PLATINUM PROMOTIONS

WE'RE [illegible] THE ROAD A[illegible]!

Throughout the year we attend most of the major U.S. shows including:
Chicago Sun Times, **Shriners Show** (MA), **National Sports Collector's Convention**, **SportsFest**, **Gibraltar Trade Center** (MI) ***and others***...

We will be at these locations prior to each show to give your collection the time it deserves.

Canadian Customers Please Call:

902-835-1048

U.S. Customers Please Call:

502-526-8056

Call us to arrange a meeting either before, during or after the show!

For large collections we will travel to your location!

Selling! Selling! Selling! Selling! Selling!

- **All Hockey Sets 1910-1972**
- **All Hockey Singles 1910-1972**
- We have a huge inventory of many of the highest graded singles from the '50's and '60's, plus Pre-war Cards! We also have a large number of discounted cards for bargain hunters.

Fill your want lists by faxing or phoning me. Our product is backed by a full money-back guarantee, no questions asked. We can provide you with references from many satisfied U.S. customers.

CHECK OUT ONE OF EBAY'S LARGEST AND BEST AUCTION SITES AND OUR GREAT EBAY STORE

To find us on Ebay, go to "Sellers" and type in **potts39** or e-mail at **potts39@bellsouth.net.** We list a very small portion of our inventory on Ebay, so please contact Steve or Len with your requests.

Almost every dealer claims to be the biggest "this" or the largest "that". We make no claims and try not to compete with anyone. What we do claim is that we deal with honesty, integrity and fairness. We enjoy this hobby and try to make it fun. We'd like very much for you to try dealing with us and our products. We look forward to your call!

BECKETT®

THE #1 AUTHORITY ON COLLECTIBLES

HOCKEY CARD PRICE GUIDE

NUMBER 28

THE HOBBY'S MOST RELIABLE AND RELIED UPON SOURCE™

Founder & Advisor: Dr. James Beckett III • Edited by the staff of Beckett Hockey

Prices in this guide reflect current retail rates determined just prior to printing. They do not reflect for-sale prices by the author, publisher, distributors, advertisers, or any card dealers associated with this guide. Every effort has been made to eliminate errors. Readers are invited to write us noting any errors which may be researched and corrected in subsequent printings. The publisher will not be held responsible for losses which may occur in the sale or purchase of cards because of information contained herein.

BECKETT is a registered trademark of BECKETT MEDIA LLC, DALLAS, TEXAS
Manufactured in the United States of America | Published by Beckett Media LLC

Beckett Media LLC
4635 McEwen Dr. • Dallas, TX 75244
(972) 991-6657 • beckett.com

First Printing ISBN: 978-1-936681-17-4

CONTENTS

HOW TO USE AND CONDITION GUIDE

Isn't it great? Every year this book gets bigger and better with all the new sets coming out. But even more exciting is that every year there are more attractive choices and, subsequently, more interest in the cards we love so much. This edition has been enhanced and expanded from the previous edition. The cards you collect–who appears on them, what they look like, where they are from, and (most important to most of you) what their current values are–are enumerated within. Many of the features contained in the other Beckett Price Guides have been incorporated into this volume since condition grading, terminology, and many other aspects of collecting are common to the card hobby in general. We hope you find the book both interesting and useful in your collecting pursuits.

The Beckett Hockey Card Price Guide has been successful where other attempts have failed because it is complete, current, and valid. This Price Guide contains not just one, but two prices by condition for all hockey cards listed. These account for most of the hockey cards in existence. The prices were added to the card lists just prior to printing and reflect not the author's opinions or desires, but the going retail prices for each card based on the active market (sports memorabilia conventions and shows, sports card shops, mail-order catalogs, local club meetings, auction results, and other firsthand reports of actual realized prices).

What is the best price guide available on the market today? Of course card sellers will prefer the price guide with the highest prices, while card buyers will naturally prefer the one with the lowest prices. Accuracy, however, is the true test. Use the price guide used by more collectors and dealers than all the others combined because it's not the lowest and not the highest – but the most accurate guide, and is produced with integrity.

To facilitate your use of this book, read the complete introductory section on the following pages before going to the pricing pages. Every collectible field has its own terminology; we've tried to capture most of these terms and definitions in our glossary. Please read carefully the section on grading and the condition of your cards, as you will not be able to determine which price column is appropriate for a given card without first knowing its condition.

HOW TO COLLECT

Each collection is personal and reflects the individuality of its owner. There are no set rules on how to collect cards. Since card collecting is a hobby or leisure pastime, what you collect, how much you collect, and how much time and money you spend collecting are entirely up to you. The funds you have available for collecting and your own personal taste should determine how you collect.

It is impossible to collect every card ever produced. Therefore, beginners as well as intermediate and advanced collectors usually specialize in some way. One of the reasons this hobby is popular is that individual collectors can define and tailor their collecting methods to match their own tastes.

Many collectors select complete sets from particular years, acquire only certain players, some collectors are only interested in the first cards or Rookie Cards of certain players, and others collect cards by team.

Remember, this is a hobby so pick a style of collecting that appeals to you.

DETERMINING VALUE

Why are some cards more valuable than others? Obviously, the economic laws of supply and demand are applicable to card collecting just as they are to any other field where a commodity is bought, sold or traded in a free, unregulated market.

Supply (the number of cards available on the market) is less than the total number of cards originally produced since attrition diminishes that original quantity. Each year a percentage of cards is typically thrown away, destroyed or otherwise lost to collectors. This percentage is much, much smaller today than it was in the past because more and more people have become increasingly aware of the value of their cards.

For those who collect only Mint condition cards, the supply of older cards can be quite small indeed. Until recently, collectors were not so conscious of the need to preserve the condition of their cards. For this reason, it is difficult to know exactly how many 1953 Topps are currently available, Mint or otherwise. It is generally accepted that there are fewer 1953 Topps available than 1963, 1973 or 1983 Topps cards. If demand were equal for each of these sets, the law of supply and demand would increase the price for the least available sets. Demand, however, is never equal for all sets, so price correlations can be complicated. The demand for a card is influenced by many factors. These include: (1) the age of the card; (2) the number of cards printed; (3) the player(s) portrayed on the card; (4) the attractiveness and popularity of the set; and (5) the physical condition of the card.

In general, (1) the older the card, (2) the fewer the number of the cards printed, (3) the more famous, popular and talented the player, (4) the more attractive and popular the set, and (5) the better the condition of the card, the higher the value of the card will be. There are exceptions to all but one of these factors: the condition of the card. Given two cards similar in all respects except condition, the one in the best condition will always be valued higher.

While those guidelines help to establish the value of a card, the countless exceptions and peculiarities make any simple, direct mathematical formula to determine card values impossible.

REGIONAL VARIATION

Since the market varies from region to region, card prices of local players may be higher. This is known as a regional premium. How significant the premium is and if there is any premium at all depends on the local popularity of the team and the player.

The largest regional premiums usually do not apply to superstars, who often are so well-known nationwide that the prices of their key cards are too high for local dealers to realize a premium.

Lesser stars often command the strongest premiums. Their popularity is concentrated in their home region, creating local demand that greatly exceeds overall demand.

Regional premiums can apply to popular retired players and sometimes can be found in the areas where the players grew up or starred in college.

A regional discount is the converse of a regional premium. Regional discounts occur when a player has been so popular in his region for so long that local collectors and dealers have accumulated quantities of his key cards. The abundant supply may make the cards available in that area at the lowest prices anywhere.

SET PRICES

A somewhat paradoxical situation exists in the price of a complete set vs. the combined cost of the individual cards in the set. In nearly every case, the sum of the prices for the individual cards is higher than the cost for the complete set. This is prevalent especially in the cards of the last few years. The reasons for this apparent anomaly stem from the habits of collectors and from the carrying costs to dealers. Today, each card in a set normally is produced in the same quantity as all other cards in its set.

Many collectors pick up only stars, superstars and particular teams. As a result, the dealer is left with a shortage of certain player cards and an abundance of others. He therefore incurs an expense in simply "carrying" these less desirable cards in stock. On the other hand, if he sells a complete set, he gets rid of large numbers of cards at one time. For this reason, he generally is willing to receive less money for a complete set. By doing this, he recovers all of his costs and also makes a profit.

The disparity between the price of the complete set and the sum of the individual cards also has been influenced by the fact that some of the major manufacturers now are pre-collating card sets. Since "pulling" individual cards from the sets involves a specific type of labor (and cost), the singles or star card market is not affected significantly by pre-collation.

Set prices also do not include rare card varieties, unless specifically stated. Of course, the prices for sets do include one example of each type for the given set, but this is the least expensive variety.

CONDITION GUIDE

The most widely used grades are defined on page 45. Obviously, many cards will not perfectly fit one of the definitions. Therefore, categories between the major grades known as in-between grades are used, such as Good to Very Good (G-Vg), Very Good to Excellent (VgEx), and Excellent-Mint to Near Mint (ExMt-NrMt). Such grades indicate a card with all qualities of the lower category but with at least a few qualities of the higher category.

This Price Guide book lists each card and set in three grades, with the middle grade valued at about 40-45% of the top grade, and the bottom grade valued at about 10-15% of the top grade.

The value of cards that fall between the listed columns can also be calculated using a percentage of the top grade. For example, a card that falls between the top and middle grades (Ex,

Price Guide Percentage by Grade

	1933/34-1940/41	1951/52-1967/68	1968/69-1979/80	1980/81-1989/90	1990/91-Present
MT	300%+	300%+	250%+	125-150%	100-125%
NrMt-Mt	150-300%	150-250%	200%+	100%	10▲%
NrMt	100-150%	100%	100%	40-60%	30-50%
Ex-Mt	100%	50-75%	40-60%	25-40%	20-30%
Ex	50-75%	30-50%	20-40%	15-25%	10-20%
VG	30-50%	15-30%	10-20%	5-15%	5-10%
G/F/P	15-30%	5-15%	5-10%	5%	5%

ExMt or NrMt in most cases) will generally be valued at anywhere from 50% to 90% of the top grade.

Similarly, a card that falls between the middle and bottom grades (G-Vg, Vg or VgEx in most cases) will generally be valued at anywhere from 20% to 40% of the top grade.

There are also cases where cards are in better condition than the top grade or worse than the bottom grade. Cards that grade worse than the lowest grade are generally valued at 5-10% of the top grade.

When a card exceeds the top grade by one – such as NrMt-Mt when the top grade is NrMt, or Mint when the top grade is NrMt-Mt – a premium of up to 50% is possible, with 10-20% the usual norm.

When a card exceeds the top grade by two – such as Mint when the top grade is NrMt, or NrMt-Mt when the top grade is ExMt – a premium of 25-50% is the usual norm. But certain condition sensitive cards or sets, particularly those from the pre-war era, can bring premiums of up to 100% or even more.

Unopened packs, boxes and factory-collated sets are considered Mint in their unknown (and presumed perfect) state. Once opened, however, each card can be graded (and valued) in its own right by taking into account any defects that may be present in spite of the fact that the card has never been handled.

GENERAL CARD FLAWS

CENTERING

Current centering terminology uses numbers representing the percentage of border on either side of the main design. Obviously, centering is diminished in importance for borderless cards.

SLIGHTLY OFF-CENTER (60/40)

A slightly off-center card is one that upon close inspection is found to have one border bigger than the opposite border. This degree once was offensive to only purists, but now some hobbyists try to avoid cards that are anything other than perfectly centered.

OFF-CENTER (70/30)

An off-center card has one border that is noticeably more than twice as wide as the opposite border.

BADLY OFF-CENTER (80/20 OR WORSE)

A badly off-center card has virtually no border on one side of the card.

MISCUT

A miscut card actually shows part of the adjacent card in its larger border and consequently a corresponding amount of its card is cut off.

CORNER WEAR

Corner wear is the most scrutinized grading criteria in the hobby.

CORNER WITH A SLIGHT TOUCH OF WEAR

The corner still is sharp, but there is a slight touch of wear showing. On a dark-bordered card, this shows as a dot of white.

FUZZY CORNER

The corner still comes to a point, but the point has just begun to fray. A slightly "dinged" corner is considered the same as a fuzzy corner.

SLIGHTLY ROUNDED CORNER

The fraying of the corner has increased to where there is only a hint of a point. Mild layering may be evident. A "dinged" corner is considered the same as a slightly rounded corner.

ROUNDED CORNER

The point is completely gone. Some layering is noticeable.

BADLY ROUNDED CORNER

The corner is completely round and rough. Severe layering is evident.

CREASES

A third common defect is the crease. The degree of creasing in a card is difficult to show in a drawing or picture. On giving the specific condition of an expensive card for sale, the seller should note any creases additionally. Creases can be categorized as to severity according to the following scale.

LIGHT CREASE

A light crease is a crease that is barely noticeable upon close inspection. In fact, when cards are in plastic sheets or holders, a light crease may not be seen (until the card is taken out of the holder). A light crease on the front is much more serious than a light crease on the card back only.

MEDIUM CREASE

A medium crease is noticeable when held and studied at arm's length by the naked eye, but does not overly detract from the appearance of the card. It is an obvious crease, but not one that breaks the picture surface of the card.

HEAVY CREASE

A heavy crease is one that has torn or broken through the card's picture surface, e.g., puts a tear in the photo surface.

ALTERATIONS

DECEPTIVE TRIMMING

This occurs when someone alters the card in order (1) to shave off edge wear, (2) to improve the sharpness of the corners, or (3) to improve centering – obviously their objective is to falsely increase the perceived value of the card to an unsuspecting buyer. The shrinkage usually is evident only if the trimmed card is compared to an adjacent full-sized card or if the trimmed card is itself measured.

OBVIOUS TRIMMING

Obvious trimming is noticeable and unfortunate. It is usually performed by non-collectors who give no thought to the present or future value of their cards.

DECEPTIVELY RETOUCHED BORDERS

This occurs when the borders (especially on those cards with dark borders) are touched up on the edges and corners with magic marker or crayons of appropriate color in order to make the card appear to be Mint.

MISCELLANEOUS CARD FLAWS

The following are common minor flaws that, depending on severity, lower a card's condition by one to four grades and often render it no better than Excellent-Mint: bubbles (lumps in surface), gum and wax stains, diamond cutting (slanted borders), notching, off-centered backs, paper wrinkles, scratched-off cartoons or puzzles on back, rubber band marks, scratches, surface impressions and warping.

The following are common serious flaws that, depending on severity, lower a card's condition at least four grades and often render it no better than Good: chemical or sun fading, erasure marks, mildew, miscutting (severe off-centering), holes, bleached or retouched borders, tape marks, tears, trimming, water or coffee stains and writing.

GRADES

MINT (MT)

A card with no flaws or wear. The card has four perfect corners, 55/45 or better centering from top to bottom and from left to right, original gloss, smooth edges and original color borders. A Mint card does not have print spots, color or focus imperfections.

NEAR MINT-MINT (NRMT-MT)

A card with one minor flaw. Any one of the following would lower a Mint card to Near Mint-Mint: one corner with a slight touch of wear, barely noticeable print spots, color or focus imperfections. The card must have 60/40 or better centering in both directions, original gloss, smooth edges and original color border.

NEAR MINT (NRMT)

A card with one minor flaw. Any one of the following would lower a Mint card to Near Mint: one fuzzy corner or two to four corners with slight touches of wear, 70/30 to 60/40 centering, slightly rough edges, minor print spots, color or focus imperfections. The card must have original gloss and original color borders.

EXCELLENT-MINT (EXMT)

A card with two or three fuzzy, but not rounded, corners and centering no worse than 80/20. The card may have no more than two of the following: slightly rough edges, very slightly discolored borders, minor print spots, color or focus imperfections. The card must have original gloss.

EXCELLENT (EX)

A card with four fuzzy but definitely not rounded corners and centering no worse than 70/30. The card may have a small amount of original gloss lost, rough edges, slightly discolored borders and minor print spots, color or focus imperfections.

VERY GOOD (VG)

A card that has been handled but not abused: slightly rounded corners with slight layering, slight notching on edges, a significant amount of gloss lost from the surface but no scuffing and moderate discoloration of borders. The card may have a few light creases.

GOOD (G), FAIR (F), POOR (P)

A well-worn, mishandled or abused card: badly rounded and layered corners, scuffing, most or all original gloss missing, seriously discolored borders, moderate or heavy creases, and one or more serious flaws. The grade of Good, Fair or Poor depends on the severity of wear and flaws. Good, Fair and Poor cards generally are used only as fillers.

2013-14 Absolute

Card	Low	High
COMP.SET w/o SPs (35)	15.00	40.00
36-40 ROOKIE JSY PRINT RUN 99		
1 Sidney Crosby	1.50	4.00
2 Sven Baertschi	.30	.75
3 Patrick Kane	.75	2.00
4 Gabriel Landeskog	.30	.75
5 Tyler Seguin	.60	1.50
6 Pavel Datsyuk	.50	1.25
7 Ryan Nugent-Hopkins	.40	1.00
8 P.K. Subban	.60	1.50
9 John Tavares	.75	2.00
10 Rick Nash	.40	1.00
11 Bobby Ryan	.40	1.00
12 Claude Giroux	.40	1.00
13 Dustin Brown	.40	1.00
14 Joe Thornton	.40	1.00
15 Steven Stamkos	.75	2.00
16 Nazem Kadri	.40	1.00
17 D.Sedin/H.Sedin	.40	1.00
18 Alex Ovechkin	1.50	4.00
19 Andrew Ladd	.40	1.00
20 Zdeno Chara	.40	1.00
21 Filip Forsberg	1.50	4.00
22 Tomas Hertl	.75	2.00
23 Damien Brunner	.50	1.25
24 Brendan Gallagher	2.00	5.00
25 Mikhail Grigorenko	.75	2.00
26 Sean Monahan	1.00	2.50
27 Valeri Nichushkin	.60	1.50
28 Jacob Trouba	1.00	2.50
29 Aleksander Barkov	1.50	4.00
30 Seth Jones	.60	1.50
31 Danny Dekeyser	.75	2.00
32 Ryan Murray	1.00	2.50
33 Boone Jenner	.60	1.50
34 Morgan Rielly	1.50	4.00
35 Mathew Dumba	.60	1.50
36 Nail Yakupov JSY	6.00	15.00
37 Nathan MacKinnon JSY	15.00	40.00
38 Jonathan Huberdeau JSY	5.00	12.00
39 Alex Galchenyuk JSY	10.00	25.00
40 Anthony Bennett BK JSY	4.00	10.00

2013-14 Absolute Holo Lava Flow

VETS/25: 1X TO 2.5X BASIC CARDS
ROOKIES/25: 1X TO 2.5X BASIC CARDS
LAVA FLOW JSY/25*: .5X TO 1.2X BASIC JSY/99

2013-14 Absolute Draft Day Materials

Card	Low	High
*LAVA FLOW/25: .5X TO 1.2X BASIC JSY		
1 Nathan MacKinnon	10.00	25.00
2 Jacob Trouba	8.00	20.00
3 Aleksander Barkov	6.00	15.00
4 Seth Jones	2.50	6.00
5 Sean Monahan	4.00	10.00
6 Ryan Murray	4.00	10.00
7 Valeri Nichushkin	2.50	6.00

2013-14 Absolute Happy Holidays Materials

Card	Low	High
*LAVA FLOW/25: .5X TO 1.2X BASIC JSY		
NM Nathan MacKinnon	10.00	25.00

2013-14 Absolute Ink

Card	Low	High
CK Carl Klingberg	2.00	5.00
JF Justin Faulk	2.00	5.00
JM John Moore	2.00	5.00
RE Ryan Ellis	2.00	5.00
SD Simon Despres	2.50	6.00
TE Tim Erixon	2.00	5.00
OEL Oliver Ekman-Larsson	2.50	6.00

2013-14 Absolute Logo Patch Autographs

Card	Low	High
CP Chet Pickard	2.50	6.00
DH Dougie Hamilton	12.00	30.00
JA Jake Allen	6.00	15.00
JS Jaden Schwartz	5.00	12.00
JS Jordan Schroeder	4.00	10.00
JT Jarred Tinordi	8.00	20.00
MR Morgan Rielly	10.00	25.00
NB Nathan Beaulieu	8.00	20.00
NY Nail Yakupov	15.00	40.00
RM Ryan Murray	15.00	40.00
TB Tyson Barrie	4.00	10.00

2013-14 Absolute NHL Icons

Card	Low	High
*LAVA FLOW/25: X TO X BASIC INSERTS		
1 Jaromir Jagr	4.00	10.00
2 Jarome Iginla	1.50	4.00
3 Teemu Selanne	3.00	8.00
4 Martin Brodeur	3.00	8.00
5 Daniel Alfredsson	1.50	4.00

2013-14 Absolute Retired

Card	Low	High
*LAVA FLOW/25: .5X TO 1.2X BASIC INSERTS		
1 Gordie Howe	3.00	8.00
2 Mario Lemieux	5.00	12.00
3 Ray Bourque	2.50	6.00
4 Chris Chelios	1.50	4.00
5 Eric Lindros	2.50	6.00
6 Steve Yzerman	3.00	8.00
7 Mark Messier	2.00	5.00
8 Brendan Shanahan	2.00	5.00

2013-14 Absolute Rookie Roundup Materials

Card	Low	High
*LAVA FLOW/25: .5X TO 1.2X BASIC JSY		
1 Justin Schultz	3.00	8.00
2 Tom Wilson	5.00	12.00
3 Petr Mrazek	6.00	15.00
4 Charlie Coyle	3.00	8.00
5 Jarred Tinordi	3.00	8.00
6 Cory Conacher	2.00	5.00
7 Nicklas Jensen	2.50	6.00
8 Morgan Rielly	8.00	20.00
9 Beau Bennett	4.00	10.00
10 Ryan Murray	5.00	12.00

2013-14 Absolute Rookie Showcase Materials

Card	Low	High
*LAVA FLOW/25: .5X TO 1.2X BASIC JSY		
1 Chris Kreider	2.50	6.00
2 Tyson Barrie	2.50	6.00
3 Jake Allen	3.00	8.00
4 Jussi Rynnas	1.50	4.00
5 Jaden Schwartz	3.00	8.00
6 Ryan Nugent-Hopkins	2.50	6.00
7 Gabriel Landeskog	6.00	15.00
8 Adam Henrique	2.50	6.00

2013-14 Absolute Rookie Tool of the Trade

Card	Low	High
*LAVA FLOW/25: .5X TO 1.2X BASIC JSY		
1 Jonathan Toews	10.00	25.00
2 Steven Stamkos	10.00	25.00
3 Alex Ovechkin	12.00	30.00
4 Sidney Crosby	20.00	50.00

1989-90 Action Packed Prototypes

This three-card set was produced by Action Packed to show the NHL and NHLPA a sample in order to obtain a license for hockey cards. The cards are unnumbered and listed below in alphabetical order. Reportedly only 1000 cards of Gretzky and Lemieux were produced and only 300 of Yzerman. These cards are standard size with the rounded corners.

Card	Low	High
COMPLETE SET (4)	125.00	300.00
1 Wayne Gretzky	50.00	100.00
2 Mario Lemieux	30.00	75.00
3 Mario Lemieux White border	30.00	75.00
4 Steve Yzerman	50.00	100.00

1990 Action Packed Promos Gold

Action Packed produced these cards in order to show the NBA what they could do with basketball cards. These unnumbered cards are numbered alphabetically for convenience in the checklist below. The cards are standard size, 2 1/2" by 3 1/2" with rounded corners. There is some question as to whether this is a legitimate set since Action Packed did not intend these to be sold.

Card	Low	High
COMPLETE SET (4)	100.00	200.00
*SILVER: .4X TO 1X GOLD		
5 Mario Lemieux	15.00	40.00
6 Wayne Gretzky	25.00	60.00

1993 Action Packed HOF Induction

This special limited edition standard-size set was produced by Action Packed to commemorate the 1993 Hockey Hall Of Fame induction on November 16, 1993, and honors the ten inductees. It was given to attendees at the induction and was on sale at the Hockey Hall of Fame. This set was released in a special black cardboard display featuring all ten cards (in two rows of five) and which could be placed in a black cardboard sleeve with the Hall of Fame logo and the words "1993 Hockey Hall of Fame Induction, November 16, 1993" printed in silver letters on the front. The back of the sleeve gives the set serial number out of a total of 5,000 sets produced.

Card	Low	High
COMPLETE SET (10)	8.00	20.00
1 Edgar Laprade	.75	2.00
2 Guy Lapointe	2.00	5.00
3 Billy Smith	3.00	8.00
4 Steve Shutt	2.00	5.00
5 John D'Amico	.40	1.00
6 Al Shaver	.20	.50
7 Seymour Knox III	.20	.50
8 Frank Griffiths	.20	.50
9 Fred Page	.20	.50
10 Al Strachan	.20	.50

1993 Action Packed Prototypes

Both prototype cards measure the standard size and feature Bobby Hull. The first card has a borderless embossed color photo, while the second card has the same design but is all in gold. Both cards feature a silver Stanley Cup in the upper right corner. The horizontal backs carry biographical (in English and French) and statistical information, the Blackhawks logo on a puck, and the word "Prototype" printed vertically on the left. The cards are numbered on the back with a "BH" prefix.

Card	Low	High
COMPLETE SET (2)	3.00	8.00
1 Bobby Hull (Color)	1.50	4.00
2 Bobby Hull (Gold)	2.00	5.00

1994 Action Packed Badge of Honor Promos

Issued to herald the release of a new product, each of these four pins measures approximately 1 1/2" by 1". They were packaged together in a cardboard sleeve which carries a checklist on its back. On a bronze background, the fronts feature color player portraits with a gold border. The player's last name appears in gold lettering at the bottom. The Action Packed logo is above the picture, while the year 1994 inside a puck and hockey sticks icon is below. The backs carry the copyrights "Action Packed 1994" and "NHL 1994", and "NHLPA 1994." The pins are unnumbered and checklisted below in alphabetical order. By all accounts, the actual set these pins were designed to promote never was released.

Card	Low	High
COMPLETE SET (4)	10.00	25.00
1 Sergei Fedorov	4.00	10.00
2 Doug Gilmour	2.00	5.00
3 Mike Modano	3.00	8.00
4 Patrick Roy	5.00	12.00

1994-95 Action Packed Big Picture Promos

These four standard-size cards were issued to preview a proposed (but never released) Action Packed product: "Big Picture" cards. The fronts have borderless embossed color action photos. On a team color-coded background, the backs have a color close-up inside a gold foil circle, the player's name and team in gold foil lettering, and player profile. The front and back are hinged at the top, and the card opens up to reveal a 5 3/4" by 6 1/2" mini-poster, with a movie-frame design.

Card	Low	High
COMPLETE SET (4)	8.00	20.00
BP1 Jeremy Roenick	1.25	3.00
BP2 John Vanbiesbrouck	1.25	3.00
BP3 Jaromir Jagr	4.00	10.00
BP4 Steve Yzerman	4.00	10.00

1994-95 Action Packed Mammoth

The cards measure approximately 7 1/2" by 10 1/2". The fronts have borderless embossed color action photos with rounded corners. The player's last name is gold foil stamped on the bottom. The backs carry a color player cutout superimposed over the team logo. Player biography, profile and career totals are superimposed over the cutout. The player's name, team and position appear in a black bar alongside the left. The cards were issued in a plastic sleeve and are indivdiually numbered out of 25,000 on the back.

Card	Low	High
COMPLETE SET (16)	10.00	25.00
MM1 Pavel Bure	1.25	3.00
MM2 Chris Chelios	1.00	2.50
MM3 Sergei Fedorov	1.25	3.00
MM4 Doug Gilmour	.75	2.00
MM5 Wayne Gretzky	2.50	6.00
MM6 Brett Hull	1.25	3.00
MM7 Jaromir Jagr	1.00	2.50
MM8 Eric Lindros	1.25	3.00
MM9 Mark Messier	1.00	2.50
MM9 Felix Potvin	1.25	3.00
MM10 Alexander Mogilny	1.00	2.50
MM11 Adam Oates	1.00	2.50
MM13 Jeremy Roenick	1.25	3.00
MM14 Patrick Roy	1.50	4.00
MM15 John Vanbiesbrouck	1.00	2.50
MM16 Alexei Yashin	.75	2.00

2010-11 Adrenalyn XL

Card	Low	High
1 Ilya Kovalchuk	.25	.60
2 Zach Parise	.25	.60
3 Travis Zajac	.20	.50
4 Patrik Elias	.25	.60
5 Dainius Zubrus	.12	.30
6 Jason Arnott	.20	.50
7 Colin White	.15	.40
8 Anton Volchenkov	.15	.40
9 Andy Greene	.15	.40
10 Martin Brodeur	.50	1.25
11 John Tavares	.50	1.25
12 Matt Moulson	.20	.50
13 Rob Schremp	.15	.40
14 Trent Hunter	.15	.40
15 Josh Bailey	.20	.50
16 Kyle Okposo	.20	.50
17 Mark Streit	.15	.40
18 Bruno Gervais	.15	.40
19 Jack Hillen	.15	.40
20 Dwayne Roloson	.20	.50
21 Marian Gaborik	.30	.75
22 Chris Drury	.20	.50
23 Ryan Callahan	.25	.60
24 Brandon Dubinsky	.20	.50
25 Vinny Prospal	.15	.40
26 Alexander Frolov	.15	.40
27 Michael Del Zotto	.20	.50
28 Daniel Girardi	.15	.40
29 Marc Staal	.25	.60
30 Henrik Lundqvist	.40	1.00
31 Mike Richards	.25	.60
32 Jeff Carter	.25	.60
33 Nikolai Zherdev	.15	.40
34 Daniel Briere	.25	.60
35 Claude Giroux	.25	.60
36 Ville Leino	.20	.50
37 Matt Carle	.20	.50
38 Kimmo Timonen	.15	.40
39 Chris Pronger	.20	.50
40 Michael Leighton	.20	.50
41 Evgeni Malkin	.75	2.00
42 Sidney Crosby	1.00	2.50
43 Jordan Staal	.25	.60
44 Chris Kunitz	.25	.60
45 Pascal Dupuis	.15	.40
46 Max Talbot	.25	.60
47 Paul Martin	.15	.40
48 Zbynek Michalek	.15	.40
49 Kristopher Letang	.25	.60
50 Marc-Andre Fleury	.40	1.00
51 Marc Savard	.15	.40
52 Nathan Horton	.20	.50
53 Milan Lucic	.25	.60
54 Patrice Bergeron	.30	.75
55 David Krejci	.25	.60
56 Tyler Seguin RC	2.00	5.00
57 Zdeno Chara	.20	.50
58 Dennis Seidenberg	.20	.50
59 Johnny Boychuk	.15	.40
60 Tuukka Rask	.25	.60
61 Thomas Vanek	.25	.60
62 Jason Pominville	.25	.60
63 Tim Connolly	.15	.40
64 Derek Roy	.25	.60
65 Jochen Hecht	.15	.40
66 Nathan Gerbe	.15	.40
67 Craig Rivet	.15	.40
68 Tyler Myers	.25	.60
69 Jordan Leopold	.15	.40
70 Ryan Miller	.25	.60
71 Scott Gomez	.20	.50
72 Michael Cammalleri	.25	.60
73 Brian Gionta	.20	.50
74 Benoit Pouliot	.15	.40
75 Andrei Kostitsyn	.20	.50
76 Tomas Plekanec	.25	.60
77 Josh Gorges	.15	.40
78 P.K. Subban RC	1.50	4.00
79 Andrei Markov	.25	.60
80 Carey Price	1.00	2.50
81 Jason Spezza	.15	.40
82 Daniel Alfredsson	.25	.60
83 Milan Michalek	.15	.40
84 Mike Fisher	.25	.60
85 Alex Kovalev	.25	.60
86 Peter Regin	.20	.50
87 Sergei Gonchar	.15	.40
88 Chris Phillips	.15	.40
89 Erik Karlsson	.50	1.25
90 Brian Elliott	.20	.50
91 Phil Kessel	.30	.75
92 Tyler Bozak	.25	.60
93 Mikhail Grabovski	.20	.50
94 Kris Versteeg	.20	.50
95 Colby Armstrong	.15	.40
96 Nikolai Kulemin	.20	.50
97 Tomas Kaberle	.15	.40
98 Dion Phaneuf	.25	.60
99 Luke Schenn	.20	.50
100 Jonas Gustavsson	.30	.75
101 Evander Kane	.25	.60
102 Dustin Byfuglien	.25	.60
103 Nik Antropov	.20	.50
104 Rich Peverley	.25	.60
105 Bryan Little	.25	.60
106 Nicklas Bergfors	.20	.50
107 Andrew Ladd	.25	.60
108 Zach Bogosian	.20	.50
109 Tobias Enstrom	.15	.40
110 Ondrej Pavelec	.25	.60
111 Eric Staal	.30	.75
112 Tuomo Ruutu	.20	.50
113 Erik Cole	.20	.50
114 Chad LaRose	.15	.40
115 Brandon Sutter	.20	.50
116 Zach Boychuk	.20	.50
117 Joni Pitkanen	.20	.50
118 Jamie McBain RC	.50	1.25
119 Joe Corvo	.15	.40
120 Cam Ward	.25	.60
121 Stephen Weiss	.20	.50
122 David Booth	.15	.40
123 Cory Stillman	.15	.40
124 Rostislav Olesz	.15	.40
125 Michael Frolik	.15	.40
126 Steve Reinprecht	.15	.40
127 Dmitry Kulikov	.20	.50
128 Bryan McCabe	.15	.40
129 Dennis Wideman	.15	.40
130 Tomas Vokoun	.20	.50
131 Vincent Lecavalier	.20	.50
132 Steven Stamkos	.50	1.25
133 Martin St. Louis	.25	.60
134 Ryan Malone	.15	.40
135 Steve Downie	.15	.40
136 Simon Gagne	.25	.60
137 Mattias Ohlund	.15	.40
138 Victor Hedman	.30	.75
139 Pavel Kubina	.15	.40
140 Mike Smith	.25	.60
141 Alex Ovechkin	1.00	2.50
142 Alexander Semin	.25	.60
143 Nicklas Backstrom	.40	1.00
144 Mike Knuble	.15	.40
145 Eric Fehr	.15	.40
146 Marcus Johansson RC	.75	2.00
147 Mike Green	.25	.60
148 Jeff Schultz	.15	.40
149 John Carlson	.30	.75
150 Semyon Varlamov	.25	.60
151 Marian Hossa	.20	.50
152 Patrick Sharp	.25	.60
153 Patrick Kane	.50	1.25
154 Jonathan Toews	.50	1.25
155 Dave Bolland	.20	.50
156 Troy Brouwer	.25	.60
157 Brent Seabrook	.25	.60
158 Duncan Keith	.25	.60
159 Brian Campbell	.15	.40
160 Marty Turco	.25	.60
161 Rick Nash	.25	.60
162 Kristian Huselius	.15	.40
163 R.J. Umberger	.15	.40
164 Antoine Vermette	.15	.40
165 Jakub Voracek	.25	.60
166 Derick Brassard	.25	.60
167 Mike Commodore	.15	.40
168 Kris Russell	.15	.40
169 Jan Hejda	.15	.40
170 Steve Mason	.20	.50
171 Pavel Datsyuk	.30	.75
172 Henrik Zetterberg	.30	.75
173 Tomas Holmstrom	.15	.40
174 Johan Franzen	.25	.60
175 Valtteri Filppula	.25	.60
176 Mike Modano	.40	1.00
177 Nicklas Lidstrom	.25	.60
178 Brian Rafalski	.15	.40
179 Niklas Kronwall	.15	.40
180 Jimmy Howard	.30	.75
181 Martin Erat	.15	.40
182 Patric Hornqvist	.20	.50
183 Matthew Lombardi	.15	.40
184 J.P. Dumont	.15	.40
185 Steve Sullivan	.15	.40
186 David Legwand	.20	.50
187 Shea Weber	.20	.50
188 Ryan Suter	.15	.40
189 Kevin Klein	.15	.40
190 Pekka Rinne	.30	.75
191 T.J. Oshie	.40	1.00
192 Andy McDonald	.20	.50
193 Brad Boyes	.15	.40
194 David Backes	.25	.60
195 Alex Steen	.25	.60
196 David Perron	.15	.40
197 Erik Johnson	.15	.40
198 Barret Jackman	.15	.40
199 Carlo Colaiacovo	.15	.40
200 Jaroslav Halak	.25	.60
201 Jarome Iginla	.25	.60
202 Daymond Langkow	.15	.40
203 Rene Bourque	.15	.40
204 Olli Jokinen	.20	.50
205 Matt Stajan	.20	.50
206 Mikael Backlund	.20	.50
207 Jay Bouwmeester	.30	.75
208 Robyn Regehr	.15	.40
209 Mark Giordano	.20	.50
210 Miikka Kiprusoff	.20	.50
211 Paul Stastny	.25	.60
212 Milan Hejduk	.20	.50
213 Matt Duchene	.25	.60
214 Peter Mueller	.20	.50
215 Chris Stewart	.20	.50
216 Brandon Yip RC	.50	1.25
217 Adam Foote	.15	.40
218 John-Michael Liles	.15	.40
219 Kyle Cumiskey	.15	.40
220 Craig Anderson	.25	.60
221 Dustin Penner	.15	.40
222 Sam Gagner	.20	.50
223 Ales Hemsky	.20	.50
224 Taylor Hall RC	2.00	5.00
225 Jordan Eberle RC	1.25	3.00
226 Gilbert Brule	.25	.60
227 Kurtis Foster	.15	.40
228 Tom Gilbert	.15	.40
229 Ryan Whitney	.15	.40
230 Jeff Deslauriers	.15	.40
231 Mikko Koivu	.25	.60
232 Martin Havlat	.20	.50
233 Andrew Brunette	.15	.40
234 Matt Cullen	.15	.40
235 Chuck Kobasew	.15	.40
236 Guillaume Latendresse	.20	.50
237 Brent Burns	.30	.75
238 Greg Zanon	.15	.40
239 Cam Barker	.15	.40
240 Niklas Backstrom	.25	.60
241 Henrik Sedin	.25	.60
242 Daniel Sedin	.25	.60
243 Alexandre Burrows	.25	.60
244 Mason Raymond	.20	.50
245 Ryan Kesler	.25	.60
246 Mikael Samuelsson	.15	.40
247 Christian Ehrhoff	.15	.40
248 Dan Hamhuis	.20	.50
249 Keith Ballard	.15	.40
250 Roberto Luongo	.25	.60
251 Nick Bonino RC	.60	1.50
252 Saku Koivu	.25	.60
253 Ryan Getzlaf	.40	1.00
254 Corey Perry	.25	.60
255 Bobby Ryan	.25	.60
256 Teemu Selanne	.50	1.25
257 Luca Sbisa	.20	.50
258 Toni Lydman	.15	.40
259 Lubomir Visnovsky	.15	.40
260 Jonas Hiller	.20	.50
261 Brad Richards	.25	.60
262 Brenden Morrow	.20	.50
263 Loui Eriksson	.20	.50
264 Steve Ott	.20	.50
265 Jamie Benn	.30	.75
266 James Neal	.25	.60
267 Trevor Daley	.15	.40
268 Stephane Robidas	.15	.40
269 Nicklas Grossman	.15	.40
270 Kari Lehtonen	.20	.50
271 Anze Kopitar	.40	1.00
272 Ryan Smyth	.20	.50
273 Dustin Brown	.25	.60
274 Alexei Ponikarovsky	.15	.40
275 Justin Williams	.20	.50
276 Wayne Simmonds	.30	.75
277 Drew Doughty	.25	.60
278 Rob Scuderi	.15	.40
279 Jack Johnson	.15	.40
280 Jonathan Quick	.40	1.00
281 Wojtek Wolski	.15	.40
282 Shane Doan	.20	.50
283 Ray Whitney	.20	.50
284 Radim Vrbata	.20	.50
285 Scottie Upshall	.15	.40
286 Martin Hanzal	.15	.40
287 Adrian Aucoin	.15	.40
288 Keith Yandle	.25	.60
289 Ed Jovanovski	.15	.40
290 Ilya Bryzgalov	.20	.50
291 Joe Thornton	.25	.60
292 Joe Pavelski	.25	.60
293 Patrick Marleau	.25	.60
294 Dany Heatley	.20	.50
295 Devin Setoguchi	.20	.50
296 Logan Couture	.25	.60
297 Marc-Edouard Vlasic	.15	.40
298 Dan Boyle	.20	.50
299 Jason Demers	.15	.40
300 Antti Niemi	.20	.50

2010-11 Adrenalyn XL Extra

Card	Low	High
STATED ODDS 1:8 BOOSTER		
E1 Zach Parise	1.50	4.00
E2 Dwayne Roloson	1.25	3.00
E3 Marc Staal	1.50	4.00
E4 Jeff Carter	1.50	4.00
E5 Jordan Staal	1.50	4.00
E6 Nathan Horton	1.25	3.00
E7 Derek Roy	1.50	4.00
E8 Brian Gionta	1.25	3.00
E9 Sergei Gonchar	1.00	2.50
E10 Phil Kessel	2.00	5.00
E11 Rich Peverley	1.50	4.00
E12 Brandon Sutter	1.25	3.00
E13 Cory Stillman	1.00	2.50
E14 Vincent Lecavalier	1.25	3.00
E15 Mike Green	1.50	4.00
E16 Patrick Kane	3.00	8.00
E17 R.J. Umberger	1.00	2.50
E18 Nicklas Lidstrom	1.50	4.00
E19 Patric Hornqvist	1.25	3.00
E20 Andy McDonald	1.25	3.00
E21 Jay Bouwmeester	2.00	5.00
E22 Matt Duchene	1.50	4.00
E23 Ales Hemsky	1.25	3.00
E24 Andrew Brunette	1.00	2.50
E25 Roberto Luongo	1.50	4.00
E26 Bobby Ryan	1.50	4.00
E27 James Neal	1.50	4.00
E28 Jonathan Quick	2.50	6.00
E29 Ray Whitney	1.25	3.00
E30 Patrick Marleau	1.50	4.00

2010-11 Adrenalyn XL Extra Signature

Card	Low	High
STATED ODDS 1:8 BOOSTER		
ES1 Martin Brodeur	5.00	12.00
ES2 John Tavares	5.00	12.00
ES3 Henrik Lundqvist	4.00	10.00
ES4 Mike Richards	2.50	6.00
ES5 Evgeni Malkin	8.00	20.00
ES6 Zdeno Chara	2.00	5.00
ES7 Tyler Myers	2.50	6.00
ES8 Michael Cammalleri	2.50	6.00
ES9 Jason Spezza	1.50	4.00
ES10 Tomas Kaberle	1.50	4.00
ES11 Niclas Bergfors	2.00	5.00
ES12 Cam Ward	2.50	6.00
ES13 Stephen Weiss	2.00	5.00
ES14 Martin St. Louis	2.50	6.00
ES15 Nicklas Backstrom	4.00	10.00
ES16 Duncan Keith	2.50	6.00
ES17 Antoine Vermette	1.50	4.00
ES18 Henrik Zetterberg	3.00	8.00
ES19 Pekka Rinne	3.00	8.00
ES20 Erik Johnson	1.50	4.00
ES21 Miikka Kiprusoff	2.00	5.00
ES22 Craig Anderson	2.50	6.00
ES23 Jordan Eberle	5.00	12.00
ES24 Niklas Backstrom	2.50	6.00
ES25 Daniel Sedin	2.50	6.00
ES26 Teemu Selanne	5.00	12.00
ES27 Loui Eriksson	2.00	5.00
ES28 Anze Kopitar	4.00	10.00
ES29 Shane Doan	2.00	5.00
ES30 Dany Heatley	2.00	5.00

2010-11 Adrenalyn XL Special

Card	Low	High
STATED ODDS 1:2 BOOSTER		
S1 Andy Greene	.50	1.25
S2 Patrik Elias	.75	2.00
S3 Kyle Okposo	.75	2.00
S4 Matt Moulson	.60	1.50
S5 Brandon Dubinsky	.60	1.50
S6 Vinny Prospal	.50	1.25
S7 Claude Giroux	.75	2.00
S8 Kimmo Timonen	.50	1.25
S9 Marc-Andre Fleury	1.25	3.00
S10 Zbynek Michalek	.50	1.25
S11 Marc Savard	.50	1.25
S12 Patrice Bergeron	1.00	2.50
S13 Tim Connolly	.50	1.25
S14 Thomas Vanek	.75	2.00
S15 Carey Price	3.00	8.00
S16 P.K. Subban	2.00	5.00
S17 Alex Kovalev	.75	2.00
S18 Milan Michalek	.50	1.25
S19 Kris Versteeg	.60	1.50
S20 Jonas Gustavsson	1.00	2.50
S21 Ondrej Pavelec	.75	2.00
S22 Dustin Byfuglien	.75	2.00
S23 Jamie McBain	.60	1.50
S24 Joe Corvo	.50	1.25
S25 David Booth	.50	1.25
S26 Bryan McCabe	.50	1.25
S27 Ryan Malone	.50	1.25
S28 Simon Gagne	.75	2.00
S29 Semyon Varlamov	.75	2.00
S30 Alexander Semin	.75	2.00
S31 Marian Hossa	.60	1.50
S32 Brent Seabrook	.75	2.00
S33 Steve Mason	.60	1.50
S34 Jakub Voracek	.75	2.00
S35 Johan Franzen	.75	2.00
S36 Jimmy Howard	1.00	2.50
S37 David Legwand	.60	1.50
S38 Ryan Suter	.50	1.25
S39 Alex Steen	.75	2.00
S40 T.J. Oshie	1.25	3.00
S41 Olli Jokinen	.60	1.50
S42 Robyn Regehr	.50	1.25
S43 Chris Stewart	.60	1.50
S44 Milan Hejduk	.60	1.50
S45 Sam Gagner	.60	1.50
S46 Dustin Penner	.50	1.25
S47 Martin Havlat	.60	1.50
S48 Brent Burns	1.00	2.50
S49 Alexandre Burrows	.75	2.00
S50 Keith Ballard	.50	1.25
S51 Saku Koivu	.75	2.00
S52 Corey Perry	.75	2.00
S53 Stephane Robidas	.50	1.25
S54 Steve Ott	.60	1.50
S55 Dustin Brown	.75	2.00
S56 Ryan Smyth	.60	1.50
S57 Keith Yandle	.75	2.00
S58 Ed Jovanovski	.50	1.25
S59 Joe Pavelski	.75	2.00
S60 Dan Boyle	.60	1.50

2010-11 Adrenalyn XL Ultimate Signature

Card	Low	High
STATED ODDS 1:23		
U1 Ilya Kovalchuk	4.00	10.00
U2 Mark Streit	2.50	6.00
U3 Marian Gaborik	5.00	12.00
U4 Chris Pronger	3.00	8.00
U5 Sidney Crosby	12.00	30.00
U6 Tuukka Rask	4.00	10.00
U7 Ryan Miller	4.00	10.00
U8 Andrei Markov	4.00	10.00
U9 Daniel Alfredsson	4.00	10.00
U10 Dion Phaneuf	4.00	10.00
U11 Zach Bogosian	3.00	8.00
U12 Eric Staal	5.00	12.00
U13 Tomas Vokoun	3.00	8.00
U14 Steven Stamkos	8.00	20.00
U15 Alex Ovechkin	15.00	40.00
U16 Jonathan Toews	8.00	20.00
U17 Rick Nash	6.00	15.00
U18 Pavel Datsyuk	5.00	12.00
U19 Shea Weber	3.00	8.00
U20 Jaroslav Halak	4.00	10.00
U21 Jarome Iginla	4.00	10.00
U22 Paul Stastny	4.00	10.00
U23 Taylor Hall	12.00	30.00
U24 Mikko Koivu	4.00	10.00
U25 Henrik Sedin	4.00	10.00
U26 Ryan Getzlaf	6.00	15.00
U27 Brad Richards	4.00	10.00
U28 Drew Doughty	4.00	10.00
U29 Ilya Bryzgalov	3.00	8.00
U30 Joe Thornton	4.00	10.00

1956 Adventure R749

The Adventure series produced by Gum Products in 1956, contains a wide variety of subject matter. Cards in the set measure the standard size. The color drawings are printed on a heavy thickness of cardboard and have large white borders. The backs contain the card number, the caption, and a short text. The most expensive cards in the series of 100 are those associated with sports (Louis, Tunney, etc.). In addition, card number 86 (Schmelling) is notorious and sold at a premium price because of the Nazi symbol printed on the card. Although this set is considered by many to be a topical or non-sport set, several boxers are featured (cards 11, 22, 31-35, 41-44, 76-80, 86-90). One of the few cards of Boston-area legend Harry Agannis is in this set. The sports-related cards are in greater demand than the non-sport cards. These cards came in one-card penny packs where were packed 240 to a box.

Card	Low	High
COMPLETE SET (100)	225.00	450.00
63 Hockey's Hardy Perennials Chuck Rayner Gordie Howe	20.00	40.00

1990-91 Alberta International Team Canada

This 24-card set features the Canadian National Team and a bonus card of Vladislav Tretiak, the honorary captain of the Soviet Olympic team during the Pre-Olympic Hockey Tour. The cards are slightly smaller than standard size, measuring approximately 2 7/16" by 3 1/2".

Card	Low	High
COMPLETE SET (24)	6.00	15.00
1 Craig Billington	.40	1.00
2 Doug Dadswell	.40	1.00
3 Greg Andrusak	.25	.60
4 Karl Dykhuis	.25	.60
5 Gord Hynes	.25	.60
6 Ken MacArthur	.25	.60
7 Jim Paek	.25	.60
8 Brad Schlegel	.25	.60
9 Dave Archibald	.25	.60
10 Stu Barnes	.40	1.00
11 Brad Bennett	.25	.60
12 Todd Brost	.25	.60
13 Jose Charbonneau	.25	.60
14 Jason Lafreniere	.25	.60
15 Chris Lindberg	.25	.60
16 Ken Priestlay	.25	.60
17 Stephane Roy	.25	.60
18 Randy Smith	.25	.60
19 Todd Strueby	.25	.60
20 Vladislav Tretiak	1.50	4.00
21 Dave King CO	.25	.60
23 Checklist Card	.04	.10
NNO Title Card	.04	.10

1991-92 Alberta International Team Canada

Sponsored by Alberta Lotteries, this 24-card standard-size set features the Canadian National Team. The fronts feature posed player photos on the ice that are full-bleed on the left and bottom. The cards are unnumbered and checklisted below in alphabetical order.

Card	Low	High
COMPLETE SET (24)	4.80	12.00
1 Dave Archibald	.20	.50
2 Todd Brost	.20	.50
3 Sean Burke	.75	2.00
4 Terry Crisp ACO	.20	.50
5 Kevin Dahl	.20	.50
6 Karl Dykhuis	.20	.50
7 Wayne Fleming AGM/ACO	.02	.10
8 Curt Giles	.20	.50
9 Gord Hynes	.20	.50
10 Fabian Joseph	.20	.50
11 Joe Juneau	.40	1.00
12 Trevor Kidd	.40	1.00
13 Dave King GM/CO	.20	.50
14 Chris Kontos	.20	.50
15 Chris Lindberg	.20	.50
16 Kent Manderville	.20	.50
17 Adrien Plavsic	.20	.50
18 Dan Ratushny	.20	.50
19 Stephane Roy	.20	.50
20 Brad Schlegel	.20	.50
21 Scott Scissons	.20	.50
22 Randy Smith	.20	.50
23 Jason Woolley	.30	.75
24 Title Card	.02	.10

1992-93 Alberta International Team Canada

This 22-card set features the Canadian National Team as well as bonus cards of Mike Myers, honorary captain of the team, and of Vladislav Tretiak, honorary captain of Russia's National Team. The cards are slightly smaller than standard size, measuring 2 1/2" by 3 7/16". The cards are unnumbered and checklisted below in alphabetical order.

Card	Low	High
COMPLETE SET (22)	8.00	20.00
1 Dominic Amodeo	.20	.50
2 Mark Astley	.20	.50

3 Adrian Aucoin .40 1.00
4 Mark Bassen .20 .50
5 Eric Bellerose .20 .50
6 Mike Brewer .20 .50
7 Dany Dube CO .02 .10
8 Mike Fountain .30 .75
9 Todd Hlushko .20 .50
10 Hank Lammens .20 .50
11 Derek Laxdal .20 .50
12 Derek Mayer .20 .50
13 Keith Morris .20 .50
14 Mike Myers SNL 4.00 10.00
15 Jackson Penney .20 .50
16 Garth Premak .20 .50
17 Tom Renney CO .20 .50
18 Allain Roy .30 .75
19 Stephane Roy .20 .50
20 Trevor Sim .20 .50
21 Vladislav Tretiak 1.25 3.00
22 Title Card .02 .10

1993-94 Alberta International Team Canada

This 23-card standard-size set features players on the 1994 Canadian National Hockey Team. The cards are unnumbered and checklisted below in alphabetical order.

COMPLETE SET (23) 12.00 30.00
1 Adrian Aucoin .30 .75
2 Todd Brost .20 .50
3 Dany Dube .02 .10
4 David Harlock .20 .50
5 Corey Hirsch .30 .75
6 Todd Hlushko .20 .50
7 Fabian Joseph .20 .50
8 Paul Kariya 6.00 15.00
9 Chris Kontos .20 .50
10 Manny Legace 2.00 5.00
11 Brett Lindros .20 .50
12 Ken Lovsin .20 .50
13 Jason Marshall .20 .50
14 Derek Mayer .20 .50
15 Dwayne Norris .20 .50
16 Tom Renney CO .20 .50
17 Russ Romaniuk .20 .50
18 Brian Savage .60 1.50
19 Trevor Sim .20 .50
20 Chris Therien .30 .75
21 Todd Warriner .20 .50
22 Craig Woodcroft .20 .50
23 Title Card .02 .10

2008 All-Star Collection Series 1

COMPLETE SET (7) 10.00 20.00
1 Bobby Hull 2.50 6.00
2 Johnny Bower 1.50 4.00
3 Dick Duff 1.25 3.00
4 Dennis Hull 1.50 4.00
5 Pierre Pilote 1.50 4.00
6 Tony Esposito 1.50 4.00
7 Bobby Hull HOF 2.50 6.00

2008 All-Star Collection Series 1 Autographs

AUBH1 Bobby Hull 30.00 60.00
AUDD3 Dick Duff 10.00 20.00
AUDH4 Dennis Hull 12.50 25.00
AUJB2 Johnny Bower 15.00 30.00
AUPP5 Pierre Pilote 20.00 40.00
AUTE6 Tony Esposito 20.00 40.00

1992-93 All World Mario Lemieux Promos

This set consists of six standard-size cards. All cards feature the same color action photo of Mario Lemieux, skating with stick in both hands. On the first three cards, the top of the photo is oval-shaped and framed by yellow stripes. The space above the oval as well as the stripe at the bottom carrying player information are purple. The outer border is green. Inside green borders, the horizontal back has a color close-up photo, biography and statistics. On the second three cards listed below, the player photo is tilted slightly to the right and framed by a thin green border. Yellow stripes above and below the picture carry information, and the outer border is black-and-white speckled. The back has a similar design and displays a close-up color head shot and biographical and statistical information on a pastel green panel. All cards are numbered as number 1. The cards were issued three different ways, in Spanish, French, and English. The design and concept of these cards is very similar to the 1992 All World Troy Aikman promos.

COMPLETE SET (6) 10.00 25.00
COMMON CARD (1A-1F) 2.00 5.00

1993 American Licorice Sour Punch Caps

Printed in Canada and sponsored by the American Licorice Co., these individually wrapped cards were inserted in specially-marked packages of 4 1/2 oz. Sour Punch Candy Straws. Each package contained one card, measuring the standard size with two punch-out caps, each measuring 1 1/2" in diameter. One cap carries the Sour Punch logo and where appropriate, a flavor, while the other cap features a color player portrait with a black border. The cards are numbered on the front, and the backs are blank. There is a special promotion cap featuring Bobby Hull with no number, but the letter "P." This promo cap was used by the American Licorice sales brokerage as a sales sample.

COMPLETE SET (8) 4.80 12.00
1 Theo Fleury .50 1.25
2 Guy Lafleur 1.00 2.50
Blue Raspbe
3 Chris Chelios .50 1.25
Strawberr
4 Stan Mikita .50 1.25
Sour Apple Cap
5 Rocket Richard 1.00 2.50
Strawber
6 Steve Thomas .20 .50
Blue Raspberry Cap
7 Checklist 1 .08 .25
Sour Punch Cap Logo
8 Checklist 2 .08 .25
Sour Punch Cap Logo
P Bobby Hull 1.00 2.50
Sour Punch C

2007 Americana Promos

DISTRIBUTED AT TRADE SHOWS
PR Patrick Roy SL 1.25 3.00

2007 Americana Sports Legends

RANDOM INSERTS IN PACKS
STATED PRINT RUN 500 SERIAL #'d SETS
6 Tony Esposito 1.50 4.00
9 Patrick Roy 4.00 10.00

2007 Americana Sports Legends Material

RANDOM INSERTS IN PACKS
PRINT RUNS B/WN 25-500 COPIES PER
6 Tony Esposito Jsy/500 4.00 10.00

2007 Americana Sports Legends Signature

RANDOM INSERTS IN PACKS
PRINT RUNS B/WN 25-50 COPIES PER
6 Tony Esposito/25 15.00 40.00
9 Patrick Roy/25 50.00 100.00

2007 Americana Sports Legends Signature Material

*MTL: .5X TO 1.2X BASIC SIG
RANDOM INSERTS IN PACKS
PRINT RUNS B/WN 25-50 COPIES PER

1993 Anti-Gambling Postcards

COMPLETE SET (13) 6.00 15.00
11 Chris Chelios HK .50 1.25
12 Andy Moog HK .40 1.00

2005-06 Artifacts

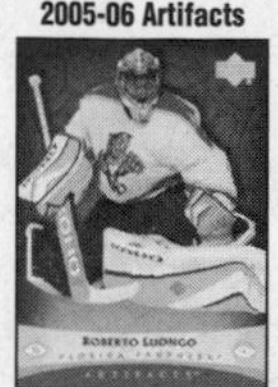

This 342-card set was released in a mix of product specific unopened and through inserts in Rookie Update. Cards numbered 1-242 were in the unopened product while cards 243-342 were inserts in Rookie Update. The unopened product came in five-card packs, with a $9.99 SRP, which came 10 packs to a box. Cards numbered 1-100 feature veterans in team alphabetical order while cards 101-150 feature retired greats in alphabetical order and All-Stars (151-200) in team alphabetical order. All cards 101-200 were issued to a stated print run of 899 serial numbered sets. Cards numbered 201-342 are all Rookie Cards amd all issued to 750 serial numbered sets with cards 201-242 in the unopened product and cards 243-342 in the Rookie Update packs.

COMP.SET w/o SPs (100) 15.00 30.00
101-200 AL/AS PRINT RUN 899
201-342 ROOKIE PRINT RUN 750
243-342 ISSUED IN ROOKIE UPDATE
1 Jean-Sebastien Giguere .30 .75
2 Sergei Fedorov .50 1.25
3 Joffrey Lupul .25 .60
4 Dany Heatley .30 .75
5 Ilya Kovalchuk .30 .75
6 Kari Lehtonen .25 .60
7 Andrew Raycroft .25 .60
8 Joe Thornton .40 1.00
9 Glen Murray .25 .60
10 Sergei Samsonov .25 .60
11 Patrice Bergeron .40 1.00
12 Martin Biron .25 .60
13 Maxim Afinogenov .20 .50
14 Chris Drury .25 .60
15 Jarome Iginla .30 .75
16 Miikka Kiprusoff .25 .60
17 Jordan Leopold .20 .50
18 Eric Staal .40 1.00
19 Justin Williams .25 .60
20 Erik Cole .25 .60
21 Tuomo Ruutu .30 .75
22 Eric Daze .25 .60
23 Tyler Arnason .20 .50
24 Joe Sakic .50 1.25
25 Rob Blake .30 .75
26 David Aebischer .25 .60
27 Milan Hejduk .25 .60
28 Alex Tanguay .30 .75
29 Geoff Sanderson .20 .50
30 Rick Nash .30 .75
31 Nikolai Zherdev .20 .50
32 Mike Modano .50 1.25
33 Bill Guerin .30 .75
34 Brenden Morrow .25 .60
35 Marty Turco .30 .75
36 Manny Legace .30 .75
37 Pavel Datsyuk .40 1.00
38 Brendan Shanahan .40 1.00
39 Steve Yzerman .75 2.00
40 Henrik Zetterberg .40 1.00
41 Ty Conklin .25 .60
42 Ryan Smyth .25 .60
43 Stephen Weiss .20 .50
44 Roberto Luongo .50 1.25
45 Olli Jokinen .30 .75
46 Alexander Frolov .20 .50
47 Dustin Brown .30 .75
48 Luc Robitaille .30 .75
49 Dwayne Roloson .25 .60
50 Marian Gaborik .50 1.25
51 Mike Ribeiro .25 .60
52 Michael Ryder .25 .60
53 Jose Theodore .30 .75
54 Saku Koivu .30 .75
55 Steve Sullivan .20 .50
56 Jordin Tootoo .30 .75
57 Tomas Vokoun .25 .60
58 Martin Brodeur .60 1.50
59 Scott Gomez .25 .60
60 Jeff Friesen .20 .50
61 Patrik Elias .30 .75
62 Tom Poti .20 .50
63 Mark Messier .50 1.25
64 Jaromir Jagr .75 2.00
65 Mark Parrish .20 .50
66 Rick DiPietro .25 .60
67 Alexei Yashin .25 .60
68 Daniel Alfredsson .30 .75
69 Dominik Hasek .50 1.25
70 Marian Hossa .25 .60
71 Jason Spezza .30 .75
72 Martin Havlat .30 .75
73 Robert Esche .25 .60
74 Keith Primeau .30 .75
75 Simon Gagne .30 .75
76 Michal Handzus .25 .60
77 Brett Hull .40 1.00
78 Mike Comrie .25 .60
79 Shane Doan .25 .60
80 Marc-Andre Fleury .50 1.25
81 Mario Lemieux 1.00 2.50
82 Mark Recchi .40 1.00
83 Evgeni Nabokov .25 .60
84 Patrick Marleau .30 .75
85 Jonathan Cheechoo .30 .75
86 Mike Sillinger .20 .50
87 Doug Weight .30 .75
88 Keith Tkachuk .30 .75
89 Brad Richards .30 .75
90 Fredrik Modin .20 .50
91 Martin St. Louis .30 .75
92 Vincent Lecavalier .25 .60
93 Ed Belfour .30 .75
94 Owen Nolan .25 .60
95 Mats Sundin .30 .75
96 Nik Antropov .25 .60
97 Ed Jovanovski .25 .60
98 Markus Naslund .30 .75
99 Trevor Linden .30 .75
100 Olaf Kolzig .30 .75
101 Glenn Anderson AL 1.00 2.50
102 Bill Barber AL .75 2.00
103 Jean Beliveau AL 1.00 2.50
104 Mike Bossy AL 1.00 2.50
105 Johnny Bower AL 1.25 3.00
106 Scotty Bowman AL .75 2.00
107 Johnny Bucyk AL .75 2.00
108 Wayne Cashman AL .60 1.50
109 Gerry Cheevers AL 2.00 5.00
110 Don Cherry AL 1.00 2.50
111 Bobby Clarke AL 1.00 2.50
112 Gordie Howe AL 3.00 8.00
113 Wayne Gretzky AL 5.00 12.00
114 Marcel Dionne AL 1.25 3.00
115 Phil Esposito AL 1.50 4.00
116 Tony Esposito AL 1.00 2.50
117 Grant Fuhr AL 1.00 2.50
118 Bernie Geoffrion AL .75 2.00
119 Clark Gillies AL 1.00 2.50
120 Butch Goring AL .60 1.50
121 Glenn Hall AL .60 1.50
122 Paul Henderson AL .75 2.00
123 Ron Hextall AL 1.50 4.00
124 Al Iafrate AL .75 2.00
125 Red Kelly AL 1.00 2.50
126 Jari Kurri AL 1.00 2.50
127 Guy LaFleur AL 1.25 3.00
128 Igor Larionov AL 1.00 2.50
129 Reggie Leach AL .60 1.50
130 Hakan Loob AL .60 1.50
131 Frank Mahovlich AL 1.00 2.50
132 Rick Martin AL .60 1.50
133 Lanny McDonald AL 1.00 2.50
134 Stan Mikita AL 1.25 3.00
135 Dickie Moore AL .60 1.50
136 Ken Morrow AL .60 1.50
137 Larry Murphy AL .75 2.00
138 Cam Neely AL 1.00 2.50
139 Mats Naslund AL 1.00 2.50
140 Bob Nystrom AL .60 1.50
141 Terry O'Reilly AL .75 2.00
142 Brad Park AL .75 2.00
143 Gilbert Perreault AL 1.00 2.50
144 Rene Robert AL .60 1.50
145 Derek Sanderson AL .60 1.50
146 Denis Savard AL 1.25 3.00
147 Peter Stastny AL 1.00 2.50
148 Thomas Steen AL .60 1.50
149 Dave Taylor AL .75 2.00
150 Bryan Trottier AL 1.25 3.00
151 Sergei Fedorov AS 1.50 4.00
152 Ilya Kovalchuk AS 1.00 2.50
153 Dany Heatley AS 1.00 2.50
154 Joe Thornton AS 1.25 3.00
155 Glen Murray AS .75 2.00
156 Jarome Iginla AS 1.00 2.50
157 Eric Daze AS .75 2.00
158 Joe Sakic AS 1.50 4.00
159 Rob Blake AS 1.00 2.50
160 Milan Hejduk AS .75 2.00
161 Alex Tanguay AS 1.00 2.50
162 Rick Nash AS 1.00 2.50
163 Mike Modano AS 1.50 4.00
164 Bill Guerin AS 1.00 2.50
165 Marty Turco AS 1.00 2.50
166 Brendan Shanahan AS 1.25 3.00
167 Steve Yzerman AS 2.50 6.00
168 Pavel Datsyuk AS 1.25 3.00
169 Roberto Luongo AS 1.50 4.00
170 Luc Robitaille AS 1.00 2.50
171 Marian Gaborik AS 1.50 4.00
172 Jose Theodore AS 1.00 2.50
173 Saku Koivu AS 1.00 2.50
174 Tomas Vokoun AS .75 2.00
175 Martin Brodeur AS 2.00 5.00
176 Scott Gomez AS .75 2.00
177 Patrik Elias AS 1.00 2.50
178 Mark Messier AS 1.50 4.00
179 Jaromir Jagr AS 2.50 6.00
180 Alexei Yashin AS .75 2.00
181 Mark Parrish AS .60 1.50
182 Dominik Hasek AS 1.50 4.00
183 Marian Hossa AS .75 2.00
184 Daniel Alfredsson AS 1.00 2.50
185 Keith Primeau AS 1.00 2.50
186 Simon Gagne AS 1.00 2.50
187 Brett Hull AS 1.25 3.00
188 Shane Doan AS .75 2.00
189 Mario Lemieux AS 3.00 8.00
190 Mark Recchi AS 1.25 3.00
191 Evgeni Nabokov AS .75 2.00
192 Keith Tkachuk AS 1.00 2.50
193 Martin St. Louis AS 1.00 2.50
194 Vincent Lecavalier AS .75 2.00
195 Ed Belfour AS 1.00 2.50
196 Mats Sundin AS 1.00 2.50
197 Owen Nolan AS .75 2.00
198 Markus Naslund AS 1.00 2.50
199 Ed Jovanovski AS .75 2.00
200 Olaf Kolzig AS 1.00 2.50
201 Corey Perry RC 7.50 15.00
202 Braydon Coburn RC 3.00 8.00
203 Hannu Toivonen RC 3.00 8.00
204 Thomas Vanek RC 6.00 15.00
205 Dion Phaneuf RC 5.00 12.00
206 Cam Ward RC 5.00 12.00
207 Brent Seabrook RC 6.00 15.00
208 Wojtek Wolski RC 2.50 6.00
209 Gilbert Brule RC 3.00 8.00
210 Jussi Jokinen RC 3.00 8.00
211 Jim Howard RC 8.00 20.00
212 Brad Winchester RC 3.00 8.00
213 Rostislav Olesz RC 2.50 6.00
214 George Parros RC 2.00 5.00
215 Matt Foy RC 2.00 5.00
216 Alexander Perezhogin RC 2.50 6.00
217 Ryan Suter RC 4.00 10.00
218 Zach Parise RC 8.00 20.00
219 Henrik Lundqvist RC 12.00 30.00
220 Robert Nilsson RC 3.00 8.00
221 Andrej Meszaros RC 2.50 6.00
222 Jeff Carter RC 5.00 12.00
223 David Leneveu RC 2.50 6.00
224 Sidney Crosby RC 150.00 300.00
225 Ryane Clowe RC 4.00 10.00
226 Jeff Woywitka RC 2.00 5.00
227 Evgeny Artykuhin RC 2.50 6.00
228 Alexander Steen RC 6.00 15.00
229 Rob McVicar RC 2.50 6.00
230 Alexander Ovechkin RC 30.00 80.00
231 Peter Budaj RC 4.00 10.00
232 Rene Bourque RC 3.00 8.00
233 Yann Danis RC 2.50 6.00
234 Eric Nystrom RC 2.50 6.00
235 Mike Richards RC 6.00 15.00
236 Kevin Nastiuk RC 2.00 5.00
237 Petteri Nokelainen RC 2.00 5.00
238 Ryan Getzlaf RC 8.00 20.00
239 Johan Franzen RC 5.00 12.00
240 Brandon Bochenski RC 3.00 8.00
241 Patrick Eaves RC 3.00 8.00
242 Jim Slater RC 2.50 6.00
243 Dustin Penner RC 3.00 8.00
244 Zenon Konopka RC 2.00 5.00
245 Michael Wall RC 2.50 6.00
246 Adam Berkhoel RC 2.50 6.00
247 Andrew Alberts RC 2.00 5.00
248 Milan Jurcina RC 2.50 6.00
249 Ben Walter RC 2.00 5.00
250 Jordan Sigalet RC 2.00 5.00
251 Nathan Paetsch RC 2.50 6.00
252 Chris Thorburn RC 2.50 6.00
253 Daniel Paille RC 3.00 8.00
254 Mark Giordano RC 3.00 8.00
255 Niklas Nordgren RC 3.00 8.00
256 Andrew Ladd RC 4.00 10.00
257 Chad Larose RC 2.00 5.00
258 Danny Richmond RC 2.00 5.00
259 Duncan Keith RC 6.00 15.00
260 Cam Barker RC 2.50 6.00
261 Martin St. Pierre RC 2.00 5.00
262 Corey Crawford RC 8.00 20.00
263 James Wisniewski RC 2.50 6.00
264 Brad Richardson RC 3.00 8.00
265 Vitaly Kolesnik RC 2.50 6.00
266 Alexandre Picard RC 2.00 5.00
267 Ole-Kristian Tollefsen RC 2.50 6.00
268 Steven Goertzen RC 2.00 5.00
269 Geoff Platt RC 2.50 6.00
270 Joakim Lindstrom RC 2.00 5.00
271 Junior Lessard RC 2.00 5.00
272 Vojtech Polak RC 2.00 5.00
273 Brett Lebda RC 2.00 5.00
274 Kyle Quincey RC 2.50 6.00
275 Valtteri Filppula RC 4.00 10.00
276 Danny Syvret RC 2.00 5.00
277 Kyle Brodziak RC 2.00 5.00
278 J-F Jacques RC 2.00 5.00
279 Matt Greene RC 2.00 5.00
280 Anthony Stewart RC 2.50 6.00
281 Greg Jacina RC 2.00 5.00
282 Petr Taticek RC 2.50 6.00
283 Yanick Lehoux RC 3.00 8.00
284 Jeff Tambellini RC 2.00 5.00
285 Petr Kanko RC 2.50 6.00
286 Richard Petiot RC 2.50 6.00
287 Mikko Koivu RC 4.00 10.00
288 Derek Boogaard RC 4.00 10.00
289 Jonathan Ferland RC 2.50 6.00
290 Maxim Lapierre RC 3.00 8.00
291 Jean-Philippe Cote RC 2.00 5.00
292 Andrei Kostitsyn RC 4.00 10.00
293 Greg Zanon RC 2.50 6.00
294 Kevin Klein RC 2.00 5.00
295 Pekka Rinne RC 5.00 12.00
296 Barry Tallackson RC 2.50 6.00
297 Cam Janssen RC 2.50 6.00
298 Jason Ryznar RC 2.00 5.00
299 Jeremy Colliton RC 2.00 5.00
300 Chris Campoli RC 2.00 5.00
301 Bruno Gervais RC 2.00 5.00
302 Petr Prucha RC 3.00 8.00
303 Ryan Hollweg RC 2.00 5.00
304 Al Montoya RC 3.00 8.00
305 Brian McGrattan RC 2.00 5.00
306 Christoph Schubert RC 2.00 5.00
307 R.J. Umberger RC 3.00 8.00
308 Stefan Ruzicka RC 2.00 5.00
309 Ben Eager RC 2.50 6.00
310 Alexandre Picard RC 2.00 5.00
311 Keith Ballard RC 2.50 6.00
312 Matt Jones RC 2.00 5.00
313 Maxime Talbot RC 3.00 8.00
314 Erik Christensen RC 2.00 5.00
315 Ryan Whitney RC 3.00 8.00
316 Colby Armstrong RC 3.00 8.00
317 Josh Gorges RC 2.50 6.00
318 Dimitri Patzold RC 2.00 5.00
319 Steve Bernier RC 3.00 8.00
320 Grant Stevenson RC 2.00 5.00
321 Doug Murray RC 2.00 5.00
322 Jay McClement RC 2.00 5.00
323 Jeff Hoggan RC 2.00 5.00
324 Colin Hemingway RC 2.00 5.00
325 Dennis Wideman RC 2.00 5.00
326 Lee Stempniak RC 3.00 8.00
327 Chris Beckford-Tseu RC 2.50 6.00
328 Gerald Coleman RC 2.00 5.00
329 Nick Tarnasky RC 2.00 5.00
330 Paul Ranger RC 2.00 5.00
331 Darren Reid RC 2.00 5.00
332 Ryan Craig RC 2.00 5.00
333 Andrew Wozniewski RC 2.50 6.00
334 Staffan Kronwall RC 2.00 5.00
335 Jay Harrison RC 2.50 6.00
336 Kevin Bieksa RC 6.00 15.00
337 Rick Rypien RC 6.00 15.00
338 Rob McVicar 2.50 6.00
339 Tomas Mojzis RC 2.00 5.00
340 Tomas Fleischmann RC 3.00 8.00
341 Jakub Klepis RC 2.00 5.00
342 Mike Green RC 4.00 10.00

2005-06 Artifacts Blue

*1-100 VETS/75: 2.5X TO 6X BASIC CARDS
*101-200 AL/AS/75: .8X TO 2X AL/AS/899
STATED PRINT RUN 75 SER.#'d SETS
63 Mark Messier 4.00 10.00
178 Mark Messier 4.00 10.00

2005-06 Artifacts Green

*1-100 VETS/25: 4X TO 10X BASIC CARDS
*101-200 AL/AS/25: 1.2X TO 3X AL/AS/899
PRINT RUN 25 SER.#'d SETS
63 Mark Messier 6.00 15.00
178 Mark Messier 6.00 15.00

2005-06 Artifacts Pewter

*1-100 VETS/100: 2X TO 5X BASIC CARDS
*101-200 AL/AS/100: 6X TO 1.5X AL/AS/899
PRINT RUN 100 SER.#'d SETS
63 Mark Messier 3.00 8.00
178 Mark Messier 3.00 8.00

2005-06 Artifacts Red

*1-100 VETS/50: 3X TO 8X BASIC CARDS
*101-200 AL/AS/50: 1X TO 3X AL/AS/899
PRINT RUN 50 SER.#'d SETS
63 Mark Messier 5.00 12.00
178 Mark Messier 6.00 15.00

2005-06 Artifacts Autofacts

STATED PRINT RUN 100 SER.#'d SETS
AFAF Alexander Frolov 6.00 15.00
AFAH Ales Hemsky 6.00 15.00
AFAM Antti Miettinen 4.00 10.00
AFAR Andrew Raycroft 6.00 15.00
AFAT Alex Tanguay 6.00 15.00
AFBB Brad Boyes 4.00 10.00
AFBC Bobby Clarke 10.00 25.00
AFBI Martin Biron 6.00 15.00
AFBL Brian Leetch 8.00 20.00
AFBM Bryan McCabe 4.00 10.00
AFBO Mike Bossy 10.00 25.00
AFBR Brad Richards 6.00 15.00
AFCD Chris Drury 6.00 15.00
AFCE Christian Ehrhoff 4.00 10.00
AFCN Cam Neely 8.00 20.00
AFCO Bob Cole 4.00 10.00
AFCP Chris Pronger 6.00 15.00
AFDA David Aebischer 6.00 15.00
AFDC Don Cherry 15.00 40.00
AFDL David Legwand 4.00 10.00
AFDM Darren McCarty 8.00 20.00
AFDS Denis Savard 6.00 15.00
AFDU Dustin Brown 5.00 12.00
AFEC Erik Cole 4.00 10.00
AFES Eric Staal 10.00 25.00
AFGF Grant Fuhr 10.00 25.00
AFGL Georges Laraque 4.00 10.00
AFGW Gump Worsley 8.00 20.00
AFHE Milan Hejduk 8.00 20.00
AFHO Marcel Hossa 4.00 10.00
AFHS Marian Hossa 8.00 20.00
AFHZ Henrik Zetterberg 10.00 25.00
AFIK Ilya Kovalchuk 10.00 25.00
AFJB Jay Bouwmeester 4.00 10.00
AFJC Jonathan Cheechoo 10.00 25.00
AFJG Jean-Sebastien Giguere 6.00 15.00
AFJI Jarome Iginla 12.00 30.00
AFJK Jari Kurri 8.00 20.00
AFJL Joffrey Lupul 6.00 15.00
AFJR Jeremy Roenick 8.00 20.00
AFJS Jason Spezza 8.00 20.00
AFJT Joe Thornton 12.00 30.00
AFJW Justin Williams 4.00 10.00
AFKD Kris Draper 4.00 10.00
AFKH Ken Hodge 4.00 10.00
AFKL Kari Lehtonen 8.00 20.00
AFLN Ladislav Nagy 4.00 10.00
AFLR Luc Robitaille 6.00 15.00
AFMA Maxim Afinogenov 6.00 15.00
AFMC Mike Cammalleri 6.00 15.00
AFMF Marc-Andre Fleury 12.00 30.00
AFMG Marian Gaborik 10.00 25.00
AFMH Martin Havlat 8.00 20.00
AFML Manny Legace 6.00 15.00
AFMM Mike Modano 10.00 25.00
AFMN Markus Naslund 6.00 15.00
AFMO Brendan Morrison 4.00 10.00
AFMP Mark Popovic 4.00 10.00
AFMR Mike Ribeiro 4.00 10.00
AFMT Marty Turco 6.00 15.00
AFNA Nikolai Antropov 4.00 10.00
AFNH Nathan Horton 5.00 12.00
AFNO Mika Noronen 4.00 10.00
AFNY Bob Nystrom 4.00 10.00
AFNZ Nikolai Zherdev 4.00 10.00
AFOK Dave Taylor 4.00 10.00
AFPB Patrice Bergeron 8.00 20.00
AFPS Philippe Sauve 4.00 10.00
AFPW Peter Worrell 4.00 10.00
AFRB Rob Blake 4.00 10.00
AFRE Robert Esche 8.00 20.00
AFRF Ruslan Fedotenko 4.00 10.00
AFRH Ron Hextall 15.00 40.00
AFRK Ryan Kesler 12.00 30.00
AFRL Roberto Luongo 8.00 20.00
AFRM Ryan Miller 6.00 15.00
AFRN Rick Nash 10.00 25.00
AFRS Ryan Smyth 6.00 15.00
AFRY Michael Ryder 8.00 20.00
AFRZ Richard Zednik 4.00 10.00
AFSC Dave Schultz 6.00 15.00
AFSG Simon Gagne 8.00 20.00
AFSK Saku Koivu 8.00 20.00
AFSL Martin St. Louis 6.00 15.00
AFSS Steve Sullivan 4.00 10.00
AFST Matt Stajan 6.00 15.00
AFSU Mats Sundin 10.00 25.00
AFSW Stephen Weiss 4.00 10.00
AFTC Ty Conklin 4.00 10.00
AFTH Trent Hunter 4.00 10.00
AFTL Trevor Linden 10.00 25.00
AFTR Tuomo Ruutu 6.00 15.00
AFTS Tony Salmelainen 4.00 10.00
AFVL Vincent Lecavalier 8.00 20.00
AFWC Wayne Cashman 4.00 10.00
AFZC Zdeno Chara 6.00 15.00

2005-06 Artifacts Autofacts Copper

*COPPER/75: .5X TO 1.2X BASIC AUTO
AFDH Dominik Hasek 10.00 25.00
AFGH Gordie Howe 60.00 120.00
AFMB Martin Brodeur 40.00 100.00
AFWG Wayne Gretzky 75.00 150.00

2005-06 Artifacts Autofacts Silver

*SILVER/50: .6X TO 1.5X BASIC AUTO
STATED PRINT RUN 50 SER.#'d SETS
AFDH Dominik Hasek 12.00 30.00
AFGH Gordie Howe 50.00 100.00
AFMB Martin Brodeur 40.00 100.00
AFWG Wayne Gretzky 150.00 250.00

2005-06 Artifacts Frozen Artifacts

STATED PRINT RUN 275 SER.#'d SETS
*COPPER/125: .5X TO 1.2X JSY/275
*SILVER/50: .6X TO 1.5X JSY/275
*MAROON/25: .8X TO 2X JSY/275
*DUAL SWATCH/65: .8X TO 2X JSY/275
*DUAL COPPER/50: .8X TO 2X JSY/275
*DUAL MAROON/15: 1.2X TO 3X JSY/275
*DUAL SILVER/25: 1X TO 2.5X JSY/275
*PATCH/50: 1X TO 2.5X JSY/275
*DUAL PATCH/15: 1.5X TO 4X JSY/275
FAAF Alexander Frolov 2.50 6.00
FAAM Al MacInnis 4.00 10.00
FABC Bobby Clarke 4.00 10.00
FABG Bernie Geoffrion 2.50 6.00
FABH Brett Hull 5.00 12.00
FABM Brendan Morrison 2.50 6.00
FABO Jay Bouwmeester 4.00 10.00
FABR Brad Richards 4.00 10.00
FABS Borje Salming 4.00 10.00
FABT Bryan Trottier 5.00 12.00
FACO Chris Osgood 4.00 10.00
FADC Dan Cloutier 3.00 8.00
FADH Dominik Hasek 6.00 15.00
FADR Derek Roy 2.50 6.00
FADS Darryl Sittler 3.00 8.00
FADU Dustin Brown 4.00 10.00
FADW Doug Weight 4.00 10.00
FAEB Ed Belfour 4.00 10.00
FAEL Eric Lindros 6.00 15.00
FAGR Gary Roberts 2.50 6.00
FAGU Bill Guerin 4.00 10.00
FAHO Marcel Hossa 2.50 6.00
FAHZ Henrik Zetterberg 5.00 12.00
FAJB Jean Beliveau 4.00 10.00
FAJK Jari Kurri 4.00 10.00
FAJL Joffrey Lupul 3.00 8.00
FAJO Jose Theodore 4.00 10.00
FAJT Jocelyn Thibault 3.00 8.00
FAJW Justin Williams 3.00 8.00
FAKD Kris Draper 5.00 12.00
FAMG Marian Gaborik 6.00 15.00
FAMH Martin Havlat 4.00 10.00
FAML Mario Lemieux 12.00 30.00
FAMO Alexander Mogilny 3.00 8.00
FAMR Mike Ribeiro 3.00 8.00
FAMT Marty Turco 4.00 10.00
FANH Nathan Horton 4.00 10.00
FAON Owen Nolan 3.00 8.00
FAPK Paul Kariya 5.00 12.00
FARA Bill Ranford 4.00 10.00
FARB Ray Bourque 4.00 10.00
FARD Rick DiPietro 3.00 8.00
FARE Mark Recchi 5.00 12.00
FARH Ron Hextall 6.00 15.00
FARL Roberto Luongo 6.00 15.00
FASA Denis Savard 5.00 12.00
FASL Martin St. Louis 4.00 10.00
FATE Tony Esposito 4.00 10.00
FAWG Wayne Gretzky 20.00 50.00

2005-06 Artifacts Goalie Gear

STATED PRINT RUN 50 SER.#'d SETS
*DUAL PATCH/15: 1X TO 2.5X JSY/50
FGCO Chris Osgood 6.00 15.00
FGDH Dominik Hasek 10.00 25.00
FGEB Ed Belfour 6.00 15.00
FGGC Gerry Cheevers 12.00 30.00
FGJO Jose Theodore 6.00 15.00
FGJT Jocelyn Thibault 5.00 12.00
FGMT Marty Turco 6.00 15.00
FGRA Bill Ranford 6.00 15.00
FGRD Rick DiPietro 5.00 12.00
FGRL Roberto Luongo 10.00 25.00
FGTE Tony Esposito 6.00 15.00

2005-06 Artifacts Treasured Patches

TPAT Alex Tanguay 6.00 15.00
TPBL Brian Leetch 6.00 15.00
TPBS Brendan Shanahan 8.00 20.00
TPCJ Curtis Joseph 6.00 15.00
TPCP Chris Pronger 5.00 12.00
TPDA Daniel Alfredsson 6.00 15.00
TPDH Dany Heatley 6.00 15.00
TPEB Ed Belfour 6.00 15.00
TPHA Dominik Hasek 10.00 25.00
TPHO Marian Hossa 5.00 12.00
TPIK Ilya Kovalchuk 6.00 15.00
TPJG Jean-Sebastien Giguere 6.00 15.00
TPJI Jarome Iginla 6.00 15.00
TPJJ Jaromir Jagr 15.00 40.00
TPJO Jose Theodore 6.00 15.00
TPJR Jeremy Roenick 6.00 15.00
TPJS Joe Sakic 10.00 25.00
TPJT Joe Thornton 8.00 20.00
TPKP Keith Primeau 6.00 15.00
TPMB Martin Brodeur 12.00 30.00
TPMD Marc Denis 5.00 12.00
TPMG Marian Gaborik 10.00 25.00
TPMH Milan Hejduk 5.00 12.00
TPML Mario Lemieux 20.00 50.00
TPMM Mike Modano 10.00 25.00
TPMN Markus Naslund 6.00 15.00
TPMS Mark Messier 10.00 25.00
TPNK Nikolai Khabibulin 6.00 15.00
TPPD Pavel Datsyuk 8.00 20.00
TPPE Patrik Elias 6.00 15.00
TPPF Peter Forsberg 8.00 20.00
TPRN Rick Nash 6.00 15.00
TPSD Shane Doan 5.00 12.00
TPSF Sergei Fedorov 10.00 25.00
TPSK Saku Koivu 6.00 15.00
TPSL Martin St. Louis 6.00 15.00
TPSP Jason Spezza 6.00 15.00
TPSS Scott Stevens 6.00 15.00
TPSU Mats Sundin 6.00 15.00
TPSY Steve Yzerman 15.00 40.00
TPTB Todd Bertuzzi 6.00 15.00
TPTR Tuomo Ruutu 6.00 15.00
TPTS Teemu Selanne 12.00 30.00
TPWG Wayne Gretzky 30.00 80.00
TPZP Zigmund Palffy 6.00 15.00

2005-06 Artifacts Treasured Swatches

STATED PRINT RUN 275 SER.#'d SETS
*COPPER/125: .5X TO 1.2X BASIC JSY/275
*SILVER/50: .6X TO 1.5X BASIC JSY/275
*MAROON/25: .8X TO 2X BASIC JSY/275
*DUAL PATCH/15: 1.5X TO 4X BASIC JSY/275
*DUAL SWATCH/65: .8X TO 2X JSY/275
*DUAL COPPER/50: .8X TO 2X JSY/275
*DUAL MAROON/15: 1.2X TO 3X JSY/275
*DUAL SILVER/25: 1X TO 2.5X JSY/275
*PATCH/50: 1X TO 2.5X BASIC JSY/275
TSAT Alex Tanguay 4.00 10.00
TSBL Brian Leetch 4.00 10.00
TSBS Brendan Shanahan 5.00 12.00
TSCJ Curtis Joseph 4.00 10.00
TSCP Chris Pronger 3.00 8.00
TSDA Daniel Alfredsson 4.00 10.00
TSDH Dany Heatley 4.00 10.00
TSEB Ed Belfour 4.00 10.00
TSHA Dominik Hasek 6.00 15.00
TSHO Marian Hossa 3.00 8.00
TSIK Ilya Kovalchuk 4.00 10.00
TSJG Jean-Sebastien Giguere 4.00 10.00
TSJI Jarome Iginla 4.00 10.00
TSJJ Jaromir Jagr 10.00 25.00
TSJO Jose Theodore 4.00 10.00
TSJR Jeremy Roenick 4.00 10.00
TSJS Joe Sakic 6.00 15.00
TSJT Joe Thornton 5.00 12.00
TSKP Keith Primeau 4.00 10.00
TSMB Martin Brodeur 8.00 20.00
TSMD Marc Denis 3.00 8.00
TSMG Marian Gaborik 6.00 15.00
TSMH Milan Hejduk 3.00 8.00
TSML Mario Lemieux 12.00 30.00
TSMM Mike Modano 6.00 15.00
TSMN Markus Naslund 4.00 10.00
TSMP Michael Peca 3.00 8.00
TSMS Mark Messier 6.00 15.00
TSNK Nikolai Khabibulin 4.00 10.00
TSPD Pavel Datsyuk 5.00 12.00
TSPE Patrik Elias 4.00 10.00
TSPF Peter Forsberg 5.00 12.00
TSRN Rick Nash 4.00 10.00
TSRS Ryan Smyth 3.00 8.00
TSSD Shane Doan 3.00 8.00
TSSF Sergei Fedorov 6.00 15.00
TSSK Saku Koivu 4.00 10.00
TSSL Martin St. Louis 4.00 10.00
TSSP Jason Spezza 4.00 10.00
TSSS Scott Stevens 4.00 10.00
TSST Matt Stajan 3.00 8.00
TSSU Mats Sundin 4.00 10.00
TSSY Steve Yzerman 10.00 25.00
TSTB Todd Bertuzzi 4.00 10.00
TSTR Tuomo Ruutu 4.00 10.00
TSTS Teemu Selanne 8.00 20.00
TSVL Vincent Lecavalier 3.00 8.00
TSWG Wayne Gretzky 20.00 50.00
TSZP Zigmund Palffy 4.00 10.00

2006-07 Artifacts

This 272-card set was issued in four-card packs which came 10 to a box. Cards numbered 1-100 featured NHL veterans while cards 101-150 featured retired greats and cards 151-200 featured NHL all-stars. All cards between 101 and 200 were issued to a stated print run of 999 serial numbered sets. Cards numbered 201-272 feature NHL rookies and those were broken down into cards 201-230 with a print run of 999 serial numbered sets and cards 231-272 with a stated print run of 599 serial numbered sets. Those cards 231-272 were issued as redemptions from cards in packs.

COMP.SET w/o SPs (100) 12.00 30.00
101-200 AS/LEGEND PRINT RUN 999
201-230 ROOKIE PRINT RUN 999
231-272 ROOKIE PRINT RUN 599
1 Alexander Ovechkin 1.50 4.00
2 Olaf Kolzig .40 1.00
3 Roberto Luongo .60 1.50
4 Markus Naslund .30 .75
5 Brendan Morrison .25 .60
6 Mats Sundin .40 1.00
7 Darcy Tucker .30 .75
8 Alexander Steen .40 1.00
9 Andrew Raycroft .30 .75
10 Michael Peca .30 .75
11 Brad Richards .40 1.00
12 Vincent Lecavalier .30 .75
13 Martin St. Louis .40 1.00
14 Keith Tkachuk .40 1.00
15 Doug Weight .40 1.00
16 Patrick Marleau .40 1.00
17 Joe Thornton .50 1.25
18 Jonathan Cheechoo .40 1.00
19 Vesa Toskala .30 .75
20 Mark Recchi .50 1.25
21 Sidney Crosby 1.50 4.00
22 Marc-Andre Fleury .60 1.50
23 Colby Armstrong .30 .75
24 Shane Doan .30 .75
25 Curtis Joseph .40 1.00
26 Jeremy Roenick .40 1.00
27 Mike Richards .40 1.00
28 Peter Forsberg .50 1.25
29 Simon Gagne .40 1.00
30 Jeff Carter .40 1.00
31 Jason Spezza .40 1.00
32 Dany Heatley .40 1.00
33 Daniel Alfredsson .40 1.00
34 Martin Gerber .30 .75
35 Brendan Shanahan .50 1.25
36 Jaromir Jagr 1.00 2.50
37 Henrik Lundqvist .75 2.00
38 Petr Prucha .30 .75
39 Miroslav Satan .30 .75
40 Rick DiPietro .30 .75
41 Alexei Yashin .30 .75
42 Patrik Elias .40 1.00
43 Martin Brodeur .75 2.00
44 Brian Gionta .30 .75
45 Paul Kariya .50 1.25
46 Tomas Vokoun .30 .75
47 Saku Koivu .40 1.00
48 Cristobal Huet .30 .75
49 Michael Ryder .25 .60
50 Alex Kovalev .30 .75
51 Pavol Demitra .50 1.25
52 Marian Gaborik .50 1.25
53 Manny Fernandez .30 .75
54 Alexander Frolov .25 .60
55 Rob Blake .40 1.00
56 Nathan Horton .40 1.00
57 Olli Jokinen .40 1.00
58 Todd Bertuzzi .40 1.00
59 Ed Belfour .40 1.00
60 Ales Hemsky .30 .75
61 Joffrey Lupul .30 .75
62 Ryan Smyth .30 .75
63 Henrik Zetterberg .50 1.25
64 Pavel Datsyuk .50 1.25
65 Nicklas Lidstrom .40 1.00
66 Dominik Hasek .50 1.25
67 Mike Modano .60 1.50
68 Marty Turco .40 1.00
69 Brenden Morrow .30 .75
70 Eric Lindros .60 1.50
71 Fredrik Modin .25 .60
72 Rick Nash .40 1.00
73 Sergei Fedorov .60 1.50
74 Joe Sakic .60 1.50
75 Milan Hejduk .30 .75
76 Jose Theodore .40 1.00
77 Marek Svatos .25 .60
78 Martin Havlat .25 .60
79 Nikolai Khabibulin .40 1.00
80 Tuomo Ruutu .40 1.00
81 Eric Staal .50 1.25
82 Cam Ward .40 1.00
83 Rod Brind'Amour .40 1.00
84 Jarome Iginla .40 1.00
85 Miikka Kiprusoff .30 .75
86 Dion Phaneuf .40 1.00
87 Alex Tanguay .25 .60
88 Ryan Miller .40 1.00
89 Chris Drury .30 .75
90 Daniel Briere .40 1.00
91 Brad Boyes .25 .60
92 Patrice Bergeron .50 1.25
93 Zdeno Chara .40 1.00
94 Marc Savard .25 .60
95 Ilya Kovalchuk .40 1.00
96 Marian Hossa .30 .75
97 Kari Lehtonen .30 .75
98 Teemu Selanne .75 2.00
99 Jean-Sebastien Giguere .40 1.00
100 Chris Pronger .30 .75
101 Glenn Anderson 1.25 3.00
102 Jean Beliveau 1.25 3.00
103 Bob Bourne .75 2.00

104 Mike Bossy 1.25 3.00
105 Richard Brodeur 1.00 2.50
106 Johnny Bucyk 1.25 3.00
107 Gerry Cheevers 1.25 3.00
108 Don Cherry 2.00 5.00
109 Wendel Clark 1.25 3.00
110 Bobby Clarke 1.25 3.00
111 Phil Esposito 2.00 5.00
112 Tony Esposito 1.25 3.00
113 Grant Fuhr 1.25 3.00
114 Doug Gilmour 1.50 4.00
115 Peter Stastny 1.25 3.00
116 Glenn Hall 2.00 5.00
117 Ron Hextall 2.00 5.00
118 Guy Lafleur 1.50 4.00
119 Guy Lapointe 1.00 2.50
120 Reggie Leach .75 2.00
121 Ted Lindsay 1.00 2.50
122 Lanny McDonald 1.25 3.00
123 Joe Mullen 1.00 2.50
124 Kirk Muller .75 2.00
125 Cam Neely 1.25 3.00
126 Bob Nystrom .75 2.00
127 Terry O'Reilly .75 2.00
128 Bernie Parent 1.25 3.00
129 Gilbert Perreault 1.25 3.00
130 Denis Potvin 1.25 3.00
131 Bill Ranford 1.25 3.00
132 Derek Sanderson 1.00 2.50
133 Denis Savard 1.50 4.00
134 Steve Shutt 1.25 3.00
135 Darryl Sittler 1.25 3.00
136 Billy Smith 1.25 3.00
137 Thomas Steen .75 2.00
138 Rick Vaive .75 2.00
139 Ron Ellis .75 2.00
140 Doug Wilson 1.00 2.50
141 Wayne Gretzky 6.00 15.00
142 Patrick Roy 3.00 8.00
143 Gordie Howe 4.00 10.00
144 Ray Bourque 2.00 5.00
145 Al MacInnis 1.25 3.00
146 Mike Krushelnyski .75 2.00
147 Mario Lemieux 4.00 10.00
148 Bob Probert 1.00 2.50
149 Tiger Williams 1.00 2.50
150 Clark Gillies 1.25 3.00
151 Teemu Selanne 2.50 6.00
152 Ilya Kovalchuk 1.25 3.00
153 Marian Hossa 1.00 2.50
154 Patrice Bergeron 1.50 4.00
155 Cristobal Huet 1.00 2.50
156 Ryan Miller 1.25 3.00
157 Miikka Kiprusoff 1.00 2.50
158 Jarome Iginla 1.25 3.00
159 Eric Staal 1.50 4.00
160 Nikolai Khabibulin 1.25 3.00
161 Joe Sakic 2.00 5.00
162 Alex Tanguay .75 2.00
163 Rick Nash 1.25 3.00
164 Mike Modano 2.00 5.00
165 Marty Turco 1.25 3.00
166 Henrik Zetterberg 1.50 4.00
167 Pavel Datsyuk 1.50 4.00
168 Brendan Shanahan 1.50 4.00
169 Ales Hemsky 1.00 2.50
170 Chris Pronger 1.00 2.50
171 Roberto Luongo 2.00 5.00
172 Olli Jokinen 1.25 3.00
173 Alexander Frolov .75 2.00
174 Marian Gaborik 1.50 4.00
175 Saku Koivu 1.25 3.00
176 Michael Ryder .75 2.00
177 Paul Kariya 1.50 4.00
178 Tomas Vokoun 1.00 2.50
179 Martin Brodeur 2.50 6.00
180 Patrik Elias 1.25 3.00
181 Brian Gionta 1.00 2.50
182 Miroslav Satan 1.00 2.50
183 Jaromir Jagr 3.00 8.00
184 Henrik Lundqvist 2.50 6.00
185 Dany Heatley 1.25 3.00
186 Ed Belfour 1.25 3.00
187 Jason Spezza 1.25 3.00
188 Peter Forsberg 1.50 4.00
189 Simon Gagne 1.25 3.00
190 Shane Doan 1.00 2.50
191 Sidney Crosby 5.00 12.00
192 Marc-Andre Fleury 2.00 5.00
193 Joe Thornton 1.50 4.00
194 Patrick Marleau 1.25 3.00
195 Jonathan Cheechoo 1.25 3.00
196 Martin St. Louis 1.25 3.00
197 Vincent Lecavalier 1.00 2.50
198 Brad Richards 1.25 3.00
199 Mats Sundin 1.25 3.00
200 Markus Naslund 1.00 2.50
201 Dustin Byfuglien RC 5.00 12.00
202 Yan Stastny RC 2.00 5.00
203 Mark Stuart RC 2.00 5.00
204 Eric Fehr RC 3.00 8.00
205 Bill Thomas RC 2.00 5.00
206 Joel Perrault RC 2.00 5.00
207 Carsen Germyn RC 2.00 5.00
208 Ryan Potulny RC 2.00 5.00
209 David Printz RC 2.00 5.00
210 Rob Collins RC 2.00 5.00
211 Steve Regier RC 2.00 5.00
212 Matt Koalska RC 2.00 5.00
213 Masi Marjamaki RC 2.00 5.00
214 Konstantin Pushkarev RC 2.50 6.00
215 Ben Ondrus RC 2.00 5.00
216 Brendan Bell RC 2.00 5.00
217 Ian White RC 2.50 6.00
218 Jeremy Williams RC 2.00 5.00
219 Marc-Antoine Pouliot RC 2.00 5.00
220 Noah Welch RC 2.00 5.00
221 Michel Ouellet RC 2.50 6.00
222 Shea Weber RC 5.00 12.00
223 Jarkko Immonen RC 2.00 5.00
224 David Liffiton RC 2.00 5.00
225 Tomas Kopecky RC 2.50 6.00
226 Billy Thompson RC 2.00 5.00
227 Filip Novak RC 2.00 5.00
228 Matt Carle RC 2.00 5.00
229 Erik Reitz RC 2.00 5.00
230 Miroslav Kopriva RC 2.00 5.00
231 Ryan Shannon RC 2.50 6.00
232 Benoit Pouliot RC 3.00 8.00
233 Phil Kessel RC 6.00 15.00
234 Drew Stafford RC 4.00 10.00
235 Dustin Boyd RC 2.50 6.00
236 Josh Hennessey RC 2.50 6.00
237 Dave Bolland RC 4.00 10.00
238 Paul Stastny RC 6.00 15.00
239 Fredrik Norrena RC 2.50 6.00
240 Loui Eriksson RC 4.00 10.00
241 Derek Meech RC 2.50 6.00
242 Ladislav Smid RC 2.50 6.00
243 Janis Sprukts RC 2.50 6.00
244 Anze Kopitar RC 10.00 25.00
245 Niklas Backstrom RC 5.00 12.00
246 G. Latendresse RC 4.00 10.00
247 Alexander Radulov RC 5.00 12.00
248 Travis Zajac RC 5.00 12.00
249 Blake Comeau RC 4.00 10.00
250 Nigel Dawes RC 2.50 6.00
251 Alexei Kaigorodov RC 2.50 6.00
252 Martin Houle RC 3.00 8.00
253 Enver Lisin RC 2.50 6.00
254 Evgeni Malkin RC 15.00 40.00
255 M-E Vlasic RC 2.50 6.00
256 Marek Schwarz RC 4.00 10.00
257 Karri Ramo RC 2.50 6.00
258 Kris Newbury RC 2.50 6.00
259 Luc Bourdon RC 4.00 10.00
260 Darren Machesney RC 2.50 6.00
261 Jordan Staal RC 6.00 15.00
262 Patrick O'Sullivan RC 4.00 10.00
263 Patrik Thoresen RC 2.50 6.00
264 Mikhail Grabovski RC 5.00 12.00
265 Jesse Schultz RC 2.50 6.00
266 Michael Blunden RC 2.50 6.00
267 David Booth RC 3.00 8.00
268 Brandon Prust RC 2.50 6.00
269 Matt Lashoff RC 2.50 6.00
270 Niklas Grossman RC 4.00 10.00
271 Joe Pavelski RC 12.00 30.00
272 Clarke MacArthur RC 3.00 8.00

2006-07 Artifacts Gold

*1-100 VETS/50: 3X TO 8X BASIC CARDS
*101-200 L/S/50: 1X TO 2.5X L/S/999
*201-230 ROOKIES/50: .6X TO 1.5X RC/999
STATED PRINT RUN 50 SER. #'d SETS

2006-07 Artifacts Bronze

*1-100 VETS/25: 4X TO 10X BASIC CARDS
*101-200 L/S/25: 1.2X TO 3X L/S/999
*201-230 ROOKIES/25: 1.2X TO 3X RC/999
BRONZE PRINT RUN 25 SER.#'d SETS

2006-07 Artifacts Silver

*1-100 VETS/100: 2X TO 5X BASIC CARDS
*101-200 L/S/100: .6X TO 1.5X L/S/999
*201-230 ROOKIES/100: .5X TO 1.2X RC/999
PRINT RUN 100 SER.#'d SETS

2006-07 Artifacts Autofacts

STATED ODDS 1:10
AFAA Adrian Aucoin 3.00 8.00
AFAH Ales Hemsky 6.00 15.00
AFAK Andrei Kostitsyn 8.00 20.00
AFAO Alexander Ovechkin SP 60.00 120.00
AFAP Alexandre Picard 3.00 8.00
AFBB Bob Bourne 3.00 8.00
AFBC Bobby Clarke 10.00 25.00
AFBE Jean Beliveau SP 50.00 100.00
AFBI Martin Biron 3.00 8.00
AFBL Brett Lebda 3.00 8.00
AFBN Bob Nystrom 5.00 12.00
AFBO Jay Bouwmeester 10.00 25.00
AFBP Bob Probert 15.00 40.00
AFBR Brad Boyes 3.00 8.00
AFBS Billy Smith UER 8.00 20.00
(Chico Resch pictured)
AFBU Johnny Bucyk SP 6.00 15.00
AFBW Ben Walter 3.00 8.00
AFBY Mike Bossy 6.00 15.00
AFCA Jeff Carter 6.00 15.00
AFCD Chris Drury 5.00 12.00
AFCG Clark Gillies 5.00 12.00
AFCK Chuck Kobasew 3.00 8.00
AFCN Cam Neely 10.00 25.00
AFCP Corey Perry 6.00 15.00
AFDA David Aebischer 5.00 12.00
AFDB Doug Bodger 3.00 8.00
AFDE Derek Boogaard 20.00 40.00
AFDP Dion Phaneuf 12.00 30.00
AFDR Dwayne Roloson 5.00 12.00
AFDS Denis Savard 5.00 12.00
AFDW Doug Wilson 3.00 8.00
AFFP Fernando Pisani 3.00 8.00
AFGA Glenn Anderson SP 6.00 15.00
AFGF Grant Fuhr SP 15.00 40.00
AFGL Guy Lafleur SP 20.00 50.00
AFHO Gordie Howe 40.00 80.00
AFHR Ryan Hollweg 3.00 8.00
AFHZ Henrik Zetterberg SP 15.00 40.00
AFIK Ilya Kovalchuk SP 15.00 40.00
AFJB Jaroslav Balastik 3.00 8.00
AFJC Jonathan Cheechoo 8.00 20.00
AFJH Jeff Halpern 3.00 8.00
AFJI Jarome Iginla SP 15.00 40.00
AFJL Joffrey Lupul SP 8.00 20.00
AFJM Joe Mullen 4.00 10.00
AFJT Jose Theodore SP 12.00 30.00
AFKD Kris Draper 3.00 8.00
AFKM Kirk Muller 5.00 12.00
AFLE Reggie Leach 8.00 20.00
AFLN Ladislav Nagy 3.00 8.00
AFLS Lee Stempniak 3.00 8.00
AFMA Marian Gaborik SP 15.00 40.00
AFMB Martin Brodeur SP 50.00 125.00
AFMC Mike Cammalleri 4.00 10.00
AFMG Martin Gerber 5.00 12.00
AFMI Mike Richards 8.00 20.00
AFMK Miikka Kiprusoff SP 15.00 40.00
AFML Mario Lemieux SP 150.00 300.00
AFMR Michael Ryder 5.00 12.00
AFMS Marek Svatos 5.00 12.00
AFMT Mikael Tellqvist 5.00 12.00
AFNH Nathan Horton 5.00 12.00
AFOJ Olli Jokinen 4.00 10.00
AFPB Pierre-Marc Bouchard SP 25.00 50.00
AFPE Phil Esposito SP 40.00 100.00
AFPM Patrick Marleau 8.00 20.00
AFRA Ray Bourque SP 25.00 60.00
AFRB Rob Blake SP 12.00 30.00
AFRE Ron Ellis 5.00 12.00
AFRF Ruslan Fedotenko 3.00 8.00
AFRG Ryan Getzlaf 6.00 15.00
AFRH Ron Hextall SP 20.00 50.00
AFRI Richard Brodeur 5.00 12.00
AFRK Rostislav Klesla 3.00 8.00
AFRL Rod Langway 4.00 10.00
AFRM Ryan Malone SP 12.00 30.00
AFRO Mike Ribeiro 4.00 10.00
AFRS Ryan Smyth EXCH 12.00 30.00
AFRY Ryan Miller 15.00 30.00
AFSC Sidney Crosby 90.00 200.00
AFSG Scott Gomez 4.00 10.00
AFSH Scott Hartnell 5.00 12.00
AFSS Steve Shutt 4.00 10.00
AFSW Stephen Weiss 3.00 8.00
AFTE Tony Esposito SP 20.00 50.00
AFTH Joe Thornton SP 10.00 25.00
AFTL Ted Lindsay 8.00 20.00
AFTS Thomas Steen 3.00 8.00
AFTV Thomas Vanek 10.00 25.00
AFVO Tomas Vokoun 5.00 12.00
AFWC Wendel Clark 20.00 50.00
AFWG Wayne Gretzky SP 125.00 200.00
AFWI Tiger Williams 5.00 12.00
AFWR Wade Redden SP 15.00 40.00
AFZC Zdeno Chara 8.00 20.00

2006-07 Artifacts Frozen Artifacts

STATED PRINT RUN 250 SER.#'d SETS
*BLUE/50 .6X TO 1.5X BASIC JSY
*GOLD/25 .8X TO 2X BASIC JSY
*RED/100 .5X TO 1.2X BASIC JSY
*PATCH BLUE/25: 1.2X TO 3X BASIC JSY
*PATCH RED/35: 1.2X TO 3X BASIC JSY
FAAO Adam Oates 3.00 8.00
FAAT Alex Tanguay 2.00 5.00
FABG Brian Gionta 2.50 6.00
FABM Brenden Morrow 2.50 6.00
FABP Brad Park 2.50 6.00
FABR Bill Ranford 3.00 8.00
FABS Brad Stuart 2.00 5.00
FACC Chris Chelios 3.00 8.00
FACD Chris Drury 2.50 6.00
FACK Chuck Kobasew 2.00 5.00
FACP Chris Pronger 2.50 6.00
FACW Cam Ward 3.00 8.00
FADA Daniel Alfredsson 3.00 8.00
FADS Darryl Sittler 3.00 8.00
FAES Eric Staal 4.00 10.00
FAGA Glenn Anderson 3.00 8.00
FAHZ Henrik Zetterberg 4.00 10.00
FAJB Jay Bouwmeester 3.00 8.00
FAJC Jeff Carter 3.00 8.00
FAJI Jarome Iginla 3.00 8.00
FAJL Joffrey Lupul 2.50 6.00
FAJO Jonathan Cheechoo 3.00 8.00
FAJS Joe Sakic 5.00 12.00
FALM Lanny McDonald 3.00 8.00
FAMC Bryan McCabe 2.00 5.00
FAMH Milan Hejduk 2.50 6.00
FAMK Miikka Kiprusoff 2.50 6.00
FAMM Mike Modano 5.00 12.00
FAMO Brendan Morrison 2.00 5.00
FAMR Mark Recchi 4.00 10.00
FANL Nicklas Lidstrom 3.00 8.00
FAPB Patrice Bergeron 4.00 10.00
FAPD Pavol Demitra 4.00 10.00
FAPE Patrik Elias 3.00 8.00
FAPM Patrick Marleau 3.00 8.00
FAPR Patrick Roy 8.00 20.00
FAPS Peter Stastny 3.00 8.00
FARB Rod Brind'Amour 3.00 8.00
FARL Roberto Luongo 5.00 12.00
FARM Ryan Miller 3.00 8.00
FARS Ryan Smyth 2.50 6.00
FASG Simon Gagne 3.00 8.00
FASK Saku Koivu 3.00 8.00
FASP Jason Spezza 3.00 8.00
FASS Steve Shutt 3.00 8.00
FASU Steve Sullivan 2.00 5.00
FASW Stephen Weiss 2.00 5.00
FATS Teemu Selanne 6.00 15.00
FATV Tomas Vokoun 2.50 6.00
FAWC Wendel Clark 3.00 8.00

2006-07 Artifacts Treasured Swatches

STATED PRINT RUN 250 SER.#'d SETS
*GOLD/25: 1X TO 2.5X BASIC JSY
*RED/100: .5X TO 1.2X BASIC JSY
*SILVER/50: .6X TO 1.5X BASIC JSY
*PATCH BLUE/25: 1.2X TO 3X BASIC JSY
*PATCH RED/35: 1.2X TO 3X BASIC JSY
TSAF Alexander Frolov 2.00 5.00
TSAH Ales Hemsky 2.50 6.00
TSAK Alex Kovalev 2.50 6.00
TSAM Al MacInnis 3.00 8.00
TSAO Alexander Ovechkin 8.00 20.00
TSAR Jason Arnott 2.50 6.00
TSBB Bob Bourne 2.00 5.00
TSBC Bobby Clarke 3.00 8.00
TSBG Bill Guerin 3.00 8.00
TSBL Rob Blake 3.00 8.00
TSBN Bob Nystrom 2.00 5.00
TSBP Bob Probert 5.00 12.00
TSBS Borje Salming 3.00 8.00
TSCJ Curtis Joseph 3.00 8.00
TSCN Cam Neely 3.00 8.00
TSDG Doug Gilmour 4.00 10.00
TSDW Tiger Williams 2.50 6.00
TSEB Ed Belfour 3.00 8.00
TSEL Eric Lindros 5.00 12.00
TSGF Grant Fuhr 3.00 8.00
TSIK Ilya Kovalchuk 3.00 8.00
TSJA Jason Allison 2.50 6.00
TSJG Jean-Sebastien Giguere 3.00 8.00
TSJJ Jaromir Jagr 8.00 20.00
TSJN Joe Nieuwendyk 3.00 8.00
TSJT Joe Thornton 4.00 10.00
TSKP Keith Primeau 3.00 8.00
TSKT Keith Tkachuk 3.00 8.00
TSMB Martin Brodeur 6.00 15.00
TSMF Manny Fernandez 2.50 6.00
TSMH Marian Hossa 2.50 6.00
TSML Mario Lemieux 10.00 25.00
TSMM Mike Modano 4.00 10.00
TSMN Markus Naslund 2.50 6.00
TSMR Mark Recchi 4.00 10.00
TSMT Marty Turco 3.00 8.00
TSNK Nikolai Khabibulin 3.00 8.00
TSOK Olaf Kolzig 3.00 8.00
TSPF Peter Forsberg 4.00 10.00
TSPK Paul Kariya 4.00 10.00
TSRB Ray Bourque 5.00 12.00
TSRN Rick Nash 3.00 8.00
TSRV Rick Vaive 2.00 5.00
TSRY Michael Ryder 2.00 5.00
TSSC Sidney Crosby 12.00 30.00
TSSF Sergei Fedorov 5.00 12.00
TSSG Scott Gomez 2.50 6.00
TSSK Saku Koivu 3.00 8.00
TSSN Scott Niedermayer 3.00 8.00
TSWE Doug Weight 3.00 8.00

2006-07 Artifacts Tundra Tandems

*BLUE/25: .6X TO 1.5X BASIC TANDEM/125
*BLUE/25: .5X TO 1.2X BASIC TANDEM/50
*PATCH RED/25: 1X TO 2.5X TANDEM/125
*PATCH RED/25: .8X TO 2X TANDEM/50
*RED/50: .5X TO 1.2X BASIC TANDEM/125
*RED/50: .4X TO 1X BASIC TANDEM/50
TTAB A.Raycroft/B.McCabe 3.00 8.00
TTAD M.Afinogenov/C.Drury 3.00 8.00
TTAG Anderson/Gretzky/50 25.00 60.00
TTAK G.Anderson/M.Krushelnyski 4.00 10.00
TTAM M.Stajan/A.Steen 4.00 10.00
TTAS S.Samsonov/A.Kovalev 3.00 8.00
TTBB Boyes/Bergeron 5.00 12.00
TTBE M.Brodeur/P.Elias 8.00 20.00
TTBJ Shanahan/Jagr 10.00 25.00
TTBN B.Nystrom/B.Bourne 2.50 6.00
TTBO Bucyk/Bourque 6.00 15.00
TTBR B.Rolston/P.Bouchard 4.00 10.00
TTCA C.Neely/A.Oates 4.00 10.00
TTCE C.Joseph/E.Jovo 4.00 10.00
TTCG W.Clark/D.Gilmour 6.00 15.00
TTCL D.Ciccarelli/R.Langway 4.00 10.00
TTCN M.Comrie/L.Nagy 3.00 8.00
TTCR C.Neely/R.Bourque 6.00 15.00
TTDB D.Sittler/B.Salming 6.00 15.00
TTDD Alfredsson/Heatley 4.00 10.00
TTDH T.Holmstrom/P.Datsyuk 5.00 12.00
TTDO T.Daley/S.Ott 3.00 8.00
TTDR R.Brodeur/T.Williams 3.00 8.00
TTDW K.Draper/J.Williams 2.50 6.00
TTEJ E.Belfour/J.Bouwmeester 4.00 10.00
TTFB R.Blake/A.Frolov 4.00 10.00
TTFG P.Forsberg/S.Gagne 5.00 12.00
TTFP M.Fernandez/M.Parrish 3.00 8.00
TTFR G.Fuhr/B.Ranford 4.00 10.00
TTGC S.Gagne/J.Carter 4.00 10.00
TTGD M.Gaborik/P.Demitra 5.00 12.00
TTGG S.Gomez/B.Gionta 3.00 8.00
TTGP G.Lafleur/P.Stastny 5.00 12.00
TTHD H.Sedin/D.Sedin 4.00 10.00
TTHK Hossa/Kovalchuk 4.00 10.00
TTHO D.Hasek/C.Osgood 5.00 12.00
TTHP M.Hossa/P.Prucha 3.00 8.00
TTHS M.Hejduk/M.Svatos 3.00 8.00
TTHU S.Harnell/S.Upshall 4.00 10.00
TTIT J.Iginla/A.Tanguay 4.00 10.00
TTJA J.Mullen/A.MacInnis 3.00 8.00
TTJH J.Spezza/D.Heatley 4.00 10.00
TTJJ J.Lupul/J.Stoll 3.00 8.00
TTKA P.Kariya/J.Arnott 5.00 12.00
TTKH N.Khabibulin/M.Havlat 4.00 10.00
TTKK S.Koivu/A.Kovalev 4.00 10.00
TTKL I.Kovalchuk/K.Lehtonen 4.00 10.00
TTKO O.Kolzig/A.Ovechkin 15.00 40.00
TTKP Kiprusoff/Phaneuf 6.00 15.00
TTLB Lafleur/Beliveau 15.00 40.00
TTLC M.Lemieux/S.Crosby 40.00 80.00
TTLM J.LeClair/M.Recchi 5.00 12.00
TTLN M.Naslund/R.Luongo 6.00 15.00
TTLR V.Lecavalier/B.Richards 4.00 10.00
TTLS G.Lafleur/S.Shutt 5.00 12.00
TTLZ L.Robitaille/Z.Palffy 4.00 10.00
TTMB R.Miller/M.Biron 4.00 10.00
TTMC L.Murphy/C.Chelios 4.00 10.00
TTME L.McDonald/R.Ellis 4.00 10.00
TTML M.Modano/E.Lindros 6.00 15.00
TTMM L.McDonald/A.MacInnis 4.00 10.00
TTMR M.Satan/R.DiPietro 3.00 8.00
TTMS G.Murray/M.Savard 3.00 8.00
TTMT B.McCabe/D.Tucker 3.00 8.00
TTNF R.Nash/S.Federov 6.00 15.00
TTNG S.Niedermayer/J.Giguere 4.00 10.00
TTNH N.Lidstrom/H.Zetter 5.00 12.00
TTNO M.Naslund/M.Ohlund 3.00 8.00
TTNP C.Pronger/S.Niedermayer 4.00 10.00
TTNR J.Nieuwendyk/G.Roberts 4.00 10.00
TTNY M.York/T.Hunter 2.50 6.00
TTOT O.Jokinen/T.Bertuzzi 4.00 10.00
TTPJ P.Roy/J.Sakic 10.00 25.00
TTPK P.Roy/K.Muller 10.00 25.00
TTPM P.Marleau/M.Bell 4.00 10.00
TTPT P.Leclaire/T.Conklin 3.00 8.00
TTRB P.Roy/R.Bourque 10.00 25.00
TTRD S.Doan/J.Roenick 4.00 10.00
TTRK T.Ruutu/N.Khabibulin 4.00 10.00
TTRM M.Recchi/R.Malone 5.00 12.00
TTRR M.Ribeiro/M.Ryder 3.00 8.00
TTRS R.Smyth/S.Horcoff 3.00 8.00
TTSF M.St.Louis/R.Fedotenko 4.00 10.00
TTSJ S.Kapanen/J.Pitkanen 2.50 6.00
TTSM M.Denis/S.Burke 3.00 8.00
TTSP T.Selanne/C.Perry 8.00 20.00
TTST Sakic/Theodore 6.00 15.00
TTSV D.Sittler/R.Vaive 4.00 10.00
TTSW E.Staal/C.Ward 5.00 12.00
TTTC J.Thornton/J.Cheechoo 6.00 15.00
TTTG K.Tkachuk/B.Guerin 4.00 10.00
TTTM M.Turco/B.Morrow 4.00 10.00
TTTO M.Sundin/M.Peca 4.00 10.00
TTTW D.Weight/K.Tkachuk 4.00 10.00
TTVE T.Vokoun/M.Erat 3.00 8.00
TTWA W.Redden/A.Meszaros 2.50 6.00
TTWB J.Williams/R.Brind'Amour 4.00 10.00
TTWG D.Weight/B.Guerin 4.00 10.00
TTWS D.Savard/D.Wilson 5.00 12.00
TTZM Z.Chara/M.Jurcina 4.00 10.00

2007-08 Artifacts

COMP.SET w/o SPs (100) 12.00 30.00
101-140 STARS/LEG PRINT RUN 1499
141-200 ROOKIES PRINT RUN 999
201-242 ROOKIES PRINT RUN 599
1 Ryan Miller .40 1.00
2 Thomas Vanek .50 1.25
3 Chris Drury .30 .75
4 Daniel Briere .40 1.00
5 Zach Parise .50 1.25
6 Patrik Elias .40 1.00
7 Martin Brodeur .75 2.00
8 Marian Hossa .30 .75
9 Ilya Kovalchuk .40 1.00
10 Kari Lehtonen .30 .75
11 Dany Heatley .40 1.00
12 Ray Emery .30 .75
13 Jason Spezza .40 1.00
14 Daniel Alfredsson .40 1.00
15 Sidney Crosby 1.50 4.00
16 Evgeni Malkin 1.25 3.00
17 Marc-Andre Fleury .60 1.50
18 Jordan Staal .40 1.00
19 Jaromir Jagr 1.00 2.50
20 Henrik Lundqvist .50 1.25
21 Martin Straka .25 .60
22 Vincent Lecavalier .30 .75
23 Brad Richards .40 1.00
24 Martin St. Louis .40 1.00
25 Alexei Yashin .30 .75
26 Rick DiPietro .30 .75
27 Miroslav Satan .30 .75
28 Mats Sundin .40 1.00
29 Andrew Raycroft .30 .75
30 Darcy Tucker .30 .75
31 Alexander Steen .40 1.00
32 Saku Koivu .40 1.00
33 Guillaume Latendresse .30 .75
34 Cristobal Huet .30 .75
35 Michael Ryder .25 .60
36 Eric Staal .50 1.25
37 Cam Ward .40 1.00
38 Ray Whitney .30 .75
39 Nathan Horton .40 1.00
40 Olli Jokinen .30 .75
41 Tomas Vokoun .30 .75
42 Patrice Bergeron .50 1.25
43 Marc Savard .25 .60
44 Tim Thomas .50 1.25
45 Alexander Ovechkin 1.50 4.00
46 Olaf Kolzig .40 1.00
47 Alexander Semin .40 1.00
48 Simon Gagne .40 1.00
49 Martin Biron .30 .75
50 Jeff Carter .40 1.00
51 Henrik Zetterberg .50 1.25
52 Pavel Datsyuk .50 1.25
53 Nicklas Lidstrom .40 1.00
54 Tomas Holmstrom .30 .75
55 Jean-Sebastien Giguere .40 1.00
56 Chris Pronger .30 .75
57 Ryan Getzlaf .60 1.50
58 Teemu Selanne .75 2.00
59 Markus Naslund .40 1.00
60 Roberto Luongo .50 1.25
61 Henrik Sedin .40 1.00
62 Daniel Sedin .40 1.00
63 Chris Mason .30 .75
64 Alexander Radulov .40 1.00
65 Paul Kariya .50 1.25
66 Peter Forsberg .50 1.25
67 Jonathan Cheechoo .40 1.00
68 Joe Thornton .50 1.25
69 Evgeni Nabokov .30 .75
70 Mike Modano .60 1.50
71 Marty Turco .40 1.00
72 Mike Ribeiro .30 .75
73 Marian Gaborik .50 1.25
74 Pavol Demitra .50 1.25
75 Pierre-Marc Bouchard .40 1.00
76 Jarome Iginla .40 1.00
77 Dion Phaneuf .40 1.00
78 Miikka Kiprusoff .30 .75
79 Alex Tanguay .25 .60
80 Joe Sakic .60 1.50
81 Milan Hejduk .30 .75
82 Paul Stastny .40 1.00
83 Brad Boyes .25 .60
84 Manny Legace .30 .75
85 Doug Weight .40 1.00
86 Rick Nash .40 1.00
87 Pascal Leclaire .30 .75
88 Sergei Fedorov .60 1.50
89 Ales Hemsky .30 .75
90 Dwayne Roloson .30 .75
91 Shawn Horcoff .25 .60
92 Martin Havlat .40 1.00
93 Nikolai Khabibulin .40 1.00
94 Tuomo Ruutu .40 1.00
95 Anze Kopitar .60 1.50
96 Alexander Frolov .25 .60
97 Mike Cammalleri .30 .75
98 Shane Doan .30 .75
99 Mikael Tellqvist .30 .75
100 Zbynek Michalek .25 .60
101 Wayne Gretzky L 6.00 15.00
102 Mario Lemieux L 4.00 10.00
103 Gordie Howe L 3.00 8.00
104 Bobby Orr L 4.00 10.00
105 Mark Messier L 2.00 5.00
106 Patrick Roy L 3.00 8.00
107 Ray Bourque L 2.00 5.00
108 Gilbert Perreault L 1.25 3.00
109 Bobby Clarke L 1.25 3.00
110 Guy Lafleur L 1.50 4.00
111 Don Cherry L 1.50 4.00
112 Ron Hextall L 2.00 5.00
113 Grant Fuhr L 1.25 3.00
114 Larry Robinson L 1.25 3.00
115 Cam Neely L 1.25 3.00
116 Bernie Parent L 1.25 3.00
117 Frank Mahovlich L 1.50 4.00
118 Tony Esposito L 1.25 3.00
119 Phil Esposito L 2.00 5.00
120 Stan Mikita L 1.50 4.00
121A Sidney Crosby S 5.00 12.00
121B Joe Sakic S 2.00 5.00
123 Martin Brodeur S 2.50 6.00
124 Dany Heatley S 1.25 3.00
125 Joe Thornton S 1.50 4.00
126 Henrik Zetterberg S 1.50 4.00
127 Jaromir Jagr S 3.00 8.00
128 Simon Gagne S 1.25 3.00
129 Jarome Iginla S 1.25 3.00
130 Roberto Luongo S 1.50 4.00
131 Alexander Ovechkin S 5.00 12.00
132 Ilya Kovalchuk S 1.25 3.00
133 Mats Sundin S 1.25 3.00
134 Rick Nash S 1.25 3.00
135 Patrice Bergeron S 1.50 4.00
136 Saku Koivu S 1.25 3.00
137 Henrik Lundqvist S 1.50 4.00
138 Evgeni Malkin S 4.00 10.00
139 Vincent Lecavalier S 1.00 2.50
140 Ryan Miller S 1.25 3.00
141 Jeff Finger RC 2.00 5.00
142 Colin Fraser RC 2.00 5.00
143 Pierre Parenteau RC 2.50 6.00
144 David Koci RC 2.00 5.00
145 Bryan Bickell RC 4.00 10.00
146 Jonas Nordqvist RC 2.00 5.00
147 Tomas Popperle RC 2.50 6.00
148 Curtis Glencross RC 3.00 8.00
149 Marc Methot RC 2.00 5.00
150 David Krejci RC 6.00 15.00
151 Jonathan Sigalet RC 2.00 5.00
152 Petr Kalus RC 2.00 5.00
153 Jaroslav Halak RC 6.00 15.00
154 Duncan Milroy RC 2.00 5.00
155 Jannik Hansen RC 2.50 6.00
156 Jeff Schultz RC 2.50 6.00
157 Jamie Hunt RC 2.00 5.00
158 Daniel Carcillo RC 2.50 6.00
159 Andy Greene RC 2.50 6.00
160 Mark Fraser RC 2.00 5.00
161 Rod Pelley RC 2.00 5.00
162 David Clarkson RC 3.00 8.00
163 Aaron Rome RC 2.50 6.00
164 Kent Huskins RC 2.00 5.00
165 Bjorn Melin RC 2.00 5.00
166 Drew Miller RC 2.50 6.00
167 David Moss RC 3.00 8.00
168 Tomi Maki RC 2.00 5.00
169 Scott Munroe RC 2.00 5.00
170 Nathan Guenin RC 2.50 6.00
171 Ryan Parent RC 2.00 5.00
172 Frans Nielsen RC 3.00 8.00
173 Lauri Tukonen RC 2.00 5.00
174 Yutaka Fukufuji RC 2.50 6.00
175 John Zeiler RC 2.00 5.00
176 Gabe Gauthier RC 2.00 5.00
177 Shay Stephenson RC 2.00 5.00
178 Joe Piskula RC 2.00 5.00
179 Jack Johnson RC 2.50 6.00
180 Tom Gilbert RC 2.50 6.00
181 Mathieu Roy RC 2.00 5.00
182 Zack Stortini RC 2.00 5.00
183 Bryan Young RC 2.00 5.00
184 Sebastien Bisaillon RC 2.00 5.00
185 Rob Schremp RC 2.50 6.00
186 Martin Lojek RC 2.00 5.00
187 Rich Peverley RC 3.00 8.00
188 Ryan Callahan RC 4.00 10.00
189 Daniel Girardi RC 2.50 6.00
190 Brandon Dubinsky RC 4.00 10.00
191 Matt Ellis RC 2.50 6.00
192 Patrick Kaleta RC 2.00 5.00
193 Mark Mancari RC 2.50 6.00
194 Danny Bois RC 2.00 5.00
195 Thomas Plihal RC 2.50 6.00
196 Tobias Stephan RC 2.50 6.00
197 Joel Lundqvist RC 2.00 5.00
198 Chris Conner RC 2.00 5.00
199 Krys Barch RC 2.50 6.00
200 Joel Ward RC 3.00 8.00
201 T.J. Hensick RC 4.00 10.00
202 Jonathan Toews RC 25.00 50.00
203 Kris Russell RC 4.00 10.00
204 Tuukka Rask RC 12.00 30.00
205 Carey Price RC 25.00 50.00
206 Mason Raymond RC 5.00 12.00
207 Nicklas Backstrom RC 10.00 25.00
208 Peter Mueller RC 4.00 10.00
209 Nicklas Bergfors RC 3.00 8.00
210 Bobby Ryan RC 8.00 20.00
211 Curtis McElhinney RC 5.00 12.00
212 Steve Downie RC 4.00 10.00
213 Casey Borer RC 3.00 8.00
214 Martin Hanzal RC 4.00 10.00
215 Jonathan Bernier RC 8.00 20.00
216 Matt Smaby RC 3.00 8.00
217 Sam Gagner RC 6.00 15.00
218 Stefan Meyer RC 4.00 10.00
219 Ville Koistinen RC 3.00 8.00
220 Marc Staal RC 5.00 12.00
221 Kyle Chipchura RC 5.00 12.00
222 Mike Weber RC 3.00 8.00
223 Nick Foligno RC 6.00 15.00
224 Devin Setoguchi RC 5.00 12.00
225 Matt Niskanen RC 5.00 12.00
226 James Sheppard RC 3.00 8.00
227 Bryan Little RC 5.00 12.00
228 Tyler Kennedy RC 5.00 12.00
229 Erik Johnson RC 5.00 12.00
230 Jiri Tlusty RC 5.00 12.00
231 Patrick Kane RC 20.00 50.00
232 Andrew Cogliano RC 5.00 12.00
233 David Jones RC 3.00 8.00
234 Anton Stralman RC 3.00 8.00
235 Brian Elliott RC 6.00 15.00
236 Tobias Enstrom RC 5.00 12.00
237 David Perron RC 5.00 12.00
238 Chris Bourque RC 4.00 10.00
239 Ondrej Pavelec RC 6.00 15.00
240 Milan Lucic RC 15.00 40.00
241 Jack Skille RC 4.00 10.00
242 Sergei Kostitsyn RC 4.00 10.00

2007-08 Artifacts Blue

*1-100 VETS/25: 5X TO 12X BASIC CARDS
*101-140 S/L/25: 1.5X TO 4X S/L/1499
*141-200 ROOKIES/25: 1.2X TO 3X RC/999
*201-242 ROOKIES/25: .8X TO 2X RC/599
STATED PRINT RUN 25 #'d SETS

2007-08 Artifacts Gold

*1-100 VETS/50: 4X TO 10X BASIC CARDS
*101-140 S/L/50: 1.2X TO 3X S/L/1499
*141-200 ROOKIES/50: 1X TO 2.5X RC/999
*201-242 ROOKIES/50: .6X TO 1.5X RC/599
STATED PRINT RUN 50 SER.#'d SETS

2007-08 Artifacts Silver

*1-100 VETS/100: 2.5X TO 6X BASIC CARDS
*101-140 S/L/100: .8X TO 2X S/L/1499
*141-200 ROOKIES/100: .8X TO 2X RC/999
*201-242 ROOKIES/100: .5X TO 1.2X RC/599
STATED PRINT RUN 100 #'d SETS

2007-08 Artifacts Autofacts

STATED ODDS: 1:10
AFAF Alexander Frolov 4.00 10.00
AFAK Andrei Kostitsyn 5.00 12.00
AFAL Andrew Ladd 6.00 15.00
AFAM Al MacInnis 6.00 15.00
AFAN Andrew Raycroft 5.00 12.00
AFAO Alex Ovechkin SP 60.00 120.00
AFAT Alex Tanguay 4.00 10.00
AFBC Bobby Clarke 8.00 20.00
AFBG Butch Goring 4.00 10.00
AFBI Martin Biron 5.00 12.00
AFBM Brendan Morrison 4.00 10.00
AFBO Ray Bourque SP 15.00 40.00
AFBP Bernie Parent SP 10.00 25.00
AFBR Brad Richardson 5.00 12.00
AFBS Borje Salming SP 10.00 25.00
AFBY Brad Boyes 4.00 10.00
AFCH Erik Christensen 4.00 10.00
AFCM Clarke MacArthur 4.00 10.00
AFCP Chris Pronger 5.00 12.00
AFDB Daniel Briere 6.00 15.00
AFDE Denis Potvin 6.00 15.00
AFDL David Leneveu 5.00 12.00
AFDP Dion Phaneuf 6.00 15.00
AFDS Drew Stafford 5.00 12.00
AFDT Darcy Tucker SP 8.00 20.00
AFDU Dustin Brown 6.00 15.00
AFEC Erik Cole 5.00 12.00
AFEM Evgeni Malkin 20.00 50.00
AFES Eric Staal 8.00 20.00
AFGA Glenn Anderson 6.00 15.00
AFGB Gilbert Brule SP 8.00 20.00
AFGC Gerry Cheevers 6.00 15.00
AFGH Gordie Howe SP 30.00 60.00
AFGL Guillaume Latendresse 5.00 12.00
AFGP Gilbert Perreault 6.00 15.00
AFHA Dale Hawerchuk 8.00 20.00
AFHE Milan Hejduk 5.00 12.00
AFHL Henrik Lundqvist 8.00 20.00
AFHZ Henrik Zetterberg 8.00 20.00
AFIK Ilya Kovalchuk 8.00 20.00
AFJA Jason Arnott 5.00 12.00
AFJB Johnny Bucyk 5.00 12.00
AFJC Jeff Carter 6.00 15.00
AFJK Jari Kurri SP
AFJR Jeremy Roenick 6.00 15.00
AFJS Jarret Stoll 5.00 12.00
AFKL Kari Lehtonen 5.00 12.00
AFKM Kirk Muller 4.00 10.00
AFLA Guy Lafleur 8.00 20.00
AFLM Lanny McDonald SP
AFLR Luc Robitaille 6.00 15.00
AFMB Martin Brodeur SP 60.00 120.00
AFMC Mike Cammalleri 5.00 12.00
AFMG Marian Gaborik 8.00 20.00
AFMH Martin Havlat 6.00 15.00
AFMI Mike Bossy 6.00 15.00
AFMK Miikka Kiprusoff 12.00 30.00
AFML Mario Lemieux SP 60.00 150.00
AFMM Mark Messier SP 150.00 250.00
AFMR Mike Richards 6.00 15.00
AFNB Niklas Backstrom 6.00 15.00
AFNZ Nikolai Zherdev 4.00 10.00
AFOR Bobby Orr SP
AFPE Corey Perry 6.00 15.00
AFPK Phil Kessel 8.00 20.00
AFPO Patrick O'Sullivan 5.00 12.00
AFPR Patrick Roy SP 50.00 100.00
AFPS Paul Stastny 6.00 15.00
AFRA Bill Ranford 10.00 25.00
AFRB Richard Brodeur 5.00 12.00
AFRE Ron Ellis 4.00 10.00
AFRH Ron Hextall 10.00 25.00
AFRM Ryan Malone 4.00 10.00
AFRN Rick Nash 6.00 15.00
AFSC Sidney Crosby 75.00 150.00
AFSG Scott Gomez 5.00 12.00
AFST Peter Stastny 5.00 12.00
AFTL Ted Lindsay SP 10.00 25.00
AFTV Tomas Vokoun 5.00 12.00
AFTW Tiger Williams 5.00 12.00
AFWC Wayne Cashman 5.00 12.00
AFWG Wayne Gretzky SP 150.00 300.00
AFZC Zdeno Chara 6.00 15.00

2007-08 Artifacts Frozen Artifacts

STATED PRINT RUN 299 #'d SETS
FAAK Alex Kovalev 3.00 8.00
FAAO Alexander Ovechkin 15.00 40.00
FAAR Andrew Raycroft 3.00 8.00
FAAS Alexander Steen 4.00 10.00
FAAT Alex Tanguay 2.50 6.00
FAAY Alexei Yashin 3.00 8.00
FABB Brad Boyes 2.50 6.00
FABF Bernie Federko 2.50 6.00
FABG Brian Gionta 3.00 8.00
FABM Brendan Morrison 2.50 6.00
FABR Bill Ranford 4.00 10.00
FABS Billy Smith 4.00 10.00
FACC Chris Chelios 4.00 10.00
FACD Chris Drury 3.00 8.00
FACI Dino Ciccarelli 4.00 10.00
FACJ Curtis Joseph 4.00 10.00
FACN Cam Neely 4.00 10.00
FACP Chris Pronger 3.00 8.00
FACW Cam Ward 4.00 10.00
FADA Daniel Alfredsson 4.00 10.00
FADC Dan Cloutier 3.00 8.00
FADH Dale Hawerchuk 5.00 12.00
FADL David Legwand 3.00 8.00
FADP Rick DiPietro 3.00 8.00
FADS Darryl Sittler 3.00 8.00
FADW Doug Weight 4.00 10.00
FAEB Ed Belfour 4.00 10.00
FAEM Evgeni Malkin 12.00 30.00
FAES Eric Staal 5.00 12.00
FAGA Glenn Anderson 4.00 10.00
FAGL Guy Lafleur 5.00 12.00
FAHA Dominik Hasek 5.00 12.00
FAHZ Henrik Zetterberg 5.00 12.00
FAIK Ilya Kovalchuk 4.00 10.00
FAJB Jay Bouwmeester 4.00 10.00
FAJC Jonathan Cheechoo 4.00 10.00
FAJI Jarome Iginla 4.00 10.00
FAJL Jere Lehtinen 2.50 6.00
FAJO Joe Sakic 6.00 15.00
FAJS Jason Spezza 4.00 10.00
FAKL Kari Lehtonen 3.00 8.00
FAKT Keith Tkachuk 4.00 10.00
FALM Lanny McDonald 4.00 10.00
FALR Larry Robinson 4.00 10.00
FAMC Bryan McCabe 2.50 6.00
FAMH Marian Hossa 3.00 8.00
FAML Mario Lemieux 12.00 30.00
FAMO Brenden Morrow 3.00 8.00
FARI Brad Richards 4.00 10.00
FASA Borje Salming 4.00 10.00
FASH Brendan Shanahan 5.00 12.00

2007-08 Artifacts Frozen Artifacts Gold

*GOLD: .6X TO 1.5X BASE
STATED PRINT RUN 50 #'d SETS

2007-08 Artifacts Frozen Artifacts Icy Blue

*ICY BLUE: .8X TO 2X BASE
STATED PRINT RUN 25 #'d SETS

2007-08 Artifacts Frozen Artifacts Silver

*SILVER: .5X TO 1.2X BASE
STATED PRINT RUN 100 #'d SETS

2007-08 Artifacts Frozen Artifacts Patches Bronze

STATED PRINT RUN 50 SERIAL #'d SETS
FAAK Alex Kovalev 8.00 20.00
FAAO Alexander Ovechkin 40.00 100.00
FAAR Andrew Raycroft 8.00 20.00
FAAS Alexander Steen 10.00 25.00
FAAT Alex Tanguay 6.00 15.00
FABB Brad Boyes 6.00 15.00
FABF Bernie Federko 6.00 15.00
FABG Brian Gionta 8.00 20.00
FABM Brendan Morrison 6.00 15.00
FABR Bill Ranford 10.00 25.00
FABS Billy Smith 10.00 25.00
FACC Chris Chelios 10.00 25.00
FACD Chris Drury 8.00 20.00
FACI Dino Ciccarelli 10.00 25.00
FACJ Curtis Joseph 10.00 25.00
FACN Cam Neely 10.00 25.00
FACP Chris Pronger 8.00 20.00
FACW Cam Ward 10.00 25.00
FADA Daniel Alfredsson 10.00 25.00
FADC Dan Cloutier 8.00 20.00
FADH Dale Hawerchuk 12.00 30.00
FADL David Legwand 8.00 20.00
FADP Rick DiPietro 8.00 20.00
FADW Doug Weight 10.00 25.00
FAEB Ed Belfour 10.00 25.00
FAEM Evgeni Malkin 30.00 80.00
FAES Eric Staal 12.00 30.00
FAGA Glenn Anderson 10.00 25.00
FAHA Dominik Hasek 12.00 30.00
FAHZ Henrik Zetterberg 12.00 30.00
FAIK Ilya Kovalchuk 10.00 25.00
FAJB Jay Bouwmeester 10.00 25.00
FAJC Jonathan Cheechoo 10.00 25.00
FAJI Jarome Iginla 10.00 25.00
FAJL Jere Lehtinen 6.00 15.00
FAJO Joe Sakic 15.00 40.00
FAJS Jason Spezza 10.00 25.00

FAKL Kari Lehtonen 8.00 20.00
FAKT Keith Tkachuk 10.00 25.00
FALM Lanny McDonald 10.00 25.00
FALR Larry Robinson 10.00 25.00
FAMC Bryan McCabe 6.00 15.00
FAMH Marian Hossa 8.00 20.00
FAML Mario Lemieux 30.00 80.00
FAMO Brenden Morrow 8.00 20.00
FARI Brad Richards 10.00 25.00
FASA Borje Salming 10.00 25.00
FASH Brendan Shanahan 12.00 30.00

2007-08 Artifacts Frozen Artifacts Patches Gold

*GOLD: .5X TO 1.2X BASE
STATED PRINT RUN 25 SERIAL #'d SETS

2007-08 Artifacts Treasured Patches Bronze

*PATCHES BRONZE: .8X TO 2X SWATCHES
STATED PRINT RUN 50 SERIAL #'d SETS

2007-08 Artifacts Treasured Patches Gold

*PATCHES GOLD: 1.5X TO 4X SWATCHES
STATED PRINT RUN 50 SERIAL #'d SETS

2007-08 Artifacts Treasured Swatches

STATED PRINT RUN 299 SERIAL #'d SETS
TSAF Alexander Frolov 3.00 8.00
TSAH Ales Hemsky 4.00 10.00
TSAK Alex Kovalev 4.00 10.00
TSAM Al MacInnis 5.00 12.00
TSAO Alexander Ovechkin 20.00 50.00
TSBB Bob Bourne 3.00 8.00
TSBG Bill Guerin 5.00 12.00
TSBL Rob Blake 5.00 12.00
TSBN Bob Nystrom 3.00 8.00
TSBR Brad Richards 5.00 12.00
TSBS Borje Salming 5.00 12.00
TSCJ Curtis Joseph 6.00 15.00
TSCN Cam Neely 5.00 12.00
TSDB Daniel Briere 5.00 12.00
TSDG Doug Gilmour 6.00 15.00
TSDH Dany Heatley 5.00 12.00
TSDW Doug Weight 5.00 12.00
TSEB Ed Belfour 5.00 12.00
TSEL Eric Lindros 8.00 20.00
TSGO Scott Gomez 4.00 10.00
TSIK Ilya Kovalchuk 5.00 12.00
TSJG Jean-Sebastien Giguere 5.00 12.00
TSJJ Jaromir Jagr 12.00 30.00
TSJT Joe Thornton 6.00 15.00
TSKT Keith Tkachuk 5.00 12.00
TSMB Martin Brodeur 10.00 25.00
TSMF Manny Fernandez 4.00 10.00
TSMH Marian Hossa 4.00 10.00
TSMM Mike Modano 8.00 20.00
TSMN Markus Naslund 5.00 12.00
TSMR Mark Recchi 6.00 15.00
TSMT Marty Turco 5.00 12.00
TSNK Nikolai Khabibulin 5.00 12.00
TSOK Olaf Kolzig 5.00 12.00
TSPF Peter Forsberg 6.00 15.00
TSPK Paul Kariya 6.00 15.00
TSRB Ray Bourque 8.00 20.00
TSRN Rick Nash 5.00 12.00
TSRY Michael Ryder 3.00 8.00
TSSC Sidney Crosby 12.00 30.00
TSSF Sergei Fedorov 8.00 20.00
TSSG Simon Gagne 5.00 12.00
TSSK Saku Koivu 5.00 12.00
TSSN Scott Niedermayer 5.00 12.00
TSSS Steve Shutt 5.00 12.00
TSTH Tomas Holmstrom 4.00 10.00
TSTS Teemu Selanne 10.00 25.00
TSTW Tiger Williams 4.00 10.00
TSVL Vincent Lecavalier 4.00 10.00
TSWG Wayne Gretzky 25.00 60.00

2007-08 Artifacts Treasured Swatches Gold

*GOLD: .6X TO 1.5X BASE
STATED PRINT RUN 50 SERIAL #'d SETS

2007-08 Artifacts Treasured Swatches Icy Blue

*ICY BLUE: .8X TO 2X BASE
STATED PRINT RUN 25 SERIAL #'d SETS

2007-08 Artifacts Treasured Swatches Silver

*SILVER: .5X TO 1.2X BASE
STATED PRINT RUN 100 SERIAL #'d SETS

2007-08 Artifacts Tundra Tandems

STATED PRINT RUN 125 SER.#'d SETS
TTAL A.MacInnis/L.McDonald 6.00 15.00
TTAM A.Steen/M.Stajan 6.00 15.00
TTBB Belfour/Bouwmeester 6.00 15.00
TTBC S.Bernier/M.Carle 4.00 10.00
TTBE M.Biron/R.Esche 5.00 12.00
TTBK P.Bergeron/P.Kessel 8.00 20.00
TTBM R.Bourque/A.MacInnis 10.00 25.00
TTBO K.Bieksa/M.Ohlund 5.00 12.00
TTBP B.Salming/P.Forsberg 8.00 20.00
TTBS M.Brodeur/S.Stevens 6.00 15.00
TTBT P.Budaj/J.Theodore 6.00 15.00
TTCF S.Crosby/M.Fleury 15.00 40.00
TTCG J.Cheechoo/B.Guerin 6.00 15.00
TTCM S.Crosby/E.Malkin 25.00 60.00
TTCR C.Perry/R.Getzlaf 10.00 25.00
TTDG C.Drury/S.Gomez 5.00 12.00
TTDH D.Sedin/H.Sedin 6.00 15.00
TTDJ S.Doan/E.Jovanovski 5.00 12.00
TTDL P.Datsyuk/N.Lidstrom 8.00 20.00
TTDR P.Demitra/B.Rolston 8.00 20.00
TTER E.Staal/R.Brind'Amour 8.00 20.00
TTFM B.Federko/J.Mullen 5.00 12.00
TTFT M.Fernandez/T.Thomas 8.00 20.00
TTFV P.Forsberg/T.Vokoun 8.00 20.00
TTGC S.Gagne/J.Carter 6.00 15.00
TTGE B.Gionta/P.Elias 6.00 15.00
TTGK M.Gaborik/M.Koivu 8.00 20.00
TTGL W.Gretzky/M.Lemieux 30.00 80.00
TTGS J.Giguere/T.Selanne 12.00 30.00
TTHA D.Heatley/D.Alfredsson 6.00 15.00
TTHB M.Havlat/P.Bondra 6.00 15.00
TTHC Hawerchuk/Ciccarelli 8.00 20.00
TTHL G.Howe/M.Lemieux 20.00 50.00
TTHO D.Hasek/C.Osgood 8.00 20.00
TTHR A.Hemsky/D.Roloson 5.00 12.00
TTHS M.Hejduk/M.Svatos 5.00 12.00
TTHW N.Horton/S.Weiss 6.00 15.00
TTIH I.Kovalchuk/M.Hossa 6.00 15.00
TTIT J.Iginla/A.Tanguay 6.00 15.00
TTJJ C.Joseph/E.Jovanovski 6.00 15.00
TTJL J.Jokinen/J.Lehtinen 4.00 10.00
TTJM J.Sakic/M.Hejduk 10.00 25.00
TTJP J.Sakic/P.Roy 15.00 40.00
TTJS J.Jagr/M.Straka 15.00 40.00
TTKA J.Kurri/G.Anderson 6.00 15.00
TTKF A.Kopitar/A.Frolov 10.00 25.00
TTKK A.Kovalev/A.Kostitsyn 5.00 12.00
TTKP M.Kiprusoff/D.Phaneuf 6.00 15.00
TTKR S.Koivu/M.Ryder 6.00 15.00
TTKT P.Kariya/K.Tkachuk 8.00 20.00
TTLA D.Legwand/J.Arnott 5.00 12.00
TTLC N.Lidstrom/C.Chelios 6.00 15.00
TTLH K.Lehtonen/M.Hossa 5.00 12.00
TTLN R.Luongo/M.Naslund 8.00 20.00
TTLR V.Lecavalier/B.Richards 6.00 15.00
TTLS M.Legace/C.Sanford 5.00 12.00
TTLV P.Leclaire/D.Vyborny 5.00 12.00
TTMB M.Sundin/B.Salming 6.00 15.00
TTML B.Morrison/T.Linden 6.00 15.00
TTMM M.Modano/J.Mullen 5.00 12.00
TTMO G.Lafleur/L.Robinson 8.00 20.00
TTMP M.Brodeur/P.Elias 10.00 25.00
TTMR M.Modano/M.Ribeiro 10.00 25.00
TTMS G.Murray/M.Savard 5.00 12.00
TTMW B.McCabe/I.White 4.00 10.00
TTNF R.Nash/S.Fedorov 10.00 25.00
TTNT E.Nabokov/V.Toskala 5.00 12.00
TTNY B.Witt/T.Hunter 4.00 10.00
TTOK A.Ovechkin/O.Kolzig 25.00 60.00
TTOM A.Ovechkin/E.Malkin 25.00 60.00
TTPA P.Stastny/A.Stastny 5.00 12.00
TTPB G.Perreault/D.Briere 6.00 15.00
TTPG Z.Parise/B.Gionta 8.00 20.00
TTPN C.Pronger/S.Niedermayer 6.00 15.00
TTPP F.Pisani/M.Pouliot 4.00 10.00
TTRB P.Roy/R.Bourque 15.00 40.00
TTRG W.Redden/M.Gerber 5.00 12.00
TTRH M.Ryder/C.Higgins 4.00 10.00
TTRJ R.Bourque/J.Bucyk 10.00 25.00
TTSB B.Smith/B.Bourne 6.00 15.00
TTSD M.St. Louis/M.Denis 6.00 15.00
TTSE J.Spezza/P.Eaves 6.00 15.00
TTSF M.Sundin/P.Forsberg 8.00 20.00
TTSG M.Satan/B.Guerin 6.00 15.00
TTSH J.Stoll/S.Horcoff 5.00 12.00
TTSK B.Seabrook/D.Keith 6.00 15.00
TTSL Shanahan/Lundqvist 8.00 20.00
TTSR M.Sundin/A.Raycroft 6.00 15.00
TTSS D.Sittler/B.Salming 6.00 15.00
TTST J.Sakic/P.Turgeon 10.00 25.00
TTSW D.Savard/D.Wilson 8.00 20.00
TTTM J.Thornton/P.Marleau 8.00 20.00
TTTS R.Smyth/J.Theodore 6.00 15.00
TTTZ M.Turco/S.Zubov 6.00 15.00
TTWB D.Weight/B.Boyes 6.00 15.00
TTWP T.Williams/B.Probert 5.00 12.00
TTWW C.Ward/J.Williams 6.00 15.00
TTYS A.Yashin/M.Satan 5.00 12.00
TTZH H.Zetterberg/T.Holmstrom 8.00 20.00

2007-08 Artifacts Tundra Tandems Icy Blue

*ICY BLUE: .5X TO 1.2X BASE
STATED PRINT RUN 50 SERIAL #'d SETS

2007-08 Artifacts Tundra Tandems Metallic Purple

*SINGLES: .4X TO 1X BASIC CARDS
RANDOM INSERTS IN RETAIL PACKS

2007-08 Artifacts Tundra Tandems Red

*RED: .6X TO 1.5X BASE
STATED PRINT RUN 25 SERIAL #'d SETS

2007-08 Artifacts Tundra Tandems Patches Icy Blue

*SILVER: 1X TO 2.5X BASIC TANDEMS
STATED PRINT RUN 25 SERIAL #'d SETS

2007-08 Artifacts Tundra Tandems Patches Silver

*SILVER: .8X TO 2 X BASIC TANDEMS
STATED PRINT RUN 35 SERIAL #'d SETS

2007-08 Artifacts Tundra Trios Blue

STATED PRINT RUN 75 #'d SETS
T3AMV Vanek/Afino/Miller 12.00 30.00
T3ASD Arnott/Sulli/Dumont 8.00 20.00
T3ASH Heat/Spezza/Alfred 10.00 25.00
T3BLK Brod/Luongo/Kipr 15.00 40.00
T3BWH Horton/Bouw/Weiss 10.00 25.00
T3CHD Hasek/Dats/Chelios 12.00 30.00
T3CMS Crosby/Staal/Malkin 40.00 100.00
T3DGK Gab/Koivu/Demitra 12.00 30.00
T3FCK Frolov/Kopitar/Camm 15.00 40.00
T3GEP Gionta/Elias/Parise 12.00 30.00
T3GRC Gagne/Cart/Richards 10.00 25.00
T3GYS Guerin/Satan/Yashin 10.00 25.00
T3HRK Havlat/Khabi/Ruutu 10.00 25.00
T3ITK Iginla/Kipr/Tanguay 10.00 25.00
T3JJD Doan/Joseph/Jovo 10.00 25.00
T3KHL Kovy/Hossa/Lehton 10.00 25.00
T3KPK Kovalev/Kostit/Perez 8.00 20.00
T3KRH Koivu/Ryder/Higgins 10.00 25.00
T3LBS Laraque/Shell/Brash 8.00 20.00
T3LGH Gretz/Howe/Lemieux 50.00 125.00
T3LHZ Zett/Lidstrom/Holms 12.00 30.00
T3LMK Linden/Morr/Kesler 12.00 30.00
T3LRC Lem/Crosby/Recchi 40.00 100.00
T3LRS Lecav/St. Lou/Rich 10.00 25.00
T3LTC Crosby/Thorn/Lecav 30.00 80.00
T3LZB Leclair/Brule/Zherd 8.00 20.00
T3MCB Marleau/Carle/Bernier 10.00 25.00
T3MCT Murray/Chara/Thomas 12.00 30.00
T3MGM McD/Gilmour/MacIn 12.00 30.00
T3MLR Modano/Lindros/Rib 15.00 40.00
T3MRM Mo/Mullen/Roenick 15.00 40.00
T3MSW Salming/McD/Williams 10.00 25.00
T3NBO Bourque/Neely/Oates 10.00 25.00
T3NPG Getzlaf/Nied/Perry 15.00 40.00
T3NSS Nasl/Sedin/Sedin 10.00 25.00
T3OGF Ovech/Green/Fehr 40.00 100.00
T3PRB Bouch/Rolston/Parrish 10.00 25.00
T3PSB Smith/Potvin/Bourne 10.00 25.00
T3RBB Roy/Belfour/Brodeur 20.00 50.00
T3REE Emery/Redden/Eaves 8.00 20.00
T3RLR Roy/Lafleur/Robinson 25.00 60.00
T3RSS Raycroft/Steen/Stajan 10.00 25.00
T3SBK Berg/Kessel/Savard 12.00 30.00
T3SDG Straka/Drury/Gomez 8.00 20.00
T3SHB Sakic/Hejduk/Budaj 15.00 40.00
T3SJL Shan/Jagr/Lundqvist 25.00 60.00
T3SNF Sundin/Forsberg/Nasl 12.00 30.00
T3SPG Selanne/Gig/Pronger 20.00 50.00
T3SRH Hem/Roloson/Stoll 8.00 20.00
T3STM Sundin/Tuck/McCabe 10.00 25.00
T3TCM Thorn/Cheech/Michal 12.00 30.00
T3TKL Kipr/Leht/Toskala 8.00 20.00
T3TKS Tkach/Kariya/Stemp 12.00 30.00
T3VHB Hasek/Vok/Budaj 12.00 30.00
T3VNF Nash/Fed/Vyborny 15.00 40.00
T3WLB Weight/Legace/Boyes 10.00 25.00
T3WPP Williams/Probert/Plett 8.00 20.00
T3WSW Staal/Ward/Williams 12.00 30.00
T3ZLT Turco/Zubov/Leht 10.00 25.00

2008-09 Artifacts

This set was released on October 28, 2008. The base set consists of 302 cards. Cards 1-200 feature veterans, with cards 101-200 serial numbered of 999. Cards 201-260 are rookies serial numbered of 999, and cards 271-312 were issued in packs as exchange cards with an announced print run of 750, but actually released with a print run of 999.

COMP.SET w/o SPs (100) 12.00 30.00
101-200 LEG/S PRINT RUN 999
201-312 ROOKIE PRINT RUN 999
1 Alexander Ovechkin 1.50 4.00
2 Nicklas Backstrom .60 1.50
3 Markus Naslund .30 .75
4 Roberto Luongo .50 1.25
5 Daniel Sedin .40 1.00
6 Henrik Sedin .40 1.00
7 Mats Sundin .40 1.00
8 Vesa Toskala .30 .75
9 Alexander Steen .40 1.00
10 Vincent Lecavalier .30 .75
11 Martin St. Louis .40 1.00
12 Paul Kariya .50 1.25
13 Manny Legace .40 1.00
14 Brad Boyes .25 .60
15 Joe Thornton .50 1.25
16 Patrick Marleau .40 1.00
17 Evgeni Nabokov .30 .75
18 Jonathan Cheechoo .40 1.00
19 Peter Stastny .40 1.00
20 Mario Lemieux 1.25 3.00
21 Sidney Crosby 1.50 4.00
22 Marc-Andre Fleury .60 1.50
23 Evgeni Malkin 1.25 3.00
24 Jordan Staal .40 1.00
25 Peter Mueller .30 .75
26 Shane Doan .30 .75
27 Daniel Briere .40 1.00
28 Simon Gagne .40 1.00
29 Mike Richards .40 1.00
30 Jason Spezza .40 1.00
31 Dany Heatley .40 1.00
32 Daniel Alfredsson .40 1.00
33 Mark Messier .50 1.25
34 Marian Hossa .30 .75
35 Henrik Lundqvist .50 1.25
36 Brendan Shanahan .50 1.25
37 Brian Leetch .40 1.00
38 Rick DiPietro .30 .75
39 Bill Guerin .40 1.00
40 Mike Bossy .40 1.00
41 Zach Parise .40 1.00
42 Martin Brodeur .75 2.00
43 Jason Arnott .30 .75
44 J.P. Dumont .25 .60
45 Patrick Roy 1.00 2.50
46 Carey Price 1.50 4.00
47 Saku Koivu .40 1.00
48 Alex Tanguay .25 .60
49 Alex Kovalev .30 .75
50 Larry Robinson .40 1.00
51 Marian Gaborik .50 1.25
52 Josh Harding .40 1.00
53 Anze Kopitar .60 1.50
54 Jack Johnson .25 .60
55 Tomas Vokoun .30 .75
56 Nathan Horton .30 .75
57 Wayne Gretzky 2.00 5.00
58 Andrew Cogliano .30 .75
59 Sam Gagner .30 .75
60 Ales Hemsky .30 .75
61 Dustin Penner .30 .75
62 Jari Kurri .40 1.00
63 Gordie Howe 1.00 2.50
64 Nicklas Lidstrom .40 1.00
65 Henrik Zetterberg .50 1.25
66 Pavel Datsyuk .50 1.25
67 Dominik Hasek .50 1.25
68 Mike Modano .60 1.50
69 Brad Richards .40 1.00
70 Marty Turco .40 1.00
71 Rick Nash .40 1.00
72 Nikolai Zherdev .25 .60
73 Paul Stastny .40 1.00
74 Joe Sakic .60 1.50
75 Peter Forsberg .50 1.25
76 Ryan Smyth .30 .75
77 Patrick Kane .75 2.00
78 Jonathan Toews 1.00 2.50
79 Patrick Sharp .40 1.00
80 Bobby Hull .60 1.50
81 Eric Staal .50 1.25
82 Cam Ward .40 1.00
83 Miikka Kiprusoff .30 .75
84 Jarome Iginla .40 1.00
85 Dion Phaneuf .40 1.00
86 Mike Cammalleri .30 .75
87 Thomas Vanek .40 1.00
88 Ryan Miller .40 1.00
89 Drew Stafford .30 .75
90 Gilbert Perreault .40 1.00
91 Bobby Orr 1.25 3.00
92 Tim Thomas .40 1.00
93 Phil Kessel .50 1.25
94 Marc Savard .25 .60
95 Ilya Kovalchuk .40 1.00
96 Kari Lehtonen .30 .75
97 Teemu Selanne .75 2.00
98 Jean-Sebastien Giguere .40 1.00
99 Scott Niedermayer .40 1.00
100 Ryan Getzlaf .60 1.50
101 Dale Hawerchuk LEG 1.50 4.00
102 Rod Langway LEG 1.00 2.50
103 Johnny Bower LEG 1.50 4.00
104 Borje Salming LEG 1.25 3.00
105 Frank Mahovlich LEG 1.25 3.00
106 Bernie Federko LEG 1.00 2.50
107 Al MacInnis LEG 1.25 3.00
108 Peter Stastny LEG 1.25 3.00
109 Mario Lemieux LEG 4.00 10.00
110 Joe Mullen LEG 1.00 2.50
111 Bobby Clarke LEG 1.25 3.00
112 Ron Hextall LEG 2.00 5.00
113 Andy Bathgate LEG 1.25 3.00
114 Brian Leetch LEG 1.25 3.00
115 Walt Tkaczuk LEG .75 2.00
116 Mike Bossy LEG 1.25 3.00
117 Bob Bourne LEG .75 2.00
118 Clark Gillies LEG 1.25 3.00
119 Jean Beliveau LEG 1.25 3.00
120 Scotty Bowman LEG 1.25 3.00
121 Guy Lafleur LEG 1.50 4.00
122 Steve Shutt LEG 1.25 3.00
123 Larry Robinson LEG 1.25 3.00
124 Patrick Roy LEG 3.00 8.00
125 Dino Ciccarelli LEG 1.25 3.00
126 Marcel Dionne LEG 1.50 4.00
127 Bernie Nicholls LEG 1.00 2.50
128 Luc Robitaille LEG 1.25 3.00
129 Grant Fuhr LEG 1.25 3.00
130 Wayne Gretzky LEG 6.00 15.00
131 Jari Kurri LEG 1.25 3.00
132 Alex Delvecchio LEG 1.50 4.00
133 Gordie Howe LEG 3.00 8.00
134 Red Kelly LEG 1.50 4.00
135 Ted Lindsay LEG 1.25 3.00
136 Doug Wilson LEG 1.00 2.50
137 Tony Esposito LEG 1.25 3.00
138 Bobby Hull LEG 2.00 5.00
139 Denis Savard LEG 1.50 4.00
140 Stan Mikita LEG 1.50 4.00
141 Lanny McDonald LEG 1.25 3.00
142 Gilbert Perreault LEG 1.25 3.00
143 Ray Bourque LEG 2.00 5.00
144 Johnny Bucyk LEG 1.25 3.00
145 Don Cherry LEG 3.00 8.00
146 Phil Esposito LEG 2.00 5.00
147 Cam Neely LEG 1.25 3.00
148 Willie O'Ree LEG 1.25 3.00
149 Bobby Orr LEG 4.00 10.00
150 Terry O'Reilly LEG 1.00 2.50
151 Alexander Ovechkin S 5.00 12.00
152 Roberto Luongo S 1.50 4.00
153 Henrik Sedin S 1.25 3.00
154 Mats Sundin S 1.25 3.00
155 Vincent Lecavalier S 1.00 2.50
156 Martin St. Louis S 1.25 3.00
157 Paul Kariya S 1.50 4.00
158 Joe Thornton S 1.50 4.00
159 Patrick Marleau S 1.25 3.00
160 Sidney Crosby S 5.00 12.00
161 Evgeni Malkin S 4.00 10.00
162 Marc-Andre Fleury S 2.00 5.00
163 Simon Gagne S 1.25 3.00
164 Daniel Briere S 1.25 3.00
165 Dany Heatley S 1.25 3.00
166 Jason Spezza S 1.25 3.00
167 Daniel Alfredsson S 1.25 3.00
168 Markus Naslund S 1.00 2.50
169 Brendan Shanahan S 1.50 4.00
170 Martin Brodeur S 2.50 6.00
171 Zach Parise S 1.25 3.00
172 Carey Price S 5.00 12.00
173 Saku Koivu S 1.25 3.00
174 Marian Gaborik S 1.50 4.00
175 Josh Harding S 1.25 3.00
176 Anze Kopitar S 2.00 5.00
177 Sam Gagner S 1.00 2.50
178 Andrew Cogliano S 1.00 2.50
179 Henrik Zetterberg S 1.50 4.00
180 Chris Osgood S 1.25 3.00
181 Pavel Datsyuk S 1.50 4.00
182 Mike Modano S 2.00 5.00
183 Marty Turco S 1.25 3.00
184 Rick Nash S 1.25 3.00
185 Joe Sakic S 2.00 5.00
186 Peter Forsberg S 1.50 4.00
187 Paul Stastny S 1.25 3.00
188 Patrick Kane S 2.50 6.00
189 Jonathan Toews S 3.00 8.00
190 Eric Staal S 1.50 4.00
191 Jarome Iginla S 1.25 3.00
192 Miikka Kiprusoff S 1.00 2.50
193 Ryan Miller S 1.25 3.00
194 Thomas Vanek S 1.25 3.00
195 Patrice Bergeron S 1.50 4.00
196 Ilya Kovalchuk S 1.25 3.00
197 Teemu Selanne S 2.50 6.00
198 Jean-Sebastien Giguere S 1.25 3.00
199 Ryan Getzlaf S 2.00 5.00
200 Scott Niedermayer S 1.25 3.00
201 Derick Brassard RC 2.50 6.00
202 Mark Fistric RC 2.50 6.00
203 Alex Goligoski RC 4.00 10.00
204 Claude Giroux RC 6.00 15.00
205 Jon Filewich RC 2.50 6.00
206 Robbie Earl RC 2.00 5.00
207 Ilya Zubov RC 2.50 6.00
208 Steve Mason RC 5.00 12.00
209 Brian Boyle RC 2.50 6.00
210 Shawn Matthias RC 3.00 8.00
211 Ryan Stone RC 2.00 5.00
212 Teddy Purcell RC 4.00 10.00
213 Mike Iggulden RC 2.50 6.00
214 Tim Ramholt RC 2.50 6.00
215 Kyle Okposo RC 3.00 8.00
216 Sami Lepisto RC 2.50 6.00
217 Colin Stuart RC 2.50 6.00
218 Brandon Nolan RC 2.50 6.00
219 Andrew Murray RC 2.50 6.00
220 Kevin Doell RC 2.00 5.00
221 Tim Conboy RC 2.50 6.00
222 Pascal Pelletier RC 2.00 5.00
223 Chris Minard RC 3.00 8.00
224 Joey Mormina RC 2.50 6.00
225 Peter Vandermeer RC 2.00 5.00
226 Darryl Boyce RC 2.50 6.00
227 Cody McLeod RC 2.50 6.00
228 Corey Locke RC 2.50 6.00
229 Jordan Hendry RC 2.50 6.00
230 Mike Brown RC 4.00 10.00
231 B.J. Crombeen RC 2.00 5.00
232 David Brine RC 2.00 5.00
233 Joe Jensen RC 3.00 8.00
234 Kyle Greentree RC 3.00 8.00
235 Zach Fitzgerald RC 3.00 8.00
236 Marc-Andre Gragnani RC 2.50 6.00
237 Andrew Ebbett RC 2.00 5.00
238 Erik Ersberg RC 2.50 6.00
239 Jonathan Ericsson RC 3.00 8.00
240 Theo Peckham RC 3.00 8.00
241 Tyler Plante RC 2.50 6.00
242 Niklas Hjalmarsson RC 5.00 12.00
243 Tom Sestito RC 3.00 8.00
244 Tom Cavanagh RC 2.50 6.00
245 Alex Foster RC 2.50 6.00
246 Kyle Turris RC 5.00 12.00
247 Brian Lee RC 2.50 6.00
248 Justin Abdelkader RC 5.00 12.00
249 Adam Pineault RC 2.50 6.00
250 Boris Valabik RC 3.00 8.00
251 Darren Helm RC 3.00 8.00
252 Matt D'Agostini RC 2.50 6.00
253 Mattias Ritola RC 2.50 6.00
254 Dan LaCosta RC 3.00 8.00
255 Danny Taylor RC 2.50 6.00
256 Clay Wilson RC 2.00 5.00
257 Jordan LaVallee RC 3.00 8.00
258 Mike Mole RC 2.50 6.00
259 Jack Hillen RC 2.50 6.00
260 Garrett Stafford RC 3.00 8.00
271 Karl Alzner RC 2.00 5.00
272 Cory Schneider RC 8.00 20.00
273 Luke Schenn RC 4.00 10.00
274 Steven Stamkos RC 12.00 30.00
275 Alex Pietrangelo RC 4.00 10.00
276 Jamie McGinn RC 3.00 8.00
277 Dustin Jeffery RC 3.00 8.00
278 Mikkel Boedker RC 4.00 10.00
279 Luca Sbisa RC 2.00 5.00
280 Zach Smith RC 2.50 6.00
281 Corey Potter RC 5.00 12.00
282 Josh Bailey RC 4.00 10.00
283 Petr Vrana RC 2.00 5.00
284 Patric Hornqvist RC 3.00 8.00
285 Max Pacioretty RC 20.00 40.00
286 Colton Gillies RC 2.50 6.00
287 Drew Doughty RC 8.00 20.00
288 Michael Frolik RC 3.00 8.00
289 Tim Sestito RC 2.50 6.00
290 Patrik Berglund RC 2.50 6.00
291 Fabian Brunnstrom RC 2.50 6.00
292 Jakub Voracek RC 6.00 15.00
293 Chris Stewart RC 3.00 8.00
294 Viktor Tikhonov RC 2.50 6.00
295 Brandon Sutter RC 3.00 8.00
296 Brett Sutter RC 3.00 8.00
297 Tim Kennedy RC 3.00 8.00
298 Blake Wheeler RC 8.00 20.00
299 Zach Bogosian RC 3.00 8.00
300 Brendan Mikkelson RC 2.00 5.00
301 Justin Pogge RC 3.00 8.00
302 Zach Boychuk RC 3.00 8.00
303 Nathan Gerbe RC 3.00 8.00
304 Nikita Filatov RC 3.00 8.00
305 James Neal RC 6.00 15.00
306 Kenndal McArdle RC 2.50 6.00
307 Ben Maxwell RC 3.00 8.00
308 T.J. Oshie RC 6.00 15.00
309 Ty Wishart RC 2.50 6.00
310 Nikolai Kulemin RC 3.00 8.00
311 Simeon Varlamov RC 6.00 15.00
312 Michal Repik RC 3.00 8.00
P1 Cover Card Promo .75 2.00

2008-09 Artifacts Blue

*1-100 VETS/50: 3X TO 8X BASIC CARDS
*101-200 L/S/50: 1X TO 2.5X L/S/999
*201-260 ROOKIES/50: .8X TO 2X RC/999
STATED PRINT RUN 50 SER.#'d SETS
2 Nicklas Backstrom 5.00 12.00

2008-09 Artifacts Copper Spectrum

*1-100 VETS/25: 4X TO 10X BASIC CARDS
*101-200 L/S/25: 1.2X TO 3X L/S/999
*201-260 ROOKIES/25: 1X TO 2.5X RC/999
STATED PRINT RUN 25 SER.#'d SETS
2 Nicklas Backstrom 6.00 15.00

2008-09 Artifacts Gold

*1-100 VETS/75: 2.5X TO 6X BASIC CARDS
*101-200 L/S/75: .8X TO 2X L/S/999
*201-260 ROOKIES/75: .6X TO 1.5X RC/999
STATED PRINT RUN 75 SER.#'d SETS
2 Nicklas Backstrom 4.00 10.00

2008-09 Artifacts Silver

*1-100 VETS/100: 2X TO 5X BASIC CARDS
*101-200 L/S/100: .6X TO 1.5X L/S/999
*201-260 ROOKIES/100: .5X TO 1.2X RC/999
STATED PRINT RUN 100 SER.#'d SETS
2 Nicklas Backstrom 3.00 8.00

2008-09 Artifacts Autofacts

STATED ODDS 1:10
AFAK Anze Kopitar 12.00 30.00
AFAO Alexander Ovechkin 50.00 100.00
AFAP Alexandre Picard 4.00 10.00
AFAR Andrew Raycroft 5.00 12.00
AFBB Brian Boyle 4.00 10.00
AFBC Chris Bourque 5.00 12.00
AFBJ Johnny Bower 8.00 20.00
AFBL Michael Blunden 4.00 10.00
AFBN Bob Nystrom 4.00 10.00
AFBO Bobby Orr 100.00 200.00
AFBR Bobby Ryan 6.00 15.00
AFCA Daniel Carcillo 4.00 10.00
AFCB Casey Borer 6.00 15.00
AFCD Chris Drury 12.00 30.00
AFCG Claude Giroux 20.00 50.00
AFCH Kyle Chipchura 5.00 12.00
AFCK Chris Kunitz 6.00 15.00
AFCM Clarke MacArthur 4.00 10.00
AFCN Cam Neely 15.00 40.00
AFCP Corey Perry 6.00 15.00
AFCW Cam Ward 10.00 25.00
AFDA David Perron 5.00 12.00
AFDB Dan Boyle 5.00 12.00
AFDC Dan Cleary 5.00 12.00
AFDE Derick Brassard 4.00 10.00
AFDH Dany Heatley 6.00 15.00
AFDP Dustin Penner 5.00 12.00
AFDR Drew Stafford 5.00 12.00
AFDS Daniel Sedin 6.00 15.00
AFEJ Erik Johnson 5.00 12.00
AFEM Evgeni Malkin 25.00 50.00
AFEN Eric Nystrom 4.00 10.00
AFES Tony Esposito 10.00 25.00
AFGH Gordie Howe 60.00 120.00
AFGL Guillaume Latendresse 4.00 10.00
AFGP Gilbert Perreault 6.00 15.00
AFHA Dominik Hasek 20.00 40.00
AFHS Henrik Sedin 6.00 15.00
AFHZ Henrik Zetterberg 20.00 40.00
AFIK Ilya Kovalchuk 12.00 30.00
AFIZ Ilya Zubov 4.00 10.00
AFJA Jared Boll 4.00 10.00
AFJB Johnny Bucyk 6.00 15.00
AFJC Jeff Carter 6.00 15.00
AFJF Jon Filewich 4.00 10.00
AFJH Josh Harding 6.00 15.00
AFJI Jarome Iginla SP 25.00 60.00
AFJJ Jack Johnson 4.00 10.00
AFJL Joffrey Lupul 5.00 12.00
AFJO Johnny Boychuk 6.00 15.00
AFJP Jason Pominville 6.00 15.00
AFJS Jack Skille 5.00 12.00
AFJT Jonathan Toews 25.00 50.00
AFKA Patrick Kane 20.00 50.00
AFKC Kyle Calder 4.00 10.00
AFLE Mario Lemieux 75.00 150.00
AFLK Lukas Kaspar 4.00 10.00
AFMA Martin Brodeur 60.00 120.00
AFMB Mike Bossy 6.00 15.00
AFME Mark Messier 40.00 80.00
AFMH Marian Hossa 5.00 12.00
AFML Matt Lashoff 4.00 10.00
AFMM Mike Modano 10.00 25.00
AFMR Mike Ribeiro 5.00 12.00
AFMT Maxime Talbot 6.00 15.00
AFNA Evgeni Nabokov 5.00 12.00
AFNF Nick Foligno 6.00 15.00
AFNH Nathan Horton 5.00 12.00
AFNK Niklas Kronwall 5.00 12.00
AFOP Ondrej Pavelec 8.00 20.00
AFPB Peter Budaj 5.00 12.00
AFPE Patrik Elias 6.00 15.00
AFPK Phil Kessel 8.00 20.00
AFPR Carey Price 25.00 60.00
AFPS Paul Stastny 6.00 15.00
AFRB Ray Bourque 20.00 50.00
AFRE Robbie Earl 3.00 8.00
AFRG Ryan Getzlaf 10.00 25.00
AFRL Rod Langway 5.00 12.00
AFRN Rick Nash 12.00 30.00
AFRO Dwayne Roloson 5.00 12.00
AFRS Ryan Smyth 5.00 12.00
AFSC Sidney Crosby 75.00 150.00
AFSD Steve Downie 6.00 15.00
AFSE Devin Setoguchi 5.00 12.00
AFSG Sam Gagner 5.00 12.00
AFSH James Sheppard 4.00 10.00
AFSK Sergei Kostitsyn 4.00 10.00
AFSM Steve Mason 10.00 25.00
AFST Jordan Staal 10.00 25.00
AFTE Tobias Enstrom 4.00 10.00
AFTH T.J. Hensick 5.00 12.00
AFTJ Joe Thornton 15.00 40.00
AFTK Tyler Kennedy 5.00 12.00
AFTL Jiri Tlusty 5.00 12.00
AFTO Tomas Kaberle 4.00 10.00
AFTR Tuukka Rask 15.00 30.00
AFTV Tomas Vokoun 5.00 12.00
AFVL Vincent Lecavalier 10.00 25.00
AFWG Wayne Gretzky 150.00 250.00

2008-09 Artifacts Frozen Artifacts Retail

*SINGLES: .4X TO 1X BASIC INSERTS
RANDOM INSERTS IN RETAIL PACKS

2008-09 Artifacts Frozen Artifacts Dual

STATED PRINT RUN 199 SERIAL #'d SETS
FADAK Anze Kopitar 6.00 15.00
FADAM Al MacInnis 4.00 10.00
FADAO Adam Oates 4.00 10.00
FADAS Alexander Semin 4.00 10.00
FADAT Alex Tanguay 2.50 6.00
FADBB Brad Boyes 2.50 6.00
FADBG Bill Guerin 4.00 10.00
FADBS Brendan Shanahan 5.00 12.00
FADCC Chris Chelios 4.00 10.00
FADCN Cam Neely 4.00 10.00
FADCW Cam Ward 4.00 10.00
FADDA Daniel Alfredsson 4.00 10.00
FADDB Daniel Briere 4.00 10.00
FADDC Dino Ciccarelli 4.00 10.00
FADDH Dominik Hasek 5.00 12.00
FADDP Dion Phaneuf 4.00 10.00
FADDS Daniel Sedin 4.00 10.00
FADDT Darcy Tucker 3.00 8.00
FADEM Evgeni Malkin 12.00 30.00
FADEN Evgeni Nabokov 3.00 8.00
FADES Eric Staal 5.00 12.00
FADHA Dale Hawerchuk 5.00 12.00
FADHE Dany Heatley 4.00 10.00
FADHL Henrik Lundqvist 5.00 12.00
FADHS Henrik Sedin 4.00 10.00
FADIK Ilya Kovalchuk 4.00 10.00
FADJC Jonathan Cheechoo 4.00 10.00
FADJG Jean-Sebastien Giguere 4.00 10.00
FADJS Joe Sakic 6.00 15.00
FADJT Joe Thornton 5.00 12.00
FADKO Alex Kovalev 3.00 8.00
FADMB Martin Brodeur 8.00 20.00
FADMF Manny Fernandez 3.00 8.00
FADMG Marian Gaborik 5.00 12.00
FADMK Miikka Kiprusoff 3.00 8.00
FADMM Mark Messier 5.00 12.00
FADMN Markus Naslund 3.00 8.00
FADMO Mike Modano 6.00 15.00
FADMS Marc Savard 2.50 6.00
FADOV Alexander Ovechkin 15.00 40.00
FADPF Peter Forsberg 5.00 12.00
FADPR Patrick Roy 8.00 20.00
FADRB Ray Bourque 6.00 15.00
FADSA Borje Salming 4.00 10.00
FADSC Sidney Crosby 10.00 25.00
FADSP Jason Spezza 4.00 10.00
FADSU Mats Sundin 4.00 10.00
FADTV Thomas Vanek 4.00 10.00

2008-09 Artifacts Frozen Artifacts Dual Blue

*BLUE: .8X TO 2X BASE
STATED PRINT RUN 50 SERIAL #'d SETS

2008-09 Artifacts Frozen Artifacts Jersey Patch Combo

STATED PRINT RUN 50 SER.#'d SETS
*GOLD/25: .6X TO 1.5X BASE COMBO/50
*SILVER/35: .5X TO 1.2X BASE COMBO/50
FADAK Anze Kopitar 10.00 25.00
FADAM Al MacInnis 6.00 15.00
FADAO Adam Oates 6.00 15.00
FADAS Alexander Semin 6.00 15.00
FADAT Alex Tanguay 4.00 10.00
FADBB Brad Boyes 4.00 10.00
FADBG Bill Guerin 6.00 15.00
FADBS Brendan Shanahan 8.00 20.00
FADCC Chris Chelios 6.00 15.00
FADCN Cam Neely 6.00 15.00
FADCW Cam Ward 6.00 15.00
FADDA Daniel Alfredsson 6.00 15.00
FADDB Daniel Briere 6.00 15.00
FADDC Dino Ciccarelli 6.00 15.00
FADDH Dominik Hasek 8.00 20.00
FADDP Dion Phaneuf 6.00 15.00
FADDS Daniel Sedin 6.00 15.00
FADDT Darcy Tucker 5.00 12.00
FADEM Evgeni Malkin 20.00 50.00
FADEN Evgeni Nabokov 5.00 12.00
FADES Eric Staal 8.00 20.00
FADHA Dale Hawerchuk 8.00 20.00
FADHE Dany Heatley 6.00 15.00
FADHL Henrik Lundqvist 8.00 20.00
FADHS Henrik Sedin 6.00 15.00
FADIK Ilya Kovalchuk 6.00 15.00
FADJC Jonathan Cheechoo 6.00 15.00
FADJG Jean-Sebastien Giguere 6.00 15.00
FADJS Joe Sakic 10.00 25.00
FADJT Joe Thornton 8.00 20.00
FADKO Alex Kovalev 5.00 12.00
FADMB Martin Brodeur 12.00 30.00
FADMF Manny Fernandez 5.00 12.00
FADMG Marian Gaborik 8.00 20.00
FADMK Miikka Kiprusoff 5.00 12.00
FADMM Mark Messier 8.00 20.00
FADMN Markus Naslund 5.00 12.00
FADMO Mike Modano 10.00 25.00
FADMS Marc Savard 4.00 10.00
FADOV Alexander Ovechkin 25.00 60.00
FADPF Peter Forsberg 8.00 20.00
FADPR Patrick Roy 15.00 40.00
FADRB Ray Bourque 10.00 25.00
FADSA Borje Salming 6.00 15.00
FADSC Sidney Crosby 25.00 60.00
FADSP Jason Spezza 6.00 15.00
FADSU Mats Sundin 6.00 15.00
FADTV Thomas Vanek 6.00 15.00

2008-09 Artifacts Treasured Swatches Retail

TSAK Alex Kovalev 3.00 8.00
TSAM Andrej Meszaros 2.50 6.00
TSAO Adam Oates 4.00 10.00
TSAS Alexander Steen 4.00 10.00
TSBS Borje Salming 4.00 10.00
TSCW Cam Ward 4.00 10.00
TSDP David Perron 3.00 8.00
TSDT Darcy Tucker 3.00 8.00
TSEM Evgeni Malkin 12.00 30.00
TSES Eric Staal 5.00 12.00
TSGA Glenn Anderson 4.00 10.00
TSGE Martin Gerber 3.00 8.00
TSGH Gordie Howe SP 15.00 30.00
TSIK Ilya Kovalchuk 4.00 10.00
TSJG Jean-Sebastien Giguere 4.00 10.00
TSJL Jere Lehtinen 2.50 6.00
TSJM Joe Mullen 3.00 8.00
TSJO Jussi Jokinen 2.50 6.00
TSJP Joni Pitkanen 2.50 6.00
TSJW Justin Williams 3.00 8.00
TSKC Kyle Calder 2.50 6.00
TSKL Kari Lehtonen 3.00 8.00
TSKO Anze Kopitar 6.00 15.00
TSKT Keith Tkachuk 4.00 10.00
TSLI John-Michael Liles 2.50 6.00
TSLM Lanny McDonald 4.00 10.00
TSLR Larry Robinson 4.00 10.00
TSLS Lee Stempniak 2.50 6.00
TSLU Joffrey Lupul 3.00 8.00
TSMG Marian Gaborik 5.00 12.00
TSMK Mikko Koivu 3.00 8.00
TSMN Markus Naslund 3.00 8.00
TSMR Mark Recchi 5.00 12.00
TSMS Marc Savard 2.50 6.00
TSMT Marty Turco 4.00 10.00
TSNL Nicklas Lidstrom 4.00 10.00
TSOV Alexander Ovechkin 15.00 40.00
TSPB Patrice Bergeron 5.00 12.00
TSPF Peter Forsberg 5.00 12.00
TSPH Dion Phaneuf 4.00 10.00
TSPK Paul Kariya 5.00 12.00
TSPM Patrick Marleau 4.00 10.00
TSPS Peter Stastny 4.00 10.00
TSRA Andrew Raycroft 3.00 8.00
TSRI Mike Richards 4.00 10.00
TSSU Mats Sundin 4.00 10.00
TSWG Wayne Gretzky SP 20.00 40.00

2008-09 Artifacts Treasured Swatches Dual

STATED PRINT RUN 199 SER.#'d SETS
*BLUE/50: .8X TO 2X BASIC JSY/199
*GOLD/75: .6X TO 1.5X BASIC JSY/199
*SILVER/100: .5X TO 1.2X BASIC JSY/199
TSDAH Ales Hemsky 3.00 8.00
TSDAO Alexander Ovechkin 15.00 40.00
TSDAS Alexander Steen 4.00 10.00
TSDBB Bob Bourne 2.50 6.00
TSDBL Brian Leetch 4.00 10.00
TSDBM Brendan Morrison 2.50 6.00
TSDBR Brad Richards 4.00 10.00
TSDBS Brendan Shanahan 5.00 12.00
TSDCD Chris Drury 3.00 8.00
TSDCP Chris Pronger 3.00 8.00
TSDCW Cam Ward 4.00 10.00
TSDDH Dany Heatley 4.00 10.00
TSDDS Daniel Sedin 4.00 10.00
TSDES Eric Staal 5.00 12.00
TSDGA Glenn Anderson 4.00 10.00
TSDGP Gilbert Perreault 4.00 10.00
TSDHS Henrik Sedin 4.00 10.00
TSDJC Jonathan Cheechoo 4.00 10.00
TSDJI Jarome Iginla 4.00 10.00
TSDJM Joe Mullen 3.00 8.00
TSDJR Jeremy Roenick 4.00 10.00
TSDJS Jordan Staal 4.00 10.00
TSDJT Jonathan Toews 8.00 20.00
TSDKA Paul Kariya 5.00 12.00
TSDKL Kari Lehtonen 3.00 8.00
TSDKT Keith Tkachuk 4.00 10.00
TSDLM Lanny McDonald 4.00 10.00
TSDLR Luc Robitaille 4.00 10.00
TSDLU Roberto Luongo 5.00 12.00
TSDMB Martin Brodeur 8.00 20.00
TSDMO Brenden Morrow 3.00 8.00
TSDMS Mats Sundin 4.00 10.00
TSDMT Marty Turco 4.00 10.00
TSDNB Nicklas Backstrom 6.00 15.00
TSDPB Pierre-Marc Bouchard 4.00 10.00
TSDPD Pavol Demitra 5.00 12.00
TSDPE Patrik Elias 4.00 10.00
TSDPK Patrick Kane 8.00 20.00
TSDPL Pascal Leclaire 3.00 8.00
TSDPM Patrick Marleau 4.00 10.00
TSDPS Paul Stastny 4.00 10.00
TSDRD Rick DiPietro 3.00 8.00
TSDRG Ryan Getzlaf 6.00 15.00
TSDRN Rick Nash 6.00 15.00
TSDSA Miroslav Satan 4.00 10.00
TSDSD Shane Doan 3.00 8.00
TSDST Peter Stastny 4.00 10.00
TSDTS Teemu Selanne 8.00 20.00

2008-09 Artifacts Treasured Swatches Jersey Patch Combo

STATED PRINT RUN 50 SER.#'d SETS
*GOLD/25: .8X TO 2X BASE COMBO/50
*SILVER/35: .6X TO 1.5X BASE COMBO/50
TSDAH Ales Hemsky 5.00 12.00
TSDAO Alexander Ovechkin 25.00 60.00
TSDAS Alexander Steen 6.00 15.00
TSDBB Bob Bourne 4.00 10.00
TSDBL Brian Leetch 6.00 15.00
TSDBM Brendan Morrison 4.00 10.00
TSDBR Brad Richards 6.00 15.00
TSDBS Brendan Shanahan 8.00 20.00
TSDCD Chris Drury 5.00 12.00
TSDCP Chris Pronger 5.00 12.00
TSDCW Cam Ward 6.00 15.00
TSDDH Dany Heatley 6.00 15.00
TSDDS Daniel Sedin 6.00 15.00
TSDES Eric Staal 8.00 20.00
TSDGA Glenn Anderson 6.00 15.00
TSDGP Gilbert Perreault 6.00 15.00
TSDHS Henrik Sedin 6.00 15.00
TSDJC Jonathan Cheechoo 6.00 15.00
TSDJI Jarome Iginla 6.00 15.00

TSDJM Joe Mullen 5.00 12.00
TSDJR Jeremy Roenick 6.00 15.00
TSDJS Jordan Staal 6.00 15.00
TSDJT Jonathan Toews 12.00 30.00
TSDKA Paul Kariya 8.00 20.00
TSDKL Kari Lehtonen 5.00 12.00
TSDKT Keith Tkachuk 6.00 15.00
TSDLM Lanny McDonald 6.00 15.00
TSDLR Luc Robitaille 6.00 15.00
TSDLU Roberto Luongo 8.00 20.00
TSDMB Martin Brodeur 12.00 30.00
TSDMO Brenden Morrow 5.00 12.00
TSDMS Mats Sundin 6.00 15.00
TSDMT Marty Turco 6.00 15.00
TSDNB Nicklas Backstrom 10.00 25.00
TSDPB Pierre-Marc Bouchard 6.00 15.00
TSDPD Pavol Demitra 8.00 20.00
TSDPE Patrik Elias 6.00 15.00
TSDPK Patrick Kane 12.00 30.00
TSDPL Pascal Leclaire 5.00 12.00
TSDPM Patrick Marleau 6.00 15.00
TSDPS Paul Stastny 6.00 15.00
TSDRD Rick DiPietro 5.00 12.00
TSDRG Ryan Getzlaf 10.00 25.00
TSDRN Rick Nash 6.00 15.00
TSDSA Miroslav Satan 6.00 15.00
TSDSD Shane Doan 5.00 12.00
TSDST Peter Stastny 6.00 15.00
TSDTS Teemu Selanne 12.00 30.00

2008-09 Artifacts Tundra Tandems

STATED PRINT RUN 100 SERIAL #'d SETS
*BRONZE/75: .4X TO 1X BASE
*GOLD/25: .6X TO 1.5X BASE
*SILVER/50: .5X TO 1.2X BASE
TTAR S.Weber/J.Arnott 5.00 12.00
TTAS D.Alfredsson/J.Spezza 6.00 15.00
TTBD B.Seabrook/D.Keith 6.00 15.00
TTBJ J.Johnson/R.Blake 6.00 15.00
TTBL M.Brodeur/R.Luongo 12.00 30.00
TTBN M.Biron/A.Niittymaki 5.00 12.00
TTBR M.Richards/D.Briere 6.00 15.00
TTBS D.Stafford/S.Bernier 5.00 12.00
TTBT D.Tucker/J.Blake 5.00 12.00
TTCL N.Lidstrom/C.Chelios 6.00 15.00
TTCM S.Crosby/E.Malkin 15.00 40.00
TTCR J.Cheechoo/M.Ryder 6.00 15.00
TTDF P.Datsyuk/S.Fedorov 10.00 25.00
TTDG M.Gaborik/P.Demitra 8.00 20.00
TTDM S.Doan/P.Mueller 5.00 12.00
TTDS M.Modano/D.Weight 10.00 25.00
TTDZ P.Datsyuk/H.Zetterberg 8.00 20.00
TTEC E.Staal/C.Ward 8.00 20.00
TTEM E.Staal/M.Staal 8.00 20.00
TTEP P.Elias/Z.Parise 6.00 15.00
TTFB P.Forsberg/N.Backstrom 10.00 25.00
TTFM M.Fleury/E.Malkin 20.00 50.00
TTFS P.Forsberg/B.Salming 8.00 20.00
TTGB S.Gagne/D.Briere 6.00 15.00
TTGD S.Gomez/C.Drury 5.00 12.00
TTGH S.Gagne/D.Heatley 6.00 15.00
TTGK M.Gaborik/M.Koivu 8.00 20.00
TTGL W.Gretzky/M.Lemieux 20.00 50.00
TTGM W.Gretzky/M.Messier 30.00 80.00
TTGS M.Satan/B.Guerin 6.00 15.00
TTHG A.Hemsky/S.Gagner 5.00 12.00
TTHM G.Howe/M.Messier 15.00 40.00
TTHO D.Hasek/C.Osgood 8.00 20.00
TTHV N.Horton/T.Vokoun 5.00 12.00
TTIK J.Iginla/M.Kiprusoff 6.00 15.00
TTJJ E.Johnson/B.Jackman 5.00 12.00
TTJL H.Lundqvist/V.Toskala 8.00 20.00
TTJR J.Staal/R.Malone 6.00 15.00
TTJS O.Jokinen/S.Koivu 6.00 15.00
TTKB P.Kariya/B.Boyes 8.00 20.00
TTKF S.Fedorov/V.Kozlov 8.00 20.00
TTKJ A.Kopitar/J.Johnson 10.00 25.00
TTKK A.Kovalev/A.Kostitsyn 5.00 12.00
TTKL I.Kovalchuk/K.Lehtonen 6.00 15.00
TTKP S.Koivu/C.Price 12.00 30.00
TTKT M.Kiprusoff/V.Toskala 5.00 12.00
TTLG R.Langway/M.Green 6.00 15.00
TTLH N.Lidstrom/T.Holmstrom 6.00 15.00
TTLM M.Lemieux/E.Malkin 20.00 50.00
TTLN R.Nash/P.Leclaire 6.00 15.00
TTLS S.Shutt/L.Robinson 6.00 15.00
TTLT J.Thornton/V.Lecavalier 8.00 20.00
TTMC P.Marleau/J.Cheechoo 6.00 15.00
TTMK R.Kesler/B.Morrison 8.00 20.00
TTMP M.Modano/Z.Parise 10.00 25.00
TTMR M.Modano/B.Richards 10.00 25.00
TTMS L.McDonald/B.Salming 6.00 15.00
TTMT J.Thornton/P.Marleau 8.00 20.00
TTMV R.Miller/T.Vanek 6.00 15.00
TTMW M.Gaborik/P.Bouchard 8.00 20.00
TTNK C.Neely/P.Kessel 8.00 20.00
TTNL R.Luongo/M.Naslund 8.00 20.00
TTNY R.DiPietro/B.Guerin 6.00 15.00
TTOE A.Edler/M.Ohlund 4.00 10.00
TTOM A.Ovechkin/E.Malkin 25.00 60.00
TTOS A.Oates/M.Savard 6.00 15.00
TTPF S.Gagne/M.Biron 6.00 15.00
TTPN S.Niedermayer/C.Pronger 6.00 15.00
TTPP P.Stastny/P.Stastny 6.00 15.00
TTPR P.Stastny/R.Smyth 6.00 15.00
TTPS D.Stafford/D.Paille 5.00 12.00
TTRC W.Redden/M.Commodore 4.00 10.00
TTRD M.Dionne/L.Robitaille 8.00 20.00
TTRL M.Ryder/G.Latendresse 4.00 10.00
TTRM M.Ribeiro/B.Morrow 5.00 12.00
TTRP P.Roy/C.Price 25.00 60.00
TTRS L.Robitaille/S.Shutt 6.00 15.00
TTSA S.Sullivan/J.Arnott 5.00 12.00
TTSB P.Bergeron/M.Savard 8.00 20.00
TTSF J.Sakic/P.Forsberg 10.00 25.00
TTSG T.Selanne/J.Giguere 12.00 30.00
TTSH S.Horcoff/J.Stoll 5.00 12.00
TTSJ J.Cheechoo/M.Michalek 6.00 15.00
TTSK J.Kurri/T.Selanne 12.00 30.00
TTSM S.Koivu/M.Koivu 6.00 15.00
TTSO A.Ovechkin/A.Semin 25.00 60.00
TTSR J.Sakic/P.Roy 12.00 30.00
TTSS H.Sedin/D.Sedin 6.00 15.00
TTSW M.Svatos/W.Wolski 5.00 12.00
TTTB P.Budaj/J.Theodore 6.00 15.00
TTTK P.Kane/J.Toews 12.00 30.00
TTTL M.Legace/K.Tkachuk 6.00 15.00
TTTM M.Sundin/A.Steen 6.00 15.00
TTTT J.Thornton/J.Toews 15.00 40.00
TTVB T.Vokoun/J.Bouwmeester 6.00 15.00
TTVP V.Lecavalier/P.Ranger 5.00 12.00
TTWB R.Brind'Amour/J.Williams 6.00 15.00
TTWH S.Weiss/N.Horton 5.00 12.00
TTWL R.Whitney/K.Letang 6.00 15.00
TTZG S.Gonchar/S.Zubov 5.00 12.00

2008-09 Artifacts Tundra Tandems Bronze

*BRONZE/75: .4X TO 1X BASE
STATED PRINT RUN 75 SERIAL #'d SETS
TTFB P.Forsberg/N.Backstrom 10.00 25.00

2008-09 Artifacts Tundra Tandems Gold

*GOLD/25: .6X TO 1.5X BASE
STATED PRINT RUN 25 SERIAL #'d SETS
TTFB P.Forsberg/N.Backstrom 15.00 40.00

2008-09 Artifacts Tundra Trios Gold

STATED PRINT RUN 75 SERIAL #'d SETS
T3ASE Spezza/Alfredsson/Redden 10.00 25.00
T3ASR Weber/Arnott/Sullivan 8.00 20.00
T3BEP Elias/Parise/Brodeur 20.00 50.00
T3BKJ Kopitar/Brown/Johnson 15.00 40.00
T3BSW Staal/Brind'Amour/Ward 12.00 30.00
T3CLO Ciccarelli/Oates/Lngwy 10.00 25.00
T3FCM Crosby/Malkin/Fleury 40.00 100.00
T3FKM Messier/Kurri/Fuhr 10.00 25.00
T3GBK Gabrk/Koiv/Bouchrd 12.00 30.00
T3GBR Gagne/Richards/Biron 10.00 25.00
T3GSD Satan/Guerin/DiPietro 10.00 25.00
T3HKL Koval/Holik/Leht 10.00 25.00
T3HLD Datsyuk/Lidstrom/Hasek 12.00 30.00
T3ICK Iginla/Cammllr/Kiprsff 10.00 25.00
T3JDM Doan/Mueller/Jovanovski 8.00 20.00
T3KKP Koivu/Kovalev/Price 40.00 100.00
T3KLB Kariya/Boyes/Legace 12.00 30.00
T3KOM Ovech/Malkin/Koval 15.00 40.00
T3KTK Kane/Toews/Khabibulin 25.00 60.00
T3LAM Messier/Leetch/Anderson 12.00 30.00
T3LBR Bourq/Robnsn/Lngwy 15.00 40.00
T3LGM Gretz/Mario/Mess 50.00 125.00
T3LNB Nash/Brule/Leclaire 10.00 25.00
T3LSD Lecavlr/St.Louis/Denis 10.00 25.00
T3MMM McDon/MacInn/Mulln 10.00 25.00
T3MRM Modano/Roenick/Mullen 15.00 40.00
T3MRT Modano/Richards/Turco 15.00 40.00
T3MVS Vanek/Stafford/Miller 10.00 25.00
T3NBO Neely/Oates/Bourque 10.00 25.00
T3NLS Naslund/Sedin/Bourque 12.00 30.00
T3RBL Roy/Brodeur/Luongo 25.00 60.00
T3RHG Hemsky/Gagner/Roloson 8.00 20.00
T3SBS Sakic/Stastny/Budaj 15.00 40.00
T3SBT Bergern/Savrd/Thoms 12.00 30.00
T3SJL Shanh/Staal/Lundqvst 12.00 30.00
T3SNG Selanne/Nieder/Giguere 20.00 50.00
T3STS Sundin/Steen/Toskala 10.00 25.00
T3STT Thornton/Sakic/Toews 25.00 60.00
T3SWV Savard/Vaive/Wilson 12.00 30.00
T3TNC Thornton/Chee/Nabok 12.00 30.00
T3TSB Trottier/Smith/Bourne 12.00 30.00
T3VWH Weiss/Horton/Vokoun 8.00 20.00

2009-10 Artifacts

COMP.SET w/o SPs (100) 12.00 30.00
101-150 LEG/STAR PRINT RUN 999
151-200 ROOKIE PRINT RUN 999
201-242 ROOKIE PRINT RUN 699
1 Henrik Lundqvist .60 1.50
2 Chris Osgood .40 1.00
3 Jason Spezza .40 1.00
4 Brian Campbell .30 .75
5 Kris Versteeg .40 1.00
6 Wojtek Wolski .25 .60
7 Simon Gagne .40 1.00
8 Phil Kessel .50 1.25
9 Eric Staal .50 1.25
10 Doug Weight .40 1.00
11 Pavel Datsyuk .50 1.25
12 Niklas Backstrom .40 1.00
13 Zach Parise .40 1.00
14 Steven Stamkos .75 2.00
15 Olli Jokinen .30 .75
16 Jonas Hiller .30 .75
17 Cam Ward .40 1.00
18 Henrik Zetterberg .50 1.25
19 Miikka Kiprusoff .30 .75
20 Roberto Luongo .50 1.25
21 Andrei Kostitsyn .30 .75
22 Patrice Bergeron .50 1.25
23 Jeff Carter .40 1.00
24 Carey Price 1.50 4.00
25 Teemu Selanne .75 2.00
26 Chris Drury .30 .75
27 Thomas Vanek .40 1.00
28 Patrick Kane .75 2.00
29 Peter Budaj .30 .75
30 Daniel Alfredsson .40 1.00
31 Joe Thornton .40 1.00
32 Patrick Marleau .40 1.00
33 Tim Thomas .40 1.00
34 Blake Wheeler .40 1.00
35 Jason Arnott .30 .75
36 Shane Doan .30 .75
37 Nathan Horton .40 1.00
38 Jonathan Toews .75 2.00
39 Ryan Kesler .40 1.00
40 Patrick O'Sullivan .30 .75
41 Tomas Kaberle .25 .60
42 Jordan Staal .40 1.00
43 Tomas Vokoun .30 .75
44 Dany Heatley .40 1.00
45 Patrik Berglund .25 .60
46 Vincent Lecavalier .30 .75
47 David Backes .40 1.00
48 Derick Brassard .40 1.00
49 Patrik Elias .40 1.00
50 Martin St. Louis .40 1.00
51 Ray Whitney .30 .75
52 Evgeni Nabokov .30 .75
53 Martin Brodeur .75 2.00
54 Evgeni Malkin 1.25 3.00
55 Pierre-Marc Bouchard .40 1.00
56 Nicklas Backstrom .60 1.50
57 Shea Weber .30 .75
58 Bobby Ryan .40 1.00
59 Mikhail Grabovski .40 1.00
60 Sidney Crosby 1.50 4.00
61 Nicklas Lidstrom .40 1.00
62 Brad Richards .40 1.00
63 Jason Pominville .40 1.00
64 Rick DiPietro .30 .75
65 Ales Hemsky .30 .75
66 Marty Turco .40 1.00
67 Mason Raymond .40 1.00
68 Ilya Kovalchuk .40 1.00
69 Mike Modano .60 1.50
70 Ryan Getzlaf .60 1.50
71 Alexander Frolov .30 .75
72 Steve Mason .30 .75
73 Zach Bogosian .30 .75
74 Bryan Little .40 1.00
75 David Booth .25 .60
76 Nikolai Zherdev .25 .60
77 Alexander Ovechkin 1.50 4.00
78 Mike Richards .40 1.00
79 Ryan Miller .40 1.00
80 J.P. Dumont .25 .60
81 Jarome Iginla .40 1.00
82 Sam Gagner .30 .75
83 Anze Kopitar .60 1.50
84 Milan Hejduk .30 .75
85 Drew Doughty .50 1.25
86 Peter Mueller .30 .75
87 Marc Staal .40 1.00
88 Andrei Markov .40 1.00
89 Simeon Varlamov .40 1.00
90 Rick Nash .30 .75
91 Marc-Andre Fleury .60 1.50
92 Dion Phaneuf .50 1.25
93 Paul Stastny .40 1.00
94 Tomas Plekanec .40 1.00
95 Andrew Cogliano .30 .75
96 Mikko Koivu .40 1.00
97 Jakub Voracek .40 1.00
98 Luke Schenn .30 .75
99 Devin Setoguchi .30 .75
100 Paul Kariya .50 1.25
101 Denis Potvin L 1.25 3.00
102 Steve Shutt L 1.25 3.00
103 Dale Hawerchuk L 1.50 4.00
104 Stan Mikita L 1.50 4.00
105 Mario Lemieux L 4.00 10.00
106 Denis Savard L 1.50 4.00
107 Alex Delvecchio L 1.50 4.00
108 Johnny Bucyk L 2.00 5.00
109 Ted Lindsay L 1.00 2.50
110 Clark Gillies L 1.25 3.00
111 Red Kelly L 1.25 3.00
112 Gilbert Perreault L 1.25 3.00
113 Jean Beliveau L 1.25 3.00
114 Mark Messier L 1.50 4.00
115 Guy Carbonneau L 2.00 5.00
116 Steve Yzerman L 3.00 8.00
117 Frank Mahovlich L 1.50 4.00
118 Lanny McDonald L 1.25 3.00
119 Peter Stastny L 1.25 3.00
120 Larry Robinson L 1.25 3.00
121 Bobby Orr L 4.00 10.00
122 Cam Neely L 1.25 3.00
123 Rogie Vachon L 1.50 4.00
124 Phil Esposito L 2.00 5.00
125 Johnny Bower L 1.50 4.00
126 Luc Robitaille L 1.25 3.00
127 Patrick Roy L 3.00 8.00
128 Doug Gilmour L 1.50 4.00
129 Mike Bossy L 1.25 3.00
130 Bobby Clarke L 1.25 3.00
131 Ray Bourque L 2.00 5.00
132 Al MacInnis L 1.25 3.00
133 Bobby Hull L 1.50 4.00
134 Gordie Howe L 3.00 8.00
135 Wayne Gretzky L 6.00 15.00
136 Alexander Ovechkin S 5.00 12.00
137 Jonathan Toews S 2.50 6.00
138 Henrik Zetterberg S 1.50 4.00
139 Joe Thornton S 1.25 3.00
140 Evgeni Malkin S 4.00 10.00
141 Henrik Lundqvist S 2.00 5.00
142 Pavel Datsyuk S 1.50 4.00
143 Martin Brodeur S 2.50 6.00
144 Ilya Kovalchuk S 1.25 3.00
145 Patrick Kane S 2.50 6.00
146 Carey Price S 5.00 12.00
147 Jeff Carter S 1.25 3.00
148 Vincent Lecavalier S 1.00 2.50
149 Jarome Iginla S 1.25 3.00
150 Sidney Crosby S 5.00 12.00
151 Chris Durno RC 2.00 5.00
152 Peter Regin RC 2.00 5.00
153 Kevin Quick RC 1.50 4.00
154 Kurtis McLean RC 2.00 5.00
155 Mike Santorelli RC 2.50 6.00
156 Alexander Sulzer RC 1.50 4.00
157 Troy Bodie RC 2.00 5.00
158 Matt Beleskey RC 2.00 5.00
159 Kevin Westgarth RC 2.00 5.00
160 John Scott RC 2.50 6.00
161 Mikael Backlund RC 2.50 6.00
162 Byron Bitz RC 2.00 5.00
163 Bryan Rodney RC 2.00 5.00
164 Tim Wallace RC 1.50 4.00
165 Ben Lovejoy RC 2.50 6.00
166 Riley Armstrong RC 2.00 5.00
167 Jaime Sifers RC 2.00 5.00
168 Sean Collins RC 2.00 5.00
169 Riku Helenius RC 2.50 6.00
170 Ville Leino RC 2.00 5.00
171 Michal Neuvirth RC 4.00 10.00
172 Artem Anisimov RC 2.50 6.00
173 Davis Drewiske RC 2.50 6.00
174 David Schlemko RC 2.00 5.00
175 Luca Caputi RC 2.50 6.00
176 Jakub Petruzalek RC 2.50 6.00
177 Ryan Vesce RC 2.00 5.00
178 Jay Beagle RC 3.00 8.00
179 Jhonas Enroth RC 3.00 8.00
180 Brandon Segal RC 2.00 5.00
181 Tim Stapleton RC 2.50 6.00
182 Jesse Joensuu RC 2.00 5.00
183 David Van Der Gulik RC 2.00 5.00
184 Antti Niemi RC 4.00 10.00
185 Grant Lewis RC 2.00 5.00
186 Cal O'Reilly RC 2.00 5.00
187 Brian Salcido RC 2.00 5.00
188 Phil Oreskovic RC 2.50 6.00
189 Kris Chucko RC 2.00 5.00
190 Joel Rechlicz RC 1.50 4.00
191 Andrew MacDonald RC 1.50 4.00
192 Spencer Machacek RC 2.50 6.00
193 T.J. Galiardi RC 2.50 6.00
194 Michael Sauer RC 2.00 5.00
195 Yannick Weber RC 2.50 6.00
196 Christian Hanson RC 2.50 6.00
197 Ivan Vishnevskiy RC 2.00 5.00
198 Taylor Chorney RC 2.50 6.00
199 John Negrin RC 2.50 6.00
200 Matt Pelech RC 2.50 6.00
201 John Carlson RC 4.00 10.00
202 Michael Grabner RC 2.50 6.00
203 Jonas Gustavsson RC 3.00 8.00
204 Victor Hedman RC 5.00 12.00
205 Lars Eller RC 2.50 6.00
206 Logan Couture RC 5.00 12.00
207 Mark Letestu RC 2.50 6.00
208 Shawn Heshka RC 2.50 6.00
209 James van Riemsdyk RC 5.00 12.00
210 Erik Karlsson RC 8.00 20.00
211 Michael Del Zotto RC 2.50 6.00
212 John Tavares RC 12.00 30.00
213 Matthew Corrente RC 2.00 5.00
214 Colin Wilson RC 2.50 6.00
215 Mathieu Carle RC 2.50 6.00
216 Danny Irmen RC 1.50 4.00
217 Andrei Loktionov RC 3.00 8.00
218 Dmitry Kulikov RC 2.50 6.00
219 Devan Dubnyk RC 5.00 12.00
220 Jakub Kindl RC 2.50 6.00
221 Jamie Benn RC 8.00 20.00
222 Ryan Stoa RC 2.00 5.00
223 Matt Duchene RC 5.00 12.00
224 Matt Gilroy RC 2.50 6.00
225 Viktor Stalberg RC 2.50 6.00
226 Sergei Shirokov RC 1.50 4.00
227 Tyler Myers RC 4.00 10.00
228 Brad Marchand RC 6.00 15.00
229 Evander Kane RC 5.00 12.00
230 MacGregor Sharp RC 2.50 6.00
231 Ryan Oâ€™Reilly RC 4.00 10.00
232 Daniel Larsson RC 2.00 5.00
233 Ryan O'Marra RC 1.50 4.00
234 Bobby Sanguinetti RC 1.50 4.00
235 Jason Demers RC 4.00 10.00
236 Tyler Ennis RC 3.00 8.00
237 Tyler Bozak RC 4.00 10.00
238 Benn Ferriero RC 2.50 6.00
239 Mikko Lehtonen RC 4.00 10.00
240 Anton Khudobin RC 2.50 6.00
241 Tyler Eckford RC 2.00 5.00
242 James Reimer RC 6.00 15.00

2009-10 Artifacts Gold

*1-100 VETS/75: 3X TO 8X BASIC CARDS
*101-150 L/S/75: 1X TO 2.5X L/S/999
*151-200 ROOKIES/75: .8X TO 2X RC/999
STATED PRINT RUN 50 SER.#'d SETS

2009-10 Artifacts Silver

*1-100 VETS/75: 2.5X TO 6X BASIC CARDS
*101-150 L/S/75: .8X TO 2X L/S/999
*151-200 ROOKIES/75: .6X TO 1.5X RC/999
STATED PRINT RUN 75 SER.#'d SETS

2009-10 Artifacts Silver Spectrum

*1-100 VETS/25: 4X TO 10X BASIC CARDS
*101-150 L/S/25: 1.2X TO 3X L/S/999
*151-200 ROOKIES/25: 1X TO 2.5X RC/999
STATED PRINT RUN 25 SER.#'d SETS

2009-10 Artifacts Autofacts

AFAC Andrew Cogliano 5.00 12.00
AFAE Andrew Ebbett 4.00 10.00
AFAM Al MacInnis 6.00 15.00
AFAO Adam Oates 6.00 15.00
AFAT Alex Tanguay 4.00 10.00
AFBB Bob Bourne 5.00 12.00
AFBG Brian Gionta 5.00 12.00
AFBL Brian Lee 6.00 15.00
AFBM Brenden Morrow 5.00 12.00
AFBO Brian Boyle 4.00 10.00
AFBP Pierre-Marc Bouchard 6.00 15.00
AFCA Mike Cammalleri 5.00 12.00
AFCG Clark Gillies 6.00 15.00
AFCH Don Cherry 15.00 40.00
AFCR Sidney Crosby 75.00 150.00
AFCS Cory Stillman 5.00 12.00
AFDA Matt D'Agostini 5.00 12.00
AFDB David Booth 4.00 10.00
AFDC David Clarkson 5.00 12.00
AFDD Drew Doughty 8.00 20.00
AFDG Daniel Girardi 4.00 10.00
AFDH Dale Hawerchuk 15.00 30.00
AFDJ David Jones 4.00 10.00
AFDL Dan LaCosta 5.00 12.00
AFDP David Perron 4.00 10.00
AFDS Darryl Sittler 8.00 20.00
AFDU Dustin Boyd 4.00 10.00
AFDW Doug Weight 6.00 15.00
AFEL Patrik Elias 6.00 15.00
AFEM Evgeni Malkin 40.00 80.00
AFEN Evgeni Nabokov 5.00 12.00
AFES Phil Esposito 10.00 25.00
AFFB Fabian Brunnstrom 5.00 12.00
AFFI Mark Fistric 4.00 10.00
AFFM Frank Mahovlich 15.00 30.00
AFGA Glenn Anderson 6.00 15.00
AFGH Gordie Howe 30.00 60.00
AFHE Dany Heatley 6.00 15.00
AFHM Milan Hejduk 5.00 12.00
AFJB Jean Beliveau 60.00 120.00
AFJD Jeff Drouin-Deslauriers 4.00 10.00
AFJE Jonathan Ericsson 5.00 12.00
AFJG Jean-Sebastien Giguere 6.00 15.00
AFJJ Jack Johnson 4.00 10.00
AFJK Jari Kurri 8.00 20.00
AFJM Joe Mullen 5.00 12.00
AFJP Jason Pominville 6.00 15.00
AFJS Jack Skille 4.00 10.00
AFJT Joe Thornton 6.00 15.00
AFKC Kyle Chipchura 5.00 12.00
AFKD Kris Draper 4.00 10.00
AFKL Kari Lehtonen 5.00 12.00
AFKT Kyle Turris 6.00 15.00
AFLI Bryan Little 6.00 15.00
AFLR Larry Robinson 6.00 15.00
AFLS Luke Schenn 5.00 12.00
AFMB Mike Bossy 8.00 20.00
AFMC Bryan McCabe 5.00 12.00
AFMD Marcel Dionne 10.00 25.00
AFMF Marc-Andre Fleury 12.00 30.00
AFMH Martin Havlat 5.00 12.00
AFMI Mike Iggulden 4.00 10.00
AFMK Miikka Kiprusoff
AFML Milan Lucic 5.00 12.00
AFMM Milan Michalek 4.00 10.00
AFMO Mike Modano 8.00 20.00
AFMP Michael Peca 5.00 12.00
AFMR Mason Raymond 6.00 15.00
AFNK Nikolai Khabibulin 6.00 15.00
AFNZ Nikolai Zherdev 4.00 10.00
AFPB Peter Budaj 5.00 12.00
AFPE Dustin Penner 4.00 10.00
AFPI Alex Pietrangelo 5.00 12.00
AFPK Phil Kessel 8.00 20.00
AFPM Patrick Marleau 10.00 25.00
AFPO Denis Potvin 6.00 15.00
AFPR Patrick Roy 50.00 100.00
AFRB Rob Blake 6.00 15.00
AFRC Ryane Clowe 5.00 12.00
AFRH Ron Hextall 10.00 25.00
AFRI Mattias Ritola 5.00 12.00
AFRK Rostislav Klesla 6.00 15.00
AFRM Mike Ribeiro 5.00 12.00
AFRV Rogie Vachon 8.00 20.00
AFRY Ryan Miller 6.00 15.00
AFSA Derek Sanderson 5.00 12.00
AFSC Marek Schwarz 4.00 10.00
AFSE Devin Setoguchi 5.00 12.00
AFSH James Sheppard 4.00 10.00
AFSS Steven Stamkos 12.00 30.00
AFTG Tom Gilbert 4.00 10.00
AFTS Tom Sestito 4.00 10.00
AFTV Thomas Vanek 6.00 15.00
AFTW Ty Wishart 5.00 12.00
AFVF Valtteri Filppula 6.00 15.00
AFWI Doug Wilson 5.00 12.00
AFZB Zach Boychuk 5.00 12.00

2009-10 Artifacts Frozen Artifacts

STATED PRINT RUN 199 SER.#'d SETS
*BLUE/25: .6X TO 1.5X BASIC JSY
*COPPER/50: .5X TO 1.2X BASIC JSY
*JSY-PATCH/35: .8X TO 2X BASIC JSY
*BLU JSY-PTCH/25: 1X TO 2.5X BASIC JSY
*RETAIL JSY: .4X TO 1X BASIC JSY
FAAM Al MacInnis 5.00 12.00
FABC Bobby Clarke 5.00 12.00
FABL Brian Leetch 8.00 20.00
FABN Bernie Nicholls 3.00 8.00
FABO Mike Bossy 5.00 12.00
FABR Rob Blake 5.00 12.00
FABS Borje Salming 5.00 12.00
FABU Johnny Bucyk 8.00 20.00
FACJ Curtis Joseph 6.00 15.00
FACN Cam Neely 5.00 12.00
FADC Dino Ciccarelli 5.00 12.00
FADG Doug Gilmour 6.00 15.00
FADH Dale Hawerchuk 6.00 15.00
FADW Doug Weight 5.00 12.00
FAFM Frank Mahovlich 6.00 15.00
FAGA Glenn Anderson 5.00 12.00
FAGC Guy Carbonneau 8.00 20.00
FAGF Grant Fuhr 5.00 12.00
FAGH Gordie Howe 12.00 30.00
FAGP Gilbert Perreault 5.00 12.00
FAJK Jari Kurri 5.00 12.00
FAJS Joe Sakic 8.00 20.00
FALM Lanny McDonald 5.00 12.00
FALR Larry Robinson 5.00 12.00
FAMB Martin Brodeur 10.00 25.00
FAML Mario Lemieux 15.00 40.00
FAMM Mark Messier 6.00 15.00
FAMO Mike Modano 8.00 20.00
FAMS Mats Sundin 5.00 12.00
FANI Scott Niedermayer 5.00 12.00
FANL Nicklas Lidstrom 5.00 12.00
FAPE Phil Esposito 8.00 20.00
FAPK Paul Kariya 6.00 15.00
FAPR Patrick Roy 12.00 30.00
FAPS Peter Stastny 5.00 12.00
FARB Ray Bourque 8.00 20.00
FARH Ron Hextall 8.00 20.00
FARL Rod Langway 4.00 10.00
FARO Luc Robitaille 5.00 12.00
FASF Sergei Fedorov 8.00 20.00
FASH Brendan Shanahan 6.00 15.00
FASK Saku Koivu 5.00 12.00
FASS Steve Shutt 5.00 12.00
FATE Tony Esposito 5.00 12.00
FATS Teemu Selanne 10.00 25.00
FAWG Wayne Gretzky 25.00 60.00
FAWI Doug Wilson 4.00 10.00

2009-10 Artifacts Treasured Swatches

STATED PRINT RUN 199 SER.#'d SETS
*BLUE/25: .6X TO 1.5X BASIC JSY
*COPPER/50: .5X TO 1.2X BASIC JSY
*JSY-PATCH/35: .8X TO 2X BASIC JSY
*BLU JSY-PTCH/25: 1X TO 2.5X BASIC JSY
*RETAIL: .3X TO .8X BASIC JSY
TSAK Alex Kovalev 5.00 12.00
TSAO Alexander Ovechkin 8.00 20.00
TSBR Brad Richards 5.00 12.00
TSBW Blake Wheeler 5.00 12.00
TSCD Chris Drury 4.00 10.00
TSCP Carey Price 20.00 50.00
TSDD Drew Doughty 6.00 15.00
TSDH Dany Heatley 5.00 12.00
TSDP Dion Phaneuf 6.00 15.00
TSDS Daniel Sedin 5.00 12.00
TSEM Evgeni Malkin 15.00 40.00
TSEN Evgeni Nabokov 4.00 10.00
TSES Eric Staal 6.00 15.00
TSGA Marian Gaborik 6.00 15.00
TSHL Henrik Lundqvist 8.00 20.00
TSIK Ilya Kovalchuk 5.00 12.00
TSJB Jay Bouwmeester 5.00 12.00
TSJC Duncan Keith 5.00 12.00
TSJI Jarome Iginla 5.00 12.00
TSJP Jason Pominville 5.00 12.00
TSJS Jason Spezza 5.00 12.00
TSJT Jonathan Toews 10.00 25.00
TSKO Anze Kopitar 8.00 20.00
TSLS Luke Schenn 4.00 10.00
TSMA Patrick Marleau 5.00 12.00
TSMF Marc-Andre Fleury 8.00 20.00
TSMG Mike Green 5.00 12.00
TSMH Marian Hossa 4.00 10.00
TSMK Miikka Kiprusoff 4.00 10.00
TSMN Markus Naslund 4.00 10.00
TSMR Mike Richards 5.00 12.00
TSMS Marc Savard 3.00 8.00
TSMT Marty Turco 5.00 12.00
TSNB Nicklas Backstrom 8.00 20.00
TSOJ Olli Jokinen 4.00 10.00
TSPD Pavel Datsyuk 6.00 15.00
TSPL Pascal Leclaire 5.00 12.00
TSPM Peter Mueller 4.00 10.00
TSPS Paul Stastny 5.00 12.00
TSRD Rick DiPietro 4.00 10.00
TSRG Ryan Getzlaf 8.00 20.00
TSRL Roberto Luongo 6.00 15.00
TSRM Ryan Miller 5.00 12.00
TSRN Rick Nash 4.00 10.00
TSSC Sidney Crosby 20.00 50.00
TSSE Devin Setoguchi 4.00 10.00
TSSM Martin St. Louis 5.00 12.00
TSST Jordan Staal 5.00 12.00
TSSV Marek Svatos 3.00 8.00
TSWR Wade Redden 3.00 8.00

2009-10 Artifacts Tundra Tandems

STATED PRINT RUN 100 SER.#'d SETS
*RED/50: .5X TO 1.2X BASIC DUAL
*SILVER/25: .6X TO 1.5X BASIC DUAL
*PATCH/35: .8X TO 2X BASIC DUAL
*PATCH RED/15: 1X TO 2.5X BASIC DUAL
TTBE Brodeur/Elias 10.00 25.00
TTBK Kopitar/Brown 8.00 20.00
TTCM Malkin/Crosby 20.00 50.00
TTCR Chelios/Rafalski 5.00 12.00
TTDM Mueller/Doan 4.00 10.00
TTDT Selanne/Hawerchuk 10.00 25.00
TTED Perron/Johnson 4.00 10.00
TTFM Federko/Mullen 4.00 10.00
TTFS Fleury/Staal 8.00 20.00
TTFT Thomas/Fernandez 5.00 12.00
TTGA Zherdev/Gaborik 6.00 15.00
TTGF Gilmour/Fleury 8.00 20.00
TTGR Richards/Gagne 5.00 12.00
TTGS Selanne/Getzlaf 10.00 25.00
TTHB Booth/Horton 5.00 12.00
TTHH Hextall/Howe 8.00 20.00
TTHZ Zetterberg/Holmstrom 6.00 15.00
TTIB Bouwmeester/Iginla 5.00 12.00
TTJD Doughty/Johnson 6.00 15.00
TTJK Jokinen/Kiprusoff 4.00 10.00
TTJP Leclaire/Spezza 5.00 12.00
TTKL Kovalchuk/Little 6.00 15.00
TTKT Kariya/Tkachuk 6.00 15.00
TTKW Kessel/Wheeler 6.00 15.00
TTLC Crosby/Lemieux 20.00 50.00
TTLD Datsyuk/Lidstrom 6.00 15.00
TTLM Messier/Leetch 6.00 15.00
TTLS Stamkos/Lecavalier 10.00 25.00
TTMF Fuhr/Messier 6.00 15.00
TTMS Marleau/Setoguchi 5.00 12.00
TTMT Modano/Turco 8.00 20.00
TTNB Bourque/Neely 8.00 20.00
TTNK Kurri/Nicholls 5.00 12.00
TTNL Naslund/Lundqvist 8.00 20.00
TTNU Nash/Umberger 4.00 10.00
TTOB Backstrom/Ovechkin 8.00 20.00
TTOD Draper/Osgood 5.00 12.00
TTOG Gagner/O'Sullivan 4.00 10.00
TTPB Seabrook/Sharp 5.00 12.00
TTPC Clarkson/Parise 5.00 12.00
TTPS Stafford/Pominville 5.00 12.00
TTPW Stastny/Wolski 5.00 12.00
TTRG Robitaille/Gretzky 20.00 50.00
TTRS Savard/Roy 12.00 30.00
TTRV Roy/Vanek 5.00 12.00
TTSB Sakic/Bourque 8.00 20.00
TTSG Gilmour/Sundin 6.00 15.00
TTSH Spezza/Heatley 5.00 12.00
TTSL Sundin/Luongo 6.00 15.00
TTSS Sundin/Salming 5.00 12.00
TTSW Ward/Staal 6.00 15.00
TTTG Theodore/Green 5.00 12.00
TTTK Kane/Toews 10.00 25.00
TTWD DiPietro/Weight 5.00 12.00
TTWS Weber/Sullivan 4.00 10.00

2009-10 Artifacts Tundra Trios

STATED PRINT RUN 75 SER.#'d SETS
TRIASW Arnott/Sullivan/Weber 8.00 20.00
TRIBEP Parise/Elias/Brodeur 20.00 50.00
TRIBHS Weiss/Horton/Booth 10.00 25.00
TRIBKP Phaneuf/Kiprsf/Bouwm 12.00 30.00
TRIBSW Staal/Brind`Amour/Ward 12.00 30.00
TRICGM Crosby/Mess/Gretzky 40.00 100.00
TRICMS Crosby/Staal/Malkin 40.00 100.00
TRIDMB Mueller/Doan/Boedker 8.00 20.00
TRIEJM Staal/Staal/Staal 12.00 30.00
TRIFCT Fernndz/Thomas/Chara 10.00 25.00
TRIFKD Frolov/Doughty/Kopitar 15.00 40.00
TRIGCK Gomez/Kostits/Cammall 8.00 20.00
TRIGFL Letang/Fleury/Gonchar 10.00 25.00
TRIGOB Green/Bckstrm/Ovech 40.00 100.00
TRIGRC Richards/Gagne/Carter 10.00 25.00
TRIHOD Holmstrm/Datsyk/Osgd 12.00 30.00
TRIJIB Bouwmstr/Jokin/Iginla 10.00 25.00
TRIKGG Giguere/Koivu/Getzlaf 15.00 40.00
TRIKLL Little/Kovalchk/Lehtnen 10.00 25.00
TRIKTP Tkachuk/Kariya/Perron 12.00 30.00
TRILBE Edler/Bieksa/Luongo 12.00 30.00
TRILGH Howe/Gretzky/Lemieux 50.00 125.00
TRILHZ Holmstrm/Zetter/Lidstrm 12.00 30.00
TRILSS Stamkos/Lecav/St.L 20.00 50.00
TRIMGP Price/Markov/Gionta 40.00 100.00
TRIMNC Cheech/Nabkv/Marleau 12.00 30.00
TRIMRT Turco/Richards/Modano 15.00 40.00
TRINLZ Naslund/Lundq/Zhrdev 15.00 40.00
TRINSS Sundin/Sakic/Nolan 15.00 40.00
TRIOCG O'Sulli/Cogliano/Gagner 8.00 20.00
TRIPMV Vanek/Pominville/Miller 10.00 25.00
TRIPRS Pominville/Roy/Stafford 10.00 25.00
TRISHS Stastny/Hejduk/Sakic 15.00 40.00
TRISJK Jokinen/Selanne/Kurri 20.00 50.00
TRISLH Spezza/Leclaire/Heatley 10.00 25.00
TRISTK Kane/Toews/Sharp 20.00 50.00
TRITSS Toskala/Stajan/Schenn 10.00 25.00
TRIWDT Weight/DiPietro/Tamblini 10.00 25.00

2010-11 Artifacts

COMP.SET w/o SPs (100) 12.00 30.00
101-150 ROOKIE PRINT RUN 999
151-200 L/S PRINT RUN 999
201-242 ROOKIE REDMP/699 ODDS 1:24
1 Brad Richards .40 1.00
2 Henrik Lundqvist .60 1.50
3 Jonathan Toews .75 2.00
4 Thomas Vanek .40 1.00
5 Andrew Cogliano .25 .60
6 Patrick Kane .75 2.00
7 Carey Price 1.50 4.00
8 Miikka Kiprusoff .30 .75
9 John Tavares .75 2.00
10 Jimmy Howard .50 1.25
11 Ryan Miller .40 1.00
12 Ilya Kovalchuk .40 1.00
13 Vincent Lecavalier .30 .75
14 Pascal Leclaire .30 .75
15 Kyle Okposo .40 1.00
16 Matt Duchene .40 1.00
17 Nicklas Backstrom .60 1.50
18 Shane Doan .30 .75
19 Tomas Vokoun .30 .75
20 Patrik Elias .40 1.00
21 Patrick Marleau .40 1.00
22 Marc-Andre Fleury .60 1.50
23 Alexander Ovechkin 1.50 4.00
24 Mike Cammalleri .40 1.00
25 Dustin Penner .25 .60
26 Marc Savard .25 .60
27 Cam Ward .40 1.00
28 Martin St. Louis .40 1.00
29 Patrik Berglund .25 .60
30 Evander Kane .40 1.00
31 Andrei Markov .40 1.00
32 Mike Green .40 1.00
33 Brandon Sutter .30 .75
34 Derick Brassard .40 1.00
35 Claude Giroux .40 1.00
36 Phil Kessel .50 1.25
37 Chris Stewart .30 .75
38 Joe Pavelski .40 1.00
39 Jonas Gustavsson .50 1.25
40 Ryan Kesler .40 1.00
41 Daniel Briere .40 1.00
42 Brandon Dubinsky .30 .75
43 Jeff Carter .40 1.00
44 Anze Kopitar .60 1.50
45 Milan Lucic .40 1.00
46 Bobby Ryan .40 1.00
47 Dion Phaneuf .40 1.00
48 Steven Stamkos .75 2.00
49 Rene Bourque .25 .60
50 Jason Spezza .25 .60
51 James Neal .40 1.00
52 Tuukka Rask .40 1.00
53 Eric Staal .50 1.25
54 Evgeni Malkin 1.25 3.00
55 Stephen Weiss .30 .75
56 Tyler Myers .40 1.00
57 Rich Peverley .40 1.00
58 Henrik Sedin .40 1.00
59 Mikko Koivu .40 1.00
60 Ilya Bryzgalov .30 .75
61 Roberto Luongo .40 1.00
62 Sidney Crosby 1.50 4.00
63 Zach Parise .40 1.00
64 Joe Thornton .40 1.00
65 J.P. Dumont .25 .60
66 Paul Stastny .40 1.00
67 Ryan Getzlaf .60 1.50
68 David Perron .25 .60
69 Rick Nash .40 1.00
70 Michael Frolik .25 .60
71 Zach Bogosian .30 .75
72 Dany Heatley .30 .75
73 Jamie Benn .50 1.25
74 David Backes .40 1.00
75 Antti Niemi .30 .75
76 Sam Gagner .30 .75
77 Daniel Alfredsson .40 1.00
78 Jack Johnson .25 .60
79 Scottie Upshall .25 .60
80 Patric Hornqvist .30 .75
81 Jordan Staal .40 1.00
82 Corey Perry .40 1.00
83 Mike Richards .40 1.00
84 Jarome Iginla .40 1.00
85 Shea Weber .30 .75
86 Tyler Bozak .40 1.00
87 Niklas Backstrom .40 1.00
88 Drew Doughty .40 1.00
89 Daniel Sedin .40 1.00
90 Pavel Datsyuk .50 1.25
91 Derek Roy .40 1.00
92 Duncan Keith .40 1.00
93 Martin Brodeur .75 2.00
94 Josh Bailey .30 .75
95 Nicklas Lidstrom .40 1.00
96 Jakub Voracek .40 1.00
97 Zdeno Chara .30 .75
98 Marian Gaborik .50 1.25
99 Henrik Zetterberg .50 1.25
100 Guillaume Latendresse .30 .75
101 Nick Palmieri RC 2.00 5.00
102 Zach Hamill RC 2.00 5.00
103 Jamie McBain RC 2.00 5.00
104 Nick Johnson RC 1.50 4.00
105 Dean Arsene RC 2.00 5.00
106 P.K. Subban RC 12.00 30.00
107 Jared Cowen RC 2.00 5.00
108 Justin Mercier RC 2.00 5.00
109 Grant Clitsome RC 2.00 5.00
110 Kaspars Daugavins RC 2.50 6.00
111 Kyle Wilson RC 2.50 6.00
112 Alex Plante RC 2.00 5.00
113 Nate Prosser RC 2.00 5.00
114 Dylan Reese RC 2.00 5.00
115 Brock Trotter RC 4.00 10.00
116 Raymond Sawada RC 1.50 4.00
117 Arturs Kulda RC 2.00 5.00
118 Tomas Kana RC 2.00 5.00
119 Jerome Samson RC 2.00 5.00
120 Chad Kolarik RC 2.00 5.00
121 Corey Elkins RC 1.50 4.00
122 Derek Smith RC 2.00 5.00
123 Brayden Irwin RC 2.00 5.00
124 Charles Linglet RC 2.00 5.00
125 Matt Zaba RC 2.50 6.00
126 Bobby Butler RC 2.00 5.00
127 Cody Almond RC 2.00 5.00
128 Dustin Tokarski RC 2.00 5.00
129 Casey Wellman RC 2.00 5.00
130 Alexander Pechurski RC 2.50 6.00
131 Francis Wathier 2.00 5.00
132 Matt Martin RC 3.00 8.00
133 Ilkka Heikkinen RC 3.00 8.00
134 Maxim Noreau RC 1.50 4.00
135 Jeff Penner RC 3.00 8.00
136 Adam McQuaid RC 2.50 6.00
137 Nick Bonino RC 2.50 6.00
138 Dustin Kohn RC 2.00 5.00
139 Eric Tangradi RC 2.00 5.00
140 Andrew Bodnarchuk RC 2.00 5.00
141 Brandon Yip RC 2.00 5.00
142 Evgeny Dadonov RC 2.50 6.00
143 Justin Falk RC 1.50 4.00
144 J.T. Wyman RC 2.00 5.00
145 Richard Clune RC 2.50 6.00
146 Johan Motin RC 1.50 4.00
147 Nick Spaling RC 2.00 5.00
148 Nazem Kadri RC 6.00 15.00
149 Philip Larsen RC 2.00 5.00
150 Maxime Fortunus RC 1.50 4.00
151 Patrick Kane S 2.50 6.00
152 Jaroslav Halak S 1.25 3.00
153 Sidney Crosby S 5.00 12.00
154 Nicklas Backstrom S 2.00 5.00
155 Joe Thornton S 1.25 3.00
156 Eric Staal S 1.50 4.00
157 Matt Duchene S 1.25 3.00
158 Jonathan Toews S 2.50 6.00
159 Ilya Kovalchuk S 1.25 3.00
160 Evgeni Malkin S 4.00 10.00
161 Marian Gaborik S 1.50 4.00
162 Martin Brodeur S 2.50 6.00
163 Drew Doughty S 1.25 3.00
164 Daniel Sedin S 1.25 3.00
165 Jeff Carter S 1.25 3.00
166 Ryan Miller S 1.25 3.00
167 Marc-Andre Fleury S 2.00 5.00
168 Thomas Vanek S 1.25 3.00
169 Henrik Lundqvist S 2.00 5.00
170 Steven Stamkos S 2.50 6.00
171 Mike Richards S 1.25 3.00
172 Henrik Zetterberg S 1.50 4.00
173 Jonas Gustavsson S 1.50 4.00
174 Vincent Lecavalier S 1.00 2.50
175 Pavel Datsyuk S 1.50 4.00
176 Antti Niemi S 1.00 2.50
177 John Tavares S 2.50 6.00
178 Alexander Ovechkin S 5.00 12.00
179 Jarome Iginla S 1.25 3.00
180 Anze Kopitar S 2.00 5.00
181 Jean Beliveau L 1.25 3.00
182 Luc Robitaille L 1.25 3.00
183 Cam Neely L 1.25 3.00
184 Mike Modano L 2.00 5.00
185 Jari Kurri L 1.25 3.00
186 Bobby Clarke L 1.25 3.00
187 Gordie Howe L 3.00 8.00

188 Mark Messier L 2.00 5.00
189 Gilbert Perreault L 1.25 3.00
190 Ron Hextall L 1.50 4.00
191 Bobby Hull L 1.25 3.00
192 Steve Yzerman L 3.00 8.00
193 Denis Potvin L 1.25 3.00
194 Dale Hawerchuk L 1.50 4.00
195 Bobby Orr L 4.00 10.00
196 Mario Lemieux L 4.00 10.00
197 Patrick Roy L 3.00 8.00
198 Phil Esposito L 2.00 5.00
199 Brian Leetch L 1.25 3.00
200 Wayne Gretzky L 6.00 15.00
201 Cam Fowler RC 4.00 10.00
202 Alexander Burmistrov RC 3.00 8.00
203 Tyler Seguin RC 15.00 30.00
204 Luke Adam RC 3.00 8.00
205 Henrik Karlsson RC 3.00 8.00
206 Jeff Skinner RC 6.00 15.00
207 Nick Leddy RC 3.00 8.00
208 Kevin Shattenkirk RC 6.00 15.00
209 Nick Holden RC 3.00 8.00
210 Philip Larsen RC 3.00 8.00
211 Alexander Vasyunov RC 3.00 8.00
212 Taylor Hall RC 12.00 30.00
213 Jamie Arniel RC 3.00 8.00
214 Brayden Schenn RC 5.00 12.00
215 Marco Scandella RC 3.00 8.00
216 Stefan Della Rovere RC 8.00 20.00
217 Anders Lindback RC 3.00 8.00
218 Jacob Josefson RC 3.00 8.00
219 Nino Niederreiter RC 4.00 10.00
220 Derek Stepan RC 6.00 15.00
221 Robin Lehner RC 6.00 15.00
222 Sergei Bobrovsky RC 10.00 25.00
223 Oliver Ekman-Larsson RC 5.00 12.00
224 Kyle Palmieri RC 6.00 15.00
225 Justin Braun RC 3.00 8.00
226 Ian Cole RC 3.00 8.00
227 Dana Tyrell RC 3.00 8.00
228 Keith Aulie RC 3.00 8.00
229 Matt Kassian RC 3.00 8.00
230 Marcus Johansson RC 5.00 12.00
231 Jordan Eberle RC 8.00 20.00
232 Magnus Paajarvi RC 4.00 10.00
233 Jordan Caron RC 5.00 12.00
234 Brandon Pirri RC 3.00 8.00
235 Jeremy Morin RC 5.00 12.00
236 Evgeny Grachev RC 3.00 8.00
237 Mattias Tedenby RC 2.50 6.00
238 Mark Olver RC 3.00 8.00
239 Eric Wellwood RC 4.00 10.00
240 Kyle Clifford RC 3.00 8.00
241 Zac Dalpe RC 3.00 8.00
242 Travis Hamonic RC 4.00 10.00

2010-11 Artifacts Emerald

*1-100 VETS/50: 3X TO 8X BASIC CARDS
*101-150 ROOKIES/50: .8X TO 2X RC/999
*151-200 L/S/50: 1X TO 2.5X L/S/999
106 P.K. Subban 20.00 50.00

2010-11 Artifacts Gold

*1-100 VETS/35: 3X TO 8X BASIC CARDS
*101-150 ROOKIES/35: .8X TO 2X RC/999
*151-200 L/S/35: 1X TO 2.5X L/S/999
106 P.K. Subban 40.00 80.00

2010-11 Artifacts Silver

*1-100 VETS/25: 4X TO 10X BASIC CARDS
*101-150 ROOKIES: 1X TO 2.5X RC/999
*151-200 L/S/25: 1.2X TO 3X L/S/999
106 P.K. Subban 50.00 100.00
148 Nazem Kadri 20.00 50.00

2010-11 Artifacts Autofacts

AFAE Andrew Ebbett 2.50 6.00
AFAF Alexander Frolov
AFAG Alex Goligoski 5.00 12.00
AFAK Anze Kopitar 8.00 20.00
AFAM Al MacInnis 5.00 12.00
AFAN Andrei Markov 4.00 10.00
AFAO Alexander Ovechkin 40.00 80.00
AFAP Alex Pietrangelo 6.00 15.00
AFAT Alex Tanguay 5.00 12.00
AFBA Mikael Backlund 2.50 6.00
AFBD Brandon Dubinsky 5.00 12.00
AFBF Benn Ferriero 2.50 6.00
AFBH Bobby Hull 30.00 60.00
AFBM Brad Marchand 6.00 15.00
AFBO Bobby Orr 50.00 100.00
AFBR Bobby Ryan 6.00 15.00
AFBS Billy Smith 4.00 10.00
AFBW Blake Wheeler 6.00 15.00
AFCA Luca Caputi 3.00 8.00
AFCG Claude Giroux 12.50 30.00
AFCH Don Cherry 15.00 40.00
AFCO Cal O'Reilly 3.00 8.00
AFCS Cory Schneider 3.00 8.00
AFDA Darren Helm 3.00 8.00
AFDB David Backes 4.00 10.00
AFDC Daniel Carcillo 5.00 12.00
AFDD Drew Doughty 4.00 10.00
AFDH Dale Hawerchuk 6.00 15.00
AFDP Denis Potvin 5.00 12.00
AFDS Denis Savard 5.00 12.00
AFEK Evander Kane 4.00 10.00
AFEM Evgeni Malkin 15.00 40.00
AFER Jonathan Ericsson 2.50 6.00
AFES Eric Staal 10.00 25.00
AFET Eric Tangradi 3.00 8.00
AFFE Bernie Federko 8.00 20.00
AFGB Gilbert Brule 4.00 10.00
AFGH Gordie Howe 50.00 100.00
AFHE Dany Heatley 8.00 20.00
AFIK Ilya Kovalchuk 6.00 15.00
AFJC Jared Cowen 3.00 8.00
AFJD J.P. Dumont 2.50 6.00
AFJE Jhonas Enroth 4.00 10.00
AFJG Jonas Gustavsson 5.00 12.00
AFJI Jarome Iginla 15.00 40.00
AFJS Jordan Staal 6.00 15.00
AFJT Joe Thornton 4.00 10.00
AFJV Jakub Voracek 4.00 10.00
AFKC Kris Chucko 2.50 6.00
AFKE Phil Kessel 6.00 15.00
AFLC Logan Couture 4.00 10.00
AFLR Luc Robitaille
AFMA Alec Martinez 5.00 12.00
AFMB Martin Brodeur 40.00 80.00
AFMD Matt Duchene 4.00 10.00
AFME Matt Ellis 2.50 6.00
AFMF Mark Fraser 2.50 6.00
AFMI Mike Bossy 10.00 25.00
AFML Mario Lemieux 50.00 100.00
AFMM Mark Messier 20.00 50.00
AFMN Michal Neuvirth 8.00 20.00
AFMP Matt Pelech 2.50 6.00
AFMR Mike Ribeiro 3.00 8.00
AFMS Marek Svatos 2.50 6.00
AFNG Nathan Gerbe 2.50 6.00
AFNH Nathan Horton 3.00 8.00
AFNI Antti Niemi 3.00 8.00
AFNK Nazem Kadri 10.00 25.00
AFPE Phil Esposito 10.00 25.00
AFPK Patrick Kane 15.00 40.00
AFPO Patrick O'Sullivan 2.50 6.00
AFPS P.K. Subban 15.00 40.00
AFRH Ron Hextall 10.00 25.00
AFRM Ryan Miller 8.00 20.00
AFRN Rick Nash 20.00 50.00
AFRV Rogie Vachon 5.00 12.00
AFSA Bobby Sanguinetti 2.50 6.00
AFSC Sidney Crosby 75.00 150.00
AFSE Devin Setoguchi 3.00 8.00
AFSG Simon Gagne 4.00 10.00
AFSH Steve Shutt 6.00 15.00
AFSM Steve Mason 6.00 15.00
AFSP Spencer Machacek 2.50 6.00
AFSS Steven Stamkos 20.00 50.00
AFST Martin St. Louis
AFSU Brandon Sutter 3.00 8.00
AFSV Sergei Shirokov 3.00 8.00
AFSY Steve Yzerman 100.00 175.00
AFTA John Tavares 20.00 50.00
AFTE Tyler Ennis 6.00 15.00
AFTG T.J. Galiardi 3.00 8.00
AFTM Tyler Myers 4.00 10.00
AFTO Jonathan Toews 20.00 40.00
AFVA James van Riemsdyk 6.00 15.00
AFVH Victor Hedman 5.00 12.00
AFWG Wayne Gretzky 100.00 200.00
AFYW Yannick Weber 3.00 8.00
AFZA Zach Boychuk 3.00 8.00
AFZB Zach Bogosian 3.00 8.00

2010-11 Artifacts Frozen Artifacts

STATED PRINT RUN 150 SER.#'d SETS
*BLUE/35: .6X TO 1.5X BASIC JSY
*EMERALD/15: 1X TO 2.5X BASIC JSY
FAAF Alexander Frolov 2.50 6.00
FAAK Anze Kopitar 6.00 15.00
FAAM Andrei Markov 4.00 10.00
FABB Bob Bourne 2.50 6.00
FABG Brian Gionta 3.00 8.00
FABR Derick Brassard 4.00 10.00
FACG Claude Giroux 4.00 10.00
FACO Chris Osgood 4.00 10.00
FACP Carey Price 8.00 20.00
FACW Cam Ward 4.00 10.00
FADB David Backes 4.00 10.00
FADD Drew Doughty 4.00 10.00
FADH Dany Heatley 3.00 8.00
FADR Derek Roy 4.00 10.00
FADS Devin Setoguchi 3.00 8.00
FAEL Patrik Elias 4.00 10.00
FAES Eric Staal 5.00 12.00
FAGL Guillaume Latendresse 3.00 8.00
FAHS Henrik Sedin 4.00 10.00
FAJC Jeff Carter 4.00 10.00
FAJJ Jack Johnson 2.50 6.00
FAJO Jordan Staal 4.00 10.00
FAJP Jason Pominville 4.00 10.00
FAJS Jason Spezza 2.50 6.00
FAJT Joe Thornton 4.00 10.00
FAJV Jakub Voracek 4.00 10.00
FALR Luc Robitaille 4.00 10.00
FAMF Marc-Andre Fleury 6.00 15.00
FAMG Mike Green 4.00 10.00
FAMK Miikka Kiprusoff 3.00 8.00
FAMR Mike Richards 4.00 10.00
FAMS Martin St. Louis 4.00 10.00
FAMT Marty Turco 4.00 10.00
FAMU Peter Mueller 3.00 8.00
FAPE Corey Perry 4.00 10.00
FAPM Patrick Marleau 4.00 10.00
FAPS Paul Stastny 4.00 10.00
FARL Roberto Luongo 6.00 15.00
FARM Ryan Miller 4.00 10.00
FARN Rick Nash 4.00 10.00
FASC Sidney Crosby 15.00 40.00
FASG Scott Gomez 3.00 8.00
FASM Steve Mason 3.00 8.00
FAST Drew Stafford 4.00 10.00
FASW Shea Weber 3.00 8.00
FATP Tomas Plekanec 6.00 15.00
FATV Thomas Vanek 4.00 10.00
FAVL Vincent Lecavalier 3.00 8.00
FAWG Wayne Gretzky 20.00 50.00
FAZP Zach Parise 4.00 10.00

2010-11 Artifacts Frozen Artifacts Retail

*RETAIL: .4X TO 1X BASIC INSERTS
STATED ODDS 1: RETAIL

2010-11 Artifacts Frozen Artifacts Silver

*SILVER: .5X TO 1.2X BASIC INSERTS
STATED PRINT RUN 50 SER.#'d SETS

2010-11 Artifacts Jerseys Bronze

STATED PRINT RUN 150 SER.#'d SETS
1 Brad Richards 4.00 10.00
2 Henrik Lundqvist 6.00 15.00
3 Jonathan Toews 8.00 20.00
4 Thomas Vanek 4.00 10.00
6 Patrick Kane 8.00 20.00
7 Carey Price 15.00 40.00
8 Miikka Kiprusoff 3.00 8.00
9 John Tavares 8.00 20.00
11 Ryan Miller 4.00 10.00
12 Ilya Kovalchuk 4.00 10.00
13 Vincent Lecavalier 3.00 8.00
14 Pascal Leclaire 3.00 8.00
15 Kyle Okposo 4.00 10.00
16 Matt Duchene 4.00 10.00
17 Nicklas Backstrom 6.00 15.00
18 Shane Doan 3.00 8.00
19 Tomas Vokoun 3.00 8.00
20 Patrik Elias 4.00 10.00
21 Patrick Marleau 4.00 10.00
22 Marc-Andre Fleury 6.00 15.00
23 Alexander Ovechkin 15.00 40.00
24 Mike Cammalleri 8.00 20.00
27 Cam Ward 4.00 10.00
28 Martin St. Louis 4.00 10.00
29 Patrik Berglund 3.00 8.00
30 Evander Kane 4.00 10.00
31 Andrei Markov 4.00 10.00
32 Mike Green 4.00 10.00
34 Derick Brassard 4.00 10.00
35 Claude Giroux 4.00 10.00
36 Phil Kessel 5.00 12.00
38 Joe Pavelski 4.00 10.00
40 Ryan Kesler 12.00 30.00
41 Daniel Briere 4.00 10.00
43 Jeff Carter 4.00 10.00
44 Anze Kopitar 6.00 15.00
45 Milan Lucic 4.00 10.00
46 Bobby Ryan 4.00 10.00
47 Dion Phaneuf 4.00 10.00
48 Steven Stamkos 8.00 20.00
49 Rene Bourque 2.50 6.00
50 Jason Spezza 2.50 6.00
51 James Neal 4.00 10.00
53 Eric Staal 5.00 12.00
54 Evgeni Malkin 12.00 30.00
55 Stephen Weiss 3.00 8.00
58 Henrik Sedin 4.00 10.00
59 Mikko Koivu 4.00 10.00
60 Ilya Bryzgalov 3.00 8.00
61 Roberto Luongo 4.00 10.00
62 Sidney Crosby 15.00 40.00
63 Zach Parise 4.00 10.00
64 Joe Thornton 4.00 10.00
65 J.P. Dumont 2.50 6.00
66 Paul Stastny 4.00 10.00
67 Ryan Getzlaf 6.00 15.00
69 Rick Nash 4.00 10.00
70 Michael Frolik 2.50 6.00
71 Zach Bogosian 3.00 8.00
72 Dany Heatley 3.00 8.00
74 David Backes 4.00 10.00
75 Antti Niemi 3.00 8.00
76 Sam Gagner 3.00 8.00
77 Daniel Alfredsson 4.00 10.00
78 Jack Johnson 2.50 6.00
81 Jordan Staal 4.00 10.00
82 Corey Perry 4.00 10.00
83 Mike Richards 4.00 10.00
84 Jarome Iginla 4.00 10.00
85 Shea Weber 3.00 8.00
87 Niklas Backstrom 4.00 10.00
88 Drew Doughty 4.00 10.00
89 Daniel Sedin 4.00 10.00
90 Pavel Datsyuk 5.00 12.00
91 Derek Roy 4.00 10.00
92 Duncan Keith 4.00 10.00
93 Martin Brodeur 8.00 20.00
94 Josh Bailey 3.00 8.00
95 Nicklas Lidstrom 4.00 10.00
96 Jakub Voracek 4.00 10.00
98 Marian Gaborik 5.00 12.00
99 Henrik Zetterberg 5.00 12.00
100 Guillaume Latendresse 3.00 8.00

2010-11 Artifacts Jerseys Patches Emerald

*EMER.PATCH/50: .8X TO 2X BASIC JSY
STATED PRINT RUN 50 SER.#'d SETS
22 Marc-Andre Fleury 10.00 25.00
40 Ryan Kesler 15.00 40.00

2010-11 Artifacts Jerseys Patches Gold

*GOLD PATCH/15: 1.2X TO 3X BASIC JSY
STATED PRINT RUN 15 SER.#'d SETS
5 Andrew Cogliano 8.00 20.00
25 Dustin Penner 8.00 20.00
26 Marc Savard 8.00 20.00
42 Brandon Dubinsky 10.00 25.00
52 Tuukka Rask 12.00 30.00
68 David Perron 8.00 20.00
79 Scottie Upshall 8.00 20.00
97 Zdeno Chara 10.00 25.00

2010-11 Artifacts Treasured Swatches

STATED PRINT RUN 150 SER.#'d SETS
*BLUE/35: .6X TO 1.5X BASIC JSY
*EMERALD/15: 1X TO 2.5X BASIC JSY
*RETAIL: .4X TO 1X BASIC JSY
*SILVER/50: .5X TO 1.2X BASIC JSY
*BLUE PATCH/50: .8X TO 2X BASIC JSY
*EMER.PATCH/25: 1X TO 2.5X BASIC JSY
*GOLD PATCH/15: 1.2X TO 3X BASIC JSY
TSAF Alexander Frolov 2.50 6.00
TSAK Anze Kopitar 6.00 15.00
TSAO Alexander Ovechkin 8.00 20.00
TSBG Brian Gionta 3.00 8.00
TSCG Claude Giroux 4.00 10.00
TSCO Chris Osgood 4.00 10.00
TSCP Corey Perry 4.00 10.00
TSDB Derick Brassard 4.00 10.00
TSDD Drew Doughty 4.00 10.00
TSDR Derek Roy 4.00 10.00
TSDS Drew Stafford 4.00 10.00
TSEM Evgeni Malkin 12.00 30.00
TSES Eric Staal 5.00 12.00
TSGL Guillaume Latendresse 3.00 8.00
TSHS Henrik Sedin 4.00 10.00
TSHZ Henrik Zetterberg 5.00 12.00
TSJA Jason Arnott 3.00 8.00
TSJC Jeff Carter 4.00 10.00
TSJI Jarome Iginla 4.00 10.00
TSJJ Jack Johnson 2.50 6.00
TSJP Jason Pominville 4.00 10.00
TSJS Jason Spezza 2.50 6.00
TSJT Jonathan Toews 8.00 20.00
TSJV Jakub Voracek 4.00 10.00
TSMD Matt Duchene 4.00 10.00
TSMG Mike Green 4.00 10.00
TSMK Miikka Kiprusoff 3.00 8.00
TSMM Mark Messier 6.00 15.00
TSMR Mike Richards 4.00 10.00
TSMT Marty Turco 4.00 10.00
TSPD Pavel Datsyuk 5.00 12.00
TSPE Patrik Elias 4.00 10.00
TSPK Patrick Kane 8.00 20.00
TSPS Paul Stastny 4.00 10.00
TSRG Ryan Getzlaf 6.00 15.00
TSRL Roberto Luongo 4.00 10.00
TSRM Ryan Miller 4.00 10.00
TSRN Rick Nash 4.00 10.00
TSSC Sidney Crosby 15.00 40.00
TSSE Daniel Sedin 4.00 10.00
TSSG Scott Gomez 3.00 8.00
TSSM Steve Mason 3.00 8.00
TSSS Steven Stamkos 8.00 20.00
TSST Jordan Staal 4.00 10.00
TSSW Shea Weber 3.00 8.00
TSTA John Tavares 8.00 20.00
TSTP Tomas Plekanec 4.00 10.00
TSTV Thomas Vanek 4.00 10.00
TSZP Zach Parise 4.00 10.00

2010-11 Artifacts Tundra Tandems Bronze

STATED PRINT RUN 125 SER.#'d SETS
*EMERALD/35: .6X TO 1.5X BASIC JSY
*SILVER/75: .5X TO 1.2X BASIC JSY
*EMER.PATCH/40: .8X TO 2X BASIC JSY
*GOLD PATCH/15: 1.2X TO 3X BASIC JSY
TT2ANA R.Getzlaf/C.Perry 6.00 15.00
TT2ATL Z.Bogosian/E.Kane 4.00 10.00
TT2AVS P.Stastny/M.Duchene 4.00 10.00
TT2BOS M.Lucic/M.Ryder 4.00 10.00
TT2CBJ J.Voracek/S.Mason 4.00 10.00
TT2CHI J.Toews/P.Kane 8.00 20.00
TT2CZE T.Vokoun/J.Voracek 4.00 10.00
TT2DET Datsyuk/H.Zetterberg 5.00 12.00
TT2EDM B.Ranford/B.Nicholls 4.00 10.00
TT2FLA D.Booth/S.Weiss 3.00 8.00
TT2FLY Briere/van Riemsdyk 6.00 15.00
TT2NJD Z.Parise/M.Brodeur 8.00 20.00
TT2OTT Alfredsson/J.Spezza 4.00 10.00
TT2SJS D.Heatley/R.Blake 4.00 10.00
TT2SVK M.Hossa/M.Gaborik 5.00 12.00
TT2SWE Lundqvist/Zetterberg 6.00 15.00
TT2TBL S.Yzerman/S.Stamkos 10.00 25.00
TT22004 A.Ovechkin/E.Malkin 15.00 40.00
TT22005 S.Crosby/B.Ryan 10.00 25.00
TT22007 P.Kane/van Riemsdyk 6.00 15.00
TT22008 S.Stamkos/D.Doughty 8.00 20.00
TT22009 J.Tavares/V.Hedman 8.00 20.00
TT2BUFF D.Stafford/T.Vanek 4.00 10.00
TT2CALG R.Bourque/J.Iginla 4.00 10.00
TT2CALI J.Thornton/R.Getzlaf 6.00 15.00
TT2CAPS Backstrom/Ovechkin 6.00 15.00
TT2CNAO A.Oates/C.Neely 4.00 10.00
TT2COLO D.Tucker/A.Foote 3.00 8.00
TT2DEER D.Phaneuf/C.Ward 4.00 10.00
TT2DRUM Briere/G.Latendresse 4.00 10.00
TT2FLAM J.Iginla/Bouwmeester 5.00 12.00
TT2FLYR D.Briere/C.Giroux 4.00 10.00
TT2NEWJ van Riemsdyk/B.Ryan 6.00 15.00
TT2PENS S.Crosby/M.Fleury 10.00 25.00
TT2PORT M.Hossa/C.Neely 4.00 10.00
TT2RMDR R.Miller/D.Roy 4.00 10.00
TT2RUSD S.Gonchar/A.Markov 4.00 10.00
TT2RUSG Bryzgalov/E.Nabokov 3.00 8.00
TT2SCAO S.Crosby/A.Ovechkin 10.00 25.00
TT2SSMA Thornton/W.Gretzky 20.00 50.00
TT2WILD Backstrom/M.Koivu 6.00 15.00
TT2BLUES D.Backes/P.Kariya 5.00 12.00
TT2CANES T.Ruutu/E.Staal 5.00 12.00
TT2FNGOL M.Kiprusoff/A.Niemi 3.00 8.00
TT2GIANT E.Kane/M.Lucic 4.00 10.00
TT2HAWKD B.Campbell/D.Keith 4.00 10.00
TT2KINGD J.Johnson/D.Doughty 4.00 10.00
TT2KOIVU S.Koivu/M.Koivu 8.00 20.00
TT2LEAFS J.Giguere/P.Kessel 8.00 20.00
TT2PREDS S.Sullivan/S.Weber 3.00 8.00
TT2STAAL J.Staal/E.Staal 5.00 12.00
TT2SWEDE Backstrom/J.Franzen 6.00 15.00
TT2TWINS D.Sedin/H.Sedin 4.00 10.00
TT2VALDOR J.Dumont/R.Luongo 4.00 10.00

2010-11 Artifacts Tundra Trios Bronze

STATED PRINT RUN 75 SER.#'d SETS
*EMERALD/15: .8X TO 2X BASIC TRIO
*SILVER/50: .5X TO 1.2X BASIC TRIO
*GOLD PATCH/15: 1X TO 2.5X BASIC TRIO
*EMER.PATCH/40: .8X TO 2X BASIC TRIO
TT3CBJ Nash/Mason/Voracek 5.00 12.00
TT3DEF Bouwme/Phanf/Hedmn 6.00 15.00
TT3FLA Vokoun/Weiss/Frolik 4.00 10.00
TT3N01 Crosby/Tavres/Stmkos 12.00 30.00
TT3OSH Horton/Arnott/Tavares 10.00 25.00
TT3TRI Tavres/Brodr/Gaborik 10.00 25.00
TT3BRAM Spezza/Wolski/Duch 5.00 12.00
TT3BRNS Thomas/Ryder/Whler 5.00 12.00
TT3BUDS Kessel/Kulemin/Schenn 6.00 15.00
TT3BUFF Roy/Vanek/Miller 5.00 12.00
TT3CALG Bourque/Igla/Kiprsoff 5.00 12.00
TT3CAPS Ovechkin/Semin/Green 10.00 25.00
TT3DEVS Parise/Brodeur/Elias 10.00 25.00
TT3DUCK Koivu/Perry/Lupul 5.00 12.00
TT3FLYS Richards/Carter/Giroux 10.00 25.00
TT3HABS Cammi/Markov/Gionta 10.00 25.00
TT3HAWK Kane/Hossa/Toews 10.00 25.00
TT3HERO Howe/Lemieux/Gretzky 40.00 80.00
TT3JCKT Mason/Voracek/Brass 5.00 12.00
TT3KING Brown/Doughty/Kopitar 8.00 20.00
TT3LEAF Kaberle/Giguere/Kessel 8.00 20.00
TT3LOND Nash/Kane/Perry 6.00 15.00
TT3MICH Camm/Johnson/Turco 5.00 12.00
TT3PENS Fleury/Staal/Malkin 15.00 40.00
TT3PNTH Vokoun/Booth/Frolik 4.00 10.00
TT3SABS Miller/Stafford/Pomin 5.00 12.00
TT3SBRS Roy/Pominville/Vanek 5.00 12.00
TT3SENS Kovalev/Alfred/Foligno 5.00 12.00
TT3SSMA Thornt/P.Espo/Carter 8.00 20.00
TT3VANC Luongo/Sedin/Sedin 5.00 12.00
TT3WILD Koivu/Backstr/Latend 5.00 12.00
TT3WING Datsyuk/Zetter/Osgood 6.00 15.00
TT3WISC Heatley/Pavelski/Brque 5.00 12.00
TT3LOOPS Tucker/Doan/Iginla 5.00 12.00
TT3NODAK Stafford/Parise/Toews 10.00 25.00
TT3PETES Pronger/Yzerman/Staal 10.00 25.00
TT3RMSKI Crosby/Lecav/Richards 12.00 30.00
TT3SHARK Heatley/Thorn/Marleau 5.00 12.00

2011-12 Artifacts

COMP.SET w/o SPs (100) 12.00 30.00
101-151 L/S PRINT RUN 999
152-200 ROOKIE PRINT RUN 999
201-230 ROOKIE RED.ODDS 1:12H 1:135R
231-242 WILD CARD RED.ODDS 1:30H 1:336R
201-242 ROOKIE PRINT RUN 699
1 Roberto Luongo .40 1.00
2 Matt Stajan .30 .75
3 Marian Hossa .30 .75
4 Taylor Hall .75 2.00
5 Nicklas Lidstrom .40 1.00
6 Shea Weber .30 .75
7 Tim Thomas .40 1.00
8 Alexander Ovechkin 1.50 4.00
9 Zach Parise .40 1.00
10 Marian Gaborik .50 1.25
11 Mark Messier .50 1.25
12 Patrick Marleau .40 1.00
13 Pavel Datsyuk .50 1.25
14 Jordan Eberle .40 1.00
15 Paul Coffey .40 1.00
16 Evander Kane .40 1.00
17 Ryan Kesler .40 1.00
18 Nathan Horton .40 1.00
19 Jonathan Toews .75 2.00
20 Luc Robitaille .40 1.00
21 Derek Stepan .40 1.00
22 Brian Boyle .25 .60
23 Milan Hejduk .30 .75
24 Jonas Hiller .30 .75
25 Chris Stewart .30 .75
26 Thomas Vanek .40 1.00
27 Scott Niedermayer .40 1.00
28 Claude Giroux .40 1.00
29 Tomas Vokoun .30 .75
30 Ryan Miller .40 1.00
31 Carey Price 1.25 3.00
32 Kris Versteeg .30 .75
33 Patrick Roy 1.00 2.50
34 Patrick Kane .75 2.00
35 Brad Richards .40 1.00
36 Lars Eller .30 .75
37 Patrice Bergeron .50 1.25
38 Chris Drury .30 .75
39 Derek Roy .30 .75
40 Tuukka Rask .40 1.00
41 Jaroslav Halak .40 1.00
42 David Backes .40 1.00
43 Drew Stafford .40 1.00
44 Jay Bouwmeester .40 1.00
45 Jonathan Bernier .40 1.00
46 Anze Kopitar .60 1.50
47 Henrik Lundqvist .50 1.25
48 Guillaume Latendresse .30 .75
49 Dustin Byfuglien .40 1.00
50 Tyler Ennis .30 .75
51 Brendan Shanahan .50 1.25
52 Mike Green .40 1.00
53 Ales Hemsky .30 .75
54 Jean-Sebastien Giguere .30 .75
55 Maxime Talbot .30 .75
56 Stephen Weiss .30 .75
57 Tyler Myers .40 1.00
58 Cam Ward .40 1.00
59 Martin Brodeur .75 2.00
60 Logan Couture .40 1.00
61 Jakub Voracek .40 1.00
62 Brandon Dubinsky .30 .75
63 Nikita Filatov .25 .60
64 Alex Tanguay .25 .60
65 Erik Karlsson .75 2.00
66 Mario Lemieux 1.25 3.00
67 Alex Pietrangelo .30 .75
68 Jeff Carter .40 1.00
69 Vincent Lecavalier .30 .75
70 Tyler Seguin .75 2.00
71 Evgeni Malkin 1.25 3.00
72 Marc-Andre Fleury .60 1.50
73 Marc Staal .40 1.00
74 Jamie Benn .50 1.25
75 Jarome Iginla .40 1.00
76 P.K. Subban .75 2.00
77 Victor Hedman .50 1.25
78 Ilya Kovalchuk .40 1.00
79 Andrei Markov .40 1.00
80 Paul Stastny .40 1.00
81 Phil Kessel .50 1.25
82 Mike Richards .40 1.00
83 Kyle Okposo .40 1.00
84 Drew Doughty .40 1.00
85 Matt Duchene .40 1.00
86 Ondrej Pavelec .40 1.00
87 Sidney Crosby 1.50 4.00
88 Eric Lindros .60 1.50
89 Sam Gagner .30 .75
90 Mike Modano .60 1.50
91 Steven Stamkos .75 2.00
92 Joe Thornton .40 1.00
93 Bill Ranford .40 1.00
94 Daniel Carcillo .25 .60
95 Jason Spezza .40 1.00
96 Ryan Getzlaf .60 1.50
97 Robin Lehner .30 .75
98 Pekka Rinne .50 1.25
99 Wayne Gretzky 2.00 5.00
100 Joe Sakic .60 1.50
101 Bobby Orr L 4.00 10.00
102 Gilbert Perreault L 1.25 3.00
103 Bobby Hull L 1.25 3.00
104 Wayne Gretzky L 6.00 15.00
105 Igor Larionov L 1.25 3.00
106 Mario Lemieux L 4.00 10.00
107 Gordie Howe L 2.50 6.00
108 Grant Fuhr L 1.25 3.00
109 Jari Kurri L 1.25 3.00
110 Ron Francis L 1.50 4.00
111 Marcel Dionne L 1.50 4.00
112 Luc Robitaille L 1.25 3.00
113 Larry Robinson L 1.25 3.00
114 Guy Lafleur L 1.50 4.00
115 Clark Gillies L 1.25 3.00
116 Mike Bossy L 1.25 3.00
117 Denis Potvin L 1.25 3.00
118 Brian Leetch L 1.25 3.00
119 Bobby Clarke L 1.25 3.00
120 Markus Naslund L 1.00 2.50
121 Alexander Ovechkin S 5.00 12.00
122 Nicklas Backstrom S 2.00 5.00
123 Ryan Kesler S 1.25 3.00
124 Henrik Sedin S 1.25 3.00
125 Jaroslav Halak S 1.25 3.00
126 Patrick Marleau S 1.25 3.00
127 Dany Heatley S 1.00 2.50
128 Evgeni Malkin S 4.00 10.00
129 Sidney Crosby S 5.00 12.00
130 Mike Richards S 1.25 3.00
131 Jeff Carter S 1.25 3.00
132 Erik Karlsson S 2.50 6.00
133 Marian Gaborik S 1.50 4.00
134 Henrik Lundqvist S 1.50 4.00
135 John Tavares S 2.50 6.00
136 Ryan Getzlaf S 2.00 5.00
137 Dustin Byfuglien S 1.25 3.00
138 Martin Brodeur S 2.50 6.00
139 Carey Price S 4.00 10.00
140 P.K. Subban S 2.50 6.00
141 Anze Kopitar S 2.00 5.00
142 Drew Doughty S 1.25 3.00
143 Nicklas Lidstrom S 1.25 3.00
144 Brad Richards S 1.25 3.00
145 Rick Nash S 1.25 3.00
146 Matt Duchene S 1.25 3.00
147 Jonathan Toews S 2.50 6.00
148 Patrick Kane S 2.50 6.00
149 Eric Staal S 1.50 4.00
150 Jarome Iginla S 1.25 3.00
151 Tim Thomas S 1.25 3.00
152 Timo Pielmeier 2.50 6.00
153 Jean-Philippe Levasseur 2.00 5.00
154 Greg Nemisz RC 2.00 5.00
155 Lance Bouma RC 2.00 5.00
156 Marcus Kruger RC 3.00 8.00
157 Hugh Jessiman RC 2.00 5.00
158 Cameron Gaunce RC 1.50 4.00
159 John Moore RC 2.00 5.00
160 Tomas Kubalik RC 2.00 5.00
161 Tomas Vincour RC 2.00 5.00
162 Colton Sceviour RC 2.00 5.00
163 Teemu Hartikainen RC 2.00 5.00
164 Chris Vande Velde RC 3.00 8.00
165 Scott Timmins RC 2.00 5.00
166 Drew Bagnall RC 2.00 5.00
167 Carson McMillan RC 2.50 6.00
168 Aaron Palushaj RC 2.00 5.00
169 Brendon Nash RC 2.00 5.00
170 Jonathon Blum RC 2.00 5.00
171 Blake Geoffrion RC 2.00 5.00
172 Adam Henrique RC 5.00 12.00
173 Matt Campanale RC 2.00 5.00
174 Shane Sims RC 2.00 5.00
175 Mikko Koskinen RC 2.50 6.00
176 Jamie Doornbosch RC 2.00 5.00
177 Mark Katic RC 2.00 5.00
178 Justin DiBenedetto RC 1.50 4.00
179 Cam Talbot RC 5.00 12.00
180 Patrick Wiercioch RC 2.00 5.00
181 Erik Condra RC 2.00 5.00
182 Roman Wick RC 2.50 6.00
183 Colin Greening RC 2.00 5.00
184 Andre Benoit RC 2.50 6.00
185 Stephane Da Costa RC 2.00 5.00
186 Erik Gustafsson RC 2.50 6.00
187 Ben Holmstrom RC 2.00 5.00
188 Zac Rinaldo RC 2.00 5.00
189 Joe Vitale RC 2.00 5.00
190 Brian Strait RC 2.50 6.00
191 Alex Stalock 2.00 5.00
192 Joe Colborne RC 2.00 5.00
193 Ben Scrivens RC 3.00 8.00
194 Matt Frattin RC 2.00 5.00
195 Cody Hodgson RC 4.00 10.00
196 Yann Sauve RC 2.00 5.00
197 Todd Ford RC 2.50 6.00
198 Paul Postma RC 2.00 5.00
199 Andrei Zubarev RC 2.50 6.00
200 Carl Klingberg RC 2.00 5.00
201 Devante Smith-Pelly RC 5.00 12.00
202 Mark Scheifele RC 8.00 20.00
203 Anton Lander RC 6.00 15.00
204 Zack Kassian RC 4.00 10.00
205 Roman Horak RC 3.00 8.00
206 Justin Faulk RC 4.00 10.00
207 Brandon Saad RC 6.00 15.00
208 Gabriel Landeskog RC 6.00 15.00
209 Ryan Johansen RC 6.00 15.00
210 Kevin Marshall RC 5.00 12.00
211 Brendan Smith RC 3.00 8.00
212 Ryan Nugent-Hopkins RC 15.00 40.00
213 Erik Gudbranson RC 4.00 10.00
214 Viatcheslav Voynov RC 3.00 8.00
215 Brett Bulmer RC 4.00 10.00
216 Louis Leblanc RC 6.00 15.00
217 Craig Smith RC 4.00 10.00
218 Adam Larsson RC 4.00 10.00
219 David Ullstrom RC 3.00 8.00
220 Tim Erixon RC 4.00 10.00
221 Sean Couturier RC 6.00 15.00
222 David Rundblad RC 3.00 8.00
223 Andy Miele RC 4.00 10.00
224 Robert Bortuzzo RC 3.00 8.00
225 Harri Sateri RC 4.00 10.00
226 Cade Fairchild RC 4.00 10.00
227 Brett Connolly RC 3.00 8.00
228 Jake Gardiner RC 5.00 12.00
229 Eddie Lack RC 3.00 8.00
230 Cody Eakin RC 4.00 10.00
231 Matt Read RC 8.00 20.00
232 Mika Zibanejad RC 8.00 20.00
233 Gustav Nyquist RC 8.00 20.00
234 Lennart Petrell RC 4.00 10.00
235 Dmitry Orlov RC 4.00 10.00
236 Raphael Diaz RC 3.00 8.00
237 Alexei Emelin RC 3.00 8.00
238 Peter Holland RC 3.00 8.00
239 Colten Teubert RC 3.00 8.00
240 Corey Tropp RC 3.00 8.00
241 Stefan Elliott RC 5.00 12.00
242 David Savard RC 5.00 12.00

2011-12 Artifacts Emerald

*1-100 VETS/25: 2.5X TO 6X BASIC CARDS
*101-120 LEG/25: .8X TO 2X LEG/999
*121-151 STAR/25: .8X TO 2X STAR/999
*152-200 ROOKIE/25: .6X TO 1.5X RC/999
STATED PRINT RUN 99 SER.#'d SETS

2011-12 Artifacts Spectrum

*1-100 VETS/25: 4X TO 10X BASIC CARDS
*101-120 LEG/25: 1.2X TO 3X LEG/999
*121-151 STAR/25: 1.2X TO 3X STAR/999
*152-200 ROOKIE/25: 1X TO 2.5X RC/999
STATED PRINT RUN 25 SER.#'d SETS

2011-12 Artifacts Autofacts

GROUP A STATED ODDS 1:8472 H
GROUP B STATED ODDS 1:1017 H
GROUP C STATED ODDS 1:398 H
GROUP D STATED ODDS 1:140 H
GROUP E STATED ODDS 1:103 H
GROUP F STATED ODDS 1:16 H
OVERALL STATED ODDS 1:10 H 1:1000 R
AAB Andrew Bodnarchuk F 3.00 8.00
AAD Luke Adam E 4.00 10.00
AAH Ales Hemsky B 12.00 30.00
AAK Arturs Kulda F 3.00 8.00
AAL Karl Alzner F 3.00 8.00
AAO Alexander Ovechkin B 40.00 100.00
AAP Alex Pietrangelo C 5.00 12.00
ABA Andy Bathgate E 5.00 12.00
ABB Brian Boyle F 3.00 8.00
ABI Brayden Irwin F 3.00 8.00
ABM Brett MacLean F 3.00 8.00
ABN Brent Burns F 6.00 15.00
ABO Butch Bouchard C 12.00 30.00
ABR Derick Brassard E 5.00 12.00
ABS Brandon Sutter F 4.00 10.00
ABU Bobby Butler F 4.00 10.00
ACA Cal O'Reilly F 3.00 8.00
ACE Corey Elkins F 3.00 8.00
ACG Colton Gillies E 3.00 8.00
ACL Dan Cleary D 5.00 12.00
ACM Clarke MacArthur F 3.00 8.00
ACO Chris Osgood D 5.00 12.00
ACS Chris Stewart D 4.00 10.00
ADA David Backes F 5.00 12.00
ADB Dan Boyle F 4.00 10.00
ADC Daniel Carcillo F 3.00 8.00
ADE Michael Del Zotto F 3.00 8.00
ADS Duane Sutter E 3.00 8.00
AEB Jordan Eberle D 15.00 40.00
AEK Evander Kane C 20.00 40.00
AEM Evgeni Malkin B 40.00 80.00
AEN Eric Nystrom F 3.00 8.00
AEW Eric Wellwood D 3.00 8.00
AFW Francis Wathier D 6.00 15.00
AGH Gordie Howe A 125.00 200.00
AIL Igor Larionov B 8.00 20.00
AJB Jamie Benn F 6.00 15.00
AJC Jared Cowen D 5.00 12.00
AJD J.P. Dumont D 3.00 8.00
AJE Jhonas Enroth E 5.00 12.00
AJF Justin Falk F 3.00 8.00
AJG Jonas Gustavsson C 6.00 15.00
AJM Jacob Markstrom F 5.00 12.00
AJO Jim O'Brien F 3.00 8.00
AJP Jeff Penner E 4.00 10.00
AJS James Sheppard F 3.00 8.00
AJT Joe Thornton B 12.00 30.00
AJV Jakub Voracek D 5.00 12.00
AJW J.T. Wyman D 3.00 8.00
AKA Keith Aulie F 4.00 10.00
AKD Kaspars Daugavins F 3.00 8.00
AKT Kyle Turris E 3.00 8.00
AKU Nikolai Kulemin D 5.00 12.00
ALA Andrew Ladd F 5.00 12.00
ALE Lars Eller F 4.00 10.00
ALS Luke Schenn C 5.00 12.00
AMA Rick MacLeish B 25.00 50.00
AMD Matt Beleskey F 3.00 8.00
AMC Thomas McCollum F 4.00 10.00
AMD Matt Duchene C 10.00 25.00
AME Barry Melrose E 4.00 10.00
AMG Matt Gilroy F 3.00 8.00
AMM Mark Messier A 40.00 80.00
AMN Michal Neuvirth E 4.00 10.00
AMS Marco Scandella F 3.00 8.00
AMT Mattias Tedenby E 3.00 8.00
AMZ Mats Zuccarello-Aasen E 5.00 12.00
ANA Markus Naslund C 12.00 30.00
ANH Nathan Horton C 6.00 15.00
ANK Nazem Kadri C 10.00 25.00
ANZ Nikolay Zherdev D 5.00 12.00
AOR Bobby Orr B 90.00 150.00
APA Patrick Marleau B 10.00 25.00
APB Patrice Bergeron B 60.00 120.00
APC Patrice Cormier F 3.00 8.00
APH Patric Hornqvist F 4.00 10.00
APJ Joe Pavelski C 6.00 15.00
APL Perttu Lindgren E 3.00 8.00
APM Peter Mueller C 5.00 12.00
ARB Richard Bachman F 4.00 10.00
ARE Ray Emery D 4.00 10.00
ARM Ryan McDonagh F 8.00 20.00
ARY Bobby Ryan E 5.00 12.00
ASA Jerome Samson F 3.00 8.00
ASC Brayden Schenn D 5.00 12.00
ASD Stefan Della Rovere F 3.00 8.00
ASM Stefan Meyer F 3.00 8.00
ASR Michael Sauer F 3.00 8.00
ASS Steve Shutt D 10.00 25.00
AST Marc Staal C 10.00 25.00
ASW Shea Weber C 8.00 20.00
ATA Maxime Talbot D 4.00 10.00
ATE Tyler Ennis F 4.00 10.00
ATL Jiri Tlusty F 4.00 10.00
ATM Tyler Myers D 5.00 12.00
ATT Tomas Tatar F 4.00 10.00
AVS Viktor Stalberg D 3.00 8.00
AWC Wendel Clark B 15.00 40.00
AWG Wayne Gretzky A 150.00 250.00
AZA Matt Zaba D 3.00 8.00

2011-12 Artifacts Frozen Artifacts Jerseys Blue

STATED PRINT RUN 135 SER.#'d SETS
*EMERALD/35: .8X TO 2X BLUE/135
*PURPLE RETAIL: .4X TO 1X BLUE/135
FAAK Anze Kopitar 6.00 15.00
FAAS Alexander Semin 4.00 10.00
FABR Daniel Briere 4.00 10.00
FABY Dustin Byfuglien 4.00 10.00
FACA Craig Anderson 4.00 10.00
FACN Cam Neely 4.00 10.00
FACP Carey Price 12.00 30.00
FADB David Backes 4.00 10.00
FADC Dino Ciccarelli 4.00 10.00
FADD Drew Doughty 4.00 10.00
FADP Dion Phaneuf 4.00 10.00
FADR Derek Roy 3.00 8.00
FADS Drew Stafford 4.00 10.00
FADU Dustin Brown 4.00 10.00
FAEM Evgeni Malkin 12.00 30.00
FAHL Henrik Lundqvist 5.00 12.00
FAHZ Henrik Zetterberg 5.00 12.00
FAIK Ilya Kovalchuk 4.00 10.00
FAJB Jay Bouwmeester 4.00 10.00
FAJC Jeff Carter 4.00 10.00
FAJE Jonathan Ericsson 3.00 8.00
FAJG Jean-Sebastien Giguere 3.00 8.00
FAJI Jarome Iginla 4.00 10.00
FAJS Jordan Staal 4.00 10.00
FAJV James van Riemsdyk 4.00 10.00
FAKL Kristopher Letang 6.00 15.00
FAKR David Krejci 4.00 10.00
FALE Lars Eller 3.00 8.00
FAMB Martin Brodeur 8.00 20.00
FAMG Mike Green 4.00 10.00
FAML Mario Lemieux 12.00 30.00
FAMR Mike Richards 4.00 10.00
FANH Nathan Horton 4.00 10.00
FANK Nikolai Kulemin 4.00 10.00
FAPE Corey Perry 4.00 10.00
FAPK Phil Kessel 5.00 12.00
FAPS Paul Stastny 4.00 10.00
FARB Rene Bourque 2.50 6.00
FARH Ron Hextall 5.00 12.00
FARI Brad Richards 4.00 10.00
FARL Roberto Luongo 4.00 10.00
FARY Bobby Ryan 4.00 10.00
FASB Sergei Bobrovsky 4.00 10.00
FASC Sidney Crosby 15.00 40.00
FATE Tyler Ennis 3.00 8.00
FATH Taylor Hall 5.00 12.00
FATP Tomas Plekanec 4.00 10.00
FATS Tyler Seguin 8.00 20.00
FATV Thomas Vanek 4.00 10.00
FAZC Zdeno Chara 4.00 10.00

2011-12 Artifacts Horizontal Jerseys

STATED PRINT RUN 50 SER.#'d SETS
*EMERALD/35: .8X TO 2X BASIC JSY/50
1 Roberto Luongo 5.00 12.00
2 Matt Stajan 4.00 10.00
3 Marian Hossa 4.00 10.00
4 Taylor Hall 10.00 25.00
5 Nicklas Lidstrom 5.00 12.00
6 Shea Weber 4.00 10.00
7 Tim Thomas 6.00 15.00
8 Alexander Ovechkin 20.00 50.00
9 Zach Parise 5.00 12.00
10 Marian Gaborik 6.00 15.00
11 Mark Messier 6.00 15.00
12 Patrick Marleau 5.00 12.00
13 Pavel Datsyuk 6.00 15.00
14 Jordan Eberle 5.00 12.00
15 Paul Coffey 5.00 12.00
16 Evander Kane 5.00 12.00
17 Ryan Kesler 5.00 12.00
18 Nathan Horton 5.00 12.00
19 Jonathan Toews 10.00 25.00
20 Luc Robitaille 5.00 12.00
21 Derek Stepan 5.00 12.00
22 Brian Boyle 3.00 8.00
23 Milan Hejduk
24 Jonas Hiller 4.00 10.00
25 Chris Stewart 4.00 10.00
26 Thomas Vanek 5.00 12.00
27 Scott Niedermayer 5.00 12.00
28 Claude Giroux 6.00 15.00

29 Tomas Vokoun 4.00 10.00
30 Ryan Miller 5.00 12.00
31 Carey Price 15.00 40.00
32 Kris Versteeg 4.00 10.00
33 Patrick Roy 12.00 30.00
34 Patrick Kane 10.00 25.00
35 Brad Richards 5.00 12.00
36 Lars Eller
37 Patrice Bergeron 6.00 15.00
38 Chris Drury 4.00 10.00
39 Derek Roy 4.00 10.00
40 Tuukka Rask 5.00 12.00
41 Jaroslav Halak 5.00 12.00
42 David Backes 5.00 12.00
43 Drew Stafford 5.00 12.00
44 Jay Bouwmeester 5.00 12.00
45 Jonathan Bernier
46 Anze Kopitar 8.00 20.00
47 Henrik Lundqvist 6.00 15.00
48 Guillaume Latendresse 4.00 10.00
49 Dustin Byfuglien 5.00 12.00
50 Tyler Ennis 4.00 10.00
52 Mike Green
53 Ales Hemsky 4.00 10.00
54 Jean-Sebastien Giguere 6.00 15.00
55 Maxime Talbot 4.00 10.00
56 Stephen Weiss 4.00 10.00
57 Tyler Myers
58 Cam Ward 5.00 12.00
59 Martin Brodeur 10.00 25.00
60 Logan Couture 5.00 12.00
61 Jakub Voracek 5.00 12.00
62 Brandon Dubinsky 4.00 10.00
63 Nikita Filatov
64 Alex Tanguay 3.00 8.00
65 Erik Karlsson 8.00 20.00
66 Mario Lemieux 15.00 40.00
67 Alex Pietrangelo 4.00 10.00
68 Jeff Carter 5.00 12.00
69 Vincent Lecavalier 4.00 10.00
70 Tyler Seguin 8.00 20.00
71 Evgeni Malkin 15.00 40.00
72 Marc-Andre Fleury 8.00 20.00
73 Marc Staal 5.00 12.00
74 Jamie Benn 6.00 15.00
75 Jarome Iginla 5.00 12.00
76 P.K. Subban 10.00 25.00
77 Victor Hedman 6.00 15.00
78 Ilya Kovalchuk 5.00 12.00
79 Andrei Markov 5.00 12.00
80 Paul Stastny 5.00 12.00
81 Phil Kessel 6.00 15.00
82 Mike Richards 5.00 12.00
83 Kyle Okposo 5.00 12.00
84 Drew Doughty 5.00 12.00
85 Matt Duchene 5.00 12.00
86 Ondrej Pavelec 5.00 12.00
87 Sidney Crosby 12.00 30.00
88 Eric Lindros 6.00 15.00
89 Sam Gagner 4.00 10.00
90 Mike Modano 8.00 20.00
91 Steven Stamkos 10.00 25.00
92 Joe Thornton 5.00 12.00
93 Bill Ranford 5.00 12.00
94 Daniel Carcillo 3.00 8.00
95 Jason Spezza 5.00 12.00
96 Ryan Getzlaf 8.00 20.00
97 Robin Lehner 4.00 10.00
98 Pekka Rinne 6.00 15.00
100 Joe Sakic 8.00 20.00

2011-12 Artifacts Jerseys

STATED PRINT RUN 125 SER.#'d SETS
*EMERALD/65: .8X TO 2X JERSEY/125
1 Roberto Luongo 4.00 10.00
2 Matt Stajan 3.00 8.00
3 Marian Hossa 3.00 8.00
4 Taylor Hall 10.00 25.00
5 Nicklas Lidstrom 4.00 10.00
6 Shea Weber 3.00 8.00
7 Tim Thomas 6.00 15.00
8 Alexander Ovechkin 15.00 40.00
9 Zach Parise 4.00 10.00
10 Marian Gaborik 5.00 12.00
11 Mark Messier 5.00 12.00
12 Patrick Marleau 4.00 10.00
13 Pavel Datsyuk 5.00 12.00
14 Jordan Eberle 4.00 10.00
15 Paul Coffey 4.00 10.00
16 Evander Kane 4.00 10.00
17 Ryan Kesler 4.00 10.00
18 Nathan Horton 4.00 10.00
19 Jonathan Toews 8.00 20.00
20 Luc Robitaille 6.00 15.00
21 Derek Stepan 4.00 10.00
22 Brian Boyle 2.50 6.00
23 Milan Hejduk 3.00 8.00
24 Jonas Hiller 3.00 8.00
25 Chris Stewart 3.00 8.00
26 Thomas Vanek 4.00 10.00
27 Scott Niedermayer 4.00 10.00
28 Claude Giroux 4.00 10.00
29 Tomas Vokoun 5.00 12.00
30 Ryan Miller 4.00 10.00
31 Carey Price 12.00 30.00
32 Kris Versteeg 3.00 8.00
33 Patrick Roy 10.00 25.00
34 Patrick Kane 8.00 20.00
35 Brad Richards 4.00 10.00
36 Lars Eller 3.00 8.00
37 Patrice Bergeron 5.00 12.00
38 Chris Drury 3.00 8.00
39 Derek Roy 3.00 8.00
40 Tuukka Rask 4.00 10.00
41 Jaroslav Halak 4.00 10.00
42 David Backes 4.00 10.00
43 Drew Stafford 4.00 10.00
44 Jay Bouwmeester 4.00 10.00
45 Jonathan Bernier 4.00 10.00
46 Anze Kopitar 6.00 15.00
47 Henrik Lundqvist 5.00 12.00
48 Guillaume Latendresse 3.00 8.00
49 Dustin Byfuglien 4.00 10.00
50 Tyler Ennis 3.00 8.00
52 Mike Green 4.00 10.00
53 Ales Hemsky 3.00 8.00
54 Jean-Sebastien Giguere
55 Maxime Talbot 3.00 8.00
56 Stephen Weiss 3.00 8.00
57 Tyler Myers 4.00 10.00
59 Martin Brodeur 8.00 20.00
60 Logan Couture 4.00 10.00
61 Jakub Voracek 4.00 10.00
62 Brandon Dubinsky 3.00 8.00
63 Nikita Filatov 2.50 6.00
64 Alex Tanguay 2.50 6.00
65 Erik Karlsson 6.00 15.00
66 Mario Lemieux 12.00 30.00
67 Alex Pietrangelo 3.00 8.00
68 Jeff Carter 4.00 10.00
69 Vincent Lecavalier 3.00 8.00
70 Tyler Seguin 8.00 20.00
71 Evgeni Malkin 12.00 30.00
72 Marc-Andre Fleury 6.00 15.00
73 Marc Staal 4.00 10.00
74 Jamie Benn 5.00 12.00
75 Jarome Iginla 4.00 10.00
76 P.K. Subban 8.00 20.00
77 Victor Hedman 5.00 12.00
78 Ilya Kovalchuk 5.00 12.00
79 Andrei Markov 4.00 10.00
80 Paul Stastny 4.00 10.00
81 Phil Kessel 5.00 12.00
82 Mike Richards 4.00 10.00
83 Kyle Okposo 4.00 10.00
84 Drew Doughty 4.00 10.00
85 Matt Duchene 4.00 10.00
86 Ondrej Pavelec 4.00 10.00
87 Sidney Crosby 15.00 40.00
88 Eric Lindros 6.00 15.00
89 Sam Gagner 3.00 8.00
90 Mike Modano 6.00 15.00
91 Steven Stamkos 8.00 20.00
92 Joe Thornton 4.00 10.00
93 Bill Ranford 6.00 15.00
94 Daniel Carcillo 2.50 6.00
95 Jason Spezza 4.00 10.00
96 Ryan Getzlaf 6.00 15.00
97 Robin Lehner 3.00 8.00
98 Pekka Rinne 5.00 12.00
100 Joe Sakic 8.00 20.00

2011-12 Artifacts Jerseys Patch Spectrum

*PATCH/15: 1X TO 2.5X BASIC JSY
PATCH STATED PRINT RUN 15
51 Brendan Shanahan 12.00 30.00
58 Cam Ward 15.00 40.00

2011-12 Artifacts Rookie Autographs Redemptions

AUTO EXCH STATED ODDS 1:160H
STATED PRINT RUN 99 SER.#'d SETS
EXCH EXPIRATION: 9/9/2013
REDA1 Ryan Nugent-Hopkins 100.00 200.00
REDA2 Gabriel Landeskog 25.00 60.00
REDA3 Cody Hodgson 30.00 80.00
REDA4 Sean Couturier 30.00 80.00
REDA5 Brett Connolly 15.00 40.00
REDA6 Mark Scheifele 50.00 100.00
REDA7 Ryan Johansen 30.00 80.00
REDA8 Adam Larsson 20.00 50.00
REDA9 Mika Zibanejad 15.00 40.00
REDA10 Jake Gardiner 20.00 50.00
REDA11 Erik Gudbranson 15.00 40.00
REDA12 Matt Read 20.00 50.00
REDA13 Teemu Hartikainen 15.00 40.00
REDA14 Joe Colborne 20.00 50.00
REDA15 Matt Frattin 30.00 60.00
REDA16 Craig Smith 15.00 40.00

2011-12 Artifacts Treasured Swatches Blue

BLUE PRINT RUN 135 SER.#'d SETS
*EMERALD/35: .8X TO 2X BLUE/135
*PURPLE RETAIL: .4X TO 1X BLUE/135
TSAB Alexandre Burrows 5.00 12.00
TSAO Alexander Ovechkin 15.00 40.00
TSCG Claude Giroux 4.00 10.00
TSCM Clarke MacArthur 2.50 6.00
TSCO Chris Osgood 4.00 10.00
TSCP Chris Pronger 3.00 8.00
TSDG Doug Gilmour 5.00 12.00
TSDS Daniel Sedin 4.00 10.00
TSEK Evander Kane 4.00 10.00
TSHO Marian Hossa 3.00 8.00
TSHS Henrik Sedin 4.00 10.00
TSIB Ilya Bryzgalov 4.00 10.00
TSIL Igor Larionov 6.00 15.00
TSJB Jamie Benn 5.00 12.00
TSJC John Carlson 5.00 12.00
TSJE Jordan Eberle 4.00 10.00
TSJH Jonas Hiller 3.00 8.00
TSJJ Jack Johnson 2.50 6.00
TSJN James Neal 6.00 15.00
TSJQ Jonathan Quick 6.00 15.00
TSJT Jonathan Toews 8.00 20.00
TSKO Kyle Okposo 4.00 10.00
TSKS Kevin Shattenkirk 3.00 8.00
TSMB Mike Bossy 4.00 10.00
TSMD Matt Duchene 4.00 10.00
TSMF Marc-Andre Fleury 6.00 15.00
TSMG Marian Gaborik 5.00 12.00
TSMH Milan Hejduk 3.00 8.00
TSMI Ryan Miller 4.00 10.00
TSMK Miikka Kiprusoff 4.00 10.00
TSMM Mark Messier 5.00 12.00
TSMS Martin St. Louis 4.00 10.00
TSNL Nicklas Lidstrom 4.00 10.00
TSOP Ondrej Pavelec 4.00 10.00
TSPB Patrik Berglund 3.00 8.00
TSPK Patrick Kane 8.00 20.00
TSPS P.K. Subban 8.00 20.00
TSRB Ray Bourque 6.00 15.00
TSRG Ryan Getzlaf 6.00 15.00
TSRK Ryan Kesler 4.00 10.00
TSRS Ryan Smyth 3.00 8.00
TSSH Scott Hartnell 4.00 10.00
TSSS Steven Stamkos 8.00 20.00
TSTT Tim Thomas 6.00 15.00
TSTV Thomas Vanek 4.00 10.00
TSTZ Travis Zajac 3.00 8.00
TSVL Vincent Lecavalier 3.00 8.00
TSZP Zach Parise 4.00 10.00

2011-12 Artifacts Tundra Tandems Jerseys Blue

BLUE PRINT RUN 225 SER.#'d SETS
*EMERALD/50: .8X TO 2X BLUE/225
TT2AS J.Spezza/D.Alfredsson 5.00 12.00
TT2BB D.Backes/P.Berglund 5.00 12.00
TT2BP P.Berglund/A.Pietrangelo 4.00 10.00
TT2BQ J.Quick/J.Bernier 8.00 20.00
TT2CD P.Datsyuk/D.Cleary 6.00 15.00
TT2CM S.Crosby/E.Malkin 20.00 50.00
TT2CP C.Price/P.Subban 15.00 40.00
TT2CR C.Anderson/R.Lehner 5.00 12.00
TT2DD D.Stafford/D.Roy 5.00 12.00
TT2DE D.Byfuglien/E.Kane 5.00 12.00
TT2DS M.Staal/B.Dubinsky 5.00 12.00
TT2EH T.Hall/J.Eberle 10.00 25.00
TT2EZ T.Zajac/P.Elias 5.00 12.00
TT2FH C.Fowler/J.Hiller 4.00 10.00
TT2FL M.Fleury/K.Letang 8.00 20.00
TT2GD M.Gaborik/B.Dubinsky 6.00 15.00
TT2GS N.Gerbe/D.Stafford 5.00 12.00
TT2HC J.Carter/S.Hartnell 5.00 12.00
TT2HK N.Horton/D.Krejci 5.00 12.00
TT2IB J.Iginla/R.Bourque 5.00 12.00
TT2JM J.Staal/M.Staal 5.00 12.00
TT2KD D.Doughty/A.Kopitar 8.00 20.00
TT2KJ K.Letang/J.Neal 8.00 20.00
TT2KK P.Kessel/N.Kulemin 6.00 15.00
TT2LE N.Lidstrom/J.Ericsson 5.00 12.00
TT2LG V.Lecavalier/S.Gagne 5.00 12.00
TT2LK R.Luongo/R.Kesler 5.00 12.00
TT2LM M.Lemieux/M.Messier 15.00 40.00
TT2MB J.Bailey/M.Moulson 4.00 10.00
TT2MH M.Modano/B.Hull 8.00 20.00
TT2MJ Kiprusoff/Bouwmeester 5.00 12.00
TT2MK A.Markov/A.Kostitsyn 5.00 12.00
TT2MM R.Miller/T.Myers 5.00 12.00
TT2MS D.Setoguchi/P.Marleau 5.00 12.00
TT2MZ M.Brodeur/Z.Parise 10.00 25.00
TT2OB Ovechkin/Backstrom 20.00 50.00
TT2OH J.Howard/C.Osgood 5.00 12.00
TT2PE T.Plekanec/L.Eller 5.00 12.00
TT2PG R.Getzlaf/C.Perry 8.00 20.00
TT2PS D.Phaneuf/L.Schenn 5.00 12.00
TT2RB B.Richards/J.Benn 6.00 15.00
TT2RG M.Richards/C.Giroux 6.00 15.00
TT2RH P.Rinne/P.Hornqvist 6.00 15.00
TT2RJ R.Smyth/J.Williams 4.00 10.00
TT2RO M.Ribeiro/S.Ott 4.00 10.00
TT2SB E.Staal/P.Bergeron 6.00 15.00
TT2SD M.Duchene/P.Stastny 5.00 12.00
TT2SG W.Gretzky/J.Sakic 15.00 40.00
TT2SM S.Stamkos/M.St. Louis 10.00 25.00
TT2SS H.Sedin/D.Sedin 5.00 12.00
TT2SV S.Varlamov/A.Semin 5.00 12.00
TT2SW S.Weber/R.Suter 4.00 10.00
TT2TK J.Toews/P.Kane 10.00 25.00
TT2TR T.Thomas/T.Rask 8.00 20.00
TT2UF R.Umberger/N.Filatov 3.00 8.00
TT2VE T.Ennis/T.Vanek 5.00 12.00
TT2WB D.Booth/S.Weiss 4.00 10.00
TT2ZH Zetterberg/Holmstrom 6.00 15.00

2011-12 Artifacts Tundra Trios Jerseys Blue

STATED PRINT RUN 149 SER.#'d SETS
TT3ANA Perry/Getzlaf/Fowler 8.00 20.00
TT3AVS Sakic/Roy/Bourque 15.00 40.00
TT3BOS Rask/Thomas/Chara 10.00 25.00
TT3BUF Ennis/Vanek/Gerbe 6.00 15.00
TT3CAN Thornton/Staal/Berg 8.00 20.00
TT3CBJ Vorack/Filatv/Brassard 6.00 15.00
TT3CGY Iginla/Kipru/Bouwmstr 6.00 15.00
TT3CHI Kane/Toews/Hossa 12.00 30.00
TT3COL Duchene/Stastny/Liles 6.00 15.00
TT3DAL Richards/Benn/Eriksson 8.00 20.00
TT3DET Zetter/Lidstrm/Franzn 8.00 20.00
TT3DRW Datsyk/Cleary/Osgd 8.00 20.00
TT3EDM Hall/Eberle/Paajarvi 12.00 30.00
TT3LAK Dghty/Kopitar/Quick 12.50 30.00
TT3NJD Parise/Zajac/Elias 6.00 15.00
TT3NSH Weber/Suter/Rinne 8.00 20.00
TT3NYI Mlson/Okposo/Bailey 6.00 15.00
TT3NYR Staal/Dubinsky/Gaborik 8.00 20.00
TT3OTT Spezza/Alfred/Foligno 6.00 15.00
TT3PHI Giroux/Richrds/Bobrov 6.00 15.00
TT3SJS Marleau/Setog/Thrntn 6.00 15.00
TT3VAN Kesler/Sedin/Sedin 6.00 15.00
TT3WPG Byfuglien/Kane/Pavelec 6.00 15.00
TT3BEES Chara/Thomas/Seguin 12.00 30.00
TT3BOLT Stamk/St. Louis/Lecav 12.00 30.00
TT3BUFF Pomin/Vanek/Stafford 6.00 15.00
TT3CAPS Bckstrm/Ovech/Semin 10.00 25.00
TT3FLYR Carter/Hartnell/Briere 6.00 15.00
TT3LBBR Subban/Price/Plekanec 20.00 50.00
TT3PENS Fleury/Letang/Neal 12.00 30.00
TT3PITT Malkin/Crosby/Staal 25.00 60.00
TT3SABR Myers/Miller/Stafford 6.00 15.00
TT3STAR Ribeiro/Lehtn/Goligoski 5.00 12.00
TT3WILD Gonchar/Spez/Andersn 6.00 15.00
TT3BLUES Back/Halak/Berglund 6.00 15.00
TT3KINGS Williams/Smyth/Bernier 6.00 15.00
TT3LEAFS Kulemin/Kessel/Phanf 8.00 20.00
TT3NUCKS Luongo/Kesler/Edler 6.00 15.00

2011-12 Artifacts Tundra Trios Patches Emerald

*EMERALD/20: 1X TO 2.5X BLUE/149
STATED PRINT RUN 20 SER.#'d SETS
TT3GR8 Mess/Lemieux/Yzer 50.00 120.00
TT3DEVILS Nieder/ShnHn/Brodr 30.00 80.00

2012-13 Artifacts

COMP.SET w/o SP's (100) 12.00 30.00
101-150 STATED PRINT RUN 999
151-198 ROOKIE PRINT RUN 999
199-240 ROOKIE RED./699 ODDS 1:10H, 1:96R
1 Alex Tanguay .25 .60
2 Alexander Ovechkin 1.50 4.00
3 Anze Kopitar .60 1.50
4 Bobby Orr 1.25 3.00
5 Bobby Ryan .40 1.00
6 Brandon Dubinsky .30 .75
7 Brendan Shanahan .50 1.25
8 Brett Hull .40 1.00
9 Cam Neely .40 1.00
10 Chris Drury .30 .75
11 Claude Giroux .40 1.00
12 Colton Orr .40 1.00
13 Cam Fowler .30 .75
14 Dale Hawerchuk .50 1.25
15 Daniel Alfredsson .40 1.00
16 Daniel Sedin .40 1.00
17 Denis Savard .50 1.25
18 Derek Roy .30 .75
19 Derek Stepan .40 1.00
20 Dino Ciccarelli .40 1.00
21 Doug Wilson .30 .75
22 Drew Doughty .40 1.00
23 Drew Stafford .40 1.00
24 Duncan Keith .40 1.00
25 Eric Lindros .60 1.50
26 Eric Staal .50 1.25
27 Erik Karlsson .75 2.00
28 Evgeni Malkin 1.25 3.00
29 George Parros .30 .75
30 Henrik Sedin .40 1.00
31 Henrik Zetterberg .50 1.25
32 Ilya Kovalchuk .40 1.00
33 Jari Kurri .40 1.00
34 Jarome Iginla .40 1.00
35 Jaromir Jagr 1.00 2.50
36 Jason Spezza .40 1.00
37 Jean Beliveau .40 1.00
38 Jeff Carter .40 1.00
39 Joe Sakic .60 1.50
40 Joe Thornton .40 1.00
41 Johan Franzen .40 1.00
42 John Tavares .75 2.00
43 Dustin Brown .40 1.00
44 Jonathan Toews .75 2.00
45 Jordan Eberle .40 1.00
46 Jordan Staal .40 1.00
47 Keith Yandle .40 1.00
48 Kristopher Letang .40 1.00
49 Larry Robinson .40 1.00
50 Logan Couture .40 1.00
51 Luc Robitaille .40 1.00
52 Kevin Shattenkirk .40 1.00
53 Marian Gaborik .40 1.00
54 Marian Hossa .30 .75
55 Sam Gagner .30 .75
56 Mario Lemieux 1.25 3.00
57 Mark Messier .50 1.25
58 Markus Naslund .30 .75
59 Matt Duchene .40 1.00
60 Matt Moulson .30 .75
61 Maxime Talbot .30 .75
62 Mike Green .40 1.00
63 Mike Modano .60 1.50
64 Mike Richards .40 1.00
65 Milan Lucic .40 1.00
66 Nathan Horton .40 1.00
67 Nicklas Backstrom .60 1.50
68 Nicklas Lidstrom .40 1.00
69 P.K. Subban .60 1.50
70 Patrice Bergeron .50 1.25
71 Patrick Kane .75 2.00
72 Patrick Sharp .40 1.00
73 Paul Coffey .40 1.00
74 Paul Stastny .40 1.00
75 Pavel Datsyuk .50 1.25
76 Rene Bourque .25 .60
77 Ray Bourque .60 1.50
78 Nikolai Kulemin .30 .75
79 Rick Nash .40 1.00
80 Ron Francis .50 1.25
81 Ryan Callahan .40 1.00
82 Ryan Getzlaf .60 1.50
83 Ryan Kesler .40 1.00
84 Ryan Nugent-Hopkins .40 1.00
85 Shane Doan .30 .75
86 Sidney Crosby 1.50 4.00
87 Stephen Weiss .30 .75
88 Steve Ott .30 .75
89 Steven Stamkos .75 2.00
90 Taylor Hall .75 2.00
91 Teemu Selanne .75 2.00
92 Tony Twist .25 .60
93 Trevor Linden .40 1.00
94 Tyler Ennis .30 .75
95 Tyler Myers .30 .75
96 Tyler Seguin .60 1.50
97 Vincent Lecavalier .30 .75
98 Wayne Gretzky 4.00 10.00
99 Zach Parise .40 1.00
100 Zdeno Chara .40 1.00
101 Antti Niemi 1.25 3.00
102 Carey Price 4.00 10.00
103 Cory Schneider 1.25 3.00
104 Corey Crawford 2.00 5.00
105 Curtis Joseph 1.50 4.00
106 Dominik Hasek 2.00 5.00
107 Ed Belfour 1.50 4.00
108 Pekka Rinne 2.00 5.00
109 Jean-Sebastien Giguere 1.25 3.00
110 Jim Howard 1.50 4.00
111 Johnny Bower 1.50 4.00
112 Ondrej Pavelec 1.50 4.00
113 Jonathan Quick 2.50 6.00
114 Kari Lehtonen 1.25 3.00
115 Marc-Andre Fleury 2.50 6.00
116 Martin Brodeur 3.00 8.00
117 Miikka Kiprusoff 1.25 3.00
118 Patrick Roy 4.00 10.00
119 Semyon Varlamov 1.50 4.00
120 Ryan Miller 1.50 4.00
121 Steve Mason 1.25 3.00
122 Tim Thomas 1.50 4.00
123 Tomas Vokoun 1.25 3.00
124 Tony Esposito 1.50 4.00
125 Tuukka Rask 1.50 4.00
126 Alex Pietrangelo TC 1.25 3.00
127 Brayden Schenn TC 1.50 4.00
128 Brenden Morrow TC 1.25 3.00
129 Brent Seabrook TC 1.50 4.00
130 Calvin de Haan TC 1.25 3.00
131 Chris Pronger TC 1.25 3.00
132 Cody Eakin TC 1.25 3.00
133 Corey Perry TC 1.50 4.00
134 Dale Hawerchuk TC 2.00 5.00
135 Dan Boyle TC 1.25 3.00
136 Drew Doughty TC 1.50 4.00
137 Duncan Keith TC 1.50 4.00
138 Erik Gudbranson TC 1.50 4.00
139 Dustin Tokarski TC 1.25 3.00
140 Jarome Iginla TC 1.50 4.00
141 Louis Leblanc TC 1.50 4.00
142 Marcus Foligno TC 1.25 3.00
143 Patrice Bergeron TC 2.00 5.00
144 Roberto Luongo TC 1.50 4.00
145 Ryan Ellis TC 1.00 2.50
146 Ryan Getzlaf TC 2.50 6.00
147 Shea Weber TC 1.25 3.00
148 Simon Despres TC 1.25 3.00
149 Wayne Gretzky TC 8.00 20.00
150 Zack Kassian TC 1.25 3.00
151 Mat Clark RC 2.00 5.00
152 Carter Camper RC 1.50 4.00
153 Maxime Sauve RC 2.00 5.00
154 Lane MacDermid RC 2.00 5.00
155 Torey Krug RC 8.00 20.00
156 Michael Hutchinson RC 4.00 10.00
157 Travis Turnbull RC 2.00 5.00
158 Sven Baertschi RC 2.50 6.00
159 Akim Aliu RC 2.00 5.00
160 Jeremy Welsh RC 2.00 5.00
161 Brandon Bollig RC 2.00 5.00
162 Tyson Barrie RC 4.00 10.00
163 Mike Connolly RC 2.00 5.00
164 Dalton Prout RC 2.00 5.00
165 Cody Goloubef RC 2.00 5.00
166 Shawn Hunwick RC 2.00 5.00
167 Andrew Joudrey RC 2.00 5.00
168 Ryan Garbutt RC 2.00 5.00
169 Reilly Smith RC 4.00 10.00
170 Brenden Dillon RC 2.00 5.00
171 Scott Glennie RC 2.00 5.00
172 Riley Sheahan RC 2.00 5.00
173 Philippe Cornet RC 2.00 5.00
174 Colby Robak RC 2.00 5.00
175 Jordan Nolan RC 2.00 5.00
176 Kristopher Foucault RC 2.00 5.00
177 Jason Zucker RC 2.50 6.00
178 Tyler Cuma RC 2.00 5.00
179 Chay Genoway RC 2.00 5.00
180 Gabriel Dumont RC 2.00 5.00
181 Robert Mayer RC 2.50 6.00
182 Chet Pickard RC 2.00 5.00
183 Aaron Ness RC 2.00 5.00
184 Casey Cizikas RC 2.00 5.00
185 Matt Donovan RC 2.00 5.00
186 Chris Kreider RC 8.00 20.00
187 Jakob Silfverberg RC 4.00 10.00
188 Mark Stone RC 4.00 10.00
189 Brandon Manning RC 2.00 5.00
190 Michael Stone RC 2.00 5.00
191 Matt Watkins RC 2.00 5.00
192 Tyson Sexsmith RC 2.00 5.00
193 Jake Allen RC 6.00 15.00
194 Jaden Schwartz RC 4.00 10.00
195 J.T. Brown RC 2.00 5.00
196 Carter Ashton RC 1.50 4.00
197 Ryan Hamilton RC 2.00 5.00
198 Jussi Rynnas RC 2.00 5.00
RED199 Viktor Fasth XRC 4.00 10.00
RED200 Dougie Hamilton XRC 8.00 20.00
RED201 Mikhail Grigorenko XRC 8.00 20.00
RED202 Max Reinhart XRC 4.00 10.00
RED203 Ryan Murphy XRC 4.00 10.00
RED204 Drew LeBlanc XRC 3.00 8.00
RED205 Michael Sgarbossa XRC 3.00 8.00
RED206 J.Audy-Marchessault XRC
RED207 Jack Campbell XRC 4.00 10.00
RED208 Damien Brunner XRC 4.00 10.00
RED209 Nail Yakupov XRC 12.00 30.00
RED210 Jonathan Huberdeau XRC 10.00 25.00
RED211 Tyler Toffoli XRC 6.00 15.00
RED212 Mikael Granlund XRC 8.00 20.00
RED213 Alex Galchenyuk XRC 8.00 20.00
RED214 Filip Forsberg XRC 8.00 20.00
RED215 Stefan Matteau XRC 4.00 10.00
RED216 Brock Nelson XRC 4.00 10.00
RED217 J.T. Miller XRC 4.00 10.00
RED218 Cory Conacher XRC 4.00 10.00
RED219 Scott Laughton XRC 4.00 10.00
RED220 Chris Brown XRC 3.00 8.00
RED221 Beau Bennett XRC 6.00 15.00
RED222 Matthew Irwin XRC 4.00 10.00
RED223 Vladimir Tarasenko XRC 10.00 25.00
RED224 Richard Panik XRC 5.00 12.00
RED225 Mike Kostka XRC 4.00 10.00
RED226 Jordan Schroeder XRC 4.00 10.00
RED227 Tom Wilson XRC 6.00 15.00
RED228 Zach Redmond XRC 4.00 10.00
RED229 Brendan Gallagher XRC 12.00 30.00
RED230 Justin Schultz XRC 6.00 15.00
RED231 Charlie Coyle XRC 6.00 15.00
RED232 Nathan Beaulieu XRC 4.00 10.00
RED233 Emerson Etem XRC 5.00 12.00
RED234 Ryan Spooner XRC 6.00 15.00
RED235 Petr Mrazek XRC 8.00 20.00
RED236 Jonas Brodin XRC 8.00 20.00
RED237 Jarred Tinordi XRC 4.00 10.00
RED238 Jean-Gabriel Pageau XRC 4.00 10.00
RED239 Nicklas Jensen XRC 4.00 10.00
RED240 Nick Bjugstad XRC 4.00 10.00

2012-13 Artifacts Emerald

*1-100 VETS/99: 3X TO 8X BASIC CARDS
*101-150 VET/99: 1X TO 2.5X BASIC/999
*151-198 ROOK/99: .6X TO 1.5X RC/999
STATED PRINT RUN 99 SER.#'d SETS

2012-13 Artifacts Gold Spectrum

*1-100 VETS/25: 5X TO 12X BASIC CARDS
*101-150 VET/25: 2X TO 5X BASIC/999
*151-198 ROOK/25: 1X TO 2.5X RC/999
STATED PRINT RUN 25 SER.#'d SETS

2012-13 Artifacts Sapphire

*1-100 VETS/85: 3X TO 8X BASIC CARDS
*101-150 VET/85: 1.2X TO 3X BASIC/999
*151-198 ROOK/85: .6X TO 1.5X RC/999
STATED PRINT RUN 85 SER.#'d SETS

2012-13 Artifacts Autofacts

AAG Aaron Gagnon E 4.00 10.00
AAM Adam McQuaid E 6.00 15.00
AAO Alexander Ovechkin C 30.00 60.00
AAS Anthony Stewart D 3.00 8.00
ABH Bobby Hull A 40.00 80.00
ABL Brian Lee E 4.00 10.00
ABM Brendan Mikkelson E 3.00 8.00
ABO Bobby Orr C 50.00 100.00
ABT Bryan Trottier B 10.00 25.00
ACE Cody Eakin TC E 4.00 10.00
ACF Cam Fowler E 4.00 10.00
ACH Cody Hodgson E 6.00 15.00
ACJ Curtis Joseph A 40.00 80.00
ACK Chris Kunitz B 12.00 30.00
ADB Drayson Bowman E 3.00 8.00
ADG Daniel Girardi E 3.00 8.00
ADP David Perron B 12.00 30.00
ADU Dustin Brown C 6.00 15.00
AEL Eric Lindros A 30.00 60.00
AEN Evgeni Nabokov D 4.00 10.00
AFW Francis Wathier E 4.00 10.00
AGL Gabriel Landeskog B 25.00 50.00
AJB Jamie Benn B 12.00 30.00
AJD Jason Demers E 4.00 10.00
AJE Jordan Eberle B 10.00 25.00
AJJ Jaromir Jagr A 40.00 80.00
AJM John Moore E 3.00 8.00
AJN James Neal D 10.00 25.00
AJO Johan Motin E 4.00 10.00
AKC Kyle Clifford E 3.00 8.00
AKT Kimmo Timonen E 3.00 8.00
ALA Guillaume Latendresse B 15.00 30.00
ALE Mario Lemieux A 40.00 80.00
AMB Mike Bossy B 12.00 30.00
AML Maxim Lapierre E 4.00 10.00
AMM Mark Messier A 40.00 80.00
AMN Michal Neuvirth E 4.00 10.00
AMS Matt Stajan E 4.00 10.00
ANF Nick Foligno E 4.00 10.00
ANG Nicklas Grossman E 4.00 10.00
APC Paul Coffey A 30.00 60.00
APL Pascal Leclaire TC E 4.00 10.00
APR Patrick Roy A 50.00 100.00
ARA Tuukka Rask B 20.00 40.00
ARJ Ryan Jones E 4.00 10.00
ARL Robin Lehner C 5.00 12.00
ARN Ryan Nugent-Hopkins A 30.00 60.00
ARO Ryan O'Reilly E 5.00 12.00
ASC Sidney Crosby A 75.00 150.00
ASG Sam Gagner D 4.00 10.00
ASS Steven Stamkos C 20.00 40.00
AST Marco Sturm E 4.00 10.00
ASW Stephen Weiss B 8.00 20.00
ATL Trevor Lewis E 5.00 12.00
ATR Tuomo Ruutu B 10.00 25.00
ATS Tim Stapleton E 3.00 8.00
ATW Tom Wandell E 3.00 8.00
AVF Valtteri Filppula E 5.00 12.00
AWG Wayne Gretzky A 125.00 200.00
AZK Zack Kassian E 4.00 10.00

2012-13 Artifacts Frozen Artifacts Jerseys Blue

GROUP A STATED ODDS 1:5152
GROUP B STATED ODDS 1:1717
GROUP C STATED ODDS 1:48
OVERALL ODDS 1:48 HOB, 1:72 RET
*EMERALD/36: .8X TO 2X BLUE GRP B-C
*EMERALD/36: .6X TO 1.5X BLUE GRP B
FAAK Anze Kopitar C 6.00 15.00
FAAO Alexander Ovechkin C 15.00 40.00
FAAS Alexander Semin C 4.00 10.00
FAAT Alex Tanguay B 3.00 8.00
FABD Brandon Dubinsky A
FABH Brett Hull C 5.00 12.00
FABS Brendan Shanahan C 5.00 12.00
FACD Chris Drury C 3.00 8.00
FACF Cam Fowler C 3.00 8.00
FACG Claude Giroux C 4.00 10.00
FADA Daniel Alfredsson C 4.00 10.00
FADD Drew Doughty C 4.00 10.00
FADP David Perron C 2.50 6.00
FADR Derek Roy C 3.00 8.00
FADS Daniel Sedin C 4.00 10.00
FAGR Mike Green C 4.00 10.00
FAJC Jeff Carter C 4.00 10.00
FAJC Jean-Sebastien Giguere C 3.00 8.00
FAJI Jarome Iginla C 4.00 10.00
FAJQ Jonathan Quick C 6.00 15.00
FAJS Jason Spezza C 4.00 10.00
FALC Logan Couture C 4.00 10.00
FALO Linus Omark C 3.00 8.00
FALR Larry Robinson AS C 4.00 10.00
FAMG Michael Grabner C 3.00 8.00
FAMN Markus Naslund C 4.00 10.00
FAMS Marc Staal C 3.00 8.00
FAST Derek Stepan C 4.00 10.00
FATS Tyler Seguin C 6.00 15.00

2012-13 Artifacts Horizontal Jerseys

COMMON CARD/36 4.00 10.00
UNLISTED STARS/36 5.00 12.00
STATED PRINT RUN 36
*EMERALD/24: .8X TO 2X HORIZ.JSY/36
2 Alexander Ovechkin 15.00 40.00
3 Anze Kopitar 8.00 20.00
5 Bobby Ryan 5.00 12.00
6 Brandon Dubinsky 4.00 10.00
7 Brendan Shanahan 6.00 15.00
8 Brett Hull 6.00 15.00
11 Claude Giroux 5.00 12.00
12 Colton Orr 5.00 12.00
13 Cam Fowler 4.00 10.00
15 Daniel Alfredsson 5.00 12.00
16 Daniel Sedin 5.00 12.00
17 Denis Savard 6.00 15.00
18 Derek Roy 4.00 10.00
19 Derek Stepan 5.00 12.00
20 Dino Ciccarelli 5.00 12.00
21 Doug Wilson 4.00 10.00
22 Drew Doughty 5.00 12.00
23 Drew Stafford 5.00 12.00
24 Duncan Keith AS 5.00 12.00
25 Eric Lindros AS 6.00 15.00
27 Erik Karlsson 10.00 25.00
28 Evgeni Malkin 15.00 40.00
31 Henrik Zetterberg 6.00 15.00
32 Ilya Kovalchuk 5.00 12.00
34 Jarome Iginla 6.00 15.00
35 Jaromir Jagr AS 10.00 25.00
36 Jason Spezza 5.00 12.00
38 Jeff Carter 5.00 12.00
41 Johan Franzen 5.00 12.00
42 John Tavares 10.00 25.00
45 Jordan Eberle 15.00 40.00
46 Jordan Staal 5.00 12.00
47 Keith Yandle 5.00 12.00
48 Kristopher Letang 8.00 20.00
49 Larry Robinson AS 5.00 12.00
50 Logan Couture
51 Luc Robitaille 5.00 12.00
52 Kevin Shattenkirk 5.00 12.00
53 Marian Gaborik 5.00 12.00
54 Marian Hossa AS 4.00 10.00
55 Sam Gagner 4.00 10.00
56 Mario Lemieux AS 15.00 40.00
58 Markus Naslund AS 4.00 10.00
59 Matt Duchene 5.00 12.00
60 Matt Moulson 4.00 10.00
61 Maxime Talbot 4.00 10.00
62 Mike Green 5.00 12.00
63 Mike Modano 8.00 20.00
64 Mike Richards 5.00 12.00
65 Milan Lucic 5.00 12.00
66 Nathan Horton 5.00 12.00
67 Nicklas Backstrom 8.00 20.00
69 P.K. Subban 8.00 20.00
70 Patrice Bergeron 6.00 15.00
72 Patrick Sharp 5.00 12.00
74 Paul Stastny 5.00 12.00
75 Pavel Datsyuk 6.00 15.00
77 Ray Bourque 8.00 20.00
78 Nikolai Kulemin 4.00 10.00
79 Rick Nash AS 5.00 12.00
80 Ron Francis 6.00 15.00
81 Ryan Callahan 5.00 12.00
82 Ryan Getzlaf 8.00 20.00
83 Ryan Kesler 5.00 12.00
85 Shane Doan 4.00 10.00
86 Sidney Crosby 15.00 40.00
87 Stephen Weiss 4.00 10.00
94 Tyler Ennis 4.00 10.00
95 Tyler Myers 4.00 10.00
96 Tyler Seguin 8.00 20.00
97 Vincent Lecavalier 4.00 10.00
98 Wayne Gretzky AS 30.00 60.00
99 Zach Parise 5.00 12.00
100 Zdeno Chara 5.00 12.00
105 Curtis Joseph 5.00 12.00
107 Ed Belfour 8.00 20.00
109 Jean-Sebastien Giguere 4.00 10.00
110 Jim Howard 6.00 15.00
113 Jonathan Quick 8.00 20.00
115 Marc-Andre Fleury
116 Martin Brodeur 10.00 25.00
117 Miikka Kiprusoff 4.00 10.00
118 Patrick Roy 15.00 40.00
119 Semyon Varlamov 5.00 12.00
122 Tim Thomas 5.00 12.00
123 Tomas Vokoun 6.00 15.00
126 Alex Pietrangelo TC 6.00 15.00
127 Brayden Schenn TC 6.00 15.00
133 Corey Perry TC 5.00 12.00
134 Dale Hawerchuk TC 6.00 15.00
136 Drew Doughty TC 5.00 12.00
137 Duncan Keith TC 5.00 12.00
140 Jarome Iginla TC 5.00 12.00
141 Louis Leblanc TC 5.00 12.00
143 Patrice Bergeron TC 6.00 15.00
145 Ryan Ellis TC 3.00 8.00
146 Ryan Getzlaf TC 8.00 20.00
150 Zack Kassian TC 4.00 10.00

2012-13 Artifacts Jerseys

STATED PRINT RUN 25-125
*EMERALD/75: .8X TO 2X BASIC JSY/125
*EMERALD/75: .4X TO 1X BASIC JSY/35
*EMERALD/50: .5X TO 1.2X BASIC JSY/25
*GOLD/15: 1.2X TO 3X BASIC JSY/125
*GOLD/15: .8X TO 2X BASIC JSY/35
*GOLD/15: .8X TO 2X BASIC JSY/25
1 Alex Tanguay AS/125 2.50 6.00
2 Alexander Ovechkin/125 15.00 40.00
3 Anze Kopitar/125 6.00 15.00
5 Bobby Ryan/125 4.00 10.00
6 Brandon Dubinsky/125 3.00 8.00
7 Brendan Shanahan/125 5.00 12.00
8 Brett Hull/125 5.00 12.00
9 Cam Neely/125 4.00 10.00
10 Chris Drury/125 3.00 8.00
11 Claude Giroux/125 4.00 10.00
12 Colton Orr/125 4.00 10.00
13 Cam Fowler/125 3.00 8.00
14 Dale Hawerchuk/125 5.00 12.00
15 Daniel Alfredsson/125 4.00 10.00
16 Daniel Sedin/125 4.00 10.00
17 Denis Savard/125 5.00 12.00
18 Derek Roy/125 3.00 8.00
19 Derek Stepan/125 4.00 10.00
20 Dino Ciccarelli/125 4.00 10.00
21 Doug Wilson/125 3.00 8.00
22 Drew Doughty/125 4.00 10.00
23 Drew Stafford/125 4.00 10.00
24 Duncan Keith AS/125 4.00 10.00
25 Eric Lindros AS/125 5.00 12.00
26 Eric Staal/125 5.00 12.00
27 Erik Karlsson/125 8.00 20.00
28 Evgeni Malkin/125 12.00 30.00
29 George Parros/125 3.00 8.00
30 Henrik Sedin/125 4.00 10.00
31 Henrik Zetterberg/125 5.00 12.00
32 Ilya Kovalchuk/125 4.00 10.00
33 Jari Kurri/125 4.00 10.00
34 Jarome Iginla/125 4.00 10.00
35 Jaromir Jagr AS/125 6.00 15.00
36 Jason Spezza/125 4.00 10.00
37 Jean Beliveau AS/65 20.00 50.00
38 Jeff Carter/125 4.00 10.00
40 Joe Thornton/125 4.00 10.00
41 Johan Franzen/125 3.00 8.00
42 John Tavares/25 15.00 40.00
43 Dustin Brown/125 4.00 10.00
44 Jonathan Toews/125 8.00 20.00
45 Jordan Eberle/125 4.00 10.00
46 Jordan Staal/125 4.00 10.00
47 Keith Yandle/125 4.00 10.00
48 Kristopher Letang/125 4.00 10.00
49 Larry Robinson AS/125 4.00 10.00
50 Logan Couture/125 4.00 10.00
51 Luc Robitaille/125 4.00 10.00
52 Kevin Shattenkirk/125 6.00 15.00
53 Marian Gaborik/125 4.00 10.00
54 Marian Hossa AS/125 3.00 8.00
55 Sam Gagner/125 3.00 8.00
56 Mario Lemieux AS/125 12.00 30.00
57 Mark Messier/125 5.00 12.00
58 Markus Naslund AS/125 3.00 8.00
59 Matt Duchene/125 4.00 10.00
60 Matt Moulson/125 3.00 8.00
61 Maxime Talbot/125 3.00 8.00
62 Mike Green/125 4.00 10.00
63 Mike Modano/125 6.00 15.00
64 Mike Richards/125 4.00 10.00
65 Milan Lucic/125 5.00 12.00
66 Nathan Horton/125 4.00 10.00
67 Nicklas Backstrom/125 6.00 15.00
68 Nicklas Lidstrom/125 4.00 10.00
69 P.K. Subban/125 6.00 15.00
70 Patrice Bergeron/125 5.00 12.00
71 Patrick Kane/125 8.00 20.00
72 Patrick Sharp/125 4.00 10.00
73 Paul Coffey/125 4.00 10.00
74 Paul Stastny/125 4.00 10.00
75 Pavel Datsyuk/125 5.00 12.00
76 Rene Bourque/125 3.00 8.00
77 Ray Bourque/125 6.00 15.00
78 Nikolai Kulemin/125 6.00 15.00
79 Rick Nash AS/125 4.00 10.00
80 Ron Francis/125 5.00 12.00
81 Ryan Callahan/125 3.00 8.00
82 Ryan Getzlaf/125 6.00 15.00
83 Ryan Kesler/125 4.00 10.00
85 Shane Doan/125 3.00 8.00
86 Sidney Crosby/125 15.00 40.00
87 Stephen Weiss/125 3.00 8.00
88 Steve Ott/125 3.00 8.00
89 Steven Stamkos/125 8.00 20.00
90 Taylor Hall/125 8.00 20.00
91 Teemu Selanne AS/35 8.00 20.00
92 Tony Twist/125 4.00 10.00
93 Trevor Linden/125 5.00 12.00
94 Tyler Ennis/125 3.00 8.00
95 Tyler Myers/125 3.00 8.00
96 Tyler Seguin/125 6.00 15.00
97 Vincent Lecavalier/125 3.00 8.00
98 Wayne Gretzky AS/125 20.00 50.00
99 Zach Parise/125 4.00 10.00
100 Zdeno Chara/125 4.00 10.00
101 Antti Niemi/125 3.00 8.00
102 Carey Price/125 8.00 20.00
103 Cory Schneider/125 3.00 8.00
104 Corey Crawford/125 5.00 12.00
105 Curtis Joseph/125 4.00 10.00
106 Dominik Hasek/125 5.00 12.00
107 Ed Belfour/125 4.00 10.00
108 Pekka Rinne/125 5.00 12.00
109 Jean-Sebastien Giguere/125 3.00 8.00
110 Jim Howard/125 5.00 12.00
111 Johnny Bower/125 10.00 25.00
112 Ondrej Pavelec/125 4.00 10.00
113 Jonathan Quick/125 10.00 25.00
114 Kari Lehtonen/125 3.00 8.00
115 Marc-Andre Fleury/125 6.00 15.00
116 Martin Brodeur/125 8.00 20.00
117 Miikka Kiprusoff/125 3.00 8.00
118 Patrick Roy/125 10.00 25.00
119 Semyon Varlamov/125 4.00 10.00
120 Ryan Miller/125 4.00 10.00
121 Steve Mason/125 3.00 8.00
122 Tim Thomas/125 6.00 15.00
123 Tomas Vokoun/125 8.00 20.00
124 Tony Esposito/125 5.00 12.00
125 Tuukka Rask/125 4.00 10.00
126 Alex Pietrangelo TC/125 4.00 10.00
127 Brayden Schenn TC/125 5.00 12.00
128 Brenden Morrow TC/125 4.00 10.00
129 Brent Seabrook TC/125 5.00 12.00
130 Calvin de Haan TC/125 4.00 10.00
131 Chris Pronger TC/125 4.00 10.00
132 Cody Eakin TC/125 4.00 10.00
133 Corey Perry TC/125 5.00 12.00
134 Dale Hawerchuk TC/125 6.00 15.00
135 Dan Boyle TC/125 4.00 10.00
136 Drew Doughty TC/125 5.00 12.00
137 Duncan Keith TC/125 5.00 12.00
138 Erik Gudbranson TC/125 5.00 12.00
139 Dustin Tokarski TC/125 4.00 10.00
140 Jarome Iginla TC/125 5.00 12.00
141 Louis Leblanc TC/125 5.00 12.00
142 Marcus Foligno TC/125 4.00 10.00
143 Patrice Bergeron TC/125 6.00 15.00
144 Roberto Luongo TC/125 4.00 10.00
145 Ryan Ellis TC/125 3.00 8.00
146 Ryan Getzlaf TC/125 8.00 20.00
147 Shea Weber TC/125 4.00 10.00
148 Simon Despres TC/125 4.00 10.00
149 Wayne Gretzky TC/125 25.00 60.00
150 Zack Kassian TC/125 4.00 10.00

2012-13 Artifacts Rookie Autographs Redemptions

AUTO EXCH ODDS 1:160 HOBBY
EXCH EXPIRATION: 9/15/2014
I Alex Galchenyuk 60.00 120.00
II Beau Bennett 15.00 40.00
III Brendan Gallagher 20.00 50.00
IV Charlie Coyle 12.00 30.00
V Cory Conacher 12.00 30.00
VI Damien Brunner 30.00 80.00
VII Dougie Hamilton 20.00 50.00
VIII Vladimir Tarasenko 60.00 120.00
IX Filip Forsberg 25.00 50.00
X Mikhail Grigorenko 15.00 40.00
XI Jonathan Huberdeau 20.00 50.00
XII Justin Schultz 15.00 40.00
XIII Mikael Granlund 20.00 50.00
XIV J.T. Miller 15.00 40.00
XV Nail Yakupov 60.00 120.00
XVI Nathan Beaulieu 15.00 40.00
XVII Tyler Toffoli 15.00 40.00
XVIII Emerson Etem 12.00 30.00

2012-13 Artifacts Treasured Swatches Jerseys Blue

GROUP A STATED ODDS 1:5152
GROUP B STATED ODDS 1:1717
GROUP C STATED ODDS 1:48
OVERALL ODDS 1:48 HOB, 1:72 RET
*EMERALD/36: .8X TO 2X BLUE GRP B-C
TSBE Patrice Bergeron C 5.00 12.00
TSEK Evander Kane C 4.00 10.00
TSEL Eric Lindros C 6.00 15.00
TSGA Sam Gagner C 3.00 8.00
TSIK Ilya Kovalchuk C 4.00 10.00
TSJF Johan Franzen C 4.00 10.00
TSJV James van Riemsdyk C 4.00 10.00
TSMH Milan Hejduk C 3.00 8.00
TSML Mario Lemieux AS C 12.00 30.00
TSMM Mike Modano C 6.00 15.00
TSMR Mike Richards C 4.00 10.00
TSNB Nicklas Backstrom C 6.00 15.00
TSNK Nikolai Kulemin C 3.00 8.00
TSPB Patrik Berglund C 2.50 6.00
TSPD Pavel Datsyuk C 5.00 12.00
TSRB Ray Bourque C 6.00 15.00
TSRG Ryan Getzlaf C 6.00 15.00
TSSC Sidney Crosby C 15.00 40.00
TSSD Shane Doan C 3.00 8.00
TSSG Simon Gagne C 4.00 10.00
TSST Jordan Staal C 4.00 10.00
TSTE Tyler Ennis C 3.00 8.00
TSTM Tyler Myers C 3.00 8.00
TSTS Teemu Selanne A
TSTV Tomas Vokoun C 3.00 8.00
TSVA Thomas Vanek C 4.00 10.00
TSVL Vincent Lecavalier C 3.00 8.00
TSZC Zdeno Chara C 4.00 10.00
TSZP Zach Parise B 4.00 10.00

2012-13 Artifacts Tundra Tandems Jerseys Blue

STATED ODDS 1:16 HOBBY
*EMERALD/36: 1X TO 2.5X BASIC TANDEM
*EMERALD/20: 1.2X TO 3X BASIC TANDEM
TTBE B.Shanahan/E.Lindros 5.00 12.00
TTBH P.Bergeron/N.Horton 5.00 12.00
TTBK E.Kane/D.Byfuglien 4.00 10.00
TTBL M.Brodeur/R.Luongo 8.00 20.00
TTBQ J.Bernier/J.Quick 10.00 25.00
TTBS D.Backes/C.Stewart 4.00 10.00
TTCD B.Dubinsky/R.Callahan 4.00 10.00
TTDD D.Wilson/D.Savard 5.00 12.00
TTDY S.Doan/K.Yandle 4.00 10.00
TTEB J.Benn/L.Eriksson 5.00 12.00
TTEH J.Eberle/T.Hall 8.00 20.00
TTEJ E.Staal/J.Staal 5.00 12.00
TTEL C.Eakin/L.Leblanc TC 8.00 20.00
TTFK Kassian/M.Foligno TC 6.00 15.00
TTFS M.Fleury/J.Staal 6.00 15.00
TTGB M.Green/N.Backstrom 6.00 15.00
TTGF R.Getzlaf/C.Fowler 6.00 15.00
TTGR R.Getzlaf/B.Ryan 6.00 15.00
TTGS M.Gaborik/D.Stepan 4.00 10.00
TTHB B.Hull/E.Belfour 6.00 15.00
TTHG S.Hartnell/C.Giroux 4.00 10.00
TTHH D.Hasek/J.Howard 5.00 12.00
TTJP Thornton/P.Marleau TC 4.00 10.00
TTKB Kiprusoff/Bouwmeester 4.00 10.00
TTKC K.Shattenkirk/C.Stewart 4.00 10.00
TTKD A.Kopitar/D.Doughty 8.00 20.00
TTKE N.Kronwall/J.Ericsson 3.00 8.00
TTKP I.Kovalchuk/Z.Parise 4.00 10.00
TTLD N.Lidstrom/P.Datsyuk 5.00 12.00
TTLH N.Lidstrom/J.Howard 4.00 10.00
TTLJ M.Lemieux/J.Jagr 10.00 25.00
TTLK R.Luongo/R.Kesler 4.00 10.00
TTMB Bergeron/B.Morrow TC 5.00 12.00
TTME T.Myers/T.Ennis 3.00 8.00
TTMG M.Messier/M.Gartner 5.00 12.00
TTMJ Bouwmeester/Kiprusoff 4.00 10.00
TTMV R.Miller/T.Vanek 4.00 10.00
TTNF M.Naslund/R.Francis 5.00 12.00
TTNM R.Nash/S.Mason 4.00 10.00
TTPB C.Pronger/I.Bryzgalov 4.00 10.00
TTPD P.Sharp/D.Keith 4.00 10.00
TTPE T.Plekanec/L.Eller 4.00 10.00
TTPO M.Paajarvi/L.Omark 3.00 8.00
TTRC M.Richards/J.Carter 4.00 10.00
TTRO M.Ribeiro/S.Ott 3.00 8.00
TTRS L.Robinson/P.Subban 6.00 15.00
TTSA C.Anderson/J.Spezza 4.00 10.00
TTSC Shanahan/Ciccarelli 5.00 12.00
TTSD P.Stastny/M.Duchene 4.00 10.00
TTSL J.Staal/K.Letang 4.00 10.00
TTSO A.Semin/A.Ovechkin 15.00 40.00
TTSS H.Sedin/D.Sedin 4.00 10.00
TTSW S.Weber/R.Suter 3.00 8.00
TTTR T.Rask/T.Thomas 4.00 10.00
TTVN T.Vokoun/M.Neuvirth 5.00 12.00
TTWK Khabibulin/R.Whitney 4.00 10.00
TTWV S.Weiss/K.Versteeg 3.00 8.00
TTYE Yandle/Ekman-Larsson 4.00 10.00
TTZF H.Zetterberg/J.Franzen 5.00 12.00

2012-13 Artifacts Tundra Trios Jerseys Blue

GROUP A ODDS 1:2385 HOB
GROUP B ODDS 1:32 HOB
*EMERALD/18: 1X TO 2.5X BLUE GRP B
TT3ASA Alfrdsn/Spezza/Andrsn B 5.00 12.00
TT3BHP Backs/Halk/Pietran B 6.00 15.00
TT3BJB Brodr/Belfr/Josph B 10.00 25.00
TT3BKM Bergrn/Mrchnd/Krejci B 6.00 15.00
TT3BMH Belfour/Hull/Modano A 6.00 15.00
TT3BPK Pavelc/Kane/Byfug B 8.00 20.00
TT3BQD Quick/Dghty/Bernr B 8.00 20.00
TT3BSS Backes/Stwart/Shatt B 5.00 12.00
TT3CBP Bourque/Park/Chara B 8.00 20.00
TT3CTR Thomas/Rask/Chara B 8.00 20.00
TT3DYE Doan/Yndle/Ek-Lars B 5.00 12.00
TT3DZF Franzn/Datsyk/Zettr B 8.00 20.00
TT3EGO Ellis/Gdbmsn/Olsn TC B 5.00 12.00
TT3FMS Staal/Fleury/Malkin B 15.00 40.00
TT3GRF Getzlaf/Ryan/Fowler B 8.00 20.00
TT3GSD Giguere/Ststny/Duch B 6.00 15.00
TT3GSS Staal/Stepan/Boyle B 5.00 12.00
TT3GSV Gigre/Varlmv/Ststny B 8.00 20.00
TT3HVV van Rms/Hrtnll/Vrack B 5.00 12.00
TT3IKC Kiprsff/Iginla/Camml B 5.00 12.00
TT3KMK Kessel/Kulmin/McArt B 6.00 15.00
TT3KPC Koval/Parise/Clarksn B 5.00 12.00
TT3LJG Gretzky/Jagr/Lindros B 12.00 30.00
TT3LSS Lecav/StLoui/Stamk B 10.00 25.00
TT3MOT Mlsn/Okpso/Tavres B 10.00 25.00
TT3NBM Brassard/Mason/Nash B 5.00 12.00
TT3OPC Orr/Parros/Carkner B 5.00 12.00
TT3PBG Pronger/Giroux/Bryz B 5.00 12.00
TT3PPS Price/Subban/Plek B 15.00 40.00
TT3PSK Seabrk/Keith/Prngr TC B 6.00 15.00
TT3RCK Kopitr/Richrds/Cartr B 8.00 20.00
TT3RMV Miller/Vanek/Roy B 10.00 25.00
TT3SLJ Jagr/Lindros/Shanhn B 10.00 25.00
TT3SOB Semn/Ovech/Bckstrm B 8.00 20.00
TT3SSK Sedin/Sedin/Kesler B 5.00 12.00
TT3SSS Staal/Staal/Staal B 6.00 15.00
TT3TMB Mrrw/Thrntn/Berg TC B 6.00 15.00
TT3VME Vanek/Myers/Ennis B 5.00 12.00

2013-14 Artifacts

COMP.SET w/o SP's (100) 12.00 30.00
101-200 STATED PRINT RUN 999
101-200 STATED PRINT RUN 899
*ROOK.EXCH: .3X TO .8X ROOKIE/899
ROOKIE EXCH ODDS 1:10 HOB
1 Adam Henrique .40 1.00
2 Adam Larsson .40 1.00
3 Alex Tanguay .25 .60
4 Alexander Ovechkin 1.50 4.00
5 Alexandre Burrows .40 1.00
6 Andrei Markov .40 1.00
7 Blake Wheeler .40 1.00
8 Bob Nystrom .25 .60
9 Bobby Ryan .40 1.00
10 Brad Marchand .50 1.25
11 Brayden Schenn .40 1.00
12 Bryan Little .40 1.00
13 Bryan Trottier .50 1.25
14 Claude Lemieux .30 .75
15 Colin Greening .25 .60
16 Corey Perry .40 1.00
17 Dale Hawerchuk .50 1.25
18 Daniel Briere .40 1.00
19 David Perron .25 .60
20 Dion Phaneuf .40 1.00
21 Doug Gilmour .50 1.25
22 Drew Doughty .40 1.00
23 Drew Stafford .40 1.00
24 Duncan Keith .40 1.00
25 Dustin Brown .40 1.00
26 Eric Lindros .60 1.50
27 Evgeni Malkin 1.25 3.00
28 Gabriel Landeskog .30 .75
29 Harold Snepsts .25 .60
30 Henrik Zetterberg .50 1.25
31 Ilya Kovalchuk .40 1.00
32 Jacques Lemaire .40 1.00
33 James Neal .40 1.00
34 Jamie McBain .25 .60
35 Jaromir Jagr 1.00 2.50
36 Jason Pominville .30 .75
37 Jason Spezza .40 1.00
38 Jay Bouwmeester .40 1.00
39 Jeff Carter .40 1.00
40 Jeff Skinner .30 .75
41 Joe Sakic .60 1.50
42 Jonathan Toews .75 2.00
43 Jordan Eberle .40 1.00
44 Justin Williams .30 .75
45 Keith Yandle .40 1.00
46 Kevin Shattenkirk .40 1.00
47 Kris Letang .40 1.00
48 Larry Murphy .40 1.00
49 Lars Eller .30 .75
50 Luke Adam .30 .75
51 Luke Schenn .25 .60
52 Marc Staal .30 .75
53 Marian Gaborik .40 1.00
54 Mario Lemieux 1.25 3.00
55 Markus Naslund .30 .75
56 Mats Sundin .40 1.00
57 Matt Duchene .40 1.00
58 Matt Read .25 .60
59 Matt Stajan .30 .75
60 Maxime Talbot .30 .75
61 Michael Cammalleri .30 .75
62 Michael Frolik .25 .60
63 Michel Goulet .30 .75
64 Mike Gartner .40 1.00
65 Mike Green .40 1.00
66 Mike Modano .60 1.50
67 Mike Ribeiro .30 .75
68 Mike Richards .40 1.00
69 Milan Hejduk .30 .75
70 Milan Lucic .40 1.00
71 Nathan Horton .40 1.00
72 Nick Foligno .30 .75
73 Nicklas Lidstrom .40 1.00
74 Slava Voynov .40 1.00
75 Niklas Kronwall .30 .75
76 Oliver Ekman-Larsson .30 .75
77 P.K. Subban .60 1.50
78 Patric Hornqvist .30 .75
79 Patrice Bergeron .50 1.25
80 Patrick Marleau .40 1.00
81 Patrik Elias .40 1.00
82 Paul Coffey .40 1.00
83 Paul Stastny .40 1.00
84 Pavel Bure .50 1.25
85 Peter Mueller .25 .60
86 Ron Francis .50 1.25
87 Ryan Getzlaf .60 1.50
88 Ryan Nugent-Hopkins .40 1.00
89 Scott Hartnell .40 1.00
90 Scott Niedermayer .40 1.00
91 Shea Weber .30 .75
92 Sidney Crosby 1.50 4.00
93 Taylor Hall .75 2.00
94 Theoren Fleury .50 1.25
95 Tomas Plekanec .40 1.00
96 Tyler Seguin .60 1.50
97 Valtteri Filppula .40 1.00
98 Wayne Gretzky 2.00 5.00
99 Zach Parise .40 1.00
100 Zdeno Chara .40 1.00
101 Bernie Parent G 1.50 4.00
102 Bill Ranford G 1.50 4.00
103 Braden Holtby G 2.50 6.00
104 Carey Price G 5.00 12.00
105 Chris Osgood G 1.50 4.00
106 Corey Crawford G 2.00 5.00
107 Cory Schneider G 1.25 3.00
108 Craig Anderson G 1.50 4.00
109 Curtis Joseph G 1.50 4.00
110 Dominik Hasek G 2.00 5.00
111 Ed Belfour G 1.50 4.00
112 Ilya Bryzgalov G 1.50 4.00
113 Jean-Sebastien Giguere G 1.25 3.00
114 Jim Howard G 1.50 4.00
115 Jonathan Quick G 2.50 6.00
116 Kari Lehtonen G 1.25 3.00
117 Marc-Andre Fleury G 2.50 6.00
118 Martin Brodeur G 3.00 8.00
119 Miikka Kiprusoff G 1.25 3.00
120 Ondrej Pavelec G 1.50 4.00
121 Patrick Roy G 4.00 10.00
122 Pekka Rinne G 2.00 5.00
123 Roberto Luongo G 1.50 4.00
124 Robin Lehner G 1.25 3.00
125 Tuukka Rask G 1.50 4.00
126 Brett Connolly TC 1.00 2.50
127 Bryan Trottier TC 2.00 5.00
128 Carter Ashton TC 1.00 2.50
129 Chet Pickard TC 1.00 2.50
130 Cody Goloubef TC 1.00 2.50
131 Colten Teubert TC 1.00 2.50
132 Corey Perry TC 1.50 4.00
133 Dany Heatley TC 1.25 3.00
134 Devante Smith-Pelly TC 1.25 3.00
135 Duncan Keith TC 1.50 4.00
136 Evander Kane TC 1.50 4.00
137 Jaden Schwartz TC 2.00 5.00
138 Jamie Benn TC 2.00 5.00
139 Jared Cowen TC 1.00 2.50
140 Joe Sakic TC 2.50 6.00
141 Joe Thornton TC 1.50 4.00
142 Keith Aulie TC 1.00 2.50
143 Mark Stone TC 1.25 3.00
144 Patrice Cormier TC 1.00 2.50
145 Ryan Johansen TC 2.00 5.00
146 Stefan Della Rovere TC 1.00 2.50
147 Steve Shutt TC 1.25 3.00
148 Tyler Ennis TC 1.25 3.00
149 Wayne Gretzky TC 8.00 20.00
150 Zach Boychuk TC 1.00 2.50
151 Alex Chiasson RC 2.00 5.00
152 Alex Galchenyuk RC 6.00 15.00
153 Austin Watson RC 1.50 4.00
154 Beau Bennett RC 2.50 6.00
155 Brendan Gallagher RC 6.00 15.00
156 Calvin Pickard RC 2.00 5.00
157 Charlie Coyle RC 2.00 5.00
158 Chris Brown RC 1.25 3.00
159 Christian Thomas RC 1.50 4.00
160 Cory Conacher RC 1.25 3.00
161 Cristopher Nilstorp RC 1.50 4.00
162 Damien Brunner RC 1.50 4.00
163 Dougie Hamilton RC 4.00 10.00
164 Drew Shore RC 1.50 4.00
165 Emerson Etem RC 2.00 5.00
166 Filip Forsberg RC 5.00 12.00
167 Jack Campbell RC 1.50 4.00
168 Jamie Oleksiak RC 1.50 4.00
169 Jared Staal RC 2.00 5.00
170 Jarred Tinordi RC 2.00 5.00
171 Johan Larsson RC 1.50 4.00
172 Jonas Brodin RC 1.50 4.00
173 Jonathan Huberdeau RC 5.00 12.00
174 Jordan Schroeder RC 2.00 5.00
175 Justin Schultz RC 2.00 5.00
176 Leo Komarov RC 2.00 5.00
177 Mark Pysyk RC 2.00 5.00
178 Max Reinhart RC 2.00 5.00
179 Mikael Granlund RC 3.00 8.00
180 Mikhail Grigorenko RC 2.50 6.00
181 Nail Yakupov RC 6.00 15.00
182 Nathan Beaulieu RC 1.50 4.00
183 Nick Bjugstad RC 2.50 6.00
184 Nick Petrecki RC 1.25 3.00
185 Nicklas Jensen RC 1.50 4.00
186 Petr Mrazek RC 4.00 10.00
187 Quinton Howden RC 1.50 4.00
188 Richard Panik RC 2.00 5.00
189 Rickard Rakell RC 2.00 5.00
190 Roman Cervenka RC 1.50 4.00
191 Ryan Murphy RC 2.00 5.00
192 Ryan Spooner RC 2.00 5.00
193 Scott Laughton RC 2.00 5.00
194 Stefan Matteau RC 1.50 4.00
195 Thomas Hickey RC 1.50 4.00
196 Tye McGinn RC 2.00 5.00
197 Tyler Toffoli RC 4.00 10.00
198 Viktor Fasth RC 2.00 5.00
199 Vladimir Tarasenko RC 8.00 20.00
200 Zach Redmond RC 1.50 4.00
RED201 Hampus Lindholm RC 3.00 8.00
RED202 Carl Soderberg RC 2.00 5.00
RED203 Zemgus Girgensons RC 4.00 10.00
RED204 Sean Monahan RC 3.00 8.00
RED205 Elias Lindholm RC 3.00 8.00
RED206 Antti Raanta RC 2.50 6.00
RED207 Nathan MacKinnon RC 15.00 40.00
RED208 Ryan Murray RC 3.00 8.00
RED209 Valeri Nichushkin RC 2.00 5.00
RED210 Danny DeKeyser RC 2.50 6.00
RED211 Mark Arcobello RC 2.00 5.00
RED212 Aleksander Barkov RC 5.00 12.00
RED213 Linden Vey RC 1.25 3.00
RED214 Mathew Dumba RC 2.00 5.00
RED215 Michael Bournival RC 2.00 5.00
RED216 Seth Jones RC 2.00 5.00
RED217 Reid Boucher RC 2.00 5.00
RED218 Ryan Strome RC 2.50 6.00
RED219 Dylan McIlrath RC 1.25 3.00
RED220 Cody Ceci RC 1.50 4.00
RED221 Michael Raffl RC 1.50 4.00
RED222 Lucas Lessio RC 1.25 3.00
RED223 Olli Maatta RC 3.00 8.00
RED224 Tomas Hertl RC 2.50 6.00
RED225 Dmitrij Jaskin RC 2.00 5.00
RED226 Nikita Kucherov RC 5.00 12.00
RED227 Morgan Rielly RC 5.00 12.00
RED228 Joacim Eriksson RC 2.00 5.00
RED229 Philipp Grubauer RC 2.00 5.00
RED230 Jacob Trouba RC 3.00 8.00
RED231 Josh Leivo RC 2.00 5.00
RED232 Boone Jenner RC 2.00 5.00
RED233 Tyler Johnson RC 5.00 12.00
RED234 Frederik Andersen RC 3.00 8.00
RED235 Jon Merrill RC 2.00 5.00
RED236 Marek Mazanec RC 2.00 5.00
RED237 Freddie Hamilton RC 2.00 5.00
RED238 Rasmus Ristolainen RC 3.00 8.00
RED239 Martin Jones RC 5.00 12.00
RED240 Justin Fontaine RC 2.00 5.00
RED241 John Gibson RC 6.00 15.00
RED242 Tomas Jurco RC 3.00 8.00

2013-14 Artifacts Emerald

*1-100 VETS/99: 3X TO 8X BASIC CARDS
*101-150 G/TC/99: 1X TO 2.5X BASIC G/TC
*151-200 ROOKIES/99: .6X TO 1.5X BASIC RC
STATED PRINT RUN 99 SER.#'d SETS
152 Alex Galchenyuk 12.00 30.00
181 Nail Yakupov 20.00 50.00

2013-14 Artifacts Ruby

*1-100 VETS/399: 2X TO 5X BASIC CARDS
1-100 STATED PRINT RUN 399
*101-150 G/TC/299: .6X TO 1.5X BASIC G/TC
*151-200 ROOKIES/299: .5X TO 1.2X BASIC RC
101-200 STATED PRINT RUN 299

2013-14 Artifacts Sapphire

*1-100 VETS/85: 3X TO 8X BASIC CARDS
*101-150 G/TC/85: 1X TO 2.5X BASIC G/TC
*151-200 ROOKIES/85: .8X TO 2X BASIC RC
STATED PRINT RUN 85 SER.#'d SETS
152 Alex Galchenyuk 15.00 40.00

2013-14 Artifacts Spectrum

*1-100 VETS/25: 6X TO 15X BASIC CARDS
*101-150 G/TC/25: 1.5X TO 4X BASIC G/TC
*151-200 ROOKIES/25: 1.2X TO 3X BASIC RC
STATED PRINT RUN 25 SER.#'d SETS
152 Alex Galchenyuk 60.00 120.00
155 Brendan Gallagher 40.00 80.00
181 Nail Yakupov 40.00 100.00

2013-14 Artifacts Autofacts

GROUP A ODDS 1:12,806 HOB
GROUP B ODDS 1:1577 HOB
GROUP C ODDS 1:1053 HOB
GROUP D ODDS 1:59 HOB
GROUP E ODDS 1:38 HOB
GROUP F ODDS 1:28 HOB
OVERALL ODDS 1:13 HOB, 1:1000 RET
AAG Alex Goligoski E 2.50 6.00
ABB Brett Bulmer D 2.50 6.00
ABL Brian Lee F 2.50 6.00
ABM Brendan Mikkelson F 2.50 6.00
ABN Brendon Nash D 2.50 6.00
ABO Bobby Orr B 75.00 125.00
ABS Brayden Schenn D 4.00 10.00
ACG Cameron Gaunce D 2.50 6.00
ACO Cal O'Reilly F 2.50 6.00
ACP Corey Perry C 5.00 12.00
ACW Colin Wilson E 3.00 8.00
ADA Stephane Da Costa E 2.50 6.00
ADB Drayson Bowman E 2.50 6.00
ADS David Savard F 2.50 6.00
AEN Evgeni Nabokov E 3.00 8.00
AET Eric Tangradi D 2.50 6.00
AGR Andy Greene D 2.50 6.00
AJB Josh Bailey E 3.00 8.00
AJC Jared Cowen F 2.50 6.00
AJE Jonathan Ericsson F 3.00 8.00
AJF Justin Falk D 2.50 6.00
AJG Jake Gardiner D 4.00 10.00
AJH Josh Harding E 4.00 10.00
AJR Jay Rosehill F 2.50 6.00
ALI Leland Irving F 3.00 8.00
AMA Shawn Matthias D 2.50 6.00
AMH Matthew Halischuk F 2.50 6.00
AML Mario Lemieux B 60.00 100.00
AMM Matt Martin D 2.50 6.00
AMS Marco Sturm E 2.50 6.00
ANG Nicklas Grossman E 2.50 6.00
APB Pavel Bure B
APE Patrik Elias C 5.00 12.00
APO Patrick O'Sullivan F 2.50 6.00
ARO Ryan O'Marra D 2.50 6.00
ASD Simon Despres F 3.00 8.00
ASM Brendan Smith E 3.00 8.00
ASS Steven Stamkos B 30.00 60.00
AST Mark Streit F 2.50 6.00
ASU Mats Sundin B 20.00 50.00
ATE Tim Erixon E 2.50 6.00
ATL Trevor Lewis F 2.50 6.00
ATR Tuomo Ruutu E 3.00 8.00
ATS Tim Stapleton E 2.50 6.00
ATV Tomas Vincour E 2.50 6.00
ATW Tommy Wingels D 2.50 6.00
AVS Viktor Stalberg E 2.50 6.00
AWG Wayne Gretzky A 150.00 250.00

2013-14 Artifacts Buyback Autographs

STATED PRINT RUN 5-40
1 S.Crosby/40 '09-10ART 75.00 125.00
2 T.Rask/5 '07-08ART
3 S.Stamkos/25 '10-11ART 30.00 80.00
4 J.Tavares/18 '09-10ART 50.00 100.00

2013-14 Artifacts Frozen Artifacts Jerseys Blue

GROUP A ODDS 1:200 HOBBY
GROUP B ODDS 1:40 HOBBY
*GREEN PATCH/36: .8X TO 2X BLUE JSY
FAAL Adam Larsson B 4.00 10.00
FABE Patrik Berglund A 4.00 10.00
FABO Pierre-Marc Bouchard A 5.00 12.00
FABS Brayden Schenn B 4.00 10.00
FACG Colin Greening A 3.00 8.00
FADD David Desharnais B 4.00 10.00
FAGA Simon Gagne B 4.00 10.00
FAGO Michel Goulet B 3.00 8.00
FAGR Mike Green B 4.00 10.00
FAJS Joe Sakic A 5.00 12.00
FALE Lars Eller A 4.00 10.00
FALS Luke Schenn B 2.50 6.00
FAMG Marian Gaborik B 4.00 10.00
FAMR Mike Richards B 4.00 10.00
FAMR Matt Duchene B 4.00 10.00
FANG Nathan Gerbe B 2.50 6.00
FANK Nikolai Khabibulin B 4.00 10.00
FAOE Oliver Ekman-Larsson B 3.00 8.00
FAPB Patrice Bergeron B 5.00 12.00
FAPE Patrik Elias B 4.00 10.00
FAPM Peter Mueller B 2.50 6.00
FAPR Pekka Rinne B 5.00 12.00
FAPS P.K. Subban B 6.00 15.00
FAPS Paul Stastny B 4.00 10.00
FARD Raphael Diaz A 3.00 8.00
FASG Sam Gagner B 3.00 8.00
FASW Shea Weber B 3.00 8.00
FAWE Stephen Weiss A 4.00 10.00

2013-14 Artifacts Jerseys

STATED PRINT RUN 125 SER.#'d SETS
*EMERALD/75: .8X TO 2X BASIC JSY/125
*SPECTRUM/15: 1.2X TO 3X BASIC JSY/125
*HORIZNTL/36: 1X TO 2.5X BASIC JSY/125
*HRZN EMERALD/24: 1X TO 2.5X JSY/125
1 Adam Henrique 4.00 10.00
2 Adam Larsson 4.00 10.00
4 Alexander Ovechkin 8.00 20.00
5 Alexandre Burrows 4.00 10.00
6 Andrei Markov 4.00 10.00
8 Bob Nystrom 2.50 6.00
9 Bobby Ryan 4.00 10.00
10 Brad Marchand 5.00 12.00
11 Brayden Schenn 4.00 10.00
13 Bryan Trottier 5.00 12.00
14 Claude Lemieux 5.00 12.00
15 Colin Greening 2.50 6.00
16 Corey Perry 4.00 10.00
17 Dale Hawerchuk 5.00 12.00
18 Daniel Briere 4.00 10.00
19 David Perron 2.50 6.00
20 Dion Phaneuf 4.00 10.00
21 Doug Gilmour 5.00 12.00
22 Drew Doughty 4.00 10.00
23 Drew Stafford 4.00 10.00
24 Duncan Keith 4.00 10.00
25 Dustin Brown 4.00 10.00
26 Eric Lindros 6.00 15.00
27 Evgeni Malkin 12.00 30.00
28 Gabriel Landeskog 3.00 8.00
29 Harold Snepsts 2.50 6.00
30 Henrik Zetterberg 5.00 12.00
31 Ilya Kovalchuk 4.00 10.00
32 Jacques Lemaire 6.00 15.00
34 Jamie McBain 2.50 6.00
35 Jaromir Jagr 10.00 25.00
36 Jason Pominville 3.00 8.00
37 Jason Spezza 4.00 10.00
38 Jay Bouwmeester 4.00 10.00
39 Jeff Carter 4.00 10.00
40 Jeff Skinner 3.00 8.00
41 Joe Sakic 6.00 15.00
42 Jonathan Toews 10.00 25.00
43 Jordan Eberle 4.00 10.00
44 Justin Williams 3.00 8.00
45 Keith Yandle 4.00 10.00
46 Kevin Shattenkirk 4.00 10.00
47 Kris Letang 4.00 10.00
48 Larry Murphy 4.00 10.00
49 Lars Eller 3.00 8.00
50 Luke Adam 3.00 8.00
51 Luke Schenn 2.50 6.00
53 Marian Gaborik 4.00 10.00
54 Mario Lemieux 6.00 15.00
55 Markus Naslund 3.00 8.00
56 Mats Sundin 5.00 12.00
57 Matt Duchene 4.00 10.00
58 Matt Read 2.50 6.00
59 Matt Stajan 3.00 8.00
60 Maxime Talbot 3.00 8.00
61 Michael Cammalleri 3.00 8.00
62 Michael Frolik 2.50 6.00
63 Michel Goulet 3.00 8.00
64 Mike Gartner 4.00 10.00
65 Mike Green 4.00 10.00
66 Mike Modano 6.00 15.00
67 Mike Ribeiro 3.00 8.00
68 Mike Richards 4.00 10.00
69 Milan Hejduk 3.00 8.00
70 Milan Lucic 4.00 10.00
71 Nathan Horton 4.00 10.00
72 Nick Foligno 3.00 8.00
73 Nicklas Lidstrom 4.00 10.00
74 Slava Voynov 3.00 8.00
75 Niklas Kronwall 3.00 8.00
76 Oliver Ekman-Larsson 3.00 8.00
77 P.K. Subban 6.00 15.00
78 Patric Hornqvist 3.00 8.00
79 Patrice Bergeron 6.00 15.00
80 Patrick Marleau 4.00 10.00
81 Patrik Elias 4.00 10.00
82 Paul Coffey 4.00 10.00
83 Paul Stastny 4.00 10.00
84 Pavel Bure 5.00 12.00
85 Peter Mueller 3.00 8.00
86 Ron Francis 5.00 12.00
87 Ryan Getzlaf 6.00 15.00
88 Ryan Nugent-Hopkins 4.00 10.00
90 Scott Niedermayer 4.00 10.00
91 Shea Weber 3.00 8.00
92 Sidney Crosby 15.00 40.00
93 Taylor Hall 8.00 20.00
94 Theoren Fleury 5.00 12.00
95 Tomas Plekanec 4.00 10.00
96 Tyler Seguin 6.00 15.00
97 Valtteri Filppula 5.00 12.00
98 Wayne Gretzky 15.00 40.00
99 Zach Parise 4.00 10.00
100 Zdeno Chara 5.00 12.00
101 Bernie Parent G 6.00 15.00
102 Bill Ranford G 5.00 12.00
103 Braden Holtby G 8.00 20.00
104 Carey Price G 6.00 15.00
106 Corey Crawford G 6.00 15.00
107 Cory Schneider G 4.00 10.00
108 Craig Anderson G 5.00 12.00
109 Curtis Joseph G 5.00 12.00
110 Dominik Hasek G 6.00 15.00
111 Ed Belfour G 5.00 12.00
112 Ilya Bryzgalov G 5.00 12.00
113 Jean-Sebastien Giguere G 4.00 10.00
114 Jim Howard G 5.00 12.00
115 Jonathan Quick G 8.00 20.00
116 Kari Lehtonen G 4.00 10.00
117 Marc-Andre Fleury G 8.00 20.00
118 Martin Brodeur G 6.00 15.00
119 Miikka Kiprusoff G 4.00 10.00
120 Ondrej Pavelec G 5.00 12.00
121 Patrick Roy G 15.00 40.00
122 Pekka Rinne G 6.00 15.00
123 Roberto Luongo G 5.00 12.00
124 Robin Lehner G 4.00 10.00
125 Tuukka Rask G 5.00 12.00
126 Brett Connolly TC 3.00 8.00
127 Bryan Trottier TC 6.00 15.00
129 Chet Pickard TC 3.00 8.00
130 Cody Goloubef TC 3.00 8.00
131 Colten Teubert TC 3.00 8.00
132 Corey Perry TC 5.00 12.00
133 Dany Heatley TC 4.00 10.00
134 Devante Smith-Pelly TC 4.00 10.00
135 Duncan Keith TC 5.00 12.00
136 Evander Kane TC 5.00 12.00
137 Jaden Schwartz TC 6.00 15.00
138 Jamie Benn TC 6.00 15.00
139 Jared Cowen TC 3.00 8.00
140 Joe Sakic TC 8.00 20.00
141 Joe Thornton TC 5.00 12.00
142 Keith Aulie TC 3.00 8.00
144 Patrice Cormier TC 3.00 8.00
145 Ryan Johansen TC 4.00 10.00
146 Stefan Della Rovere TC 3.00 8.00
147 Steve Shutt TC 4.00 10.00
148 Tyler Ennis TC 4.00 10.00
149 Wayne Gretzky TC 25.00 50.00
150 Zach Boychuk TC 3.00 8.00
152 Alex Galchenyuk 12.00 30.00
153 Austin Watson 3.00 8.00
154 Beau Bennett 5.00 12.00
155 Brendan Gallagher 10.00 25.00
156 Calvin Pickard 4.00 10.00
157 Charlie Coyle 4.00 10.00
158 Chris Brown 3.00 8.00
159 Christian Thomas 3.00 8.00
160 Cory Conacher 2.50 6.00
161 Cristopher Nilstorp 3.00 8.00
162 Damien Brunner 5.00 12.00
163 Dougie Hamilton 5.00 12.00
164 Drew Shore 3.00 8.00
165 Emerson Etem 4.00 10.00
167 Jack Campbell 3.00 8.00
168 Jamie Oleksiak 3.00 8.00
169 Jared Staal 4.00 10.00
170 Jarred Tinordi 4.00 10.00
172 Jonas Brodin 3.00 8.00
173 Jonathan Huberdeau 6.00 15.00
174 Jordan Schroeder 4.00 10.00
175 Justin Schultz 4.00 10.00
177 Mark Pysyk 4.00 10.00
180 Mikhail Grigorenko 6.00 15.00
181 Nail Yakupov 10.00 25.00
182 Nathan Beaulieu 3.00 8.00
184 Nick Petrecki 2.50 6.00
185 Nicklas Jensen 3.00 8.00
186 Petr Mrazek 8.00 20.00
187 Quinton Howden 3.00 8.00
189 Rickard Rakell 4.00 10.00
190 Roman Cervenka 3.00 8.00
191 Ryan Murphy 4.00 10.00
192 Ryan Spooner 4.00 10.00
193 Scott Laughton 4.00 10.00
194 Stefan Matteau 3.00 8.00
195 Thomas Hickey 3.00 8.00
197 Tyler Toffoli 5.00 12.00
198 Viktor Fasth 5.00 12.00
199 Vladimir Tarasenko 12.50 25.00
200 Zach Redmond 3.00 8.00

2013-14 Artifacts Rookie Autographs Redemptions

ISSUED VIA MAIL REDEMPTION
EXCH CARD ODDS 1:160 HOBBY
EXCH EXPIRATION: 9/15/2015
I Nathan MacKinnon 100.00 200.00
II Tomas Hertl 30.00 60.00
III Sean Monahan 30.00 80.00
IV Seth Jones 40.00 80.00
V Valeri Nichushkin 25.00 50.00
VI Morgan Rielly 25.00 50.00
VII Aleksander Barkov 20.00 50.00
VIII Jacob Trouba 25.00 50.00
IX Elias Lindholm 12.00 30.00
X Ryan Murray 12.00 30.00
XI Rasmus Ristolainen 15.00 40.00
XII Boone Jenner 15.00 40.00
XIII Olli Maatta 15.00 40.00
XIV Matt Nieto 10.00 25.00
XV Freddie Hamilton 12.00 30.00
XVI Mathew Dumba 10.00 25.00
XVII Michael Bournival 15.00 40.00
XVIII Nikita Zadorov 12.00 30.00
XIX Zemgus Girgensons 15.00 40.00
XX Danny DeKeyser 12.00 30.00
XXI Mark Arcobello 10.00 25.00
XXII Sami Vatanen 12.00 30.00
XXIII Joakim Nordstrom 10.00 25.00
XXIV Hampus Lindholm 10.00 25.00

2013-14 Artifacts Top 12 Rookie Signatures

STATED ODDS 1:100 HOBBY
EXCH EXPIRATION: 9/20/2015
RSAG Alex Galchenyuk EXCH
RSBB Beau Bennett 10.00 25.00
RSBG Brendan Gallagher 25.00 60.00
RSCC Charlie Coyle 8.00 20.00
RSCO Cory Conacher 5.00 12.00
RSDH Dougie Hamilton 40.00 80.00
RSEE Emerson Etem 8.00 20.00
RSJH Jonathan Huberdeau 15.00 40.00
RSJS Justin Schultz 8.00 20.00
RSNY Nail Yakupov EXCH 25.00 60.00
RSTT Tyler Toffoli 15.00 40.00
RSVT Vladimir Tarasenko 30.00 80.00

2013-14 Artifacts Treasured Swatches Jerseys Blue

GROUP A ODDS 1:3700 HOB
GROUP B ODDS 1:86 HOB
GROUP C ODDS 1:46 HOB
OVERALL ODDS 1:36 HOB, 1:48 RET
*EMERALD/36: .8X TO 2X BASIC JSY
TSAH Ales Hemsky B 2.50 6.00
TSBO Ray Bourque C 6.00 15.00
TSCS Craig Smith B 2.50 6.00
TSEB Ed Belfour C 4.00 10.00
TSGA Sam Gagner C 3.00 8.00
TSJC Jeff Carter C 4.00 10.00
TSJH Jim Howard C 4.00 10.00
TSMB Martin Brodeur C 8.00 20.00
TSMK Miikka Kiprusoff C 3.00 8.00
TSMR Mike Richards B 4.00 10.00
TSMS Matt Stajan B 3.00 8.00
TSPR Pekka Rinne C 5.00 12.00
TSPS Paul Stastny B 4.00 10.00
TSRB Rene Bourque B 3.00 8.00
TSRD Raphael Diaz B 2.50 6.00
TSRG Ryan Getzlaf B 6.00 15.00
TSRJ Ryan Johansen A 8.00 20.00
TSRL Roberto Luongo C 4.00 10.00
TSSC Sean Couturier C 4.00 10.00
TSSG Simon Gagne B 4.00 10.00
TSSH Scott Hartnell C 4.00 10.00
TSSO Steve Ott B 3.00 8.00
TSSV Semyon Varlamov B 4.00 10.00
TSSW Stephen Weiss B 3.00 8.00
TSTR Tuukka Rask C 4.00 10.00
TSTV Thomas Vanek C 4.00 10.00
TSZC Zdeno Chara B 4.00 10.00
TSZP Zach Parise C 4.00 10.00

2013-14 Artifacts Tundra Sixes Jerseys Blue

STATED ODDS 1:160 HOBBY
T6AVS Colorado Avalanche 10.00 25.00
T6BOS Boston Bruins 12.00 30.00
T6HOF 1990s Stars 30.00 80.00
T62010 Young Stars 15.00 40.00
T62011 Young Stars 10.00 25.00
T6BEES Boston Bruins 15.00 40.00
T6LBBR Montreal Canadiens 30.00 80.00
T6ASTAR All Star Greats 15.00 40.00
T6LEAFS Toronto Maple Leafs 15.00 40.00
T6WINGS Detroit Red Wings 12.00 30.00
T6CHAMPS Los Angeles Kings 12.00 30.00
T6FLYERS Philadelphia Flyers 12.00 30.00
T6OILERS Edmonton Oilers 12.00 30.00

2013-14 Artifacts Tundra Tandems Jerseys Blue

GROUP A ODDS 1:736 HOB
GROUP B ODDS 1:24 HOB
GROUP C ODDS 1:53 HOB
OVERALL ODDS 1:16 HOB
*EMERALD/36: 1X TO 2.5X BLUE TANDEM
TTAG A.Hemsky/S.Gagner B 3.00 8.00
TTBL P.Bergeron/M.Lucic B 5.00 12.00
TTBM E.Belfour/M.Modano B 6.00 15.00
TTBP R.Bourque/B.Park C 6.00 15.00
TTCD D.Alfredsson/C.Greening B 4.00 10.00
TTCR T.Rask/Z.Chara B 4.00 10.00
TTDZ P.Datsyuk/H.Zetterberg B 5.00 12.00
TTEH T.Hall/J.Eberle B 8.00 20.00
TTEK P.Elias/I.Kovalchuk A 5.00 12.00
TTFL K.Letang/M.Fleury B 6.00 15.00
TTGB M.Green/N.Backstrom C 6.00 15.00
TTGC R.Callahan/M.Gartner C 4.00 10.00
TTGH M.Green/B.Holtby B 6.00 15.00
TTHB S.Hartnell/D.Briere B 5.00 12.00
TTHG S.Hartnell/C.Giroux B 4.00 10.00
TTHM N.Horton/B.Marchand B 5.00 12.00
TTHS P.Hornqvist/C.Smith D 3.00 8.00
TTJD J.Carter/D.Doughty B 4.00 10.00
TTKC D.Keith/C.Crawford B 5.00 12.00
TTKO A.Ovechkin/I.Kovalchuk B 15.00 40.00
TTLG E.Lindros/C.Giroux B 6.00 15.00
TTLJ M.Lemieux/J.Jagr B 12.00 30.00
TTLK R.Luongo/R.Kesler B 4.00 10.00
TTLS R.Luongo/C.Schneider C 4.00 10.00
TTMA R.Miller/L.Adam B 4.00 10.00
TTMC P.Marleau/L.Couture B 4.00 10.00
TTNH M.Neuvirth/B.Holtby B 6.00 15.00
TTNK E.Nabokov/N.Khabibulin B 4.00 10.00
TTPE T.Plekanec/L.Eller B 4.00 10.00
TTPK O.Pavelec/E.Kane C 4.00 10.00
TTPO M.Paajarvi/L.Omark B 4.00 10.00
TTPS P.Subban/T.Plekanec B 6.00 15.00
TTRB R.Getzlaf/B.Ryan B 6.00 15.00
TTRC J.Carter/M.Richards B 4.00 10.00
TTRD M.Richards/D.Doughty B 4.00 10.00
TTRW P.Rinne/S.Weber B 5.00 12.00
TTSA C.Anderson/J.Spezza B 4.00 10.00
TTSD M.Duchene/P.Stastny C 4.00 10.00
TTSG M.Sundin/D.Gilmour C 5.00 12.00
TTSH J.Sakic/M.Hejduk A 6.00 15.00
TTSS C.Stewart/K.Shattenkirk B 5.00 12.00
TTVS T.Vanek/D.Stafford C 4.00 10.00
TTWM S.Weiss/P.Mueller C 3.00 8.00
TTWP J.Williams/D.Penner C 3.00 8.00
TTWS S.Weber/C.Smith B 3.00 8.00

2013-14 Artifacts Tundra Trios Jerseys Blue

GROUP A ODDS 1:3597 HOB
GROUP B ODDS 1:710 HOB
GROUP C ODDS 1:62 HOB
GROUP D ODDS 1:101 HOB
OVERALL ODDS 1:36 HOB
*EMERALD/18: 1X TO 2.5X BLUE GRP C-D
*EMERALD/18: .8X TO 2X BLUE GRP B
*EMERALD/18: .6X TO 1.5X BLUE GRP A
T3ASK Spezza/Karlsson/Alfredsson C 8.00 20.00
T3BEK Brodeur/Elias/Kovlchk C 8.00 20.00
T3BJB Brodeur/Belfour/Josph D 8.00 20.00
T3BLM Marchand/Bergeron/Lucic C 5.00 12.00
T3BPK Pavelec/Kane/Byfuglien C 4.00 10.00
T3CBP Chara/Bourque/Park C 6.00 15.00
T3CHR Rask/Chara/Horton C 4.00 10.00
T3EHN Eberle/Hall/RNH C 8.00 20.00
T3GRH Ryan/Hiller/Getzlaf B 8.00 20.00
T3GSD Duchene/Giguere/Stastny D 4.00 10.00
T3GSV Giguere/Varlamov/Stastny D 4.00 10.00
T3HBB Hartnell/Briere/Bryzgalov C 4.00 10.00
T3HSS Hartnell/Schenn/Schenn C 4.00 10.00
T3HVG Hartnell/Voracek/Gagne C 4.00 10.00
T3IKS Kiprusoff/Stajan/Iginla B 5.00 12.00
T3LJG Lindros/Jagr/Gartner A 12.00 30.00
T3LLJ Lemieux/Lindros/Jagr C 12.00 30.00
T3LSG Gretzky/Lemieux/Sakic B 20.00 50.00
T3OGH Holtby/Green/Ovchkn D 15.00 40.00
T3PED Plekanec/Eller/Desharnais C 4.00 10.00
T3RCD Richards/Carter/Doughty C 4.00 10.00
T3RCP Carter/Penner/Richards D 4.00 10.00
T3RWH Rinne/Weber/Hornqvist C 5.00 12.00
T3SDG Gilmour/Sundin/Domi D 6.00 15.00
T3SGT Sundin/Twist/Goulet C 6.00 15.00
T3SHS Sakic/Hull/Sundin C 8.00 20.00
T3TMB Thorntn/Morrw/Bergrn C 6.00 15.00
T3VEA Ennis/Adam/Vanek C 4.00 10.00
T3VYE Yandle/Ekman-Lar/Vermte C 4.00 10.00

2014-15 Artifacts

COMP.SET w/o SP's (100) 12.00 30.00
ROOKIE EXCH ODDS 1:10 HOB
ROOKIE EXCH EXP. 9/15/2016
1 Ryan McDonagh .40 1.00
2 Brendan Gallagher .40 1.00
3 Jason Spezza .40 1.00
4 Kyle Turris .40 1.00
5 Peter Forsberg .40 1.00
6 Cody Hodgson .40 1.00
7 Larry Murphy .40 1.00
8 Cody Eakin .25 .60
9 Henrik Zetterberg .50 1.25
10 Jaromir Jagr 1.00 2.50
11 Hampus Lindholm .30 .75
12 Georges Laraque .25 .60
13 Slava Voynov .40 1.00
14 Sam Gagner .30 .75
15 Sean Couturier .40 1.00
16 Joe Thornton .40 1.00
17 Chris Pronger .30 .75
18 Dustin Byfuglien .40 1.00
19 Mike Green .40 1.00
20 Eric Lindros .60 1.50
21 Luc Robitaille .40 1.00
22 Max Pacioretty .40 1.00
23 Mats Sundin .40 1.00
24 Paul Coffey .40 1.00
25 Markus Naslund .30 .75
26 Josh Gorges .25 .60
27 Doug Harvey .40 1.00
28 Brett Hull .40 1.00
29 Cam Fowler .30 .75
30 Eddie Shack .40 1.00
31 Trevor Linden .40 1.00
32 Rob Brown .30 .75
33 Jeremy Roenick .40 1.00
34 Alex Chiasson .30 .75
35 Nicklas Backstrom .60 1.50
36 Brad Park .30 .75
37 Jakub Voracek .40 1.00
38 Rick Nash .40 1.00
39 Tyler Seguin .60 1.50
40 Paul Stastny .40 1.00
41 Wayne Gretzky 2.00 5.00
42 Wayne Simmonds .50 1.25
43 Olli Maatta .40 1.00
44 Simon Despres .40 1.00
45 Anze Kopitar .60 1.50
46 Jonathan Toews .75 2.00
47 Travis Zajac .30 .75
48 Brian Campbell .25 .60
49 Ron Francis .50 1.25
50 Eric Lindros .60 1.50
51 Mike Richards .40 1.00
52 Dustin Brown .30 .75
53 Patrice Bergeron .50 1.25
54 Adam Oates .40 1.00
55 John Tavares .75 2.00
56 Jordan Eberle .40 1.00
57 Brian Bellows .30 .75

Join the Fun!

GET IN ON THE ACTION WITH THESE OUTSTANDING CASE BREAKERS

Contact Ted Barker at tbarker@beckett.com or 972.448.9147 to advertise!

58 Larry Robinson .40 1.00
59 Chris Kreider .40 1.00
60 Brent Seabrook .40 1.00
61 John Carlson .50 1.25
62 Corey Perry .40 1.00
63 Matt Read .25 .60
64 Shea Weber .30 .75
65 Alexander Ovechkin 1.50 4.00
66 John LeClair .40 1.00
67 Marcel Dionne .50 1.25
68 Milan Lucic .40 1.00
69 Victor Hedman .50 1.25
70 Vincent Damphousse .30 .75
71 Kyle Okposo .40 1.00
72 Bill Guerin .40 1.00
73 Rob Blake .40 1.00
74 Steve Yzerman .75 2.00
75 Ryan Nugent-Hopkins .40 1.00
76 Teemu Selanne .75 2.00
77 Duncan Keith .40 1.00
78 Erik Karlsson .75 2.00
79 Niklas Kronwall .30 .75
80 Ryan Kesler .40 1.00
81 Pierre Turgeon .40 1.00
82 Dan Boyle .30 .75
83 Brad Richards .40 1.00
84 Scott Hartnell .40 1.00
85 Alexander Edler .25 .60
86 Alex Tanguay .25 .60
87 Drew Doughty .40 1.00
88 Michel Goulet .30 .75
89 Cody Eakin .25 .60
90 Sidney Crosby 1.50 4.00
91 Ryan Getzlaf .60 1.50
92 Logan Couture .40 1.00
93 Brian Gionta .30 .75
94 Jeff Carter .40 1.00
95 Drew Stafford .40 1.00
96 Josh Bailey .30 .75
97 Cam Neely .40 1.00
98 Bryan Bickell .25 .60
99 Andrew Ladd .40 1.00
100 Nikolai Kulemin .30 .75
101 Henrik Lundqvist G 2.00 5.00
102 Marc-Andre Fleury G 2.50 6.00
103 Antti Niemi G 1.25 3.00
104 Dominik Hasek G 2.00 5.00
105 Bill Ranford G 1.50 4.00
106 Marty Turco G 1.50 4.00
107 Jonathan Quick G 2.50 6.00
108 Olaf Kolzig G 1.50 4.00
109 Carey Price G 5.00 12.00
110 Cory Schneider G 1.25 3.00
111 Semyon Varlamov G 1.50 4.00
112 Cam Ward G 1.50 4.00
113 Ed Belfour G 1.50 4.00
114 Tony Esposito G 1.50 4.00
115 Pekka Rinne G 2.00 5.00
116 Jonas Hiller G 1.25 3.00
117 Ondrej Pavelec G 1.50 4.00
118 Grant Fuhr G 1.50 4.00
119 Pelle Lindbergh G 1.50 4.00
120 Richard Brodeur G 1.50 4.00
121 Evgeny Kuznetsov RC 6.00 15.00
122 Mark Visentin RC 1.50 4.00
123 Greg McKegg RC 1.25 3.00
124 Matt Lindblad RC 1.25 3.00
125 Teuvo Teravainen RC 2.50 6.00
126 Colton Sissons RC 1.50 4.00
127 Ty Rattie RC 2.00 5.00
128 Andrey Makarov RC 1.50 4.00
129 Calle Jarnkrok RC 1.50 4.00
130 Jake McCabe RC 1.50 4.00
131 Brandon Gormley RC 1.50 4.00
132 Bill Arnold RC 1.25 3.00
133 Alexander Khokhlachev RC 1.50 4.00
134 Jonathan Racine RC 1.50 4.00
135 Patrik Nemeth RC 1.50 4.00
136 Corban Knight RC 1.50 4.00
137 Laurent Brossoit RC 1.50 4.00
138 Joey Hishon RC 2.00 5.00
139 Teemu Pulkkinen RC 2.00 5.00
140 Scott Mayfield RC 1.25 3.00
141 Joni Ortio RC 2.00 5.00
142 Vladislav Namestnikov RC 2.50 6.00
143 Markus Granlund RC 2.50 6.00
144 Cedric Paquette RC 1.50 4.00
145 Oscar Klefbom RC 3.00 8.00
146 Johnny Gaudreau RC 6.00 15.00
147 Simon Moser RC 1.00 2.50
148 Ryan Sproul RC 1.50 4.00
149 Tyler Wotherspoon RC 1.50 4.00
150 Vincent Trocheck RC 2.00 5.00
151 William Karlsson RC 4.00 10.00
152 Seth Griffith RC 3.00 8.00
153 Sam Reinhart RC 8.00 20.00
154 Josh Jooris RC 4.00 10.00
155 Victor Rask RC 2.50 6.00
156 Adam Clendening RC 2.50 6.00
157 Dennis Everberg RC 4.00 10.00
158 Alexander Wennberg RC 5.00 12.00
159 Curtis McKenzie RC 2.00 5.00
160 Landon Ferraro RC 1.50 4.00
161 Leon Draisaitl RC 12.00 30.00
162 Aaron Ekblad RC 10.00 25.00
163 Andy Andreoff RC 2.50 6.00
164 Christian Folin RC 2.50 6.00
165 Jiri Sekac RC 2.50 6.00
166 Mark Van Guilder RC 2.50 6.00
167 Damon Severson RC 2.50 6.00
168 Griffin Reinhart RC 3.00 8.00
169 Anthony Duclair RC 4.00 10.00
170 Curtis Lazar RC 3.00 8.00
171 Shayne Gostisbehere RC 10.00 25.00
172 Tobias Rieder RC 2.50 6.00
173 Adam Payerl RC 2.00 5.00
174 Chris Tierney RC 2.50 6.00
175 Jori Lehtera RC 3.00 8.00
176 Jonathan Drouin RC 8.00 20.00
177 Stuart Percy RC 2.50 6.00
178 Bo Horvat RC 8.00 20.00
179 Andre Burakovsky RC 4.00 10.00
180 Adam Lowry RC 3.00 8.00
181 Darnell Nurse RC 8.00 20.00
182 Kerby Rychel RC 2.00 5.00
183 Kevin Hayes RC 8.00 20.00
184 Marko Dano RC 2.50 6.00
185 Brandon Kozun RC 4.00 10.00
186 Mirco Mueller RC 2.50 6.00
187 Phillip Danault RC 2.50 6.00
188 Joe Morrow RC 4.00 10.00
189 Seth Helgeson RC 2.00 5.00
190 Rocco Grimaldi RC 4.00 10.00
191 Justin Hodgman RC 3.00 8.00
192 Barclay Goodrow RC 2.50 6.00

2014-15 Artifacts Emerald

*1-100 VETS/99: 3X TO 8X BASIC CARDS
*101-120 G/99: 1X TO 2.5X BASIC G
*121-150 ROOKIES/99: .8X TO 2X BASIC RC

2014-15 Artifacts Ruby

*1-100 VETS/399: 2X TO 5X BASIC CARDS
1-100 STATED PRINT RUN 399
*101-120 G/299: .6X TO 1.5X BASIC G
*121-150 ROOKIES/299: .6X TO 1.5X BASIC RC

2014-15 Artifacts Sapphire

*1-100 VETS/85: 3X TO 8X BASIC CARDS
*101-120 G/85: 1X TO 2.5X BASIC G
*121-150 ROOKIES/85: 1X TO 2.5X BASIC RC

2014-15 Artifacts Spectrum

*1-100 VETS/25: 6X TO 15X BASIC CARDS
*101-120 G/25: 1.5X TO 4X BASIC G
*121-150 ROOKIES/25: 1.5X TO 4X BASIC RC
125 Teuvo Teravainen 30.00 60.00

2014-15 Artifacts Autofacts

GROUP A ODDS 1:3,489 HOB
GROUP B ODDS 1:1,191 HOB
GROUP C ODDS 1:651 HOB
GROUP D ODDS 1:360 HOB
GROUP E ODDS 1:299 HOB
GROUP F ODDS 1:85 HOB
GROUP G ODDS 1:77 HOB
GROUP H ODDS 1:24 HOB
OVERALL ODDS 1:13 HOB, 1:1000 RET
AAL Anders Lindback F 2.50 6.00
AAR Antti Raanta G 6.00 15.00
ABD Brenden Dillon G 2.50 6.00
ABH Braden Holtby D 15.00 40.00
ABO Bobby Orr B 75.00 150.00
ABR Mike Brown H 3.00 8.00
ACC Casey Cizikas H 2.50 6.00
ACF Cam Fowler F 3.00 8.00
ACG Cody Goloubef F 2.50 6.00
ACK Chris Kreider C 5.00 12.00
ADL Drew LeBlanc H 2.50 6.00
ADM Dylan McIlrath H 3.00 8.00
AFM Frazer McLaren G 2.50 6.00
AJA Jake Allen G 5.00 12.00
AJB J.T. Brown H 2.50 6.00
AJH Josh Harding E 3.00 8.00
AJJ Jaromir Jagr A 50.00 100.00
AJL Johan Larsson H 3.00 8.00
AJS Jeff Skinner D 4.00 10.00
AJT John Tavares D 15.00 40.00
ALA Luke Adam F 3.00 8.00
AMB Mike Bossy B 10.00 25.00
AMC Ryan McDonagh H 4.00 10.00
AMF Marc-Andre Fleury C 6.00 15.00
AMG Michel Goulet C 4.00 10.00
AMH Milan Hejduk C 4.00 10.00
AML Mario Lemieux A 40.00 80.00
ANF Nick Foligno F 3.00 8.00
APD Pavel Datsyuk D 10.00 25.00
APK Patrick Kane B 20.00 40.00
ARP Richard Panik G 2.50 6.00
ARS Riley Sheahan E 4.00 10.00
ASA Brandon Saad H 6.00 15.00
ASB Sergei Bobrovsky D 6.00 15.00
ASC Scotty Bowman C 8.00 20.00
ATB Tyler Bozak E 3.00 8.00
ATJ Tomas Jurco H 4.00 10.00
ATK Tim Kennedy F 2.50 6.00
ATM Tye McGinn D 2.50 6.00
ATT Tomas Tatar H 6.00 15.00
ATW Tom Wilson H 4.00 10.00
AWG Wayne Gretzky B 75.00 150.00

2014-15 Artifacts Frozen Artifacts Jerseys Blue

*EMERALD PATCH/36: .75X TO 2X BASIC JSY
FAAM Andrei Markov 4.00 10.00
FAAO Adam Oates 4.00 10.00
FABB Brian Bellows 3.00 8.00
FABH Brett Hull 5.00 12.00
FABM Brad Marchand 5.00 12.00
FABO Brooks Orpik 3.00 8.00
FABR Richard Brodeur 4.00 10.00
FABS Brandon Saad 4.00 10.00
FACO Colton Orr 2.50 6.00
FADB Dave Bolland 2.50 6.00
FADC David Clarkson 2.50 6.00
FADD David Desharnais 4.00 10.00
FADP David Perron 2.50 6.00
FADS Denis Savard 5.00 12.00
FAJL John LeClair 4.00 10.00
FAMG Michael Grabner 3.00 8.00
FAMK Marcus Kruger 4.00 10.00
FAMN Matt Niskanen 3.00 8.00
FAOK Olaf Kolzig 4.00 10.00
FAPC Paul Coffey 4.00 10.00
FAPF Peter Forsberg 4.00 10.00
FAPS P.K. Subban 6.00 15.00
FAPT Pierre Turgeon 4.00 10.00
FARB Ray Bourque 6.00 15.00
FASC Sean Couturier 4.00 10.00
FATR Tuukka Rask 4.00 10.00
FATS Tyler Seguin 6.00 15.00
FAVH Victor Hedman 5.00 12.00

2014-15 Artifacts Jerseys

*EMERALD/75: .8X TO 2X BASIC JSY/125
*EMERALD/25: 1X TO 2.5X BASIC JSY/125
*EMRLD ROOK/75: 1X TO 2.5X ROOK JSY/399
*SPECTRUM/15: 1.2X TO 3X BASIC JSY/125
*ROOK SPEC/15: 1.5X TO 4X ROOK JSY/399
1 Ryan McDonagh 4.00 10.00
2 Brendan Gallagher 4.00 10.00
4 Kyle Turris 4.00 10.00
5 Peter Forsberg 4.00 10.00
6 Cody Hodgson 4.00 10.00
7 Larry Murphy 4.00 10.00
8 Cody Eakin 2.50 6.00
9 Henrik Zetterberg 5.00 12.00
11 Hampus Lindholm 3.00 8.00
12 Georges Laraque 2.50 6.00
13 Slava Voynov 4.00 10.00
14 Sam Gagner 3.00 8.00
15 Sean Couturier 4.00 10.00
16 Joe Thornton 4.00 10.00
17 Chris Pronger 3.00 8.00
19 Mike Green 4.00 10.00
21 Luc Robitaille 4.00 10.00
22 Max Pacioretty 4.00 10.00
23 Mats Sundin 4.00 10.00
25 Markus Naslund 3.00 8.00
26 Josh Gorges 2.50 6.00
28 Brett Hull 4.00 10.00
29 Cam Fowler 3.00 8.00
30 Eddie Shack 4.00 10.00
31 Trevor Linden 4.00 10.00
32 Rob Brown 3.00 8.00
33 Jeremy Roenick 4.00 10.00
34 Alex Chiasson 3.00 8.00
35 Nicklas Backstrom 6.00 15.00
37 Jakub Voracek 4.00 10.00
38 Rick Nash 4.00 10.00
39 Tyler Seguin 6.00 15.00
41 Wayne Gretzky 20.00 40.00
42 Wayne Simmonds 5.00 12.00
43 Olli Maatta 4.00 10.00
44 Simon Despres 4.00 10.00
45 Anze Kopitar 6.00 15.00
46 Jonathan Toews 8.00 20.00
47 Travis Zajac 3.00 8.00
49 Ron Francis 5.00 12.00
50 Eric Lindros 6.00 15.00
51 Mike Richards 4.00 10.00
52 Dustin Brown 3.00 8.00
53 Patrice Bergeron 5.00 12.00
54 Adam Oates 4.00 10.00
55 John Tavares 8.00 20.00
56 Jordan Eberle 4.00 10.00
57 Brian Bellows 3.00 8.00
58 Larry Robinson 2.50 6.00
59 Chris Kreider 4.00 10.00
60 Brent Seabrook 4.00 10.00
62 Corey Perry 4.00 10.00
63 Matt Read 2.50 6.00
64 Shea Weber 3.00 8.00
65 Alexander Ovechkin 5.00 12.00
66 John LeClair 4.00 10.00
67 Marcel Dionne 5.00 12.00
68 Milan Lucic 6.00 15.00
69 Victor Hedman 5.00 12.00
70 Vincent Damphousse 3.00 8.00
73 Rob Blake 4.00 10.00
74 Steve Yzerman 6.00 15.00
75 Ryan Nugent-Hopkins 4.00 10.00
77 Duncan Keith 4.00 10.00
78 Erik Karlsson 8.00 20.00
79 Niklas Kronwall 3.00 8.00
80 Ryan Kesler 4.00 10.00
81 Pierre Turgeon 4.00 10.00
82 Dan Boyle 3.00 8.00
83 Brad Richards 4.00 10.00
85 Alexander Edler 2.50 6.00
87 Drew Doughty 4.00 10.00
88 Michel Goulet 3.00 8.00
89 Cody Eakin 2.50 6.00
90 Sidney Crosby 15.00 40.00
91 Ryan Getzlaf 6.00 15.00
92 Logan Couture 4.00 10.00
93 Brian Gionta 3.00 8.00
94 Jeff Carter 4.00 10.00
95 Drew Stafford 4.00 10.00
97 Cam Neely 4.00 10.00
98 Bryan Bickell 2.50 6.00
99 Andrew Ladd 4.00 10.00
100 Nikolai Kulemin 3.00 8.00
101 Henrik Lundqvist 5.00 12.00
102 Marc-Andre Fleury 6.00 15.00
103 Antti Niemi 3.00 8.00
104 Dominik Hasek 5.00 12.00
105 Bill Ranford 4.00 10.00
106 Marty Turco 4.00 10.00
107 Jonathan Quick 6.00 15.00
108 Olaf Kolzig 4.00 10.00
109 Carey Price 10.00 25.00
110 Cory Schneider 3.00 8.00
111 Semyon Varlamov 4.00 10.00
112 Cam Ward 4.00 10.00
113 Ed Belfour 4.00 10.00
114 Tony Esposito 4.00 10.00
115 Pekka Rinne 5.00 12.00
116 Jonas Hiller 3.00 8.00
117 Ondrej Pavelec 4.00 10.00
118 Grant Fuhr 10.00 25.00
120 Richard Brodeur 4.00 10.00
121 Evgeny Kuznetsov 12.00 30.00
122 Mark Visentin 3.00 8.00
123 Greg McKegg 2.50 6.00
125 Teuvo Teravainen 5.00 12.00
126 Colton Sissons 3.00 8.00
127 Ty Rattie 4.00 10.00
130 Jake McCabe 3.00 8.00
131 Brandon Gormley 3.00 8.00
136 Corban Knight 4.00 10.00
138 Joey Hishon 4.00 10.00
140 Scott Mayfield 2.50 6.00
142 Vladislav Namestnikov 5.00 12.00
143 Markus Granlund 5.00 12.00
145 Oscar Klefbom 6.00 15.00
146 Johnny Gaudreau 12.00 30.00
148 Ryan Sproul 3.00 8.00
149 Tyler Wotherspoon 3.00 8.00
150 Vincent Trocheck 4.00 10.00

2014-15 Artifacts Stick to Stick Duos

STATED ODDS 1:480 HOBBY
SSCB Z.Chara/P.Bergeron 15.00 40.00
SSDJ D.Hasek/J.Howard 15.00 40.00
SSFC P.Coffey/G.Fuhr 12.00 30.00
SSFM G.Fuhr/A.Moog 25.00 50.00
SSGG D.Gilmour/M.Gartner 15.00 40.00
SSHH D.Hasek/D.Hasek 15.00 40.00
SSKC A.Kopitar/J.Carter 20.00 50.00
SSLC M.Lemieux/P.Coffey 40.00 100.00
SSLN R.Nash/H.Lundqvist 25.00 50.00
SSME T.Ennis/T.Myers 10.00 25.00
SSOB A.Ovechkin/N.Backstrom 40.00 100.00
SSSS H.Sedin/D.Sedin 15.00 40.00
SSYH S.Yzerman/B.Hull 25.00 60.00
SSZF J.Franzen/H.Zetterberg 20.00 50.00

2014-15 Artifacts Stick to Stick Trios

STATED ODDS 1:360 HOBBY
STGK Fhr/Moog/Brdr
STTC Nsh/St.Ls/Dghty 30.00 60.00
STAVS Roy/Frsbrg/Skc
STBUF Hwrchk/Hsk/Fhr 20.00 50.00
STCAN Lmx/Rbtlle/Mssr 50.00 120.00
STDET Frnzn/Zttrbrg/Hwrd 20.00 50.00
STDRW Yzrmn/Hll/Zttrbrg 25.00 60.00
STLAK Krri/Grtzky/Rbtlle 80.00 200.00
STMON Blveau/Glmr/Bllws 20.00 50.00
STMTL Bllws/Dmphse/LClr 15.00 40.00
STNET Prce/Qck/Hwrd 20.00 50.00
STPHI Lndrs/Hwrchk/LClr 25.00 60.00
STRAN Lflr/Lndrs/Mssr 40.00 80.00
STTOR Mrphy/Grtnr/Glmr 30.00 80.00
STUSA Kssl/Kne/Qck
STKING Dghty/Rchrds/Crtr 30.00 60.00
STLBBR Crbneau/Dmphse/Svrd 20.00 50.00
STKINGS Qck/Kptr/Dghty 25.00 60.00
STWINGS Rbtlle/Hll/Yzrmn 25.00 60.00
STNETUSA Qck/Mllr/Hwrd 25.00 60.00

2014-15 Artifacts Top 12 Rookie Signatures

RSCK Corban Knight 8.00 20.00
RSEK Evgeny Kuznetsov 60.00 120.00
RSGM Greg McKegg 6.00 15.00
RSTR Ty Rattie 10.00 25.00
RSTT Teuvo Teravainen 12.00 30.00
RSVN Vladislav Namestnikov 12.00 30.00

2014-15 Artifacts Treasured Swatches Jerseys Blue

*PATCH EMERALD/36: .8X TO 2X BASIC JSY
TSAK Anze Kopitar C 6.00 15.00
TSAN Antti Niemi C 3.00 8.00
TSCF Cody Franson C 2.50 6.00
TSCH Carl Hagelin B 4.00 10.00
TSCK Chris Kreider C 4.00 10.00
TSCN Cam Neely C 4.00 10.00
TSCS Cory Schneider C 3.00 8.00
TSDB Daniel Briere C 3.00 8.00
TSJH Jonas Hiller C 3.00 8.00
TSKL Kari Lehtonen C 3.00 8.00
TSMG Mike Green C 4.00 10.00
TSNB Nicklas Backstrom C 6.00 15.00
TSNL Nicklas Lidstrom B 4.00 10.00
TSPB Patrik Berglund B 2.50 6.00
TSPF Peter Forsberg C 4.00 10.00
TSRF Ron Francis C 5.00 12.00
TSRG Ryan Getzlaf C 6.00 15.00
TSRM Ryan McDonagh B 4.00 10.00
TSRN Ryan Nugent-Hopkins A 6.00 15.00
TSSG Sam Gagner B 3.00 8.00
TSSK Saku Koivu C 4.00 10.00
TSSM Steve Mason C 3.00 8.00
TSSV Slava Voynov C 4.00 10.00
TSTL Trevor Linden C 4.00 10.00
TSTP Tomas Plekanec A 6.00 15.00
TSVA Semyon Varlamov C 4.00 10.00
TSZB Zach Bogosian C 3.00 8.00

2014-15 Artifacts Tundra Sixes Jerseys Blue

STATED ODDS 1:160 HOBBY
T6AS All Stars A 15.00 40.00
T6TC Team Canada B 20.00 50.00
T6LAK LA Kings Stars B 12.00 30.00
T6MON Canadiens Stars B 30.00 80.00
T6LOSANA Ducks/Kings Stars B 15.00 40.00
T6NJDNYR Devils/Rangers Stars A 20.00 50.00
T6NYINJD Devils/Islanders Stars A 20.00 50.00
T6NYRNYI Rangers/Islanders Stars A 10.00 25.00
T6OTTBUF Senators/Sabres Stars B 10.00 25.00
T6STLCHI Blackhawks/Blues Stars B 12.00 30.00

2014-15 Artifacts Tundra Tandems Jerseys Blue

GROUP A STATED ODDS 1:6522
GROUP B STATED ODDS 1:255 HOBBY
GROUP C STATED ODDS 1:22 HOBBY
OVERALL STATED ODDS 1:20 HOBBY
TTAT C.Anderson/K.Turris C 4.00 10.00
TTBD D.Briere/D.Desharnais C 4.00 10.00
TTBH D.Brunner/A.Henrique C 4.00 10.00
TTBN D.Brown/J.Nolan C 4.00 10.00
TTBV Bobrovsky/Varlamov C 4.00 10.00
TTCD J.Carter/D.Doughty C 4.00 10.00
TTCE G.Cheevers/P.Esposito C 5.00 12.00
TTEC C.Eakin/A.Chiasson C 3.00 8.00
TTEH J.Eberle/RNH B 5.00 12.00
TTFB C.Fowler/N.Bonino C 3.00 8.00
TTGD J.Gorges/Desharnais C 4.00 10.00
TTGG Galchenyuk/Gallagher C 6.00 15.00
TTGR M.Greene/M.Richards C 4.00 10.00
TTGS B.Gallagher/P.Subban C 6.00 15.00
TTHG T.Hall/S.Gagner C 8.00 20.00
TTKB Kronwall/Backstrom C 6.00 15.00
TTKL Karlsson/Landeskog B 10.00 25.00
TTKN D.Keith/R.Nash C 4.00 10.00
TTKS E.Karlsson/J.Spezza C 8.00 20.00
TTLC Lehtonen/A.Chiasson C 3.00 8.00
TTLM M.Naslund/L.Murphy B 5.00 12.00
TTMH T.Myers/C.Hodgson C 4.00 10.00
TTMN M.Green/N.Backstrom B 8.00 20.00
TTOM A.Ovechkin/E.Malkin C 15.00 40.00
TTQM R.Miller/J.Quick C 6.00 15.00
TTQP J.Quick/C.Price C 12.00 30.00
TTRR Robitaille/L.Robinson A 10.00 25.00
TTSB C.Schneider/M.Brodeur C 8.00 20.00
TTSH Schneider/A.Henrique C 4.00 10.00
TTSL M.Sundin/E.Lindros C 6.00 15.00
TTSP P.Subban/M.Pacioretty C 6.00 15.00
TTSZ Stepan/Zuccarello C 4.00 10.00
TTVK J.Voracek/D.Krejci C 4.00 10.00
TTVR J.Voracek/M.Read C 4.00 10.00
TTWR S.Weber/P.Rinne C 5.00 12.00

2014-15 Artifacts Tundra Tandems Patches Emerald

TTAT Craig Anderson 10.00 25.00
Kyle Turris
TTBD Daniel Briere 10.00 25.00
David Desharnais
TTBL Dustin Byfuglien 10.00 25.00
Andrew Ladd
TTBN Dustin Brown 10.00 25.00
Jordan Nolan
TTBV Sergei Bobrovsky 10.00 25.00
Semyon Varlamov
TTCD Jeff Carter 10.00 25.00
Drew Doughty
TTCE G.Cheevers/P.Esposito 12.00 30.00
TTDB Vincent Damphousse 8.00 20.00
Brian Bellows
TTDT Vincent Damphousse 10.00 25.00
Pierre Turgeon
TTEC Cody Eakin 8.00 20.00
Alex Chiasson
TTES Alexander Edler 10.00 25.00
Daniel Sedin
TTFB Cam Fowler 8.00 20.00
Nick Bonino
TTGG Galchenyuk/Gallagher 15.00 40.00
TTGL Michel Goulet 12.00 30.00
Guy Lafleur
TTGR Matt Greene 10.00 25.00
Mike Richards
TTGS B.Gallagher/P.Subban 15.00 40.00
TTHC Scott Hartnell 10.00 25.00
Braydon Coburn
TTHG Taylor Hall 20.00 50.00
Sam Gagner
TTHR Scott Hartnell 10.00 25.00
Jeremy Roenick
TTKB Niklas Kronwall 15.00 40.00
Nicklas Backstrom
TTKN Duncan Keith 10.00 25.00
Rick Nash
TTLC Kari Lehtonen 8.00 20.00
Alex Chiasson
TTLM Markus Naslund 10.00 25.00
Larry Murphy
TTMH Tyler Myers 10.00 25.00
Cody Hodgson
TTMN Mike Green 15.00 40.00
Nicklas Backstrom
TTOB Kyle Okposo 10.00 25.00
Josh Bailey
TTOM Ovechkin/Malkin 40.00 100.00
TTQM R.Miller/J.Quick 15.00 40.00
TTQP J.Quick/C.Price 30.00 80.00
TTRR Luc Robitaille 10.00 25.00
Larry Robinson
TTSB Schneider/M.Brodeur 20.00 50.00
TTSG Teemu Selanne 20.00 50.00
Ryan Getzlaf
TTSH Cory Schneider 10.00 25.00
Adam Henrique
TTSL M.Sundin/E.Lindros 15.00 40.00
TTSP P.Subban/Pacioretty 15.00 40.00
TTSZ Derek Stepan 10.00 25.00
Mats Zuccarello-Aasen
TTVK Jakub Voracek 10.00 25.00
David Krejci
TTVR Jakub Voracek 10.00 25.00
Matt Read
TTWR Shea Weber 12.00 30.00
Pekka Rinne

2014-15 Artifacts Tundra Trios Patches Emerald

*BLUE TRIO: .15X TO .4X PATCH/18
T3MC Markov/Price/Subban 20.00 50.00
T3ANA Fowler/Lindholm/Perry 10.00 25.00
T3BOS Bergeron/Lucic/Rask 25.00 60.00
T3BUF Hodgson/Stafford/Myers 10.00 25.00
T3CAN Brodeur/Weber/Richards 20.00 50.00
T3CBJ Bobrvsky/Hortn/Schultz 10.00 25.00
T3CZE Voracek/Krejci/Elias 10.00 25.00
T3EDM Gagner/Eberle/Hall 20.00 50.00
T3FIN Koivu/Rask/Selanne 20.00 50.00
T3LAK Richards/Brown/Carter 12.00 30.00
T3MON Subban/Pacrty/Dshrns 15.00 40.00
T3MTL Desharn/Briere/Gionta 12.00 30.00
T3NET Quick/Niemi/Hiller 15.00 40.00
T3NYI Okposo/Bailey/Nielsen 12.00 30.00
T3NYR McDonagh/Staal/Hagelin 10.00 25.00
T3PHI Hartnell/Voracek/Read 10.00 25.00
T3RUS Markov/Voynov/Semin 25.00 50.00
T3STL Elliott/Berglund/Jackman 8.00 20.00
T3SVK Palffy/Handzus/Chara 40.00 80.00
T3USA Kesler/Stepan/McDonagh 10.00 25.00
T3VAN Kesler/Edler/Sedin 20.00 40.00
T3WAS Green/Carlson/Ovechkin 40.00 100.00
T3LBBR Lafleur/Carbon/Robinson
T3GOALIE Schneider/Howard/Rinne 12.00 30.00

2014-15 Artifacts Upper Deck Ice Previews

RANDOM INSERTS IN BLASTER PACKS
P1 Sidney Crosby 6.00 15.00
P2 Henrik Lundqvist 2.00 5.00
P3 P.K. Subban 2.50 6.00
P4 Jonathan Bernier 1.50 4.00
P5 Jonathan Toews 3.00 8.00
P6 Tuukka Rask 1.50 4.00

2014-15 Artifacts Rookie Autographs Redemptions

EXCH EXPIRATION: 9/15/2016
I Jonathon Drouin 40.00 80.00
II Aaron Ekblad 30.00 60.00
III Sam Reinhart 30.00 60.00
IV Leon Draisaitl 25.00 50.00
V Bo Horvat 25.00 50.00
VI Andre Burakovsky 15.00 40.00
VII Curtis Lazar 15.00 40.00
VIII Alexander Wennberg 20.00 50.00
IX Anthony Duclair 15.00 40.00
X Seth Griffith 12.00 30.00
XI Jiri Sekac 10.00 25.00
XII Griffin Reinhart 12.00 30.00
XIII David Pastrnak 40.00 80.00
XIV Damon Severson 10.00 25.00
XV Adam Clendening 10.00 25.00
XVI Shayne Gostisbehere 40.00 80.00
XVII Stuart Percy 10.00 25.00
XVIII Kerby Rychel 8.00 20.00

2015-16 Artifacts

101-130 STAR PRINT RUN 999
131-160 LEGEND PRINT RUN 499
161-180 ROOKIE PRINT RUN 999
DRAFT EXCH ODDS 1:9 H, 1:96 R/BL
DRAFT EXCH EXPIRATON: 9/15/2017
1 Gabriel Landeskog .40 1.00
2 Brandon Dubinsky .30 .75
3 Marian Gaborik .40 1.00
4 Sam Gagner .30 .75
5 John Gibson .40 1.00
6 Alex Galchenyuk .50 1.25
7 Jakub Voracek .40 1.00
8 Cam Ward .40 1.00
9 P.K. Subban .60 1.50
10 Calle Jarnkrok .30 .75
11 Tomas Hertl .40 1.00
12 Jeff Carter .40 1.00
13 Jason Pominville .30 .75
14 Ondrej Pavelec .40 1.00
15 Semyon Varlamov .40 1.00
16 Mike Smith .40 1.00
17 Kari Lehtonen .30 .75
18 Morgan Rielly .30 .75
19 Tanner Pearson .25 .60
20 Alexandre Burrows .30 .75
21 Ondrej Palat .30 .75
22 Wayne Simmonds .50 1.25
23 Chris Kunitz .40 1.00
24 Scott Hartnell .40 1.00
25 Corey Perry .40 1.00
26 Craig Anderson .40 1.00
27 David Backes .40 1.00
28 Nick Bjugstad .30 .75
29 Bobby Ryan .30 .75
30 Frederik Andersen .30 .75
31 Charlie Coyle .30 .75
32 Elias Lindholm .25 .60
33 Gustav Nyquist .40 1.00
34 Paul Stastny .40 1.00
35 Jori Lehtera .30 .75
36 Jonathan Drouin .50 1.25
37 Sam Reinhart .40 1.00
38 Daniel Sedin .40 1.00
39 Tomas Jurco .40 1.00
40 John Carlson .50 1.25
41 James Neal .40 1.00
42 Roberto Luongo .40 1.00
43 Sean Monahan .40 1.00
44 Duncan Keith .40 1.00
45 Victor Hedman .50 1.25
46 Nicklas Backstrom .60 1.50
47 Corey Crawford .50 1.25
48 Henrik Lundqvist .50 1.25
49 Olli Maatta .40 1.00
50 Erik Karlsson .75 2.00
51 Henrik Zetterberg .50 1.25
52 Thomas Vanek .40 1.00
53 Marian Hossa .30 .75
54 Darcy Kuemper .30 .75
55 Patrick Kane .75 2.00
56 Mats Zuccarello .30 .75
57 Ryan Kesler .40 1.00
58 Patrik Elias .40 1.00
59 Jamie Benn .50 1.25
60 Brayden Schenn .40 1.00
61 Ryan Strome .30 .75
62 Nazem Kadri .30 .75
63 Leon Draisaitl .40 1.00
64 Johan Franzen .40 1.00
65 Brendan Gallagher .50 1.25
66 Dustin Brown .30 .75
67 Griffin Reinhart .30 .75
68 Adam Henrique .40 1.00
69 Michael Cammalleri .30 .75
70 Patrick Marleau .40 1.00
71 Tyler Johnson .30 .75
72 Brian Elliott .30 .75
73 Pekka Rinne .50 1.25
74 Kyle Okposo .40 1.00
75 Ryan McDonagh .30 .75
76 Zdeno Chara .40 1.00
77 Jeff Skinner .30 .75
78 David Krejci .30 .75
79 Nail Yakupov .30 .75
80 Cody Hodgson .40 1.00
81 Ryan Murray .25 .60
82 Henrik Sedin .40 1.00
83 Sean Couturier .40 1.00
84 Jacob Trouba .30 .75
85 Phil Kessel .60 1.50
86 Chris Kreider .40 1.00
87 Matt Moulson .30 .75
88 Evgeni Malkin 1.25 3.00
89 Joe Pavelski .40 1.00
90 Jason Spezza .30 .75
91 Jonathan Huberdeau .40 1.00
92 Oliver Ekman-Larsson .30 .75
93 Evgeny Kuznetsov .60 1.50
94 Jarome Iginla .40 1.00
95 Ryan Johansen .50 1.25
96 Mark Scheifele .50 1.25
97 Ryan Nugent-Hopkins .40 1.00
98 Jiri Hudler .30 .75
99 Milan Lucic .30 .75
100 Jonas Hiller .30 .75
101 Pavel Datsyuk S 2.00 5.00
102 Logan Couture S 1.50 4.00
103 Anze Kopitar S 2.50 6.00
104 Jonathan Bernier S 1.50 4.00
105 Johnny Gaudreau S 2.50 6.00
106 Ryan Miller S 1.50 4.00
107 Tyler Seguin S 2.50 6.00
108 Ryan Getzlaf S 2.50 6.00
109 Zemgus Girgensons S 1.25 3.00
110 Blake Wheeler S 1.50 4.00
111 Sergei Bobrovsky S 1.50 4.00
112 Eric Staal S 2.00 5.00
113 John Tavares S 3.00 8.00
114 Alexander Ovechkin S 6.00 15.00
115 Jonathan Toews S 3.00 8.00
116 Zach Parise S 1.50 4.00
117 Shane Doan S 1.25 3.00
118 Sidney Crosby S 6.00 15.00
119 Nathan MacKinnon S 3.00 8.00
120 Shea Weber S 1.25 3.00
121 Tuukka Rask S 1.50 4.00
122 Cory Schneider S 1.25 3.00
123 Carey Price S 5.00 12.00
124 Aaron Ekblad S 1.50 4.00
125 Taylor Hall S 3.00 8.00
126 Vladimir Tarasenko S 2.50 6.00
127 Kyle Turris S 1.25 3.00
128 Steven Stamkos S 3.00 8.00
129 Claude Giroux S 1.50 4.00
130 Rick Nash S 1.50 4.00
131 Mats Sundin LEG 2.00 5.00
132 Mike Gartner LEG 2.00 5.00
133 Pierre Turgeon LEG 2.00 5.00
134 Marty Turco LEG 2.00 5.00
135 Wendel Clark LEG 2.00 5.00
136 Rod Brind'Amour LEG 1.50 4.00
137 Mario Lemieux LEG 6.00 15.00
138 Dale Hawerchuk LEG 2.50 6.00
139 Tony Esposito LEG 2.00 5.00
140 Jari Kurri LEG 2.00 5.00
141 Lanny McDonald LEG 2.00 5.00
142 Martin Brodeur LEG 4.00 10.00
143 Mike Keane LEG 1.50 4.00
144 Tom Barrasso LEG 2.00 5.00
145 John Vanbiesbrouck LEG 2.00 5.00
146 Patrick Roy LEG 5.00 12.00
147 Joe Sakic LEG 3.00 8.00
148 Owen Nolan LEG 1.50 4.00
149 Glen Murray LEG 1.50 4.00
150 Theoren Fleury LEG 2.50 6.00
151 Glenn Hall LEG 1.50 4.00
152 Pelle Lindbergh LEG 2.00 5.00
153 Marcel Dionne LEG 2.50 6.00
154 Wayne Gretzky LEG 10.00 25.00
155 Doug Weight LEG 2.00 5.00
156 Ron Francis LEG 2.50 6.00
157 Steve Larmer LEG 1.50 4.00
158 Steve Yzerman LEG 3.00 8.00
159 Gerry Cheevers LEG 2.00 5.00
160 Rob Blake LEG 2.00 5.00
161 Henrik Samuelsson RC 1.25 3.00
162 Antoine Bibeau RC 1.50 4.00
163 Slater Koekkoek RC 1.25 3.00
164 Ryan Hartman RC 2.00 5.00
165 Shane Prince RC 1.25 3.00
166 Nick Shore RC 1.50 4.00
167 Stefan Noesen RC 1.25 3.00
168 Emile Poirier RC 1.50 4.00
169 Anthony Stolarz RC 1.50 4.00
170 Josh Anderson RC 1.50 4.00
171 Nick Cousins RC 1.50 4.00
172 Matt Puempel RC 1.25 3.00
173 Kevin Fiala RC 1.50 4.00
174 Brendan Ranford RC 1.25 3.00
175 Kyle Baun RC 1.50 4.00
176 Jacob de la Rose RC 1.50 4.00
177 Connor Hellebuyck RC 4.00 10.00
178 Ronalds Kenins RC 1.50 4.00
179 Sam Bennett RC 2.00 5.00
180 Malcolm Subban RC 4.00 10.00
181 Canadiens/Fucale EXCH 3.00 8.00
182 Blues/Fabbri EXCH 4.00 10.00
183 Rangers/Lindberg EXCH 3.00 8.00
184 Ducks/Ritchie EXCH 3.00 8.00
185 Lightning/Vermin EXCH 2.50 6.00
186 Predators/Saros EXCH 4.00 10.00
187 Capitals/Stephenson EXCH 3.00 8.00
188 Canucks/Virtanen EXCH 4.00 10.00
189 Red Wings/Larkin EXCH 10.00 25.00
190 Blackhawks/Panarin EXCH 10.00 25.00
191 Islanders/Pelech EXCH 2.50 6.00
192 Flames/Kulak EXCH 2.50 6.00
193 Senators/Wideman EXCH 3.00 8.00
194 Wild/Olofsson EXCH 3.00 8.00
195 Penguins/Sprong EXCH 6.00 15.00
196 Kings/Mersch EXCH 3.00 8.00
197 Bruins/Miller EXCH 2.50 6.00
198 Jets/Ehlers EXCH 6.00 15.00
199 Blue Jackets EXCH 4.00 10.00
200 Sharks/Goldobin EXCH 3.00 8.00
201 Stars/Janmark EXCH 3.00 8.00
202 Maple Leafs/Sparks EXCH 4.00 10.00
203 Avalanche/Rantanen EXCH 6.00 15.00
204 Flyers/Leier EXCH 3.00 8.00
205 Connor McDavid RC 80.00 150.0
206 Sabres/Eichel EXCH 12.00 30.
207 Coyotes/Domi EXCH 6.00 15.
208 Devils/Kalinin EXCH 2.50 6.
209 Panthers/Brickley EXCH 2.50 6.
210 Hurricanes/Hanifin EXCH 4.00 10.
211 Wild Card/McCann EXCH 3.00 8.
212 Wild Card/Ullmark EXCH 4.00 10.
213 Wild Card/Shinkaruk EXCH 3.00 8.
214 Wild Card/Parayko EXCH 4.00 10.
215 Wild Card/Petan EXCH 3.00 8.
216 Wild Card/Condon EXCH 3.00 8.
217 Wild Card/Hudon EXCH 3.00 8.
218 Wild Card/McCarron EXCH 4.00 10.
219 Wild Card/Murray EXCH 15.00 40.
220 Wild Card/Hutton EXCH 3.00 8.

2015-16 Artifacts Emerald

*1-100 VETS/99: 2.5X TO 6X BASIC CARDS
*101-130 S/99: .6X TO 1.5X BASIC S/999
*131-160 LEG/99: .6X TO 1.5X BASIC LEG/499
*161-180 ROOKIES/99: .6X TO 1.5X BASIC RC/999
164 Ryan Hartman 3.00 8.

2015-16 Artifacts Ruby

*1-100 VETS/399: 2X TO 5X BASIC CARDS
*101-130 S/399: .5X TO 1.2X BASIC S/999
*131-160 LEG/399: .4X TO 1X BASIC LEG/499
*161-180 ROOKIES/399: .5X TO 1.2X BASIC RC/999
164 Ryan Hartman 2.50 6.
205 Connor McDavid 80.00 150.

2015-16 Artifacts Sapphire

*1-100 VETS/85: 2.5X TO 6X BASIC CARDS
*101-130 S/85: .6X TO 1.5X BASIC S/999
*131-160 LEG/85: .6X TO 1.5X BASIC LEG/499
*161-180 ROOKIES/85: .6X TO 1.5X BASIC RC/999
164 Ryan Hartman 3.00 8.

2015-16 Artifacts Spectrum

*1-100 VETS/25: 5X TO 12X BASIC CARDS
*101-130 S/25: 1.2X TO 3X BASIC S/999
*131-160 LEG/25: 1.2X TO 3X BASIC LEG/499
*161-180 ROOKIES/25: 1.2X TO 3X BASIC RC/999
154 Wayne Gretzky LEG 30.00 60.
164 Ryan Hartman 6.00 15.

2015-16 Artifacts Autofacts

GROUP A ODDS 1:3869
GROUP B ODDS 1:774
GROUP C ODDS 1:387
GROUP D ODDS 1:277
GROUP E ODDS 1:69
OVERALL ODDS 1:45 H, 1:1000 BL
AAG Alex Goligoski E 3.00 8.
AAN Andrej Nestrasil E 3.00 8.
AAP Alex Pietrangelo B 5.00 12.
ABR Brett Ritchie D 4.00 10.
ABS Brendan Smith E 4.00 10.
ACJ Calle Jarnkrok E 4.00 10.
ACN Cam Neely A 8.00 20.
ADH Dougie Hamilton C 6.00 15.
AEL Elias Lindholm C 4.00 10.
AJB Jonathan Bernier B 6.00 15.
AJM Jon Merrill E 3.00 8.
AJO Joni Ortio E 5.00 12.
AML Michael Latta E 3.00 8.
AMM Mirco Mueller D 4.00 10.
AMP Mark Pysyk E 3.00 8.
ANY Nail Yakupov B 5.00 12.
APB Pierre-Edouard Bellemare E 4.00 10.
APN Patrik Nemeth E 3.00 8.
ARJ Ryan Johansen B 8.00 20.
ARN Ryan Nugent-Hopkins B 8.00 20.
ARS Reilly Smith D 6.00 15.
ASB Sven Baertschi D 5.00 12.
ASC Brayden Schenn C 6.00 15.
ASG Shayne Gostisbehere E 20.00 50.
AST Ryan Strome C 6.00 15.
ATB Tyson Barrie E 5.00 12.
ATT Tomas Tatar C 5.00 12.
AVR Victor Rask E 3.00 8.
AWC Wendel Clark A 8.00 20.
AWG Wayne Gretzky A 125.00 200.
AWK William Karlsson E 10.00 25.
AZG Zemgus Girgensons D 5.00 12.

2015-16 Artifacts Frozen Artifacts Jerseys Blue

GROUP A ODDS 1:144
GROUP B ODDS 1:64
GROUP C ODDS 1:52
OVERALL ODDS 1:24H, 1:48R, 1:80BL
FAAB Aleksander Barkov B 3.00 8.
FAAG Alex Galchenyuk C 4.00 10.
FABD Brandon Dubinsky B 2.50 6.
FABE Brian Elliott B 2.50 6.
FABR Bobby Ryan C 2.50 6.
FABS Brandon Saad C 3.00 8.
FABU Alexandre Burrows B 2.50 6.
FACC Charlie Coyle B 2.50 6.
FACK Chris Kunitz C 3.00 8
FAEK Evgeny Kuznetsov C 5.00 12
FAGI John Gibson B 3.00 8
FAJC Jeff Carter B 3.00 8
FAJD Jonathan Drouin A 5.00 12
FAJG Johnny Gaudreau A 6.00 15
FAJI Jarome Iginla C 3.00 8
FAJN James Neal B 3.00 8
FAKL Kari Lehtonen C 2.50 6
FAML Milan Lucic C 2.50 6
FAMS Martin St. Louis A 4.00 10
FANY Nail Yakupov B 2.50 6
FAPK Phil Kessel C 5.00 12
FAPM Patrick Marleau C 3.00 8
FARS Ryan Strome C 2.50 6
FASC Sean Couturier B 3.00 8
FASM Mike Smith A 4.00 10
FASR Sam Reinhart A 4.00 10
FATJ Tomas Jurco A 4.00 10

2015-16 Artifacts Honoured Members Relics

STATED PRINT RUN 27 SER.#'d SETS
HMRAO Adam Oates Stick 40.00 80
HMRBC Bobby Clarke Stick 30.00 60
HMRBH Brett Hull Patch 30.00 60
HMRBL Brian Leetch Stick 20.00 50
HMRBO Ray Bourque GLV-STK 30.00 60
HMRBP Brad Park PTCH-STK 20.00 50
HMRCC Chris Chelios Patch 20.00 50
HMRCN Cam Neely Stick 30.00 60
HMRDG Doug Gilmour Stick 20.00 50
HMRDP Denis Potvin Stick 20.00 50
HMREB Ed Belfour Patch 30.00 60
HMRGA Glenn Anderson Stick 15.00 40
HMRGF Grant Fuhr PTCH-STK 40.00 80
HMRHU Bobby Hull Stick 30.00 60
HMRJB Jean Beliveau GLV-STK 90.00 150
HMRJS Joe Sakic Patch 40.00 80
HMRMD Marcel Dionne Stick 30.00 60
HMRME Mark Messier PTCH-STK 20.00 50
HMRML Mario Lemieux PTCH-GLV 60.00 100
HMRMM Mike Modano Patch 30.00 60

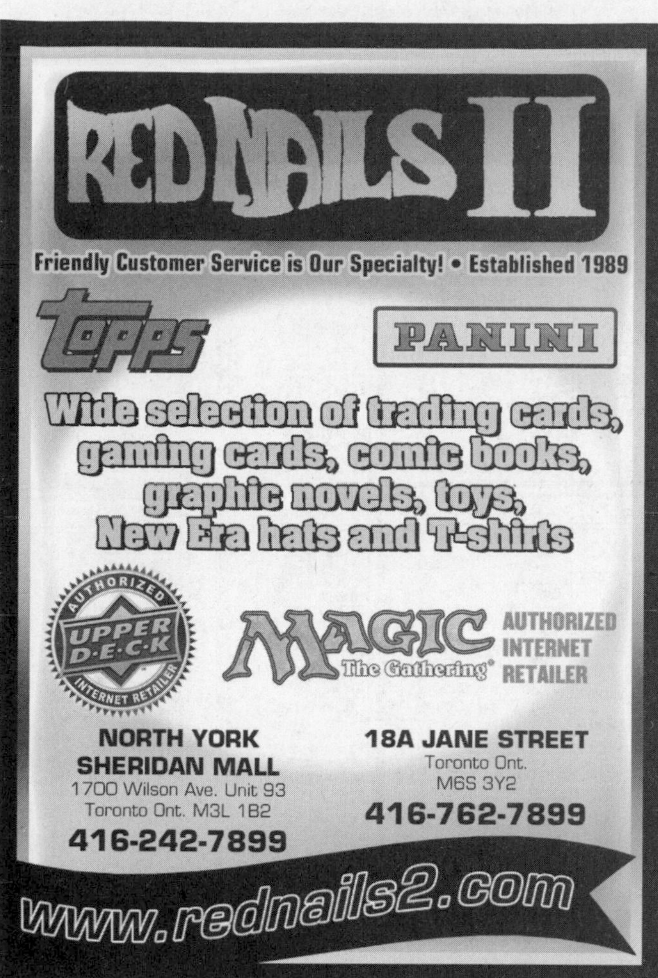
RED NAILS II
Friendly Customer Service is Our Specialty! • Established 1989
topps
PANINI
Wide selection of trading cards, gaming cards, comic books, graphic novels, toys, New Era hats and T-shirts
AUTHORIZED UPPER DECK INTERNET RETAILER
MAGIC The Gathering
AUTHORIZED INTERNET RETAILER
NORTH YORK SHERIDAN MALL
1700 Wilson Ave. Unit 93
Toronto Ont. M3L 1B2
416-242-7899
18A JANE STREET
Toronto Ont.
M6S 3Y2
416-762-7899
www.rednails2.com

PRISTINE
AUCTION

PRICING and CHECKLISTS updated daily | Great tool for trading with instant access to card values | Free Organize to catalog your entire collection
OPG subscriptions start at only $8.25/month*
*with a 1-year subscription
For more information, visit www.beckett.com/hk
BECKETT MEDIA

HMRMS Mats Sundin PTCH-STK 40.00 80.00
HMRPC Paul Coffey Stick 40.00 80.00
HMRPE Phil Esposito Stick 40.00 80.00
HMRRB Rob Blake Pants-STK 30.00 60.00
HMRSI Darryl Sittler Stick 15.00 40.00
HMRSY Steve Yzerman PTCH-STK 50.00 100.00
HMRTS Terry Sawchuk Stick 30.00 60.00

2015-16 Artifacts Honoured Members Signatures

STATED PRINT RUN 27 SER.#'d SETS
HMSBH Brett Hull 40.00 80.00
HMSBO Bobby Orr 125.00 200.00
HMSGF Grant Fuhr 40.00 80.00
HMSMB Mike Bossy 30.00 60.00
HMSPR Patrick Roy 75.00 135.00

2015-16 Artifacts Jerseys

1-130 STATED PRINT RUN 125
131-160 STATED PRINT RUN 99
161-180 STATED PRINT RUN 399
*1-100 EMERALD/75: .6X TO 1.5X JSY/125
*101-130 EMERALD/49: .5X TO 1.2X JSY/125
*131-160 EMERALD/25: .6X TO 1.5X JSY/99
*161-179 EMERALD/199: .6X TO 1.5X JSY/399
*161-179 SPECTRUM/99: .8X TO 2X JSY/399
1 Gabriel Landeskog 4.00 10.00
2 Brandon Dubinsky 3.00 8.00
3 Marian Gaborik 4.00 10.00
4 Sam Gagner 3.00 8.00
5 John Gibson 4.00 10.00
6 Alex Galchenyuk 5.00 12.00
7 Jakub Voracek 4.00 10.00
8 Cam Ward 4.00 10.00
9 P.K. Subban 6.00 15.00
10 Calle Jarnkrok 3.00 8.00
11 Tomas Hertl 4.00 10.00
12 Jeff Carter 4.00 10.00
13 Jason Pominville 3.00 8.00
14 Ondrej Pavelec 4.00 10.00
15 Semyon Varlamov 4.00 10.00
16 Mike Smith 4.00 10.00
17 Kari Lehtonen 3.00 8.00
18 Morgan Rielly 3.00 8.00
19 Tanner Pearson 2.50 6.00
20 Alexandre Burrows 3.00 8.00
21 Ondrej Palat 3.00 8.00
23 Chris Kunitz 4.00 10.00
24 Scott Hartnell 4.00 10.00
25 Corey Perry 4.00 10.00
26 Craig Anderson 4.00 10.00
27 David Backes 4.00 10.00
28 Nick Bjugstad 3.00 8.00
29 Bobby Ryan 3.00 8.00
30 Frederik Andersen 3.00 8.00
31 Charlie Coyle 3.00 8.00
32 Elias Lindholm 2.50 6.00
33 Gustav Nyquist 4.00 10.00
34 Paul Stastny 4.00 10.00
36 Jonathan Drouin 5.00 12.00
37 Sam Reinhart 4.00 10.00
38 Daniel Sedin 4.00 10.00
39 Tomas Jurco 4.00 10.00
40 John Carlson 5.00 12.00
41 James Neal 4.00 10.00
42 Roberto Luongo 6.00 15.00
43 Sean Monahan 4.00 10.00
44 Duncan Keith 4.00 10.00
45 Victor Hedman 5.00 12.00
46 Nicklas Backstrom 6.00 15.00
47 Corey Crawford 5.00 12.00
48 Henrik Lundqvist 5.00 12.00
49 Olli Maatta 4.00 10.00
50 Erik Karlsson 8.00 20.00
51 Henrik Zetterberg 5.00 12.00
52 Thomas Vanek 4.00 10.00
53 Marian Hossa 3.00 8.00
54 Darcy Kuemper 3.00 8.00
55 Patrick Kane 8.00 20.00
56 Mats Zuccarello 3.00 8.00
57 Ryan Kesler 4.00 10.00
58 Patrik Elias 4.00 10.00
59 Jamie Benn 5.00 12.00
60 Brayden Schenn 4.00 10.00
61 Ryan Strome 3.00 8.00
62 Nazem Kadri 3.00 8.00
63 Leon Draisaitl 4.00 10.00
64 Johan Franzen 4.00 10.00
65 Brendan Gallagher 5.00 12.00
66 Dustin Brown 3.00 8.00
70 Patrick Marleau 4.00 10.00
72 Brian Elliott 3.00 8.00
73 Pekka Rinne 5.00 12.00
74 Kyle Okposo 4.00 10.00
75 Ryan McDonagh 3.00 8.00
76 Zdeno Chara 4.00 10.00
77 Jeff Skinner 3.00 8.00
78 David Krejci 3.00 8.00
79 Nail Yakupov 3.00 8.00
80 Cody Hodgson 4.00 10.00
82 Henrik Sedin 4.00 10.00
83 Sean Couturier 4.00 10.00
84 Jacob Trouba 3.00 8.00
85 Phil Kessel 6.00 15.00
86 Chris Kreider 4.00 10.00
87 Matt Moulson 3.00 8.00
88 Evgeni Malkin 12.00 30.00
89 Joe Pavelski 4.00 10.00
90 Jason Spezza 4.00 10.00
91 Jonathan Huberdeau 4.00 10.00
92 Oliver Ekman-Larsson 3.00 8.00
93 Evgeny Kuznetsov 6.00 15.00
94 Jarome Iginla 4.00 10.00
95 Ryan Johansen 5.00 12.00
96 Mark Scheifele 4.00 10.00
97 Ryan Nugent-Hopkins 4.00 10.00
98 Jiri Hudler 3.00 8.00
99 Milan Lucic 3.00 8.00
100 Jonas Hiller 3.00 8.00
101 Pavel Datsyuk S 6.00 15.00
102 Logan Couture S 5.00 12.00
103 Anze Kopitar S 8.00 20.00
104 Jonathan Bernier S 5.00 12.00
105 Johnny Gaudreau S 8.00 20.00
106 Ryan Miller S 5.00 12.00
107 Tyler Seguin S 8.00 20.00
108 Ryan Getzlaf S 8.00 20.00
109 Zemgus Girgensons S 4.00 10.00
110 Blake Wheeler S 5.00 12.00
111 Sergei Bobrovsky S 5.00 12.00
112 Eric Staal S 6.00 15.00
113 John Tavares S 10.00 25.00
114 Alexander Ovechkin S 20.00 50.00
115 Jonathan Toews S 10.00 25.00
116 Zach Parise S 5.00 12.00
117 Shane Doan S 4.00 10.00
118 Sidney Crosby S 20.00 50.00
119 Nathan MacKinnon S 10.00 25.00
120 Shea Weber S 5.00 12.00
121 Tuukka Rask S 5.00 12.00
123 Carey Price S 15.00 40.00
124 Aaron Ekblad S 5.00 12.00
125 Taylor Hall S 10.00 25.00
126 Vladimir Tarasenko S 6.00 15.00
127 Kyle Turris S 4.00 10.00
128 Steven Stamkos S 10.00 25.00
129 Claude Giroux S 5.00 12.00
130 Rick Nash S 5.00 12.00
131 Mats Sundin LEG 5.00 12.00
132 Mike Gartner LEG 5.00 12.00
134 Marty Turco LEG 5.00 12.00
135 Wendel Clark LEG 5.00 12.00
136 Rod Brind'Amour LEG 4.00 10.00
137 Mario Lemieux LEG 8.00 20.00
138 Dale Hawerchuk LEG 6.00 15.00
139 Tony Esposito LEG 5.00 12.00
140 Jari Kurri LEG 5.00 12.00
141 Lanny McDonald LEG 5.00 12.00
142 Martin Brodeur LEG 10.00 25.00
143 Mike Keane LEG 4.00 10.00
146 Patrick Roy LEG 12.00 30.00
148 Owen Nolan LEG 4.00 10.00
149 Glen Murray LEG 4.00 10.00
150 Theoren Fleury LEG 6.00 15.00
151 Glenn Hall LEG 6.00 15.00
152 Pelle Lindbergh LEG 8.00 20.00
153 Marcel Dionne LEG 8.00 20.00
154 Wayne Gretzky LEG 20.00 50.00
156 Ron Francis LEG 6.00 15.00
158 Steve Yzerman LEG 8.00 20.00
159 Gerry Cheevers LEG 8.00 20.00
160 Rob Blake LEG 5.00 12.00
161 Henrik Samuelsson 2.50 6.00
162 Antoine Bibeau 3.00 8.00
163 Slater Koekkoek 2.50 6.00
165 Shane Prince 2.50 6.00
168 Emile Poirier 3.00 8.00
170 Josh Anderson 3.00 8.00
171 Nick Cousins 3.00 8.00
172 Matt Puempel 2.50 6.00
173 Kevin Fiala 3.00 8.00
176 Jacob de la Rose 3.00 8.00
177 Connor Hellebuyck 8.00 20.00
178 Ronalds Kenins 3.00 8.00
179 Sam Bennett 5.00 12.00
180 Malcolm Subban 8.00 20.00
182 Robby Fabbri 2.50 6.00
Issued in SPx
188 Jake Virtanen 4.00 10.00
Issued in SPx
189 Dylan Larkin 8.00 20.00
190 Artemi Panarin 8.00 20.00
206 Jack Eichel 12.00 30.00
Issued in SPx
210 Noah Hanifin 3.00 8.00
Issued in SPx

2015-16 Artifacts Jerseys Autographs

*161-179 EMER/49: .6X TO 1.5X AU/125
*161-179 SPECT/15: .8X TO 2X AU/125
1 Gabriel Landeskog/49 8.00 20.00
2 Brandon Dubinsky/49 6.00 15.00
3 Marian Gaborik/49 12.00 30.00
4 Sam Gagner/49 6.00 15.00
5 John Gibson/49 8.00 20.00
6 Alex Galchenyuk/49 12.00 30.00
8 Cam Ward/49 8.00 20.00
9 P.K. Subban/49 15.00 40.00
10 Calle Jarnkrok/49 6.00 15.00
11 Tomas Hertl/49 12.00 30.00
13 Jason Pominville/49 6.00 15.00
15 Semyon Varlamov/49 8.00 20.00
17 Kari Lehtonen/49 6.00 15.00
18 Morgan Rielly/49 8.00 20.00
19 Tanner Pearson/49 6.00 15.00
20 Alexandre Burrows/49 10.00 25.00
23 Chris Kunitz/49 8.00 20.00
24 Scott Hartnell/49 8.00 20.00
25 Corey Perry/49 8.00 20.00
27 David Backes/49 8.00 20.00
29 Bobby Ryan/49 6.00 15.00
30 Frederik Andersen/49 6.00 15.00
31 Charlie Coyle/49 6.00 15.00
32 Elias Lindholm/49 5.00 12.00
33 Gustav Nyquist/49 8.00 20.00
34 Paul Stastny/49 6.00 15.00
37 Sam Reinhart/49 8.00 20.00
39 Tomas Jurco/49 8.00 20.00
43 Sean Monahan/49 8.00 20.00
49 Olli Maatta/49 8.00 20.00
56 Mats Zuccarello/49 8.00 20.00
57 Ryan Kesler/49 8.00 20.00
58 Patrik Elias/49 8.00 20.00
59 Jamie Benn/49 12.00 30.00
60 Brayden Schenn/49 8.00 20.00
61 Ryan Strome/49 8.00 20.00
63 Leon Draisaitl/49 10.00 25.00
64 Johan Franzen/49 8.00 20.00
65 Brendan Gallagher/49 15.00 30.00
70 Patrick Marleau/49 8.00 20.00
73 Pekka Rinne/49 10.00 25.00
74 Kyle Okposo/49 6.00 15.00
75 Ryan McDonagh/49 6.00 15.00
77 Jeff Skinner/49 6.00 15.00
78 David Krejci/49 12.50 25.00
79 Nail Yakupov/49 15.00 30.00
80 Cody Hodgson/49 8.00 20.00
83 Sean Couturier/49 8.00 20.00
84 Jacob Trouba/49 6.00 15.00
86 Chris Kreider/49 10.00 25.00
87 Matt Moulson/49 6.00 15.00
88 Evgeni Malkin/49 20.00 40.00
89 Joe Pavelski/49 8.00 20.00
90 Jason Spezza/49 8.00 20.00
91 Jonathan Huberdeau/49 8.00 20.00
93 Evgeny Kuznetsov/49 15.00 30.00
94 Jarome Iginla/49 12.50 25.00
95 Ryan Johansen/49 8.00 20.00
96 Mark Scheifele/49 10.00 25.00
97 Ryan Nugent-Hopkins/49 20.00 40.00
100 Jonas Hiller/49 6.00 15.00
102 Logan Couture/25 8.00 20.00
103 Anze Kopitar/25 20.00 50.00
104 Jonathan Bernier/25 8.00 20.00
105 Johnny Gaudreau/25 20.00 50.00
106 Ryan Miller/25 8.00 20.00
109 Zemgus Girgensons/25 12.00 30.00
111 Sergei Bobrovsky/25 12.00 30.00
112 Eric Staal/25 15.00 40.00
113 John Tavares/25 20.00 50.00
114 Alexander Ovechkin/25 40.00 80.00
115 Jonathan Toews/25 30.00 60.00
116 Zach Parise/25 20.00 50.00
120 Shea Weber/25 10.00 25.00
121 Tuukka Rask/25 12.00 30.00
123 Carey Price/25 50.00 100.00
124 Aaron Ekblad/25 12.00 30.00
127 Kyle Turris/25 10.00 25.00
129 Claude Giroux/25 15.00 40.00
130 Rick Nash/25 12.00 30.00
132 Mike Gartner/25 15.00 40.00
133 Pierre Turgeon/25 25.00 50.00
134 Marty Turco/25 15.00 40.00
135 Wendel Clark/25 12.00 30.00
136 Rod Brind'Amour/25 10.00 25.00
137 Mario Lemieux/25 60.00 100.00
138 Dale Hawerchuk/25 20.00 50.00
139 Tony Esposito/25 15.00 40.00
140 Jari Kurri/25 15.00 40.00
141 Lanny McDonald/25 15.00 40.00
142 Martin Brodeur/25 40.00 80.00
143 Mike Keane/25 12.00 30.00
146 Patrick Roy/25 40.00 80.00
148 Owen Nolan/25 12.00 30.00
149 Glen Murray/25 10.00 25.00
150 Theoren Fleury/25 20.00 50.00
153 Marcel Dionne/25 25.00 50.00
154 Wayne Gretzky/25 150.00 250.00
158 Steve Yzerman/25 40.00 80.00
160 Rob Blake/25 15.00 40.00
161 Henrik Samuelsson/125 5.00 12.00
162 Antoine Bibeau/125 6.00 15.00
163 Slater Koekkoek/125 6.00 15.00
165 Shane Prince/125 5.00 12.00
168 Emile Poirier/125 6.00 15.00
170 Josh Anderson/125 6.00 15.00
171 Nick Cousins/125 6.00 15.00
172 Matt Puempel/125 5.00 12.00
176 Jacob de la Rose/125 6.00 15.00
177 Connor Hellebuyck/125 12.00 30.00
179 Sam Bennett/125 20.00 40.00
180 Malcolm Subban/125 25.00 50.00
182 Robby Fabbri/125 8.00 20.00
Issued in SPx
188 Jake Virtanen/125 8.00 20.00
Issued in SPx
205 Connor McDavid/125
210 Noah Hanifin/125 8.00 20.00
Issued in SPx
211 Jared McCann/125 6.00 15.00
Issued in SPx

2015-16 Artifacts Lord Stanley's Legacy Relics

GROUP A ODDS 1:1,007
GROUP B ODDS 1:234
GROUP C ODDS 1:168
GROUP D ODDS 1:60
OVERALL STATED ODDS 1:36 HOB
LSLRAK Anze Kopitar D 6.00 15.00
LSLRBH Brett Hull A 5.00 12.00
LSLRCC Corey Crawford D 5.00 12.00
LSLRCH Chris Chelios D 4.00 10.00
LSLRCP Corey Perry C 4.00 10.00
LSLRDD Drew Doughty D 4.00 10.00
LSLREM Evgeni Malkin C 12.00 30.00
LSLREP Patrik Elias D 4.00 10.00
LSLRES Eric Staal D 5.00 12.00
LSLRGC Gerry Cheevers A 10.00 25.00
LSLRGF Grant Fuhr B 6.00 15.00
LSLRJQ Jonathan Quick C 6.00 15.00
LSLRJT Jonathan Toews B 6.00 15.00
LSLRLM Lanny McDonald B 5.00 12.00
LSLRMH Marian Hossa D 3.00 8.00
LSLRML Mario Lemieux A 20.00 50.00
LSLRMM Mark Messier A 8.00 20.00
LSLRPB Patrice Bergeron D 5.00 12.00
LSLRPC Paul Coffey C 5.00 12.00
LSLRPD Pavel Datsyuk C 5.00 12.00
LSLRPF Peter Forsberg B 5.00 12.00
LSLRPK Patrick Kane D 8.00 20.00
LSLRPR Patrick Roy B 12.00 30.00
LSLRRF Ron Francis C 5.00 12.00
LSLRRG Ryan Getzlaf D 6.00 15.00
LSLRSC Sidney Crosby B 20.00 50.00
LSLRSY Steve Yzerman B 8.00 20.00
LSLRZC Zdeno Chara D 4.00 10.00

2015-16 Artifacts Lord Stanley's Legacy Signatures

UNPRICED GRP A ODDS 1:13,097
GROUP B ODDS 1:467
GROUP C ODDS 1:489
GROUP D ODDS 1:733
OVERALL STATED ODDS 1:240 HOB
LSAK Anze Kopitar C 15.00 40.00
LSBO Bobby Orr B 100.00 175.00
LSBS Brandon Saad D 10.00 25.00
LSCC Chris Chelios C 12.00 30.00
LSDS Dave Schultz D 12.00 30.00
LSJS Joe Sakic B 20.00 40.00
LSMB Mike Bossy B 12.00 30.00
LSMM Mark Messier A 60.00 100.00
LSMS Martin St. Louis C 10.00 25.00
LSNL Nicklas Lidstrom B 20.00 40.00
LSTS Teemu Selanne B 20.00 40.00
LSTT Tyler Toffoli C 12.00 30.00
LSWG Wayne Gretzky C 150.00 250.00

2015-16 Artifacts Rookie Autographs Redemptions

EXCH STATED ODDS 1:105
EXCH EXPIRATON: 9/15/2017
I Auto EXCH I/McDavid 350.00 600.00
II Auto EXCH II/Larkin 90.00 150.00
III Auto EXCH III/Domi 60.00 100.00
IV Auto EXCH IV/Ehlers 25.00 50.00
V Auto EXCH V/Panarin 75.00 125.00
VI Auto EXCH VI/Virtanen 12.00 30.00
VII Auto EXCH VII/Fabbri 12.00 30.00
VIII Auto EXCH VIII/Hanifin 12.00 30.00
IX Auto EXCH IX/McCann 10.00 25.00
X Auto EXCH X/Lindberg 10.00 25.00
XI Auto EXCH XI/Fucale 25.00 50.00
XII Auto EXCH XII/Rantanen 20.00 50.00
XIII Auto EXCH XIII/Ritchie 12.00 30.00
XIV Auto EXCH XIV/Condon 25.00 50.00
XV Auto EXCH XV/Rask 12.00 30.00
XVI Auto EXCH XVI/Sparks 12.00 30.00
XVII Auto EXCH XVII/Parayko 12.00 30.00
XVIII Auto EXCH XVIII/Hutton 20.00 40.00
XIX Auto EXCH XIX/Ullmark 20.00 50.00
XX Auto EXCH XX/Petan 12.00 30.00

2015-16 Artifacts Rookie Jersey Autographs Redemptions

STATED ODDS 1:435 HOB
*EMERALD: .6X TO 1.5X BASIC JSY AU EXCH
EXCH EXPIRATON: 9/15/2017
I Rdmpt I/McDavid EXCH 400.00 750.00
II Rdmpt II/Larkin EXCH 125.00 250.00
III Rdmpt III/Domi EXCH 50.00 100.00
IV Rdmpt IV/Ehlers EXCH 30.00 60.00
V Rdmpt V/Panarin EXCH 100.00 175.00

2015-16 Artifacts Rookie Jersey Redemptions

STATED ODDS 1:137 HOB
*EMERALD: .5X TO 1.2X BASIC JSY EXCH
*SPECTRUM: .6X TO 1.5X BASIC JSY EXCH
EXCH EXPIRATON: 9/15/2017
I Rdmpt I/McDavid EXCH 60.00 150.00
II Rdmpt II/Larkin EXCH 40.00 80.00
III Rdmpt III/Domi EXCH 20.00 50.00
IV Rdmpt IV/Ehlers EXCH 10.00 25.00
V Rdmpt V/Panarin EXCH 15.00 40.00

2015-16 Artifacts Rookie Redemption Ruby

*EMERALD: .5X TO 1.2X BASIC JSY EXCH
*SAPPHIRE: .6X TO 1.5X RUBY
*SPECTRUM: .8X TO 2X BASIC JSY EXCH
EXCH EXPIRATION: 9/15/2017
I Rdmpt I/McDavid EXCH 100.00 175.00
II Rdmpt II/Larkin EXCH 30.00 60.00
III Rdmpt III/Domi EXCH 20.00 50.00
IV Rdmpt IV/Ehlers EXCH 10.00 25.00
V Rdmpt V/Panarin EXCH 15.00 40.00

2015-16 Artifacts Stick to Stick Green

STATED ODDS 1:640
STSBC Bobby Clarke 12.00 30.00
STSCP Carey Price 25.00 60.00
STSDD Drew Doughty 8.00 20.00
STSDG Doug Gilmour 12.00 30.00
STSGL Guy Lafleur 12.00 30.00
STSJB Jean Beliveau 25.00 50.00
STSML Milan Lucic 8.00 20.00
STSRM Ryan McDonagh
STSTB Tom Barrasso 10.00 25.00
STSVD Vincent Damphousse 8.00 20.00

2015-16 Artifacts Stick to Stick Duos Green

STATED ODDS 1:960
STS2CP F.Potvin/W.Clark 25.00 50.00
STS2GC J.Carlson/M.Green 12.00 30.00
STS2GL D.Gilmour/M.Liut 12.00 30.00
STS2LR M.Richter/G.Lafleur 12.00 30.00
STS2SF P.Forsberg/J.Sakic 12.00 30.00
STS2SS H.Sedin/D.Sedin 10.00 25.00
STS2YL S.Yzerman/N.Lidstrom 15.00 40.00
STS2YZ H.Zetterberg/S.Yzerman 15.00 40.00

2015-16 Artifacts Stick to Stick Trios Green

STATED ODDS 1:720
STS3LAK Carter/Pearson/Toffoli 12.00 30.00
STS3LOS Blake/Gretzky/Kurri 40.00 80.00
STS3NYR Richter/Vanbiesbrouck/Park 12.00 30.00
STS3TML Bernier/Kessel/van Riemsdyk 20.00 50.00
STS3WAS Backstrom/Ovechkin/Green 50.00 125.00
STS3BLUES Joseph/Hull/Oates 25.00 50.00
STS3KINGS Gaborik/Williams/Quick 25.00 50.00

2015-16 Artifacts Top 12 Rookie Signatures

STATED ODDS 1:480 HOB
RSCM Connor McDavid EXCH
(inserted in 2016-17 Artifacts)
RSDL Dylan Larkin B
(inserted in 2016-17 Artifacts)
RSEP Emile Poirier 5.00 12.00
RSHS Henrik Samuelsson 4.00 10.00
RSJR Jacob de la Rose 5.00 12.00
RSMS Malcolm Subban 12.00 30.00
RSNE Nikolaj Ehlers C
(inserted in 2016-17 Artifacts)
RSRF Robby Fabbri C
(inserted in 2016-17 Artifacts)
RSRH Ryan Hartman 6.00 15.00
RSSB Sam Bennett 6.00 15.00

2015-16 Artifacts Treasured Swatches Jerseys Blue

GROUP A ODDS 1:106
GROUP B ODDS 1:31
OVERALL ODDS 1:24H, 1:48R, 1:80BL
TSAS Alexander Semin B 3.00 8.00
TSBG Brendan Gallagher A 4.00 10.00
TSBH Braden Holtby B 5.00 12.00
TSBS Brayden Schenn B 3.00 8.00
TSCJ Calle Jarnkrok B 2.50 6.00
TSCK Chris Kreider B 3.00 8.00
TSDK David Krejci A 2.50 6.00
TSFA Frederik Andersen B 2.50 6.00
TSJH Jiri Hudler A 2.50 6.00
TSKA Nazem Kadri B 2.50 6.00
TSKU Darcy Kuemper B 2.50 6.00
TSLD Leon Draisaitl B 3.00 8.00
TSMM Matt Moulson A 2.50 6.00
TSMS Mark Scheifele B 4.00 10.00
TSMZ Mika Zibanejad B 3.00 8.00
TSNB Nick Bjugstad B 2.50 6.00
TSOE Oliver Ekman-Larsson B 2.50 6.00
TSOM Olli Maatta A 3.00 8.00
TSPE Patrik Elias B 3.00 8.00
TSPS Paul Stastny A 3.00 8.00
TSSE Brent Seabrook B 3.00 8.00
TSSV Semyon Varlamov B 3.00 8.00
TSTH Tomas Hertl A 3.00 8.00
TSTT Tyler Toffoli B 3.00 8.00
TSVH Victor Hedman B 3.00 8.00
TSZK Zack Kassian B 2.00 5.00

2015-16 Artifacts Tundra Sixes Jerseys Blue

T6TC Pit/Cnly/Sch/Myr/Schf/Hck 10.00 25.00
T6CAR Stl/Stl/Sknr/Wrd/Lnd/Smn 10.00 25.00
T6CHI Sbrk/Kth/Crwf/Hsa/Shp/Sd 10.00 25.00
T6LAK Crtr/Tffi/Prs/Brw/Kptr/Wlms 12.00 30.00
T6RC1 Bnt/Prl/Ros/Csn/Sms/Fla 6.00 15.00
T6RC2 Pm/M.Sb/Hlk/Kn/Bu/An
T6VAN Mlr/Sdn/Brw/Sdn/Edlr/Ksn 8.00 20.00
T6BLUES Bck/Trs/Ell/Osh/Stsl/Aln 12.00 30.00

2015-16 Artifacts Tundra Tandems Jerseys Blue

STATED PRINT RUN 399 SER.#'d SETS
*EMERALD/15: 1.2X TO 3X BLUE/399
TTBB N.Bjugstad/A.Barkov 3.00 8.00
TTBH B.Bishop/V.Hedman 4.00 10.00
TTBK N.Backstrom/E.Kuznetsov 5.00 12.00
TTBL P.Bergeron/M.Lucic 4.00 10.00
TTBS T.Seguin/J.Benn 5.00 12.00
TTCT J.Carter/T.Toffoli 3.00 8.00
TTDP J.Drouin/O.Palat 4.00 10.00
TTGA F.Andersen/J.Gibson 3.00 8.00
TTGR Z.Girgensons/S.Reinhart 3.00 8.00
TTHN T.Hall/R.Nugent-Hopkins 6.00 15.00
TTMG S.Monahan/J.Gaudreau 5.00 12.00
TTNJ T.Jurco/G.Nyquist 3.00 8.00
TTPC L.Couture/J.Pavelski 3.00 8.00
TTPG M.Pacioretty/A.Galchenyuk 4.00 10.00
TTSB D.Backes/P.Stastny 3.00 8.00
TTSS D.Sedin/H.Sedin 3.00 8.00
TTTK K.Turris/E.Karlsson 6.00 15.00
TTVC S.Couturier/J.Voracek 3.00 8.00
TTVK J.van Riemsdyk/N.Kadri 3.00 8.00
TTWJ S.Weber/S.Jones 2.50 6.00
TTWS B.Wheeler/M.Scheifele 4.00 10.00
TTYD N.Yakupov/L.Draisaitl 3.00 8.00

2015-16 Artifacts Tundra Trios Jerseys Blue

T3AZ Gagner/Boedker/Ekmn-Lrsn 3.00 8.00
T3ANA Gibson/Kesler/Andersen 4.00 10.00
T3BUF Hodgson/Girgensons/Reinhart 4.00 10.00
T3CAN Sedin/Miller/Sedin 4.00 10.00
T3CBJ Hartnell/Dubinsky/Johansen 5.00 12.00
T3FLA Ekblad/Huberdeau/Barkov 4.00 10.00
T3LAK Quick/Kopitar/Doughty 6.00 15.00
T3NYI Okposo/Tavares/Strome 5.00 12.00
T3NYR Nash/Kreider/St. Louis 4.00 10.00
T3OIL RNH/Eberle/Draisaitl 4.00 10.00
T3TBL Drouin/Palat/Hedman 5.00 12.00
T3TOR Kessel/Rielly/Kadri
T3CAPS Ovchkn/Bckstrm/Kzntsv 5.00 12.00
T3JETS Wheeler/Pavelec/Scheifele 5.00 12.00
T3NASH Jones/Neal/Jarnkrok 4.00 10.00
T3WILD Coyle/Pominville/Kuemper 3.00 8.00
T3BLUES Backes/Stastny/Oshie 6.00 15.00

2015-16 Artifacts Year One Rookie Sweaters

STATED ODDS 1:60 HOB
*EMERALD/16: 1.2X TO 3X BASIC JSY
RGAE Aaron Ekblad 4.00 10.00
RGBR Brett Ritchie 2.50 6.00
RGCJ Calle Jarnkrok 3.00 8.00
RGEK Evgeny Kuznetsov 6.00 15.00
RGJD Jonathan Drouin 5.00 12.00
RGJG Johnny Gaudreau 5.00 12.00
RGKL Kari Lehtonen 3.00 8.00
RGLD Leon Draisaitl 4.00 10.00
RGSR Sam Reinhart 4.00 10.00

2016-17 Artifacts

1 Evgeni Malkin 1.25 3.00
2 Evgeny Kuznetsov .60 1.50
3 Sam Reinhart .30 .75
4 Sergei Bobrovsky .40 1.00
5 Jonathan Toews .75 2.00
6 Ryan Strome .30 .75
7 Victor Hedman .50 1.25
8 Matt Beleskey .30 .75
9 Marian Gaborik .40 1.00
10 Johnny Gaudreau .60 1.50
11 Derek Stepan .30 .75
12 Patrick Marleau .40 1.00
13 Michael Raffl .25 .60
14 Shea Weber .30 .75
15 Tyler Seguin .60 1.50
16 Frederik Andersen .30 .75
17 Gustav Nyquist .40 1.00
18 Nazem Kadri .30 .75
19 Gabriel Landeskog .30 .75
20 Vladimir Tarasenko .60 1.50
21 Kyle Turris .30 .75
22 Zach Parise .40 1.00
23 Alex Galchenyuk .50 1.25
24 Cam Ward .40 1.00
25 Taylor Hall .75 2.00
26 Michael Cammalleri .30 .75
27 Dustin Byfuglien .40 1.00
28 Matt Murray .60 1.50
29 Mike Smith .40 1.00
30 Aaron Ekblad .40 1.00
31 Kyle Palmieri .30 .75
32 Evander Kane .40 1.00
33 Nicklas Backstrom .60 1.50
34 Sam Bennett .50 1.25
35 Anders Lee .40 1.00
36 Ryan Miller .40 1.00
37 Tomas Hertl .40 1.00
38 Roberto Luongo .60 1.50
39 T.J. Oshie .60 1.50
40 Drew Doughty .50 1.25
41 Duncan Keith .50 1.25
42 Kevin Shattenkirk .30 .75
43 Kevin Hayes .30 .75
44 Steven Stamkos .75 2.00
45 Jonathan Huberdeau .40 1.00
46 Scott Hartnell .30 .75
47 Justin Faulk .30 .75
48 Mike Hoffman .30 .75
49 James van Riemsdyk .40 1.00
50 Ryan Kesler .40 1.00
51 Tomas Tatar .30 .75
52 David Krejci .40 1.00
53 Phil Kessel .50 1.25
54 Pekka Rinne .50 1.25
55 Max Domi .50 1.25
56 Brendan Gallagher .50 1.25
57 Claude Giroux .40 1.00
58 Cory Schneider .40 1.00
59 Nathan MacKinnon .75 2.00
60 Jason Spezza .40 1.00
61 Brent Burns .50 1.25
62 Kris Letang .40 1.00
63 Devan Dubnyk .40 1.00
64 Anze Kopitar .60 1.50
65 Jarome Iginla .50 1.25
66 Tyler Johnson .30 .75
67 Mark Stone .40 1.00
68 Nikolaj Ehlers .40 1.00
69 Corey Crawford .50 1.25
70 Jake Allen .40 1.00
71 Jaroslav Halak .40 1.00
72 Rick Nash .30 .75
73 Carey Price 1.25 3.00
74 John Klingberg .40 1.00
75 Jordan Eberle .40 1.00
76 Wayne Simmonds .50 1.25
77 Tyler Toffoli .40 1.00
78 Cam Talbot .50 1.25
79 Dougie Hamilton .40 1.00
80 Henrik Zetterberg .50 1.25
81 Artemi Panarin .50 1.25
82 Nino Niederreiter .30 .75
83 Nick Foligno .30 .75
84 Roman Josi .40 1.00
85 Ryan O'Reilly .40 1.00
86 Noah Hanifin .40 1.00
87 Henrik Lundqvist .60 1.50
88 Anthony Duclair .40 1.00
89 Bobby Ryan .30 .75
90 Patrick Sharp .30 .75
91 Joe Thornton .60 1.50
92 Petr Mrazek .40 1.00
93 Aleksander Barkov .50 1.25
94 Loui Eriksson .40 1.00
95 Bo Horvat .60 1.50
96 Braden Holtby .60 1.50
97 Leon Draisaitl .50 1.25
98 Tomas Plekanec .40 1.00
99 Ryan Getzlaf .60 1.50
100 Blake Wheeler .50 1.25
101 Patrick Kane S 4.00 10.00
102 Jonathan Quick S 3.00 8.00
103 Mats Zuccarello S 2.00 5.00
104 Mikael Granlund S 1.50 4.00
105 Alexander Ovechkin S 8.00 20.00
106 Corey Perry S 2.00 5.00
107 Patrice Bergeron S 2.50 6.00
108 Sean Monahan S 2.00 5.00
109 Matt Duchene S 2.00 5.00
110 Connor McDavid S 10.00 25.00
111 Jaromir Jagr S 5.00 12.00
112 P.K. Subban S 3.00 8.00
113 Jeff Skinner S 2.00 5.00
114 Nikita Kucherov S 3.00 8.00
115 John Tavares S 4.00 10.00
116 Jakub Voracek S 2.00 5.00
117 Erik Karlsson S 4.00 10.00
118 Adam Henrique S 2.00 5.00
119 Filip Forsberg S 2.50 6.00
120 Jack Eichel S 4.00 10.00
121 Oliver Ekman-Larsson S 1.50 4.00
122 Mark Scheifele S 2.50 6.00
123 Morgan Rielly S 1.50 4.00
124 Joe Pavelski S 2.00 5.00
125 Sidney Crosby S 8.00 20.00
126 Brandon Saad S 2.00 5.00
127 Alexander Steen S 2.00 5.00
128 Jamie Benn S 2.50 6.00
129 Daniel Sedin S 2.00 5.00
130 Dylan Larkin S 3.00 8.00
131 Steve Yzerman LEG 2.50 6.00
132 Pavel Bure LEG 2.00 5.00
133 Larry Murphy LEG 2.00 5.00
134 Jeremy Roenick LEG 2.00 5.00
135 Paul Coffey LEG 2.00 5.00
136 John LeClair LEG 2.00 5.00
137 Bob Bourne LEG 2.00 5.00
138 Trevor Linden LEG 2.00 5.00
139 Mike Bossy LEG 2.00 5.00
140 Ron Hextall LEG 2.00 5.00
141 Chris Chelios LEG 2.00 5.00
142 Denis Savard LEG 2.50 6.00
143 Grant Fuhr LEG 2.00 5.00
144 Larry Robinson LEG 2.00 5.00
145 Wayne Gretzky LEG 10.00 25.00
146 Johnny Bucyk LEG 2.00 5.00
147 Kirk McLean LEG 2.00 5.00
148 Borje Salming LEG 2.00 5.00
149 Martin Brodeur LEG 4.00 10.00
150 Mark Messier LEG 2.50 6.00
151 Dominik Hasek LEG 2.00 5.00
152 Patrick Roy LEG 5.00 12.00
153 Peter Forsberg LEG 2.00 5.00
154 Pierre Turgeon LEG 2.00 5.00
155 Joe Sakic LEG 3.00 8.00
156 Mike Richter LEG 2.00 5.00
157 Brett Hull LEG 3.00 8.00
158 Mario Lemieux LEG 6.00 15.00
159 Teemu Selanne LEG 4.00 10.00
160 Guy Lafleur LEG 2.50 6.00
161 William Nylander RC 6.00 15.00
162 Sonny Milano RC 1.50 4.00
163 Kasperi Kapanen RC 3.00 8.00
164 Josh Morrissey RC 2.00 5.00
165 Trevor Carrick RC 1.50 4.00
166 Anthony Mantha RC 4.00 10.00
167 Michael Matheson RC 1.50 4.00
168 Hudson Fasching RC 1.25 3.00
169 Oliver Bjorkstrand RC 1.50 4.00
170 Brendan Leipsic RC 1.50 4.00
171 Pavel Zacha RC 2.00 5.00
172 Justin Bailey RC 1.50 4.00
173 Esa Lindell RC 1.50 4.00
174 Steven Santini RC 1.25 3.00
175 Nikita Soshnikov RC 1.00 2.50
176 Sergey Tolchinsky RC 1.25 3.00
177 Ryan Pulock RC 1.50 4.00
178 Jason Dickinson RC 1.25 3.00
179 Connor Brown RC 2.50 6.00
180 Charlie Lindgren RC 2.50 6.00
181 Nick Sorensen RC 1.25 3.00
182 Dylan Strome RC 5.00 12.00
183 Brandon Carlo RC 2.50 6.00
184 Nick Baptiste RC 2.50 6.00
185 Matthew Tkachuk RC 8.00 20.00
186 Sebastian Aho RC 5.00 12.00
187 Tyler Motte RC 2.50 6.00
188 A.J. Greer RC 2.50 6.00
189 Zach Werenski RC 5.00 12.00
190 Gemel Smith RC 2.50 6.00
191 Tyler Bertuzzi RC 3.00 8.00
192 Jesse Puljujarvi RC 6.00 15.00
193 Denis Malgin RC 2.50 6.00
194 Nic Dowd RC 2.50 6.00
195 Joel Eriksson Ek RC 5.00 12.00
196 Mikhail Sergachev RC 5.00 12.00
197 Pontus Aberg RC 2.50 6.00
198 Nick Lappin RC 2.50 6.00
199 Anthony Beauvillier RC 5.00 12.00
200 Jimmy Vesey RC 5.00 12.00
201 Thomas Chabot RC 5.00 12.00
202 Travis Konecny RC 5.00 12.00
203 Tristan Jarry RC 5.00 12.00
204 Kevin Labanc RC 2.50 6.00
205 Alex Friesen RC 2.50 6.00
206 Brayden Point RC 8.00 20.00
207 Auston Matthews RC 30.00 80.00
208 Troy Stecher RC 2.50 6.00
209 Zach Sanford RC 2.50 6.00
210 Patrik Laine RC 10.00 25.00
211 Mitch Marner RC 12.00 30.00
212 Ivan Provorov RC 5.00 12.00
213 Kyle Connor RC 6.00 15.00
214 Christian Dvorak RC 2.50 6.00
215 Pavel Buchnevich RC 4.00 10.00
216 Jakub Vrana RC 2.50 6.00
217 Brendan Perlini RC 2.50 6.00
218 Drake Caggiula RC 2.50 6.00
219 Julius Honka RC 2.50 6.00
220 Mathew Barzal RC 8.00 20.00

2016-17 Artifacts Aurum

A1 Alexander Ovechkin 10.00 25.00
A2 Oliver Ekman-Larsson 2.00 5.00
A3 Jamie Benn 3.00 8.00
A4 Vladimir Tarasenko 4.00 10.00
A5 Derick Brassard 2.50 6.00
A6 Jussi Jokinen 2.00 5.00
A7 Anze Kopitar 4.00 10.00
A8 Ryan Getzlaf 4.00 10.00
A9 Brad Marchand 4.00 10.00
A10 Connor McDavid 12.00 30.00
A11 Victor Rask 2.00 5.00
A12 John Tavares 5.00 12.00
A13 Logan Couture 2.50 6.00
A14 Cam Atkinson 2.50 6.00
A15 Sidney Crosby 10.00 25.00
A16 Filip Forsberg 3.00 8.00
A17 Braden Holtby 4.00 10.00
A18 Patrick Kane 5.00 12.00
A19 Matt Murray 4.00 10.00
A20 Max Domi 3.00 8.00
A21 Erik Karlsson 5.00 12.00
A22 Carey Price 8.00 20.00
A23 Henrik Zetterberg 3.00 8.00
A24 Daniel Sedin 2.50 6.00
A25 Kyle Palmieri 2.00 5.00
A26 Joe Thornton 2.50 6.00
A27 Johnny Gaudreau 4.00 10.00
A28 Mikko Koivu 2.00 5.00
A29 Steven Stamkos 5.00 12.00
A30 Artemi Panarin 3.00 8.00
A31 Matt Duchene 2.50 6.00
A32 Shayne Gostisbehere 3.00 8.00
A33 Patric Hornqvist 2.50 6.00
A34 Jaromir Jagr 6.00 15.00
A35 Jack Eichel 5.00 12.00
A36 William Nylander 10.00 25.00
A37 Anthony Mantha 6.00 15.00
A38 Kasperi Kapanen 5.00 12.00
A39 Pavel Zacha 3.00 8.00
A40 Hudson Fasching 2.50 6.00
A41 Wayne Gretzky 12.00 30.00
A42 Mark Messier 3.00 8.00
A43 Steve Yzerman 3.00 8.00
A44 Doug Harvey 2.00 5.00
A45 Mario Lemieux 8.00 20.00
A46 Luc Robitaille 2.50 6.00
A47 Kirk McLean 2.50 6.00
A48 Curtis Joseph 2.50 6.00
A49 Patrick Roy 6.00 15.00
A50 Bobby Orr 8.00 20.00

2016-17 Artifacts Autofacts

AAE Aaron Ekblad A 12.00 30.00
AAK Anze Kopitar A 15.00 40.00
AAL Anders Lee C 8.00 20.00
AAW Alexander Wennberg C 6.00 15.00
ABJ Boone Jenner C 8.00 20.00
ACO Chris Osgood B 12.00 30.00
AEP Emile Poirier D 6.00 15.00
AJG John Gibson D 8.00 20.00
AJH Jiri Hudler B 6.00 15.00
AJW Jordan Weal D 6.00 15.00
AJZ Jason Zucker B 6.00 15.00
AMG Mikhail Grigorenko D 5.00 12.00
AMM Mike McCarron D 8.00 20.00
ANB Nick Bjugstad C 6.00 15.00
ANS Nick Shore D 6.00 15.00
ARB Rod Brind'Amour C 8.00 20.00
ARS Ryan Spooner D 6.00 15.00
ATL Trevor Linden A 12.00 30.00
AVN Vladislav Namestnikov D 5.00 12.00
AWG Wayne Gretzky A 125.00 200.00

2016-17 Artifacts Autograph Materials Silver

1 Evgeni Malkin/25 50.00 125.00
3 Sam Reinhart/49 6.00 15.00
4 Sergei Bobrovsky/25 15.00 40.00
6 Ryan Strome/75 5.00 12.00
8 Matt Beleskey/75 5.00 12.00
9 Marian Gaborik/25 15.00 40.00
11 Derek Stepan/25 12.00 30.00
12 Patrick Marleau/25 15.00 40.00
16 Frederik Andersen/75 6.00 15.00
19 Gabriel Landeskog/25 12.00 30.00
21 Kyle Turris/49 6.00 15.00
22 Zach Parise/25 15.00 40.00
23 Alex Galchenyuk/25 20.00 50.00
24 Cam Ward/49 8.00 20.00
25 Taylor Hall/25 30.00 80.00
30 Aaron Ekblad/25 15.00 40.00
34 Sam Bennett/49 10.00 25.00
35 Anders Lee/75 6.00 15.00
36 Ryan Miller/25 15.00 40.00
37 Tomas Hertl/25 15.00 40.00
43 Kevin Hayes/75 5.00 12.00
45 Jonathan Huberdeau/49 8.00 20.00
48 Mike Hoffman/75 5.00 12.00
49 James van Riemsdyk/49 8.00 20.00
51 Tomas Tatar/49 6.00 15.00
52 David Krejci/25 15.00 40.00
54 Pekka Rinne/49 20.00 50.00
56 Brendan Gallagher/25 20.00 50.00
57 Claude Giroux/25 15.00 40.00
58 Cory Schneider/49 6.00 15.00
60 Jason Spezza/25 15.00 40.00
64 Anze Kopitar/25 25.00 60.00
65 Jarome Iginla/25 15.00 40.00
66 Tyler Johnson/49 6.00 15.00
67 Mark Stone/75 6.00 15.00
68 Nikolaj Ehlers/49 8.00 20.00
70 Jake Allen/75 6.00 15.00
71 Jaroslav Halak/75 6.00 15.00
72 Rick Nash/25 15.00 40.00
73 Carey Price/25 50.00 125.00
74 John Klingberg/49 8.00 20.00
77 Tyler Toffoli/25 15.00 40.00
84 Roman Josi/49 8.00 20.00
86 Noah Hanifin/49 8.00 20.00
87 Henrik Lundqvist/25 15.00 40.00
88 Anthony Duclair/75 6.00 15.00
89 Bobby Ryan/25 12.00 30.00
93 Aleksander Barkov/49 8.00 20.00
94 Loui Eriksson/25 15.00 40.00
95 Bo Horvat/75 10.00 25.00
102 Jonathan Quick 25.00 60.00
105 Alexander Ovechkin 60.00 150.00
106 Corey Perry 15.00 40.00
108 Sean Monahan 15.00 40.00
109 Matt Duchene 15.00 40.00
110 Connor McDavid 80.00 200.00
111 Jaromir Jagr 40.00 100.00
112 P.K. Subban 25.00 60.00
113 Jeff Skinner 15.00 40.00
115 John Tavares 30.00 80.00
116 Jakub Voracek 15.00 40.00
118 Adam Henrique 15.00 40.00
122 Mark Scheifele 20.00 50.00
123 Morgan Rielly 15.00 40.00
124 Joe Pavelski 20.00 50.00
128 Jamie Benn 20.00 50.00
131 Steve Yzerman 20.00 50.00
132 Pavel Bure 15.00 40.00
134 Jeremy Roenick 15.00 40.00
135 Paul Coffey 15.00 40.00
136 John LeClair 15.00 40.00
137 Bob Bourne 15.00 40.00
138 Trevor Linden 20.00 50.00
139 Mike Bossy 15.00 40.00
140 Ron Hextall 15.00 40.00
141 Chris Chelios 15.00 40.00
142 Denis Savard 15.00 40.00
143 Grant Fuhr 15.00 40.00
144 Larry Robinson 15.00 40.00
145 Wayne Gretzky 80.00 200.00
146 Johnny Bucyk 15.00 40.00
147 Kirk McLean 15.00 40.00
149 Martin Brodeur 30.00 80.00
152 Patrick Roy 40.00 100.00
154 Pierre Turgeon 15.00 40.00
157 Brett Hull 20.00 50.00
158 Mario Lemieux 50.00 120.00
162 Sonny Milano 12.00 30.00
163 Kasperi Kapanen 20.00 50.00
164 Josh Morrissey 12.00 30.00
165 Trevor Carrick 10.00 25.00

166 Anthony Mantha 25.00 60.00
167 Michael Matheson 10.00 25.00
168 Hudson Fasching 10.00 25.00
169 Oliver Bjorkstrand 8.00 20.00
170 Brendan Leipsic 10.00 25.00
171 Pavel Zacha 12.00 30.00
172 Justin Bailey 10.00 25.00
173 Esa Lindell 10.00 25.00
174 Steven Santini 8.00 20.00
175 Nikita Soshnikov 6.00 15.00
177 Ryan Pulock 10.00 25.00
178 Jason Dickinson 8.00 20.00
179 Connor Brown 15.00 40.00
180 Charlie Lindgren 20.00 50.00

2016-17 Artifacts Frozen Artifacts

FAAH Andrew Hammond C 4.00 10.00
FABB Bob Bourne A 5.00 12.00
FACA Jeff Carter B 5.00 12.00
FACK Chris Kreider C 5.00 12.00
FAHS Henrik Sedin C 5.00 12.00
FAJC John Carlson C 6.00 15.00
FAJJ Jack Johnson C 3.00 8.00
FAJS Jakob Silfverberg B 5.00 12.00
FAJT Jacob Trouba C 4.00 10.00
FAJZ Jason Zucker C 4.00 10.00
FAKL Kris Letang B 5.00 12.00
FAMH Martin Hanzal C 4.00 10.00
FAMJ Martin Jones C 5.00 12.00
FAMP Max Pacioretty B 5.00 12.00
FANL Nick Leddy C 3.00 8.00
FAOP Ondrej Palat C 4.00 10.00
FAPE Patrik Elias C 5.00 12.00
FAPT Pierre Turgeon A 5.00 12.00
FARH Ron Hextall A 5.00 12.00
FARL Roberto Luongo B 4.00 10.00
FARR Rasmus Ristolainen C 4.00 10.00
FASM Steve Mason C 4.00 10.00
FASV Semyon Varlamov C 5.00 12.00
FAZC Zdeno Chara C 5.00 12.00

2016-17 Artifacts Honoured Members Relics

HMRBH Brett Hull 30.00 80.00
HMRBO Johnny Bower 30.00 80.00
HMRBS Borje Salming 30.00 80.00
HMRDH Doug Harvey 25.00 60.00
HMRDS Denis Savard UER 40.00 100.00
HMRGL Guy Lafleur 40.00 100.00
HMRJB Johnny Bucyk 30.00 80.00
HMRLM Lanny McDonald 30.00 80.00
HMRLR Luc Robitaille 30.00 80.00
HMRMU Larry Murphy 30.00 80.00
HMRPF Peter Forsberg 30.00 80.00
HMRPR Patrick Roy 80.00 200.00
HMRRB Rob Blake 30.00 80.00
HMRTE Tony Esposito 30.00 80.00
HMRWG Wayne Gretzky 150.00 400.00

2016-17 Artifacts Lord Stanley's Legacy Relics

LSLRCW Cam Ward C 5.00 12.00
LSLRDK Duncan Keith B 5.00 12.00
LSLRHZ Henrik Zetterberg A 6.00 15.00
LSLRJC Jeff Carter B 5.00 12.00
LSLRLR Larry Robinson A 5.00 12.00
LSLRMB Martin Brodeur A 10.00 25.00
LSLRMF Marc-Andre Fleury C 8.00 20.00
LSLRPB Patrice Bergeron B 6.00 15.00

2016-17 Artifacts Lord Stanley's Legacy Signatures

LSLSCP Corey Perry D 20.00 50.00
LSLSJK Jari Kurri D 20.00 50.00
LSLSML Mario Lemieux B 60.00 150.00
LSLSPE Phil Esposito C 30.00 80.00
LSLSPR Patrick Roy B 50.00 125.00
LSLSRB Ray Bourque C 30.00 80.00
LSLSSY Steve Yzerman B 25.00 60.00
LSLSWY Wayne Gretzky A

2016-17 Artifacts Piece de Resistance

PRCM Connor McDavid B 25.00 60.00
PRCP Corey Perry C 5.00 12.00
PRDS Daniel Sedin C 5.00 12.00
PRGF Grant Fuhr A 5.00 12.00
PRJJ Jaromir Jagr C 12.00 30.00
PRJQ Jonathan Quick C 8.00 20.00
PRJS Jason Spezza C 5.00 12.00
PRLM Larry Murphy A 5.00 12.00
PRMD Max Domi C 6.00 15.00
PRMH Marian Hossa C 4.00 10.00
PRML Mario Lemieux A 15.00 40.00
PROV Alexander Ovechkin A 20.00 50.00
PRPC Paul Coffey A 5.00 12.00
PRPK Patrick Kane B 10.00 25.00
PRSC Sidney Crosby A 20.00 50.00
PRSS Steven Stamkos C 10.00 25.00
PRVN Valeri Nichushkin C 4.00 10.00

2016-17 Artifacts Rookie Autograph Relics Redemptions Emerald

Auston Matthews 400.00 600.00
I Patrik Laine 60.00 150.00
II Jesse Puljujarvi 25.00 60.00
V Jimmy Vesey 25.00 60.00
Zach Werenski 25.00 60.00

2016-17 Artifacts Rookie Autograph Relics Redemptions Silver

Auston Matthews 300.00 500.00
I Patrik Laine 80.00 150.00
I Jesse Puljujarvi 30.00 80.00
V Jimmy Vesey 30.00 80.00
Zach Werenski 25.00 60.00

2016-17 Artifacts Rookie Autographs Redemptions

Mikhail Sergachev 20.00 50.00
Auston Matthews 250.00 350.00
Patrik Laine 40.00 100.00
I Jesse Puljujarvi 25.00 60.00
Jimmy Vesey 20.00 50.00
Zach Werenski 20.00 50.00
I Travis Konecny 20.00 50.00
II Ivan Provorov 20.00 50.00
III Kyle Connor 25.00 60.00
I Dylan Strome 20.00 50.00
Matthew Tkachuk 30.00 80.00
V Jakub Vrana 10.00 25.00
X Anthony DeAngelo 10.00 25.00
II Sebastian Aho 20.00 50.00
IV Tyler Motte 10.00 25.00
IX John Quenneville 10.00 25.00
VI Joel Eriksson Ek 10.00 25.00
III Christian Dvorak 10.00 25.00
VII Brendan Perlini 10.00 25.00
VIII Julius Honka 10.00 25.00

2016-17 Artifacts Rookie Relics Redemptions Emerald

I Auston Matthews 90.00 150.00
II Patrik Laine 25.00 60.00
III Jesse Puljujarvi 20.00 50.00
IV Jimmy Vesey 15.00 40.00
V Zach Werenski 20.00 50.00

2016-17 Artifacts Rookie Relics Redemptions Silver

I Auston Matthews 50.00 125.00
II Patrik Laine 30.00 80.00
III Jesse Puljujarvi 20.00 50.00
IV Jimmy Vesey 15.00 40.00
V Zach Werenski 15.00 40.00

2016-17 Artifacts Top 12 Rookie Signatures

RSAM Anthony Mantha A 25.00 60.00
RSHF Hudson Fasching B 15.00 40.00
RSKK Kasperi Kapanen B 12.00 30.00
RSPZ Pavel Zacha B 20.00 50.00
RSSM Sonny Milano B 25.00 60.00

2016-17 Artifacts Tundra Teammates Quads Materials

T4ANA Perry/Kesler/Silfverberg/Gibson 6.00 15.00
T4CHB Kane/Keith/Toews/Hossa 12.00 30.00
T4EDM McDavid/Draisaitl/Eberle/Talbot 30.00 80.00
T4FLA Jagr/Barkov/Ekblad/Luongo 15.00 40.00
T4OTT Karlsson/Stone/Hoffman/Anderson 6.00 15.00
T4SJS Pavelski/Burns/Thornton/Jones 8.00 20.00
T4VAN Linden/Sedin/Bure/Sedin 8.00 20.00
T4CAPS Ovechkin/Backstrom Kuznetsov/Holtby 25.00 60.00
T4STAR Benn/Seguin/Spezza/Klingberg 10.00 25.00
T4WINGS Chelios/Coffey Yzerman/Zetterberg 8.00 20.00

2016-17 Artifacts Year One Rookie Sweaters

RSCM Connor McDavid B 40.00 100.00
RSJE Jack Eichel B 15.00 40.00
RSJV Jake Virtanen B 10.00 25.00
RSMC Mike Condon B 8.00 20.00
RSMD Max Domi B 10.00 25.00
RSNE Nikolaj Ehlers B 8.00 20.00
RSPB Pavel Bure A 30.00 80.00
RSSB Sam Bennett B 10.00 25.00

2017-18 Artifacts

1 Adam Henrique .30 .75
2 Steven Stamkos .75 2.00
3 Eric Staal .50 1.25
4 Braden Holtby .60 1.50
5 Johnny Gaudreau .60 1.50
6 Aaron Ekblad .40 1.00
7 Charlie Coyle .30 .75
8 Patrice Bergeron .50 1.25
9 Sebastian Aho .40 1.00
10 Drew Doughty .40 1.00
11 Filip Forsberg .50 1.25
12 Nino Niederreiter .30 .75
13 Victor Rask .40 1.00
14 Dylan Larkin .40 1.00
15 Daniel Sedin .40 1.00
16 Morgan Rielly .40 1.00
17 Frans Nielsen .30 .75
18 James Neal .30 .75
19 Cory Schneider .30 .75
20 Jordan Eberle .40 1.00
21 Andrew Ladd .40 1.00
22 Zach Werenski .40 1.00
23 John Carlson .50 1.25
24 Ivan Provorov .40 1.00
25 Derek Stepan .30 .75
26 Brayden Schenn .40 1.00
27 Nick Leddy .25 .60
28 Robby Fabbri .40 1.00
29 Shea Weber .30 .75
30 Oliver Ekman-Larsson .40 1.00
31 Mark Stone .40 1.00
32 Max Pacioretty .40 1.00
33 Nikita Kucherov .60 1.50
34 Brad Marchand .50 1.25
35 Jamie Benn .50 1.25
36 Pavel Zacha .40 1.00
37 Ryan O'Reilly .40 1.00
38 Brandon Saad .40 1.00
39 Nazem Kadri .30 .75
40 Tyler Seguin .60 1.50
41 Mark Scheifele .50 1.25
42 Evgeni Malkin 1.25 3.00
43 Jason Spezza .40 1.00
44 Leon Draisaitl .60 1.50
45 Jonathan Toews .75 2.00
46 Rickard Rakell .30 .75
47 Andreas Athanasiou .40 1.00
48 Alexander Wennberg .30 .75
49 Erik Karlsson .50 1.25
50 Frederik Andersen .30 .75
51 Tuukka Rask .40 1.00
52 Mats Zuccarello .40 1.00
53 Claude Giroux .40 1.00
54 Blake Wheeler .40 1.00
55 Jaromir Jagr 1.00 2.50
56 Gustav Nyquist .40 1.00
57 Gabriel Landeskog .30 .75
58 Bo Horvat .40 1.00
59 Jonathan Drouin .40 1.00
60 Nathan MacKinnon .75 2.00
61 Jack Eichel .60 1.50
62 Milan Lucic .40 1.00
63 Mike Smith .40 1.00
64 Joe Thornton .40 1.00
65 T.J. Oshie .60 1.50
66 Joe Pavelski .40 1.00
67 Patrick Kane .75 2.00
68 Jake Allen .50 1.25
69 Ryan Spooner .30 .75
70 Roberto Luongo .40 1.00
71 Alex Pietrangelo .30 .75
72 Carey Price 1.25 3.00
73 Jake Muzzin .30 .75
74 Logan Couture .40 1.00
75 John Gibson .40 1.00
76 Kyle Palmieri .30 .75
77 Jimmy Vesey .40 1.00
78 David Pastrnak .60 1.50
79 Teuvo Teravainen .30 .75
80 Cam Atkinson .40 1.00
81 Artemi Panarin .40 1.00
82 Ryan Getzlaf .40 1.00
83 Jaden Schwartz .50 1.25
84 Christian Dvorak .30 .75
85 Sean Monahan .40 1.00
86 Anze Kopitar .60 1.50
87 Nicklas Backstrom .60 1.50
88 Matt Murray .60 1.50
89 Nick Bjugstad .30 .75
90 Ryan Johansen .40 1.00
91 Matt Duchene .40 1.00
92 Vincent Trocheck .30 .75
93 Matthew Tkachuk .40 1.00
94 Kyle Okposo .30 .75
95 Kris Letang .40 1.00
96 Loui Eriksson .30 .75
97 Nikolaj Ehlers .40 1.00
98 Anders Lee .40 1.00
99 Tyler Toffoli .30 .75
100 Derick Brassard .40 1.00
101 P.K. Subban S 2.00 5.00
102 Ryan Kesler S 2.00 5.00
103 Henrik Zetterberg S 2.00 5.00
104 Taylor Hall S 4.00 10.00
105 Mike Hoffman S 1.50 4.00
106 Alex Galchenyuk S 2.50 6.00
107 Wayne Simmonds S 2.50 6.00
108 Aleksander Barkov S 2.00 5.00
109 Devan Dubnyk S 2.00 5.00
110 Auston Matthews S 8.00 20.00
111 John Klingberg S 1.50 4.00
112 Max Domi S 2.00 5.00
113 Corey Crawford S 2.50 6.00
114 Jeff Carter S 2.00 5.00
115 Sidney Crosby S 8.00 20.00
116 Tyson Barrie S 2.00 5.00
117 Justin Faulk S 1.50 4.00
118 Mark Giordano S 1.50 4.00
119 Henrik Lundqvist S 3.00 8.00
120 Henrik Sedin S 2.00 5.00
121 David Krejci S 1.50 4.00
122 Alexander Ovechkin S 8.00 20.00
123 Brent Burns S 2.50 6.00
124 John Tavares S 4.00 10.00
125 Connor McDavid S 8.00 20.00
126 Sam Reinhart S 1.50 4.00
127 Patrik Laine S 3.00 8.00
128 Sergei Bobrovsky S 2.00 5.00
129 Victor Hedman S 2.50 6.00
130 Vladimir Tarasenko S 3.00 8.00
131 Mario Lemieux LEG 6.00 15.00
132 Dave Taylor LEG 1.50 4.00
133 Martin Brodeur LEG 4.00 10.00
134 Owen Nolan LEG 2.00 5.00
135 Ed Belfour LEG 2.50 6.00
136 Larry Murphy LEG 1.50 4.00
137 Mark Recchi LEG 2.50 6.00
138 Tom Barrasso LEG 1.50 4.00
139 Vincent Damphousse LEG 1.50 4.00
140 Felix Potvin LEG 2.00 5.00
141 Lanny McDonald LEG 2.00 5.00
142 Nicklas Lidstrom LEG 1.50 4.00
143 Teemu Selanne LEG 2.50 6.00
144 Marcel Dionne LEG 2.50 6.00
145 Bob Probert LEG 2.00 5.00
146 Igor Larionov LEG 2.00 5.00
147 Guy Lafleur LEG 2.50 6.00
148 Pelle Lindbergh LEG 2.00 5.00
149 Theoren Fleury LEG 2.00 5.00
150 Rod Brind'Amour LEG 2.00 5.00
151 Dale Hawerchuk LEG 2.50 6.00
152 Patrick Roy LEG 5.00 12.00
153 Doug Gilmour LEG 2.50 6.00
154 Brett Hull LEG 2.00 5.00
155 Paul Coffey LEG 2.00 5.00
156 Dominik Hasek LEG 2.00 5.00
157 Wayne Gretzky LEG 10.00 25.00
158 Joe Sakic LEG 2.50 6.00
159 Mike Gartner LEG 2.00 5.00
160 Ray Bourque LEG 3.00 8.00
161 Ivan Barbashev RC 1.50 4.00
162 Vladislav Kamenev RC 2.50 6.00
163 Jonny Brodzinski RC 1.50 4.00
164 Tyson Jost RC 3.00 8.00
165 Evgeny Svechnikov RC 3.00 8.00
166 J.T. Compher RC 2.00 5.00
167 Jon Gillies RC 1.50 4.00
168 Adrian Kempe RC 2.00 5.00
169 Lucas Wallmark RC 1.50 4.00
170 Alexander Nylander RC 2.50 6.00
171 Brock Boeser RC 10.00 25.00
172 Nikita Scherbak RC 3.00 8.00
173 Christian Fischer RC 2.00 5.00
174 Colin White RC 1.50 4.00
175 Charlie McAvoy RC 8.00 20.00
176 Josh Ho-Sang RC 2.00 5.00
177 Samuel Morin RC 1.50 4.00
178 Jack Roslovic RC 2.00 5.00
179 Clayton Keller RC 4.00 10.00
180 Alex Tuch RC 4.00 10.00
181 Anaheim Ducks EXCH 8.00 20.00
182 Arizona Coyotes EXCH 8.00 20.00
183 Boston Bruins EXCH 8.00 20.00
184 Buffalo Sabres EXCH 5.00 12.00
185 Calgary Flames EXCH 5.00 12.00
186 Carolina Hurricanes EXCH 8.00 20.00
187 Chicago Blackhawks EXCH 8.00 20.00
188 Colorado Avalanche EXCH 4.00 10.00
189 Columbus Blue Jackets EXCH 4.00 10.00
190 Dallas Stars EXCH 3.00 8.00
191 Detroit Red Wings EXCH 4.00 10.00
192 Edmonton Oilers EXCH 10.00 25.00
193 Florida Panthers EXCH 6.00 15.00
194 Los Angeles Kings EXCH 8.00 20.00
195 Minnesota Wild EXCH 6.00 15.00
196 Montreal Canadiens EXCH 8.00 20.00
197 Nashville Predators EXCH 3.00 8.00
198 New Jersey Devils EXCH 20.00 50.00
199 New York Islanders EXCH 8.00 20.00
200 New York Rangers EXCH 6.00 15.00
201 Ottawa Senators EXCH 8.00 20.00
202 Philadelphia Flyers EXCH 20.00 50.00
203 Pittsburgh Penguins EXCH 10.00 25.00
204 San Jose Sharks EXCH 6.00 15.00
205 St. Louis Blues EXCH 6.00 15.00
206 Tampa Bay Lightning EXCH 6.00 15.00
207 Toronto Maple Leafs EXCH 12.00 30.00
208 Vancouver Canucks EXCH 5.00 12.00
209 Washington Capitals EXCH 6.00 15.00
210 Winnipeg Jets EXCH 3.00 6.00
211 Wild Card EXCH 6.00 15.00
212 Wild Card EXCH 6.00 15.00
213 Wild Card EXCH 6.00 15.00
214 Wild Card EXCH 6.00 15.00
215 Wild Card EXCH 6.00 15.00
216 Wild Card EXCH 6.00 15.00
217 Wild Card EXCH 6.00 15.00
218 Wild Card EXCH 6.00 15.00
219 Wild Card EXCH 6.00 15.00
220 Wild Card EXCH 6.00 15.00

2017-18 Artifacts Emerald

*VETS/99: 2.5X TO 6X BASIC INSERTS
*RC/99: 1X TO 2.5X BASIC INSERTS
175 Charlie McAvoy 25.00 60.00
176 Josh Ho-Sang 8.00 20.00
179 Clayton Keller 12.00 30.00

2017-18 Artifacts Orange

*VETS/55: 4X TO 10X BASIC CARDS
*S.LEG/55: .75X TO 2X BASIC CARDS
*ROOKIES: 1X TO 2.5X BASIC CARDS
165 Evgeny Svechnikov 15.00 40.00
170 Alexander Nylander 15.00 40.00
171 Brock Boeser 30.00 80.00
175 Charlie McAvoy 30.00 80.00
176 Josh Ho-Sang 15.00 40.00
179 Clayton Keller 15.00 40.00

2017-18 Artifacts Purple

*VETS/55: 6X TO 15X BASIC CARDS
*S.LEG/55: 1.25X TO 3X BASIC CARDS
*ROOKIES: 2X TO 5X BASIC CARDS
171 Brock Boeser 90.00 150.00
175 Charlie McAvoy 60.00 150.00
179 Clayton Keller 50.00 125.00

2017-18 Artifacts Aurum

A1 Ace Bailey 8.00 20.00
A2 Frank Mahovlich 2.50 6.00
A3 Darryl Sittler 2.50 6.00
A4 Charlie Conacher 2.00 5.00
A5 Doug Gilmour 3.00 8.00
A6 Wendel Clark 3.00 8.00
A7 Alexander Ovechkin 10.00 25.00
A8 Aleksander Barkov 2.50 6.00
A9 Alex Pietrangelo 2.00 5.00
A10 John Tavares 5.00 12.00
A11 Leon Draisaitl 4.00 10.00
A12 Alexander Wennberg 2.00 5.00
A13 Sean Monahan 2.50 6.00
A14 Connor McDavid 10.00 25.00
A15 Brent Burns 3.00 8.00
A16 Rickard Rakell 2.00 5.00
A17 Cam Atkinson 2.50 6.00
A18 Claude Giroux 2.50 6.00
A19 Sidney Crosby 10.00 25.00
A20 Tyler Seguin 4.00 10.00
A21 Jeff Carter 2.50 6.00
A22 Mats Zuccarello 2.50 6.00
A23 Tuukka Rask 2.50 6.00
A24 P.K. Subban 2.50 6.00
A25 Henrik Sedin 2.50 6.00
A26 Auston Matthews 15.00 40.00
A27 Mike Hoffman 2.00 5.00
A28 Corey Crawford 3.00 8.00
A29 Ryan O'Reilly 2.50 6.00
A30 Marc-Andre Fleury 4.00 10.00
A31 Jeff Skinner 2.00 5.00
A32 Mike Green 2.00 5.00
A33 Devan Dubnyk 2.50 6.00
A34 Victor Hedman 3.00 8.00
A35 Carey Price 8.00 20.00
A36 Nicklas Backstrom 4.00 10.00
A37 Taylor Hall 5.00 12.00
A38 Jonathan Drouin 2.50 6.00
A39 Jake Guentzel 3.00 8.00
A40 Craig Anderson 2.50 6.00
A41 Mark Scheifele 3.00 8.00
A42 Pekka Rinne 3.00 8.00
A43 Ryan Getzlaf 2.50 6.00
A44 Nikita Kucherov 4.00 10.00
A45 Tyson Jost 5.00 12.00
A46 Charlie McAvoy 20.00 50.00
A47 Brock Boeser 30.00 80.00
A48 Alexander Nylander 10.00 25.00
A49 Clayton Keller 15.00 40.00
A50 Josh Ho-Sang 8.00 20.00

2017-18 Artifacts Autofacts

AAL Artturi Lehkonen D 4.00 10.00
ABR Bobby Ryan A 12.00 30.00
ADF Derek Forbort D 4.00 10.00
ADS Derek Sanderson A 8.00 20.00
AEK Evander Kane C 5.00 12.00
AFA Radek Faksa B 4.00 10.00
AJE Joel Edmundson D 4.00 10.00
AJF Justin Falk D 4.00 10.00
AJN Joakim Nordstrom D 4.00 10.00
AJS Jason Spezza A 8.00 20.00
AON Owen Nolan C 6.00 15.00
APH Phil Housley C 4.00 10.00
ARU Bryan Rust C 5.00 12.00
ASA Sebastian Aho B 5.00 12.00
ATW Tom Wilson C 5.00 12.00
AVA Viktor Arvidsson D 4.00 10.00
AVH Victor Hedman C 6.00 15.00
AWK William Karlsson D 10.00 25.00
AZP Zach Parise A 8.00 20.00

2017-18 Artifacts Autograph Materials Emerald

*VETS/25: 12X TO 30X BASIC CARDS
*ROOKIES: 3X TO 10X BASIC CARDS
44 Leon Draisaitl/25 30.00 80.00
50 Frederik Andersen/25 30.00 80.00
58 Bo Horvat/25 30.00 80.00
164 Tyson Jost/35 40.00 100.00
166 J.T. Compher/35 20.00 50.00
167 Jon Gillies/35 25.00 60.00
168 Adrian Kempe/35 40.00 100.00
170 Alexander Nylander/35 30.00 80.00
171 Brock Boeser/35 50.00 125.00
172 Nikita Scherbak/35 25.00 60.00
175 Charlie McAvoy/35 150.00 250.00
176 Josh Ho-Sang/35 80.00 150.00
177 Samuel Morin/35 25.00 60.00
179 Clayton Keller/35 80.00 150.00

2017-18 Artifacts Autograph Materials Silver

*VETS/25: 12X TO 30X BASIC CARDS
*VETS/35: 10X TO 25X BASIC CARDS
*ROOKIES: 2.5X TO 6X BASIC CARDS
164 Tyson Jost/99 30.00 80.00
165 Evgeny Svechnikov/99 30.00 80.00
168 Adrian Kempe/99 20.00 50.00
170 Alexander Nylander/99 20.00 50.00
171 Brock Boeser/99 40.00 100.00
176 Josh Ho-Sang/99 50.00 125.00
179 Clayton Keller/99 50.00 125.00

2017-18 Artifacts Centennial Remnants

CRAM Auston Matthews C 20.00 50.00
CRCM Connor McDavid B 30.00 80.00
CREK Erik Karlsson C 6.00 15.00
CRJJ Jaromir Jagr C 12.00 30.00
CRJT Joe Thornton C 5.00 12.00
CRMB Martin Brodeur B 10.00 25.00
CRMD Marcel Dionne A 12.00 30.00
CRML Mario Lemieux A 15.00 40.00
CRPK Patrick Kane C 10.00 25.00
CRPR Patrick Roy A 15.00 40.00
CRRB Ray Bourque B 12.00 30.00
CRSC Sidney Crosby B 15.00 40.00
CRSY Steve Yzerman B 25.00 60.00
CRWG Wayne Gretzky A 30.00 80.00

2017-18 Artifacts Frozen Artifacts

FAAA Andreas Athanasiou C 4.00 10.00
FAAS Andrew Shaw C 3.00 8.00
FAAW Alexander Wennberg B 3.00 8.00
FABH Braden Holtby A 6.00 15.00
FACP Colton Parayko B 4.00 10.00
FADB Dustin Byfuglien A 4.00 10.00
FADD Devan Dubnyk B 4.00 10.00
FADH Dale Hawerchuk A 5.00 12.00
FADP David Pastrnak B 6.00 15.00
FAEK Erik Karlsson A 5.00 12.00
FAJN James Neal B 3.00 8.00
FAJP Joe Pavelski A 4.00 10.00
FAKO Kyle Okposo C 3.00 8.00
FAKP Kyle Palmieri C 3.00 8.00
FAML Milan Lucic B 4.00 10.00
FAMZ Mats Zuccarello B 4.00 10.00
FANB Nicklas Backstrom A 6.00 15.00
FANK Nikita Kucherov A 6.00 15.00
FANL Nick Leddy C 2.50 6.00
FAPR Pekka Rinne B 5.00 12.00
FARI Mike Richter A 4.00 10.00
FARK Ryan Kesler B 4.00 10.00
FARR Rickard Rakell C 3.00 8.00
FASG Shayne Gostisbehere C 4.00 10.00
FASR Sam Reinhart C 3.00 8.00
FAVR Victor Rask C 4.00 10.00
FAVT Vincent Trocheck C 3.00 8.00

2017-18 Artifacts Honoured Hopefuls Relics

HHDS Daniel Sedin 30.00 80.00
HHEK Erik Karlsson
HHHL Henrik Lundqvist 80.00 150.00
HHHS Henrik Sedin 60.00 150.00
HHJI Jarome Iginla
HHJJ Jaromir Jagr 150.00 250.00
HHJT Joe Thornton 40.00 100.00
HHMH Marian Hossa 80.00 150.00
HHPK Patrick Kane
HH-SC Sidney Crosby

2017-18 Artifacts Honoured Hopefuls Signatures

HHSCP Carey Price 100.00 250.00
HHS-RL Roberto Luongo 100.00 200.00

2017-18 Artifacts Honoured Members Relics

HMRAL Al MacInnis
HMRBL Brian Leetch 60.00 150.00
HMRHA Dale Hawerchuk 40.00 100.00
HMRIL Igor Larionov 80.00 150.00
HMRJB Johnny Bower 80.00 150.00
HMRMB Martin Brodeur
HMRPL Pat LaFontaine 40.00 100.00
HMRSE Teemu Selanne
HMRSM Stan Mikita

2017-18 Artifacts Honoured Members Signatures

HMSEB Ed Belfour 80.00 150.00
HMSGA Glenn Anderson 30.00 80.00
HMSMB Martin Brodeur
HMSMG Mike Gartner 25.00 60.00
HMSNL Nicklas Lidstrom
HMSRV Rogie Vachon 40.00 100.00
HMSWG Wayne Gretzky

2017-18 Artifacts Lord Stanley's Legacy Relics

LSLRBM Brad Marchand C 10.00 25.00
LSLRBM Vincent Damphousse B 6.00 15.00
LSLRDD Drew Doughty C 8.00 20.00
LSLREB Ed Belfour B 10.00 25.00
LSLRKL Kris Letang C 8.00 20.00
LSLRLM Lanny McDonald A 8.00 20.00
LSLRPR Patrick Kane B 15.00 40.00
LSLRRG Patrick Roy A 20.00 50.00
LSLRSY Ryan Getzlaf C 8.00 20.00
LSLRVD Steve Yzerman A 10.00 25.00

2017-18 Artifacts Materials Emerald

*VETS/65: 8X TO 20X BASIC INSERTS
*VETS/25: 2X TO 5X BASIC INSERTS
*RC/99: 2X TO 5X BASIC INSERTS
165 Evgeny Svechnikov 20.00 50.00
171 Brock Boeser 25.00 60.00
176 Josh Ho-Sang 20.00 50.00
179 Clayton Keller 20.00 50.00

2017-18 Artifacts Materials Purple

*RC/49: 3X TO 8X BASIC CARDS
171 Brock Boeser 50.00 125.00

2017-18 Artifacts Rookie Autograph Redemptions

III TBD Rookie 20.00 50.00
IV TBD Rookie 20.00 50.00
V TBD Rookie 20.00 50.00
VI TBD Rookie 20.00 50.00
VII TBD Rookie 15.00 40.00
VIII TBD Rookie 15.00 40.00
IX TBD Rookie 12.00 30.00
X TBD Rookie 12.00 30.00
XI TBD Rookie 12.00 30.00
XII TBD Rookie 12.00 30.00
XIII TBD Rookie 10.00 25.00
XIV TBD Rookie 10.00 25.00
XIX TBD Rookie 15.00 40.00
XV TBD Rookie 10.00 25.00
XVI TBD Rookie 8.00 20.00
XVII TBD Rookie 12.00 30.00
XVIII TBD Rookie 15.00 40.00
XX TBD Rookie 10.00 25.00

2017-18 Artifacts Rookie Autograph Relic Redemptions Silver

III TBD Rookie 15.00 40.00
IV TBD Rookie 8.00 20.00
V TBD Rookie 12.00 30.00
VI TBD Rookie 8.00 20.00
VII TBD Rookie 8.00 20.00

2017-18 Artifacts Top 12 Rookie Signatures

RSAN Alexander Nylander B 8.00 20.00
RSBB Brock Boeser A 40.00 100.00
RSCK Clayton Keller A
RSCW Colin White B 8.00 20.00
RSNS Nikita Scherbak B 8.00 20.00
RSTJ Tyson Jost A 20.00 50.00

2017-18 Artifacts Tundra Teammates Duo Materials

T2ANA R.Rakell/J.Gibson 4.00 10.00
T2CBJ A.Wennberg/S.Jones 3.00 8.00
T2CHI B.Seabrook/C.Crawford 5.00 12.00
T2DET D.Larkin/A.Athanasiou 4.00 10.00
T2FLA A.Ekblad/V.Trocheck 4.00 10.00
T2MIN E.Staal/N.Niederreiter 5.00 12.00
T2NJD T.Hall/C.Schneider 8.00 20.00
T2NYI J.Tavares/B.Nelson 8.00 20.00
T2OTT E.Karlsson/M.Hoffman 5.00 12.00
T2PHI S.Gostisbehere/B.Schenn 4.00 10.00
T2PIT K.Letang/P.Kessel 5.00 12.00
T2SAN B.Burns/L.Couture 5.00 12.00
T2TBL V.Hedman/N.Kucherov 6.00 15.00
T2WAS E.Kuznetsov/A.Burakovsky 6.00 15.00

2017-18 Artifacts Tundra Teammates Quad Materials

T4BOS Bergeron/Pastrnak Marchand/Spooner 10.00 25.00
T4BUF Eichel/Reinhart/O'Reilly Ristolainen 10.00 25.00
T4CAR Staal/Teravainen/Lindholm/Rask 6.00 15.00
T4DAS Benn/Klingberg/Seguin/Spezza 10.00 25.00
T4MON Price/Weber/Pacioretty Galchenyuk 20.00 50.00
T4NAS Subban/Forsberg/Johansen/Josi 8.00 20.00
T4STL Tarasenko/Pietrangelo Fabbri/Parayko 10.00 25.00
T4WIN Scheifele/Byfuglien/Wheeler/Laine 10.0025.00

2017-18 Artifacts Year One Rookie Sweaters

RSAM Auston Matthews A 30.00 80.00
RSCD Christian Dvorak C 6.00 15.00
RSIP Ivan Provorov C 8.00 20.00
RSJG Jake Guentzel A 25.00 60.00
RSJV Jimmy Vesey C 8.00 20.00
RSMM Mitch Marner B 12.00 30.00
RSPL Patrik Laine A 12.00 30.00
RSPZ Pavel Zacha C 8.00 20.00
RSWN William Nylander B 12.00 30.00
RSZW Zach Werenski B 8.00 20.00

2017-18 Artifacts Year One Rookie Sweaters Red

*RED/25: .5X TO 1.25X BASIC INSERTS
RSAM Auston Matthews 80.00 150.00

2001-02 Atomic

Released in late November 2001, this 125-card base set featured die-cut cards printed on styrene stock and carried an SRP of $5.99 for a 5-card hobby pack. Rookies subset cards (101-125) were short printed to just 500 copies each and were inserted at a rate of 1:21. Retail packs contained 3 cards.

COMP.SET w/o SP's (100) 15.00 40.00
1 Paul Kariya .40 1.00
2 Steve Shields .25 .60
3 Milan Hnilicka .25 .60
4 Patrik Stefan .25 .60
5 Jason Allison .25 .60
6 Byron Dafoe .25 .60
7 Bill Guerin .30 .75
8 Sergei Samsonov .25 .60
9 Joe Thornton .40 1.00
10 Martin Biron .25 .60
11 Tim Connolly .20 .50
12 J-P Dumont .20 .50
13 Jarome Iginla .30 .75
14 Marc Savard .20 .50
15 Roman Turek .25 .60
16 Ron Francis .40 1.00
17 Arturs Irbe .25 .60
18 Jeff O'Neill .20 .50
19 Tony Amonte .25 .60
20 Steve Sullivan .20 .50
21 Jocelyn Thibault .25 .60
22 Rob Blake .30 .75
23 Chris Drury .25 .60
24 Peter Forsberg .40 1.00
25 Milan Hejduk .25 .60
26 Patrick Roy .75 2.00
27 Joe Sakic .50 1.25
28 Alex Tanguay .25 .60
29 Marc Denis .25 .60
30 Geoff Sanderson .20 .50
31 Ed Belfour .30 .75
32 Mike Modano .50 1.25
33 Joe Nieuwendyk .30 .75
34 Pierre Turgeon .30 .75
35 Sergei Fedorov .50 1.25
36 Dominik Hasek .50 1.25
37 Brett Hull .40 1.00
38 Luc Robitaille .30 .75
39 Brendan Shanahan .40 1.00
40 Steve Yzerman 1.00 2.50
41 Mike Comrie .25 .60
42 Tommy Salo .25 .60
43 Ryan Smyth .25 .60
44 Pavel Bure .40 1.00
45 Valeri Bure .20 .50
46 Roberto Luongo .50 1.25
47 Zigmund Palffy .30 .75
48 Felix Potvin .50 1.25
49 Manny Fernandez .25 .60
50 Marian Gaborik .50 1.25
51 Saku Koivu .30 .75
52 Yanic Perreault .20 .50
53 Jose Theodore .30 .75
54 Mike Dunham .25 .60
55 David Legwand .25 .60
56 Jason Arnott .25 .60
57 Martin Brodeur .60 1.50
58 Patrik Elias .30 .75
59 Mariusz Czerkawski .20 .50
60 Rick DiPietro .25 .60
61 Michael Peca .25 .60
62 Alexei Yashin .25 .60
63 Theo Fleury .40 1.00
64 Brian Leetch .30 .75
65 Eric Lindros .50 1.25
66 Mark Messier .50 1.25
67 Daniel Alfredsson .30 .75
68 Martin Havlat .25 .60
69 Marian Hossa .25 .60
70 Patrick Lalime .25 .60
71 Roman Cechmanek .25 .60
72 John LeClair .30 .75
73 Mark Recchi .40 1.00
74 Jeremy Roenick .30 .75
75 Sean Burke .20 .50
76 Daymond Langkow .25 .60
77 Johan Hedberg .25 .60
78 Alexei Kovalev .25 .60
79 Mario Lemieux 1.00 2.50
80 Martin Straka .20 .50
81 Brent Johnson .25 .60
82 Chris Pronger .25 .60
83 Keith Tkachuk .30 .75
84 Doug Weight .30 .75
85 Evgeni Nabokov .25 .60
86 Owen Nolan .30 .75
87 Teemu Selanne .60 1.50
88 Nikolai Khabibulin .30 .75
89 Vincent Lecavalier .25 .60
90 Brad Richards .30 .75
91 Curtis Joseph .30 .75
92 Alexander Mogilny .25 .60
93 Mats Sundin .30 .75
94 Markus Naslund .30 .75
95 Daniel Sedin .30 .75
96 Henrik Sedin .30 .75
97 Peter Bondra .30 .75
98 Jaromir Jagr .75 2.00
99 Olaf Kolzig .30 .75
100 Adam Oates .30 .75
101 Ilja Bryzgalov RC 8.00 20.00
102 Timo Parssinen RC 4.00 10.00
103 Dany Heatley 5.00 12.00
104 Ilya Kovalchuk RC 15.00 40.00
105 Kamil Piros RC 3.00 8.00
106 Erik Cole RC 6.00 15.00
107 Vaclav Nedorost RC 3.00 8.00
108 Pavel Datsyuk RC 12.00 30.00
109 Niklas Hagman RC 4.00 10.00
110 Kristian Huselius RC 5.00 12.00
111 Jaroslav Bednar RC 3.00 8.00
112 Pascal Dupuis RC 5.00 12.00
113 Martin Erat RC 5.00 12.00
114 Scott Clemmensen RC 3.00 8.00
115 Radek Martinek RC 3.00 8.00
116 Dan Blackburn RC 4.00 10.00
117 Ivan Ciernik RC 3.00 8.00
118 Chris Neil RC 4.00 10.00
119 Pavel Brendl 3.00 8.00
120 Jiri Dopita RC 3.00 8.00
121 Krystofer Kolanos RC 3.00 8.00
122 Mark Rycroft RC 4.00 10.00
123 Jeff Jillson RC 3.00 8.00
124 Nikita Alexeev RC 3.00 8.00
125 Brian Sutherby RC 3.00 8.00
NNO Johan Hedberg Promo .50 1.25
NNO Mats Sundin Promo .50 1.25
NNO Keith Tkachuk Promo .50 1.25

2001-02 Atomic Blue

*BLUE/60-97: 5X TO 12X BASIC CARDS
*BLUE/40-44: 6X TO 15X BASIC CARDS
*BLUE/30-39: 8X TO 20X BASIC CARDS
*BLUE/17-27: 10X TO 25X BASIC CARDS
STATED ODDS 1:161
BLUE PRINT RUN 1-97

2001-02 Atomic Gold

*1-100 GOLD/200: 4X TO 10X BASIC CARDS
GOLD/200 ODDS 2:21 HOBBY
66 Mark Messier 4.00 10.00

2001-02 Atomic Premiere Date

*1-100 VETS/90: 6X TO 15X BASIC CARDS
*101-125 ROOKIES/90: .5X TO 1.2X SP/500
PREM.DATE/90 ODDS 1:21 HOBBY PACKS
66 Mark Messier 6.00 15.00

2001-02 Atomic Red

*1-100 RED/290: 3X TO 8X BASIC CARDS
RED/290 ODDS 4:25 RETAIL
66 Mark Messier 3.00 8.00

2001-02 Atomic Blast

BLAST/55 ODDS 1:321 HOB/1:481 RET
1 Paul Kariya 8.00 20.00
2 Peter Forsberg 12.50 30.00
3 Joe Sakic 10.00 25.00
4 Steve Yzerman 25.00 60.00
5 Mike Comrie 8.00 20.00
6 Pavel Bure 8.00 20.00
7 Alexei Yashin 8.00 20.00
8 Eric Lindros 10.00 25.00
9 Mario Lemieux 30.00 80.00
10 Jaromir Jagr 8.00 20.00

2001-02 Atomic Core Players

COMPLETE SET (20) 30.00 80.00
STATED ODDS 1:21 HOB/1:25 RET
1 Paul Kariya 1.25 3.00
2 Joe Thornton 2.00 5.00
3 Patrick Roy 6.00 15.00
4 Mike Modano 1.25 3.00
5 Steve Yzerman 6.00 15.00
6 Pavel Bure 1.25 3.00
7 Zigmund Palffy 1.00 2.50
8 Marian Gaborik 2.50 6.00
9 Saku Koivu 1.25 3.00
10 Martin Brodeur 3.00 8.00
11 Alexei Yashin 1.00 2.50
12 Mark Messier 1.50 4.00
13 Marian Hossa 1.25 3.00
14 John LeClair 1.25 3.00
15 Mario Lemieux 8.00 20.00
16 Chris Pronger 1.00 2.50
17 Teemu Selanne 1.25 3.00
18 Vincent Lecavalier 1.25 3.00
19 Curtis Joseph 1.25 3.00
20 Jaromir Jagr 2.00 5.00

2001-02 Atomic Jerseys

STATED ODDS 3:21
1 Jean-Sebastien Giguere 4.00 10.00
2 Steve Rucchin 3.00 8.00
3 Byron Dafoe 3.00 8.00
4 Erik Rasmussen 3.00 8.00
5 Phil Housley 3.00 8.00
6 Marc Savard 4.00 10.00
7 Jeff Shantz 3.00 8.00
8 Tony Amonte 4.00 10.00
9 Eric Daze 3.00 8.00
10 Jocelyn Thibault 4.00 10.00
11 Peter Forsberg 6.00 15.00
12 Dave Reid 3.00 8.00
13 Patrick Roy 12.00 30.00
14 Joe Sakic 8.00 20.00
15 Lyle Odelein 3.00 8.00
16 Ed Belfour 5.00 12.00
17 Benoit Hogue 3.00 8.00
18 Jyrki Lumme 3.00 8.00
19 Mike Modano 5.00 12.00
20 Sergei Zubov 4.00 10.00
21 Mathieu Dandenault 3.00 8.00
22 Dominik Hasek 8.00 20.00
23 Darren McCarty 3.00 8.00
24 Chris Osgood 4.00 10.00
25 Brendan Shanahan 5.00 12.00
26 Steve Yzerman 10.00 25.00
27 Valeri Bure 3.00 8.00
28 Wade Flaherty 3.00 8.00
29 Felix Potvin 5.00 12.00
30 Sergei Zholtok 3.00 8.00
31 Benoit Brunet 3.00 8.00
32 Jeff Hackett 3.00 8.00
33 Saku Koivu 5.00 12.00
34 Mike Dunham 3.00 8.00
35 Tom Fitzgerald 3.00 8.00
36 Scott Walker 3.00 8.00
37 Scott Niedermayer 4.00 10.00
38 Mariusz Czerkawski 3.00 8.00
39 Chris Terreri 3.00 8.00
40 Guy Hebert 4.00 10.00
41 Mike York 3.00 8.00
42 Mika Alatalo 3.00 8.00
43 Rene Corbet 3.00 8.00
44 Jan Hrdina 3.00 8.00
45 Mario Lemieux 12.00 30.00
47 Teemu Selanne 5.00 12.00
48 Mats Sundin 4.00 10.00
49 Dimitri Yushkevich 3.00 8.00
50 Jaromir Jagr 6.00 15.00

2001-02 Atomic Patches
PATCH/16-503 ODDS 1:21 HOBBY
1 Jean-Sebastien Giguere/403 6.00 15.00
2 Steve Rucchin/303 6.00 15.00
3 Byron Dafoe/128 6.00 15.00
4 Erik Rasmussen/153 6.00 15.00
5 Phil Housley/106 6.00 15.00
6 Marc Savard/403 6.00 15.00
7 Jeff Shantz/203 6.00 15.00
8 Tony Amonte/403 6.00 15.00
9 Eric Daze/328 6.00 15.00
10 Jocelyn Thibault/328 6.00 15.00
12 Dave Reid/328 6.00 15.00
13 Patrick Roy/53 40.00 100.00
14 Joe Sakic/303 10.00 25.00
15 Lyle Odelein/153 8.00 20.00
16 Ed Belfour/48 20.00 50.00
17 Benoit Hogue/123 6.00 15.00
18 Jyrki Lumme/303 6.00 15.00
19 Mike Modano/128 12.00 30.00
20 Sergei Zubov/268 6.00 15.00
21 Mathieu Dandenault/178 6.00 15.00
22 Dominik Hasek/283 10.00 25.00
23 Darren McCarty/16 20.00 50.00
24 Chris Osgood/203 6.00 15.00
26 Steve Yzerman/53 30.00 80.00
27 Valeri Bure/428 6.00 15.00
28 Wade Flaherty/302 6.00 15.00
29 Felix Potvin/103 10.00 25.00
30 Sergei Zholtok/138 6.00 15.00
33 Saku Koivu/53 15.00 40.00
34 Mike Dunham/193 6.00 15.00
35 Tom Fitzgerald/378 6.00 15.00
36 Scott Walker/428 6.00 15.00
37 Scott Niedermayer/478 6.00 15.00
38 Mariusz Czerkawski/503 6.00 15.00
39 Chris Terreri/153 6.00 15.00
40 Guy Hebert/115 6.00 15.00
41 Mike York/403 6.00 15.00
42 Mika Alatalo/228 6.00 15.00
43 Rene Corbet/53 12.00 30.00
44 Jan Hrdina/353 6.00 15.00
46 Kevin Stevens/353 6.00 15.00
47 Teemu Selanne/153 8.00 20.00
48 Mats Sundin/203 8.00 20.00
49 Dimitri Yushkevich/128 6.00 15.00
50 Jaromir Jagr/78 15.00 40.00

2001-02 Atomic Power Play
COMPLETE SET (36) 15.00 30.00
STATED ODDS 1:1
1 Paul Kariya .50 1.25
2 Patrik Stefan .30 .75
3 Sergei Samsonov .40 1.00
4 Joe Thornton .75 2.00
5 Jarome Iginla .50 1.25
6 Jeff O'Neill .30 .75
7 Tony Amonte .40 1.00
8 Peter Forsberg .50 1.25
9 Milan Hejduk .50 1.25
10 Joe Sakic 1.00 2.50
11 Mike Modano .50 1.25
12 Sergei Fedorov .75 2.00
13 Brendan Shanahan .50 1.25
14 Steve Yzerman 2.50 6.00
15 Mike Comrie .40 1.00
16 Pavel Bure .50 1.25
17 Zigmund Palffy .40 1.00
18 Marian Gaborik 1.25 3.00
19 Saku Koivu .50 1.25
20 Jason Arnott .30 .75
21 Alexei Yashin .30 .75
22 Theo Fleury .30 .75
23 Eric Lindros .50 1.25
24 Mark Messier .50 1.25
25 Marian Hossa .50 1.25
26 John LeClair .50 1.25
27 Mario Lemieux 3.00 8.00
28 Chris Pronger .40 1.00
29 Keith Tkachuk .50 1.25
30 Teemu Selanne .50 1.25
31 Vincent Lecavalier .50 1.25
32 Mats Sundin .50 1.25
33 Daniel Sedin .30 .75
34 Henrik Sedin .30 .75
35 Peter Bondra .50 1.25
36 Jaromir Jagr .75 2.00

2001-02 Atomic Rookie Reaction
COMPLETE SET (10) 10.00 25.00
STATED ODDS 1:41
1 Dany Heatley 2.00 5.00
2 Ilya Kovalchuk 6.00 15.00
3 Vaclav Nedorost .40 1.00
4 Rostislav Klesla .75 2.00
5 Rick DiPietro 2.00 5.00
6 Pavel Brendl .40 1.00
7 Jiri Dopita .40 1.00
8 Kris Beech .40 1.00
9 Johan Hedberg .75 2.00
10 Nikita Alexeev .40 1.00

2001-02 Atomic Statosphere
COMPLETE SET (20) 40.00 80.00
STATED ODDS 1:21 HOB/1:25 RET
1-10 ISSUED IN HOBBY PACKS
11-20 ISSUED IN RETAIL PACKS
1 Patrick Roy 6.00 15.00
2 Ed Belfour 1.25 3.00
3 Dominik Hasek 2.50 6.00
4 Martin Brodeur 3.00 8.00
5 Rick DiPietro 1.00 2.50
6 Mike Richter 1.25 3.00
7 Roman Cechmanek 1.00 2.50
8 Johan Hedberg 1.00 2.50
9 Evgeni Nabokov 1.00 2.50
10 Curtis Joseph 1.25 3.00
11 Peter Forsberg 3.00 8.00
12 Joe Sakic 2.50 6.00
13 Brett Hull 1.50 4.00
14 Pavel Bure 1.50 4.00
15 Zigmund Palffy 1.00 2.50
16 Alexei Yashin 1.00 2.50
17 Alexei Kovalev 1.00 2.50
18 Mario Lemieux 8.00 20.00
19 Martin Straka 1.00 2.50
20 Jaromir Jagr 2.00 5.00

2001-02 Atomic Team Nucleus
COMPLETE SET (15) 30.00 60.00
STATED ODDS 1:21 HOB/1:25 RET
1 Boston Bruins 2.00 5.00
2 Calgary Flames 2.00 5.00
3 Carolina Hurricanes 2.00 5.00
4 Colorado Avalanche 4.00 10.00
5 Dallas Stars 2.00 5.00
6 Detroit Red Wings 4.00 10.00
7 Edmonton Oilers 2.00 5.00
8 New Jersey Devils 2.00 5.00
9 New York Islanders 2.00 5.00
10 New York Rangers 2.00 5.00
11 Pittsburgh Penguins 2.00 5.00
12 San Jose Sharks 2.00 5.00
13 Toronto Maple Leafs 2.00 5.00
14 Vancouver Canucks 2.00 5.00
15 Washington Capitals 2.00 5.00

2001-02 Atomic Toronto Fall Expo
Available only by wrapper redemption at the 2001 Toronto Fall Expo, this 25-card set paralleled the Atomic rookies, but carried a Fall Expo gold stamp. Each card was serial numbered out of 500.
COMPLETE SET (25) 30.00 80.00
*EXPO/500: .3X TO .8X BASIC RC/500
STATED PRINT RUN 500 SETS

2002-03 Atomic
Released in mid-November, this 125-card set sported a die-cut design. Cards 101-125 were shortprinted to just 1300 copies each. Cards 126-131 were available in packs of Private Stock Reserve at a rate of 1:9 hobby packs and 1:49 retail.
101-125 ROOKIE SP PRINT RUN 1300
1 Jean-Sebastien Giguere .25 .60
2 Paul Kariya .30 .75
3 Adam Oates .25 .60
4 Dany Heatley .25 .60
5 Ilya Kovalchuk .30 .75
6 Glen Murray .20 .50
7 Sergei Samsonov .20 .50
8 Joe Thornton .30 .75
9 Martin Biron .20 .50
10 J-P Dumont .15 .40
11 Miroslav Satan .25 .60
12 Craig Conroy .15 .40
13 Jarome Iginla .25 .60
14 Roman Turek .25 .60
15 Erik Cole .20 .50
16 Ron Francis .30 .75
17 Arturs Irbe .20 .50
18 Jeff O'Neill .15 .40
19 Mark Bell .15 .40
20 Eric Daze .15 .40
21 Jocelyn Thibault .20 .50
22 Rob Blake .25 .60
23 Chris Drury .25 .60
24 Peter Forsberg .30 .75
25 Steven Reinprecht .15 .40
26 Patrick Roy .60 1.50
27 Joe Sakic .40 1.00
28 Marc Denis .20 .50
29 Espen Knutsen .15 .40
30 Ray Whitney .20 .50
31 Jason Arnott .20 .50
32 Bill Guerin .25 .60
33 Mike Modano .40 1.00
34 Marty Turco .25 .60
35 Pavel Datsyuk .30 .75
36 Sergei Fedorov .40 1.00
37 Brett Hull .30 .75
38 Curtis Joseph .25 .60
39 Nicklas Lidstrom .25 .60
40 Brendan Shanahan .30 .75
41 Steve Yzerman .50 1.25
42 Mike Comrie .25 .60
43 Tommy Salo .20 .50
44 Ryan Smyth .20 .50
45 Kristian Huselius .15 .40
46 Roberto Luongo .40 1.00
47 Stephen Weiss .25 .60
48 Jason Allison .20 .50
49 Zigmund Palffy .25 .60
50 Felix Potvin .40 1.00
51 Andrew Brunette .15 .40
52 Manny Fernandez .20 .50
53 Marian Gaborik .40 1.00
54 Doug Gilmour .30 .75
55 Saku Koivu .25 .60
56 Yanic Perreault .15 .40
57 Jose Theodore .25 .60
58 Denis Arkhipov .15 .40
59 Mike Dunham .20 .50
60 Martin Brodeur .50 1.25
61 Patrik Elias .25 .60
62 Joe Nieuwendyk .25 .60
63 Chris Osgood .25 .60
64 Michael Peca .20 .50
65 Alexei Yashin .20 .50
66 Dan Blackburn .20 .50
67 Pavel Bure .30 .75
68 Eric Lindros .40 1.00
69 Mike Richter .25 .60
70 Daniel Alfredsson .25 .60
71 Marian Hossa .20 .50
72 Patrick Lalime .20 .50
73 Roman Cechmanek .20 .50
74 Simon Gagne .25 .60
75 Jeremy Roenick .25 .60
76 Tony Amonte .20 .50
77 Daniel Briere .20 .50
78 Sean Burke .15 .40
79 Johan Hedberg .25 .60
80 Mario Lemieux .75 2.00
81 Alexei Morozov .15 .40
82 Brent Johnson .20 .50
83 Chris Pronger .20 .50
84 Keith Tkachuk .25 .60
85 Patrick Marleau .25 .60
86 Evgeni Nabokov .20 .50
87 Owen Nolan .25 .60
88 Teemu Selanne .50 1.25
89 Nikolai Khabibulin .25 .60
90 Vincent Lecavalier .20 .50
91 Ed Belfour .25 .60
92 Alexander Mogilny .20 .50
93 Gary Roberts .15 .40
94 Mats Sundin .25 .60
95 Todd Bertuzzi .25 .60
96 Dan Cloutier .20 .50
97 Markus Naslund .20 .50
98 Peter Bondra .25 .60
99 Jaromir Jagr .60 1.50
100 Olaf Kolzig .25 .60
101 Stanislav Chistov RC .75 2.00
102 Martin Gerber RC 1.25 3.00
103 Alexei Smirnov RC 1.00 2.50
104 Chuck Kobasew RC 1.00 2.50
105 Rick Nash RC 6.00 15.00
106 Dmitri Bykov RC .75 2.00
107 Henrik Zetterberg RC 8.00 20.00
108 Kari Haakana RC .75 2.00
109 Ales Hemsky RC 3.00 8.00
110 Alex Henry RC 1.00 2.50
111 Jay Bouwmeester RC 2.50 6.00
112 Alexander Frolov RC 1.50 4.00
113 P-M Bouchard RC 1.25 3.00
114 Sylvain Blouin RC .75 2.00
115 Ron Hainsey RC .75 2.00
116 Adam Hall RC .75 2.00
117 Scottie Upshall RC 1.00 2.50
118 Mike Danton .75 2.00
119 Ray Schultz RC .75 2.00
120 Anton Volchenkov RC .75 2.00
121 Dennis Seidenberg RC 1.25 3.00
122 Patrick Sharp RC 2.50 6.00
123 Dick Tarnstrom RC .75 2.00
124 Alexander Svitov RC .75 2.00
125 Steve Eminger RC .75 2.00
126 Jordan Leopold RC 1.25 3.00
127 Stephane Veilleux RC .75 2.00
128 Jason Spezza RC 5.00 12.00
129 Radovan Somik RC .75 2.00
130 Jeff Taffe RC .75 2.00
131 Tom Koivisto RC .75 2.00

2002-03 Atomic Blue
*1-100 VETS/175: 2X TO 5X BASIC CARDS
*101-125 ROOKIES/175: .5X TO 1.2X
BLUE/175 ODDS 1:6 US

2002-03 Atomic Gold
*1-100 VETS/99: 2.5X TO 6X BASIC CARDS
*101-125 ROOKIES/99: .6X TO 1.5X
GOLD/99 ODDS 1:11 HOBBY

2002-03 Atomic Red
*1-100 VETS/125: 2.5X TO 6X BASIC CARDS
*101-25 ROOKIES/125: .6X TO 1.5X
RED/125 STATED ODDS 1:6

2002-03 Atomic Cold Fusion
COMPLETE SET (24) 30.00 60.00
STATED ODDS 1:11
1 Paul Kariya .75 2.00
2 Dany Heatley 1.00 2.50
3 Ilya Kovalchuk 1.00 2.50
4 Joe Thornton 1.25 3.00
5 Jarome Iginla 1.00 2.50
6 Jeff O'Neill .60 1.50
7 Eric Daze .60 1.50
8 Peter Forsberg 2.00 5.00
9 Joe Sakic 1.50 4.00
10 Pavel Datsyuk .75 2.00
11 Brendan Shanahan 1.25 3.00
12 Steve Yzerman 3.00 8.00
13 Mike Comrie .60 1.50
14 Kristian Huselius .60 1.50
15 Saku Koivu .75 2.00
16 Pavel Bure 1.00 2.50
17 Eric Lindros .75 2.00
18 Daniel Alfredsson .60 1.50
19 Simon Gagne .75 2.00
20 Mario Lemieux 5.00 12.00
21 Teemu Selanne .75 2.00
22 Mats Sundin .75 2.00
23 Markus Naslund .75 2.00
24 Jaromir Jagr 1.25 3.00

2002-03 Atomic Denied
COMPLETE SET (20) 15.00 40.00
STATED ODDS 1:41
1 Jean-Sebastien Giguere .75 2.00
2 Roman Turek .75 2.00
3 Arturs Irbe .75 2.00
4 Jocelyn Thibault .75 2.00
5 Patrick Roy 5.00 12.00
6 Marty Turco .75 2.00
7 Curtis Joseph 1.00 2.50
8 Roberto Luongo 1.50 4.00
9 Felix Potvin 1.00 2.50
10 Jose Theodore 1.00 2.50
11 Martin Brodeur 2.50 6.00
12 Chris Osgood .75 2.00
13 Mike Richter .75 2.00
14 Patrick Lalime .75 2.00
15 Roman Cechmanek .75 2.00
16 Sean Burke .75 2.00
17 Brent Johnson .75 2.00
18 Evgeni Nabokov .75 2.00
19 Nikolai Khabibulin 1.00 2.50
20 Ed Belfour 1.00 2.50

2002-03 Atomic Hobby Parallel
*1-100 VETS/775: 1.2X TO 3X BASIC CARDS
*101-125 ROOKIES/775: .4X TO 1X
HOBBY/775 STATED ODDS 3:4

2002-03 Atomic Jerseys
OVERALL STATED ODDS 4:21
*GOLD/25: 1.2X TO 3X BASIC JSY
GOLD PRINT RUN 25 SER.#'d SETS
*PATCH/164-339: .8X TO 2X BASIC JSY
*PATCH/61-70: 1X TO 2.5X BASIC JSY
PATCH STATED PRINT RUN 61-339
1 Adam Oates 2.50 6.00
2 Roman Turek 2.50 6.00
3 Jason Arnott 2.50 6.00
4 Bill Guerin 2.50 6.00
5 Scott Young 2.50 6.00
6 Dominik Hasek 8.00 20.00
7 Brett Hull 4.00 10.00
8 Curtis Joseph 3.00 8.00
9 Luc Robitaille 3.00 8.00
10 Ryan Smyth 2.50 6.00
11 Jose Theodore 6.00 15.00
12 Jeff Friesen 2.50 6.00
13 Oleg Tverdovsky 2.50 6.00
14 Alexei Yashin 2.50 6.00
15 Pavel Bure 4.00 10.00
16 Mark Messier 4.00 10.00
17 John LeClair 2.50 6.00
18 Daymond Langkow 2.50 6.00
19 Mario Lemieux 12.00 30.00
20 Pavol Demitra 2.50 6.00
21 Ray Ferraro 2.50 6.00
22 Tom Barrasso 3.00 8.00
23 Darcy Tucker 2.50 6.00
24 Jaromir Jagr 8.00 20.00
25 Robert Lang 2.50 6.00

2002-03 Atomic National Pride
COMP.CANADA SET (10) 20.00 40.00
COMP.US SET (10) 8.00 15.00
OVERALL STATED ODDS 1:21
C1-C10 ISSUED IN CANADA PACKS
U1-U10 ISSUED IN US PACKS
C1 Paul Kariya .75 2.00
C2 Jarome Iginla 1.00 2.50
C3 Rob Blake .60 1.50
C4 Joe Sakic 1.50 4.00
C5 Curtis Joseph .75 2.00
C6 Brendan Shanahan 1.00 2.50
C7 Steve Yzerman 4.00 10.00
C8 Martin Brodeur 2.00 5.00
C9 Mario Lemieux 5.00 12.00
C10 Chris Pronger .60 1.50
U1 Bill Guerin .60 1.50
U2 Mike Modano 1.25 3.00
U3 Chris Chelios .75 2.00
U4 Brett Hull 1.00 2.50
U5 Brian Leetch .60 1.50
U6 Mike Richter .60 1.50
U7 Jeremy Roenick 1.00 2.50
U0 Tony Amonte .80 1.50
U9 Keith Tkachuk .75 2.00
U10 Tom Barrasso .60 1.50

2002-03 Atomic Power Converters
COMPLETE SET (20) 15.00 40.00
STATED ODDS 1:21
1 Dany Heatley 1.50 4.00
2 Ilya Kovalchuk 1.50 4.00
3 Miroslav Satan 1.25 3.00
4 Jarome Iginla 1.50 4.00
5 Ron Francis 1.25 3.00
6 Sami Kapanen .75 2.00
7 Nicklas Lidstrom 1.25 3.00
8 Luc Robitaille 1.25 3.00
9 Jason Allison .75 2.00
10 Zigmund Palffy .75 2.00
11 Andrew Brunette .75 2.00
12 Alexei Yashin .75 2.00
13 Pavel Bure 1.25 3.00
14 Eric Lindros 1.25 3.00
15 Daniel Briere .75 2.00
16 Pavol Demitra .75 2.00
17 Keith Tkachuk 1.25 3.00
18 Todd Bertuzzi 1.25 3.00
19 Markus Naslund 1.25 3.00
20 Peter Bondra 1.25 3.00

2002-03 Atomic Super Colliders
COMPLETE SET (16) 12.00 30.00
STATED ODDS 1:21
1 Ilya Kovalchuk 2.00 5.00
2 Joe Thornton 2.00 5.00
3 Jarome Iginla 2.00 5.00
4 Erik Cole .75 2.00
5 Jason Arnott .75 2.00
6 Brendan Shanahan 1.25 3.00
7 Ryan Smyth .75 2.00
8 Jason Allison .75 2.00
9 Michael Peca .75 2.00
10 Eric Lindros 1.25 3.00
11 Jeremy Roenick 1.25 3.00
12 Chris Pronger .75 2.00
13 Keith Tkachuk .75 2.00
14 Owen Nolan .75 2.00
15 Gary Roberts .75 2.00
16 Todd Bertuzzi 1.25 3.00

1998-99 Aurora
The 1998-99 Pacific Aurora set was issued in one series with a total of 200 standard size cards. The six-card packs retail for $2.99 each. The fronts feature color game-action photos with a smaller head-shot of the featured player in the upper right hand corner. The super-thick card also offers a challenging trivia question on the back.
COMPLETE SET (200) 25.00 50.00
1 Travis Green .12 .30
2 Guy Hebert .15 .40
3 Paul Kariya .25 .60
4 Steve Rucchin .12 .30
5 Tomas Sandstrom .12 .30
6 Teemu Selanne .40 1.00
7 Jason Allison .15 .40
8 Ray Bourque .30 .75
9 Anson Carter .15 .40
10 Byron Dafoe .15 .40
11 Ted Donato .12 .30
12 Dave Ellett .15 .40
13 Dimitri Khristich .12 .30
14 Sergei Samsonov .15 .40
15 Matthew Barnaby .12 .30
16 Michal Grosek .12 .30
17 Dominik Hasek .40 1.00
18 Brian Holzinger .12 .30
19 Michael Peca .12 .30
20 Miroslav Satan .15 .40
21 Dixon Ward .15 .40
22 Alexei Zhitnik .12 .30
23 Andrew Cassels .12 .30
24 Theo Fleury .25 .60
25 Jarome Iginla .40 1.00
26 Marty McInnis .12 .30
27 Derek Morris .12 .30
28 Michael Nylander .15 .40
29 Cory Stillman .12 .30
30 Kevin Dineen .12 .30
31 Nelson Emerson .12 .30
32 Martin Gelinas .12 .30
33 Sami Kapanen .12 .30
34 Trevor Kidd .12 .30
35 Robert Kron .12 .30
36 Jeff O'Neill .12 .30
37 Keith Primeau .12 .30
38 Tony Amonte .15 .40
39 Chris Chelios .20 .50
40 Eric Daze .15 .40
41 Jeff Hackett .12 .30
42 Jean-Yves Leroux .15 .40
43 Jeff Shantz .12 .30
44 Alexei Zhamnov .12 .30
45 Adam Deadmarsh .12 .30
46 Peter Forsberg 1.00 2.50
47 Valeri Kamensky .12 .30
48 Claude Lemieux .15 .40
49 Eric Messier .12 .30
50 Sandis Ozolinsh .12 .30
51 Patrick Roy 1.00 2.50
52 Joe Sakic .30 .75
53 Ed Belfour .20 .50
54 Derian Hatcher .12 .30
55 Brett Hull .30 .75
56 Jamie Langenbrunner .12 .30
57 Jere Lehtinen .15 .40
58 Mike Modano .30 .75
59 Joe Nieuwendyk .20 .50
60 Darryl Sydor .12 .30
61 Sergei Zubov .12 .30
62 Sergei Fedorov .30 .75
63 Vyacheslav Kozlov .15 .40
64 Igor Larionov .20 .50
65 Nicklas Lidstrom .25 .60
66 Darren McCarty .12 .30
67 Chris Osgood .20 .50
68 Brendan Shanahan .25 .60
69 Steve Yzerman .60 1.50
70 Kelly Buchberger .12 .30
71 Mike Grier .12 .30
72 Bill Guerin .20 .50
73 Roman Hamrlik .12 .30
74 Boris Mironov .12 .30
75 Janne Niinimaa .12 .30
76 Ryan Smyth .15 .40
77 Doug Weight .20 .50
78 Dino Ciccarelli .20 .50
79 Dave Gagner .12 .30
80 Ed Jovanovski .15 .40
81 Viktor Kozlov .15 .40
82 Paul Laus .15 .40
83 Scott Mellanby .12 .30
84 Ray Whitney .12 .30
85 Rob Blake .20 .50
86 Stephane Fiset .15 .40
87 Yanic Perreault .12 .30
88 Luc Robitaille .20 .50
89 Jamie Storr .15 .40
90 Jozef Stumpel .15 .40
91 Vladimir Tsyplakov .12 .30
92 Shayne Corson .15 .40
93 Vincent Damphousse .15 .40
94 Saku Koivu .20 .50
95 Mark Recchi .25 .60
96 Martin Rucinsky .12 .30
97 Brian Savage .12 .30
98 Jocelyn Thibault .15 .40
99 Andrew Brunette .15 .40
100 Mike Dunham .15 .40
101 Tom Fitzgerald .15 .40
102 Sergei Krivokrasov .12 .30
103 Denny Lambert .15 .40
104 Mikhail Shtalenkov .12 .30
105 Darren Turcotte .15 .40
106 Dave Andreychuk .20 .50
107 Jason Arnott .15 .40
108 Martin Brodeur .40 1.00
109 Patrik Elias .20 .50
110 Bobby Holik .12 .30
111 Randy McKay .15 .40
112 Scott Niedermayer .20 .50
113 Scott Stevens .20 .50
114 Bryan Berard .15 .40
115 Jason Dawe .12 .30
116 Trevor Linden .15 .40
117 Zigmund Palffy .20 .50
118 Robert Reichel .12 .30
119 Tommy Salo .15 .40
120 Bryan Smolinski .12 .30
121 Adam Graves .12 .30
122 Wayne Gretzky 1.50 4.00
123 Alexei Kovalev .12 .30
124 Brian Leetch .20 .50
125 Mike Richter .20 .50
126 Ulf Samuelsson .15 .40
127 Kevin Stevens .12 .30
128 Daniel Alfredsson .20 .50
129 Andreas Dackell .12 .30
130 Igor Kravchuk .12 .30
131 Shawn McEachern .12 .30
132 Chris Phillips .12 .30
133 Damian Rhodes .20 .50
134 Alexei Yashin .15 .40
135 Rod Brind'Amour .20 .50
136 Alexandre Daigle .12 .30
137 Eric Desjardins .15 .40
138 Chris Gratton .15 .40
139 Ron Hextall .20 .50
140 John LeClair .20 .50
141 Eric Lindros .30 .75
142 John Vanbiesbrouck .15 .40
143 Dainius Zubrus .12 .30
144 Brad Isbister .12 .30
145 Nikolai Khabibulin .20 .50
146 Jeremy Roenick .30 .75
147 Cliff Ronning .12 .30
148 Keith Tkachuk .20 .50
149 Rick Tocchet .15 .40
150 Oleg Tverdovsky .20 .50
151 Stu Barnes .12 .30
152 Tom Barrasso .15 .40
153 Kevin Hatcher .12 .30
154 Jaromir Jagr .50 1.25
155 Darius Kasparaitis .12 .30
156 Alexei Morozov .12 .30
157 Martin Straka .12 .30
158 Jim Campbell .12 .30
159 Geoff Courtnall .15 .40
160 Grant Fuhr .20 .50
161 Al MacInnis .20 .50
162 Jamie McLennan .15 .40
163 Chris Pronger .15 .40
164 Pierre Turgeon .20 .50
165 Tony Twist .12 .30
166 Jeff Friesen .12 .30
167 Tony Granato .12 .30
168 Patrick Marleau .20 .50
169 Marty McSorley .12 .30
170 Owen Nolan .20 .50
171 Marco Sturm .12 .30
172 Mike Vernon .15 .40
173 Karl Dykhuis .12 .30
174 Mikael Renberg .15 .40
175 Stephane Richer .12 .30
176 Alexander Selivanov .12 .30
177 Paul Ysebaert .12 .30
178 Rob Zamuner .12 .30
179 Sergei Berezin .15 .40
180 Tie Domi .15 .40
181 Mike Johnson .12 .30
182 Curtis Joseph .20 .50
183 Igor Korolev .12 .30
184 Mathieu Schneider .12 .30
185 Mats Sundin .20 .50
186 Todd Bertuzzi .20 .50
187 Donald Brashear .12 .30
188 Pavel Bure .25 .60
189 Mark Messier .30 .75
190 Alexander Mogilny .15 .40
191 Mattias Ohlund .12 .30
192 Garth Snow .15 .40
193 Brian Bellows .15 .40
194 Peter Bondra .15 .40
195 Sergei Gonchar .12 .30
196 Calle Johansson .12 .30
197 Joe Juneau .15 .40
198 Olaf Kolzig .20 .50
199 Adam Oates .20 .50
200 Richard Zednik .12 .30
S108 Martin Brodeur SAMPLE .40 1.00

1998-99 Aurora Atomic Laser Cuts
COMPLETE SET (20) 25.00 50.00
STATED ODDS 4:37 HOBBY
1 Paul Kariya .75 2.00
2 Teemu Selanne .75 2.00
3 Sergei Samsonov .60 1.50
4 Dominik Hasek 1.50 4.00
5 Peter Forsberg 2.00 5.00
6 Patrick Roy 4.00 10.00
7 Joe Sakic 1.50 4.00
8 Mike Modano 1.25 3.00
9 Sergei Fedorov 1.25 3.00
10 Brendan Shanahan .75 2.00
11 Steve Yzerman 4.00 10.00
12 Martin Brodeur 2.00 5.00
13 Wayne Gretzky 5.00 12.00
14 John LeClair .75 2.00
15 Eric Lindros .75 2.00
16 Jaromir Jagr 1.25 3.00
17 Mats Sundin .75 2.00
18 Pavel Bure .75 2.00
19 Mark Messier .75 2.00
20 Peter Bondra .60 1.50

1998-99 Aurora Championship Fever
COMPLETE SET (50) 15.00 40.00
STATED ODDS 1:1
*COPPER/20: 10X TO 25X BASIC INSERTS
*ICE BLUE/100: 5X TO 12X BASIC INSERTS
*RED: .8X TO 2X BASIC INSERTS
RED STATED ODDS 1:4 TREAT
*SILVER/250: 2X TO 5X BASIC INSERTS
1 Paul Kariya .40 1.00
2 Teemu Selanne .40 1.00
3 Ray Bourque .50 1.25
4 Byron Dafoe .25 .60
5 Sergei Samsonov .30 .75
6 Dominik Hasek .60 1.50
7 Michael Peca .30 .75
8 Theo Fleury .30 .75
9 Keith Primeau .30 .75
10 Chris Chelios .40 1.00
11 Peter Forsberg .40 1.00
12 Patrick Roy 1.50 4.00
13 Joe Sakic .60 1.50
14 Ed Belfour .40 1.00
15 Mike Modano .50 1.25
16 Sergei Fedorov .50 1.25
17 Nicklas Lidstrom .40 1.00
18 Chris Osgood .30 .75
19 Brendan Shanahan .40 1.00
20 Steve Yzerman 1.50 4.00
21 Doug Weight .30 .75
22 Dino Ciccarelli .30 .75
23 Rob Blake .30 .75
24 Saku Koivu .30 .75
25 Mark Recchi .25 .60
26 Martin Brodeur .75 2.00
27 Patrik Elias .30 .75
28 Trevor Linden .30 .75
29 Zigmund Palffy .30 .75
30 Wayne Gretzky 2.00 5.00
31 Mike Richter .40 1.00
32 Daniel Alfredsson .30 .75
33 Damian Rhodes .25 .60
34 Alexei Yashin .30 .75
35 John LeClair .30 .75
36 Eric Lindros .40 1.00
37 Dainius Zubrus .30 .75
38 Keith Tkachuk .30 .75
39 Tom Barrasso .30 .75
40 Jaromir Jagr .50 1.25
41 Grant Fuhr .30 .75
42 Pierre Turgeon .30 .75
43 Patrick Marleau .30 .75
44 Mike Vernon .30 .75
45 Rob Zamuner .25 .60
46 Mats Sundin .30 .75
47 Pavel Bure .40 1.00
48 Mark Messier .40 1.00
49 Peter Bondra .25 .60
50 Olaf Kolzig .30 .75
NNO M.Brodeur Gold AU/97 75.00 150.00

1998-99 Aurora Cubes
COMPLETE SET (20) 40.00 100.00
ONE PER HOBBY BOX
1 Paul Kariya 1.50 4.00
2 Teemu Selanne 1.50 4.00
3 Dominik Hasek 3.00 8.00
4 Peter Forsberg 3.00 8.00
5 Patrick Roy 6.00 15.00
6 Joe Sakic 3.00 8.00
7 Mike Modano 2.50 6.00
8 Sergei Fedorov 2.50 6.00
9 Brendan Shanahan 1.50 4.00
10 Steve Yzerman 5.00 12.00
11 Martin Brodeur 4.00 10.00
12 Wayne Gretzky 8.00 20.00
13 John LeClair 1.50 4.00
14 Eric Lindros 1.50 4.00
15 Jaromir Jagr 2.50 6.00
16 Mats Sundin 1.50 4.00
17 Pavel Bure 1.50 4.00
18 Mark Messier 1.50 4.00
19 Peter Bondra 1.25 3.00
20 Olaf Kolzig 1.25 3.00

1998-99 Aurora Front Line Copper
COPPER/80 ODDS 1:97 CANADIAN
*ICE BLUE/15: .8X TO 2X COPPER/80
1 Dominik Hasek 15.00 40.00
2 Peter Forsberg 10.00 25.00
3 Patrick Roy 25.00 60.00
4 Joe Sakic 15.00 40.00
5 Steve Yzerman 25.00 60.00
6 Daniel Alfredsson 10.00 25.00
7 Eric Lindros 12.00 30.00
8 Jaromir Jagr 12.00 30.00
9 Wayne Gretzky 40.00 100.00
10 Tie Domi 8.00 20.00

1998-99 Aurora Man Advantage
COMPLETE SET (20) 50.00 100.00
STATED ODDS 1:73
1 Paul Kariya 2.00 5.00
2 Teemu Selanne 2.00 5.00
3 Ray Bourque 3.00 8.00
4 Michael Peca .75 2.00
5 Peter Forsberg 5.00 12.00
6 Joe Sakic 4.00 10.00
7 Mike Modano 3.00 8.00
8 Joe Nieuwendyk 1.50 4.00
9 Brendan Shanahan 2.00 5.00
10 Steve Yzerman 10.00 25.00
11 Shayne Corson .75 2.00
12 Zigmund Palffy 1.50 4.00
13 Wayne Gretzky 12.50 30.00
14 John LeClair 2.00 5.00
15 Eric Lindros 2.00 5.00
16 Jaromir Jagr 3.00 8.00
17 Mats Sundin 2.00 5.00
18 Pavel Bure 2.00 5.00
19 Mark Messier 2.00 5.00
20 Peter Bondra 1.50 4.00

1998-99 Aurora NHL Command
STATED ODDS 1:361
1 Teemu Selanne 3.00 8.00
2 Dominik Hasek 6.00 15.00
3 Peter Forsberg 8.00 20.00
4 Patrick Roy 15.00 40.00
5 Mike Modano 5.00 12.00
6 Steve Yzerman 15.00 40.00
7 Martin Brodeur 8.00 20.00
8 Wayne Gretzky 20.00 50.00
9 Eric Lindros 3.00 8.00
10 Jaromir Jagr 5.00 12.00

1999-00 Aurora
Cards feature one large color action photo, and one small color action photo on each cardfront. Card backs feature current statistics with another color action photo. Cardstock is thicker than most cards and were available at both hobby and retail outlets.
*STRIPED: .4X TO 1X BASIC CARDS
1 Guy Hebert .20 .50
2 Paul Kariya .25 .60
3 Marty McInnis .12 .30
4 Steve Rucchin .12 .30
5 Teemu Selanne .40 1.00
6 Andrew Brunette .12 .30
7 Kelly Buchberger .12 .30
8 Damian Rhodes .12 .30
9 Jason Allison .15 .40
10 Ray Bourque .30 .75
11 Anson Carter .15 .40
12 Byron Dafoe .12 .30
13 Sergei Samsonov .15 .40
14 Joe Thornton .30 .75
15 Curtis Brown .12 .30
16 Dominik Hasek .30 .75
17 Joe Juneau .15 .40
18 Michael Peca .15 .40
19 Miroslav Satan .15 .40
20 Valeri Bure .12 .30
21 Jean-Sebastien Giguere .20 .50
22 Phil Housley .12 .30
23 Jarome Iginla .20 .50
24 Cory Stillman .12 .30
25 Ron Francis .25 .60
26 Arturs Irbe .15 .40
27 Sami Kapanen .12 .30
28 Keith Primeau .12 .30
29 Ray Sheppard .12 .30
30 Tony Amonte .15 .40
31 J-P Dumont .15 .40
32 Doug Gilmour .25 .60
33 Jocelyn Thibault .15 .40
34 Alexei Zhamnov .12 .30
35 Adam Deadmarsh .12 .30
36 Chris Drury .15 .40
37 Theo Fleury .25 .60
38 Peter Forsberg .20 .50
39 Milan Hejduk .15 .40
40 Claude Lemieux .15 .40
41 Patrick Roy .75 2.00
42 Joe Sakic .30 .75
43 Ed Belfour .20 .50
44 Brett Hull .30 .75
45 Jamie Langenbrunner .12 .30
46 Jere Lehtinen .15 .40
47 Mike Modano .30 .75
48 Joe Nieuwendyk .20 .50
49 Chris Chelios .20 .50
50 Sergei Fedorov .30 .75
51 Nicklas Lidstrom .20 .50
52 Darren McCarty .12 .30
53 Chris Osgood .20 .50
54 Brendan Shanahan .25 .60
55 Steve Yzerman .60 1.50
56 Bill Guerin .20 .50
57 Mike Grier .12 .30
58 Tommy Salo .15 .40
59 Ryan Smyth .15 .40
60 Doug Weight .20 .50
61 Pavel Bure .25 .60
62 Sean Burke .12 .30
63 Viktor Kozlov .12 .30
64 Rob Niedermayer .12 .30
65 Mark Parrish .12 .30
66 Ray Whitney .15 .40
67 Donald Audette .12 .30
68 Rob Blake .20 .50
69 Zigmund Palffy .20 .50
70 Luc Robitaille .20 .50
71 Jamie Storr .12 .30
72 Jozef Stumpel .12 .30
73 Shayne Corson .12 .30
74 Jeff Hackett .12 .30
75 Saku Koivu .20 .50
76 Martin Rucinsky .12 .30
77 Brian Savage .12 .30
78 Mike Dunham .12 .30
79 Sergei Krivokrasov .12 .30
80 David Legwand .12 .30
81 Cliff Ronning .12 .30
82 Scott Walker .12 .30
83 Jason Arnott .15 .40
84 Martin Brodeur .40 1.00
85 Patrik Elias .20 .50
86 Bobby Holik .12 .30
87 Brendan Morrison .15 .40
88 Petr Sykora .15 .40
89 Mariusz Czerkawski .12 .30
90 Kenny Jonsson .12 .30
91 Felix Potvin .30 .75
92 Mike Watt .12 .30
93 Adam Graves .15 .40
94 Brian Leetch .20 .50
95 John MacLean .15 .40
96 Petr Nedved .12 .30
97 Mike Richter .20 .50
98 Magnus Arvedson .12 .30
99 Marian Hossa .15 .40
100 Shawn McEachern .12 .30
101 Ron Tugnutt .15 .40
102 Alexei Yashin .15 .40
103 Rod Brind'Amour .20 .50
104 Eric Desjardins .15 .40
105 John LeClair .20 .50
106 Eric Lindros .30 .75
107 Mark Recchi .25 .60
108 John Vanbiesbrouck .15 .40
109 Nikolai Khabibulin .15 .40
110 Teppo Numminen .12 .30
111 Jeremy Roenick .20 .50
112 Rick Tocchet .15 .40
113 Keith Tkachuk .20 .50

114 Matthew Barnaby .15 .40
115 Tom Barrasso .20 .50
116 Jaromir Jagr .50 1.25
117 Alexei Kovalev .15 .40
118 Martin Straka .12 .30
119 Vincent Damphousse .15 .40
120 Jeff Friesen .15 .40
121 Patrick Marleau .20 .50
122 Steve Shields .15 .40
123 Mike Vernon .15 .40
124 Pavol Demitra .25 .60
125 Grant Fuhr .20 .50
126 Al MacInnis .20 .50
127 Chris Pronger .15 .40
128 Pierre Turgeon .20 .50
129 Chris Gratton .12 .30
130 Kevin Hodson .12 .30
131 Vincent Lecavalier .15 .40
132 Paul Mara .12 .30
133 Darcy Tucker .12 .30
134 Sergei Berezin .12 .30
135 Mike Johnson .15 .40
136 Curtis Joseph .20 .50
137 Yanic Perreault .12 .30
138 Mats Sundin .20 .50
139 Steve Thomas .12 .30
140 Mark Messier .30 .75
141 Bill Muckalt .12 .30
142 Alexander Mogilny .15 .40
143 Markus Naslund .20 .50
144 Mattias Ohlund .15 .40
145 Garth Snow .15 .40
146 Peter Bondra .15 .40
147 Sergei Gonchar .12 .30
148 Benoit Gratton RC .12 .30
149 Olaf Kolzig .20 .50
150 Adam Oates .20 .50

1999-00 Aurora Premiere Date

PREMIERE DATE/60: 15X TO 40X BASIC CARDS
PREMIERE DATE PRINT RUN 60
*STRIPED/60: .4X TO 1X BASIC PD/60

1999-00 Aurora Canvas Creations

COMPLETE SET (10) 60.00 120.00
STATED ODDS 1:193
1 Paul Kariya 4.00 10.00
2 Teemu Selanne 4.00 10.00
3 Dominik Hasek 8.00 20.00
4 Peter Forsberg 5.00 12.00
5 Patrick Roy 10.00 25.00
6 Steve Yzerman 10.00 25.00
7 Pavel Bure 4.00 10.00
8 John LeClair 3.00 8.00
9 Eric Lindros 5.00 12.00
10 Jaromir Jagr 6.00 15.00

1999-00 Aurora Championship Fever

Martin Brodeur autographed 197 copies of his insert card and one each of the parallel cards; these were inserted randomly.
COMPLETE SET (20) 40.00 80.00
STATED ODDS 4:25
ICE BLUE/100: 3X TO 8X BASIC INSERTS
COPPER/20: 5X TO 12X BASIC INSERTS
SILVER/250: 1X TO 2.5X BASIC INSERTS
1 Paul Kariya .60 1.50
2 Teemu Selanne .60 1.50
3 Ray Bourque 1.00 2.50
4 Dominik Hasek 1.25 3.00
5 Michael Peca .50 1.25
6 Theo Fleury .50 1.25
7 Peter Forsberg 1.50 4.00
8 Patrick Roy 3.00 8.00
9 Joe Sakic 1.50 4.00
10 Ed Belfour .60 1.50
11 Mike Modano 1.00 2.50
12 Brendan Shanahan .60 1.50
13 Steve Yzerman 3.00 8.00
14 Pavel Bure .60 1.50
15 Martin Brodeur 1.50 4.00
16 John LeClair .60 1.50
17 Eric Lindros .60 1.50
18 Jaromir Jagr 1.00 2.50
19 Curtis Joseph .60 1.50
20 Mats Sundin .60 1.50
NNO Martin Brodeur AU/197 30.00 80.00

1999-00 Aurora Complete Players

COMPLETE SET (10) 150.00 300.00
HOBBY/RETAIL PRINT RUN 299
HOBBY PARALLEL 25: 2.5X TO 6X BASIC INSERTS
RETAIL/25: 2.5X TO 6X BASIC INSERTS
HOB/RET PARALLEL PRINT RUN 25
1 Paul Kariya 10.00 25.00
2 Teemu Selanne 10.00 25.00
3 Dominik Hasek 12.50 30.00
4 Peter Forsberg 15.00 40.00
5 Patrick Roy 25.00 60.00
6 Mike Modano 12.50 30.00
7 Steve Yzerman 30.00 80.00
8 John LeClair 10.00 25.00
9 Eric Lindros 10.00 25.00
10 Jaromir Jagr 10.00 25.00

1999-00 Aurora Glove Unlimited

COMPLETE SET (20) 50.00 100.00
STATED ODDS 2:25
1 Guy Hebert 1.50 4.00
2 Byron Dafoe 1.50 4.00
3 Dominik Hasek 4.00 10.00
4 Arturs Irbe 1.50 4.00
5 Jocelyn Thibault 1.50 4.00
6 Patrick Roy 12.50 25.00
7 Ed Belfour 2.00 5.00
8 Chris Osgood 1.50 4.00
9 Tommy Salo 1.50 4.00
10 Jeff Hackett 1.50 4.00
11 Martin Brodeur 6.00 12.00
12 Felix Potvin 2.00 5.00
13 Mike Richter 2.00 5.00
14 Ron Tugnutt 1.50 4.00
15 John Vanbiesbrouck 1.50 4.00
16 Nikolai Khabibulin 1.50 4.00
17 Grant Fuhr 1.50 4.00
18 Steve Shields 1.50 4.00
19 Curtis Joseph 2.00 5.00
20 Olaf Kolzig 1.50 4.00

1999-00 Aurora Styrotechs

COMPLETE SET (20) 25.00 60.00
STATED ODDS 1:25
1 Paul Kariya 1.25 3.00
2 Teemu Selanne 1.25 3.00
3 Dominik Hasek 3.00 8.00
4 Theo Fleury .75 2.00
5 Peter Forsberg 3.00 8.00
6 Patrick Roy 8.00 20.00
7 Ed Belfour 1.25 3.00
8 Mike Modano 2.00 5.00
9 Brendan Shanahan 1.25 3.00
10 Steve Yzerman 6.00 15.00
11 Pavel Bure 1.25 3.00
12 Martin Brodeur 5.00 12.00
13 Alexei Yashin .40 1.00
14 John LeClair .40 1.00
15 Eric Lindros 1.25 3.00
16 Keith Tkachuk .75 2.00
17 Jaromir Jagr 3.00 8.00
18 Curtis Joseph 1.25 3.00
19 Mats Sundin 1.25 3.00
20 Mark Messier 1.50 4.00

2000-01 Aurora

Released as a 150-card set, Aurora base cards feature a white borderd card with two player photos on the card front. A full color action photo appears set against a background that fades from green to blue, top to bottom, and a smaller brown tone player action photo set against a blue triangle. Cards are highlighted with bronze foil. Aurora was packaged in 36-pack boxes with each pack containing six cards. A parallel with a striped background was also created and inserted randomly. The striped set was complete at 50 cards and was skip numbered.
COMPLETE SET (150) 20.00 40.00
*PINSTRIPE: .8X TO 2X BASIC CARDS
1 Guy Hebert .20 .50
2 Paul Kariya .30 .75
3 Steve Rucchin .15 .40
4 Teemu Selanne .50 1.25
5 Andrew Brunette .15 .40
6 Scott Fankhouser .15 .40
7 Damian Rhodes .15 .40
8 Patrik Stefan .20 .50
9 Jason Allison .20 .50
10 Anson Carter .20 .50
11 Paul Coffey .25 .60
12 Byron Dafoe .20 .50
13 John Grahame .15 .40
14 Sergei Samsonov .20 .50
15 Joe Thornton .40 1.00
16 Maxim Afinogenov .15 .40
17 Martin Biron .20 .50
18 Doug Gilmour .30 .75
19 Dominik Hasek .40 1.00
20 Michael Peca .20 .50
21 Miroslav Satan .15 .40
22 Fred Brathwaite .20 .50
23 Valeri Bure .20 .50
24 Jarome Iginla .25 .60
25 Derek Morris .15 .40
26 Marc Savard .20 .50
27 Rod Brind'Amour .25 .60
28 Ron Francis .30 .75
29 Arturs Irbe .20 .50
30 Sami Kapanen .15 .40
31 Tony Amonte .20 .50
32 Eric Daze .20 .50
33 Steve Sullivan .15 .40
34 Jocelyn Thibault .20 .50
35 Alexei Zhamnov .20 .50
36 Ray Bourque .40 1.00
37 Chris Drury .20 .50
38 Peter Forsberg .30 .75
39 Milan Hejduk .20 .50
40 Patrick Roy .60 1.50
41 Joe Sakic .40 1.00
42 Alex Tanguay .20 .50
43 Ed Belfour .25 .60
44 Brett Hull .40 1.00
45 Mike Modano .40 1.00
46 Brenden Morrow .20 .50
47 Joe Nieuwendyk .25 .60
48 Chris Chelios .25 .60
49 Sergei Fedorov .40 1.00
50 Nicklas Lidstrom .25 .60
51 Chris Osgood .25 .60
52 Brendan Shanahan .30 .75
53 Pat Verbeek .20 .50
54 Steve Yzerman .75 2.00
55 Mike Grier .15 .40
56 Bill Guerin .25 .60
57 Tommy Salo .20 .50
58 Ryan Smyth .20 .50
59 Doug Weight .25 .60
60 Pavel Bure .30 .75
61 Trevor Kidd .15 .40
62 Viktor Kozlov .20 .50
63 Roberto Luongo .40 1.00
64 Ray Whitney .20 .50
65 Rob Blake .25 .60
66 Stephane Fiset .15 .40
67 Zigmund Palffy .25 .60
68 Luc Robitaille .25 .60
69 Jamie Storr .20 .50
70 Jozef Stumpel .15 .40
71 Jeff Hackett .15 .40
72 Saku Koivu .25 .60
73 Trevor Linden .25 .60
74 Martin Rucinsky .15 .40
75 Jose Theodore .30 .75
76 Mike Dunham .15 .40
77 Patric Kjellberg .15 .40
78 David Legwand .25 .60
79 Cliff Ronning .15 .40
80 Jason Arnott .20 .50
81 Martin Brodeur .50 1.25
82 Patrik Elias .25 .60
83 Scott Gomez .20 .50
84 John Madden .20 .50
85 Scott Stevens .25 .60
86 Petr Sykora .20 .50
87 Tim Connolly .15 .40
88 Mariusz Czerkawski .15 .40
89 Brad Isbister .15 .40
90 Mark Parrish .15 .40
91 John Vanbiesbrouck .20 .50
92 Theo Fleury .30 .75
93 Adam Graves .20 .50
94 Jan Hlavac .15 .40
95 Brian Leetch .25 .60
96 Mark Messier .40 1.00
97 Petr Nedved .20 .50
98 Mike Richter .25 .60
99 Daniel Alfredsson .25 .60
100 Radek Bonk .20 .50
101 Marian Hossa .20 .50
102 Shawn McEachern .15 .40
103 Vaclav Prospal .15 .40
104 Brian Boucher .20 .50
105 Eric Desjardins .20 .50
106 Simon Gagne .25 .60
107 John LeClair .25 .60
108 Eric Lindros .40 1.00
109 Mark Recchi .30 .75
110 Shane Doan .20 .50
111 Joe Juneau .20 .50
112 Jeremy Roenick .25 .60
113 Keith Tkachuk .25 .60
114 Jean-Sebastien Aubin .20 .50
115 Jan Hrdina .15 .40
116 Jaromir Jagr .60 1.50
117 Alexei Kovalev .20 .50
118 Martin Straka .20 .50
119 Pavol Demitra .30 .75
120 Dallas Drake .15 .40
121 Michal Handzus .15 .40
122 Al MacInnis .25 .60
123 Chris Pronger .20 .50
124 Roman Turek .20 .50
125 Pierre Turgeon .25 .60
126 Vincent Damphousse .20 .50
127 Jeff Friesen .15 .40
128 Patrick Marleau .25 .60
129 Owen Nolan .25 .60
130 Steve Shields .15 .40
131 Dan Cloutier .20 .50
132 Matt Elich RC .20 .50
133 Mike Johnson .15 .40
134 Vincent Lecavalier .20 .50
135 Kevin Weekes .15 .40
136 Nikolai Antropov .20 .50
137 Tie Domi .40 1.00
138 Jeff Farkas .15 .40
139 Curtis Joseph .30 .75
140 Mats Sundin .25 .60
141 Steve Thomas .15 .40
142 Andrew Cassels .15 .40
143 Steve Kariya .15 .40
144 Markus Naslund .20 .50
145 Felix Potvin .40 1.00
146 Peter Bondra .20 .50
147 Jeff Halpern .15 .40
148 Olaf Kolzig .25 .60
149 Adam Oates .25 .60
150 Chris Simon .15 .40

2000-01 Aurora Premiere Date

*PREM.DATE/50: 12X TO 30X BASIC CARDS
STATED PRINT RUN 50 SER.#'d SETS
*PINSTRIPES: .4X TO 1X BASIC INSERTS
96 Mark Messier 12.00 30.00

2000-01 Aurora Autographs

STATED PRINT RUN 197-500
23 Valeri Bure/300 6.00 15.00
37 Chris Drury/250 8.00 20.00
42 Alex Tanguay/500 8.00 20.00
46 Brenden Morrow/500 6.00 15.00
55 Mike Grier/500 6.00 15.00
75 Jose Theodore/500 12.50 30.00
78 David Legwand/500 8.00 20.00
81 Martin Brodeur/197 40.00 100.00
115 Jean-Sebastien Aubin/500 8.00 20.00
135 Nikolai Antropov/500 6.00 15.00
148 Olaf Kolzig/250 8.00 20.00

2000-01 Aurora Canvas Creations

COMPLETE SET (10) 60.00 100.00
STATED ODDS 1:361
1 Paul Kariya 4.00 10.00
2 Peter Forsberg 5.00 12.00
3 Patrick Roy 12.50 30.00
4 Mike Modano 4.00 10.00
5 Steve Yzerman 10.00 25.00
6 Pavel Bure 4.00 10.00
7 Martin Brodeur 10.00 25.00
8 John LeClair 3.00 8.00
9 Jaromir Jagr 4.00 10.00
10 Curtis Joseph 3.00 8.00

2000-01 Aurora Championship Fever

COMPLETE SET (20) 30.00 60.00
STATED ODDS 4:37
*COPPER/90: 10X TO 25X BASIC INSERT
COPPER PRINT RUN 90 SER.#'d SETS
*BLUE/92: 10X TO 25X BASIC INSERT
BLUE PRINT RUN 92 SER.#'d SETS
*SILVER/221: 6X TO 15X BASIC INSERT
SILVER PRINT RUN 221 SER.#'d SETS
1 Paul Kariya .75 2.00
2 Teemu Selanne .75 2.00
3 Dominik Hasek 1.50 4.00
4 Ray Bourque 1.50 4.00
5 Peter Forsberg 2.00 5.00
6 Patrick Roy 4.00 10.00
7 Ed Belfour .75 2.00
8 Brett Hull 1.00 2.50
9 Mike Modano 1.25 3.00
10 Sergei Fedorov 1.25 3.00
11 Brendan Shanahan .75 2.00
12 Steve Yzerman 4.00 10.00
13 Pavel Bure .75 2.00
14 Martin Brodeur 1.50 4.00
15 Scott Gomez .75 2.00
16 Mark Messier .75 2.00
17 Brian Boucher .75 2.00
18 John LeClair .75 2.00
19 Jaromir Jagr 1.25 3.00
20 Curtis Joseph .75 2.00
NNO John LeClair AU/197 15.00 40.00

2000-01 Aurora Dual Game-Worn Jerseys

STATED PRINT RUN 200 SER.#'d SETS
1 P.Sykora/S.Koivu 12.00 30.00
2 J.Vanbiesbrouck/R.Luongo 20.00 40.00
3 S.Yzerman/B.Shanahan 20.00 50.00
4 J.Jagr/P.Bondra 12.00 30.00

2000-01 Aurora Game Worn Jerseys

1 Paul Coffey 5.00 12.00
2 Brendan Shanahan 6.00 15.00
3 Steve Yzerman 12.50 30.00
4 Steve Yzerman 15.00 40.00
5 Saku Koivu 5.00 12.00
6 John Vanbiesbrouck 5.00 12.00
7 Mark Messier 10.00 25.00
8 Petr Sykora 5.00 12.00
9 Eric Lindros 6.00 15.00
10 Peter Bondra 5.00 12.00

2000-01 Aurora Scouting Reports

COMPLETE SET (20) 30.00 80.00
STATED ODDS 2:37 HOBBY
1 Paul Kariya 2.00 5.00
2 Teemu Selanne 2.00 5.00
3 Patrik Stefan 1.50 4.00
4 Joe Thornton 2.50 6.00
5 Peter Forsberg 3.00 8.00
6 Milan Hejduk 2.00 5.00
7 Brett Hull 2.00 5.00
8 Ed Belfour 2.00 5.00
9 Sergei Fedorov 2.50 6.00
10 Brendan Shanahan 2.50 6.00
11 Pavel Bure 2.00 5.00
12 Roberto Luongo 2.50 6.00
13 Martin Brodeur 4.00 10.00
14 Scott Gomez 1.50 4.00
15 Marian Hossa 1.50 4.00
16 Brian Boucher 1.50 4.00
17 John LeClair 2.00 5.00
18 Vincent Lecavalier 2.00 5.00
19 Curtis Joseph 2.00 5.00
20 Mats Sundin 2.00 5.00

2000-01 Aurora Styrotechs

COMPLETE SET (20) 12.00 30.00
A VERSION ODDS 1:37 HOBBY
B VERSION ODDS 1:37 RETAIL
1A Paul Kariya 1.00 2.50
1B Teemu Selanne 1.00 2.50
2A Doug Gilmour 1.00 2.50
2B Dominik Hasek 2.50 6.00
3A Peter Forsberg 2.50 6.00
3B Patrick Roy 6.00 15.00
4A Joe Sakic 2.50 6.00
4B Ray Bourque 2.00 5.00
5A Brett Hull 1.00 2.50
5B Mike Modano 2.00 5.00
6A Brendan Shanahan 1.00 2.50
6B Steve Yzerman 6.00 15.00
7A Scott Gomez .40 1.00
7B Martin Brodeur 4.00 10.00
8A John LeClair .40 1.00
8B Brian Boucher .40 1.00
9A Jaromir Jagr 3.00 8.00
9B Jean-Sebastien Aubin .40 1.00
10A Curtis Joseph 1.00 2.50
10B Mats Sundin 1.00 2.50

1996 Avalanche Photo Pucks

COMPLETE SET (5) 6.00 15.00
1 Claude Lemieux 2.00 5.00
Peter Forsberg
2 Joe Sakic 1.50 4.00
Adam Deadmarsh
3 Patrick Roy 2.00 5.00
Adam Foote
4 Valeri Kamensky 1.25 3.00
Mike Ricci
5 Colorado Avalanche 1.25 3.00

1997 Avalanche Pins

This set of promotional giveaway pins was sponsored by Denver Post. One pin was given out per special event night.
1 Team Logo .40 1.00
2 Joe Sakic 1.50 4.00
3 Patrick Roy 2.50 6.00
4 Marc Crawford CO .40 1.00
5 Peter Forsberg 1.50 4.00
6 Claude Lemieux .40 1.00
7 Olympic Break .40 1.00
8 Sandiz Ozolinsh .40 1.00
9 Adam Foote .75 2.00

1999-00 Avalanche Pins

Released as a limited edition set in conjunction with the Denver Post, this 8-pin set commemorates the innagural season of the Pepsi Center. These pins were available for purchase on April 2 at the Pepsi Center vs. the Dallas Stars. Each pin was shrinkwraped with an oversized card featuring the respective player and logos of both the Pepsi Center and The Denver Post.
COMPLETE SET (8)
1 Joe Sakic 1.50 4.00
2 Adam Foote 1.25 3.00
3 Adam Deadmarsh .40 1.00
4 Patrick Roy 2.50 6.00
5 Peter Forsberg 2.00 5.00
6 Sandis Ozolinsh .40 1.00
7 Chris Drury .40 1.00
8 Milan Hejduk 1.25 3.00

1999-00 Avalanche Team Issue

This set was issued as a promotional giveaway by the Avs. Each card in this set measures 3 1/2" x 5" and card backs are blank. The cards are unnumbered, so are listed below alphabetically.
COMPLETE SET (24) 8.00 20.00
1 Greg DeVries .08 .25
2 Adam Deadmarsh .20 .50
3 Marc Denis .40 1.00
4 Chris Dingman .08 .25
5 Chris Drury .40 1.00
6 Adam Foote .20 .50
7 Peter Forsberg 1.25 3.00
8 Alexei Gusarov .08 .25
9 Milan Hejduk .60 1.50
10 Sami Helenius .08 .25
11 Dan Hinote .30 .75
12 Jon Klemm .15 .40
13 Eric Messier .08 .25
14 Aaron Miller .08 .25
15 Jeff Odgers .08 .25
16 Sandis Ozolinsh .20 .50
17 Shjon Podein .08 .25
18 Dave Reid .08 .25
19 Brian Rolston .20 .50
20 Patrik Roy 2.00 5.00
21 Joe Sakic .75 2.00
22 Martin Skoula .20 .50
23 Alex Tanguay .60 1.50
24 Stephane Yelle .15 .40

2001-02 Avalanche Team Issue

This 23-card set measured approx. 3 1/2" X 5". Each card carried the players jersey number, name and position diagonally along the bottom of the card with the team logo at the top.
COMPLETE SET (22) 15.00 30.00
1 David Aebischer .75 2.00
2 Stephane Yelle .40 1.00
3 Rob Blake .75 2.00
4 Shjon Podein .40 1.00
5 Scott Parker .40 1.00
6 Brian Willsie .40 1.00
7 Brad Larsen .40 1.00
8 Radim Vrbata .40 1.00
9 Rick Berry .40 1.00
10 Adam Foote .40 1.00
11 Chris Drury .40 1.00
12 Alex Tanguay .75 2.00
13 Dan Hinote .40 1.00
14 Eric Messier .40 1.00
15 Joe Sakic 1.25 3.00
16 Pascal Trepanier .40 1.00
17 Martin Skoula .40 1.00
18 Steven Reinprecht .40 1.00
19 Patrick Roy 2.00 5.00
20 Milan Hejduk .75 2.00
21 Todd Gill .40 1.00
22 Greg DeVries .40 1.00
23 Peter Forsberg 1.50 4.00

2002-03 Avalanche Postcards

This postcard sized set was used as a promotional item by the team and featured player action photos on team colored card fronts. Card backs were blank.
COMPLETE SET (18) 10.00 25.00
1 Mike Keane .40 1.00
2 Riku Hahl .60 1.50
3 Scott Parker .60 1.50
4 David Aebischer .60 1.50
5 Steven Reinprecht .40 1.00
6 Greg deVries .40 1.00
7 Eric Messier .40 1.00
8 Peter Forsberg 2.00 5.00
9 Joe Sakic 2.00 5.00
10 Martin Skoula .40 1.00
11 Adam Foote .40 1.00
12 Derek Morris .40 1.00
13 Brian Willsie .40 1.00
14 Jeff Shantz .40 1.00
15 Milan Hejduk .60 1.50
16 Rob Blake .60 1.50
17 Dan Hinote .40 1.00
18 Bryan Muir .40 1.00

2003-04 Avalanche Team Issue

These team issued cards were sponsored by Conoco and each was handed out at one home game.
COMPLETE SET (20) 10.00 25.00
1 David Aebischer .40 1.00
2 Rob Blake .75 2.00
3 Jim Cummins .40 1.00
4 Adam Foote .40 1.00
5 Peter Forsberg 1.25 3.00
6 Chris Gratton .40 1.00
7 Riku Hahl .40 1.00
8 Milan Hejduk .75 2.00
9 Dan Hinote .40 1.00
10 Paul Kariya .75 2.00
11 Steve Konowalchuk .40 1.00
12 John-Michael Liles .40 1.00
13 Andrei Nikolishin .40 1.00
14 Joe Sakic 1.25 3.00
15 Phil Sauve .40 1.00
16 Teemu Selanne .75 2.00
17 Karlis Skrastins .40 1.00
18 Marek Svatos .75 2.00
19 Alex Tanguay .75 2.00
20 Peter Worrell .40 1.00

2006-07 Avalanche Postcards

COMPLETE SET (21) 15.00 30.00
1 Tyler Arnason .40 1.00
2 Patrice Brisebois .40 1.00
3 Andrew Brunette .40 1.00
4 Peter Budaj .75 2.00
5 Brett Clark .40 1.00
6 Milan Hejduk .75 2.00
7 Ken Klee .40 1.00
8 Ian Laperriere .40 1.00
9 Jordan Leopold .40 1.00
10 Brett McLean .40 1.00
11 Brad Richardson .40 1.00
12 Mark Rycroft .40 1.00
13 Joe Sakic 2.00 5.00
14 Kurt Sauer .40 1.00
15 Karlis Skrastins .40 1.00
16 Paul Stastny 2.00 5.00
17 Marek Svatos .75 2.00
18 Jose Theodore .75 2.00
19 Pierre Turgeon .40 1.00
20 Ossi Vaananen .40 1.00
21 Wojtek Wolski .75 2.00
22 Ken Klee .40 1.00
23 Paul Stastny 2.00 5.00
24 Antii Laaksonen .75 2.00
25 Brett Clark .75 2.00
26 Brad May .40 1.00
27 Pierre Lacroix .75 2.00
28 Jeff Hackett .75 2.00
29 Tony Granato .75 2.00
30 Jacques Cloutier .75 2.00
31 Francois Giguere .75 2.00
32 Joel Quenneville .40 1.00

2003-04 Backcheck: A Hockey Retrospective

Produced by the National Library of Canada, this sepia-toned set features a look back at some early photos from hockey's history.
COMPLETE SET (20) 8.00 20.00
1 Choosing Sides .20 .50
2 Outdoor Game .20 .50
3 Early Skating .20 .50
4 Ottawa Rebels .40 1.00
5 Renfrew hockey team .40 1.00
6 Oxford Canadian Hockey Club .40 1.00
7 Gore Bay Hockey Club .40 1.00
8 Ottawa Silver Seven .75 2.00
9 Maurice Richard 2.00 5.00
10 Clarence Campbell .40 1.00
11 Bodychecking .20 .50
12 Asahi Athletic Club .40 1.00
13 Lester B. Pearson .20 .50
Swiss game
14 Prisoners' hockey team .40 1.00
15 Sydney Millionaires .40 1.00
16 Jacques Plante 2.00 5.00
Quebec Citadelles
17 Shinny .20 .50
18 Montreal Canadiens 1942 .75 2.00
19 Eva Ault .20 .50
20 Orillia Hockey Club .40 1.00

1995-96 Bashan Imperial Super Stickers

This set of 136 stickers was released in five-sticker packs (plus one stick of gum) late in the 1995-96 season. The stickers measured the standard size and featured color player photos and name on the front, and playing information on the back. Collation of this product was extremely poor, making set building somewhat arduous.
COMPLETE SET (136) 15.00 30.00
1 Ducks Logo .08 .25
2 Paul Kariya .60 1.50
3 Chad Kilger .08 .25
4 Oleg Tverdovsky .08 .25
5 Bruins Logo .08 .25
6 Ray Bourque .60 1.50
7 Cam Neely .60 1.50
8 Adam Oates .20 .50
9 Kevin Stevens .20 .50
10 Sabres Logo .08 .25
11 Pat LaFontaine .20 .50
12 Dominik Hasek .75 2.00
13 Alexei Zhitnik .08 .25
14 Flames Logo .08 .25
15 Theo Fleury .40 1.00
16 Phil Housley .08 .25
17 Trevor Kidd .20 .50
18 Joe Nieuwendyk .20 .50
19 Zarley Zalapski .08 .25
20 Blackhawks Logo .08 .25
21 Jeremy Roenick .60 1.50
22 Chris Chelios .40 1.00
23 Ed Belfour .60 1.50
24 Joe Murphy .08 .25
25 Patrick Poulin .08 .25
26 Avalanche Logo .08 .25
27 Joe Sakic .75 2.00
28 Peter Forsberg 1.00 2.50
29 Sandis Ozolinsh .08 .25
30 Mike Ricci .08 .25
31 Valeri Kamensky .08 .25
32 Stars Logo .08 .25
33 Mike Modano .60 1.50
34 Kevin Hatcher .08 .25
35 Andy Moog .20 .50
36 Red Wings Logo .08 .25
37 Steve Yzerman 1.25 3.00
38 Sergei Fedorov .60 1.50
39 Paul Coffey .40 1.00
40 Keith Primeau .08 .25
41 Nicklas Lidstrom .40 1.00
42 Oilers Logo .08 .25
43 Doug Weight .08 .25
44 Jason Arnott .08 .25
45 Bill Ranford .20 .50
46 Panthers Logo .08 .25
47 John Vanbiesbrouck .40 1.00
48 Stu Barnes .08 .25
49 Scott Mellanby .08 .25
50 Rob Niedermayer .08 .25
51 Whalers Logo .08 .25
52 Brendan Shanahan .40 1.00
53 Geoff Sanderson .08 .25
54 Sean Burke .20 .50
55 Jeff O'Neill .08 .25
56 Kings Logo .08 .25
57 Wayne Gretzky 2.00 5.00
58 Rob Blake .20 .50
59 Rick Tocchet .20 .50
60 Dimitri Khristich .08 .25
61 Kelly Hrudey .20 .50
62 Canadiens Logo .08 .25
63 Pierre Turgeon .08 .25
64 Mark Recchi .20 .50
65 Saku Koivu .40 1.00
66 Patrick Roy 1.50 4.00
67 Vincent Damphousse .08 .25
68 Devils Logo .08 .25
69 Stephane Richer .08 .25
70 Martin Brodeur 1.25 3.00
71 Scott Niedermayer .08 .25
72 Scott Stevens .08 .25
73 Islander Logo .08 .25
74 Kirk Muller .08 .25
75 Mathieu Schneider .08 .25
76 Derek King .08 .25
77 Wendel Clark .20 .50
78 Ranger Logo .08 .25
79 Brian Leetch .40 1.00
80 Mark Messier .60 1.50
81 Alexei Kovalev .08 .25
82 Luc Robitaille .40 1.00
83 Mike Richter .40 1.00
84 Senators Logo .08 .25
85 Dan Quinn .08 .25
86 Alexandre Daigle .08 .25
87 Steve Duchesne .08 .25
88 Radek Bonk .08 .25
89 Flyers Logo .08 .25
90 Eric Lindros .60 1.50
91 Mikael Renberg .08 .25
92 John LeClair .20 .50
93 Eric Desjardins .08 .25
94 Rod Brind'Amour .08 .25
95 Penguins Logo .08 .25
96 Jaromir Jagr .75 2.00
97 Mario Lemieux 1.50 4.00
98 Ron Francis .20 .50
99 Sergei Zubov .08 .25
100 Blues Logo .08 .25
101 Brett Hull .60 1.50
102 Al MacInnis .20 .50
103 Dale Hawerchuk .20 .50
104 Chris Pronger .40 1.00
105 Sharks Logo .08 .25
106 Craig Janney .08 .25
107 Pat Falloon .08 .25
108 Arturs Irbe .40 1.00
109 Ulf Dahlen .08 .25
110 Owen Nolan .20 .50
111 Lightning Logo .08 .25
112 Roman Hamrlik .08 .25
113 Brian Bradley .08 .25
114 Chris Gratton .08 .25
115 Brian Bellows .08 .25
116 Maple Leafs Logo .08 .25
117 Doug Gilmour .40 1.00
118 Mats Sundin .60 1.50
119 Dave Andreychuk .08 .25
120 Felix Potvin .40 1.00
121 Larry Murphy .08 .25
122 Canucks Logo .08 .25
123 Pavel Bure .40 1.00
124 Alexander Mogilny .20 .50
125 Trevor Linden .20 .50
126 Jeff Brown .08 .25
127 Kirk McLean .20 .50
128 Capitals Logo .08 .25
129 Joe Juneau .08 .25
130 Peter Bondra .20 .50
131 Jim Carey .20 .50
132 Calle Johansson .08 .25
133 Jets Logo .08 .25
134 Teemu Selanne .60 1.50
135 Alexei Zhamnov .08 .25
136 Keith Tkachuk .40 1.00

1995-96 Bashan Imperial Super Stickers Die Cut

These die-cut stickers were randomly inserted in packs at indeterminate odds. They featured player's image is over a starburst background.
COMPLETE SET (25) 8.00 20.00
1 Pierre Turgeon .08 .25
2 Patrick Roy 1.50 4.00
3 Pat LaFontaine .20 .50
4 Joe Sakic 1.00 2.50
5 Paul Coffey .40 1.00
6 Ray Bourque .60 1.50
7 Brian Leetch .40 1.00
8 Joe Juneau .08 .25
9 Jeremy Roenick .60 1.50
10 Chris Chelios .40 1.00
11 Brett Hull .60 1.50
12 Paul Kariya .40 1.00
13 Jason Arnott .08 .25
14 Pavel Bure .40 1.00
15 Steve Duchesne .08 .25
16 Martin Brodeur 1.25 3.00
17 Eric Lindros .60 1.50
18 Mikael Renberg .08 .25
19 Felix Potvin .40 1.00
20 Roman Hamrlik .08 .25
21 Wayne Gretzky 2.00 5.00
22 Brendan Shanahan .60 1.50
23 Jaromir Jagr .75 2.00
24 Mario Lemieux 1.50 4.00
25 Steve Yzerman 1.25 3.00

1968 Bauer Ads

These oversized cards are approximately 8" x 10" and feature full color fronts, with blank backs. They were issued as premiums with Bauer skates. Since they are unnumbered, they are checklisted below in alphabetical order.
COMPLETE SET (21) 300.00 600.00
1 Andy Bathgate 12.50 25.00
2 Gary Bergman 12.50 25.00
3 Charlie Burns 12.50 25.00
4 Ray Cullen 12.50 25.00
5 Gary Dornhoeffer 12.50 25.00
6 Kent Douglas 12.50 25.00
7 Tim Ecclestone 12.50 25.00
8 Bill Flett 12.50 25.00
9 Ed Giacomin 20.00 40.00
10 Ted Harris 12.50 25.00
11 Paul Henderson 20.00 40.00
12 Ken Hodge 12.50 25.00
13 Harry Howell 12.50 25.00
14 Earl Ingarfield 12.50 25.00
15 Gilles Marotte 12.50 25.00
16 Doug Mohns 12.50 25.00
17 Bobby Orr 75.00 150.00
18 Claude Provost 12.50 25.00
19 Gary Sabourin 12.50 25.00
20 Brian Smith 12.50 25.00
21 Bob Woytowich 12.50 25.00

1991-92 BayBank Bobby Orr

These promotional cards were sponsored by BayBank and measure approximately 2 1/2" by 3 1/2". A player card and a sponsor advertisement were packaged inside a hockey puck-shaped holder (bearing the Bruins logo) and passed out to ticket holders on BayBank Night at the Bruins game. The fronts of the first two cards have a color action player photo framed by a blue and green inner border design. The white outer border on card 1 is slightly thicker than on card 2, and the positions of the player's name and the sponsor name are reversed when one compares the two cards. The third card has a green border. Against a pale green background, the back presents biography, statistics (career and playoffs), and career awards. The card number appears in a green box in the upper left corner.
COMPLETE SET (4) 12.00 30.00
1 Bobby Orr 3.00 8.00
(Skating with Flyer in pursuit)
2 Bobby Orr 3.00 8.00
(Skating alone with puck)
3 Bobby Orr 3.00 8.00
(Skating behind the net)
NNO Bobby Orr 8 1/2 x 11 4.00 10.00

1995 BayBank Bobby Orr

This set consists of a 10" by 8" sheet, featuring a color action photo of Bobby Orr, and a standard-size card carrying the same picture. The sheet has a blank back; the card back salutes the Boston Bruins on the 25th Anniversary of the 1970 Stanley Cup Championship.
COMPLETE SET (2) 6.00 15.00
1 Bobby Orr 4.00 10.00
(Oversized card)
2 Bobby Orr 2.00 5.00
(Regular size card)

1971-72 Bazooka

The 1971-72 Bazooka set contains 36 cards. The cards, nearly identical in design to the 1971-72 Topps and O-Pee-Chee hockey cards, were distributed in 12 three-card panels as the bottoms of Bazooka bubble gum boxes. The cards are numbered at the bottom of each obverse. The cards are blank backed and are about 2/3 the size of standard cards. The panels of three are in numerical order, e.g., cards 1-3 are a panel, cards 4-6 form a panel, etc. The prices below refer to cut-apart individual cards; values for panels are 50 percent more than the values below. This is a very scarce set with limited confirmed sales.
COMPLETE SET (36) 4500.00 9000.00
1 Phil Esposito 375.00 750.00
2 Frank Mahovlich 200.00 400.00
3 Ed Van Impe 25.00 50.00
4 Bobby Hull 500.00 1000.00
5 Henri Richard 150.00 300.00
6 Gilbert Perreault 375.00 750.00
7 Alex Delvecchio 125.00 250.00
8 Denis DeJordy 75.00 150.00
9 Ted Harris 30.00 60.00
10 Gilles Villemure 75.00 150.00
11 Dave Keon 150.00 300.00
12 Derek Sanderson 150.00 300.00
13 Orland Kurtenbach 30.00 60.00
14 Bob Nevin 30.00 60.00
15 Yvan Cournoyer 100.00 200.00
16 Andre Boudrias 25.00 50.00
17 Frank St.Marseille 25.00 50.00
18 Norm Ullman 100.00 200.00
19 Garry Unger 40.00 80.00
20 Pierre Bouchard 25.00 50.00
21 Roy Edwards 75.00 150.00
22 Ralph Backstrom 30.00 60.00
23 Guy Trottier 25.00 50.00
24 Serge Bernier 25.00 50.00
25 Bert Marshall 25.00 50.00
26 Wayne Hillman 25.00 50.00
27 Tim Ecclestone 25.00 50.00
28 Walt McKechnie 25.00 50.00
29 Tony Esposito 375.00 750.00
30 Rod Gilbert 100.00 200.00
31 Walt Tkaczuk 30.00 60.00
32 Roger Crozier 75.00 150.00
33 Ken Schinkel 25.00 50.00
34 Ron Ellis 25.00 50.00
35 Stan Mikita 300.00 600.00
36 Bobby Orr 1800.00 3000.00

1994 Be A Player Magazine

Cards were inserted into the NHLPA's Be A Player magazine. Cards are full color and are larger than standard size.

COMPLETE SET (4) 4.00 10.00
1 Paul Kariya 2.00 5.00
2 Felix Potvin .60 1.50
3 Joe Sakic 1.25 3.00
4 Teemu Selanne .75 2.00

1994-95 Be A Player

This set was issued by Upper Deck in conjunction with the NHL Players Association. The set contained 180 standard-size cards, each numbered with an "R" prefix. The card backs contained text and personal information. The set was released in hobby (blue) and retail (purple) packaging. Production total for both was announced at 1,995 cases. Each box was individually numbered on the side. Each pack included 11 cards and one autographed card. Suggested retail was $5.95 per pack. The NNO Wayne Gretzky promo card was included as a premium in an NHLPA hockey tips video. The card is slightly different from his R99 regular issue card. This set was not licensed by the National Hockey League and did not use any NHL team logos.

R1 Doug Gilmour .20 .50
R2 Joel Otto .10 .25
R3 Kirk Muller .10 .25
R4 Marty McInnis .10 .25
R5 Dave Gagner .12 .30
R6 Geoff Courtnall .10 .25
R7 Dale Hawerchuk .20 .50
R8 Mike Modano .25 .60
R9 Roman Hamrlik .12 .30
R10 Marty McSorley .10 .25
R11 Teemu Selanne .30 .75
R12 Jeremy Roenick .30 .75
R13 Glenn Healy .12 .30
R14 Darren Turcotte .10 .25
R15 Derian Hatcher .10 .25
R16 Enrico Ciccone .10 .25
R17 Tony Amonte .12 .30
R18 Mark Recchi .20 .50
R19 Eric Weinrich .10 .25
R20 John Vanbiesbrouck .12 .30
R21 Nick Kypreos .10 .25
R22 Gilbert Dionne .10 .25
R23 Theo Fleury .15 .40
R24 Todd Gill .10 .25
R25 Jari Kurri .12 .30
R26 Brad May .10 .25
R27 Russ Courtnall .10 .25
R28 Bill Ranford .12 .30
R29 Steve Yzerman .40 1.00
R30 Alexandre Daigle .10 .25
R31 Mike Hudson .10 .25
R32 Ray Bourque .25 .60
R33 Dave Andreychuk .15 .40
R34 Jason Arnott .12 .30
R35 Pavel Bure .15 .40
R36 Keith Tkachuk .15 .40
R37 Scott Niedermayer .15 .40
R38 Johan Garpenlov .10 .25
R39 Dino Ciccarelli .12 .30
R40 Rob Blake .15 .40
R41 Dave Manson .10 .25
R42 Adam Foote .10 .25
R43 Chris Pronger .15 .40
R44 Scott Lachance .10 .25
R45 Adam Oates .15 .40
R46 Brian Leetch .15 .40
R47 Guy Hebert .12 .30
R48 Brett Hull .30 .75
R49 Mike Ricci .10 .25
R50 Dave Ellett .10 .25
R51 Owen Nolan .15 .40
R52 Craig Janney .12 .30
R53 Trevor Linden .12 .30
R54 Ray Sheppard .12 .30
R55 Rob Niedermayer .12 .30
R56 Kevin Haller .10 .25
R57 Jeff Norton .10 .25
R58 Martin Brodeur .40 1.00
R59 Robb Stauber .10 .25
R60 Sylvain Turgeon .10 .25
R61 Pat Verbeek .12 .30
R62 Steve Smith .10 .25
R63 Jaromir Jagr .40 1.00
R64 Steve Duchesne .10 .25
R65 Tie Domi .12 .30
R66 Sylvain Lefebvre .10 .25
R67 Guy Carbonneau .10 .25
R68 Alexander Mogilny .12 .30
R69 Mario Lemieux .60 1.50
R70 Neil Wilkinson .10 .25
R71 Curtis Joseph .25 .60
R72 Wendel Clark .12 .30
R73 Kirk McLean .12 .30
R74 Mikael Renberg .12 .30
R75 Shawn McEachern .10 .25
R76 Mats Sundin .12 .30
R77 Craig Simpson .10 .25
R78 Phil Housley .12 .30
R79 Pat LaFontaine .15 .40
R80 Pierre Turgeon .12 .30
R81 Felix Potvin .15 .40
R82 Kevin Stevens .10 .25
R83 Steve Chiasson .10 .25
R84 Robert Petrovicky .10 .25
R85 Joe Juneau .12 .30
R86 Brendan Shanahan .20 .50
R87 Joe Sacco .10 .25
R88 David Reid .10 .25
R89 Louie DeBrusk .10 .25
R90 Darryl Sydor .10 .25
R91 Paul Coffey .15 .40
R92 Alexei Yashin .15 .40
R93 Jason Arnott .12 .30
R94 Gary Suter TT .10 .25
R95 Luc Robitaille TT .15 .40
R96 Joe Sakic .30 .75
R97 Chris Chelios .15 .40
R98 Tony Granato TT .10 .25
R99 Wayne Gretzky .75 2.00
R100 Joe Juneau .12 .30
R101 Curtis Joseph .25 .60
R102 Vincent Damphousse TT .12 .30
R103 Paul Kariya .20 .50
R104 Brendan Shanahan .20 .50
R105 Eric Desjardins TT .12 .30
R106 Eric Lindros .15 .40
R107 Kirk McLean SS .12 .30
R108 Mike Ricci SS .10 .25
R109 Chris Chelios .15 .40
R110 Chris Gratton SS .10 .25
R111 Doug Gilmour .20 .50
R112 Vincent Damphousse SS .12 .30
R113 Mark Osborne SS .10 .25
R114 Mike Modano .25 .60
R115 Steve Yzerman .40 1.00
R116 Garry Valk SS .10 .25
R117 Adam Graves SS .10 .25
R118 Doug Weight SS .12 .30
R119 Rob Niedermayer SS .12 .30
R120 Craig Simpson SS .10 .25
R121 Patrick Roy .40 1.00
R122 Ronnie Stern SS .10 .25
R123 Jiri Slegr SS .10 .25
R124 Darren Turcotte SS .10 .25
R125 Vladimir Malakhov SS .10 .25
R126 Paul Kariya TN .20 .50
R127 Mike Gartner TN .15 .40
R128 Scott Niedermayer TN .15 .40
R129 Dino Ciccarelli TN .12 .30
R130 Martin Brodeur TN .40 1.00
R131 Kevin Hatcher TN .10 .25
R132 Pat LaFontaine TN .15 .40
R133 Joel Otto TN .10 .25
R134 Jason Arnott .12 .30
R135 John Vanbiesbrouck TN .12 .30
R136 Derian Hatcher TN .10 .25
R137 Brendan Shanahan TN .20 .50
R138 Felix Potvin .15 .40
R139 Trevor Linden TN .12 .30
R140 Ken Baumgartner TN .12 .30
R141 Denis Leary .10 .25
R142 Wendel Clark DLO .12 .30
R143 Cam Neely .15 .40
R144 Jeremy Roenick .30 .75
R145 Sergei Fedorov .25 .60
R146 Scott Stevens DLO .15 .40
R147 Wayne Gretzky .75 2.00
R148 Darius Kasparaitis DLO .10 .25
R149 Brian Leetch DLO .15 .40
R150 Marty McSorley DLO .10 .25
R151 Paul Kariya .20 .50
R152 Peter Forsberg .40 1.00
R153 Brett Lindros .10 .25
R154 Kenny Jonsson .10 .25
R155 Jason Allison .12 .30
R156 Aaron Gavey .10 .25
R157 Jamie Storr .12 .30
R158 Viktor Kozlov .10 .25
R159 Valeri Bure .10 .25
R160 Oleg Tverdovsky .12 .30
R161 Brent Gretzky RH .10 .25
R162 Todd Harvey .10 .25
R163 Todd Warriner RH .10 .25
R164 Jeff Friesen .10 .25
R165 Adam Deadmarsh .10 .25
R166 Ken Baumgartner NHLPA .12 .30
R167 Terry Carkner NHLPA .10 .25
R168 Tie Domi NHLPA .12 .30
R169 Steve Larmer NHLPA .12 .30
R170 Larry Murphy NHLPA .12 .30
R171 Steve Thomas NHLPA .10 .25
R172 Alexei Yashin .15 .40
R173 Felix Potvin .15 .40
R174 Curtis Joseph .25 .60
R175 Rob Zamuner NHLPA .10 .25
R176 Wayne Gretzky FAN .75 2.00
R177 Pavel Bure FAN .15 .40
R178 Eric Lindros FAN .15 .40
R179 Patrick Roy FAN .40 1.00
R180 Doug Gilmour FAN .20 .50
NNO Wayne Gretzky PROMO 4.00 10.00

1994-95 Be A Player 99 All-Stars

COMPLETE SET (19) 30.00 80.00
G1 Wayne Gretzky 10.00 25.00
G2 Paul Coffey 2.00 5.00
G3 Rob Blake 2.00 5.00
G4 Pat Conacher 1.00 2.50
G5 Russ Courtnall 1.00 2.50
G6 Sergei Fedorov 2.00 5.00
G7 Grant Fuhr 2.00 5.00
G8 Todd Gill 1.00 2.50
G9 Tony Granato 1.00 2.50
G10 Brett Hull 3.00 8.00
G11 Charlie Huddy 1.00 2.50
G12 Steve Larmer 2.00 5.00
G13 Kelly Hrudey 2.00 5.00
G14 Al MacInnis 2.00 5.00
G15 Marty McSorley 2.00 5.00
G16 Jari Kurri 2.00 5.00
G17 Kirk Muller 1.00 2.50
G18 Rick Tocchet 2.00 5.00
G19 Steve Yzerman 6.00 15.00

1994-95 Be A Player Autographs

These authentic signature cards were issued one per foil pack. All autographs were guaranteed by the National Hockey League Players Association. The Jiri Slegr card (#119) was only available through a mail-in offer. The set is considered complete without it. Reportedly, most players signed approximately 2,400 of each card (including Slegr). Players who signed fewer are indicated below.

ONE SIGNATURE CARD PER PACK
1 Doug Gilmour/1250* 8.00 20.00
2 Adam Foote 2.00 5.00
3 Martin Brodeur 20.00 50.00
4 Alexander Semak 2.00 5.00
5 Dale Hawerchuk 4.00 10.00
6 Derek King 2.00 5.00
7 Mark Recchi 4.00 10.00
8 Fredrik Olausson 2.00 5.00
9 Dave McLlwain 2.00 5.00
10 Marc Bergevin 2.00 5.00
11 Teemu Selanne/600* 30.00 80.00
12 Jeremy Roenick/600* 15.00 40.00
13 Eric Lacroix 3.00 8.00
14 Marty McInnis 2.00 5.00
15 Kris King 2.00 5.00
16 Bill Ranford 2.50 6.00
17 Gary Roberts 2.00 5.00
18 Mark Osborne 2.00 5.00
19 Dmitri Mironov 2.00 5.00
20 John Vanbiesbrouck/600* 30.00 80.00
21 Alexei Zhamnov 2.50 6.00
22 Brad May 2.00 5.00
23 Doug Lidster 2.00 5.00
24 Mikael Renberg 2.50 6.00
25 Kris Draper 2.00 5.00
26 Darryl Sydor 2.00 5.00
27 Claude Lemieux 3.00 8.00
28 Doug Brown 2.00 5.00
29 Louie DeBrusk 2.00 5.00
30 Andy Moog 5.00 12.00
31 Donald Audette 2.00 5.00
32 Ray Bourque/600* 20.00 50.00
33 Brian Rolston 2.00 5.00
34 Ted Drury 2.00 5.00
35 Darren Turcotte 2.00 5.00
36 Gary Shuchuk 2.50 6.00
37 Mike Ricci 2.00 5.00
38 Kirk Maltby 2.00 5.00
39 Doug Bodger 2.00 5.00
40 Kirk Muller 2.00 5.00
41 Sylvain Lefebvre 2.00 5.00
42 Brent Grieve 2.00 5.00
43 Bill Houlder 2.00 5.00
44 Neil Wilkinson 2.00 5.00
45 Donald Dufresne 2.00 5.00
46 Brian Leetch/600* 12.00 30.00
47 Bryan Smolinski 2.00 5.00
48 Kevin Hatcher 2.00 5.00
49 Steven Rice 2.00 5.00
50 Bill Guerin 2.50 6.00
51 Grant Jennings 2.00 5.00
52 Dave Andreychuk 3.00 8.00
53 Sean Burke 2.50 6.00
54 Nick Kypreos 2.00 5.00
55 Drake Berehowsky 2.00 5.00
56 Kevin Haller 2.00 5.00
57 Bill Berg 2.00 5.00
58 Chris Simon 2.00 5.00
59 Owen Nolan UER 3.00 8.00
60 Don Sweeney 2.00 5.00
61 Johan Garpenlov 2.00 5.00
62 Garry Galley 2.00 5.00
63 Pat LaFontaine 5.00 12.00
64 Craig Berube 2.00 5.00
65 Dave Ellett 2.00 5.00
66 Robert Kron 2.00 5.00
67 Alexander Godynyuk 2.00 5.00
68 Markus Naslund 3.00 8.00
69 Joel Otto 2.00 5.00
70 Igor Ulanov 2.00 5.00
71 Pat Verbeek 2.50 6.00
72 Craig MacTavish 2.00 5.00
73 Gary Leeman 2.00 5.00
74 Kevin Todd 2.00 5.00
75 Mike Sullivan 2.00 5.00
76 Rob Pearson 2.00 5.00
77 Dave Gagner 2.50 6.00
78 Dirk Graham 2.00 5.00
79 Joe Sacco 2.00 5.00
80 Jassen Cullimore 2.00 5.00
81 Glen Featherstone 2.00 5.00
82 Scott Lachance 2.00 5.00
83 Kerry Huffman 2.00 5.00
84 Troy Loney 2.00 5.00
85 Rob Gaudreau 2.00 5.00
86 Brendan Shanahan/600* 20.00 50.00
87 Joe Murphy 2.00 5.00
88 Scott Niedermayer 3.00 8.00
89 Dan Quinn 2.50 6.00
90 Jeff Norton 2.00 5.00
91 Jim Dowd 2.00 5.00
92 Ray Ferraro 2.00 5.00
93 Shawn Burr 2.00 5.00
94 Denis Savard 4.00 10.00
95 Dave Manson 2.00 5.00
96 Joe Nieuwendyk 5.00 12.00
97 Tony Amonte 2.50 6.00
98 James Patrick 2.00 5.00
99 Guy Hebert 2.50 6.00
100 Peter Zezel 2.00 5.00
101 Shawn McEachern 2.00 5.00
102 Dave Lowry 2.00 5.00
103 David Reid 2.00 5.00
104 Todd Gill 2.00 5.00
105 John Cullen 2.00 5.00
106 Guy Carbonneau 2.00 5.00
107 Jeff Beukeboom 2.00 5.00
108 Wayne Gretzky/300* 300.00 500.00
109 Curtis Joseph 5.00 12.00
110 Jason Arnott 2.50 6.00
111 Eric DeSjardins 2.50 6.00
112 Gary Suter 2.00 5.00
113 Luc Robitaille 6.00 15.00
114 Tony Granato 2.00 5.00
115 Steve Yzerman/600* 30.00 80.00
116 Chris Gratton 2.00 5.00
117 Doug Weight 2.50 6.00
118 Garry Valk 2.00 5.00
119 Jiri Slegr 8.00 20.00
120 Vincent Damphousse 2.50 6.00
121 Vladimir Malakhov 2.00 5.00
122 Craig Simpson 2.00 5.00
123 Theo Fleury 6.00 15.00
124 Dave Poulin 2.00 5.00
125 Derian Hatcher 2.00 5.00
126 Jimmy Waite 2.00 5.00
127 Norm Maciver 2.00 5.00
128 Glenn Healy 2.50 6.00
129 Jocelyn Lemieux 2.00 5.00
130 Steve Chiasson 2.00 5.00
131 Keith Jones 2.00 5.00
132 Enrico Ciccone 2.00 5.00
133 Martin Lapointe 2.00 5.00
134 John MacLean 2.50 6.00
135 Geoff Courtnall 2.00 5.00
136 David Shaw 2.00 5.00
137 Steve Duchesne 2.00 5.00
138 Dean Evason 2.00 5.00
139 Eric Weinrich 2.00 5.00
140 Kelly Hrudey 2.50 6.00
141 Ted Donato 2.00 5.00
142 Darius Kasparaitis 2.00 5.00
143 Tie Domi 2.50 6.00
144 Terry Carkner 2.00 5.00
145 Steve Thomas 2.00 5.00
146 Steve Larmer 2.50 6.00
147 Rob Zamuner 2.00 5.00
148 Larry Murphy 2.50 6.00
149 Ken Baumgartner 2.50 6.00
150 Alexei Yashin/600* 3.00 8.00
151 Paul Kariya/600* 25.00 60.00
152 Todd Harvey 2.00 5.00
153A V.Kozlov VK 4.00 10.00
153B V.Kozlov full auto 20.00 50.00
154 Brent Gretzky 2.00 5.00
155 Petr Klima 2.00 5.00
156 Kent Manderville 2.00 5.00
157 Mike Eagles 2.00 5.00
158 Valeri Kamensky 2.50 6.00
159 Thomas Steen 2.00 5.00
160 Michal Pivonka 2.50 6.00
161 Steve Heinze 2.00 5.00
162 Nicklas Lidstrom 6.00 15.00
163 Uwe Krupp 2.00 5.00
164 Pat Elynuik 2.00 5.00
165 Mike Peca 2.50 6.00
166 Sylvain Cote 2.00 5.00
167 Trevor Kidd 2.50 6.00
168 Patrick Poulin 2.00 5.00
169 Shane Churla 2.00 5.00
170 Scott Mellanby 2.50 6.00
171 Mike Sillinger 2.00 5.00
172 Shayne Corson 2.00 5.00
173 Micah Aivazoff 2.00 5.00
174 Robert Lang 2.00 5.00
175 Rod Brind'Amour 2.50 6.00
176 Troy Murray 2.00 5.00
177 Mike Krushelnyski 2.00 5.00
178 Sergio Momesso 3.00 8.00

1994-95 Be A Player Up Close and Personal

This 10-card set was inserted two per box (1:8 packs) in Be A Player product. The cards featured an "Up Close" photo of the player and Roy Firestone, a popular ESPN show host. The text on the back was written by Firestone. The cards are numbered with an "UC" prefix.

COMPLETE SET (10) 20.00 50.00
UC1 Wayne Gretzky 6.00 15.00
UC2 Eric Lindros 1.00 2.50
UC3 Pavel Bure 1.00 2.50
UC4 Teemu Selanne 1.00 2.50
UC5 Steve Yzerman 4.00 10.00
UC6 Jeremy Roenick 1.25 3.00
UC7 Sergei Fedorov 1.50 4.00
UC8 Patrick Roy 6.00 15.00
UC9 Paul Kariya 1.00 2.50
UC10 Doug Gilmour .50 1.25

1995-96 Be A Player

This 225-card set was released in June 1996. It was released by Upper Deck, in conjunction with the NHLPA. The set was not licensed by the NHL, hence the absence of logos and insignia from player uniforms, and the color changes on the sweaters of players from Colorado and the Islanders. Suggested retail was $7.99 per ten-card pack, although packs tended to sell for more due to the allure of the one-per-pack autographs.

1 Brett Hull .12 .30
2 Jyrki Lumme .05 .15
3 Shean Donovan .05 .15
4 Yuri Khmylev .05 .15
5 Stephane Matteau .05 .15
6 Basil McRae .05 .15
7 Dimitri Yushkevich .05 .15
8 Ron Francis .12 .30
9 Keith Carney .05 .15
10 Brad Dalgarno .05 .15
11 Bob Carpenter .05 .15
12 Kevin Stevens .07 .20
13 Patrick Flatley .05 .15
14 Craig Muni .05 .15
15 Travis Green .07 .20
16 Derek Plante .05 .15
17 Mike Craig .05 .15
18 Chris Pronger .10 .25
19 Bret Hedican .05 .15
20 Mathieu Schneider .05 .15
21 Chris Therien .05 .15
22 Greg Adams .05 .15
23 Arturs Irbe .07 .20
24 Zigmund Palffy .10 .25
25 Peter Douris .05 .15
26 Bob Sweeney .05 .15
27 Chris Terreri .07 .20
28 Alexei Zhitnik .05 .15
29 Jay Wells .05 .15
30 Andrew Cassels .05 .15
31 Radek Bonk .05 .15
32 Brian Bellows .07 .20
33 Frantisek Kucera .05 .15
34 Valeri Bure .05 .15
35 Randy Wood .05 .15
36 Dimitri Khristich .05 .15
37 Randy Ladouceur .05 .15
38 Nelson Emerson .05 .15
39 Bryan Marchment .05 .15
40 Kevin Lowe .07 .20
41 Trevor Linden .10 .25
42 Neal Broten .07 .20
43 Tom Chorske .05 .15
44 Patrice Brisebois .05 .15
45 Wayne Presley .05 .15
46 Murray Craven .05 .15
47 Craig Janney .05 .15
48 Ken Daneyko .05 .15
49 Dino Ciccarelli .07 .20
50 Jason Dawe .05 .15
51 Brad McCrimmon .05 .15
52 Randy McKay .05 .15
53 Rudy Poeschek .05 .15
54 Calle Johansson .05 .15
55 Wendel Clark .10 .25
56 Rob Ray .05 .15
57 Garth Snow .07 .20
58 Joe Juneau .07 .20
59 Craig Wolanin .05 .15
60 Ray Sheppard .07 .20
61 Oleg Tverdovsky .10 .25
62 Geoff Sanderson .05 .15
63 Mike Ridley .05 .15
64 David Oliver .05 .15
65 Russ Courtnall .05 .15
66 Joe Reekie .05 .15
67 Ken Wregget .07 .20
68 Teppo Numminen .05 .15
69 Mikhail Shtalenkov .05 .15
70 Luke Richardson .05 .15
71 Brent Gilchrist .05 .15
72 Phil Housley .07 .20
73 Greg Johnson .05 .15
74 Sean Hill .05 .15
75 Karl Dykhuis .05 .15
76 Tim Cheveldae .07 .20
77 Shjon Podein .05 .15
78 Rene Corbet .05 .15
79 Ronnie Stern .05 .15
80 Mike Donnelly .05 .15
81 Randy Cunneyworth .05 .15
82 Rick Tocchet .07 .20
83 Dallas Drake .05 .15
84 Cam Russell .05 .15
85 Daren Puppa .07 .20
86 Benoit Brunet .05 .15
87 Paul Ranheim .05 .15
88 Bob Rouse .05 .15
89 Todd Elik .05 .15
90 Darcy Wakaluk .05 .15
91 Cliff Ronning .05 .15
92 Pat Conacher .05 .15
93 Todd Krygier .05 .15
94 Dave Babych .05 .15
95 Pat Falloon .05 .15
96 Don Beaupre .07 .20
97 Wayne Gretzky .50 1.25
98 Chris Joseph .05 .15
99 Vyacheslav Kozlov .07 .20
100 Brent Fedyk .05 .15
101 Tim Taylor .05 .15
102 Mike Eastwood .05 .15
103 Mike Keane .05 .15
104 Grant Ledyard .05 .15
105 Rob Dimaio .05 .15
106 Martin Straka .05 .15
107 Scott Young .05 .15
108 Zarley Zalapski .05 .15
109 Steve Leach .05 .15
110 Jody Hull .05 .15
111 Lyle Odelein .05 .15
112 Rob Corkum .05 .15
113 Rob Blake .07 .20
114 Randy Burridge .05 .15
115 Keith Primeau .05 .15
116 Glen Wesley .05 .15
117 Brian Bradley .07 .20
118 Andrei Kovalenko .05 .15
119 Patrik Juhlin .05 .15
120 John Tucker .05 .15
121 Stephane Fiset .07 .20
122 Mike Hough .05 .15
123 Steve Smith .05 .15
124 Tom Barrasso .07 .20
125 Ray Whitney .07 .20
126 Benoit Hogue .05 .15
127 Stu Barnes .05 .15
128 Craig Ludwig .05 .15
129 Curtis Leschyshyn .05 .15
130 John LeClair .10 .25
131 Dennis Vial .05 .15
132 Cory Stillman .05 .15
133 Roman Hamrlik .05 .15
134 Al MacInnis .10 .25
135 Igor Korolev .05 .15
136 Rick Zombo .05 .15
137 Zdeno Ciger .07 .20
138 Brian Savage .05 .15
139 Paul Ysebaert .05 .15
140 Brent Sutter .05 .15
141 Ed Olczyk .05 .15
142 Adam Creighton .05 .15
143 Jesse Belanger .05 .15
144 Glen Murray .05 .15
145 Alexander Selivanov .07 .20
146 Trent Yawney .05 .15
147 Bruce Driver .05 .15
148 Michael Nylander .05 .15
149 Martin Gelinas .05 .15
150 Yanic Perreault .05 .15
151 Craig Billington .07 .20
152 Pierre Turgeon .10 .25
153 Mike Modano .15 .40
154 Joe Mullen .07 .20
155 Todd Ewen .05 .15
156 Petr Nedved .07 .20
157 Dominic Roussel .05 .15
158 Murray Baron .05 .15
159 Robert Dirk .05 .15
160 Tomas Sandstrom .07 .20
161 Brian Holzinger RC .20 .50
162 Ken Klee RC .05 .15
163 Radek Dvorak RC .12 .30
164 Marcus Ragnarsson RC .12 .30
165 Aaron Gavey .05 .15
166 Jeff O'Neill .10 .25
167 Chad Kilger RC .10 .25
168 Todd Bertuzzi RC .12 .30
169 Robert Svehla .05 .15
170 Eric Daze .20 .50
171 Daniel Alfredsson RC .50 1.25
172 Shane Doan RC .30 .75
173 Kyle McLaren .05 .15
174 Saku Koivu .10 .25
175 Jere Lehtinen .07 .20
176 Nikolai Khabibulin .07 .20
177 Niklas Sundstrom .10 .25
178 Ed Jovanovski .10 .25
179 Jason Bonsignore .05 .15
180 Kenny Jonsson .10 .25
181 Vitali Yachmenev .10 .25
182 Alexei Kovalev .05 .15
183 Sandis Ozolinsh .07 .20
184 Rob Niedermayer .07 .20
185 Richard Park .10 .25
186 Adam Deadmarsh .05 .15
187 Sergei Krivokrasov .05 .15
188 Alexandre Daigle .05 .15
189 Jim Carey .07 .20
190 Todd Marchant .05 .15
191 Mike Richter .10 .25
192 Dominik Hasek .12 .30
193 Chris Osgood .07 .20
194 Ed Belfour .07 .20
195 Felix Potvin .10 .25
196 Grant Fuhr .10 .25
197 Patrick Roy .25 .60
198 Ron Hextall .10 .25
199 Jocelyn Thibault .07 .20
200 Kirk McLean .07 .20
201 Jari Kurri .10 .25
202 Bobby Holik .05 .15
203 Mats Sundin .10 .25
204 Alexander Mogilny .07 .20
205 Valeri Karpov .05 .15
206 Igor Larionov .05 .15
207 Valeri Zelepukin .05 .15
208 Jozef Stumpel .05 .15
209 Sergei Nemchinov .05 .15
210 Peter Bondra .10 .25
211 Chris Chelios .10 .25
212 Adam Graves .07 .20
213 Dale Hunter .07 .20
214 Tony Twist .05 .15
215 Keith Tkachuk .10 .25
216 Vladimir Konstantinov .07 .20
217 Sandy McCarthy .05 .15
218 Jamie Macoun .05 .15
219 Scott Stevens .10 .25
220 Mark Tinordi .05 .15
221 Bob Probert .07 .20
222 Gino Odjick .05 .15
223 Ulf Samuelsson .05 .15
224 Stu Grimson .05 .15
225 Marty McSorley .05 .15

1995-96 Be A Player Autographs

These authentic signed cards were inserted at a rate of one per pack. Every seventh pack featured a special signed card which was distinguished by unique die-cut corners. The card fronts are the same as the regular cards, but the backs of the signed cards feature a certificate of authenticity. Although production numbers were not officially revealed, documents suggest approximately 3,000 regular and 400 die-cut versions of each signed card were released. The quantities of the Wayne Gretzky cards (#S97) were intially reported at 802 signed and 99 die-cut copies. Upper Deck later announced the actual numbers as being 648 regular and 234 die-cut. The Mike Richter card (#191) was not inserted in packs, but was made available through a mail-in offer. The set is considered complete without this card.

S1 Brett Hull 6.00 15.00
S2 Jyrki Lumme 2.50 6.00
S3 Shean Donovan 2.50 6.00
S4 Yuri Khmylev 2.50 6.00
S5 Stephane Matteau 2.50 6.00
S6 Basil McRae 2.50 6.00
S7 Dimitri Yushkevich 2.50 6.00
S8 Ron Francis 6.00 15.00
S9 Keith Carney 2.50 6.00
S10 Brad Dalgarno 2.50 6.00
S11 Bob Carpenter 2.50 6.00
S12 Kevin Stevens 2.50 6.00
S13 Pat Flatley 2.50 6.00
S14 Craig Muni 2.50 6.00
S15 Travis Green 2.50 6.00
S16 Derek Plante 2.50 6.00
S17 Mike Craig 2.50 6.00
S18 Chris Pronger 6.00 15.00
S19 Bret Hedican 2.50 6.00
S20 Mathieu Schneider 2.50 6.00
S21 Chris Therien 2.50 6.00
S22 Greg Adams 2.50 6.00
S23 Arturs Irbe 4.00 10.00
S24 Zigmund Palffy 4.00 10.00
S25 Peter Douris 2.50 6.00
S26 Bob Sweeney 2.50 6.00
S27 Chris Terreri 2.50 6.00
S28 Alexei Zhitnik 2.50 6.00
S29 Jay Wells 2.50 6.00
S30 Andrew Cassels 2.50 6.00
S31 Radek Bonk 4.00 10.00
S32 Brian Bellows 2.50 6.00
S33 Frantisek Kucera 2.50 6.00
S34 Valeri Bure 4.00 10.00
S35 Randy Wood 2.50 6.00
S36 Dimitri Khristich 2.50 6.00
S37 Randy Ladouceur 2.50 6.00
S38 Nelson Emerson 2.50 6.00
S39 Bryan Marchment 4.00 10.00
S40 Kevin Lowe 4.00 10.00
S41 Trevor Linden 6.00 15.00
S42 Neal Broten 4.00 10.00
S43 Tom Chorske 2.50 6.00
S44 Patrice Brisebois 2.50 6.00
S45 Wayne Presley 2.50 6.00
S46 Murray Craven 2.50 6.00
S47 Craig Janney 2.50 6.00
S48 Ken Daneyko 2.50 6.00
S49 Dino Ciccarelli 4.00 10.00
S50 Jason Dawe 2.50 6.00
S51 Brad McCrimmon 8.00 20.00
S52 Randy McKay 2.50 6.00
S53 Rudy Poeschek 2.50 6.00
S54 Calle Johansson 2.50 6.00
S55 Wendel Clark 6.00 15.00
S56 Rob Ray 4.00 10.00
S57 Garth Snow 4.00 10.00
S58 Joe Juneau 4.00 10.00
S59 Craig Wolanin 2.50 6.00
S60 Ray Sheppard 2.50 6.00
S61 Oleg Tverdovsky 2.50 6.00
S62 Geoff Sanderson 2.50 6.00
S63 Mike Ridley 2.50 6.00
S64 David Oliver 2.50 6.00
S65 Russ Courtnall 2.50 6.00
S66 Joe Reekie 2.50 6.00
S67 Ken Wregget 5.00 12.00
S68 Teppo Numminen 2.50 6.00
S69 Mikhail Shtalenkov 2.50 6.00
S70 Luke Richardson 2.50 6.00
S71 Brent Gilchrist 2.50 6.00
S72 Phil Housley 2.50 6.00
S73 Greg Johnson 2.50 6.00
S74 Sean Hill 2.50 6.00
S75 Karl Dykhuis 2.50 6.00
S76 Tim Cheveldae 2.50 6.00
S77 Shjon Podein 2.50 6.00
S78 Rene Corbet 2.50 6.00
S79 Ron Stern 2.50 6.00
S80 Mike Donnelly 2.50 6.00
S81 Randy Cunneyworth 2.50 6.00
S82 Rick Tocchet 4.00 10.00
S83 Dallas Drake 2.50 6.00
S84 Cam Russell 2.50 6.00
S85 Daren Puppa 2.50 6.00
S86 Benoit Brunet 2.50 6.00
S87 Paul Ranheim 2.50 6.00
S88 Bob Rouse 2.50 6.00
S89 Todd Elik 2.50 6.00
S90 Darcy Wakaluk 2.50 6.00
S91 Cliff Ronning 2.50 6.00
S92 Pat Conacher 2.50 6.00
S93 Todd Krygier 2.50 6.00
S94 Dave Babych 2.50 6.00
S95 Pat Falloon 2.50 6.00
S96 Don Beaupre 4.00 10.00
S97 Wayne Gretzky/648* 125.00 250.00
S98 Chris Joseph 2.50 6.00
S99 Vyacheslav Kozlov 4.00 10.00
S100 Brent Fedyk 2.50 6.00
S101 Tim Taylor 2.50 6.00
S102 Mike Eastwood 2.50 6.00
S103 Mike Keane 2.50 6.00
S104 Grant Ledyard 2.50 6.00
S105 Rob Dimaio 2.50 6.00
S106 Martin Straka 2.50 6.00
S107 Scott Young 2.50 6.00
S108 Zarley Zalapski 3.00 8.00
S109 Steve Leach 2.50 6.00
S110 Jody Hull 2.50 6.00
S111 Lyle Odelein 2.50 6.00
S112 Bob Corkum 2.50 6.00
S113 Rob Blake 4.00 10.00
S114 Randy Burridge 2.50 6.00
S115 Keith Primeau 4.00 10.00
S116 Glen Wesley 2.50 6.00
S117 Brian Bradley 2.50 6.00
S118 Andrei Kovalenko 2.50 6.00
S119 Patrik Juhlin 2.50 6.00
S120 John Tucker 2.50 6.00
S121 Stephane Fiset 4.00 10.00
S122 Mike Hough 2.50 6.00
S123 Steve Smith 2.50 6.00
S124 Tom Barrasso 4.00 10.00
S125 Ray Whitney 2.50 6.00
S126 Benoit Hogue 2.50 6.00
S127 Stu Barnes 2.50 6.00
S128 Craig Ludwig 4.00 10.00
S129 Curtis Leschyshyn 2.50 6.00
S130 John LeClair 6.00 15.00
S131 Dennis Vial 2.50 6.00
S132 Cory Stillman 2.50 6.00
S133 Roman Hamrlik 2.50 6.00
S134 Al MacInnis 6.00 15.00
S135 Igor Korolev 2.50 6.00
S136 Rick Zombo 2.50 6.00
S137 Zdeno Ciger 2.50 6.00
S138 Brian Savage 2.50 6.00
S139 Paul Ysebaert 2.50 6.00
S140 Brent Sutter 4.00 10.00
S141 Ed Olczyk 2.50 6.00
S142 Adam Creighton 2.50 6.00
S143 Jesse Belanger 2.50 6.00
S144 Glen Murray 2.50 6.00
S145 Alexander Selivanov 2.50 6.00
S146 Trent Yawney 2.50 6.00
S147 Bruce Driver 2.50 6.00
S148 Michael Nylander 2.50 6.00
S149 Martin Gelinas 3.00 8.00
S150 Yanic Perreault 2.50 6.00
S151 Craig Billington 4.00 10.00
S152 Pierre Turgeon 4.00 10.00
S153 Mike Modano 10.00 25.00
S154 Joe Mullen 4.00 10.00
S155 Todd Ewen 2.50 6.00
S156 Petr Nedved 2.50 6.00
S157 Dominic Roussel 2.50 6.00
S158 Murray Baron 2.50 6.00
S159 Robert Dirk 2.50 6.00
S160 Tomas Sandstrom 2.50 6.00
S161 Brian Holzinger 2.50 6.00
S162 Ken Klee 2.50 6.00
S163 Radek Dvorak 2.50 6.00
S164 Marcus Ragnarsson 2.50 6.00
S165 Aaron Gavey 2.50 6.00
S166 Jeff O'Neill 2.50 6.00
S167 Chad Kilger 2.50 6.00
S168 Todd Bertuzzi 6.00 15.00
S169 Robert Svehla 2.50 6.00
S170 Eric Daze 2.50 6.00
S171 Daniel Alfredsson 6.00 15.00
S172 Shane Doan 4.00 10.00
S173 Kyle McLaren 2.50 6.00
S174 Saku Koivu 6.00 15.00
S175 Jere Lehtinen 4.00 10.00
S176 Nikolai Khabibulin 4.00 10.00
S177 Niklas Sundstrom 2.50 6.00
S178 Ed Jovanovski 4.00 10.00
S179 Jason Bonsignore 2.50 6.00
S180 Kenny Jonsson 2.50 6.00
S181 Vitali Yachmenev 2.50 6.00
S182 Alexei Kovalev 4.00 10.00
S183 Sandis Ozolinsh 2.50 6.00
S184 Rob Niedermayer 6.00 15.00
S185 Richard Park 2.50 6.00
S186 Adam Deadmarsh 2.50 6.00
S187 Sergei Krivokrasov 2.50 6.00
S188 Alexandre Daigle 4.00 10.00
S189 Jim Carey 4.00 10.00
S190 Todd Marchant 4.00 10.00
S191 Mike Richter Mail In 60.00 120.00
S192 Dominik Hasek 10.00 25.00
S193 Chris Osgood 6.00 15.00
S194 Ed Belfour 6.00 15.00
S195 Felix Potvin 8.00 20.00
S196 Grant Fuhr 6.00 15.00
S197 Patrick Roy 20.00 50.00
S198 Ron Hextall 6.00 15.00
S199 Jocelyn Thibault 4.00 10.00
S200 Kirk McLean 4.00 10.00
S201 Jari Kurri 6.00 15.00
S202 Bobby Holik 4.00 10.00
S203 Mats Sundin 8.00 20.00
S204 Alexander Mogilny 5.00 12.00
S205 Valeri Karpov 2.50 6.00
S206 Igor Larionov 4.00 10.00
S207 Valeri Zelepukin 2.50 6.00
S208 Jozef Stumpel 2.50 6.00
S209 Sergei Nemchinov 2.50 6.00
S210 Peter Bondra 4.00 10.00
S211 Chris Chelios 6.00 15.00
S212 Adam Graves 2.50 6.00
S213 Dale Hunter 4.00 10.00
S214 Tony Twist 5.00 12.00
S215 Keith Tkachuk 4.00 10.00
S216 Vladimir Konstantinov 25.00 60.00
S217 Sandy McCarthy 2.50 6.00
S218 Jamie Macoun 2.50 6.00
S219 Scott Stevens 6.00 15.00
S220 Mark Tinordi 2.50 6.00
S221 Bob Probert 8.00 20.00
S222 Gino Odjick 2.50 6.00
S223 Ulf Samuelsson 2.50 6.00
S224 Stu Grimson 4.00 10.00
S225 Marty McSorley 2.50 6.00

1995-96 Be A Player Autographs Die Cut

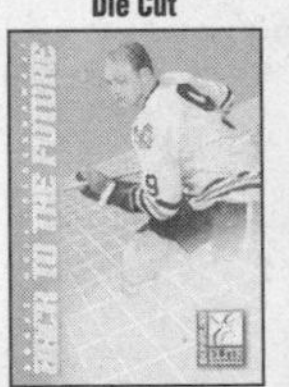

*DIE CUT: .6X TO 1.5X BASE AU/3000
ONE AUTOGRAPH PER PACK
S97 Wayne Gretzky/234* 300.00 500.00

1995-96 Be A Player Gretzky's Great Memories

COMPLETE SET (10) 40.00 80.00
COMMON GRETZKY (GM1-GM10) 4.00 10.00

1995-96 Be A Player Lethal Lines

COMPLETE SET (15) 20.00 50.0
LL1 Keith Tkachuk 1.50 4.0
LL2 Wayne Gretzky 5.00 12.0
LL3 Brett Hull 2.00 5.0
LL4 Eric Daze 1.50 4.0
LL5 Saku Koivu 1.50 4.0
LL6 Daniel Alfredsson 1.50 4.0
LL7 Pavel Bure 1.50 4.0
LL8 Sergei Fedorov 1.50 4.0
LL9 Alexander Mogilny 1.50 4.0
LL10 Paul Kariya 1.50 4.0
LL11 Mario Lemieux 3.00 8.0
LL12 Jaromir Jagr 2.00 5.0
LL13 Brendan Shanahan 1.50 4.0
LL14 Eric Lindros 1.50 4.0
LL15 Alexei Kovalev 1.25 3.0

1996-97 Be A Player

This 220-card set was issued by Pinnacle in two seri and was distributed in eight-card packs with a suggested retail price of $6.99. For the first time, the series was licensed by the NHL, as well as the NHLP and thus the players were allowed to be seen in their own uniforms. Promotional cards were issued to dealers in six-card and two-card packs. These cards mirror those in the regular set save for the addition o the word PROMO written on the card back. The numbering, however, is the same as the base cards. The P prefix has been added for checklist purposes only.

COMPLETE SET (220)	10.00	25.00
COMP.SERIES 1 (110)	6.00	15.00
COMP.SERIES 2 (110)	6.00	15.00
1 Todd Gill	.25	.60
2 Dave Andreychuk	.30	.75
3 Igor Kravchuk	.20	.50
4 Tom Fitzgerald	.20	.50
5 Jeremy Roenick	.40	1.00
6 Peter Popovic	.20	.50
7 Andy Moog	.30	.75
8 Steven Rice	.20	.50
9 Darren Langdon	.20	.50
10 Mark Fitzpatrick	.20	.50
11 Alexei Zhamnov	.25	.60
12 Luc Robitaille	.30	.75
13 Michal Pivonka	.20	.50
14 Kevin Hatcher	.20	.50
15 Stephane Yelle	.20	.50
16 Bill Ranford	.25	.60
17 Jamie Baker	.20	.50
18 Sean Burke	.20	.50
19 Al Iafrate	.20	.50
20 Mark Recchi	.40	1.00
21 Rod Brind'Amour	.30	.75
22 Doug Gilmour	.40	1.00
23 Mike Wilson	.20	.50
24 Barry Potomski RC	.20	.50
25 Mike Gartner	.30	.75
26 Jason Wiemer	.20	.50
27 Scott Lachance	.20	.50
28 Joe Murphy	.20	.50
29 Bill Guerin	.30	.75
30 Byron Dafoe	.20	.50
31 Esa Tikkanen	.20	.50
32 Ken Baumgartner	.20	.50
33 Valeri Kamensky	.25	.60
34 J.J. Daigneault	.20	.50
35 Ulf Dahlen	.20	.50
36 Jason Allison	.25	.60
37 Ted Donato	.20	.50
38 Pat Verbeek	.20	.50
39 Miroslav Satan	.20	.50
40 Eric Desjardins	.25	.60
41 Dave Karpa	.20	.50
42 Jeff Hackett	.25	.60
43 Doug Brown	.20	.50
44 Gord Murphy	.20	.50
45 Kelly Hrudey	.25	.60
46 Kelly Miller	.20	.50
47 Tie Domi	.25	.60
48 Alexei Yashin	.25	.60
49 German Titov	.20	.50
50 Stephane Richer	.25	.60
51 Corey Hirsch	.25	.60
52 Brad May	.20	.50
53 Joe Nieuwendyk	.30	.75
54 Sylvain Lefebvre	.20	.50
55 Brian Leetch	.30	.75
56 Petr Svoboda	.20	.50
57 Dave Manson	.20	.50
58 Jason Woolley	.20	.50
59 Scott Niedermayer	.30	.75
60 Kelly Chase	.20	.50
61 Guy Hebert	.25	.60
62 Shayne Corson	.20	.50
63 Jon Casey	.25	.60
64 Rob Zettler	.20	.50
65 Mikael Andersson	.20	.50
66 Tony Amonte	.25	.60
67 Johan Garpenlov	.20	.50
68 Denny Lambert	.20	.50
69 Jim McKenzie	.20	.50
70 Darren Turcotte	.20	.50
71 Eric Weinrich	.20	.50
72 Troy Mallette	.20	.50
73 Donald Audette	.20	.50
74 Philippe Boucher	.20	.50
75 Shawn Chambers	.20	.50
76 Joel Otto	.20	.50
77 Tommy Salo	.25	.60
78 Olaf Kolzig	.30	.75
79 Adrian Aucoin	.20	.50
80 Alek Stojanov	.20	.50
81 Robert Reichel	.20	.50
82 Marc Bureau	.20	.50
83 Alexander Godynyuk	.20	.50
84 Bill Berg	.20	.50
85 Marc Bergevin	.20	.50
86 Kevin Kaminski	.20	.50
87 Uwe Krupp	.20	.50
88 Boris Mironov	.20	.50
89 Bob Bassen	.20	.50
90 Darryl Shannon	.20	.50
91 Mikael Renberg	.25	.60
92 Mike Stapleton	.20	.50
93 David Roberts	.20	.50
94 Peter Zezel	.20	.50
95 Mathieu Dandenault	.20	.50
96 Bobby Dollas	.20	.50
97 Don Sweeney	.20	.50
98 Niklas Andersson	.20	.50
99 Pat Jablonski	.25	.60
100 John Slaney	.20	.50
101 Kevin Todd	.20	.50
102 Jamie Pushor	.20	.50
103 Andreas Johansson RC	.20	.50
104 Corey Schwab	.25	.60
105 Todd Simpson RC	.20	.50
106 Landon Wilson	.20	.50
107 Daniel Goneau RC	.30	.75
108 David Wilkie	.20	.50
109 Andreas Dackell RC	.30	.75
110 Marek Malik	.20	.50
111 Mark Messier	.30	.75
112 Francois Leroux	.20	.50
113 Michal Sykora	.20	.50
114 Rob Zamuner	.20	.50
115 Craig Berube	.20	.50
116 Mike Ricci	.20	.50
117 Adam Burt	.20	.50
118 Alexander Karpovtsev	.20	.50
119 Shawn McEachern	.20	.50
120 Shawn Antoski	.20	.50
121 Dave Reid	.20	.50
122 Todd Warriner	.20	.50
123 Markus Naslund	.30	.75
124 Martin Rucinsky	.20	.50
125 Bob Carpenter	.20	.50
126 Dean McAmmond	.20	.50
127 Trevor Kidd	.20	.50
128 Martin Lapointe	.20	.50
129 Enrico Ciccone	.20	.50
130 Dixon Ward	.20	.50
131 Jason Muzzatti	.25	.60
132 Bryan Smolinski	.20	.50
133 Norm Maciver	.20	.50
134 Fredrik Olausson	.20	.50
135 Daniel Lacroix	.20	.50
136 Mike Peluso	.20	.50
137 Andrei Nikolishin	.20	.50
138 Rhett Warrener	.20	.50
139 Ray Ferraro	.20	.50
140 Glenn Healy	.25	.60
141 Steve Duchesne	.20	.50
142 Tony Granato	.20	.50
143 Cory Cross	.20	.50
144 Jon Klemm	.20	.50
145 Sami Kapanen	.20	.50
146 Grant Marshall	.20	.50
147 Matthew Barnaby	.20	.50
148 Lyle Odelein	.20	.50
149 Joe Dziedzic	.20	.50
150 Sergei Gonchar	.20	.50
151 Doug Zmolek	.20	.50
152 Sean O'Donnell RC	.20	.50
153 Scott Thornton	.20	.50
154 Steve Heinze	.20	.50
155 Garry Valk	.20	.50
156 Jeff Finley	.20	.50
157 Trent Klatt	.20	.50
158 Jeff Beukeboom	.20	.50
159 Theo Fleury	.60	1.50
160 Dana Murzyn	.20	.50
161 Tommy Albelin	.25	.60
162 Bryan McCabe	.20	.50
163 Shaun Van Allen	.20	.50
164 Rick Tabaracci	.25	.60
165 Kevin Miller	.20	.50
166 Mariusz Czerkawski	.20	.50
167 Gerald Diduck	.20	.50
168 Brad McCrimmon	.20	.50
169 Stephane Matteau	.20	.50
170 Scott Daniels	.20	.50
171 Scott Mellanby	.25	.60
172 Sandy Moger	.20	.50
173 Steve Konowalchuk	.20	.50
174 Doug Weight	.30	.75
175 Darren McCarty	.20	.50
176 Darryl Sydor	.20	.50
177 Dave Ellett	.20	.50
178 Bob Boughner RC	.20	.50
179 Derek Armstrong	.20	.50
180 Gary Suter	.20	.50
181 Donald Brashear	.20	.50
182 Chris Tamer	.20	.50
183 Darrin Shannon	.20	.50
184 Stanislav Neckar	.20	.50
185 Brent Severyn	.20	.50
186 Steve Rucchin	.20	.50
187 Jeff Norton	.25	.60
188 Steven Finn	.20	.50
189 Kjell Samuelsson	.20	.50
190 Jeff Friesen	.20	.50
191 Shawn Burr	.20	.50
192 Paul Laus	.20	.50
193 Jeff Odgers	.20	.50
194 Keith Jones	.20	.50
195 Richard Matvichuk	.20	.50
196 Adam Foote	.20	.50
197 Bob Errey	.20	.50
198 Ryan Smyth	.25	.60
199 Mark Janssens	.20	.50
200 Claude Lapointe	.20	.50
201 Brian Noonan	.20	.50
202 Damian Rhodes	.25	.60
203 Dale Hawerchuk	.40	1.00
204 Bill Lindsay	.20	.50
205 Brian Skrudland	.20	.50
206 Curtis Joseph	.30	.75
207 Jon Rohloff	.20	.50
208 Doug Bodger	.20	.50
209 Steve Sullivan RC	.25	.60
210 Ricard Persson	.20	.50
211 Dwayne Roloson RC	2.00	5.00
212 Mike Dunham	.20	.50
213 Marcel Cousineau RC	.20	.50
214 Eric Fichaud	.25	.60
215 Matt Johnson	.20	.50
216 Fredrik Modin RC	.75	2.00
217 Denis Pederson	.20	.50
218 Kevin Hodson RC	.30	.75
219 Drew Bannister	.20	.50
220 Mike Grier RC	.50	1.25
P44 Gord Murphy PROMO	.20	.50
P52 Brad May PROMO	.20	.50
P55 Brian Leetch PROMO	.30	.75
P67 Johan Garpenlov PROMO	.20	.50
P89 Bob Bassen PROMO	.20	.50
P91 Mikael Renberg PROMO	.25	.60
P119 Shawn MacEachern PROMO	.20	.50
P176 Darryl Sydor PROMO	.20	.50
P181 Donald Brashear PROMO	.20	.50
P217 Denis Pederson PROMO	.20	.50
P218 Kevin Hodson PROMO	.30	.75
P219 Drew Bannister PROMO	.20	.50

1996-97 Be A Player Autographs

These autographs were inserted one per pack. Gold foil distinguishes them from base cards. Alexei Zhamnov did not sign, and thus the set is considered complete at 219 cards. A silver parallel version of the autograph set existed as well. The cards were distinguishable by the silver foil backing on the card fronts. Although no odds were published, these cards were inserted at a rate of about 1:30 packs.

ONE AUTO CARD PER PACK
*SILVER AUTO: .6X TO 1.5X BASIC AU

1 Todd Gill	2.50	6.00
2 Dave Andreychuk	3.00	8.00
3 Igor Kravchuk	2.00	5.00
4 Tom Fitzgerald	2.00	5.00
5 Jeremy Roenick	5.00	12.00
6 Peter Popovic	2.00	5.00
7 Andy Moog	3.00	8.00
8 Steven Rice	2.00	5.00
9 Darren Langdon	2.00	5.00
10 Mark Fitzpatrick	2.00	5.00
12 Luc Robitaille	3.00	8.00
13 Michal Pivonka	2.00	5.00
14 Kevin Hatcher	2.00	5.00
15 Stephane Yelle	2.00	5.00
16 Bill Ranford	2.50	6.00
17 Jamie Baker	2.00	5.00
18 Sean Burke	2.00	5.00
19 Al Iafrate	2.00	5.00
20 Mark Recchi	4.00	10.00
21 Rod Brind'Amour	3.00	8.00
22 Doug Gilmour	4.00	10.00
23 Mike Wilson	2.00	5.00
24 Barry Potomski	2.00	5.00
25 Mike Gartner	3.00	8.00
26 Jason Wiemer	2.00	5.00
27 Scott Lachance	2.00	5.00
28 Joe Murphy	2.00	5.00
29 Bill Guerin	3.00	8.00
30 Byron Dafoe	2.00	5.00
31 Esa Tikkanen	2.00	5.00
32 Ken Baumgartner	2.00	5.00
33 Valeri Kamensky	2.50	6.00
34 J.J. Daigneault	2.00	5.00
35 Ulf Dahlen	2.00	5.00
36 Jason Allison	2.50	6.00
37 Ted Donato	2.00	5.00
38 Pat Verbeek	2.00	5.00
39 Miroslav Satan	2.00	5.00
40 Eric Desjardins	2.50	6.00
41 Dave Karpa	2.00	5.00
42 Jeff Hackett	2.50	6.00
43 Doug Brown	2.00	5.00
44 Gord Murphy	2.00	5.00
45 Kelly Hrudey	2.50	6.00
46 Kelly Miller	2.00	5.00
47 Tie Domi	2.50	6.00
48 Alexei Yashin	2.50	6.00
49 German Titov	2.00	5.00
50 Stephane Richer	2.50	6.00
51 Corey Hirsch	2.50	6.00
52 Brad May	2.00	5.00
53 Joe Nieuwendyk	3.00	8.00
54 Sylvain Lefebvre	2.00	5.00
55 Brian Leetch	3.00	8.00
56 Petr Svoboda	2.00	5.00
57 Dave Manson	2.00	5.00
58 Jason Woolley	2.00	5.00
59 Scott Niedermayer	3.00	8.00
60 Kelly Chase	2.00	5.00
61 Guy Hebert	2.50	6.00
62 Shayne Corson	2.00	5.00
63 Jon Casey	2.50	6.00
64 Rob Zettler	2.00	5.00
65 Mikael Andersson	2.00	5.00
66 Tony Amonte	2.50	6.00
67 Johan Garpenlov	2.00	5.00
68 Denny Lambert	2.00	5.00
69 Jim McKenzie	2.00	5.00
70 Darren Turcotte	2.00	5.00
71 Eric Weinrich	2.00	5.00
72 Troy Mallette	2.00	5.00
73 Donald Audette	2.00	5.00
74 Philippe Boucher	2.00	5.00
75 Shawn Chambers	2.00	5.00
76 Joel Otto	2.00	5.00
77 Tommy Salo	2.50	6.00
78 Olaf Kolzig	3.00	8.00
79 Adrian Aucoin	2.00	5.00
80 Alek Stojanov	2.00	5.00
81 Robert Reichel	2.00	5.00
82 Marc Bureau	2.00	5.00
83 Alexander Godynyuk	2.00	5.00
84 Bill Berg	2.00	5.00
85 Marc Bergevin	2.00	5.00
86 Kevin Kaminski	2.00	5.00
87 Uwe Krupp	2.00	5.00
88 Boris Mironov	2.00	5.00
89 Bob Bassen	2.00	5.00
90 Darryl Shannon	2.00	5.00
91 Mikael Renberg	2.50	6.00
92 Mike Stapleton	2.00	5.00
93 David Roberts	2.00	5.00
94 Peter Zezel	2.00	5.00
95 Mathieu Dandenault	2.00	5.00
96 Bobby Dollas	2.00	5.00
97 Don Sweeney	2.00	5.00
98 Niklas Andersson	2.00	5.00
99 Pat Jablonski	2.50	6.00
100 John Slaney	2.00	5.00
101 Kevin Todd	2.00	5.00
102 Jamie Pushor	2.00	5.00
103 Andreas Johansson	2.00	5.00
104 Corey Schwab	2.50	6.00
105 Todd Simpson	2.00	5.00
106 Landon Wilson	2.00	5.00
107 Daniel Goneau	3.00	8.00
108 David Wilkie	2.00	5.00
109 Andreas Dackell	3.00	8.00
110 Marek Malik	2.00	5.00
111 Mark Messier	12.00	30.00
112 Francois Leroux	2.00	5.00
113 Michal Sykora	2.00	5.00
114 Rob Zamuner	2.00	5.00
115 Craig Berube	2.00	5.00
116 Mike Ricci	2.00	5.00
117 Adam Burt	2.00	5.00
118 Alexander Karpovtsev	2.00	5.00
119 Shawn McEachern	2.00	5.00
120 Shawn Antoski	2.00	5.00
121 Dave Reid	2.00	5.00
122 Todd Warriner	2.00	5.00
123 Markus Naslund	3.00	8.00
124 Martin Rucinsky	2.00	5.00
125 Bob Carpenter	2.00	5.00
126 Dean McAmmond	2.00	5.00
127 Trevor Kidd	2.00	5.00
128 Martin Lapointe	2.00	5.00
129 Enrico Ciccone	2.00	5.00
130 Dixon Ward	2.00	5.00
131 Jason Muzzatti	2.50	6.00
132 Bryan Smolinski	2.00	5.00
133 Norm Maciver	2.00	5.00
134 Fredrik Olausson	2.00	5.00
135 Daniel Lacroix	2.00	5.00
136 Mike Peluso	2.00	5.00
137 Andrei Nikolishin	2.00	5.00
138 Rhett Warrener	2.00	5.00
139 Ray Ferraro	2.00	5.00
140 Glenn Healy	2.50	6.00
141 Steve Duchesne	2.00	5.00
142 Tony Granato	2.00	5.00
143 Cory Cross	2.00	5.00
144 Jon Klemm	2.00	5.00
145 Sami Kapanen	2.00	5.00
146 Grant Marshall	2.00	5.00
147 Matthew Barnaby	2.00	5.00
148 Lyle Odelein	2.00	5.00
149 Joe Dziedzic	2.00	5.00
150 Sergei Gonchar	2.00	5.00
151 Doug Zmolek	2.00	5.00
152 Sean O'Donnell	2.00	5.00
153 Scott Thornton	2.00	5.00
154 Steve Heinze	2.00	5.00
155 Garry Valk	2.00	5.00
156 Jeff Finley	2.00	5.00
157 Trent Klatt	2.00	5.00
158 Jeff Beukeboom	2.00	5.00
159 Theo Fleury	6.00	15.00
160 Dana Murzyn	2.00	5.00
161 Tommy Albelin	2.50	6.00
162 Bryan McCabe	2.00	5.00
163 Shaun Van Allen	2.00	5.00
164 Rick Tabaracci	2.50	6.00
165 Kevin Miller	2.00	5.00
166 Mariusz Czerkawski	2.00	5.00
167 Gerald Diduck	2.00	5.00
168 Brad McCrimmon	2.00	5.00
169 Stephane Matteau	2.00	5.00
170 Scott Daniels	2.00	5.00
171 Scott Mellanby	2.50	6.00
172 Sandy Moger	2.00	5.00
173 Steve Konowalchuk	2.00	5.00
174 Doug Weight	3.00	8.00
175 Darren McCarty	2.00	5.00
176 Darryl Sydor	2.00	5.00
177 Dave Ellett	2.00	5.00
178 Bob Boughner	2.00	5.00
179 Derek Armstrong	2.00	5.00
180 Gary Suter	2.00	5.00
181 Donald Brashear	2.00	5.00
182 Chris Tamer	2.00	5.00
183 Darrin Shannon	2.00	5.00
184 Stanislav Neckar	2.00	5.00
185 Brent Severyn	2.00	5.00
186 Steve Rucchin	2.00	5.00
187 Jeff Norton	2.50	6.00
188 Steven Finn	2.00	5.00
189 Kjell Samuelsson	2.00	5.00
190 Jeff Friesen	2.00	5.00
191 Shawn Burr	2.00	5.00
192 Paul Laus	2.00	5.00
193 Jeff Odgers	2.00	5.00
194 Keith Jones	2.00	5.00
195 Richard Matvichuk	2.00	5.00
196 Adam Foote	2.00	5.00
197 Bob Errey	2.00	5.00
198 Ryan Smyth	2.50	6.00
199 Mark Janssens	2.00	5.00
200 Claude Lapointe	2.00	5.00
201 Brian Noonan	2.00	5.00
202 Damian Rhodes	2.50	6.00
203 Dale Hawerchuk	4.00	10.00
204 Bill Lindsay	2.00	5.00
205 Brian Skrudland	2.00	5.00
206 Curtis Joseph	8.00	20.00
207 Jon Rohloff	2.00	5.00
208 Doug Bodger	2.00	5.00
209 Steve Sullivan	2.50	6.00
210 Ricard Persson	2.00	5.00
211 Dwayne Roloson	2.00	5.00
212 Mike Dunham	2.00	5.00
213 Marcel Cousineau	2.00	5.00
214 Eric Fichaud	2.50	6.00
215 Matt Johnson	2.00	5.00
216 Fredrik Modin	8.00	20.00
217 Denis Pederson	2.00	5.00
218 Kevin Hodson	3.00	8.00
219 Drew Bannister	2.00	5.00
220 Mike Grier	4.00	10.00

1996-97 Be A Player Biscuit In The Basket

COMPLETE SET (25)	25.00	60.00
1 Wayne Gretzky	6.00	15.00
2 Mario Lemieux	4.00	10.00
3 Eric Lindros	2.00	5.00
4 Theo Fleury	2.50	6.00
5 Peter Forsberg	2.00	5.00
6 Keith Tkachuk	1.25	3.00
7 Sergei Fedorov	2.00	5.00
8 Mike Modano	2.00	5.00
9 Jaromir Jagr	3.00	8.00
10 Brendan Shanahan	1.50	4.00
11 Teemu Selanne	2.50	6.00
12 Mats Sundin	1.25	3.00
13 Steve Yzerman	3.00	8.00
14 Brett Hull	6.00	15.00
15 Zigmund Palffy	1.25	3.00
16 Joe Sakic	2.00	5.00
17 John LeClair	1.25	3.00
18 Pavel Bure	1.50	4.00
19 Mark Messier	2.00	5.00
20 Paul Kariya	1.50	4.00
21 Jason Arnott	1.00	2.50
22 Saku Koivu	1.25	3.00
23 Daniel Alfredsson	1.25	3.00
24 Alexander Mogilny	1.00	2.50
25 Owen Nolan	1.25	3.00

1996-97 Be A Player Lemieux Die Cut

This two-card set commemorated the career of future Hall-of-Famer, Mario Lemieux, with a special interlocking, all-foil Dufex, die-cut insert. The first card was randomly inserted in Series 1 packs with it's matching, interlocking counterpart inserted in Series 2 packs. Only 66 of each card was produced and sequentially numbered.

STATED PRINT RUN 66 SER.#'d SETS

1 Mario Lemieux	100.00	200.00
2 Mario Lemieux	100.00	200.00

1996-97 Be A Player Lindros Die Cut

This two-card set honored the superstar center, Eric Lindros, with a special interlocking, all-foil Dufex, die-cut insert. Each card carried an authentic autograph. The first card was randomly inserted in Series 1 packs with it's matching, interlocking counterpart inserted in Series 2 packs. Only 88 of each card was produced and sequentially numbered.

STATED PRINT RUN 88 SER.#'d SETS

1 Eric Lindros AU	60.00	150.00
2 Eric Lindros AU	60.00	150.00

1996-97 Be A Player Link to History

Randomly inserted at an approximate rate of 1:2 packs, cards from this 20-card set featured ten top rookie standouts matched with their 10 mega-star veteran counterparts. The first five rookie "Links" appeared in Series I with the second five veteran "Links" and featured silver foil with blue accents. The second five rookie "Links" appeared in Series II with the first five veteran "Links" and featured silver foil with red accents.

COMPLETE SET (20)	8.00	20.00
COMP.SERIES 1 (10)	4.00	10.00
COMP.SERIES 2 (10)	4.00	10.00
1A Jarome Iginla	.75	2.00
1B Teemu Selanne	1.25	3.00
2A Harry York	.60	1.50
2B Peter Forsberg	1.00	2.50
3A Sergei Berezin	1.00	2.50
3B Brendan Shanahan	.75	2.00
4A Ethan Moreau	.60	1.50
4B Pavel Bure	.75	2.00
5A Rem Murray	.60	1.50
5B Jason Arnott	.50	1.25
6A Jamie Langenbrunner	.40	1.00
6B Paul Kariya	.75	2.00
7A Jim Campbell	.40	1.00
7B Eric Lindros	1.00	2.50
8A Jonas Hoglund	.40	1.00
8B Pat LaFontaine	.60	1.50
9A Wade Redden	.40	1.00
9B Steve Yzerman	1.50	4.00
10A Patrick Lalime	.75	2.00
10B John Vanbiesbrouck	.60	1.50
2B Peter Forsberg PROMO	1.00	2.50

1996-97 Be A Player Link to History Autographs

An authentic autograph and gold foil on each card front make these parallel cards easy to identify from their more common Link to History counterparts. Exact odds per pack were not released, but they're significantly tougher to pull than the non-autographed cards. Because of a delayed return, Ethan Moreau's cards were inserted in Series II packs only; Teemu Selanne's autographed cards replaced them in Series I packs. A silver parallel version of the autograph was also created. The cards were distinguishable by the silver foil backing on the card fronts. Although no odds were published, these cards were inserted at a rate of about 1:30 packs.

*SILVER AUTO: .8X TO 2X BASIC AU

1A Jarome Iginla	6.00	15.00
1B Teemu Selanne	8.00	20.00
2A Harry York	5.00	12.00
2B Peter Forsberg	12.00	30.00
3A Sergei Berezin	8.00	20.00
3B Brendan Shanahan	6.00	15.00
4A Ethan Moreau	5.00	12.00
4B Pavel Bure	10.00	25.00
5A Rem Murray	5.00	12.00
5B Jason Arnott	4.00	10.00
6A Jamie Langenbrunner	3.00	8.00
6B Paul Kariya	12.00	30.00
7A Jim Campbell	3.00	8.00
7B Eric Lindros	15.00	40.00
8A Jonas Hoglund	3.00	8.00
8B Pat LaFontaine	5.00	12.00
9A Wade Redden	3.00	8.00
9B Steve Yzerman	15.00	40.00
10A Patrick Lalime	6.00	15.00
10B John Vanbiesbrouck	5.00	12.00

1996-97 Be A Player Stacking the Pads

COMPLETE SET (15)	12.00	30.00
1 Patrick Lalime	.75	2.00
2 Chris Osgood	.60	1.50
3 Ron Hextall	.50	1.25
4 John Vanbiesbrouck	.60	1.50
5 Martin Brodeur	4.00	10.00
6 Felix Potvin	1.50	4.00
7 Nikolai Khabibulin	.50	1.25
8 Jim Carey	.60	1.50
9 Grant Fuhr	.60	1.50
10 Mike Richter	.60	1.50
11 Dominik Hasek	1.25	3.00
12 Andy Moog	.60	1.50
13 Patrick Roy	4.00	10.00
14 Curtis Joseph	.60	1.50
15 Jocelyn Thibault	.60	1.50

1997-98 Be A Player

The 1997-98 Be A Player set was issued by Pinnacle in two series totalling 250 cards and was distributed in eight-card packs with a suggested retail price of $6.99. The fronts featured color action photos of players with a heavy emphasis on rookies and Calder Trophy candidates in a white and net-shadow border. The backs carried a head photo with player information and career statistics.

COMPLETE SET (250)	6.00	15.00
1 Eric Lindros	.50	1.25
2 Martin Brodeur	.60	1.50
3 Saku Koivu	.30	.75
4 Felix Potvin	.30	.75
5 Adam Oates	.30	.75
6 Rob DiMaio	.20	.50
7 Jari Kurri	.30	.75
8 Andrew Cassels	.20	.50
9 Trevor Linden	.25	.60
10 Jocelyn Thibault	.20	.50
11 Chris Chelios	.30	.75
12 Paul Coffey	.30	.75
13 Nikolai Khabibulin	.30	.75
14 Robert Lang	.20	.50
15 Brett Hull	.40	1.00
16 Mike Sillinger	.20	.50
17 Lyle Odelein	.20	.50
18 Bryan Berard	.20	.50
19 Craig Muni	.20	.50
20 Kris Draper	.20	.50
21 Ed Jovanovski	.20	.50
22 Keith Tkachuk	.30	.75
23 Dean Malkoc	.25	.60
24 Cory Stillman	.25	.60
25 Chris Osgood	.30	.75
26 Dainius Zubrus	.25	.60
27 Yves Racine	.25	.60
28 Eric Cairns RC	.30	.75
29 Dan Bylsma	.25	.60
30 Chris Terreri	.20	.50
31 Bill Huard	.25	.60
32 Warren Rychel	.25	.60
33 Scott Walker	.25	.60
34 Brian Holzinger	.25	.60
35 Roman Turek	.25	.60
36 Ron Tugnutt	.30	.75
37 Mike Richter	.30	.75
38 Mattias Norstrom	.25	.60
39 Joe Sacco	.25	.60
40 Derek King	.25	.60
41 Brad Werenka	.20	.50
42 Paul Kruse	.25	.60
43 Mike Knuble RC	.30	.75
44 Mike Peca	.25	.60
45 Jean-Yves Leroux RC	.30	.75
46 Ray Sheppard	.25	.60
47 Reid Simpson	.25	.60
48 Rob Brown	.25	.60
49 Dave Babych	.20	.50
50 Scott Pellerin	.20	.50
51 Bruce Gardiner RC	.25	.60
52 Adam Deadmarsh	.20	.50
53 Curtis Brown	.20	.50
54 Jason Marshall	.20	.50
55 Gerald Diduck	.20	.50
56 Mick Vukota	.20	.50
57 Kevin Dean	.20	.50
58 Adam Graves	.20	.50
59 Craig Conroy	.20	.50
60 Cale Hulse	.25	.60
61 Dimitri Khristich	.25	.60
62 Chris Wells	.25	.60
63 Travis Green	.25	.60
64 Tyler Wright	.25	.60
65 Chris Simon	.25	.60
66 Mikhail Shtalenkov	.25	.60
67 Anson Carter	.20	.50
68 Zarley Zalapski	.20	.50
69 Per Gustafsson	.25	.60
70 Jayson More	.25	.60
71 Steve Thomas	.25	.60
72 Todd Marchant	.25	.60
73 Gary Roberts	.25	.60
74 Richard Smehlik	.20	.50
75 Aaron Miller	.20	.50
76 Daren Puppa	.25	.60
77 Garth Snow	.25	.60
78 Greg DeVries	.25	.60
79 Randy Burridge	.20	.50
80 Jim Cummins	.25	.60
81 Rich Pilon	.25	.60
82 Chris McAlpine	.20	.50
83 Joe Sakic	.50	1.25
84 Ted Drury	.25	.60
85 Brent Gilchrist	.30	.75
86 Dallas Eakins RC	.30	.75
87 Bruce Driver	.25	.60
88 Jamie Huscroft	.25	.60
89 Jeff Brown	.25	.60
90 Janne Laukkanen	.25	.60
91 Ken Klee	.25	.60
92 Peter Bondra	.25	.60
93 Ian Moran	.25	.60
94 Stephane Quintal	.25	.60
95 Jason York	.25	.60
96 Todd Harvey	.25	.60
97 Slava Kozlov	.25	.60
98 Kevin Haller	.25	.60
99 Alexei Zhamnov	.20	.50
100 Craig Johnson	.20	.50
101 Mike Keane	.20	.50
102 Craig Rivet	.25	.60
103 Roman Vopat	.25	.60
104 Jim Johnson	.25	.60
105 Ray Whitney	.25	.60
106 Ron Sutter	.25	.60
107 Jamie McLennan	.20	.50
108 Kris King	.20	.50
109 Lance Pitlick RC	.30	.75
110 Mike Dunham	.25	.60
111 Jim Dowd	.25	.60
112 Geoff Sanderson	.25	.60
113 Vladimir Vujtek	.25	.60
114 Tim Taylor	.25	.60
115 Sandis Ozolinsh	.25	.60
116 Scott Daniels	.25	.60
117 Bob Corkum	.25	.60
118 Kirk McLean	.25	.60
119 Darcy Tucker	.30	.75
120 Dennis Vaske	.25	.60
121 Kirk Muller	.20	.50
122 Jay McKee	.20	.50
123 Jere Lehtinen	.25	.60
124 Ruslan Salei	.25	.60
125 Al MacInnis	.30	.75
126 Ulf Samuelsson	.30	.75
127 Rick Tocchet	.20	.50
128 Nick Kypreos	.20	.50
129 Joel Bouchard	.20	.50
130 Jeff O'Neill	.25	.60
131 Daniel McGillis RC	.25	.60
132 Sean Pronger	.20	.50
133 Vladimir Malakhov	.20	.50
134 Petr Sykora	.20	.50
135 Zigmund Palffy	.30	.75
136 Joe Reekie	.20	.50
137 Chris Gratton	.20	.50
138 Craig Billington	.20	.50
139 Steve Washburn	.20	.50
140 Robert Kron	.20	.50
141 Larry Murphy	.30	.75
142 Shean Donovan	.25	.60
143 Scott Young	.25	.60
144 Janne Niinimaa	.25	.60
145 Ken Belanger RC	.30	.75
146 Pavol Demitra	.40	1.00
147 Roman Hamrlik	.25	.60
148 Lonny Bohonos	.25	.60
149 Mike Eagles	.25	.60
150 Kelly Buchberger	.25	.60
151 Mattias Timander	.25	.60
152 Benoit Hogue	.25	.60
153 Joey Kocur	.20	.50
154 Mats Lindgren	.20	.50
155 Aki Berg	.20	.50
156 Tim Sweeney	.20	.50
157 Vincent Damphousse	.25	.60
158 Dan Kordic	.25	.60
159 Darius Kasparaitis	.25	.60
160 Randy McKay	.25	.60
161 Steve Staios	.25	.60
162 Brendan Witt	.25	.60
163 Paul Ysebaert	.25	.60
164 Greg Adams	.25	.60
165 Kent Manderville	.20	.50
166 Steve Dubinsky	.20	.50
167 David Nemirovsky	.20	.50
168 Todd Bertuzzi	.30	.75
169 Frederic Chabot RC	.25	.60
170 Dmitri Mironov	.25	.60
171 Pat Peake	.25	.60
172 Ed Ward	.25	.60
173 Jeff Shantz	.25	.60
174 Dave Gagner	.20	.50
175 Randy Cunneyworth	.20	.50
176 Daymond Langkow	.20	.50
177 Alex Hicks	.20	.50
178 Darby Hendrickson	.20	.50
179 Mike Sullivan	.20	.50
180 Anders Eriksson	.25	.60
181 Turner Stevenson	.25	.60
182 Shane Churla	.25	.60
183 Dave Lowry	.20	.50
184 Joe Juneau	.25	.60
185 Bob Essensa	.25	.60
186 James Black	.20	.50
187 Michal Grosek	.20	.50
188 Tomas Holmstrom	.20	.50
189 Ian Laperriere	.20	.50
190 Terry Yake	.20	.50
191 Jason Smith	.20	.50
192 Sergei Zholtok	.25	.60
193 Doug Houda	.25	.60
194 Guy Carbonneau	.30	.75
195 Terry Carkner	.25	.60
196 Alexei Gusarov	.25	.60
197 Vladimir Tsyplakov	.25	.60
198 Jarrod Skalde	.25	.60
199 Marty Murray	.25	.60
200 Aaron Ward	.20	.50
201 Bobby Holik	.20	.50
202 Steve Chiasson	.20	.50
203 Brantt Myhres	.20	.50
204 Eric Messier RC	.30	.75
205 Rene Corbet	.25	.60
206 Mathieu Schneider	.25	.60
207 Tom Chorske	.25	.60
208 Doug Lidster	.25	.60
209 Igor Ulanov	.25	.60
210 Blair Atcheynum RC	.30	.75
211 Sebastien Bordeleau	.25	.60
212 Alexei Morozov	.25	.60
213 Vaclav Prospal RC	.25	.60
214 Brad Bombardir RC	.25	.60
215 Mattias Ohlund	.25	.60
216 Chris Dingman RC	.30	.75
217 Erik Rasmussen	.25	.60
218 Mike Johnson RC	.25	.60
219 Chris Phillips	.25	.60
220 Sergei Samsonov	.20	.50
221 Patrick Marleau	.40	1.00
222 Alyn McCauley	.25	.60
223 Ryan Vandenbussche RC	.25	.60
224 Daniel Cleary	.25	.60
225 Magnus Arvedson RC	.30	.75
226 Brad Isbister	.25	.60
227 Pascal Rheaume RC	.25	.60
228 Patrik Elias RC	.50	1.25
229 Krzysztof Oliwa RC	.30	.75
230 Tyler Moss RC	.25	.60
231 Jamie Rivers	.25	.60
232 Joe Thornton	.30	.75
233 Steve Shields RC	.30	.75
234 Dave Scatchard RC	.25	.60
235 Patrick Cote RC	.25	.60
236 Rich Brennan RC	.25	.60
237 Boyd Devereaux	.25	.60
238 Per Johan Axelsson RC	.30	.75
239 Craig Millar RC	.25	.60
240 Juha Ylonen	.25	.60
241 Donald MacLean RC	.30	.75
242 Jaroslav Svejkovsky	.25	.60
243 Marco Sturm RC	.30	.75
244 Steve McKenna RC	.40	1.00
245 Derek Morris RC	.30	.75
246 Dean Chynoweth	.25	.60
247 Alexander Mogilny	.25	.60
248 Ray Bourque	.50	1.25
249 Ed Belfour	.30	.75
250 John LeClair	.30	.75
P3 Saku Koivu PROMO	.30	.75

1997-98 Be A Player Autographs

Inserted one per pack, this 250-card set was an autographed gold foil enhanced parallel version of the base set. Die-cut and limited prismatic die-cut parallel autographed versions of the base set were also produced. Die-cut auto stated odds were 1:7. The prismatic parallel had a stated print run of 100 sets.

ONE AUTO PER PACK
*DIE CUT: .8X TO 2X BASIC AUTO
*DIE CUT: .5X TO 1.2X BASIC AU SP
*PRISM/100: 1.2X TO 3X BASIC AUTO
*PRISM/100: .6X TO 1.5X BASIC AU SP

1 Eric Lindros SP	5.00	12.00
2 Martin Brodeur SP	20.00	50.00
3 Saku Koivu	3.00	8.00
4 Felix Potvin	5.00	12.00
5 Adam Oates	3.00	8.00
6 Rob DiMaio	2.00	5.00
7 Jari Kurri	3.00	8.00
8 Andrew Cassels	2.00	5.00
9 Trevor Linden	2.50	6.00
10 Jocelyn Thibault	2.00	5.00
11 Chris Chelios	3.00	8.00
12 Paul Coffey	3.00	8.00
13 Nikolai Khabibulin	3.00	8.00
14 Robert Lang	2.00	5.00
15 Brett Hull SP	15.00	40.00
16 Mike Sillinger	2.00	5.00
17 Lyle Odelein	2.00	5.00
19 Craig Muni	2.00	5.00
20 Kris Draper	2.00	5.00
21 Ed Jovanovski	2.00	5.00
22 Keith Tkachuk	3.00	8.00
23 Dean Malkoc	2.50	6.00
24 Cory Stillman	2.50	6.00
25 Chris Osgood	3.00	8.00
26 Dainius Zubrus	2.50	6.00
27 Yves Racine	2.50	6.00
28 Eric Cairns	3.00	8.00
29 Dan Bylsma	2.50	6.00
30 Chris Terreri	2.00	5.00
31 Bill Huard	2.50	6.00
32 Warren Rychel	2.50	6.00
33 Scott Walker	2.50	6.00
34 Brian Holzinger	2.50	6.00
35 Roman Turek	2.50	6.00
36 Ron Tugnutt	3.00	8.00
37 Mike Richter	5.00	12.00
38 Mattias Norstrom	2.50	6.00
39 Joe Sacco	2.50	6.00
40 Derek King	2.50	6.00
41 Brad Werenka	2.00	5.00
42 Paul Kruse	2.50	6.00
43 Mike Knuble	3.00	8.00
44 Mike Peca	2.50	6.00
45 Jean-Yves Leroux	3.00	8.00
46 Ray Sheppard	2.50	6.00
47 Reid Simpson	2.50	6.00
48 Rob Brown	2.50	6.00
49 Dave Babych	2.00	5.00
50 Scott Pellerin	2.00	5.00
51 Bruce Gardiner	2.50	6.00
52 Adam Deadmarsh	2.00	5.00
53 Curtis Brown	2.00	5.00
54 Jason Marshall	2.00	5.00
55 Gerald Diduck	2.00	5.00
56 Mick Vukota	2.00	5.00
57 Kevin Dean	2.00	5.00
58 Adam Graves	2.00	5.00
59 Craig Conroy	2.00	5.00
60 Cale Hulse	2.50	6.00
61 Dimitri Khristich	2.50	6.00
62 Chris Wells	2.50	6.00
63 Travis Green	2.50	6.00
64 Tyler Wright	2.50	6.00
65 Chris Simon	2.50	6.00
66 Mikhail Shtalenkov	2.50	6.00
67 Anson Carter	2.00	5.00
68 Zarley Zalapski	2.00	5.00
69 Per Gustafsson	2.50	6.00
70 Jayson More	2.50	6.00
71 Steve Thomas	2.50	6.00
72 Todd Marchant	2.50	6.00
73 Gary Roberts	2.50	6.00
74 Richard Smehlik	2.00	5.00
75 Aaron Miller	2.00	5.00
76 Daren Puppa	2.50	6.00
77 Garth Snow	2.50	6.00
78 Greg DeVries	2.50	6.00
79 Randy Burridge	2.00	5.00
80 Jim Cummins	2.50	6.00
81 Rich Pilon	2.50	6.00
82 Chris McAlpine	2.00	5.00
83 Joe Sakic SP	25.00	60.00
84 Ted Drury	2.50	6.00
85 Brent Gilchrist	3.00	8.00
86 Dallas Eakins	3.00	8.00
87 Bruce Driver	2.50	6.00
88 Jamie Huscroft	2.50	6.00
89 Jeff Brown	2.50	6.00
90 Janne Laukkanen	2.50	6.00
91 Ken Klee	2.50	6.00
92 Peter Bondra	2.50	6.00
93 Ian Moran	2.50	6.00
94 Stephane Quintal	2.50	6.00
95 Jason York	2.50	6.00
96 Todd Harvey	2.50	6.00
97 Slava Kozlov	2.50	6.00
98 Kevin Haller	2.50	6.00
99 Alexei Zhamnov	2.00	5.00
100 Craig Johnson	2.00	5.00
101 Mike Keane	2.00	5.00

HOCKEY **DEALER DIRECTORY**

ALASKA

BOSCO'S
2301 Spenard Road,
Anchorage, AK 99503
907-274-4112
patmoe@boscos.com

DON'S SPORTSCARDS
9900 Old Seward Hwy., Ste 8, Anchorage, AK 99515
907-349-8804
donssports@aol.com

ARIZONA

PHOENIX SPORTS CARDS
5870 West Thunderbird Road, Suite A2, Glendale, AZ 85306
602-548-1254
phxsportscards@cox.net

CALIFORNIA

A & N SPORTS CARDS
105 W Arrow Highway, Suite #7, San Dimas, CA 91773
909-394-2375
ansportscard@yahoo.com

CLAIREMONT SPORTCARDS
3949 Clairemont Drive Suite 4, San Diego, CA 92117
858-270-4945
clairemontsc@netscape.net

PSA RESEARCH DEPARTMENT
1610 E. St Andrew Place, Santa Ana, CA 92705
949-567-1246
VLopez@collectors.com

COLORADO

BILL'S SPORTS COLLECTIBLES
2335 S Broadway, Denver, CO 80210
303-733-4878
billssportscolo@aol.com

FLORIDA

BIG LEAGUE
920 State Road 436, Casselberry, FL 32707
407-834-2273

ORLANDO SPORTSCARDS SOUTH
9476 S Orange Blossom Trl., Orlando, FL 32837
407-240-0384
orlandosportscards@hotmail.com

GEORGIA

J & J'S SPORTS CARDS
2135 E Main St. SW, Snellville , GA 30078
770-736-9998
gotbaseballcards@bellsouth.net

ILLINOIS

GIZMO'S SPORTSCARDS
P.O. Box #134, Davis Junction, IL 61020
815-540-5206
pirate8@aol.com

THE BASEBALL CARD KING
1002 Geneva Street, Shorewood, IL 60404
815-609-7777
foxforce5@outlook.com

INDIANA

BASEBALL CARD EXCHANGE INC.
2412 U.S Highway 41, Schererville, IN 46375
219-515-6907

MORE FUN SPORTSCARDS
706 Joliet St., Dyer, IN 46311
219-322-5080

MASSACHUSETTS

BAYSTATE SPORTS CARDS
861 Edgell Rd., Framingham, MA 01701
508-877-2273

NEWSBREAK, INC.
Route 6 Target Plaza, Swansea, MA 02777
508-675-9380
newsbreak@cox.net

MICHIGAN

S & F SPORT CARDS
26019 Lorelei Dr., Flat Rock, MI 48134
734-782-5462
frankmio@provide.net

THE STADIUM
3980 East Wilder Rd., Bay City, MI 48706
989-667-0450
dumars1935@charter.net

MINNESOTA

BLUE LINE SPORTS CARDS
35751 678th Street, Hill City, MN 55748
218-838-8136
JKimball56401@yahoo.com

COLLECTORS CONNECTION
2220 Mountain Shadow Drive, Duluth, MN 55811
218-726-1360
adavis@bizDuluth.com

THREE STARS SPORTSCARDS
2825 Hamline Ave N, Roseville, MN 55113
651-633-6041
dan@threestarssportscards.com

MISSOURI

SPORTS CARD DUGOUT
8041b Watson Rd., St. Louis, MO 63119
314-963-9666
RFauthSCD@sbcglobal.net

NEVADA

LEGACY SPORTS CARDS
8125 W Sahara Ave Ste 160, Las Vegas, NV 89117
702-341-6525
marcel@legacysportscards.com

NEW HAMPSHIRE
Diamond King Sports
1 Bayside Rd., Ste 114, Greenland, NH 03840
603-431-8311

NEW YORK

A&S Sports LLC.
825 Carman Ave., Westbury, NY 11590
516-398-7800

BP SPORTSCARDS & MEMORABILIA
38 N Main St., Florida, NY 10921
845-651-1660

CENTER ICE SPORTS CARDS
11 Glenalby Road (Corner of Blvd.), Tonawanda, NY 14150,
716-957-3742
www.centericesportscards.com

MONTASY COMICS NYC
431 5th Avenue, 2nd Floor, New York, NY 10016
212-683-2018
info@montasycomicsnyc.com

NIAGRA SPORTS CARDS
5154 Townline Rd., Sanborn, NY 14132
716-550-2946
cmworczak@yahoo.com

OHIO

TRIPLE PLAY SPORTSCARDS
399 S State St., Suite 15,

Westerville, OH 43081
614-899-7066
tripleplayohio@gmail.com

PENNSYLVANIA

BASEBALL CARD CASTLE
20555 Route 19, Cranberry Twp, PA 16066, USA
724-772-0490
bbcardcas@aol.com

SPORTS AMERICA SPORTS CARDS
6 State Rd., Suite 101, Mechanicsburg, PA 17050
717-422-6716
sportsamerica@comcast.net

SPORTSCARDS ETC.
Robinson Twp. 5629-B Steubenville Pike, McKees Rocks, PA 15136
412-787-3235
scerob@comcast.net

RHODE ISLAND

BASEBALL CARDS OF RHODE ISLAND
6861 Post Rd., North Kingstown, RI 02852
401-885-7340
baseballcardsofri@gmail.com

CENTRAL SPORTS CARDS
791 Central Ave., Pawtucket, RI 02861
401-724-2040

WASHINGTON

KNUTSEN'S NORTHWEST SPORTSCARDS
5510 6th Ave., Suite A, Tacoma, WA 98406
253-564-9204
northwestsportscards@yahoo.com

BRITISH COLUMBIA

SPORTS CARD ALLEY
5-2220 Bowen Road, Nanaimo, BC V9S 1H9
250-758-1484
sportsca@telus.net

MANITOBA

SPORTS CARD CONNECTION
51 D St. Annes Rd., Winnipeg, MB R2M 2Y6
204-256-7080
sportscc1@gmail.com

NOVA SCOTIA

D & M SPORTS CARDS
201 Chain Lake Dr. Unit 16, Halifax, NS B3S 1C8
902-468-1895

ONTARIO

PRINCE WHOLESALERS
614 Gordon Baker Rd., North York, ON M2H 3B4
416-492-1280
info@princewholesalers.com

QUEBEC

GESTION IMAGINAIRE INC.
2700 Blvd. Laurier, Centre d'achat Laurier, Quebec, QC G1V 4P7, CANADA
418-658-5639
sport@imaginaire.com

SASKATCHEWAN

AJW Sportscards
Unit 33-134 Primrose Dr., Saskatoon, SK S7K 5S6
306-384-3838
lawson@ajwsportscards.com

HOCKEY HEAVEN AB
Kungsgatan 6, 65224 Karlstad, SWEDEN
465-415-7870

RICHARD F. REA INC.
734-425-6780
reabros@aol.com

102 Craig Rivet 2.50 6.00
103 Roman Vopat 2.50 6.00
104 Jim Johnson 2.50 6.00
105 Ray Whitney 2.50 6.00
106 Ron Sutter 2.50 6.00
107 Jamie McLennan 2.00 5.00
108 Kris King 2.00 5.00
109 Lance Pitlick 3.00 8.00
110 Mike Dunham 2.50 6.00
111 Jim Dowd 2.50 6.00
112 Geoff Sanderson 2.50 6.00
113 Vladimir Vujtek 2.50 6.00
114 Tim Taylor 2.50 6.00
115 Sandis Ozolinsh 2.50 6.00
116 Scott Daniels 2.50 6.00
117 Bob Corkum 2.50 6.00
118 Kirk McLean 2.50 6.00
119 Darcy Tucker 3.00 8.00
120 Dennis Vaske 2.50 6.00
121 Kirk Muller 2.00 5.00
122 Jay McKee 2.00 5.00
123 Jere Lehtinen 2.50 6.00
124 Ruslan Salei 2.50 6.00
125 Al MacInnis SP 8.00 20.00
126 Ulf Samuelsson 3.00 8.00
127 Rick Tocchet 2.00 5.00
128 Nick Kypreos 2.00 5.00
129 Joel Bouchard 2.00 5.00
130 Jeff O'Neill 2.50 6.00
131 Daniel McGillis 2.50 6.00
132 Sean Pronger 2.00 5.00
133 Vladimir Malakhov 2.00 5.00
134 Petr Sykora 2.00 5.00
135 Zigmund Palffy 3.00 8.00
136 Joe Reekie 2.00 5.00
137 Chris Gratton 2.00 5.00
138 Craig Billington 2.00 5.00
139 Steve Washburn 2.00 5.00
140 Robert Kron 2.00 5.00
141 Larry Murphy 3.00 8.00
142 Shean Donovan 2.50 6.00
143 Scott Young 2.50 6.00
144 Janne Niinimaa 2.50 6.00
145 Ken Belanger 3.00 8.00
146 Pavol Demitra 4.00 10.00
147 Roman Hamrlik 2.50 6.00
148 Lonny Bohonos 2.50 6.00
149 Mike Eagles 2.50 6.00
150 Kelly Buchberger 2.50 6.00
151 Mattias Timander 2.50 6.00
152 Benoit Hogue 2.50 6.00
153 Joey Kocur 2.00 5.00
154 Mats Lindgren 2.00 5.00
155 Aki Berg 2.00 5.00
156 Tim Sweeney 2.00 5.00
157 Vincent Damphousse 2.50 6.00
158 Dan Kordic 2.50 6.00
159 Darius Kasparaitis 2.50 6.00
160 Randy McKay 2.50 6.00
161 Steve Staios 2.50 6.00
162 Brendan Witt 2.50 6.00
163 Paul Ysebaert 2.50 6.00
164 Greg Adams 2.50 6.00
165 Kent Manderville 2.00 5.00
166 Steve Dubinsky 2.00 5.00
167 David Nemirovsky 2.00 5.00
168 Todd Bertuzzi 3.00 8.00
169 Frederic Chabot 2.50 6.00
170 Dmitri Mironov 2.50 6.00
171 Pat Peake 2.50 6.00
172 Ed Ward 2.50 6.00
173 Jeff Shantz 2.50 6.00
174 Dave Gagner 2.00 5.00
175 Randy Cunneyworth 2.00 5.00
176 Daymond Langkow 2.00 5.00
177 Alex Hicks 2.00 5.00
178 Darby Hendrickson 2.00 5.00
179 Mike Sullivan 2.00 5.00
180 Anders Eriksson 2.50 6.00
181 Turner Stevenson 2.50 6.00
182 Shane Churla 2.50 6.00
183 Dave Lowry 2.00 5.00
184 Joe Juneau 2.50 6.00
185 Bob Essensa 2.50 6.00
186 James Black 2.00 5.00
187 Michal Grosek 2.00 5.00
188 Tomas Holmstrom 2.00 5.00
189 Ian Laperriere 2.00 5.00
190 Terry Yake 2.00 5.00
191 Jason Smith 2.00 5.00
192 Sergei Zholtok 2.50 6.00
193 Doug Houda 2.50 6.00
194 Guy Carbonneau 3.00 8.00
195 Terry Carkner 2.50 6.00
196 Alexei Gusarov 2.50 6.00
197 Vladimir Tsyplakov 2.50 6.00
198 Jarrod Skalde 2.50 6.00
199 Marty Murray 2.50 6.00
200 Aaron Ward 2.00 5.00
201 Bobby Holik 2.00 5.00
202 Steve Chiasson 2.00 5.00
203 Brantt Myhres 2.00 5.00
204 Eric Messier 3.00 8.00
205 Rene Corbet 2.50 6.00
206 Mathieu Schneider 2.50 6.00
207 Tom Chorske 2.50 6.00
208 Doug Lidster 2.50 6.00
209 Igor Ulanov 2.50 6.00
210 Blair Atcheynum 3.00 8.00
211 Sebastien Bordeleau 2.50 6.00
212 Alexei Morozov 2.50 6.00
213 Vaclav Prospal 2.50 6.00
214 Brad Bombardir 2.50 6.00
215 Mattias Ohlund 2.50 6.00
216 Chris Dingman 3.00 8.00
217 Erik Rasmussen 2.50 6.00
218 Mike Johnson 2.50 6.00
219 Chris Phillips 2.50 6.00
220 Sergei Samsonov 2.00 5.00
221 Patrick Marleau 4.00 10.00
222 Alyn McCauley 2.50 6.00
223 Ryan Vandenbussche 2.50 6.00
224 Daniel Cleary 2.50 6.00
225 Magnus Arvedson 3.00 8.00
226 Brad Isbister 2.50 6.00
227 Pascal Rheaume 2.50 6.00
228 Patrik Elias 5.00 12.00
229 Krzysztof Oliwa 3.00 8.00
230 Tyler Moss 2.50 6.00
231 Jamie Rivers 2.50 6.00
232 Joe Thornton 3.00 8.00
233 Steve Shields 3.00 8.00
234 Dave Scatchard 2.50 6.00
235 Patrick Cote 2.50 6.00
236 Rich Brennan 2.50 6.00
237 Boyd Devereaux 2.50 6.00
238 Per Johan Axelsson 3.00 8.00
239 Craig Millar 2.50 6.00
240 Juha Ylonen 2.50 6.00
241 Donald MacLean 3.00 8.00
242 Jaroslav Svejkovsky 2.50 6.00
243 Marco Sturm 3.00 8.00
244 Steve McKenna 4.00 10.00
245 Derek Morris 3.00 8.00
246 Dean Chynoweth 2.50 6.00
247 Alexander Mogilny SP 12.00 30.00
248 Ray Bourque SP 25.00 60.00
249 Ed Belfour SP 15.00 40.00
250 John LeClair SP 12.00 30.00

1997-98 Be A Player One Timers

COMPLETE SET (20) 12.50 30.00
STATED ODDS 1:7
1 Wayne Gretzky 3.00 8.00
2 Keith Tkachuk .60 1.50
3 Eric Lindros 1.00 2.50
4 Brendan Shanahan .75 2.00
5 Paul Kariya .75 2.00
6 Brett Hull .75 2.00
7 Jaromir Jagr 1.50 4.00
8 Teemu Selanne 1.25 3.00
9 John LeClair .60 1.50
10 Mike Modano 1.00 2.50
11 Peter Forsberg .75 2.00
12 Pavel Bure .75 2.00
13 Peter Bondra .50 1.25
14 Saku Koivu .60 1.50
15 Pat LaFontaine .60 1.50
16 Patrik Elias 1.00 2.50
17 Richard Zednik .50 1.25
18 Mike Johnson .50 1.25
19 Marco Sturm .60 1.50
20 Joe Thornton .60 1.50

1997-98 Be A Player Stacking the Pads

COMPLETE SET (15) 12.00 30.00
STATED ODDS 1:15
1 Guy Hebert .50 1.25
2 Dominik Hasek 3.00 8.00
3 Felix Potvin .60 1.50
4 Patrick Roy 3.00 8.00
5 Ed Belfour .60 1.50
6 Chris Osgood .60 1.50
7 Curtis Joseph .60 1.50
8 John Vanbiesbrouck .60 1.50
9 Jocelyn Thibault .40 1.00
10 Mike Richter .60 1.50
11 Martin Brodeur 3.00 8.00
12 Garth Snow .50 1.25
13 Nikolai Khabibulin .60 1.50
14 Tommy Salo .40 1.00
15 Byron Dafoe .40 1.00

1997-98 Be A Player Take A Number

COMPLETE SET (20) 30.00 60.00
STATED ODDS 1:15
TN1 Ray Bourque 2.00 5.00
TN2 Eric Daze .75 2.00
TN3 Ed Belfour 1.00 2.50
TN4 Patrick Roy 5.00 12.00
TN5 Sergei Fedorov 1.25 3.00
TN6 John Vanbiesbrouck .75 2.00
TN7 Doug Gilmour .75 2.00
TN8 Wayne Gretzky 6.00 15.00
TN9 Bryan Berard .75 2.00
TN10 Eric Lindros 1.00 2.50
TN11 Paul Coffey 1.00 2.50
TN12 Jeremy Roenick 1.25 3.00
TN13 Brett Hull 1.25 3.00
TN14 Pierre Turgeon .75 2.00
TN15 Keith Primeau .75 2.00
TN16 Daren Puppa .75 2.00
TN17 Mark Messier 1.00 2.50
TN18 Alexander Mogilny .75 2.00
TN19 Joe Sakic 2.00 5.00
TN20 Jaromir Jagr 1.50 4.00

1998-99 Be A Player

The 1998-99 Be A Player set was issued in two series totalling 300 cards and was distributed in eight-card packs with an SRP of $6.99. The fronts featured color action photos of players with a heavy emphasis on rookies and Calder Trophy candidates printed on 30 pt. card stock with a full foil treatment. The backs carried a head photo with player information and career statistics. A gold-foiled parallel version was also created and inserted into random packs.

COMPLETE SET (300) 60.00 120.00
COMP.SERIES 1 (150) 25.00 60.00
COMP.SERIES 2 (150) 25.00 60.00
1 Jason Marshall .25 .60
2 Paul Kariya .50 1.25
3 Teemu Selanne .75 2.00
4 Guy Hebert .30 .75
5 Ted Drury .25 .60
6 Byron Dafoe .30 .75
7 Rob Dimaio .25 .60
8 Ray Bourque .60 1.50
9 Joe Thornton .75 2.00
10 Sergei Samsonov .30 .75
11 Dimitri Khristich .25 .60
12 Michael Peca .25 .60
13 Jason Woolley .25 .60
14 Matthew Barnaby .25 .60
15 Brian Holzinger .25 .60
16 Dixon Ward .30 .75
17 Tyler Moss .25 .60
18 Jarome Iginla .75 2.00
19 Marty McInnis .25 .60
20 Andrew Cassels .25 .60
21 Jason Wiemer .25 .60
22 Trevor Kidd .25 .60
23 Keith Primeau .25 .60
24 Sami Kapanen .25 .60
25 Robert Kron .25 .60
26 Glen Wesley .25 .60
27 Jeff Hackett .25 .60
28 Tony Amonte .30 .75
29 Alexei Zhamnov .25 .60
30 Eric Weinrich .25 .60
31 Jeff Shantz .25 .60
32 Christian Laflamme .25 .60
33 Adam Foote .25 .60
34 Patrick Roy 1.00 2.50
35 Peter Forsberg .60 1.50
36 Adam Deadmarsh .25 .60
37 Joe Sakic .60 1.50
38 Eric Lacroix .25 .60
39 Guy Carbonneau .25 .60
40 Mike Modano .60 1.50
41 Roman Turek .25 .60
42 Mike Keane .25 .60
43 Sergei Zubov .25 .60
44 Jere Lehtinen .30 .75
45 Sergei Fedorov .60 1.50
46 Steve Yzerman 1.25 3.00
47 Chris Osgood .40 1.00
48 Larry Murphy .30 .75
49 Vyacheslav Kozlov .25 .60
50 Darren McCarty .25 .60
51 Boris Mironov .25 .60
52 Roman Hamrlik .25 .60
53 Bill Guerin .40 1.00
54 Mike Grier .25 .60
55 Todd Marchant .25 .60
56 Ray Whitney .25 .60
57 Dave Gagner .25 .60
58 Scott Mellanby .25 .60
59 Robert Svehla .25 .60
60 Viktor Kozlov .30 .75
61 Luc Robitaille .40 1.00
62 Yanic Perreault .25 .60
63 Jozef Stumpel .30 .75
64 Sandy Moger .25 .60
65 Ian Laperriere .25 .60
66 Jocelyn Thibault .30 .75
67 Dave Manson .25 .60
68 Mark Recchi .50 1.25
69 Patrick Poulin .25 .60
70 Benoit Brunet .25 .60
71 Turner Stevenson .25 .60
72 Mike Dunham .30 .75
73 Tom Fitzgerald .30 .75
74 Darren Turcotte .30 .75
75 Brad Smyth .25 .60
76 J.J. Daigneault .25 .60
77 Dave Andreychuk .40 1.00
78 Jason Arnott .30 .75
79 Martin Brodeur .75 2.00
80 Randy McKay .30 .75
81 Patrik Elias .40 1.00
82 Kevin Dean .25 .60
83 Tommy Salo .30 .75
84 Scott Lachance .25 .60
85 Bryan Berard .30 .75
86 Robert Reichel .25 .60
87 Kenny Jonsson .25 .60
88 Kevin Stevens .25 .60
89 Mike Richter .40 1.00
90 Wayne Gretzky 2.00 5.00
91 Adam Graves .25 .60
92 Alexei Kovalev .25 .60
93 Ulf Samuelsson .30 .75
94 Radek Bonk .25 .60
95 Wade Redden .25 .60
96 Damian Rhodes .40 1.00
97 Bruce Gardiner .25 .60
98 Daniel Alfredsson .40 1.00
99 Ron Hextall .40 1.00
100 Eric Lindros .60 1.50
101 Chris Gratton .30 .75
102 Dainius Zubrus .25 .60
103 Luke Richardson .25 .60
104 Petr Svoboda .25 .60
105 Rick Tocchet .30 .75
106 Teppo Numminen .25 .60
107 Jeremy Roenick .60 1.50
108 Nikolai Khabibulin .40 1.00
109 Brad Isbister .25 .60
110 Peter Skudra .25 .60
111 Alexei Morozov .25 .60
112 Kevin Hatcher .25 .60
113 Darius Kasparaitis .25 .60
114 Stu Barnes .25 .60
115 Martin Straka .25 .60
116 Andrei Zyuzin .25 .60
117 Marcus Ragnarsson .25 .60
118 Murray Craven .25 .60
119 Marco Sturm .25 .60
120 Patrick Marleau .40 1.00
121 Shawn Burr .25 .60
122 Grant Fuhr .40 1.00
123 Chris Pronger .30 .75
124 Geoff Courtnall .30 .75
125 Jim Campbell .25 .60
126 Pavol Demitra .50 1.25
127 Todd Gill .25 .60
128 Cory Cross .25 .60
129 Daymond Langkow .25 .60
130 Alexander Selivanov .25 .60
131 Mikael Renberg .30 .75
132 Rob Zamuner .25 .60
133 Stephane Richer .25 .60
134 Fredrik Modin .25 .60
135 Derek King .25 .60
136 Mats Sundin .40 1.00
137 Mike Johnson .25 .60
138 Alyn McCauley .25 .60
139 Jason Smith .25 .60
140 Markus Naslund .40 1.00
141 Alexander Mogilny .30 .75
142 Mattias Ohlund .25 .60
143 Donald Brashear .25 .60
144 Garth Snow .30 .75
145 Brian Bellows .30 .75
146 Peter Bondra .30 .75
147 Joe Juneau .30 .75
148 Steve Konowalchuk .25 .60
149 Ken Klee .25 .60
150 Michal Pivonka .25 .60
151 Steve Rucchin .25 .60
152 Stu Grimson .25 .60
153 Tomas Sandstrom .25 .60
154 Fredrik Olausson .25 .60
155 Travis Green .25 .60
156 Jason Allison .30 .75
157 Steve Heinze .25 .60
158 Rob Tallas .25 .60
159 Darren Van Impe .25 .60
160 Ken Baumgartner .25 .60
161 Peter Ferraro .25 .60
162 Dominik Hasek .75 2.00
163 Geoff Sanderson .25 .60
164 Miroslav Satan .30 .75
165 Rob Ray .25 .60
166 Alexei Zhitnik .25 .60
167 Phil Housley .30 .75
168 Theo Fleury .50 1.25
169 Ken Wregget .30 .75
170 Valeri Bure .25 .60
171 Rico Fata .30 .75
172 Arturs Irbe .30 .75
173 Sean Hill .25 .60
174 Ron Francis .50 1.25
175 Jeff O'Neill .25 .60
176 Paul Ranheim .25 .60
177 Paul Coffey .40 1.00
178 Doug Gilmour .50 1.25
179 Eric Daze .30 .75
180 Chris Chelios .40 1.00
181 Bob Probert .25 .60
182 Mark Fitzpatrick .25 .60
183 Alexei Gusarov .25 .60
184 Sylvain Lefebvre .25 .60
185 Craig Billington .25 .60
186 Valeri Kamensky .25 .60
187 Milan Hejduk RC .60 1.50
188 Sandis Ozolinsh .25 .60
189 Brett Hull .60 1.50
190 Ed Belfour .40 1.00
191 Darryl Sydor .25 .60
192 Sergei Gusev RC .25 .60
193 Joe Nieuwendyk .40 1.00
194 Derian Hatcher .25 .60
195 Brendan Shanahan .50 1.25
196 Tomas Holmstrom .25 .60
197 Nicklas Lidstrom .50 1.25
198 Martin Lapointe .25 .60
199 Igor Larionov .40 1.00
200 Kris Draper .25 .60
201 Kelly Buchberger .25 .60
202 Andrei Kovalenko .25 .60
203 Josef Boranok .25 .60
204 Mikhail Shtalenkov .25 .60
205 Pat Falloon .25 .60
206 Mark Parrish RC .60 1.50
207 Terry Carkner .25 .60
208 Rob Niedermayer .25 .60
209 Sean Burke .25 .60
210 Oleg Kvasha RC .40 1.00
211 Pavel Bure .50 1.25
212 Rob Blake .40 1.00
213 Vladimir Tsyplakov .25 .60
214 Stephane Fiset .30 .75
215 Steve Duchesne .30 .75
216 Patrice Brisebois .25 .60
217 Vincent Damphousse .30 .75
218 Saku Koivu .40 1.00
219 Jose Theodore .50 1.25
220 Brett Clark RC .25 .60
221 Martin Rucinsky .25 .60
222 Vladimir Malakhov .25 .60
223 Sergei Krivokrasov .25 .60
224 Scott Walker .25 .60
225 Greg Johnson .25 .60
226 Cliff Ronning .25 .60
227 Eric Fichaud .25 .60
228 Bob Carpenter .25 .60
229 Scott Daniels .25 .60
230 Brian Rolston .30 .75
231 Sergei Brylin .25 .60
232 Scott Niedermayer .40 1.00
233 Bryan Smolinski .25 .60
234 Trevor Linden .30 .75
235 Eric Brewer .40 1.00
236 Zigmund Palffy .40 1.00
237 Sergei Nemchinov .25 .60
238 Brian Leetch .40 1.00
239 Mathieu Schneider .25 .60
240 Niklas Sundstrom .25 .60
241 Manny Malhotra .40 1.00
242 Jeff Beukeboom .25 .60
243 Petr Nedved .25 .60
244 Ron Tugnutt .25 .60
245 Shaun Van Allen .25 .60
246 Alexei Yashin .30 .75
247 Jason York .25 .60
248 Shawn McEachern .25 .60
249 Marian Hossa .30 .75
250 John LeClair .40 1.00
251 Rod Brind'Amour .40 1.00
252 John Vanbiesbrouck .30 .75
253 Eric Desjardins .30 .75
254 Valeri Zelepukin .25 .60
255 Karl Dykhuis .25 .60
256 Keith Tkachuk .40 1.00
257 Dallas Drake .25 .60
258 Oleg Tverdovsky .40 1.00
259 Jyrki Lumme .25 .60
260 Jimmy Waite .25 .60
261 Jaromir Jagr 1.00 2.50
262 German Titov .25 .60
263 Robert Lang .25 .60
264 Brad Werenka .25 .60
265 Rob Brown .25 .60
266 Bobby Dollas .25 .60
267 Jeff Friesen .25 .60
268 Andy Sutton RC .25 .60
269 Steve Shields .25 .60
270 Mike Ricci .25 .60
271 Joe Murphy .25 .60
272 Tony Granato .25 .60
273 Jamie McLennan .30 .75
274 Al MacInnis .40 1.00
275 Pierre Turgeon .40 1.00
276 Kelly Chase .25 .60
277 Craig Conroy .25 .60
278 Scott Young .25 .60
279 Vincent Lecavalier .75 2.00
280 Wendel Clark .30 .75
281 Daren Puppa .30 .75
282 Sandy McCarthy .25 .60
283 Daniil Markov .25 .60
284 Curtis Joseph .40 1.00
285 Sergei Berezin .30 .75
286 Steve Sullivan .25 .60
287 Tomas Kaberle RC .50 1.25
288 Kris King .25 .60
289 Igor Korolev .25 .60
290 Mark Messier .60 1.50
291 Bill Muckalt RC .25 .60
292 Todd Bertuzzi .40 1.00
293 Brad May .25 .60
294 Peter Zezel .25 .60
295 Dmitri Mironov .25 .60
296 Adam Oates .40 1.00
297 Calle Johansson .25 .60
298 Craig Berube .25 .60
299 Sergei Gonchar .25 .60
300 Andrei Nikolishin .25 .60

1998-99 Be A Player Press Release

This 300-card set paralleled the basic series, but carried a gold foil "Press Release" stamp on the card fronts. The cards were rumored to be available only to members of the media.

*SINGLES: 12X TO 30X BASIC CARDS
ISSUED AS MEDIA PROMOS

1998-99 Be A Player Gold

*VETERANS: 2X TO 5X BASIC CARDS
*ROOKIES: 1.2X TO 3X BASIC CARDS

1998-99 Be A Player Autographs

Inserted one per pack, this 300-card set was an autographed version of the base set. SP's had an announced print run of 450 except for the Gretzky card which was reported to be limited to 90 copies. A gold-foil parallel to the set was also created and inserted in random packs. Gold SP's had an announced print run of 50 except for the Gretzky gold parallel which was numbered out of 9.

ONE AUTO PER PACK
SILVER SP ANNOUNCED PRINT RUN 90-450
1 Jason Marshall 2.50 6.00
2 Paul Kariya SP 10.00 25.00
3 Teemu Selanne SP 15.00 40.00
4 Guy Hebert 4.00 10.00
5 Ted Drury 2.50 6.00
6 Byron Dafoe 2.50 6.00
7 Rob Dimaio 2.50 6.00
8 Ray Bourque SP 15.00 40.00
9 Joe Thornton 10.00 25.00
10 Sergei Samsonov 4.00 10.00
11 Dimitri Khristich 2.50 6.00
12 Michael Peca 2.50 6.00
13 Jason Woolley 2.50 6.00
14 Matthew Barnaby 2.50 6.00
15 Brian Holzinger 2.50 6.00
16 Dixon Ward 2.50 6.00
17 Tyler Moss 2.50 6.00
18 Jarome Iginla 8.00 20.00
19 Marty McInnis 2.50 6.00
20 Andrew Cassels 2.50 6.00
21 Jason Wiemer 2.50 6.00
22 Trevor Kidd 4.00 10.00
23 Keith Primeau 2.50 6.00
24 Sami Kapanen 2.50 6.00
25 Robert Kron 2.50 6.00
26 Glen Wesley 2.50 6.00
27 Jeff Hackett 4.00 10.00
28 Tony Amonte SP 6.00 15.00
29 Alexei Zhamnov 2.50 6.00
30 Eric Weinrich 2.50 6.00
31 Jeff Shantz 2.50 6.00
32 Christian Laflamme 2.50 6.00
33 Adam Foote 2.50 6.00
34 Patrick Roy SP 30.00 80.00
35 Peter Forsberg SP 20.00 40.00
36 Adam Deadmarsh 3.00 8.00
37 Joe Sakic SP 20.00 50.00
38 Eric Lacroix 2.50 6.00
39 Guy Carbonneau 3.00 8.00
40 Mike Modano SP 12.00 30.00
41 Roman Turek 2.50 6.00
42 Mike Keane 2.50 6.00
43 Sergei Zubov 3.00 8.00
44 Jere Lehtinen 4.00 10.00
45 Sergei Fedorov SP 10.00 25.00
46 Steve Yzerman SP 40.00 100.00
47 Chris Osgood 5.00 12.00
48 Larry Murphy 2.50 6.00
49 Vyacheslav Kozlov 4.00 10.00
50 Darren McCarty 4.00 10.00
51 Boris Mironov 2.50 6.00
52 Roman Hamrlik 2.50 6.00
53 Bill Guerin 2.50 6.00
54 Mike Grier 2.50 6.00
55 Todd Marchant 2.50 6.00
56 Ray Whitney 2.50 6.00
57 Dave Gagner 2.50 6.00
58 Scott Mellanby 2.50 6.00
59 Robert Svehla 2.50 6.00
60 Viktor Kozlov 2.50 6.00
61 Luc Robitaille 8.00 20.00
62 Yanic Perreault 2.50 6.00
63 Jozef Stumpel 2.50 6.00
64 Sandy Moger 2.50 6.00
65 Ian Laperriere 2.50 6.00
66 Jocelyn Thibault 4.00 10.00
67 Dave Manson 2.50 6.00
68 Mark Recchi SP 6.00 15.00
69 Patrick Poulin 2.50 6.00
70 Benoit Brunet 2.50 6.00
71 Turner Stevenson 2.50 6.00
72 Mike Dunham 4.00 10.00
73 Tom Fitzgerald 2.50 6.00
74 Darren Turcotte 2.50 6.00
75 Brad Smyth 2.50 6.00
76 J.J. Daigneault 2.50 6.00
77 Dave Andreychuk 4.00 10.00
78 Jason Arnott 3.00 8.00
79 Martin Brodeur SP 25.00 60.00
80 Randy McKay 2.50 6.00
81 Patrik Elias 4.00 10.00
82 Kevin Dean 2.50 6.00
83 Tommy Salo 4.00 10.00
84 Scott Lachance 2.50 6.00
85 Bryan Berard 2.50 6.00
86 Robert Reichel 2.50 6.00
87 Kenny Jonsson 2.50 6.00
88 Kevin Stevens 2.50 6.00
89 Mike Richter SP 10.00 25.00
90 Wayne Gretzky/90* 200.00 400.00
91 Adam Graves 4.00 10.00
92 Alexei Kovalev 4.00 10.00
93 Ulf Samuelsson 2.50 6.00
94 Radek Bonk 2.50 6.00
95 Wade Redden 2.50 6.00
96 Damian Rhodes 2.50 6.00
97 Bruce Gardiner 2.50 6.00
98 Daniel Alfredsson 6.00 15.00
99 Ron Hextall 6.00 15.00
100 Eric Lindros SP 15.00 30.00
101 Chris Gratton 2.50 6.00
102 Dainius Zubrus 2.50 6.00
103 Luke Richardson 2.50 6.00
104 Petr Svoboda 2.50 6.00
105 Rick Tocchet 4.00 10.00
106 Teppo Numminen 2.50 6.00
107 Jeremy Roenick SP 12.00 30.00
108 Nikolai Khabibulin 4.00 10.00
109 Brad Isbister 2.50 6.00
110 Peter Skudra 2.50 6.00
111 Alexei Morozov 2.50 6.00
112 Kevin Hatcher 2.50 6.00
113 Darius Kasparaitis 4.00 10.00
114 Stu Barnes 2.50 6.00
115 Martin Straka 2.50 6.00
116 Andrei Zyuzin 2.50 6.00
117 Marcus Ragnarsson 2.50 6.00
118 Murray Craven 2.50 6.00
119 Marco Sturm 2.50 6.00
120 Patrick Marleau 4.00 10.00
121 Shawn Burr 2.50 6.00
122 Grant Fuhr 5.00 12.00
123 Chris Pronger 4.00 10.00
124 Geoff Courtnall 2.50 6.00
125 Jim Campbell 2.50 6.00
126 Pavol Demitra 6.00 15.00
127 Todd Gill 2.50 6.00
128 Cory Cross 2.50 6.00
129 Daymond Langkow 2.50 6.00
130 Alexander Selivanov 2.50 6.00
131 Mikael Renberg 2.50 6.00
132 Rob Zamuner 2.50 6.00
133 Stephane Richer 2.50 6.00
134 Fredrik Modin 2.50 6.00
135 Derek King 2.50 6.00
136 Mats Sundin SP 15.00 40.00
137 Mike Johnson 2.50 6.00
138 Alyn McCauley 2.50 6.00
139 Jason Smith 2.50 6.00
140 Markus Naslund 6.00 15.00
141 Alexander Mogilny SP 10.00 25.00
142 Mattias Ohlund 2.50 6.00
143 Donald Brashear 2.50 6.00
144 Garth Snow 3.00 8.00
145 Brian Bellows 2.50 6.00
146 Peter Bondra SP 8.00 20.00
147 Joe Juneau 2.50 6.00
148 Steve Konowalchuk 2.50 6.00
149 Ken Klee 2.50 6.00
150 Michal Pivonka 2.50 6.00
151 Steve Rucchin 2.50 6.00
152 Stu Grimson 2.50 6.00
153 Tomas Sandstrom 2.50 6.00
154 Fredrik Olausson 2.50 6.00
155 Travis Green 2.50 6.00
156 Jason Allison 2.50 6.00
157 Steve Heinze 2.50 6.00
158 Rob Tallas 2.50 6.00
159 Darren Van Impe 2.50 6.00
160 Ken Baumgartner 2.50 6.00
161 Peter Ferraro 2.50 6.00
162 Dominik Hasek SP 25.00 60.00
163 Geoff Sanderson 2.50 6.00
164 Miroslav Satan 4.00 10.00
165 Rob Ray 4.00 10.00
166 Alexei Zhitnik 2.50 6.00
167 Phil Housley 2.50 6.00
168 Theo Fleury SP 10.00 25.00
169 Ken Wregget 2.50 6.00
170 Valeri Bure 2.50 6.00
171 Rico Fata 2.50 6.00
172 Arturs Irbe 4.00 10.00
173 Sean Hill 2.50 6.00
174 Ron Francis SP 10.00 25.00
175 Jeff O'Neill 2.50 6.00
176 Paul Ranheim 2.50 6.00
177 Paul Coffey SP 12.00 30.00
178 Doug Gilmour SP 12.00 30.00
179 Eric Daze 2.50 6.00
180 Chris Chelios SP 10.00 25.00
181 Bob Probert 10.00 20.00
182 Mark Fitzpatrick 2.50 6.00
183 Alexei Gusarov 2.50 6.00
184 Sylvain Lefebvre 2.50 6.00
185 Craig Billington 2.50 6.00
186 Valeri Kamensky 2.50 6.00
187 Milan Hejduk 6.00 15.00
188 Sandis Ozolinsh 2.50 6.00
189 Brett Hull SP 15.00 40.00
190 Ed Belfour SP 12.00 30.00
191 Darryl Sydor 2.50 6.00
192 Sergei Gusev 2.50 6.00
193 Joe Nieuwendyk SP 6.00 15.00
194 Derian Hatcher 2.50 6.00
195 Brendan Shanahan SP 8.00 20.00
196 Tomas Holmstrom 5.00 12.00
197 Nicklas Lidstrom 5.00 12.00
198 Martin Lapointe 4.00 10.00
199 Igor Larionov 5.00 12.00
200 Kris Draper 3.00 8.00
201 Kelly Buchberger 2.50 6.00
202 Andrei Kovalenko 2.50 6.00
203 Josef Beranek 2.50 6.00
204 Mikhail Shtalenkov 2.50 6.00
205 Pat Falloon 2.50 6.00
206 Mark Parrish 2.50 6.00
207 Terry Carkner 2.50 6.00
208 Rob Niedermayer 4.00 10.00
209 Sean Burke 4.00 10.00
210 Oleg Kvasha 2.50 6.00
211 Pavel Bure SP 15.00 40.00
212 Rob Blake 4.00 10.00
213 Vladimir Tsyplakov 2.50 6.00
214 Stephane Fiset 2.50 6.00
215 Steve Duchesne 2.50 6.00
216 Patrice Brisebois 2.50 6.00
217 Vincent Damphousse 2.50 6.00
218 Saku Koivu 6.00 15.00
219 Jose Theodore 8.00 20.00
220 Brett Clark 2.50 6.00
221 Martin Rucinsky 2.50 6.00
222 Vladimir Malakhov 2.50 6.00
223 Sergei Krivokrasov 2.50 6.00
224 Scott Walker 2.50 6.00
225 Greg Johnson 2.50 6.00
226 Cliff Ronning 2.50 6.00
227 Eric Fichaud 2.50 6.00
228 Bob Carpenter 2.50 6.00
229 Scott Daniels 2.50 6.00
230 Brian Rolston 2.50 6.00
231 Sergei Brylin 2.50 6.00
232 Scott Niedermayer 5.00 12.00
233 Bryan Smolinski 2.50 6.00
234 Trevor Linden 4.00 10.00
235 Eric Brewer 2.50 6.00
236 Zigmund Palffy SP 6.00 15.00
237 Sergei Nemchinov 2.50 6.00
238 Brian Leetch SP 8.00 20.00
239 Mathieu Schneider 2.50 6.00
240 Niklas Sundstrom 2.50 6.00
241 Manny Malhotra 2.50 6.00
242 Jeff Beukeboom 2.50 6.00
243 Petr Nedved 2.50 6.00
244 Ron Tugnutt 3.00 8.00
245 Shawn Van Allen 2.50 6.00
246 Alexei Yashin 3.00 8.00
247 Jason York 2.50 6.00
248 Shawn McEachern 2.50 6.00
249 Marian Hossa 6.00 15.00
250 John LeClair SP 8.00 20.00
251 Rod Brind'Amour 4.00 10.00
252 John Vanbiesbrouck 4.00 10.00
253 Eric Desjardins 3.00 8.00
254 Valeri Zelepukin 2.50 6.00
255 Karl Dykhuis 2.50 6.00
256 Keith Tkachuk 5.00 12.00
257 Dallas Drake 2.50 6.00
258 Oleg Tverdovsky 2.50 6.00
259 Jyrki Lumme 2.50 6.00
260 Jimmy Waite 2.50 6.00
261 Jaromir Jagr SP 20.00 50.00
262 German Titov 2.50 6.00
263 Robert Lang 2.50 6.00
264 Brad Werenka 2.50 6.00
265 Rob Brown 2.50 6.00
266 Bobby Dollas 2.50 6.00
267 Jeff Friesen 2.50 6.00
268 Andy Sutton 2.50 6.00
269 Steve Shields 4.00 10.00
270 Mike Ricci 2.50 6.00
271 Joe Murphy 2.50 6.00
272 Tony Granato 2.50 6.00
273 Jamie McLennan 2.50 6.00
274 Al MacInnis SP 8.00 20.00
275 Pierre Turgeon 3.00 8.00
276 Kelly Chase 2.50 6.00
277 Craig Conroy 2.50 6.00
278 Scott Young 2.50 6.00
279 Vincent Lecavalier 8.00 20.00
280 Wendel Clark 4.00 10.00
281 Daren Puppa 2.50 6.00
282 Sandy McCarthy 2.50 6.00
283 Daniil Markov 2.50 6.00
284 Curtis Joseph SP 15.00 30.00
285 Sergei Berezin 2.50 6.00
286 Steve Sullivan 2.50 6.00
287 Tomas Kaberle 2.50 6.00
288 Kris King 2.50 6.00
289 Igor Korolev 2.50 6.00
290 Mark Messier SP 20.00 50.00
291 Bill Muckalt 2.50 6.00
292 Todd Bertuzzi 6.00 15.00
293 Brad May 3.00 8.00
294 Peter Zezel 2.50 6.00
295 Dmitri Mironov 2.50 6.00
296 Adam Oates SP 10.00 25.00
297 Calle Johansson 2.50 6.00
298 Craig Berube 2.50 6.00
299 Sergei Gonchar 2.50 6.00
300 Andrei Nikolishin 2.50 6.00

1998-99 Be A Player Autographs Gold

*GOLD: .8X TO 2X SILVER AU
*GOLD: .6X TO 1.5X SILVER AU SP
GOLD SP ANNC'd PRINT RUN 50

1998-99 Be A Player All-Star Game Used Sticks

ANNOUNCED PRINT RUN 100 SETS
S1 Eric Lindros 15.00 40.00
S2 Peter Forsberg 25.00 60.00
S3 Teemu Selanne 20.00 50.00
S4 Mike Modano 15.00 40.00
S5 Mats Sundin 15.00 40.00
S6 Patrick Roy 40.00 100.00
S7 Paul Kariya 15.00 40.00
S8 Martin Brodeur 25.00 60.00
S9 Steve Yzerman 40.00 100.00
S10 Mark Messier 15.00 40.00
S11 Brett Hull 15.00 40.00
S12 Joe Sakic 25.00 60.00
S13 Alexander Mogilny 15.00 40.00
S14 Sergei Fedorov 20.00 50.00
S15 Ray Bourque 25.00 60.00
S16 Jeremy Roenick 15.00 40.00
S17 Jaromir Jagr 30.00 80.00
S18 Dominik Hasek 15.00 40.00
S19 Chris Chelios 15.00 40.00
S20 John LeClair 15.00 40.00
S21 Brendan Shanahan 15.00 40.00
S22 Ed Belfour 15.00 40.00
S23 Wayne Gretzky 50.00 100.00

1998-99 Be A Player All-Star Game Used Jerseys

ANNOUNCED PRINT RUN 100 SETS
AS1 Eric Lindros 12.50 30.00
AS2 Peter Forsberg 15.00 40.00
AS3 Teemu Selanne 12.50 30.00
AS4 Mike Modano 12.50 30.00
AS5 Mats Sundin 12.50 30.00
AS6 Patrick Roy 20.00 50.00
AS7 Paul Kariya 12.50 30.00
AS8 Martin Brodeur 25.00 60.00
AS9 Steve Yzerman 30.00 80.00
AS10 Mark Messier 12.50 30.00
AS11 Paul Coffey 12.50 30.00
AS12 Brett Hull 12.50 30.00
AS13 Joe Sakic 20.00 50.00
AS14 Alexander Mogilny 8.00 20.00
AS15 Sergei Fedorov 15.00 40.00
AS16 Ray Bourque 15.00 40.00
AS17 Jeremy Roenick 12.50 30.00
AS18 Jaromir Jagr 15.00 40.00
AS19 Pavel Bure 12.50 30.00
AS20 Dominik Hasek 20.00 50.00
AS21 Chris Chelios 12.50 30.00
AS22 John LeClair 12.50 30.00
AS23 Brendan Shanahan 12.50 30.00
AS24 Ed Belfour 12.50 30.00
AS25 Wayne Gretzky 50.00 100.00

1998-99 Be A Player All-Star Legend Gordie Howe

Randomly inserted in packs, this two-card set honored Hall-of-Famer Gordie Howe. One card in the set carried a piece of Howe's Detroit Red Wings jerseys embedded in the cards. Each card was autographed by Gordie Howe and eachc ard was limited to just 90 copies.

ANNOUNCED PRINT RUN 90
GH1 G.Howe GJ AU 125.00 250.00
GH2 Gordie Howe AU 100.00 200.00

1998-99 Be A Player All-Star Milestones

COMPLETE SET (22) 50.00 100.00
M1 Wayne Gretzky 4.00 10.00
M2 Mark Messier 2.00 5.00
M3 Dino Ciccarelli 1.50 4.00
M4 Steve Yzerman 4.00 10.00
M5 Dave Andreychuk 1.50 4.00
M6 Brett Hull 2.50 6.00
M7 Wayne Gretzky 4.00 10.00
M8 Mark Messier 2.00 5.00
M9 Dino Ciccarelli 1.50 4.00
M10 Steve Yzerman 3.00 8.00
M11 Bernie Nicholls 1.50 4.00
M12 Ron Francis 1.50 4.00
M13 Ray Bourque 2.50 6.00
M14 Paul Coffey 2.00 5.00
M15 Adam Oates 1.50 4.00
M16 Phil Housley 1.50 4.00
M17 Dale Hunter 1.50 4.00
M18 Luc Robitaille 1.50 4.00
M19 Doug Gilmour 1.50 4.00
M20 Larry Murphy 1.50 4.00
M21 Dave Andreychuk 1.50 4.00
M22 Al MacInnis 1.50 4.00

1998-99 Be A Player Playoff Game Used Jerseys

ANNOUNCED PRINT RUN 100 SETS
G1 Wayne Gretzky 50.00 100.00
G2 Mats Sundin 12.50 30.00
G3 Jeremy Roenick 12.50 30.00
G4 Eric Lindros 12.50 30.00
G5 John LeClair 12.50 30.00
G6 Joe Sakic 25.00 50.00
G7 Peter Forsberg 12.00 30.00
G8 Patrick Roy 30.00 80.00
G9 Martin Brodeur 25.00 60.00
G10 Pavel Bure 12.50 30.00
G11 Teemu Selanne 12.50 30.00
G12 Paul Kariya 12.50 30.00
G13 Ray Bourque 20.00 50.00
G14 Brendan Shanahan 12.50 30.00
G15 Steve Yzerman 30.00 80.00
G16 Sergei Fedorov 15.00 40.00

G17 Mike Modano 12.50 30.00
G18 Brett Hull 12.50 30.00
G19 Ed Belfour 12.50 30.00
G20 Mark Messier 15.00 40.00
G21 Alexander Mogilny 8.00 20.00
G22 Tony Amonte 8.00 20.00
G23 Jaromir Jagr 20.00 50.00
G24 Alexei Yashin 8.00 20.00

1998-99 Be A Player Playoff Highlights

COMPLETE SET (18) 40.00 100.00
H1 Mark Messier 2.00 5.00
H2 Peter Forsberg 5.00 12.00
H3 Wayne Gretzky 12.50 30.00
H4 Martin Brodeur 5.00 12.00
H5 Jaromir Jagr 3.00 8.00
H6 Mike Richter 2.00 5.00
H7 Steve Yzerman 10.00 25.00
H8 Patrick Roy 8.00 20.00
H9 Paul Coffey 2.00 5.00
H10 Joe Sakic 4.00 10.00
H11 John Vanbiesbrouck 2.00 5.00
H12 Pavel Bure 2.00 5.00
H13 Chris Osgood 2.00 5.00
H14 Chris Chelios 2.00 5.00
H15 Curtis Joseph 2.00 5.00
H16 Brian Leetch 2.00 5.00
H17 Sergei Fedorov 3.00 8.00
H18 Doug Gilmour 2.00 5.00

1998-99 Be A Player Playoff Legend Mario Lemieux

Randomly inserted in packs, this 4-card set was limited to a print run of just 66 sets. Each card featured one or two pieces of game-used memorabilia and an autograph from Mario Lemieux.
STATED PRINT RUN 66 CARDS
L1 All-Star Jersey AU 150.00 300.00
L2 Penguins Jersey AU 150.00 300.00
L3 All-Star Jsy/Stick AU 200.00 400.00
L4 Penguins Jsy/Stick AU 200.00 400.00

1998-99 Be A Player Playoff Practice Used Jerseys

ANNOUNCED PRINT RUN 100 SETS
P1 Brett Hull 8.00 20.00
P2 Alexander Mogilny 6.00 15.00
P3 Ray Bourque 15.00 40.00
P4 Pavel Bure 10.00 25.00
P5 Steve Yzerman 25.00 60.00
P6 Ed Belfour 10.00 25.00
P7 Jaromir Jagr 12.50 30.00
P8 Sergei Fedorov 12.50 30.00
P9 Teemu Selanne 10.00 25.00
P10 Eric Lindros 10.00 25.00
P11 Tony Amonte 8.00 20.00
P12 Jeremy Roenick 10.00 25.00
P13 John LeClair 10.00 25.00
P14 Mike Modano 10.00 25.00
P15 Joe Sakic 12.50 30.00
P16 Patrick Roy 30.00 80.00
P17 Mark Messier 10.00 25.00
P18 Paul Kariya 10.00 25.00
P19 Martin Brodeur 20.00 50.00
P20 Mats Sundin 25.00 60.00
P21 Brendan Shanahan 10.00 25.00
P22 Peter Forsberg 15.00 40.00
P23 Alexei Yashin 6.00 15.00
P24 Wayne Gretzky 100.00 150.00

1998-99 Be A Player Atlanta National

*SINGLES: 1.2X TO 3X BASIC CARDS
AVAILABLE AT ATLANTA NATIONAL '99
AVAILABLE VIA PACK REDEMPTION ONLY

1998-99 Be A Player Toronto Spring Expo

Available via wrapper redemption at the Be A Player booth during the 1999 Toronto Spring Expo Show. Each wrapper was exchanged for one random card from 1998-99 Be A Player Series II that was serial-numbered out of 25 and embossed with the Spring Expo logo.
*SINGLES: 15X TO 40X BASIC CARDS

1998-99 Be A Player Tampa Bay All-Star Game

These cards were only available to children during the special kid's preview at the 1999 NHL All-Star Game in Tampa Bay. These cards parallel the 1998-99 Be A Player Series I set, and each card was hand serial-numbered to 50 with an embossed silver All-Star logo.

*SINGLES: 10X TO 25X BASIC CARDS

2005-06 Be A Player

Released in August 2005, Be A Player was produced by Upper Deck for the first time. Each pack contained 5 cards including one autograph card and carried a $20 SRP, each box carried 10 packs.
COMPLETE SET (90) 15.00 40.00
1 Jean-Sebastien Giguere .60 1.50
2 Joffrey Lupul .50 1.25
3 Ilya Kovalchuk .60 1.50
4 Dany Heatley .60 1.50
5 Kari Lehtonen .50 1.25
6 Glen Murray .50 1.25
7 Joe Thornton .75 2.00
8 Andrew Raycroft .50 1.25
9 Miroslav Satan .50 1.25
10 Chris Drury .50 1.25
11 Daniel Briere .60 1.50
12 Jarome Iginla .60 1.50
13 Miikka Kiprusoff .50 1.25
14 Martin Gelinas .40 1.00
15 Erik Cole .50 1.25
16 Eric Staal .75 2.00
17 Tuomo Ruutu .60 1.50
18 Eric Daze .50 1.25
19 Joe Sakic 1.00 2.50
20 Peter Forsberg .75 2.00
21 Milan Hejduk .50 1.25
22 Rob Blake .60 1.50
23 Alex Tanguay .60 1.50
24 Rick Nash .60 1.50
25 Nikolai Zherdev .40 1.00
26 Todd Marchant .40 1.00
27 Marty Turco .60 1.50
28 Brenden Morrow .50 1.25
29 Mike Modano 1.00 2.50
30 Brendan Shanahan .75 2.00
31 Nicklas Lidstrom .60 1.50
32 Pavel Datsyuk .75 2.00
33 Steve Yzerman 1.50 4.00
34 Curtis Joseph .60 1.50
35 Ryan Smyth .50 1.25
36 Jason Smith .40 1.00
37 Ty Conklin .50 1.25
38 Olli Jokinen .60 1.50
39 Roberto Luongo 1.00 2.50
40 Jay Bouwmeester .60 1.50
41 Zigmund Palffy .60 1.50
42 Luc Robitaille .60 1.50
43 Alexander Frolov .40 1.00
44 Marian Gaborik 1.00 2.50
45 Dwayne Roloson .50 1.25
46 Saku Koivu .60 1.50
47 Jose Theodore .60 1.50
48 Michael Ryder .50 1.25
49 Tomas Vokoun .50 1.25
50 Steve Sullivan .40 1.00
51 Jordin Tootoo .60 1.50
52 Martin Brodeur 1.25 3.00
53 Patrik Elias .60 1.50
54 Scott Gomez .50 1.25
55 Rick DiPietro .50 1.25
56 Mike Peca .50 1.25
57 Trent Hunter .40 1.00
58 Jaromir Jagr 1.50 4.00
59 Bobby Holik .40 1.00
60 Dan Blackburn .30 .75
61 Marian Hossa .50 1.25
62 Jason Spezza .60 1.50
63 Daniel Alfredsson .60 1.50
64 Keith Primeau .60 1.50
65 Simon Gagne .60 1.50
66 Robert Esche .50 1.25
67 Brett Hull .75 2.00
68 Shane Doan .50 1.25
69 Mike Comrie .50 1.25
70 Marc-Andre Fleury 1.00 2.50
71 Mark Recchi .75 2.00
72 Mario Lemieux 2.00 5.00
73 Patrick Marleau .60 1.50
74 Jonathan Cheechoo .60 1.50
75 Evgeni Nabokov .50 1.25
76 Chris Pronger .50 1.25
77 Doug Weight .60 1.50
78 Keith Tkachuk .60 1.50
79 Martin St. Louis .60 1.50
80 Vincent Lecavalier .50 1.25
81 Nikolai Khabibulin .60 1.50
82 Brad Richards .60 1.50
83 Dave Andreychuk .60 1.50
84 Gary Roberts .40 1.00
85 Mats Sundin .60 1.50
86 Joe Nieuwendyk .60 1.50
87 Markus Naslund .60 1.50
88 Brendan Morrison .40 1.00
89 Ed Jovanovski .50 1.25
90 Olaf Kolzig .60 1.50

2005-06 Be A Player First Period

*STARS: 2X TO 5X
PRINT RUN 100 SER.#'d SETS

2005-06 Be A Player Second Period

*STARS: 5X TO 12X
PRINT RUN 50 SER.#'d SETS

2005-06 Be A Player Class Action

PRINT RUN 299 SER.#'d SETS
CA1 Keith Tkachuk 3.00 8.00
CA2 Dany Heatley 3.00 8.00
CA3 Ilya Kovalchuk 3.00 8.00
CA4 Joe Thornton 4.00 10.00
CA5 Jarome Iginla 3.00 8.00
CA6 Peter Forsberg 4.00 10.00
CA7 Joe Sakic 5.00 12.00
CA8 Rick Nash 3.00 8.00
CA9 Mike Modano 5.00 12.00
CA10 Steve Yzerman 8.00 20.00
CA11 Mats Sundin 3.00 8.00
CA12 Martin St. Louis 3.00 8.00
CA13 Jose Theodore 3.00 8.00
CA14 Miikka Kiprusoff 2.50 6.00
CA15 Martin Brodeur 6.00 15.00
CA16 Mark Messier 5.00 12.00
CA17 Markus Naslund 3.00 8.00
CA18 Jeremy Roenick 3.00 8.00
CA19 Brett Hull 4.00 10.00
CA20 Mario Lemieux 10.00 25.00

2005-06 Be A Player Dual Signatures

STATED ODDS 1:10
AR D.Andreychuk/L.Robitaille 8.00 20.00
BD D.Briere/C.Drury 8.00 20.00
BF M. Brodeur/M.Fleury 40.00 80.00
BS B.Rafalski/S.Niedermayer 5.00 12.00
DK D.Heatley/K.Lehtonen 10.00 25.00
DL K.Draper/N.Lidstrom SP 20.00 50.00
DR M.Denis/D.Roloson 8.00 20.00
DT E.Daze/J.Thibault 5.00 12.00
FL M.Fleury/R.Luongo 15.00 40.00
GB B.Guerin/B.Morrow 5.00 12.00
GD B.Guerin/C.Drury 5.00 12.00
HH M.Hossa/D.Hasek 12.00 30.00
HR M.Hossa/W.Redden 8.00 20.00
HT G.Howe/J.Thornton SP 75.00 150.00
IM J.Iginla/P.Marleau 10.00 25.00
JE J.Spezza/E.Staal 12.00 30.00
KC K.Tkachuk/C.Pronger 10.00 25.00
LI M.St. Louis/J.Iginla 12.00 30.00
LL M.St.Louis/V.Lecavalier 12.00 30.00
LP N.Lidstrom/C.Pronger 20.00 50.00
LW R.Luongo/S.Weiss 8.00 20.00
MA M.Peca/A.Aucoin 5.00 12.00
MC P.Marleau/J.Cheechoo 8.00 20.00
ND R.Nash/M.Denis 12.00 30.00
NL M.Naslund/T.Linden 12.00 30.00
NT R.Nash/J.Thornton 15.00 40.00
PA P.Kariya/A.Tanguay 12.00 30.00
PE K.Primeau/R.Esche 5.00 12.00
PP M.Peca/M.Parrish 5.00 12.00
RB L.Robitaille/D.Brown 10.00 25.00
RJ R.Blake/J.Bouwmeester 5.00 12.00
RL R.Luongo/K.Lehtonen 15.00 40.00
RR M.Ryder/M.Ribeiro 6.00 15.00
RT M.Ryder/J.Theodore 8.00 20.00
SB J.Sakic/R.Blake SP 20.00 50.00
SR J.Spezza/M.Ryder 12.00 30.00
SS R.Smyth/J.Smith 8.00 20.00
ST M.Sillinger/K.Tkachuk 5.00 12.00
TL M.Turco/R.Luongo 10.00 25.00
TM J.Thornton/G.Murray 10.00 25.00
TP J.Thornton/K.Primeau 10.00 25.00
TR J.Theodore/M.Ribeiro 8.00 20.00
VR V.Lecavalier/R.Fedotenko 10.00 25.00

2005-06 Be A Player Ice Icons

PRINT RUN 99 SER.#'d SETS
ICE1 Martin Brodeur 10.00 25.00
ICE2 Mario Lemieux 15.00 40.00
ICE3 Joe Sakic 8.00 20.00
ICE4 Peter Forsberg 6.00 15.00
ICE5 Steve Yzerman 12.00 30.00

2005-06 Be A Player Outtakes

PRINT RUN 499 SER.#'d SETS
OT1 Jean-Sebastien Giguere 6.00 15.00
OT2 Sergei Fedorov 10.00 25.00
OT3 Dany Heatley 6.00 15.00
OT4 Ilya Kovalchuk 6.00 15.00
OT5 Andrew Raycroft 5.00 12.00
OT6 Joe Thornton 8.00 20.00
OT7 Chris Drury 5.00 12.00
OT8 Jarome Iginla 6.00 15.00
OT9 Miikka Kiprusoff 5.00 12.00
OT10 Eric Staal 8.00 20.00
OT11 Tuomo Ruutu 6.00 15.00
OT12 Peter Forsberg 8.00 20.00
OT13 Rob Blake 6.00 15.00
OT14 Alex Tanguay 6.00 15.00
OT15 Joe Sakic 10.00 25.00
OT16 Nikolai Zherdev 4.00 10.00
OT17 Rick Nash 6.00 15.00
OT18 Mike Modano 10.00 25.00
OT19 Marty Turco 6.00 15.00
OT20 Pavel Datsyuk 8.00 20.00
OT21 Brendan Shanahan 8.00 20.00
OT22 Steve Yzerman 15.00 40.00
OT23 Ryan Smyth 5.00 12.00
OT24 Roberto Luongo 10.00 25.00
OT25 Luc Robitaille 6.00 15.00
OT26 Marian Gaborik 10.00 25.00
OT27 Saku Koivu 6.00 15.00
OT28 Jose Theodore 6.00 15.00
OT29 Tomas Vokoun 5.00 12.00
OT30 Steve Sullivan 4.00 10.00
OT31 Martin Brodeur 12.00 30.00
OT32 Jaromir Jagr 15.00 40.00
OT33 Mark Messier 10.00 25.00
OT34 Michael Peca 5.00 12.00
OT35 Daniel Alfredsson 6.00 15.00
OT36 Jason Spezza 6.00 15.00
OT37 Jeremy Roenick 6.00 15.00
OT38 Simon Gagne 6.00 15.00
OT39 Shane Doan 5.00 12.00
OT40 Mario Lemieux 20.00 50.00
OT41 Patrick Marleau 6.00 15.00
OT42 Keith Tkachuk 6.00 15.00
OT43 Chris Pronger 5.00 12.00
OT44 Vincent Lecavalier 5.00 12.00
OT45 Martin St. Louis 6.00 15.00
OT46 Mats Sundin 6.00 15.00
OT47 Ed Belfour 6.00 15.00
OT48 Markus Naslund 6.00 15.00
OT49 Ed Jovanovski 5.00 12.00
OT50 Olaf Kolzig 6.00 15.00

2005-06 Be A Player Quad Signatures

STATED ODDS 1:180
BLTG Brodr/Lngo/Theo/Ggy 250.00 500.00
BLUE Prng/Tkchk/Wnrch/Silln 30.00 80.00
BOST Thorn/Ray/Murry/Berg 60.00 150.00
COLO Tangy/Sakc/Absh/Dmph 75.00 150.00
GDEF Prongr/Ldstrm/Blke/J-Bo 100.00 200.00
GOAL Brodr/Theo/Giggy/Flry 150.00 300.00
HAWK Rutu/Dze/Thiblt/Berard 30.00 80.00
HSNT Heatly/Sakc/Nash/Thrn
IMPL Iginla/Marl/Prmeau/St.Ls 50.00 100.00
ITLB Iginla/Tangy/St.Lu/Bergr 50.00 125.00
MAPL Sundn/Stjn/McCbe/Rbrts 40.00 100.00
MONT Theo/Ryder/Ribro/Sray 125.00 250.00
OTWA Hossa/Rddn/Bndr/Hask 100.00 200.00
RBSS Rutu/Brgrn/Staal/Stjan 60.00 125.00
SCCH Andry/St.Lu/Rchr/Stllm 60.00 100.00
SDPH Smyth/Dze/Prmu/Hlik 30.00 80.00
SHSL Sakc/Htly/Sndn/St.Lu 60.00 125.00
SSIR Smyth/Smth/Ignla/Rghr 100.00 200.00
TLAL Trco/Lngo/Absch/Lhtnn 60.00 150.00

2005-06 Be A Player Signatures

STATED ODDS ONE PER PACK
AA Adrian Aucoin 2.50 6.00
AB Andrew Brunette 2.50 6.00
AC Andrew Cassels 2.50 6.00
AE David Aebischer 3.00 8.00
AH Adam Hall 2.50 6.00
AL Andreas Lilja 2.50 6.00
AM Alyn McCauley 2.50 6.00
AN Dave Andreychuk 4.00 10.00
AR Andrew Raycroft 5.00 12.00
AT Alex Tanguay 4.00 10.00
AV Sean Avery 2.50 6.00
BA Matthew Barnaby 3.00 8.00
BB Bryan Berard 2.50 6.00
BD Boyd Devereaux 2.50 6.00
BE Brenden Morrow 4.00 10.00
BG Bill Guerin SP 8.00 20.00
BH Bobby Holik 2.50 6.00
BI Martin Biron 3.00 8.00
BJ Barret Jackman 2.50 6.00
BM Brendan Morrison 4.00 10.00
BN Brian Boucher 3.00 8.00
BO Bob Boughner 2.50 6.00
BR Brian Rolston 2.50 6.00
BS Brendan Shanahan 10.00 25.00
BT Brent Sopel 2.50 6.00
BW Brendan Witt 2.50 6.00
BY Bryan McCabe 2.50 6.00
CC Carlo Colaiacovo 2.50 6.00
CD Chris Drury SP 30.00 80.00
CO Craig Conroy 2.50 6.00
CP Chris Pronger 4.00 10.00
CR Craig Rivet 2.50 6.00
CS Cory Stillman 2.50 6.00
DB Daniel Briere 6.00 15.00
DC Daniel Cleary 3.00 8.00
DD Dallas Drake 2.50 6.00
DE Derian Hatcher 3.00 8.00
DI Daniel Alfredsson 5.00 12.00
DL David Legwand 3.00 8.00
DN Dan Cloutier 3.00 8.00
DO Shean Donovan 2.50 6.00
DR Dwayne Roloson 4.00 10.00
DT Mathieu Schneider 2.50 6.00
DU Dustin Brown 6.00 15.00
DY Darryl Sydor 2.50 6.00
EB Eric Brewer 2.50 6.00
EC Erik Cole 4.00 10.00
EI Eric Staal 8.00 20.00
EL Eric Lindros 8.00 20.00
ER Eric Belanger 2.50 6.00
ES Robert Esche 3.00 8.00
EW Eric Weinrich 2.50 6.00
FA Brian Rafalski 2.50 6.00
FE Ruslan Fedotenko 2.50 6.00
GI Brian Gionta 2.50 6.00
GL Martin Gelinas 2.50 6.00
GM Glen Murray 2.50 6.00
GS Garth Snow 2.50 6.00
HA Dominik Hasek 15.00 40.00
HE Bret Hedican 2.50 6.00
HF Shawn Horcoff 2.50 6.00
HO Gordie Howe SP 250.00 400.00
HT Dany Heatley 8.00 20.00
HZ Henrik Zetterberg 10.00 25.00
IG Jarome Iginla 12.00 30.00
IL Ian Laperriere 2.50 6.00
JA Jason Arnott 2.50 6.00
JB Jay Bouwmeester 5.00 12.00
JC Jonathan Cheechoo 4.00 10.00
JD Jody Shelley 2.50 6.00
JG Jean-Sebastien Giguere 4.00 10.00
JI Jim Dowd 2.50 6.00
JL Joffrey Lupul 3.00 8.00
JM John-Michael Liles 2.50 6.00
JO Jeff O'Neill 2.50 6.00
JP J-P Dumont 2.50 6.00
JS Jason Smith 2.50 6.00
JT Jocelyn Thibault 4.00 10.00
JW Justin Williams 2.50 6.00
KA Trent Klatt 2.50 6.00
KD Kris Draper 4.00 10.00
KE Kevyn Adams 2.50 6.00
KL Kari Lehtonen 12.00 30.00
KP Keith Primeau SP 8.00 20.00
KT Keith Tkachuk SP 20.00 50.00
KW Kevin Weekes 3.00 8.00
LA Robert Lang 2.50 6.00
LE Jordan Leopold 2.50 6.00
LU Luc Robitaille SP 20.00 50.00
LW Daymond Langkow 2.50 6.00
MA Brad May 3.00 8.00
MD Mathieu Dandenault 2.50 6.00
ME Mike Knuble 2.50 6.00
MF Marc-Andre Fleury 8.00 20.00
MH Marian Hossa 8.00 20.00
MI Mike Comrie 4.00 10.00
ML Martin Lapointe 2.50 6.00
MO Mattias Ohlund 2.50 6.00
MP Mark Parrish 2.50 6.00
MR Marc Denis 4.00 10.00
MS Matt Stajan 3.00 8.00
MT Martin Brodeur SP 150.00 250.00
MU Bryan Muir 2.50 6.00
MW Mattias Weinhandl 2.50 6.00
NA Markus Naslund SP 12.00 30.00
NB Nick Boynton 2.50 6.00
ND Niko Dimitrakos 2.50 6.00
NH Nathan Horton 5.00 12.00
NI Rob Niedermayer 3.00 8.00
NL Nicklas Lidstrom SP 25.00 60.00
OK Olaf Kolzig 5.00 12.00
OR Brooks Orpik 4.00 10.00
OT Steve Ott 3.00 8.00
PA Paul Martin 2.50 6.00
PB Peter Bondra 4.00 10.00
PC Patrice Bergeron 8.00 20.00
PD Pascal Dupuis 2.50 6.00
PE Mike Peca 4.00 10.00
PK Paul Kariya 12.00 30.00
PM Patrick Marleau SP 25.00 60.00
PT Pierre Turgeon 3.00 8.00
RA Rod Brind'Amour 4.00 10.00
RB Rob Blake 4.00 10.00
RC Brad Richards 5.00 12.00
RD Rick DiPietro 5.00 12.00
RF Rico Fata 2.50 6.00
RI Mike Ribeiro 3.00 8.00
RK Ryan Kesler 6.00 15.00
RL Roberto Luongo SP 25.00 60.00
RN Rick Nash 10.00 25.00
RO Gary Roberts 2.50 6.00
RR Robyn Regehr 2.50 6.00
RS Ryan Smyth 3.00 8.00
RU Tuomo Ruutu 3.00 8.00
RW Ray Whitney 2.50 6.00
RY Michael Ryder SP 8.00 20.00
SA Joe Sakic 25.00 60.00
SB Sean Burke 4.00 10.00
SC Scott Niedermayer 4.00 10.00
SD Shane Doan 2.50 6.00
SE Steve Sullivan 2.50 6.00
SG Mike Sillinger 2.50 6.00
SH Shawn McEachern 2.50 6.00
SI Steve Shields 3.00 8.00
SJ Joe Thornton 15.00 40.00
SL Martin St. Louis 4.00 10.00
SM Scott Mellanby 2.50 6.00
SN Geoff Sanderson 3.00 8.00
SO Steve Staios 2.50 6.00
SP Jason Spezza 12.00 30.00
SQ Stephane Quintal 2.50 6.00
SR Steve Rucchin 2.50 6.00
SS Sheldon Souray 2.50 6.00
SU Mats Sundin 25.00 60.00
TE Mikael Tellqvist 3.00 8.00
TH Jose Theodore 5.00 12.00
TI Mattias Timander 2.50 6.00
TL Trevor Linden 6.00 15.00
TM Todd Marchant 2.50 6.00
TN Tyson Nash 2.50 6.00
TO Steve Thomas 2.50 6.00
TP Tom Poti 2.50 6.00
TR Trent Hunter 2.50 6.00
TT Tim Taylor 2.50 6.00
TU Marty Turco 4.00 10.00
TW Todd White 2.50 6.00
VD Vincent Damphousse 3.00 8.00
VL Vincent Lecavalier 20.00 50.00
WA Scott Walker 2.50 6.00
WE Stephen Weiss 2.50 6.00
WR Wade Redden 2.50 6.00
YO Scott Young 2.50 6.00
ZE Eric Daze 2.50 6.00

2005-06 Be A Player Triple Signatures

STATED ODDS 1:90
AVS Sakic/Tanguay/Kariya SP 30.00 80.00
BSH Bondra/Spezza/Hossa SP 40.00 100.00
BUF Drury/Briere/Biron 20.00 50.00
DAL Turco/Morrow/Guerin SP 20.00 50.00
DEV Brodeur/Niedrmyr/Rafalski SP 125.00 250.00
DRL Dipietro/Raycroft/Luongo SP 30.00 80.00
FGR Fleury/Giguere/Raycroft SP 30.00 80.00
HGT Howe/Guerin/Tkachuk SP 100.00 200.00
HSN Hossa/Sundin/Naslund SP 40.00 100.00
IBM Iginla/Bergeron/Marleau SP 20.00 50.00
LBP Lidstrom/Blake/Pronger SP 30.00 80.00
LLA Luongo/Lehtnen/Aebischr SP 30.00 80.00
MTL Theodore/Ryder/Ribeiro SP 30.00 80.00
NKI Naslund/Kariya/Iginla SP 50.00 100.00
NMS Naslund/Morrison/Sopel 20.00 50.00
PAN Weiss/Horton/Bouwmeester 20.00 50.00
PDL Primeau/Daze/Lindros SP 20.00 50.00
PTS Primeau/Thornton/Sundin SP 30.00 80.00
SIS Sakic/Iginla/Sundin SP 75.00 150.00
SNL Sundin/Naslund/Lidstrom SP 20.00 50.00
STL Tkachuk/Pronger/Drake SP 20.00 50.00
STS Sakic/Thornton/Spezza SP 100.00 200.00
TBL St.Louis/Richards/Lecavlr SP 60.00 120.00
TGR Turco/Giguere/Raycroft 25.00 60.00
TLP Thorntn/Lecavalr/Primeau SP 25.00 60.00

2005-06 Be A Player World Cup Salute

PRINT RUN 199 SER.#'d SETS
WCS1 Fredrik Modin 2.50 6.00
WCS2 Vincent Lecavalier 3.00 8.00
WCS3 Keith Tkachuk 4.00 10.00
WCS4 Joe Sakic 6.00 15.00
WCS5 Martin Havlat 4.00 10.00
WCS6 Kimmo Timonen 10.00 25.00
WCS7 Joe Thornton 5.00 12.00
WCS8 Mike Modano 6.00 15.00
WCS9 Daniel Alfredsson 4.00 10.00
WCS10 Patrik Elias 4.00 10.00
WCS11 Martin Brodeur 8.00 20.00
WCS12 Tomas Vokoun 3.00 8.00
WCS13 Miikka Kiprusoff 3.00 8.00
WCS14 Robert Esche 3.00 8.00
WCS15 Bill Guerin 4.00 10.00

2006-07 Be A Player

COMP.SET w/o SPs (170) 20.00 50.00
RC STATED PRINT RUN 999 #'d SETS
1 Dainius Zubrus .20 .50
2 Nikolai Zherdev .20 .50
3 Alexei Yashin .25 .60
4 Curtis Joseph .30 .75
5 Justin Williams .25 .60
6 Todd White .20 .50
7 Kyle Wellwood .25 .60
8 Doug Weight .30 .75
9 Cam Ward .30 .75
10 Aaron Ward .20 .50
11 Scott Walker .20 .50
12 David Vyborny .20 .50
13 Radim Vrbata .25 .60
14 Antoine Vermette .25 .60
15 Stephane Veilleux .20 .50
16 Thomas Vanek .40 1.00
17 Mike Van Ryn .20 .50
18 R.J. Umberger .20 .50
19 Marty Turco .30 .75
20 Darcy Tucker .25 .60
21 Vesa Toskala .25 .60
22 Kimmo Timonen .20 .50
23 Joe Thornton .40 1.00
24 Jose Theodore .30 .75
25 Tim Taylor .20 .50
26 Alex Tanguay .20 .50
27 Steve Sullivan .20 .50
28 Brad Stuart .20 .50
29 Martin Straka .20 .50
30 Jarret Stoll .25 .60
31 Lee Stempniak .20 .50
32 Matt Stajan .25 .60
33 Eric Staal .40 1.00
34 Martin St. Louis .30 .75
35 Jason Spezza .30 .75
36 Sheldon Souray .20 .50
37 Ryan Smyth .25 .60
38 Jason Smith .20 .50
39 Chris Simon .20 .50
40 Mike Sillinger .20 .50
41 Jody Shelley .20 .50
42 Teemu Selanne .60 1.50
43 Henrik Sedin .30 .75
44 Brent Seabrook .30 .75
45 Nick Schultz .20 .50
46 Marc Savard .20 .50
47 Sergei Samsonov .25 .60
48 Sami Salo .20 .50
49 Joe Sakic .50 1.25
50 Michael Ryder .20 .50
51 Tuomo Ruutu .30 .75
52 Derek Roy .20 .50
53 Dwayne Roloson .25 .60
54 Mike Richards .30 .75
55 Brad Richards .30 .75
56 Robyn Regehr .20 .50
57 Wade Redden .20 .50
58 Andrew Raycroft .25 .60
59 Brian Rafalski .25 .60
60 Petr Prucha .25 .60
61 Wayne Primeau .20 .50
62 Tom Poti .20 .50
63 Joni Pitkanen .20 .50
64 Dion Phaneuf .30 .75
65 Andrew Peters .20 .50
66 Yanic Perreault .20 .50
67 Dustin Penner .25 .60
68 Michael Peca .25 .60
69 Mark Parrish .20 .50
70 Alexander Ovechkin 1.25 3.00
71 Steve Ott .25 .60
72 Michael Nylander .20 .50
73 Mattias Norstrom .20 .50
74 Antero Niittymaki .25 .60
75 Scott Niedermayer .30 .75
76 Markus Naslund .25 .60
77 Glen Murray .25 .60
78 Bryan Muir .20 .50
79 Brendan Morrison .20 .50
80 Steve Montador .20 .50
81 Ryan Miller .30 .75
82 Milan Michalek .20 .50
83 Andrej Meszaros .20 .50
84 Andy McDonald .25 .60
85 Jamal Mayers .20 .50
86 Patrick Marleau .30 .75
87 Andrei Markov .30 .75
88 Ryan Malone .20 .50
89 Manny Malhotra .20 .50
90 Roberto Luongo .50 1.25
91 Henrik Lundqvist .60 1.50
92 John-Michael Liles .20 .50
93 Nicklas Lidstrom .30 .75
94 Jordan Leopold .20 .50
95 Jere Lehtinen .20 .50
96 David Legwand .25 .60
97 Vincent Lecavalier .25 .60
98 Georges Laraque .25 .60
99 Andrew Ladd .30 .75
100 Chris Kunitz .30 .75
101 Slava Kozlov .20 .50
102 Alexei Kovalev .25 .60
103 Olaf Kolzig .30 .75
104 Saku Koivu .30 .75
105 Chuck Kobasew .20 .50
106 Mike Knuble .20 .50
107 Nikolai Khabibulin .30 .75
108 Duncan Keith .40 1.00
109 Olli Jokinen .30 .75
110 Jarome Iginla .30 .75
111 Trent Hunter .20 .50
112 Cristobal Huet .25 .60
113 Marian Hossa .25 .60
114 Shawn Horcoff .20 .50
115 Bobby Holik .20 .50
116 Chris Higgins .20 .50
117 Dany Heatley .30 .75
118 Martin Havlat .20 .50
119 Dan Hamhuis .25 .60
120 Bill Guerin .30 .75
121 Mike Green .30 .75
122 Hal Gill .20 .50
123 Martin Gerber .25 .60
124 Simon Gagne .30 .75
125 Alexander Frolov .20 .50
126 Kurtis Foster .20 .50
127 Peter Forsberg .40 1.00
128 Marc-Andre Fleury .50 1.25
129 Ruslan Fedotenko .20 .50
130 Sergei Federov .50 1.25
131 Garnet Exelby .20 .50
132 Robert Esche .25 .60
133 Steve Eminger .20 .50
134 Patrik Elias .30 .75
135 Patrick Eaves .20 .50
136 J.P. Dumont .20 .50
137 Chris Drury .25 .60
138 Shane Doan .25 .60
139 Marc Denis .25 .60
140 Craig Conroy .20 .50
141 Erik Cole .25 .60
142 Chris Clark .20 .50
143 Jonathan Cheechoo .30 .75
144 Zdeno Chara .30 .75
145 Jeff Carter .30 .75
146 Brian Campbell .25 .60
147 Mike Cammalleri .20 .50
148 Kyle Calder .20 .50
149 Brent Burns .40 1.00
150 Gilbert Brule .25 .60
151 Dustin Brown .30 .75
152 Curtis Brown .20 .50
153 Rod Brind`Amour .30 .75
154 Daniel Briere .30 .75
155 Eric Brewer .20 .50
156 Dan Boyle .25 .60
157 Brad Boyes .20 .50
158 Jay Bouwmeester .30 .75
159 Pierre-Marc Bouchard .30 .75
160 Rob Blake .30 .75
161 Steve Bernier .20 .50
162 Patrice Bergeron .40 1.00
163 Mark Bell .20 .50
164 Keith Ballard .20 .50
165 Sean Avery .20 .50
166 Adrian Aucoin .20 .50
167 Daniel Alfredsson .30 .75
168 Maxim Afinogenov .20 .50
169 Kevyn Adams .20 .50
170 Shawn Bates .20 .50
201 Evgeni Malkin RC 15.00 30.00
202 Phil Kessel RC 8.00 20.00
203 Luc Bourdon RC 5.00 12.00
204 Dustin Boyd RC 3.00 8.00
205 Patrick O'Sullivan RC 5.00 12.00
206 Blake Comeau RC 5.00 12.00
207 Shea Weber RC 8.00 20.00
208 Matt Carle RC 3.00 8.00
209 Loui Eriksson RC 5.00 12.00
210 Mark Stuart RC 3.00 8.00
211 Eric Fehr RC 5.00 12.00
212 Travis Zajac RC 6.00 15.00
213 Anze Kopitar RC 12.00 30.00
214 Ladislav Smid RC 3.00 8.00
215 Noah Welch RC 3.00 8.00
216 Jordan Staal RC 8.00 20.00
217 Alexander Radulov RC 6.00 15.00
218 Drew Stafford RC 5.00 12.00
219 Paul Stastny RC 8.00 20.00
220 Dave Bolland RC 5.00 12.00
221 Marek Schwarz RC 5.00 12.00
222 Ryan Potulny RC 3.00 8.00
223 Marc-Antoine Pouliot RC 3.00 8.00
224 Jarkko Immonen RC 3.00 8.00
225 Josh Hennessy RC 3.00 8.00
226 Benoit Pouliot RC 4.00 10.00
227 Nigel Dawes RC 3.00 8.00
228 Matt Lashoff RC 3.00 8.00
229 Keith Yandle RC 6.00 15.00
230 Karri Ramo RC 3.00 8.00
231 Guillaume Latendresse RC 5.00 12.00
232 Marc-Edouard Vlasic RC 3.00 8.00
233 Patrick Thoresen RC 3.00 8.00
234 Niklas Grossman RC 5.00 12.00
235 Ian White RC 4.00 10.00
236 Clarke MacArthur RC 4.00 10.00
237 Jesse Schultz RC 3.00 8.00
238 David Booth RC 4.00 10.00
239 Joe Pavelski RC 15.00 40.00
240 Martin Houle RC 4.00 10.00
241 Mikhail Grabovski RC 6.00 15.00
242 David McKee RC 3.00 8.00
243 Brandon Prust RC 3.00 8.00
244 Kristopher Letang RC 10.00 25.00
245 Shawn Belle RC 3.00 8.00

2006-07 Be A Player Autographs

OVERALL AUTO ODDS ONE PER PACK
1-170 UNPRICED PRINT RUN 10
202 Phil Kessel 8.00 20.00
203 Luc Bourdon 15.00 30.00
205 Patrick O'Sullivan 5.00 12.00
207 Shea Weber 8.00 20.00
208 Matt Carle 3.00 8.00
216 Jordan Staal 8.00 20.00
219 Paul Stastny 10.00 25.00
227 Nigel Dawes 3.00 8.00
231 Guillaume Latendresse 5.00 12.00
233 Patrick Thoresen 3.00 8.00

2006-07 Be A Player Profiles

COMPLETE SET (30) 50.00 100.00
STATED PRINT RUN 499 SER.#'d SETS
PP1 Vincent Lecavalier 1.25 3.00
PP2 Thomas Vanek 2.00 5.00
PP3 Teemu Selanne 3.00 8.00
PP4 Simon Gagne 1.50 4.00
PP5 Sergei Federov 2.50 6.00
PP6 Scott Niedermayer 1.50 4.00
PP7 Saku Koivu 1.50 4.00
PP8 Ryan Smyth 1.25 3.00
PP9 Pierre-Marc Bouchard 1.50 4.00
PP10 Phil Kessel 2.50 6.00
PP11 Peter Forsberg 2.00 5.00
PP12 Paul Stastny 2.50 6.00
PP13 Patrice Bergeron 2.00 5.00
PP14 Nicklas Lidstrom 1.50 4.00
PP15 Markus Naslund 1.25 3.00
PP16 Marian Hossa 1.25 3.00
PP17 Marc-Andre Fleury 2.50 6.00
PP18 Jordan Staal 2.00 5.00
PP19 Jonathan Cheechoo 1.50 4.00
PP20 Joe Thornton 2.00 5.00
PP21 Joe Sakic 2.50 6.00
PP22 Jay Bouwmeester 1.50 4.00
PP23 Jarome Iginla 1.50 4.00
PP24 Guillaume Latendresse 1.25 3.00
PP25 Eric Staal 2.00 5.00
PP26 Dion Phaneuf 1.50 4.00
PP27 Dany Heatley 1.50 4.00
PP28 Daniel Alfredsson 1.50 4.00
PP29 Alexander Ovechkin 5.00 12.00
PP30 Alexander Frolov 1.00 2.50

2006-07 Be A Player Signatures

This 170-card set was released in July, 2007. The set was issued in five-card packs with a $12.99 SRP which came eight packs to a box and 15 boxes to a case.
AA Adrian Aucoin 4.00 10.00
AD Daniel Alfredsson 6.00 15.00
AF Alexander Frolov 4.00 10.00
AK Alexei Kovalev 5.00 12.00
AL Andrew Ladd 6.00 15.00
AM Andrei Markov 6.00 15.00
AN Antero Niittymaki 5.00 12.00
AO Alexander Ovechkin 30.00 60.00
AP Andrew Peters 4.00 10.00
AR Andrew Raycroft 5.00 12.00
AS Sean Avery 4.00 10.00
AT Alex Tanguay 4.00 10.00
AV Antoine Vermette 5.00 12.00
AW Aaron Ward 4.00 10.00
AY Alexei Yashin 5.00 12.00
BA Shawn Bates 4.00 10.00
BB Brad Boyes 4.00 10.00
BC Brian Campbell 5.00 12.00
BD Daniel Briere 6.00 15.00
BE Patrice Bergeron 8.00 20.00
BG Bill Guerin 6.00 15.00
BH Bobby Holik 4.00 10.00
BL Rob Blake 6.00 15.00
BM Bryan Muir 4.00 10.00
BO Dan Boyle 5.00 12.00
BR Brad Richards 6.00 15.00
BS Brad Stuart 4.00 10.00
BU Brent Burns 8.00 20.00
CA Jeff Carter 6.00 15.00
CB Curtis Brown 4.00 10.00
CC Craig Conroy 4.00 10.00
CD Chris Drury 5.00 12.00
CH Chuck Kobasew 4.00 10.00
CJ Curtis Joseph 6.00 15.00
CK Chris Kunitz 6.00 15.00
CL Chris Clark 4.00 10.00
CM Mike Cammalleri 4.00 10.00
CR Cristobal Huet 5.00 12.00
CS Chris Simon 4.00 10.00
CW Cam Ward 6.00 15.00
DA Dan Hamhuis 5.00 12.00
DB Dustin Brown 6.00 15.00
DH Dany Heatley 6.00 15.00
DK Duncan Keith 8.00 20.00
DL David Legwand 5.00 12.00
DP Dion Phaneuf 6.00 15.00
DR Derek Roy 4.00 10.00
DT Darcy Tucker 5.00 12.00
DV David Vyborny 4.00 10.00
DW Doug Weight 6.00 15.00
DZ Dainius Zubrus 4.00 10.00
EA Patrick Eaves 4.00 10.00
EB Eric Brewer 4.00 10.00
EC Erik Cole 5.00 12.00
EL Patrik Elias 6.00 15.00
EM Steve Eminger 4.00 10.00
ES Eric Staal 8.00 20.00
EX Garnet Exelby 4.00 10.00
GA Simon Gagne 6.00 15.00
GB Gilbert Brule 5.00 12.00
GE Martin Gerber 5.00 12.00
GL Georges Laraque 5.00 12.00
GM Glen Murray 5.00 12.00
HA Martin Havlat 4.00 10.00
HG Hal Gill 4.00 10.00
HI Chris Higgins 4.00 10.00
HL Henrik Lundqvist 12.00 30.00
HO Shawn Horcoff 4.00 10.00
HS Henrik Sedin 6.00 15.00
HU Trent Hunter 4.00 10.00
JA Jason Smith 4.00 10.00
JB Jay Bouwmeester 6.00 15.00
JC Jonathan Cheechoo 6.00 15.00
JD J.P. Dumont 4.00 10.00
JE Jere Lehtinen 4.00 10.00
JI Jarome Iginla 6.00 15.00
JL John-Michael Liles 4.00 10.00
JM Jamal Mayers 4.00 10.00
JO Joe Sakic 12.00 30.00
JP Joni Pitkanen 4.00 10.00
JS Jarret Stoll 5.00 12.00
JT Joe Thornton SP 100.00 200.00
JW Justin Williams 5.00 12.00
KA Kevyn Adams 4.00 10.00
KB Keith Ballard 4.00 10.00
KC Kyle Calder 4.00 10.00
KF Kurtis Foster 4.00 10.00
KN Mike Knuble 4.00 10.00
KO Saku Koivu 6.00 15.00
KT Kimmo Timonen 4.00 10.00
KW Kyle Wellwood 5.00 12.00
KZ Slava Kozlov 4.00 10.00
LE Jordan Leopold 4.00 10.00
LS Lee Stempniak 4.00 10.00
MA Manny Malhotra 4.00 10.00
MB Mark Bell 4.00 10.00
MC Andy McDonald 5.00 12.00
MD Marc Denis 5.00 12.00
MF Marc-Andre Fleury 10.00 25.00
MG Mike Green 6.00 15.00
MH Marian Hossa 5.00 12.00
MI Milan Michalek 4.00 10.00
MN Michael Nylander 4.00 10.00
MO Brendan Morrison 4.00 10.00
MP Michael Peca 5.00 12.00
MS Marc Savard 4.00 10.00
MT Marty Turco 6.00 15.00
MV Mike Van Ryn 4.00 10.00
MX Maxim Afinogenov 4.00 10.00
MZ Andrej Meszaros 4.00 10.00
NA Markus Naslund 5.00 12.00
NK Nikolai Khabibulin 6.00 15.00
NL Nicklas Lidstrom 8.00 20.00
NO Mattias Norstrom 4.00 10.00
NS Nick Schultz 4.00 10.00
NZ Nikolai Zherdev 4.00 10.00
OJ Olli Jokinen 6.00 15.00
OK Olaf Kolzig 6.00 15.00
OT Steve Ott 5.00 12.00
PA Mark Parrish 4.00 10.00
PB Pierre-Marc Bouchard 6.00 15.00
PE Dustin Penner 5.00 12.00
PF Peter Forsberg 30.00 60.00
PM Patrick Marleau 6.00 15.00
PP Petr Prucha 5.00 12.00

RA Brian Rafalski 5.00 12.00
RB Rod Brind`Amour 6.00 15.00
RD Michael Ryder 4.00 10.00
RE Robert Esche 5.00 12.00
RF Ruslan Fedotenko 4.00 10.00
RI Mike Richards 6.00 15.00
RL Roberto Luongo 20.00 50.00
RM Ryan Malone 4.00 10.00
RO Dwayne Roloson 5.00 12.00
RR Robyn Regehr 4.00 10.00
RS Ryan Smyth 5.00 12.00
RU R.J. Umberger 4.00 10.00
RV Radim Vrbata 5.00 12.00
RY Ryan Miller 6.00 15.00
SB Steve Bernier 4.00 10.00
SD Shane Doan 5.00 12.00
SE Sergei Samsonov 5.00 12.00
SF Sergei Federov 8.00 20.00
SH Jody Shelley 4.00 10.00
SI Mike Sillinger 4.00 10.00
SJ Matt Stajan 5.00 12.00
SK Brent Seabrook 6.00 15.00
SL Martin St. Louis 6.00 15.00
SM Steve Montador 4.00 10.00
SN Scott Niedermayer 6.00 15.00
SO Sheldon Souray 4.00 10.00
SP Jason Spezza 6.00 15.00
SS Sami Salo 4.00 10.00
ST Martin Straka 4.00 10.00
SU Steve Sullivan 4.00 10.00
TH Jose Theodore 6.00 15.00
TP Tom Poti 4.00 10.00
TR Tuomo Ruutu 6.00 15.00
TS Teemu Selanne 15.00 40.00
TT Tim Taylor 4.00 10.00
TV Thomas Vanek 8.00 20.00
TW Todd White 4.00 10.00
VE Stephane Veilleux 4.00 10.00
VL Vincent Lecavalier 5.00 12.00
VT Vesa Toskala 5.00 12.00
WA Scott Walker 4.00 10.00
WP Wayne Primeau 4.00 10.00
WR Wade Redden 4.00 10.00
YP Yanic Perreault 4.00 10.00
ZC Zdeno Chara 6.00 15.00

2006-07 Be A Player Signatures 25

STATED PRINT RUN 25 SER.#'d SETS
AL Andrew Ladd 15.00 40.00
AM Andy McDonald 12.00 30.00
AO Alexander Ovechkin 60.00 150.00
AP Andrew Peters 10.00 25.00
AR Andrew Raycroft 12.00 30.00
AT Alex Tanguay 10.00 25.00
AY Alexei Yashin 12.00 30.00
BC Brian Campbell 12.00 30.00
BG Bill Guerin 15.00 40.00
BH Bobby Holik 10.00 25.00
BR Brad Richards 15.00 40.00
BS Brad Stuart 10.00 25.00
CC Craig Conroy 10.00 25.00
CD Chris Drury 12.00 30.00
CH Chuck Kobasew 10.00 25.00
CK Chris Kunitz 15.00 40.00
CL Chris Clark 10.00 25.00
CR Cristobal Huet 12.00 30.00
DA Daniel Alfredsson 15.00 40.00
DB Dustin Brown 15.00 40.00
DH Dany Heatley 15.00 40.00
DK Duncan Keith 20.00 50.00
DP Dion Phaneuf 15.00 40.00
DR Derek Roy 10.00 25.00
DT Darcy Tucker 12.00 30.00
DV David Vyborny 10.00 25.00
DW Doug Weight 15.00 40.00
EA Patrik Elias 15.00 40.00
EB Eric Brewer 10.00 25.00
ES Eric Staal 20.00 50.00
GL Guillaume Latendresse 15.00 40.00
GM Glen Murray 12.00 30.00
HI Chris Higgins 10.00 25.00
HL Henrik Lundqvist 30.00 80.00
HO Shawn Horcoff 10.00 25.00
JA Jason Smith 10.00 25.00
JC Jonathan Cheechoo 15.00 40.00
JI Jarome Iginla 15.00 40.00
JL John-Michael Liles 10.00 25.00
JO Joe Sakic 25.00 60.00
JS Jarret Stoll 12.00 30.00
JW Justin Williams 12.00 30.00
KC Kyle Calder 10.00 25.00
KO Saku Koivu 15.00 40.00
KT Kimmo Timonen 10.00 25.00
KW Kyle Wellwood 12.00 30.00
KZ Slava Kozlov 10.00 25.00
LE Jordan Leopold 10.00 25.00
MA Maxim Afinogenov 10.00 25.00
MF Marc-Andre Fleury 25.00 60.00
MH Marian Hossa 12.00 30.00
MK Mike Knuble 10.00 25.00
MN Michael Nylander 10.00 25.00
MP Michael Peca 12.00 30.00
MS Martin St. Louis 15.00 40.00
MT Marty Turco 15.00 40.00
MV Mike Van Ryn 10.00 25.00
NA Markus Naslund 12.00 30.00
ND Nigel Dawes 10.00 25.00
NL Nicklas Lidstrom 15.00 40.00
OJ Olli Jokinen 15.00 40.00
PB Patrice Bergeron 20.00 50.00
PE Dustin Penner 12.00 30.00
PF Peter Forsberg 75.00 150.00
PK Phil Kessel 25.00 60.00
PM Patrick Marleau 15.00 40.00
PS Paul Stastny 25.00 60.00
PT Patrick Thoresen 10.00 25.00
RB Rob Blake 15.00 40.00
RD Michael Ryder 10.00 25.00
RF Ruslan Fedotenko 10.00 25.00
RL Roberto Luongo 50.00 120.00
RM Ryan Miller 15.00 40.00
RO Dwayne Roloson 12.00 30.00
RS Ryan Smyth 12.00 30.00
RU R.J. Umberger 10.00 25.00
SE Sergei Samsonov 12.00 30.00
SF Sergei Federov 25.00 60.00
SG Simon Gagne 15.00 40.00
SH Jody Shelley 10.00 25.00
SK Brent Seabrook 15.00 40.00
SN Scott Niedermayer 15.00 40.00
SP Jason Spezza 15.00 40.00
SS Sami Salo 10.00 25.00
ST Jordan Staal 25.00 60.00
SU Steve Sullivan 10.00 25.00
SW Shea Weber 25.00 60.00
TH Trent Hunter 10.00 25.00
TP Tom Poti 10.00 25.00
TS Teemu Selanne 40.00 100.00
VL Vincent Lecavalier 12.00 30.00
WA Scott Walker 10.00 25.00

2006-07 Be A Player Signatures Duals

DAS C.Simon/S.Avery 4.00 10.00
DBC R.Blake/M.Cammalleri 6.00 15.00
DBK P.Bergeron/P.Kessel 15.00 40.00
DBO M.Savard/G.Murray 5.00 12.00
DBP M.Parrish/P.Bouchard 6.00 15.00
DBU D.Briere/T.Vanek 8.00 20.00
DBV D.Vyborny/G.Brule 5.00 12.00
DCA C.Conroy/A.Tanguay 4.00 10.00
DCB S.Bernier/M.Carle 4.00 10.00
DCH B.Seabrook/D.Keith 15.00 30.00
DCW A.Ward/Z.Chara 6.00 15.00
DDR C.Drury/D.Roy 5.00 12.00
DED J.Smith/D.Roloson 5.00 12.00
DER B.Rafalski/P.Elias 6.00 15.00
DEV A.Vermette/P.Eaves 5.00 12.00
DFL N.Lidstrom/P.Forsberg 15.00 40.00
DFS M.Fleury/J.Staal 10.00 25.00
DFZ N.Zherdev/S.Federov 10.00 25.00
DGC S.Gagne/J.Carter 6.00 15.00
DGE S.Eminger/M.Green 6.00 15.00
DHK S.Koivu/C.Huet 6.00 15.00
DHM M.Straka/H.Lundqvist 12.00 30.00
DHS J.Spezza/D.Heatley 6.00 15.00
DIH J.Iginla/D.Heatley 6.00 15.00
DIP J.Iginla/D.Phaneuf 6.00 15.00
DJS J.Stoll/S.Horcoff 5.00 12.00
DKH M.Hossa/S.Kozlov 5.00 12.00
DKR T.Ruutu/N.Khabibulin 6.00 15.00
DKS S.Samsonov/A.Kovalev 5.00 12.00
DLN M.Naslund/R.Luongo 10.00 25.00
DLS V.Lecavalier/M.St. Louis 8.00 20.00
DMB B.Morrison/L.Bourdon(((((6.00 15.00
DMC B.Campbell/R.Miller 6.00 15.00
DMG P.Marleau/B.Guerin 6.00 15.00
DMK A.McDonald/C.Kunitz 6.00 15.00
DMS M.Malhotra/J.Shelley 4.00 10.00
DNA D.Legwand/S.Sullivan 5.00 12.00
DNE R.Esche/A.Niittymaki 5.00 12.00
DOC A.Ovechkin/C.Clark 25.00 50.00
DPL G.Laraque/A.Peters 5.00 12.00
DRF B.Richards/R.Fedotenko 6.00 15.00
DRH M.Ryder/C.Higgins 4.00 10.00
DRM W.Redden/A.Meszaros 4.00 10.00
DRS R.Regehr/B.Stuart 4.00 10.00
DRT D.Tucker/A.Raycroft 5.00 12.00
DRU M.RIchards/R.Umberger 6.00 15.00
DSA D.Alfredsson/J.Spezza 12.00 30.00
DSB R.Brind'Amour/E.Staal 8.00 20.00
DSH M.Sillinger/T.Hunter 4.00 10.00
DSK T.Selanne/S.Koivu 12.00 30.00
DSM A.Markov/S.Souray 6.00 15.00
DSN T.Selanne/S.Niedermayer 12.00 30.00
DSO J.Shelley/S.Ott 5.00 12.00
DSS J.Sakic/P.Stastny 10.00 25.00
DSY A.Yashin/R.Smyth 5.00 12.00
DTL J.Lehtinen/M.Turco 6.00 15.00
DVB M.Van Ryn/J.Bouwmeester 6.00 15.00
DWB D.Weight/B.Boyes 6.00 15.00
DWS K.Wellwood/M.Stajan 5.00 12.00

2006-07 Be A Player Signatures Trios

STATED PRINT RUN 25 SER.#'d SETS
TBKS Savard/Bergeron/Kessel 40.00 100.00
TCWB Weber/Carle/Bourdon 40.00 100.00
TDBV Drury/Briere/Vanek 30.00 80.00
TFCO Frolov/Cam/O'Sully 25.00 60.00
TFLS Sully/Leg/Forsberg 30.00 80.00
TFSM Malone/Fleury/Staal 40.00 100.00
TFVB Vyborny/Federov/Brule
TGCR Gagne/Richards/Carter 25.00 60.00
THHK Huet/Higgins/Kovalev 20.00 50.00
THKH Hossa/Holik/Kozlov 20.00 50.00
TIPT Iginla/Tanguay/Phaneuf 25.00 60.00
TJBM Jokin/Bouw/Montador
TKRL Koivu/Ryder/Laten 25.00 60.00
TLNM Naslund/Luongo/Morris 40.00 100.00
TLRS Lecav/Richards/St. Lou 40.00 100.00
TMAR Afinogenov/Roy/Miller 25.00 60.00
TOKC Kolzig/Ovechkin/Clark 300.00 500.00
TRKS Ruutu/Seabrook/Khabi 25.00 60.00
TRPP Peca/Perr/Raycroft 20.00 50.00
TRSH Stoll/Horcoff/Roloson 20.00 50.00
TSAH Alfred/Spezza/Heatley
TSBC Cole/Brind'Amour/Staal 30.00 80.00
TSNP Straka/Nylander/Prucha 20.00 50.00
TSTS Sakic/Theodore/Stastny 40.00 100.00
TTBM Toskala/Michal/Bernier 20.00 50.00
TTCM Marleau/Thorn/Cheech 30.00 80.00
TTLO Lehtinen/Turco/Ott 25.00 60.00
TTWS Tucker/Wellw/Stajan 20.00 50.00
TWBS Weight/Boyes/Stemp 25.00 60.00
TYSS Yashin/Smyth/Sillinger 20.00 50.00

2006-07 Be A Player Unmasked Warriors

STATED PRINT RUN 99 SER.#'d SETS
UM1 Ryan Miller 6.00 15.00
UM2 Jose Theodore 6.00 15.00
UM3 Marty Turco 6.00 15.00
UM4 Dwayne Roloson 5.00 12.00
UM5 Cristobal Huet 5.00 12.00
UM6 Henrik Lundqvist 12.00 30.00
UM7 Cam Ward 6.00 15.00
UM8 Marc-Andre Fleury 10.00 25.00
UM9 Andrew Raycroft 5.00 12.00
UM10 Roberto Luongo 10.00 25.00

2006-07 Be A Player Up Close and Personal

STATED PRINT RUN 999 SER.#'d SETS
UC1 Alex Tanguay .60 1.50
UC2 Justin Williams .75 2.00
UC3 Alexander Ovechkin 4.00 10.00
UC4 Alexei Yashin .75 2.00
UC5 Andrew Raycroft .75 2.00
UC6 Andy McDonald .75 2.00
UC7 Bill Guerin 1.00 2.50
UC8 Brad Richards 1.00 2.50
UC9 Brian Campbell .75 2.00
UC10 Chris Drury .75 2.00
UC11 Cristobal Huet .75 2.00
UC12 Dany Heatley 1.00 2.50
UC13 Darcy Tucker .75 2.00
UC14 Ryan Miller 1.00 2.50
UC15 Dion Phaneuf 1.00 2.50
UC16 Doug Weight 1.00 2.50
UC17 Dwayne Roloson .75 2.00
UC18 Eric Staal 1.25 3.00
UC19 Henrik Lundqvist 2.00 5.00
UC20 Henrik Sedin 1.00 2.50
UC21 Jarome Iginla 1.00 2.50
UC22 Jason Spezza 1.00 2.50
UC23 Jonathan Cheechoo 1.00 2.50
UC24 Daniel Briere 1.00 2.50
UC25 Joe Sakic 1.50 4.00
UC26 Joe Thornton 1.25 3.00
UC27 Lee Stempniak .60 1.50
UC28 Marc Savard .60 1.50
UC29 Marc-Andre Fleury 1.50 4.00
UC30 Marian Hossa .75 2.00
UC31 Mark Parrish .60 1.50
UC32 Markus Naslund .75 2.00
UC33 Martin St. Louis 1.00 2.50
UC34 Martin Straka .60 1.50
UC35 Marty Turco 1.00 2.50
UC36 Michael Peca .75 2.00
UC37 Michael Ryder .60 1.50
UC38 Nicklas Lidstrom 1.00 2.50
UC39 Nikolai Khabibulin 1.00 2.50
UC40 Olaf Kolzig 1.00 2.50
UC41 Martin Havlat .60 1.50
UC42 Patrice Bergeron 1.25 3.00
UC43 Patrick Marleau 1.00 2.50
UC44 Patrik Elias 1.00 2.50
UC45 Paul Stastny 1.50 4.00
UC46 Peter Forsberg 1.25 3.00
UC47 Rob Blake 1.00 2.50
UC48 Roberto Luongo 1.50 4.00
UC49 Rod Brind`Amour 1.00 2.50
UC50 Ryan Smyth .75 2.00
UC51 Saku Koivu 1.00 2.50
UC52 Scott Niedermayer 1.00 2.50
UC53 Sergei Federov 1.50 4.00
UC54 Simon Gagne 1.00 2.50
UC55 Kimmo Timonen .60 1.50
UC56 Teemu Selanne 2.00 5.00
UC57 Jordan Staal 1.50 4.00
UC58 Vincent Lecavalier .75 2.00
UC59 Wade Redden .60 1.50
UC60 Zdeno Chara 1.00 2.50

2007-08 Be A Player

This set featured 360 cards with cards 1-200 as the basic veterans, 201-300 short-printed rookies serial numbered to 99 and 301-360 were released as exchange cards. Cards 301-360 featured cards with players from the 2008-09 rookie class and they were short-printed and serial numbered to 99.

COMP.SET w/o SPs (200) 20.00 50.00
201-300 ROOKIE PRINT RUN 99
301-360 XRC STATED PRINT RUN 99
1 Ryan Getzlaf .50 1.25
2 Jean-Sebastien Giguere .30 .75
3 Corey Perry .30 .75
4 Teemu Selanne .60 1.50
5 Chris Pronger .25 .60
6 Chris Kunitz .30 .75
7 Scott Niedermayer .30 .75
8 Ilya Kovalchuk .30 .75
9 Eric Perrin .20 .50
10 Colby Armstrong .20 .50
11 Kari Lehtonen .25 .60
12 Mark Recchi .40 1.00
13 Slava Kozlov .20 .50
14 Patrice Bergeron .40 1.00
15 Marc Savard .20 .50
16 Tim Thomas .40 1.00
17 Zdeno Chara .30 .75
18 Marco Sturm .20 .50
19 Phil Kessel .40 1.00
20 Glen Murray .25 .60
21 Thomas Vanek .40 1.00
22 Ryan Miller .30 .75
23 Derek Roy .20 .50
24 Jason Pominville .30 .75
25 Drew Stafford .25 .60
26 Steve Bernier .20 .50
27 Miikka Kiprusoff .25 .60
28 Jarome Iginla .30 .75
29 Daymond Langkow .20 .50
30 Dion Phaneuf .30 .75
31 Alex Tanguay .20 .50
32 Kristian Huselius .20 .50
33 Matthew Lombardi .20 .50
34 Curtis Joseph .30 .75
35 Eric Staal .40 1.00
36 Rod Brind'Amour .30 .75
37 Cam Ward .30 .75
38 Justin Williams .25 .60
39 Ray Whitney .25 .60
40 Erik Cole .25 .60
41 Jason Williams .20 .50
42 Nikolai Khabibulin .30 .75
43 Patrick Sharp .30 .75
44 Brent Seabrook .30 .75
45 Robert Lang .20 .50
46 Martin Havlat .30 .75
47 Duncan Keith .30 .75
48 Joe Sakic .50 1.25
49 Jose Theodore .30 .75
50 Ryan Smyth .25 .60
51 Milan Hejduk .25 .60
52 Marek Svatos .20 .50
53 Paul Stastny .30 .75
54 Wojtek Wolski .25 .60
55 Rick Nash .30 .75
56 Gilbert Brule .25 .60
57 Pascal Leclaire .25 .60
58 Nikolai Zherdev .20 .50
59 Rostislav Klesla .20 .50
60 Michael Peca .25 .60
61 Mike Modano .50 1.25
62 Brad Richards .30 .75
63 Marty Turco .30 .75
64 Mike Ribeiro .25 .60
65 Brenden Morrow .25 .60
66 Jere Lehtinen .20 .50
67 Dominik Hasek .40 1.00
68 Nicklas Lidstrom .30 .75
69 Pavel Datsyuk .40 1.00
70 Chris Osgood .30 .75
71 Henrik Zetterberg .40 1.00
72 Dan Cleary .25 .60
73 Tomas Holmstrom .25 .60
74 Valtteri Filppula .30 .75
75 Jarret Stoll .25 .60
76 Ales Hemsky .25 .60
77 Mathieu Garon .25 .60
78 Shawn Horcoff .20 .50
79 Dustin Penner .25 .60
80 Joni Pitkanen .20 .50
81 Dwayne Roloson .25 .60
82 Olli Jokinen .25 .60
83 Tomas Vokoun .25 .60
84 Nathan Horton .30 .75
85 David Booth .20 .50
86 Stephen Weiss .20 .50
87 Jay Bouwmeester .30 .75
88 Anze Kopitar .50 1.25
89 Rob Blake .30 .75
90 Alexander Frolov .20 .50
91 Dustin Brown .30 .75
92 Mike Cammalleri .25 .60
93 Patrick O'Sullivan .25 .60
94 Marian Gaborik .40 1.00
95 Niklas Backstrom .30 .75
96 Pierre-Marc Bouchard .30 .75
97 Brian Rolston .25 .60
98 Josh Harding .30 .75
99 Mikko Koivu .25 .60
100 Saku Koivu .30 .75
101 Mark Streit .20 .50
102 Tomas Plekanec .30 .75
103 Michael Ryder .20 .50
104 Alex Kovalev .25 .60
105 Chris Higgins .20 .50
106 Andrei Markov .30 .75
107 Guillaume Latendresse .25 .60
108 Alexander Radulov .30 .75
109 Jason Arnott .25 .60
110 Chris Mason .25 .60
111 Martin Erat .20 .50
112 J.P. Dumont .20 .50
113 David Legwand .25 .60
114 Martin Brodeur .60 1.50
115 Zach Parise .40 1.00
116 Patrik Elias .30 .75
117 Brian Gionta .25 .60
118 John Madden .20 .50
119 Travis Zajac .25 .60
120 Rick DiPietro .25 .60
121 Mike Comrie .25 .60
122 Bill Guerin .30 .75
123 Miroslav Satan .25 .60
124 Trent Hunter .20 .50
125 Ruslan Fedotenko .20 .50
126 Jaromir Jagr .75 2.00
127 Henrik Lundqvist .40 1.00
128 Chris Drury .25 .60
129 Scott Gomez .25 .60
130 Brendan Shanahan .40 1.00
131 Michal Rozsival .20 .50
132 Sean Avery .20 .50
133 Jason Spezza .30 .75
134 Dany Heatley .30 .75
135 Ray Emery .25 .60
136 Antoine Vermette .20 .50
137 Mike Fisher .20 .50
138 Daniel Alfredsson .30 .75
139 Wade Redden .20 .50
140 Martin Gerber .25 .60
141 Mike Richards .30 .75
142 Martin Biron .25 .60
143 Daniel Briere .30 .75
144 Simon Gagne .30 .75
145 Mike Knuble .20 .50
146 Jeff Carter .30 .75
147 R.J. Umberger .20 .50
148 Steven Reinprecht .20 .50
149 Shane Doan .25 .60
150 Ilya Bryzgalov .30 .75
151 Ed Jovanovski .25 .60
152 Radim Vrbata .25 .60
153 Keith Ballard .20 .50
154 Petr Sykora .25 .60
155 Marc-Andre Fleury .50 1.25
156 Marian Hossa .25 .60
157 Evgeni Malkin 1.00 2.50
158 Sergei Gonchar .20 .50
159 Ryan Malone .20 .50
160 Jordan Staal .30 .75
161 Ryan Whitney .25 .60
162 Joe Thornton .40 1.00
163 Evgeni Nabokov .25 .60
164 Jonathan Cheechoo .30 .75
165 Milan Michalek .20 .50
166 Brian Campbell .25 .60
167 Patrick Marleau .30 .75
168 Paul Kariya .40 1.00
169 Manny Legace .25 .60
170 Andy McDonald .25 .60
171 Brad Boyes .20 .50
172 Lee Stempniak .20 .50
173 Keith Tkachuk .30 .75
174 Vincent Lecavalier .25 .60
175 Mike Smith .30 .75
176 Jussi Jokinen .20 .50
177 Martin St. Louis .30 .75
178 Paul Ranger .20 .50
179 Karri Ramo .30 .75
180 Mats Sundin .30 .75
181 Vesa Toskala .25 .60
182 Alexander Steen .30 .75
183 Darcy Tucker .25 .60
184 Tomas Kaberle .20 .50
185 Nikolai Antropov .25 .60
186 Matt Stajan .25 .60
187 Jason Blake .20 .50
188 Roberto Luongo .40 1.00
189 Daniel Sedin .30 .75
190 Markus Naslund .30 .75
191 Ryan Kesler .40 1.00
192 Alexander Edler .20 .50
193 Brendan Morrison .20 .50
194 Henrik Sedin .30 .75
195 Alexander Ovechkin 1.25 3.00
196 Olaf Kolzig .30 .75
197 Michael Nylander .20 .50
198 Sergei Fedorov .50 1.25
199 Mike Green .30 .75
200 Alexander Semin .30 .75
201 Bobby Ryan RC 12.00 30.00
202 Drew Miller RC 6.00 15.00
203 Ryan Carter RC 5.00 12.00
204 Kent Huskins RC 5.00 12.00
205 Petteri Wirtanen RC 5.00 12.00
206 Ondrej Pavelec RC 10.00 25.00
207 Bryan Little RC 8.00 20.00
208 Brett Sterling RC 5.00 12.00
209 Tobias Enstrom RC 8.00 20.00
210 Tuukka Rask RC 20.00 50.00
211 David Krejci RC 15.00 40.00
212 Vladimir Sobotka RC 6.00 15.00
213 Milan Lucic RC 25.00 60.00
214 Matt Hunwick RC 6.00 15.00
215 Mike Weber RC 5.00 12.00
216 Patrick Kaleta RC 5.00 12.00
217 Curtis McElhinney RC 8.00 20.00
218 Matt Keetley RC 6.00 15.00
219 Casey Borer RC 5.00 12.00
220 Patrick Kane RC 40.00 100.00
221 Jack Skille RC 6.00 15.00
222 Jonathan Toews RC 80.00 150.00
223 Kris Versteeg RC 15.00 40.00
224 Petri Kontiola RC 5.00 12.00
225 Jake Dowell RC 5.00 12.00
226 David Koci RC 5.00 12.00
227 T.J. Hensick RC 6.00 15.00
228 Tyler Weiman RC 6.00 15.00
229 David Jones RC 5.00 12.00
230 Jaroslav Hlinka RC 6.00 15.00
231 Johnny Boychuk RC 8.00 20.00
232 Jared Boll RC 6.00 15.00
233 Kris Russell RC 6.00 15.00
234 Matt Niskanen RC 8.00 20.00
235 Tobias Stephan RC 6.00 15.00
236 Sam Gagner RC 10.00 25.00
237 Andrew Cogliano RC 8.00 20.00
238 Tom Gilbert RC 6.00 15.00
239 Rob Schremp RC 6.00 15.00
240 Liam Reddox RC 5.00 12.00
241 Cory Murphy RC 5.00 12.00
242 Stefan Meyer RC 6.00 15.00
243 Tanner Glass RC 5.00 12.00
244 Jack Johnson RC 6.00 15.00
245 Jonathan Bernier RC 12.00 30.00
246 Lauri Tukonen RC 5.00 12.00
247 Jonathan Quick RC 150.00 300.00
248 Matt Moulson RC 8.00 20.00
249 Brady Murray RC 5.00 12.00
250 James Sheppard RC 5.00 12.00
251 Aaron Voros RC 5.00 12.00
252 Cal Clutterbuck RC 8.00 20.00
253 Carey Price RC 75.00 135.00
254 Jaroslav Halak RC 12.00 30.00
255 Kyle Chipchura RC 8.00 20.00
256 Sergei Kostitsyn RC 6.00 15.00
257 Ryan O'Byrne RC 8.00 20.00
258 Ville Koistinen RC 5.00 12.00
259 Antti Pihlstrom RC 6.00 15.00
260 Nicklas Bergfors RC 5.00 12.00
261 David Clarkson RC 8.00 20.00
262 Andy Greene RC 6.00 15.00
263 Olli Malmivaara RC 5.00 12.00
264 Frans Nielsen RC 8.00 20.00
265 Marc Staal RC 8.00 20.00
266 Brandon Dubinsky RC 10.00 25.00
267 Ryan Callahan RC 10.00 25.00
268 Ivan Baranka RC 6.00 15.00
269 Greg Moore RC 6.00 15.00
270 Daniel Girardi RC 6.00 15.00
271 Nick Foligno RC 10.00 25.00
272 Brian Elliott RC 10.00 25.00
273 Alexander Nikulin RC 6.00 15.00
274 Steve Downie RC 6.00 15.00
275 Riley Cote RC 6.00 15.00
276 Ryan Parent RC 5.00 12.00
277 Denis Tolpeko RC 5.00 12.00
278 Peter Mueller RC 6.00 15.00
279 Martin Hanzal RC 6.00 15.00
280 Daniel Carcillo RC 6.00 15.00
281 Daniel Winnik RC 6.00 15.00
282 Craig Weller RC 5.00 12.00
283 Tyler Kennedy RC 8.00 20.00
284 Devin Setoguchi RC 8.00 20.00
285 Thomas Greiss RC 10.00 25.00
286 Torrey Mitchell RC 6.00 15.00
287 Lukas Kaspar RC 5.00 12.00
288 Tomas Plihal RC 6.00 15.00
289 Erik Johnson RC 8.00 20.00
290 David Perron RC 8.00 20.00
291 Steve Wagner RC 5.00 12.00
292 Matt Smaby RC 5.00 12.00
293 Mike Lundin RC 5.00 12.00
294 Jiri Tlusty RC 8.00 20.00
295 Anton Stralman RC 5.00 12.00
296 Mason Raymond RC 8.00 20.00
297 Jannik Hansen RC 6.00 15.00
298 Drew MacIntyre RC 6.00 15.00
299 Nicklas Backstrom RC 20.00 50.00
300 Chris Bourque RC 6.00 15.00
301 Steven Stamkos XRC 40.00 100.00
302 Michael Frolik XRC 8.00 20.00
303 Alex Pietrangelo XRC 15.00 40.00
304 Zach Bogosian XRC 15.00 40.00
305 Oscar Moller XRC 8.00 20.00
306 Colton Gillies XRC 10.00 25.00
307 Viktor Tikhonov XRC 10.00 25.00
308 Luke Schenn XRC 12.00 30.00
309 Andreas Nodl XRC 8.00 20.00
310 Blake Wheeler XRC 20.00 40.00
311 Fabian Brunnstrom XRC 12.00 30.00
312 Drew Doughty XRC 25.00 50.00
313 Kyle Okposo XRC 15.00 40.00
314 Kyle Turris XRC 30.00 60.00
315 Zach Boychuk XRC 10.00 25.00
316 Nikita Filatov XRC 8.00 20.00
317 Petr Vrana XRC 8.00 20.00
318 Luca Sbisa XRC 6.00 15.00
319 Mikkel Boedker XRC 12.00 30.00
320 Patric Hornqvist XRC 6.00 15.00
321 T.J. Oshie XRC 20.00 50.00
322 Nikolai Kulemin XRC 6.00 15.00
323 Brandon Sutter XRC 10.00 25.00
324 Derick Brassard XRC 8.00 20.00
325 James Neal XRC 15.00 40.00
326 Claude Giroux XRC 30.00 60.00
327 Vladimir Mihalik XRC 6.00 15.00
328 Patrik Berglund XRC 15.00 40.00
329 Adam Pardy XRC 6.00 15.00
330 Jonas Frogren XRC 8.00 20.00
331 Jakub Voracek XRC 10.00 25.00
332 Mark Fistric XRC 8.00 20.00
333 Marc-Andre Gragnani XRC 8.00 20.00
334 Justin Abdelkader XRC 12.00 30.00
335 Brian Boyle XRC 12.00 30.00
336 Shawn Matthias XRC 6.00 15.00
337 Lauri Korpikoski XRC 6.00 15.00
338 Robbie Earl XRC 6.00 15.00
339 Steve Mason XRC 25.00 60.00
340 Brian Lee XRC 12.00 30.00
341 Kevin Porter XRC 6.00 15.00
342 Alex Goligoski XRC 12.00 30.00
343 Ryan Jones XRC 10.00 25.00
344 Boris Valabik XRC 8.00 20.00
345 Darren Helm XRC 10.00 25.00
346 Derek Dorsett XRC 6.00 15.00
347 Wayne Simmonds XRC 10.00 25.00
348 Ben Bishop XRC 15.00 40.00
349 John Mitchell XRC 6.00 15.00
350 Jonathan Ericsson XRC 8.00 20.00
351 Tyler Plante XRC 8.00 20.00
352 Andrew Ebbett XRC 6.00 15.00
353 Tom Sestito XRC 8.00 20.00
354 Jonathan Filewich XRC 6.00 15.00
355 Ilya Zubov XRC 8.00 20.00
356 Anssi Salmela XRC 8.00 20.00
357 Dane Byers XRC 6.00 15.00
358 Adam Pineault XRC 6.00 15.00
359 Mike Iggulden XRC 8.00 20.00
360 Matt D'Agostini XRC 6.00 15.00

2007-08 Be A Player Player's Club

*PLAYER'S CLUB: 2.5X TO 6X BASE
STATED PRINT RUN 99 SERIAL #'d SETS

2007-08 Be A Player Player's Club Platinum

*PLATINUM: 10X TO 25X BASE
(1-200) PRINT RUN 25 SERIAL #'d SETS
(201-300) PRINT RUN 1 SERIAL #'d SET

2007-08 Be A Player Signatures

OVERALL AUTO ODDS 1 PER PACK
SAA Adrian Aucoin 4.00 10.00
SAF Andrew Ference 4.00 10.00
SAK Anze Kopitar 8.00 20.00
SAM Andrei Markov 6.00 15.00
SAO Alexander Ovechkin 25.00 60.00
SAP Andrew Peters 4.00 10.00
SAR Jason Arnott 5.00 12.00
SAS Alexander Semin 6.00 15.00
SAT Alex Tanguay 4.00 10.00
SAV Aaron Voros 4.00 10.00
SBA Nicklas Backstrom 8.00 20.00
SBB Brad Boyes 4.00 10.00
SBC Brian Campbell 5.00 12.00
SBD Daniel Briere 6.00 15.00
SBM Brendan Morrison 4.00 10.00
SBO Dan Boyle 5.00 12.00
SBP Brian Pothier 4.00 10.00
SBR Brian Rafalski 5.00 12.00
SBS Brent Seabrook 8.00 20.00
SBW Brendan Witt 4.00 10.00
SCA Mike Cammalleri 5.00 12.00
SCC Chris Clark 4.00 10.00
SCH Chris Higgins 4.00 10.00
SCI Chris Campoli 4.00 10.00
SCK Chuck Kobasew 4.00 10.00
SCL David Clarkson 6.00 15.00
SCM Chris Mason 5.00 12.00
SCN Chris Neil 4.00 10.00
SCO Mike Commodore 4.00 10.00
SCP Carey Price 25.00 50.00
SCR Chris Conner 4.00 10.00
SCS Cory Stillman 4.00 10.00
SCW Cam Ward 6.00 15.00
SCY Dan Cleary 5.00 12.00
SDA Dan Hamhuis 5.00 12.00
SDB Dustin Brown 6.00 15.00
SDC Daniel Carcillo 5.00 12.00
SDE Derian Hatcher 5.00 12.00
SDH Dominik Hasek 12.00 30.00
SDK Duncan Keith 6.00 15.00
SDM David Moss 6.00 15.00
SDO Donald Brashear 4.00 10.00
SDP Dion Phaneuf 6.00 15.00
SDR Derek Roy 4.00 10.00
SDS Daniel Sedin 6.00 15.00
SDT Darcy Tucker 5.00 12.00
SDV David Vyborny 4.00 10.00
SEC Erik Cole 5.00 12.00
SES Eric Staal 8.00 20.00
SFI Mike Fisher 4.00 10.00
SFR Alexander Frolov 4.00 10.00
SGA Simon Gagne 6.00 15.00
SGC Gregory Campbell 4.00 10.00
SGE Garnet Exelby 4.00 10.00
SHA Josh Harding 6.00 15.00
SHE Dany Heatley 6.00 15.00
SHM Martin Hanzal 5.00 12.00
SHO Marian Hossa 5.00 12.00
SHS Henrik Sedin 6.00 15.00
SHU Cristobal Huet 5.00 12.00
SIB Ilya Bryzgalov 6.00 15.00
SJB Jay Bouwmeester 6.00 15.00
SJC Jonathan Cheechoo 6.00 15.00
SJE Jeff Carter 6.00 15.00
SJH Johan Hedberg 5.00 12.00
SJI Jarome Iginla 6.00 15.00
SJJ Jack Johnson 5.00 12.00
SJL Jamie Langenbrunner 4.00 10.00
SJM Jamal Mayers 4.00 10.00
SJO Joe Thornton 12.00 30.00
SJP Jason Pominville 6.00 15.00
SJR Jarkko Ruutu 4.00 10.00
SJS Joe Sakic 25.00 50.00
SJT Jonathan Toews 25.00 60.00
SJW Jason Williams 4.00 10.00
SKB Keith Ballard 4.00 10.00
SKC Kyle Chipchura 6.00 15.00
SKD Kris Draper 4.00 10.00
SKE Tyler Kennedy 6.00 15.00
SKI Miikka Kiprusoff 5.00 12.00
SKM Kimmo Timonen 4.00 10.00
SKN Mike Knuble 4.00 10.00
SKO Saku Koivu 6.00 15.00
SKQ Kyle Quincey 4.00 10.00
SKR Kris Russell 5.00 12.00
SKS Phil Kessel 8.00 20.00
SLE Jere Lehtinen 4.00 10.00
SLJ Andreas Lilja 4.00 10.00
SLS Lee Stempniak 4.00 10.00
SLU Milan Lucic 20.00 50.00
SMA Manny Malhotra 4.00 10.00
SMC Matt Carle 4.00 10.00
SMF Marc-Andre Fleury 12.00 30.00
SMI Milan Michalek 4.00 10.00
SMK Mike Komisarek 4.00 10.00
SML Mike Lundin 4.00 10.00
SMM Mike Modano
SMN Markus Naslund 6.00 15.00
SMP Michael Peca 5.00 12.00
SMU Peter Mueller 5.00 12.00
SMY Cory Murphy 4.00 10.00
SNA Nikolai Antropov 5.00 12.00
SNB Niklas Backstrom 6.00 15.00
SNI Matt Niskanen 6.00 15.00
SNL Nicklas Lidstrom 8.00 20.00
SNS Nick Schultz 4.00 10.00
SOJ Olli Jokinen 5.00 12.00
SOK Olaf Kolzig 6.00 15.00
SOS Chris Osgood 6.00 15.00
SPA Mark Parrish 4.00 10.00
SPD David Perron 6.00 15.00
SPH Chris Phillips 4.00 10.00
SPI Pierre-Marc Bouchard 6.00 15.00
SPK Patrick Kane 30.00 60.00
SPM Patrick Marleau 6.00 15.00
SPN Paul Martin 4.00 10.00
SPR Paul Ranger 4.00 10.00
SPS Paul Stastny 6.00 15.00
SRB Rod Brind'Amour 6.00 15.00
SRD Rob Davison 4.00 10.00
SRI Mike Richards 6.00 15.00
SRK Ryan Kesler 8.00 20.00
SRL Roberto Luongo 12.00 30.00
SRN Rick Nash 6.00 15.00
SRO Rostislav Olesz 4.00 10.00
SRR Robyn Regehr 4.00 10.00
SRS Ryan Smyth 5.00 12.00
SRW Ryan Whitney 5.00 12.00
SSA Marc Savard 4.00 10.00
SSF Sergei Fedorov 10.00 25.00
SSG Sergei Gonchar 4.00 10.00
SSH James Sheppard 4.00 10.00
SSI Mike Sillinger 4.00 10.00
SSJ Matt Stajan 5.00 12.00
SSK Slava Kozlov 4.00 10.00
SSM Martin St. Louis 6.00 15.00
SSO Steve Ott 4.00 10.00
SSP Jason Spezza 6.00 15.00
SSR Steven Reinprecht 4.00 10.00
SST Jordan Staal 6.00 15.00
SSW Stephen Weiss 4.00 10.00
SSY Petr Sykora 5.00 12.00
STC Tim Connolly 4.00 10.00
STE Tobias Enstrom 6.00 15.00
STI Tim Thomas 8.00 20.00
STL Trevor Linden 6.00 15.00
STM Torrey Mitchell 5.00 12.00
STO Jordin Tootoo 6.00 15.00
STP Tomas Plekanec 6.00 15.00
STR Tuomo Ruutu 6.00 15.00
STT Tim Taylor 4.00 10.00
STV Thomas Vanek 8.00 20.00
STW Todd White 4.00 10.00
STZ Travis Zajac 5.00 12.00
SVL Vincent Lecavalier 5.00 12.00
SWA Scott Walker 4.00 10.00
SWE Shea Weber 5.00 12.00
SWH Ray Whitney 5.00 12.00
SWI Justin Williams 5.00 12.00
SWR Wade Redden 4.00 10.00
SWW Wojtek Wolski 5.00 12.00
SZP Zach Parise 6.00 15.00

2007-08 Be A Player Signatures Duals

OVERALL AUTO ODDS 1 PER PACK
2SAM J.Arnott/C.Mason 6.00 15.00
2SBD B.Seabrook/D.Keith 15.00 30.00
2SBH J.Harding/N.Backstrom 8.00 20.00
2SBL D.Boyle/M.Lundin 6.00 15.00
2SBS E.Staal/R.Brind'Amour 10.00 25.00
2SCB J.Carter/D.Briere 8.00 20.00
2SCK A.Kopitar/M.Cammalleri 12.00 30.00
2SCR D.Roy/T.Connolly 5.00 12.00
2SCV D.Carcillo/A.Voros 6.00 15.00
2SCW E.Cole/R.Whitney 6.00 15.00
2SDC D.Cleary/K.Draper 8.00 20.00
2SEJ E.Staal/J.Staal 12.00 30.00
2SEN T.Enstrom/M.Miskanen 8.00 20.00
2SEP Z.Parise/P.Elias
2SFS M.Fleury/J.Staal 10.00 25.00
2SGW S.Gonchar/R.Whitney 6.00 15.00
2SHO D.Hasek/C.Osgood 15.00 40.00
2SHS M.Hossa/P.Sykora 6.00 15.00
2SIM J.Iginla/D.Moss 12.00 30.00
2SJB Jokinen/Bouwmeester 8.00 20.00
2SJP J.Sakic/P.Stastny 20.00 50.00
2SJR J.Johnson/K.Russell 6.00 15.00
2SJT J.Sheppard/T.Kennedy 8.00 20.00
2SKL M.Kiprusoff/R.Luongo 10.00 25.00
2SKR M.Richards/M.Knuble 8.00 20.00
2SLH M.Lucic/M.Hanzal 8.00 20.00
2SLS Lecavalier/M.St. Louis 8.00 20.00
2SMC P.Marleau/J.Cheechoo 8.00 20.00
2SMK A.Markov/M.Komisarek 8.00 20.00
2SMT T.Thomas/G.Murray 10.00 25.00
2SNL M.Naslund/R.Luongo 10.00 25.00
2SNV R.Nash/D.Vyborny 8.00 20.00
2SOT J.Spezza/M.Fisher 8.00 20.00
2SPP C.Price/T.Plekanec 25.00 60.00
2SPV T.Vanek/J.Pominville 10.00 25.00
2SRA R.Regehr/A.Aucoin 5.00 12.00
2SRC W.Radden/M.Commodore 5.00 12.00
2SRQ B.Rafalski/K.Quincey 6.00 15.00
2SSB L.Stempniak/B.Boyes 5.00 12.00
2SSH S.Fedorov/C.Huet 12.00 30.00
2SSK M.Savard/P.Kessel 10.00 25.00
2SSS H.Sedin/D.Sedin 8.00 20.00
2STC J.Thornton/B.Campbell 10.00 25.00
2STK J.Toews/P.Kane 75.00 150.00
2STM J.Toews/P.Mueller 20.00 50.00
2SWC B.Witt/C.Campoli 5.00 12.00

2007-08 Be A Player Signatures Trios

STATED PRINT RUN 25 SERIAL #'d SETS
3SASF Heatley/Spezza/Fisher 20.00 50.00
3SBTP Toews/Mueller/Price 100.00 200.00
3SCAP Carcillo/Peters/Neil 15.00 40.00
3SCPV Vanek/Connolly/Pominville 15.00 40.00
3SCWS Williams/Staal/Cole 25.00 60.00
3SEGP Parise/Elias/Gionta
3SHKS Kennedy/Hossa/Staal 20.00 50.00
3SHPK Plekanec/Higgins/Koivu 20.00 50.00
3SIKT Tanguay/Kiprusoff/Iginla 20.00 50.00
3SKBR Knuble/Richards/Briere 20.00 50.00
3SKPL Kiprusoff/Price/Luongo 100.00 200.00
3SKSM Kane/Mitchell/Sheppard 40.00 100.00
3SLMH Michalek/Hanzal/Lucic 60.00 150.00
3SMBS Mayers/Boyes/Stempniak 12.00 30.00
3SMHF Fleury/Mason/Huet 15.00 40.00
3SNRL Russell/Niskanen/Lundin
3SNSS Naslund/Sedin/Sedin 20.00 50.00
3SPDB Brind'Amour/Draper/Peca 30.00 60.00
3SPRC Redden/Phillips/Commodore 12.00 30.00
3SSBH Sheppard/Bouchard/Harding 20.00 50.00
3SSHN St. Louis/Nash/Heatley 20.00 50.00
3SSMK Savard/Murray/Kessel 30.00 60.00
3SSSS Sakic/Stastny/Smyth 30.00 60.00
3SSTT Sakic/Thornton/Toews 100.00 200.00
3STCM Thornton/Cheech/Michalek 25.00 60.00

2008-09 Be A Player

COMP.SET w/o SPs (180) 25.00 60.00
181-280 ROOKIE PRINT RUN 99
RR281-RR340 ROOKIE PRINT RUN 99
1 Ryan Getzlaf .60 1.50
2 Corey Perry .40 1.00
3 Chris Pronger .30 .75
4 Teemu Selanne .75 2.00
5 Bobby Ryan .40 1.00
6 Scott Niedermayer .40 1.00
7 Jean-Sebastien Giguere .40 1.00
8 Ilya Kovalchuk .40 1.00
9 Bryan Little .30 .75
10 Kari Lehtonen .30 .75

11 Slava Kozlov .25 .60
12 Todd White .25 .60
13 Patrice Bergeron .50 1.25
14 Marc Savard .25 .60
15 David Krejci .40 1.00
16 Phil Kessel .50 1.25
17 Zdeno Chara .40 1.00
18 Tim Thomas .40 1.00
19 Michael Ryder .25 .60
20 Derek Roy .25 .60
21 Thomas Vanek .40 1.00
22 Jason Pominville .40 1.00
23 Ryan Miller .40 1.00
24 Drew Stafford .30 .75
25 Jarome Iginla .40 1.00
26 Mike Cammalleri .30 .75
27 Daymond Langkow .25 .60
28 Todd Bertuzzi .40 1.00
29 Dion Phaneuf .40 1.00
30 Miikka Kiprusoff .30 .75
31 Rene Bourque .25 .60
32 Ray Whitney .30 .75
33 Cam Ward .40 1.00
34 Eric Staal .50 1.25
35 Tuomo Ruutu .40 1.00
36 Rod Brind`Amour .40 1.00
37 Sergei Samsonov .30 .75
38 Patrick Kane .75 2.00
39 Jonathan Toews 1.00 2.50
40 Kris Versteeg .50 1.25
41 Patrick Sharp .40 1.00
42 Brian Campbell .30 .75
43 Nikolai Khabibulin .40 1.00
44 Cristobal Huet .30 .75
45 Paul Stastny .40 1.00
46 Milan Hejduk .30 .75
47 Ryan Smyth .30 .75
48 Wojtek Wolski .30 .75
49 Joe Sakic .60 1.50
50 Peter Budaj .30 .75
51 Rick Nash .40 1.00
52 Kristian Huselius .25 .60
53 R.J. Umberger .25 .60
54 Mike Commodore .25 .60
55 Fredrik Modin .25 .60
56 Brenden Morrow .30 .75
57 Brad Richards .40 1.00
58 Mike Ribeiro .30 .75
59 Loui Eriksson .40 1.00
60 Mike Modano .60 1.50
61 Marty Turco .40 1.00
62 Pavel Datsyuk .50 1.25
63 Marian Hossa .30 .75
64 Henrik Zetterberg .50 1.25
65 Nicklas Lidstrom .40 1.00
66 Tomas Holmstrom .30 .75
67 Johan Franzen .40 1.00
68 Chris Osgood .40 1.00
69 Sam Gagner .30 .75
70 Ales Hemsky .30 .75
71 Sheldon Souray .25 .60
72 Andrew Cogliano .30 .75
73 Shawn Horcoff .25 .60
74 Dwayne Roloson .30 .75
75 Stephen Weiss .25 .60
76 David Booth .25 .60
77 Jay Bouwmeester .40 1.00
78 Nathan Horton .30 .75
79 Tomas Vokoun .30 .75
80 Anze Kopitar .60 1.50
81 Dustin Brown .40 1.00
82 Alexander Frolov .25 .60
83 Patrick O'Sullivan .30 .75
84 Jarret Stoll .30 .75
85 Marek Zidlicky .25 .60
86 Mikko Koivu .30 .75
87 Antti Miettinen .25 .60
88 Andrew Brunette .25 .60
89 Pierre-Marc Bouchard .40 1.00
90 Niklas Backstrom .40 1.00
91 Robert Lang .25 .60
92 Alex Kovalev .30 .75
93 Andrei Markov .40 1.00
94 Alex Tanguay .25 .60
95 Carey Price 1.50 4.00
96 Andrei Kostitsyn .30 .75
97 Saku Koivu .40 1.00
98 J.P. Dumont .25 .60
99 Shea Weber .30 .75
100 Martin Erat .25 .60
101 Jason Arnott .30 .75
102 Dan Ellis .25 .60
103 Martin Brodeur .75 2.00
104 Patrik Elias .40 1.00
105 Zach Parise .40 1.00
106 Brian Gionta .30 .75
107 Travis Zajac .30 .75
108 Scott Clemmensen .25 .60
109 Mark Streit .25 .60
110 Doug Weight .40 1.00
111 Bill Guerin .40 1.00
112 Trent Hunter .25 .60
113 Joey MacDonald .40 1.00
114 Rick DiPietro .30 .75
115 Nikolai Zherdev .25 .60
116 Scott Gomez .30 .75
117 Markus Naslund .30 .75
118 Chris Drury .30 .75
119 Brandon Dubinsky .30 .75
120 Henrik Lundqvist .50 1.25
121 Wade Redden .25 .60
122 Dany Heatley .40 1.00
123 Daniel Alfredsson .40 1.00
124 Jason Spezza .40 1.00
125 Nick Foligno .40 1.00
126 Antoine Vermette .25 .60
127 Alex Auld .25 .60
128 Jeff Carter .40 1.00
129 Mike Richards .40 1.00
130 Simon Gagne .40 1.00
131 Scott Hartnell .40 1.00
132 Mike Knuble .25 .60
133 Martin Biron .30 .75
134 Peter Mueller .30 .75
135 Shane Doan .30 .75
136 Olli Jokinen .30 .75
137 Ed Jovanovski .30 .75
138 Martin Hanzal .30 .75
139 Ilya Bryzgalov .30 .75
140 Sidney Crosby 1.50 4.00
141 Jordan Staal .40 1.00
142 Evgeni Malkin 1.25 3.00
143 Petr Sykora .30 .75
144 Miroslav Satan .40 1.00
145 Marc-Andre Fleury .60 1.50
146 Ruslan Fedotenko .25 .60
147 Joe Thornton .50 1.25
148 Devin Setoguchi .30 .75
149 Patrick Marleau .40 1.00
150 Milan Michalek .25 .60
151 Dan Boyle .30 .75
152 Jonathan Cheechoo .40 1.00
153 Evgeni Nabokov .30 .75
154 David Backes .40 1.00
155 Brad Boyes .25 .60
156 Keith Tkachuk .40 1.00
157 David Perron .30 .75
158 Paul Kariya .50 1.25
159 Manny Legace .40 1.00
160 Martin St. Louis .40 1.00
161 Vincent Lecavalier .30 .75
162 Vaclav Prospal .25 .60
163 Mark Recchi .50 1.25
164 Mike Smith .40 1.00
165 Nik Antropov .30 .75
166 Matt Stajan .30 .75
167 Alexei Ponikarovsky .25 .60
168 Tomas Kaberle .25 .60
169 Lee Stempniak .25 .60
170 Vesa Toskala .30 .75
171 Daniel Sedin .40 1.00
172 Henrik Sedin .40 1.00
173 Pavol Demitra .50 1.25
174 Kyle Wellwood .30 .75
175 Roberto Luongo .50 1.25
176 Alexander Ovechkin 1.50 4.00
177 Nicklas Backstrom .60 1.50
178 Alexander Semin .40 1.00
179 Mike Green .40 1.00
180 Jose Theodore .40 1.00
181 Zach Bogosian RC 6.00 15.00
182 Brandon Sutter RC 6.00 15.00
183 Jakub Voracek RC 12.00 30.00
184 Fabian Brunnstrom RC 5.00 12.00
185 Drew Doughty RC 15.00 40.00
186 Colton Gillies RC 5.00 12.00
187 Josh Bailey RC 8.00 20.00
188 Kyle Okposo RC 6.00 15.00
189 Kyle Turris RC 10.00 25.00
190 Patrik Berglund RC 5.00 12.00
191 Steven Stamkos RC 60.00 120.00
192 Luke Schenn RC 8.00 20.00
193 Cory Schneider RC 15.00 40.00
194 Karl Alzner RC 4.00 10.00
195 Blake Wheeler RC 15.00 40.00
196 Zach Boychuk RC 6.00 15.00
197 Derick Brassard RC 5.00 12.00
198 James Neal RC 12.00 30.00
199 Max Pacioretty RC 40.00 80.00
200 Patric Hornqvist RC 6.00 15.00
201 Mikkel Boedker RC 8.00 20.00
202 T.J. Oshie RC 12.00 30.00
203 Nikolai Kulemin RC 6.00 15.00
204 Tim Kennedy RC 6.00 15.00
205 Nikita Filatov RC 6.00 15.00
206 Mark Fistric RC 5.00 12.00
207 Michael Frolik RC 6.00 15.00
208 Oscar Moller RC 5.00 12.00
209 Brian Lee RC 5.00 12.00
210 Claude Giroux RC 30.00 60.00
211 Alex Goligoski RC 8.00 20.00
212 Jamie McGinn RC 6.00 15.00
213 Alex Pietrangelo RC 8.00 20.00
214 Justin Pogge RC 6.00 15.00
215 Simeon Varlamov RC 25.00 60.00
216 Chris Stewart RC 6.00 15.00
217 Michal Repik RC 6.00 15.00
218 Jon Filewich RC 5.00 12.00
219 Dustin Jeffrey RC 6.00 15.00
220 Robbie Earl RC 4.00 10.00
221 Tom Cavanagh RC 5.00 12.00
222 Nathan Gerbe RC 6.00 15.00
223 Steve Mason RC 10.00 25.00
224 Brian Boyle RC 5.00 12.00
225 Ben Maxwell RC 6.00 15.00
226 Ilya Zubov RC 5.00 12.00
227 Brendan Mikkelson RC 4.00 10.00
228 Justin Abdelkader RC 10.00 25.00
229 Trevor Smith RC 5.00 12.00
230 Ty Wishart RC 5.00 12.00
231 Oskar Osala RC 6.00 15.00
232 Theo Peckham RC 6.00 15.00
233 Shawn Matthias RC 6.00 15.00
234 Tyler Plante RC 5.00 12.00
235 Kenndal McArdle RC 5.00 12.00
236 Derek Joslin RC 5.00 12.00
237 Ben Bishop RC 10.00 25.00
238 Adam Pineault RC 5.00 12.00
239 Brett Carson RC 8.00 20.00
240 Jonathan Ericsson RC 6.00 15.00
241 Trevor Lewis RC 6.00 15.00
242 Lauri Korpikoski RC 4.00 10.00
243 Ryan Stone RC 4.00 10.00
244 Boris Valabik RC 6.00 15.00
245 John Curry RC 6.00 15.00
246 Niklas Hjalmarsson RC 10.00 25.00
247 Darren Helm RC 6.00 15.00
248 Teddy Purcell RC 8.00 20.00
249 Radek Smolenak RC 8.00 20.00
250 Andrew Gordon RC 10.00 25.00
251 Josh Tordjman RC 12.50 30.00
252 Justin Peters RC 6.00 15.00
253 Tom Sestito RC 6.00 15.00
254 Matt D'Agostini RC 5.00 12.00
255 Martins Karsums RC 12.00 30.00
256 Paul Szczechura RC 6.00 15.00
257 Andrew Ebbett RC 4.00 10.00
258 Dan LaCosta RC 6.00 15.00
259 Jonas Junland RC 10.00 25.00
260 Maxsim Mayorov RC 6.00 15.00
261 Mattias Ritola RC 5.00 12.00
262 Corey Potter RC 10.00 25.00
263 Sami Lepisto RC 5.00 12.00
264 Danny Taylor RC 5.00 12.00
265 Brett Sutter RC 6.00 15.00
266 Derek Dorsett RC 8.00 20.00
267 Tim Sestito RC 5.00 12.00
268 Wayne Simmonds RC 6.00 15.00
269 Ryan Jones RC 6.00 15.00
270 Zack Smith RC 5.00 12.00
271 Luca Sbisa RC 4.00 10.00
272 Jonathon Kalinski RC 6.00 15.00
273 Viktor Tikhonov RC 5.00 12.00
274 Kevin Porter RC 5.00 12.00
275 Chris Porter RC 6.00 15.00
276 Vladimir Mihalik RC 4.00 10.00
277 Jonas Frogren RC 4.00 10.00
278 John Mitchell RC 5.00 12.00
279 Andreas Nodl RC 4.00 10.00
280 Janne Pesonen RC 5.00 12.00
RR281 John Tavares XRC 30.00 80.00
RR282 Victor Hedman XRC 10.00 25.00
RR283 Matt Duchene XRC 12.00 30.00
RR284 Jonas Gustavsson XRC 15.00 40.00
RR285 Oskars Bartulis XRC 8.00 20.00
RR286 Daniel Larsson XRC 12.00 30.00
RR287 Ryan O'Marra XRC 8.00 20.00
RR288 Mathieu Perreault XRC 10.00 25.00
RR289 Lars Eller XRC 8.00 20.00
RR290 Mathieu Carle XRC 8.00 20.00
RR291 Brad Marchand XRC 20.00 50.00
RR292 Logan Couture XRC 15.00 40.00
RR293 Perttu Lindgren XRC 6.00 15.00
RR294 Braden Holtby XRC 20.00 40.00
RR295 Michael Grabner XRC 8.00 20.00
RR296 Cody Franson XRC 6.00 15.00
RR297 James Reimer XRC 15.00 40.00
RR298 Jason Demers XRC 8.00 20.00
RR299 Sergei Shirokov XRC 8.00 20.00
RR300 Viktor Stalberg XRC 8.00 20.00
RR301 Benn Ferriero XRC 8.00 20.00
RR302 Tyler Bozak XRC 12.00 30.00
RR303 James van Riemsdyk XRC 12.00 30.00
RR304 Erik Karlsson XRC 15.00 40.00
RR305 Matt Gilroy XRC 8.00 20.00
RR306 Colin Wilson XRC 8.00 20.00
RR307 Alec Martinez XRC 10.00 25.00
RR308 Dmitry Kulikov XRC 8.00 20.00
RR309 Jamie Benn XRC 15.00 40.00
RR310 Ryan O'Reilly XRC 10.00 25.00
RR311 Tyler Myers XRC 8.00 20.00
RR312 Evander Kane XRC 12.00 30.00
RR313 Antti Niemi XRC 20.00 50.00
RR314 Frazer McLaren XRC 5.00 12.00
RR315 Michael Del Zotto XRC 6.00 15.00
RR316 Ville Leino XRC 10.00 25.00
RR317 Michal Neuvirth XRC 10.00 25.00
RR318 Matt Pelech XRC 10.00 25.00
RR319 Riku Helenius XRC 6.00 15.00
RR320 Ivan Vishnevskiy XRC 6.00 15.00
RR321 Jhonas Enroth XRC 6.00 15.00
RR322 Artem Anisimov XRC 6.00 15.00
RR323 Mikael Backlund XRC 8.00 20.00
RR324 Christian Hanson XRC 8.00 20.00
RR325 Yannick Weber XRC 8.00 20.00
RR326 T.J. Galiardi XRC 6.00 15.00
RR327 Spencer Machacek XRC 5.00 12.00
RR328 Luca Caputi XRC 8.00 20.00
RR329 Brian Salcido XRC 10.00 25.00
RR330 Tyler Ennis XRC 10.00 25.00
RR331 Carl Gunnarsson XRC 8.00 20.00
RR332 Alexander Salak XRC 8.00 20.00
RR333 Scott Parse XRC 5.00 12.00
RR334 Matt Beleskey XRC 10.00 25.00
RR335 Cal O'Reilly XRC 6.00 15.00
RR336 Taylor Chorney XRC 6.00 15.00
RR337 Mike Santorelli XRC 6.00 15.00
RR338 Peter Regin XRC 8.00 20.00
RR339 Kris Chucko XRC 6.00 15.00
RR340 John Scott XRC 5.00 12.00

2008-09 Be A Player Player's Club

*1-180 VETS/15: 5X TO 12X BASIC CARDS
1-180 VETERAN PRINT RUN 15
177 Nicklas Backstrom 8.00 20.00

2008-09 Be A Player Rookie Jerseys

STATED ODDS 1:9
STATED PRINT RUN 299 SER.#'d SETS
RJAP Alex Pietrangelo 5.00 12.00
RJBM Ben Maxwell 4.00 10.00
RJBS Brandon Sutter 4.00 10.00
RJBW Blake Wheeler 10.00 25.00
RJCG Colton Gillies 3.00 8.00
RJCS Cory Schneider 10.00 25.00
RJDB Derick Brassard 3.00 8.00
RJDD Drew Doughty 10.00 25.00
RJFB Fabian Brunnstrom 3.00 8.00
RJGI Claude Giroux 8.00 20.00
RJJB Josh Bailey 5.00 12.00
RJJN James Neal 8.00 20.00
RJJP Justin Pogge 4.00 10.00
RJJV Jakub Voracek 8.00 20.00
RJKA Karl Alzner 2.50 6.00
RJKO Kyle Okposo 4.00 10.00
RJKT Kyle Turris 6.00 15.00
RJLS Luke Schenn 5.00 12.00
RJMB Mikkel Boedker 5.00 12.00
RJMF Michael Frolik 4.00 10.00
RJMP Max Pacioretty 15.00 40.00
RJNF Nikita Filatov 4.00 10.00
RJNK Nikolai Kulemin 4.00 10.00
RJPB Patrik Berglund 3.00 8.00
RJSB Luca Sbisa 2.50 6.00
RJSM Steve Mason 15.00 40.00
RJSS Steven Stamkos 15.00 40.00
RJST Chris Stewart 4.00 10.00
RJTO T.J. Oshie 8.00 20.00
RJVT Viktor Tikhonov 3.00 8.00
RJZB Zach Bogosian 4.00 10.00

2008-09 Be A Player Rookie Redemption Bonus

Due to a computer error that caused Upper Deck to send the wrong redemption cards out initially, these were produced. These new cards had a foil shift and a jersey swatch to all but seven cards. The seven cards without the jersey swatches look like the 2009-10 Be A Player Rookie Cards, but the photos are different and on the card back it reads 2008-09 Be A Player. These were shipped to the correct customers in October, 2010.

STATED PRINT RUN 99 SER.#'d SETS
RR281 John Tavares 25.00 60.00
RR282 Victor Hedman 12.00 30.00
RR283 Matt Duchene 12.00 30.00
RR284 Jonas Gustavsson 12.00 30.00
RR285 Oskars Bartulis 6.00 15.00
RR286 Daniel Larsson 6.00 15.00
RR287 Ryan O'Marra 6.00 15.00
RR288 Mathieu Perreault 5.00 12.00
RR289 Lars Eller 6.00 15.00
RR290 Mathieu Carle 4.00 10.00
RR291 Brad Marchand 15.00 40.00
RR292 Logan Couture 12.00 30.00
RR293 Perttu Lindgren 5.00 12.00
RR294 Braden Holtby 20.00 40.00
RR295 Michael Grabner 6.00 15.00
RR296 Cody Franson 5.00 12.00
RR297 James Reimer 30.00 60.00
RR298 Jason Demers 6.00 15.00
RR299 Sergei Shirokov 6.00 15.00
RR300 Viktor Stalberg 6.00 15.00
RR301 Benn Ferriero 6.00 15.00
RR302 Tyler Bozak 10.00 25.00
RR303 James van Riemsdyk 10.00 25.00
RR304 Erik Karlsson 12.00 30.00
RR305 Matt Gilroy 6.00 15.00
RR306 Colin Wilson 6.00 15.00
RR307 Alec Martinez 8.00 20.00
RR308 Dmitry Kulikov 6.00 15.00
RR309 Jamie Benn 12.00 30.00
RR310 Ryan O'Reilly 8.00 20.00
RR311 Tyler Myers 6.00 15.00
RR312 Evander Kane 10.00 25.00
RR313 Antti Niemi 15.00 40.00
RR314 Frazer McLaren 4.00 10.00
RR315 Michael Del Zotto 5.00 12.00
RR316 Ville Leino 8.00 20.00
RR317 Michal Neuvirth 8.00 20.00
RR318 Matt Pelech 8.00 20.00
RR319 Riku Helenius 5.00 12.00
RR320 Ivan Vishnevskiy 5.00 12.00
RR321 Jhonas Enroth 6.00 15.00
RR322 Artem Anisimov 5.00 12.00
RR323 Mikael Backlund 6.00 15.00
RR324 Christian Hanson 6.00 15.00
RR325 Yannick Weber 6.00 15.00
RR326 T.J. Galiardi 5.00 12.00
RR327 Spencer Machacek 4.00 10.00
RR328 Luca Caputi 6.00 15.00
RR329 Brian Salcido 8.00 20.00
RR330 Tyler Ennis 8.00 20.00
RR331 Carl Gunnarsson 4.00 10.00
RR332 Alexander Salak 4.00 10.00
RR333 Scott Parse 4.00 10.00
RR334 Matt Beleskey 8.00 20.00
RR335 Cal O'Reilly 5.00 12.00
RR336 Taylor Chorney 5.00 12.00
RR337 Mike Santorelli 5.00 12.00
RR338 Peter Regin 6.00 15.00
RR339 Kris Chucko 5.00 12.00
RR340 John Scott 8.00 20.00

2008-09 Be A Player Signatures

STATED ODDS 1 PER PACK
SAA Adrian Aucoin 3.00 8.00
SAB Adam Burish 4.00 10.00
SAE Alexander Edler 3.00 8.00
SAF Andrew Ference 3.00 8.00
SAK Anze Kopitar 8.00 20.00
SAL Andreas Lilja 3.00 8.00
SAM Andy McDonald 4.00 10.00
SAP Andrew Peters 3.00 8.00
SBA Bryan Allen 3.00 8.00
SBB Brad Boyes 3.00 8.00
SBC Brian Campbell 4.00 10.00
SBE Patrik Berglund 3.00 8.00
SBG Ben Guite 3.00 8.00
SBI Kevin Bieksa 4.00 10.00
SBJ Josh Bailey 5.00 12.00
SBK Rob Blake 5.00 12.00
SBL Brian Lee 3.00 8.00
SBO David Booth 3.00 8.00
SBR Derick Brassard 3.00 8.00
SBRI Daniel Briere 5.00 12.00
SBS Brian Sutherby 3.00 8.00
SBU Alexandre Burrows 5.00 12.00
SBUR Brent Burns 6.00 15.00
SBY Dan Boyle 4.00 10.00
SCD Chris Drury 4.00 10.00
SCG Colton Gillies 3.00 8.00
SCH Cristobal Huet 4.00 10.00
SCL David Clarkson 4.00 10.00
SCO Chris Osgood 5.00 12.00
SCP Corey Perry 5.00 12.00
SCS Cory Stillman 3.00 8.00
SDA Daniel Sedin 5.00 12.00
SDB Dustin Boyd 3.00 8.00
SDC Dan Cleary 4.00 10.00
SDE Dan Ellis 3.00 8.00
SDH Dan Hamhuis 4.00 10.00
SDK Duncan Keith 8.00 20.00
SDM Darren McCarty 5.00 12.00
SDO Dominic Moore 3.00 8.00
SDP Daniel Paille 3.00 8.00
SDR Derek Roy 3.00 8.00
SDU Dustin Brown 5.00 12.00
SDV Devin Setoguchi 4.00 10.00
SDW Doug Weight 5.00 12.00
SEB Eric Brewer 3.00 8.00
SEM Evgeni Malkin 25.00 60.00
SEN Evgeni Nabokov 4.00 10.00
SES Eric Staal 8.00 20.00
SFL Marc-Andre Fleury 10.00 25.00
SFM Fredrik Modin 3.00 8.00
SFR Alexander Frolov 3.00 8.00
SGA Simon Gagne 5.00 12.00
SGI Brian Gionta 4.00 10.00
SGP George Parros 3.00 8.00
SGU Bill Guerin 5.00 12.00
SHA Scott Hartnell 5.00 12.00
SHE Dany Heatley 5.00 12.00
SHO Patric Hornqvist 4.00 10.00
SHS Henrik Sedin 5.00 12.00
SIB Ilya Bryzgalov 4.00 10.00
SJA Jason Arnott 4.00 10.00
SJB Jay Bouwmeester 5.00 12.00
SJC Jeff Carter 5.00 12.00
SJD J.P. Dumont 3.00 8.00
SJF Johan Franzen 6.00 15.00
SJH Josh Harding 10.00 25.00
SJO John Oduya 4.00 10.00
SJP Jason Pominville 5.00 12.00
SJS Joe Sakic 15.00 40.00
SJV Jakub Voracek 8.00 20.00
SJW James Wisniewski 3.00 8.00
SKB Keith Ballard 3.00 8.00
SKE Ryan Kesler 6.00 15.00
SKT Kyle Turris 6.00 15.00
SLA Brooks Laich 3.00 8.00
SLO Matthew Lombardi 3.00 8.00
SLS Luca Sbisa 2.50 6.00
SLU Brad Lukowich 3.00 8.00
SMA Paul Martin 3.00 8.00
SMAR Andrei Markov 5.00 12.00
SMB Martin Biron 4.00 10.00
SMC Mike Commodore 3.00 8.00
SMF Mike Fisher 3.00 8.00
SMH Marian Hossa 4.00 10.00
SMI Mikkel Boedker 5.00 12.00
SMK Mike Komisarek 3.00 8.00
SMM Milan Michalek 3.00 8.00
SMN Markus Naslund 4.00 10.00
SMO Derek Morris 3.00 8.00
SMR Mason Raymond 5.00 12.00
SMT Maxime Talbot 5.00 12.00
SMU Peter Mueller 4.00 10.00
SMV Marc-Edouard Vlasic 3.00 8.00
SMY Manny Malhotra 3.00 8.00
SNA Nik Antropov 4.00 10.00
SNB Niklas Backstrom 5.00 12.00
SNF Nick Foligno 5.00 12.00
SNH Nathan Horton 4.00 10.00
SNK Nikolai Kulemin 4.00 10.00
SNL Nicklas Lidstrom 15.00 30.00
SNS Nick Schultz 3.00 8.00
SOJ Olli Jokinen 4.00 10.00
SOK Kyle Okposo 4.00 10.00
SOM Oscar Moller 3.00 8.00
SPA Paul Kariya 8.00 20.00
SPC Chris Phillips 3.00 8.00
SPD David Perron 4.00 10.00
SPE Patrik Elias 5.00 12.00
SPH Dion Phaneuf 5.00 12.00
SPM Patrick Marleau 5.00 12.00
SPO Patrick O'Sullivan 4.00 10.00
SPS Paul Stastny 5.00 12.00
SRA Brian Rafalski 4.00 10.00
SRB Rod Brind`Amour 5.00 12.00
SRG Ryan Getzlaf 8.00 20.00
SRI Mike Richards SP 50.00 120.00
SRK Rostislav Klesla 3.00 8.00
SRO Rostislav Olesz 3.00 8.00
SRR Robyn Regehr 3.00 8.00
SRS Ryan Smyth 4.00 10.00
SRT Raffi Torres 3.00 8.00
SRU R.J. Umberger 3.00 8.00
SRW Ray Whitney 4.00 10.00
SSC Sidney Crosby 60.00 120.00
SSD Shane Doan 4.00 10.00
SSE Brent Seabrook 5.00 12.00
SSF Sergei Fedorov 10.00 25.00
SSG Scott Gomez 4.00 10.00
SSH James Sheppard 3.00 8.00
SSI Mike Sillinger 3.00 8.00
SSJ Jordan Staal 5.00 12.00
SSL Luke Schenn 5.00 12.00
SSN Scott Niedermayer 5.00 12.00
SSP Jason Spezza 5.00 12.00
SST Matt Stajan 4.00 10.00
SSTA Marc Staal 5.00 12.00
SSU Ryan Suter 4.00 10.00
SSW Scott Walker 3.00 8.00
STA Jeff Tambellini 3.00 8.00
STG Tim Gleason 3.00 8.00
STH Jose Theodore 5.00 12.00
STM Travis Moen 3.00 8.00
STN Teppo Numminen 4.00 10.00
STO T.J. Oshie 8.00 20.00
STP Tom Preissing 3.00 8.00
STR Tuomo Ruutu 5.00 12.00
STT Tim Thomas 10.00 25.00
STV Thomas Vanek 5.00 12.00
STZ Travis Zajac 4.00 10.00
SVO Tomas Vokoun 4.00 10.00
SWF Stephen Weiss 3.00 8.00
SWM Willie Mitchell 3.00 8.00
SWS Shea Weber 4.00 10.00
SWW Wojtek Wolski 4.00 10.00
SZP Zach Parise 5.00 12.00

2008-09 Be A Player Signatures Dual

STATED ODDS 1:8
S2AD Dumont/Arnott 6.00 15.00
S2AK Kulemin/Antropov 8.00 20.00
S2BB Blake/Boyle 8.00 20.00
S2BH Harding/Backstrom 8.00 20.00
S2BS Brind`Amour/Staal 10.00 25.00
S2BV Voracek/Brassard 10.00 25.00
S2CH Huet/Campbell 6.00 15.00
S2FM M-A Fleury/Malkin 15.00 40.00
S2GB Briere/Gagne 6.00 15.00
S2GP Gionta/Parise 8.00 20.00
S2HB Horton/Booth 6.00 15.00
S2HC Cleary/Hossa 15.00 40.00
S2JK Bouwmeester/Ballard 8.00 20.00
S2JP Stastny/Sakic 20.00 50.00
S2KB Kariya/Boyes 12.00 30.00
S2KJ Okposo/Bailey 10.00 25.00
S2LB Boyd/Lombardi 5.00 12.00
S2ME Edler/Mitchell 5.00 12.00
S2MK Markov/Komisarek 8.00 20.00
S2MS Setoguchi/Marleau 8.00 20.00
S2MT Mueller/Turris 12.00 30.00
S2NG Getzlaf/Niedermayer 12.00 30.00
S2OK Kopitar/O'Sullivan 12.00 30.00
S2PV Vanek/Pominville 8.00 20.00
S2RC Carter/Richards 25.00 60.00
S2SG Sheppard/Gillies 6.00 15.00
S2SH Heatley/Spezza 8.00 20.00
S2SK Seabrook/Keith 25.00 50.00
S2SS Sedin/Sedin 15.00 30.00
S2SW Weber/Suter 6.00 15.00
S2TP Berglund/Oshie 8.00 20.00
S2WG Guerin/Weight 8.00 20.00

2008-09 Be A Player Signatures Trios

STATED PRINT RUN 35 SER.#'d SETS
S3AWE Arnott/Weber/Ellis 15.00 40.00
S3BRC Briere/Richrds/Carter 100.00 175.00
S3BSG Bckstm/Shpprd/Gillis 20.00 50.00
S3EGP Elias/Gionta/Parise 20.00 50.00
S3FMS Fleury/Malkin/Staal 30.00 80.00
S3FSH Fisher/Spezza/Heatley 20.00 50.00
S3HOF Hossa/Osgood/Franzen 20.00 50.00
S3JDM Jokinen/Doan/Mueller 15.00 40.00
S3KBM Kariya/Boyes/McDonald 25.00 60.00
S3MNB Marleau/Nabokov/Boyle 20.00 50.00
S3SSE Sedin/Sedin/Edler 20.00 50.00
S3SSS Sakic/Smyth/Stastny 30.00 80.00
S3TOB Tambellini/Okposo/Bailey 30.00 80.00
S3VBH Vokoun/Bouwm/Horton 20.00 50.00
S3WBS Whitney/Brind/Staal 25.00 60.00

2009-10 Be A Player

COMP.SET w/o SPs (200) 25.00 50.00
201-300 ROOKIE PRINT RUN 99
301-360 ROOKIE EXCH PRINT RUN 99
1 Sidney Crosby 1.50 4.00
2 Joe Thornton .40 1.00
3 Jamal Mayers .25 .60
4 Ryan Getzlaf .60 1.50
5 Pierre-Marc Bouchard .40 1.00
6 Eric Staal .50 1.25
7 Mikkel Boedker .25 .60
8 Daniel Sedin .40 1.00
9 Patric Hornqvist .30 .75
10 Zdeno Chara .40 1.00
11 Mike Richards .40 1.00
12 Nicklas Lidstrom .40 1.00
13 Patrick Kane .75 2.00
14 Mark Stuart .25 .60
15 Oscar Moller .25 .60
16 Josh Bailey .30 .75
17 Luca Sbisa .40 1.00
18 Ethan Moreau .25 .60
19 Phil Kessel .50 1.25
20 Ondrej Pavelec .50 1.25
21 Mike Sillinger .25 .60
22 Boyd Gordon .25 .60
23 Kristopher Letang .40 1.00
24 Brad Richards .40 1.00
25 Nathan McIver .25 .60
26 Martin Brodeur .75 2.00
27 Zach Parise .40 1.00
28 Dany Heatley .40 1.00
29 Mike Cammalleri .30 .75
30 Tomas Vokoun .30 .75
31 Scott Hartnell .40 1.00
32 Roberto Luongo .50 1.25
33 Wojtek Wolski .25 .60
34 Ryan Callahan .40 1.00
35 Aaron Voros .25 .60
36 Bobby Ryan .40 1.00
37 Nick Schultz .25 .60
38 Henrik Zetterberg .50 1.25
39 Nick Foligno .30 .75
40 Patrick O'Sullivan .30 .75
41 Dan Hamhuis .30 .75
42 Scott Walker .25 .60
43 Eric Brewer .25 .60
44 Simon Gagne .40 1.00
45 Paul Martin .25 .60
46 Milan Lucic .30 .75
47 Rostislav Klesla .40 1.00
48 Adrian Aucoin .25 .60
49 Ryan Kesler .40 1.00
50 Brad Boyes .25 .60
51 Ryan Suter .40 1.00
52 Mike Komisarek .30 .75
53 Tim Gleason .25 .60
54 Brooks Laich .40 1.00
55 Dustin Brown .30 .75
56 Blake Wheeler .40 1.00
57 Ilya Bryzgalov .30 .75
58 Manny Malhotra .25 .60
59 Jason Spezza .40 1.00
60 Rich Peverley .30 .75
61 Paul Stastny .40 1.00
62 Tim Connolly .25 .60
63 Jeff Halpern .25 .60
64 Nathan Horton .40 1.00
65 Kris Versteeg .40 1.00
66 Andrew Cogliano .30 .75
67 Jonathan Quick .75 2.00
68 Nik Antropov .30 .75
69 David Perron .25 .60
70 Krys Barch .25 .60
71 Derek Roy .30 .75
72 Jordan Staal .40 1.00
73 Evgeni Malkin 1.25 3.00
74 Mark Streit .25 .60
75 Carey Price 1.50 4.00
76 Jean-Sebastien Giguere .40 1.00
77 Cal Clutterbuck .25 .60
78 Mike Modano .60 1.50
79 Jay Bouwmeester .40 1.00
80 Pavel Datsyuk .50 1.25
81 Jeff Carter .40 1.00
82 Marc Savard .25 .60
83 Luke Schenn .30 .75
84 Patrick Marleau .40 1.00
85 R.J. Umberger .30 .75
86 Marc Staal .40 1.00
87 Drew Doughty .50 1.25
88 Erik Johnson .30 .75
89 Patrik Elias .40 1.00
90 Alexandre Burrows .40 1.00
91 Niklas Backstrom .40 1.00
92 David Krejci .40 1.00
93 Ryan Malone .25 .60
94 J.P. Dumont .25 .60
95 Mike Commodore .25 .60
96 Daniel Alfredsson .40 1.00
97 Johan Franzen .40 1.00
98 Erik Cole .30 .75
99 Peter Budaj .30 .75
100 Bryan McCabe .30 .75
101 Jonathan Toews .75 2.00
102 Nikolai Kulemin .30 .75
103 Mikko Koivu .40 1.00
104 Robert Lang .25 .60
105 Tomas Plekanec .40 1.00
106 Marty Turco .40 1.00
107 Chris Campoli .25 .60
108 Mike Knuble .25 .60
109 Vincent Lecavalier .30 .75
110 Jussi Jokinen .25 .60
111 Matt Greene .25 .60
112 Willie Mitchell .25 .60
113 Thomas Vanek .40 1.00
114 Scott Niedermayer .40 1.00
115 Shea Weber .30 .75
116 Bryan Little .40 1.00
117 Pascal Leclaire .40 1.00
118 Brian Rafalski .25 .60
119 Olli Jokinen .30 .75
120 Shawn Horcoff .25 .60
121 Rene Bourque .25 .60
122 Joni Pitkanen .30 .75
123 Matt Bradley .25 .60
124 Matt Moulson .30 .75
125 Raffi Torres .25 .60
126 Miikka Kiprusoff .30 .75
127 Shane Doan .30 .75
128 Patrice Bergeron .50 1.25
129 Scott Hannan .25 .60
130 Evgeni Nabokov .30 .75
131 Steven Stamkos .75 2.00
132 Corey Perry .40 1.00
133 T.J. Oshie .60 1.50
134 Mikael Samuelsson .25 .60
135 Steve Mason .30 .75
136 Drew Stafford .40 1.00
137 Chris Pronger .30 .75
138 Jonas Hiller .30 .75
139 Robyn Regehr .30 .75
140 Bryan Allen .25 .60
141 Andrei Markov .40 1.00
142 David Backes .40 1.00
143 Derick Brassard .40 1.00
144 Tuukka Rask .40 1.00
145 Martin Havlat .30 .75
146 Mike Grier .25 .60
147 Dan Boyle .30 .75
148 Shawn Thornton .25 .60
149 Marc-Andre Fleury .60 1.50
150 Matt Stajan .30 .75
151 Daniel Briere .40 1.00
152 Maxim Afinogenov .25 .60
153 Duncan Keith .40 1.00
154 Dan Cleary .40 1.00
155 Anze Kopitar .60 1.50
156 Kyle Okposo .40 1.00
157 Brent Burns .50 1.25
158 Brenden Morrow .30 .75
159 Ryan Miller .40 1.00
160 Henrik Sedin .40 1.00
161 Darcy Tucker .30 .75
162 Ray Whitney .30 .75
163 Jakub Voracek .40 1.00
164 Tomas Fleischmann .25 .60
165 Braydon Coburn .25 .60
166 Saku Koivu .40 1.00
167 Adam Burish .50 1.25
168 George Parros .25 .60
169 Jarome Iginla .40 1.00
170 Brandon Sutter .30 .75
171 Pekka Rinne .50 1.25
172 Sam Gagner .30 .75
173 Chris Drury .30 .75
174 Niklas Kronwall .30 .75
175 Dion Phaneuf .50 1.25
176 Zach Bogosian .30 .75
177 Maxime Talbot .40 1.00
178 Daniel Winnik .25 .60
179 Scott Gomez .30 .75
180 Cam Ward .40 1.00
181 Ilya Kovalchuk .40 1.00
182 Devin Setoguchi .30 .75
183 Mike Fisher .25 .60
184 James Neal .40 1.00
185 Ryan Smyth .30 .75
186 Loui Eriksson .30 .75
187 Stephen Weiss .25 .60
188 Mason Raymond .40 1.00
189 Jason Pominville .40 1.00
190 Teemu Selanne .75 2.00
191 Martin St. Louis .40 1.00
192 Rod Brind`Amour .40 1.00
193 Brent Seabrook .30 .75
194 Ron Hainsey .25 .60
195 Milan Hejduk .30 .75
196 Tim Thomas .40 1.00
197 David Legwand .30 .75
198 Jeff Tambellini .25 .60
199 Georges Laraque .30 .75
200 Alexander Ovechkin 1.50 4.00
201 John Tavares RC 40.00 80.00
202 Devan Dubnyk RC 12.00 30.00
203 Andrei Loktionov RC 8.00 20.00
204 Lars Eller RC 6.00 15.00
205 Tyler Eckford RC 5.00 12.00
206 Drayson Bowman RC 6.00 15.00
207 Artem Anisimov RC 6.00 15.00
208 Mikko Lehtonen RC 10.00 25.00
209 Dan Sexton RC 8.00 20.00
210 Ryan O'Reilly RC 10.00 25.00
211 Kris Chucko RC 5.00 12.00
212 Cal O'Reilly RC 5.00 12.00
213 Victor Hedman RC 12.00 30.00
214 Mike Brodeur RC 15.00 40.00
215 Carl Gunnarsson RC 5.00 12.00
216 Luca Caputi RC 6.00 15.00
217 Danny Irmen RC 4.00 10.00
218 Antti Niemi RC 10.00 25.00
219 Benn Ferriero RC 6.00 15.00
220 Jhonas Enroth RC 8.00 20.00
221 Keaton Ellerby RC 5.00 12.00
222 James Wright RC 6.00 15.00
223 Michael Del Zotto RC 6.00 15.00
224 Alexander Salak RC 5.00 12.00
225 Jonas Gustavsson RC 8.00 20.00
226 David Desharnais RC 12.00 30.00
227 Ville Leino RC 5.00 12.00
228 Riku Helenius RC 6.00 15.00
229 Braden Holtby RC 20.00 40.00
230 Joel Rechlicz RC 4.00 10.00
231 Ivan Vishnevskiy RC 5.00 12.00
232 Peter Regin RC 5.00 12.00
233 MacGregor Sharp RC 6.00 15.00
234 Michael Grabner RC 6.00 15.00
235 Alexander Sulzer RC 4.00 10.00
236 David Laliberte RC 10.00 25.00
237 Logan Couture RC 12.00 30.00
238 Vladimir Zharkov RC 6.00 15.00
239 Colin McDonald RC 5.00 12.00
240 Matt Hendricks RC 5.00 12.00
241 Brad Marchand RC 15.00 40.00
242 Taylor Chorney RC 6.00 15.00
243 T.J. Galiardi RC 6.00 15.00
244 Erik Karlsson RC 20.00 50.00
245 Perttu Lindgren RC 5.00 12.00
246 Ryan Keller RC 6.00 15.00
247 Tyler Ennis RC 8.00 20.00
248 Michael Sauer RC 5.00 12.00
249 Teemu Laakso RC 4.00 10.00
250 James van Riemsdyk RC 12.00 30.00
251 John Negrin RC 6.00 15.00
252 Ryan Stoa RC 5.00 12.00
253 Tom Wandell RC 6.00 15.00
254 Michal Neuvirth RC 15.00 40.00
255 John Carlson RC 25.00 60.00
256 Mike Santorelli RC 6.00 15.00
257 Anton Khudobin RC 6.00 15.00
258 Brian Salcido RC 5.00 12.00
259 James Reimer RC 15.00 40.00
260 Colin Wilson RC 6.00 15.00
261 Deryk Engelland RC 8.00 20.00
262 Scott Parse RC 6.00 15.00
263 Tyler Bozak RC 12.00 30.00
264 Yannick Weber RC 6.00 15.00
265 Andrew MacDonald RC 4.00 10.00
266 Matthew Corrente RC 5.00 12.00
267 Shaun Heshka RC 6.00 15.00
268 Jakub Kindl RC 6.00 15.00
269 Mark Letestu RC 6.00 15.00
270 Oskars Bartulis RC 8.00 20.00
271 Viktor Stalberg RC 6.00 15.00
272 Frazer McLaren RC 5.00 12.00
273 Jason Demers RC 10.00 25.00
274 Ryan Wilson RC 6.00 15.00
275 Evander Kane RC 12.00 30.00
276 Sergei Shirokov RC 4.00 10.00
277 Aaron Gagnon RC 4.00 10.00
278 Cody Franson RC 6.00 15.00
279 Ryan O'Marra RC 4.00 10.00
280 Mikael Backlund RC 6.00 15.00
281 Jamie Benn RC 25.00 50.00
282 Andreas Thuresson RC 5.00 12.00
283 Christian Hanson RC 6.00 15.00
284 Mathieu Carle RC 6.00 15.00
285 Phil Oreskovic RC 6.00 15.00
286 Matt Beleskey RC 5.00 12.00
287 Tyler Myers RC 10.00 25.00
288 Ryan Vesce RC 5.00 12.00
289 Bobby Sanguinetti RC 4.00 10.00
290 Mario Bliznak RC 6.00 15.00
291 Spencer Machacek RC 6.00 15.00
292 Tom Pyatt RC 6.00 15.00
293 Byron Bitz RC 5.00 12.00
294 Dmitry Kulikov RC 6.00 15.00
295 Mathieu Perreault RC 10.00 25.00
296 Chad Johnson RC 8.00 20.00
297 Daniel Larsson RC 5.00 12.00
298 Matt Pelech RC 6.00 15.00
299 Matt Gilroy RC 6.00 15.00
300 Matt Duchene RC 12.00 30.00
301 Taylor Hall XRC 25.00 60.00
302 Jordan Caron XRC 6.00 15.00
303 Nino Niederreiter XRC 6.00 15.00
304 Cody Almond XRC 6.00 15.00
305 Nick Leddy XRC 6.00 15.00
306 J.T. Wyman XRC 6.00 15.00
307 Alexander Burmistrov XRC 6.00 15.00
308 Jeff Penner XRC 6.00 15.00
309 Brandon Yip XRC 6.00 15.00
310 Anders Lindback XRC 6.00 15.00
311 Bryan Pitton XRC 6.00 15.00
312 Magnus Paajarvi XRC 6.00 15.00
313 Maxime Fortunus XRC 6.00 15.00
314 Philip Larsen XRC 6.00 15.00
315 Tommy Wingels XRC 6.00 15.00
316 Tyler Seguin XRC 25.00 50.00
317 Brayden Schenn XRC 12.00 30.00
318 Arturs Kulda XRC 6.00 15.00
319 Mark Olver XRC 6.00 15.00
320 Eric Tangradi XRC 6.00 15.00
321 Brayden Irwin XRC 6.00 15.00
322 Derek Stepan XRC 10.00 25.00
323 Zach Hamill XRC 6.00 15.00
324 Alex Plante XRC 6.00 15.00
325 Henrik Karlsson XRC 6.00 15.00
326 Clayton Stoner XRC 6.00 15.00

327 Kyle Clifford XRC 6.00 15.00
328 Oliver Ekman-Larsson XRC 8.00 20.00
329 Matt Martin XRC 8.00 20.00
330 Andrew Bodnarchuk XRC 6.00 15.00
331 Evan Oberg XRC 6.00 15.00
332 Dustin Kohn XRC 6.00 15.00
333 Jordan Eberle XRC 30.00 60.00
334 Dana Tyrell XRC 6.00 15.00
335 Jake Muzzin XRC 6.00 15.00
336 Justin Falk XRC 6.00 15.00
337 Jared Cowen XRC 6.00 15.00
338 Nazem Kadri XRC 15.00 30.00
339 Dean Arsene XRC 6.00 15.00
340 Justin Mercier XRC 6.00 15.00
341 Sergei Bobrovsky XRC 8.00 20.00
342 Casey Wellman XRC 6.00 15.00
343 Derek Smith XRC 6.00 15.00
344 Jeff Skinner XRC 10.00 25.00
345 Nick Bonino XRC 6.00 15.00
346 Alexander Pechurski XRC 6.00 15.00
347 Cam Fowler XRC 6.00 15.00
348 Dustin Tokarski XRC 6.00 15.00
349 Alexander Urbom XRC 6.00 15.00
350 Nick Palmieri XRC 6.00 15.00
351 Kevin Shattenkirk XRC 6.00 15.00
352 Zac Dalpe XRC 6.00 15.00
353 Brandon Pirri XRC 6.00 15.00
354 Jacob Josefson XRC 5.00 12.00
355 Nick Holden XRC 5.00 12.00
356 Jamie McBain XRC 6.00 15.00
357 Evgeny Dadonov XRC 6.00 15.00
358 Matt Taormina XRC 6.00 15.00
359 Marcus Johansson XRC 8.00 20.00
360 P.K. Subban XRC 20.00 50.00

2009-10 Be A Player Player's Club

*1-200 VETS/25: 2.5X TO 6X BASIC CARDS
1-200 VETERAN PRINT RUN 25
*201-300 ROOK/15: .6X TO 1.5X BASIC RC
201-300 ROOKIE PRINT RUN 15

2009-10 Be A Player Goalies Unmasked

COMPLETE SET (30) 60.00 120.00
STATED PRINT RUN 499 SER.#'d SETS
GU1 Martin Brodeur 4.00 10.00
GU2 Ryan Miller 2.00 5.00
GU3 Marc-Andre Fleury 3.00 8.00
GU4 Carey Price 8.00 20.00
GU5 Jose Theodore 2.00 5.00
GU6 Brian Elliott 1.50 4.00
GU7 Antero Niittymaki 2.00 5.00
GU8 Ray Emery 1.50 4.00
GU9 Tim Thomas 2.00 5.00
GU10 Henrik Lundqvist 3.00 8.00
GU11 Ondrej Pavelec 2.50 6.00
GU12 Tomas Vokoun 1.50 4.00
GU13 Dwayne Roloson 1.50 4.00
GU14 Cam Ward 2.00 5.00
GU15 Jean-Sebastien Giguere 2.00 5.00
GU16 Evgeni Nabokov 1.50 4.00
GU17 Cristobal Huet 2.00 5.00
GU18 Roberto Luongo 4.00 10.00
GU19 Jonathan Quick 4.00 10.00
GU20 Ilya Bryzgalov 1.50 4.00
GU21 Craig Anderson 2.00 5.00
GU22 Miikka Kiprusoff 1.50 4.00
GU23 Pekka Rinne 2.50 6.00
GU24 Chris Osgood 2.00 5.00
GU25 Marty Turco 2.00 5.00
GU26 Niklas Backstrom 2.00 5.00
GU27 Jonas Hiller 1.50 4.00
GU28 Chris Mason 1.50 4.00
GU29 Steve Mason 1.50 4.00
GU30 Nikolai Khabibulin 2.00 5.00

2009-10 Be A Player Meet The Rookies

COMPLETE SET (10) 40.00 80.00
STATED PRINT RUN 499 SER.#'d SETS
MR1 John Tavares 8.00 20.00
MR2 Victor Hedman 3.00 8.00
MR3 Matt Duchene 3.00 8.00
MR4 James van Riemsdyk 3.00 8.00
MR5 Mikael Backlund 1.50 4.00
MR6 Jonas Gustavsson 2.00 5.00
MR7 Colin Wilson 1.50 4.00
MR8 Logan Couture 3.00 8.00
MR9 Bobby Sanguinetti 1.00 2.50
MR10 Tyler Bozak 2.50 6.00

2009-10 Be A Player Rookie Jerseys

STATED PRINT RUN 250 SER.#'d SETS
*PATCH/15: .8X TO 2X BASIC JSY/250
RJAA Artem Anisimov 4.00 10.00
RJAM Andrew MacDonald 2.50 6.00
RJAN Antti Niemi 6.00 15.00
RJBA Mikael Backlund 4.00 10.00
RJBB Byron Bitz 3.00 8.00
RJBF Benn Ferriero 4.00 10.00
RJBM Brad Marchand 10.00 25.00
RJBO Tyler Bozak 6.00 15.00
RJBS Brian Salcido 3.00 8.00
RJCF Cody Franson 4.00 10.00
RJCH Christian Hanson 4.00 10.00
RJCM Colin McDonald 3.00 8.00
RJCO Cal O'Reilly 3.00 8.00
RJCW Colin Wilson 4.00 10.00
RJDD Devan Dubnyk 10.00 25.00
RJDE Michael Del Zotto 4.00 10.00
RJDI Danny Irmen 2.50 6.00
RJDK Dmitry Kulikov 4.00 10.00
RJEK Evander Kane 8.00 20.00
RJFM Frazer McLaren 3.00 8.00
RJGR Michael Grabner 4.00 10.00
RJIV Ivan Vishnevskiy 3.00 8.00
RJJB Jamie Benn 12.00 30.00
RJJD Jason Demers 6.00 15.00
RJJE Jhonas Enroth 5.00 12.00
RJJG Jonas Gustavsson 5.00 12.00
RJJK Jakub Kindl 4.00 10.00
RJJT John Tavares 20.00 50.00
RJJV James van Riemsdyk 8.00 20.00
RJKA Erik Karlsson 12.00 30.00
RJKE Keaton Ellerby 3.00 8.00
RJLC Luca Caputi 4.00 10.00
RJLE Lars Eller 4.00 10.00
RJLO Logan Couture 8.00 20.00
RJMB Matt Beleskey 3.00 8.00
RJMC Matthew Corrente 3.00 8.00
RJMD Matt Duchene 8.00 20.00
RJMG Matt Gilroy 4.00 10.00
RJMN Michal Neuvirth 6.00 15.00
RJMP Matt Pelech 4.00 10.00
RJMS Mike Santorelli 4.00 10.00
RJOB Oskars Bartulis 4.00 10.00
RJOM Ryan O'Marra 2.50 6.00
RJPL Perttu Lindgren 3.00 8.00
RJPR Peter Regin 3.00 8.00
RJRH Riku Helenius 4.00 10.00
RJRS Ryan Stoa 3.00 8.00
RJSA Bobby Sanguinetti 2.50 6.00
RJSM Spencer Machacek 4.00 10.00
RJSS Sergei Shirokov 2.50 6.00
RJTC Taylor Chorney 4.00 10.00
RJTG T.J. Galiardi 4.00 10.00
RJTM Tyler Myers 6.00 15.00
RJVH Victor Hedman 8.00 20.00
RJVL Ville Leino 3.00 8.00
RJVS Viktor Stalberg 4.00 10.00
RJYW Yannick Weber 4.00 10.00

2009-10 Be A Player Rookie Jerseys Autographs

RJAA Artem Anisimov 10.00 25.00
RJCF Cody Franson 10.00 25.00
RJEK Evander Kane 15.00 40.00
RJJB Jamie Benn 15.00 40.00
RJJV James van Riemsdyk 30.00 60.00
RJKA Erik Karlsson 20.00 50.00
RJMD Matt Duchene 40.00 80.00
RJMG Matt Gilroy 10.00 25.00
RJVH Victor Hedman 20.00 50.00

2009-10 Be A Player Sidelines

COMPLETE SET (60) 60.00 120.00
STATED ODDS 1:4
S1 Alexander Ovechkin 3.00 8.00
S2 Anze Kopitar 1.25 3.00
S3 Brad Richards .75 2.00
S4 Cam Ward .75 2.00
S5 Carey Price 3.00 8.00
S6 Daniel Alfredsson .75 2.00
S7 Dany Heatley .75 2.00
S8 Dion Phaneuf 1.00 2.50
S9 Drew Doughty 1.00 2.50
S10 Dustin Penner .50 1.25
S11 Eric Staal 1.00 2.50
S12 Evander Kane 1.50 4.00
S13 Evgeni Malkin 2.50 6.00
S14 Henrik Lundqvist 1.25 3.00
S15 Henrik Sedin .75 2.00
S16 Henrik Zetterberg 1.00 2.50
S17 Ilya Kovalchuk .75 2.00
S18 Jarome Iginla .75 2.00
S19 Jason Spezza .75 2.00
S20 Jay Bouwmeester .75 2.00
S21 Jean-Sebastien Giguere .75 2.00
S22 Jeff Carter .75 2.00
S23 Joe Thornton .75 2.00
S24 John Tavares 4.00 10.00
S25 Jonathan Toews 1.50 4.00
S26 Marc-Andre Fleury 1.25 3.00
S27 Marian Gaborik 1.00 2.50
S28 Martin Brodeur 1.50 4.00
S29 Marty Turco .75 2.00
S30 Matt Duchene 1.50 4.00
S31 Miikka Kiprusoff .60 1.50
S32 Mike Cammalleri .60 1.50
S33 Mike Green .75 2.00
S34 Mike Modano 1.25 3.00
S35 Mike Richards .75 2.00
S36 Mikko Koivu .75 2.00
S37 Nicklas Backstrom 1.25 3.00
S38 Nicklas Lidstrom .75 2.00
S39 Patrick Kane 1.50 4.00
S40 Patrick Marleau .75 2.00
S41 Paul Kariya 1.00 2.50
S42 Paul Stastny .75 2.00
S43 Pavel Datsyuk 1.00 2.50
S44 Phil Kessel 1.00 2.50
S45 Rick DiPietro .60 1.50
S46 Rick Nash .60 1.50
S47 Roberto Luongo 1.00 2.50
S48 Ryan Getzlaf 1.25 3.00
S49 Ryan Miller .75 2.00
S50 Sam Gagner .60 1.50
S51 Scott Niedermayer .75 2.00
S52 Shane Doan .60 1.50
S53 Shea Weber .60 1.50
S54 Sidney Crosby 3.00 8.00
S55 Steve Mason .60 1.50
S56 Steven Stamkos 1.50 4.00
S57 Thomas Vanek .75 2.00
S58 Vincent Lecavalier .60 1.50
S59 Zach Parise .75 2.00
S60 Zdeno Chara .75 2.00

2009-10 Be A Player Signatures

SAA Adrian Aucoin 3.00 8.00
SAB Adam Burish 6.00 15.00
SAK Anze Kopitar 8.00 20.00
SAL Bryan Allen 3.00 8.00
SAM Andrei Markov 5.00 12.00
SAN Artem Anisimov 5.00 12.00
SAV Aaron Voros 3.00 8.00
SAX Alexandre Burrows 5.00 12.00
SBB Brent Burns 6.00 15.00
SBE Jamie Benn 15.00 40.00
SBG Boyd Gordon 3.00 8.00
SBK David Backes 5.00 12.00
SBL Brooks Laich 5.00 12.00
SBM Brenden Morrow 4.00 10.00
SBO Bobby Ryan 5.00 12.00
SBR Derick Brassard 5.00 12.00
SBS Brent Seabrook 4.00 10.00
SBU Peter Budaj 4.00 10.00
SBY Brad Boyes 3.00 8.00
SCA Chris Campoli 3.00 8.00
SCD Chris Drury 4.00 10.00
SCF Cody Franson 5.00 12.00
SCK David Clarkson 4.00 10.00
SCL Ryan Callahan 5.00 12.00
SCO Mike Commodore 3.00 8.00
SCP Carey Price 20.00 50.00
SCY Corey Perry 5.00 12.00
SDA Daniel Briere 5.00 12.00
SDB Dustin Brown 4.00 10.00
SDC Dan Cleary 5.00 12.00
SDH Dan Hamhuis 4.00 10.00
SDN Dan Boyle 4.00 10.00
SDP Dion Phaneuf 6.00 15.00
SDR Derek Roy SP 4.00 10.00
SDS Daniel Sedin 5.00 12.00
SDT Darcy Tucker 4.00 10.00
SDV David Perron 3.00 8.00
SDW Daniel Winnik 3.00 8.00
SEB Eric Brewer 3.00 8.00
SEC Erik Cole 4.00 10.00
SEK Erik Karlsson 15.00 40.00
SEM Evgeni Malkin SP/1*
SFI Mike Fisher 3.00 8.00
SGI Matt Gilroy 5.00 12.00
SGL Georges Laraque 4.00 10.00
SGP George Parros 3.00 8.00
SHA Scott Hannan 3.00 8.00
SHE Milan Hejduk 4.00 10.00
SHI Jonas Hiller 4.00 10.00
SHS Henrik Sedin 5.00 12.00
SHT Dany Heatley 5.00 12.00
SHZ Henrik Zetterberg SP 20.00 50.00
SIB Ilya Bryzgalov SP 20.00 50.00
SJB Jay Bouwmeester 5.00 12.00
SJC Jeff Carter SP 5.00 12.00
SJF Johan Franzen SP 5.00 12.00
SJH Jeff Halpern 3.00 8.00
SJI Jarome Iginla 15.00 40.00
SJM Jamal Mayers 3.00 8.00
SJN James Neal 5.00 12.00
SJO Joe Thornton 5.00 12.00
SJP Joni Pitkanen 4.00 10.00
SPO Jason Pominville 5.00 12.00
SJS Jason Spezza 5.00 12.00
SJT Jeff Tambellini 3.00 8.00
SJV Jakub Voracek 5.00 12.00
SKA Evander Kane 10.00 25.00
SKB Krys Barch 3.00 8.00
SKE Ryan Kesler 5.00 12.00
SKL Kristopher Letang 5.00 12.00
SKN Mike Knuble 3.00 8.00
SKU Nikolai Kulemin 4.00 10.00
SLS Luca Sbisa 5.00 12.00
SLU Roberto Luongo 6.00 15.00
SMB Mikkel Boedker 3.00 8.00
SMC Mike Cammalleri 4.00 10.00
SMD Matt Duchene 10.00 25.00
SMF Marc-Andre Fleury 15.00 40.00
SMM Manny Malhotra 3.00 8.00
SMN Matt Moulson 4.00 10.00
SMR Mike Richards SP 5.00 12.00
SMS Mike Sillinger 3.00 8.00
SMT Maxime Talbot 5.00 12.00
SMY Matt Bradley 3.00 8.00
SNB Niklas Backstrom 5.00 12.00
SNF Nick Foligno 4.00 10.00
SNK Niklas Kronwall 4.00 10.00
SNL Nicklas Lidstrom 5.00 12.00
SNM Nathan McIver 3.00 8.00
SNS Nick Schultz 3.00 8.00
SOJ Olli Jokinen 4.00 10.00
SOK Kyle Okposo 5.00 12.00
SOM Oscar Moller 3.00 8.00
SOP Ondrej Pavelec 6.00 15.00
SOS Patrick O'Sullivan 4.00 10.00
SPB Patrice Bergeron 6.00 15.00
SPB Pierre-Marc Bouchard 5.00 12.00
SPD Pavel Datsyuk 6.00 15.00
SPE Patrik Elias 5.00 12.00
SPH Patric Hornqvist 4.00 10.00
SPK Patrick Kane 20.00 50.00
SPL Pascal Leclaire 5.00 12.00
SPM Paul Martin 3.00 8.00
SPR Chris Pronger 4.00 10.00
SPS Paul Stastny SP 5.00 12.00
SPT Patrick Marleau 5.00 12.00
SPV Rich Peverley 4.00 10.00
SRA Mason Raymond 5.00 12.00
SRB Rene Bourque 3.00 8.00
SRC Brad Richards 5.00 12.00
SRE Peter Regin 4.00 10.00
SRF Brian Rafalski 3.00 8.00
SRG Ryan Getzlaf 8.00 20.00
SRH Ron Hainsey 3.00 8.00
SRI Pekka Rinne 6.00 15.00
SRK Rostislav Klesla 5.00 12.00
SRO Ryan O'Reilly 8.00 20.00
SRR Robyn Regehr 4.00 10.00
SRS Ryan Suter SP 5.00 12.00
SRT Raffi Torres 3.00 8.00
SRU R.J. Umberger 4.00 10.00
SRY Ryan Smyth 4.00 10.00
SSA Marc Staal 5.00 12.00
SSC Luke Schenn 4.00 10.00
SSD Shane Doan 4.00 10.00
SSE Devin Setoguchi 4.00 10.00
SSG Scott Gomez 4.00 10.00
SSH Scott Hartnell 5.00 12.00
SSI Sidney Crosby 80.00 150.00
SSK Saku Koivu 5.00 12.00
SSM Steve Mason 4.00 10.00
SSR Mark Stuart 3.00 8.00
SST Martin St. Louis 5.00 12.00
SSU Brandon Sutter 4.00 10.00
SSW Shea Weber 4.00 10.00
STF Tomas Fleischmann 3.00 8.00
STG Tim Gleason 3.00 8.00
STH Shawn Thornton 3.00 8.00
STJ T.J. Oshie SP 8.00 20.00
STM Tyler Myers 8.00 20.00
STP Tomas Plekanec 5.00 12.00
STT Tim Thomas 5.00 12.00
STU Marty Turco 5.00 12.00
STV Thomas Vanek 5.00 12.00
STZ Travis Zajac 4.00 10.00
SVA James van Riemsdyk 10.00 25.00
SVH Victor Hedman 10.00 25.00
SVL Vincent Lecavalier 4.00 10.00
SVO Tomas Vokoun 4.00 10.00
SWE Stephen Weiss 3.00 8.00
SWK Scott Walker 3.00 8.00
SWM Willie Mitchell 3.00 8.00
SWW Wojtek Wolski 3.00 8.00
SZB Zach Bogosian 4.00 10.00
SZC Zdeno Chara SP 5.00 12.00
SZP Zach Parise 5.00 12.00

2009-10 Be A Player Signatures Duals

STATED ODDS 1:8
S2BB Boedker/Bryzgalov 6.00 15.00
S2BC Briere/Carter 8.00 20.00
S2BK Kane/Bogosian 12.00 30.00
S2BM Mason/Brassard 8.00 20.00
S2CP Price/Cammalleri 20.00 40.00
S2CS Staal/Cole 10.00 25.00
S2DJ Drury/Jokinen 6.00 15.00
S2DO O'Reilly/Duchene 12.00 30.00
S2DZ Datsyuk/Zetterberg 10.00 25.00
S2GP Gomez/Plekanec 10.00 25.00
S2GR Getzlaf/Ryan 12.00 30.00
S2HM Hedman/Myers 10.00 25.00
S2HR Richards/Hartnell 8.00 20.00
S2HS Hejduk/Stastny 8.00 20.00
S2IB Bourque/Iginla 8.00 20.00
S2KV Kane/van Riemsdyk 15.00 40.00
S2LK Kronwall/Lidstrom 15.00 30.00
S2MH Marleau/Heatley 10.00 25.00
S2MT Marleau/Thornton 8.00 20.00
S2NB Neal/Benn 8.00 20.00
S2PO Oshie/Perron 12.00 30.00
S2RB Regehr/Bouwmeester 8.00 20.00
S2RM Morrow/Richards 8.00 20.00
S2RV Roy/Vanek 8.00 20.00
S2SF Spezza/Foligno 8.00 20.00
S2SG Staal/Gilroy 8.00 20.00
S2SS Sedin/Sedin 8.00 20.00
S2SW Weber/Suter 8.00 20.00

2009-10 Be A Player Signatures Foursomes

STATED PRINT RUN 25 SER.#'d SETS
S4SWE2 Hornqvst/Franz/Kron/Lids 75.00 150.00

2009-10 Be A Player Signatures Trios

STATED ODDS 1:24
S3BPO Boyes/Perron/Oshie 15.00 40.00
S3CSS Staal/Sutter/Cole 12.00 30.00
S3DZF Datsyk/Zetter/Franzn 30.00 60.00
S3GCP Plekan/Gomz/Camm 8.00 20.00
S3HWS Stastny/Wolski/Hejduk 10.00 25.00
S3IMB Bourqe/Mayers/Igin 10.00 25.00
S3MKH Hedmn/Karlssn/Myers 15.00 40.00
S3MTH Thorntn/Heatly/Marleu 20.00 50.00
S3PRV Vanek/Pominville/Roy 12.00 30.00
S3RCV Richrds/Carter/Riemsdyk 15.00 40.00
S3RMB Richrds/Morrw/Benn 12.50 30.00
S3SBK Kopitar/Smyth/Brown 15.00 40.00
S3SSK Kesler/Sedin/Sedin 12.00 30.00
S3UBV Brassard/Voracek/Umberger 10.00 25.00

2002-03 BAP All-Star Edition

Released to coincide with the 2003 NHL All-Star game, this 150-card set featured players who made appearances in past all-star games. Cards 101-150 were short-printed to just 100 copies each and featured rookies.

101-150 SP/ROOKIE PRINT RUN 100
1 Daniel Alfredsson .25 .60
2 Tony Amonte .20 .50
3 Ed Belfour .25 .60
4 Rob Blake .25 .60
5 Peter Bondra .25 .60
6 Radek Bonk .20 .50
7 Martin Brodeur .50 1.25
8 Martin Brodeur .50 1.25
9 Martin Brodeur .50 1.25
10 Valeri Bure .20 .50
11 Pavel Bure .30 .75
12 Pavel Bure .30 .75
13 Sean Burke .15 .40
14 Roman Cechmanek .20 .50
15 Chris Chelios .25 .60
16 Vincent Damphousse .20 .50
17 Eric Daze .15 .40
18 Pavol Demitra .30 .75
19 Patrik Elias .25 .60
20 Sergei Fedorov .40 1.00
21 Sergei Fedorov .40 1.00
22 Theo Fleury .30 .75
23 Peter Forsberg .30 .75
24 Peter Forsberg .30 .75
25 Peter Forsberg .30 .75
26 Simon Gagne .25 .60
27 Scott Gomez .20 .50
28 Bill Guerin .25 .60
29 Milan Hejduk .20 .50
30 Phil Housley .20 .50
31 Brett Hull .30 .75
32 Jarome Iginla .25 .60
33 Arturs Irbe .20 .50
34 Jaromir Jagr .60 1.50
35 Jaromir Jagr .60 1.50
36 Jaromir Jagr .60 1.50
37 Curtis Joseph .25 .60
38 Ed Jovanovski .20 .50
39 Tomas Kaberle .15 .40
40 Sami Kapanen .15 .40
41 Paul Kariya .30 .75
42 Paul Kariya .30 .75
43 Paul Kariya .30 .75
44 Nikolai Khabibulin .25 .60
45 Saku Koivu .25 .60
46 Olaf Kolzig .25 .60
47 Alexei Kovalev .25 .60
48 John LeClair .25 .60
49 Brian Leetch .25 .60
50 Brian Leetch .25 .60
51 Mario Lemieux .75 2.00
52 Mario Lemieux .75 2.00
53 Mario Lemieux .75 2.00
54 Nicklas Lidstrom .25 .60
55 Nicklas Lidstrom .25 .60
56 Eric Lindros .40 1.00
57 Al MacInnis .25 .60
58 Mark Messier .40 1.00
59 Mark Messier .40 1.00
60 Mike Modano .40 1.00
61 Mike Modano .40 1.00
62 Alexander Mogilny .20 .50
63 Evgeni Nabokov .20 .50
64 Markus Naslund .20 .50
65 Scott Niedermayer .25 .60
66 Owen Nolan .25 .60
67 Teppo Numminen .20 .50
68 Chris Osgood .25 .60
69 Sandis Ozolinsh .20 .50
70 Zigmund Palffy .25 .60
71 Felix Potvin .40 1.00
72 Chris Pronger .20 .50
73 Mark Recchi .30 .75
74 Mike Richter .25 .60
75 Luc Robitaille .25 .60
76 Jeremy Roenick .25 .60
77 Patrick Roy .60 1.50
78 Patrick Roy .60 1.50
79 Patrick Roy .60 1.50
80 Joe Sakic .40 1.00
81 Joe Sakic .40 1.00
82 Tommy Salo .20 .50
83 Teemu Selanne .50 1.25
84 Brendan Shanahan .30 .75
85 Brendan Shanahan .30 .75
86 Brendan Shanahan .30 .75
87 Scott Stevens .25 .60
88 Mats Sundin .25 .60
89 Mats Sundin .25 .60
90 Darryl Sydor .15 .40
91 Jose Theodore .25 .60
92 Joe Thornton .30 .75
93 Keith Tkachuk .25 .60
94 Ron Tugnutt .20 .50
95 Roman Turek .25 .60
96 Doug Weight .25 .60
97 Alexei Yashin .20 .50
98 Steve Yzerman .50 1.25
99 Steve Yzerman .50 1.25
100 Alexei Zhamnov .20 .50
101 Dany Heatley SP 3.00 8.00
102 Ilya Kovalchuk SP 4.00 10.00
103 Marian Gaborik SP 5.00 12.00
104 Marty Turco SP 3.00 8.00
105 Mike Comrie SP 3.00 8.00
106 Cody Rudkowsky RC 2.00 5.00
107 Levente Szuper RC 3.00 8.00
108 Alex Henry RC 2.50 6.00
109 Lynn Loyns RC 2.00 5.00
110 Tomi Pettinen RC 2.00 5.00
111 Micki Dupont RC 2.00 5.00
112 Shaone Morrisonn RC 2.00 5.00
113 Ryan Miller RC 20.00 50.00
114 Mikael Tellqvist RC 2.00 5.00
115 Dany Sabourin RC 2.00 5.00
116 Tim Thomas RC 12.00 30.00
117 Kurt Sauer RC 2.00 5.00
118 Kari Haakana RC 2.00 5.00
119 Lasse Pirjeta RC 2.00 5.00
120 Shawn Thornton RC 2.50 6.00
121 Curtis Sanford RC 3.00 8.00
122 Dick Tarnstrom RC 2.00 5.00
123 Radovan Somik RC 2.00 5.00
124 Martin Gerber RC 3.00 8.00
125 Dennis Seidenberg RC 3.00 8.00
126 P-M Bouchard RC 3.00 8.00
127 Alexei Smirnov RC 2.50 6.00
128 Ales Hemsky RC 8.00 20.00
129 Stephane Veilleux RC 2.00 5.00
130 Tom Koivisto RC 2.00 5.00
131 Jeff Taffe RC 2.00 5.00
132 Jordan Leopold RC 3.00 8.00
133 Stanislav Chistov RC 2.00 5.00
134 Rick Nash RC 25.00 60.00
135 Chuck Kobasew RC 2.50 6.00
136 Alexander Svitov RC 2.00 5.00
137 Carlo Colaiacovo RC 3.00 8.00
138 Jason Spezza RC 20.00 50.00
139 Henrik Zetterberg RC 30.00 80.00
140 Anton Volchenkov RC 2.00 5.00
141 Ron Hainsey RC 2.00 5.00
142 Jay Bouwmeester RC 6.00 15.00
143 Adam Hall RC 2.00 5.00
144 Steve Eminger RC 2.00 5.00
145 Mike Cammalleri RC 6.00 15.00
146 Dmitri Bykov RC 2.00 5.00
147 Ivan Majesky RC 2.00 5.00
148 Alexander Frolov RC 4.00 10.00
149 Scottie Upshall RC 2.50 6.00
150 Patrick Sharp RC 6.00 15.00

2002-03 BAP All-Star Edition Silver

*101-105 SILVER/20: .8X TO 2X BASIC SP
*106-150 SILVER/20: .8X TO 2X BASIC ROOKIE
SILVER PRINT RUN 20 SER.#'d SETS

2002-03 BAP All-Star Edition Bobble Heads

ONE PER BOX
1 Mario Lemieux/1066 20.00 50.00
2 Jose Theodore/1560 10.00 25.00
3 Pavel Bure/2010 10.00 25.00
4 Curtis Joseph/1031 10.00 25.00
5 Martin Brodeur/1530 12.50 30.00
6 Peter Forsberg/2031 12.50 30.00
7 Steve Yzerman/2019 12.50 30.00
8 Jaromir Jagr/2068 10.00 25.00
9 Joe Sakic/1519 10.00 25.00
10 Patrick Roy/1033 20.00 50.00

2002-03 BAP All-Star Edition He Shoots He Score Prizes

ONE PER PACK
1 Brian Leetch 1 pt. .15 .40
2 Eric Lindros 1 pt. .25 .60
3 Mark Messier 1 pt. .25 .60
4 Owen Nolan 1 pt. .15 .40
5 Teemu Selanne 1 pt. .30 .75
6 Brendan Shanahan 1 pt. .20 .50
7 Mats Sundin 1 pt. .15 .40
8 Alexei Yashin 1 pt. .12 .30
9 Martin Brodeur 2 pt. .40 1.00
10 Pavel Bure 2 pt. .25 .60
11 Sergei Fedorov 2 pt. .30 .75
12 Jaromir Jagr 2 pt. .50 1.25
13 Curtis Joseph 2 pt. .20 .50
14 Nicklas Lidstrom 2 pt. .20 .50
15 Mike Modano 2 pt. .30 .75
16 Patrick Roy 2 pt. .50 1.25
17 Joe Sakic 2 pt. .30 .75
18 Peter Forsberg 3 pt. .25 .60
19 Mario Lemieux 3 pt. .60 1.50
20 Steve Yzerman 3 pt. .40 1.00

2002-03 BAP All-Star Edition He Shoots He Scores Prizes

ANNOUNCED PRINT RUN 20 SETS
1 Tony Amonte 8.00 20.00
2 Ed Belfour 10.00 25.00
3 Martin Brodeur 20.00 50.00
4 Pavel Bure 12.00 30.00
5 Chris Chelios 10.00 25.00
6 Sergei Fedorov 15.00 40.00
7 Peter Forsberg 12.00 30.00
8 Jaromir Jagr 25.00 60.00
9 Curtis Joseph 10.00 25.00
10 Paul Kariya 12.00 30.00
11 Nikolai Khabibulin 10.00 25.00
12 John LeClair 10.00 25.00
13 Brian Leetch 10.00 25.00
14 Mario Lemieux 30.00 80.00
15 Nicklas Lidstrom 10.00 25.00
16 Eric Lindros 15.00 40.00
17 Al MacInnis 10.00 25.00
18 Mark Messier 15.00 40.00
19 Mike Modano 30.00 60.00
20 Markus Naslund 8.00 20.00
21 Owen Nolan 10.00 25.00
22 Chris Pronger 8.00 20.00
23 Mark Recchi 12.00 30.00
24 Patrick Roy 25.00 60.00
25 Joe Sakic 15.00 40.00
26 Teemu Selanne 20.00 50.00
27 Brendan Shanahan 12.00 30.00
28 Mats Sundin 10.00 25.00
29 Alexei Yashin 8.00 20.00
30 Steve Yzerman 20.00 50.00

2002-03 BAP All-Star Edition Jerseys

STATED PRINT RUN 100 SETS
*SILVER/30: .5X TO 1.2X BASE HI
1 Daniel Alfredsson 6.00 15.00
2 Tony Amonte 6.00 15.00
3 Ed Belfour 8.00 20.00
4 Rob Blake 6.00 15.00
5 Peter Bondra 6.00 15.00
6 Radek Bonk 4.00 10.00
7 Martin Brodeur 15.00 40.00
8 Martin Brodeur 15.00 40.00
9 Martin Brodeur 15.00 40.00
10 Valeri Bure 4.00 10.00
11 Pavel Bure 8.00 20.00
12 Pavel Bure 8.00 20.00
13 Sean Burke 4.00 10.00
14 Roman Cechmanek 4.00 10.00
15 Chris Chelios 8.00 20.00
16 Vincent Damphousse 4.00 10.00
17 Eric Daze 4.00 10.00
18 Pavol Demitra 4.00 10.00
19 Patrik Elias 4.00 10.00
20 Sergei Fedorov 8.00 20.00
21 Sergei Fedorov 8.00 20.00
22 Theo Fleury 10.00 25.00
23 Peter Forsberg 10.00 25.00
24 Peter Forsberg 10.00 25.00
25 Peter Forsberg 10.00 25.00
26 Simon Gagne 8.00 20.00
27 Scott Gomez 6.00 15.00
28 Bill Guerin 6.00 15.00
29 Milan Hejduk 8.00 20.00
30 Phil Housley 4.00 10.00
31 Brett Hull 10.00 25.00
32 Jarome Iginla 10.00 25.00
33 Arturs Irbe 6.00 15.00
34 Jaromir Jagr 10.00 25.00
35 Jaromir Jagr 10.00 25.00
36 Jaromir Jagr 10.00 25.00
37 Curtis Joseph 8.00 20.00
38 Ed Jovanovski 4.00 10.00
39 Tomas Kaberle 4.00 10.00
40 Sami Kapanen 4.00 10.00
41 Paul Kariya 8.00 20.00
42 Paul Kariya 8.00 20.00
43 Paul Kariya 8.00 20.00
44 Nikolai Khabibulin 8.00 20.00
45 Saku Koivu 8.00 20.00
46 Olaf Kolzig 6.00 15.00
47 Alexei Kovalev 4.00 10.00
48 John LeClair 6.00 15.00
49 Brian Leetch 6.00 15.00
50 Brian Leetch 6.00 15.00
51 Mario Lemieux 15.00 40.00
52 Mario Lemieux 15.00 40.00
53 Mario Lemieux 15.00 40.00
54 Nicklas Lidstrom 8.00 20.00
55 Nicklas Lidstrom 8.00 20.00
56 Eric Lindros 8.00 20.00
57 Al MacInnis 6.00 15.00
58 Mark Messier 12.00 30.00
59 Mark Messier 12.00 30.00
60 Mike Modano 8.00 20.00
61 Mike Modano 8.00 20.00
62 Alexander Mogilny 6.00 15.00
63 Evgeni Nabokov 6.00 15.00
64 Markus Naslund 8.00 20.00
65 Scott Niedermayer 6.00 15.00
66 Owen Nolan 6.00 15.00
67 Teppo Numminen 4.00 10.00
68 Chris Osgood 6.00 15.00
69 Sandis Ozolinsh 4.00 10.00
70 Zigmund Palffy 6.00 15.00
71 Felix Potvin 10.00 25.00
72 Chris Pronger 6.00 15.00
73 Mark Recchi 6.00 15.00
74 Mike Richter 6.00 15.00
75 Luc Robitaille 6.00 15.00
76 Jeremy Roenick 10.00 25.00
77 Patrick Roy 20.00 50.00
78 Patrick Roy 20.00 50.00
79 Patrick Roy 20.00 50.00
80 Joe Sakic 15.00 40.00
81 Joe Sakic 15.00 40.00
82 Tommy Salo 4.00 10.00
83 Teemu Selanne 8.00 20.00
84 Brendan Shanahan 8.00 20.00
85 Brendan Shanahan 8.00 20.00
86 Brendan Shanahan 8.00 20.00
87 Scott Stevens 4.00 10.00
88 Mats Sundin 8.00 20.00
89 Mats Sundin 8.00 20.00
90 Darryl Sydor 4.00 10.00
91 Jose Theodore 8.00 20.00
92 Joe Thornton 12.00 30.00
93 Keith Tkachuk 8.00 20.00
94 Ron Tugnutt 4.00 10.00
95 Roman Turek 4.00 10.00
96 Doug Weight 4.00 10.00
97 Alexei Yashin 4.00 10.00
98 Steve Yzerman 15.00 40.00
99 Steve Yzerman 15.00 40.00
100 Alexei Zhamnov 4.00 10.00

2002-03 BAP First Edition

This 440-card set contained several different subsets. The draft picks cards featured different players in retail and hobby packs and are noted below with "H" or "R" suffixes. Cards 426-440 (both retail and hobby) were available by a mail-in redemption found in packs only.

1 Mario Lemieux .75 2.00
2 Sergei Gonchar .20 .50
3 Brian Leetch .25 .60
4 Felix Potvin .40 1.00
5 Sandis Ozolinsh .20 .50
6 Steven Reinprecht .15 .40
7 Byron Dafoe .20 .50
8 Mark Bell .15 .40
9 Jeff O'Neill .15 .40
10 Sean Burke .15 .40
11 Darcy Tucker .15 .40
12 Scott Stevens .25 .60
13 David Aebischer .20 .50
14 Jocelyn Thibault .20 .50
15 Radek Bonk .20 .50
16 Milan Hejduk .20 .50
17 Zigmund Palffy .25 .60
18 Luc Robitaille .25 .60
19 Tomas Kaberle .15 .40
20 Rostislav Klesla .15 .40
21 Alexei Zhamnov .20 .50
22 Ron Francis .30 .75
23 Mike Fisher .15 .40
24 Dany Heatley .25 .60
25 Kyle McLaren .15 .40
26 Doug Weight .25 .60
27 Henrik Sedin .25 .60
28 Roman Turek .25 .60
29 Adam Deadmarsh .20 .50
30 Sami Kapanen .15 .40
31 Sergei Samsonov .20 .50
32 Kristian Huselius .15 .40
33 Dimitri Yushkevich .15 .40
34 Patrik Elias .25 .60
35 Nick Boynton .15 .40
36 Martin Biron .20 .50
37 Brad Richards .25 .60
38 Alyn McCauley .15 .40
39 Daniel Sedin .25 .60
40 Teppo Numminen .20 .50
41 Luke Richardson .15 .40
42 Manny Fernandez .20 .50
43 Vincent Lecavalier .20 .50
44 Mattias Ohlund .15 .40
45 Milan Kraft .15 .40
46 Mike Dunham .20 .50
47 Derian Hatcher .20 .50
48 Oleg Tverdovsky .15 .40
49 Shane Doan .20 .50
50 Martin Skoula .15 .40
51 John LeClair .25 .60
52 Tommy Salo .20 .50
53 Miroslav Satan .25 .60
54 Bryan Berard .15 .40
55 Roman Cechmanek .20 .50
56 Alexei Morozov .15 .40
57 Jean-Sebastien Giguere .25 .60
58 Pierre Turgeon .25 .60
59 Martin Straka .20 .50
60 Stephane Yelle .15 .40
61 Marc Savard .15 .40
62 Sergei Zubov .20 .50
63 Jeff Friesen .15 .40
64 Daniel Briere .20 .50
65 Patrik Stefan .20 .50
66 Pavol Demitra .30 .75
67 Radek Dvorak .20 .50
68 Marty Turco .25 .60
69 Keith Tkachuk .25 .60
70 Maxim Afinogenov .15 .40
71 Mika Noronen .20 .50
72 Evgeni Nabokov .20 .50
73 Todd Bertuzzi .25 .60
74 Valeri Bure .20 .50
75 Marian Hossa .20 .50
76 J-P Dumont .15 .40
77 Niklas Sundstrom .15 .40
78 Eric Daze .15 .40
79 Brian Boucher .20 .50
80 Nikolai Khabibulin .25 .60
81 Darren McCarty .20 .50
82 Pavel Brendl .15 .40
83 Mark Recchi .30 .75
84 Dan Cloutier .20 .50
85 Manny Legace .25 .60
86 Keith Primeau .25 .60
87 Alex Tanguay .20 .50
88 Ed Jovanovski .20 .50
89 Roberto Luongo .40 1.00
90 Andreas Johansson .15 .40
91 Steve Shields .20 .50
92 Saku Koivu .25 .60
93 Chris Drury .25 .60
94 Olaf Kolzig .25 .60
95 Jan Hrdina .15 .40
96 Ivan Novoseltsev .15 .40
97 Kenny Jonsson .15 .40
98 Martin Havlat .20 .50
99 Scott Niedermayer .25 .60
100 Chris Phillips .15 .40
101 Tony Amonte .20 .50
102 Alexander Mogilny .20 .50
103 Chris Pronger .20 .50
104 Chris Gratton .15 .40
105 Sergei Fedorov .40 1.00
106 David Legwand .20 .50
107 Ron Tugnutt .20 .50
108 Steven McCarthy .15 .40
109 Brian Rolston .20 .50
110 Bobby Holik .15 .40
111 Darryl Sydor .15 .40
112 Steve Sullivan .15 .40
113 Toby Petersen .15 .40
114 Scott Gomez .20 .50
115 Adam Foote .15 .40
116 Rob Niedermayer .20 .50
117 Arturs Irbe .20 .50
118 Al MacInnis .25 .60
119 Jeff Hackett .20 .50
120 Pavel Bure .30 .75
121 Patrick Lalime .20 .50
122 Vincent Damphousse .20 .50
123 Steve Passmore .15 .40
124 Simon Gagne .25 .60
125 Shawn McEachern .15 .40
126 Bryan McCabe .15 .40
127 Jamie Storr .20 .50
128 Mike Richter .25 .60
129 Petr Sykora .20 .50
130 Trevor Kidd .15 .40
131 Jaromir Jagr .60 1.50
132 Bill Guerin .25 .60
133 Mark Messier .40 1.00
134 Ilya Kovalchuk .30 .75
135 Teemu Selanne .50 1.25
136 Dominik Hasek .40 1.00
137 Mats Sundin .25 .60
138 Jose Theodore .25 .60
139 Brendan Shanahan .30 .75
140 Daniel Alfredsson .25 .60
141 Martin Brodeur .50 1.25
142 Jarome Iginla .25 .60
143 Peter Bondra .25 .60
144 Peter Forsberg .30 .75
145 Curtis Joseph .25 .60
146 Alexei Yashin .20 .50
147 Patrick Roy .60 1.50
148 Markus Naslund .20 .50
149 Jeremy Roenick .25 .60
150 Eric Lindros .40 1.00
151 Steve Yzerman .50 1.25
152 Marian Gaborik .40 1.00
153 Mike Modano .40 1.00
154 Joe Sakic .40 1.00
155 Paul Kariya .30 .75
156 Owen Nolan .25 .60
157 Rob Blake .25 .60

158 Nicklas Lidstrom .25 .60
159 Joe Thornton .30 .75
160 Mario Lemieux .75 2.00
161 Magnus Arvedson .15 .40
162 Chris Clark .15 .40
163 Don Sweeney .15 .40
164 Fredrik Modin .15 .40
165 Matt Cooke .15 .40
166 Rhett Warrener .15 .40
167 Tim Taylor .15 .40
168 Viktor Kozlov .15 .40
169 Michal Rozsival .20 .50
170 Mathieu Schneider .15 .40
171 Matt Cullen .15 .40
172 Vladimir Malakhov .15 .40
173 Mattias Norstrom .15 .40
174 Greg Johnson .15 .40
175 Eric Desjardins .15 .40
176 Damian Rhodes .15 .40
177 Stephane Quintal .15 .40
178 Sami Salo .15 .40
179 Craig Rivet .15 .40
180 Oleg Saprykin .15 .40
181 Chris Therien .15 .40
182 Robyn Regehr .15 .40
183 Erik Cole .20 .50
184 Ed Belfour .25 .60
185 Chris Chelios .25 .60
186 Pavel Datsyuk .30 .75
187 Mike Comrie .25 .60
188 Doug Gilmour .30 .75
189 Johan Hedberg .25 .60
190 Brett Hull .30 .75
191 Theo Fleury .30 .75
192 Rick DiPietro .20 .50
193 Marcus Ragnarsson .15 .40
194 Mike Peca .20 .50
195 Ryan Smyth .20 .50
196 Ruslan Salei .15 .40
197 Anson Carter .20 .50
198 Eric Brewer .15 .40
199 Alexei Kovalev .25 .60
200 Gary Roberts .15 .40
201 Micki Dupont RC .15 .40
202 Pat Verbeek .15 .40
203 Dmitri Kalinin .15 .40
204 Brad Stuart .15 .40
205 Brent Johnson .20 .50
206 Todd White .15 .40
207 Andy McDonald .25 .60
208 Glen Murray .20 .50
209 Chris Osgood .25 .60
210 Tim Connolly .15 .40
211 Scott Hartnell .25 .60
212 Radim Vrbata .20 .50
213 Dimitri Khristich .15 .40
214 Brendan Morrison .20 .50
215 Matt Henderson RC .15 .40
216 Jason Allison .20 .50
217 Ray Whitney .20 .50
218 Niklas Hagman .15 .40
219 Andrew Brunette .15 .40
220 Brian Rafalski .15 .40
221 Mark Parrish .15 .40
222 Dave Andreychuk .25 .60
223 Dainius Zubrus .15 .40
224 P.J. Stock .15 .40
225 Espen Knutsen .15 .40
226 Jiri Dopita .15 .40
227 Jeff Jillson .15 .40
228 Tie Domi .20 .50
229 Milan Hnilicka .20 .50
230 Martin Lapointe .20 .50
231 Taylor Pyatt .15 .40
232 Kyle Calder .15 .40
233 Marc Denis .20 .50
234 Brenden Morrow .20 .50
235 Cliff Ronning .15 .40
236 Wade Redden .15 .40
237 Kris Beech .15 .40
238 Patrick Marleau .25 .60
239 Corey Schwab .20 .50
240 Nikita Alexeev .15 .40
241 Miikka Kiprusoff .20 .50
242 Jason Arnott .20 .50
243 Joe Nieuwendyk .25 .60
244 Adam Oates .25 .60
245 Darius Kasparaitis .15 .40
246 Mike York .15 .40
247 Donald Brashear .15 .40
248 Kevin Weekes .20 .50
249 Jaroslav Spacek .15 .40
250 Alex Auld .15 .40
251 Denis Arkhipov .15 .40
252 Cory Stillman .15 .40
253 Craig Conroy .15 .40
254 Dan Blackburn .20 .50
255 Vaclav Nedorost .15 .40
256 Ladislav Nagy .15 .40
257 Lukas Krajicek .20 .50
258 Raffi Torres .15 .40
259 Richard Zednik .15 .40
260 Brad Bombardir .15 .40
261 Ilja Bryzgalov .20 .50
262 Frederic Cassivi .15 .40
263 Geoff Sanderson .20 .50
264 Dwayne Roloson .15 .40
265 Jani Hurme .20 .50
266 Sebastien Centomo .15 .40
267 Jeff Halpern .15 .40
268 Mikael Renberg .15 .40
269 Vaclav Prospal .15 .40
270 Sylvain Blouin RC .15 .40
271 Olivier Michaud .15 .40
272 Pascal Dupuis .15 .40
273 Michael Nylander .15 .40
274 Daymond Langkow .20 .50
275 Mike Sillinger .15 .40
276 Yanic Perreault .15 .40
277 Oleg Petrov .15 .40
278 Rod Brind'Amour .25 .60
279 Scott Clemmensen .15 .40
280 Jason Smith .15 .40
281 Vladimir Orszagh .15 .40
282 Stephen Weiss .25 .60
283 Tony Hrkac .15 .40
284 Ty Conklin .20 .50
285 Ulf Dahlen .15 .40
286 Karel Pilar .15 .40
287 Krys Kolanos .15 .40
288 Marcel Hossa .15 .40
289 Martin Prusek .15 .40
290 Robert Svehla .15 .40
291 Radoslav Suchy .15 .40
292 Alexander Khavanov .15 .40
293 Andy Delmore .15 .40
294 Adrian Aucoin .15 .40
295 Bates Battaglia .15 .40
296 Jussi Markkanen .15 .40
297 Martin Erat .15 .40
298 Jim Dowd .15 .40
299 Mark Hartigan .15 .40
300 Neil Little .15 .40
301 Markus Naslund UC .25 .60
302 Bill Guerin UC .30 .75
303 Nicklas Lidstrom UC .30 .75
304 Sergei Fedorov UC .50 1.25
305 Mats Sundin UC .30 .75
306 Teemu Selanne UC .60 1.50
307 Sergei Gonchar UC .25 .60
308 Brian Leetch UC .30 .75
309 Jeremy Roenick UC .30 .75
310 Jaromir Jagr UC .75 2.00
311 Mark Recchi UC .40 1.00
312 Sandis Ozolinsh UC .25 .60
313 Jarome Iginla UC .30 .75
314 Jose Theodore UC .30 .75
315 Steve Yzerman UC .60 1.50
316 Paul Kariya UC .40 1.00
317 Eric Daze UC .20 .50
318 Ilya Kovalchuk UC .40 1.00
319 Brendan Shanahan UC .40 1.00
320 Marian Gaborik UC .50 1.25
321 Joe Sakic UC .50 1.25
322 Peter Forsberg UC .40 1.00
323 Mario Lemieux UC 1.00 2.50
324 Luc Robitaille UC .30 .75
325 Eric Lindros UC .50 1.25
326 Mike Modano UC .50 1.25
327 Patrick Roy UC .75 2.00
328 Dominik Hasek UC .50 1.25
329 Scott Stevens UC .30 .75
330 Martin Brodeur UC .60 1.50
331 Keith Tkachuk UC .30 .75
332 Rostislav Klesla UC .20 .50
333 Joe Thornton UC .40 1.00
334 Alexei Yashin UC .25 .60
335 Brett Hull UC .40 1.00
336 Olaf Kolzig UC .30 .75
337 Roberto Luongo UC .50 1.25
338 Pavel Bure UC .40 1.00
339 Chris Chelios UC .30 .75
340 Owen Nolan UC .30 .75
341 Paul Kariya FP .40 1.00
342 Ilya Kovalchuk FP .40 1.00
343 Joe Thornton FP .40 1.00
344 Miroslav Satan FP .30 .75
345 Jarome Iginla FP .30 .75
346 Jeff O'Neill FP .20 .50
347 Eric Daze FP .20 .50
348 Patrick Roy FP .75 2.00
349 Rostislav Klesla FP .20 .50
350 Mike Modano FP .50 1.25
351 Steve Yzerman FP .60 1.50
352 Mike Comrie FP .30 .75
353 Roberto Luongo FP .50 1.25
354 Zigmund Palffy FP .30 .75
355 Marian Gaborik FP .50 1.25
356 Jose Theodore FP .30 .75
357 Scott Hartnell FP .30 .75
358 Martin Brodeur FP .60 1.50
359 Alexei Yashin FP .25 .60
360 Pavel Bure FP .40 1.00
361 Marian Hossa FP .25 .60
362 Simon Gagne FP .30 .75
363 Daniel Briere FP .25 .60
364 Mario Lemieux FP 1.00 2.50
365 Chris Pronger FP .25 .60
366 Owen Nolan FP .30 .75
367 Nikolai Khabibulin FP .30 .75
368 Mats Sundin FP .30 .75
369 Markus Naslund FP .25 .60
370 Jaromir Jagr FP .75 2.00
371 Iginla/Naslund/Bertuzzi SL .30 .75
372 Iginla/Sundin/Mury/Grin SL .30 .75
373 Oates/Allison/Sakic SL .30 .75
374 Chel/Rnick/Mury/Gqne SL .30 .75
375 Worrell/Ference/Neil SL .20 .50
376 Roy/Cechmanek/Turco SL .75 2.00
377 Theo/Roy/Cech./Turco SL .75 2.00
378 Demitra/Murray/Sundin SL .40 1.00
379 Rolston/Peca/Satan SL .30 .75
380 Hasek/Brodeur/Nabokv SL .60 1.50
381 Svehla/Kaspar/Hatcher SL .25 .60
382 Lidstrom/Gonchar SL .30 .75
383 Htley/Kovalchuk/Huslius SL .40 1.00
384 Koval/Heatley/Huselius SL .40 1.00
385 Aucoin/Pronger/Lidstrom SL .30 .75
386 Perreault/Brind/Francis SL .40 1.00
387 Bondra/Iginla SL .30 .75
388 Briere/Ddmrsh/Hrdina SL .25 .60
389 Patrick Roy AS .75 2.00
390 Chris Pronger AS .25 .60
391 Rob Blake AS .30 .75
392 Vincent Damphousse AS .25 .60
393 Owen Nolan AS .30 .75
394 Brendan Shanahan AS .40 1.00
395 Dominik Hasek AS .50 1.25
396 Nicklas Lidstrom AS .30 .75
397 Sandis Ozolinsh AS .25 .60
398 Sergei Fedorov AS .50 1.25
399 Jaromir Jagr AS .75 2.00
400 Teemu Selanne AS .60 1.50
401H Mike Modano Draft .50 1.25
401R Trevor Linden Draft .30 .75
402H Jeremy Roenick Draft .30 .75
402R Mats Sundin Draft .30 .75
403H Bill Guerin Draft .30 .75
403R Olaf Kolzig Draft .30 .75
404H Owen Nolan Draft .30 .75
404R Jaromir Jagr Draft .75 2.00
405H Martin Brodeur Draft .60 1.50
405R Eric Lindros Draft .50 1.25
406H Scott Niedermayer Draft .30 .75
406R Peter Forsberg Draft .40 1.00
407H Markus Naslund Draft .25 .60
407R Alexei Yashin Draft .25 .60
408H Chris Pronger Draft .25 .60
408R Paul Kariya Draft .40 1.00
409H Jason Arnott Draft .25 .60
409R Jocelyn Thibault Draft .25 .60
410H Adam Deadmarsh Draft .25 .60
410R Jason Allison Draft .25 .60
411H Todd Bertuzzi Draft .30 .75
411R Ed Jovanovski Draft .25 .60
412H Jeff O'Neill Draft .20 .50
412R Ryan Smyth Draft .25 .60
413H Dan Cloutier Draft .25 .60
413R Jarome Iginla Draft .30 .75
414H Jean-Sebastien Giguere Draft .30 .75
414R Martin Biron Draft .25 .60
415H Petr Sykora Draft .25 .60
415R Brian Boucher Draft .25 .60
416H Marc Denis Draft .25 .60
416R Joe Thornton Draft .40 1.00
417H Roberto Luongo Draft .50 1.25
417R Eric Brewer Draft .20 .50
418H Sergei Samsonov Draft .25 .60
418R Marian Hossa Draft .25 .60
419H Vincent Lecavalier Draft .25 .60
419R Mark Bell Draft .20 .50
420H Alex Tanguay Draft .25 .60
420R Simon Gagne Draft .30 .75
421H Martin Havlat Draft .25 .60
421R Rick DiPietro Draft .25 .60
422H Dany Heatley Draft .30 .75
422R Marian Gaborik Draft .50 1.25
423H Rostislav Klesla Draft .20 .50
423R Scott Hartnell Draft .30 .75
424H Ilya Kovalchuk Draft .40 1.00
424R Stephen Weiss Draft .30 .75
425H Dan Blackburn Draft .25 .60
425R Lukas Krajicek Draft .25 .60
426H Steve Yzerman Draft 5.00 12.00
426R Mario Lemieux Draft 5.00 12.00
427H Gary Roberts Draft .20 .50
427R Brian Leetch Draft .30 .75
428H Brendan Shanahan Draft .40 1.00
428R Pierre Turgeon Draft .30 .75
429H Joe Sakic Draft 1.50 4.00
429R Teemu Selanne Draft .60 1.50
430H Keith Tkachuk Draft .30 .75
430R Sedin/Sedin Draft .30 .75
431H Steve Ott Draft RC 1.50 4.00
431R Brooks Orpik Draft RC 1.25 3.00
432H Pascal Leclaire Draft RC 1.00 2.50
432R Shaone Morrisonn Draft RC .75 2.00
433H Alexei Smirnov Draft RC 1.00 2.50
433R Ron Hainsey Draft RC .75 2.00
434H Alexander Frolov Draft RC 1.50 4.00
434R Anton Volchenkov Draft RC .75 2.00
435H Jeff Taffe Draft RC .75 2.00
435R Jason Spezza Draft RC 5.00 12.00
436H Alexander Svitov Draft RC .75 2.00
436R Stanislav Chistov Draft RC .75 2.00
437H Chuck Kobasew Draft RC 1.00 2.50
437R Ales Hemsky Draft RC 3.00 8.00
438H Carlo Colaiacovo Draft RC 1.25 3.00
438R Jay Bouwmeester Draft RC 2.50 6.00
439H Rick Nash Draft RC 6.00 15.00
439R Scottie Upshall Draft RC 1.00 2.50
440H P-M Bouchard Draft RC 1.25 3.00
440R Steve Eminger Draft RC .75 2.00

2002-03 BAP First Edition Debut Jerseys

This 160-card set was inserted at a overall rate for memorabilia of 1:36 hobby and 1:48 retail. Each card was limited to a production run of 50 copies.
OVERALL MEM.ODDS 1:36 HBBY/1:48 RET.
ANNCD PRINT RUN 50 SETS
1 Pavel Bure 15.00 40.00
2 Patrick Roy 20.00 50.00
3 Curtis Joseph 15.00 40.00
4 Mats Sundin 12.00 30.00
5 Ed Belfour 15.00 40.00
6 Teemu Selanne 20.00 50.00
7 Martin Brodeur 25.00 60.00
8 Owen Nolan 10.00 25.00
9 Jarome Iginla 20.00 50.00
10 Steve Yzerman 25.00 60.00
11 Marian Gaborik 20.00 50.00
12 Jaromir Jagr 12.00 30.00
13 Eric Lindros 12.00 30.00
14 Ilya Kovalchuk 15.00 40.00
15 Nicklas Lidstrom 12.00 30.00
16 Paul Kariya 15.00 40.00
17 Joe Thornton 20.00 50.00
18 Mark Messier 20.00 50.00
19 Keith Tkachuk 10.00 25.00
20 Joe Sakic 15.00 40.00

2002-03 BAP First Edition He Shoots He Scores Points

ONE PER PACK
1 Ron Francis 1 pt. .20 .50
2 Sergei Fedorov 1 pt. .25 .60
3 Milan Hejduk 1 pt. .12 .30
3 Saku Koivu 1 pt. .15 .40
4 Dany Heatley 1 pt. .15 .40
5 Ilya Kovalchuk 1 pt. .20 .50
7 Teemu Selanne 1 pt. .30 .75
8 Eric Lindros 1 pt. .25 .60
9 Mark Messier 1 pt. .25 .60
10 Owen Nolan 1 pt.. .15 .40
11 Joe Thornton 1 pt. .20 .50
12 Pavel Bure 2 pts. .25 .60
13 Jarome Iginla 2 pts. .20 .50
14 Paul Kariya 2 pts. .25 .60
15 Joe Sakic 2 pts. .30 .75
16 Steve Yzerman 2 pts. .40 1.00
17 Mike Modano 2 pts. .30 .75
18 Peter Forsberg 3 pts. .25 .60
19 Mats Sundin 3 pts. .20 .50
20 Mario Lemieux 3 pts. .60 1.50

2002-03 BAP First Edition He Shoots He Scores Prizes

PRINT RUN 20 SER. #'d SETS
1 Peter Forsberg 12.00 30.00
2 Mario Lemieux 30.00 80.00
3 Mats Sundin 10.00 25.00
4 Jarome Iginla 10.00 25.00
5 Pavel Bure 12.00 30.00
6 Joe Sakic 15.00 40.00
7 Steve Yzerman 20.00 50.00
8 Paul Kariya 12.00 30.00
9 Mike Modano 15.00 40.00
10 Mark Messier 15.00 40.00
11 Milan Hejduk 8.00 20.00
12 Ron Francis 12.00 30.00
13 Saku Koivu 10.00 25.00
14 Owen Nolan 10.00 25.00
15 Joe Thornton 12.00 30.00
16 Ilya Kovalchuk 12.00 30.00
17 Dany Heatley 10.00 25.00
18 Eric Lindros 15.00 40.00
19 Teemu Selanne 20.00 50.00
20 Sergei Fedorov 15.00 40.00
21 Brendan Shanahan 12.00 30.00
22 Marian Gaborik 15.00 40.00
23 Patrick Roy 25.00 60.00
24 Martin Brodeur 20.00 50.00
25 Jose Theodore 10.00 25.00
26 Dominik Hasek 15.00 40.00
27 Jeremy Roenick 10.00 25.00
28 Jaromir Jagr 25.00 60.00
29 Keith Tkachuk 10.00 25.00
30 Markus Naslund 8.00 20.00

2002-03 BAP First Edition Jerseys

CARDS 1-130 AVAIL. RETAIL/HOBBY
CARDS 131-160 AVAIL.HOBBY ONLY
ANNCD PRINT RUN 100 SETS
1 Mario Lemieux 15.00 40.00
2 Sergei Gonchar 5.00 12.00
3 Brian Leetch 5.00 12.00
4 Felix Potvin 8.00 20.00
5 Sandis Ozolinsh 5.00 12.00
6 Steven Reinprecht 5.00 12.00
7 Byron Dafoe 5.00 12.00
8 Mark Bell 5.00 12.00
9 Jeff O'Neill 5.00 12.00
10 Sean Burke 5.00 12.00
11 Darcy Tucker 5.00 12.00
12 Scott Stevens 5.00 12.00
13 David Aebischer 5.00 12.00
14 Jocelyn Thibault 5.00 12.00
15 Radek Bonk 5.00 12.00
16 Milan Hejduk 6.00 15.00
17 Zigmund Palffy 5.00 12.00
18 Luc Robitaille 5.00 12.00
19 Tomas Kaberle 5.00 12.00
20 Rostislav Klesla 5.00 12.00
21 Alexei Zhamnov 5.00 12.00
22 Ron Francis 5.00 12.00
23 Mike Fisher 5.00 12.00
24 Dany Heatley 8.00 20.00
25 Kyle McLaren 5.00 12.00
26 Doug Weight 5.00 12.00
27 Henrik Sedin 5.00 12.00
28 Roman Turek 5.00 12.00
29 Adam Deadmarsh 5.00 12.00
30 Sami Kapanen 5.00 12.00
31 Sergei Samsonov 5.00 12.00
32 Kristian Huselius 5.00 12.00
33 Dimitri Yushkevich 5.00 12.00
34 Patrik Elias 5.00 12.00
35 Nick Boynton 5.00 12.00
36 Martin Biron 5.00 12.00
37 Brad Richards 5.00 12.00
38 Alyn McCauley 5.00 12.00
39 Daniel Sedin 5.00 12.00
40 Teppo Numminen 5.00 12.00
41 Luke Richardson 5.00 12.00
42 Manny Fernandez 5.00 12.00
43 Vincent Lecavalier 6.00 15.00
44 Mattias Ohlund 5.00 12.00
45 Milan Kraft 5.00 12.00
46 Mike Dunham 5.00 12.00
47 Derian Hatcher 5.00 12.00
48 Oleg Tverdovsky 5.00 12.00
49 Shane Doan 5.00 12.00
50 Martin Skoula 5.00 12.00
51 John LeClair 6.00 15.00
52 Tommy Salo 5.00 12.00
53 Miroslav Satan 5.00 12.00
54 Bryan Berard 5.00 12.00
55 Roman Cechmanek 5.00 12.00
56 Alexei Morozov 5.00 12.00
57 Jean-Sebastien Giguere 5.00 12.00
58 Pierre Turgeon 5.00 12.00
59 Martin Straka 5.00 12.00
60 Stephane Yelle 5.00 12.00
61 Marc Savard 5.00 12.00
62 Sergei Zubov 5.00 12.00
63 Jeff Friesen 5.00 12.00
64 Daniel Briere 5.00 12.00
65 Patrik Stefan 5.00 12.00
66 Pavol Demitra 5.00 12.00
67 Radek Dvorak 5.00 12.00
68 Marty Turco 5.00 12.00
69 Keith Tkachuk 6.00 15.00
70 Maxim Afinogenov 5.00 12.00
71 Mika Noronen 5.00 12.00
72 Evgeni Nabokov 5.00 12.00
73 Todd Bertuzzi 6.00 15.00
74 Valeri Bure 5.00 12.00
75 Marian Hossa 6.00 15.00
76 J-P Dumont 5.00 12.00
77 Niklas Sundstrom 5.00 12.00
78 Eric Daze 5.00 12.00
79 Brian Boucher 5.00 12.00
80 Nikolai Khabibulin 6.00 15.00
81 Darren McCarty 5.00 12.00
82 Pavel Brendl 5.00 12.00
83 Mark Recchi 5.00 12.00
84 Dan Cloutier 5.00 12.00
85 Manny Legace 5.00 12.00
86 Keith Primeau 5.00 12.00
87 Alex Tanguay 5.00 12.00
88 Ed Jovanovski 5.00 12.00
89 Roberto Luongo 10.00 25.00
90 Andreas Johansson 5.00 12.00
91 Steve Shields 5.00 12.00
92 Saku Koivu 6.00 15.00
93 Chris Drury 5.00 12.00
94 Olaf Kolzig 5.00 12.00
95 Jan Hrdina 5.00 12.00
96 Ivan Novoseltsev 5.00 12.00
97 Kenny Jonsson 5.00 12.00
98 Martin Havlat 5.00 12.00
99 Scott Niedermayer 5.00 12.00
100 Chris Phillips 5.00 12.00
101 Tony Amonte 5.00 12.00
102 Alexander Mogilny 5.00 12.00
103 Chris Pronger 5.00 12.00
104 Chris Gratton 5.00 12.00
105 Sergei Fedorov 8.00 20.00
106 David Legwand 5.00 12.00
107 Ron Tugnutt 5.00 12.00
108 Steven McCarthy 5.00 12.00
109 Brian Rolston 5.00 12.00
110 Bobby Holik 5.00 12.00
111 Darryl Sydor 5.00 12.00
112 Steve Sullivan 5.00 12.00
113 Toby Petersen 5.00 12.00
114 Scott Gomez 5.00 12.00
115 Adam Foote 5.00 12.00
116 Rob Niedermayer 5.00 12.00
117 Arturs Irbe 5.00 12.00
118 Al MacInnis 5.00 12.00
119 Jeff Hackett 5.00 12.00
120 Pavel Bure 6.00 15.00
121 Patrick Lalime 5.00 12.00
122 Vincent Damphousse 5.00 12.00
123 Steve Passmore 5.00 12.00
124 Simon Gagne 6.00 15.00
125 Shawn McEachern 5.00 12.00
126 Bryan McCabe 5.00 12.00
127 Jamie Storr 5.00 12.00
128 Mike Richter 6.00 15.00
129 Petr Sykora 5.00 12.00
130 Trevor Kidd 5.00 12.00
131 Jaromir Jagr 10.00 25.00
132 Bill Guerin 5.00 12.00
133 Mark Messier 6.00 15.00
134 Ilya Kovalchuk 10.00 25.00
135 Teemu Selanne 6.00 15.00
136 Dominik Hasek 15.00 40.00
137 Mats Sundin 6.00 15.00
138 Jose Theodore 10.00 25.00
139 Brendan Shanahan 6.00 15.00
140 Daniel Alfredsson 5.00 12.00
141 Martin Brodeur 12.00 30.00
142 Jarome Iginla 10.00 25.00
143 Peter Bondra 6.00 15.00
144 Peter Forsberg 15.00 40.00
145 Curtis Joseph 6.00 15.00
146 Alexei Yashin 5.00 12.00
147 Patrick Roy 20.00 50.00
148 Markus Naslund 6.00 15.00
149 Jeremy Roenick 10.00 25.00
150 Eric Lindros 6.00 15.00
151 Steve Yzerman 10.00 25.00
152 Marian Gaborik 12.50 30.00
153 Mike Modano 8.00 20.00
154 Joe Sakic 12.50 30.00
155 Paul Kariya 6.00 15.00
156 Owen Nolan 5.00 12.00
157 Rob Blake 5.00 12.00
158 Nicklas Lidstrom 6.00 15.00
159 Joe Thornton 10.00 25.00
160 Mario Lemieux 15.00 40.00

2002-03 BAP First Edition Magnificent Inserts

This 10-card set featured game-used equipment from the career of Mario Lemieux. Cards MI1-MI5 had a print run of 40 copies each and cards MI6-MI10 were limited to just 10 copies each. Cards MI6-MI10 are not priced due to scarcity.
CARDS MI1-MI5 PRINT RUN 40 SETS
CARDS MI6-MI10 PRINT RUN 10 SETS
MI1 2000-01 Jersey 30.00 80.00
MI2 1985-86 Jersey 30.00 80.00
MI3 2002 All-Star Jersey 30.00 80.00
MI4 1987 Canada Cup Jersey 30.00 80.00
MI5 Dual Jersey 50.00 125.00
MI6 Number
MI7 Emblem
MI8 Triple Jersey
MI9 Quad Jersey
MI10 Complete Package

2002-03 BAP First Edition Scoring Leaders

ANNCD PRINT RUN 50 SETS
1 Paul Kariya 12.50 30.00
2 Dany Heatley 20.00 50.00
3 Sergei Samsonov 12.50 30.00
4 Jarome Iginla 15.00 40.00
5 Ron Francis 12.50 30.00
6 Eric Daze 12.50 30.00
7 Joe Sakic 20.00 50.00
8 Mike Modano 15.00 40.00
9 Brendan Shanahan 12.50 30.00
10 Patrik Elias 12.50 30.00
11 Alexei Yashin 12.50 30.00
12 Eric Lindros 12.50 30.00
13 Daniel Alfredsson 12.50 30.00
14 Jeremy Roenick 15.00 40.00
15 Alexei Kovalev 12.50 30.00
16 Owen Nolan 12.50 30.00
17 Brad Richards 12.50 30.00
18 Mats Sundin 12.50 30.00
19 Markus Naslund 12.50 30.00
20 Jaromir Jagr 15.00 40.00

1999-00 BAP Memorabilia

Released as two series, the base 300-card set was released under Be A Player Memorabilia, and the last 100-cards were released as Be A Player Memorabilia AS Update. Base cards feature color action photos and are enhanced with blue foil highlights. Gold and silver parallels of the set were also created and inserted into random packs. Gold parallels had a stated print run of 100 sets and silver parallels had a stated print run of 1000 sets. Be A Player Memorabilia was packaged in 24-pack boxes with packs containing eight cards and carried a suggested retail price of $3.29 US and $4.99 CAN.
1 Patrik Stefan RC .15 .40
2 Glen Murray .12 .30
3 Nicklas Lidstrom .15 .40
4 Arturs Irbe .12 .30
5 Viktor Kozlov .10 .25
6 Dimitri Yushkevich .10 .25
7 Byron Ritchie RC .10 .25
8 Robert Svehla .10 .25
9 Jeremy Roenick .15 .40
10 Ron Francis .20 .50
11 Oleg Kvasha .10 .25
12 Marian Hossa .12 .30
13 Mark Recchi .20 .50
14 Scott Mellanby .10 .25
15 Adam Graves .12 .30
16 Boris Mironov .10 .25
17 Derian Hatcher .12 .30
18 Brian Leetch .15 .40
19 Mattias Ohlund .12 .30
20 Ray Whitney .12 .30
21 Mike Richter .15 .40
22 Paul Mara .10 .25
23 Todd Bertuzzi .12 .30
24 Sergei Zubov .10 .25
25 Cliff Ronning .10 .25
26 Anson Carter .12 .30
27 Dmitri Mironov .10 .25
28 Shane Willis .10 .25
29 Shayne Corson .10 .25
30 Chris Chelios .15 .40
31 Pavel Kubina .10 .25
32 Michal Grosek .10 .25
33 Gary Suter .10 .25
34 Greg Adams .10 .25
35 Joe Thornton .25 .60
36 Matt Higgins .10 .25
37 Chris Gratton .10 .25
38 Ray Bourque .25 .60
39 Tommy Salo .12 .30
40 Igor Kravchuk .10 .25
41 Byron Dafoe .10 .25
42 Larry Murphy .12 .30
43 Bryan McCabe .12 .30
44 John Vanbiesbrouck .12 .30
45 Brett Hull .25 .60
46 Christian Dube .10 .25
47 Kyle McLaren .10 .25
48 Jere Lehtinen .12 .30
49 Petr Nedved .10 .25
50 Jason Allison .12 .30
51 Brad Lukowich RC .12 .30
52 Scott Stevens .15 .40
53 Sergei Krivokrasov .10 .25
54 Olaf Kolzig .15 .40
55 Sami Kapanen .10 .25
56 Sami Salo .12 .30
57 Cory Stillman .10 .25
58 Darcy Tucker .10 .25
59 Rod Brind'Amour .15 .40
60 John Jakopin RC .10 .25
61 Martin Brodeur .30 .75
62 Jiri Slegr .10 .25
63 Rem Murray .10 .25
64 Jason Arnott .12 .30
65 Jon Sim RC .15 .40
66 Cory Sarich .10 .25
67 Brian Rafalski RC .15 .40
68 Kevin Hatcher .10 .25
69 Ted Donato .10 .25
70 Dan LaCouture .10 .25
71 Alexei Kovalev .12 .30
72 Peter Bondra .12 .30
73 John LeClair .15 .40
74 Matthew Barnaby .12 .30
75 Adam Oates .15 .40
76 Janne Niinimaa .10 .25
77 Tom Barrasso .15 .40
78 Sergei Gonchar .10 .25
79 Alex Tanguay .12 .30
80 Jean-Luc Grand-Pierre RC .10 .25
81 Alexei Tezikov RC .15 .40
82 Doug Gilmour .20 .50
83 Sergei Brylin .10 .25
84 Ron Tugnutt .12 .30
85 Stephane Richer .12 .30
86 Marc Denis .12 .30
87 Sergei Fedorov .25 .60
88 Brian Rolston .12 .30
89 Chris Pronger .12 .30
90 Dan Cloutier .10 .25
91 Anders Eriksson .10 .25
92 Donald Audette .10 .25
93 Ed Jovanovski .12 .30
94 Tony Amonte .12 .30
95 Jamie Storr .10 .25
96 German Titov .10 .25
97 Eric Daze .12 .30
98 Zigmund Palffy .15 .40
99 Dan McGillis .10 .25
100 Nikolai Khabibulin .12 .30
101 Mathieu Schneider .10 .25
102 Magnus Arvedson .10 .25
103 Joe Sakic .25 .60
104 Brian Campbell RC .15 .40
105 Wade Redden .10 .25
106 Andrei Nikolishin .10 .25
107 Steve Rucchin .10 .25
108 Shawn McEachern .10 .25
109 Alexander Karpovtsev .10 .25
110 Miroslav Satan .12 .30
111 Andreas Dackell .10 .25
112 Niklas Sundstrom .10 .25
113 Scott Niedermayer .15 .40
114 Ken Wregget .10 .25
115 Olli Jokinen .12 .30
116 Vincent Lecavalier .12 .30
117 Paul Kariya .20 .50
118 Alexei Zhamnov .10 .25
119 Martin Rucinsky .10 .25
120 Daniel Cleary .10 .25
121 Yanic Perreault .10 .25
122 Alexei Zhitnik .10 .25
123 Vadim Sharifijanov .10 .25
124 Derek King .10 .25
125 Jason Woolley .10 .25
126 Pavel Bure .20 .50
127 Darius Kasparaitis .12 .30
128 Stu Barnes .12 .30
129 Josef Beranek .10 .25
130 Milan Hejduk .12 .30
131 Michael Peca .12 .30
132 Tomas Holmstrom .10 .25
133 Patrick Marleau .15 .40
134 Dominik Hasek .25 .60
135 Chris Osgood .15 .40
136 Radek Bonk .10 .25
137 Martin Biron .12 .30
138 Igor Larionov .15 .40
139 Felix Potvin .25 .60
140 Oleg Tverdovsky .10 .25
141 Steve Yzerman .50 1.25
142 Bobby Holik .10 .25
143 Landon Wilson .10 .25
144 Marty McInnis .10 .25
145 Remi Royer .10 .25
146 Brendan Morrison .12 .30
147 Jaromir Jagr .40 1.00
148 Steve Thomas .10 .25
149 Rico Fata .10 .25
150 John Madden RC .15 .40
151 Miroslav Guren .10 .25
152 Jochen Hecht RC .25 .60
153 Gary Roberts .10 .25
154 Patrik Elias .15 .40
155 Al MacInnis .15 .40
156 Jonathan Girard .10 .25
157 Jan Hlavac .10 .25
158 Pierre Turgeon .15 .40
159 Matt Cullen .10 .25
160 Trevor Letowski .10 .25
161 Roman Turek .12 .30
162 Luc Robitaille .15 .40
163 Marcus Nilsson .10 .25
164 Pavol Demitra .20 .50
165 Fredrik Olausson .10 .25
166 Blake Sloan .12 .30
167 Eric Lindros .25 .60
168 Guy Hebert .15 .40
169 Adam Deadmarsh .10 .25
170 Mike Leclerc .10 .25
171 Teemu Selanne .30 .75
172 Ty Jones .10 .25
173 Calle Johansson .10 .25
174 Ed Belfour .15 .40
175 Craig MacDonald RC .15 .40
176 Todd Harvey .10 .25
177 Martin Straka .10 .25
178 Mariusz Czerkawski .10 .25
179 Grant Fuhr .15 .40
180 Mark Parrish .10 .25
181 Sandis Ozolinsh .10 .25
182 Patrice Brisebois .10 .25
183 Geoff Courtnall .12 .30
184 Chris Drury .12 .30
185 Saku Koivu .15 .40
186 Teppo Numminen .10 .25
187 Alexei Morozov .12 .30
188 Stephane Quintal .10 .25
189 Eric Desjardins .12 .30
190 Pavel Patera RC .10 .25
191 Vladimir Malakhov .10 .25
192 Jean-Sebastien Giguere .15 .40
193 Niclas Havelid RC .15 .40
194 Trevor Linden .15 .40
195 Simon Gagne .15 .40
196 Kevin Weekes .10 .25
197 Joe Nieuwendyk .15 .40
198 Cameron Mann .10 .25
199 Adam Mair RC .10 .25
200 Kim Johnsson RC .10 .25
201 Mikael Renberg .10 .25
202 Curtis Joseph .15 .40
203 Juha Lind .10 .25
204 Doug Weight .15 .40
205 Mats Lindgren .10 .25
206 Marcus Ragnarsson .10 .25
207 Igor Korolev .10 .25
208 Claude Lemieux .12 .30
209 Jeff Hackett .10 .25
210 Brendan Witt .10 .25
211 Steve Kariya RC .15 .40
212 Jarome Iginla .15 .40
213 Pavel Rosa .10 .25
214 Andrei Zyuzin .10 .25
215 Oleg Saprykin RC .15 .40
216 Sean Burke .10 .25
217 Mike Modano .25 .60
218 Phil Housley .10 .25
219 Ryan Smyth .12 .30
220 Daren Puppa .10 .25
221 Aki Berg .10 .25
222 Mike Grier .10 .25
223 Keith Jones .10 .25
224 Marc Savard .10 .25
225 Bill Guerin .15 .40
226 Theo Fleury .20 .50
227 Shawn Heins RC .10 .25
228 Tom Poti .10 .25
229 Tim Connolly .10 .25
230 Glen Wesley .10 .25
231 Brendan Shanahan .20 .50
232 Kenny Jonsson .10 .25
233 Mats Sundin .15 .40
234 Damian Rhodes .10 .25
235 Martin Lapointe .12 .30
236 David Legwand .10 .25
237 Rob Niedermayer .10 .25
238 Bill Muckalt .10 .25
239 Valeri Bure .10 .25
240 Manny Malhotra .12 .30
241 Jozef Stumpel .10 .25
242 Brad Stuart .12 .30
243 Curtis Brown .10 .25
244 Alexei Yashin .12 .30
245 Owen Nolan .15 .40
246 Shawn Bates .10 .25
247 Jan Hrdina .10 .25
248 Marco Sturm .12 .30
249 Nelson Emerson .10 .25
250 Stephane Fiset .12 .30
251 Mike Vernon .12 .30
252 Jason Botterill .10 .25
253 Marty Reasoner .10 .25
254 Roman Hamrlik .12 .30
255 Ray Ferraro .10 .25
256 Jamie Langenbrunner .10 .25
257 Brian Holzinger .10 .25
258 Andrew Brunette .10 .25
259 Peter Forsberg .15 .40
260 Jyrki Lumme .10 .25
261 Keith Primeau .10 .25
262 Patrick Roy .60 1.50
263 Dmitri Nabokov .10 .25
264 Darryl Laplante .10 .25
265 Mark Messier .25 .60
266 Benoit Gratton RC .10 .25
267 Bryan Berard .10 .25
268 Wendel Clark .12 .30
269 Vincent Damphousse .12 .30
270 J-P Dumont .12 .30
271 Darryl Sydor .12 .30
272 Darren Turcotte .10 .25
273 Sergei Berezin .10 .25
274 Jeff Friesen .12 .30
275 Ville Peltonen .10 .25
276 Rick Tocchet .12 .30
277 Darren McCarty .10 .25
278 Greg Johnson .10 .25
279 Dan Smith RC .10 .25
280 Sergei Samsonov .12 .30
281 Petr Sykora .12 .30
282 Dallas Drake .10 .25
283 Steve Konowalchuk .10 .25
284 Yan Golubovsky .10 .25
285 Dan Boyle RC .12 .30
286 Alexander Mogilny .12 .30
287 Daniel Alfredsson .15 .40
288 Steve Shields .12 .30
289 Markus Naslund .15 .40
290 Vyacheslav Kozlov .10 .25
291 Keith Tkachuk .15 .40
292 Adrian Aucoin .10 .25
293 Jocelyn Thibault .12 .30
294 Kevin Stevens .12 .30
295 John MacLean .12 .30
296 Mike Ricci .12 .30
297 Rob Blake .15 .40
298 Radek Dvorak .10 .25
299 Mike Dunham .10 .25
300 Richard Matvichuk .10 .25
301 Scott Gomez .12 .30
302 Nikolai Antropov RC .40 1.00
303 Glen Metropolit RC .10 .25
304 Robyn Regehr .10 .25
305 Mathieu Biron .10 .25
306 Nathan Dempsey RC .10 .25
307 Roberto Luongo .20 .50
308 Andreas Karlsson RC .10 .25
309 Ray Bourque .25 .60
310 Artem Chubarov .10 .25
311 Mike Fisher RC .15 .40
312 Andrew Ference .10 .25
313 Todd Reirden RC .10 .25
314 Martin Skoula RC .10 .25
315 Radislav Suchy RC .10 .25
316 Joel Prpic RC .10 .25
317 Yuri Butsayev RC .10 .25
318 Andy Delmore RC .10 .25
319 Steve McCarthy .10 .25
320 Brian Rolston .12 .30
321 Dimitri Kalinin RC .10 .25
322 Brenden Morrow .15 .40
323 Mike Vernon .12 .30
324 Nils Ekman RC .10 .25
325 Felix Potvin .25 .60
326 Jan Nemecek RC .10 .25
327 Michael York .10 .25
328 Evgeni Nabokov RC .60 1.50
329 Rick Tocchet .12 .30
330 Vitali Vishnevsky .12 .30
331 Francis Bouillon RC .15 .40
332 Robert Esche RC .15 .40
333 Ray Giroux RC .10 .25
334 Per Svartvadet RC .10 .25
335 Kyle Calder RC .12 .30
336 Brian Boucher .15 .40
337 Dan Hinote RC .12 .30
338 Darrel Scoville RC .10 .25
339 Ivan Novoseltsev RC .20 .50
340 Petr Schastlivy RC .10 .25
341 Andre Savage RC .10 .25
342 Michal Grosek .10 .25
343 Richard Lintner RC .10 .25
344 Tyson Nash RC .10 .25
345 Tommy Westlund RC .10 .25
346 Jason Krog RC .10 .25
347 Jarkko Ruutu RC .10 .25
348 Mike Ribeiro .12 .30
349 Alexander Mogilny .12 .30
350 Maxim Afinogenov .10 .25
351 Ron Tugnutt .12 .30
352 Jaroslav Spacek .10 .25
353 Petr Buzek .10 .25
354 Sami Helenius RC .12 .30
355 Peter Schaefer .10 .25
356 Alan Letang RC .15 .40

357 Keith Primeau .10 .25
358 Jay Henderson RC .10 .25
359 Dave Tanabe .10 .25
360 Fred Brathwaite .10 .25
361 Chris Gratton .10 .25
362 Maxim Balmochnyk .10 .25
363 John Emmons .10 .25
364 Mark Eaton RC .10 .25
365 Kevyn Adams .10 .25
366 Alfie Michaud RC .10 .25
367 Chris Herperger RC .10 .25
368 Scott Langkow .10 .25
369 Marquis Mathieu RC .10 .25
370 Milan Hnilicka RC .10 .25
371 Michal Rozsival RC .10 .25
372 Sergei Krivokrasov .10 .25
373 Brad Chartrand RC .10 .25
374 Ryan Bonni RC .10 .25
375 Roman Lyashenko .10 .25
376 Denis Hamel RC .10 .25
377 Stephane Robidas RC .10 .25
378 Jeff Halpern RC .10 .25
379 Karlis Skrastins RC .10 .25
380 Jeff Zehr RC .10 .25
381 Brian Holzinger .10 .25
382 Josef Beranek .10 .25
383 Harold Druken .10 .25
384 Doug Gilmour .20 .50
385 Ladislav Nagy RC .10 .25
386 Bert Robertsson RC .10 .25
387 Scott Fankhouser RC .10 .25
388 Brian Willsie .10 .25
389 Eric Boguniecki RC .10 .25
390 Dmitri Yakushin RC .10 .25
391 Chris Clark RC .10 .25
392 Paul Comrie RC .25 .60
393 John Grahame RC .12 .30
394 Rod Brind'Amour .15 .40
395 Vladimir Malakhov .10 .25
396 Jiri Fischer .10 .25
397 Kimmo Timonen .10 .25
398 Brad Ference .10 .25
399 Marc Lamothe RC .10 .25
400 Radek Dvorak .10 .25
DT5 Dimitri Tertyshny TRIB .10 .25
SC3 Steve Chiasson TRIB .10 .25

1999-00 BAP Memorabilia Gold

*VETERANS: 12X TO 30X BASIC CARDS
*TRIBUTE: 4X TO 10X BASIC TRIB
*ROOKIES: 8X TO 20X BASIC RC
STATED PRINT RUN 100 SER.#'d SETS

1999-00 BAP Memorabilia Silver

*VETERANS: 1.5X TO 4X BASIC CARDS
*ROOKIES: 1X TO 2.5X
STATED PRINT RUN 1000 SER.#'d SETS

1999-00 BAP Memorabilia Jersey

JERSEY STATED ODDS 1:250
*JSY AND STICK: .6X TO 1.5X BASIC JSY
JERSEY AND STICK ODDS 1:999
*JSY EMBLEMS: .8X TO 2X BASIC JSY
JERSEY EMBLEM ODDS 1:999
*JSY NUMBERS: .8X TO 2X BASIC JSY
JERSEY NUMBERS ODDS 1:999
J1 Eric Lindros 10.00 25.00
J2 Peter Forsberg 8.00 20.00
J3 Teemu Selanne 10.00 25.00
J4 Mike Modano 8.00 20.00
J5 Mats Sundin 10.00 25.00
J6 Patrick Roy 15.00 40.00
J7 Paul Kariya 8.00 20.00
J8 Martin Brodeur 10.00 25.00
J9 Ray Bourque 15.00 40.00
J10 Mark Messier 10.00 25.00
J11 Curtis Joseph 8.00 20.00
J12 Brett Hull 8.00 20.00
J13 Al MacInnis 6.00 15.00
J14 Theo Fleury 8.00 20.00
J15 Sergei Fedorov 8.00 20.00
J16 Brian Leetch 6.00 15.00
J17 Alexei Yashin 6.00 15.00
J18 Jaromir Jagr 10.00 25.00
J19 Pavel Bure 8.00 20.00
J20 Dominik Hasek 6.00 15.00
J21 Chris Chelios 6.00 15.00
J22 John LeClair 6.00 15.00
J23 Brendan Shanahan 8.00 20.00
J24 Ed Belfour 8.00 20.00
J25 Wayne Gretzky 30.00 80.00
J26 Saku Koivu 6.00 15.00
J27 Tony Amonte 6.00 15.00
J28 Peter Bondra 6.00 15.00

1999-00 BAP Memorabilia All-Star Selects Silver

COMPLETE SET (24) 20.00 40.00
SILVER STATED ODDS 1:25
*GOLD: 2X TO 5X SILVER
GOLD STATED ODDS 1:250
SL1 Peter Forsberg 2.50 6.00
SL2 Pavol Demitra .75 2.00
SL3 Jaromir Jagr 1.50 4.00
SL4 Sandis Ozolinsh .50 1.25
SL5 Nicklas Lidstrom 1.00 2.50
SL6 Dominik Hasek 2.00 5.00
SL7 Eric Lindros 1.00 2.50
SL8 Paul Kariya 1.00 2.50
SL9 Tony Amonte .75 2.00
SL10 Brian Leetch 1.00 2.50
SL11 Al MacInnis 1.00 2.50
SL12 Martin Brodeur 2.50 6.00
SL13 Petr Sykora .50 1.25
SL14 Sergei Samsonov .75 2.00
SL15 Marian Hossa 1.00 2.50
SL16 Andrei Zyuzin .50 1.25
SL17 Sami Salo .50 1.25
SL18 Roman Turek 1.00 2.50
SL19 Chris Drury .75 2.00
SL20 Vincent Lecavalier 1.00 2.50
SL21 J-P Dumont .75 2.00
SL22 Kyle McLaren .50 1.25
SL23 Adrian Aucoin .50 1.25
SL24 Marc Denis 1.00 2.50

1999-00 BAP Memorabilia AS American Hobby

Randomly inserted in American hobby packs at the rate of 1:32, this 12-card set featured former NHL greats from the New York Rangers and the Boston Bruins.
COMPLETE SET (12) 15.00 30.00
STATED ODDS 1:32
AH1 Ken Hodge 1.25 3.00
AH2 Cam Neely 2.50 6.00
AH3 Derek Sanderson 2.00 5.00
AH4 Gerry Cheevers 2.00 5.00
AH5 Johnny Bucyk 1.25 3.00
AH6 Wayne Cashman 1.25 3.00
AH7 Vic Hadfield 1.25 3.00
AH8 Andy Bathgate 1.25 3.00
AH9 Brad Park 1.25 3.00
AH10 Ed Giacomin 1.50 4.00
AH11 John Davidson 1.50 4.00
AH12 Rod Gilbert 1.25 3.00

1999-00 BAP Memorabilia AS American Hobby Autographs

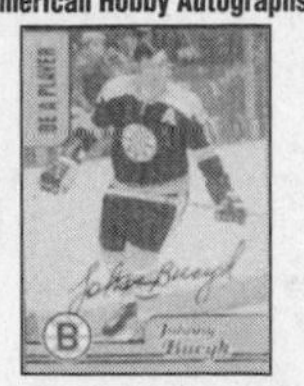

Randomly inserted in American hobby packs at the rate of 1:320, this 12-card set paralleled the base Channel Specific American insert set in an autographed version.
STATED ODDS 1:320
AH1 Ken Hodge 10.00 25.00
AH2 Cam Neely 25.00 60.00
AH3 Derek Sanderson 25.00 60.00
AH4 Gerry Cheevers 25.00 60.00
AH5 Johnny Bucyk 15.00 40.00
AH6 Wayne Cashman 15.00 40.00
AH7 Vic Hadfield 15.00 40.00
AH8 Andy Bathgate 15.00 40.00
AH9 Brad Park 15.00 40.00
AH10 Ed Giacomin 20.00 50.00
AH11 John Davidson 20.00 50.00
AH12 Rod Gilbert 15.00 40.00

1999-00 BAP Memorabilia AS Canadian Hobby

Randomly inserted in Canadian hobby packs at the rate of 1:32, this 12-card set featured former NHL greats from the Toronto Maple Leafs and the Montreal Canadians.
COMPLETE SET (12) 15.00 30.00
STATED ODDS 1:32
CH1 Borje Salming 1.50 4.00
CH2 Dave Keon 2.00 5.00
CH3 Darryl Sittler 2.00 5.00
CH4 Frank Mahovlich 2.00 5.00
CH5 Johnny Bower 2.00 5.00
CH6 Lanny McDonald 1.25 3.00
CH7 Peter Mahovlich 1.25 3.00
CH8 Dickie Moore 1.25 3.00
CH9 John Ferguson 1.25 3.00
CH10 Larry Robinson 1.25 3.00
CH11 Yvan Cournoyer 1.25 3.00
CH12 Serge Savard 1.25 3.00

1999-00 BAP Memorabilia AS Canadian Hobby Autographs

Randomly inserted in Canadian Hobby packs at the rate of 1:320, this 12-card set paralleled the base Channel Specific Canadian insert set in an autographed version.
STATED ODDS 1:320
CH1 Borje Salming 20.00 50.00
CH2 Dave Keon 25.00 60.00
CH3 Darryl Sittler 25.00 60.00
CH4 Frank Mahovlich 25.00 60.00
CH5 Johnny Bower 25.00 60.00
CH6 Lanny McDonald 15.00 40.00
CH7 Peter Mahovlich 15.00 40.00
CH8 Dickie Moore 15.00 40.00
CH9 John Ferguson 15.00 40.00
CH10 Larry Robinson 15.00 40.00
CH11 Yvan Cournoyer 15.00 40.00
CH12 Serge Savard 15.00 40.00

1999-00 BAP Memorabilia AS Retail

Randomly inserted in retail packs at the rate of 1:32, this 12-card set featured former NHL greats from the Chicago Blackhawks and the Detroit Red Wings.
COMPLETE SET (12) 20.00 40.00
STATED ODDS 1:32
R1 Bobby Hull 4.00 10.00
R2 Dennis Hull 1.25 3.00
R3 Denis Savard 1.25 3.00
R4 Pierre Pilote 1.25 3.00
R5 Stan Mikita 2.50 6.00
R6 Tony Esposito 2.00 5.00
R7 Alex Delvecchio 1.50 4.00
R8 Bill Gadsby 1.25 3.00
R9 Mickey Redmond 2.00 5.00
R10 Norm Ullman 1.25 3.00
R11 Red Kelly 1.50 4.00
R12 Ted Lindsay 1.50 4.00

1999-00 BAP Memorabilia AS Retail Autographs

Randomly inserted in retail packs at the rate of 1:320, this 12-card set paralleled the base Channel Specific Retail insert set in an autographed version.
STATED ODDS 1:320
R1 Bobby Hull 30.00 80.00
R2 Dennis Hull 20.00 40.00
R3 Denis Savard 20.00 40.00
R4 Pierre Pilote 20.00 40.00
R5 Stan Mikita 30.00 80.00
R6 Tony Esposito 30.00 80.00
R7 Alex Delvecchio 20.00 40.00
R8 Bill Gadsby 20.00 40.00
R9 Mickey Redmond 25.00 60.00
R10 Norm Ullman 20.00 40.00
R11 Red Kelly 20.00 40.00
R12 Ted Lindsay 25.00 50.00

1999-00 BAP Memorabilia AS Heritage Ruby

Randomly inserted in packs, this 24-card set featured NHL stars in their first team uniform and their current team uniform. The base set was red and sequentially numbered to 1000. Sapphire and emerald parallels were also created. Sapphire parallels were blue in color and had a stated print run of 100 sets. Emerald parallels were green in color and had a stated print run of 10 sets.
COMPLETE SET (24) 60.00 125.00
RUBY PRINT RUN 1000 SER.#'d SETS
*SAPPHIRE/100: 3X TO 8X RUBY/1000
SAPPHIRE STATED PRINT RUN 100
H1 Brendan Shanahan 2.00 5.00
H2 John LeClair 2.00 5.00
H3 Jeremy Roenick 2.00 5.00
H4 John Vanbiesbrouck 1.50 4.00
H5 Dominik Hasek 4.00 10.00
H6 Adam Oates 1.50 4.00
H7 Teemu Selanne 2.00 5.00
H8 Ron Francis 1.50 4.00
H9 Al MacInnis 1.50 4.00
H10 Patrick Roy 8.00 20.00
H11 Doug Gilmour 1.50 4.00
H12 Brett Hull 2.50 6.00
H13 Curtis Joseph 2.00 5.00
H14 Mark Messier 2.00 5.00
H15 Paul Coffey 2.00 5.00
H16 Byron Dafoe 1.50 4.00
H17 Ed Belfour 2.00 5.00
H18 Wayne Gretzky 10.00 25.00
H19 Pavel Bure 2.00 5.00
H20 Chris Chelios 2.00 5.00
H21 Mats Sundin 2.00 5.00
H22 Joe Nieuwendyk 1.50 4.00
H23 Pavol Demitra 1.50 4.00
H24 Grant Fuhr 2.00 5.00

1999-00 BAP Update Double All Star Jerseys

Randomly inserted in Update Factory Sets at the rate of 1:5, this 20-card set featured player photos coupled with two swatches of game-worn jerseys.
ODDS 1:5 UPDATE FACTORY SETS
D1 Jaromir Jagr 15.00 40.00
D2 Eric Lindros 15.00 40.00
D3 Peter Forsberg 20.00 50.00
D4 Patrick Roy 20.00 50.00
D5 Paul Kariya 15.00 40.00
D6 Mats Sundin 15.00 40.00
D7 Ray Bourque 20.00 50.00
D8 Ed Belfour 12.00 30.00
D9 Wayne Gretzky 75.00 200.00
D10 Teemu Selanne 15.00 40.00
D11 Brendan Shanahan 15.00 40.00
D12 Dominik Hasek 25.00 60.00
D13 Pavel Bure 15.00 40.00
D14 John LeClair 15.00 40.00
D15 Al MacInnis 10.00 25.00
D16 Brett Hull 12.00 30.00
D17 Brian Leetch 15.00 40.00
D18 Mark Messier 15.00 40.00
D19 Martin Brodeur 20.00 50.00
D20 Sergei Fedorov 20.00 50.00

1999-00 BAP Update Teammates Jerseys

ODDS 1:5 UPDATE FACTORY SETS
TM1 C.Joseph/J.Roenick 12.50 30.00
TM2 W.Gretzky/R.Blake 25.00 60.00
TM3 P.Roy/M.Messier 15.00 40.00
TM4 T.Selanne/B.Hull 12.50 30.00
TM5 B.Shanahan/S.Fedorov 15.00 40.00
TM6 R.Bourque/B.Leetch 15.00 40.00
TM7 E.Lindros/J.LeClair 12.50 30.00
TM8 J.Jagr/M.Messier 15.00 40.00
TM9 M.Brodeur/B.Shanahan 15.00 40.00
TM10 P.Forsberg/P.Kariya 15.00 40.00
TM11 E.Belfour/C.Chelios 12.50 30.00
TM12 T.Selanne/P.Kariya 12.50 30.00
TM13 D.Hasek/P.Bondra 15.00 40.00
TM14 S.Yzerman/P.Bure 15.00 40.00
TM15 J.LeClair/R.Bourque 20.00 50.00
TM16 T.Fleury/O.Nolan 12.50 30.00
TM17 M.Brodeur/P.Coffey 20.00 50.00
TM18 J.LeClair/E.Lindros 12.50 30.00
TM19 J.Jagr/P.Bure 20.00 50.00
TM20 D.Hasek/N.Khabibulin 15.00 40.00
TM21 P.Roy/B.Leetch 20.00 50.00
TM22 W.Gretzky/M.Modano 30.00 80.00
TM23 P.Forsberg/S.Ozolinsh 15.00 40.00
TM24 C.Chelios/R.Bourque 15.00 40.00
TM25 M.Sundin/N.Lidstrom 12.50 30.00
TM26 P.Kariya/M.Modano 12.50 30.00
TM27 T.Fleury/T.Amonte 12.50 30.00
TM28 P.Forsberg/T.Selanne 12.00 30.00
TM29 E.Lindros 12.50 30.00
D.Sydor
TM30 P.Bure/M.Sundin 12.50 30.00
TM31 J.Roenick/S.Stevens 12.50 30.00
TM32 J.Jagr/O.Kolzig 15.00 40.00
TM33 M.Richter/T.Amonte 12.50 30.00
TM34 C.Pronger/A.MacInnis 12.50 30.00
TM35 B.Shanahan/M.Brodeur 15.00 40.00
TM36 A.Mogilny/M.Messier 12.50 30.00
TM37 S.Yzerman/S.Fedorov 25.00 60.00
TM38 B.Shanahan/S.Fedorov 15.00 40.00
TM39 S.Yzerman/C.Chelios 20.00 50.00
TM40 S.Yzerman/B.Shanahan 15.00 40.00
TM41 M.Sundin/C.Joseph 12.50 30.00
TM42 P.Forsberg/P.Roy 20.00 50.00
TM43 P.Forsberg/J.Sakic 15.00 40.00
TM44 J.Sakic/P.Roy 20.00 50.00
TM45 T.Selanne/P.Kariya 12.50 30.00
TM46 B.Hull/M.Modano 15.00 40.00
TM47 B.Hull/E.Belfour 12.50 30.00
TM48 E.Belfour/M.Modano 12.00 30.00
TM49 E.Lindros/J.LeClair 12.50 30.00
TM50 B.Leetch/T.Fleury 15.00 40.00

2000-01 BAP Memorabilia

Released as a 521-card base set, including two update sets, Be A Player Memorabilia cards featured full color player action shots with white borders on three sides and black lettering. Be A Player was packaged in 24-pack boxes with packs containing eight cards and carried an American SRP of $3.29 and a Canadian SRP of $4.99. A Trevor Linden Autograph redemption card was randomly inserted in series one packs. For a $20.00 donation to the Trevor Linden foundation, an autographed card was returned. Be A Player Memorabilia Update, card numbers 397-497 and inserts were issued in factory set form only. Be A Player Final Update was issued by mail redemption as a 24-card set numbered 498-521.
COMPLETE SET (521) 40.00 100.00
COMP.SER 1 (396) 30.00 80.00
COMP.UPDATE SET (101) 15.00 30.00
COMP. FINAL UPD.SET (24) 15.00 30.00
1 Jaromir Jagr 1.00 2.50
2 Scott Mellanby .25 .60
3 Mike Fisher .30 .75
4 Slava Kozlov .30 .75
5 Steve Valiquette RC .30 .75
6 Simon Gagne .40 1.00
7 Alexei Morozov .25 .60
8 Alexei Zhitnik .30 .75
9 Jochen Hecht .25 .60
10 Jamie Allison .25 .60
11 Olli Jokinen .30 .75
12 Bobby Holik .25 .60
13 Keith Primeau .30 .75
14 Bryan McCabe .25 .60
15 Tim Connolly .25 .60
16 Marco Sturm .30 .75
17 Craig Darby .25 .60
18 Jeff Cowan RC .25 .60
19 Brad Stuart .30 .75
20 Sean O'Donnell .25 .60
21 Mike Minard RC .40 1.00
22 Rob Blake .40 1.00
23 Marek Malik .25 .60
24 Marek Posmyk .25 .60
25 Alex Tanguay .30 .75
26 Steven McCarthy .25 .60
27 Bill Guerin .40 1.00
28 Ed Jovanovski .30 .75
29 Martin Skoula .30 .75
30 Jeff Hackett .25 .60
31 Vladimir Tsyplakov .25 .60
32 Sergei Zubov .30 .75
33 Damian Rhodes .25 .60
34 Brent Sopel RC .40 1.00
35 Frantisek Kaberle .25 .60
36 Michael Peca .30 .75
37 Steve Kelly .25 .60
38 Geoff Sanderson .30 .75
39 Petr Svoboda .25 .60
40 Martin Brodeur .75 2.00
41 Markus Naslund .30 .75
42 Steve Thomas .25 .60
43 Anson Carter .30 .75
44 Theo Fleury .50 1.25
45 Felix Potvin .60 1.50
46 Adam Deadmarsh .30 .75
47 Dave Tanabe .25 .60
48 Trevor Kidd .25 .60
49 Jeff Friesen .25 .60
50 Marc Moro RC .25 .60
51 Luc Robitaille .40 1.00
52 Mike Richter .40 1.00
53 Eric Desjardins .30 .75
54 Jean-Sebastien Aubin .30 .75
55 Paul Laus .25 .60
56 Kimmo Timonen .25 .60
57 Steve Sullivan .25 .60
58 Eric Cairns .25 .60
59 Scott Stevens .40 1.00
60 Andy Delmore .25 .60
61 Jeff Nielsen .25 .60
62 Mathieu Biron .25 .60
63 Juha Lind .25 .60
64 Maxim Afinogenov .25 .60
65 Guy Hebert .30 .75
66 Sergei Brylin .25 .60
67 Mike Modano .60 1.50
68 Tommy Salo .30 .75
69 Bryan Smolinski .30 .75
70 Sergei Varlamov .25 .60
71 Paul Mara .25 .60
72 Peter Forsberg .50 1.25
73 Doug Weight .40 1.00
74 Peter Bondra .30 .75
75 Marc Denis .30 .75
76 Jamie Storr .30 .75
77 Alexei Kovalev .30 .75
78 Dainius Zubrus .25 .60
79 Mike Grier .25 .60
80 Olaf Kolzig .40 1.00
81 Bryan Adams RC .25 .60
82 Scott Niedermayer .40 1.00
83 David Gosselin RC .30 .75
84 Boris Mironov .25 .60
85 Kyle McLaren .25 .60
86 Steve Kariya .25 .60
87 Dimitri Yushkevich .25 .60
88 Paul Kariya .50 1.25
89 Brian Leetch .40 1.00
90 Jeff Daniels .25 .60
91 Brendan Morrison .40 1.00
92 Brian Campbell .25 .60
93 Ray Whitney .30 .75
94 Marian Hossa .30 .75
95 Sergei Samsonov .30 .75
96 Mike York .25 .60
97 Mark Eaton .25 .60
98 Ryan VandenBussche .25 .60
99 Vladimir Malakhov .25 .60
100 Jeff Finley .25 .60
101 John Vanbiesbrouck .30 .75
102 Brad Isbister .25 .60
103 John Madden .30 .75
104 Patrick Roy 1.00 2.50
105 Radek Bonk .30 .75
106 Brett Hull .60 1.50
107 Andreas Dackell .25 .60
108 Pierre Turgeon .40 1.00
109 Jason Woolley .25 .60
110 Jeff O'Neill .30 .75
111 John LeClair .40 1.00
112 Darryl Sydor .30 .75
113 Ryan Smyth .30 .75
114 Curtis Joseph .50 1.25
115 Gary Roberts .25 .60
116 Pavel Kubina .25 .60
117 Roman Hamrlik .30 .75
118 Sandis Ozolinsh .30 .75
119 Manny Fernandez .30 .75
120 Adam Oates .40 1.00
121 Darby Hendrickson .25 .60
122 Glen Murray .25 .60
123 Jiri Slegr .25 .60
124 Steve Yzerman 1.25 3.00
125 Mats Lindgren .25 .60
126 Sergei Gonchar .25 .60
127 Joe Thornton .60 1.50
128 Petr Sykora .30 .75
129 Pavol Demitra .50 1.25
130 Tyler Wright .25 .60
131 Johan Davidsson .25 .60
132 Brian Rolston .30 .75
133 Mark Messier .60 1.50
134 Darcy Tucker .25 .60
135 Oleg Tverdovsky .25 .60
136 Petr Nedved .30 .75
137 Harold Druken .25 .60
138 Valeri Bure .30 .75
139 Mikael Andersson .25 .60
140 Evgeni Nabokov .30 .75
141 Janne Laukkanen .25 .60
142 Radek Dvorak .30 .75
143 Brian Boucher .30 .75
144 Eric Daze .30 .75
145 Dan Cloutier .30 .75
146 Scott Gomez .30 .75
147 Dallas Drake .25 .60
148 Shawn McEachern .25 .60
149 Joe Nieuwendyk .40 1.00
150 Kenny Jonsson .25 .60
151 Saku Koivu .40 1.00
152 Roman Turek .30 .75
153 Chris Gratton .25 .60
154 Steve Rucchin .25 .60
155 Teppo Numminen .25 .60
156 Jamie Langenbrunner .30 .75
157 Johnathan Aitken RC .25 .60
158 Nikolai Antropov .30 .75
159 Stephane Fiset .25 .60
160 Manny Malhotra .25 .60
161 Pavel Bure .50 1.25
162 Chris Drury .30 .75
163 Roberto Luongo .60 1.50
164 Norm Maracle .25 .60
165 Brendan Shanahan .50 1.25
166 Calle Johansson .25 .60
167 Cory Stillman .25 .60
168 Jozef Stumpel .25 .60
169 Ron Tugnutt .30 .75
170 Brian Savage .25 .60
171 Viktor Kozlov .30 .75
172 Chris Simon .25 .60
173 Chris Joseph .25 .60
174 Willie Mitchell RC .40 1.00
175 Randy Robitaille .25 .60
176 Sami Kapanen .25 .60
177 Jonathan Girard .25 .60
178 Andrew Cassels .25 .60
179 Jani Hurme RC .25 .60
180 Maxim Balmochnyk .25 .60
181 Adam Graves .30 .75
182 Steve Shields .25 .60
183 Marc Savard .30 .75
184 Zigmund Palffy .40 1.00
185 Magnus Arvedson .25 .60
186 Byron Dafoe .30 .75
187 Jan Hlavac .25 .60
188 Len Barrie .25 .60
189 Jocelyn Thibault .30 .75
190 Fred Brathwaite .30 .75
191 Fredrik Modin .25 .60
192 Shane Doan .30 .75
193 Petr Mika RC .25 .60
194 Larry Murphy .30 .75
195 Daniel Alfredsson .40 1.00
196 Brenden Morrow .30 .75
197 Martin Rucinsky .25 .60
198 Michal Handzus .25 .60
199 Dominik Hasek .60 1.50
200 Rod Brind'Amour .40 1.00
201 Trevor Letowski .25 .60
202 Derian Hatcher .30 .75
203 Phil Housley .30 .75
204 Martin Biron .30 .75
205 Sergei Berezin .25 .60
206 Ron Francis .50 1.25
207 Cliff Ronning .25 .60
208 Robert Svehla .25 .60
209 Vincent Lecavalier .30 .75
210 Kent Manderville .25 .60
211 Andrew Brunette .25 .60
212 Chris Chelios .40 1.00
213 Alexander Karpovtsev .25 .60
214 Robyn Regehr .25 .60
215 Mika Alatalo .25 .60
216 Jan Hrdina .25 .60
217 Nicklas Lidstrom .40 1.00
218 Ivan Novoseltsev .25 .60
219 Alexander Mogilny .30 .75
220 Chris Pronger .30 .75
221 Paul Coffey .40 1.00
222 John Grahame .25 .60
223 Jeff Farkas .25 .60
224 Eric Lindros .60 1.50
225 Jorgen Jonsson .25 .60
226 Jean-Francois Labbe RC .25 .60
227 Owen Nolan .40 1.00
228 Oleg Saprykin .25 .60
229 Patrick Marleau .40 1.00
230 Aaron Downey RC .25 .60
231 Chris Osgood .40 1.00
232 Mike Wilson .25 .60
233 Joe Sakic .60 1.50
234 Dieter Kochan RC .25 .60
235 Jeremy Roenick .40 1.00
236 Alexei Zhamnov .30 .75
237 Sergei Fedorov .60 1.50
238 Petr Schastlivy .25 .60
239 Milan Hejduk .30 .75
240 Patrice Brisebois .25 .60
241 Marty Reasoner .25 .60
242 Ed Belfour .40 1.00
243 Vitali Vishnevsky .25 .60
244 Keith Tkachuk .40 1.00
245 Petr Buzek .25 .60
246 Miroslav Satan .25 .60
247 Adam Mair .25 .60
248 Jere Karalahti .25 .60
249 Mike Dunham .25 .60
250 Mike Sillinger .25 .60
251 Andrei Skopintsev RC .25 .60
252 S.Vyshedkevich RC .25 .60
253 Steve Duchesne .25 .60
254 Tomas Kaberle .25 .60
255 Arturs Irbe .30 .75
256 Niklas Sundstrom .25 .60
257 Al MacInnis .40 1.00
258 Mike Ribeiro .30 .75
259 Rob Niedermayer .30 .75
260 Jean-Guy Trudel RC .25 .60
261 Martin Straka .30 .75
262 Jason Arnott .30 .75
263 David Legwand .40 1.00
264 Tony Amonte .30 .75
265 Jason Allison .30 .75
266 Patrik Elias .40 1.00
267 Mark Recchi .50 1.25
268 Patrik Stefan .30 .75
269 Mariusz Czerkawski .25 .60
270 Vincent Damphousse .30 .75
271 Sergei Krivokrasov .25 .60
272 Teemu Selanne .75 2.00
273 Patrick Lalime .30 .75
274 Nick Boynton .25 .60
275 Darren McCarty .25 .60
276 Jaroslav Spacek .25 .60
277 Chris Dingman .25 .60
278 Jarome Iginla .40 1.00
279 Andrei Zyuzin .25 .60
280 Jyrki Lumme .25 .60
281 Michal Grosek .25 .60
282 Janne Niinimaa .25 .60
283 Wade Redden .25 .60
284 Ray Bourque .60 1.50
285 Trevor Linden .40 1.00
286 Ladislav Nagy .25 .60
287 Jose Theodore .50 1.25
288 Bates Battaglia .25 .60
289 Mikael Renberg .25 .60
290 Donald Audette .30 .75
291 Doug Gilmour .50 1.25
292 Yanic Perreault .25 .60
293 Anders Eriksson .25 .60
294 Gary Suter .30 .75
295 Brad Ference .25 .60
296 Mats Sundin .40 1.00
297 Ray Ferraro .25 .60
298 Jiri Fischer .25 .60
299 Todd Bertuzzi .30 .75
300 Derek Morris .25 .60
301 Patric Kjellberg .25 .60
302 Pat Verbeek .30 .75
303 Kip Miller .25 .60
304 Alexei Vasilyev .25 .60
305 Marcus Ragnarsson .25 .60
306 Arron Asham .25 .60
307 Sylvain Cote .25 .60
308 Vaclav Prospal .25 .60
309 Aki Berg .25 .60
310 Alexander Selivanov .25 .60
311 Wayne Primeau .25 .60
312 Brian Rafalski .25 .60
313 Jonas Hoglund .25 .60
314 Adam Foote .30 .75
315 Steve Konowalchuk .25 .60
316 Robert Dome .25 .60
317 Antti Laaksonen .25 .60
318 Mike Ricci .30 .75
319 Gino Odjick .25 .60
320 Eric Weinrich .25 .60
321 Jason Strudwick .25 .60
322 Kim Johnsson .25 .60
323 Dimitri Kalinin .25 .60
324 Daymond Langkow .25 .60
325 Todd Marchant .25 .60
326 Richard Matvichuk .25 .60
327 Travis Green .25 .60
328 Igor Larionov .40 1.00
329 Mattias Ohlund .25 .60
330 Igor Kravchuk .25 .60
331 Richard Zednik .25 .60
332 Curtis Brown .25 .60
333 Krzysztof Oliwa .25 .60
334 Darius Kasparaitis .30 .75
335 Michael Nylander .25 .60
336 Stan Drulia .25 .60
337 Nelson Emerson .25 .60
338 Greg Johnson .25 .60
339 Sean Hill .25 .60
340 Keith Jones .25 .60
341 Bill Muckalt .25 .60
342 Randy McKay .25 .60
343 Stu Grimson .25 .60
344 Tyson Nash .25 .60
345 Dan Hinote .25 .60
346 Mike Rathje .25 .60
347 Brian Holzinger .25 .60
348 Eric Nickulas RC .25 .60
349 Alexandre Daigle .30 .75
350 Jan Bulis .25 .60
351 Tom Poti .25 .60
352 Kevyn Adams .25 .60
353 Scott Thornton .30 .75
354 Sean Burke .25 .60
355 Peter Worrell .25 .60
356 Josef Beranek .25 .60
357 Matt Cullen .25 .60
358 Sandy McCarthy .25 .60
359 Sergei Zholtok .25 .60
360 Darren Langdon .25 .60
361 Martin Lapointe .30 .75
362 Adrian Aucoin .25 .60
363 Dmitri Nabokov .25 .60
364 Jason Blake .25 .60
365 Jeff Halpern .25 .60
366 Rico Fata .25 .60
367 Dave Reid .25 .60
368 Vitali Yachmenev .25 .60
369 Hnat Domenichelli .25 .60
370 Rick Tocchet .30 .75
371 Tommy Westlund .25 .60
372 Chris Phillips .25 .60
373 Claude Lemieux .30 .75
374 Greg Adams .25 .60
375 Todd Simpson .25 .60
376 Ken Klee .25 .60
377 Andre Savage .25 .60
378 Bryan Marchment .30 .75
379 Dean McAmmond .25 .60
380 Mike Johnson .25 .60
381 Tomas Holmstrom .30 .75
382 Robert Lang .25 .60
383 Dan McGillis .25 .60
384 Jamie Rivers .25 .60
385 Dave Andreychuk .40 1.00
386 Marty McInnis .30 .75
387 Sami Salo .25 .60
388 Daniel Cleary .30 .75
389 Robert Esche .25 .60
390 Aaron Gavey .25 .60
391 Andrei Nikolishin .25 .60
392 Jason Krog .25 .60
393 Stu Barnes .30 .75
394 Tomas Vokoun .30 .75
395 Peter Schaefer .25 .60
396 Daniil Markov .25 .60
397 Daniel Sedin .75 2.00
398 Kris Beech .25 .60
399 Samuel Pahlsson .25 .60
400 Gary Roberts .25 .60
401 Marian Gaborik RC .75 2.00
402 Oleg Kvasha .25 .60
403 Martin Havlat RC .75 2.00
404 Roman Simicek RC .25 .60
405 Dallas Drake .25 .60
406 Jakub Cutta RC .25 .60
407 German Titov .25 .60
408 Jarno Kultanen RC .25 .60
409 Sandis Ozolinsh .30 .75
410 David Vyborny .25 .60
411 Olli Jokinen .30 .75
412 Maxim Sushinski .25 .60
413 John Vanbiesbrouck .30 .75
414 Shane Hnidy RC .25 .60
415 Milan Kraft .25 .60
416 Alexander Kharitonov RC .25 .60
417 Andrei Nazarov .25 .60
418 Dave Andreychuk .40 1.00
419 Niclas Wallin RC .30 .75
420 Rostislav Klesla RC .60 1.50
421 Denis Shvidki .25 .60
422 Mathieu Garon .25 .60
423 Taylor Pyatt .25 .60
424 Roman Cechmanek RC .30 .75
425 Mark Smith RC .25 .60
426 Shayne Corson .25 .60
427 Jonas Ronnqvist RC .25 .60
428 J-P Dumont .25 .60
429 Josef Vasicek RC .60 1.50
430 Tyler Bouck RC .25 .60
431 Matt Schneider .25 .60
432 Andrei Markov .50 1.25
433 Vladimir Malakhov .25 .60
434 Maxime Ouellet .40 1.00
435 Matt Bradley .25 .60
436 Dave Manson .25 .60
437 Brad Tapper RC .25 .60
438 Eric Boulton RC .25 .60
439 Brent Johnson .30 .75
440 Marty Turco RC .50 1.25
441 Tomas Vlasak .25 .60
442 Greg Classen RC .25 .60
443 Mark Messier .60 1.50
444 Justin Williams RC .60 1.50
445 Sean Hill .25 .60
446 Bryan McCabe .25 .60
447 Andreas Karlsson .25 .60
448 Mika Noronen .25 .60
449 Alexander Karpovtsev .25 .60
450 Boyd Devereaux .25 .60
451 Lubomir Visnovsky RC .50 1.25
452 Scott Hartnell RC .60 1.50
453 Jason Labarbera RC .30 .75
454 Petr Hubacek RC .25 .60
455 Alexander Khavanov RC .25 .60
456 Petr Svoboda RC .30 .75
457 Tomi Kallio .25 .60
458 Mike Vernon .30 .75
459 Reto Von Arx RC .30 .75
460 Maxim Kuznetsov .30 .75
461 Steven Reinprecht RC .40 1.00
462 Turner Stevenson .25 .60
463 Roberto Luongo .60 1.50
464 Brad Richards .40 1.00
465 Bryce Salvador RC .30 .75
466 Kevin Hatcher .25 .60
467 Paul Coffey .40 1.00
468 Marty Murray .25 .60
469 Todd Fedoruk RC .25 .60
470 Brian Swanson RC .25 .60
471 Christian Matte .25 .60
472 Sascha Goc RC .25 .60
473 Dale Purinton RC .25 .60
474 Brad May .25 .60
475 Brad Brown .30 .75
476 Petteri Nummelin RC .25 .60
477 Ruslan Fedotenko RC .25 .60
478 Ronald Petrovicky RC .25 .60
479 David Aebischer RC .50 1.25
480 Michel Riesen RC .30 .75
481 Ladislav Benysek RC .25 .60
482 Mark Parrish .25 .60
483 Mike Mottau .25 .60
484 Ossi Vaananen RC .30 .75
485 Andrew Raycroft RC .60 1.50
486 Sylvain Cote .25 .60
487 Richard Jackman .25 .60
488 Toni Lydman .25 .60
489 Ron Tugnutt .30 .75
490 Igor Larionov .40 1.00
491 Lubomir Sekeras RC .25 .60
492 Roman Hamrlik .30 .75
493 Johan Holmqvist RC .25 .60
494 Josef Melichar RC .25 .60
495 Sheldon Keefe .25 .60
496 Henrik Sedin .60 1.50
497 Rick DiPietro RC 1.00 2.50
498 Teemu Selanne .75 2.00
499 Keith Tkachuk .40 1.00
500 Rob Blake .40 1.00
501 Mario Lemieux 1.25 3.00
502 Johan Hedberg RC .30 .75
503 Felix Potvin .60 1.50
504 Branislav Mezei .25 .60
505 Mike Comrie RC .60 1.50
506 Miikka Kiprusoff .40 1.00
507 Petr Tenkrat RC .25 .60
508 Mark Bell .25 .60
509 Steve Gainey RC .25 .60
510 Jason Williams RC .40 1.00
511 Shawn Horcoff RC .50 1.25
512 Eric Chouinard .25 .60
513 Derek Gustafson RC .25 .60
514 Bryan Allen .25 .60
515 Kristian Kudroc .25 .60
516 Gregg Naumenko RC .25 .60
517 Pierre Dagenais .25 .60
518 Juraj Kolnik RC .25 .60
519 Tomas Kloucek RC .25 .60
520 Andreas Lilja RC .25 .60
521 Alexei Ponikarovsky RC .40 1.00
NNO Trevor Linden AU 15.00 25.00

2000-01 BAP Memorabilia Ruby

*RUBY/200: 2.5X TO 6X BASIC CARDS
STATED PRINT RUN 200 SER.#'d SETS

2000-01 BAP Memorabilia Sapphire

*SAPPHIRE/100: 4X TO 10X BASIC CARDS
STATED PRINT RUN 100 SER.#'d SETS

2000-01 BAP Memorabilia All-Star Tickets

Randomly seeded in packs at the rate of 1:864, this 10-card set featured swatches of All-Star Game tickets with the respective year's All-Star Game logo faded into the background.
COMPLETE SET (10) 150.00 300.00
STATED ODDS 1:864
AST1 1990 All-Star Game 12.50 30.00
AST2 1991 All-Star Game 12.50 30.00
AST3 1992 All-Star Game 12.50 30.00
AST4 1993 All-Star Game 12.50 30.00
AST5 1994 All-Star Game 12.50 30.00
AST6 1996 All-Star Game 12.50 30.00
AST7 1997 All-Star Game 12.50 30.00
AST8 1998 All-Star Game 12.50 30.00
AST9 1999 All-Star Game 12.50 30.00
AST10 2000 All-Star Game 12.50 30.00

2000-01 BAP Memorabilia Georges Vezina

Randomly inserted in packs at the rate of 1:2400, this 16-card set features today's top goalies coupled with a swatch of a Georges Vezina goalie pad. The Vezina pad used was believed to be the only one in existance.
V1 Olaf Kolzig 125.00 250.00
V2 Dominik Hasek 150.00 300.00
V3 Dominik Hasek 150.00 300.00
V4 Dominik Hasek 150.00 300.00
V5 Jim Carey 125.00 250.00
V6 Dominik Hasek 150.00 300.00
V7 Dominik Hasek 150.00 300.00
V8 Ed Belfour 125.00 250.00
V9 Patrick Roy 225.00 400.00
V10 Ed Belfour 125.00 250.00
V11 Patrick Roy 225.00 400.00
V12 Patrick Roy 225.00 400.00
V13 Grant Fuhr 125.00 250.00
V14 John Vanbiesbrouck 125.00 250.00
V15 Tom Barrasso 125.00 250.00
V16 Georges Vezina 500.00 800.00

2000-01 BAP Memorabilia Goalie Memorabilia

Randomly inserted in packs at the rate of 1:999, this 30-card set featured swatches of goalie worn jerseys, sticks, pads and gloves. Cards G1-G11 were single player cards with two swatches of memorabilia, card numbers G12-G28 were dual player cards with two swatches of memorabilia, and card numbers G29 and G30 were triple player cards with three swatches of memorabilia.
STATED ODDS 1:999
G1 Mike Richter J/S 20.00 50.00
G2 Patrick Roy G/S 100.00 200.00
G3 Dominik Hasek G/S 75.00 150.00
G4 Ed Belfour J/S 20.00 50.00
G5 Curtis Joseph G/S 25.00 60.00
G6 Terry Sawchuk G/S 75.00 150.00
G7 Vladislav Tretiak J/G 100.00 200.00

G8 Gerry Cheevers S/P 20.00 50.00
G9 Felix Potvin G/J 25.00 60.00
G10 Frank Brimsek G/J 20.00 50.00
G11 Bernie Parent P/J 20.00 50.00
G12 B.Parent/T.Esposito J/J 40.00 100.00
G13 J.Bower/C.Joseph S/S 75.00 150.00
G14 Brimsek/Cheevers G/S 40.00 100.00
G15 P.Roy/J.Plante S/G 75.00 150.00
G16 V.Tretiak/T.Esposito J/J 75.00 150.00
G17 Sawchuk/C.Joseph S/J 75.00 150.00
G18 T.Broda/C.Joseph G/J 40.00 100.00
G19 J.Bower/T.Broda S/G 40.00 100.00
G20 F.Potvin/C.Joseph G/S 75.00 150.00
G21 E.Belfour/P.Roy J/J 40.00 100.00
G22 E.Belfour/V.Tretiak J/J 40.00 100.00
G23 Sawchuk/J.Plante S/G 100.00 200.00
G24 J.Bower/T.Sawchuk S/S 75.00 150.00
G25 T.Esposito/Cheevers S/S 25.00 60.00
G26 F.Brimsek/Cheevers G/P 30.00 80.00
G27 C.Joseph/T.Broda G/G 40.00 100.00
G28 P.Roy/T.Sawchuk G/G 100.00 200.00
G29 Joseph/Bower/Sawch S 75.00 150.00
G30 Cheev/Parent/Espo S 75.00 150.00

2000-01 BAP Memorabilia Jersey

STATED ODDS 1:360
*NUMBERS: .6X TO 1.5X JERSEY CARDS
*JSY/STICK: .5X TO 1.2X BASIC JSY
*EMBLEMS: .8X TO 2X BASIC JSY
J1 Jeremy Roenick 8.00 20.00
J2 Mats Sundin 8.00 20.00
J3 Pavel Bure 10.00 25.00
J4 Martin Brodeur 15.00 40.00
J5 Mike Richter 8.00 20.00
J6 Brendan Shanahan 10.00 25.00
J7 Chris Pronger 6.00 15.00
J8 Al MacInnis 8.00 20.00
J9 Jaromir Jagr 20.00 50.00
J10 Olaf Kolzig 8.00 20.00
J11 Tony Amonte 6.00 15.00
J12 Scott Stevens 8.00 20.00
J13 Dominik Hasek 12.00 30.00
J14 Peter Forsberg 10.00 25.00
J15 Teemu Selanne 15.00 40.00
J16 Eric Lindros 12.00 30.00
J17 Nicklas Lidstrom 8.00 20.00
J18 Theo Fleury 10.00 25.00
J19 Darryl Sydor 6.00 15.00
J20 Mike Modano 12.00 30.00
J21 Nikolai Khabibulin 12.00 30.00
J22 Sandis Ozolinsh 6.00 15.00
J23 Mark Messier 12.00 30.00
J24 Joe Sakic 12.00 30.00
J25 Wayne Gretzky 40.00 100.00
J26 Owen Nolan 8.00 20.00
J27 Daniel Alfredsson 8.00 20.00
J28 Paul Coffey 8.00 20.00
J29 Steve Yzerman 25.00 60.00
J30 Brett Hull 12.00 30.00
J31 Paul Kariya 10.00 25.00
J32 John LeClair 8.00 20.00
J33 Ed Belfour 8.00 20.00
J34 Patrick Roy 20.00 50.00
J35 Sergei Fedorov 12.00 30.00
J36 Mark Recchi 10.00 25.00
J37 Ray Bourque 12.00 30.00
J38 Brian Leetch 8.00 20.00
J39 Rob Blake 8.00 20.00
J40 Curtis Joseph 10.00 25.00

2000-01 BAP Memorabilia Mario Lemieux Legends

Randomly inserted in packs at the rate of 1:4800, this 10-card set featured game-used memorabilia swatches from Mario Lemieux. Memorabilia combinations are listed below. The stated print run on each card was an estimated 30 sets.
STATED ODDS 1:2400
STATED PRINT RUN 30 SETS
L1 1987-88 Jsy 50.00 125.00
L2 1991-92 Jsy 50.00 125.00
L3 1987 Jsy 1991 Glove 60.00 150.00
L4 1991-92 Jsy-Glove 60.00 150.00
L5 1991-92 Jsy Emblem 90.00 150.00
L6 1991-92 Jsy Number 50.00 125.00
L7 1991-92 Glove 50.00 125.00
L8 1996 AS Jsy 50.00 125.00
L9 1987 Jsy/1996 AS Jsy 60.00 150.00
L10 1991 Jsy/1996 Jsy 90.00 150.00

2000-01 BAP Memorabilia Patent Power Jerseys

STATED ODDS 1:4800
PP1 M.Lemieux/W.Gretzky 200.00 350.00
PP2 P.Kariya/S.Yzerman 60.00 120.00
PP3 P.Bure/J.Jagr 30.00 80.00
PP4 M.Sundin/P.Forsberg 20.00 50.00
PP5 T.Selanne/B.Hull 30.00 80.00
PP6 B.Shanahan/J.LeClair 30.00 80.00

2000-01 BAP Memorabilia Update Heritage Jerseys

Inserts were placed in the Be A Player Memorabilia Update set on top of the sealed 100 cards along with the DiPietro Rookie card. Sets contained either four random insert cards, or one memorabilia card. Memorabilia cards were inserted at approximately one in five sets. The Heritage Jersey Cards featured a gold background, full color player action photography and a swatch of a game-used jersey in the upper right hand corner of the card front. Gold parallels numbered 1/1 were also created and inserted randomly, but are not priced due to scarcity.
MEMORABILIA STATED ODDS 1:5 FACT.SETS
H1 Mark Messier 12.00 30.00
H2 Pavel Bure 15.00 40.00
H3 Paul Coffey 15.00 40.00
H4 Mats Sundin 15.00 40.00
H5 Curtis Joseph 15.00 40.00
H6 Ed Belfour 15.00 40.00
H7 Mike Modano 20.00 50.00
H8 Brett Hull 15.00 40.00
H9 Teemu Selanne 20.00 50.00
H10 Keith Tkachuk 10.00 25.00
H11 Patrick Roy 30.00 80.00
H12 Chris Chelios 10.00 25.00
H13 Al MacInnis 10.00 25.00
H14 Theo Fleury 10.00 25.00
H15 Keith Primeau 10.00 25.00
H16 Ray Bourque 20.00 50.00
H17 Brendan Shanahan 20.00 50.00
H18 Owen Nolan 10.00 25.00
H19 Felix Potvin 20.00 50.00
H20 Trevor Linden 15.00 40.00
H21 Scott Stevens 10.00 25.00
H22 Adam Oates 10.00 25.00

2000-01 BAP Memorabilia Update Record Breakers

Inserts were placed in the Be A Player Memorabilia Update set on top of the sealed 100 cards along with the DiPietro Rookie card. Sets contained either four random insert cards, or one memorabilia card. Memorabilia cards were inserted at approximately one in five sets. This 2-card set featured full color player action photography on a white card stock with two swatches of game used memorabilia. Gold parallels numbered 1/1 were also created and inserted randomly, but are not priced due to scarcity.
MEMORABILIA STATED ODDS 1:5 FACT.SETS
BB1 P.Bure/V.Bure 25.00 60.00
RB1 P.Roy/T.Sawchuk/33 100.00 250.00

2000-01 BAP Memorabilia Update Teammates

MEMORABILIA STATED ODDS 1:5 FACT.SETS
TM1 P.Sykora/M.Brodeur 15.00 40.00
TM2 S.Gonchar/A.Oates 10.00 25.00
TM3 J.Jagr/M.Lemieux 40.00 100.00
TM4 T.Amonte/B.Probert 12.50 30.00
TM5 J.Roenick/K.Tkachuk 10.00 25.00
TM6 M.Peca/D.Hasek 10.00 25.00
TM7 M.Messier/B.Leetch 20.00 50.00
TM8 P.Bure/P.Laus 10.00 25.00
TM9 T.Domi/M.Sundin 10.00 25.00
TM10 M.Brodeur/S.Niedermayer 20.00 50.00
TM11 K.McLaren/B.Dafoe 10.00 25.00
TM12 N.Lidstrom/C.Chelios 20.00 50.00
TM13 D.McCarty/S.Yzerman 20.00 50.00
TM14 D.Sydor/E.Belfour 10.00 25.00
TM15 B.Hull/M.Modano 12.00 30.00
TM16 B.Shanahan/S.Fedorov 20.00 50.00
TM17 N.Lidstrom/S.Kozlov 10.00 25.00
TM18 P.Roy/P.Forsberg 40.00 100.00
TM19 M.Richter/T.Fleury 10.00 25.00
TM20 M.Straka/J.Jagr 10.00 25.00
TM21 J.Arnott/S.Stevens 10.00 25.00
TM22 B.Shanahan/C.Osgood 10.00 25.00
TM23 P.Kariya/G.Hebert 10.00 25.00
TM24 C.Joseph/M.Sundin 10.00 25.00
TM25 T.Amonte/E.Daze 10.00 25.00
TM26 T.Selanne/P.Kariya 10.00 25.00
TM27 P.Sykora/J.Arnott 10.00 25.00
TM28 P.Roy/J.Sakic 30.00 80.00
TM29 S.Yzerman/S.Fedorov 20.00 50.00
TM30 K.Tkachuk/T.Numminen 10.00 25.00
TM31 S.Niedermayer/S.Stevens 10.00 25.00
TM32 M.Messier/M.Richter 10.00 25.00
TM33 T.Numminen/N.Khabibulin 10.00 25.00
TM34 P.Forsberg/J.Sakic 20.00 50.00
TM35 C.Osgood/S.Kozlov 10.00 25.00
TM36 E.Belfour/M.Modano 12.50 30.00
TM37 T.Domi/C.Joseph 10.00 25.00
TM38 J.Roenick/N.Khabibulin 10.00 25.00
TM39 G.Hebert/T.Selanne 10.00 25.00
TM40 T.Fleury/B.Leetch 10.00 25.00

2000-01 BAP Memorabilia Update Tough Materials

MEMORABILIA STATED ODDS 1:5 FACT.SETS
T1 Bob Probert 20.00 50.00
T2 Tie Domi 30.00 80.00
T3 Stu Grimson 25.00 60.00
T4 Eric Cairns 8.00 20.00
T5 Paul Laus 8.00 20.00
T6 Donald Brashear 15.00 40.00
T7 Rob Ray 15.00 40.00
T8 Wade Belak 8.00 20.00
T9 Kelly Chase 8.00 20.00
T10 Peter Worrell 8.00 20.00
T11 Darren McCarty 20.00 50.00
T12 Todd Simpson 8.00 20.00
T13 Krzysztof Oliwa 12.00 30.00
T14 Sandy McCarthy 8.00 20.00
T15 Brad Brown 8.00 20.00
T16 Luke Richardson 8.00 20.00
T17 Jeff Odgers 8.00 20.00
T18 Chris Dingman 8.00 20.00
T19 Enrico Ciccone 8.00 20.00
T20 Ryan VandenBussche 12.00 30.00
T21 Bob Boughner 8.00 20.00
T22 Gino Odjick 8.00 20.00
T23 Matt Johnson 8.00 20.00
T24 Jean-Luc Grand-Pierre 8.00 20.00
T25 Craig Berube 15.00 40.00
T26 Ian Laperriere 8.00 20.00

2001-02 BAP Memorabilia

Released in August 2001, this 300-card set featured color action photos on gray and black bordered card fronts. The final 200-cards were released in BAP Update packs.
COMPLETE SET (500) 75.00 200.00
COMP.SERIES 1 (300) 30.00 80.00
1 Rick DiPietro .15 .40
2 Radek Dvorak .15 .40
3 Radek Bonk .12 .30
4 Evgeni Nabokov .15 .40
5 Roman Turek .15 .40
6 Daniel Sedin .20 .50
7 Jeff Halpern .12 .30
8 Joe Thornton .25 .60
9 Maxim Afinogenov .12 .30
10 Oleg Saprykin .12 .30
11 Shane Willis .12 .30
12 Jocelyn Thibault .15 .40
13 Alex Tanguay .15 .40
14 Brenden Morrow .15 .40
15 Steve Yzerman .60 1.50
16 Anson Carter .15 .40
17 Brad Richards .20 .50
18 Mike York .12 .30
19 Brian Rafalski .12 .30
20 Maxime Ouellet .20 .50
21 Ruslan Fedotenko .12 .30
22 Brad Stuart .12 .30
23 Daniel Corso .12 .30
24 Mika Noronen .12 .30
25 Jason Williams .12 .30
26 Scott Stevens .20 .50
27 Patrick Lalime .15 .40
28 Johan Hedberg .15 .40
29 Vincent Damphousse .15 .40
30 Jochen Hecht .12 .30
31 Ed Jovanovski .15 .40
32 Jean-Sebastien Giguere .15 .40
33 Fred Brathwaite .15 .40
34 Arturs Irbe .15 .40
35 Ron Tugnutt .15 .40
36 Ed Belfour .20 .50
37 Chris Osgood .20 .50
38 Mike Comrie .15 .40
39 Aaron Miller .12 .30
40 Martin Brodeur .40 1.00
41 Martin Havlat .15 .40
42 Roman Cechmanek .15 .40
43 Teppo Numminen .12 .30
44 Milan Kraft .12 .30
45 Pavol Demitra .25 .60
46 Henrik Sedin .20 .50
47 Byron Dafoe .15 .40
48 Dave Tanabe .12 .30
49 Chris Drury .15 .40
50 Tommy Salo .15 .40
51 Lubomir Visnovsky .12 .30
52 Andrei Markov .20 .50
53 Jason Arnott .15 .40
54 Adam Foote .15 .40
55 Vitali Vishnevski .12 .30
56 Ville Nieminen .12 .30
57 Mike Mottau .12 .30
58 Brendan Morrison .15 .40
59 Lee Goren .12 .30
60 Scott Gomez .15 .40
61 Tim Connolly .12 .30
62 Daniel Alfredsson .20 .50
63 Owen Nolan .20 .50
64 Chris Pronger .15 .40
65 Fredrik Modin .12 .30
66 Mario Lemieux .60 1.50
67 Olaf Kolzig .20 .50
68 Jeff Friesen .12 .30
69 Patrik Stefan .15 .40
70 Sergei Samsonov .15 .40
71 J-P Dumont .12 .30
72 Sandis Ozolinsh .12 .30
73 Milan Hejduk .15 .40
74 Sergei Zubov .15 .40
75 Sergei Fedorov .30 .75
76 Janne Niinimaa .12 .30
77 Roberto Luongo .30 .75
78 Felix Potvin .30 .75
79 Petr Sykora .12 .30
80 Petr Nedved .15 .40
81 Shawn McEachern .12 .30
82 Simon Gagne .20 .50
83 Sean Burke .12 .30
84 Al MacInnis .20 .50
85 Vincent Lecavalier .15 .40
86 Sergei Gonchar .12 .30
87 Oleg Tverdovsky .12 .30
88 Bill Guerin .20 .50
89 Miroslav Satan .15 .40
90 Marc Savard .12 .30
91 Peter Forsberg .25 .60
92 Brett Hull .25 .60
93 Nicklas Lidstrom .20 .50
94 Ryan Smyth .15 .40
95 Luc Robitaille .20 .50
96 Alexander Mogilny .15 .40
97 Mark Messier .30 .75
98 Marian Hossa .15 .40
99 Keith Primeau .15 .40
100 Todd Bertuzzi .20 .50
101 Justin Williams .12 .30
102 Ossi Vaananen .12 .30
103 Robert Lang .12 .30
104 Pavel Bure .25 .60
105 Tomas Kaberle .12 .30
106 Nikolai Antropov .12 .30
107 Tomi Kallio .12 .30
108 David Vyborny .12 .30
109 Denis Shvidki .12 .30
110 Jozef Stumpel .12 .30
111 Dimitri Kalinin .12 .30
112 Stephane Robidas .12 .30
113 Scott Walker .12 .30
114 Jamie Langenbrunner .12 .30
115 Maxim Kuznetsov .12 .30
116 Mike Grier .12 .30
117 Michael Nylander .12 .30
118 Derian Hatcher .12 .30
119 Scott Niedermayer .12 .30
120 Petr Schastlivy .12 .30
121 Tomas Divisek RC .30 .75
122 Toby Petersen .12 .30
123 Jarkko Ruutu .12 .30
124 Chris Chelios .20 .50
125 Andrew Raycroft .15 .40
126 Jason Woolley .12 .30
127 Derek Morris .12 .30
128 David Legwand .15 .40
129 Jaromir Jagr .50 1.25
130 Serge Aubin .12 .30
131 Jere Lehtinen .12 .30
132 Manny Legace .15 .40
133 Patrick Roy .50 1.25
134 Glen Murray .15 .40
135 Jan Bulis .12 .30
136 Mike Dunham .15 .40
137 Jan Hlavac .12 .30
138 Wade Redden .12 .30
139 Jan Hrdina .12 .30
140 Keith Tkachuk .20 .50
141 Yanic Perreault .12 .30
142 Jonas Ronnqvist .12 .30
143 John Madden .15 .40
144 Jani Hurme .15 .40
145 Chris Gratton .12 .30
146 Toni Lydman .12 .30
147 Mike Modano .30 .75
148 Boris Mironov .12 .30
149 Joe Sakic .30 .75
150 Chris Nielsen .12 .30
151 Marty Turco .20 .50
152 Bryan Smolinski .12 .30
153 Daniel Cleary .15 .40
154 Anders Eriksson .12 .30
155 Pierre Dagenais .12 .30
156 Wes Walz .12 .30
157 Brian Savage .12 .30
158 Stu Barnes .12 .30
159 Eric Desjardins .15 .40
160 Juraj Kolnik .12 .30
161 Brendan Shanahan .25 .60
162 Karel Rachunek .12 .30
163 Marc Denis .12 .30
164 Martin Straka .12 .30
165 Alexander Kharitonov .12 .30
166 Sergei Brylin .12 .30
167 Eric Daze .20 .50
168 Alexei Kovalev .15 .40
169 Jiri Slegr .12 .30
170 Brian Rolston .12 .30
171 Phil Housley .12 .30
172 Josef Vasicek .12 .30
173 Patrick Marleau .20 .50
174 Steven Reinprecht .12 .30
175 Gary Roberts .12 .30
176 Darryl Sydor .12 .30
177 Michel Riesen .12 .30
178 Kevyn Adams .12 .30
179 Andreas Lilja .12 .30
180 Roman Hamrlik .12 .30
181 Mathieu Garon .15 .40
182 Scott Hartnell .20 .50
183 Kenny Jonsson .12 .30
184 Jeff Ulmer .12 .30
185 Petr Hubacek .12 .30
186 Jeremy Roenick .20 .50
187 Scott Young .12 .30
188 Sergei Berezin .12 .30
189 Steve Konowalchuk .12 .30
190 Curtis Joseph .20 .50
191 Jonathan Girard .12 .30
192 Brian Campbell .12 .30
193 Markus Naslund .20 .50
194 David Aebischer .15 .40
195 Peter Bondra .20 .50
196 Paul Kariya .25 .60
197 Jason Allison .15 .40
198 Dominik Hasek .30 .75
199 Branislav Mezei .12 .30
200 Peter Smrek RC .25 .60
201 Miikka Kiprusoff .20 .50
202 Kristian Kudroc .12 .30
203 Kyle McLaren .12 .30
204 Calle Johansson .15 .40
205 Gregg Naumenko .12 .30
206 Damian Rhodes .15 .40
207 Willie Mitchell .12 .30
208 Daniel Tkaczuk .12 .30
209 Mike Ribeiro .15 .40
210 Rostislav Klesla .12 .30
211 Denis Arkhipov .12 .30
212 Andy McDonald .12 .30
213 Ivan Novoseltsev .12 .30
214 Manny Fernandez .15 .40
215 Reto Von Arx .12 .30
216 Ray Bourque .30 .75
217 Mike Jefferson RC .25 .60
218 Jason Chimera RC .25 .60
219 Mattias Ohlund .12 .30
220 Rico Fata .12 .30
221 Brad Tapper .12 .30
222 Mike Richter .20 .50
223 Nick Boynton .12 .30
224 Harold Druken .12 .30
225 Chris Clark .12 .30
226 Colin White .12 .30
227 Tyler Bouck .12 .30
228 Jesse Wallin .12 .30
229 Jeff Hackett .15 .40
230 Greg Classen .12 .30
231 Adam Mair .12 .30
232 Ivan Ciernik RC .25 .60
233 Marc Chouinard .12 .30
234 Chris Mason .12 .30
235 Ronald Petrovicky .12 .30
236 Kyle Calder .12 .30
237 Rick Berry .12 .30
238 Mathieu Darche RC .40 1.00
239 Theo Fleury .25 .60
240 Mike Commodore .12 .30
241 Michal Handzus .12 .30
242 Bill Tibbetts RC .25 .60
243 Cory Stillman .12 .30
244 Valeri Bure .12 .30
245 Matt Pettinger .12 .30
246 Rod Brind'Amour .20 .50
247 Pascal Dupuis RC .40 1.00
248 Martin Rucinsky .12 .30
249 Cliff Ronning .12 .30
250 Brad Isbister .12 .30
251 Anti-Jussi Niemi .12 .30
252 Mark Bell .12 .30
253 Martin Spanhel RC .25 .60
254 Andrew Cassels .12 .30
255 Andrew Brunette .12 .30
256 Ron Francis .25 .60
257 Tony Amonte .15 .40
258 Espen Knutsen .12 .30
259 Viktor Kozlov .12 .30
260 Sergei Krivokrasov .12 .30
261 Richard Zednik .15 .40
262 Bubba Berenzweig .12 .30
263 Pavel Patera .12 .30
264 Mike Johnson .12 .30
265 Teemu Selanne .40 1.00
266 John LeClair .20 .50
267 Adam Deadmarsh .15 .40
268 Herbert Vasilijevs .12 .30
269 Steven McCarthy .12 .30
270 Mathieu Schneider .12 .30
271 Peter Bartos .12 .30
272 Ray Ferraro .12 .30
273 Eric Chouinard .12 .30
274 Marian Cisar .12 .30
275 Jarome Iginla .20 .50
276 Jeff O'Neill .12 .30
277 Steve Sullivan .12 .30
278 Rob Blake .20 .50
279 Geoff Sanderson .12 .30
280 Niclas Wallin .12 .30
281 Vitali Yeremeyev .12 .30
282 Doug Weight .20 .50
283 Martin Skoula .15 .40
284 Zigmund Palffy .20 .50
285 Marian Gaborik .30 .75
286 Saku Koivu .20 .50
287 Joe Nieuwendyk .20 .50
288 Patrik Elias .20 .50
289 Mariusz Czerkawski .12 .30
290 Brian Leetch .20 .50
291 Alexei Yashin .15 .40
292 Mark Recchi .20 .50
293 Shane Doan .15 .40
294 Brian Holzinger .12 .30
295 Mikael Samuelsson RC .30 .75
296 Pierre Turgeon .20 .50
297 Sheldon Keefe .12 .30
298 Mats Sundin .20 .50
299 Bryan Allen .12 .30
300 Adam Oates .20 .50
301 Ilja Bryzgalov RC .60 1.50
302 Erik Cole RC .50 1.25
303 Pavel Datsyuk RC 2.00 5.00
304 Nikolai Khabibulin .20 .50
305 Dan Blackburn RC .30 .75
306 Jeff Jillson RC .25 .60
307 Brian Sutherby RC .25 .60
308 Vaclav Nedorost RC .25 .60
309 Byron Ritchie .12 .30
310 Martin Erat RC .40 1.00
311 Vaclav Pletka RC .25 .60
312 Karel Pilar RC .25 .60
313 Jaroslav Obsut RC .25 .60
314 Jason Allison .15 .40
315 Eric Lindros .30 .75
316 Mike Farrell RC .25 .60
317 Doug Gilmour .25 .60
318 Bruno St. Jacques RC .25 .60
319 Martin Lapointe .12 .30
320 Dan Focht RC .25 .60
321 Ben Simon RC .30 .75
322 Mike Peluso RC .25 .60
323 Martin Cibak RC .25 .60
324 Marcel Hossa RC .40 1.00
325 Chris Neil .15 .40
326 Mark Rycroft RC .30 .75
327 Timo Parssinen RC .30 .75
328 Sebastien Charpentier RC .25 .60
329 Kip Brennan RC .25 .60
330 Christian Berglund RC .30 .75
331 Tom Kostopoulos RC .25 .60
332 Pat Kavanagh RC .30 .75
333 Sebastien Centomo RC .25 .60
334 Andrew Brunette .12 .30
335 Toni Dahlman RC .25 .60
336 Kamil Piros RC .25 .60
337 Robert Schnabel RC .25 .60
338 Radim Vrbata .12 .30
339 Chris Osgood .20 .50
340 Steve Montador RC .25 .60
341 Reinhard Divis RC .25 .60
342 Steve Moore RC .40 1.00
343 Branko Radivojevic RC .25 .60
344 Zdenek Kutlak RC .25 .60
345 Jiri Dopita RC .25 .60
346 Josef Boumedienne RC .25 .60
347 Phil Housley .15 .40
348 Niko Kapanen RC .40 1.00
349 Travis Roche RC .25 .60
350 Raffi Torres RC .40 1.00
351 Randy Robitaille .12 .30
352 Chris Corrinet RC .25 .60
353 Pierre Turgeon .20 .50
354 Pavel Skrbek RC .25 .60
355 Jeremy Roenick .20 .50
356 Riku Hahl RC .25 .60
357 Stanislav Gron RC .25 .60
358 Pasi Nurminen RC .25 .60
359 Nick Smith RC .25 .60
360 Shane Endicott RC .25 .60
361 Ales Kotalik RC .50 1.25
362 Blake Bellefeuille RC .25 .60
363 Jaroslav Bednar RC .25 .60
364 Andreas Salomonsson RC .25 .60
365 Krystofer Kolanos RC .25 .60
366 Tim Connolly .12 .30
367 Ivan Huml RC .25 .60
368 Sean Avery RC .25 .60
369 Trent Hunter RC .50 1.25
370 Richard Scott RC .25 .60
371 Doug Weight .20 .50
372 Ilya Kovalchuk RC 1.25 3.00
373 Dominik Hasek .30 .75
374 Scott Clemmensen RC .25 .60
375 Nikita Alexeev RC .25 .60
376 Luc Robitaille .20 .50
377 Mike Peca .15 .40
378 Brett Hull .25 .60
379 Valeri Bure .12 .30
380 Pavel Brendl .12 .30
381 Jukka Hentunen RC .25 .60
382 John Erskine RC .25 .60
383 Nick Schultz RC .25 .60
384 Radek Martinek RC .25 .60
385 Dany Heatley .20 .50
386 Alex Auld .25 .60
387 Tyler Arnason RC .30 .75
388 Ty Conklin RC .40 1.00
389 Olivier Michaud RC .40 1.00
390 Sandis Ozolinsh .12 .30
391 Evgeny Konstantinov RC .25 .60
392 Roman Turek .15 .40
393 Kristian Huselius RC .40 1.00
394 Alexei Yashin .15 .40
395 Alexander Mogilny .15 .40
396 Eric Meloche RC .25 .60
397 Andy McDonald .12 .30
398 Niklas Hagman RC .30 .75
399 Ryan Flinn RC .25 .60
400 Mike Weaver RC .25 .60
401 Nolan Yonkman .12 .30
402 Ryan Jardine .12 .30
403 Andrej Nedorost RC .25 .60
404 Andrej Podkonicky RC .25 .60
405 Hnat Domenichelli .12 .30
406 Bob Wren RC .25 .60
407 Brad Norton RC .25 .60
408 Brian Pothier RC .25 .60
409 Trevor Letowski .12 .30
410 Chris Bala RC .25 .60
411 Tom Fitzgerald .12 .30
412 Petr Tenkrat .12 .30
413 Dan Snyder RC .30 .75
414 David Cullen RC .25 .60
415 David Ling RC .25 .60
416 Dean Melanson RC .25 .60
417 Duvie Westcott RC .25 .60
418 Eric Beaudoin RC .25 .60
419 Marty McInnis .15 .40
420 Francis Lessard RC .25 .60
421 Frederic Cassivi RC .25 .60
422 Bill Lindsay .12 .30
423 Kim Johnsson .12 .30
424 Daniil Markov .12 .30
425 Guillaume Lefebvre RC .25 .60
426 Hannes Hyvonen RC .25 .60
427 Jeff Daw RC .25 .60
428 Jody Shelley RC .30 .75
429 Joel Kwiatkowski RC .25 .60
430 Josh Langfeld RC .25 .60
431 Kelly Fairchild RC .25 .60
432 Kevin Sawyer RC .25 .60
433 Kriby Law RC .25 .60
434 Kyle Rossiter RC .25 .60
435 Lukas Krajicek RC .25 .60
436 Mark Hartigan RC .25 .60
437 Martin Prusek RC .25 .60
438 Matt Davidson RC .25 .60
439 Andre Roy .12 .30
440 Chris Kelleher RC .25 .60
441 Mike Matteucci RC .25 .60
442 Nathan Perrott RC .25 .60
443 Neil Little RC .25 .60
444 Rocky Thompson RC .25 .60
445 Ryan Tobler RC .30 .75
446 Scott Nichol RC .25 .60
447 Jiri Slegr .12 .30
448 Stephen Weiss RC .60 1.50
449 Jeff Cowan .12 .30
450 Thomas Ziegler RC .30 .75
451 Todd Rohloff RC .25 .60
452 Blake Sloan .12 .30
453 Tony Tuzzolino RC .25 .60
454 Tony Virta RC .25 .60
455 Adam Oates .20 .50
456 Benoit Brunet .12 .30
457 Benoit Hogue .12 .30
458 Brian Savage .12 .30
459 Cliff Ronning .12 .30
460 Darius Kasparaitis .12 .30
461 Dean McAmmond .12 .30
462 Donald Brashear .12 .30
463 Glen Murray .15 .40
464 Jamie Allison .12 .30
465 Jamie Langenbrunner .12 .30
466 Jan Hlavac .12 .30
467 Jason Arnott .15 .40
468 Joe Nieuwendyk .20 .50
469 Jozef Stumpel .12 .30
470 Juha Ylonen .12 .30
471 Kevin Weekes .15 .40
472 Kirill Safronov .12 .30
473 Manny Malhotra .15 .40
474 Martin Rucinsky .12 .30
475 Matthew Barnaby .12 .30
476 Mike Keane .15 .40
477 Mike York .12 .30
478 Mikko Eloranta .12 .30
479 Pascal Rheaume .12 .30
480 Pavel Bure .25 .60
481 Pierre Dagenais .12 .30
482 Randy McKay .12 .30
483 Ray Ferraro .12 .30
484 Rem Murray .15 .40
485 Rick Berry .12 .30
486 Sean Brown .12 .30
487 Sean Hill .12 .30
488 Sergei Berezin .12 .30
489 Shane Willis .12 .30
490 Stephane Fiset .15 .40
491 Stephane Richer .12 .30
492 Steve Thomas .12 .30
493 Tom Barrasso .15 .40
494 Tom Poti .12 .30
495 Trevor Linden .20 .50
496 Valeri Kamensky .12 .30
497 Ville Nieminen .12 .30
498 Zdeno Chara .20 .50
499 Shjon Podein .12 .30
500 Shaun Van Allen .12 .30

2001-02 BAP Memorabilia Ruby

*VETS/200: 3X TO 8X BASIC CARDS
*ROOKIES/200: 2X TO 5X BASIC RC
RUBY PRINT RUN 200 SER.#'d SETS
97 Mark Messier 4.00 10.00

2001-02 BAP Memorabilia Sapphire

*VETS/100: 5X TO 12X BASIC CARDS
*ROOKIES/100: 3X TO 8X BASIC RC
STATED PRINT RUN 100 SER.#'d SETS
6 Daniel Sedin 4.00 10.00
97 Mark Messier 6.00 15.00

2001-02 BAP Memorabilia All-Star Jerseys

ANNOUNCED PRINT RUN 98
*DOUBLE/60: .6X TO 1.5X BASIC JSY
ASJ1 Evgeni Nabokov 6.00 15.00
ASJ2 Paul Kariya 6.00 15.00
ASJ3 Zigmund Palffy 6.00 15.00
ASJ4 Milan Hejduk 6.00 15.00
ASJ5 Patrick Roy 12.00 30.00
ASJ6 Rob Blake 6.00 15.00
ASJ7 Nicklas Lidstrom 6.00 15.00
ASJ8 Martin Brodeur 15.00 40.00
ASJ9 Doug Weight 4.00 10.00
ASJ10 Bill Guerin 4.00 10.00
ASJ11 Dominik Hasek 12.50 30.00
ASJ12 Joe Sakic 12.50 30.00
ASJ13 Alexei Kovalev 4.00 10.00
ASJ14 Roman Cechmanek 4.00 10.00
ASJ15 Pavel Bure 6.00 15.00
ASJ16 Mario Lemieux 20.00 50.00
ASJ17 Ray Bourque 10.00 25.00
ASJ18 Teppo Numminen 4.00 10.00
ASJ19 Sandis Ozolinsh 4.00 10.00
ASJ20 Tony Amonte 6.00 15.00
ASJ21 Peter Forsberg 10.00 25.00
ASJ22 Brian Leetch 6.00 15.00
ASJ23 Radek Bonk 4.00 10.00
ASJ24 Theo Fleury 12.00 30.00
ASJ25 Simon Gagne 6.00 15.00
ASJ26 Valeri Bure 4.00 10.00
ASJ27 Pavol Demitra 4.00 10.00
ASJ28 Scott Gomez 6.00 15.00
ASJ29 Curtis Joseph 6.00 15.00
ASJ30 Viktor Kozlov 4.00 10.00
ASJ31 Mark Messier 8.00 20.00
ASJ32 Mike Modano 8.00 20.00
ASJ33 Owen Nolan 6.00 15.00
ASJ34 Tommy Salo 4.00 10.00
ASJ35 Roman Turek 4.00 10.00
ASJ36 Steve Yzerman 15.00 40.00
ASJ37 Jaromir Jagr 10.00 25.00
ASJ38 Mats Sundin 6.00 15.00
ASJ39 Nikolai Khabibulin 6.00 15.00
ASJ40 Markus Naslund 6.00 15.00
ASJ41 Keith Tkachuk 6.00 15.00
ASJ42 Alexei Yashin 4.00 10.00
ASJ43 Chris Pronger 6.00 15.00
ASJ44 Al MacInnis 6.00 15.00
ASJ45 Peter Bondra 4.00 10.00
ASJ46 Arturs Irbe 6.00 15.00
ASJ47 Eric Lindros 6.00 15.00
ASJ48 Teemu Selanne 6.00 15.00
ASJ49 Daniel Alfredsson 6.00 15.00
ASJ50 Brett Hull 10.00 25.00

2001-02 BAP Memorabilia All-Star Starting Lineup

With a print run of just 70 sets, this 12-card set featured game-worn jersey swatches from starters of the 2001 NHL All-Star Game.
STATED PRINT RUN 70 SETS
S1 Dominik Hasek 12.50 30.00
S2 Nicklas Lidstrom 12.00 30.00
S3 Sandis Ozolinsh 10.00 25.00
S4 Milan Hejduk 10.00 25.00
S5 Peter Forsberg 15.00 40.00
S6 Pavel Bure 10.00 25.00
S7 Patrick Roy 30.00 80.00
S8 Ray Bourque 20.00 50.00
S9 Rob Blake 10.00 25.00
S10 Paul Kariya 10.00 25.00
S11 Theo Fleury 15.00 40.00
S12 Joe Sakic 20.00 50.00

2001-02 BAP Memorabilia All-Star Teammates

This 50-card set highlighted players who were teammates at either the 1994, 1996, 1997, 1998, 1999, 2000, or 2001 NHL All-Star Game. Each card carried a swatch of All-Star Game jersey from each player depicted. Each card was limited to just 80 copies.
ANNOUNCED PRINT RUN 80
AST1 Nabokov/Hejduk/Palffy 12.50 30.00
AST2 Kariya/Lemieux/Gagne 30.00 80.00
AST3 Blake/Roy/Sakic 30.00 80.00
AST4 Brodeur/Weight/Leetch 20.00 50.00
AST5 Cechmanek/Bure/Forsberg 20.00 50.00
AST6 Nabokov/Hejduk/Palffy 12.50 30.00
AST7 Bourque/Leetch/Fleury 20.00 50.00
AST8 Amonte/Guerin/Weight 12.50 30.00
AST9 Nabokov/Cech/Hasek 15.00 40.00
AST10 Kariya/Sakic/Fleury 20.00 50.00
AST11 P.Forsberg/M.Hejduk 15.00 40.00
AST12 P.Roy/M.Lemieux 25.00 60.00
AST13 R.Bourque/R.Blake 20.00 50.00
AST14 P.Bure/V.Bure/Kozlov 12.50 30.00
AST15 Brodeur/Gomez/Stevens 20.00 50.00
AST16 C.Pronger/A.MacInnis 12.50 30.00
AST17 Amnte/Modno/Roenck 12.00 30.00
AST18 Kolzig/Salo/Turek 12.50 30.00
AST19 B.Shanahan/S.Yzerman 20.00 50.00
AST20 M.Sundin/T.Salo 15.00 40.00
AST21 J.Jagr/P.Bure 12.50 30.00
AST22 Modno/Joseph/Yzrmn 20.00 50.00
AST23 P.Bure/V.Bure 12.50 30.00
AST24 Yzerman/Messier/Gomez 20.00 50.00
AST25 M.Modano/E.Lindros 12.50 30.00
AST26 P.Forsberg/T.Selanne 20.00 50.00
AST27 Naslund/Yashin/Bondra 12.50 30.00
AST28 Hasek/Irbe/Khab 15.00 40.00
AST29 Sundin/Lidstrom/Naslund 12.50 30.00
AST30 C.Pronger/A.MacInnis 12.50 30.00
AST31 P.Kariya/T.Amonte 12.50 30.00
AST32 P.Forsberg/J.Jagr 20.00 50.00
AST33 M.Modano/J.LeClair 12.50 30.00
AST34 Grtzky/Modno/Lndros 40.00 100.00
AST35 P.Roy/J.Sakic 25.00 60.00
AST36 Jagr/Forsberg/Bure 25.00 60.00
AST37 W.Gretzky/P.Roy 60.00 150.00
AST38 Bourque/Chelios/Leetch 20.00 50.00
AST39 E.Lindros/M.Messier 12.50 30.00
AST40 D.Hasek/N.Khabibulin 12.50 30.00
AST41 J.Sakic/M.Modano 15.00 40.00
AST42 D.Hasek/R.Bourque 15.00 40.00
AST43 S.Yzerman/M.Sundin 20.00 50.00
AST44 P.Kariya/P.Bure 12.50 30.00
AST45 M.Sundin/T.Selanne 12.50 30.00
AST46 B.Hull/E.Belfour 12.50 30.00
AST47 J.Jagr/E.Lindros 12.50 30.00
AST48 P.Forsberg/P.Kariya 15.00 40.00
AST49 W.Gretzky/C.Joseph 25.00 60.00
AST50 P.Roy/R.Bourque 15.00 40.00

2001-02 BAP Memorabilia Draft Redemptions

Inserted randomly in packs, this 30-card set featured cards representing the top thirty draft picks in 2001. Each card was redeemable for the player it represented once that player made his NHL debut. Collectors had six months to redeem the cards once the player was available. The redemption cards themselves were hand-numbered out of 100 but none were fully redeemed. BAP did announce the print runs for many of the cards that did get redeemed and since some were issued more than a year after initial release, slightly different card styles were used. If by 11/1/2005, the player has still not played in the NHL, the collector has the choice of redeeming the card for others in the set or continuing to wait.
ANNOUNCED FINAL PRINT RUN 31-100
1 Ilya Kovalchuk/74* 60.00 150.00
2 Jason Spezza/55* 125.00 250.00
3 Alexander Svitov/52* 20.00 50.00
4 Stephen Weiss/55* 40.00 80.00
5 Stanislav Chistov/53* 15.00 40.00
6 Mikko Koivu/56* 10.00 25.00
7 Mike Komisarek/47* 25.00 60.00
8 Pascal LeClaire/49* 30.00 60.00
9 Tuomo Ruutu/64* 30.00 60.00
10 Dan Blackburn/67* 15.00 40.00
11 Fredrik Sjostrom/100 10.00 25.00
12 Dan Hamhuis/63* 25.00 60.00
13 Ales Hemsky/52* 40.00 100.00
14 Chuck Kobasew/50* 25.00 50.00
16 R.J. Umberger/58* 10.00 25.00
17 Carlo Colaiacovo/50* 25.00 60.00
19 Shaone Morrisonn/48* 20.00 50.00
20 Marcel Goc/57* 10.00 25.00
21 Colby Armstrong/45* 10.00 25.00
22 Jiri Novotny/45*
23 Tim Gleason/61* 15.00 40.00
24 Lukas Krajicek/31* 25.00 60.00
25 Alexander Perezhogin/47* 10.00 25.00
26 Jason Bacashihua/46* 25.00 60.00
27 Jeff Woywitka/48* 8.00 20.00
29 Adam Munro/100 8.00 20.00
30 Dave Steckel/35* 8.00 20.00

2001-02 BAP Memorabilia 500 Goal Scorers

This 28-card set featured players who hit the milestone of 500 goals in their career. Each card featured an action photo of the given player alongside a game-worn swatch of his jersey on the card front. Each card was printed in quantities of 99,50,40 or 20 only. The Shanahan and Francis cards were available in random BAP Update packs only. Cards with print runs of 20 or less are not priced due to scarcity.
JSY/20-99 STATED ODDS 1:269
GS1 Wayne Gretzky/20 125.00 250.00
GS2 Gordie Howe/20 75.00 150.00
GS3 Marcel Dionne/50 20.00 50.00
GS4 Phil Esposito/40 25.00 60.00
GS5 Mike Gartner/99 10.00 25.00
GS6 Mark Messier/99 25.00 60.00
GS7 Steve Yzerman/99 30.00 80.00
GS8 Brett Hull/99 25.00 60.00
GS9 Mario Lemieux/20 75.00 150.00
GS10 Dino Ciccarelli/99 10.00 25.00
GS11 Jari Kurri/99 12.50 30.00
GS12 Luc Robitaille/99 10.00 25.00
GS13 Mike Bossy/50 12.50 30.00
GS14 Dave Andreychuk/99 10.00 25.00
GS15 Guy Lafleur/50 25.00 60.00
GS16 John Bucyk/99 10.00 25.00
GS17 Maurice Richard/20 60.00 150.00
GS18 Stan Mikita/40 25.00 60.00
GS19 Frank Mahovlich/40 25.00 60.00
GS20 Bryan Trottier/99 10.00 25.00
GS21 Dale Hawerchuk/99 10.00 25.00
GS22 Gilbert Perreault/99 15.00 40.00
GS23 Jean Beliveau/20 90.00 150.00
GS24 Pat Verbeek/99 10.00 25.00

GS25 Michel Goulet/99 10.00 25.00
GS26 Joe Mullen/99 12.00 30.00
GS27 Lanny McDonald/99 12.00 30.00
GS28 Bobby Hull/40 30.00 80.00
NNO Brendan Shanahan/25 25.00 60.00
NNO Ron Francis/25 20.00 50.00

2001-02 BAP Memorabilia Goalies Jerseys

STATED PRINT RUN 80 SETS
GJ1 Byron Dafoe 10.00 25.00
GJ2 Dominik Hasek 15.00 40.00
GJ3 Mike Vernon 10.00 25.00
GJ4 Arturs Irbe 10.00 25.00
GJ5 Jocelyn Thibault 10.00 25.00
GJ6 Patrick Roy 15.00 40.00
GJ7 Ed Belfour 10.00 25.00
GJ8 Chris Osgood 10.00 25.00
GJ9 Johan Hedberg 10.00 25.00
GJ10 R.Luongo/T.Kid 10.00 25.00
GJ11 J.Theodore/J.Hackett 12.00 30.00
GJ12 Mike Dunham 10.00 25.00
GJ13 Martin Brodeur 20.00 50.00
GJ14 Mike Richter 10.00 25.00
GJ15 R.Cechmanek/B.Boucher 10.00 25.00
GJ16 Jean-Sebastien Aubin 10.00 25.00
GJ17 Roman Turek 10.00 25.00
GJ18 Curtis Joseph 10.00 25.00
GJ19 Olaf Kolzig 10.00 25.00
GJ20 Felix Potvin 15.00 40.00

2001-02 BAP Memorabilia Goalie Traditions

This 42-card set featured game-worn goalie gear swatches of one, two or three goalies from the past and present. Single player cards were limited to 60 sets, two player cards were limited to 50 sets, and three player cards were limited to 20 sets.
GT1-GT18 SINGLE PRINT RUN 60
GT19-GT36 DOUBLE PRINT RUN 50
GT1 Curtis Joseph 12.50 30.00
GT2 Johnny Bower 20.00 50.00
GT3 Turk Broda 30.00 80.00
GT4 Patrick Roy 25.00 60.00
GT5 Jacques Plante 25.00 60.00
GT6 Jose Theodore 15.00 40.00
GT7 Glenn Hall 12.50 30.00
GT8 Tony Esposito 12.50 30.00
GT9 Jocelyn Thibault 12.50 30.00
GT10 Chuck Rayner 12.50 30.00
GT11 Ed Giacomin 15.00 40.00
GT12 Mike Richter 12.50 30.00
GT13 Frank Brimsek 12.50 30.00
GT14 Gerry Cheevers 12.50 30.00
GT15 Byron Dafoe 12.50 30.00
GT16 Terry Sawchuk 30.00 80.00
GT17 Glenn Hall 12.50 30.00
GT18 Chris Osgood 12.50 30.00
GT19 C.Joseph/T.Broda 40.00 100.00
GT20 C.Joseph/J.Bower 30.00 80.00
GT21 J.Bower/T.Broda 20.00 50.00
GT22 T.Sawchuk/G.Hall 50.00 125.00
GT23 G.Hall/C.Osgood 20.00 50.00
GT24 T.Sawchuck/C.Osgood 40.00 100.00
GT25 G.Hall/J.Thibault 12.00 30.00
GT26 G.Hall/T.Esposito 20.00 50.00
GT27 T.Esposito/J.Thibault 20.00 50.00
GT28 J.Plante/P.Roy 50.00 125.00
GT29 J.Plante/J.Theodore 30.00 80.00
GT30 P.Roy/J.Theodore 50.00 125.00
GT31 F.Brimsek/B.Dafoe 20.00 50.00
GT32 F.Brimsek/G.Cheevers 20.00 50.00
GT33 G.Cheevers/B.Dafoe 12.00 30.00
GT34 C.Rayner/E.Giacomin 20.00 50.00
GT35 C.Rayner/M.Richter 20.00 50.00
GT36 E.Giacomin/M.Richter 20.00 50.00
GT37 Joseph/Bower/Broda
GT38 Sawchuk/Hall/Osgood 60.00 120.00
GT39 Esposito/Hall/Thibault
GT40 Plante/Roy/Theodore 90.00 150.00
GT41 Brimsek/Cheevers/Dafoe
GT42 Richter/Rayner/Giacomin

2001-02 BAP Memorabilia He Shoots He Scores Points

ONE PER PACK
1 Roman Cechmanek 1 pt. .25 .60
2 Martin Havlat 1 pt. .25 .60
3 Milan Hejduk 1 pt. .30 .75
4 Curtis Joseph 1 pt. .30 .75
5 Saku Koivu 1 pt. .30 .75
6 Mark Messier 1 pt. .30 .75
7 Mike Modano 1 pt. .50 1.25
8 Evgeni Nabokov 1 pt. .25 .60
9 Chris Pronger 1 pt. .25 .60
10 Mats Sundin 1 pt. .30 .75
11 Martin Brodeur 2 pts. .75 2.00
12 Peter Forsberg 2 pts. .60 1.50
13 Paul Kariya 2 pts. .30 .75
14 Vincent Lecavalier 2 pts. .30 .75
15 Patrick Roy 2 pts. 1.50 4.00
16 Joe Sakic 2 pts. .60 1.50
17 Steve Yzerman 2 pts. 1.50 4.00
18 Pavel Bure 3 pts. .30 .75
19 Mario Lemieux 3 pts. 2.00 5.00
20 Teemu Selanne 3 pts. .30 .75

2001-02 BAP Memorabilia Patented Power

This six card set featured game-worn jersey swatches from both player's featured. Each card was limited to just 20 copies.
STATED PRINT RUN 20 SETS
PP1 J.Jagr/M.Sundin 25.00 60.00
PP2 M.Lemieux/W.Gretzky 100.00 200.00
PP3 P.Bure/M.Hejduk 40.00 100.00
PP4 M.Modano/C.Pronger 25.00 60.00
PP5 P.Kariya/J.Sakic 60.00 150.00
PP6 P.Forsberg/S.Yzerman 75.00 200.00

2001-02 BAP Memorabilia Rocket's Mates

This 10-card set featured game-used jersey swatches from player's who played with Hall-of-Famer Maurice "Rocket" Richard. The card fronts carried a small action photo of the featured player on the right side and a black-and-white head shot of Richard on the left. Each card was limited to 50 copies.
STATED PRINT RUN 50 SETS
RM1 Jacques Plante 50.00 125.00
RM2 Doug Harvey 25.00 60.00
RM3 Jean Beliveau 30.00 80.00
RM4 Henri Richard 25.00 60.00
RM5 Bernie Geoffrion 30.00 80.00
RM6 Dollard St. Laurent 25.00 60.00
RM7 Elmer Lach 25.00 60.00
RM8 Dickie Moore 25.00 60.00
RM9 Butch Bouchard 25.00 60.00
RM10 Jean-Guy Talbot 25.00 60.00

2001-02 BAP Memorabilia Stanley Cup Champions

This 14-card set honored the winners of the 2001 Stanley Cup, the Colorado Avalanche. Each card carried a full-color photo of the featured player and a swatch of game-used jersey on the card front. Each card was limited to just 40 copies.
STATED PRINT RUN 40 SETS
CA1 Patrick Roy 75.00 150.00
CA2 Adam Foote 12.00 30.00
CA3 Ray Bourque 60.00 120.00
CA4 Martin Skoula 15.00 40.00
CA5 Shjon Podein 15.00 40.00
CA6 Alex Tanguay 15.00 40.00
CA7 Chris Dingman 15.00 40.00
CA8 Milan Hejduk 15.00 40.00
CA9 Peter Forsberg 20.00 50.00
CA10 Joe Sakic 30.00 80.00
CA11 Eric Messier 15.00 40.00
CA12 Jon Klemm 15.00 40.00
CA13 Dave Reid 15.00 40.00
CA14 Chris Drury 15.00 40.00

2001-02 BAP Memorabilia Stanley Cup Playoffs

This 32-card set featured players who participated in the 2001 Stanley Cup Playoffs. Each card carried a full-color photo and a swatch of game-used jersey on the card front. Cards SC1-16 were limited to 95 copies each, cards SC17-24 were limited to 80, cards SC25-60 were limited to 40, and cards SC31-SC32 were limited to just 10 copies each.
SC1 Mats Sundin/95 10.00 25.00
SC2 Daniel Alfredsson/95 10.00 25.00
SC3 Scott Stevens/95 10.00 25.00
SC4 Arturs Irbe/95 6.00 15.00
SC5 Martin Straka/95 10.00 25.00
SC6 Olaf Kolzig/95 10.00 25.00
SC7 Doug Gilmour/95 10.00 25.00
SC8 Roman Cechmanek/95 10.00 25.00
SC9 Joe Sakic/95 15.00 40.00
SC10 Daniel Sedin/95 10.00 25.00
SC11 Zigmund Palffy/95 10.00 25.00
SC12 Sergei Fedorov/95 10.00 25.00
SC13 Ed Belfour/95 10.00 25.00
SC14 Tommy Salo/95 10.00 25.00
SC15 Roman Turek/95 10.00 25.00
SC16 Owen Nolan/95 10.00 25.00
SC17 Patrick Roy/80 20.00 50.00
SC18 Luc Robitaille/80 10.00 25.00
SC19 Chris Pronger/80 10.00 25.00
SC20 Mike Modano/80 12.50 30.00
SC21 Martin Brodeur/80 20.00 50.00
SC22 Curtis Joseph/80 10.00 25.00
SC23 Dominik Hasek/80 12.50 30.00
SC24 Mario Lemieux/80 30.00 80.00
SC25 Jason Arnott/60 10.00 25.00
SC26 Johan Hedberg/60 10.00 25.00
SC27 Ray Bourque/60 15.00 40.00
SC28 Al MacInnis/60 10.00 25.00
SC29 Scott Gomez/40 10.00 25.00
SC30 Chris Drury/40 10.00 25.00
SC31 R.Bourque/10 Cup Winners
SC32 Patrick Roy/10 Conn Smythe

2002-03 BAP Memorabilia

Released in mid-November 2002, this 300-card base set featured 200 veteran cards, 30 shortprinted rookie cards and the following shortprinted subsets: Franchise Players (201-230) and the Big Deal (231-270). Shortprinted cards were inserted at a rate of one per pack. Cards 301-400 were only available via mail-in offer found in packs.
CARDS 301-400 AVAIL.VIA MAIL-IN
1 Steve Yzerman .50 1.25
2 Steve Reinprecht .15 .40
3 Jean-Sebastien Giguere .25 .60
4 Chris Simon .15 .40
5 Dany Heatley .25 .60
6 Brendan Morrison .20 .50
7 Bill Guerin .25 .60
8 Alexander Mogilny .20 .50
9 Martin Biron .20 .50
10 Brad Richards .25 .60
11 Craig Conroy .15 .40
12 Al MacInnis .25 .60
13 Arturs Irbe .20 .50
14 Evgeni Nabokov .20 .50
15 Alexei Zhamnov .20 .50
16 Daniel Briere .20 .50
17 Alex Tanguay .20 .50
18 Milan Kraft .15 .40
19 Marc Denis .20 .50
20 Adam Oates .25 .60
21 Darryl Sydor .15 .40
22 Daniel Alfredsson .25 .60
23 Brendan Shanahan .30 .75
24 Brian Leetch .25 .60
25 Anson Carter .20 .50
26 Adrian Aucoin .15 .40
27 Kristian Huselius .15 .40
28 Jamie Langenbrunner .20 .50
29 Adam Deadmarsh .20 .50
30 Denis Arkhipov .15 .40
31 Andrew Brunette .15 .40
32 Donald Audette .15 .40
33 Rob Blake .25 .60
34 Jaromir Jagr .60 1.50
35 Felix Potvin .40 1.00
36 Dan Cloutier .20 .50
37 Niklas Hagman .15 .40
38 Alyn McCauley .15 .40
39 Eric Brewer .15 .40
40 Nikolai Khabibulin .25 .60
41 Brett Hull .30 .75
42 Brent Johnson .20 .50
43 Brenden Morrow .20 .50
44 Mike Ricci .20 .50
45 Ray Whitney .20 .50
46 Alexei Kovalev .25 .60
47 Chris Drury .25 .60
48 Daymond Langkow .20 .50
49 Eric Daze .15 .40
50 Pavel Brendl .15 .40
51 Bates Battaglia .15 .40
52 Jani Hurme .20 .50
53 Dean McAmmond .15 .40
54 Dan Blackburn .20 .50
55 Maxim Afinogenov .15 .40
56 Alexei Yashin .20 .50
57 Steve Shields .20 .50
58 Joe Nieuwendyk .25 .60
59 Frantisek Kaberle .15 .40
60 Jan Lasak .20 .50
61 Ron Francis .30 .75
62 Jeff Friesen .15 .40
63 Doug Gilmour .30 .75
64 Jeff Halpern .15 .40
65 Ilya Kovalchuk .30 .75
66 Daniel Sedin .25 .60
67 Glen Murray .20 .50
68 Bryan McCabe .15 .40
69 Miroslav Satan .25 .60
70 Pavel Kubina .15 .40
71 Derek Morris .15 .40
72 Chris Pronger .20 .50
73 Erik Cole .20 .50
74 Owen Nolan .25 .60
75 Jocelyn Thibault .20 .50
76 Jan Hrdina .15 .40
77 Greg DeVries .15 .40
78 Krystofer Kolanos .15 .40
79 David Vyborny .15 .40
80 Jeremy Roenick .25 .60
81 Jason Arnott .20 .50
82 Mike Leclerc .15 .40
83 Marian Hossa .20 .50
84 Chris Chelios .25 .60
85 Eric Lindros .40 1.00
86 Jochen Hecht .15 .40
87 Chris Osgood .25 .60
88 Roberto Luongo .40 1.00
89 Martin Brodeur .50 1.25
90 Jaroslav Modry .15 .40
91 Martin Erat .15 .40
92 Manny Fernandez .20 .50
93 Jose Theodore .25 .60
94 Olaf Kolzig .25 .60
95 Ed Jovanovski .20 .50
96 Sandis Ozolinsh .20 .50
97 Corey Schwab .20 .50
98 Sami Kapanen .15 .40
99 Mike Comrie .25 .60
100 Shane Willis .15 .40
101 Dominik Hasek .40 1.00
102 Jason Allison .20 .50
103 Doug Weight .25 .60
104 Marty Turco .25 .60
105 Patrick Marleau .25 .60
106 Rostislav Klesla .15 .40
107 Johan Hedberg .25 .60
108 Joe Sakic .40 1.00
109 Marian Gaborik .40 1.00
110 Sean Burke .15 .40
111 Mark Bell .15 .40
112 John LeClair .25 .60
113 Jaroslav Svoboda .15 .40
114 Todd Bertuzzi .25 .60
115 Martin Havlat .20 .50
116 Pavel Datsyuk .30 .75
117 Jarome Iginla .25 .60
118 Mark Messier .40 1.00
119 Stu Barnes .15 .40
120 Shayne Corson .15 .40
121 Mark Parrish .15 .40
122 Joe Thornton .30 .75
123 Patrik Elias .25 .60
124 Milan Hnilicka .20 .50
125 Mike Dunham .20 .50
126 Oleg Tverdovsky .15 .40
127 Richard Zednik .15 .40
128 Peter Forsberg .30 .75
129 Mikko Eloranta .15 .40
130 Zdeno Chara .25 .60
131 Curtis Joseph .25 .60
132 Steve Rucchin .15 .40
133 Sergei Fedorov .40 1.00
134 Josef Vasicek .15 .40
135 Ryan Smyth .20 .50
136 Scott Niedermayer .25 .60
137 Shane Doan .20 .50
138 Steve Sullivan .15 .40
139 Stephen Weiss .25 .60
140 Alexander Daigle .15 .40
141 Fred Brathwaite .20 .50
142 Peter Bondra .25 .60
143 Patrik Stefan .20 .50
144 Tony Amonte .20 .50
145 Valeri Bure .20 .50
146 Rick DiPietro .20 .50
147 Martin Straka .20 .50
148 Jeff O'Neill .15 .40
149 Milan Hejduk .20 .50
150 Kirk Maltby .15 .40
151 Mike York .15 .40
152 Scott Gomez .20 .50
153 Mike Peca .20 .50
154 Mike Richter .25 .60
155 Patrick Lalime .20 .50
156 Justin Williams .20 .50
157 Mario Lemieux .75 2.00
158 Kevin Weekes .20 .50
159 Scott Young .15 .40
160 Tommy Salo .20 .50
161 Steve Webb .15 .40
162 Teemu Selanne .50 1.25
163 Jozef Stumpel .15 .40
164 Patrick Roy .60 1.50
165 Zigmund Palffy .25 .60
166 Pavel Bure .30 .75
167 Vincent Damphousse .20 .50
168 Sergei Gonchar .20 .50
169 Sergei Samsonov .20 .50
170 Luc Robitaille .25 .60
171 Scott Stevens .25 .60
172 Robert Lang .15 .40
173 Henrik Sedin .25 .60
174 Tim Connolly .15 .40
175 Pierre Turgeon .25 .60
176 Yanic Perreault .15 .40
177 Radek Bonk .20 .50
178 Keith Tkachuk .25 .60
179 Paul Kariya .30 .75
180 Mike Modano .40 1.00
181 Saku Koivu .25 .60
182 Mark Recchi .30 .75
183 Roman Turek .25 .60
184 Kris Draper .15 .40
185 Scott Hartnell .25 .60
186 Keith Primeau .25 .60
187 Vincent Lecavalier .20 .50
188 Darcy Tucker .15 .40
189 Markus Naslund .20 .50
190 Pavol Demitra .30 .75
191 Gary Roberts .15 .40
192 Rod Brind'Amour .25 .60
193 Radim Vrbata .20 .50
194 Nicklas Lidstrom .25 .60
195 Tom Poti .15 .40
196 Roman Cechmanek .20 .50
197 Scott Mellanby .15 .40
198 Mats Sundin .25 .60
199 Filip Kuba .15 .40
200 Simon Gagne .25 .60
201 Paul Kariya FP .50 1.25
202 Ilya Kovalchuk FP .50 1.25
203 Joe Thornton FP .50 1.25
204 Miroslav Satan FP .40 1.00
205 Jarome Iginla FP .40 1.00
206 Ron Francis FP .50 1.25
207 Eric Daze FP .25 .60
208 Patrick Roy FP 1.00 2.50
209 Rostislav Klesla FP .25 .60
210 Mike Modano FP .60 1.50
211 Steve Yzerman FP .75 2.00
212 Mike Comrie FP .40 1.00
213 Roberto Luongo FP .60 1.50
214 Zigmund Palffy FP .40 1.00
215 Marian Gaborik FP .60 1.50
216 Jose Theodore FP .40 1.00
217 Scott Hartnell FP .40 1.00
218 Martin Brodeur FP .75 2.00
219 Alexei Yashin FP .30 .75
220 Pavel Bure FP .50 1.25
221 Marian Hossa FP .30 .75
222 Simon Gagne FP .40 1.00
223 Daniel Briere FP .30 .75
224 Mario Lemieux FP 1.25 3.00
225 Chris Pronger FP .30 .75
226 Owen Nolan FP .40 1.00
227 Nikolai Khabibulin FP .40 1.00
228 Mats Sundin FP .40 1.00
229 Markus Naslund FP .30 .75
230 Jaromir Jagr FP 1.00 2.50
231 P.Forsberg/E.Lindros .60 1.50
232 P.Roy/J.Thibault 1.00 2.50
233 T.Sawchuk/J.Bucyk .75 2.00
234 J.Plante/G.Worsley .50 1.25
235 C.Pronger/B.Shanahan .50 1.25
236 E.Lindros/P.Brendl .60 1.50
237 K.Beech/J.Jagr 1.00 2.50
238 E.Jovanovski/P.Bure .50 1.25
239 J.Iginla/J.Nieuwendyk .40 1.00
240 D.Hasek/E.Daze .60 1.50
241 D.Savard/C.Chelios .50 1.25
242 A.Oates/J.Allison .40 1.00
243 D.Hasek/S.Kozlov .60 1.50
244 R.Svehla/D.Yushkevich .25 .60
245 T.Linden/T.Bertuzzi .40 1.00
246 G.Lafleur/S.Zubov .50 1.25
247 J.Arnott/B.Guerin .40 1.00
248 A.Mogilny/M.Peca .30 .75
249 B.Shanahan/K.Primeau .50 1.25
250 J.LeClair/M.Recchi .50 1.25
251 R.Blake/A.Deadmarsh .40 1.00
252 J.Roenick/A.Zhamnov .40 1.00
253 M.Peca/T.Connolly .30 .75
254 S.Ozolinsh/O.Nolan .40 1.00
255 C.Drury/M.Fernandez .40 1.00
256 R.Turek/F.Braithwaite .40 1.00
257 J.Arnott/J.Nieuwendyk .40 1.00
258 D.Andreychuk/B.Rolston .40 1.00
259 B.Berard/F.Potvin .60 1.50
260 V.Bure/R.Niedermayer .30 .75
261 B.Boucher/M.Handzus .30 .75
262 Adam Oates .40 1.00
263 Bobby Holik .25 .60
264 Robert Lang .25 .60
265 Curtis Joseph .40 1.00
266 Ed Belfour .40 1.00
267 Darius Kasparaitis .25 .60
268 Bill Guerin .40 1.00
269 Petr Sykora .30 .75
Oleg Tverdovsky
270 Tony Amonte .30 .75
271 P-M Bouchard RC .75 2.00
272 Rick Nash RC 4.00 10.00
273 Dennis Seidenberg RC .75 2.00
274 Jay Bouwmeester RC 2.50 6.00
275 Stanislav Chistov RC .50 1.25
276 Kurt Sauer RC .50 1.25
277 Ivan Majesky RC .50 1.25
278 Chuck Kobasew RC .60 1.50
279 Jeff Taffe RC .50 1.25
280 Mikael Tellqvist RC .50 1.25
281 Ales Hemsky RC 2.00 5.00
282 Patrick Sharp RC 1.50 4.00
283 Jordan Leopold RC .75 2.00
284 Dmitri Bykov RC .50 1.25
285 Alex Henry RC .60 1.50
286 Henrik Zetterberg RC 5.00 12.00
287 Alexander Frolov RC 1.00 2.50
288 Steve Eminger RC .50 1.25
289 Carlo Colaiacovo RC .75 2.00
290 Tom Koivisto RC .50 1.25
291 Shawn Thornton RC .60 1.50
292 Ron Hainsey RC .50 1.25
293 Martin Gerber RC .75 2.00
294 Adam Hall RC .50 1.25
295 Jason Spezza RC 3.00 8.00
296 Anton Volchenkov RC .50 1.25
297 Jeff Paul RC .50 1.25
298 Scottie Upshall RC .60 1.50
299 Alexander Svitov RC .50 1.25
300 Alexei Smirnov RC .60 1.50
301 Ed Belfour .75 2.00
302 Ryan Bayda RC .50 1.25
303 Jerred Smithson RC .50 1.25
304 Mike Komisarek RC .75 2.00
305 Jarret Stoll RC 2.00 5.00
306 Radovan Somik RC .50 1.25
307 Rob Davison RC .50 1.25
308 Jason King RC .75 2.00
309 Tony Amonte .20 .50
310 Cam Severson RC .50 1.25
311 Matt Walker RC .50 1.25
312 Jesse Fibiger RC .50 1.25
313 Ray Emery RC 1.50 4.00
314 Vernon Fiddler RC .60 1.50
315 Alex Kovalev .25 .60
316 Marc-Andre Bergeron RC .60 1.50
317 Jason Elliott RC .50 1.25
318 Craig Andersson RC 2.50 6.00
319 Sandis Ozolinsh .20 .50
320 Ryan Miller RC 3.00 8.00
321 Chris Osgood .25 .60
322 Michael Garnett RC .50 1.25
323 Bobby Allen RC .50 1.25
324 Cristobal Huet RC 1.00 2.50
325 Curtis Murphy RC .50 1.25
326 Darren Haydar RC .50 1.25
327 Mathieu Schneider .15 .40
328 Ray Schultz RC .50 1.25
329 Jim Vandermeer RC .50 1.25
330 Miroslav Zalesak RC .50 1.25
331 Christian Backman RC .50 1.25
332 John Craighead RC .50 1.25
333 Doug Gilmour .30 .75
334 Dick Tarnstrom RC .50 1.25
335 Chad Wiseman RC .50 1.25
336 John Tripp RC .50 1.25
337 Ari Ahonen RC .50 1.25
338 Rickard Wallin RC .50 1.25
339 Jonathan Hedstrom RC .50 1.25
340 Daniel Briere .20 .50
341 Paul Manning RC .50 1.25
342 Igor Radulov RC .50 1.25
343 Tomas Malec RC .50 1.25
344 Sean McMorrow RC .50 1.25
345 Dany Sabourin RC .50 1.25
346 Steve Thomas .15 .40
347 Shaone Morrisonn RC .50 1.25
348 Brad Defauw RC .50 1.25
349 Michael Leighton RC .75 2.00
350 Pascal Leclaire RC .60 1.50
351 Chris Schmidt RC .50 1.25
352 Stephane Veilleux RC .50 1.25
353 Jim Fahey RC .50 1.25
354 Konstantin Koltsov RC .60 1.50
355 Cody Rudkowsky RC .60 1.50
356 Anson Carter .20 .50
357 Francois Beauchemin RC .75 2.00
358 Patrick Boileau RC .50 1.25
359 Sylvain Blouin RC .50 1.25
360 Eric Bertrand RC .50 1.25
361 Jamie Hodson RC .50 1.25
362 Curtis Sanford RC .75 2.00
363 Ryan Kraft RC .50 1.25
364 Owen Nolan .25 .60
365 Niko Dimitrakos RC .50 1.25
366 Simon Gamache RC .50 1.25
367 Doug Janik RC .50 1.25
368 Tomas Kurka UER RC .50 1.25
369 Josh Harding RC 6.00 15.00
370 Radoslav Hecl RC .50 1.25
371 Kris Vernarsky RC .50 1.25
372 Steve Ott RC 1.00 2.50
373 Frederic Cloutier RC .50 1.25
374 Eric Godard RC .50 1.25
375 Kari Haakana RC .50 1.25
376 Tomi Pettinen RC .50 1.25
377 Brooks Orpik RC .75 2.00
378 Lynn Loyns RC .50 1.25
379 Radim Vrbata .20 .50
380 Fernando Pisani RC .60 1.50
381 Alexei Semenov RC .50 1.25
382 Burke Henry RC .50 1.25
383 Tim Thomas RC 2.50 6.00
384 Mike Siklenka RC 1.25 3.00
385 Lasse Pirjeta RC .50 1.25
386 Tomas Zizka RC .50 1.25
387 Tomas Surovy RC .50 1.25
388 Paul Gaustad RC .50 1.25
389 Martin Samuelsson RC .50 1.25
390 Matt Henderson RC .50 1.25
391 Mike Dunham .20 .50
392 Levente Szuper RC .75 2.00
393 Jared Aulin RC .50 1.25
394 Brandon Reid RC .50 1.25
395 Mike Cammalleri RC 1.50 4.00
396 Ian MacNeil RC .50 1.25
397 Brad Isbister .15 .40
398 Garnet Exelby RC .50 1.25
399 Jason Bacashihua RC .60 1.50
400 Sami Kapanen .15 .40

2002-03 BAP Memorabilia Ruby

*1-200 VETS: 2X TO 5X BASE HI
*201-270 VETS: 1X TO 2.5X BASE SP
*271-300 ROOKIES: .6X TO 1.5X
RUBY PRINT RUN 200 SER.#'d SETS

2002-03 BAP Memorabilia Sapphire

*1-200 VETS: 4X TO 10X BASE HI
*201-270 VETS: 5X TO 5X BASE SP
*271-300 ROOKIES: 1.2X TO 3X
SAPPHIRE PRINT RUN 100 SER.#'d SETS

2002-03 BAP Memorabilia All-Star Jerseys

This 60-card set featured swatches of all-star game-used jerseys. Each card was limited to just 90 copies each.
STATED PRINT RUN 90 SETS
ASJ1 Daniel Alfredsson 6.00 15.00
ASJ2 Tony Amonte 6.00 15.00
ASJ3 Ed Belfour 6.00 15.00
ASJ4 Rob Blake 6.00 15.00
ASJ5 Peter Bondra 6.00 15.00
ASJ6 Martin Brodeur 12.50 30.00
ASJ7 Pavel Bure 6.00 15.00
ASJ8 Chris Chelios 6.00 15.00
ASJ9 Eric Daze 6.00 15.00
ASJ10 Pavol Demitra 6.00 15.00
ASJ11 Patrik Elias 6.00 15.00
ASJ12 Sergei Fedorov 10.00 25.00
ASJ13 Theo Fleury 6.00 15.00
ASJ14 Peter Forsberg 12.50 30.00
ASJ15 Simon Gagne 6.00 15.00
ASJ16 Bill Guerin 6.00 15.00
ASJ17 Dominik Hasek 12.50 30.00
ASJ18 Milan Hejduk 6.00 15.00
ASJ19 Brett Hull 12.50 30.00
ASJ20 Jarome Iginla 8.00 20.00
ASJ21 Arturs Irbe 8.00 20.00
ASJ22 Jaromir Jagr 12.50 30.00
ASJ23 Curtis Joseph 6.00 15.00
ASJ24 Ed Jovanovski 6.00 15.00
ASJ25 Paul Kariya 6.00 15.00
ASJ26 Nikolai Khabibulin 6.00 15.00
ASJ27 Saku Koivu 6.00 15.00
ASJ28 Alexei Kovalev 6.00 15.00
ASJ29 John LeClair 6.00 15.00
ASJ30 Brian Leetch 6.00 15.00
ASJ31 Mario Lemieux 15.00 40.00
ASJ32 Nicklas Lidstrom 6.00 15.00
ASJ33 Eric Lindros 6.00 15.00
ASJ34 Al MacInnis 6.00 15.00
ASJ35 Mark Messier 6.00 15.00
ASJ36 Mike Modano 8.00 20.00
ASJ37 Alexander Mogilny 6.00 15.00
ASJ38 Evgeni Nabokov 6.00 15.00
ASJ39 Markus Naslund 6.00 15.00
ASJ40 Scott Niedermayer 6.00 15.00
ASJ41 Owen Nolan 6.00 15.00
ASJ42 Felix Potvin 8.00 20.00
ASJ43 Sandis Ozolinsh 6.00 15.00
ASJ44 Zigmund Palffy 6.00 15.00
ASJ45 Chris Pronger 6.00 15.00
ASJ46 Mark Recchi 6.00 15.00
ASJ47 Mike Richter 6.00 15.00
ASJ48 Luc Robitaille 6.00 15.00
ASJ49 Jeremy Roenick 8.00 20.00
ASJ50 Patrick Roy 20.00 50.00
ASJ51 Joe Sakic 12.50 30.00
ASJ52 Teemu Selanne 6.00 15.00
ASJ53 Brendan Shanahan 6.00 15.00
ASJ54 Mats Sundin 6.00 15.00
ASJ55 Jose Theodore 8.00 20.00
ASJ56 Joe Thornton 8.00 20.00
ASJ57 Keith Tkachuk 6.00 15.00
ASJ58 Doug Weight 6.00 15.00
ASJ59 Alexei Yashin 6.00 15.00
ASJ60 Steve Yzerman 15.00 40.00

2002-03 BAP Memorabilia All-Star Starting Lineup

This 12-card set featured swatches of all-star game jerseys and was limited to just 40 copies each.
STATED PRINT RUN 40 SETS
AS1 Patrick Roy 60.00 125.00
AS2 Chris Pronger 20.00 50.00
AS3 Rob Blake 20.00 50.00
AS4 Vincent Damphousse 20.00 50.00
AS5 Owen Nolan 20.00 50.00
AS6 Brendan Shanahan 20.00 50.00
AS7 Dominik Hasek 30.00 80.00
AS8 Nicklas Lidstrom 20.00 50.00
AS9 Sandis Ozolinsh 20.00 50.00
AS10 Sergei Fedorov 20.00 50.00
AS11 Jaromir Jagr 25.00 60.00
AS12 Teemu Selanne 20.00 50.00

2002-03 BAP Memorabilia All-Star Teammmates

STATED PRINT RUN 75 SETS
AST1 S.Fedorov/T.Selanne 12.50 30.00
AST2 C.Joseph/J.Roenick 12.50 30.00
AST3 P.Roy/M.Messier 20.00 50.00
AST4 M.Lemieux/M.Messier 25.00 60.00
AST5 B.Shanahan/J.Jagr 12.50 30.00
AST6 A.Mogilny/P.Kariya 12.50 30.00
AST7 S.Yzerman/O.Nolan 25.00 60.00
AST8 T.Fleury/M.Sundin 12.50 30.00
AST9 M.Brodeur/D.Hasek 25.00 60.00
AST10 P.Bure/P.Forsberg 12.50 30.00
AST11 J.Jagr/D.Hasek 12.50 30.00
AST12 E.Lindros/M.Modano 12.50 30.00
AST13 E.Lindros/K.Tkachuk 12.50 30.00
AST14 P.Forsberg/D.Hasek 15.00 40.00
AST15 A.Yashin/T.Selanne 12.50 30.00
AST16 J.Jagr/M.Sundin 12.50 30.00
AST17 S.Yzerman/J.Roenick 20.00 50.00
AST18 M.Brodeur/C.Joseph 20.00 50.00
AST19 C.Pronger/T.Amonte 12.50 30.00
AST20 E.Lindros/M.Messier 15.00 40.00
AST21 J.Sakic/B.Guerin 12.50 30.00
AST22 M.Lemieux/P.Roy 30.00 80.00
AST23 E.Nabokov/D.Hasek 12.50 30.00
AST24 P.Forsberg/P.Bure 20.00 50.00
AST25 P.Kariya/M.Brodeur 20.00 50.00
AST26 J.Theodore/P.Roy 30.00 80.00
AST27 B.Shanahan/O.Nolan 12.50 30.00
AST28 J.Iginla/M.Lemieux 25.00 60.00
AST29 J.Jagr/N.Lidstrom 12.50 30.00
AST30 T.Selanne/S.Fedorov 12.50 30.00

2002-03 BAP Memorabilia All-Star Triple Jerseys

Limited to just 50 copies, this 20-card set featured triple swatches of jerseys from three different all-star games.
STATED PRINT RUN 50 SETS
ASTJ1 Rob Blake 12.50 30.00
ASTJ2 Martin Brodeur 30.00 80.00
ASTJ3 Pavel Bure 12.50 30.00
ASTJ4 Peter Forsberg 25.00 60.00
ASTJ5 Dominik Hasek 15.00 40.00
ASTJ6 Jaromir Jagr 15.00 40.00
ASTJ7 Paul Kariya 12.50 30.00
ASTJ8 John LeClair 12.50 30.00
ASTJ9 Brian Leetch 12.50 30.00
ASTJ10 Mario Lemieux 40.00 100.00
ASTJ11 Nicklas Lidstrom 12.50 30.00
ASTJ12 Eric Lindros 12.50 30.00
ASTJ13 Al MacInnis 12.50 30.00
ASTJ14 Mark Messier 25.00 60.00
ASTJ15 Mike Modano 15.00 40.00
ASTJ16 Owen Nolan 12.50 30.00
ASTJ17 Patrick Roy 50.00 100.00
ASTJ18 Teemu Selanne 12.50 30.00
ASTJ19 Brendan Shanahan 12.50 30.00
ASTJ20 Mats Sundin 12.50 30.00

2002-03 BAP Memorabilia Draft Redemptions

Inserted randomly in packs, this 30-card set featured cards representing the top thirty draft picks in 2002. Each card was redeemable for the player it represented once that player made his NHL debut. Collectors had six months to redeem the cards once the player was available. The redemption cards themselves were hand-numbered out of 100.
ANNOUNCED FINAL PRINT RUN 36-100
1 Rick Nash/67* 60.00 120.00
2 Kari Lehtonen/64* 40.00 80.00
3 Jay Bouwmeester/63* 25.00 60.00
4 Joni Pitkanen/100 20.00 50.00
5 Ryan Whitney/63* 15.00 40.00
6 Scottie Upshall/52* 12.00 30.00
7 Joffrey Lupul/56* 20.00 50.00
8 P-M Bouchard/50* 25.00 60.00
9 Petr Taticek/40* 8.00 20.00
10 Eric Nystrom/54* 6.00 15.00
11 Keith Ballard/45* 6.00 15.00
12 Steve Eminger/51* 12.00 30.00
13 Alexander Semin/45* 25.00 60.00
14 Chris Higgins/61* 15.00 40.00
16 Jakub Klepis/38* 8.00 20.00
17 Boyd Gordon/54* 10.00 25.00
18 Denis Grebeshkov/44* 10.00 25.00
20 Daniel Paille/46* 20.00 50.00
21 Anton Babchuk/38* 10.00 25.00
22 Sean Bergenheim/45* 12.50 30.00
23 Ben Eager/44* 10.00 25.00
24 Alexander Steen/49* 20.00 40.00
25 Cam Ward/57* 15.00 40.00
28 Jones Johansson/36* 8.00 20.00
29 Hannu Toivonen/59* 12.00 30.00
30 Jim Slater/48* 6.00 15.00

2002-03 BAP Memorabilia Franchise Players

STATED PRINT RUN 40 SETS
FP1 Paul Kariya 10.00 25.00
FP2 Ilya Kovalchuk 15.00 40.00
FP3 Joe Thornton 15.00 40.00
FP4 Miroslav Satan 10.00 25.00
FP5 Jarome Iginla 12.50 30.00
FP6 Ron Francis 10.00 25.00
FP7 Eric Daze 10.00 25.00
FP8 Patrick Roy 15.00 40.00
FP9 Rostislav Klesla 10.00 25.00
FP10 Mike Modano 12.50 30.00
FP11 Steve Yzerman 20.00 50.00
FP12 Mike Comrie 10.00 25.00
FP13 Roberto Luongo 12.50 30.00
FP14 Zigmund Palffy 10.00 25.00
FP15 Marian Gaborik 15.00 40.00
FP16 Jose Theodore 12.50 30.00
FP17 Scott Hartnell 12.50 30.00
FP18 Martin Brodeur 15.00 40.00
FP19 Alexei Yashin 10.00 25.00
FP20 Pavel Bure 10.00 25.00
FP21 Marian Hossa 10.00 25.00
FP22 Simon Gagne 12.50 30.00
FP23 Daniel Briere 10.00 25.00
FP24 Mario Lemieux 25.00 60.00
FP25 Chris Pronger 10.00 25.00
FP26 Owen Nolan 10.00 25.00
FP27 Nikolai Khabibulin 10.00 25.00
FP28 Mats Sundin 10.00 25.00
FP29 Markus Naslund 10.00 25.00
FP30 Jaromir Jagr 12.50 30.00

2002-03 BAP Memorabilia Future of the Game

STATED PRINT RUN 30 SETS
FG1 Pavel Datsyuk 15.00 40.00
FG2 Dan Blackburn 12.50 30.00
FG3 Ilya Kovalchuk 20.00 50.00
FG4 Roberto Luongo 20.00 50.00
FG5 Dany Heatley 20.00 50.00
FG6 Jose Theodore 15.00 40.00
FG7 Mike Comrie 12.50 30.00
FG8 Marian Gaborik 25.00 60.00
FG9 Simon Gagne 15.00 40.00
FG10 Joe Thornton 25.00 60.00
FG11 Trent Hunter 12.50 30.00
FG12 Martin Havlat 12.50 30.00
FG13 Scott Hartnell 15.00 40.00
FG14 Kristian Huselius 12.50 30.00
FG15 Rick DiPietro 12.50 30.00
FG16 Kyle Calder 12.50 30.00
FG17 Alex Tanguay 12.50 30.00
FG18 Brad Richards 12.50 30.00
FG19 Rostislav Klesla 12.50 30.00
FG20 Justin Williams 12.50 30.00
FG21 Jason Spezza 30.00 80.00
FG22 Jay Bouwmeester 12.50 30.00

2002-03 BAP Memorabilia He Shoots He Scores Points

ONE PER PACK
1 Mike Modano 1 pt. .25 .60
2 Jeremy Roenick 1 pt. .15 .40
3 Owen Nolan 1 pt. .15 .40
4 Chris Pronger 1 pt. .12 .30
5 Ron Francis 1 pt. .20 .50
6 Jose Theodore 1 pt. .15 .40
7 Brendan Shanahan 1 pt. .20 .50
8 Dany Heatley 1 pt. .15 .40
9 Paul Kariya 2 pts. .25 .60
10 Pavel Bure 2 pts. .25 .60
11 Peter Forsberg 2 pts. .25 .60
12 Joe Sakic 2 pts. .30 .75
13 Dominik Hasek 2 pts. .30 .75
14 Martin Brodeur 2 pts. .40 1.00
15 Eric Lindros 2 pts. .30 .75
16 Ilya Kovalchuk 2 pts. .25 .60
17 Jaromir Jagr 2 pts. .50 1.25
18 Patrick Roy 3 pts. .50 1.25
19 Mario Lemieux 3 pts. .60 1.50
20 Steve Yzerman 3 pts. .40 1.00

2002-03 BAP Memorabilia He Shoots He Scores Prizes

ANNOUNCED PRINT RUN 20 SETS
1 Steve Yzerman 20.00 50.00
2 Mario Lemieux 30.00 80.00
3 Patrick Roy 25.00 60.00
4 Jaromir Jagr 25.00 60.00
5 Ilya Kovalchuk 12.00 30.00
6 Eric Lindros 15.00 40.00
7 Martin Brodeur 20.00 50.00
8 Dominik Hasek 15.00 40.00
9 Joe Sakic 15.00 40.00
10 Peter Forsberg 12.00 30.00
11 Pavel Bure 12.00 30.00
12 Paul Kariya 12.00 30.00
13 Dany Heatley 10.00 25.00
14 Brendan Shanahan 12.00 30.00
15 Jose Theodore 10.00 25.00
16 Ron Francis 12.00 30.00
17 Chris Pronger 8.00 20.00
18 Owen Nolan 10.00 25.00
19 Jeremy Roenick 10.00 25.00
20 Mike Modano 15.00 40.00
21 Roberto Luongo 15.00 40.00
22 Marian Gaborik 15.00 40.00
23 Todd Bertuzzi 10.00 25.00
24 Pavel Datsyuk 12.00 30.00
25 Jarome Iginla 10.00 25.00
26 Mats Sundin 10.00 25.00
27 Mark Messier 15.00 40.00
28 Sergei Fedorov 15.00 40.00
29 Nicklas Lidstrom 10.00 25.00
30 Teemu Selanne 20.00 50.00

2002-03 BAP Memorabilia Magnificent Inserts

This 10-card set featured game-used equipment from the career of Mario Lemieux. Cards MI1-MI5 had a print run of 40 copies each and cards MI6-MI10 were limited to just 10 copies each. Cards MI6-MI10 are not priced due to scarcity.
MI1-M15 PRINT RUN 40 SETS
MI1 2000-01 Jersey 30.00 80.00
MI2 1985-86 Jersey 30.00 80.00
MI3 2002 All-Star Jersey 30.00 80.00
MI4 1987 Canada Cup Jersey 30.00 80.00
MI5 Dual Jersey 50.00 125.00
MI6 Number
MI7 Emblem
MI8 Triple Jersey
MI9 Quad Jersey
MI10 Complete Package

2002-03 BAP Memorabilia Magnificent Inserts Autographs

MI1 Mario Lemieux 75.00 150.00
MI2 Mario Lemieux 75.00 150.00
MI3 Mario Lemieux 75.00 150.00
MI4 Mario Lemieux 75.00 150.00
MI5 Mario Lemieux Dual 100.00 200.00

2002-03 BAP Memorabilia Mini Stanley Cups

Inserted one per hobby box, these miniature Stanley Cup replicas featured a player picture from a cup winning team on the front.
ONE PER HOBBY BOX
1 Johnny Bower 8.00 20.00
2 Tim Horton 12.00 30.00
3 Jean Beliveau 15.00 40.00
4 Lorne Worsley 8.00 20.00
5 Terry Sawchuk 12.00 30.00
6 Serge Savard 8.00 20.00
7 Henri Richard 8.00 20.00
8 Phil Esposito 8.00 20.00
9 Frank Mahovlich 8.00 20.00
10 Gerry Cheevers 8.00 20.00
11 Yvan Cournoyer 8.00 20.00
12 Bobby Clarke 8.00 20.00

13 Bernie Parent 8.00 20.00
14 Steve Shutt 8.00 20.00
15 Larry Robinson 8.00 20.00
16 Guy Lafleur 15.00 40.00
17 Guy Lapointe 8.00 20.00
18 Bryan Trottier 8.00 20.00
19 Mike Bossy 10.00 25.00
20 Denis Potvin 8.00 20.00
21 Bob Nystrom 8.00 20.00
22 Mark Messier 8.00 20.00
23 Andy Moog 8.00 20.00
24 Patrick Roy 20.00 50.00
25 Jari Kurri 10.00 25.00
26 Grant Fuhr 8.00 20.00
27 Doug Gilmour 8.00 20.00
28 Adam Graves 8.00 20.00
29 Mario Lemieux 20.00 50.00
30 Jaromir Jagr 15.00 40.00
31 John LeClair 8.00 20.00
32 Brian Leetch 8.00 20.00
33 Martin Brodeur 15.00 40.00
34 Peter Forsberg 12.00 30.00
35 Steve Yzerman 15.00 40.00
36 Nicklas Lidstrom 12.00 30.00
37 Mike Modano 12.00 30.00
38 Scott Stevens 8.00 20.00
39 Joe Sakic 12.00 30.00
40 Dominik Hasek 12.00 30.00

2002-03 BAP Memorabilia Stanley Cup Champions

This 15-card set featured swatches of game-worn jersey from the 2002 Stanley Cup Champion Detroit Red Wings. Cards were limited to just 40 copies each.
STATED PRINT RUN 40 SETS
SCC1 Jiri Fischer 15.00 40.00
SCC2 Mathieu Dandenault 15.00 40.00
SCC3 Chris Chelios 15.00 40.00
SCC4 Dominik Hasek 25.00 50.00
SCC5 Steve Yzerman 20.00 50.00
SCC6 Brendan Shanahan 15.00 40.00
SCC7 Luc Robitaille 15.00 40.00
SCC8 Nicklas Lidstrom 15.00 40.00
SCC9 Manny Legace 20.00 40.00
SCC10 Sergei Fedorov 30.00 60.00
SCC11 Darren McCarty 15.00 40.00
SCC12 Jason Williams 15.00 40.00
SCC13 Pavel Datsyuk 15.00 40.00
SCC14 Tomas Holmstrom 15.00 40.00
SCC15 Brett Hull 12.00 30.00

2002-03 BAP Memorabilia Stanley Cup Playoffs

This 32-card set featured swatches of game-worn jersey. Print runs are listed below.
STATED PRINT RUNS 10 - 90
SC1 Roman Cechmanek/90 8.00 20.00
SC2 Patrick Lalime/90 8.00 20.00
SC3 Gary Roberts/90 8.00 20.00
SC4 Alexei Yashin/90 8.00 20.00
SC5 Joe Thornton/90 12.00 30.00
SC6 Jose Theodore/90 15.00 40.00
SC7 Ron Francis/90 12.00 30.00
SC8 Martin Brodeur/90 20.00 50.00
SC9 Owen Nolan/90 8.00 20.00
SC10 Sean Burke/90 8.00 20.00
SC11 Felix Potvin/90 15.00 40.00
SC12 Peter Forsberg/90 15.00 40.00
SC13 Todd Bertuzzi/90 8.00 20.00
SC14 Steve Yzerman/90 20.00 50.00
SC15 Eric Daze/90 8.00 20.00
SC16 Brent Johnson/90 8.00 20.00
SC17 Teemu Selanne/60 15.00 40.00
SC18 Chris Drury/60 8.00 20.00
SC19 Alexander Mogilny/60 8.00 20.00
SC20 Daniel Alfredsson/60 8.00 20.00
SC21 Sergei Fedorov/60 15.00 40.00
SC22 Keith Tkachuk/60 8.00 20.00
SC23 Saku Koivu/60 8.00 20.00
SC24 Jeff O'Neill/60 8.00 20.00
SC25 Curtis Joseph/40 15.00 40.00
SC26 Arturs Irbe/40 15.00 40.00
SC27 Dominik Hasek/40 30.00 80.00
SC28 Patrick Roy/40 30.00 80.00
SC29 Ron Francis/30 25.00 60.00
SC30 Dominik Hasek/30 20.00 50.00
SC31 Steve Yzerman/10
SC32 Nicklas Lidstrom/10

2002-03 BAP Memorabilia Teammates

STATED PRINT RUN 70 SETS
TM1 D.Hasek/S.Yzerman 25.00 60.00
TM2 S.Fedorov/B.Shanahan 15.00 40.00
TM3 L.Robitaille/B.Hull 15.00 40.00
TM4 J.Sakic/P. Forsberg 25.00 60.00
TM5 R.Blake/P.Roy 15.00 40.00
TM6 P.Bure/E.Lindros 12.50 30.00
TM7 B.Leetch/M.Messier 15.00 40.00
TM8 M.Sundin/C.Joseph 12.50 30.00
TM9 J.Roenick/R.Cechmanek 12.50 30.00
TM10 M.Recchi/S.Gagne 12.50 30.00
TM11 J.Jagr/P. Bondra 12.50 30.00
TM12 J.Theodore/S.Koivu 12.50 30.00
TM13 Z.Palffy/F.Potvin 12.50 30.00
TM14 M.Brodeur/P.Elias 20.00 50.00
TM15 M.Lemieux/A.Kovalev 25.00 60.00
TM16 C.Pronger/A.MacInnis 12.50 30.00
TM17 D.Weight/K.Tkachuk 12.50 30.00
TM18 T.Selanne/O.Nolan 12.50 30.00
TM19 E.Jovanovski/M.Naslund 12.50 30.00
TM20 J.Iginla/R.Turek 15.00 40.00

2003-04 BAP Memorabilia

This 250-card set came in packs as a 200-card base set including 100 veteran skaters, a 70-card Between the Pipes subset, and 30 rookies that were short-printed. Cards 201-250 were available via an online offer only for $29 US.
COMP. SET w/o UPDATE (200) 20.00 50.00
COMP.SET w/o SP's (170) 10.00 25.00
201-250 AVAIL.VIA ONLINE OFFER ONLY
1 Al MacInnis .30 .75
2 Alexei Morozov .20 .50
3 Ales Hemsky .30 .75
4 Ales Kotalik .20 .50
5 Alex Kovalev .25 .60
6 Alexander Frolov .25 .60
7 Alexander Mogilny .25 .60
8 Alexei Yashin .25 .60
9 Alexei Zhamnov .25 .60
10 Anson Carter .25 .60
11 Barret Jackman .20 .50
12 Bill Guerin .30 .75
13 Brad Richards .30 .75
14 Brad Stuart .20 .50
15 Brendan Shanahan .40 1.00
16 Chris Drury .25 .60
17 Brett Hull .40 1.00
18 Daniel Alfredsson .30 .75
19 Daniel Briere .30 .75
20 Dany Heatley .30 .75
21 David Legwand .25 .60
22 Daymond Langkow .20 .50
23 Derian Hatcher .20 .50
24 Doug Weight .30 .75
25 Ed Jovanovski .30 .75
26 Eric Daze .25 .60
27 Eric Lindros .50 1.25
28 Geoff Sanderson .20 .50
29 Glen Murray .25 .60
30 Henrik Zetterberg .40 1.00
31 Ilya Kovalchuk .30 .75
32 Jamie Langenbrunner .25 .60
33 Jarome Iginla .30 .75
34 Jaromir Jagr .75 2.00
35 Jason Allison .25 .60
36 Jason Spezza .30 .75
37 Jay Bouwmeester .30 .75
38 Jeff O'Neill .20 .50
39 Jere Lehtinen .25 .60
40 Jeremy Roenick .30 .75
41 Joe Sakic .50 1.25
42 Joe Thornton .40 1.00
43 John LeClair .30 .75
44 Keith Tkachuk .30 .75
45 Kristian Huselius .25 .60
46 Marian Gaborik .50 1.25
47 Marian Hossa .25 .60
48 Mario Lemieux 1.00 2.50
49 Mark Messier .50 1.25
50 Markus Naslund .30 .75
51 Martin Havlat .30 .75
52 Martin St. Louis .30 .75
53 Mats Sundin .30 .75
54 Michael Peca .25 .60
55 Mike Comrie .25 .60
56 Mike Johnson .20 .50
57 Mike Komisarek .20 .50
58 Mike Modano .50 1.25
59 Milan Hejduk .25 .60
60 Miroslav Satan .25 .60
61 Nicklas Lidstrom .30 .75
62 Olli Jokinen .30 .75
63 Owen Nolan .25 .60
64 Pascal Dupuis .20 .50
65 Patrick Marleau .30 .75
66 Patrik Elias .30 .75
67 Patrik Stefan .20 .50
68 Paul Kariya .40 1.00
69 Pavel Bure .40 1.00
70 Pavol Demitra .40 1.00
71 Peter Bondra .25 .60
72 Peter Forsberg .40 1.00
73 Petr Sykora .25 .60
74 Ray Whitney .25 .60
75 Richard Zednik .20 .50
76 Rick Nash .30 .75
77 Rob Blake .30 .75
78 Ron Francis .40 1.00
79 Ryan Smyth .25 .60
80 Saku Koivu .30 .75
81 Sandis Ozolinsh .20 .50
82 Scott Hartnell .30 .75
83 Scott Niedermayer .25 .60
84 Scottie Upshall .25 .60
85 Sergei Fedorov .50 1.25
86 Sergei Gonchar .20 .50
87 Sergei Samsonov .25 .60
88 Sergei Zubov .25 .60
89 Simon Gagne .30 .75
90 Zdeno Chara .25 .60
91 Chuck Kobasew .20 .50
92 Steve Yzerman .75 2.00
93 Teemu Selanne .60 1.50
94 Todd Bertuzzi .30 .75
95 Tony Amonte .25 .60
96 Vaclav Prospal .20 .50
97 Vincent Lecavalier .25 .60
98 Slava Kozlov .25 .60
99 Sylvester Flis .50 1.25
100 Zigmund Palffy .30 .75
101 Alex Auld .20 .50
102 Andrew Raycroft .25 .60
103 Ari Ahonen .20 .50
104 Brent Johnson .25 .60
105 Brian Boucher .25 .60
106 Brian Finley .20 .50
107 Byron Dafoe .25 .60
108 Chris Osgood .30 .75
109 Cristobal Huet .25 .60
110 Corey Schwab .20 .50
111 Curtis Joseph .30 .75
112 Curtis Sanford .20 .50
113 Dan Blackburn .25 .60
114 Dan Cloutier .25 .60
115 David Aebischer .25 .60
116 Dwayne Roloson .25 .60
117 Ed Belfour .30 .75
118 Evgeni Nabokov .25 .60
119 Felix Potvin .50 1.25
120 Fred Brathwaite .25 .60
121 Garth Snow .25 .60
122 Jani Hurme .20 .50
123 Jason Bacashihua .20 .50
124 Jean-Sebastien Giguere .30 .75
125 Jeff Hackett .25 .60
126 Jocelyn Thibault .25 .60
127 Johan Hedberg .25 .60
128 John Grahame .20 .50
129 Jose Theodore .25 .60
130 Josh Harding .25 .60
131 Jussi Markkanen .20 .50
132 Kevin Weekes .25 .60
133 Manny Fernandez .25 .60
134 Manny Legace .25 .60
135 Marc Denis .25 .60
136 Martin Biron .25 .60
137 Martin Brodeur .60 1.50
138 Martin Gerber .20 .50
139 Martin Prusek .25 .60
140 Marty Turco .30 .75
141 Mathieu Garon .20 .50
142 Maxime Ouellet .25 .60
143 Michael Leighton .20 .50
144 Miikka Kiprusoff .25 .60
145 Mika Noronen .20 .50
146 Mikael Tellqvist .20 .50
147 Mike Dunham .25 .60
148 Nikolai Khabibulin .25 .60
149 Olaf Kolzig .25 .60
150 Pascal Leclaire .20 .50
151 Pasi Nurminen .25 .60
152 Patrick Lalime .25 .60
153 Patrick Roy .75 2.00
154 Ray Emery .20 .50
155 Rick DiPietro .25 .60
156 Robert Esche .20 .50
157 Roberto Luongo .50 1.25
158 Roman Cechmanek .25 .60
159 Roman Turek .25 .60
160 Ron Tugnutt .25 .60
161 Ryan Miller .30 .75
162 Sean Burke .20 .50
163 Sebastien Caron .25 .60
164 Sebastien Charpentier .20 .50
165 Steve Shields .25 .60
166 Tomas Vokoun .25 .60
167 Tommy Salo .25 .60
168 Trevor Kidd .20 .50
169 Vesa Toskala .20 .50
170 Zac Bierk .20 .50
171 Tuomo Ruutu RC .75 2.00
172 Jordin Tootoo RC 1.00 2.50
173 Joni Pitkanen RC .75 2.00
174 Peter Sejna RC .60 1.50
175 Dan Hamhuis RC .60 1.50
176 Eric Staal RC 2.50 6.00
177 Dan Fritsche RC .50 1.25
178 Dustin Brown RC 1.00 2.50
179 Christopher Higgins RC 1.00 2.50
180 Nathan Horton RC 1.25 3.00
181 Milan Michalek RC 1.00 2.50
182 Boyd Gordon RC .60 1.50
183 Marc-Andre Fleury RC 3.00 8.00
184 Joffrey Lupul RC 1.25 3.00
185 David Hale RC .50 1.25
186 Sean Bergenheim RC .60 1.50
187 Tim Gleason RC .60 1.50
188 Pavel Vorobiev RC .60 1.50
189 Paul Martin RC .60 1.50
190 Marek Svatos RC 1.00 2.50
191 Antoine Vermette RC 1.00 2.50
192 Matt Stajan RC .75 2.00
193 Alexander Semin RC 1.50 4.00
194 Brent Burns RC 1.25 3.00
195 Jiri Hudler RC 1.25 3.00
196 Matthew Lombardi RC .60 1.50
197 Maxim Kondratiev RC .50 1.25
198 Brent Krahn RC .50 1.25
199 Antti Miettinen RC .75 2.00
200 Patrice Bergeron RC 2.50 6.00
201 Cover Card .20 .50
Checklist
202 Marek Zidlicky XRC .30 .75
203 John-Michael Liles XRC .40 1.00
204 Ryan Malone XRC .60 1.50
205 Tom Preissing XRC .40 1.00
206 Rastislav Stana XRC .50 1.25
207 Mike Commodore .20 .50
208 Jaromir Jagr .75 2.00
209 Fredrik Sjostrom XRC .50 1.25
210 Nikolai Zherdev XRC .60 1.50
211 Derek Roy XRC .60 1.50
212 Marcus Nilsson .20 .50
213 Milan Michalek XRC .60 1.50
214 Tomas Plekanec XRC 1.00 2.50
215 Mark Popovic XRC .40 1.00
216 Frederic Henry XRC .40 1.00
217 Nolan Schaefer XRC .40 1.00
218 Colton Orr XRC .40 1.00
219 Mike Smith XRC 1.00 2.50
220 Cory Stillman .20 .50
221 Carl Corazzini XRC .30 .75
222 Eric Heffler XRC .40 1.00
223 Dimitri Afanasenkov .25 .60
224 Garth Murray .25 .60
225 Matt Ellison XRC .30 .75
226 Ville Nieminen .20 .50
227 Brooks Laich XRC .50 1.25
228 Sergei Gonchar .20 .50
229 Fedor Tyutin XRC .30 .75
230 Ron Francis .40 1.00
231 Phil Osaer XRC .30 .75
232 Miikka Kiprusoff .25 .60
233 Michal Barinka XRC .30 .75
234 Brad Boyes XRC .50 1.25
235 Erik Westrum XRC .30 .75
236 Kari Lehtonen XRC 1.50 4.00
237 Chad Alban XRC .50 1.25
238 Thomas Pock XRC .40 1.00
239 Darryl Sydor .20 .50
240 Greg Mauldin XRC .40 1.00
241 Eric Perrin XRC .30 .75
242 Michael Ryder .25 .60
243 Esa Pirnes XRC .30 .75
244 Matt Murley XRC .40 1.00
245 Trevor Daley XRC .50 1.25
246 Libor Pivko XRC .30 .75
247 John Pohl XRC .30 .75
248 Seamus Kotyk XRC .30 .75
249 Sergei Zinovjev XRC .30 .75
250 Joe Nieuwendyk .30 .75

2003-04 BAP Memorabilia Ruby

*1-170 VETS/200: 2X TO 5X BASIC CARDS
*171-200 ROOKIES/200: .8X TO 2X
PRINT RUN 200 SER.#'d SETS

2003-04 BAP Memorabilia Sapphire

*1-170 VETS/100: 3X TO 8X BASIC CARDS
*171-200 ROOKIE/100 : 1.2X TO 3X
PRINT RUN 100 SER.#'d SETS

2003-04 BAP Memorabilia All-Star Jerseys

SEMISTARS 6.00 15.00
UNLISTED STARS 8.00 20.00
STATED PRINT RUN 90 SETS
ASJ1 Peter Forsberg 10.00 25.00
ASJ2 Jaromir Jagr 10.00 25.00
ASJ3 Mike Modano 8.00 20.00
ASJ4 Bill Guerin 6.00 15.00
ASJ5 Paul Kariya 6.00 15.00
ASJ6 Nicklas Lidstrom 6.00 15.00
ASJ7 Teemu Selanne 6.00 15.00
ASJ8 Patrick Roy 15.00 40.00
ASJ9 Alex Kovalev 6.00 15.00
ASJ10 Dany Heatley MVP
ASJ11 Sergei Fedorov 10.00 25.00
ASJ12 Jaromir Jagr 10.00 25.00
ASJ13 Brian Leetch 6.00 15.00
ASJ14 Joe Thornton 8.00 20.00
ASJ15 Jose Theodore 8.00 20.00
ASJ16 Brendan Shanahan 6.00 15.00
ASJ17 Patrick Roy 15.00 40.00
ASJ18 Chris Pronger 6.00 15.00
ASJ19 Nicklas Lidstrom 6.00 15.00
ASJ20 Eric Daze MVP
ASJ21 Martin Brodeur 15.00 40.00
ASJ22 Pavel Bure 6.00 15.00
ASJ23 Peter Forsberg 12.50 30.00
ASJ24 Paul Kariya 6.00 15.00
ASJ25 Brian Leetch 6.00 15.00
ASJ26 Teemu Selanne 6.00 15.00
ASJ27 Markus Naslund 6.00 15.00
ASJ28 Patrick Roy 15.00 40.00
ASJ29 Joe Sakic 10.00 25.00
ASJ30 Bill Guerin MVP
ASJ31 Al MacInnis 6.00 15.00
ASJ32 Jaromir Jagr 10.00 25.00
ASJ33 John LeClair 6.00 15.00
ASJ34 Martin Brodeur 15.00 40.00
ASJ35 Mike Modano 8.00 20.00
ASJ36 Jeremy Roenick 8.00 20.00
ASJ37 Brendan Shanahan 6.00 15.00
ASJ38 Mats Sundin 6.00 15.00
ASJ39 Steve Yzerman 12.50 30.00
ASJ40 Pavel Bure MVP

2003-04 BAP Memorabilia All-Star Staring Lineup

1 Nikolai Khabibulin 8.00 20.00
2 Brian Leetch 8.00 20.00
3 Sandis Ozolinsh 8.00 20.00
4 Mario Lemieux 15.00 40.00
5 Jaromir Jagr 10.00 25.00
6 Alex Kovalev 8.00 20.00
7 Patrick Roy 15.00 40.00
8 Nicklas Lidstrom 8.00 20.00
9 Rob Blake 8.00 20.00
10 Mike Modano 10.00 25.00
11 Bill Guerin 8.00 20.00
12 Teemu Selanne 8.00 20.00

2003-04 BAP Memorabilia All-Star Teammates

STATED PRINT RUN 30 SETS
AST1 P.Forsberg/P.Roy 30.00 80.00
AST2 D.Heatley/J.Jagr 20.00 50.00
AST3 M.Modano/B.Guerin 20.00 50.00
AST4 N.Lidstrom/P.Kariya 20.00 50.00
AST5 B.Leetch/J.Thornton 25.00 60.00
AST6 J.Theodore/P.Roy 40.00 100.00
AST7 B.Shanahan/B.Leetch 20.00 50.00
AST8 M.Brodeur/P.Roy 40.00 100.00
AST9 P.Forsberg/N.Lidstrom 25.00 60.00
AST10 J.Sakic/B.Leetch 30.00 80.00

2003-04 BAP Memorabilia Brush with Greatness

This 25-card set featured artist renderings on the card fronts along with foil highlights. Foil cards were inserted at one per box. A contest entry parallel without the foil effect was also created and more entry plentiful. On the back of the contest cards were rules and instructions for entering a drawing for a jersey of the given player with the artist's rendering painted on the jersey. Some of the jerseys also included the player's autograph. Entry deadlines were staggered, but the last deadline was August 2004.
FOIL ODDS 1 PER BOX
COMMON CONTEST CARD .60 1.50
1 Mario Lemieux 6.00 15.00
2 Martin Brodeur 5.00 12.00
3 Marian Gaborik 3.00 8.00
4 Paul Kariya 2.00 5.00
5 Peter Forsberg 5.00 12.00
6 Jason Spezza 3.00 6.00
7 Maurice Richard 4.00 10.00
8 Jacques Plante 3.00 8.00
9 Henrik Zetterberg 3.00 6.00
10 Ed Belfour 2.00 5.00
11 Nicklas Lidstrom 2.00 5.00
12 Rick Nash 2.50 6.00
13 Bill Barilko 2.00 5.00
14 Jean-Sebastien Giguere 2.00 5.00
15 Jose Theodore 2.00 5.00
16 Pavel Bure 2.00 5.00
17 Ilya Kovalchuk 2.50 6.00
18 Mats Sundin 2.00 5.00
19 Terry Sawchuk 3.00 8.00
20 Joe Thornton 3.00 8.00
21 Dominik Hasek 4.00 10.00
22 Joe Sakic 4.00 10.00
23 Dany Heatley 2.50 6.00
24 Steve Yzerman 5.00 12.00
25 Patrick Roy 6.00 15.00

2003-04 BAP Memorabilia Deep in the Crease

COMPLETE SET (15) 12.00 30.00
D1 Atlanta Thrashers .75 2.00
D2 Chicago Blackhawks .75 2.00
D3 Montreal Canadiens .75 2.00
D4 New Jersey Devils .75 2.00
D5 New York Rangers .75 2.00
D6 Nashville Predators .75 2.00
D7 Anaheim Mighty Ducks .75 2.00
D8 Detroit Red Wings 2.50 6.00
D9 Toronto Maple Leafs 1.25 3.00
D10 Vancouver Canucks .75 2.00
D11 Minnesota Wild .75 2.00
D12 St.Louis Blues .75 2.00
D13 Buffalo Sabres 1.25 3.00
D14 Florida Panthers 1.25 3.00
D15 Pittsburgh Penguins 2.00 5.00

2003-04 BAP Memorabilia Draft Redemptions

Inserted randomly in packs, this 30-card set featured cards representing the top thirty draft picks in 2003. Each card was redeemable for the player it represented once that player made his NHL debut. Collectors had six months to redeem the cards once the player was available. The redemption cards themselves were hand-numbered out of 100.
ANNOUNCED FINAL PRINT RUN 27-66
1 Marc-Andre Fleury/56* 40.00 100.00
2 Eric Staal/51* 40.00 100.00
3 Nathan Horton/48* 25.00 60.00
4 Nikolai Zherdev/52* 25.00 60.00
5 Thomas Vanek/66* 20.00 50.00
6 Milan Michalek/41* 25.00 60.00
7 Ryan Suter/46* 15.00 40.00
8 Braydon Coburn/56* 15.00 40.00
9 Dion Phaneuf/65* 25.00 60.00
10 Andrei Kostitsyn/55* 12.50 30.00
11 Jeff Carter/52* 30.00 60.00
13 Dustin Brown/43* 15.00 40.00
14 Brent Seabrook/46* 12.50 30.00
15 Robert Nilsson/49* 12.50 30.00
16 Steve Bernier/56* 12.50 30.00
17 Zach Parise/57* 25.00 60.00
18 Eric Fehr/43* 12.50 30.00
19 Ryan Getzlaf/59* 40.00 80.00
20 Brent Burns/46* 15.00 40.00
21 Mark Stuart/36* 8.00 20.00
22 Marc-Antoine Pouliot/35* 8.00 20.00
23 Ryan Kesler/40* 20.00 50.00
24 Mike Richards/60* 20.00 50.00
25 Anthony Stewart/51* 12.50 30.00
27 Jeff Tambellini/50* 8.00 20.00
28 Corey Perry/57* 25.00 60.00
29 Patrick Eaves/52* 10.00 25.00
30 Shawn Belle/27* 8.00 20.00

2003-04 BAP Memorabilia Future of the Game

STATED PRINT RUN 30 SETS
FG1 Scottie Upshall 10.00 25.00
FG2 Ray Emery 10.00 25.00
FG3 Rick Nash 25.00 60.00
FG4 Stanislav Chistov 8.00 20.00
FG5 Ryan Miller 15.00 40.00
FG6 Henrik Zetterberg 20.00 50.00
FG7 Alexander Frolov 8.00 20.00
FG8 Barret Jackman 8.00 20.00
FG9 Brandon Reid 8.00 20.00
FG10 Mike Komisarek 8.00 20.00
FG11 Alexei Smirnov 8.00 20.00
FG12 Steve Ott 10.00 25.00
FG13 Mike Cammalleri 10.00 25.00
FG14 Jason Spezza 25.00 60.00
FG15 Carlo Colaiacovo 8.00 20.00
FG16 Jared Aulin 8.00 20.00
FG17 Ales Hemsky 12.00 30.00
FG18 Marc-Andre Fleury 20.00 50.00
FG19 Jay Bouwmeester 20.00 50.00
FG20 Dustin Brown 12.00 30.00

2003-04 BAP Memorabilia Future Wave

STATED PRINT RUN 60 SETS
FW1 Marc-Andre Fleury 25.00 60.00
FW2 Ray Emery 12.00 30.00
FW3 David Aebischer 12.00 30.00
FW4 Rick DiPietro 12.00 30.00
FW5 Dan Blackburn 8.00 20.00
FW6 Mathieu Garon 8.00 20.00
FW7 Ryan Miller 15.00 40.00
FW8 Brian Finley 8.00 20.00
FW9 Alex Auld 8.00 20.00
FW10 Mika Noronen 8.00 20.00
FW11 Mikael Tellqvist 12.00 30.00
FW12 Andrew Raycroft 12.00 30.00

2003-04 BAP Memorabilia Gloves

STATED PRINT RUN 30 SETS
GUG1 Jean Sebastien Giguere 15.00 40.00
GUG2 Patrick Roy 30.00 60.00
GUG3 Marty Turco 15.00 40.00
GUG4 Olaf Kolzig 12.00 30.00
GUG5 Patrick Lalime 15.00 40.00
GUG6 Jacques Plante 30.00 80.00
GUG7 Bill Durnan 15.00 40.00
GUG8 Bernie Parent 15.00 40.00
GUG9 Vladislav Tretiak 25.00 60.00
GUG10 Charlie Hodge 15.00 40.00
GUG11 Keith Tkachuk 15.00 40.00
GUG12 Mario Lemieux 30.00 60.00
GUG13 Eric Lindros 15.00 40.00
GUG14 Sergei Samsonov 15.00 40.00
GUG15 Jarome Iginla 15.00 40.00
GUG16 Wendel Clark 15.00 40.00
GUG17 Dickie Moore 15.00 40.00
GUG18 Bill Gadsby 30.00 60.00
GUG19 Bernie Geoffrion 15.00 40.00
GUG20 Eddie Shore 30.00 60.00

2003-04 BAP Memorabilia He Shoots He Scores Points

ONE PER PACK
1 Jose Theodore 1 Pt. .40 1.00
2 Jeremy Roenick 1 Pt. .40 1.00
3 Chris Pronger 1 Pt. .40 1.00
4 Markus Naslund 1 Pt. .40 1.00
5 Nicklas Lidstrom 1 Pt. .40 1.00
6 Dany Heatley 1 Pt. .40 1.00
7 Bill Guerin 1 Pt. .40 1.00
8 Pavel Bure 1 Pt. .40 1.00
9 Steve Yzerman 2 Pts. .40 1.00
10 Joe Thornton 2 Pts. .40 1.00
11 Mats Sundin 2 Pts. .40 1.00
12 Brendan Shanahan 2 Pts. .40 1.00
13 Teemu Selanne 2 Pts. .40 1.00
14 Joe Sakic 2 Pts. .40 1.00
15 Mike Modano 2 Pts. .40 1.00
16 Paul Kariya 2 Pts. .40 1.00
17 Sergei Fedorov 2 Pts. .40 1.00
18 Patrick Roy 3 Pts. .40 1.00
19 Peter Forsberg 3 Pts. .40 1.00
20 Martin Brodeur 3 Pts. .40 1.00

2003-04 BAP Memorabilia Jersey and Stick

STATED PRINT RUN 90 SETS
SJ1 Joe Thornton 12.00 30.00
SJ2 Sergei Samsonov 8.00 20.00
SJ3 Jarome Iginla 10.00 25.00
SJ4 Ron Francis 8.00 20.00
SJ5 Jocelyn Thibault 8.00 20.00
SJ6 Mats Sundin 8.00 20.00
SJ7 Rob Blake 8.00 20.00
SJ8 Al MacInnis 8.00 20.00
SJ9 Rick Nash 15.00 40.00
SJ10 Marty Turco 8.00 20.00
SJ11 Bill Guerin 8.00 20.00
SJ12 Chris Chelios 8.00 20.00
SJ13 Luc Robitaille 8.00 20.00
SJ14 Mike Comrie 8.00 20.00
SJ15 Markus Naslund 8.00 20.00
SJ16 Roberto Luongo 10.00 25.00
SJ17 Peter Bondra 8.00 20.00
SJ18 John LeClair 8.00 20.00
SJ19 Rick DiPietro 8.00 20.00
SJ20 Tony Amonte 8.00 20.00
SJ21 Eric Lindros 8.00 20.00
SJ22 Jeremy Roenick 10.00 25.00
SJ23 Ilya Kovalchuk 12.50 30.00
SJ24 Dany Heatley 8.00 20.00
SJ25 Patrick Roy 15.00 40.00
SJ26 Joe Sakic 15.00 40.00
SJ27 Peter Forsberg 12.50 30.00
SJ28 Mike Modano 12.50 30.00
SJ29 Steve Yzerman 20.00 50.00
SJ30 Nicklas Lidstrom 8.00 20.00
SJ31 Brett Hull 8.00 20.00
SJ32 Jose Theodore 8.00 20.00
SJ33 Martin Brodeur 15.00 40.00
SJ34 Pavel Bure 8.00 20.00
SJ35 Mario Lemieux 20.00 50.00
SJ36 Jaromir Jagr 12.50 30.00
SJ37 Marian Gaborik 20.00 50.00
SJ38 Brendan Shanahan 8.00 20.00
SJ39 Dominik Hasek 12.50 30.00
SJ40 Todd Bertuzzi 8.00 20.00

2003-04 BAP Memorabilia Jerseys

STATED PRINT RUN 90 SETS
GJ1 Joe Thornton 10.00 25.00
GJ2 Dominik Hasek 10.00 25.00
GJ3 Jarome Iginla 10.00 25.00
GJ4 Ron Francis 6.00 15.00
GJ5 Henrik Zetterberg 8.00 20.00
GJ6 Mats Sundin 6.00 15.00
GJ7 Rob Blake 6.00 15.00
GJ8 Al MacInnis 6.00 15.00
GJ9 Milan Hejduk 6.00 15.00
GJ10 Rick Nash 10.00 25.00
GJ11 Marty Turco 6.00 15.00
GJ12 Jean-Sebastien Giguere 6.00 15.00
GJ13 Jason Spezza 8.00 20.00
GJ14 Luc Robitaille 6.00 15.00
GJ15 Alexander Mogilny 6.00 15.00
GJ16 Mike Comrie 6.00 15.00
GJ17 Markus Naslund 6.00 15.00
GJ18 Roberto Luongo 10.00 25.00
GJ19 Jay Bouwmeester 6.00 15.00
GJ20 Marian Hossa 6.00 15.00
GJ21 Todd Bertuzzi 6.00 15.00
GJ22 Saku Koivu 6.00 15.00
GJ23 Curtis Joseph 6.00 15.00
GJ24 Rick DiPietro 6.00 15.00
GJ25 Ed Belfour 6.00 15.00
GJ26 Eric Lindros 6.00 15.00
GJ27 Jeremy Roenick 8.00 20.00
GJ28 Brian Leetch 6.00 15.00
GJ29 Owen Nolan 6.00 15.00
GJ30 Simon Gagne 6.00 15.00
GJ31 Brendan Shanahan 6.00 15.00
GJ32 Ilya Kovalchuk 10.00 25.00
GJ33 Dany Heatley 10.00 25.00
GJ34 Patrick Roy 15.00 40.00
GJ35 Joe Sakic 12.00 30.00
GJ36 Peter Forsberg 8.00 20.00
GJ37 Mike Modano 8.00 20.00
GJ38 Steve Yzerman 15.00 40.00
GJ39 Nicklas Lidstrom 6.00 15.00
GJ40 Brett Hull 6.00 15.00
GJ41 Jose Theodore 8.00 20.00
GJ42 Martin Brodeur 12.00 30.00
GJ43 Pavel Bure 6.00 15.00
GJ44 Mark Messier 6.00 15.00
GJ45 Mario Lemieux 20.00 50.00
GJ46 Jaromir Jagr 10.00 25.00
GJ47 Marian Gaborik 12.00 30.00
GJ48 Teemu Selanne 6.00 15.00
GJ49 Paul Kariya 6.00 15.00
GJ50 Sergei Fedorov 8.00 20.00

2003-04 BAP Memorabilia Masks III

COMPLETE SET (20) 15.00 40.00
1 Jean-Sebastien Giguere 4.00 10.00
2 Roman Cechmanek 3.00 8.00
3 Dominik Hasek 5.00 12.00
4 Roberto Luongo 5.00 12.00
5 Ryan Miller 6.00 15.00
6 Sean Burke 3.00 8.00
7 Kevin Weekes 3.00 8.00
8 Mike Dunham 3.00 8.00
9 Jeff Hackett 3.00 8.00
10 Martin Prusek 3.00 8.00
11 Olaf Kolzig 3.00 8.00
12 Nikolai Khabibulin 3.00 8.00
13 Pasi Nurminen 3.00 8.00
14 Johan Hedberg 3.00 8.00
15 Marty Turco 3.00 8.00
16 Felix Potvin 3.00 8.00
17 Marc Denis 3.00 8.00
18 Marc-Andre Fleury 8.00 20.00
19 David Aebischer 3.00 8.00
20 Jocelyn Thibault 3.00 8.00

2003-04 BAP Memorabilia Masks III Gold

*GOLD: 2.5X TO 6X BASIC MASKS
STATED PRINT RUN 30 SETS

2003-04 BAP Memorabilia Masks III Silver

*SILVER: 1X TO 2.5X BASIC MASKS
PRINT RUN SERIAL 300 SETS

2003-04 BAP Memorabilia Practice Jerseys

STATED PRINT RUN 40 SETS
PMP1 Curtis Joseph 10.00 25.00
PMP2 Martin Brodeur 15.00 40.00
PMP3 Ed Jovanovski 10.00 25.00
PMP4 Scott Neidermayer 10.00 25.00
PMP5 Al MacInnis 10.00 25.00
PMP6 Rob Blake 10.00 25.00
PMP7 Chris Pronger 10.00 25.00
PMP8 Owen Nolan 10.00 25.00
PMP9 Eric Lindros 10.00 25.00
PMP10 Paul Kariya 10.00 25.00
PMP11 Steve Yzerman 15.00 40.00
PMP12 Brendan Shanahan 10.00 25.00
PMP13 Theo Fleury 10.00 25.00
PMP14 Ryan Smyth 10.00 25.00
PMP15 Joe Nieuwendyk 10.00 25.00
PMP16 Jarome Iginla 12.50 30.00

2003-04 BAP Memorabilia Stanley Cup Champions

STATED PRINT RUN 40 SETS
SCC1 Martin Brodeur 40.00 100.00
SCC2 Jamie Langenbrunner 12.50 30.00
SCC3 Scott Gomez 12.50 30.00
SCC4 Joe Nieuwendyk 12.50 30.00
SCC5 John Madden 12.50 30.00
SCC6 Scott Niedermayer 12.50 30.00
SCC7 Jeff Friesen 12.50 30.00
SCC8 Scott Stevens 25.00 60.00
SCC9 Patrik Elias 12.50 30.00
SCC10 Corey Schwab 12.50 30.00

2003-04 BAP Memorabilia Stanley Cup Playoffs

CARDS 1-16 PRINT RUN 90 SETS
CARDS 17-24 PRINT RUN 80 SETS
CARDS 25-28 PRINT RUN 50 SETS
CARDS 29-30 PRINT RUN 20 SETS
CARDS 31-32 PRINT RUN 10 SETS
29-32 NOT PRICED DUE TO SCARCITY
SCP1 Steve Yzerman 15.00 40.00
SCP2 Jean-Sebastien Giguere 6.00 15.00
SCP3 Doug Weight 6.00 15.00
SCP4 Ed Jovanovski 6.00 15.00
SCP5 Joe Sakic 12.00 30.00
SCP6 Marian Gaborik 10.00 25.00
SCP7 Mike Modano 10.00 25.00
SCP8 Georges Laraque 6.00 15.00
SCP9 Marian Hossa 8.00 20.00
SCP10 Alexei Yashin 6.00 15.00
SCP11 Scott Niedermayer 6.00 15.00
SCP12 Jeff Hackett 6.00 15.00
SCP13 Martin St.Louis 6.00 15.00
SCP14 Jaromir Jagr 10.00 25.00
SCP15 Mark Recchi 6.00 15.00
SCP16 Alex Mogilny 6.00 15.00
SCP17 Paul Kariya 8.00 20.00
SCP18 Marty Turco 6.00 15.00
SCP19 Dwayne Roloson 6.00 15.00
SCP20 Markus Naslund 8.00 20.00
SCP21 Daniel Alfredsson 6.00 15.00
SCP22 Jeremy Roenick 8.00 20.00
SCP23 Vincent Lecavalier 8.00 20.00
SCP24 Jamie Langenbrunner 6.00 15.00
SCP25 Jean-Sebastien Giguere 6.00 15.00
SCP26 Manny Fernandez 6.00 15.00
SCP27 Jason Spezza 12.50 30.00
SCP28 John Madden 6.00 15.00
SCP29 Paul Kariya
SCP30 Martin Brodeur
SCP31 Scott Stevens Cup Winners
SCP32 Jean-Sebastien Giguere Conn Smythe

2003-04 BAP Memorabilia Super Rookies

This 12-card set was randomly inserted and featured rookies from the 2003-04 season. A silver parallel serial-numbered out of 100 and gold parallel 1/1s were also created. Prices for the silver parallel can be found by using the multiplier below.
COMPLETE SET (12) 20.00 50.00
*SILVER: .75X TO 2X BASE HI
SILVER PRINT RUN 100 SER.#'d SETS
SR1 Tuomo Ruutu 4.00 10.00
SR2 Joffrey Lupul 4.00 10.00
SR3 Brent Burns 2.00 5.00
SR4 David Hale 2.00 5.00
SR5 Patrice Bergeron 5.00 12.00
SR6 Joni Pitkanen 2.50 6.00
SR7 Sean Bergenheim 2.50 6.00
SR8 Boyd Gordon 2.00 5.00
SR9 Eric Staal 4.00 10.00
SR10 Nathan Horton 4.00 10.00
SR11 Dustin Brown 3.00 8.00
SR12 Tim Gleason 2.00 5.00
SR13 Dan Hamhuis 2.00 5.00
SR14 Jordin Tootoo 4.00 10.00
SR15 Jiri Hudler 4.00 10.00
SR16 Marc-Andre Fleury 8.00 20.00
SR17 Christopher Higgins 2.00 5.00
SR18 Pavel Vorobiev 2.00 5.00
SR19 Alexander Semin 2.50 6.00
SR20 Brent Krahn 2.00 5.00

2003-04 BAP Memorabilia Tandems

STATED PRINT RUN 60 SETS
T1 D.Roloson/M.Fernandez 10.00 25.00
T2 P.Lalime/M.Prusek 12.50 30.00
T3 D.Hasek/M.Legace 25.00 60.00
T4 M.Biron/R.Miller 12.50 30.00
T5 M.Brodeur/C.Schwab 15.00 40.00
T6 M.Turco/R.Tugnutt 10.00 25.00
T7 J.Giguere/M.Gerber 10.00 25.00
T8 J.Theodore/M.Garon 12.50 30.00
T9 R.Luongo/J.Hurme 12.50 30.00
T10 E.Belfour/T.Kidd 12.50 30.00

1999-00 BAP Millennium Prototypes

This 8-card set was issued to dealers as a promo to introduce the Be A Player Millennium brand.
COMPLETE SET (8) 4.80 12.00
1 Teemu Selanne 1.25 3.00
2 Sergei Samsonov .60 1.50
3 Mike Modano .75 2.00
4 Sergei Fedorov 1.25 3.00
5 Saku Koivu .60 1.50
6 John Vanbiesbrouck .60 1.50
7 Sergei Berezin .20 .50
8 Olaf Kolzig .60 1.50

1999-00 BAP Millennium

Released as a 250-card set, Be A Player Millennium featured all silver foil base cards with full color action photography. Ruby, sapphire and emerald parallels were also created and inserted randomly. Ruby parallels are red in color and have a stated print run of 1000 sets. Sapphire parallels are blue in color and have a stated print run of 100 sets. Emerald parallels are green in color and have a stated print run of 10 sets. Emerald parallels are not priced due to scarcity. Millennium was packaged in 12-pack boxes with packs containing five cards. Each pack contained one authentic autograph card. Due to a difficulty in obtaining the Jaromir Jagr Signature cards, BAP offered a special Game Jersey card to those that sent in the redemption for the autographed card. The jersey card has been added to the bottom of the checklist.
COMPLETE SET (250) 125.00 250.00
JAGR GJ ISSUED VIA EXCH.SIG. CARD
1 Paul Kariya .30 .75
2 Teemu Selanne .50 1.25
3 Oleg Tverdovsky .15 .40
4 Niclas Havelid RC .25 .60
5 Guy Hebert .25 .60
6 Stu Grimson .20 .50
7 Pavel Trnka .15 .40
8 Ladislav Kohn .15 .40
9 Matt Cullen .12 .30
10 Steve Rucchin .15 .40
11 Dominic Roussel .15 .40
12 Patrik Stefan RC .25 .60
13 Damian Rhodes .15 .40
14 Ray Ferraro .15 .40
15 Andrew Brunette .15 .40
16 Johan Garpenlov .15 .40
17 Nelson Emerson .15 .40
18 Jason Botterill .15 .40
19 Kelly Buchberger .15 .40
20 Ray Bourque .40 1.00
21 Ken Belanger .15 .40
22 Sergei Samsonov .20 .50
23 Byron Dafoe .15 .40
24 Joe Thornton .40 1.00
25 Kyle McLaren .15 .40
26 Cameron Mann .15 .40
27 Mikko Eloranta RC .20 .50
28 Jonathan Girard .15 .40
29 Dominik Hasek .40 1.00
30 Michael Peca .20 .50
31 Erik Rasmussen .15 .40
32 Brian Campbell RC .25 .60
33 Miroslav Satan .20 .50
34 Vaclav Varada .15 .40
35 Martin Biron .20 .50
36 Dixon Ward .15 .40
37 Cory Sarich .15 .40
38 Grant Fuhr .25 .60
39 Jarome Iginla .25 .60
40 Valeri Bure .15 .40
41 Oleg Saprykin RC .25 .60
42 Rene Corbet .15 .40
43 Cory Stillman .15 .40
44 Denis Gauthier .15 .40
45 Steve Dubinsky .15 .40
46 Rico Fata .15 .40
47 Steve Halko RC .15 .40
48 Keith Primeau .15 .40

49 Sami Kapanen .15 .40
50 Arturs Irbe .20 .50
51 Jeff O'Neill .15 .40
52 Kent Manderville .15 .40
53 Gary Roberts .15 .40
54 Nolan Pratt .15 .40
55 Brad Brown .15 .40
56 Tony Amonte .20 .50
57 J-P Dumont .20 .50
58 Anders Eriksson .15 .40
59 Bryan Muir .15 .40
60 Dean McAmmond .15 .40
61 Jocelyn Thibault .20 .50
62 Eric Daze .20 .50
63 Shean Donovan .15 .40
64 Scott Parker .15 .40
65 Peter Forsberg .25 .60
66 Patrick Roy 1.00 2.50
67 Joe Sakic .40 1.00
68 Sandis Ozolinsh .15 .40
69 Chris Drury .20 .50
70 Milan Hejduk .20 .50
71 Shjon Podein .15 .40
72 Marc Denis .20 .50
73 Alex Tanguay .20 .50
74 Blake Sloan .20 .50
75 Jamie Langenbrunner .15 .40
76 Mike Modano .40 1.00
77 Derian Hatcher .20 .50
78 Joe Nieuwendyk .25 .60
79 Ed Belfour .25 .60
80 Brad Lukowich RC .20 .50
81 Jere Lehtinen .20 .50
82 Brett Hull .40 1.00
83 Shawn Chambers .15 .40
84 Pavel Patera RC .15 .40
85 Darryl Sydor .20 .50
86 Jiri Fischer .15 .40
87 Nicklas Lidstrom .25 .60
88 Steve Yzerman .75 2.00
89 Sergei Fedorov .40 1.00
90 Brendan Shanahan .30 .75
91 Chris Chelios .25 .60
92 Aaron Ward .15 .40
93 Kirk Maltby .15 .40
94 Yuri Butsayev RC .15 .40
95 Mathieu Dandenault .15 .40
96 Doug Weight .25 .60
97 Bill Guerin .25 .60
98 Tom Poti .15 .40
99 Wayne Gretzky 1.25 3.00
100 Georges Laraque RC .50 1.25
101 Sean Brown .15 .40
102 Mike Grier .15 .40
103 Tommy Salo .20 .50
104 Rem Murray .15 .40
105 Paul Comrie RC .40 1.00
106 Pavel Bure .30 .75
107 Rob Niedermayer .15 .40
108 Oleg Kvasha .15 .40
109 Filip Kuba RC .15 .40
110 Viktor Kozlov .15 .40
111 Radek Dvorak .15 .40
112 Ray Whitney .20 .50
113 Mark Parrish .15 .40
114 Dan Boyle RC .20 .50
115 Marcus Nilsson .15 .40
116 Lance Pitlick .15 .40
117 Paul Laus .15 .40
118 Rob Blake .25 .60
119 Stephane Fiset .20 .50
120 Zigmund Palffy .25 .60
121 Donald Audette .15 .40
122 Luc Robitaille .25 .60
123 Jamie Storr .15 .40
124 Dan Bylsma .15 .40
125 Pavel Rosa .15 .40
126 Jason Blake RC .20 .50
127 Mattias Norstrom .15 .40
128 Saku Koivu .25 .60
129 Trevor Linden .25 .60
130 Arron Asham .15 .40
131 Matt Higgins .15 .40
132 Martin Rucinsky .15 .40
133 Brian Savage .15 .40
134 Jeff Hackett .15 .40
135 Scott Thornton .15 .40
136 David Legwand .15 .40
137 Cliff Ronning .15 .40
138 Ville Peltonen .15 .40
139 Tomas Vokoun .25 .60
140 Sergei Krivokrasov .15 .40
141 Greg Johnson .15 .40
142 Mike Dunham .15 .40
143 Martin Brodeur .50 1.25
144 Scott Niedermayer .25 .60
145 Petr Sykora .20 .50
146 Vadim Sharifijanov .15 .40
147 Denis Pederson .15 .40
148 Jason Arnott .20 .50
149 Brendan Morrison .20 .50
150 Bobby Holik .15 .40
151 Brian Rafalski RC .25 .60
152 Olli Jokinen .20 .50
153 Tim Connolly .15 .40
154 Gino Odjick .15 .40
155 Zdeno Chara .25 .60
156 Kenny Jonsson .15 .40
157 Mariusz Czerkawski .15 .40
158 Kim Johnsson RC .15 .40
159 Brian Leetch .25 .60
160 Theo Fleury .30 .75
161 Petr Nedved .15 .40
162 John MacLean .20 .50
163 Manny Malhotra .20 .50
164 Jan Hlavac .15 .40
165 Valeri Kamensky .15 .40
166 Adam Graves .20 .50
167 Michael York .15 .40
168 Mike Richter .25 .60
169 Chris Phillips .15 .40
170 Marian Hossa .20 .50
171 Magnus Arvedson .15 .40
172 Ron Tugnutt .20 .50
173 Vaclav Prospal .15 .40
174 Sami Salo .20 .50
175 Jason York .15 .40
176 Shawn McEachern .15 .40
177 Rob Zamuner .15 .40
178 Eric Lindros .40 1.00
179 John LeClair .25 .60
180 Eric Desjardins .20 .50
181 Rod Brind'Amour .25 .60
182 Mark Recchi .30 .75
183 Simon Gagne .25 .60
184 Sandy McCarthy .15 .40
185 John Vanbiesbrouck .20 .50
186 Dan McGillis .15 .40
187 Keith Jones .15 .40
188 Keith Tkachuk .25 .60
189 Teppo Numminen .15 .40
190 Jeremy Roenick .25 .60
191 Nikolai Khabibulin .20 .50
192 Deron Quint .15 .40
193 Trevor Letowski .15 .40
194 Jaromir Jagr .60 1.50
195 Jan Hrdina .15 .40
196 Andrew Ference .15 .40
197 Alexei Kovalev .20 .50
198 Martin Straka .15 .40
199 Kip Miller .15 .40
200 Martin Sonnenberg RC .15 .40
201 Alexei Morozov .20 .50
202 Chris Pronger .20 .50
203 Al MacInnis .25 .60
204 Pavol Demitra .30 .75
205 Pierre Turgeon .25 .60
206 Jamal Mayers .15 .40
207 Chris McAlpine .15 .40
208 Ron Sutter .15 .40
209 Mike Rathje .15 .40
210 Patrick Marleau .25 .60
211 Jeff Friesen .20 .50
212 Niklas Sundstrom .15 .40
213 Steve Shields .20 .50
214 Brad Stuart .20 .50
215 Alexander Korolyuk .15 .40
216 Mike Ricci .20 .50
217 Paul Mara .15 .40
218 Fredrik Modin .15 .40
219 Dan Cloutier .15 .40
220 Vincent Lecavalier .20 .50
221 Pavel Kubina .15 .40
222 Chris Gratton .15 .40
223 Mike Sillinger .15 .40
224 Nikolai Antropov RC .60 1.50
225 Todd Warriner .15 .40
226 Mats Sundin .25 .60
227 Curtis Joseph .25 .60
228 Chris McAllister RC .15 .40
229 Bryan Berard .15 .40
230 Tomas Kaberle .15 .40
231 Igor Korolev .15 .40
232 Sergei Berezin .15 .40
233 Artem Chubarov .15 .40
234 Ed Jovanovski .20 .50
235 Mark Messier .40 1.00
236 Bill Muckalt .15 .40
237 Brad May .15 .40
238 Adrian Aucoin .15 .40
239 Mattias Ohlund .20 .50
240 Greg Hawgood .15 .40
241 Steve Kariya RC .25 .60
242 Markus Naslund .25 .60
243 Alexander Mogilny .20 .50
244 Jamie Huscroft .15 .40
245 Peter Bondra .20 .50
246 Olaf Kolzig .25 .60
247 Brendan Witt .15 .40
248 Adam Oates .25 .60
249 Sergei Gonchar .15 .40
250 Jan Bulis .12 .30
NNO J.Jagr GJ Special 30.00 80.00

1999-00 BAP Millennium Ruby

*VETERANS: 1.5X TO 4X BASIC CARDS
*ROOKIES: 1.2X TO 3X BASIC CARDS
STATED PRINT RUN 1000 SER.#'d SETS

1999-00 BAP Millennium Sapphire

*VETERANS: 10X TO 25X BASIC CARDS
*ROOKIES: 8X TO 20X BASIC CARD
SAPPHIRE PRINT RUN 100 SER.#'d SETS

1999-00 BAP Millennium Autographs

Inserted one per pack, this 250-card set paralleled the base set with player autographs and a congratulatory note on the back. Gold parallels were also created and inserted randomly into packs. Gold SP's had a print run of 50 sets.

1 Paul Kariya SP 20.00 50.00
2 Teemu Selanne SP 15.00 40.00
3 Oleg Tverdovsky 2.50 6.00
4 Niclas Havelid 4.00 10.00
5 Guy Hebert 4.00 10.00
6 Stu Grimson 3.00 8.00
7 Pavel Trnka 2.50 6.00
8 Ladislav Kohn 2.50 6.00
9 Matt Cullen 2.50 6.00
10 Steve Rucchin 2.50 6.00
11 Dominic Roussel 2.50 6.00
12 Patrik Stefan 4.00 10.00
13 Damian Rhodes 2.50 6.00
14 Ray Ferraro 2.50 6.00
15 Andrew Brunette 2.50 6.00
16 Johan Garpenlov 2.50 6.00
17 Nelson Emerson 2.50 6.00
18 Jason Botterill 2.50 6.00
19 Kelly Buchberger 2.50 6.00
20 Ray Bourque SP 15.00 40.00
21 Ken Belanger 2.50 6.00
22 Sergei Samsonov SP 3.00 8.00
23 Byron Dafoe SP 6.00 15.00
24 Joe Thornton 6.00 15.00
25 Kyle McLaren 2.50 6.00
26 Cameron Mann 2.50 6.00
27 Mikko Eloranta 3.00 8.00
28 Jonathan Girard 2.50 6.00
29 Dominik Hasek SP 150.00 250.00
30 Michael Peca SP 5.00 12.00
31 Erik Rasmussen 2.50 6.00
32 Brian Campbell 4.00 10.00
33 Miroslav Satan 3.00 8.00
34 Vaclav Varada 2.50 6.00
35 Martin Biron 3.00 8.00
36 Dixon Ward 2.50 6.00
37 Cory Sarich 2.50 6.00
38 Grant Fuhr SP 8.00 20.00
39 Jarome Iginla 8.00 20.00
40 Valeri Bure 2.50 6.00
41 Oleg Saprykin 4.00 10.00
42 Rene Corbet 2.50 6.00
43 Cory Stillman 2.50 6.00
44 Denis Gauthier 2.50 6.00
45 Steve Dubinsky 2.50 6.00
46 Rico Fata 2.50 6.00
47 Steve Halko 2.50 6.00
48 Keith Primeau SP 2.50 6.00
49 Sami Kapanen 2.50 6.00
50 Arturs Irbe 3.00 8.00
51 Jeff O'Neill 2.50 6.00
52 Kent Manderville 2.50 6.00
53 Gary Roberts 2.50 6.00
54 Nolan Pratt 2.50 6.00
55 Brad Brown 2.50 6.00
56 Tony Amonte SP 3.00 8.00
57 J-P Dumont 3.00 8.00
58 Anders Eriksson 2.50 6.00
59 Bryan Muir 2.50 6.00
60 Dean McAmmond 2.50 6.00
61 Jocelyn Thibault 3.00 8.00
62 Eric Daze 3.00 8.00
63 Shean Donovan 2.50 6.00
64 Scott Parker 2.50 6.00
65 Peter Forsberg SP 20.00 50.00
66 Patrick Roy SP 15.00 40.00
67 Joe Sakic SP 15.00 40.00
68 Sandis Ozolinsh 2.50 6.00
69 Chris Drury 3.00 8.00
70 Milan Hejduk 3.00 8.00
71 Shjon Podein 2.50 6.00
72 Marc Denis 3.00 8.00
73 Alex Tanguay 3.00 8.00
74 Blake Sloan 3.00 8.00
75 Jamie Langenbrunner 2.50 6.00
76 Mike Modano SP 12.00 30.00
77 Derian Hatcher 3.00 8.00
78 Joe Nieuwendyk SP 4.00 10.00
79 Ed Belfour SP 12.00 30.00
80 Brad Lukowich 3.00 8.00
81 Jere Lehtinen 3.00 8.00
82 Brett Hull SP 12.00 30.00
83 Shawn Chambers 2.50 6.00
84 Pavel Patera 2.50 6.00
85 Darryl Sydor 3.00 8.00
86 Jiri Fischer 2.50 6.00
87 Nicklas Lidstrom 8.00 20.00
88 Steve Yzerman SP 30.00 80.00
89 Sergei Fedorov SP 10.00 25.00
90 Brendan Shanahan SP 8.00 20.00
91 Chris Chelios SP 8.00 20.00
92 Aaron Ward 2.50 6.00
93 Kirk Maltby 2.50 6.00
94 Yuri Butsayev 2.50 6.00
95 Mathieu Dandenault 2.50 6.00
96 Doug Weight SP 4.00 10.00
97 Bill Guerin 4.00 10.00
98 Tom Poti 2.50 6.00
99 Wayne Gretzky SP 350.00 450.00
100 Georges Laraque 8.00 20.00
101 Sean Brown 2.50 6.00
102 Mike Grier 2.50 6.00
103 Tommy Salo 3.00 8.00
104 Rem Murray 2.50 6.00
105 Paul Comrie 6.00 15.00
106 Pavel Bure SP 8.00 20.00
107 Rob Niedermayer 2.50 6.00
108 Oleg Kvasha 2.50 6.00
109 Filip Kuba 2.50 6.00
110 Viktor Kozlov 2.50 6.00
111 Radek Dvorak 2.50 6.00
112 Ray Whitney 3.00 8.00
113 Mark Parrish 2.50 6.00
114 Dan Boyle 3.00 8.00
115 Marcus Nilsson 2.50 6.00
116 Lance Pitlick 2.50 6.00
117 Paul Laus 2.50 6.00
118 Rob Blake 4.00 10.00
119 Stephane Fiset 3.00 8.00
120 Zigmund Palffy SP 4.00 10.00
121 Donald Audette 2.50 6.00
122 Luc Robitaille 4.00 10.00
123 Jamie Storr 2.50 6.00
124 Dan Bylsma 2.50 6.00
125 Pavel Rosa 2.50 6.00
126 Jason Blake 3.00 8.00
127 Mattias Norstrom 2.50 6.00
128 Saku Koivu SP 6.00 15.00
129 Trevor Linden 4.00 10.00
130 Arron Asham 2.50 6.00
131 Matt Higgins 2.50 6.00
132 Martin Rucinsky 2.50 6.00
133 Brian Savage 2.50 6.00
134 Jeff Hackett 2.50 6.00
135 Scott Thornton 2.50 6.00
136 David Legwand 2.50 6.00
137 Cliff Ronning 2.50 6.00
138 Ville Peltonen 2.50 6.00
139 Tomas Vokoun 4.00 10.00
140 Sergei Krivokrasov 2.50 6.00
141 Greg Johnson 2.50 6.00
142 Mike Dunham 2.50 6.00
143 Martin Brodeur SP 15.00 40.00
144 Scott Niedermayer SP 6.00 15.00
145 Petr Sykora 3.00 8.00
146 Vadim Sharifijanov 2.50 6.00
147 Denis Pederson 2.50 6.00
148 Jason Arnott SP 3.00 8.00
149 Brendan Morrison 3.00 8.00
150 Bobby Holik 2.50 6.00
151 Brian Rafalski 4.00 10.00
152 Olli Jokinen 3.00 8.00
153 Tim Connolly 2.50 6.00
154 Gino Odjick 2.50 6.00
155 Zdeno Chara 4.00 10.00
156 Kenny Jonsson 2.50 6.00
157 Mariusz Czerkawski 2.50 6.00
158 Kim Johnsson 2.50 6.00
159 Brian Leetch SP 4.00 10.00
160 Theo Fleury SP 8.00 20.00
161 Petr Nedved 2.50 6.00
162 John MacLean 3.00 8.00
163 Manny Malhotra 3.00 8.00
164 Jan Hlavac 2.50 6.00
165 Valeri Kamensky 2.50 6.00
166 Adam Graves 3.00 8.00
167 Michael York 2.50 6.00
168 Mike Richter SP 4.00 10.00
169 Chris Phillips 2.50 6.00
170 Marian Hossa 3.00 8.00
171 Magnus Arvedson 2.50 6.00
172 Ron Tugnutt 3.00 8.00
173 Vaclav Prospal 2.50 6.00
174 Sami Salo 3.00 8.00
175 Jason York 2.50 6.00
176 Shawn McEachern 2.50 6.00
177 Rob Zamuner 2.50 6.00
178 Eric Lindros SP 10.00 25.00
179 John LeClair SP 4.00 10.00
180 Eric Desjardins 3.00 8.00
181 Rod Brind'Amour 4.00 10.00
182 Mark Recchi 5.00 12.00
183 Simon Gagne 4.00 10.00
184 Sandy McCarthy 2.50 6.00
185 John Vanbiesbrouck SP 6.00 15.00
186 Dan McGillis 2.50 6.00
187 Keith Jones 2.50 6.00
188 Keith Tkachuk SP 6.00 15.00
189 Teppo Numminen 2.50 6.00
190 Jeremy Roenick SP 8.00 20.00
191 Nikolai Khabibulin 3.00 8.00
192 Deron Quint 2.50 6.00
193 Trevor Letowski 2.50 6.00
194 Jaromir Jagr SP 30.00 80.00
195 Jan Hrdina 2.50 6.00
196 Andrew Ference 2.50 6.00
197 Alexei Kovalev 3.00 8.00
198 Martin Straka 2.50 6.00
199 Kip Miller 2.50 6.00
200 Martin Sonnenberg 2.50 6.00
201 Alexei Morozov 3.00 8.00
202 Chris Pronger SP 3.00 8.00
203 Al MacInnis SP 4.00 10.00
204 Pavol Demitra 5.00 12.00
205 Pierre Turgeon 4.00 10.00
206 Jamal Mayers 2.50 6.00
207 Chris McAlpine 2.50 6.00
208 Ron Sutter 2.50 6.00
209 Mike Rathje 2.50 6.00
210 Patrick Marleau 4.00 10.00
211 Jeff Friesen SP 6.00 15.00
212 Niklas Sundstrom 2.50 6.00
213 Steve Shields 3.00 8.00
214 Brad Stuart 3.00 8.00
215 Alexander Korolyuk 2.50 6.00
216 Mike Ricci 3.00 8.00
217 Paul Mara 2.50 6.00
218 Fredrik Modin 2.50 6.00
219 Dan Cloutier 2.50 6.00
220 Vincent Lecavalier 3.00 8.00
221 Pavel Kubina 2.50 6.00
222 Chris Gratton SP 6.00 15.00
223 Mike Sillinger 2.50 6.00
224 Nikolai Antropov 10.00 25.00
225 Todd Warriner 2.50 6.00
226 Mats Sundin SP 6.00 15.00
227 Curtis Joseph SP 6.00 15.00
228 Chris McAllister 2.50 6.00
229 Bryan Berard SP 6.00 15.00
230 Tomas Kaberle 2.50 6.00
231 Igor Korolev 2.50 6.00
232 Sergei Berezin 2.50 6.00
233 Artem Chubarov 2.50 6.00
234 Ed Jovanovski 3.00 8.00
235 Mark Messier SP 12.00 30.00
236 Bill Muckalt 2.50 6.00
237 Brad May 2.50 6.00
238 Adrian Aucoin 2.50 6.00
239 Mattias Ohlund 3.00 8.00
240 Greg Hawgood 2.50 6.00
241 Steve Kariya 4.00 10.00
242 Markus Naslund 4.00 10.00
243 Alexander Mogilny SP 3.00 8.00
244 Jamie Huscroft 2.50 6.00
245 Peter Bondra SP 6.00 15.00
246 Olaf Kolzig SP 6.00 15.00
247 Brendan Witt 2.50 6.00
248 Adam Oates SP 6.00 15.00
249 Sergei Gonchar 2.50 6.00
250 Jan Bulis 2.50 6.00

1999-00 BAP Millennium Autographs Gold

Randomly inserted at approximately two per box, this 250-card set parallels the Signatures set in gold foil. Announced print run for the short prints in this set is 50 cards.

*GOLD: 1X TO 2.5X BASIC AU
GOLD/50: .8X TO 2X BASIC AU
29 Dominik Hasek/50* 200.00 350.00
99 Wayne Gretzky/50* 400.00 800.00

1999-00 BAP Millennium Calder Candidates Ruby

Randomly inserted in packs, this 50-card set featured top Calder trophy prospects. Cards contained full-color action photography and were set off by a red border. Ruby versions were serial numbered 0101/1000 to 1000/1000. Sapphire and emerald parallels were also created and randomly inserted. Sapphire parallels were blue in color and had a stated print run of 100 sets. Emerald parallels were green in color and had a stated print run of 10 sets.

COMPLETE SET (50) 100.00 200.00
STATED PRINT RUN 1000 SETS
*SAPPHIRE/100: 1.5X TO 4X RUBY/1000
SAPPHIRE PRINT RUN 100 SETS
*EMERALD/10: 4X TO 10X RUBY/1000
EMERALD STATED PRINT RUN 10
C1 Alex Tanguay 2.50 6.00
C2 Simon Gagne 3.00 8.00
C3 Kyle Calder 2.00 5.00
C4 Ryan Johnson 2.00 5.00
C5 Dave Tanabe 2.00 5.00
C6 Scott Gomez 2.00 5.00
C7 Patrik Stefan 2.00 5.00
C8 Jiri Fischer 2.00 5.00
C9 Blake Sloan 2.00 5.00
C10 Trevor Letowski 2.00 5.00
C11 Michael York 2.00 5.00
C12 Mike Ribeiro 2.00 5.00
C13 Ladislav Kohn 2.00 5.00
C14 Martin Skoula 2.00 5.00
C15 Steve Kariya 2.00 5.00
C16 Nikolai Antropov 2.00 5.00
C17 David Legwand 2.50 6.00
C18 J-P Dumont 2.00 5.00
C19 Filip Kuba 2.00 5.00
C20 Mike Fisher 2.00 5.00
C21 Tim Connolly 2.00 5.00
C22 Martin Biron 2.50 6.00
C23 Oleg Saprykin 2.00 5.00
C24 Maxim Afinogenov 2.00 5.00
C25 Petr Buzek 2.00 5.00
C26 Paul Comrie 2.00 5.00
C27 Brian Boucher 2.50 6.00
C28 Peter Schaefer 2.00 5.00
C29 Alex Tezikov 2.00 5.00
C30 Milan Hnilicka 2.50 6.00
C31 Brian Rafalski 2.00 5.00
C32 Sami Helenius 2.00 5.00
C33 Frantisek Kaberle 2.00 5.00
C34 Jochen Hecht 2.00 5.00
C35 Mathieu Biron 2.00 5.00
C36 Randy Robitaille 2.00 5.00
C37 Roberto Luongo 4.00 10.00
C38 Steve McCarthy 2.00 5.00
C39 Brad Lukowich 2.00 5.00
C40 Kim Johnsson 2.00 5.00
C41 Brad Stuart 2.00 5.00
C42 Glen Metropolit 2.00 5.00
C43 Marc Denis 2.50 6.00
C44 Robyn Regehr 2.00 5.00
C45 Per Svartvadet 2.00 5.00
C46 Jonathan Girard 2.00 5.00
C47 Mark Eaton 2.00 5.00
C48 Ivan Novoseltsev 2.00 5.00
C49 Jan Hlavac 2.00 5.00
C50 Richard Jackman 2.00 5.00

1999-00 BAP Millennium Goalie Memorabilia

STATED PRINT RUN 30 SETS
G1 Curtis Joseph 75.00 200.00
G2 Patrick Roy 60.00 150.00
G3 Grant Fuhr 60.00 150.00
G4 Garth Snow 40.00 100.00
G5 Jeff Hackett 30.00 80.00
G6 Chris Osgood 25.00 60.00
G7 Dominik Hasek 40.00 100.00
G8 Arturs Irbe 30.00 80.00

1999-00 BAP Millennium Jerseys

STATED PRINT RUN 100 SETS
*JSY NUMBER: .6X TO 1.5X BASIC JSY
JSY NUMBER PRINT RUN 30 SETS
*JSY EMBLEMS: .8X TO 2X BASIC JSY
JSY EMBLEM PRINT RUN 20 SETS
*JSY AND STICK: .5X TO 1.2X BASIC JSY
JERSEY AND STICK PRINT RUN 40
J1 Theo Fleury 8.00 20.00
J2 Brendan Shanahan 12.00 30.00
J3 Curtis Joseph 12.00 30.00
J4 Saku Koivu 12.00 30.00
J5 Dominik Hasek 25.00 60.00
J6 Al MacInnis 8.00 20.00
J7 John LeClair 12.00 30.00
J8 Teemu Selanne 15.00 40.00
J9 Wayne Gretzky 40.00 100.00
J10 Pavel Bure 12.00 30.00
J11 Mark Messier 12.00 30.00
J12 Jaromir Jagr 15.00 40.00
J13 Ray Bourque 20.00 50.00
J14 Chris Chelios 12.00 30.00
J15 Mats Sundin 12.00 30.00
J16 Paul Kariya 12.00 30.00
J17 Peter Bondra 8.00 20.00
J18 Eric Lindros 12.00 30.00
J19 Sergei Fedorov 15.00 40.00
J20 Peter Forsberg 20.00 50.00
J21 Brett Hull 12.00 30.00
J22 Tony Amonte 8.00 20.00
J23 Patrick Roy 30.00 80.00
J24 Ed Belfour 12.00 30.00
J25 Martin Brodeur 25.00 60.00
J26 Brian Leetch 8.00 20.00
J27 Mike Modano 12.00 30.00
J28 Joe Sakic 15.00 40.00
J29 Jeremy Roenick 15.00 40.00
J30 Steve Yzerman 25.00 60.00
J31 Alexander Mogilny 8.00 20.00
J32 Paul Coffey 12.00 30.00

1999-00 BAP Millennium Pearson

Randomly inserted in packs, this 16-card set features recipients of the Lester B. Pearson Trophy for outstanding play. Cards are foil and picture the Pearson trophy in the lower right hand corner. Stated print run for this set is 300 cards.

COMPLETE SET (16) 125.00 250.00
STATED PRINT RUN 300 SETS
P1 Jaromir Jagr 10.00 25.00
P2 Dominik Hasek 10.00 25.00
P3 Mario Lemieux 20.00 50.00
P4 Eric Lindros 2.50 6.00
P5 Sergei Fedorov 8.00 20.00
P6 Mark Messier 2.50 6.00
P7 Brett Hull 6.00 15.00
P8 Steve Yzerman 15.00 40.00
P9 Wayne Gretzky 25.00 60.00
P10 Mike Liut 2.50 6.00
P11 Marcel Dionne 4.00 10.00
P12 Guy Lafleur 5.00 12.00
P13 Bobby Orr 25.00 60.00
P14 Phil Esposito 6.00 15.00
P15 Bobby Clarke 6.00 15.00
P16 Jean Ratelle 2.50 6.00

1999-00 BAP Millennium Pearson Autographs

Randomly seeded in packs, this 16-card set parallels the base Be A Player Millennium Pearson set and is enhanced with player autographs. Players signed 30 cards each.

FIRST 30 CARDS OF PRINT RUN SIGNED
P1 Jaromir Jagr 75.00 200.00
P2 Dominik Hasek 75.00 200.00
P3 Mario Lemieux 125.00 250.00
P4 Eric Lindros 40.00 80.00
P5 Sergei Fedorov 40.00 100.00
P6 Mark Messier 75.00 200.00
P7 Brett Hull 40.00 100.00
P8 Steve Yzerman 75.00 200.00
P9 Wayne Gretzky 300.00 600.00
P10 Mike Liut 30.00 60.00
P11 Marcel Dionne 40.00 80.00
P12 Guy Lafleur 60.00 150.00
P13 Bobby Orr 250.00 500.00
P14 Phil Esposito 40.00 80.00
P15 Bobby Clarke 40.00 100.00
P16 Jean Ratelle 30.00 60.00

1999-00 BAP Millennium Players of the Decade

Randomly inserted in packs, this 10-card set features top players from the last two decades. Base cards contain full color action photography set against a blue foil background. Stated print run for this set is 1000 cards.

COMPLETE SET (10) 60.00 120.00
STATED PRINT RUN 1000 SETS
D1 Wayne Gretzky 15.00 40.00
D2 Mark Messier 3.00 8.00
D3 Patrick Roy 12.50 30.00
D4 Dominik Hasek 5.00 12.00
D5 Jaromir Jagr 4.00 10.00
D6 Eric Lindros 5.00 10.00
D7 Sergei Fedorov 5.00 12.00
D8 Brett Hull 3.00 8.00
D9 Ray Bourque 4.00 10.00
D10 Steve Yzerman 15.00 40.00

1999-00 BAP Millennium Players of the Decade Autographs

Randomly inserted in packs, this 10-card set parallels the base Players of the Decade insert set and is enhanced with player autographs. The first 90 cards in the 1000 set print run were autographed. Jagr, Hull, and Yzerman were exchange cards.

FIRST 90 CARDS OF PRINT RUN SIGNED
D1 Wayne Gretzky 125.00 300.00
D2 Mark Messier 40.00 100.00
D3 Patrick Roy 75.00 200.00
D4 Dominik Hasek 60.00 150.00
D5 Jaromir Jagr 60.00 150.00
D6 Eric Lindros 25.00 60.00
D7 Sergei Fedorov 40.00 100.00
D8 Brett Hull 30.00 80.00
D9 Ray Bourque 40.00 100.00
D10 Steve Yzerman 75.00 200.00

2000-01 BAP Parkhurst 2000

Randomly inserted in packs of Be A Player Memorabilia, Be A Player Memorabilia Update, and Be A Player Signature Series at the rate of 1:5, this 250-card set features the Parkhurst name and logo. Player action shots are framed by a green and gray border along the left and bottom of the card. Each card is enhanced with a Parkhurst 50th anniversary gold foil stamp.

COMPLETE SET (250) 50.00 125.00
COMP.SERIES 1 (100) 20.00 50.00
COMP.UPDATE SET (50) 10.00 25.00
COMP.SIG.SERIES SET (100) 20.00 50.00
STATED ODDS 1:5 SER.1/SIG.SERIES
P1 Pavel Bure .50 1.25
P2 Tony Amonte .30 .75
P3 Chris Pronger .30 .75
P4 John Madden .30 .75
P5 Kimmo Timonen .25 .60
P6 Marc Savard .30 .75
P7 Peter Forsberg .50 1.25
P8 Arturs Irbe .30 .75
P9 Mike York .25 .60
P10 Brendan Shanahan .50 1.25
P11 Simon Gagne .40 1.00
P12 Maxim Afinogenov .25 .60
P13 Joe Sakic .60 1.50
P14 Curtis Joseph .50 1.25
P15 Jozef Stumpel .25 .60
P16 Vitali Vishnevsky .25 .60
P17 Owen Nolan .40 1.00
P18 Jan Hrdina .25 .60
P19 Brenden Morrow .30 .75
P20 Todd Bertuzzi .30 .75
P21 Vincent Lecavalier .30 .75
P22 Andrew Brunette .25 .60
P23 Brendan Morrison .40 1.00
P24 Rod Brind'Amour .40 1.00
P25 Patrik Elias .40 1.00
P26 Joe Thornton .60 1.50
P27 Roman Turek .30 .75
P28 Fred Brathwaite .30 .75
P29 Brian Leetch .40 1.00
P30 Trevor Linden .40 1.00
P31 Janne Niinimaa .25 .60
P32 Nikolai Antropov .30 .75
P33 Teemu Selanne .75 2.00
P34 Calle Johansson .25 .60
P35 Boris Mironov .25 .60
P36 Eric Desjardins .30 .75
P37 Mark Parrish .25 .60
P38 Alex Tanguay .30 .75
P39 Jason Arnott .30 .75
P40 Vincent Damphousse .30 .75
P41 Dominik Hasek .60 1.50
P42 Teppo Numminen .25 .60
P43 Patrick Lalime .30 .75
P44 Valeri Bure .30 .75
P45 Adam Oates .40 1.00
P46 Sergei Zubov .30 .75
P47 Tim Connolly .25 .60
P48 Pavel Kubina .25 .60
P49 Nicklas Lidstrom .40 1.00
P50 Mark Recchi .50 1.25
P51 Chris Drury .30 .75
P52 Kyle McLaren .25 .60
P53 Steve Kariya .25 .60
P54 Scott Gomez .30 .75
P55 Rob Blake .40 1.00
P56 Miroslav Satan .25 .60
P57 Cliff Ronning .25 .60
P58 Radek Dvorak .30 .75
P59 Jeff O'Neill .30 .75
P60 Dainius Zubrus .25 .60
P61 Brad Ference .25 .60
P62 Jarome Iginla .40 1.00
P63 Chris Simon .25 .60
P64 Darryl Sydor .30 .75
P65 Daniel Alfredsson .40 1.00
P66 Sandis Ozolinsh .30 .75
P67 Brian Rafalski .25 .60
P68 Ryan Smyth .30 .75
P69 John LeClair .40 1.00
P70 Patrik Stefan .30 .75
P71 Patrick Marleau .40 1.00
P72 Roberto Luongo .60 1.50
P73 Chris Osgood .40 1.00
P74 Pierre Turgeon .40 1.00
P75 Zigmund Palffy .40 1.00
P76 Jeff Farkas .25 .60
P77 Milan Hejduk .30 .75
P78 Ray Whitney .30 .75
P79 Felix Potvin .60 1.50
P80 Chris Gratton .25 .60
P81 Brad Stuart .30 .75
P82 Ron Francis .50 1.25
P83 Oleg Tverdovsky .25 .60
P84 Alexei Kovalev .30 .75
P85 Sergei Fedorov .60 1.50
P86 Nick Boynton .25 .60
P87 David Legwand .40 1.00
P88 Robyn Regehr .25 .60
P89 Brian Boucher .30 .75
P90 Roman Hamrlik .30 .75
P91 Jochen Hecht .25 .60
P92 Alexei Zhamnov .30 .75
P93 Olaf Kolzig .40 1.00
P94 Jose Theodore .50 1.25
P95 Jeremy Roenick .40 1.00
P96 Theo Fleury .50 1.25
P97 Patrick Roy 1.00 2.50
P98 Marian Hossa .30 .75
P99 Martin Brodeur .75 2.00
P100 Brett Hull .60 1.50
P101 Daniel Sedin .75 2.00
P102 Paul Coffey .40 1.00
P103 Ray Bourque .60 1.50
P104 Glen Murray .25 .60
P105 Mariusz Czerkawski .25 .60
P106 Jeff Friesen .25 .60
P107 Sergei Samsonov .30 .75
P108 Tyler Wright .25 .60
P109 Manny Fernandez .30 .75
P110 Mike Richter .40 1.00
P111 Pavol Demitra .50 1.25
P112 Brian Rolston .30 .75
P113 Ron Tugnutt .30 .75
P114 Alexander Mogilny .30 .75
P115 Radek Bonk .30 .75
P116 Al MacInnis .40 1.00
P117 J-P Dumont .25 .60
P118 Ed Belfour .40 1.00
P119 Jeff Hackett .25 .60
P120 Shawn McEachern .25 .60
P121 Dan Cloutier .30 .75
P122 Mika Noronen .25 .60
P123 Derian Hatcher .30 .75
P124 Saku Koivu .40 1.00
P125 Keith Primeau .30 .75
P126 Mats Sundin .40 1.00
P127 Damian Rhodes .25 .60
P128 Chris Chelios .40 1.00
P129 Mike Dunham .25 .60
P130 Keith Tkachuk .40 1.00
P131 Steve Thomas .25 .60
P132 Phil Housley .30 .75
P133 Doug Weight .40 1.00
P134 Kris Beech .25 .60
P135 Jyrki Lumme .25 .60
P136 Guy Hebert .30 .75
P137 Sami Kapanen .25 .60
P138 Trevor Kidd .25 .60
P139 Marian Gaborik .75 2.00
P140 Martin Straka .30 .75
P141 Ed Jovanovski .30 .75
P142 Jean-Sebastien Aubin .30 .75
P143 Viktor Kozlov .30 .75
P144 Scott Stevens .40 1.00
P145 Jiri Slegr .25 .60
P146 Steve Yzerman 1.25 3.00
P147 Jocelyn Thibault .30 .75
P148 Stephane Fiset .25 .60
P149 Kenny Jonsson .25 .60
P150 Steve Shields .25 .60
P151 Paul Kariya .50 1.25
P152 Shane Willis .25 .60
P153 Martin Lapointe .30 .75
P154 Brian Savage .25 .60
P155 Alexei Yashin .30 .75
P156 Marcus Ragnarsson .25 .60
P157 Petr Tenkrat .25 .60
P158 Sandis Ozolinsh .30 .75
P159 Anson Carter .30 .75
P160 Scott Hartnell .60 1.50
P161 Rick Tocchet .30 .75
P162 Brad Richards .40 1.00
P163 Byron Dafoe .30 .75
P164 Marc Denis .30 .75
P165 Steve Reinprecht .40 1.00
P166 Mario Lemieux 1.25 3.00
P167 Taylor Pyatt .25 .60
P168 Mike Vernon .30 .75
P169 Scott Niedermayer .40 1.00
P170 Milan Kraft .25 .60
P171 Donald Audette .30 .75
P172 Steve Sullivan .25 .60
P173 Todd Marchant .25 .60
P174 Scott Walker .25 .60
P175 Daymond Langkow .25 .60
P176 Fredrik Modin .25 .60
P177 Ray Ferraro .25 .60
P178 Michael Nylander .25 .60
P179 Robert Svehla .25 .60
P180 Petr Sykora .30 .75
P181 Claude Lemieux .30 .75
P182 Sergei Berezin .25 .60
P183 Doug Gilmour .50 1.25
P184 Jere Lehtinen .30 .75
P185 Maxim Sushinski .25 .60
P186 Jan Hlavac .25 .60
P187 Michal Handzus .25 .60
P188 Jamie Langenbrunner .30 .75
P189 John Vanbiesbrouck .30 .75
P190 Brent Johnson .30 .75
P191 Jason Allison .30 .75
P192 Adam Deadmarsh .30 .75
P193 Scott Mellanby .25 .60
P194 Sergei Brylin .25 .60
P195 Shane Doan .30 .75
P196 Jonas Hoglund .25 .60
P197 Bill Guerin .40 1.00
P198 Espen Knutsen .25 .60
P199 Bryan Smolinski .30 .75
P200 Brad Isbister .25 .60
P201 Robert Lang .25 .60
P202 Andrew Cassels .25 .60
P203 Daniel Tkaczuk .30 .75
P204 Igor Larionov .40 1.00
P205 Andrei Markov .50 1.25
P206 Magnus Arvedson .25 .60
P207 Henrik Sedin .60 1.50
P208 Manny Legace .25 .60
P209 Adam Graves .30 .75
P210 Marty Turco .50 1.25
P211 Stu Barnes .30 .75
P212 Geoff Sanderson .30 .75
P213 Luc Robitaille .40 1.00
P214 Roman Hamrlik .30 .75
P215 Jaromir Jagr 1.00 2.50
P216 Markus Naslund .30 .75
P217 Alexei Zhitnik .30 .75
P218 Joe Nieuwendyk .40 1.00
P219 Lubomir Sekeras .25 .60
P220 Petr Nedved .30 .75
P221 Dallas Drake .25 .60
P222 Sergei Gonchar .25 .60
P223 Dave Tanabe .25 .60
P224 Tommy Salo .30 .75
P225 Rick DiPietro 1.00 2.50
P226 Justin Williams .60 1.50
P227 Dimitri Khristich .25 .60
P228 Lubomir Visnovsky .50 1.25
P229 Jani Hurme .25 .60
P230 Roman Cechmanek .30 .75
P231 Cory Stillman .25 .60
P232 Mike Modano .60 1.50
P233 Scott Pellerin .25 .60
P234 Mark Messier .60 1.50
P235 Scott Young .25 .60
P236 Peter Bondra .30 .75
P237 Oleg Saprykin .25 .60
P238 Pat Verbeek .30 .75
P239 Martin Rucinsky .25 .60
P240 Martin Havlat .75 2.00
P241 Evgeni Nabokov .30 .75
P242 Tomi Kallio .25 .60
P243 Eric Daze .30 .75
P244 Roberto Luongo .60 1.50
P245 Bobby Holik .25 .60
P246 Sean Burke .25 .60
P247 Martin Biron .30 .75
P248 Mathieu Garon .25 .60
P249 Jamie Storr .30 .75
P250 Maxime Ouellet .40 1.00

2006-07 Be A Player Portraits

COMP.SET w/o SPs (100) 12.00 30.00
1 Jean-Sebastien Giguere .30 .75

2 Chris Pronger .25 .60
3 Teemu Selanne .60 1.50
4 Scott Niedermayer .30 .75
5 Ilya Kovalchuk .30 .75
6 Kari Lehtonen .25 .60
7 Marian Hossa .25 .60
8 Marc Savard .20 .50
9 Brad Boyes .20 .50
10 Patrice Bergeron .40 1.00
11 Hannu Toivonen .25 .60
12 Zdeno Chara .30 .75
13 Daniel Briere .30 .75
14 Chris Drury .25 .60
15 Ryan Miller .30 .75
16 Jarome Iginla .30 .75
17 Miikka Kiprusoff .25 .60
18 Dion Phaneuf .30 .75
19 Alex Tanguay .20 .50
20 Rod Brind'Amour .30 .75
21 Erik Cole .25 .60
22 Eric Staal .40 1.00
23 Cam Ward .30 .75
24 Nikolai Khabibulin .30 .75
25 Martin Havlat .20 .50
26 Tuomo Ruutu .30 .75
27 Marek Svatos .20 .50
28 Joe Sakic .50 1.25
29 Jose Theodore .30 .75
30 Milan Hejduk .25 .60
31 Rick Nash .30 .75
32 Nikolai Zherdev .20 .50
33 Sergei Federov .50 1.25
34 Gilbert Brule .25 .60
35 Mike Modano .50 1.25
36 Marty Turco .30 .75
37 Brenden Morrow .25 .60
38 Eric Lindros .50 1.25
39 Dominik Hasek .40 1.00
40 Pavel Datsyuk .40 1.00
41 Nicklas Lidstrom .30 .75
42 Henrik Zetterberg .40 1.00
43 Ales Hemsky .25 .60
44 Ryan Smyth .25 .60
45 Joffrey Lupul .25 .60
46 Shawn Horcoff .20 .50
47 Ed Belfour .30 .75
48 Olli Jokinen .30 .75
49 Nathan Horton .30 .75
50 Todd Bertuzzi .30 .75
51 Rob Blake .30 .75
52 Alexander Frolov .20 .50
53 Pavol Demitra .40 1.00
54 Manny Fernandez .25 .60
55 Marian Gaborik .40 1.00
56 Cristobal Huet .25 .60
57 Sergei Samsonov .25 .60
58 Saku Koivu .30 .75
59 Michael Ryder .20 .50
60 Paul Kariya .40 1.00
61 Tomas Vokoun .25 .60
62 Martin Brodeur .60 1.50
63 Patrik Elias .30 .75
64 Brian Gionta .25 .60
65 Alexei Yashin .25 .60
66 Miroslav Satan .25 .60
67 Rick DiPietro .25 .60
68 Jaromir Jagr .75 2.00
69 Henrik Lundqvist .60 1.50
70 Brendan Shanahan .40 1.00
71 Dany Heatley .30 .75
72 Jason Spezza .30 .75
73 Wade Redden .20 .50
74 Daniel Alfredsson .30 .75
75 Peter Forsberg .40 1.00
76 Antero Niittymaki .25 .60
77 Jeff Carter .30 .75
78 Simon Gagne .30 .75
79 Curtis Joseph .30 .75
80 Jeremy Roenick .30 .75
81 Shane Doan .25 .60
82 Marc-Andre Fleury .50 1.25
83 Sidney Crosby 1.25 3.00
84 Joe Thornton .40 1.00
85 Patrick Marleau .30 .75
86 Jonathan Cheechoo .30 .75
87 Keith Tkachuk .30 .75
88 Doug Weight .30 .75
89 Brad Richards .30 .75
90 Vincent Lecavalier .25 .60
91 Martin St. Louis .30 .75
92 Mats Sundin .30 .75
93 Alexander Steen .30 .75
94 Michael Peca .25 .60
95 Andrew Raycroft .25 .60
96 Markus Naslund .25 .60
97 Brendan Morrison .20 .50
98 Roberto Luongo .50 1.25
99 Alexander Ovechkin 1.25 3.00
100 Olaf Kolzig .30 .75
101 Yan Stastny RC 1.25 3.00
102 Mark Stuart RC 1.25 3.00
103 Evgeni Malkin RC 8.00 20.00
104 Patrick Thoresen RC 1.25 3.00
105 Patrick O'Sullivan RC 2.00 5.00
106 Tomas Kopecky RC 1.50 4.00
107 M-A Pouliot RC 1.25 3.00
108 Konstantin Pushkarev RC 1.50 4.00
109 Phil Kessel RC 3.00 8.00
110 Luc Bourdon RC 2.00 5.00
111 Shea Weber RC 3.00 8.00
112 G. Latendresse RC 2.00 5.00
113 Jordan Staal RC 3.00 8.00
114 Paul Stastny RC 3.00 8.00
115 Anze Kopitar RC 5.00 12.00
116 Jarkko Immonen RC 1.25 3.00
117 Travis Zajac RC 2.50 6.00
118 Nigel Dawes RC 1.25 3.00
119 Kristopher Letang RC 4.00 10.00
120 Ryan Potulny RC 1.25 3.00
121 Ryan Shannon RC 1.25 3.00
122 Marc-Edouard Vlasic RC 1.25 3.00
123 Noah Welch RC 1.25 3.00
124 Ladislav Smid RC 1.25 3.00
125 Matt Carle RC 1.25 3.00
126 Loui Eriksson RC 2.00 5.00
127 Brendan Bell RC 1.25 3.00
128 Ian White RC 1.50 4.00
129 Jeremy Williams RC 1.25 3.00
130 Eric Fehr RC 2.00 5.00

2006-07 Be A Player Portraits First Exposures

ODDS 1 PER PACK
FEAK Andrei Kostitsyn 3.00 8.00
FEAL Andrew Ladd 4.00 10.00
FEAM Andrej Meszaros 2.50 6.00
FEAO Alexander Ovechkin 10.00 25.00
FEAP Alexander Perezhogin 2.50 6.00
FEAS Alexander Steen 4.00 10.00
FEBB Brandon Bochenski 2.50 6.00
FEBW Brad Winchester 2.50 6.00
FECB Cam Barker 2.50 6.00
FECP Corey Perry 4.00 10.00
FECW Cam Ward 4.00 10.00
FEDB Derek Boogaard 6.00 15.00
FEDP Daniel Paille 3.00 8.00
FEDP Dion Phaneuf 4.00 10.00
FEEN Eric Nystrom 2.50 6.00
FEGB Gilbert Brule 3.00 8.00
FEHL Henrik Lundqvist 8.00 20.00
FEHT Hannu Toivonen 3.00 8.00
FEJC Jeff Carter 4.00 10.00
FEJF Johan Franzen 4.00 10.00
FEJG Josh Gorges 2.50 6.00
FEJH Jim Howard 6.00 15.00
FEJJ Jussi Jokinen 3.00 8.00
FEJK Jakub Klepis 2.50 6.00
FEJT Jeff Tambellini 2.50 6.00
FEMJ Milan Jurcina 2.50 6.00
FEMK Mikko Koivu 3.00 8.00
FEMR Mike Richards 4.00 10.00
FEPB Peter Budaj 3.00 8.00
FEPN Petteri Nokelainen 2.50 6.00
FEPP Petr Prucha 3.00 8.00
FERG Ryan Getzlaf 6.00 15.00
FERO Rostislav Olesz 2.50 6.00
FERS Ryan Suter 3.00 8.00
FERU R.J. Umberger 2.50 6.00
FERW Ryan Whitney 3.00 8.00
FESC Sidney Crosby 15.00 40.00
FETV Thomas Vanek 5.00 12.00
FEVF Valtteri Filppula 4.00 10.00
FEWW Wojtek Wolski 3.00 8.00
FEYD Yann Danis 3.00 8.00
FEZP Zach Parise 5.00 12.00

2006-07 Be A Player Portraits Signature Portraits

OVERALL ODDS ONE PER PACK
SPAL Andrew Ladd 12.00 30.00
SPAO Alexander Ovechkin 50.00 125.00
SPAT Alex Tanguay 8.00 20.00
SPBB Brad Boyes 8.00 20.00
SPBG Bill Guerin 12.00 30.00
SPBH Bobby Holik 8.00 20.00
SPBL Brian Leetch 12.00 30.00
SPBM Brenden Morrow 10.00 25.00
SPBR Brian Rolston 10.00 25.00
SPBS Brent Seabrook 12.00 30.00
SPBW Brad Winchester 8.00 20.00
SPCA Colby Armstrong 10.00 25.00
SPCB Cam Barker 8.00 20.00
SPCD Chris Drury SP 15.00 40.00
SPCH Jonathan Cheechoo 12.00 30.00
SPCW Cam Ward 12.00 30.00
SPDB Daniel Briere SP 20.00 50.00
SPDH Dany Heatley 12.00 30.00
SPDP Daniel Paille 10.00 25.00
SPDR Dwayne Roloson 10.00 25.00
SPDW Doug Weight SP 20.00 50.00
SPEJ Ed Jovanovski 10.00 25.00
SPEM Evgeni Malkin 30.00 80.00
SPEN Evgeni Nabokov 10.00 25.00
SPES Robert Esche 10.00 25.00
SPGM Glen Murray 10.00 25.00
SPHA Jeff Halpern 8.00 20.00
SPHE Milan Hejduk 10.00 25.00
SPHK Dominik Hasek 15.00 40.00
SPHL Henrik Lundqvist 25.00 60.00
SPHT Hannu Toivonen 10.00 25.00
SPJB Jay Bouwmeester SP 20.00 50.00
SPJC Jeff Carter 12.00 30.00
SPJG Jean-Sebastien Giguere SP 20.00 50.00
SPJI Jarome Iginla 12.00 30.00
SPJJ Jussi Jokinen 10.00 25.00
SPJO Joe Thornton 15.00 40.00
SPJP Joni Pitkanen 8.00 20.00
SPJS Joe Sakic 20.00 50.00
SPKB Keith Ballard 8.00 20.00
SPKL Kari Lehtonen 10.00 25.00
SPKO Mikko Koivu 10.00 25.00
SPKP Keith Primeau 12.00 30.00
SPLE John LeClair 12.00 30.00
SPLS Lee Stempniak 8.00 20.00
SPMA Marc-Andre Fleury 20.00 50.00
SPMB Mark Bell 8.00 20.00
SPMG Martin Gerber 10.00 25.00
SPMH Marian Hossa 10.00 25.00
SPMJ Milan Jurcina 8.00 20.00
SPMK Miikka Kiprusoff 10.00 25.00
SPMM Mike Modano SP 30.00 80.00
SPMN Markus Naslund 10.00 25.00
SPMO Brendan Morrison 8.00 20.00
SPMS Marek Svatos 8.00 20.00
SPMT Marty Turco 12.00 30.00
SPNH Nathan Horton 12.00 30.00
SPNK Nikolai Khabibulin SP 20.00 50.00
SPNL Nicklas Lidstrom 12.00 30.00
SPNZ Nikolai Zherdev 8.00 20.00
SPOJ Olli Jokinen SP 20.00 50.00
SPOK Olaf Kolzig 12.00 30.00
SPPB Patrice Bergeron 15.00 40.00
SPPK Paul Kariya 15.00 40.00
SPPM Patrick Marleau 12.00 30.00
SPPP Petr Prucha 10.00 25.00
SPRB Rob Blake 12.00 30.00
SPRD Mike Richards 12.00 30.00
SPRJ R.J. Umberger 8.00 20.00
SPRL Roberto Luongo 20.00 50.00
SPRM Ryan Miller 12.00 30.00
SPRN Rick Nash 12.00 30.00
SPRO Rostislav Olesz 8.00 20.00
SPRW Ryan Whitney 10.00 25.00
SPSB Steve Bernier 8.00 20.00
SPSC Sidney Crosby SP 300.00 450.00
SPSD Shane Doan 10.00 25.00
SPSF Sergei Fedorov SP 30.00 80.00
SPSG Simon Gagne SP 20.00 50.00
SPSJ Matt Stajan 10.00 25.00
SPSK Saku Koivu 12.00 30.00
SPSM Mats Sundin 12.00 30.00
SPSN Scott Niedermayer 12.00 30.00
SPSP Jason Spezza 12.00 30.00
SPSR Ryan Suter 10.00 25.00
SPSS Steve Sullivan 8.00 20.00
SPST Eric Staal 15.00 40.00
SPTP Tom Poti 8.00 20.00
SPTR Tuomo Ruutu 12.00 30.00
SPTV Thomas Vanek 15.00 40.00
SPVO Tomas Vokoun 10.00 25.00
SPWR Wade Redden 8.00 20.00
SPWW Wojtek Wolski 10.00 25.00
SPZC Zdeno Chara 12.00 30.00

2006-07 Be A Player Portraits Dual Signature Portraits

STATED ODDS 1:6
DSBB B.Boyes/P.Bergeron 12.00 30.00
DSCJ Z.Chara/M.Jurcina 10.00 25.00
DSCT J.Thornton/J.Cheech SP 40.00 80.00
DSDB C.Drury/D.Briere 10.00 25.00
DSDJ J.Spezza/D.Heatley 10.00 25.00
DSFN R.Nash/S.Fedorov 15.00 40.00
DSFW M.Fleury/R.Whitney 15.00 40.00
DSGC S.Gagne/J.Carter 10.00 25.00
DSGN S.Nieder/J.Giguere 10.00 25.00
DSHL D.Hasek/N.Lidstrom 12.00 30.00
DSHS M.Hejduk/M.Svatos 8.00 20.00
DSIT J.Iginla/A.Tanguay 10.00 25.00
DSJB O.Jokinen/J.Bouwmeester 10.00 25.00
DSKK S.Koivu/M.Koivu 10.00 25.00
DSKV P.Kariya/T.Vokoun 12.00 30.00
DSLN M.Naslund/R.Luongo 15.00 40.00
DSLP H.Lundqvist/P.Prucha 20.00 50.00
DSMT M.Modano/M.Turco 15.00 40.00
DSNT T.Ruutu/N.Khabibulin 10.00 25.00
DSOK O.Kolzig/A.Ovechkin 40.00 100.00
DSRU M.Richards/R.Umberger 10.00 25.00
DSSM J.Sakic/M.Modano SP 50.00 100.00
DSWG D.Weight/B.Guerin 10.00 25.00
DSWS E.Staal/C.Ward 12.00 30.00

2006-07 Be A Player Portraits Triple Signature Portraits

PRINT RUN 25 SER.#'d SETS
TBOS Murray/Boyes/Berg 50.00 120.00
TBUF Drury/Briere/Miller 40.00 100.00
TCGY Tang/Kipper/Iginla
TCLB Nash/Zherd/Fed 60.00 150.00
TCOL Sakic/Hejd/Svat 60.00 150.00
TLWF Luongo/Fleury/Ward 60.00 150.00
TNSS Spezza/Nash/Staal 50.00 125.00
TOTT Heat/Redd/Spezza 40.00 100.00
TSJS Thorn/Bell/Cheech 50.00 125.00
TSSM Sakic/Mo/Sundin 60.00 150.00

2000-01 BAP Signature Series

Released in February 2001 as a 300-card set with 5 cards per pack, Be A Player Signature Series featured full color action photos on silver metallic stock with the set name on the left border and the players name in the lower right corner. Cards 251-275 were short-printed to just 1000 serial-numbered sets, and cards 276-300 were short-printed to just 500 serial-numbered sets.

COMP.SET w/o SP's (250) 50.00 100.00
251-275 SP PRINT RUN 1000
276-300 SP PRINT RUN 500
1 Doug Gilmour .75 2.00
2 Todd Reirden .40 1.00
3 Mike Johnson .40 1.00
4 Scott Walker .40 1.00
5 Mike York .40 1.00
6 Roman Turek .50 1.25
7 Sergei Zubov .50 1.25
8 Brad Stuart .50 1.25
9 Michael Peca .50 1.25
10 Jyrki Lumme .40 1.00
11 Steve Yzerman 2.00 5.00
12 Olaf Kolzig .60 1.50
13 Ray Bourque 1.00 2.50
14 Clarke Wilm .40 1.00
15 Eric Desjardins .50 1.25
16 Rod Brind'Amour .60 1.50
17 Marc Savard .50 1.25
18 Jarome Iginla .60 1.50
19 Daniel Alfredsson .60 1.50
20 Alexei Yashin .50 1.25
21 Keith Tkachuk .60 1.50
22 Jaromir Jagr 1.50 4.00
23 Trevor Kidd .40 1.00
24 Alexei Kovalev .50 1.25
25 Jan Hrdina .40 1.00
26 Tom Poti .40 1.00
27 Jere Karalahti .40 1.00
28 Janne Niinimaa .40 1.00
29 Ray Whitney .50 1.25
30 Nicklas Lidstrom .60 1.50
31 Martin Lapointe .50 1.25
32 Matt Cullen .40 1.00
33 Theo Fleury .75 2.00
34 Mats Sundin .60 1.50
35 Kimmo Timonen .40 1.00
36 Joe Thornton 1.00 2.50
37 Adam Graves .50 1.25
38 Andrei Zyuzin .40 1.00
39 Michal Handzus .40 1.00
40 Jamie Storr .50 1.25
41 Teemu Selanne 1.25 3.00
42 Brian Rafalski .40 1.00
43 Aaron Gavey .40 1.00
44 Jose Theodore .75 2.00
45 Tyler Wright .40 1.00
46 Alexander Mogilny .50 1.25
47 Brad Isbister .40 1.00
48 Guy Hebert .50 1.25
49 Chris Simon .40 1.00
50 Dominik Hasek 1.00 2.50
51 Dan Cloutier .50 1.25
52 Brian Holzinger .40 1.00
53 Dimitri Khristich .40 1.00
54 Tyson Nash .40 1.00
55 Patrick Marleau .60 1.50
56 Marty Reasoner .40 1.00
57 Manny Fernandez .50 1.25
58 Brenden Morrow .50 1.25
59 Darren McCarty .40 1.00
60 Milan Hejduk .50 1.25
61 Darius Kasparaitis .50 1.25
62 Jere Lehtinen .50 1.25
63 Andrew Brunette .40 1.00
64 Wayne Gretzky 3.00 8.00
65 Robyn Regehr .40 1.00
66 Travis Green .40 1.00
67 John Grahame .40 1.00
68 Mike Fisher .50 1.25
69 Josef Marha .40 1.00
70 Randy McKay .40 1.00
71 Brett Hull 1.00 2.50
72 Anson Carter .50 1.25
73 Owen Nolan .60 1.50
74 Sean Burke .40 1.00
75 Mario Lemieux 2.00 5.00
76 Brian Savage .40 1.00
77 Jason Ward .40 1.00
78 Patrick Lalime .50 1.25
79 Glen Murray .40 1.00
80 Mathieu Biron .40 1.00
81 Todd Bertuzzi .50 1.25
82 Chris Drury .50 1.25
83 Maxim Afinogenov .40 1.00
84 Michal Rozsival .40 1.00
85 Glen Metropolit .40 1.00
86 Mariusz Czerkawski .40 1.00
87 Byron Dafoe .50 1.25
88 Mark Recchi .75 2.00
89 Mike Modano 1.00 2.50
90 Felix Potvin 1.00 2.50
91 Saku Koivu .60 1.50
92 Jay Pandolfo .40 1.00
93 Todd Simpson .40 1.00
94 Calle Johansson .40 1.00
95 Bill Guerin .60 1.50
96 Oleg Tverdovsky .40 1.00
97 Kyle McLaren .40 1.00
98 Mark Messier 1.00 2.50
99 Chris Gratton .40 1.00
100 Sergei Brylin .40 1.00
101 David Legwand .60 1.50
102 Jason Allison .50 1.25
103 Daniel Cleary .50 1.25
104 Curtis Joseph .75 2.00
105 Sergei Fedorov 1.00 2.50
106 Jeremy Roenick .60 1.50
107 Frantisek Kaberle .40 1.00
108 Chris Pronger .50 1.25
109 Martin Skoula .50 1.25
110 Jiri Slegr .40 1.00
111 Trevor Letowski .40 1.00
112 Colin Forbes .40 1.00
113 Sergei Zholtok .40 1.00
114 David Harlock .40 1.00
115 Scott Stevens .60 1.50
116 Dave Tanabe .40 1.00
117 Mattias Timander .40 1.00
118 Stu Barnes .50 1.25
119 Simon Gagne .60 1.50
120 Paul Coffey .60 1.50
121 Peter Bondra .50 1.25
122 Ed Jovanovski .50 1.25
123 J-P Dumont .40 1.00
124 Pavol Demitra .75 2.00
125 Mike Vernon .50 1.25
126 Brendan Morrison .60 1.50
127 Dainius Zubrus .40 1.00
128 Al MacInnis .60 1.50
129 Kevyn Adams .40 1.00
130 Petr Buzek .40 1.00
131 Steve Kariya .40 1.00
132 Keith Primeau .50 1.25
133 Kenny Jonsson .40 1.00
134 Lance Pitlick .40 1.00
135 Randy Robitaille .40 1.00
136 Brian Rolston .50 1.25
137 Alex Tanguay .50 1.25
138 Alexei Zhamnov .50 1.25
139 Peter Forsberg .75 2.00
140 Cam Stewart .40 1.00
141 Vitali Vishnevsky .40 1.00
142 Tim Connolly .40 1.00
143 Tie Domi 1.00 2.50
144 Jaroslav Modry .40 1.00
145 Jarno Kultanen RC .40 1.00
146 Igor Larionov .60 1.50
147 Derian Hatcher .50 1.25
148 Scott Niedermayer .60 1.50
149 Shawn McEachern .40 1.00
150 Sergei Berezin .40 1.00
151 Rob Blake .60 1.50
152 Steve Thomas .40 1.00
153 Ryan Smyth .50 1.25
154 Petr Nedved .50 1.25
155 Jochen Hecht .40 1.00
156 Richard Zednik .40 1.00
157 Tommy Salo .50 1.25
158 Ed Belfour .60 1.50
159 Lyle Odelein .40 1.00
160 Steve Sullivan .40 1.00
161 Vincent Damphousse .50 1.25
162 Andy Delmore .40 1.00
163 Harold Druken .40 1.00
164 Martin Brodeur 1.25 3.00
165 Mike Richter .60 1.50
166 Radek Bonk .50 1.25
167 Joe Sakic 1.00 2.50
168 John Vanbiesbrouck .50 1.25
169 Jeff Shantz .40 1.00
170 Jean-Sebastien Aubin .50 1.25
171 Shayne Corson .40 1.00
172 Jeff Friesen .40 1.00
173 Jeff Hackett .40 1.00
174 Jozef Stumpel .40 1.00
175 Daymond Langkow .40 1.00
176 Nikolai Antropov .50 1.25
177 Ron Tugnutt .50 1.25
178 Viktor Kozlov .50 1.25
179 Adam Oates .60 1.50
180 Steve Webb .40 1.00
181 Pierre Turgeon .60 1.50
182 Fred Brathwaite .50 1.25
183 Martin Biron .50 1.25
184 John LeClair .60 1.50
185 Steve Rucchin .40 1.00
186 Patrik Elias .60 1.50
187 Boris Mironov .40 1.00
188 Mika Alatalo .40 1.00
189 Jocelyn Thibault .50 1.25
190 Jason York .40 1.00
191 Zigmund Palffy .60 1.50
192 Paul Kariya .75 2.00
193 Stu Grimson .40 1.00
194 Jeff Halpern .40 1.00
195 Scott Gomez .50 1.25
196 Tomas Vlasak .40 1.00
197 Roman Hamrlik .50 1.25
198 Radek Dvorak .50 1.25
199 Martin Straka .50 1.25
200 Martin Rucinsky .40 1.00
201 Valeri Bure .50 1.25
202 Scott Mellanby .40 1.00
203 Steve McKenna .40 1.00
204 Luc Robitaille .60 1.50
205 Joe Nieuwendyk .60 1.50
206 Brendan Shanahan .75 2.00
207 Robert Lang .40 1.00
208 Todd Marchant .40 1.00
209 Doug Weight .60 1.50
210 Andre Roy .40 1.00
211 Patrick Roy 1.50 4.00
212 Vincent Lecavalier .50 1.25
213 Trevor Linden .60 1.50
214 Patrik Stefan .50 1.25
215 Jan Hlavac .40 1.00
216 Ron Francis .75 2.00
217 Brian Boucher .50 1.25
218 Tony Hrkac .40 1.00
219 Brian Leetch .60 1.50
220 Tony Amonte .50 1.25
221 Nikolai Khabibulin 1.00 2.50
222 Sandis Ozolinsh .50 1.25
223 Darryl Sydor .50 1.25
224 Bobby Holik .40 1.00
225 Sami Kapanen .40 1.00
226 Pavel Bure .75 2.00
227 Steve Konowalchuk .40 1.00
228 Brent Gilchrist .40 1.00
229 Jeff O'Neill .50 1.25
230 Andre Savage .40 1.00
231 Pavel Kubina .40 1.00
232 Jason Arnott .50 1.25
233 Petr Sykora .50 1.25
234 Miroslav Satan .40 1.00
235 Chris Osgood .60 1.50
236 Sergei Samsonov .50 1.25
237 Marian Hossa .50 1.25
238 Arturs Irbe .50 1.25
239 Josh Holden .40 1.00
240 Phil Housley .50 1.25
241 Dimitri Yushkevich .40 1.00
242 Cliff Ronning .40 1.00
243 John Madden .50 1.25
244 Jaroslav Spacek .40 1.00
245 Craig Darby .40 1.00
246 Eric Lindros 1.00 2.50
247 Markus Naslund .50 1.25
248 Sergei Gonchar .40 1.00
249 Gary Roberts .40 1.00
250 Steve Shields .40 1.00
251 Petteri Nummelin RC 1.00 2.50
252 Mika Noronen SP 1.00 2.50
253 Andrew Raycroft RC 2.50 6.00
254 Taylor Pyatt SP 1.00 2.50
255 Toni Lydman SP 1.00 2.50
256 Matt Bradley SP 1.00 2.50
257 Petr Hubacek RC 1.00 2.50
258 Ossi Vaananen RC 1.25 3.00
259 Dimitri Kalinin SP 1.00 2.50
260 Justin Williams RC 2.50 6.00
261 Jeff Farkas SP 1.00 2.50
262 Brent Sopel RC 1.50 4.00
263 Samuel Pahlsson SP 1.00 2.50
264 Josef Vasicek RC 2.50 6.00
265 Shane Willis SP 1.00 2.50
266 Petr Svoboda RC 1.25 3.00
267 Petr Schastlivy SP 1.00 2.50
268 Roman Simicek RC 1.00 2.50
269 Reto Von Arx RC 1.25 3.00
270 Colin White RC 1.00 2.50
271 Lubomir Sekeras RC 1.00 2.50
272 Alexander Kharitonov RC 1.00 2.50
273 Maxim Sushinski SP 1.00 2.50
274 Sergei Vyshedkevich RC 1.00 2.50
275 Brad Ference SP 1.00 2.50
276 Martin Havlat RC 5.00 12.00
277 Maxime Ouellet SP 2.50 6.00
278 Roberto Luongo SP 4.00 10.00
279 Marian Gaborik RC 8.00 20.00
280 Daniel Sedin SP 5.00 12.00
281 Henrik Sedin SP 4.00 10.00
282 Milan Kraft SP 1.50 4.00
283 Denis Shvidki SP 1.50 4.00
284 Kris Beech SP 1.50 4.00
285 Rostislav Klesla RC 4.00 10.00
286 Jani Hurme RC 1.50 4.00
287 Oleg Saprykin SP 1.50 4.00
288 Marty Turco RC 3.00 8.00
289 Brad Richards SP 2.50 6.00
290 Steve McCarthy SP 1.50 4.00
291 Tomi Kallio SP 1.50 4.00
292 Evgeni Nabokov SP 2.00 5.00
293 Steven Reinprecht RC 2.50 6.00
294 Andrei Markov SP 3.00 8.00
295 Brent Johnson SP 2.00 5.00
296 Rick DiPietro RC 6.00 15.00
297 Roman Cechmanek RC 2.00 5.00
298 Daniel Tkaczuk SP 2.00 5.00
299 Mathieu Garon SP 1.50 4.00
300 Scott Hartnell RC 4.00 10.00

2000-01 BAP Signature Series Ruby

*1-250 VETS/200: 1.5X TO 4X BASIC CARDS
*251-275 SP/200: .5X TO 1.5X BASIC SP/1000
*276-230 SP/200: .5X TO 1X BASIC SP/500
STATED PRINT RUN 200 SER.#'d SETS
98 Mark Messier 4.00 10.00

2000-01 BAP Signature Series Sapphire

*STARS: 2X TO 6X BASIC CARDS
*SP's 251-275: .4X TO 1X
*SP's 276-300: .3X TO .8X
STATED PRINT RUN 100 SER.#'d SETS

2000-01 BAP Signature Series Autographs

Randomly inserted in packs at the rate of one in one, this 250-card set paralleld the base set with player autographs.

*GOLD: .6X TO 1.2X SILVER AU
*GOLD: .4X TO 1X SILVER AU SP
OVERALL AUTO ODDS 1:1
1 Pavel Bure SP 12.00 30.00
2 Valeri Bure SP 8.00 20.00
3 Mike Johnson 2.50 6.00
4 Rob Blake 4.00 10.00
5 Brendan Morrison 4.00 10.00
6 David Legwand 4.00 10.00
7 Dimitri Kalinin 2.50 6.00
8 Jeff Farkas 2.50 6.00
9 Brian Savage 2.50 6.00
10 Dan Cloutier 3.00 8.00
11 Tom Poti 2.50 6.00
12 Doug Gilmour SP 12.00 30.00
13 Steve Konowalchuk 2.50 6.00
14 Scott Mellanby 2.50 6.00
15 Brent Sopel 4.00 10.00
16 Ron Tugnutt SP 8.00 20.00
17 Steve Thomas 2.50 6.00
18 Dainius Zubrus 2.50 6.00
19 Jason Allison SP 8.00 20.00
20 Jason Ward 2.50 6.00
21 Brian Holzinger 2.50 6.00
22 Jere Karalahti 2.50 6.00
23 Todd Reirden 2.50 6.00
24 Brent Gilchrist 2.50 6.00
25 Steve McKenna 2.50 6.00
26 Viktor Kozlov 3.00 8.00
27 Ryan Smyth 3.00 8.00
28 Al MacInnis SP 10.00 25.00
29 Daniel Cleary 3.00 8.00
30 Patrick Lalime 3.00 8.00
31 Dimitri Khristich 2.50 6.00
32 Janne Niinimaa 2.50 6.00
33 Mike Johnson 2.50 6.00
34 Jeff O'Neill SP 8.00 20.00
35 Luc Robitaille SP 10.00 25.00
36 Adam Oates SP 10.00 25.00
37 Petr Nedved 3.00 8.00
38 Kevyn Adams 2.50 6.00
39 Curtis Joseph SP 12.00 30.00
40 Glen Murray 2.50 6.00
41 Tyson Nash 2.50 6.00
42 Ray Whitney 3.00 8.00
43 Scott Walker 2.50 6.00
44 Andre Savage 2.50 6.00
45 Joe Nieuwendyk SP 10.00 25.00
46 Steve Webb 2.50 6.00
47 Jochen Hecht 2.50 6.00
48 Petr Buzek 2.50 6.00
49 Sergei Fedorov SP 25.00 60.00
50 Mathieu Biron 2.50 6.00
51 Patrick Marleau 4.00 10.00
52 Nicklas Lidstrom SP 10.00 25.00
53 Mike York 2.50 6.00
54 Pavel Kubina 2.50 6.00
55 Brendan Shanahan SP 20.00 50.00
56 Pierre Turgeon SP 10.00 25.00
57 Richard Zednik 2.50 6.00
58 Steve Kariya 2.50 6.00
59 Jeremy Roenick SP 10.00 25.00
60 Todd Bertuzzi 3.00 8.00
61 Marty Reasoner 2.50 6.00
62 Martin Lapointe 3.00 8.00
63 Roman Turek 3.00 8.00
64 Jason Arnott SP 8.00 20.00
65 Robert Lang 2.50 6.00
66 Fred Brathwaite 3.00 8.00
67 Tommy Salo 3.00 8.00
68 Keith Primeau SP 8.00 20.00
69 Frantisek Kaberle 2.50 6.00
70 Chris Drury 3.00 8.00
71 Manny Fernandez 3.00 8.00
72 Shane Willis 2.50 6.00
73 Matt Cullen 2.50 6.00
74 Sergei Zubov 3.00 8.00
75 Petr Sykora 3.00 8.00
76 Todd Marchant 2.50 6.00
77 Martin Biron 3.00 8.00
78 Ed Belfour SP 20.00 50.00
79 Kenny Jonsson SP 6.00 15.00
80 Chris Pronger SP 8.00 20.00
81 Maxim Afinogenov 2.50 6.00
82 Brenden Morrow 3.00 8.00
83 Theo Fleury SP 12.00 30.00
84 Brad Stuart 3.00 8.00
85 Miroslav Satan 2.50 6.00
86 Doug Weight SP 10.00 25.00
87 John LeClair SP 10.00 25.00
88 Lyle Odelein 2.50 6.00
89 Lance Pitlick 2.50 6.00
90 Martin Skoula 3.00 8.00
91 Michal Rozsival 2.50 6.00
92 Darren McCarty 2.50 6.00
93 Mats Sundin SP 10.00 25.00
94 Michael Peca 3.00 8.00
95 Chris Osgood SP 15.00 40.00
96 Andre Roy 2.50 6.00
97 Steve Rucchin 2.50 6.00
98 Steve Sullivan 2.50 6.00
99 Randy Robitaille 2.50 6.00
100 Jiri Slegr 2.50 6.00
101 Glen Metropolit 2.50 6.00
102 Milan Hejduk 3.00 8.00
103 Kimmo Timonen 2.50 6.00
104 Jyrki Lumme 2.50 6.00
105 Sergei Samsonov SP 8.00 20.00
106 Patrick Roy SP 25.00 60.00
107 Patrik Elias 4.00 10.00
108 Vincent Damphousse 3.00 8.00
109 Brian Rolston 3.00 8.00
110 Peter Forsberg SP 12.00 30.00
111 Mariusz Czerkawski 2.50 6.00
112 Darius Kasparaitis 3.00 8.00
113 Joe Thornton 6.00 15.00
114 Steve Yzerman SP 30.00 80.00
115 Marian Hossa 3.00 8.00
116 Vincent Lecavalier 3.00 8.00
117 Colin White 2.50 6.00
118 Boris Mironov 2.50 6.00
119 Andy Delmore 2.50 6.00
120 Alex Tanguay 3.00 8.00
121 Colin Forbes 2.50 6.00
122 Byron Dafoe 3.00 8.00
123 Jere Lehtinen 3.00 8.00
124 Adam Graves 3.00 8.00
125 Olaf Kolzig SP 10.00 25.00
126 Arturs Irbe 3.00 8.00
127 Trevor Linden 4.00 10.00
128 Mika Alatalo 2.50 6.00
129 Harold Druken 2.50 6.00
130 Alexei Zhamnov 3.00 8.00
131 Sergei Zholtok 2.50 6.00
132 Mark Recchi SP 12.00 30.00
133 Andrew Brunette 2.50 6.00
134 Andrei Zyuzin 2.50 6.00
135 Ray Bourque SP 15.00 40.00
136 Josh Holden 2.50 6.00
137 Patrik Stefan 3.00 8.00
138 Jocelyn Thibault 3.00 8.00
139 Martin Brodeur SP 20.00 50.00
140 Trevor Letowski 2.50 6.00
141 David Harlock 2.50 6.00
142 Mike Modano SP 15.00 40.00
143 Wayne Gretzky SP 300.00 600.00
144 Michal Handzus 2.50 6.00
145 Clarke Wilm 2.50 6.00
146 Phil Housley 3.00 8.00
147 Jan Hlavac 2.50 6.00
148 Jason York 2.50 6.00
149 Mike Richter SP 10.00 25.00
150 Sergei Vyshedkevich 2.50 6.00
151 Cam Stewart 2.50 6.00
152 Scott Stevens SP 10.00 25.00
153 Felix Potvin 6.00 15.00
154 Robyn Regehr 2.50 6.00
155 Jamie Storr 3.00 8.00
156 Eric Desjardins 3.00 8.00
157 Dimitri Yushkevich 2.50 6.00
158 Ron Francis SP 12.00 30.00
159 Zigmund Palffy SP 10.00 25.00
160 Radek Bonk 3.00 8.00
161 Vitali Vishnevsky 2.50 6.00
162 Dave Tanabe 2.50 6.00
163 Saku Koivu 4.00 10.00
164 Travis Green 2.50 6.00
165 Teemu Selanne SP 20.00 50.00
166 Rod Brind'Amour 4.00 10.00
167 Cliff Ronning 2.50 6.00
168 Brian Boucher 3.00 8.00
169 Paul Kariya SP 12.00 30.00
170 Joe Sakic SP 15.00 40.00
171 Tim Connolly 2.50 6.00
172 Mattias Timander 2.50 6.00
173 Jay Pandolfo 2.50 6.00
174 John Grahame 2.50 6.00
175 Brian Rafalski 2.50 6.00
176 Marc Savard 3.00 8.00
177 John Madden 3.00 8.00
178 Tony Hrkac 2.50 6.00
179 Stu Grimson 2.50 6.00
180 John Vanbiesbrouck SP 8.00 20.00
181 Tie Domi 6.00 15.00
182 Stu Barnes 3.00 8.00
183 Todd Simpson 2.50 6.00
184 Mike Fisher 3.00 8.00
185 Aaron Gavey 2.50 6.00
186 Jarome Iginla 4.00 10.00
187 Jaroslav Spacek 2.50 6.00
188 Brian Leetch SP 10.00 25.00
189 Jeff Halpern 2.50 6.00
190 Jeff Shantz 2.50 6.00
191 Jaroslav Modry 2.50 6.00
192 Simon Gagne 4.00 10.00
193 Calle Johansson 2.50 6.00
194 Josef Marha 2.50 6.00
195 Jose Theodore 5.00 12.00
196 Daniel Alfredsson 4.00 10.00
197 Craig Darby 2.50 6.00
198 Tony Amonte SP 8.00 20.00
199 Scott Gomez 3.00 8.00
200 Jean-Sebastien Aubin 3.00 8.00
201 Jarno Kultanen 2.50 6.00
202 Paul Coffey SP 10.00 25.00
203 Bill Guerin SP 10.00 25.00
204 Roberto Luongo 6.00 15.00
205 Randy McKay 2.50 6.00
206 Tyler Wright 2.50 6.00
207 Alexei Yashin 3.00 8.00
208 Eric Lindros SP 25.00 60.00
209 Nikolai Khabibulin 6.00 15.00
210 Tomas Vlasak 2.50 6.00
211 Shayne Corson 2.50 6.00
212 Igor Larionov SP 10.00 25.00
213 Peter Bondra SP 8.00 20.00
214 Mika Noronen 2.50 6.00
215 Andrew Raycroft 6.00 15.00
216 Taylor Pyatt 2.50 6.00
217 Toni Lydman 2.50 6.00
218 Matt Bradley 2.50 6.00
219 Brad Richards 4.00 10.00
220 Steve McCarthy 2.50 6.00
221 Tomi Kallio 2.50 6.00
222 Justin Williams 6.00 15.00
223 Brad Ference 2.50 6.00
224 Steven Reinprecht 4.00 10.00
225 Samuel Pahlsson 2.50 6.00
226 Josef Vasicek 6.00 15.00
227 Jani Hurme 2.50 6.00
228 Petr Svoboda 3.00 8.00
229 Petr Schastlivy 2.50 6.00
230 Roman Simicek 2.50 6.00
231 Reto Von Arx 3.00 8.00
232 Oleg Saprykin 2.50 6.00
233 Lubomir Sekeras 2.50 6.00
234 Alexander Kharitonov 2.50 6.00
235 Maxim Sushinski 2.50 6.00
236 Andrei Markov 5.00 12.00
237 Scott Hartnell 6.00 15.00
238 Martin Havlat 8.00 20.00
239 Maxime Ouellet 4.00 10.00
240 Petteri Nummelin 2.50 6.00
241 Marian Gaborik 8.00 20.00
242 Daniel Sedin 8.00 20.00
243 Henrik Sedin 6.00 15.00
244 Milan Kraft 2.50 6.00
245 Denis Shvidki 2.50 6.00
246 Kris Beech 2.50 6.00
247 Rostislav Klesla 6.00 15.00
248 Petr Hubacek 2.50 6.00
249 Ossi Vaananen 3.00 8.00
250 Marty Turco 5.00 12.00

2000-01 BAP Signature Series Department of Defense

Randomly inserted in packs, this 20-card set featured a game-used swatch of jersey and a action player photo on a background of computer generated steel girders and rivets. Each card had a stated print run of 100 each.

ANNOUNCED PRINT RUN 100
DD1 Brian Leetch 10.00 25.00
DD2 Ray Bourque 20.00 50.00
DD3 Chris Chelios 12.50 30.00
DD4 Nicklas Lidstrom 20.00 50.00
DD5 Sandis Ozolinsh 8.00 20.00
DD6 Scott Stevens 10.00 25.00
DD7 Al MacInnis 10.00 25.00
DD8 Kyle McLaren 8.00 20.00
DD9 Kenny Jonsson 8.00 20.00
DD10 Teppo Numminen 8.00 20.00
DD11 Sergei Zubov 8.00 20.00
DD12 Scott Niedermayer 8.00 20.00
DD13 Paul Coffey 15.00 40.00
DD14 Adam Foote 8.00 20.00
DD15 Sergei Gonchar 8.00 20.00
DD16 Phil Housley 8.00 20.00
DD17 Eric Desjardins 8.00 20.00
DD18 Dimitri Yushkevich 8.00 20.00
DD19 Chris Pronger 10.00 25.00
DD20 Rob Blake 10.00 25.00

2000-01 BAP Signature Series Franchise Players

ANNOUNCED PRINT RUN 30
F1 Paul Kariya 6.00 15.00
F2 Patrik Stefan 4.00 10.00
F3 Joe Thornton 8.00 20.00
F4 Dominik Hasek 12.00 30.00
F5 Jarome Iginla 5.00 12.00
F6 Jeff O'Neill 4.00 10.00
F7 Tony Amonte 4.00 10.00
F8 Peter Forsberg 6.00 15.00
F9 Ron Tugnutt 4.00 10.00
F10 Mike Modano 8.00 20.00
F11 Steve Yzerman 15.00 40.00
F12 Doug Weight 5.00 12.00
F13 Pavel Bure 6.00 15.00
F14 Rob Blake 5.00 12.00
F15 Marian Gaborik 10.00 25.00
F16 Saku Koivu 5.00 12.00
F17 David Legwand 5.00 12.00
F18 Martin Brodeur 10.00 25.00
F19 Mariusz Czerkawski 3.00 8.00
F20 Brian Leetch 5.00 12.00
F21 Marian Hossa 4.00 10.00
F22 John LeClair 5.00 12.00
F23 Keith Tkachuk 5.00 12.00
F24 Jaromir Jagr 12.00 30.00
F25 Chris Pronger 4.00 10.00
F26 Owen Nolan 5.00 12.00
F27 Vincent Lecavalier 4.00 10.00
F28 Curtis Joseph 6.00 15.00
F29 Daniel Sedin 10.00 25.00
F30 Olaf Kolzig 5.00 12.00

2000-01 BAP Signature Series Goalie Memorabilia Autographs

Randomly inserted in packs, this 5-card set featured a game-used swatch of equipment and an autograph beside a color action photo of the player. The player's name was printed along the left border and the words "Goalie Legend" appeared on the top of each card. Each card had a stated print run of 150 sets.

ANNOUNCED PRINT RUN 150 SETS
GLS1 Gerry Cheevers 50.00 125.00
GLS2 Vladislav Tretiak 90.00 150.00
GLS3 Tony Esposito 40.00 100.00
GLS4 Johnny Bower 40.00 100.00
GLS5 Bernie Parent 50.00 125.00

2000-01 BAP Signature Series He Shoots He Scores Points

ONE PER PACK
1 P.Bure 3pts. .50 1.25
2 M.Brodeur 1pts. .75 2.00
3 T.Fleury 3pts. .50 1.25
4 P.Forsberg 1pts. .50 1.25
5 P.Forsberg 3pts. .50 1.25
6 D.Hasek 2pts. .60 1.50
7 B.Hull 2pts. .60 1.50
8 J.Jagr 3pts 1.00 2.50
9 C.Joseph 1pts. .50 1.25
10 P.Kariya 2pts. .50 1.25
11 M.Lemieux 3pts. 1.25 3.00
12 M.Messier 2pts. .60 1.50
13 M.Modano 2pts. .60 1.50
14 Z.Palffy 1pts. .40 1.00
15 L.Robitaille 2pts. .40 1.00
16 P.Roy 2pts. 1.00 2.50
17 J.Sakic 2pts. .60 1.50
18 B.Shanahan 1pts. .50 1.25
19 M.Sundin 1pts. .40 1.00
20 S.Yzerman 3pts. 1.25 3.00

2000-01 BAP Signature Series Jersey

STATED PRINT RUN 100 SER.#'d SETS
*JSY/STICK/100: .5X TO 1.2X BASIC JSY
J1 Theo Fleury 10.00 25.00
J2 Brendan Shanahan 10.00 25.00
J3 Curtis Joseph 10.00 25.00
J4 Saku Koivu 10.00 25.00
J5 Dominik Hasek 20.00 50.00
J6 Al MacInnis 10.00 25.00
J7 John LeClair 10.00 25.00
J8 Teemu Selanne 10.00 25.00
J9 Scott Niedermayer 10.00 25.00
J10 Pavel Bure 10.00 25.00
J11 Mark Messier 10.00 25.00
J12 Jaromir Jagr 12.00 30.00
J13 Chris Pronger 10.00 25.00
J14 Chris Osgood 10.00 25.00
J15 Mats Sundin 10.00 25.00
J16 Paul Kariya 10.00 25.00
J17 Scott Stevens 10.00 25.00
J18 Kenny Jonsson 10.00 25.00
J19 Sergei Fedorov 12.50 30.00
J20 Peter Forsberg 15.00 40.00
J21 Brett Hull 12.50 30.00
J22 Tony Amonte 10.00 25.00
J23 Patrick Roy 12.00 30.00
J24 Ed Belfour 10.00 25.00
J25 Martin Brodeur 25.00 60.00
J26 Brian Leetch 10.00 25.00
J27 Mike Modano 12.50 30.00
J28 Jeff Friesen 10.00 25.00
J29 Jeremy Roenick 12.50 30.00
J30 Steve Yzerman 30.00 80.00
J31 Joe Sakic 20.00 50.00
J32 Mike Peca 10.00 25.00
J33 Luc Robitaille 10.00 25.00
J34 Adam Oates 10.00 25.00
J35 Valeri Bure 10.00 25.00
J36 Kyle McLaren 10.00 25.00
J37 Nicklas Lidstrom 10.00 25.00
J38 Jason Arnott 10.00 25.00
J39 Mike Richter 10.00 25.00
J40 Keith Tkachuk 10.00 25.00

2000-01 BAP Signature Series Mario Lemieux Legend

Randomly inserted in packs, this 5-card set features two swatches of game-used equipment per card, accompanied by a photo of Mario Lemieux. Each card has a stated print run of 30, but the cards are not serial numbered.
ANNOUNCED PRINT RUN 30
LM1 Mario Lemieux EMB 80.00 200.00
LM2 Mario Lemieux Jsy/Glv 100.00 250.00
LM3 Mario Lemieux Jsy/Glv 100.00 250.00
LM4 Mario Lemieux Jsy/Jsy 100.00 250.00
LM5 Mario Lemieux Jsy/Jsy/Jsy 250.00 500.00

2000-01 BAP Signature Series Mario Lemieux Retrospective

Randomly inserted in packs, this 20-card set highlights the career of Mario Lemieux. Each card portrays a specific milestone in his career.
COMPLETE SET (20) 30.00 80.00
R1 M.Lemieux-Laval Juniors 2.00 5.00
R2 M.Lemieux-NHL Draft 2.00 5.00
R3 M.Lemieux-1st NHL Game 2.00 5.00
R4 M.Lemieux-1st NHL Season 2.00 5.00
R5 M.Lemieux-'85-'86 Season HL 2.00 5.00
R6 M.Lemieux-'86-'87 Season HL 2.00 5.00
R7 M.Lemieux-'87 Canada Cup 2.00 5.00
R8 M.Lemieux-'87-'88 Season HL 2.00 5.00
R9 M.Lemieux-'88-'89 Season HL 2.00 5.00
R10 M.Lemieux-'90-'91 Season HL 2.00 5.00
R11 M.Lemieux-'91-'92 Season HL 2.00 5.00
R12 M.Lemieux-'92-'93 Season HL 2.00 5.00
R13 M.Lemieux-'93-'94 Season HL 2.00 5.00
R14 M.Lemieux-'95-'96 Season HL 2.00 5.00
R15 M.Lemieux-'96 All-Star Game 2.00 5.00
R16 M.Lemieux-Final NHL Game 2.00 5.00
R17 M.Lemieux-Pitts.retires 66 2.00 5.00
R18 M.Lemieux-HOF induction 2.00 5.00
R19 M.Lemieux-Mario Returns 2.00 5.00
R20 M.Lemieux-1500th Point 2.00 5.00

2001-02 BAP Signature Series

This 250-card set featured full-color action photos on silver-mirrored card fronts. Cards 226-250 were available in BAP Update packs only.
COMP.SER. 1 SET (225) 100.00 200.00
225-250 ISSUED IN BAP UPDATE
1 Rick DiPietro .30 .75
2 Patrik Stefan .30 .75
3 Hal Gill .25 .60
4 J-P Dumont .25 .60
5 Jarome Iginla .40 1.00
6 Shane Willis .25 .60
7 Chris Phillips .25 .60
8 Rostislav Klesla .25 .60
9 Brenden Morrow .30 .75
10 Manny Legace .30 .75
11 Anson Carter .30 .75
12 Roberto Luongo .60 1.50
13 Aaron Miller .25 .60
14 Wayne Primeau .25 .60
15 Brian Savage .25 .60
16 John Jakopin .25 .60
17 Greg Johnson .25 .60
18 Marc Chouinard .25 .60
19 Steve Martins .25 .60
20 Marian Hossa .30 .75
21 Brent Johnson .30 .75
22 Sean Burke .25 .60
23 Jan Hrdina .25 .60
24 Evgeni Nabokov .30 .75
25 Adam Deadmarsh .30 .75
26 Brad Richards .40 1.00
27 Wade Redden .25 .60
28 David Legwand .30 .75
29 Jean-Sebastien Giguere .30 .75
30 Ray Ferraro .25 .60
31 Denis Hamel .25 .60
32 Marc Savard .25 .60
33 Craig Adams .25 .60
34 Landon Wilson .25 .60
35 Marc Denis .30 .75
36 Roman Lyashenko .25 .60
37 Tomas Holmstrom .25 .60
38 Mike Comrie .30 .75
39 Scott Hartnell .40 1.00
40 Sergei Krivokrasov .25 .60
41 Mathieu Garon .30 .75
42 Denis Arkhipov .25 .60
43 Roman Hamrlik .25 .60
44 Mike Mottau .25 .60
45 Shawn McEachern .25 .60
46 Peter White .25 .60
47 Shane Doan .30 .75
48 Janne Laukkanen .25 .60
49 Martin St. Louis .40 1.00
50 Tomas Kaberle .25 .60
51 Daniel Sedin .40 1.00
52 Jonas Ronnqvist .25 .60
53 Damian Rhodes .30 .75
54 Vaclav Varada .25 .60
55 Ronald Petrovicky .25 .60
56 Tommy Westlund .25 .60
57 Michael Nylander .25 .60
58 Serge Aubin .25 .60
59 Jiri Fischer .30 .75
60 Shawn Horcoff .30 .75
61 Peter Worrell .25 .60
62 Willie Mitchell .25 .60
63 Oleg Petrov .25 .60
64 Scott Walker .25 .60
65 Tomi Kallio .25 .60
66 Jason Strudwick .25 .60
67 Magnus Arvedson .25 .60
68 Eric Daze .30 .75
69 Johan Hedberg .30 .75
70 Fredrik Modin .25 .60
71 Nathan Dempsey .25 .60
72 Henrik Sedin .40 1.00
73 Mike LeClerc .25 .60
74 Hnat Domenichelli .25 .60
75 Jeff Cowan .25 .60
76 Brad Stuart .25 .60
77 Bryan Allen .25 .60
78 Wes Walz .25 .60
79 Patrick Traverse .25 .60
80 Markus Naslund .40 1.00
81 Brad Isbister .25 .60
82 Jan Hlavac .25 .60
83 Steve Sullivan .25 .60
84 Marian Gaborik .60 1.50
85 Kristian Kudroc .25 .60
86 Peter Schaefer .25 .60
87 Pascal Trepanier .25 .60
88 Milan Hnilicka .30 .75
89 Dave Lowry .25 .60
90 Jamie Allison .25 .60
91 Jeff Nielsen .25 .60
92 Sheldon Souray .25 .60
93 Mike Dunham .30 .75
94 Branislav Mezei .25 .60
95 Dale Purinton .25 .60
96 Cory Sarich .25 .60
97 Jarkko Ruutu .25 .60
98 Kyle Calder .25 .60
99 Frantisek Musil .25 .60
100 Tomas Kloucek .25 .60
101 Karel Rachunek .25 .60
102 Darcy Tucker .25 .60
103 Alex Tanguay .30 .75
104 Patrick Lalime .30 .75
105 Ossi Vaananen .25 .60
106 Martin Skoula .30 .75
107 Lubomir Visnovsky .25 .60
108 Richard Zednik .30 .75
109 Jani Hurme .30 .75
110 Teppo Numminen .25 .60
111 Scott Young .25 .60
112 Robert Reichel .25 .60
113 Dave Tanabe .25 .60
114 Steven Reinprecht .25 .60
115 Ryan Smyth .30 .75
116 Jozef Stumpel .25 .60
117 Martin Rucinsky .25 .60
118 Radek Dvorak .30 .75
119 Chris Herperger .25 .60
120 Eric Weinrich .25 .60
121 Claude Lemieux .30 .75
122 Mike Ricci .30 .75
123 Cory Stillman .25 .60
124 Alyn McCauley .25 .60
125 Trevor Linden .40 1.00
126 Vitali Vishnevsky .25 .60
127 Tim Connolly .25 .60
128 Oleg Saprykin .25 .60
129 Arturs Irbe .30 .75
130 Ville Nieminen .25 .60
131 David Vyborny .25 .60
132 Janne Niinimaa .25 .60
133 Joey Tetarenko .25 .60
134 Bryan Smolinski .25 .60
135 Stacy Roest .25 .60
136 Mikael Renberg .25 .60
137 Gino Odjick .25 .60
138 Petr Sykora .25 .60
139 Alexei Yashin .30 .75
140 Martin Havlat .30 .75
141 Rick Tocchet .25 .60
142 Daymond Langkow .30 .75
143 Kevin Stevens .25 .60
144 Patrick Marleau .40 1.00
145 Reed Low .25 .60
146 Bryan McCabe .30 .75
147 Dimitri Khristich .25 .60
148 Oleg Tverdovsky .25 .60
149 Yannick Tremblay .25 .60
150 Martin Biron .30 .75
151 Rob Niedermayer .30 .75
152 Rod Brind'Amour .40 1.00
153 Adam Foote .30 .75
154 Geoff Sanderson .25 .60
155 Pat Verbeek .30 .75
156 Nicklas Lidstrom .40 1.00
157 Jochen Hecht .25 .60
158 Robert Svehla .25 .60
159 Mathieu Schneider .25 .60
160 Antti Laaksonen .25 .60
161 Jeff Hackett .30 .75
162 Scott Niedermayer .40 1.00
163 Sandis Ozolinsh .25 .60
164 Radek Bonk .25 .60
165 Roman Cechmanek .30 .75
166 Mike Johnson .25 .60
167 Milan Kraft .25 .60
168 Adam Graves .30 .75
169 Pavol Demitra .50 1.25
170 Kevin Weekes .30 .75
171 Travis Green .25 .60
172 Jeff Halpern .25 .60
173 Steve Shields .30 .75
174 Lubos Bartecko .25 .60
175 P.J. Stock .25 .60
176 Maxim Afinogenov .25 .60
177 Derek Morris .25 .60
178 Bates Battaglia .25 .60
179 Boris Mironov .25 .60
180 David Aebischer .30 .75
181 Espen Knutsen .25 .60
182 Darryl Sydor .25 .60
183 Igor Larionov .40 1.00
184 Eric Brewer .25 .60
185 Trevor Kidd .25 .60
186 Eric Belanger .25 .60
187 Manny Fernandez .30 .75
188 Francois Bouillon .25 .60
189 Patrik Elias .40 1.00
190 Mariusz Czerkawski .25 .60
191 Daniel Alfredsson .40 1.00
192 Brian Boucher .30 .75
193 Sergei Berezin .25 .60
194 Kris Beech .25 .60
195 Vincent Damphousse .30 .75
196 Fred Brathwaite .30 .75
197 Ben Clymer .25 .60
198 Wade Belak .30 .75
199 Ed Jovanovski .30 .75
200 Sergei Gonchar .25 .60
201 Dan Blackburn RC .60 1.50
202 Daniel Tjarnqvist .50 1.25
203 Andreas Salomonsson RC .50 1.25
204 Vaclav Nedorost RC .50 1.25
205 Justin Kurtz RC .75 2.00
206 Jiri Dopita RC .50 1.25
207 Ilya Kovalchuk RC 4.00 10.00
208 Richard Jackman .60 1.50
209 Scott Nichol RC .50 1.25
210 Brad Larsen .50 1.25
211 Jason Williams .50 1.25
212 Kristian Huselius RC .75 2.00
213 Andreas Lilja .50 1.25
214 Nick Schultz RC .50 1.25
215 Marc Moro .50 1.25
216 Scott Clemmensen RC .50 1.25
217 Brad Tapper .50 1.25
218 Barrett Heisten .50 1.25
219 Chris Neil RC .60 1.50
220 Pavel Brendl .50 1.25
221 Miikka Kiprusoff .75 2.00
222 Jimmie Olvestad .50 1.25
223 Brian Sutherby RC .50 1.25
224 Timo Parssinen RC .60 1.50
225 Sascha Goc .50 1.25
226 Dany Heatley .75 2.00
227 Nick Boynton .50 1.25
228 Steve Begin .50 1.25
229 Erik Cole RC 1.00 2.50
230 Mark Bell .50 1.25
231 Rick Berry .50 1.25
232 Niko Kapanen RC .75 2.00
233 Pavel Datsyuk RC 4.00 10.00
234 Niklas Hagman RC .60 1.50
235 Jaroslav Bednar RC .50 1.25
236 Pascal Dupuis RC .75 2.00
237 Mike Ribeiro .60 1.50
238 Martin Erat RC .75 2.00
239 Jiri Bicek .50 1.25
240 Radek Martinek RC .50 1.25
241 Ivan Ciernik RC .50 1.25
242 Jesse Boulerice .50 1.25
243 Krys Kolanos RC .50 1.25
244 Toby Petersen .50 1.25
245 Jeff Jillson RC .50 1.25
246 Mark Rycroft RC .60 1.50
247 Kamil Piros RC .50 1.25
248 Nikita Alexeev RC .50 1.25
249 Stephen Peat .50 1.25
250 Pierre Dagenais .50 1.25

2001-02 BAP Signature Series Certified 100

This 60-card set resembled the base set, but carried a light purple background and the words "Signature Series Certified" on the card front and was numbered on the back "1 of 100". Players featured in this set were not included in the base set.
ANNOUNCED PRINT RUN 100
*CERTIFIED 50: .8X TO 2X CERT/100
C1 Al MacInnis 4.00 10.00
C2 Adam Oates 4.00 10.00
C3 Byron Dafoe 4.00 10.00
C4 Bill Guerin 4.00 10.00
C5 Brian Leetch 4.00 10.00
C6 Brendan Shanahan 3.00 8.00
C7 Chris Drury 4.00 10.00
C8 Chris Gratton 2.50 6.00
C9 Curtis Joseph 3.00 8.00
C10 Chris Pronger 2.50 6.00
C11 Donald Audette 2.50 6.00
C12 Doug Weight 2.50 6.00
C13 Ed Belfour 3.00 8.00
C14 Eric Lindros 3.00 8.00
C15 Jason Allison 2.50 6.00
C16 Jason Arnott 2.50 6.00
C17 John LeClair 3.00 8.00
C18 Jeff O'Neill 2.50 6.00
C19 Jeremy Roenick 3.00 8.00
C20 Joe Sakic 5.00 12.00
C21 Joe Thornton 4.00 10.00
C22 Kyle McLaren 2.50 6.00
C23 Luc Robitaille 4.00 10.00
C24 Martin Brodeur 8.00 20.00
C25 Milan Hejduk 3.00 8.00
C26 Martin Lapointe 2.50 6.00
C27 Mike Modano 4.00 10.00
C28 Mark Recchi 2.50 6.00
C29 Mats Sundin 3.00 8.00
C30 Olaf Kolzig 2.50 6.00
C31 Peter Bondra 3.00 8.00
C32 Pavel Bure 3.00 8.00
C33 Paul Kariya 3.00 8.00
C34 Pierre Turgeon 2.50 6.00
C35 Rob Blake 2.50 6.00
C36 Ron Francis 2.50 6.00
C37 Roman Turek 2.50 6.00
C38 Sergei Fedorov 4.00 10.00
C39 Scott Gomez 2.50 6.00
C40 Sami Kapanen 2.50 6.00
C41 Saku Koivu 3.00 8.00
C42 Sergei Samsonov 2.50 6.00
C43 Scott Stevens 2.50 6.00
C44 Steve Yzerman 8.00 20.00
C45 Tony Amonte 4.00 10.00
C46 Theo Fleury 2.50 6.00
C47 Teemu Selanne 3.00 8.00
C48 Tommy Salo 2.50 6.00
C49 Vincent Lecavalier 3.00 8.00
C50 Zigmund Palffy 4.00 10.00
C51 Brett Hull 3.00 8.00
C52 Dominik Hasek 5.00 12.00
C53 Jaromír Jagr 4.00 10.00
C54 Mario Lemieux 12.50 30.00
C55 Mark Messier 3.00 8.00
C56 Mike Vernon 2.50 6.00
C57 Owen Nolan 2.50 6.00
C58 Peter Forsberg 8.00 20.00
C59 Patrick Roy 8.00 20.00
C60 Wayne Gretzky 12.50 30.00

2001-02 BAP Signature Series Autographs

This 297-card set partially paralleled the base set but carried player autographs in a muted area on the card front. The first 250 cards have numbers that match the base set and the remainder feature the player's initials and a prefix on them. Those that carried an "L" or "XL" prefix were announced as short printed. Cards 226-250 and numbers LTS, LPF, LSY, LSF, LTA, LJR and XLMM were available in BAP Update packs only. A few additional cards were released after the company merged with Leaf Trading Cards in 2015, such as Curtis Joseph and Patrick Roy.
OVERALL AUTO ODDS 1:1
1 Rick DiPietro 6.00 15.00
2 Patrik Stefan 3.00 8.00
3 Hal Gill 3.00 8.00
4 J-P Dumont 3.00 8.00
5 Jarome Iginla 10.00 25.00
6 Shane Willis 3.00 8.00
7 Chris Phillips 3.00 8.00
8 Rostislav Klesla 3.00 8.00
9 Brenden Morrow 4.00 10.00
10 Manny Legace 4.00 10.00
11 Anson Carter SP 12.50 30.00
12 Roberto Luongo 8.00 20.00
13 Aaron Miller 3.00 8.00
14 Wayne Primeau 3.00 8.00
15 Brian Savage 3.00 8.00
16 John Jakopin 3.00 8.00
17 Greg Johnson 3.00 8.00
18 Marc Chouinard 3.00 8.00
19 Steve Martins 3.00 8.00
20 Marian Hossa 6.00 15.00
21 Brent Johnson SP 40.00 100.00
22 Sean Burke 4.00 10.00
23 Jan Hrdina 3.00 8.00
24 Evgeni Nabokov 4.00 10.00
25 Adam Deadmarsh 3.00 8.00
26 Brad Richards 4.00 10.00
27 Wade Redden 3.00 8.00
28 David Legwand 3.00 8.00
29 Jean-Sebastien Giguere 4.00 10.00
30 Ray Ferraro 3.00 8.00
31 Denis Hamel 3.00 8.00
32 Marc Savard 3.00 8.00
33 Craig Adams 3.00 8.00
34 Landon Wilson 3.00 8.00
35 Marc Denis 4.00 10.00
36 Roman Lyashenko 3.00 8.00
37 Tomas Holmstrom 3.00 8.00
38 Mike Comrie 3.00 8.00
39 Scott Hartnell 3.00 8.00
40 Sergei Krivokrasov 3.00 8.00
41 Mathieu Garon 4.00 10.00
42 Denis Arkhipov 3.00 8.00
43 Roman Hamrlik 3.00 8.00
44 Mike Mottau 3.00 8.00
45 Shawn McEachern 3.00 8.00
46 Peter White SP 50.00 100.00
47 Shane Doan 3.00 8.00
48 Janne Laukkanen 3.00 8.00
49 Martin St. Louis 10.00 25.00
50 Tomas Kaberle 3.00 8.00
51 Daniel Sedin 8.00 20.00
52 Jonas Ronnqvist 3.00 8.00
53 Damian Rhodes 4.00 10.00
54 Vaclav Varada 3.00 8.00
55 Ronald Petrovicky 3.00 8.00
56 Tommy Westlund 3.00 8.00
57 Michael Nylander 3.00 8.00
58 Serge Aubin 3.00 8.00
59 Jiri Fischer SP 25.00 60.00
60 Shawn Horcoff 3.00 8.00
61 Peter Worrell 3.00 8.00
62 Willie Mitchell 3.00 8.00
63 Oleg Petrov 3.00 8.00
64 Scott Walker 3.00 8.00
65 Tomi Kallio 3.00 8.00
66 Jason Strudwick 3.00 8.00
67 Magnus Arvedson 3.00 8.00
68 Eric Daze 4.00 10.00
69 Johan Hedberg 4.00 10.00
70 Fredrik Modin 3.00 8.00
71 Nathan Dempsey 3.00 8.00
72 Henrik Sedin 8.00 20.00
73 Mike LeClerc 3.00 8.00
74 Hnat Domenichelli 3.00 8.00
75 Jeff Cowan 3.00 8.00
76 Brad Stuart 3.00 8.00
77 Bryan Allen 3.00 8.00
78 Wes Walz 3.00 8.00
79 Patrick Traverse 3.00 8.00
80 Markus Naslund 4.00 10.00
81 Brad Isbister 3.00 8.00
82 Jan Hlavac SP 30.00 80.00
83 Steve Sullivan 3.00 8.00
84 Marian Gaborik 12.50 30.00
85 Kristian Kudroc 3.00 8.00
86 Peter Schaefer 3.00 8.00
87 Pascal Trepanier 3.00 8.00
88 Milan Hnilicka 4.00 10.00
89 Dave Lowry 3.00 8.00
90 Jamie Allison 3.00 8.00
91 Jeff Nielsen 3.00 8.00
92 Sheldon Souray 3.00 8.00
93 Mike Dunham 4.00 10.00
94 Branislav Mezei 3.00 8.00
95 Dale Purinton 3.00 8.00
96 Cory Sarich 3.00 8.00
97 Jarkko Ruutu 3.00 8.00
98 Kyle Calder 3.00 8.00
99 Frantisek Musil 3.00 8.00
100 Tomas Kloucek 3.00 8.00
101 Karel Rachunek 3.00 8.00
102 Darcy Tucker 3.00 8.00
103 Alex Tanguay 4.00 10.00
104 Patrick Lalime 4.00 10.00
105 Ossi Vaananen 3.00 8.00
106 Martin Skoula 3.00 8.00
107 Lubomir Visnovsky 3.00 8.00
108 Richard Zednik 3.00 8.00
109 Jani Hurme 4.00 10.00
110 Teppo Numminen 3.00 8.00
111 Scott Young 3.00 8.00
112 Robert Reichel 4.00 10.00
113 Dave Tanabe 3.00 8.00
114 Steven Reinprecht 3.00 8.00
115 Ryan Smyth 3.00 8.00
116 Jozef Stumpel 3.00 8.00
117 Martin Rucinsky 3.00 8.00
118 Radek Dvorak 3.00 8.00
119 Chris Herperger 3.00 8.00
120 Eric Weinrich 3.00 8.00
121 Claude Lemieux 4.00 10.00
122 Mike Ricci 4.00 10.00
123 Cory Stillman 3.00 8.00
124 Alyn McCauley 3.00 8.00
125 Trevor Linden 4.00 10.00
126 Vitaly Vishnevsky 3.00 8.00
127 Tim Connolly 3.00 8.00
128 Oleg Saprykin 3.00 8.00
129 Arturs Irbe 6.00 15.00
130 Ville Nieminen 3.00 8.00
131 David Vyborny 3.00 8.00
132 Janne Niinimaa 3.00 8.00
133 Joey Tetarenko 3.00 8.00
134 Bryan Smolinski 3.00 8.00
135 Stacy Roest 3.00 8.00
136 Mikael Renberg 3.00 8.00
137 Gino Odjick 3.00 8.00
138 Petr Sykora 3.00 8.00
139 Alexei Yashin 4.00 10.00
140 Martin Havlat 4.00 10.00
141 Rick Tocchet 3.00 8.00
142 Daymond Langkow 3.00 8.00
143 Kevin Stevens 3.00 8.00
144 Patrick Marleau 4.00 10.00
145 Reed Low 3.00 8.00
146 Bryan McCabe 3.00 8.00
147 Dimitri Khristich 3.00 8.00
148 Oleg Tverdovsky 3.00 8.00
149 Yannick Tremblay 3.00 8.00
150 Martin Biron 4.00 10.00
151 Rob Niedermayer 3.00 8.00
152 Rod Brind'Amour 4.00 10.00
153 Adam Foote 3.00 8.00
154 Geoff Sanderson 3.00 8.00
155 Pat Verbeek 3.00 8.00
156 Nicklas Lidstrom 10.00 25.00
157 Jochen Hecht 3.00 8.00
158 Robert Svehla 3.00 8.00
159 Mathieu Schneider 3.00 8.00
160 Antti Laaksonen 3.00 8.00
161 Jeff Hackett 4.00 10.00
162 Scott Niedermayer 3.00 8.00
163 Sandis Ozolinsh 3.00 8.00
164 Radek Bonk 3.00 8.00
165 Roman Cechmanek 4.00 10.00
166 Mike Johnson 3.00 8.00
167 Milan Kraft 3.00 8.00
168 Adam Graves 3.00 8.00
169 Pavol Demitra 8.00 20.00
170 Kevin Weekes 4.00 10.00
171 Travis Green 3.00 8.00
172 Jeff Halpern 3.00 8.00
173 Steve Shields 4.00 10.00
174 Lubos Bartecko 3.00 8.00
175 P.J. Stock 4.00 10.00
176 Maxim Afinogenov 3.00 8.00
177 Derek Morris 3.00 8.00
178 Bates Battaglia 4.00 10.00
179 Boris Mironov 3.00 8.00
180 David Aebischer 8.00 20.00
181 Espen Knutsen 3.00 8.00
182 Darryl Sydor 3.00 8.00
183 Igor Larionov 12.00 30.00
184 Eric Brewer 3.00 8.00
185 Trevor Kidd 4.00 10.00
186 Eric Belanger 3.00 8.00
187 Manny Fernandez 15.00 40.00
188 Francois Bouillon 3.00 8.00
189 Patrik Elias 4.00 10.00
190 Mariusz Czerkawski 3.00 8.00
191 Daniel Alfredsson 4.00 10.00
192 Brian Boucher 4.00 10.00
193 Sergei Berezin 3.00 8.00
194 Kris Beech 3.00 8.00
195 Vincent Damphousse 3.00 8.00
196 Fred Brathwaite 4.00 10.00
197 Ben Clymer 3.00 8.00
198 Wade Belak 6.00 15.00
199 Ed Jovanovski 4.00 10.00
200 Sergei Gonchar 3.00 8.00
201 Dan Blackburn 4.00 10.00
202 Daniel Tjarnqvist 3.00 8.00
203 Andreas Salomonsson 5.00 12.00
204 Vaclav Nedorost 3.00 8.00
205 Justin Kurtz 3.00 8.00
206 Jiri Dopita 3.00 8.00
207 Ilya Kovalchuk 8.00 20.00
208 Richard Jackman 3.00 8.00
209 Scott Nichol 3.00 8.00
210 Brad Larsen 3.00 8.00
211 Jason Williams 3.00 8.00
212 Kristian Huselius 3.00 8.00
213 Andreas Lilja 3.00 8.00
214 Nick Schultz 3.00 8.00
215 Marc Moro 3.00 8.00
216 Scott Clemmensen 4.00 10.00
217 Brad Tapper 3.00 8.00
218 Barrett Heisten 3.00 8.00
219 Chris Neil 3.00 8.00
220 Pavel Brendl 3.00 8.00
221 Miikka Kiprusoff 8.00 20.00
222 Jimmie Olvestad 3.00 8.00
223 Brian Sutherby 5.00 12.00
224 Timo Parssinen 3.00 8.00
225 Sascha Goc 3.00 8.00
226 Dany Heatley 6.00 15.00
227 Nick Boynton 3.00 8.00
228 Steve Begin 3.00 8.00
229 Erik Cole 5.00 12.00
230 Mark Bell 3.00 8.00
231 Rick Berry 3.00 8.00
232 Niko Kapanen 3.00 8.00
233 Pavel Datsyuk 15.00 40.00
234 Niklas Hagman 3.00 8.00
235 Jaroslav Bednar 3.00 8.00
236 Pascal Dupuis 4.00 10.00
237 Mike Ribeiro 3.00 8.00
238 Martin Erat 3.00 8.00
239 Jiri Bicek 3.00 8.00
240 Radek Martinek 3.00 8.00
241 Ivan Ciernik 3.00 8.00
242 Jesse Boulerice 3.00 8.00
243 Krystofer Kolanos 3.00 8.00
244 Toby Petersen 3.00 8.00
245 Jeff Jillson 3.00 8.00
246 Mark Rycroft 3.00 8.00
247 Kamil Piros 3.00 8.00
248 Nikita Alexeev 3.00 8.00
249 Stephen Peat 3.00 8.00
250 Pierre Dagenais 3.00 8.00
LAM Al MacInnis SP 8.00 20.00
LBD Byron Dafoe SP 10.00 25.00
LBG Bill Guerin SP 8.00 20.00
LBL Brian Leetch SP 12.50 30.00
LBS Brendan Shanahan SP 20.00 50.00
LCD Chris Drury SP 8.00 20.00
LCG Chris Gratton SP 8.00 20.00
LCJ Curtis Joseph SP 20.00 40.00
LCP Chris Pronger SP 8.00 20.00
LDA Donald Audette SP 8.00 20.00
LDW Doug Weight SP 10.00 25.00
LEB Ed Belfour SP 20.00 50.00
LJAL Jason Allison SP 8.00 20.00
LJL John LeClair SP 12.50 30.00
LJO Jeff O'Neill SP 8.00 20.00
LJR Jeremy Roenick SP 15.00 40.00
LJS Joe Sakic SP 25.00 60.00
LJT Joe Thornton SP 12.50 30.00
LKM Kyle McLaren SP 8.00 20.00
LLR Luc Robitaille SP 10.00 25.00
LMH Milan Hejduk SP 12.50 30.00
LML Martin Lapointe SP 8.00 20.00
LMR Mark Recchi SP 8.00 20.00
LOK Olaf Kolzig SP 8.00 20.00
LPBO Peter Bondra SP 8.00 20.00
LPBU Pavel Bure SP 12.50 30.00
LPK Paul Kariya SP 15.00 40.00
LPT Pierre Turgeon SP 8.00 20.00
LRB Rob Blake SP 8.00 20.00
LRF Ron Francis SP 8.00 20.00
LRT Roman Turek SP 8.00 20.00
LSF Sergei Fedorov SP 15.00 40.00
LSK Sami Kapanen SP 8.00 20.00
LSSA Sergei Samsonov SP 8.00 20.00
LSST Scott Stevens SP 12.00 30.00
LSY Steve Yzerman SP 40.00 80.00
LTA Tony Amonte SP 8.00 20.00
LTS Teemu Selanne SP 12.50 30.00
LTSA Tommy Salo SP 8.00 20.00
LVL Vincent Lecavalier SP 12.50 30.00
LZP Zigmund Palffy SP 10.00 25.00
XLDH Dominik Hasek SP 100.00 200.00
XLML Mario Lemieux SP 200.00 350.00
XLMM Mark Messier SP 75.00 150.00
XLMV Mike Vernon SP 25.00 60.00
XLON Owen Nolan SP 30.00 80.00
XLPF Peter Forsberg SP 75.00 125.00
XLPR Patrick Roy SP 200.00 350.00
XLWG Wayne Gretzky SP 250.00 400.00

2001-02 BAP Signature Series Autographs Gold

This 297-card set paralleled the base autograph set but carried a gold tone card front. Gold cards were advertised as being more scarce, but no information on production numbers is known at this time.
*GOLD: .5X TO 1.2X BASE AUTO
11 Anson Carter 25.00 60.00
21 Brent Johnson 40.00 100.00
46 Peter White 50.00 100.00
59 Jiri Fischer 40.00 100.00
82 Jan Hlavac 25.00 60.00
XLDH Dominik Hasek SP 250.00 400.00
XLML Mario Lemieux SP 250.00 400.00
XLWG Wayne Gretzky SP 350.00 600.00

2001-02 BAP Signature Series Department of Defense

STATED PRINT RUN 40 SETS
DD1 Rob Blake 10.00 25.00
DD2 Brian Leetch 10.00 25.00
DD3 Nicklas Lidstrom 12.00 30.00
DD4 Oleg Tverdovsky 10.00 25.00
DD5 Chris Pronger 10.00 25.00
DD6 Al MacInnis 10.00 25.00
DD7 Kyle McLaren 10.00 25.00
DD8 Sergei Gonchar 10.00 25.00
DD9 Tomas Kaberle 10.00 25.00
DD10 Sandis Ozolinsh 10.00 25.00
DD11 Darius Kasparaitis 10.00 25.00
DD12 Rostislav Klesla 10.00 25.00

2001-02 BAP Signature Series 500 Goal Scorers

This 28-card set featured game-worn jersey swatches of members of the exclusive 500-goal club. Print runs were varied and are listed below. Cards ML, MM and SY were available in random packs of BAP Update. All cards carried a S500 prefix.
STATED PRINT RUN 10-90
1 Gordie Howe/10
2 Steve Yzerman/30 50.00 120.00
3 Jean Beliveau/20 40.00 80.00
4 Frank Mahovlich/30 40.00 80.00
5 Stan Mikita/30 40.00 80.00
6 Guy Lafleur/30 25.00 60.00
7 Marcel Dionne/30 15.00 40.00
8 Bobby Hull/20 25.00 60.00
9 Phil Esposito/30 40.00 80.00
10 Mike Bossy/50 20.00 50.00
11 Luc Robitaille/30 25.00 60.00
12 Jari Kurri/90 10.00 25.00
13 Dave Andreychuk/90 10.00 25.00
14 Mike Gartner/90 10.00 25.00
15 John Bucyk/30 25.00 60.00
16 Michel Goulet/90 10.00 25.00
17 Dino Ciccarelli/90 10.00 25.00
18 Pat Verbeek/90 10.00 25.00
19 Bryan Trottier/50 10.00 25.00
20 Dale Hawerchuk/90 10.00 25.00
21 Gilbert Perreault/90 12.00 30.00
22 Joe Mullen/90 12.00 30.00
23 Lanny McDonald/90 10.00 25.00
24 Brett Hull/30 30.00 80.00
25 Mark Messier/30 30.00 80.00
26 Mario Lemieux/20 100.00 200.00
27 Maurice Richard/10
28 Ron Francis/10
29 Brendan Shanahan/10
ML Mario Lemieux/10 AU
MM Mark Messier/10 AU
SY Steve Yzerman/10 AU

2001-02 BAP Signature Series Franchise Jerseys

STATED PRINT RUN 28 SETS
FP1 Paul Kariya 12.50 30.00
FP2 Ilya Kovalchuk 20.00 50.00
FP3 Joe Thornton 15.00 40.00
FP4 Miroslav Satan 12.50 30.00
FP5 Jarome Iginla 15.00 40.00
FP6 Sami Kapanen 12.50 30.00
FP7 Tony Amonte 12.50 30.00
FP8 Joe Sakic 20.00 50.00
FP9 Rostislav Klesla 12.50 30.00
FP10 Mike Modano 20.00 50.00
FP11 Steve Yzerman 15.00 40.00
FP12 Tommy Salo 15.00 40.00
FP13 Pavel Bure 12.50 30.00
FP14 Zigmund Palffy 12.50 30.00
FP15 Marian Gaborik 15.00 40.00
FP16 Jose Theodore 15.00 40.00
FP17 David Legwand 12.50 30.00
FP18 Martin Brodeur 20.00 50.00
FP19 Eric Lindros 12.50 30.00
FP20 Alexei Yashin 12.50 30.00
FP21 Daniel Alfredsson 12.50 30.00
FP22 John LeClair 12.50 30.00
FP23 Sean Burke 12.50 30.00
FP24 Mario Lemieux 30.00 80.00
FP25 Owen Nolan 12.50 30.00
FP26 Doug Weight 12.50 30.00
FP27 Vincent Lecavalier 12.50 30.00
FP28 Mats Sundin 12.50 30.00
FP29 Markus Naslund 12.50 30.00
FP30 Jaromir Jagr 20.00 50.00

2001-02 BAP Signature Series He Shoots He Scores Points

ONE PER PACK
1 Tony Amonte 1pt. .20 .50
2 Sergei Fedorov 1pt. .30 .75
3 Bill Guerin 1pt. .25 .60
4 John Leclair 1pt. .25 .60
5 Eric Lindros 1pt. .30 .75
6 Mark Messier 1 pt. .30 .75
7 Mike Modano 1pt. .30 .75
8 Luc Robitaille 1pt. .20 .50
9 Jeremy Roenick 1pt. .25 .60
10 Teemu Selanne 1pt. .25 .60
11 Mats Sundin 1pt. .20 .50
12 Pavel Bure 2 pts. .30 .75
13 Jarome Iginla 2 pts. .30 .75
14 Jaromir Jagr 2 pts. .30 .75
15 Paul Kariya 2 pts. .25 .60
16 Ilya Kovalchuk 2 pts. .30 .75
17 Brendan Shanahan 2 pts. .30 .75
18 Mario Lemieux 3 pts. 1.50 4.00
19 Joe Sakic 3 pts. .30 .75
20 Steve Yzerman 3 pts. .50 1.25

2001-02 BAP Signature Series International Medals

Limited to just 30 copies each, this 42-card set features game-worn jersey swatches from NHL players who participated in the 2002 Winter Olympics. The card fronts carried a color head shot photo of the featured player along with the jersey swatch under the player to appear as if it was a medal around his neck.
ANNOUNCED PRINT RUN 30
IB1 Nikolai Khabibulin 12.50 30.00
IB2 Sergei Samsonov 12.50 30.00
IB3 Darius Kasparaitis 12.50 30.00
IB4 Alexei Yashin 12.50 30.00
IB5 Oleg Tverdovsky 12.50 30.00
IB6 Pavel Bure 12.50 30.00
IB7 Ilya Kovalchuk 15.00 40.00
IB8 Alexei Kovalev 12.50 30.00
IS1 Mike Richter 12.50 30.00
IS2 Tony Amonte 12.50 30.00
IS3 Chris Chelios 12.50 30.00
IS4 Doug Weight 12.50 30.00
IS5 John LeClair 12.50 30.00
IS6 Mike Modano 15.00 40.00
IS7 Bill Guerin 12.50 30.00
IS8 Brian Rolston 12.50 30.00
IG1 Martin Brodeur 20.00 50.00
IG2 Rob Blake 12.50 30.00
IG3 Al MacInnis 12.50 30.00
IG4 Theo Fleury 25.00 60.00
IG5 Paul Kariya 12.50 30.00
IG6 Mario Lemieux 30.00 80.00
IG7 Eric Lindros 15.00 40.00
IG8 Steve Yzerman 30.00 80.00

2001-02 BAP Signature Series Jerseys

GJ1-GJ70 ANNC'D PRINT RUN 60
GJ71-GJ98 ANNC'D PRINT RUN 90
GJ1 Paul Kariya 10.00 25.00
GJ2 Rostislav Klesla 4.00 10.00
GJ3 Joe Thornton 12.50 30.00
GJ4 Martin Havlat 10.00 25.00
GJ5 Byron Dafoe 10.00 25.00
GJ6 Dominik Hasek 15.00 40.00
GJ7 Miroslav Satan 10.00 25.00
GJ8 Teemu Selanne 10.00 25.00
GJ9 Jarome Iginla 8.00 20.00
GJ10 Ron Francis 10.00 25.00
GJ11 Pierre Turgeon 10.00 25.00
GJ12 Tony Amonte 10.00 25.00
GJ13 Henrik Sedin 6.00 15.00
GJ14 Alex Tanguay 10.00 25.00
GJ15 Marian Gaborik 12.00 30.00
GJ16 Joe Sakic 15.00 40.00
GJ17 Patrick Roy 25.00 60.00
GJ18 Chris Drury 10.00 25.00
GJ19 Rob Blake 10.00 25.00
GJ20 Mike Modano 12.50 30.00
GJ21 Sergei Fedorov 12.50 30.00
GJ22 Nicklas Lidstrom 10.00 25.00
GJ23 Steve Yzerman 20.00 50.00
GJ24 Milan Hejduk 8.00 20.00
GJ25 Jeff O'Neill 4.00 10.00
GJ26 Luc Robitaille 10.00 25.00
GJ27 Brendan Shanahan 10.00 25.00
GJ28 Pavel Bure 10.00 25.00
GJ29 Roberto Luongo 12.50 30.00
GJ30 Zigmund Palffy 10.00 25.00
GJ31 Brian Savage 4.00 10.00
GJ32 Saku Koivu 10.00 25.00
GJ33 Scott Stevens 10.00 25.00
GJ34 Scott Gomez 8.00 20.00
GJ35 Martin Brodeur 20.00 50.00
GJ36 Jason Arnott 4.00 10.00
GJ37 Scott Niedermayer 8.00 20.00
GJ38 Eric Lindros 10.00 25.00
GJ39 Brian Leetch 10.00 25.00
GJ40 Mark Messier 10.00 25.00
GJ41 Mike Richter 10.00 25.00
GJ42 Kenny Jonsson 8.00 20.00

GJ43 Alexei Yashin 8.00 20.00
GJ44 Radek Bonk 8.00 20.00
GJ45 Ilya Kovalchuk 12.00 30.00
GJ46 Marian Hossa 10.00 25.00
GJ47 Roman Cechmanek 4.00 10.00
GJ48 Mark Recchi 10.00 25.00
GJ49 John LeClair 10.00 25.00
GJ50 Brian Boucher 10.00 25.00
GJ51 Keith Primeau 8.00 20.00
GJ52 Jeremy Roenick 12.00 30.00
GJ53 Jaromir Jagr 15.00 40.00
GJ54 Mario Lemieux 25.00 60.00
GJ55 Owen Nolan 10.00 25.00
GJ56 Doug Weight 10.00 25.00
GJ57 Chris Pronger 10.00 25.00
GJ58 Al MacInnis 10.00 25.00
GJ59 Vincent Lecavalier 10.00 25.00
GJ60 Brad Richards 10.00 25.00
GJ61 Curtis Joseph 10.00 25.00
GJ62 Mats Sundin 10.00 25.00
GJ63 Daniel Sedin 8.00 20.00
GJ64 Peter Bondra 10.00 25.00
GJ65 Adam Oates 10.00 25.00
GJ66 Olaf Kolzig 10.00 25.00
GJ67 Sergei Gonchar 8.00 20.00
GJ68 Todd Bertuzzi 10.00 25.00
GJ69 Theo Fleury 8.00 20.00
GJ70 Markus Naslund 10.00 25.00
GJ71 Alexander Mogilny 8.00 20.00
GJ72 Nikolai Khabibulin 10.00 25.00
GJ73 Ed Belfour 10.00 25.00
GJ74 Petr Sykora 4.00 10.00
GJ75 Peter Forsberg 10.00 25.00
GJ76 Patrick Lalime 8.00 20.00
GJ77 Keith Tkachuk 10.00 25.00
GJ78 Daniel Alfredsson 8.00 20.00
GJ79 Chris Chelios 10.00 25.00
GJ80 Sean Burke 4.00 10.00
GJ81 Eric Daze 4.00 10.00
GJ82 Patrik Elias 4.00 10.00
GJ83 Adam Foote 4.00 10.00
GJ84 Bill Guerin 8.00 20.00
GJ85 Jose Theodore 12.00 30.00
GJ86 Sandis Ozolinsh 4.00 10.00
GJ87 Felix Potvin 10.00 25.00
GJ88 Tommy Salo 8.00 20.00
GJ89 Martin Straka 4.00 10.00
GJ90 Jocelyn Thibault 8.00 20.00
GJ91 Pavel Bure 10.00 25.00
GJ92 Roman Turek 4.00 10.00
GJ93 Sergei Samsonov 8.00 20.00
GJ94 Dan Cloutier 8.00 20.00
GJ95 Kristian Huselius 4.00 10.00
GJ96 Arturs Irbe 8.00 20.00
GJ97 Sami Kapanen 4.00 10.00
GJ98 Evgeni Nabokov 8.00 20.00

2001-02 BAP Signature Series Teammates Jerseys

STATED PRINT RUN 40 SETS
TM1 P.Kariya/J.Friesen 12.50 30.00
TM2 P.Stefan/I.Kovalchuk 12.50 30.00
TM3 B.Guerin/B.Dafoe 8.00 20.00
TM4 M.Biron/M.Satan 8.00 20.00
TM5 J.Iginla/R.Turek 12.50 30.00
TM6 R.Francis/S.Kapanen 8.00 20.00
TM7 T.Amonte/E.Daze 8.00 20.00
TM8 J.Sakic/P.Roy 40.00 100.00
TM9 C.Drury/M.Hejduk 12.50 30.00
TM10 M.Modano/E.Belfour 15.00 40.00
TM11 S.Yzerman/B.Shanahan 20.00 50.00
TM12 L.Robitaille/D.Hasek 25.00 60.00
TM13 P.Bure/R.Luongo 12.50 30.00
TM14 Z.Palffy/F.Potvin 15.00 40.00
TM15 M.Gaborik/M.Fernandez 12.50 30.00
TM16 B.Savage/J.Theodore 15.00 40.00
TM17 J.Arnott/M.Brodeur 20.00 50.00
TM18 S.Niedermayer/S.Stevens 8.00 20.00
TM19 M.Messier/E.Lindros 15.00 40.00
TM20 K. Jonsson/A.Yashin 8.00 20.00
TM21 D.Alfredsson/P.Lalime 12.50 30.00
TM22 M.Recchi/J.Roenick 12.50 30.00
TM23 J.LeClair/B.Boucher 8.00 20.00
TM24 M.Lemieux/M.Kraft 25.00 60.00
TM25 O.Nolan/T.Selanne 12.50 30.00
TM26 D.Weight/K.Tkachuk 8.00 20.00
TM27 V.Lecavalier/N.Khabibulin 12.50 30.00
TM28 M.Sundin/C.Joseph 12.50 30.00
TM29 D.Sedin/M.Naslund 12.50 30.00
TM30 P.Bondra/J.Jagr 20.00 50.00

2001-02 BAP Signature Series Vintage Autographs

This 40-card set featured autographs of retired NHL stars. Autographs were positioned beneath a full-color player photo on the card fronts. Print runs for each card are listed below. Card #VA16 was supposed to be Woody Dumart, but he passed away before he could sign, therefore that card does not exist.
STATED PRINT RUN 20-90
VA1 Tony Esposito/60 20.00 50.00
VA2 Phil Esposito/40 30.00 80.00
VA3 Gordie Howe/20 75.00 200.00
VA4 Gordie Howe/20 75.00 200.00
VA5 Jean Beliveau/40 25.00 60.00
VA6 Jean Beliveau/40 25.00 60.00
VA7 Bobby Hull/40 20.00 50.00
VA8 Bobby Hull/40 20.00 50.00
VA9 Ted Lindsay/40 15.00 40.00
VA10 Johnny Bower/60 12.50 30.00
VA11 Milt Schmidt/80 20.00 50.00
VA12 Red Kelly/80 12.50 30.00
VA13 Glenn Hall/40 15.00 40.00
VA14 Chuck Rayner/40 20.00 50.00
VA15 Elmer Lach/80 15.00 40.00
VA17 Gerry Cheevers/40 20.00 50.00
VA18 Gump Worsley/40 30.00 80.00
VA19 Butch Bouchard/80 12.00 30.00
VA20 Henri Richard/80 12.00 30.00
VA21 Henri Richard/80 12.00 30.00
VA22 Bernie Geoffrion/80 20.00 50.00
VA23 Dollard St. Laurent/80 12.50 30.00
VA24 Dickie Moore/70 12.50 30.00
VA25 Jean-Guy Talbot/80 12.50 30.00
VA26 Bill Gadsby/80 12.50 30.00
VA27 Frank Mahovlich/40 25.00 60.00
VA28 Dino Ciccarelli/70 12.50 30.00
VA29 Jari Kurri/70 15.00 40.00
VA30 Mike Bossy/70 12.50 30.00
VA31 Johnny Bucyk/90 12.50 30.00
VA32 Michel Goulet/90 10.00 25.00
VA33 Stan Mikita/40 20.00 50.00
VA34 Bryan Trottier/70 12.50 30.00
VA35 Dale Hawerchuk/70 15.00 40.00
VA36 Gilbert Perreault/40 15.00 40.00
VA37 Marcel Dionne/40 20.00 50.00
VA38 Mike Gartner/70 12.50 30.00
VA39 Lanny McDonald/70 12.50 30.00
VA40 Guy Lafleur/40 40.00 100.00

2001-02 BAP Signature Series Beckett Promos

Inserted into issues of Beckett Hockey Collector #140, this 250-card set paralleled the basic Bap Signature Series set but carried a "Beckett" stamp on the card backs.
*SINGLES: 1.5X TO 4X BASIC CARDS

2002-03 BAP Signature Series

Released in mid-May, this 200-card base set consisted of 177 veterans and 23 rookies.
1 Dany Heatley .30 .75
2 Alexei Zhamnov .25 .60
3 Mike Comrie .30 .75
4 Dwayne Roloson .20 .50
5 Mike Dunham .25 .60
6 Simon Gagne .30 .75
7 Evgeni Nabokov .25 .60
8 Bryan McCabe .20 .50
9 Todd Bertuzzi .30 .75
10 Alex Kovalev .30 .75
11 Dave Andreychuk .30 .75
12 Daniel Alfredsson .30 .75
13 Marian Gaborik .50 1.25
14 J-S Aubin .20 .50
15 Andy McDonald .30 .75
16 Brad Richards .30 .75
17 Henrik Sedin .30 .75
18 Mark Bell .20 .50
19 Adam Deadmarsh .25 .60
20 Marc Denis .25 .60
21 Mike York .20 .50
22 Johan Hedberg .30 .75
23 Vincent Damphousse .25 .60
24 Marian Hossa .25 .60
25 Richard Zednik .20 .50
26 Alexei Yashin .25 .60
27 Sergei Gonchar .25 .60
28 Martin Straka .25 .60
29 Ed Jovanovski .25 .60
30 Robert Lang .20 .50
31 Markus Naslund .25 .60
32 Mike Sillinger .20 .50
33 Jamie Storr .25 .60
34 Kimmo Timonen .20 .50
35 Patrick Lalime .25 .60
36 Alyn McCauley .20 .50
37 Scott Walker .20 .50
38 Trevor Linden .30 .75
39 Ilya Kovalchuk .40 1.00
40 Jarome Iginla .30 .75
41 Alex Tanguay .25 .60
42 Yanic Perreault .20 .50
43 Jocelyn Thibault .25 .60
44 Eric Brewer .20 .50
45 Ray Whitney .25 .60
46 Ryan Smyth .25 .60
47 Steven Reinprecht .20 .50
48 Phil Housley .25 .60
49 Milan Hnilicka .25 .60
50 Maxim Afinogenov .20 .50
51 Andrew Brunette .20 .50
52 Miroslav Satan .30 .75
53 Glen Murray .25 .60
54 Mark Parrish .20 .50
55 Daniel Sedin .30 .75
56 Brendan Morrison .25 .60
57 Brian Rafalski .20 .50
58 Dan Cloutier .25 .60
59 Espen Knutsen .20 .50
60 Radim Vrbata .25 .60
61 Patrik Stefan .25 .60
62 Eric Daze .20 .50
63 Felix Potvin .50 1.25
64 Darcy Tucker .20 .50
65 Jose Theodore .30 .75
66 Scott Hartnell .30 .75
67 Martin Havlat .25 .60
68 Radek Bonk .25 .60
69 Patrick Marleau .30 .75
70 Andy Delmore .20 .50
71 Rostislav Klesla .20 .50
72 David Aebischer .25 .60
73 Steve Shields .25 .60
74 Stu Barnes .20 .50
75 Tim Connolly .20 .50
76 Jean-Sebastien Giguere .30 .75
77 Shane Doan .25 .60
78 Brian Rolston .25 .60
79 Shawn McEachern .20 .50
80 Martin Biron .25 .60
81 Craig Conroy .20 .50
82 Mika Noronen .25 .60
83 Brian Boucher .25 .60
84 Kyle Calder .20 .50
85 Cliff Ronning .20 .50
86 Brian Gionta .25 .60
87 Shawn Bates .20 .50
88 Michal Handzus .25 .60
89 Daniel Briere .25 .60
90 Adam Graves .25 .60
91 Martin St. Louis .30 .75
92 Ladislav Nagy .20 .50
93 Oleg Tverdovsky .20 .50
94 Pavel Brendl .20 .50
95 Alexei Morozov .20 .50
96 Daymond Langkow .25 .60
97 Krys Kolanos .20 .50
98 Sean Burke .20 .50
99 Chris Drury .30 .75
100 Steve Sullivan .20 .50
101 Paul Kariya .40 1.00
102 Peter Forsberg .40 1.00
103 Ron Tugnutt .25 .60
104 Manny Legace .30 .75
105 Tommy Salo .25 .60
106 Kristian Huselius .20 .50
107 Jason Allison .25 .60
108 Mariusz Czerkawski .20 .50
109 Jeff Friesen .20 .50
110 Chris Osgood .30 .75
111 Martin Prusek .20 .50
112 Steve Yzerman .60 1.50
113 John LeClair .30 .75
114 Jan Hrdina .20 .50
115 Tony Amonte .25 .60
116 Teemu Selanne .60 1.50
117 Cory Stillman .20 .50
118 Nikolai Khabibulin .30 .75
119 Mats Sundin .30 .75
120 Olaf Kolzig .30 .75
121 Petr Sykora .25 .60
122 Joe Thornton .40 1.00
123 Roman Turek .30 .75
124 Derek Morris .20 .50
125 Bill Guerin .30 .75
126 Brendan Shanahan .40 1.00
127 Roberto Luongo .50 1.25
128 Zigmund Palffy .30 .75
129 Pavol Demitra .40 1.00
130 Saku Koivu .30 .75
131 Joe Nieuwendyk .30 .75
132 Mike Peca .25 .60
133 Petr Schastlivy .20 .50
134 Jeremy Roenick .30 .75
135 Mario Lemieux 1.00 2.50
136 Petr Cajanek .20 .50
137 Vincent Lecavalier .25 .60
138 Peter Bondra .30 .75
139 Brent Johnson .25 .60
140 Sergei Samsonov .25 .60
141 Joe Sakic .50 1.25
142 Brenden Morrow .25 .60
143 Arturs Irbe .25 .60
144 Chris Chelios .30 .75
145 Sandis Ozolinsh .25 .60
146 Doug Gilmour .40 1.00
147 Scott Stevens .30 .75
148 Sergei Fedorov .50 1.25
149 Keith Primeau .30 .75
150 Eric Boguniecki .20 .50
151 Shane Willis .20 .50
152 Rob Blake .30 .75
153 Luc Robitaille .30 .75
154 Pierre Turgeon .30 .75
155 Curtis Joseph .30 .75
156 Stephen Weiss .30 .75
157 Patrik Elias .30 .75
158 Mark Recchi .40 1.00
159 Al MacInnis .30 .75
160 Patrick Roy .75 2.00
161 Darryl Sydor .20 .50
162 Nicklas Lidstrom .30 .75
163 Doug Weight .30 .75
164 Roman Cechmanek .25 .60
165 Marty Turco .30 .75
166 Pavel Datsyuk .40 1.00
167 Chris Pronger .25 .60
168 Scott Young .20 .50
169 Igor Larionov .30 .75
170 Keith Tkachuk .30 .75
171 Ron Francis .40 1.00
172 Dan Blackburn .25 .60
173 Jeff O'Neill .20 .50
174 Bobby Holik .20 .50
175 Erik Cole .25 .60
176 Pavel Bure .40 1.00
177 Brian Leetch .30 .75
178 Curtis Sanford RC .60 1.50
179 Carlo Colaiacovo RC .60 1.50
180 Dennis Seidenberg RC .60 1.50
181 Adam Hall RC .40 1.00
182 Ivan Majesky RC .40 1.00
183 Rick Nash RC 3.00 8.00
184 Alexei Smirnov RC .50 1.25
185 Chuck Kobasew RC .50 1.25
186 Ron Hainsey RC .40 1.00
187 Stephane Veilleux RC .40 1.00
188 Scottie Upshall RC .50 1.25
189 Lasse Pirjeta RC .40 1.00
190 Henrik Zetterberg RC 4.00 10.00
191 Jay Bouwmeester RC 1.25 3.00
192 Alexander Frolov RC .75 2.00
193 Dmitri Bykov RC .40 1.00
194 Stanislav Chistov RC .40 1.00
195 Jordan Leopold RC .60 1.50
196 P-M Bouchard RC .60 1.50
197 Mike Cammalleri RC 1.25 3.00
198 Anton Volchenkov RC .40 1.00
199 Lynn Loyns RC .40 1.00
200 Steve Eminger RC .40 1.00

2002-03 BAP Signature Series All-Rookie

This 12-card set featured game-worn equipment from some of the leagues most promising young players. Each card was limited to just 50 copies.
STATED PRINT RUN 50 SETS
AR1 Ryan Miller 15.00 40.00
AR2 Jay Bouwmeester 12.50 30.00
AR3 Dennis Seidenberg 10.00 25.00
AR4 Stephen Weiss 12.50 30.00
AR5 Marcel Hossa 12.50 30.00
AR6 Radovan Somik 10.00 25.00
AR7 Jan Lasak 10.00 25.00
AR8 Jordan Leopold 10.00 25.00
AR9 Barret Jackman 10.00 25.00
AR10 Mike Cammalleri 15.00 40.00
AR11 Henrik Zetterberg Skate 20.00 50.00
AR12 Rick Nash 20.00 50.00

2002-03 BAP Signature Series Autographs

This 200-card set paralleled the base set but carried certified autographs on the card fronts. They were inserted one per pack and short prints are designated below.
ONE PER PACK
*GOLD: .75X TO 1.25X
1 Dany Heatley 4.00 10.00
2 Alexei Zhamnov 2.50 6.00
3 Mike Comrie 2.50 6.00
4 Dwayne Roloson 3.00 8.00
5 Mike Dunham 2.00 5.00
6 Simon Gagne 6.00 15.00
7 Evgeni Nabokov 4.00 10.00
8 Bryan McCabe 2.00 5.00
9 Todd Bertuzzi 4.00 10.00
10 Alexei Kovalev 3.00 8.00
11 Dave Andreychuk 3.00 8.00
12 Daniel Alfredsson 3.00 8.00
13 Marian Gaborik 6.00 15.00
14 J-S Aubin 2.00 5.00
15 Andy McDonald 2.00 5.00
16 Brad Richards 3.00 8.00
17 Henrik Sedin 5.00 12.00
18 Mark Bell 2.00 5.00
19 Adam Deadmarsh 2.00 5.00
20 Marc Denis 4.00 10.00
21 Mike York 2.00 5.00
22 Johan Hedberg 2.00 5.00
23 Vincent Damphousse 2.00 5.00
24 Marian Hossa 5.00 12.00
25 Richard Zednik 2.00 5.00
26 Alexei Yashin 2.00 5.00
27 Sergei Gonchar 2.00 5.00
28 Martin Straka 2.00 5.00
29 Ed Jovanovski 4.00 10.00
30 Robert Lang 2.00 5.00
31 Markus Naslund 6.00 15.00
32 Mike Sillinger 2.00 5.00
33 Jamie Storr 2.00 5.00
34 Kimmo Timonen 2.00 5.00
35 Patrick Lalime 2.00 5.00
36 Alyn McCauley 2.00 5.00
37 Scott Walker 2.00 5.00
38 Trevor Linden 4.00 10.00
39 Ilya Kovalchuk 12.50 30.00
40 Jarome Iginla 8.00 20.00
41 Alex Tanguay 4.00 10.00
42 Yanic Perreault 2.00 5.00
43 Jocelyn Thibault 2.00 5.00
44 Eric Brewer 2.00 5.00
45 Ray Whitney 2.00 5.00
46 Ryan Smyth 2.00 5.00
47 Steven Reinprecht 2.00 5.00
48 Phil Housley 2.00 5.00
49 Milan Hnilicka 2.00 5.00
50 Maxim Afinogenov 2.00 5.00
51 Andrew Brunette 2.00 5.00
52 Miroslav Satan 4.00 10.00
53 Glen Murray 2.00 5.00
54 Mark Parrish 2.00 5.00
55 Daniel Sedin 5.00 12.00
56 Brendan Morrison 2.00 5.00
57 Brian Rafalski 2.00 5.00
58 Dan Cloutier 4.00 10.00
59 Espen Knutsen 2.00 5.00
60 Radim Vrbata 2.00 5.00
61 Patrik Stefan 2.00 5.00
62 Eric Daze 2.00 5.00
63 Felix Potvin 6.00 15.00
64 Darcy Tucker 2.00 5.00
65 Jose Theodore 6.00 15.00
66 Scott Hartnell 3.00 8.00
67 Martin Havlat 4.00 10.00
68 Radek Bonk 2.00 5.00
69 Patrick Marleau 4.00 10.00
70 Andy Delmore 2.00 5.00
71 Rostislav Klesla 2.00 5.00
72 David Aebischer 4.00 10.00
73 Steve Shields 2.00 5.00
74 Stu Barnes 2.00 5.00
75 Tim Connolly 2.00 5.00
76 Jean-Sebastien Giguere 4.00 10.00
77 Shane Doan 3.00 8.00
78 Brian Rolston 2.00 5.00
79 Shawn McEachern 2.00 5.00
80 Martin Biron 2.00 5.00
81 Craig Conroy 2.00 5.00
82 Mika Noronen 2.00 5.00
83 Brian Boucher 2.00 5.00
84 Kyle Calder 2.00 5.00
85 Cliff Ronning 2.00 5.00
86 Brian Gionta 2.00 5.00
87 Shawn Bates 2.00 5.00
88 Michal Handzus 2.00 5.00
89 Daniel Briere 4.00 10.00
90 Adam Graves 2.00 5.00
91 Martin St. Louis 6.00 15.00
92 Ladislav Nagy 2.00 5.00
93 Oleg Tverdovsky 2.00 5.00
94 Pavel Brendl 2.00 5.00
95 Alexei Morozov 2.00 5.00
96 Daymond Langkow 2.00 5.00
97 Krys Kolanos 2.00 5.00
98 Sean Burke 4.00 10.00
99 Chris Drury 4.00 10.00
100 Steve Sullivan 2.00 5.00
101 Paul Kariya SP 15.00 40.00
102 Peter Forsberg SP 25.00 60.00
103 Ron Tugnutt SP 8.00 20.00
104 Manny Legace 4.00 10.00
105 Tommy Salo SP 8.00 20.00
106 Kristian Huselius 2.00 5.00
107 Jason Allison SP 8.00 20.00
108 Mariusz Czerkawski 2.00 5.00
109 Jeff Friesen SP 8.00 20.00
110 Chris Osgood SP 8.00 20.00
111 Martin Prusek 2.00 5.00
112 Steve Yzerman SP 30.00 80.00
113 John LeClair SP 8.00 20.00
114 Jan Hrdina 2.00 5.00
115 Tony Amonte SP 8.00 20.00
116 Teemu Selanne SP 8.00 20.00
117 Cory Stillman 2.00 5.00
118 Nikolai Khabibulin SP 10.00 25.00
119 Mats Sundin SP 20.00 50.00
120 Olaf Kolzig SP 12.00 30.00
121 Petr Sykora 8.00 20.00
122 Joe Thornton SP 15.00 40.00
123 Roman Turek SP 8.00 20.00
124 Derek Morris SP 8.00 20.00
125 Bill Guerin SP 8.00 20.00
126 Brendan Shanahan SP 15.00 40.00
127 Roberto Luongo 8.00 20.00
128 Zigmund Palffy SP 8.00 20.00
129 Pavol Demitra SP 8.00 20.00
130 Saku Koivu SP 6.00 15.00
131 Joe Nieuwendyk SP 8.00 20.00
132 Mike Peca SP 8.00 20.00
133 Petr Schastlivy 2.00 5.00
134 Jeremy Roenick SP 15.00 40.00
135 Mario Lemieux SP 125.00 250.00
136 Petr Cajanek 2.00 5.00
137 Vincent Lecavalier SP 10.00 25.00
138 Peter Bondra SP 8.00 20.00
139 Brent Johnson SP 6.00 15.00
140 Sergei Samsonov SP 8.00 20.00
141 Joe Sakic SP 20.00 50.00
142 Brenden Morrow 4.00 10.00
143 Arturs Irbe 2.00 5.00
144 Chris Chelios SP 12.50 30.00
145 Sandis Ozolinsh 2.00 5.00
146 Doug Gilmour SP 8.00 20.00
147 Scott Stevens SP 10.00 25.00
148 Sergei Fedorov SP 12.50 30.00
149 Keith Primeau SP 8.00 20.00
150 Eric Boguniecki 2.00 5.00
151 Shane Willis 2.00 5.00
152 Rob Blake SP 8.00 20.00
153 Luc Robitaille SP 12.50 30.00
154 Pierre Turgeon SP 8.00 20.00
155 Curtis Joseph SP 12.50 30.00
156 Stephen Weiss 3.00 8.00
157 Patrik Elias SP 8.00 20.00
158 Mark Recchi SP 8.00 20.00
159 Al MacInnis SP 8.00 20.00
160 Patrick Roy SP 30.00 80.00
161 Darryl Sydor SP 8.00 20.00
162 Nicklas Lidstrom SP 12.00 30.00
163 Doug Weight SP 8.00 20.00
164 Roman Cechmanek 2.00 5.00
165 Marty Turco 4.00 10.00
166 Pavel Datsyuk 12.50 30.00
167 Chris Pronger SP 8.00 20.00
168 Scott Young 2.00 5.00
169 Igor Larionov SP 10.00 25.00
170 Keith Tkachuk SP 8.00 20.00
171 Ron Francis SP 8.00 20.00
172 Dan Blackburn 2.00 5.00
173 Jeff O'Neill SP 8.00 20.00
174 Bobby Holik SP 8.00 20.00
175 Erik Cole 2.00 5.00
176 Pavel Bure SP 10.00 25.00
177 Brian Leetch SP 8.00 20.00
178 Curtis Sanford 4.00 10.00
179 Carlo Colaiacovo 2.00 5.00
180 Dennis Seidenberg 3.00 8.00
181 Adam Hall 2.00 5.00
182 Ivan Majesky 2.00 5.00
183 Rick Nash 10.00 25.00
184 Alexei Smirnov 2.00 5.00
185 Chuck Kobasew 2.00 5.00
186 Ron Hainsey 2.00 5.00
187 Stephane Veilleux 2.00 5.00
188 Scottie Upshall 4.00 10.00
189 Lasse Pirjeta 2.00 5.00
190 Henrik Zetterberg 20.00 40.00
191 Jay Bouwmeester 6.00 15.00
192 Alexander Frolov 6.00 15.00
193 Dmitri Bykov 2.00 5.00
194 Stanislav Chistov 2.00 5.00
195 Jordan Leopold 2.00 5.00
196 P-M Bouchard 4.00 10.00
197 Mike Cammalleri 4.00 10.00
198 Anton Volchenkov 2.00 5.00
199 Lynn Loyns 2.00 5.00
200 Steve Eminger 2.00 5.00

2002-03 BAP Signature Series Autograph Buybacks 1998

Available randomly in packs of 2002-03 BAP Signature Series, these cards were older BAP autograph cards that were "bought back" by ITG and inserted into the product on a average of two per box. These cards are distinguishable by the silver foil "10th Anniversary" stamp they carry on the card fronts. Several different years are represented in this buyback series.
*BUYBACKS: .6X TO 1.5X ORIGINAL VALUES

2002-03 BAP Signature Series Autograph Buybacks 1999

*BUYBACKS: .6X TO 1.5X ORIGINAL VALUES

2002-03 BAP Signature Series Autograph Buybacks 2000

*BUYBACKS: .6X TO 1.5X ORIGINAL VALUES

2002-03 BAP Signature Series Autograph Buybacks 2001

*BUYBACKS: .6X TO 1.5X ORIGINAL VALUES

2002-03 BAP Signature Series Defensive Wall

This 10-card set featured pieces of game-used jersey from starting defensive trios. Each card was limited to 50 copies each.
STATED PRINT RUN 50 SETS
DW1 Colorado Avalanche 40.00 100.00
DW2 Toronto Maple Leafs 25.00 60.00
DW3 Philadelphia Flyers 15.00 40.00
DW4 NY Rangers 15.00 40.00
DW5 Dallas Stars 20.00 50.00
DW6 NJ Devils 20.00 50.00
DW7 St. Louis Blues 15.00 40.00
DW8 Ottawa Senators 15.00 40.00
DW9 Washington Capitals 15.00 40.00
DW10 Vancouver Canucks 15.00 40.00

2002-03 BAP Signature Series Famous Scraps

This 12-card set highlighted two players who have "mixed it up" at various times during their careers. Each card was limted to just 50 copies and carried pieces of jersey from each player.
ANNOUNCED PRINT RUN 50 SETS
FS1 D.Schultz/T.Williams 20.00 50.00
FS2 B.Probert/W.Clark 25.00 60.00
FS3 I.Laperriere/B.Guerin 12.00 30.00
FS4 P.Worrell/C.Gratton 15.00 40.00
FS5 B.Guerin/J.Iginla 15.00 40.00
FS6 T.Domi/R.Ray 30.00 80.00
FS7 M.Comrie/I.Kovalchuk 20.00 50.00
FS8 F.Potvin/R.Hextall 20.00 50.00
FS9 O.Nolan/B.Probert 20.00 50.00
FS10 P.Roy/C.Osgood 30.00 80.00
FS11 D.Brashear/G.Laraque 20.00 50.00
FS12 M.Johnson/S.McCarthy 15.00 40.00

2002-03 BAP Signature Series Franchise Players

STATED PRINT RUN 50 SETS
FJ1 Paul Kariya 8.00 20.00
FJ2 Dany Heatley 12.50 30.00
FJ3 Joe Thornton 15.00 40.00
FJ4 Miroslav Satan 8.00 20.00
FJ5 Jarome Iginla 10.00 25.00
FJ6 Ron Francis 8.00 20.00
FJ7 Jocelyn Thibault 8.00 20.00
FJ8 Rick Nash 15.00 40.00
FJ9 Joe Sakic 15.00 40.00
FJ10 Mike Modano 12.50 30.00
FJ11 Steve Yzerman 20.00 50.00
FJ12 Mike Comrie 8.00 20.00
FJ13 Roberto Luongo 12.50 30.00
FJ14 Jason Allison 8.00 20.00
FJ15 Marian Gaborik 15.00 40.00
FJ16 Jose Theodore 8.00 20.00
FJ17 David Legwand 8.00 20.00
FJ18 Martin Brodeur 20.00 50.00
FJ19 Mike Peca 8.00 20.00
FJ20 Pavel Bure 8.00 20.00
FJ21 Marian Hossa 8.00 20.00
FJ22 Jeremy Roenick 10.00 25.00
FJ23 Daniel Briere 8.00 20.00
FJ24 Mario Lemieux 15.00 40.00
FJ25 Teemu Selanne 8.00 20.00
FJ26 Chris Pronger 8.00 20.00
FJ27 Vincent Lecavalier 8.00 20.00
FJ28 Mats Sundin 8.00 20.00
FJ29 Markus Naslund 8.00 20.00
FJ30 Jaromir Jagr 12.50 30.00

2002-03 BAP Signature Series Golf

This 100-card set was inserted one per pack and pictured players enjoying the game of golf.
COMPLETE SET (100) 50.00 100.00
ONE PER PACK
GS1 Adam Foote .50 1.25
GS2 Adam Oates .50 1.25
GS3 Adrian Aucoin .30 .75
GS4 Alex Tanguay .50 1.25
GS5 Alexander Mogilny .50 1.25
GS6 Alexei Yashin .30 .75
GS7 Alyn McCauley .30 .75
GS8 Andy McDonald .30 .75
GS9 Brian Leetch .50 1.25
GS10 Bates Battaglia .30 .75
GS11 Bobby Holik .30 .75
GS12 Brad Isbister .30 .75
GS13 Brendan Morrison .50 1.25
GS14 Arturs Irbe .50 1.25
GS15 Brian Savage .30 .75
GS16 Bryan Marchment .30 .75
GS17 Bryan McCabe .30 .75
GS18 Carlo Colaiacovo .30 .75
GS19 Chris Drury .50 1.25
GS20 Chris Gratton .30 .75
GS21 Chris Neil .30 .75
GS22 Chris Osgood .50 1.25
GS23 Chris Simon .30 .75
GS24 Curtis Joseph .60 1.50
GS25 Daniel Sedin .30 .75
GS26 Darius Kasparaitis .30 .75
GS27 Darren McCarty .30 .75
GS28 Darryl Sittler .60 1.50
GS29 David Aebischer .50 1.25
GS30 David Legwand .50 1.25
GS31 Denis Arkhipov .30 .75
GS32 Derek Morris .30 .75
GS33 Donald Brashear .30 .75
GS34 Doug Gilmour .50 1.25
GS35 Ed Belfour .60 1.50
GS36 Ed Jovanovski .50 1.25
GS37 Erik Cole .30 .75
GS38 Eric Lindros .60 1.50
GS39 Grant Fuhr .50 1.25
GS40 Jaroslav Svoboda .30 .75
GS41 Jeff O'Neill .30 .75
GS42 Jarome Iginla .75 2.00
GS43 Joe Sakic 1.25 3.00
GS44 Johan Hedberg .50 1.25
GS45 Josef Vasicek .30 .75
GS46 Jean-Sebastien Giguere .50 1.25
GS47 Kenny Jonsson .30 .75
GS48 Luc Robitaille .50 1.25
GS49 Mario Lemieux 4.00 10.00
GS50 Mark Parrish .30 .75
GS51 Martin Brodeur 1.50 4.00
GS52 Martin Erat .30 .75
GS53 Martin Skoula .30 .75
GS54 Mats Sundin .60 1.50
GS55 Matt Cooke .30 .75
GS56 Mattias Ohlund .30 .75
GS57 Mike Dunham .50 1.25
GS58 Mike Fisher .30 .75
GS59 Mike Keane .30 .75
GS60 Mike Peca .30 .75
GS61 Mike Ricci .30 .75
GS62 Milan Hejduk .60 1.50
GS63 Miroslav Satan .50 1.25
GS64 Nik Antropov .30 .75
GS65 Olaf Kolzig .50 1.25
GS66 Owen Nolan .50 1.25
GS67 Pat Verbeek .30 .75
GS68 Patrick Marleau .50 1.25
GS69 Patrick Roy 3.00 8.00
GS70 Paul Kariya .60 1.50
GS71 Peter Bondra .50 1.25
GS72 Peter Forsberg 1.50 4.00
GS73 Petr Sykora .30 .75
GS74 Radek Dvorak .30 .75
GS75 Rick DiPietro .50 1.25
GS76 Rob Blake .50 1.25
GS77 Robert Lang .30 .75
GS78 Roman Hamrlik .30 .75
GS79 Dany Heatley .50 1.25
GS80 Ron Francis .50 1.25
GS81 Ryan Smyth .30 .75
GS82 Sami Kapanen .30 .75
GS83 Scott Hartnell .30 .75
GS84 Scott Stevens .50 1.25
GS85 Scott Walker .30 .75
GS86 Stan Mikita .75 2.00
GS87 Stanislav Chistov .30 .75
GS88 Steve Konowalchuk .30 .75
GS89 Steve Rucchin .30 .75
GS90 Steve Yzerman 3.00 8.00
GS91 Stephen Peat .30 .75
GS92 Steven Reinprecht .30 .75
GS93 Teemu Selanne .60 1.50
GS94 Tie Domi .50 1.25
GS95 Todd Bertuzzi .60 1.50
GS96 Todd White .30 .75
GS97 Tom Poti .30 .75
GS98 Trent Klatt .30 .75
GS99 Trevor Kidd .50 1.25
GS100 Wade Redden .30 .75

2002-03 BAP Signature Series Jerseys

STATED PRINT RUN 90 SETS
SGJ1 Mario Lemieux 20.00 50.00
SGJ2 Steve Yzerman 20.00 50.00
SGJ3 Peter Forsberg 12.50 30.00
SGJ4 Patrick Roy 20.00 50.00
SGJ5 Jarome Iginla 10.00 25.00
SGJ6 Pavel Bure 8.00 20.00
SGJ7 Jaromir Jagr 10.00 25.00
SGJ8 Eric Lindros 8.00 20.00
SGJ9 Paul Kariya 8.00 20.00
SGJ10 Ilya Kovalchuk 10.00 25.00
SGJ11 Mike Modano 10.00 25.00
SGJ12 Joe Thornton 12.50 30.00
SGJ13 Jose Theodore 8.00 20.00
SGJ14 Jeremy Roenick 10.00 25.00
SGJ15 Martin Brodeur 15.00 40.00
SGJ16 Mats Sundin 8.00 20.00
SGJ17 Mark Messier 8.00 20.00
SGJ18 Alexei Yashin 6.00 15.00
SGJ19 Marian Gaborik 12.50 30.00
SGJ20 Brendan Shanahan 8.00 20.00
SGJ21 Owen Nolan 6.00 15.00
SGJ22 Joe Sakic 12.50 30.00
SGJ23 Daniel Alfredsson 6.00 15.00
SGJ24 Teemu Selanne 8.00 20.00
SGJ25 Nicklas Lidstrom 8.00 20.00
SGJ26 John LeClair 8.00 20.00
SGJ27 Keith Tkachuk 8.00 20.00
SGJ28 Brian Leetch 6.00 15.00
SGJ29 Milan Hejduk 8.00 20.00
SGJ30 Dany Heatley 10.00 25.00
SGJ31 Sergei Samsonov 6.00 15.00
SGJ32 Todd Bertuzzi 8.00 20.00
SGJ33 Markus Naslund 8.00 20.00
SGJ34 Chris Chelios 8.00 20.00
SGJ35 Rob Blake 6.00 15.00
SGJ36 Sergei Fedorov 10.00 25.00
SGJ37 Al MacInnis 6.00 15.00
SGJ38 Luc Robitaille 6.00 15.00
SGJ39 Martin Havlat 6.00 15.00
SGJ40 Ron Francis 6.00 15.00
SGJ41 Alexander Mogilny 6.00 15.00
SGJ42 Chris Pronger 6.00 15.00
SGJ43 Doug Weight 6.00 15.00
SGJ44 Zigmund Palffy 8.00 20.00
SGJ45 Peter Bondra 6.00 15.00
SGJ46 Mike Comrie 6.00 15.00
SGJ47 Pavel Datsyuk 12.50 30.00
SGJ48 Marian Hossa 8.00 20.00
SGJ49 Saku Koivu 8.00 20.00
SGJ50 Dan Blackburn 6.00 15.00
SGJ51 Steve Shields 6.00 15.00
SGJ52 Bill Guerin 6.00 15.00
SGJ53 Doug Gilmour 6.00 15.00
SGJ54 Jason Spezza 12.50 30.00
SGJ55 Jay Bouwmeester 6.00 15.00
SGJ56 Alexei Smirnov 6.00 15.00
SGJ57 Stanislav Chistov 6.00 15.00
SGJ58 Chuck Kobasew 6.00 15.00
SGJ59 Jordan Leopold 6.00 15.00
SGJ60 Niko Kapanen 6.00 15.00
SGJ61 Scottie Upshall 6.00 15.00
SGJ62 Ron Hainsey 6.00 15.00
SGJ63 Alexander Frolov 6.00 15.00
SGJ64 Mike Cammalleri 6.00 15.00
SGJ65 Dennis Seidenberg 6.00 15.00
SGJ66 Rick Nash 10.00 25.00
SGJ67 Carlo Colaiacovo 6.00 15.00
SGJ68 Marty Turco 6.00 15.00
SGJ69 Alex Kovalev 6.00 15.00
SGJ70 Vincent Lecavalier 6.00 15.00

2002-03 BAP Signature Series Magnificent Inserts

This 10-card set featured game-used equipment from the career of Mario Lemieux. Cards MI1-MI5 had a print run of 40 copies each and cards MI6-MI10 were limited to just 10 copies each. Cards MI6-MI10 are not priced due to scarcity.
MI1-MI5 PRINT RUN 40 SETS
MI1 2000-01 Season 30.00 80.00
MI2 1985-86 Season 30.00 80.00
MI3 2002 NHL All-Star 30.00 80.00
MI4 1987 Canada Cup 30.00 80.00
MI5 Dual Jersey 50.00 125.00
MI6 Number
MI7 Emblem
MI8 Triple Jersey
MI9 Quad Jersey
MI10 Complete Package

2002-03 BAP Signature Series Phenoms

This 12-card set featured players in their 4th year in the league and included swatches of game jerseys. Cards were limited to just 40 copies each.
ANNOUNCED PRINT RUN 40
YP1 Simon Gagne 12.00 30.00
YP2 Scott Gomez 12.00 30.00
YP3 David Legwand 10.00 25.00
YP4 Patrik Stefan 10.00 25.00
YP5 Brad Stuart 10.00 25.00
YP6 Alex Tanguay 10.00 25.00
YP7 Brent Johnson 8.00 20.00
YP8 Roberto Luongo 20.00 50.00
YP9 Evgeni Nabokov 12.00 30.00
YP10 Nik Antropov 12.00 30.00

2002-03 BAP Signature Series Triple Memorabilia

STATED PRINT RUN 30 SETS
TM1 Mario Lemieux 100.00 250.00
TM2 Mats Sundin 20.00 50.00
TM3 Steve Yzerman 50.00 120.00
TM4 Joe Thornton 30.00 80.00
TM5 Eric Lindros 20.00 50.00
TM6 Patrick Roy 50.00 125.00
TM7 Brett Hull 30.00 80.00
TM8 Sergei Fedorov 30.00 80.00
TM9 Martin Brodeur 50.00 125.00
TM10 Joe Sakic 30.00 80.00

2000-01 BAP Ultimate Memorabilia Autographs

Be A Player Ultimate Memorabilia was released in May 2001 and boasted one memorabilia card per pack and a SRP of approximately $100 per pack. There were 5 packs in a box and 1 card per pack. This 50-card set featured certified player autographs under color action photos on silver and purple die-cut card stock. Each card in Ultimate Memorabilia was sealed in a clear plastic slab with a descriptive label at the top.
ANNOUNCED PRINT RUN 90
1 Theo Fleury 15.00 40.00
2 Brendan Shanahan 15.00 40.00
3 Curtis Joseph 15.00 40.00
4 Saku Koivu 15.00 40.00
5 Olaf Kolzig 10.00 25.00
6 Al MacInnis 12.00 30.00
7 John LeClair 15.00 40.00
8 Teemu Selanne 15.00 40.00
9 Wayne Gretzky 150.00 300.00
10 Pavel Bure 15.00 40.00
11 Mario Lemieux 100.00 200.00
12 Milan Hejduk 15.00 40.00
13 Ray Bourque 25.00 60.00
14 Daniel Alfredsson 10.00 25.00
15 Mats Sundin 20.00 50.00
16 Paul Kariya 15.00 40.00
17 Scott Gomez 10.00 25.00
18 Eric Lindros 15.00 40.00
19 Sergei Fedorov 20.00 50.00
20 Peter Forsberg 25.00 60.00
21 Vincent Lecavalier 12.00 30.00
22 Tony Amonte 10.00 25.00
23 Patrick Roy 60.00 150.00
24 Ed Belfour 15.00 40.00
25 Martin Brodeur 40.00 100.00
26 Brian Leetch 10.00 25.00
27 Mike Modano 20.00 50.00
28 Joe Sakic 30.00 80.00
29 Jeremy Roenick 15.00 40.00
30 Steve Yzerman 60.00 150.00
31 Nikolai Khabibulin 10.00 25.00
32 Roman Turek 10.00 25.00
33 Keith Primeau 12.00 30.00
34 Mike Richter 15.00 40.00
35 Patrik Stefan 10.00 25.00
36 Scott Stevens 10.00 25.00
37 Valeri Bure 10.00 25.00
38 Doug Weight 10.00 25.00
39 Nicklas Lidstrom 15.00 40.00
40 Chris Drury 10.00 25.00
41 Mike Peca 10.00 25.00
42 Chris Pronger 12.00 30.00
43 Rob Blake 10.00 25.00
44 Luc Robitaille 12.00 30.00
45 Joe Thornton 25.00 60.00
46 Jason Arnott 10.00 25.00
47 Daniel Sedin 20.00 40.00
48 Pierre Turgeon 10.00 25.00
49 Brad Stuart 10.00 25.00
50 Adam Oates 10.00 25.00

2000-01 BAP Ultimate Memorabilia Active Eight

This 8-card set featured three players on each card along with a game-used jersey swatch of each. Each card recognized the three statistical leaders in a featured category. Each card was sealed in a clear plastic slab with a descriptive label at the top. Stated print run on these cards was 30 sets.

ANNOUNCED PRINT RUN 30
AE1 Messier/Yzerman/Lemieux 200.00 400.00
AE2 Messier/Yzerman/Francis 60.00 150.00
AE3 Lemieux/Hull/Bure 75.00 200.00
AE4 Lemieux/Lindros/Jagr 100.00 200.00
AE5 Roy/Vernon/VBK 60.00 150.00
AE6 Belfour/Roy/Hasek 60.00 150.00
AE7 Brodeur/Hasek/Osgood 60.00 150.00
AE8 Hasek/Brodeur/Hebert 60.00 150.00

2000-01 BAP Ultimate Memorabilia Dynasty Jerseys

This 20-card set featured a swatch of game-used jersey of the depicted player and commemorates that player's time with a championship team. The jersey swatch was affixed on the card in the shape of the Stanley Cup. Each card was sealed in a clear plastic slab with a descriptive label at the top. Stated print run on these cards was 50 sets.

ANNOUNCED PRINT RUN 50
D1 Wayne Gretzky 150.00 300.00
D2 Mark Messier 40.00 100.00
D3 Grant Fuhr 30.00 80.00
D4 Paul Coffey 25.00 60.00
D5 Bill Ranford 30.00 80.00
D6 Mario Lemieux 100.00 200.00
D7 Paul Coffey 25.00 60.00
D8 Jaromir Jagr 40.00 100.00
D9 Tom Barrasso 25.00 60.00
D10 Ron Francis 25.00 60.00
D11 Larry Murphy 25.00 60.00
D12 Ulf Samuelsson 25.00 60.00
D13 Steve Yzerman 60.00 120.00
D14 Chris Osgood 25.00 60.00
D15 Nicklas Lidstrom 25.00 60.00
D16 Sergei Fedorov 30.00 80.00
D17 Brendan Shanahan 25.00 60.00
D18 Darren McCarty 25.00 60.00
D19 Slava Kozlov 20.00 50.00
D20 Mike Vernon 25.00 60.00

2000-01 BAP Ultimate Memorabilia Game-Used Jerseys

JERSEY ANNOUNCED PRINT RUN 60
*STICK/90: .4X TO 1X JERSEY/60
GJ1 Theo Fleury 15.00 40.00
GJ2 Brendan Shanahan 10.00 25.00
GJ3 Curtis Joseph 10.00 25.00
GJ4 Roman Turek 10.00 25.00
GJ5 Dominik Hasek 20.00 50.00
GJ6 Al MacInnis 10.00 25.00
GJ7 John LeClair 10.00 25.00
GJ8 Teemu Selanne 10.00 25.00
GJ9 Wayne Gretzky 50.00 120.00
GJ10 Pavel Bure 10.00 25.00
GJ11 Mark Messier 10.00 25.00
GJ12 Jaromir Jagr 15.00 40.00
GJ13 Arturs Irbe 8.00 20.00
GJ14 Vincent Lecavalier 10.00 25.00
GJ15 Mats Sundin 12.50 30.00
GJ16 Paul Kariya 10.00 25.00
GJ17 Marian Hossa 10.00 25.00
GJ18 Owen Nolan 8.00 20.00
GJ19 Sergei Fedorov 12.00 30.00
GJ20 Peter Forsberg 20.00 50.00
GJ21 Brett Hull 12.50 30.00
GJ22 Tony Amonte 8.00 20.00
GJ23 Patrick Roy 30.00 80.00
GJ24 Ed Belfour 10.00 25.00
GJ25 Martin Brodeur 30.00 80.00
GJ26 Brian Leetch 8.00 20.00
GJ27 Mike Modano 15.00 40.00
GJ28 Joe Sakic 20.00 50.00
GJ29 Jeremy Roenick 12.50 30.00
GJ30 Steve Yzerman 30.00 80.00
GJ31 Jason Allison 8.00 20.00
GJ32 Milan Hejduk 10.00 25.00
GJ33 Mike Richter 10.00 25.00
GJ34 Patrik Stefan 8.00 20.00
GJ35 Kyle McLaren 8.00 20.00
GJ36 Valeri Bure 8.00 20.00
GJ37 Felix Potvin 20.00 50.00
GJ38 Chris Pronger 8.00 20.00
GJ39 Scott Stevens 8.00 20.00
GJ40 Luc Robitaille 8.00 20.00
GJ41 Roberto Luongo 15.00 40.00
GJ42 Chris Osgood 8.00 20.00
GJ43 Olaf Kolzig 8.00 20.00
GJ44 Scott Gomez 8.00 20.00
GJ45 Jason Arnott 8.00 20.00
GJ46 Rob Blake 8.00 20.00
GJ47 Keith Tkachuk 10.00 25.00
GJ48 Saku Koivu 8.00 20.00
GJ49 Alexei Yashin 8.00 20.00
GJ50 Nicklas Lidstrom 10.00 25.00

2000-01 BAP Ultimate Memorabilia Goalie Memorabilia

This 20-card set featured swatches of game-used equipment from each of the depicted goalies on the card. Each card was sealed in a clear plastic slab with a descriptive label at the top. Stated print run on these cards was 30 sets.

ANNOUNCED PRINT RUN 30
GM1 J.Plante/P.Roy 60.00 150.00
GM2 T.Sawchuk/P.Roy 60.00 150.00
GM3 M.Vernon/C.Osgood 25.00 60.00
GM4 C.Joseph/F.Potvin 40.00 100.00
GM5 T.Esposito/E.Belfour 25.00 60.00
GM6 T.Broda/J.Bower 30.00 80.00
GM7 B.Parent/B.Boucher 25.00 60.00
GM8 T.Esposito/G.Cheevers 30.00 80.00
GM9 B.Parent/G.Cheevers 40.00 100.00
GM10 Jacques Plante G/J 60.00 150.00
GM11 P.Roy/E.Belfour 60.00 150.00
GM12 C.Joseph/D.Hasek 30.00 80.00
GM13 R.Turek/E.Belfour 25.00 60.00
GM14 M.Brodeur/J.Plante 60.00 150.00
GM15 M.Richter/J.Vanbiesbrouck 25.00 60.00
GM16 Jacques Plante G/S/J 60.00 150.00
GM17 T.Esposito/Parent/Tretiak 60.00 150.00
GM18 Brimsek/Dafoe/Cheevers 50.00 125.00
GM19 Bower/Broda/Sawchuk 75.00 200.00
GM20 Roy/Vezina/Sawchuk 250.00 400.00

2000-01 BAP Ultimate Memorabilia Goalie Memorabilia Autographed

This 5-card set featured a swatch of game-used equipment and an autograph from the depicted goalie. Each card was sealed in a clear plastic slab with a descriptive label at the top. Stated print run on these cards was 50 sets.

ANNOUNCED PRINT RUN 50
UG1 Gerry Cheevers 40.00 100.00
UG2 Vladislav Tretiak 75.00 200.00
UG3 Tony Esposito 40.00 100.00
UG4 Johnny Bower 40.00 100.00
UG5 Bernie Parent 50.00 125.00

2000-01 BAP Ultimate Memorabilia Goalie Sticks

ANNOUNCED PRINT RUN 50
G1 Guy Hebert 12.50 30.00
G2 Damian Rhodes 12.50 30.00
G3 Byron Dafoe 12.50 30.00
G4 Dominik Hasek 15.00 40.00
G5 Mike Vernon 12.50 30.00
G6 Arturs Irbe 12.50 30.00
G7 Jocelyn Thibault 12.50 30.00
G8 Patrick Roy 50.00 125.00
G9 Marc Denis 12.50 30.00
G10 Ed Belfour 12.50 30.00
G11 Chris Osgood 12.50 30.00
G12 Tommy Salo 12.50 30.00
G13 Roberto Luongo 15.00 40.00
G14 Jamie Storr 12.50 30.00
G15 Manny Fernandez 12.50 30.00
G16 Jeff Hackett 12.50 30.00
G17 Mike Dunham 12.50 30.00
G18 Martin Brodeur 30.00 80.00
G19 John Vanbiesbrouck 20.00 50.00
G20 Mike Richter 12.50 30.00
G21 Patrick Lalime 12.50 30.00
G22 Brian Boucher 12.50 30.00
G23 Nikolai Khabibulin 12.50 30.00
G24 J-S Aubin 12.50 30.00
G25 Roman Turek 12.50 30.00
G26 Steve Shields 12.50 30.00
G27 Dan Cloutier 12.50 30.00
G28 Curtis Joseph 12.50 30.00
G29 Felix Potvin 15.00 40.00
G30 Olaf Kolzig 12.50 30.00

2000-01 BAP Ultimate Memorabilia Gordie Howe No. 9

This 3-card set featured swatches of game-used jerseys of Gordie Howe from one of the three professional teams he played for during his career. The cards carried a color action photo of Howe in the team's jersey in the forefront and the shape of the number 9 in the background with another action shot and a head shot on it. The jersey swatch was affixed in the shape of the hollow of the number 9. Each card was sealed in a clear plastic slab with a descriptive label at the top. Stated print run on these cards was 50 sets.

ANNOUNCED PRINT RUN 50
COMMON JSY/AU/20 125.00 250.00
JSY/AUTO ANNC'D PRINT RUN 20
9-1 Detroit 50.00 125.00
9-2 New England 50.00 125.00
9-3 Houston 50.00 125.00

2000-01 BAP Ultimate Memorabilia Gordie Howe Retrospective Jerseys

This 7-card set featured game-used swatches of Gordie Howe's jerseys from the three teams he played for during his professional career. The cards carried a color action photo of Howe in the team's jersey in the forefront and the words "Howe Legend" in the background. Cards with one or two jersey swatches also carried larger headshots and the depicted team logo in the background. Each card was sealed in a clear plastic slab with a descriptive label at the top. Stated print run on these cards was 50 sets.

ANNOUNCED PRINT RUN 50
HL1 Detroit 60.00 150.00
HL2 New England 60.00 150.00
HL3 Houston 60.00 150.00
HL4 Detroit/New England 75.00 200.00
HL5 Houston/Detroit 75.00 200.00
HL6 Houston/New England 75.00 200.00
HL7 Detroit/Houston/N.Eng. 100.00 250.00

2000-01 BAP Ultimate Memorabilia Gordie Howe Retrospective Jerseys Autograph

This set paralleled the Be A Player Ultimate Memorabilia Gordie Howe Retrospective Jerseys set except that each card carries an autograph of Gordie Howe along with the words "Mr. Hockey" in his handwriting. Each card was sealed in a clear plastic slab with a descriptive label at the top. Stated print run on these cards was 20 sets.

ANNOUNCED PRINT RUN 20
GH1 Detroit 125.00 250.00
GH2 New England 125.00 250.00
GH3 Houston 125.00 250.00
GH4 Detroit/New England 125.00 250.00
GH5 Houston/Detroit 125.00 250.00
GH6 Houston/New England 125.00 250.00
GH7 Detroit/Houston/N.England 400.00 800.00

2000-01 BAP Ultimate Memorabilia Hart Trophy

This 20-card set featured game-used jersey swatches of past winners of the Hart trophy. Each card carried a color action photo of the given player and a picture of the trophy alongside the jersey swatch. Some players in the set have multiple cards to mirror the amount times they have won the trophy. Each card was sealed in a clear plastic slab with a descriptive label at the top. Stated print run on these cards was 30 sets.

ANNOUNCED PRINT RUN 30
H1 Chris Pronger 20.00 50.00
H2 Jaromir Jagr 40.00 100.00
H3 Dominik Hasek 30.00 80.00
H4 Dominik Hasek 30.00 80.00
H5 Mario Lemieux 60.00 150.00
H6 Eric Lindros 30.00 80.00
H7 Sergei Fedorov 30.00 80.00
H8 Mario Lemieux 60.00 150.00
H9 Mark Messier 50.00 125.00
H10 Brett Hull 25.00 60.00
H11 Mark Messier 50.00 125.00
H12 Wayne Gretzky 75.00 150.00
H13 Mario Lemieux 60.00 120.00
H14 Wayne Gretzky 60.00 120.00
H15 Wayne Gretzky 60.00 120.00
H16 Wayne Gretzky 60.00 120.00
H17 Wayne Gretzky 60.00 120.00
H18 Wayne Gretzky 60.00 120.00
H19 Wayne Gretzky 60.00 120.00
H20 Wayne Gretzky 60.00 120.00

2000-01 BAP Ultimate Memorabilia Jacques Plante Jerseys

This 15-card set featured a game-used jersey swatch of goalie great Jacques Plante. Each card also carried a photo of a current day goalie and the cards are listed below based on those players. Each card was sealed in a clear plastic slab with a descriptive label at the top. Stated print run on these cards was 30 sets.

ANNOUNCED PRINT RUN 30
*SKATES/20: .6X TO 1.5X JSY/30
SKATES ANNOUNCED PRINT RUN 20
PJ1 Patrick Roy 75.00 200.00
PJ2 Ed Belfour 25.00 60.00
PJ3 Martin Brodeur 50.00 120.00
PJ4 Dominik Hasek 40.00 100.00
PJ5 Chris Osgood 25.00 60.00
PJ6 Curtis Joseph 25.00 60.00
PJ7 Tommy Salo 25.00 60.00
PJ8 Mike Richter 25.00 60.00
PJ9 Byron Dafoe 25.00 60.00
PJ10 Roberto Luongo 25.00 60.00
PJ11 Roman Turek 25.00 60.00
PJ12 Olaf Kolzig 25.00 60.00
PJ13 Felix Potvin 25.00 60.00
PJ14 Jocelyn Thibault 25.00 60.00
PJ15 Brian Boucher 20.00 50.00

2000-01 BAP Ultimate Memorabilia Jacques Plante Skate

ANNOUNCED PRINT RUN 20
PS1 Patrick Roy 75.00 200.00
PS2 Ed Belfour 40.00 100.00
PS3 Martin Brodeur 75.00 200.00
PS4 Dominik Hasek 60.00 150.00
PS5 Chris Osgood 40.00 100.00
PS6 Curtis Joseph 40.00 80.00
PS7 Jeff Hackett 40.00 80.00
PS8 Mike Richter 25.00 60.00
PS9 Guy Hebert 30.00 80.00
PS10 Roberto Luongo 40.00 100.00
PS11 Roman Turek 40.00 100.00
PS12 Olaf Kolzig 30.00 80.00
PS13 Felix Potvin 60.00 125.00
PS14 Jocelyn Thibault 40.00 80.00
PS15 Brian Boucher 25.00 60.00

2000-01 BAP Ultimate Memorabilia Journey Jerseys

This 20-card set features game-used jersey swatches of players who played for at least two different franchises during their career. Each card carries a swatch of the player's jersey for both teams depicted as well as photos of the player in each team's jersey. Each card was sealed in a clear plastic slab with a descriptive label at the top. Stated print run on these cards was 50 sets.

ANNOUNCED PRINT RUN 50
JJ1 Wayne Gretzky 150.00 350.00
JJ2 Mark Messier 25.00 60.00
JJ3 Pavel Bure 20.00 50.00
JJ4 Jeff Hackett 20.00 50.00
JJ5 Mats Sundin 20.00 50.00
JJ6 Curtis Joseph 20.00 50.00
JJ7 Ed Belfour 20.00 50.00
JJ8 Mike Modano 20.00 50.00
JJ9 Brett Hull 25.00 60.00
JJ10 Teemu Selanne 20.00 50.00
JJ11 Keith Tkachuk 20.00 50.00
JJ12 Patrick Roy 125.00 300.00
JJ13 Chris Chelios 20.00 50.00
JJ14 Al MacInnis 20.00 50.00
JJ15 Theo Fleury 25.00 60.00
JJ16 Jason Allison 20.00 50.00
JJ17 Jeremy Roenick 25.00 60.00
JJ18 Brendan Shanahan 20.00 50.00
JJ19 Owen Nolan 15.00 40.00
JJ20 Felix Potvin 30.00 80.00

2000-01 BAP Ultimate Memorabilia Magnificent Ones

This 10-card set featured game-used jersey swatches from Mario Lemieux and another star player on each card. The cards carry a small headshot of Lemieux beside his jersey swatch on the right side of the card and an action shot of the other player on the left beside his jersey swatch. The words "Magnificent Ones" is printed across the top border. Each card was sealed in a clear plastic slab with a descriptive label at the top. Stated print run on these cards was 40 sets.

ANNOUNCED PRINT RUN 40
ML1 S.Yzerman/M.Lemieux 60.00 150.00
ML2 J.Jagr/M.Lemieux 50.00 120.00
ML3 M.Brodeur/M.Lemieux 60.00 150.00
ML4 M.Messier/M.Lemieux 40.00 100.00
ML5 P.Roy/M.Lemieux 50.00 120.00
ML6 R.Bourque/M.Lemieux 60.00 150.00
ML7 R.Francis/M.Lemieux 25.00 60.00
ML8 D.Hasek/M.Lemieux 60.00 150.00
ML9 W.Gretzky/M.Lemieux 125.00 300.00
ML10 P.Coffey/M.Lemieux 30.00 80.00

2000-01 BAP Ultimate Memorabilia Maurice Richard Autographs

This 5-card set remembers one of the greats of the game, Rocket Richard. Each card features a photo of Richard and a cut autograph. The autographs were originally on 8x10 reprints of Richard's 1953-54 Parkhurst card. In the Game, Inc. obtained the autographs through a private signing with Richard. The autographs were then cut and affixed to the cards in this set as swatches. Each card was sealed in a clear plastic slab with a descriptive label at the top. Stated print run on these cards was 10 sets.

R1 Maurice Richard 200.00 400.00
R2 Maurice Richard 200.00 400.00
R3 Maurice Richard 200.00 400.00
R4 Maurice Richard 200.00 400.00
R5 Maurice Richard 200.00 400.00

2000-01 BAP Ultimate Memorabilia NHL Records

This 10-card set recognized 10 different players who hold various NHL records. Each card featured a photo and a swatch of game-used jersey of that player. A brief explanation of the record was on the back of each card. Each card was sealed in a clear plastic slab with a descriptive label at the top. Stated print run on these cards was 30 sets.

ANNOUNCED PRINT RUN 30
R1 Terry Sawchuk 50.00 120.00
R2 Patrick Roy 40.00 100.00
R3 Tony Esposito 25.00 60.00
R4 Jacques Plante 40.00 100.00
R5 Bill Mosienko 25.00 60.00
R6 Teemu Selanne 25.00 60.00
R7 Mario Lemieux 40.00 100.00
R8 Ray Bourque 30.00 80.00
R9 Gordie Howe 40.00 100.00
R10 Wayne Gretzky 60.00 150.00

2000-01 BAP Ultimate Memorabilia Norris Trophy

This 10-card set featured game-used jersey swatches of winners of the Norris trophy. The cards carried an action photo of the given player, a picture of the Norris trophy, and a square piece of jersey. Each card was sealed in a clear plastic slab with a descriptive label at the top. Stated print run on these cards was 50 sets.

ANNOUNCED PRINT RUN 50
N1 Chris Pronger 15.00 40.00
N2 Al MacInnis 20.00 50.00
N3 Rob Blake 15.00 40.00
N4 Brian Leetch 15.00 40.00
N5 Chris Chelios 20.00 50.00
N6 Paul Coffey 20.00 50.00
N7 Ray Bourque 30.00 80.00
N8 Chris Chelios 20.00 50.00
N9 Brian Leetch 15.00 40.00
N10 Ray Bourque 30.00 80.00

2000-01 BAP Ultimate Memorabilia Retro-Active

This 10-card set featured a player from the past and from the present who have both won the same award. Each card carries a photo of each player along side a game-used jersey swatch of each. A photo of the shared award is in the middle of the two swatches. Each card was sealed in a clear plastic slab with a descriptive label at the top. Stated print run on these cards was 30 sets.

ANNOUNCED PRINT RUN 30
RA1 G.Howe/C.Pronger 40.00 100.00
RA2 T.Sawchuk/P.Roy 100.00 200.00
RA3 T.Esposito/M.Lemieux 40.00 100.00
RA4 T.Esposito/E.Belfour 30.00 80.00
RA5 B.Parent/S.Yzerman 50.00 125.00
RA6 G.Howe/M.Lemieux 100.00 200.00
RA7 B.Mosienko/P.Kariya 40.00 100.00
RA8 J.Plante/P.Roy 100.00 200.00
RA9 G.Howe/J.Jagr 40.00 100.00
RA10 W.Gretzky/M.Messier 150.00 400.00

2000-01 BAP Ultimate Memorabilia Teammates

ANNOUNCED PRINT RUN 70
TM1 S.Yzerman/S.Fedorov 20.00 50.00
TM2 B.Shanahan/S.Kozlov 12.00 30.00
TM3 S.Yzerman/C.Chelios 20.00 50.00
TM4 S.Yzerman/B.Shanahan 30.00 80.00
TM5 J.Roenick/K.Tkachuk 12.00 30.00
TM6 N.Lidstom/S.Fedorov 15.00 40.00
TM7 N.Lidstrom/C.Osgood 12.00 30.00
TM8 N.Lidstrom/B.Shanahan 15.00 40.00
TM9 C.Osgood/S.Fedorov 12.00 30.00
TM10 N.Khabibulin/J.Roenick 8.00 20.00
TM11 S.Gonchar/A.Oates 8.00 20.00
TM12 C.Joseph/M.Sundin 12.00 30.00
TM13 C.Joseph/T.Domi 8.00 20.00
TM14 M.Sundin/T.Domi 8.00 20.00
TM15 P.Forsberg/P.Roy 40.00 100.00
TM16 P.Forsberg/J.Sakic 20.00 50.00
TM17 J.Sakic/P.Roy 40.00 100.00
TM18 B.Mironov/T.Amonte 8.00 20.00
TM19 P.Bure/P.Laus 8.00 20.00
TM20 M.Peca/D.Hasek 15.00 40.00
TM21 P.Kariya/T.Selanne 15.00 40.00
TM22 T.Selanne/G.Hebert 8.00 20.00
TM23 P.Kariya/G.Hebert 8.00 20.00
TM24 B.Hull/M.Modano 15.00 40.00
TM25 B.Hull/E.Belfour 12.00 30.00
TM26 E.Belfour/M.Modano 15.00 40.00
TM27 S.Zubov/E.Belfour 8.00 20.00
TM28 B.Hull/D.Sydor 8.00 20.00
TM29 E.Desjardins/J.LeClair 8.00 20.00
TM30 J.Arnott/M.Brodeur 15.00 40.00
TM31 S.Yzerman/M.Vernon 20.00 50.00
TM32 B.Hull/C.Joseph 20.00 50.00
TM33 K.Tkachuk/T.Selanne 12.00 30.00
TM34 M.Sundin/O.Nolan 12.00 30.00
TM35 E.Belfour/C.Chelios 12.00 30.00
TM36 M.Messier/W.Gretzky 100.00 250.00
TM37 T.Fleury/A.MacInnis 10.00 25.00
TM38 F.Potvin/M.Sundin 15.00 40.00
TM39 M.Lemieux/J.Jagr 40.00 100.00
TM40 R.Bourque/A.Oates 20.00 50.00

2001-02 BAP Ultimate Memorabilia Active Eight

All cards in this product were graded by Beckett Grading Services and available only in graded form. Due to the various amount of grading ranges, only a median price for Mint/NmMt+ copies was assigned below.

STATED PRINT RUN 30 SER.#'d SETS
1 Kariya/Lemieux/Sakic 60.00 150.00
2 Roy/Vernon/Barrasso 50.00 100.00
3 Francis/Messier/Yzerman 40.00 100.00
4 Lemieux/Robitaille/Jagr 50.00 125.00
5 Messier/Hull/Lemieux 60.00 150.00
6 Selanne/Nieuwendyk/Robitaille 40.00 100.00
7 Messier/Francis/Stevens 40.00 100.00
8 Lemieux/Sundin/Yzerman 40.00 100.00

2001-02 BAP Ultimate Memorabilia All-Star History

STATED PRINT RUN 40 SER.#'d SETS
1 Turk Broda 20.00 50.00
2 Frank Brimsek 15.00 40.00
3 Ted Kennedy 15.00 40.00
4 Maurice Richard 60.00 120.00
5 Chuck Rayner 15.00 40.00
6 Bill Mosienko 15.00 40.00
7 Jean Beliveau 30.00 80.00
8 Doug Harvey 15.00 40.00
9 Ted Lindsay 15.00 40.00
10 Henri Richard 20.00 50.00
11 Jacques Plante 30.00 80.00
12 Glenn Hall 15.00 40.00
13 Terry Sawchuk 40.00 100.00
14 Bobby Hull 15.00 40.00
15 Johnny Bower 15.00 40.00
16 Tim Horton 40.00 100.00
17 Johnny Bucyk 12.50 30.00
18 Stan Mikita 15.00 40.00
19 Bill Gadsby 15.00 40.00
20 Gordie Howe 40.00 100.00
21 Ed Giacomin 15.00 40.00
22 Bernie Parent 40.00 80.00
23 Bobby Clarke 15.00 40.00
24 Gilbert Perreault 12.50 30.00
25 Frank Mahovlich 15.00 40.00
26 Tony Esposito 25.00 60.00
27 Denis Potvin 15.00 40.00
28 Guy Lafleur 25.00 60.00
29 Bryan Trottier 15.00 40.00
30 Lanny McDonald 12.50 30.00
31 Marcel Dionne 15.00 40.00
32 Wayne Gretzky 80.00 200.00
33 Mike Bossy 15.00 40.00
34 Mark Messier 15.00 40.00
35 Paul Coffey 25.00 60.00
36 Steve Yzerman 40.00 100.00
37 Mario Lemieux 40.00 100.00
38 Grant Fuhr 15.00 40.00
39 Patrick Roy 40.00 100.00
40 Brett Hull 25.00 60.00
41 Brian Leetch 15.00 40.00
42 Jeremy Roenick 20.00 50.00
43 Jaromir Jagr 25.00 60.00
44 Luc Robitaille 15.00 40.00
45 Joe Sakic 30.00 80.00
46 Eric Lindros 15.00 40.00
47 Paul Kariya 15.00 40.00
48 Mike Modano 15.00 40.00
49 Peter Forsberg 25.00 60.00
50 Pavel Bure 15.00 40.00
51 Milan Hejduk 15.00 40.00
52 Mats Sundin 15.00 40.00

2001-02 BAP Ultimate Memorabilia Autographs

STATED PRINT RUN 20-40
1 Alexei Yashin/40 15.00 40.00
2 Brian Leetch/40 25.00 60.00
3 Daniel Alfredsson/40 15.00 40.00
4 Keith Tkachuk/40 25.00 60.00
5 Milan Hejduk/40 25.00 60.00
6 Mark Recchi/40 15.00 40.00
7 Paul Kariya/40 25.00 60.00
8 Scott Stevens/40 15.00 40.00
9 Joe Sakic/40 40.00 100.00
10 Al MacInnis/30 15.00 40.00
11 Peter Bondra/40 15.00 40.00
12 John LeClair/40 25.00 60.00
13 Brendan Shanahan/40 25.00 60.00
14 Rob Blake/40 15.00 40.00
15 Luc Robitaille/40 15.00 40.00
16 Jarome Iginla/40 30.00 80.00
17 Pavel Bure/40 25.00 60.00
18 Marcel Dionne/40 15.00 40.00
19 Gordie Howe/40 50.00 125.00
20 Phil Esposito/40 15.00 40.00
21 Guy Lafleur/40 30.00 80.00
22 Gilbert Perreault/40 15.00 40.00
23 Bobby Hull/40 30.00 80.00
24 Jean Beliveau/40 25.00 60.00
25 Stan Mikita/40 30.00 80.00
26 Ted Lindsay/20 25.00 60.00
27 Frank Mahovlich/30 25.00 60.00
28 Mario Lemieux/30 100.00 250.00
29 Tony Amonte/30 15.00 40.00
30 Jeremy Roenick/30 30.00 80.00
31 Owen Nolan/40 15.00 40.00
32 Mark Messier/40 40.00 100.00
33 Steve Yzerman/40 60.00 120.00
34 Sergei Fedorov/40 30.00 80.00
35 Wayne Gretzky/30 200.00 400.00

2001-02 BAP Ultimate Memorabilia Calder Trophy

STATED PRINT RUN 30 SER.#'d SETS
1 Evgeni Nabokov 15.00 40.00
2 Scott Gomez 15.00 40.00
3 Chris Drury 10.00 25.00
4 Sergei Samsonov 15.00 40.00
5 Bryan Berard 10.00 25.00
6 Daniel Alfredsson 15.00 40.00
7 Peter Forsberg 25.00 60.00
8 Martin Brodeur 40.00 100.00
9 Teemu Selanne 20.00 50.00
10 Pavel Bure 20.00 50.00
11 Ed Belfour 20.00 50.00
12 Tom Barrasso 15.00 40.00
13 Brian Leetch 15.00 40.00
14 Joe Nieuwendyk 15.00 40.00
15 Luc Robitaille 15.00 40.00
16 Mario Lemieux 40.00 100.00
17 Dale Hawerchuk 15.00 40.00
18 Mike Bossy 20.00 50.00
19 Bryan Trottier 15.00 40.00
20 Denis Potvin 20.00 50.00
21 Gilbert Perreault 15.00 40.00
22 Tony Esposito 20.00 50.00
23 Glenn Hall 20.00 50.00
24 Terry Sawchuk 40.00 100.00
25 Frank Brimsek 20.00 50.00

2001-02 BAP Ultimate Memorabilia Decades

STATED PRINT RUN 50 SER.#'d SETS
1 Chuck Rayner 20.00 50.00
2 Frank Brimsek 20.00 50.00
3 Terry Sawchuk 40.00 100.00
4 Jacques Plante 50.00 125.00
5 Doug Harvey 20.00 50.00
6 Bill Gadsby 20.00 50.00
7 Gordie Howe 40.00 100.00
8 Ted Lindsay 20.00 50.00
9 Johnny Bower 20.00 50.00
10 Glenn Hall 20.00 50.00
11 Bobby Hull 25.00 60.00
12 Stan Mikita 20.00 50.00
13 Tony Esposito 25.00 60.00
14 Gerry Cheevers 20.00 50.00
15 Guy Lafleur 25.00 60.00
16 Bobby Clarke 20.00 50.00
17 Denis Potvin 20.00 50.00
18 Serge Savard 20.00 50.00
19 Patrick Roy 40.00 100.00
20 Grant Fuhr 20.00 50.00
21 Larry Robinson 20.00 50.00
22 Al MacInnis 20.00 50.00
23 Cam Neely 30.00 80.00
24 Mike Bossy 20.00 50.00

2001-02 BAP Ultimate Memorabilia Dynamic Duos

STATED PRINT RUN 30 SER.#'d SETS
1 M.Modano/W.Gretzky 50.00 125.00
2 J.Jagr/J.LeClair 20.00 50.00
3 L.Robitaille/J.Sakic 25.00 60.00
4 M.Hejduk/B.Hull 25.00 60.00
5 P.Bure/Yahsin 20.00 50.00
6 S.Yzerman/M.Sundin 30.00 80.00
7 P.Kariya/P.Forsberg 25.00 60.00
8 Selanne/Shanahan 20.00 50.00
9 M.Messier/J.Iginla 25.00 60.00
10 Mogilny/Recchi 20.00 50.00
11 Bondra/Fleury 20.00 50.00
12 Roenick/Lemieux 60.00 150.00
13 E.Lindros/I.Kovalchuk 25.00 60.00
14 Tkachuk/Amonte 20.00 50.00
15 Weight/Alfredsson 20.00 50.00
16 Damphousse/Fedorov 20.00 50.00

2001-02 BAP Ultimate Memorabilia Dynasty Jerseys

STATED PRINT RUN 50 SER.#'d SETS
1 Bill Barber 20.00 50.00
2 Mike Bossy 20.00 50.00
3 Bobby Clarke 20.00 50.00
4 Yvan Cournoyer 20.00 50.00
5 Bob Gainey 20.00 50.00
6 Guy Lafleur 25.00 60.00
7 Guy Lapointe 20.00 50.00
8 Reggie Leach 20.00 50.00
9 Bob Nystrom 20.00 50.00
10 Bernie Parent 20.00 50.00
11 Denis Potvin 20.00 50.00
12 Larry Robinson 20.00 50.00
13 Serge Savard 20.00 50.00
14 Dave Schultz 20.00 50.00
15 Steve Shutt 20.00 50.00
16 Billy Smith 20.00 50.00
17 Bryan Trottier 20.00 50.00
18 Joe Watson 20.00 50.00

2001-02 BAP Ultimate Memorabilia 500 Goal Scorers

STATED PRINT RUN 10-30
1 Wayne Gretzky/10
2 Gordie Howe/10
3 Mario Lemieux/10
4 Bobby Hull/10
5 Mike Bossy/30 20.00 50.00
6 Guy Lafleur/30 30.00 80.00
7 Jean Beliveau/10
8 Stan Mikita/30 20.00 50.00
9 Marcel Dionne/30 20.00 50.00
10 Phil Esposito/30 30.00 80.00
11 Frank Mahovlich/10
12 Mark Messier/30 20.00 50.00
13 Steve Yzerman/30 60.00 150.00
14 Brett Hull/30 40.00 100.00
15 Mike Gartner/30 20.00 50.00
16 Bryan Trottier/30 20.00 50.00
17 Gilbert Perreault/30 20.00 50.00
18 Lanny McDonald/30 25.00 60.00
19 Jari Kurri/30 30.00 80.00
20 Dale Hawerchuk/30 20.00 50.00
21 Luc Robitaille/30 20.00 50.00
22 Dave Andreychuk/30 20.00 50.00
23 John Bucyk/30 25.00 60.00
24 Michel Goulet/30 20.00 50.00
25 Joe Mullen/30 20.00 50.00
26 Dino Ciccarelli/30 20.00 50.00
27 Pat Verbeek/30 20.00 50.00
28 Maurice Richard/10
29 Ron Francis/30 20.00 50.00
30 Brendan Shanahan/30 30.00 80.00

2001-02 BAP Ultimate Memorabilia 500 Goal Scorers Autographs

ANNOUNCED PRINT RUN 10-30
1 Bobby Hull/25 75.00 150.00
2 Bryan Trottier/15 15.00 40.00
3 Dale Hawerchuk/25 30.00 60.00
4 Dave Andreychuk/30 30.00 60.00
6 Frank Mahovlich/25 40.00 100.00
7 Gilbert Perreault/15
8 Guy Lafleur/20 40.00 80.00
9 Jari Kurri/20
10 Jean Beliveau/15 40.00 80.00
11 John Bucyk/25 30.00 60.00
12 Lanny McDonald/20 25.00 50.00
13 Luc Robitaille/15
14 Marcel Dionne/25 30.00 60.00
16 Michel Goulet/30 25.00 50.00
17 Mike Bossy/25 50.00 125.00
18 Mike Gartner/30 30.00 60.00
19 Gordie Howe/20
21 Phil Esposito/15 60.00 100.00
23 Stan Mikita/25 30.00 60.00
24 Steve Yzerman/15
25 Joe Mullen/20 15.00 40.00

2001-02 BAP Ultimate Memorabilia 500 Goal Scorers Jerseys and Sticks

*JSY/STICK/40: .5X TO 1.2X JSY/30
STATED PRINT RUN 20-40
7 Jean Beliveau/40 25.00 60.00
11 Frank Mahovlich/40 25.00 60.00

2001-02 BAP Ultimate Memorabilia Gloves Are Off

STATED PRINT RUN 30 SER.#'d SETS
1 Rocket Richard 30.00 80.00
2 Gordie Howe 40.00 100.00
3 Mario Lemieux 30.00 80.00
4 Wayne Gretzky 40.00 100.00
5 Bill Gadsby 20.00 50.00
6 Doug Harvey 15.00 40.00
7 Ted Kennedy 20.00 50.00
8 King Clancy 25.00 60.00
9 Joe Sakic 30.00 80.00
10 Guy Lafleur 25.00 60.00
11 Eric Lindros 15.00 40.00
13 Mats Sundin 15.00 40.00
14 Al MacInnis 15.00 40.00
15 Doug Weight 15.00 40.00
16 Simon Gagne 15.00 40.00
17 Scott Niedermayer 15.00 40.00
18 Sergei Samsonov 15.00 40.00
19 Alexei Yashin 15.00 40.00
20 John LeClair 15.00 40.00
21 Sergei Fedorov 25.00 60.00
22 Chris Chelios 15.00 40.00
23 Jarome Iginla 25.00 60.00
24 Ace Bailey 30.00 80.00
25 Dickie Moore 15.00 40.00

2001-02 BAP Ultimate Memorabilia Jerseys

STATED PRINT RUN 50 SER.#'d SETS
*JSY-STICK/50: .5X TO 1.2X JSY/50
1 Paul Kariya 12.50 30.00
2 Martin Brodeur 25.00 60.00
3 John LeClair 12.50 30.00
4 Ilya Kovalchuk 15.00 40.00
5 Bill Guerin 10.00 25.00
6 Dominik Hasek 15.00 40.00
7 Keith Tkachuk 12.50 30.00
8 Pavel Bure 12.50 30.00
9 Brian Leetch 10.00 25.00
10 Mario Lemieux 25.00 60.00
11 Mats Sundin 12.50 30.00
12 Owen Nolan 10.00 25.00
13 Mark Messier 12.50 30.00
14 Jaromir Jagr 15.00 40.00
15 Joe Sakic 20.00 50.00
16 Rob Blake 10.00 25.00
17 Brendan Shanahan 12.50 30.00
18 Eric Lindros 12.50 30.00
19 Mike Modano 15.00 40.00
20 Sergei Fedorov 15.00 40.00
21 Nicklas Lidstrom 12.50 30.00
22 Steve Yzerman 25.00 60.00
23 Teemu Selanne 12.50 30.00
24 Alexei Yashin 10.00 25.00
25 Doug Weight 10.00 25.00
26 Chris Pronger 10.00 25.00
27 Patrick Roy 25.00 60.00
28 Curtis Joseph 12.50 30.00
29 Jeremy Roenick 15.00 40.00
30 Luc Robitaille 10.00 25.00

2001-02 BAP Ultimate Memorabilia Journey Jerseys

STATED PRINT RUN 50 SER.#'d SETS
1 Mark Messier 15.00 40.00
2 Curtis Joseph 15.00 40.00
3 Alexei Yashin 12.50 30.00
4 Gordie Howe 50.00 125.00
5 Felix Potvin 15.00 40.00
6 Rob Blake 12.50 30.00
7 Pavel Bure 20.00 50.00
8 Mats Sundin 15.00 40.00
9 Ed Belfour 15.00 40.00
10 Mike Modano 20.00 50.00
11 Brett Hull 20.00 50.00
12 Brendan Shanahan 15.00 40.00
13 Teemu Selanne 15.00 40.00
14 Keith Tkachuk 12.50 30.00
15 Patrick Roy 60.00 150.00
16 Luc Robitaille 15.00 40.00
17 Jeremy Roenick 20.00 50.00
18 Alexander Mogilny 12.50 30.00
19 Dominik Hasek 20.00 50.00
20 Jaromir Jagr 25.00 60.00
21 Roman Turek 12.50 30.00
22 Wayne Gretzky 150.00 350.00

2001-02 BAP Ultimate Memorabilia Legend Terry Sawchuk

All cards in this product were graded by Beckett Grading Services and were initially available only in graded form. Prices below reflect raw cards that have been broken out of the case or the most common lower tiered grades on the market. Cards in this 16-card set honored legendary goalie Terry Sawchuk by combining a swatch of his game-worn jersey with a swatch of game jersey from a current NHL goalie. Cards from this set were serial-numbered out of 20 on the back of the grading label but not on the card themselves. The cards were unnumbered and are listed below in checklist order.

1 Patrick Roy 40.00 80.00
Terry Sawchuk
2 Martin Brodeur 40.00 80.00
Terry Sawchuk
3 Dominik Hasek
Terry Sawchuk
4 Curtis Joseph
Terry Sawchuk
5 Nikolai Khabibulin
Terry Sawchuk
6 Johan Hedberg
Terry Sawchuk
7 Ed Belfour 20.00 40.00
Terry Sawchuk
8 Mike Richter 25.00 50.00
Terry Sawchuk
9 Felix Potvin 30.00 60.00
Terry Sawchuk
10 Tommy Salo
Terry Sawchuk
11 Roberto Luongo 20.00 40.00
Terry Sawchuk
12 Byron Dafoe
Terry Sawchuk
13 Jose Theodore
Terry Sawchuk
14 Jocelyn Thibault 20.00 40.00
Terry Sawchuk
15 Evgeni Nabokov 20.00 40.00
Terry Sawchuk
16 Olaf Kolzig 20.00 40.00
Terry Sawchuk

2001-02 BAP Ultimate Memorabilia Les Canadiens

STATED PRINT RUN 40 SER.#'d SETS
1 Mark Recchi 20.00 50.00
2 Yvan Cournoyer 20.00 50.00
3 Steve Shutt 20.00 50.00
4 Maurice Richard 75.00 200.00
5 Bob Gainey 25.00 60.00
6 Larry Robinson 20.00 50.00
7 Henri Richard 20.00 50.00
8 Jose Theodore 25.00 60.00
9 Saku Koivu 20.00 50.00
10 Patrick Roy 50.00 125.00
11 Jean Beliveau 30.00 80.00
12 Doug Harvey 20.00 50.00
13 Frank Mahovlich 20.00 50.00
14 Peter Mahovlich 20.00 50.00
15 Guy Lafleur 25.00 60.00
16 Serge Savard 20.00 50.00
17 Guy Lapointe 20.00 50.00
18 Jacques Plante 50.00 125.00

2001-02 BAP Ultimate Memorabilia Name Plates

STATED PRINT RUN 40-50
1 Wayne Gretzky LA/40 100.00 200.00
2 Mario Lemieux/50 40.00 100.00
3 Paul Kariya/40 15.00 40.00
4 Pavel Bure/40 15.00 40.00
5 Mats Sundin/40 15.00 40.00
6 Mark Recchi/40 10.00 25.00
7 Dominik Hasek/40 20.00 50.00
8 Luc Robitaille/50 10.00 25.00
9 Bill Guerin/50 10.00 25.00
10 Eric Lindros/50 15.00 40.00
11 Patrick Roy/40 30.00 80.00
12 Nikolai Khabibulin/50 15.00 40.00
13 Teemu Selanne/50 15.00 40.00
14 Mark Messier/50 15.00 40.00
15 Steve Yzerman/50 30.00 80.00
16 Brian Leetch/50 10.00 25.00
17 Owen Nolan/50 10.00 25.00
18 Jarome Iginla/50 20.00 50.00
19 Gordie Howe Aeros/50 30.00 80.00
20 Roman Cechmanek/50 10.00 25.00
21 Joe Thornton/50 20.00 50.00
22 Ilya Kovalchuk/50 20.00 50.00
23 Curtis Joseph/50 15.00 40.00
24 Jeremy Roenick/50 20.00 50.00
25 Keith Tkachuk/50 15.00 40.00
26 Joe Sakic/50 15.00 40.00
27 Jaromir Jagr/50 20.00 50.00
28 Rob Blake/40 10.00 25.00
29 Mike Modano/50 20.00 50.00
30 Martin Brodeur/50 30.00 80.00
31 Nicklas Lidstrom/50 15.00 40.00
32 John LeClair/50 15.00 40.00
33 Gordie Howe NE/50 30.00 80.00
34 Chris Pronger/50 10.00 25.00
35 Sergei Fedorov/50 20.00 50.00
36 Jason Arnott/50 10.00 25.00
37 Marcel Dionne/40 10.00 25.00
38 Phil Esposito/50 20.00 50.00

39 Wayne Gretzky NYR/50 75.00 200.00
40 Doug Weight/40 10.00 25.00

2001-02 BAP Ultimate Memorabilia Playoff Records

STATED PRINT RUN 10-50
1 Patrick Roy/50 20.00 50.00
2 Patrick Roy/50 20.00 50.00
3 Larry Robinson/50 12.00 30.00
4 Mark Messier/50 15.00 40.00
5 Wayne Gretzky/50 40.00 80.00
6 Reggie Leach/50 12.00 30.00
7 Jari Kurri/50 15.00 40.00
8 Jari Kurri/50 15.00 40.00
9 Wayne Gretzky/50 40.00 80.00
10 Wayne Gretzky/10
11 Wayne Gretzky/10
12 Wayne Gretzky/10
13 Wayne Gretzky/50 40.00 80.00
14 Wayne Gretzky/10
15 Mario Lemieux/50 30.00 60.00
16 Mike Bossy/50 12.00 30.00
17 Mark Messier/50 15.00 40.00
18 Wayne Gretzky/10
19 Joe Sakic/50 30.00 60.00
20 Maurice Richard/10

2001-02 BAP Ultimate Memorabilia Prototypical Players

STATED PRINT RUN 40 SER.#'d SETS
1 J.Plante/P.Roy 40.00 100.00
2 J.Plante/M.Brodeur 40.00 100.00
3 J.Plante/D.Hasek 40.00 100.00
4 D.Harvey/C.Pronger 20.00 50.00
5 D.Harvey/R.Blake 20.00 50.00
6 D.Harvey/N.Lidstrom 25.00 60.00
7 J.Beliveau/S.Yzerman 40.00 100.00
8 J.Beliveau/M.Lemieux 40.00 100.00
9 J.Beliveau/J.Sakic 25.00 60.00
10 Bo.Hull/L.Robitaille 25.00 60.00
11 Bo.Hull/P.Kariya 25.00 60.00
12 Bo.Hull/B.Shanahan 25.00 60.00
13 G.Howe/J.Jagr 30.00 80.00
14 G.Howe/P.Bure 25.00 60.00
15 G.Howe/Br. Hull 25.00 60.00

2001-02 BAP Ultimate Memorabilia Retro Trophies

STATED PRINT RUN 25 SER.#'d SETS
1 W.Gretzky/J.Sakic 60.00 150.00
2 G.Howe/J.Jagr 40.00 100.00
3 W.Gretzky/J.Jagr 60.00 150.00
4 W.Gretzky/M.Lemieux 75.00 200.00
5 B.Clarke/M.Lemieux 50.00 125.00
6 M.Bossy/J.Sakic 30.00 80.00
7 J.Kurri/P.Kariya 25.00 60.00
8 L.McDonald/C.Joseph 25.00 60.00
9 T.Sawchuk/D.Hasek 40.00 100.00
10 G.Hall/P.Roy 40.00 100.00
11 T.Sawchuk/E.Nabokov 30.00 80.00
12 T.Esposito/M.Brodeur 40.00 100.00
13 B.Clarke/S.Yzerman 30.00 80.00
14 G.Hall/P.Roy 30.00 80.00
15 B.Parent/P.Roy 40.00 80.00
16 W.Gretzky/M.Lemieux 75.00 200.00
17 G.Lafleur/M.Lemieux 50.00 125.00
18 D.Harvey/N.Lidstrom 25.00 60.00
19 W.Gretzky/M.Lemieux 75.00 200.00
20 G.Lafleur/J.Sakic 30.00 80.00

2001-02 BAP Ultimate Memorabilia Retro Teammates

STATED PRINT RUN 10-30
1 Beliveau/H.Richard/M.Richard/10
2 M.Richard/Plante/Harvey/10
3 Howe/Lindsay/Sawchuk/30 100.00 250.00
4 Gretzky/Messier/Coffey/10
5 Bossy/Trottier/Potvin/30 40.00 80.00
6 Clarke/Barber/Schultz/30 40.00 80.00
7 Hull/Hall/Mikita/30 75.00 150.00
8 Horton/Bower/Sawchuk/30 75.00 150.00
9 Lapointe/Savard/Mahovlich/30 40.00 80.00
10 Lafleur/Cournoyer/Beliveau/30 60.00 120.00
11 Lemieux/Coffey/Jagr/30 50.00 100.00
12 Gretzky/Leetch/Messier/30 125.00 250.00
13 Gretzky/Kurri/Robitaille/30 100.00 200.00
14 H.Richard/Harvey/M.Richard/10

2001-02 BAP Ultimate Memorabilia Scoring Leaders

STATED PRINT RUN 40 SER.#'d SETS
1 Wayne Gretzky 1982 75.00 150.00
2 Wayne Gretzky 1983 75.00 150.00
3 Wayne Gretzky 1984 75.00 150.00
4 Wayne Gretzky 1985 75.00 150.00
5 Jari Kurri 1986 25.00 60.00
6 Wayne Gretzky 1987 75.00 150.00
7 Mario Lemieux 1988 30.00 80.00
8 Mario Lemieux 1989 30.00 80.00
9 Brett Hull 1990 12.00 30.00
10 Brett Hull 1991 12.00 30.00
11 Brett Hull 1992 12.00 30.00
12 T.Selanne 15.00 40.00
A.Mogilny 1993
13 Pavel Bure 1994 15.00 40.00
14 Peter Bondra 1995 15.00 40.00
15 Mario Lemieux 1996 30.00 80.00
16 Keith Tkachuk 1997 15.00 40.00
17 T.Selanne 20.00 50.00
P.Bondra 1998
18 Teemu Selanne 1999 20.00 50.00
19 Pavel Bure 2000 15.00 40.00
20 Pavel Bure 2001 15.00 40.00
21 Jarome Iginla 2002 20.00 50.00

2001-02 BAP Ultimate Memorabilia Stanley Cup Winners

STATED PRINT RUN 10-50
1 Henri Richard 25.00 60.00
2 Jean Beliveau 30.00 80.00
3 Yvan Cournoyer 20.00 50.00
4 Red Kelly 20.00 50.00
5 Maurice Richard 60.00 150.00
6 Serge Savard 20.00 50.00
7 Jacques Plante/10
8 Johnny Bower 20.00 50.00
9 Bryan Trottier 20.00 50.00
10 Larry Robinson 20.00 50.00
11 Mark Messier 30.00 80.00
12 Jacques Laperriere 20.00 50.00
13 Doug Harvey 20.00 50.00
14 Frank Mahovlich 20.00 50.00
15 Guy Lapointe 12.00 30.00
16 Jari Kurri 25.00 60.00
17 Guy Lafleur 25.00 60.00
18 Bob Gainey 30.00 80.00
19 Grant Fuhr 20.00 50.00
20 Turk Broda/10
21 Ted Kennedy 20.00 50.00
22 Steve Shutt 20.00 50.00
23 Wayne Gretzky 75.00 200.00
24 Terry Sawchuk 40.00 100.00
25 Denis Potvin 20.00 50.00
26 Ted Lindsay 20.00 50.00
27 Billy Smith 20.00 50.00
28 Gordie Howe/10

2001-02 BAP Ultimate Memorabilia Waving the Flag

STATED PRINT RUN 30 SER.#'d SETS
1 Mario Lemieux 30.00 80.00
2 Joe Sakic 20.00 50.00
3 Steve Yzerman 25.00 60.00
4 Paul Kariya 15.00 40.00
5 Curtis Joseph 12.50 30.00
6 Martin Brodeur 25.00 60.00
7 Eric Lindros 12.50 30.00
8 Chris Pronger 10.00 25.00
9 Jaromir Jagr 15.00 40.00
10 Milan Hejduk 12.50 30.00
11 Dominik Hasek 20.00 50.00
12 Martin Havlat 10.00 25.00
13 Teemu Selanne 15.00 40.00
14 Jani Hurme 10.00 25.00
15 Miikka Kiprusoff 15.00 40.00
16 Sami Kapanen 10.00 25.00
17 Mats Sundin 12.50 30.00
18 Nicklas Lidstrom 12.50 30.00
19 Tommy Salo 10.00 25.00
20 Markus Naslund 12.50 30.00
21 Jeremy Roenick 15.00 40.00
22 Doug Weight 10.00 25.00
23 Tony Amonte 10.00 25.00
24 Brian Leetch 12.00 30.00
25 Mike Modano 15.00 40.00
26 Brett Hull 15.00 40.00
27 John Leclair 12.50 30.00
28 Keith Tkachuk 12.50 30.00
29 Alexei Yashin 10.00 25.00
30 Pavel Bure 12.50 30.00
31 Nikolai Khabibulin 12.50 30.00
32 Darius Kasparaitis 10.00 25.00

2002-03 BAP Ultimate Memorabilia

Released in May 2003, BAP Ultimate Memorabilia contained a BGS graded rookie, carrying a stated print run of 250, and an encapsulated memorabilia card per pack. The cards were not numbered and are listed below in original checklist order. Prices below generally reflect those of raw cards broken out of cases or BGS graded Mint 9 or lower.

COMPLETE SET (100)
1 P-M Bouchard 3.00 8.00
2 Rick Nash 15.00 40.00
3 Dennis Seidenberg 3.00 8.00
4 Jay Bouwmeester 6.00 15.00
5 Stanislav Chistov 2.00 5.00
6 Kurt Sauer 2.00 5.00
7 Ivan Majesky 2.00 5.00
8 Chuck Kobasew 2.50 6.00
9 Jordan Leopold 3.00 8.00
10 Steve Ott 4.00 10.00
11 Ales Hemsky 8.00 20.00
12 Patrick Sharp 6.00 15.00
13 Kari Haakana 2.00 5.00
14 Dmitri Bykov 2.00 5.00
15 Alex Henry 2.50 6.00
16 Henrik Zetterberg 20.00 50.00
17 Alexander Frolov 4.00 10.00
18 Steve Eminger 2.00 5.00
19 Scottie Upshall 2.50 6.00
20 Tom Koivisto 2.00 5.00
21 Ari Ahonen 2.00 5.00
22 Ron Hainsey 2.00 5.00
23 Martin Gerber 3.00 8.00
24 Adam Hall 2.00 5.00
25 Lasse Pirjeta 2.00 5.00
26 Anton Volchenkov 2.00 5.00
27 Jeff Paul 2.00 5.00
28 Carlo Colaiacovo 3.00 8.00
29 Alexander Svitov 2.00 5.00
30 Alexei Smirnov 2.50 6.00
31 Jeff Taffe 2.00 5.00
32 Mikael Tellqvist 2.00 5.00
33 Radovan Somik 2.00 5.00
34 Mike Komisarek 3.00 8.00
35 Chris Schmidt 2.00 5.00
36 Dick Tarnstrom 2.00 5.00
37 Ryan Bayda 2.00 5.00
38 Sylvain Blouin 2.00 5.00
39 Ray Emery 6.00 15.00
40 Stephane Veilleux 2.00 5.00
41 Curtis Sanford 3.00 8.00
42 Eric Godard 2.00 5.00
43 Pascal Leclaire 2.50 6.00
44 Patrick Boileau 2.00 5.00
45 Tim Thomas 8.00 20.00
46 Mike Cammalleri 6.00 15.00
47 Jason Spezza 12.00 30.00
48 Cody Rudkowsky 2.00 5.00
49 Darren Haydar 2.00 5.00
50 Ryan Miller 12.00 30.00
51 Brandon Reid 2.00 5.00
52 Christian Backman 2.00 5.00
53 Niko Dimitrakos 2.00 5.00
54 Garnet Exelby 2.00 5.00
55 Jason King 3.00 8.00
56 Martin Samuelsson 2.00 5.00
57 Miroslav Zalesak 2.00 5.00
58 Tomas Malec 2.00 5.00
59 Michael Garnett 2.00 5.00
60 Matt Walker 2.00 5.00
61 Shaone Morrisonn 2.00 5.00
62 Chad Wiseman 2.00 5.00
63 Michael Leighton 3.00 8.00
64 Tomas Surovy 2.00 5.00
65 Jason Bacashihua 2.50 6.00
66 Jim Vandermeer 2.00 5.00
67 Konstantin Koltsov 2.50 6.00
68 Fernando Pisani 2.00 5.00
69 Rickard Wallin 2.00 5.00
70 Brooks Orpik 3.00 8.00
71 Tomas Zizka 2.00 5.00
72 Jarret Stoll 8.00 20.00
73 Cristobal Huet 4.00 10.00
74 Levente Szuper 3.00 8.00
75 Jared Aulin 2.00 5.00
76 Simon Gamache 2.00 5.00
77 Kris Vernarsky 2.00 5.00
78 Radoslav Hecl 2.00 5.00
79 Jamie Hodson 2.00 5.00
80 Marc-Andre Bergeron 2.50 6.00
81 Mike Siklenka 5.00 12.00
82 Igor Radulov 2.00 5.00
83 Paul Manning 2.00 5.00
84 John Tripp 2.00 5.00
85 Ian MacNeil 2.00 5.00
86 Jim Fahey 2.00 5.00
87 Dany Sabourin 2.00 5.00
88 Alexei Semenov 2.00 5.00
89 Curtis Murphy 2.00 5.00
90 Jerred Smithson 2.00 5.00
91 Francois Beauchemin 3.00 8.00
92 Vernon Fiddler 2.50 6.00
93 Cam Severson 2.00 5.00
94 Burke Henry 2.00 5.00
95 Brad Defauw 2.00 5.00
96 Craig Andersson 6.00 15.00
97 Frederic Cloutier 2.00 5.00
98 Tomas Kurka 2.00 5.00
99 Jonathan Hedstrom 2.00 5.00
100 Valeri Kharlamov 6.00 15.00

2002-03 BAP Ultimate Memorabilia Active Eight

PRINT RUN 30 SER.#'d SETS
1 Messier/Francis/Yzerman 40.00 100.00
2 Lemieux/Forsberg/Oates 40.00 100.00
3 Roy/Belfour/Brodeur 50.00 120.00
4 Hull/Messier/Yzerman 40.00 100.00
5 Messier/Francis/Yzerman 40.00 100.00
6 Roy/Belfour/Joseph 50.00 120.00
7 Lemieux/Sakic/Leetch 50.00 120.00
8 Lemieux/Yzerman/Oates 60.00 150.00

2002-03 BAP Ultimate Memorabilia All-Star MVP

PRINT RUN 40 SER.#'d SETS
1 Bill Guerin 12.50 30.00
2 Bobby Hull 15.00 40.00
3 Bobby Hull 15.00 40.00
4 Brett Hull 20.00 50.00
5 Dany Heatley 15.00 40.00
6 Eric Daze 12.50 30.00
7 Frank Mahovlich 15.00 40.00
8 Grant Fuhr 15.00 40.00
9 Henri Richard 12.50 30.00
10 Jean Beliveau 25.00 60.00
11 Mario Lemieux 25.00 60.00
12 Mario Lemieux 25.00 60.00
13 Mario Lemieux 25.00 60.00
14 Mark Recchi 12.50 30.00
15 Mike Bossy 12.50 30.00
16 Mike Gartner 12.50 30.00
17 Mike Richter 12.50 30.00
18 Pavel Bure 12.50 30.00
19 Peter Mahovlich 15.00 40.00
20 Reggie Leach 12.50 30.00
21 Vincent Damphousse 12.50 30.00
22 Teemu Selanne 15.00 40.00

2002-03 BAP Ultimate Memorabilia Autographs

COMMON CARD (1-30) 12.50 30.00
PRINT RUN 30 SER.#'d SETS
1 Alexander Frolov 15.00 35.00
2 Alexei Smirnov 12.50 30.00
3 Anton Volchenkov 12.50 30.00
4 Carlo Colaiacovo 12.50 30.00
5 Chuck Kobasew 12.50 30.00
6 Jay Bouwmeester 20.00 50.00
7 Jordan Leopold 12.50 30.00
8 Mike Cammalleri 12.50 30.00
9 P-M Bouchard 15.00 35.00
10 Rick Nash 40.00 80.00
11 Ron Hainsey 12.50 30.00
12 Scottie Upshall 12.50 30.00
13 Stanislav Chistov 12.00 30.00
14 Sergei Fedorov 25.00 60.00
15 Patrick Roy 100.00 250.00
16 Mario Lemieux 100.00 250.00
17 Brian Leetch 20.00 50.00
18 Dany Heatley 20.00 50.00
19 Jarome Iginla 25.00 60.00
20 Joe Sakic 50.00 125.00
21 Joe Thornton 30.00 80.00
22 Jose Theodore 25.00 60.00
23 Pavel Bure 20.00 50.00
24 Peter Forsberg 40.00 100.00
25 Saku Koivu 20.00 50.00
26 Alexander Svitov 12.50 30.00
27 Stephane Veilleux 12.50 30.00
28 Adam Hall 12.50 30.00
29 Henrik Zetterberg 40.00 100.00
30 Steve Eminger 12.50 30.00

2002-03 BAP Ultimate Memorabilia Calder Candidates

COMMON CARD (1-20) 12.50 30.00
PRINT RUN 40 SER.#'d SETS
1 Henrik Zetterberg 30.00 80.00
2 Niko Kapanen 12.50 30.00
3 Ron Hainsey 12.50 30.00
4 Jason Spezza 30.00 80.00
5 Anton Volchenkov 12.50 30.00
6 Ivan Huml 12.50 30.00
7 Tyler Arnason 12.50 30.00
8 Dennis Seidenberg 12.50 30.00
9 Alexander Frolov 12.50 30.00
10 Alexei Smirnov 12.50 30.00
11 Jay Bouwmeester 15.00 30.00
12 Ales Hemsky 15.00 35.00
13 Rick Nash 30.00 80.00
14 Jordan Leopold 12.50 30.00
15 Stephen Weiss 12.50 30.00
16 Ryan Miller 20.00 30.00
17 Chuck Kobasew 12.50 30.00
18 Alexander Svitov 12.50 30.00
19 Adam Hall 12.50 30.00
20 Stanislav Chistov 12.50 30.00

2002-03 BAP Ultimate Memorabilia Conn Smythe

PRINT RUN 30 SER.#'d SETS
1 Jean Beliveau 30.00 80.00
2 Roger Crozier 15.00 40.00
3 Glenn Hall 20.00 50.00
4 Serge Savard 15.00 40.00
5 Yvan Cournoyer 15.00 40.00
6 Bernie Parent 20.00 50.00
7 Bernie Parent 20.00 50.00
8 Reggie Leach 15.00 40.00
9 Guy Lafleur 25.00 60.00
10 Larry Robinson 15.00 40.00
11 Bryan Trottier 15.00 40.00
12 Mike Bossy 15.00 40.00
13 Billy Smith 15.00 40.00
14 Mark Messier 25.00 60.00
15 Patrick Roy 40.00 100.00
16 Ron Hextall 20.00 50.00
17 Al MacInnis 15.00 40.00
18 Bill Ranford 15.00 40.00
19 Mario Lemieux 40.00 100.00
20 Mario Lemieux 40.00 100.00
21 Patrick Roy 40.00 100.00
22 Brian Leetch 20.00 50.00
23 Claude Lemieux 15.00 40.00
24 Joe Sakic 30.00 80.00
25 Mike Vernon 25.00 60.00
26 Steve Yzerman 30.00 80.00
27 Joe Nieuwendyk 15.00 40.00
28 Scott Stevens 15.00 40.00
29 Patrick Roy 40.00 100.00
30 Nicklas Lidstrom 20.00 40.00

2002-03 BAP Ultimate Memorabilia Cup Duels

STATED PRINT RUN 40 SER.#'d SETS
1 G.Hainsworth/T.Thompson 30.00 80.00
2 T.Sawchuk/J.Plante 60.00 150.00
3 J.Plante/J.Bower 25.00 60.00
4 G.Hall/T.Sawchuk 30.00 80.00
5 J.Bower/T.Sawchuk 25.00 60.00
6 R.Crozier/G.Worsley 15.00 40.00
7 G.Cheevers/E.Giacomin 15.00 40.00
8 G.Gilbert/B.Parent 15.00 40.00
9 B.Smith/G.Fuhr 15.00 40.00
10 P.Roy/M.Vernon 30.00 80.00
11 R.Hextall/G.Fuhr 15.00 40.00
12 A.Moog/G.Fuhr 20.00 50.00
13 P.Roy/M.Vernon 30.00 80.00
14 A.Moog/B.Ranford 15.00 40.00
15 T.Barrasso/E.Belfour 20.00 50.00
16 M.Brodeur/M.Vernon 30.00 80.00
17 J.Vanbiesbrouck/P.Roy 30.00 80.00
18 O.Kolzig/C.Osgood 20.00 50.00
19 M.Brodeur/E.Belfour 30.00 80.00
20 P.Roy/M.Brodeur 50.00 125.00

2002-03 BAP Ultimate Memorabilia Customer Appreciation

This special memorabilia card was only available to collectors who held a Henrik Zetterberg autograph redemption card. The card was sent back along with the autograph card as a token of appreciation. The card was serial-numbered to just 31 copies and was sealed in a plastic card slab.

1 Henrik Zetterberg 40.00 100.00

2002-03 BAP Ultimate Memorabilia Dynamic Duos

PRINT RUN 30 SER.#'d SETS
1 M.Lemieux/J.Thornton 25.00 60.00
2 P.Forsberg/M.Sundin 20.00 50.00
3 I.Kovalchuk/S.Fedorov 25.00 60.00
4 S.Yzerman/D.Heatley 30.00 80.00
5 M.Modano/B.Hull 25.00 60.00
6 B.Shanahan/P.Kariya 20.00 50.00
7 J.Sakic/E.Lindros 20.00 50.00
8 S.Koivu/T.Selanne 20.00 50.00
9 J.Jagr/M.Gaborik 25.00 60.00
10 P.Bure/S.Samsonov 20.00 50.00

2002-03 BAP Ultimate Memorabilia Dynasty Jerseys

COMMON CARD (1-20) 15.00 50.00
PRINT RUN 50 SER.#'d SETS
1 Brendan Shanahan 25.00 60.00
2 Brett Hull 30.00 80.00
3 Chris Chelios 25.00 60.00
4 Chris Osgood 15.00 40.00
5 Darren McCarty 15.00 50.00
6 Igor Larionov 15.00 50.00
7 Jiri Fischer 15.00 50.00
8 Kirk Maltby 15.00 40.00
9 Kris Draper 15.00 50.00
10 Luc Robitaille 20.00 50.00
11 Manny Legace 20.00 50.00
12 Martin Lapointe 15.00 50.00
13 Mathieu Dandenault 15.00 40.00
14 Mike Vernon 20.00 50.00
15 Nicklas Lidstrom 25.00 60.00
16 Pavel Datsyuk 25.00 60.00
17 Sergei Fedorov 25.00 60.00
18 Steve Yzerman 40.00 100.00
19 Tomas Holmstrom 20.00 50.00
20 Slava Kozlov 15.00 40.00

2002-03 BAP Ultimate Memorabilia Finals Showdown

This 40-card set featured jersey swatches from players who have faced off in the finals in years past. Cards were serial-numbered to just 40 and each card was encapsulated in a clear plastic slab with a descriptive label encased at the top. The set is unnumbered and listed below in checklist order.

PRINT RUN 40 SER.#'d SETS
1 A.Delvecchio/D.Harvey 20.00 50.00
2 B.Geoffrion/T.Lindsay 20.00 50.00
3 H.Richard/T.Horton 30.00 80.00
4 M.Richard/F.Mahovlich 40.00 100.00
5 S.Mikita/T.Sawchuk 30.00 80.00
6 F.Mahovlich/B.Hull 20.00 50.00
7 R.Kelly/T.Sawchuk 25.00 60.00
8 T.Horton/A.Delvecchio 30.00 80.00
9 J.Beliveau/G.Hall 20.00 50.00
10 J.Beliveau/R.Crozier 20.00 50.00
11 J.Bower/J.Ferguson 20.00 50.00
12 P.Mahovlich/B.Hull 20.00 50.00
13 G.Cheevers/R.Gilbert 20.00 50.00
14 Y.Cournoyer/B.Hull 20.00 50.00
15 B.Parent/J.Bucyk 20.00 50.00
16 B.Clarke/G.Perreault 20.00 50.00
17 S.Shutt/D.Schultz 20.00 50.00
18 G.Lapointe/G.Cheevers 20.00 50.00
19 L.Robinson/G.Cheevers 15.00 40.00
20 G.Lafleur/P.Esposito 40.00 100.00
21 B.Smith/B.Clarke 25.00 60.00
22 B.Trottier/G.Fuhr 25.00 60.00
23 M.Messier/D.Potvin 20.00 50.00
24 P.Roy/L.McDonald 30.00 80.00
25 J.Kurri/R.Hextall 30.00 80.00
26 K.Lowe/C.Neely 20.00 50.00
27 A.MacInnis/P.Roy 30.00 80.00
28 M.Messier/C.Neely 20.00 50.00
29 M.Lemieux/M.Modano 40.00 100.00
30 J.Jagr/J.Roenick 25.00 60.00
31 P.Roy/L.Robitaille 30.00 80.00
32 M.Messier/P.Bure 30.00 80.00
33 M.Brodeur/S.Yzerman 40.00 100.00
34 P.Roy/R.Niedermayer 40.00 100.00
35 S.Yzerman/E.Lindros 40.00 100.00
36 S.Fedorov/O.Kolzig 20.00 50.00
37 B.Hull/M.Peca 20.00 50.00
38 J.Arnott/E.Belfour 20.00 50.00
39 J.Sakic/M.Brodeur 30.00 80.00
40 N.Lidstrom/R.Francis 20.00 50.00

2002-03 BAP Ultimate Memorabilia 500 Goal Scorers

This 3-card set honored the 3 latest players to hit the 500 goal mark. Cards were serial-numbered to just 30 and each card was encapsulated in a clear plastic slab with a descriptive label encased at the top. The set is unnumbered and listed below in checklist order.

PRINT RUN 30 SER.#'d SETS
1 Joe Nieuwendyk 15.00 40.00
2 Joe Sakic 30.00 80.00
3 Jaromir Jagr 25.00 60.00

2002-03 BAP Ultimate Memorabilia 500 Goal Scorers Jersey and Stick

This 3-card set paralleled the regular insert set but included piece of stick with the swatch of jersey. Cards were serial-numbered to just 30 and were encapsulated in a clear plastic holder with a descriptive label encased at the top. Cards were unnumbered and are listed in checklist order.

*JSY/STK: .5X TO 1.25X JERSEY
PRINT RUN 30 SER.#'d SETS
1 Joe Nieuwendyk 20.00 50.00
2 Joe Sakic 40.00 100.00
3 Jaromir Jagr 30.00 80.00

2002-03 BAP Ultimate Memorabilia Global Dominators

This 10-card set featured game-worn jersey swatches of players who regularly represent their nation in competition. Cards were serial-numbered to just 30 and each card was encapsulated in a clear plastic slab with a descriptive label encased at the top. The set is unnumbered and listed below in checklist order. Unpriced gold one of ones were also created.

COMMON CARD (1-10) 15.00 40.00
PRINT RUN 30 SER.#'d SETS
1 Mario Lemieux 40.00 100.00
2 Al MacInnis 10.00 25.00
3 Rob Blake 15.00 40.00
4 Peter Forsberg 15.00 40.00
5 Igor Larionov 15.00 40.00
6 Joe Sakic 30.00 80.00
7 Steve Yzerman 40.00 100.00
8 Alexander Mogilny 15.00 40.00
9 Theo Fleury 15.00 40.00
10 Brendan Shanahan 20.00 50.00

2002-03 BAP Ultimate Memorabilia Gloves Are Off

COMMON CARD (1-20) 15.00 40.00
PRINT RUN 30 SER.#'d SETS
1 Ace Bailey 40.00 100.00
2 Mario Lemieux 30.00 80.00
3 Joe Sakic 20.00 50.00
4 Aurel Joliat 40.00 100.00
5 Guy Lafleur 30.00 80.00
6 Al MacInnis 15.00 40.00
7 Dickie Moore 15.00 40.00
8 Chris Chelios 15.00 40.00
9 Sergei Fedorov 20.00 50.00
10 Eddie Shore 20.00 50.00
11 Ted Kennedy 25.00 60.00
12 Eric Lindros 15.00 40.00
13 Mats Sundin 15.00 40.00
14 Doug Harvey 12.00 30.00
15 Bill Gadsby 20.00 50.00
16 Jarome Iginla 20.00 50.00
17 Joe Thornton 20.00 50.00
18 Maurice Richard 30.00 80.00
19 Brett Hull 15.00 40.00
20 King Clancy 25.00 60.00

2002-03 BAP Ultimate Memorabilia Great Moments

This 17-card set reflected on some of the best moments in NHL history and included pieces of game-used memorabilia from the featured play. Cards were serial-numbered to just 30 unless otherwise noted below and each card was encapsulated in a clear plastic slab with a descriptive label encased at the top. The set is unnumbered and listed below in checklist order.

COMMON CARD (1-20) 25.00 60.00
PRINT RUN 30 SER.#'d SETS/
1 Teeder Kennedy/10
2 E.Shore/A.Bailey/10
3 M.Richard/J.Henry/10
4 Mario Lemieux 50.00 125.00
5 Darryl Sittler/27 50.00 125.00
6 Bill Barilko/10
7 Frank Brimsek 25.00 60.00
8 Teemu Selanne 25.00 60.00
9 Mark Messier 25.00 60.00
10 Patrick Roy 50.00 125.00
11 Jacques Plante 30.00 80.00
12 Jean Beliveau 30.00 80.00
13 Glenn Hall 25.00 60.00
14 M.Richard/Five Playoff Goals 40.00 100.00
15 George Hainsworth/20
16 M.Richard/Habs 5th Cup 40.00 100.00
17 Bill Mosienko 25.00 60.00
18 M.Richard/Fifty in Fifty 40.00 100.00
19 Terry Sawchuk 40.00 100.00
20 Stan Mikita 25.00 60.00

2002-03 BAP Ultimate Memorabilia Hat Tricks

This 20-card set featured 3 different swatches of game-used memorabilia from the featured player. Cards were serial-numbered to just 30 and each card was encapsulated in a clear plastic slab with a descriptive label encased at the top. The set is unnumbered and listed below in checklist order.

COMMON CARD (1-20) 10.00 25.00
UNLISTED STARS 15.00 40.00
PRINT RUN 30 SER.#'d SETS
1 Simon Gagne 20.00 50.00
2 John LeClair 15.00 40.00
3 Adam Deadmarsh 10.00 25.00
4 Jeff O'Neill 10.00 25.00
5 Keith Tkachuk 15.00 40.00
6 Joe Thornton 25.00 60.00
7 Rob Blake 10.00 25.00
8 Alexei Yashin 10.00 25.00
9 Sergei Fedorov 25.00 60.00
10 Mario Lemieux 60.00 150.00
11 Jarome Iginla 25.00 60.00
12 Doug Weight 15.00 40.00
13 Brett Hull 30.00 80.00
14 Joe Sakic 50.00 125.00
15 Sergei Samsonov 10.00 25.00
16 Al MacInnis 15.00 40.00
17 Eric Lindros 20.00 50.00
18 Steve Yzerman 60.00 150.00
19 Mats Sundin 20.00 50.00
20 Chris Chelios 20.00 50.00

2002-03 BAP Ultimate Memorabilia Jerseys

COMMON CARD (1-40) 10.00 25.00
PRINT RUN 50 SER.#'d SETS
1 Bill Guerin 10.00 25.00
2 Jarome Iginla 20.00 50.00
3 Jose Theodore 15.00 40.00
4 Mario Lemieux 30.00 80.00
5 Martin Brodeur 20.00 50.00
6 Brendan Shanahan 25.00 60.00
7 Brett Hull 20.00 50.00
8 Dany Heatley 12.50 30.00
9 Ed Belfour 8.00 20.00
10 Eric Lindros 10.00 25.00
11 Ilya Kovalchuk 15.00 40.00
12 Jaromir Jagr 15.00 40.00
13 Jason Spezza 15.00 40.00
14 Jay Bouwmeester 15.00 40.00
15 Jeremy Roenick 12.50 30.00
16 Joe Sakic 15.00 40.00
17 Joe Thornton 15.00 40.00
18 John LeClair 10.00 25.00
19 Marian Gaborik 20.00 50.00
20 Marian Hossa 10.00 25.00
21 Mark Messier 10.00 25.00
22 Markus Naslund 10.00 25.00
23 Marty Turco 10.00 25.00
24 Mats Sundin 10.00 25.00
25 Mike Modano 12.50 30.00
26 Milan Hejduk 10.00 25.00
27 Nicklas Lidstrom 15.00 40.00
28 Patrick Roy 30.00 75.00
29 Paul Kariya 10.00 25.00
30 Pavel Bure 10.00 25.00
31 Peter Forsberg 25.00 60.00
32 Rick Nash 25.00 60.00
33 Saku Koivu 10.00 25.00
34 Sergei Fedorov 15.00 40.00
35 Sergei Samsonov 10.00 25.00
36 Steve Yzerman 25.00 60.00
37 Teemu Selanne 15.00 40.00
38 Todd Bertuzzi 10.00 25.00
39 Valeri Kharlamov 25.00 60.00
40 Vincent Lecavalier 15.00 40.00

2002-03 BAP Ultimate Memorabilia Jersey and Stick

COMMON CARD (1-30) 12.50 30.00
SEMISTARS 15.00 40.00
*JSY/STK: .5X TO 1.25X JSY
PRINT RUN 50 SER.#'d SETS
1 Patrick Roy 20.00 50.00
2 Mike Modano 12.50 40.00
3 Peter Forsberg 20.00 50.00
4 Mark Messier 15.00 40.00
5 Brett Hull 25.00 60.00
6 Martin Brodeur 30.00 80.00
7 Joe Thornton 15.00 40.00
8 Ilya Kovalchuk 20.00 50.00
9 Pavel Bure 12.50 30.00
10 Rick Nash 25.00 60.00
11 Marty Turco 12.50 30.00
12 Jay Bouwmeester 12.50 30.00
13 Nicklas Lidstrom 15.00 40.00
14 Jaromir Jagr 20.00 50.00
15 Mario Lemieux 40.00 100.00
16 Markus Naslund 12.50 30.00
17 Brendan Shanahan 15.00 40.00
18 Paul Kariya 12.50 30.00
19 Roberto Luongo 20.00 50.00
20 Joe Sakic 15.00 40.00
21 Mats Sundin 12.50 30.00
22 Steve Yzerman 30.00 80.00
23 Dany Heatley 15.00 40.00
24 Jose Theodore 12.50 30.00
25 Saku Koivu 12.50 30.00
26 Marian Hossa 12.50 30.00
27 Marian Gaborik 25.00 60.00
28 Sergei Fedorov 15.00 40.00
29 Todd Bertuzzi 15.00 30.00
30 Teemu Selanne 12.50 30.00

2002-03 BAP Ultimate Memorabilia Journey Jerseys

This 10-card set featured swatches of game-worn jerseys from every team the given player played for. Cards were serial-numbered to just 50 and each card was encapsulated in a clear plastic slab with a descriptive label encased at the top. The set is unnumbered and listed below in checklist order. Unpriced gold one of ones were also created.

COMMON CARD (1-10) 15.00 40.00
PRINT RUN 50 SER.#'d SETS
1 Patrick Roy 40.00 100.00
2 Ed Belfour 20.00 60.00
3 Jaromir Jagr 20.00 50.00
4 Brett Hull 30.00 80.00
5 Adam Oates 15.00 40.00
6 Eric Lindros 20.00 50.00
7 Bill Guerin 15.00 40.00
8 Jeremy Roenick 20.00 50.00
9 Pavel Bure 15.00 40.00
10 Alexander Mogilny 15.00 40.00

2002-03 BAP Ultimate Memorabilia Lifetime Achievers

This 20-card set featured swatches of game-worn jerseys. Cards were serial-numbered to just 40 and each card was encapsulated in a clear plastic slab with a descriptive label encased at the top. The set is unnumbered and listed below in checklist order.

COMMON CARD (1-20) 10.00 25.00
UNLISTED STARS 12.50 30.00
PRINT RUN 40 SER.#'d SETS
1 Sergei Fedorov 15.00 40.00
2 Nicklas Lidstrom 12.50 25.00
3 Brendan Shanahan 10.00 25.00
4 Ed Belfour 12.50 25.00
5 Doug Gilmour 10.00 25.00
6 Jaromir Jagr 20.00 50.00
7 Patrick Roy 30.00 80.00
8 Eric Lindros 12.50 25.00
9 Brian Leetch 12.50 30.00
10 Pavel Bure 12.50 30.00
11 Brett Hull 20.00 50.00
12 Martin Brodeur 30.00 80.00
13 Curtis Joseph 12.50 30.00
14 Mario Lemieux 30.00 80.00
15 Steve Yzerman 30.00 80.00
16 Luc Robitaille 12.50 30.00
17 Mark Messier 12.50 30.00
18 Chris Chelios 12.50 30.00
19 Ron Francis 10.00 25.00
20 Joe Sakic 25.00 60.00

2002-03 BAP Ultimate Memorabilia Magnificent Inserts

This 10-card set featured game-used equipment from the career of Mario Lemieux. Cards 1-5 had a print run of 30 copies each and cards 6-10 were limited to just 10 copies each. Cards 6-10 are not priced due to scarcity. Each card was encapsulated in a clear plastic slab with a descriptive label encased at the top.

1-5 ANNOUNCED PRINT RUN 30
6-10 UNPIRCED PRINT RUN 10
1 1985-86 Season 40.00 100.00
2 2000-01 Season 40.00 100.00
3 2002 NHL All-Star 40.00 100.00
4 1987 Canada Cup 40.00 100.00
5 Dual Jersey 50.00 120.00
6 Number
7 Emblem
8 Triple Jersey
9 Quad Jersey
10 Complete Package

2002-03 BAP Ultimate Memorabilia Magnificent Ones

This 10-card set featured dual swatches of jerseys from Mario Lemieux and a player he recognized as one of the best in the game. Cards were serial-numbered to just 30 and each card was encapsulated in a clear plastic slab with a descriptive label encased at the top. The set is unnumbered and listed below in checklist order.

PRINT RUN 30 SER.#'d SETS
1 M.Lemieux/P.Roy 60.00 120.00
2 M.Lemieux/S.Yzerman 50.00 100.00
3 M.Lemieux/J.Jagr 25.00 60.00
4 M.Lemieux/M.Modano 25.00 60.00
5 M.Lemieux/M.Brodeur 50.00 100.00
6 M.Lemieux/P.Kariya 25.00 60.00
7 M.Lemieux/J.Sakic 25.00 60.00
8 M.Lemieux/P.Forsberg 30.00 80.00
9 M.Lemieux/P.Bure 25.00 60.00
10 M.Lemieux/B.Shanahan 30.00 80.00

2002-03 BAP Ultimate Memorabilia Nameplates

COMMON CARD (1-20) 10.00 25.00
UNLISTED STARS 12.50 30.00
PRINT RUN 40 SER.#'d SETS
1 Jaromir Jagr 30.00 80.00
2 Mike Modano 15.00 40.00
3 Joe Thornton 20.00 50.00
4 Nicklas Lidstrom 12.50 30.00
5 Jay Bouwmeester 10.00 25.00
6 Jason Spezza 25.00 60.00
7 Patrick Roy 40.00 100.00
8 Peter Forsberg 25.00 60.00
9 Steve Yzerman 40.00 100.00
10 Marian Hossa 10.00 25.00
11 Ilya Kovalchuk 25.00 60.00
12 Ed Belfour 12.50 30.00
13 Mario Lemieux 40.00 100.00
14 Joe Sakic 25.00 60.00
15 Marian Gaborik 25.00 60.00
16 Pavel Bure 12.50 30.00
17 Martin Brodeur 25.00 60.00
18 Markus Naslund 10.00 25.00
19 Curtis Joseph 12.50 30.00
20 Paul Kariya 10.00 25.00

2002-03 BAP Ultimate Memorabilia Numerology

This 30-card set featured dual swatches of game-used jersey from the 2 featured players; who both wore the same jersey number. Cards were serial-numbered to just 40 and each card was encapsulated in a clear plastic slab with a descriptive label encased at the top. The set is unnumbered and listed below in checklist order.

COMMON CARD (1-30) 12.50 30.00
PRINT RUN 40 SER.#'d SETS
1 G.Hall/J.Hedberg 12.50 30.00
2 T.Sawchuk/R.Turek 30.00 80.00
3 J.Plante/S.Burke 20.00 50.00
4 B.Parent/R.Luongo 20.00 50.00
5 D.Harvey/B.Leetch 12.50 30.00
6 J.Beliveau/V.Lecavalier 30.00 80.00
7 R.Kelly/R.Blake 12.50 30.00
8 D.Potvin/N.Lidstrom 12.50 30.00
9 P.Esposito/K.Tkachuk 30.00 80.00
10 R.Gilbert/G.Roberts 12.50 30.00
11 M.Richard/P.Kariya 40.00 100.00
12 B.Hull/M.Modano 15.00 40.00
13 J.Bucyk/P.Bure 12.50 30.00
14 G.Lafleur/M.Gaborik 40.00 100.00
15 A.Delvecchio/R.Francis 12.50 30.00
16 G.Perreault/M.Messier 15.00 40.00
17 Y.Cournoyer/J.Iginla 15.00 40.00
18 M.Dionne/T.Linden 15.00 40.00
19 V.Kharlamov/I.Kovalchuk 40.00 100.00
20 S.Savard/M.Hossa 12.50 30.00
21 L.Robinson/S.Yzerman 30.00 80.00
22 B.Trottier/J.Sakic 15.00 40.00
23 V.Tretiak/E.Belfour 25.00 60.00
24 S.Mikita/P.Forsberg 15.00 40.00
25 M.Bossy/K.Huselius 12.50 30.00
26 B.Nystrom/M.Hejduk 12.50 30.00
27 F.Mahovlich/M.Peca 12.50 30.00
28 B.Smith/C.Joseph 15.00 40.00
29 G.Fuhr/D.Blackburn 40.00 100.00
30 T.Esposito/M.Turco 15.00 40.00

2002-03 BAP Ultimate Memorabilia Playoff Scorers

PRINT RUN 30 SER.#'d SETS
1 Peter Forsberg 15.00 40.00
2 Joe Sakic 25.00 60.00
3 Brett Hull 20.00 50.00
4 Peter Forsberg 20.00 50.00
5 Steve Yzerman 30.00 80.00
6 Eric Lindros 15.00 40.00
7 Joe Sakic 25.00 60.00
8 Sergei Fedorov 20.00 50.00
9 Brian Leetch 15.00 40.00
10 Mario Lemieux 30.00 80.00
11 Mark Messier 15.00 40.00
12 Mike Bossy 20.00 50.00
13 Maurice Richard 40.00 100.00
14 Jean Beliveau 20.00 50.00
15 Brett Hull 25.00 60.00
16 Bryan Trottier 15.00 40.00
17 Mario Lemieux 40.00 100.00
18 Bobby Hull 20.00 50.00
19 Phil Esposito 20.00 50.00
20 Steve Yzerman 20.00 50.00

2002-03 BAP Ultimate Memorabilia Retro Teammates

PRINT RUN 30 SER.#'d SETS
1 Sittler/McDonald/Williams 30.00 80.00

2 G.Gilbert/Cheevers/Bucyk 30.00 80.00
3 Hull/Mikita/Hall 30.00 80.00
4 Lafleur/Cournoyer/Savard 75.00 200.00
5 R.Gilbert/Giacomin/P.Esposito 30.00 80.00
6 Lemieux/Jagr/Francis 75.00 200.00
7 Richard/Plante/Beliveau 75.00 200.00
8 Horton/Bower/Kelly 60.00 150.00
9 Schultz/Clarke/Parent 30.00 80.00
10 Delvecchio/Sawchuk/Abel 30.00 80.00

2002-03 BAP Ultimate Memorabilia Retro Trophies

COMMON CARD (1-20) 20.00 50.00
PRINT RUN 40 SER.#'d SETS
1 D.Heatley/M.Lemieux 30.00 80.00
2 P.Roy/T.Sawchuk 75.00 150.00
3 M.Peca/B.Clarke 20.00 50.00
4 S.Koivu/H.Richard 20.00 50.00
5 P.Kariya/M.Dionne 20.00 50.00
6 J.Jagr/S.Mikita 20.00 50.00
7 S.Yzerman/J.Beliveau 25.00 60.00
8 E.Belfour/G.Hall 20.00 50.00
9 M.Lemieux/H.Morenz/10
10 J.Theodore/J.Plante 30.00 80.00
11 N.Lidstrom/L.Robinson 20.00 50.00
12 M.Lemieux/P.Esposito 40.00 100.00
13 J.Iginla/B.Hull 20.00 50.00
14 M.Messier/R.Hextall 20.00 50.00
15 M.Brodeur/F.Brimsek 40.00 100.00
16 N.Lidstrom/R.Crozier 20.00 50.00
17 M.Lemieux/L.McDonald 40.00 100.00
18 P.Forsberg/B.Trottier 20.00 50.00
19 Br.Hull/Bo.Hull 30.00 80.00
20 J.Sakic/M.Richard 40.00 100.00

2002-03 BAP Ultimate Memorabilia Scoring Leaders

ANNOUNCED PRINT RUN 40
1 Peter Forsberg 2002-03 25.00 60.00
2 Jarome Iginla 2001-02 15.00 40.00
3 Jaromir Jagr 2000-01 15.00 40.00
4 Jaromir Jagr 1999-00 15.00 40.00
5 Jaromir Jagr 1998-99 15.00 40.00
6 Jaromir Jagr 1997-98 15.00 40.00
7 Mario Lemieux 1996-97 20.00 50.00
8 Mario Lemieux 1995-96 20.00 50.00
9 Jaromir Jagr 1994-95 15.00 40.00
10 Mario Lemieux 1992-93 20.00 50.00
11 Mario Lemieux 1991-92 20.00 50.00
12 Mario Lemieux 1988-89 20.00 50.00
13 Mario Lemieux 1987-88 20.00 50.00
14 Marcel Dionne 1979-80 12.50 30.00
15 Bryan Trottier 1978-79 12.50 30.00
16 Guy Lafleur 1977-78 12.50 30.00
17 Guy Lafleur 1976-77 12.50 30.00
18 Guy Lafleur 1975-76 12.50 30.00
19 Phil Esposito 1973-74 20.00 50.00
20 Phil Esposito 1972-73 20.00 50.00
21 Phil Esposito 1971-72 20.00 50.00
22 Phil Esposito 1970-71 20.00 50.00
23 Phil Esposito 1968-69 12.00 30.00
24 Stan Mikita 1967-68 12.50 30.00
25 Stan Mikita 1966-67 12.50 30.00
26 Bobby Hull 1965-66 20.00 50.00
27 Stan Mikita 1964-65 12.50 30.00
28 Stan Mikita 1963-64 12.50 30.00
29 Bobby Hull 1961-62 20.00 50.00
30 Bernie Geoffrion 1960-61 12.50 30.00
31 Bobby Hull 1959-60 20.00 50.00
32 Dickie Moore 1958-59 12.50 30.00
33 Dickie Moore 1957-58 12.50 30.00
34 Jean Beliveau 1956-57 20.00 50.00
35 Bernie Geoffrion 1955-56 12.50 30.00

2002-03 BAP Ultimate Memorabilia Vintage Jerseys

This 40-card set featured jersey swatches from past hockey greats. Cards were serial-numbered to just 40 and each card was encapsulated in a clear plastic slab with a descriptive label encased at the top. The set is unnumbered and listed below in checklist order. Unpriced gold one of one's exist.
PRINT RUN 40 SER.#'d SETS
1 Stan Mikita 15.00 40.00
2 Alex Delvecchio 15.00 40.00
3 Aurel Joliat 30.00 80.00
4 Bernie Parent 15.00 40.00
5 Bill Barber 12.50 30.00
6 Bobby Clarke 12.50 30.00
7 Bobby Hull 12.50 30.00
8 Bryan Trottier 12.50 30.00
9 Dennis Hull 12.50 30.00
10 Doug Harvey 12.50 30.00
11 Ed Giacomin 12.50 30.00
12 Frank Brimsek 12.50 30.00
13 Frank Mahovlich 12.50 30.00
14 George Hainsworth 20.00 50.00
15 Gerry Cheevers 12.50 30.00
16 Gilbert Perreault 12.50 30.00
17 Glenn Hall 12.50 30.00
18 Guy Lafleur 12.50 30.00
19 Harry Lumley 20.00 50.00
20 Henri Richard 12.50 30.00
21 Jacques Plante 30.00 80.00
22 Jean Beliveau 25.00 60.00
23 John Bucyk 12.50 30.00
24 Lanny McDonald 12.50 30.00
25 Larry Robinson 12.50 30.00
26 Marcel Dionne 12.50 30.00
27 Maurice Richard 30.00 80.00
28 Mike Bossy 12.50 30.00
29 Peter Mahovlich 12.50 30.00
30 Phil Esposito 12.50 30.00
31 Red Kelly 20.00 50.00
32 Roger Crozier 12.50 30.00
33 Roy Worters 20.00 50.00
34 Sid Abel 12.50 30.00
35 Ted Lindsay 12.50 30.00
36 Terry Sawchuk 50.00 125.00
37 Tim Horton 30.00 80.00
38 Tony Esposito 12.50 30.00
39 Valeri Kharlamov 25.00 60.00
40 Vladislav Tretiak 40.00 100.00

2003-04 BAP Ultimate Memorabilia Autographs

Each pack of Ultimate contained one memorabilia card that was slabbed by BGS and one unslabbed card of either an auto, gold auto, auto/jersey, auto/stick, auto/emblem or auto/number. The auto/memorabilia cards were found in sealed toploaders.
1-89 ANNOUNCED PRINT RUN 135
90-130 ANNOUNCED PRINT RUN 100
131-165 ANNOUNCED PRINT RUN 19
1 Alexei Kovalev 6.00 15.00
2 Shane Doan 6.00 15.00
3 Ales Hemsky 6.00 15.00
4 Ray Whitney 6.00 15.00
5 Alexander Frolov 6.00 15.00
6 Mike Peca 6.00 15.00
7 Chris Drury 6.00 15.00
8 Chris Osgood 6.00 15.00
9 Andrew Raycroft 8.00 20.00
10 Rick DiPietro 6.00 15.00
11 Chuck Kobasew 6.00 15.00
12 Vincent Lecavalier 8.00 20.00
13 Olaf Kolzig 8.00 20.00
14 Erik Cole 6.00 15.00
15 Ryan Smyth 6.00 15.00
16 Anson Carter 6.00 15.00
17 Jocelyn Thibault 6.00 15.00
18 Alexei Yashin 6.00 15.00
19 David Aebischer 6.00 15.00
20 Chris Pronger 6.00 15.00
21 Ron Francis 10.00 25.00
22 Markus Naslund 8.00 20.00
23 Tommy Salo 6.00 15.00
24 Patrick Lalime 6.00 15.00
25 Joe Nieuwendyk 8.00 20.00
26 Vincent Damphousse 6.00 15.00
27 Bill Guerin 6.00 15.00
28 Jeremy Roenick 12.00 30.00
29 Barret Jackman 6.00 15.00
30 Curtis Joseph 8.00 20.00
31 Jason Spezza 15.00 40.00
32 Sergei Fedorov 15.00 40.00
33 Gary Roberts 6.00 15.00
34 Glen Murray 6.00 15.00
35 Adam Oates 6.00 15.00
36 Felix Potvin 10.00 25.00
37 Eric Brewer 6.00 15.00
38 Jeff O'Neill 6.00 15.00
39 Tomas Vokoun 8.00 20.00
40 Olli Jokinen 6.00 15.00
41 Martin Prusek 6.00 15.00
42 Sergei Gonchar 6.00 15.00
43 Kevin Weekes 6.00 15.00
44 Roman Cechmanek 6.00 15.00
45 Scott Stevens 6.00 15.00
46 Dwayne Roloson 6.00 15.00
47 Martin Biron 6.00 15.00
48 Keith Tkachuk 6.00 15.00
49 Pasi Nurminen 6.00 15.00
50 Saku Koivu 8.00 20.00
51 David Legwand 6.00 15.00
52 Jay Bouwmeester 6.00 15.00
53 Patrik Elias 6.00 15.00
54 Zigmund Palffy 6.00 15.00
55 Tyler Arnason 6.00 15.00
56 Sergei Samsonov 6.00 15.00
57 Ryan Miller 15.00 40.00
58 Mike Dunham 6.00 15.00
59 Nikolai Khabibulin 8.00 20.00
60 Roman Turek 6.00 15.00
61 Marian Hossa 8.00 20.00
62 Marc Denis 6.00 15.00
63 Peter Bondra 8.00 20.00
64 Marty Turco 8.00 20.00
65 John LeClair 8.00 20.00
66 Johan Hedberg 6.00 15.00
67 Sean Burke 6.00 15.00
68 Ed Jovanovski 6.00 15.00
69 Tony Amonte 6.00 15.00
70 Daymond Langkow 6.00 15.00
71 Miroslav Satan 6.00 15.00
72 Jean-Sebastien Giguere 6.00 15.00
73 Evgeni Nabokov 8.00 20.00
74 Rostislav Klesla 6.00 15.00
75 Al MacInnis 6.00 15.00
76 Niko Kapanen 6.00 15.00
77 Manny Fernandez 6.00 15.00
78 Milan Hejduk 8.00 20.00
79 Doug Weight 6.00 15.00
80 Jarome Iginla 12.50 30.00
81 Martin St. Louis 8.00 20.00
82 Daniel Alfredsson 6.00 15.00
83 Marian Gaborik 12.50 30.00
84 Rob Blake 6.00 15.00
85 Dan Cloutier 6.00 15.00
86 Simon Gagne 10.00 25.00
87 Mark Recchi 6.00 15.00
88 Teemu Selanne 10.00 25.00
89 Todd Bertuzzi 8.00 20.00
90 Chris Kunitz 10.00 25.00
91 Eric Staal 40.00 100.00
92 Nathan Horton 12.50 30.00
93 Andrew Peters 8.00 20.00
94 Alexander Semin 25.00 60.00
95 Matthew Lombardi 8.00 20.00
96 Joffrey Lupul 12.50 30.00
97 John-Michael Liles 10.00 25.00
98 Jiri Hudler 12.50 30.00
99 Tuomo Ruutu 12.50 30.00
100 Anton Babchuk 8.00 20.00
101 Dan Fritsche 8.00 20.00
102 Derek Roy 8.00 20.00
103 Paul Martin 8.00 20.00
104 Pavel Vorobiev 8.00 20.00
105 Matthew Spiller 8.00 20.00
106 Patrice Bergeron 25.00 60.00
107 Chris Higgins 10.00 25.00
108 Noah Clarke 8.00 20.00
109 Nikolai Zherdev 15.00 30.00
110 Brent Burns 10.00 25.00
111 Dustin Brown 12.00 30.00
112 Michael Ryder 20.00 50.00
113 Joni Pitkanen 8.00 20.00
114 Jordin Tootoo 20.00 50.00
115 Ryan Malone 10.00 25.00
116 David Hale 8.00 20.00
117 Antti Miettinen 8.00 20.00
118 Doug Lynch 8.00 20.00
119 Tim Gleason 8.00 20.00
120 Dan Hamhuis 10.00 25.00
121 Fredrik Sjostrom 8.00 20.00
122 Kari Lehtonen 30.00 80.00
123 Marc-Andre Fleury 30.00 80.00
124 Marek Zidlicky 10.00 25.00
125 Milan Michalek 15.00 40.00
126 Matt Stajan 10.00 25.00
127 Peter Sarno 8.00 20.00
128 Antoine Vermette 10.00 25.00
129 Boyd Gordon 8.00 20.00
130 Kyle Wellwood 10.00 25.00
131 Steve Yzerman 100.00 200.00
132 Rick Nash 50.00 100.00
133 Roberto Luongo 25.00 50.00
134 Joe Thornton 40.00 80.00
135 Joe Sakic 50.00 100.00
136 Pavel Datsyuk 40.00 80.00
137 Martin Brodeur
138 Mike Modano 30.00 60.00
139 Brian Leetch 40.00 80.00
140 Peter Forsberg 50.00 100.00
141 Owen Nolan 25.00 50.00
142 Brett Hull 50.00 100.00
143 Jaromir Jagr 40.00 80.00
144 Dominik Hasek 40.00 80.00
145 Ilya Kovalchuk 40.00 80.00
146 Jose Theodore 75.00 125.00
147 Mario Lemieux 100.00 200.00
148 Mats Sundin 40.00 80.00
149 Eric Lindros 50.00 100.00
150 Henrik Zetterberg 50.00 100.00
151 Dany Heatley 30.00 80.00
152 Nicklas Lidstrom 40.00 80.00
153 Bobby Orr 75.00 150.00
154 Ted Kennedy 40.00 80.00
155 Ray Bourque 40.00 80.00
156 Jean Beliveau 40.00 80.00
157 Tony Esposito 30.00 60.00
158 Patrick Roy 150.00 300.00
159 Ted Lindsay 40.00 80.00
160 Frank Mahovlich 30.00 60.00
161 Guy Lafleur 30.00 60.00
162 Henri Richard 25.00 50.00
163 Maurice Richard 100.00 200.00
164 Phil Esposito 30.00 60.00
165 Johnny Bower 25.00 50.00

2003-04 BAP Ultimate Memorabilia Autographs Gold

*1-89 GOLD/35: 1X TO 2.5X BASIC AU
1-89 ANNOUNCED PRINT RUN 35
*90-130 GOLD/20: .6X TO 1.5X BASIC AU
90-130 ANNOUNCED PRINT RUN 20
131-165 UNPRICED PRINT RUN 1

2003-04 BAP Ultimate Memorabilia Autographed Jerseys

10-89/131-165 PRINT RUN 30
91-129 PRINT RUN 20 SER.#'d SETS
10 Rick DiPietro 20.00 50.00
12 Vincent Lecavalier 30.00 80.00
13 Olaf Kolzig 25.00 60.00
17 Jocelyn Thibault 20.00 50.00
19 David Aebischer 20.00 50.00
20 Chris Pronger 20.00 50.00
21 Ron Francis 40.00 80.00
22 Markus Naslund 20.00 50.00
24 Patrick Lalime 20.00 50.00
27 Bill Guerin 20.00 50.00
28 Jeremy Roenick 25.00 60.00
29 Barret Jackman 20.00 50.00
30 Curtis Joseph 15.00 40.00
31 Jason Spezza 25.00 60.00
33 Gary Roberts 20.00 50.00
39 Tomas Vokoun 20.00 50.00
48 Keith Tkachuk 25.00 60.00
50 Saku Koivu 25.00 60.00
52 Jay Bouwmeester 20.00 50.00
56 Sergei Samsonov 25.00 60.00
57 Ryan Miller 25.00 60.00
58 Mike Dunham 20.00 50.00
59 Nikolai Khabibulin 25.00 60.00
60 Roman Turek 20.00 50.00
61 Marian Hossa 25.00 60.00
62 Marc Denis 20.00 50.00
65 John LeClair 25.00 60.00
66 Johan Hedberg 20.00 50.00
68 Ed Jovanovski 20.00 50.00
69 Tony Amonte 20.00 50.00
72 Jean-Sebastien Giguere 20.00 50.00
75 Al MacInnis 20.00 50.00
77 Manny Fernandez 20.00 50.00
78 Milan Hejduk 25.00 60.00
79 Doug Weight 20.00 50.00
81 Martin St.Louis 25.00 60.00
82 Daniel Alfredsson 20.00 50.00
83 Marian Gaborik 25.00 60.00
85 Dan Cloutier 20.00 50.00
86 Simon Gagne 20.00 50.00
87 Mark Recchi 20.00 50.00
88 Teemu Selanne 60.00 125.00
89 Todd Bertuzzi 25.00 60.00
91 Eric Staal 30.00 80.00
92 Nathan Horton
94 Alexander Semin
95 Matthew Lombardi
96 Joffrey Lupul 15.00 40.00
99 Tuomo Ruutu
101 Dan Fritsche
102 Derek Roy
106 Patrice Bergeron 50.00 100.00
107 Christopher Higgins 20.00 50.00
109 Nikolai Zherdev 40.00 100.00
110 Brent Burns 12.00 30.00
111 Dustin Brown 10.00 25.00
112 Michael Ryder 20.00 50.00
113 Joni Pitkanen 12.00 30.00
114 Jordin Tootoo
115 Ryan Malone
119 Tim Gleason
120 Dan Hamhuis
126 Matt Stajan
128 Antoine Vermette
129 Boyd Gordon
131 Steve Yzerman 50.00 125.00
132 Rick Nash 30.00 80.00
133 Roberto Luongo 25.00 60.00
134 Joe Thornton 25.00 60.00
135 Joe Sakic 40.00 100.00
136 Pavel Datsyuk 30.00 80.00
137 Martin Brodeur 100.00 200.00
138 Mike Modano 25.00 60.00
139 Brian Leetch 20.00 50.00
140 Peter Forsberg 40.00 100.00
141 Owen Nolan 20.00 50.00
142 Brett Hull 25.00 60.00
144 Dominik Hasek 40.00 100.00
145 Ilya Kovalchuk 20.00 50.00
146 Jose Theodore 20.00 50.00
147 Mario Lemieux 75.00 200.00
148 Mats Sundin 25.00 60.00
149 Eric Lindros 25.00 60.00
150 Henrik Zetterberg 25.00 60.00
151 Dany Heatley 30.00 80.00
152 Nicklas Lidstrom 25.00 60.00
153 Bobby Orr 125.00 250.00
155 Ray Bourque 40.00 100.00
157 Tony Esposito 50.00 100.00
158 Patrick Roy 125.00 250.00
165 Johnny Bower 30.00 80.00

2003-04 BAP Ultimate Memorabilia Autographed Sticks

PRINT RUN 30 SER.#'d SETS
32 Sergei Fedorov 25.00 60.00
45 Scott Stevens 25.00 60.00
56 Sergei Samsonov 12.00 30.00
86 Simon Gagne 20.00 50.00
123 Marc-Andre Fleury 30.00 80.00
131 Steve Yzerman 60.00 150.00
132 Rick Nash 25.00 60.00
134 Joe Thornton 25.00 60.00
135 Joe Sakic 30.00 80.00
136 Pavel Datsyuk 30.00 80.00
138 Mike Modano 20.00 50.00
140 Peter Forsberg 25.00 60.00
142 Brett Hull 25.00 60.00
143 Jaromir Jagr 30.00 80.00
145 Ilya Kovalchuk 25.00 60.00
147 Mario Lemieux 75.00 200.00
151 Dany Heatley 25.00 60.00
153 Bobby Orr 125.00 250.00
158 Patrick Roy 75.00 200.00
165 Johnny Bower 25.00 60.00

2003-04 BAP Ultimate Memorabilia Active Eight

PRINT RUN 30 SER.#'d SETS
1 Belfour/Brodeur/Hasek 40.00 100.00
2 Belfour/Joseph/Brodeur 40.00 100.00
3 Lemieux/Hull/Mogilny 30.00 80.00
4 Sundin/Lidstrom/Forsberg 25.00 60.00
5 Lemieux/Messier/Forsberg 40.00 100.00
6 Yzerman/Sakic/Stevens 30.00 80.00
7 Roenick/Modano/Leetch 25.00 60.00
8 Lemieux/Hull/Yzerman 40.00 100.00

2003-04 BAP Ultimate Memorabilia Always An All-Star

PRINT RUN 50 SER.#'d SETS
1 Martin Brodeur 25.00 60.00
2 Mike Modano 15.00 40.00
3 Brian Leetch 12.50 30.00
4 Brett Hull 20.00 50.00
5 Al MacInnis 12.50 30.00
6 Paul Kariya 12.50 30.00
7 Eric Lindros 12.50 30.00
8 Teemu Selanne 12.50 30.00
9 Nicklas Lidstrom 12.50 30.00
10 Sergei Fedorov 20.00 50.00
11 Patrick Roy 30.00 80.00
12 Peter Forsberg 20.00 50.00
13 Mark Messier 20.00 50.00
14 Jaromir Jagr 15.00 40.00
15 Ray Bourque 25.00 60.00
16 Mario Lemieux 40.00 100.00
17 Brendan Shanahan 12.50 30.00
18 Chris Pronger 12.50 30.00
19 Dominik Hasek 15.00 40.00
20 Mats Sundin 12.50 30.00

2003-04 BAP Ultimate Memorabilia Blades of Steel

This 7-card set featured swatches of game-used skates. Each card was limited to just 20 copies.
ANNOUNCED PRINT RUN 20
1 Mario Lemieux
2 Henrik Zetterberg 15.00 40.00
3 Al MacInnis 12.00 30.00
4 Pavel Bure 20.00 50.00
5 Jarome Iginla 12.00 30.00
6 Raymond Bourque 20.00 50.00
7 Pavel Datsyuk 20.00 50.00

2003-04 BAP Ultimate Memorabilia Calder Candidates

PRINT RUN 50 SER.#'d SETS
1 Andrew Raycroft 8.00 20.00
2 Eric Staal 10.00 25.00
3 Michael Ryder 10.00 25.00
4 Marc-Andre Fleury 20.00 50.00
5 Ryan Malone 8.00 20.00
6 Trent Hunter 8.00 20.00
7 Patrice Bergeron 12.00 30.00
8 Joni Pitkanen 8.00 20.00
9 Matthew Lombardi 8.00 20.00
10 Nikolai Zherdev 12.50 30.00
11 Tuomo Ruutu 8.00 20.00
12 Joffrey Lupul 10.00 25.00

2003-04 BAP Ultimate Memorabilia Career Year

PRINT RUN 40 SER.#'d SETS
1 Martin Brodeur 30.00 80.00
2 Cam Neely 15.00 40.00
3 Ray Bourque 15.00 40.00
4 Patrick Roy 30.00 80.00
5 Rick Nash 15.00 40.00
6 Steve Yzerman 30.00 80.00
7 Bobby Orr 60.00 125.00
8 Mario Lemieux 40.00 100.00

2003-04 BAP Ultimate Memorabilia Complete Jersey

PRINT RUN 30 SER.#'d SETS
1 Joe Thornton 30.00 80.00
2 Mario Lemieux 100.00 200.00
3 Marian Gaborik 40.00 100.00
4 Brett Hull 30.00 80.00
5 Dany Heatley 30.00 80.00
6 Joe Sakic 50.00 120.00
7 Paul Kariya 25.00 60.00
8 Steve Yzerman 50.00 120.00
9 Rick Nash 40.00 100.00
10 Nicklas Lidstrom 25.00 60.00
11 Sergei Fedorov 25.00 60.00
12 Patrick Roy 50.00 120.00
13 Peter Forsberg 40.00 100.00
14 Henrik Zetterberg 25.00 60.00
15 Dominik Hasek 30.00 80.00
16 Martin Brodeur 50.00 120.00
17 Mike Modano 25.00 60.00
18 Brendan Shanahan 25.00 60.00
19 Ilya Kovalchuk 40.00 100.00
20 Saku Koivu 25.00 60.00

2003-04 BAP Ultimate Memorabilia Cornerstones

PRINT RUN 20 SER.#'d SETS
1 Vezina/Plnt/Roy/Theodre 100.00 200.00
2 Plante/Richrd/Harve/Belivu 75.00 150.00
3 H.Richard/Laflr/Rbnsn/Svrd 40.00 80.00
4 Bower/F.Mahvlch/Kelly/Hrtn 50.00 100.00
5 Shore/Orr/Bourq/Thrntn 75.00 150.00
6 Brimsk/Lumly/Hall/Espo 40.00 80.00
7 Lndsy/Swchk/Delvc/Yzrmn 40.00 100.00
8 Bossy/Trottr/Potvn/Smith 50.00 80.00

2003-04 BAP Ultimate Memorabilia Dynamic Duos

PRINT RUN 30 SER.#'d SETS
1 T.Selanne 20.00 50.00
S.Koivu
2 M.Sundin/P.Forsberg 20.00 50.00
3 M.Lemieux/S.Yzerman 40.00 100.00
4 J.Sakic/B.Shanahan 20.00 50.00
5 E.Lindros/P.Kariya 20.00 50.00
6 J.Roenick/K.Tkachuk 20.00 50.00
7 I.Kovalchuk/S.Fedorov 20.00 50.00
8 R.Nash/J.Thornton 20.00 50.00
9 B.Hull/M.Modano 15.00 40.00
10 M.Messier/J.Spezza 20.00 50.00

2003-04 BAP Ultimate Memorabilia Franchise Present and Future

PRINT RUN 40 SER.#'d SETS
1 S.Fedorov/J.Lupul 15.00 40.00
2 I.Kovalchuk/D.Heatley 25.00 60.00
3 J.Thornton/P.Bergeron 20.00 50.00
4 M.Satan/D.Roy 12.50 30.00
5 J.Iginla/M.Lombardi 15.00 40.00
6 J.O'Neill/E.Staal 15.00 40.00
7 J.Thibault/T.Ruutu 12.50 30.00
8 P.Forsberg/D.Aebischer 15.00 40.00
9 R.Nash/N.Zherdev 20.00 50.00
10 M.Modano/S.Ott 15.00 40.00
11 S.Yzerman/P.Datsyuk 30.00 80.00
12 R.Smyth/A.Hemsky 12.50 30.00
13 R.Luongo/J.Bouwmeester 20.00 50.00
14 Z.Palffy/A.Frolov 15.00 40.00
15 M.Gaborik/P.Bouchard 15.00 40.00
16 J.Theodore/M.Ryder 15.00 40.00
17 D.Legwand/J.Tootoo 15.00 40.00
18 M.Brodeur/P.Martin 30.00 80.00
19 A.Yashin/R.DiPietro 15.00 40.00
20 M.Messier/F.Tyutin 15.00 40.00
21 M.Hossa/J.Spezza 20.00 50.00
22 J.LeClair/J.Pitkanen 12.50 30.00
23 S.Doan/B.Boucher 12.50 30.00
24 M.Lemieux/M.Fleury 50.00 125.00
25 C.Pronger/B.Jackman 12.50 30.00
26 E.Nabokov/J.Cheechoo 15.00 40.00
27 N.Khabibulin/V.Lecavalier 15.00 40.00
28 M.Sundin/M.Stajan 15.00 40.00
29 M.Naslund/A.Auld 15.00 40.00
30 O.Kolzig/A.Semin 15.00 40.00

2003-04 BAP Ultimate Memorabilia Gloves Are Off

PRINT RUN 25 SER.#'d SETS
1 Joe Thornton 20.00 50.00
2 Brett Hull 20.00 50.00
3 Mario Lemieux 30.00 80.00
4 Joe Sakic 20.00 50.00
5 Jarome Iginla 20.00 50.00
6 Sergei Samsonov 15.00 40.00
7 Mats Sundin 15.00 40.00
8 Eric Lindros 15.00 40.00
9 Rob Blake 15.00 40.00
10 John LeClair 15.00 40.00
11 Stan Mikita 15.00 40.00
12 Bill Gadsby 15.00 40.00
13 Aurel Joliat 25.00 60.00
14 Bernie Geoffrion 15.00 40.00
15 Dickie Moore 15.00 40.00
16 Howie Morenz 50.00 125.00
17 Doug Harvey 20.00 50.00
18 King Clancy 30.00 80.00
19 Ray Bourque 15.00 40.00
20 Eddie Shore 30.00 80.00

2003-04 BAP Ultimate Memorabilia Great Moments

COMMON CARD(1-12) 12.50 30.00
UNLISTED STARS 15.00
PRINT RUN 40 SER.#'d SETS
1 Bobby Orr 40.00 100.00
2 S.Mikita 25.00 60.00
B.Hull
3 Patrick Roy 30.00 80.00
4 Steve Yzerman 25.00 60.00
5 M.Messier 25.00 60.00
J.Theodore
6 Ray Bourque 15.00 40.00
7 B.Clarke 15.00 40.00
B.Barber
8 Henri Richard 12.50 30.00
9 Mike Bossy 15.00 40.00
10 Maurice Richard 30.00 80.00
11 Mark Messier 25.00 60.00
12 Cam Neely 15.00 40.00

2003-04 BAP Ultimate Memorabilia Hat Tricks

This 20-card set featured three different pieces of memorabilia. Cards were limited to 30 cards each.
PRINT RUN 30 SER.#'d SETS
1 Keith Tkachuk 15.00 40.00
2 Henrik Zetterberg 25.00 60.00
3 Alexei Yashin 12.50 30.00
4 Mats Sundin 15.00 40.00
5 Joe Thornton 25.00 60.00
6 Pavel Datsyuk 30.00 80.00
7 Joe Sakic 25.00 60.00
8 Mario Lemieux 50.00 125.00
9 Milan Hejduk 15.00 40.00
10 Eric Lindros 15.00 40.00
11 Jarome Iginla 25.00 60.00
12 Steve Yzerman 40.00 100.00
13 Sergei Samsonov 12.50 30.00
14 Brett Hull 15.00 40.00
15 Chris Chelios 15.00 40.00
16 Al MacInnis 12.50 30.00
17 Doug Weight 12.50 30.00
18 John LeClair 15.00 40.00
19 Rob Blake 12.50 30.00
20 Scott Niedermayer 15.00 40.00

2003-04 BAP Ultimate Memorabilia Heroes

PRINT RUN 30 SER.#'d SETS
1 I.Kovalchuk/V.Kharlamov 30.00 80.00
2 J.Thornton/S.Yzerman 25.00 60.00
3 J.Iginla/M.Messier 20.00 50.00
4 S.Yzerman/B.Trottier 25.00 60.00
5 M.Lemieux/G.Lafleur 40.00 100.00
6 R.Nash/M.Sundin 20.00 50.00
7 D.Heatley/B.Hull 20.00 50.00
8 P.Roy/J.Plante 50.00 125.00
9 T.Sawchuk/G.Hainsworth 40.00 100.00
10 J.Theodore/P.Roy 40.00 100.00
11 R.Luongo/P.Roy 40.00 100.00
12 E.Belfour/V.Tretiak 30.00 80.00
13 M.Brodeur/P.Roy 40.00 100.00
14 M.Richter/G.Cheevers 20.00 50.00
15 T.Selanne/J.Kurri 30.00 80.00
16 A.Tanguay/J.Sakic 20.00 50.00
17 P.Marleau/M.Lemieux 30.00 80.00
18 V.Lecavalier/S.Yzerman 25.00 60.00
19 M.St.Louis/M.Lemieux 30.00 80.00
20 T.Ruutu/P.Forsberg 20.00 50.00

2003-04 BAP Ultimate Memorabilia Hometown Heroes

PRINT RUN 50 SER.#'d SETS
1 M.Richard 30.00 80.00
H.Richard
2 M.Brodeur/R.Luongo 25.00 60.00
3 R.Bourque/D.Harvey 20.00 50.00
4 P.Forsberg/M.Naslund 15.00 40.00
5 M.Gaborik/Z.Chara 15.00 40.00
6 G.Hainsworth/B.Park 15.00 40.00
7 M.Dionne/Y.Cournoyer 12.50 30.00
8 E.Staal/A.Delvecchio 20.00 50.00
9 F.Mahovlich/P.Mahovlich 15.00 40.00
10 R.Blake/R.Kelly 15.00 40.00
11 B.Hull/A.Raycroft 15.00 40.00
12 J.Theodore/M.St.Louis 20.00 50.00
13 J.Thornton/E.Lindros 15.00 40.00
14 M.Messier/J.Iginla 15.00 40.00
15 B.Durnan/C.Conacher 20.00 50.00
16 P.Esposito/T.Esposito 20.00 50.00
17 J.Kurri/K.Lehtonen 25.00 60.00
18 T.Sawchuk/B.Mosienko 25.00 60.00
19 A.Joliat/D.Potvin 20.00 50.00
20 M.Bossy/M.Lemieux 30.00 80.00

2003-04 BAP Ultimate Memorabilia Jerseys

PRINT RUN 50 SER.#'d SETS
1 Paul Kariya 10.00 25.00
2 Teemu Selanne 10.00 25.00
3 Sergei Fedorov 12.50 30.00
4 Mario Lemieux 25.00 60.00
5 Dany Heatley 15.00 40.00
6 Joe Thornton 15.00 40.00
7 Steve Yzerman 25.00 60.00
8 Bill Guerin 8.00 20.00
9 Ilya Kovalchuk 15.00 40.00
10 Chris Pronger 8.00 20.00
11 Mats Sundin 10.00 25.00
12 Peter Forsberg 12.50 30.00
13 Rick Nash 15.00 40.00
14 Mike Modano 12.50 30.00
15 Martin Brodeur 25.00 60.00
16 Jason Spezza 15.00 40.00
17 Brett Hull 12.50 30.00
18 Jeremy Roenick 12.50 30.00
19 Joe Sakic 12.50 30.00
20 Ed Belfour 10.00 25.00
21 Jose Theodore 12.50 30.00
22 Roberto Luongo 12.50 30.00
23 Henrik Zetterberg 15.00 40.00
24 Dominik Hasek 12.50 30.00
25 Jarome Iginla 12.50 30.00
26 Eric Lindros 10.00 25.00
27 Keith Tkachuk 10.00 25.00
28 Marian Gaborik 12.50 30.00
29 Nicklas Lidstrom 10.00 25.00
30 John LeClair 10.00 25.00
31 Pavel Datsyuk 15.00 30.00
32 Vincent Lecavalier 10.00 25.00
33 Markus Naslund 10.00 25.00
34 Milan Hejduk 10.00 25.00
35 Todd Bertuzzi 10.00 25.00
36 Marty Turco 8.00 20.00
37 Rob Blake 8.00 20.00
38 Andrew Raycroft 8.00 20.00
39 Martin St. Louis 8.00 20.00
40 Saku Koivu 10.00 25.00

2003-04 BAP Ultimate Memorabilia Jersey and Stick

PRINT RUN 50 SER.#'d SETS
1 Jason Spezza 15.00 40.00
2 Brian Leetch 10.00 25.00
3 Dany Heatley 12.00 30.00
4 Mario Lemieux 30.00 80.00
5 Mats Sundin 10.00 25.00
6 Jarome Iginla 20.00 50.00
7 Mike Modano 12.00 30.00
8 Rick Nash 15.00 40.00
9 Steve Yzerman 30.00 80.00
10 Keith Tkachuk 15.00 40.00
11 Joe Thornton 15.00 40.00
12 Martin Brodeur 30.00 80.00
13 Dominik Hasek 20.00 50.00
14 Nikolai Khabibulin 15.00 40.00
15 Joe Sakic 15.00 40.00
16 Vincent Lecavalier 15.00 40.00
17 Peter Forsberg 15.00 40.00
18 Brendan Shanahan 12.00 30.00
19 Marc-Andre Fleury 20.00 50.00
20 Chris Pronger 10.00 25.00
21 Patrick Roy 30.00 80.00
22 Johnny Bower 25.00 60.00
23 Ray Bourque 20.00 50.00
24 Jacques Plante 25.00 60.00
25 Jean Beliveau 20.00 50.00
26 Gump Worsley 25.00 60.00
27 Gilbert Perreault 15.00 40.00
28 Bryan Trottier 12.00 30.00
29 Mike Bossy 12.00 30.00
30 Marcel Dionne 10.00 25.00

2003-04 BAP Ultimate Memorabilia Journey Jerseys

PRINT RUN 50 SER.#'d SETS
1 Sergei Fedorov 12.50 30.00
2 Paul Kariya 12.50 30.00
3 Teemu Selanne 12.50 30.00
4 Ed Belfour 20.00 50.00
5 Brian Leetch 12.50 30.00
6 Patrick Roy 40.00 100.00
7 Brett Hull 20.00 50.00
8 Mark Messier 20.00 50.00
9 Jeremy Roenick 15.00 40.00
10 Ray Bourque 25.00 60.00

2003-04 BAP Ultimate Memorabilia Lifetime Achievers

PRINT RUN 30 SER.#'d SETS
1 Mario Lemieux 30.00 80.00
2 Patrick Roy 30.00 80.00
3 Bobby Orr 50.00 125.00
4 Ray Bourque 15.00 40.00
5 Mark Messier 25.00 60.00
6 Brett Hull 15.00 40.00
7 Brian Leetch 15.00 40.00
8 Steve Yzerman 30.00 80.00

2003-04 BAP Ultimate Memorabilia Magnificent Career

PRINT RUN 40 SER.#'d SETS
AUTO PRINT RUN 10 SETS
AUTOS NOT PRICED DUE TO SCARCITY
1 Mario Lemieux 30.00 80.00
A Grand Entrance
2 Mario Lemieux 30.00 80.00
Twice Is Nice
3 Mario Lemieux 30.00 80.00
A Scoring Machine
4 Mario Lemieux 30.00 80.00
A Canadian Hero
5 Mario Lemieux 30.00 80.00
A Hoard Of Hardware
6 Mario Lemieux 30.00 80.00
Farewell For Now
7 Mario Lemieux/600-Goal Man 30.00 80.00
8 Mario Lemieux 30.00 80.00
International Star
9 Mario Lemieux/1,700th Point 30.00 80.00
10 Quad Jersey 75.00 150.00

2003-04 BAP Ultimate Memorabilia Magnificent Prospects

PRINT RUN 30 SER.#'d SETS
AUTO PRINT RUN 10 SETS
AUTOS NOT PRICED DUE TO SCARCITY
AUTOS SIGNED BY LEMIEUX ONLY
1 M.Lemieux/M.Fleury 75.00 150.00
2 M.Lemieux/E.Staal 30.00 80.00
3 M.Lemieux/P.Bergeron 40.00 100.00
4 M.Lemieux/M.Ryder 30.00 80.00
5 M.Lemieux/R.Malone 30.00 80.00
6 M.Lemieux/T.Ruutu 30.00 80.00
7 M.Lemieux/J.Lupul 30.00 80.00
8 M.Lemieux/J.Tootoo 30.00 80.00
9 M.Lemieux/A.Raycroft 30.00 80.00
10 M.Lemieux/N.Zherdev 30.00 80.00

2003-04 BAP Ultimate Memorabilia Nameplates

PRINT RUN 40 SER.#'d SETS
1 Sergei Fedorov 15.00 40.00
2 Dominik Hasek 15.00 40.00
3 Dany Heatley 15.00 40.00
4 Markus Naslund 12.50 30.00
5 Curtis Joseph 12.50 30.00
6 Mike Modano 15.00 40.00
7 Paul Kariya 12.50 30.00
8 Mark Messier 20.00 50.00
9 Teemu Selanne 12.50 30.00
10 Martin Brodeur 30.00 80.00
11 Brian Leetch 15.00 40.00
12 Joe Thornton 15.00 40.00
13 Mario Lemieux 40.00 100.00
14 Steve Yzerman 25.00 60.00
15 Eric Lindros 12.50 30.00
16 Peter Forsberg 25.00 60.00
17 Zigmund Palffy 12.50 30.00
18 Jeremy Roenick 15.00 40.00
19 Chris Pronger 12.50 30.00
20 Nicklas Lidstrom 15.00 40.00
21 Mats Sundin 12.50 30.00
22 Brendan Shanahan 12.50 30.00
23 Henrik Zetterberg 20.00 50.00
24 Jose Theodore 15.00 40.00
25 Marc-Andre Fleury 25.00 60.00
26 Kari Lehtonen 15.00 40.00
27 Andrew Raycroft 15.00 40.00
28 Ray Bourque 25.00 60.00
29 Cam Neely 15.00 40.00
30 Patrick Roy/20 50.00 120.00

2003-04 BAP Ultimate Memorabilia Perennial Powerhouse Jersey

PRINT RUN 30 SER.#'d SETS
1 Patrick Roy 30.00 80.00
2 Joe Sakic 20.00 50.00
3 Peter Forsberg 15.00 40.00
4 Ray Bourque 20.00 50.00
5 Rob Blake 12.50 30.00
6 Alex Tanguay 12.50 30.00
7 Milan Hejduk 12.50 30.00
8 David Aebischer 12.50 30.00
9 Paul Kariya 12.50 30.00
10 Teemu Selanne 12.50 30.00

2003-04 BAP Ultimate Memorabilia Perennial Powerhouse Jersey and Stick

*JSY/STK: .6X TO 1.5X JSY HI
PRINT RUN 30 SER.#'d SETS

2003-04 BAP Ultimate Memorabilia Raised to the Rafters

This 20-card set commemorated past stars who's respective teams have retired their jersey numbers. Cards were limited to just 30 copies each.
PRINT RUN 30 SER.#'d SETS
1 Cam Neely 25.00 60.00
2 Doug Harvey 25.00 60.00
3 Mike Richter 25.00 60.00
4 Bobby Orr 100.00 200.00
5 Johnny Bower 20.00 50.00
6 Ray Bourque 25.00 60.00
7 Sid Abel 20.00 50.00
8 Ted Lindsay 20.00 50.00
9 Rod Gilbert 20.00 50.00
10 Maurice Richard 30.00 80.00
11 Jean Beliveau 30.00 80.00
12 Bobby Hull 20.00 50.00
13 Stan Mikita 15.00 40.00
14 Bobby Clarke 25.00 60.00
15 Bernie Parent 25.00 60.00
16 Jacques Plante 30.00 80.00
17 Mike Bossy 20.00 50.00
18 Marcel Dionne 20.00 50.00
19 Bryan Trottier 20.00 50.00
20 Eddie Shore 30.00 80.00

2003-04 BAP Ultimate Memorabilia Retro Teammates

PRINT RUN 30 SER.#'d SETS
1 Bourque/Neely/Oates 40.00 100.00
2 M.Richard/Harvey/Plante 75.00 200.00
3 Sawchuk/Lindsay/Abel 40.00 100.00
4 Messier/Richter/Leetch 60.00 150.00
5 Orr/Cheevers/Bucyk 125.00 300.00
6 Trottier/Bossy/Potvin 40.00 100.00
7 Beliveau/H.Richard/Worsley 40.00 100.00
8 Clarke/Barber/Parent 40.00 100.00
9 Sittler/McDonald/Salming 40.00 100.00
10 Shore/Thomspon/Stewart 40.00 100.00

2003-04 BAP Ultimate Memorabilia Retro-Active Trophies

PRINT RUN 50 SER.#'d SETS
1 T.Lindsay/J.Iginla 15.00 40.00
2 B.Orr/P.Forsberg 30.00 80.00
3 J.Beliveau/M.Lemieux 30.00 80.00
4 R.Bourque/P.Forsberg 25.00 60.00
5 B.Orr/M.Lemieux 75.00 200.00
6 T.Sawchuk/M.Brodeur 30.00 80.00
7 R.Worters/D.Hasek 15.00 40.00
8 E.Shore/M.Messier 15.00 40.00
9 M.Richard/M.Lemieux 40.00 100.00
10 D.Harvey/N.Lidstrom 15.00 40.00
11 B.Orr/B.Leetch 40.00 100.00
12 R.Bourque/C.Pronger 15.00 40.00
13 B.Mosienko/J.Sakic 20.00 50.00
14 M.Dionne/Br.Hull 15.00 40.00
15 J.Plante/M.Brodeur 30.00 80.00
16 J.Bower/E.Belfour 15.00 40.00
17 P.Roy/J.Theodore 30.00 80.00
18 J.Beliveau/S.Yzerman 25.00 60.00
19 P.Roy/J.Sakic 30.00 80.00
20 G.Lafleur/M.Lemieux 30.00 80.00

2003-04 BAP Ultimate Memorabilia Seams Unbelievable

ANNOUNCED PRINT RUN 20
1 Mario Lemieux 25.00 60.00
2 Patrick Roy 25.00 60.00
3 Steve Yzerman 30.00 60.00
4 Bobby Orr 20.00 50.00
5 Raymond Bourque 20.00 50.00
6 Martin Brodeur 25.00 60.00
7 Ilya Kovalchuk 12.00 30.00
8 Rick Nash 20.00 50.00

2003-04 BAP Ultimate Memorabilia The Goal

This 14-card set commemorated probably the most famous goal in hockey history. Known now as "The Goal", this image of Bobby Orr flying through the air after being tripped by Noel Picard and scoring on Glenn Hall to lead the Bruins to a defeat over the Blues to win the Stanley Cup is probably one of the most recognizable in hockey. Single jersey and stick cards were limited to 35 copies. Jersey autographs were limited to 10 copies each. All other print runs are listed below.

SINGLE JSY PRINT RUN 35 SER.#'d SETS
SINGLE STK PRINT RUN 35 SER.#'d SETS
JSY AU PRINT RUN 10 SER.#'d SETS
1 Bobby Orr JSY 50.00 120.00
2 B.Orr JSY AU
3 Noel Picard JSY 20.00 50.00
4 Glenn Hall JSY 20.00 50.00
5 B.Orr/N.Picard JSY/30 100.00 250.00
6 B.Orr/G.Hall JSY/30 125.00 250.00
7 B.Orr/G.Hall JSY AU
8 Bobby Orr STK 75.00 200.00
9 Glenn Hall STK 25.00 60.00
10 Noel Picard STK 20.00 50.00
11 Orr/Hall/Picard STK/10
12 Orr/Hall/Picard JSY/10
13 Orr/Hall/Picard JSY AU/10
14 N.Picard/G.Hall JSY/29 25.00 60.00

2003-04 BAP Ultimate Memorabilia Triple Threads

PRINT RUN 40 SER.#'d SETS
1 Brodeur/Potvin/DiPietro 40.00 100.00
2 Hasek/Cloutier/Aebischer 25.00 60.00
3 Jean-Sebastien Giguere 20.00 50.00
4 Belfour/Turco/Cechmanek 15.00 40.00
5 Theodore/Osgood/Luongo 20.00 50.00
6 Kolzig/Biron/Nabokov 15.00 40.00
7 Roy/Crozier/Bower 20.00 50.00
8 Sawchuk/Lumley/Plante 40.00 100.00
9 Hainsworth/Brimsek/Worters 30.00 80.00
10 Blake/Bouwmeester/Pronger 12.50 30.00
11 Lidstrom/Brewer/MacInnis 12.50 30.00
12 Leetch/Chara/Foote 15.00 40.00
13 Orr/T.Horton/Robinson 75.00 200.00
14 Harvey/Bourque/Salming 20.00 50.00
15 Sundin/Modano/Alfredsson 15.00 40.00
16 Lemieux/Hossa/Hull 40.00 100.00
17 St.Louis/Mogilny/Kovalchuk 20.00 50.00
18 Heatley/Thornton/Koivu 30.00 80.00
19 Weight/Palffy/Kariya 12.50 30.00
20 Selanne/Lindros/Tkachuk 15.00 40.00
21 Sakic/Bertuzzi/Yzerman 30.00 80.00
22 Forsberg/Amonte/Naslund 20.00 50.00
23 Nolan/Roenick/Zetterberg 12.00 30.00
24 Nash/Shanahan/Arnott 15.00 40.00
25 Gaborik/Elias/LeClair 15.00 40.00
26 Beliveau/F.Mahovlich/Bossy 25.00 60.00
27 Lindsay/H.Richard/Clarke 20.00 50.00
28 Neely/P.Esposito/McDonald 30.00 80.00
29 Bergeron/Horton/Bergenheim 25.00 60.00
30 Hunter/Gordon/Hale 12.50 30.00
31 Ruutu/Semin/Martin 12.50 30.00
32 Tootoo/Lombardi/Pitkanen 12.00 30.00
33 Staal/Ryder/Brown 25.00 60.00
34 Fleury/Zherdev/Raycroft 25.00 60.00

2003-04 BAP Ultimate Memorabilia Ultimate Goaltender

PRINT RUN 20 SER.#'d SETS
AUTO PRINT RUN 3 SER.#'d SETS
1 Patrick Roy 30.00 60.00
Jersey
2 Patrick Roy 30.00 60.00
Jersey
3 Patrick Roy 50.00 100.00
Jersey
Stick
4 Patrick Roy 40.00 80.00
Number
5 Patrick Roy 40.00 80.00
Pad
6 Patrick Roy 40.00 100.00
Triple Memorabilia

2003-04 BAP Ultimate Memorabilia Vintage Blades of Steel

ANNOUNCED PRINT RUN 20
1 Bill Barilko 40.00 80.00
2 Georges Vezina 175.00 300.00
3 Rocket Richard 40.00 80.00
4 Cyclone Taylor 50.00 100.00
5 Frank Patrick 40.00 80.00
6 Frank Nighbor 30.00 60.00
7 Hap Day 50.00 100.00
8 Clint Benedict 40.00 80.00
9 Elmer Lach 30.00 60.00
10 Busher Jackson 30.00 60.00
11 Eddie Shore 30.00 60.00
12 Jacques Plante 40.00 80.00
13 Toe Blake 40.00 80.00
14 Jack Adams 30.00 60.00
15 Bobby Orr 75.00 150.00
16 Tim Horton 40.00 80.00
17 Aurel Joliat 40.00 80.00
18 Nels Stewart 30.00 60.00
19 Paddy Moran 30.00 60.00
20 Jean Beliveau 25.00 50.00

2003-04 BAP Ultimate Memorabilia Vintage Jerseys

PRINT RUN 40 SER.#'d SETS
1 Aurel Joliat 30.00 80.00
2 Bobby Orr 75.00 150.00
3 Doug Harvey 12.50 30.00
4 Roy Worters 20.00 50.00
5 Jacques Plante 20.00 50.00
6 Jean Beliveau 25.00 60.00
7 Johnny Bower 15.00 40.00
8 George Hainsworth 15.00 40.00
9 Frank Brimsek 15.00 40.00
10 Roger Crozier 12.50 30.00
11 Harry Lumley 20.00 50.00
12 Sid Abel 12.50 30.00
13 Bill Mosienko 12.50 30.00
14 John Bucyk 12.50 30.00
15 Ted Lindsay 12.50 30.00
16 Alex Delvecchio 12.50 30.00
17 Phil Esposito 15.00 40.00
18 Frank Mahovlich 12.50 30.00
19 Maurice Richard 30.00 80.00
20 Dennis Hull 12.50 30.00
21 Marcel Dionne 12.50 30.00
22 Terry O'Reilly 15.00 40.00
23 Vladislav Tretiak 25.00 60.00
24 Henri Richard 12.50 30.00
25 Larry Robinson 12.50 30.00
26 Mike Bossy 12.50 30.00
27 Bryan Trottier 12.50 30.00
28 Gump Worsley 12.50 30.00
29 Bobby Clarke 12.50 30.00
30 Red Kelly 15.00 40.00
31 Gilbert Perreault 12.50 30.00
32 Lanny McDonald 12.50 30.00
33 Ray Bourque 15.00 40.00
34 Ed Giacomin 12.50 30.00
35 Valeri Kharlamov 20.00 50.00
36 Stan Mikita 12.50 30.00
37 Denis Potvin 12.50 30.00
38 Bobby Hull 20.00 50.00
39 Patrick Roy 15.00 40.00
40 Cam Neely 12.50 30.00

2003-04 BAP Ultimate Memorabilia Vintage Lumber

PRINT RUN 30 SER.#'d SETS
1 Bernie Geoffrion 15.00 40.00
2 Henri Richard 20.00 50.00
3 Joe Primeau 15.00 40.00
4 Georges Vezina 100.00 250.00
5 Jean Beliveau 15.00 40.00
6 Maurice Richard 50.00 125.00
7 Tim Horton 30.00 80.00
8 Doug Harvey 15.00 40.00
9 Terry Sawchuk 30.00 80.00
10 Jacques Plante 25.00 60.00
11 Harry Lumley 20.00 50.00
12 Howie Morenz 40.00 100.00

2001-02 BAP Update He Shoots He Scores Points

Inserted one per pack, these cards carried a value of 1, 2 or 3 points. The points could be redeemed for special memorabilia cards. The cards are unnumbered and are listed below in alphabetical order by point value. Redemption cards expired May 2003.

ONE PER PACK
1 Todd Bertuzzi 1 pt. .20 .50
2 Theo Fleury 1 pt. .25 .60
3 Marian Gaborik 1 pt. .25 .60
4 Bill Guerin 1 pt. .25 .60
5 Martin Havlat 1 pt. .20 .50
6 Marian Hossa 1 pt. .25 .60
7 Nicklas Lidstrom 1 pt. .30 .75
8 Joe Thornton 1 pt. .25 .60
9 Alexei Yashin 1 pt. .20 .50
10 Ed Belfour 2 pts. .25 .60
11 Martin Brodeur 2 pts. .40 1.00
12 Pavel Bure 2 pts. .30 .75
13 Ron Francis 2 pts. .25 .60
14 Luc Robitaille 2 pts. .20 .50
15 Jose Theodore 2 pts. .25 .60
16 Peter Forsberg 3 pts. .30 .75
17 Dominik Hasek 3 pts. .60 1.50
18 Curtis Joseph 3 pts. .60 1.50
19 Patrick Roy 3 pts. 1.50 4.00

2001-02 BAP Update Heritage

Randomly inserted into packs of BAP Update, this 30-card set featured game-worn jersey swatches of the featured players affixed beside a color action photo of the player on a blue card front. Cards in this set were limited to 90 copies each.

STATED PRINT RUN 90 SETS
H1 Wayne Gretzky 30.00 80.00
H2 Curtis Joseph 10.00 25.00
H3 Felix Potvin 12.00 30.00
H4 Mark Messier 12.50 30.00
H5 Doug Gilmour 10.00 25.00
H6 Keith Tkachuk 10.00 25.00
H7 Teemu Selanne 8.00 20.00
H8 Adam Oates 10.00 25.00
H9 Pavel Bure 6.00 15.00
H10 Mats Sundin 10.00 25.00
H11 Ed Belfour 10.00 25.00
H12 Mike Modano 8.00 20.00
H13 Brett Hull 12.50 30.00
H14 Brendan Shanahan 10.00 25.00
H15 Al MacInnis 10.00 25.00
H16 Theo Fleury 10.00 25.00
H17 Ed Jovanovski 6.00 15.00
H18 Keith Primeau 6.00 15.00
H19 Patrick Roy 20.00 50.00
H20 Jeff Hackett 6.00 15.00
H21 Owen Nolan 10.00 25.00
H22 Jeremy Roenick 12.50 30.00
H23 Mark Recchi 10.00 25.00
H24 Roman Turek 10.00 25.00
H25 Alexander Mogilny 10.00 25.00
H26 Jason Allison 6.00 15.00
H27 Luc Robitaille 10.00 25.00
H28 Bill Guerin 10.00 25.00
H29 Rob Blake 10.00 25.00
H30 Gary Roberts 6.00 15.00

2001-02 BAP Update Passing the Torch

Randomly inserted into packs of BAP Update, this 6-card set featured game-worn swatches from the three players featured on each card. Two black-and-white photos flanked a smaller color photo on the card front with the jersey swatches under each photo. Cards from this set were limited to 25 copies each.

STATED PRINT RUN 25 SETS
PTT1 Bucyk/Neely/Thornton 20.00 50.00
PTT2 Hull/Goulet/Amonte 20.00 50.00
PTT3 Abel/Howe/Yzerman 60.00 150.00
PTT4 Richard/Lafleur/Koivu 60.00 150.00
PTT5 Giacomin/Gilbert/Leetch 20.00 50.00
PTT6 Clancy/Horton/Sundin 60.00 150.00

2001-02 BAP Update Rocket's Rivals

Randomly inserted into packs of BAP Update, this 10-card set featured game-worn jersey swatches of the featured player. Each card carried a black-and-white photo of Rocket Richard on the left side and a color photo of the featured player on the right. The jersey swatch was affixed in the middle. Exact print runs for each card are printed below.

STATED PRINT RUN 10-40
RR1 Gordie Howe/10
RR2 Ted Lindsay/30 40.00 100.00
RR3 Johnny Bower/30 40.00 100.00
RR4 Terry Sawchuk/30 40.00 100.00
RR5 Frank Brimsek/40 20.00 50.00
RR6 Turk Broda/10
RR7 Bill Gadsby/30 15.00 40.00
RR8 Chuck Rayner/10
RR9 Glenn Hall/30 20.00 50.00
RR10 Bill Mosienko/40 30.00 80.00

2001-02 BAP Update Tough Customers

This 40-card set was randomly inserted into packs of BAP Update. Each card carried two jersey swatches from some of the league's most notorious enforcers. Jersey swatches were affixed under color photos of each player. Cards from this set were limited to 90 copies each.

STATED PRINT RUN 90 SETS
TC1 D.Schultz/T.Williams 20.00 50.00
TC2 B.Probert/T.Domi 15.00 40.00
TC3 I.Laperriere/S.Grimson 10.00 25.00
TC4 P.Worrell/C.Berube 8.00 20.00
TC5 J.Mayers/K.Belanger 8.00 20.00
TC6 S.Grimson/B.Probert 25.00 60.00
TC7 P.Laus/M.Johnson 8.00 20.00
TC8 R.Ray/C.Neil 12.00 30.00
TC9 A.Nazarov/B.Brown 8.00 20.00
TC10 J.Tetarenko/D.Langdon 8.00 20.00
TC11 T.Domi/R.Ray 12.00 30.00
TC12 K.Oliwa/P.Worrell 8.00 20.00
TC13 L.Richardson/J.Odgers 8.00 20.00
TC14 P.J.Stock/M.Barnaby 8.00 20.00
TC15 W.Belak/S.McCarthy 8.00 20.00
TC16 D.Brashear/G.Laraque 15.00 40.00
TC17 A.Roy/J.Odgers 8.00 20.00
TC18 A.Roy/T.Domi 8.00 20.00
TC19 D.Brashear/B.Probert 15.00 40.00
TC20 D.Langdon/R.Thompson 8.00 20.00
TC21 R.Vandenbussche/C.Simon 10.00 25.00
TC22 M.Johnson/C.Berube 8.00 20.00
TC23 S.Parker/D.Lambert 8.00 20.00
TC24 G.Laraque/J.Odgers 8.00 20.00
TC25 L.Richardson/W.Belak 8.00 20.00
TC26 C.Dingman/P.Laus 8.00 20.00
TC27 G.Odjick/C.Simon 8.00 20.00
TC28 I.Laperriere/A.Nazarov 8.00 20.00
TC29 G.Laraque/P.Laus 8.00 20.00
TC30 K.Oliwa/E.Cairns 8.00 20.00
TC31 M.Richard/T.Lindsay 50.00 125.00
TC32 G.Howe/S.Mikita 75.00 150.00
TC33 D.Lambert/A.Roy 8.00 20.00
TC34 W.Clark/B.Probert 20.00 50.00
TC35 R.Vandenbussche/J.Mayers 8.00 20.00
TC36 R.Thompson/P.J.Stock 8.00 20.00
TC37 S.Parker/K.Belanger 8.00 20.00
TC38 C.Neil/M.Barnaby 8.00 20.00
TC39 C.Dingman/S.McCarthy 15.00 40.00
TC40 G.Odjick/E.Cairns 8.00 20.00

2001-02 BAP Update Travel Plans

Randomly inserted into packs of BAP Update, this 16-card set featured game-worn jersey swatches of the featured player from two different teams. Each card carried small color photos of the player in the two different uniforms alongside the two jersey swatches. Cards in this set were limited to 50 copies each.

STATED PRINT RUN 50 SETS
TP1 Jaromir Jagr 20.00 50.00
TP2 Dominik Hasek 20.00 50.00
TP3 Roman Turek 8.00 20.00
TP4 Teemu Selanne 15.00 40.00
TP5 Keith Tkachuk 12.50 30.00
TP6 Rob Blake 12.50 30.00
TP7 Alexander Mogilny 8.00 20.00
TP8 Luc Robitaille 12.50 30.00
TP9 Alexei Yashin 8.00 20.00
TP10 Eric Lindros 15.00 40.00
TP11 Jeremy Roenick 15.00 40.00
TP12 Doug Weight 8.00 20.00
TP13 Felix Potvin 15.00 40.00
TP14 Nikolai Khabibulin 15.00 40.00
TP15 Dave Andreychuk 8.00 20.00
TP16 Dan Cloutier 8.00 20.00

1934-44 Beehive Group I Photos

The 1934-44 Beehive photos are the first of three groups. Production was suspended in 1944 due to wartime priorities. The photos include a facsimile autograph, small script or occasionally block letters. Complete set price is not given due to an ongoing debate over what constitutes a complete set. A number of unconfirmed photos are scattered throughout the Beehive master checklist. If anyone has information to corroborate the existence of any of these cards, please forward it to Beckett Publications.

COMMON PHOTO 7.50 15.00
1 Bobby Bauer 7.50 15.00
2 Red Beattie 12.50 25.00
3 Buzz Boll
(Unconfirmed)
4 Yank Boyd 75.00 150.00
5A Frankie Brimsek 12.50 25.00
(With Net)
5B Frankie Brimsek 15.00 30.00
(Without Net)
8 Dit Clapper 10.00 20.00
9 Roy Conacher 10.00 20.00
10 Bun Cook 10.00 20.00
11 Bill Cowley 10.00 20.00
12 John Crawford 7.50 15.00
13 Woody Dumart 12.50 25.00
14 Don Gallinger 87.50 175.00
15 Ray Getiffe 15.00 30.00
17 Bep Guidolin 50.00 100.00
18 Red Hamill 15.00 30.00
19 Mel Hill 10.00 20.00
24 Pat McReavy 7.50 15.00
25 Alex Motter 15.00 30.00
26 Peggy O'Neil 10.00 20.00
29 Charlie Sands 10.00 20.00
30 Jackie Schmidt 87.50 175.00
31 Milt Schmidt 10.00 20.00
32 Jack Shewchuk 10.00 20.00
33 Eddie Shore 50.00 100.00
35 Tiny Thompson 25.00 50.00
36 Cooney Weiland 10.00 20.00
38 George Allen 12.50 25.00
39 Doug Bentley 15.00 30.00
40 Max Bentley 20.00 40.00
42 Glenn Brydson 62.50 125.00
43 Marty Burke 7.50 15.00
44 Bill Carse 7.50 15.00
45 Bob Carse 7.50 15.00
46 Lorne Chabot 25.00 50.00
47 John Chad 15.00 30.00
49 Les Cunningham 15.00 30.00
50 Cully Dahlstrom 10.00 20.00
53 Leroy Goldsworthy 12.50 25.00
54 Paul Goodman 20.00 40.00
55 Johnny Gottselig 12.50 25.00
56 Philip Hergesheimer 7.50 15.00
58 George(Wingy) Johnston 87.50 175.00
59 Alex Kaleta 15.00 30.00
60 Mike Karakas 15.00 30.00
63 Alex Levinsky 12.50 25.00
64 Sam LoPresti 25.00 50.00
65 Dave Mackay 125.00 250.00
66 Bill MacKenzie
(Unconfirmed)
67 Mush March 7.50 15.00
68 John Mariucci 25.00 50.00
69 Joe Matte 62.50 125.00
70 Red Mitchell UER 87.50 175.00
(Name misspelled Mitchel)
72 Peter Palangio 40.00 80.00
73 Joe Papike 50.00 100.00
75 Cliff Purpur 87.50 175.00
77 Doc Romnes 25.00 50.00
78 Earl Seibert 10.00 20.00
81 Paul Thompson 15.00 30.00
83 Louis Trudel UER 20.00 40.00
(Name misspelled Trudell)
84 Audley Tuten 87.50 175.00
85 Art Wiebe 12.50 25.00
86 Sid Abel 15.00 30.00
87 Larry Aurie 7.50 15.00
88 Marty Barry 12.50 25.00
89 Ralph Bowman 12.50 25.00
90 Adam Brown 40.00 80.00
91 Connie Brown 50.00 100.00
92 Jerry Brown 150.00 300.00
93 Mud Bruneteau 10.00 20.00
94 Eddie Bush 125.00 250.00
95 Joe Carveth 7.50 15.00
99 Les Douglas 50.00 100.00
100 Gus Biesebrecht UER 7.50 15.00
(Name misspelled Geisebrech)
101 Ebbie Goodfellow 10.00 20.00
102 Don Grosso 7.50 15.00
104 Syd Howe 10.00 20.00
105 Bill Jennings 40.00 80.00
106 Jack Keating 15.00 30.00
107 Pete Kelly 10.00 20.00
108 Hec Kilrea 10.00 20.00
109 Ken Kilrea 10.00 20.00
110 Wally Kilrea 10.00 20.00
111 Herb Lewis 10.00 20.00
112 Carl Liscombe 7.50 15.00
114 Douglas McCaig 40.00 80.00
115A Bucko McDonald 50.00 100.00
(Ice photo)
115B Bucko McDonald 50.00 100.00
(Dressing room photo)
116 Pat McReavy 40.00 80.00
118 Johnny Mowers 12.50 25.00
119 Jimmy Orlando 7.50 15.00
120 Gord Pettinger 20.00 40.00
121 John Sherf 20.00 40.00
123 Norm Smith 15.00 30.00
124 John Sorrell 12.50 25.00
125 Jack Stewart 20.00 40.00
128 Carl Voss 50.00 100.00
129 Eddie Wares 12.00 30.00
131 Arch Wilder 12.50 25.00
132 Douglas Young 12.50 25.00
133 Jack Adams 12.50 25.00
134 Marty Barry 200.00 400.00
135 Joe Benoit 10.00 20.00
136 Paul Bibeault 25.00 50.00
137 Toe Blake 15.00 30.00
138 Butch Bouchard 7.50 15.00
139 Claude Bourque 20.00 40.00
140 George Allan Brown 62.50 125.00
141 Walt Buswell 20.00 40.00
143 Murph Chamberlain 25.00 50.00
144 Wilf Cude 15.00 30.00
145 Bunny Dame 25.00 50.00
146 Tony DeMeres UER 7.50 15.00
(Name misspelled Dremers)
147 Joffre Desilets 10.00 20.00
148 Gordie Drillon 350.00 700.00
149 Polly Drouin 7.50 15.00
151 Johnny Gagnon 7.50 15.00
152 Bert Gardiner 15.00 30.00
153 Ray Getiffe 40.00 80.00
154 Red Goupille 10.00 20.00
155 Tony Graboski 10.00 20.00
157 Paul Haynes 7.50 15.00
158 Gerry Heffernan 75.00 150.00
160 Roger Jenkins 30.00 60.00
161 Aurel Joliat 20.00 40.00
162 Elmer Lach 20.00 40.00
163 Leo Lamoreux UER 62.50 125.00
(Name misspelled Camoreaux)
164 Pit Lepine 7.50 15.00
165 Rod Lorraine 15.00 30.00
166 Georges Mantha 10.00 20.00
167 Sylvio Mantha 10.00 20.00
169 Armand Mondou 7.50 15.00
170 Howie Morenz 375.00 750.00
171 Pete Morin 75.00 150.00
172 Buddy O'Connor 75.00 150.00
175 Jack Portland 7.50 15.00
176 John Quilty 12.50 25.00
177 Ken Reardon 20.00 40.00
178 Terry Reardon 50.00 100.00
179 Maurice Richard 20.00 40.00
180 Earl Robinson 200.00 400.00
181 Charlie Sands 30.00 60.00
182 Babe Siebert 20.00 40.00
183 Alex Singbush 50.00 100.00
184 Bill Summerhill 87.50 175.00
185 Louis Trudel 40.00 80.00
187 Cy Wentworth 1500.00 3000.00
188 Douglas Young 50.00 100.00
189 Bill Beveridge 30.00 60.00
190 Russ Blinco 20.00 40.00
191 Herb Cain 30.00 60.00
192 Gerry Carson UER 87.50 175.00
(Name misspelled Jerry)
194 Alex Connell 30.00 60.00
195 Tom Cook 20.00 40.00
196 Stewart Evans 15.00 30.00
197 Bob Gracie 50.00 100.00
198 Max Kaminsky 87.50 175.00
199 Bill MacKenzie 62.50 125.00
200 Gus Marker 100.00 200.00
201 Baldy Northcott 30.00 60.00
202 Earl Robinson 25.00 50.00
203 Paul Runge 87.50 175.00
204 Gerry Shannon UER 87.50 175.00
(Name misspelled Jerry)
206 Des Smith 20.00 40.00
207 Hooley Smith 20.00 40.00
208 Dave Trottier 50.00 100.00
209 Jimmy Ward 20.00 40.00
210 Cy Wentworth 25.00 50.00
211 Viv Allen 30.00 60.00
212 Tom Anderson 20.00 40.00
215 Bill Benson 25.00 50.00
218 Lorne Carr 25.00 50.00
219 Art Chapman 20.00 40.00
222 Red Dutton 25.00 50.00
223 Pat Egan 20.00 40.00
224 Happy Emms 40.00 80.00
225 Wilf Field 20.00 40.00
226 John Gallagher 20.00 40.00
232 Joe Jerwa 25.00 50.00
234 Jim Klein 50.00 100.00
236 Joe Krol 625.00 1250.00
237 Joe Lamb 40.00 80.00
238 Red Heron 20.00 40.00
241 Hazen McAndrew 750.00 1500.00
243 Ken Mosdell 200.00 400.00
244 Al Murray 15.00 30.00
245 John O'Flaherty 30.00 60.00
246 Chuck Rayner 100.00 200.00
247 Earl Robertson 25.00 50.00
249 Sweeny Schriner 20.00 40.00
250 Al Shields 50.00 100.00
252 Pete Slobodzian UER 30.00 60.00
(Name misspelled Slobodian)
255 Nels Stewart 25.00 50.00
256 Fred Thurier 62.50 125.00
257 Harry Watson 112.50 225.00
258 Eddie Wiseman 15.00 30.00
259 Roy Worters 30.00 60.00
260 Ralph Wycherly 30.00 60.00
261 Frank Boucher 20.00 40.00
263 Norm Burns 50.00 100.00
265 Mac Colville 7.50 15.00
266 Neil Colville 10.00 20.00
267 Bill Cook 12.50 25.00
268 Joe Cooper 7.50 15.00
269 Art Coulter 7.50 15.00
270 Gord Davidson 30.00 60.00
271 Cecil Dillon 10.00 20.00
272 Jim Franks 100.00 200.00
273 Red Garrett 75.00 150.00
275 Ott Heller 7.50 15.00
276A Jim Henry 50.00 100.00
(Vertical photo)
276B Jim Henry 30.00 60.00
(Horizontal photo)
277 Bryan Hextall Sr. 15.00 30.00
278 Dutch Hiller 10.00 20.00
279 Ching Johnson 12.50 25.00
280 Bill Juzda 10.00 20.00
281 Butch Keeling 10.00 20.00
282 Davey Kerr 15.00 30.00
283 Bobby Kirk 50.00 100.00
284 Bob Kirkpatrick 50.00 100.00
285 Kilby MacDonald 10.00 20.00
286 Larry Molyneaux 15.00 30.00
287 John Murray Murdoch 20.00 40.00
288 Vic Myles 87.50 175.00
289 Lynn Patrick 10.00 20.00
290 Murray Patrick 7.50 15.00
291 Alf Pike 7.50 15.00
292 Babe Pratt 12.50 25.00
293 Alex Shibicky 7.50 15.00
294 Clint Smith 7.50 15.00
295 Norman Tustin 50.00 100.00
296 Grant Warwick 50.00 100.00
297 Phil Watson 7.50 15.00
298 Syl Apps Sr. 12.50 25.00
299 Murray Armstrong 7.50 15.00
300 Andy Blair 10.00 20.00
301 Buzz Boll 10.00 20.00
302 George Boothman 125.00 250.00
303 Turk Broda 12.50 25.00
304 Lorne Carr 30.00 60.00
305 Murph Chamberlain 7.50 15.00
306 Lex Chisholm 10.00 20.00
307 Jack Church 10.00 20.00
308 Francis Clancy 15.00 30.00
309 Charlie Conacher 12.50 25.00
310 Bob Copp 30.00 60.00
311 Baldy Cotton 10.00 20.00
312 Bob Davidson 7.50 15.00
313 Hap Day 7.50 15.00
314 Ernie Dickens 100.00 200.00
315 Gordie Drillon 7.50 15.00
316 Frank Finnigan 12.50 25.00
317 Jack Forsey 100.00 200.00
318 Jimmy Fowler UER 7.50 15.00
(Name misspelled Jimmie)
319 Bob Goldham 100.00 200.00
320 Hank Goldup 7.50 15.00
321 George Hainsworth 20.00 40.00
322 Reg Hamilton 7.50 15.00
323 Red Heron 10.00 20.00
324 Mel Hill 150.00 300.00
325 Frank Hollett 7.50 15.00
326 Red Horner 10.00 20.00
327 Art Jackson 7.50 15.00
328 Harvey Jackson 7.50 15.00
329 Bingo Kampman 20.00 40.00
330 Reg Kelly 10.00 20.00
331 William Kendall 40.00 80.00
332 Hec Kilrea 25.00 50.00
333 Pete Langelle 10.00 20.00
334 Bucko McDonald 10.00 20.00
335A Norm Mann 12.50 25.00
335B Norm Mann 87.50 175.00
(Name overlaps stick)
336 Gus Marker 7.50 15.00
337 Johnny McCreedy 20.00 40.00
338 Jack McLean 50.00 100.00
339 Don Metz 7.50 15.00
340 Nick Metz 7.50 15.00
341 George Parsons 12.50 25.00
342 Bud Poile 87.50 175.00
343 Babe Pratt 125.00 250.00
344 Joe Primeau 12.50 25.00
345 Doc Romnes 25.00 50.00
346 Sweeny Schriner 15.00 30.00
347 Jack Shill 12.50 25.00
348 Wally Stanowski UER 7.50 15.00
(Name misspelled Stanowsky)
349 Phil Stein 25.00 50.00
350A Gaye Stewart 175.00 350.00
(Home Sweater)
350B Gaye Stewart 100.00 200.00
(Away Sweater)
351 Billy Taylor 7.50 15.00
352 Rhys Thompson 200.00 400.00
353 Bill Thoms 7.50 15.00
354 1944-45 Maple Leafs 150.00 300.00
355 1937 Winnipeg Monarchs 75.00 150.00
356 Foster Hewitt 40.00 80.00
357 Wes McKnight 62.50 125.00
358A Allan Cup 30.00 60.00
(Dated on back)
358B Allan Cup 62.50 125.00
(Blank Back)
359A Lady Byng Trophy 30.00 60.00
(Dated on back)
359B Lady Byng Trophy 62.50 125.00
(Blank back)
360A Calder Trophy 30.00 60.00
(Dated on back)
360B Calder Trophy 62.50 125.00
(Blank back)
361A Hart Trophy 30.00 60.00
(Dated on back)
361B Hart Trophy 62.50 125.00
(Blank back)
362A Memorial Cup 40.00 80.00
(Dated on back)
362B Memorial Cup 75.00 150.00
(Blank back)
363A Prince of Wales Trophy 87.50 175.00
(Dated on back)
363B Prince of Wales Trophy 100.00 200.00
(Blank back)
364A Stanley Cup 30.00 60.00
(Dated on back)
364B Stanley Cup 50.00 100.00
(Blank back)
364C Stanley Cup 50.00 100.00
(Name horizontal)
365A Georges Vezina Trophy 30.00 60.00
(Dated on back)
365B Georges Vezina Trophy 62.50 125.00
(Blank back)

1944-63 Beehive Group II Photos

The 1944-63 Beehive photos are the second of three groups. Issued after World War II, this group generally had new photos and a larger script than was typical of Group I. Facsimile autographs were again featured. There are a number of unconfirmed photos that appeared on the Beehive checklist, among these are the Allan and Memorial Cup trophies in either of their varieties.

1 Bob Armstrong 5.00 10.00
2 Pete Babando 25.00 50.00
3 Ray Barry 25.00 50.00
4 Gus Bodnar 40.00 80.00
5 Leo Boivin 6.00 12.00
6 Frankie Brimsek 12.50 25.00
8 John Bucyk 7.50 15.00
9 Charlie Burns 5.00 10.00
10 Jack Caffery 30.00 60.00
11 Real Chevrefils 5.00 10.00
12A Wayne Connelly 10.00 20.00
12B Wayne Connelly 30.00 60.00
(Name overlaps skate)
14 John Crawford 10.00 20.00
15A Dave Creighton 6.00 12.00
(White sweater)
15B Dave Creighton 30.00 60.00
(Photo on ice)
16 Woody Dumart 12.50 25.00
17 Pat Egan 15.00 30.00
19 Lorne Ferguson 6.00 12.00
20 Fern Flaman 5.00 10.00
21 Bruce Gamble 6.00 12.00
22 Cal Gardner 6.00 12.00
23 Ray Gariepy 10.00 20.00
24 Jack Gelineau 12.50 25.00
25 Jean-Guy Gendron 5.00 10.00
26A Warren Godfrey 6.00 12.00
(A on sweater)
26B Warren Godfrey 30.00 60.00
(With puck)
26C Warren Godfrey 50.00 100.00
(Without puck)
27 Ed Harrison 5.00 10.00
28 Don Head 5.00 10.00
29 Andy Hebenton 7.50 15.00
30 Murray Henderson 7.50 15.00
31 Jim Henry 15.00 30.00
32 Larry Hillman 20.00 40.00
33 Pete Horeck 10.00 20.00
34 Bronco Horvath 5.00 10.00
35 Tom Johnson 6.00 12.00
36 Eddie Johnston 7.50 15.00
38 Joe Klukay 90.00 175.00
39 Edward Kryznowski 6.00 12.00
40 Orland Kurtenbach 20.00 40.00
41 Leo Labine 5.00 10.00
42 Hal Laycoe 5.00 10.00
43 Harry Lumley 7.50 15.00
44 Pentti Lund 500.00 1000.00
45 Fleming Mackell 5.00 10.00
46 Phil Maloney 10.00 20.00
47 Frank Martin 10.00 20.00
48 Jack McIntyre 10.00 20.00
49 Don McKenney 5.00 10.00
50 Dick Meissner 5.00 10.00
51 Doug Mohns 5.00 10.00
52 Murray Oliver 5.00 10.00
53 Willie O'Ree 7.50 15.00
54A John Peirson 6.00 12.00
54B Johnny Peirson 50.00 100.00
55A Cliff Pennington 10.00 20.00
(Name away from skate)
55B Cliff Pennington 50.00 100.00
(Name near skate)
56A Bob Perreault 12.50 25.00
(Name away from skate)
56B Bob Perreault 50.00 100.00
(Name overlaps skate)
57 Jim Peters 10.00 20.00
58 Dean Prentice 6.00 12.00
59 Andre Pronovost 5.00 10.00
60 Bill Quackenbush 10.00 20.00
61 Larry Regan 25.00 50.00
62 Earl Reibel 20.00 40.00
63 Paul Ronty 6.00 12.00
64 Ed Sandford 5.00 10.00
65 Terry Sawchuk 60.00 125.00
66A Norm Defelice ERR 75.00 150.00
(name on front is Don Simmons)
66B Norm Defelice COR 5.00 10.00
67 Kenny Smith 6.00 12.00
68A Pat Stapleton 10.00 20.00
(Name away from skate)
68B Pat Stapleton 50.00 100.00
(Name near skate)
69 Vic Stasiuk 7.50 15.00
70 Red Sullivan 12.50 25.00
71 Jerry Toppazzini 5.00 10.00
72 Zellio Toppazzini 6.00 12.00
73 Grant Warwick 20.00 40.00
74 Tom Williams 5.00 10.00
75 Al Arbour 6.00 12.00
76 Pete Babando 10.00 20.00
77 Earl Balfour 5.00 10.00
78 Murray Balfour 5.00 10.00
79 Jim Bedard 10.00 20.00
80 Doug Bentley 12.50 25.00
81 Gus Bodnar 6.00 12.00
82 Frankie Brimsek 20.00 40.00
83 Adam Brown 10.00 20.00
84 Hank Ciesla 20.00 40.00
85 Jim Conacher 7.50 15.00
86 Pete Conacher 5.00 10.00
87 Roy Conacher 5.00 10.00
88 Joe Conn 40.00 80.00
89 Murray Costello 40.00 80.00
90 Gerry Couture 12.50 25.00
91 Al Dewsbury 6.00 12.00
92 Ernie Dickens 5.00 10.00
93 Jack Evans 5.00 10.00
94 Reggie Fleming 5.00 10.00
95 Lee Fogolin 7.50 15.00
96 Bill Gadsby 5.00 10.00
97 George Gee 6.00 12.00
98 Bob Goldham 12.50 25.00
99 Bep Guidolin 6.00 12.00
100 Glenn Hall 6.00 12.00
101 Murray Hall 15.00 30.00
102 Red Hamill 15.00 30.00
103 Bill Hay 5.00 10.00
104 Jim Henry 15.00 30.00
105 Wayne Hillman 12.50 25.00
107 Bronco Horvath 6.00 12.00
108 Fred Hucul 12.50 25.00
109A Bobby Hull 100.00 200.00
(Jersey 9)
109B Bobby Hull 15.00 30.00
(Jersey 16)
110 Lou Jankowski 12.50 25.00
111 Forbes Kennedy 25.00 50.00
112 Ted Lindsay 7.50 15.00
113 Ed Litzenberger 5.00 10.00
114 Harry Lumley Goalie 20.00 40.00
115A Len Lunde 30.00 60.00
(Name away from stick)
115B Len Lunde 10.00 20.00
(Name overlaps stick)
116 Pat Lundy 7.50 15.00
118A Al MacNeil 20.00 40.00
(Name overlaps stick and skate)
118B Al MacNeil 6.00 12.00
(Name overlaps stick)
119A Chico Maki 7.50 15.00
(Name away from stick)
119B Chico Maki 60.00 125.00
(Name overlaps stick)
120 Doug McCaig 12.50 25.00
121 Ab McDonald 5.00 10.00
122 Jim McFadden 20.00 40.00
124 Gerry Melnyk UER 5.00 10.00
(Name misspelled Jerry)
125 Stan Mikita 6.00 12.00
127 Gus Mortson 5.00 10.00
128 Bill Mosienko 7.50 15.00
129 Ron Murphy 5.00 10.00
130 Ralph Nattrass 12.50 25.00
131 Eric Nesterenko 5.00 10.00
132 Bert Olmstead 12.50 25.00
133 Jim Peters 20.00 40.00
134 Pierre Pilote 5.00 10.00
135 Metro Prystai 6.00 12.00
137 Clare Raglan 15.00 30.00
138A Al Rollins 50.00 100.00
(Vertical photo)
138B Al Rollins 15.00 30.00
(Horizontal photo)
139 Tod Sloan 5.00 10.00
140 Dollard St. Laurent 5.00 10.00
141 Gaye Stewart 10.00 20.00
142 Jack Stewart 20.00 40.00
143A Bob Turner 25.00 50.00
(Name away from stick)
143B Bob Turner 15.00 30.00
(Name overlaps stick)
144 Elmer Vasko 5.00 10.00
145 Kenny Wharram 5.00 10.00
146 Larry Wilson 10.00 20.00
147 Howie Young 12.50 25.00
149 Sid Abel 10.00 20.00
150 Al Arbour 20.00 40.00
151 Pete Babando 12.50 25.00
152A Doug Barkley 30.00 60.00
(Stick blade showing)
152B Doug Barkley 10.00 20.00
(No blade showing)
153 Hank Bassen 6.00 12.00
154 Stephen Black 15.00 30.00
155 Marcel Bonin 7.50 15.00
156 John Bucyk 25.00 50.00
157 John Conacher 100.00 200.00
158 Gerry Couture UER 6.00 12.00
(Name misspelled Jerry)
159 Billy Dea 12.50 25.00
160B Alex Delvecchio COR 5.00 10.00
162 Bill Dineen 5.00 10.00
163 Jim Enio 30.00 60.00
164 Alex Faulkner 25.00 50.00
165 Lee Fogolin 6.00 12.00
166 Val Fonteyne 5.00 10.00
167 Bill Gadsby 7.50 15.00
168 Fern Gauthier 20.00 40.00
169 George Gee 7.50 15.00
170 Fred Glover 5.00 10.00
171 Howie Glover 5.00 10.00
172 Warren Godfrey 5.00 10.00
173 Peter Goegan 5.00 10.00
174 Bob Goldham 6.00 12.00
175 Glenn Hall 40.00 80.00
176 Larry Hillman 25.00 50.00
177 Pete Horeck 20.00 40.00
178A Gordie Howe 25.00 50.00
178B Gordie Howe 40.00 80.00
(C on sweater)
179 Ron Ingram 20.00 40.00
180 Larry Jeffrey 15.00 30.00
181 Al Johnson 5.00 10.00
182 Red Kelly 5.00 10.00
183 Forbes Kennedy 5.00 10.00
184 Leo Labine 5.00 10.00
185 Tony Leswick 5.00 10.00
186 Ted Lindsay 6.00 12.00
187 Ed Litzenberger 15.00 30.00
188 Harry Lumley 12.50 25.00
189 Len Lunde 5.00 10.00
190 Parker MacDonald 5.00 10.00
191 Bruce MacGregor 5.00 10.00
192 Clare Martin 12.50 25.00
193 Jim McFadden 7.50 15.00
194 Max McNab 12.50 25.00
195 Gerry Melnyk UER 5.00 10.00
(Name misspelled Jerry)
196 Don Morrison 12.50 25.00
197 Rud Morrison 25.00 50.00
198 Gerry Odrowski 5.00 10.00
199 Murray Oliver 5.00 10.00
200 Marty Pavelich 5.00 10.00
201 Jim Peters 25.00 50.00
202 Bud Poile 75.00 150.00
203 Andre Pronovost 6.00 12.00
204 Marcel Pronovost 5.00 10.00
205 Metro Prystai 5.00 10.00
206 Bill Quackenbush 25.00 50.00

207 Earl Reibel 5.00 10.00
208 Leo Reise Jr. 6.00 12.00
209A Terry Sawchuk ERR 20.00 40.00
(name misspelled Sawchuck)
209B Terry Sawchuk COR 20.00 40.00
(name spelled correctly; different photo)
210 Glen Skov 5.00 10.00
211 Floyd Smith 6.00 12.00
212A Vic Stasiuk 12.50 25.00
(Home sweater;
full stick showing)
212B Vic Stasiuk 20.00 40.00
(Home sweater;
partial stick showing)
212C Vic Stasiuk 7.50 15.00
(Away sweater)
213 Gaye Stewart 15.00 30.00
214 Jack Stewart 15.00 30.00
215 Norm Ullman 5.00 10.00
216 Johnny Wilson 5.00 10.00
217 Benny Woit 5.00 10.00
218 Howie Young 6.00 12.00
219 Larry Zeidel 12.50 25.00
220 Ralph Backstrom 5.00 10.00
221 Dave Balon 5.00 10.00
222 Jean Beliveau 10.00 20.00
223A Red Berenson 12.50 25.00
(White script)
223B Red Berenson 100.00 200.00
(Black script)
224 Marcel Bonin 5.00 10.00
225 Butch Bouchard 5.00 10.00
226 Tod Campeau 50.00 100.00
227 Joe Carveth 6.00 12.00
228 Murph Chamberlain 25.00 50.00
229 Doc Couture 20.00 40.00
230 Floyd Curry UER 5.00 10.00
(Name misspelled Currie)
231 Ian Cushenan 7.50 15.00
232 Lorne Davis 6.00 12.00
233 Eddie Dorohoy 12.50 25.00
234 Gilles Dube 30.00 60.00
235 Bill Durnan 20.00 40.00
236 Norm Dussault 12.50 25.00
237 John Ferguson 6.00 12.00
238 Bob Fillion 7.50 15.00
239 Louie Fontinato 5.00 10.00
240 Dick Gamble 10.00 20.00
241 Bernard Geoffrion 7.50 15.00
242 Phil Goyette 5.00 10.00
243 Leo Gravelle 12.50 25.00
244 John Hanna 30.00 60.00
245 Glen Harmon 10.00 20.00
246 Terry Harper 5.00 10.00
247 Doug Harvey 7.50 15.00
248 Bill Hicke 5.00 10.00
251A Charlie Hodge 40.00 80.00
(White script)
251B Charlie Hodge 6.00 12.00
(Black script)
252 Tom Johnson 6.00 12.00
253 Vern Kaiser 20.00 40.00
254 Frank King 20.00 40.00
255 Elmer Lach 6.00 12.00
256 Al Langlois 5.00 10.00
257 Jacques Laperriere 5.00 10.00
258 Hal Laycoe 6.00 12.00
259 Jackie Leclair 5.00 10.00
260 Roger Leger 10.00 20.00
261 Ed Litzenberger 12.50 25.00
262 Ross Lowe 20.00 40.00
263 Al MacNeil 5.00 10.00
264 Bud MacPherson 5.00 10.00
265 Cesare Maniago 6.00 12.00
266 Don Marshall 5.00 10.00
267 Paul Masnick 5.00 10.00
268 Eddie Mazur 10.00 20.00
269 John McCormack 6.00 12.00
270 Alvin McDonald 5.00 10.00
271 Calum MacKay 6.00 12.00
272 Gerry McNeil 7.50 15.00
273 Paul Meger 10.00 20.00
274 Dickie Moore 6.00 12.00
275 Kenny Mosdell 10.00 20.00
276 Bert Olmstead 5.00 10.00
277 Gerry Plamondon 10.00 20.00
278 Jacques Plante 20.00 40.00
279 Andre Pronovost 5.00 10.00
280 Claude Provost 5.00 10.00
281 Ken Reardon 12.50 25.00
282 Billy Reay 6.00 12.00
283 Henri Richard 10.00 20.00
284 Maurice Richard 20.00 40.00
285 Rip Riopelle 15.00 30.00
286 George Robertson 50.00 100.00
287 Bobby Rousseau 5.00 10.00
288 Dollard St. Laurent 5.00 10.00
289 Jean-Guy Talbot 5.00 10.00
290A Gilles Tremblay 5.00 10.00
(Dark background)
290B Gilles Tremblay 100.00 200.00
(Light background)
291A J.C. Tremblay 5.00 10.00
(Dark background)
291B J.C. Tremblay 100.00 200.00
(Light background)
292 Bob Turner 5.00 10.00
293 Grant Warwick 20.00 40.00
294 Gump Worsley 12.50 25.00
295 Clint Albright 6.00 12.00
296A Dave Balon 12.50 25.00
(Name high on photo)
296B Dave Balon 5.00 10.00
(Name low on photo)
297A Andy Bathgate 6.00 12.00
(Home sweater)
297B Andy Bathgate 10.00 20.00
(Away sweater)
298 Max Bentley 25.00 50.00
299 Johnny Bower 25.00 50.00
300 Hy Buller 10.00 20.00
301A Larry Cahan 6.00 12.00
(Home sweater)
301B Larry Cahan 12.50 25.00
(Away sweater)
302 Bob Crystal 15.00 30.00
304 Brian Cullen 5.00 10.00
305 Ian Cushenan 5.00 10.00
306 Billy Dea 15.00 30.00
307 Frank Eddolls 5.00 10.00
308 Pat Egan 20.00 40.00
309A Jack Evans 5.00 10.00
(Name parallel to bottom)
309B Jack Evans 20.00 40.00
(Name printed diagonally)
310 Dunc Fisher 7.50 15.00
311 Louie Fontinato 5.00 10.00
312 Bill Gadsby 5.00 10.00
313 Jean-Guy Gendron 5.00 10.00
314 Rod Gilbert 6.00 12.00
315 Howie Glover 20.00 40.00
317 Phil Goyette 5.00 10.00
318 Aldo Guidolin 25.00 50.00
319 Vic Hadfield 6.00 12.00
320 Ted Hampson 5.00 10.00
321 Doug Harvey 6.00 12.00
322 Andy Hebenton 5.00 10.00
323 Camille Henry 5.00 10.00
324 Wally Hergesheimer 5.00 10.00
325 Ike Hildebrand 15.00 30.00
326 Bronco Horvath 6.00 12.00
327 Harry Howell 5.00 10.00
328A Earl Ingarfield Sr. 5.00 10.00
(Name away from stick)
328B Earl Ingarfield Sr. 12.50 25.00
(Name near stick)
329 Bing Juckes 15.00 30.00
330 Alex Kaleta 7.50 15.00
331 Stephen Kraftcheck 20.00 40.00
332 Eddie Kullman 7.50 15.00
333 Gus Kyle 6.00 12.00
334 Gord Labossiere 25.00 50.00
335 Al Langlois 5.00 10.00
336 Edgar Laprade 7.50 15.00
337 Tony Leswick 6.00 12.00
338 Danny Lewicki 5.00 10.00
339 Pentti Lund 10.00 20.00
340 Don Marshall 12.50 25.00
341 Jack McCartan 6.00 12.00
342 Bill McDonagh 12.50 25.00
343 Don McKenney 10.00 20.00
344 Jackie McLeod 10.00 20.00
345 Nick Mickoski 6.00 12.00
346 Billy Moe 7.50 15.00
348 Ron Murphy 5.00 10.00
349 Buddy O'Connor 7.50 15.00
350 Marcel Paille 50.00 100.00
351 Jacques Plante 50.00 100.00
352 Bud Poile 20.00 40.00
353 Larry Popein 5.00 10.00
354A Dean Prentice 5.00 10.00
(Home sweater)
354B Dean Prentice 7.50 15.00
(Away sweater)
355 Don Raleigh 7.50 15.00
356A Jean Ratelle ERR 25.00 50.00
(Name misspelled John)
356B Jean Ratelle COR 20.00 40.00
357 Chuck Rayner 12.50 25.00
358 Leo Reise Jr. 6.00 12.00
359 Paul Ronty 6.00 12.00
360 Ken Schinkel 5.00 10.00
361 Eddie Shack 15.00 30.00
362 Fred Shero 15.00 30.00
363 Reg Sinclair 20.00 40.00
364 Eddie Slowinski 7.50 15.00
365 Allan Stanley 5.00 10.00
366 Wally Stanowski 6.00 12.00
367 Red Sullivan 5.00 10.00
369 Gump Worsley 5.00 10.00
370 Gary Aldcorn 10.00 20.00
371 Syl Apps Sr. 90.00 175.00
372 Al Arbour 5.00 10.00
373A George Armstrong 6.00 12.00
373B George Armstrong 12.50 25.00
(Dark background)
373C George Armstrong 100.00 200.00
(Light background)
374 Bob Bailey 20.00 40.00
375 Earl Balfour 10.00 20.00
376 Bill Barilko 25.00 50.00
377 Andy Bathgate 25.00 50.00
378 Bob Baun 5.00 10.00
379 Max Bentley 12.50 25.00
380 Jack Bionda 75.00 150.00
381 Garth Boesch 6.00 12.00
382 Leo Boivin 7.50 15.00
383 Hugh Bolton 5.00 10.00
384 Johnny Bower 10.00 20.00
385 Carl Brewer 5.00 10.00
386 Turk Broda 12.50 25.00
387 Larry Cahan 7.50 15.00
388 Ray Ceresino 50.00 100.00
389 Ed Chadwick 6.00 12.00
390 Pete Conacher 50.00 100.00
391 Les Costello 20.00 40.00
392 Dave Creighton 10.00 20.00
393 Barry Cullen 12.50 25.00
394 Brian Cullen 5.00 10.00
395 Robert Dawes 12.50 25.00
396 Kent Douglas 5.00 10.00
397 Dick Duff 5.00 10.00
398 Gary Edmundson 5.00 10.00
399 Gerry Ehman 5.00 10.00
400 Bill Ezinicki 10.00 20.00
401 Fern Flaman 25.00 50.00
402 Cal Gardner 10.00 20.00
403 Ted Hampson 5.00 10.00
404 Gord Hannigan 10.00 20.00
405 Billy Harris 5.00 10.00
406 Bob Hassard 40.00 80.00
407 Larry Hillman 5.00 10.00
408 Tim Horton 12.50 25.00
409 Bronco Horvath 10.00 20.00
410 Ron Hurst 75.00 150.00
411 Gerry James UER 15.00 30.00
(Name misspelled Jerry)
412 Bill Juzda 7.50 15.00
413A Red Kelly 6.00 12.00
(Bare-headed)
413B Red Kelly 15.00 30.00
(Wearing helmet)
414 Ted Kennedy 10.00 20.00
415 Dave Keon 7.50 15.00
416 Joe Klukay 6.00 12.00
417 Stephen Kraftcheck 20.00 40.00
418 Danny Lewicki 12.50 25.00
419 Ed Litzenberger 6.00 12.00
420 Harry Lumley 12.50 25.00
421 Vic Lynn 6.00 12.00
422 Fleming MacKell 7.50 15.00
423 John MacMillan 5.00 10.00
424 Al MacNeil 10.00 20.00
425 Frank Mahovlich 12.50 25.00
426 Phil Maloney 75.00 150.00
427 Cesare Maniago 6.00 12.00
428 Frank Mathers 20.00 40.00
429 John McCormack 30.00 60.00
430 Parker MacDonald 12.50 25.00
431 Don McKenney 20.00 40.00
432 Howie Meeker 7.50 15.00
433 Don Metz 150.00 300.00
434 Nick Metz 100.00 200.00
435 Rudy Migay 5.00 10.00
436 Jim Mikol 5.00 10.00
437 Jim Morrison 5.00 10.00
438 Gus Mortson 6.00 12.00
439 Eric Nesterenko 7.50 15.00
440 Bob Nevin 5.00 10.00
441 Mike Nykoluk 25.00 50.00
442 Bert Olmstead 6.00 12.00
443 Bob Pulford 5.00 10.00
444 Marc Reaume 7.50 15.00
445 Larry Regan 5.00 10.00
446 Dave Reid 75.00 150.00
447 Al Rollins 15.00 30.00
448 Eddie Shack 6.00 15.00
449 Don Simmons 6.00 12.00
450 Tod Sloan 5.00 10.00
451 Sid Smith 5.00 10.00
452 Bob Solinger 30.00 60.00
453A Allan Stanley ERR 6.00 12.00
(Name misspelled Alan;
dark background)
453B Allan Stanley COR 12.50 25.00
(Light background)
454 Wally Stanowski 200.00 400.00
455 Ron Stewart 5.00 10.00
456 Harry Taylor 20.00 40.00
457 Jim Thomson 6.00 12.00
458 Ray Timgren 7.50 15.00
459 Harry Watson 6.00 12.00
460 Johnny Wilson 5.00 10.00
461 1962-63 Maple Leafs 200.00 400.00
(Team picture)
462A Lady Byng Trophy 150.00 300.00
(Four white borders)
462B Lady Byng Trophy 60.00 125.00
(White bottom
border only)
463A Calder Memorial Trophy 150.00 300.00
(Four white borders)
463B Calder Memorial Trophy 60.00 125.00
(White bottom
border only)
464A Hart Trophy 150.00 300.00
(Four white borders)
464B Hart Trophy 60.00 125.00
(White bottom
border only)
465A James Norris 150.00 300.00
Memorial Trophy
(Four white borders)
465B James Norris 60.00 125.00
Memorial Trophy
(White bottom
border only)
466A Prince of Wales Trophy 150.00 300.00
(Four white borders)
466B Prince of Wales Trophy 60.00 125.00
(White bottom
border only)
467A Art Ross Trophy 150.00 300.00
(Four white borders)
467B Art Ross Trophy 60.00 125.00
(White bottom
border only)
468A Stanley Cup 150.00 300.00
(Four white borders)
468B Stanley Cup 60.00 125.00
(White bottom
border only)
469A Georges Vezina Trophy 150.00 300.00
(Four white borders)
469B Georges Vezina Trophy 60.00 125.00
(White bottom
border only)

1964-67 Beehive Group III Photos

The 1964-67 Beehive photo set is the third of three groups. These photos were issued by St. Lawrence Starch and measure 5 3/8" by 8". The fronts display black-and-white action poses inside a white inner border and a simulated wood-grain outer border. The player's name is displayed on an plaque in the lower wooden border. The backs are blank. A number of unconfirmed photos are part of the Beehive checklist, but have yet to be confirmed.and therefore are not listed below.

1 Murray Balfour 12.50 25.00
2 Leo Boivin 6.00 12.00
3 John Bucyk 7.50 15.00
4 Wayne Connelly 75.00 150.00
5 Bob Dillabough 6.00 12.00
6 Gary Dornhoefer 7.50 15.00
7 Reggie Fleming 6.00 12.00
8 Guy Gendron 60.00 125.00
9 Warren Godfrey 150.00 300.00
10 Ted Green 6.00 12.00
11 Andy Hebenton 90.00 175.00
12 Eddie Johnston 7.50 15.00
13 Tom Johnson 7.50 15.00
14 Forbes Kennedy 10.00 20.00
15 Orland Kurtenbach 20.00 40.00
16 Bobby Leiter 6.00 12.00
17 Parker MacDonald 6.00 12.00
18 Bob McCord 10.00 20.00
19 Ab McDonald 6.00 12.00
20 Murray Oliver 6.00 12.00
21 Bernie Parent 40.00 80.00
22 Cliff Pennington 100.00 225.00
23 Bob Perreault 175.00 350.00
24 Dean Prentice 6.00 12.00
25 Ron Schock UER 6.00 12.00
26 Pat Stapleton 25.00 50.00
27 Ron Stewart 7.50 15.00
28 Ed Westfall 6.00 12.00
29 Tom Williams 6.00 12.00
30 Lou Angotti 6.00 12.00
31 Wally Boyer 6.00 12.00
32 Denis DeJordy 7.50 15.00
33 Dave Dryden 15.00 30.00
34A Phil Esposito 40.00 80.00
34B Phil Esposito 10.00 20.00
35 Glenn Hall ERR 10.00 20.00
36 Murray Hall 100.00 225.00
37 Bill Hay 6.00 12.00
38 Camille Henry 10.00 20.00
39 Wayne Hillman 75.00 150.00
40 Ken Hodge Sr. 7.50 15.00
41A Bobby Hull 100.00 225.00
41B Bobby Hull 200.00 400.00
41C Bobby Hull 15.00 30.00
41D Bobby Hull 15.00 30.00
41E Bobby Hull 200.00 400.00
41F Bobby Hull 15.00 30.00
42 Dennis Hull 6.00 12.00
43 Doug Jarrett 6.00 12.00
44 Len Lunde 6.00 12.00
45 Al MacNeil 6.00 12.00
46A Chico Maki 50.00 100.00
46B Chico Maki 6.00 12.00
47 John McKenzie 15.00 30.00
49 Stan Mikita 10.00 20.00
50 Doug Mohns 6.00 12.00
51A Eric Nesterenko 100.00 225.00
51B Eric Nesterenko 6.00 12.00
52A Pierre Pilote 125.00 250.00
52B Pierre Pilote 7.50 15.00
53 Matt Ravlich 6.00 12.00
55A Fred Stanfield 75.00 150.00
55B Fred Stanfield 50.00 100.00
56 Pat Stapleton 6.00 12.00
57 Bob Turner 125.00 250.00
58 Ed Van Impe 6.00 12.00
59 Elmer Vasko 7.50 15.00
60 Kenny Wharram 6.00 12.00
61 Doug Barkley 6.00 12.00
62 Hank Bassen 7.50 15.00
63A Andy Bathgate 6.00 12.00
63B Andy Bathgate 6.00 12.00
64 Gary Bergman 6.00 12.00
65 Leo Boivin 7.50 15.00
66 Roger Crozier 7.50 15.00
67A Alex Delvecchio 10.00 20.00
67B Alex Delvecchio 150.00 300.00
68 Alex Faulkner 175.00 350.00
69 Val Fonteyne 6.00 12.00
70 Bill Gadsby 6.00 12.00
71 Warren Godfrey 12.50 25.00
72 Pete Goegan 12.50 25.00
73 Murray Hall 6.00 12.00
74 Ted Hampson 6.00 12.00
75 Billy Harris 15.00 30.00
76 Paul Henderson 10.00 20.00
77A Gordie Howe 20.00 40.00
77B Gordie Howe 100.00 225.00
78 Ron Ingram 150.00 300.00
79A Larry Jeffrey 50.00 100.00
79B Larry Jeffrey 30.00 60.00
80A Eddie Joyal 12.50 25.00
80B Eddie Joyal 100.00 225.00
81 Al Langlois 6.00 12.00
82 Ted Lindsay 10.00 20.00
83 Parker MacDonald 6.00 12.00
84A Bruce MacGregor 7.50 15.00
84B Bruce MacGregor 50.00 100.00
85 Pete Mahovlich 6.00 12.00
86 Bert Marshall 6.00 12.00
87 Pit Martin 6.00 12.00
89 Ab McDonald 6.00 12.00
90 Ron Murphy 6.00 12.00
91 Dean Prentice 6.00 12.00
92 Andre Pronovost 10.00 20.00
93 Marcel Pronovost 5.00 10.00
94A Floyd Smith 7.50 15.00
94B Floyd Smith 100.00 225.00
94C Floyd Smith 90.00 175.00
95 Norm Ullman 10.00 20.00
96 Bob Wall 6.00 12.00
97 Ralph Backstrom 6.00 12.00
98 Dave Balon 6.00 12.00
99 Jean Beliveau 12.50 25.00
100 Red Berenson 6.00 12.00
101 Yvan Cournoyer 10.00 20.00
102 Dick Duff 7.50 15.00
103 John Ferguson 6.00 12.00
104 John Hanna 100.00 200.00
105A Terry Harper 6.00 12.00
105B Terry Harper IA 100.00 225.00
106 Ted Harris 6.00 12.00
107 Bill Hicke 7.50 15.00
108 Charlie Hodge 10.00 20.00
109 Jacques Laperriere 6.00 12.00
110A Claude Larose 6.00 12.00
110B Claude Larose 300.00 500.00
111 Claude Provost 6.00 12.00
112 Henri Richard 12.50 25.00
113 Maurice Richard 30.00 60.00
114 Jim Roberts 6.00 12.00
115 Bobby Rousseau 6.00 12.00
116 Jean-Guy Talbot 6.00 12.00
117A Gilles Tremblay 6.00 12.00
117B Gilles Tremblay 50.00 100.00
118 J.C. Tremblay 6.00 12.00
119 Gump Worsley 10.00 20.00
120 Lou Angotti 6.00 12.00
121 Arnie Brown 6.00 12.00
122 Larry Cahan 150.00 300.00
124 Reggie Fleming 6.00 12.00
125 Bernie Geoffrion 10.00 20.00
126 Ed Giacomin 12.50 25.00
127 Rod Gilbert 10.00 20.00
128 Phil Goyette 6.00 12.00
129 Vic Hadfield 7.50 15.00
131 Camille Henry 75.00 150.00
132 Bill Hicke 6.00 12.00
133 Wayne Hillman 6.00 12.00
134 Harry Howell 7.50 15.00
135 Earl Ingarfield Sr. 6.00 12.00
137 Orland Kurtenbach 10.00 20.00
138 Gord Labossiere 75.00 150.00
139 Al MacNeil 6.00 12.00
140 Cesare Maniago 10.00 20.00
141 Don Marshall 6.00 12.00
143 Jim Neilson 6.00 12.00
144 Bob Nevin 6.00 12.00
145 Marcel Paille 20.00 40.00
146 Jacques Plante 40.00 80.00
147 Jean Ratelle 12.50 25.00
148 Rod Seiling 6.00 12.00
151 George Armstrong 10.00 20.00
152 Andy Bathgate 10.00 20.00
153A Bob Baun 60.00 125.00
153B Bob Baun 10.00 20.00
154A Johnny Bower 90.00 175.00
154B Johnny Bower 12.50 25.00
155 Wally Boyer 15.00 30.00
156 John Brenneman 6.00 12.00
157 Carl Brewer 12.50 25.00
158 Turk Broda 15.00 30.00
159 Brian Conacher 6.00 12.00
160 Kent Douglas 6.00 12.00
161 Ron Ellis 6.00 12.00
162 Bruce Gamble 10.00 20.00
163A Billy Harris 50.00 100.00
163B Billy Harris 100.00 225.00
164 Larry Hillman 12.50 25.00
165A Tim Horton 90.00 175.00
165B Tim Horton 15.00 30.00
166 Bronco Horvath 90.00 175.00
167 Larry Jeffrey 15.00 30.00
168 Eddie Joyal 20.00 40.00
169 Red Kelly 10.00 20.00
170 Ted Kennedy 10.00 20.00
171A Dave Keon 75.00 150.00
171B Dave Keon 12.50 25.00
172 Orland Kurtenbach 7.50 20.00
173 Ed Litzenberger 10.00 20.00
174A Frank Mahovlich 90.00 175.00
174B Frank Mahovlich 15.00 30.00
175A Don McKenney 50.00 100.00
175B Don McKenney 10.00 20.00
176 Dickie Moore 10.00 20.00
177 Jim Pappin 6.00 12.00
178A Marcel Pronovost 7.50 15.00
178B Marcel Pronovost 15.00 30.00
180A Bob Pulford 50.00 100.00
180B Bob Pulford 10.00 20.00
181 Terry Sawchuk 15.00 30.00
182 Brit Selby 6.00 12.00
183 Eddie Shack 12.50 25.00
184 Don Simmons 12.50 25.00
185 Allan Stanley 10.00 20.00
186 Pete Stemkowski 6.00 12.00
187A Ron Stewart 90.00 175.00
187B Ron Stewart 30.00 60.00
188 Mike Walton 15.00 30.00
189 Bernie Geoffrion 25.00 50.00
190 Byng Trophy 60.00 125.00
191 Calder Memorial Trophy 60.00 125.00
192 Hart Trophy 60.00 125.00
193 Prince of Wales Trophy 60.00 125.00
194 James Norris Trophy 60.00 125.00
195 Art Ross Trophy 60.00 125.00
196 Stanley Cup 60.00 125.00
197 Vezina Trophy 60.00 125.00

1997-98 Beehive

The Beehives set was issued in one series totaling 75 cards and was distributed in four-card packs with a suggested retail price of $4.99. This set is a revival of the 1934-67 Beehive Photos sets produced by the St. Lawrence Starch Co. of Port Credit, Ontario. This new version features color player portraits printed on 5" by 7" cards. The backs carry a black-and-white action player photos with player information and career statistics. The player information as well as a trivia question is printed in both French and English. The set contains the topical subsets: Golden Originals (57-62), and Junior League Stars (63-74).

COMPLETE SET (75) 25.00 60.00
1 Eric Lindros 1.00 2.50
2 Teemu Selanne 1.25 3.00
3 Brendan Shanahan .75 2.00
4 Joe Sakic 1.00 2.50
5 John LeClair .60 1.50
6 Brett Hull .75 2.00
7 Jaromir Jagr 1.50 4.00
8 Bryan Berard .40 1.00
9 Peter Forsberg .75 2.00
10 Ed Belfour .60 1.50
11 Steve Yzerman 1.25 3.00
12 Curtis Joseph .60 1.50
13 Saku Koivu .60 1.50
14 Keith Tkachuk .60 1.50
15 Pavel Bure .75 2.00
16 Felix Potvin .60 1.50
17 Ray Bourque 1.00 2.50
18 Theo Fleury .75 2.00
19 Patrick Roy 1.50 4.00
20 Joe Nieuwendyk .60 1.50
21 Alexei Yashin .50 1.25
22 Owen Nolan .60 1.50
23 Mark Recchi .75 2.00
24 Dominik Hasek 1.00 2.50
25 Chris Chelios .60 1.50
26 Mike Modano 1.00 2.50
27 John Vanbiesbrouck .60 1.50
28 Brian Leetch .60 1.50
29 Dino Ciccarelli .60 1.50
30 Mark Messier 1.00 2.50
31 Paul Kariya .75 2.00
32 Jocelyn Thibault .40 1.00
33 Wayne Gretzky 3.00 8.00
34 Doug Weight .60 1.50
35 Yanic Perreault .50 1.25
36 Luc Robitaille .60 1.50
37 Chris Osgood .60 1.50
38 Adam Oates .60 1.50
39 Mats Sundin .60 1.50
40 Trevor Linden .50 1.25
41 Mike Richter .60 1.50
42 Zigmund Palffy .60 1.50
43 Pat LaFontaine .60 1.50
44 Grant Fuhr .60 1.50
45 Martin Brodeur 1.25 3.00
46 Sergei Fedorov 1.00 2.50
47 Doug Gilmour .75 2.00
48 Daniel Alfredsson .60 1.50
49 Ron Francis .75 2.00
50 Geoff Sanderson .50 1.25
51 Joe Thornton .60 1.50
52 Vaclav Prospal RC .50 1.25
53 Patrik Elias RC 1.00 2.50
54 Mike Johnson RC .50 1.25
55 Alyn McCauley .50 1.25
56 Brendan Morrison RC .75 2.00
57 Johnny Bower GO .60 1.50
58 John Bucyk GO .60 1.50
59 Stan Mikita GO .75 2.00
60 Ted Lindsay GO .60 1.50
61 Maurice Richard GO 1.00 2.50
62 Andy Bathgate GO .60 1.50
63 Stefan Cherneski JLS RC .50 1.25
64 Craig Hillier JLS RC .60 1.50
65 Daniel Tkaczuk JLS .60 1.50
66 Josh Holden JLS .50 1.25
67 Marian Cisar JLS RC .60 1.50
68 J-P Dumont JLS RC .60 1.50
69 Roberto Luongo JLS RC 6.00 15.00
70 Aren Miller JLS RC .60 1.50
71 Mathieu Garon JLS .60 1.50
72 Charlie Stephens JLS RC .60 1.50
73 Sergei Varlamov JLS RC .50 1.25
74 Pierre Dagenais JLS RC .60 1.50
75 Willie O'Ree CC RC 1.00 2.50
P1 Eric Lindros PROMO
R1 Redemption EXPIRED .08 .25

1997-98 Beehive Authentic Autographs

Randomly inserted in packs at the rate of 1:12, this 19-card set features autographed cards of CHL stars that seem to have an outstanding chance of becoming NHL stars as well as some of the NHL's top rookies.
STATED ODDS 1:12
51 Joe Thornton 10.00 25.00
52 Vaclav Prospal 3.00 8.00
53 Patrik Elias 6.00 15.00
54 Mike Johnson 2.00 5.00
55 Alyn McCauley 15.00 40.00
56 Brendan Morrison 4.00 10.00
63 Stefan Cherneski 2.00 5.00
64 Craig Hillier 2.00 5.00
65 Daniel Tkaczuk 2.00 5.00
66 Josh Holden 2.00 5.00
67 Marian Cisar 2.00 5.00
68 J-P Dumont 4.00 10.00
69 Roberto Luongo 12.00 30.00
70 Aren Miller 2.00 5.00
71 Mathieu Garon 4.00 10.00
72 Charlie Stephens 2.00 5.00
73 Sergei Varlamov 2.00 5.00
74 Pierre Dagenais 2.00 5.00
75 Willie O'Ree 12.00 30.00

1997-98 Beehive Golden Portraits

Randomly inserted in packs at the rate of 1:3, this 75-card set is a gold-foil parallel version of the base set.
*VETS: 2X TO 5X BASIC CARDS
*ROOKIES: 1X TO 2.5X BASIC CARD
STATED ODDS 1:3

1997-98 Beehive Golden Originals Autographs

Randomly inserted in packs at the rate of 1:36, this six-card set features autographed color photos of six top retired players.
STATED ODDS 1:36
57 Johnny Bower 8.00 20.00
58 John Bucyk 8.00 20.00
59 Stan Mikita 15.00 30.00
60 Ted Lindsay 8.00 20.00
61 Maurice Richard 50.00 100.00
62 Andy Bathgate 8.00 20.00

1997-98 Beehive Team

Randomly inserted in packs at the rate of 1:11, this 25-card set features color photos of some of Hockey's best players. The backs carry player information. A Beehive Gold Team set was also produced which is a parallel version to this insert set and has an insertion rate of 1:49.
COMPLETE SET (25) 60.00 150.00
STATED ODDS 1:11
*GOLD TEAM: 1X TO 2.5X BASIC INSERTS
GOLD TEAM ODDS 1:49
1 Paul Kariya 2.50 6.00
2 Mark Messier 3.00 8.00
3 Mike Modano 3.00 8.00
4 Brendan Shanahan 3.00 8.00
5 John Vanbiesbrouck 2.50 6.00
6 Martin Brodeur 6.00 15.00
7 Wayne Gretzky 12.00 30.00
8 Eric Lindros 3.00 8.00
9 Peter Forsberg 2.50 6.00
10 Jaromir Jagr 4.00 10.00
11 Teemu Selanne 2.50 6.00
12 John LeClair 2.50 6.00
13 Saku Koivu 2.50 6.00
14 Brett Hull 3.00 8.00
15 Patrick Roy 8.00 20.00
16 Steve Yzerman 8.00 20.00
17 Keith Tkachuk 2.00 5.00
18 Pat LaFontaine 2.00 5.00
19 Joe Sakic 5.00 12.00
20 Patrik Elias 2.00 5.00
21 Vaclav Prospal 1.50 4.00
22 Joe Thornton 4.00 10.00
23 Sergei Samsonov 2.00 5.00
24 Alexei Morozov UER 1.50 4.00
25 Marco Sturm 1.50 4.00

2003-04 Beehive

This 250-card set was designed to reflect the design of the original Beehive photos with "woodgrain" borders and color player photos. The set consisted of 200 veterans and 50 short-printed rookies inserted at 1:5 packs.
COMPLETE SET (250) 30.00 80.00
COMP.SET w/o SP's (200) 8.00 20.00
201-250 ROOKIE ODDS 1:5
1 Petr Sykora .25 .60
2 Martin Gerber .20 .50
3 Vaclav Prospal .20 .50
4 Jean-Sebastien Giguere .30 .75
5 Sergei Fedorov .50 1.25
6 Stanislav Chistov .20 .50
7 Sandis Ozolinsh .20 .50
8 Pasi Nurminen .25 .60
9 Marc Savard .25 .60
10 Vyacheslav Kozlov .25 .60
11 Dany Heatley .30 .75
12 Ilya Kovalchuk .30 .75
13 Andrew Raycroft .25 .60
14 Glen Murray .25 .60
15 Brian Rolston .25 .60
16 Jeff Jillson .20 .50
17 Don Cherry .60 1.50
18 Nick Boynton .20 .50
19 Felix Potvin .50 1.25
20 Joe Thornton .40 1.00
21 Sergei Samsonov .25 .60
22 Ales Kotalik .20 .50
23 Alexei Zhitnik .25 .60
24 Maxim Afinogenov .20 .50
25 Chris Drury .25 .60
26 Daniel Briere .30 .75
27 Martin Biron .25 .60
28 Steve Reinprecht .20 .50
29 Jamie McLennan .20 .50
30 Martin Gelinas .20 .50
31 Jarome Iginla .30 .75
32 Roman Turek .25 .60
33 Jeff O'Neill .20 .50
34 Danny Markov .20 .50
35 Erik Cole .25 .60
36 Rod Brind'Amour .30 .75
37 Jamie Storr .25 .60
38 Ron Francis .40 1.00
39 Bryan Berard .25 .60
40 Eric Daze .25 .60
41 Kyle Calder .20 .50
42 Michael Leighton .20 .50
44 Jocelyn Thibault .25 .60
45 Tyler Arnason .20 .50
46 Philippe Sauve .25 .60
47 Teemu Selanne .60 1.50
48 Alex Tanguay .25 .60
49 Derek Morris .20 .50
50 Milan Hejduk .25 .60
51 Patrick Roy .75 2.00
52 David Aebischer .25 .60
53 Joe Sakic .50 1.25
54 Paul Kariya .40 1.00
55 Peter Forsberg .40 1.00
56 Darryl Sydor .20 .50
57 Trevor Letowski .20 .50
58 Marc Denis .25 .60
59 Rick Nash .30 .75
60 Todd Marchant .20 .50
61 Brenden Morrow .25 .60
62 Jere Lehtinen .25 .60
63 Sergei Zubov .25 .60
64 Stu Barnes .20 .50
65 Teppo Numminen .20 .50
66 Bill Guerin .30 .75
67 Marty Turco .30 .75
68 Mike Modano .50 1.25
69 Gordie Howe 1.00 2.50
70 Brendan Shanahan .40 1.00
71 Brett Hull .40 1.00
72 Nicklas Lidstrom .30 .75
73 Dominik Hasek .50 1.25
74 Henrik Zetterberg .40 1.00
75 Steve Yzerman .75 2.00
76 Eric Brewer .20 .50
77 Adam Oates .30 .75
78 Ryan Smyth .25 .60
79 Ales Hemsky .30 .75
80 Raffi Torres .20 .50
81 Wayne Gretzky 1.50 4.00
82 Tommy Salo .25 .60
83 Steve Shields .25 .60
84 Jay Bouwmeester .30 .75
85 Olli Jokinen .30 .75
86 Roberto Luongo .50 1.25
87 Marcel Dionne .40 1.00
88 Alexander Frolov .25 .60
89 Adam Deadmarsh .25 .60
90 Jason Allison .25 .60
91 Luc Robitaille .30 .75
92 Roman Cechmanek .25 .60
93 Zigmund Palffy .30 .75
94 Andrew Brunette .20 .50
95 Dwayne Roloson .25 .60
96 Pascal Dupuis .20 .50
97 Wes Walz .20 .50
98 Manny Fernandez .25 .60
99 Marian Gaborik .50 1.25
100 Pierre-Marc Bouchard .30 .75
101 Andrei Markov .30 .75
102 Guy Lafleur .40 1.00
103 Mike Ribeiro .25 .60
104 Jose Theodore .30 .75
105 Marcel Hossa .20 .50
106 Michael Ryder .25 .60
107 Saku Koivu .30 .75
108 Greg Johnson .20 .50
109 David Legwand .25 .60
110 Tomas Vokoun .25 .60
111 Jamie Langenbrunner .25 .60
112 Jeff Friesen .20 .50
113 John Madden .20 .50
114 Scott Niedermayer .30 .75
115 Martin Brodeur .60 1.50
116 Patrik Elias .30 .75
117 Scott Gomez .25 .60
118 Scott Stevens .30 .75
119 Brian Gionta .25 .60
119B Alexei Zhamnov .25 .60
120 Mariusz Czerkawski .20 .50
121 Eric Godard .20 .50
122 Jason Blake .20 .50
123 Mark Parrish .20 .50
124 Alexei Yashin .25 .60
125 Michael Peca .25 .60
126 Rick DiPietro .25 .60
127 Alex Kovalev .25 .60
128 Anson Carter .25 .60
129 Brian Leetch .30 .75
130 Petr Nedved .20 .50
131 Eric Lindros .50 1.25
132 Mark Messier .50 1.25
133 Mike Dunham .25 .60
134 Daniel Alfredsson .30 .75
135 Zdeno Chara .30 .75
136 Jason Spezza .30 .75
137 Marian Hossa .25 .60
138 Patrick Lalime .25 .60
139 Bobby Clarke .30 .75
140 John LeClair .30 .75
141 Justin Williams .25 .60
142 Mark Recchi .40 1.00
143 Robert Esche .20 .50
144 Tony Amonte .25 .60
145 Jeff Hackett .25 .60
146 Jeremy Roenick .30 .75
147 Simon Gagne .30 .75
148 Brian Boucher .25 .60
149 Chris Gratton .20 .50
150 David Tanabe .20 .50
151 Jan Hrdina .20 .50
152 Mike Johnson .20 .50
153 Sean Burke .20 .50
154 Brooks Orpik .25 .60
155 Konstantin Koltsov .20 .50
156 Rico Fata .20 .50
157 Sebastien Caron .25 .60
158 Mario Lemieux 1.00 2.50
159 Martin Straka .20 .50
160 Jonathan Cheechoo .25 .60
161 Kyle McLaren .20 .50
162 Niko Dimitrakos .20 .50
163 Evgeni Nabokov .25 .60
164 Patrick Marleau .30 .75
165 Vincent Damphousse .25 .60
166 Chris Pronger .25 .60
167 Reed Low .20 .50
168 Chris Osgood .30 .75
169 Doug Weight .30 .75
170 Keith Tkachuk .30 .75
171 Pavol Demitra .40 1.00
172 Dave Andreychuk .30 .75
173 Martin St. Louis .30 .75
174 Nikolai Khabibulin .30 .75
175 Vincent Lecavalier .25 .60
176 Brad Richards .30 .75
177 Fredrik Modin .20 .50
178 Gary Roberts .20 .50
179 Joe Nieuwendyk .30 .75
180 Tie Domi .25 .60
181 Alexander Mogilny .25 .60
182 Ed Belfour .30 .75
183 Mats Sundin .30 .75
184 Owen Nolan .25 .60
185 Daniel Sedin .30 .75
186 Magnus Arvedson .20 .50
187 Dan Cloutier .25 .60
188 Henrik Sedin .30 .75
189 Brendan Morrison .25 .60
190 Jason King .20 .50
191 Trevor Linden .30 .75
192 Ed Jovanovski .25 .60
193 Johan Hedberg .25 .60
194 Markus Naslund .30 .75
195 Todd Bertuzzi .30 .75
196 Robert Lang .20 .50
197 Sergei Gonchar .20 .50
198 Jaromir Jagr .75 2.00
199 Olaf Kolzig .30 .75
200 Peter Bondra .25 .60
201 Joffrey Lupul RC 2.00 5.00
202 Patrice Bergeron RC 4.00 10.00
203 Niklas Kronwall RC 1.50 4.00
204 Eric Staal RC 4.00 10.00
205 Pavel Vorobiev RC 1.00 2.50
206 Tuomo Ruutu RC 1.25 3.00
207 Tomas Plekanec RC 2.50 6.00
208 Timofei Shishkanov RC .75 2.00
209 Tuomas Pihlman RC 1.00 2.50
210 Dan Fritsche RC .75 2.00

211 Antti Miettinen RC 1.25 3.00
212 Jiri Hudler RC 2.00 5.00
213 Nathan Horton RC 2.00 5.00
214 Dustin Brown RC 1.50 4.00
215 Kyle Wellwood RC 1.25 3.00
216 Mike Smith RC 2.50 6.00
217 Ryan Kesler RC 4.00 10.00
218 Fredrik Sjostrom RC 1.25 3.00
219 Chris Higgins RC 1.50 4.00
220 Dan Hamhuis RC 1.00 2.50
221 Jordin Tootoo RC 1.50 4.00
222 Carl Corazzini RC .75 2.00
223 Tony Martensson RC .75 2.00
224 Aaron Johnson RC .75 2.00
225 Anton Babchuk RC .75 2.00
226 Jozef Balej RC .75 2.00
227 Joni Pitkanen RC 1.25 3.00
228 Aleksander Suglobov RC .75 2.00
229 Marc-Andre Fleury RC 5.00 12.00
230 Nikolai Zherdev RC 1.50 4.00
231 Gavin Morgan RC 1.00 2.50
232 Milan Michalek RC 1.50 4.00
233 Peter Sejna RC 1.00 2.50
234 Matt Stajan RC 1.25 3.00
235 Maxim Kondratiev RC .75 2.00
236 Alexander Semin RC 2.50 6.00
237 Zbynek Michalek RC .75 2.00
238 Jeff Hamilton RC .75 2.00
239 Andrew Hutchinson RC .75 2.00
240 Mikhail Yakubov RC .75 2.00
241 Sergei Zinovjev RC .75 2.00
242 Noah Clarke RC .75 2.00
243 Tim Jackman RC 1.00 2.50
244 Jason Pominville RC 2.00 5.00
245 Tony Salmelainen RC .75 2.00
246 Rastislav Stana RC 1.25 3.00
247 Darryl Bootland RC 1.00 2.50
248 Trevor Daley RC 1.25 3.00
249 Peter Sarno RC .75 2.00
250 Nathan Smith RC .75 2.00
NNO Checklist Card .08 .20

2003-04 Beehive Variations

This partial parallel set featured varying photos from the base set and could be distinguished by the lighter borders.

STATED ODDS 1:3
5 Sergei Fedorov 1.00 2.50
12 Ilya Kovalchuk .60 1.50
17 Don Cherry 1.25 3.00
20 Joe Thornton .75 2.00
21 Sergei Samsonov .50 1.25
25 Chris Drury .50 1.25
31 Jarome Iginla .60 1.50
35 Erik Cole .50 1.25
44 Jocelyn Thibault .50 1.25
51 Patrick Roy 1.50 4.00
53 Joe Sakic 1.00 2.50
55 Peter Forsberg .75 2.00
59 Rick Nash .60 1.50
67 Marty Turco .60 1.50
68 Mike Modano 1.00 2.50
69 Gordie Howe 2.00 5.00
74 Henrik Zetterberg .75 2.00
75 Steve Yzerman 1.50 4.00
79 Ales Hemsky .60 1.50
80 Raffi Torres .40 1.00
81 Wayne Gretzky 3.00 8.00
86 Roberto Luongo 1.00 2.50
87 Marcel Dionne .75 2.00
91 Luc Robitaille .60 1.50
93 Zigmund Palffy .60 1.50
99 Marian Gaborik 1.00 2.50
102 Guy Lafleur .75 2.00
104 Jose Theodore .60 1.50
107 Saku Koivu .60 1.50
110 Tomas Vokoun .50 1.25
115 Martin Brodeur 1.25 3.00
120 Mariusz Czerkawski .40 1.00
126 Rick DiPietro .50 1.25
132 Mark Messier 1.00 2.50
136 Jason Spezza .60 1.50
137 Marian Hossa .50 1.25
139 Bobby Clarke .60 1.50
144 Tony Amonte .50 1.25
146 Jeremy Roenick .60 1.50
153 Sean Burke .40 1.00
158 Mario Lemieux 2.00 5.00
164 Patrick Marleau .60 1.50
170 Keith Tkachuk .60 1.50
174 Nikolai Khabibulin .60 1.50
175 Vincent Lecavalier .50 1.25
182 Ed Belfour .60 1.50
183 Mats Sundin .60 1.50
190 Jason King .40 1.00
195 Todd Bertuzzi .60 1.50
198 Jaromir Jagr 1.50 4.00

2003-04 Beehive Gold

*1-200 VETS/15: 8X TO 20X BASIC CARDS
*201-250 ROOKIE/15: 2X TO 5X BASIC RC
STATED PRINT RUN 15 SER.#'d SETS

2003-04 Beehive Silver

*1-200 VETS/67: 5X TO 12X BASIC CARDS
*201-250 ROOKIE/67: 1.2X TO 3X BASIC RC

2003-04 Beehive Jumbos

These large box toppers were found one per box in an indivdual "jumbo" pack that carried a jumbo jersey and a jumbo base or variation card.

ONE PER BOX
1 Jean-Sebastien Giguere 1.00 2.50
2 Sergei Fedorov 1.25 3.00
3 Ilya Kovalchuk 1.50 4.00
4 Joe Thornton 2.00 5.00
5 Don Cherry 3.00 8.00
6 Ron Francis 1.00 2.50
7 Jocelyn Thibault 1.00 2.50
8 Peter Forsberg 3.00 8.00
9 Rick Nash 1.50 4.00
10 Marty Turco 1.00 2.50
11 Gordie Howe 4.00 10.00
12 Steve Yzerman 4.00 10.00
13 Roberto Luongo 1.50 4.00
14 Don Cherry 2.50 6.00
15 Marian Gaborik 2.50 6.00
16 Guy Lafleur 1.50 4.00
17 Scotty Bowman 1.50 4.00
18 Martin Brodeur 4.00 10.00
19 Jason Spezza 2.00 5.00
20 Marian Hossa 1.00 2.50
21 Jeremy Roenick 1.50 4.00
22 Mario Lemieux 5.00 12.00
23 Ed Belfour 1.25 3.00
24 Markus Naslund 1.00 2.50
25 Todd Bertuzzi 1.00 2.50

2003-04 Beehive Jumbo Variations

STATED ODDS 1:3
1 Joffrey Lupul 3.00 8.00
2 Sergei Fedorov 4.00 10.00
3 Ilya Kovalchuk 4.00 10.00
4 Joe Thornton 5.00 12.00
5 Don Cherry 8.00 20.00
6 Eric Staal 4.00 10.00
7 Tuomo Ruutu 2.50 6.00
8 Peter Forsberg 8.00 20.00
9 Rick Nash 4.00 10.00
10 Marty Turco 2.50 6.00
11 Gordie Howe 10.00 25.00
12 Jiri Hudler 4.00 10.00
13 Nathan Horton 4.00 10.00
14 Don Cherry 8.00 20.00
15 Marian Gaborik 6.00 15.00
16 Guy Lafleur 4.00 10.00
17 Scotty Bowman 4.00 10.00
18 Martin Brodeur 10.00 25.00
19 Jason Spezza 3.00 8.00
20 Marian Hossa 3.00 8.00
21 Joni Pitkanen 3.00 8.00
22 Marc-Andre Fleury 8.00 20.00
23 Ed Belfour 3.00 8.00
24 Markus Naslund 3.00 8.00
25 Todd Bertuzzi 3.00 8.00

2003-04 Beehive Jumbo Jerseys

These large box toppers were found one per box in an indivdual "jumbo" pack that carried a jumbo jersey and a jumbo base or variation card. Each card carried two jersey swatches.

ONE PER JUMBO PACK
BH1 Jeremy Roenick 6.00 15.00
BH2 Marty Turco 5.00 12.00
BH3 Mario Lemieux 40.00 100.00
BH4 Todd Bertuzzi 5.00 12.00
BH5 Jarome Iginla 6.00 15.00
BH6 Dominik Hasek 10.00 25.00
BH7 Chris Drury 5.00 12.00
BH8 Jose Theodore 8.00 20.00
BH9 Joe Sakic 8.00 20.00
BH10 Mike Modano 6.00 15.00
BH11 Mats Sundin 6.00 15.00
BH12 Sergei Fedorov 6.00 15.00
BH13 Keith Tkachuk 6.00 15.00
BH14 Ed Belfour 6.00 15.00
BH15 Sean Burke 5.00 12.00
BH16 Tony Amonte 5.00 12.00
BH17 Joe Thornton 8.00 20.00
BH18 Vincent Lecavalier 5.00 12.00
BH19 Roberto Luongo 8.00 20.00
BH20 Steve Yzerman 15.00 40.00
BH21 Jason Spezza 8.00 20.00
BH22 Rick Nash 8.00 20.00

2003-04 Beehive Jerseys

STATED ODDS 1:15
JT1 Mike Modano 5.00 12.00
JT2 Zigmund Palffy 3.00 8.00
JT3 Jason Spezza 5.00 12.00
JT4 Tony Amonte 3.00 8.00
JT5 Jeremy Roenick 5.00 12.00
JT6 Vincent Lecavalier 3.00 8.00
JT7 Marian Gaborik 8.00 20.00
JT8 Alexei Yashin 3.00 8.00
JT9 Ilya Kovalchuk 5.00 12.00
JT10 Keith Tkachuk 4.00 10.00
JT11 Markus Naslund 4.00 10.00
JT12 Bill Guerin 3.00 8.00
JT13 Brendan Shanahan 4.00 10.00
JT14 Dominik Hasek 6.00 15.00
JT15 Jose Theodore 5.00 12.00
JT16 Eric Lindros 4.00 10.00
JT17 Martin Brodeur 10.00 25.00
JT18 Patrick Lalime 3.00 8.00
JT19 Rick Nash 5.00 12.00
JT20 Ryan Smyth 3.00 8.00
JT21 Marty Turco 3.00 8.00
JT22 Roberto Luongo 5.00 12.00
JT23 Jean-Sebastien Giguere 3.00 8.00
JT24 Ed Belfour 6.00 15.00
JT25 Joe Thornton 5.00 12.00
JT26 Todd Bertuzzi 4.00 10.00
JT27 Steve Yzerman 10.00 25.00
JT28 Saku Koivu 4.00 10.00
JT29 Jarome Iginla 5.00 12.00
JT30 Chris Drury 3.00 8.00
JT31 Joe Sakic 8.00 20.00
JT32 Paul Kariya 4.00 10.00
JT33 Marian Hossa 4.00 10.00
JT34 Doug Weight 3.00 8.00
JT35 Sergei Fedorov 5.00 12.00
JT36 Mats Sundin 4.00 10.00
JT37 Mario Lemieux 12.50 30.00
JT38 Teemu Selanne 4.00 10.00
JT39 Jocelyn Thibault 4.00 10.00
JT40 Ron Francis 3.00 8.00

2003-04 Beehive Jersey Autographs

STATED ODDS 1:240
SJ1 Martin Brodeur/20 75.00 125.00
SJ2 Saku Koivu/25 30.00 80.00
SJ3 Ilya Kovalchuk/25 30.00 80.00
SJ4 Eric Lindros/25 60.00 120.00
SJ5 Patrick Roy/25 100.00 200.00
SJ6 Jason Spezza/25 50.00 125.00
SJ7 Marty Turco/25 20.00 50.00
SJ8 Jarome Iginla/30 20.00 50.00
SJ9 Wayne Gretzky/10
SJ10 Marian Hossa/50 20.00 50.00
SJ11 Gordie Howe
SJ12 Roberto Luongo/50 20.00 50.00
SJ13 Zigmund Palffy/25 15.00 40.00
SJ14 Jeremy Roenick/50 25.00 60.00
SJ15 Jose Theodore/25 25.00 60.00
SJ16 Joe Thornton/50 40.00 100.00
SJ17 David Aebischer/50 15.00 40.00
SJ18 Todd Bertuzzi/75 15.00 40.00
SJ19 Mike Comrie/75 12.50 30.00
SJ20 Marcel Hossa/75 12.50 30.00
SJ21 Markus Naslund/75 15.00 40.00
SJ22 Rick DiPietro/50 25.00 60.00
SJ23 Scott Hartnell/50 15.00 40.00
SJ24 Ales Hemsky/90 12.00 30.00
SJ25 Henrik Zetterberg/90 15.00 40.00

2003-04 Beehive Signatures

STATED ODDS 1:240
STATED PRINT RUN 10-100
RF1 Martin Brodeur
RF2 Patrick Roy
RF3 Jason Spezza/25 75.00 150.00
RF4 Wayne Gretzky/10
RF5 Gordie Howe/10
RF6 Jose Theodore/25 30.00 80.00
RF7 David Aebischer/25 15.00 40.00
RF8 Marian Gaborik/25 15.00 40.00
RF9 Jarome Iginla/25 50.00 125.00
RF10 Marian Hossa/50 25.00 60.00
RF11 Joe Thornton/100 15.00 40.00
RF12 Anson Carter/25 15.00 40.00
RF13 Chuck Kobasew/50 12.50 30.00
RF14 Roberto Luongo/25 20.00 50.00
RF15 Jeremy Roenick/25 50.00 125.00
RF16 Mike Comrie/100 8.00 20.00
RF17 Markus Naslund/100 12.50 30.00
RF18 Rick DiPietro/50 25.00 60.00
RF19 Henrik Zetterberg/100 15.00 40.00
RF20 Jared Aulin/50 12.50 30.00
RF21 Rick Nash/25 25.00 60.00
RF22 Owen Nolan/25 15.00 40.00
RF23 Marcel Hossa/50 6.00 15.00
RF24 Scott Hartnell/90 12.50 30.00
RF25 Ales Hemsky/75 6.00 15.00

2003-04 Beehive Sticks Beige Border

BEIGE ODDS 1:30
BE1 Jarome Iginla 5.00 12.00
BE2 Jean-Sebastien Giguere 2.50 6.00
BE3 Keith Tkachuk 4.00 10.00
BE4 Jocelyn Thibault 2.50 6.00
BE5 Martin Brodeur 10.00 25.00
BE6 Joe Sakic 8.00 20.00
BE7 Mike Modano 6.00 15.00
BE8 Johan Hedberg 2.50 6.00
BE9 Mats Sundin 4.00 10.00
BE10 Brendan Shanahan 4.00 10.00
BE11 Owen Nolan 2.50 6.00
BE12 Marc Denis 2.50 6.00
BE13 Teemu Selanne 4.00 10.00
BE14 Curtis Joseph 4.00 10.00
BE15 Patrik Stefan 2.50 6.00
BE16 Mike Comrie 2.50 6.00
BE17 Milan Hejduk 6.00 15.00
BE18 Ed Jovanovski 2.50 6.00
BE19 Luc Robitaille 2.50 6.00
BE20 Olaf Kolzig 2.50 6.00
BE21 Mika Noronen 2.50 6.00
BE22 Jeremy Roenick 6.00 15.00
BE23 Mike Dunham 2.50 6.00
BE24 Rick DiPietro 2.50 6.00
BE25 Peter Bondra 2.50 6.00
BE26 Ed Belfour 4.00 10.00
BE27 Felix Potvin 4.00 10.00
BE28 Peter Forsberg 10.00 25.00
BE29 Gordie Howe 10.00 25.00
BE30 Brian Boucher 2.50 6.00
BE31 Brett Hull 6.00 15.00
BE32 Sean Burke 2.50 6.00
BE33 Ilya Kovalchuk 6.00 15.00
BE34 Roman Cechmanek 2.50 6.00
BE35 Jaromir Jagr 6.00 15.00
BE36 David Aebischer 2.50 6.00
BE37 Dominik Hasek 8.00 20.00
BE38 Tommy Salo 2.50 6.00
BE39 Guy Lafleur 2.50 6.00
BE40 Jose Theodore 5.00 12.00
BE41 Marcel Dionne 2.50 6.00
BE42 Vincent Lecavalier 4.00 10.00

2003-04 Beehive Sticks Blue Border

STATED ODDS 1:60
BL1 Sean Burke 3.00 8.00
BL2 Zigmund Palffy 3.00 8.00
BL3 Simon Gagne 5.00 12.00
BL4 Justin Williams 3.00 8.00
BL5 Jean-Sebastien Giguere 4.00 10.00
BL6 Chris Chelios 5.00 12.00
BL7 John LeClair 5.00 12.00
BL8 Rick DiPietro 3.00 8.00
BL9 Peter Bondra 3.00 8.00
BL10 Pavel Bure 8.00 20.00
BL11 Mark Messier 6.00 15.00
BL12 Olaf Kolzig 3.00 8.00
BL13 Martin Brodeur 12.50 30.00
BL14 Felix Potvin 6.00 15.00
BL15 Owen Nolan 3.00 8.00
BL16 Patrik Stefan 3.00 8.00
BL17 Jaromir Jagr 8.00 20.00
BL18 Tommy Salo 3.00 8.00
BL19 Mark Recchi 3.00 8.00
BL20 Ed Belfour 5.00 12.00
BL21 Roman Cechmanek 3.00 8.00

2003-04 Beehive Sticks Red Border

STATED ODDS 1:60
RE1 Dominik Hasek 10.00 25.00
RE2 Brett Hull 8.00 20.00
RE3 Peter Forsberg 12.50 30.00
RE4 Jose Theodore 6.00 15.00
RE5 Marc Denis 3.00 8.00
RE6 Mike Modano 10.00 25.00
RE7 Mark Messier 6.00 15.00
RE8 Mats Sundin 5.00 12.00
RE9 Brendan Shanahan 5.00 12.00
RE10 Eric Lindros 5.00 12.00
RE11 Ron Francis 6.00 15.00
RE12 Jeremy Roenick 8.00 20.00
RE13 Ilya Kovalchuk 8.00 20.00
RE14 Martin Brodeur 12.50 30.00
RE15 Joe Sakic 10.00 25.00
RE16 Keith Tkachuk 5.00 12.00
RE17 David Aebischer 3.00 8.00
RE18 Marcel Dionne 3.00 8.00
RE19 Owen Nolan 3.00 8.00
RE20 Sergei Fedorov 8.00 20.00
RE21 Gordie Howe 12.50 30.00

2003-04 Beehive UD Promos

*UD PROMOS: 1X TO 2.5X BASIC CARDS
132 Mark Messier 1.25 3.00

2005-06 Beehive

This 250-card set was issued into the hobby in five-card (four regular and one jumbo) packs which came 15 packs to a box. Cards numbered 1-90 feature veterans in team alphabetical order while cards 91-180 feature Rookie Cards and cards 181-250 are all jumbo cards. The Rookie Cards were inserted at a stated rate of one in four.

COMP.SET w/o SP's (90) 10.00 25.00
91-180 ROOKIE ODDS 1:4
ONE JUMBO PER PACK
1 Teemu Selanne .75 2.00
2 Joffrey Lupul .30 .75
3 Jean-Sebastien Giguere .40 1.00
4 Ilya Kovalchuk .40 1.00
5 Kari Lehtonen .30 .75
6 Marian Hossa .30 .75
7 Patrice Bergeron .50 1.25
8 Sergei Samsonov .30 .75
9 Andrew Raycroft .30 .75
10 Brian Leetch .40 1.00
11 Glen Murray .30 .75
12 Chris Drury .30 .75
13 Daniel Briere .40 1.00
14 Jarome Iginla .40 1.00
15 Miikka Kiprusoff .30 .75
16 Tony Amonte .30 .75
17 Erik Cole .30 .75
18 Eric Staal .50 1.25
19 Nikolai Khabibulin .40 1.00
20 Tuomo Ruutu .40 1.00
21 Eric Daze .30 .75
22 Joe Sakic .60 1.50
23 Milan Hejduk .30 .75
24 Alex Tanguay .40 1.00
25 Rob Blake .40 1.00
26 Rick Nash .40 1.00
27 Sergei Fedorov .60 1.50
28 Mike Modano .60 1.50
29 Bill Guerin .40 1.00
30 Marty Turco .40 1.00
31 Steve Yzerman 1.00 2.50
32 Brendan Shanahan .50 1.25
33 Pavel Datsyuk .50 1.25
34 Nicklas Lidstrom .40 1.00
35 Ty Conklin .30 .75
36 Chris Pronger .30 .75
37 Ryan Smyth .30 .75
38 Roberto Luongo .60 1.50
39 Jay Bouwmeester .40 1.00
40 Olli Jokinen .40 1.00
41 Luc Robitaille .40 1.00
42 Jeremy Roenick .40 1.00
43 Pavol Demitra .50 1.25
44 Marian Gaborik .60 1.50
45 Dwayne Roloson .30 .75
46 Saku Koivu .40 1.00
47 Jose Theodore .40 1.00
48 Michael Ryder .30 .75
49 Mike Ribeiro .30 .75
50 Paul Kariya .50 1.25
51 Tomas Vokoun .30 .75
52 Martin Brodeur .75 2.00
53 Patrik Elias .40 1.00
54 Scott Gomez .30 .75
55 Alexander Mogilny .30 .75
56 Miroslav Satan .30 .75
57 Alexei Yashin .30 .75
58 Rick DiPietro .30 .75
59 Jaromir Jagr 1.00 2.50
60 Dominik Hasek .60 1.50
61 Dany Heatley .40 1.00
62 Martin Havlat .40 1.00
63 Jason Spezza .40 1.00
64 Daniel Alfredsson .40 1.00
65 Peter Forsberg .50 1.25
66 Robert Esche .30 .75
67 Keith Primeau .40 1.00
68 Simon Gagne .40 1.00
69 Curtis Joseph .40 1.00
70 Shane Doan .30 .75
71 Mario Lemieux 1.25 3.00
72 Mark Recchi .50 1.25
73 Zigmund Palffy .40 1.00
74 Joe Thornton .50 1.25
75 Patrick Marleau .40 1.00
76 Jonathan Cheechoo .40 1.00
77 Evgeni Nabokov .30 .75
78 Doug Weight .40 1.00
79 Keith Tkachuk .40 1.00
80 Martin St. Louis .40 1.00
81 Vincent Lecavalier .30 .75
82 Brad Richards .40 1.00
83 Mats Sundin .40 1.00
84 Ed Belfour .40 1.00
85 Eric Lindros .60 1.50
86 Jason Allison .30 .75
87 Markus Naslund .40 1.00
88 Brendan Morrison .25 .60
89 Todd Bertuzzi .40 1.00
90 Olaf Kolzig .40 1.00
91 Brandon Bochenski RC 2.00 5.00
92 Patrick Eaves RC 2.00 5.00
93 Derek Boogaard RC 2.50 6.00
94 Brad Richardson RC 2.00 5.00
95 Ole-Kristian Tollefsen RC 1.50 4.00
96 Dennis Wideman RC 1.25 3.00
97 Lee Stempniak RC 2.00 5.00
98 Maxim Lapierre RC 2.00 5.00
99 Andrei Kostsitsyn RC 2.50 6.00
100 Rob McVicar RC 1.50 4.00
101 Sidney Crosby RC 25.00 50.00
102 Alexander Ovechkin RC 12.00 30.00
103 Jeff Carter RC 3.00 8.00
104 Corey Perry RC 8.00 20.00
105 Rostislav Olesz RC 1.50 4.00
106 Gilbert Brule RC 2.00 5.00
107 Zach Parise RC 5.00 12.00
108 Alexander Perezhogin RC 1.50 4.00
109 Hannu Toivonen RC 2.00 5.00
110 Wojtek Wolski RC 1.50 4.00
111 Jeff Woywitka RC 1.25 3.00
112 Alexander Steen RC 4.00 10.00
113 Ryan Getzlaf RC 5.00 12.00
114 Dion Phaneuf RC 3.00 8.00
115 Ryan Suter RC 2.50 6.00
116 Mike Richards RC 4.00 10.00
117 Cam Ward RC 3.00 8.00
118 Robert Nilsson RC 2.00 5.00
119 Jim Howard RC 5.00 12.00
120 Thomas Vanek RC 4.00 10.00
121 Braydon Coburn RC 2.00 5.00
122 Brent Seabrook RC 4.00 10.00
123 Peter Budaj RC 2.50 6.00
124 Yann Danis RC 1.50 4.00
125 David Leneveu RC 1.50 4.00
126 Henrik Lundqvist RC 8.00 20.00
127 Johan Franzen RC 3.00 8.00
128 Andrej Meszaros RC 1.50 4.00
129 Jussi Jokinen RC 2.00 5.00
130 Rene Bourque RC 2.00 5.00
131 Jay McClement RC 1.25 3.00
132 Keith Ballard RC 1.50 4.00
133 Evgeny Artyukhin RC 1.50 4.00
134 R.J. Umberger RC 2.00 5.00
135 Petteri Nokelainen RC 1.25 3.00
136 Petr Prucha RC 2.00 5.00
137 Ryan Whitney RC 2.00 5.00
138 Matt Foy RC 1.25 3.00
139 Ryane Clowe RC 2.50 6.00
140 Andrew Wozniewski RC 1.50 4.00
141 Maxime Talbot RC 2.00 5.00
142 Anthony Stewart RC 1.50 4.00
143 Andrew Alberts RC 1.25 3.00
144 Jakub Klepis RC 1.25 3.00
145 Mikko Koivu RC 2.50 6.00
146 Ryan Hollweg RC 1.25 3.00
147 Jim Slater RC 1.50 4.00
148 Chris Campoli RC 1.25 3.00
149 Jordan Sigalet RC 1.25 3.00
150 Steve Bernier RC 2.00 5.00
151 Tomas Fleischmann RC 2.00 5.00
152 Matt Jones RC 1.25 3.00
153 Barry Tallackson RC 1.50 4.00
154 Ben Eager RC 1.50 4.00
155 Danny Richmond RC 1.25 3.00
156 Andrew Ladd RC 2.50 6.00
157 Jeremy Colliton RC 1.25 3.00
158 Bruno Gervais RC 1.25 3.00
159 Jeff Tambellini RC 1.25 3.00
160 Gerald Coleman RC 1.25 3.00
161 Paul Ranger RC 1.25 3.00
162 Staffan Kronwall RC 1.25 3.00
163 Dustin Penner RC 2.00 5.00
164 Kyle Brodziak RC 1.25 3.00
165 Greg Jacina RC 1.25 3.00
166 Erik Christensen RC 1.25 3.00
167 Kyle Quincey RC 1.50 4.00
168 Chris Thorburn RC 1.50 4.00
169 Christoph Schubert RC 1.25 3.00
170 Dimitri Patzold RC 1.25 3.00
171 Junior Lessard RC 1.25 3.00
172 Vojtech Polak RC 1.25 3.00
173 Adam Berkhoel RC 1.50 4.00
174 Cam Barker RC 1.50 4.00
175 Kevin Dallman RC 1.50 4.00
176 Milan Jurcina RC 1.50 4.00
177 Brad Winchester RC 2.00 5.00
178 George Parros RC 1.25 3.00
179 Al Montoya RC 2.00 5.00
180 Brett Lebda RC 1.25 3.00
181 Joe Sakic 1.50 4.00
182 Alex Tanguay 1.00 2.50
183 Milan Hejduk .75 2.00
184 Rick Nash 1.00 2.50
185 Mike Modano 1.50 4.00
186 Bill Guerin 1.00 2.50
187 Steve Yzerman 2.50 6.00
188 Brendan Shanahan 1.25 3.00
189 Chris Pronger .75 2.00
190 Roberto Luongo 1.50 4.00
191 Jeremy Roenick 1.00 2.50
192 Luc Robitaille 1.00 2.50
193 Marian Gaborik 1.50 4.00
194 Saku Koivu 1.00 2.50
195 Jose Theodore 1.00 2.50
196 Paul Kariya 1.25 3.00
197 Martin Brodeur 2.00 5.00
198 Patrik Elias 1.00 2.50
199 Miroslav Satan .75 2.00
200 Alexei Yashin .75 2.00
201 Jaromir Jagr 2.50 6.00
202 Dominik Hasek 1.50 4.00
203 Dany Heatley 1.00 2.50
204 Jason Spezza 1.00 2.50
205 Peter Forsberg 1.25 3.00
206 Keith Primeau 1.00 2.50
207 Curtis Joseph 1.00 2.50
208 Brett Hull 1.25 3.00
209 Mario Lemieux 3.00 8.00
210 Evgeni Nabokov .75 2.00
211 Jonathan Cheechoo 1.00 2.50
212 Keith Tkachuk 1.00 2.50
213 Doug Weight 1.00 2.50
214 Martin St. Louis 1.00 2.50
215 Vincent Lecavalier .75 2.00
216 Mats Sundin 1.00 2.50
217 Ed Belfour 1.00 2.50
218 Eric Lindros 1.50 4.00
219 Markus Naslund 1.00 2.50
220 Olaf Kolzig 1.00 2.50
221 Mike Bossy 1.00 2.50
222 Wayne Cashman .60 1.50
223 Gerry Cheevers 2.00 5.00
224 Bobby Clarke 1.00 2.50
225 Phil Esposito 1.50 4.00
226 Tony Esposito 1.00 2.50
227 Grant Fuhr 1.00 2.50
228 Glenn Hall .60 1.50
229 Jari Kurri 1.00 2.50
230 Guy Lafleur 1.25 3.00
231 Lanny McDonald 1.00 2.50
232 Gilbert Perreault 1.00 2.50
233 Jean Beliveau 1.00 2.50
234 Johnny Bucyk .75 2.00
235 Gordie Howe 3.00 8.00
236 Wayne Gretzky 5.00 12.00
237 Bernie Geoffrion .75 2.00
238 Red Kelly 1.00 2.50
239 Stan Mikita 1.25 3.00
240 Bryan Trottier 1.25 3.00
241 Jean-Sebastien Giguere 1.00 2.50
242 Sergei Fedorov 1.50 4.00
243 Teemu Selanne 2.00 5.00
244 Ilya Kovalchuk 1.00 2.50
245 Marian Hossa .75 2.00
246 Patrice Bergeron 1.25 3.00
247 Joe Thornton 1.25 3.00
248 Jarome Iginla 1.00 2.50
249 Miikka Kiprusoff .75 2.00
250 Nikolai Khabibulin 1.00 2.50

2005-06 Beehive Beige

*1-90 VETS: 5X TO 12X BASIC CARDS
*101-150 ROOKIES: 1X TO 2.5X RC
BEIGE ODDS 1:15

2005-06 Beehive Blue

*1-90 VETS: 4X TO 10X BASIC CARDS
*101-150 ROOKIES: .6X TO 1.5X RC
BLUE ODDS 1:5

2005-06 Beehive Gold

*1-90 VETS: 5X TO 12X BASIC CARDS
*101-150 ROOKIES: 1X TO 2.5X RC
STATED ODDS 1:240

2005-06 Beehive Red

*1-90 VETS: 2X TO 5X BASIC CARDS
*101-150 ROOKIES: .4X TO 1X BASIC RC
STATED ODDS 1:2

2005-06 Beehive Rookie Jumbos

COMPLETE SET (5) 20.00 40.00
COMMON CARD (R1-R5) 1.50 4.00
R1 Sidney Crosby 8.00 20.00
R2 Alexander Ovechkin 4.00 10.00
R3 Jeff Carter 2.50 6.00
R4 Alexander Perezhogin 1.50 4.00
R5 Corey Perry 2.50 6.00

2005-06 Beehive Matte

*1-90 VETS: 6X TO 15X BASIC CARDS
1-100 VET PRINT RUN 100
*91-180 ROOKIES: 1.5X TO 4X
101-180 ROOKIE PRINT RUN 25
101 Sidney Crosby 400.00 700.00

2005-06 Beehive Matted Materials

STATED ODDS 1:7.5
MMAF Adam Foote 3.00 8.00
MMAH Ales Hemsky 4.00 10.00
MMAK Alex Kovalev 4.00 10.00
MMAR Andrew Raycroft 4.00 10.00
MMAY Alexei Yashin 4.00 10.00
MMBG Bill Guerin 5.00 12.00
MMBM Brendan Morrison 3.00 8.00
MMBR Brad Richards 5.00 12.00
MMBW Brendan Witt 3.00 8.00
MMCD Chris Drury 4.00 10.00
MMCJ Curtis Joseph 5.00 12.00
MMCO Chris Osgood 5.00 12.00
MMDA Daniel Alfredsson 5.00 12.00
MMDB Dustin Brown 5.00 12.00
MMDC Dan Cloutier 4.00 10.00
MMDE Pavol Demitra 6.00 15.00
MMDH Dany Heatley 5.00 12.00
MMDR Dwayne Roloson 4.00 10.00
MMDW Doug Weight 5.00 12.00
MMEL Eric Lindros 8.00 20.00
MMGA Mathieu Garon 4.00 10.00
MMGI Brian Gionta 4.00 10.00
MMGL Guy Lafleur 6.00 15.00
MMGM Glen Murray 4.00 10.00
MMGO Scott Gomez 4.00 10.00
MMHJ Milan Hejduk 4.00 10.00
MMHO Marian Hossa 4.00 10.00
MMHS Henrik Sedin 5.00 12.00
MMHZ Henrik Zetterberg 6.00 15.00
MMIK Ilya Kovalchuk 5.00 12.00
MMJB Jay Bouwmeester 5.00 12.00
MMJG Jean-Sebastien Giguere 5.00 12.00
MMJO Jose Theodore 5.00 12.00
MMJR Jeremy Roenick 5.00 12.00
MMJS Jason Spezza 5.00 12.00
MMJT Joe Thornton 6.00 15.00
MMJW Jason Williams 3.00 8.00
MMKP Keith Primeau 5.00 12.00
MMKT Keith Tkachuk 5.00 12.00
MMLN Ladislav Nagy 3.00 8.00
MMLR Luc Robitaille 5.00 12.00
MMLU Joffrey Lupul 4.00 10.00
MMMB Martin Brodeur 8.00 20.00
MMMC Bryan McCabe 3.00 8.00
MMMD Marc Denis 4.00 10.00
MMMF Manny Fernandez 4.00 10.00
MMMG Martin Gerber 4.00 10.00
MMMH Marcel Hossa 3.00 8.00
MMMI Milan Michalek 3.00 8.00
MMMK Miikka Kiprusoff 4.00 10.00
MMML Mario Lemieux 15.00 40.00
MMMM Mike Modano 8.00 20.00
MMMN Markus Naslund 5.00 12.00
MMMP Mark Parrish 3.00 8.00
MMMR Michael Ryder 4.00 10.00
MMMS Mats Sundin 5.00 12.00
MMMT Marty Turco 5.00 12.00
MMMW Brenden Morrow 4.00 10.00
MMNA Nik Antropov 4.00 10.00
MMNH Nathan Horton 5.00 12.00
MMNK Nikolai Khabibulin 5.00 12.00
MMOJ Olli Jokinen 5.00 12.00
MMPA Patrik Elias 5.00 12.00
MMPB Pierre-Marc Bouchard 5.00 12.00
MMPD Pavel Datsyuk 6.00 15.00
MMPE Michael Peca 4.00 10.00
MMPF Peter Forsberg 6.00 15.00
MMRB Rob Blake 5.00 12.00
MMRE Robert Esche 4.00 10.00
MMRM Ryan Miller 5.00 12.00
MMRN Rick Nash 5.00 12.00
MMSA Joe Sakic 8.00 20.00
MMSC Sidney Crosby 15.00 40.00
MMSF Sergei Fedorov 8.00 20.00
MMSG Simon Gagne 5.00 12.00
MMSK Saku Koivu 5.00 12.00
MMSL Martin St. Louis 5.00 12.00
MMSS Sergei Samsonov 4.00 10.00
MMST Matt Stajan 4.00 10.00
MMSY Steve Yzerman 10.00 25.00
MMTB Todd Bertuzzi 5.00 12.00
MMTC Ty Conklin 4.00 10.00
MMWG Wayne Gretzky 30.00 60.00

2005-06 Beehive Matted Materials Remarkable

UNLISTED STARS 12.00 30.00
STATED PRINT RUN 50 SER.#'d SETS
RMBM Brendan Morrison 12.00 30.00
RMBR Brad Richards 10.00 25.00
RMCO Chris Osgood 15.00 40.00
RMDH Dany Heatley 25.00 60.00
RMDW Doug Weight 12.00 30.00
RMGL Guy Lafleur 30.00 80.00
RMHO Marian Hossa 12.00 30.00
RMHZ Henrik Zetterberg 15.00 40.00
RMIK Ilya Kovalchuk 40.00 100.00
RMJO Jose Theodore 15.00 40.00
RMJR Jeremy Roenick 15.00 40.00
RMJS Jason Spezza 25.00 60.00
RMJT Joe Thornton 12.50 30.00
RMLR Luc Robitaille 25.00 60.00
RMMB Martin Brodeur 40.00 100.00
RMMH Marcel Hossa 15.00 40.00
RMMN Markus Naslund 25.00 60.00
RMMP Mark Parrish 12.00 30.00
RMPE Michael Peca 12.00 30.00
RMRB Rob Blake 15.00 40.00
RMRN Rick Nash 25.00 60.00
RMSC Sidney Crosby 400.00 700.00
RMSL Martin St. Louis 20.00 50.00
RMTB Todd Bertuzzi 15.00 40.00
RMWG Wayne Gretzky 150.00 300.00

2005-06 Beehive PhotoGraphs

STATED ODDS 1:60
PGAO Alexander Ovechkin 40.00 100.00
PGBH Bobby Hull 40.00 80.00
PGCO Corey Perry 8.00 20.00
PGCP Chris Pronger 10.00 25.00
PGDW Doug Weight 8.00 20.00
PGES Eric Staal 8.00 20.00
PGGH Gordie Howe 50.00 125.00
PGGL Guy LaFleur 30.00 80.00
PGJC Jeff Carter 10.00 25.00
PGJI Jarome Iginla 15.00 40.00
PGJS Jason Spezza 10.00 25.00
PGJT Joe Thornton 8.00 20.00
PGLA Guy Lapointe 8.00 20.00
PGMB Mike Bossy 10.00 25.00
PGMD Marcel Dionne 10.00 25.00
PGMM Mike Modano 12.00 30.00
PGMN Markus Naslund 8.00 20.00
PGMT Marty Turco 6.00 15.00
PGPE Phil Esposito SP 40.00 80.00
PGRB Ray Bourque 30.00 80.00
PGRN Rick Nash 8.00 20.00
PGSC Sidney Crosby 100.00 200.00
PGSL Martin St. Louis 8.00 20.00
PGTE Tony Esposito 15.00 40.00
PGWG Wayne Gretzky SP 200.00 300.00

2005-06 Beehive Signature Scrapbook

STATED ODDS 1:30
SSAA Andrew Alberts 3.00 8.00
SSAM Andrej Meszaros 3.00 8.00
SSAO Alexander Ovechkin 60.00 120.00
SSAP Alexander Perezhogin 6.00 15.00
SSAR Andrew Raycroft 6.00 15.00
SSAS Anthony Stewart 8.00 20.00
SSBA Matthew Barnaby 3.00 8.00
SSBB Brandon Bochenski 3.00 8.00
SSBC Bobby Clarke 15.00 40.00
SSBE Steve Bernier 8.00 20.00
SSBM Brenden Morrow 8.00 20.00
SSBO Mike Bossy SP 20.00 50.00
SSBP Brad Park 6.00 15.00
SSBR Brad Richards 6.00 15.00
SSBS Borje Salming 8.00 20.00
SSBU Peter Budaj 6.00 15.00
SSCB Cam Barker 3.00 8.00
SSCC Chris Campoli 3.00 8.00
SSCH Jonathan Cheechoo 8.00 20.00
SSCK Chris Kunitz 6.00 15.00
SSCL Ryane Clowe 5.00 12.00
SSCN Craig Conroy 3.00 8.00
SSCO Braydon Coburn 10.00 25.00
SSCP Corey Perry 8.00 20.00
SSCS Cory Stillman 3.00 8.00
SSCW Cam Ward 15.00 40.00
SSDA Daniel Alfredsson 8.00 20.00
SSDC Don Cherry 12.00 30.00
SSDF Dan Fritsche 3.00 8.00
SSDH Dany Heatley SP 20.00 50.00
SSDI Dickie Moore 6.00 15.00
SSDK Duncan Keith 3.00 8.00
SSDL David Leneveu 8.00 20.00
SSDM Darren McCarty 6.00 15.00
SSDP Dion Phaneuf 12.00 30.00
SSDS Derek Sanderson 8.00 20.00
SSDT Dave Taylor 5.00 12.00
SSEA Patrick Eaves 6.00 15.00
SSED Eric Daze 3.00 8.00
SSFC Fred Cusick 8.00 25.00
SSFT Fedor Tyutin 3.00 8.00
SSGB Gilbert Brule 5.00 12.00
SSGH Gordie Howe SP 60.00 150.00
SSGL Guy Lafleur SP 50.00 100.00
SSGP Gilbert Perreault 10.00 25.00
SSHO Marian Hossa 8.00 20.00
SSHV Martin Havlat 10.00 25.00
SSHZ Henrik Zetterberg 10.00 25.00
SSJB Jay Bouwmeester SP 15.00 40.00
SSJC Jeff Carter 10.00 25.00
SSJF Johan Franzen 8.00 20.00
SSJH Jim Howard 25.00 60.00
SSJI Jarome Iginla SP 10.00 25.00
SSJM Jay McClement 3.00 8.00
SSJO Jeff O'Neill 3.00 8.00
SSJR Jeremy Roenick 20.00 50.00
SSJS Jason Spezza SP 30.00 60.00
SSJT Joe Thornton SP 20.00 40.00
SSJV Josef Vasicek 3.00 8.00
SSKM Ken Morrow 3.00 8.00
SSKN Kevin Nastiuk 6.00 15.00
SSKP Keith Primeau SP 8.00 20.00
SSLM Lanny McDonald 5.00 12.00
SSLR Luc Robitaille SP 25.00 60.00
SSLS Lee Stempniak 3.00 8.00
SSLU Roberto Luongo SP 25.00 60.00
SSMB Martin Brodeur SP 75.00 150.00
SSMC Mike Cammalleri 8.00 20.00
SSMD Marcel Dionne SP 20.00 50.00
SSMG Marian Gaborik SP 30.00 60.00
SSMH Marcel Hossa 3.00 8.00
SSMI Miroslav Satan 3.00 8.00
SSMJ Milan Jurcina 3.00 8.00
SSMK Mikko Koivu 8.00 20.00
SSMM Mike Modano SP 20.00 50.00
SSMN Markus Naslund SP 10.00 25.00
SSMP Michael Peca 3.00 8.00
SSMR Mike Ribeiro SP 8.00 20.00
SSMS Marco Sturm 3.00 8.00
SSMT Marty Turco 6.00 15.00
SSMU Larry Murphy 3.00 8.00
SSNH Nathan Horton 4.00 10.00
SSNK Nikolai Khabibulin 8.00 20.00
SSNY Michael Nylander 3.00 8.00
SSNZ Nikolai Zherdev 6.00 15.00
SSON Owen Nolan 8.00 20.00
SSPB Patrice Bergeron SP 10.00 25.00
SSPE Phil Esposito SP 25.00 50.00
SSPN Petteri Nokelainen 3.00 8.00
SSPP Petr Prucha 8.00 20.00
SSRB Rob Blake 10.00 25.00
SSRE Robert Esche 3.00 8.00
SSRI Mike Richards 10.00 25.00
SSRL Reggie Leach 5.00 12.00
SSRM Ryan Miller 8.00 20.00
SSRN Rick Nash SP 15.00 40.00
SSRS Ryan Smyth 10.00 25.00
SSRV Rogie Vachon 8.00 20.00
SSRW Ryan Whitney 6.00 15.00
SSRY Michael Ryder 6.00 15.00
SSSB Scotty Bowman SP 20.00 40.00
SSSC Sidney Crosby SP 300.00 450.00
SSSD Shane Doan 3.00 8.00
SSSE Brent Seabrook 5.00 12.00
SSSG Simon Gagne 10.00 25.00
SSSL Martin St. Louis SP 10.00 25.00
SSST Alexander Steen 15.00 30.00
SSSZ Sergei Zubov 3.00 8.00
SSTA Tyler Arnason 3.00 8.00
SSTB Todd Bertuzzi SP 10.00 25.00
SSTE Tony Esposito SP 20.00 40.00
SSTO Terry O'Reilly 6.00 15.00
SSTV Thomas Vanek 20.00 50.00
SSVP Vaclav Prospal 3.00 8.00
SSWC Wayne Cashman 6.00 15.00
SSYD Yann Danis 6.00 15.00
SSZC Zdeno Chara 10.00 25.00
SSZP Zach Parise 8.00 20.00

2006-07 Beehive

This 235-card set was released in April, 2007. The set was issued into the hobby in five card packs (four regular size and a jumbo card), with a $4.99 SRP, which came 15 packs to a box and 16 boxes to a case. Cards numbered 1-100 feature veterans, while cards 101-160 feature Rookie Cards and cards 161-235 feature a mix of veterans and retired greats in a 5" by 7" form.

COMPLETE SET w/o SPs (100) 10.00 25.00
5 X 7 ONE PER PACK
1 Alexander Ovechkin 1.50 4.00
2 Olaf Kolzig .40 1.00
3 Markus Naslund .30 .75
4 Roberto Luongo .60 1.50
5 Mats Sundin .40 1.00
6 Michael Peca .30 .75
7 Alexander Steen .40 1.00
8 Andrew Raycroft .30 .75

9 Vincent Lecavalier .30 .75
10 Brad Richards .40 1.00
11 Martin St. Louis .40 1.00
12 Manny Legace .30 .75
13 Keith Tkachuk .40 1.00
14 Doug Weight .40 1.00
15 Joe Thornton .50 1.25
16 Patrick Marleau .40 1.00
17 Jonathan Cheechoo .40 1.00
18 Vesa Toskala .30 .75
19 Sidney Crosby 1.50 4.00
20 Mark Recchi .50 1.25
21 Marc-Andre Fleury .60 1.50
22 Colby Armstrong .30 .75
23 Shane Doan .30 .75
24 Ed Jovanovski .30 .75
25 Jeremy Roenick .40 1.00
26 Owen Nolan .30 .75
27 Peter Forsberg .50 1.25
28 Simon Gagne .40 1.00
29 Jeff Carter .40 1.00
30 Joni Pitkanen .25 .60
31 Jason Spezza .40 1.00
32 Dany Heatley .40 1.00
33 Martin Gerber .30 .75
34 Daniel Alfredsson .40 1.00
35 Jaromir Jagr 1.00 2.50
36 Brendan Shanahan .50 1.25
37 Henrik Lundqvist .75 2.00
38 Alexei Yashin .30 .75
39 Rick DiPietro .30 .75
40 Miroslav Satan .30 .75
41 Martin Brodeur .75 2.00
42 Patrik Elias .40 1.00
43 Brian Gionta .30 .75
44 Paul Kariya .50 1.25
45 Tomas Vokoun .30 .75
46 Jason Arnott .30 .75
47 Saku Koivu .40 1.00
48 Cristobal Huet .30 .75
49 Michael Ryder .25 .60
50 Alexei Kovalev .30 .75
51 Marian Gaborik .50 1.25
52 Manny Fernandez .30 .75
53 Pavol Demitra .50 1.25
54 Mark Parrish .25 .60
55 Alexander Frolov .25 .60
56 Rob Blake .40 1.00
57 Ed Belfour .40 1.00
58 Todd Bertuzzi .40 1.00
59 Olli Jokinen .40 1.00
60 Ales Hemsky .30 .75
61 Jarret Stoll .30 .75
62 Ryan Smyth .30 .75
63 Joffrey Lupul .30 .75
64 Henrik Zetterberg .50 1.25
65 Dominik Hasek .50 1.25
66 Pavel Datsyuk .50 1.25
67 Nicklas Lidstrom .40 1.00
68 Mike Modano .60 1.50
69 Marty Turco .40 1.00
70 Eric Lindros .60 1.50
71 Rick Nash .40 1.00
72 Pascal LeClaire .30 .75
73 Gilbert Brule .30 .75
74 Sergei Fedorov .60 1.50
75 Joe Sakic .60 1.50
76 Milan Hejduk .30 .75
77 Jose Theodore .40 1.00
78 Marek Svatos .25 .60
79 Nikolai Khabibulin .40 1.00
80 Tuomo Ruutu .40 1.00
81 Martin Havlat .25 .60
82 Eric Staal .50 1.25
83 Cam Ward .40 1.00
84 Rod Brind`Amour .40 1.00
85 Jarome Iginla .40 1.00
86 Miikka Kiprusoff .30 .75
87 Alex Tanguay .25 .60
88 Dion Phaneuf .40 1.00
89 Chris Drury .30 .75
90 Ryan Miller .40 1.00
91 Patrice Bergeron .50 1.25
92 Hannu Toivonen .30 .75
93 Brad Boyes .25 .60
94 Zdeno Chara .40 1.00
95 Ilya Kovalchuk .40 1.00
96 Kari Lehtonen .30 .75
97 Marian Hossa .30 .75
98 Teemu Selanne .75 2.00
99 Chris Pronger .30 .75
100 Jean-Sebastien Giguere .40 1.00
101 David McKee RC 1.25 3.00
102 Ryan Shannon RC 1.25 3.00
103 Shane O'Brien RC 1.25 3.00
104 Matt Lashoff RC 1.25 3.00
105 Phil Kessel RC 3.00 8.00
106 Mark Stuart RC 1.25 3.00
107 Yan Stastny RC 1.25 3.00
108 Clarke MacArthur RC 1.50 4.00
109 Drew Stafford RC 2.00 5.00
110 Brandon Prust RC 1.25 3.00
111 Dustin Boyd RC 1.25 3.00
112 Michael Blunden RC 1.25 3.00
113 Dave Bolland RC 2.00 5.00
114 Paul Stastny RC 3.00 8.00
115 Fredrik Norrena RC 1.25 3.00
116 Loui Eriksson RC 2.00 5.00
117 Tomas Kopecky RC 1.50 4.00
118 Stefan Liv RC 1.25 3.00
119 Jeff Drouin-Deslauriers RC 1.25 3.00
120 Alexei Mikhnov RC 1.25 3.00
121 Ladislav Smid RC 1.25 3.00
122 Patrick Thoresen RC 1.25 3.00
123 Marc-Antoine Pouliot RC 1.25 3.00
124 David Booth RC 1.50 4.00
125 Anze Kopitar RC 5.00 12.00
126 Patrick O'Sullivan RC 2.00 5.00
127 Konstantin Pushkarev RC 1.50 4.00
128 Benoit Pouliot RC 1.50 4.00
129 Mikhail Grabovski RC 2.50 6.00
130 Guillaume Latendresse RC 2.00 5.00
131 Alexander Radulov RC 2.50 6.00
132 Shea Weber RC 3.00 8.00
133 Travis Zajac RC 2.50 6.00
134 Johnny Oduya RC 2.00 5.00
135 Blake Comeau RC 2.00 5.00
136 Nigel Dawes RC 1.25 3.00
137 Jarkko Immonen RC 1.25 3.00
138 Josh Hennessy RC 1.25 3.00
139 Kelly Guard RC 1.50 4.00
140 Martin Houle RC 1.50 4.00
141 Ryan Potulny RC 1.25 3.00
142 Enver Lisin RC 1.25 3.00
143 Keith Yandle RC 2.50 6.00
144 Evgeni Malkin RC 8.00 20.00
145 Kristopher Letang RC 4.00 10.00
146 Jordan Staal RC 3.00 8.00
147 Michel Ouellet RC 1.50 4.00
148 Noah Welch RC 1.25 3.00
149 Joe Pavelski RC 6.00 15.00
150 Marc-Edouard Vlasic RC 1.25 3.00
151 Matt Carle RC 1.25 3.00
152 Marek Schwarz RC 2.00 5.00
153 Blair Jones RC 1.25 3.00
154 Ian White RC 1.50 4.00
155 Brendan Bell RC 1.25 3.00
156 Kris Newbury RC 1.25 3.00
157 Jesse Schultz RC 1.25 3.00
158 Alexander Edler RC 2.00 5.00
159 Luc Bourdon RC 2.00 5.00
160 Eric Fehr RC 2.00 5.00
161 Alexander Ovechkin 5.00 12.00
162 Roberto Luongo 2.00 5.00
163 Markus Naslund 1.00 2.50
164 Michael Peca 1.00 2.50
165 Mats Sundin 1.25 3.00
166 Vincent Lecavalier 1.00 2.50
167 Joe Thornton 1.50 4.00
168 Jonathan Cheechoo 1.25 3.00
169 Sidney Crosby 5.00 12.00
170 Mario Lemieux 4.00 10.00
171 Marc-Andre Fleury 2.00 5.00
172 Jeremy Roenick 1.25 3.00
173 Shane Doan 1.00 2.50
174 Bobby Clarke 1.25 3.00
175 Peter Forsberg 1.50 4.00
176 Simon Gagne 1.25 3.00
177 Jason Spezza 1.25 3.00
178 Dany Heatley 1.25 3.00
179 Jaromir Jagr 3.00 8.00
180 Brendan Shanahan 1.50 4.00
181 Henrik Lundqvist 2.50 6.00
182 Mike Bossy 1.25 3.00
183 Billy Smith 1.25 3.00
184 Miroslav Satan 1.00 2.50
185 Martin Brodeur 2.50 6.00
186 Patrik Elias 1.25 3.00
187 Paul Kariya 1.50 4.00
188 Tomas Vokoun 1.00 2.50
189 Patrick Roy 3.00 8.00
190 Michael Ryder .75 2.00
191 Saku Koivu 1.25 3.00
192 Guy Lafleur 1.50 4.00
193 Marian Gaborik 1.50 4.00
194 Manny Fernandez 1.00 2.50
195 Rob Blake 1.25 3.00
196 Alexander Frolov .75 2.00
197 Luc Robitaille 1.25 3.00
198 Marcel Dionne 1.50 4.00
199 Ed Belfour 1.25 3.00
200 Todd Bertuzzi 1.25 3.00
201 Ryan Smyth 1.00 2.50
202 Ales Hemsky 1.00 2.50
203 Grant Fuhr 1.25 3.00
204 Gordie Howe 4.00 10.00
205 Henrik Zetterberg 1.50 4.00
206 Nicklas Lidstrom 1.25 3.00
207 Dominik Hasek 1.50 4.00
208 Mike Modano 2.00 5.00
209 Marty Turco 1.25 3.00
210 Eric Lindros 2.00 5.00
211 Rick Nash 1.25 3.00
212 Pascal LeClaire 1.00 2.50
213 Joe Sakic 2.00 5.00
214 Milan Hejduk 1.00 2.50
215 Jose Theodore 1.25 3.00
216 Ray Bourque 2.00 5.00
217 Bobby Hull 2.00 5.00
218 Tony Esposito 1.25 3.00
219 Martin Havlat .75 2.00
220 Cam Ward 1.25 3.00
221 Eric Staal 1.50 4.00
222 Jarome Iginla 1.25 3.00
223 Dion Phaneuf 1.25 3.00
224 Miikka Kiprusoff 1.00 2.50
225 Alex Tanguay .75 2.00
226 Chris Drury 1.00 2.50
227 Ryan Miller 1.25 3.00
228 Patrice Bergeron 1.50 4.00
229 Cam Neely 1.25 3.00
230 Brad Boyes .75 2.00
231 Bobby Orr 4.00 10.00
232 Ilya Kovalchuk 1.25 3.00
233 Kari Lehtonen 1.00 2.50
234 Teemu Selanne 2.50 6.00
235 Chris Pronger 1.00 2.50

2006-07 Beehive Blue

*BLUE (1-100): 2.5X TO 6X
*BLUE (101-160): .6X TO 1.5X
STATED ODDS 1:15

2006-07 Beehive Gold

*GOLD (1-100): 5X TO 12X
*GOLD (101-160): 2X TO 5X
COMMON TROPHY 15.00 40.00
STATED ODDS 1:240

2006-07 Beehive Matte

*MATTE (1-100): 4X TO 10X
*MATTER (101-160): 1X TO 2.5X
PRINT RUN 100 SER.#'d SETS

2006-07 Beehive Red Facsimile Signatures

*RED (1-100): 2X TO 5X
*RED (101-160): .5X TO 1.2XI
STATED ODDS 1:8

2006-07 Beehive Wood

*STARS: 1.5X TO 4X BASE HI
*RCs: .15X TO .4X BASE HI
STATED ODDS 1:2

2006-07 Beehive 5x7 Black and White

STATED ODDS 1:15
5 Mats Sundin 2.50 6.00
17 Jonathan Cheechoo 2.50 6.00
28 Simon Gagne 2.50 6.00
45 Tomas Vokoun 2.00 5.00
47 Saku Koivu 2.50 6.00
49 Michael Ryder 1.50 4.00
51 Marian Gaborik 3.00 8.00
57 Ed Belfour 2.50 6.00
67 Nicklas Lidstrom 2.50 6.00
74 Sergei Fedorov 4.00 10.00
83 Cam Ward 2.50 6.00
85 Jarome Iginla 2.50 6.00
91 Patrice Bergeron 3.00 8.00
96 Kari Lehtonen 2.00 5.00
98 Teemu Selanne 5.00 12.00
100 Jean-Sebastien Giguere 2.50 6.00
174 Bobby Clarke 2.00 5.00
182 Mike Bossy 2.00 5.00
183 Billy Smith 2.00 5.00
192 Guy Lafleur 2.50 6.00
203 Grant Fuhr 2.00 5.00
216 Ray Bourque 3.00 8.00
217 Bobby Hull 3.00 8.00
218 Tony Esposito 2.00 5.00
229 Cam Neely 2.00 5.00

2006-07 Beehive 5x7 Cherry Wood

STATED ODDS 1:240
PT President's Trophy 12.00 30.00
SC Stanley Cup 40.00 80.00
VT Vezina Trophy 25.00 50.00
ART Art Ross Trophy 40.00 80.00
BMT Masterton Trophy 12.00 30.00
CCT Campbell Trophy 12.00 30.00
CMT Calder Trophy 12.00 30.00
CST Conn Smythe Trophy 12.00 30.00
FST Selke Trophy 12.00 30.00
HMT Hart Memorial Trophy
JAA Jack Adams Award 12.00 30.00
JNT James Norris Trophy 15.00 40.00
KCT King Clancy Trophy 20.00 50.00
LBP Pearson Award 12.00 30.00
LBT Lady Byng Trophy 12.00 30.00
MRT Rocket Richard Trophy 12.00 30.00
PWT Prince of Wales Trophy 12.00 30.00
WJT Jennings Trophy 12.00 30.00

2006-07 Beehive 5x7 Dark Wood

STATED ODDS 1:150
3 Markus Naslund 5.00 12.00
4 Roberto Luongo 10.00 25.00
9 Vincent Lecavalier 5.00 12.00
19 Sidney Crosby 25.00 60.00
21 Marc-Andre Fleury 10.00 25.00
31 Jason Spezza 6.00 15.00
32 Dany Heatley 6.00 15.00
36 Brendan Shanahan 8.00 20.00
37 Henrik Lundqvist 12.00 30.00
44 Paul Kariya 8.00 20.00
64 Henrik Zetterberg 8.00 20.00
68 Mike Modano 10.00 25.00
71 Rick Nash 6.00 15.00
82 Eric Staal 8.00 20.00
86 Miikka Kiprusoff 5.00 12.00
90 Ryan Miller 6.00 15.00
95 Ilya Kovalchuk 6.00 15.00
105 Phil Kessel 8.00 20.00
144 Evgeni Malkin 20.00 50.00
146 Jordan Staal 8.00 20.00
170 Mario Lemieux 15.00 40.00
189 Patrick Roy 12.00 30.00
198 Marcel Dionne 6.00 15.00
204 Gordie Howe 15.00 40.00
231 Bobby Orr 15.00 40.00

2006-07 Beehive Matted Materials

STATED ODDS 1:8
MMAE David Aebischer 5.00 12.00
MMAF Alexander Frolov 4.00 10.00
MMAH Ales Hemsky 5.00 12.00
MMAO Alexander Ovechkin 25.00 60.00
MMAS Alexander Steen 6.00 15.00
MMAT Alex Tanguay 4.00 10.00
MMBB Brad Boyes 4.00 10.00
MMBO Pierre-Marc Bouchard 6.00 15.00
MMCD Chris Drury 5.00 12.00
MMCN Cam Neely 6.00 15.00
MMCP Corey Perry 6.00 15.00
MMCS Cory Stillman 4.00 10.00
MMCW Cam Ward 6.00 15.00
MMDA Daniel Alfredsson 6.00 15.00
MMDH Dany Heatley 6.00 15.00
MMDR Dwayne Roloson 5.00 12.00
MMEB Ed Belfour 6.00 15.00
MMES Eric Staal 8.00 20.00
MMHA Martin Havlat 4.00 10.00
MMHT Hannu Toivonen 5.00 12.00
MMHZ Henrik Zetterberg 8.00 20.00
MMIK Ilya Kovalchuk 6.00 15.00
MMJB Jay Bouwmeester 6.00 15.00
MMJC Jeff Carter 6.00 15.00
MMJI Jarome Iginla 6.00 15.00
MMJJ Jaromir Jagr 15.00 40.00
MMJL Joffrey Lupul 5.00 12.00
MMJS Joe Sakic 10.00 25.00
MMJT Joe Thornton 8.00 20.00
MMLE Jere Lehtinen 4.00 10.00
MMLN Ladislav Nagy 4.00 10.00
MMMB Martin Brodeur 12.00 30.00
MMMG Marian Gaborik 8.00 20.00
MMMH Milan Hejduk 5.00 12.00
MMML Mario Lemieux SP 15.00 40.00
MMMM Mike Modano 10.00 25.00
MMMP Michael Peca 5.00 12.00
MMMS Mats Sundin 6.00 15.00
MMMT Marty Turco 6.00 15.00
MMNL Nicklas Lidstrom 6.00 15.00
MMPB Patrice Bergeron 8.00 20.00
MMPF Peter Forsberg 8.00 20.00
MMPK Paul Kariya 8.00 20.00
MMPM Patrick Marleau 6.00 15.00
MMRB Ray Bourque 10.00 25.00
MMRL Roberto Luongo 10.00 25.00
MMRM Ryan Miller 6.00 15.00
MMRN Rick Nash 6.00 15.00
MMRS Ryan Smyth 5.00 12.00
MMSA Marc Savard 4.00 10.00
MMSC Sidney Crosby SP 25.00 60.00
MMSG Scott Gomez 5.00 12.00
MMSK Saku Koivu 6.00 15.00
MMSS Sergei Samsonov 5.00 12.00
MMST Jarret Stoll 5.00 12.00
MMSV Marek Svatos 4.00 10.00
MMSZ Sergei Zubov 5.00 12.00
MMTH Tomas Holmstrom 5.00 12.00
MMTV Tomas Vokoun 5.00 12.00
MMZC Zdeno Chara 6.00 15.00

2006-07 Beehive PhotoGraphs

STATED ODDS 1:240
PGAR Andrew Raycroft 8.00 20.00
PGBO Bobby Orr SP 100.00 200.00
PGDH Dominik Hasek SP 60.00 125.00
PGES Eric Staal 12.00 30.00
PGGH Gordie Howe 75.00 125.00
PGGL Guy Lafleur 12.00 30.00
PGHE Dany Heatley 10.00 25.00
PGJI Jarome Iginla 10.00 25.00
PGJT Joe Thornton 12.00 30.00
PGKL Kari Lehtonen 8.00 20.00
PGMB Martin Brodeur 50.00 100.00
PGMG Marian Gaborik 12.00 30.00
PGML Mario Lemieux SP
PGMM Mike Modano 15.00 40.00
PGMR Michael Ryder 6.00 15.00
PGNL Nicklas Lidstrom 15.00 30.00
PGPB Patrice Bergeron 12.00 30.00
PGPR Patrick Roy 60.00 125.00
PGRB Ray Bourque 15.00 40.00
PGRL R. Luongo EXCH 15.00 40.00
PGRN Rick Nash 10.00 25.00
PGSC Sidney Crosby 75.00 150.00
PGTE Tony Esposito 10.00 25.00
PGVL Vincent Lecavalier 8.00 20.00
PGWG W. Gretzky EXCH 150.00 250.00

2006-07 Beehive Signature Scrapbook

STATED ODDS 1:15
SSAF Alexander Frolov 3.00 8.00
SSAH Ales Hemsky 4.00 10.00
SSBB Brad Boyes 3.00 8.00
SSBG Brian Gionta 4.00 10.00
SSBO Bobby Orr SP
SSCA Colby Armstrong 4.00 10.00
SSCC Chris Campoli 3.00 8.00
SSCH Chris Higgins 3.00 8.00
SSCP Chris Phillips 3.00 8.00
SSDC Don Cherry 12.00 30.00
SSDL David Leneveu 4.00 10.00
SSDR Dwayne Roloson 4.00 10.00
SSDS Darryl Sittler 6.00 15.00
SSDT Darcy Tucker 4.00 10.00
SSES Eric Staal SP 20.00 50.00
SSGE Martin Gerber 4.00 10.00
SSGH Gordie Howe SP 40.00 80.00
SSHE Milan Hejduk 4.00 10.00
SSHU Cristobal Huet 4.00 10.00
SSJA Jason Arnott 4.00 10.00
SSJB Johnny Bucyk 5.00 12.00
SSJC J. Cheechoo EXCH 5.00 12.00
SSJI Jarome Iginla 5.00 12.00
SSJP Joni Pitkanen 3.00 8.00
SSJS Jarret Stoll 4.00 10.00
SSJT Jose Theodore SP 15.00 40.00
SSKD Kris Draper 3.00 8.00
SSLN Ladislav Nagy 3.00 8.00
SSMB Mike Bossy SP 15.00 40.00
SSMC Mike Cammalleri 3.00 8.00
SSMF Marc-Andre Fleury 6.00 15.00
SSMG Marian Gaborik 6.00 15.00
SSMH Martin Havlat 3.00 8.00
SSMP Michael Peca 4.00 10.00
SSMR Mike Richards 5.00 12.00
SSMS Marek Svatos 3.00 8.00
SSPA J.P. Parise 3.00 8.00
SSPB Pierre-Marc Bouchard 5.00 12.00
SSPE Patrik Elias 5.00 12.00
SSPM Patrick Marleau SP 15.00 40.00
SSPP Petr Prucha 4.00 10.00
SSPR Patrick Roy SP 75.00 150.00
SSPS Peter Stastny 5.00 12.00
SSRB Rene Bourque 3.00 8.00
SSRM Ryan Miller 5.00 12.00
SSRW Ryan Whitney 4.00 10.00
SSSA Marc Savard 3.00 8.00
SSSB Steve Bernier 3.00 8.00
SSSS Sergei Samsonov SP 12.00 30.00
SSTH Tomas Holmstrom 4.00 10.00
SSTL Ted Lindsay SP 12.00 30.00
SSTO Terry O'Reilly SP 10.00 25.00
SSVT Vesa Toskala SP 12.00 30.00
SSWG Wayne Gretzky SP 150.00 300.00

2001-02 Between the Pipes

Released in late February, this 170-card set was the first to focus exclusively on the netminders of the past and present NHL. Subsets included trophy winners and netcam photography. The last twenty cards in the set were available in BAP Update packs only. Total production for this product was limited to 800 cases.

COMPLETE SET (150) 50.00 100.00
COMP.SET w/UPDATE (170) 75.00 150.00
151-170 ISSUED IN BAP UPDATE
1 Patrick Roy 1.50 4.00
2 Jean-Sebastien Giguere .50 1.25
3 Ron Tugnutt .50 1.25
4 Rick DiPietro .50 1.25
5 Milan Hnilicka .50 1.25
6 Jean-Sebastien Aubin .50 1.25
7 Craig Billington .40 1.00
8 Byron Dafoe .50 1.25
9 Maxime Ouellet .60 1.50
10 Ed Belfour .60 1.50
11 John Grahame .50 1.25
12 Mathieu Garon .50 1.25
13 Martin Biron .50 1.25
14 Dan Cloutier .50 1.25
15 Tomas Vokoun .50 1.25
16 Arturs Irbe .50 1.25
17 Curtis Joseph .60 1.50
18 Jocelyn Thibault .50 1.25
19 Roman Cechmanek .50 1.25
20 Miikka Kiprusoff .60 1.50
21 Olaf Kolzig .60 1.50
22 Jani Hurme .50 1.25
23 David Aebischer .50 1.25
24 Damian Rhodes .50 1.25
25 Marc Denis .50 1.25
26 Marty Turco .60 1.50
27 Evgeni Nabokov .50 1.25
28 Manny Legace .50 1.25
29 Mike Dunham .50 1.25
30 Tommy Salo .50 1.25
31 Sean Burke .40 1.00
32 Andrew Raycroft .50 1.25
33 Roberto Luongo 1.00 2.50
34 Johan Holmqvist .50 1.25
35 Felix Potvin 1.00 2.50
36 Martin Brodeur 1.25 3.00
37 Gregg Naumenko .40 1.00
38 Travis Scott .40 1.00
39 Manny Fernandez .50 1.25
40 Kevin Weekes .50 1.25
41 Steve Passmore .40 1.00
42 Johan Hedberg .50 1.25
43 Patrick Lalime .50 1.25
44 Jose Theodore .60 1.50
45 Mika Noronen .40 1.00
46 Brent Johnson .50 1.25
47 Chris Mason .40 1.00
48 Mike Fountain .40 1.00
49 Jamie McLennan .40 1.00
50 Mike Richter .60 1.50
51 Eric Fichaud .40 1.00
52 Steve Shields .50 1.25
53 Rich Parent .40 1.00
54 Mike Vernon .50 1.25
55 Jason LaBarbera .40 1.00
56 Dominik Hasek 1.00 2.50
57 Dan Blackburn RC 2.00 5.00
58 Robert Esche .40 1.00
59 Joaquin Gage .40 1.00
60 Jamie Storr .50 1.25
61 Brian Boucher .50 1.25
62 Trevor Kidd .40 1.00
63 Nikolai Khabibulin .60 1.50
64 Norm Maracle .40 1.00
65 Roman Turek .50 1.25
66 Tyler Moss .40 1.00
67 Fred Brathwaite .50 1.25
68 Garth Snow .50 1.25
69 Dieter Kochan .40 1.00
70 Bob Essensa .50 1.25
71 Kirk McLean .50 1.25
72 Chris Osgood .60 1.50
73 Jeff Hackett .50 1.25
74 Stephane Fiset .50 1.25
75 Dominic Roussel .40 1.00
76 Corey Hirsch .40 1.00
77 Vitali Yeremeyev .40 1.00
78 Tom Barrasso .50 1.25
79 Scott Clemmensen RC 1.50 4.00
80 Martin Brochu .40 1.00
81 Corey Schwab .40 1.00
82 Ty Conklin RC 2.50 6.00
83 Dwayne Roloson .50 1.25
84 Ilja Bryzgalov RC 4.00 10.00
85 Olivier Michaud RC 2.50 6.00
86 Vesa Toskala .40 1.00
87 Jussi Markkanen .40 1.00
88 Patrick Desrochers .40 1.00
89 Peter Skudra .50 1.25
90 J-F Damphousse .40 1.00
91 Mike Dunham .50 1.25
92 Mike Richter .60 1.50
93 Brian Boucher .50 1.25
94 Patrick Roy 1.50 4.00
95 Martin Biron .50 1.25
96 Jean-Sebastien Aubin .50 1.25
97 Curtis Joseph .60 1.50
98 Martin Brodeur 1.25 3.00
99 Arturs Irbe .50 1.25
100 Jeff Hackett .50 1.25
101 Ed Belfour .60 1.50
102 Jocelyn Thibault .50 1.25
103 Roman Cechmanek .50 1.25
104 Patrick Lalime .50 1.25
105 Olaf Kolzig .60 1.50
106 Byron Dafoe .50 1.25
107 Johan Hedberg .50 1.25
108 Dan Cloutier .50 1.25
109 Dominik Hasek 1.00 2.50
110 Olaf Kolzig .60 1.50
111 Patrick Roy 2.00 5.00
112 Ed Belfour .75 2.00
113 Grant Fuhr .75 2.00
114 Ron Hextall .75 2.00
115 Pelle Lindbergh .75 2.00
116 Tom Barrasso .60 1.50
117 Billy Smith .75 2.00
118 Bernie Parent .75 2.00
119 Tony Esposito 1.25 3.00
120 Gump Worsley 1.00 2.50
121 Glenn Hall 1.00 2.50
122 Jacques Plante 1.25 3.00
123 Johnny Bower .75 2.00
124 Terry Sawchuk 1.25 3.00
125 Harry Lumley .75 2.00
126 Bill Durnan .75 2.00
127 Turk Broda .60 1.50
128 Frank Brimsek .60 1.50
129 Tiny Thompson .60 1.50
130 George Hainsworth .60 1.50
131 Gump Worsley 1.00 2.50
132 Georges Vezina 1.25 3.00
133 Vladislav Tretiak 1.25 3.00
134 Tiny Thompson .60 1.50
135 Terry Sawchuk 1.25 3.00
136 Jacques Plante 1.25 3.00
137 Chuck Rayner .50 1.25
138 Bernie Parent .75 2.00
139 Harry Lumley .75 2.00
140 Glenn Hall 1.00 2.50
141 George Hainsworth .60 1.50
142 Ed Giacomin .75 2.00
143 Charlie Gardiner .50 1.25
144 Tony Esposito 1.25 3.00
145 Bill Durnan .75 2.00
146 Gerry Cheevers 1.25 3.00
147 Turk Broda .60 1.50
148 Frank Brimsek .60 1.50
149 Johnny Bower .75 2.00
150 Roy Worters .60 1.50
151 Pasi Nurminen RC 1.50 4.00
152 Alex Auld .40 1.00
153 John Vanbiesbrouck .60 1.50
154 Wade Flaherty .40 1.00
155 Kevin Weekes .50 1.25
156 Tom Barrasso .50 1.25
157 Stephane Fiset .50 1.25
158 Sebastien Centomo RC 1.50 4.00
159 Jean-Francois Labbe .50 1.25
160 Simon Lajeunesse .40 1.00
161 Frederic Cassivi RC 1.50 4.00
162 Martin Prusek RC 1.50 4.00
163 Dominik Hasek 1.00 2.50
164 David Aebischer .50 1.25
165 Dan Cloutier .50 1.25
166 Byron Dafoe .50 1.25
167 Curtis Joseph .60 1.50
168 Ed Belfour .60 1.50
169 Tommy Salo .50 1.25
170 Jose Theodore .60 1.50

2001-02 Between the Pipes All-Star Jerseys

Limited to just 60 copies each, this 16-card set featured goalies who played in the last several All-Star Games alongside a swatch of their jersey from the game.

STATED PRINT RUN 60 SETS
ASJ1 Ed Belfour 10.00 25.00
ASJ2 Arturs Irbe 10.00 25.00
ASJ3 Martin Brodeur 25.00 60.00
ASJ4 Roman Cechmanek 10.00 25.00
ASJ5 Dominik Hasek 15.00 40.00
ASJ6 Olaf Kolzig 10.00 25.00
ASJ7 Curtis Joseph 10.00 25.00
ASJ8 Mike Richter 10.00 25.00
ASJ9 Patrick Roy 30.00 80.00
ASJ10 Evgeni Nabokov 10.00 25.00
ASJ11 Tommy Salo 10.00 25.00
ASJ12 Curtis Joseph 10.00 25.00
ASJ13 Dominik Hasek 12.00 30.00
ASJ14 Roman Turek 10.00 25.00
ASJ15 Nikolai Khabibulin 10.00 25.00
ASJ16 Patrick Roy 15.00 30.00

2001-02 Between the Pipes Double Memorabilia

This 30-card set featured both a game-worn jersey swatch and a stick or pad swatch from the featured goalie. Each card was limited to 50 copies.

STATED PRINT RUN 50 SETS
DM1 Felix Potvin 15.00 40.00
DM2 Mike Vernon 15.00 40.00
DM3 Johan Hedberg 15.00 40.00
DM4 Olaf Kolzig 15.00 40.00
DM5 Jeff Hackett 15.00 40.00
DM6 Martin Brodeur 20.00 50.00
DM7 Mike Dunham 15.00 40.00
DM8 Trevor Kidd 12.00 30.00
DM9 Damian Rhodes 15.00 40.00
DM10 John Grahame 15.00 40.00
DM11 Roberto Luongo 15.00 40.00
DM12 Manny Legace 15.00 40.00
DM13 Evgeni Nabokov 15.00 40.00
DM14 Jose Theodore 15.00 40.00
DM15 Robert Esche 15.00 40.00
DM16 Chris Osgood 12.00 30.00
DM17 Sean Burke 15.00 40.00
DM18 Martin Biron 15.00 40.00
DM19 Jocelyn Thibault 15.00 40.00
DM20 Brian Boucher 20.00 40.00
DM21 Curtis Joseph 12.00 30.00
DM22 Roman Turek 15.00 40.00
DM23 Gerry Cheevers 15.00 40.00
DM24 Terry Sawchuk 75.00 150.00
DM25 Grant Fuhr 15.00 40.00
DM26 Bernie Parent 20.00 50.00
DM27 Ron Hextall 15.00 40.00
DM28 Gump Worsley 30.00 80.00
DM29 Tony Esposito 40.00 100.00
DM30 Ed Giacomin 15.00 40.00

2001-02 Between the Pipes Future Wave

This 10-card set featured younger goalies from around the league alongside a game-worn jersey swatch. The word "Future Wave" were printed vertically on the right border and the player's name is printed in the right bottom corner. Each card was limited to just 22 copies.

FW1 Johan Hedberg 20.00 50.00
FW2 Martin Biron 15.00 40.00
FW3 Patrick Lalime 30.00 60.00
FW4 Roberto Luongo 30.00 60.00
FW5 J.Holmqvist 25.00 50.00
D.Blackburn
FW6 Dan Cloutier 12.50 30.00
FW7 M.Kiprusoff 12.50 30.00
E.Nabokov
FW8 Brian Boucher 12.50 30.00
FW9 Mathieu Garon 20.00 50.00
FW10 Rick DiPietro 25.00 60.00

2001-02 Between the Pipes Goalie Gear

This 30-card set featured an up close color photo beside a game-used swatch of goalie pad or glove. The word "goalie" was printed vertically along the right border and the goalie's name was printed under the photo. Cards from this set were limited to just 20-70 copies.

STATED PRINT RUN 20-70
GG1 Felix Potvin 12.50 30.00
GG2 Jeff Hackett 10.00 25.00
GG3 Mike Vernon 10.00 25.00
GG4 Sean Burke 10.00 25.00
GG5 Johan Hedberg 12.50 30.00
GG6 Jose Theodore 12.50 30.00
GG7 Robert Esche 10.00 25.00
GG8 Dan Cloutier 10.00 25.00
GG9 Olaf Kolzig 12.50 30.00
GG10 Roberto Luongo 15.00 40.00
GG11 Manny Legace 10.00 25.00
GG12 Martin Brodeur 25.00 60.00
GG13 Marty Turco 12.50 30.00
GG14 Arturs Irbe 12.50 30.00
GG15 Damian Rhodes 10.00 25.00
GG16 Trevor Kidd 10.00 25.00
GG17 Mike Dunham 10.00 25.00
GG18 Evgeni Nabokov 12.50 30.00
GG19 Roman Turek 10.00 25.00
GG20 Brian Boucher 10.00 25.00
GG21 Jocelyn Thibault 10.00 25.00
GG22 Dominik Hasek/20 15.00 40.00
GG23 Patrick Roy/20 25.00 50.00
GG24 Curtis Joseph/20 50.00 100.00
GG25 Brent Johnson 10.00 25.00
GG26 Patrick Lalime 10.00 25.00
GG27 J-S Aubin 10.00 25.00
GG28 Martin Biron 10.00 25.00
GG29 Chris Osgood 12.50 30.00
GG30 Rick DiPietro 12.50 30.00

2001-02 Between the Pipes He Shoots He Saves Points

Inserted one per pack, these cards carry a value of 1, 2 or 3 points. The points could be redeemed for special memorabilia cards. The cards are unnumbered and are listed below in alphabetical order by point value. The redemption program ended November 2002.

ONE PER PACK
1 Brian Boucher 1pt. .20 .50
2 Sean Burke 1pt. .20 .50
3 Byron Dafoe 1pt. .20 .50
4 Nikoali Khabibulin 1pt. .25 .60
5 Olaf Kolzig 1pt. .20 .50
6 Roberto Luongo 1pt. .25 .60
7 Evgeni Nabokov 1pt. .20 .50
8 Jose Theodore 1pt. .30 .75
9 Jocelyn Thibault 1 pt. .25 .60
10 Roman Turek 1pt. .20 .50
11 Ed Belfour 2 pts. .25 .60
12 Martin Brodeur 2 pts. .40 1.00
13 Grant Fuhr 2 pts. .30 .75
14 Glenn Hall 2 pts. .20 .50
15 Jacques Plante 2 pts. .25 .60
16 Tommy Salo 2 pts. .20 .50
17 Dominik Hasek 3 pts. .50 1.25
18 Curtis Joseph 3 pts. .30 .75
19 Patrick Roy 3 pts. 1.50 4.00
20 Terry Sawchuk 3 pts. .30 .75

2001-02 Between the Pipes Jerseys

This 42-card set featured game-worn jersey swatches affixed to the right of full-color action photos on a two color background. The words "game used jersey" are printed at the card top and the player's name is printed on the right hand border. Each card was limited to 90 copies.

STATED PRINT RUN 90 SETS
*JSY-STICK/90: .5X TO 1.2X BASIC JSY
GJ1 Byron Dafoe 6.00 15.00
GJ2 Dominik Hasek 12.50 30.00
GJ3 Mike Vernon 10.00 25.00
GJ4 Arturs Irbe 10.00 25.00
GJ5 Jocelyn Thibault 6.00 15.00
GJ6 Patrick Roy 25.00 60.00
GJ7 Ed Belfour 10.00 25.00
GJ8 Chris Osgood 10.00 25.00
GJ9 Johan Hedberg 6.00 15.00
GJ10 Roberto Luongo 12.50 30.00
GJ11 Jose Theodore 12.50 30.00
GJ12 Mike Dunham 6.00 15.00
GJ13 Martin Brodeur 20.00 50.00
GJ14 Mike Richter 10.00 25.00
GJ15 Roman Cechmanek 6.00 15.00
GJ16 J-S Aubin 6.00 15.00
GJ17 Roman Turek 6.00 15.00
GJ18 Curtis Joseph 10.00 25.00
GJ19 Olaf Kolzig 10.00 25.00
GJ20 Felix Potvin 25.00 60.00
GJ21 Trevor Kidd 8.00 20.00
GJ22 Tommy Salo 6.00 15.00
GJ23 Jeff Hackett 8.00 20.00
GJ24 Brian Boucher 6.00 15.00
GJ25 Dan Cloutier 6.00 15.00
GJ26 Damian Rhodes 6.00 15.00
GJ27 Ron Tugnutt 6.00 15.00
GJ28 Marty Turco 8.00 20.00
GJ29 Manny Fernandez 6.00 15.00
GJ30 Marc Denis 6.00 15.00
GJ31 Evgeni Nabokov 10.00 25.00
GJ32 Nikolai Khabibulin 10.00 25.00
GJ33 Sean Burke 6.00 15.00
GJ34 Gregg Naumenko 6.00 15.00
GJ35 Steve Shields 6.00 15.00
GJ36 Mathieu Garon 6.00 15.00
GJ37 Manny Legace 6.00 15.00
GJ38 Johan Holmqvist 6.00 15.00
GJ39 Martin Biron 6.00 15.00
GJ40 David Aebischer 6.00 15.00
GJ41 Miikka Kiprusoff 10.00 25.00
GJ42 John Grahame 6.00 15.00

2001-02 Between the Pipes Emblems

This 10-card set featured swatches of jersey emblem of the featured player. The words "game-used emblem is printed along the card top and the player's name is printed vertically along the left hand border. Each card was limited to just 20 copies.

GUE1 Dominik Hasek 50.00 120.00
GUE2 Jocelyn Thibault 25.00 60.00
GUE3 Patrick Roy 50.00 120.00
GUE4 Johan Hedberg 75.00 150.00
GUE5 Roman Turek 25.00 60.00
GUE6 Curtis Joseph 25.00 60.00
GUE7 Olaf Kolzig 25.00 60.00
GUE8 Tommy Salo 30.00 80.00
GUE9 Brian Boucher 25.00 60.00
GUE10 Evgeni Nabokov 30.00 80.00

2001-02 Between the Pipes Numbers

Limited to just 20 copies each, this 10 card set featured game-worn swatches from the featured player's jersey number. The words "in the numbers" appear vertically along the right hand border and the player's name appears along the left hand border.

ITN1 Dominik Hasek 60.00 125.00
ITN2 Jocelyn Thibault
ITN3 Patrick Roy 60.00 125.00
ITN4 Johan Hedberg 40.00 80.00
ITN5 Roman Turek 25.00 60.00
ITN6 Curtis Joseph 40.00 80.00
ITN7 Olaf Kolzig 25.00 60.00
ITN8 Tommy Salo 15.00 40.00
ITN9 Brian Boucher 15.00 40.00
ITN10 Evgeni Nabokov 25.00 60.00

2001-02 Between the Pipes Masks

This 40-card set featured some of the more memorable goalie masks from the past and present NHL. Dufex technology was used to give the cards an overall foil effect. The cards were unnumbered and are listed below in alphabetical order by series. Series One (#1-30) were inserts in Between the Pipes and cards #31-40 were available in Be a Player Update packs only.

COMPLETE SET (40) 75.00 150.00
CARDS 31-40 AVAIL.IN BAP UPD.PACKS
SILVER/300: .8X TO 2X BASIC INSERT
GOLD/30: 2X TO 5X BASIC INSERT
1 Murray Bannerman 2.50 6.00
2 Ed Belfour Stars 5.00 12.00
3 Martin Biron 3.00 8.00
4 Sean Burke 3.00 8.00
5 Roman Cechmanek 2.50 6.00
6 Gerry Cheevers 6.00 15.00
7 Byron Dafoe 3.00 8.00
8 Mike Dunham 2.50 6.00
9 Manny Fernandez 3.00 8.00
10 Ed Giacomin 5.00 12.00
11 Gilles Gratton 2.50 6.00
12 Johan Hedberg 3.00 8.00
13 Brent Johnson 3.00 8.00
14 Curtis Joseph Blues 5.00 12.00
15 Curtis Joseph Leafs 5.00 12.00
16 Olaf Kolzig 3.00 8.00
17 Patrick Lalime 3.00 8.00
18 Manny Legace 2.50 6.00
19 Roberto Luongo 5.00 12.00
20 Evgeni Nabokov 4.00 10.00
21 Jacques Plante 8.00 20.00
22 Felix Potvin 6.00 15.00
23 Damian Rhodes 2.50 6.00
24 Mike Richter 5.00 12.00
25 Patrick Roy 8.00 20.00
26 Tommy Salo 3.00 8.00
27 Steve Shields 2.50 6.00
28 Jose Theodore 4.00 10.00
29 Roman Turek 3.00 8.00
30 John Vanbiesbrouck 4.00 10.00
31 Ed Belfour Blackhawks 5.00 12.00
32 Rick DiPietro 3.00 8.00
33 Grant Fuhr 4.00 10.00
34 Jeff Hackett 3.00 8.00
35 Brian Hayward 2.50 6.00
36 Milan Hnilicka 2.50 6.00
37 Nikolai Khabibulin 4.00 10.00
38 Miikka Kiprusoff 3.00 8.00
39 Jocelyn Thibault 3.00 8.00
40 Ron Tugnutt 4.00 10.00

2001-02 Between the Pipes Record Breakers

This 20-card set featured record setting goalies along side swatches of game-used jerseys. The words "Record Breakers" appeared along the top left border

nd the goalie's feat was printed in the bottom right order. Each card was limited to just 50 copies each.
NNOUNCED PRINT RUN 50
31 Patrick Roy 25.00 60.00
32 Sawchuk/Brodeur/Plante 150.00 300.00
33 Jacques Plante 25.00 60.00
34 Martin Brodeur 25.00 60.00
35 Terry Sawchuk 30.00 80.00
36 Bernie Parent 15.00 40.00
37 Tony Esposito 15.00 40.00
38 Ed Belfour 15.00 40.00
39 Grant Fuhr 15.00 40.00
310 Patrick Roy 25.00 60.00
311 Patrick Roy 25.00 60.00
312 Ed Belfour 15.00 40.00
313 Jacques Plante 25.00 60.00
314 Gerry Cheevers 15.00 40.00
315 Terry Sawchuk 30.00 80.00
316 Patrick Roy 25.00 60.00
317 Patrick Roy 25.00 60.00
318 Chris Osgood 15.00 40.00
319 Tony Esposito 15.00 40.00
320 Glenn Hall 15.00 40.00

2001-02 Between the Pipes Tandems

his 13-card set featured goalie duos from specific ams around the league. Each card included a full-olor photo of each goalie and a game-worn jersey watch on the card front. The words "Goalie Tandems" ere printed on the bottom border of each card. This t was limited to just 50 copies of each card.
NNOUNCED PRINT RUN 50
T1 E.Nabokov 30.00 80.00
M.Kiprusoff
T2 R.Cechmanek/B.Boucher 12.00 30.00
T3 J.Theodore/J.Hackett 20.00 50.00
T4 R.Luongo/T.Kidd 15.00 40.00
T5 P.Roy/D.Aebischer 50.00 125.00
T6 S.Shields/J.Giguere 15.00 40.00
T7 E.Belfour/M.Turco 15.00 40.00
T8 R.Turek/M.Vernon 15:00 40.00
T9 D.Hasek/M.Legace 15.00 40.00
T10 B.Dafoe/J.Grahame 12.00 30.00
T11 S.Burke/R.Esche 12.00 30.00
T12 J.Thibault/S.Passmore 20.00 50.00
T13 J.Aubin/J.Hedberg 15.00 40.00

2001-02 Between the Pipes Trophy Winners

his 24-card set honored goalies who have won rious league awards through the years. Each card atured a color photo in the card center accompanied a swatch of game-used jersey. On the right side of e card front the player's name and the trophy he won as printed vertically. On the left side of the card was a cture of the award itself. Each card was limited to 50 pies.
TATED PRINT RUN 40 SETS
W1 Patrick Roy 50.00 125.00
W2 Dominik Hasek 20.00 50.00
W3 Evgeni Nabokov 30.00 80.00
W4 Jacques Plante 40.00 100.00
W5 Olaf Kolzig 15.00 40.00
W6 Terry Sawchuk 60.00 150.00
W7 Glenn Hall 15.00 40.00
W8 Billy Smith 15.00 40.00
W9 Turk Broda 40.00 100.00
W10 Ron Hextall 15.00 40.00
W11 Tiny Thompson 30.00 80.00
W12 Bill Durnan 15.00 40.00
W13 Glenn Hall 15.00 40.00
W14 Terry Sawchuk 40.00 100.00
W15 Tony Esposito 20.00 50.00
W16 Glenn Hall 15.00 40.00
W17 Martin Brodeur 25.00 60.00
W18 Jacques Plante 25.00 60.00
W19 Dominik Hasek 20.00 50.00
W20 Billy Smith 15.00 40.00
W21 Bernie Parent 15.00 40.00
W22 Ed Belfour 20.00 50.00
W23 Frank Brimsek 15.00 40.00
W24 Dominik Hasek 20.00 50.00

2001-02 Between the Pipes Vintage Memorabilia

his 20-card set featured game-used equipment from tired goalies. Each card carried a full color photo of e featured goalie on the right side of the card front d a larger black-and-white up close photo on the left de of the card front. The game-used swatch was fixed in the center of the two photos. Each card was nited to just 40 sets.
TATED PRINT RUN 40 SETS
M1 Grant Fuhr 15.00 40.00
M2 Turk Broda 25.00 60.00
M3 Gerry Cheevers 15.00 40.00
M4 Bernie Parent 15.00 40.00
M5 Jacques Plante 30.00 80.00
M6 Terry Sawchuk 40.00 100.00
M7 Frank Brimsek 20.00 50.00
M8 Glenn Hall 15.00 40.00
M9 Tony Esposito 15.00 40.00
M10 Vladislav Tretiak 30.00 80.00
M11 Billy Smith 15.00 40.00
M12 Johnny Bower 40.00 100.00
M13 Georges Vezina 300.00 600.00
M14 Ron Hextall 15.00 40.00
M15 Ed Giacomin 15.00 40.00
M16 Gump Worsley 20.00 50.00
M17 Bill Durnan 20.00 50.00
M18 Rogie Vachon 25.00 60.00
M19 Tiny Thompson 15.00 40.00
M20 Charlie Gardner 15.00 40.00

2002-03 Between the Pipes

his 150-card set highlighted the goal keepers, past d present, of the NHL. The set included two subsets; nshrined", which featured retired goalies, and "home d away", which featured goalies in their home and ad uniforms.
OMPLETE SET (150) 20.00 50.00
Patrick Roy 1.00 2.50
Jose Theodore .40 1.00
Olaf Kolzig .40 1.00
Roberto Luongo .60 1.50
Tommy Salo .30 .75
Dan Blackburn .30 .75
Patrick Lalime .30 .75
Martin Brodeur .75 2.00
Evgeni Nabokov .30 .75
) Jani Hurme .30 .75
Dan Cloutier .30 .75
2 Mike Dunham .30 .75
3 Miikka Kiprusoff .30 .75
Rick DiPietro .30 .75
Martin Biron .30 .75
Steve Passmore .25 .60
Curtis Joseph .40 1.00
3 Manny Fernandez .30 .75
9 Kevin Weekes .30 .75
) Stephane Fiset .25 .60
21 Jocelyn Thibault .30 .75
22 David Aebischer .30 .75
23 Marty Turco .40 1.00
24 Jamie Storr .30 .75
25 Marc Denis .30 .75
26 Arturs Irbe .30 .75
27 Felix Potvin .60 1.50
28 Manny Legace .40 1.00
29 Mike Richter .40 1.00
30 J-S Aubin .25 .60
31 Sean Burke .25 .60
32 Milan Hnilicka .30 .75
33 Ed Belfour .40 1.00
34 Roman Turek .40 1.00
35 Frederic Cassivi .25 .60
36 Tomas Vokoun .30 .75
37 Travis Scott .25 .60
38 Dwayne Roloson .25 .60
39 Roman Cechmanek .30 .75
40 Johan Hedberg .40 1.00
41 Neil Little .25 .60
42 Jeff Hackett .30 .75
43 John Grahame .25 .60
44 Norm Maracle .25 .60
45 Ty Conklin .30 .75
46 Trevor Kidd .25 .60
47 Nikolai Khabibulin .40 1.00
48 Dieter Kochan .25 .60
49 Robert Esche .25 .60
50 Chris Osgood .40 1.00
51 Jean-Sebastien Giguere .40 1.00
52 Steve Shields .30 .75
53 Wade Flaherty .25 .00
54 Peter Skudra .25 .60
55 Brent Johnson .30 .75
56 Brian Boucher .30 .75
57 Garth Snow .30 .75
58 Fred Brathwaite .30 .75
59 Ron Tugnutt .30 .75
60 Craig Billington .25 .60
61 Martin Brochu .25 .60
62 Corey Schwab .30 .75
63 Tim Thomas RC 2.50 6.00
64 J-F Labbe .25 .60
65 Damian Rhodes .25 .60
66 Kevin Hodson .25 .60
67 Jamie McLennan .25 .60
68 Tyler Moss .25 .60
69 Tom Barrasso .30 .75
70 Corey Hirsch .25 .60
71 Eric Fichaud .25 .60
72 Byron Dafoe .30 .75
73 Mika Noronen .30 .75
74 Alex Auld .25 .60
75 Curtis Sanford RC 1.00 2.50
76 Martin Gerber RC 1.00 2.50
77 Mikael Tellqvist RC .60 1.50
78 J-M Pelletier .25 .60
79 J-F Damphousse .30 .75
80 Johan Holmqvist .25 .60
81 Mathieu Garon .30 .75
82 Martin Prusek .25 .60
83 Ilya Bryzgalov .30 .75
84 Andrew Raycroft .30 .75
85 Derek Gustafson .25 .60
86 Jason LaBarbera .25 .60
87 Marc Lamothe .30 .75
88 Scott Clemmensen .25 .60
89 Cody Rudkowsky RC .60 1.50
90 Craig Andersson RC 2.00 5.00
91 Maxime Ouellet .30 .75
92 Jan Lasak .30 .75
93 Patrick DesRochers .25 .60
94 Pasi Nurminen .25 .60
95 Sebastien Centomo .25 .60
96 Jussi Markkanen .25 .60
97 Sebastien Charpentier .25 .60
98 Reinhard Divis .25 .60
99 Simon Lajeunesse .25 .60
100 Vesa Toskala .25 .60
101 Olivier Michaud .25 .60
102 Levente Szuper RC 1.00 2.50
103 Philippe Sauve .25 .60
104 Dany Sabourin RC .60 1.50
105 Ryan Miller RC 4.00 10.00
106 Chris Mason .25 .60
107 Steve Valiquette .25 .60
108 Pascal Leclaire RC .75 2.00
109 Jason Elliott RC .60 1.50
110 Michael Garnett RC .60 1.50
111 Tiny Thompson EN .50 1.25
112 Frank Brimsek EN .40 1.00
113 Jacques Plante EN .75 2.00
114 Terry Sawchuk EN 1.25 3.00
115 Georges Vezina EN .60 1.50
116 Chuck Rayner EN .50 1.25
117 Glenn Hall EN .60 1.50
118 Turk Broda EN .50 1.25
119 George Hainsworth EN .50 1.25
120 Roy Worters EN .50 1.25
121 Jean-Sebastien Giguere HA .40 1.00
122 Milan Hnilicka HA .30 .75
123 Steve Shields HA .30 .75
124 Martin Biron HA .30 .75
125 Roman Turek HA .40 1.00
126 Arturs Irbe HA .30 .75
127 Jocelyn Thibault HA .30 .75
128 Patrick Roy HA 1.00 2.50
129 Marc Denis HA .30 .75
130 Marty Turco HA .40 1.00
131 Curtis Joseph HA .40 1.00
132 Tommy Salo HA .30 .75
133 Roberto Luongo HA .60 1.50
134 Felix Potvin HA .60 1.50
135 Manny Fernandez HA .30 .75
136 Jose Theodore HA .40 1.00
137 Tomas Vokoun HA .30 .75
138 Martin Brodeur HA .75 2.00
139 Chris Osgood HA .40 1.00
140 Mike Richter HA .40 1.00
141 Patrick Lalime HA .30 .75
142 Roman Cechmanek HA .30 .75
143 Sean Burke HA .25 .60
144 Johan Hedberg HA .40 1.00
145 Brent Johnson HA .30 .75
146 Evgeni Nabokov HA .30 .75
147 Nikolai Khabibulin HA .40 1.00
148 Ed Belfour HA .40 1.00
149 Dan Cloutier HA .30 .75
150 Olaf Kolzig HA .40 1.00

2002-03 Between the Pipes Silver

This 110-card set paralleled the first 110 cards of the base set but carried silver foil backgrounds on the card fronts. Each card was individually numbered out of 100.
*STARS: 3X TO 8X BASE HI
*ROOKIES: .75X TO 2X
SILVER PRINT RUN 100 SER.#'d SETS

2002-03 Between the Pipes All-Star Stick and Jersey

Limited to just 40-copies each, this 16-card set featured pieces of all-star game jerseys and sticks.
COMMON CARD (1-16) 10.00 25.00
STATED PRINT RUN 40 SETS
1 Ed Belfour 15.00 40.00
2 Curtis Joseph 15.00 40.00
3 Martin Brodeur 30.00 80.00
4 Patrick Roy 40.00 100.00
5 Mike Richter 15.00 40.00
6 Evgeni Nabokov 15.00 40.00
7 Olaf Kolzig 15.00 40.00
8 Felix Potvin 15.00 40.00
9 Tommy Salo 15.00 40.00
10 Jose Theodore 15.00 40.00
11 Nikolai Khabibulin 15.00 40.00
12 Roman Turek 10.00 25.00
13 Sean Burke 15.00 40.00
14 Roman Cechmanek 10.00 25.00
15 Arturs Irbe 15.00 40.00
16 Chris Osgood 15.00 40.00

2002-03 Between the Pipes Behind the Mask

This 20-card set featured swatches of game jerseys. Cards were limited to 30 copies each.
COMMON CARD (1-20) 12.50 30.00
STATED PRINT RUN 30 SETS
1 Marty Turco 12.50 30.00
2 Martin Brodeur 20.00 40.00
3 Patrick Roy 25.00 60.00
4 Roberto Luongo 20.00 50.00
5 Tommy Salo 12.50 30.00
6 Nikolai Khabibulin 12.50 30.00
7 Sean Burke 12.50 30.00
8 Patrick Lalime 12.50 30.00
9 Arturs Irbe 12.50 30.00
10 Jocelyn Thibault 12.50 30.00
11 Jose Theodore 15.00 40.00
12 Rick DiPietro 15.00 40.00
13 Marc Denis 12.50 30.00
14 Mike Dunham 12.50 30.00
15 Johan Hedberg 12.50 30.00
16 Olaf Kolzig 15.00 40.00
17 Dan Cloutier 12.50 30.00
18 Felix Potvin 20.00 50.00
19 Ed Belfour 15.00 40.00
20 Steve Shields 12.50 30.00

2002-03 Between the Pipes Blockers

Limited to just 50 copies each, this 18-card set featured pieces of game-used goalie blockers.
COMMON CARD (1-18) 8.00 20.00
STATED PRINT RUN 50 SETS
1 Curtis Joseph 10.00 40.00
2 Jani Hurme 8.00 20.00
3 Evgeni Nabokov 10.00 25.00
4 Felix Potvin 15.00 40.00
5 Jean-Sebastien Giguere 10.00 25.00
6 Jocelyn Thibault 8.00 25.00
7 Marty Turco 12.50 30.00
8 Mike Dunham 8.00 25.00
9 Johan Hedberg 8.00 20.00
10 Roman Cechmanek 8.00 25.00
11 Olaf Kolzig 10.00 25.00
12 Patrick Lalime 8.00 25.00
13 Roberto Luongo 15.00 30.00
14 Roman Turek 8.00 25.00
15 Nikolai Khabibulin 10.00 25.00
16 Tommy Salo 8.00 25.00
17 Trevor Kidd 8.00 25.00
18 Sean Burke 10.00 25.00

2002-03 Between the Pipes Complete Package

Limited to just 10 copies each, this 12-card set featured four pieces of game-used memorabilia. This set is not priced due to scarcity.
CP1 Patrick Roy
CP2 Curtis Joseph
CP3 Terry Sawchuk
CP4 Jacques Plante
CP5 Marty Turco
CP6 Johan Hedberg
CP7 Sean Burke
CP8 Jocelyn Thibault
CP9 Bernie Parent
CP10 Nikolai Khabibulin
CP11 Grant Fuhr
CP12 Roman Cechmanek

2002-03 Between the Pipes Double Memorabilia

This 20-card set carried dual swatches of game-used memorabillia. Each card was limited to just 40 copies each.
COMMON CARD (1-20) 10.00 25.00
STATED PRINT RUN 40 SETS
1 Martin Brodeur 30.00 80.00
2 Sean Burke 12.50 30.00
3 Dan Cloutier 10.00 25.00
4 Chris Osgood 15.00 40.00
5 Jose Theodore 20.00 50.00
6 Olaf Kolzig 12.50 30.00
7 Patrick Roy 30.00 80.00
8 Tommy Salo 10.00 25.00
9 Marty Turco 10.00 25.00
10 Roman Turek 10.00 25.00
11 Mike Dunham 10.00 25.00
12 Manny Legace 12.00 30.00
13 Jocelyn Thibault 10.00 25.00
14 Nikolai Khabibulin 12.50 30.00
15 Johan Hedberg 10.00 25.00
16 Trevor Kidd 10.00 25.00
17 J-S Aubin 12.50 30.00
18 Jacques Plante 40.00 100.00
19 Terry Sawchuk 40.00 100.00
20 Roger Crozier 12.50 30.00

2002-03 Between the Pipes Emblems

Limited to 10 copies each, this 30-card set carried pieces of jersey emblems on the card fronts. This set is not priced due to scarcity.

2002-03 Between the Pipes Future Wave

COMMON CARD (1-12) 8.00 20.00
STATED PRINT RUN 60 SETS
1 Miikka Kiprusoff 10.00 30.00
2 Jose Theodore 8.00 25.00
3 Roberto Luongo 20.00 50.00
4 Rick DiPietro 10.00 30.00
5 Dan Blackburn 8.00 20.00
6 Mathieu Garon 8.00 20.00
7 Johan Hedberg 8.00 20.00
8 Dan Cloutier 8.00 20.00
9 Martin Biron 8.00 20.00
10 Marty Turco 10.00 30.00
11 Alex Auld 10.00 25.00
12 Brent Johnson 8.00 20.00

2002-03 Between the Pipes Goalie Autographs

1 Martin Biron/50* 12.50 30.00
2 Dan Blackburn/50* 12.50 30.00
3 Sean Burke/50* 12.50 30.00
4 Dan Cloutier/50* 12.50 30.00
5 Marc Denis/50* 12.50 30.00
6 Jean-Sebastien Giguere/50* 12.50 30.00
7 Johan Hedberg/50* 12.50 30.00
8 Milan Hnilicka/50* 12.50 30.00
9 Arturs Irbe/50* 25.00 50.00
10 Brent Johnson/50* 12.50 30.00
11 Curtis Joseph/50* 15.00 40.00
12 Nikolai Khabibulin/50* 15.00 40.00
13 Olaf Kolzig/50* 12.50 30.00
14 Patrick Lalime/50* 12.50 30.00
15 Roberto Luongo/50* 20.00 50.00
16 Evgeni Nabokov/50* 12.50 30.00
17 Chris Osgood/50* 15.00 40.00
18 Felix Potvin/50* 20.00 50.00
19 Dwayne Roloson/50* 15.00 40.00
20 Tommy Salo/50* 12.50 30.00
21 Steve Shields/50* 12.50 30.00
22 Jose Theodore/50* 20.00 50.00
23 Jocelyn Thibault/50* 12.50 30.00
24 Marty Turco/50* 12.50 30.00
25 Roman Turek/50* 12.50 30.00
26 Johnny Bower/90* 15.00 40.00
27 Bernie Parent/90* 15.00 40.00
28 Ed Giacomin/90* 15.00 40.00
29 Gerry Cheevers/90* 15.00 40.00
30 Vladislav Tretiak/90* 40.00 100.00
31 Gump Worsley/40* 25.00 60.00
32 Tony Esposito/90* 20.00 50.00
33 John Davidson/90* 15.00 40.00
34 Glenn Hall/90* 15.00 40.00
35 Charlie Hodge/90* 15.00 40.00
36 Rogie Vachon/90* 15.00 40.00

2002-03 Between the Pipes He Shoots He Saves Points

Inserted one per pack, these cards carried a value of 1, 2 or 3 points. The points could be redeemed for special memorabilia cards. The cards are unnumbered and are listed below in alphabetical order by point value. The redemption program ended December 31, 2003.
ONE PER PACK
1 Sean Burke 1 pt. .40 1.00
2 Roman Cechmanek 1 pt. .40 1.00
3 Dan Cloutier 1 pt. .40 1.00
4 Johan Hedberg 1 pt. .40 1.00
5 Arturs Irbe 1 pt. .40 1.00
6 Patrick Lalime 1 pt. .40 1.00
7 Evgeni Nabokov 1 pt. .40 1.00
8 Felix Potvin 1 pt. .40 1.00
9 Mike Richter 1 pt. .40 1.00
10 Marty Turco 1 pt. .40 1.00
11 Roman Turek 1 pt. .40 1.00
12 Dan Blackburn 2 pt. .40 1.00
13 Nikolai Khabibulin 2 pt. .40 1.00
14 Olaf Kolzig 2 pt. .40 1.00
15 Roberto Luongo 2 pt. .40 1.00
16 Tommy Salo 2 pt. .40 1.00
17 Jocelyn Thibault 2 pt. .40 1.00
18 Martin Brodeur 3 pt. .40 1.00
19 Patrick Roy 3 pt. .40 1.00
20 Jose Theodore 3 pt. .40 1.00

2002-03 Between the Pipes Inspirations

These dual jersey cards were limited to just 40 copies each.
STATED PRINT RUN 40 SETS
I1 P.Roy/J.Plante 30.00 80.00
I2 T.Sawchuk/G.Hainsworth 50.00 125.00
I3 J.Theodore/P.Roy 40.00 100.00
I4 R.Luongo/P.Roy 20.00 50.00
I5 S.Burke/B.Parent 20.00 50.00
I6 E.Belfour/V.Tretiak 25.00 60.00
I7 D.Blackburn/C.Joseph 20.00 50.00
I8 M.Brodeur/P.Roy 25.00 60.00
I9 M.Richter/G.Cheevers 25.00 60.00
I10 R.DiPietro/R.Hextall 20.00 50.00

2002-03 Between the Pipes Jerseys

*STK/JSY: .5X TO 1.25X BASE JERSEY
STATED PRINT RUN 90 SETS
1 Arturs Irbe 8.00 20.00
2 Miikka Kiprusoff 8.00 20.00
3 Rick DiPietro 10.00 25.00
4 Dan Blackburn 8.00 20.00
5 Dan Cloutier 8.00 20.00
6 David Aebischer 8.00 20.00
7 Evgeni Nabokov 8.00 20.00
8 Felix Potvin 8.00 20.00
9 Manny Fernandez 8.00 20.00
10 J-S Aubin 10.00 25.00
11 Jean-Sebastien Giguere 10.00 25.00
12 Jani Hurme 8.00 20.00
13 Jocelyn Thibault 8.00 20.00
14 Jose Theodore 12.50 30.00
15 Mike Dunham 8.00 20.00
16 Martin Biron 8.00 20.00
17 Johan Hedberg 8.00 20.00
18 Martin Brodeur 15.00 40.00
19 Marty Turco 8.00 20.00
20 Mika Noronen 8.00 20.00
21 Mike Richter 10.00 25.00
22 Nikolai Khabibulin 10.00 25.00
23 Olaf Kolzig 10.00 25.00
24 Patrick Lalime 8.00 20.00
25 Patrick Roy 15.00 40.00
26 Roberto Luongo 15.00 40.00
27 Roman Cechmanek 8.00 20.00
28 Roman Turek 8.00 20.00
29 Sean Burke 10.00 25.00
30 Tommy Salo 8.00 20.00
31 Maxime Ouellet 8.00 20.00
32 Ed Belfour 10.00 25.00
33 Sebastien Charpentier 8.00 20.00
34 Robert Esche 8.00 20.00
35 Curtis Sanford 8.00 20.00
36 Milan Hnilicka 8.00 20.00
37 Steve Shields 8.00 20.00
38 Tim Thomas 12.50 30.00
39 Trevor Kidd 8.00 20.00
40 Fred Brathwaite 8.00 20.00
41 Martin Prusek 8.00 20.00
42 John Grahame 8.00 20.00
43 Jamie Storr 8.00 20.00
44 Sebastien Centomo 8.00 20.00
45 Ron Tugnutt 8.00 20.00
46 Martin Gerber 8.00 20.00
47 Jussi Markkanen 8.00 20.00
48 Simon Lajeunesse 8.00 20.00
49 Reinhard Divis 8.00 20.00
50 Jeff Hackett 8.00 20.00

2002-03 Between the Pipes Masks II

Created on Dufex card stock, this 30-card set featured artist renderings of the masks made famous by the goalies who wore them.
COMPLETE SET (30) 30.00 60.00
*SILVER: 1.25X TO 3X BASE HI
SILVER PRINT RUN 300 SETS
*GOLD: 3X TO 8X BASE HI
GOLD PRINT RUN 30 SETS
1 Jean-Sebastien Giguere 2.00 5.00
2 Milan Hnilicka 2.00 5.00
3 Steve Shields 2.00 5.00
4 Martin Biron 2.00 5.00
5 Roman Turek 2.00 5.00
6 Kevin Weekes 2.00 5.00
7 Jocelyn Thibault 2.00 5.00
8 Patrick Roy 4.00 10.00
9 Marc Denis 2.00 5.00
10 Marty Turco 2.00 5.00
11 Curtis Joseph 3.00 8.00
12 Tommy Salo 2.00 5.00
13 Roberto Luongo 4.00 10.00
14 Felix Potvin 3.00 8.00
15 Manny Fernandez 2.00 5.00
16 Jose Theodore 3.00 8.00
17 Mike Dunham 2.00 5.00
18 Mike Richter 2.50 6.00
19 Rick DiPietro 2.00 5.00
20 Patrick Lalime 2.00 5.00
21 Roman Cechmanek 2.00 5.00
22 Sean Burke 2.00 5.00
23 Johan Hedberg 2.00 5.00
24 Evgeni Nabokov 2.00 5.00
25 Miikka Kiprusoff 3.00 8.00
26 Brent Johnson 2.00 5.00
27 Nikolai Khabibulin 2.50 6.00
28 Ed Belfour 3.00 8.00
29 Jeff Hackett 2.00 5.00
30 Olaf Kolzig 2.00 5.00

2002-03 Between the Pipes Nightmares

This 10-card set featured jersey swatches from NHL goalies and shooters who had a history of scoring against them. Production was limited to 60 copies each.
STATED PRINT RUN 60 SETS
GN1 D.Blackburn/I.Kovalchuk 12.50 30.00
GN2 M.Richter/M.Lemieux 20.00 50.00
GN3 T.Salo/J.Jagr 12.50 30.00
GN4 F.Potvin/S.Yzerman 25.00 60.00
GN5 S.Fiset/P.Bure 10.00 25.00
GN6 M.Richter/J.Iginla 12.50 30.00
GN7 T.Salo/P.Forsberg 12.50 30.00
GN8 C.Joseph/J.Sakic 15.00 40.00
GN9 O.Kolzig/E.Lindros 12.50 30.00
GN10 T.Barrasso/M.Sundin 10.00 25.00

2002-03 Between the Pipes Pads

Limited to just 50 copies each, this 14-card set featured pieces of game-used goalie pads.
STAT.PRINT RUN 50 SETS
1 Martin Brodeur 15.00 40.00
2 Patrick Roy 20.00 50.00
3 Marty Turco 8.00 20.00
4 Curtis Joseph 15.00 40.00
5 Ed Belfour 12.50 30.00
6 Jose Theodore 10.00 25.00
7 Sean Burke 8.00 20.00
8 Dan Cloutier 8.00 20.00
9 Chris Osgood 10.00 25.00
10 Nikolai Khabibulin 10.00 25.00
11 J-S Aubin 10.00 25.00
12 Steve Shields 8.00 20.00
13 Mike Dunham 8.00 20.00
14 Jocelyn Thibault 8.00 20.00

2002-03 Between the Pipes Record Breakers

This 16-card memorabilia set was limited to just 40 copies each.
STATED PRINT RUN 40 SETS
1 Terry Sawchuk 30.00 80.00
2 Patrick Roy 15.00 40.00
3 George Hainsworth 20.00 50.00
4 Jacques Plante 25.00 60.00
5 Patrick Roy 20.00 50.00
6 Glenn Hall 12.50 30.00
7 Tony Esposito 12.50 30.00
8 Gerry Cheevers 12.50 30.00
9 Martin Brodeur 20.00 50.00
10 Bernie Parent 25.00 60.00
11 Terry Sawchuk 30.00 80.00
12 Patrick Roy 20.00 50.00
13 Johnny Bower 12.50 30.00
14 Ed Belfour 12.50 30.00
15 Patrick Roy 15.00 40.00
16 Terry Sawchuk 30.00 80.00

2002-03 Between the Pipes Stick and Jerseys

This 30-card set partially paralleled the base jersey set but also carried a piece of game-used stick. Print run was 90 copies each.
1 Arturs Irbe 10.00 25.00
2 Miikka Kiprusoff 10.00 25.00
3 Rick DiPietro 10.00 25.00
4 Dan Blackburn 10.00 25.00
5 Dan Cloutier 10.00 25.00
6 David Aebischer 10.00 25.00
7 Evgeni Nabokov 10.00 25.00
8 Felix Potvin 12.50 30.00
9 Manny Fernandez 10.00 25.00
10 J-S Aubin 10.00 25.00
11 Jean-Sebastien Giguere 10.00 25.00
12 Jani Hurme 10.00 25.00
13 Jocelyn Thibault 10.00 25.00
14 Jose Theodore 15.00 40.00
15 Mike Dunham 10.00 25.00
16 Martin Biron 10.00 25.00
17 Johan Hedberg 10.00 25.00
18 Martin Brodeur 15.00 40.00
19 Marty Turco 10.00 25.00
20 Mika Noronen 10.00 25.00
21 Mike Richter 10.00 25.00
22 Nikolai Khabibulin 10.00 25.00
23 Olaf Kolzig 10.00 25.00
24 Patrick Lalime 10.00 25.00
25 Patrick Roy 25.00 60.00
26 Roberto Luongo 12.00 30.00
27 Roman Cechmanek 10.00 25.00
28 Roman Turek 10.00 25.00
29 Sean Burke 10.00 25.00
30 Tommy Salo 10.00 25.00

2002-03 Between the Pipes Tandems

This 20-card memorabilia set featured starting goalies and their backups. Each card was limited to 30 copies.
STATED PRINT RUN 30 SETS
1 M.Richter/D.Blackburn 10.00 25.00
2 P.Roy/D.Aebischer 50.00 100.00
3 J.Thibault/S.Passmore 10.00 25.00
4 E.Nabokov/M.Kiprusoff 12.50 30.00
5 P.Lalime/M.Prusek 10.00 25.00
6 M.Biron/M.Noronen 10.00 25.00
7 J.Hedberg/J-S Aubin 10.00 25.00
8 R.Cechmanek/R.Esche 10.00 25.00
9 J.Theodore/J.Hackett 12.50 30.00
10 F.Potvin/J.Storr 15.00 40.00
11 M.Dunham/T.Voukon 10.00 25.00
12 D.Cloutier/A.Auld 10.00 25.00
13 J-S Giguere/M.Gerber 12.50 30.00
14 E.Belfour/T.Kidd 12.50 30.00
15 B.Johnson/F.Brathwaite 10.00 25.00
16 C.Osgood/R.Dipietro 30.00 80.00
17 S.Shields/J.Grahame 12.00 30.00
18 T.Salo/J.Markkanen 10.00 25.00
19 M.Turco/R.Tugnutt 10.00 25.00
20 O.Kolzig/M.Ouellet 12.50 30.00

2002-03 Between the Pipes Trappers

Limited to just 60 copies each, this 18-card set featured pieces of game-used goalie trappers.
STATED PRINT RUN 60 SETS
GT1 Vladislav Tretiak 20.00 50.00
GT2 Bill Durnan 20.00 50.00
GT3 Dan Cloutier 8.00 20.00
GT4 Byron Dafoe 8.00 20.00
GT5 Johan Hedberg 8.00 20.00
GT6 Charlie Hodge 20.00 50.00
GT7 Nikolai Khabibulin 8.00 20.00
GT8 Jacques Plante 30.00 80.00
GT9 Olaf Kolzig 12.00 30.00
GT10 Harry Lumley 12.00 30.00
GT11 Bernie Parent 20.00 60.00
GT12 Patrick Roy 25.00 60.00
GT13 Terry Sawchuk 30.00 80.00
GT14 Jocelyn Thibault 8.00 20.00
GT15 Marty Turco 8.00 20.00
GT16 Roger Crozier 15.00 40.00
GT17 Sean Burke 8.00 20.00
GT18 Grant Fuhr 20.00 50.00

2002-03 Between the Pipes Vintage Memorabilia

This 20-card memorabilia set was limited to just 20 copies per card.
ANNOUNCED PRINT RUN 20 SETS
1 Johnny Bower 30.00 60.00
2 Harry Lumley 25.00 50.00
3 Roger Crozier 30.00 60.00
4 Ed Giacomin 30.00 60.00
5 Bill Durnan 25.00 60.00
6 George Hainsworth 30.00 60.00
7 Gerry Cheevers 40.00 80.00
8 Bernie Parent 30.00 60.00
9 Tony Esposito 20.00 50.00
10 Jacques Plante 30.00 60.00
11 Charlie Hodge 25.00 50.00
12 Glenn Hall 30.00 80.00
13 Roy Worters 25.00 60.00
14 Tiny Thompson 40.00 80.00
15 Charlie Gardiner 25.00 50.00
16 Terry Sawchuk 50.00 120.00
17 Frank Brimsek 25.00 50.00
18 Vladislav Tretiak 30.00 60.00
19 Bernie Parent 30.00 60.00
20 Ed Giacomin 75.00 150.00

2005-06 Between the Pipes

COMPLETE SET (25) 6.00 15.00
1 Johnny Bower .40 1.00
2 Turk Broda .40 1.00
3 Martin Brodeur 1.25 3.00
4 Richard Brodeur .20 .50
5 Gerry Cheevers .40 1.00
6 Tony Esposito .40 1.00
7 Grant Fuhr .40 1.00
8 Ed Giacomin .30 .75
9 Glenn Hall .30 .75
10 Ron Hextall .40 1.00
11 Charlie Hodge .20 .50
12 Mike Palmateer .30 .75
13 Bernie Parent .40 1.00
14 Jacques Plante .75 2.00
15 Bill Ranford .20 .50
16 Chico Resch .20 .50
17 Patrick Roy 1.25 3.00
18 Terry Sawchuk .75 2.00
19 Billy Smith .40 1.00
20 Jose Theodore .40 1.00
21 Tiny Thompson .40 1.00
22 Vladislav Tretiak .40 1.00
23 Rogie Vachon .30 .75
24 Georges Vezina .40 1.00
25 Gump Worsley .40 1.00

2005-06 Between the Pipes Autographs

RANDOM INSERTS IN BTP BOX SETS
ABP Bernie Parent 12.00 30.00
ABR Bill Ranford 6.00 15.00
ABS Billy Smith 10.00 25.00
ACH Charlie Hodge 8.00 20.00
ACR Chico Resch 6.00 15.00
AEG Ed Giacomin 10.00 25.00
AGC Gerry Cheevers 10.00 25.00
AGH Glenn Hall 10.00 25.00
AGR Grant Fuhr 10.00 25.00
AGW Gump Worsley 10.00 25.00
AJB Johnny Bower 12.00 30.00
AJT Jose Theodore 10.00 25.00
AMB Martin Brodeur 60.00 100.00
AMP Mike Palmateer 10.00 25.00
APR Patrick Roy 60.00 100.00
ARB Richard Brodeur 6.00 15.00
ARH Ron Hextall 10.00 25.00
ARV Rogie Vachon 8.00 20.00
ATO Tony Esposito 12.00 30.00
AVT Vladislav Tretiak 15.00 40.00

2005-06 Between the Pipes Complete Package

RANDOM INSERTS IN BTP BOX SETS
CP1 Grant Fuhr 30.00 60.00
CP2 Patrick Roy 40.00 80.00
CP3 Jacques Plante 60.00 120.00
CP4 Gerry Cheevers 25.00 60.00
CP5 Terry Sawchuk 40.00 100.00
CP6 Bernie Parent 40.00 80.00
CP7 Jose Theodore 25.00 60.00

2005-06 Between the Pipes Double Memorabilia

PRINT RUN 40 SER. #'d SETS
DM1 Patrick Roy 20.00 50.00
DM2 Patrick Roy 20.00 50.00
DM3 Martin Brodeur 15.00 40.00
DM4 Ron Hextall 10.00 25.00
DM5 Tony Esposito 10.00 25.00
DM6 Gerry Cheevers 10.00 25.00
DM7 Vladislav Tretiak 20.00 50.00
DM8 Jose Theodore 12.00 30.00

2005-06 Between the Pipes Gloves

RANDOM INSERTS IN BTP BOX SETS
GUG1 Tony Esposito 10.00 25.00
GUG2 Patrick Roy 15.00 40.00
GUG3 Gilles Gilbert 10.00 25.00
GUG4 Vladislav Tretiak 20.00 50.00
GUG5 Jose Theodore 10.00 25.00
GUG6 Rogie Vachon 8.00 20.00
GUG7 Charlie Hodge 8.00 20.00
GUG8 Grant Fuhr 10.00 25.00

2005-06 Between the Pipes Jerseys

RANDOM INSERTS IN BTP BOX SETS
GOLD/20: .8X TO 2X BASIC JSY
GUJ1 Patrick Roy 12.00 30.00
GUJ2 Patrick Roy 12.00 30.00
GUJ3 Martin Brodeur 12.00 30.00
GUJ4 Tony Esposito 8.00 20.00
GUJ5 Vladislav Tretiak 8.00 20.00
GUJ6 Glenn Hall 8.00 20.00
GUJ7 Mike Richter 8.00 20.00
GUJ8 Jose Theodore 8.00 20.00
GUJ9 Billy Smith 8.00 20.00
GUJ10 Grant Fuhr 8.00 20.00
GUJ11 Bill Ranford 5.00 12.00
GUJ12 Richard Brodeur 5.00 12.00

2005-06 Between the Pipes Jersey and Sticks

RANDOM INSERTS IN BTP BOX SETS
SJ1 Patrick Roy 15.00 40.00
SJ2 Patrick Roy 15.00 40.00
SJ3 Martin Brodeur 15.00 40.00
SJ4 Ed Giacomin 10.00 25.00
SJ5 Johnny Bower 10.00 25.00
SJ6 Tony Esposito 10.00 25.00
SJ7 Mike Richter 10.00 25.00
SJ8 Ron Hextall 10.00 25.00
SJ9 Jose Theodore 10.00 25.00
SJ10 Grant Fuhr 10.00 25.00

2005-06 Between the Pipes Pads

ANNOUNCED PRINT RUN 20
GUP1 Bernie Parent 12.00 30.00
GUP2 Grant Fuhr 12.00 30.00
GUP3 Gerry Cheevers 12.00 30.00
GUP4 Ron Hextall 12.00 30.00
GUP5 Martin Brodeur 15.00 40.00
GUP6 Patrick Roy 20.00 50.00
GUP7 Jacques Plante 25.00 60.00
GUP8 Jose Theodore 12.00 30.00

2005-06 Between the Pipes Signed Memorabilia

RANDOM INSERTS IN BTP BOX SETS
SM1 Patrick Roy 50.00 100.00
SM2 Patrick Roy 50.00 100.00
SM3 Martin Brodeur 40.00 80.00
SM4 Glenn Hall 20.00 40.00
SM5 Johnny Bower 20.00 40.00
SM6 Gerry Cheevers 20.00 40.00
SM7 Ed Giacomin 20.00 40.00
SM8 Jose Theodore 20.00 40.00
SM9 Grant Fuhr 40.00 80.00
SM10 Bernie Parent 30.00 60.00

2006-07 Between The Pipes

This 150-card set was released in March, 2007. The set was issued into the hobby in five-card packs with came 24 packs to a box and 24 boxes to a case. With some exceptions, the set is broken down thusly: Minor league goalies in first name Alpabetical order (1-55); current NHL goalies in 1st name alphabetical order (56-77); retired greats in 1st name alphabetical order (78-104); Current NHL goalies again in 1st name alphabetical order (105-118) and more retired goalies (127-150).
COMPLETE SET (150) 15.00 40.00
1 Al Montoya .30 .75
2 Andrew Penner .25 .60
3 Barry Brust .25 .60
4 Brent Krahn .25 .60
5 Bryan Pitton .25 .60
6 Brian Finley .25 .60
7 Carey Price 1.25 3.00
8 Chris Beckford-Tseu .30 .75
9 Corey Crawford .30 .75
10 Craig Anderson .30 .75
11 Curtis McElhinney .25 .60
12 David LeNeveu .25 .60
13 Frank Doyle .25 .60
14 Frederic Cassivi .25 .60
15 Gerald Coleman .25 .60
16 Hannu Toivonen .25 .60
17 Jaroslav Halak .60 1.50
18 Jason Bacashihua .25 .60
19 Jason LaBarbera .25 .60
20 Jeff Glass .25 .60
21 J-F Racine .25 .60
22 Jimmy Howard .50 1.25
23 John Murray .25 .60
24 Jonathan Bernier .60 1.50
25 Jordan Parise .50 1.25
26 Josh Harding .30 .75
27 J-P Levasseur .25 .60
28 Julien Ellis .25 .60
29 Justin Leclerc .25 .60
30 Justin Pogge .30 .75
31 Kelly Guard .25 .60
32 Kevin Lalande .25 .60
33 Kurt Mucha .25 .60
34 Kyle Moir .25 .60
35 Leland Irving .40 1.00
36 Marek Schwarz .30 .75
37 Martin Houle .25 .60
38 Michael Leighton .25 .60
39 Mikael Tellqvist .30 .75
40 Mike Smith .50 1.25
41 Nicola Riopel .25 .60
42 Pekka Rinne .40 1.00
43 Philippe Sauve .25 .60
44 Rejean Beauchemin .25 .60
45 Ryan Daniels .25 .60
46 Stefan Liv .20 .50
47 Tobias Stephan .25 .60

48 Steve Mason .60 1.50
49 Trevor Cann .25 .60
50 Tuukka Rask .75 2.00
51 Tyler Plante .25 .60
52 Tyson Sexsmith .25 .60
53 Wade Dubielewicz .25 .60
54 Yann Danis .25 .60
55 Yutaka Fukufuji .25 .60
56 Alex Auld .20 .50
57 Antero Niittymaki .25 .60
58 Cam Ward .30 .75
59 Cristobal Huet .25 .60
60 Peter Budaj .25 .60
61 Dominik Hasek .40 1.00
62 Dwayne Roloson .25 .60
63 Henrik Lundqvist .60 1.50
64 Ilya Bryzgalov .30 .75
65 Ed Belfour .30 .75
66 Johan Holmqvist .30 .75
67 Kari Lehtonen .25 .60
68 Manny Fernandez .25 .60
69 Marc-Andre Fleury .50 1.25
70 Martin Brodeur .60 1.50
71 Martin Gerber .25 .60
72 Pascal Leclaire .25 .60
73 Ray Emery .25 .60
74 Rick DiPietro .25 .60
75 Roberto Luongo .50 1.25
76 Ryan Miller .30 .75
77 Tim Thomas .40 1.00
78 Andy Moog .30 .75
79 Bernie Parent .30 .75
80 Billy Smith .30 .75
81 Brian Hayward .25 .60
82 Charlie Hodge .40 1.00
83 Chico Resch .30 .75
84 Dan Bouchard .30 .75
85 Doug Favell .30 .75
86 Ed Giacomin .50 1.25
87 Emile Francis .30 .75
88 Felix Potvin .50 1.25
89 Gerry Cheevers .30 .75
90 Gilles Gilbert .30 .75
91 Glenn Hall .50 1.25
92 Grant Fuhr .30 .75
93 Gump Worsley .30 .75
94 John Davidson .30 .75
95 Johnny Bower .50 1.25
96 Ken Wregget .25 .60
97 Mike Palmateer .30 .75
98 Patrick Roy .75 2.00
99 Richard Brodeur .25 .60
100 Rogie Vachon .40 1.00
101 Ron Hextall .50 1.25
102 Tom Barrasso .30 .75
103 Tony Esposito .30 .75
104 Vladislav Tretiak .50 1.25
105 Al Montoya .30 .75
106 Cam Ward .30 .75
107 Carey Price 1.25 3.00
108 Grant Fuhr .30 .75
109 Hannu Toivonen .25 .60
110 Kari Lehtonen .25 .60
111 Leland Irving .40 1.00
112 Marc-Andre Fleury .50 1.25
113 Marek Schwarz .30 .75
114 Martin Brodeur .60 1.50
115 Rick DiPietro .25 .60
116 Tuukka Rask .75 2.00
117 Martin Brodeur .60 1.50
118 Patrick Roy .75 2.00
119 Roberto Luongo .50 1.25
120 Marc-Andre Fleury .50 1.25
121 Carey Price 1.25 3.00
122 Justin Pogge .30 .75
123 Jeff Glass .25 .60
124 Bill Ranford .30 .75
125 Ed Belfour .30 .75
126 George Hainsworth .30 .75
127 Georges Vezina .50 1.25
128 Jacques Plante .50 1.25
129 Pelle Lindbergh .40 1.00
130 Roger Crozier .30 .75
131 Roy Worters .30 .75
132 Terry Sawchuk .40 1.00
133 Tiny Thompson .30 .75
134 Turk Broda .30 .75
135 Bower/Sawchuk .50 1.25
136 Parent/Favell .30 .75
137 Smith/Resch .30 .75
138 Worsley/Vachon .40 1.00
139 Belfour/Hasek .40 1.00
140 Giacomin/Davidson .50 1.25
141 Plante/Hall .50 1.25
142 Hasek/Fuhr .40 1.00
143 Patrick Roy .75 2.00
144 Terry Sawchuk .40 1.00
145 Bernie Parent .30 .75
146 George Hainsworth .30 .75
147 Glenn Hall .50 1.25
148 Grant Fuhr .30 .75
149 Martin Brodeur .60 1.50
150 Gerry Cheevers .30 .75

2006-07 Between The Pipes Aspiring

STATED PRINT RUN 50 SER.#'d SETS
AS01 M.Brodeur/C.Ward 15.00 40.00
AS02 P.Roy/C.Huet 20.00 50.00
AS03 D.Hasek/R.Miller 12.00 30.00
AS04 R.Luongo/L.Irving 10.00 25.00
AS05 P.Roy/C.Price 30.00 80.00
AS06 D.Hasek/M.Schwarz 10.00 25.00
AS07 G.Fuhr/R.Emery 8.00 20.00
AS08 P.Lindbergh/H.Lundqvist 20.00 50.00
AS09 M.Brodeur/J.Glass 15.00 40.00
AS10 P.Roy/J.Bernier 20.00 50.00

2006-07 Between The Pipes Autographs

COMMON CARD 3.00 8.00
SEMISTARS 4.00 10.00
UNLISTED STARS 5.00 12.00
STATED ODDS 1:24
AAA Alex Auld 3.00 8.00
AAM Al Montoya 5.00 12.00
AAM2 Al Montoya SP 12.00 30.00
AAMO Andy Moog 5.00 12.00
AAN Antero Niittymaki 4.00 10.00
AAP Andrew Penner 4.00 10.00
ABB Barry Brust 4.00 10.00
ABF Brian Finley 4.00 10.00
ABH Brian Hayward 4.00 10.00
ABK Brent Krahn 4.00 10.00
ABP Bernie Parent 8.00 20.00
ABPI Bryan Pitton 4.00 10.00
ABR Bill Ranford 8.00 20.00
ABS Billy Smith 5.00 12.00
ACA Craig Anderson 5.00 12.00
ACBT Chris Beckford-Tseu 5.00 12.00
ACC Corey Crawford 8.00 20.00
ACH Cristobal Huet 4.00 10.00
ACHO Charlie Hodge 6.00 15.00
ACM Curtis McElhinney 4.00 10.00
ACP Carey Price 25.00 50.00
ACP2 Carey Price SP 50.00 100.00
ACP3 Carey Price 60.00 125.00
ACR Chico Resch 5.00 12.00
ACW Cam Ward 5.00 12.00
ACW2 Cam Ward SP 12.00 30.00
ADB Dan Bouchard 5.00 12.00
ADD Devan Dubnyk 6.00 15.00
ADF Doug Favell 5.00 12.00
ADH Dominik Hasek 15.00 40.00
ADL David LeNeveu 4.00 10.00
ADR Dwayne Roloson 4.00 10.00
AEB Ed Belfour 25.00 50.00
AEB2 Ed Belfour 25.00 50.00
AEF Emile Francis 5.00 12.00
AEG Ed Giacomin 8.00 20.00
AFC Frederic Cassivi 4.00 10.00
AFD Frank Doyle 4.00 10.00
AFP Felix Potvin 8.00 20.00
AGC Gerry Cheevers 5.00 12.00
AGF Grant Fuhr 5.00 12.00
AGF2 Grant Fuhr SP 12.00 30.00
AGG Gilles Gilbert 5.00 12.00
AGH Glenn Hall 8.00 20.00
AGW Gump Worsley 8.00 20.00
AHL Henrik Lundqvist 15.00 40.00
AHT Hannu Toivonen 4.00 10.00
AHT2 Hannu Toivonen SP 8.00 20.00
AIB Ilya Bryzgalov 5.00 12.00
AJB Johnny Bower 8.00 20.00
AJBA Jason Bacashihua 4.00 10.00
AJBE Jonathan Bernier 10.00 25.00
AJD John Davidson 8.00 20.00
AJDL Jeff Deslauriers 3.00 8.00
AJE Julien Ellis 4.00 10.00
AJFR J-F Racine 4.00 10.00
AJG Jeff Glass 4.00 10.00
AJG2 Jeff Glass 8.00 20.00
AJH Jimmy Howard 10.00 25.00
AJHA Jaroslav Halak 10.00 25.00
AJHO Johan Holmqvist 5.00 12.00
AJHR Josh Harding 5.00 12.00
AJL Justin Leclerc 4.00 10.00
AJLB Jason LaBarbera 4.00 10.00
AJM John Murray 4.00 10.00
AJP Justin Pogge 5.00 12.00
AJP2 Justin Pogge 25.00 50.00
AJPA Jordan Parise 8.00 20.00
AJPL J-P Levasseur 4.00 10.00
AJV John Vanbiesbrouck 12.00 30.00
AKG Kelly Guard 4.00 10.00
AKL Kari Lehtonen 4.00 10.00
AKL2 Kari Lehtonen 15.00 40.00
AKLA Kevin Lalande 4.00 10.00
AKM Kyle Moir 4.00 10.00
AKMU Kurt Mucha 4.00 10.00
AKW Ken Wregget 4.00 10.00
ALI Leland Irving 6.00 15.00
ALI2 Leland Irving SP 25.00 60.00
AMB Martin Brodeur 60.00 120.00
AMB2 Martin Brodeur 60.00 120.00
AMB3 Martin Brodeur 40.00 100.00
AMF Marc-Andre Fleury 40.00 80.00
AMF2 Marc-Andre Fleury SP 40.00 80.00
AMF3 Marc-Andre Fleury 40.00 80.00
AMFR Manny Fernandez 4.00 10.00
AMG Martin Gerber 4.00 10.00
AMH Martin Houle 4.00 10.00
AML Michael Leighton 4.00 10.00
AMP Mike Palmateer 5.00 12.00
AMS Marek Schwarz 5.00 12.00
AMS2 Marek Schwarz 25.00 50.00
AMSM Mike Smith 8.00 20.00
ANR Nicola Riopel 4.00 10.00
APL Pascal Leclaire 4.00 10.00
APR Patrick Roy 60.00 120.00
APR2 Patrick Roy 60.00 120.00
APRI Pekka Rinne 6.00 15.00
APS Philippe Sauve 4.00 10.00
ARB Rejean Beauchemin 4.00 10.00
ARBR Richard Brodeur 4.00 10.00
ARD Ryan Daniels 4.00 10.00
ARDI Rick DiPietro 25.00 50.00
ARE Ray Emery 4.00 10.00
ARH Ron Hextall 8.00 20.00
ARL Roberto Luongo 8.00 20.00
ARL2 Roberto Luongo 25.00 60.00
ARM Ryan Miller 12.00 30.00
ARV Rogie Vachon 6.00 15.00
ASL Stefan Liv 6.00 15.00
ASM Steve Mason 8.00 20.00
ATB Tom Barrasso 12.00 30.00
ATC Trevor Cann 4.00 10.00
ATE Tony Esposito 8.00 20.00
ATM Thomas McCollum 5.00 12.00
ATP Tyler Plante 4.00 10.00
ATR Tuukka Rask 12.00 30.00
ATR2 Tuukka Rask 30.00 60.00
ATS Tyson Sexsmith 4.00 10.00
ATST Tobias Stephan 4.00 10.00
ATT Tim Thomas 10.00 25.00
AVT Vladislav Tretiak 25.00 60.00
AWD Wade Dubielewicz 4.00 10.00
AYD Yann Danis 4.00 10.00
AYFA Yutaka Fukufuji ENG 20.00 50.00
AYFB Yutaka Fukufuji KANJI 60.00 150.00

2006-07 Between The Pipes Double Jerseys

ANNOUNCED PRINT RUN 40
DJ01 A.Montoya/J.Davidson 10.00 25.00
DJ02 D.Roloson/M.Fernandez 8.00 20.00
DJ03 R.Hextall/B.Parent 20.00 50.00
DJ04 C.Ward/M.Brodeur 15.00 40.00
DJ05 C.Huet/P.Roy 20.00 50.00
DJ06 D.Hasek/R.Miller 15.00 40.00
DJ07 D.Hasek/T.Sawchuk 15.00 40.00
DJ08 E.Giacomin/H.Lundqvist 25.00 60.00
DJ09 V.Tretiak/V.Myshkin 15.00 40.00
DJ10 G.Cheevers/T.Thomas 12.00 30.00
DJ11 G.Hall/T.Esposito 12.00 30.00
DJ12 G.Fuhr/B.Ranford 15.00 40.00
DJ13 J.Plante/G.Worsley 25.00 50.00
DJ14 J.Davidson/M.Richter 12.00 30.00
DJ15 F.Potvin/J.Pogge 20.00 50.00
DJ16 A.Niittymaki/K.Lehtonen 8.00 20.00
DJ17 D.Bouchard/P.Roy 25.00 60.00
DJ18 M.Fleury/T.Barrasso 15.00 40.00
DJ19 M.Brodeur/T.Sawchuk 25.00 60.00
DJ20 I.Bryzgalov/V.Tretiak 15.00 40.00
DJ21 P.Roy/C.Price 25.00 60.00
DJ22 P.Roy/M.Brodeur 30.00 80.00
DJ23 R.Emery/D.Hasek 12.00 30.00
DJ24 R.DiPietro/B.Smith 12.00 30.00
DJ25 R.Luongo/M.Brodeur 15.00 40.00
DJ26 R.Worters/F.Brimsek 8.00 20.00
DJ27 J.Vanbiesbrouck/M.Richter 20.00 50.00
DJ28 F.Potvin/A.Raycroft 15.00 40.00
DJ29 R.Luongo/P.Roy 25.00 60.00

2006-07 Between The Pipes Double Memorabilia

COMMON CARD 8.00 20.00
SEMISTARS 10.00 25.00
UNLISTED STARS 12.00 30.00
STATED PRINT RUN 40 SER.#'d SETS
DM01 Rogie Vachon 10.00 25.00
DM02 Martin Brodeur 20.00 50.00
DM03 Gerry Cheevers 12.00 30.00
DM04 Tony Esposito 8.00 20.00
DM05 Marc-Andre Fleury 10.00 25.00
DM06 Ed Giacomin 15.00 40.00
DM07 Dominik Hasek 12.00 30.00
DM08 Ron Hextall 15.00 40.00
DM09 Leland Irving 12.00 30.00
DM10 Roberto Luongo 10.00 25.00
DM11 Al Montoya 8.00 20.00
DM12 Bernie Parent 12.00 30.00
DM13 Jacques Plante 15.00 40.00
DM14 Patrick Roy (COL) 20.00 50.00
DM15 Patrick Roy (MTL) 20.00 50.00
DM16 Terry Sawchuk 20.00 50.00
DM17 Tiny Thompson 10.00 25.00
DM18 Hannu Toivonen 8.00 20.00
DM19 Vladislav Tretiak 15.00 40.00
DM20 Felix Potvin 15.00 40.00

2006-07 Between The Pipes Forgotten Franchises

COMPLETE SET (10) 10.00 25.00
COMMON CARD 1.50 4.00
ODDS 1:12 PACKS
FF01 Chuck Rayner 1.50 4.00
FF02 Hap Holmes 1.50 4.00
FF03 Alex Connell 1.50 4.00
FF04 Vernon Jake Forbes 1.50 4.00
FF05 Lorne Chabot 1.50 4.00
FF06 Earl Robertson 1.50 4.00
FF07 Clint Benedict 1.50 4.00
FF08 Wilf Cude 1.50 4.00
FF09 Roy Worters 1.50 4.00
FF10 Paddy Moran 1.50 4.00

2006-07 Between The Pipes Gloves

STATED PRINT RUN 50 SER.#'d SETS
GG01 Martin Brodeur 15.00 40.00
GG02 Rick DiPietro 10.00 25.00
GG03 Tony Esposito 10.00 25.00
GG04 Marc-Andre Fleury 12.00 30.00
GG05 Grant Fuhr 12.00 30.00
GG06 Ed Giacomin 20.00 50.00
GG07 Gilles Gilbert 12.00 30.00
GG08 David LeNeveu 8.00 20.00
GG09 Dominik Hasek 15.00 40.00
GG10 Charlie Hodge 10.00 25.00
GG11 Leland Irving 10.00 25.00
GG12 Curtis Joseph 12.00 30.00
GG13 Felix Potvin 15.00 40.00
GG14 Al Montoya 8.00 20.00
GG15 Jacques Plante
GG16 Patrick Roy 30.00 80.00
GG17 Hannu Toivonen 10.00 25.00
GG18 Gump Worsley 12.00 30.00
GG19 Glenn Hall

2006-07 Between The Pipes Jerseys

ANNOUNCED PRINT RUN 90
GUJ01 Rogie Vachon 6.00 15.00
GUJ02 Marc-Andre Fleury 10.00 25.00
GUJ03 Henrik Lundqvist 10.00 25.00
GUJ04 Tony Esposito 6.00 15.00
GUJ05 Manny Fernandez 5.00 12.00
GUJ06 Jeff Glass 5.00 12.00
GUJ07 Kelly Guard 5.00 12.00
GUJ08 Ron Hextall 6.00 15.00
GUJ09 Kari Lehtonen 5.00 12.00
GUJ10 Roberto Luongo 10.00 25.00
GUJ11 Antero Niittymaki 5.00 12.00
GUJ12 Billy Smith 6.00 15.00
GUJ13 Mike Smith 6.00 15.00
GUJ14 Hannu Toivonen 5.00 12.00
GUJ15 Gump Worsley 10.00 25.00
GUJ16 Tom Barrasso 6.00 15.00
GUJ17 Richard Brodeur 5.00 12.00
GUJ18 Barry Brust 5.00 12.00
GUJ19 Dwayne Roloson 5.00 12.00
GUJ20 Martin Gerber 5.00 12.00
GUJ21 Jason Bacashihua 5.00 12.00
GUJ22 Jonathan Bernier 8.00 20.00
GUJ23 Rejean Beauchemin 5.00 12.00
GUJ24 Ryan Daniels 5.00 12.00
GUJ25 Yann Danis 5.00 12.00
GUJ26 Curtis McElhinney 5.00 12.00
GUJ27 Brian Finley 5.00 12.00
GUJ28 Mathieu Garon 5.00 12.00
GUJ29 Johan Holmqvist 6.00 15.00
GUJ30 Mikael Tellqvist 6.00 15.00
GUJ31 Pekka Rinne 6.00 15.00
GUJ32 Bill Ranford 6.00 15.00
GUJ33 Andrew Penner 5.00 12.00
GUJ34 Corey Crawford 6.00 15.00
GUJ35 Andy Moog 6.00 15.00
GUJ36 Jimmy Howard 6.00 15.00
GUJ37 Josh Harding 6.00 15.00
GUJ38 Martin Houle 5.00 12.00
GUJ39 Pascal Leclaire 5.00 12.00
GUJ40 Vladislav Tretiak 10.00 25.00
GUJ41 Leland Irving 5.00 12.00
GUJ42 Philippe Sauve 5.00 12.00
GUJ43 Brent Krahn 5.00 12.00
GUJ44 Maxime Ouellet 5.00 12.00
GUJ45 Grant Fuhr 10.00 25.00
GUJ46 Cristobal Huet 8.00 20.00
GUJ47 Ryan Miller 6.00 15.00
GUJ48 Carey Price 12.00 30.00
GUJ49 Terry Sawchuk 10.00 25.00
GUJ50 Tim Thomas 6.00 15.00
GUJ51 Justin Pogge 4.00 10.00
GUJ52 Ed Giacomin 10.00 25.00
GUJ53 Andrew Raycroft 5.00 12.00
GUJ54 Frank Brimsek 5.00 12.00
GUJ55 Glenn Hall 6.00 15.00
GUJ56 Ray Emery 5.00 12.00
GUJ57 J-S Aubin 5.00 12.00
GUJ58 Ilya Bryzgalov 6.00 15.00
GUJ59 Marek Schwarz 6.00 15.00
GUJ60 Peter Budaj 5.00 12.00
GUJ61 Dominik Hasek 10.00 25.00
GUJ62 Curtis Joseph 6.00 15.00
GUJ63 Felix Potvin 6.00 15.00
GUJ64 Cam Ward 6.00 15.00
GUJ65 Mike Richter 6.00 15.00
GUJ66 Patrick Roy 15.00 40.00
GUJ67 David LeNeveu 5.00 12.00
GUJ68 Alex Auld 4.00 10.00
GUJ69 Rick DiPietro 5.00 12.00
GUJ70 Martin Brodeur 12.00 30.00
GUJ71 Ed Belfour 6.00 15.00

2006-07 Between The Pipes Pads

COMMON CARD 8.00 20.00
SEMISTARS 10.00 25.00
UNLISTED STARS 12.00 30.00
STATED ANNCD PRINT RUN 70
GP01 Martin Brodeur 12.00 30.00
GP02 Gerry Cheevers 8.00 20.00
GP03 Grant Fuhr 8.00 20.00
GP04 Bernie Parent 8.00 20.00
GP05 Jacques Plante 12.00 30.00
GP06 Patrick Roy 15.00 40.00
GP07 Tiny Thompson 8.00 20.00
GP08 Vladislav Tretiak 25.00 60.00
GP09 Curtis Joseph 10.00 25.00
GP10 Ron Hextall 10.00 25.00
GP11 Ed Belfour 10.00 25.00

2006-07 Between The Pipes Playing For Your Country

STATED PRINT RUN 40 SER.#'d SETS
PC01 Jonathan Bernier 15.00 40.00
PC02 Martin Brodeur 12.00 30.00
PC03 Ilya Bryzgalov 8.00 20.00
PC04 Roberto Luongo 12.00 30.00
PC05 Tom Barrasso 10.00 25.00
PC06 Vladimir Dzurilla 8.00 20.00
PC07 Grant Fuhr 12.00 30.00
PC08 Dominik Hasek 10.00 25.00
PC09 Cristobal Huet 8.00 20.00
PC10 Marc-Andre Fleury 10.00 25.00
PC11 Carey Price 15.00 40.00
PC12 John Vanbiesbrouck 8.00 20.00
PC13 Henrik Lundqvist 10.00 25.00
PC14 Rogie Vachon 8.00 20.00
PC15 Al Montoya 8.00 20.00
PC16 Vladimir Myshkin 12.00 30.00
PC17 Antero Niittymaki 8.00 20.00
PC18 Justin Pogge 10.00 25.00
PC19 Tony Esposito 10.00 25.00
PC20 Mike Richter 8.00 20.00
PC21 Patrick Roy 12.00 30.00
PC22 Marek Schwarz 6.00 15.00
PC23 Hannu Toivonen 8.00 20.00
PC24 Vladislav Tretiak 15.00 40.00
PC25 Curtis Joseph 8.00 20.00
PC26 Kari Lehtonen 8.00 20.00

2006-07 Between The Pipes Prospect Trios

STATED PRINT RUN 40 SER.#'d SETS
PT01 Thomas/Finley/Toivo 12.00 30.00
PT02 Leclaire/Budaj/Hard 12.00 30.00
PT03 Emery/Glass/Guard 15.00 40.00
PT04 Niitty/Houle/Beauch 15.00 40.00
PT05 McEl/Lalande/Irving 10.00 25.00
PT06 Irving/Bernier/Cann 15.00 40.00
PT07 Price/Levass/Mason 20.00 50.00
PT08 Ellis/LaCosta/Peters 8.00 20.00
PT09 Price/Westblom/Irving 20.00 50.00
PT10 Lalande/Plante/Moir 10.00 25.00
PT11 Daniels/Vincent/Ellis 10.00 25.00
PT12 Price/Boutin/Bernier 20.00 50.00
PT13 Fleury/Auld/Lehtonen 15.00 40.00
PT14 Bernier/Brust/Labarb 12.00 30.00
PT15 Huet/Price/Danis 20.00 50.00
PT16 Beck/Schwarz/Baca 10.00 25.00
PT17 Aubin/Coleman/Craw 12.00 30.00
PT18 Pogge/Bryz/Montoya 10.00 25.00
PT19 Thomp/Boutin/Munro 10.00 25.00
PT20 LeNev/Cassivi/Ouellet 10.00 25.00

2006-07 Between The Pipes Roy vs. Brodeur

RB1-RB6 DUAL JERSEY PRINT RUN 25
RB01 Roy (MTL)/Brodeur JSY 40.00 80.00
RB02 Roy (COL)/Brodeur JSY 40.00 80.00
RB03 Roy (MTL)/Brodeur JSY 40.00 80.00
RB04 Roy (COL)/Brodeur JSY 40.00 80.00
RB05 Roy/Brodeur JSY 40.00 80.00
RB06 Roy/Brodeur GLV 40.00 80.00
RB07 Roy/Brodeur Patch/10
RB08 Roy/Brodeur Patch/10
RB09 Roy (MTL)/Brodeur AU/10
RB10 Roy (COL)/Brodeur AU/10

2006-07 Between The Pipes Shooting Gallery

STATED PRINT RUN 30 SER.#'d SETS
SG01 Vezina/Plante/Vach etc 250.00 400.00
SG02 Bower/Sawch/Palm etc 125.00 250.00
SG03 Thomp/Cheev/Gilb etc 75.00 175.00
SG04 Gard/Francis/Brims etc 75.00 175.00
SG05 Giac/Davids/VBK etc 150.00 300.00
SG06 Sawch/Croz/Giac etc 100.00 200.00
SG07 Parent/Lind/Hexy etc 125.00 250.00
SG08 Tret/Hasek/Richt etc 125.00 250.00
SG09 Sawch/Plant/Bow etc 75.00 150.00
SG10 Durn/Plante/Hall etc 200.00 350.00

2006-07 Between The Pipes Stick and Jersey

STATED PRINT RUN 40 SER.#'d SETS
SJ01 Manny Fernandez 10.00 25.00
SJ02 Johnny Bower 10.00 25.00
SJ03 Martin Brodeur 15.00 40.00
SJ04 Gerry Cheevers 12.00 30.00
SJ05 John Davidson 10.00 25.00
SJ06 Rick DiPietro 12.50 30.00
SJ07 Ray Emery 8.00 20.00
SJ08 Tony Esposito 12.00 30.00
SJ09 Marc-Andre Fleury 15.00 40.00
SJ10 Grant Fuhr 12.00 30.00
SJ11 Ed Giacomin 12.00 30.00
SJ12 Glenn Hall 12.00 30.00
SJ13 Dominik Hasek 12.00 30.00
SJ14 Ron Hextall 15.00 40.00
SJ15 Cristobal Huet 10.00 25.00
SJ16 Leland Irving 12.00 30.00
SJ17 Jason LaBarbera 10.00 25.00
SJ18 Roberto Luongo 15.00 40.00
SJ19 Henrik Lundqvist 12.00 30.00
SJ20 Ryan Miller 12.50 30.00
SJ21 Al Montoya 10.00 25.00
SJ22 Antero Niittymaki 10.00 25.00
SJ23 Felix Potvin 10.00 40.00
SJ24 Bernie Parent 15.00 40.00
SJ25 Jacques Plante 25.00 60.00
SJ26 Andrew Raycroft 10.00 25.00
SJ27 Mike Richter 10.00 25.00
SJ28 Pekka Rinne 10.00 25.00
SJ29 Patrick Roy (COL) 15.00 40.00
SJ30 Patrick Roy (MTL) 20.00 50.00
SJ31 Terry Sawchuk 20.00 50.00
SJ32 Billy Smith 12.00 30.00
SJ33 Roger Crozier 10.00 25.00
SJ34 Tim Thomas 10.00 25.00
SJ35 Hannu Toivonen 10.00 25.00
SJ36 Rogie Vachon 12.00 30.00
SJ37 John Vanbiesbrouck 12.00 30.00
SJ38 Gump Worsley 12.00 30.00
SJ39 Richard Brodeur 12.00 30.00
SJ40 Tom Barrasso 12.00 30.00

2006-07 Between The Pipes Stick Work

STATED PRINT RUN 50 SER.#'d SETS
SW01 Roy/Brodeur/Luongo 50.00 120.00
SW02 Crozier/Hasek/Miller 40.00 80.00
SW03 Parent/Lind/Hextall 40.00 80.00
SW04 Worsley/Roy/Huet 40.00 100.00
SW05 Espo/Cheesy/Giaco 12.00 30.00
SW06 Bower/Palma/Potvin 60.00 120.00

2006-07 Between The Pipes The Mask

COMPLETE SET (40) 125.00 250.00
ODDS 1:24
M01 Al Montoya 4.00 10.00
M02 Kari Lehtonen 5.00 12.00
M03 Miikka Kiprusoff 5.00 12.00
M04 Antero Niittymaki 3.00 8.00
M05 Ray Emery 3.00 8.00
M06 Andrew Raycroft 3.00 8.00
M07 Ryan Miller 5.00 12.00
M08 Martin Gerber 3.00 8.00
M09 Ken Dryden 8.00 20.00
M10 Marc-Andre Fleury 6.00 15.00
M11 Joey MacDonald 3.00 8.00
M12 Henrik Lundqvist 5.00 12.00
M13 Cam Ward 4.00 10.00
M14 Cristobal Huet 5.00 12.00
M15 Rick DiPietro 4.00 10.00
M16 Ilya Bryzgalov 3.00 8.00
M17 Jose Theodore 4.00 10.00
M18 Dominik Hasek 8.00 20.00
M19 Nikolai Khabibulin 4.00 10.00
M20 Marty Turco 4.00 10.00
M21 Marek Schwarz 3.00 8.00
M22 Patrick Roy 10.00 25.00
M23 Dominik Hasek 8.00 20.00
M24 Ed Belfour 4.00 10.00
M25 Manny Legace 3.00 8.00
M26 Curtis Joseph 5.00 12.00
M27 Hannu Toivonen 3.00 8.00
M28 Martin Biron 3.00 8.00
M29 Dan Cloutier 3.00 8.00
M30 Kevin Weekes 3.00 8.00
M31 Jimmy Howard 4.00 10.00
M32 Devan Dubnyk 3.00 8.00
M33 Mikael Tellqvist 3.00 8.00
M34 Jacques Plante 6.00 15.00
M35 Jeff Glass 3.00 8.00
M36 Henrik Lundqvist 5.00 12.00
M37 Vesa Toskala 3.00 8.00
M38 Johan Hedberg 3.00 8.00
M39 Tomas Vokoun 4.00 10.00
M40 Carey Price 10.00 25.00

2006-07 Between The Pipes The Mask Silver

*SILVER: .5X to 1.5X MASK HI
STATED PRINT RUN 100 SER.#'d SETS

2006-07 Between The Pipes The Mask Game-Used

STATED PRINT RUN 25 SER.#'d SETS
MGU01 Martin Biron 15.00 40.00
MGU02 Ilya Bryzgalov 15.00 40.00
MGU03 Rick DiPietro 20.00 50.00
MGU04 Ken Dryden 100.00 200.00
MGU05 Ray Emery 15.00 40.00
MGU06 Marc-Andre Fleury 30.00 60.00
MGU07 Dominik Hasek 40.00 80.00
MGU08 Cristobal Huet 20.00 50.00
MGU09 Miikka Kiprusoff 40.00 80.00
MGU10 Kari Lehtonen 20.00 50.00
MGU11 Henrik Lundqvist 30.00 60.00
MGU12 Ryan Miller 20.00 50.00
MGU13 Al Montoya 15.00 40.00
MGU14 Antero Niittymaki 15.00 40.00
MGU15 Jacques Plante 30.00 80.00
MGU16 Andrew Raycroft 20.00 50.00
MGU17 Patrick Roy 40.00 100.00
MGU18 Marty Turco 15.00 40.00
MGU19 Cam Ward 15.00 40.00
MGU20 Hannu Toivonen 15.00 40.00

2007-08 Between The Pipes

COMPLETE SET (100) 12.00 30.00
1 Adam Courchaine .25 .60
2 Adam Dennis .25 .60
3 Al Montoya .25 .60
4 Antoine Lafleur .25 .60
5 Braden Holtby .75 2.00
6 Brian Elliott .40 1.00
7 Carey Price 2.00 5.00
8 Corey Crawford .30 .75
9 Cory Schneider .60 1.50
10 Curtis McElhinney .30 .75
11 Daren Machesney .25 .60
12 Devan Dubnyk .40 1.00
13 Dustin Tokarski .30 .75
14 Erik Ersberg .30 .75
15 Hannu Toivonen .25 .60
16 Jaroslav Halak .50 1.25
17 Jeff Deslauriers .25 .60
18 Jeff Glass .25 .60
19 Jeremy Smith .30 .75
20 Jimmy Howard .50 1.25
21 John Murray .25 .60
22 Jonas Hiller .40 1.00
23 Jonathan Bernier .50 1.25
24 Jordan Parise .30 .75
25 Jordan Sigalet .25 .60
26 Josh Tordjman .50 1.25
27 Josh Unice .30 .75
28 Justin Peters .25 .60
29 Justin Pogge .30 .75
30 Karri Ramo .30 .75
31 Kevin Desfosses .25 .60
32 Kevin Poulin .30 .75
33 Kyle Gajewski .25 .60
34 Leland Irving .30 .75
35 Linden Rowat .30 .75
36 Marek Schwarz .30 .75
37 Matt Keetley .25 .60
38 Maxime Daigneault .25 .60
39 Michal Neuvirth .40 1.00
40 Mike Murphy .30 .75
41 Ondrej Pavelec .40 1.00
42 Pekka Rinne .40 1.00
43 Peter Delmas .20 .50
44 Riku Helenius .25 .60
45 Robert Mayer .30 .75
46 Ryan Munce .25 .60
47 Scott Monroe .25 .60
48 Simeon Varlamov .60 1.50
49 Steve Mason 2.50 6.00
50 Taylor Dakers .25 .60
51 Thomas Greiss .40 1.00
52 Thomas McCollum .30 .75
53 Tobias Stephan .25 .60
54 Tomas Popperle .25 .60
55 Tomi Karhunen .25 .60
56 Torrie Jung .25 .60
57 Trevor Cann .25 .60
58 Tuukka Rask .75 2.00
59 Tyler Weiman .25 .60
60 Tyson Sexsmith .25 .60
61 Cam Ward .30 .75
62 Dan Cloutier .25 .60
63 Dominik Hasek .40 1.00
64 Jean-Sebastien Giguere .30 .75
65 Kari Lehtonen .25 .60
66 Tim Thomas .40 1.00
67 Martin Brodeur .60 1.50
68 Marty Turco .30 .75
69 Pascal Leclaire .25 .60
70 Peter Budaj .25 .60
71 Ray Emery .25 .60
72 Roberto Luongo .40 1.00
73 Ryan Miller .30 .75
74 Tomas Vokoun .25 .60
75 Terry Sawchuk .40 1.00
76 Billy Smith .30 .75
77 Felix Potvin .50 1.25
78 Glenn Hall .40 1.00
79 Grant Fuhr .30 .75
80 Gump Worsley .40 1.00
81 John Davidson .25 .60
82 Johnny Bower .30 .75
83 Mike Palmateer .30 .75
84 Patrick Roy .75 2.00
85 Rogie Vachon .40 1.00
86 Ron Hextall .50 1.25
87 Tom Barrasso .30 .75
88 Ed Giacomin .30 .75
89 Tony Esposito .30 .75
90 Gerry Cheevers .30 .75
91 Joe Daley .30 .75
92 Gilles Gratton .30 .75
93 Richard Brodeur .25 .60
94 Bernie Parent .30 .75
95 Les Binkley .25 .60
96 Ernie Wakely .25 .60
97 Michel Dion .25 .60
98 John Garrett .25 .60
99 Mike Liut .25 .60
100 Ed Mio .25 .60

2007-08 Between The Pipes Autographs

AAC Adam Courchaine 4.00 10.00
AAD Adam Dennis 4.00 10.00
AAL Antoine Lafleur 4.00 10.00
AAM Al Montoya 4.00 10.00
ABE Brian Elliott 6.00 15.00
ABH Braden Holtby 12.00 30.00
ABP Bernie Parent SP 25.00 60.00
ABS Billy Smith SP 15.00 40.00
ACC Corey Crawford 12.00 30.00
ACM Curtis McElhinney 5.00 12.00
ACO Chris Osgood SP 5.00 12.00
ACP Carey Price 30.00 80.00
ACS Cory Schneider 10.00 25.00
ACW Cam Ward 5.00 12.00
ADC Dan Cloutier 4.00 10.00
ADD Devan Dubnyk 6.00 15.00
ADH Dominik Hasek SP 10.00 25.00
ADMA1 Daren Machesney 4.00 10.00
ADMA2 Drew MacIntyre 4.00 10.00
ADT Dustin Tokarski 5.00 12.00
AEE Erik Ersberg 5.00 12.00
AEM Ed Mio 4.00 10.00
AEW Ernie Wakely 4.00 10.00
AFP Felix Potvin SP 8.00 20.00
AGC Gerry Cheevers SP 15.00 40.00
AGE Grant Fuhr SP 5.00 12.00
AGG Gilles Gratton 5.00 12.00
AGH Glenn Hall SP 20.00 50.00
AGW Gump Worsley SP 20.00 50.00
AHT Hannu Toivonen 4.00 10.00
AJB Johnny Bower SP 8.00 20.00
AJBE Jonathan Bernier 8.00 20.00
AJD Jeff Deslauriers 4.00 10.00
AJDA Joe Daley 5.00 12.00
AJG Jeff Glass 4.00 10.00
AJGA John Garrett 4.00 10.00
AJH Jaroslav Halak 8.00 20.00
AJHA Josh Harding SP 15.00 40.00
AJHI Jonas Hiller 6.00 15.00
AJHO Jimmy Howard 8.00 20.00
AJM John Murray 4.00 10.00
AJP Justin Pogge 5.00 12.00
AJPA Jordan Parise 5.00 12.00
AJPE Justin Peters 4.00 10.00
AJS Jordan Sigalet 4.00 10.00
AJSG Jean-Sebastien Giguere SP 5.00 12.00
AJSM Jeremy Smith 5.00 12.00
AJT Josh Tordjman 8.00 20.00
AJU Josh Unice 5.00 12.00
AKD Kevin Desfosses 4.00 10.00
AKG Kyle Gajewski 4.00 10.00
AKL Kari Lehtonen 4.00 10.00
AKP Kevin Poulin 5.00 12.00
AKR Karri Ramo 5.00 12.00
ALB Les Binkley 4.00 10.00
ALI Leland Irving 5.00 12.00
ALR Linden Rowat 5.00 12.00
AMB Martin Brodeur SP 25.00 60.00
AMD Michel Dion 4.00 10.00
AMDA Maxime Daigneault 4.00 10.00
AMG Martin Gerber SP 4.00 10.00
AMK Matt Keetley 4.00 10.00
AML Mike Liut 4.00 10.00
AMM Mike Murphy 5.00 12.00
AMN Michal Neuvirth 6.00 15.00
AMP Mike Palmateer SP 12.00 30.00
AMS Marek Schwarz 5.00 12.00
AMT Marty Turco SP 5.00 12.00
AOP Ondrej Pavelec 6.00 15.00
APB Peter Budaj 4.00 10.00
APD Peter Delmas 3.00 8.00
APL Pascal Leclaire 4.00 10.00
APR Patrick Roy SP 30.00 80.00
APRI Pekka Rinne 8.00 20.00
ARB Richard Brodeur 4.00 10.00
ARE Ray Emery SP 8.00 20.00
ARH Riku Helenius 4.00 10.00
ARHE Ron Hextall SP 8.00 20.00
ARL Roberto Luongo SP 10.00 25.00
ARM Ryan Miller SP 12.00 30.00
ARMA Robert Mayer 5.00 12.00
ARMU Ryan Munce 4.00 10.00
ARV Rogie Vachon SP 12.00 30.00
ASM Scott Monroe 4.00 10.00
ASMA Steve Mason 10.00 25.00
ATB Tom Barrasso SP 8.00 20.00
ATC Trevor Cann 4.00 10.00
ATD Taylor Dakers 4.00 10.00
ATE Tony Esposito SP 12.00 30.00
ATG Thomas Greiss 6.00 15.00
ATJ Torrie Jung 4.00 10.00
ATK Tomi Karhunen 4.00 10.00
ATMC Thomas McCollum 5.00 12.00
ATP Tomas Popperle 4.00 10.00
ATR Tuukka Rask 15.00 40.00
ATS Tobias Stephan 4.00 10.00
ATSE Tyson Sexsmith 4.00 10.00
ATT Tim Thomas SP 10.00 25.00
ATV Tomas Vokoun SP 8.00 20.00
ATW Tyler Weiman 4.00 10.00
AVT Vladislav Tretiak SP 20.00 50.00
AYD Yann Danis 4.00 10.00
AJDAV John Davidson SP 4.00 10.00

2007-08 Between The Pipes First Round Goalies Jerseys

STATED PRINT RUN 90 SER.#'d SETS
FRG01 Leland Irving 5.00 12.00
FRG02 John Davidson 4.00 10.00
FRG03 Jonathan Bernier 8.00 20.00
FRG04 Tuukka Rask 12.00 30.00
FRG05 Carey Price 30.00 80.00
FRG06 Marek Schwarz 5.00 12.00
FRG07 Devan Dubnyk 6.00 15.00
FRG08 Al Montoya 4.00 10.00
FRG09 Marc-Andre Fleury 8.00 20.00
FRG10 Cam Ward 5.00 12.00
FRG11 Kari Lehtonen 4.00 10.00
FRG12 Adam Munro 4.00 10.00
FRG13 Hannu Toivonen 4.00 10.00
FRG14 Pascal Leclaire 4.00 10.00
FRG15 Dan Cloutier 4.00 10.00
FRG16 Jean-Sebastien Giguere 5.00 12.00
FRG17 Roberto Luongo 6.00 15.00
FRG18 Grant Fuhr 5.00 12.00
FRG19 Tom Barrasso 5.00 12.00
FRG20 Martin Brodeur 10.00 25.00

2007-08 Between The Pipes Flashbacks

COMPLETE SET (10) 15.00 40.00
FB01 Martin Brodeur 4.00 10.00
FB02 Dominik Hasek 2.50 6.00
FB03 Ray Emery 1.50 4.00
FB04 Patrick Roy 5.00 12.00
FB05 Ryan Miller 2.00 5.00
FB06 Ed Belfour 2.00 5.00
FB07 Jean-Sebastien Giguere 2.00 5.00
FB08 Roberto Luongo 2.50 6.00
FB09 Cam Ward 2.00 5.00
FB10 Kari Lehtonen 1.50 4.00

2007-08 Between The Pipes Goaltending Traditions

COMPLETE SET (10) 20.00 50.00
GT01 J.Bernier/R.Vachon 2.50 6.00
GT02 C.Price/P.Roy 12.00 30.00
GT03 T.Cann/P.Roy 5.00 12.00
GT04 J.Howard/D.Hasek 3.00 8.00
GT05 L.Irving/M.Vernon 2.50 6.00
GT06 A.Montoya/M.Richter 4.00 10.00
GT07 C.Schneider/R.Luongo 4.00 10.00
GT08 J.Pogge/F.Potvin 3.00 8.00
GT09 T.Rask/G.Cheevers 5.00 12.00
GT10 M.Schwarz/G.Hall 2.50 6.00

2007-08 Between The Pipes Jerseys

STATED PRINT RUN 90 SETS
CCJ01 Adam Munro 4.00 10.00
CCJ02 Barry Brust 4.00 10.00
CCJ03 Brian Elliott 6.00 15.00
CCJ04 Cam Ward 5.00 12.00
CCJ05 Carey Price 15.00 40.00
CCJ06 Corey Crawford 5.00 12.00
CCJ07 David LeNeveu 4.00 10.00
CCJ08 Gerald Coleman 4.00 10.00
CCJ09 Jeremy Smith 5.00 12.00
CCJ10 John Murray 4.00 10.00
CCJ11 Jonathan Boutin 4.00 10.00
CCJ12 Karri Ramo 5.00 12.00
CCJ13 Kevin Nastiuk 4.00 10.00
CCJ14 Leland Irving 5.00 12.00
CCJ15 Linden Rowat 5.00 12.00
CCJ16 Michael Leighton 4.00 10.00
CCJ17 Pascal Leclaire 4.00 10.00
CCJ18 Pekka Rinne 6.00 15.00
CCJ19 Peter Budaj 4.00 10.00
CCJ20 Ray Emery 4.00 10.00
CCJ21 Roberto Luongo 6.00 15.00
CCJ22 Steve Mason 10.00 25.00
CCJ23 Thomas McCollum 5.00 12.00
CCJ24 Trevor Cann 4.00 10.00
CCJ25 Tuukka Rask 12.00 30.00
CCJ26 Tyson Sexsmith 4.00 10.00
CCJ27 Adam Dennis 4.00 10.00
CCJ28 Curtis McElhinney 5.00 12.00
CCJ29 Dan Cloutier 4.00 10.00
CCJ30 Hannu Toivonen 4.00 10.00
CCJ31 Jason Bacashihua 4.00 10.00
CCJ32 Jonathan Bernier 8.00 20.00
CCJ33 Manny Fernandez 4.00 10.00
CCJ34 Marty Turco 5.00 12.00
CCJ35 Patrick Roy (MON) 12.00 30.00
CCJ36 Patrick Roy (COL) 12.00 30.00
CCJ37 Richard Brodeur 4.00 10.00
CCJ38 Ryan Miller 6.00 15.00
CCJ39 Tim Thomas 6.00 15.00
CCJ40 Tyler Weiman 4.00 10.00
CCJ41 Dominik Hasek 6.00 15.00
CCJ42 Felix Potvin 8.00 20.00
CCJ43 Grant Fuhr 5.00 12.00
CCJ44 Josh Harding 5.00 12.00
CCJ45 Jean-Sebastien Giguere 5.00 12.00
CCJ46 Kari Lehtonen 4.00 10.00
CCJ47 Marek Schwarz 5.00 12.00
CCJ48 Martin Brodeur 10.00 25.00
CCJ49 Mike Richter 10.00 25.00
CCJ50 Ron Hextall 8.00 20.00
CCJ51 Ed Belfour 6.00 15.00
CCJ52 Dan Bouchard 4.00 10.00
CCJ53 Curtis Sanford 4.00 10.00
CCJ54 Tomas Vokoun 4.00 10.00
CCJ55 Philippe Sauve 4.00 10.00
CCJ56 Brent Krahn 4.00 10.00
CCJ57 Kevin Lalande 4.00 10.00
CCJ58 Alex Auld 3.00 8.00

CCJ59 Ryan Daniels 4.00 10.00
CCJ60 John Vanbiesbrouck 5.00 12.00
CCJ61 Mathieu Garon 4.00 10.00
CCJ62 Mike Smith 5.00 12.00
CCJ63 Ilya Bryzgalov 5.00 12.00
CCJ64 Vladislav Tretiak 10.00 25.00

2007-08 Between The Pipes Tandem Threads

STATED PRINT RUN 90 SER.#'d SETS
TT01 D.Hasek/R.Miller 10.00 25.00
TT02 R.Luongo/D.Cloutier
TT03 F.Potvin/J.Pogge 15.00 40.00
TT04 P.Roy/C.Price 30.00 80.00
TT05 C.McElhinney/L.Irving 6.00 15.00
TT06 G.Cheevers/T.Thomas 10.00 25.00
TT07 P.Roy/P.Budaj 15.00 40.00
TT08 G.Worsley/R.Vachon 12.00 30.00
TT09 E.Giacomin/A.Montoya 10.00 25.00
TT10 M.Turco/M.Smith 6.00 15.00
TT11 P.Roy/M.Brodeur 20.00 40.00
TT12 B.Parent/R.Hextall 20.00 40.00
TT13 T.Vokoun/R.Luongo 10.00 20.00
TT14 Beezer/Richter 10.00 25.00
TT15 T.Esposito/E.Belfour 10.00 25.00
TT16 T.Sawchuk/J.Bernier 10.00 25.00
TT17 G.Fuhr/M.Garon 10.00 25.00
TT18 M.Gerber/R.Emery 6.00 15.00
TT19 C.Ward/M.Leighton 6.00 15.00
TT20 J.Giguere/K.Lehtonen 6.00 15.00

2007-08 Between The Pipes The Future of Goaltending

COMPLETE SET (10) 6.00 15.00
FOG01 Carey Price 4.00 10.00
FOG02 Leland Irving .60 1.50
FOG03 Trevor Cann .50 1.25
FOG04 Tuukka Rask 1.50 4.00
FOG05 Jaroslav Halak 1.00 2.50
FOG06 Al Montoya .50 1.25
FOG07 Justin Pogge .60 1.50
FOG08 Jonathan Bernier 1.00 2.50
FOG09 Marek Schwarz .60 1.50
FOG10 Tyson Sexsmith .50 1.25

2007-08 Between The Pipes The Mask

COMPLETE SET (30) 75.00 150.00
M1 Nikolai Khabibulin 3.00 8.00
M2 Manny Legace 2.50 6.00
M3 Dominik Hasek 4.00 10.00
M4 Carey Price 20.00 50.00
M5 Roberto Luongo 4.00 10.00
M6 Jean-Sebastien Giguere 3.00 8.00
M7 Mathieu Garon 2.50 6.00
M8 Marc-Andre Fleury 5.00 12.00
M9 Marc Denis 2.50 6.00
M10 Evgeni Nabokov 2.50 6.00
M11 Manny Fernandez 2.50 6.00
M12 Niklas Backstrom 3.00 8.00
M13 Josh Harding 3.00 8.00
M14 Miikka Kiprusoff 2.50 6.00
M15 Martin Biron 2.50 6.00
M16 Chris Mason 2.50 6.00
M17 Cam Ward 3.00 8.00
M18 Tim Thomas 5.00 12.00
M19 Marty Turco 3.00 8.00
M20 Johan Hedberg 2.50 6.00
M21 Henrik Lundqvist 4.00 10.00
M22 Martin Gerber 2.50 6.00
M23 Johan Holmqvist 2.50 6.00
M24 Pascal Leclaire 2.50 6.00
M25 Cristobal Huet 2.50 6.00
M26 David Aebischer 2.50 6.00
M27 Peter Budaj 2.50 6.00
M28 Mikael Tellqvist 2.50 6.00
M29 Ryan Miller 3.00 8.00
M30 Ty Conklin 2.50 6.00

2007-08 Between The Pipes The Mask Game-Used

ANNOUNCED PRINT RUN 60 SETS
MGU01 Manny Legace 8.00 20.00
MGU02 Dominik Hasek 12.00 30.00
MGU03 Ryan Miller 10.00 25.00
MGU04 Roberto Luongo 12.00 30.00
MGU05 Jean-Sebastien Giguere 10.00 25.00
MGU06 Cristobal Huet 8.00 20.00
MGU07 Marc-Andre Fleury 15.00 40.00
MGU08 Evgeni Nabokov 8.00 20.00
MGU09 Miikka Kiprusoff 8.00 20.00
MGU10 Martin Biron 6.00 15.00
MGU11 Chris Mason 8.00 20.00
MGU12 Cam Ward 10.00 25.00
MGU13 Tim Thomas 12.00 30.00
MGU14 Pascal Leclaire 8.00 20.00
MGU15 Marty Turco 10.00 25.00
MGU16 Jacques Plante 25.00 60.00
MGU17 Henrik Lundqvist 12.00 30.00
MGU18 Martin Gerber 8.00 20.00
MGU19 Peter Budaj 8.00 20.00
MGU20 Carey Price 30.00 60.00

2008-09 Between The Pipes

This set was released on March 26, 2009. The base set consists of 100 cards.
COMPLETE SET (100) 12.00 30.00
Adam Courchaine .20 .50
Al Montoya .20 .50
Andrew Engelage .20 .50
Antoine Lafleur .20 .50
Ben Bishop .40 1.00
Braden Holtby .60 1.50
Brian Elliott .20 .50
Simeon Varlamov .50 1.25
Chet Pickard .25 .60
0 Chris Carrozzi .20 .50
1 Corey Crawford .30 .75
2 Cory Schneider .60 1.50
3 Curtis McElhinney .20 .50
4 Daren Machesney .20 .50
5 Dustin Tokarski .25 .60
6 Erik Ersberg .20 .50
7 Jacob DeSerres .20 .50
8 Jake Allen .40 1.00
9 Jaroslav Janus .20 .50
0 Jeremy Smith .25 .60
1 Jimmy Howard .40 1.00
2 John Curry .25 .60
3 Jonathan Bernier .30 .75
4 Jonathan Quick .50 1.25
5 Josh Unice .20 .50
6 Justin Pogge .25 .60
7 Kevin Poulin .25 .60
8 Kurtis Mucha .20 .50
9 Kyle Gajewski .20 .50
0 Leland Irving .25 .60
1 Linden Rowat .20 .50
2 Marek Schwarz .25 .60
3 Michael Hutchinson .30 .75
4 Miika Wiikman .25 .60
5 Mike Murphy .25 .60
36 Nolan Schaefer .20 .50
37 Ondrej Pavelec .30 .75
38 Patrick Killeen .20 .50
39 Pekka Rinne .30 .75
40 Peter Delmas .25 .60
41 Raffaele D'Orso .20 .50
42 Robert Mayer .25 .60
43 Steve Mason .40 1.00
44 Steven Stanford .20 .50
45 Thomas McCollum .25 .60
46 Tobias Stephan .20 .50
47 Trevor Cann .20 .50
48 Tuukka Rask .25 .60
49 Tyler Beskorowany .20 .50
50 Tyson Sexsmith .30 .75
51 Nicola Riopel .20 .50
52 Peter Di Salvo .20 .50
53 Jhonas Enroth .20 .50
54 Brandon Foote .20 .50
55 Alain Valiquette .20 .50
56 Jamie Tucker .20 .50
57 J.P. Anderson .20 .50
58 Travis Yonkman .20 .50
59 Timo Pielmeier .20 .50
60 Evgeni Nabokov .20 .50
61 Chris Osgood .25 .60
62 Jonas Hiller .20 .50
63 Carey Price 1.00 2.50
64 Jean-Sebastien Giguere .25 .60
65 Vesa Toskala .20 .50
66 Martin Brodeur .50 1.25
67 Niklas Backstrom .25 .60
68 Manny Fernandez .20 .50
69 Tim Thomas .25 .60
70 Olaf Kolzig .25 .60
71 Cristobal Huet .20 .50
72 Roberto Luongo .30 .75
73 Bill Durnan .25 .60
74 Glenn Hall .20 .50
75 Gump Worsley .20 .50
76 Jacques Plante .40 1.00
77 Johnny Bower .30 .75
78 Roger Crozier .20 .50
79 Terry Sawchuk .30 .75
80 Turk Broda .25 .60
81 Bernie Parent .25 .60
82 Rogie Vachon .30 .75
83 Dominik Hasek .30 .75
84 Ed Giacomin .30 .75
85 Gerry Cheevers .25 .60
86 Grant Fuhr .25 .60
87 John Vanbiesbrouck .25 .60
88 Patrick Roy .60 1.50
89 Pelle Lindbergh .30 .75
90 Tony Esposito .25 .60
91 Ed Belfour .25 .60
92 Gary Smith .20 .50
93 Gerry Desjardins .20 .50
94 Jacques Plante .40 1.00
95 Al Smith .20 .50
96 Gilles Gratton .25 .60
97 Marcel Paille .20 .50
98 George Gardner .20 .50
99 Les Binkley .40 1.00
100 Ernie Wakely .25 .60

2008-09 Between The Pipes Autographs

STATED ODDS 1:12
AAA Alain Valiquette 4.00 10.00
AAC Adam Courchaine 4.00 10.00
AAE Andrew Engelage 4.00 10.00
AAL Antoine Lafleur 4.00 10.00
AAM Al Montoya 4.00 10.00
ABE Brian Elliott 4.00 10.00
ABF Brandon Foote 4.00 10.00
ABH Braden Holtby 12.00 30.00
ABP Bernie Parent SP 8.00 20.00
ACC Chris Carrozzi 4.00 10.00
ACCR Corey Crawford 12.00 30.00
ACH Cristobal Huet 4.00 10.00
ACM Curtis McElhinney 4.00 10.00
ACO Chris Osgood SP 12.00 30.00
ACP Carey Price SP 20.00 50.00
ACPI Chet Pickard 5.00 12.00
ACPR Carey Price SP 20.00 50.00
ACS Cory Schneider 12.00 30.00
ADH Dominik Hasek 15.00 40.00
ADM Daren Machesney 4.00 10.00
ADT Dustin Tokarski 5.00 12.00
AEB Ed Belfour SP
AEE Erik Ersberg 4.00 10.00
AEW Ernie Wakely 5.00 12.00
AFP Felix Potvin SP
AGC Gerry Cheevers 5.00 12.00
AGD Gerry Desjardins 4.00 10.00
AGF Grant Fuhr 12.00 30.00
AGG Gilles Gratton 5.00 12.00
AGS Gary Smith 4.00 10.00
AJA Jake Allen 8.00 20.00
AJB Jonathan Bernier 6.00 15.00
AJC John Curry 5.00 12.00
AJD Jacob DeSerres 4.00 10.00
AJH Jimmy Howard 8.00 20.00
AJHI Jonas Hiller SP 4.00 10.00
AJJ Jaroslav Janus 4.00 10.00
AJP Justin Pogge 5.00 12.00
AJPA J.P. Anderson 4.00 10.00
AJQ Jonathan Quick 20.00 50.00
AJS Jeremy Smith 5.00 12.00
AJSG Jean-Sebastien Giguere SP 12.00 30.00
AJT Jamie Tucker 4.00 10.00
AJU Josh Unice 4.00 10.00
AJV John Vanbiesbrouck SP
AKM Kurtis Mucha 4.00 10.00
AKP Kevin Poulin 5.00 12.00
ALB Les Binkley 8.00 20.00
ALI Leland Irving 5.00 12.00
ALR Linden Rowat 4.00 10.00
AMB Martin Brodeur SP 40.00 80.00
AMF Manny Fernandez SP 4.00 10.00
AMH Michael Hutchinson 6.00 15.00
AMM Mike Murphy 5.00 12.00
AMS Marek Schwarz 5.00 12.00
AMT Marty Turco 5.00 12.00
AMW Miika Wiikman 5.00 12.00
ANR Niklas Backstrom SP 15.00 40.00
ANS Nolan Schaefer 4.00 10.00
AOK Olaf Kolzig 5.00 12.00
AOP Ondrej Pavelec 6.00 15.00
APB Peter Budaj 4.00 10.00
APD Peter Delmas 5.00 12.00
APDI Peter Di Salvo 4.00 10.00
APK Patrick Killeen 4.00 10.00
APR Pekka Rinne 6.00 15.00
APRO Patrick Roy SP 60.00 120.00
ARD Raffaele D'Orso 4.00 10.00
ARG Ed Giacomin SP 12.00 30.00
ARL Roberto Luongo SP 15.00 40.00
ARM Robert Mayer 5.00 12.00
ARV Rogie Vachon SP 10.00 25.00
ASM Steve Mason 8.00 20.00
ASS Steven Stanford 4.00 10.00
ASV Simeon Varlamov 10.00 25.00
ATB Tyler Beskorowany 4.00 10.00
ATC Trevor Cann 4.00 10.00
ATE Tony Esposito SP 20.00 50.00
ATM Thomas McCollum 5.00 12.00
ATR Tuukka Rask 10.00 25.00
ATS Tobias Stephan 4.00 10.00
ATSE Tyson Sexsmith 6.00 15.00
ATT Tim Thomas SP 15.00 40.00
ATY Travis Yonkman 4.00 10.00
AVT Vesa Toskala SP 10.00 25.00
AVTR Vladislav Tretiak 15.00 40.00

2008-09 Between The Pipes Draft Day Duos

OVERALL G-U ODDS 1:20
ANNOUNCED PRINT RUN 50
DDD01 C.Pickard/T.McCollum 6.00 15.00
DDD02 T.Cann/T.Sexsmith
DDD03 J.Bernier/L.Irving 8.00 20.00
DDD04 S.Mason/S.Varlamov 12.00 30.00
DDD05 C.Price/T.Rusk 25.00 60.00
DDD06 A.Montoya/M.Schwarz 6.00 15.00
DDD07 C.Crawford/J.Howard 10.00 25.00
DDD08 J.Harding/H.Toivonen 6.00 15.00
DDD09 P.Leclaire/P.Budaj 5.00 12.00
DDD10 P.Sauve/J.LeBarbera 5.00 12.00
DDD11 R.Luongo/S.Clemmensen 8.00 20.00
DDD12 J.Giguere/B.Boucher 6.00 15.00
DDD13 M.Turco/D.Cloutier
DDD14 G.Fuhr/M.Vernon 6.00 15.00
DDD15 M.Brodeur/F.Potvin 12.00 30.00
DDD16 M.Richter/S.Burke 6.00 15.00
DDD17 P.Roy/K.McLean 15.00 40.00
DDD18 D.Hasek/V.Tretiak 12.50 30.00
DDD19 K.Wregget/R.Hextall 10.00 25.00
DDD20 T.Thomas/E.Nabokov 6.00 15.00

2008-09 Between The Pipes Emblems

OVERALL G-U ODDS 1:20
ANNOUNCED PRINT RUN 19
GUE01 Martin Brodeur 25.00 60.00
GUE02 Peter Budaj 20.00 50.00
GUE03 Corey Crawford 15.00 40.00
GUE04 John Curry 12.00 30.00
GUE05 Peter Delmas 12.00 30.00
GUE06 Brian Elliott 10.00 25.00
GUE07 Tony Esposito
GUE08 Manny Fernandez
GUE09 Jean-Sebastien Giguere 12.00 30.00
GUE10 Jaroslav Halak 12.00 30.00
GUE11 Dominik Hasek
GUE12 Riku Helenius 10.00 25.00
GUE13 Jonas Hiller 20.00 50.00
GUE14 Braden Holtby 25.00 60.00
GUE15 Tim Thomas 20.00 50.00
GUE16 Torrie Jung 8.00 20.00
GUE17 Kris Lazaruk 12.00 30.00
GUE18 Pelle Lindbergh 50.00 100.00
GUE19 Roberto Luongo 25.00 60.00
GUE20 Daren Machesney 10.00 25.00
GUE21 Steve Mason 20.00 50.00
GUE22 Cristobal Huet 10.00 25.00
GUE23 Drew MacIntyre
GUE24 Simeon Varlamov 25.00 60.00
GUE25 Mike Murphy 12.00 30.00
GUE26 Chris Osgood 20.00 50.00
GUE27 Chet Pickard 12.00 30.00
GUE28 Justin Pogge 12.00 30.00
GUE29 Felix Potvin 40.00 100.00
GUE30 Carey Price 25.00 60.00
GUE31 Jonathan Quick 20.00 50.00
GUE32 Pekka Rinne 20.00 50.00
GUE33 Olivier Roy 12.00 30.00
GUE34 Patrick Roy 40.00 100.00
GUE35 Patrick Roy 40.00 100.00
GUE36 Marek Schwarz 12.00 30.00
GUE37 Dustin Tokarski 12.00 30.00
GUE38 Vesa Toskala 10.00 25.00
GUE39 Vladislav Tretiak 40.00 80.00
GUE40 Marty Turco 12.00 30.00
GUE41 Josh Unice 10.00 25.00
GUE42 John Vanbiesbrouck 25.00 60.00
GUE43 Kristofer Westblom 10.00 25.00
GUE44 Miika Wiikman 12.00 30.00
GUE45 Evgeni Nabokov 10.00 25.00

2008-09 Between The Pipes Goaltending Evolution

OVERALL G-U ODDS 1:20
ANNOUNCED PRINT RUN 50
GE01 Roy/Price/Halak 40.00 100.00
GE02 Hasek/Elliott/Glass 12.00 30.00
GE03 Potvin/Toskala/Pogge 15.00 40.00
GE04 Cheevers/Thomas/Rask 10.00 25.00
GE05 Roy/Budaj/Delmas 25.00 60.00
GE06 Belfour/Turco/Stephan 10.00 25.00
GE07 Plante/Price/Halak 40.00 100.00
GE08 Sawchuk/Osgood/Howard 15.00 40.00
GE09 Brodeur/Luongo/Ellis 12.00 30.00
GE10 Sawchuk/Quick/Bernier 20.00 50.00

2008-09 Between The Pipes Great Moments

OVERALL G-U ODDS 1:20
ANNOUNCED PRINT RUN 40
GM01 Jacques Plante 12.00 30.00
GM02 Glenn Hall 6.00 15.00
GM03 Billy Smith 8.00 20.00
GM04 Vladislav Tretiak 10.00 25.00
GM05 Terry Sawchuk 10.00 25.00
GM06 Patrick Roy 20.00 50.00
GM07 Martin Brodeur 15.00 40.00
GM08 Clint Benedict 12.00 30.00

2008-09 Between The Pipes He Shoots He Saves

STATED PRINT RUN 20 SER.#'d SETS
1PT 1 Point EXCH
HSHS01 P.Roy/M.Brodeur 30.00 80.00
HSHS02 O.Kolzig/Varlamov 30.00 80.00
HSHS03 Cheevers/Fernandez 15.00 40.00
HSHS04 T.Esposito/C.Huet 15.00 40.00
HSHS05 T.Thompson/Gardiner 12.00 30.00
HSHS06 R.Brodeur/R.Luongo 20.00 50.00
HSHS07 D.Tokarski/C.Pickard 15.00 40.00
HSHS08 F.Potvin/V.Toskala 30.00 80.00
HSHS09 D.Hasek/C.Osgood 20.00 50.00
HSHS10 Lindbergh/B.Parent 20.00 50.00
HSHS11 P.Roy/C.Price 30.00 80.00
HSHS12 Tretiak/E.Nabokov 25.00 60.00
HSHS13 E.Belfour/M.Turco 15.00 40.00
HSHS14 J.Bower/J.Pogge 20.00 50.00
HSHS15 T.Thomas/T.Rask 20.00 50.00
HSHS16 J.Plante/P.Roy 30.00 80.00
HSHS17 S.Mason/J.Quick 25.00 60.00
HSHS18 P.Roy/P.Budaj 20.00 50.00
HSHS19 Sawchuk/J.Bernier 20.00 50.00
HSHS20 D.Hasek/B.Elliott 20.00 50.00
HSHS21 J.Plante/J.Halak 25.00 60.00
HSHS22 R.Hextall/J.Vanbies 20.00 50.00
HSHS23 G.Hall/C.Crawford 20.00 50.00
HSHS24 M.Brodeur/T.Sawchuk 25.00 60.00
HSHS25 R.Luongo/E.Nabokov 20.00 50.00
HSHS26 J.Giguere/J.Hiller 15.00 40.00
HSHS27 R.Crozier/J.Howard 25.00 60.00
HSHS28 Hainsworth/R.Worters 20.00 50.00
HSHS29 S.Mason/S.Varlamov 30.00 80.00
HSHS30 C.Price/R.Vachon 25.00 60.00

2008-09 Between The Pipes Jerseys

OVERALL G-U ODDS 1:20
ANNOUNCED PRINT RUN 90 SETS
GUJ01 Martin Brodeur SP 20.00 50.00
GUJ02 Peter Budaj 6.00 15.00
GUJ03 Corey Crawford 10.00 25.00
GUJ04 John Curry 8.00 20.00
GUJ05 Peter Delmas 8.00 20.00
GUJ06 Brian Elliott 6.00 15.00
GUJ07 Tony Esposito 8.00 20.00
GUJ08 Manny Fernandez 6.00 15.00
GUJ09 Jean-Sebastien Giguere 8.00 20.00
GUJ10 Jaroslav Halak 8.00 20.00
GUJ11 Dominik Hasek 10.00 25.00
GUJ12 Riku Helenius
GUJ13 Jonas Hiller 6.00 15.00
GUJ14 Braden Holtby 20.00 50.00
GUJ15 Tim Thomas 8.00 20.00
GUJ16 Torrie Jung
GUJ17 Kris Lazaruk 8.00 20.00
GUJ18 Pelle Lindbergh SP 25.00 60.00
GUJ19 Roberto Luongo SP 15.00 40.00
GUJ20 Daren Machesney 6.00 15.00
GUJ21 Steve Mason 25.00 60.00
GUJ22 Cristobal Huet
GUJ23 Drew MacIntyre 8.00 20.00
GUJ24 Simeon Varlamov 12.00 30.00
GUJ25 Mike Murphy 8.00 20.00
GUJ26 Chris Osgood 8.00 20.00
GUJ27 Chet Pickard 8.00 20.00
GUJ28 Justin Pogge 10.00 25.00
GUJ29 Felix Potvin
GUJ30 Carey Price 25.00 60.00
GUJ31 Jonathan Quick 15.00 40.00
GUJ32 Pekka Rinne 10.00 25.00
GUJ33 Olivier Roy 8.00 20.00
GUJ34 Patrick Roy SP 20.00 50.00
GUJ35 Patrick Roy SP 15.00 40.00
GUJ36 Marek Schwarz 8.00 20.00
GUJ37 Dustin Tokarski 8.00 20.00
GUJ38 Vesa Toskala 6.00 15.00
GUJ39 Vladislav Tretiak 15.00 40.00
GUJ40 Marty Turco 8.00 20.00
GUJ41 Josh Unice 6.00 15.00
GUJ42 John Vanbiesbrouck 12.00 30.00
GUJ43 Kristofer Westblom 6.00 15.00
GUJ44 Miika Wiikman 8.00 20.00
GUJ45 Evgeni Nabokov 6.00 15.00

2008-09 Between The Pipes Masked Men

MM01 Chet Pickard 3.00 8.00
MM02 Timo Pielmeier 2.50 6.00
MM03 Carey Price 12.00 30.00
MM04 Corey Crawford 4.00 10.00
MM05 Cory Schneider 8.00 20.00
MM06 Jimmy Howard 5.00 12.00
MM07 Jonathan Bernier 4.00 10.00
MM08 Marek Schwarz 3.00 8.00
MM09 Robert Mayer 3.00 8.00
MM10 Thomas McCollum 3.00 8.00
MM11 Antoine Tardif 3.00 8.00
MM12 Gabriel Girard 2.50 6.00
MM13 Karel St. Laurent 3.00 8.00
MM14 Brent Krahn 4.00 10.00
MM15 Jean-Philippe Levasseur 4.00 10.00
MM16 Peter Delmas 3.00 8.00
MM17 Cristobal Huet 2.50 6.00
MM18 Evgeni Nabokov 2.50 6.00
MM19 Jean-Sebastien Giguere 3.00 8.00
MM20 Martin Brodeur 6.00 15.00
MM21 Patrick Roy 8.00 20.00
MM22 Patrick Roy 8.00 20.00
MM23 Steve Mason 5.00 12.00
MM24 Vesa Toskala 2.50 6.00
MM25 Manny Fernandez 2.50 6.00
MM26 Marty Turco 3.00 8.00
MM27 Justin Pogge 3.00 8.00
MM28 Niklas Backstrom 3.00 8.00
MM29 Olivier Roy 3.00 8.00
MM30 Tim Thomas 3.00 8.00
MM31 Travis Fullerton 2.50 6.00
MM32 Devan Dubnyk 4.00 10.00
MM33 Jacob DeSerres 2.50 6.00
MM34 Marek Benda 3.00 8.00
MM35 Nathan Dunnett 2.50 6.00
MM36 Linden Rowat 2.50 6.00
MM37 Adam Courchaine 2.50 6.00
MM38 Dustin Tokarski 3.00 8.00
MM39 Daniel Larsson 5.00 12.00
MM40 Josh Tordjman 5.00 12.00
MM41 Roberto Luongo 4.00 10.00
MM42 Brian Elliott 2.50 6.00
MM43 Trevor Cann 2.50 6.00
MM44 Ed Belfour 3.00 8.00
MM45 Felix Potvin 5.00 12.00
MM46 Dominik Hasek 4.00 10.00
MM47 Frederic Piche 2.50 6.00
MM48 Jhonas Enroth 2.50 6.00
MM49 Kurtis Mucha 2.50 6.00
MM50 Nolan Schaefer 2.50 6.00

2008-09 Between The Pipes Numbers

ANNOUNCED PRINT RUN 19 SETS
GUN01 Martin Brodeur 20.00 50.00
GUN02 Peter Budaj
GUN03 Corey Crawford 12.00 30.00
GUN04 John Curry 10.00 25.00
GUN05 Peter Delmas 10.00 25.00
GUN06 Brian Elliott
GUN07 Tony Esposito 25.00 50.00
GUN08 Manny Fernandez 8.00 20.00
GUN09 Jean-Sebastien Giguere 10.00 25.00
GUN10 Jaroslav Halak 10.00 25.00
GUN11 Dominik Hasek
GUN12 Riku Helenius 8.00 20.00
GUN13 Jonas Hiller 8.00 20.00
GUN14 Braden Holtby 25.00 60.00
GUN15 Tim Thomas 10.00 25.00
GUN16 Torrie Jung 6.00 15.00
GUN17 Kris Lazaruk 10.00 25.00
GUN18 Pelle Lindbergh 40.00 80.00
GUN19 Roberto Luongo 12.00 30.00
GUN20 Daren Machesney
GUN21 Steve Mason 15.00 40.00
GUN22 Cristobal Huet 15.00 40.00
GUN23 Drew MacIntyre 10.00 25.00
GUN24 Simeon Varlamov 20.00 50.00
GUN25 Mike Murphy
GUN26 Chris Osgood
GUN27 Chet Pickard 10.00 25.00
GUN28 Justin Pogge 10.00 25.00
GUN29 Felix Potvin 15.00 40.00
GUN30 Carey Price 20.00 40.00
GUN31 Jonathan Quick 15.00 40.00
GUN32 Pekka Rinne 12.00 30.00
GUN33 Olivier Roy 10.00 25.00
GUN34 Patrick Roy 25.00 60.00
GUN35 Patrick Roy 25.00 60.00
GUN36 Marek Schwarz 10.00 25.00
GUN37 Dustin Tokarski 10.00 25.00
GUN38 Vesa Toskala 8.00 20.00
GUN39 Vladislav Tretiak 8.00 20.00
GUN40 Marty Turco 10.00 25.00
GUN41 Josh Unice 8.00 20.00
GUN42 John Vanbiesbrouck 10.00 25.00
GUN43 Kristofer Westblom 8.00 20.00
GUN44 Miika Wiikman
GUN45 Evgeni Nabokov 8.00 20.00

2008-09 Between The Pipes Prospect Combos

ANNOUNCED PRINT RUN 90 SETS
PC01 J.Pogge/M.Murphy 5.00 12.00
PC02 B.Elliott/T.Cann 4.00 10.00
PC03 J.Howard/T.McCollum 8.00 20.00
PC04 J.Halak/B.Holtby 10.00 25.00
PC05 M.Schwarz/K.Westblom 5.00 12.00
PC06 P.Rinne/T.Sexsmith 6.00 15.00
PC07 S.Varlamov/N.Riopel 10.00 25.00
PC08 J.Harding/D.Tokarski 5.00 12.00
PC09 J.Quick/O.Roy 10.00 25.00
PC10 C.Crawford/C.Pickard 6.00 15.00
PC11 A.Montoya/S.Mason 8.00 20.00
PC12 L.Irving/K.Lazaruk 5.00 12.00

2008-09 Between The Pipes Super-Sized Pads

OVERALL G-U ODDS 1:20
ANNOUNCED PRINT RUN 30 SETS
SSP01 Patrick Roy 30.00 80.00
SSP02 Patrick Roy 30.00 80.00
SSP03 Martin Brodeur 25.00 60.00
SSP04 Pelle Lindbergh 60.00 120.00
SSP05 Ed Belfour 12.00 30.00
SSP06 Gerry Cheevers 20.00 50.00
SSP07 Grant Fuhr 12.00 30.00
SSP08 Chris Osgood 25.00 60.00
SSP09 Marty Turco 12.00 30.00
SSP10 Vladislav Tretiak 40.00 100.00
SSP11 Ron Hextall 25.00 60.00
SSP12 Bernie Parent 40.00 100.00

2008-09 Between The Pipes Super Glove

ANNOUNCED PRINT RUN 20 SETS
SG01 Martin Brodeur 30.00 80.00
SG02 Peter Budaj 8.00 20.00
SG03 Rick DiPietro 15.00 40.00
SG04 Marc-Andre Fleury 15.00 40.00
SG05 Jean-Sebastien Giguere 10.00 25.00
SG06 Dominik Hasek 12.00 30.00
SG07 Miikka Kiprusoff 15.00 40.00
SG08 Chris Osgood 15.00 40.00
SG09 Felix Potvin 15.00 40.00
SG10 Jose Theodore 10.00 25.00
SG11 Jocelyn Thibault 8.00 20.00
SG12 Vesa Toskala 20.00 50.00
SG13 Marty Turco 10.00 25.00
SG14 Tomas Vokoun 8.00 20.00
SG15 Cam Ward 10.00 25.00
SG16 Roberto Luongo 15.00 40.00
SG17 Patrick Roy 60.00 120.00
SG18 Sean Burke 6.00 15.00
SG19 Olaf Kolzig 15.00 40.00
SG20 Evgeni Nabokov 8.00 20.00

2009-10 Between The Pipes

COMPLETE SET (150) 20.00 50.00
1 Alexander Salak .20 .50
2 Alex Stalock .25 .60
3 Anton Khudobin .25 .60
4 Ben Bishop .25 .60
5 Cedrick Desjardins .40 1.00
6 Chad Johnson .25 .60
7 Chet Pickard .30 .75
8 Cory Schneider .30 .75
9 Daniel Larsson .20 .50
10 Devan Dubnyk .50 1.25
11 Dustin Tokarski .25 .60
12 James Reimer .60 1.50
13 Jhonas Enroth .30 .75
14 Joe Fallon .20 .50
15 Johan Backlund .25 .60
16 John Curry .20 .50
17 Jonathan Bernier .25 .60
18 Justin Pogge .25 .60
19 Kevin Lalande .20 .50
20 Leland Irving .25 .60
21 Mark Dekanich .20 .50
22 Matt Climie .20 .50
23 Michal Neuvirth .40 1.00
24 Mike Brodeur .25 .60
25 Mike McKenna .20 .50
26 Mike Murphy .25 .60
27 Nathan Lawson .20 .50
28 Thomas McCollum .25 .60
29 Trevor Cann .30 .75
30 Tyler Weiman .25 .60
31 Andrew Hayes .20 .50
32 Adam Brown .20 .50
33 Adam Morrison .20 .50
34 Calvin Pickard .40 1.00
35 Darcy Kuemper .25 .60
36 Drew Owsley .20 .50
37 Garrett Zemlak .20 .50
38 James Reid .25 .60
39 Jamie Tucker .20 .50
40 Kent Simpson .20 .50
41 Linden Rowat .20 .50
42 Martin Jones .40 1.00
43 Nathan Lieuwen .30 .75
44 Torrie Jung .20 .50
45 Tyler Bunz .20 .50
46 Antoine Tardif .20 .50
47 Jake Allen .40 1.00
48 Kevin Poulin .25 .60
49 Louis Domingue .30 .75
50 Marc-Antoine Gelinas .25 .60
51 Marco Cousineau .20 .50
52 Mathieu Corbeil-Theriault .20 .50
53 Matthew Dopud .20 .50
54 Maxime Clermont .20 .50
55 Mickael Audette .20 .50
56 Nathan Dunnett .20 .50
57 Nicolas Champion .20 .50
58 Olivier Roy .25 .60
59 Peter Delmas .20 .50
60 Jacob Markstrom .40 1.00
61 Brandon Maxwell .20 .50
62 Chris Carrozzi .25 .60
63 Edward Pasquale .25 .60
64 Jason Missiaen .20 .50
65 J.P. Anderson .20 .50
66 Matt Hackett .30 .75
67 Michael Houser .30 .75
68 Michael Hutchinson .30 .75
69 Patrick Killeen .20 .50
70 Peter Di Salvo .25 .60
71 Philipp Grubauer .30 .75
72 Robin Lehner .20 .50
73 Scott Stajcer .20 .50
74 Troy Passingham .20 .50
75 Tyler Beskorowany .20 .50
76 Antti Niemi .40 1.00
77 Cam Ward .25 .60
78 Carey Price 1.00 2.50
79 Chris Osgood .25 .60
80 Evgeni Nabokov .20 .50
81 Ilya Bryzgalov .20 .50
82 Jean-Sebastien Giguere .25 .60
83 Jaroslav Halak .25 .60
84 Jimmy Howard .30 .75
85 Jonas Hiller .20 .50
86 Josh Harding .25 .60
87 Kari Lehtonen .20 .50
88 Manny Legace .20 .50
89 Marc-Andre Fleury .40 1.00
90 Martin Brodeur .50 1.25
91 Marty Turco .25 .60
92 Miikka Kiprusoff .20 .50
93 Niklas Backstrom .25 .60
94 Tuukka Rask .25 .60
95 Ondrej Pavelec .30 .75
96 Pascal Leclaire .25 .60
97 Ray Emery .20 .50
98 Rick DiPietro .20 .50
99 Roberto Luongo .30 .75
100 Ryan Miller .25 .60
101 Scott Clemmensen .20 .50
102 Simeon Varlamov .25 .60
103 Cristobal Huet .25 .60
104 Tim Thomas .25 .60
105 Tomas Vokoun .20 .50
106 Vesa Toskala .25 .60
107 Allan Bester .20 .50
108 Andy Moog .40 1.00
109 Bernie Parent .25 .60
110 Bill Durnan .25 .60
111 Billy Smith .25 .60
112 Brian Hayward .20 .50
113 Bunny Larocque .20 .50
114 Dan Bouchard .20 .50
115 Dominik Hasek .30 .75
116 Charlie Hodge .20 .50
117 Ed Giacomin .30 .75
118 Ed Johnston .40 1.00
119 Felix Potvin .40 1.00
120 Gerry Cheevers .25 .60
121 Gilles Meloche .25 .60
122 Gilles Villemure .30 .75
123 Glenn Hall .50 1.25
124 Grant Fuhr .25 .60
125 Gump Worsley .40 1.00
126 Harry Lumley .25 .60
127 Jacques Plante .40 1.00
128 Georges Vezina .30 .75
129 Johnny Bower .30 .75
130 Mike Liut .30 .75
131 Patrick Roy .60 1.50
132 Pelle Lindbergh .30 .75
133 Pete Peeters .40 1.00
134 Richard Brodeur .25 .60
135 Rogie Vachon .30 .75
136 Ron Hextall .40 1.00
137 Terry Sawchuk .30 .75
138 Tony Esposito .25 .60
139 Turk Broda .25 .60
140 Vladislav Tretiak .25 .60
141 Don McLeod .25 .60
142 Pat Riggin .30 .75
143 Jim Corsi .30 .75
144 Gary Bromley .30 .75
145 George Gardner .20 .50
146 Ron Grahame .20 .50
147 Gary Inness .40 1.00
148 Mike Curran .20 .50
149 Ken Brown .20 .50
150 Wayne Rutledge .20 .50

2009-10 Between The Pipes AHL Rookies

COMPLETE SET (9) 15.00 40.00
STATED ODDS 1:8
AR01 Chad Johnson 2.50 6.00
AR02 Braden Holtby 6.00 15.00
AR03 Anton Khudobin 2.50 6.00
AR04 Dustin Tokarski 2.50 6.00
AR05 Alexander Salak 2.00 5.00
AR06 Alex Stalock 2.50 6.00
AR07 Chet Pickard 3.00 8.00
AR08 Mike Murphy 2.50 6.00
AR09 Thomas McCollum 2.50 6.00

2009-10 Between The Pipes Autographs

OVERALL STATED ODDS 1:8
AAA Alex Auld SP 8.00 20.00
AAB Allan Bester SP 8.00 20.00
AAK Anton Khudobin 5.00 12.00
AAM Andy Moog 8.00 20.00
AAN Antero Niittymaki SP 10.00 25.00
AAS Alexander Salak 4.00 10.00
ABB Ben Bishop 5.00 12.00
ABH Brian Hayward 4.00 10.00
ABM Brandon Maxwell 4.00 10.00
ABP Bernie Parent SP 10.00 25.00
ABS Billy Smith 5.00 12.00
ACC Chris Carrozzi SP 10.00 25.00
ACD Cedrick Desjardins 8.00 20.00
ACH Cristobal Huet 5.00 12.00
ACJ Chad Johnson 5.00 12.00
ACO Chris Osgood 5.00 12.00
ACP Chet Pickard SP 12.00 30.00
ACS Cory Schneider 6.00 15.00
ADB Dan Bouchard 4.00 10.00
ADH Dominik Hasek SP 20.00 50.00
ADL Daniel Larsson 4.00 10.00
ADM Don McLeod 6.00 15.00
ADO Drew Owsley 4.00 10.00
ADT Dustin Tokarski SP 10.00 25.00
AEE Erik Ersberg 4.00 10.00
AEG Ed Giacomin SP 12.00 30.00
AEJ Ed Johnston 8.00 20.00
AEN Evgeni Nabokov 4.00 10.00
AEP Edward Pasquale 5.00 12.00
AFP Felix Potvin SP 25.00 50.00
AGB Gary Bromley 6.00 15.00
AGC Gerry Cheevers SP 10.00 25.00
AGF Grant Fuhr 5.00 12.00
AGH Glenn Hall SP 20.00 50.00
AGI Gary Inness 8.00 20.00
AGM Gilles Meloche 5.00 12.00
AGV Gilles Villemure 6.00 15.00
AGW Gump Worsley SP 15.00 40.00
AGZ Garrett Zemlak 4.00 10.00
AHT Hannu Toivonen 5.00 12.00
AJA Jake Allen 8.00 20.00
AJB Johan Backlund 5.00 12.00
AJC Jim Corsi 6.00 15.00
AJE Jhonas Enroth 6.00 15.00
AJG Jean-Sebastien Giguere 5.00 12.00
AJL Jason Labarbera 4.00 10.00
AJM Jason Missiaen 4.00 10.00
AJP Justin Pogge SP 10.00 25.00
AJQ Jonathan Quick 12.00 30.00
AJR James Reimer 12.00 30.00
AJT Jamie Tucker SP 8.00 20.00
AKP Kevin Poulin 5.00 12.00
AKS Kent Simpson 4.00 10.00
ALD Louis Domingue 6.00 15.00
ALI Leland Irving 5.00 12.00
ALR Linden Rowatt SP
AMA Mickael Audette 4.00 10.00
AMC Matt Climie 4.00 10.00
AMG Marc-Antoine Gelinas 5.00 12.00
AMH Matt Hackett 6.00 15.00
AMJ Martin Jones 6.00 15.00
AMK Miikka Kiprusoff 4.00 10.00
AML Mike Liut 6.00 15.00
AMM Mike McKenna 4.00 10.00
AMN Michal Neuvirth 8.00 20.00
AMT Marty Turco 5.00 12.00
ANB Niklas Backstrom 6.00 15.00
ANL Nathan Lawson 4.00 10.00
AOP Ondrej Pavelec 6.00 15.00
AOR Olivier Roy 5.00 12.00
APB Peter Budaj 4.00 10.00
APD Peter Delmas 4.00 10.00
APG Philipp Grubauer 6.00 15.00
APK Patrick Killeen 4.00 10.00
APP Pete Peeters 8.00 20.00
APR Patrick Roy SP 30.00 60.00
ARB Richard Brodeur SP 10.00 25.00
ARE Ray Emery 4.00 10.00
ARG Ron Grahame 4.00 10.00
ARH Ron Hextall 8.00 20.00
ARL Robin Lehner 4.00 10.00
ARV Rogie Vachon SP 12.00 30.00
ASS Scott Stajcer 4.00 10.00
ASV Simeon Varlamov 5.00 12.00
ATB Tyler Beskorowany 4.00 10.00
ATC Trevor Cann SP 12.00 30.00
ATE Tony Esposito SP 15.00 40.00
ATM Thomas McCollum SP 10.00 25.00
ATP Troy Passingham 4.00 10.00
ATR Tuukka Rask SP 10.00 25.00
ATT Tim Thomas SP 15.00 30.00
ATV Tomas Vokoun 4.00 10.00
ATW Tyler Weiman 5.00 12.00
AVT Vesa Toskala 5.00 12.00
AAM2 Andy Moog 8.00 20.00
AAST Alex Stalock 5.00 12.00
ABH2 Brian Hayward 4.00 10.00
ABP2 Bernie Parent SP 10.00 25.00
ACHO Charlie Hodge SP 8.00 20.00
ACPI Calvin Pickard 8.00 20.00
ACPR Carey Price 15.00 40.00
ADB2 Dan Bouchard 4.00 10.00
ADH2 Dominik Hasek SP 20.00 50.00
AEG2 Ed Giacomin SP 12.00 30.00
AGB2 Gary Bromley 6.00 15.00
AGC2 Gerry Cheevers SP 10.00 25.00
AGH2 Glenn Hall SP 20.00 50.00
AGI2 Gary Inness 8.00 20.00
AGM2 Gilles Meloche 5.00 12.00
AGW2 Gump Worsley SP 15.00 40.00
AJAN J.P. Anderson SP 8.00 20.00
AJBE Jonathan Bernier 5.00 12.00
AJBO Johnny Bower SP 12.00 30.00
AJMA Jacob Markstrom 25.00 50.00
AJRE James Reid 5.00 12.00
AMBR Martin Brodeur SP 40.00 100.00
AMCL Maxime Clermont 4.00 10.00
AMCO Marco Cousineau 4.00 10.00
AMHU Michael Hutchinson 6.00 15.00
AML2 Mike Liut 6.00 15.00
ANLI Nathan Lieuwen 6.00 15.00
APDI Peter Di Salvo 5.00 12.00
APP2 Pete Peeters 8.00 20.00
APR2 Pat Riggin 6.00 15.00
APRI Pat Riggin 6.00 15.00
ARB2 Richard Brodeur SP 10.00 25.00
ARLU Roberto Luongo SP 12.00 30.00
ARV2 Rogie Vachon SP 12.00 30.00
ATE2 Tony Esposito SP 15.00 40.00
AVTR Vladislav Tretiak 20.00 50.00
ACHO2 Charlie Hodge SP 8.00 20.00
AJBO2 Johnny Bower SP 12.00 30.00

2009-10 Between The Pipes Brodeur Tribute

COMPLETE SET (9) 25.00 50.00
COMMON BRODEUR 3.00 8.00
OVERALL STATED ODDS 1:8

2009-10 Between The Pipes CHL Rookies

COMPLETE SET (9) 15.00 40.00
STATED ODDS 1:8
CR01 Michael Houser 3.00 8.00
CR02 Petr Mrazek 6.00 15.00
CR03 Tyson Teichmann 2.00 5.00
CR04 Brandon Anderson 2.00 5.00
CR05 Hudson Stremmel 3.00 8.00
CR06 Jordan Binnington 2.00 5.00
CR07 Guillaume Nadeau 3.00 8.00
CR08 Philippe Tremblay 2.00 5.00
CR09 Robin Gusse 2.50 6.00

2009-10 Between The Pipes Glove Save Black

STATED PRINT RUN 30 SER.#'d SETS
GS01 Cam Ward 12.00 30.00
GS02 Chris Osgood 12.00 30.00
GS03 Dominik Hasek 15.00 40.00
GS04 Ed Belfour 12.00 30.00
GS05 Evgeni Nabokov 10.00 25.00
GS06 Felix Potvin 20.00 50.00
GS07 Gerry Cheevers 12.00 30.00

GS08 Grant Fuhr 12.00 30.00
GS09 Hannu Toivonen 12.00 30.00
GS10 Jose Theodore 12.00 30.00
GS11 Jean-Sebastien Giguere 12.00 30.00
GS12 Kirk McLean 25.00 60.00
GS13 Leland Irving 12.00 30.00
GS14 Manny Fernandez 10.00 25.00
GS15 Manny Legace 10.00 25.00
GS16 Marc-Andre Fleury 20.00 50.00
GS17 Martin Brodeur 25.00 60.00
GS18 Marty Turco
GS19 Miikka Kiprusoff 10.00 25.00
GS20 Olaf Kolzig 12.00 30.00
GS21 Patrick Roy 15.00 40.00
GS22 Peter Budaj 10.00 25.00
GS23 Rick DiPietro 10.00 25.00
GS24 Roberto Luongo 15.00 40.00
GS25 Ron Hextall 20.00 50.00
GS26 Ryan Miller 25.00 50.00
GS27 Sean Burke 8.00 20.00
GS28 Tomas Vokoun 10.00 25.00
GS29 Tony Esposito 12.00 30.00
GS30 Vesa Toskala 12.00 30.00

2009-10 Between The Pipes Gold Medal Masks

COMPLETE SET (9) 30.00 60.00
OVERALL STATED ODDS 1:8
GMM01 Tomas Vokoun 2.50 6.00
GMM02 Martin Brodeur 5.00 12.00
GMM03 Ilya Bryzgalov 2.50 6.00
GMM04 Jonas Hiller 2.50 6.00
GMM05 Miikka Kiprusoff 2.50 6.00
GMM06 Ryan Miller 3.00 8.00
GMM07 Roberto Luongo 4.00 10.00
GMM08 Jaroslav Halak 3.00 8.00
GMM09 Evgeni Nabokov 2.50 6.00

2009-10 Between The Pipes He Shoots He Saves Prizes

STATED PRINT RUN 30 SER.#'d SETS
HS01 Billy Smith
HS02 Ron Hextall 40.00 80.00
HS03 Ron Hextall 40.00 80.00
HS04 Chris Osgood 15.00 30.00
HS05 Martin Brodeur 40.00 80.00
HS06 Damian Rhodes 15.00 30.00
HS07 Martin Brodeur 40.00 80.00
HS08 Jose Theodore 15.00 40.00
HS09 Evgeni Nabokov 12.00 30.00
HS10 Mika Noronen 10.00 25.00
HS11 Chris Mason 15.00 40.00

2009-10 Between The Pipes Homegrown Black

STATED PRINT RUN 60 SER.#'d SETS
HG1 Martin Brodeur 12.00 30.00
HG2 Marc-Andre Fleury 12.00 30.00
HG3 Marty Turco 6.00 15.00
HG4 Roberto Luongo 8.00 20.00
HG5 Carey Price 25.00 60.00
HG6 Tomas Vokoun 5.00 12.00
HG7 Kari Lehtonen 5.00 12.00
HG8 Tuukka Rask 6.00 15.00
HG9 Miikka Kiprusoff 5.00 12.00
HG10 Niklas Backstrom 12.00 30.00
HG11 Vesa Toskala 6.00 15.00
HG12 Olaf Kolzig 6.00 15.00
HG13 Peter Budaj 5.00 12.00
HG14 Jaroslav Halak 6.00 15.00
HG15 Jacob Markstrom 15.00 40.00
HG16 Pelle Lindbergh 25.00 60.00
HG17 Evgeni Nabokov 5.00 12.00
HG18 Jonas Hiller 5.00 12.00
HG19 Tim Thomas 6.00 15.00
HG20 Rick DiPietro 5.00 12.00
HG21 Ryan Miller 15.00 40.00
HG22 Jonathan Quick 12.00 30.00
HG23 Ilya Bryzgalov 5.00 12.00
HG24 Simeon Varlamov 6.00 15.00

2009-10 Between The Pipes International Crease Black

STATED PRINT RUN 60 SER.#'d SETS
IC01 Brodeur/Luongo/Roy 30.00 80.00
IC02 Thomas/Miller/Craig 25.00 60.00
IC03 Markstrom/Lundqvist/Lindbergh 25.00 60.00
IC04 Kiprusoff/Lehtonen/Toskala 20.00 50.00
IC05 Varlamov/Bryzgalov/Tretiak 15.00 40.00
IC06 Pavelec/Vokoun/Hasek 15.00 40.00

2009-10 Between The Pipes Jerseys Black

M1-M45 ANNOUNCED PRINT RUN 130
M01 J.P. Anderson 4.00 10.00
M02 Martin Brodeur 10.00 25.00
M03 Peter Budaj 4.00 10.00
M04 Trevor Cann 6.00 15.00
M05 Maxime Clermont 4.00 10.00
M06 John Curry 4.00 10.00
M07 Peter Delmas 4.00 10.00
M08 Cedrick Desjardins 8.00 20.00
M09 Louis Domingue 6.00 15.00
M10 Brian Elliott 4.00 10.00
M11 Andrew Engelage 10.00 25.00
M12 Marc-Andre Fleury 10.00 25.00
M13 Jean-Sebastien Giguere 8.00 20.00
M14 Jacob Markstrom 8.00 20.00
M15 Dominik Hasek 10.00 25.00
M16 Riku Helenius 5.00 12.00
M17 Braden Holtby 12.00 30.00
M18 Torrie Jung 4.00 10.00
M19 Anton Khudobin 5.00 12.00
M20 Kari Lehtonen 4.00 10.00
M21 Nathan Lieuwen 6.00 15.00
M22 Roberto Luongo 6.00 15.00
M23 Daren Machesney 4.00 10.00
M24 Drew MacIntyre 8.00 20.00
M25 Ryan Miller 8.00 20.00
M26 Mike Murphy 5.00 12.00
M27 Evgeni Nabokov 4.00 10.00
M28 Edward Pasquale 5.00 12.00
M29 Calvin Pickard 8.00 20.00
M30 Chet Pickard 6.00 15.00
M31 Felix Potvin 8.00 20.00
M32 Carey Price 20.00 50.00
M33 Jonathan Quick 10.00 25.00
M34 Nicola Riopel 4.00 10.00
M35 Olivier Roy 5.00 12.00
M36 Patrick Roy 12.00 30.00
M37 Patrick Roy 12.00 30.00
M38 Scott Stajcer 4.00 10.00
M39 Tim Thomas 5.00 12.00
M40 Dustin Tokarski 5.00 12.00
M41 Jamie Tucker 4.00 10.00
M42 Simeon Varlamov 5.00 12.00
M43 Mark Visentin 4.00 10.00
M44 Cam Ward 5.00 12.00
M45 Miika Wiikman 5.00 12.00
M46 Tony Esposito/40* 8.00 20.00
M47 Bernie Parent/40* 8.00 20.00
M48 Glenn Hall/40* 15.00 40.00
M49 Ed Giacomin/40* 10.00 25.00
M50 Ron Hextall/40* 12.00 30.00

2009-10 Between The Pipes Jerseys Silver

M1-M45 ANNOUNCED PRINT RUN 19
M46-M50 UNPRICED ANNOUNCED PRINT RUN 9
M02 Martin Brodeur 15.00 40.00
M03 Peter Budaj 6.00 15.00
M04 Trevor Cann 10.00 25.00
M05 Maxime Clermont 6.00 15.00
M06 John Curry 6.00 15.00
M07 Peter Delmas 6.00 15.00
M08 Cedrick Desjardins 12.00 30.00
M09 Louis Domingue 10.00 25.00
M10 Brian Elliott 6.00 15.00
M11 Andrew Engelage 15.00 40.00
M13 Jean-Sebastien Giguere 8.00 20.00
M14 Jacob Markstrom 12.00 30.00
M15 Dominik Hasek 10.00 25.00
M16 Riku Helenius 8.00 20.00
M17 Braden Holtby 20.00 50.00
M20 Kari Lehtonen 6.00 15.00
M21 Nathan Lieuwen 10.00 25.00
M22 Roberto Luongo 10.00 25.00
M23 Daren Machesney 6.00 15.00
M25 Ryan Miller 8.00 20.00
M27 Evgeni Nabokov 6.00 15.00
M28 Edward Pasquale 8.00 20.00
M31 Felix Potvin 12.00 30.00
M32 Carey Price 30.00 80.00
M33 Jonathan Quick 15.00 40.00
M35 Olivier Roy 8.00 20.00
M37 Patrick Roy 20.00 50.00
M39 Tim Thomas 8.00 20.00
M40 Dustin Tokarski 8.00 20.00
M41 Jamie Tucker 6.00 15.00
M42 Simeon Varlamov 8.00 20.00
M44 Cam Ward 8.00 20.00
M45 Miika Wiikman 8.00 20.00

2009-10 Between The Pipes Masked Men II

*GOLD/20: 1.5X TO 4X BASIC INSERTS
MM01 Gilles Gratton 3.00 8.00
MM02 Brian Hayward 2.50 6.00
MM03 Denis Herron 2.50 6.00
MM04 Patrick Roy 8.00 20.00
MM05 Felix Potvin 5.00 12.00
MM06 Ed Belfour 3.00 8.00
MM07 Ron Hextall 5.00 12.00
MM08 Martin Brodeur 6.00 15.00
MM09 Jimmy Howard 4.00 10.00
MM10 Evgeni Nabokov 2.50 6.00
MM11 Michael Houser 4.00 10.00
MM12 Mike McKenna 2.50 6.00
MM13 Tuukka Rask 2.50 6.00
MM14 Michal Neuvirth 5.00 12.00
MM15 Chet Pickard 4.00 10.00
MM16 James Reimer 8.00 20.00
MM17 Jean-Francois Berube 2.50 6.00
MM18 Evan Mosher 2.50 6.00
MM19 Olivier Roy 3.00 8.00
MM20 Frederic Piche 2.50 6.00
MM21 Patrick Roy 8.00 20.00
MM22 Jacques Plante 5.00 12.00
MM23 Grant Fuhr 3.00 8.00
MM24 Mark Dekanich 2.50 6.00
MM25 Chris Carrozzi 3.00 8.00
MM26 Riku Helenius 3.00 8.00
MM27 Braden Holtby 8.00 20.00
MM28 Dan LaCosta 2.50 6.00
MM29 Peter Mannino 3.00 8.00
MM30 Kevin Regan 3.00 8.00
MM31 Jeff Zatkoff 3.00 8.00
MM32 Jean-Philipp Gagnon 2.50 6.00
MM33 Tim Thomas 3.00 8.00
MM34 Miikka Kiprusoff 2.50 6.00
MM35 Roberto Luongo 4.00 10.00
MM36 Carey Price 12.00 30.00
MM37 Cristobal Huet 3.00 8.00
MM38 Ilya Bryzgalov 2.50 6.00
MM39 Scott Clemmensen 2.50 6.00
MM40 Louis Domingue 4.00 10.00
MM41 Craig Anderson 3.00 8.00
MM42 Ed Giacomin 4.00 10.00
MM43 Jason LaBarbera 2.50 6.00
MM44 Marc-Andre Fleury 5.00 12.00
MM45 Simeon Varlamov 3.00 8.00
MM46 Ryan Miller 3.00 8.00
MM47 Matthew Hackett 4.00 10.00
MM48 Chris Perugini 2.50 6.00
MM49 Cody St. Jacques 2.50 6.00
MM50 Doug Favell 3.00 8.00

2009-10 Between The Pipes Mega Stars Black

STATED PRINT RUN 60 SER.#'d SETS
MS01 Patrick Roy 20.00 50.00
MS02 Felix Potvin 12.00 30.00
MS03 Chris Osgood 8.00 20.00
MS04 Ed Belfour 8.00 20.00
MS05 Martin Brodeur 15.00 40.00
MS06 Dominik Hasek 12.00 30.00
MS07 Martin Brodeur 15.00 40.00
MS08 Ed Belfour 8.00 20.00
MS09 Dominik Hasek 12.00 30.00
MS10 Patrick Roy 20.00 50.00
MS11 Arturs Irbe 8.00 20.00
MS12 Dominik Hasek 12.00 30.00
MS13 Olaf Kolzig 8.00 20.00
MS14 Martin Brodeur 15.00 40.00
MS15 Mike Richter 12.00 30.00
MS16 Tommy Salo 6.00 15.00
MS17 Dominik Hasek 12.00 30.00
MS18 Martin Brodeur 15.00 40.00
MS19 Patrick Roy 20.00 50.00
MS20 Evgeni Nabokov 6.00 15.00
MS21 Patrick Roy 20.00 50.00
MS22 Dominik Hasek 12.00 30.00
MS23 Patrick Roy 12.00 30.00
MS24 Rick DiPietro 6.00 15.00

2009-10 Between The Pipes Net Brawlers

COMPLETE SET (9) 40.00 80.00
OVERALL STATED ODDS 1:8
NB01 A.Montoya/R.DiPietro 4.00 10.00
NB02 T.Conklin/P.Nurminen 3.00 8.00
NB03 C.Osgood/P.Roy 10.00 25.00
NB04 J.Hurme/F.Potvin 6.00 15.00
NB05 O.Kolzig/B.Dafoe 4.00 10.00
NB06 T.Voukon/M.Kiprusoff 3.00 8.00
NB07 C.Crawford/A.Montoya 5.00 12.00
NB08 M.Leighton/J.Howard 5.00 12.00
NB09 R.Hextall/F.Potvin 6.00 15.00

2009-10 Between The Pipes Origins Black

STATED PRINT RUN 40 SER.#'d SETS
O01 Gerry Cheevers 8.00 20.00
O02 Tony Esposito 8.00 20.00
O03 Bernie Parent 8.00 20.00
O04 Billy Smith 8.00 20.00
O05 Rogie Vachon 10.00 25.00
O06 Ed Belfour 8.00 20.00
O07 Miikka Kiprusoff 6.00 15.00
O08 Dominik Hasek 10.00 25.00
O09 Roberto Luongo 10.00 25.00
O10 Jean-Sebastien Giguere 8.00 20.00

2009-10 Between The Pipes Pad Save Black

STATED PRINT RUN 60 SER.#'d SETS
PS01 David Aebischer 12.00 30.00
PS02 Ed Belfour 10.00 25.00
PS03 Brian Boucher 8.00 20.00
PS04 Martin Brodeur 20.00 50.00
PS05 Sean Burke 6.00 15.00
PS06 Gerry Cheevers 10.00 25.00
PS07 Dan Cloutier 8.00 20.00
PS08 Robert Esche 10.00 25.00
PS09 Grant Fuhr 10.00 25.00
PS10 Ron Hextall 15.00 40.00
PS11 Leland Irving 10.00 25.00
PS12 Curtis Joseph 12.00 30.00
PS13 Nikolai Khabibulin 10.00 25.00
PS14 Patrick Lalime 8.00 20.00
PS15 Pelle Lindbergh 40.00 100.00
PS16 Chris Osgood 10.00 25.00
PS17 Bernie Parent 20.00 50.00
PS18 Patrick Roy 15.00 40.00
PS19 Patrick Roy 15.00 40.00
PS20 Jose Theodore 10.00 25.00
PS21 Tim Thomas 10.00 25.00
PS22 Vladislav Tretiak 30.00 80.00
PS23 Marty Turco 10.00 25.00
PS24 Mike Vernon 8.00 20.00
PS25 Tomas Vokoun 8.00 20.00

2009-10 Between The Pipes Stick Save Black

STATED PRINT RUN 20 SER.#'d SETS
SS01 Carey Price 30.00 60.00
SS02 Chris Osgood 20.00 40.00
SS03 Evgeni Nabokov 20.00 40.00
SS04 Steve Mason 20.00 40.00
SS05 Ilya Bryzgalov 25.00 50.00
SS06 Jimmy Howard 25.00 50.00
SS07 John Vanbiesbrouck 25.00 60.00
SS08 Jonas Gustavsson 20.00 40.00
SS09 Jonas Hiller 20.00 40.00
SS10 Mike Richter 25.00 50.00
SS11 Jean-Sebastien Giguere 20.00 40.00
SS12 Cristobal Huet 20.00 40.00
SS13 Ken Dryden 100.00 200.00
SS14 Marc-Andre Fleury 40.00 80.00
SS15 Martin Brodeur 40.00 80.00
SS16 Marty Turco 20.00 40.00
SS17 Miikka Kiprusoff 20.00 40.00
SS18 Mike Smith 20.00 40.00
SS19 Niklas Backstrom 20.00 40.00
SS20 Pascal Leclaire 20.00 40.00
SS21 Patrick Roy 60.00 120.00
SS22 Pekka Rinne 25.00 50.00
SS23 Pelle Lindbergh 60.00 120.00
SS24 Roberto Luongo 25.00 50.00
SS25 Ed Belfour 25.00 50.00
SS26 Nikolai Khabibulin 25.00 50.00
SS27 Tim Thomas 25.00 50.00
SS28 Tomas Vokoun 20.00 40.00
SS29 Tuukka Rask 20.00 40.00
SS30 Vesa Toskala 20.00 40.00

2010-11 Between The Pipes

COMPLETE SET (200) 20.00 50.00
1 Adam Brown .20 .50
2 Mickael Audette .20 .50
3 Antonio Mastropietro .20 .50
4 Brandon Maxwell .20 .50
5 Calvin Pickard .25 .60
6 Cam Lanigan .20 .50
7 Christopher Gibson .30 .75
8 Darcy Kuemper .25 .60
9 David Honzik .20 .50
10 Drew Owsley .20 .50
11 Evan Mosher .20 .50
12 Frederic Piche .20 .50
13 Gabriel Girard .20 .50
14 Guillaume Nadeau .25 .60
15 Igor Bobkov .40 1.00
16 Jack Campbell .25 .60
17 James Reid .20 .50
18 Jean-Francois Berube .25 .60
19 Jordan Binnington .20 .50
20 J.P. Anderson .25 .60
21 Kent Simpson .20 .50
22 Liam Liston .20 .50
23 Louis Domingue .25 .60
24 Mac Carruth .20 .50
25 Malcolm Subban .50 1.25
26 Mark Friesen .20 .50
27 Mark Segal .20 .50
28 Mark Visentin .25 .60
29 Mavric Parks .20 .50
30 Maxime Clermont .20 .50
31 Michael Houser .20 .50
32 Nathan Lieuwen .20 .50
33 Nicolas Champion .20 .50
34 Olivier Roy .25 .60
35 Petr Mrazek .50 1.25
36 Philipp Grubauer .30 .75
37 Ramis Sadikov .25 .60
38 Robin Gusse .25 .60
39 Scott Stajcer .20 .50
40 Scott Wedgewood .20 .50
41 Steven Stanford .20 .50
42 Thomas Heemskerk .20 .50
43 Ty Rimmer .20 .50
44 Tyler Bunz .20 .50
45 Tyson Teichmann .20 .50
46 Alec Richards .20 .50
47 Alex Stalock .25 .60
48 Anton Khudobin .20 .50
49 Ben Bishop .25 .60
50 Brad Thiessen .25 .60
51 Braden Holtby .50 1.25
52 Carter Hutton .40 1.00
53 Cedrick Desjardins .25 .60
54 Chad Johnson .20 .50
55 Chet Pickard .20 .50
56 David Leggio .20 .50
57 Dustin Tokarski .20 .50
58 Eddie Lack .25 .60
59 Jacob Markstrom .30 .75
60 Jake Allen .40 1.00
61 James Reimer .25 .60
62 Jean-Philippe Levasseur .20 .50
63 Jeff Deslauriers .15 .40
64 Jeff Frazee .30 .75
65 Jeff Zatkoff .25 .60
66 Jeremy Smith .25 .60
67 Jhonas Enroth .25 .60
68 Johan Backlund .20 .50
69 John Curry .20 .50
70 Jussi Rynnas .25 .60
71 Justin Pogge .20 .50
72 Kevin Poulin .25 .60
73 Leland Irving .25 .60
74 Mark Dekanich .20 .50
75 Martin Jones .40 1.00
76 Matt Climie .20 .50
77 Matt Hackett .25 .60
78 Michael Hutchinson .30 .75
79 Mike Murphy .25 .60
80 Mikko Koskinen .25 .60
81 Richard Bachman .25 .60
82 Robert Mayer .25 .60
83 Robin Lehner .40 1.00
84 Thomas McCollum .25 .60
85 Timo Pielmeier RC .25 .60
86 Tyler Weiman .20 .50
87 Alex Auld .20 .50
88 Andrew Raycroft .20 .50
89 Antero Niittymaki .20 .50
90 Antti Niemi .20 .50
91 Brian Boucher .20 .50
92 Brian Elliott .20 .50
93 Cam Ward .25 .60
94 Carey Price 1.00 2.50
95 Chris Mason .20 .50
96 Chris Osgood .25 .60
97 Corey Crawford .30 .75
98 Cory Schneider .20 .50
99 Craig Anderson .25 .60
100 Curtis McElhinney .20 .50
101 Dan Ellis .20 .50
102 Devan Dubnyk .25 .60
103 Dwayne Roloson .20 .50
104 Evgeni Nabokov .20 .50
105 Henrik Lundqvist .40 1.00
106 Ilya Bryzgalov .20 .50
107 Jean-Sebastien Giguere .20 .50
108 Jaroslav Halak .25 .60
109 Jason LaBarbera .20 .50
110 Jimmy Howard .30 .75
111 Johan Hedberg .20 .50
112 Jonas Hiller .20 .50
113 Jonathan Bernier .25 .60
114 Jonathan Quick .40 1.00
115 Josh Harding .25 .60
116 Justin Peters .20 .50
117 Kari Lehtonen .20 .50
118 Marc-Andre Fleury .40 1.00
119 Martin Biron .20 .50
120 Martin Brodeur .50 1.25
121 Martin Gerber .20 .50
122 Marty Turco .25 .60
123 Mathieu Garon .20 .50
124 Michal Neuvirth .20 .50
125 Miikka Kiprusoff .20 .50
126 Mike Brodeur .25 .60
127 Mike Smith .25 .60
128 Niklas Backstrom .25 .60
129 Ondrej Pavelec .25 .60
130 Pascal Leclaire .20 .50
131 Patrick Lalime .20 .50
132 Pekka Rinne .30 .75
133 Peter Budaj .20 .50
134 Rick DiPietro .20 .50
135 Roberto Luongo .25 .60
136 Ryan Miller .25 .60
137 Scott Clemmensen .20 .50
138 Semyon Varlamov .25 .60
139 Sergei Bobrovsky .50 1.25
140 Tim Thomas .20 .50
141 Tomas Vokoun .20 .50
142 Tuukka Rask .25 .60
143 Ty Conklin .20 .50
144 Andy Moog .25 .60
145 Rick Wamsley .25 .60
146 Bernie Parent .25 .60
147 Billy Smith .25 .60
148 Murray Bannerman .25 .60
149 Bob Sauve .25 .60
150 Cesare Maniago .30 .75
151 Chico Resch .25 .60
152 Curtis Joseph .30 .75
153 Dan Bouchard .20 .50
154 Darren Pang .25 .60
155 Denis Herron .20 .50
156 Dominik Hasek .40 1.00
157 Don Beaupre .20 .50
158 Ed Giacomin .40 1.00
159 Felix Potvin .40 1.00
160 Frank Pietrangelo .30 .75
161 Gerry Cheevers .25 .60
162 Gilles Gilbert .20 .50
163 Glenn Hall .25 .60
164 Grant Fuhr .25 .60
165 Greg Millen .20 .50
166 John Garrett .25 .60
167 John Vanbiesbrouck .30 .75
168 Johnny Bower .30 .75
169 Kelly Hrudey .20 .50
170 Kirk McLean .25 .60
171 Michel Dion .20 .50
172 Mike Richter .25 .60
173 Mike Vernon .20 .50
174 Olaf Kolzig .25 .60
175 Patrick Roy .60 1.50
176 Phil Myre .20 .50
177 Pokey Reddick .20 .50
178 Richard Brodeur .25 .60
179 Roger Crozier .20 .50
180 Rogie Vachon .30 .75
181 Ron Low .25 .60
182 Sean Burke .15 .40
183 Steve Penney .25 .60
184 Tom Barrasso .25 .60
185 Tony Esposito .25 .60
186 Vladislav Tretiak .30 .75
187 Sami Jo Small .30 .75
188 Kim St. Pierre .40 1.00
189 Charline Labonte .30 .75
190 Manon Rheaume .50 1.25
191 Terry Sawchuk .30 .75
192 George Hainsworth .25 .60
193 Georges Vezina .30 .75
194 Gump Worsley .25 .60
195 Jacques Plante .30 .75
196 Pelle Lindbergh .40 1.00
197 Clint Benedict .20 .50
198 Tiny Thompson .25 .60
199 Turk Broda .25 .60
200 Tom Fenton .30 .75

2010-11 Between The Pipes Autographs

K Anton Khudobin 4.00 10.00
AAM Andy Moog 5.00 12.00
AAR Alec Richards 4.00 10.00
AAS Alex Stalock 5.00 12.00
ABH Braden Holtby 10.00 25.00
ABP Bernie Parent SP 10.00 25.00
ABS Billy Smith SP 10.00 25.00
ABT Brad Thiessen 5.00 12.00
ACC Corey Crawford SP 12.00 30.00
ACD Cedrick Desjardins 5.00 12.00
ACG Christopher Gibson 6.00 15.00
ACJ Chad Johnson 4.00 10.00
ACL Charline Labonte 6.00 15.00
ACO Chris Osgood SP 10.00 25.00
ACP Calvin Pickard 5.00 12.00
ACR Chico Resch 5.00 12.00
ACS Cory Schneider SP 8.00 20.00
ADB Dan Bouchard 4.00 10.00
ADH Denis Herron 4.00 10.00
ADK Darcy Kuemper 5.00 12.00
ADL David LeNeveu SP 8.00 20.00
ADR Dwayne Roloson SP 8.00 20.00
ADT Dustin Tokarski 4.00 10.00
AEG Ed Giacomin SP 12.00 30.00
AEL Eddie Lack 5.00 12.00
AEM Evan Mosher 4.00 10.00
AFP Frederic Piche 4.00 10.00
AGC Gerry Cheevers SP 15.00 40.00
AGF Grant Fuhr SP 10.00 25.00
AGH Glenn Hall SP 10.00 25.00
AGM Greg Millen 4.00 10.00
AGN Guillaume Nadeau 5.00 12.00
AGW Gump Worsley SP 12.00 30.00
AHL Henrik Lundqvist SP 15.00 40.00
AIB Igor Bobkov 8.00 20.00
AJA Jake Allen 8.00 20.00
AJB Johan Backlund 4.00 10.00
AJC Jack Campbell 5.00 12.00
AJE Jhonas Enroth 5.00 12.00
AJF Jeff Frazee 6.00 15.00
AJG John Garrett 5.00 12.00
AJH Jaroslav Halak SP 10.00 25.00
AJM Jacob Markstrom 6.00 15.00
AJQ Jonathan Quick SP 15.00 30.00
AJR Jussi Rynnas 5.00 12.00
AJZ Jeff Zatkoff 5.00 12.00
AKH Kelly Hrudey 4.00 10.00
AKM Kirk McLean SP 10.00 25.00
AKS Kent Simpson 4.00 10.00
ALD Louis Domingue 5.00 12.00
ALI Leland Irving 5.00 12.00
AMC Matt Climie 4.00 10.00
AMD Mark Dekanich 4.00 10.00
AMG Martin Gerber SP 8.00 20.00
AMH Michael Hutchinson 6.00 15.00
AML Mike Liut SP 6.00 15.00
AMM Mike Murphy 5.00 12.00
AMN Michal Neuvirth SP 8.00 20.00
AMR Manon Rheaume SP 40.00 80.00
AMR Mike Richter SP 10.00 25.00
AMS Malcolm Subban 10.00 25.00
AMT Marty Turco 5.00 12.00
AMV Mark Visentin 5.00 12.00
ANB Niklas Backstrom SP 10.00 25.00
ANK Nikolai Khabibulin SP 8.00 20.00
AOK Olaf Kolzig 5.00 12.00
AOP Ondrej Pavelec 5.00 12.00
AOR Olivier Roy 5.00 12.00
APB Peter Budaj SP 8.00 20.00
APG Philipp Grubauer 6.00 15.00
APL Patrick Lalime SP 8.00 20.00
APM Phil Myre 4.00 10.00
APR Pekka Rinne SP 12.00 30.00
ARB Richard Brodeur 5.00 12.00
ARE Ray Emery SP 8.00 20.00
ARG Robin Gusse 5.00 12.00
ARH Ron Hextall SP 12.00 30.00
ARL Roberto Luongo SP 10.00 25.00
ARM Robert Mayer 5.00 12.00
ARS Ramis Sadikov 5.00 12.00
ARW Rick Wamsley 6.00 15.00
ASB Sergei Bobrovsky SP 15.00 40.00
ASP Steve Penney 6.00 15.00
ASS Steven Stanford 4.00 10.00
ASV Semyon Varlamov SP 12.00 30.00
ASW Scott Wedgewood 4.00 10.00
ATB Tyler Bunz 4.00 10.00
ATE Tony Esposito SP 15.00 30.00
ATF Tom Fenton 6.00 15.00
ATP Timo Pielmeier 5.00 12.00
ATR Tuukka Rask 10.00 25.00
ATT Tyson Teichmann 4.00 10.00
ATV Tomas Vokoun SP 8.00 20.00
AVT Vladislav Tretiak SP 15.00 40.00
AANI Antti Niemi SP 8.00 20.00
AARA Andrew Raycroft SP
ABSA Bob Sauve 5.00 12.00
ACJO Curtis Joseph SP 12.00 30.00
ACMA Cesare Maniago 6.00 15.00
ACME Curtis McElhinney SP 8.00 20.00
ACPR Carey Price SP 20.00 50.00
ACSA Curtis Sanford 4.00 10.00
ADBE Don Beaupre SP 8.00 20.00
ADHA Dominik Hasek SP 15.00 40.00
AFPI Frank Pietrangelo 6.00 15.00
AFPO Felix Potvin SP 15.00 40.00
AJBE Jonathan Bernier 5.00 12.00
AJBI Jordan Binnington 4.00 10.00
AJBO Johnny Bower SP 12.00 30.00
AJFB Jean-Francois Berube 5.00 12.00
AJHE Johan Hedberg 5.00 12.00
AJHI Jonas Hiller 4.00 10.00
AJHO Jimmy Howard SP 12.00 30.00
AJPA J.P. Anderson 5.00 12.00
AJPO Justin Pogge 4.00 10.00
AJSG Jean-Sebastien Giguere SP 12.00 30.00
AJSM Jeremy Smith 5.00 12.00
AKSP Kim St. Pierre 8.00 20.00
AMAF Marc-Andre Fleury SP 15.00 40.00
AMBA Murray Bannerman 5.00 12.00
AMBR Martin Brodeur SP 20.00 50.00
AMCL Maxime Clermont 4.00 10.00
AMDI Michel Dion 4.00 10.00
AMIB Mike Brodeur 5.00 12.00
AMSE Mark Segal 4.00 10.00
AMVE Mike Vernon 4.00 10.00
APMR Petr Mrazek 10.00 25.00
APRE Pokey Reddick SP 8.00 20.00
APRO Patrick Roy SP 40.00 100.00
ARBA Richard Bachman 5.00 12.00
ARLO Ron Low 5.00 12.00
ASBU Sean Burke SP 6.00 15.00
ASJS Sami Jo Small 6.00 15.00
ATBA Tom Barrasso SP 12.00 30.00
ATMC Thomas McCollum 5.00 12.00
ATRI Ty Rimmer 4.00 10.00
ATTH Tim Thomas SP 8.00 20.00

2010-11 Between The Pipes Countrymen Quad Memorabilia Silver

ANNOUNCED PRINT RUN 50
CM01 Flry/Fuhr/Josph/Price 60.00 150.00
CM02 Vachn/Roy/Brdr/Longo 20.00 50.00
CM03 T.Espo/Barrso/Rchtr/Mllr 30.00 80.00
CM04 DiPtr/Vnbies/Thmas/Qck 30.00 80.00
CM05 Kipr/Lhtn/Bckstrm/Rask 15.00 40.00
CM06 Lndbrg/Hdbrg/Lndq/Mrkst 25.00 60.00
CM07 Trtk/Vrlmv/Bryz/Bbrvsky 20.00 50.00
CM08 Dzrilla/Hsek/Vokn/Halak 30.00 80.00

2010-11 Between The Pipes Deep In The Crease

COMPLETE SET (30) 50.00 100.00
STATED ODDS 1:8
DC01 Hiller/Lvsur/Emry/Bobkv 4.00 10.00
DC02 Pav/Masn/Mnno/Psqle 2.50 6.00
DC03 Thmas/Rask/Dltn/Htch 3.00 8.00
DC04 Miller/Llme/Enrth/Leggio 2.50 6.00
DC05 Kipr/Ktley/Irvng/Lamr 2.50 6.00
DC06 Ward/Petrs/Pgge/Mrphy 2.50 6.00
DC07 Crwfrd/Trco/Rchrds/Smp 3.00 8.00
DC08 Budaj/Elliott/Grhme/Pick 2.50 6.00
DC09 Garn/Wsl/LNv/Corbl-Thr 2.00 5.00
DC10 Leht/Rycrft/Bchmn/Cmp 2.50 6.00
DC11 Howrd/Osgd/McCl/Mrz 5.00 12.00
DC12 Khab/Dbnyk/Dslr/Roy 2.50 6.00
DC13 Vokn/Clmsn/Mrks/Plnte 3.00 8.00
DC14 Quick/Bernr/Jns/Berb 4.00 10.00
DC15 Bckstr/Hrdng/Hcktt/Kmpr 2.50 6.00
DC16 Price/Auld/Sanford/Mayer 10.00 25.00
DC17 Brodr/Hdbrg/Frze/Wdge 5.00 12.00
DC18 Rinn/Dknch/Smth/Pckrd 3.00 8.00
DC19 DiPietro/Plin/Lwsn/Kskn 2.50 6.00
DC20 Lndqv/Birn/Jhnsn/Stjcr 4.00 10.00
DC21 Andrsn/Lclre/Brdr/Lhnr 4.00 10.00
DC22 Bobrvs/Bchr/Lghtn/Bcklnd 5.00 12.00
DC23 Bryz/LaBrb/Clim/Dmig 2.50 6.00
DC24 Flry/Jhnsn/Crry/Thsen 4.00 10.00
DC25 Nimi/Niitty/Stlck/Andr 2.50 6.00
DC26 Halk/Cnkln/Alln/Bshp 4.00 10.00
DC27 Rolsn/Smth/Tkrsk/Jnus 2.50 6.00
DC28 Gigre/Gustv/Rmer/Ryns 3.00 8.00
DC29 Lungo/Schn/Lck/Wman 2.50 6.00
DC30 Varlmv/Nvith/Hltby/Grbr 5.00 12.00

2010-11 Between The Pipes Franchise Leaders Jerseys Silver

STATED PRINT RUN 9-29
FL01 Jean-Sebastien Giguere 10.00 25.00
FL02 Kari Lehtonen 5.00 12.00
FL03 Tiny Thompson/9
FL04 Dominik Hasek 10.00 25.00
FL05 Mike Vernon 5.00 12.00
FL06 Cam Ward 6.00 15.00
FL07 Tony Esposito 6.00 15.00
FL08 Patrick Roy 15.00 40.00
FL09 Marc Denis
FL10 Marty Turco 6.00 15.00
FL11 Terry Sawchuk/9
FL12 Grant Fuhr 6.00 15.00
FL13 Roberto Luongo 6.00 15.00
FL14 Rogie Vachon 8.00 20.00
FL15 Niklas Backstrom 10.00 25.00
FL16 Jacques Plante/9
FL17 Tomas Vokoun 10.00 25.00
FL18 Martin Brodeur 12.00 30.00
FL19 Billy Smith 6.00 15.00
FL20 Mike Richter 10.00 25.00
FL21 Patrick Lalime 5.00 12.00
FL22 Ron Hextall 8.00 20.00
FL23 Ilya Bryzgalov 5.00 12.00
FL24 Tom Barrasso 6.00 15.00
FL25 Evgeni Nabokov
FL26 Mike Liut 15.00 40.00
FL27 Nikolai Khabibulin 8.00 20.00
FL28 Turk Broda/9
FL29 Kirk McLean 15.00 40.00
FL30 Olaf Kolzig 6.00 15.00

2010-11 Between The Pipes Full Gear Silver

STATED PRINT RUN 29 SER.#'d SETS
FG01 Martin Brodeur 25.00 60.00
FG02 Carey Price 30.00 80.00
FG03 Patrick Roy 30.00 80.00
FG04 Niklas Backstrom 20.00 50.00
FG05 Curtis Joseph 20.00 50.00
FG06 Pelle Lindbergh 40.00 80.00

2010-11 Between The Pipes Golden Goalies Jerseys Black

STATED PRINT RUN 30-80
SILVER/20: .6X TO 1.5X BLACK/80*
GG01 Charline Labonte 6.00 15.00
GG02 Kim St. Pierre 8.00 20.00
GG03 Sami-Jo Small 6.00 15.00
GG04 Roberto Luongo 5.00 12.00
GG05 Martin Brodeur 10.00 25.00
GG06 Ed Belfour 5.00 12.00
GG07 Dominik Hasek 8.00 20.00
GG08 Vladimir Myshkin 5.00 12.00
GG09 Vladislav Tretiak/30* 12.00 30.00
GG10 Jim Craig/30* 15.00 40.00
GG11 Tomas Vokoun 4.00 10.00
GG12 Evgeni Nabokov 4.00 10.00
GG13 Henrik Lundqvist 8.00 20.00
GG14 Bill Ranford 5.00 12.00
GG15 Curtis Joseph 6.00 15.00
GG16 Vladimir Dzurilla 10.00 25.00
GG17 Jonas Hiller 4.00 10.00
GG18 Ilya Bryzgalov 4.00 10.00
GG19 Dwayne Roloson 4.00 10.00
GG20 Cam Ward 5.00 12.00
GG21 Jean-Sebastien Giguere 4.00 10.00
GG22 Marc Denis 4.00 10.00
GG23 Martin Biron 4.00 10.00
GG24 Johan Hedberg 4.00 10.00
GG25 Carey Price 20.00 50.00
GG26 Justin Pogge 4.00 10.00
GG27 Leland Irving 5.00 12.00
GG28 Dustin Tokarski 4.00 10.00
GG29 Mike Richter 5.00 12.00
GG30 Chet Pickard 4.00 10.00
GG31 Jonathan Bernier 5.00 12.00
GG32 Devan Dubnyk 5.00 12.00
GG33 Grant Fuhr 5.00 12.00

2010-11 Between The Pipes Guarding the Bleu Blanc et Rouge Net

COMPLETE SET (10) 25.00 60.00
BBR01 Georges Vezina 3.00 8.00
BBR02 George Hainsworth 2.50 6.00
BBR03 Wilf Cude 3.00 8.00
BBR04 Bill Durnan 2.50 6.00
BBR05 Gerry McNeil 1.50 4.00
BBR06 Jacques Plante 3.00 8.00
BBR07 Rogie Vachon 3.00 8.00
BBR08 Gump Worsley 2.50 6.00
BBR09 Patrick Roy 6.00 15.00
BBR10 Carey Price 10.00 25.00

2010-11 Between The Pipes Guarding the Blue and White Net

COMPLETE SET (10) 15.00 40.00
BW01 Lorne Chabot 2.00 5.00
BW02 Turk Broda 2.50 6.00
BW03 Harry Lumley 2.50 6.00
BW04 Johnny Bower 3.00 8.00
BW05 Mike Palmateer 2.50 6.00
BW06 Allan Bester 2.00 5.00
BW07 Felix Potvin 4.00 10.00
BW08 Curtis Joseph 3.00 8.00
BW09 Jean-Sebastien Giguere 2.00 5.00
BW10 James Reimer 2.50 6.00

2010-11 Between The Pipes Inspired Mask

COMPLETE SET (13) 60.00 120.00
IM01 Ray Emery 5.00 12.00
IM02 Tim Thomas 5.00 12.00
IM03 James Reimer 6.00 15.00
IM04 Antero Niittymaki 5.00 12.00
IM05 Jason Labarbera 5.00 12.00
IM06 Jaroslav Halak 6.00 15.00
IM07 Alex Auld 5.00 12.00
IM08 Carey Price 15.00 40.00
IM09 Mikael Tellqvist 6.00 15.00
IM10 Kari Lehtonen 5.00 12.00
IM11 Wade Dubielewicz 5.00 12.00
IM12 Carey Price 15.00 40.00
IM13 Ray Emery 5.00 12.00

2010-11 Between The Pipes Jerseys Black

STATED PRINT RUN 120 SER.#'d SETS
M01 Antti Niemi 4.00 10.00
M02 Brian Boucher 4.00 10.00
M03 Calvin Pickard 5.00 12.00
M04 Chet Pickard 4.00 10.00
M05 Chris Osgood 5.00 12.00
M06 Christopher Gibson 6.00 15.00
M07 Corey Crawford 6.00 15.00
M08 Cory Schneider 4.00 10.00
M09 Darcy Kuemper 5.00 12.00
M10 Darren Pang 5.00 12.00
M11 David Honzik 4.00 10.00
M12 Devan Dubnyk 5.00 12.00
M13 Don Beaupre 4.00 10.00
M14 Ed Johnston/30* 12.00 30.00
M15 Evgeni Nabokov 4.00 10.00
M16 Felix Potvin 8.00 20.00
M17 Gilles Meloche 5.00 12.00
M18 Henrik Lundqvist 8.00 20.00
M19 Ilya Bryzgalov 4.00 10.00
M20 Jack Campbell 5.00 12.00
M21 Jacob Markstrom 6.00 15.00
M22 Jake Allen 8.00 20.00
M23 James Reimer 12.00 30.00
M24 Jamie Tucker 4.00 10.00
M25 Jeff Deslauriers 3.00 8.00
M26 Jean-Francois Berube 5.00 12.00
M27 Jhonas Enroth 5.00 12.00
M28 Ty Conklin 4.00 10.00
M29 Jonas Gustavsson 6.00 15.00
M30 Jonas Hiller 4.00 10.00
M31 Jonathan Quick 8.00 20.00
M32 Jordan Binnington 4.00 10.00
M33 Michael Leighton 4.00 10.00
M34 J.P. Anderson 5.00 12.00
M35 Kari Lehtonen 4.00 10.00
M36 Kent Simpson 4.00 10.00
M37 Mike Richter 5.00 12.00
M38 Liam Liston 4.00 10.00
M39 Marc-Andre Fleury 8.00 20.00
M40 Mark Visentin 5.00 12.00
M41 Martin Brodeur 10.00 25.00
M42 Mike Brodeur 5.00 12.00
M43 Mike Murphy 5.00 12.00
M44 Miikka Kiprusoff 4.00 10.00
M45 Mikko Koskinen 5.00 12.00
M46 Olivier Roy 5.00 12.00
M47 Pascal Leclaire 4.00 10.00
M48 Pekka Rinne 6.00 15.00
M49 Philipp Grubauer 6.00 15.00
M50 Pokey Reddick 4.00 10.00
M51 Roberto Luongo 5.00 12.00
M52 Roger Crozier/30* 6.00 15.00
M53 Ryan Miller 5.00 12.00
M54 Scott Stajcer 4.00 10.00
M55 Cam Ward 5.00 12.00
M56 Carey Price 20.00 50.00
M57 Jaroslav Halak 5.00 12.00
M58 Jean-Sebastien Giguere 4.00 10.00
M59 Niklas Backstrom 5.00 12.00
M60 Keith Hamilton 4.00 10.00
M61 Rick DiPietro 4.00 10.00
M62 Robin Lehner 8.00 20.00
M63 Semyon Varlamov 5.00 12.00
M64 Sergei Bobrovsky 10.00 25.00
M65 Tim Thomas 6.00 15.00
M66 Tom Barrasso 5.00 12.00
M67 Tuukka Rask 5.00 12.00
M68 Dominik Hasek/30* 12.00 30.00
M69 Ed Giacomin/30* 12.00 30.00
M70 Andy Moog/30* 12.00 30.00
M71 Grant Fuhr/30* 12.00 30.00
M72 Billy Smith/30 8.00 20.00
M73 John Vanbiesbrouck/30* 10.00 25.00
M74 Patrick Roy/30* 20.00 50.00
M75 Patrick Roy/30* 20.00 50.00
M76 Rogie Vachon/30* 10.00 25.00
M77 Tony Esposito/30* 10.00 25.00
M78 Ron Hextall/30* 10.00 25.00

2010-11 Between The Pipes Jerseys Silver

SILVER/20-30: .5X TO 1.2X BLACK
ANNOUNCED PRINT RUN 20-30

2010-11 Between The Pipes Leaders Jerseys Silver

STATED PRINT RUN 39 SER.#'d SETS
L01 Martin Brodeur 12.00 30.00
L02 Martin Brodeur 12.00 30.00
L03 Dominik Hasek 10.00 25.00
L04 Patrick Roy 15.00 40.00
L05 Tom Barrasso 6.00 15.00
L06 Patrick Roy 12.00 30.00
L07 Ron Hextall 8.00 20.00
L08 Martin Brodeur 12.00 30.00
L09 Glenn Hall 6.00 15.00
L10 Jacques Plante 8.00 20.00

2010-11 Between The Pipes Masked Men III Emerald

rds from this set were initially intended to carry a print run of just one. They were serial numbered to one, however, a printing error occurred and ITG announced that 340 of each card were actually produced and inserted into packs. To make amends, ITG later offered two different redemption deals for collectors in which they would receive a limited edition memorabilia version of one the players in exchange for 17 copies of the below listed cards.

STATED PRINT RUN 340 SER.#'d SETS
MM01 Alex Auld 2.50 6.00
MM02 Andrew Raycroft 2.50 6.00
MM03 Antero Niittymaki 2.50 6.00
MM04 Antti Niemi 2.50 6.00
MM05 Brent Johnson 2.50 6.00
MM06 Brian Boucher 2.50 6.00
MM07 Brian Elliott 2.50 6.00
MM08 Cam Ward 3.00 8.00
MM09 Carey Price 12.00 30.00
MM10 Chris Mason 2.50 6.00
MM11 Corey Crawford 4.00 10.00
MM12 Cory Schneider 2.50 6.00
MM13 Craig Anderson 3.00 8.00
MM14 Scott Clemmensen 2.50 6.00
MM15 Ty Conklin 2.50 6.00
MM16 Devan Dubnyk 3.00 8.00
MM17 Dwayne Roloson 2.50 6.00
MM18 Henrik Lundqvist 5.00 12.00
MM19 Ilya Bryzgalov 2.50 6.00
MM20 James Reimer 8.00 20.00
MM21 Jaroslav Halak 3.00 8.00
MM22 Jason LaBarbera 2.50 6.00
MM23 Jean-Sebastien Giguere 2.50 6.00
MM24 Jimmy Howard 4.00 10.00
MM25 Johan Hedberg 2.50 6.00
MM26 Jhonas Enroth 3.00 8.00
MM27 Jonas Hiller 2.50 6.00
MM28 Jonathan Bernier 3.00 8.00
MM29 Jonathan Quick 5.00 12.00
MM30 Kari Lehtonen 2.50 6.00
MM31 Marc-Andre Fleury 5.00 12.00
MM32 Martin Brodeur 6.00 15.00
MM33 Marty Turco 6.00 15.00
MM34 Mathieu Garon 2.50 6.00
MM35 Michal Neuvirth 2.50 6.00
MM36 Miikka Kiprusoff 2.50 6.00
MM37 Niklas Backstrom 3.00 8.00
MM38 Ondrej Pavelec 3.00 8.00
MM39 Pascal Leclaire 2.50 6.00
MM40 Patrick Lalime 2.50 6.00
MM41 Pekka Rinne 4.00 10.00
MM42 Peter Budaj 2.50 6.00
MM43 Rick DiPietro 2.50 6.00
MM44 Roberto Luongo 3.00 8.00
MM45 Ryan Miller 3.00 8.00
MM46 Semyon Varlamov 4.00 10.00
MM47 Sergei Bobrovsky 6.00 15.00
MM48 Tim Thomas 2.50 6.00
MM49 Tomas Vokoun 2.50 6.00
MM50 Tuukka Rask 3.00 8.00

2010-11 Between The Pipes Masked Men III Silver

*SILVER: .5X TO 1.2X EMERALD
STATED PRINT RUN 100 SER.#'d SETS

2010-11 Between The Pipes Ready Willing and Able Jerseys Black

STATED PRINT RUN 80 SER.#'d SETS
SILVER/30: .5X TO 1.2X BLACK
RWA01 C.Price/A.Auld 30.00 80.00
RWA02 T.Thomas/T.Rask 8.00 20.00
RWA03 R.Miller/J.Enroth 8.00 20.00
RWA04 M.Fleury/B.Johnson 12.00 30.00
RWA05 R.Luongo/C.Schneider 8.00 20.00
RWA06 J.Quick/J.Bernier 12.00 30.00
RWA07 I.IBryzgalov/J.LaBarbera 6.00 15.00
RWA08 J-S Giguere/J.Reimer 12.00 30.00
RWA09 M.Brodeur/J.Hedberg 12.00 30.00
RWA10 B.Boucher/S.Bobrovsky 12.00 30.00
RWA11 C.Ward/J.Peters 8.00 20.00
RWA12 J.Halak/T.Conklin 8.00 20.00

2010-11 Between The Pipes School Is Out Jerseys Silver

STATED PRINT RUN 49 SER.#'d SETS
SO01 K.McLean/P.Budaj 6.00 15.00
SO02 R.Wamsley/P.Leclaire 6.00 15.00
SO03 B.Parent/P.Lindbergh 25.00 60.00
SO04 G.Hall/M.Vernon 6.00 15.00
SO05 V.Tretiak/E.Belfour 8.00 20.00
SO06 A.Moog/M.Turco 6.00 15.00
SO07 G.Fuhr/I.Bryzgalov 6.00 15.00
SO08 P.Peeters/J.Hiller 6.00 15.00
SO09 T.Barrasso/C.Ward 6.00 15.00
SO10 B.Ranford/J.Quick 10.00 25.00
SO11 G.Meloche/M.Fleury 10.00 25.00
SO12 J.Plante/B.Parent 8.00 20.00

2010-11 Between The Pipes Showdown Dual Jerseys Silver

STATED PRINT RUN 39 SER.#'d SETS
SD01 P.Roy/J.Vanbiesbrouck 20.00 50.00
SD02 R.Luongo/R.Miller 8.00 20.00
SD03 K.McLean/M.Richter 15.00 40.00
SD04 G.Fuhr/R.Hextall 10.00 25.00
SD05 M.Vernon/P.Roy 20.00 50.00
SD06 M.Brodeur/J.Giguere 15.00 40.00
SD07 B.Parent/G.Gilbert 10.00 25.00
SD08 V.Tretiak/T.Esposito 12.00 30.00

2010-11 Between The Pipes Stick Save Silver

STATED PRINT RUN 24 SER.#'d SETS
SS01 Bernie Parent 15.00 40.00
SS02 Brent Johnson 12.00 30.00
SS03 Chris Osgood 15.00 40.00
SS04 Felix Potvin 25.00 60.00
SS05 Jaroslav Halak 15.00 40.00
SS06 John Vanbiesbrouck 20.00 50.00
SS07 Jonas Gustavsson 15.00 40.00
SS08 Kari Lehtonen 12.00 30.00
SS09 Mark Visentin 15.00 40.00
SS10 Martin Brodeur 30.00 80.00
SS11 Olaf Kolzig 15.00 40.00
SS12 Patrick Roy 40.00 100.00
SS13 Patrick Roy 40.00 100.00
SS14 Rick DiPietro 12.00 30.00
SS15 Ryan Miller 15.00 40.00
SS16 Tim Thomas 12.00 30.00
SS17 Tom Barrasso 15.00 40.00
SS18 Tomas Vokoun 12.00 30.00

2010-11 Between The Pipes Their Country's Finest

COMPLETE SET (9) 15.00 40.00
CF01 Martin Brodeur 5.00 12.00
CF02 Ryan Miller 2.50 6.00
CF03 Henrik Lundqvist 4.00 10.00
CF04 Miikka Kiprusoff 2.00 5.00
CF05 Ilya Bryzgalov 2.00 5.00
CF06 Tomas Vokoun 2.00 5.00
CF07 Jaroslav Halak 2.50 6.00
CF08 Jonas Hiller 2.00 5.00
CF09 Olaf Kolzig 2.50 6.00

2011-12 Between The Pipes

COMPLETE SET (200) 15.00 40.00
1 Jimmy Appleby .20 .50
2 J.P. Anderson .25 .60
3 Jordan Binnington .20 .50
4 Laurent Brossoit .25 .60
5 Tyler Bunz .20 .50
6 Jack Campbell .25 .60
7 Mac Carruth .20 .50
8 Cole Cheveldave .20 .50
9 Mathieu Corbeil .20 .50
10 Andrew D'Agostini .20 .50
11 Louis Domingue .15 .40
12 Chris Driedger .20 .50
13 Alex Dubeau .25 .60
14 Christopher Gibson .25 .60
15 Gabriel Girard .20 .50
16 Domenic Graham .20 .50
17 Keith Hamilton .20 .50
18 Matt Hewitt .20 .50
19 David Honzik .25 .60
20 Michael Houser .20 .50
21 Nathan Liuewen .25 .60
22 Andrey Makarov .20 .50
23 Brandon Maxwell .20 .50
24 Adam Morrison .20 .50
25 Petr Mrazek .50 1.25
26 Matt Murray .30 .75
27 Mathias Niederberger .20 .50
28 Drew Owsley .20 .50
29 Calvin Pickard .25 .60
30 Ty Rimmer .20 .50
31 Luke Siemens .20 .50
32 Malcolm Subban .40 1.00
33 Francois Tremblay .15 .40
34 Mark Visentin .20 .50
35 Scott Wedgewood .25 .60
36 Roman Will .15 .40
37 Jake Allen .40 1.00
38 Richard Bachman .20 .50
39 Cedrick Desjardins .20 .50
40 Matt Hackett .25 .60
41 Braden Holtby .50 1.25
42 Leland Irving .20 .50
43 Chad Johnson .20 .50
44 Martin Jones .40 1.00
45 Anton Khudobin .20 .50
46 Keith Kinkaid .20 .50
47 Darcy Kuemper .25 .60
48 Eddie Lack .20 .50
49 Robin Lehner .20 .50
50 Jacob Markstrom .25 .60
51 Robert Mayer .25 .60
52 Mike Murphy .20 .50
53 Edward Pasquale .20 .50
54 Jordan Pearce .20 .50
55 Timo Pielmeier .25 .60
56 Alec Richards .20 .50
57 Jussi Rynnas .25 .60
58 Harri Sateri .20 .50
59 Ben Scrivens .30 .75
60 Tyson Sexsmith .20 .50
61 Jeremy Smith .25 .60
62 Iiro Tarkki .25 .60
63 Jeff Zatkoff .25 .60
64 Craig Anderson SG .25 .60
65 Niklas Backstrom SG .25 .60
66 Jonathan Bernier SG .25 .60
67 Sergei Bobrovsky SG .25 .60
68 Ilya Bryzgalov SG .25 .60
69 Peter Budaj SG .20 .50
70 Corey Crawford SG .30 .75
71 Brian Elliott SG .20 .50
72 Dan Ellis SG .20 .50
73 Ray Emery SG .20 .50
74 Jhonas Enroth SG .25 .60
75 Marc-Andre Fleury SG .40 1.00
76 Mathieu Garon SG .20 .50
77 Thomas Greiss SG .20 .50
78 Jonas Gustavsson SG .25 .60
79 Jaroslav Halak SG .25 .60
80 Jonas Hiller SG .20 .50
81 Jimmy Howard SG .25 .60
82 Kari Lehtonen SG .20 .50
83 Henrik Lundqvist SG .30 .75
84 Roberto Luongo SG .25 .60
85 Tim Thomas SG .25 .60
86 Ryan Miller SG .25 .60
87 Michal Neuvirth SG .20 .50
88 Antti Niemi SG .20 .50
89 Antero Niittymaki SG .20 .50
90 Carey Price SG .75 2.00
91 Jonathan Quick SG .40 1.00
92 Tuukka Rask SG .25 .60
93 James Reimer SG .25 .60
94 Pekka Rinne SG .30 .75
95 Dwayne Roloson SG .20 .50
96 Cory Schneider SG .20 .50
97 Mike Smith SG .25 .60
98 Semyon Varlamov SG .25 .60
99 Tomas Vokoun SG .20 .50
100 Don Beaupre DEC .20 .50
101 Ed Belfour DEC .25 .60
102 Dan Bouchard DEC .20 .50
103 Johnny Bower DEC .25 .60
104 Richard Brodeur DEC .25 .60
105 Gary Bromley DEC .30 .75
106 Sean Burke DEC .15 .40
107 Jim Carey DEC .20 .50
108 Ed Chadwick DEC .25 .60
109 Gerry Cheevers DEC .25 .60
110 Dan Cloutier DEC .20 .50
111 Byron Dafoe DEC .25 .60
112 Joe Daley DEC .20 .50
113 Denis DeJordy DEC .20 .50
114 Michel Dion DEC .20 .50
115 Tony Esposito DEC .25 .60
116 Emile Francis DEC .20 .50
117 Grant Fuhr DEC .25 .60
118 Ed Giacomin DEC .25 .60
119 Gilles Gilbert DEC .20 .50
120 Glenn Hall DEC .25 .60
121 Glen Hanlon DEC .20 .50
122 Dominik Hasek DEC .30 .75
123 Denis Herron DEC .20 .50
124 Charlie Hodge DEC .20 .50
125 Arturs Irbe DEC .20 .50
126 Curtis Joseph DEC .25 .60
127 Reggie Lemelin DEC .30 .75
128 Mike Liut DEC .20 .50
129 Cesare Maniago DEC .25 .60
130 Jack McCartan DEC .25 .60
131 Rollie Melanson DEC .15 .40
132 Gilles Meloche DEC .25 .60
133 Greg Millen DEC .20 .50
134 Phil Myre DEC .20 .50
135 Chris Osgood DEC .25 .60
136 Darren Pang DEC .25 .60
137 Bernie Parent DEC .25 .60
138 Pete Peeters DEC .25 .60
139 Felix Potvin DEC .40 1.00
140 Bill Ranford DEC .25 .60
141 Chico Resch DEC .25 .60
142 Damian Rhodes DEC .25 .60
143 Mike Richter DEC .25 .60
144 Patrick Roy DEC .60 1.50
145 Gary Simmons DEC .25 .60
146 Billy Smith DEC .25 .60
147 Doug Soetaert DEC .15 .40
148 Greg Stefan DEC .15 .40
149 Rogie Vachon DEC .30 .75
150 John Vanbiesbrouck DEC .25 .60
151 Mike Veisor DEC .15 .40
152 Mike Vernon DEC .20 .50
153 Gilles Villemure DEC .20 .50
154 Rick Wamsley DEC .25 .60
155 Craig Anderson SS .25 .60
156 Tom Barrasso SS .25 .60
157 Brian Boucher SS .20 .50
158 Jim Carey SS .20 .50
159 Ty Conklin SS .20 .50
160 Jim Craig SS .40 1.00
161 Jimmy Howard SS .25 .60
162 Brent Johnson SS .20 .50
163 Ryan Miller SS .25 .60
164 Jonathan Quick SS .40 1.00
165 Damian Rhodes SS .25 .60
166 Mike Richter SS .25 .60
167 Cory Schneider SS .20 .50
168 Tim Thomas SS .25 .60
169 John Vanbiesbrouck SS .25 .60
170 Jonathan Bernier LBP .25 .60
171 Dan Bouchard LBP .20 .50
172 Richard Brodeur LBP .25 .60
173 Dan Cloutier LBP .20 .50
174 Corey Crawford LBP .30 .75
175 Denis DeJordy LBP .20 .50
176 Michel Dion LBP .20 .50
177 Gilles Gilbert LBP .20 .50
178 Denis Herron LBP .20 .50
179 Charlie Hodge LBP .20 .50
180 Reggie Lemelin LBP .30 .75
181 Roberto Luongo LBP .25 .60
182 Gilles Meloche LBP .25 .60
183 Phil Myre LBP .20 .50
184 Bernie Parent LBP .25 .60
185 Felix Potvin LBP .40 1.00
186 Patrick Roy LBP .60 1.50
187 Rogie Vachon LBP .30 .75
188 Georges Vezina LBP .25 .60
189 Gilles Villemure LBP .20 .50
190 T.Sawchuk ET/W.Rutledge .25 .60
191 C.Maniago ET/G.Bauman .25 .60
192 C.Hodge ET/G.Smith .20 .50
193 L.Binkley ET/H.Bassen .20 .50
194 B.Parent ET/D.Favell .25 .60
195 G.Hall ET/S.Martin .25 .60
196 Jack McCartan IP .25 .60
197 Seth Martin IP .25 .60
198 Leif Holmqvist IP .20 .50
199 Vladimir Dzurilla IP .25 .60
200 Paul Deutsch OGW .25 .60

2011-12 Between The Pipes 10th Anniversary

STATED ODDS 1:8
BTPA01 Jonas Hiller 1.50 4.00
BTPA02 Tim Thomas 2.00 5.00
BTPA03 Ryan Miller 2.00 5.00
BTPA04 Miikka Kiprusoff 2.00 5.00
BTPA05 Cam Ward 2.00 5.00
BTPA06 Corey Crawford 2.50 6.00
BTPA07 Semyon Varlamov 2.00 5.00
BTPA08 Kari Lehtonen 1.50 4.00
BTPA09 Jim Howard 2.00 5.00
BTPA10 Nikolai Khabibulin 1.50 4.00
BTPA11 Jose Theodore 2.00 5.00
BTPA12 Jonathan Quick 3.00 8.00
BTPA13 Niklas Backstrom 2.00 5.00
BTPA14 Carey Price 6.00 15.00
BTPA15 Pekka Rinne 2.50 6.00
BTPA16 Evgeni Nabokov 1.50 4.00
BTPA17 Henrik Lundqvist 2.50 6.00
BTPA18 Craig Anderson 2.00 5.00
BTPA19 Ilya Bryzgalov 2.00 5.00
BTPA20 Mike Smith 2.00 5.00
BTPA21 Marc-Andre Fleury 3.00 8.00
BTPA22 Brian Elliott 1.50 4.00
BTPA23 Jaroslav Halak 2.00 5.00
BTPA24 Antti Niemi 1.50 4.00
BTPA25 Dwayne Roloson 1.50 4.00
BTPA26 Jonas Gustavsson 2.00 5.00
BTPA27 James Reimer 2.00 5.00
BTPA28 Roberto Luongo 2.00 5.00
BTPA29 Tomas Vokoun 1.50 4.00
BTPA30 Ondrej Pavelec 2.00 5.00
BTPA31 Bernie Parent 2.00 5.00
BTPA32 Curtis Joseph 2.00 5.00
BTPA33 Dominik Hasek 2.50 6.00
BTPA34 Ed Belfour 2.00 5.00
BTPA35 Georges Vezina 2.00 5.00
BTPA36 Gerry Cheevers 2.00 5.00
BTPA37 Glenn Hall 2.00 5.00
BTPA38 Grant Fuhr 2.00 5.00
BTPA39 Jacques Plante 2.50 6.00
BTPA40 Johnny Bower 2.00 5.00
BTPA41 Patrick Roy 5.00 12.00
BTPA42 Pelle Lindbergh 3.00 8.00
BTPA43 Terry Sawchuk 2.00 5.00
BTPA44 Tony Esposito 2.00 5.00
BTPA45 Turk Broda 2.00 5.00

2011-12 Between The Pipes Aspire Jerseys Silver

SILVER ANNOUNCED PRINT RUN 140
AS01 N.Lieuwen/R.Miller 6.00 15.00
AS02 L.Irving/M.Kiprusoff 6.00 15.00
AS03 A.Khudobin/T.Thomas 12.00 30.00
AS04 T.Cann/P.Roy 12.00 30.00
AS05 L.Brossoit/M.Kiprusoff 6.00 15.00
AS06 M.Murphy/C.Ward 6.00 15.00
AS07 K.Simpson/C.Crawford 6.00 15.00
AS08 J.Campbell/K.Lehtonen 6.00 15.00
AS09 P.Mrazek/J.Howard 12.00 30.00
AS10 J.Markstrom/H.Lundqvist 6.00 15.00
AS11 O.Roy/D.Dubnyk 6.00 15.00
AS12 C.Gibson/J.Quick 10.00 25.00
AS13 M.Hackett/N.Backstrom 6.00 15.00
AS14 R.Mayer/C.Price 20.00 50.00
AS15 C.Pickard/P.Rinne 8.00 20.00
AS16 S.Stajcer/H.Lundqvist 6.00 15.00
AS17 R.Lehner/C.Anderson 6.00 15.00
AS18 M.Visentin/M.Smith 6.00 15.00
AS19 J.Binnington/J.Halak 6.00 15.00
AS20 J.Anderson/A.Niemi 6.00 15.00
AS21 D.Honzik/R.Luongo 6.00 15.00
AS22 B.Holtby/T.Vokoun 8.00 20.00
AS23 J.Gervais-Chouinard/P.Roy 8.00 20.00
AS24 M.Koskinen/E.Nabokov 6.00 15.00
AS25 T.Bunz/N.Khabibulin 5.00 12.00
AS26 T.Rimmer/C.Price 10.00 25.00
AS27 S.Wedgewood/R.Luongo 6.00 15.00
AS28 E.Pasquale/O.Pavelec 8.00 20.00
AS29 M.Jones/J.Bernier 10.00 25.00
AS30 D.Tokarski/D.Roloson 6.00 15.00

2011-12 Between The Pipes Autographs

OVERALL AUTO STATED ODDS 1:8
AAD Andrew D'Agostini 4.00 10.00
AADU Alex Dubeau 5.00 12.00
AAI Arturs Irbe DEC 6.00 15.00
AAK Anton Khudobin 4.00 10.00
AAM Adam Morrison 4.00 10.00
AAN Antti Niemi SG 6.00 15.00
AANI Antero Niittymaki SG 4.00 10.00
AAR Alec Richards 4.00 10.00
ABD Byron Dafoe DEC 6.00 15.00
ABM Brandon Maxwell 4.00 10.00
ABP Bernie Parent DEC 10.00 25.00
ABP2 Bernie Parent LBP SP 15.00 40.00
ABR Bill Ranford DEC 6.00 15.00
ABS Ben Scrivens 6.00 15.00
ABSM Billy Smith DEC 6.00 15.00
ACC Corey Crawford SG 8.00 20.00
ACC2 Corey Crawford LBP SP 12.00 30.00
ACD Cedrick Desjardins 4.00 10.00
ACG Christopher Gibson 5.00 12.00
ACH Charlie Hodge DEC 8.00 20.00
ACH2 Charlie Hodge LBP SP 12.00 30.00
ACJ Chad Johnson 4.00 10.00
ACJO Curtis Joseph DEC SP 8.00 20.00
ACM Cesare Maniago DEC 6.00 15.00
ACO Chris Osgood DEC 8.00 20.00
ACP Calvin Pickard
ACPR Carey Price SG 10.00 25.00
ACR Chico Resch DEC 6.00 15.00
ACS Curtis Sanford 4.00 10.00
ACS2 Cory Schneider SS 4.00 10.00
ADB Don Beaupre DEC 5.00 12.00
ADBO Dan Bouchard DEC 5.00 12.00
ADBO2 Dan Bouchard LBP SP 8.00 20.00
ADC Dan Cloutier DEC 4.00 10.00
ADC2 Dan Cloutier LBP SP 8.00 20.00
ADD Denis DeJordy DEC 5.00 12.00
ADD2 Denis DeJordy LBP SP 10.00 25.00
ADF Doug Favell DEC 5.00 12.00
ADG Domenic Graham 4.00 10.00
ADH David Honzik 5.00 12.00
ADH2 D.Herron LBP SP UER 8.00 20.00
ADHA Dominik Hasek DEC SP 25.00 60.00
ADHE Denis Herron DEC 6.00 15.00
ADM Drew MacIntyre 5.00 12.00
ADO Drew Owsley 4.00 10.00
ADP Darren Pang DEC 6.00 15.00
ADR Dwayne Roloson SG 4.00 10.00
ADR1 Damian Rhodes DEC 5.00 12.00
ADR2 Damian Rhodes SS SP 10.00 25.00
ADS Doug Soetaert DEC 8.00 20.00
AEB Ed Belfour DEC 15.00 30.00
AEC Ed Chadwick DEC 6.00 15.00
AEF Emile Francis DEC 6.00 15.00
AEG Ed Giacomin DEC 8.00 20.00
AEL Eddie Lack 4.00 10.00
AEP Edward Pasquale 4.00 10.00
AFP Felix Potvin DEC 15.00 30.00
AFP2 Felix Potvin LBP SP 25.00 50.00
AFT Francois Tremblay 3.00 8.00
AGB Gary Bromley DEC 8.00 20.00
AGC Gerry Cheevers DEC 8.00 20.00
AGF Grant Fuhr DEC 6.00 15.00
AGG Gilles Gilbert DEC 6.00 15.00
AGG2 Gilles Gilbert LBP SP 10.00 25.00
AGH Glenn Hall DEC 10.00 25.00
AGHA Glen Hanlon DEC 5.00 12.00
AGM Gilles Meloche DEC 8.00 20.00
AGM2 Gilles Meloche LBP SP 12.00 30.00
AGMI Greg Millen DEC 5.00 12.00
AGS Gary Simmons DEC 6.00 15.00
AGST Greg Stefan DEC 5.00 12.00
AGV Gilles Villemure DEC 6.00 15.00
AGV2 Gilles Villemure LBP SP 10.00 25.00
AHL Henrik Lundqvist SG 15.00 40.00
AIB Ilya Bryzgalov SG 6.00 15.00
AJA Jake Allen 8.00 20.00
AJB Jordan Binnington 4.00 10.00
AJBA Jason Bacashihua 4.00 10.00
AJBA2 Jason Bacashihua SS SP 8.00 20.00
AJBE Jonathan Bernier SG SP 10.00 25.00
AJBE2 Jonathan Bernier LBP SP 10.00 25.00
AJBO Johnny Bower DEC 12.00 30.00
AJC Jack Campbell 5.00 12.00
AJCA Jim Carey DEC 8.00 20.00
AJCA2 Jim Carey SS 8.00 20.00
AJCR Jim Craig SS 15.00 30.00
AJD Joe Daley DEC 5.00 12.00
AJE Jhonas Enroth SG 5.00 12.00
AJH Jaroslav Halak SG 8.00 20.00
AJHI Jonas Hiller SG 4.00 10.00
AJHO Jimmy Howard SG 6.00 15.00
AJHO2 Jimmy Howard SS SP 12.00 30.00
AJM Jacob Markstrom 5.00 12.00
AJMC Jack McCartan DEC 8.00 20.00
AJMC2 Jack McCartan IP SP 10.00 25.00
AJP Jordan Pearce 4.00 10.00
AJQ Jonathan Quick SG 12.00 30.00
AJQ2 Jonathan Quick SS SP 25.00 50.00
AJR Jussi Rynnas 5.00 12.00
AJV John Vanbiesbrouck DEC SP 20.00 40.00
AJV2 John Vanbiesbrouck SS SP 20.00 40.00
AJZ Jeff Zatkoff 5.00 12.00
AKH Keith Hamilton 4.00 10.00
AKK Keith Kinkaid 4.00 10.00
AKL Kari Lehtonen SG 4.00 10.00
AKS Kent Simpson 5.00 12.00
ALB Laurent Brossoit 5.00 12.00
ALD Louis Domingue 3.00 8.00
ALI Leland Irving 4.00 10.00
AMAF Marc-Andre Fleury SG SP 15.00 40.00
AMC Mac Carruth 4.00 10.00
AMCO Mathieu Corbeil 4.00 10.00
AMD Michel Dion DEC 6.00 15.00
AMD2 Michel Dion LBP SP 20.00 40.00
AMDE Mark Dekanich 3.00 8.00
AMG Mathieu Garon SG
AMH Michael Houser 4.00 10.00
AMHA Matt Hackett 5.00 12.00
AMJ Martin Jones 8.00 20.00
AML Michael Leighton 4.00 10.00
AMLI Mike Liut DEC 5.00 12.00
AMM Matt Murray 6.00 15.00
AMMU Mike Murphy 4.00 10.00
AMN Mathias Niederberger 4.00 10.00
AMR Mike Richter DEC SP 15.00 40.00
AMR2 Mike Richter SS SP 20.00 50.00
AMS Malcolm Subban 8.00 20.00
AMV Mike Veisor DEC 4.00 10.00
AMVE Mike Vernon DEC 8.00 20.00
AMVI Mark Visentin 4.00 10.00
ANL Nathan Lieuwen 3.00 8.00
APD Paul Deutsch OGW 10.00 25.00
APM Petr Mrazek 10.00 25.00
APM2 Phil Myre LBP SP 8.00 20.00
APMY Phil Myre DEC 5.00 12.00
APP Pete Peeters DEC 6.00 15.00
APR Patrick Roy DEC SP 50.00 120.00
APR2 Patrick Roy LBP SP 50.00 120.00
ARB Richard Bachman 4.00 10.00
ARBR Richard Brodeur DEC 6.00 15.00
ARBR2 Richard Brodeur LBP 10.00 25.00
ARE Ray Emery SG 4.00 10.00
ARG Robin Gusse 3.00 8.00
ARL Roberto Luongo SG SP 12.00 30.00
ARL2 Roberto Luongo LBP SP 15.00 30.00
ARLE Reggie Lemelin DEC 6.00 15.00
ARLE2 Reggie Lemelin LBP SP 20.00 40.00
ARM Rollie Melanson DEC 4.00 10.00
ARMA Robert Mayer 5.00 12.00
ARV Rogie Vachon DEC 8.00 20.00
ARV2 Rogie Vachon LBP 12.00 30.00
ARW Rick Wamsley DEC 6.00 15.00
ARW2 Roman Will 4.00 10.00
ASB Sean Burke DEC 5.00 12.00
ASBO Sergei Bobrovsky SG 5.00 12.00
ASM Seth Martin IP 6.00 15.00
ASV Semyon Varlamov SG 5.00 12.00
ASW Scott Wedgewood 5.00 12.00
ATB Tom Barrasso SS SP
ATB Tyler Bunz 4.00 10.00
ATE Tony Esposito DEC SP 15.00 30.00
ATG Thomas Greiss SG 4.00 10.00
ATP Timo Pielmeier 5.00 12.00
ATR Ty Rimmer 4.00 10.00
ATRA Tuukka Rask SG 5.00 12.00
ATS Tyson Sexsmith 4.00 10.00
ATT Tim Thomas SS SP 15.00 30.00
ATV Tomas Vokoun SG SP 12.00 30.00

2011-12 Between The Pipes Countrymen Quad Memorabilia Silver

SILVER ANNOUNCED PRINT RUN 50
CM01 Miikka Kiprusoff 8.00 20.00
CM02 Mike Richter 8.00 20.00
CM03 Roberto Luongo 8.00 20.00
CM04 Henrik Lundqvist 10.00 25.00
CM05 Olaf Kolzig 8.00 20.00
CM06 Ilya Bryzgalov 8.00 20.00
CM07 Jonas Hiller 6.00 15.00
CM08 Vladislav Tretiak 15.00 40.00
CM09 Vladimir Dzurilla 10.00 25.00

2011-12 Between The Pipes Cup Tandems Jerseys Silver

SILVER ANNOUNCED PRINT RUN 50
CT01 P.Roy/D.Soetaert 20.00 50.00
CT02 B.Ranford/G.Fuhr 15.00 40.00
CT03 P.Roy/A.Racicot 20.00 50.00
CT04 P.Roy/S.Fiset 20.00 50.00
CT05 M.Vernon/C.Osgood 12.00 30.00
CT06 E.Belfour/R.Turek 8.00 20.00
CT07 P.Roy/D.Aebischer 10.00 25.00
CT08 D.Hasek/M.Legace 8.00 20.00
CT09 N.Khabibulin/J.Grahame 6.00 15.00
CT10 C.Ward/M.Gerber 8.00 20.00
CT11 J.Giguere/I.Bryzgalov 8.00 20.00
CT12 C.Osgood/D.Hasek 10.00 25.00
CT13 M.Fleury/M.Garon 12.00 30.00
CT14 A.Niemi/C.Huet 10.00 25.00
CT15 T.Thomas/T.Rask 8.00 20.00

2011-12 Between The Pipes Franchise Jerseys Silver

SILVER ANNOUNCED PRINT RUN 50
F01 Hiller/Bryzgalov/Giguere 12.00 30.00
F02 Thomas/Moog/Cheevers 12.00 30.00
F03 Miller/Hasek/Barrasso 12.00 30.00
F04 Kiprusoff/Giguere/Vernon 12.50 30.00
F05 Crawford/Belfour/Esposito 10.00 25.00
F06 Lehtonen/Smith/Belfour 8.00 20.00
F07 Howard/Hasek/Crozier 12.00 30.00
F08 Dubnyk/Ranford/Fuhr 8.00 20.00
F09 Quick/Cloutier/Vachon 12.00 30.00
F10 Price/Roy/Vachon 25.00 60.00
F11 Lundqvist/Richter/Giacomin 12.00 30.00
F12 Bryzgalov/Hextall/Parent 10.00 25.00
F13 Fleury/Aubin/Barrasso 12.00 30.00
F14 Niemi/Nabokov/Vernon 15.00 40.00
F15 Halak/Joseph/Hall 15.00 40.00
F16 Reimer/Joseph/Potvin 15.00 40.00
F17 Luongo/Cloutier/Brodeur 8.00 20.00
F18 Vokoun/Varlamov/Riggin 10.00 25.00

2011-12 Between The Pipes Full Gear Silver

SILVER ANNOUNCED PRINT RUN 19
FG01 Miikka Kiprusoff 15.00 40.00
FG02 Patrick Roy 30.00 80.00
FG03 Dominik Hasek 25.00 60.00
FG04 Patrick Roy 30.00 80.00
FG05 Curtis Joseph 20.00 50.00
FG06 Carey Price 30.00 80.00

2011-12 Between The Pipes He Shoots He Saves Points

EACH HAS NINE CARDS OF EQUAL VALUE
CJ1 Curtis Joseph UL .25 .60
CP1 Carey Price UL .75 2.00
GC1 Gerry Cheevers UL .30 .75
GV1 Georges Vezina UL .30 .75
HL1 Henrik Lundqvist UL .30 .75
JB1 Johnny Bower UL .30 .75
JP1 Jacques Plante UL .40 1.00
PR1 Patrick Roy UL .60 1.50
RL1 Roberto Luongo UL .25 .60
TE1 Tony Esposito UL .30 .75
TS1 Terry Sawchuk UL .30 .75

2011-12 Between The Pipes He Shoots He Saves Prizes

ISSUED VIA MAIL REDEMPTION
ANNOUNCED PRINT RUN 20
HSHS-01 Ilya Bryzgalov 10.00 25.00
HSHS-02 J.Reimer/J.Gustavsson 12.00 30.00
HSHS-03 Hltby/Vkoun/Klzig 25.00 60.00
HSHS-04 Jaroslav Halak 10.00 25.00
HSHS-05 J.Quick/J.Bernier 20.00 50.00
HSHS-06 Price/Mayer/Roy 40.00 100.00
HSHS-07 Roberto Luongo 10.00 25.00
HSHS-08 C.Crawford/R.Emery 15.00 40.00
HSHS-09 Thmas/Rask/Chvers 20.00 50.00
HSHS-10 Nikolai Khabibulin 8.00 20.00
HSHS-11 I.Bryzgalov/S.Bobrovsky 12.00 30.00
HSHS-12 Rmer/Gstvssn/Ptvin 20.00 50.00
HSHS-13 Braden Holtby 20.00 50.00
HSHS-14 J.Halak/B.Elliott 12.00 30.00
HSHS-15 Quick/Brnier/Vchon 20.00 50.00
HSHS-16 Carey Price 30.00 80.00
HSHS-17 R.Luongo/C.Schneider 12.00 30.00
HSHS-18 Crwfrd/Emery/Espsto 15.00 40.00
HSHS-19 Tim Thomas 10.00 25.00
HSHS-20 N.Khabibulin/D.Dubnyk 12.00 30.00
HSHS-21 Bryzglv/Bbrvsky/Prent 30.00 60.00
HSHS-22 James Reimer 10.00 25.00
HSHS-23 B.Hltby/Vkoun 25.00 60.00
HSHS-24 Hlak/Elltt/Jseph 12.00 30.00
HSHS-25 Jonathan Quick 15.00 40.00
HSHS-26 C.Price/R.Mayer 40.00 100.00
HSHS-27 Lngo/Schnder/Brdeur 12.00 30.00
HSHS-28 Corey Crawford 12.00 30.00
HSHS-29 T.Thomas/T.Rask 12.00 30.00
HSHS-30 Khbbln/Dbnyk/Fuhr 12.00 30.00

2011-12 Between The Pipes Jerseys Silver

SILVER ANNOUNCED PRINT RUN 140
SILVER PATCH/19: .8X TO 2X BASIC JSY
M01 Alex Auld 4.00 10.00
M02 Antero Niittymaki 4.00 10.00
M03 Antti Niemi 6.00 15.00
M04 Carey Price 15.00 40.00
M05 Kent Simpson 5.00 12.00
M06 Cory Schneider 4.00 10.00
M07 Craig Anderson 5.00 12.00
M08 Henrik Lundqvist 6.00 15.00
M09 Ilya Bryzgalov 5.00 12.00
M10 James Reimer 8.00 20.00
M11 Jaroslav Halak 5.00 12.00
M12 John Vanbiesbrouck 5.00 12.00
M13 Jonas Gustavsson 5.00 12.00
M14 Mikko Koskinen 5.00 12.00
M15 Jonathan Quick 8.00 20.00
M16 Josh Harding 5.00 12.00
M17 Kevin Bailie 5.00 12.00
M18 Niklas Backstrom 5.00 12.00
M19 Roberto Luongo 5.00 12.00
M20 Jonathan Bernier 5.00 12.00
M21 Tim Thomas 6.00 15.00
M22 Tomas Vokoun 4.00 10.00
M23 Patrick Roy 12.00 30.00
M24 Ed Belfour 6.00 15.00
M25 Dominik Hasek 6.00 15.00
M26 Grant Fuhr 5.00 12.00
M27 Keith Hamilton 4.00 10.00
M28 Marc-Andre Fleury 8.00 20.00
M29 Jonas Hiller 4.00 10.00
M30 Devan Dubnyk 5.00 12.00
M31 Ryan Miller 5.00 12.00
M32 J.P. Anderson 5.00 12.00
M33 Jack Campbell 5.00 12.00
M34 Sean Burke 3.00 8.00
M35 Curtis Joseph 6.00 15.00
M36 Don Beaupre 4.00 10.00
M37 Greg Stefan 3.00 8.00
M38 Byron Dafoe 5.00 12.00
M39 Arturs Irbe 8.00 20.00
M40 Dan Cloutier 4.00 10.00
M41 Thomas Greiss 4.00 10.00
M42 Robert Mayer 5.00 12.00
M43 Jacob Markstrom 5.00 12.00
M44 Jake Allen 8.00 20.00
M45 Darcy Kuemper 5.00 12.00
M46 Mike Murphy 4.00 10.00
M47 Robin Lehner 4.00 10.00
M48 Martin Jones 8.00 20.00
M49 Laurent Brossoit 5.00 12.00
M50 Tyler Bunz 6.00 15.00
M51 J.P. Cesario 4.00 10.00
M52 Andrew D'Agostini 4.00 10.00
M53 Mac Engel 3.00 8.00
M54 Jacob Gervais-Chouinard 3.00 8.00
M55 Maxime Lagace 5.00 12.00
M56 Petr Mrazek 10.00 25.00
M57 Matt Murray 6.00 15.00
M58 Drew Owsley 4.00 10.00
M59 Ty Rimmer 4.00 10.00
M60 Anthony Terenzio 3.00 8.00

2011-12 Between The Pipes Journey Dual Jerseys Silver

SILVER ANNOUNCED PRINT RUN 40
JJ01 Curtis Joseph 12.00 30.00
JJ02 Dominik Hasek 10.00 25.00
JJ03 Roberto Luongo 8.00 20.00
JJ04 John Vanbiesbrouck 8.00 20.00
JJ05 Ilya Bryzgalov 8.00 20.00
JJ06 J-S Giguere 8.00 20.00
JJ07 Chris Osgood 8.00 20.00
JJ08 Miikka Kiprusoff 8.00 20.00
JJ09 Tomas Vokoun 6.00 15.00
JJ10 Kari Lehtonen 6.00 15.00
JJ11 Glenn Hall 10.00 25.00
JJ12 Damian Rhodes 8.00 20.00
JJ13 Patrick Roy 20.00 50.00
JJ14 Rogie Vachon 10.00 25.00
JJ15 Ed Belfour 8.00 20.00
JJ16 Phil Myre 8.00 20.00
JJ17 Felix Potvin 12.00 30.00
JJ18 Mike Vernon 6.00 15.00
JJ19 Don Beaupre 8.00 20.00
JJ20 Grant Fuhr 8.00 20.00
JJ21 Jaroslav Halak 8.00 20.00

2011-12 Between The Pipes Masked Men IV Ruby Die Cuts

MASKED MEN OVERALL ODDS 1:6
SILVER/90: .8X TO 2X BASIC INSERTS
MM01 Craig Anderson 2.50 6.00
MM02 Alex Auld 2.00 5.00
MM03 Niklas Backstrom 2.50 6.00
MM04 Murray Bannerman 2.00 5.00
MM05 Ed Belfour 2.50 6.00
MM06 Jonathan Bernier 2.50 6.00
MM07 Martin Biron 2.00 5.00
MM08 Sergei Bobrovsky 2.50 6.00
MM09 Gary Bromley 3.00 8.00
MM10 Ilya Bryzgalov 2.50 6.00
MM11 Jack Campbell 2.50 6.00
MM12 Scott Clemmensen 2.00 5.00
MM13 Corey Crawford 3.00 8.00
MM14 Rick DiPietro 2.00 5.00
MM15 Devan Dubnyk 2.50 6.00
MM16 Ray Emery 2.00 5.00
MM17 Marc-Andre Fleury 4.00 10.00
MM18 Grant Fuhr 2.50 6.00
MM19 Mathieu Garon 2.00 5.00
MM20 Martin Gerber 2.00 5.00
MM21 Ed Giacomin 2.50 6.00
MM22 Jonas Hiller 2.00 5.00
MM23 Jim Howard 2.50 6.00
MM24 Curtis Joseph 2.50 6.00
MM25 Miikka Kiprusoff 2.50 6.00
MM26 Kari Lehtonen 2.00 5.00
MM27 Henrik Lundqvist 3.00 8.00
MM28 Roberto Luongo 2.50 6.00
MM29 Chris Mason 2.00 5.00
MM30 Kirk McLean 2.00 5.00
MM31 Ryan Miller 2.50 6.00
MM32 Evgeni Nabokov 2.00 5.00
MM33 Bernie Parent 2.50 6.00
MM34 Felix Potvin 4.00 10.00
MM35 Carey Price 8.00 20.00
MM36 Jonathan Quick 4.00 10.00
MM37 James Reimer 2.50 6.00
MM38 Mike Richter 2.50 6.00
MM39 Dwayne Roloson 2.00 5.00
MM40 Patrick Roy 4.00 10.00
MM41 Patrick Roy 4.00 10.00
MM42 Curtis Sanford 2.00 5.00
MM43 Mike Smith 2.50 6.00
MM44 Tim Thomas 2.50 6.00
MM45 Rogie Vachon 3.00 8.00
MM46 John Vanbiesbrouck 2.50 6.00
MM47 Semyon Varlamov 2.50 6.00
MM48 Tomas Vokoun 2.00 5.00
MM49 Cam Ward 2.50 6.00
MM50 Gerry Cheevers 2.50 6.00

2011-12 Between The Pipes Stick and Jersey Silver

SILVER ANNOUNCED PRINT RUN 19
SJ01 Patrick Roy 40.00 100.00
SJ02 Billy Smith 15.00 40.00
SJ03 Mike Richter 15.00 40.00
SJ04 Felix Potvin 25.00 60.00
SJ05 Bill Ranford 15.00 40.00
SJ06 Chris Osgood 15.00 40.00
SJ07 John Vanbiesbrouck 25.00 60.00
SJ08 Pelle Lindbergh 30.00 75.00
SJ09 Ryan Miller 15.00 40.00
SJ10 Henrik Lundqvist 15.00 40.00
SJ11 Roberto Luongo 15.00 40.00
SJ12 Curtis Joseph 15.00 40.00
SJ13 Arturs Irbe 12.00 30.00
SJ14 Rogie Vachon 20.00 50.00
SJ15 Dominik Hasek 20.00 50.00
SJ16 Ed Belfour 15.00 40.00
SJ17 Marc-Andre Fleury 25.00 60.00
SJ18 Tony Esposito 15.00 40.00
SJ19 Rick DiPietro 12.00 30.00
SJ20 Carey Price 50.00 120.00
SJ21 Mike Vernon 12.00 30.00

2012-13 Between The Pipes

COMPLETE SET (200) 25.00 50.00
1 Jacob Brennan .20 .50
2 Philippe Cadorette .20 .50
3 Mathias Niederberger .20 .50
4 Malcolm Subban .30 .75
5 Etienne Marcoux .20 .50
6 Storm Phaneuf .20 .50
7 Matej Machovsky .20 .50
8 Corbin Boes .20 .50
9 Chris Driedger .20 .50
10 Alex Bureau .20 .50
11 Christopher Gibson .25 .60
12 Louis-Philip Guindon .15 .40
13 Domenic Graham .20 .50
14 Laurent Brossoit .25 .60
15 Tristan Jarry .25 .60
16 Devin Williams .15 .40
17 Oscar Dansk .40 1.00
18 Austin Lotz .15 .40
19 Daniel Cotton .15 .40
20 Robert Steeves .15 .40
21 Garret Sparks .30 .75
22 Jaroslav Pavelka .20 .50
23 Zachary Fucale .50 1.25
24 Cole Cheveldave .30 .75
25 Taran Kozun .15 .40
26 Jackson Whistle .15 .40
27 Jordon Cooke .20 .50
28 Mike Morrison .15 .40
29 Joel Vienneau .20 .50
30 John Gibson .40 1.00
31 Mackenzie Skapski .20 .50
32 Ty Rimmer .20 .50
33 Anthony Stolarz .30 .75
34 Jake Patterson .30 .75
35 Marek Langhamer .25 .60
36 Spencer Martin .20 .50
37 Alex Dubeau .25 .60
38 Justin Paulic .15 .40
39 Daniel Wapple .15 .40
40 Christopher Festarini .15 .40
41 Daniel Altshuller .20 .50
42 Clint Windsor .15 .40
43 Jacob Blair .15 .40
44 Brandon Hope .15 .40
45 Jordan Binnington .25 .60
46 Antoine Bibeau .15 .40
47 Maxime Lagace .20 .50
48 Andrew D'Agostini .20 .50
49 Michael Giugovaz .15 .40
50 Matt Mahalak .20 .50
51 Brendan Burke .20 .50
52 Mac Carruth .20 .50
53 Luke Siemens .20 .50
54 Brett Zarowny .15 .40
55 Mac Engel .25 .60
56 Francois Brassard .15 .40
57 Patrik Bartosak .25 .60
58 Matt Hewitt .20 .50
59 Philippe Desrosiers .20 .50
60 Robin Gusse .20 .50
61 Alexandre Belanger .20 .50
62 Jake Paterson .30 .75
63 Nikita Serebryakov .25 .60
64 Sebastien Auger .20 .50
65 J.P. Anderson .20 .50
66 Andrey Makarov .25 .60
67 Matt Murray .25 .60
68 Brandon Glover .25 .60
69 Marvin Cupper .15 .40
70 Jacob Gervais-Chouinard .20 .50
71 Eric Williams .15 .40
72 Franky Palazzese .15 .40
73 Eetu Laurikainen .25 .60
74 Eric Comrie .25 .60
75 Francois Tremblay .20 .50
76 Brandon Whitney .25 .60
77 Payton Lee .15 .40
78 Patrik Polivka .25 .60
79 Ondrej Pavelec SG .25 .60
80 Semyon Varlamov SG .25 .60
81 Antti Niemi SG .20 .50
82 Brian Elliott SG .20 .50
83 Carey Price SG .75 2.00
84 Corey Crawford SG .30 .75
85 Evgeni Nabokov SG .20 .50
86 Henrik Lundqvist SG .30 .75
87 Ilya Bryzgalov SG .25 .60
88 Jonas Hiller SG .20 .50
89 Jonathan Quick SG .40 1.00
90 Kari Lehtonen SG .20 .50
91 Marc-Andre Fleury SG .40 1.00
92 Jimmy Howard SG .25 .60
93 Nikolai Khabibulin SG .25 .60
94 Rick DiPietro SG .20 .50
95 Roberto Luongo SG .25 .60
96 Tomas Vokoun SG .20 .50

97 Arturs Irbe DEC .20 .50
98 Bill Ranford DEC .25 .60
99 Bob Essensa DEC .25 .60
100 Brian Hayward DEC .20 .50
101 Byron Dafoe DEC .25 .60
102 Chris Osgood DEC .25 .60
103 Chris Terreri DEC .20 .50
104 Craig Billington DEC .15 .40
105 Curtis Joseph DEC .25 .60
106 Damian Rhodes DEC .25 .60
107 Dan Cloutier DEC .20 .50
108 Dominik Hasek DEC .30 .75
109 Ed Belfour DEC .25 .60
110 Garth Snow DEC .20 .50
111 Jim Carey DEC .20 .50
112 John Vanbiesbrouck DEC .25 .60
113 Kirk McLean DEC .20 .50
114 Mike Richter DEC .25 .60
115 Olaf Kolzig DEC .25 .60
116 Peter Sidorkiewicz DEC .20 .50
117 Rick Wamsley DEC .25 .60
118 Ron Tugnutt DEC .20 .50
119 Sean Burke DEC .15 .40
120 Tim Cheveldae DEC .25 .60
121 Wendell Young DEC .15 .40
122 Allan Bester DEC .20 .50
123 Andy Moog DEC .25 .60
124 Billy Smith DEC .25 .60
125 Bob Froese DEC .20 .50
126 Corrado Micalef DEC .15 .40
127 Don Beaupre DEC .20 .50
128 Ed Mio DEC .25 .60
129 Glen Hanlon DEC .20 .50
130 Grant Fuhr DEC .25 .60
131 Jim Craig DEC .30 .75
132 Jiri Crha DEC .15 .40
133 John Garrett DEC .25 .60
134 Kelly Hrudey DEC .20 .50
135 Michel Dion DEC .20 .50
136 Mike Liut DEC .20 .50
137 Patrick Roy DEC .60 1.50
138 Rejean Lemelin DEC .25 .60
139 Richard Brodeur DEC .25 .60
140 Richard Sevigny DEC .20 .50
141 Rick St. Croix DEC .15 .40
142 Ron Hextall DEC .25 .60
143 Doug Favell DEC .25 .60
144 Bernie Parent DEC .25 .60
145 Chico Resch DEC .25 .60
146 Gary Bromley DEC .20 .50
147 Gary Inness DEC .25 .60
148 Gerry Cheevers DEC .25 .60
149 Gilles Gilbert DEC .20 .50
150 Gilles Gratton DEC .25 .60
151 Gilles Meloche DEC .25 .60
152 Gilles Villemure DEC .20 .50
153 Bobby Taylor DEC .15 .40
154 Mike Palmateer DEC .25 .60
155 Rogie Vachon DEC .30 .75
156 Ron Grahame DEC .20 .50
157 Ron Low DEC .20 .50
158 Tony Esposito DEC .25 .60
159 Vladislav Tretiak DEC .30 .75
160 Cesare Maniago DEC .25 .60
161 Charlie Hodge DEC .20 .50
162 Denis DeJordy DEC .20 .50
163 Ed Giacomin DEC .25 .60
164 Glenn Hall DEC .25 .60
165 Johnny Bower DEC .25 .60
166 Roger Crozier DEC .20 .50
167 Gump Worsley DEC .25 .60
168 Jacques Plante DEC .30 .75
169 Terry Sawchuk DEC .25 .60
170 Bill Durnan DEC .25 .60
171 Chuck Rayner DEC .15 .40
172 Emile Francis DEC .20 .50
173 Frank Brimsek DEC .20 .50
174 Harry Lumley DEC .25 .60
175 Turk Broda DEC .25 .60
176 Charlie Gardiner DEC .20 .50
177 George Hainsworth DEC .25 .60
178 Lorne Chabot DEC .20 .50
179 Roy Worters DEC .25 .60
180 Tiny Thompson DEC .25 .60
181 Patrick Roy RB .60 1.50
182 Grant Fuhr RB .25 .60
183 Glenn Hall RB .25 .60
184 George Hainsworth RB .25 .60
185 Henrik Lundqvist RB .30 .75
186 Gerry Cheevers RB .25 .60
187 Alec Connell RB .20 .50
188 Sam LoPresti RB .15 .40
189 Dominik Hasek RB .30 .75
190 Ron Tugnutt RB .20 .50
191 Vladislav Tretiak IS .30 .75
192 Tony Esposito IS .25 .60
193 Rogie Vachon IS .30 .75
194 Jim Craig IS .30 .75
195 Grant Fuhr IS .25 .60
196 Bill Ranford IS .25 .60
197 Mike Richter IS .25 .60
198 Dominik Hasek IS .30 .75
199 Henrik Lundqvist IS .30 .75
200 Roberto Luongo IS .25 .60

2012-13 Between The Pipes Aspire Jerseys Silver

ANNOUNCED PRINT RUN 140
ASP01 E.Comrie/C.Price 20.00 50.00
ASP02 J.Binnington/C.Joseph 8.00 20.00
ASP03 J.Gibson/J.Hiller 6.00 15.00
ASP04 O.Dansk/H.Lundqvist 10.00 25.00
ASP05 J.Anderson/A.Niemi 5.00 12.00
ASP06 M.Murray/M.Fleury 10.00 25.00
ASP07 C.Gibson/J.Quick 8.00 20.00
ASP08 G.Sparks/F.Potvin 8.00 20.00
ASP09 J.Paterson/J.Howard 6.00 15.00
ASP10 B.Whitney/E.Belfour 6.00 15.00
ASP11 L.Brossoit/M.Vernon 6.00 15.00
ASP12 M.Subban/A.Moog 6.00 15.00
ASP13 M.Lagace/K.Lehtonen 5.00 12.00
ASP14 D.Honzik/R.Luongo 6.00 15.00
ASP15 D.Altshuller/A.Irbe 8.00 20.00
ASP16 R.DiPietro/B.Smith 6.00 15.00
ASP17 I.Bryzgalov/R.Hextall 6.00 15.00
ASP18 C.Price/P.Roy 15.00 40.00
ASP19 H.Lundqvist/M.Richter 6.00 15.00
ASP20 P.Roy/D.Bouchard 10.00 25.00

2012-13 Between The Pipes Autographs

ONE AUTO PER BOX
AABE Allan Bester DEC 6.00 15.00
AABI Antoine Bibeau 3.00 8.00
AAD Alex Dubeau 5.00 12.00
AAI Arturs Irbe DEC 10.00 25.00
AAM Andrey Makarov 5.00 12.00
AAMO Andy Moog DEC 6.00 15.00
AAN Antti Niemi SG 5.00 12.00
AAS Anthony Stolarz 6.00 15.00
ABB Brendan Burke 4.00 10.00
ABBI Ben Bishop SG SP 10.00 25.00
ABD Byron Dafoe DEC 5.00 12.00
ABE Bob Essensa DEC 6.00 15.00
ABEL Brian Elliott SG SP 10.00 25.00
ABF Bob Froese DEC 5.00 12.00
ABH Brian Hayward DEC 5.00 12.00
ABP Bernie Parent DEC SP 20.00 40.00
ABT Bobby Taylor DEC 4.00 10.00
ABW Brandon Whitney 5.00 12.00
ACB Corbin Boes 4.00 10.00
ACDI Craig Billington DEC 4.00 10.00
ACC Cole Cheveldave 6.00 15.00
ACCR Corey Crawford SG SP 20.00 40.00
ACD Chris Driedger 4.00 10.00
ACG Christopher Gibson 5.00 12.00
ACJ Curtis Joseph DEC SP 20.00 40.00
ACM Corrado Micalef DEC 4.00 10.00
ACMA Cesare Maniago DEC SP 12.00 30.00
ACP Carey Price SG SP 30.00 80.00
ACR Chico Resch DEC SP 10.00 25.00
ACT Chris Terreri DEC SP 8.00 20.00
ADA Daniel Altshuller 4.00 10.00
ADB Don Beaupre DEC 5.00 12.00
ADC Dan Cloutier DEC SP 10.00 25.00
ADD Denis DeJordy DEC SP 8.00 20.00
ADF Doug Favell DEC SP 25.00 50.00
ADG Domenic Graham 4.00 10.00
ADH Denis Herron DEC 5.00 12.00
ADHA Dominik Hasek DEC SP 20.00 40.00
ADR Damian Rhodes DEC 6.00 15.00
ADRI Dennis Riggin DEC 6.00 15.00
AEC Eric Comrie 5.00 12.00
AEF Emile Francis DEC SP 15.00 40.00
AEG Ed Giacomin DEC 8.00 20.00
AEL Eetu Laurikainen 5.00 12.00
AEM Etienne Marcoux 4.00 10.00
AEMI Ed Mio DEC 6.00 15.00
AEN Evgeni Nabokov SG SP 8.00 20.00
AFB Francois Brassard 3.00 8.00
AFT Francois Tremblay 4.00 10.00
AGB Gary Bromley DEC 5.00 12.00
AGG Gilles Gilbert DEC 5.00 12.00
AGGR Gilles Gratton DEC 6.00 15.00
AGH Glen Hanlon DEC 5.00 12.00
AGHE Guy Hebert DEC SP 15.00 30.00
AGI Gary Inness DEC 6.00 15.00
AGM Gilles Meloche DEC 6.00 15.00
AGS Greg Stefan DEC 5.00 12.00
AGSN Garth Snow DEC 5.00 12.00
AGSP Garret Sparks 6.00 15.00
AGV Gilles Villemure DEC 5.00 12.00
AHL Henrik Lundqvist SG SP 15.00 40.00
AIB Ilya Bryzgalov SG SP 25.00 50.00
AJA J.P. Anderson 4.00 10.00
AJB Jacob Brennan 4.00 10.00
AJBI Jordan Binnington 5.00 12.00
AJBO Johnny Bower DEC SP 20.00 40.00
AJC Jordon Cooke 4.00 10.00
AJCA Jim Carey DEC SP 10.00 25.00
AJCR Jiri Crha DEC 6.00 15.00
AJCRA Jim Craig DEC SP 20.00 40.00
AJG John Gibson 8.00 20.00
AJGA John Garrett DEC 6.00 15.00
AJGC Jacob Gervais-Chouinard 4.00 10.00
AJH Jonas Hiller SG 5.00 12.00
AJHO Jimmy Howard SG 10.00 25.00
AJP Jake Paterson 6.00 15.00
AJPA Jaroslav Pavelka 4.00 10.00
AJPAT Jake Patterson 6.00 15.00
AJQ Jonathan Quick SG 12.00 30.00
AJV John Vanbiesbrouck DEC SP 25.00 50.00
AKB Kevin Bailie 5.00 12.00
AKH Kelly Hrudey DEC 5.00 12.00
AKL Kari Lehtonen SG 6.00 15.00
AKM Kirk McLean DEC 8.00 20.00
ALB Laurent Brossoit 5.00 12.00
ALL Liam Liston 4.00 10.00
AMC Mac Carruth SP 8.00 20.00
AMD Michel Dion DEC 5.00 12.00
AME Mac Engel 5.00 12.00
AMF Marc-Andre Fleury SG SP 12.00 30.00
AMH Matt Hewitt 4.00 10.00
AML Manny Legace DEC 6.00 15.00
AMLI Mike Liut DEC SP 20.00 40.00
AMM Matt Mahalak 4.00 10.00
AMMU Matt Murray 5.00 12.00
AMN Mathias Niederberger 4.00 10.00
AMP Mike Palmateer DEC SP 30.00 60.00
AMS Malcolm Subban 8.00 20.00
ANK Nikolai Khabibulin SG SP 15.00 30.00
AOD Oscar Dansk 6.00 15.00
AOK Olaf Kolzig DEC SP 20.00 40.00
AOP Ondrej Pavelec SG 8.00 20.00
APB Patrik Bartosak 5.00 12.00
APC Philippe Cadorette 4.00 10.00
APD Philippe Desrosiers 4.00 10.00
APP Patrik Polivka 5.00 12.00
APR Patrick Roy DEC SP 40.00 80.00
APS Peter Sidorkiewicz DEC 5.00 12.00
ARB Richard Brodeur DEC SP 10.00 25.00
ARD Rick DiPietro SG SP 8.00 20.00
ARE Ray Emery SG SP 20.00 40.00
ARG Robin Gusse 4.00 10.00
ARGR Ron Grahame DEC SP 8.00 20.00
ARH Ron Hextall DEC SP 20.00 40.00
ARL Rejean Lemelin DEC 6.00 15.00
ARLO Ron Low DEC 5.00 12.00
ARLU Roberto Luongo SG SP 10.00 25.00
ARS Richard Sevigny DEC 5.00 12.00
ARST Rick St. Croix DEC SP 8.00 20.00
ART Ron Tugnutt DEC 8.00 20.00
ASA Sebastien Auger 5.00 12.00
ASB Sean Burke DEC 4.00 10.00
ASM Spencer Martin 4.00 10.00
ASP Storm Phaneuf 4.00 10.00
ASV Semyon Varlamov SG SP 10.00 25.00
ATC Tim Cheveldae DEC 6.00 15.00
ATE Tony Esposito DEC SP 25.00 50.00
ATJ Tristan Jarry 5.00 12.00
ATR Ty Rimmer 4.00 10.00
ATV Tomas Vokoun SG 5.00 12.00
AVT Vladislav Tretiak DEC SP 20.00 40.00
AWY Wendell Young DEC 4.00 10.00
AZF Zachary Fucale 12.00 30.00

2012-13 Between The Pipes Big League Debut Jerseys Silver

BL1-BL30 ANNOUNCED PRINT RUN 100
BL31-BL40 ANNOUNCED PRINT RUN 19
BL01 Carey Price/100* 20.00 50.00
BL02 Chris Osgood/100* 6.00 15.00
BL03 Curtis Joseph/100* 8.00 20.00
BL04 Dan Cloutier/100* 5.00 12.00
BL05 Ed Belfour/100* 6.00 15.00
BL06 Evgeni Nabokov/100* 6.00 15.00
BL07 Felix Potvin/100* 8.00 20.00
BL08 Don Beaupre/100* 5.00 12.00
BL09 Jimmy Howard/100* 6.00 15.00
BL10 Jonathan Quick/100* 10.00 25.00
BL11 Kari Lehtonen/100* 5.00 12.00
BL12 Marc-Andre Fleury/100* 10.00 25.00
BL13 Mike Richter/100* 5.00 12.00
BL14 Nikolai Khabibulin/100* 6.00 15.00
BL15 Olaf Kolzig/100* 6.00 15.00
BL16 Ondrej Pavelec/100* 6.00 15.00
BL17 Ray Emery/100* 5.00 12.00
BL18 Rick DiPietro/100* 5.00 12.00
BL19 Ron Hextall/100* 6.00 15.00
BL20 Ron Tugnutt/100* 5.00 12.00
BL21 Brian Elliott/100* 5.00 12.00
BL22 Antti Niemi/100* 5.00 12.00
BL23 Jonas Hiller/100* 5.00 12.00
BL24 John Vanbiesbrouck/100* 10.00 25.00
BL25 Chris Terreri/100* 5.00 12.00
BL26 Mike Vernon/100* 6.00 15.00
BL27 Patrick Roy/100* 15.00 40.00
BL28 Tim Cheveldae/100* 6.00 15.00
BL29 Allan Bester/100* 5.00 12.00
BL30 Tom Barrasso/100* 6.00 15.00
BL31 Ed Giacomin/19* 12.00 30.00
BL32 Jacques Plante/19* 20.00 50.00
BL33 Rogie Vachon/19* 20.00 50.00
BL34 Terry Sawchuk/19* 12.00 30.00
BL35 Grant Fuhr/19* 15.00 40.00
BL36 Mike Palmateer/19* 15.00 40.00
BL37 Tony Esposito/19* 15.00 40.00
BL38 Bernie Parent/19* 15.00 40.00
BL39 Corey Crawford/19* 15.00 40.00
BL40 Henrik Lundqvist/19* 10.00 25.00

2012-13 Between The Pipes Draft Day Jerseys Silver

ANNOUNCED PRINT RUN 100
DD01 M.Subban/D.Altshuller 10.00 25.00
DD02 M.Murray/J.Paterson 8.00 20.00
DD03 O.Dansk/B.Whitney 8.00 20.00
DD04 J.Gibson/C.Gibson 6.00 15.00
DD05 L.Brossoit/J.Binnington 8.00 20.00
DD06 D.Honzik/G.Sparks 8.00 20.00
DD07 C.Price/J.Quick 20.00 50.00
DD08 B.Bishop/O.Pavelec 6.00 15.00
DD09 M.Fleury/J.Howard 10.00 25.00
DD10 I.Bryzgalov/H.Lundqvist 8.00 20.00
DD11 E.Nabokov/D.Cloutier 5.00 12.00
DD12 O.Kolzig/A.Irbe 10.00 25.00
DD13 S.Burke/M.Richter 8.00 20.00
DD14 P.Roy/K.McLean 15.00 40.00
DD15 V.Tretiak/T.Barrasso 20.00 40.00
DD16 A.Bester/D.Hasek 10.00 25.00
DD17 G.Fuhr/M.Vernon 12.00 30.00
DD18 J.Vanbiesbrouck/G.Stefan 8.00 20.00
DD19 R.Lemelin/M.Palmateer 6.00 15.00
DD20 G.Meloche/B.Smith 8.00 20.00

2012-13 Between The Pipes He Shoots He Saves Points

EACH HAS NINE CARDS OF EQUAL VALUE
BP1 Bernie Parent UL .25 .60
CP1 Carey Price UL .75 2.00
DH1 Dominik Hasek UL .30 .75
EB1 Ed Belfour UL .25 .60
FP1 Felix Potvin UL .40 1.00
GF1 Grant Fuhr UL .25 .60
HL1 Henrik Lundqvist UL .30 .75
JQ1 Jonathan Quick UL .40 1.00
PR1 Patrick Roy UL .60 1.50
RL1 Roberto Luongo UL .25 .60
MAF1 Marc-Andre Fleury UL .40 1.00

2012-13 Between The Pipes He Shoots He Saves Prizes

ANNOUNCED PRINT RUN 20
ISSUED VIA MAIL REDEMPTION
HSHS01 Bernie Parent 30.00 80.00
HSHS02 John Vanbiesbrouck 20.00 50.00
HSHS03 Curtis Joseph 15.00 40.00
HSHS04 Chris Osgood 20.00 50.00
HSHS05 Dominik Hasek 25.00 60.00
HSHS06 Nikolai Khabibulin 20.00 50.00
HSHS07 Terry Sawchuk 30.00 80.00
HSHS08 Mike Vernon 40.00 80.00
HSHS09 Felix Potvin 25.00 60.00
HSHS10 Ron Hextall 25.00 60.00
HSHS11 Carey Price 60.00 150.00
HSHS12 Tony Esposito 30.00 80.00
HSHS13 Henrik Lundqvist 20.00 50.00
HSHS14 Rick DiPietro 15.00 40.00
HSHS15 Patrick Roy
HSHS16 Ed Giacomin 25.00 60.00
HSHS17 Sean Burke 25.00 60.00
HSHS18 Arturs Irbe 25.00 60.00
HSHS19 Marc-Andre Fleury 30.00 80.00
HSHS20 Mike Richter 20.00 50.00
HSHS21 Jacques Plante 50.00 100.00
HSHS22 Dan Cloutier 15.00 40.00
HSHS23 Vladislav Tretiak 20.00 40.00
HSHS24 Jonas Hiller 15.00 40.00
HSHS25 Pelle Lindbergh 30.00 80.00
HSHS26 Bill Ranford 50.00 100.00
HSHS27 Ilya Bryzgalov 20.00 50.00
HSHS28 Grant Fuhr 20.00 50.00
HSHS29 Patrick Roy 25.00 60.00
HSHS30 Kirk McLean 20.00 50.00

2012-13 Between The Pipes Jerseys Silver

ANNOUNCED PRINT RUN 140
PATCH/19: .8X TO 2X BASIC JSY/140*
M01 Daniel Altshuller 3.00 8.00
M02 J.P. Anderson 3.00 8.00
M03 Kevin Bailie 4.00 10.00
M04 Don Beaupre 3.00 8.00
M05 Ed Belfour 4.00 10.00
M06 Jordan Binnington 4.00 10.00
M07 Laurent Brossoit 4.00 10.00
M08 Ilya Bryzgalov 4.00 10.00
M09 Sean Burke 2.50 6.00
M10 Tim Cheveldae 4.00 10.00
M11 Cole Cheveldave 5.00 12.00
M12 Dan Cloutier 3.00 8.00
M13 Eric Comrie 4.00 10.00
M14 Jordon Cooke 3.00 8.00
M15 Andrew D'Agostini 3.00 8.00
M16 Byron Dafoe 4.00 10.00
M17 Oscar Dansk 5.00 12.00
M18 Rick DiPietro 4.00 10.00
M19 Alex Dubeau 4.00 10.00
M20 Mac Engel 4.00 10.00
M21 Marc-Andre Fleury 5.00 12.00
M22 Zachary Fucale 6.00 15.00
M23 Grant Fuhr 4.00 10.00
M24 John Garrett 4.00 10.00
M25 Jacob Gervais-Chouinard 3.00 8.00
M26 Christopher Gibson 4.00 10.00
M27 John Gibson 6.00 15.00
M28 Michael Giugovaz 2.50 6.00
M29 Robin Gusse 3.00 8.00
M30 Dominik Hasek 5.00 12.00
M31 David Honzik 4.00 10.00
M32 Gary Inness 4.00 10.00
M33 Arturs Irbe 6.00 15.00
M34 Tristan Jarry 4.00 10.00
M35 Curtis Joseph 6.00 15.00
M36 Nikolai Khabibulin 4.00 10.00
M37 Olaf Kolzig 6.00 15.00
M38 Maxime Lagace 3.00 8.00
M39 Manny Legace 3.00 8.00
M40 Kari Lehtonen 3.00 8.00
M41 Rejean Lemelin 5.00 12.00
M42 Liam Liston 3.00 8.00
M43 Henrik Lundqvist 5.00 12.00
M44 Roberto Luongo 4.00 10.00
M45 Spencer Martin 3.00 8.00
M46 Matt Murray 4.00 10.00
M47 Antti Niemi 3.00 8.00
M48 Jake Paterson 5.00 12.00
M49 Ondrej Pavelec 5.00 12.00
M50 Storm Phaneuf 3.00 8.00
M51 Carey Price 12.00 30.00
M52 Jonathan Quick 6.00 15.00
M53 Ty Rimmer 3.00 8.00
M54 Patrick Roy 10.00 25.00
M55 Garret Sparks 5.00 12.00
M56 Malcolm Subban 5.00 12.00
M57 Francois Tremblay 6.00 15.00
M58 John Vanbiesbrouck 5.00 12.00
M59 Brandon Whitney 4.00 10.00
M60 Ray Emery 4.00 10.00

2012-13 Between The Pipes Junior Gems Silver

ANNOUNCED PRINT RUN 100
JG01 M.Subban/J.Gibson 12.00 30.00
JG02 J.Binnington/G.Sparks 6.00 15.00
JG03 M.Engel/T.Rimmer 5.00 12.00
JG04 M.Lagace/A.Dubeau 5.00 12.00
JG05 J.Anderson/M.Murray 5.00 12.00
JG06 C.Cheveldave/J.Cooke 6.00 15.00
JG07 A.D'Agostini/M.Giugovaz 4.00 10.00
JG08 S.Phaneuf/B.Whitney 5.00 12.00
JG09 L.Brossoit/T.Jarry 5.00 12.00
JG10 E.Comrie/Z.Fucale 10.00 25.00

2012-13 Between The Pipes Masked Men V Rainbow

SILVER/50: .8X TO 2X RAINBOW
MM1 Murray Bannerman 2.50 6.00
MM2 Ed Belfour 4.00 10.00
MM3 Dan Bouchard 2.50 6.00
MM4 Gary Bromley 2.50 6.00
MM5 Gerry Cheevers 3.00 8.00
MM6 Michel Dion 2.50 6.00
MM7 Ray Emery 2.50 6.00
MM8 Doug Favell 3.00 8.00
MM9 Marc-Andre Fleury 5.00 12.00
MM10 Marc-Andre Fleury 5.00 12.00
MM11 Grant Fuhr 4.00 10.00
MM12 Corey Crawford 4.00 10.00
MM13 John Garrett 3.00 8.00
MM14 Gilles Gratton 3.00 8.00
MM15 Dominik Hasek 4.00 10.00
MM16 Brian Hayward 2.50 6.00
MM17 Rick DiPietro 2.50 6.00
MM18 Ron Hextall 4.00 10.00
MM19 Jimmy Howard 3.00 8.00
MM20 Arturs Irbe 2.50 6.00
MM21 Curtis Joseph 4.00 10.00
MM22 Nikolai Khabibulin 3.00 8.00
MM23 Olaf Kolzig 3.00 8.00
MM24 Manny Legace 2.50 6.00
MM25 Ron Low 2.50 6.00
MM26 Denis Herron 2.50 6.00
MM27 Roberto Luongo 3.00 8.00
MM28 Kirk McLean 2.50 6.00
MM29 Gilles Meloche 3.00 8.00
MM30 Ed Mio 3.00 8.00
MM31 Andy Moog 3.00 8.00
MM32 Evgeni Nabokov 2.50 6.00
MM33 Mike Palmateer 3.00 8.00
MM34 Bernie Parent 4.00 10.00
MM35 Ondrej Pavelec 3.00 8.00
MM36 Felix Potvin 5.00 12.00
MM37 Carey Price 10.00 25.00
MM38 Jonathan Quick 5.00 12.00
MM39 Bill Ranford 3.00 8.00
MM40 Chico Resch 3.00 8.00
MM41 Damian Rhodes 3.00 8.00
MM43 Mike Richter 3.00 8.00
MM43 Patrick Roy 8.00 20.00
MM44 Gary Simmons 3.00 8.00
MM45 Billy Smith 3.00 8.00
MM46 Garth Snow 2.50 6.00
MM47 Wayne Stephenson 2.50 6.00
MM48 Rogie Vachon 4.00 10.00
MM49 John Vanbiesbrouck 3.00 8.00
MM50 Semyon Varlamov 3.00 8.00

2012-13 Between The Pipes Masked Men V Memorabilia

ANNOUNCED PRINT RUN 19
MM01 Ed Belfour 10.00 25.00
MM02 Gerry Cheevers 12.00 30.00
MM03 Ray Emery 10.00 25.00
MM04 Marc-Andre Fleury 15.00 40.00
MM05 Grant Fuhr 15.00 40.00
MM06 Dominik Hasek 12.00 30.00
MM07 Rick DiPietro 12.00 30.00
MM08 Ron Hextall 12.00 30.00
MM09 Jimmy Howard 10.00 25.00
MM10 Arturs Irbe 15.00 40.00
MM11 Curtis Joseph 12.00 30.00
MM12 Olaf Kolzig 12.00 30.00
MM13 Henrik Lundqvist 12.00 30.00
MM14 Roberto Luongo 10.00 25.00
MM15 Andy Moog 12.00 30.00
MM16 Evgeni Nabokov 10.00 25.00
MM17 Felix Potvin 15.00 40.00
MM18 Carey Price 30.00 80.00
MM19 Jonathan Quick 15.00 40.00
MM20 Bill Ranford 12.00 30.00
MM21 Patrick Roy 20.00 50.00
MM22 Billy Smith 10.00 25.00
MM23 Garth Snow 8.00 20.00
MM24 John Vanbiesbrouck 15.00 40.00

2012-13 Between The Pipes Rivals Silver

ANNOUNCED PRINT RUN 70
R01 P.Roy/R.Tugnutt 12.00 30.00
R02 M.Richter/R.Hextall 12.00 30.00
R03 A.Bester/G.Stefan 6.00 15.00
R04 R.Lemelin/G.Fuhr 10.00 25.00
R05 E.Belfour/C.Joseph 10.00 25.00
R06 F.Potvin/P.Roy 20.00 50.00
R07 A.Moog/P.Roy 12.00 30.00
R08 J.Vanbiesbrouck/B.Smith 8.00 20.00
R09 A.Niemi/R.Luongo 8.00 20.00
R10 P.Roy/C.Osgood 20.00 50.00

2012-13 Between The Pipes Stick and Jersey Silver

ANNOUNCED PRINT RUN 19
SJ01 Mike Vernon 10.00 25.00
SJ02 John Vanbiesbrouck 20.00 50.00
SJ03 Rogie Vachon 15.00 40.00
SJ04 Patrick Roy 30.00 80.00
SJ05 Bill Ranford 12.00 30.00
SJ06 Chris Osgood 12.00 30.00
SJ07 Grant Fuhr 15.00 40.00
SJ08 Dominik Hasek 20.00 50.00
SJ09 Arturs Irbe
SJ10 Curtis Joseph 12.00 30.00
SJ11 Olaf Kolzig 20.00 50.00
SJ12 Allan Bester 10.00 25.00
SJ13 Roger Crozier 10.00 25.00
SJ14 Billy Smith 12.00 30.00
SJ15 Sean Burke 12.00 30.00
SJ16 Rick DiPietro 15.00 40.00
SJ17 Marc-Andre Fleury 15.00 40.00
SJ18 Richard Brodeur 12.00 30.00
SJ19 Bernie Parent 25.00 50.00
SJ20 Henrik Lundqvist 15.00 40.00

2013-14 Between the Pipes

COMPLETE SET (150) 15.00 40.00
1 Antti Niemi SG .20 .50
2 Antti Raanta SG .30 .75
3 Ben Bishop SG .25 .60
4 Carey Price SG .75 2.00
5 Corey Crawford SG .30 .75
6 Eddie Lack SG .20 .50
7 Evgeni Nabokov SG .20 .50
8 Jake Allen SG .30 .75
9 Jimmy Howard SG .25 .60
10 Jonas Hiller SG .20 .50
11 Marc-Andre Fleury SG .40 1.00
12 Martin Jones SG .40 1.00
13 Mike Smith SG .25 .60
14 Ray Emery SG .20 .50
15 Semyon Varlamov SG .25 .60
16 Steve Mason SG .20 .50
17 Tomas Vokoun SG .20 .50
18 Tuukka Rask SG .25 .60
19 Viktor Fasth SG .25 .60
20 Ondrej Pavelec SG .25 .60
21 Jonas Gustavsson SG .20 .50
22 Nikolai Khabibulin SG .25 .60
23 Peter Budaj SG .20 .50
24 Andrew D'Agostini CHL .20 .50
25 Sebastien Auger CHL .20 .50
26 Robert Steeves CHL .15 .40
27 Troy Trombley CHL .15 .40
28 Jake Patterson CHL .25 .60
29 Franky Palazzese CHL .15 .40
30 Danny Mumaugh CHL .20 .50
31 Alex Bureau CHL .20 .50
32 Alex Dubeau CHL .20 .50
33 Alex Nedeljkovic CHL .25 .60
34 Alexandre Belanger CHL .20 .50
35 Anthony Brodeur CHL .40 1.00
36 Anthony Stolarz CHL .15 .40
37 Antoine Bibeau CHL .15 .40
38 Austin Lotz CHL .15 .40
39 Brandon Hope CHL .15 .40
40 Brandon Whitney CHL .25 .60
41 Brendan Burke CHL .15 .40
42 Brent Moran CHL .20 .50
43 Charlie Graham CHL .15 .40
44 Chris Driedger CHL .20 .50
45 Daniel Altshuller CHL .20 .50
46 Dawson MacAuley CHL .20 .50
47 Eetu Laurikainen CHL .25 .60
48 Eric Comrie CHL .20 .50
49 Eric Williams CHL .15 .40
50 Etienne Marcoux CHL .15 .40
51 Francois Brassard CHL .15 .40
52 Francois Tremblay CHL .20 .50
53 Jake Paterson CHL .25 .60
54 Jake Smith CHL .20 .50
55 Jordon Cooke CHL .15 .40
56 Julio Billia CHL .25 .60
57 Justin Nichols CHL .20 .50
58 Justin Paulic CHL .25 .60
59 Louis-Philip Guindon CHL .15 .40
60 Mackenzie Blackwood CHL .25 .60
61 Mackenzie Skapski CHL .20 .50
62 Marek Langhamer CHL .25 .60
63 Mason McDonald CHL .25 .60
64 Matt Mahalak CHL .20 .50
65 Matt Murray CHL .25 .60
66 Michael Giugovaz CHL .25 .60
67 Nikita Serebryakov CHL .25 .60
68 Oscar Dansk CHL .30 .75
69 Patrik Bartosak CHL .15 .40
70 Patrik Polivka CHL .25 .60
71 Payton Lee CHL .20 .50
72 Philippe Cadorette CHL .20 .50
73 Philippe Desrosiers CHL .20 .50
74 Spencer Martin CHL .25 .60
75 Storm Phaneuf CHL .15 .40
76 Taylor Dupuis CHL .15 .40
77 Tristan Jarry CHL .20 .50
78 Ty Edmonds CHL .25 .60
79 Zachary Fucale CHL .30 .75
80 Coleman Vollrath CHL .25 .60
81 Andre Racicot GOTG .15 .40
82 Arturs Irbe GOTG .20 .50
83 Bernie Parent GOTG .25 .60
84 Bill Ranford GOTG .25 .60
85 Billy Smith GOTG .25 .60
86 Blaine Lacher GOTG .15 .40
87 Byron Dafoe GOTG .25 .60
88 Charlie Hodge GOTG .20 .50
89 Chris Osgood GOTG .25 .60
90 Clint Malarchuk GOTG .15 .40
91 Corey Hirsch GOTG .15 .40
92 Cristobal Huet GOTG .20 .50
93 Curt Ridley GOTG .15 .40
94 Curtis Joseph GOTG .25 .60
95 Dan Bouchard GOTG .20 .50
96 Daniel Berthiaume GOTG .15 .40
97 Andy Moog GOTG .25 .60
98 Dominic Roussel GOTG .15 .40
99 Dominik Hasek GOTG .30 .75
100 Doug Soetaert GOTG .15 .40
101 Dwayne Roloson GOTG .15 .40
102 Ed Belfour GOTG .25 .60
103 Ed Giacomin GOTG .25 .60
104 Ed Staniowski GOTG .15 .40
105 Emile Francis GOTG .20 .50
106 Felix Potvin GOTG .40 1.00
107 Gerry Cheevers GOTG .25 .60
108 Gilles Villemure GOTG .20 .50
109 Glenn Hall GOTG .25 .60
110 Grant Fuhr GOTG .25 .60
111 Guy Hebert GOTG .20 .50
112 Hardy Astrom GOTG .15 .40
113 Jamie Storr GOTG .15 .40
114 Jeff Hackett GOTG .20 .50
115 Jim Rutherford GOTG .20 .50
116 Jimmy Waite GOTG .20 .50
117 Mike Palmateer GOTG .25 .60
118 Johan Hedberg GOTG .20 .50
119 John Blue GOTG .15 .40
120 John Garrett GOTG .25 .60
121 John Vanbiesbrouck GOTG .25 .60
122 Johnny Bower GOTG .30 .75
123 Kelly Hrudey GOTG .20 .50
124 Tim Cheveldae GOTG .25 .60
125 Kirk McLean GOTG .20 .50
126 Mario Gosselin GOTG .15 .40
127 Mario Lessard GOTG .15 .40
128 Martin Prusek GOTG .15 .40
129 Marty Turco GOTG .25 .60
130 Mike Liut GOTG .20 .50
131 Mike Richter GOTG .25 .60
132 Olaf Kolzig GOTG .25 .60
133 Patrick Lalime GOTG .20 .50
134 Patrick Roy GOTG .60 1.50
135 Pete LoPresti GOTG .15 .40
136 Pete Peeters GOTG .20 .50
137 Richard Brodeur GOTG .25 .60
138 Tommy Salo GOTG .20 .50
139 Rick Wamsley GOTG .25 .60
140 Rogie Vachon GOTG .30 .75
141 Roman Turek GOTG .20 .50
142 Ron Grahame GOTG .20 .50
143 Ron Hextall GOTG .25 .60
144 Sean Burke GOTG .15 .40
145 Steve Baker GOTG .15 .40
146 Steve Penney GOTG .15 .40
147 Tom Barrasso GOTG .25 .60
148 Tony Esposito GOTG .25 .60
149 Ty Conklin GOTG .20 .50
150 Vladislav Tretiak GOTG .30 .75

2013-14 Between the Pipes Aspire Jerseys Silver

ANNOUNCED PRINT RUN 180
ASP01 Z.Fucale/C.Price 15.00 40.00
ASP02 S.Martin/S.Varlamov 5.00 12.00
ASP03 B.Burke/M.Smith 5.00 12.00
ASP04 A.Stolarz/S.Mason 4.00 10.00
ASP05 M.Murray/M.A.Fleury 8.00 20.00
ASP06 J.Paterson/J.Howard 5.00 12.00
ASP07 T.Jarry/M.A.Fleury 8.00 20.00
ASP08 B.Whitney/C.Crawford 6.00 15.00

2013-14 Between the Pipes Autographs

AAB Alex Bureau 4.00 10.00
AABI Antoine Bibeau 3.00 8.00
AABR Anthony Brodeur 8.00 20.00
AAD Alex Dubeau 4.00 10.00
AAI Arturs Irbe 8.00 20.00
AAL Austin Lotz 3.00 8.00
AAN Alex Nedeljkovic 5.00 12.00
AAR Antti Raanta 8.00 20.00
AARA Andre Racicot 4.00 10.00
AAS Anthony Stolarz 3.00 8.00
ABB Ben Bishop 5.00 12.00
ABBR Brendan Burke 3.00 8.00
ABD Byron Dafoe SP 20.00 40.00
ABL Blaine Lacher 5.00 12.00
ABM Brent Moran 3.00 8.00
ABP Bernie Parent SP 25.00 50.00
ABS Billy Smith 5.00 12.00
ACC Corey Crawford 8.00 20.00
ACD Chris Driedger 4.00 10.00
ACG Charlie Graham 3.00 8.00
ACH Charlie Hodge SP 12.50 25.00
ACHI Corey Hirsch 3.00 8.00
ACHI2 Corey Hirsch 3.00 8.00
ACHU Cristobal Huet 5.00 12.00
ACHU2 Cristobal Huet 5.00 12.00
ACJ Curtis Joseph 8.00 20.00
ACM Clint Malarchuk 5.00 12.00
ACM2 Clint Malarchuk 5.00 12.00
ACO Chris Osgood SP 12.00 30.00
ACO2 Chris Osgood SP 12.00 30.00
ACP Carey Price 10.00 25.00
ACR Curt Ridley 8.00 20.00
ACR2 Curt Ridley 8.00 20.00
ACV Coleman Vollrath 5.00 12.00
ADA Daniel Altshuller 3.00 8.00
ADBE Daniel Berthiaume 6.00 15.00
ADBE2 Daniel Berthiaume 6.00 15.00
ADH Denis Herron 6.00 15.00
ADHA Dominik Hasek SP 25.00 50.00
ADR Dominic Roussel 3.00 8.00
ADS Doug Soetaert 3.00 8.00
AEB Ed Belfour SP 30.00 60.00
AEC Eric Comrie 4.00 10.00
AEF Emile Francis SP 12.00 30.00
AEG Ed Giacomin SP 20.00 40.00
AEL Eddie Lack 4.00 10.00
AEM Etienne Marcoux 3.00 8.00
AEN Evgeni Nabokov 4.00 10.00
AES Ed Staniowski 6.00 15.00
AES2 Ed Staniowski 6.00 15.00
AGC Gerry Cheevers SP
AGF Grant Fuhr SP 12.50 25.00
AGH Glenn Hall SP 20.00 40.00
AGV Gilles Villemure 5.00 12.00
AHA Hardy Astrom 5.00 12.00
AHA2 Hardy Astrom 5.00 12.00
AHL Henrik Lundqvist 10.00 25.00
AIB Ilya Bryzgalov SP
AJB Julio Billia 5.00 12.00
AJBL John Blue 4.00 10.00
AJBO Johnny Bower 8.00 20.00
AJC Jordon Cooke 3.00 8.00
AJG John Garrett 6.00 15.00
AJGU Jonas Gustavsson 4.00 10.00
AJH Jimmy Howard 6.00 15.00
AJHA Jeff Hackett 4.00 10.00
AJHE1 Johan Hedberg 4.00 10.00
AJHE2 Johan Hedberg 4.00 10.00
AJHI Jonas Hiller 4.00 10.00
AJN Justin Nichols 4.00 10.00
AJP Jake Patterson 5.00 12.00
AJPA Justin Paulic 5.00 12.00
AJR Jim Rutherford 6.00 15.00
AJR2 Jim Rutherford 6.00 15.00
AJS Jamie Storr 3.00 8.00
AJT Jocelyn Thibault SP 10.00 25.00
AJV John Vanbiesbrouck SP 25.00 50.00
AJW Jimmy Waite 4.00 10.00
AKM Kirk McLean SP 25.00 50.00
ALG Louis-Philip Guindon 3.00 8.00
AMF Marc-Andre Fleury 6.00 15.00
AMG Michael Giugovaz 5.00 12.00
AMGO Mario Gosselin 4.00 10.00
AMGO2 Mario Gosselin 4.00 10.00
AMJ Martin Jones 6.00 15.00
AMLE Mario Lessard 6.00 15.00
AMM Matt Murray 20.00 50.00
AMMA Mason McDonald 5.00 12.00
AMP Martin Prusek 4.00 10.00
AMSK Mackenzie Skapski 4.00 10.00
AMT Marty Turco 5.00 12.00
ANK Nikolai Khabibulin 6.00 15.00
ANS Nikita Serebryakov 5.00 12.00
AOD Oscar Dansk 5.00 12.00
AOK Olaf Kolzig 6.00 15.00
AOP Ondrej Pavelec 8.00 20.00
APB Patrik Bartosak 3.00 8.00
APC Philippe Cadorette 4.00 10.00
APD Philippe Desrosiers 4.00 10.00
APL Payton Lee 4.00 10.00
APLA Patrick Lalime 4.00 10.00
APLO Pete LoPresti 4.00 10.00
APLO2 Pete LoPresti 4.00 10.00
APP Pete Peeters 4.00 10.00
APR Patrick Roy SP 50.00 100.00
APR2 Patrick Roy SP 50.00 100.00
ARB Richard Brodeur SP 25.00 50.00
ARD Rick DiPietro 4.00 10.00
ARE Ray Emery 4.00 10.00
ARG Ron Grahame 5.00 12.00
ARL Roberto Luongo 5.00 12.00
ART Roman Turek SP
ARV Rogie Vachon SP 25.00 50.00
ARW Rick Wamsley SP 15.00 40.00
ASBA Steve Baker 4.00 10.00
ASM Steve Mason 8.00 20.00
ASMA Spencer Martin 5.00 12.00
ASP Storm Phaneuf 3.00 8.00
ASPE Steve Penney 5.00 12.00
ASV Semyon Varlamov 6.00 15.00
ATB Tom Barrasso SP 15.00 40.00
ATB2 Tom Barrasso SP 15.00 40.00
ATC Ty Conklin 4.00 10.00
ATC2 Ty Conklin 4.00 10.00
ATE Tony Esposito SP 20.00 50.00
ATJ Tristan Jarry 4.00 10.00
AVF Viktor Fasth 5.00 12.00
AVT Vladislav Tretiak 15.00 30.00
AZF Zachary Fucale 6.00 15.00

2013-14 Between the Pipes Big League Debut Jerseys Silver

BLD1-BLD18 ANNC'D PRINT RUN 180
BLD19-BLD30 UNPRICED ANNC'D PRINT RUN 9
BLD01 Steve Mason/180* 5.00 12.00
BLD02 Ed Belfour/180* 6.00 15.00
BLD03 Evgeni Nabokov/180* 5.00 12.00
BLD04 Patrick Roy/180* 15.00 40.00
BLD05 Ron Hextall/180* 6.00 15.00
BLD06 Mike Richter/180* 6.00 15.00
BLD07 Mike Vernon/180* 5.00 12.00
BLD08 Carey Price/180* 20.00 50.00
BLD09 Dan Cloutier/180* 5.00 12.00
BLD10 Semyon Varlamov/180* 6.00 15.00
BLD11 Viktor Fasth/180* 6.00 15.00
BLD12 Marty Turco/180* 6.00 15.00
BLD13 Marc-Andre Fleury/180* 10.00 25.00
BLD14 Don Beaupre/180* 4.00 10.00
BLD15 Cristobal Huet/180* 5.00 12.00
BLD16 Ray Emery/180* 5.00 12.00
BLD17 Olaf Kolzig/180* 6.00 15.00
BLD18 Rick Wamsley/180* 6.00 15.00

2013-14 Between the Pipes Current Crop Jerseys Silver

ANNOUNCED PRINT RUN 180
CC01 Corey Crawford 8.00 20.00
CC02 Ray Emery 4.00 10.00
CC03 Viktor Fasth 5.00 12.00
CC04 Marc-Andre Fleury 8.00 20.00
CC05 Antti Niemi 4.00 10.00
CC06 Steve Mason 4.00 10.00
CC07 Carey Price 6.00 15.00
CC08 Tuukka Rask 5.00 12.00
CC09 Evgeni Nabokov 4.00 10.00
CC10 Semyon Varlamov 5.00 12.00

2013-14 Between the Pipes Draft Day Jerseys Silver

ANNOUNCED PRINT RUN 90
DD01 Marc-Andre Fleury 5.00 12.00
DD02 Tuukka Rask 5.00 12.00
DD03 Carey Price 8.00 20.00
DD04 Corey Crawford 6.00 15.00
DD05 Ray Emery 4.00 10.00
DD06 Steve Mason 4.00 10.00
DD07 Ben Bishop 5.00 12.00
DD08 Jimmy Howard
DD09 Jake Allen 6.00 15.00

2013-14 Between the Pipes He Shoots He Saves Points

RANDOM INSERTS IN PACKS
AN1 Antti Niemi UL .20 .50
AN2 Antti Niemi UM .20 .50
AN3 Antti Niemi UR .20 .50
AN4 Antti Niemi CL .20 .50
AN5 Antti Niemi C .20 .50
AN6 Antti Niemi CR .20 .50
AN7 Antti Niemi LL .20 .50
AN8 Antti Niemi LM .20 .50
AN9 Antti Niemi LR .20 .50
AR1 Antti Raanta UL .30 .75
AR2 Antti Raanta UM .30 .75
AR3 Antti Raanta UR .30 .75
AR4 Antti Raanta CL .30 .75
AR5 Antti Raanta C .30 .75
AR6 Antti Raanta CR .30 .75
AR7 Antti Raanta LL .30 .75
AR8 Antti Raanta LM .30 .75
AR9 Antti Raanta LR .30 .75
CC1 Corey Crawford UL .30 .75
CC2 Corey Crawford UM .30 .75
CC3 Corey Crawford UR .30 .75
CC4 Corey Crawford CL .30 .75
CC5 Corey Crawford C .30 .75
CC6 Corey Crawford CR .30 .75
CC7 Corey Crawford LL .30 .75
CC8 Corey Crawford LM .30 .75
CC9 Corey Crawford LR .30 .75
CP1 Carey Price UL .75 2.00
CP2 Carey Price UM .75 2.00
CP3 Carey Price UR .75 2.00
CP4 Carey Price CL .75 2.00
CP5 Carey Price C .75 2.00
CP6 Carey Price CR .75 2.00
CP7 Carey Price LL .75 2.00
CP8 Carey Price LM .75 2.00
CP9 Carey Price LR .75 2.00
EL1 Eddie Lack UL .20 .50
EL2 Eddie Lack UM .20 .50
EL3 Eddie Lack UR .20 .50
EL4 Eddie Lack CL .20 .50
EL5 Eddie Lack C .20 .50
EL6 Eddie Lack CR .20 .50
EL7 Eddie Lack LL .20 .50
EL8 Eddie Lack LM .20 .50
EL9 Eddie Lack LR .20 .50
JH1 Jimmy Howard UL .25 .60
JH2 Jimmy Howard UM .25 .60
JH3 Jimmy Howard UR .25 .60
JH4 Jimmy Howard CL .25 .60
JH5 Jimmy Howard C .25 .60
JH6 Jimmy Howard CR .25 .60
JH7 Jimmy Howard LL .25 .60
JH8 Jimmy Howard LM .25 .60
JH9 Jimmy Howard LR .25 .60
MS1 Mike Smith UL .25 .60
MS2 Mike Smith UM .25 .60

S3 Mike Smith UR .25 .60
S4 Mike Smith CL .25 .60
S5 Mike Smith C .25 .60
S6 Mike Smith CR .25 .60
S7 Mike Smith LL .25 .60
S8 Mike Smith LM .25 .60
S9 Mike Smith LR .25 .60
M1 Steve Mason UL .20 .50
M2 Steve Mason UM .20 .50
M3 Steve Mason UR .20 .50
M4 Steve Mason CL .20 .50
M5 Steve Mason C .20 .50
M6 Steve Mason CR .20 .50
M7 Steve Mason LL .20 .50
M8 Steve Mason LM .20 .50
M9 Steve Mason LR .20 .50
V1 Semyon Varlamov UL .25 .60
V2 Semyon Varlamov UM .25 .60
V3 Semyon Varlamov UR .25 .60
V4 Semyon Varlamov CL .25 .60
V5 Semyon Varlamov C .25 .60
V6 Semyon Varlamov CR .25 .60
V7 Semyon Varlamov LL .25 .60
V8 Semyon Varlamov LM .25 .60
V9 Semyon Varlamov LR .25 .60
R1 Tuukka Rask UL .25 .60
R2 Tuukka Rask UM .25 .60
R3 Tuukka Rask UR .25 .60
R4 Tuukka Rask CL .25 .60
R5 Tuukka Rask C .25 .60
R6 Tuukka Rask CR .25 .60
R7 Tuukka Rask LL .25 .60
R8 Tuukka Rask LM .25 .60
R9 Tuukka Rask LR .25 .60
AF1 Marc-Andre Fleury UL .40 1.00
AF2 Marc-Andre Fleury UM .40 1.00
AF3 Marc-Andre Fleury UR .40 1.00
AF4 Marc-Andre Fleury CL .40 1.00
AF5 Marc-Andre Fleury C .40 1.00
AF6 Marc-Andre Fleury CR .40 1.00
AF7 Marc-Andre Fleury LL .40 1.00
AF8 Marc-Andre Fleury LM .40 1.00
AF9 Marc-Andre Fleury LR .40 1.00

2013-14 Between the Pipes Immortals

Georges Vezina 1.00 2.50
Clint Benedict .75 2.00
Hap Holmes .75 2.00
Hugh Lehman .75 2.00
Alec Connell .75 2.00
John Ross Roach .75 2.00
Doc Stewart 1.25 3.00
Lorne Chabot .75 2.00
George Hainsworth 1.00 2.50
Charlie Gardiner .75 2.00
Hal Winkler .75 2.00
Tiny Thompson 1.00 2.50
Roy Worters 1.00 2.50
Wilf Cude 1.25 3.00
Andy Aitkenhead 1.00 2.50
Norm Smith .75 2.00
Dave Kerr .60 1.50
Mike Karakas .60 1.50
Turk Broda 1.00 2.50
Bill Beveridge .60 1.50
Frank Brimsek .75 2.00
Bill Durnan 1.00 2.50
Paul Bibeault .75 2.00
Johnny Mowers .60 1.50
Chuck Rayner .75 2.00
Steve Buzinski 1.00 2.50
Frank McCool .75 2.00
Ken McAuley .60 1.50
Harry Lumley 1.00 2.50
Jim Henry .60 1.50
Jack Gelineau 1.25 3.00
Al Rollins .75 2.00
Gerry McNeil .60 1.50
Terry Sawchuk 1.00 2.50
Gump Worsley 1.00 2.50
Jacques Plante 1.25 3.00
Bruce Gamble .60 1.50
Hank Bassen .75 2.00
Roger Crozier .75 2.00
Wayne Rutledge .75 2.00
Gary Bauman .75 2.00
Al Smith .60 1.50
Roy Edwards .60 1.50
Bunny Larocque .75 2.00
Pelle Lindbergh 1.00 2.50

2013-14 Between the Pipes Jerseys Silver

NNOUNCED PRINT RUN 180
JM01 Alex Nedeljkovic 4.00 10.00
JM02 Alex Dubeau 3.00 8.00
JM03 Andrew D'Agostini 3.00 8.00
JM04 Anthony Brodeur 6.00 15.00
JM05 Anthony Stolarz 2.50 6.00
JM06 Antoine Bibeau 2.50 6.00
JM07 Brandon Whitney 4.00 10.00
JM08 Brendan Burke 2.50 6.00
JM09 Cole Cheveldave 4.00 10.00
JM10 Daniel Altshuller 3.00 8.00
JM11 Eric Comrie 3.00 8.00
JM12 Etienne Marcoux 2.50 6.00
JM13 Francois Tremblay 3.00 8.00
JM14 Jake Patterson 4.00 10.00
JM15 Jordon Cooke 2.50 6.00
JM16 Julio Billia 4.00 10.00
JM17 Matt Murray 4.00 10.00
JM18 Michael Giugovaz 4.00 10.00
JM19 Oscar Dansk 5.00 12.00
JM20 Patrik Bartosak 2.50 6.00
JM21 Payton Lee 3.00 8.00
JM22 Philippe Desrosiers 3.00 8.00
JM23 Spencer Martin 4.00 10.00
JM24 Storm Phaneuf 2.50 6.00
JM25 Tristan Jarry 4.00 10.00
JM26 Arturs Irbe 3.00 8.00
JM27 Mike Vernon 3.00 8.00
JM28 Bill Ranford 4.00 10.00
JM29 Chris Osgood 4.00 10.00
JM30 Cristobal Huet 5.00 12.00
JM31 Corey Hirsch 4.00 10.00
JM32 Ron Hextall 4.00 10.00
JM33 Andy Moog 4.00 10.00
JM34 Daniel Berthiaume 4.00 10.00
JM35 Dominic Roussel 2.50 6.00
JM36 Dominik Hasek 5.00 12.00
JM37 Ed Belfour 4.00 10.00
JM38 Don Beaupre 3.00 8.00
JM39 Grant Fuhr 4.00 10.00
JM40 Jamie Storr 2.50 6.00
JM41 Jim Rutherford 4.00 10.00
JM42 Johan Hedberg 3.00 8.00
JM43 John Vanbiesbrouck 4.00 10.00
JM44 Kirk McLean 10.00 25.00
JM45 Marty Turco 4.00 10.00
JM46 Mike Richter 6.00 15.00
GUM47 Patrick Lalime 3.00 8.00
GUM48 Patrick Roy 6.00 15.00
GUM49 Tim Cheveldae 4.00 10.00
GUM50 Chico Resch 5.00 12.00
GUM51 Rick Wamsley 4.00 10.00
GUM52 Ty Conklin 3.00 8.00
GUM53 Dwayne Roloson 3.00 8.00
GUM54 Jeff Hackett 3.00 8.00

2013-14 Between the Pipes Pack Your Bags Jerseys Silver

ANNOUNCED PRINT RUN 90
PYB01 Curtis Joseph 6.00 15.00
PYB02 Curtis Joseph 6.00 15.00
PYB03 Dan Cloutier 5.00 12.00
PYB04 Dominik Hasek 8.00 20.00
PYB05 Dominik Hasek 8.00 20.00
PYB06 Ed Belfour 6.00 15.00
PYB07 Semyon Varlamov 6.00 15.00
PYB08 Evgeni Nabokov 5.00 12.00
PYB09 Felix Potvin 10.00 25.00
PYB10 Johan Hedberg 6.00 15.00
PYB11 Grant Fuhr 6.00 15.00
PYB12 Chris Osgood 6.00 15.00
PYB13 John Vanbiesbrouck 6.00 15.00
PYB14 Mike Vernon 5.00 12.00
PYB15 Byron Dafoe 6.00 15.00
PYB16 Patrick Roy 8.00 20.00
PYB17 Ray Emery 5.00 12.00
PYB18 Damian Rhodes 4.00 10.00
PYB19 Manny Fernandez 6.00 15.00
PYB20 Steve Mason 5.00 12.00
PYB21 Tom Barrasso 6.00 15.00

2013-14 Between the Pipes Rivals Jerseys Silver

ANNOUNCED PRINT RUN 90
R01 E.Belfour/D.Hasek 6.00 15.00
R02 J.Howard/C.Crawford 6.00 15.00
R03 C.Price/T.Rask 15.00 40.00
R04 P.Roy/C.Osgood 12.00 30.00
R05 R.Hextall/F.Potvin 8.00 20.00
R06 C.Joseph/P.Lalime 5.00 12.00

2013-14 Between the Pipes Top Prospects Jerseys Silver

ANNOUNCED PRINT RUN 90
TP01 Corey Crawford 5.00 12.00
TP02 Marc-Andre Fleury 6.00 15.00
TP03 Carey Price 12.00 30.00
TP04 Zachary Fucale 5.00 12.00
TP05 Tristan Jarry 3.00 8.00
TP06 Spencer Martin 4.00 10.00
TP07 Ty Edmonds 4.00 10.00
TP08 Mason McDonald 4.00 10.00
TP09 Alex Nedeljkovic 4.00 10.00

1951 Berk Ross

The 1951 Berk Ross set consists of 72 cards (each measuring approximately 2 1/16" by 2 1/2") with tinted photographs, divided evenly into four series (designated in the checklist as 1, 2, 3 and 4). The cards were marketed in boxes containing two card panels, without gum, and the set includes stars of other sports as well as baseball players. The set is sometimes still found in the original packaging. Intact panels command a premium over the listed prices. The catalog designation for this set is W532-1. In every series the first ten cards are baseball players; the set has a heavy emphasis on Yankees and Phillies players as they were in the World Series the year before. The set includes the first card of Bob Cousy as well as a card of Whitey Ford in his Rookie Card year.

COMPLETE SET (72) 900.00 1500.00
1-17 Bill Durnan Hockey 50.00 100.00
1-18 Bill Quackenbush Hockey 40.00 80.00
2-16 Jack Stewart Hockey 20.00 40.00
3-16 Sid Abel Hockey 40.00 80.00

1996-97 Black Diamond

This hobby-only set was issued in one series totaling 180 cards, with three varying levels of difficulty: Single Black Diamond (1-90), Double Black Diamond (91-150), and Triple Black Diamond (151-180). Doubles were inserted 1:4 packs and Triples 1:30 packs. Packs of six cards retailed for $3.49. This set is most noteworthy because of the inclusion of one of the most sought after RCs to date: #160 Joe Thornton. The Gretzky promo mirrors the regular issue, aside from the word SAMPLE which runs across his portrait on the card back.

COMPLETE SET (180) 350.00 600.00
COMP.SINGLE SET (90) 10.00 25.00
1 Roman Turek RC .40 1.00
2 Slava Fetisov .25 .60
3 Mike Dunham .25 .60
4 Jean-Francois Fortin RC .40 1.00
5 Keith Primeau .25 .60
6 Zigmund Palffy .40 1.00
7 Curtis Leschyshyn .25 .60
8 Vladimir Tsyplakov RC .40 1.00
9 Adam Graves .25 .60
10 Ian Laperriere .40 1.00
11 Bill Lindsay .25 .60
12 Brian Leetch .40 1.00
13 Martin Lapointe .25 .60
14 Scott Barney RC .40 1.00
15 Mike Grier RC .50 1.25
16 Vladimir Konstantinov .30 .75
17 Rem Murray RC .40 1.00
18 Ed Jovanovski .30 .75
19 Chris O'Sullivan .25 .60
20 Steve Rucchin .25 .60
21 Jay Pandolfo .40 1.00
22 Nick Boynton RC .40 1.00
23 Greg Adams .25 .60
24 Adam Colagiacomo RC .40 1.00
25 Vincent Damphousse .30 .75
26 Shane Willis RC .40 1.00
27 Alexei Kovalev .25 .60
28 Doug Gilmour .50 1.25
29 Joel Otto .25 .60
30 Donald Audette .25 .60
31 Tommy Salo .30 .75
32 Rob Ray .40 1.00
33 Kris Draper .25 .60
34 Ed Belfour .40 1.00
35 Mike Richter .40 1.00
36 Nikolai Khabibulin .30 .75
37 Eric Desjardins .30 .75
38 Daniel Tkaczuk RC .40 1.00
39 Keith Jones .25 .60
40 Per Gustafsson RC .40 1.00
41 Jocelyn Thibault .40 1.00
42 Mike Gartner .40 1.00
43 Vitali Yachmenev .25 .60
44 Jonas Hoglund .25 .60
45 Craig Janney .30 .75
46 Daymond Langkow .30 .75
47 Mattias Timander RC .40 1.00
48 Scott Young .25 .60
49 Mikael Renberg .30 .75
50 Nicklas Lidstrom .50 1.25
51 Andrei Kovalenko .25 .60
52 Adam Foote .25 .60
53 Guy Hebert .30 .75
54 Kevin Hatcher .25 .60
55 Rick Tocchet .30 .75
56 Sergei Zubov .25 .60
57 Chris Phillips .40 1.00
58 Denis Savard .50 1.25
59 Bernie Nicholls .25 .60
60 Jozef Stumpel .25 .60
61 Darius Kasparaitis .25 .60
62 Kelly Hrudey .30 .75
63 Marcel Cousineau RC .25 .60
64 Brian Skrudland .25 .60
65 Byron Dafoe .25 .60
66 Ray Sheppard .30 .75
67 Chris Simon .25 .60
68 Dainius Zubrus RC .50 1.25
69 Ethan Moreau RC .40 1.00
70 Theo Fleury .75 2.00
71 Damian Rhodes .30 .75
72 Kevin Dineen .25 .60
73 Kenny Jonsson .25 .60
74 Ray Ferraro .25 .60
75 Jaromir Jagr 1.00 2.50
76 Wayne Primeau .25 .60
77 Chris Gratton .30 .75
78 Alyn McCauley .40 1.00
79 Christian Dube .25 .60
80 Bill Ranford .30 .75
81 Adam Deadmarsh .25 .60
82 Dale Hunter .30 .75
83 Derek Plante .25 .60
84 Todd Bertuzzi .40 1.00
85 Stephane Fiset .30 .75
86 Boyd Devereaux RC .40 1.00
87 Jere Lehtinen .25 .60
88 Peter Schaefer RC .30 .75
89 Alexander Mogilny .30 .75
90 Joe Juneau .25 .60
91 Alexandre Daigle .50 1.25
92 Jeff O'Neill .50 1.25
93 Todd Warriner .50 1.25
94 Sergei Berezin RC 1.25 3.00
95 Petr Nedved .60 1.50
96 Phil Housley .60 1.50
97 Jason Arnott .60 1.50
98 Sandis Ozolinsh .50 1.25
99 Mike Modano 1.25 3.00
100 Mark Messier 1.25 3.00
101 Ron Francis 1.00 2.50
102 Oleg Tverdovsky .60 1.50
103 Patrick Marleau RC 8.00 20.00
104 Brian Bellows .60 1.50
105 Eric Fichaud .60 1.50
106 Alexei Zhamnov .60 1.50
107 Wendel Clark .60 1.50
108 Dimitri Khristich .50 1.25
109 Mike Ricci .50 1.25
110 John LeClair .75 2.00
111 Owen Nolan .75 2.00
112 Bill Guerin .75 2.00
113 Vyacheslav Kozlov .50 1.25
114 Brendan Shanahan 1.00 2.50
115 Trevor Linden .60 1.50
116 Jose Theodore 1.00 2.50
117 Rod Brind'Amour .75 2.00
118 Brian Holzinger .60 1.50
119 Shayne Corson .50 1.25
120 Bryan Smolinski .50 1.25
121 Tony Granato .50 1.25
122 Mariusz Czerkawski .50 1.25
123 Andrew Cassels .50 1.25
124 Scott Stevens .75 2.00
125 Mike Ridley .50 1.25
126 Jamie Langenbrunner .50 1.25
127 Scott Mellanby .60 1.50
128 Grant Fuhr .75 2.00
129 Felix Potvin .75 2.00
130 Marc Denis .75 2.00
131 Corey Hirsch .60 1.50
132 Chris Osgood .75 2.00
133 Peter Bondra .60 1.50
134 Martin Brodeur 1.50 4.00
135 Pierre Turgeon .75 2.00
136 Pat Verbeek .50 1.25
137 Scott Niedermayer .75 2.00
138 Geoff Sanderson .60 1.50
139 Jason Dawe .50 1.25
140 Rob Niedermayer .60 1.50
141 Daniel Alfredsson .75 2.00
142 Jim Campbell .50 1.25
143 Roman Hamrlik .60 1.50
144 Rob Blake .75 2.00
145 Chris Chelios .75 2.00
146 Teemu Selanne 1.50 4.00
147 Jim Carey .75 2.00
148 Dino Ciccarelli .75 2.00
149 Mark Recchi 1.00 2.50
150 Chris Pronger .60 1.50
151 Paul Coffey 10.00 25.00
152 Adam Oates 10.00 25.00
153 Keith Tkachuk 10.00 25.00
154 Janne Niinimaa 10.00 25.00
155 Sergei Fedorov 15.00 40.00
156 Dominik Hasek 15.00 40.00
157 Eric Lindros 15.00 40.00
158 Curtis Joseph 10.00 25.00
159 Alexei Yashin 8.00 20.00
160 Joe Thornton RC 60.00 150.00
161 Bryan Berard 10.00 25.00
162 Steve Yzerman 25.00 60.00
163 Mats Sundin 10.00 25.00
164 Jarome Iginla 12.00 30.00
165 John Vanbiesbrouck 10.00 25.00
166 Mario Lemieux 30.00 80.00
167 Jeremy Roenick 15.00 40.00
168 Patrick Lalime RC 15.00 40.00
169 Joe Sakic 15.00 40.00
170 Brett Hull 50.00 120.00
171 Peter Forsberg 15.00 40.00
172 Doug Weight 10.00 25.00
173 Tony Amonte 8.00 20.00
174 Patrick Roy 25.00 60.00
175 Paul Kariya 12.00 30.00
176 Pavel Bure 12.00 30.00
177 Ray Bourque 15.00 40.00
178 Saku Koivu 10.00 25.00
179 Wade Redden 6.00 15.00
180 Wayne Gretzky 50.00 120.00
P180 Wayne Gretzky Promo 2.00 5.00

1996-97 Black Diamond Gold

This was a gold-foil parallel to the three-tiered Upper Deck Black Diamond set. Single golds were inserted 1:15 packs, Doubles 1:46, and Triples, for which an insertion ratio was not announced, were limited to just 50 sets.

*SINGLE VETS: 3X TO 8X BASIC CARDS
*SINGLE ROOKIES: 1.2X TO 3X
*DOUBLE VETS: 1.2X TO 3X BASIC CARDS
*DOUBLE ROOKIES: .8X TO 2X
*TRIPLE VETS: 1.5X TO 4X BASIC CARDS
*TRIPLE ROOKIES: 1.2X TO 3X
151-180 TRIPLE ANNOUNCED PRINT RUN 50

1996-97 Black Diamond Run for the Cup

Each card in this set was individually numbered to just 100 sets, printed on cel-chrome, and feature high profile players.

STATED PRINT RUN 100 SERIAL #'d SETS
RC1 Wayne Gretzky 200.00 350.00
RC2 Saku Koivu 30.00 80.00
RC3 Mario Lemieux 150.00 250.00
RC4 Patrick Roy 150.00 250.00
RC5 Jaromir Jagr 50.00 120.00
RC6 John Vanbiesbrouck 20.00 50.00
RC7 Peter Forsberg 30.00 80.00
RC8 Paul Kariya 40.00 100.00
RC9 Steve Yzerman 125.00 250.00
RC10 Joe Sakic 75.00 150.00
RC11 Mark Messier 40.00 100.00
RC12 Sergei Fedorov 40.00 100.00
RC13 Mats Sundin 30.00 80.00
RC14 Pavel Bure 60.00 120.00
RC15 Ed Jovanovski 25.00 60.00
RC16 Mike Modano 30.00 80.00
RC17 Curtis Joseph 25.00 60.00
RC18 Teemu Selanne 30.00 80.00
RC19 Jarome Iginla 30.00 80.00
RC20 Eric Lindros 60.00 120.00

1997-98 Black Diamond

The 1997-98 Upper Deck Black Diamond set was issued in one series totaling 150 cards and distributed in six-card packs with a suggested retail price of $3.49. The fronts feature color action player photos reproduced on Light F/X card stock with foil treatment and one, two, three, or four Black Diamonds on the front designating its rarity. The backs carry player information and statistics.

COMPLETE SET (150) 50.00 100.00
1 Alexei Zhitnik .25 .60
2 Adam Graves .25 .60
3 Keith Primeau .30 .75
4 Mike Richter .40 1.00
5 Felix Potvin .40 1.00
6 Valeri Bure .25 .60
7 Mark Messier .60 1.50
8 Dainius Zubrus .30 .75
9 Owen Nolan .40 1.00
10 Kenny Jonsson .30 .75
11 Ron Francis .50 1.25
12 Bryan Berard .25 .60
13 Eric Messier RC .40 1.00
14 Paul Kariya .50 1.25
15 Teemu Elomo RC .30 .75
16 Joe Nieuwendyk .40 1.00
17 Scott Stevens .40 1.00
18 Zigmund Palffy .40 1.00
19 Brett Hull .50 1.25
20 Dominik Hasek .60 1.50
21 Dino Ciccarelli .40 1.00
22 Rob Niedermayer .25 .60
23 Mark Recchi .50 1.25
24 Brad Isbister .30 .75
25 Timo Vertala RC .30 .75
26 Mika Noronen RC .30 .75
27 Sandis Ozolinsh .30 .75
28 Chris Phillips .30 .75
29 Chris Chelios .40 1.00
30 Jason Dawe .30 .75
31 Kirk McLean .30 .75
32 Jason Allison .30 .75
33 Brian Leetch .40 1.00
34 Guy Hebert .30 .75
35 David Legwand RC .50 1.25
36 Pierre Hedin RC .30 .75
37 Sergei Samsonov .25 .60
38 Bill Guerin .40 1.00
39 Chris Osgood .40 1.00
40 Jere Lehtinen .30 .75
41 Patrick Roy 1.00 2.50
42 John Vanbiesbrouck .40 1.00
43 Maxim Afinogenov RC .50 1.25
44 Patrik Elias RC 1.50 4.00
45 Josh Holden .30 .75
46 Saku Koivu .40 1.00
47 Maxim Balmochnykh RC .50 1.25
48 Pasi Petrilainen .25 .60
49 Robert Reichel .30 .75
50 Wade Redden .25 .60
51 Richard Zednik .30 .75
52 Ty Jones RC .30 .75
53 Nikolai Khabibulin .40 1.00
54 Kyle McLaren .25 .60
55 Daniel Tkaczuk .40 1.00
56 Alexei Zhamnov .25 .60
57 Donald MacLean RC .40 1.00
58 Dave Gagner .25 .60
59 Jeremy Roenick .50 1.25
60 Ray Bourque .60 1.50
61 Rod Brind'Amour .40 1.00
62 Miroslav Satan .25 .60
63 Eric Daze .25 .60
64 Mike Ricci .30 .75
65 John LeClair .40 1.00
66 Bryan Marchment .40 1.00
67 Henrik Petre RC .30 .75
68 John MacLean .25 .60
69 Artem Chubarov RC .30 .75
70 Doug Gilmour .50 1.25
71 Marco Sturm RC .40 1.00
72 Jaromir Jagr 1.00 2.50
73 Daniel Alfredsson .40 1.00
74 Daren Puppa .30 .75
75 Adam Deadmarsh .25 .60
76 Luc Robitaille .40 1.00
77 Mats Sundin .40 1.00
78 Dan Cloutier .25 .60
79 Manny Malhotra RC .50 1.25
80 Mike Modano .60 1.50
81 Espen Knutsen RC .40 1.00
82 Sergei Fedorov .60 1.50
83 Chris Pronger .30 .75
84 Doug Weight .40 1.00
85 Dmitri Nabokov .30 .75
86 Gary Roberts .30 .75
87 Peter Bondra .30 .75
88 Robert Dome RC .25 .60
89 Jan Bulis RC .40 1.00
90 Eric Brewer RC .50 1.25
91 Nikos Tselios RC .30 .75
92 Scott Mellanby .30 .75
93 Vitali Vishnevsky RC .50 1.25
94 Derian Hatcher .30 .75
95 Teemu Selanne .75 2.00
96 Joe Sakic .60 1.50
97 Alexander Mogilny .30 .75
98 Jesse Boulerice RC .50 1.25
99 Johan Forsander RC .30 .75
100 Pierre Turgeon .40 1.00
101 Tony Amonte .30 .75
102 Timo Ahmaoja RC .30 .75
103 Rob Blake .40 1.00
104 Derek Morris RC .40 1.00
105 Alex Tanguay RC 1.00 2.50
106 Peter Forsberg .50 1.25
107 Shayne Corson .25 .60
108 Tyler Moss RC .30 .75
109 Adam Oates .40 1.00
110 Keith Tkachuk .40 1.00
111 Alexei Yashin .30 .75
112 Joe Thornton .40 1.00
113 Andy Moog .40 1.00
114 Daniel Sedin RC 4.00 10.00
115 Pavel Bure .50 1.25
116 Denis Shvidki RC .50 1.25
117 Jason Arnott .30 .75
118 Mike Johnson RC .30 .75
119 Nicklas Lidstrom .40 1.00
120 Mattias Ohlund .30 .75
121 Alexander Selivanov .25 .60
122 Martin Brodeur .75 2.00
123 Steve Yzerman .75 2.00
124 Dimitri Vlassenkov RC .40 1.00
125 Jeff Farkas RC .50 1.25
126 Curtis Joseph .40 1.00
127 Yanic Perreault .30 .75
128 Alyn McCauley .30 .75
129 Vyacheslav Kozlov .30 .75
130 Alexei Morozov .30 .75
131 Roberto Luongo RC 3.00 8.00
132 Jarome Iginla .40 1.00
133 Pat LaFontaine .40 1.00
134 Ed Belfour .40 1.00
135 Toby Petersen RC .50 1.25
136 Henrik Sedin RC 8.00 20.00
137 Marcus Nilson .30 .75
138 Cameron Mann .30 .75
139 Eero Somervuori RC .30 .75
140 Patrick Marleau .50 1.25
141 Ed Jovanovski .25 .60
142 Roman Hamrlik .30 .75
143 Theo Fleury .50 1.25
144 Wayne Gretzky 2.00 5.00
145 Eric Lindros .60 1.50
146 Boyd Deveraux .30 .75
147 Sami Kapanen .30 .75
148 Grant Fuhr .40 1.00
149 Brendan Shanahan .50 1.25
150 Vincent Lecavalier RC 2.50 6.00

1997-98 Black Diamond Double Diamond

Inserted one in every pack, this 150-card set is a two black diamond parallel version of the Upper Deck Black Diamond base set.

*VETS: .75X TO 2X BASIC CARDS
*ROOKIES: .6X TO 1.5X
STATED ODDS 1:1

1997-98 Black Diamond Triple Diamond

Randomly inserted in packs at the rate of 1:3, this 150-card set is an all-gold Light F/X parallel version of the base set with three black diamonds printed on the card fronts.

*VETS: 3X TO 8X BASIC CARDS
*ROOKIES: 1.2X TO 3X
STATED ODDS 1:3

1997-98 Black Diamond Quadruple Diamond

Randomly inserted in packs, this 150-card set is an all-black Light F/X parallel version of the base set with four black diamonds printed on the card fronts. Only 50 sets were produced.

*VETS: 15X TO 40X BASIC CARDS
*ROOKIES: 4X TO 10X

1997-98 Black Diamond Premium Cut

Randomly inserted in packs at the rate of 1:7, this 30-card set features color action photos of top stars printed in a Light F/X card design with a single black diamond.

COMPLETE SET (30) 30.00 80.00
SINGLE DIAMOND ODDS 1:7
*DOUBLE DIAM: .5X TO 1.2X SINGLE
DOUBLE DIAMOND ODDS 1:15
*TRIPLE DIAM: .8X TO 2X SINGLE
*QUAD VERTICAL: 3X TO 8X SINGLE
QUAD VERTICAL ODDS 1:180
PC1 Wayne Gretzky 10.00 25.00
PC2 Patrick Roy 6.00 15.00
PC3 Brendan Shanahan 1.50 4.00
PC4 Ray Bourque 1.50 4.00
PC5 Alexei Morozov 1.00 2.50
PC6 John LeClair 1.50 4.00
PC7 Steve Yzerman 4.00 10.00
PC8 Patrik Elias 1.00 2.50
PC9 Pavel Bure 1.50 4.00
PC10 Brian Leetch 1.50 4.00
PC11 Peter Forsberg 2.00 5.00
PC12 Marco Sturm 1.00 2.50
PC13 Eric Lindros 1.50 4.00
PC14 Keith Tkachuk 1.00 2.50
PC15 Teemu Selanne 1.50 4.00
PC16 Bryan Berard 1.00 2.50
PC17 Joe Thornton 2.50 6.00
PC18 Brett Hull 2.00 5.00
PC19 Nicklas Lidstrom 1.50 4.00
PC20 Jaromir Jagr 2.50 6.00
PC21 Vaclav Prospal 1.00 2.50
PC22 Pat LaFontaine 1.50 4.00
PC23 Mark Messier 1.50 4.00
PC24 Martin Brodeur 4.00 10.00
PC25 Mike Modano 2.50 6.00
PC26 Paul Kariya 1.50 4.00
PC27 Mike Johnson 1.00 2.50
PC28 Sergei Samsonov 1.00 2.50
PC29 Joe Sakic 2.50 6.00
PC30 Mats Sundin 1.50 4.00

1997-98 Black Diamond Premium Cut Quadruple Diamond Horizontal

This 30-card hobby only set is a special black Light F/X, embossed, horizontal, die-cut version of the regular insert set with various insertion rates. Cards #8, 10, 16, 17, 18, 19, 23, 27, 29 and 30 have an insertion rate of 1:30; #4, 5, 7, 12, 14, 15, 21, 22, 25 and 26 have a 1:90 insertion rate; #6, 9, 11, 20, 24 and 28 have a 1:2000 insertion rate; #3 and 13 have a 1:15,000 insertion rate; and #1 and 2 have a 1:30,000 insertion rate.

*HORIZONTAL 1:30: .8X TO 2X SINGLE
8/10/16/17/18/19/23/27/29/30 ODDS 1:30
*HORIZONTAL 1:90: 1.2X TO 3X SINGLE
4/5/7/12/14/15/21/22/25/26 ODDS 1:90
*HORIZONTAL 1:2000: 6X TO 15X SINGLE
6/9/11/20/24/28 ODDS 1:2000
3/13 ODDS 1:15,000
1/2 ODDS 1:30,000
PC1 Wayne Gretzky 300.00 800.00
PC2 Patrick Roy 200.00 400.00
PC13 Eric Lindros 60.00 150.00

1998-99 Black Diamond

The 1998-99 Upper Deck Black Diamond set was issued in one series for a total of 120 cards and was distributed in six-card packs with a suggested retail price of $3.99. The fronts feature color action player photos reproduced on Light F/X card stock with foil treatment and one, two, three, or four Black Diamonds designating its rarity. Cards 1-90 are regular player cards with cards 91-120 displaying top prospect players and an insertion rate of 1:4 for the single diamond cards. The backs carry player information and statistics. Only 2,000 Double Diamond sets were produced, 1,000 Triple Diamond sets, and 100 Quadruple Diamond sets.

COMPLETE SET (120) 30.00 80.00
COMP.SET w/o SP's (90) 10.00 20.00
SP 91-120 STATED ODDS 1:4
1 Paul Kariya .25 .60
2 Teemu Selanne .25 .60
3 Johan Davidsson .08 .25
4 Ray Bourque .40 1.00
5 Sergei Samsonov .20 .50
6 Jason Allison .08 .25
7 Joe Thornton .40 1.00
8 Miroslav Satan .20 .50
9 Brian Holzinger .08 .25
10 Dominik Hasek .50 1.25
11 Rico Fata .08 .25
12 Jarome Iginla .30 .75
13 Theo Fleury .08 .25
14 Ron Francis .20 .50
15 Gary Roberts .08 .25
16 Keith Primeau .08 .25
17 Sami Kapanen .08 .25
18 Doug Gilmour .20 .50
19 Chris Chelios .25 .60
20 Tony Amonte .20 .50
21 Peter Forsberg .60 1.50
22 Patrick Roy 1.25 3.00
23 Joe Sakic .50 1.25
24 Chris Drury .20 .50
25 Brett Hull .30 .75
26 Ed Belfour .25 .60
27 Mike Modano .40 1.00
28 Darryl Sydor .08 .25
29 Sergei Fedorov .40 1.00
30 Steve Yzerman 1.25 3.00
31 Nicklas Lidstrom .25 .60
32 Chris Osgood .20 .50
33 Brendan Shanahan .25 .60
34 Doug Weight .20 .50
35 Bill Guerin .08 .25
36 Tom Poti .08 .25
37 Pavel Bure .25 .60
38 Mark Parrish RC .75 2.00
39 Rob Niedermayer .08 .25
40 Pavel Rosa RC .08 .25
41 Rob Blake .08 .25
42 Olli Jokinen .20 .50
43 Vincent Damphousse .08 .25
44 Mark Recchi .20 .50
45 Terry Ryan .08 .25
46 Saku Koivu .25 .60
47 Mike Dunham .20 .50
48 Sergei Krivokrasov .08 .25
49 Scott Stevens .20 .50
50 Martin Brodeur .60 1.50
51 Brendan Morrison .20 .50
52 Eric Brewer .08 .25
53 Zigmund Palffy .20 .50
54 Felix Potvin .25 .60
55 Wayne Gretzky 1.50 4.00
56 Brian Leetch .25 .60
57 Manny Malhotra .08 .25
58 Mike Richter .25 .60
59 Alexei Yashin .08 .25
60 Wade Redden .08 .25
61 Daniel Alfredsson .20 .50
62 Eric Lindros .25 .60
63 John LeClair .25 .60
64 John Vanbiesbrouck .20 .50
65 Rod Brind'Amour .20 .50
66 Keith Tkachuk .25 .60
67 Daniel Briere .08 .25
68 Jeremy Roenick .30 .75
69 Jaromir Jagr .40 1.00
70 German Titov .08 .25
71 Alexei Morozov .20 .50
72 Patrick Marleau .20 .50
73 Andrei Zyuzin .08 .25
74 Mike Vernon .20 .50
75 Owen Nolan .20 .50
76 Marty Reasoner .20 .50
77 Al MacInnis .20 .50
78 Chris Pronger .20 .50
79 Wendel Clark .20 .50
80 Vincent Lecavalier .60 1.50
81 Craig Janney .08 .25
82 Tomas Kaberle RC .60 1.50
83 Curtis Joseph .25 .60
84 Mats Sundin .25 .60
85 Mark Messier .25 .60
86 Bill Muckalt RC .20 .50
87 Mattias Ohlund .20 .50
88 Peter Bondra .20 .50
89 Olaf Kolzig .20 .50
90 Richard Zednik .08 .25
91 Harold Druken SP 1.25 3.00
92 Roberto Luongo SP 1.25 3.00
93 Daniel Tkaczuk SP 1.00 2.50
94 Brenden Morrow SP RC 2.00 5.00
95 Mike Van Ryn SP 1.00 2.50
96 Brian Finley SP RC 1.00 2.50
97 Jani Rita SP RC 1.25 3.00
98 Iikka Mikkola SP RC 1.25 3.00
99 Mikko Jokela SP RC 1.25 3.00
100 Tommi Santala SP RC 1.25 3.00
101 Teemu Virkkunen SP RC 1.25 3.00
102 Arto Laatikainen SP RC 1.25 3.00
103 Kirill Safronov SP RC 1.25 3.00
104 Alexei Volkov SP RC 1.25 3.00
105 Denis Arkhipov SP RC 1.25 3.00
106 Alexander Zevakhin SP RC 1.25 3.00
107 Denis Shvidki SP 1.25 3.00
108 Maxim Afinogenov SP 1.25 3.00
109 Daniel Sedin SP 1.25 3.00
110 Henrik Sedin SP 1.25 3.00
111 Jimmie Olvestad SP RC 1.25 3.00
112 Mattias Weinhandl SP RC 1.25 3.00
113 Mathias Tjarnqvist SP RC 1.25 3.00
114 Jakob Johansson SP RC 1.25 3.00
115 David Legwand SP 1.25 3.00
116 Barrett Heisten SP RC 1.25 3.00
117 Tim Connolly SP RC 1.50 4.00
118 Andy Hilbert SP RC 1.25 3.00
119 Joe Blackburn SP RC 1.25 3.00
120 Dave Tanabe SP RC 1.25 3.00

1998-99 Black Diamond Double Diamond

Randomly inserted into packs, this 120-card set is a parallel version of the base set displaying two black diamonds on the card fronts. Only 2,000 sets were made.

*1-90 SINGLES: 2X TO 5X BASIC CARDS
*91-120 SINGLES: .6X TO 1.5X BASIC SP
STATED PRINT RUN 2000 SER.#'d SETS

1998-99 Black Diamond Triple Diamond

Randomly inserted into packs, this 120-card set is a parallel version of the base set displaying three black diamonds on the card fronts. Only 1,000 sets were made.

*1-90 TRIPLE: 3X TO 8X BASIC CARDS
*91-120 TRIPLE: 1.2X TO 3X BASIC SP
STATED PRINT RUN 1000 SER.#'d SETS

1998-99 Black Diamond Quadruple Diamond

Randomly inserted into packs, this 120-card set is a parallel version of the base set displaying four black diamonds on the card fronts. Only 100 sets were made.

*1-90 QUADS: 30X TO 80X BASIC CARDS
*91-120 QUADS: 4X TO 10X BASIC SP
STATED PRINT RUN 100 SER.#'d SETS

1998-99 Black Diamond Myriad

Randomly inserted into packs, this 30-card set features color action photos of the current top NHL's superstars. Only 1,500 serially numbered sets were produced. A limited edition parallel version of this set, Myriad 2, was produced and numbered 1 of 1.

COMPLETE SET (30)
STATED PRINT RUN 1500 SER.#'d SETS
M1 Vincent Lecavalier 6.00 15.00
M2 John Vanbiesbrouck 2.00 5.00
M3 Paul Kariya 2.50 6.00
M4 Keith Tkachuk 2.50 6.00
M5 Mike Modano 4.00 10.00
M6 Dominik Hasek 5.00 12.00
M7 Teemu Selanne 2.50 6.00
M8 Manny Malhotra 1.00 2.50
M9 Brendan Shanahan 2.50 6.00
M10 Pavel Bure 2.50 6.00
M11 Chris Drury 2.00 5.00
M12 Curtis Joseph 2.50 6.00
M13 Joe Sakic 5.00 12.00
M14 Eric Lindros 2.50 6.00
M15 Peter Bondra 2.00 5.00
M16 Brett Hull 4.00 10.00
M17 Ray Bourque 4.00 10.00
M18 Jaromir Jagr 4.00 10.00
M19 Steve Yzerman 12.50 30.00
M20 Mark Parrish 4.00 10.00
M21 Martin Brodeur 6.00 15.00
M22 Saku Koivu 2.50 6.00
M23 Patrick Roy 12.50 30.00
M24 John LeClair 2.50 6.00
M25 Doug Gilmour 2.00 5.00
M26 Sergei Fedorov 4.00 10.00
M27 Wayne Gretzky 15.00 40.00
M28 Peter Forsberg 6.00 15.00
M29 Eric Brewer 1.00 2.50
M30 Sergei Samsonov 2.00 5.00

1998-99 Black Diamond Winning Formula Gold

Randomly inserted into hobby packs only, this 30-card set features color photos of top players and goalies. Each card is sequentially numbered to the pictured player's goals or goalie's wins multiplied times 50.

COMPLETE SET (30) 125.00 250.00
STATED PRINT RUN 800-2600
WF1 Paul Kariya/850 3.00 8.00
WF2 Teemu Selanne/2600 3.00 8.00
WF3 Sergei Samsonov/1100 2.50 6.00
WF4 Dominik Hasek/1650 6.00 15.00
WF5 Vincent Lecavalier/2200 5.00 12.00
WF6 Patrick Roy/1550 15.00 40.00
WF7 Peter Forsberg/1250 8.00 20.00
WF8 Joe Sakic/1350 5.00 12.00
WF9 Ed Belfour/1850 3.00 8.00
WF10 Brendan Shanahan/1400 3.00 8.00
WF11 Steve Yzerman/1200 20.00 50.00
WF12 Chris Osgood/1650 2.50 6.00
WF13 Curtis Joseph/1450 3.00 8.00
WF14 Manny Malhotra/800 2.50 6.00
WF15 Martin Brodeur/2150 6.00 15.00
WF16 Chris Drury/1400 2.50 6.00
WF17 Zigmund Palffy/2250 2.50 6.00
WF18 Wayne Gretzky/1150 15.00 40.00
WF19 Theo Fleury/1350 2.50 6.00
WF20 Alexei Yashin/1650 2.50 6.00
WF21 Eric Lindros/1500 3.00 8.00
WF22 John LeClair/2550 2.50 6.00
WF23 Keith Tkachuk/2000 3.00 8.00
WF24 Mark Messier/1100 3.00 8.00
WF25 Jaromir Jagr/1750 5.00 12.00
WF26 Brett Hull/1350 5.00 12.00
WF27 Mats Sundin/1650 3.00 8.00
WF28 Pavel Bure/2550 3.00 8.00
WF29 Peter Bondra/2600 2.50 6.00
WF30 Mike Modano/1050 8.00 20.00

1998-99 Black Diamond Winning Formula Platinum

Randomly inserted into packs, this 30-card set is a platinum foil parallel version of the regular Winning Formula set. Each card is numbered to the player's actual accomplishments. Scarcer cards are not priced.

STATED PRINT RUN 16-52
WF1 Paul Kariya/17
WF2 Teemu Selanne/52 50.00 100.00
WF3 Sergei Samsonov/22
WF4 Dominik Hasek/33 100.00 200.00
WF5 Vincent Lecavalier/44 100.00 200.00
WF6 Patrick Roy/31 250.00 500.00

WF7 Peter Forsberg/25
WF8 Joe Sakic/27
WF9 Ed Belfour/37 60.00 120.00
WF10 Brendan Shanahan/28
WF11 Steve Yzerman/24
WF12 Chris Osgood/33 75.00 150.00
WF13 Curtis Joseph/29
WF14 Manny Malhotra/16 25.00 60.00
WF15 Martin Brodeur/43 100.00 200.00
WF16 Chris Drury/28
WF17 Zigmund Palffy/45 60.00 120.00
WF18 Wayne Gretzky/23
WF19 Theo Fleury/27
WF20 Alexei Yashin/33 25.00 60.00
WF21 Eric Lindros/30 50.00 100.00
WF22 John LeClair/51 40.00 100.00
WF23 Keith Tkachuk/40 75.00 150.00
WF24 Mark Messier/22
WF25 Jaromir Jagr/35 60.00 150.00
WF26 Brett Hull/27
WF27 Mats Sundin/33 50.00 100.00
WF28 Pavel Bure/51 50.00 100.00
WF29 Peter Bondra/52 50.00 100.00
WF30 Mike Modano/21

1998-99 Black Diamond Year of the Great One

Randomly inserted into packs, this 99-card set features color photos of the great Wayne Gretzky. Cards 1-45 are marked with a single diamond; 46-75 display double diamonds; 76-90 show triple diamonds; and 91-99 carry quadruple diamonds. Each card is sequentially numbered to 99.
COMMON YOTG (1-99) 125.00 250.00
STATED PRINT RUN 99 SER. #'d SETS

1999-00 Black Diamond

The 1999-00 Black Diamond set was released as 120-card set comprised of 90 veteran cards and 30 Diamonds in the Rough cards, short printed and inserted at one in three packs, which feature future NHL stars. Player action shots are set against a card background where the middle 2/3 is silver foil and the top and bottom are colored to match the player's team colors. Black Diamond was packaged in 24-pack boxes with 6-card packs, carried an SRP of $3.99, and was released as both hobby and retail.
1 Paul Kariya .30 .75
2 Teemu Selanne .50 1.25
3 Guy Hebert .25 .60
4 Damian Rhodes .15 .40
5 Patrik Stefan RC .25 .60
6 Dean Sylvester RC .15 .40
7 Sergei Samsonov .20 .50
8 Byron Dafoe .15 .40
9 Ray Bourque .40 1.00
10 Joe Thornton .40 1.00
11 Dominik Hasek .40 1.00
12 Michael Peca .20 .50
13 Miroslav Satan .20 .50
14 Martin Biron .20 .50
15 Oleg Saprykin RC .25 .60
16 Valeri Bure .15 .40
17 Robyn Regehr .15 .40
18 Dave Tanabe .15 .40
19 Arturs Irbe .20 .50
20 Sami Kapanen .15 .40
21 Kyle Calder RC .20 .50
22 Tony Amonte .20 .50
23 Doug Gilmour .30 .75
24 Patrick Roy 1.00 2.50
25 Joe Sakic .40 1.00
26 Peter Forsberg .25 .60
27 Chris Drury .20 .50
28 Milan Hejduk .20 .50
29 Mike Modano .40 1.00
30 Brett Hull .40 1.00
31 Ed Belfour .25 .60
32 Jon Sim RC .25 .60
33 Nicklas Lidstrom .25 .60
34 Sergei Fedorov .40 1.00
35 Brendan Shanahan .30 .75
36 Steve Yzerman .75 2.00
37 Chris Osgood .25 .60
38 Paul Comrie RC .40 1.00
39 Bill Guerin .25 .60
40 Doug Weight .25 .60
41 Pavel Bure .30 .75
42 Ivan Novoseltsev RC .30 .75
43 Trevor Kidd .15 .40
44 Zigmund Palffy .25 .60
45 Luc Robitaille .25 .60
46 Stephane Fiset .20 .50
47 Mike Ribeiro .20 .50
48 Saku Koivu .25 .60
49 David Legwand .15 .40
50 Rob Valicevic RC .20 .50
51 Martin Brodeur .50 1.25
52 Scott Gomez .20 .50
53 Brian Rafalski RC .25 .60
54 Tim Connolly .15 .40
55 Jorgen Jonsson RC .15 .40
56 Theo Fleury .30 .75
57 Brian Leetch .25 .60
58 Mike Richter .25 .60
59 Marian Hossa .20 .50
60 Radek Bonk .15 .40
61 Mike Fisher RC .25 .60
62 Eric Lindros .40 1.00
63 Keith Primeau .15 .40
64 John LeClair .25 .60
65 Jeremy Roenick .25 .60
66 Keith Tkachuk .25 .60
67 Mika Alatalo RC .20 .50
68 Jaromir Jagr .60 1.50
69 Martin Straka .15 .40
70 Alexei Kovalev .20 .50
71 Jochen Hecht RC .40 1.00
72 Pavol Demitra .30 .75
73 Chris Pronger .20 .50
74 Patrick Marleau .25 .60
75 Owen Nolan .25 .60
76 Jeff Friesen .20 .50
77 Steve Shields .20 .50
78 Vincent Lecavalier .20 .50
79 Dan Cloutier .15 .40
80 Adam Mair RC .15 .40
81 Mike Johnson .20 .50
82 Mats Sundin .25 .60
83 Nikolai Antropov RC .60 1.50
84 Curtis Joseph .25 .60
85 Steve Kariya RC .25 .60
86 Mark Messier .40 1.00
87 Alexander Mogilny .20 .50
88 Olaf Kolzig .25 .60
89 Peter Bondra .20 .50
90 Alexandre Volchkov RC .15 .40
91 Pavel Brendl SP RC .40 1.00
92 Jamie Lundmark SP .20 .50
93 Kris Beech SP .15 .40
94 Michael Zigomanis SP .15 .40
95 Branislav Mezei SP RC .15 .40
96 Sheldon Keefe SP RC .25 .60
97 Brian Finley SP .25 .60
98 Taylor Pyatt SP .15 .40
99 Denis Shvidki SP .20 .50
100 Barret Jackman SP .15 .40
101 Maxime Ouellet SP .25 .60
102 Milan Kraft SP RC .20 .50
103 Brad Ralph SP RC .20 .50
104 Alexei Volkov SP .20 .50
105 Mathieu Chouinard SP .15 .40
106 Mark Bell SP .15 .40
107 Ryan Jardine SP RC .20 .50
108 Kristian Kudroc SP RC .15 .40
109 Norm Milley SP .15 .40
110 Jeff Heerema SP .15 .40
111 Jaroslav Kristek SP RC .20 .50
112 Luke Sellars SP RC .25 .60
113 Bryan Kazarian SP RC .20 .50
114 Brett Lysak SP RC .20 .50
115 Andrei Shefer SP RC .20 .50
116 Michal Sivek SP RC .20 .50
117 Justin Papineau SP .15 .40
118 Mattias Weinhandl SP .15 .40
119 Daniel Sedin SP .60 1.50
120 Henrik Sedin SP .60 1.50

1999-00 Black Diamond Diamond Cut

The 90-card Diamond Cut set parallels the Black Diamond base 90-card set in a die cut version and is seeded at 1:6 packs; and the 30-card Diamond Cut Diamonds in the Rough set parallels the 30 prospect cards in a die cut version and is seeded at 1:11 packs. On the front of these parallels, the words "Diamond Cut" appear just above the player's name.
*VETERANS 1-90: 2X TO 5X BASIC CARDS
*ROOKIES 1-90: 1.2X TO 3X BASIC CARDS
1-90 STATED ODDS 1:6
*ROOKIES 91-20: .8X TO 2X BASIC CARDS
91-120 STATED ODDS 1:3

1999-00 Black Diamond Final Cut

The 90-card Final Cut set parallels the Black Diamond base 90-card set in a die cut holographic foil version and is numbered on the back out of 100; and the 30-card Final Cut Diamonds in the Rough set parallels the 30 prospect cards at the end of the set in a die cut holographic foil version and is numbered on the back out of 50. On the front of these parallels, the words "Final Cut" appear just above the player's name.
*VETERANS 1-90: 10X TO 25X BASIC CARDS
*ROOKIES 1-90: 5X TO 12X
*ROOKIES 91-120: 4X TO 10X
1-90 STATED PRINT RUN 100
91-120 SP STATED PRINT RUN 50

1999-00 Black Diamond A Piece of History

Randomly inserted in hobby packs at 1:179 and retail packs at 1:336, this 20-card set features NHL players with a single diamond-cut swatch of a game-used stick. Hobby cards feature a red foil shift, and retail cards feature a blue foil shift. Double and triple diamond parallels of this set were also created. These parallels carry two or three swatches of memorabilia respectively. Double diamonds were seeded at 1:1008, and triple diamonds were numbered one of one. Triple diamonds not priced due to scarcity.
SINGLE STATED ODDS 1:336
*DOUBLE: .8X TO 2X SINGLE
DOUBLE ODDS 1:864 HOB, 1:1008 RET
BH Brett Hull 8.00 20.00
DH Dominik Hasek 10.00 25.00
EB Ed Belfour 10.00 25.00
EL Eric Lindros 10.00 25.00
GH Gordie Howe 20.00 50.00
JJ Jaromir Jagr 12.00 30.00
JL John LeClair 10.00 25.00
JS Joe Sakic 12.00 30.00
KT Keith Tkachuk 10.00 25.00
MB Martin Brodeur 12.00 30.00
MM Mike Modano 10.00 25.00
PB Pavel Bure 10.00 25.00
PF Peter Forsberg 10.00 25.00
PK Paul Kariya 10.00 25.00
PR Patrick Roy 20.00 50.00
RB Ray Bourque 10.00 25.00
SY Steve Yzerman 20.00 50.00
TC Tim Connolly 8.00 20.00
TS Teemu Selanne 10.00 25.00
WG Wayne Gretzky 30.00 80.00

1999-00 Black Diamond Diamonation

Randomly inserted in packs at 1:4, this 20-card set showcases NHL's most collectible players on a foil card with laser-etched diamonds in the background.
COMPLETE SET (20) 12.00 30.00
STATED ODDS 1:4
D1 Paul Kariya .50 1.25
D2 Patrik Stefan .75 2.00
D3 Sergei Samsonov .50 1.25
D4 Teemu Selanne .50 1.25
D5 Patrick Roy 2.50 6.00
D6 Mike Modano .75 2.00
D7 Sergei Fedorov 1.00 2.50
D8 Pavel Bure .60 1.50
D9 David Legwand .50 1.25
D10 Martin Brodeur 1.25 3.00
D11 Theo Fleury .50 1.25
D12 Eric Lindros .75 2.00
D13 Keith Tkachuk .50 1.25
D14 Jaromir Jagr .75 2.00
D15 Mats Sundin .50 1.25
D16 Steve Kariya .60 1.50
D17 Peter Bondra .50 1.25
D18 Peter Forsberg 1.25 3.00
D19 Steve Yzerman 2.50 6.00
D20 Zigmund Palffy .50 1.25

1999-00 Black Diamond Diamond Might

Randomly inserted in packs at 1:9, this 10-card set pictures NHL's toughest players set against a colored foil background.
COMPLETE SET (10) 8.00 15.00
STATED ODDS 1:9
DM1 Peter Forsberg 1.50 4.00
DM2 Brendan Shanahan 1.00 2.50
DM3 Eric Lindros 1.00 2.50
DM4 John LeClair .75 2.00
DM5 Jaromir Jagr 1.00 2.50
DM6 Keith Tkachuk .60 1.50
DM7 Teemu Selanne .60 1.50
DM8 Mats Sundin .60 1.50
DM9 Mark Messier .75 2.00
DM10 Theo Fleury .60 1.50

1999-00 Black Diamond Diamond Skills

Randomly inserted in packs at 1:24, this 10-card set features top players who make the highlight reel night after night. Action player photos on a foil-front card are set against a centered diamond background that is framed by horizontal laser-etched lines.
COMPLETE SET (10) 25.00 50.00
STATED ODDS 1:24
DS1 Teemu Selanne 1.25 3.00
DS2 Paul Kariya 3.00 8.00
DS3 Patrick Roy 6.00 15.00
DS4 Pavel Bure 1.50 4.00
DS5 Sergei Fedorov 2.50 6.00
DS6 Eric Lindros 2.00 5.00
DS7 Jaromir Jagr 2.00 5.00
DS8 Martin Brodeur 3.00 8.00
DS9 Theo Fleury 1.25 3.00
DS10 Curtis Joseph 1.25 3.00

1999-00 Black Diamond Gordie Howe Gallery

Randomly inserted in packs at 1:12, this 10-card set pays tribute to one of hockey's greatest legends. A centered picture framed by a diamond is centered on a holographic foil background. Card backs carry a "GH" prefix.
COMPLETE SET (10) 30.00 80.00
COMMON HOWE (GH1-GH10) 5.00 12.00
STATED ODDS 1:12

1999-00 Black Diamond Myriad

Randomly inserted in packs at 1:24, this 10-card set showcases 10 of the NHL's most collectible stars in action.
COMPLETE SET (10) 20.00 40.00
STATED ODDS 1:24
M1 Patrik Stefan 2.00 5.00
M2 Teemu Selanne 1.25 3.00
M3 Sergei Samsonov 1.25 3.00
M4 Joe Sakic 2.50 6.00
M5 Brett Hull 1.50 4.00
M6 Pavel Bure 1.50 4.00
M7 Steve Yzerman 6.00 15.00
M8 Jaromir Jagr 2.00 5.00
M9 Eric Lindros 2.00 5.00
M10 Paul Kariya 3.00 8.00

2000-01 Black Diamond

Released in early December 2000, Black Diamond featured a 132-card base set consisting of 82 regular issue cards and 50 short printed Precious Gems cards divided up into three tiers. Tier 1, numbers 61-75 and 112-132, were sequentially numbered to 1999, tier 2, card numbers 76-84, were sequentially numbered to 1250, and tier 3, card numbers 85-90, were sequentially numbered to 500. Cards 91-132 were only available in packs of Upper Deck Rookie Update. Base cards were all foil and have colored borders along the top and bottom of the card to match each respective player's team colors. Black Diamond was packaged in 24-pack boxes with packs containing six cards and carried a suggested retail price of $3.99.
COMPLETE SET (90) 300.00 600.00
COMP.SET w/o SP's (82) 15.00 30.00
61-75/112-132 ROOK.PRINT RUN 1999
76-84 ROOKIE PRINT RUN 1250
85-90 PREC.GEMS PRINT RUN 500
91-132 ISSUED IN UD ROOK.UPDATE
1 Paul Kariya .40 1.00
2 Teemu Selanne .60 1.50
3 Patrik Stefan .25 .60
4 Joe Thornton .50 1.25
5 Sergei Samsonov .25 .60
6 Dominik Hasek .50 1.25
7 Maxim Afinogenov .20 .50
8 Valeri Bure .25 .60
9 Marc Savard .25 .60
10 Ron Francis .40 1.00
11 Jeff O'Neill .25 .60
12 Tony Amonte .25 .60
13 Michal Grosek .20 .50
14 Patrick Roy .75 2.00
15 Ray Bourque .50 1.25
16 Milan Hejduk .25 .60
17 Peter Forsberg .40 1.00
18 Brett Hull .50 1.25
19 Ed Belfour .30 .75
20 Mike Modano .50 1.25
21 Brendan Shanahan .40 1.00
22 Chris Osgood .30 .75
23 Steve Yzerman 1.00 2.50
24 Doug Weight .30 .75
25 Tommy Salo .25 .60
26 Pavel Bure .40 1.00
27 Trevor Kidd .20 .50
28 Rob Blake .30 .75
29 Luc Robitaille .30 .75
30 Jose Theodore .40 1.00
31 Saku Koivu .30 .75
32 David Legwand .30 .75
33 Martin Brodeur .60 1.50
34 Scott Gomez .25 .60
35 Scott Stevens .30 .75
36 Tim Connolly .20 .50
37 Mariusz Czerkawski .20 .50
38 Mark Messier .50 1.25
39 Theo Fleury .40 1.00
40 Marian Hossa .25 .60
41 Radek Bonk .25 .60
42 Brian Boucher .25 .60
43 John LeClair .30 .75
44 Simon Gagne .30 .75
45 Jeremy Roenick .30 .75
46 Keith Tkachuk .30 .75
47 Jaromir Jagr .75 2.00
48 Martin Straka UER .25 .60
49 Steve Shields .20 .50
50 Jeff Friesen .20 .50
51 Chris Pronger .25 .60
52 Roman Turek .25 .60
53 Vincent Lecavalier .25 .60
54 Dan Cloutier .25 .60
55 Curtis Joseph .40 1.00
56 Mats Sundin .30 .75
57 Markus Naslund .25 .60
58 Felix Potvin .50 1.25
59 Olaf Kolzig .30 .75
60 Jeff Halpern .20 .50
61 Matt Pettinger RC 1.50 4.00
62 Chris Nielsen RC 1.50 4.00
63 Dany Heatley RC 6.00 15.00
64 Matt Zultek RC 1.50 4.00
65 Dmitri Afanasenkov RC 1.50 4.00
66 Tyler Bouck RC 1.50 4.00
67 Jonas Andersson RC 1.50 4.00
68 Marc-Andre Thinel RC 1.50 4.00
69 Jaroslav Svoboda RC 1.50 4.00
70 Josef Vasicek RC 4.00 10.00
71 Andrew Raycroft RC 4.00 10.00
72 Juraj Kolnik RC 1.50 4.00
73 Zdenek Blatny RC 1.50 4.00
74 Sebastien Caron RC 2.00 5.00
75 Michael Ryder RC 6.00 15.00
76 Eric Nickulas RC 2.00 5.00
77 Jeff Cowan RC 2.00 5.00
78 Steven Reinprecht RC 3.00 8.00
79 David Gosselin RC 2.50 6.00
80 Colin White RC 2.00 5.00
81 Stove Valiquette RC 2.50 6.00
82 Jani Hurme RC 2.00 5.00
83 Jean-Guy Trudel RC 2.00 5.00
84 Dieter Kochan RC 2.00 5.00
85 Paul Kariya PG 6.00 15.00
86 Patrick Roy PG 15.00 40.00
87 Steve Yzerman PG 12.00 30.00
88 Pavel Bure PG 6.00 15.00
89 Martin Brodeur PG 8.00 20.00
90 Jaromir Jagr PG 10.00 25.00
91 Samuel Pahlsson .20 .50
92 Eric Boulton RC .30 .75
93 Daniel Tkaczuk .25 .60
94 Rob Shearer RC .40 1.00
95 David Vyborny .20 .50
96 Tyler Bouck .20 .50
97 Mike Comrie RC 3.00 8.00
98 Anson Carter .25 .60
99 Roman Simicek RC .30 .75
100 Andrei Markov .40 1.00
101 Jason Arnott .25 .60
102 Mike Mottau .20 .50
103 Taylor Pyatt .20 .50
104 Alexei Yashin .25 .60
105 Todd Fedoruk RC .30 .75
106 Milan Kraft .20 .50
107 Mario Lemieux 1.00 2.50
108 Evgeni Nabokov .25 .60
109 Brad Richards .30 .75
110 Daniel Sedin .60 1.50
111 Henrik Sedin .50 1.25
112 Petr Tenkrat RC 1.50 4.00
113 Lee Goren RC 1.50 4.00
114 David Aebischer RC 3.00 8.00
115 Yuri Babenko RC 1.50 4.00
116 Rostislav Klesla RC 4.00 10.00
117 Marty Turco RC 3.00 8.00
118 Jason Williams RC 2.50 6.00
119 Michel Riesen RC 2.00 5.00
120 Lubomir Visnovsky RC 3.00 8.00
121 Travis Scott RC 2.00 5.00
122 Peter Bartos RC 2.00 5.00
123 Marian Gaborik RC 6.00 15.00
124 Scott Hartnell RC 4.00 10.00
125 Rick DiPietro RC 6.00 15.00
126 Vitali Yeremeyev RC 2.00 5.00
127 Martin Havlat RC 5.00 12.00
128 Roman Cechmanek RC 2.00 5.00
129 Justin Williams RC 4.00 10.00
130 Ruslan Fedotenko RC 1.50 4.00
131 Alexander Kharitonov RC 1.50 4.00
132 Alexei Ponikarovsky RC 2.50 6.00

2000-01 Black Diamond Gold

Randomly inserted in hobby packs, this 90-card set paralleled the base set enhanced with a gold stamp across the middle of the card reading "Diamond Gold." Each card was sequentially numbered to 100.
*1-60/91-111 VETS/100: 8X TO 20X
*61-75 ROOK/100: 1X TO 2.5X RC/1999
*76-84 ROOK/100: .8X TO 2X RC/1250
*85-90 PG/100: .6X TO 1.5X PG/500
GOLD PRINT RUN 100 SER.#'d SETS

2000-01 Black Diamond Diamonation

Randomly inserted in packs at the rate of 1:12, this nine card set features full color player action photography set against a red and silver foil background with gold foil highlights.
COMPLETE SET (9) 15.00 30.00
STATED ODDS 1:12
IG1 Paul Kariya 1.00 2.50
IG2 Patrick Roy 5.00 12.00
IG3 Sergei Fedorov 2.00 5.00
IG4 Pavel Bure 1.25 3.00
IG5 Scott Gomez 1.00 2.50
IG6 John LeClair 1.25 3.00
IG7 Jaromir Jagr 1.50 4.00
IG8 Vincent Lecavalier 1.00 2.50
IG9 Curtis Joseph 1.00 2.50

2000-01 Black Diamond Diamond Might

Randomly seeded in packs at the rate of 1:12, this nine card set features full color action photography set on an all foil card with red highlights along the card bottom in the shape of a "V." Cards have gold foil stamping highlights.
COMPLETE SET (9) 15.00 30.00
STATED ODDS 1:12
FP1 Teemu Selanne 1.25 3.00
FP2 Peter Forsberg 2.50 6.00
FP3 Ray Bourque 2.00 5.00
FP4 Mike Modano 1.50 4.00
FP5 Brendan Shanahan 1.50 4.00
FP6 Pavel Bure 1.25 3.00
FP7 Martin Brodeur 2.50 6.00
FP8 John LeClair 1.25 3.00
FP9 Jaromir Jagr 1.50 4.00

2000-01 Black Diamond Diamond Skills

Randomly inserted in packs at the rate of 1:17, this six card set features full color action photography set against a foil backdrop with cardboard borders along the top and bottom left hand corners. Cards contain gold foil stamping highlights.
COMPLETE SET (6) 20.00 40.00
STATED ODDS 1:17
IC1 Patrick Roy 6.00 15.00
IC2 Mike Modano 2.00 5.00
IC3 Steve Yzerman 6.00 15.00
IC4 Martin Brodeur 3.00 8.00
IC5 John LeClair 1.50 4.00
IC6 Jaromir Jagr 2.00 5.00

2000-01 Black Diamond Game Gear

Randomly inserted in Black Diamond packs at the rate of 1:23 and 1:30 in UD Update packs, this 32-card set features player action shots coupled with a swatch of game used memorabilia. Update cards are marked below.
STATED ODDS 1:23/1:30 UPDATE
BJV J.Vanbiesbrouck Blocker 8.00 20.00
BSB Sean Burke Blocker 6.00 15.00
BTB Tom Barrasso Blocker 6.00 15.00
BTS Tommy Salo Blocker 6.00 15.00
CJV J.Vanbiesbrouck Glove 6.00 15.00
CKM Kirk McLean Glove 6.00 15.00
CSB Sean Burke Glove 6.00 15.00
CTB Tom Barrasso Glove 6.00 15.00
CTS Tommy Salo Glove 6.00 15.00
GEL Eric Lindros Glove SP 8.00 20.00
GTS Teemu Selanne Glove SP 10.00 25.00
GWG Wayne Gretzky Glove SP 40.00 100.00
LBD Byron Dafoe Pad 6.00 15.00
LCJ Curtis Joseph Pad 6.00 15.00
LDH Dominik Hasek Pad 10.00 25.00
LGF Grant Fuhr Pad 20.00 50.00
LJV J.Vanbiesbrouck Pad 6.00 15.00
LMB Martin Biron Pad 6.00 15.00
LOK Olaf Kolzig Pad 6.00 15.00
LRL Roberto Luongo Pad 8.00 20.00
LSS Steve Shields Pad 6.00 15.00
SMM Mark Messier Skate SP 30.00 80.00
GDR Chris Drury Glove Upd 6.00 15.00
GFE S.Fedorov Glove Upd 20.00 50.00
GSA Joe Sakic Glove Upd 12.50 30.00
GTH J.Thornton Glove Upd 8.00 20.00
GYA Alexei Yashin Glove Upd 6.00 15.00
LAU J-S Aubin Pad Upd 6.00 15.00
LDE Marc Denis Pad Upd 6.00 15.00
LOS Chris Osgood Pad Upd 6.00 15.00
LTU Roman Turek Pad Upd 6.00 15.00
SJA J.Jagr Skate Upd 15.00 40.00

2000-01 Black Diamond Myriad

Randomly inserted in packs at the rate of 1:17, this six card set features player action photography set against a blue and silver foil background with a black and silver border along the left side of the card. Cards contain gold foil highlights.
COMPLETE SET (6) 12.00 25.00
STATED ODDS 1:17
CC1 Paul Kariya 1.50 4.00
CC2 Peter Forsberg 3.00 8.00
CC3 Pavel Bure 1.50 4.00
CC4 Scott Gomez 1.50 4.00
CC5 Jaromir Jagr 2.00 5.00
CC6 Curtis Joseph 1.50 4.00

2003-04 Black Diamond

This 198-card set consisted of four distinct tiers. Single diamond cards (1-84); double diamond cards (85-126) inserted at 1:2; triple diamond cards (127-168) inserted at 1:8 and quadruple diamond cards inserted at 1:24. An oversized 5X7 Joe Thornton card with the sales sheet information on the back of the card was distributed to hobby shops and distributors before the release of the product.
COMPLETE SET (198) 200.00 400.00
COMP.SET w/o SP's (126) 40.00 80.00
85-126 DOUBLE ODDS 1:2
127-168 TRIPLE ODDS 1:8
169-198 QUAD ODDS 1:24
1 Mike York .25 .60
2 Pavel Bure .50 1.25
3 Steve Reinprecht .25 .60
4 Vincent Lecavalier .30 .75
5 Alex Auld .25 .60
6 Eric Daze .30 .75
7 Jeff Hackett .30 .75
8 Manny Fernandez .30 .75
9 Alexei Zhamnov .30 .75
10 Bryan Marchment .25 .60
11 Jason Allison .30 .75
12 Tony Amonte .30 .75
13 David Legwand .30 .75
14 Geoff Sanderson .25 .60
15 Olaf Kolzig .40 1.00
16 Vaclav Prospal .25 .60
17 Sebastien Caron .30 .75
18 Daniel Alfredsson .40 1.00
19 Martin Biron .30 .75
20 Jay Bouwmeester .40 1.00
21 Nikolai Khabibulin .40 1.00
22 Keith Tkachuk .40 1.00
23 Miroslav Satan .30 .75
24 Rick DiPietro .30 .75
25 Ryan Smyth .30 .75
26 Alexander Mogilny .30 .75
27 Daniil Markov .25 .60
28 Jason Spezza .40 1.00
29 Roman Cechmanek .30 .75
30 Brendan Morrison .30 .75
31 Chris Gratton .25 .60
32 Joe Sakic .60 1.50
33 Jose Theodore .40 1.00
34 Dwayne Roloson .30 .75
35 Ed Jovanovski .30 .75
36 Peter Forsberg .50 1.25
37 Robert Esche .25 .60
38 Daniel Briere .40 1.00
39 Doug Weight .40 1.00
40 Mike Comrie .30 .75
41 Michael Peca .30 .75
42 Ales Kotalik .25 .60
43 Alexei Kovalev .30 .75
44 Tommy Salo .30 .75
45 Pavol Demitra .50 1.25
46 Alex Tanguay .30 .75
47 Johan Hedberg .30 .75
48 Jan Hrdina .25 .60
49 Mike Komisarek .25 .60
50 Petr Sykora .30 .75
51 Ilya Kovalchuk .40 1.00
52 Mike Modano .60 1.50
53 Scottie Upshall .30 .75
54 Rico Fata .25 .60
55 Sergei Gonchar .25 .60
56 Mike Dunham .30 .75
57 Olli Jokinen .40 1.00
58 Roman Turek .30 .75
59 Alexander Svitov .25 .60
60 Bill Guerin .40 1.00
61 Byron Dafoe .30 .75
62 Patrick Marleau .40 1.00
63 Patrik Elias .40 1.00
64 Brett Hull .50 1.25
65 Marco Sturm .25 .60
66 Andrew Raycroft .30 .75
67 Scott Gomez .30 .75
68 John LeClair .40 1.00
69 Kyle Calder .25 .60
70 Pierre-Marc Bouchard .40 1.00
71 Nikolai Antropov .30 .75
72 Jean-Sebastien Giguere .40 1.00
73 Marc Denis .30 .75
74 Martin Straka .25 .60
75 Peter Bondra .30 .75
76 Ron Hainsey .25 .60
77 Brendan Shanahan .50 1.25
78 Evgeni Nabokov .30 .75
79 Glen Murray .30 .75
80 Martin Brodeur .75 2.00
81 Adam Deadmarsh .30 .75
82 Kevin Weekes .30 .75
03 Owen Nolan .30 .75
84 Zdeno Chara .40 1.00
85 Andrew Cassels .50 1.25
86 Simon Gagne .75 2.00
87 Derian Hatcher .50 1.25
88 Mats Sundin .75 2.00
89 Chris Osgood .75 2.00
90 Henrik Zetterberg 1.00 2.50
91 Saku Koivu .75 2.00
92 Sergei Samsonov .60 1.50
93 Arron Asham .50 1.25
94 Teppo Numminen .50 1.25
95 Philippe Sauve .60 1.50
96 Jeff O'Neill .50 1.25
97 Luc Robitaille .75 2.00
98 Marty Turco .75 2.00
99 Niko Dimitrakos .50 1.25
100 Markus Naslund .75 2.00
101 Stephen Weiss .50 1.25
102 Ed Belfour .75 2.00
103 Roberto Luongo 1.25 3.00
104 Eric Lindros 1.25 3.00
105 Jocelyn Thibault .60 1.50
106 Marian Hossa .60 1.50
107 Teemu Selanne 1.50 4.00
108 Jaromir Jagr 2.00 5.00
109 Stanislav Chistov .50 1.25
110 Zigmund Palffy .75 2.00
111 P.J. Axelsson .50 1.25
112 Denis Arkhipov .50 1.25
113 Sean Burke .50 1.25
114 Todd Marchant .50 1.25
115 Maxim Afinogenov .50 1.25
116 Tomas Vokoun .60 1.50
117 Jason Blake .50 1.25
118 Jordan Leopold .50 1.25
119 Martin St. Louis .75 2.00
120 Pavel Datsyuk 1.00 2.50
121 Marc Savard .60 1.50
122 Marian Gaborik 1.25 3.00
123 Jamie Langenbrunner .60 1.50
124 Jarome Iginla .75 2.00
125 Al MacInnis .75 2.00
126 Nicklas Lidstrom .75 2.00
127 Georges Laraque 2.00 5.00
128 Justin Williams 2.00 5.00
129 Anson Carter 2.00 5.00
130 Chris Drury 2.00 5.00
131 Willie Mitchell 1.50 4.00
132 Rick Nash 2.50 6.00
133 Scott Stevens 2.50 6.00
134 Chris Pronger 2.00 5.00
135 Mario Lemieux 8.00 20.00
136 Steve Ott 2.00 5.00
137 Steve Yzerman 6.00 15.00
138 Dany Heatley 2.50 6.00
139 Ron Francis 3.00 8.00
140 Alexander Frolov 2.00 5.00
141 Tyler Arnason 1.50 4.00
142 Rob Blake 2.50 6.00
143 Patrick Lalime 2.00 5.00
144 Joe Thornton 3.00 8.00
145 David Aebischer 2.00 5.00
146 Alexei Yashin 2.00 5.00
147 Felix Potvin 4.00 10.00
148 Boyd Gordon RC 2.50 6.00
149 Tom Preissing RC 2.50 6.00
150 Brent Burns RC 5.00 12.00
151 Antoine Vermette RC 4.00 10.00
152 Antti Miettinen RC 3.00 8.00
153 Maxim Kondratiev RC 2.00 5.00
154 Christian Ehrhoff RC 2.50 6.00
155 Jiri Hudler RC 5.00 12.00
156 David Hale RC 2.00 5.00
157 Marek Svatos RC 4.00 10.00
158 Matthew Lombardi RC 2.50 6.00
159 Alexander Semin RC 6.00 15.00
160 John-Michael Liles RC 2.50 6.00
161 Dan Fritsche RC 2.00 5.00
162 Esa Pirnes RC 2.00 5.00
163 Cody McCormick RC 2.50 6.00
164 Lasse Kukkonen RC 2.00 5.00
165 Tim Gleason RC 2.50 6.00
166 Marek Zidlicky RC 2.00 5.00
167 Christoph Brandner RC 2.50 6.00
168 Sean Bergenheim RC 2.50 6.00
169 Mike Johnson 3.00 8.00
170 Erik Cole 4.00 10.00
171 Barret Jackman 3.00 8.00
172 Marcel Hossa 3.00 8.00
173 Tie Domi 4.00 10.00
174 Michael Rupp 3.00 8.00
175 Jeremy Roenick 5.00 12.00
176 Sergei Fedorov 8.00 20.00
177 Paul Kariya 6.00 15.00
178 Mike Ricci 4.00 10.00
179 Brenden Morrow 4.00 10.00
180 Dominik Hasek 8.00 20.00
181 P.J. Stock 3.00 8.00
182 Ales Hemsky 5.00 12.00
183 Todd Bertuzzi 5.00 12.00
184 Patrice Bergeron RC 10.00 25.00
185 Pavel Vorobiev RC 4.00 10.00
186 Milan Michalek RC 6.00 15.00
187 Matt Stajan RC 5.00 12.00
188 Dan Hamhuis RC 4.00 10.00
189 Joffrey Lupul RC 8.00 20.00
190 Eric Staal RC 12.00 30.00
191 Tuomo Ruutu RC 5.00 12.00
192 Nathan Horton RC 8.00 20.00
193 Dustin Brown RC 6.00 15.00
194 Jordin Tootoo RC 6.00 15.00
195 Joni Pitkanen RC 5.00 12.00
196 Peter Sejna RC 4.00 10.00
197 Chris Higgins RC 6.00 15.00
198 Marc-Andre Fleury RC 15.00 40.00
NNO Joe Thornton 5X7 PREVIEW 1.50 4.00

2003-04 Black Diamond Green

This set is also referred to as the "Color" parallel.
*1-84 SINGLE/100: 4X TO 10X
*85-126 DOUBLE/100: 2X TO 5X
*127-147 TRIPLE/100: .6X TO 1.5X
*148-168 TRIP.ROOK/100: .5X TO 1.2X
*169-183 QUAD/100: .3X TO .8X
*184-198 QUAD ROOK/100: .4X TO 1X
STATED PRINT RUN 100 SER.#'d SETS

2003-04 Black Diamond Red

This set is also referred to as the "Cut" parallel.
*1-84 SINGLE/50: 6X TO 15X
*85-126 DOUBLE/50: 3X TO 8X
*127-147 TRIPLE/50: 1X TO 2.5X
*148-168 TRIP.ROOK/50: .8X TO 2X
*169-183 QUAD/50: .5X TO 1.2X
*184-198 QUAD ROOK/50: .6X TO 1.5X
STATED PRINT RUN 50 SER.#'d SETS

2003-04 Black Diamond Signature Gems

This 36-card autograph set featured certified autographs on diamond-mirrored stickers affixed to th cards.
STATED ODDS 1:48
SG1 Maxim Afinogenov 6.00 15.0
SG2 Ray Bourque 15.00 40.0
SG4 Pavel Bure 10.00 25.0
SG5 Erik Cole 6.00 15.0
SG6 Mike Comrie 6.00 15.0
SG7 Simon Gagne 8.00 20.0
SG8 Rick Nash 12.50 30.0
SG9 Wayne Gretzky 100.00 200.0
SG10 Scott Hartnell 8.00 20.0
SG11 Martin Havlat 6.00 15.0
SG12 Ilya Kovalchuk 8.00 20.0
SG13 Gordie Howe 50.00 125.0
SG14 Curtis Joseph 8.00 20.0
SG15 Alexander Svitov 6.00 15.0
SG16 John LeClair 6.00 15.0
SG17 Steve Ott 6.00 15.0
SG18 Bobby Orr 100.00 200.0
SG19 Joe Thornton 15.00 40.0
SG20 Henrik Zetterberg 10.00 25.0
SG21 Marty Turco 8.00 20.0
SG22 Marian Hossa 12.00 30.0
SG23 Patrick Roy/24 200.00 400.0
SG24 Jean-Sebastien Giguere 6.00 15.0
SG25 Marian Gaborik 10.00 25.0
SG26 Todd Bertuzzi 8.00 20.0
SG27 Jason Spezza 12.50 30.0
SG28 Jarome Iginla 15.00 40.0
SG29 Sergei Samsonov 6.00 15.0
SG30 Jose Theodore 12.50 30.0
SG31 Justin Williams 6.00 15.0
SG32 Alexander Frolov 6.00 15.0
SG33 Brooks Orpik 6.00 15.0
SG34 Kurt Sauer 6.00 15.0
SG35 Steve Yzerman 25.00 60.0
SG36 Ed Belfour 20.00 50.0
SG37 Jeff Taffe 6.00 15.0

2003-04 Black Diamond Thread

STATED ODDS 1:12
*GREEN/99: .6X TO 1.5X BASIC JSY
*RED/50: 1X TO 2.5X BASIC JSY
DTDH Dany Heatley 8.00 20.0
DTPF Peter Forsberg 8.00 20.0
DTRN Rick Nash 8.00 20.0
DTIK Ilya Kovalchuk 8.00 20.0
DTJS Jason Spezza 6.00 15.0
DTJT Joe Thornton 8.00 20.0
DTML Mario Lemieux 10.00 25.0
DTMB Martin Brodeur 10.00 25.0
DTMO Mike Modano 8.00 20.0
DTAZ Alexei Zhamnov 5.00 12.0
DTAF Alexander Frolov 5.00 12.0
DTAS Alexander Svitov 5.00 12.0
DTKC Kyle Calder 5.00 12.0
DTMA Maxim Afinogenov 5.00 12.0
DTSN Scott Niedermayer 5.00 12.0
DTDB Daniel Briere 5.00 12.0
DTJB Jay Bouwmeester 5.00 12.0
DTMT Marty Turco 6.00 15.0
DTEJ Ed Jovanovski 5.00 12.0
DTED Eric Daze 5.00 12.0
DTJG Jean-Sebastien Giguere 5.00 12.0
DTTH Jocelyn Thibault 5.00 12.0
DTKP Keith Primeau 5.00 12.0
DTMD Marc Denis 5.00 12.0
DTDU Mike Dunham 5.00 12.0
DTCP Chris Pronger 5.00 12.0
DTDA David Aebischer 5.00 12.0
DTDW Doug Weight 5.00 12.0
DTAT Alex Tanguay 5.00 12.0
DTBM Brenden Morrow 5.00 12.0
DTPB Peter Bondra 5.00 12.0
DTJR Jeremy Roenick 6.00 15.0
DTMM Mark Messier 12.50 30.0
DTEB Ed Belfour 6.00 15.0
DTRL Roberto Luongo 8.00 20.0
DTTE Jose Theodore 8.00 20.0
DTPK Paul Kariya 6.00 15.0
DTEL Eric Lindros 6.00 15.0
DTMS Mats Sundin 6.00 15.0
DTBS Brendan Shanahan 6.00 15.0
DTMH Marian Hossa 6.00 15.0
DTMN Markus Naslund 6.00 15.0

2005-06 Black Diamond

This 294-card set was issued both in product specific unopened and as an insert in Rookie Update packs. The unopened product had five-card packs which car 24 to a box. Those cards covered cards 1-210 while cards 211-294 were available in the Rookie Update packs. In the pack issued cards: Cards numbered 85-126 were issued at a stated rate of one in four; cards 127-168 were issued at a stated rate of one in eight and cards 169-210 were issued at a stated rate of one in 24.
COMP.SET w/o SP's (84) 10.00 20.0
85-126 DOUBLE ODDS 1:4
127-168 TRIPLE ODDS 1:8
169-210 QUAD ODDS 1:24
211-294 ISSUED IN ROOKIE UPDATE PACKS
1 Joffrey Lupul .20 .5
2 Steve Rucchin .15 .4
3 Riku Hahl .15 .4
4 Shawn McEachern .15 .4
5 Marc Savard .15 .4
6 Philippe Sauve .20 .5
7 Nick Boynton .15 .4
8 Martin Lapointe .15 .4
9 Maxim Afinogenov .15 .4
10 Chris Drury .20 .5
11 Mike Grier .15 .4
12 Jordan Leopold .15 .4
13 Darren McCarty .15 .4
14 Martin Gelinas .15 .4
15 Eric Staal .30 .7
16 Jeff O'Neill .15 .4
17 Erik Cole .20 .5
18 Rod Brind'Amour .25 .6
19 Jocelyn Thibault .20 .5
20 Tyler Arnason .15 .4
21 Bryan Berard .15 .4
22 Eric Daze .20 .5
23 Rob Blake .25 .6
24 Nikolai Zherdev .15 .4
25 Marc Denis .20 .5
26 Justin Williams .20 .5
27 Brenden Morrow .20 .5
28 Sergei Zubov .20 .5
29 Jere Lehtinen .20 .5
30 Henrik Zetterberg .30 .7
31 Ty Conklin .20 .5
32 Ryan Smyth .20 .5
33 Jason Smith .15 .4

4 Chris Chelios .25 .60
5 Stephen Weiss .15 .40
6 Olli Jokinen .25 .60
7 Gary Roberts .15 .40
8 Alexander Frolov .15 .40
9 Mathieu Garon .20 .50
0 Lubomir Visnovsky .15 .40
1 Dwayne Roloson .20 .50
2 Pascal Dupuis .15 .40
3 Brian Rolston .20 .50
4 Filip Kuba .15 .40
5 Richard Zednik .15 .40
6 Sheldon Souray .15 .40
7 Steve Sullivan .15 .40
8 Jordin Tootoo .25 .60
9 Tomas Vokoun .20 .50
0 Scott Walker .15 .40
1 Martin Brodeur .50 1.25
2 Scott Niedermayer .25 .60
3 Brian Rafalski .20 .50
4 Alexander Mogilny .20 .50
5 Bobby Holik .15 .40
6 Kevin Weekes .20 .50
7 Jamie Lundmark .15 .40
8 Michael Peca .20 .50
9 Mark Parrish .15 .40
0 Adrian Aucoin .15 .40
1 Wade Redden .15 .40
2 Zdeno Chara .25 .60
3 Simon Gagne .25 .60
4 Robert Esche .20 .50
5 Mike Comrie .20 .50
6 Shane Doan .20 .50
7 Derian Hatcher .15 .40
8 Ladislav Nagy .15 .40
9 Milan Kraft .15 .40
0 Ryan Malone .15 .40
Marco Sturm .15 .40
2 Brad Stuart .15 .40
3 Alyn McCauley .15 .40
4 Patrick Lalime .20 .50
5 Dustin Brown .25 .60
6 Fredrik Modin .15 .40
7 Dave Andreychuk .25 .60
8 Brian Leetch .25 .60
9 Tie Domi .20 .50
0 Ed Jovanovski .20 .50
Brendan Morrison .15 .40
2 Dan Cloutier .20 .50
3 Brendan Witt .15 .40
4 Martin Biron .20 .50
5 Manny Legace 1.00 2.50
6 Jean-Sebastien Giguere 1.00 2.50
7 Sergei Fedorov 1.50 4.00
8 Andrew Raycroft .75 2.00
9 Sergei Samsonov .75 2.00
0 Miroslav Satan .75 2.00
Miikka Kiprusoff .75 2.00
2 David Aebischer .75 2.00
3 Milan Hejduk .75 2.00
4 Marty Turco 1.00 2.50
Curtis Joseph 1.00 2.50
6 Nicklas Lidstrom 1.00 2.50
7 Roberto Luongo 1.50 4.00
8 Zigmund Palffy 1.00 2.50
9 Luc Robitaille 1.00 2.50
00 Mike Ribeiro .75 2.00
01 Michael Ryder .75 2.00
02 Scott Gomez .75 2.00
03 Patrik Elias 1.00 2.50
04 Alexei Yashin .75 2.00
05 Daniel Alfredsson 1.00 2.50
06 Martin Havlat 1.00 2.50
07 Tony Amonte .75 2.00
08 John LeClair 1.00 2.50
09 Brett Hull 1.25 3.00
0 Marc-Andre Fleury 1.50 4.00
1 Mark Recchi 1.25 3.00
2 Patrick Marleau 1.00 2.50
3 Jonathan Cheechoo 1.00 2.50
4 Chris Pronger .75 2.00
5 Doug Weight 1.00 2.50
6 Brad Richards 1.00 2.50
7 Glen Murray .75 2.00
8 Tuomo Ruutu 1.00 2.50
9 Pavol Demitra 1.25 3.00
20 David Legwand .75 2.00
21 Eric Lindros 1.50 4.00
2 Rick DiPietro .75 2.00
3 Al MacInnis 1.00 2.50
4 Joe Nieuwendyk 1.00 2.50
5 Trevor Linden 1.00 2.50
6 Olaf Kolzig 1.00 2.50
7 Dany Heatley 2.00 5.00
8 Kari Lehtonen 1.50 4.00
9 Patrice Bergeron 2.50 6.00
0 Alex Tanguay 2.00 5.00
1 Paul Kariya 2.50 6.00
2 Mike Modano 3.00 8.00
3 Bill Guerin 2.00 5.00
4 Pavel Datsyuk 2.50 6.00
5 Brendan Shanahan 2.50 6.00
6 Saku Koivu 2.00 5.00
7 Marian Hossa 1.50 4.00
8 Jason Spezza 2.00 5.00
9 Jeremy Roenick 2.00 5.00
0 Keith Primeau 2.00 5.00
1 Evgeni Nabokov 1.50 4.00
2 Vincent Lecavalier 1.50 4.00
3 Ed Belfour 2.00 5.00
4 Jason Allison 1.50 4.00
5 Markus Naslund 2.00 5.00
6 Keith Tkachuk 2.00 5.00
7 Nikolai Khabibulin 2.00 5.00
8 Andrew Alberts RC 2.00 5.00
9 Andy Wozniewski RC 2.50 6.00
0 Brandon Bochenski RC 3.00 8.00
1 Brent Seabrook RC 6.00 15.00
2 Cam Ward RC 5.00 12.00
3 Chris Campoli RC 2.00 5.00
4 David Leneveu RC 2.50 6.00
5 Duncan Keith RC 6.00 15.00
6 Henrik Lundqvist RC 12.00 30.00
7 Jay McClement RC 2.00 5.00
8 Johan Franzen RC 5.00 12.00
9 Jussi Jokinen RC 3.00 8.00
0 Keith Ballard RC 2.50 6.00
1 Kevin Dallman RC 2.50 6.00
2 Maxime Talbot RC 3.00 8.00
3 Niklas Nordgren RC 3.00 8.00
4 Peter Budaj RC 4.00 10.00
5 Petteri Nokelainen RC 2.00 5.00
6 Rene Bourque RC 3.00 8.00
7 Jeff Woywitka RC 2.00 5.00
8 Ryan Hollweg RC 2.00 5.00
9 Ilya Kovalchuk 3.00 8.00
0 Joe Thornton 4.00 10.00
1 Jarome Iginla 3.00 8.00
2 Joe Sakic 5.00 12.00
3 Peter Forsberg 4.00 10.00
4 Rick Nash 3.00 8.00

175 Steve Yzerman 8.00 20.00
176 Marian Gaborik 5.00 12.00
177 Jose Theodore 3.00 8.00
178 Jaromir Jagr 8.00 20.00
179 Mark Messier 5.00 12.00
180 Dominik Hasek 5.00 12.00
181 Mario Lemieux 10.00 25.00
182 Martin St. Louis 3.00 8.00
183 Mats Sundin 3.00 8.00
184 Wayne Gretzky 15.00 40.00
185 Gordie Howe 10.00 25.00
186 Ray Bourque 5.00 12.00
187 Patrick Roy 8.00 20.00
188 Bryan Trottier 4.00 10.00
189 Cam Neely 3.00 8.00
190 Gilbert Brule RC 5.00 12.00
191 Alexander Ovechkin RC 30.00 80.00
192 Zach Parise RC 8.00 20.00
193 Sidney Crosby RC 200.00 300.00
194 Dion Phaneuf RC 8.00 20.00
195 Jeff Carter RC 8.00 20.00
196 Corey Perry RC 8.00 20.00
197 Thomas Vanek RC 10.00 25.00
198 Ryan Getzlaf RC 12.00 30.00
199 Mike Richards RC 10.00 25.00
200 Robert Nilsson RC 5.00 12.00
201 Alexander Steen RC 10.00 25.00
202 Rostislav Olesz RC 4.00 10.00
203 Wojtek Wolski RC 4.00 10.00
204 Ryan Suter RC 6.00 15.00
205 Hannu Toivonen RC 5.00 12.00
206 Yann Danis RC 4.00 10.00
207 Jim Howard RC 8.00 20.00
208 Andrej Meszaros RC 4.00 10.00
209 Braydon Coburn RC 5.00 12.00
210 Alexander Perezhogin RC 4.00 10.00
211 Dustin Penner RC 5.00 12.00
212 Zenon Konopka RC 2.00 5.00
213 Jim Slater RC 2.50 6.00
214 Adam Berkhoel RC 2.50 6.00
215 Jordan Sigalet RC 2.00 5.00
216 Milan Jurcina RC 2.50 6.00
217 Ben Walter RC 2.00 5.00
218 Chris Thorburn RC 2.50 6.00
219 Daniel Paille RC 3.00 8.00
220 Nathan Paetsch RC 2.50 6.00
221 Andrew Ladd RC 4.00 10.00
222 Kevin Nastiuk RC 2.00 5.00
223 Danny Richmond RC 2.00 5.00
224 Cam Barker RC 2.50 6.00
225 Corey Crawford RC 10.00 25.00
226 James Wisniewski RC 2.50 6.00
227 Brad Richardson RC 3.00 8.00
228 Vitaly Kolesnik RC 2.50 6.00
229 Ole-Kristian Tollefsen RC 2.50 6.00
230 Jaroslav Balastik RC 2.00 5.00
231 Geoff Platt RC 2.50 6.00
232 Alexandre Picard RC 2.00 5.00
233 Joakim Lindstrom RC 2.00 5.00
234 Junior Lessard RC 2.00 5.00
235 Vojtech Polak RC 2.00 5.00
236 Kyle Quincey RC 2.50 6.00
237 Valtteri Filppula RC 4.00 10.00
238 Brett Lebda RC 2.00 5.00
239 Kyle Brodziak RC 2.00 5.00
240 Brad Winchester RC 3.00 8.00
241 Danny Syvret RC 2.00 5.00
242 Matt Greene RC 2.00 5.00
243 J-F Jacques RC 2.00 5.00
244 Anthony Stewart RC 2.50 6.00
245 Rob Globke RC 2.00 5.00
246 Petr Taticek RC 2.50 6.00
247 Jeff Tambellini RC 2.00 5.00
248 Petr Kanko RC 3.00 8.00
249 George Parros RC 2.00 5.00
250 Yanick Lehoux RC 3.00 8.00
251 Richard Petiot RC 2.50 6.00
252 Mikko Koivu RC 4.00 10.00
253 Derek Boogaard RC 4.00 10.00
254 Matt Foy RC 2.00 5.00
255 Andrei Kostitsyn RC 4.00 10.00
256 Maxim Lapierre RC 3.00 8.00
257 Kevin Klein RC 2.00 5.00
258 Pekka Rinne RC 5.00 12.00
259 Barry Tallackson RC 2.50 6.00
260 Jason Ryznar RC 2.00 5.00
261 Jeremy Colliton RC 2.00 5.00
262 Bruno Gervais RC 2.00 5.00
263 Petr Prucha RC 3.00 8.00
264 Al Montoya RC 3.00 8.00
265 Christoph Schubert RC 2.00 5.00
266 Patrick Eaves RC 3.00 8.00
267 R.J. Umberger RC 3.00 8.00
268 Ben Eager RC 2.50 6.00
269 Alexandre Picard RC 2.00 5.00
270 Stefan Ruzicka RC 2.00 5.00
271 Ryan Whitney RC 3.00 8.00
272 Erik Christensen RC 2.00 5.00
273 Colby Armstrong RC 3.00 8.00
274 Steve Bernier RC 3.00 8.00
275 Dimitri Patzold RC 2.00 5.00
276 Ryane Clowe RC 4.00 10.00
277 Josh Gorges RC 2.50 6.00
278 Grant Stevenson RC 2.00 5.00
279 Lee Stempniak RC 3.00 8.00
280 Colin Hemingway RC 2.00 5.00
281 Dennis Wideman RC 2.00 5.00
282 Evgeny Artyukhin RC 2.50 6.00
283 Ryan Craig RC 2.00 5.00
284 Paul Ranger RC 2.00 5.00
285 Darren Reid RC 2.00 5.00
286 Gerald Coleman RC 2.00 5.00
287 Staffan Kronwall RC 2.00 5.00
288 Jay Harrison RC 2.50 6.00
289 Kevin Bieksa RC 4.00 10.00
290 Rob McVicar RC 3.00 8.00
291 Tomas Mojzis RC 2.00 5.00
292 Jakub Klepis RC 2.00 5.00
293 Tomas Fleischmann RC 3.00 8.00
294 Mike Green RC 4.00 10.00

2005-06 Black Diamond Emerald

*1-84 VET/25.: 12X TO 30X BASIC SNGL
*85-126 VET/25.: 3X TO 8X BASIC DBLE
*127-147 VET/25: 1.5X TO 4X BASIC TRPL
*148-168 ROOK/25: 1.5X TO 4X BASIC RC
*169-189 VET/25: 1X TO 2.5X BASIC QUAD
*QUAD ROOKIE: 1X TO 2.5X
STATED PRINT RUN 25 SER.#'d SETS
156 Henrik Lundqvist 75.00 150.00
191 Alexander Ovechkin 200.00 350.00
193 Sidney Crosby 300.00 600.00
194 Dion Phaneuf 40.00 100.00

2005-06 Black Diamond Ruby

*1-84 VET/100: 8X TO 20X BASIC SINGL
*85-126 VET/100: 2X TO 5X BASIC DBLE
*127-147 VET/100: 1X TO 2.5X BASIC TRPL
*148-168 ROOK/100: .8X TO 2X BASIC RC
*169-189 VET/100: .6X TO 1.5X BASIC QUAD
*190-210 ROOK/100: .5X TO 1.2X BASIC RC
PRINT RUN 100 SER.#'d SETS

191 Alexander Ovechkin 125.00 250.00
193 Sidney Crosby 200.00 400.00

2005-06 Black Diamond Gemography

COMMON CARD 4.00 10.00
SEMISTARS 5.00 12.00
UNLISTED STARS 6.00 15.00
STATED ODDS 1:62
GAC Anson Carter 5.00 12.00
GAV Antoine Vermette 6.00 12.00
GBA Milan Bartovic 4.00 10.00
GBB Brad Boyes 6.00 12.00
GBI Martin Biron 6.00 12.00
GCD Chris Drury 6.00 12.00
GDB Dustin Brown 6.00 15.00
GDH Dany Heatley 12.00 30.00
GEC Erik Cole 6.00 15.00
GFS Fredrik Sjostrom 4.00 10.00
GGH Gordie Howe 40.00 100.00
GHA Dominik Hasek 15.00 40.00
GHO Marcel Hossa 4.00 10.00
GIK Ilya Kovalchuk 15.00 40.00
GJC Jonathan Cheechoo 12.50 30.00
GJI Jarome Iginla 15.00 40.00
GJR Jeremy Roenick 10.00 25.00
GJT Joe Thornton 20.00 50.00
GKD Kris Draper 5.00 12.00
GLR Luc Robitaille 10.00 25.00
GMB Martin Brodeur 50.00 125.00
GMC Mike Comrie 4.00 10.00
GMF Marc-Andre Fleury 15.00 40.00
GMG Marian Gaborik 20.00 50.00
GMH Martin Havlat 6.00 15.00
GMN Markus Naslund 6.00 12.00
GMP Mark Popovic 4.00 10.00
GMR Michael Ryder 8.00 15.00
GNK Nikolai Khabibulin 8.00 15.00
GNZ Nikolai Zherdev 4.00 10.00
GPB Patrice Bergeron 6.00 15.00
GRB Ray Bourque 30.00 80.00
GRE Robert Esche 4.00 10.00
GRK Ryan Kesler 10.00 25.00
GSB Sean Bergenheim 4.00 10.00
GSL Martin St. Louis 6.00 15.00
GSP Jason Spezza 12.00 30.00
GSS Sheldon Souray 4.00 10.00
GTM Travis Moen 4.00 10.00
GTR Tuomo Ruutu 6.00 12.00
GTS Timofei Shishkanov 4.00 10.00
GWG Wayne Gretzky 150.00 300.00

2005-06 Black Diamond Gemography Emerald

*EMERALD: .6X TO 1.5X
PRINT RUN 25 SER.#'d SETS
GWG Wayne Gretzky 250.00 500.00

2005-06 Black Diamond Gemography Ruby

*RUBY: .5X TO 1.2X
PRINT RUN 50 SER.#'d SETS

2005-06 Black Diamond Jerseys

STATED ODDS 1:12
*RUBY/100: .5X TO 1.2X BASIC JSY
JAM Al MacInnis 4.00 10.00
JBH Brett Hull 5.00 12.00
JBO Mike Bossy 5.00 12.00
JBS Brendan Shanahan 5.00 12.00
JCC Chris Chelios 5.00 12.00
JCJ Curtis Joseph 5.00 12.00
JEB Ed Belfour 5.00 12.00
JEJ Ed Jovanovski 3.00 8.00
JGL Guy Lafleur 6.00 15.00
JHA Dominik Hasek 6.00 15.00
JJF Jeff Friesen 3.00 8.00
JJI Jarome Iginla 6.00 15.00
JJJ Jaromir Jagr 6.00 15.00
JJN Joe Nieuwendyk 3.00 8.00
JJO Jose Theodore 4.00 10.00
JJR Jeremy Roenick 5.00 12.00
JJS Joe Sakic 8.00 20.00
JJT Joe Thornton 6.00 15.00
JKP Keith Primeau 3.00 8.00
JMB Martin Brodeur 10.00 25.00
JMG Marian Gaborik 6.00 15.00
JMH Milan Hejduk 3.00 8.00
JML Mario Lemieux 15.00 40.00
JMM Mike Modano 5.00 12.00
JMS Mark Messier 8.00 20.00
JOJ Olli Jokinen 3.00 8.00
JON Owen Nolan 4.00 8.00
JPB Pavel Bure 5.00 12.00
JPE Peter Bondra 4.00 10.00
JPF Peter Forsberg 6.00 15.00
JPK Paul Kariya 5.00 12.00
JPL Patrick Lalime 3.00 8.00
JRL Roberto Luongo 6.00 15.00
JRN Rick Nash 5.00 12.00
JSF Sergei Fedorov 5.00 12.00
JSK Saku Koivu 5.00 12.00
JSL Martin St. Louis 4.00 10.00
JSU Mats Sundin 5.00 12.00
JSY Steve Yzerman 12.00 30.00
JTS Teemu Selanne 5.00 12.00
JWG Wayne Gretzky 15.00 40.00

2005-06 Black Diamond Jersey Duals

*DUAL: 1.25X TO 3X SINGLE
PRINT RUN 25 SER.#'d SETS
DJDH Dany Heatley 12.50 30.00

2006-07 Black Diamond

This 210-card set was issued into the hobby in five-card packs, with an $3.99 SRP, which came 24 packs to a box. Cards numbered 1-84 feature veterans in team alphabetical order while cards 85-126 also features another grouping of veterans in team alphabetical order. Cards numbered 148-168 exist in two versions, one of which is a Rookie Card and the other is a veteran player. The set concludes with more Rookie Cards from 190-210. Please note that no cards 169-189 exist in this set.

1 Corey Perry .30 .75
2 Ilya Bryzgalov .30 .75
3 Scott Niedermayer .30 .75
4 Slava Kozlov .20 .50
5 Jim Slater .20 .50
6 Hannu Toivonen .25 .60
7 Marc Savard .20 .50
8 Zdeno Chara .30 .75
9 Glen Murray .25 .60
10 Daniel Briere .30 .75
11 Maxim Afinogenov .20 .50
12 Thomas Vanek .40 1.00
13 Daymond Langkow .20 .50
14 Chuck Kobasew .20 .50
15 Rod Brind'Amour .30 .75
16 Justin Williams .25 .60
17 Mike Commodore .20 .50
18 Michal Handzus .25 .60
19 Brent Seabrook .30 .75
20 Nikolai Khabibulin .30 .75
21 Peter Budaj .25 .60
22 Wojtek Wolski .25 .60
23 Fredrik Modin .20 .50
24 Pascal Leclaire .25 .60
25 Bryan Berard .20 .50
26 Brenden Morrow .25 .60
27 Sergei Zubov .25 .60
28 Jere Lehtinen .20 .50
29 Kris Draper .20 .50
30 Tomas Holmstrom .25 .60
31 Dwayne Roloson .25 .60
32 Jarret Stoll .25 .60
33 Shawn Horcoff .20 .50
34 Fernando Pisani .20 .50
35 Olli Jokinen .30 .75
36 Nathan Horton .30 .75
37 Todd Bertuzzi .30 .75
38 Mike Cammalleri .20 .50
39 Craig Conroy .20 .50
40 Pavol Demitra .40 1.00
41 Mark Parrish .20 .50
42 Manny Fernandez .25 .60
43 Pierre-Marc Bouchard .30 .75
44 Sergei Samsonov .25 .60
45 Alex Kovalev .25 .60
46 Jason Arnott .25 .60
47 Steve Sullivan .20 .50
48 Scott Hartnell .30 .75
49 Scott Gomez .25 .60
50 Brian Gionta .25 .60
51 Zach Parise .40 1.00
52 Rick DiPietro .25 .60
53 Robert Nilsson .20 .50
54 Jason Blake .20 .50
55 Petr Prucha .25 .60
56 Martin Straka .20 .50
57 Martin Gerber .25 .60
58 Wade Redden .20 .50
59 Patrick Eaves .20 .50
60 Joni Pitkanen .20 .50
61 Mike Richards .30 .75
62 Antero Niittymaki .25 .60
63 Curtis Joseph .30 .75
64 Ladislav Nagy .20 .50
65 Ed Jovanovski .25 .60
66 Colby Armstrong .25 .60
67 Ryan Whitney .25 .60
68 Ryan Malone .20 .50
69 Steve Bernier .20 .50
70 Evgeni Nabokov .25 .60
71 Vesa Toskala .25 .60
72 Keith Tkachuk .30 .75
73 Bill Guerin .30 .75
74 Manny Legace .25 .60
75 Vaclav Prospal .20 .50
76 Marc Denis .25 .60
77 Martin St. Louis .30 .75
78 Andrew Raycroft .25 .60
79 Darcy Tucker .25 .60
80 Daniel Sedin .30 .75
81 Henrik Sedin .30 .75
82 Brendan Morrison .20 .50
83 Dainius Zubrus .20 .50
84 Olaf Kolzig .30 .75
85 Teemu Selanne 2.50 6.00
86 Jean-Sebastien Giguere 1.25 3.00
87 Chris Pronger 1.00 2.50
88 Marian Hossa 1.00 2.50
89 Brad Boyes .75 2.00
90 Chris Drury 1.00 2.50
91 Ryan Miller 1.25 3.00
92 Alex Tanguay .75 2.00
93 Erik Cole 1.00 2.50
94 Tuomo Ruutu 1.25 3.00
95 Martin Havlat .75 2.00
96 Jose Theodore 1.25 3.00
97 Marek Svatos .75 2.00
98 Sergei Fedorov 2.00 5.00
99 Gilbert Brule 1.00 2.50
100 Eric Lindros 2.00 5.00
101 Marty Turco 1.25 3.00
102 Pavel Datsyuk 1.50 4.00
103 Ales Hemsky 1.00 2.50
104 Ryan Smyth 1.00 2.50
105 Jay Bouwmeester 1.25 3.00
106 Rob Blake 1.25 3.00
107 Alexander Frolov .75 2.00
108 Mikko Koivu 1.00 2.50
109 Cristobal Huet 1.00 2.50
110 Mike Ribeiro 1.00 2.50
111 Tomas Vokoun 1.00 2.50
112 Patrik Elias 1.25 3.00
113 Alexei Yashin 1.00 2.50
114 Miroslav Satan 1.00 2.50
115 Henrik Lundqvist 2.50 6.00
116 Daniel Alfredsson 1.25 3.00
117 Simon Gagne 1.25 3.00
118 Jeff Carter 1.25 3.00
119 Shane Doan 1.00 2.50
120 Jeremy Roenick 1.25 3.00
121 Mark Recchi 1.50 4.00
122 Patrick Marleau 1.25 3.00
123 Doug Weight 1.25 3.00
124 Brad Richards 1.25 3.00
125 Alexander Steen 1.25 3.00
126 Michael Peca 1.00 2.50
127 Kari Lehtonen 1.50 4.00
128 Patrice Bergeron 2.50 6.00
129 Miikka Kiprusoff 1.50 4.00
130 Dion Phaneuf 2.00 5.00
131 Eric Staal 2.50 6.00
132 Cam Ward 2.00 5.00
133 Milan Hejduk 1.50 4.00
134 Mike Modano 3.00 8.00
135 Henrik Zetterberg 2.50 6.00
136 Nicklas Lidstrom 2.00 5.00
137 Ed Belfour 2.00 5.00
138 Saku Koivu 2.00 5.00
139 Michael Ryder 1.25 3.00
140 Paul Kariya 2.50 6.00
141 Brendan Shanahan 2.50 6.00
142 Dany Heatley 2.00 5.00
143 Marc-Andre Fleury 3.00 8.00
144 Jonathan Cheechoo 2.00 5.00
145 Vincent Lecavalier 1.50 4.00
146 Markus Naslund 1.50 4.00
147 Roberto Luongo 3.00 8.00
148A Roman Polak RC 1.50 4.00
148B Ilya Kovalchuk 2.50 6.00
149A Joel Perrault RC 1.25 3.00
149B Ray Bourque 4.00 10.00
150A Yan Stastny RC 1.25 3.00
150B Cam Neely 2.50 6.00
151A Konstantin Pushkarev RC 1.50 4.00
151B Jarome Iginla 2.50 6.00
152A Jarkko Immonen RC 1.25 3.00
152B Joe Sakic 4.00 10.00
153A Marc-Antoine Pouliot RC 1.25 3.00
153B Patrick Roy 6.00 15.00
154A Jeremy Williams RC 1.25 3.00
154B Rick Nash 2.50 6.00
155A Michel Ouellet RC 1.50 4.00
155B Dominik Hasek 3.00 8.00
156A Tomas Kopecky RC 1.50 4.00
156B Gordie Howe 5.00 12.00
157A Keith Yandle RC 2.50 6.00
157B Wayne Gretzky 8.00 20.00
158A Marc-Edouard Vlasic RC 1.25 3.00
158B Marian Gaborik 3.00 8.00
159A Shane O'Brien RC 1.25 3.00
159B Jean Beliveau 2.50 6.00
160A Ryan Shannon RC 1.25 3.00
160B Martin Brodeur 5.00 12.00
161A John Oduya RC 2.00 5.00
161B Jaromir Jagr 6.00 15.00
162A Fredrik Norrena RC 1.25 3.00
162B Jason Spezza 2.50 6.00
163A Kristopher Letang RC 4.00 10.00
163B Peter Forsberg 3.00 8.00
164A Niklas Backstrom RC 2.50 6.00
164B Sidney Crosby 10.00 25.00
165A D.J. King RC 1.25 3.00
165B Mario Lemieux 8.00 20.00
166A Patrick Thoresen RC 1.25 3.00
166B Joe Thornton 3.00 8.00
167A Patrick Fischer RC 1.25 3.00
167B Mats Sundin 2.50 6.00
168A Mikko Lehtonen RC 1.50 4.00
168B Alexander Ovechkin 10.00 25.00
190 Mark Stuart RC 2.50 6.00
191 Eric Fehr RC 4.00 10.00
192 Ryan Potulny RC 2.50 6.00
193 Ian White RC 3.00 8.00
194 Alexei Kaigorodov RC 2.50 6.00
195 Noah Welch RC 2.50 6.00
196 Shea Weber RC 6.00 15.00
197 Enver Lisin RC 2.50 6.00
198 Matt Carle RC 2.50 6.00
199 Patrick O'Sullivan RC 4.00 10.00
200 Anze Kopitar RC 10.00 25.00
201 Travis Zajac RC 5.00 12.00
202 Phil Kessel RC 8.00 20.00
203 G. Latendresse RC 4.00 10.00
204 Nigel Dawes RC 2.50 6.00
205 Jordan Staal RC 8.00 20.00
206 Paul Stastny RC 6.00 15.00
207 Luc Bourdon RC 4.00 10.00
208 Ladislav Smid RC 2.50 6.00
209 Loui Eriksson RC 4.00 10.00
210 Evgeni Malkin RC 25.00 60.00

2006-07 Black Diamond Ruby

*1-84 VETS/100: 6X TO 15X BASIC CARDS
*85-126 VET/100: 1.5X TO 4X BASIC CARDS
*86-147 VET/100: 1X TO 2.5X BASIC CARDS
*148-210 VET/100: 1.2X TO 3X BASIC CARD
*148-210 ROOK/100: 1.5X TO 4X BASIC RC
STATED PRINT RUN 100 #'d SETS

2006-07 Black Diamond Gemography

STATED ODDS 1:48
GAB Adam Berkhoel 3.00 8.00
GAL Andrew Ladd 3.00 8.00
GAO Alexander Ovechkin SP 125.00 250.00
GBB Brandon Bochenski 3.00 8.00
GBL Brian Leetch SP 25.00 60.00
GBM Bryan McCabe EXCH 3.00 8.00
GBW Brad Winchester 3.00 8.00
GCA Jeff Carter 6.00 15.00
GCB Cam Barker 3.00 8.00
GCK Chuck Kobasew 3.00 8.00
GCP Chris Phillips 3.00 8.00
GCS Cory Stillman 3.00 8.00
GDA David Aebischer 4.00 10.00
GDP Dion Phaneuf 8.00 20.00
GDR Danny Richmond 3.00 8.00
GDW Doug Weight 3.00 8.00
GEC Erik Christensen 4.00 10.00
GGH Gordie Howe SP 50.00 100.00
GGL Georges Laraque 3.00 8.00
GGM Glen Murray 4.00 10.00
GHA Scott Hartnell 3.00 8.00
GHZ Henrik Zetterberg SP 10.00 25.00
GJC Jonathan Cheechoo 6.00 15.00
GJG Josh Gorges 3.00 8.00
GJH Jim Howard 6.00 15.00
GJI Jarome Iginla SP 12.00 30.00
GJJ Jussi Jokinen 4.00 10.00
GJO Jeff O'Neill 3.00 8.00
GJP Joni Pitkanen SP 8.00 20.00
GJS Jim Slater 3.00 8.00
GJT Jose Theodore 6.00 15.00
GKD Kris Draper SP 10.00 25.00
GKL Kari Lehtonen SP 10.00 25.00
GKT Kimmo Timonen 3.00 8.00
GMG Marian Gaborik SP 15.00 40.00
GMH Marian Hossa SP 10.00 25.00
GMK Miikka Kiprusoff SP 15.00 40.00
GML Mario Lemieux SP 60.00 120.00
GMP Mark Parrish 3.00 8.00
GMR Mike Ribeiro 3.00 8.00
GMS Miroslav Satan 4.00 10.00
GMT Marty Turco SP 10.00 25.00
GMV Mike Van Ryn 3.00 8.00
GMZ Marek Zidlicky 3.00 8.00
GNH Nathan Horton 5.00 12.00
GPB Patrice Bergeron SP 10.00 25.00
GPM Patrick Marleau 5.00 12.00
GPP Petr Prucha 3.00 8.00
GPR Paul Ranger 3.00 8.00
GRB Rene Bourque 3.00 8.00
GRM Ryan Miller SP 10.00 25.00
GRN Rick Nash SP 15.00 40.00
GSC Sidney Crosby 75.00 150.00
GSH Shawn Horcoff 3.00 8.00
GTC Ty Conklin 4.00 10.00
GVT Vesa Toskala 4.00 10.00
GWG Wayne Gretzky SP 125.00 250.00

2006-07 Black Diamond Jerseys

JAA Arron Asham 2.50 6.00
JAF Alexander Frolov 2.50 6.00
JAH Ales Hemsky 3.00 8.00
JAK Alex Kovalev 3.00 8.00
JAL Jason Allison 3.00 8.00
JAM Andrej Meszaros 2.50 6.00
JAO Alexander Ovechkin SP 15.00 40.00
JAS Alexander Steen 4.00 10.00
JAT Alex Tanguay 2.50 6.00
JBB Brad Boyes 2.50 6.00
JBE Patrice Bergeron 5.00 12.00
JBG Bill Guerin 4.00 10.00
JBJ Barret Jackman 2.50 6.00
JBL Brian Leetch 4.00 10.00
JBM Brendan Morrison 2.50 6.00
JBO Brandon Bochenski 2.50 6.00
JBR Martin Brodeur 8.00 20.00
JBS Brad Stuart 2.50 6.00
JBU Peter Budaj 3.00 8.00
JCD Chris Drury 3.00 8.00
JCJ Curtis Joseph 4.00 10.00
JCK Chuck Kobasew 2.50 6.00
JCO Mike Comrie 3.00 8.00
JCP Corey Perry 4.00 10.00
JCW Cam Ward 4.00 10.00
JDB Donald Brashear 2.50 6.00
JDC Dan Cloutier 3.00 8.00
JDE Pavol Demitra 5.00 12.00
JDH Dan Hamhuis 3.00 8.00
JDK Duncan Keith 5.00 12.00
JDP Dion Phaneuf 4.00 10.00
JDW Doug Weight 4.00 10.00
JEA Evgeni Artyukhin 2.50 6.00
JEB Ed Belfour 4.00 10.00
JEL Eric Lindros 6.00 15.00
JGA Simon Gagne 4.00 10.00
JHE Milan Hejduk 3.00 8.00
JHZ Henrik Zetterberg 5.00 12.00
JIK Ilya Kovalchuk 4.00 10.00
JJA Jason Arnott 3.00 8.00
JJB Jay Bouwmeester 4.00 10.00
JJF Jeff Friesen 2.50 6.00
JJG Jean-Sebastien Giguere 4.00 10.00
JJH Jeff Hoggan 2.50 6.00
JJJ Jaromir Jagr 10.00 25.00
JJK Jakub Klepis 2.50 6.00
JJL Joffrey Lupul 3.00 8.00
JJN Joe Nieuwendyk 4.00 10.00
JJS Joe Sakic 6.00 15.00
JJT Joe Thornton 5.00 12.00
JKD Kris Draper 2.50 6.00
JKO Andrei Kostitsyn 3.00 8.00
JKT Keith Tkachuk 4.00 10.00
JLA Andrew Ladd 4.00 10.00
JLE Jere Lehtinen 2.50 6.00
JMA Mark Bell 2.50 6.00
JMB Martin Biron 3.00 8.00
JMC Mike Cammalleri 2.50 6.00
JMH Marian Hossa 3.00 8.00
JMI Mike Komisarek 2.50 6.00
JMJ Milan Jurcina 2.50 6.00
JMK Miikka Kiprusoff 3.00 8.00
JMM Mike Modano 6.00 15.00
JMN Markus Naslund 3.00 8.00
JMO Shaone Morrisonn 2.50 6.00
JMP Michael Peca 3.00 8.00
JMR Mark Recchi 5.00 12.00
JMS Marek Svatos 2.50 6.00
JNH Nathan Horton 4.00 10.00
JNK Nikolai Khabibulin 4.00 10.00
JPA Daniel Paille 3.00 8.00
JPB Peter Bondra 2.50 6.00
JPD Pavel Datsyuk 5.00 12.00
JPF Peter Forsberg 5.00 12.00
JPK Paul Kariya 5.00 12.00
JRB Rod Brind'Amour 4.00 10.00
JRC Ryan Craig 2.50 6.00
JRD Rick DiPietro 3.00 8.00
JRH Ryan Hollweg 2.50 6.00
JRK Rostislav Klesla 2.50 6.00
JRM Ryan Miller 4.00 10.00
JRO Rob Blake 4.00 10.00
JRU R.J. Umberger 2.50 6.00
JRY Michael Ryder 2.50 6.00
JSA Miroslav Satan 3.00 8.00
JSC Sidney Crosby SP 25.00 60.00
JSF Sergei Fedorov 6.00 15.00
JSG Scott Gomez 3.00 8.00
JSH Jody Shelley 2.50 6.00
JSM Mats Sundin 4.00 10.00
JSN Brendan Shanahan 5.00 12.00
JSS Sergei Samsonov 3.00 8.00
JST Matt Stajan 3.00 8.00
JSU Scottie Upshall 2.50 6.00
JSW Stephen Weiss 2.50 6.00
JTC Ty Conklin 3.00 8.00
JTH Tomas Holmstrom 3.00 8.00
JTP Tom Poti 2.50 6.00
JVN Ville Nieminen 2.50 6.00
JWG Wayne Gretzky 25.00 60.00

2006-07 Black Diamond Jerseys Ruby

*RUBY: .5X TO 1.5X BASE HI
STATED PRINT RUN 100 SER.#'d SETS
JSC Sidney Crosby/25 75.00 150.00
JWG Wayne Gretzky/25 80.00 200.00

2007-08 Black Diamond

COMP.SET w/o SPs (84) 15.00 40.00
85-126 DOUBLE DIAMOND ODDS 1:4
127-147 TRIPLE VETERAN ODDS 1:8
127-147 TRIPLE ROOKIE ODDS 1:8
COMMON QUAD (169-189) 3.00 8.00
169-210 QUAD DIAMOND ODDS 1:24
1 Scott Niedermayer .30 .75
2 Andy McDonald .25 .60
3 Bobby Holik .20 .50
4 Marc Savard .20 .50
5 Zdeno Chara .30 .75
6 Glen Murray .25 .60
7 Tim Thomas .40 1.00
8 Manny Fernandez .25 .60
9 Jason Pominville .30 .75
10 Derek Roy .20 .50
11 Daymond Langkow .20 .50
12 Matthew Lombardi .20 .50
13 Justin Williams .25 .60
14 Rod Brind`Amour .30 .75
15 Erik Cole .25 .60
16 Nikolai Khabibulin .30 .75
17 Duncan Keith .30 .75
18 Brent Seabrook .30 .75
19 Tuomo Ruutu .30 .75
20 Peter Budaj .25 .60
21 Marek Svatos .20 .50
22 Wojtek Wolski .25 .60
23 Pascal LeClaire .25 .60
24 David Vyborny .20 .50
25 Gilbert Brule .25 .60
26 Brenden Morrow .25 .60
27 Mike Ribeiro .25 .60
28 Jussi Jokinen .20 .50
29 Jere Lehtinen .20 .50
30 Tomas Holmstrom .25 .60
31 Kris Draper .20 .50
32 Jarret Stoll .25 .60
33 Shawn Horcoff .20 .50
34 Joni Pitkanen .20 .50
35 Stephen Weiss .20 .50
36 Nathan Horton .30 .75
37 Jozef Stumpel .20 .50
38 Jay Bouwmeester .30 .75
39 Mike Cammalleri .25 .60
40 Rob Blake .30 .75
41 Patrick O'Sullivan .25 .60
42 Ladislav Nagy .20 .50
43 Pierre-Marc Bouchard .30 .75
44 Pavol Demitra .40 1.00
45 Brian Rolston .25 .60
46 Alexei Kovalev .25 .60
47 Chris Higgins .20 .50
48 Cristobal Huet .25 .60
49 Steve Sullivan .20 .50
50 Jason Arnott .25 .60
51 Travis Zajac .25 .60
52 Bill Guerin .30 .75
53 Scott Gomez .25 .60
54 Martin Straka .20 .50
55 Wade Redden .20 .50
56 Antoine Vermette .20 .50
57 Joffrey Lupul .25 .60
58 Mike Richards .30 .75
59 Martin Biron .25 .60
60 Mike Knuble .20 .50
61 Ed Jovanovski .25 .60
62 David Aebischer .25 .60
63 Keith Ballard .20 .50
64 Mark Recchi .40 1.00
65 Colby Armstrong .20 .50
66 Milan Michalek .20 .50
67 Steve Bernier .20 .50
68 Joe Pavelski .30 .75
69 Keith Tkachuk .30 .75
70 Lee Stempniak .20 .50
71 Brad Boyes .20 .50
72 Johan Holmqvist .25 .60
73 Marc Denis .25 .60
74 Alexander Steen .30 .75
75 Tomas Kaberle .20 .50
76 Jason Blake .20 .50
77 Henrik Sedin .30 .75
78 Daniel Sedin .30 .75
79 Brendan Morrison .20 .50
80 Mattias Ohlund .20 .50
81 Michael Nylander .20 .50
82 Alexander Semin .30 .75
83 Olaf Kolzig .30 .75
84 Viktor Kozlov .20 .50
85 Ryan Getzlaf 2.00 5.00
86 Chris Pronger 1.00 2.50
87 Phil Kessel 1.50 4.00
88 Drew Stafford 1.00 2.50
89 Alex Tanguay .75 2.00
90 Dion Phaneuf 1.25 3.00
91 Cam Ward 1.25 3.00
92 Martin Havlat 1.25 3.00
93 Milan Hejduk 1.00 2.50
94 Paul Stastny 1.25 3.00
95 Sergei Fedorov 2.00 5.00
96 Marty Turco 1.25 3.00
97 Nicklas Lidstrom 1.25 3.00
98 Pavel Datsyuk 1.50 4.00
99 Dwayne Roloson 1.00 2.50
100 Ales Hemsky 1.00 2.50
101 Olli Jokinen 1.00 2.50
102 Tomas Vokoun 1.00 2.50
103 Anze Kopitar 2.00 5.00
104 Alexander Frolov .75 2.00
105 Mikko Koivu 1.00 2.50
106 Guillaume Latendresse 1.00 2.50
107 Alexander Radulov 1.25 3.00
108 Patrik Elias 1.25 3.00
109 Brian Gionta 1.00 2.50
110 Zach Parise 1.50 4.00
111 Rick DiPietro 1.00 2.50
112 Miroslav Satan 1.00 2.50
113 Chris Drury 1.00 2.50
114 Ray Emery 1.00 2.50
115 Daniel Alfredsson 1.25 3.00
116 Daniel Briere 1.25 3.00
117 Jeff Carter 1.25 3.00
118 Shane Doan 1.00 2.50
119 Jordan Staal 1.25 3.00
120 Patrick Marleau 1.25 3.00
121 Doug Weight 1.25 3.00
122 Manny Legace 1.00 2.50
123 Brad Richards 1.25 3.00
124 Andrew Raycroft 1.00 2.50
125 Darcy Tucker 1.00 2.50
126 Markus Naslund 1.25 3.00
127 Jean-Sebastien Giguere 2.00 5.00
128 Teemu Selanne 4.00 10.00
129 Marian Hossa 1.50 4.00
130 Kari Lehtonen 1.50 4.00
131 Patrice Bergeron 2.50 6.00
132 Thomas Vanek 2.50 6.00
133 Miikka Kiprusoff 1.50 4.00
134 Rick Nash 2.00 5.00
135 Mike Modano 3.00 8.00
136 Dominik Hasek 2.50 6.00
137 Henrik Zetterberg 2.50 6.00
138 Marian Gaborik 2.50 6.00
139 Saku Koivu 2.00 5.00
140 Michael Ryder 1.25 3.00
141 Henrik Lundqvist 2.50 6.00
142 Jason Spezza 2.00 5.00
143 Simon Gagne 2.00 5.00
144 Evgeni Malkin 6.00 15.00
145 Jonathan Cheechoo 2.00 5.00
146 Paul Kariya 2.50 6.00
147 Martin St. Louis 2.00 5.00
148 Petr Kalus RC 1.25 3.00
149 Rob Schremp RC 1.50 4.00
150 Matt Smaby RC 1.25 3.00
151 Andy Greene RC 1.50 4.00
152 Drew Miller RC 1.50 4.00
153 Daniel Winnik RC 1.50 4.00
154 Frans Nielsen RC 2.00 5.00
155 Lauri Tukonen RC 1.25 3.00
156 Ryan Callahan RC 2.50 6.00
157 Jaroslav Halak RC 6.00 15.00
158 David Krejci RC 4.00 10.00
159 Mason Raymond RC 2.00 5.00
160 Curtis McElhinney RC 2.00 5.00
161 Jared Boll RC 1.50 4.00
162 Torrey Mitchell RC 1.50 4.00
163 David Perron RC 2.00 5.00
164 Milan Lucic RC 6.00 15.00
165 Jaroslav Hlinka RC 1.50 4.00
166 Brandon Dubinsky RC 2.50 6.00
167 Brian Elliott RC 2.50 6.00
168 Brett Sterling RC 1.25 3.00
169 Ilya Kovalchuk 3.00 8.00
170 Bobby Orr 10.00 25.00
171 Ryan Miller 3.00 8.00
172 Jarome Iginla 3.00 8.00
173 Eric Staal 4.00 10.00

174 Joe Sakic 5.00 12.00
175 Gordie Howe 8.00 20.00
176 Wayne Gretzky 12.00 30.00
177 Mark Messier 5.00 12.00
178 Peter Forsberg 4.00 10.00
179 Martin Brodeur 6.00 15.00
180 Jaromir Jagr 8.00 20.00
181 Dany Heatley 3.00 8.00
182 Sidney Crosby 8.00 20.00
183 Marc-Andre Fleury 5.00 12.00
184 Mario Lemieux 10.00 25.00
185 Joe Thornton 4.00 10.00
186 Vincent Lecavalier 2.50 6.00
187 Mats Sundin 3.00 8.00
188 Roberto Luongo 4.00 10.00
189 Alexander Ovechkin 12.00 30.00
190 Jack Johnson RC 4.00 10.00
191 Jonathan Toews RC 25.00 60.00
192 Bobby Ryan RC 8.00 20.00
193 Sam Gagner RC 6.00 15.00
194 Carey Price RC 30.00 80.00
195 Erik Johnson RC 5.00 12.00
196 Nicklas Bergfors RC 3.00 8.00
197 Jonathan Bernier RC 8.00 20.00
198 Nicklas Backstrom RC 10.00 25.00
199 Bryan Little RC 5.00 12.00
200 Patrick Kane RC 20.00 40.00
201 Andrew Cogliano RC 5.00 12.00
202 Marc Staal RC 5.00 12.00
203 Nick Foligno RC 6.00 15.00
204 Peter Mueller RC 4.00 10.00
205 Devin Setoguchi RC 5.00 12.00
206 Kris Russell RC 4.00 10.00
207 James Sheppard RC 3.00 8.00
208 Matt Niskanen RC 5.00 12.00
209 Kyle Chipchura RC 5.00 12.00
210 Martin Hanzal RC 4.00 10.00

2007-08 Black Diamond Ruby

*SINGLE RUBY: 5X TO 12X BASE
*DOUBLE RUBY: 1.5X TO 4X BASE DOUBLE
*TRIPLE RUBY: 1X TO 2.5X BASE TRIPLE
*TRIPLE RUBY ROOKIE: 1.2X TO 3X BASE
*DOUBLE RUBY: .8X TO 2X BASE QUADS
*DOUBLE RUBY ROOK: .6X TO 1.5X BASE
STATED PRINT RUN 100 SER.#'d SETS
191 Jonathan Toews 100.00 200.00
194 Carey Price 100.00 200.00
198 Nicklas Backstrom 12.00 30.00
200 Patrick Kane 60.00 150.00
204 Peter Mueller 20.00 50.00

2007-08 Black Diamond Gemography

OVERALL STATED ODDS 1:48
GAF Maxim Afinogenov 3.00 8.00
GAH Ales Hemsky 4.00 10.00
GAK Andrei Kostitsyn 4.00 10.00
GAO Alexander Ovechkin SP 75.00 150.00
GAT Alex Tanguay SP
GBG Brian Gionta SP
GBL Michael Blunden 3.00 8.00
GBM Brenden Morrow 4.00 10.00
GBP Benoit Pouliot SP 15.00 40.00
GBR Martin Brodeur SP 60.00 120.00
GCA Colby Armstrong 3.00 8.00
GCB Cam Barker SP 5.00 12.00
GCH Jonathan Cheechoo 5.00 12.00
GCK Chuck Kobasew 3.00 8.00
GCO Erik Cole 4.00 10.00
GCP Corey Perry 5.00 12.00
GCT Chris Thorburn 3.00 8.00
GCW Cam Ward SP
GDB Daniel Briere 5.00 12.00
GDH Dominik Hasek SP 15.00 40.00
GDL David Leneveu 4.00 10.00
GDP Dion Phaneuf 5.00 12.00
GDR Dwayne Roloson SP 6.00 15.00
GDU Dustin Brown 5.00 12.00
GEC Erik Christensen 3.00 8.00
GEF Eric Fehr 3.00 8.00
GEM Evgeni Malkin 25.00 60.00
GEN Evgeni Nabokov 4.00 10.00
GES Eric Staal 6.00 15.00
GFO Matt Foy 3.00 8.00
GFP Fernando Pisani 3.00 8.00
GGB Gilbert Brule 4.00 10.00
GGE Martin Gerber 4.00 10.00
GGL Georges Laraque 4.00 10.00
GGO Scott Gomez 4.00 10.00
GHZ Henrik Zetterberg 6.00 15.00
GIK Ilya Kovalchuk 5.00 12.00
GJC Jeff Carter 5.00 12.00
GJH Josh Hennessy 3.00 8.00
GJI Jarome Iginla SP 25.00 60.00
GJL John-Michael Liles 3.00 8.00
GJM Jay McClement 3.00 8.00
GJP Joni Pitkanen SP 5.00 12.00
GJS Jarret Stoll 4.00 10.00
GJW Justin Williams SP 6.00 15.00
GKC Kyle Calder 3.00 8.00
GKG Kelly Guard 3.00 8.00
GKL Kristopher Letang 10.00 25.00
GKO Mikko Koivu 4.00 10.00
GKQ Kyle Quincey 3.00 8.00
GLA Guillaume Latendresse 4.00 10.00
GLE Loui Eriksson 6.00 15.00
GLN Ladislav Nagy 3.00 8.00
GMA Mario Lemieux SP
GMB Martin Biron 4.00 10.00
GMC Mike Cammalleri 4.00 10.00
GMF Marc-Andre Fleury SP 10.00 25.00
GMG Marian Gaborik SP 25.00 60.00
GMH Milan Hejduk 4.00 10.00
GMI Mike Richards 5.00 12.00
GMK Miikka Kiprusoff 4.00 10.00
GML Matt Lashoff 3.00 8.00
GMP Mark Parrish 3.00 8.00
GMR Mike Ribeiro 4.00 10.00
GMT Marty Turco 5.00 12.00
GND Nigel Dawes 3.00 8.00
GNH Nathan Horton 5.00 12.00
GPB Patrice Bergeron 8.00 20.00
GPE Patrik Elias 5.00 12.00
GPK Phil Kessel 6.00 15.00
GPM Paul Mara 3.00 8.00
GPO Patrick O'Sullivan 4.00 10.00
GPP Petr Prucha 3.00 8.00
GRB Rene Bourque SP 5.00 12.00
GRF Ruslan Fedotenko 3.00 8.00
GRI Brad Richardson 4.00 10.00
GRK Rostislav Klesla 3.00 8.00
GRM Ryan Malone 3.00 8.00
GRN Rick Nash 5.00 12.00
GSB Steve Bernier 3.00 8.00
GSC Sidney Crosby 100.00 175.00
GSG Simon Gagne 5.00 12.00
GSS Steve Sullivan 3.00 8.00
GST Mark Stuart 3.00 8.00
GSW Stephen Weiss 3.00 8.00
GTH Tomas Holmstrom 4.00 10.00
GVF Valtteri Filppula 5.00 12.00
GVT Vesa Toskala SP 6.00 15.00
GWI Jeremy Williams 3.00 8.00
GWR Wade Redden 3.00 8.00
GZC Zdeno Chara 8.00 20.00

2007-08 Black Diamond Jerseys

STATED ODDS 1:13
BDJAA Arron Asham 3.00 8.00
BDJAE David Aebischer 4.00 10.00
BDJAF Alexander Frolov 3.00 8.00
BDJAH Adam Hall 3.00 8.00
BDJAK Alexei Kovalev 4.00 10.00
BDJAM Andrej Meszaros 3.00 8.00
BDJAO Alex Ovechkin SP 20.00 50.00
BDJAR Alexander Radulov 5.00 12.00
BDJAS Alexander Steen 5.00 12.00
BDJAT Alex Tanguay 3.00 8.00
BDJAU Alexander Auld 3.00 8.00
BDJBB Brad Boyes 3.00 8.00
BDJBE Patrice Bergeron 6.00 15.00
BDJBG Bill Guerin 5.00 12.00
BDJBI Martin Biron 4.00 10.00
BDJBJ Barret Jackman 3.00 8.00
BDJBL Jason Blake 3.00 8.00
BDJBM Brendan Morrison 3.00 8.00
BDJBO Brandon Bochenski 3.00 8.00
BDJBR Brad Richards 5.00 12.00
BDJBS Brad Stuart 3.00 8.00
BDJCD Chris Drury 4.00 10.00
BDJCH Chris Higgins 3.00 8.00
BDJCK Chuck Kobasew 3.00 8.00
BDJCO Chris Osgood 5.00 12.00
BDJCP Chris Phillips 3.00 8.00
BDJDA Daniel Alfredsson 5.00 12.00
BDJDE Pavol Demitra 6.00 15.00
BDJDH Dany Heatley SP 5.00 12.00
BDJDL David Legwand 4.00 10.00
BDJDR Dwayne Roloson 4.00 10.00
BDJDT Darcy Tucker 4.00 10.00
BDJDW Doug Weight 5.00 12.00
BDJEB Ed Belfour 5.00 12.00
BDJEJ Ed Jovanovski 4.00 10.00
BDJEN Evgeni Nabokov 4.00 10.00
BDJES Eric Staal 6.00 15.00
BDJFP Fernando Pisani 3.00 8.00
BDJGE Martin Gerber 4.00 10.00
BDJGM Glen Murray 4.00 10.00
BDJHA Dominik Hasek SP 6.00 15.00
BDJHE Milan Hejduk 4.00 10.00
BDJHM Martin Havlat 5.00 12.00
BDJHS Henrik Sedin 5.00 12.00
BDJHT Hannu Toivonen 4.00 10.00
BDJIK Ilya Kovalchuk 5.00 12.00
BDJJA Jason Arnott 4.00 10.00
BDJJB Jay Bouwmeester 5.00 12.00
BDJJC Jeff Carter 5.00 12.00
BDJJG Jean-Sebastien Giguere 5.00 12.00
BDJJI Jarome Iginla 5.00 12.00
BDJJJ Jaromir Jagr 12.00 30.00
BDJJL Jere Lehtinen 3.00 8.00
BDJJO Jonathan Cheechoo 5.00 12.00
BDJJS Jarret Stoll 4.00 10.00
BDJJT Joe Thornton 6.00 15.00
BDJJU Jussi Jokinen 3.00 8.00
BDJJW Jason Williams 3.00 8.00
BDJKC Kyle Calder 3.00 8.00
BDJKT Keith Tkachuk 5.00 12.00
BDJLU Joffrey Lupul 4.00 10.00
BDJMA Martin Brodeur 10.00 25.00
BDJMB Mark Bell 3.00 8.00
BDJMC Bryan McCabe 3.00 8.00
BDJMD Marc Denis 4.00 10.00
BDJMF Manny Fernandez 4.00 10.00
BDJMG Marian Gaborik SP 6.00 15.00
BDJMH Marian Hossa 4.00 10.00
BDJMI Michael Peca 4.00 10.00
BDJMJ Milan Jurcina 3.00 8.00
BDJML Manny Legace 4.00 10.00
BDJMM Milan Michalek 3.00 8.00
BDJMN Markus Naslund 5.00 12.00
BDJMO Brenden Morrow 4.00 10.00
BDJMP Mark Parrish 3.00 8.00
BDJMR Mike Ribeiro 4.00 10.00
BDJMS Marc Savard 3.00 8.00
BDJMT Marty Turco 5.00 12.00
BDJNL Nicklas Lidstrom 5.00 12.00
BDJNZ Nikolai Zherdev 3.00 8.00
BDJOH Mattias Ohlund 3.00 8.00
BDJOJ Olli Jokinen 4.00 10.00
BDJPB Pierre-Marc Bouchard 5.00 12.00
BDJPC Corey Perry 5.00 12.00
BDJPD Pavel Datsyuk SP 6.00 15.00
BDJPE Patrik Elias 5.00 12.00
BDJPF Peter Forsberg 6.00 15.00
BDJPM Patrick Marleau 5.00 12.00
BDJRA Andrew Raycroft 4.00 10.00
BDJRL Roberto Luongo 6.00 15.00
BDJRM Ryan Miller 5.00 12.00
BDJRN Rick Nash SP 5.00 12.00
BDJSA Joe Sakic 8.00 20.00
BDJSC Sidney Crosby SP 12.00 30.00
BDJSG Simon Gagne 5.00 12.00
BDJSH Brendan Shanahan 6.00 15.00
BDJSP Jason Spezza SP 5.00 12.00
BDJSU Mats Sundin 5.00 12.00
BDJTH Jose Theodore 5.00 12.00
BDJWI Justin Williams 4.00 10.00

2007-08 Black Diamond Jerseys Ruby Dual

*RUBY DUAL: .5X TO 1.2X
STATED PRINT RUN 100 SER.#'d SETS

2007-08 Black Diamond Jerseys Gold Triple

*GOLD TRIPLE: 1X TO 2.5X
STATED PRINT RUN 25 SER.#'d SETS

2007-08 Black Diamond Run for the Cup

STATED ODDS 1:288
CUP1 Jean-Sebastien Giguere 10.00 25.00
CUP2 Ilya Kovalchuk 10.00 25.00
CUP3 Thomas Vanek 12.00 30.00
CUP4 Jarome Iginla 10.00 25.00
CUP5 Eric Staal 12.00 30.00
CUP6 Joe Sakic 15.00 40.00
CUP7 Mike Modano 15.00 40.00
CUP8 Henrik Zetterberg 12.00 30.00
CUP9 Ales Hemsky 8.00 20.00
CUP10 Marian Gaborik 12.00 30.00
CUP11 Saku Koivu 10.00 25.00
CUP12 Martin Brodeur 15.00 40.00
CUP13 Jaromir Jagr 12.00 30.00
CUP14 Dany Heatley 10.00 25.00
CUP15 Sidney Crosby 25.00 60.00
CUP16 Joe Thornton 12.00 30.00
CUP17 Paul Kariya 12.00 30.00
CUP18 Vincent Lecavalier 8.00 20.00
CUP19 Mats Sundin 10.00 25.00
CUP20 Roberto Luongo 12.00 30.00
CUP21 Alexander Ovechkin 40.00 100.00

2008-09 Black Diamond

This set was released on December 17, 2008. The base set consists of 210 cards. Cards 1-147 and 169-189 feature veterans, and cards 148-168 as well as 190-210 are rookies
COMP.SET w/o SPs (84) 10.00 25.00
DOUBLE STATED ODDS 1:4
TRIPLE STATED ODDS 1:8
QUAD STATED ODDS 1:24
1 Bobby Ryan .25 .60
2 Corey Perry .25 .60
3 Bryan Little .20 .50
4 Marco Sturm .15 .40
5 Patrice Bergeron .30 .75
6 Tim Thomas .25 .60
7 Zdeno Chara .25 .60
8 Jason Pominville .25 .60
9 Daymond Langkow .15 .40
10 Mike Cammalleri .20 .50
11 Justin Williams .20 .50
12 Ray Whitney .20 .50
13 Rod Brind'Amour .25 .60
14 Brian Campbell .20 .50
15 Cristobal Huet .20 .50
16 Dustin Byfuglien .25 .60
17 Darcy Tucker .20 .50
18 Marek Svatos .15 .40
19 Wojtek Wolski .20 .50
20 Pascal Leclaire .20 .50
21 Brenden Morrow .20 .50
22 Sean Avery .15 .40
23 Sergei Zubov .20 .50
24 Valtteri Filppula .25 .60
25 Dan Cleary .20 .50
26 Johan Franzen .25 .60
27 Niklas Kronwall .20 .50
28 Dustin Penner .20 .50
29 Dwayne Roloson .20 .50
30 Erik Cole .20 .50
31 Gilbert Brule .15 .40
32 Mathieu Garon .20 .50
33 Andrew Cogliano .20 .50
34 Jay Bouwmeester .25 .60
35 Dustin Brown .25 .60
36 Jack Johnson .15 .40
37 Josh Harding .25 .60
38 Pierre-Marc Bouchard .25 .60
39 Alex Kovalev .20 .50
40 Jaroslav Halak .25 .60
41 Andrei Markov .25 .60
42 Guillaume Latendresse .15 .40
43 Sergei Kostitsyn .15 .40
44 Tomas Plekanec .25 .60
45 Dan Ellis .15 .40
46 Brian Gionta .20 .50
47 Brian Rolston .20 .50
48 Patrik Elias .25 .60
49 Bill Guerin .25 .60
50 Mark Streit .15 .40
51 Mike Comrie .20 .50
52 Brendan Shanahan .30 .75
53 Chris Drury .20 .50
54 Marc Staal .25 .60
55 Nikolai Zherdev .15 .40
56 Scott Gomez .20 .50
57 Wade Redden .15 .40
58 Antoine Vermette .15 .40
59 Martin Gerber .20 .50
60 Jeff Carter .25 .60
61 Mike Knuble .15 .40
62 Scott Hartnell .25 .60
63 Daniel Carcillo .15 .40
64 Ed Jovanovski .20 .50
65 Ilya Bryzgalov .20 .50
66 Sergei Gonchar .15 .40
67 Milan Michalek .15 .40
68 Patrick Marleau .25 .60
69 Andy McDonald .20 .50
70 Brad Boyes .15 .40
71 Manny Legace .25 .60
72 Paul Kariya .30 .75
73 Radim Vrbata .20 .50
74 Ryan Malone .15 .40
75 Vaclav Prospal .15 .40
76 Jason Blake .15 .40
77 Nikolai Antropov .20 .50
78 Tomas Kaberle .15 .40
79 Kevin Bieksa .20 .50
80 Mattias Ohlund .15 .40
81 Alexander Semin .25 .60
82 Jose Theodore .25 .60
83 Michael Nylander .15 .40
84 Mike Green .25 .60
85 Chris Pronger .30 .75
86 Teemu Selanne .75 2.00
87 Kari Lehtonen .30 .75
88 Marc Savard .25 .60
89 Derek Roy .25 .60
90 Cam Ward .40 1.00
91 Patrick Kane .75 2.00
92 Patrick Sharp .40 1.00
93 Milan Hejduk .30 .75
94 Brad Richards .40 1.00
95 Marty Turco .40 1.00
96 Mike Ribeiro .30 .75
97 Mike Modano .60 1.50
98 Chris Osgood .40 1.00
99 Ales Hemsky .30 .75
100 Shawn Horcoff .25 .60
101 Nathan Horton .30 .75
102 Tomas Vokoun .30 .75
103 Anze Kopitar .60 1.50
104 Alexander Frolov .25 .60
105 Niklas Backstrom .40 1.00
106 Andrei Kostitsyn .30 .75
107 Sam Gagner .30 .75
108 Jason Arnott .30 .75
109 J.P. Dumont .25 .60
110 Zach Parise .40 1.00
111 Rick DiPietro .30 .75
112 Markus Naslund .30 .75
113 Simon Gagne .40 1.00
114 Daniel Briere .40 1.00
115 Mike Richards .40 1.00
116 Martin Biron .30 .75
117 Shane Doan .30 .75
118 Peter Mueller .30 .75
119 Olli Jokinen .30 .75
120 Jordan Staal .40 1.00
121 Evgeni Nabokov .30 .75
122 Jonathan Cheechoo .40 1.00
123 Erik Johnson .30 .75
124 Vesa Toskala .30 .75
125 Daniel Sedin .40 1.00
126 Henrik Sedin .40 1.00
127 Ryan Getzlaf 1.50 4.00
128 Jean-Sebastien Giguere 1.00 2.50
129 Ryan Miller 1.00 2.50
130 Thomas Vanek 1.00 2.50
131 Dion Phaneuf 1.00 2.50
132 Miikka Kiprusoff .75 2.00
133 Eric Staal 1.25 3.00
134 Jonathan Toews 2.50 6.00
135 Peter Forsberg 1.25 3.00
136 Paul Stastny 1.00 2.50
137 Rick Nash 1.00 2.50
138 Marian Hossa .75 2.00
139 Pavel Datsyuk 1.25 3.00
140 Nicklas Lidstrom 1.00 2.50
141 Marian Gaborik 1.25 3.00
142 Saku Koivu 1.00 2.50
143 Dany Heatley 1.00 2.50
144 Jason Spezza 1.00 2.50
145 Daniel Alfredsson 1.00 2.50
146 Martin St. Louis 1.00 2.50
147 Nicklas Backstrom 1.50 4.00
148 Viktor Tikhonov RC 1.50 4.00
149 Steve Mason RC 3.00 8.00
150 Mark Fistric RC 1.50 4.00
151 Justin Abdelkader RC 3.00 8.00
152 Mattias Ritola RC 1.50 4.00
153 Darren Helm RC 2.00 5.00
154 Claude Giroux RC 6.00 15.00
155 Tom Sestito RC 2.00 5.00
156 Shawn Matthias RC 2.00 5.00
157 Luca Sbisa RC 1.25 3.00
158 Oscar Moller RC 1.50 4.00
159 Erik Ersberg RC 1.50 4.00
160 Patric Hornqvist RC 2.00 5.00
161 Brian Lee RC 1.50 4.00
162 Ilya Zubov RC 1.50 4.00
163 Alex Goligoski RC 2.50 6.00
164 Jon Filewich RC 1.50 4.00
165 Vladimir Mihalik RC 1.25 3.00
166 Nikolai Kulemin RC 2.00 5.00
167 Robbie Earl RC 1.25 3.00
168 Mike Brown RC 2.50 6.00
169 Ilya Kovalchuk 3.00 8.00
170 Bobby Orr 10.00 25.00
171 Jarome Iginla 3.00 8.00
172 Joe Sakic 5.00 12.00
173 Gordie Howe 8.00 20.00
174 Henrik Zetterberg 4.00 10.00
175 Wayne Gretzky 15.00 40.00
176 Mark Messier 4.00 10.00
177 Patrick Roy 8.00 20.00
178 Carey Price 12.00 30.00
179 Martin Brodeur 6.00 15.00
180 Henrik Lundqvist 4.00 10.00
181 Mario Lemieux 10.00 25.00
182 Sidney Crosby 12.00 30.00
183 Evgeni Malkin 10.00 25.00
184 Marc-Andre Fleury 5.00 12.00
185 Joe Thornton 4.00 10.00
186 Vincent Lecavalier 2.50 6.00
187 Mats Sundin 3.00 8.00
188 Roberto Luongo 4.00 10.00
189 Alexander Ovechkin 12.00 30.00
190 Zach Bogosian RC 5.00 12.00
191 Blake Wheeler RC 12.00 30.00
192 Brandon Sutter RC 5.00 12.00
193 Jakub Voracek RC 10.00 25.00
194 Derick Brassard RC 4.00 10.00
195 James Neal RC 10.00 25.00
196 Michael Frolik RC 5.00 12.00
197 Drew Doughty RC 10.00 25.00
198 Colton Gillies RC 4.00 10.00
199 Kyle Okposo RC 5.00 12.00
200 Lauri Korpikoski RC 3.00 8.00
201 Fabian Brunnstrom RC 4.00 10.00
202 Zach Boychuk RC 5.00 12.00
203 Mikkel Boedker RC 6.00 15.00
204 Kyle Turris RC 8.00 20.00
205 Nikita Filatov RC 5.00 12.00
206 Alex Pietrangelo RC 6.00 15.00
207 T.J. Oshie RC 6.00 15.00
208 Patrik Berglund RC 4.00 10.00
209 Steven Stamkos RC 15.00 40.00
210 Luke Schenn RC 6.00 15.00

2008-09 Black Diamond Ruby

*RUBY (1-84): 6X TO 15X BASE
*RUBY (85-126): 4X TO 10X BASE
*RUBY (127-147): 1.5X TO 4X BASE
*RUBY RCs (148-168): .6X TO 1.5X BASE
*RUBY (169-189): .5X TO 1.2X BASE
*RUBY RCs (190-210): .6X TO 1.5X BASE
STATED PRINT RUN 100 SERIAL #'d SETS
147 Nicklas Backstrom 6.00 15.00
209 Steven Stamkos 50.00 120.00

2008-09 Black Diamond Gemography

GAC Andrew Cogliano 5.00 12.00
GAO Alexander Ovechkin
GAT Alex Tanguay 4.00 10.00
GBA Cam Barker 4.00 10.00
GBB Brendan Bell 4.00 10.00
GBC Blake Comeau 4.00 10.00
GBD Brandon Dubinsky 8.00 20.00
GBE Jonathan Bernier 8.00 20.00
GBO Brad Boyes 4.00 10.00
GBR Bobby Ryan 6.00 15.00
GCA Ryan Carter 4.00 10.00
GCB Casey Borer 6.00 15.00
GCD Chris Drury 5.00 12.00
GCK Chris Kunitz 6.00 15.00
GCO Corey Perry 6.00 15.00
GCP Chris Phillips 4.00 10.00
GDC Dan Cleary 5.00 12.00
GDG Daniel Girardi
GDH Dany Heatley
GDM Drew Miller 6.00 15.00
GDP Daniel Paille 4.00 10.00
GDS Daniel Sedin 6.00 15.00
GDU Dustin Penner 5.00 12.00
GEJ Erik Johnson 5.00 12.00
GHA Josh Harding 6.00 15.00
GHS Henrik Sedin 6.00 15.00
GJB Jay Bouwmeester 6.00 15.00
GJG Jean-Sebastien Giguere 6.00 15.00
GJH Jannik Hansen 6.00 15.00
GJI Jarome Iginla 20.00 40.00
GJL John-Michael Liles 4.00 10.00
GJO Johnny Boychuk 4.00 10.00
GJS Jordan Staal 20.00 40.00
GJT Joe Thornton 25.00 50.00
GJW Justin Williams 5.00 12.00
GKD Kris Draper 4.00 10.00
GKE Phil Kessel 8.00 20.00
GKQ Kyle Quincey 8.00 20.00
GLE Loui Eriksson 6.00 15.00
GLK Lukas Kaspar 4.00 10.00
GLT Lauri Tukonen 4.00 10.00
GMA Drew MacIntyre 6.00 15.00
GMB Martin Biron 5.00 12.00
GMC Marco Sturm 4.00 10.00
GMG Martin Gerber 5.00 12.00
GMH Michal Handzus 5.00 12.00
GMK Mike Knuble 4.00 10.00
GML Milan Lucic 8.00 20.00
GMM Mark Mancari 5.00 12.00
GMN Markus Naslund 5.00 12.00
GMO Mike Modano 15.00 30.00
GMP Marc-Antoine Pouliot 4.00 10.00
GMR Mason Raymond 6.00 15.00
GMS Matt Stajan 5.00 12.00
GNB Nicklas Bergfors
GNI Nicklas Backstrom 10.00 25.00
GNW Noah Welch 4.00 10.00
GNZ Nikolai Zherdev 4.00 10.00
GPB Pierre-Marc Bouchard 6.00 15.00
GPE Rod Pelley 4.00 10.00
GPJ Jason Pominville 6.00 15.00
GPK Patrick Kane 25.00 60.00
GPO Ryan Potulny 4.00 10.00
GPR Carey Price 25.00 50.00
GPS Paul Stastny SP 12.00 30.00
GRC Ryane Clowe 5.00 12.00
GRG Ryan Getzlaf
GRI Mike Richards SP 25.00 60.00
GRK Rostislav Klesla 4.00 10.00
GRO Rob Schremp 5.00 12.00
GRP Rich Peverley 5.00 12.00
GRS Ryan Smyth 5.00 12.00
GSC Sidney Crosby 75.00 150.00
GSE Devin Setoguchi 5.00 12.00
GSM Stefan Meyer 4.00 10.00
GST Drew Stafford 5.00 12.00
GSW Stephen Weiss 4.00 10.00
GSZ Marek Schwarz 6.00 15.00
GTG Tom Gilbert 4.00 10.00
GTH Tomas Holmstrom 5.00 12.00
GTI Jussi Timonen 4.00 10.00
GTK Tyler Kennedy
GTL Jiri Tlusty 5.00 12.00
GTP Tomas Plihal 5.00 12.00
GTV Thomas Vanek SP 15.00 40.00
GTZ Travis Zajac 5.00 12.00

2008-09 Black Diamond Jerseys Quad

*GOLD/25: .6X TO 1.5X BASIC QUAD
*RUBY/100: .5X TO 1.2X BASIC QUAD
BDJAK Anze Kopitar 10.00 25.00
BDJAM Andrej Meszaros 4.00 10.00
BDJAO Alexander Ovechkin 12.00 30.00
BDJAR Andrew Raycroft 5.00 12.00
BDJAS Alexander Semin 6.00 15.00
BDJBB Brad Boyes 4.00 10.00
BDJBD Brandon Dubinsky 5.00 12.00
BDJBG Brian Gionta 5.00 12.00
BDJBM Brenden Morrow 5.00 12.00
BDJBO Brandon Bochenski 4.00 10.00
BDJBR Brad Richardson 5.00 12.00
BDJBW Brendan Witt 4.00 10.00
BDJCA Jeff Carter 6.00 15.00
BDJCC Chris Chelios 6.00 15.00
BDJCD Chris Drury 5.00 12.00
BDJCH Chris Higgins 4.00 10.00
BDJCK Chuck Kobasew 4.00 10.00
BDJCW Cam Ward 6.00 15.00
BDJDA Daniel Alfredsson 6.00 15.00
BDJDB Daniel Briere 6.00 15.00
BDJDH Dany Heatley 6.00 15.00
BDJDP Dion Phaneuf 6.00 15.00
BDJDR Dwayne Roloson 5.00 12.00
BDJDT Darcy Tucker 5.00 12.00
BDJDW Doug Weight 6.00 15.00
BDJEC Erik Cole 5.00 12.00
BDJEF Eric Fehr 4.00 10.00
BDJEJ Ed Jovanovski 5.00 12.00
BDJEN Evgeni Nabokov 5.00 12.00
BDJES Eric Staal 8.00 20.00
BDJGB Gilbert Brule 4.00 10.00
BDJGE Martin Gerber 5.00 12.00
BDJGL Guillaume Latendresse 4.00 10.00
BDJGU Bill Guerin 6.00 15.00
BDJHL Henrik Lundqvist 8.00 20.00
BDJHZ Henrik Zetterberg 8.00 20.00
BDJIK Ilya Kovalchuk 6.00 15.00
BDJIW Ian White 4.00 10.00
BDJJA Jason Arnott 5.00 12.00
BDJJB Jay Bouwmeester 6.00 15.00
BDJJC Jonathan Cheechoo 6.00 15.00
BDJJG Jean-Sebastien Giguere 6.00 15.00
BDJJI Jarome Iginla 6.00 15.00
BDJJM John-Michael Liles 4.00 10.00
BDJJP Joni Pitkanen 4.00 10.00
BDJJS Joe Sakic 10.00 25.00
BDJJT Joe Thornton 8.00 20.00
BDJKL Kari Lehtonen 5.00 12.00
BDJKO Alex Kovalev 5.00 12.00
BDJLE Manny Legace 6.00 15.00
BDJLS Lee Stempniak 4.00 10.00
BDJMA Mark Stuart 4.00 10.00
BDJMB Martin Brodeur 10.00 25.00
BDJMC Mike Cammalleri 5.00 12.00
BDJMF Manny Fernandez 5.00 12.00
BDJMG Marian Gaborik 8.00 20.00
BDJMI Milan Michalek 4.00 10.00
BDJML Mario Lemieux 12.00 30.00
BDJMM Mark Messier 8.00 20.00
BDJMN Markus Naslund 5.00 12.00
BDJMO Mike Modano 10.00 25.00
BDJMR Michael Ryder 4.00 10.00
BDJMS Martin St. Louis 6.00 15.00
BDJMU Joe Mullen 5.00 12.00
BDJMV Andrei Markov 6.00 15.00
BDJMZ Marek Zidlicky 4.00 10.00
BDJNZ Nikolai Zherdev 4.00 10.00
BDJOJ Olli Jokinen 5.00 12.00
BDJPB Patrice Bergeron 8.00 20.00
BDJPD Pavel Datsyuk 8.00 20.00
BDJPF Peter Forsberg 8.00 20.00
BDJPI Pierre-Marc Bouchard 6.00 15.00
BDJPK Paul Kariya 8.00 20.00
BDJPL Pascal Leclaire 5.00 12.00
BDJPR Patrick Roy 15.00 40.00
BDJPS Paul Stastny 6.00 15.00
BDJRD Rick DiPietro 5.00 12.00
BDJRE Mark Recchi 8.00 20.00
BDJRI Mike Richards 6.00 15.00
BDJRJ R.J. Umberger 4.00 10.00
BDJRL Roberto Luongo 8.00 20.00
BDJRN Rick Nash 6.00 15.00
BDJSA Marc Savard 4.00 10.00
BDJSC Sidney Crosby 15.00 40.00
BDJSG Simon Gagne 6.00 15.00
BDJSH Jody Shelley 4.00 10.00
BDJSP Jason Spezza 6.00 15.00
BDJST Alexander Steen 6.00 15.00
BDJSU Mats Sundin 5.00 12.00
BDJSW Shea Weber 5.00 12.00
BDJTH Jose Theodore 6.00 15.00
BDJTK Keith Tkachuk 6.00 15.00
BDJTP Tomas Plekanec 6.00 15.00
BDJTS Teemu Selanne 12.00 30.00
BDJTT Tim Thomas 6.00 15.00
BDJTV Thomas Vanek 6.00 15.00
BDJWG Wayne Gretzky 30.00 80.00
BDJZP Zach Parise 6.00 15.00

2008-09 Black Diamond Premier Die-Cut

STATED ODDS 1:1015
PDC1 Scott Niedermayer 6.00 15.00
PDC2 Marian Hossa 5.00 12.00
PDC3 Jason Spezza 6.00 15.00
PDC4 Daniel Alfredsson 6.00 15.00
PDC5 Ryan Getzlaf 10.00 25.00
PDC6 Chris Pronger 5.00 12.00
PDC7 Ryan Malone 4.00 10.00
PDC8 Brenden Morrow 5.00 12.00
PDC9 Mike Ribeiro 5.00 12.00
PDC10 Alex Kovalev 5.00 12.00
PDC11 Alexander Frolov 4.00 10.00
PDC12 Mike Richards 6.00 15.00
PDC13 Daniel Briere 6.00 15.00
PDC14 Peter Mueller 5.00 12.00
PDC15 Shane Doan 5.00 12.00
PDC16 Olli Jokinen 5.00 12.00
PDC17 Henrik Sedin 6.00 15.00
PDC18 Daniel Sedin 6.00 15.00
PDC19 Patrick Marleau 6.00 15.00
PDC20 J.P. Dumont 4.00 10.00
PDC21 Zach Parise 6.00 15.00
PDC22 Andrew Cogliano 5.00 12.00
PDC23 Brad Richards 6.00 15.00
PDC24 Chris Drury 5.00 12.00
PDC25 Chris Osgood 6.00 15.00
PDC26 Dany Heatley 6.00 15.00
PDC27 Dion Phaneuf 6.00 15.00
PDC28 Eric Staal 8.00 20.00
PDC29 Henrik Lundqvist 8.00 20.00
PDC30 Jean-Sebastien Giguere 6.00 15.00
PDC31 Jonathan Cheechoo 6.00 15.00
PDC32 Marc-Andre Fleury 10.00 25.00
PDC33 Marian Gaborik 8.00 20.00
PDC34 Martin St. Louis 6.00 15.00
PDC35 Nicklas Lidstrom 6.00 15.00
PDC36 Patrik Elias 6.00 15.00
PDC37 Paul Stastny 6.00 15.00
PDC38 Rick Nash 6.00 15.00
PDC39 Roberto Luongo 8.00 20.00
PDC40 Ryan Miller 6.00 15.00
PDC41 Sam Gagner 5.00 12.00
PDC42 Thomas Vanek 6.00 15.00
PDC43 Carey Price 25.00 60.00
PDC44 Evgeni Malkin 12.00 30.00
PDC45 Henrik Zetterberg 8.00 20.00
PDC46 Ilya Kovalchuk 6.00 15.00
PDC47 Jarome Iginla 6.00 15.00
PDC48 Joe Thornton 8.00 20.00
PDC49 Jonathan Toews 15.00 40.00
PDC50 Mark Messier 8.00 20.00
PDC51 Martin Brodeur 12.00 30.00
PDC52 Nicklas Backstrom 10.00 25.00
PDC53 Patrick Kane 12.00 30.00
PDC54 Patrick Roy 15.00 40.00
PDC55 Alexander Ovechkin 25.00 60.00
PDC56 Bobby Orr 20.00 50.00
PDC57 Gordie Howe 15.00 40.00
PDC58 Mario Lemieux 20.00 50.00
PDC59 Sidney Crosby 25.00 60.00
PDC60 Wayne Gretzky 30.00 80.00

2008-09 Black Diamond Run for the Cup

STATED PRINT RUN 100 SERIAL #'d SETS
CUP1 Jean-Sebastien Giguere 8.00 20.00
CUP2 Ilya Kovalchuk 8.00 20.00
CUP3 Marc Savard 5.00 12.00
CUP4 Ryan Miller 8.00 20.00
CUP5 Dion Phaneuf 8.00 20.00
CUP6 Jarome Iginla 8.00 20.00
CUP7 Eric Staal 10.00 25.00
CUP8 Jonathan Toews 20.00 50.00
CUP9 Patrick Kane 15.00 40.00
CUP10 Paul Stastny 8.00 20.00
CUP11 Joe Sakic 12.00 30.00
CUP12 Rick Nash 8.00 20.00
CUP13 Marty Turco 8.00 20.00
CUP14 Mike Modano 12.00 30.00
CUP15 Pavel Datsyuk 10.00 25.00
CUP16 Marian Hossa 6.00 15.00
CUP17 Henrik Zetterberg 12.00 30.00
CUP18 Shawn Horcoff 5.00 12.00
CUP19 Tomas Vokoun 6.00 15.00
CUP20 Anze Kopitar 12.00 30.00
CUP21 Marian Gaborik 10.00 25.00
CUP22 Carey Price 30.00 80.00
CUP23 Saku Koivu 8.00 20.00
CUP24 Martin Brodeur 15.00 40.00
CUP25 Rick DiPietro 6.00 15.00
CUP26 Daniel Alfredsson 8.00 20.00
CUP27 Jason Spezza 8.00 20.00
CUP28 Dany Heatley 8.00 20.00
CUP29 Mike Richards 8.00 20.00
CUP30 Shane Doan 6.00 15.00
CUP31 Olli Jokinen 6.00 15.00
CUP32 Peter Mueller 6.00 15.00
CUP33 Evgeni Malkin 25.00 60.00
CUP34 Marc-Andre Fleury 12.00 30.00
CUP35 Sidney Crosby 30.00 80.00
CUP36 Joe Thornton 10.00 25.00
CUP37 Paul Kariya 10.00 25.00
CUP38 Vincent Lecavalier 6.00 15.00
CUP39 Martin St. Louis 8.00 20.00
CUP40 Roberto Luongo 10.00 25.00
CUP41 Nicklas Backstrom 12.00 30.00
CUP42 Alexander Ovechkin 30.00 80.00

2009-10 Black Diamond

COMP.SET w/o SP's (90) 10.00 25.00
DOUBLE STATED ODDS 1:4
TRIPLE STATED ODDS 1:8
QUAD STATED ODDS 1:12
1 Jonas Hiller .20 .50
2 Sean Avery .20 .50
3 Peter Mueller .20 .50
4 Alexander Frolov .20 .50
5 Phil Kessel .30 .75
6 Mikhail Grabovski .25 .60
7 Teemu Selanne .50 1.25
8 Justin Abdelkader .20 .50
9 Daniel Sedin .25 .60
10 Brent Burns .30 .75
11 Sheldon Souray .15 .40
12 Scott Gomez .20 .50
13 Evgeni Nabokov .20 .50
14 Joe Pavelski .25 .60
15 Kyle Turris .25 .60
16 Martin Havlat .20 .50
17 Andrew Cogliano .20 .50
18 Marian Gaborik .30 .75
19 Darren Helm .20 .50
20 Niklas Kronwall .20 .50
21 Ryan Suter .25 .60
22 Mike Knuble .15 .40
23 Shea Weber .20 .50
24 Semyon Varlamov .25 .60
25 Chris Kunitz .25 .60
26 Nik Antropov .20 .50
27 Mikkel Boedker .15 .40
28 Ryan Malone .15 .40
29 Ilya Bryzgalov .20 .50
30 Drew Doughty .30 .75
31 Tim Thomas .25 .60
32 Andrei Kostitsyn .20 .50
33 Paul Kariya .30 .75
34 Sam Gagner .20 .50
35 Patrik Elias .25 .60
36 Devin Setoguchi .20 .50
37 Scott Hartnell .25 .60
38 Derek Roy .20 .50
39 Brian Campbell .20 .50
41 Todd White .15 .40
42 Jack Johnson .15 .40
43 Milan Hejduk .20 .50
44 Andrei Markov .25 .60
45 Marc Savard .15 .40
46 Jean-Sebastien Giguere .25 .60
47 Chris Mason .20 .50
48 Niklas Backstrom .25 .60
49 Jussi Jokinen .15 .40
50 Steve Ott .15 .40
51 Jonathan Cheechoo .25 .60
52 Pekka Rinne .30 .75
53 Ian Laperriere .15 .40
54 Steve Mason .20 .50
55 Kari Lehtonen .20 .50
56 Zdeno Chara .25 .60
57 Matt Stajan .20 .50
58 Dan Ellis .15 .40
59 Antti Miettinen .15 .40
60 Brian Gionta .20 .50
61 Sergei Gonchar .15 .40
62 Ryan Kesler .25 .60
63 Rene Bourque .15 .40
64 R.J. Umberger .20 .50
65 Alex Kovalev .25 .60
66 Tomas Kaberle .15 .40
67 Jaroslav Halak .25 .60
68 Chris Pronger .20 .50
69 David Booth .15 .40
70 Valtteri Filppula .25 .60
71 Henrik Sedin .25 .60
72 Erik Cole .20 .50
73 Mike Ribeiro .20 .50
74 Daniel Carcillo .15 .40
75 Jamie Langenbrunner .15 .40
76 Jason Pominville .25 .60
77 Patrick Sharp .25 .60
78 Mike Cammalleri .20 .50
79 Jakub Voracek .25 .60
80 Scott Niedermayer .25 .60
81 David Krejci .25 .60
82 Marian Hossa .20 .50
83 Dustin Penner .15 .40
84 Tomas Vokoun .20 .50
85 Nikolai Khabibulin .25 .60
86 Loui Eriksson .20 .50
87 Rob Blake .25 .60
88 Martin St. Louis .25 .60
89 Ethan Moreau .15 .40
90 Dan Boyle .20 .50
91 Ales Hemsky .30 .75
92 Johan Franzen .40 1.00
93 Ryan Smyth .30 .75
94 Pascal Leclaire .40 1.00
95 Simon Gagne .40 1.00
96 Brenden Morrow .30 .75
97 Vincent Lecavalier .30 .75
98 Mikko Koivu .40 1.00
99 Jean Beliveau .40 1.00
100 Zach Parise .40 1.00
101 Patrick Marleau .40 1.00
102 Luc Robitaille .40 1.00
103 Paul Stastny .40 1.00
104 Chris Drury .30 .75
105 Doug Gilmour .50 1.25
106 Bobby Ryan .40 1.00
107 Shane Doan .30 .75
108 Corey Perry .40 1.00
109 Jason Arnott .30 .75
110 Henrik Lundqvist .60 1.50
111 Milan Lucic .30 .75
112 Ryan Getzlaf .60 1.50
113 Anze Kopitar .60 1.50
114 Guy Carbonneau .60 1.50
115 Mats Sundin .40 1.00
116 Jason Spezza .40 1.00
117 Olli Jokinen .30 .75
118 Ryan Miller .40 1.00
119 Mike Green .40 1.00
120 Marty Turco .40 1.00
121 Rogie Vachon .50 1.25
122 Alexandre Burrows .40 1.00
123 Alexander Semin .40 1.00
124 Johnny Bucyk .60 1.50
125 Daniel Alfredsson .40 1.00
126 Brendan Shanahan .50 1.25
127 J.P. Dumont .25 .60
128 Clark Gillies .40 1.00
129 Dion Phaneuf .50 1.25
130 David Backes .40 1.00
131 Eric Staal .50 1.25
132 Luke Schenn .30 .75
133 Bob Bourne .30 .75
134 Pavel Datsyuk .50 1.25
135 Cam Ward .40 1.00
136 Dale Hawerchuk 1.25 3.00
137 Stan Mikita 1.25 3.00
138 Jeff Carter 1.00 2.50
139 Ilya Kovalchuk 1.00 2.50
140 Steven Stamkos 2.00 5.00
141 Dany Heatley 1.00 2.50
142 Carey Price 4.00 10.00
143 Henrik Zetterberg 1.25 3.00
144 Mike Richards 1.00 2.50
145 Harry Howell .75 2.00
146 Rick Nash .75 2.00
147 Gilbert Perreault 1.00 2.50
148 Patrick Kane 2.00 5.00
149 Joe Thornton 1.00 2.50
150 Miikka Kiprusoff .75 2.00
151 Jordan Staal 1.00 2.50
152 Tony Esposito 1.00 2.50

53 Nicklas Lidstrom 1.00 2.50
54 Nicklas Backstrom 1.50 4.00
55 Thomas Vanek 1.00 2.50
56 Phil Esposito 1.50 4.00
57 Marc-Andre Fleury 1.50 4.00
58 Brian Salcido RC 1.50 4.00
59 Luca Caputi RC 2.00 5.00
60 Yannick Weber RC 2.00 5.00
61 Kris Chucko RC 1.50 4.00
62 Riku Helenius RC 2.00 5.00
63 Ivan Vishnevskiy RC 1.50 4.00
64 T.J. Galiardi RC 2.00 5.00
65 Benn Ferriero RC 2.00 5.00
66 Cody Franson RC 2.00 5.00
67 Byron Bitz RC 1.50 4.00
68 Taylor Chorney RC 2.00 5.00
69 John Negrin RC 2.00 5.00
70 Jesse Joensuu RC 1.50 4.00
71 Cal O'Reilly RC 1.50 4.00
72 Spencer Machacek RC 2.00 5.00
73 Christian Hanson RC 2.00 5.00
74 Matt Beleskey RC 1.50 4.00
75 Jay Rosehill RC 2.00 5.00
76 Michael Sauer RC 1.50 4.00
77 Michael Grabner RC 2.00 5.00
78 Dmitry Kulikov RC 2.00 5.00
79 Alec Martinez RC 2.50 6.00
80 Matt Hendricks RC 1.50 4.00
81 Peter Stastny 2.50 6.00
82 Bobby Hull 3.00 8.00
83 Joe Sakic 4.00 10.00
84 Jarome Iginla 2.50 6.00
85 Don Cherry 2.50 6.00
86 Roberto Luongo 3.00 8.00
87 Jonathan Toews 5.00 12.00
88 Jari Kurri 2.50 6.00
89 Evgeni Malkin 8.00 20.00
90 Scotty Bowman 2.50 6.00
91 Martin Brodeur 5.00 12.00
92 Ray Bourque 4.00 10.00
93 Steve Yzerman 6.00 15.00
94 Sidney Crosby 10.00 25.00
95 Alexander Ovechkin 10.00 25.00
96 Bobby Orr 8.00 20.00
97 Mark Messier 3.00 8.00
98 Patrick Roy 6.00 15.00
99 Mario Lemieux 8.00 20.00
0 Gordie Howe 6.00 15.00
1 Wayne Gretzky 10.00 25.00
2 Tyler Bozak RC 4.00 10.00
3 Michael Del Zotto RC 2.50 6.00
4 Colin Wilson RC 2.50 6.00
5 Tyler Myers RC 4.00 10.00
6 Jamie Benn RC 8.00 20.00
7 Erik Karlsson RC 8.00 20.00
8 Viktor Stalberg RC 2.50 6.00
9 Matt Gilroy RC 2.50 6.00
0 Antti Niemi RC 4.00 10.00
1 Jhonas Enroth RC 3.00 8.00
2 Artem Anisimov RC 2.50 6.00
3 Ryan O'Reilly RC 4.00 10.00
4 Mikael Backlund RC 2.50 6.00
5 Ville Leino RC 2.00 5.00
6 Jonas Gustavsson RC 8.00 20.00
7 Sergei Shirokov RC 1.50 4.00
8 Victor Hedman RC 5.00 12.00
9 Evander Kane RC 5.00 12.00
0 James van Riemsdyk RC 5.00 12.00
1 Matt Duchene RC 5.00 12.00
2 John Tavares RC 20.00 50.00
Derick Brassard .25 .60

2009-10 Black Diamond Ruby

UBY SINGLE DIAMOND: 8X TO 20X BASE
UBY DOUBLE DIAMOND: 5X TO 12X BASE
UBY TRIPLE DIAMOND: 4X TO 10X BASE
UBY TRIPLE D ROOKIES: 1X TO 2.5X BASE
UBY QUAD DIAMOND: .6X TO 1.5X BASE
UBY QUAD D ROOKIES: .5X TO 1.2X BASE
ATED PRINT RUN 100 SER.#'d SETS
0 Zach Parise 5.00 12.00
4 Nicklas Backstrom 8.00 20.00
9 Luca Caputi 5.00 12.00
0 Yannick Weber 5.00 12.00
7 Michael Grabner 5.00 12.00
0 Antti Niemi 15.00 40.00
6 Jonas Gustavsson 15.00 40.00
0 James van Riemsdyk 12.00 30.00
1 Matt Duchene 25.00 60.00
2 John Tavares 40.00 100.00

2009-10 Black Diamond Gemography

E Andrew Ebbett 4.00 10.00
F Alexander Frolov 5.00 12.00
M Al MacInnis 8.00 20.00
O Adam Oates 6.00 15.00
T Alex Tanguay 4.00 10.00
B Brian Boyle 4.00 10.00
D Brandon Dubinsky 5.00 12.00
E Brendan Bell 4.00 10.00
M Bryan McCabe 5.00 12.00
O Bobby Orr 75.00 150.00
W Blake Wheeler 6.00 15.00
P Carey Price 25.00 60.00
B David Backes 6.00 15.00
D Drew Doughty 8.00 20.00
H Darren Helm 5.00 12.00
L Dan LaCosta 5.00 12.00
U J.P. Dumont 4.00 10.00
L Patrik Elias 6.00 15.00
M Evgeni Malkin 30.00 80.00
L Marc-Andre Fleury 12.00 30.00
R Mark Fraser 4.00 10.00
H Gordie Howe 75.00 150.00
Z Henrik Zetterberg 15.00 40.00
A Jason Arnott 5.00 12.00
D Jeff Drouin-Deslauriers 4.00 10.00
E Jonathan Ericsson 5.00 12.00
G Jean-Sebastien Giguere 6.00 15.00
Jarome Iginla 6.00 15.00
K Jari Kurri 6.00 15.00
O Joel Perrault 4.00 10.00
T Jiri Tlusty 5.00 12.00
N Patrick Kane 30.00 60.00
T Kyle Turris 6.00 15.00
D Matt D'Agostini 5.00 12.00
F Mark Fistric 4.00 10.00
H Michal Handzus 6.00 15.00
P Michael Peca 5.00 12.00
R Mattias Ritola 5.00 12.00
S Miroslav Satan 5.00 12.00
G Nathan Gerbe 5.00 12.00
K Nikolai Khabibulin 6.00 15.00
W Noah Welch 4.00 10.00
V Alexander Ovechkin 75.00 150.00
A Max Pacioretty 8.00 20.00
Joni Pitkanen 5.00 12.00
K Phil Kessel 8.00 20.00
O Marc-Antoine Pouliot 5.00 12.00
R Patrick Roy 100.00 200.00

GRC Ryane Clowe 5.00 12.00
GRK Rostislav Klesla 6.00 15.00
GRP Rich Peverley 5.00 12.00
GSC Sidney Crosby 60.00 120.00
GSM Stefan Meyer 5.00 12.00
GSS Steven Stamkos 20.00 50.00
GTO Jonathan Toews 12.00 30.00
GTV Thomas Vanek 8.00 20.00
GTZ Travis Zajac 5.00 12.00
GWG Wayne Gretzky 150.00 250.00
GYZ Steve Yzerman 125.00 250.00
GZB Zach Bogosian 5.00 12.00

2009-10 Black Diamond Hardware Heroes

COMPLETE SET (42) 500.00 1000.00
STATED PRINT RUN 100 SER.#'d SETS
HH1 Patrick Kane 10.00 25.00
HH2 Evgeni Malkin 15.00 40.00
HH3 Dale Hawerchuk 6.00 15.00
HH4 Peter Stastny 5.00 12.00
HH5 Luc Robitaille 5.00 12.00
HH6 Mike Bossy 8.00 20.00
HH7 Gilbert Perreault 5.00 12.00
HH8 Steve Mason 4.00 10.00
HH9 Evgeni Malkin 15.00 40.00
HH10 Henrik Zetterberg 6.00 15.00
HH11 Steve Yzerman 12.00 30.00
HH12 Brad Richards 5.00 12.00
HH13 Wayne Gretzky 25.00 60.00
HH14 Wayne Gretzky 25.00 60.00
HH15 Mario Lemieux 15.00 40.00
HH16 Mark Messier 6.00 15.00
HH17 Mark Messier 6.00 15.00
HH18 Joe Sakic 8.00 20.00
HH19 Sidney Crosby 20.00 50.00
HH20 Phil Esposito 8.00 20.00
HH21 Gordie Howe 12.00 30.00
HH22 Bobby Hull 6.00 15.00
HH23 Stan Mikita 6.00 15.00
HH24 Bobby Clarke 5.00 12.00
HH25 Alexander Ovechkin 20.00 50.00
HH26 Steve Yzerman 12.00 30.00
HH27 Jarome Iginla 5.00 12.00
HH28 Sidney Crosby 20.00 50.00
HH29 Bobby Orr 20.00 50.00
HH30 Nicklas Lidstrom 5.00 12.00
HH31 Ray Bourque 8.00 20.00
HH32 Brian Leetch 5.00 12.00
HH33 Zdeno Chara 6.00 15.00
HH34 Pavel Datsyuk 6.00 15.00
HH35 Martin Brodeur 10.00 25.00
HH36 Patrick Roy 12.00 30.00
HH37 Ron Hextall 8.00 20.00
HH38 Grant Fuhr 5.00 12.00
HH39 Miikka Kiprusoff 4.00 10.00
HH40 Jose Theodore 5.00 12.00
HH41 Teemu Selanne 10.00 25.00
HH42 Tim Thomas 5.00 12.00

2009-10 Black Diamond Horizontal

*HORIZ: .5X TO 1.2X DIE-CUTS
STATED ODDS 1:48

2009-10 Black Diamond Horizontal Perimeter Die-Cut

STATED ODDS 1:12
BD1 Ilya Kovalchuk 2.50 6.00
BD2 Steven Stamkos 4.00 10.00
BD3 Carey Price 10.00 25.00
BD4 Henrik Zetterberg 3.00 8.00
BD5 Patrick Kane 5.00 12.00
BD6 Joe Thornton 2.50 6.00
BD7 Miikka Kiprusoff 2.00 5.00
BD8 Nicklas Lidstrom 2.50 6.00
BD9 Phil Esposito 4.00 10.00
BD10 Peter Stastny 2.50 6.00
BD11 Bobby Hull 5.00 12.00
BD12 Joe Sakic 4.00 10.00
BD13 Jarome Iginla 2.50 6.00
BD14 Don Cherry 2.50 6.00
BD15 Roberto Luongo 5.00 12.00
BD16 Jonathan Toews 5.00 12.00
BD17 Jari Kurri 2.50 6.00
BD18 Evgeni Malkin 5.00 12.00
BD19 Scotty Bowman 2.50 6.00
BD20 Ray Bourque 4.00 10.00
BD21 Martin Brodeur SP 8.00 20.00
BD22 Steve Yzerman SP 12.00 30.00
BD23 Sidney Crosby SP 15.00 40.00
BD24 Alexander Ovechkin SP 15.00 40.00
BD25 Bobby Orr SP 15.00 40.00
BD26 Mark Messier SP 5.00 12.00
BD27 Patrick Roy SP 15.00 40.00
BD28 Mario Lemieux SP 10.00 25.00
BD29 Gordie Howe SP 10.00 25.00
BD30 Wayne Gretzky SP 20.00 50.00

2009-10 Black Diamond Jerseys Quad

*GOLD/25: .8X TO 2X BASIC JSY
*RUBY/50: .5X TO 1.2X BASIC JSY
QJAF Alexander Frolov 4.00 10.00
QJAK Anze Kopitar 8.00 20.00
QJAO Alexander Ovechkin 10.00 25.00
QJBD Brandon Dubinsky 4.00 10.00
QJBR Derick Brassard 5.00 12.00
QJCH Cristobal Huet 5.00 12.00
QJCP Carey Price 20.00 50.00
QJDB David Booth 3.00 8.00
QJDD Drew Doughty 6.00 15.00
QJDH Dale Hawerchuk 6.00 15.00
QJDP David Perron 3.00 8.00
QJDS Drew Stafford 5.00 12.00
QJDU Dustin Brown
QJEM Evgeni Malkin 15.00 40.00
QJFB Francis Bouillon 3.00 8.00
QJGA Glenn Anderson 5.00 12.00
QJJB Jay Bouwmeester 5.00 12.00
QJJL Jordan Leopold 3.00 8.00
QJJP Jason Pominville 5.00 12.00
QJJT Jeff Tambellini 3.00 8.00
QJJV Jakub Voracek 5.00 12.00
QJKA Sami Kapanen 4.00 10.00
QJLM Lanny McDonald 5.00 12.00
QJMB Martin Brodeur 10.00 25.00
QJMH Marian Hossa 4.00 10.00
QJMK Mike Komisarek 4.00 10.00
QJMS Marc Staal 5.00 12.00
QJNH Nathan Horton 5.00 12.00
QJPH Dion Phaneuf 6.00 15.00
QJPK Patrick Kane
QJPO Patrick O'Sullivan 4.00 10.00
QJPS Patrick Sharp 5.00 12.00
QJRD Rick DiPietro 4.00 10.00
QJRM Ryan Miller 5.00 12.00
QJRN Rick Nash 4.00 10.00
QJSC Sidney Crosby 15.00 40.00
QJSD Shane Doan 4.00 10.00
QJSG Simon Gagne 5.00 12.00
QJSK Saku Koivu 5.00 12.00
QJSS Steve Shutt 5.00 12.00
QJST Jordan Staal 5.00 12.00
QJSW Shea Weber 4.00 10.00
QJTO Jonathan Toews 10.00 25.00
QJTV Thomas Vanek 5.00 12.00
QJVL Vincent Lecavalier 4.00 10.00
QJVO Tomas Vokoun 4.00 10.00
QJWE Stephen Weiss 3.00 8.00
QJWR Wade Redden
QJZB Zach Bogosian 4.00 10.00
QJZP Zach Parise 5.00 12.00

2010-11 Black Diamond

COMP.SET w/o SPS (90) 8.00 20.00
91-130 DOUBLE DIAMOND ODDS 1:4
131-180 TRIPLE DIAMOND ODDS 1:4
181-222 QUAD DIAMOND ODDS 1:12
1 Ales Hemsky .20 .50
2 Craig Anderson .25 .60
3 Tomas Plekanec .25 .60
4 Wojtek Wolski .15 .40
5 Olli Jokinen .20 .50
6 Mike Smith .25 .60
7 Ville Leino .20 .50
8 Marty Turco .25 .60
9 Daniel Alfredsson .25 .60
10 Nathan Horton .20 .50
11 Martin Havlat .20 .50
12 Steve Mason .20 .50
13 Mike Knuble .15 .40
14 Dustin Brown .25 .60
15 Bryan McCabe .15 .40
16 J.P. Dumont .15 .40
17 Mike Modano .40 1.00
18 Loui Eriksson .20 .50
19 Brandon Dubinsky .20 .50
20 Nik Antropov .20 .50
21 Patrick Sharp .25 .60
22 Lee Stempniak .15 .40
23 Brad Boyes .15 .40
24 Claude Giroux .25 .60
25 Mark Streit .15 .40
26 Dustin Penner .15 .40
27 Jason Pominville .25 .60
28 Devin Setoguchi .20 .50
29 Evander Kane .25 .60
30 Andrew Brunette .15 .40
31 Tomas Holmstrom .15 .40
32 Sam Gagner .20 .50
33 Alex Tanguay .15 .40
34 Blake Wheeler .25 .60
35 Brent Seabrook .25 .60
36 Ryan Kesler .25 .60
37 Jonas Hiller .20 .50
38 Jonathan Quick .40 1.00
39 Nikolai Kulemin .20 .50
40 Pekka Rinne .30 .75
41 Brian Elliott .20 .50
42 Brenden Morrow .20 .50
43 Rich Peverley .25 .60
44 Kari Lehtonen .20 .50
45 Shawn Horcoff .15 .40
46 Tim Gleason .15 .40
47 Jamie Langenbrunner .15 .40
48 Antoine Vermette .15 .40
49 Milan Hejduk .20 .50
50 Alexander Semin .25 .60
51 Kyle Okposo .25 .60
52 Jean-Sebastien Giguere .20 .50
53 Pascal Dupuis .15 .40
54 Milan Michalek .15 .40
55 Bryan Little .25 .60
56 David Booth .15 .40
57 Michael Leighton .20 .50
58 Milan Lucic .25 .60
59 Andy McDonald .20 .50
60 Semyon Varlamov .25 .60
61 Andrei Markov .25 .60
62 Rene Bourque .15 .40
63 Josh Bailey .20 .50
64 Victor Hedman .30 .75
65 Tomas Kaberle .15 .40
66 Patric Hornqvist .20 .50
67 Mike Fisher .25 .60
68 Joe Pavelski .25 .60
69 Guillaume Latendresse .20 .50
70 Stephen Weiss .20 .50
71 Travis Zajac .20 .50
72 Jakub Voracek .25 .60
73 Alexandre Burrows .25 .60
74 David Backes .25 .60
75 James van Riemsdyk .40 1.00
76 Rick DiPietro .20 .50
77 Ryan Smyth .20 .50
78 Ryan Suter .15 .40
79 Alex Kovalev .25 .60
80 Mike Ribeiro .20 .50
81 Scott Hartnell .25 .60
82 Ryan Malone .15 .40
83 T.J. Oshie .40 1.00
84 Mikael Samuelsson .15 .40
85 Jay Bouwmeester .30 .75
86 Vaclav Prospal .15 .40
87 Valtteri Filppula .25 .60
88 Saku Koivu .25 .60
89 Jussi Jokinen .15 .40
90 Brian Gionta .20 .50
91 Chris Pronger .50 1.25
92 Antti Niemi .50 1.25
93 Cam Ward .60 1.50
94 Zdeno Chara .50 1.25
95 Shane Doan .50 1.25
96 Tomas Vokoun .50 1.25
97 Tyler Myers .60 1.50
98 Chris Drury .50 1.25
99 Dion Phaneuf .60 1.50
100 Niklas Backstrom .60 1.50
101 Drew Doughty .60 1.50
102 Miikka Kiprusoff .50 1.25
103 Vincent Lecavalier .50 1.25
104 Mike Cammalleri .60 1.50
105 Marian Hossa .50 1.25
106 Matt Duchene .60 1.50
107 Ilya Bryzgalov .50 1.25
108 Corey Perry .60 1.50
109 Phil Kessel .75 2.00
110 Shea Weber .50 1.25
111 Dan Boyle .50 1.25
112 Luke Schenn .50 1.25
113 Patrice Bergeron .75 2.00
114 Daniel Briere .60 1.50
115 Johan Franzen .60 1.50
116 Patrick Marleau .60 1.50
117 Brad Richards .60 1.50
118 Tuukka Rask .60 1.50
119 Teemu Selanne 1.25 3.00
120 Duncan Keith .60 1.50
121 Patrik Elias .60 1.50
122 Jordan Staal .60 1.50
123 Jimmy Howard .75 2.00
124 Anze Kopitar 1.00 2.50
125 Bobby Ryan .60 1.50
126 Derek Roy .60 1.50
127 Jason Spezza .40 1.00
128 Carey Price 2.50 6.00
129 Marc Savard .40 1.00
130 Scott Gomez .50 1.25
131 Daniel Sedin 1.00 2.50
132 Nicklas Lidstrom 1.00 2.50
133 John Tavares 2.00 5.00
134 Nicklas Backstrom 1.50 4.00
135 Tony Esposito 1.00 2.50
136 Mike Green 1.00 2.50
137 Zach Parise 1.00 2.50
138 Pavel Datsyuk 1.25 3.00
139 Paul Stastny 1.00 2.50
140 Ilya Kovalchuk 1.00 2.50
141 Henrik Sedin 1.00 2.50
142 Mark Messier 1.50 4.00
143 Luc Robitaille 1.00 2.50
144 Henrik Lundqvist 1.50 4.00
145 Ryan Getzlaf 1.50 4.00
146 Patrick Kane 2.00 5.00
147 Phil Esposito 1.50 4.00
148 Martin St. Louis 1.00 2.50
149 Mike Bossy 1.00 2.50
150 Marc-Andre Fleury 1.50 4.00
151 Marian Gaborik 1.25 3.00
152 Dany Heatley .75 2.00
153 Ryan Miller 1.00 2.50
154 Mikko Koivu 1.00 2.50
155 Thomas Vanek 1.00 2.50
156 Maxim Noreau RC 1.25 3.00
157 Arturs Kulda RC 1.50 4.00
158 Jacob Josefson RC 1.50 4.00
159 Brayden Irwin RC 1.50 4.00
160 Cody Almond RC 1.50 4.00
161 Alexander Urbom RC 1.50 4.00
162 Matt Taormina RC 1.50 4.00
163 Tommy Wingels RC 1.50 4.00
164 Nick Palmieri RC 1.50 4.00
165 Nick Johnson RC 1.25 3.00
166 T.J. Brodie RC 1.50 4.00
167 Casey Wellman RC 1.50 4.00
168 Alex Plante RC 1.50 4.00
169 Philip Larsen RC 1.50 4.00
170 Dustin Tokarski RC 1.50 4.00
171 Justin Falk RC 1.25 3.00
172 Anders Lindback RC 1.50 4.00
173 Brandon Pirri RC 1.50 4.00
174 Jake Muzzin RC 1.50 4.00
175 Kyle Clifford RC 1.50 4.00
176 Dana Tyrell RC 1.50 4.00
177 Mark Olver RC 1.50 4.00
178 Henrik Karlsson RC 1.50 4.00
179 Nick Leddy RC 1.50 4.00
180 Jamie McBain RC 1.50 4.00
181 Joe Thornton 2.50 6.00
182 Bobby Orr 8.00 20.00
183 Eric Staal 3.00 8.00
184 Steve Yzerman 6.00 15.00
185 Mario Lemieux 8.00 20.00
186 Jarome Iginla 2.50 6.00
187 Patrick Roy 6.00 15.00
188 Jonathan Toews 5.00 12.00
189 Jeff Carter 2.50 6.00
190 Steven Stamkos 5.00 12.00
191 Henrik Zetterberg 3.00 8.00
192 Alexander Ovechkin 10.00 25.00
193 Martin Brodeur 5.00 12.00
194 Guy Lafleur 3.00 8.00
195 Rick Nash 2.50 6.00
196 Mike Richards 2.50 6.00
197 Evgeni Malkin 8.00 20.00
198 Roberto Luongo 2.50 6.00
199 Sidney Crosby 10.00 25.00
200 Wayne Gretzky 12.00 30.00
201 Gordie Howe 6.00 15.00
202 Jared Cowen RC 2.50 6.00
203 Marcus Johansson RC 4.00 10.00
204 Sergei Bobrovsky RC 6.00 15.00
205 Zac Dalpe RC 2.50 6.00
206 Cam Fowler RC 3.00 8.00
207 Alexander Burmistrov RC 2.50 6.00
208 Nino Niederreiter RC 3.00 8.00
209 Oliver Ekman-Larsson RC 4.00 10.00
210 Zach Hamill RC 2.50 6.00
211 Brandon Yip RC 2.50 6.00
212 Jordan Caron RC 4.00 10.00
213 Jeff Skinner RC 10.00 25.00
214 Magnus Paajarvi RC 3.00 8.00
215 Brayden Schenn RC 4.00 10.00
216 Eric Tangradi RC 2.50 6.00
217 Derek Stepan RC 5.00 12.00
218 P.K. Subban RC 12.00 30.00
219 Nazem Kadri RC 8.00 20.00
220 Jordan Eberle RC 6.00 15.00
221 Tyler Seguin RC 20.00 40.00
222 Taylor Hall RC 10.00 25.00

2010-11 Black Diamond Ruby

*1-90 SINGLE: 8X TO 20X BASIC CARDS
*91-130 DOUBLE: 3X TO 8X BASIC CARDS
*131-155 TRIPLE: 2X TO 5X BASIC CARDS
*156-180 TRIP.ROOK: 1X TO 2.5X BASIC RC
*181-201 QUAD: .6X TO 1.5X BASIC CARDS
*202-222 QUAD ROOK: .6X TO 1.5X BASIC RC
STATED PRINT RUN 100 SER.#'d SETS
213 Jeff Skinner 30.00 60.00
218 P.K. Subban 30.00 60.00
220 Jordan Eberle 15.00 40.00
221 Tyler Seguin 30.00 80.00
222 Taylor Hall 30.00 80.00

2010-11 Black Diamond Gemography

STATED ODDS 1:60
GBM Barry Melrose 5.00 12.00
GBO Bobby Orr 125.00 200.00
GBS Bobby Sanguinetti 4.00 10.00
GBU Peter Budaj 5.00 12.00
GCG Clark Gillies 6.00 15.00
GCL David Clarkson 4.00 10.00
GDC Daniel Carcillo 4.00 10.00
GEK Erik Karlsson 12.00 30.00
GEN Eric Nystrom 4.00 10.00
GET Eric Tangradi 5.00 12.00
GFR Mark Fraser 4.00 10.00
GGF Grant Fuhr SP 15.00 40.00
GGH Gordie Howe 60.00 120.00
GGI Claude Giroux 15.00 40.00
GHS Henrik Sedin 6.00 15.00
GIV Ivan Vishnevskiy 4.00 10.00
GJB Jamie Benn 10.00 25.00
GJC Jared Cowen 5.00 12.00
GJG Jean-Sebastien Giguere 10.00 25.00
GJK Jari Kurri 6.00 15.00
GJT John Tavares 15.00 30.00
GJV Jakub Voracek 6.00 15.00
GKA Evander Kane 8.00 20.00
GKC Kris Chucko 4.00 10.00
GLR Luc Robitaille 12.00 30.00
GMB Mikael Backlund
GMD Matt Duchene 20.00 50.00
GMF Mark Fistric 4.00 10.00
GMG Matt Gilroy 4.00 10.00
GMM Mark Messier 50.00 100.00
GMN Michal Neuvirth 5.00 12.00
GMP Matt Pelech 4.00 10.00
GMS Marek Svatos 4.00 10.00
GNG Nathan Gerbe 4.00 10.00
GNH Nathan Horton 5.00 12.00
GNK Nazem Kadri 15.00 40.00
GPB Patrice Bergeron 8.00 20.00
GPE Phil Esposito 15.00 30.00
GPH Patric Hornqvist 5.00 12.00
GPM Peter Mueller 5.00 12.00
GPS P.K. Subban 30.00 80.00
GRP Ryan Parent 4.00 10.00
GSC Sidney Crosby 60.00 120.00
GSG Simon Gagne 6.00 15.00
GSM Spencer Machacek 4.00 10.00
GSS Steven Stamkos 25.00 50.00
GST Peter Stastny 5.00 12.00
GSV Sergei Shirokov 5.00 12.00
GSW Stephen Weiss 5.00 12.00
GTE Tony Esposito
GTJ T.J. Galiardi 5.00 12.00
GTM Tyler Myers 8.00 20.00
GVL Ville Leino 10.00 25.00
GVR James van Riemsdyk 10.00 25.00
GWG Wayne Gretzky 150.00 250.00
GYW Yannick Weber 5.00 12.00
GZH Zach Hamill 8.00 20.00

2010-11 Black Diamond Hardware Heroes

STATED ODDS 1:160
STATED PRINT RUN 100 SER.#'d SETS
HHAO Alexander Ovechkin 20.00 50.00
HHBC Bobby Clarke 12.00 30.00
HHBL Brian Leetch 5.00 12.00
HHBO Bobby Orr 20.00 50.00
HHBR Martin Brodeur 10.00 25.00
HHCP Chris Pronger 4.00 10.00
HHCR Sidney Crosby 25.00 50.00
HHDC Don Cherry 5.00 12.00
HHDK Duncan Keith 5.00 12.00
HHGH Gordie Howe 10.00 25.00
HHGL Guy Lafleur 10.00 25.00
HHGR Wayne Gretzky 40.00 80.00
HHHS Henrik Sedin 12.00 30.00
HHJT Jonathan Toews 12.00 30.00
HHLG Guy Lafleur 10.00 25.00
HHLM Lanny McDonald 5.00 12.00
HHLR Larry Robinson 5.00 12.00
HHMB Martin Brodeur 10.00 25.00
HHML Mario Lemieux 15.00 40.00
HHMM Mark Messier 8.00 20.00
HHMS Martin St. Louis 5.00 12.00
HHOV Alexander Ovechkin 20.00 50.00
HHPD Pavel Datsyuk 6.00 15.00
HHPE Phil Esposito 8.00 20.00
HHPK Patrick Kane 10.00 25.00
HHPR Patrick Roy 12.00 30.00
HHRB Ray Bourque 8.00 20.00
HHRK Red Kelly 5.00 12.00
HHRM Ryan Miller 8.00 20.00
HHSB Scotty Bowman 4.00 10.00
HHSC Sidney Crosby 25.00 60.00
HHSD Shane Doan 4.00 10.00
HHSE Henrik Sedin 12.00 30.00
HHSM Stan Mikita 8.00 20.00
HHSS Steven Stamkos 10.00 25.00
HHSY Steve Yzerman 15.00 40.00
HHTE Tony Esposito 6.00 15.00
HHTH Jose Theodore 8.00 20.00
HHTM Tyler Myers 5.00 12.00
HHTS Teemu Selanne 10.00 25.00
HHWG Wayne Gretzky 40.00 80.00
HHYS Steve Yzerman 15.00 40.00

2010-11 Black Diamond Jerseys Quad

STATED ODDS 1:13
OVERALL G-U STATED ODDS 1:12
QJAK Alex Kovalev 4.00 10.00
QJAO Alexander Ovechkin 8.00 20.00
QJBL Brian Leetch 4.00 10.00
QJBR Bobby Ryan 4.00 10.00
QJBW Blake Wheeler 4.00 10.00
QJCC Chris Campoli 2.50 6.00
QJCN Cam Neely 4.00 10.00
QJCP Carey Price 15.00 40.00
QJDG Doug Gilmour 5.00 12.00
QJDH Dale Hawerchuk 5.00 12.00
QJDR Derek Roy 4.00 10.00
QJES Eric Staal 5.00 12.00
QJGA Glenn Anderson 4.00 10.00
QJHL Henrik Lundqvist 6.00 15.00
QJHZ Henrik Zetterberg 5.00 12.00
QJIB Ilya Bryzgalov 3.00 8.00
QJIK Ilya Kovalchuk 4.00 10.00
QJJA Jason Arnott 3.00 8.00
QJJC Jeff Carter 4.00 10.00
QJJT John Tavares 8.00 20.00
QJJV Jakub Voracek 4.00 10.00
QJJW Justin Williams 3.00 8.00
QJLM Lanny McDonald 4.00 10.00
QJMA Ryan Malone 2.50 6.00
QJMF Michael Frolik 2.50 6.00
QJMG Marian Gaborik 5.00 12.00
QJMJ Milan Jurcina 2.50 6.00
QJMK Mikko Koivu 4.00 10.00
QJML Mario Lemieux 8.00 20.00
QJNB Nicklas Backstrom 6.00 15.00
QJNH Nathan Horton 3.00 8.00
QJNK Nikolai Kulemin 3.00 8.00
QJPD Pavel Datsyuk 5.00 12.00
QJPM Peter Mueller 3.00 8.00
QJPS Peter Stastny 3.00 8.00
QJRB Ray Bourque 8.00 20.00
QJRM Ryan Miller 4.00 10.00
QJRN Rick Nash 4.00 10.00
QJSB Steve Bernier 2.50 6.00
QJSC Sidney Crosby 15.00 40.00
QJSG Scott Gomez 3.00 8.00
QJSM Steve Mason 6.00 15.00
QJSV Steve Shutt 4.00 10.00
QJSW Stephen Weiss 3.00 8.00
QJTB Todd Bertuzzi 3.00 8.00
QJTO Jonathan Toews 6.00 15.00
QJTT Tim Thomas 5.00 12.00
QJTV Thomas Vanek 4.00 10.00
QJVO Tomas Vokoun 3.00 8.00
QJWG Wayne Gretzky 20.00 50.00

2010-11 Black Diamond Jerseys Quad Gold

*SINGLES: .6X TO 1.5X BASIC INSERTS
STATED PRINT RUN 25 SER.#'d SETS

2010-11 Black Diamond Jerseys Quad Ruby

*SINGLES: .5X TO 1.2X BASIC INSERTS
STATED PRINT RUN 50 SER.#'d SETS

2010-11 Black Diamond Team Canada Die Cuts

COMPLETE SET (16) 150.00 300.00
STATED ODDS 1:64
TCBO Bobby Orr 12.00 30.00
TCDD Drew Doughty 4.00 10.00
TCDK Duncan Keith 4.00 10.00
TCGH Gordie Howe 8.00 20.00
TCJI Jarome Iginla 4.00 10.00
TCMB Martin Brodeur 8.00 20.00
TCMF Marc-Andre Fleury 6.00 15.00
TCML Mario Lemieux 12.00 30.00
TCMM Mark Messier 6.00 15.00
TCMR Mike Richards 4.00 10.00
TCPM Patrick Marleau 4.00 10.00
TCRL Roberto Luongo 4.00 10.00
TCSC Sidney Crosby 15.00 40.00
TCTO Jonathan Toews 8.00 20.00
TCWG Wayne Gretzky 12.00 30.00
TCYZ Steve Yzerman 8.00 20.00

2011-12 Black Diamond

COMP.SET w/o SPs (100) 8.00 20.00
101-150 DOUBLE DIAMOND ODDS 1:4
151-200 TRIPLE DIAMOND ODDS 1:4
201-250 QUAD DIAMOND ODDS 1:12
1 Wayne Gretzky 1.25 3.00
2 Saku Koivu .25 .60
3 Nathan Gerbe .15 .40
4 Rene Bourque .15 .40
5 Patrik Elias .25 .60
6 Dustin Brown .25 .60
7 Brian Gionta .20 .50
8 Craig Anderson .25 .60
9 Chris Kunitz .25 .60
10 Bobby Orr .75 2.00
11 Kevin Shattenkirk .20 .50
12 Tobias Enstrom .15 .40
13 Michael Grabner .20 .50
14 Travis Zajac .20 .50
15 Guillaume Latendresse .20 .50
16 Ryan Smyth .20 .50
17 Loui Eriksson .20 .50
18 Patrick Sharp .25 .60
19 Alex Tanguay .15 .40
20 Gordie Howe .50 1.25
21 Tuukka Rask .25 .60
22 Tyler Myers .25 .60
23 Jussi Jokinen .15 .40
24 Semyon Varlamov .25 .60
25 Ales Hemsky .20 .50
26 Stephen Weiss .20 .50
27 Lars Eller .20 .50
28 Matt Moulson .20 .50
29 Milan Michalek .15 .40
30 Pascal Dupuis .15 .40
31 Martin Havlat .20 .50
32 Dwayne Roloson .20 .50
33 Tomas Vokoun .20 .50
34 Chris Pronger .20 .50
35 Marc Staal .25 .60
36 Kyle Okposo .25 .60
37 Patric Hornqvist .20 .50
38 Jonathan Bernier .25 .60
39 Sam Gagner .20 .50
40 Patrick Roy .60 1.50
41 Mike Ribeiro .20 .50
42 Steve Mason .20 .50
43 Milan Hejduk .20 .50
44 Brent Seabrook .25 .60
45 Matt Stajan .20 .50
46 Olli Jokinen .20 .50
47 Tyler Ennis .20 .50
48 Drew Stafford .25 .60
49 Mario Lemieux .75 2.00
50 Mark Messier .30 .75
51 Jean-Sebastien Giguere .20 .50
52 Erik Johnson .15 .40
53 Valtteri Filppula .25 .60
54 Tomas Plekanec .25 .60
55 Derek Stepan .25 .60
56 Josh Bailey .20 .50
57 Ryan Callahan .25 .60
58 Daniel Briere .25 .60
59 James Neal .25 .60
60 Teemu Selanne .50 1.25
61 Dustin Penner .20 .50
62 Scott Clemmensen .20 .50
63 Ville Leino .20 .50
64 Nikolai Kulemin .25 .60
65 Antoine Vermette .15 .40
66 Milan Lucic .25 .60
67 Ryan Suter .15 .40
68 Jay Bouwmeester .25 .60
69 Ryane Clowe .15 .40
70 Jonathan Toews .50 1.25
71 Alexandre Burrows .25 .60
72 Jordan Eberle .25 .60
73 Dennis Seidenberg .20 .50
74 Brandon Dubinsky .20 .50
75 Corey Crawford .30 .75
76 Jason Pominville .20 .50
77 Rich Peverley .25 .60
78 David Booth .15 .40
79 Henrik Sedin .25 .60
80 Carey Price .75 2.00
81 T.J. Oshie .40 1.00
82 Cam Fowler .20 .50
83 Thomas Vanek .25 .60
84 Bobby Ryan .25 .60
85 James van Riemsdyk .25 .60
86 Simon Gagne .25 .60
87 David Perron .15 .40
88 Travis Hamonic .20 .50
89 Michael Frolik .15 .40
90 Alexander Ovechkin 1.00 2.50
91 Nicklas Backstrom .40 1.00
92 Darren Helm .20 .50
93 Daniel Sedin .25 .60
94 Sergei Bobrovsky .25 .60
95 Andrei Markov .25 .60
96 Scott Hartnell .25 .60
97 Tyler Seguin .50 1.25
98 Patrik Berglund .20 .50
99 Jonathan Ericsson .20 .50
100 Sidney Crosby 1.00 2.50
101 Evander Kane .60 1.50
102 Jordan Staal .60 1.50
103 Antti Niemi .50 1.25
104 Mikko Koivu .50 1.25
105 Chris Stewart .50 1.25
106 Erik Karlsson 1.25 3.00
107 Phil Kessel .75 2.00
108 Shea Weber .50 1.25
109 Duncan Keith .60 1.50
110 Brenden Morrow .50 1.25
111 Eric Staal .75 2.00
112 Dany Heatley .50 1.25
113 Jim Howard .60 1.50
114 Jaroslav Halak .60 1.50
115 Ilya Bryzgalov .60 1.50
116 Shane Doan .50 1.25
117 Jacob Markstrom .60 1.50
118 Alex Goligoski .50 1.25
119 Patrice Bergeron .75 2.00
120 Claude Giroux .60 1.50
121 Joe Pavelski .60 1.50
122 Victor Hedman .75 2.00
123 David Backes .60 1.50
124 Kristopher Letang .60 1.50
125 David Krejci .60 1.50
126 Jeff Skinner .60 1.50
127 Marian Hossa .50 1.25
128 Pekka Rinne .75 2.00
129 Jakub Voracek .60 1.50
130 Alexander Semin .60 1.50
131 Marc-Andre Fleury 1.00 2.50
132 Anze Kopitar 1.00 2.50
133 Johan Franzen .60 1.50
134 Joe Thornton .60 1.50
135 Mike Green .60 1.50
136 Michael Cammalleri .50 1.25
137 Jonas Hiller .50 1.25
138 Vincent Lecavalier .50 1.25
139 Devin Setoguchi .50 1.25
140 Cam Ward .60 1.50
141 Ondrej Pavelec .60 1.50
142 Nathan Horton .60 1.50
143 Matt Duchene .60 1.50
144 Daniel Alfredsson .60 1.50
145 Jonathan Quick 1.00 2.50
146 Ryan Getzlaf 1.00 2.50
147 Kari Lehtonen .50 1.25
148 Paul Stastny .60 1.50
149 Marian Gaborik .75 2.00
150 James Reimer .60 1.50
151 Corey Perry 1.00 2.50
152 Zach Parise 1.00 2.50
153 Miikka Kiprusoff 1.00 2.50
154 Pavel Datsyuk 1.25 3.00
155 Ryan Kesler 1.00 2.50
156 Ryan Miller 1.00 2.50
157 Henrik Lundqvist 1.25 3.00
158 Brad Marchand 1.25 3.00
159 Jeff Carter 1.00 2.50
160 Logan Couture 1.00 2.50
161 Patrick Kane 2.00 5.00
162 Zdeno Chara 1.00 2.50
163 Dustin Byfuglien 1.00 2.50
164 Rick Nash 1.00 2.50
165 Brayden Schenn 1.00 2.50
166 P.K. Subban 2.00 5.00
167 Jarome Iginla 1.00 2.50
168 Drew Doughty 1.00 2.50
169 John Tavares 2.00 5.00
170 Mike Richards 1.00 2.50
171 Dion Phaneuf 1.00 2.50
172 Ilya Kovalchuk 1.00 2.50
173 Taylor Hall 2.00 5.00
174 Henrik Zetterberg 1.25 3.00
175 Jason Spezza 1.00 2.50
176 Roman Horak RC 1.50 4.00
177 Maxime Macenauer RC 1.50 4.00
178 John Moore RC 1.50 4.00
179 Colin Greening RC 1.50 4.00
180 Cam Atkinson RC 4.00 10.00
181 Tomas Vincour RC 1.50 4.00
182 Yann Sauve RC 1.50 4.00
183 Alexei Emelin RC 1.50 4.00
184 Erik Condra RC 1.50 4.00
185 Justin Faulk RC 2.50 6.00
186 Cameron Gaunce RC 1.25 3.00
187 Joe Vitale RC 1.50 4.00
188 David Rundblad RC 1.50 4.00
189 Erik Gustafsson RC 2.00 5.00
190 Raphael Diaz RC 1.50 4.00
191 David Savard RC 1.50 4.00
192 Tim Erixon RC 1.50 4.00
193 Teemu Hartikainen RC 1.50 4.00
194 Ben Scrivens RC 2.50 6.00
195 Paul Postma RC 1.50 4.00
196 Craig Smith RC 2.00 5.00
197 Patrick Wiercioch RC 1.50 4.00
198 Alex Stalock 1.50 4.00
199 Brett Bulmer RC 1.50 4.00
200 Stephane Da Costa RC 1.50 4.00
201 Sidney Crosby AS 10.00 25.00
202 Alexander Ovechkin AS 10.00 25.00
203 Martin Brodeur AS 5.00 12.00
204 Steven Stamkos AS 5.00 12.00
205 Jonathan Toews AS 5.00 12.00
206 Carey Price AS 8.00 20.00
207 Tim Thomas AS 2.50 6.00
208 Nicklas Lidstrom AS 2.50 6.00
209 Roberto Luongo AS 2.50 6.00
210 Jaromir Jagr AS 6.00 15.00
211 Evgeni Malkin AS 8.00 20.00
212 Teemu Selanne AS 5.00 12.00
213 Mike Gartner AS 2.50 6.00
214 Brett Hull AS 3.00 8.00
215 Jari Kurri AS 2.50 6.00
216 Brendan Shanahan AS 3.00 8.00
217 Joe Sakic AS 4.00 10.00
218 Eric Lindros AS 4.00 10.00
219 Paul Coffey AS 2.50 6.00
220 Patrick Roy AS 6.00 15.00
221 Mark Messier AS 3.00 8.00
222 Mario Lemieux AS 8.00 20.00
223 Gordie Howe AS 5.00 12.00
224 Bobby Orr AS 8.00 20.00
225 Wayne Gretzky AS 12.00 30.00
226 Cody Hodgson RC 8.00 20.00
227 Jake Gardiner RC 5.00 12.00
228 Carl Klingberg RC 3.00 8.00
229 Mika Zibanejad RC 8.00 20.00
230 Mark Scheifele RC 8.00 20.00
231 Aaron Palushaj RC 3.00 8.00
232 Adam Larsson RC 4.00 10.00
233 Matt Read RC 6.00 15.00
234 Matt Frattin RC 3.00 8.00
235 Blake Geoffrion RC 3.00 8.00
236 Devante Smith-Pelly RC 5.00 12.00
237 Erik Gudbranson RC 4.00 10.00

238 Jonathon Blum RC 3.00 8.00
239 Anton Lander RC 3.00 8.00
240 Brandon Saad RC 6.00 15.00
241 Adam Henrique RC 8.00 20.00
242 Brett Connolly RC 3.00 8.00
243 Harri Sateri RC 3.00 8.00
244 Joe Colborne RC 3.00 8.00
245 Marcus Kruger RC 5.00 12.00
246 Greg Nemisz RC 3.00 8.00
247 Ryan Johansen RC 6.00 15.00
248 Sean Couturier RC 6.00 15.00
249 Gabriel Landeskog RC 8.00 20.00
250 Ryan Nugent-Hopkins RC 15.00 30.00

2011-12 Black Diamond Ruby

*1-100 SINGLE: 8X TO 20X BASIC CARDS
*101-150 DOUBLE: 3X TO 8X BASIC DBLE
*151-175 TRIPLE: 2X TO 5X BASIC TRIPLE
*176-200 TRIPLE ROOKIE: 1X TO 2.5X BASE
*201-225 QUAD: .8X TO 2X BASIC QUAD
*226-250 QUAD ROOKIE: .6X TO 1.5X BASE
STATED PRINT RUN 100 SER. #'d SETS
226 Cody Hodgson 30.00 60.00
249 Gabriel Landeskog 25.00 60.00
250 Ryan Nugent-Hopkins 40.00 100.00

2011-12 Black Diamond All-Time Greats Championship Rings

STATED ODDS 1:168
ATG1 Duncan Keith 12.00 30.00
ATG2 Jonathan Toews 12.00 30.00
ATG3 Patrick Kane 15.00 40.00
ATG4 Patrick Sharp 10.00 25.00
ATG5 Henrik Zetterberg 12.00 30.00
ATG6 Johan Franzen 10.00 25.00
ATG7 Nicklas Lidstrom 10.00 25.00
ATG8 Pavel Datsyuk 12.00 30.00
ATG9 Glenn Anderson 10.00 25.00
ATG10 Grant Fuhr 10.00 25.00
ATG11 Jari Kurri 10.00 25.00
ATG12 Mark Messier 10.00 25.00
ATG13 Paul Coffey 10.00 25.00
ATG14 Wayne Gretzky 20.00 50.00
ATG15 Evgeni Malkin 10.00 25.00
ATG16 Jaromir Jagr 25.00 60.00
ATG17 Mario Lemieux 15.00 40.00
ATG18 Sidney Crosby 40.00 100.00

2011-12 Black Diamond Boston Bruins Championship Rings

STATED ODDS 1:126
CRB1 Tim Thomas 25.00 50.00
CRB2 Patrice Bergeron 20.00 50.00
CRB3 Zdeno Chara 15.00 40.00
CRB4 Brad Marchand 20.00 50.00
CRB5 Milan Lucic 15.00 40.00
CRB6 Nathan Horton 8.00 20.00
CRB7 David Krejci 12.00 30.00
CRB8 Michael Ryder 8.00 20.00
CRB9 Chris Kelly 12.00 30.00
CRB10 Dennis Seidenberg 12.00 30.00
CRB11 Mark Recchi 20.00 50.00
CRB12 Rich Peverley 15.00 40.00
CRB13 Tyler Seguin 15.00 40.00
CRB14 Andrew Ference 6.00 15.00
CRB15 Tomas Kaberle 10.00 25.00
CRB16 Johnny Boychuk 10.00 25.00
CRB17 Adam McQuaid 12.00 30.00
CRB18 Daniel Paille 6.00 15.00
CRB19 Gregory Campbell 6.00 15.00
CRB20 Shawn Thornton 10.00 25.00
CRB21 Shane Hnidy 10.00 25.00
CRB22 Steve Kampfer 10.00 25.00
CRB23 Jordan Caron 15.00 40.00
CRB24 Tuukka Rask 20.00 50.00

2011-12 Black Diamond Dual Jerseys

OVERALL JERSEY ODDS 1:12 HOB, 1:48 RET
GROUP A ANNC'D ODDS 1:4,274
GROUP B ANNC'D ODDS 1:647
GROUP C ANNC'D ODDS 1:220
GROUP D ANNC'D ODDS 1:144
GROUP E ANNC'D ODDS 1:43
GROUP F ANNC'D ODDS 1:18
09TCCH Cody Hodgson C 4.00 10.00
09TCDT Dustin Tokarski E 4.00 10.00
09TCJE Jordan Eberle D 8.00 20.00
09TCJT John Tavares B 10.00 25.00
09TCPK P.K. Subban E 8.00 20.00
09TCTM Tyler Myers E 4.00 10.00
BOSNH Nathan Horton F 4.00 10.00
BOSTR Tuukka Rask F 4.00 10.00
BOSTT Tim Thomas F 5.00 12.00
BOSZC Zdeno Chara F 4.00 10.00
CGYJB Jay Bouwmeester F 4.00 10.00
CGYJI Jarome Iginla D 5.00 12.00
CGYMK Miikka Kiprusoff F 4.00 10.00
CGYRB Rene Bourque F 2.50 6.00
DETHZ Henrik Zetterberg F 5.00 12.00
DETJE Jonathan Ericsson F 3.00 8.00
DETJH Jim Howard E 4.00 10.00
DETNK Niklas Kronwall E 3.00 8.00
GR8GP Gilbert Perreault E 4.00 10.00
GR8ML Mario Lemieux C 12.00 30.00
GR8MM Mark Messier C 5.00 12.00
GR8WG Wayne Gretzky A 40.00 80.00
MTLAK Andrei Kostitsyn F 3.00 8.00
MTLAM Andrei Markov F 4.00 10.00
MTLCP Carey Price A 20.00 50.00
MTLPK P.K. Subban B 8.00 20.00
PHICG Claude Giroux F 4.00 10.00
PHICP Chris Pronger E 3.00 8.00
PHIJV James van Riemsdyk E 4.00 10.00
PHISH Scott Hartnell F 4.00 10.00
TORJG Jonas Gustavsson F 4.00 10.00
TORNK Nikolai Kulemin F 4.00 10.00
TORPK Phil Kessel E 5.00 12.00
TORTB Tyler Bozak F 4.00 10.00
VANAE Alexander Edler E 2.50 6.00
VANDS Daniel Sedin D 4.00 10.00
VANRK Ryan Kesler F 4.00 10.00
VANRL Roberto Luongo F 4.00 10.00
PITTJS Jordan Staal F 4.00 10.00
PITTKL Kristopher Letang D 5.00 12.00
PITTMF Marc-Andre Fleury E 6.00 15.00
PITTSC Sidney Crosby D 15.00 40.00
WASHAS Alexander Semin C 4.00 10.00
WASHMG Mike Green F 4.00 10.00
WASHNB Nicklas Backstrom C 6.00 15.00
WASHOV Alexander Ovechkin C 15.00 40.00
GOALIEMB Martin Brodeur E 6.00 15.00
GOALIEPR Patrick Roy E 6.00 15.00
GOALIERB Richard Brodeur F 4.00 10.00
GOALIETE Tony Esposito B 8.00 20.00

2011-12 Black Diamond Gemography

OVERALL ODDS 1:60 HOB, 1:1200 RET
GROUP A ANNC'D ODDS 1:14,246
GROUP B ANNC'D ODDS 1:1006
GROUP C ANNC'D ODDS 1:570
GROUP D ANNC'D ODDS 1:68
GEMAB Andy Bathgate B 50.00 100.00
GEMAH Ales Hemsky C 8.00 20.00
GEMAK Arturs Kulda D 4.00 10.00
GEMAO Alexander Ovechkin B 30.00 80.00
GEMBA Josh Bailey C 5.00 12.00
GEMBE Patrice Bergeron B 20.00 40.00
GEMBH Brett Hull B 30.00 60.00
GEMBL Brian Lee D 5.00 12.00
GEMBM Brett MacLean D 4.00 10.00
GEMBO Bobby Orr A 125.00 200.00
GEMBS Brayden Schenn C 8.00 20.00
GEMCA Cody Almond D 4.00 10.00
GEMCH Cody Hodgson B 40.00 80.00
GEMCN Cam Neely B 20.00 40.00
GEMCO Cal O'Reilly D 4.00 10.00
GEMCS Cory Schneider C 6.00 15.00
GEMDB Drayson Bowman D 4.00 10.00
GEMDC Daniel Carcillo C 8.00 20.00
GEMGH Gordie Howe B 60.00 120.00
GEMGL Guillaume Latendresse B 8.00 20.00
GEMJA Jamie Arniel D 5.00 12.00
GEMJB Jonathon Blum C 5.00 12.00
GEMJC John Carlson D 8.00 20.00
GEMJD Jason Demers D 4.00 10.00
GEMJE Jordan Eberle C 20.00 50.00
GEMJM Jacob Markstrom D 6.00 15.00
GEMJN John Negrin D 5.00 12.00
GEMKA Keith Aulie D 6.00 15.00
GEMKD Kaspars Daugavins D 5.00 12.00
GEMKT Kyle Turris C 4.00 10.00
GEMLC Luca Caputi D 4.00 10.00
GEMLO Logan Couture B 12.00 30.00
GEMMA Rick MacLeish B 30.00 60.00
GEMMH Matthew Halischuk D 4.00 10.00
GEMMM Mark Messier A 50.00 120.00
GEMMN Markus Naslund B 25.00 50.00
GEMMO Mark Olver D 4.00 10.00
GEMMS Marco Scandella D 4.00 10.00
GEMMZ Mats Zuccarello-Aasen D 6.00 15.00
GEMNP Nick Palmieri D 5.00 12.00
GEMOB Oskars Bartulis D 5.00 12.00
GEMPB Patrik Berglund D 5.00 12.00
GEMPC Patrice Cormier D 4.00 10.00
GEMPK Patrick Kane B 25.00 60.00
GEMPL Philip Larsen D 4.00 10.00
GEMPM Peter Mueller B 8.00 20.00
GEMRB Richard Bachman D 5.00 12.00
GEMRM Ryan McDonagh D 5.00 12.00
GEMSC Sidney Crosby B 75.00 150.00
GEMSH Steve Shutt A 50.00 100.00
GEMSS Steven Stamkos B 50.00 100.00
GEMST Chris Stewart C 5.00 12.00
GEMTE Tyler Ennis C 8.00 20.00
GEMTL Trevor Lewis D 5.00 12.00
GEMTM Thomas McCollum D 5.00 12.00
GEMTT Tomas Tatar D 6.00 15.00
GEMVH Victor Hedman B 12.00 30.00
GEMWG Wayne Gretzky B 150.00 250.00

2011-12 Black Diamond Hardware Heroes

STATED PRINT RUN 100
SOME PLAYERS HAVE MULT. CARDS WITH SAME VALUE
HHBH Brett Hull 10.00 25.00
HHBO Bobby Orr 30.00 60.00
HHBP Bernie Parent 10.00 25.00
HHCP Corey Perry 10.00 25.00
HHCS Cory Schneider 8.00 20.00
HHDS Daniel Sedin 10.00 25.00
HHDW Doug Weight 8.00 20.00
HHEL Eric Lindros 15.00 40.00
HHHM Howie Morenz 12.00 30.00
HHIL Ian Laperriere 6.00 15.00
HHJA Jaromir Jagr 12.00 30.00
HHJG Jaromir Jagr 12.00 30.00
HHJJ Jaromir Jagr 12.00 30.00
HHJS Jeff Skinner 10.00 25.00
HHML Mario Lemieux 15.00 40.00
HHMS Martin St. Louis 10.00 25.00
HHNL Nicklas Lidstrom 10.00 25.00
HHPE Corey Perry 10.00 25.00
HHRK Ryan Kesler 10.00 25.00
HHSC Milt Schmidt 8.00 20.00
HHSE Daniel Sedin 8.00 20.00
HHTH Tim Thomas 12.00 30.00
HHTT Tim Thomas 12.00 30.00
HHWG Wayne Gretzky 50.00 100.00

2011-12 Black Diamond Lustrous Rookies

STATED ODDS 1:288 HOBBY
LR1 Devante Smith-Pelly 12.00 30.00
LR2 Greg Nemisz 8.00 20.00
LR3 Brandon Saad 15.00 40.00
LR4 Marcus Kruger 10.00 25.00
LR5 Gabriel Landeskog 25.00 60.00
LR6 Ryan Johansen 15.00 40.00
LR7 Anton Lander 8.00 20.00
LR8 Ryan Nugent-Hopkins 75.00 150.00
LR9 Erik Gudbranson 10.00 25.00
LR10 Adam Larsson 10.00 25.00
LR11 Adam Henrique 20.00 50.00
LR12 Mika Zibanejad 20.00 50.00
LR13 Sean Couturier 12.00 30.00
LR14 Brett Connolly 8.00 20.00
LR15 Jake Gardiner 10.00 25.00
LR16 Joe Colborne 8.00 20.00
LR17 Cody Hodgson 12.00 30.00
LR18 Mark Scheifele 20.00 50.00

2012-13 Black Diamond

COMP.SET w/o SP's (100) 10.00 25.00
101-150 DOUBLE DIAMOND ODDS 1:4
151-200 TRIPLE DIAMOND ODDS 1:8
201-250 QUAD DIAMOND ODDS 1:24
1 Sidney Crosby .75 2.00
2 Jonathan Ericsson .20 .50
3 Patrik Berglund .15 .40
4 Tyler Seguin .40 1.00
5 Scott Hartnell .25 .60
6 Tomas Fleischmann .15 .40
7 Ilya Bryzgalov .25 .60
8 Daniel Sedin .25 .60
9 Darren Helm .20 .50
10 Alexander Ovechkin 1.00 2.50
11 Nicklas Backstrom .40 1.00
12 Eric Staal .30 .75
13 Evgeni Nabokov .20 .50
14 David Perron .15 .40
15 Jeff Carter .25 .60
16 James van Riemsdyk .25 .60
17 Bobby Ryan .25 .60
18 Thomas Vanek .25 .60
19 Scott Niedermayer .25 .60
20 Jonathan Quick .40 1.00
21 Joe Thornton .25 .60
22 Henrik Sedin .25 .60
23 Dustin Byfuglien .25 .60
24 Jonas Hiller .20 .50
25 Jason Pominville .20 .50
26 Corey Crawford .30 .75
27 Jason Spezza .25 .60
28 Nathan Horton .25 .60
29 Taylor Hall .50 1.25
30 Jonathan Toews .50 1.25
31 Alexandre Burrows .25 .60
32 Joe Pavelski .25 .60
33 Jay Bouwmeester .25 .60
34 Ryan Suter .15 .40
35 Phil Esposito .40 1.00
36 Mikkel Boedker .15 .40
37 Phil Kessel .30 .75
38 P.A. Parenteau .15 .40
39 Jacob Markstrom .25 .60
40 Jeff Skinner .25 .60
41 Dany Heatley .20 .50
42 Kristopher Letang .25 .60
43 Daniel Briere .25 .60
44 Ondrej Pavelec .25 .60
45 Andrew Ladd .25 .60
46 Derek Stepan .25 .60
47 Tomas Plekanec .25 .60
48 Valtteri Filppula .25 .60
49 Erik Johnson .15 .40
50 Steven Stamkos .50 1.25
51 Steve Ott .20 .50
52 James Neal .25 .60
53 Cody Hodgson .25 .60
54 Tyler Ennis .20 .50
55 Olli Jokinen .20 .50
56 Matt Stajan .20 .50
57 Kari Lehtonen .20 .50
58 Derek Roy .20 .50
59 Steve Mason .20 .50
60 Patrick Roy .60 1.50
61 Mike Ribeiro .20 .50
62 Sam Gagner .20 .50
63 Jack Johnson .15 .40
64 Patric Hornqvist .20 .50
65 Kyle Okposo .25 .60
66 Marc Staal .20 .50
67 Brian Elliott .20 .50
68 Mike Green .15 .40
69 Vincent Lecavalier .20 .50
70 Mario Lemieux .75 2.00
71 Mike Smith .25 .60
72 Milan Michalek .15 .40
73 Matt Moulson .20 .50
74 Lars Eller .20 .50
75 Stephen Weiss .20 .50
76 Ales Hemsky .20 .50
77 Semyon Varlamov .25 .60
78 Jordan Staal .25 .60
79 Tyler Myers .20 .50
80 Joe Sakic .40 1.00
81 Zdeno Chara .25 .60
82 Alex Tanguay .15 .40
83 Patrick Sharp .25 .60
84 Loui Eriksson .20 .50
85 Ryan Smyth .20 .50
86 Zach Parise .25 .60
87 Travis Zajac .20 .50
88 Michael Grabner .20 .50
89 Evander Kane .25 .60
90 Bobby Orr .75 2.00
91 Logan Couture .25 .60
92 Chris Kunitz .25 .60
93 Craig Anderson .25 .60
94 Niklas Backstrom .20 .50
95 Dustin Brown .25 .60
96 Patrik Elias .25 .60
97 Cam Ward .25 .60
98 Nathan Gerbe .15 .40
99 Ryan Getzlaf .40 1.00
100 Wayne Gretzky 1.25 3.00
101 Tuukka Rask .60 1.50
102 Johnny Bucyk .50 1.25
103 Shea Weber .50 1.25
104 Saku Koivu .60 1.50
105 Ryan Miller .60 1.50
106 Ryan Callahan .60 1.50
107 Roberto Luongo .60 1.50
108 Rick Nash .60 1.50
109 Pekka Rinne .75 2.00
110 Paul Coffey .60 1.50
111 Patrick Marleau .60 1.50
112 Patrick Kane 1.25 3.00
113 Patrice Bergeron .75 2.00
114 P.K. Subban 1.00 2.50
115 Niklas Backstrom .50 1.25
116 Milan Lucic .60 1.50
117 Mikko Koivu .50 1.25
118 Mike Richards .60 1.50
119 Braden Holtby 1.00 2.50
120 Matt Duchene .60 1.50
121 Jordan Eberle .60 1.50
122 Marian Hossa .50 1.25
123 Marian Gaborik .60 1.50
124 Marcel Dionne .75 2.00
125 Marc-Andre Fleury 1.00 2.50
126 Luc Robitaille .60 1.50
127 Johan Franzen .60 1.50
128 Jim Howard .60 1.50
129 Jaroslav Halak .60 1.50
130 Jaromir Jagr 1.50 4.00
131 Joe Mullen .50 1.25
132 Jari Kurri .60 1.50
133 Jamie Benn .75 2.00
134 Jacob Markstrom .60 1.50
135 Henrik Zetterberg .75 2.00
136 Ryan Nugent-Hopkins .60 1.50
137 Gilbert Perreault .60 1.50
138 Paul Stastny .60 1.50
139 Erik Karlsson 1.25 3.00
140 Duncan Keith .60 1.50
141 Drew Doughty .60 1.50
142 Dion Phaneuf .60 1.50
143 David Clarkson .40 1.00
144 Daniel Alfredsson .60 1.50
145 Ron Hextall .60 1.50
146 Brendan Smith .50 1.25
147 Brayden Schenn .60 1.50
148 Bill Ranford .60 1.50
149 Anze Kopitar 1.00 2.50
150 Adam Henrique .60 1.50
151 Bobby Hull 1.00 2.50
152 Brad Park .75 2.00
153 Brendan Shanahan 1.25 3.00
154 Dino Ciccarelli 1.00 2.50
155 Dominik Hasek 1.25 3.00
156 Doug Gilmour 1.25 3.00
157 Gabriel Landeskog 1.00 2.50
158 Guy Lafleur 1.25 3.00
159 Jean Beliveau 1.00 2.50
160 Howie Morenz .75 2.00
161 Brian Leetch 1.00 2.50
162 Miikka Kiprusoff .75 2.00
163 Mike Gartner 1.00 2.50
164 John Tavares 2.00 5.00
165 Mike Modano 1.50 4.00
166 Neal Broten .75 2.00
167 Pelle Lindbergh 2.00 5.00
168 Mark Messier 1.25 3.00
169 Antti Niemi .75 2.00
170 Ron Francis 1.25 3.00
171 Claude Giroux 1.00 2.50
172 Martin St. Louis 1.00 2.50
173 Stan Mikita 1.25 3.00
174 Ted Lindsay 1.00 2.50
175 Tony Esposito 1.00 2.50
176 Mat Clark RC 1.50 4.00
177 Carter Camper RC 1.25 3.00
178 Lane MacDermid RC 1.50 4.00
179 Torey Krug RC 3.00 8.00
180 Michael Hutchinson RC 3.00 8.00
181 Travis Turnbull RC 1.50 4.00
182 Jeremy Welsh RC 1.50 4.00
183 Brandon Bollig RC 1.50 4.00
184 Mike Connolly RC 1.50 4.00
185 Dalton Prout RC 1.50 4.00
186 Andrew Joudrey RC 1.50 4.00
187 Shawn Hunwick RC 2.50 6.00
188 Ryan Garbutt RC 1.50 4.00
189 Mark Messier RG 1.25 3.00
190 Philippe Cornet RC 1.50 4.00
191 Colby Robak RC 1.50 4.00
192 Kristopher Foucault RC 1.50 4.00
193 Chay Genoway RC 1.50 4.00
194 Robert Mayer RC 2.00 5.00
195 Aaron Ness RC 1.50 4.00
196 Matt Donovan RC 1.50 4.00
197 Brandon Manning RC 1.50 4.00
198 Michael Stone RC 1.50 4.00
199 Matt Watkins RC 1.50 4.00
200 Tyson Sexsmith RC 1.50 4.00
201 Alexander Ovechkin AS 8.00 20.00
202 Bobby Clarke AS 2.50 6.00
203 Bobby Orr AS 8.00 20.00
204 Brett Hull AS 2.50 6.00
205 Carey Price AS 8.00 20.00
206 Curtis Joseph AS 2.50 6.00
207 Ed Belfour AS 2.50 6.00
208 Eric Lindros AS 4.00 10.00
209 Evgeni Malkin AS 8.00 20.00
210 Henrik Lundqvist AS 3.00 8.00
211 Ilya Kovalchuk AS 2.50 6.00
212 Jarome Iginla AS 2.50 6.00
213 Jeff Skinner AS 4.00 10.00
214 Joe Sakic AS 4.00 10.00
215 Jonathan Quick AS 4.00 10.00
216 Jonathan Toews AS 5.00 12.00
217 Mario Lemieux AS 8.00 20.00
218 Martin Brodeur AS 5.00 12.00
219 Nicklas Lidstrom AS 2.50 6.00
220 Patrick Roy AS 6.00 15.00
221 Pavel Datsyuk AS 3.00 8.00
222 Sidney Crosby AS 8.00 20.00
223 Steven Stamkos AS 5.00 12.00
224 Teemu Selanne AS 5.00 12.00
225 Wayne Gretzky AS 8.00 20.00
226 Maxime Sauve RC 3.00 8.00
227 Sven Baertschi RC 4.00 10.00
228 Akim Aliu RC 3.00 8.00
229 Tyson Barrie RC 6.00 15.00
230 Cody Goloubef RC 3.00 8.00
231 Brenden Dillon RC 3.00 8.00
232 Reilly Smith RC 6.00 15.00
233 Scott Glennie RC 3.00 8.00
234 Riley Sheahan RC 3.00 8.00
235 Wayne Gretzky RG 12.00 30.00
236 Jordan Nolan RC 3.00 8.00
237 Jason Zucker RC 4.00 10.00
238 Tyler Cuma RC 3.00 8.00
239 Gabriel Dumont RC 3.00 8.00
240 Chet Pickard RC 3.00 8.00
241 Casey Cizikas RC 3.00 8.00
242 Chris Kreider RC 12.00 30.00
243 Mark Stone RC 6.00 15.00
244 Jakob Silfverberg RC 8.00 20.00
245 Jake Allen RC 10.00 25.00
246 Jaden Schwartz RC 6.00 15.00
247 J.T. Brown RC 3.00 8.00
248 Ryan Hamilton RC 3.00 8.00
249 Carter Ashton RC 2.50 6.00
250 Jussi Rynnas RC 3.00 8.00

2012-13 Black Diamond Ruby

*1-100 SINGLE: 6X TO 15X BASIC CARDS
*101-150 DOUBLE: 3X TO 8X BASIC DBLE
*151-175 TRIPLE: 2X TO 5X BASIC TRIPLE
*176-200 TRIPLE ROOKIE: 1X TO 2.5X
*201-225 QUAD: .8X TO 2X BASIC QUAD
*226-250 QUAD ROOKIE: .6X TO 1.5X
STATED PRINT RUN 100
242 Chris Kreider 15.00 40.00
246 Jaden Schwartz 10.00 25.00

2012-13 Black Diamond All-Time Greats Championship Rings

STATED ODDS 1:126
ATG1 Jean Beliveau 15.00 40.00
ATG2 Guy Lafleur 12.00 30.00
ATG3 Howie Morenz 15.00 40.00
ATG4 Patrick Roy 25.00 60.00
ATG5 Brendan Shanahan 20.00 50.00
ATG6 Brett Hull 15.00 40.00
ATG7 Nicklas Lidstrom 15.00 40.00
ATG8 Luc Robitaille 15.00 40.00
ATG9 Mike Bossy 12.00 30.00
ATG10 Clark Gillies 15.00 40.00
ATG11 Bryan Trottier 20.00 50.00
ATG12 Denis Potvin 15.00 40.00
ATG13 Patrick Roy 15.00 40.00
ATG14 Joe Sakic 15.00 40.00
ATG15 Ray Bourque 15.00 40.00
ATG16 Chris Drury 12.00 30.00
ATG17 Milan Hejduk 12.00 30.00
ATG18 Alex Tanguay 10.00 25.00
CRB1 Drew Doughty 15.00 40.00
CRB2 Jonathan Quick 12.00 30.00
CRB3 Anze Kopitar 12.00 30.00
CRB4 Jeff Carter 10.00 25.00
CRB5 Mike Richards 10.00 25.00
CRB6 Simon Gagne 15.00 40.00
CRB7 Rob Scuderi 10.00 25.00
CRB8 Matt Greene 10.00 25.00
CRB9 Dwight King 10.00 25.00
CRB10 Jordan Nolan 12.00 30.00
CRB11 Viatcheslav Voynov 15.00 40.00
CRB12 Justin Williams 15.00 40.00
CRB13 Dustin Brown 12.00 30.00
CRB14 Jarret Stoll 12.00 30.00
CRB15 Dustin Penner 10.00 25.00
CRB16 Trevor Lewis 15.00 40.00
CRB17 Jonathan Bernier 15.00 40.00
CRB18 Brad Richardson 12.00 30.00
CRB19 Kyle Clifford 10.00 25.00
CRB20 Colin Fraser 10.00 25.00
CRB21 Willie Mitchell 12.00 30.00
CRB22 Alec Martinez 10.00 25.00
CRB23 Andrei Loktionov 12.00 30.00
CRB24 Luc Robitaille 15.00 40.00

2012-13 Black Diamond Dual Jerseys

OVERALL JSY ODDS 1:12 H,1:48 R, 1:48 B
GROUP A ANNC'D ODDS 1:5,080
GROUP B ANNC'D ODDS 1:874
GROUP C ANNC'D ODDS 1:121
GROUP D ANNC'D ODDS 1:69
GROUP E ANNC'D ODDS 1:39
GROUP F ANNC'D ODDS 1:30
84BH Brett Hull C 10.00 25.00
84LR Luc Robitaille B 25.00 50.00
84ML Mario Lemieux B 30.00 60.00
84PR Patrick Roy B 25.00 50.00
ANABR Bobby Ryan F 4.00 10.00
ANACP Corey Perry D 4.00 10.00
ANAJH Jonas Hiller E 3.00 8.00
ANARG Ryan Getzlaf F 6.00 15.00
BEESBP Brad Park C 5.00 12.00
BEESCN Cam Neely F 4.00 10.00
BEESPE Phil Esposito C 15.00 30.00
BEESRB Ray Bourque D 6.00 15.00
BOSBM Brad Marchand F 5.00 12.00
BOSML Milan Lucic C 4.00 10.00
BOSPB Patrice Bergeron D 8.00 20.00
BOSTR Tuukka Rask F 4.00 10.00
BOSTS Tyler Seguin D 6.00 15.00
BOSZC Zdeno Chara D 4.00 10.00
BUFFCH Cody Hodgson E 4.00 10.00
BUFFDS Drew Stafford F 4.00 10.00
BUFFRM Ryan Miller F 4.00 10.00
BUFFTM Tyler Myers D 3.00 8.00
CBJDB Derick Brassard F 4.00 10.00
CBJJJ Jack Johnson B 5.00 12.00
CBJRJ Ryan Johansen F 5.00 12.00
CBJSM Steve Mason E 3.00 8.00
DALLJB Jamie Benn A
DALLKL Kari Lehtonen C 8.00 20.00
DALLLE Loui Eriksson F 3.00 8.00
DALLMR Michael Ryder C 6.00 15.00
DETHZ Henrik Zetterberg C 5.00 12.00
DETJF Johan Franzen D 4.00 10.00
DETJH Jim Howard D 4.00 10.00
DETNK Niklas Kronwall C 4.00 10.00
DETNL Nicklas Lidstrom E 4.00 10.00
DETPV Pavel Datsyuk C 6.00 15.00
EDMJE Jordan Eberle C 8.00 20.00
EDMLO Linus Omark C 3.00 8.00
EDMMP Magnus Paajarvi D 6.00 15.00
EDMRN Ryan Nugent-Hopkins C 10.00 25.00
EDMTH Taylor Hall D 8.00 20.00
EDMWG Wayne Gretzky A 75.00 125.00
GOALIEMB Martin Brodeur C 8.00 20.00
GOALIEPR Pekka Rinne D 5.00 12.00
GOALIERL Roberto Luongo B 5.00 12.00
LAKAK Anze Kopitar F 6.00 15.00
LAKDB Dustin Brown F 5.00 12.00
LAKJQ Jonathan Quick D 6.00 15.00
LAKJW Justin Williams F 3.00 8.00
NYRBB Brian Boyle D 3.00 8.00
NYRCK Chris Kreider C 5.00 12.00
NYRHL Henrik Lundqvist C 8.00 20.00
NYRMG Marian Gaborik C 5.00 12.00
NYRMS Marc Staal D 4.00 10.00
NYRRC Ryan Callahan E 4.00 10.00
PHICG Claude Giroux E 4.00 10.00
PHICP Chris Pronger E 3.00 8.00
PHIIB Ilya Bryzgalov D 4.00 10.00
PHISH Scott Hartnell D 4.00 10.00
PITTEM Evgeni Malkin E 8.00 20.00
PITTJN James Neal A
PITTKL Kristopher Letang C 12.00 30.00
PITTMF Marc-Andre Fleury D 6.00 15.00
PITTML Mario Lemieux B 12.00 30.00
PITTSC Sidney Crosby E 15.00 40.00
STARAO Alexander Ovechkin C 15.00 40.00
STARIK Ilya Kovalchuk C 4.00 10.00
STARJI Jarome Iginla B 5.00 12.00
STARJT Jonathan Toews C 8.00 20.00
STARSC Sidney Crosby D 10.00 25.00
STARSS Steven Stamkos D 6.00 15.00
STLCS Chris Stewart F 3.00 8.00
STLDB David Backes F 4.00 10.00
STLJH Jaroslav Halak E 4.00 10.00
STLPB Patrik Berglund D 2.50 6.00
TC1BC Brett Connolly TC E 6.00 15.00
TC1BS Brayden Schenn TC E 8.00 20.00
TC1CA Carter Ashton TC E 6.00 15.00
TC1CC Casey Cizikas TC E 4.00 10.00
TC1CE Cody Eakin TC E 6.00 15.00
TC1DO Dylan Olsen TC E 5.00 12.00
TC2EG Erik Gudbranson TC E 4.00 10.00
TC2JS Jaden Schwartz TC E 6.00 15.00
TC2LL Louis Leblanc TC C 8.00 20.00
TC2RE Ryan Ellis TC E 6.00 15.00
TC2SD Simon Despres TC E 6.00 15.00
TC2TB Tyson Barrie TC E 8.00 20.00
TORCO Colton Orr D 4.00 10.00
TORDP Dion Phaneuf A 12.50 25.00
TORNK Nikolai Kulemin E 3.00 8.00
TORPK Phil Kessel C 10.00 25.00
TOUGHCO Colton Orr E 4.00 10.00
TOUGHDC Daniel Carcillo F 4.00 10.00
TOUGHGP George Parros F 3.00 8.00
TOUGHMC Matt Carkner D 3.00 8.00
VANAB Alexandre Burrows C 4.00 10.00
VANDS Daniel Sedin C 4.00 10.00
VANRK Ryan Kesler C 8.00 20.00
VANRL Roberto Luongo D 4.00 10.00
GOALIERM Ryan Miller E 4.00 10.00

2012-13 Black Diamond Gemography

OVERALL ODDS 1:60 H, 1:1200 R, 1:200 B
GROUP A ANNC'D ODDS 1:3,818
GROUP B ANNC'D ODDS 1:1,374
GROUP C ANNC'D ODDS 1:599
GROUP D ANNC'D ODDS 1:99
GEMAO Alexander Ovechkin A
GEMBM Brendan Mikkelson D 4.00 10.00
GEMBO Bobby Orr A 60.00 120.00
GEMBT Bryan Trottier A 40.00 80.00
GEMCA Carter Ashton D 4.00 10.00
GEMCE Cody Eakin D 5.00 12.00
GEMCF Cam Fowler D 5.00 12.00
GEMCJ Curtis Joseph B 25.00 60.00
GEMCK Chris Kunitz B 10.00 20.00
GEMCP Chet Pickard C 5.00 12.00
GEMCZ Casey Cizikas C 5.00 12.00
GEMDB Drayson Bowman D 4.00 10.00
GEMDG Daniel Girardi D 4.00 10.00
GEMDP David Perron B
GEMEN Evgeni Nabokov D 6.00 15.00
GEMGL Gabriel Landeskog A
GEMJB Jamie Benn B 12.00 30.00
GEMJE Jordan Eberle B 10.00 25.00
GEMJK Jake Allen C 15.00 40.00
GEMJM John Moore D 4.00 10.00
GEMKR Chris Kreider B 15.00 40.00
GEMLA Maxim Lapierre D 4.00 10.00
GEMMN Michal Neuvirth D 5.00 12.00
GEMMS Matt Stajan B 8.00 20.00
GEMNG Nicklas Grossman D 5.00 12.00
GEMRN Ryan Nugent-Hopkins A 75.00 135.00
GEMRY Jussi Rynnas C 10.00 25.00
GEMSC Sidney Crosby A 90.00 150.00
GEMSG Scott Glennie B
GEMSH Jaden Schwartz C 10.00 25.00
GEMSS Steven Stamkos A
GEMSV Sven Baertschi B 10.00 25.00
GEMSW Stephen Weiss C 5.00 12.00
GEMTA John Tavares A 25.00 50.00
GEMTS Tim Stapleton D 4.00 10.00
GEMTW Tom Wandell D 4.00 10.00
GEMVF Valtteri Filppula D 6.00 15.00
GEMWG Wayne Gretzky A
GEMZK Zack Kassian B 8.00 20.00

2012-13 Black Diamond Hardware Heroes

STATED PRINT RUN 100
HHBC Brian Campbell 6.00 15.00
HHBE Brian Elliott 8.00 20.00
HHBH Bobby Hull 10.00 25.00
HHBT Bryan Trottier 10.00 25.00
HHDA Daniel Alfredsson 10.00 25.00
HHDP Denis Potvin 10.00 25.00
HHEK Erik Karlsson 20.00 50.00
HHEM Evgeni Malkin Ross 10.00 25.00
HHEV Evgeni Malkin Lindsay 10.00 25.00
HHGL Gabriel Landeskog 12.00 30.00
HHHL Henrik Lundqvist 12.00 30.00
HHJQ Jonathan Quick 15.00 40.00
HHMA Evgeni Malkin 30.00 80.00
HHMB Mike Bossy 10.00 25.00
HHMP Max Pacioretty 10.00 25.00
HHPB Patrice Bergeron 12.00 30.00
HHSS Steven Stamkos 12.00 30.00
HHWG Wayne Gretzky 25.00 60.00

2012-13 Black Diamond Lustrous

GREATS ODDS 1:1728 HOBBY
STARS ODDS 1:864 HOBBY
ROOKIES ODDS 1:288 HOBBY
LGBO Bobby Orr G 75.00 150.00
LGML Mario Lemieux G 40.00 80.00
LGPR Patrick Roy G 50.00 100.00
LGWG Wayne Gretzky G 100.00 150.00
LRCA Carter Ashton R 4.00 10.00
LRCC Casey Cizikas R 5.00 12.00
LRCG Cody Goloubef R 5.00 12.00
LRCK Chris Kreider R 15.00 40.00
LRJA Jake Allen R 15.00 40.00
LRJR Jussi Rynnas R 6.00 15.00
LRJS Jakob Silfverberg R 6.00 15.00
LRJZ Jason Zucker R 6.00 15.00
LRSB Sven Baertschi R 6.00 15.00
LRSC Jaden Schwartz R 8.00 20.00
LRSG Scott Glennie R 5.00 12.00
LRTB Tyson Barrie R 10.00 25.00
LSAO Alexander Ovechkin S 40.00 80.00
LSCP Carey Price S 20.00 50.00
LSJE Jordan Eberle S 10.00 25.00
LSJS Jeff Skinner S 10.00 25.00
LSJT Jonathan Toews S 20.00 50.00
LSSC Sidney Crosby S 25.00 60.00
LSSS Steven Stamkos S 10.00 25.00
LSTH Taylor Hall S 6.00 15.00

2013-14 Black Diamond

COMP.SET w/o SP's (100) 10.00 25.00
101-150 DOUBLE ODDS 1:3 HOB, 1:4 BLST
151-200 TRIPLE ODDS 1:6 HOB, 1:8 BLST
201-250 QUAD ODDS 1:13 HOB, 1:24 BLST
1 Brad Richards .25 .60
2 Alex Tanguay .15 .40
3 Derek Roy .20 .50
4 Max Pacioretty .25 .60
5 Sergei Kostitsyn .15 .40
6 Ray Whitney .20 .50
7 Paul Stastny .25 .60
8 Cory Schneider .20 .50
9 Nicklas Backstrom .40 1.00
10 Slava Voynov .20 .50
11 Jack Johnson .15 .40
12 Jonathan Bernier .25 .60
13 Devin Setoguchi .20 .50
14 David Krejci .25 .60
15 Jim Howard .25 .60
16 Martin Hanzal .15 .40
17 Mikael Backlund .20 .50
18 Dustin Jeffrey .15 .40
19 Alexander Semin .25 .60
20 David Backes .25 .60
21 Kyle Turris .15 .40
22 Sam Gagner .20 .50
23 Teddy Purcell .25 .60
24 Michael Ryder .15 .40
25 Bobby Ryan .25 .60
26 Andrew Ladd .25 .60
27 Raffi Torres .15 .40
28 Logan Couture .25 .60
29 David Clarkson .15 .40
30 Shea Weber .20 .50
31 Nathan Horton .25 .60
32 Steve Ott .20 .50
33 Joe Pavelski .25 .60
34 Ryan Suter .15 .40
35 Zdeno Chara .25 .60
36 Wayne Simmonds .30 .75
37 Ryan O'Reilly .25 .60
38 Jakob Silfverberg .20 .50
39 Jakub Voracek .25 .60
40 Alexandre Burrows .25 .60
41 Frazer McLaren .15 .40
42 Dan Boyle .20 .50
43 Kris Versteeg .20 .50
44 Evgeni Nabokov .20 .50
45 Henrik Sedin .25 .60
46 Patrick Marleau .25 .60
47 Jeff Skinner .20 .50
48 Michael Grabner .20 .50
49 Johan Franzen .25 .60
50 Andrew Shaw .25 .60
51 Ryan Johansen .30 .75
52 Lars Eller .20 .50
53 Tyler Ennis .20 .50
54 Niklas Kronwall .20 .50
55 Ales Hemsky .15 .40
56 Brent Seabrook .25 .60
57 Mike Ribeiro .20 .50
58 Tomas Vokoun .20 .50
59 Adam Henrique .25 .60
60 Justin Williams .20 .50
61 Justin Faulk .15 .40
62 Jiri Tlusty .20 .50
63 Mike Fisher .20 .50
64 Shawn Horcoff .15 .40
65 Chris Kunitz .25 .60
66 Kari Lehtonen .20 .50
67 Simon Despres .20 .50
68 Marian Hossa .20 .50
69 Cody Hodgson .25 .60
70 Brandon Saad .25 .60
71 Derek Stepan .25 .60
72 P.A. Parenteau .15 .40
73 Sergei Bobrovsky .25 .60
74 Lee Stempniak .15 .40
75 David Legwand .20 .50
76 Oliver Ekman-Larsson .20 .50
77 Jake Muzzin .15 .40
78 Eric Staal .30 .75
79 Alex Pietrangelo .20 .50
80 Evander Kane .25 .60
81 Jonas Hiller .20 .50
82 Tyler Bozak .20 .50
83 Saku Koivu .25 .60
84 Matt Duchene .25 .60
85 Jacob Markstrom .20 .50
86 Martin St. Louis .25 .60
87 Ray Emery .20 .50
88 Matt Moulson .20 .50
89 Craig Anderson .25 .60
90 Pascal Dupuis .15 .40
91 Jason Pominville .20 .50
92 Joe Thornton .25 .60
93 Ondrej Pavelec .25 .60
94 Chris Stewart .20 .50
95 Jamie Benn .30 .75
96 Brian Elliott .20 .50
97 Blake Wheeler .25 .60
98 James van Riemsdyk .25 .60
99 Patrik Elias .25 .60
100 Tomas Fleischmann .15 .40
101 Daniel Sedin .60 1.50
102 Andy Moog .60 1.50
103 Antti Niemi .50 1.25
104 Anze Kopitar 1.00 2.50
105 Bill Ranford .60 1.50
106 Brad Marchand .75 2.00
107 Braden Holtby 1.00 2.50
108 Brayden Schenn .60 1.50
109 Cam Neely .60 1.50
110 Roberto Luongo .60 1.50
111 Daniel Alfredsson .60 1.50
112 Dave Schultz .60 1.50
113 Dion Phaneuf .60 1.50
114 Corey Crawford .75 2.00
115 Erik Karlsson 1.25 3.00
116 Gabriel Landeskog .75 2.00
117 Grant Fuhr .60 1.50
118 Steve Mason .50 1.25
119 James Neal .60 1.50
120 Jari Kurri .60 1.50
121 Jarome Iginla .60 1.50
122 Jaroslav Halak .60 1.50
123 Jason Spezza .60 1.50
124 Jeff Carter .60 1.50
125 Jordan Staal .60 1.50
126 Kris Letang .60 1.50
127 Larry Robinson .60 1.50
128 Luc Robitaille .60 1.50
129 Marc-Andre Fleury 1.00 2.50
130 Marian Gaborik .60 1.50
131 Markus Naslund .50 1.25
132 Mike Richards .60 1.50
133 Milan Hejduk .50 1.25
134 Dany Heatley .50 1.25
135 Pekka Rinne .75 2.00
136 Peter Stastny .50 1.25
137 Phil Kessel .75 2.00
138 Ron Hextall .60 1.50
139 Terry O'Reilly .50 1.25
140 Ryan Getzlaf 1.00 2.50
141 Ryan Kesler .60 1.50
142 Ryan Smyth .50 1.25
143 Corey Perry .60 1.50
144 Scott Hartnell .60 1.50
145 Thomas Vanek .60 1.50
146 Tony Esposito .60 1.50
147 Tuukka Rask .60 1.50
148 Vincent Damphousse .50 1.25
149 Vincent Lecavalier .50 1.25
150 Wendel Clark .60 1.50
151 Bobby Hull 1.00 2.50
152 Gilbert Perreault 1.00 2.50
153 Carey Price 3.00 8.00
154 Chris Kunitz 1.00 2.50
155 Claude Giroux 1.00 2.50
156 P.K. Subban 1.50 4.00
157 Peter Forsberg 1.00 2.50
158 Doug Gilmour 1.25 3.00
159 Guy Lafleur 1.25 3.00
160 Felix Potvin 1.50 4.00
161 Jonathan Quick 1.50 4.00
162 Jordan Eberle 1.00 2.50
163 Mikko Koivu .75 2.00
164 Nicklas Lidstrom 1.00 2.50
165 Patrice Bergeron 1.25 3.00
166 Paul Coffey 1.25 3.00
167 Pavel Datsyuk 1.25 3.00
168 Phil Esposito 1.50 4.00
169 Rick Nash 1.00 2.50
170 Rogie Vachon 1.25 3.00
171 Ron Francis 1.25 3.00
172 Taylor Hall 2.00 5.00
173 Teemu Selanne 2.00 5.00
174 Tyler Seguin 1.50 4.00
175 Zach Parise 1.00 2.50
176 Charlie Coyle RC 1.50 4.00
177 Jack Campbell RC 1.25 3.00
178 Drew Shore RC 1.25 3.00
179 Lucas Lessio RC 1.00 2.50
180 Eric Gelinas RC 1.50 4.00
181 Igor Bobkov RC 1.25 3.00
182 Ryan Murphy RC 1.50 4.00
183 Beau Bennett RC 2.00 5.00
184 Tom Wilson RC 2.50 6.00
185 Nathan Beaulieu RC 1.25 3.00
186 Carl Soderberg RC 1.50 4.00
187 Tanner Pearson RC 1.50 4.00
188 Emerson Etem RC 1.50 4.00
189 Frank Corrado RC 1.00 2.50
190 Zach Redmond RC 1.25 3.00
191 Rickard Rakell RC 1.50 4.00
192 Scott Laughton RC 1.50 4.00
193 Johan Larsson RC 1.50 4.00
194 Austin Watson RC 1.25 3.00
195 Michael Sgarbossa RC 1.50 4.00
196 Joakim Nordstrom RC 2.00 5.00
197 Sami Vatanen RC 1.50 4.00
198 Filip Forsberg RC 5.00 12.00
199 Seth Jones RC 1.50 4.00
200 Nicklas Jensen RC 1.25 3.00
201 Alexander Ovechkin AS 8.00 20.00
202 Bobby Orr AS 6.00 15.00
203 Brett Hull AS 2.00 5.00
204 Dale Hawerchuk AS 2.50 6.00
205 Eric Lindros AS 3.00 8.00
206 Evgeni Malkin AS 6.00 15.00
207 Steve Yzerman AS 4.00 10.00
208 Jean Beliveau AS 2.00 5.00
209 Joe Sakic AS 3.00 8.00
210 John Tavares AS 4.00 10.00
211 Jonathan Toews AS 4.00 10.00

212 Mario Lemieux AS 6.00 15.00
213 Mark Messier AS 2.50 6.00
214 Martin Brodeur AS 4.00 10.00
215 Mats Sundin AS 2.00 5.00
216 Mike Bossy AS 2.50 6.00
217 Dominik Hasek AS 2.50 6.00
218 Patrick Kane AS 4.00 10.00
219 Patrick Roy AS 5.00 12.00
220 Pavel Bure AS 2.50 6.00
221 Ryan Miller AS 2.00 5.00
222 Sidney Crosby AS 8.00 20.00
223 Steven Stamkos AS 4.00 10.00
224 Theoren Fleury AS 2.50 6.00
225 Wayne Gretzky AS 6.00 15.00
226 Nail Yakupov RC 6.00 15.00
227 Tomas Hertl RC 2.50 6.00
228 Elias Lindholm RC 3.00 8.00
229 Nathan MacKinnon RC 12.00 30.00
230 Morgan Rielly RC 5.00 12.00
231 Brendan Gallagher RC 6.00 15.00
232 Cory Conacher RC 1.25 3.00
233 Justin Schultz RC 2.00 5.00
234 Mikael Granlund RC 3.00 8.00
235 Vladimir Tarasenko RC 8.00 20.00
236 Zemgus Girgensons RC 4.00 10.00
237 Alex Galchenyuk RC 8.00 20.00
238 Jonathan Huberdeau RC 5.00 12.00
239 Jonas Brodin RC 1.50 4.00
240 J.T. Miller RC 2.00 5.00
241 Dougie Hamilton RC 4.00 10.00
242 Boone Jenner RC 2.00 5.00
243 Tyler Toffoli RC 4.00 10.00
244 Aleksander Barkov RC 5.00 12.00
245 Rasmus Ristolainen RC 3.00 8.00
246 Ryan Murray RC 2.00 5.00
247 Valeri Nichushkin RC 2.00 5.00
248 Mikhail Grigorenko RC 2.50 6.00
249 Jacob Trouba RC 3.00 8.00
250 Sean Monahan RC 3.00 8.00

2013-14 Black Diamond Emerald

1-175/201-225 UNPRICED PRINT RUN 10
*176-200 ROOK/25: 2.5X TO 6X BASIC RC
*227-250 ROOK/25: 1.5X TO 4X BASIC RC
183 Beau Bennett AU 12.00 30.00
184 Tom Wilson AU 25.00 60.00
187 Tanner Pearson AU 15.00 40.00
192 Scott Laughton AU 15.00 40.00
194 Austin Watson AU 12.00 30.00
227 Tomas Hertl AU 20.00 50.00
229 Nathan MacKinnon AU 250.00 400.00
230 Morgan Rielly AU 60.00 120.00
231 Brendan Gallagher AU 40.00 100.00
232 Cory Conacher AU 10.00 25.00
233 Justin Schultz AU 15.00 40.00
237 Alex Galchenyuk AU 75.00 150.00
238 Jonathan Huberdeau AU 40.00 100.00
241 Dougie Hamilton AU 50.00 100.00
242 Boone Jenner AU 15.00 40.00
243 Tyler Toffoli AU 30.00 80.00
244 Aleksander Barkov AU 60.00 120.00
246 Ryan Murray AU 15.00 40.00
248 Mikhail Grigorenko AU 20.00 50.00
250 Sean Monahan AU 60.00 120.00

2013-14 Black Diamond Ruby

*1-100 VETS/50: 8X TO 20X BASIC CARD
*101-150 VETS/50: 3X TO 8X BASIC CARD
*151-175 VETS/50: 2X TO 5X BASIC CARD
*201-225 VET AS/50: 1.2X TO 3X BASIC CARD
*176-200 ROOK/150: 1.2X TO 3X BASIC RC
*226-250 ROOK/150: .8X TO 2X BASIC RC
114 Corey Crawford 6.00 15.00
229 Nathan MacKinnon 40.00 80.00

2013-14 Black Diamond All-Time Greats Championship Rings

STATED ODDS 1:210
ATG19 Wayne Gretzky 15.00 40.00
ATG20 Steve Yzerman 15.00 40.00
ATG21 Grant Fuhr 8.00 20.00
ATG22 Ron Francis 10.00 25.00
ATG23 Mike Bossy 8.00 20.00
ATG24 Bobby Hull 8.00 20.00
ATG25 Martin Brodeur 15.00 40.00
ATG26 Andy Moog 8.00 20.00
ATG27 Mark Messier 10.00 25.00

2013-14 Black Diamond Dual Jerseys

OVERALL ODDS 1:10 HOB, 1:48 BLST
UNPRICED GRP A ODDS 1:76,730
GROUP B ODDS 1:2074
GROUP C ODDS 1:1177
GROUP D ODDS 1:262
GROUP E ODDS 1:217
GROUP F ODDS 1:97
GROUP G ODDS 1:30
GROUP H ODDS 1:21
984BH Brett Hull F 5.00 12.00
984LR Luc Robitaille D 4.00 10.00
984ML Mario Lemieux D 10.00 25.00
984PR Patrick Roy C 15.00 40.00
SBH Brett Hull B 15.00 30.00
SJJ Jaromir Jagr F 5.00 12.00
SMB Martin Brodeur F 8.00 20.00
SML Mario Lemieux D 10.00 25.00
SPR Patrick Roy D 10.00 25.00
SWG Wayne Gretzky B 40.00 80.00
EESBP Brad Park G 3.00 8.00
EESBR Bill Ranford B
EESCN Cam Neely H 4.00 10.00
EESGM Glen Murray H 3.00 8.00
EESPE Phil Esposito D 6.00 15.00
EESRB Ray Bourque G 6.00 15.00
RUINSDH Dougie Hamilton H 4.00 10.00
RUINSPB Patrice Bergeron G 5.00 12.00
RUINSTR Tuukka Rask C 6.00 15.00
RUINSZC Zdeno Chara G 4.00 10.00
UFFCH Cody Hodgson G 4.00 10.00
UFFMG Mikhail Grigorenko G 2.50 6.00
UFFRM Ryan Miller G 4.00 10.00
UFFTV Thomas Vanek B 6.00 15.00
ALLJB Jamie Benn F 5.00 12.00
ALLJC Jack Campbell H 1.50 4.00
ALLJO Jamie Oleksiak G 3.00 8.00
ALLKL Kari Lehtonen H 3.00 8.00
DMDD Devan Dubnyk H 4.00 10.00
DMJE Jordan Eberle G 4.00 10.00
DMJS Justin Schultz H 2.00 5.00
DMNY Nail Yakupov G 6.00 15.00
DMRN Ryan Nugent-Hopkins E 6.00 15.00
DMTH Taylor Hall H 8.00 20.00
AKAK Anze Kopitar F 6.00 15.00
AKDB Dustin Brown F 4.00 10.00
AKDD Drew Doughty E 4.00 10.00
AKJQ Jonathan Quick D 6.00 15.00
BBRCP Carey Price G 12.00 30.00
BBRLR Larry Robinson F 4.00 10.00
BBRPK P.K. Subban G 6.00 15.00
BBRPR Patrick Roy C 10.00 25.00
ETCP Carey Price G 12.00 30.00

NETMB Martin Brodeur D 8.00 20.00
NETPR Pekka Rinne G 5.00 12.00
NETRM Ryan Miller F 4.00 10.00
NYRHL Henrik Lundqvist D 5.00 12.00
NYRJT J.T. Miller H 2.00 5.00
NYRRC Ryan Callahan B 10.00 25.00
NYRRN Rick Nash G 4.00 10.00
PENSBB Beau Bennett H 2.50 6.00
PENSEM Evgeni Malkin E 12.00 30.00
PENSJN James Neal G 4.00 10.00
PENSKL Kris Letang E 5.00 12.00
PENSMF Marc-Andre Fleury F 6.00 15.00
PENSML Mario Lemieux D 10.00 25.00
PHICG Claude Giroux F 4.00 10.00
PHIEL Eric Lindros D 6.00 15.00
PHIPF Peter Forsberg G 4.00 10.00
PHISH Scott Hartnell C
PHISL Scott Laughton H 2.00 5.00
PHIWS Wayne Simmonds G 5.00 12.00
RFWDAG Alex Galchenyuk H 8.00 20.00
RFWDJH Jonathan Huberdeau H 4.00 10.00
RFWDNY Nail Yakupov G 6.00 15.00
RFWDVT Vladimir Tarasenko G 8.00 20.00
ROOKBG Brendan Gallagher H 6.00 15.00
ROOKDDH Dougie Hamilton H 4.00 10.00
ROOKDH Dougie Hamilton H 4.00 10.00
ROOKDJS Justin Schultz H 2.00 5.00
ROOKDJT Jarred Tinordi H 2.00 5.00
ROOKDNB Nathan Beaulieu H 1.50 4.00
ROOKJH Jonathan Huberdeau H 4.00 10.00
ROOKJO Jamie Oleksiak H 2.50 6.00
ROOKMP Mark Pysyk H 2.50 6.00
ROOKNB Nathan Beaulieu H 1.50 4.00
STARAO Alexander Ovechkin E 15.00 40.00
STARCG Claude Giroux A
STARIK Ilya Kovalchuk G 4.00 10.00
STARJT Jonathan Toews G 5.00 12.00
STARRG Ryan Getzlaf D 6.00 15.00
STLCS Chris Stewart H 3.00 8.00
STLJH Jaroslav Halak F 4.00 10.00
STLPB Patrik Berglund D 2.50 6.00
STLVT Vladimir Tarasenko G 6.00 15.00
TORDP Dion Phaneuf G 4.00 10.00
TORNK Nikolai Kulemin D 3.00 8.00
TORPK Phil Kessel G 5.00 12.00
VANHS Henrik Sedin F 4.00 10.00
VANJS Jordan Schroeder H 2.50 6.00
VANRL Roberto Luongo G 4.00 10.00
WINGSDB Damien Brunner H 4.00 10.00
WINGSJF Johan Franzen E 4.00 10.00
WINGSJH Jim Howard G 4.00 10.00
WINGSNK Niklas Kronwall E 3.00 8.00
WINGSPV Pavel Datsyuk E 5.00 12.00
WINGSZT Henrik Zetterberg E 4.00 10.00

2013-14 Black Diamond Gemography

OVERALL ODDS 1:100 H,1:1200 BLST
GROUP A ODDS 1:8906 HOB
GROUP B ODDS 1:6412 HOB
GROUP C ODDS 1:2748 HOB
GROUP D ODDS 1:811 HOB
GROUP E ODDS 1:123 HOB
GEMAB Adam Burish E 4.00 10.00
GEMAK Arturs Kulda E 4.00 10.00
GEMAL Anders Lindback E 4.00 10.00
GEMAO Alexander Ovechkin A 75.00 125.00
GEMBO Bobby Orr C 50.00 100.00
GEMBS Brandon Saad E 8.00 20.00
GEMCS Clayton Stoner E 4.00 10.00
GEMDJ Dustin Jeffrey E 4.00 10.00
GEMDP Daniel Paille E 5.00 12.00
GEMEG Erik Gudbranson D 5.00 12.00
GEMEN Evgeni Nabokov A
GEMFB Fabian Brunnstrom D 4.00 10.00
GEMFM Frazer McLaren E 5.00 12.00
GEMJT John Tavares B 15.00 40.00
GEMKE Keaton Ellerby E 4.00 10.00
GEMML Mario Lemieux A
GEMMS Mats Sundin A 40.00 80.00
GEMPB Pavel Bure A
GEMPO Patrick O'Sullivan D 5.00 12.00
GEMPP Paul Postma E 4.00 10.00
GEMRE Ray Emery E 5.00 12.00
GEMRM Ryan McDonagh E 6.00 15.00
GEMSA Michael Sauer E 4.00 10.00
GEMSC Sidney Crosby A
GEMSK Sergei Kostitsyn E 4.00 10.00
GEMSS Steven Stamkos B
GEMTK Tim Kennedy E 4.00 10.00
GEMTR Tuukka Rask C 12.00 30.00
GEMWG Wayne Gretzky B
GEMZK Zenon Konopka D 8.00 20.00

2013-14 Black Diamond Hardware Heroes

STATED PRINT RUN 100 SER.#'d SETS
HHAL Alexander Ovechkin 30.00 80.00
HHAO Alexander Ovechkin 30.00 80.00
HHBO Bobby Orr 12.00 30.00
HHCC Corey Crawford 10.00 25.00
HHDK Duncan Keith 8.00 20.00
HHHZ Henrik Zetterberg 8.00 20.00
HHJH Jonathan Huberdeau 10.00 25.00
HHJT Jonathan Toews 15.00 40.00
HHKA Patrick Kane 12.00 30.00
HHMB Martin Brodeur 15.00 40.00
HHPB Pavel Bure 10.00 25.00
HHPC Paul Coffey 8.00 20.00
HHPF Peter Forsberg 10.00 25.00
HHPK P.K. Subban 15.00 40.00
HHPR Patrick Roy 20.00 50.00
HHSB Sergei Bobrovsky 8.00 20.00
HHSC Sidney Crosby 30.00 80.00
HHZC Zdeno Chara 8.00 20.00

2013-14 Black Diamond Lustrous

L1-L12 ROOKIE ODDS 1:240 HOB
L13-L20 STARS ODDS 1:720 HOB
L21-L24 GREATS ODDS 1:1440 HOB
L1 Nathan MacKinnon R 40.00 80.00
L2 Justin Schultz R 5.00 12.00
L3 Seth Jones R 10.00 25.00
L4 Jonathan Huberdeau R 10.00 25.00
L5 Cory Conacher R 3.00 8.00
L6 Nail Yakupov R 15.00 40.00
L7 Damien Brunner R 4.00 10.00
L8 Tyler Toffoli R 10.00 25.00
L9 Brendan Gallagher R 12.00 30.00
L10 Dougie Hamilton R 10.00 25.00
L11 Vladimir Tarasenko R 20.00 50.00
L12 Alex Galchenyuk R 20.00 50.00
L13 Sidney Crosby S 15.00 40.00
L14 Alexander Ovechkin S 30.00 80.00
L15 Steven Stamkos S 10.00 25.00
L16 Jonathan Toews S 10.00 25.00
L17 John Tavares S 15.00 40.00
L18 Patrice Bergeron S 10.00 25.00
L19 Henrik Lundqvist S 10.00 25.00
L20 Phil Kessel S 10.00 25.00
L21 Wayne Gretzky G 30.00 80.00
L22 Bobby Orr G 50.00 120.00
L23 Dominik Hasek G 20.00 50.00
L24 Bobby Hull G 15.00 40.00

2013-14 Black Diamond Stanley Cup Champs Championship Rings

STATED ODDS 1:158
CRB1 Andrew Shaw 10.00 25.00
CRB2 Ben Smith 8.00 20.00
CRB3 Brandon Bollig 8.00 20.00
CRB4 Brandon Saad 12.00 30.00
CRB5 Brent Seabrook 10.00 25.00
CRB6 Bryan Bickell 10.00 25.00
CRB7 Corey Crawford 12.00 30.00
CRB8 Daniel Carcillo 5.00 12.00
CRB9 Dave Bolland 6.00 15.00
CRB10 Duncan Keith 10.00 25.00
CRB11 Jamal Mayers 6.00 15.00
CRB12 Johnny Oduya 8.00 20.00
CRB13 Jonathan Toews 20.00 50.00
CRB14 Marcus Kruger 10.00 25.00
CRB15 Marian Hossa 10.00 25.00
CRB16 Michael Frolik 6.00 15.00
CRB17 Michal Handzus 8.00 20.00
CRB18 Michal Rozsival 6.00 15.00
CRB19 Nick Leddy 6.00 15.00
CRB20 Niklas Hjalmarsson 8.00 20.00
CRB21 Patrick Kane 20.00 50.00
CRB22 Patrick Sharp 10.00 25.00
CRB23 Ray Emery 8.00 20.00
CRB24 Viktor Stalberg 6.00 15.00

2014-15 Black Diamond

COMP.SET w/o SP's (100) 12.00 30.00
101-150 DOUBLE ODDS 1:3 HOB, 1:4 BLST
151-200 TRIPLE ODDS 1:6 HOB, 1:8 BLST
201-250 QUAD ODDS 1:13 HOB, 1:24 BLST
1 Valtteri Filppula .25 .60
2 Jiri Hudler .20 .50
3 Claude Lemieux .20 .50
4 Brandon Dubinsky .20 .50
5 Ryan Callahan .25 .60
6 Joe Pavelski .25 .60
7 Wayne Simmonds .30 .75
8 Mike Smith .25 .60
9 Chris Kreider .25 .60
10 Jack Johnson .15 .40
11 Nathan MacKinnon .50 1.25
12 Morgan Rielly .25 .60
13 Brandon Saad .25 .60
14 Evander Kane .25 .60
15 Justin Williams .20 .50
16 Jordan Eberle .25 .60
17 Eddie Lack .20 .50
18 Oliver Ekman-Larsson .20 .50
19 Marc-Andre Fleury .40 1.00
20 Andrew Ladd .25 .60
21 Pascal Dupuis .15 .40
22 Carter Hutton .25 .60
23 Patrik Berglund .15 .40
24 Matt Moulson .20 .50
25 Pierre Turgeon .25 .60
26 Mikko Koivu .20 .50
27 Alex Pietrangelo .20 .50
28 Niklas Kronwall .20 .50
29 Tomas Plekanec .25 .60
30 Johan Franzen .25 .60
31 Cam Fowler .20 .50
32 Blake Wheeler .25 .60
33 Cody Hodgson .25 .60
34 Mike Fisher .20 .50
35 Braden Holtby .40 1.00
36 Tyler Johnson .25 .60
37 Nick Bjugstad .20 .50
38 Andrew Cogliano .15 .40
39 Mike Richards .25 .60
40 Aleksander Barkov .25 .60
41 Glen Murray .20 .50
42 Alex Stalock .20 .50
43 Olli Maatta .25 .60
44 Tomas Hertl .25 .60
45 Jay Bouwmeester .25 .60
46 Brian Elliott .20 .50
47 Tyler Ennis .20 .50
48 Alec Martinez .15 .40
49 Zdeno Chara .25 .60
50 Travis Zajac .20 .50
51 Ryan McDonagh .25 .60
52 Jeff Skinner .25 .60
53 Slava Voynov .25 .60
54 Milan Lucic .25 .60
55 Doug Wilson .20 .50
56 Craig Smith .15 .40
57 Adam Henrique .25 .60
58 T.J. Oshie .40 1.00
59 Tyler Toffoli .25 .60
60 Jason Pominville .20 .50
61 Matt Carle .15 .40
62 Kyle Turris .25 .60
63 John Carlson .30 .75
64 Antoine Vermette .15 .40
65 Bryan Little .25 .60
66 Ben Scrivens .20 .50
67 Patrik Elias .25 .60
68 Bill Barber .25 .60
69 Eric Staal .30 .75
70 Josh Bailey .20 .50
71 Daniel Sedin .25 .60
72 Kari Lehtonen .20 .50
73 Dion Phaneuf .25 .60
74 Patrick Marleau .25 .60
75 Derek Stepan .25 .60
76 Clarke MacArthur .15 .40
77 Vladimir Tarasenko .40 1.00
78 David Perron .15 .40
79 Brayden Schenn .25 .60
80 Valeri Nichushkin .20 .50
81 Dustin Brown .20 .50
82 Erik Johnson .15 .40
83 Drew Stafford .25 .60
84 Shane Doan .20 .50
85 Marian Hossa .20 .50
86 Bryan Bickell .15 .40
87 Semyon Varlamov .25 .60
88 Sergei Bobrovsky .25 .60
89 Mike Green .25 .60
90 Dwayne Roloson .15 .40
91 Jonathan Huberdeau .25 .60
92 Doug Harvey .25 .60
93 Kevin Shattenkirk .25 .60
94 Patrick Sharp .25 .60
95 Chris Higgins .15 .40
96 Colin Greening .15 .40
97 Vincent Damphousse .20 .50
98 Max Pacioretty .25 .60
99 Ryan O'Reilly .25 .60
100 Sean Monahan .25 .60
101 Nathan Horton .60 1.50
102 Nicklas Backstrom 1.00 2.50
103 Ryan Suter .60 1.50
104 Erik Karlsson 1.25 3.00
105 Jeff Carter .60 1.50
106 Henrik Sedin .60 1.50
107 Keith Yandle .60 1.50
108 Roberto Luongo .60 1.50
109 Bobby Ryan .60 1.50
110 Brian Bellows .50 1.25
111 Jakub Voracek .60 1.50
112 Jamie Benn .75 2.00
113 Antti Niemi .50 1.25
114 P.K. Subban 1.00 2.50
115 Tony Esposito .60 1.50
116 John LeClair .60 1.50
117 Taylor Hall 1.25 3.00
118 Brent Seabrook .60 1.50
119 Corey Crawford .75 2.00
120 Logan Couture .60 1.50
121 Pekka Rinne .75 2.00
122 Kyle Okposo .60 1.50
123 Zach Parise .60 1.50
124 Cory Schneider .50 1.25
125 Nazem Kadri .60 1.50
126 Mike Richter .60 1.50
127 Joe Thornton .60 1.50
128 David Backes .60 1.50
129 Trevor Linden .60 1.50
130 Brad Marchand .75 2.00
131 Doug Gilmour .75 2.00
132 Rick Nash .60 1.50
133 Ben Bishop .60 1.50
134 Guy Lafleur .75 2.00
135 Vincent Lecavalier .50 1.25
136 Jim Howard .60 1.50
137 Mike Modano 1.00 2.50
138 Corey Perry .60 1.50
139 Chris Kunitz .60 1.50
140 Phil Esposito 1.00 2.50
141 Arturs Irbe .50 1.25
142 Dustin Byfuglien .60 1.50
143 Duncan Keith .60 1.50
144 Nicklas Lidstrom .60 1.50
145 James van Riemsdyk .60 1.50
146 Alexander Steen .60 1.50
147 Craig Anderson .60 1.50
148 Gabriel Landeskog .50 1.25
149 Adam Oates .60 1.50
150 John Gibson .75 2.00
151 Pavel Datsyuk 1.25 3.00
152 Patrice Bergeron 1.25 3.00
153 Ron Francis 1.25 3.00
154 Jonathan Quick 1.50 4.00
155 Tyler Seguin 1.50 4.00
156 Jonathan Bernier 1.00 2.50
157 Grant Fuhr 1.00 2.50
158 Patrick Kane 2.00 5.00
159 Jari Kurri 1.00 2.50
160 Henrik Zetterberg 1.25 3.00
161 Phil Kessel 1.25 3.00
162 Shea Weber .75 2.00
163 Martin St. Louis 1.00 2.50
164 Ryan Getzlaf 1.50 4.00
165 Bobby Hull 1.00 2.50
166 Carey Price 3.00 8.00
167 Jeremy Roenick 1.00 2.50
168 Drew Doughty 1.00 2.50
169 Anze Kopitar 1.50 4.00
170 Ryan Nugent-Hopkins 1.00 2.50
171 Felix Potvin 1.50 4.00
172 Tuukka Rask 1.00 2.50
173 Matt Duchene 1.00 2.50
174 Theoren Fleury 1.25 3.00
175 Claude Giroux 1.00 2.50
176 Trevor van Riemsdyk RC 2.50 6.00
177 Nicolas Deslauriers RC 1.50 4.00
178 Vincent Trocheck RC 2.00 5.00
179 Mark Visentin RC 1.50 4.00
180 Mirco Mueller RC 1.50 4.00
181 Kristers Gudlevskis RC 1.50 4.00
182 Markus Granlund RC 2.50 6.00
183 Greg McKegg RC 1.25 3.00
184 Colton Sissons RC 1.50 4.00
185 Ryan Sproul RC 1.50 4.00
186 Andrey Makarov RC 1.50 4.00
187 William Karlsson RC 6.00 15.00
188 Laurent Brossoit RC 1.50 4.00
189 Pierre-Edouard Bellemare RC 1.50 4.00
190 Christian Folin RC 1.50 4.00
191 Corban Knight RC 1.50 4.00
192 Teemu Pulkkinen RC 2.00 5.00
193 Michael Zalewski RC 1.25 3.00
194 Jake McCabe RC 1.50 4.00
195 Patrick Brown RC 1.50 4.00
196 Patrik Nemeth RC 1.50 4.00
197 Brandon Kozun RC 1.25 3.00
198 Jori Lehtera RC 2.00 5.00
199 Dennis Everberg RC 1.50 4.00
200 Marko Dano RC 1.50 4.00
201 Jonathan Toews AS 4.00 10.00
202 Teemu Selanne AS 4.00 10.00
203 Peter Forsberg AS 2.00 5.00
204 John Tavares AS 4.00 10.00
205 Mats Sundin AS 2.00 5.00
206 Mario Lemieux AS 6.00 15.00
207 Stan Mikita AS 2.50 6.00
208 Martin Brodeur AS 4.00 10.00
209 Pavel Bure AS 2.50 6.00
210 Mark Messier AS 2.00 5.00
211 Bobby Orr AS 4.00 10.00
212 Mike Bossy AS 2.00 5.00
213 Steven Stamkos AS 4.00 10.00
214 Joe Sakic AS 3.00 8.00
215 Ray Bourque AS 3.00 8.00
216 Patrick Roy AS 5.00 12.00
217 Henrik Lundqvist AS 2.50 6.00
218 Evgeni Malkin AS 6.00 15.00
219 Sidney Crosby AS 5.00 12.00
220 Wayne Gretzky AS 10.00 25.00
221 Dominik Hasek AS 2.50 6.00
222 Jarome Iginla AS 2.00 5.00
223 Steve Yzerman AS 4.00 10.00
224 Jaromir Jagr AS 5.00 12.00
225 Alexander Ovechkin AS 8.00 20.00
226 Sam Reinhart RC 8.00 20.00
227 Brandon Gormley RC 2.50 6.00
228 Adam Lowry RC 2.50 6.00
229 Evgeny Kuznetsov RC 10.00 25.00
230 Vladislav Namestnikov RC 4.00 10.00
231 Johnny Gaudreau RC 12.00 30.00
232 Anthony Duclair RC 4.00 10.00
233 Damon Severson RC 2.50 6.00
234 Jiri Sekac RC 2.50 6.00
235 Teuvo Teravainen RC 4.00 10.00
236 Oscar Klefbom RC 5.00 12.00
237 Calle Jarnkrok RC 2.50 6.00
238 Alexander Khokhlachev RC 2.50 6.00
239 Griffin Reinhart RC 3.00 8.00
240 Andre Burakovsky RC 4.00 10.00
241 Ty Rattie RC 3.00 8.00
242 Alexander Wennberg RC 5.00 12.00
243 Aaron Ekblad RC 5.00 12.00
244 Joey Hishon RC 3.00 8.00
245 Jonathan Drouin RC 8.00 20.00
246 Chris Tierney RC 2.50 6.00
247 Victor Rask RC 2.50 6.00
248 Leon Draisaitl RC 12.00 30.00
249 Stuart Percy RC 2.50 6.00
250 Curtis Lazar RC 3.00 8.00

2014-15 Black Diamond Emerald

*176-200 ROOK/25: 2.5X TO 6X BASIC RC
*227-250 ROOK/25: 1.5X TO 4X BASIC RC
178 Vincent Trocheck AU 20.00 50.00
179 Mark Visentin AU 25.00 50.00
180 Mirco Mueller AU 15.00 40.00
182 Markus Granlund AU 25.00 60.00
183 Greg McKegg AU 12.00 30.00
184 Colton Sissons AU 15.00 40.00
185 Ryan Sproul AU 15.00 40.00
188 Laurent Brossoit AU 15.00 40.00
191 Corban Knight AU 15.00 40.00
194 Jake McCabe AU 15.00 40.00
226 Sam Reinhart AU 100.00 200.00
227 Brandon Gormley AU 15.00 40.00
229 Evgeny Kuznetsov AU 50.00 100.00
230 Vladislav Namestnikov AU 25.00 60.00
231 Johnny Gaudreau AU 150.00 250.00
235 Teuvo Teravainen AU 100.00 175.00
236 Oscar Klefbom AU 30.00 80.00
238 Alexander Khokhlachev AU 15.00 40.00
239 Griffin Reinhart AU 20.00 50.00
240 Andre Burakovsky AU 50.00 100.00
241 Ty Rattie AU 20.00 50.00
242 Alexander Wennberg AU 30.00 80.00
243 Aaron Ekblad AU 100.00 200.00
244 Joey Hishon AU 20.00 50.00
245 Jonathan Drouin AU 125.00 200.00
246 Chris Tierney AU 15.00 40.00
250 Curtis Lazar AU

2014-15 Black Diamond Orange

*1-100 VETS: 3X TO 8X BASIC CARD
*101-150 VETS: 2X TO 5X BASIC CARD
*151-175 VET: 1.5X TO 4X BASIC CARD
*176-200 ROOK: 1X TO 2.5X BASIC RC
*201-225 VET AS: 1X TO 2.5X BASIC CARD
*226-250 ROOK: .8X TO 2X BASIC RC
1-100 STATED ODDS 1:1 BONUS PACK
101-150 STATED ODDS 1:2 BONUS PACK
151-175 STATED ODDS 1:4 BONUS PACK
201-225 STATED ODDS 1:5 BONUS PACK
102 Nicklas Backstrom 5.00 12.00
220 Wayne Gretzky AS 25.00 50.00
231 Johnny Gaudreau 20.00 50.00

2014-15 Black Diamond Ruby

*1-100 VETS/50: 6X TO 15X BASIC CARD
*101-150 VETS/50: 2.5X TO 6X BASIC CARD
*151-175 VETS/50: 1.5X TO 4X BASIC CARD
*176-200 ROOK/150: 1X TO 2.5X BASIC RC
*201-225 VET AS/50: 1.2X TO 3X BASIC CARD
*226-250 ROOK/150: .6X TO 1.5X BASIC RC
102 Nicklas Backstrom 6.00 15.00
220 Wayne Gretzky AS 25.00 50.00
231 Johnny Gaudreau 30.00 80.00
243 Aaron Ekblad 20.00 50.00
245 Jonathan Drouin 20.00 50.00

2014-15 Black Diamond Championship Rings

CRB1 Drew Doughty 10.00 25.00
CRB2 Anze Kopitar 15.00 40.00
CRB3 Willie Mitchell 6.00 15.00
CRB4 Kyle Clifford 6.00 15.00
CRB5 Slava Voynov 10.00 25.00
CRB6 Tanner Pearson 6.00 15.00
CRB7 Trevor Lewis 6.00 15.00
CRB8 Dustin Brown 8.00 20.00
CRB9 Mike Richards 10.00 25.00
CRB10 Matt Greene 6.00 15.00
CRB11 Tyler Toffoli 10.00 25.00
CRB12 Jeff Schultz 6.00 15.00
CRB13 Jeff Carter 10.00 25.00
CRB14 Jarret Stoll 8.00 20.00
CRB15 Jonathan Quick 15.00 40.00
CRB16 Jake Muzzin 6.00 15.00
CRB17 Alec Martinez 6.00 15.00
CRB18 Justin Williams 8.00 20.00
CRB19 Robyn Regehr 6.00 15.00
CRB20 Dwight King 6.00 15.00
CRB21 Marian Gaborik 10.00 25.00

2014-15 Black Diamond Dual Jerseys

UNPRICED GRP A ODDS 1:9704
GROUP B ODDS 1:1071
GROUP C ODDS 1:746
GROUP D ODDS 1:267
GROUP E ODDS 1:20
GROUP F ODDS 1:23
ASEM Evgeni Malkin E 5.00 12.00
ASLC Logan Couture E 4.00 10.00
ASRN Rick Nash F 4.00 10.00
ASVL Vincent Lecavalier F 3.00 8.00
ANABL Ben Lovejoy F 2.50 6.00
ANACF Cam Fowler E 3.00 8.00
ANACP Corey Perry D 4.00 10.00
ANARG Ryan Getzlaf E 6.00 15.00
CHIBS Brent Seabrook F 4.00 10.00
CHIJT Jonathan Toews C 12.00 30.00
CHIPS Patrick Sharp F 4.00 10.00
CHISA Brandon Saad E 4.00 10.00
DALCE Cody Eakin E 2.50 6.00
DALKL Kari Lehtonen E 3.00 8.00
DALPN Patrik Nemeth F 4.00 10.00
DALTS Tyler Seguin E 6.00 15.00
LAKCF Colin Fraser E 2.50 6.00
LAKJM Jake Muzzin E 2.50 6.00
LAKJN Jordan Nolan E 4.00 10.00
LAKKC Kyle Clifford F 2.50 6.00
MONAG Alex Galchenyuk F 6.00 15.00
MONBG Brendan Gallagher E 4.00 10.00
MONCP Carey Price F 10.00 25.00
MONMP Max Pacioretty E 4.00 10.00
NJDAG Andy Greene F 2.50 6.00
NJDAH Adam Henrique E 4.00 10.00
NJDCS Cory Schneider E 3.00 8.00
NJDSG Stephen Gionta E 2.50 6.00
NYIFN Frans Nielsen F 2.50 6.00
NYIMD Matt Donovan F 2.50 6.00
NYIMG Michael Grabner E 3.00 8.00
NYITH Thomas Hickey E 2.50 6.00
OTTBR Bobby Ryan E 4.00 10.00
OTTEK Erik Karlsson E 8.00 20.00
OTTKT Kyle Turris A
OTTRL Robin Lehner E 3.00 8.00
PHIBC Braydon Coburn D 2.50 6.00
PHIJV Jakub Voracek B 6.00 15.00
PHIMR Matt Read B 4.00 10.00
PHISC Sean Couturier E 4.00 10.00
PHISM Steve Mason E 3.00 8.00
PHIWS Wayne Simmonds E 5.00 12.00
PITBG Brian Gibbons F 2.50 6.00
PITBS Brandon Sutter E 3.00 8.00
PITCK Chris Kunitz F 4.00 10.00
PITJZ Jeff Zatkoff E 3.00 8.00
PITMF Marc-Andre Fleury F 6.00 15.00
PITOM Olli Maatta F 4.00 10.00
TOREB Ed Belfour F 4.00 10.00
TORJB Jonathan Bernier E 4.00 10.00
TORPK Phil Kessel E 5.00 12.00
TORRF Ron Francis F 5.00 12.00
WASAO Alexander Ovechkin E 15.00 40.00
WASJC John Carlson D 5.00 12.00
WASMG Mike Green E 4.00 10.00
WASNB Nicklas Backstrom D 6.00 15.00
BUFFDS Drew Stafford C 6.00 15.00
BUFFMM Matt Moulson F 3.00 8.00
BUFFTE Tyler Ennis E 3.00 8.00
BUFFTM Tyler Myers E 3.00 8.00
LBBRBB Brian Bellows F 3.00 8.00
LBBRLR Larry Robinson F 4.00 10.00
LBBRPT Pierre Turgeon E 4.00 10.00
LBBRVD Vincent Damphousse F 3.00 8.00
DUCKSCP Corey Perry E 4.00 10.00
DUCKSHL Hampus Lindholm E 3.00 8.00
DUCKSRG Ryan Getzlaf E 6.00 15.00
DUCKSTS Teemu Selanne F 8.00 20.00
KINGSAK Anze Kopitar F 6.00 15.00
KINGSDB Dustin Brown E 3.00 8.00
KINGSDD Drew Doughty F 4.00 10.00
KINGSSV Slava Voynov E 4.00 10.00
WINGSJH Jim Howard E 4.00 10.00
WINGSNK Niklas Kronwall C 5.00 12.00
WINGSPD Pavel Datsyuk E 5.00 12.00
WINGSSY Steve Yzerman E 8.00 20.00
KINGS2JC Jeff Carter B 6.00 15.00
KINGS2JW Justin Williams E 3.00 8.00
KINGS2MG Matt Greene F 2.50 6.00
KINGS2MR Mike Richards E 4.00 10.00

2014-15 Black Diamond Gemography

OVERALL ODDS 1:120 H, 1:1200 BLST
GROUP A ODDS 1:33,564 HOB
GROUP B ODDS 1:2238 HOB
GROUP C ODDS 1:455 HOB
GROUP D ODDS 1:177 HOB
GEMAW Austin Watson C 4.00 10.00
GEMBD Brenden Dillon D 3.00 8.00
GEMBO Bobby Orr B 90.00 150.00
GEMBR Bobby Ryan B 10.00 25.00
GEMBS Brandon Sutter C 5.00 12.00
GEMCC Connor Carrick D 3.00 8.00
GEMCK Chris Kreider C 6.00 15.00
GEMCT Colten Teubert C 5.00 12.00
GEMDB David Backes C 6.00 15.00
GEMDS Drew Shore D 3.00 8.00
GEMHS Harri Sateri D 20.00 40.00
GEMJB Johnny Bucyk B 15.00 40.00
GEMJC Jared Cowen C 4.00 10.00
GEMJG John Gibson D 6.00 15.00
GEMJM Jon Merrill D 3.00 8.00
GEMJO Jamie Oleksiak C 5.00 12.00
GEMJT Jarred Tinordi D 8.00 20.00
GEMLE Lars Eller C 5.00 12.00
GEMLL Lucas Lessio D 4.00 10.00
GEMLS Luke Schenn C 4.00 10.00
GEMML Michael Latta D 5.00 12.00
GEMPP Paul Postma D 3.00 8.00
GEMRF Ron Francis B 15.00 40.00
GEMRM Ryan Murphy D 3.00 8.00
GEMRP Richard Panik D 3.00 8.00
GEMSB Sergei Bobrovsky C 6.00 15.00
GEMTA John Tavares B 30.00 60.00
GEMTW Tom Wilson A 50.00 100.00
GEMWG Wayne Gretzky B 150.00 250.00

2014-15 Black Diamond Hardware Heroes

HHAO Alexander Ovechkin 30.00 80.00
HHDH Dominik Hasek 12.00 30.00
HHJS Joe Sakic 12.00 30.00
HHJT Joe Thornton 8.00 20.00
HHJW Justin Williams 8.00 20.00
HHMS Martin St. Louis 8.00 20.00
HHNM Nathan MacKinnon 15.00 40.00
HHPD Pavel Datsyuk 10.00 25.00
HHPF Peter Forsberg 12.00 30.00
HHRO Ryan O'Reilly 8.00 20.00
HHSC Sidney Crosby 30.00 80.00
HHTR Tuukka Rask 8.00 20.00
HHWG Wayne Gretzky 40.00 100.00

2014-15 Black Diamond UD Black Lustrous Rookies Previews

STATED ODDS 1:240 HOBBY
LRP1 Aaron Ekblad 15.00 40.00
LRP2 Evgeny Kuznetsov 8.00 20.00
LRP3 Curtis Lazar 8.00 20.00
LRP4 Leon Draisaitl 30.00 80.00
LRP5 Sam Reinhart 15.00 40.00
LRP6 Jonathan Drouin 15.00 40.00
LRP7 Alexander Wennberg 12.00 30.00
LRP8 Anthony Duclair 6.00 15.00

2015-16 Black Diamond

BDBAE Aaron Ekblad 3.00 8.00
BDBAK Anze Kopitar 5.00 12.00
BDBAL Andrew Ladd 3.00 8.00
BDBAO Alexander Ovechkin 12.00 30.00
BDBBD Brandon Dubinsky 2.50 6.00
BDBBE Jamie Benn 4.00 10.00
BDBBO Bobby Orr 6.00 15.00
BDBCG Claude Giroux 3.00 8.00
BDBCP Carey Price 6.00 15.00
BDBCS Cory Schneider 2.50 6.00
BDBEK Erik Karlsson 6.00 15.00
BDBEM Evgeni Malkin 10.00 25.00
BDBES Eric Staal 4.00 10.00
BDBFF Filip Forsberg 4.00 10.00
BDBHL Henrik Lundqvist 4.00 10.00
BDBHS Henrik Sedin 3.00 8.00
BDBHZ Henrik Zetterberg 4.00 10.00
BDBJB Jonathan Bernier 3.00 8.00
BDBJJ Jaromir Jagr 8.00 20.00
BDBJP Joe Pavelski 3.00 8.00
BDBJQ Jonathan Quick 5.00 12.00
BDBJT Jonathan Toews 6.00 15.00
BDBMD Matt Duchene 3.00 8.00
BDBML Mario Lemieux 10.00 25.00
BDBNA Rick Nash 3.00 8.00
BDBNB Nicklas Backstrom 5.00 12.00
BDBNM Nathan MacKinnon 6.00 15.00
BDBPB Patrice Bergeron 4.00 10.00
BDBPD Pavel Datsyuk 4.00 10.00
BDBPE Corey Perry 3.00 8.00
BDBPK Patrick Kane 6.00 15.00
BDBPR Patrick Roy 6.00 15.00
BDBPS P.K. Subban 5.00 12.00
BDBRG Ryan Getzlaf 5.00 12.00
BDBRM Ryan Miller 3.00 8.00
BDBRN Ryan Nugent-Hopkins 3.00 8.00
BDBSC Sidney Crosby 12.00 30.00
BDBSD Shane Doan 2.50 6.00
BDBSM Sean Monahan 3.00 8.00
BDBSS Steven Stamkos 6.00 15.00
BDBSW Shea Weber 2.50 6.00
BDBSY Steve Yzerman 5.00 12.00
BDBTA John Tavares 6.00 15.00
BDBTH Taylor Hall 6.00 15.00
BDBTR Tuukka Rask 3.00 8.00
BDBTS Tyler Seguin 5.00 12.00
BDBVT Vladimir Tarasenko 5.00 12.00
BDBWG Wayne Gretzky 15.00 40.00
BDBZG Zemgus Girgensons 2.50 6.00
BDBZP Zach Parise 3.00 8.00
BDRAC Andrew Copp RC 25.00 60.00
BDRAP Artemi Panarin RC 150.00 250.00
BDRCH Connor Hellebuyck RC 60.00 150.00
BDRCM Connor McDavid RC 1500.00 2200.00
BDRDL Dylan Larkin RC 350.00 500.00
BDRDS Daniel Sprong RC 50.00 125.00
BDREP Emile Poirier RC 25.00 60.00
BDRHS Henrik Samuelsson RC 20.00 50.00
BDRJE Jack Eichel RC 450.00 700.00
BDRJR Jacob de la Rose RC 25.00 60.00
BDRJV Jake Virtanen RC 90.00 150.00
BDRKF Kevin Fiala RC 25.00 60.00
BDRMD Max Domi RC 125.00 225.00
BDRMP Matt Puempel RC 20.00 50.00
BDRMS Malcolm Subban RC 50.00 100.00
BDRNE Nikolaj Ehlers RC 75.00 135.00
BDRNG Nikolay Goldobin RC 25.00 60.00
BDRNH Noah Hanifin RC 30.00 80.00
BDRNR Nick Ritchie RC 25.00 60.00
BDRNS Nick Shore RC 25.00 60.00
BDRRA Mikko Rantanen RC 50.00 125.00
BDRRF Robby Fabbri RC 30.00 80.00
BDRRH Ryan Hartman RC 30.00 80.00
BDRRK Ronalds Kenins RC 25.00 60.00
BDRSB Sam Bennett RC 150.00 225.00
BDRSP Shane Prince RC 20.00 50.00
BDRRWG Wayne Gretzky RR 300.00 500.00

2015-16 Black Diamond Pure Black

*UNSIGNED/99: .5X TO 1.2X BASE CRD/199
EXCH EXPIRATION: 11/10/2017
BDBAE Aaron Ekblad AU/99 6.00 15.00
BDBAK Anze Kopitar AU/99 10.00 25.00
BDBAL Andrew Ladd AU/99 6.00 15.00
BDBAO Alexander Ovechkin AU/25 40.00 80.00
BDBBD Brandon Dubinsky AU/99 5.00 12.00
BDBBO Bobby Orr AU/25 100.00 175.00
BDBCP Carey Price AU/25 100.00 175.00
BDBEM Evgeni Malkin AU/99 12.00 30.00
BDBES Eric Staal AU/99 8.00 20.00
BDBJB Jonathan Bernier AU/99 6.00 15.00
BDBJP Joe Pavelski AU/99 6.00 15.00
BDBJT Jonathan Toews AU/25 30.00 60.00
BDBMD Matt Duchene AU/99 6.00 15.00
BDBML Mario Lemieux AU/25 75.00 125.00
BDBNA Rick Nash AU/99 6.00 15.00
BDBNM Nathan MacKinnon AU/99 10.00 25.00
BDBPD Pavel Datsyuk AU/99 8.00 20.00
BDBPR Patrick Roy AU/25 50.00 100.00
BDBSC Sidney Crosby AU/25 EXCH 75.00 135.00
BDBSW Shea Weber AU/99 6.00 15.00
BDBSY Steve Yzerman AU/25 40.00 80.00
BDBTA John Tavares AU/99 12.00 30.00
BDBTH Taylor Hall AU/99 10.00 25.00
BDBWG Wayne Gretzky AU/25 150.00 250.00
BDBZG Zemgus Girgensons AU/99 5.00 12.00

2015-16 Black Diamond Championship Rings

STATED ODDS 1:5
CRAD Andrew Desjardins 4.00 10.00
CRAS Andrew Shaw 6.00 15.00
CRAV Antoine Vermette 4.00 10.00
CRBB Bryan Bickell 4.00 10.00
CRBR Brad Richards 6.00 15.00
CRBS Brent Seabrook 6.00 15.00
CRCC Corey Crawford 8.00 20.00
CRDK Duncan Keith 10.00 25.00
CRDR David Rundblad 6.00 15.00
CRJN Joakim Nordstrom 6.00 15.00
CRJO Johnny Oduya 6.00 15.00
CRJT Jonathan Toews 12.00 30.00
CRKC Kyle Cumiskey 5.00 12.00
CRKT Kimmo Timonen 5.00 12.00
CRKV Kris Versteeg 5.00 12.00
CRMH Marian Hossa 8.00 20.00
CRMK Marcus Kruger 6.00 15.00
CRMR Michal Rozsival 5.00 12.00
CRNH Niklas Hjalmarsson 5.00 12.00
CRPK Patrick Kane 20.00 40.00
CRPS Patrick Sharp 6.00 15.00
CRSA Brandon Saad 6.00 15.00
CRSD Scott Darling 6.00 15.00
CRTR Trevor van Riemsdyk 6.00 15.00
CRTT Teuvo Teravainen 6.00 15.00

2015-16 Black Diamond Diamond Mine Memorabilia

STATED PRINT RUN 5-125
DMAG Alex Galchenyuk Ptch/50 6.00 15.00
DMAK Anze Kopitar Glv/25 15.00 40.00
DMAO Alexander Ovechkin Ptch/25 40.00 100.00
DMAT Alex Tanguay Ptch/75 2.50 6.00
DMBG Brendan Gallagher Ptch/25 12.00 30.00
DMBL Rob Blake Pants/75 4.00 10.00
DMBR Bill Ranford Pads/75 6.00 15.00
DMCC Chris Chelios Ptch/50 5.00 12.00
DMCG Claude Giroux Jsy/125 4.00 10.00
DMCP Carey Price Pants/25 30.00 60.00
DMCR Corey Crawford Ptch/50 6.00 15.00
DMDB Dustin Brown Glv/25 8.00 20.00
DMDG Doug Gilmour Stk/25 12.00 30.00
DMDS Daniel Sedin Ptch/50 5.00 12.00
DMEM Evgeni Malkin Skate/25 10.00 25.00
DMGM Glen Murray Ptch/75 3.00 8.00
DMGR Wayne Gretzky Socks/25 40.00 80.00
DMHL Henrik Lundqvist Jsy/125 5.00 12.00
DMHS Henrik Sedin Stk/50 5.00 12.00
DMHZ Henrik Zetterberg Ptch/25 12.00 30.00
DMJA James van Riemsdyk Jsy/125 4.00 10.00
DMJC Jeff Carter Glv/25 10.00 25.00
DMJG Johnny Gaudreau Jsy/125 6.00 15.00
DMJP Jason Spezza Ptch/25 8.00 20.00
DMJQ Jonathan Quick Blkr/50 8.00 20.00
DMJR Jeremy Roenick Ptch/50 5.00 12.00
DMJT Jonathan Toews Jsy/125 8.00 20.00
DMJV John Vanbiesbrouck Stk/15 20.00 40.00
DMMD Marcel Dionne Skate/25 12.00 30.00
DMMF Marc-Andre Fleury Pads/50 10.00 25.00
DMNM Nathan MacKinnon Jsy/125 8.00 20.00
DMPB Patrice Bergeron Jsy/125 5.00 12.00
DMPD Pavel Datsyuk Pads/25 25.00 50.00
DMPR Patrick Roy Pads/15 25.00 50.00
DMPS P.K. Subban Jsy/125 6.00 15.00
DMPT Pierre Turgeon Ptch/50 5.00 12.00
DMRG Ryan Getzlaf Jsy/125 6.00 15.00
DMRL Roberto Luongo Glv/25 10.00 25.00
DMRN Rick Nash Jsy/125 4.00 10.00
DMRO Rod Brind'Amour Ptch/75 3.00 8.00
DMRY Bobby Ryan Ptch/50 4.00 10.00
DMSC Sidney Crosby Ptch/15 30.00 60.00

DMSH Scott Hartnell Ptch/50 5.00 12.00
DMSS Steven Stamkos Jsy/125 8.00 20.00
DMTA John Tavares Jsy/125 8.00 20.00
DMTE Tony Esposito Pads/15 20.00 40.00
DMTS Tyler Seguin Jsy/125 6.00 15.00
DMVT Vladimir Tarasenko Jsy/125 6.00 15.00
DMWG Wayne Gretzky Glv/15 30.00 80.00
DMZC Zdeno Chara Ptch/50 5.00 12.00
DMZP Zach Parise Skate/25 10.00 25.00

2015-16 Black Diamond Double Diamond Jersey Booklets

DDBBK J.Bernier/N.Kadri/99 8.00 20.00
DDBBS J.Benn/T.Seguin/99 15.00 40.00
DDBBT D.Backes/Tarasenko/99 12.00 30.00
DDBCB R.Bourque/Z.Chara/99 15.00 40.00
DDBCT J.Carter/T.Toffoli/99 8.00 20.00
DDBFI T.Fleury/J.Iginla/99 8.00 20.00
DDBID J.Iginla/M.Duchene/99 8.00 20.00
DDBKM E.Malkin/C.Kunitz/99 10.00 25.00
DDBMC Brodeur/Schneider/99 15.00 40.00
DDBMG Monahan/Gaudreau/99 10.00 25.00
DDBNZ R.Nash/M.Zuccarello/99 8.00 20.00
DDBPG R.Getzlaf/C.Perry/99 12.00 30.00
DDBPP Z.Parise/J.Pominville/99 8.00 20.00
DDBPS C.Price/P.Subban/99 25.00 50.00
DDBRF B.Ranford/G.Fuhr/99 15.00 30.00
DDBRG W.Gretzky/R.Blake/25 40.00 80.00
DDBSK D.Savard/M.Keane/99 10.00 25.00
DDBSS D.Sedin/H.Sedin/99 8.00 20.00
DDBVG C.Giroux/J.Voracek/99 8.00 20.00

2015-16 Black Diamond Jerseys

*PRIME/25-35: .8X TO 2X JSY/85
*PRIME/25: .6X TO 1.5X JSY/35
BDBAE Aaron Ekblad/85 4.00 10.00
BDBAK Anze Kopitar/85 6.00 15.00
BDBAL Andrew Ladd/85 4.00 10.00
BDBAO Alexander Ovechkin/35 20.00 50.00
BDBBD Brandon Dubinsky/85 3.00 8.00
BDBBE Jamie Benn/85 5.00 12.00
BDBCG Claude Giroux/85 4.00 10.00
BDBCP Carey Price/35 20.00 40.00
BDBCS Cory Schneider/85 3.00 8.00
BDBEK Erik Karlsson/85 8.00 20.00
BDBEM Evgeni Malkin/35 15.00 40.00
BDBES Eric Staal/85 5.00 12.00
BDBHL Henrik Lundqvist/35 6.00 15.00
BDBHS Henrik Sedin/85 4.00 10.00
BDBHZ Henrik Zetterberg/85 5.00 12.00
BDBJB Jonathan Bernier/85 4.00 10.00
BDBJP Joe Pavelski/85 4.00 10.00
BDBJQ Jonathan Quick/85 6.00 15.00
BDBJT Jonathan Toews/35 10.00 25.00
BDBMD Matt Duchene/85 4.00 10.00
BDBML Mario Lemieux/35 15.00 40.00
BDBNA Rick Nash/85 4.00 10.00
BDBNB Nicklas Backstrom/85 6.00 15.00
BDBNM Nathan MacKinnon/35 10.00 25.00
BDBPB Patrice Bergeron/85 5.00 12.00
BDBPD Pavel Datsyuk/35 6.00 15.00
BDBPE Corey Perry/85 4.00 10.00
BDBPK Patrick Kane/35 10.00 25.00
BDBPR Patrick Roy/35 12.00 30.00
BDBPS P.K. Subban/85 6.00 15.00
BDBRG Ryan Getzlaf/35 8.00 20.00
BDBRM Ryan Miller/85 4.00 10.00
BDBSC Sidney Crosby/35 20.00 50.00
BDBSD Shane Doan/85 3.00 8.00
BDBSM Sean Monahan/85 4.00 10.00
BDBSS Steven Stamkos/85 8.00 20.00
BDBSW Shea Weber/85 3.00 8.00
BDBSY Steve Yzerman/35 8.00 20.00
BDBTA John Tavares/35 6.00 15.00
BDBTR Tuukka Rask/85 4.00 10.00
BDBTS Tyler Seguin/85 6.00 15.00
BDBVT Vladimir Tarasenko/85 6.00 15.00
BDBWG Wayne Gretzky/35 30.00 60.00
BDBZG Zemgus Girgensons/85 3.00 8.00
BDBZP Zach Parise/85 4.00 10.00

2015-16 Black Diamond Retired Numbers

RNBC Bobby Clarke/84 8.00 20.00
RNBH Bobby Hull/80 6.00 15.00
RNBO Bobby Orr/79 20.00 40.00
RNBS Borje Salming/90 6.00 15.00
RNDG Doug Gilmour/103 8.00 20.00
RNGF Grant Fuhr/100 6.00 15.00
RNHU Brett Hull/106 8.00 20.00
RNJS Joe Sakic/109 10.00 25.00
RNLR Larry Robinson/92 6.00 15.00
RNMB Mike Bossy/87 6.00 15.00
RNMD Marcel Dionne/89 8.00 20.00
RNME Mark Messier/104 8.00 20.00
RNMG Mike Gartner/98 6.00 15.00
RNML Mario Lemieux/106 20.00 50.00
RNMM Mike Modano/111 10.00 25.00
RNMN Markus Naslund/109 5.00 12.00
RNPR Patrick Roy/103 12.00 30.00
RNRB Ray Bourque/101 10.00 25.00
RNSA Terry Sawchuk/70 8.00 20.00
RNTS Teemu Selanne/114 12.00 30.00
RNWG Wayne Gretzky/99 30.00 60.00

2015-16 Black Diamond Retired Numbers Autographs

RNBC Bobby Clarke/49 20.00 50.00
RNBH Bobby Hull/25 40.00 80.00
RNBO Bobby Orr/10
RNBS Borje Salming/49 20.00 50.00
RNDG Doug Gilmour/49 25.00 60.00
RNGF Grant Fuhr/49 30.00 60.00
RNHU Brett Hull/25 25.00 60.00
RNJS Joe Sakic/25 40.00 100.00
RNLR Larry Robinson/25 25.00 60.00
RNMB Mike Bossy/49 20.00 50.00
RNMD Marcel Dionne/49 25.00 60.00
RNME Mark Messier/10
RNMG Mike Gartner/49 20.00 50.00
RNML Mario Lemieux/10
RNMM Mike Modano/25 40.00 100.00
RNMN Markus Naslund/49 15.00 40.00
RNPR Patrick Roy/10
RNRB Ray Bourque/25 40.00 80.00
RNTS Teemu Selanne/25 75.00 125.00
RNWG Wayne Gretzky/10

2015-16 Black Diamond Rookie Gems

STATED PRINT RUN 399 SER.#'d SETS
RGCH Connor Hellebuyck 8.00 20.00
RGCM Connor McDavid 75.00 125.00
RGDL Dylan Larkin 25.00 50.00
RGEP Emile Poirier 3.00 8.00
RGHS Henrik Samuelsson 2.50 6.00
RGJE Jack Eichel 30.00 60.00
RGJR Jacob de la Rose 3.00 8.00
RGKF Kevin Fiala 3.00 8.00
RGMD Max Domi 6.00 15.00
RGMS Malcolm Subban 8.00 20.00
RGNE Nikolaj Ehlers 6.00 15.00
RGNH Noah Hanifin 4.00 10.00
RGRH Ryan Hartman 4.00 10.00
RGRK Ronalds Kenins 3.00 8.00
RGSB Sam Bennett 4.00 10.00
RGSG Stanislav Galiev 3.00 8.00

2015-16 Black Diamond Rookie Gems Pure Black

*BLACK/25: .8X TO 2X BASIC INSERTS/399
RGCM Connor McDavid 300.00 500.00
RGDL Dylan Larkin 125.00 200.00
RGJE Jack Eichel 75.00 150.00
RGRH Ryan Hartman 8.00 20.00

2015-16 Black Diamond Rookie Gems Pure Black Autographs

EXCH EXPIRATION: 11/10/2017
RGCM Connor McDavid/49 EXCH 450.00 700.00
RGEP Emile Poirier/99 8.00 20.00
RGJR Jacob de la Rose/99 8.00 20.00
RGKF Kevin Fiala/99 8.00 20.00
RGMD Max Domi/99 30.00 60.00
RGMS Malcolm Subban/99 20.00 50.00
RGNE Nikolaj Ehlers/99 15.00 40.00
RGNH Noah Hanifin/99 10.00 25.00
RGRH Ryan Hartman/99 10.00 25.00
RGSB Sam Bennett/49 30.00 60.00

2015-16 Black Diamond Rookie Jersey Booklets

STATED PRINT RUN 299 SER.#'d SETS
RBRCH Connor Hellebuyck 12.00 30.00
RBRCM Connor McDavid 50.00 100.00
RBREP Emile Poirier 5.00 12.00
RBRJD Jacob de la Rose 5.00 12.00
RBRJE Jack Eichel 20.00 50.00
RBRJV Jake Virtanen 6.00 15.00
RBRKF Kevin Fiala 5.00 12.00
RBRMD Max Domi 10.00 25.00
RBRMP Matt Puempel 4.00 10.00
RBRNE Nikolaj Ehlers 8.00 20.00
RBRNH Noah Hanifin 6.00 15.00
RBRRH Ryan Hartman 6.00 15.00
RBRSB Sam Bennett 6.00 15.00
RBRSP Shane Prince 4.00 10.00

2015-16 Black Diamond Rookie Jersey Booklets Patch

STATED PRINT RUN 25 SER.#'d SETS
RBRCH Connor Hellebuyck AU 75.00 150.00
RBRCM Connor McDavid AU 450.00 800.00
RBREP Emile Poirier AU 20.00 50.00
RBRJD Jacob de la Rose AU 20.00 50.00
RBRJE Jack Eichel 100.00 200.00
RBRJV Jake Virtanen AU 25.00 60.00
RBRKF Kevin Fiala AU 20.00 50.00
RBRMD Max Domi AU 125.00 200.00
RBRMP Matt Puempel AU 15.00 40.00
RBRNE Nikolaj Ehlers AU 75.00 150.00
RBRNH Noah Hanifin AU 25.00 60.00
RBRRH Ryan Hartman AU 25.00 60.00
RBRSB Sam Bennett AU 75.00 150.00
RBRSP Shane Prince AU 30.00 60.00

2015-16 Black Diamond Rookie Jersey Placards

*PATCH/25: .8X TO 2X BASIC JSY/299
RMPCM Connor McDavid 30.00 80.00
RMPJE Jack Eichel 12.00 30.00
RMPJR Jacob de la Rose 3.00 8.00
RMPKF Kevin Fiala 3.00 8.00
RMPMD Max Domi 6.00 15.00
RMPSB Sam Bennett 4.00 10.00

2015-16 Black Diamond Rookie Jersey Placards Autographs

*PATCH/15: X TO X BASIC AUTO/125
RMPCM Connor McDavid 150.00 250.00
RMPJR Jacob de la Rose 5.00 12.00
RMPKF Kevin Fiala 5.00 12.00
RMPMD Max Domi 10.00 25.00
RMPNE Nikolaj Ehlers 10.00 25.00
RMPSB Sam Bennett 6.00 15.00

2015-16 Black Diamond Rookie Signature Placards

RSPCM Connor McDavid/149 175.00 300.00
RSPEP Emile Poirier/249 5.00 12.00
RSPJR Jacob de la Rose/249 5.00 12.00
RSPKF Kevin Fiala/249 5.00 12.00
RSPMC Nikolaj Ehlers/149 10.00 25.00
RSPMD Max Domi/249 10.00 25.00
RSPMS Malcolm Subban/249 12.00 30.00
RSPNH Noah Hanifin/249 6.00 15.00
RSPRH Ryan Hartman/249 6.00 15.00
RSPSB Sam Bennett/249 6.00 15.00

2015-16 Black Diamond Rookie Team Logo Jumbos

STATED ODDS 1:2.5
RTLCM Connor McDavid 50.00 100.00
RTLJD Jacob de la Rose 6.00 15.00
RTLJE Jack Eichel 25.00 50.00
RTLJV Jake Virtanen 8.00 20.00
RTLKF Kevin Fiala 10.00 25.00
RTLMD Max Domi 12.00 30.00
RTLMP Matt Puempel 5.00 12.00
RTLMS Malcolm Subban 15.00 40.00
RTLNE Nikolaj Ehlers 12.00 30.00
RTLRH Ryan Hartman 8.00 20.00
RTLSB Sam Bennett 8.00 20.00

2015-16 Black Diamond Rookie Team Logo Jumbos Autographs Gold

STATED PRINT RUN 25 SER.#'d SETS
RTLCM Connor McDavid
RTLJD Jacob de la Rose 12.00 30.00
RTLJV Jake Virtanen 15.00 40.00
RTLKF Kevin Fiala 12.00 30.00
RTLMD Max Domi 25.00 60.00
RTLMP Matt Puempel 10.00 25.00
RTLMS Malcolm Subban 30.00 80.00
RTLNE Nikolaj Ehlers 25.00 60.00
RTLRH Ryan Hartman 15.00 40.00
RTLSB Sam Bennett 15.00 40.00

2015-16 Black Diamond Signature Placards

GROUP A ODDS 1:61
GROUP B ODDS 1:22
GROUP C ODDS 1:25
GROUP D ODDS 1:15
GROUP E ODDS 1:12
OVERALL ODDS 1:4
SPAG Alex Galchenyuk B 12.00 30.00
SPAL Anders Lee E 5.00 12.00
SPBB Brent Burns C 6.00 15.00
SPBG Brendan Gallagher B 12.00 30.00
SPBH Bo Horvat D 8.00 20.00
SPBS Brandon Saad C 6.00 15.00
SPCN Cam Neely A
SPCO Chris Osgood B 10.00 25.00
SPCP Carey Price A 30.00 60.00
SPDH Dougie Hamilton C 10.00 25.00
SPFA Frederik Andersen E 5.00 12.00
SPGA Glenn Anderson A
SPGN Gustav Nyquist C 6.00 15.00
SPJC John Carlson D 8.00 20.00
SPJG Johnny Gaudreau D 20.00 40.00
SPJK John Klingberg E 8.00 20.00
SPJP Joe Pavelski A
SPJV James van Riemsdyk B 10.00 25.00
SPMK Mike Keane B 8.00 20.00
SPMM Marty McSorley B 10.00 25.00
SPON Owen Nolan B 8.00 20.00
SPTA Tomas Tatar E 5.00 12.00
SPTK Torey Krug E 6.00 15.00
SPTT Tyler Toffoli D 6.00 15.00
SPZG Zemgus Girgensons D 5.00 12.00
SPZP Zach Parise A

2015-16 Black Diamond Silver on Black Autographs

SBAK Anze Kopitar/50 20.00 50.00
SBAO Alexander Ovechkin/20 40.00 80.00
SBFP Felix Potvin/65 20.00 50.00
SBJB Jamie Benn/50 15.00 40.00
SBJT Jonathan Toews/35 60.00 100.00
SBKY Keith Yandle/65 10.00 25.00
SBMF Marc-Andre Fleury/35 20.00 50.00
SBMM Mark Messier/20 30.00 60.00
SBMP Max Pacioretty/65 10.00 25.00
SBNL Nicklas Lidstrom/35 12.00 30.00
SBPE Phil Esposito/35 25.00 50.00
SBRB Ray Bourque/35 25.00 50.00
SBSY Steve Yzerman/20 40.00 80.00
SBTH Taylor Hall/65 20.00 40.00

2015-16 Black Diamond Silver on Black Rookie Autographs

SBRSCM Connor McDavid/99 300.00 500.00
SBRSEP Emile Poirier/199 5.00 12.00
SBRSJR Jacob de la Rose/199 5.00 12.00
SBRSKF Kevin Fiala/199 5.00 12.00
SBRSMD Max Domi/199 15.00 40.00
SBRSMS Malcolm Subban/199 12.00 30.00
SBRSNE Nikolaj Ehlers/99 12.00 30.00
SBRSNH Noah Hanifin/199 6.00 15.00
SBRSRH Ryan Hartman/199 6.00 15.00
SBRSSB Sam Bennett/199 6.00 15.00

2015-16 Black Diamond Team Logo Jumbos

STATED ODDS 1:5
TLBBAO Adam Oates 8.00 20.00
TLBBBO Bobby Orr 30.00 60.00
TLBBCN Cam Neely 15.00 40.00
TLBBGC Gerry Cheevers 20.00 50.00
TLBBPB Patrice Bergeron 12.00 30.00
TLBBPE Phil Esposito 12.00 30.00
TLBBRB Ray Bourque 12.00 30.00
TLBBTR Tuukka Rask 8.00 20.00
TLBBZC Zdeno Chara 12.00 30.00
TLCBBH Bobby Hull 12.00 30.00
TLCBCC Chris Chelios 8.00 20.00
TLCBCR Corey Crawford 10.00 25.00
TLCBDK Duncan Keith 8.00 20.00
TLCBDS Denis Savard 10.00 25.00
TLCBGH Glenn Hall 6.00 15.00
TLCBJR Jeremy Roenick 40.00 80.00
TLCBJT Jonathan Toews 15.00 40.00
TLCBSL Steve Larmer 8.00 20.00
TLMCAG Alex Galchenyuk 10.00 25.00
TLMCBG Brendan Gallagher 10.00 25.00
TLMCCA Carey Price 40.00 80.00
TLMCGL Guy Lafleur 12.00 30.00
TLMCLR Larry Robinson 8.00 20.00
TLMCMP Max Pacioretty 12.00 30.00
TLMCPR Patrick Roy 15.00 40.00
TLMCPS P.K. Subban 10.00 25.00
TLMCVD Vincent Damphousse 6.00 15.00
TLNYBL Brian Leetch 8.00 20.00
TLNYDS Derek Stepan 8.00 20.00
TLNYHL Henrik Lundqvist 12.00 30.00
TLNYJV John Vanbiesbrouck 12.00 30.00
TLNYMG Mike Gartner 8.00 20.00
TLNYMM Mark Messier 12.00 30.00
TLNYMR Mike Richter 8.00 20.00
TLNYRN Rick Nash 8.00 20.00
TLNYWG Wayne Gretzky 40.00 80.00
TLPPCK Chris Kunitz 10.00 25.00
TLPPEM Evgeni Malkin 25.00 60.00
TLPPJJ Jaromir Jagr 20.00 50.00
TLPPKL Kris Letang 8.00 20.00
TLPPMF Marc-Andre Fleury 12.00 30.00
TLPPML Mario Lemieux 25.00 60.00
TLPPPC Paul Coffey 12.00 30.00
TLPPSC Sidney Crosby 30.00 80.00
TLPPTB Tom Barrasso 10.00 25.00
TLRWCC Chris Chelios 12.00 30.00
TLRWCO Chris Osgood 12.00 30.00
TLRWGN Gustav Nyquist 8.00 20.00
TLRWHZ Henrik Zetterberg 10.00 25.00
TLRWNL Nicklas Lidstrom 12.00 30.00
TLRWPD Pavel Datsyuk 10.00 25.00
TLRWSY Steve Yzerman 15.00 40.00
TLRWTS Terry Sawchuk 8.00 20.00
TLRWTT Tomas Tatar 6.00 15.00

2015-16 Black Diamond Team Logo Jumbos Gold Black Diamond

TLBBAO Adam Oates 8.00 20.00
TLBBBO Bobby Orr 40.00 80.00
TLBBCN Cam Neely 8.00 20.00
TLBBGC Gerry Cheevers 15.00 40.00
TLBBPB Patrice Bergeron 10.00 25.00
TLBBPE Phil Esposito 12.00 30.00
TLBBRB Ray Bourque 15.00 40.00
TLBBTR Tuukka Rask 8.00 20.00
TLBBZC Zdeno Chara 8.00 20.00
TLCBBH Bobby Hull 8.00 20.00
TLCBCC Chris Chelios 8.00 20.00
TLCBCR Corey Crawford 10.00 25.00
TLCBDK Duncan Keith 8.00 20.00
TLCBDS Denis Savard 10.00 25.00
TLCBGH Glenn Hall 6.00 15.00
TLCBJR Jeremy Roenick 8.00 20.00
TLCBJT Jonathan Toews 15.00 40.00
TLCBSL Steve Larmer 6.00 15.00
TLMCAG Alex Galchenyuk 10.00 25.00
TLMCBG Brendan Gallagher 10.00 25.00
TLMCCA Carey Price 20.00 40.00
TLMCGL Guy Lafleur 10.00 25.00
TLMCLR Larry Robinson 8.00 20.00
TLMCMP Max Pacioretty 8.00 20.00
TLMCPR Patrick Roy 25.00 50.00
TLMCPS P.K. Subban 12.00 30.00
TLMCVD Vincent Damphousse 6.00 15.00
TLNYBL Brian Leetch 8.00 20.00
TLNYDS Derek Stepan 8.00 20.00
TLNYHL Henrik Lundqvist 10.00 25.00
TLNYJV John Vanbiesbrouck 8.00 20.00
TLNYMG Mike Gartner 8.00 20.00
TLNYMM Mark Messier 12.00 30.00
TLNYMR Mike Richter 8.00 20.00
TLNYRN Rick Nash 8.00 20.00
TLNYWG Wayne Gretzky 50.00 100.00
TLPPCK Chris Kunitz 8.00 20.00
TLPPEM Evgeni Malkin 25.00 60.00
TLPPJJ Jaromir Jagr 20.00 50.00
TLPPKL Kris Letang 8.00 20.00
TLPPMF Marc-Andre Fleury 12.00 30.00
TLPPML Mario Lemieux 25.00 50.00
TLPPPC Paul Coffey 8.00 20.00
TLPPSC Sidney Crosby 25.00 50.00
TLPPTB Tom Barrasso 8.00 20.00
TLRWCC Chris Chelios 8.00 20.00
TLRWCO Chris Osgood 8.00 20.00
TLRWGN Gustav Nyquist 8.00 20.00
TLRWHZ Henrik Zetterberg 10.00 25.00
TLRWNL Nicklas Lidstrom 8.00 20.00
TLRWPD Pavel Datsyuk 10.00 25.00
TLRWSY Steve Yzerman 12.00 30.00
TLRWTS Terry Sawchuk 8.00 20.00
TLRWTT Tomas Tatar 6.00 15.00

2016-17 Black Diamond

BDBAH Adam Henrique 3.00 8.00
BDBAK Anze Kopitar 5.00 12.00
BDBAO Alexander Ovechkin 12.00 30.00
BDBBB Brent Burns 4.00 10.00
BDBBH Braden Holtby 5.00 12.00
BDBBS Brandon Saad 3.00 8.00
BDBBW Blake Wheeler 3.00 8.00
BDBCG Claude Giroux 3.00 8.00
BDBCM Connor McDavid 15.00 40.00
BDBCP Carey Price 10.00 25.00
BDBCS Cory Schneider 2.50 6.00
BDBDD Drew Doughty 3.00 8.00
BDBDK David Krejci 3.00 8.00
BDBEK Erik Karlsson 6.00 15.00
BDBEM Evgeni Malkin 10.00 25.00
BDBGI John Gibson 3.00 8.00
BDBHL Henrik Lundqvist 3.00 8.00
BDBHO Bo Horvat 5.00 12.00
BDBHZ Henrik Zetterberg 4.00 10.00
BDBJA Jake Allen 4.00 10.00
BDBJB Jamie Benn 4.00 10.00
BDBJE Jack Eichel 6.00 15.00
BDBJG Johnny Gaudreau 5.00 12.00
BDBJJ Jaromir Jagr 8.00 20.00
BDBJK John Klingberg 3.00 8.00
BDBJO Roman Josi 3.00 8.00
BDBJP Joe Pavelski 3.00 8.00
BDBJS Jeff Skinner 3.00 8.00
BDBJT Jonathan Toews 6.00 15.00
BDBKA Patrick Kane 6.00 15.00
BDBML Mario Lemieux 10.00 25.00
BDBMP Max Pacioretty 3.00 8.00
BDBMR Morgan Rielly 2.50 6.00
BDBMS Mark Scheifele 4.00 10.00
BDBNK Nikita Kucherov 5.00 12.00
BDBNM Nathan MacKinnon 6.00 15.00
BDBOE Oliver Ekman-Larsson 2.50 6.00
BDBPR Patrick Roy 8.00 20.00
BDBRB Ray Bourque 5.00 12.00
BDBRJ Ryan Johansen 4.00 10.00
BDBRN Rick Nash 3.00 8.00
BDBRO Ryan O'Reilly 3.00 8.00
BDBSC Sidney Crosby 12.00 30.00
BDBSG Shayne Gostisbehere 4.00 10.00
BDBSS Steven Stamkos 6.00 15.00
BDBSY Steve Yzerman 4.00 10.00
BDBTA John Tavares 6.00 15.00
BDBVT Vladimir Tarasenko 5.00 12.00
BDBWG Wayne Gretzky 15.00 40.00
BDBZP Zach Parise 3.00 8.00
BDRAM Auston Matthews RC 1000.00 1500.00
BDRBA Mathew Barzal RC 150.00 300.00
BDRBL Brendan Leipsic RC 25.00 60.00
BDRCB Connor Brown RC 40.00 100.00
BDRCD Christian Dvorak RC 25.00 60.00
BDRCL Charlie Lindgren RC 50.00 125.00
BDRDS Dylan Strome RC 80.00 200.00
BDRHF Hudson Fasching RC 25.00 60.00
BDRIP Ivan Provorov RC 100.00 200.00
BDRJB Justin Bailey RC 25.00 60.00
BDRJD Jason Dickinson RC 20.00 50.00
BDRJE Joel Eriksson Ek RC 25.00 60.00
BDRJP Jesse Puljujarvi RC 60.00 150.00
BDRKC Kyle Connor RC 60.00 150.00
BDRKK Kasperi Kapanen RC 50.00 125.00
BDRLC Lawson Crouse RC 20.00 50.00
BDRMA Anthony Mantha RC 60.00 150.00
BDRMM Mitch Marner RC 200.00 400.00
BDRMO Tyler Motte RC 25.00 60.00
BDRMS Mikhail Sergachev RC 60.00 150.00
BDRMT Matthew Tkachuk RC 60.00 150.00
BDRMW Miles Wood RC 20.00 50.00
BDRNS Nikita Soshnikov RC 15.00 40.00
BDROB Oliver Bjorkstrand RC 20.00 50.00
BDRPB Pavel Buchnevich RC 40.00 100.00
BDRPL Patrik Laine RC 350.00 500.00
BDRPZ Pavel Zacha RC 30.00 80.00
BDRSA Sebastian Aho RC 50.00 125.00
BDRSC Nick Schmaltz RC 25.00 60.00
BDRSM Sonny Milano RC 30.00 80.00
BDRSS Steven Santini RC 20.00 50.00
BDRTK Travis Konecny RC 50.00 125.00
BDRVE Jimmy Vesey RC 50.00 125.00
BDRWN William Nylander RC 150.00 300.00
BDRZW Zach Werenski RC 50.00 120.00

2016-17 Black Diamond Championship Banners

CBAK Anze Kopitar/112 8.00 20.00
CBBC Bobby Clarke/74 10.00 25.00
CBCP Corey Perry/107 5.00 12.00
CBCW Cam Ward/106 5.00 12.00
CBGH Glenn Hall/61 5.00 12.00
CBIL Igor Larionov/97 5.00 12.00
CBJK Jari Kurri/87 5.00 12.00
CBJL John LeClair/93 5.00 12.00
CBJT Jonathan Toews/110 10.00 25.00
CBLM Lanny McDonald/89 5.00 12.00
CBLR Larry Robinson/79 5.00 12.00
CBMB Martin Brodeur/95 10.00 25.00
CBMF Marc-Andre Fleury/109 8.00 20.00
CBML Mario Lemieux/92 15.00 40.00
CBMM Mark Messier/94 6.00 15.00
CBMS Milt Schmidt/39 5.00 12.00
CBNL Nicklas Lidstrom/98 5.00 12.00
CBPR Patrick Roy/86 12.00 30.00
CBST Martin St. Louis/104 5.00 12.00
CBWG Wayne Gretzky/84 25.00 60.00

2016-17 Black Diamond Diamond Mine Relics

DMAE Aaron Ekblad/50 8.00 20.00
DMAO Alexander Ovechkin/15 60.00 150.00
DMAS Alexander Steen/50 8.00 20.00
DMBB Brent Burns/199 8.00 20.00
DMBE Patrice Bergeron/199 8.00 20.00
DMBR Bill Ranford/35 10.00 25.00
DMCC Corey Crawford/199 8.00 20.00
DMCS Cory Schneider/50 6.00 15.00
DMDK Duncan Keith/199 6.00 15.00
DMDS Daniel Sedin/199 6.00 15.00
DMEM Evgeni Malkin/35 30.00 80.00
DMFF Filip Forsberg/50 10.00 25.00
DMHS Henrik Sedin/50 8.00 20.00
DMJB Jamie Benn/50 10.00 25.00
DMJC Jeff Carter/35 10.00 25.00
DMJH Jonathan Huberdeau/50 8.00 20.00
DMJO Joe Thornton/35 10.00 25.00
DMJR Jeremy Roenick/199 6.00 15.00
DMJW Justin Williams/50 6.00 15.00
DMKU Evgeny Kuznetsov/199 10.00 25.00
DMLR Larry Robinson/15 15.00 40.00
DMLU Luc Robitaille/15 15.00 40.00
DMMB Martin Brodeur/199 12.00 30.00
DMMF Marc-Andre Fleury/50 12.00 30.00
DMMH Marian Hossa/35 8.00 20.00
DMMM Mark Messier/15 20.00 50.00
DMMR Morgan Rielly/50 6.00 15.00
DMOE Oliver Ekman-Larsson/199 5.00 12.00
DMPB Pavel Bure/199 6.00 15.00
DMPC Paul Coffey/199 6.00 15.00
DMPF Peter Forsberg/15 15.00 40.00
DMRG Ryan Getzlaf/199 10.00 25.00
DMRL Roberto Luongo/35 10.00 25.00
DMRN Rick Nash/50 8.00 20.00
DMSB Sam Bennett/199 8.00 20.00
DMSK Jeff Skinner/50 8.00 20.00
DMSS Steven Stamkos/15 30.00 80.00
DMTA John Tavares/35 20.00 50.00
DMTE Tony Esposito/15 15.00 40.00
DMTL Trevor Linden/15 20.00 50.00
DMVH Victor Hedman/35 12.00 30.00
DMVT Vladimir Tarasenko/35 15.00 40.00

2016-17 Black Diamond Pure Black

COMMON CARD 5.00 12.00
SEMISTARS 6.00 15.00
UNLISTED STARS 8.00 20.00
BDBCP Carey Price AU/25 50.00 125.00
BDBHL Henrik Lundqvist AU/25 50.00 125.00
BDBJJ Jaromir Jagr AU/25 40.00 100.00
BDBJT Jonathan Toews AU/25 40.00 100.00
BDBML Mario Lemieux AU/25 60.00 150.00
BDBPR Patrick Roy AU/25 50.00 125.00
BDBRB Ray Bourque AU/25 25.00 60.00
BDBSC Sidney Crosby AU/25 150.00 250.00
BDBSY Steve Yzerman AU/25 50.00 125.00
BDBWG Wayne Gretzky AU/25 200.00 400.00

2016-17 Black Diamond Rookie Booklet Relics

RBRAM Auston Matthews 30.00 80.00
RBRCD Christian Dvorak 5.00 12.00
RBRDS Dylan Strome 10.00 25.00
RBRHF Hudson Fasching 5.00 12.00
RBRIP Ivan Provorov 10.00 25.00
RBRJD Jason Dickinson 4.00 10.00
RBRJM Josh Morrissey 6.00 15.00
RBRJP Jesse Puljujarvi 12.00 30.00
RBRKK Kasperi Kapanen 10.00 25.00
RBRMA Anthony Mantha 12.00 30.00
RBRMM Mitch Marner 25.00 60.00
RBRMT Matthew Tkachuk 15.00 40.00
RBRPL Patrik Laine 20.00 50.00
RBRPZ Pavel Zacha 6.00 15.00
RBRSM Sonny Milano 6.00 15.00
RBRWN William Nylander 20.00 50.00

2016-17 Black Diamond Rookie Booklet Relics Jersey Autographs

RBRAM Auston Matthews 200.00 400.00
RBRCD Christian Dvorak 10.00 25.00
RBRDS Dylan Strome 20.00 50.00
RBRHF Hudson Fasching 10.00 25.00
RBRIP Ivan Provorov 20.00 50.00
RBRJD Jason Dickinson 8.00 20.00
RBRJM Josh Morrissey 12.00 30.00
RBRJP Jesse Puljujarvi 25.00 60.00
RBRKK Kasperi Kapanen 20.00 50.00
RBRMA Anthony Mantha 25.00 60.00
RBRMM Mitch Marner 50.00 125.00
RBRMT Matthew Tkachuk 30.00 80.00
RBRPL Patrik Laine 40.00 100.00
RBRPZ Pavel Zacha 12.00 30.00
RBRSM Sonny Milano 12.00 30.00
RBRWN William Nylander 50.00 125.00

2016-17 Black Diamond Rookie Gems

RGAM Auston Matthews 40.00 100.00
RGCL Charlie Lindgren 6.00 15.00
RGDS Dylan Strome 6.00 15.00
RGHF Hudson Fasching 3.00 8.00
RGIP Ivan Provorov 6.00 15.00
RGJD Jason Dickinson 2.50 6.00
RGJP Jesse Puljujarvi 8.00 20.00
RGJV Jimmy Vesey 6.00 15.00
RGLC Lawson Crouse 2.50 6.00
RGMA Anthony Mantha 8.00 20.00
RGMM Mitch Marner 15.00 40.00
RGNS Nikita Soshnikov 2.00 5.00
RGOB Oliver Bjorkstrand 2.50 6.00
RGPL Patrik Laine 12.00 30.00
RGPZ Pavel Zacha 4.00 10.00
RGTM Tyler Motte 3.00 8.00
RGWN William Nylander 12.00 30.00
RGZW Zach Werenski 6.00 15.00

2016-17 Black Diamond Rookie Gems Pure Black

*BLACK/25: 1X TO 2.5X BASIC INSERTS
RGAM Auston Matthews 150.00 300.00
RGPL Patrik Laine 80.00 200.00

2016-17 Black Diamond Rookie Gems Pure Black Signatures

RGCL Charlie Lindgren/199 15.00 40.00
RGDS Dylan Strome/199 15.00 40.00
RGHF Hudson Fasching/199 8.00 20.00
RGIP Ivan Provorov/199 15.00 40.00
RGJD Jason Dickinson/199 6.00 15.00
RGJP Jesse Puljujarvi/199 20.00 50.00
RGJV Jimmy Vesey/199 15.00 40.00
RGLC Lawson Crouse/199 6.00 15.00
RGMA Anthony Mantha/99 20.00 50.00
RGMM Mitch Marner/99 40.00 100.00
RGNS Nikita Soshnikov/199 5.00 12.00
RGOB Oliver Bjorkstrand/199 6.00 15.00
RGPL Patrik Laine/99 60.00 150.00
RGPZ Pavel Zacha/99 10.00 25.00
RGTM Tyler Motte/199 8.00 20.00
RGWN William Nylander/99 30.00 80.00
RGZW Zach Werenski/199 15.00 40.00

2016-17 Black Diamond Rookie Team Logo Jumbos Autographs Alternate Logo

RTLAM Auston Matthews 400.00 650.00
RTLDS Dylan Strome
RTLHF Hudson Fasching
RTLIP Ivan Provorov 60.00 150.00
RTLMA Anthony Mantha 60.00 150.00
RTLPL Patrik Laine
RTLPZ Pavel Zacha
RTLSM Sonny Milano 40.00 100.00
RTLWN William Nylander 60.00 150.00

2016-17 Black Diamond Run for the Cup

RUNAK Anze Kopitar 8.00 20.00
RUNAM Auston Matthews 60.00 150.00
RUNAO Alexander Ovechkin 20.00 50.00
RUNAP Alex Pietrangelo 4.00 10.00
RUNBH Braden Holtby 8.00 20.00
RUNCM Connor McDavid 25.00 60.00
RUNCP Carey Price 15.00 40.00
RUNDD Drew Doughty 5.00 12.00
RUNDL Dylan Larkin 8.00 20.00
RUNEK Erik Karlsson 10.00 25.00
RUNFF Filip Forsberg 6.00 15.00
RUNHL Henrik Lundqvist 5.00 12.00
RUNJB Jamie Benn 6.00 15.00
RUNJE Jack Eichel 10.00 25.00
RUNJP Joe Pavelski 5.00 12.00
RUNJT John Tavares 10.00 25.00
RUNMA Anthony Mantha 12.00 30.00
RUNML Mario Lemieux 15.00 40.00
RUNNK Nikita Kucherov 8.00 20.00
RUNPA Artemi Panarin 6.00 15.00
RUNPK Patrick Kane 10.00 25.00
RUNRG Ryan Getzlaf 8.00 20.00
RUNSC Sidney Crosby 20.00 50.00
RUNSM Sean Monahan 5.00 12.00
RUNSS Steven Stamkos 10.00 25.00
RUNSY Steve Yzerman 6.00 15.00
RUNTH Joe Thornton 5.00 12.00
RUNTS Tyler Seguin 8.00 20.00
RUNVT Vladimir Tarasenko 8.00 20.00
RUNWG Wayne Gretzky 25.00 60.00

2016-17 Black Diamond Signature Placards

SPAH Andrew Hammond D 5.00 12.00
SPBC Bobby Clarke B 20.00 50.00
SPBG Brendan Gallagher B 12.00 30.00
SPBH Brett Hull A
SPBO Bo Horvat D 10.00 25.00
SPCG Clark Gillies A
SPCH Carl Hagelin D 12.00 30.00
SPGN Gustav Nyquist B 10.00 25.00
SPHL Henrik Lundqvist B 30.00 80.00
SPHU Jonathan Huberdeau C 15.00 40.00
SPJK Jari Kurri C 15.00 40.00
SPJT Jacob Trouba D 8.00 20.00
SPKP Kyle Palmieri D 6.00 15.00
SPMD Matt Duchene A 25.00 60.00
SPMG Mikael Granlund D 10.00 25.00
SPMS Mark Stone C 6.00 15.00
SPNF Nick Foligno C 10.00 25.00
SPNL Nicklas Lidstrom A
SPPR Pekka Rinne B 10.00 25.00
SPRJ Roman Josi D 8.00 20.00
SPRO Ryan O'Reilly D 8.00 20.00
SPTL Trevor Linden C 12.00 30.00
SPTT Tyler Toffoli C 15.00 40.00
SPZP Zach Parise B 12.00 30.00

2016-17 Black Diamond Signature Rookie Materials Jersey

SRJAM Auston Matthews/25 200.00 400.00
SRJDS Dylan Strome/99 15.00 40.00
SRJDV Christian Dvorak/99 8.00 20.00
SRJHF Hudson Fasching/99 8.00 20.00
SRJIP Ivan Provorov/99 15.00 40.00
SRJJD Jason Dickinson/99 6.00 15.00
SRJJP Jesse Puljujarvi/99 20.00 50.00
SRJKK Kasperi Kapanen/99 15.00 40.00
SRJLC Lawson Crouse/99 6.00 15.00
SRJMA Anthony Mantha/99 20.00 50.00
SRJMI Michael Matheson/99 8.00 20.00
SRJMM Mitch Marner/99 40.00 100.00
SRJMR Mike Reilly/99 6.00 15.00
SRJOB Oliver Bjorkstrand/99 6.00 15.00
SRJPL Patrik Laine/99 30.00 80.00
SRJPZ Pavel Zacha/99 10.00 25.00
SRJSM Sonny Milano/99 10.00 25.00
SRJWN William Nylander/99 30.00 80.00

2016-17 Black Diamond Silver on Black Signatures

SBAH Adam Henrique/125 10.00 25.00
SBBP Peter Bondra/125 10.00 25.00
SBCM Connor McDavid/25 200.00 300.00
SBCP Carey Price/25 100.00 200.00
SBDA Dave Andreychuk/125 10.00 25.00
SBJG John Gibson/125 10.00 25.00
SBPM Patrick Marleau/125 10.00 25.00
SBRN Rick Nash/125 10.00 25.00
SBSB Sam Bennett/125 12.00 30.00
SBSM Sean Monahan/125 10.00 25.00
SBTA John Tavares/125 20.00 50.00

2016-17 Black Diamond Team Logo Jumbos

TLEOCM Connor McDavid 40.00 100.00
TLEOGF Grant Fuhr 8.00 20.00
TLEOJE Jordan Eberle 8.00 20.00
TLEOJK Jari Kurri 8.00 20.00
TLEOLD Leon Draisaitl 10.00 25.00
TLEOMM Mark Messier 10.00 25.00
TLEOPC Paul Coffey 8.00 20.00
TLEORN Ryan Nugent-Hopkins 8.00 20.00
TLEOWG Wayne Gretzky SP 60.00 150.00
TLNIBB Bob Bourne 8.00 20.00
TLNIBN Bob Nystrom 6.00 15.00
TLNIBS Billy Smith 8.00 20.00
TLNICG Clark Gillies 8.00 20.00
TLNIJT John Tavares 15.00 40.00
TLNIMB Mike Bossy SP 15.00 40.00
TLNINE Brock Nelson 6.00 15.00
TLNINL Nick Leddy 5.00 12.00
TLNITH Travis Hamonic 5.00 12.00
TLSBAM Al MacInnis 8.00 20.00
TLSBAP Alex Pietrangelo 6.00 15.00
TLSBAS Alexander Steen 8.00 20.00
TLSBBH Brett Hull SP 15.00 40.00
TLSBCP Colton Parayko 8.00 20.00
TLSBDG Doug Gilmour 10.00 25.00
TLSBJA Jake Allen 10.00 25.00
TLSBRF Robby Fabbri 8.00 20.00
TLSBVT Vladimir Tarasenko 12.00 30.00
TLVCAE Alexander Edler 5.00 12.00
TLVCBO Bo Horvat 12.00 30.00
TLVCDS Daniel Sedin 8.00 20.00
TLVCHS Henrik Sedin 8.00 20.00
TLVCJV Jake Virtanen 10.00 25.00
TLVCKM Kirk McLean 8.00 20.00
TLVCPB Pavel Bure SP 30.00 80.00
TLVCRL Roberto Luongo 8.00 20.00
TLVCTL Trevor Linden 10.00 25.00
TLWCAB Andre Burakovsky 6.00 15.00
TLWCAO Alexander Ovechkin SP 20.00 50.00
TLWCBH Braden Holtby 12.00 30.00
TLWCEK Evgeny Kuznetsov 12.00 30.00
TLWCJC John Carlson 10.00 25.00
TLWCJW Justin Williams 6.00 15.00
TLWCMG Mike Gartner 8.00 20.00
TLWCNB Nicklas Backstrom 12.00 30.00
TLWCPB Peter Bondra 8.00 20.00
TLWJBL Bryan Little 6.00 15.00
TLWJBW Blake Wheeler SP 20.00 50.00
TLWJCH Connor Hellebuyck 12.00 30.00
TLWJDB Dustin Byfuglien 8.00 20.00
TLWJJT Jacob Trouba 6.00 15.00
TLWJMP Mathieu Perreault 6.00 15.00
TLWJMS Mark Scheifele 10.00 25.00
TLWJNE Nikolaj Ehlers 8.00 20.00
TLWJTM Tyler Myers 6.00 15.00

2017-18 Black Diamond

BDBAM Auston Matthews 12.00 30.00
BDBAO Alexander Ovechkin 12.00 30.00
BDBBM Brad Marchand 4.00 10.00
BDBBO Bobby Orr 10.00 25.00
BDBCM Connor McDavid 12.00 30.00
BDBCP Carey Price 10.00 25.00
BDBDD Devan Dubnyk 3.00 8.00
BDBDH Dale Hawerchuk 4.00 10.00
BDBDO Max Domi 3.00 8.00
BDBEK Erik Karlsson 4.00 10.00
BDBEM Evgeni Malkin 10.00 25.00
BDBFA Frederik Andersen 2.50 6.00
BDBGL Guy Lafleur 4.00 10.00
BDBHL Henrik Lundqvist 5.00 12.00
BDBHS Henrik Sedin 3.00 8.00
BDBHZ Henrik Zetterberg 3.00 8.00
BDBJC Jeff Carter 3.00 8.00
BDBJD Jonathan Drouin 3.00 8.00
BDBJE Jack Eichel 5.00 12.00
BDBJG Jake Guentzel 4.00 10.00
BDBJP Joe Pavelski 3.00 8.00
BDBJS Jaden Schwartz 4.00 10.00
BDBJT John Tavares 6.00 15.00
BDBLC Logan Couture 3.00 8.00
BDBLD Leon Draisaitl 5.00 12.00
BDBMA Mitch Marner 5.00 12.00
BDBMF Marc-Andre Fleury 8.00 20.00
BDBMH Mike Hoffman 2.50 6.00
BDBML Mario Lemieux 10.00 25.00
BDBMM Matt Murray 5.00 12.00
BDBMT Matthew Tkachuk 3.00 8.00
BDBNE Nikolaj Ehlers 3.00 8.00
BDBNK Nikita Kucherov 5.00 12.00
BDBNM Nathan MacKinnon 6.00 15.00
BDBPK Patrick Kane 6.00 15.00
BDBPL Patrik Laine 5.00 12.00
BDBPS P.K. Subban 3.00 8.00
BDBRG Ryan Getzlaf 3.00 8.00
BDBRL Roberto Luongo 3.00 8.00
BDBSB Sergei Bobrovsky 3.00 8.00
BDBSC Sidney Crosby 12.00 30.00
BDBSS Steven Stamkos 6.00 15.00
BDBTH Taylor Hall 6.00 15.00
BDBTS Tyler Seguin 5.00 12.00
BDBVH Victor Hedman 4.00 10.00
BDBVR Victor Rask 3.00 8.00
BDBVT Vladimir Tarasenko 5.00 12.00
BDBWG Wayne Gretzky 15.00 40.00
BDBWN William Nylander 5.00 12.00
BDBWS Wayne Simmonds 4.00 10.00
BDRAB Anders Bjork RC 40.00 100.00
BDRAD Alex DeBrincat RC 60.00 150.00
BDRAK Adrian Kempe RC 30.00 80.00
BDRAN Alexander Nylander RC 40.00 100.00
BDRBB Brock Boeser RC 450.00 600.00
BDRCF Christian Fischer RC 30.00 80.00
BDRCK Clayton Keller RC 150.00 300.00
BDRCM Charlie McAvoy RC 200.00 400.00
BDRCW Colin White RC 25.00 60.00
BDRDG Denis Gurianov RC 25.00 60.00
BDREC Eric Comrie RC 20.00 50.00
BDRES Evgeny Svechnikov RC 50.00 125.00
BDRIB Ivan Barbashev RC 25.00 60.00
BDRJC J.T. Compher RC 30.00 80.00
BDRJD Jake DeBrusk RC 40.00 100.00
BDRJF Jakob Forsbacka-Karlsson RC 25.00 60.00
BDRJG Jon Gillies RC 25.00 60.00
BDRJH Josh Ho-Sang RC 30.00 80.00
BDRJR Jack Roslovic RC 40.00 100.00
BDRLK Luke Kunin RC 25.00 60.00
BDRMB Madison Bowey RC 20.00 50.00
BDRNH Nico Hischier RC 300.00 600.00
BDRNP Nolan Patrick RC 50.00 125.00
BDRNS Nikita Scherbak RC 50.00 125.00
BDROT Owen Tippett RC 50.00 125.00
BDRPC Peter Cehlarik RC 25.00 60.00
BDRPD Pierre-Luc Dubois RC 60.00 150.00
BDRSM Samuel Morin RC 25.00 60.00
BDRTJ Tyson Jost RC 50.00 125.00
BDRTS Travis Sanheim RC 25.00 60.00
BDRVK Vladislav Kamenev RC 40.00 100.00
BDRVS Vadim Shipachyov RC 80.00 200.00
BDRRMR Maurice Richard RR 350.00 400.00

2017-18 Black Diamond Championship Banners

CBBO Bobby Orr/70 30.00 80.00
CBDA Dave Andreychuk/104 10.00 25.00
CBDG Doug Gilmour/89 12.00 30.00
CBDP Denis Potvin/81 10.00 25.00
CBEB Ed Belfour/99 12.00 30.00
CBJB Johnny Bower/64 10.00 25.00
CBJM Jake Muzzin/114 8.00 20.00
CBJS Joe Sakic/96 12.00 30.00
CBMU Matt Murray/116 15.00 40.00
CBVD Vincent Damphousse/93 8.00 20.00

2017-18 Black Diamond Championship Banners Gold

CBDA Dave Andreychuk AU/99 20.00 50.00
CBDG Doug Gilmour AU/25 25.00 60.00
CBJB Johnny Bower AU/25 40.00 100.00
CBJM Jake Muzzin AU/99 15.00 40.00
CBVD Vincent Damphousse AU/99 15.00 40.00

2017-18 Black Diamond Championship Rings

CRBR Bryan Rust 10.00 25.00
CRCH Carl Hagelin 10.00 25.00
CRCK Chris Kunitz 10.00 25.00
CRCS Conor Sheary 10.00 25.00
CREM Evgeni Malkin 12.00 30.00
CRJG Jake Guentzel 12.00 30.00
CRJS Justin Schultz 10.00 25.00
CRMC Matt Cullen 8.00 20.00
CRMF Marc-Andre Fleury 15.00 40.00
CRMM Matt Murray 15.00 40.00
CRNB Nick Bonino 8.00 20.00
CRPH Patric Hornqvist 8.00 20.00
CRPK Phil Kessel 12.00 30.00

CRRH Ron Hainsey 8.00 20.00
CRSC Sidney Crosby 40.00 100.00

2017-18 Black Diamond Diamond Cutters

DCBH Braden Holtby 15.00 40.00
DCBM Brad Marchand 12.00 30.00
DCCM Connor McDavid 40.00 100.00
DCEK Erik Karlsson 12.00 30.00
DCNM Nathan MacKinnon 20.00 50.00
DCVT Vladimir Tarasenko 15.00 40.00
DCRCW Colin White 20.00 50.00
DCRES Evgeny Svechnikov 40.00 100.00
DCRJH Josh Ho-Sang 25.00 60.00
CRJR Jack Roslovic 25.00 60.00
CRNH Nico Hischier 60.00 150.00
CRNP Nolan Patrick 40.00 100.00

2017-18 Black Diamond Diamond Debut Relics

DAN Alexander Nylander 3.00 8.00
DBB Brock Boeser 10.00 25.00
DCK Clayton Keller 5.00 12.00
DCM Charlie McAvoy 6.00 15.00
DCW Colin White 2.00 5.00
DNH Nico Hischier 6.00 15.00
DNP Nolan Patrick 4.00 10.00
DNS Nikita Scherbak 4.00 10.00
DPD Pierre-Luc Dubois 4.00 10.00

2017-18 Black Diamond Hardware Heroes

HAD Alex Delvecchio 10.00 25.00
HAM Auston Matthews 40.00 100.00
HBB Brent Burns 12.00 30.00
HBH Braden Holtby 15.00 40.00
HCM Connor McDavid 40.00 100.00
HCP Carey Price 30.00 80.00
HEB Ed Belfour 12.00 30.00
HES Eddie Shore 10.00 25.00
HJB Johnny Bower 10.00 25.00
HMR Maurice Richard 10.00 25.00
HPK Patrick Kane 20.00 50.00
HSC Sidney Crosby 40.00 100.00

2017-18 Black Diamond Pure Black

PURE BLACK/25-99: .6X TO 1.50X BASIC CARDS
DBDD Devan Dubnyk AU/99 8.00 20.00
DBEM Evgeni Malkin AU/99 25.00 60.00
DBGL Guy Lafleur AU/25 40.00 100.00
DBJG Jake Guentzel AU/99 25.00 60.00
DBJP Joe Pavelski AU/99 8.00 20.00
DBJT John Tavares AU/99 12.00 30.00
DBLC Logan Couture AU/99 8.00 20.00
DBMF Marc-Andre Fleury AU/99 25.00 60.00
DBML Mario Lemieux AU/25 60.00 150.00
DBNK Nikita Kucherov AU/99 12.00 30.00
DBPL Patrik Laine AU/99 30.00 80.00
DBRL Roberto Luongo AU/25 20.00 50.00
DBSS Steven Stamkos AU/99 15.00 40.00
DBTS Tyler Seguin AU/99 10.00 25.00
DBWN William Nylander AU/99 30.00 80.00

2017-18 Black Diamond Relics Pure Black Premium

BLACK/50: .75X TO 2X BASIC CARDS
BLACK/25: 2X TO 5X BASIC CARDS
DBJG Jake Guentzel/50 20.00 50.00

2017-18 Black Diamond Rookie Booklet Relics

BRAN Alexander Nylander 6.00 15.00
BRBB Brock Boeser 20.00 50.00
BRCK Clayton Keller 10.00 25.00
BRCM Charlie McAvoy 12.00 30.00
BRES Evgeny Svechnikov 8.00 20.00
BRHF Haydn Fleury 4.00 10.00
BRIB Ivan Barbashev 4.00 10.00
BRJH Josh Ho-Sang 5.00 12.00
BRLK Luke Kunin 4.00 10.00
BRMB Madison Bowey 3.00 8.00
BRNH Nico Hischier 12.00 30.00
BRNP Nolan Patrick 8.00 20.00
BRNS Nikita Scherbak 8.00 20.00
BRPD Pierre-Luc Dubois 8.00 20.00
BRTJ Tyson Jost 8.00 20.00
BRVS Vadim Shipachyov 12.00 30.00

2017-18 Black Diamond Rookie Booklet Relics Patch Autographs

BRBB Brock Boeser 100.00 200.00
BRCK Clayton Keller 100.00 200.00
BRCM Charlie McAvoy 30.00 80.00
BRES Evgeny Svechnikov 20.00 50.00
BRHF Haydn Fleury 10.00 25.00
BRIB Ivan Barbashev 10.00 25.00
BRJH Josh Ho-Sang 12.00 30.00
BRLK Luke Kunin 10.00 25.00
BRMB Madison Bowey 8.00 20.00
BRNS Nikita Scherbak 30.00 80.00
BRPD Pierre-Luc Dubois 20.00 50.00
BRTJ Tyson Jost 20.00 50.00
BRVS Vadim Shipachyov 30.00 80.00

2017-18 Black Diamond Rookie Gems

GAN Alexander Nylander 5.00 12.00
GBB Brock Boeser 30.00 80.00
GCK Clayton Keller 20.00 50.00
GCM Charlie McAvoy 20.00 50.00
GCW Colin White 3.00 8.00
GES Evgeny Svechnikov 6.00 15.00
GIB Ivan Barbashev 3.00 8.00
GJH Josh Ho-Sang 4.00 10.00
GJR Jack Roslovic 4.00 10.00
GLK Luke Kunin 3.00 8.00
GNH Nico Hischier 10.00 25.00
GNP Nolan Patrick 25.00 60.00
GNS Nikita Scherbak 6.00 15.00
GOT Owen Tippett 6.00 15.00
GPD Pierre-Luc Dubois 6.00 15.00
GTJ Tyson Jost 6.00 15.00
GVS Vadim Shipachyov 10.00 25.00

2017-18 Black Diamond Rookie Team Logo Jumbos

LBB Brock Boeser 25.00 60.00
LCK Clayton Keller 12.00 30.00
LCM Charlie McAvoy 15.00 40.00
LES Evgeny Svechnikov 10.00 25.00
LIB Ivan Barbashev 5.00 12.00
LJH Josh Ho-Sang 6.00 15.00
LNH Nico Hischier 15.00 40.00
LNP Nolan Patrick 10.00 25.00
LTJ Tyson Jost 10.00 25.00
LVS Vadim Shipachyov 15.00 40.00

2017-18 Black Diamond Run for the Cup

NCK Clayton Keller 12.00 30.00
RUNNH Nico Hischier 15.00 40.00
RUNNP Nolan Patrick 10.00 25.00

2017-18 Black Diamond Signature Placards

SPAM Anthony Mantha C 12.00 30.00
SPCD Christian Dvorak C 6.00 15.00
SPDD Devan Dubnyk B 8.00 20.00
SPDS Derek Sanderson C 20.00 50.00
SPJC John Carlson B 10.00 25.00
SPMD Matt Duchene A 8.00 20.00
SPMT Matthew Tkachuk A 8.00 20.00
SPNE Nikolaj Ehlers B 8.00 20.00
SPWS Wayne Simmonds A 10.00 25.00
SPZW Zach Werenski B 8.00 20.00

2017-18 Black Diamond Silver on Black Rookie Signatures

SBRSAB Anders Bjork/125 10.00 25.00
SBRSAD Alex DeBrincat/125 40.00 100.00
SBRSBB Brock Boeser/49 100.00 200.00
SBRSCK Clayton Keller/49 100.00 200.00
SBRSCM Charlie McAvoy/49 100.00 200.00
SBRSCW Colin White/125 8.00 20.00
SBRSHS Josh Ho-Sang/49 10.00 25.00
SBRSOT Owen Tippett/125 15.00 40.00
SBRSTJ Tyson Jost/49 15.00 40.00
SBRSVS Vadim Shipachyov/125 25.00 60.00

2017-18 Black Diamond Silver on Black Signatures

SBCM Connor McDavid/50 150.00 250.00
SBFM Frank Mahovlich/99 12.00 30.00
SBJJ Joe Thornton/99 12.00 30.00
SBJT John Tavares/99 12.00 30.00
SBPP Pierre Pilote/99 10.00 25.00
SBRV Rogie Vachon/50 12.00 30.00

2017-18 Black Diamond Team Logo Jumbos

SCFLBR Martin Brodeur 30.00 80.00
SCFLJT Jonathan Toews 30.00 80.00
SCFLMB Mike Bossy 25.00 60.00
SCFLML Mario Lemieux 50.00 120.00
SCFLMM Mark Messier 25.00 60.00
SCFLPR Patrick Roy 40.00 100.00
SCFLSC Sidney Crosby 60.00 150.00
SCFLTS Teemu Selanne 20.00 50.00
SCFLWG Wayne Gretzky 80.00 200.00
TLCFDG Doug Gilmour 20.00 50.00
TLCFJG Johnny Gaudreau 25.00 60.00
TLCFJI Jarome Iginla 15.00 40.00
TLCFLM Lanny McDonald 15.00 40.00
TLCFMG Mark Giordano 12.00 30.00
TLCFMT Matthew Tkachuk 15.00 40.00
TLCFSB Sam Bennett 12.00 30.00
TLCFSM Sean Monahan 15.00 40.00
TLCFTF Theoren Fleury 15.00 40.00
TLLAAK Anze Kopitar 25.00 60.00
TLLACS Charlie Simmer 15.00 40.00
TLLADD Drew Doughty 15.00 40.00
TLLADT Dave Taylor 12.00 30.00
TLLAJQ Jonathan Quick 25.00 60.00
TLLAMD Marcel Dionne 20.00 50.00
TLLARB Rob Blake 15.00 40.00
TLLARV Rogie Vachon 20.00 50.00
TLLAWG Wayne Gretzky 80.00 200.00
TLMLAM Auston Matthews 60.00 150.00
TLMLDG Doug Gilmour 20.00 50.00
TLMLDS Darryl Sittler 15.00 40.00
TLMLFM Frank Mahovlich 15.00 40.00
TLMLFP Felix Potvin 15.00 40.00
TLMLJB Johnny Bower 15.00 40.00
TLMLKC King Clancy 12.00 30.00
TLMLSA Syl Apps 12.00 30.00
TLMLWC Wendel Clark 20.00 50.00

1968-69 Blackhawks Team Issue

This 8-card set measures approximately 4" by 6".
COMPLETE SET (8) 25.00 50.00
1 Dennis Hull 4.00 8.00
2 Doug Jarrett 2.50 5.00
3 Chico Maki 3.00 6.00
4 Gilles Marotte 2.50 5.00
5 Stan Mikita 10.00 20.00
6 Jim Pappin 2.50 5.00
7 Pat Stapleton 2.50 5.00
8 Ken Wharram 3.00 6.00

1970-71 Blackhawks Postcards

This 14-card set measures approximately 4" by 6". T
COMPLETE SET (14) 25.00 50.00
1 Lou Angotti 1.50 3.00
2 Bryan Campbell 1.50 3.00
3 Bobby Hull 10.00 20.00
Bill Wirtz
Stan Mikita
4 Dennis Hull 3.00 6.00
5 Tommy Ivan GM 1.50 3.00
Billy Reay CO
6 Doug Jarrett 1.50 3.00
7 Keith Magnuson 2.50 5.00
8 Pit Martin 1.50 3.00
9 Stan Mikita 5.00 10.00
10 Eric Nesterenko 2.50 5.00
11 Jim Pappin 2.00 4.00
12 Allan Pinder 1.50 3.00
13 Paul Shmyr 1.50 3.00
14 Bill White 2.00 4.00

1979-80 Blackhawks Postcards

COMPLETE SET (22) 12.50 25.00
1 Keith Brown .50 1.00
2 J.P. Bordeleau .50 1.00
3 Ted Bully .50 1.00
4 Alain Daigle .50 1.00
5 Tony Esposito 3.00 6.00
6 Greg Fox .50 1.00
7 Tim Higgins .50 1.00
8 Eddie Johnston CO .40 1.00
9 Reggie Kerr .50 1.00
10 Cliff Koroll .50 1.00
11 Tom Lysiak .50 1.00
12 Keith Magnuson 1.00 2.00
13 John Marks .50 1.00
14 Stan Mikita 4.00 8.00
15 Grant Mulvey 1.00 2.00
16 Bob Murray 1.00 2.00
17 Mike O'Connell .50 1.00
18 Rich Preston .50 1.00
19 Bob Pulford 1.00 2.00
20 Terry Ruskowski .50 1.00
21 Mike Veisor .50 1.00
22 Doug Wilson 2.00 4.00

1980-81 Blackhawks Postcards

These postcard-size cards measure approximately 4" by 6".
COMPLETE SET (16) 12.50 25.00
1 Keith Brown .75 2.00
2 Greg Fox .40 1.00
3 Dave Hutchison .40 1.00
4 Cliff Koroll ACO .40 1.00
5 Keith Magnuson CO .60 1.50
6 Peter Marsh .60 1.50
7 Grant Mulvey .60 1.50
8 Rich Preston .40 1.00
9 Florent Robidoux .40 1.00
10 Terry Ruskowski .60 1.50
11 Denis Savard 2.50 5.00
12 Al Secord .75 2.00
13 Ron Sedlbauer .40 1.00
14 Glen Sharpley .40 1.00
15 Darryl Sutter .75 2.00
16 Miles Zaharko .40 1.00

1980-81 Blackhawks White Border

These 14 blank-backed photos measure approximately 5 1/2" by 8 1/2".
COMPLETE SET (14) 10.00 20.00
1 Murray Bannerman .60 1.50
2 J.P. Bordeleau .40 1.00
3 Keith Brown .75 2.00
4 Tony Esposito 2.50 5.00
5 Greg Fox .40 1.00
6 Tim Higgins .40 1.00
7 Doug Lecuyer .40 1.00
8 John Marks .40 1.00
9 Grant Mulvey .60 1.50
10 Rich Preston .40 1.00
11 Terry Ruskowski .60 1.50
12 Denis Savard 2.50 5.00
13 Darryl Sutter .75 2.00
14 Tim Trimper .40 1.00

1981-82 Blackhawks Borderless Postcards

These 28 postcards measure approximately 3 1/2" by 5 1/2"..
COMPLETE SET (28) 12.00 30.00
1 Murray Bannerman .60 1.50
2 Keith Brown .60 1.50
3 Ted Bulley .30 .75
4 Doug Crossman .60 1.50
5 Jerome Dupont .30 .75
6 Tony Esposito 2.00 5.00
7 Greg Fox .30 .75
8 Bill Gardner .30 .75
9 Tim Higgins .30 .75
10 Dave Hutchison .30 .75
11 Reg Kerr .30 .75
12 Cliff Koroll ACO .30 .75
13 Tom Lysiak .60 1.50
14 Keith Magnuson CO .60 1.50
15 John Marks .30 .75
16 Peter Marsh .30 .75
17 Grant Mulvey .30 .75
18 Bob Murray .30 .75
19 Rick Paterson .30 .75
20 Rich Preston .30 .75
21 Bob Pulford GM .60 1.50
22 Terry Ruskowski .30 .75
23 Denis Savard 2.00 5.00
24 Al Secord .75 2.00
25 Glen Sharpley .30 .75
26 Darryl Sutter .75 2.00
27 Toni Tanti .75 2.00
28 Doug Wilson 1.25 3.00

1981-82 Blackhawks Brown Background

These 17 postcards measure approximately 4" by 6"..
COMPLETE SET (17) 10.00 25.00
1 Keith Brown .75 2.00
2 Greg Fox .40 1.00
3 Dave Hutchison .40 1.00
4 Cliff Koroll ACO .40 1.00
5 Keith Magnuson CO .75 2.00
6 Peter Marsh .75 2.00
7 Grant Mulvey .75 2.00
8 Bob Pulford GM 1.25 3.00
CO
9 Rich Preston .40 1.00
10 Florent Robidoux .40 1.00
11 Terry Ruskowski .75 2.00
12 Denis Savard 3.00 8.00
13 Al Secord .75 2.00
14 Ron Sedlbauer .40 1.00
15 Glen Sharpley .40 1.00
16 Darryl Sutter 1.25 3.00
17 Miles Zaharko .40 1.00

1982-83 Blackhawks Postcards

.
COMPLETE SET (23) 12.00 30.00
1 Murray Bannerman .50 1.25
2 Keith Brown .50 1.25
3 Doug Crossman .40 1.00
4 Dennis Cyr .30 .75
5 Tony Esposito 1.50 4.00
6 Dave Feamster .30 .75
7 Bill Gardner .30 .75
8 Greg Fox .30 .75
9 Tim Higgins .30 .75
10 Steve Larmer 2.00 5.00
11 Steve Ludzik .60 1.50
12 Tom Lysiak .50 1.25
13 Peter Marsh .30 .75
14 Grant Mulvey .30 .75
15 Bob Murray .30 .75
16 Troy Murray .40 1.00
17 Rick Paterson .30 .75
18 Rich Preston .30 .75
19 Denis Savard 1.50 4.00
20 Al Secord .75 2.00
21 Darryl Sutter .60 1.50
22 Orval Tessier CO .40 1.00
23 Doug Wilson 1.00 2.50

1983-84 Blackhawks Postcards

These 27 postcards measure approximately 3 1/2" by 5 1/2".
COMPLETE SET (27) 14.00 35.00
1 Murray Bannerman .60 1.50
2 Keith Brown .40 1.00
3 Denis Cyr .30 .75
4 Jerome Dupont .30 .75
5 Tony Esposito 1.50 4.00
6 Dave Feamster .30 .75
7 Curt Fraser .40 1.00
8 Bill Gardner .30 .75
9 Bob Janecyk .60 1.50
10 Cliff Koroll ACO .20 .50
11 Steve Larmer 3.00 8.00
12 Steve Ludzik .60 1.50
13 Tom Lysiak .60 1.50
14 Peter Marsh .30 .75
15 Bob Murray .30 .75
16 Troy Murray .60 1.50
17 Jack O'Callahan .30 .75
18 Rick Paterson .30 .75
19 Rich Preston .30 .75
20 Denis Savard 1.50 4.00
21 Al Secord .75 2.00
22 Darryl Sutter .75 2.00
23 Orval Tessier CO .20 .50
24 Behn Wilson .30 .75
25 Doug Wilson 1.00 2.50
26 Ken Yaremchuk .30 .75
27 Title Card .20 .50

1985-86 Blackhawks Team Issue

COMPLETE SET (26) 20.00 40.00
1 Steve Larmer 1.25 3.00
2 Keith Brown .75 2.00
3 Cliff Koroll .40 1.00
4 Roger Neilson .40 1.00
5 Bob Pulford .40 1.00
6 Behn Wilson .75 2.00
7 Jerome Dupont .75 2.00
8 Rick Paterson .40 1.00
9 Al Secord 1.25 3.00
10 Marc Bergevin .40 1.00
11 Darryl Sutter 1.25 3.00
12 Murray Bannerman .75 2.00
13 Bruce Cassidy .40 1.00
14 Bill Watson .40 1.00
15 Curt Fraser .40 1.00
16 Warren Skorodenski .75 2.00
17 Troy Murray .40 1.00
18 Bill Gardner .40 1.00
19 Ken Yaremchuk .40 1.00
20 Steve Ludzik .40 1.00
21 Jack O'Callahan .75 2.00
22 Tom Lysiak .40 1.00
23 Bob Murray .40 1.00
24 Ed Olczyk .75 2.00
25 Denis Savard 1.25 3.00
26 Doug Wilson 1.25 3.00

1986-87 Blackhawks Coke

The cards measure approximately 3 1/2" by 6 1/2".
COMPLETE SET (24) 8.00 20.00
1 Murray Bannerman .40 1.00
2 Marc Bergevin .30 .75
3 Keith Brown .30 .75
4 Dave Donnelly .30 .75
5 Curt Fraser .30 .75
6 Steve Larmer 1.25 3.00
7 Steve Ludzik .30 .75
8 Dave Manson .60 1.50
9 Bob Murray .30 .75
10 Troy Murray .30 .75
11 Gary Nylund .30 .75
12 Jack O'Callahan .30 .75
13 Ed Olczyk .40 1.00
14 Rick Paterson .30 .75
15 Wayne Presley .30 .75
16 Rich Preston .30 .75
17 Bob Sauve .40 1.00
18 Denis Savard 1.25 3.00
19 Al Secord .40 1.00
20 Mike Stapleton .30 .75
21 Darryl Sutter .40 1.00
22 Bill Watson .30 .75
23 Behn Wilson .30 .75
24 Doug Wilson .60 1.50

1987-88 Blackhawks Coke

The cards measure approximately 3 1/2" by 6 1/2".
COMPLETE SET (30) 8.00 20.00
1 Murray Bannerman .40 1.00
2 Marc Bergevin .30 .75
3 Keith Brown .30 .75
4 Glen Cochrane .30 .75
5 Curt Fraser .30 .75
6 Steve Larmer 1.00 2.50
7 Mark LaVarre .30 .75
8 Steve Ludzik .30 .75
9 Dave Manson .60 1.50
10 Bob Mason .40 1.00
11 Bob McGill .30 .75
12 Bob Murdoch CO .30 .75
13 Bob Murray .30 .75
14 Troy Murray .40 1.00
15 Brian Noonan .30 .75
16 Gary Nylund .30 .75
17 Darren Pang .60 1.50
18 Wayne Presley .30 .75
19 Everett Sanipass .30 .75
20 Denis Savard 1.00 2.50
21 Mike Stapleton .30 .75
22 Darryl Sutter CO .30 .75
23 Duane Sutter .40 1.00
24 Steve Thomas .50 1.25
25 Wayne Thomas CO .30 .75
26 Rick Vaive .40 1.00
27 Dan Vincelette .30 .75
28 Bill Watson .30 .75
29 Behn Wilson .30 .75
30 Doug Wilson .60 1.50

1988-89 Blackhawks Coke

The cards measure approximately 3 1/2" by 6 1/2".
COMPLETE SET (25) 8.00 20.00
1 Ed Belfour 4.00 10.00
2 Keith Brown .20 .50
3 Bruce Cassidy .20 .50
4 Mike Eagles .20 .50
5 Dirk Graham .40 1.00
6 Mike Hudson .20 .50
7 Mike Keenan CO .60 1.50
8 Steve Larmer .60 1.50
9 Dave Manson .40 1.00
10 Jacques Martin CO .08 .25
11 Bob McGill .20 .50
12 E.J. McGuire CO .08 .25
13 Troy Murray .40 1.00
14 Brian Noonan .20 .50
15 Darren Pang .30 .75
16 Wayne Presley .20 .50
17 Everett Sanipass .20 .50
18 Denis Savard .75 2.00
19 Duane Sutter .30 .75
20 Steve Thomas .40 1.00
21 Rick Vaive .30 .75
22 Dan Vincelette .20 .50
23 Jimmy Waite .30 .75
24 Doug Wilson .40 1.00
25 Trent Yawney .20 .50

1989-90 Blackhawks Coke

This 27-card set was issued in a photo album consisting of five unperforated sheets measuring approximately 12" by 12". The first four sheets have six players each, while the last sheet features the three coaches.
COMPLETE SET (27) 8.00 20.00
1 Denis Savard .75 2.00
2 Troy Murray .30 .75
3 Steve Larmer .60 1.50
4 Doug Wilson .60 1.50
5 Bob Murray .20 .50
6 Jeremy Roenick 3.00 8.00
7 Duane Sutter .30 .75
8 Greg Gilbert .20 .50
9 Trent Yawney .20 .50
10 Bob McGill .20 .50
11 Jacques Cloutier .30 .75
12 Bob Bassen .20 .50
13 Steve Thomas .40 1.00
14 Adam Creighton .30 .75
15 Wayne Van Dorp .20 .50
16 Dirk Graham .40 1.00
17 Mike Hudson .20 .50
18 Al Secord .30 .75
19 Alain Chevrier .30 .75
20 Wayne Presley .20 .50
21 Steve Konroyd .20 .50
22 Everett Sanipass .20 .50
23 Keith Brown .20 .50
24 Dave Manson .40 1.00
25 Mike Keenan CO .40 1.00
26 E.J. McGuire CO .08 .25
27 Jacques Martin CO .08 .25

1990-91 Blackhawks Coke

This 28-card set was issued in a photo album consisting of five unperforated sheets measuring approximately 11 3/4" by 12 1/4".
COMPLETE SET (28) 8.00 20.00
1 Dirk Graham .30 .75
2 Troy Murray .30 .75
3 Steve Larmer .40 1.00
4 Doug Wilson .40 1.00
5 Chris Chelios 1.00 2.50
6 Jeremy Roenick 2.00 5.00
7 Steve Thomas .30 .75
8 Greg Gilbert .20 .50
9 Trent Yawney .20 .50
10 Bob McGill .20 .50
11 Jacques Cloutier .25 .60
12 Jocelyn Lemieux .20 .50
13 Michel Goulet .40 1.00
14 Adam Creighton .25 .60
15 Mike McNeill .20 .50
16 Ed Belfour 2.50 6.00
17 Mike Hudson .20 .50
18 Greg Millen .30 .75
19 Stu Grimson .30 .75
20 Wayne Presley .20 .50
21 Steve Konroyd .20 .50
22 Mike Peluso .30 .75
23 Keith Brown .20 .50
24 Dave Manson .30 .75
25 Mike Keenan CO .30 .75
26 Darryl Sutter CO .30 .75
27 E.J. McGuire CO .08 .25
28 Vladislav Tretiak CO 1.00 2.50

1991-92 Blackhawks Coke

This photo album measured approximately 11 5/8" by 12 1/4".
COMPLETE SET (28) 8.00 20.00
1 Ed Belfour 1.25 3.00
2 Keith Brown .20 .50
3 Rod Buskas .20 .50
4 Chris Chelios .75 2.00
5 Karl Dykhuis .20 .50
6 Greg Gilbert .20 .50
7 Michel Goulet .30 .75
8 Dirk Graham .30 .75
9 Stu Grimson .40 1.00
10 Mike Hudson .20 .50
11 Mike Keenan GM/CO .40 1.00
12 Steve Konroyd .20 .50
13 Frantisek Kucera .20 .50
14 Steve Larmer .40 1.00
15 Brad Lauer .20 .50
16 Jocelyn Lemieux .20 .50
17 Bryan Marchment .20 .50
18 Dave McDowall CO .08 .25
19 Brian Noonan .20 .50
20 Mike Peluso .20 .50
21 Rich Preston CO .08 .25
22 Jeremy Roenick 1.25 3.00
23 Steve Smith .30 .75
24 Mike Stapleton .20 .50
25 Brent Sutter .30 .75
26 Darryl Sutter CO .30 .75
27 John Tonelli .30 .75
28 Jimmy Waite .30 .75

1992-93 Blackhawks Coke

COMPLETE SET (20) 10.00 25.00
1 Adam Bennett .30 .75
2 Cam Russell .30 .75
3 Christian Ruuttu .30 .75
4 Stu Grimson .75 2.00
5 Brent Sutter .75 2.00
6 Dave Christian .40 1.00
7 Mike Hudson .30 .75
8 Rob Brown .30 .75
9 Steve Larmer .75 2.00
10 Bryan Marchment .30 .75
11 Igor Kravchuk .30 .75
12 Paul Baxter .30 .75
13 Vladislav Tretiak .75 2.00
14 Rich Preston .30 .75
15 Darryl Sutter .75 2.00
16 Keith Brown .30 .75
17 Bob Pulford .30 .75
18 Jimmy Waite .40 1.00
19 Ed Belfour 1.25 3.00
20 Jeremy Roenick 1.25 3.00

1993-94 Blackhawks Coke

This team photo album measured approximately 11 1/2" by 12 1/4". Each of the four glossy pages features two rows with three player cards per row; the final six player cards are printed on the inside of the back cover.

COMPLETE SET (30) 6.00 15.00
1 Joe Murphy .30 .75
2 Chris Chelios .75 2.00
3 Rich Sutter .20 .50
4 Frantisek Kucera .20 .50
5 Jeff Shantz .20 .50
6 Brian Noonan .20 .50
7 Michel Goulet .30 .75
8 Jeremy Roenick .75 2.00
9 Dave Christian .20 .50
10 Patrick Poulin .20 .50
11 Brent Sutter .20 .50
12 Cam Russell .20 .50
13 Stephane Matteau .20 .50
14 Ed Belfour 1.00 2.50
15 Neil Wilkinson .20 .50
16 Eric Weinrich .20 .50
17 Christian Ruuttu .20 .50
18 Kevin Todd .20 .50
19 Jeff Hackett .40 1.00
20 Steve Smith .25 .60
21 Jocelyn Lemieux .20 .50
22 Keith Carney .20 .50
23 Troy Murray .20 .50
24 Darin Kimble .20 .50
25 Dirk Graham .30 .75
26 Bob Pulford GM .20 .50
27 Darryl Sutter CO .20 .50
28 Paul Baxter ACO .08 .25
29 Rich Preston ACO .08 .25
30 Phil Myre ACO .08 .25

1994-95 Blackhawks Coke

These cards are more like oversized photos, and came complete with an album.
COMPLETE SET(21) 6.00 15.00
1 Tony Amonte .75 2.00
2 Ed Belfour 1.00 2.50
3 Keith Carney .20 .50
4 Chris Chelios .75 2.00
5 Dirk Graham .30 .75
6 Brent Grieve .20 .50
7 Jeff Hackett .40 1.00
8 Roger Johansson .20 .50
9 Darin Kimble .20 .50
10 Sergei Krivokrasov .20 .50
11 Joe Murphy .20 .50
12 Bernie Nicholls .40 1.00
13 Patrick Poulin .20 .50
14 Bob Probert .40 1.00
15 Cam Russell .20 .50
16 Jeff Shantz .20 .50
17 Steve Smith .20 .50
18 Greg Smyth .20 .50
19 Gary Suter .30 .75
20 Brent Sutter .20 .50
21 Eric Weinrich .20 .50

1995-96 Blackhawks Coke

COMPLETE SET (19) 6.00 15.00
1 Tony Amonte .75 2.00
2 Ed Belfour 1.00 2.50
3 Keith Carney .20 .50
4 Chris Chelios .75 2.00
5 Murray Craven .20 .50
6 Jim Cummins .20 .50
7 Eric Daze .40 1.00
8 Jeff Hackett .40 1.00
9 Sergei Krivokrasov .20 .50
10 Joe Murphy .20 .50
11 Bernie Nicholls .40 1.00
12 Bob Probert .40 1.00
13 Cam Russell .20 .50
14 Denis Savard .40 1.00
15 Jeff Shantz .20 .50
16 Steve Smith .20 .50
17 Gary Suter .20 .50
18 Brent Sutter .20 .50
19 Eric Weinrich .20 .50

1998 Blackhawks Legends

Made and distributed by Pizza Hut in 1998, these cards feature rounded corners, and full color photos on the front.
COMPLETE SET (5) 4.80 12.00
1 Tony Esposito 1.25 3.00
2 Glenn Hall 1.25 3.00
3 Bobby Hull 2.00 5.00
4 Steve Larmer .60 1.50
5 Denis Savard .60 1.50

1998-99 Blackhawks Chicago Sun-Times

These full-page color player profiles ran in the Chicago Sun-Times during the 1998-99 season. Each page contains a action photo along with player stats and career highlights. The pages are unnumbered and are listed below in alphabetical order.
COMPLETE SET 3.00 8.00
1 Chris Chelios 1.25 3.00
2 Mark Fitzpatrick .40 1.00
3 Doug Gilmour .75 2.00
4 Christian Laflamme .40 1.00
5 Bob Probert 1.25 3.00
6 Jocelyn Thibault .40 1.00

1999-00 Blackhawks Chicago Sun-Times

These full-page color player profiles ran in the Chicago Sun-Times during the 1999-2000 season. Each page contains a action photo along with player stats and career highlights. The pages are unnumbered and are listed below in alphabetical order.
COMPLETE SET (12) 4.00 10.00
1 Tony Amonte .75 2.00
2 Brad Brown .40 1.00
3 Mark Janssens .40 1.00
4 Jean-Yves Leroux .40 1.00
5 Dave Manson .40 1.00
6 Bryan McCabe .40 1.00
7 Boris Mironov .40 1.00
8 Michael Nylander .40 1.00
9 Doug Zmolek .40 1.00
10 Coaches .40 1.00
11 Team photo .40 1.00

1999-00 Blackhawks Lineup Cards

These 8X10 items were inserted in the first 4,000 copies of each Blackhawks game program.
COMPLETE SET (10) 8.00 20.00
1 Tony Amonte 1.50 4.00
2 Brad Brown .40 1.00
3 Eric Daze 1.25 3.00
4 Doug Gilmour 1.50 4.00
5 Dean McAmmond .40 1.00
6 Bryan McCabe .40 1.00
7 Boris Mironov .40 1.00
8 Steve Sullivan .75 2.00
9 Jocelyn Thibault 1.25 3.00
10 Alexei Zhamnov .40 1.00

2002-03 Blackhawks Postcards

These are standard postcard size and feature blank backs.
1 Eric Daze .40 1.00
2 Steve Poapst .40 1.00
3 Jason Strudwick .40 1.00
4 Brian Sutter CO .40 1.00
5 Jocelyn Thibault .75 2.00
6 Ryan Vandenbussche .40 1.00
7 Alexei Zhamnov .40 1.00

2003-04 Blackhawks Postcards

COMPLETE SET (31) 10.00 25.00
1 Craig Andersson .40 1.00
2 Tyler Arnason .30 .75
3 Anton Babchuk .20 .50
4 Mark Bell .40 1.00
5 Kyle Calder .40 1.00
6 Eric Daze .40 1.00
7 Nathan Dempsey .20 .50
8 Alexander Karpovtsev .20 .50
9 Igor Korolev .20 .50
10 Lasse Kukkonen .20 .50
11 Michael Leighton .40 1.00
12 Al MacAdam ACO .04 .10
13 Steve McCarthy .20 .50
14 Brett McLean .20 .50
15 Travis Moen .20 .50
16 Scott Nichol .20 .50
17 Ville Nieminen .20 .50
18 Steve Passmore .40 1.00
19 Steve Poapst .20 .50
20 Deron Quint .20 .50
21 Igor Radulov .40 1.00
22 Tuomo Ruutu 2.00 5.00
23 Denis Savard ACO .30 .75
24 Jason Strudwick .20 .50
25 Steve Sullivan .40 1.00
26 Brent Sutter CO .10 .25
27 Jocelyn Thibault .75 2.00
28 Vladislav Tretiak ACO .40 1.00
29 Ryan VandenBussche .20 .50
30 Pavel Vorobiev .20 .50
31 Alexei Zhamnov .20 .50

2006-07 Blackhawks Postcards

COMPLETE SET (23) 10.00 20.00
1 Adrian Aucoin .40 1.00
2 Denis Arkhipov .40 1.00
3 Jeff Hamilton .40 1.00
4 Martin Lapointe .40 1.00
5 Tony Salmelainen .40 1.00
6 Jassen Cullimore .40 1.00
7 Martin Havlat .60 1.50
8 Patrick Sharp .40 1.00
9 Michael Holmqvist .40 1.00
10 Brent Seabrook .40 1.00
11 Rene Bourque .40 1.00
12 Jim Vandermeer .40 1.00
13 Duncan Keith .40 1.00
14 Nikolai Khabibulin .75 2.00
15 Michal Handzus .40 1.00
16 Tuomo Ruutu .75 2.00
17 Radim Vrbata .40 1.00
18 Brian Boucher .60 1.50
19 Bryan Smolinski .40 1.00
20 Lasse Kukkonen .40 1.00
21 Denis Savard CO .75 2.00
22 Mark Hardy CO .20 .50
23 Stephane Waite ACO .20 .50

2006-07 Blackhawks Postcards Glossy

It is believed that there are other singles not yet catalogued. Please forward any additional information to hockeymag@beckett.com.
1 Troy Brouwer .75 2.00
2 Peter Bondra 1.00 2.50
3 James Wisniewski .75 2.00
4 Karl Stewart .75 2.00
5 Ryan Stewart CO .75 2.00

2007-08 Blackhawks Team Issue

COMPLETE SET (28) 8.00 20.00
1 Kevyn Adams .30 .75
2 Rene Bourque .30 .75
3 Adam Burish .30 .75
4 Martin Havlat .30 .75
5 Magnus Johansson .30 .75
6 Patrick Kane 1.50 4.00
7 Duncan Keith .30 .75
8 Nikolai Khabibulin .40 1.00
9 David Koci .75 2.00
10 Patrick Lalime .40 1.00
11 Robert Lang .30 .75
12 Martin Lapointe .30 .75
13 Yanic Perreault .30 .75
14 Danny Richmond .30 .75
15 Tuomo Ruutu .40 1.00
16 Sergei Samsonov .30 .75
17 Brent Seabrook .30 .75
18 Patrick Sharp .30 .75
19 Brent Sopel .30 .75
20 Jonathan Toews 1.50 4.00
21 Jason Williams .30 .75
22 James Wisniewski .30 .75
23 Andrei Zyuzin .30 .75
24 Denis Savard HC .30 .75
25 Mark Hardy AC .10 .25
26 Ryan Stewart AC .10 .25
27 John Torchetti AC .10 .25
28 Stephane Waite CO .10 .25

2012-13 Blackhawks Upper Deck Stanley Cup Champions

COMPLETE SET (31) 12.00 20.00
1 Bryan Bickell .25 .60
2 Dave Bolland .30 .75
3 Brandon Bollig .30 .75
4 Sheldon Brookbank .25 .60
5 Daniel Carcillo .25 .60
6 Corey Crawford .50 1.25
7 Ray Emery .30 .75
8 Michael Frolik .25 .60
9 Michal Handzus .25 .60
10 Niklas Hjalmarsson .25 .60
11 Marian Hossa .30 .75
12 Patrick Kane .75 2.00
13 Duncan Keith .40 1.00
14 Marcus Kruger .50 1.25
15 Nick Leddy .25 .60
16 Jamal Mayers .25 .60
17 Johnny Oduya .30 .75
18 Michal Rozsival .25 .60
19 Brandon Saad .40 1.00
20 Brent Seabrook .40 1.00
21 Patrick Sharp .40 1.00
22 Andrew Shaw .40 1.00
23 Ben Smith .30 .75
24 Viktor Stalberg .25 .60
25 Jonathan Toews .75 2.00
26 No Loss SH .25 .60
27 Marian Hossa SH .30 .75
28 Brent Seabrook SH .40 1.00
29 Patrick Kane SH .75 2.00
30 Corey Crawford SH .50 1.25
CB Celebration Photo 1.25 3.00

1993 Bleachers 23K Manon Rheaume

This four-card standard-size set featured 23 Karat gold borders. The production run was reportedly 10,000 numbered sets and 1,500 uncut numbered strips.
COMPLETE SET (4) 8.00 20.00
COMMON CARD 2.00 5.00

1996 Bleachers Lemieux

This one-card set featured an embossed image of Mario Lemieux on a 23 Karat all-gold sculptured card. The card was packaged in a clear acrylic holder along

with a Certificate of Authenticity inside a collectible foil-stamped box. Only 10,000 of the card were produced and are serially numbered.
1 Mario Lemieux 2.00 5.00

2001-02 Blizzak Kim St. Pierre

This single card was issued as a promotional premium with the purchase of a set of Bridgestone Blizzak tires in the province of Quebec during the winter of 2001-02. The card features a photo of Canadian National Women's team goalie St-Pierre wearing a Bridgestone jersey on the tront, and features personal and statistical data on the back in French. It is believed that 2,000 of these cards were produced, but less than 500 were actually given out in the promotion.

NNO Kim St. Pierre 2.00 5.00

2001-02 Blue Jackets Donatos Pizza

Sponsored by Donatos Pizza, this 24-card set was issued in sheets containing 6 cards, a pizza coupon and a merchandise coupon.

COMPLETE SET (24) 5.00 12.00
1 Geoff Sanderson .20 .50
2 Grant Marshall .20 .50
3 Serge Aubin .20 .50
4 Robert Kron .20 .50
5 Blake Sloan .20 .50
6 Mattias Timander .20 .50
7 Tyler Wright .20 .50
8 Espen Knutsen .40 1.00
9 Rostislav Klesla .40 1.00
10 Kevin Dineen .20 .50
11 Deron Quint .20 .50
12 Ron Tugnutt .40 1.00
13 Marc Denis .40 1.00
14 David Vyborny .20 .50
15 Lyle Odelein .20 .50
16 Jean-Luc Grand-Pierre .20 .50
17 Radim Bicanek .20 .50
18 Geoff Sanderson .20 .50
19 Ron Tugnutt .40 1.00
20 Ray Whitney .20 .50
21 Mike Sillinger .20 .50
22 Chris Nielsen .20 .50
23 Jamie Pushor .20 .50
24 Jamie Heward .20 .50

2013-14 Blue Jackets Buffalo Wild Wings

COMPLETE SET (8)
1 Sergei Bobrovsky
2 Brandon Dubinsky
3 Nick Foligno
4 Marian Gaborik SP
5 Jack Johnson
6 Mark Letestu
7 R.J. Umberger
8 James Wisniewski

1970-71 Blues Postcards

This 20-card set measures approximately 3 1/2" by 5 1/2" and was issued by the team.

COMPLETE SET (20) 20.00 40.00
1 Red Berenson 1.50 3.00
2 Chris Bordeleau 1.00 2.00
3 Craig Cameron 1.00 2.00
4 Tim Ecclestone 1.00 2.00
5 Glenn Hall 5.00 10.00
6 Fran Huck 1.00 2.00
7 Jim Lorentz 1.00 2.00
8 Bill McCreary AGM 1.00 2.00
9 Ab McDonald 1.50 3.00
10 George Morrison 1.00 2.00
11 Noel Picard 1.50 3.00
12 Barclay Plager 2.00 4.00
13 Bill Plager 1.50 3.00
14 Bob Plager 2.00 4.00
15 Jim Roberts 1.00 2.00
16 Gary Sabourin 1.00 2.00
17 Frank St. Marseille 1.50 3.00
18 Bill Sutherland 1.00 2.00
19 Ernie Wakely 1.50 3.00
20 Bob Wall 1.00 2.00

1971-72 Blues Postcards

This 30-card set measures approximately 3 1/2" by 5 1/2".

COMPLETE SET (30) 35.00 70.00
1 Al Arbour CO 2.50 5.00
2 John Arbour 1.00 2.00
3 Curt Bennett 1.00 2.00
4 Chris Bordeleau 1.00 2.00
5 Carl Brewer 1.50 3.00
6 Jacques Caron 1.00 2.00
7 Terry Crisp 2.00 4.00
8 Andre Dupont 1.50 3.00
9 Jack Egers 1.00 2.00
10 Larry Hornung 1.00 2.00
11 Brian Lavender 1.00 2.00
11 Mike Murphy 1.00 2.00
12 G.Marchant/A.McPherson 1.00 2.00
12 Gerry Odrowski 1.00 2.00
13 Bill McCreary AGM .50 1.00
14 Danny O'Shea 1.00 2.00
15 Mike Parizeau 1.00 2.00
16 Noel Picard 1.50 3.00
17 Barclay Plager 2.00 4.00
18 Bill Plager 1.50 3.00
19 Bob Plager 2.00 4.00
20 Phil Roberto 1.50 3.00
21 Gary Sabourin 1.00 2.00
22 Jim Shires 1.00 2.00
23 Frank St. Marseille 1.50 3.00
24 Floyd Thomson 1.00 2.00
25 Garry Unger 2.50 5.00
26 Garry Unger action 2.50 5.00
27 Ernie Wakely 1.50 3.00
28 Tom Woodcock TR 1.00 2.00

1972-73 Blues White Border

Printed on thin white stock, this set of 22 photos measures approximately 6 7/8" by 8 3/4".

COMPLETE SET (22) 30.00 60.00
1 Jacques Caron 1.50 3.00
2 Steve Durbano 2.00 4.00
3 Jack Egers 1.50 3.00
4 Chris Evans 1.50 3.00
5 Jean Hamel 1.50 3.00
6 Fran Huck 1.50 3.00
7 Brent Hughes 1.50 3.00
8 Bob Johnson 2.00 4.00
9 Mike Lampman 1.50 3.00
10 Bob McCord 1.50 3.00
11 Wayne Merrick 2.00 4.00
12 Mike Murphy 1.50 3.00
13 Danny O'Shea 1.50 3.00
14 Barclay Plager 2.50 5.00
15 Bob Plager 2.50 5.00
16 Pierre Plante 1.50 3.00
17 Phil Roberto 2.00 4.00
18 Gary Sabourin 1.50 3.00
19 Wayne Stephenson 2.50 5.00
20 Jean-Guy Talbot CO 1.50 3.00
21 Floyd Thomson 1.50 3.00
22 Garry Unger 2.50 5.00
AC1 Garry Unger 2.50 5.00
AC2 Phil Roberto 2.00 4.00

1973-74 Blues White Border

Printed on thin white stock, this set of 24 photos measures approximately 6 7/8" by 8 3/4". The set is dated by the Glen Sather photo; 1973-74 was his only season with the team.

COMPLETE SET (24) 25.00 50.00
1 Lou Angotti .75 1.50
2 Don Awrey .75 1.50
3 John Davidson 2.50 5.00
4 Ab Demarco .75 1.50
5 Steve Durbano .75 1.50
6 Chris Evans .75 1.50
7 Larry Giroux .75 1.50
8 Jean Hamel .75 1.50
9 Nick Harbaruk .75 1.50
10 J.Bob Kelly 1.00 2.00
11 Mike Lampman .75 1.50
12 Wayne Merrick .75 1.50
13 Barclay Plager 2.00 4.00
14 Bob Plager 2.00 4.00
15 Pierre Plante 1.50 3.00
16 Phil Roberto 2.50 5.00
17 Gary Sabourin .75 1.50
18 Glen Sather 2.00 4.00
19 Wayne Stephenson 2.00 4.00
20 Jean-Guy Talbot CO .75 1.50
21 Floyd Thomson .75 1.50
22 Garry Unger 1.25 2.50
23 Garry Unger action 1.25 2.50
24 Team Photo 1.50 3.00
(1972-73 team)

1978-79 Blues Postcards

This 21-postcard set of the St. Louis Blues measures approximately 3 1/2" by 5 1/2".

COMPLETE SET (24) 15.00 30.00
1 Wayne Babych 1.00 2.00
2 Curt Bennett 1.00 2.00
3 Harvey Bennett .50 1.00
4 Red Berenson 1.50 3.00
5 Blue Angels 1.00 2.00
6 Jack Brownschidle 1.00 2.00
7 Mike Crombeen .50 1.00
8 Tony Currie .50 1.00
9 Fanvan .10 .25
10 Bernie Federko 2.00 4.00
11 Barry Gibbs .50 1.00
12 Larry Giroux .50 1.00
13 Inge Hammarstrom 1.00 2.00
14 Neil Labatte .50 1.00
15 Bob Murdoch .50 1.00
16 Phil Myre 1.00 2.00
17 Larry Patey .50 1.00
18 Barclay Plager CO 1.00 2.00
19 Rick Shinske .50 1.00
20 John Smrke .50 1.00
21 Ed Staniowski .50 1.00
22 Bob Stewart .50 1.00
23 Brian Sutter 2.00 4.00
24 Garry Unger 1.50 3.00

1987-88 Blues Team Photos

The 20 team photos in this set each measure approximately 8 1/2" by 11".

COMPLETE SET (20) 6.00 15.00
1 1967-68 Team Photo .60 1.50
2 1968-69 Team Photo .40 1.00
3 1969-70 Team Photo .40 1.00
4 1970-71 Team Photo .40 1.00
5 1971-72 Team Photo .40 1.00
6 1972-73 Team Photo .40 1.00
7 1973-74 Team Photo .40 1.00
8 1974-75 Team Photo .40 1.00
9 1975-76 Team Photo .40 1.00
10 1976-77 Team Photo .40 1.00
11 1977-78 Team Photo .40 1.00
12 1978-79 Team Photo .40 1.00
13 1979-80 Team Photo .40 1.00
14 1980-81 Team Photo .40 1.00
15 1981-82 Team Photo .40 1.00
16 1982-83 Team Photo .40 1.00
17 1983-84 Team Photo .40 1.00
18 1984-85 Team Photo .40 1.00
19 1985-86 Team Photo .40 1.00
20 1986-87 Team Photo .40 1.00

1987-88 Blues Kodak

The 1987-88 St. Louis Blues Team Photo Album was sponsored by Kodak in conjunction with KMOX Radio. The set consists of three large sheets, each measuring approximately 11" by 8 1/4" and joined together to form one continuous sheet.

COMPLETE SET (26) 12.00 30.00
1 Brian Benning .40 1.00
2 Tim Bothwell .30 .75
3 Charlie Bourgeois .30 .75
4 Paul Cavallini .40 1.00
5 Gino Cavallini .40 1.00
6 Michael Dark .30 .75
7 Doug Evans .30 .75
8 Todd Ewen .60 1.50
9 Bernie Federko 1.25 3.00
10 Ron Flockhart .30 .75
11 Doug Gilmour 2.50 6.00
12 Gaston Gingras .30 .75
13 Tony Hrkac .40 1.00
14 Mark Hunter .40 1.00
15 Jocelyn Lemieux .30 .75
16 Tony McKegney .40 1.00
17 Rick Meagher .40 1.00
18 Greg Millen .60 1.50
19 Robert Nordmark .30 .75
20 Greg Paslawski .30 .75
21 Herb Raglan .30 .75
22 Rob Ramage .40 1.00
23 Cliff Ronning 1.00 2.50
24 Brian Sutter .60 1.50
25 Perry Turnbull .30 .75
26 Rick Wamsley .60 1.50

1987-88 Blues Team Issue

This 24-card set measures 3 1/2" by 5 1/2".

COMPLETE SET (24) 14.00 35.00
1 Brian Benning .40 1.00
2 Mike Bullard .75 2.00
3 Gino Cavallini .40 1.00
4 Paul Cavallini .40 1.00
5 Craig Coxe .30 .75
6 Robert Dirk .30 .75
7 Doug Evans .30 .75
8 Todd Ewen .60 1.50
9 Bernie Federko 1.25 3.00
10 Gaston Gingras .30 .75
11 Tony Hrkac .40 1.00
12 Brett Hull 6.00 15.00
13 Tony McKegney .40 1.00
14 Rick Meagher .40 1.00
15 Greg Millen .60 1.50
16 Sergio Momesso .30 .75
17 Greg Paslawski .30 .75
18 Herb Raglan .30 .75
19 Dave Richter .30 .75
20 Vincent Riendeau .40 1.00
21 Gordie Roberts .40 1.00
22 Brian Sutter CO .60 1.50
23 Tom Tilley .30 .75
24 Steve Tuttle .30 .75

1988-89 Blues Kodak

The 1988-89 St. Louis Blues Team Photo Album was sponsored by Kodak. It consists of three large sheets, each measuring approximately 11" by 8 1/4" and joined together to form one continuous sheet.

COMPLETE SET (25) 10.00 25.00
1 Brian Benning .30 .75
2 Tim Bothwell .30 .75
3 Gino Cavallini .30 .75
4 Paul Cavallini .30 .75
5 Craig Coxe .30 .75
6 Doug Evans .30 .75
7 Todd Ewen .40 1.00
8 Bernie Federko .75 2.00
9 Gaston Gingras .30 .75
10 Tony Hrkac .40 1.00
11 Brett Hull 5.00 12.00
12 Mike Lalor .30 .75
13 Tony McKegney .40 1.00
14 Rick Meagher .30 .75
15 Greg Millen .40 1.00
16 Sergio Momesso .30 .75
17 Greg Paslawski .30 .75
18 Herb Raglan .30 .75
19 Vincent Riendeau .40 1.00
20 Dave Richter .30 .75
21 Gordie Roberts .30 .75
22 Cliff Ronning .75 2.00
23 Tom Tilley .30 .75
24 Steve Tuttle .30 .75
25 Peter Zezel .40 1.00

1988-89 Blues Team Issue

This 24-card set measures approximately 3 1/2" by 5 1/4".

COMPLETE SET (24) 10.00 25.00
1 Brian Benning .30 .75
2 Mike Bullard .60 1.50
3 Gino Cavallini .30 .75
4 Paul Cavallini .30 .75
5 Craig Coxe .30 .75
6 Robert Dirk .30 .75
7 Doug Evans .30 .75
8 Todd Ewen .40 1.00
9 Bernie Federko .75 2.00
10 Gaston Gingras .30 .75
11 Tony Hrkac .40 1.00
12 Brett Hull 5.00 12.00
13 Tony McKegney .40 1.00
14 Rick Meagher .30 .75
15 Greg Millen .40 1.00
16 Sergio Momesso .30 .75
17 Greg Paslawski .30 .75
18 Herb Raglan .30 .75
19 Dave Richter .30 .75
20 Vincent Riendeau .40 1.00
21 Gordie Roberts .30 .75
22 Brian Sutter CO .40 1.00
23 Tom Tilley .30 .75
24 Steve Tuttle .30 .75

1989-90 Blues Kodak

This 25-card set of St. Louis Blues measures approximately 2 3/8" by 3 1/2" and has a portrait shot of the player surrounded by yellow borders. The set was supposedly passed out to the first 15,000 ticket-holders at the Blues vs. Buffalo Sabres game on February 27th.

COMPLETE SET (25) 10.00 25.00
1 Pat Jablonski .40 1.00
4 Gordie Roberts .20 .50
6 Tony Twist .60 1.50
9 Peter Zezel .30 .75
10 Dave Lowry .20 .50
12 Adam Oates 1.25 3.00
14 Paul Cavallini .20 .50
15 Paul MacLean .30 .75
16 Brett Hull 2.00 5.00
17 Gino Cavallini .20 .50
19 Rod Brind'Amour 1.25 3.00
20 Tom Tilley .20 .50
21 Jeff Brown .40 1.00
22 Rick Meagher .20 .50
23 Adrien Plavsic .20 .50
25 Herb Raglan .20 .50
26 Mike Lalor .20 .50
27 Sergio Momesso .20 .50
30 Vincent Riendeau .40 1.00
31 Curtis Joseph 4.00 10.00
35 Steve Tuttle .20 .50
38 Dominic Lavoie .20 .50
39 Kelly Chase .20 .50
40 Dave Thomlinson .20 .50
NNO Brian Sutter CO .30 .75

1990-91 Blues Kodak

This 25-card standard-size set was sponsored by Kodak in conjunction with KMOX Radio.

COMPLETE SET (25) 10.00 25.00
1 Bob Bassen .20 .50
2 Rod Brind'Amour 1.25 3.00
3 Jeff Brown .30 .75
4 David Bruce .20 .50
5 Gino Cavallini .20 .50
6 Paul Cavallini .20 .50
7 Geoff Courtnall .40 1.00
8 Robert Dirk .20 .50
9 Glen Featherstone .20 .50
10 Brett Hull 2.00 5.00
11 Curtis Joseph 1.25 3.00
12 Dave Lowry .20 .50
13 Paul MacLean .20 .50
14 Mario Marois .20 .50
15 Rick Meagher .20 .50
16 Sergio Momesso .20 .50
17 Adam Oates 1.25 3.00
18 Vincent Riendeau .30 .75
19 Cliff Ronning .50 1.25
20 Harold Snepsts .40 1.00
21 Scott Stevens .60 1.50
22 Brian Sutter CO .20 .50
23 Rich Sutter .20 .50
24 Steve Tuttle .20 .50
25 Ron Wilson .20 .50

1991-92 Blues Postcards

This 22-card set measures approximately 3 1/2" by 5 1/2".

COMPLETE SET (22) 8.00 20.00
1 Murray Baron .20 .50
2 Bob Bassen .20 .50
3 Jeff Brown .40 1.00
4 Garth Butcher .30 .75
5 Gino Cavallini .20 .50
6 Paul Cavallini .20 .50
7 Kelly Chase .25 .60
8 Dave Christian .30 .75
9 Nelson Emerson .30 .75
10 Brett Hull 1.50 4.00
11 Pat Jablonski .30 .75
12 Curtis Joseph 1.25 3.00
13 Darin Kimble .20 .50
14 Dave Lowry .20 .50
15 Michel Mongeau .20 .50
16 Adam Oates .75 2.00
17 Rob Robinson .20 .50
18 Brendan Shanahan 1.50 4.00
19 Rich Sutter .30 .75
20 Ron Sutter .30 .75
21 Ron Wilson .20 .50
22 Rick Zombo .20 .50

1992-93 Blues UD Best of the Blues

This 28-card standard-size set, subtitled "Best of the Blues" was distributed at McDonald's restaurants of St. Louis and Metro East and showcases St. Louis Blues' players from the past 25 years.

COMPLETE SET (28) 12.00 30.00
1 Glenn Hall 1.25 3.00
2 Doug Gilmour 1.25 3.00
3 Al Arbour .40 1.00
4 Mike Liut .40 1.00
5 Blake Dunlop .20 .50
6 Noel Picard .20 .50
7 Bob Plager .40 1.00
8 Ab McDonald .20 .50
9 Curtis Joseph 2.00 5.00
10 Wayne Babych .20 .50
11 Red Berenson .40 1.00
12 Brett Hull 1.50 4.00
13 Bob Gassoff .40 1.00
14 Bernie Federko .40 1.00
15 Gary Sabourin .20 .50
16 Joe Mullen .40 1.00
17 Adam Oates .75 2.00
18 Jorgen Pettersson .20 .50
19 Frank St. Marseille .30 .75
20 Scott Stevens .60 1.50
21 Rob Ramage .40 1.00
22 Jacques Plante 1.25 3.00
23 Rick Meagher .20 .50
24 Barclay Plager .40 1.00
25 Brian Sutter .40 1.00
26 Perry Turnbull .20 .50
27 Garry Unger .40 1.00
28 Checklist SP 2.00 5.00
NNO Brett Hull AU 60.00 150.00

1996-97 Blues Dispatch 30th Anniversary

This set was created by the St. Louis Post-Dispatch to commemorate the 30th anniversary of the Blues joining the NHL.

COMPLETE SET (5) 4.00 10.00
1 Grant Fuhr .75 2.00
2 Brett Hull 1.50 4.00
3 Al MacInnis .75 2.00
4 Chris Pronger .75 2.00
5 Tony Twist .75 2.00

1999-00 Blues Taco Bell

Released by In the Game in conjunction with Taco Bell, this 24-card set features the 1999-2000 St. Louis Blues on four different six card sheets with a Taco Bell coupon.

COMPLETE SET (24) 6.00 15.00
1 Marc Bergevin .08 .25
2 Jochen Hecht .20 .50
3 Jamie McLennan .20 .50
4 Pierre Turgeon .30 .75
5 Scott Young .20 .50
6 Dave Ellett .08 .25
7 Lubos Bartecko .08 .25
8 Pavol Demitra .40 1.00
9 Michal Handzus .20 .50
10 Jeff Finley .08 .25
11 Ricard Persson .08 .25
12 Bob Bassen .08 .25
13 Craig Conroy .08 .25
14 Mike Eastwood .08 .25
15 Scott Pellerin .08 .25
16 Chris Pronger 1.25 3.00
17 Todd Reirden .08 .25
18 Roman Turek .30 .75
19 Kelly Chase .20 .50
20 Al MacInnis .75 2.00
21 Jamal Mayers .20 .50
22 Pascal Rheaume .08 .25
23 Tyson Nash .75 2.00
24 Stephane Richer .08 .25

2002-03 Blues Magnets

These magnets were handed out at home games throughout the 2002-03 season.

1 Pavol Demitra 2.00 5.00
2 Martin Rucinsky 1.25 3.00
3 Doug Weight 2.00 5.00

2002-03 Blues Team Issue

This set was handed out at a home game during the 2002-03 season. The cards came attached in a large foldout format.

COMPLETE SET (24) 8.00 20.00
1 Fred Brathwaite .30 .75
2 Petr Cajanek .20 .50
3 Daniel Corso .20 .50
4 Pavol Demitra .40 1.00
5 Dallas Drake .20 .50
6 Mike Eastwood .20 .50
7 Jeff Finley .20 .50
8 Barret Jackman .75 2.00
9 Brent Johnson .40 1.00
10 Alexander Khavanov .20 .50
11 Tom Koivisto .20 .50
12 Christian Laflamme .20 .50
13 Reed Low .20 .50
14 Al MacInnis .60 1.50
15 Jamal Mayers .30 .75
16 Scott Mellanby .20 .50
17 Tyson Nash .40 1.00
18 Shjon Podein .20 .50
19 Chris Pronger .60 1.50
20 Bryce Salvador .20 .50
21 Cory Stillman .20 .50
22 Keith Tkachuk .75 2.00
23 Mike Van Ryn .20 .50
24 Doug Weight .60 1.50

2005-06 Blues Team Set

COMPLETE SET (24) 6.00 15.00
1 Christian Backman .30 .75
2 Eric Doguniecki .30 .75
3 Eric Brewer .30 .75
4 Petr Cajanek .30 .75
5 Aaron Downey .30 .75
6 Dallas Drake .30 .75
7 Jeff Hoggan .30 .75
8 Barret Jackman .30 .75
9 Ryan Johnson .30 .75
10 Patrick LaLime .40 1.00
11 Jamal Mayers .30 .75
12 Dean McAmmond .30 .75
13 Jay McClement .30 .75
14 Mark Rycroft .30 .75
15 Bryce Salvador .30 .75
16 Curtis Sanford .40 1.00
17 Mike Sillinger .30 .75
18 Lee Stempniak .50 1.25
19 Keith Tkachuk .50 1.25
20 Matt Walker .30 .75
21 Doug Weight .50 1.25
22 Eric Weinrich .30 .75
23 Dennis Wideman .30 .75
24 Scott Young .30 .75

1938 Bocnal Tobacco Luminous

Cards measure 1 3/8 x 2 1/2 and feature white design on a black background. They are meant to glow in the dark. Produced for Newgent Cigarettes in London.

19 Field Hockey 15.00 30.00
20 Ice Hockey 25.00 50.00

1990-91 Bowman

The 1990-91 Bowman set contains 264 standard-size cards.

COMPLETE SET (264) 8.00 20.00
COMP.FACT.SET (264) 10.00 25.00
1 Jeremy Roenick RC .50 1.25
2 Doug Wilson .15 .40
3 Greg Millen .12 .30
4 Steve Thomas .10 .25
5 Steve Larmer .12 .30
6 Denis Savard .20 .50
7 Ed Belfour RC .50 1.25
8 Dirk Graham .12 .30
9 Adam Creighton .10 .25
10 Keith Brown .12 .30
11 Jacques Cloutier RC .12 .30
12 Al Secord .12 .30
13 Troy Murray .12 .30
14 Kelly Chase RC .30 .75
15 Dave Lowry RC .12 .30
16 Adam Oates .15 .40
17 Sergio Momesso RC .12 .30
18 Paul MacLean .12 .30
19 Peter Zezel .15 .40
20 Vincent Riendeau RC .15 .40
21 Dave Thomlinson RC .12 .30
22 Paul Cavallini .12 .30
23 Rod Brind'Amour RC .30 .75
24 Brett Hull .30 .75
25 Jeff Brown .15 .40
26 Dominic Lavoie RC .12 .30
27 Andy Brickley .10 .25
28 Bob Sweeney .10 .25
29 Cam Neely .15 .40
30 Bob Carpenter .12 .30
31 Ray Bourque .25 .60
32 Rejean Lemelin .12 .30
33 Craig Janney .15 .40
34 Bob Beers RC .12 .30
35 Andy Moog .15 .40
36 Dave Poulin .15 .40
37 Brian Propp .15 .40
38 John Byce RC .12 .30
39 John Carter RC .12 .30
40 Dave Christian .12 .30
41 Shayne Corson .12 .30
42 Chris Chelios .15 .40
43 Mike McPhee .12 .30
44 Guy Carbonneau .10 .25
45 Stephane Richer .15 .40
46 Petr Svoboda .15 .40
Chris Chelios actually pictured
47 Russ Courtnall .15 .40
48 Sylvain Lefebvre RC .12 .30
49 Brian Skrudland .12 .30
50 Patrick Roy .40 1.00
51 Bobby Smith .12 .30
52 Mathieu Schneider RC .12 .30
53 Stephan Lebeau RC .12 .30
54 Petri Skriko .15 .40
55 Jim Sandlak .15 .40
56 Doug Lidster .15 .40
57 Kirk McLean .10 .25
58 Brian Bradley .12 .30
59 Greg Adams .10 .25
60 Paul Reinhart .15 .40
61 Trevor Linden .12 .30
62 Adrien Plavsic RC .15 .40
63 Igor Larionov RC .30 .75
64 Steve Bozek .12 .30
65 Dan Quinn .12 .30
66 Mike Liut .12 .30
67 Nick Kypreos RC .15 .40
68 Michal Pivonka RC .12 .30
69 Dino Ciccarelli .15 .40
70 Kevin Hatcher .12 .30
71 Dale Hunter .15 .40
72 Don Beaupre .10 .25
73 Geoff Courtnall .12 .30
74 Rob Murray RC .10 .25
75 Calle Johansson .15 .40
76 Kelly Miller .10 .25
77 Mike Ridley .10 .25
78 Alan May RC .10 .25
79 Bob Brooke .10 .25
80 Slava Fetisov RC .30 .75
81 Sylvain Turgeon .12 .30
82 Kirk Muller .12 .30
83 John MacLean .12 .30
84 Jon Morris RC .10 .25
85 Brendan Shanahan .20 .50
86 Peter Stastny .12 .30
87 Bruce Driver .15 .40
88 Neil Brady RC .12 .30
89 Patrik Sundstrom .15 .40
90 Eric Weinrich RC .15 .40
91 Joe Nieuwendyk .10 .25
92 Sergei Makarov RC .30 .75
93 Al MacInnis .12 .30
94 Mike Vernon .15 .40
95 Gary Roberts .15 .40
96 Doug Gilmour .20 .50
97 Joe Mullen .12 .30
98 Rick Wamsley .15 .40
99 Joel Otto .12 .30
100 Paul Ranheim RC .15 .40
101 Gary Suter .15 .40
102 Theo Fleury .20 .50
103 Sergei Priakin RC .10 .25
104 Tony Horacek RC .10 .25
105 Ron Hextall .12 .30
106 Gord Murphy RC .15 .40
107 Pelle Eklund .10 .25
108 Rick Tocchet .15 .40
109 Murray Craven .15 .40
110 Doug Sulliman .12 .30
111 Kjell Samuelsson .12 .30
112 Ilkka Sinisalo .12 .30
113 Keith Acton .15 .40
114 Mike Bullard .12 .30
115 Doug Crossman .12 .30
116 Tom Fitzgerald RC .12 .30
117 Don Maloney .15 .40
118 Alan Kerr .12 .30
119 Mark Fitzpatrick RC .12 .30
120 Hubie McDonough RC .12 .30
121 Randy Wood .10 .25
122 Jeff Norton .15 .40
123 Pat LaFontaine .15 .40
124 Pat Flatley .15 .40
125 Joe Reekie RC .10 .25
126 Brent Sutter .12 .30
127 David Volek .15 .40
128 Shawn Cronin RC .10 .25
129 Dale Hawerchuk .20 .50
130 Brent Ashton .15 .40
131 Bob Essensa RC .25 .60
132 Dave Ellett .10 .25
133 Thomas Steen .12 .30
134 Doug Smail .12 .30
135 Fredrik Olausson .12 .30
136 Dave McLlwain .15 .40
137 Pat Elynuik .12 .30
138 Teppo Numminen RC .30 .75
139 Paul Fenton .15 .40
140 Tony Granato .12 .30
141 Tomas Sandstrom .15 .40
142 Rob Blake RC .25 .60
143 Wayne Gretzky .75 2.00
144 Kelly Hrudey .10 .25
145 Mike Krushelnyski .15 .40
146 Steve Duchesne .10 .25
147 Steve Kasper .12 .30
148 John Tonelli .12 .30
149 Dave Taylor .15 .40
150 Larry Robinson .12 .30
151 Todd Elik RC .15 .40
152 Luc Robitaille .15 .40
153 Al lafrate .10 .25
154 Allan Bester .15 .40
155 Gary Leeman .12 .30
156 Mark Osborne .12 .30
157 Tom Fergus .12 .30
158 Brad Marsh .12 .30
159 Wendel Clark .15 .40
160 Daniel Marois .12 .30
161 Ed Olczyk .15 .40
162 Rob Ramage .15 .40
163 Vincent Damphousse .12 .30
164 Lou Franceschetti RC .15 .40
165 Paul Gillis .12 .30
166 Craig Wolanin RC .12 .30
167 Marc Fortier .12 .30
168 Tony McKegney .10 .25
169 Joe Sakic .50 1.25
170 Michel Petit .12 .30
171 Scott Gordon RC .10 .25
172 Tony Hrkac .10 .25
173 Bryan Fogarty RC .10 .25
174 Mike Hough .12 .30
175 Claude Loiselle RC .10 .25
176 Ulf Dahlen .15 .40
177 Larry Murphy .12 .30
178 Neal Broten .10 .25
179 Don Barber RC .12 .30
180 Shawn Chambers .12 .30
181 Clark Donatelli RC .10 .25
182 Brian Bellows .12 .30
183 Jon Casey .15 .40
184 Neil Wilkinson RC .12 .30
185 Aaron Broten .12 .30
186 Dave Gagner .15 .40
187 Basil McRae .12 .30
188 Mike Modano RC .50 1.25
189 Grant Fuhr .15 .40
190 Martin Gelinas RC .30 .75
191 Jari Kurri .20 .50
192 Geoff Smith RC .15 .40
193 Craig MacTavish .12 .30
194 Esa Tikkanen .12 .30
195 Glenn Anderson .15 .40
196 Joe Murphy RC .12 .30
197 Petr Klima .10 .25
198 Kevin Lowe .15 .40
199 Mark Messier .30 .75
200 Steve Smith .12 .30
201 Craig Simpson .12 .30
202 Rob Brown .30 .75
203 Wendell Young RC .15 .40
204 Mario Lemieux .60 1.50
205 Phil Bourque .12 .30
206 Mark Recchi RC .50 1.25
207 Zarley Zalapski .12 .30
208 Kevin Stevens RC .30 .75
209 Tom Barrasso .12 .30
210 John Cullen .15 .40
211 Paul Coffey .15 .40
212 Bob Errey .12 .30
213 Tony Tanti .12 .30
214 Carey Wilson .12 .30
215A Brian Leetch ERR .20 .50
215B Brian Leetch COR .20 .50
216 Darren Turcotte RC .12 .30
217 Brian Mullen .15 .40
218 Mike Richter RC .50 1.25
219 Troy Mallette RC .12 .30
220 Mike Gartner .15 .40
221 Bernie Nicholls .15 .40
222 John Vanbiesbrouck .12 .30
223 John Ogrodnick .15 .40
224 Paul Broten .12 .30
225 James Patrick .15 .40
226 Mark Janssens RC .15 .40
227 Randy McKay RC .12 .30
228 Marc Habscheid .12 .30
229 Jimmy Carson .12 .30
230 Yves Racine RC .15 .40
231 Dave Barr .15 .40
232 Shawn Burr .12 .30
233 Steve Yzerman .50 1.25
234 Steve Chiasson .10 .25
235 Daniel Shank RC .15 .40
236 John Chabot .15 .40
237 Gerard Gallant .10 .25
238 Bernie Federko .12 .30
239 Phil Housley .12 .30
240 Alexander Mogilny RC .50 1.25
241 Pierre Turgeon .12 .30
242 Daren Puppa .12 .30
243 Scott Arniel .10 .25
244 Christian Ruuttu .12 .30
245 Doug Bodger .12 .30
246 Dave Andreychuk .15 .40
247 Mike Foligno .12 .30
248 Dean Kennedy RC .10 .25
249 Dave Snuggerud RC .12 .30
250 Rick Vaive .12 .30
251 Todd Krygier RC .12 .30
252 Adam Burt RC .12 .30
253 Scott Young .10 .25
254 Ron Francis .20 .50
255 Peter Sidorkiewicz .15 .40
256 Dave Babych .10 .25
257 Pat Verbeek .12 .30
258 Ray Ferraro .12 .30
259 Chris Govedaris RC .12 .30
260 Brad Shaw RC .12 .30
261 Kevin Dineen .15 .40
262 Dean Evason .12 .30
263 Checklist 1-132 .10 .25
264 Checklist 133-264 .10 .25

1990-91 Bowman Tiffany

Bowman Tiffany cards parallel the base set and Topps announced a production run of only 3000 sets. The cards can be distinguished by a glossy coating not found on regular issued cards.

COMPLETE SET (264) 50.00 100.00
*TIFFANY: 5X TO 12X BASIC CARDS

1990-91 Bowman Hat Tricks

This 22-card standard size set was issued as an insert in the 1990-91 Bowman hockey wax packs. This set honored the 14 players (1-14) who scored three or more goals (a hat trick) in a game at least twice during the 1989-90 regular season and the eight players (15-22) who performed the feat during the 1990 NHL playoffs. The fronts of the cards have a glossy sheen to them while the backs talk about the hat tricks of the players. There are two Mike Gartner cards as he had hat tricks for two different teams.

COMPLETE SET (22) 2.50 6.00
*TIFFANY: 3X TO 8X BASIC INSERTS
1 Brett Hull .30 .75
2 Mario Lemieux .75 2.00
3 Rob Brown .30 .75
4 Mark Messier .30 .75
5 Steve Yzerman .75 2.00
6 Vincent Damphousse .12 .30
7 Kevin Dineen .15 .40
8 Mike Gartner .15 .40
9 Pat LaFontaine .15 .40
10 Gary Leeman .12 .30
11 Stephane Richer .15 .40
12 Luc Robitaille .15 .40
13 Steve Thomas .10 .25
14 Rick Tocchet .15 .40
15 Dino Ciccarelli .15 .40
16 John Druce .15 .40
17 Mike Gartner .15 .40
18 Tony Granato .12 .30
19 Jari Kurri .20 .50
20 Bernie Nicholls .15 .40
21 Tomas Sandstrom .15 .40
22 Dave Taylor .15 .40

1991-92 Bowman

The 1991-92 Bowman hockey set contains 429 standard-size cards. On a white card face, the fronts display color action player photos enclosed by blue and tan border stripes. The player's name appears in a purple stripe below the picture. The backs are colorful (displaying blue, green, and red fading to yellow sections) and present biography and statistics (career and for the 1990-91 season). The season statistics are broken down to show the player's performance against each NHL team. The cards are numbered on the back and checklisted below according to teams. The only Rookie Card worthy of note is John LeClair.

1 John Cullen .07 .20
2 Todd Krygier .07 .20
3 Kay Whitmore .07 .20
4 Terry Yake .07 .20
5 Randy Ladouceur .07 .20
6 Kevin Dineen .07 .20
7 Jim McKenzie RC .10 .25
8 Brad Shaw .05 .15
9 Mark Hunter .07 .20
10 Dean Evason .07 .20
11 Mikael Andersson .07 .20
12 Pat Verbeek .07 .20
13 Peter Sidorkiewicz .07 .20
14 Mike Tomlak .07 .20
15 Zarley Zalapski .07 .20
16 Rob Brown .07 .20
17 Sylvain Cote .07 .20
18 Bobby Holik .10 .25
19 Daryl Reaugh .07 .20
20 Paul Cyr .07 .20
21 Doug Bodger .07 .20
22 Dave Andreychuk .10 .25
23 Clint Malarchuk .07 .20
24 Darrin Shannon .07 .20
25 Christian Ruuttu .07 .20
26 Uwe Krupp .07 .20
27 Pierre Turgeon .07 .20
28 Kevin Haller RC .10 .25
29 Dave Snuggerud .05 .15
30 Alexander Mogilny .07 .2
31 Dale Hawerchuk .12 .3
32 Mike Ramsey .07 .2
33 Darcy Wakaluk RC .10 .2
34 Tony Tanti .07 .2
35 Jay Wells .07 .2
36 Mikko Makela .07 .2
37 Daren Puppa .07 .2
38 Benoit Hogue .07 .2
39 Rick Vaive .05 .1
40 Grant Ledyard .07 .2
41 Steve Yzerman HT .30 .7
42 Steve Yzerman .30 .7
43 Shawn Burr .07 .2
44 Yves Racine .07 .2
45 Johan Garpenlov .07 .2
46 Keith Primeau .07 .2
47 Tim Cheveldae .07 .2
48 Brad McCrimmon .07 .2
49 Dave Barr .07 .2
50 Sergei Fedorov .15 .4
51 Brent Fedyk .07 .2
52 Jimmy Carson .07 .2
53 Paul Ysebaert .07 .2
54 Rick Zombo .07 .2

Bob Probert .07 .20
Gerard Gallant .05 .15
Kevin Miller .07 .20
Randy Moller .07 .20
Kris King .07 .20
Corey Millen RC .10 .25
Brian Mullen .07 .20
Darren Turcotte .07 .20
Ray Sheppard .07 .20
David Shaw .07 .20
Troy Mallette .07 .20
James Patrick .07 .20
Mark Janssens .07 .20
John Vanbiesbrouck .07 .20
Joey Kocur .07 .20
Mike Richter .10 .25
John Ogrodnick .07 .20
Kelly Kisio .07 .20
Normand Rochefort .07 .20
Mike Gartner .07 .20
Brian Leetch .07 .20
Bernie Nicholls .07 .20
Jan Erixon .07 .20
Larry Murphy .07 .20
Joe Mullen .07 .20
Tom Barrasso .07 .20
Paul Coffey .07 .20
Jiri Hrdina .07 .20
Mark Recchi .12 .30
Randy Gilhen .07 .20
Bob Errey .07 .20
Scott Young .07 .20
Mario Lemieux .40 1.00
Ulf Samuelsson .07 .20
Frank Pietrangelo .07 .20
Ron Francis .12 .30
Paul Stanton .07 .20
Kevin Stevens .07 .20
Bryan Trottier .12 .30
Phil Bourque .07 .20
Jaromir Jagr .25 .60
Petr Klima HT .07 .20
Adam Graves .07 .20
Esa Tikkanen .07 .20
Norm Maciver RC .10 .25
Craig MacTavish .07 .20
Bill Ranford .07 .20
Martin Gelinas .07 .20
Charlie Huddy .07 .20
Petr Klima .07 .20
Ken Linseman .07 .20
Steve Smith .10 .25
Craig Simpson .05 .15
Chris Joseph .07 .20
Joe Murphy .07 .20
Jeff Beukeboom .07 .20
Grant Fuhr .10 .25
Geoff Smith .07 .20
Anatoli Semenov .07 .20
Mark Messier .25 .60
Kevin Lowe .07 .20
Glenn Anderson .10 .25
Bobby Smith .07 .20
Doug Smail .07 .20
Jon Casey .07 .20
Gaetan Duchesne .05 .15
Neal Broten .07 .20
Brian Hayward .07 .20
Brian Propp .07 .20
Mark Tinordi .07 .20
Mike Modano .20 .50
Marc Bureau .07 .20
Ulf Dahlen .07 .20
Chris Dahlquist .07 .20
Brian Bellows .07 .20
Mike Craig .07 .20
Dave Gagner .07 .20
Brian Glynn .07 .20
Joe Sakic .30 .75
Owen Nolan .10 .25
Everett Sanipass .07 .20
Jamie Baker RC .07 .20
Mats Sundin .10 .25
Craig Wolanin .07 .20
Kip Miller .07 .20
Steven Finn .07 .20
Tony Hrkac .07 .20
Curtis Leschyshyn .07 .20
Mike McNeil .07 .20
Mike Hough .07 .20
Alexei Gusarov RC .07 .20
Jacques Cloutier .07 .20
Shawn Anderson .07 .20
Stephane Morin .07 .20
Bryan Fogarty .07 .20
Scott Pearson .07 .20
Ron Tugnutt .07 .20
Randy Velischek .07 .20
David Reid .05 .15
Rob Ramage .07 .20
Dave Hannan .07 .20
Wendel Clark .10 .25
Peter Ing .07 .20
Michel Petit .07 .20
Brian Bradley .07 .20
Rob Cimetta .07 .20
Gary Leeman .07 .20
Aaron Broten .07 .20
Dave Ellett .07 .20
Peter Zezel .05 .15
Daniel Marois .07 .20
Mike Krushelnyski .07 .20
Luke Richardson .07 .20
Scott Thornton .07 .20
Mike Foligno .10 .25
Vincent Damphousse .07 .20
Todd Gill .07 .20
Kevin Maguire .07 .20
Wayne Gretzky HT .50 1.25
Tomas Sandstrom HT .07 .20
John Tonelli .07 .20
Wayne Gretzky .50 1.25
Larry Robinson .05 .15
Jay Miller .07 .20
Tomas Sandstrom .07 .20
John McIntyre .07 .20
Brad Jones .07 .20
Rob Blake .10 .25
Kelly Hrudey .07 .20
Marty McSorley .07 .20
Todd Elik .07 .20
Dave Taylor .07 .20
Steve Kasper .07 .20
Luc Robitaille .07 .20
Bob Kudelski .05 .15
Daniel Berthiaume .07 .20
Steve Duchesne .05 .15
Tony Granato .07 .20
Bob Essensa .07 .20
Phil Sykes .07 .20
Paul MacDermid .07 .20
196 Dave McLlwain .07 .20
197 Phil Housley .07 .20
198 Pat Elynuik .07 .20
199 Randy Carlyle .07 .20
200 Thomas Steen .07 .20
201 Teppo Numminen .07 .20
202 Danton Cole .05 .15
203 Doug Evans .05 .15
204 Ed Olczyk .07 .20
205 Moe Mantha .07 .20
206 Scott Arniel .07 .20
207 Rick Tabaracci .07 .20
208 Bryan Marchment RC .07 .20
209 Mark Osborne .07 .20
210 Fredrik Olausson .07 .20
211 Brent Ashton .07 .20
212 Ray Ferraro .07 .20
213 Mark Fitzpatrick .07 .20
214 Hubie McDonough .07 .20
215 Joe Reekie .07 .20
216 Bill Berg .07 .20
217 Wayne McBean .05 .15
218 Pat Flatley .07 .20
219 Jeff Hackett .07 .20
220 Derek King .05 .15
221 Craig Ludwig .07 .20
222 Pat LaFontaine .10 .25
223 David Volek .07 .20
224 Glenn Healy .10 .25
225 Jeff Norton .07 .20
226 Brent Sutter .07 .20
227 Randy Wood .07 .20
228 Gary Nylund .07 .20
229 Dave Chyzowski .05 .15
230 Rick Tocchet .07 .20
231 Ken Wregget .07 .20
232 Terry Carkner .07 .20
233 Martin Hostak .05 .15
234 Ron Hextall .10 .25
235 Gord Murphy .07 .20
236 Scott Mellanby .07 .20
237 Pete Peeters .05 .15
238 Ron Sutter .07 .20
239 Murray Craven .07 .20
240 Kjell Samuelsson .07 .20
241 Pelle Eklund .07 .20
242 Mark Pederson .07 .20
243 Murray Baron .07 .20
244 Keith Acton .07 .20
245 Derrick Smith .07 .20
246 Mike Ricci .10 .25
247 Dale Kushner .07 .20
248 Normand Lacombe .07 .20
249 Theo Fleury HT .07 .20
250 Sergei Makarov HT .07 .20
251 Paul Ranheim .10 .25
252 Joe Nieuwendyk .07 .20
253 Mike Vernon .07 .20
254 Gary Suter .07 .20
255 Doug Gilmour .20 .50
256 Paul Fenton .07 .20
257 Roger Johansson .07 .20
258 Stephane Matteau .07 .20
259 Frank Musil .07 .20
260 Joel Otto .07 .20
261 Tim Sweeney .07 .20
262 Al MacInnis .07 .20
263 Gary Roberts .07 .20
264 Sergei Makarov .07 .20
265 Carey Wilson .07 .20
266 Ric Nattress .07 .20
267 Robert Reichel .20 .50
268 Rick Wamsley .05 .15
269 Brian MacLellan .07 .20
270 Theo Fleury .07 .20
271 Claude Lemieux .07 .20
272 John MacLean .07 .20
273 Slava Fetisov .07 .20
274 Kirk Muller .05 .15
275 Sean Burke .10 .25
276 Alexei Kasatonov .05 .15
277 Claude Lemieux .07 .20
278 Eric Weinrich .10 .25
279 Patrik Sundstrom .07 .20
280 Zdeno Ciger .07 .20
281 Bruce Driver .07 .20
282 Laurie Boschman .07 .20
283 Chris Terreri .07 .20
284 Ken Daneyko .07 .20
285 Doug Brown .07 .20
286 Jon Morris .07 .20
287 Peter Stastny .07 .20
288 Brendan Shanahan .12 .30
289 John MacLean .07 .20
290 Mike Liut .07 .20
291 Michal Pivonka .07 .20
292 Kelly Miller .07 .20
293 John Druce .07 .20
294 Calle Johansson .07 .20
295 Alan May .07 .20
296 Kevin Hatcher .07 .20
297 Tim Bergland .07 .20
298 Mikhail Tatarinov .07 .20
299 Peter Bondra .07 .20
300 Al Iafrate .07 .20
301 Nick Kypreos .07 .20
302 Dino Ciccarelli .07 .20
303 Dale Hunter .07 .20
304 Don Beaupre .07 .20
305 Jim Hrivnak .07 .20
306 Stephen Leach .07 .20
307 Dimitri Khristich FBC .07 .20
308 Mike Ridley .07 .20
309 Sergio Momesso .07 .20
310 Kirk McLean .07 .20
311 Greg Adams .07 .20
312 Adrien Plavsic .07 .20
313 Cliff Ronning .07 .20
314 Garry Valk .07 .20
315 Troy Gamble .05 .15
316 Gino Odjick .07 .20
317 Doug Lidster .07 .20
318 Geoff Courtnall .07 .20
319 Tom Kurvers .07 .20
320 Robert Kron .07 .20
321 Jyrki Lumme .07 .20
322 Jay Mazur .05 .15
323 Dave Capuano .07 .20
324 Petr Nedved .07 .20
325 Steve Bozek .07 .20
326 Igor Larionov .07 .20
327 Trevor Linden .07 .20
328 Shayne Corson .07 .20
329 Eric Desjardins .10 .25
330 Stephane Richer .07 .20
331 Brian Skrudland .07 .20
332 Sylvain Lefebvre .07 .20
333 Stephan Lebeau .07 .20
334 Mike Keane .05 .15
335 Patrick Roy UER .25 .60
336 Brent Gilchrist .07 .20
337 Andre Racicot RC .07 .20
338 Guy Carbonneau .07 .20
339 Mike McPhee .07 .20
340 Andrew Cassels .07 .20
341 Petr Svoboda .07 .20
342 Denis Savard .12 .30
343 Mathieu Schneider .07 .20
344 John LeClair RC .25 .60
345 Tom Chorske .07 .20
346 Russ Courtnall .07 .20
347 Ken Hodge Jr. HT .10 .25
348 Cam Neely HT .10 .25
349 Randy Burridge .07 .20
350 Glen Wesley .07 .20
351 Chris Nilan .07 .20
352 Jeff Lazaro .07 .20
353 Wes Walz .07 .20
354 Rejean Lemelin .07 .20
355 Craig Janney .07 .20
356 Ray Bourque .15 .40
357 Bob Sweeney .07 .20
358 Dave Christian .07 .20
359 Dave Poulin .07 .20
360 Garry Galley .07 .20
361 Andy Moog .07 .20
362 Ken Hodge Jr. .10 .25
363 Jim Wiemer .07 .20
364 Petri Skriko .05 .15
365 Don Sweeney .07 .20
366 Cam Neely .10 .25
367 Brett Hull HT .15 .40
368 Gino Cavallini .07 .20
369 Scott Stevens .10 .25
370 Rich Sutter .07 .20
371 Glen Featherstone .05 .15
372 Vincent Riendeau .07 .20
373 Dave Lowry .07 .20
374 Rod Brind'Amour .07 .20
375 Brett Hull .15 .40
376 Dan Quinn .07 .20
377 Tom Tilley .05 .15
378 Paul Cavallini .07 .20
379 Bob Bassen .07 .20
380 Mario Marois .07 .20
381 Darin Kimble .07 .20
382 Ron Wilson .07 .20
383 Garth Butcher .07 .20
384 Adam Oates .10 .25
385 Jeff Brown .07 .20
386 Jeremy Roenick HT .25 .60
387 Tony McKegney .07 .20
388 Troy Murray .07 .20
389 Dave Manson .07 .20
390 Ed Belfour .25 .60
391 Steve Thomas .07 .20
392 Michel Goulet .07 .20
393 Trent Yawney .07 .20
394 Adam Creighton .07 .20
395 Steve Larmer .07 .20
396 Jim Waite .07 .20
397 Dirk Graham .07 .20
398 Chris Chelios .10 .25
399 Mike Hudson .07 .20
400 Doug Wilson .07 .20
401 Greg Gilbert .07 .20
402 Wayne Presley .07 .20
403 Jeremy Roenick .25 .60
404 Frantisek Kucera .07 .20
405 Blackhawks .07 .20
North Stars
406 Blues .10 .25
Red Wings
407 Flames .10 .25
Oilers
408 Penguins .07 .20
Devils
409 Rangers .07 .20
Capitals
410 Bruins .05 .15
Whalers
411 Canadiens .07 .20
Sabres
412 Kings .05 .15
Canucks
413 Penguins .07 .20
Capitals
414 Bruins .07 .20
Canadiens
415 North Stars .20 .50
Blues
416 Kings .05 .15
Oilers
417 North Stars .10 .25
Oilers
418 Bruins .07 .20
Penguins
419 Game 1 Cup Finals .07 .20
420 Game 2 Cup Finals .07 .20
421 Game 3 Cup Finals .07 .20
422 Game 4 Cup Finals .07 .20
423 Game 5 Cup Finals .07 .20
424 Game 6 Cup Finals .07 .20
425 Mario Lemieux Smythe .40 1.00
426 Checklist 1-108 .05 .15
427 Checklist 109-216 .05 .15
428 Checklist 217-324 .05 .15
429 Checklist 325-429 .05 .15

1992-93 Bowman

The 1992-93 Bowman hockey set contains 442 standard-size cards. Reportedly only 2,000 16-box wax cases were produced. One of 45 gold-foil engraved cards was inserted in each 15-card pack. These gold-foil cards feature 44 All-Stars (Campbell Conference on cards 199-220 and Wales Conference on cards 222-243) and a special card commemorating Mario Lemieux as the winner of the Conn Smythe trophy (440). The 18 gold-foil All-Stars that were single printed are listed in the checklist below as SP. The basic card fronts feature color action player photos with white borders. A magenta bar at the top left corner carries the Bowman "B". A gradated turquoise bar at the bottom right displays the player's name. The backs have a burlap-textured background and carry a close-up photo, a yellow and white statistics box presenting the player's performance vs. other teams, and biography. The only noteworthy Rookie Card in the set is Guy Hebert. There are a number of non glossy Eric Lindros (No. 442) cards on the market. These are unauthorized releases and should be avoided by collectors.

1 Wayne Gretzky 2.50 6.00
2 Mike Krushelnyski .10 .25
3 Ray Bourque .50 1.25
4 Keith Brown .12 .30
5 Bob Sweeney .10 .25
6 Dave Christian .10 .25
7 Frantisek Kucera .12 .30
8 John LeClair .25 .60
9 Jamie Macoun .12 .30
10 Bob Carpenter .10 .25
11 Garry Galley .10 .25
12 Bob Kudelski .12 .30
13 Doug Bodger .10 .25
14 Craig Janney .12 .30
15 Glen Wesley .10 .25
16 Daren Puppa .12 .30
17 Andy Brickley .12 .30
18 Steve Konroyd .12 .30
19 Dave Poulin .10 .25
20 Phil Housley .10 .25
21 Kevin Todd .10 .25
22 Tomas Sandstrom .12 .30
23 Pierre Turgeon .12 .30
24 Steve Smith .10 .25
25 Ray Sheppard .10 .25
26 Stu Barnes .10 .25
27 Grant Ledyard .10 .25
28 Benoit Hogue .10 .25
29 Randy Burridge .10 .25
30 Clint Malarchuk .10 .25
31 Steve Duchesne .10 .25
32 Guy Hebert RC 2.00 5.00
33 Steve Kasper .12 .30
34 Alexander Mogilny .12 .30
35 Marty McSorley .10 .25
36 Doug Weight .30 .75
37 Dave Taylor .12 .30
38 Guy Carbonneau .12 .30
39 Brian Benning .10 .25
40 Nelson Emerson .10 .25
41 Craig Wolanin .10 .25
42 Kelly Hrudey .12 .30
43 Chris Chelios .15 .40
44 Dave Andreychuk .15 .40
45 Russ Courtnall .10 .25
46 Stephane Richer .12 .30
47 Petr Svoboda .12 .30
48 Barry Pederson .10 .25
49 Claude Lemieux .10 .25
50 Tony Granato .10 .25
51 Al MacInnis .12 .30
52 Luciano Borsato .10 .25
53 Sergei Makarov .10 .25
54 Bobby Smith .12 .30
55 Gary Suter .10 .25
56 Tom Draper .10 .25
57 Corry Millen .10 .25
58 Joe Mullen .12 .30
59 Joe Nieuwendyk .12 .30
60 Brian Hayward .10 .25
61 Steve Larmer .10 .25
62 Cam Neely .15 .40
63 Ric Nattress .12 .30
64 Denis Savard .20 .50
65 Gerald Diduck .12 .30
66 Pat Jablonski .12 .30
67 Brad McCrimmon .10 .25
68 Dirk Graham .10 .25
69 Joel Otto .10 .25
70 Luc Robitaille .12 .30
71 Dana Murzyn .10 .25
72 Jocelyn Lemieux .10 .25
73 Mike Hudson .10 .25
74 Patrick Roy 2.00 6.00
75 Doug Wilson .12 .30
76 Wayne Presley .10 .25
77 Felix Potvin .30 .75
78 Jeremy Roenick .25 .60
79 Andy Moog .12 .30
80 Joey Kocur .12 .30
81 Neal Broten .12 .30
82 Shayne Corson .10 .25
83 Doug Gilmour .20 .50
84 Rob Zettler .10 .25
85 Bob Probert .12 .30
86 Mike Vernon .12 .30
87 Rick Zombo .10 .25
88 Adam Creighton .10 .25
89 Mike McPhee .10 .25
90 Ed Belfour .15 .40
91 Steve Chiasson .10 .25
92 Dominic Roussel .12 .30
93 Troy Murray .10 .25
94 Jari Kurri .15 .40
95 Geoff Smith .10 .25
96 Paul Ranheim .10 .25
97 Rick Wamsley .10 .25
98 Brian Noonan .10 .25
99 Kevin Lowe .12 .30
100 Josef Beranek .10 .25
101 Michel Petit .10 .25
102 Craig Billington .12 .30
103 Steve Yzerman .75 2.00
104 Glenn Anderson .15 .40
105 Perry Berezan .10 .25
106 Bill Ranford .12 .30
107 Randy Ladouceur .10 .25
108 Jimmy Carson .10 .25
109 Gary Roberts .10 .25
110 Checklist 1-110 .08 .25
111 Brad Shaw .10 .25
112 Pat Verbeek .10 .25
113 Mark Messier .25 .60
114 Grant Fuhr .15 .40
115 Sylvain Cote .12 .30
116 Mike Sullivan .10 .25
117 Steve Thomas .12 .30
118 Craig MacTavish .10 .25
119 Dave Babych .12 .30
120 Jim Waite .12 .30
121 Kevin Dineen .10 .25
122 Shawn Burr .10 .25
123 Ron Francis .20 .50
124 Garth Butcher .12 .30
125 Jarmo Myllys .10 .25
126 Doug Brown .12 .30
127 James Patrick .10 .25
128 Ray Ferraro .10 .25
129 Terry Carkner .12 .30
130 John MacLean .12 .30
131 Randy Velischek .10 .25
132 John Vanbiesbrouck .12 .30
133 Dean Evason .10 .25
134 Patrick Flatley .12 .30
135 Petr Klima .10 .25
136 Geoff Sanderson .12 .30
137 Joe Reekie .10 .25
138 Kirk Muller .10 .25
139 Brian Mullen .10 .25
140 Daniel Berthiaume .12 .30
141 David Shaw .12 .30
142 Pat LaFontaine .15 .40
143 Ulf Dahlen .10 .25
144 Esa Tikkanen .10 .25
145 Slava Fetisov .10 .25
146 Mike Gartner .12 .30
147 Brent Sutter .10 .25
148 Darcy Wakaluk .12 .30
149 Brian Leetch .12 .30
150 Craig Simpson .10 .25
151 Mike Modano .40 1.00
152 Bryan Trottier .20 .50
153 Larry Murphy .12 .30
154 Pavel Bure .30 .75
155 Kay Whitmore .12 .30
156 Darren Turcotte .10 .25
157 Frank Musil .12 .30
158 Mikael Andersson .10 .25
159 Rick Tocchet .12 .30
160 Scott Stevens .15 .40
161 Bernie Nicholls .10 .25
162 Peter Sidorkiewicz .10 .25
163 Scott Mellanby .10 .25
164 Alexander Semak .10 .25
165 Kjell Samuelsson .12 .30
166 Kelly Kisio .12 .30
167 Sylvain Turgeon .10 .25
168 Rob Brown .10 .25
169 Gerard Gallant .10 .25
170 Jyrki Lumme .10 .25
171 Dave Gagner .12 .30
172 Tony Tanti .10 .25
173 Zarley Zalapski .10 .25
174 Joe Murphy .10 .25
175 Ron Sutter .10 .25
176 Dino Ciccarelli .12 .30
177 Jim Johnson .12 .30
178 Mike Hough .12 .30
179 Pelle Eklund .12 .30
180 John Druce .10 .25
181 Paul Coffey .15 .40
182 Ken Wregget .12 .30
183 Brendan Shanahan .20 .50
184 Keith Acton .12 .30
185 Steven Finn .10 .25
186 Brett Hull .25 .60
187 Rollie Melanson .10 .25
188 Derek King .10 .25
189 Mario Lemieux .60 1.50
190 Mathieu Schneider .10 .25
191 Claude Vilgrain .12 .30
192 Gary Leeman .10 .25
193 Paul Cavallini .10 .25
194 John Cullen .10 .25
195 Ron Hextall .12 .30
196 David Volek .10 .25
197 Gordie Roberts .12 .30
198 Dale Craigwell .10 .25
199 Ed Belfour FOIL 2.00 6.00
200 Brian Bellows FOIL SP .12 .30
201 Chris Chelios FOIL .15 .40
202 Tim Cheveldae FOIL SP .10 .25
203A V.Damphousse FOIL ERR .12 .30
203B V.Damphousse FOIL COR .12 .30
204 Dave Ellett FOIL .10 .25
205 Sergei Fedorov FOIL SP 4.00 10.00
206 Theo Fleury FOIL 1.50 4.00
207 Wayne Gretzky FOIL 6.00 15.00
208 Phil Housley FOIL .10 .25
209 Brett Hull FOIL 2.00 5.00
210 Trevor Linden FOIL SP .12 .30
211 Al MacInnis FOIL .12 .30
212 Kirk McLean FOIL SP .10 .25
213 Adam Oates FOIL .15 .40
214 Gary Roberts FOIL SP .10 .25
215 Larry Robinson FOIL .15 .40
216 Luc Robitaille FOIL .12 .30
217 Jeremy Roenick FOIL SP 3.00 8.00
218 Mark Tinordi FOIL .10 .25
219 Doug Wilson FOIL .12 .30
220 Steve Yzerman FOIL 3.00 8.00
221 Checklist 111-220 .08 .25
222 Don Beaupre FOIL SP .12 .30
223 Ray Bourque FOIL 2.00 5.00
224 Rod Brind'Amour FOIL SP .10 .25
225 Randy Burridge FOIL SP .10 .25
226 Paul Coffey FOIL SP .15 .40
227 John Cullen FOIL .10 .25
228 Eric Desjardins FOIL SP .12 .30
229 Ray Ferraro FOIL .10 .25
230 Kevin Hatcher FOIL .10 .25
231 Jaromir Jagr FOIL 2.50 6.00
232 Brian Leetch FOIL SP .12 .30
233 Mario Lemieux FOIL 3.00 8.00
234 Mark Messier FOIL .25 .60
235 Alexander Mogilny FOIL .12 .30
236 Kirk Muller FOIL .10 .25
237 Owen Nolan FOIL .10 .25
238 Mike Richter FOIL .15 .40
239 Patrick Roy FOIL 4.00 10.00
240 Joe Sakic FOIL SP 4.00 10.00
241 Kevin Stevens FOIL .10 .25
242 Scott Stevens FOIL .15 .40
243 Bryan Trottier FOIL SP .20 .50
244 Joe Sakic .40 1.00
245 Daniel Marois .10 .25
246 Randy Wood .10 .25
247 Jeff Brown .12 .30
248 Peter Bondra .12 .30
249 Peter Stastny .12 .30
250 Tom Barrasso .12 .30
251 Al Iafrate .12 .30
252 James Black .10 .25
253 Jan Erixon .12 .30
254 Brian Lawton .12 .30
255 Luke Richardson .12 .30
256 Rich Sutter .10 .25
257 Jeff Chychrun .10 .25
258 Adam Oates .15 .40
259 Tom Kurvers .10 .25
260 Brian Bellows .12 .30
261 Trevor Linden .12 .30
262 Vincent Riendeau .12 .30
263 Peter Zezel .10 .25
264 Rich Pilon .10 .25
265 Paul Broten .10 .25
266 Gaetan Duchesne .10 .25
267 Doug Lidster .12 .30
268 Rod Brind'Amour .10 .25
269 Jon Casey .10 .25
270 Pat Elynuik .10 .25
271 Kevin Hatcher .10 .25
272 Brian Propp .10 .25
273 Tom Fergus .12 .30
274 Steve Weeks .10 .25
275 Calle Johansson .10 .25
276 Russ Romaniuk .10 .25
277 Greg Paslawski .10 .25
278 Ed Olczyk .10 .25
279 Rod Langway .12 .30
280 Murray Craven .10 .25
281 Guy Larose .10 .25
282 Paul MacDermid .12 .30
283 Brian Bradley .10 .25
284 Paul Stanton .10 .25
285 Kirk McLean .10 .25
286 Andrei Lomakin .10 .25
287 Randy Carlyle .12 .30
288 Donald Audette .12 .30
289 Dan Quinn .12 .30
290 Mike Keane .10 .25
291 Dave Ellett .10 .25
292 Joe Juneau UER .10 .25
293 Phil Bourque .10 .25
294 Michal Pivonka .10 .25
295 Fredrik Olausson .10 .25
296 Randy McKay .12 .30
297 Don Beaupre .12 .30
298 Steve Leach .10 .25
299 Teppo Numminen .10 .25
300 Slava Kozlov .12 .30
301 Kevin Haller .10 .25
302 Jaromir Jagr .40 1.00
303 Dale Hunter .12 .30
304 Bob Errey .12 .30
305 Nicklas Lidstrom .12 .30
306 Bob Essensa .12 .30
307 Sylvain Lefebvre .10 .25
308 Dale Hawerchuk .20 .50
309 Dave Snuggerud .10 .25
310 Michel Goulet .12 .30
311 Eric Desjardins .12 .30
312 Thomas Steen .10 .25
313 Scott Niedermayer .15 .40
314 Mark Recchi .20 .50
315 Gord Murphy .12 .30
316 Sergio Momesso .10 .25
317 Todd Elik .10 .25
318 Louie DeBrusk .10 .25
319 Mike Lalor .12 .30
320 Jamie Leach .10 .25
321 Darryl Sydor .10 .25
322 Brent Gilchrist .10 .25
323 Alexei Kasatonov .10 .25
324 Rick Tabaracci .10 .25
325 Wendel Clark .12 .30
326 Vladimir Konstantinov .15 .40
327 Randy Gilhen .10 .25
328 Owen Nolan .10 .25
329 Vincent Damphousse .12 .30
330 Checklist 221-331 .08 .25
331 Yves Racine .10 .25
332 Jacques Cloutier .12 .30
333 Greg Adams .10 .25
334 Mike Craig .10 .25
335 Curtis Leschyshyn .12 .30
336 John McIntyre .10 .25
337 Stephane Quintal .10 .25
338 Kelly Miller .10 .25
339 Dave Manson .10 .25
340 Stephane Matteau .10 .25
341 Christian Ruuttu .10 .25
342 Mike Donnelly .10 .25
343 Eric Weinrich .10 .25
344 Mats Sundin .15 .40
345 Geoff Courtnall .10 .25
346 Stephan Lebeau .10 .25
347 Jeff Beukeboom .10 .25
348 Jeff Hackett .12 .30
349 Uwe Krupp .10 .25
350 Igor Larionov .10 .25
351 Ulf Samuelsson .10 .25
352 Marty McInnis .10 .25
353 Peter Ahola .10 .25
354 Mike Richter .15 .40
355 Theo Fleury .25 .60
356 Dan Lambert .10 .25
357 Brent Ashton .10 .25
358 David Bruce .10 .25
359 Chris Dahlquist .12 .30
360 Mike Ridley .10 .25
361 Pat Falloon .10 .25
362 Doug Smail .10 .25
363 Adrien Plavsic .10 .25
364 Ron Wilson .12 .30
365 Derian Hatcher .10 .25
366 Kevin Stevens .10 .25
367 Rob Blake .12 .30
368 Curtis Joseph .15 .40
369 Tom Fitzgerald .10 .25
370 Dave Lowry .12 .30
371 J.J. Daigneault .10 .25
372 Jim Hrivnak .12 .30
373 Adam Graves .10 .25
374 Brad May .10 .25
375 Todd Gill .10 .25
376 Paul Ysebaert .10 .25
377 David Williams RC .10 .25
378 Bob Bassen .10 .25
379 Brian Glynn .10 .25
380 Kris King .10 .25
381 Rob Pearson .10 .25
382 Marc Bureau .12 .30
383 Jim Paek .12 .30
384 Tomas Forslund .10 .25
385 Darrin Shannon .10 .25
386 Chris Terreri .12 .30
387 Andrew Cassels .10 .25
388 Jay More .10 .25
389 Tony Amonte .12 .30
390 Mark Pederson .10 .25
391 Kevin Miller .10 .25
392 Igor Ulanov .10 .25
393 Kelly Buchberger .10 .25
394 Mark Fitzpatrick .12 .30
395 Mikhail Tatarinov .10 .25
396 Petr Nedved .12 .30
397 Jeff Odgers .10 .25
398 Stephane Fiset .10 .25
399 Mark Tinordi .10 .25
400 Johan Garpenlov .10 .25
401 Robert Reichel .10 .25
402 Don Sweeney UER .10 .25
403 Rob DiMaio .10 .25
404 Bill Lindsay RC .10 .25
405 Steph Beauregard .12 .30
406 Mike Ricci .12 .30
407 Bobby Holik .12 .30
408 Igor Kravchuk .10 .25
409 Murray Baron .10 .25
410 Troy Gamble .10 .25
411 Cliff Ronning .10 .25
412 Jeff Reese .10 .25
413 Robert Kron .10 .25
414 Benoit Brunet .10 .25
415 Shawn McEachern .10 .25
416 Sergei Fedorov .25 .60
417 Joe Sacco .10 .25
418 Bryan Marchment .12 .30
419 John LeBlanc RC .12 .30
420 Tim Cheveldae .10 .25
421 Claude LaPointe .10 .25
422 Ken Sutton .10 .25
423 Anatoli Semenov .10 .25
424 Mike McNeil .12 .30
425 Norm Maciver .10 .25
426 Sergei Nemchinov .10 .25
427 Dimitri Khristich .10 .25
428 Dominik Hasek .30 .75
429 Bob McGill .10 .25
430 Valeri Zelepukin .10 .25
431 Vladimir Ruzicka .10 .25
432 Valeri Kamensky .10 .25
433 Pat MacLeod .10 .25
434 Glenn Healy .12 .30
435 Patrice Brisebois .10 .25
436 James Baker .10 .25
437 Michel Picard .12 .30
438 Scott Lachance UER .10 .25
439 Gilbert Dionne .10 .25
440 M.Lemieux Smythe FOIL 3.00 8.00
441 Checklist 332-441 .08 .25
442 Eric Lindros UER .50 1.25

1995-96 Bowman

The 1995-96 Bowman set - the first hockey release under that name by the Topps company since 1992-93 - was issued in one series totaling 165 cards. The 9-card packs had a suggested retail price of $2.00. The highlight of the set is an extended Rookies subset (91-165). Rookie Cards in the set include Daniel Alfredsson and Petr Sykora. The Cool Trade redemption offer expired on October 15, 1996.

1 Wayne Gretzky .50 1.25
2 Ray Bourque .15 .40
3 Craig Janney .05 .15
4 Andrew Cassels .05 .15
5 Alexander Mogilny .07 .20
6 Pierre Turgeon .10 .25
7 Dave Andreychuk .10 .25
8 Mark Messier .15 .40
9 Igor Korolev .05 .15
10 Tomas Sandstrom .07 .20
11 Shayne Corson .05 .15
12 Chris Chelios .10 .25
13 Claude Lemieux .10 .25
14 Stephane Richer .07 .20
15 Patrick Roy .25 .60
16 Al MacInnis .10 .25
17 Cam Neely .10 .25
18 Doug Gilmour .12 .30
19 Steve Thomas .07 .20
20 Jeremy Roenick .12 .30
21 Steve Yzerman .12 .30
22 Petr Klima .05 .15
23 Luc Robitaille .10 .25
24 Bill Ranford .07 .20
25 Grant Fuhr .10 .25
26 Sean Burke .05 .15
27 John MacLean .07 .20
28 Brendan Shanahan .12 .30
29 Pat LaFontaine .10 .25
30 John Vanbiesbrouck .07 .20
31 Ron Francis .12 .30
32 Brian Leetch .10 .25
33 Dave Gagner .05 .15
34 Larry Murphy .10 .25
35 Mike Modano .15 .40
36 Rick Tocchet .07 .20
37 Scott Mellanby .07 .20
38 Ron Hextall .10 .25
39 Joe Juneau .07 .20
40 Mario Lemieux .30 .75
41 Paul Coffey .10 .25
42 Joe Sakic .15 .40
43 Brett Hull .12 .30
44 Adam Oates .10 .25
45 Wendel Clark .10 .25
46 Trevor Linden .10 .25
47 Tom Barrasso .07 .20
48 Kevin Hatcher .07 .20
49 Mats Sundin .10 .25
50 Scott Stevens .10 .25
51 Mark Recchi .12 .30
52 Theo Fleury .12 .30
53 Ed Belfour .07 .20
54 Adam Graves .07 .20
55 Peter Bondra .10 .25
56 Dominik Hasek .12 .30
57 Jaromir Jagr .25 .60
58 Owen Nolan .10 .25
59 Kevin Stevens .07 .20
60 Alexei Zhamnov .10 .25
61 Dimitri Khristich .05 .15
62 Chris Pronger .10 .25
63 John LeClair .10 .25
64 Scott Niedermayer .10 .25
65 Pavel Bure .12 .30
66 Chris Osgood .07 .20
67 Geoff Sanderson .05 .15
68 Doug Weight .10 .25
69 Keith Tkachuk .10 .25
70 Martin Brodeur .25 .60
71 Eric Lindros .15 .40
72 Martin Straka .05 .15
73 Alexander Selivanov .07 .20
74 Jim Carey .07 .20
75 Teemu Selanne .20 .50
76 Rob Niedermayer .07 .20
77 Vyacheslav Kozlov .07 .20
78 Todd Harvey .05 .15
79 Felix Potvin .10 .25
80 Sergei Fedorov .15 .40
81 Mathieu Schneider .05 .15
82 Roman Hamrlik .05 .15
83 Mikael Renberg .07 .20
84 Jeff Friesen .05 .15
85 Peter Forsberg .25 .60
86 Kenny Jonsson .10 .25
87 Brian Savage .05 .15
88 Oleg Tverdovsky .10 .25
89 Nikolai Khabibulin .07 .20
90 Paul Kariya .12 .30
91 Zdenek Nedved .05 .15
92 Darren Langdon RC .20 .50
93 Lonny Bohonos RC .07 .20
94 Mike Wilson RC .20 .50
95 Landon Wilson RC .05 .15
96 Bryan McCabe .10 .25
97 Byron Dafoe .07 .20
98 Denny Lambert RC .07 .20
99 Craig Mills .05 .15
100 Ed Jovanovski .10 .25
101 Jason Bonsignore .05 .15
102 Clayton Beddoes UER RC .07 .20
103 Jamie Pushor .07 .20
104 Drew Bannister .07 .20
105 Ed Ward .07 .20
106 Todd Warriner .07 .20
107 Deron Quint .07 .20

108 Rhett Warrener .05 .15
109 Marko Kiprusoff .07 .20
110 Daniel Alfredsson RC .50 1.25
111 Marcus Ragnarsson UER RC .12 .30
112 Miroslav Satan RC .12 .30
113 Niklas Sundstrom .10 .25
114 Mathieu Dandenault .20 .50
115 Vitali Yachmenev .10 .25
116 Petr Sykora RC .25 .60
117 Antti Tormanen .05 .15
118 Jeff O'Neill .10 .25
119 David Nemirovsky RC .07 .20
120 Jason Doig .10 .25
121 Aaron Gavey .05 .15
122 Ladislav Kohn .07 .20
123 Richard Park .10 .25
124 Stephane Yelle .07 .20
125 Eric Daze .20 .50
126 Niclas Andersson .07 .20
127 Brendan Witt .10 .25
128 Jamie Storr .07 .20
129 Darby Hendrickson .05 .15
130 Radek Dvorak RC .12 .30
131 Cory Stillman .05 .15
132 Jamie Rivers .05 .15
133 Ville Peltonen .05 .15
134 Peter Ferraro .07 .20
135 Trent McCleary RC .07 .20
136 Chris Wells .07 .20
137 Chad Kilger RC .10 .25
138 Denis Pederson .05 .15
139 Roman Vopat .05 .15
140 Shean Donovan .05 .15
141 Alex Stojanov .05 .15
142 Mark Kolesar RC .07 .20
143 Scott Walker RC .05 .15
144 Dave Roche RC .07 .20
145 Corey Hirsch .07 .20
146 Aki Berg .10 .25
147 Stefan Ustorf .05 .15
148 Saku Koivu .10 .25
149 Shane Doan RC .30 .75
150 Jere Lehtinen .07 .20
151 Kyle McLaren RC .05 .15
152 Marty Murray .10 .25
153 Sean Pronger RC .07 .20
154 Joaquin Gage RC .07 .20
155 Eric Fichaud .07 .20
156 Todd Bertuzzi RC .12 .30
157 Wayne Primeau .05 .15
158 Scott Bailey RC .12 .30
159 Viktor Kozlov .07 .20
160 Valeri Bure .05 .15
161 Dody Wood .05 .15
162 Grant Marshall .05 .15
163 Ken Klee RC .05 .15
164 Corey Schwab RC .20 .50
165 Brian Holzinger RC .20 .50

1995-96 Bowman Foil

The 1995-96 Bowman All-Foil set is a 165-card parallel of the regular version. The cards, which were inserted one per pack, feature a stylish metallicized front, while the backs remain the same as the basic cards.
*VETS: 3X TO 8X BASIC CARDS
*ROOKIES: 1.2X TO 3X BASIC CARDS
ONE PER PACK

1995-96 Bowman Draft Prospects

Inserted one in every pack, this 40-card set features the players who participated in the first annual 1996 CHL Draft Prospects game in Toronto. Fourteen of the players pictured went on to become first-round selections in the 1996 NHL entry draft.
COMPLETE SET (40) 4.00 10.00
ONE PER PACK
P1 Johnathan Aitken .08 .25
P2 Chris Allen .08 .25
P3 Matt Bradley .08 .25
P4 Daniel Briere 1.00 2.50
P5 Jeff Brown .08 .25
P6 Jan Bulis .08 .25
P7 Daniel Corso .08 .25
P8 Luke Curtin .08 .25
P9 Matthieu Descoteaux .08 .25
P10 Boyd Devereaux .08 .25
P11 Jason Doyle .08 .25
P12 Etienne Drapeau .08 .25
P13 J-P Dumont .40 1.00
P14 Mathieu Garon .40 1.00
P15 Josh Green .08 .25
P16 Chris Hajt .08 .25
P17 Matt Higgins .08 .25
P18 Craig Hillier .08 .25
P19 Josh Holden .08 .25
P20 Dan Focht .08 .25
P21 Henry Kuster .08 .25
P22 Francis Larivee .08 .25
P23 Mario Larocque .08 .25
P24 Wes Mason .08 .25
P25 Francois Methot .08 .25
P26 Geoff Peters .08 .25
P27 Randy Petruk .08 .25
P28 Chris Phillips .40 1.00
P29 Boris Protsenko .08 .25
P30 Remi Royer .08 .25
P31 Cory Sarich .08 .25
P32 Jaroslav Svejkovsky .08 .25
P33 Curtis Tipler .08 .25
P34 Darren Van Oene .08 .25
P35 Jesse Wallin .08 .25
P36 Kurt Walsh .08 .25
P37 Lance Ward .08 .25
P38 Steve Wasylko .08 .25
P39 Trevor Wasyluk .08 .25
P40 Jon Zukiwsky .08 .25

1995-96 Bowman Bowman's Best

Randomly inserted in packs at a rate of 1:12, this 30-card set is dedicated to the finest stars and up'n'comers in the NHL. A refractor parallel to this set was also created and inserted at a rate of 1:36.
COMPLETE SET (30) 40.00 100.00
*REFRACTOR: 1X TO 2.5X BASIC INSERTS
BB1 Peter Forsberg 3.00 8.00
BB2 Teemu Selanne 1.50 4.00
BB3 Eric Lindros 1.50 4.00
BB4 Scott Stevens .75 2.00
BB5 Wayne Gretzky 8.00 20.00
BB6 Mark Messier 1.50 4.00
BB7 Jaromir Jagr 2.50 6.00
BB8 Martin Brodeur 4.00 10.00
BB9 Alexander Mogilny .75 2.00
BB10 Mario Lemieux 6.00 15.00
BB11 Joe Sakic 3.00 8.00
BB12 Sergei Fedorov 2.00 5.00
BB13 Pavel Bure 1.50 4.00
BB14 Brian Leetch .75 2.00
BB15 Paul Kariya 1.50 4.00
BB16 Daniel Alfredsson 2.00 5.00
BB17 Saku Koivu 1.50 4.00
BB18 Eric Daze .40 1.00
BB19 Ed Jovanovski 1.50 4.00
BB20 Vitali Yachmenev .40 1.00
BB21 Niklas Sundstrom .40 1.00
BB22 Radek Dvorak .40 1.00
BB23 Byron Dafoe .75 2.00
BB24 Shane Doan 1.50 4.00
BB25 Chad Kilger .40 1.00
RR26 Jeff O'Neill .40 1.00
BB27 Cory Stillman .40 1.00
BB28 Valeri Bure .40 1.00
BB29 Marcus Ragnarsson .40 1.00
BB30 Todd Bertuzzi 2.00 5.00

1998-99 Bowman's Best

This 150-card set was distributed in six-card packs with a suggested retail price of $5. The set features color action photos of 100 key veterans printed on cards with a gold design and 35 top NHL rookies and 14 CHL stars showcased on silver-designed cards. The cards are all printed on thick 26-pt. stock. The backs carry player information and career statistics.
COMPLETE SET (150) 50.00 125.00
COMP.SET w/o SP's (100) 10.00 25.00
1 Steve Yzerman 1.50 4.00
2 Paul Kariya .30 .75
3 Wayne Gretzky 2.00 5.00
4 Jaromir Jagr .50 1.25
5 Mark Messier .30 .75
6 Keith Tkachuk .30 .75
7 John LeClair .30 .75
8 Martin Brodeur .75 2.00
9 Rob Blake .25 .60
10 Brett Hull .40 1.00
11 Dominik Hasek .60 1.50
12 Peter Forsberg .75 2.00
13 Doug Gilmour .25 .60
14 Vincent Damphousse .08 .25
15 Zigmund Palffy .25 .60
16 Daniel Alfredsson .25 .60
17 Mike Vernon .25 .60
18 Chris Pronger .25 .60
19 Wendel Clark .25 .60
20 Curtis Joseph .30 .75
21 Peter Bondra .25 .60
22 Grant Fuhr .25 .60
23 Nikolai Khabibulin .25 .60
24 Kevin Hatcher .08 .25
25 Brian Leetch .30 .75
26 Patrik Elias .25 .60
27 Chris Osgood .25 .60
28 Patrick Roy 1.50 4.00
29 Chris Chelios .30 .75
30 Trevor Kidd .08 .25
31 Theo Fleury .08 .25
32 Michael Peca .08 .25
33 Ray Bourque .50 1.25
34 Ed Belfour .30 .75
35 Sergei Fedorov .50 1.25
36 Adrian Aucoin .08 .25
37 Alexei Yashin .08 .25
38 Rick Tocchet .25 .60
39 Mats Sundin .30 .75
40 Alexander Mogilny .25 .60
41 Jeff Friesen .08 .25
42 Eric Lindros .30 .75
43 Mike Richter .30 .75
44 Saku Koivu .30 .75
45 Teemu Selanne .30 .75
46 Doug Weight .25 .60
47 Nicklas Lidstrom .30 .75
48 Mike Modano .50 1.25
49 Joe Sakic .60 1.50
50 Ron Francis .25 .60
51 Jason Allison .08 .25
52 Brendan Shanahan .30 .75
53 Bobby Holik .08 .25
54 Damian Rhodes .25 .60
55 Jeremy Roenick .40 1.00
56 Tom Barrasso .08 .25
57 Al MacInnis .25 .60
58 Pavel Bure .30 .75
59 Olaf Kolzig .25 .60
60 Patrick Marleau .15 .40
61 Cliff Ronning .08 .25
62 Joe Nieuwendyk .25 .60
63 Jeff Hackett .25 .60
64 Keith Primeau .08 .25
65 Jarome Iginla .40 1.00
66 Sergei Samsonov .25 .60
67 Rod Brind'Amour .25 .60
68 Dino Ciccarelli .25 .60
69 Ryan Smyth .25 .60
70 Owen Nolan .25 .60
71 Mike Johnson .08 .25
72 Adam Oates .25 .60
73 Mattias Ohlund .25 .60
74 Jamie Heward RC .08 .25
75 Mike Dunham .25 .60
76 Jere Lehtinen .25 .60
77 Tony Amonte .25 .60
78 Derek Morris .08 .25
79 Darren McCarty .08 .25
80 Bryan Berard .25 .60
81 Adam Graves .08 .25
82 John Vanbiesbrouck .25 .60
83 Marco Sturm .08 .25
84 Joe Thornton .50 1.25
85 Wade Redden .08 .25
86 Pierre Turgeon .25 .60
87 Bill Ranford .25 .60
88 Alexei Zhitnik .08 .25
89 Valeri Kamensky .08 .25
90 Dean McAmmond .08 .25
91 Jozef Stumpel .25 .60
92 Jocelyn Thibault .25 .60
93 Joe Juneau .25 .60
94 Craig Janney .25 .60
95 Robert Reichel .25 .60
96 Mark Recchi .25 .60
97 Sami Kapanen .08 .25
98 Shayne Corson .08 .25
99 Scott Niedermayer .08 .25
100 Trevor Linden .25 .60
101 Olli Jokinen SP 1.25 3.00
102 Chris Drury SP 2.00 5.00
103 Daniel Cleary SP 1.00 2.50
104 Yan Golubovsky SP RC 1.25 3.00
105 Brendan Morrison SP 1.25 3.00
106 Manny Malhotra SP 1.00 2.50
107 Marian Hossa SP 1.00 2.50
108 Daniel Briere SP 1.00 2.50
109 Vincent Lecavalier SP 1.50 4.00
110 Milan Hejduk SP RC 3.00 8.00
111 Tom Poti SP 1.00 2.50
112 Mike Maneluk SP RC 1.25 3.00
113 Marty Reasoner SP 1.00 2.50
114 Rico Fata SP 1.00 2.50
115 Eric Brewer SP 1.00 2.50
116 Dan Cloutier SP 1.00 2.50
117 Mike Leclerc SP 1.00 2.50
118 Dimitri Tertyshny SP RC 1.00 2.50
119 Josh Green SP RC 1.50 4.00
120 Mark Parrish SP RC 1.50 4.00
121 Jamie Wright SP 1.00 2.50
122 Fred Lindquist SP RC 1.00 2.50
123 Daniil Markov SP RC 1.00 2.50
124 Bill Muckalt SP RC 1.25 3.00
125 Johan Davidsson SP 1.00 2.50
126 Oleg Kvasha SP RC 1.25 3.00
127 Cameron Mann SP 1.00 2.50
128 Pascal Trepanier SP RC 1.00 2.50
129 Clarke Wilm SP RC 1.00 2.50
130 Alain Nasreddine SP RC 1.00 2.50
131 Bryan Helmer SP RC 1.00 2.50
132 Michal Handzus SP RC 2.00 5.00
133 Pavel Kubina SP RC 1.25 3.00
134 Zdeno Chara SP 1.00 2.50
135 Matt Higgins SP RC 1.00 2.50
136 David Legwand SP 1.50 4.00
137 Brad Stuart SP RC 2.00 5.00
138 Mark Bell SP RC 2.00 5.00
139 Eric Chouinard SP 1.00 2.50
140 Simon Gagne SP 1.50 4.00
141 Ramzi Abid SP RC 2.00 5.00
142 Sergei Varlamov SP 1.25 3.00
143 Mike Ribeiro SP 1.00 2.50
144 Derrick Walser SP RC 1.00 2.50
145 Mathieu Garon SP 1.00 2.50
146 Daniel Tkaczuk SP 1.00 2.50
147 Jeff Heerema SP RC 1.50 4.00
148 Sebastien Roger SP RC 1.00 2.50
149 Bret DeCecco SP 1.00 2.50
150 Checklist SP 1.25 3.00

1998-99 Bowman's Best Refractors

Randomly inserted in packs at the rate of 1:52, this 150-card set is a refractive parallel version of the base set. Only 400 of each card were produced and sequentially numbered.
*1-100 REFRACTOR: 8X TO 20X BASIC CARDS
*101-150 REFRACTOR: 3X TO 6X BASIC SP
REFRACTOR STATED ODDS 1:387

1998-99 Bowman's Best Atomic Refractors

Randomly inserted into packs at the rate of 1:1549, this 150-card set is a parallel version of the base set and is similar in design. The difference is seen in the special sparkling refractive sheen of the cards. Only 100 of each card was produced and sequentially numbered.
*1-100 ATOMIC REF: 20X TO 50X BASIC CARDS
*101-150 ATOMIC REF: 6X TO 15X BASIC SP
ATOMIC REFRACTOR/100 ODDS 1:1549
ATOMIC REF PRINT RUN 100 SER.#'d SETS
1 Steve Yzerman 40.00 100.00
3 Wayne Gretzky 60.00 150.00
28 Patrick Roy 40.00 100.00

1998-99 Bowman's Best Autographs

Randomly inserted in packs at the rate of 1:97, this 20-card set displays autographed color photos of five rookie and five veteran players each featured in two different photos. Both versions of the rookies carry silver backgrounds, with gold backgrounds for the veterans. Each card is stamped with the Topps "Certified Autograph Issue" logo.
STATED ODDS 1:97
*REFRACTOR: .8X TO 2X BASIC AUTO
REFRACTOR STATED ODDS 1:516
*ATOMIC REF: 1.5X TO 4X BASIC AUTO
ATOMIC REFRACTOR ODDS 1:1549
A1A Dominik Hasek 15.00 40.00
A1B Dominik Hasek 15.00 40.00
A2A Jaromir Jagr 15.00 40.00
A2B Jaromir Jagr 15.00 40.00
A3A Peter Bondra 6.00 15.00
A3B Peter Bondra 6.00 15.00
A4A Sergei Fedorov 15.00 40.00
A4B Sergei Fedorov 15.00 40.00
A5A Ray Bourque 20.00 50.00
A5B Ray Bourque 20.00 50.00
A6A Bill Muckalt 3.00 8.00
A6B Bill Muckalt 3.00 8.00
A7A Brendan Morrison 6.00 15.00
A7B Brendan Morrison 6.00 15.00
A8A Chris Drury 6.00 15.00
A8B Chris Drury 6.00 15.00
A9A Mark Parrish 3.00 8.00
A9B Mark Parrish 3.00 8.00
A10A Manny Malhotra 3.00 8.00
A10B Manny Malhotra 3.00 8.00

1998-99 Bowman's Best Mirror Image Fusion

Randomly inserted in packs at the rate of 1:12, this 20-card set features color action photos of Western and Eastern Conference players printed on die-cut, double-sided cards. Each card features a veteran on one side and a rising star on the other and can be married to its die-cut counterpart from the opposite conference.
COMPLETE SET (20) 60.00 125.00
STATED ODDS 1:12
*REFRACTOR/100: 4X TO 10X BASIC INSERTS
REFRACTOR/100 STATED ODDS 1:387
REFRACTOR PRINT RUN 100 SER.#'d SETS
*ATOMIC REF/25: 10X TO 25X BASIC INSERTS
ATOMIC REFRACTOR/25 ODDS 1:1549
ATOMIC REF.PRINT RUN 25 SER.#'d SETS
F1 J.LeClair/B.Battaglia 2.00 5.00
F2 P.Kariya/M.LeClerc 2.00 5.00
F3 J.Jagr/M.Parrish 4.00 10.00
F4 Selanne/Lindquist 2.00 5.00
F5 Lindros/Lecavalier 2.00 5.00
F6 P.Forsberg/O.Jokinen 5.00 12.00
F7 B.Leetch/D.Markov 1.25 3.00
F8 Lidstrom/Golubovsky 2.00 5.00
F9 D.Hasek/D.Cloutier 4.00 10.00
F10 P.Roy/T.Moss 8.00 20.00
F11 S.Samsonov/M.Watt 1.25 3.00
F12 K.Tkachuk/J.Wright 2.50 6.00
F13 P.Bondra/M.Hossa 2.50 6.00
F14 P.Bure/B.Muckalt 2.00 5.00
F15 Gretzky/Morrison 12.00 30.00
F16 Fedorov/Reasoner 2.00 5.00
F17 R.Bourque/E.Brewer 3.00 8.00
F18 C.Pronger/T.Poti 1.25 3.00
F19 Brodeur/Theodore 5.00 12.00
F20 C.Osgood/J.Storr 1.25 3.00

1998-99 Bowman's Best Performers

Randomly inserted in packs at the rate of 1:12, this 10-card set features action color photos of top young stars and rookies.
COMPLETE SET (10) 10.00 25.00
STATED ODDS 1.12
*REFRACTOR/200: 4X TO 10X BASIC INSERTS
REFRACTOR/200 STATED ODDS 1:387
REFRACTOR PRINT RUN 200 SER.#'d SETS
*ATOMIC REF/50: 10X TO 25X BASIC INSERTS
ATOMIC REFRACTOR/50 ODDS 1:1549
ATOMTC REFRACTOR PRINT RUN 50
BP1 Mike Johnson .75 2.00
BP2 Sergei Samsonov 1.25 3.00
BP3 Patrik Elias .75 2.00
BP4 Patrick Marleau 1.25 3.00
BP5 Mattias Ohlund .75 2.00
BP6 Manny Malhotra .75 2.00
BP7 Chris Drury .75 2.00
BP8 Daniel Briere 1.25 3.00
BP9 Brendan Morrison .75 2.00
BP10 Vincent Lecavalier 4.00 10.00

1998-99 Bowman's Best Scotty Bowman's Best

Randomly inserted into packs at the rate of 1:6, this 11-card set features color photos of ten of the best present day players in the NHL according to Scotty Bowman who is one of the greatest coaches of all time. Card #11 is a card of the coach himself and 100 of these cards were autographed with an insertion rate of 1:7,745.
COMPLETE SET (11) 25.00 50.00
STATED ODDS 1:6
*REFRACT/200: 2.5X TO 6X BASIC INSERTS
REFRACTOR/200 STATED ODDS 1:704
REFRACTOR PRINT RUN 200 SER.#'d SETS
*ATOMIC REF/50: 5X TO 12X BASIC INSERTS
ATOMIC REFRACTOR/50 ODDS 1:2816
ATOMIC REF.PRINT RUN 50 SER.#'d SETS
SB1 Dominik Hasek 2.50 6.00
SB2 Martin Brodeur 3.00 8.00
SB3 Chris Osgood 1.25 3.00
SB4 Nicklas Lidstrom 2.00 5.00
SB5 Eric Lindros 2.00 5.00
SB6 Jaromir Jagr 2.00 5.00
SB7 Steve Yzerman 4.00 10.00
SB8 Peter Forsberg 2.00 5.00
SB9 Paul Kariya 1.25 3.00
SB10 Ray Bourque 2.00 5.00
SB11 Scotty Bowman 1.25 3.00
SB11S Scotty Bowman AU/100 40.00 100.00

2001-02 Bowman YoungStars

Released in late May, this 165-card set carried an SRP of $3.00. Card fronts carried gold foil accents and black borders on full-color action photos. The Topps/NHL Young Stars logo appeared in the bottom left hand corner.
COMPLETE SET (165) 75.00 150.00
1 Patrick Roy 1.25 3.00
2 Brett Hull .60 1.50
3 Mario Lemieux 1.50 4.00
4 Jaromir Jagr 1.25 3.00
5 Mats Sundin .50 1.25
6 Mike Modano .75 2.00
7 Jarome Iginla .50 1.25
8 Jason Allison .40 1.00
9 Mike Richter .50 1.25
10 Chris Pronger .40 1.00
11 Patrik Elias .50 1.25
12 Tommy Salo .40 1.00
13 Tony Amonte .40 1.00
14 Joe Thornton .60 1.50
15 Joe Sakic .75 2.00
16 Pavel Bure .60 1.50
17 Teemu Selanne 1.00 2.50
18 Markus Naslund .50 1.25
19 Nikolai Khabibulin .50 1.25
20 Paul Kariya .60 1.50
21 Dominik Hasek .75 2.00
22 Ron Francis .60 1.50
23 Ray Ferraro .30 .75
24 Miroslav Satan .40 1.00
25 Milan Hejduk .40 1.00
26 Jose Theodore .50 1.25
27 Daniel Alfredsson .50 1.25
28 Michael Peca .40 1.00
29 Keith Primeau .40 1.00
30 Doug Weight .50 1.25
31 Sean Burke .30 .75
32 Adam Oates .50 1.25
33 Brian Rolston .40 1.00
34 Rob Blake .50 1.25
35 Steve Yzerman 1.50 4.00
36 Eric Lindros .75 2.00
37 Keith Tkachuk .50 1.25
38 Dan Cloutier .40 1.00
39 Chris Osgood .50 1.25
40 Zigmund Palffy .50 1.25
41 Jocelyn Thibault .40 1.00
42 Roman Turek .40 1.00
43 Ed Belfour .50 1.25
44 Adam Deadmarsh .40 1.00
45 Marian Hossa .40 1.00
46 Owen Nolan .50 1.25
47 Curtis Joseph .50 1.25
48 Peter Bondra .50 1.25
49 Jeremy Roenick .50 1.25
50 Brendan Shanahan .60 1.50
51 Eric Daze .40 1.00
52 J-P Dumont .30 .75
53 Bill Guerin .50 1.25
54 Jukka Hentunen RC .50 1.25
55 Brian Leetch .50 1.25
56 Alexei Kovalev .40 1.00
57 Olaf Kolzig .50 1.25
58 Mike York .30 .75
59 Felix Potvin .75 2.00
60 Pierre Turgeon .50 1.25
61 Luc Robitaille .50 1.25
62 Sami Kapanen .30 .75
63 Byron Dafoe .40 1.00
64 Ryan Smyth .40 1.00
65 John LeClair .50 1.25
66 Pavol Demitra .60 1.50
67 Alexei Yashin .40 1.00
68 Vincent Lecavalier .40 1.00
69 Chris Drury .40 1.00
70 Mike Dunham .40 1.00
71 Patrick Lalime .40 1.00
72 Derek Morris .30 .75
73 Peter Forsberg .60 1.50
74 Sergei Fedorov .75 2.00
75 Mark Parrish .30 .75
76 Simon Gagne .50 1.25
77 Jeff O'Neill .30 .75
78 Alexander Mogilny .40 1.00
79 Johan Hedberg .40 1.00
80 Martin Brodeur 1.00 2.50
81 Claude Lemieux .40 1.00
82 Mark Messier .75 2.00
83 Nicklas Lidstrom .50 1.25
84 Stu Barnes .40 1.00
85 Steve Sullivan .30 .75
86 Jeff Friesen .30 .75
87 Brent Johnson .40 1.00
88 Marc Denis .40 1.00
89 Jason Arnott .40 1.00
90 Brendan Morrison .40 1.00
91 Jere Lehtinen .40 1.00
92 Craig Conroy .30 .75
93 Petr Sykora .30 .75
94 Gary Roberts .30 .75
95 Saku Koivu .50 1.25
96 Scott Stevens .50 1.25
97 Radek Bonk .30 .75
98 Roman Cechmanek .40 1.00
99 Robert Lang .30 .75
100 Tom Barrasso .40 1.00
101 Yanic Perreault .30 .75
102 Joe Nieuwendyk .50 1.25
103 Al MacInnis .50 1.25
104 Vincent Damphousse .40 1.00
105 Anson Carter .40 1.00
106 Sergei Samsonov .40 1.00
107 Theo Fleury .60 1.50
108 Mark Recchi .60 1.50
109 Marco Sturm .30 .75
110 Jiri Dopita RC .50 1.25
111 Tim Connolly .30 .75
112 Mike Fisher .30 .75
113 Alex Tanguay .40 1.00
114 Christian Berglund RC .60 1.50
115 Olivier Michaud RC .75 2.00
116 John Erskine RC .50 1.25
117 Mikael Samuelsson RC .60 1.50
118 Radek Martinek RC .50 1.25
119 Mark Rycroft RC .60 1.50
120 Mike Ribeiro .40 1.00
121 Vaclav Pletka RC .50 1.25
122 Toni Dahlman RC .50 1.25
123 Brian Sutherby RC .50 1.25
124 Karel Rachunek .30 .75
125 Robyn Regehr .30 .75
126 Martin Erat RC .75 2.00
127 Nick Boynton .30 .75
128 Nick Schultz RC .50 1.25
129 Timo Parssinen RC .60 1.50
130 Jaroslav Bednar RC .50 1.25
131 Roberto Luongo .75 2.00
132 Pascal Dupuis RC .75 2.00
133 Dave Tanabe .30 .75
134 Dany Heatley .50 1.25
135 Jeff Jillson RC .50 1.25
136 Marian Gaborik .75 2.00
137 Radim Vrbata .30 .75
138 Andrew Ference .30 .75
139 Rostislav Klesla .30 .75
140 Dan Blackburn RC .60 1.50
141 Andy Hilbert .30 .75
142 Martin Havlat .40 1.00
143 Niko Kapanen RC .75 2.00
144 Brenden Morrow .40 1.00
145 Scott Hartnell .50 1.25
146 Raffi Torres RC .75 2.00
147 Vaclav Nedorost RC .50 1.25
148 Krys Kolanos RC .50 1.25
149 Kyle Calder .30 .75
150 Niklas Hagman RC .60 1.50
151 Brian Gionta .40 1.00
152 Kristian Huselius RC .75 2.00
153 Mike Comrie .40 1.00
154 Ty Conklin RC .75 2.00
155 Justin Williams .30 .75
156 Erik Cole RC 1.00 2.50
157 Nikita Alexeev RC .50 1.25
158 Paul Mara .30 .75
159 Ilya Kovalchuk RC 4.00 10.00
160 David Legwand .40 1.00
161 Ilja Bryzgalov RC 1.25 3.00
162 Brad Richards .50 1.25
163 Evgeni Nabokov .40 1.00
164 Kris Beech .30 .75
165 Pavel Datsyuk RC 3.00 8.00

2001-02 Bowman YoungStars Gold

This 165-card set paralleled the base set, but card fronts had a gold glitter effect added. Each card was serial-numbered out of 250.
*VETS/250: 1.5X TO 4X BASIC CARDS
*ROOKIES/250: 1X TO 2.5X BASIC CARDS
STATED PRINT RUN 250 SER.#'d SETS

2001-02 Bowman YoungStars Ice Cubed

This 165-card set paralleled the base set, but the card stock was approximately 3 times thicker and the card fronts were high gloss. These cards were inserted into every pack that did not contain a memorabilia card to prevent pack searching.
*ICE CUBED: .5X TO 1.2X BASIC CARDS
ONE PER NON-MEMORABILIA PACK

2001-02 Bowman YoungStars Autographs

This 23-card set featured certified autographs of players who participated in the 2002 Topps/NHL Young Stars Game. All cards carried a YSA prefix.
STATED ODDS 1:478
AF Andrew Ference 10.00 25.00
BM Brenden Morrow 15.00 40.00
BR Brad Richards 25.00 60.00
DB Dan Blackburn 10.00 25.00
DH Dany Heatley 25.00 60.00
DL David Legwand 10.00 25.00
DT Dave Tanabe 10.00 25.00
IK Ilya Kovalchuk 30.00 80.00
JW Justin Williams 10.00 25.00
KC Kyle Calder 10.00 25.00
KH Kristian Huselius 10.00 25.00
KR Karel Rachunek 10.00 25.00
MC Mike Comrie 10.00 25.00
MF Mike Fisher 10.00 25.00
MG Marian Gaborik 25.00 60.00
MR Mike Ribeiro 10.00 25.00
NB Nick Boynton 10.00 25.00
PD Pavel Datsyuk 30.00 60.00
PM Paul Mara 10.00 25.00
RL Roberto Luongo 20.00 50.00
RR Robyn Regehr 10.00 25.00
SH Scott Hartnell 10.00 25.00
TC Tim Connolly 10.00 25.00

2001-02 Bowman YoungStars Relics

This 69-card set featured swatches of jerseys and sticks used in the 2002 Topps/NHL Young Stars Game. Jersey swatches were inserted at a rate of one in six. Stick swatches were inserted at a rate of 1:193. Combo cards with both jersey and stick swatches were serial-numbered out of 25. All cards carried a FF prefix.
JERSEY STATED ODDS 1:6
STICK STATED ODDS 1:193
JERSEY-STICK PRINT RUN 25
JAF Andrew Ference J 2.00 5.00
JBM Brenden Morrow J 3.00 8.00
JBR Brad Richards J 3.00 8.00
JDB Dan Blackburn J 2.00 5.00
JDH Dany Heatley J 4.00 10.00
JDL David Legwand J 2.00 5.00
JDT Dave Tanabe J 2.00 5.00
JIK Ilya Kovalchuk J 6.00 15.00
JJW Justin Williams J 2.00 5.00
JKC Kyle Calder J 2.00 5.00
JKH Kristian Huselius J 2.00 5.00
JKR Karel Rachunek J 2.00 5.00
JMC Mike Comrie J 2.00 5.00
JMF Mike Fisher J 2.00 5.00
JMG Marian Gaborik J 12.00 30.00
JMR Mike Ribeiro J 2.00 5.00
JNB Nick Boynton J 2.00 5.00
JPD Pavel Datsyuk J 8.00 20.00
JPM Paul Mara J 2.00 5.00
JRL Roberto Luongo J 4.00 10.00
JRR Robyn Regehr J 2.00 5.00
JSH Scott Hartnell J 2.00 5.00
JTC Tim Connolly J 2.00 5.00
SAF Andrew Ference S 8.00 20.00
SBM Brenden Morrow S 10.00 25.00
SBR Brad Richards S 8.00 20.00
SDB Dan Blackburn S 8.00 20.00
SDH Dany Heatley S 10.00 25.00
SDL David Legwand S 8.00 20.00
SDT Dave Tanabe S 8.00 20.00
SIK Ilya Kovalchuk S 20.00 50.00
SJW Justin Williams S 10.00 25.00
SKC Kyle Calder S 8.00 20.00
SKH Kristian Huselius S 8.00 20.00
SKR Karel Rachunek S 8.00 20.00
SMC Mike Comrie S 8.00 20.00
SMF Mike Fisher S 8.00 20.00
SMG Marian Gaborik S 10.00 25.00
SMR Mike Ribeiro S 8.00 20.00
SNB Nick Boynton S 8.00 20.00
SPD Pavel Datsyuk S 12.00 30.00
SPM Paul Mara S 8.00 20.00
SRL Roberto Luongo S 10.00 25.00
SRR Robyn Regehr S 8.00 20.00
SSH Scott Hartnell S 8.00 20.00
STC Tim Connolly S 8.00 20.00
DSAF Andrew Ference J-S 15.00 40.00
DSBM Brenden Morrow J-S 15.00 40.00
DSBR Brad Richards J-S 25.00 60.00
DSDB Dan Blackburn J-S 25.00 60.00
DSDH Dany Heatley J-S 50.00 125.00
DSDL David Legwand J-S 12.00 30.00
DSDT Dave Tanabe J-S 15.00 40.00
DSIK Ilya Kovalchuk J-S 75.00 200.00
DSJW Justin Williams J-S 15.00 40.00
DSKC Kyle Calder J-S 15.00 40.00
DSKH Kristian Huselius J-S 15.00 40.00
DSKR Karel Rachunek J-S 15.00 40.00
DSMC Mike Comrie J-S 25.00 60.00
DSMF Mike Fisher J-S 15.00 40.00
DSMG Marian Gaborik J-S 50.00 125.00
DSMR Mike Ribeiro J-S 25.00 60.00
DSNB Nick Boynton J-S 15.00 40.00
DSPD Pavel Datsyuk J-S 50.00 125.00
DSPM Paul Mara J-S 15.00 40.00
DSRL Roberto Luongo J-S 40.00 100.00
DSRR Robyn Regehr J-S 15.00 40.00
DSSH Scott Hartnell J-S 15.00 40.00
DSTC Tim Connolly J-S 15.00 40.00

2001-02 Bowman YoungStars Rivals

This 11-card set featured dual game-worn swatches from players who participated in the 2002 Topps Young Stars game. Each card was serial-numbered out of 250. All cards carried a FF prefix.
STATED PRINT RUN 250 SER.#'d SETS
R1 R.Luongo/D.Blackburn 15.00 40.00
R2 K.Rachunek/B.Richards 12.00 30.00
R3 A.Ference/D.Tanabe 10.00 25.00
R4 N.Boynton/R.Regehr 12.00 30.00
R5 M.Gaborik/I.Kovalchuk 20.00 50.00
R6 M.Comrie/D.Heatley 15.00 40.00
R7 M.Ribeiro/J.Williams 10.00 25.00
R8 T.Connolly/D.Legwand 10.00 25.00
R9 M.Fisher/P.Datsyuk 15.00 40.00
R10 S.Hartnell/B.Morrow 12.00 30.00
R11 K.Huselius/K.Calder 10.00 25.00

2002 Bowman Toronto Spring Expo

This 10-card set was part of a wrapper redemption program at the Topps booth during the 2002 Toronto Spring Expo. A total of 500 sets were made available, with the first 300 including a card autographed by top prospect Ilya Kovalchuk. The remaining 200 sets included a non-signed Kovalchuk card.
COMPLETE SET (10) 10.00 25.00
1 Ilya Kovalchuk/200* 6.00 15.00
1B Ilya Kovalchuk AU/300* 15.00 40.00
2 Curtis Joseph .80 2.00
3 Pavel Datsyuk 2.00 5.00
4 Jose Theodore .80 2.00
5 Jarome Iginla .40 1.00
6 Martin Brodeur .80 2.00
7 Patrick Roy 1.20 3.00
8 Dany Heatley 1.20 3.00
9 Dan Blackburn 1.20 3.00
10 Mats Sundin .40 1.00

2002-03 Bowman YoungStars

Released in April 2003, this 165-card set featured color action photos on black-bordered card fronts. The set highlighted the annual Topps YoungStars game held on All-Star weekend.
1 Nicklas Lidstrom .25 .60
2 Martin Brodeur .50 1.25
3 Tony Amonte .20 .50
4 Todd Bertuzzi .25 .60
5 Joe Thornton .30 .75
6 Ron Francis .30 .75
7 Paul Kariya .30 .75
8 Eric Lindros .40 1.00
9 John LeClair .25 .60
10 Doug Weight .25 .60
11 Jaromir Jagr .60 1.50
12 Mats Sundin .25 .60
13 Saku Koivu .25 .60
14 Peter Forsberg .30 .75
15 Alexei Yashin .20 .50
16 Mike Modano .40 1.00
17 Chris Drury .25 .60
18 Ryan Smyth .20 .50
19 Tomas Vokoun .20 .50
20 Marian Hossa .20 .50
21 Owen Nolan .25 .60
22 Vincent Lecavalier .20 .50
23 Jocelyn Thibault .20 .50
24 Marc Denis .20 .50
25 Roberto Luongo .40 1.00
26 Mario Lemieux .75 2.00
27 Keith Tkachuk .25 .60
28 Radek Bonk .20 .50
29 Bill Guerin .25 .60
30 Jason Allison .20 .50
31 Jeff O'Neill .15 .40
32 Alexei Zhamnov .20 .50
33 Scott Stevens .25 .60
34 Mark Recchi .30 .75
35 Alexander Mogilny .20 .50
36 Olaf Kolzig .25 .60
37 Sean Burke .15 .40
38 Brett Hull .30 .75
39 Andrew Cassels .15 .40
40 Jarome Iginla .25 .60
41 Joe Sakic .40 1.00
42 Brian Leetch .25 .60
43 Simon Gagne .25 .60
44 Dan Cloutier .20 .50
45 Brian Rolston .20 .50
46 Milan Hejduk .20 .50
47 Steve Yzerman .50 1.25
48 Martin Havlat .20 .50
49 Alexei Kovalev .25 .60
50 Pavol Demitra .30 .75
51 Mark Parrish .15 .40
52 Felix Potvin .40 1.00
53 Brenden Morrow .20 .50
54 Steve Sullivan .15 .40
55 Patrick Roy .60 1.50
56 Manny Fernandez .20 .50
57 Vincent Damphousse .20 .50
58 Michael Peca .20 .50
59 Anson Carter .20 .50
60 Kevin Weekes .20 .50
61 Peter Bondra .25 .60
62 Brad Richards .25 .60
63 Johan Hedberg .25 .60
64 Olli Jokinen .25 .60
65 Miroslav Satan .25 .60
66 Petr Sykora .20 .50
67 Al MacInnis .25 .60
68 Markus Naslund .20 .50
69 Mark Messier .40 1.00
70 Rob Blake .25 .60
71 Sergei Samsonov .20 .50
72 Jose Theodore .25 .60
73 Eric Boguniecki .15 .40
74 Nikolai Khabibulin .25 .60
75 Marco Sturm .15 .40
76 Patrick Lalime .20 .5
77 Jeremy Roenick .25 .6
78 John Madden .15 .4
79 Steve Rucchin .15 .4
80 Jere Lehtinen .25 .6
81 Stu Barnes .15 .4
82 Roman Turek .25 .60
83 Curtis Joseph .25 .60
84 Evgeni Nabokov .20 .50
85 Daniel Alfredsson .25 .60
86 Brendan Morrison .20 .5
87 Roman Cechmanek .20 .5
88 Chris Osgood .25 .6
89 Tommy Salo .20 .5
90 Craig Conroy .15 .4
91 Zigmund Palffy .25 .6
92 Pavel Bure .30 .7
93 Brent Johnson .20 .5
94 Ed Belfour .25 .6
95 Shane Doan .20 .5
96 David Legwand .20 .5
97 Sergei Fedorov .40 1.0
98 Jason Arnott .20 .5
99 Keith Primeau .25 .6
100 Martin St. Louis .25 .6
101 Teemu Selanne .50 1.2
102 Patrik Elias .25 .6
103 Ray Whitney .20 .5
104 Brendan Shanahan .30 .7
105 Taylor Pyatt .15 .4
106 Niklas Hagman .15 .4
107 Henrik Tallinder .15 .4
108 Rostislav Klesla .15 .4
109 David Aebischer .20 .5
110 Marcel Hossa .15 .4
111 Pavel Brendl .15 .4
112 Ossi Vaananen .15 .4
113 Erik Cole .20 .5
114 Marian Gaborik .40 1.0
115 Alexander Svitov RC .15 .4
116 Stanislav Chistov RC .15 .4
117 Jordan Leopold RC .25 .6
118 Ryan Miller RC 1.00 2.5
119 Kurt Sauer RC .15 .4
120 Jonathan Cheechoo .20 .5
121 Radovan Somik RC .15 .4
122 Anton Volchenkov RC .15 .4
123 Pavel Datsyuk .30 .7
124 Alexander Frolov RC .30 .7
125 Steve Ott RC .30 .7
126 Jason Spezza RC 1.00 2.5
127 Barret Jackman .20 .5
128 Steve Eminger RC .15 .4
129 Pascal Dupuis .15 .4
130 Brian Sutherby .15 .4
131 Dan Blackburn .20 .5
132 Ron Hainsey RC .15 .4
133 Jay Bouwmeester RC .50 1.2
134 Adam Hall RC .15 .4
135 Mike Comrie .25 .6
136 Nick Schultz .15 .4
137 Henrik Zetterberg RC 1.50 4.0
138 Radim Vrbata .20 .5
139 Jaroslav Svoboda .15 .4
140 Tyler Arnason .25 .6
141 Dany Heatley .25 .6
142 Ivan Huml .15 .4
143 Kristian Huselius .15 .4
144 Martin Gerber RC .25 .6
145 Tom Koivisto RC .15 .4
146 Mikael Tellqvist RC .15
147 Dennis Seidenberg RC .25 .6
148 Mike Cammalleri RC .50 1.2
149 Niko Kapanen .20
150 Shawn Thornton RC .20
151 Alexei Smirnov RC .20
152 Jamie Lundmark .20
153 Shawn Horcoff .20
154 Branko Radivojevic .15 .4
155 Rick Nash RC 1.25 3.
156 Mattias Weinhandl .15
157 Stephen Weiss .25
158 Dmitri Bykov RC .15
159 Ales Hemsky RC .60 1.
160 Chuck Kobasew RC .20
161 P-M Bouchard RC .25

162 Scottie Upshall RC .20 .50
163 Patrick Sharp RC .50 1.25
164 Derrick Walser .15 .40
165 Ilya Kovalchuk .30 .75
NNO Jerry Walsh .08 .25
Honorary Eqmt. Mgr.

2002-03 Bowman YoungStars Gold

Inserted at 1:11, this 165-card set paralleled the base ste but carried a gold "glitter" effect on the card fronts. Each card was serial-numbered out of 250 on the card back.

*VETS/250: 2X TO 5X BASIC CARDS
*ROOKIES/250: 1.5X TO 4X BASIC RC
STATED ODDS 1:11
STATED PRINT RUN 250 SER.#'d SETS
69 Mark Messier 2.50 6.00

2002-03 Bowman YoungStars Silver

Inserted one per non-memorabilia pack, this 165-card set paralleled the base set but carried a silver "glitter" effect on the card fronts.

*VETS: .8X TO 2X BASIC CARDS
*ROOKIES: .6X TO 1.5X
ONE PER PACK
69 Mark Messier 1.00 2.50

2002-03 Bowman YoungStars Autographs

Inserted at 1:333, this 27-card set featured certified autographs of players who competed in the annual Topps YoungStars game.

COMMON CARD 10.00 30.00
STATED ODDS 1:333
STATED PRINT RUN 50 SER.#'d SETS
AF Alexander Frolov 15.00 40.00
AH Adam Hall 10.00 30.00
AS Alexander Svitov 10.00 30.00
AV Anton Volchenkov 10.00 30.00
BJ Barret Jackman 10.00 30.00
BR Branko Radivojevic 10.00 30.00
BS Brian Sutherby 10.00 30.00
DA David Aebischer 20.00 50.00
DS Dennis Seidenberg 10.00 30.00
HT Henrik Tallinder 10.00 30.00
JB Jay Bouwmeester 20.00 60.00
JL Jordan Leopold 10.00 30.00
MH Marcel Hossa 10.00 30.00
MW Mattias Weinhandl 10.00 30.00
NH Niklas Hagman 10.00 30.00
NK Niko Kapanen 10.00 30.00
NS Nick Schultz 10.00 30.00
OV Ossi Vaananen 10.00 30.00
PB Pavel Brendl 10.00 30.00
RK Rostislav Klesla 10.00 30.00
RM Ryan Miller 40.00 100.00
RN Rick Nash 40.00 100.00
SC Stanislav Chistov 10.00 30.00
SH Shawn Horcoff 10.00 30.00
SW Stephen Weiss 15.00 40.00
TA Tyler Arnason 10.00 30.00
TP Taylor Pyatt 10.00 30.00

2002-03 Bowman YoungStars Jerseys

Inserted at 1:7, this 27-card set featured a swatch of player jersey worn during the annual Topps YoungStars game. All cards carried a "FFJ" prefix on the card back.

COMMON CARD 3.00 8.00
STATED ODDS 1:7
*PATCH/50: 1.2X TO 3X BASE JSY
*DBL.STUFF/25: 3X TO 8X BASE JSY
*STICKS: 1X TO 2.5X BASE JSY
AF Alexander Frolov 4.00 10.00
AH Adam Hall 3.00 8.00
AS Alexander Svitov 3.00 8.00
AV Anton Volchenkov 3.00 8.00
BJ Barret Jackman 3.00 8.00
BR Branko Radivojevic 3.00 8.00
BS Brian Sutherby 3.00 8.00
DA David Aebischer 3.00 8.00
DS Dennis Seidenberg 3.00 8.00
HT Henrik Tallinder 3.00 8.00
JB Jay Bouwmeester 4.00 10.00
JL Jordan Leopold 3.00 8.00
MH Marcel Hossa 3.00 8.00
MW Mattias Weinhandl 3.00 8.00
NH Niklas Hagman 3.00 8.00
NK Niko Kapanen 3.00 8.00
NS Nick Schultz 3.00 8.00
OV Ossi Vaananen 3.00 8.00
PB Pavel Brendl 3.00 8.00
RK Rostislav Klesla 3.00 8.00
RM Ryan Miller 5.00 12.00
RN Rick Nash 6.00 15.00
SC Stanislav Chistov 3.00 8.00
SH Shawn Horcoff 3.00 8.00
SW Stephen Weiss 4.00 10.00
TA Tyler Arnason 3.00 8.00
TP Taylor Pyatt 3.00 8.00

2002-03 Bowman YoungStars MVP Puck Relic

Inserted at 1:1340, this 1-card set featured a piece of puck used during the Topps YoungStars game during the 2003 NHL All-Star weekend. The card front pictured the game MVP, Brian Sutherby and Topps representative J.Peter Sawkins. Each card was serial-numbered out of 100.

STATED ODDS 1:1340
STATED PRINT RUN 100 SER.#'d SETS
1 Brian Sutherby 20.00 50.00

2002-03 Bowman YoungStars Rivals

Inserted at 1:139, this 13-card set featured game-worn jersey swatches of the two players pictured. All cards carry a "FFR" prefix on the card backs and were serial-numbered out of 250.

STATED ODDS 1:139
STATED PRINT RUN 250 SER.#'d SETS
AFAS A.Frolov/A.Svitov 6.00 15.00
AHMW A.Hall/M.Weinhandl 6.00 15.00
BJDS B.Jackman/D.Seidenberg 6.00 15.00
BRPB B.Radivojevic/P.Brendl 6.00 15.00
DARM D.Aebischer/R.Miller 10.00 25.00
JLTP J.Leopold/T.Pyatt 6.00 15.00
NKMH N.Kapanen/M.Hossa 8.00 20.00
NSNH N.Schultz/N.Hagman 6.00 15.00
OVHT O.Vaananen/H.Tallinder 6.00 15.00
RKAV R.Klesla/A.Volchenkov 6.00 15.00
RNJB R.Nash/J.Bouwmeester 10.00 25.00
SCSW S.Chistov/S.Weiss 8.00 20.00
TABS T.Arnason/B.Sutherby 6.00 15.00

2003-04 Bowman

2003-04 Bowman/Bowman Chrome was packaged as one product consisting of two distinct brands.

COMP.SET w/o SP's (110) 20.00 40.00
1 Rick Nash .25 .60
2 Brian Leetch .25 .60
3 Pasi Nurminen .20 .50
4 Vincent Lecavalier .20 .50
5 Nicklas Lidstrom .25 .60
6 Barret Jackman .15 .40
7 Stanislav Chistov .15 .40
8 Patrick Marleau .25 .60
9 Paul Kariya .30 .75
10 Joe Thornton .30 .75
11 Daniel Alfredsson .25 .60
12 Bill Guerin .25 .60
13 Tyler Arnason .15 .40
14 Dwayne Roloson .20 .50
15 Dany Heatley .25 .60
16 Brett Hull .30 .75
17 Ilya Kovalchuk .25 .60
18 Marian Hossa .20 .50
19 Joe Sakic .40 1.00
20 Henrik Zetterberg .30 .75
21 Peter Forsberg .30 .75
22 Ales Kotalik .15 .40
23 Jamie Lundmark .15 .40
24 Brian Sutherby .15 .40
25 Patrik Elias .25 .60
26 Tomas Vokoun .20 .50
27 Jeremy Roenick .25 .60
28 Alexander Svitov .15 .40
29 Josef Vasicek .15 .40
30 Martin Brodeur .50 1.25
31 Chuck Kobasew .15 .40
32 Kyle Calder .15 .40
33 Daymond Langkow .15 .40
34 Marc Denis .20 .50
35 Sergei Samsonov .20 .50
36 Chris Pronger .20 .50
37 Sebastien Caron .20 .50
38 Markus Naslund .25 .60
39 Dominik Hasek .40 1.00
40 Alex Kovalev .20 .50
41 Roman Turek .20 .50
42 Petr Sykora .20 .50
43 Niko Kapanen .15 .40
44 Todd Bertuzzi .25 .60
45 Aleksey Morozov .15 .40
46 Ed Belfour .25 .60
47 David Aebischer .20 .50
48 Mike Johnson .15 .40
49 Jose Theodore .25 .60
50 Marian Gaborik .40 1.00
51 Evgeni Nabokov .20 .50
52 Eric Brewer .15 .40
53 Chris Osgood .25 .60
54 Sergei Gonchar .15 .40
55 Michael Rupp .15 .40
56 Olaf Kolzig .25 .60
57 Jan Bulis .15 .40
58 Dan Cloutier .20 .50
59 Nik Antropov .20 .50
60 Roberto Luongo .40 1.00
61 Ales Hemsky .25 .60
62 Robert Esche .15 .40
63 Adam Hall .15 .40
64 Chris Drury .20 .50
65 Alyn McCauley .15 .40
66 Mario Lemieux .75 2.00
67 Pierre-Marc Bouchard .25 .60
68 Jaromir Jagr .60 1.50
69 Alexei Yashin .20 .50
70 Patrick Lalime .20 .50
71 Miroslav Satan .20 .50
72 Michael Peca .20 .50
73 Ziggy Palffy .25 .60
74 Jason Spezza .25 .60
75 Jay Bouwmeester .25 .60
76 Tommy Salo .20 .50
77 Simon Gagne .25 .60
78 Nick Schultz .15 .40
79 Scott Stevens .25 .60
80 Jarome Iginla .25 .60
81 Roman Cechmanek .20 .50
82 Alexander Mogilny .20 .50
83 Ron Francis .30 .75
84 Mike Dunham .20 .50
85 Glen Murray .20 .50
86 Rick DiPietro .20 .50
87 David Legwand .20 .50
88 Nikolai Khabibulin .25 .60
89 Mike Comrie .20 .50
90 Marty Turco .25 .60
91 Sergei Fedorov .40 1.00
92 Brian Boucher .20 .50
93 Kristian Huselius .15 .40
94 Saku Koivu .25 .60
95 Justin Papineau .15 .40
96 Martin Biron .20 .50
97 Derian Hatcher .15 .40
98 Martin St. Louis .25 .60
99 Mike Modano .40 1.00
100 Jean-Sebastien Giguere .25 .60
101 Pavol Demitra .30 .75
102 Olli Jokinen .25 .60
103 Kevin Weekes .20 .50
104 Steve Shields .20 .50
105 Mats Sundin .25 .60
106 Artem Chubarov .15 .40
107 Alexander Frolov .20 .50
108 Jocelyn Thibault .20 .50
109 Martin Havlat .25 .60
110 Milan Hejduk .20 .50
111 Nathan Horton RC 1.50 4.00
112 Joffrey Lupul RC 1.50 4.00
113 Tuomo Ruutu RC 1.00 2.50
114 Jiri Hudler RC 1.50 4.00
115 Marek Svatos RC 1.25 3.00
116 Milan Michalek RC 1.25 3.00
117 Maxim Kondratiev RC .60 1.50
118 Dan Hamhuis RC .75 2.00
119 Boyd Gordon RC .75 2.00
120 Eric Staal RC 5.00 12.00
121 Dan Fritsche RC .60 1.50
122 Matthew Spiller RC .75 2.00
123 Ryan Malone RC 1.25 3.00
124 Cody McCormick RC .75 2.00
125 Tom Preissing RC .75 2.00
126 Dominic Moore RC .60 1.50
127 Matthew Lombardi RC .75 2.00
128 Chris Higgins RC 1.25 3.00
129 Pavel Vorobiev RC .75 2.00
130 Wade Brookbank RC .75 2.00
131 Tim Gleason RC .75 2.00
132 Matt Murley RC .75 2.00
133 Andrew Peters RC .75 2.00
134 Gregory Campbell RC .60 1.50
135 John-Michael Liles RC .75 2.00
136 Sergei Zinovjev RC .60 1.50
137 Alexander Semin RC 2.00 5.00
138 Lasse Kukkonen RC .60 1.50
139 Marek Zidlicky RC .60 1.50
140 Tony Salmelainen RC .60 1.50
141 Travis Moen RC .75 2.00
142 Nikolai Zherdev RC 1.25 3.00
143 Paul Martin RC .75 2.00
144 Peter Sarno RC .60 1.50
145 David Hale RC .60 1.50
146 Dustin Brown RC 1.25 3.00
147 Matt Stajan AU RC 6.00 15.00
148 Peter Sejna AU RC 5.00 12.00
149 S.Bergenheim AU RC 5.00 12.00
150 Antti Miettinen AU RC 6.00 15.00
151 Patrice Bergeron AU RC 20.00 50.00
152 Marc-Andre Fleury AU RC 20.00 50.00
153 Antoine Vermette AU RC 8.00 20.00
154 Jordin Tootoo AU RC 8.00 20.00
155 Rick Mrozik AU RC 4.00 10.00
156 Joni Pitkanen AU RC 6.00 15.00

2003-04 Bowman Gold

*1-110 VETS: 2.5X TO 6X BASIC CARDS
*111-146 ROOKIES: .5X TO 1.2X BASIC RC
ONE GOLD PER PACK
147 Matt Stajan 1.50 4.00
148 Peter Sejna 1.25 3.00
149 Sean Bergenheim 1.25 3.00
150 Antti Miettinen 1.50 4.00
151 Patrice Bergeron 5.00 12.00
152 Marc-Andre Fleury 6.00 15.00
153 Antoine Vermette 2.00 5.00
154 Jordin Tootoo 2.00 5.00
155 Rick Mrozik 1.00 2.50
156 Joni Pitkanen 1.50 4.00

2003-04 Bowman Future Fabrics

STATED ODDS 1:178
FFDA David Aebischer 5.00 12.00
FFAF Alexander Frolov 5.00 12.00
FFJS Jason Spezza 8.00 20.00
FFDB Dan Blackburn 4.00 10.00
FFRM Ryan Miller 8.00 20.00
FFSHO Shawn Horcoff 3.00 8.00
FFMW Mattias Weinhandl 3.00 8.00
FFNK Niko Kapanen 3.00 8.00
FFAH Adam Hall 3.00 8.00
FFAS Alexander Svitov 3.00 8.00
FFKH Kristian Huselius 3.00 8.00
FFNH Niklas Hagman 3.00 8.00
FFJB Jay Bouwmeester 3.00 8.00
FFJL Jordan Leopold 3.00 8.00
FFBS Brian Sutherby 3.00 8.00
FFSC Stanislav Chistov 3.00 8.00
FFSH Scott Hartnell 3.00 8.00
FFBJ Barret Jackman 3.00 8.00
FFTA Tyler Arnason 3.00 8.00
FFJLU Jamie Lundmark 3.00 8.00

2003-04 Bowman Future Rivals

STATED ODDS 1:187
AK T.Arnason/N.Kapanen 4.00 10.00
AT D.Aebischer/M.Turco 6.00 15.00
CH S.Chistov/M.Hejduk 4.00 10.00
CI M.Comrie/J.Iginla 8.00 20.00
GH M.Gaborik/D.Heatley 12.00 30.00
HD M.Hejduk/P.Datsyuk 10.00 25.00
HG K.Huselius/S.Gagne 4.00 10.00
HH S.Horcoff/A.Hall 4.00 10.00
JF B.Jackman/A.Frolov 4.00 10.00
KD N.Kapanen/P.Datsyuk 6.00 15.00
LK V. Lecavalier/I.Kovalchuk 10.00 25.00
LT P.Lalime/J.Theodore 6.00 15.00
ML R.Miller/R.Luongo 10.00 25.00
MM P.Marleau/B.Morrison 6.00 15.00
NC R.Nash/S.Chistov 10.00 25.00
NG R.Nash/M.Gaborik 12.00 30.00
RS B.Richards/B.Sutherby 6.00 15.00
SH J.Spezza/N.Hagman 8.00 20.00
WL M. Weinhandl/J.Lundmark 4.00 10.00

2003-04 Bowman Goal to Goal

This 9-card set featured swatches of game-worn jerseys of both players featured along with a piece of all-star goal net.

STATED ODDS 1:299
AY D.Alfredsson/A.Yashin 12.00 30.00
GC M.Gaborik/S.Chistov 15.00 40.00
HG D.Heatley/B.Guerin 12.00 30.00
JH J.Jagr/M.Hejduk 20.00 50.00
KN N.Kapanen/R.Nash 15.00 40.00
MN M.Modano/M.Naslund 15.00 40.00
SG J.Spezza/S.Gagne 15.00 40.00
SI M.Satan/J.Iginla 12.00 30.00
TK J.Thornton/I.Kovalchuk 25.00 60.00

2003-04 Bowman Premier Performance Jerseys

STATED ODDS 1:28
PPMSTO Matt Stajan 4.00 10.00
PPNH Nathan Horton 4.00 10.00
PPPS Peter Sejna 2.50 6.00
PPAM Antti Miettinen 2.50 6.00
PPMS Marek Svatos 5.00 12.00
PPJP Joni Pitkanen 2.50 6.00
PPJL Joffrey Lupul 3.00 8.00
PPAV Antoine Vermette 2.50 6.00
PPDH Dan Hamhuis 2.50 6.00
PPSB Sean Bergenheim 3.00 8.00

2003-04 Bowman Premier Performance Patches

*PATCHES: .75X TO 2X JSY HI
PRINT RUN 50 SER.#'d SETS

2003-04 Bowman Signs of the Future

STATED ODDS 1:81
SOFES Eric Staal 8.00 20.00
SOFMS Matt Stajan 8.00 20.00
SOFRN Rick Nash 10.00 25.00
SOFMAF Marc-Andre Fleury 15.00 40.00
SOFAM Antti Miettinen 4.00 10.00
SOFAV Antoine Vermette 4.00 10.00
SOFMZ Miroslav Zalesak 4.00 10.00
SOFPMB Pierre-Marc Bouchard 5.00 12.00
SOFPS Peter Sejna 4.00 10.00

2003-04 Bowman Chrome

2003-04 Bowman/Bowman Chrome was packaged as one product consisting of two distinct brands.

COMP.SET w/o SP's (110) 30.00 60.00
RC AUTO PRINT RUN 250 SER.#'d SETS
1 Rick Nash .40 1.00
2 Brian Leetch .40 1.00
3 Pasi Nurminen .30 .75
4 Vincent Lecavalier .30 .75
5 Nicklas Lidstrom .40 1.00
6 Barret Jackman .25 .60
7 Stanislav Chistov .25 .60
8 Patrick Marleau .40 1.00
9 Paul Kariya .50 1.25
10 Joe Thornton .50 1.25
11 Daniel Alfredsson .40 1.00
12 Bill Guerin .40 1.00
13 Tyler Arnason .25 .60
14 Dwayne Roloson .30 .75
15 Dany Heatley .40 1.00
16 Brett Hull .50 1.25
17 Ilya Kovalchuk .40 1.00
18 Marian Hossa .30 .75
19 Joe Sakic .60 1.50
20 Henrik Zetterberg .50 1.25
21 Peter Forsberg .50 1.25
22 Ales Kotalik .25 .60
23 Jamie Lundmark .25 .60
24 Brian Sutherby .25 .60
25 Patrik Elias .40 1.00
26 Tomas Vokoun .30 .75
27 Jeremy Roenick .40 1.00
28 Alexander Svitov .25 .60
29 Josef Vasicek .25 .60
30 Martin Brodeur .75 2.00
31 Chuck Kobasew .25 .60
32 Kyle Calder .25 .60
33 Daymond Langkow .25 .60
34 Marc Denis .30 .75
35 Sergei Samsonov .30 .75
36 Chris Pronger .30 .75
37 Sebastien Caron .30 .75
38 Markus Naslund .40 1.00
39 Dominik Hasek .60 1.50
40 Alex Kovalev .30 .75
41 Roman Turek .30 .75
42 Petr Sykora .30 .75
43 Niko Kapanen .25 .60
44 Todd Bertuzzi .40 1.00
45 Aleksey Morozov .25 .60
46 Ed Belfour .40 1.00
47 David Aebischer .30 .75
48 Mike Johnson .25 .60
49 Jose Theodore .40 1.00
50 Marian Gaborik .60 1.50
51 Evgeni Nabokov .30 .75
52 Eric Brewer .25 .60
53 Chris Osgood .40 1.00
54 Sergei Gonchar .25 .60
55 Michael Rupp .25 .60
56 Olaf Kolzig .40 1.00
57 Jan Bulis .25 .60
58 Dan Cloutier .30 .75
59 Nik Antropov .30 .75
60 Roberto Luongo .60 1.50
61 Ales Hemsky .40 1.00
62 Robert Esche .25 .60
63 Adam Hall .25 .60
64 Chris Drury .30 .75
65 Alyn McCauley .25 .60
66 Mario Lemieux 1.25 3.00
67 Pierre-Marc Bouchard .40 1.00
68 Jaromir Jagr 1.00 2.50
69 Alexei Yashin .30 .75
70 Patrick Lalime .30 .75
71 Miroslav Satan .30 .75
72 Michael Peca .30 .75
73 Ziggy Palffy .40 1.00
74 Jason Spezza .40 1.00
75 Jay Bouwmeester .40 1.00
76 Tommy Salo .30 .75
77 Simon Gagne .40 1.00
78 Nick Schultz .25 .60
79 Scott Stevens .40 1.00
80 Jarome Iginla .40 1.00
81 Roman Cechmanek .30 .75
82 Alexander Mogilny .30 .75
83 Ron Francis .50 1.25
84 Mike Dunham .30 .75
85 Glen Murray .30 .75
86 Rick DiPietro .30 .75
87 David Legwand .30 .75
88 Nikolai Khabibulin .40 1.00
89 Mike Comrie .30 .75
90 Marty Turco .40 1.00
91 Sergei Fedorov .60 1.50
92 Brian Boucher .30 .75
93 Kristian Huselius .25 .60
94 Saku Koivu .40 1.00
95 Justin Papineau .25 .60
96 Martin Biron .30 .75
97 Derian Hatcher .25 .60
98 Martin St. Louis .40 1.00
99 Mike Modano .60 1.50
100 Jean-Sebastien Giguere .40 1.00
101 Pavol Demitra .50 1.25
102 Olli Jokinen .40 1.00
103 Kevin Weekes .30 .75
104 Steve Shields .30 .75
105 Mats Sundin .40 1.00
106 Artem Chubarov .25 .60
107 Alexander Frolov .30 .75
108 Jocelyn Thibault .30 .75
109 Martin Havlat .40 1.00
110 Milan Hejduk .30 .75
111 Nathan Horton RC 2.00 5.00
112 Joffrey Lupul RC 2.00 5.00
113 Tuomo Ruutu RC 1.25 3.00
114 Jiri Hudler RC 2.00 5.00
115 Marek Svatos RC 1.50 4.00
116 Milan Michalek RC 1.50 4.00
117 Maxim Kondratiev RC .75 2.00
118 Dan Hamhuis RC 1.00 2.50
119 Boyd Gordon RC 1.00 2.50
120 Eric Staal RC 4.00 10.00
121 Dan Fritsche RC .75 2.00
122 Matthew Spiller RC 1.00 2.50
123 Ryan Malone RC 1.50 4.00
124 Cody McCormick RC 1.00 2.50
125 Tom Preissing RC 1.00 2.50
126 Dominic Moore RC .75 2.00
127 Matthew Lombardi RC 1.00 2.50
128 Chris Higgins RC 1.50 4.00
129 Pavel Vorobiev RC 1.00 2.50
130 Wade Brookbank RC 1.00 2.50
131 Tim Gleason RC 1.00 2.50
132 Matt Murley RC 1.00 2.50
133 Andrew Peters RC 1.00 2.50
134 Gregory Campbell RC .75 2.00
135 John-Michael Liles RC 1.00 2.50
136 Sergei Zinovjev RC .75 2.00
137 Alexander Semin RC 2.50 6.00
138 Lasse Kukkonen RC .75 2.00
139 Marek Zidlicky RC .75 2.00
140 Tony Salmelainen RC .75 2.00
141 Travis Moen RC 1.00 2.50
142 Nikolai Zherdev RC 1.50 4.00
143 Paul Martin RC 1.00 2.50
144 Peter Sarno RC .75 2.00
145 David Hale RC .75 2.00
146 Dustin Brown RC 1.50 4.00
147 Matt Stajan AU RC 8.00 20.00
148 Peter Sejna AU RC 6.00 15.00
149 Sean Bergenheim AU RC 6.00 15.00
150 Antti Miettinen AU RC 8.00 20.00
151 Patrice Bergeron AU RC 20.00 50.00
152 Marc-Andre Fleury AU RC 30.00 80.00
153 Antoine Vermette AU RC 10.00 25.00
154 Jordin Tootoo AU RC 10.00 25.00
155 Rick Mrozik AU RC 5.00 12.00
156 Joni Pitkanen AU RC 8.00 20.00

2003-04 Bowman Chrome Refractors

*1-110 VETS/300: 2.5X TO 6X BASIC CARDS
*111-146 ROOKIE/300: .8X TO 2X BASIC RC
*ROOKIE AU/50: .5X TO 1.2X BASIC AU
151 Patrice Bergeron 50.00 100.00
152 Marc-Andre Fleury 40.00 100.00

2003-04 Bowman Chrome Gold Refractors

*1-110 VETS/50: 6X TO 15X BASIC CARDS
*111-146 ROOKIES/50: 2X TO 5X BASIC RC

2003-04 Bowman Chrome Xfractors

*1-110 VETS/150: 4X TO 10X BASIC CARDS
*111-146 ROOKIE/150: 1.2X TO 3X BASIC RC
*ROOKIE AU/25: .6X TO 1.5X BASIC AU
151 Patrice Bergeron AU 75.00 135.00
152 Marc-Andre Fleury AU 80.00 150.00

1938-39 Bruins Garden Magazine Supplement

These large (8 X 10") photos were printed on very thin, sepia-toned stock and inserted in game programs issued at the Boston Gardens. Any additional information would be appreciated.

COMPLETE SET (9) 350.00 700.00
1 Red Beattie 20.00 40.00
2 Walter Galbraith 20.00 40.00
3 Lionel Hitchman 40.00 80.00
4 Joseph Lamb 20.00 40.00
5 Harry Oliver 20.00 40.00
6 Art Ross 75.00 150.00
7 Eddie Shore 125.00 250.00
8 Nels Stewart 40.00 80.00
9 Tiny Thompson 50.00 100.00

1955-56 Bruins Photos

These black and white photos measure approximately 6" x 8" and were distributed in an envelope bearing the Bruins logo.

COMPLETE SET (17) 100.00 200.00
1 Bob Armstrong 5.00 10.00
2 Marcel Bonin 5.00 10.00
3 Leo Boivin 7.50 15.00
4 Real Chevrefils 5.00 10.00
5 Fern Flaman 7.50 15.00
6 Cal Gardner 2.50 5.00
7 Lionel Heinrich 2.50 5.00
8 Leo Labine 7.50 15.00
9 Hal Laycoe 5.00 10.00
10 Fleming Mackell 5.00 10.00
11 Don McKenney 5.00 10.00
12 Doug Mohns 7.50 15.00
13 Bill Quackenbush 7.50 15.00
14 Johnny Peirson 5.00 10.00
15 Terry Sawchuk 25.00 50.00
16 Vic Stasiuk 5.00 10.00
17 Jerry Toppazzini 5.00 10.00
NNO Envelope 10.00 20.00

1957-58 Bruins Photos

This 14-card set measures approximately 6 5/8" by 8 1/8".

COMPLETE SET (20) 100.00 200.00
1 Bob Armstrong 5.00 10.00
2 Jack Bionda 2.50 5.00
3 Leo Boivin 5.00 10.00
4 Johnny Bucyk 25.00 50.00
5 Real Chevrefils 4.00 8.00
6 Fern Flaman 6.00 12.00
7 Jean-Guy Gendron 5.00 10.00
8 Larry Hillman 5.00 10.00
9 Bronco Horvath 6.00 12.00
10 Norm Johnson 6.00 12.00
11 Leo Labine 5.00 10.00
12 Fleming Mackell 4.00 8.00
13 Don McKenney 4.00 8.00
14 Doug Mohns 6.00 12.00
15 Jim Morrison 2.50 5.00
16 Johnny Peirson 2.50 5.00
17 Larry Regan 2.50 5.00
18 Milt Schmidt CO 10.00 20.00
19 Vic Stasiuk 6.00 12.00
20 Jerry Toppazzini 2.50 5.00

1958-59 Bruins Photos

These 6X8 photos were issued by the team.

COMPLETE SET (15) 75.00 150.00
1 Bob Armstrong 5.00 10.00
2 Johnny Bucyk 15.00 30.00
3 Real Chevrefils 5.00 10.00
4 Fern Flaman 6.00 12.00
5 Jean-Guy Gendron 5.00 10.00
6 Larry Hillman 5.00 10.00
7 Leo Labine 5.00 10.00
8 Fleming MacKell 5.00 10.00
9 Don McKenney 5.00 10.00
10 Jim Morrison 5.00 10.00
11 Larry Regan 5.00 10.00
12 Dutch Reibel 5.00 10.00
13 Don Simmons 10.00 20.00
14 Vic Stasiuk 5.00 10.00
15 Jerry Toppazzini 5.00 10.00

1970-71 Bruins Postcards

Cards are standard postcard size and were issued in a binder with perforations.

COMPLETE SET (21) 75.00 150.00
1 Team Photo 2.50 5.00
2 Ed Johnston 2.50 5.00
3 Gerry Cheevers 7.50 15.00
4 Wayne Cashman 2.50 5.00
5 Garnet Bailey 5.00 10.00
6 Don Marcotte 1.50 3.00
7 John Bucyk 5.00 10.00
8 Wayne Carleton 1.50 3.00
9 Reggie Leach 4.00 8.00
10 Ken Hodge 2.50 5.00
11 Ed Westfall 2.00 4.00
12 John McKenzie 2.00 4.00
13 Phil Esposito 10.00 20.00
14 Fred Stanfield 1.50 3.00
15 Derek Sanderson 5.00 10.00
16 Bobby Orr 25.00 50.00
17 Dallas Smith 2.00 4.00
18 Rick Smith 1.50 3.00
19 Ted Green 2.00 4.00
20 Don Awrey 1.50 3.00
21 Tom Johnson CO 2.00 4.00

1970-71 Bruins Team Issue

This set of 18 team-issue photos commemorates the Boston Bruins as 1970 Stanley Cup Champions. The set was issued in two different photo packs of nine photos each. The photos measure approximately 6" by 8".

COMPLETE SET (18) 50.00 100.00
1 Garnet Bailey 5.00 10.00
2 Johnny Bucyk 5.00 10.00
3 Gary Doak 2.00 4.00
4 Phil Esposito 10.00 20.00
5 Ed Johnston 2.50 5.00
6 Don Marcotte 1.50 3.00
7 Derek Sanderson 5.00 10.00
8 Dallas Smith 2.00 4.00
9 Ed Westfall 2.00 4.00
10 Don Awrey 1.50 3.00
11 Wayne Carleton 1.50 3.00
12 Wayne Cashman 2.50 5.00
13 Gerry Cheevers 7.50 15.00
14 Ken Hodge 2.50 5.00
15 John McKenzie 2.00 4.00
16 Bobby Orr 25.00 50.00
17 Rick Smith 1.50 3.00
18 Fred Stanfield 1.50 3.00

1971-72 Bruins Postcards

Originally issued in booklet form, these 20 photo cards measure 3 1/2" by 5 1/2". The cards have perforated tops that allow them to be detached from the yellow booklet, which bears the Bruins logo and crossed hockey sticks on its front.

COMPLETE SET (20) 50.00 100.00
1 Ed Johnston 2.00 4.00
2 Bobby Orr 20.00 40.00
3 Teddy Green 1.50 3.00
4 Phil Esposito 10.00 20.00
5 Ken Hodge 2.00 4.00
6 John Bucyk 4.00 8.00
7 Rick Smith 1.00 2.00
8 Mike Walton 1.50 3.00
9 Wayne Cashman 2.00 4.00
10 Ace Bailey 5.00 10.00
11 Derek Sanderson 4.00 8.00
12 Fred Stanfield 1.00 2.00
13 Ed Westfall 1.50 3.00
14 John McKenzie 1.50 3.00
15 Dallas Smith 1.00 2.00
16 Don Marcotte 1.00 2.00
17 Garry Peters 1.00 2.00
18 Don Awrey 1.00 2.00
19 Reggie Leach 2.00 4.00
20 Gerry Cheevers 5.00 10.00

1983-84 Bruins Team Issue

This 17-card set measures approximately 3 1/8" by 4 1/8".

COMPLETE SET (17) 10.00 25.00
1 Ray Bourque 4.00 10.00
2 Bruce Crowder .40 1.00
3 Keith Crowder .60 1.50
4 Luc Dufour .40 1.00
5 Tom Fergus .40 1.00
6 Randy Hillier .40 1.00
7 Steve Kasper .60 1.50
8 Gord Kluzak .60 1.50
9 Mike Krushelnyski .40 1.00
10 Peter McNab .60 1.50
11 Rick Middleton 1.25 3.00
12 Mike Milbury .60 1.50
13 Mike O'Connell .60 1.50
14 Terry O'Reilly .75 2.00
15 Brad Palmer .40 1.00
16 Barry Pederson .60 1.50
17 Pete Peeters .75 2.00

1984-85 Bruins Postcards

This set features 20 postcard-size issues of the Bruins. It is believed they were issued as giveaways at player signing appearances.

COMPLETE SET (20) 12.00 30.00
1 Pete Peeters .75 2.00
2 Lou Sleigher .60 1.50
3 Ray Bourque 3.00 8.00
4 Mike Milbury .60 1.50
5 Keith Crowder .60 1.50
6 Steve Kasper .60 1.50
7 Mats Thelin .40 1.00
8 Ken Linseman .60 1.50
9 Terry O'Reilly 1.25 3.00
10 Barry Pederson .60 1.50
11 Nevin Markwart .60 1.50
12 Mike O'Connell .40 1.00
13 Geoff Courtnall .75 2.00
14 Doug Keans .60 1.50
15 Charlie Simmer .60 1.50
16 Rick Middleton 1.25 3.00
17 Tom Fergus .40 1.00
18 Mike Gillis .40 1.00
19 Gord Kluzak .60 1.50
20 Lyndon Byers 1.25 3.00

1988-89 Bruins Sports Action

This 24-card set measures the standard size and was issued by Sports Action.

COMPLETE SET (24) 6.00 15.00
1 Ray Bourque 1.25 3.00
2 Randy Burridge .15 .40
3 Lyndon Byers .40 1.00
4 Keith Crowder .20 .50
5 Craig Janney .20 .50
6 Bob Joyce .08 .25
7 Steve Kasper .20 .50
8 Gord Kluzak .20 .50
9 Reed Larson .08 .25
10 Rejean Lemelin .30 .75
11 Ken Linseman .20 .50
12 Tom McCarthy .08 .25
13 Rick Middleton .60 1.50
14 Jay Miller .40 1.00
15 Andy Moog .60 1.50
16 Cam Neely 1.00 2.50
17 Terry O'Reilly CO .20 .50
18 Allen Pederson .08 .25
19 Willi Plett .08 .25
20 Bob Sweeney .08 .25
21 Michael Thelven .08 .25
22 Glen Wesley .20 .50
23 Bob Joyce .20 .50
Craig Janney
24 Dynamic Duo .75 2.00
Ray Bourque
Cam Neely

1988-89 Bruins Sports Action Postcards

This 20-postcard set of the Boston Bruins was produced by Sports Action Marketing.

COMPLETE SET (20) 8.00 20.00
1 Ray Bourque 1.50 4.00
2 Andy Brickley .20 .50
3 John Carter .20 .50
4 Garry Galley .30 .75
5 Craig Janney .60 1.50
6 Greg Johnston .20 .50
7 Bob Joyce .20 .50
8 Steve Kasper .30 .75
9 Gord Kluzak .30 .75
10 Rejean Lemelin .40 1.00
11 Ken Linseman .30 .75
12 Rick Middleton .60 1.50
13 Andy Moog 1.00 2.50
14 Cam Neely 1.50 4.00
15 Bill O'Dwyer .20 .50
16 Allen Pedersen .20 .50
17 Stephane Quintal .20 .50
18 Bob Sweeney .20 .50
19 Michael Thelven .20 .50
20 Glen Wesley .40 1.00

1989-90 Bruins Sports Action

This standard sized 24-card set was issued by Sports Action.

COMPLETE SET (24) 4.80 12.00
1 Ray Bourque .75 2.00
2 Andy Brickley .20 .50
3 Randy Burridge .20 .50
4 Lyndon Byers .20 .50
5 Bob Carpenter .20 .50
6 John Carter .20 .50
7 Rob Cimetta .20 .50
8 Garry Galley .30 .75
9 Bob Gould .20 .50
10 Greg Hawgood .20 .50
11 Craig Janney .30 .75
12 Bob Joyce .20 .50
13 Rejean Lemelin .30 .75
14 Ken Linseman .20 .50
15 Andy Moog .40 1.00
16 Nevin Markwart .20 .50
17 Cam Neely .60 1.50
18 Allen Pedersen .20 .50
19 Stephane Quintal .20 .50
20 Bob Sweeney .20 .50
21 Michael Thelven .20 .50
22 Glen Wesley .30 .75
23 Bruins Top 10 Scorers .40 1.00
24 Stanley Cup Champions .40 1.00

1989-90 Bruins Sports Action Update

This 12-card standard-size set was issued by Sports Action.

COMPLETE SET (12) 3.00 8.00
1 Ray Bourque .75 2.00
2 Dave Christian .30 .75
3 Peter Douris .20 .50
4 Gord Kluzak .30 .75
5 Brian Lawton .20 .50
6 Mike Millar .20 .50
7 Dave Poulin .30 .75
8 Brian Propp .30 .75
9 Don Sweeney .30 .75
10 Graeme Townshend .20 .50
11 Jim Wiemer .20 .50
12 Bruins Leaders .75 2.00
Ray Bourque
Rejean Lemelin
Cam Neely

1990-91 Bruins Sports Action

The Markwart and Quintal cards were reportedly only issued in the first print run of 400 24-card sets. In the second and larger print run, these cards were replaced by Byers and Hodge. Consequently, the Markwart and Quintal cards are more difficult to find than the Byers and Hodge cards.

COMPLETE SET (26) 8.00 20.00
1 Bob Beers .20 .50
2 Ray Bourque 1.25 3.00
3 Andy Brickley .20 .50
4 Randy Burridge .25 .60
5 John Byce .20 .50
6 Lyndon Byers .30 .75
7 Bob Carpenter .20 .50
8 John Carter .20 .50
9 Dave Christian .25 .60
10 Peter Douris .20 .50
11 Garry Galley .20 .50
12 Ken Hodge Jr. .20 .50
13 Craig Janney .30 .75
14 Rejean Lemelin .30 .75
15 Nevin Markwart SP 1.25 3.00
16 Andy Moog .60 1.50
17 Cam Neely .75 2.00
18 Chris Nilan .25 .60
19 Allen Pedersen .20 .50
20 Dave Poulin .25 .60
21 Stephane Quintal SP 1.25 3.00
22 Bob Sweeney .20 .50
23 Don Sweeney .25 .60
24 Wes Walz .20 .50
25 Glen Wesley .30 .75
26 Rejean Lemelin .40 1.00
Andy Moog

1991-92 Bruins Sports Action

This 24-card standard-size set was issued by Sports Action.

COMPLETE SET (24) 4.80 12.00
1 Brent Ashton .15 .40
2 Bob Beers .15 .40
3 Daniel Berthiaume .20 .50
4 Ray Bourque 1.00 2.50
5 Bob Carpenter .15 .40
6 Peter Douris .08 .25
7 Glen Featherstone .08 .25
8 Ken Hodge Jr. .08 .25
9 Jeff Lazaro .08 .25
10 Stephen Leach .15 .40
11 Andy Moog .40 1.00
12 Gord Murphy .08 .25
13 Cam Neely .75 2.00
14 Adam Oates .40 1.00
15 Dave Poulin .20 .50
16 David Reid .15 .40
17 Vladimir Ruzicka .15 .40
18 Bob Sweeney .15 .40
19 Don Sweeney .15 .40
20 Jim Vesey .08 .25
21 Glen Wesley .15 .40
22 Jim Wiemer .08 .25
23 Chris Winnes .08 .25
24 The Big Three .60 1.50
Andy Moog
Ray Bourque
Cam Neely

1991-92 Bruins Sports Action Legends

Card	Low	High
COMPLETE SET (36)	6.00	15.00
1 Bob Armstrong	.08	.25
2 Leo Boivin	.15	.40
3 Ray Bourque	.75	2.00
4 Frank Brimsek	.30	.75
5 Johnny Bucyk	.40	1.00
6 Wayne Cashman	.08	.25
7 Gerry Cheevers	.40	1.00
8 Dit Clapper	.30	.75
9 Bill Cowley	.08	.25
10 Phil Esposito	.50	1.25
11 Fernie Flaman	.15	.40
12 Mel Hill	.15	.40
Bill Cowley		
Roy Conacher		
13 Lionel Hitchman	.15	.40
14 Fleming Mackell	.08	.25
15 Don Marcotte	.08	.25
16 Don McKenney	.08	.25
17 Rick Middleton	.20	.50
18 Doug Mohns	.08	.25
19 Terry O'Reilly	.15	.40
20 Bobby Orr	1.25	3.00
21 Brad Park	.30	.75
22 John Peirson	.08	.25
23 Bill Quackenbush	.20	.50
24 Jean Ratelle	.30	.75
25 Art Ross CO	.20	.50
GM		
26 Ed Sandford	.08	.25
27 Terry Sawchuk	.60	1.50
28 Milt Schmidt	.40	1.00
29 Milt Schmidt	.20	.50
Cooney Weiland		
Bill Cowley		
30 Eddie Shore	.40	1.00
31 Harry Sinden CO	.20	.50
GM		
and President		
32 Tiny Thompson	.15	.40
33 Cooney Weiland	.15	.40
34 Ed Westfall	.08	.25
35 Bruins Defense/1955-56	.20	.50
Bill Quackenbush		
Fern Flaman		
Terry Sawchuk		
Bob Armstrong		
Leo Boivin		
36 The Kraut Line	.30	.75
Milt Schmidt		
Woody Dumart		
Bobby Bauer		

1992-93 Bruins Postcards

This set measures approximately 3 1/2" by 5 1/2".

Card	Low	High
COMPLETE SET (12)	4.00	10.00
1 Ray Bourque	1.25	3.00
2 Ted Donato	.20	.50
3 Joe Juneau	.30	.75
4 Dimitri Kvartalnov	.20	.50
5 Stephen Leach	.20	.50
6 Andy Moog	.75	2.00
7 Adam Oates	.75	2.00
8 Dave Poulin	.30	.75
9 Gordie Roberts	.20	.50
10 Vladimir Ruzicka	.20	.50
11 Don Sweeney	.30	.75
12 Glen Wesley	.30	.75

1998 Bruins Alumni

Released for sale at the Fleet Center, this 35-card set features Boston Bruins from the past. The sets were sold for $18, and each set contained one autographed card.

Card	Low	High
COMPLETE SET (35)	8.00	20.00
1 Reggie Lemelin	.20	.50
2 Harry Sinden	.08	.25
3 Jim Craig	.20	.50
4 Bobby Orr	2.00	5.00
5 Ferny Flaman	.20	.50
6 Bob Beers	.08	.25
7 Ken Hodge	.20	.50
8 Cam Neely	1.25	3.00
9 John Bucyk	.40	1.00
10 Jean Ratelle	.20	.50
11 Bob Miller	.02	.10
12 Ed Sandford	.02	.10
13 Ken Linseman	.20	.50
14 Woody Dumart	.20	.50
15 Milt Schmidt	.30	.75
16 Derek Sanderson	.40	1.00
17 Fred Stanfield	.08	.25
18 Garnet Bailey	.75	2.00
19 John McKenzie	.20	.50
20 Dallas Smith	.08	.25
21 Don Marcotte	.08	.25
22 Brad Park	.30	.75
23 Matt Glennon	.02	.10
24 Terry O'Reilly	.40	1.00
25 Gary Doak	.08	.25
26 Don Awrey	.08	.25
27 Billy O'Dwyer	.02	.10
28 Dave Hynes	.02	.10
29 Tom Songin	.02	.10
30 Gerry Cheevers	.40	1.00
31 Don McKenney	.08	.25
32 Frank Simonetti	.02	.10
33 Bronco Horvath	.08	.25
34 Doug Mohns	.08	.25
35 Header Card	.02	.10

1998 Bruins Alumni Autographs

One autographed card was inserted in each set of 1998 Boston Bruins Alumni. Since so many sets would need to be purchase to complete a set, it's quite possible that no complete sets exist. The autographs of Bobby Orr and Cam Neely have not yet been confirmed, and so prices are not listed (nor are they included in the complete set value). If you can confirm either of these cards, please write to hockeymag@beckett.com. The Ace Bailey card is believed to be his only certified autographed single. Bailey was killed in the 9/11 plane hijackings.

Card	Low	High
COMPLETE SET (35)	120.00	300.00
1 Reggie Lemelin	4.00	10.00
2 Harry Sinden	4.00	10.00
3 Jim Craig	6.00	15.00
4 Bobby Orr		
5 Ferny Flaman	2.00	5.00
6 Bob Beers	.75	2.00
7 Ken Hodge	3.00	8.00
8 Cam Neely		
9 John Bucyk	10.00	25.00
10 Jean Ratelle	8.00	20.00
11 Bob Miller	.40	1.00
12 Ed Sandford	.40	1.00
13 Ken Linseman	2.00	5.00
14 Woody Dumart	15.00	40.00
15 Milt Schmidt	10.00	25.00
16 Derek Sanderson	15.00	40.00
17 Fred Stanfield	1.25	3.00
18 Garnet Bailey	15.00	40.00
19 John McKenzie	3.00	8.00
20 Dallas Smith	4.00	10.00
21 Don Marcotte	1.25	3.00
22 Brad Park	6.00	15.00
23 Matt Glennon	.40	1.00
24 Terry O'Reilly	15.00	40.00
25 Gary Doak	1.25	3.00
26 Don Awrey	1.25	3.00
27 Billy O'Dwyer	.40	1.00
28 Dave Hynes	.40	1.00
29 Tom Songin	.40	1.00
30 Gerry Cheevers	10.00	25.00
31 Don McKenney	1.25	3.00
32 Frank Simonetti	.40	1.00
33 Bronco Horvath	4.00	10.00
34 Doug Mohns	2.00	5.00
35 Header Card	.40	1.00

1999-00 Bruins Season Ticket Offer

This two card set was mailed to Bruins season ticket holders in an effort to bolster the renewal rate. The cards were perforated at the end of the offer. They are regular card stock and, because of the nature of distribution, are extremely rare in the hobby.

Card	Low	High
COMPLETE SET (2)	25.00	60.00
1 Joe Thornton	20.00	50.00
2 Sergei Samsonov	6.00	15.00

2002-03 Bruins Team Issue

These oversized (4X6) player photos feature action photos on the front and blank backs. They were distributed through the Bruins marketing department and were used mainly for autograph signings.

Card	Low	High
COMPLETE SET (8)	6.00	15.00
1 Blades MASCOT	.20	.50
2 Nick Boynton	.40	1.00
3 Hal Gill	.40	1.00
4 Glen Murray	.75	2.00
5 Brian Rolston	.75	2.00
6 Sergei Samsonov	1.25	3.00
7 P.J. Stock	1.25	3.00
8 Joe Thornton	2.00	5.00

2003-04 Bruins Team Issue

These oversized,very thin cards were available only in singles form at team events or through by-mail requests. It's possible that the checklist not complete. Send additional info to hockeymag@beckett.com

Card	Low	High
COMPLETE SET (14)	8.00	20.00
1 Nick Boynton	.40	1.00
2 Hal Gill	.40	1.00
3 Mike Knuble	.40	1.00
4 Martin Lapointe	.60	1.50
5 Dan McGillis	.40	1.00
6 Glen Murray	.60	1.50
7 Sean O'Donnell	.40	1.00
8 Felix Potvin	.40	1.00
9 Andrew Raycroft	1.25	3.00
10 Sergei Samsonov	1.25	3.00
11 Mike Sullivan CO	.10	.25
12 Joe Thornton	2.00	5.00
13 Blades MASCOT	.10	.25
14 Team photo	.40	1.00

2005-06 Bruins Boston Globe

Produced by Upper Deck, this set was distributed in two unperforated sheets with the purchase of a Sunday Boston Globe newspaper on consecutive weekends in late 2005.

Card	Low	High
COMPLETE SET (24)	8.00	20.00
1 Glen Murray	.20	.50
2 Hannu Toivonen	1.00	2.50
3 Andrew Alberts	.20	.50
4 Hal Gill	.20	.50
5 Tom Fitzgerald	.20	.50
6 Milan Jurcina	.20	.50
7 Brad Boyes	.30	.75
8 David Tanabe	.20	.50
9 Wayne Primeau	.20	.50
10 Brad Stuart	.20	.50
11 Alexei Zhamnov	.20	.50
12 Brian Leetch	.75	2.00
13 Patrice Bergeron	.75	2.00
14 Marco Sturm	.20	.50
15 Nick Boynton	.20	.50
16 Brad Isbister	.20	.50
17 Sergei Samsonov	.40	1.00
18 Pat Leahy	.20	.50
19 Andrew Raycroft	.40	1.00
20 Tim Thomas	.75	2.00
21 Travis Green	.20	.50
22 Josh Langfeld	.20	.50
23 Dan LaCouture	.20	.50
24 P.J. Axelsson	.20	.50

2010-11 Bruins Upper Deck Stanley Cup Champions

Card	Low	High
COMPLETE SET (31)	8.00	20.00
1 Patrice Bergeron	.30	.75
2 Tim Thomas	.20	.50
3 Zdeno Chara	.20	.50
4 Brad Marchand	.40	1.00
5 Milan Lucic	.25	.60
6 Nathan Horton	.20	.50
7 David Krejci	.25	.60
8 Michael Ryder	.15	.40
9 Chris Kelly	.20	.50
10 Dennis Seidenberg	.20	.50
11 Mark Recchi	.30	.75
12 Rich Peverley	.25	.60
13 Tyler Seguin	.75	2.00
14 Andrew Ference	.15	.40
15 Tomas Kaberle	.15	.40
16 Johnny Boychuk	.15	.40
17 Adam McQuaid	.25	.60
18 Daniel Paille	.15	.40
19 Gregory Campbell	.15	.40
20 Shawn Thornton	.15	.40
21 Shane Hnidy	.15	.40
22 Marc Savard	.15	.40
23 Steve Kampfer	.30	.75
24 Jordan Caron	.30	.75
25 Tuukka Rask	.25	.60
26 Milan Lucic HL	.25	.60
27 Tim Thomas HL	.20	.50
28 Zdeno Chara HL	.20	.50
29 Tim Thomas HL	.20	.50
30 Tyler Seguin HL	.75	2.00
BOS Team Photo	2.00	5.00

1932 Bulgaria Zigaretten Sport Photos

Card	Low	High
142 Field Hockey	5.00	10.00
143 Field Hockey	5.00	10.00
144 Field Hockey	5.00	10.00
148 Ice Hockey	12.50	25.00
149 Dr. B. Watson Canada	10.00	20.00
150 Ice Hockey Goalie	12.50	25.00

1911-12 C55

The C55 Hockey set, probably issued during the 1911-12 season, contains 45 numbered cards. Being one of the early Canadian cigarette cards, the issuer of this set is unknown, although there is speculation that it may have been Imperial Tobacco. These small cards measure approximately 1 1/2" by 2 1/2". The line drawing, color portrait on the front of the card is framed by two hockey sticks. The number of the card appears on both the front and back as does the player's name. The players in the set were members of the NHA: Quebec Bulldogs, Ottawa Senators, Montreal Canadiens, Montreal Wanderers, and Renfrew Millionaires. This set is prized highly by collectors but is the easiest of the three early sets (C55, C56, or C57) to find. The complete set price includes either variety of the Small variation.

Card	Low	High
COMPLETE SET (45)	7500.00	15000.00
1 Paddy Moran	300.00	600.00
2 Joe Hall RC	250.00	500.00
3 Barney Holden	150.00	250.00
4 Joe Malone RC	500.00	1000.00
5 Ed Oatman RC	150.00	250.00
6 Tom Dunderdale	200.00	350.00
7 Ken Mallen RC	150.00	250.00
8 Jack MacDonald RC	150.00	250.00
9 Fred Lake	150.00	250.00
10 Albert Kerr RC	175.00	300.00
11 Marty Walsh	175.00	300.00
12 Hamby Shore RC	150.00	250.00
13 Alex Currie RC	150.00	250.00
14 Bruce Ridpath	175.00	300.00
15 Bruce Stuart	175.00	300.00
16 Percy Lesueur	175.00	300.00
17 Jack Darragh RC	250.00	400.00
18 Steve Vair RC	150.00	250.00
19 Don Smith RC	150.00	250.00
20 Cyclone Taylor	600.00	1200.00
21 Bert Lindsay RC	175.00	300.00
22 H.L. Gilmour RC	175.00	300.00
23 Bobby Rowe RC	150.00	250.00
24 Sprague Cleghorn RC	250.00	500.00
25 Odie Cleghorn RC	175.00	300.00
26 Skene Ronan RC	150.00	250.00
27A Walter Smaill RC	350.00	700.00
27B Walter Smaill RC	400.00	800.00
28 Ernest Johnson	250.00	400.00
29 Jack Marshall	175.00	300.00
30 Harry Hyland	175.00	300.00
31 Art Ross	750.00	1500.00
32 Riley Hern	175.00	300.00
33 Gordon Roberts	250.00	400.00
34 Frank Glass	150.00	250.00
35 Ernest Russell	250.00	400.00
36 James Gardner UER RC	175.00	300.00
37 Art Bernier	150.00	250.00
38 Georges Vezina RC	3000.00	6000.00
39 Henri Dallaire RC	175.00	300.00
40 R.(Rocket) Power RC	175.00	300.00
41 Didier Pitre	175.00	300.00
42 Newsy Lalonde	750.00	1500.00
43 Eugene Payan RC	150.00	250.00
44 George Poulin RC	150.00	250.00
45 Jack Laviolette	250.00	400.00

1910-11 C56

One of the first hockey sets to appear (circa 1910-11), this full-color set of unknown origin (although there is speculation that the issuer was Imperial Tobacco) features 36 cards. The card numbering appears in the upper left part of the front of the card. These small cards measure approximately 1 1/2" by 2 5/8". The player's name and affiliation appear at the bottom within the border. The backs feature the player's name and career affiliations below crossed hockey sticks, a puck and the words "Hockey Series." In 2007, three copies of card number 37 Newsy Lalonde were discovered along with the printing stone that was used to print these cards from 1910. It's not known exactly how many copies were produced, but three is the most common number used.

Card	Low	High
COMPLETE SET (36)	5000.00	10000.00
1 Frank Patrick RC	500.00	800.00
2 Percy Lesueur RC	300.00	500.00
3 Gordon Roberts RC	150.00	300.00
4 Barney Holden RC	100.00	200.00
5 Frank Glass RC	100.00	200.00
6 Edgar Dey RC	100.00	200.00
7 Marty Walsh RC	150.00	300.00
8 Art Ross RC	500.00	1000.00
9 Angus Campbell RC	125.00	250.00
10 Harry Hyland RC	175.00	350.00
11 Herb Clark RC	75.00	150.00
12 Art Ross RC	500.00	1000.00
13 Ed Decary RC	75.00	150.00
14 Tom Dunderdale RC	200.00	400.00
15 Cyclone Taylor RC	800.00	1200.00
16 Joseph Cattarinich RC	100.00	200.00
17 Bruce Stuart RC	175.00	350.00
18 Nick Bawlf RC	75.00	150.00
19 Joseph Jones RC	100.00	200.00
20 Ernest Russell RC	175.00	350.00
21 Jack Laviolette RC	125.00	250.00
22 Riley Hern RC	150.00	300.00
23 Didier Pitre RC	150.00	300.00
24 Skinner Poulin RC	75.00	150.00
25 Art Bernier RC	75.00	150.00
26 Lester Patrick RC	400.00	700.00
27 Fred Lake RC	75.00	150.00
28 Paddy Moran RC	300.00	600.00
29 C.Toms RC	75.00	150.00
30 Ernest Johnson RC	275.00	550.00
31 Horace Gaul RC	75.00	150.00
32 Harold McNamara RC	75.00	150.00
33 Jack Marshall RC	125.00	250.00
34 Bruce Ridpath RC	75.00	150.00
35 Jack Marshall RC	125.00	250.00
36 Newsy Lalonde RC	500.00	1000.00
37 Newsy Lalonde		

1912-13 C57

This set of 50 black and white cards was produced circa 1912-13. These small cards measure approximately 1 1/2" by 2 5/8". The player's name and affiliation are printed on both the front and back. The card number appears on the back only with the words "Series of 50." Although the origin of the set is unknown, it is safe to assume that the producer who issued the C56 series issued this as well, as the backs of the cards are quite similar. A brief career outline in English is contained on the back. This set is considered to be the toughest to find of the three early hockey sets.

Card	Low	High
COMPLETE SET (50)	12000.00	20000.00
1 Georges Vezina	2500.00	5000.00
2 Punch Broadbent RC	350.00	600.00
3 Clint Benedict RC	350.00	600.00
4 A. Atchinson RC	150.00	300.00
5 Tom Dunderdale	200.00	400.00
6 Art Bernier	150.00	300.00
7 Henri Dallaire	150.00	300.00
8 George Poulin	150.00	300.00
9 Eugene Payan	150.00	300.00
10 Steve Vair	150.00	300.00
11 Bobby Rowe	150.00	300.00
12 Don Smith	150.00	300.00
13 Bert Lindsay	150.00	300.00
14 Skene Ronan	150.00	300.00
15 Sprague Cleghorn	350.00	600.00
16 Joe Hall	200.00	400.00
17 Jack MacDonald	150.00	300.00
18 Paddy Moran	300.00	500.00
19 Harry Hyland	150.00	300.00
20 Art Ross	800.00	1200.00
21 Frank Glass	150.00	300.00
22 Walter Smaill	150.00	300.00
23 Gordon Roberts	150.00	300.00
24 James Gardner	200.00	400.00
25 Ernest Johnson	200.00	400.00
26 Ernie Russell	200.00	400.00
27 Percy Lesueur	300.00	500.00
28 Bruce Ridpath	150.00	300.00
29 Jack Darragh	200.00	400.00
30 Hamby Shore	150.00	300.00
31 Fred Lake	150.00	300.00
32 Alex Currie	150.00	300.00
33 Albert Kerr	150.00	300.00
34 Eddie Gerard RC	200.00	400.00
35 Carl Kendall RC	150.00	300.00
36 Jack Fournier RC	150.00	300.00
37 Goldie Prodgers RC	200.00	400.00
38 Jack Marks RC	150.00	300.00
39 George Broughton RC	150.00	300.00
40 Arthur Boyce RC	150.00	300.00
41 Lester Patrick	500.00	1000.00
42 Joe Dennison RC	150.00	300.00
43 Cyclone Taylor	700.00	1200.00
44 Newsy Lalonde	800.00	1200.00
45 Didier Pitre	150.00	300.00
46 Jack Laviolette	150.00	300.00
47 Ed Oatman	150.00	300.00
48 Joe Malone	500.00	1000.00
49 Marty Walsh	300.00	600.00
50 Odie Cleghorn	400.00	1000.00

1912 Imperial Tobacco Lacrosse C61

This set, produced by Imperial Tobacco, features prominent lacrosse stars of the day, but is included in this book because it features several prominent hockey players of the day, including Newsy Lalonde, Jack Laviolette and Clint Benedict.

Card	Low	High
1 Charlie Querrie	150.00	400.00
2 Dolly Durkin	60.00	150.00
3 Fred Rowntree	60.00	150.00
4 Fred Graydon	60.00	150.00
5 Kid Kinsman	60.00	150.00
6 Al Dade	60.00	150.00
7 Jimmy Hogan	60.00	150.00
8 A. Kenna	60.00	150.00
9 W. O'Kane	60.00	150.00
10 F. Scott	60.00	150.00
11 Newsy Lalonde	500.00	800.00
12 Mickey Ions	100.00	200.00
13 Mag MacGregor	60.00	150.00
14 Dot Phelan	60.00	150.00
15 Spike Griffiths	60.00	150.00
16 Whitey Eastwood	60.00	150.00
17 Red McCarthy	60.00	150.00
18 Jack Shea	60.00	150.00
19 Clint Benedict	250.00	500.00
20 Bobby Pringle	60.00	150.00
21 A. Ranson	60.00	150.00
22 Lawrence Degray	60.00	150.00
23 Francis Cummings	60.00	150.00
24 Fred Degan	60.00	150.00
25 Don Cameron	60.00	150.00
26 James Gifford	60.00	150.00
27 Archie Hall	60.00	150.00
28 W. Turnbull	60.00	150.00
29 Punk Wintermute	60.00	150.00
30 Tom Gifford	60.00	150.00
31 O. Secours	60.00	150.00
32 Dr. Lachapelle	60.00	150.00
33 Joe Cattarinich	100.00	200.00
34 Dare Devil Gauthier	60.00	150.00
35 Jack Laviolette	100.00	200.00
36 George Roberts	60.00	150.00
37 Steve Rochford	60.00	150.00
38 Henry Scott	60.00	150.00
39 J. McIlwane	60.00	150.00
40 Nick Neville	60.00	150.00
41 P.J. Brennan	60.00	150.00
42 Howie McIntyre	60.00	150.00
43 Gus Dillon	60.00	150.00
44 J. Barry	60.00	150.00
45 Johnny Howard	60.00	150.00
46 Eddie Powers	60.00	150.00
47 Art Warwick	60.00	150.00
48 Ernie Menary	60.00	150.00
49 Georgie Kalls	60.00	150.00
50 Fred Stagg	60.00	150.00

1924-25 C144 Champ's Cigarettes

This unnumbered 60-card set was issued during the 1924-25 season by Champ's Cigarettes. There is a brief biography on the card back written in English. The cards are sepia tone and measure approximately 1 1/2" by 2 1/2". Since the cards are unnumbered, they are checklisted in alphabetical order by subject.

Card	Low	High
COMPLETE SET (60)	10000.00	20000.00
1 Jack Adams	150.00	250.00
2 Lloyd Andrews RC	125.00	200.00
3 Clint Benedict	250.00	400.00
4 Louis Berlinquette RC	125.00	200.00
5 Eddie Bouchard	125.00	200.00
6 Billy Boucher	150.00	250.00
7 Bob Boucher RC	125.00	200.00
8 Punch Broadbent	200.00	350.00
9 Billy Burch	200.00	350.00
10 Dutch Cain RC	125.00	200.00
11 Earl Campbell RC	125.00	200.00
12 George Carroll RC	125.00	200.00
13 King Clancy	1000.00	1750.00
14 Odie Cleghorn	150.00	250.00
15 Sprague Cleghorn	250.00	400.00
16 Alex Connell RC	250.00	400.00
17 Carson Cooper RC	125.00	200.00
18 Bert Corbeau	150.00	250.00
19 Billy Coutu	125.00	200.00
20 Hap Day RC	250.00	400.00
21 Cy Denneny	200.00	350.00
22 Charlie Dinsmore RC	125.00	200.00
23 Babe Dye	200.00	350.00
24 Frank Finnigan RC	200.00	350.00
25 Vernon Forbes	125.00	200.00
26 Norman Hec Fowler RC	150.00	250.00
27 Red Green	125.00	200.00
28 Shorty Green	200.00	350.00
29 Curly Headley RC	125.00	200.00
30 Jim Herberts RC	125.00	200.00
31 Fred Hitchman RC	125.00	200.00
32 Albert Holway RC	125.00	200.00
33 Stan Jackson	125.00	200.00
34 Aurel Joliat	800.00	1400.00
35 Louis C. Langlois RC	125.00	200.00
36 Fred Lowrey RC	125.00	200.00
37 Sylvio Mantha	200.00	350.00
38 Albert McCaffrey RC	125.00	200.00
39 Robert McKinnon RC	125.00	200.00
40 Herbie Mitchell RC	125.00	200.00
41 Howie Morenz	2000.00	3500.00
42 Dunc Munro RC	150.00	250.00
43 Gerald J.M. Munro RC	125.00	200.00
44 Frank Nighbor	250.00	400.00
45 Reg Noble	200.00	350.00
46 Mickey O'Leary RC	125.00	200.00
47 Goldie Prodgers	125.00	200.00
48 Ken Randall	125.00	200.00
49 George Redding RC	125.00	200.00
50 John Ross Roach	150.00	250.00
51 Mickey Roach	125.00	200.00
52 Sam Rothschild RC	150.00	250.00
53 Werner Schnarr RC	125.00	200.00
54 Ganton Scott RC	125.00	200.00
55 Alf Skinner RC	125.00	200.00
56 Hooley Smith RC	200.00	350.00
57 Chris Speyers RC	125.00	200.00
58 Jesse Spring	125.00	200.00
59 The Stanley Cup	350.00	600.00
60 Georges Vezina	1200.00	2000.00

1932 Briggs Chocolate

This set was issued by C.A. Briggs Chocolate company in 1932. The cards feature 31-different sports with each card including an artist's rendering of a sporting event. Although players are not named, it is thought that most were modeled after famous athletes of the time. The cardbacks include a written portion about the sport and an offer from Briggs for free baseball equipment for building a compete set of cards.

Card	Low	High
2 Hockey	125.00	250.00

1930 Campbell's Soup

Measures approximately 2" x 7" and is black and white. Lower portion of card features a Campbell's slogan. The player pictured is unidentified.

Card	Low	High
COMPLETE SET (1)	50.00	100.00
NNO Hockey Player	50.00	100.00

1994-95 Canada Games NHL POGS

Produced by Canada Games Company Limited, this set includes 376 POGS and 8 checklist cards. Each POG measures 1 5/8" in diameter; the checklist cards measure 2 3/8" by 3 1/2". Each cello pack featured 5 POGS and one checklist card; also one in every five packs contained a bonus kini. The fronts display color action head shots framed by foil and color geometric designs. The team name, player's name, and his position are printed on the fronts. In black on white, the backs carry biography, 1993-94 season statistics, NHL totals, and various logos. The POGS are numbered on the back.

Card	Low	High
COMPLETE SET (376)	40.00	100.00
1 Kini-Kings	.20	.50
2 Kini-Rangers	.20	.50
3 Kini-Penguins	.20	.50
4 Kini-Stars	.20	.50
5 Kini-Senators	.20	.50
6 Kini-Jets	.20	.50
7 Kini-Canucks	.20	.50
8 Kini-Capitals	.20	.50
9 Kini-Ducks	.20	.50
10 Kini-Bruins	.20	.50
11 Kini-Sabres	.20	.50
12 Kini-Flames	.20	.50
13 Kini-Blackhawks	.20	.50
14 Kini-Red Wings	.20	.50
15 Kini-Oilers	.20	.50
16 Kini-Panthers	.20	.50
17 Kini-Whalers	.20	.50
18 Kini-Canadiens	.20	.50
19 Kini-Devils	.20	.50
20 Kini-Islanders	.20	.50
21 Kini-Flyers	.20	.50
22 Kini-Nordiques	.20	.50
23 Kini-Sharks	.20	.50
24 Kini-Blues	.20	.50
25 Kini-Lightning	.20	.50
26 Kini-Leafs	.20	.50
27 Cliff Ronning	.02	.10
28 Bob Corkum	.02	.10
29 Joe Sacco	.02	.10
30 Peter Douris	.02	.10
31 Shaun Van Allen	.02	.10
32 Stephan Lebeau	.02	.10
33 Stu Grimson	.02	.10
34 Tim Sweeney	.02	.10
35 Adam Oates	.20	.50
36 Al Iafrate	.05	.15
37 Alexei Kastanov	.02	.10
38 Bryan Smolinski	.08	.25
39 Cam Neely	.30	.75
40 Don Sweeney	.02	.10
41 Glen Murray	.02	.10
42 Ray Bourque	.40	1.00
43 Ted Donato	.02	.10
44 Alexander Mogilny	.40	1.00
45 Doug Gilmour	.40	1.00
46 Dale Hawerchuk	.20	.50
47 Derek Plante	.08	.25
48 Donald Audette	.08	.25
49 Doug Bodger	.02	.10
50 Pat LaFontaine	.20	.50
51 Randy Wood	.02	.10
52 Richard Smehlik	.02	.10
53 Yuri Khmylev	.02	.10
54 Theo Fleury	.30	.75
55 Kelly Kisio	.02	.10
56 Joe Nieuwendyk	.08	.25
57 Michael Nylander	.02	.10
58 Joel Otto	.02	.10
59 James Patrick	.02	.10
60 Robert Reichel	.08	.25
61 Gary Roberts	.08	.25
62 Wes Walz	.02	.10
63 Ulf Dahlen	.02	.10
64 Zarley Zalapski	.02	.10
65 Tony Amonte	.30	.75
66 Dirk Graham	.02	.10
67 Joe Murphy	.05	.15
68 Bernie Nicholls	.08	.25
69 Patrick Poulin	.02	.10
70 Jeremy Roenick	.40	1.00
71 Christian Ruutu	.02	.10
72 Brent Sutter	.02	.10
73 Chris Chelios	.60	1.50
74 Steve Smith	.02	.10
75 Gary Suter	.02	.10
76 Neil Broten	.05	.15
77 Russ Courtnall	.02	.10
78 Dean Evason	.02	.10
79 Dave Gagner	.05	.15
80 Mike McPhee	.02	.10
81 Mike Modano	.30	.75
82 Paul Cavallini	.02	.10
83 Derian Hatcher	.02	.10
84 Grant Ledyard	.02	.10
85 Mark Tinordi	.02	.10
86 Dino Ciccarelli	.15	.40
87 Sergei Fedorov	1.25	3.00
88 Slava Kozlov	.08	.25
89 Darren McCarty	.08	.25
90 Keith Primeau	.08	.25
91 Ray Sheppard	.08	.25
92 Steve Yzerman	2.00	5.00
93 Paul Coffey	.40	1.00
94 Vladimir Konstantinov	.02	.10
95 Nicklas Lidstrom	.15	.40
96 Greg Adams	.02	.10
97 Jason Arnott	.30	.75
98 Kelly Buchberger	.02	.10
99 Shayne Corson	.02	.10
100 Scott Pearson	.02	.10
101 Doug Weight	.20	.50
102 Boris Mironov	.08	.25
103 Fredrik Olausson	.02	.10
104 Stu Barnes	.02	.10
105 Bob Kudelski	.02	.10
106 Andrei Lomakin	.02	.10
107 Dave Lowry	.02	.10
108 Scott Mellanby	.08	.25
109 Rob Niedermayer	.20	.50
110 Brian Skrudland	.02	.10
111 Brian Benning	.02	.10
112 Gord Murphy	.02	.10
113 Andrew Cassels	.02	.10
114 Robert Kron	.02	.10
115 Jocelyn Lemieux	.02	.10
116 Paul Ranheim	.02	.10
117 Geoff Sanderson	.20	.50
118 Jim Sandlak	.02	.10
119 Darren Turcotte	.02	.10
120 Pat Verbeek	.08	.25
121 Chris Pronger	.15	.40
122 Pat Conacher	.02	.10
123 Mike Donnelly	.04	.10
124 John Druce	.02	.10
125 Tony Granato	.05	.15
126 Wayne Gretzky	4.00	10.00
127 Jari Kurri	.08	.25
128 Warren Rychel	.02	.10
129 Rob Blake	.07	.20
130 Marty McSorley	.08	.25
131 Alexei Zhitnik	.02	.10
132 Brian Bellows	.02	.10
133 Vince Damphousse	.20	.50
134 Gilbert Dionne	.02	.10
135 Mike Keane	.02	.10
136 John LeClair	1.00	2.50
137 Kirk Muller	.08	.25
138 Oleg Petrov	.02	.10
139 Eric Desjardins	.02	.10
140 Lyle Odelein	.02	.10
141 Peter Popovic	.02	.10
142 Mathieu Schneider	.02	.10
143 Trent Klatt	.02	.10
144 Bobby Holik	.02	.10
145 Claude Lemieux	.15	.40
146 John MacLean	.07	.20
147 Corey Millen	.02	.10
148 Stephane Richer	.05	.15
149 Valeri Zelepukin	.02	.10
150 Bruce Driver	.02	.10
151 Gino Odjick	.02	.10
152 Scott Stevens	.08	.25
153 Brad Dalgarno	.02	.10
154 Ray Ferraro	.02	.10
155 Pat Flatley	.02	.10
156 Travis Green	.05	.15
157 Derek King	.02	.10
158 Marty McInnis	.02	.10
159 Steve Thomas	.08	.25
160 Pierre Turgeon	.20	.50
161 Darius Kasparaitis	.02	.10
162 Vladimir Malakhov	.02	.10
163 Alexei Kovalev	.08	.25
164 Steve Larmer	.08	.25
165 Stephane Matteau	.02	.10
166 Mark Messier	.75	2.00
167 Sergei Nemchinov	.02	.10
168 Brian Noonan	.02	.10
169 Petr Nedved	.08	.25
170 Brian Leetch	.60	1.50
171 Kevin Lowe	.02	.10
172 Sergei Zurbov	.02	.10
173 Sylvain Turgeon	.02	.10
174 Alexei Yashin	.20	.50
175 Norm Maciver	.02	.10
176 Brad Shaw	.02	.10
177 Brent Fedyk	.02	.10
178 Mark Lamb	.02	.10
179 Don McSween	.02	.10
180 Mark Recchi	.20	.50
181 Mikael Renberg	.30	.75
182 Gary Galley	.02	.10
183 Ron Francis	.20	.50
184 Jaromir Jagr	2.00	5.00
185 Mario Lemieux	3.00	8.00
186 Shawn McEachern	.02	.10
187 Joe Mullen	.07	.20
188 Tomas Sandstrom	.05	.15
189 Kevin Stevens	.07	.20
190 Martin Straka	.02	.10
191 Larry Murphy	.08	.25
192 Kjell Samuelsson	.02	.10
193 Ulf Samuelsson	.02	.10
194 Wendel Clark	.15	.40
195 Valeri Kamensky	.15	.40
196 Andrei Kovalenko	.02	.10
197 Owen Nolan	.20	.50
198 Mike Ricci	.02	.10
199 Joe Sakic	1.25	3.00
200 Scott Young	.02	.10
201 Uwe Krupp	.02	.10
202 Curtis Leschyshyn	.02	.10
203 Brett Hull	.75	2.00
204 Craig Janney	.08	.25
205 Kevin Miller	.02	.10
206 Vitali Prokhorov	.02	.10
207 Brendan Shanahan	1.25	3.00
208 Peter Stastny	.08	.25
209 Esa Tikkanen	.07	.20
210 Steve Duchesne	.02	.10
211 Gaeten Duchesne	.02	.10
212 Todd Elik	.02	.10
213 Pogman	.20	.50
214 Pat Falloon	.02	.10
215 Johan Garpenlov	.02	.10
216 Igor Larionov	.08	.25
217 Sergei Makarov	.05	.15
218 Jeff Norton	.02	.10
219 Sandis Ozolinsh	.20	.50
220 Mikael Andersson	.02	.10
221 Brian Bradley	.08	.25
222 Danton Cole	.02	.10
223 Chris Gratton	.20	.50
224 Petr Klima	.02	.10
225 Denis Savard	.08	.25
226 John Tucker	.02	.10
227 Shawn Chambers	.02	.10
228 Chris Joseph	.02	.10
229 Dave Andreychuk	.08	.25
230 Nikolai Borschevsky	.02	.10
231 Mike Craig	.02	.10
232 Mike Eastwood	.02	.10
233 Mike Gartner	.20	.50
234 Doug Gilmour	.40	1.00
235 Kent Manderville	.02	.10
236 Mike Ridley	.02	.10
237 Mats Sundin	.30	.75
238 Dave Ellett	.02	.10
239 Todd Gill	.02	.10
240 Jamie Macoun	.02	.10
241 Dmitri Mironov	.02	.10
242 Peter Bondra	.40	1.00
243 Randy Burridge	.02	.10
244 Dale Hunter	.02	.10
245 Joe Juneau	.15	.40
246 Dmitri Khristich	.08	.25
247 Kelly Miller	.02	.10
248 Michal Pivonka	.02	.10
249 Sylvain Cote	.02	.10
250 Tie Domi	.20	.50
251 Dallas Drake	.02	.10
252 Nelson Emerson	.02	.10
253 Teemu Selanne	1.25	3.00
254 Darrin Shannon	.02	.10
255 Thomas Steen	.02	.10
256 Keith Tkachuk	.60	1.50
257 Dave Manson	.02	.10
258 Stephane Quintal	.02	.10
259 Adam Graves AS	.08	.25
260 Brian Leetch AS	.40	1.00
261 John Vanbiesbrouck AS	.60	1.50
262 Scott Stevens AS	.08	.25
263 Ray Bourque AS	.40	1.00
264 Al MacInnis AS	.08	.25
265 Brendan Shanahan AS	1.25	3.00
266 Pavel Bure AS	1.50	4.00
267 Sergei Fedorov AS	1.25	3.00
268 Wayne Gretzky AS	4.00	10.00
269 Guy Hebert	.20	.50
270 Kirk McLean	.20	.50
271 John Blue	.08	.25
272 Vincent Riendeau	.08	.25
273 Grant Fuhr	.20	.50
274 Dominik Hasek	1.25	3.00
275 Trevor Kidd	.15	.40
276 Ed Belfour	.60	1.50
277 Andy Moog	.20	.50
278 Mike Vernon	.20	.50
279 Bill Ranford	.20	.50
280 John Vanbiesbrouck	1.00	2.50
281 Sean Burke	.20	.50
282 Kelly Hrudey	.20	.50
283 Patrick Roy	3.00	8.00
284 Martin Brodeur	1.50	4.00
285 Chris Terreri	.05	.15
286 Jamie McLennan	.07	.20
287 Glenn Healy	.08	.25
288 Mike Richter	.60	1.50
289 Craig Billington	.08	.25
290 Dominic Roussel	.07	.20
291 Tom Barrasso	.08	.25
292 Stephane Fiset	.08	.25
293 Curtis Joseph	.75	2.00
294 Arturs Irbe	.40	1.00
295 Daren Puppa	.20	.50
296 Felix Potvin	.60	1.50
297 Tim Cheveldae	.08	.25
298 Don Beaupre	.08	.25
299 Rick Tabaracci	.07	.20
300 Anaheim Mighty Ducks	.15	.40
301 Boston Bruins	.15	.40
302 Buffalo Sabres	.02	.10
303 Calgary Flames	.02	.10
304 Chicago Blackhawks	.08	.25
305 Dallas Stars	.02	.10
306 Detroit Red Wings	.15	.40
307 Edmonton Oilers	.02	.10
308 Florida Panthers	.02	.10
309 Hartford Whalers	.02	.10
310 Los Angeles Kings	.15	.40
311 Montreal Canadiens	.15	.40
312 New Jersey Devils	.02	.10
313 Jeff Brown	.02	.10
314 New York Rangers	.15	.40
315 Ottawa Senators	.02	.10
316 Philadelphia Flyers	.02	.10
317 Pittsburgh Penguins	.02	.10
318 Quebec Nordiques	.02	.10
319 St. Louis Blues	.02	.10
320 San Jose Sharks	.08	.25
321 Tampa Bay Lightning	.02	.10
322 Toronto Maple Leafs	.08	.25
323 Vancouver Canucks	.02	.10
324 Washington Capitals	.02	.10
325 Winnipeg Jets	.02	.10
326 Calder Trophy	1.50	4.00
327 Norris Trophy	.40	1.00
328 Game Winning Goals	.30	.75
329 Geoff Courtnall	.02	.10
330 Pogman	.20	.50
331 Art Ross Trophy	1.25	3.00
332 Vezina Trophy	1.25	3.00
333 Jennings Trophy	1.25	3.00
334 Brian Leetch	.40	1.00
335 Martin Gelinas	.07	.20
336 Cam Neely	.20	.50
337 Mike Richter	.60	1.50
338 Luke Richardson	.02	.10
339 Jyrkki Lumme	.02	.10
340 Nathan Lafayette	.02	.10
341 Pavel Bure	1.00	2.50
342 Sergio Momesso	.02	.10
343 Trevor Linden	.20	.50
344 Tie Domi	.15	.40
345 Scott Stevens	.08	.25
346 Teppo Numminen	.02	.10
347 Anatoli Semenov	.02	.10
348 Steve Heinze	.02	.10

349 Tom Chorske .02 .10
350 Bill Guerin .07 .20
351 Scott Niedermayer .08 .25
352 Adam Graves .08 .25
353 Alexandre Daigle .20 .50
354 Troy Mallette .02 .10
355 Dave McLlwain .02 .10
356 Josef Beranek .02 .10
357 Kevin Dineen .02 .10
358 Eric Lindros 1.50 4.00
359 Bob Rouse .02 .10
360 Sergei Fedorov AW 1.25 3.00
361 Bob Errey .02 .10
362 Brad May .02 .10
363 Kevin Hatcher .02 .10
364 New York Islanders .02 .10
365 Randy Ladouceur .02 .10
366 Bobby Dollas .02 .10
367 Igor Kravchuk .02 .10
368 Jesse Belanger .02 .10
369 Pogman .20 .50
370 Gary Valk .02 .10
371 Pogman .20 .50
372 Ron Hextall .20 .50
373 Rod Brind'Amour .20 .50
374 Benoit Hogue .02 .10
375 Alexei Zhamnov .08 .25
376 Goal Scoring Leader 1.50 4.00
NNO Checklist 1-47 .02 .10
NNO Checklist 48-94 .02 .10
NNO Checklist 95-141 .02 .10
NNO Checklist 142-188 .02 .10
NNO Checklist 189-235 .02 .10
NNO Checklist 236-282 .02 .10
NNO Checklist 283-329 .02 .10
NNO Checklist 330-376 .02 .10

1995-96 Canada Games NHL POGS

This set of 296 POGS was produced by Canada Games. The POGS were distributed in packs of five, with every fifth pack containing a bonus Kini. These Kinis are listed at the end of the checklist with a K-prefix. They do not picture the trophy mentioned. The POGS themselves feature a colorful action shot of the player, while the backs feature abbreviated stats.

COMPLETE SET (296) 32.00 80.00
1 Wayne Gretzky 2.50 6.00
2 Mario Lemieux 2.00 5.00
3 Cam Neely .40 1.00
4 Ray Bourque .75 2.00
5 Patrick Roy 1.50 4.00
6 Mark Messier .50 1.25
7 Brett Hull .50 1.25
8 Grant Fuhr .30 .75
9 Eric Lindros 1.00 2.50
10 John LeClair .60 1.50
11 Jaromir Jagr 1.25 3.00
12 Chris Chelios .40 1.00
13 Paul Coffey .40 1.00
14 Dominik Hasek .75 2.00
15 Alexei Zhamnov .30 .75
16 Keith Tkachuk .40 1.00
17 Theo Fleury .40 1.00
18 Ray Bourque .75 2.00
19 Larry Murphy .30 .75
20 Ed Belfour .40 1.00
21 Pavel Bure 1.00 2.50
22 Doug Gilmour .40 1.00
23 Brett Hull .50 1.25
24 Mark Messier .50 1.25
25 Cam Neely .40 1.00
26 Jeremy Roenick .40 1.00
27 Patrick Roy 1.50 4.00
28 Jim Carey .30 .75
29 Peter Forsberg 1.00 2.50
30 Jeff Friesen .02 .10
31 Kenny Jonsson .30 .75
32 Paul Kariya 1.25 3.00
33 Ian Laperriere .02 .10
34 David Oliver .02 .10
35 Kyle McLaren .30 .75
36 Ray Bourque .50 1.25
37 Alexei Kasatonov .02 .10
38 Blaine Lacher .30 .75
39 Brian Holzinger .30 .75
40 Derek Plante .02 .10
41 Mike Peca .02 .10
42 Pat LaFontaine .40 1.00
43 Jason Dawe .02 .10
44 Brad May .02 .10
45 Yuri Khmylev .02 .10
46 Garry Galley .02 .10
47 Alexei Zhitnik .02 .10
48 Dominik Hasek .75 2.00
49 Joe Nieuwendyk .30 .75
50 German Titov .02 .10
51 Cory Stillman .02 .10
52 Theo Fleury .40 1.00
53 Paul Kruse .02 .10
54 Michael Nylander .02 .10
55 Gary Roberts .02 .10
56 Phil Housley .02 .10
57 Steve Chiasson .02 .10
58 Zarley Zalapski .02 .10
59 Ron Stern .02 .10
60 Trevor Kidd .30 .75
61 Jeremy Roenick .40 1.00
62 Denis Savard .40 1.00
63 Tony Amonte .40 1.00
64 Bernie Nicholls .02 .10
65 Sergei Krivokrasov .02 .10
66 Joe Murphy .02 .10
67 Patrick Poulin .02 .10
68 Bob Probert .30 .75
69 Gary Suter .02 .10
70 Chris Chelios .40 1.00
71 Ed Belfour .40 1.00
72 Joe Sakic .75 2.00
73 Mike Ricci .02 .10
74 Valeri Kamensky .30 .75
75 Andrei Kovalenko .02 .10
76 Owen Nolan .30 .75
77 Peter Forsberg 1.00 2.50
78 Scott Young .02 .10
79 Uwe Krupp .02 .10
80 Curtis Leschyshyn .02 .10
81 Adam Deadmarsh .30 .75
82 Stephane Fiset .30 .75
83 Bob Bassen .02 .10
84 Corey Millen .02 .10
85 Mike Modano .50 1.25
86 Dave Gagner .30 .75
87 Mike Donnelly .02 .10
88 Trent Klatt .02 .10
89 Kevin Hatcher .02 .10
90 Grant Ledyard .02 .10
91 Greg Adams .02 .10
92 Andy Moog .30 .75
93 Keith Primeau .30 .75
94 Kris Draper .02 .10
95 Sergei Fedorov .75 2.00
96 Steve Yzerman 1.25 3.00
97 Vyacheslav Kozlov .02 .10
98 Ray Sheppard .30 .75
99 Dino Ciccarelli .30 .75
100 Slava Fetisov .02 .10
101 Nicklas Lidstrom .40 1.00
102 Paul Coffey .40 1.00
103 Darren McCarty .30 .75
104 Mike Vernon .30 .75
105 Doug Weight .30 .75
106 Jason Arnott .30 .75
107 Todd Marchant .02 .10
108 David Oliver .02 .10
109 Igor Kravchuk .02 .10
110 Jiri Slegr .02 .10
111 Kelly Buchberger .02 .10
112 Scott Thornton .02 .10
113 Bill Ranford .30 .75
114 Jesse Belanger .02 .10
115 Stu Barnes .02 .10
116 Scott Mellanby .30 .75
117 Bill Lindsay .02 .10
118 Dave Lowry .02 .10
119 Gaetan Duchesne .02 .10
120 Johan Garpenlov .02 .10
121 Paul Laus .02 .10
122 Gord Murphy .02 .10
123 John Vanbiesbrouck .40 1.00
124 Andrew Cassels .02 .10
125 Geoff Sanderson .30 .75
126 Brendan Shanahan .75 2.00
127 Paul Ranheim .02 .10
128 Steven Rice .02 .10
129 Frantisek Kucera .02 .10
130 Glen Wesley .02 .10
131 Sean Burke .30 .75
132 Wayne Gretzky 2.50 6.00
133 Dimitri Khristich .02 .10
134 Jari Kurri .30 .75
135 John Druce .02 .10
136 Pat Conacher .02 .10
137 Rick Tocchet .30 .75
138 Rob Blake .30 .75
139 Tony Granato .02 .10
140 Marty McSorley .30 .75
141 Darryl Sydor .30 .75
142 Eric Lacroix .02 .10
143 Kelly Hrudey .30 .75
144 Brian Savage .02 .10
145 Pierre Turgeon .30 .75
146 Benoit Brunet .02 .10
147 Valeri Bure .30 .75
148 Vincent Damphousse .30 .75
149 Mike Keane .02 .10
150 Mark Recchi .30 .75
151 Vladimir Malakhov .02 .10
152 Patrice Brisebois .02 .10
153 J.J. Daigneault .02 .10
154 Yves Racine .02 .10
155 Patrick Roy 1.50 4.00
156 Bob Carpenter .02 .10
157 Neal Broten .02 .10
158 Steve Thomas .30 .75
159 Bobby Holik .30 .75
160 John MacLean .30 .75
161 Mike Peluso .02 .10
162 Randy McKay .02 .10
163 Stephane Richer .30 .75
164 Scott Niedermayer .30 .75
165 Scott Stevens .30 .75
166 Bill Guerin .30 .75
167 Martin Brodeur 1.00 2.50
168 Kirk Muller .30 .75
169 Zigmund Palffy .40 1.00
170 Travis Green .02 .10
171 Brett Lindros .02 .10
172 Derek King .02 .10
173 Pat Flatley .02 .10
174 Wendel Clark .30 .75
175 Bryan McCabe .02 .10
176 Mathieu Schneider .02 .10
177 Eric Fichaud .30 .75
178 Ray Ferraro .02 .10
179 Adam Graves .30 .75
180 Mark Messier .50 1.25
181 Sergei Nemchinov .02 .10
182 Pat Verbeek .30 .75
183 Luc Robitaille .30 .75
184 Alexei Kovalev .30 .75
185 Jeff Beukeboom .02 .10
186 Brian Leetch .40 1.00
187 Ulf Samuelsson .02 .10
188 Alexander Karpovtsev .02 .10
189 Mike Richter .40 1.00
190 Alexandre Daigle .30 .75
191 Alexei Yashin .30 .75
192 Dan Quinn .02 .10
193 Martin Straka .02 .10
194 Radek Bonk .02 .10
195 Pavol Demitra .30 .75
196 Steve Duchesne .30 .75
197 Chris Dahlquist .02 .10
198 Sean Hill .02 .10
199 Stanislav Neckar .02 .10
200 Don Beaupre .30 .75
201 Eric Lindros 1.00 2.50
202 Rod Brind'Amour .30 .75
203 Shjon Podein .02 .10
204 Brent Fedyk .02 .10
205 Joel Otto .02 .10
206 John LeClair .60 1.50
207 Kevin Dineen .02 .10
208 Petr Svoboda .02 .10
209 Eric Desjardins .02 .10
210 Ron Hextall .30 .75
211 Mario Lemieux 2.00 5.00
212 Petr Nedved .30 .75
213 Bryan Smolinski .30 .75
214 Tomas Sandstrom .30 .75
215 Ron Francis .30 .75
216 Jaromir Jagr 1.25 3.00
217 Sergei Zubov .02 .10
218 Drake Berehowsky .02 .10
219 Dmitri Mironov .02 .10
220 Ken Wregget .30 .75
221 Tom Barrasso .30 .75
222 Igor Larionov .30 .75
223 Jeff Friesen .30 .75
224 Kevin Miller .02 .10
225 Ray Whitney .02 .10
226 Craig Janney .30 .75
227 Pat Falloon .02 .10
228 Ulf Dahlen .02 .10
229 Viktor Kozlov .02 .10
230 Michal Sykora .02 .10
231 Sandis Ozolinsh .30 .75
232 Jamie Baker .02 .10
233 Arturs Irbe .30 .75
234 Adam Creighton .02 .10
235 Ian Laperriere .02 .10
236 Brett Hull .50 1.25
237 Brian Noonan .02 .10
238 Dale Hawerchuk .30 .75
239 Esa Tikkanen .30 .75
240 Geoff Courtnall .02 .10
241 Shayne Corson .02 .10
242 Al MacInnis .30 .75
243 Chris Pronger .30 .75
244 Jeff Norton .02 .10
245 Grant Fuhr .30 .75
246 Brian Bradley .30 .75
247 Chris Gratton .30 .75
248 John Cullen .02 .10
249 John Tucker .02 .10
250 Paul Ysebaert .02 .10
251 Petr Klima .02 .10
252 Alexander Selivanov .02 .10
253 Brian Bellows .02 .10
254 Enrico Ciccone .02 .10
255 Roman Hamrlik .30 .75
256 Daren Puppa .30 .75
257 Doug Gilmour .40 1.00
258 Benoit Hogue .02 .10
259 Mats Sundin .40 1.00
260 Dave Andreychuk .30 .75
261 Mike Gartner .30 .75
262 Randy Wood .02 .10
263 Tie Domi .30 .75
264 Dave Ellett .02 .10
265 Todd Gill .02 .10
266 Larry Murphy .30 .75
267 Kenny Jonsson .30 .75
268 Felix Potvin .40 1.00
269 Cliff Ronning .30 .75
270 Mike Ridley .02 .10
271 Trevor Linden .30 .75
272 Alexander Mogilny .30 .75
273 Martin Gelinas .30 .75
274 Pavel Bure .75 2.00
275 Russ Courtnall .02 .10
276 Jeff Brown .02 .10
277 Jyrki Lumme .02 .10
278 Kirk McLean .30 .75
279 Steve Konowalchuk .02 .10
280 Kelly Miller .02 .10
281 Peter Bondra .40 1.00
282 Keith Jones .02 .10
283 Joe Juneau .30 .75
284 Mark Tinordi .02 .10
285 Calle Johansson .02 .10
286 Sergei Gonchar .02 .10
287 Jim Carey .30 .75
288 Dallas Drake .02 .10
289 Alexei Zhamnov .30 .75
290 Mike Eastwood .02 .10
291 Igor Korolev .02 .10
292 Teemu Selanne .75 2.00
293 Keith Tkachuk .40 1.00
294 Teppo Numminen .02 .10
295 Dave Manson .02 .10
296 Tim Cheveldae .30 .75
K1 Lester B. Pearson .30 .75
K2 Art Ross .30 .75
K3 Bill Masterton .30 .75
K4 Calder .30 .75
K5 Clarence S. Campbell .30 .75
K6 Conn Smythe .30 .75
K7 Frank J. Selke .30 .75
K8 Hart .30 .75
K9 Jack Adams .30 .75
K10 James Norris .30 .75
K11 King Clancy .30 .75
K12 Lady Byng .30 .75
K13 Prince of Wales .30 .75
K14 Stanley Cup .30 .75
K15 Vezina .30 .75
K16 William M. Jennings .30 .75

1983 Canadian National Juniors

This 21-card set features Canada's 1983 National Junior Team. The cards measure approximately 3 1/2" by 5" and feature on the fronts either color posed action shots or close-up photos, shot against a blue background. On a red card face, the photos are enclosed by white borders, and the upper right corner of the picture is cut off to allow space for the team logo. The backs are blank and the unnumbered cards are checklisted below in alphabetical order. The set includes early cards of Mario Lemieux, Steve Yzerman, Mike Vernon, Dave Andreychuk, and Pat Verbeek. Three other players on the team who were not at the photo session and therefore not represented in the set are Paul Boutillier, Marc Habscheid, and Brad Shaw. A large team card (approximately 5" by 10 1/4") featuring all the players (except Marc Habscheid) and coaches was also produced. A two-thirds size (measuring approximately 5" by 7 1/4") team card entitled Celebration '82 with Troy Murray holding the Championship Plate as well as a (7 1/4" by 10 1/4") '82 team card were also produced. These special oversized cards are not typically included as part of the complete set as listed and valued below.

COMPLETE SET (21) 50.00 125.00
1 Dave Andreychuk 3.00 8.00
2 Joe Cirella .75 2.00
3 Paul Cyr .40 1.00
4 Dale Derkatch .40 1.00
5 Mike Eagles .40 1.00
6 Pat Flatley UER .75 2.00
(Misspelled Flately)
7 Mario Gosselin .75 2.00
8 Gary Leeman .75 2.00
9 Mario Lemieux 30.00 75.00
10 Mark Morrison .40 1.00
11 James Patrick .75 2.00
12 Mike Sands .60 1.50
13 Gord Sherven .40 1.00
14 Tony Tanti .75 2.00
15 Larry Trader .40 1.00
16 Sylvain Turgeon .60 1.50
17 Pat Verbeek 3.00 8.00
18 Mike Vernon 3.00 8.00
19 Steve Yzerman 30.00 60.00
20 Checklist Card .20 .50
21 Title Card .20 .50
NNO Team Card 3.00 8.00
(Regular size
NNO Large Team Card 4.00 10.00
NNO Team Card '82 2.00 5.00
NNO Celebration '82 2.00 5.00
(Troy Murray

2003 Canada Post

Released in early 2003, this 24-card set, produced by Pacific Trading Cards, featured actual Canada Post stamps on the cards. Packs were sold exclusively at Canada Post offices and contained six cards.

COMPLETE SET (24) 30.00 60.00
1 Wayne Gretzky 4.00 10.00
2 Gordie Howe 3.00 8.00
3 Maurice Richard 2.00 5.00
4 Doug Harvey 1.25 3.00
5 Bobby Orr 3.00 8.00
6 Jacques Plante 1.50 4.00
7 Jean Beliveau 2.00 5.00
8 Terry Sawchuk 2.00 5.00
9 Eddie Shore 1.50 4.00
10 Denis Potvin 1.25 3.00
11 Bobby Hull 2.00 5.00
12 Syl Apps 1.25 3.00
13 Tim Horton 1.50 4.00
14 Guy Lafleur 1.50 4.00
15 Howie Morenz 1.50 4.00
16 Glenn Hall 1.50 4.00
17 Red Kelly 1.25 3.00
18 Phil Esposito 1.50 4.00
19 Frank Mahovlich 1.25 3.00
20 Ray Bourque 1.50 4.00
21 Serge Savard 1.25 3.00
22 Stan Mikita 1.25 3.00
23 Mike Bossy 1.25 3.00
24 Bill Durnan 1.50 4.00

2003 Canada Post Autographs

These autographed versions of the Canada Post cards were randomly inserted into packs. Each player signed just 100 cards.

COMPLETE SET (4) 150.00 300.00
7 Jean Beliveau 40.00 100.00
11 Bobby Hull 40.00 100.00
14 Guy Lafleur 40.00 80.00
16 Glenn Hall 30.00 60.00

2004 Canada Post

This 6-card set, produced by Pacific Trading Cards, updated the 2003 set and featured actual Canada Post stamps on the cards. Packs were sold exclusively at Canada Post offices.

COMPLETE SET (6) 6.00 15.00
25 Johnny Bower 1.50 4.00
26 Marcel Dionne 1.25 3.00
27 Ted Lindsay 1.25 3.00
28 Brad Park 1.25 3.00
29 Larry Robinson 1.00 2.50
30 Milt Schmidt 1.25 3.00

2004 Canada Post Autographs

Randomly inserted in Canada Post packs, found only at Canada Post outlets, at a rate of about 1:9 packs. It was reported that the autographs were limited to 300 sets.

COMPLETE SET (6) 150.00 250.00
1 Johnny Bower 25.00 50.00
2 Marcel Dionne 20.00 40.00
3 Larry Robinson 20.00 40.00
4 Milt Schmidt 20.00 40.00
5 Ted Lindsay 25.00 50.00
6 Brad Park 20.00 40.00

2005 Canada Post

This 6-card set, produced by Pacific Trading Cards, updated further the set that featured actual Canada Post stamps on the cards. Packs were sold exclusively at Canada Post offices.

COMPLETE SET (6) 6.00 15.00
31 Henri Richard 1.25 3.00
32 Grant Fuhr 1.50 4.00
33 Allan Stanley 1.00 2.50
34 Pierre Pilote 1.25 3.00
35 Bryan Trottier 1.50 4.00
36 John Bucyk 1.25 3.00

2005 Canada Post Autographs

This 6-card set was randomly inserted in Canada Post packs, found only at Canada Post outlets, at a rate of about 1:10 packs.

COMPLETE SET (6) 125.00 200.00
31 Henri Richard 12.00 30.00
32 Grant Fuhr 15.00 40.00
33 Allan Stanley 10.00 25.00
34 Pierre Pilote 15.00 40.00
35 Bryan Trottier 15.00 40.00
36 John Bucyk 15.00 40.00

2014 Canada Post Original 6 Defensemen

1 Doug Harvey 1.25 3.00
2 Tim Horton 1.25 3.00
3 Harry Howell 1.00 2.50
4 Red Kelly 1.00 2.50
5 Bobby Orr 1.50 4.00
6 Pierre Pilote 1.00 2.50

2015 Canada Post Great Canadian Goalies

1 Johnny Bower 1.00 2.50
2 Martin Brodeur 1.25 3.00
3 Ken Dryden 1.00 2.50
4 Tony Esposito 1.00 2.50
5 Bernie Parent 1.25 3.00
6 Gump Worsley 1.00 2.50

1992 Canadian Summer Olympics

Produced by Erin Maxx Cards (Toronto), this 263-card set features Canadian Summer Olympic hopefuls. The factory set was packaged in a serially-numbered large red collector's box. Fourteen-card packs were also issued. The fronts display full-bleed color or black-and-white photos accented by thin white lines that form a picture frame. The Canadian Olympic symbol appears in the upper left corner, while the player's name and event are printed on a white bar that forms the bottom of the picture frame. In a horizontal format, the bilingual backs have a closeup photo, biography, a personal note, and a list of athletic achievements.

COMPLETE SET (263) 3.00 8.00
136 Alain Cote .08 .25

2004 Canadian Women's World Championship Team

This oversized (3 3/4 by 5 1/4) series features players who competed for Team Canada at the 2004 World Women's Championships in Halifax. It's believed they were sold in set form at the event. The cards are unnumbered and so are listed in alphabetical order.

COMPLETE SET (22) 25.00
1 Dana Antal .40 1.00
2 Gillian Apps .60 1.50
3 Kelly Bechard .40 1.00
4 Jennifer Botterill .40 1.00
5 Therese Brisson .40 1.00
6 Cassie Campbell 1.25 3.00
7 Delaney Collins .40 1.00
8 Gillian Ferrari .40 1.00
9 Danielle Goyette .40 1.00
10 Jayna Hefford .75 2.00
11 Becky Kellar .40 1.00
12 Gina Kingsbury .40 1.00
13 Charline Labonte 1.25 3.00
14 Caroline Ouellette .40 1.00
15 Cherie Piper .40 1.00
16 Cheryl Pounder .40 1.00
17 Sami Jo Small .75 2.00
18 Colleen Sostorics .40 1.00
19 Kim St. Pierre .75 2.00
20 Vicky Sunohara .75 2.00
21 Sarah Vaillancourt .40 1.00
22 Hayley Wickenheiser 1.25 3.00

1964-65 Canadiens Postcards

This 24-postcard set features the Montreal Canadiens. The standard-size postcards feature action, black and white photography on the front, with the player's autograph stamped on in blue ink. The backs are blank. The set is noteworthy for including collectibles of HOFers Yvan Cournoyer and Rogatien Vachon before their RCs were issued.

COMPLETE SET (24) 100.00 200.00
1 Ralph Backstrom 2.50 5.00
2 Jean Beliveau 12.50 25.00
3 Toe Blake 5.00 10.00
4 Yvan Cournoyer 15.00 30.00
5 Dick Duff 2.50 5.00
6 John Ferguson 5.00 10.00
7 Danny Grant 2.50 5.00
8 Terry Harper 2.50 5.00
9 Ted Harris 2.50 5.00
10 Jacques Laperriere 4.00 8.00
11 Claude Larose 2.50 5.00
12 Jacques Lemaire 10.00 20.00
13 Garry Monahan 2.50 5.00
14 Claude Provost 2.50 5.00
15 Mickey Redmond 10.00 20.00
16 Henri Richard 7.50 15.00
17 Bobby Rousseau 2.50 5.00
18 Serge Savard 5.00 10.00
19 Gilles Tremblay 2.50 5.00
20 J.C. Tremblay 2.50 5.00
21 Carol Vadnais 1.50 3.00
22 Rogatien Vachon 15.00 30.00
23 Bryan Watson 1.50 3.00
24 Gump Worsley 5.00 10.00

1965-66 Canadiens Steinberg Glasses

This set of plastic glasses honoring members of the Montreal Canadiens were issued in the mid 1960's. As they are unnumbered, we are sequencing them in alphabetical order.

COMPLETE SET (12) 75.00 150.00
1 Ralph Backstrom 5.00 10.00
2 Jean Beliveau 15.00 30.00
3 John Ferguson 7.50 15.00
4 Charlie Hodge 7.50 15.00
5 Jacques Laperierre 5.00 10.00
6 Claude Provost 5.00 10.00
7 Henri Richard 10.00 20.00
8 Bob Rousseau 5.00 10.00
9 Jean Guy Talbot 5.00 10.00
10 Gilles Trembley 5.00 10.00
11 J.C. Trembley 6.00 12.00
12 Gump Worsley 10.00 20.00

1966-67 Canadiens IGA

The 1966-67 Canadiens IGA set apparently is comprised of 10 small, postage stamp sized (3/4" by 3/4") cards which likely were part of a larger coupon book. With no attention to date on the card, it has been set by the Gilles Tremblay issue. The cards feature a head shot on a pinkish-red background. If anyone knows of other cards in this set, please forward the information to Beckett Publications.

COMPLETE SET (10) 150.00 300.00
1 J.C. Tremblay 15.00 30.00
2 Ralph Backstrom 15.00 30.00
3 Dick Duff 15.00 30.00
4 Ted Harris 12.50 25.00
5 Claude Larose 12.50 25.00
6 Bobby Rousseau 15.00 30.00
7 Terry Harper 15.00 30.00
8 Gilles Tremblay 12.50 25.00
9 John Ferguson 15.00 30.00
10 Gump Worsley 40.00 80.00

1967-68 Canadiens IGA

The 1967-68 IGA Montreal Canadiens set includes 23 color cards measuring approximately 1 5/8" by 1 7/8". The cards are unnumbered other than by jersey number which is how they are listed below. The cards were part of a game involving numerous prizes. The card backs contain no personal information about the player (only information about the IGA game) and are written in French and English. The set features early cards of Jacques Lemaire and Rogatien Vachon in their Rookie Card year as well as Serge Savard two years prior to his Rookie Card year.

COMPLETE SET (30) 325.00 650.00
1 Gump Worsley 25.00 50.00
2 Jacques Laperriere 15.00 30.00
3 J.C. Tremblay 12.50 25.00
4 Jean Beliveau 40.00 80.00
5 Gilles Tremblay 10.00 20.00
6 Ralph Backstrom 10.00 20.00
8 Dick Duff 12.50 25.00
10 Ted Harris 10.00 20.00
11 Claude Larose 10.00 20.00
12 Yvan Cournoyer 20.00 40.00
14 Claude Provost 10.00 20.00
15 Bobby Rousseau 10.00 20.00
16 Henri Richard 25.00 50.00
17 Carol Vadnais 10.00 20.00
18 Serge Savard 25.00 50.00
19 Terry Harper 12.50 25.00
20 Garry Monahan 10.00 20.00
22 John Ferguson 12.50 25.00
23 Danny Grant 12.50 25.00
24 Mickey Redmond 20.00 40.00
25 Jacques Lemaire 30.00 60.00
30 Rogatien Vachon 40.00 80.00
NNO Toe Blake CO 15.00 30.00

1968-69 Canadiens IGA

The 1968-69 IGA Montreal Canadiens set includes 19 color cards measuring approximately 1 1/4" by 2 1/4". The cards are unnumbered other than by jersey number which is how they are listed below. The cards were part of a game involving numerous prizes. The card backs contain no personal information about the player (only information about the IGA game) and are written in French and English.

COMPLETE SET (30) 300.00 600.00
1 Gump Worsley 30.00 60.00
2 Jacques Laperriere 15.00 30.00
3 J.C. Tremblay 12.50 25.00
4 Jean Beliveau 40.00 80.00
5 Gilles Tremblay 10.00 20.00
6 Ralph Backstrom 12.50 25.00
8 Dick Duff 12.50 25.00
10 Ted Harris 10.00 20.00
12 Yvan Cournoyer 25.00 50.00
14 Claude Provost 10.00 20.00
15 Bobby Rousseau 12.50 25.00
16 Henri Richard 25.00 50.00
18 Serge Savard 20.00 40.00
19 Terry Harper 12.50 25.00
20 Garry Monahan 10.00 20.00
22 John Ferguson 15.00 30.00
24 Mickey Redmond 20.00 40.00
25 Jacques Lemaire 30.00 60.00
30 Rogatien Vachon 30.00 60.00

1968-69 Canadiens Postcards BW

This 20-card set of black and white postcards features full-bleed posed player photos with facsimile autographs in white. This set marks the last year the Canadiens' organization issued black and white postcards. The cards are unnumbered and checklisted below in alphabetical order. Serge Savard appears in this set prior to his Rookie Card year.

COMPLETE SET (20) 40.00 80.00
1 Ralph Backstrom 1.50 3.00
2 Jean Beliveau 7.50 15.00
3 Yvan Cournoyer 4.00 8.00
4 Dick Duff 1.50 3.00
5 John Ferguson 2.50 5.00
6 Terry Harper 1.50 3.00
7 Ted Harris 1.25 2.50
8 Jacques Laperriere 2.00 4.00
9 Jacques Lemaire 5.00 10.00
10 Garry Monahan 1.25 2.50
11 Claude Provost 1.25 2.50
12 Mickey Redmond 4.00 8.00
13 Henri Richard 4.00 8.00
14 Bobby Rousseau 1.50 3.00
15 Claude Ruel CO 1.25 2.50
16 Serge Savard 4.00 8.00
17 Gilles Tremblay 1.25 2.50
18 J.C. Tremblay 1.50 3.00
19 Rogatien Vachon 5.00 10.00
20 Gump Worsley 5.00 10.00

1969-71 Canadiens Postcards Color

This 31-card set of postcards features full-bleed posed color player photos with facsimile autographs in black across the bottom of the pictures. These postcards were also issued without facsimile autographs. For the 1969-70, 1970-71, and 1971-72 seasons, many of the same postcards were issued. The cards are unnumbered and checklisted below in alphabetical order.

COMPLETE SET (31) 50.00 100.00
1 Ralph Backstrom 1.50 3.00
2 Jean Beliveau 6.00 12.00
3 Chris Bordeleau 1.25 2.50
4 Pierre Bouchard 1.25 2.50
5 Guy Charron 1.25 2.50
6 Bill Collins 1.25 2.50
7 Yvan Cournoyer 4.00 8.00
8 John Ferguson 2.00 4.00
9 Terry Harper 1.50 3.00
10 Ted Harris 1.25 2.50
11 Rejean Houle 2.00 4.00
12 Jacques Laperriere 2.00 4.00
13 Guy Lapointe 3.00 6.00
14 Claude Larose 1.25 2.50
15 Jacques Lemaire 4.00 8.00
16 Al MacNeil CO 1.25 2.50
17 Frank Mahovlich 4.00 8.00
18 Peter Mahovlich 3.00 6.00
19 Phil Myre 2.00 4.00
20 Larry Pleau 1.50 3.00
21 Claude Provost 1.50 3.00
22 Mickey Redmond 4.00 8.00
23 Henri Richard 4.00 8.00
24 Phil Roberto 1.25 2.50
25 Jim Roberts 1.25 2.50
26 Bobby Rousseau 1.50 3.00
27 Claude Ruel CO 1.25 2.50
28 Serge Savard 4.00 8.00
29 Marc Tardif 1.50 3.00
30 J.C. Tremblay 1.50 3.00
31 Rogatien Vachon 5.00 10.00

1970-72 Canadiens Pins

This 22-pin set features members of the Montreal Canadiens. Each pin measures approximately 1 3/4" in diameter and has a black and white picture of the player. With the exception of Guy Lafleur, Frank Mahovlich, and Claude Ruel, who are pictured from the waist up, the other pictures are full body shots. The player's name appears below the picture. The pins are made of metal and have a metal clasp on the back. The pins are undated; since Bobby Rousseau's last season with the Canadiens was 1969-70 and 1971-72 was Ken Dryden, Guy Lafleur, and Frank Mahovlich's first season with Montreal, we have assigned 1970-72 to the set, meaning the set was likely issued over a period of years and may, in fact, comprise two distinct sets entirely.

COMPLETE SET (22) 75.00 150.00
1 Jean Beliveau 10.00 20.00
2 Yvan Cournoyer 4.00 8.00
3 Ken Dryden 20.00 40.00
4 John Ferguson 2.50 5.00
5 Terry Harper 2.00 4.00
6 Guy Lafleur 12.50 25.00
7 Jacques Laperriere 2.50 5.00
8 Guy Lapointe 2.50 5.00
9 Jacques Lemaire 4.00 8.00
10 Frank Mahovlich 5.00 10.00
11 Peter Mahovlich 2.50 5.00
12 Henri Richard 5.00 10.00
13 Bobby Rousseau 2.50 5.00
14 Claude Ruel CO 1.50 3.00
15 Serge Savard 2.50 5.00
16 J.C. Tremblay 2.00 4.00
17 Rogatien Vachon 4.00 8.00
18 Ted Harris 2.50 5.00
19 Claude Provost 2.50 5.00
20 Mickey Redmond 3.00 6.00
21 Ralph Backstrom 2.50 5.00
22 Gump Worsley 5.00 10.00

1971-72 Canadiens Postcards

This 25-card set of postcards features full-bleed posed color player photos with facsimile autographs in black across the pictures. For the 1969-70, 1970-71, and 1971-72 seasons, many of the same poses were issued. The cards are unnumbered and checklisted below in alphabetical order. The key cards in the set are Ken Dryden and Guy Lafleur appearing in their Rookie Card year. Also noteworthy is Coach Scotty Bowman's first card.

COMPLETE SET (25) 75.00 150.00
1 Pierre Bouchard .75 1.50
2 Scotty Bowman CO 4.00 8.00
3 Yvan Cournoyer 4.00 8.00
4 Denis DeJordy 1.50 3.00
5 Ken Dryden 20.00 40.00
6 Terry Harper 1.00 2.00
7 Dale Hoganson .75 1.50
8 Rejean Houle 1.00 2.00
9 Guy Lafleur 15.00 30.00
10 Jacques Laperriere 2.00 4.00
11 Guy Lapointe 2.00 4.00
12 Claude Larose .75 1.50
13 Jacques Lemaire 4.00 8.00
14 Frank Mahovlich 4.00 8.00
15 Peter Mahovlich 1.50 3.00
16 Phil Myre 1.50 3.00
17 Larry Pleau 1.00 2.00
18 Henri Richard 4.00 8.00
19 Phil Roberto .75 1.50
20 Jim Roberts .75 1.50
21 Leon Rochefort .75 1.50
22 Serge Savard 2.00 4.00
23 Marc Tardif 1.25 2.50
24 J.C. Tremblay 1.25 2.50
25 Rogatien Vachon 4.00 8.00

1972-73 Canadiens Postcards

This 22-card set features white bordered posed color player photos with pale green backgrounds. A facsimile autograph appears across the picture. The words "Pro Star Promotions, Inc." are printed in the border at the bottom. The Scotty Bowman card is the same as in the 1971-72 set. The cards are unnumbered and checklisted below in alphabetical order. The card of Steve Shutt predates his Rookie Card by two years.

COMPLETE SET (22) 62.50 125.00
1 Chuck Arnason 1.00 2.00
2 Pierre Bouchard 1.50 3.00
3 Scotty Bowman CO 5.00 10.00
4 Yvan Cournoyer 2.50 5.00
5 Ken Dryden 17.50 35.00
6 Rejean Houle 1.50 3.00
7 Guy Lafleur 10.00 20.00
8 Jacques Laperriere 2.00 4.00
9 Guy Lapointe 2.00 4.00
10 Claude Larose 1.00 2.00
11 Chuck Lefley 1.00 2.00
12 Jacques Lemaire 2.50 5.00
13 Frank Mahovlich 2.50 5.00
14 Peter Mahovlich 2.00 4.00
15 Bob Murdoch 1.00 2.00
16 Michel Plasse 2.00 4.00
17 Henri Richard 2.50 5.00
18 Jim Roberts 1.00 2.00
19 Serge Savard 2.00 4.00
20 Steve Shutt 4.00 8.00
21 Marc Tardif 1.50 3.00
22 Murray Wilson 1.00 2.00

1972 Canadiens Great West Life Prints

Cards measure 11" x 14" and were produced by Great West Life Insurance Company. Backs are blank. Cards are unnumbered and checklisted below in alphabetical order.

COMPLETE SET (6) 50.00 100.00
1 Pierre Bouchard 5.00 10.00
2 Yvan Cournoyer 5.00 10.00
3 Ken Dryden 20.00 40.00
4 Pete Mahovlich 5.00 10.00
5 Guy Lafleur 12.50 25.00
6 Steve Shutt 5.00 10.00

1973-74 Canadiens Postcards

This 24-card set features full-bleed color action player photos. The player's name, number and a facsimile autograph are printed on the back. Reportedly distribution problems limited sales to the public. The cards are unnumbered and checklisted below in alphabetical order. The card of Bob Gainey predates his Rookie Card by one year.

COMPLETE SET (24) 40.00 80.00
1 Jean Beliveau 6.00 12.00
(Portrait)
2 Pierre Bouchard .75 1.50
3 Scotty Bowman CO 3.00 6.00
4 Yvan Cournoyer 2.50 5.00
5 Bob Gainey 4.00 8.00
6 Dave Gardner .75 1.50
7 Guy Lafleur 5.00 10.00
8 Yvon Lambert .75 1.50
9 Jacques Laperriere 1.25 2.50
10 Guy Lapointe 1.25 2.50
11 Michel Larocque 1.50 3.00
12 Claude Larose SP 2.50 5.00
13 Chuck Lefley .75 1.50
14 Jacques Lemaire 1.50 3.00
15 Frank Mahovlich 2.50 5.00
16 Peter Mahovlich 1.25 2.50
17 Michel Plasse SP 2.50 5.00
18 Henri Richard 2.50 5.00
19 Jim Roberts SP 2.50 5.00
20 Larry Robinson 5.00 10.00
21 Serge Savard 1.25 2.50
22 Steve Shutt 2.50 5.00
23 Wayne Thomas 1.25 2.50
24 Murray Wilson SP 2.50 5.00

1974-75 Canadiens Postcards

This 27-card set features full-bleed color photos of players seated on a bench in the forum. The cards were issued with and without facsimile autographs. Claude Larose (13) and Chuck Lefley (14) went to St. Louis mid-season resulting in limited distribution of their cards. The Mario Tremblay card (25) was issued only without a facsimile autograph. The cards are unnumbered and checklisted below in alphabetical order.

COMPLETE SET (27) 37.50 75.00
1 Pierre Bouchard .75 1.50
2 Scotty Bowman CO 2.00 4.00
3 Rick Chartraw .75 1.50
4 Yvan Cournoyer 2.00 4.00
5 Ken Dryden 6.00 12.00
6 Bob Gainey 4.00 8.00
7 Glenn Goldup .75 1.50
8 Guy Lafleur 4.00 8.00
9 Yvon Lambert .75 1.50
10 Jacques Laperriere 1.00 2.00
11 Guy Lapointe 1.50 3.00
12 Michel Larocque 1.00 2.00
13 Claude Larose SP 1.50 3.00
14 Chuck Lefley SP 1.50 3.00
15 Jacques Lemaire 2.00 4.00
16 Peter Mahovlich 1.00 2.00
17 Henri Richard 2.00 4.00
18 Doug Risebrough 1.00 2.00
19 Jim Roberts SP 1.50 3.00
20 Larry Robinson 4.00 8.00
21 Glen Sather 1.50 3.00
22 Serge Savard 1.00 2.00
23 Steve Shutt 2.00 4.00
24 Wayne Thomas 1.00 2.00

25 Mario Tremblay 1.00 2.00
26 John Van Boxmeer .75 1.50
27 Murray Wilson SP 1.50 3.00

1975-76 Canadiens Postcards

This 20-card set features posed color photos of players on ice. A facsimile autograph appears in a white bottom border. The cards are unnumbered and checklisted below in alphabetical order. The Doug Jarvis card predates his Rookie Card by one year.

COMPLETE SET (20) 25.00 50.00
1 Don Awrey .75 1.50
2 Pierre Bouchard .75 1.50
3 Scotty Bowman CO 2.00 4.00
4 Yvan Cournoyer 2.00 4.00
5 Ken Dryden 6.00 12.00
6 Bob Gainey 2.00 4.00
7 Doug Jarvis 2.00 4.00
8 Guy Lafleur 4.00 8.00
9 Yvon Lambert .75 1.50
10 Guy Lapointe 1.25 2.50
11 Michel Larocque 1.00 2.00
12 Jacques Lemaire 2.00 4.00
13 Peter Mahovlich 1.00 2.00
14 Doug Risebrough .75 1.50
15 Jim Roberts .75 1.50
16 Larry Robinson 3.00 6.00
17 Serge Savard 1.25 2.50
18 Steve Shutt 2.00 4.00
19 Mario Tremblay 1.00 2.00
20 Murray Wilson .75 1.50

1976-77 Canadiens Postcards

This 23-card set features posed color photos of players seated in front of a light blue studio background. A facsimile autograph appears in a white bottom border. The cards are unnumbered and checklisted below in alphabetical order.

COMPLETE SET (23) 25.00 50.00
1 Pierre Bouchard .75 1.50
2 Scotty Bowman CO 2.00 4.00
3 Rick Chartraw .75 1.50
4 Yvan Cournoyer 1.50 3.00
5 Ken Dryden 5.00 10.00
6 Bob Gainey 2.00 4.00
7 Rejean Houle .75 1.50
8 Doug Jarvis 1.00 2.00
9 Guy Lafleur 4.00 8.00
10 Yvon Lambert .75 1.50
11 Guy Lapointe 1.00 2.00
12 Michel Larocque 1.25 2.50
13 Jacques Lemaire 1.50 3.00
14 Peter Mahovlich 1.00 2.00
15 Bill Nyrop .75 1.50
16 Doug Risebrough .75 1.50
17 Jim Roberts .75 1.50
18 Larry Robinson 2.50 5.00
19 Claude Ruel CO .50 1.00
20 Serge Savard 1.00 2.00
21 Steve Shutt 1.50 3.00
22 Mario Tremblay 1.00 2.00
23 Murray Wilson .75 1.50

1977-78 Canadiens Postcards

This 25-card set features posed action color photos of players on the ice. A facsimile autograph appears in a white bottom border. New players were photographed from the shoulders up. Many of the cards are the same as in the 1975-76 set. The cards are unnumbered and checklisted below in alphabetical order.

COMPLETE SET (25) 25.00 50.00
1 Pierre Bouchard .50 1.00
2 Scotty Bowman CO 1.50 3.00
3 Rick Chartraw .50 1.00
4 Yvan Cournoyer 1.50 3.00
5 Ken Dryden 4.50 9.00
6 Brian Engblom .75 1.50
7 Bob Gainey 1.50 3.00
8 Rejean Houle .50 1.00
9 Doug Jarvis .50 1.00
10 Guy Lafleur 3.00 6.00
11 Yvon Lambert .50 1.00
12 Guy Lapointe 1.00 2.00
13 Michel Larocque .75 1.50
14 Pierre Larouche 1.00 2.00
15 Jacques Lemaire 1.25 2.50
16 Gilles Lupien .50 1.00
17 Pierre Mondou .50 1.00
18 Bill Nyrop .50 1.00
19 Doug Risebrough .50 1.00
20 Larry Robinson 2.00 4.00
21 Claude Ruel CO .50 1.00
22 Serge Savard 1.00 2.00
23 Steve Shutt 1.50 3.00
24 Mario Tremblay .75 1.50
25 Murray Wilson .50 1.00

1978-79 Canadiens Postcards

This 26-card set features posed color player photos taken from the shoulders up. All the pictures have a red background except for Ruel and Cournoyer who are shown against blue. A facsimile autograph appears in a white bottom border. The cards are unnumbered and checklisted below in alphabetical order. The key card in the set is Rod Langway, appearing two years before his Rookie Card.

COMPLETE SET (26) 25.00 50.00
1 Scotty Bowman CO 1.50 3.00
2 Rick Chartraw .50 1.00
3 Cam Connor .50 1.00
4 Yvan Cournoyer 1.50 3.00
5 Ken Dryden 4.00 8.00
6 Brian Engblom .50 1.00
7 Bob Gainey 1.50 3.00
8 Rejean Houle .50 1.00
9 Pat Hughes .50 1.00
10 Doug Jarvis .50 1.00
11 Guy Lafleur 3.00 6.00
12 Yvon Lambert .50 1.00
13 Rod Langway 2.00 4.00
14 Guy Lapointe 1.00 2.00
15 Michel Larocque .75 1.50
16 Pierre Larouche 1.00 2.00
17 Jacques Lemaire 1.25 2.50
18 Gilles Lupien .50 1.00
19 Pierre Mondou .50 1.00
20 Mark Napier .50 1.00
21 Doug Risebrough .50 1.00
22 Larry Robinson 2.00 4.00
23 Claude Ruel CO .50 1.00
24 Serge Savard 1.00 2.00
25 Steve Shutt 1.50 3.00
26 Mario Tremblay .50 1.00

1979-80 Canadiens Postcards

This 25-card set features posed color player photos taken from the waist up. All the pictures have a red background except for Ruel who is shown against blue. A facsimile autograph appears in a white bottom border. Several cards are the same as the 1978-79 issue. Bernie Geoffrion's card was not distributed after he resigned as coach on December 12, 1980. Richard Sevigny's card received limited distribution because of late issue. The cards are unnumbered and checklisted below in alphabetical order. The cards measure approximately 3 1/2" by 5 1/2" and the backs are blank.

COMPLETE SET (25) 20.00 40.00
1 Rick Chartraw .50 1.00
2 Normand Dupont .50 1.00
3 Brian Engblom .50 1.00
4 Bob Gainey 1.50 3.00
5 Bernie Geoffrion CO SP 2.50 5.00
6 Danny Geoffrion .50 1.00
7 Denis Herron .75 1.50
8 Rejean Houle .50 1.00
9 Doug Jarvis .50 1.00
10 Guy Lafleur 2.50 5.00
11 Yvon Lambert .50 1.00
12 Rod Langway 1.00 2.00
13 Guy Lapointe 1.00 2.00
14 Michel Larocque .75 1.50
15 Pierre Larouche 1.00 2.00
16 Gilles Lupien .50 1.00
17 Pierre Mondou .50 1.00
18 Mark Napier .75 1.50
19 Doug Risebrough .75 1.50
20 Larry Robinson 1.50 3.00
21 Claude Ruel CO .50 1.00
22 Serge Savard .75 1.50
23 Richard Sevigny SP 2.50 5.00
24 Steve Shutt 1.00 2.00
25 Mario Tremblay .75 1.50

1980-81 Canadiens Postcards

This 26-card set features posed color player photos taken from the waist up against a blue background. A facsimile autograph appears in a white bottom border. The cards are unnumbered and checklisted below in alphabetical order. The cards measure approximately 3 1/2" by 5 1/2" and the backs are blank.

COMPLETE SET (26) 17.50 35.00
1 Keith Acton .60 1.50
2 Bill Baker .40 1.00
3 Rick Chartraw .40 1.00
4 Brian Engblom .40 1.00
5 Bob Gainey .75 2.00
6 Gaston Gingras .40 1.00
7 Denis Herron .75 2.00
8 Rejean Houle .60 1.50
9 Doug Jarvis .40 1.00
10 Guy Lafleur 2.50 5.00
11 Yvon Lambert .40 1.00
12 Rod Langway .60 1.50
13 Guy Lapointe .75 2.00
14 Michel Larocque .75 2.00
15 Pierre Larouche .60 1.50
16 Pierre Mondou .40 1.00
17 Mark Napier .40 1.00
18 Chris Nilan .75 2.00
19 Doug Risebrough .40 1.00
20 Larry Robinson 1.25 3.00
21 Claude Ruel CO .40 1.00
22 Serge Savard .60 1.50
23 Richard Sevigny .40 1.00
24 Steve Shutt .75 2.00
25 Mario Tremblay .60 1.50
26 Doug Wickenheiser .40 1.00

1981-82 Canadiens Postcards

This 28-card set features posed color player photos taken from the waist up against a blue or blue-white background. A facsimile autograph appears in a white bottom border. Many cards are the same as in the 1980-81 set. The Gilbert Delorme card was short-printed. The cards are unnumbered and checklisted below in alphabetical order.

COMPLETE SET (28) 14.00 35.00
1 Team Photo 1.25 3.00
2 Keith Acton .40 1.00
3 Bob Berry CO .30 .75
4 Jeff Brubaker .30 .75
5 Gilbert Delorme SP 1.50 4.00
6 Brian Engblom .30 .75
7 Bob Gainey .75 2.00
8 Gaston Gingras .30 .75
9 Denis Herron .50 1.25
10 Rejean Houle .40 1.00
11 Mark Hunter .30 .75
12 Doug Jarvis .30 .75
13 Guy Lafleur 2.00 5.00
14 Rod Langway .60 1.50
15 Jacques Laperriere .60 1.50
16 Guy Lapointe .60 1.50
17 Craig Laughlin .30 .75
18 Pierre Mondou .30 .75
19 Mark Napier .40 1.00
20 Chris Nilan .40 1.00
21 Robert Picard .30 .75
22 Doug Risebrough .30 .75
23 Larry Robinson 1.25 3.00
24 Richard Sevigny .50 1.25
25 Steve Shutt .75 2.00
26 Mario Tremblay .40 1.00
27 Rick Wamsley .50 1.25
28 Doug Wickenheiser .40 1.00

1982-83 Canadiens Postcards

This 28-card set features posed color player photos taken from the waist up against a blue background. A facsimile autograph appears in a white bottom panel. Many photos are the same as in the 1980-81 and 1981-82 sets. Player information, jersey number, and the team logo are on the back. The Richard card has the same style but it is not originally part of the set; it was issued in 1983. The Root card was issued late in the year and thus was limited in its distribution. Some color variations appear in the Gainey and Picard cards. The cards are unnumbered and checklisted below in alphabetical order. Notable cards in the set include Guy Carbonneau and Mats Naslund appearing the year before their Rookie Card.

COMPLETE SET (28) 12.00 30.00
1 Keith Acton .30 .75
2 Bob Berry CO .30 .75
3 Guy Carbonneau 1.50 4.00
4 Dan Daoust .30 .75
5 Gilbert Delorme .30 .75
6 Bob Gainey .75 2.00
7 Gaston Gingras .30 .75
8 Rick Green .30 .75
9 Rejean Houle .30 .75
10 Mark Hunter .30 .75
11 Guy Lafleur 2.00 5.00
12 Jacques Laperriere .30 .75
13 Craig Ludwig .60 1.50
14 Pierre Mondou .30 .75
15 Mark Napier .40 1.00
16 Mats Naslund 1.25 3.00
17 Ric Nattress .30 .75
18 Chris Nilan .40 1.00
19 Robert Picard .30 .75
20 Henri Richard 1.25 3.00
21 Larry Robinson 1.25 3.00
22 Bill Root SP .75 2.00
23 Richard Sevigny .50 1.25
24 Steve Shutt .75 2.00
25 Mario Tremblay .40 1.00
26 Ryan Walter .40 1.00
27 Rick Wamsley .50 1.25
28 Doug Wickenheiser .30 .75

1982-83 Canadiens Steinberg

This 24-card set was sponsored by Steinberg and the Montreal Canadiens Hockey Club as the "Follow the Play" promotion. The cards were issued in a small vinyl photo album with one card per binder and measure approximately 3 1/2" by 4 15/16". For a few of the players, the biography on the card back is written in French; those players are so noted in the checklist below. We have checklisted the cards below in alphabetical order.

COMPLETE SET (24) 10.00 25.00
1 Keith Acton .20 .50
2 Guy Carbonneau 1.25 3.00
3 Gilbert Delorme .20 .50
(French bio)
4 Bob Gainey .60 1.50
5 Rick Green .20 .50
6 Mark Hunter .20 .50
7 Rejean Houle .20 .50
8 Guy Lafleur 1.50 4.00
9 Craig Ludwig .40 1.00
10 Pierre Mondou .20 .50
11 Mark Napier .30 .75
12 Mats Naslund .75 2.00
13 Ric Nattress .20 .50
(French bio)
14 Chris Nilan .30 .75
15 Robert Picard .20 .50
16 Larry Robinson .75 2.00
17 Bill Root .20 .50
18 Richard Sevigny .40 1.00
19 Steve Shutt .60 1.50
20 Mario Tremblay .30 .75
21 Ryan Walter .30 .75
22 Rick Wamsley .40 1.00
(French bio)
23 Doug Wickenheiser .20 .50
24 Team Photo .50 1.25
xx Vinyl Card Album 2.00 5.00

1983-84 Canadiens Postcards

This 33-card set features color photos of players posed on the ice. A facsimile autograph appears at the bottom. Player information, jersey number, and the team logo are on the back. The team continued to issue cards throughout the season, so several card were distributed on a limited basis. The Laperriere card (number 14) is the same card as in the 1982-83 set. The Delorme and Wickenheiser cards were not issued as part of the set because of trade. Issued in 1984, the Beliveau card was not part of the team set but has the same style. The cards are unnumbered and checklisted below in alphabetical order. The key card in the set is Chris Chelios appearing the year before his Rookie Card.

COMPLETE SET (33) 16.00 40.00
1 Jean Beliveau 1.25 3.00
2 Bob Berry CO .30 .75
3 Guy Carbonneau .75 2.00
4 Kent Carlson .30 .75
5 John Chabot .30 .75
6 Chris Chelios 4.00 10.00
7 Gilbert Delorme SP 1.25 3.00
8 Bob Gainey .60 1.50
9 Rick Green .30 .75
10 Jean Hamel .30 .75
11 Mark Hunter .30 .75
12 Guy Lafleur 1.50 4.00
13 Jacques Lemaire .60 1.50
14 Jacques Laperriere .40 1.00
(Action shot)
15 Jacques Laperriere .40 1.00
(Head shot)
16 Craig Ludwig .40 1.00
17 Pierre Mondou .30 .75
18 Mats Naslund .75 2.00
19 Ric Nattress .30 .75
20 Chris Nilan .40 1.00
21 Steve Penney .40 1.00
22 Jacques Plante 1.25 3.00
23 Larry Robinson 1.00 2.50
24 Bill Root .30 .75
25 Richard Sevigny .40 1.00
26 Steve Shutt .60 1.50
27 Bobby Smith .60 1.50
28 Mario Tremblay .40 1.00
29 Alfie Turcotte .30 .75
30 Perry Turnbull .30 .75
31 Ryan Walter .30 .75
32 Rick Wamsley .50 1.25
33 Doug Wickenheiser SP 1.25 3.00

1984-85 Canadiens Postcards

This 31-card set features color photos of players posed on the ice. A facsimile autograph appears at the bottom. Player information, jersey number, and the team logo are on the back. Many cards are the same as in the 1983-84 set. The cards are unnumbered and checklisted below in alphabetical order.

COMPLETE SET (31) 12.00 30.00
1 Guy Carbonneau .60 1.50
(Action on ice
2 Guy Carbonneau .60 1.50
(Still
3 Kent Carlson .30 .75
4 Chris Chelios 2.50 6.00
(Same card as 1983-84&
but with facsimile auto
5 Lucien Deblois .30 .75
6 Ron Flockhart .30 .75
7 Bob Gainey .60 1.50
8 Rick Green .30 .75
9 Jean Hamel .30 .75
10 Mark Hunter .30 .75
11 Tom Kurvers .30 .75
12 Guy Lafleur 1.50 4.00
13 Jacques Laperriere .40 1.00
14 Jacques Lemaire .60 1.50
15 Craig Ludwig .40 1.00
16 Mike McPhee .60 1.50
17 Pierre Mondou .30 .75
18 Mats Naslund .75 2.00
19 Ric Nattress .30 .75
20 Chris Nilan .40 1.00
21 Steve Penney .40 1.00
(Same card as 1983-84)
22 Steve Penney .40 1.00
23 Jean Perron .30 .75
24 Larry Robinson 1.00 2.50
25 Bobby Smith .60 1.50
26 Doug Soetaert .40 1.00
27 Petr Svoboda .60 1.50
28 Mario Tremblay .40 1.00
29 Alfie Turcotte .30 .75
(Same card as 1983-84)
30 Alfie Turcotte .30 .75
(Facsimile autograph on front)
31 Ryan Walter .40 1.00

1985-86 Canadiens Placemats

Sponsored by Pepsi-Cola and 7-Up, this set of seven placemats was issued to commemorate the Montreal Canadiens as the 1984-85 Division Champions. Each placemat measures approximately 11" by 17". On an yellow-orange background with a white border, the front carries a painted portrait, action shot and a facsimile autograph of two different players. Player name, position, and number, date and place of birth, and career statistics in French and English are also found on the front. The sponsors' logos appear in the upper right corner. The backs feature a red-and-white plaid design. The placemats are unnumbered. One placemat shows portraits of all twelve players with their facsimile autographs.

COMPLETE SET (7) 8.00 20.00
1 Bob Gainey 1.50 4.00
Guy Carbonneau
2 Mats Naslund .75 2.00
Tom Kurvers
3 Chris Nilan .75 2.00
Petr Svoboda
4 Steve Penney 2.00 5.00
Chris Chelios
5 Larry Robinson 1.50 4.00
Serge Boisvert
6 Mario Tremblay .75 2.00
Bobby Smith
7 Hockey Stars 2.00 5.00
Steve Penney
Chris Chelios
Larry Robinson
Serge Boisvert
Mario Tremblay
Bobby Smith
Mats Naslund
Tom Kurvers
Bob Gainey
Guy Carbonneau
Chris Nilan
Petr Svoboda

1985-86 Canadiens Postcards

This 40-card set features color photos of players posed in red uniforms against a white background. A facsimile autograph appears on a red diagonal line in the lower right corner on most cards. However, there is some variation in the autograph location. Player information and the team logo are on the back. Several cards (1, 2, 3, 11, 14, 17, 19) were issued late in the season. The cards are unnumbered and checklisted below in alphabetical order. The key card in this set is Patrick Roy, which pre-dates his Rookie Card by one year. Other notable early cards include Claude Lemieux, Stephane Richer, and Brian Skrudland.

COMPLETE SET (40) 24.00 60.00
1 Serge Boisvert SP .60 1.50
(No red line or
autograph)
2 Serge Boisvert SP .60 1.50
(Portrait)
3 Randy Bucyk SP .60 1.50
(No red line or
autograph)
4 Guy Carbonneau .40 1.00
5 Chris Chelios 1.50 4.00
6 Kjell Dahlin .20 .50
(J in autograph on stick)
7 Kjell Dahlin .20 .50
(E in autograph on stick)
8 Lucien Deblois .20 .50
9 Bob Gainey .60 1.50
(B in autograph
on stick)
10 Bob Gainey .60 1.50
(G in autograph
on stick)
11 Gaston Gingras SP .60 1.50
12 Rick Green .20 .50
(No letters on stick)
13 Rick Green .20 .50
(C in autograph
on stick)
14 John Kordic SP 2.00 5.00
(No red line or
autograph)
15 Tom Kurvers .20 .50
16 Mike Lalor .20 .50
17 Claude Lemieux SP 3.00 8.00
(No red line or
autograph)
18 Craig Ludwig .30 .75
19 David Maley SP .60 1.50
(No red line or
autograph)
20 Mike McPhee .40 1.00
21 Sergio Momesso .30 .75
22 Mats Naslund .60 1.50
23 Chris Nilan .30 .75
(Dot from i in
Nilan touching toe)
24 Chris Nilan .30 .75
(Dot from i in
Nilan away from toe)
25 Steve Penney .30 .75
26 Jean Perron .20 .50
(Portrait)
27 Stephane Richer .75 2.00
28 Larry Robinson 1.00 2.50
29 Steve Rooney .20 .50
(Loop in R
through skate toe)
30 Steve Rooney .20 .50
(Loop in R
through skate laces)
31 Patrick Roy 10.00 25.00
32 Brian Skrudland .75 2.00
33 Bobby Smith .40 1.00
(B in autograph
touching stick)
34 Bobby Smith .40 1.00
(O in autograph
on stick)
35 Doug Soetaert .30 .75
(T at end of
name by pad)
36 Doug Soetaert .30 .75
(T at end of
name away from pad)
37 Petr Svoboda .30 .75
38 Mario Tremblay .30 .75
(T in autograph
touching blade)
39 Mario Tremblay .30 .75
(T in autograph
away from blade)
40 Ryan Walter .30 .75

1985-86 Canadiens Provigo

This 25-sticker set of the Montreal Canadiens was produced by Provigo. The puffy (Styrofoam-backed) stickers measure approximately 1 1/8" by 2 1/4" and feature a color head and shoulders photo of the player, with the player's number and name bordered by star-studded banners across the bottom of the picture. The Canadiens' logo is superimposed over the banner at its right end. The backs are blank. We have checklisted them below in alphabetical order, with the uniform number to the right of the player's name. The 25 stickers were to be attached to a cardboard poster. The poster measures approximately 20" by 11" and has 25 white spaces designated for the stickers on a red background. At the center is a picture of a goalie mask, with the Canadiens' logo above and slightly to the right. The back of the poster has a checklist, stripes in the team's colors, and two team logos. The set features early cards of Stephane Richer and Patrick Roy predating their actual Rookie Cards.

COMPLETE SET (25) 16.00 40.00
1 Guy Carbonneau 21 .50 1.25
2 Chris Chelios 24 1.50 4.00
3 Kjell Dahlin 20 .20 .50
4 Lucien Deblois 27 .20 .50
5 Bob Gainey 23 .60 1.50
6 Rick Green 5 .20 .50
7 Tom Kurvers 18 .20 .50
8 Mike Lalor 38 .20 .50
9 Craig Ludwig 17 .30 .75
10 Mike McPhee 35 .40 1.00
11 Sergio Momesso 36 .30 .75
12 Mats Naslund 26 .60 1.50
13 Chris Nilan 30 .30 .75
14 Steve Penney 37 .30 .75
15 Jean Perron CO .20 .50
16 Stephane Richer 44 .75 2.00
17 Larry Robinson 19 1.00 2.50
18 Steve Rooney 28 .20 .50
19 Patrick Roy 33 10.00 25.00
20 Brian Skrudland 39 .75 2.00
21 Bobby Smith 15 .40 1.00
22 Doug Soetaert 1 .30 .75
23 Petr Svoboda 25 .30 .75
24 Mario Tremblay 14 .30 .75
25 Ryan Walter 11 .30 .75
NNO Provigo Poster 2.00 5.00

1986-87 Canadiens Postcards

Each of the 25 cards in this set measures approximately 3 3/8" by 5 1/2". The front features a color posed photo (without borders) of the player. The information on the back has a diagonal orientation and is printed in the Canadiens' team colors red and blue. At the top on the back appears the Canadiens' logo, followed by the player's name, his signature, and brief biographical information (in French and English). Notably, the Shayne Corson card in this set pre-dates his RC by three years.

COMPLETE SET (25) 14.00 35.00
1 Guy Carbonneau 21 .40 1.00
2 Chris Chelios 24 1.25 3.00
3 Shayne Corson 34 .75 2.00
4 Kjell Dahlin 20 .20 .50
5 Bob Gainey 23 .40 1.00
6 Rick Green 5 .20 .50
7 Brian Hayward 1 .40 1.00
8 John Kordic 31 .60 1.50
9 Mike Lalor 38 .20 .50
10 Jacques Laperriere ACO .30 .75
11 Claude Lemieux 1.50 4.00
12 Craig Ludwig 17 .20 .50
13 Mike McPhee 35 .30 .75
14 Sergio Momesso 36 .20 .50
15 Mats Naslund 26 .40 1.00
16 Chris Nilan 30 .30 .75
17 Jean Perron CO .20 .50
18 Stephane Richer 44 .75 2.00
19 Larry Robinson 19 .75 2.00
20 Patrick Roy 33 6.00 15.00
21 Scott Sandelin 3 .20 .50
22 Brian Skrudland 39 .60 1.50
23 Bobby Smith 15 .30 .75
24 Petr Svoboda 25 .20 .50
25 Ryan Walter 11 .30 .75
26 Serge Savard
27 Larry Trader
28 Francois Allaire

1987 Canadiens Kodak

Little is known about this set. It is believed that the cards below represent a partial checklist for what likely was a promotional giveaway. Any additional information may be forwarded to hockeymag@beckett.com.

COMPLETE SET (7) 2.50 6.00
1 Guy Carbonneau .40 1.00
2 Bob Gainey .50 1.25
3 Mike McPhee .30 .75
4 Mats Naslund .40 1.00
5 Chris Nilan .30 .75
6 Larry Robinson .75 2.00
7 Bobby Smith .30 .75

1987-88 Canadiens Postcards

This 35-card set is in the postcard size format, with each card measuring approximately 3 1/2" by 5 1/2". The fronts feature full-bleed posed color action shots. In a diagonal format at the top of the back appears the team logo, followed by the player's name, his signature, and brief biographical information (in French and English). The cards are unnumbered and checklisted below in alphabetical order. There are two versions of the Stephane Richer postcard (#23); both are included in the complete set price.

COMPLETE SET (35) 12.00 30.00
1 Francois Allaire ACO .08 .25
2 Guy Carbonneau .40 1.00
3 Jose Charbonneau .20 .50
4 Chris Chelios 1.00 2.50
5 Shayne Corson .40 1.00
6 Kjell Dahlin .20 .50
7 Bob Gainey .50 1.25
8 Rick Green .20 .50
9 Gaston Gingras .20 .50
10 Brian Hayward .20 .50
11 John Kordic .60 1.50
12 Mike Lalor .20 .50
13 Jacques Laperriere ACO .20 .50
14 Claude Lemieux 1.25 3.00
15 Craig Ludwig .20 .50
16 David Maley .20 .50
17 Mike McPhee .30 .75
18 Sergio Momesso .20 .50
19 Claude Mouton ANN .08 .25
20 Mats Naslund .40 1.00
21 Chris Nilan .30 .75
22 Jean Perron CO .08 .25
23A Stephane Richer .60 1.50
(With moustache)
23B Stephane Richer .60 1.50
(No moustache)
24 Larry Robinson .75 2.00
25 Steve Rooney .20 .50
26 Patrick Roy 6.00 15.00
27 Scott Sandelin .20 .50
28 Serge Savard DIR .30 .75
29 Brian Skrudland .50 1.25
30 Bobby Smith .30 .75
31 Petr Svoboda .20 .50
32 Gilles Thibaudeau .20 .50
33 Larry Trader .20 .50
34 Ryan Walter .30 .75

1987-88 Canadiens Vachon Stickers

Featuring the Montreal Canadiens, this set consists of 28 panels, each measuring approximately 2 7/8" by 5 9/16". Each panel is made up of five stickers, two that measure approximately 1 1/2" by 2 5/8", and three that measure approximately 1" by 1 11/16". The larger stickers carry color action player photos or team pictures. The smaller ones are close-ups of players or action shots. The stickers appear in a variety of combinations on the panels, with one panel showing small player shots and another panel carrying the same player shots but with different action photos. All told, 88 different stickers were printed. The back of the panel explains in French and English that albums are available for 49 cents at participating supermarkets and at "Les Canadiens" souvenir boutiques, and that collectors can send in 2.00 to Super Series Vachon and receive the album through the mail. The first six stickers can be pieced together to form a composite team photo. The stickers are numbered on the front.

COMPLETE SET (88) 16.00 40.00
1 Canadiens Team Photo .08 .25
(Top left)
2 Canadiens Team Photo .08 .25
(Top middle)
3 Canadiens Team Photo .08 .25
(Top right)
4 Canadiens Team Photo .08 .25
(Bottom left)
5 Canadiens Team Photo .08 .25
(Bottom middle)
6 Canadiens Team Photo .08 .25
(Bottom right)
7 Jean Perron CO .08 .25
8 Jacques Laperriere ACO .08 .25
9 Francois Allaire ACO .08 .25
10 Jean Perron CO .08 .25
11 Jacques Laperriere .08 .25
12 Bob Gainey .30 .75
13 Bob Gainey .30 .75
14 Guy Carbonneau .15 .40
15 Guy Carbonneau .15 .40
16 Guy Carbonneau .15 .40
17 Michael McPhee .15 .40
18 Bob Gainey .30 .75
19 Chris Nilan .15 .40
20 Chris Nilan .15 .40
21 Guy Carbonneau .15 .40
22 Mike Lalor .08 .25
23 Patrick Roy and 1.50 4.00
Guy Carbonneau
24 Ryan Walter .08 .25
25 Ryan Walter .08 .25
26 Bobby Smith .15 .40
27 Mats Naslund .15 .40
28 Bobby Smith .15 .40
29 Mike McPhee .15 .40
30 Bobby Smith .15 .40
31 Claude Lemieux .75 2.00
32 Brian Skrudland .08 .25
33 Craig Ludwig .15 .40
34 Brian Skrudland .08 .25
35 Craig Ludwig .15 .40
36 Brian Skrudland .08 .25
37 Mike McPhee .15 .40
38 Mike McPhee .15 .40
39 Kjell Dahlin .08 .25
40 Kjell Dahlin .08 .25
41 Bobby Smith .15 .40
42 Patrick Roy 2.00 5.00
43 Patrick Roy 2.00 5.00
44 Larry Trader .08 .25
45 Mats Naslund .20 .50
46 Mats Naslund .20 .50
47 Mats Naslund .20 .50
48 Mats Naslund .20 .50
49 Shayne Corson .20 .50
50 Shayne Corson .20 .50
51 Stephane Richer .30 .75
52 Stephane Richer .30 .75
53 Bob Gainey .30 .75
54 Stephane Richer .30 .75
55 Sergio Momesso .08 .25
56 Sergio Momesso .08 .25
57 John Kordic .40 1.00
58 John Kordic .40 1.00
59 Mike Lalor .08 .25
60 Mike Lalor .08 .25
61 Brian Hayward .15 .40
62 Guy Carbonneau .15 .40
63 Guy Carbonneau .15 .40
64 Brian Hayward .15 .40
65 Rick Green .08 .25
66 Rick Green .08 .25
67 Brian Hayward .15 .40
68 Rick Green .08 .25
69 Patrick Roy 2.00 5.00
70 Rick Green .08 .25
71 Patrick Roy 2.00 5.00
72 Larry Robinson .40 1.00
73 Larry Robinson .40 1.00
74 Patrick Roy 2.00 5.00
75 Petr Svoboda .08 .25
76 Patrick Roy 2.00 5.00
77 Petr Svoboda .08 .25
78 Chris Chelios .60 1.50
79 Chris Chelios .60 1.50
80 Craig Ludwig .15 .40
81 Craig Ludwig .15 .40
82 Chris Chelios .60 1.50
83 Chris Chelios .60 1.50
84 Brian Hayward .15 .40
85 Craig Ludwig .15 .40
86 Bobby Smith .15 .40
87 Mats Naslund .15 .40
88 Bob Gainey .30 .75
xx Sticker Album 2.00 5.00

1988-89 Canadiens Postcards

This 30-card, team-issued set measures approximately 3 1/2" by 5 1/2" and features full-bleed color player photos. The players are posed on the ice against a white background. The coaches' cards feature color portraits against a black background. The backs are white and show the team name and logo in large red letters at the top. The player's name, number, and biography are printed in blue. A facsimile autograph at the bottom rounds out the back. The cards are unnumbered and checklisted below in alphabetical order.

COMPLETE SET (30) 10.00 25.00
1 Francois Allaire ACO .08 .25
2 Pat Burns CO .40 1.00
3 Guy Carbonneau .40 1.00
4 Jose Charbonneau .20 .50
5 Chris Chelios .75 2.00
6 Ronald Corey PRES .08 .25
7 Shayne Corson .40 1.00
8 Russ Courtnall .40 1.00
9 Eric Desjardins .60 1.50
10 Bob Gainey .40 1.00
11 Brent Gilchrist .30 .75
12 Rick Green .20 .50
13 Brian Hayward .30 .75
14 Mike Keane .40 1.00
15 Mike Lalor .20 .50
16 Jacques Laperriere ACO .20 .50
17 Claude Lemieux .60 1.50
18 Craig Ludwig .30 .75
19 Steven Martinson .20 .50
20 Mike McPhee .30 .75
21 Mats Naslund .40 1.00
22 Stephane Richer .40 1.00
23 Larry Robinson .75 2.00
24 Patrick Roy 4.00 10.00
25 Serge Savard DIR .40 1.00
26 Brian Skrudland .40 1.00
27 Bobby Smith .30 .75
28 Petr Svoboda .20 .50
30 Ryan Walter .20 .50
39 Gilles Thibaudeau .20 .50

1989-90 Canadiens Kraft

This 24-card set of Montreal Canadiens was sponsored by Le Journal de Montreal and Kraft Foods. The cards were issued as two four-card insert sheets in Les Canadiens magazine. The cards measure approximately 3 3/4" by 5 7/16". The front features a posed color photo of the player on white card stock. The cards are unnumbered and hence are listed below in alphabetical order.

COMPLETE SET (24) 10.00 25.00
1 Pat Burns CO .40 1.00
2 Guy Carbonneau .40 1.00
3 Chris Chelios 1.00 2.50
4 Shayne Corson .60 1.50
5 Russ Courtnall .30 .75
6 J.J. Daigneault .30 .75
7 Eric Desjardins .40 1.00
8 Todd Ewen .30 .75
9 Brent Gilchrist .30 .75
10 Brian Hayward .30 .75
11 Mike Keane .40 1.00
12 Stephan Lebeau .50 1.25
13 Sylvain Lefebvre .30 .75
14 Claude Lemieux .75 2.00
15 Craig Ludwig .40 1.00
16 Mike McPhee .30 .75
17 Mats Naslund .60 1.50
18 Stephane Richer .60 1.50
19 Patrick Roy 3.00 8.00
20 Mathieu Schneider .60 1.50
21 Brian Skrudland .30 .75
22 Bobby Smith .30 .75
23 Petr Svoboda .30 .75
24 Ryan Walter .30 .75

1989-90 Canadiens Postcards

This 32-card set measures approximately 3 7/16" by 5 7/16" and features borderless color player photos. The players are posed on the ice against a white background. The coaches' cards feature color portraits against a black background. The backs are white and carry the team name and logo in large red letters at the top. The player's name, jersey number, and biography are printed in blue. A facsimile autograph at the bottom rounds out the back. The cards are unnumbered and checklisted below in alphabetical order.

COMPLETE SET (32) 10.00 25.00
1 Francois Allaire ACO .08 .25
2 Pat Burns CO .40 1.00
3 Guy Carbonneau .30 .75
4 Chris Chelios .60 1.50
5 Tom Chorske .20 .50
6 Ronald Corey PR .08 .25
7 Shayne Corson .40 1.00
8 Russ Courtnall .40 1.00
9 Jean-Jacques Daigneault .20 .50
10 Eric Desjardins .40 1.00
11 Martin Desjardins .20 .50
12 Donald Dufresne .20 .50
13 Brent Gilchrist .20 .50
14 Brian Hayward .30 .75
15 Mike Keane .30 .75
16 Jacques Laperriere ACO .20 .50
17 Stephan Lebeau .40 1.00
18 Sylvain Lefebvre .40 1.00
19 Claude Lemieux .40 1.00
20 Jocelyn Lemieux .20 .50
21 Craig Ludwig .20 .50
22 Jyrki Lumme .40 1.00
23 Steven Martinson .20 .50
24 Mike McPhee .30 .75
25 Mats Naslund .40 1.00
26 Stephane Richer .40 1.00
27 Patrick Roy 2.50 6.00
28 Serge Savard DIR .20 .50
29 Brian Skrudland .40 1.00
30 Bobby Smith .30 .75
31 Petr Svoboda .30 .75
32 Ryan Walter .20 .50

1989-90 Canadiens Provigo Figurines

These 13 plastic figurines of the 1989-90 Canadiens are approximately 3" tall and show the players in their white home jerseys, wearing skates and holding white hockey sticks. The players' names and uniform numbers appear on their jersey backs. The figurines are numbered on the backs of the hockey sticks. The original issue price for these figurines was 1.99 Canadian. The figurines were distributed in a package with a coupon booklet.

COMPLETE SET (13) 28.00 70.00
6 Russ Courtnall 1.50 4.00
15 Bobby Smith 1.50 3.00
17 Craig Ludwig 1.25 3.00
21 Guy Carbonneau 1.50 4.00
23 Bob Gainey 2.00 5.00
24 Chris Chelios 3.00 8.00
25 Petr Svoboda 1.25 3.00
26 Mats Naslund 2.00 5.00
27 Shayne Corson 2.00 5.00
33 Patrick Roy 10.00 25.00
35 Mike McPhee 1.25 3.00
39 Brian Skrudland 1.50 4.00
44 Stephane Richer 2.00 5.00

1990-91 Canadiens Postcards

This 33-card set measures approximately 3 1/2" by 5

1/2" and features borderless color player photos. The players are posed on the ice against a white background. The coaches' cards feature color portraits against a black background. The backs are white and carry the team name and logo in large red letters at the top. The player's name, jersey number, and biography are printed in blue. A facsimile autograph at the bottom rounds out the back. The cards are unnumbered and checklisted below in alphabetical order.

COMPLETE SET (33) 10.00 25.00
1 Francois Allaire ACO .08 .25
2 Jean-Claude Bergeron .30 .75
3 Benoit Brunet .20 .50
4 Pat Burns CO .30 .75
5 Guy Carbonneau .30 .75
6 Andrew Cassels .30 .75
7 Tom Chorske .20 .50
8 Ronald Corey PR .08 .25
9 Shayne Corson .40 1.00
10 Russ Courtnall .30 .75
11 Jean-Jacques Daigneault .20 .50
12 Eric Desjardins .40 1.00
13 Gerald Diduck .20 .50
14 Donald Dufresne .20 .50
15 Todd Ewen .25 .60
16 Brent Gilchrist .20 .50
17 Mike Keane .30 .75
18 Jacques Laperriere ACO .20 .50
19 Stephan Lebeau .20 .50
20 Sylvain Lefebvre .30 .75
21 Mike McPhee .30 .75
22 Lyle Odelein .40 1.00
23 Mark Pederson .20 .50
24 Stephane Richer .30 .75
25 Patrick Roy 2.50 6.00
26 Denis Savard .60 1.50
27 Serge Savard DIR .30 .75
28 Mathieu Schneider .40 1.00
29 Brian Skrudland .40 1.00
30 Petr Svoboda .30 .75
31 Charles Thiffault ACO .08 .25
32 Sylvain Turgeon .20 .50
33 Ryan Walter .20 .50

1991 Canadiens Panini Team Stickers

This 32-sticker set was issued in a plastic bag that contained two 16-sticker sheets (approximately 9" by 12") and a foldout poster, "Super Poster - Hockey 91", on which the stickers could be affixed. The players' names appear only on the poster, not on the stickers. Each sticker measures about 2 1/8" by 2 7/8" and features a color player action shot on its white-bordered front. The back of the white sticker sheet is lined off into 16 panels, each carrying the logos for Panini, the NHL, and the NHLPA, as well as the same number that appears on the front of the sticker. Every Canadian NHL team was featured in this promotion. Each team set was available by mail-order from Panini Canada Ltd. for 2.99 plus 50 cents for shipping and handling.

COMPLETE SET (32) 2.00 5.00
1 Jean-Claude Bergeron .02 .10
2 Guy Carbonneau .02 .10
3 Andrew Cassels .05 .15
4 Tom Chorske .01 .05
5 Shayne Corson .05 .15
6 Russ Courtnall .05 .15
7 Jean-Jacques Daigneault .02 .10
8 Eric Desjardins .02 .10
9 Gerald Diduck .01 .05
10 Donald Dufresne .01 .05
11 Todd Ewen .01 .05
12 Brent Gilchrist .02 .10
13 Mike Keane .02 .10
14 Stephan Lebeau .02 .10
15 Sylvain Lefebvre .02 .10
16 Mike McPhee .02 .10
17 Mark Pederson .01 .05
18 Stephane Richer .08 .25
19 Patrick Roy 1.00 2.50
20 Denis Savard .15 .40
21 Mathieu Schneider .02 .10
22 Brian Skrudland .02 .10
23 Petr Svoboda .02 .10
24 Ryan Walter .02 .10
A Team Logo Left Side .05 .15
B Team Logo Right Side .05 .15
C Canadiens in Action Upper Left Corner .05 .15
D Canadiens in Action Lower Left Corner .05 .15
E Game Action Upper Right Corner .05 .15
F Game Action Lower Right Corner .05 .15
G Patrick Roy .75 2.00
H Game Action .08 .25

1991-92 Canadiens Postcards

This 31-card team-issued set measures approximately 3 1/2" by 5 1/2". The fronts feature full-bleed color photos, with the players posed in front of a white background. The backs are white and show the team name in large red letters at the top. The player's name, number, and biography (in French and English) are printed in blue. A facsimile autograph at the bottom rounds out the back. The cards are unnumbered and checklisted below in alphabetical order.

COMPLETE SET (31) 10.00 25.00
1 Francois Allaire ACO .08 .25
2 Patrice Brisebois .30 .75
3 Pat Burns CO .30 .75
4 Guy Carbonneau .30 .75
5 Ronald Corey PRES .08 .25
6 Shayne Corson .40 1.00
7 Alain Cote .20 .50
8 Russ Courtnall .40 1.00
9 Jean-Jacques Daigneault .20 .50
10 Eric Desjardins .30 .75
11 Donald Dufresne .20 .50
12 Todd Ewen .20 .50
13 Brent Gilchrist .30 .75
14 Mike Keane .30 .75
15 Jacques Laperriere ACO .20 .50
16 Stephan Lebeau .20 .50
17 John LeClair 2.50 6.00
18 Sylvain Lefebvre .30 .75
19 Mike McPhee .30 .75
20 Kirk Muller .40 1.00
21 Lyle Odelein .30 .75
22 Andre Racicot .30 .75
23 Mario Roberge .20 .50
24 Patrick Roy 2.00 5.00
25 Denis Savard .40 1.00
26 Serge Savard DIR .30 .75
27 Mathieu Schneider .30 .75
28 Brian Skrudland .30 .75
29 Petr Svoboda .20 .50
30 Charles Thiffault ACO .08 .25
31 Sylvain Turgeon .20 .50
32 Roland Melanson

1992-93 Canadiens Postcards

This 27-card team-issued set measures 3 1/2" by 5 1/2" and features full-bleed glossy color player photos. The players are posed on the ice against a white background. The backs are white and show the team name in large red letters at the top. The player's name, number, and biography are printed in blue. A facsimile autograph at the bottom rounds out the back. The cards are unnumbered and checklisted below in alphabetical order.

COMPLETE SET (27) 7.20 18.00
1 Brian Bellows .30 .75
2 Patrice Brisebois .20 .50
3 Benoit Brunet .20 .50
4 Guy Carbonneau .30 .75
5 Jean-Jacques Daigneault .20 .50
6 Vincent Damphousse .40 1.00
7 Eric Desjardins .30 .75
8 Jacques Demers CO .30 .75
9 Gilbert Dionne .20 .50
10 Donald Dufresne .20 .50
11 Todd Ewen .20 .50
12 Kevin Haller .20 .50
13 Sean Hill .20 .50
14 Mike Keane .30 .75
15 Patric Kjellberg .20 .50
16 Stephan Lebeau .20 .50
17 John LeClair 1.25 3.00
18 Kirk Muller .40 1.00
19 Lyle Odelein .30 .75
20 Oleg Petrov .20 .50
21 Andre Racicot .25 .60
22 Mario Roberge .20 .50
23 Ed Ronan .20 .50
24 Patrick Roy 1.50 4.00
25 Denis Savard .40 1.00
26 Mathieu Schneider .30 .75
27 Brian Skrudland .30 .75

1993-94 Canadiens Molson

Measuring approximately 8" by 10 1/2", this ten-card set was sponsored by Molson and was apparently distributed in conjunction with certain games throughout the season. The fronts feature full-bleed posed color photos. The photos are accented by a red line on the top and each side; at the bottom, a blue stripe carries the player's name and his uniform number. Inside a white outer border and a fading team color-coded inner border, the backs present team line-ups in English and French for the Canadiens and the respective visiting team. The cards are unnumbered and checklisted below in alphabetical order.

COMPLETE SET (10) 20.00 50.00
1 Brian Bellows 2.50 6.00
2 Benoit Brunet 2.00 5.00
3 Guy Carbonneau 2.50 6.00
4 Vincent Damphousse 4.00 10.00
5 Jean-Jacques Daigneault 3.00 8.00
6 Kevin Haller 2.00 5.00
7 Mike Keane 2.50 6.00
8 Kirk Muller 2.50 6.00
9 Peter Popovic 2.00 5.00
10 Mathieu Schneider 2.50 6.00

1993-94 Canadiens Postcards

This 26-card, team-issued set measures approximately 3 1/2" by 5 1/2" and features full-bleed glossy color player photos. The players are posed on the ice against a white background. The bilingual (French and English) backs are white and show the team name in large red letters at the top. The player's name, number, and biography are printed in blue. A facsimile autograph at the bottom rounds out the back. The cards are unnumbered and checklisted below in alphabetical order.

COMPLETE SET (26) 8.00 20.00
1 Brian Bellows .30 .75
2 Patrice Brisebois .25 .60
3 Benoit Brunet .20 .50
4 Guy Carbonneau .30 .75
5 Jean-Jacques Daigneault .20 .50
6 Vincent Damphousse .40 1.00
7 Jacques Demers CO .20 .50
8 Eric Desjardins .30 .75
9 Gilbert Dionne .20 .50
10 Paul DiPietro .20 .50
11 Kevin Haller .20 .50
12 Mike Keane .25 .60
13 Stephan LeBeau .20 .50
14 John LeClair 1.00 2.50
15 Gary Leeman .20 .50
16 Kirk Muller .30 .75
17 Lyle Odelein .30 .75
18 Peter Popovic .20 .50
19 Andre Racicot .25 .60
20 Rob Ramage .20 .50
21 Mario Roberge .20 .50
22 Ed Ronan .20 .50
23 Patrick Roy 2.00 5.00
24 Mathieu Schneider .30 .75
25 Pierre Sevigny .20 .50
26 Ron Wilson .20 .50

1994-95 Canadiens Postcards

This 27-card set measures approximately 3 1/2" by 5 1/2" and features borderless color player photos. The players are posed on the ice against a white background. The backs are white and carry the team name and logo in large red letters at the top. The player's name, jersey number, and biography are printed in blue. A facsimile autograph at the bottom rounds out the back. The cards are unnumbered and checklisted below in alphabetical order.

COMPLETE SET (27) 6.00 15.00
1 Brian Bellows .30 .75
2 Donald Brashear .20 .50
3 Patrice Brisebois .20 .50
4 Benoit Brunet .20 .50
5 Jean-Jacques Daigneault .20 .50
6 Vincent Damphousse .30 .75
7 Jacques Demers CO .20 .50
8 Eric Desjardins .30 .75
9 Gilbert Dionne .20 .50
10 Paul Dipietro .20 .50
11 Gerry Fleming .20 .50
12 Bryan Fogarty .20 .50
13 Mike Keane .20 .50
14 John LeClair .75 2.00
15 Jim Montgomery .20 .50
16 Kirk Muller .30 .75
17 Lyle Odelein .30 .75
18 Oleg Petrov .20 .50
19 Peter Popovic .20 .50
20 Yves Racine .20 .50
21 Ed Ronan .20 .50
22 Patrick Roy 1.50 4.00
23 Brian Savage .30 .75
24 Mathieu Schneider .30 .75
25 Pierre Sevigny .20 .50
26 Turner Stevenson .20 .50
27 Ron Tugnutt .40 1.00

1995-96 Canadiens Postcards

This 20-card set measures approximately 3 1/2" by 5 1/2" and features borderless color player photos. The players are posed on the ice against a white background. The backs are white and carry the team name and logo in large red letters at the top. The player's name, jersey number, and biography are printed in blue. A facsimile autograph at the bottom rounds out the back. The cards are unnumbered and checklisted below in alphabetical order.

COMPLETE SET (20) 6.00 15.00
1 Donald Brashear .20 .50
2 Patrice Brisebois .20 .50
3 Benoit Brunet .20 .50
4 Valeri Bure .20 .50
5 Marc Bureau .20 .50
6 Vincent Damphousse .40 1.00
7 Mike Keane .25 .60
8 Saku Koivu 1.50 4.00
9 Vladimir Malakhov .20 .50
10 Lyle Odelein .20 .50
11 Oleg Petrov .20 .50
12 Peter Popovic .20 .50
13 Stephane Quintal .20 .50
14 Yves Racine .20 .50
15 Mark Recchi .40 1.00
16 Patrick Roy 1.50 4.00
17 Brian Savage .25 .60
18 Turner Stevenson .20 .50
19 Mario Tremblay CO .20 .50
20 Pierre Turgeon .40 1.00

1995-96 Canadiens Sheets

These 12 sheets were inserted in Montreal Canadiens game programs during the 1995-96 season. The fronts of the 8 1/2" by 11" sheets feature black and white photos of Montreal players in construction gear, while the backs feature lineups for that evening's match. There are reports that the Bure sheet is the toughest to find; hence a premium has been attached. The cards are dated, but unnumbered, and thus have been checklisted alphabetically below.

COMPLETE SET (12) 48.00 120.00
1 Valeri Bure 8.00 20.00
2 Benoit Brunet 4.00 10.00
3 Peter Popovic 4.00 10.00
4 Saku Koivu 6.00 15.00
5 Turner Stevenson 4.00 10.00
6 Mark Recchi 5.00 12.00
7 Vladimir Malakhov 4.00 10.00
8 Stephane Quintal 4.00 10.00
9 Brian Savage 4.00 10.00
10 Patrice Brisebois 4.00 10.00
11 Vincent Damphousse 5.00 12.00
12 Pierre Turgeon 5.00 12.00

1996-97 Canadiens Postcards

This 33-card postcard set was produced by the team for distribution in set form through the club store, or as autographable handouts by the players. They are standard postcard size and feature full-bleed color photos on the front. The backs include biographical information. The unnumbered cards are listed below alphabetically.

COMPLETE SET (33) 8.00 20.00
1 Murray Baron .20 .50
2 Sebastien Bordeleau .20 .50
3 Patrice Brisebois .20 .50
4 Benoit Brunet .20 .50
5 Valeri Bure .20 .50
6 Marc Bureau .20 .50
7 Ronald Corey PRES .20 .50
8 Shayne Corson .40 1.00
9 Yvan Cournoyer .60 1.50
10 Jassen Cullimore .20 .50
11 Vincent Damphousse .40 1.00
12 Rejean Houle .20 .50
13 Pat Jablonski .30 .75
14 Saku Koivu 1.25 3.00
15 Jacques Laperierre .30 .75
16 Vladimir Malakhov .20 .50
17 Dave Manson .20 .50
18 Chris Murray .20 .50
19 Peter Popovic .20 .50
20 Stephane Qunital .20 .50
21 Mark Recchi .40 1.00
22 Stephane Richer .40 1.00
23 Craig Rivet .20 .50
24 Martin Rucinsky .30 .75
25 Brian Savage .30 .75
26 Steve Shutt .30 .75
27 Turner Stevenson .20 .50
28 Jose Theodore 4.00 10.00
29 Jocelyn Thibault .75 2.00
30 Scott Thornton .20 .50
31 Mario Trembley .20 .50
32 Darcy Tucker .40 1.00
33 David Wilkie .20 .50

1996-97 Canadiens Sheets

These large (8.5" X 11") sheets were distributed one per issue of the Montreal Canadiens game program during the exhibition and regular season. The fronts are dominated by a posed head shot, with a smaller action photo superimposed. The player's name and sweater number also appear. The back features the lineups for both teams from that evening's contest, as well as the logo of sponsor Molson Export. Unnumbered, the set is listed below in alphabetical order.

COMPLETE SET (28) 40.00 100.00
1 Patrice Brisebois 1.25 3.00
2 Benoit Brunet 1.25 3.00
3 Valeri Bure 1.50 4.00
4 Marc Bureau 1.25 3.00
5 Shayne Corson 1.50 4.00
6 Jassen Cullimore 1.25 3.00
7 Vincent Damphousse 2.00 5.00
8 Rory Fitzpatrick 1.25 3.00
9 Saku Koivu 4.00 10.00
10 Vladimir Malakhov 1.25 3.00
11 Dave Manson 1.50 4.00
12 Chris Murray 1.25 3.00
13 Peter Popovic 1.25 3.00
14 Stephane Quintal 1.25 3.00
15 Mark Recchi 2.00 5.00
16 Stephane Richer 1.50 4.00
17 Craig Rivet 1.25 3.00
18 Martin Rucinsky 1.50 4.00
19 Brian Savage 1.50 4.00
20 Turner Stevenson 1.25 3.00
21 Jose Theodore 8.00 20.00
22 Jocelyn Thibault 3.00 8.00
23 Scott Thornton 1.25 3.00
24 Darcy Tucker 1.50 4.00
25 Pierre Turgeon 2.00 5.00
26 David Wilkie 1.25 3.00
27 Centre Molson First Anniversary .40 1.00
28 Canadiens Line-up 1.25 3.00

1997-98 Canadiens Postcards

This 26-card set was produced by the team and measures the standard postcard size. The fronts feature color player photos. The backs carry player information. The cards are unnumbered and checklisted below in alphabetical order.

COMPLETE SET (26) 6.00 15.00
1 Sebastien Bordeleau .20 .50
2 Patrice Brisebois .20 .50
3 Benoit Brunet .20 .50
4 Valeri Bure .20 .50
5 Marc Bureau .20 .50
6 Brett Clark .20 .50
7 Shayne Corson .40 1.00
8 Jassen Cullimore .20 .50
9 Vincent Damphousse .40 1.00
10 Saku Koivu 1.25 3.00
11 Vladimir Malakhov .20 .50
12 Dave Manson .20 .50
13 Andy Moog .40 1.00
14 Peter Popovic .20 .50
15 Stephane Quintal .20 .50
16 Mark Recchi .30 .75
17 Stephane Richer .40 1.00
18 Craig Rivet .20 .50
19 Martin Rucinsky .30 .75
20 Brian Savage .30 .75
21 Turner Stevenson .20 .50
22 Jocelyn Thibault .40 1.00
23 Scott Thornton .20 .50
24 Darcy Tucker .20 .50
25 Alain Vigneault .20 .50
26 David Wilkie .20 .50

1998-99 Canadiens Team Issue

This 26-card set pictures the 1998-99 Montreal Canadiens team on 3.5X5.5" cards. Each card back contains a facsimile signature of the respective player. Cards are numbered alphabetically.

COMPLETE SET (26) 4.00 15.00
1 Benoit Brunet .20 .50
2 Brett Clark .20 .50
3 Shayne Corson .20 .50
4 Vincent Damphousse .40 1.00
5 Jeff Hackett .40 1.00
6 Matt Higgins .20 .50
7 Jonas Hoglund .20 .50
8 Eric Houde .20 .50
9 Saku Koivu .75 2.00
10 Vladimir Malakhov .20 .50
11 Trent McCleary .20 .50
12 Dave Morissette .20 .50
13 Alain Nasreddine .20 .50
14 Patrick Poulin .20 .50
15 Stephane Quintal .20 .50
16 Marc Recchi .30 .75
17 Craig Rivet .20 .50
18 Martin Rucinsky .20 .50
19 Brian Savage .30 .75
20 Turner Stevenson .20 .50
21 Jose Theodore 1.25 3.00
22 Scott Thornton .20 .50
23 Igor Ulanov .20 .50
24 Alain Vigneault .20 .50
25 Eric Weinrich .20 .50
26 Sergei Zholtok .20 .50

2000-01 Canadiens Postcards

This set features the Canadiens of the NHL. These postcard-like collectibles were issued by the team to each player to be used for autograph signing sessions. Sets were also available directly through the team.

COMPLETE SET (34) 8.00 20.00
1 Francois Bouillon .20 .50
2 Andrei Bashkirov .20 .50
3 Mathieu Garon .60 1.50
4 Karl Dykhuis .20 .50
5 Xavier Delisle .20 .50
6 Patrice Brisebois .20 .50
7 Benoit Brunet .20 .50
8 Jose Theodore 1.20 3.00
9 Craig Darby .20 .50
10 Eric Chouinard .30 .75
11 Jeff Hackett .40 1.00
12 Chad Kilger .20 .50
13 Jim Campbell .20 .50
14 Christian Laflamme .20 .50
15 Eric Landry .20 .50
16 Juha Lind .20 .50
17 Trevor Linden .40 1.00
18 Andrei Markov .60 1.50
19 Gino Odjick .30 .75
20 Patrick Poulin .20 .50
21 Oleg Petrov .20 .50
22 Craig Rivet .20 .50
23 Stephane Robidas .20 .50
24 Martin Rucinsky .20 .50
25 Brian Savage .40 1.00
26 Sheldon Souray .20 .50
27 Saku Koivu .60 1.50
28 Johan Witehall .20 .50
29 Eric Weinrich .20 .50
30 Dainius Zubrus .20 .50
31 Michel Therrien CO .10 .25
32 Guy Carbonneau CO .40 1.00
33 Rick Green CO .10 .25
34 Andre Savard GM .20 .50

2000-01 Canadiens Team Issue

This set is unnumbered and listed below in alphabetical order.

COMPLETE SET (22) 5.00 12.00
1 Arron Asham .40 1.00
2 Patrice Brisebois .40 1.00
3 Benoit Brunet .40 1.00
4 Craig Darby .40 1.00
5 Karl Dykhuis .40 1.00
6 Jeff Hackett .40 1.00
7 Chad Kilger .60 1.50
8 Saku Koivu 2.00 5.00
9 Christian LaFlamme .40 1.00
10 Eric Landry .40 1.00
11 Juha Lind .40 1.00
12 Andrei Markov 1.00 2.50
13 Gino Odjick .40 1.00
14 Oleg Petrov .40 1.00
15 Patrick Poulin .40 1.00
16 Craig Rivet .40 1.00
17 Stephane Robidas .40 1.00
18 Martin Rucinsky .40 1.00
19 Brian Savage .40 1.00
20 Sheldon Souray .75 2.00
21 Jose Theodore 2.00 5.00
22 Johan Witehall .40 1.00

2001-02 Canadiens Postcards

This set is a postcard-sized issue capturing the members of the 2001-02 Canadiens. The cards were available at team appearances in singles form. They were not believed to be issued in set form. The cards are unnumbered and are listed in alphabetical order.

COMPLETE SET (32) 10.00 24.44
1 Donald Audette .30 .75
2 Shaun Van Allen .30 .75
3 Patrice Brisebois .30 .75
4 Benoit Brunet .30 .75
5 Jan Bulis .30 .75
6 Andreas Dackell .30 .75
7 Karl Dykhuis .30 .75
8 Mathieu Garon .60 1.50
9 Doug Gilmour .75 2.00
10 Jeff Hackett .60 1.50
11 Joe Juneau .30 .75
12 Chad Kilger .30 .75
13 Saku Koivu .75 2.00
14 Gino Odjick .30 .75
15 Yanic Perreault .30 .75
16 Oleg Petrov .30 .75
17 Patrick Poulin .30 .75
18 Stephane Quintal .30 .75
19 Mike Ribeiro .40 1.00
20 Craig Rivet .30 .75
21 Stephane Robidas .30 .75
22 Martin Rucinsky .30 .75
23 Jose Theodore 1.25 3.00
24 Brian Savage .30 .75
25 Reid Simpson .30 .75
26 Sheldon Souray .30 .75
27 Patrick Traverse .30 .75
28 Richard Zednik .30 .75
29 Michel Therrien HCO .10 .25
30 Guy Carbonneau CO .30 .75
31 Rick Green CO .10 .25
32 Roland Melanson CO .20 .50

2002 Canadiens AGF

These four cards were distributed as a complete set inside a single package that was distributed as a promotional giveaway by Quebec-based mutual fund firm AGF. The cards mimic OPC designs from the 1970s, and feature each player involved in a typical post-retirement activity such as golfing and fishing. Although it is believed they were issued in 2002, that has not been confirmed.

COMPLETE SET (4) 2.00 5.00
NNO Henri Richard .80 2.00
NNO Rejean Houle .40 1.00
NNO Yvan Cournoyer .80 2.00
NNO Steve Shutt .80 2.00

2002-03 Canadiens Postcards

This postcard sized set resembled many of the Canadiens issues of the past with color action photos on the fronts and the player/coach's name, position, birthday, and birth place on the back in both French and English. A facsimile autograph adorned the card backs as well. Cards measured approximately 3 1/2 X 5 1/2.

COMPLETE SET (31) 7.20 18.00
1 Stephane Quintal .20 .50
2 Saku Koivu .75 2.00
3 Oleg Petrov .20 .50
4 Richard Zednik .20 .50
5 Randy McKay .20 .50
6 Bill Lindsay .20 .50
7 Andreas Dackell .20 .50
8 Chad Kilger .20 .50
9 Sylvain Blouin .20 .50
10 Mariusz Czerkawski .20 .50
11 Karl Dykhuis .20 .50
12 Mathieu Garon .40 1.00
13 Jeff Hackett .40 1.00
14 Jan Bulis .20 .50
15 Patrice Brisebois .20 .50
16 Sheldon Souray .20 .50
17 Craig Rivet .20 .50
18 Patrick Traverse .20 .50
19 Jose Theodore .75 2.00
20 Ron Hainsey .60 1.50
21 Mike Ribeiro .20 .50
22 Andrei Markov .20 .50
23 Donald Audette .20 .50
24 Joe Juneau .20 .50
25 Doug Gilmour .40 1.00
26 Yanic Perreault .20 .50
27 Michel Therrien HCO .04 .10
28 Guy Charron ACO .04 .10
29 Rick Green ACO .04 .10
30 Clement Jodoin ACO .04 .10
31 Roland Melanson ACO .10 .25

2003-04 Canadiens Postcards

Team-issued cards feature a blurred player image on the front, with player name, number, facsimile autograph and bio info in French and English on the back.

COMPLETE SET (30) 10.00 25.00
1 Donald Audette .20 .50
2 Steve Begin .20 .50
3 Francois Bouillon .20 .50
4 Patrice Brisebois .20 .50
5 Jan Bulis .20 .50
6 Andreas Dackell .20 .50
7 Karl Dykhuis .20 .50
8 Bob Gainey GM .20 .50
9 Mathieu Garon .40 1.00
10 Ron Hainsey .20 .50
11 Chris Higgins 1.00 2.50
12 Marcel Hossa .40 1.00
13 Claude Julien CO .10 .25
14 Joe Juneau .20 .50
15 Chad Kilger .20 .50
16 Saku Koivu .75 2.00
17 Mike Komisarek .40 1.00
18 Darren Langdon .40 1.00
19 Andrei Markov .20 .50
20 Yanic Perreault .20 .50
21 Stephane Quintal .20 .50
22 Mike Ribeiro .40 1.00
23 Craig Rivet .20 .50
24 Michael Ryder 1.25 3.00
25 Sheldon Souray .40 1.00
26 Niklas Sundstrom .20 .50
27 Jose Theodore 1.25 3.00
28 Jason Ward .20 .50
29 Richard Zednik .20 .50
30 Team Photo .20 .50

2005-06 Canadiens Team Issue

COMPLETE SET (25) 15.00 30.00
1 Steve Begin .40 1.00
2 Radek Bonk .40 1.00
3 Francis Bouillon .40 1.00
4 Jan Bulis .40 1.00
5 Pierre Dagenais .40 1.00
6 Mathieu Dandenault .40 1.00
7 Yann Danis .60 1.50
8 Chris Higgins .40 1.00
9 Cristobal Huet 1.00 2.50
10 Raitis Ivanans .75 2.00
11 Saku Koivu .75 2.00
12 Mike Komisarek .40 1.00
13 Alexei Kovalev .40 1.00
14 Andrei Markov .40 1.00
15 Alexander Perezhogin .40 1.00
16 Tomas Plekanec .40 1.00
17 Mike Ribeiro .40 1.00
18 Craig Rivet .40 1.00
19 Michael Ryder .75 2.00
20 Sheldon Souray .40 1.00
21 Mark Streit .40 1.00
22 Niklas Sundstrom .40 1.00
23 Jose Theodore 1.00 2.50
24 Richard Zednik .40 1.00
25 Youppi MASCOT .10 .25

2006-07 Canadiens Postcards

1 David Aebischer .60 1.50
2 Cristobal Huet .75 2.00
3 Steve Begin .40 1.00
4 Radek Bonk .40 1.00
5 Francis Bouillon .40 1.00
6 Mathieu Dandenault .40 1.00
7 Aaron Downey .60 1.50
8 Christopher Higgins .60 1.50
9 Mike Johnson .40 1.00
10 Mike Komisarek .40 1.00
11 Alex Kovalev .40 1.00
12 Guillaume Latendresse 1.25 3.00
13 Andrei Markov .40 1.00
14 Garth Murray .40 1.00
15 Janne Niinimaa .40 1.00
16 Alexander Perezhogin .40 1.00
17 Tomas Plekanec .40 1.00
18 Craig Rivet .40 1.00
19 Michael Ryder .60 1.50
20 Mark Streit .75 2.00
21 Sheldon Souray .40 1.00
22 Sergei Samsonov .40 1.00
23 Team Photo .40 1.00
24 Youppi MASCOT .10 .25

2007-08 Canadiens Postcards

COMPLETE SET (24) 7.50 15.00
1 Saku Koivu .50 1.25
2 Carey Price 3.00 8.00
3 Josh Gorges .30 .75
4 Mike Komisarek .30 .75
5 Andrei Kostitsyn .40 1.00
6 Christopher Higgins .30 .75
7 Kyle Chipchura .50 1.25
8 Steve Begin .30 .75
9 Alex Kovalev .40 1.00
10 Guillaume Latendresse .40 1.00
11 Francis Bouillon .30 .75
12 Tomas Plekanec .50 1.25
13 Mikhail Grabovski .50 1.25
14 Mark Streit .30 .75
15 Michael Ryder .30 .75
16 Roman Hamrlik .40 1.00
17 Maxim Lapierre .30 .75
18 Andrei Markov .50 1.25
19 Garth Murray .30 .75
20 Bryan Smolinski .30 .75
21 Mathieu Dandenault .30 .75
22 Tom Kostopoulos .30 .75
23 Patrice Brisebois .30 .75
24 Cristobal Huet .40 1.00

2007-08 Canadiens Team Issue

COMPLETE SET (25) 10.00 25.00
1 Steve Begin .30 .75
2 Francis Bouillon .30 .75
3 Patrice Brisebois .30 .75
4 Kyle Chipchura .50 1.25
5 Mathieu Dandenault .30 .75
6 Josh Gorges .30 .75
7 Mikhail Grabovski .50 1.25
8 Roman Hamrlik .40 1.00
9 Christopher Higgins .30 .75
10 Cristobal Huet .40 1.00
11 Saku Koivu .50 1.25
12 Mike Komisarek .30 .75
13 Andrei Kostitsyn .40 1.00
14 Tom Kostopoulos .30 .75
15 Alex Kovalev .40 1.00
16 Maxim Lapierre .30 .75
17 Guillaume Latendresse .40 1.00
18 Andrei Markov .50 1.25
19 Garth Murray .30 .75
20 Tomas Plekanec .50 1.25
21 Carey Price 3.00 8.00
22 Michael Ryder .30 .75
23 Bryan Smolinski .30 .75
24 Mark Streit .30 .75
25 Youppi! MASCOT .30 .75

2008-09 Canadiens Postcards

COMPLETE SET (24) 7.50 15.00
1 Steve Begin .30 .75
2 Francis Bouillon .40 1.00
4 Josh Gorges .30 .75
5 Jaroslav Halak .50 1.25
6 Roman Hamrlik .40 1.00
7 Chris Higgins .30 .75
8 Saku Koivu .50 1.25
9 Mike Komisarek .30 .75
10 Andrei Kostitsyn .40 1.00
11 Sergei Kostitsyn .30 .75
12 Tom Kostopoulos
13 Alex Kovalev .40 1.00
14 Ryan Lang
15 Maxim Lapierre .30 .75
16 Georges Laraque .40 1.00
17 Guillaume Latendresse .30 .75
18 Andrei Markov .50 1.25
19 Ryan O'Byrne .30 .75
20 Tomas Plekanec .50 1.25
21 Carey Price 2.00 5.00
22 Alex Tanguay .30 .75

2009-10 Canadiens Postcards

COMPLETE SET (37) 10.00 20.00
1 Marc-Andre Bergeron .30 .75
2 Mike Cammalleri .40 1.00
3 Matt D'Agostini .40 1.00
4 Hal Gill .30 .75
5 Brian Gionta .40 1.00
6 Scott Gomez .40 1.00
7 Josh Gorges .30 .75
8 Jaroslav Halak .50 1.25
9 Roman Hamrlik .30 .75
10 Andrei Kostitsyn .40 1.00
11 Maxim Lapierre .30 .75
12 Georges Laraque .40 1.00
13 Guillaume Latendresse .40 1.00
14 Paul Mara .30 .75
15 Andrei Markov .50 1.25
16 Glen Metropolit
17 Travis Moen .30 .75
18 Ryan O'Byrne
19 Max Pacioretty .60 1.50
20 Tomas Plekanec .50 1.25
21 Carey Price 2.00 5.00
22 Jaroslav Spacek .30 .75
23 Greg Stewart
24 Youppi MASCOT .30 .75
25 Mathieu Carle .50 1.25
26 Kyle Chipchura .40 1.00
27 Ben Maxwell .40 1.00
28 Benoit Pouliot .30 .75
29 Tom Pyatt .50 1.25
30 Curtis Sanford
31 P.K. Subban 1.50 4.00
32 Yannick Weber .50 1.25
33 Jacques Martin CO .30 .75
34 Perry Pearn ACO .30 .75
35 Kirk Muller ACO .30 .75
36 Pierre Groulx ACO .30 .75
37 Bob Gainey GM .40 1.00

2011-12 Canadiens Postcards

COMPLETE SET (25) 6.00 12.00
1 Peter Budaj .40 1.00
2 Mike Cammalleri .40 1.00
3 Chris Campoli .40 1.00
4 Erik Cole .40 1.00
5 Mathieu Darche .40 1.00
6 David Desharnais .60 1.50
7 Raphael Diaz .40 1.00
8 Lars Eller .40 1.00
9 Alexei Emelin .40 1.00
10 Andreas Engqvist .40 1.00
11 Hal Gill .30 .75
12 Brian Gionta .40 1.00
13 Scott Gomez .40 1.00
14 Josh Gorges .30 .75
15 Andrei Kostitsyn .40 1.00
16 Andrei Markov .50 1.25
17 Travis Moen .30 .75
18 Max Pacioretty .50 1.25
19 Aaron Palushaj .40 1.00
20 Tomas Plekanec .50 1.25
21 Carey Price 1.50 4.00
22 Jaroslav Spacek .30 .75
23 P.K. Subban 1.00 2.50
24 Yannick Weber .40 1.00
25 Ryan White .30 .75

2012-13 Canadiens Postcards

COMPLETE SET (24) 6.00 12.00
1 Colby Armstrong .30 .75
2 Mike Blunden .30 .75
3 Francis Bouillon .30 .75
4 Rene Bourque .30 .75
5 Peter Budaj .40 1.00
6 David Desharnais .50 1.25
7 Raphael Diaz .30 .75
8 Lars Eller .40 1.00
9 Alexei Emelin .50 1.25
10 Alex Galchenyuk 1.50 4.00
11 Brendan Gallagher 1.50 4.00
12 Brian Gionta .40 1.00
13 Josh Gorges .40 1.00
14 Tomas Kaberle .30 .75
15 Andrei Markov .50 1.25
16 Travis Moen .30 .75
17 Petteri Nokelainen .30 .75
18 Max Pacioretty .50 1.25
19 Carey Price 1.50 4.00
20 Brandon Prust .30 .75
21 P.K. Subban .75 2.00
22 Yannick Weber .40 1.00
23 Ryan White .30 .75
24 Youppi MASCOT .30 .75

2013-14 Canadiens Postcards

COMPLETE SET (26) 5.00 10.00
1 Francis Bouillon .30 .75
2 Michael Bournival .50 1.25
3 Rene Bourque .30 .75
4 Daniel Briere .50 1.25
5 Peter Budaj .40 1.00
6 David Desharnais .50 1.25
7 Raphael Diaz .30 .75
8 Davis Drewiske .30 .75
9 Lars Eller .40 1.00
10 Alexei Emelin .40 1.00
11 Alex Galchenyuk 2.50 6.00
12 Brendan Gallagher 1.50 4.00
13 Brian Gionta .40 1.00
14 Josh Gorges .40 1.00
15 Andrei Markov .50 1.25
16 Travis Moen .30 .75
17 Douglas Murray .30 .75
18 Max Pacioretty .50 1.25
19 George Parros .40 1.00
20 Tomas Plekanec .50 1.25
21 Carey Price 1.50 4.00
22 Brandon Prust .30 .75
23 P.K. Subban .75 2.00
24 Jarred Tinordi .50 1.25
25 Ryan White .30 .75
26 Youppi MASCOT .30 .75

2014-15 Canadiens Postcards

COMPLETE SET (24) 6.00 12.00
1 Nathan Beaulieu .40 1.00
2 Michael Bournival .40 1.00
3 Rene Bourque .30 .75
4 David Desharnais .50 1.25
5 Lars Eller .40 1.00
6 Alexei Emelin .40 1.00
7 Alex Galchenyuk .75 2.00
8 Brendan Gallagher .50 1.25
9 Tom Gilbert .30 .75
10 Manny Malhotra .30 .75
11 Andrei Markov .50 1.25
12 Travis Moen .30 .75
13 Max Pacioretty .50 1.25
14 P.A. Parenteau .30 .75
15 Tomas Plekanec .50 1.25
16 Carey Price 1.50 4.00
17 Brandon Prust .30 .75
18 Jiri Sekac .50 1.25
19 P.K. Subban .75 2.00
20 Jarred Tinordi .75 2.00
21 Dustin Tokarski .30 .75
22 Mike Weaver .30 .75
23 Dale Weise .30 .75
24 Youppi! Mascot .30 .75

2015-16 Canadiens Postcards

COMPLETE SET (25) 6.00 12.00
1 Nathan Beaulieu .40 1.00
2 Marc Bergevin .30 .75
3 Paul Byron .30 .75
4 Mike Condon .30 .75
5 David Desharnais .40 1.00
6 Lars Eller .40 1.00
7 Alexei Emelin .40 1.00
8 Tomas Fleischmann .30 .75
9 Brian Flynn .30 .75
10 Alex Galchenyuk .60 1.50
11 Brendan Gallagher .60 1.50
12 Tom Gilbert .30 .75
13 Andrei Markov .50 1.25
14 Torrey Mitchell .30 .75
15 Geoff Molson OWN .30 .75
16 Max Pacioretty .50 1.25
17 Greg Pateryn .30 .75

18 Jeff Petry	.30	.75
19 Tomas Plekanec	.50	1.25
20 Carey Price	1.50	4.00
21 Alexander Semin	.50	1.25
22 Devante Smith-Pelly	.40	1.00
23 P.K. Subban	.75	2.00
24 Dale Weise	.30	.75
25 Youppi MASCOT	.30	.75

1970-71 Canucks Royal Bank

This 20-card set of Vancouver Canucks was sponsored by Royal Bank, whose company logo appears at the lower left corner on the front. The set is subtitled Royal Bank Leo's Leaders Canucks Player of the Week. The black and white posed player photos measure approximately 5" by 7" and have white borders. The player's signature is inscribed across the bottom of the picture, and the backs are blank. The cards are unnumbered and checklisted below in alphabetical order.

COMPLETE SET (20)	30.00	60.00
1 Andre Boudrias	2.00	4.00
2 Mike Corrigan	1.50	3.00
3 Ray Cullen	2.50	5.00
4 Gary Doak	1.50	3.00
5 George Gardner	1.50	3.00
6 Murray Hall	1.50	3.00
7 Charlie Hodge	4.00	8.00
8 Danny Johnson	1.50	3.00
9 Orland Kurtenbach	2.50	5.00
10 Wayne Maki	1.50	3.00
11 Rosaire Paiement	2.00	4.00
12 Paul Popiel	2.00	4.00
13 Pat Quinn	4.00	8.00
14 Marc Reaume	1.50	3.00
15 Darryl Sly	1.50	3.00
16 Dale Tallon	2.50	5.00
17 Ted Taylor	1.50	3.00
18 Barry Wilkins	1.50	3.00
19 Dunc Wilson	2.50	5.00
20 Jim Wiste	1.50	3.00

1971-72 Canucks Royal Bank

This 20-card set of Vancouver Canucks was sponsored by Royal Bank, whose company logo appears at the lower left corner on the front. The set is subtitled Royal Bank Leo's Leaders Canucks Player of the Week. The black and white posed player photos measure approximately 5" by 7" and have white borders. The player's signature is inscribed across the bottom of the picture, and the backs are blank. The cards are numbered by week of issue. Card number 10 is unknown and may have never been issued.

COMPLETE SET (20)	25.00	50.00
1 Bobby Lalonde	1.00	2.00
2 Mike Corrigan	1.00	2.00
3 Murray Hall	1.00	2.00
4 Jocelyn Guevremont	2.00	4.00
5 Pat Quinn	3.00	6.00
6 Orland Kurtenbach	2.00	4.00
7 Paul Popiel	2.00	4.00
8 Ron Ward	1.00	2.00
9 Rosaire Paiement	1.50	3.00
11 Dale Tallon	2.00	4.00
12 Bobby Schmautz	2.00	4.00
13 Dennis Kearns	1.00	2.00
14 Barry Wilkins	1.00	2.00
15 Dunc Wilson	2.50	5.00
16 Andre Boudrias	2.00	4.00
17 Ted Taylor	1.50	3.00
18 George Gardner	1.00	2.00
19 John Schella	1.00	2.00
20 Wayne Maki	1.50	3.00
21 Gary Doak	1.00	2.00

1972-73 Canucks Nalley's

This six-card set was available on the backs of specially marked Nalley's Triple Pak Potato Chips boxes. The back yellow panel has a 6 3/4" by 5 3/8" (approximately) action shot of a Canuck player beside the goalie and net. One player card is superimposed over the lower left corner of this large action photo. The card is framed by a thin perforated line; if the card were cut out, it would measure about 3" by 3 3/4". The front features a close-up posed color player photo (from the waste up) with white borders. The player's name and position appear in white bottom border. The backs are blank. At the bottom of each back panel are miniature blue-tinted versions of all six player cards. The cards are unnumbered and checklisted below in alphabetical order.

COMPLETE SET (6)	62.50	125.00
1 Andre Boudrias	10.00	20.00
2 George Gardner	10.00	20.00
3 Wayne Maki	12.50	25.00
4 Rosaire Paiement	12.50	25.00
5 Pat Quinn	20.00	40.00
6 Barry Wilkins	10.00	20.00

1972-73 Canucks Royal Bank

This 21-card set of Vancouver Canucks was sponsored by Royal Bank, whose company logo appears at the lower left corner on the front. The set is subtitled Leo's Leaders Canucks Player of the Week. These colorful full body player photos measure approximately 5" by 7" and have white borders. The background of the photos ranges from light blue to royal blue. The player's facsimile signature is inscribed across the bottom of the picture, and the backs are blank. The cards are unnumbered on the front and checklisted below in alphabetical order.

COMPLETE SET (21)	20.00	40.00
1 Dave Balon	1.50	3.00
2 Gregg Boddy	1.00	2.00
3 Larry Bolonchuk	1.00	2.00
4 Andre Boudrias	1.00	2.00
5 Ed Dyck	1.00	2.00
6 Jocelyn Guevremont	1.50	3.00
7 James Hargreaves	1.00	2.00
8 Dennis Kearns	1.00	2.00
9 Orland Kurtenbach	1.50	3.00
10 Bobby Lalonde	1.00	2.00
11 Richard Lemieux	1.00	2.00
12 Don Lever	1.50	3.00
13 Wayne Maki	1.50	3.00
14 Bryan McSheffrey	1.00	2.00
15 Gerry O'Flaherty	1.00	2.00
16 Bobby Schmautz	1.50	3.00
17 Dale Tallon	1.50	3.00
18 Don Tannahill	1.00	2.00
19 Barry Wilkins	1.00	2.00
20 Dunc Wilson	1.50	3.00
21 John Wright	1.00	2.00

1973-74 Canucks Royal Bank

This 21-card set of Vancouver Canucks was sponsored by Royal Bank, whose company logo appears at the lower left corner on the front. The set is subtitled Royal Leaders Canucks Player of the Week. These colorful full body player photos measure approximately 5" by 7" and have white borders. The background of the photos ranges from yellowish green to green. The player's facsimile signature is inscribed across the bottom of the picture, and the backs are blank. The cards are unnumbered on the front and checklisted below in alphabetical order.

COMPLETE SET (21)	20.00	40.00
1 Paulin Bordeleau	1.00	2.00
2 Andre Boudrias	1.00	2.00
3 Jacques Caron	1.00	2.00
4 Bob Dailey	1.00	2.00
5 Dave Dunn	1.00	2.00
6 Jocelyn Guevremont	1.50	3.00
7 Dennis Kearns	1.00	2.00
8 Jerry Korab	1.00	2.00
9 Orland Kurtenbach	2.00	4.00
10 Bobby Lalonde	1.00	2.00
11 Richard Lemieux	1.00	2.00
12 Don Lever	1.50	3.00
13 Bill McCreary	1.00	2.00
14 Bryan McSheffrey	1.00	2.00
15 Gerry O'Flaherty	1.00	2.00
16 Bobby Schmautz	2.00	4.00
17 Gary Smith	2.00	4.00
18 Don Tannahill	1.00	2.00
19 Dennis Ververgaert	1.50	3.00
20 Barry Wilkins	1.00	2.00
21 John Wright	1.00	2.00

1974-75 Canucks Royal Bank

This 20-card set of Vancouver Canucks was sponsored by Royal Bank, whose company logo appears at the lower left corner on the front. The set is subtitled Royal Leaders Player of the Week. These colorful head and shoulders player photos are presented on a white background with a thin black border. The cards measure approximately 5" by 7", have white borders, and are printed on glossy paper. The player's facsimile signature is inscribed across the bottom of the picture, and the backs are blank. The cards are unnumbered on the front and checklisted below in alphabetical order.

COMPLETE SET (20)	20.00	40.00
1 Gregg Boddy	1.00	2.00
2 Paulin Bordeleau	1.50	3.00
3 Andre Boudrias	1.50	3.00
4 Bob Dailey	1.00	2.00
5 Ab DeMarco	1.00	2.00
6 John Gould	1.00	2.00
7 John Grisdale	1.00	2.00
8 Dennis Kearns	1.00	2.00
9 Bobby Lalonde	1.00	2.00
10 Don Lever	1.50	3.00
11 Ken Lockett	1.00	2.00
12 Gerry Meehan	1.50	3.00
13 Garry Monahan	1.00	2.00
14 Chris Oddleifson	1.00	2.00
15 Gerry O'Flaherty	1.00	2.00
16 Tracy Pratt	1.00	2.00
17 Mike Robitaille	1.00	2.00
18 Leon Rochefort	1.00	2.00
19 Gary Smith	1.50	3.00
20 Dennis Ververgaert	1.50	3.00

1975-76 Canucks Royal Bank

This 22-card set of Vancouver Canucks was sponsored by Royal Bank, whose company logo appears at the lower left corner on the front. The set is subtitled Royal Leaders Player of the Week. The cards measure approximately 4 3/4" by 7 1/4" and are printed on glossy paper. The fronts feature a color head and shoulders shot of the player on white background with a thin black border. The player's facsimile autograph appears below the picture. The backs are blank. The cards are unnumbered and we have checklisted them below in alphabetical order.

COMPLETE SET (22)	20.00	40.00
1 Rick Blight	1.00	2.00
2 Gregg Boddy	1.00	2.00
3 Paulin Bordeleau	1.00	2.00
4 Andre Boudrias	1.00	2.00
5 Bob Dailey	1.00	2.00
6 Ab DeMarco	1.00	2.00
7 John Gould	1.00	2.00
8 John Grisdale	1.00	2.00
9 Dennis Kearns	1.00	2.00
10 Bobby Lalonde	1.00	2.00
11 Don Lever	1.50	3.00
12 Ken Lockett	1.00	2.00
13 Garry Monahan	1.00	2.00
14 Bob Murray	1.00	2.00
15 Chris Oddleifson	1.00	2.00
16 Gerry O'Flaherty	1.00	2.00
17 Tracy Pratt	1.00	2.00
18 Mike Robitaille	1.00	2.00
19 Ron Sedlbauer	1.00	2.00
20 Gary Smith	1.50	3.00
21 Harold Snepsts	3.00	6.00
22 Dennis Ververgaert	1.50	3.00

1976-77 Canucks Royal Bank

This 23-card set of Vancouver Canucks was sponsored by Royal Bank, whose company logo appears at the lower left corner on the front. The set is subtitled Royal Leaders Player of the Week. The cards measure approximately 4 3/4" by 7 1/4" and are printed on glossy paper. The fronts feature a color head and shoulders shot of the player on white background with a thin black border. The player's facsimile autograph appears below the picture. The backs are blank. The cards are unnumbered and we have checklisted them below in alphabetical order.

COMPLETE SET (23)	20.00	40.00
1 Rick Blight	1.00	2.00
2 Bob Dailey	1.00	2.00
3 Dave Fortier	1.00	2.00
4 Brad Gassoff	1.00	2.00
5 John Gould	1.00	2.00
6 John Grisdale	1.00	2.00
7 Dennis Kearns	1.00	2.00
8 Bobby Lalonde	1.00	2.00
9 Don Lever	1.50	3.00
10 Cesare Maniago	2.00	4.00
11 Garry Monahan	1.00	2.00
12 Bob Murray	1.00	2.00
13 Chris Oddleifson	1.00	2.00
14 Gerry O'Flaherty	1.00	2.00
15 Curt Ridley	1.00	2.00
16 Mike Robitaille	1.00	2.00
17 Ron Sedlbauer	1.00	2.00
18 Harold Snepsts	2.50	5.00
19 Andy Spruce	1.00	2.00
20 Ralph Stewart	1.00	2.00
21 Dennis Ververgaert	1.50	3.00
22 Mike Walton	1.50	3.00
23 Jim Wiley	1.50	3.00

1977-78 Canucks Canada Dry Cans

This extremely scarce set features the Canucks of the NHL. Each specially-marked regular sized ginger ale can sold in the Vancouver area for a limited time featured a headshot of a player on the back side. Unopened cans sell for a premium of 100 percent.

COMPLETE SET (16)	20.00	40.00
1 Rick Blight	1.00	2.00
2 Brad Gassoff	1.00	2.00
3 Jere Gillis	1.00	2.00
4 Larry Goodenough	1.00	2.00
5 Hilliard Graves	1.00	2.00
6 Dennis Kearns	1.00	2.00
7 Don Lever	1.00	2.00
8 Cesare Maniago	2.50	5.00
9 Jack McIlhargey	1.00	2.00
10 Garry Monahan	1.00	2.00
11 Chris Oddleifson	1.00	2.00
12 Curt Ridley	1.00	2.00
13 Derek Sanderson	2.50	5.00
14 Harold Snepsts	2.00	4.00
15 Mike Walton	1.00	2.00
16 Dennis Ververgaert	1.00	2.00

1977-78 Canucks Royal Bank

This 21-card set of Vancouver Canucks was sponsored by Royal Bank, whose company logo appears at the lower left corner on the front. The set is subtitled Royal Leaders Player of the Week. The cards measure approximately 4 1/4" by 5 1/2" and are printed on thin cardboard stock. The fronts feature a color head and shoulders shot of the player on white background with a thin black border. The player's facsimile autograph appears below the picture. The backs are blank. The cards are unnumbered; they are checklisted below in alphabetical order.

COMPLETE SET (21)	20.00	40.00
1 Rick Blight	1.00	2.00
2 Larry Carriere	1.00	2.00
3 Rob Flockhart	1.00	2.00
4 Brad Gassoff	1.00	2.00
5 Jere Gillis	1.00	2.00
6 Larry Goodenough	1.00	2.00
7 Hilliard Graves	1.00	2.00
8 John Grisdale	1.00	2.00
9 Dennis Kearns	1.00	2.00
10 Don Lever	1.50	3.00
11 Cesare Maniago	2.00	4.00
12 Bob Manno	1.00	2.00
13 Jack McIlhargey	1.00	2.00
14 Garry Monahan	1.00	2.00
15 Chris Oddleifson	1.00	2.00
16 Gerry O'Flaherty	1.00	2.00
17 Curt Ridley	1.50	3.00
18 Ron Sedlbauer	1.00	2.00
19 Harold Snepsts	2.00	4.00
20 Dennis Ververgaert	1.50	3.00
21 Mike Walton	1.00	2.00

1978-79 Canucks Royal Bank

This 23-card set of Vancouver Canucks was sponsored by Royal Bank, whose company logo appears at the upper left corner on the front. The cards measure approximately 4 1/4" by 5 1/2" and are printed on thin cardboard stock. The fronts feature a color head and shoulders shot of the player on white background with a thin blue border. The player's facsimile autograph and the team logo appear above the picture. The backs present biographical and statistical information. The cards are unnumbered; they are checklisted below in alphabetical order.

COMPLETE SET (23)	20.00	40.00
1 Rick Blight	.75	1.50
2 Gary Bromley	1.00	2.00
3 Bill Derlago	.75	1.50
4 Roland Eriksson	.75	1.50
5 Curt Fraser	1.00	2.00
6 Jere Gillis	.75	1.50
7 Thomas Gradin	2.00	4.00
8 Hilliard Graves	.75	1.50
9 John Grisdale	.75	1.50
10 Glen Hanlon	1.25	2.50
11 Randy Holt	.75	1.50
12 Dennis Kearns	.75	1.50
13 Don Lever	1.00	2.00
14 Lars Lindgren	.75	1.50
15 Bob Manno	.75	1.50
16 Pit Martin	1.00	2.00
17 Jack McIlhargey	.75	1.50
18 Chris Oddleifson	.75	1.50
19 Ron Sedlbauer	.75	1.50
20 Stan Smyl	2.00	4.00
21 Harold Snepsts	2.00	4.00
22 Dennis Ververgaert	1.00	2.00
23 Lars Zetterstrom	.75	1.50

1979-80 Canucks Royal Bank

This 22-card set features posed color player photos from the shoulders up of the Vancouver Canucks. There are actually two different sets with the same value, a team-issued (no reference to Royal Bank) blank back set and a Royal Bank set; the card pictures (and values) are the same in both versions of the set. The sponsor name appears in black print at the card top, with the words "Player of the Week 1979/80" immediately below. The cards measure approximately 4 1/4" by 5 1/2". The front features a color head shot with a blue background and black and white borders. The player's jersey number, facsimile autograph, and team logo appear in the bottom white border. Since this is an unnumbered set, the cards are listed alphabetically. The Royal Bank backs carry biography, career summary, and complete statistical information (season by season, regular schedule, and playoffs).

COMPLETE SET (22)	15.00	30.00
1 Brent Ashton	1.00	2.00
2 Rick Blight	.75	1.50
3 Gary Bromley	1.00	2.00
4 Drew Callander	.75	1.50
5 Bill Derlago	1.00	2.00
6 Curt Fraser	1.00	2.00
7 Jere Gillis	.75	1.50
8 Thomas Gradin	1.50	3.00
9 Glen Hanlon	1.25	2.50
10 John Hughes	.75	1.50
11 Dennis Kearns	.75	1.50
12 Don Lever	1.00	2.00
13 Lars Lindgren	.75	1.50
14 Bob Manno	.75	1.50
15 Kevin McCarthy	.75	1.50
16 Jack McIlhargey	.75	1.50
17 Chris Oddleifson	.75	1.50
18 Curt Ridley	.75	1.50
19 Ron Sedlbauer	.75	1.50
20 Stan Smyl	1.50	3.00
21 Harold Snepsts	1.50	3.00
22 Rick Vaive	1.25	2.50

1980-81 Canucks Silverwood Dairies

This 24-card set of Vancouver Canucks was sponsored by Silverwood Dairies. The cards measure approximately 2 1/2" by 3 1/2" individually but were issued as perforated panels of three. The cards are checklisted below in alphabetical order.

COMPLETE SET (24)	20.00	40.00
1 Brent Ashton	.75	2.00
2 Ivan Boldirev	.75	2.00
3 Per-Olov Brasar	.60	1.50
4 Richard Brodeur	1.50	4.00
5 Gary Bromley	.75	2.00
6 Jerry Butler	.60	1.50
7 Colin Campbell	1.00	2.50
8 Curt Fraser	.75	2.00
9 Thomas Gradin	1.00	2.50
10 Glen Hanlon	1.00	2.50
11 Dennis Kearns	.60	1.50
12 Rick Lanz	.60	1.50
13 Lars Lindgren	.60	1.50
14 Dave Logan	.60	1.50
15 Gary Lupul	.60	1.50
16 Bob Manno	.60	1.50
17 Kevin McCarthy	.60	1.50
18 Gerry Minor	.60	1.50
19 Kevin Primeau	.60	1.50
20 Darcy Rota	.60	1.50
21 Stan Smyl	1.25	3.00
22 Harold Snepsts	1.25	3.00
23 Bobby Schmautz	.60	1.50
24 Tiger Williams	1.50	4.00

1980-81 Canucks Team Issue

This 22-card set measures approximately 3 3/4" by 4 7/8" and features posed color head and shoulder player photos against a light blue-gray background. The pictures have rounded corners and are enclosed by thick black and thin red border stripes. The player's name, uniform number, position, and the team logo appear in the thicker bottom border. A facsimile autograph runs vertically to the left of the player's head. The backs are blank.

COMPLETE SET (22)	15.00	30.00
1 Brent Ashton	.75	2.00
2 Ivan Boldirev	.75	2.00
3 Per-Olov Brasar	.60	1.50
4 Richard Brodeur	1.50	4.00
5 Gary Bromley	.75	2.00
6 Jerry Butler	.60	1.50
7 Colin Campbell	1.00	2.50
8 Curt Fraser	.75	2.00
9 Thomas Gradin	1.00	2.50
10 Glen Hanlon	1.00	2.50
11 Dennis Kearns	.60	1.50
12 Rick Lanz	.60	1.50
13 Lars Lindgren	.60	1.50
14 Dave Logan	.60	1.50
15 Gary Lupul	.60	1.50
16 Kevin McCarthy	.60	1.50
17 Gerry Minor	.60	1.50
18 Darcy Rota	.60	1.50
19 Bobby Schmautz	.60	1.50
20 Stan Smyl	1.25	3.00
21 Harold Snepsts	1.25	3.00
22 Tiger Williams	1.50	4.00

1981-82 Canucks Silverwood Dairies

This 24-card set of Vancouver Canucks was sponsored by Silverwood Dairies, and the sponsor's name and logo appear at the top of the card face. The cards measure approximately 2 7/16" by 4 1/16" and feature a color action player photo, with the team logo superimposed at the lower right corner of the picture. The cards are unnumbered and so are checklisted in alphabetical order.

COMPLETE SET (24)	10.00	25.00
1 Per-Olov Brasar	.40	1.00
2 Richard Brodeur	1.00	2.50
3 Ivan Boldirev	.50	1.25
4 Jiri Bubla	.40	1.00
5 Jerry Butler	.40	1.00
6 Colin Campbell	.60	1.50
7 Marc Crawford	.75	2.00
8 Anders Eldebrink	.40	1.00
9 Curt Fraser	.40	1.00
10 Thomas Gradin	.75	2.00
11 Doug Halward	.40	1.00
12 Darcy Rota	.40	1.00
12 Glen Hanlon	.60	1.50
13 Ivan Hlinka	.40	1.00
13 Stan Smyl	1.00	2.50
14 Rick Lanz	.40	1.00
15 Lars Lindgren	.40	1.00
16 Blair MacDonald	.40	1.00
17 Gerry Minor	.40	1.00
18 Gary Lupul	.40	1.00
22 Kevin McCarthy	.40	1.00
24 Dave(Tiger) Williams	1.00	2.50
24 Lars Molin	.40	1.00
25 Harold Snepsts	1.00	2.50

1981-82 Canucks Team Issue

This 20-card set measures approximately 3 3/4" by 4 7/8" and features posed color head and shoulder player photos against a blue background. The pictures have rounded corners and are enclosed by thick black and thin red border stripes. The player's name, uniform number, position, and the team logo appear in the thicker bottom border. A facsimile autograph runs vertically to the left of the player's head. The backs are blank. The card of Richard Brodeur is the same one used in the 1980-81 team-issued set.

COMPLETE SET (20)	8.00	20.00
1 Ivan Boldirev	.60	1.50
2 Per-Olov Brasar	.40	1.00
3 Richard Brodeur	1.00	2.50
4 Jiri Bubla	.40	1.00
5 Jerry Butler	.40	1.00
6 Colin Campbell	1.00	2.50
7 Anders Eldebrink	.40	1.00
8 Curt Fraser	.60	1.50
9 Thomas Gradin	.75	2.00
10 Doug Halward	.40	1.00
11 Glen Hanlon	.60	1.50
12 Rick Lanz	.40	1.00
13 Gary Lupul	.40	1.00
14 Blair MacDonald	.40	1.00
15 Kevin McCarthy	.40	1.00
16 Gerry Minor	.40	1.00
17 Lars Molin	.40	1.00
18 Darcy Rota	.40	1.00
19 Stan Smyl	.75	2.00
20 Tiger Williams	1.00	2.50

1982-83 Canucks Team Issue

This 23-card set of the Vancouver Canucks was issued in three panels of six cards each with a fourth panel having five cards because the team photo fills the space of two player cards. The cards measure approximately 3 3/4" by 4 7/8". The fronts feature a color posed photo of the player with rounded corners and surrounded by a thick black and a thin red border. The player's name, position, jersey number and team logo appear below the photo in a wide black border. The horizontal backs carry the player's name, position, jersey number, biographical and statistical information. The cards are unnumbered and checklisted below in alphabetical order.

COMPLETE SET (23)	8.00	20.00
1 Ivan Boldirev	.40	1.00
2 Richard Brodeur	1.00	2.50
3 Jiri Bubla	.30	.75
4 Garth Butcher	.40	1.00
5 Ron Delorme	.30	.75
6 Ken Ellacott	.30	.75
7 Curt Fraser	.30	.75
8 Thomas Gradin	.60	1.50
9 Doug Halward	.30	.75
10 Ivan Hlinka	.30	.75
11 Rick Lanz	.30	.75
12 Moe Lemay	.30	.75
13 Lars Lindgren	.30	.75
14 Kevin McCarthy	.30	.75
15 Gerry Minor	.30	.75
16 Lars Molin	.30	.75
17 Jim Nill	.30	.75
18 Darcy Rota	.30	.75
19 Stan Smyl	.60	1.50
20 Harold Snepsts	1.00	2.50
21 Patrik Sundstrom	.75	2.00
22 Tiger Williams	.75	2.00
23 Team Photo	.30	.75

1983-84 Canucks Team Issue

This 23-card set of Vancouver Canucks was issued in three panels of six cards each, with the fourth panel having 5 cards (the team photo card fills the space of two player cards). The player cards measure approximately 3 11/16" by 4 5/8". The front features a color posed photo (with rounded corners) of the player, surrounded by a thick black and a thin red border. The Canucks' logo and player information appear below the picture. The back has biographical and statistical information in a horizontal format. We have checklisted the names below in alphabetical order, with the uniform number to the right of the name.

COMPLETE SET (23)	10.00	25.00
1 Richard Brodeur 35	.75	2.00
2 Jiri Bubla 29	.20	.50
3 Garth Butcher 5	.40	1.00
4 Marc Crawford 28	.40	1.00
5 Ron Delorme 19	.20	.50
6 John Garrett 31	.40	1.00
7 Jere Gillis 4	.20	.50
8 Thomas Gradin 23	.60	1.50
9 Doug Halward 2	.20	.50
10 Mark Kirton 16	.20	.50
11 Rick Lanz 4	.20	.50
12 Gary Lupul 7	.20	.50
13 Kevin McCarthy 25	.20	.50
14 Lars Molin 26	.20	.50
15 Jim Nill 8	.20	.50
16 Michel Petit 3	.40	1.00
17 Darcy Rota 18	.20	.50
18 Stan Smyl 12	.60	1.50
19 Harold Snepsts 27	.75	2.00
20 Patrik Sundstrom 17	.60	1.50
21 Tony Tanti 9	.60	1.50
22 Tiger Williams 22	.75	2.00
23 Team Photo	.40	1.00

1984-85 Canucks Team Issue

This 26-card set of Vancouver Canucks was issued in four six-card panels plus a larger team photo card and an Air Canucks advertisement card (the latter two measure approximately 4 5/8" by 7"). The player cards measure 3 5/16" by 4 1/4". The key card in the set is Cam Neely appearing in his Rookie Card year. The cards are unnumbered and checklisted below in alphabetical order.

COMPLETE SET (26)	10.00	25.00
1 Neil Belland	.20	.50
2 Richard Brodeur	.60	1.50
3 Jiri Bubla	.20	.50
4 Garth Butcher	.30	.75
5 Frank Caprice	.30	.75
6 J.J. Daigneault	.30	.75
7 Ron Delorme	.20	.50
8 John Garrett	.40	1.00
9 Thomas Gradin	.60	1.50
10 Taylor Hall	.20	.50
11 Doug Halward	.20	.50
12 Rick Lanz	.20	.50
13 Moe Lemay	.20	.50
14 Doug Lidster	.30	.75
15 Gary Lupul	.20	.50
16 Al MacAdam	.20	.50
17 Peter McNab	.30	.75
18 Cam Neely	4.00	10.00
19 Michel Petit	.30	.75
20 Darcy Rota	.20	.50
21 Petri Skriko	.40	1.00
22 Stan Smyl	.40	1.00
23 Patrik Sundstrom	.40	1.00
24 Tony Tanti	.40	1.00
25 Team Photo (Large size)	.60	1.50
26 Air Canucks (Advertisement)	.08	.25

1985-86 Canucks Team Issue

This 25-card set of Vancouver Canucks was issued in four panels of six cards each, with a separate team photo card. The player cards measure approximately 3 3/8" by 4 1/4". The team photo measures approximately 7" by 4 5/8". The fronts feature color posed player photos (with rounded corners) surrounded by thick black and thin red borders. The Canucks' logo and player information appear below the picture. The backs are blank. The cards are unnumbered and checklisted below in alphabetical order.

COMPLETE SET (25)	7.20	18.00
1 Richard Brodeur	.60	1.50
2 Jiri Bubla	.20	.50
3 Garth Butcher	.30	.75
4 Frank Caprice	.30	.75
5 Glen Cochrane	.20	.50
6 Craig Coxe	.20	.50
7 J.J. Daigneault	.30	.75
8 Thomas Gradin	.40	1.00
9 Taylor Hall	.20	.50
10 Doug Halward	.20	.50
11 Jean-Marc Lanthier	.20	.50
12 Rick Lanz	.20	.50
13 Moe Lemay	.20	.50
14 Doug Lidster	.30	.75
15 Dave Lowry	.20	.50
16 Gary Lupul	.20	.50
17 Cam Neely	3.00	8.00
18 Brent Peterson	.20	.50
19 Jim Sandlak	.30	.75
20 Petri Skriko	.40	1.00
21 Stan Smyl	.40	1.00
22 Patrik Sundstrom	.40	1.00
23 Steve Tambellini	.20	.50
24 Tony Tanti	.40	1.00
25 Team Photo (Large size)	1.25	3.00

1986-87 Canucks Team Issue

This 24-card set of Vancouver Canucks was issued in four panels of six cards each; after perforation, the cards measure the standard size (2 1/2" by 3 1/2"). The front design has color head and shoulder shots with white borders. Below the picture the player's name and number appear between two team logos. The horizontally oriented backs have biography and career statistics. The cards are unnumbered and checklisted below in alphabetical order, with the uniform number after the name.

COMPLETE SET (24)	4.80	12.00
1 Richard Brodeur 35	.60	1.50
2 Garth Butcher 5	.30	.75
3 Frank Caprice 30	.30	.75
4 Glen Cochrane 29	.20	.50
5 Craig Coxe 32	.20	.50
6 Taylor Hall 8	.20	.50
7 Stu Kulak 16	.20	.50
8 Moe Lemay 14	.20	.50
9 Dave Lowry 22	.20	.50
10 Brad Maxwell 27	.20	.50
11 Petri Skriko 26	.30	.75
12 Barry Pederson 7	.40	1.00
13 Rick Lanz 4	.20	.50
14 Doug Lidster 3	.30	.75
15 Brent Peterson 10	.20	.50
16 Michel Petit 24	.30	.75
17 Dave Richter 6	.20	.50
18 Stan Smyl 12	.40	1.00
19 Jim Sandlak 33	.20	.50
20 Patrik Sundstrom 17	.40	1.00
21 Rich Sutter 15	.20	.50
22 Steve Tambellini 20	.20	.50
23 Tony Tanti 9	.40	1.00
24 Wendell Young 1	.40	1.00

1987-88 Canucks Shell Oil

This 24-card set of Vancouver Canucks was sponsored by Shell Oil and released only in British Columbia. It was issued as eight different three-card panels, with the cards measuring the standard size, 2 1/2" by 3 1/2", after perforation. The cards were distributed as a promotion for Shell Oil, with one panel set per week given out at participating Shell stations. Included with the cards was a coupon offering a 5.00 discount on tickets to the Canucks games. The front features a color head and shoulders shot of the player, with the Canucks' logo superimposed at the upper left hand corner of the picture. The player's name, position, and the "Formula Shell" logo appear below the picture. The back has biographical and career information on the player. The cards are unnumbered and checklisted below in alphabetical order. Kirk McLean's card predates his Rookie Card by two years.

COMPLETE SET (24)	3.00	8.00
1 Greg Adams	.30	.75
2 Jim Benning	.08	.25
3 Randy Boyd	.08	.25
4 Richard Brodeur	.40	1.00
5 David Bruce	.08	.25
6 Garth Butcher	.08	.25
7 Frank Caprice	.15	.40
8 Craig Coxe	.08	.25
9 Willie Huber	.08	.25
10 Doug Lidster	.20	.50
11 Dave Lowry	.08	.25
12 Kirk McLean	1.00	2.50
13 Larry Melnyk	.08	.25
14 Barry Pederson	.20	.50
15 Dave Richter	.08	.25
16 Jim Sandlak	.08	.25
17 Dave Saunders	.08	.25
18 Petri Skriko	.20	.50
19 Stan Smyl	.30	.75
20 Daryl Stanley	.08	.25
21 Rich Sutter	.08	.25
22 Steve Tambellini	.08	.25
23 Tony Tanti	.30	.75
24 Doug Wickenheiser	.08	.25

1988-89 Canucks Mohawk

This 24-card standard-size set of Vancouver Canucks was sponsored by Mohawk and issued in six panels of four cards each. The cards feature on the front a color head and shoulders shot of the player on white card stock. The Canucks' and Mohawk logos appear at the bottom of the card. The player's name, position, and number are given in black lettering running the bottom to top on the left side of the picture. The backs are blank. We have checklisted the cards below in alphabetical order, with the player's number to the right of his name. The cards of Trevor Linden and Kirk McLean's predate their Rookie Cards by one year.

COMPLETE SET (24)	6.00	15.00
1 Greg Adams 8	.40	1.00
2 Jim Benning 4	.20	.50
3 Ken Berry 18	.20	.50
4 Randy Boyd 29	.20	.50
5 Steve Bozek 14	.20	.50
6 Brian Bradley 10	.60	1.50
7 David Bruce 25	.20	.50
8 Garth Butcher 5	.20	.50
9 Kevan Guy 2	.20	.50
10 Doug Lidster 3	.20	.50
11 Trevor Linden 16	2.00	5.00
12 Kirk McLean 1	1.25	3.00
13 Larry Melnyk 24	.20	.50
14 Robert Nordmark 6	.20	.50
15 Barry Pederson 7	.30	.75
16 Paul Reinhart 23	.30	.75
17 Jim Sandlak 19	.20	.50
18 Petri Skriko 26	.30	.75
19 Stan Smyl 12	.30	.75
20 Harold Snepsts 27	.60	1.50
21 Ronnie Stern 20	.20	.50
22 Rich Sutter 15	.20	.50
23 Tony Tanti 9	.30	.75
24 Steve Weeks 31	.30	.75

1989-90 Canucks Mohawk

This 24-card standard-size set was sponsored by Mohawk to commemorate the Vancouver Canucks' 20th year in the NHL and was issued in six panels of four cards each. The cards feature a color head and shoulders shot of the player on white card stock. The Canucks' and Mohawk logos appear at the bottom of the card, and the Canucks' logo has the number "2" before it joining with the circular shape of the logo to suggest "20." The player's name, position, and number are given in black lettering running the bottom to top on the left side of the picture. The backs are blank. We have checklisted the cards below in alphabetical order, with the player's number to the right of his name.

COMPLETE SET (24)	6.00	15.00
1 Greg Adams 8	.30	.75
2 Jim Benning 4	.20	.50
3 Steve Bozek 14	.20	.50
4 Brian Bradley 10	.40	1.00
5 Garth Butcher 5	.20	.50
6 Craig Coxe 22	.20	.50
7 Vladimir Krutov 17	.40	1.00
8 Igor Larionov 18	.75	2.00
9 Doug Lidster 3	.20	.50
10 Trevor Linden 16	1.50	4.00
11 Kirk McLean 1	.75	2.00
12 Larry Melnyk 24	.20	.50
13 Robert Nordmark 6	.20	.50
14 Barry Pederson 7	.30	.75
15 Paul Reinhart 23	.30	.75
16 Jim Sandlak 19	.20	.50
17 Petri Skriko 26	.30	.75
18 Doug Smith	.20	.50
19 Stan Smyl 12	.40	1.00
20 Harold Snepsts 27	.40	1.00
21 Daryl Stanley 29	.20	.50
22 Rich Sutter 15	.20	.50
23 Tony Tanti 9	.30	.75
24 Steve Weeks 31	.30	.75

1990-91 Canucks Mohawk

This 29-card set of Vancouver Canucks was sponsored by Mohawk and issued in panels. After perforation, the cards measure the standard size. The front features color mug shots of the players, with thin red borders on a white card face. The player's name and position appear in black lettering above the picture, while the team logo in the lower right corner rounds out the card face. The horizontally oriented backs have biographical information and statistics (regular season and playoff). The cards are unnumbered and checklisted below in alphabetical order.

COMPLETE SET (29)	6.00	15.00
1 Greg Adams	.30	.75
2 Jim Agnew	.20	.50
3 Steve Bozek	.20	.50
4 Garth Butcher	.20	.50
5 Dave Capuano	.20	.50
6 Craig Coxe	.20	.50
7 Gerald Diduck	.20	.50
8 Troy Gamble	.30	.75
9 Don Gibson	.20	.50
10 Kevan Guy	.20	.50
11 Robert Kron	.20	.50
12 Tom Kurvers	.20	.50
13 Igor Larionov	.60	1.50
14 Doug Lidster	.20	.50
15 Trevor Linden	.75	2.00
16 Jyrki Lumme	.30	.75
17 Jay Mazur	.20	.50
18 Andrew McBain	.20	.50
19 Kirk McLean	.60	1.50
20 Rob Murphy	.20	.50
21 Petr Nedved	.60	1.50
22 Robert Nordmark	.20	.50
23 Gino Odjick	.30	.75
24 Adrien Plavsic	.20	.50
25 Dan Quinn	.20	.50
26 Jim Sandlak	.20	.50
27 Stan Smyl	.30	.75
28 Ronnie Stern	.20	.50
29 Garry Valk	.20	.50

1990-91 Canucks Molson

This set features large (approximately 8" by 10") glossy color close-up photos of Canucks, who were honored as the Molson Canadian Player of the Month. The photos are enclosed by a gold border. The player's name appears in the bottom gold border. At the bottom center is a picture of the Molson Cup. The team logo and a Molson logo in the lower corners round out the front. The backs are blank, and the unnumbered photos are checklisted below in alphabetical order.

COMPLETE SET (6)	16.00	40.00
1 Brian Bradley	2.00	5.00
2 Troy Gamble	2.00	5.00
3 Doug Lidster	2.00	5.00
4 Trevor Linden	4.00	10.00
5 Kirk McLean (Facing right)	3.00	8.00
6 Kirk McLean (Facing front)	3.00	8.00

1991 Canucks Panini Team Stickers

This 32-sticker set was issued in a plastic bag that contained two 16-sticker sheets (approximately 9" by 12") and a foldout poster, "Super Poster - Hockey 91", on which the stickers could be affixed. The players' names appear only on the poster, not on the stickers. Each sticker measures about 2 1/8" by 2 7/8" and features a color player action shot on its white-bordered front. The back of the white sticker sheet is lined off into 16 panels, each carrying the logos for Panini, the NHL, and the NHLPA, as well as the same number that appears on the front of the sticker. Every Canadian NHL team was featured in this promotion. Each team set was available by mail-order from Panini Canada Ltd. for 2.99 plus 50 cents for shipping and handling.

COMPLETE SET (32)	1.50	4.00
1 Greg Adams	.02	.10
2 Jim Agnew	.01	.05
3 Steve Bozek	.01	.05
4 Brian Bradley	.07	.20
5 Garth Butcher	.01	.05
6 Dave Capuano	.01	.05
7 Craig Coxe	.01	.05
8 Troy Gamble	.02	.10
9 Kevan Guy	.01	.05
10 Robert Kron	.01	.05
11 Igor Larionov	.08	.25
12 Doug Lidster	.02	.10
13 Trevor Linden	.20	.50
14 Jyrki Lumme	.02	.10
15 Andrew McBain	.01	.05
16 Rob Murphy	.01	.05
17 Petr Nedved	.20	.50
18 Robert Nordmark	.01	.05
19 Adrien Plavsic	.01	.05
20 Dan Quinn	.02	.10
21 Jim Sandlak	.01	.05
22 Petri Skriko	.02	.10
23 Stan Smyl	.07	.20
24 Ronnie Stern	.01	.05
A Team Logo Left Side	.05	.15
B Team Logo Right Side	.05	.15
C Canucks in Action Upper Left Corner	.05	.15
D Canucks in Action Lower Left Corner	.05	.15
E Game Action Upper Right Corner	.05	.15
F Game Action Lower Right Corner	.05	.15
G Kirk McLean	.20	.50
H Trevor Linden	.20	.50

1991-92 Canucks Autograph Cards

These autograph cards, each measuring approximately 3 3/4" by 8 1/2", were issued by the team with a large white area at the bottom for the players to sign. The front features a glossy color close-up photo, with the year and the team logo in the white border above the picture. In cursive lettering, the player's name and number appear below the picture, with his position

printed in block lettering. The unnumbered cards are blank on the back and checklisted below in alphabetical order.
COMPLETE SET (23) 10.00 25.00
1 Greg Adams .40 1.00
2 Pavel Bure 3.00 8.00
3 Dave Babych .40 1.00
4 Geoff Courtnall .40 1.00
5 Gerald Diduck .20 .50
6 Robert Dirk .20 .50
7 Troy Gamble .30 .75
8 Randy Gregg .20 .50
9 Robert Kron .20 .50
10 Igor Larionov .60 1.50
11 Doug Lidster .20 .50
12 Trevor Linden 1.00 2.50
13 Jyrki Lumme .30 .75
14 Kirk McLean 1.25 3.00
15 Sergio Momesso .20 .50
16 Rob Murphy .20 .50
17 Dana Murzyn .20 .50
18 Petr Nedved 1.25 3.00
19 Gino Odjick .30 .75
20 Adrien Plavsic .20 .50
21 Cliff Ronning .60 1.50
22 Jim Sandlak .20 .50
23 Ryan Walter .20 .50
24 Garry Valk .20 .50

1991-92 Canucks Molson

This set features large (approximately 8" by 10") glossy color close-up photos of Canucks who were honored as the Molson Canadian Player of the Month or Player of the Year. The photos are enclosed by white, red, and blue border stripes. A gold leaf appear above the picture, while a gold plaque identifying the player appears below the picture. The team logo and a Molson logo appear in the lower corners. The backs are blank, and the unnumbered photos are checklisted below in alphabetical order.
COMPLETE SET (7) 20.00 50.00
1 Greg Adams 1.50 4.00
2 Pavel Bure 6.00 15.00
(White uniform)
3 Pavel Bure POY 6.00 15.00
(Black uniform)
4 Igor Larionov 2.50 6.00
5 Trevor Linden 3.00 8.00
6 Kirk McLean 3.00 8.00
7 Cliff Ronning 2.00 5.00

1991-92 Canucks Team Issue 8x10

This set features 8" by 10" glossy color close-up photos of the Vancouver Canucks. The photos are enclosed by a thin black border. In cursive lettering, the player's name and number appear below the picture, with his position printed in block lettering. The team logo in the lower left corner completes the front. The backs carry a black and white head shot, biography, 1990-91 season summary, career highlights, personal information, and complete statistics. The cards are unnumbered and checklisted below in alphabetical order.
COMPLETE SET (23) 30.00 75.00
1 Greg Adams 1.50 4.00
2 Pavel Bure 6.00 15.00
3 Dave Babych 1.25 3.00
4 Geoff Courtnall 1.50 4.00
5 Gerald Diduck 1.25 3.00
6 Robert Dirk 1.25 3.00
7 Troy Gamble 1.50 4.00
8 Randy Gregg 1.25 3.00
9 Robert Kron 1.25 3.00
10 Igor Larionov 1.50 4.00
11 Doug Lidster 1.25 3.00
12 Trevor Linden 2.00 5.00
13 Jyrki Lumme 1.25 3.00
14 Kirk McLean 2.00 5.00
15 Sergio Momesso 1.25 3.00
16 Rob Murphy 1.25 3.00
17 Dana Murzyn 1.25 3.00
18 Petr Nedved 2.00 5.00
19 Gino Odjick 1.50 4.00
20 Adrien Plavsic 1.25 3.00
21 Cliff Ronning 2.00 5.00
22 Jim Sandlak 1.25 3.00
23 Ryan Walter 1.25 3.00

1992-93 Canucks Road Trip Art

Dubbed "Road Trip Art Cards," this set of 25 approximately 4 3/4" by 7" player portraits was available only at Subway and Payless stores. Each week for six weeks, a set of four player portraits was released at a suggested price of 2.29 per pack. Also there was a tab inside each package and one could win a pair of 1993-94 season tickets, autographed Road Trip prints, limited edition Road Trip prints, Road Trip puzzles, and Road Trip coloring books. The photos are black-and-white and picture the Canuck players dressed in western garb. A gold foil facsimile autograph is printed near the bottom. The backs carry the player's name in a wide red stripe at the top. Humorous text in the form of player quotes rests against a white background along with the team logo and the words "Road Trip." A bright yellow stripe accents the bottom of the card and contains manufacturer information. The portraits are listed below in alphabetical order with the week issued denoted.
COMPLETE SET (25) 6.00 15.00
1 Greg Adams W1 .30 .75
2 Shawn Antoski W5 .20 .50
3 Dave Babych W5 .30 .75
4 Pavel Bure W3 2.00 5.00
5 Geoff Courtnall W5 .30 .75
6 Gerald Diduck W4 .20 .50
7 Robert Dirk W5 .20 .50
8 Tom Fergus W3 .20 .50
9 Robert Kron W2 .20 .50
10 Doug Lidster W2 .20 .50
11 Trevor Linden W1 .60 1.50
12 Jyrki Lumme W1 .30 .75
13 Kirk McLean W2 .60 1.50
14 Sergio Momesso W2 .20 .50
15 Dana Murzyn W3 .20 .50
16 Petr Nedved W4 .60 1.50
17 Gino Odjick W4 .40 1.00
18 Adrien Plavsic W6 .20 .50
19 Cliff Ronning W6 .30 .75
20 Jim Sandlak W6 .20 .50
21 Jiri Slegr W1 .20 .50
22 Garry Valk W4 .20 .50
23 Ryan Walter W5 .20 .50
24 Dixon Ward W3 .20 .50
25 Kay Whitmore W6 .30 .75

1994-95 Canucks Program Inserts

Measuring approximately 8" by 10 1/2", these program inserts feature the 1994-95 Vancouver Canucks. The fronts have color action player shots with white borders. The player's name, number and position appear on the fronts, along with the words "Canucks Collector Series" in a bar at the top. The backs are blank. The inserts are unnumbered and checklisted below in alphabetical order.
COMPLETE SET (22) 32.00 80.00
1 Greg Adams 1.50 4.00
2 Shawn Antoski 1.50 4.00
3 Dave Babych 1.50 4.00
4 Jeff Brown 1.50 4.00
5 Pavel Bure 4.00 10.00
6 Geoff Courtnall 1.50 4.00
7 Gerald Diduck 1.50 4.00
8 Robert Dirk 1.50 4.00
9 Martin Gelinas 1.50 4.00
10 Brian Glynn 1.50 4.00
11 Tim Hunter 1.50 4.00
12 Nathan LaFayette 1.50 4.00
13 Trevor Linden 2.00 5.00
14 Jyrki Lumme 1.50 4.00
15 Kirk McLean 2.00 5.00
16 Dana Murzyn 1.50 4.00
17 Gino Odjick 1.50 4.00
18 Adrien Plavsic 1.50 4.00
19 Cliff Ronning 1.50 4.00
20 Jiri Slegr 1.50 4.00
21 Dixon Ward 1.50 4.00
22 Kay Whitmore 2.00 5.00

1995-96 Canucks Building the Dream Art

This 18-card set of the Vancouver Canucks features 5" by 7" borderless black-and-white player photos in construction worker poses with gold facsimile autographs at the bottom. The backs carry player information. This set continues the tradition begun in 1992-93 with the Canucks Road Trip Art set.
COMPLETE SET (18) 6.00 15.00
1 Kirk McLean .40 1.00
2 Kay Whitmore .25 .60
3 Bret Hedican .20 .50
4 Tim Hunter .20 .50
5 Dana Murzyn .20 .50
6 Jyrki Lumme .25 .60
7 Cliff Ronning .30 .75
8 Jeff Brown .30 .75
9 Martin Gelinas .40 1.00
10 Pavel Bure 2.00 5.00
11 Jiri Slegr .20 .50
12 Sergio Momesso .20 .50
13 Gino Odjick .40 1.00
14 Geoff Courtnall .20 .50
15 John McIntyre .20 .50
16 Trevor Linden .75 2.00
17 Mike Peca .40 1.00
18 Dave Babych .20 .50

1996-97 Canucks Postcards

This extremely attractive, 27-postcard set was produced by the Canucks and sponsored by IGA grocery stores as a promotional giveaway. The highly stylized fronts have an action color photo with the team name above, and a row of team logos to the right. Immediately below the photo is a strip for autographing. The backs are blank. As the postcards are unnumbered, they are listed according to their sweater number, which is displayed on the lower right hand front corner.
COMPLETE SET (27) 6.00 15.00
1 Kirk McLean .30 .75
3 Bret Hedican .08 .25
4 Mark Wotton .08 .25
5 Dana Murzyn .08 .25
6 Adrian Aucoin .08 .25
7 David Roberts .08 .25
8 Donald Brashear .08 .25
9 Russ Courtnall .20 .50
10 Esa Tikkanen .20 .50
16 Trevor Linden .30 .75
17 Mike Ridley .20 .50
18 Troy Crowder .08 .25
19 Markus Naslund .20 .50
20 Alexander Semak .08 .25
21 Jyrki Lumme .20 .50
23 Martin Gelinas .30 .75
24 Scott Walker .20 .50
26 Mike Sillinger .08 .25
27 Leif Rohlin .08 .25
29 Gino Odjick .30 .75
30 Mike Fountain .20 .50
31 Corey Hirsch .30 .75
32 Chris Joseph .08 .25
44 Dave Babych .20 .50
89 Alexander Mogilny .60 1.50
96 Pavel Bure 1.50 4.00
NNO Team Photo .20 .50

2001-02 Canucks Postcards

This is not belived to be the complete checklist
COMPLETE SET (11) 4.00 10.00
1 Todd Bertuzzi .40 1.00
2 Murray Baron .40 1.00
3 Artem Chubarov .40 1.00
4 Dan Cloutier .60 1.50
5 Matt Cooke .40 1.00
6 Ed Jovanovski .60 1.50
7 Scott Lachance .40 1.00
8 Trevor Linden .75 2.00
9 Brendan Morrison .60 1.50
10 Markus Naslund .60 1.50
11 Peter Skudra .40 1.00

2002-03 Canucks Team Issue

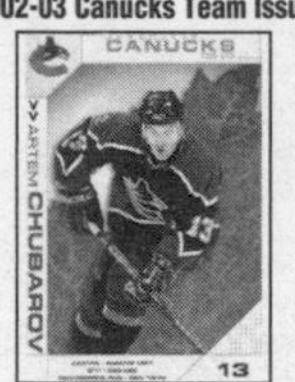

These singles were offered at team appearances. The checklist is believed to be incomplete. If you have additional information, contact us at hockeymag@beckett.com
COMPLETE SET
1 Murray Baron .40 1.00
2 Todd Bertuzzi 2.00 5.00
3 Dan Cloutier 1.25 3.00
4 Matt Cooke 1.25 3.00
5 Artem Chubarov
6 Ed Jovanovski 1.25 3.00
7 Trent Klatt
8 Trevor Linden 1.25 3.00
9 Marek Malik
10 Brendan Morrison 1.25 3.00
11 Markus Naslund 2.00 5.00
12 Mattias Ohlund .40 1.00
13 Sami Salo
14 Daniel Sedin 1.25 3.00
15 Henrik Sedin 1.25 3.00

2003-04 Canucks Postcards

COMPLETE SET (28) 20.00
1 Bryan Allen .20 .50
2 Magnus Arvedson .20 .50
3 Todd Bertuzzi .40 1.00
4 Brian Burke GM .04 .10
5 Artem Chubarov .20 .50
6 Dan Cloutier .40 1.00
7 Matt Cooke .40 1.00
8 Marc Crawford CO .10 .25
9 Johan Hedberg .20 .50
10 Mike Johnston ACO .04 .10
11 Ed Jovanovski .40 1.00
12 Mike Keane .20 .50
13 Jason King .20 .50
14 Trevor Linden .40 1.00
15 Mats Lindgren .20 .50
16 Marek Malik .20 .50
17 Brad May .20 .50
18 Jack McIlhargey ACO .04 .10
19 Brendan Morrison .40 1.00
20 Markus Naslund .75 2.00
21 Mattias Ohlund .20 .50
22 Jarkko Ruutu .20 .50
23 Sami Salo .20 .50
24 Daniel Sedin .40 1.00
25 Henrik Sedin .40 1.00
26 Jiri Slegr .20 .50
27 Brent Sopel .20 .50
28 Finn MASCOT .04 .10

2003-04 Canucks Sav-on-Foods

Created by Pacific Trading Cards, this 24-card set featured players from the Vancouver Canucks and were sold exclusively at Sav-on-Foods stores. Cards were sold in 4-card packs for an SRP of $2.99. Autographs of Markus Naslund, Todd Bertuzzi and Brendan Morrison were also randomly inserted. Because of lack of market information, they are unpriced.
COMPLETE SET (30) 6.00 15.00
1 Trevor Linden .60 1.50
2 Johan Hedberg .20 .50
3 Mike Keane .20 .50
4 Todd Bertuzzi .40 1.00
Brendan Morrison
Markus Naslund
5 Markus Naslund .60 1.50
6 Daniel Sedin .40 1.00
7 Marek Malik .20 .50
8 Brad May .20 .50
9 Brendan Morrison .20 .50
10 Mattias Ohlund .20 .50
11 Magnus Arvedson .20 .50
12 Bryan Allen .20 .50
13 Jason King .20 .50
14 Henrik Sedin .40 1.00
15 Brent Sopel .20 .50
16 Ed Jovanovski .40 1.00
Dan Cloutier
Mattias Ohlund
17 Dan Cloutier .40 1.00
18 Artem Chubarov .20 .50
19 Jarkko Ruutu .20 .50
20 Daniel Sedin .40 1.00
Henrik Sedin
Jason King
21 Ed Jovanovski .40 1.00
22 Todd Bertuzzi .40 1.00
23 Matt Cooke .40 1.00
24 Sami Salo .20 .50
NNO Markus Naslund AU
NNO Todd Bertuzzi AU
NNO Brendan Morrison AU

2006-07 Canucks Postcards

COMPLETE SET (25) 15.00 25.00
1 Kevin Bieksa .60 1.50
2 Luc Bourdon .40 1.00
3 Jan Bulis .40 1.00
4 Alexandre Burrows .40 1.00
5 Marc Chouinard .40 1.00
6 Matt Cooke .60 1.50
7 Rory Fitzpatrick .40 1.00
8 Josh Green .40 1.00
9 Ryan Kesler .40 1.00
10 Lukas Krajicek .40 1.00
11 Trevor Linden .75 2.00
12 Roberto Luongo 1.25 3.00
13 Willie Mitchell .40 1.00
14 Brendan Morrison .40 1.00
15 Markus Naslund .75 2.00
16 Mattias Ohlund .40 1.00
17 Taylor Pyatt .40 1.00
18 Dany Sabourin .40 1.00
19 Sami Salo .40 1.00
20 Tommi Santala .40 1.00
21 Daniel Sedin .75 2.00
22 Henrik Sedin .75 2.00
23 Alain Vigneault CO .10 .25
24 Fin MASCOT .10 .25
25 Logo Card .10 .25

2007-08 Canucks Team Issue

COMPLETE SET (21) 5.00 12.00
1 Logo Card .30 .75
2 Kevin Bieksa .40 1.00
3 Alexandre Burrows .50 1.25
4 Jeff Cowan .30 .75
5 Matt Cooke .30 .75
6 Brad Isbister .30 .75
7 Ryan Kesler .60 1.50
8 Lukas Krajicek .30 .75
9 Trevor Linden .50 1.25
10 Roberto Luongo .60 1.50
11 Willie Mitchell .30 .75
12 Aaron Miller .30 .75
13 Brendan Morrison .30 .75
14 Markus Naslund .50 1.25
15 Mattias Ohlund .30 .75
16 Taylor Pyatt .30 .75
17 Byron Ritchie .30 .75
18 Sami Salo .30 .75
19 Daniel Sedin .50 1.25
20 Henrik Sedin .50 1.25
21 Curtis Sanford .40 1.00

2010-11 Canucks Oversized Team Issue

COMPLETE SET (25) 60.00 120.00
1 Andrew Alberts 2.50 6.00
2 Keith Ballard 2.50 6.00
3 Kevin Bieksa 3.00 8.00
4 Alex Bolduc 2.50 6.00
5 Alexandre Burrows 4.00 10.00
6 Guillaume Desbiens 4.00 10.00
7 Christian Ehrhoff 2.50 6.00
8 Tanner Glass 2.50 6.00
9 Dan Hamhuis 3.00 8.00
10 Jannik Hansen 3.00 8.00
11 Ryan Kesler 4.00 10.00
12 Roberto Luongo 4.00 10.00
13 Manny Malhotra 3.00 8.00
14 Mason Raymond 3.00 8.00
15 Aaron Rome 2.50 6.00
16 Rick Rypien 4.00 10.00
17 Sami Salo 2.50 6.00
18 Mikael Samuelsson 2.50 6.00
19 Cory Schneider 3.00 8.00
20 Daniel Sedin 4.00 10.00
21 Henrik Sedin 4.00 10.00
22 Jeff Tambellini 2.50 6.00
23 Raffi Torres 2.50 6.00
24 Alain Vigneault 2.50 6.00
25 Kyle Wellwood 3.00 8.00

1974-75 Capitals White Borders

This 25-card set measures approximately 5" by 7" is printed on very thin paper stock. The fronts have black-and-white player portraits with white borders. The player's name and the team logo appear under the photo. The backs are blank. The cards are unnumbered and checklisted below in alphabetical order.
COMPLETE SET (25) 30.00 60.00
1 John Adams 1.00 2.00
2 Jim Anderson CO 1.00 2.00
3 Ron Anderson 1.00 2.00
4 Steve Atkinson 1.00 2.00
5 Michel Belhumeur 2.00 4.00
6 Mike Bloom 1.00 2.00
7 Gord Brooks 1.00 2.00
8 Bruce Cowick 1.00 2.00
9 Denis Dupere 1.00 2.00
10 Jack Egers 1.00 2.00
11 Jim Hrycuik 1.00 2.00
12 Greg Joly 1.50 3.00
13 Dave Kryskow 1.00 2.00
14 Yvon Labre 1.50 3.00
15 Pete Laframboise 1.00 2.00
16 Bill Lesuk 1.00 2.00
17 Ron Low 2.00 4.00
18 Joe Lundrigan 1.00 2.00
19 Mike Marson 1.50 3.00
20 Bill Mikkelson 1.00 2.00
21 Doug Mohns 2.00 4.00
22 Andre Peloffy 1.00 2.00
23 Milt Schmidt GM 2.50 5.00
24 Gord Smith 1.00 2.00
25 Tom Williams 1.50 3.00

1978-79 Capitals Team Issue

This set features the Capitals of the NHL. The oversized cards feature black and white head shots on thin paper stock. It is believed they were issued as a set to fans who requested them by mail.
COMPLETE SET (18) 7.50 15.00
1 Michel Bergeron .75 1.50
2 Greg Carroll .50 1.00
3 Guy Charron .50 1.00
4 Rolf Edberg .50 1.00
5 Rick Green .50 1.00
6 Gordie Lane .50 1.00
7 Mark Lofthouse .50 1.00
8 Jack Lynch .50 1.00
9 Dennis Maruk .75 1.50
10 Paul Mulvey .50 1.00
11 Robert Picard .50 1.00
12 Bill Riley .50 1.00
13 Tom Rowe .50 1.00
14 Bob Sirois .50 1.00
15 Gord Smith .50 1.00
16 Leif Svensson .75 1.50
17 Ryan Walter .50 1.00
18 Bernie Wolf .50 1.00

1979-80 Capitals Team Issue

This set features the Capitals of the NHL. The oversized cards feature black and white head shots on thin paper stock. It is believed they were issued as a set to fans who requested them by mail.
COMPLETE SET (23) 20.00 40.00
1 Pierre Bouchard .50 1.00
2 Guy Charron .50 1.00
3 Rolf Edberg .50 1.00
4 Mike Gartner 12.50 25.00
5 Rick Green .50 1.00
6 Bengt Gustafsson .75 1.50
7 Dennis Hextall .75 1.50
8 Gary Inness .50 1.00
9 Yvon Labre .50 1.00
10 Antero Lehtonen .50 1.00
11 Mark Lofthouse .50 1.00
12 Paul McKinnon .50 1.00
13 Dennis Maruk .75 1.50
14 Paul Mulvey .50 1.00
15 Robert Picard .75 1.50
16 Greg Polis .50 1.00
17 Errol Rausse .50 1.00
18 Tom Rowe .50 1.00
19 Peter Scamurra .50 1.00
20 Bob Surois .50 1.00
21 Wayne Stephenson .50 1.00
22 Leif Svensson .75 1.50
23 Ryan Walter .50 1.00

1981-82 Capitals Team Issue

This 21-card set measures approximately 5" by 7". The fronts have black-and-white player portraits with white borders. The player's name, position, jersey number, and the team logo appear under the photo. The backs are blank. The cards are unnumbered and checklisted below in alphabetical order.
COMPLETE SET (21) 12.00 30.00
1 Timo Blomqvist .40 1.00
2 Bobby Carpenter 1.25 3.00
3 Glen Currie .40 1.00
4 Gaetan Duchesne .60 1.50
5 Mike Gartner 4.00 10.00
6 Rick Green .60 1.50
7 Randy Holt .40 1.00
8 Wes Jarvis .40 1.00
9 Al Jensen .60 1.50
10 Dennis Maruk 1.25 3.00
11 Terry Murray .40 1.00
12 Lee Norwood .40 1.00
13 Mike Palmateer 1.25 3.00
14 Dave Parro .60 1.50
15 Torrie Robertson .60 1.50
16 Greg Theberge .40 1.00
17 Chris Valentine .40 1.00
18 Darren Veitch .40 1.00
20 Howard Walker .40 1.00
21 Ryan Walter .75 2.00

1982-83 Capitals Team Issue

This 25-card set measures approximately 5" by 7". The fronts have black-and-white player portraits with white borders. The player's name, position, jersey number, and the team logo appear under the photo. The backs are blank. The cards are unnumbered and checklisted below in alphabetical order. The card of Scott Stevens appears one year before his Rookie Card.
COMPLETE SET (25) 16.00 40.00
1 Timo Blomqvist .40 1.00
2 Ted Bulley .40 1.00
3 Bobby Carpenter .75 2.00
4 Glen Currie .40 1.00
5 Brian Engblom .60 1.50
6 Mike Gartner 3.00 8.00
7 Bob Gould .40 1.00
8 Bengt Gustafsson .75 2.00
9 Alan Haworth .40 1.00
10 Randy Holt .40 1.00
11 Ken Houston .40 1.00
12 Doug Jarvis .75 2.00
13 Rod Langway 1.50 4.00
14 Craig Laughlin .40 1.00
15 Dennis Maruk .75 2.00
16 Bryan Murray CO .40 1.00
17 Terry Murray ACO .40 1.00
18 Lee Norwood .40 1.00
19 Milan Novy .40 1.00
20 Dave Parro .60 1.50
21 David Poile GM .40 1.00
22 Pat Riggin 1.00 2.50
23 Scott Stevens 4.00 10.00
24 Chris Valentine .40 1.00
25 Darren Veitch .40 1.00

1984-85 Capitals Pizza Hut

These cards of Washington Capitals were given out to members of the Junior Capitals Club and measure approximately 4 1/2" by 6". The front features a color action photo of the player, with three blue stripes on the picture. The back has a small head shot of the player and his career statistics. The cards are unnumbered and hence are listed below alphabetically by player name.
COMPLETE SET (15) 14.00 35.00
1 Bob Carpenter .75 2.00
2 Dave Christian 1.00 2.50
3 Glen Currie .60 1.50
4 Gaetan Duchesne .60 1.50
5 Mike Gartner 3.00 8.00
6 Bob Gould .60 1.50
7 Bengt Gustafsson .75 2.00
8 Alan Haworth .60 1.50
9 Doug Jarvis .75 2.00
10 Al Jensen .75 2.00
11 Rod Langway 1.25 3.00
12 Craig Laughlin .60 1.50
13 Larry Murphy 2.00 5.00
14 Pat Riggin .75 2.00
15 Scott Stevens 3.00 8.00

1985-86 Capitals Pizza Hut

These cards of Washington Capitals were mailed three at a time to members of the Junior Capitals Club and measure approximately 4 1/2" by 6". The front features a color action photo of the player, with three red stripes on the picture. The back has a small head shot of the player and his career statistics. When Doug Jarvis, Pat Riggin, and Darren Veitch were traded, supposedly their cards were pulled and never mailed to club members. It is alleged that these cards were destroyed and only a few were kept. Consequently, these player cards are scarce.
COMPLETE SET (15) 14.00 35.00
1 Bob Carpenter .75 2.00
2 Dave Christian 1.00 2.50
3 Gaetan Duchesne .60 1.50
4 Mike Gartner 2.50 6.00
5 Bob Gould .60 1.50
6 Bengt Gustafsson .75 2.00
7 Alan Haworth .60 1.50
8 Doug Jarvis SP 1.50 4.00
9 Al Jensen .75 2.00
10 Rod Langway 1.25 3.00
11 Craig Laughlin .60 1.50
12 Larry Murphy 2.00 5.00
13 Pat Riggin SP 2.00 5.00
14 Scott Stevens 2.50 6.00
15 Darren Veitch SP 1.50 4.00

1986-87 Capitals Kodak

The 1986-87 Washington Capitals Team Photo Album was sponsored by Kodak. It consists of three large sheets joined together to form one continuous sheet. The first panel has a team photo measuring approximately 10" by 8". The second and third panels consist of player cards; after perforation, they measure approximately 2" by 2 5/8". The cards feature color posed photos, with player information below. The cards are unnumbered and we have checklisted them below in alphabetical order. Kevin Hatcher's card predates his Rookie Card by one year.
COMPLETE SET (26) 12.00 30.00
1 Greg Adams .60 1.50
2 John Barrett .30 .75
3 John Blum .30 .75
4 Dave Christian .40 1.00
5 Bob Crawford .30 .75
6 Gaetan Duchesne .30 .75
7 Lou Franceschetti .30 .75
8 Mike Gartner 1.50 4.00
9 Bob Gould .30 .75
10 Jeff Greenlaw .30 .75
11 Kevin Hatcher .75 2.00
12 Alan Haworth .30 .75
13 David A. Jensen .30 .75
14 Rod Langway .75 2.00
15 Craig Laughlin .30 .75
16 Bob Mason .40 1.00
17 Kelly Miller .40 1.00
18 Larry Murphy 1.00 2.50
19 Bryan Murray CO .30 .75
20 Pete Peeters .75 2.00
21 Michal Pivonka 1.25 3.00
22 Mike Ridley .75 2.00
23 Gary Sampson .30 .75
24 Greg Smith .30 .75
25 Scott Stevens 1.50 4.00
26 Large Team Photo .75 2.00

1986-87 Capitals Police

This 24-card police set features players of the Washington Capitals. The cards measure approximately 2 5/8" by 3 3/4" and were issued in two-card panels. The front has a color action photo on white card stock, with player information and the Capitals' logo below the picture. Inside a thin black border the back features a hockey tip ("Caps Tips"), an anti-crime tip, and logos of sponsoring police agencies. The cards are unnumbered and we have checklisted them below in alphabetical order, with the jersey number to the right of the player's name. Kevin Hatcher's card predates his Rookie Card by one year.
COMPLETE SET (24) 6.00 15.00
1 Greg Adams 22 .40 1.00
2 John Barrett 6 .20 .50
3 Bob Carpenter 10 .20 .50
4 Dave Christian 27 .30 .75
5 Yvon Corriveau 26 .20 .50
6 Gaetan Duchesne 14 .20 .50
7 Lou Franceschetti 32 .20 .50
8 Mike Gartner 11 1.25 3.00
9 Bob Gould 23 .20 .50
10 Kevin Hatcher 4 .60 1.50
11 Alan Haworth 15 .20 .50
12 Al Jensen 35 .25 .60
13 David A. Jensen 9 .20 .50
14 Rod Langway 5 .60 1.50
15 Craig Laughlin 18 .20 .50
16 Stephen Leach 21 .30 .75
17 Larry Murphy 8 .75 2.00
18 Bryan Murray CO .20 .50
19 Pete Peeters 1 .60 1.50
20 Jorgen Pettersson 12 .20 .50
21 Michal Pivonka 17 .75 2.00
22 David Poile VP .20 .50
GM
23 Greg Smith 19 .20 .50
24 Scott Stevens 3 1.25 3.00

1987-88 Capitals Kodak

The 1987-88 Washington Capitals Team Photo Album was sponsored by Kodak. It consists of three large sheets, each measuring approximately 11" by 8 1/4" and joined together to form one continuous sheet. The first panel has a team photo, with the players' names listed according to rows below the picture. While the second panel presents three rows of five cards each, the third panel presents two rows of five cards, with five Kodak coupons completing the left over portion of the panel. After perforation, the cards measure approximately 2 3/16" by 2 15/16". They feature color-posed photos bordered in red, with player information below the picture. The Capitals' logo and a picture of a Kodak film box complete the card face. The back has biographical and statistical information in a horizontal format. The cards are checklisted below by sweater number.
COMPLETE SET (26) 8.00 20.00
1 Pete Peeters .40 1.00
2 Garry Galley .40 1.00
3 Scott Stevens .75 2.00
4 Kevin Hatcher .75 2.00
5 Rod Langway .40 1.00
6 John Barrett .20 .50
8 Larry Murphy .60 1.50
10 Kelly Miller .30 .75
11 Mike Gartner 1.00 2.50
12 Peter Sundstrom .30 .75
16 Bengt Gustafsson .30 .75
17 Mike Ridley .60 1.50
18 Craig Laughlin .20 .50
19 Greg Smith .20 .50
20 Michal Pivonka .60 1.50
22 Greg Adams .40 1.00
23 Bob Gould .20 .50
25 Lou Franceschetti .20 .50
27 Dave Christian .40 1.00
29 Ed Kastelic .20 .50
30 Clint Malarchuk .40 1.00
32 Dale Hunter .60 1.50
34 Bill Houlder .30 .75
xx Bryan Murray CO .20 .50
XX Team Photo .20 .50
xx David Poile VP .20 .50
GM

1987-88 Capitals Team Issue

This 23-card set measures 5 1/4" by 8". The fronts feature autographed color action photos. The backs carry a head shot, biography, 1986-87 recap, career highlights, personal information and complete statistics with the player's name, position and jersey number at the top. The cards are unnumbered and checklisted below in alphabetical order.
COMPLETE SET (23) 10.00 25.00
1 Greg Adams .50 1.25
2 John Barrett .30 .75
3 Dave Christian .50 1.25
4 Lou Franceschetti .30 .75
5 Garry Galley .60 1.50
6 Mike Gartner 1.25 3.00
7 Bob Gould .30 .75
8 Bengt Gustafsson .40 1.00
9 Kevin Hatcher 1.25 3.00
10 Dale Hunter .75 2.00
11 David Jensen .30 .75
12 Ed Kastelic .30 .75
13 Rod Langway .50 1.25
14 Craig Laughlin .30 .75
15 Clint Malarchuk .50 1.25
16 Kelly Miller .40 1.00
17 Larry Murphy .75 2.00
18 Pete Peeters .60 1.50
19 Michal Pivonka .75 2.00
20 Mike Ridley .75 2.00
21 Greg Smith .30 .75
22 Scott Stevens 1.00 2.50
23 Peter Sundstrom .40 1.00

1988-89 Capitals Borderless

Measuring approximately 5" by 7", this 21-card set features the 1988-89 Washington Capitals. The fronts have borderless color action player photos. The backs carry player biography and statistics, season and career highlights, and short personal information. The cards are unnumbered and checklisted below in alphabetical order.
COMPLETE SET (21) 6.00 15.00
1 Dave Christian .40 1.00
2 Yvon Corriveau .30 .75
3 Geoff Courtnall .75 2.00
4 Lou Franceschetti .30 .75
5 Mike Gartner .75 2.00
6 Bob Gould .30 .75
7 Bengt Gustafsson .40 1.00
8 Kevin Hatcher .60 1.50
9 Dale Hunter .60 1.50
10 Rod Langway .60 1.50
11 Stephen Leach .30 .75
12 Grant Ledyard .30 .75
13 Clint Malarchuk .40 1.00
14 Kelly Miller .30 .75
15 Larry Murphy .60 1.50
16 Pete Peeters .40 1.00
17 Michal Pivonka .75 2.00
18 Mike Ridley .60 1.50
19 Neil Sheehy .30 .75
20 Scott Stevens .75 2.00
21 Peter Sundstrom .40 1.00

1988-89 Capitals Smokey

This 24-card safety set features players of the Washington Capitals. The cards measure approximately 2 5/8" by 3 3/4" and were issued in two-card panels. The front has a color action photo on white card stock, with player information and logos below the picture. Inside a thin black border the back features a hockey tip ("Caps Tips") and a fire prevention cartoon starring Smokey. The cards are unnumbered and we have checklisted them below in alphabetical order, with the sweater number to the right of the player's name. Geoff Courtnall's card predates his Rookie Card by a year.
COMPLETE SET (24) 6.00 15.00
1 Dave Christian 27 .30 .75
2 Yvon Corriveau 26 .20 .50
3 Geoff Courtnall 14 .60 1.50
4 Lou Franceschetti 25 .20 .50
5 Mike Gartner 11 .60 1.50
6 Bob Gould 23 .20 .50
7 Bengt Gustafsson 16 .30 .75
8 Kevin Hatcher 4 .40 1.00
9 Dale Hunter 32 .40 1.00
10 Rod Langway 5 .40 1.00
11 Stephen Leach 21 .20 .50
12 Grant Ledyard 6 .20 .50
13 Clint Malarchuk 30 .30 .75
14 Kelly Miller 10 .20 .50
15 Larry Murphy 8 .40 1.00
16 Bryan Murray CO .30 .75
17 Pete Peeters 1 .30 .75
18 Michal Pivonka 20 .60 1.50
19 David Poile VP .20 .50
GM
20 Mike Ridley 17 .40 1.00
21 Neil Sheehy 15 .20 .50
22 Scott Stevens 3 .60 1.50
23 Peter Sundstrom 12 .30 .75
24 Title Card .20 .50
Smokey the Bear

1989-90 Capitals Kodak

The 1989-90 Washington Capitals Team Photo Album was co-sponsored by Kodak and W. Bell and Co. It consists of three large sheets, each measuring approximately 11" by 8 1/4" and joined together to form one continuous sheet. The first panel has a large blue square designated for autographs. While the second panel presents three rows of five cards each, the third panel presents two rows of five cards, with Kodak advertisements completing the left over portion of the panel. After perforation, the cards measure approximately 2 3/16" by 2 1/2". They feature color action photos bordered in red, with player information below the picture. The Capitals' logo and a picture of a Kodak film box complete the card face. The back has biographical and statistical information in a horizontal format. The cards are checklisted below by sweater number.
COMPLETE SET (25) 8.00 20.00
1 Mike Liut .40 1.00
3 Scott Stevens .75 2.00
4 Kevin Hatcher .60 1.50
5 Rod Langway .60 1.50
6 Calle Johansson .40 1.00
8 Bob Rouse .30 .75
10 Kelly Miller .40 1.00
11 Tim Bergland .30 .75
12 John Tucker .30 .75
14 Geoff Courtnall .60 1.50
15 Neil Sheehy .30 .75
16 Alan May .30 .75
17 Mike Ridley .40 1.00
19 John Druce .30 .75
20 Michal Pivonka .40 1.00
21 Stephen Leach .30 .75
22 Dino Ciccarelli .75 2.00
26 Steve Maltais .30 .75
27 Bob Joyce .30 .75
29 Scot Kleinendorst .30 .75
32 Dale Hunter .60 1.50
33 Don Beaupre .40 1.00
xx Rob Laird ACO .20 .50
xx Terry Murray CO .20 .50
xx David Poile VP/GM .20 .50

1989-90 Capitals Team Issue

This 23-card set measures approximately 5" by 7". The fronts feature full-bleed, posed color photos with the player's jersey as a background. The backs are blank. The cards are unnumbered and checklisted below in alphabetical order.
COMPLETE SET (23) 7.20 18.00
1 Don Beaupre .30 .75
2 Dave Christian .30 .75
3 Dino Ciccarelli .60 1.50
4 Yvon Corriveau .20 .50
5 Geoff Courtnall .40 1.00
6 Kevin Hatcher .40 1.00
7 Bill Houlder .30 .75
8 Dale Hunter .40 1.00
9 Calle Johansson .30 .75
10 Dimitri Khristich .60 1.50
11 Scot Kleinendorst .20 .50
12 Nick Kypreos .20 .50
13 Rod Langway .40 1.00
14 Stephen Leach .20 .50
15 Bob Mason .30 .75
16 Alan May .20 .50
17 Kelly Miller .30 .75
18 Michal Pivonka .30 .75
19 Mike Ridley .30 .75
20 Bob Rouse .20 .50
21 Neil Sheehy .20 .50
22 Scott Stevens .60 1.50
23 Doug Wickenheiser .20 .50

1990-91 Capitals Kodak

The 1990-91 Washington Capitals Team Photo Album was sponsored by Kodak. It consists of three large sheets joined together to form one continuous sheet. The first panel has a team photo measuring approximately 10" by 8". The second and third panels consist of player cards; after perforation, they measure approximately 2" by 2 5/8". The cards feature color posed photos, with player information below. The cards are unnumbered and we have checklisted them below in alphabetical order.
COMPLETE SET (25) 6.00 15.00
1 Don Beaupre .40 1.00
2 Tim Bergland .20 .50
3 Peter Bondra 2.00 5.00
4 Dino Ciccarelli .40 1.00
5 John Druce .20 .50
6 Kevin Hatcher .40 1.00
7 Dale Hunter .40 1.00
8 Al Iafrate .60 1.50
9 Calle Johansson .30 .75
10 Dimitri Khristich .40 1.00
11 Nick Kypreos .20 .50
12 Mike Lalor .20 .50
13 Rod Langway .40 1.00
14 Stephen Leach .20 .50
15 Mike Liut .40 1.00
16 Alan May .20 .50
17 Kelly Miller .20 .50
18 Terry Murray CO .08 .25
19 John Perpich .20 .50
20 Michal Pivonka .40 1.00
21 David Poile VP .08 .25
GM
22 Mike Ridley .40 1.00
23 Ken Sabourin .20 .50
24 Mikhail Tatarinov .20 .50
25 Dave Tippett .20 .50

1990-91 Capitals Postcards
This 5 x 7 set features full color photos on the front and a blank back. Cards are unnumbered and checklisted below in alphabetical order.
COMPLETE SET (22) 8.00 20.00
1 Don Beaupre .40 1.00
2 Tim Bergland .20 .50
3 Peter Bondra 2.00 5.00
4 Dino Ciccarelli .40 1.00
5 John Druce .20 .50
6 Kevin Hatcher .40 1.00
7 Jim Hrivnak .25 .60
8 Dale Hunter .40 1.00
9 Al Iafrate .60 1.50
10 Calle Johansson .30 .75
11 Nick Kypreos .20 .50
12 Mike Lalor .20 .50
13 Rod Langway .40 1.00
14 Steve Leach .20 .50
15 Mike Liut .40 1.00
16 Alan May .20 .50
17 Kelly Miller .20 .50
18 Rob Murray .20 .50
19 Michal Pivonka .40 1.00
20 Mike Ridley .40 1.00
21 Neil Sheehy .20 .50
22 Dave Tippett .20 .50

1990-91 Capitals Smokey
This fire safety set contains 22 cards and features members of the Washington Capitals. The cards measure approximately 2 1/2" by 3 3/4" and were issued in two-card panels. The front has a color action photo of the player, with player information below the picture between the Smokey the Bear and team logos. The back includes Caps Tips~ and a fire prevention message from Smokey.
COMPLETE SET (22) 4.80 12.00
1 Don Beaupre .30 .75
2 Tim Bergland .15 .40
3 Peter Bondra 1.50 4.00
4 Dino Ciccarelli .40 1.00
5 John Druce .15 .40
6 Kevin Hatcher .30 .75
7 Jim Hrivnak .20 .50
8 Dale Hunter .30 .75
9 Calle Johansson .20 .50
10 Nick Kypreos .15 .40
11 Mike Lalor .15 .40
12 Rod Langway .30 .75
13 Stephen Leach .20 .50
14 Mike Liut .40 1.00
15 Alan May .15 .40
16 Kelly Miller .15 .40
17 Rob Murray .15 .40
18 Michal Pivonka .40 1.00
19 Mike Ridley .30 .75
20 Neil Sheehy .15 .40
21 Mikhail Tatarinov .15 .40
22 Dave Tippett .15 .40

1991-92 Capitals Junior 5x7
This 25-card set measures approximately 5" by 7" and features full-bleed glossy action photos; in small black type across the bottom, the uniform number, name, and position are burned in. The backs are blank.
COMPLETE SET (25) 7.20 18.00
1 Don Beaupre .40 1.00
2 Tim Bergland .20 .50
3 Peter Bondra 1.50 4.00
4 Randy Burridge .30 .75
5 Shawn Chambers .20 .50
6 Dino Ciccarelli .60 1.50
7 Sylvain Cote .30 .75
8 John Druce .20 .50
9 Jeff Greenlaw .20 .50
10 Kevin Hatcher .60 1.50
11 Dale Hunter .60 1.50
12 Al Iafrate .60 1.50
13 Calle Johansson .30 .75
14 Dimitri Khristich .60 1.50
15 Todd Krygier .20 .50
16 Nick Kypreos .20 .50
17 Mike Lalor .20 .50
18 Rod Langway .40 1.00
19 Mike Liut .40 1.00
20 Alan May .20 .50
21 Kelly Miller .20 .50
22 Michal Pivonka .60 1.50
23 Mike Ridley .40 1.00
24 Ken Sabourin .20 .50
25 Dave Tippett .20 .50

1991-92 Capitals Kodak
The 1991-92 Washington Capitals Team Photo Album was sponsored by Kodak. It consists of three large sheets joined together to form one continuous sheet. The first panel measures approximately 11" by 8," and it has blank space allotted for autographs. The second panel carries three rows with five player cards each; after perforation, they measure approximately 2 3/16" by 2 3/4." The third panel has two rows with five player cards each, and a final row consisting of two Kodak coupons. The cards feature color head shots, with player information, team logo, and a picture of a Kodak film box below. In a horizontal format, the backs have biographical and statistical information. Though the cards are unnumbered, they are arranged in alphabetical order by players' last names and checklisted below accordingly.
COMPLETE SET (25) 4.80 12.00
1 Don Beaupre .30 .75
2 Tim Bergland .15 .40
3 Peter Bondra 1.00 2.50
4 Randy Burridge .20 .50
5 Shawn Chambers .15 .40
6 Dino Ciccarelli .40 1.00
7 Sylvain Cote .20 .50
8 John Druce .15 .40
9 Kevin Hatcher .30 .75
10 Jim Hrivnak .20 .50
11 Dale Hunter .30 .75
12 Al Iafrate .40 1.00
13 Calle Johansson .20 .50
14 Dimitri Khristich .40 1.00
15 Todd Krygier .15 .40
16 Nick Kypreos .15 .40
17 Rod Langway .30 .75
18 Mike Liut .30 .75
19 Paul MacDermid .15 .40
20 Alan May .15 .40
21 Kelly Miller .15 .40
22 Michal Pivonka .40 1.00
23 Mike Ridley .30 .75
24 Brad Schlegel .15 .40
25 Dave Tippett .15 .40

1992-93 Capitals Kodak
The 1992-93 Washington Capitals Team Photo Album was sponsored by Kodak. It consists of three 8 1/4" by 11" sheets joined together to form one continuous sheet. The first panel has a slot for collecting autographs. The second and third panels consist of player cards; after perforation, they measure approximately 2 3/16" by 2 3/4". The fronts feature color action player photos with white borders. Player information and the team logo are printed in the bottom white border. The horizontal backs carry biography and complete statistical information. Though the cards are unnumbered, they are arranged alphabetically on the sheet and checklisted below accordingly.
COMPLETE SET (25) 6.00 15.00
1 Shawn Anderson .20 .50
2 Don Beaupre .40 1.00
3 Peter Bondra 1.00 2.50
4 Randy Burridge .25 .60
5 Bobby Carpenter .25 .60
6 Paul Cavallini .20 .50
7 Sylvain Cote .20 .50
8 Pat Elynuik .20 .50
9 Kevin Hatcher .30 .75
10 Jim Hrivnak .25 .60
11 Dale Hunter .40 1.00
12 Al Iafrate .40 1.00
13 Calle Johansson .25 .60
14 Keith Jones .25 .60
15 Dimitri Khristich .40 1.00
16 Steve Konowalchuk .30 .75
17 Todd Krygier .20 .50
18 Rod Langway .30 .75
19 Paul MacDermid .20 .50
20 Alan May .20 .50
21 Kelly Miller .20 .50
22 Michal Pivonka .40 1.00
23 Mike Ridley .30 .75
24 Reggie Savage .20 .50
25 Jason Woolley .25 .60

1995-96 Capitals Team Issue
This 28-card set was given away as a premium in complete sheet form at a game late in the '95-96 season. The cards -- which feature the Caps in their new sweaters -- are perforated to be removed. As the cards are unnumbered, they are listed below in alphabetical order.
COMPLETE SET (28) 4.80 12.00
1 Jason Allison .60 1.50
2 Craig Berube .15 .40
3 Peter Bondra 1.25 3.00
4 Jim Carey .20 .50
5 Sylvain Cote .15 .40
6 Mike Eagles .15 .40
7 Martin Gendron .15 .40
8 Sergei Gonchar .15 .40
9 Dale Hunter .30 .75
10 Calle Johansson .20 .50
11 Jim Johnson .15 .40
12 Keith Jones .20 .50
13 Joe Juneau .30 .75
14 Kevin Kaminski .15 .40
15 Ken Klee .15 .40
16 Olaf Kolzig .60 1.50
17 Steve Konowalchuk .30 .75
18 Kelly Miller .15 .40
19 Jeff Nelson .15 .40
20 Pat Peake .15 .40
21 Michal Pivonka .20 .50
22 Joe Reekie .15 .40
23 Jim Schoenfeld CO .08 .25
24 Slapshot Mascot .02 .10
25 Slapshot Mascot .02 .10
26 Mark Tinordi .15 .40
27 Stefan Ustorf .15 .40
28 Brendan Witt .20 .50

1998-99 Capitals Kids and Cops
This set features the Capitals of the NHL. These slightly oversized singles were given out to kids by local police officers. A completed set could be turned in at local police stations for a "special gift." If anyone knows what that gift was, we'd love to hear about it.
COMPLETE SET (7) 4.00 10.00
1 Olaf Kolzig 1.25 3.00
2 Peter Bondra 1.25 3.00
3 Adam Oates .75 2.00
4 Dale Hunter .75 2.00
5 Calle Johansson .40 1.00
6 Steve Konowalchuk .40 1.00
7 Slapshot MAS .40 1.00

2002-03 Capitals Team Issue
Checklist is incomplete. We are looking for additional information on this set.
1 Peter Bondra .60 1.50
2 Jason Doig .40 1.00
3 Sergei Gonchar .40 1.00
4 Jaromir Jagr 1.25 3.00
5 Olaf Kolzig 1.25 3.00
6 Steve Konowalchuk .40 1.00
7 Robert Lang .40 1.00
8 Brendan Witt .40 1.00
9 Dainius Zubrus .40 1.00

1949 Carrera Ltd Sports Series
Cards feature blank backs, and come from a multi-sport series of 50 cards. Each card was cutout of a tobacco pack. The Anning single recently was discovered by collector Barry Chreptyk. Based on the numbering, it's possible there may be other hockey players in the set.
44 Les Anning 15.00 40.00
46 Duke Campbell 15.00 40.00

1934-35 CCM Brown Border Photos
These lovely oversized (11 X 9) photos were issued as premiums inside boxes of CCM skates. One such premium was included per box. The photos showed teams of the day and thus are highly prized by today's collectors. They are rarely seen in high grade and when offered, typically bring prices well above those listed below. Since the photos are unnumbered, they are listed below in alphabetical order.
COMPLETE SET (12) 500.00 1000.00
1 Boston Bruins 50.00 100.00
2 Chicago Blackhawks 50.00 100.00
3 Detroit Red Wings 50.00 100.00
4 Montreal Canadiens 62.50 125.00
5 Montreal Maroons 62.50 125.00
6 New York Americans 62.50 125.00
7 New York Rangers 50.00 100.00
8 Toronto Maple Leafs 50.00 100.00
9 All-Star Game 75.00 150.00
10 Allan Cup Moncton 25.00 50.00
11 Can-Am Providence 30.00 60.00
12 Memorial Cup St. Mike's 25.00 50.00

1935-36 CCM Green Border Photos
Like the previous year's offering, singles from this set were offered as a premium with the purchase of a new pair of CCM skates. This season, however, individual players were offered, along with teams. As they are unnumbered, they are listed below in alphabetical order.
COMPLETE SET (10) 375.00 750.00
1 Boston Cubs (Can-Am champs) 25.00 50.00
2 Boston Bruins 62.50 125.00
3 Halifax (Allan Cup) 25.00 50.00
4 Montreal Maroons 75.00 150.00
5 Toronto Maple Leafs 62.50 125.00
6 Winnipeg (Memorial Cup) 25.00 50.00
7 Frank Boucher 37.50 75.00
8 Lorne Chabot 50.00 100.00
9 Charlie Conacher 50.00 100.00
10 Foster Hewitt 37.50 75.00

2008 Americana Celebrity Cuts
COMPLETE SET (100) 125.00 200.00
STATED PRINT RUN 499 SERIAL #'d SETS
*CENTURY SILVER/50: .6X TO 1.5X BASE
*CENTURY GOLD/25: .75X TO 2X BASE
UNPRICED CENTURY PLATINUM #'d TO 1
67 Patrick Roy 3.00 8.00
89 Tony Esposito 1.50 4.00

2008 Americana Celebrity Cuts Century Material
RANDOM INSERTS IN PACKS
PRINT RUNS B/WN 5-100 COPIES
NO PRICING ON QTY OF 5
67 Patrick Roy/100 6.00 15.00
89 Tony Esposito/100 4.00 10.00

2008 Americana Celebrity Cuts Century Material Combo
RANDOM INSERTS IN PACKS
PRINT RUNS B/WN 5-50 COPIES PER
NO PRICING ON QTY OF 10 OR LESS
67 Patrick Roy/50 8.00 20.00
89 Tony Esposito/50 6.00 15.00

2008 Americana Celebrity Cuts Century Signature Gold
RANDOM INSERTS IN PACKS
PRINT RUNS B/WN 1-200 COPIES PER
NO PRICING ON QTY OF 14 OR LESS
67 Patrick Roy/75 30.00 60.00
89 Tony Esposito/50 10.00 25.00

2008 Americana Celebrity Cuts Century Signature Material
RANDOM INSERTS IN PACKS
PRINT RUNS B/WN 1-50 COPIES PER
NO PRICING ON QTY OF 14 OR LESS
67 Patrick Roy/50 40.00 80.00
89 Tony Esposito/50 10.00 25.00

2008 Americana Celebrity Cuts Century Signature Material Prime
67 Patrick Roy/2

2010 Certified National Convention
COMPLETE SET (2) 3.00 6.00
AO Alex Ovechkin 1.25 3.00
SC Sidney Crosby 1.50 4.00

2010 Certified National Convention Blue
COMPLETE SET (2) 7.50 15.00
*BLUE: 1X TO 2.5X BASIC CARDS
ANNOUNCED PRINT RUN 25 SETS

2010-11 Certified
This was the first NHL release by Panini America. The product had a $10 per pack price point and it was the first 2010-11 product to include autographed Rookie Cards. Six of the base cards were released as exchange cards: 191, 194, 195, 196, 197 and 200. Card #212, BrockTrotter was unable to sign his cards after agreeing to a deal to play in Russia. All 799 were released without autographs, but they look like the other autographs in the subset, just without a signature.
COMP.SET w/o SPs (150) 20.00 50.00
IMMORTALS PRINT RUN 500 SER.#'d SETS
(171-184) PRINT RUN 1299 SER.#'d SETS
(185-188) PRINT RUN 899 SER.#'d SETS
(189-200) PRINT RUN 499 SER.#'d SETS
(201-211) PRINT RUN 799 SER.#'d SETS
1 Ryan Getzlaf .60 1.50
2 Corey Perry .40 1.00
3 Teemu Selanne .75 2.00
4 Bobby Ryan .40 1.00
5 Jonas Hiller .30 .75
6 Evander Kane .40 1.00
7 Zach Bogosian .30 .75
8 Dustin Byfuglien .40 1.00
9 Nik Antropov .30 .75
10 Ondrej Pavelec .40 1.00
11 Milan Lucic .40 1.00
12 Patrice Bergeron .50 1.25
13 Zdeno Chara .30 .75
14 Nathan Horton .30 .75
15 Tuukka Rask .40 1.00
16 Ryan Miller .40 1.00
17 Thomas Vanek .40 1.00
18 Tyler Myers .40 1.00
19 Nathan Gerbe .25 .60
20 Derek Roy .40 1.00
21 Jarome Iginla .40 1.00
22 Miikka Kiprusoff .30 .75
23 Rene Bourque .25 .60
24 Mikael Backlund .25 .60
25 Jay Bouwmeester .50 1.25
26 Brandon Sutter .30 .75
27 Eric Staal .50 1.25
28 Cam Ward .40 1.00
29 Zach Boychuk .30 .75
30 Drayson Bowman .30 .75
31 Jonathan Toews .75 2.00
32 Patrick Kane .75 2.00
33 Duncan Keith .40 1.00
34 Marty Turco .40 1.00
35 Patrick Sharp .40 1.00
36 Marian Hossa .30 .75
37 Craig Anderson .40 1.00
38 Matt Duchene .40 1.00
39 Chris Stewart .30 .75
40 Peter Mueller .30 .75
41 Paul Stastny .40 1.00
42 Rick Nash .40 1.00
43 Steve Mason .30 .75
44 Jakub Voracek .40 1.00
45 Antoine Vermette .25 .60
46 James Neal .40 1.00
47 Jamie Benn .50 1.25
48 Steve Ott .30 .75
49 Kari Lehtonen .30 .75
50 Brad Richards .40 1.00
51 Pavel Datsyuk .50 1.25
52 Henrik Zetterberg .50 1.25
53 Jimmy Howard .50 1.25
54 Nicklas Lidstrom .40 1.00
55 Johan Franzen .40 1.00
56 Tomas Holmstrom .25 .60
57 Ales Hemsky .30 .75
58 Sam Gagner .30 .75
59 Dustin Penner .25 .60
60 Jeff Deslauriers .25 .60
61 Nikolai Khabibulin .30 .75
62 Tomas Vokoun .30 .75
63 Stephen Weiss .30 .75
64 Dmitri Kulikov .30 .75
65 Michael Frolik .25 .60
66 Drew Doughty .40 1.00
67 Anze Kopitar .60 1.50
68 Jonathan Quick .60 1.50
69 Wayne Simmonds .50 1.25
70 Ryan Smyth .30 .75
71 Mikko Koivu .40 1.00
72 Cal Clutterbuck .40 1.00
73 Niklas Backstrom .40 1.00
74 Guillaume Latendresse .30 .75
75 Carey Price 1.50 4.00
76 Tomas Plekanec .40 1.00
77 Scott Gomez .30 .75
78 Michael Cammalleri .40 1.00
79 Brian Gionta .30 .75
80 Pekka Rinne .50 1.25
81 Patric Hornqvist .30 .75
82 Shea Weber .30 .75
83 Colin Wilson .30 .75
84 Jordin Tootoo .30 .75
85 Martin Brodeur .75 2.00
86 Zach Parise .40 1.00
87 Ilya Kovalchuk .40 1.00
88 Travis Zajac .30 .75
89 Andy Greene .25 .60
90 John Tavares .75 2.00
91 Matt Moulson .30 .75
92 Kyle Okposo .40 1.00
93 Josh Bailey .30 .75
94 Dwayne Roloson .30 .75
95 Henrik Lundqvist .60 1.50
96 Marian Gaborik .50 1.25
97 Artem Anisimov .30 .75
98 Michael Del Zotto .30 .75
99 Marc Staal .40 1.00
100 Daniel Alfredsson .40 1.00
101 Jason Spezza .25 .60
102 Mike Fisher .40 1.00
103 Brian Elliott .30 .75
104 Erik Karlsson .75 2.00
105 Mike Richards .40 1.00
106 Jeff Carter .40 1.00
107 Chris Pronger .30 .75
108 Claude Giroux .40 1.00
109 Simon Gagne .40 1.00
110 Michael Leighton .30 .75
111 Ilya Bryzgalov .30 .75
112 Shane Doan .30 .75
113 Wojtek Wolski .25 .60
114 Mikkel Boedker .25 .60
115 Sidney Crosby 1.50 4.00
116 Evgeni Malkin 1.25 3.00
117 Marc-Andre Fleury .60 1.50
118 Jordan Staal .40 1.00
119 Alex Goligoski .30 .75
120 Dany Heatley .30 .75
121 Joe Thornton .40 1.00
122 Dan Boyle .30 .75
123 Patrick Marleau .40 1.00
124 Joe Pavelski .40 1.00
125 T.J. Oshie .60 1.50
126 David Backes .40 1.00
127 Erik Johnson .25 .60
128 David Perron .25 .60
129 Jaroslav Halak .40 1.00
130 Steven Stamkos .75 2.00
131 Vincent Lecavalier .30 .75
132 Martin St. Louis .40 1.00
133 Steve Downie .25 .60
134 Phil Kessel .50 1.25
135 Jonas Gustavsson .50 1.25
136 Jean-Sebastien Giguere .30 .75
137 Dion Phaneuf .40 1.00
138 Luca Caputi .30 .75
139 Henrik Sedin .40 1.00
140 Daniel Sedin .40 1.00
141 Alexandre Burrows .40 1.00
142 Roberto Luongo .40 1.00
143 Ryan Kesler .40 1.00
144 Cory Schneider .30 .75
145 Alexander Ovechkin 1.50 4.00
146 Mike Green .40 1.00
147 Semyon Varlamov .40 1.00
148 John Carlson .50 1.25
149 Nicklas Backstrom .60 1.50
150 Alexander Semin .40 1.00
151 Cam Neely 2.00 5.00
152 Steve Yzerman 5.00 12.00
153 Bobby Hull 2.00 5.00
154 Ed Giacomin 3.00 8.00
155 Jean Beliveau 2.00 5.00
156 Mario Lemieux 6.00 15.00
157 Ray Bourque 3.00 8.00
158 Gilbert Perreault 2.00 5.00
159 Patrick Roy 5.00 12.00
160 Bryan Trottier 2.50 6.00
161 Stan Mikita 2.50 6.00
162 Pat LaFontaine 2.00 5.00
163 Grant Fuhr 2.00 5.00
164 Phil Esposito 3.00 8.00
165 Tony Esposito 2.00 5.00
166 Guy Lafleur 2.50 6.00
167 Glenn Hall 2.00 5.00
168 Lanny McDonald 2.00 5.00
169 Eric Lindros 3.00 8.00
170 Trevor Linden 2.00 5.00
171 Nick Bonino AU RC 3.00 8.00
172 Justin Mercier AU RC 2.50 6.00
173 Philip Larsen AU RC 2.50 6.00
174 Casey Wellman AU RC 2.50 6.00
175 Jamie McBain AU RC 2.50 6.00
176 Brandon Yip AU RC 2.50 6.00
177 Nick Palmieri AU RC 2.50 6.00
178 Maxim Noreau AU RC 2.00 5.00
179 Nick Spaling AU RC 2.50 6.00
180 Nick Johnson AU RC 2.00 5.00
181 Zach Hamill AU RC 2.50 6.00
182 Dustin Tokarski AU RC 2.50 6.00
183 Bobby Butler AU RC 2.50 6.00
184 Jared Cowen AU RC 2.50 6.00
185 Nazem Kadri AU RC 10.00 25.00
186 P.K. Subban AU RC 12.00 30.00
187 Brayden Irwin AU RC 3.00 8.00
188 Eric Tangradi AU RC 3.00 8.00
189 Taylor Hall JSY AU RC 25.00 50.00
190 Tyler Seguin JSY AU RC 25.00 50.00
191 Cam Fowler JSY AU RC 6.00 15.00
192 Jordan Eberle JSY AU RC 15.00 40.00
193 M.Paajarvi JSY AU RC 6.00 15.00
194 A.Burmistrov JSY AU RC 5.00 12.00
195 M.Tedenby JSY AU RC 4.00 10.00
196 K.Shattenkirk JSY AU RC 10.00 25.00
197 Derek Stepan JSY AU RC 10.00 25.00
198 B.Schenn JSY AU RC 8.00 20.00
199 Jeff Skinner JSY AU RC 10.00 25.00
200 N.Niederreiter JSY AU RC 6.00 15.00
201 Brad Thiessen AU RC 6.00 15.00
202 James Wyman AU RC 4.00 10.00
203 Corey Elkins AU RC 3.00 8.00
204 Jerome Samson AU RC 4.00 10.00
205 Jeremy Duchesne AU RC 5.00 12.00
206 Derek Smith AU RC 4.00 10.00
207 Bryan Pitton AU RC 5.00 12.00
208 Carter Hutton AU RC 8.00 20.00
209 Matt Martin AU RC 6.00 15.00
210 Jean-Philippe Levasseur AU RC 4.00 10.00
211 Marc-Andre Cliche AU RC 3.00 8.00
212 Brock Trotter NO AU RC 40.00 80.00
RM Ryan Miller Preview .50 1.25

2010-11 Certified Mirror Blue
*BLUE (1-150): 2.5X TO 6X BASE
*BLUE (151-170): .5X TO 1.2X BASE
*BLUE AU (171-184): .8X TO 2X BASE
*BLUE AU (185-188): .6X TO 1.5X BASE
STATED PRINT RUN 100 SER.#'d SETS
*BLUE JSY AU (189-200): .6X TO 1.5X BASE
*BLUE AU (201-212): .6X TO 1.5X BASE
189-212 PRINT RUN 50 SER.#'d SETS
149 Nicklas Backstrom 4.00 10.00
186 P.K. Subban AU 25.00 60.00
189 Taylor Hall JSY AU 30.00 80.00
192 Jordan Eberle JSY AU 20.00 50.00

2010-11 Certified Mirror Blue Materials
STATED PRINT RUN 100 SER.#'d SETS
1 Ryan Getzlaf 6.00 15.00
2 Corey Perry 4.00 10.00
3 Teemu Selanne 8.00 20.00
4 Bobby Ryan 4.00 10.00
5 Jonas Hiller 3.00 8.00
6 Evander Kane 4.00 10.00
7 Zach Bogosian 3.00 8.00
8 Dustin Byfuglien 4.00 10.00
9 Nik Antropov 3.00 8.00
10 Ondrej Pavelec 4.00 10.00
11 Milan Lucic 4.00 10.00
12 Patrice Bergeron 5.00 12.00
13 Zdeno Chara 3.00 8.00
14 Nathan Horton 3.00 8.00
15 Tuukka Rask 4.00 10.00
16 Ryan Miller 4.00 10.00
17 Thomas Vanek 4.00 10.00
18 Tyler Myers
19 Nathan Gerbe 2.50 6.00
20 Derek Roy 4.00 10.00
21 Jarome Iginla 4.00 10.00
22 Miikka Kiprusoff 3.00 8.00
23 Rene Bourque 2.50 6.00
24 Mikael Backlund 2.50 6.00
25 Jay Bouwmeester 5.00 12.00
26 Brandon Sutter 3.00 8.00
27 Eric Staal 5.00 12.00
28 Cam Ward 4.00 10.00
29 Zach Boychuk 3.00 8.00
30 Drayson Bowman 3.00 8.00
31 Jonathan Toews 8.00 20.00
32 Patrick Kane 8.00 20.00
33 Duncan Keith 4.00 10.00
34 Marty Turco 4.00 10.00
35 Patrick Sharp 4.00 10.00
36 Marian Hossa 3.00 8.00
37 Craig Anderson 4.00 10.00
38 Matt Duchene 4.00 10.00
39 Chris Stewart 3.00 8.00
40 Peter Mueller 3.00 8.00
41 Paul Stastny 4.00 10.00
42 Rick Nash 4.00 10.00
43 Steve Mason 3.00 8.00
44 Jakub Voracek 4.00 10.00
45 Antoine Vermette 2.50 6.00
46 James Neal 4.00 10.00
47 Jamie Benn 5.00 12.00
48 Steve Ott 3.00 8.00
49 Kari Lehtonen 3.00 8.00
50 Brad Richards 4.00 10.00
51 Pavel Datsyuk 5.00 12.00
52 Henrik Zetterberg 5.00 12.00
53 Jimmy Howard
54 Nicklas Lidstrom 4.00 10.00
55 Johan Franzen 4.00 10.00
56 Tomas Holmstrom 2.50 6.00
57 Ales Hemsky 3.00 8.00
58 Sam Gagner 3.00 8.00
59 Dustin Penner 2.50 6.00
60 Jeff Deslauriers 2.50 6.00
61 Nikolai Khabibulin 3.00 8.00
62 Tomas Vokoun 3.00 8.00
63 Stephen Weiss 3.00 8.00
64 Dmitri Kulikov 3.00 8.00
65 Michael Frolik 2.50 6.00
66 Drew Doughty 4.00 10.00
67 Anze Kopitar 6.00 15.00
68 Jonathan Quick 6.00 15.00
69 Wayne Simmonds 5.00 12.00
70 Ryan Smyth 3.00 8.00
71 Mikko Koivu 4.00 10.00
72 Cal Clutterbuck 4.00 10.00
73 Niklas Backstrom 4.00 10.00
74 Guillaume Latendresse 3.00 8.00
75 Carey Price 15.00 40.00
76 Tomas Plekanec 4.00 10.00
77 Scott Gomez 3.00 8.00
78 Michael Cammalleri 4.00 10.00
79 Brian Gionta 3.00 8.00
80 Pekka Rinne 5.00 12.00
81 Patric Hornqvist 3.00 8.00
82 Shea Weber 3.00 8.00
83 Colin Wilson 3.00 8.00
84 Jordin Tootoo 3.00 8.00
85 Martin Brodeur 8.00 20.00
86 Zach Parise 4.00 10.00
87 Ilya Kovalchuk 4.00 10.00
88 Travis Zajac 3.00 8.00
89 Andy Greene 2.50 6.00
90 John Tavares 6.00 15.00
91 Matt Moulson 3.00 8.00
92 Kyle Okposo 4.00 10.00
93 Josh Bailey 3.00 8.00
94 Dwayne Roloson 3.00 8.00
95 Henrik Lundqvist 6.00 15.00
96 Marian Gaborik 5.00 12.00
97 Artem Anisimov 3.00 8.00
98 Michael Del Zotto 3.00 8.00
99 Marc Staal 4.00 10.00
100 Daniel Alfredsson 4.00 10.00
101 Jason Spezza 2.50 6.00
102 Mike Fisher 4.00 10.00
103 Brian Elliott 3.00 8.00
104 Erik Karlsson 8.00 20.00
105 Mike Richards 4.00 10.00
106 Jeff Carter 4.00 10.00
107 Chris Pronger 3.00 8.00
108 Claude Giroux 4.00 10.00
109 Simon Gagne 4.00 10.00
110 Michael Leighton 3.00 8.00
111 Ilya Bryzgalov 3.00 8.00
112 Shane Doan 3.00 8.00
113 Wojtek Wolski 2.50 6.00
114 Mikkel Boedker 2.50 6.00
115 Sidney Crosby 15.00 40.00
116 Evgeni Malkin 12.00 30.00
117 Marc-Andre Fleury 6.00 15.00
118 Jordan Staal 4.00 10.00
119 Alex Goligoski 3.00 8.00
120 Dany Heatley 3.00 8.00
121 Joe Thornton
122 Dan Boyle 3.00 8.00
123 Patrick Marleau 4.00 10.00
124 Joe Pavelski 4.00 10.00
125 T.J. Oshie
126 David Backes 4.00 10.00
127 Erik Johnson 2.50 6.00
128 David Perron 2.50 6.00
129 Jaroslav Halak 4.00 10.00
130 Steven Stamkos 6.00 15.00
131 Vincent Lecavalier 3.00 8.00
132 Martin St. Louis 4.00 10.00
133 Steve Downie 2.50 6.00
134 Phil Kessel 5.00 12.00
135 Jonas Gustavsson 5.00 12.00
136 Jean-Sebastien Giguere 3.00 8.00
137 Dion Phaneuf 4.00 10.00
138 Luca Caputi 3.00 8.00
139 Henrik Sedin 4.00 10.00
140 Daniel Sedin 4.00 10.00
141 Alexandre Burrows 4.00 10.00
142 Roberto Luongo 4.00 10.00
143 Ryan Kesler 4.00 10.00
144 Cory Schneider 3.00 8.00
145 Alexander Ovechkin 15.00 40.00
146 Mike Green 4.00 10.00
147 Semyon Varlamov 4.00 10.00
148 John Carlson 5.00 12.00
149 Nicklas Backstrom 6.00 15.00
150 Alexander Semin 4.00 10.00
151 Cam Neely
152 Steve Yzerman 10.00 25.00
153 Bobby Hull 4.00 10.00
154 Ed Giacomin
155 Jean Beliveau 4.00 10.00
156 Mario Lemieux 8.00 20.00
157 Ray Bourque
158 Gilbert Perreault
159 Patrick Roy
160 Bryan Trottier
161 Stan Mikita 5.00 12.00
162 Pat LaFontaine 4.00 10.00
163 Grant Fuhr
164 Phil Esposito 6.00 15.00
165 Tony Esposito 4.00 10.00
166 Guy Lafleur
167 Glenn Hall 4.00 10.00
168 Lanny McDonald 4.00 10.00
169 Eric Lindros 6.00 15.00
170 Trevor Linden

2010-11 Certified Mirror Blue Signatures
STATED PRINT RUN 50 SER.#'d SETS
1 Ryan Getzlaf
2 Corey Perry
3 Teemu Selanne
4 Bobby Ryan
5 Jonas Hiller 5.00 12.00
6 Evander Kane
7 Zach Bogosian 5.00 12.00
8 Dustin Byfuglien 6.00 15.00
9 Nik Antropov
10 Ondrej Pavelec
11 Milan Lucic
12 Patrice Bergeron
13 Zdeno Chara
14 Nathan Horton
15 Tuukka Rask
16 Ryan Miller
17 Thomas Vanek
18 Tyler Myers
19 Nathan Gerbe 4.00 10.00
20 Derek Roy
21 Jarome Iginla
22 Miikka Kiprusoff
23 Rene Bourque
24 Mikael Backlund
25 Jay Bouwmeester
26 Brandon Sutter 5.00 12.00
27 Eric Staal
28 Cam Ward
29 Zach Boychuk 5.00 12.00
30 Drayson Bowman
31 Jonathan Toews
32 Patrick Kane
33 Duncan Keith
34 Marty Turco
35 Patrick Sharp
36 Marian Hossa
37 Craig Anderson 6.00 15.00
38 Matt Duchene
39 Chris Stewart
40 Peter Mueller 5.00 12.00
41 Paul Stastny 6.00 15.00
42 Rick Nash
43 Steve Mason
44 Jakub Voracek
45 Antoine Vermette 4.00 10.00
46 James Neal 6.00 15.00
47 Jamie Benn 8.00 20.00
48 Steve Ott
49 Kari Lehtonen 5.00 12.00
50 Brad Richards
51 Pavel Datsyuk
52 Henrik Zetterberg
53 Jimmy Howard 8.00 20.00
54 Nicklas Lidstrom
55 Johan Franzen
56 Tomas Holmstrom
57 Ales Hemsky
58 Sam Gagner 5.00 12.00
59 Dustin Penner 4.00 10.00
60 Jeff Deslauriers 4.00 10.00
61 Nikolai Khabibulin
62 Tomas Vokoun
63 Stephen Weiss
64 Dmitri Kulikov
65 Michael Frolik 4.00 10.00
66 Drew Doughty
67 Anze Kopitar
68 Jonathan Quick
69 Wayne Simmonds
70 Ryan Smyth
71 Mikko Koivu
72 Cal Clutterbuck
73 Niklas Backstrom
74 Guillaume Latendresse 5.00 12.00
75 Carey Price
76 Tomas Plekanec
77 Scott Gomez
78 Michael Cammalleri
79 Brian Gionta 5.00 12.00
80 Pekka Rinne
81 Patric Hornqvist 5.00 12.00
82 Shea Weber
83 Colin Wilson 5.00 12.00
84 Jordin Tootoo
85 Martin Brodeur
86 Zach Parise
87 Ilya Kovalchuk
88 Travis Zajac
89 Andy Greene
90 John Tavares
91 Matt Moulson 5.00 12.00
92 Kyle Okposo
93 Josh Bailey 5.00 12.00
94 Dwayne Roloson 5.00 12.00
95 Henrik Lundqvist
96 Marian Gaborik
97 Artem Anisimov 5.00 12.00
98 Michael Del Zotto
99 Marc Staal 6.00 15.00
100 Daniel Alfredsson
101 Jason Spezza
102 Mike Fisher 6.00 15.00
103 Brian Elliott 5.00 12.00
104 Erik Karlsson
105 Mike Richards
106 Jeff Carter
107 Chris Pronger
108 Claude Giroux 6.00 15.00
109 Simon Gagne
110 Michael Leighton 5.00 12.00
111 Ilya Bryzgalov
112 Shane Doan
113 Wojtek Wolski 4.00 10.00
114 Mikkel Boedker 4.00 10.00
115 Sidney Crosby
116 Evgeni Malkin
117 Marc-Andre Fleury
118 Jordan Staal
119 Alex Goligoski 5.00 12.00
120 Dany Heatley
121 Joe Thornton
122 Dan Boyle 5.00 12.00
123 Patrick Marleau
124 Joe Pavelski 6.00 15.00
125 T.J. Oshie
126 David Backes 6.00 15.00
127 Erik Johnson
128 David Perron
129 Jaroslav Halak
130 Steven Stamkos
131 Vincent Lecavalier
132 Martin St. Louis
133 Steve Downie 4.00 10.00
134 Phil Kessel
135 Jonas Gustavsson
136 Jean-Sebastien Giguere
137 Dion Phaneuf
138 Luca Caputi 5.00 12.00
139 Henrik Sedin
140 Daniel Sedin
141 Alexandre Burrows 12.00 30.00
142 Roberto Luongo
143 Ryan Kesler 6.00 15.00
144 Cory Schneider 5.00 12.00
145 Alexander Ovechkin
146 Mike Green
147 Semyon Varlamov
148 John Carlson 10.00 25.00
149 Nicklas Backstrom
150 Alexander Semin
151 Cam Neely
152 Steve Yzerman
153 Bobby Hull
154 Ed Giacomin
155 Jean Beliveau
156 Mario Lemieux
157 Ray Bourque
158 Gilbert Perreault
159 Patrick Roy
160 Bryan Trottier
161 Stan Mikita
162 Pat LaFontaine
163 Grant Fuhr
164 Phil Esposito
165 Tony Esposito
166 Guy Lafleur
167 Glenn Hall
168 Lanny McDonald
169 Eric Lindros
170 Trevor Linden

2010-11 Certified Mirror Gold
*GOLD (1-150): 4X TO 10X BASE
*GOLD (151-170): .8X TO 2X BASE
*GOLD AU (171-184): 1.2X TO 3X BASE
*GOLD AU (185-188): 1X TO 2.5X BASE
*GOLD JSY AU (189-200): 1X TO 2.5X BASE
*GOLD AU (201-212): .8X TO 2X BASE
STATED PRINT RUN 25 SER.#'d SETS
149 Nicklas Backstrom 6.00 15.00
186 P.K. Subban AU 40.00 100.00
189 Taylor Hall JSY AU 60.00 120.00
192 Jordan Eberle JSY AU 50.00 120.00

2010-11 Certified Mirror Gold Materials Prime
*GOLD: 1X TO 2.5X MIRROR BLUE MATERIALS
STATED PRINT RUN 25 SER.#'d SETS
149 Nicklas Backstrom 15.00 40.00

2010-11 Certified Mirror Gold Signatures
STATED PRINT RUN 25 SER.#'d SETS
1 Ryan Getzlaf 15.00 40.00
2 Corey Perry 8.00 20.00
3 Teemu Selanne 12.00 30.00
4 Bobby Ryan 8.00 20.00
5 Jonas Hiller 6.00 15.00
6 Evander Kane 8.00 20.00

7 Zach Bogosian 6.00 15.00
8 Dustin Byfuglien 8.00 20.00
9 Nik Antropov 6.00 15.00
13 Zdeno Chara 8.00 20.00
14 Nathan Horton 6.00 15.00
16 Ryan Miller 8.00 20.00
17 Thomas Vanek 8.00 20.00
18 Tyler Myers 8.00 20.00
19 Nathan Gerbe 5.00 12.00
20 Derek Roy 8.00 20.00
21 Jarome Iginla 15.00 40.00
23 Rene Bourque 5.00 12.00
24 Mikael Backlund 8.00 20.00
25 Jay Bouwmeester 12.00 30.00
26 Brandon Sutter 6.00 15.00
27 Eric Staal 10.00 25.00
28 Cam Ward 10.00 25.00
29 Zach Boychuk 6.00 15.00
30 Drayson Bowman 6.00 15.00
31 Jonathan Toews 10.00 25.00
32 Patrick Kane 25.00 60.00
35 Patrick Sharp 15.00 40.00
36 Marian Hossa 15.00 40.00
37 Craig Anderson 15.00 40.00
38 Matt Duchene 20.00 50.00
39 Chris Stewart 6.00 15.00
40 Peter Mueller 6.00 15.00
41 Paul Stastny 8.00 20.00
42 Rick Nash 12.00 30.00
43 Steve Mason 6.00 15.00
44 Jakub Voracek 6.00 15.00
45 Antoine Vermette 5.00 12.00
46 James Neal 8.00 20.00
47 Jamie Benn 10.00 25.00
48 Steve Ott 6.00 15.00
51 Pavel Datsyuk 15.00 40.00
53 Jimmy Howard 10.00 25.00
54 Nicklas Lidstrom 15.00 40.00
55 Johan Franzen 10.00 25.00
56 Tomas Holmstrom 12.00 30.00
57 Ales Hemsky 6.00 15.00
59 Dustin Penner 5.00 12.00
60 Jeff Deslauriers 5.00 12.00
62 Tomas Vokoun 6.00 15.00
63 Stephen Weiss 8.00 20.00
65 Michael Frolik 5.00 12.00
66 Drew Doughty 20.00 50.00
67 Anze Kopitar 12.00 30.00
68 Jonathan Quick 20.00 40.00
69 Wayne Simmonds 8.00 20.00
70 Ryan Smyth 6.00 15.00
72 Cal Clutterbuck 8.00 20.00
73 Niklas Backstrom 8.00 20.00
74 Guillaume Latendresse 6.00 15.00
75 Carey Price 20.00 50.00
77 Scott Gomez 6.00 15.00
78 Michael Cammalleri 8.00 20.00
79 Brian Gionta 6.00 15.00
80 Pekka Rinne 12.00 30.00
81 Patric Hornqvist 6.00 15.00
82 Shea Weber 6.00 15.00
84 Jordin Tootoo 6.00 15.00
85 Martin Brodeur 40.00 80.00
86 Zach Parise 10.00 30.00
87 Ilya Kovalchuk 15.00 40.00
89 Andy Greene 5.00 12.00
90 John Tavares 15.00 40.00
91 Matt Moulson 6.00 15.00
93 Josh Bailey 6.00 15.00
94 Dwayne Roloson 6.00 15.00
95 Henrik Lundqvist 12.00 30.00
97 Artem Anisimov 6.00 15.00
99 Marc Staal 8.00 20.00
100 Daniel Alfredsson 8.00 20.00
101 Jason Spezza 12.00 30.00
102 Mike Fisher 8.00 20.00
104 Erik Karlsson 15.00 40.00
105 Mike Richards 15.00 40.00
106 Jeff Carter 15.00 40.00
107 Chris Pronger 6.00 15.00
108 Claude Giroux 15.00 40.00
109 Simon Gagne 8.00 20.00
110 Michael Leighton 6.00 15.00
111 Ilya Bryzgalov 6.00 15.00
112 Shane Doan 6.00 15.00
113 Wojtek Wolski 5.00 12.00
115 Sidney Crosby 75.00 150.00
116 Evgeni Malkin 15.00 40.00
118 Jordan Staal 15.00 40.00
119 Alex Goligoski 10.00 25.00
120 Dany Heatley 6.00 15.00
121 Joe Thornton 15.00 40.00
122 Dan Boyle 6.00 15.00
123 Patrick Marleau 8.00 20.00
124 Joe Pavelski 15.00 40.00
125 T.J. Oshie 12.00 30.00
126 David Backes 8.00 20.00
127 Erik Johnson 5.00 12.00
128 David Perron 5.00 12.00
130 Steven Stamkos 25.00 60.00
131 Vincent Lecavalier 6.00 15.00
132 Martin St. Louis 12.00 30.00
133 Steve Downie 5.00 12.00
134 Phil Kessel 10.00 25.00
135 Jonas Gustavsson 10.00 25.00
137 Dion Phaneuf 8.00 20.00
138 Luca Caputi 6.00 15.00
139 Henrik Sedin 10.00 25.00
140 Daniel Sedin 12.00 30.00
141 Alexandre Burrows 15.00 40.00
143 Ryan Kesler 15.00 40.00
144 Cory Schneider 12.00 30.00
145 Alexander Ovechkin 50.00 100.00
146 Mike Green 8.00 20.00
147 Semyon Varlamov 8.00 20.00
148 John Carlson 12.00 30.00
150 Alexander Semin 8.00 20.00
151 Cam Neely 15.00 30.00
152 Steve Yzerman 50.00 100.00
153 Bobby Hull 20.00 50.00
155 Jean Beliveau 25.00 60.00
156 Mario Lemieux 60.00 120.00
157 Ray Bourque 12.00 30.00
160 Bryan Trottier 6.00 15.00
162 Pat LaFontaine 10.00 25.00
163 Grant Fuhr 10.00 25.00
164 Phil Esposito 20.00 40.00
165 Tony Esposito 12.00 30.00
166 Guy Lafleur 12.00 30.00
167 Glenn Hall 8.00 20.00
168 Lanny McDonald 8.00 20.00
169 Eric Lindros 20.00 50.00
170 Trevor Linden 25.00 60.00

2010-11 Certified Mirror Red

*RED (1-150): 2X TO 5X BASE
*RED (151-170): .4X TO 1X BASE
*RED AU (171-184): .6X TO 1.5X BASE
*RED AU (185-188): .5X TO 1.2X BASE
STATED PRINT RUN 250 SER.#'d SETS
*RED JSY AU (189-200): .5X TO 1.2X BASE
*RED AU (201-212): .5X TO 1.2X BASE
189-212 PRINT RUN 100 SER.#'d SETS
149 Nicklas Backstrom 3.00 8.00
189 Taylor Hall JSY AU 30.00 80.00
192 Jordan Eberle JSY AU 15.00 40.00

2010-11 Certified Mirror Red Materials Dual

*SINGLES: .4X TO 1X MIRROR BLUE MATERIALS
STATED PRINT RUN 150 SER.#'d SETS
149 Nicklas Backstrom 6.00 15.00

2010-11 Certified Platinum Blue

*SINGLES: 2X TO 5X BASIC CARDS
STATED PRINT RUN 250 SER.#'d SETS
149 Nicklas Backstrom 3.00 8.00

2010-11 Certified Platinum Gold

*SINGLES: 4X TO 10X BASIC CARDS
STATED PRINT RUN 25 SER.#'d SETS
149 Nicklas Backstrom 6.00 15.00

2010-11 Certified Platinum Red

*SINGLES: 1.2X TO 3X BASIC CARDS
STATED PRINT RUN 999 SER.#'d SETS
149 Nicklas Backstrom 2.00 5.00

2010-11 Certified Big Men On Campus Jerseys

STATED PRINT RUN 100-250
*PRIME/25: 1X TO 2.5X BASIC JSY/150-250
*PRIME/25: .6X TO 1.5X BASIC JSY/100
1 Joe Pavelski 4.00 10.00
2 Michael Cammalleri/100 6.00 15.00
3 Jonathan Quick 6.00 15.00
4 Brian Gionta 8.00 20.00
5 Zach Parise 4.00 10.00
6 Jonathan Toews/150 8.00 20.00
7 Ryan Miller 4.00 10.00
8 Tim Thomas 5.00 12.00
9 Kyle Okposo 4.00 10.00
10 Paul Stastny 4.00 10.00
11 Tyler Bozak 4.00 10.00
12 Travis Zajac 5.00 12.00
13 Martin St. Louis 4.00 10.00
14 Colin Wilson 3.00 8.00
15 Brett Hull 6.00 15.00

2010-11 Certified Champions

STATED PRINT RUN 500 SER.#'d SETS
1 Jonathan Toews 4.00 10.00
2 Patrick Kane 4.00 10.00
3 Antti Niemi 1.50 4.00
4 Dustin Byfuglien 2.00 5.00
5 Patrick Sharp 2.00 5.00
6 Marc-Andre Fleury 3.00 8.00
7 Sidney Crosby 6.00 15.00
8 Evgeni Malkin 6.00 15.00
9 Jordan Staal 2.00 5.00
10 Nicklas Lidstrom 2.00 5.00
11 Dan Boyle 1.50 4.00
12 Teemu Selanne 4.00 10.00
13 Ryan Getzlaf 3.00 8.00
14 Corey Perry 2.00 5.00
15 Cam Ward 2.00 5.00
16 Eric Staal 2.50 6.00
17 Martin St. Louis 2.00 5.00
18 Vincent Lecavalier 1.50 4.00
19 Nikolai Khabibulin 1.50 4.00
20 Luc Robitaille 2.50 6.00
21 Mario Lemieux 5.00 12.00
22 Tom Barrasso 2.50 6.00
23 Paul Coffey 2.50 6.00
24 Patrick Roy 6.00 15.00
25 Brett Hull 4.00 10.00
JT Jonathan Toews Preview 1.00 2.50

2010-11 Certified Champions Autographs

STATED PRINT RUN 50 SER.#'d SETS
1 Jonathan Toews 20.00 50.00
2 Patrick Kane 20.00 50.00
3 Antti Niemi
4 Dustin Byfuglien 8.00 20.00
5 Patrick Sharp 25.00 60.00
6 Marc-Andre Fleury 12.00 30.00
7 Sidney Crosby/10
8 Evgeni Malkin 20.00 50.00
9 Jordan Staal 10.00 25.00
10 Nicklas Lidstrom 12.00 30.00
11 Dan Boyle 6.00 15.00
12 Teemu Selanne 15.00 40.00
13 Ryan Getzlaf 12.00 30.00
14 Corey Perry 8.00 20.00
15 Cam Ward 8.00 20.00
16 Eric Staal 10.00 25.00
17 Martin St. Louis 8.00 20.00
18 Vincent Lecavalier/10
19 Nikolai Khabibulin
20 Luc Robitaille 12.00 30.00
21 Mario Lemieux/10
22 Tom Barrasso 10.00 25.00
23 Paul Coffey 8.00 20.00
24 Patrick Roy/10
25 Brett Hull 15.00 40.00

2010-11 Certified Champions Materials

STATED PRINT RUN 99 SER.#'d SETS
1 Jonathan Toews 10.00 25.00
2 Patrick Kane 10.00 25.00
3 Antti Niemi 4.00 10.00
4 Dustin Byfuglien
5 Patrick Sharp 10.00 25.00
6 Marc-Andre Fleury 8.00 20.00
7 Sidney Crosby 20.00 50.00
8 Evgeni Malkin 8.00 20.00
9 Jordan Staal 5.00 12.00
10 Nicklas Lidstrom 5.00 12.00
11 Dan Boyle
12 Teemu Selanne 6.00 15.00
13 Ryan Getzlaf 8.00 20.00
14 Corey Perry 5.00 12.00
15 Cam Ward
16 Eric Staal 6.00 15.00
17 Martin St. Louis 5.00 12.00
18 Vincent Lecavalier 4.00 10.00
19 Nikolai Khabibulin 4.00 10.00
20 Luc Robitaille 6.00 15.00
21 Mario Lemieux 10.00 25.00
22 Tom Barrasso 6.00 15.00
23 Paul Coffey 6.00 15.00
24 Patrick Roy 15.00 40.00
25 Brett Hull 10.00 25.00

2010-11 Certified Champions Mirror Blue

*SINGLES: .6X TO 1.5X BASIC INSERTS

2010-11 Certified Champions Mirror Gold

*SINGLES: 1X TO 2.5X BASIC INSERTS
STATED PRINT RUN 25 SER.#'d SETS

2010-11 Certified Champions Mirror Red

*SINGLES: .5X TO 1.2X BASIC INSERTS
STATED PRINT RUN 250 SER.#'d SETS

2010-11 Certified Collision Course

STATED PRINT RUN 500 SER.#'d SETS
*BLUE/100: .6X TO 1.5X BASIC INSERTS
*GOLD/25: 1X TO 2.5X BASIC INSERTS
*RED/250: .5X TO 1.2X BASIC INSERTS
1 Cal Clutterbuck 2.50 6.00
2 David Backes 2.50 6.00
3 Dustin Byfuglien 2.50 6.00
4 Steve Ott 2.00 5.00
5 Zenon Konopka 2.00 5.00
6 Colton Orr 1.50 4.00
7 Daniel Carcillo 1.50 4.00
8 George Parros 2.00 5.00
9 Milan Lucic 2.50 6.00
10 Drew Doughty 2.50 6.00

2010-11 Certified Collision Course Autographs

STATED PRINT RUN 100 SER.#'d SETS
1 Cal Clutterbuck 8.00 20.00
2 David Backes 8.00 20.00
3 Dustin Byfuglien 10.00 25.00
4 Steve Ott 6.00 15.00
5 Zenon Konopka 6.00 15.00
6 Colton Orr 12.00 30.00
7 Daniel Carcillo 10.00 25.00
8 George Parros 6.00 15.00
9 Milan Lucic 8.00 20.00
10 Drew Doughty 8.00 20.00

2010-11 Certified Fabric of the Game

STATED PRINT RUN 250 SER.#'d SETS
*PRIME/25: 1X TO 2.5X BASIC FOTG
*JSY NUM/25: .8X TO 2X BASIC FOTG
*NHL DC/25: .8X TO 2X BASIC FOTG
*TEAM DC/25: .8X TO 2X BASIC FOTG
AB Alexandre Burrows 3.00 8.00
AG Andy Greene 2.00 5.00
AGO Alex Goligoski 2.50 6.00
AH Ales Hemsky 2.50 6.00
AK Anze Kopitar 5.00 12.00
AN Antti Niemi 2.50 6.00
AO Alexander Ovechkin 8.00 20.00
AS Alexander Semin 3.00 8.00
BE Brian Elliott 2.50 6.00
BG Brian Gionta 2.50 6.00
BR Brad Richards 3.00 8.00
CA Craig Anderson 3.00 8.00
CAP Carey Price 12.00 30.00
CG Claude Giroux 3.00 8.00
COS Cory Schneider 2.50 6.00
COW Colin Wilson 2.50 6.00
CP Corey Perry 3.00 8.00
CPR Chris Pronger 2.50 6.00
CS Chris Stewart 2.50 6.00
DA Daniel Alfredsson 3.00 8.00
DD Drew Doughty 3.00 8.00
DIP Dion Phaneuf 3.00 8.00
DK Dmitri Kulikov 2.50 6.00
DR Derek Roy 3.00 8.00
DS Daniel Sedin 3.00 8.00
DUK Duncan Keith 3.00 8.00
DUP Dustin Penner 2.00 5.00
EK Erik Karlsson 6.00 15.00
EM Evgeni Malkin 10.00 25.00
ES Eric Staal 4.00 10.00
EVK Evander Kane 3.00 8.00
HL Henrik Lundqvist 5.00 12.00
HS Henrik Sedin 3.00 8.00
HZ Henrik Zetterberg 4.00 10.00
IB Ilya Bryzgalov
IK Ilya Kovalchuk 3.00 8.00
JAB Jay Bouwmeester 4.00 10.00
JB Jamie Benn 4.00 10.00
JC Jeff Carter 3.00 8.00
JD Jeff Deslauriers 2.00 5.00
JG Jean-Sebastien Giguere 2.50 6.00
JH Jaroslav Halak 3.00 8.00
JI Jarome Iginla 3.00 8.00
JN James Neal 3.00 8.00
JOB Josh Bailey 2.50 6.00
JOC John Carlson 4.00 10.00
JOG Jonas Gustavsson 4.00 10.00
JOH Jonas Hiller 2.50 6.00
JOS Jordan Staal 3.00 8.00
JP Joe Pavelski 3.00 8.00
JQ Jonathan Quick 5.00 12.00
JS Jason Spezza 2.00 5.00
JT Jordin Tootoo 2.50 6.00
JTA John Tavares 6.00 15.00
JTO Jonathan Toews 6.00 15.00
KO Kyle Okposo 3.00 8.00
LC Luca Caputi 2.50 6.00
MAB Martin Brodeur 6.00 15.00
MB Mikael Backlund 2.00 5.00
MC Michael Cammalleri 3.00 8.00
MD Matt Duchene 3.00 8.00
MF Marc-Andre Fleury 5.00 12.00
MFI Mike Fisher 3.00 8.00
MG Marian Gaborik 4.00 10.00
MID Michael Del Zotto 2.50 6.00
MIG Mike Green 3.00 8.00
MIK Miikka Kiprusoff 2.50 6.00
MLU Milan Lucic 3.00 8.00
MM Matt Moulson 2.50 6.00
MS Marc Staal 3.00 8.00
MSL Martin St. Louis 3.00 8.00
NA Nik Antropov 2.50 6.00
NCB Nicklas Backstrom 5.00 12.00
NH Nathan Horton 2.50 6.00
NL Nicklas Lidstrom 3.00 8.00
OP Ondrej Pavelec 3.00 8.00
PB Patrice Bergeron 4.00 10.00
PD Pavel Datsyuk 4.00 10.00
PEM Peter Mueller 2.50 6.00
PH Patric Hornqvist 2.50 6.00
PK Patrick Kane 6.00 15.00
PKE Phil Kessel 4.00 10.00
PM Patrick Marleau 3.00 8.00
PR Pekka Rinne 4.00 10.00
PS Patrick Sharp 3.00 8.00
PST Paul Stastny 3.00 8.00
RB Rene Bourque 2.00 5.00
RG Ryan Getzlaf 5.00 12.00
RK Ryan Kesler 3.00 8.00
RL Roberto Luongo 3.00 8.00
RM Ryan Miller 3.00 8.00
RN Rick Nash 3.00 8.00
SC Sidney Crosby 12.00 30.00
SCG Scott Gomez 2.50 6.00
SD Shane Doan 2.50 6.00
SG Sam Gagner 2.50 6.00
SM Steve Mason 2.50 6.00
SO Steve Ott 2.50 6.00
SS Steven Stamkos 6.00 15.00
STD Steve Downie 2.00 5.00
STW Stephen Weiss 2.50 6.00
SV Semyon Varlamov 3.00 8.00
SW Shea Weber 2.50 6.00
TOV Tomas Vokoun 2.50 6.00
TP Tomas Plekanec 3.00 8.00
TR Tuukka Rask 3.00 8.00
TS Teemu Selanne 5.00 12.00
TZ Travis Zajac 2.50 6.00
VL Vincent Lecavalier 2.50 6.00
ZB Zach Bogosian 2.50 6.00
ZC Zdeno Chara 2.50 6.00
ZP Zach Parise 3.00 8.00

2010-11 Certified Fabric of the Game Jersey Number Autographs

STATED PRINT RUN 5-25
AB Alexandre Burrows 15.00 40.00
AGO Alex Goligoski 25.00 60.00
AH Ales Hemsky 15.00 40.00
AK Anze Kopitar 15.00 40.00
AO Alexander Ovechkin 40.00 80.00
AS Alexander Semin 10.00 25.00
BE Brian Elliott 8.00 20.00
BG Brian Gionta 8.00 20.00
BR Brad Richards 12.00 30.00
CA Craig Anderson 20.00 50.00
CAP Carey Price 40.00 80.00
CG Claude Giroux 20.00 40.00
COS Cory Schneider 15.00 40.00
COW Colin Wilson 8.00 20.00
CP Corey Perry 10.00 25.00
CPR Chris Pronger 20.00 50.00
DA Daniel Alfredsson 10.00 25.00
DS Daniel Sedin 10.00 25.00
DUP Dustin Penner 8.00 20.00
EM Evgeni Malkin 30.00 60.00
HL Henrik Lundqvist 15.00 40.00
IK Ilya Kovalchuk 12.00 30.00
JAB Jay Bouwmeester 12.00 30.00
JB Jamie Benn 12.00 30.00
JC Jeff Carter 12.00 30.00
JD Jeff Deslauriers 6.00 15.00
JH Jaroslav Halak 10.00 25.00
JI Jarome Iginla 10.00 25.00
JOB Josh Bailey 8.00 20.00
JOG Jonas Gustavsson 12.00 30.00
JOH Jonas Hiller 8.00 20.00
JOS Jordan Staal 15.00 40.00
JP Joe Pavelski 15.00 40.00
JQ Jonathan Quick 30.00 60.00
JS Jason Spezza 15.00 40.00
JTO Jonathan Toews 20.00 50.00
MAB Martin Brodeur 40.00 80.00
MC Michael Cammalleri 15.00 40.00
MD Matt Duchene 12.00 30.00
MF Marc-Andre Fleury 20.00 50.00
MFI Mike Fisher 10.00 25.00
MG Marian Gaborik 12.00 30.00
MM Matt Moulson 8.00 20.00
MS Marc Staal 10.00 25.00
MSL Martin St. Louis 10.00 25.00
NL Nicklas Lidstrom 15.00 40.00
PEM Peter Mueller 15.00 40.00
PH Patric Hornqvist 10.00 25.00
PKE Phil Kessel 15.00 40.00
PM Patrick Marleau 10.00 25.00
PR Pekka Rinne 15.00 40.00
PS Patrick Sharp 25.00 60.00
PST Paul Stastny 10.00 25.00
RK Ryan Kesler 20.00 50.00
RM Ryan Miller 10.00 25.00
RN Rick Nash 10.00 25.00
SC Sidney Crosby 60.00 120.00
SCG Scott Gomez 8.00 20.00
SG Sam Gagner 8.00 20.00
SO Steve Ott 8.00 20.00
STD Steve Downie 6.00 15.00
TOV Tomas Vokoun 12.00 30.00
VL Vincent Lecavalier 8.00 20.00
ZB Zach Bogosian 8.00 20.00
ZP Zach Parise 12.00 30.00

2010-11 Certified Junior Legacy Combos

STATED PRINT RUN 250 SER.#'d SETS
1 Crosby/Lecavalier/50 15.00 40.00
2 C.Perry/R.Nash 4.00 10.00
3 Trottier/Sakic/50 10.00 25.00
4 J.Benn/L.Schenn 5.00 12.00
5 J.Theodore/L.Robitaille 4.00 10.00
6 D.Carcillo/S.Stamkos 8.00 20.00
7 P.Mueller/Z.Hamill 3.00 8.00
8 J.Spezza/M.Duchene 4.00 10.00
9 D.Hamhuis/Z.Chara 3.00 8.00
10 C.Armstrong/D.Phaneuf 4.00 10.00
11 J.Iginla/S.Doan 4.00 10.00
12 J.Spezza/S.Ott 3.00 8.00
13 J.Carter/P.Coffey 4.00 10.00
14 Pronger/Staal/50 8.00 20.00
15 R.Getzlaf/T.Galiardi 6.00 15.00
16 D.Roy/N.Kadri 6.00 15.00
17 C.Price/S.Gomez 15.00 40.00
18 J.Neal/S.Weiss 4.00 10.00
19 C.Anderson/D.Doughty 4.00 10.00
20 E.Lindros/J.Tavares/50 12.00 30.00

2010-11 Certified Junior Legacy Combos Prime

*SINGLES: 1X TO 2.5X BASIC INSERTS/250
*SINGLES: .6X TO 1.5X BASIC INSERTS/50
STATED PRINT RUN 25 SER.#'d SETS
5 J.Theodore/L.Robitaille 12.00 30.00
18 J.Neal/S.Weiss 10.00 25.00

2010-11 Certified Legends

STATED PRINT RUN 500 SER.#'d SETS
*BLUE/100: .6X TO 1.5X BASIC INSERTS
*GOLD/25: 1X TO 2.5X BASIC INSERTS
*RED/250: .5X TO 1.2X BASIC INSERTS
1 Ray Bourque 3.00 8.00
2 Bernie Parent 2.00 5.00
3 Bobby Clarke 2.00 5.00
4 Mario Lemieux 6.00 15.00
5 Steve Yzerman 5.00 12.00
6 Jean Beliveau 2.00 5.00
7 Henri Richard 2.00 5.00
8 Patrick Roy 5.00 12.00
9 Darryl Sittler 1.50 4.00
10 Paul Coffey 2.00 5.00
11 Bobby Hull 2.00 5.00
12 Jim Craig 1.50 4.00

2010-11 Certified Legends Autographs

STATED PRINT RUN 100 SER.#'d SETS
1 Ray Bourque/100 20.00 50.00
2 Bernie Parent/95 10.00 25.00
3 Bobby Clarke/100 10.00 25.00
4 Mario Lemieux/25 60.00 150.00
5 Steve Yzerman/25 50.00 125.00
6 Jean Beliveau/100 25.00 50.00
7 Henri Richard/100 10.00 25.00
8 Patrick Roy/25 40.00 100.00
9 Darryl Sittler/100 12.00 30.00
10 Paul Coffey/50 15.00 40.00
11 Bobby Hull/50 15.00 40.00
12 Jim Craig/99 15.00 40.00

2010-11 Certified Masked Marvels

STATED PRINT RUN 500 SER.#'d SETS
*BLUE/100: .6X TO 1.5X BASIC INSERTS
*GOLD/25: 1X TO 2.5X BASIC INSERTS
*RED/250: .5X TO 1.2X BASIC INSERTS
1 Antti Niemi 1.50 4.00
2 Semyon Varlamov 2.00 5.00
3 Jonas Gustavsson 2.50 6.00
4 Ryan Miller 2.00 5.00
5 Brian Elliott 1.50 4.00
6 Cam Ward 2.00 5.00
7 Jimmy Howard 2.50 6.00
8 Craig Anderson 2.00 5.00
9 Steve Mason 1.50 4.00
10 Jonathan Quick 3.00 8.00
11 Tuukka Rask 2.00 5.00
12 Steve Valiquette 1.50 4.00
13 Pekka Rinne 2.50 6.00
14 Henrik Lundqvist 3.00 8.00
15 Brad Thiessen 2.00 5.00
16 Ondrej Pavelec 2.00 5.00
17 Curtis McElhinney 1.50 4.00
18 Mathieu Garon 1.50 4.00
19 Carey Price 8.00 20.00
20 Pascal Leclaire 1.50 4.00
21 Michael Leighton 1.50 4.00
22 Ilya Bryzgalov 1.50 4.00
23 Jason Labarbera 1.50 4.00
24 Mike Smith 2.00 5.00
25 Michal Neuvirth 1.50 4.00
AN Antti Niemi Preview 1.00 2.50

2010-11 Certified Masked Marvels Materials

STATED PRINT RUN 99 SER.#'d SETS
1 Antti Niemi 3.00 8.00
2 Semyon Varlamov 4.00 10.00
3 Jonas Gustavsson 5.00 12.00
4 Ryan Miller 4.00 10.00
5 Brian Elliott 3.00 8.00
6 Cam Ward
7 Jimmy Howard
8 Craig Anderson 4.00 10.00
9 Steve Mason
10 Jonathan Quick 6.00 15.00
11 Tuukka Rask 8.00 20.00
12 Steve Valiquette 3.00 8.00
13 Pekka Rinne 5.00 12.00
14 Henrik Lundqvist 6.00 15.00
15 Brad Thiessen
16 Ondrej Pavelec 4.00 10.00
17 Curtis McElhinney 3.00 8.00
18 Mathieu Garon
19 Carey Price 15.00 40.00
20 Pascal Leclaire
21 Michael Leighton
22 Ilya Bryzgalov 3.00 8.00
23 Jason Labarbera
24 Mike Smith 4.00 10.00
25 Michal Neuvirth

2010-11 Certified Masked Marvels Materials Autographs

STATED PRINT RUN 25 SER.#'d SETS
1 Antti Niemi
2 Semyon Varlamov 10.00 25.00
3 Jonas Gustavsson 12.00 30.00
4 Ryan Miller 10.00 25.00
5 Brian Elliott 8.00 20.00
6 Cam Ward 10.00 25.00
7 Jimmy Howard
8 Craig Anderson 10.00 25.00
9 Steve Mason
10 Jonathan Quick 30.00 60.00
11 Tuukka Rask
12 Steve Valiquette
13 Pekka Rinne 12.00 30.00
14 Henrik Lundqvist 30.00 60.00
15 Brad Thiessen 10.00 25.00
16 Ondrej Pavelec 10.00 25.00
17 Curtis McElhinney 8.00 20.00
18 Mathieu Garon 8.00 20.00
19 Carey Price 30.00 60.00
20 Pascal Leclaire 8.00 20.00
21 Michael Leighton 8.00 20.00
22 Ilya Bryzgalov 10.00 25.00
23 Jason Labarbera
24 Mike Smith 10.00 25.00
25 Michal Neuvirth

2010-11 Certified Potential

STATED PRINT RUN 500 SER.#'d SETS
*BLUE/100: .6X TO 1.5X BASIC INSERTS
*GOLD/25: 1X TO 2.5X BASIC INSERTS
*RED/250: .5X TO 1.2X BASIC INSERTS
1 Nazem Kadri 6.00 15.00
2 Philip Larsen 1.50 4.00
3 Nick Bonino 2.00 5.00
4 Eric Tangradi 1.50 4.00
5 Bobby Butler 1.50 4.00
6 Nick Palmieri 1.50 4.00
7 Jared Cowen 1.50 4.00
8 P.K. Subban 5.00 12.00
9 Zach Hamill 1.50 4.00
10 John Tavares 4.00 10.00
11 Matt Duchene 2.00 5.00
12 Tyler Myers 2.00 5.00
13 Jimmy Howard 2.50 6.00
14 Jamie Benn 2.50 6.00
15 Tuukka Rask 2.00 5.00
16 Tyler Bozak 2.00 5.00
17 Colin Wilson 1.50 4.00
18 John Carlson 2.50 6.00
PS P.K. Subban Preview 2.00 5.00

2010-11 Certified Potential Materials

STATED PRINT RUN 99 SER.#'d SETS
1 Nazem Kadri 10.00 25.00
2 Philip Larsen 3.00 8.00
3 Nick Bonino
4 Eric Tangradi
5 Bobby Butler 3.00 8.00
6 Nick Palmieri 3.00 8.00
7 Jared Cowen 3.00 8.00
8 P.K. Subban
9 Zach Hamill 6.00 15.00
10 John Tavares 8.00 20.00
11 Matt Duchene 4.00 10.00
12 Tyler Myers
13 Jimmy Howard
14 Jamie Benn 5.00 12.00
15 Tuukka Rask 4.00 10.00
16 Tyler Bozak 4.00 10.00
17 Colin Wilson 3.00 8.00
18 John Carlson 5.00 12.00

2010-11 Certified Potential Materials Autographs

STATED PRINT RUN 25 SER.#'d SETS
1 Nazem Kadri 15.00 40.00
2 Philip Larsen 6.00 15.00
3 Nick Bonino
4 Eric Tangradi
5 Bobby Butler 6.00 15.00
6 Nick Palmieri
7 Jared Cowen
8 P.K. Subban
9 Zach Hamill
10 John Tavares 15.00 40.00
11 Matt Duchene 20.00 50.00
12 Tyler Myers
13 Jimmy Howard
14 Jamie Benn 10.00 25.00
15 Tuukka Rask
16 Tyler Bozak 12.00 30.00
17 Colin Wilson
18 John Carlson 12.00 30.00

2010-11 Certified Shirt Off My Back Combos

STATED PRINT RUN 50 SER.#'d SETS
*PRIME/25: .6X TO 1.5X BASIC INSERTS
*PRIME/25: .5X TO 1.2X BASIC INSERTS/50
1 J.Iginla/S.Crosby 15.00 40.00
2 R.Miller/S.Crosby 15.00 40.00
3 Brodeur/Luongo/100 8.00 20.00
4 R.Luongo/R.Miller 4.00 10.00
5 J.Tavares/N.Kadri 10.00 25.00
6 J.Carlson/M.Green 5.00 12.00
7 Ovechkin/Backstrom/100 15.00 40.00
8 C.Perry/R.Getzlaf 6.00 15.00
9 R.Bourque/Z.Chara 6.00 15.00
10 D.Doughty/R.Bourque 6.00 15.00
11 Miller/Parise/50 5.00 12.00
12 B.Trottier/J.Toews 8.00 20.00
13 C.Price/P.Roy/100 15.00 40.00
14 S.Crosby/S.Stamkos/51 20.00 50.00
15 Lemieux/Roy/50 15.00 40.00

2010-11 Certified Throwback Threads

STATED PRINT RUN 500 SER.#'d SETS
*BLUE/100: .6X TO 1.5X BASIC INSERTS
*GOLD/25: 1X TO 2.5X BASIC INSERTS
*RED/250: .5X TO 1.2X BASIC INSERTS
1 Ray Ferraro 2.00 5.00
2 Dale Hawerchuk 2.50 6.00
3 Peter Stastny 1.50 4.00
4 Guy Lafleur 2.50 6.00
5 Charlie Hodge 1.50 4.00
6 Dennis Maruk 1.50 4.00
7 Simon Nolet 1.50 4.00
8 Dan Bouchard 1.50 4.00
9 Lanny McDonald 2.00 5.00
10 Dino Ciccarelli 2.00 5.00

2010-11 Certified Throwback Threads Autographs

1 Ray Ferraro 10.00 25.00
2 Dale Hawerchuk 10.00 25.00
3 Peter Stastny 12.00 30.00
4 Guy Lafleur/25 40.00 100.00
5 Charlie Hodge 10.00 25.00
6 Dennis Maruk 10.00 25.00
7 Simon Nolet 10.00 25.00
8 Dan Bouchard 12.00 30.00
9 Lanny McDonald 10.00 25.00
10 Dino Ciccarelli 10.00 25.00

2010-11 Certified Top Choice

STATED PRINT RUN 500 SER.#'d SETS
*BLUE/100: .6X TO 1.5X BASIC INSERTS
*GOLD/25: 1X TO 2.5X BASIC INSERTS
*RED/250: .5X TO 1.2X BASIC INSERTS
1 John Tavares 4.00 10.00
2 Steven Stamkos 4.00 10.00
3 Patrick Kane 4.00 10.00
4 Erik Johnson 1.25 3.00
5 Sidney Crosby 6.00 15.00
6 Alexander Ovechkin 5.00 12.00
7 Marc-Andre Fleury 3.00 8.00
8 Rick Nash 2.00 5.00
9 Ilya Kovalchuk 2.00 5.00
10 Joe Thornton 2.00 5.00
11 Vincent Lecavalier 1.50 4.00
12 Mario Lemieux 6.00 15.00
SC Sidney Crosby Preview 2.00 5.00

2010-11 Certified Top Choice Materials

STATED PRINT RUN 99 SER.#'d SETS
*PRIME/25: .8X TO 2X BASIC JSY
1 John Tavares 8.00 20.00
2 Steven Stamkos 8.00 20.00
3 Patrick Kane 8.00 20.00
4 Erik Johnson 2.50 6.00
5 Sidney Crosby 15.00 40.00
6 Alexander Ovechkin 15.00 40.00
7 Marc-Andre Fleury 6.00 15.00
8 Rick Nash 4.00 10.00
9 Ilya Kovalchuk 4.00 10.00
10 Joe Thornton 4.00 10.00
11 Vincent Lecavalier 3.00 8.00
12 Mario Lemieux 12.00 30.00

2011-12 Certified

COMP.SET w/o SPs (150) 20.00 50.00
151-170 IMMORTAL PRINT RUN 500
209-225 JSY AU PRINT RUN 499
244-268 JSY AU PRINT RUN 99-299
207-208/226-268 ISSUED IN ANTHOLOGY
1 Jeff Skinner .40 1.00
2 Danny Briere .40 1.00
3 Patrice Bergeron .50 1.25
4 Patrick Sharp .40 1.00
5 Ryan Miller .40 1.00
6 Mikhail Grabovski .30 .75
7 Paul Bissonette .25 .60
8 Andy McDonald .30 .75
9 Mike Richards .40 1.00
10 Milan Lucic .40 1.00
11 Eric Staal .50 1.25
12 Patrick Kane .75 2.00
13 Jonathan Quick .60 1.50
14 Pekka Rinne .50 1.25
15 Dwayne Roloson .30 .75
16 Michael Cammalleri .30 .75
17 Cam Ward .40 1.00
18 Andrei Markov .40 1.00
19 David Backes .40 1.00
20 Matt Moulson .30 .75
21 Steve Mason .30 .75
22 Andrew Ladd .40 1.00
23 Jamie Benn .50 1.25
24 Ryan Callahan .40 1.00
25 Erik Karlsson .75 2.00
26 Drew Doughty .40 1.00
27 Nicklas Backstrom .60 1.50
28 Patrick Marleau .40 1.00
29 Cal Clutterbuck .40 1.00
30 Miikka Kiprusoff .40 1.00
31 Jeff Carter .40 1.00
32 Kris Letang .40 1.00
33 Joe Thornton .40 1.00
34 Alex Ovechkin 1.50 4.00
35 David Krejci .40 1.00
36 Rene Bourque .25 .60
37 Brandon Dubinsky .30 .75
38 Evander Kane .40 1.00
39 John Tavares .75 2.00
40 Paul Stastny .40 1.00
41 Brad Richards .40 1.00
42 Shane Doan .30 .75
43 Alex Steen .40 1.00
44 Ales Hemsky .30 .75
45 Nik Antropov .30 .75
46 Kari Lehtonen .30 .75
47 Daniel Alfredsson .40 1.00
48 Nicklas Lidstrom .40 1.00
49 Corey Perry .40 1.00
50 Jordan Eberle .40 1.00
51 Thomas Vanek .40 1.00
52 Martin Brodeur .75 2.00
53 Mark Giordano .30 .75
54 Mikko Koivu .30 .75
55 Ryan Getzlaf .60 1.50
56 Ryan Kesler .40 1.00
57 Drew Stafford .40 1.00
58 Joffrey Lupul .30 .75
59 Teddy Purcell .40 1.00
60 Sam Gagner .30 .75
61 Max Pacioretty .40 1.00
62 Ray Whitney .30 .75
63 Taylor Hall .75 2.00
64 Alexandre Burrows .40 1.00
65 Michal Neuvirth .30 .75
66 Travis Zajac .30 .75
67 Marc-Andre Fleury .60 1.50
68 Sergei Bobrovsky .40 1.00
69 Antti Niemi .30 .75
70 Sidney Crosby 1.50 4.00
71 Claude Giroux .40 1.00
72 Tyler Seguin .75 2.00
73 Ryan Smyth .30 .75
74 Mike Fisher .40 1.00
75 Michael Grabner .30 .75
76 Keith Yandle .40 1.00
77 Jacob Markstrom .40 1.00
78 Milan Hejduk .30 .75
79 Brian Gionta .30 .75
80 Kyle Okposo .40 1.00
81 Vincent Lecavalier .30 .75
82 Ondrej Pavelec .40 1.00
83 James Reimer .40 1.00
84 Brenden Morrow .30 .75
85 Sergei Kostitsyn .25 .60
86 Derek Roy .30 .75
87 Henrik Lundqvist .50 1.25
88 Cory Schneider .30 .75
89 Valtteri Filppula .40 1.00
90 Anze Kopitar .60 1.50
91 Teemu Selanne .75 2.00
92 Eric Fehr .25 .60
93 Corey Crawford .50 1.25
94 Joe Pavelski .40 1.00
95 Mattias Tedenby .25 .60
96 Tim Thomas .40 1.00
97 Brent Burns .50 1.25
98 Jordan Staal .40 1.00
99 Curtis Glencross .25 .60
100 James van Riemsdyk .40 1.00
101 Evgeni Malkin 1.25 3.00
102 Niklas Backstrom .40 1.00
103 Zach Parise .40 1.00
104 Ryane Clowe .25 .60
105 Dion Phaneuf .40 1.00
106 Ilya Bryzgalov .40 1.00
107 Erik Johnson .25 .60
108 Jaroslav Halak .40 1.00
109 Carey Price 1.25 3.00
110 Derick Brassard .40 1.00
111 Martin St. Louis .40 1.00
112 Dustin Byfuglien .40 1.00
113 Loui Eriksson .30 .75
114 Tyler Ennis .30 .75
115 Pavel Datsyuk .50 1.25
116 Jonathan Toews .75 2.00
117 Dany Heatley .30 .75
118 Ilya Kovalchuk .40 1.00
119 Martin Havlat .30 .75
120 Jarome Iginla .40 1.00
121 Mike Green .40 1.00
122 Cam Fowler .30 .75
123 Henrik Zetterberg .50 1.25
124 Marc Staal .40 1.00
125 Phil Kessel .50 1.25
126 Steven Stamkos .75 2.00
127 Antoine Vermette .25 .60
128 P.K. Subban .75 2.00
129 Matt Duchene .40 1.00
130 Stephen Weiss .30 .75
131 Daniel Sedin .40 1.00
132 Henrik Sedin .40 1.00
133 Marian Gaborik .50 1.25
134 Shea Weber .30 .75
135 Luke Schenn .30 .75
136 Brad Marchand .50 1.25
137 Marian Hossa .30 .75
138 Johan Franzen .40 1.00
139 Rick Nash .40 1.00
140 Tomas Plekanec .40 1.00
141 Brandon Sutter .30 .75
142 David Booth .25 .60
143 Barret Jackman .25 .60
144 Roberto Luongo .40 1.00
145 Jimmy Howard .40 1.00
146 Bobby Ryan .40 1.00
147 Logan Couture .40 1.00
148 Craig Anderson .40 1.00
149 Jason Spezza .40 1.00
150 Derek Stepan .40 1.00
151 Brendan Shanahan 2.00 5.00

152 Eric Lindros 2.50 6.00
153 Pat LaFontaine 1.50 4.00
154 Grant Fuhr 1.50 4.00
155 Ron Francis 2.00 5.00
156 Joe Mullen 1.25 3.00
157 Patrick Roy 4.00 10.00
158 Ray Bourque 2.50 6.00
159 Bryan Trottier 2.00 5.00
160 Darryl Sittler 1.50 4.00
161 Luc Robitaille 1.50 4.00
162 Mario Lemieux 5.00 12.00
163 Johnny Bucyk 1.50 4.00
164 Joe Sakic 2.50 6.00
165 Curtis Joseph 1.50 4.00
166 Guy Lafleur 2.00 5.00
167 Jeremy Roenick 1.50 4.00
168 Doug Gilmour 2.00 5.00
169 Mark Messier 2.00 5.00
170 Joe Nieuwendyk 1.50 4.00
171 Patrick Wiercioch AU RC 3.00 8.00
172 Brian Strait AU RC 4.00 10.00
173 Yann Sauve AU RC 3.00 8.00
174 Ben Scrivens AU RC 5.00 12.00
175 Ben Holmstrom AU RC 3.00 8.00
176 Paul Postma AU RC 3.00 8.00
177 Lance Bouma AU RC 3.00 8.00
178 Stephane Da Costa AU RC 3.00 8.00
179 Matt Frattin AU RC 3.00 8.00
180 Mark Katic AU RC 3.00 8.00
181 Brendon Nash AU RC 3.00 8.00
182 Erik Condra AU RC 3.00 8.00
183 Mikko Koskinen AU RC 4.00 10.00
184 Justin DiBenedetto AU RC 2.50 6.00
185 Brandon Saad AU SP RC 20.00 40.00
186 C.Smith AU SP RC 8.00 20.00
187 Colin Greening AU RC 3.00 8.00
188 Matt Read AU SP RC 40.00 80.00
189 Joe Vitale AU RC 3.00 8.00
190 Cam Talbot AU RC 8.00 20.00
191 Zac Rinaldo AU RC 3.00 8.00
192 Scott Timmins AU RC 3.00 8.00
193 Cameron Gaunce AU RC 2.50 6.00
194 Tomas Kubalik AU RC 3.00 8.00
195 Erik Gustafsson AU RC 4.00 10.00
196 Sean Couturier AU SP RC 20.00 50.00
197 Chris Vande Velde AU SP RC 8.00 20.00
198 Drew Bagnall AU SP RC 5.00 12.00
199 Mark Scheifele AU SP RC 10.00 25.00
200 Connie Madigan AU SP RC 12.00 30.00
201 Colton Sceviour AU SP RC 5.00 12.00
202 Teemu Hartikainen AU SP RC 5.00 12.00
203 A.Larsson AU SP RC EXCH 30.00 60.00
204 Hugh Jessiman AU SP RC 5.00 12.00
205 Carson McMillan AU SP RC 6.00 15.00
206 Tomas Vincour AU SP RC 5.00 12.00
207 Dylan Olsen AU RC 5.00 12.00
208 Colten Teubert AU RC 3.00 8.00
209 Cody Hodgson JSY AU RC 10.00 25.00
210 Blake Geoffrion JSY AU RC 5.00 12.00
211 Jonathon Blum JSY AU RC 5.00 12.00
212 Joe Colborne JSY AU RC 5.00 12.00
213 Adam Henrique JSY AU RC 12.00 30.00
214 Greg Nemisz JSY AU RC 5.00 12.00
215 Carl Klingberg JSY AU RC 5.00 12.00
216 John Moore JSY AU RC 5.00 12.00
217 Marcus Kruger JSY AU RC 8.00 20.00
218 Aaron Palushaj JSY AU RC 5.00 12.00
219 Nugent-Hopkins JSY AU RC 20.00 50.00
220 Ryan Johansen JSY AU RC 10.00 25.00
221 Brett Connolly JSY AU RC 5.00 12.00
222 Gabriel Landeskog JSY AU RC 10.00 25.00
223 Mika Zibanejad JSY AU RC 12.00 30.00
224 Jake Gardiner JSY AU RC 8.00 20.00
225 Justin Faulk JSY AU RC 8.00 20.00
226 Brett Bulmer AU RC 3.00 8.00
227 Anders Nilsson AU RC 3.00 8.00
228 Corey Tropp AU RC 3.00 8.00
229 Andy Miele AU RC 3.00 8.00
230 Anton Lander AU RC 3.00 8.00
231 T.J. Brennan AU RC 3.00 8.00
232 Brayden McNabb AU RC 3.00 8.00
233 Leland Irving AU RC 3.00 8.00
234 Roman Josi AU RC 5.00 12.00
235 Brad Malone AU RC 3.00 8.00
236 Stefan Elliott AU RC 3.00 8.00
237 Jimmy Hayes AU RC 4.00 10.00
238 Joe Finley AU RC 3.00 8.00
239 Marcus Foligno AU RC 5.00 12.00
240 Peter Holland AU RC 3.00 8.00
241 Keith Kinkaid AU RC 3.00 8.00
242 Riley Nash AU RC 3.00 8.00
243 Dmitry Orlov AU RC 4.00 10.00
244 Cody Eakin JSY AU/299 RC 8.00 20.00
245 Tim Erixon JSY AU/299 RC 6.00 15.00
246 Kassian JSY AU/299 RC 8.00 20.00
247 Ryan Ellis JSY AU/299 RC 6.00 15.00
248 D.Rundblad JSY AU/299 RC 6.00 15.00
249 B.Smith JSY AU/299 RC 6.00 15.00
250 Despres JSY AU/299 RC 6.00 15.00
251 Smith-Pelly JSY AU/99 RC 12.00 30.00
252 C.de Haan JSY AU/299 RC 6.00 15.00
253 L.Leblanc JSY AU/299 RC 6.00 15.00
254 Gudbranson JSY AU/99 RC 10.00 25.00
255 Allen York JSY AU/99 RC 10.00 25.00
256 C.Gaunce JSY AU/99 RC 6.00 15.00
257 R.Diaz JSY AU/99 RC 8.00 20.00
258 Zolnierczyk JSY AU/299 RC 6.00 15.00
259 Eddie Lack JSY AU/299 RC 6.00 15.00
260 Harri Sateri JSY AU/299 RC 6.00 15.00
261 D.Savard JSY AU/299 RC 6.00 15.00
262 Nyquist JSY AU/299 RC 15.00 40.00
263 Voynov JSY AU/299 RC 6.00 15.00
264 Hagelin JSY AU/299 RC 10.00 25.00
265 Atkinson JSY AU/150 RC 20.00 50.00
266 Emelin JSY AU/99 RC 8.00 20.00
267 R.Bortuzzo JSY AU/299 RC 6.00 15.00
268 R.Horak JSY AU/299 RC 6.00 15.00

2011-12 Certified Mirror Blue

*MIRROR BLUE/99: 2X TO 5X BASIC CARDS
*MIR.BLU IMM/99: .5X TO 1.2X BASIC CARDS
MIRROR BLUE PRINT RUN 99
93 Corey Crawford 2.50 6.00

2011-12 Certified Mirror Gold

*GOLD VETS: 4X TO 10X BASIC CARDS
*GOLD IMMORT: 1X TO 2.5X BASIC IMM
*GOLD AU: 1X TO 2.5X BASIC AU RC
*GOLD AU SP: .6X TO 1.5X BASIC AU SP
*GOLD JSY AU: 1X TO 2.5X JSY AU/499
*GOLD JSY AU: .8X TO 2X JSY AU/299
*GOLD JSY AU: .6X TO 1.5X JSY AU/99
MIRROR GOLD PRINT RUN 23-25
93 Corey Crawford 6.00 15.00
219 Nugent-Hopkins JSY AU/25 125.00 250.00

2011-12 Certified Mirror Red

*MIRROR RED/199: 1.5X TO 4X BASIC
*MIRROR RED IMM/199: .4X TO 1X BASIC
MIRROR RED PRINT RUN 199
93 Corey Crawford 2.00 5.00

2011-12 Certified Totally Silver

*TOTALLY SILVER: 1X TO 2.5X BASIC CARDS
*TOTALLY SILVER IMM: .25X TO .6X BASIC CARDS
27 Nicklas Backstrom 1.50 4.00
93 Corey Crawford 1.25 3.00

2011-12 Certified Champions

*MIRROR GOLD/25: 1.5X TO 4X BASIC INSERTS
1 Tim Thomas 1.50 4.00
2 Zdeno Chara 1.50 4.00
3 Tyler Seguin 3.00 8.00
4 Patrice Bergeron 2.00 5.00
5 Brad Marchand 2.00 5.00
6 Brent Seabrook 1.50 4.00
7 Duncan Keith 1.50 4.00
8 Sidney Crosby 6.00 15.00
9 Max Talbot 1.25 3.00
10 Pavel Datsyuk 2.00 5.00
11 Henrik Zetterberg 2.00 5.00
12 Jean-Sebastien Giguere 1.25 3.00
13 Chris Pronger 1.25 3.00
14 Tomas Holmstrom 1.00 2.50
15 Scott Niedermayer 1.50 4.00
16 Milt Schmidt 1.25 3.00
17 Al Arbour 1.25 3.00
18 Bernie Parent 1.50 4.00
19 Mark Messier 2.00 5.00
20 Jean Beliveau 1.50 4.00

2011-12 Certified Champions Autographs

STATED PRINT RUN 25-50
1 Tim Thomas/25
2 Zdeno Chara/25 25.00 50.00
3 Tyler Seguin/25 40.00 100.00
5 Brad Marchand/25 15.00 40.00
6 Brent Seabrook/25 15.00 40.00
8 Sidney Crosby/50 75.00 125.00
9 Max Talbot/25 12.00 30.00
10 Pavel Datsyuk/25 20.00 50.00
13 Chris Pronger/25
14 Tomas Holmstrom/25 20.00 50.00
15 Scott Niedermayer/25 15.00 40.00
16 Milt Schmidt/25 15.00 40.00
17 Al Arbour/25 12.00 30.00
18 Bernie Parent/25 10.00 25.00
19 Mark Messier/25
20 Jean Beliveau/25 30.00 80.00

2011-12 Certified Champions Materials

STATED PRINT RUN 99 SER.#'d SETS
*PRIME/25: .8X TO 2X MATERIAL/99
1 Tim Thomas 12.00 30.00
2 Zdeno Chara 8.00 20.00
3 Tyler Seguin 10.00 25.00
4 Patrice Bergeron 8.00 20.00
5 Brad Marchand 8.00 20.00
6 Brent Seabrook 6.00 15.00
7 Duncan Keith 6.00 15.00
8 Sidney Crosby 12.00 30.00
9 Max Talbot 5.00 12.00
10 Pavel Datsyuk 8.00 20.00
11 Henrik Zetterberg 8.00 20.00
12 Jean-Sebastien Giguere 5.00 12.00
13 Chris Pronger 5.00 12.00
14 Tomas Holmstrom 5.00 12.00
15 Scott Niedermayer 6.00 15.00
19 Mark Messier 8.00 20.00

2011-12 Certified Collision Course

*MIRROR GOLD/25: 1X TO 2.5X BASIC INSERTS
1 Tuomo Ruutu 1.25 3.00
2 Ryan Callahan 1.50 4.00
3 Brenden Morrow 1.25 3.00
4 Shea Weber 1.25 3.00
5 Tim Thomas 1.50 4.00
6 P.K. Subban 3.00 8.00
7 Ryan Kesler 1.50 4.00
8 Travis Hamonic 1.25 3.00
9 Dustin Brown 1.50 4.00
10 Alex Ovechkin 6.00 15.00

2011-12 Certified Collision Course Autographs

STATED PRINT RUN 50-100
1 Tuomo Ruutu/100 6.00 15.00
2 Ryan Callahan/100 8.00 20.00
3 Brenden Morrow/100 6.00 15.00
4 Shea Weber/100 6.00 15.00
5 Tim Thomas/100 15.00 40.00
6 P.K. Subban/100 15.00 40.00
7 Ryan Kesler/100 8.00 20.00
8 Travis Hamonic/100 6.00 15.00
9 Dustin Brown/100 8.00 20.00
10 Alex Ovechkin/50 30.00 80.00

2011-12 Certified Eternals

*MIRROR GOLD/25: 1X TO 2.5X BASIC INSERTS
1 Joe Sakic 2.50 6.00
2 Ron Francis 2.00 5.00
3 Stan Mikita 2.00 5.00
4 Tim Kerr 1.25 3.00
5 Bill Ranford 1.50 4.00
6 Mark Messier 2.00 5.00
7 Adam Graves 1.25 3.00
8 Milt Schmidt 1.25 3.00
9 Marcel Dionne 2.00 5.00
10 Denis Potvin 1.50 4.00
11 Felix Potvin 2.50 6.00
12 Emile Bouchard 1.50 4.00

2011-12 Certified Eternals Autographs

STATED PRINT RUN 5-100
1 Joe Sakic/25 50.00 100.00
2 Ron Francis/25 15.00 40.00
3 Stan Mikita/25 12.00 30.00
4 Tim Kerr/100 8.00 20.00
5 Bill Ranford/100 10.00 25.00
6 Mark Messier/5
7 Adam Graves/100 8.00 20.00
8 Milt Schmidt/100 8.00 20.00
9 Marcel Dionne/100 12.00 30.00
10 Denis Potvin/100 10.00 25.00
11 Felix Potvin/100 25.00 60.00
12 Emile Bouchard/100 10.00 25.00

2011-12 Certified Fabric of the Game

STATED PRINT RUNS 10-399
1 Corey Perry/99 4.00 10.00
2 Ryan Getzlaf/399 5.00 12.00
3 Brandon McMillan/399 2.00 5.00
4 Cam Fowler/399 2.50 6.00
5 Bobby Ryan/99 4.00 10.00
6 Andrew Ladd/399 3.00 8.00
7 Evander Kane/399 3.00 8.00
9 Ondrej Pavelec/399 3.00 8.00
10 Alexander Burmistrov/399 2.50 6.00
11 Patrice Bergeron/399 4.00 10.00
12 Milan Lucic/299 3.00 8.00
13 David Krejci/399 3.00 8.00
14 Tyler Seguin/399 6.00 15.00
15 Tim Thomas/399 4.00 10.00
16 Jordan Caron/399 4.00 10.00
17 Ryan Miller/99 4.00 10.00
18 Thomas Vanek/99 4.00 10.00
19 Drew Stafford/399 3.00 8.00
20 Derek Roy/399 2.50 6.00
21 Tyler Ennis/25 5.00 12.00
22 Nathan Gerbe/399 2.00 5.00
23 Miikka Kiprusoff/99 4.00 10.00
24 Rene Bourque/399 2.00 5.00
25 Mark Giordano/99 3.00 8.00
26 Henrik Karlsson/399 2.50 6.00
27 Jarome Iginla/99 4.00 10.00
28 Jeff Skinner/399 3.00 8.00
29 Eric Staal/99 5.00 12.00
30 Cam Ward/25 6.00 15.00
31 Brandon Sutter/399 2.50 6.00
32 Patrick Sharp/99 4.00 10.00
33 Patrick Kane/10
34 Corey Crawford/99 5.00 12.00
35 Duncan Keith/99 4.00 10.00
36 Troy Brouwer/399 2.50 6.00
37 Paul Stastny/399 3.00 8.00
38 Milan Hejduk/99 3.00 8.00
39 Ryan O'Reilly/399 3.00 8.00
40 Matt Duchene/99 4.00 10.00
41 Derick Brassard/25 6.00 15.00
42 Rick Nash/99 4.00 10.00
43 Jamie Benn/399 4.00 10.00
44 Brad Richards/399 3.00 8.00
45 Kari Lehtonen/399 2.50 6.00
46 Brenden Morrow/399 2.50 6.00
47 Loui Eriksson/399 2.50 6.00
48 Kris Draper/399 2.00 5.00
49 Nicklas Lidstrom/99 4.00 10.00
50 Valtteri Filppula/25 10.00 25.00
51 Pavel Datsyuk/399 4.00 10.00
52 Tomas Tatar/399 4.00 10.00
53 Johan Franzen/25 6.00 15.00
54 Brian Rafalski/399 2.00 5.00
55 Jimmy Howard/399 3.00 8.00
56 Shawn Horcoff/399 2.00 5.00
57 Ales Hemsky/99 3.00 8.00
58 Jordan Eberle/399 3.00 8.00
59 Sam Gagner/25 5.00 12.00
60 Taylor Hall/399 8.00 20.00
61 Magnus Paajarvi/399 2.50 6.00
62 Jacob Markstrom/399 3.00 8.00
63 Stephen Weiss/399 2.50 6.00
64 David Booth/399 3.00 8.00
65 Jonathan Quick/399 5.00 12.00
66 Drew Doughty/99 4.00 10.00
67 Ryan Smyth/399 2.50 6.00
68 Anze Kopitar/399 5.00 12.00
69 Cal Clutterbuck/99 5.00 12.00
70 Mikko Koivu/99 3.00 8.00
71 Brent Burns/399 4.00 10.00
72 Niklas Backstrom/399 3.00 8.00
73 Martin Havlat/399 2.50 6.00
74 Michael Cammalleri/25 5.00 12.00
75 Andrei Markov/399 3.00 8.00
76 Max Pacioretty/25 6.00 15.00
77 Brian Gionta/99 3.00 8.00
78 Carey Price/99 12.00 30.00
79 Lars Eller/399 2.50 6.00
80 P.K. Subban/399 6.00 15.00
81 Tomas Plekanec/399 3.00 8.00
82 Andrei Kostitsyn/399 2.50 6.00
83 Ryan Suter/399 2.00 5.00
84 Sergei Kostitsyn/399 2.00 5.00
85 Shea Weber/99 3.00 8.00
86 Martin Brodeur/99 8.00 20.00
87 Patrik Elias/399 3.00 8.00
88 Mattias Tedenby/399 2.00 5.00
89 Zach Parise/99 4.00 10.00
90 Ilya Kovalchuk/99 4.00 10.00
91 Matt Moulson/25 5.00 12.00
92 John Tavares/25 12.00 30.00
94 Kyle Okposo/399 3.00 8.00
95 Ryan Callahan/399 3.00 8.00
96 Brandon Dubinsky/399 2.50 6.00
97 Henrik Lundqvist/99 5.00 12.00
98 Marc Staal/399 3.00 8.00
99 Marian Gaborik/99 5.00 12.00
100 Erik Karlsson/25 8.00 20.00
101 Daniel Alfredsson/399 3.00 8.00
102 Bobby Butler/399 2.50 6.00
103 Jason Spezza/399 3.00 8.00
104 Danny Briere/399 3.00 8.00
105 Mike Richards/399 3.00 8.00
106 Jody Shelley/399 2.50 6.00
107 Jeff Carter/399 3.00 8.00
108 Chris Pronger/399 2.50 6.00
109 Sergei Bobrovsky/399 3.00 8.00
110 Claude Giroux/25 12.00 30.00
111 James van Riemsdyk/99 4.00 10.00
112 Shane Doan/99 3.00 8.00
113 Keith Yandle/25 6.00 15.00
114 Ilya Bryzgalov/399 3.00 8.00
115 Kris Letang/99 4.00 10.00
116 Marc-Andre Fleury/25 10.00 25.00
117 Mark Letestu/399 2.50 6.00
118 Sidney Crosby/99 15.00 40.00
119 Jordan Staal/99 4.00 10.00
120 Evgeni Malkin/99 5.00 12.00
121 Max Talbot/399 2.50 6.00
122 Patrick Marleau/25 6.00 15.00
123 Joe Thornton/25 6.00 15.00
124 Torrey Mitchell/399 2.00 5.00
125 Ryane Clowe/99 2.50 6.00
126 David Backes/99 4.00 10.00
127 T.J. Oshie/25 10.00 25.00
128 Jaroslav Halak/99 4.00 10.00
129 Victor Hedman/25 8.00 20.00
131 Teddy Purcell/399 3.00 8.00
132 Vincent Lecavalier/25 5.00 12.00
133 Martin St. Louis/99 4.00 10.00
134 Steven Stamkos/99 8.00 20.00
135 Mikhail Grabovski/399 2.50 6.00
136 Nikolai Kulemin/399 3.00 8.00
137 James Reimer/99 4.00 10.00
138 Phil Kessel/99 5.00 12.00
139 Luke Schenn/25 5.00 12.00
140 Ryan Kesler/399 3.00 8.00
142 Cory Schneider/399 2.50 6.00
143 Daniel Sedin/25 6.00 15.00
144 Henrik Sedin/399 3.00 8.00
145 Roberto Luongo/99 4.00 10.00
146 Nicklas Backstrom/99 6.00 15.00
147 Alex Ovechkin/99 6.00 15.00
148 Michal Neuvirth/399 2.50 6.00
149 Eric Fehr/399 2.00 5.00
150 Mike Green/99 4.00 10.00

2011-12 Certified Fabric of the Game Claim To Fame Die Cut

*CLAIM FAME/25: .8X TO 2X FOTG/299-399
*CLAIM FAME/25: .6X TO 1.5X FOTG/99
*CLAIM FAME/25: .5X TO 1.2X FOTG/25
CLAIM TO FAME PRINT RUNS 10-25
33 Patrick Kane 12.00 30.00

2011-12 Certified Fabric of the Game Jersey Number

*JSY NUM/25: 1X TO 2.5X FOTG/299-399
*JSY NUM/25: .8X TO 2X FOTG/99
*JSY NUM/25: .6X TO 1.5X FOTG/25
JERSEY NUMBER PRINT RUNS 1-25
33 Patrick Kane/25 15.00 40.00

2011-12 Certified Fabric of the Game National Die Cut

*NATL DC/20-25: 1X TO 2.5X FOTG/299-399
*NATL DC/20-25: .8X TO 2X FOTG/99
*NATL DC/20-25: .6X TO 1.5X FOTG/25
NATIONAL DIE CUT PRINT RUNS 1-25
33 Patrick Kane/25 15.00 40.00

2011-12 Certified Fabric of the Game NHL Die Cut

*NHL DC/20-25: 1X TO 2.5X FOTG/299-399
*NHL DC/20-25: .8X TO 2X FOTG/99
*NHL DC/20-25: .6X TO 1.5X FOTG/25
NHL DIE CUT PRINT RUNS 5-25
33 Patrick Kane 15.00 40.00

2011-12 Certified Fabric of the Game Prime

*PRIME/25: .8X TO 2X FOTG/299-399
*PRIME/25: .6X TO 1.5X FOTG/99
*PRIME/25: .5X TO 1.2X FOTG/25
PRIME STATED PRINT RUN 25
33 Patrick Kane 12.00 30.00

2011-12 Certified Fabric of the Game Jersey Number Autographs

STATED PRINT RUN 2-25
1 Corey Perry/25
3 Brandon McMillan/25 6.00 15.00
5 Bobby Ryan/25 15.00 40.00
6 Andrew Ladd/25 10.00 25.00
7 Evander Kane/25 10.00 25.00
9 Ondrej Pavelec/25 10.00 25.00
10 Alexander Burmistrov/25
14 Tyler Seguin/25 30.00 80.00
15 Tim Thomas/25 15.00 40.00
16 Jordan Caron/25 10.00 25.00
17 Ryan Miller/25
18 Thomas Vanek/25 10.00 25.00
20 Derek Roy/25 8.00 20.00
21 Tyler Ennis/25 8.00 20.00
22 Nathan Gerbe/25 6.00 15.00
24 Rene Bourque/25
26 Henrik Karlsson/25 8.00 20.00
27 Jarome Iginla/25 10.00 25.00
28 Jeff Skinner/25 12.00 30.00
29 Eric Staal/25 12.00 30.00
30 Cam Ward/10
31 Brandon Sutter/25
32 Patrick Sharp/25 20.00 50.00
33 Patrick Kane/25 30.00 60.00
36 Troy Brouwer/25 12.00 30.00
37 Paul Stastny/25 10.00 25.00
39 Ryan O'Reilly/25 10.00 25.00
40 Matt Duchene/25
41 Derick Brassard/25
42 Rick Nash/25 15.00 40.00
43 Jamie Benn/25 12.00 30.00
44 Brad Richards/25 10.00 25.00
45 Kari Lehtonen/25 8.00 20.00
46 Brenden Morrow/25 8.00 20.00
47 Loui Eriksson/25
48 Kris Draper/25
49 Nicklas Lidstrom/25 15.00 40.00
51 Pavel Datsyuk/25 30.00 60.00
52 Tomas Tatar/25 8.00 20.00
53 Johan Franzen/25 10.00 25.00
54 Brian Rafalski/25 6.00 15.00
55 Jimmy Howard/25 10.00 25.00
56 Shawn Horcoff/25 6.00 15.00
57 Ales Hemsky/25 10.00 25.00
58 Jordan Eberle/25
59 Sam Gagner/2
60 Taylor Hall/25 20.00 50.00
61 Magnus Paajarvi/25 8.00 20.00
62 Jacob Markstrom/25 20.00 50.00
63 Stephen Weiss/25 8.00 20.00
65 Jonathan Quick/25 15.00 40.00
66 Drew Doughty/25 12.00 30.00
67 Ryan Smyth/25 8.00 20.00
68 Anze Kopitar/25 15.00 40.00
69 Cal Clutterbuck/25 40.00 80.00
71 Brent Burns/25 10.00 25.00
72 Niklas Backstrom/25 10.00 25.00
73 Martin Havlat/25
74 Michael Cammalleri/25 8.00 20.00
76 Max Pacioretty/10
77 Brian Gionta/25 8.00 20.00
78 Carey Price/25 15.00 40.00
79 Lars Eller/25 20.00 40.00
80 P.K. Subban/25 20.00 50.00
82 Andrei Kostitsyn/25 8.00 20.00
83 Ryan Suter/25 6.00 15.00
85 Shea Weber/25 10.00 25.00
86 Martin Brodeur/25 50.00 100.00
87 Patrik Elias/25 10.00 25.00
88 Mattias Tedenby/25 10.00 25.00
89 Zach Parise/25 10.00 25.00
92 John Tavares/25 25.00 50.00
95 Ryan Callahan/25 15.00 40.00
96 Brandon Dubinsky/25
97 Henrik Lundqvist/25 30.00 80.00
98 Marc Staal/25 10.00 25.00
99 Marian Gaborik/25 15.00 30.00
100 Erik Karlsson/25 20.00 50.00
101 Daniel Alfredsson/24 10.00 25.00
102 Bobby Butler/25 8.00 20.00
103 Jason Spezza/25 EXCH 10.00 25.00
104 Danny Briere/25 10.00 25.00
105 Mike Richards/25 10.00 25.00
106 Jody Shelley/25 25.00 50.00
107 Jeff Carter/25
108 Chris Pronger/25 8.00 20.00
109 Sergei Bobrovsky/25 10.00 25.00
110 Claude Giroux/25 10.00 25.00
111 James van Riemsdyk/25 10.00 25.00
112 Shane Doan/25
113 Keith Yandle/25 10.00 25.00
114 Ilya Bryzgalov/25 10.00 25.00
115 Kris Letang/25 25.00 50.00
116 Marc-Andre Fleury/25 12.00 30.00
117 Mark Letestu/25 12.00 30.00
118 Sidney Crosby/25 75.00 135.00
119 Jordan Staal/25
120 Evgeni Malkin/25 30.00 80.00
121 Max Talbot/25 20.00 50.00
122 Patrick Marleau/25
123 Joe Thornton/25 12.00 30.00
124 Torrey Mitchell/25 6.00 15.00
125 Ryane Clowe/25
126 David Backes/25 10.00 25.00
127 T.J. Oshie/25 20.00 50.00
128 Jaroslav Halak/25 10.00 25.00
129 Victor Hedman/25 12.00 30.00
131 Teddy Purcell/25 10.00 25.00
132 Vincent Lecavalier/25 12.00 30.00
133 Martin St. Louis/25 10.00 25.00
134 Steven Stamkos/25 25.00 50.00
135 Mikhail Grabovski/25
136 Nikolai Kulemin/25
137 James Reimer/25 30.00 60.00
139 Luke Schenn/25 8.00 20.00
140 Ryan Kesler/25 40.00 80.00
142 Cory Schneider/10
143 Daniel Sedin/25 12.00 30.00
144 Henrik Sedin/25 12.00 30.00
145 Roberto Luongo/25 10.00 25.00
147 Alex Ovechkin/25 40.00 100.00
148 Michal Neuvirth/25 8.00 20.00
149 Eric Fehr/25 6.00 15.00
150 Mike Green/25

2011-12 Certified Gold Team

*MIR.GOLD/25: 1X TO 2.5X BASIC INSERTS
1 Martin St. Louis 1.50 4.00
2 Daniel Sedin 1.50 4.00
3 Corey Perry 1.50 4.00
4 Jarome Iginla 1.50 4.00
5 Steven Stamkos 3.00 8.00
6 Claude Giroux 1.50 4.00
7 Henrik Sedin 1.50 4.00
8 Shea Weber 1.25 3.00
9 Zdeno Chara 1.50 4.00
10 Nicklas Lidstrom 1.50 4.00
11 Tim Thomas 1.50 4.00
12 Pekka Rinne 2.00 5.00

2011-12 Certified Gold Team Autographs

STATED PRINT RUN 25 SER.#'d SETS
1 Martin St. Louis 10.00 25.00
2 Daniel Sedin 12.00 30.00
3 Corey Perry 12.00 30.00
4 Jarome Iginla 12.00 30.00
5 Steven Stamkos 25.00 60.00
6 Claude Giroux 12.00 30.00
7 Henrik Sedin 15.00 40.00
8 Shea Weber 10.00 25.00
9 Zdeno Chara
10 Nicklas Lidstrom
11 Tim Thomas 12.00 30.00
12 Pekka Rinne 15.00 40.00

2011-12 Certified Masked Marvels

*MIR.GOLD/25: 1X TO 2.5X BASIC INSERTS
1 Sergei Bobrovsky 1.50 4.00
2 Tim Thomas 1.50 4.00
3 Carey Price 5.00 12.00
4 Cam Ward 1.50 4.00
5 Corey Crawford 2.00 5.00
6 Marc-Andre Fleury 2.50 6.00
7 Pekka Rinne 2.00 5.00
8 Jonathan Quick 2.50 6.00
9 James Reimer 1.50 4.00
10 Kari Lehtonen 1.25 3.00
11 Roberto Luongo 1.50 4.00
12 Michal Neuvirth 1.25 3.00
13 Ilya Bryzgalov 1.50 4.00
14 Ondrej Pavelec 1.50 4.00
15 Henrik Lundqvist 2.00 5.00
16 Niklas Backstrom 1.50 4.00
17 Miikka Kiprusoff 1.50 4.00
18 Jonas Hiller 1.25 3.00
19 Jacob Markstrom 1.50 4.00
20 Jimmy Howard 1.50 4.00

2011-12 Certified Masked Marvels Materials

STATED PRINT RUN 99 SER.#'d SETS
*PRIME/25: .8X TO 2X BASIC MATERIAL/99
1 Sergei Bobrovsky 4.00 10.00
2 Tim Thomas 5.00 12.00
3 Carey Price 12.00 30.00
4 Cam Ward 4.00 10.00
5 Corey Crawford 5.00 12.00
6 Marc-Andre Fleury 6.00 15.00
7 Pekka Rinne 5.00 12.00
8 Jonathan Quick 6.00 15.00
9 James Reimer 4.00 10.00
10 Kari Lehtonen 3.00 8.00
11 Roberto Luongo 4.00 10.00
12 Michal Neuvirth 3.00 8.00
14 Ondrej Pavelec 4.00 10.00
15 Henrik Lundqvist 5.00 12.00
16 Niklas Backstrom 3.00 8.00
17 Miikka Kiprusoff 4.00 10.00
18 Jonas Hiller 3.00 8.00
19 Jacob Markstrom 4.00 10.00
20 Jimmy Howard 4.00 10.00

2011-12 Certified Masked Marvels Materials Autographs

STATED PRINT RUN 25 SER.#'d SETS
1 Sergei Bobrovsky 12.00 30.00
2 Tim Thomas 15.00 40.00
3 Carey Price 15.00 40.00
4 Cam Ward 12.00 30.00
6 Marc-Andre Fleury 20.00 50.00
7 Pekka Rinne 12.00 30.00
8 Jonathan Quick 15.00 40.00
10 Kari Lehtonen 10.00 25.00
11 Roberto Luongo 12.00 30.00
12 Michal Neuvirth 10.00 25.00
13 Ilya Bryzgalov 12.00 30.00
14 Ondrej Pavelec
15 Henrik Lundqvist 30.00 60.00
16 Niklas Backstrom 12.00 30.00
18 Jonas Hiller 10.00 25.00
19 Jacob Markstrom 20.00 50.00
20 Jimmy Howard 15.00 40.00

2011-12 Certified Mirror Blue Materials

STATED PRINT RUNS 2-99
1 Jeff Skinner/99 4.00 10.00
2 Danny Briere/99 4.00 10.00
3 Patrice Bergeron/99 5.00 12.00
4 Patrick Sharp/99 4.00 10.00
5 Ryan Miller/99 4.00 10.00
9 Mike Richards/99 4.00 10.00
10 Milan Lucic/99 4.00 10.00
11 Eric Staal/99 5.00 12.00
12 Patrick Kane/10
13 Jonathan Quick/99 6.00 15.00
14 Pekka Rinne/99 5.00 12.00
16 Michael Cammalleri/99 3.00 8.00
17 Cam Ward/99 4.00 10.00
18 Andrei Markov/99 4.00 10.00
19 David Backes/99 4.00 10.00
20 Matt Moulson/2
21 Steve Mason/10
22 Andrew Ladd/99 4.00 10.00
23 Jamie Benn/99 5.00 12.00
24 Ryan Callahan/99 4.00 10.00
25 Erik Karlsson/99 4.00 10.00
26 Drew Doughty/99 4.00 10.00
27 Nicklas Backstrom/99 6.00 15.00
28 Patrick Marleau/99 4.00 10.00
29 Cal Clutterbuck/99 4.00 10.00
30 Miikka Kiprusoff/99 4.00 10.00
31 Jeff Carter/99 4.00 10.00
32 Kris Letang/99 4.00 10.00
33 Joe Thornton/10
34 Alex Ovechkin/99 15.00 40.00
36 Rene Bourque/99 2.50 6.00
37 Brandon Dubinsky/99
38 Evander Kane/99 4.00 10.00
39 John Tavares/10
40 Paul Stastny/99 4.00 10.00
41 Brad Richards/99 4.00 10.00
42 Shane Doan/99 3.00 8.00
43 Zac Dalpe/99
44 Ales Hemsky/99 3.00 8.00
45 Nik Antropov/40 3.00 8.00
46 Kari Lehtonen/99 5.00 12.00
47 Daniel Alfredsson/99 4.00 10.00
48 Nicklas Lidstrom/99 5.00 12.00
49 Corey Perry/99 4.00 10.00
50 Jordan Eberle/99 6.00 15.00
51 Thomas Vanek/99 4.00 10.00
52 Martin Brodeur/99 8.00 20.00
53 Mark Giordano/99 3.00 8.00
54 Mikko Koivu/99 6.00 15.00
55 Ryan Getzlaf/99 6.00 15.00
56 Ryan Kesler/99 4.00 10.00
57 Drew Stafford/99
59 Teddy Purcell/99 4.00 10.00
60 Sam Gagner/99 3.00 8.00
62 John Carlson/99
63 Taylor Hall/99 8.00 20.00
65 Michal Neuvirth/99 3.00 8.00
66 Travis Zajac/99 3.00 8.00
67 Marc-Andre Fleury/99 6.00 15.00
68 Sergei Bobrovsky/10
69 Antti Niemi/99
70 Sidney Crosby/99 15.00 40.00
71 Claude Giroux/99 4.00 10.00
72 Tyler Seguin/99 8.00 20.00
73 Ryan Smyth/99 3.00 8.00
74 Mike Fisher/99 4.00 10.00
76 Keith Yandle/99 4.00 10.00
77 Jacob Markstrom/99 4.00 10.00
78 Milan Hejduk/99 3.00 8.00
79 Brian Gionta/10
80 Kyle Okposo/99 4.00 10.00
81 Vincent Lecavalier/99 3.00 8.00
82 Ondrej Pavelec/99 4.00 10.00
83 James Reimer/99 8.00 20.00
84 Brenden Morrow/99 3.00 8.00
85 Sergei Kostitsyn/99 2.50 6.00
86 Derek Roy/99 3.00 8.00
87 Henrik Lundqvist/99 5.00 12.00
88 Cory Schneider/99 6.00 15.00
89 Valtteri Filppula/99 20.00 50.00
90 Anze Kopitar/99 6.00 15.00
92 Eric Fehr/99 2.50 6.00
93 Corey Crawford/10
94 Joe Pavelski/99 4.00 10.00
95 Mattias Tedenby/99 2.50 6.00
96 Tim Thomas/99 4.00 10.00
97 Brent Burns/99 5.00 12.00
98 Jordan Staal/99 4.00 10.00
99 Curtis Glencross/99 2.50 6.00
100 James van Riemsdyk/99 4.00 10.00
101 Evgeni Malkin/99 12.00 30.00
102 Niklas Backstrom/99 4.00 10.00
103 Zach Parise/99 4.00 10.00
104 Ryane Clowe/10
105 Dion Phaneuf/99 4.00 10.00
106 Ilya Bryzgalov/99 4.00 10.00
107 Erik Johnson/99 2.50 6.00
108 Jaroslav Halak/99 4.00 10.00
109 Carey Price/99 8.00 20.00
110 Derick Brassard/99 4.00 10.00
111 Martin St. Louis/99 4.00 10.00
112 Dustin Byfuglien/99 4.00 10.00
113 Loui Eriksson/99 3.00 8.00
114 Tyler Ennis/99 3.00 8.00
115 Pavel Datsyuk/99 5.00 12.00
116 Jonathan Toews/10
117 Dany Heatley/99 3.00 8.00
118 Ilya Kovalchuk/99 4.00 10.00
119 Martin Havlat/99 3.00 8.00
120 Jarome Iginla/99 4.00 10.00
121 Mike Green/99 4.00 10.00
122 Cam Fowler/99 3.00 8.00
123 Henrik Zetterberg/99 5.00 12.00
124 Marc Staal/99 4.00 10.00
125 Phil Kessel/99 5.00 12.00
126 Steven Stamkos/99 8.00 20.00
127 Antoine Vermette/99 2.50 6.00
128 P.K. Subban/99 6.00 15.00
129 Matt Duchene/99 4.00 10.00
130 Stephen Weiss/99 3.00 8.00
131 Daniel Sedin/99 4.00 10.00
132 Henrik Sedin/99 4.00 10.00
133 Marian Gaborik/99 5.00 12.00
134 Shea Weber/99 3.00 8.00
135 Luke Schenn/99 3.00 8.00
136 Brad Marchand/99 5.00 12.00
137 Marian Hossa/10
138 Johan Franzen/99
139 Rick Nash/99 4.00 10.00
140 Tomas Plekanec/99 4.00 10.00
141 Brandon Sutter/99 3.00 8.00
142 David Booth/99
143 Barret Jackman/99 2.50 6.00
144 Roberto Luongo/99 4.00 10.00
145 Jimmy Howard/99 4.00 10.00
146 Bobby Ryan/99 4.00 10.00
147 Logan Couture/99 4.00 10.00
148 Craig Anderson/99 4.00 10.00
149 Jason Spezza/99 4.00 10.00
150 Derek Stepan/99 4.00 10.00
151 Brendan Shanahan/49 5.00 12.00
152 Eric Lindros/49 6.00 15.00
153 Pat LaFontaine/49 6.00 15.00
154 Grant Fuhr/49
155 Ron Francis/49 10.00 25.00
156 Joe Mullen/49 3.00 8.00
157 Patrick Roy/49 10.00 25.00
158 Ray Bourque/49 10.00 25.00
159 Bryan Trottier/49 5.00 12.00
160 Darryl Sittler/49 8.00 20.00
161 Luc Robitaille/49 4.00 10.00
162 Mario Lemieux/49 12.00 30.00
163 Johnny Bucyk/49 4.00 10.00
164 Joe Sakic/49
165 Curtis Joseph/49 4.00 10.00
166 Guy Lafleur/49 8.00 20.00
167 Jeremy Roenick/49 8.00 20.00
168 Doug Gilmour/49 6.00 15.00
169 Mark Messier/49
170 Joe Nieuwendyk/49

2011-12 Certified Mirror Gold Materials Prime

STATED PRINT RUN 25
1 Jeff Skinner 6.00 15.00
2 Danny Briere 6.00 15.00
3 Patrice Bergeron 6.00 15.00
4 Patrick Sharp 6.00 15.00
5 Ryan Miller 6.00 15.00
6 Mikhail Grabovski 10.00 25.00
9 Mike Richards 6.00 15.00
10 Milan Lucic 6.00 15.00
11 Eric Staal 8.00 20.00
12 Patrick Kane 12.00 30.00
13 Jonathan Quick 10.00 25.00
14 Pekka Rinne 8.00 20.00
16 Michael Cammalleri
17 Cam Ward 6.00 15.00
18 Andrei Markov
19 David Backes 6.00 15.00
20 Matt Moulson
21 Steve Mason
22 Andrew Ladd
23 Jamie Benn 6.00 15.00
24 Ryan Callahan 6.00 15.00
25 Erik Karlsson 12.00 30.00
26 Drew Doughty 6.00 15.00
27 Nicklas Backstrom 10.00 25.00
28 Patrick Marleau 6.00 15.00
29 Cal Clutterbuck 8.00 20.00
30 Miikka Kiprusoff 6.00 15.00
31 Jeff Carter 6.00 15.00
32 Kris Letang 6.00 15.00
33 Joe Thornton 6.00 15.00
34 Alex Ovechkin 12.00 30.00
35 David Krejci 6.00 15.00
36 Rene Bourque 4.00 10.00
37 Brandon Dubinsky 5.00 12.00
38 Evander Kane 6.00 15.00
39 John Tavares 12.00 30.00
40 Paul Stastny 6.00 15.00
41 Brad Richards 12.00 30.00
42 Shane Doan 5.00 12.00
43 Zac Dalpe
44 Ales Hemsky 5.00 12.00
45 Nik Antropov 5.00 12.00
46 Kari Lehtonen 8.00 20.00
47 Daniel Alfredsson 6.00 15.00
48 Nicklas Lidstrom 8.00 20.00
49 Corey Perry 6.00 15.00
50 Jordan Eberle 6.00 15.00
51 Thomas Vanek
52 Martin Brodeur 12.00 30.00
53 Mark Giordano 5.00 12.00
54 Mikko Koivu 5.00 12.00
55 Ryan Getzlaf
56 Ryan Kesler 6.00 15.00
57 Drew Stafford 6.00 15.00
59 Teddy Purcell 6.00 15.00
60 Sam Gagner 5.00 12.00
61 Max Pacioretty 6.00 15.00
63 Taylor Hall 12.00 30.00
64 Alexandre Burrows
65 Michal Neuvirth 5.00 12.00
66 Travis Zajac 5.00 12.00
67 Marc-Andre Fleury
68 Sergei Bobrovsky
69 Antti Niemi 5.00 12.00
70 Sidney Crosby 25.00 60.00
71 Claude Giroux
72 Tyler Seguin 12.00 30.00
73 Ryan Smyth 5.00 12.00
74 Mike Fisher 6.00 15.00
75 Michael Grabner 5.00 12.00
76 Keith Yandle 6.00 15.00
78 Milan Hejduk 5.00 12.00
79 Brian Gionta
80 Kyle Okposo 6.00 15.00
81 Vincent Lecavalier
82 Ondrej Pavelec 6.00 15.00
83 James Reimer 6.00 15.00
84 Brenden Morrow 5.00 12.00
85 Sergei Kostitsyn 4.00 10.00
86 Derek Roy 5.00 12.00
87 Henrik Lundqvist 8.00 20.00
88 Cory Schneider 5.00 12.00
89 Valtteri Filppula
90 Anze Kopitar 10.00 25.00
92 Eric Fehr
93 Corey Crawford 8.00 20.00
94 Joe Pavelski 6.00 15.00
95 Mattias Tedenby
96 Tim Thomas 8.00 20.00
97 Brent Burns 8.00 20.00
98 Jordan Staal
99 Curtis Glencross 4.00 10.00
100 James van Riemsdyk 6.00 15.00
101 Evgeni Malkin 20.00 50.00
102 Niklas Backstrom 10.00 25.00
103 Zach Parise 8.00 20.00
104 Ryane Clowe 12.00 30.00
105 Dion Phaneuf 20.00 50.00
106 Ilya Bryzgalov
107 Erik Johnson 4.00 10.00
108 Jaroslav Halak 8.00 20.00
109 Carey Price 25.00 50.00
110 Derick Brassard 6.00 15.00
111 Martin St. Louis 6.00 15.00
112 Dustin Byfuglien 15.00 40.00
113 Loui Eriksson
114 Tyler Ennis 6.00 15.00
115 Pavel Datsyuk 8.00 20.00
116 Jonathan Toews 12.00 30.00
117 Dany Heatley 5.00 12.00
118 Ilya Kovalchuk 8.00 20.00
119 Martin Havlat 5.00 12.00
120 Jarome Iginla
121 Mike Green 6.00 15.00
123 Henrik Zetterberg 8.00 20.00
124 Marc Staal
125 Phil Kessel 8.00 20.00
126 Steven Stamkos 12.00 30.00
127 Antoine Vermette
128 P.K. Subban 10.00 25.00
129 Matt Duchene 6.00 15.00
130 Stephen Weiss 5.00 12.00
131 Daniel Sedin 6.00 15.00
132 Henrik Sedin 10.00 25.00
133 Marian Gaborik 8.00 20.00
134 Shea Weber 5.00 12.00
135 Luke Schenn
136 Brad Marchand 12.00 30.00
137 Marian Hossa 5.00 12.00
138 Johan Franzen 6.00 15.00
139 Rick Nash 6.00 15.00
140 Tomas Plekanec 6.00 15.00
141 Brandon Sutter 5.00 12.00
142 David Booth 4.00 10.00
143 Barret Jackman 4.00 10.00
144 Roberto Luongo 6.00 15.00
145 Jimmy Howard 6.00 15.00

146 Bobby Ryan
147 Logan Couture 6.00 15.00
148 Craig Anderson 6.00 15.00
149 Jason Spezza
150 Derek Stepan 6.00 15.00
151 Brendan Shanahan 12.00 30.00
152 Eric Lindros 12.00 30.00
153 Pat LaFontaine 10.00 25.00
154 Grant Fuhr 6.00 15.00
155 Ron Francis 8.00 20.00
156 Joe Mullen 8.00 20.00
157 Patrick Roy 15.00 40.00
158 Ray Bourque 10.00 25.00
159 Bryan Trottier 8.00 20.00
160 Darryl Sittler 12.00 30.00
161 Luc Robitaille
162 Mario Lemieux 20.00 50.00
164 Joe Sakic 10.00 25.00
165 Curtis Joseph 8.00 20.00
166 Guy Lafleur 8.00 20.00
167 Jeremy Roenick 15.00 40.00
168 Doug Gilmour
169 Mark Messier 8.00 20.00
170 Joe Nieuwendyk

2011-12 Certified Mirror Red Materials Dual

STATED PRINT RUNS 10-150
1 Jeff Skinner/150 4.00 10.00
2 Danny Briere/150 4.00 10.00
3 Patrice Bergeron/150 5.00 12.00
4 Patrick Sharp/150 4.00 10.00
5 Ryan Miller/150 4.00 10.00
6 Mikhail Grabovski/150 3.00 8.00
9 Mike Richards/150 4.00 10.00
10 Milan Lucic/150 4.00 10.00
11 Eric Staal/150 5.00 12.00
12 Patrick Kane/25 10.00 25.00
13 Jonathan Quick/99 6.00 15.00
14 Pekka Rinne/150 5.00 12.00
16 Michael Cammalleri/150 3.00 8.00
17 Cam Ward/10
18 Andrei Markov/150 4.00 10.00
19 David Backes/150 4.00 10.00
22 Andrew Ladd/150 4.00 10.00
23 Jamie Benn/150 5.00 12.00
24 Ryan Callahan/150 4.00 10.00
25 Erik Karlsson/150 8.00 20.00
26 Drew Doughty/150 4.00 10.00
27 Nicklas Backstrom/150 6.00 15.00
28 Patrick Marleau/150 4.00 10.00
29 Cal Clutterbuck/150 4.00 10.00
30 Miikka Kiprusoff/25 5.00 12.00
31 Jeff Carter/150 4.00 10.00
32 Kris Letang/150 4.00 10.00
33 Joe Thornton/25
34 Alex Ovechkin/25 20.00 50.00
36 Rene Bourque/150 2.50 6.00
37 Brandon Dubinsky/150 3.00 8.00
38 Evander Kane/150 4.00 10.00
39 John Tavares/25 10.00 25.00
40 Paul Stastny/150 4.00 10.00
41 Brad Richards/150 4.00 10.00
42 Shane Doan/150 3.00 8.00
44 Ales Hemsky/150 3.00 8.00
45 Nik Antropov/150 3.00 8.00
46 Kari Lehtonen/150 3.00 8.00
47 Daniel Alfredsson/150 4.00 10.00
48 Nicklas Lidstrom/25
49 Corey Perry/150 4.00 10.00
50 Jordan Eberle/25 10.00 25.00
51 Thomas Vanek/150 4.00 10.00
52 Martin Brodeur/25 10.00 25.00
53 Mark Giordano/150 3.00 8.00
54 Mikko Koivu/150 3.00 8.00
55 Ryan Getzlaf/150 6.00 15.00
56 Ryan Kesler/150 4.00 10.00
57 Drew Stafford/150 4.00 10.00
59 Teddy Purcell/150 4.00 10.00
60 Sam Gagner/150 3.00 8.00
61 Max Pacioretty/25 5.00 12.00
63 Taylor Hall/25 15.00 30.00
65 Michal Neuvirth/150 3.00 8.00
66 Travis Zajac/150 3.00 8.00
67 Marc-Andre Fleury/150 6.00 15.00
68 Sergei Bobrovsky/150 4.00 10.00
69 Antti Niemi/150 3.00 8.00
70 Sidney Crosby/75 15.00 40.00
71 Claude Giroux/150 4.00 10.00
72 Tyler Seguin/25 10.00 25.00
73 Ryan Smyth/150 3.00 8.00
74 Mike Fisher/150 4.00 10.00
76 Keith Yandle/150 4.00 10.00
77 Jacob Markstrom/150 4.00 10.00
78 Milan Hejduk/25 4.00 10.00
79 Brian Gionta/150 3.00 8.00
80 Kyle Okposo/25
81 Vincent Lecavalier/150 3.00 8.00
82 Ondrej Pavelec/150 4.00 10.00
83 James Reimer/150 8.00 20.00
84 Brenden Morrow/150 3.00 8.00
85 Sergei Kostitsyn/150 2.50 6.00
86 Derek Roy/150 3.00 8.00
87 Henrik Lundqvist/150 5.00 12.00
88 Cory Schneider/25 4.00 10.00
89 Valtteri Filppula/150 20.00 50.00
90 Anze Kopitar/150 6.00 15.00
92 Eric Fehr/150 2.50 6.00
93 Corey Crawford/25 6.00 15.00
94 Joe Pavelski/150 4.00 10.00
95 Mattias Tedenby/150 2.50 6.00
96 Tim Thomas/150 5.00 12.00
97 Brent Burns/150 5.00 12.00
98 Jordan Staal/150 4.00 10.00
99 Curtis Glencross/150 2.50 6.00
100 James van Riemsdyk/150 4.00 10.00
101 Evgeni Malkin/25 15.00 40.00
102 Niklas Backstrom/150 4.00 10.00
103 Zach Parise/150 4.00 10.00
104 Ryane Clowe/150 2.50 6.00
105 Dion Phaneuf/150 4.00 10.00
106 Ilya Bryzgalov/150 4.00 10.00
107 Erik Johnson/150 2.50 6.00
108 Jaroslav Halak/150 4.00 10.00
109 Carey Price/150 6.00 15.00
110 Derick Brassard/150
111 Martin St. Louis/25
112 Dustin Byfuglien/150 4.00 10.00
113 Loui Eriksson/150 3.00 8.00
114 Tyler Ennis/25 4.00 10.00
115 Pavel Datsyuk/150 5.00 12.00
116 Jonathan Toews/25
117 Dany Heatley/150 3.00 8.00
118 Ilya Kovalchuk/150 4.00 10.00
119 Martin Havlat/150 3.00 8.00
120 Jarome Iginla/150 4.00 10.00
121 Mike Green/150 4.00 10.00
122 Cam Fowler/150 3.00 8.00
123 Henrik Zetterberg/25 6.00 15.00
124 Marc Staal/150 4.00 10.00
125 Phil Kessel/25 6.00 15.00
126 Steven Stamkos/25 10.00 25.00
127 Antoine Vermette/25 3.00 8.00
128 P.K. Subban/150 8.00 20.00
129 Matt Duchene/99 4.00 10.00
130 Stephen Weiss/25 4.00 10.00
131 Daniel Sedin/15 5.00 12.00
132 Henrik Sedin/150 4.00 10.00
133 Marian Gaborik/99 5.00 12.00
134 Shea Weber/75 3.00 8.00
135 Luke Schenn/150 3.00 8.00
136 Brad Marchand/150 5.00 12.00
137 Marian Hossa/25 4.00 10.00
138 Johan Franzen/25 5.00 12.00
139 Rick Nash/150 4.00 10.00
140 Tomas Plekanec/150 4.00 10.00
141 Brandon Sutter/150 3.00 8.00
142 David Booth/150 2.50 6.00
143 Barret Jackman/150 2.50 6.00
144 Roberto Luongo/150 4.00 10.00
145 Jimmy Howard/25
146 Bobby Ryan/150 4.00 10.00
147 Logan Couture/150 4.00 10.00
148 Craig Anderson/150 4.00 10.00
149 Jason Spezza/150 4.00 10.00
150 Derek Stepan/150 4.00 10.00
151 Brendan Shanahan/50 5.00 12.00
152 Eric Lindros/50 6.00 15.00
153 Pat LaFontaine/50 6.00 15.00
154 Grant Fuhr/50 4.00 10.00
155 Ron Francis/50 10.00 25.00
156 Joe Mullen/50 3.00 8.00
157 Patrick Roy/50 10.00 25.00
158 Ray Bourque/50 10.00 25.00
159 Bryan Trottier/50 5.00 12.00
160 Darryl Sittler/50 8.00 20.00
161 Luc Robitaille/50 4.00 10.00
162 Mario Lemieux/50 12.00 30.00
163 Johnny Bucyk/25 10.00 25.00
164 Joe Sakic/50 6.00 15.00
165 Curtis Joseph/50 4.00 10.00
166 Guy Lafleur/50 8.00 20.00
167 Jeremy Roenick/50 10.00 25.00
168 Doug Gilmour/50 6.00 15.00
169 Mark Messier/25 8.00 20.00
170 Joe Nieuwendyk/50

2011-12 Certified Mirror Blue Signatures

STATED PRINT RUN 50-99
1 Jeff Skinner/99 8.00 20.00
15 Dwayne Roloson/99 6.00 15.00
19 David Backes/99 8.00 20.00
21 Steve Mason/99 6.00 15.00
22 Andrew Ladd/99
24 Ryan Callahan/99 8.00 20.00
26 Drew Doughty/99 8.00 20.00
29 Cal Clutterbuck/99 8.00 20.00
50 Jordan Eberle/99 20.00 50.00
61 Max Pacioretty/99 8.00 20.00
65 Michal Neuvirth/99 6.00 15.00
69 Antti Niemi/99 6.00 15.00
73 Ryan Smyth/99 6.00 15.00
97 Brent Burns/99 10.00 25.00
98 Jordan Staal/99 8.00 20.00
100 James van Riemsdyk/99 8.00 20.00
103 Zach Parise/99 8.00 20.00
106 Ilya Bryzgalov/99 8.00 20.00
107 Erik Johnson/99 5.00 12.00
108 Jaroslav Halak/99 8.00 20.00
112 Dustin Byfuglien/99 8.00 20.00
117 Dany Heatley/99 6.00 15.00
124 Marc Staal/99 6.00 15.00
130 Stephen Weiss/99 6.00 15.00
131 Daniel Sedin/99 8.00 20.00
132 Henrik Sedin/99 8.00 20.00
134 Shea Weber/99 6.00 15.00
150 Derek Stepan/99 8.00 20.00
153 Pat LaFontaine/99 12.00 30.00
161 Luc Robitaille/50 20.00 40.00
168 Doug Gilmour/50 10.00 25.00

2011-12 Certified Mirror Gold Signatures

STATED PRINT RUN 1-25
1 Jeff Skinner/25 10.00 25.00
2 Danny Briere/25 10.00 25.00
4 Patrick Sharp/25 25.00 60.00
5 Ryan Miller/25 8.00 20.00
6 Mikhail Grabovski/25 6.00 15.00
11 Eric Staal/25 12.00 30.00
12 Patrick Kane/25 20.00 50.00
13 Jonathan Quick/25 25.00 50.00
14 Pekka Rinne/25 15.00 40.00
15 Dwayne Roloson/25 8.00 20.00
16 Michael Cammalleri/25 8.00 20.00
17 Cam Ward/25 8.00 20.00
19 David Backes/25
20 Matt Moulson/25 8.00 20.00
21 Steve Mason/25 8.00 20.00
22 Andrew Ladd/25
23 Jamie Benn/25 8.00 20.00
24 Ryan Callahan/25 10.00 25.00
25 Erik Karlsson/25 20.00 40.00
26 Drew Doughty/25 10.00 25.00
28 Patrick Marleau/25 10.00 25.00
29 Cal Clutterbuck/25 10.00 25.00
31 Jeff Carter/25 10.00 25.00
32 Kris Letang/25 12.00 30.00
33 Joe Thornton/25 10.00 25.00
34 Alex Ovechkin/25 40.00 100.00
36 Rene Bourque/25 10.00 25.00
37 Brandon Dubinsky/25 8.00 20.00
38 Evander Kane/25 10.00 25.00
39 John Tavares/25 20.00 50.00
40 Paul Stastny/25 10.00 25.00
41 Brad Richards/25 10.00 25.00
42 Shane Doan/25 8.00 20.00
43 Zac Dalpe/9
44 Ales Hemsky/25
46 Kari Lehtonen/25 8.00 20.00
47 Daniel Alfredsson/25 10.00 25.00
48 Nicklas Lidstrom/25 15.00 30.00
49 Corey Perry/25 10.00 25.00
50 Jordan Eberle/25 20.00 50.00
51 Thomas Vanek/25 10.00 25.00
52 Martin Brodeur/25 20.00 50.00
53 Mark Giordano/25 12.00 30.00
56 Ryan Kesler/25 10.00 25.00
57 Drew Stafford/25 10.00 25.00
59 Teddy Purcell/25 10.00 25.00
60 Sam Gagner/25 12.00 30.00
61 Max Pacioretty/25 12.00 30.00
63 Taylor Hall/25 30.00 60.00
64 Alexandre Burrows/25 15.00 40.00
65 Michal Neuvirth/25 8.00 20.00
66 Travis Zajac/25
67 Marc-Andre Fleury/25 20.00 50.00
68 Sergei Bobrovsky/25 10.00 25.00
69 Antti Niemi/25
70 Sidney Crosby/25 60.00 120.00
71 Claude Giroux/25 20.00 40.00
72 Tyler Seguin/25 20.00 50.00
73 Ryan Smyth/25 8.00 20.00
74 Mike Fisher/25 10.00 25.00
76 Keith Yandle/25
77 Jacob Markstrom/25 10.00 25.00
79 Brian Gionta/25 8.00 20.00
80 Kyle Okposo/25 10.00 25.00
81 Vincent Lecavalier/25 8.00 20.00
82 Ondrej Pavelec/25 6.00 15.00
84 Brenden Morrow/25 8.00 20.00
86 Derek Roy/25
87 Henrik Lundqvist/25 12.00 30.00
88 Cory Schneider/25 8.00 20.00
89 Valtteri Filppula/25
90 Anze Kopitar/25 10.00 25.00
91 James Neal/25
94 Joe Pavelski/25
95 Mattias Tedenby/25
96 Tim Thomas/25 15.00 40.00
97 Brent Burns/25 12.00 30.00
98 Jordan Staal/25 10.00 25.00
99 Curtis Glencross/25
100 James van Riemsdyk/25 10.00 25.00
101 Evgeni Malkin/25 25.00 50.00
102 Niklas Backstrom/25 10.00 25.00
103 Zach Parise/25 8.00 20.00
104 Ryane Clowe/25 EXCH 15.00 40.00
105 Dion Phaneuf/25 10.00 25.00
106 Ilya Bryzgalov/25 15.00 30.00
107 Erik Johnson/25 6.00 15.00
108 Jaroslav Halak/25 10.00 25.00
109 Carey Price/25 30.00 80.00
110 Derick Brassard/25 10.00 25.00
111 Martin St. Louis/25 10.00 25.00
112 Dustin Byfuglien/25 10.00 25.00
113 Loui Eriksson/25 10.00 25.00
114 Tyler Ennis/25 8.00 20.00
115 Pavel Datsyuk/25 15.00 40.00
116 Jonathan Toews/25 20.00 50.00
117 Dany Heatley/25 8.00 20.00
120 Jarome Iginla/25 10.00 25.00
124 Marc Staal/25 8.00 20.00
125 Phil Kessel/25
126 Steven Stamkos/25 25.00 50.00
127 Antoine Vermette/25 6.00 15.00
128 P.K. Subban/25 25.00 60.00
129 Matt Duchene/25 10.00 25.00
130 Stephen Weiss/25
131 Daniel Sedin/25 10.00 25.00
132 Henrik Sedin/25 10.00 25.00
133 Marian Gaborik/25 12.00 30.00
134 Shea Weber/25 8.00 20.00
135 Luke Schenn/25 8.00 20.00
136 Brad Marchand/25 15.00 40.00
137 Marian Hossa/25 12.00 30.00
138 Johan Franzen/25 10.00 25.00
139 Rick Nash/25 10.00 25.00
141 Brandon Sutter/25 10.00 25.00
144 Roberto Luongo/25 15.00 30.00
145 Jimmy Howard/25 15.00 30.00
146 Bobby Ryan/25 10.00 25.00
147 Logan Couture/25 12.00 30.00
148 Craig Anderson/25
150 Derek Stepan/25 20.00 50.00
151 Brendan Shanahan/10
152 Eric Lindros/25 30.00 80.00
153 Pat LaFontaine/25 12.00 30.00
154 Grant Fuhr/25 10.00 25.00
155 Ron Francis/25 15.00 40.00
156 Joe Mullen/25 8.00 20.00
157 Patrick Roy/25 40.00 80.00
158 Ray Bourque/20 15.00 40.00
159 Bryan Trottier/25 20.00 40.00
160 Darryl Sittler/10
161 Luc Robitaille/25 15.00 40.00
162 Mario Lemieux/25 50.00 100.00
163 Johnny Bucyk/25 10.00 25.00
164 Joe Sakic/25 20.00 50.00
165 Curtis Joseph/25 10.00 25.00
166 Guy Lafleur/25 20.00 50.00
167 Jeremy Roenick/25 20.00 50.00
168 Doug Gilmour/25 12.00 30.00
169 Mark Messier/10
170 Joe Nieuwendyk/1

2011-12 Certified Potential

*MIR.GOLD/25: 1X TO 2.5X BASIC INSERTS
1 Taylor Hall 3.00 8.00
2 Jordan Eberle 1.50 4.00
3 Jeff Skinner 1.50 4.00
4 Tyler Seguin 3.00 8.00
5 Sergei Bobrovsky 1.50 4.00
6 Blake Geoffrion 1.25 3.00
7 Cody Hodgson 2.50 6.00
8 Joe Colborne 1.25 3.00
9 Logan Couture 1.50 4.00
10 Marcus Kruger 2.00 5.00

2011-12 Certified Potential Materials

STATED PRINT RUN 99 SER.#'d SETS
*PRIME/25: 1X TO 2.5X BASIC MATERIAL/99
1 Taylor Hall 6.00 15.00
2 Jordan Eberle 3.00 8.00
3 Jeff Skinner 3.00 8.00
4 Tyler Seguin 6.00 15.00
5 Sergei Bobrovsky 3.00 8.00
6 Blake Geoffrion 2.50 6.00
7 Cody Hodgson 8.00 20.00
8 Joe Colborne 2.50 6.00
9 Logan Couture 3.00 8.00
10 Marcus Kruger 4.00 10.00

2011-12 Certified Potential Materials Autographs

STATED PRINT RUN 25-50
*PRIME AU/25: .5X TO 1.2X BASIC AU/25-50
1 Taylor Hall/50 50.00 100.00
2 Jordan Eberle/50 30.00 60.00
3 Jeff Skinner/50 15.00 40.00
4 Tyler Seguin/50 EXCH 15.00 40.00
5 Sergei Bobrovsky/50 12.00 30.00
6 Blake Geoffrion/50 6.00 15.00
7 Cody Hodgson/25 40.00 80.00
8 Joe Colborne/50 10.00 25.00
9 Logan Couture/50 10.00 25.00
10 Marcus Kruger/50 10.00 25.00

2011-12 Certified Shirt Off My Back Combos

STATED PRINT RUN 25-99
*PRIME/25: 1.2X TO 3X BASIC SHIRT 25-99
1 J.Eberle/T.Hall 8.00 20.00
3 M.St.Louis/T.Thomas 5.00 12.00
4 C.Joseph/J.Reimer 4.00 10.00
5 C.Price/J.Halak 12.00 30.00
6 S.Weber/Z.Chara 4.00 10.00
7 Yzerman/S.Stamkos/25 10.00 25.00
8 N.Leveille/R.Bourque 6.00 15.00
9 B.Leetch/M.Messier 6.00 15.00
10 J.Iginla/J.Nieuwendyk 6.00 15.00
11 J.Sakic/M.Duchene 8.00 20.00
12 M.Koivu/S.Koivu 4.00 10.00
13 G.Fuhr/J.Quick 6.00 15.00
14 C.Neely/R.Middleton 6.00 15.00
15 P.Roy/R.Vachon/25 60.00 120.00

2011-12 Certified Shirt Off My Back Combos Autographs

STATED PRINT RUN 21-25
1 J.Eberle/T.Hall/21
3 M.St.Louis/T.Thomas
4 C.Joseph/J.Reimer 50.00 100.00
5 C.Price/J.Halak 50.00 120.00
6 S.Weber/Z.Chara 15.00 40.00
7 S.Yzerman/S.Stamkos 75.00 150.00
8 N.Leveille/R.Bourque 25.00 60.00
9 B.Leetch/M.Messier 20.00 50.00
10 J.Iginla/J.Nieuwendyk 40.00 80.00
11 J.Sakic/M.Duchene 50.00 100.00
13 G.Fuhr/J.Quick 40.00 80.00
14 C.Neely/R.Middleton 25.00 60.00
15 P.Roy/R.Vachon 60.00 120.00

2011-12 Certified Stars of the NHL

STATED PRINT RUN 25 SER.#'d SETS
1 Corey Perry 8.00 20.00
2 Dustin Byfuglien 8.00 20.00
3 Milan Lucic 8.00 20.00
4 Ryan Miller 8.00 20.00
5 Jarome Iginla 8.00 20.00
6 Jeff Skinner 8.00 20.00
7 Jonathan Toews 15.00 40.00
8 Matt Duchene 8.00 20.00
9 Rick Nash 8.00 20.00
10 Jamie Benn 10.00 25.00
11 Henrik Zetterberg 10.00 25.00
12 Taylor Hall 15.00 40.00
13 Jacob Markstrom 8.00 20.00
14 Anze Kopitar 12.00 30.00
15 Niklas Backstrom 8.00 20.00
16 P.K. Subban 15.00 40.00
17 Shea Weber 6.00 15.00
18 Martin Brodeur 15.00 40.00
19 John Tavares 15.00 40.00
20 Henrik Lundqvist 10.00 25.00
21 Daniel Alfredsson 8.00 20.00
22 Claude Giroux 8.00 20.00
23 Shane Doan 6.00 15.00
24 Sidney Crosby 30.00 80.00
25 Joe Thornton 6.00 15.00
26 Chris Stewart 6.00 15.00
27 Steven Stamkos 15.00 40.00
28 James Reimer 8.00 20.00
29 Roberto Luongo 8.00 20.00
30 Alex Ovechkin 30.00 80.00

2011-12 Certified Stick Em

STATED PRINT RUN 50 SER.#'d SETS
1 Derek Stepan 10.00 25.00
2 Marian Gaborik 12.00 30.00
3 Sidney Crosby 20.00 50.00
4 Evgeni Malkin 30.00 80.00
5 Ilya Kovalchuk 10.00 25.00
6 Jarome Iginla 10.00 25.00
7 Andrei Kostitsyn 8.00 20.00
8 Alex Ovechkin 30.00 80.00
9 David Krejci 15.00 40.00
10 Tyler Seguin 10.00 25.00
11 Jaromir Jagr 15.00 40.00
12 Mario Lemieux 30.00 80.00
16 Teemu Selanne 12.00 30.00
17 Brett Hull 12.00 30.00
18 Paul Coffey 10.00 25.00
19 Pavel Datsyuk 12.00 30.00
20 Ryan Getzlaf 15.00 40.00

2011-12 Certified Throwback Threads

*MIRROR GOLD/25: .8X TO 2X BASIC INSERTS
1 Joel Quenneville 1.25 3.00
2 Randy Moller 1.25 3.00
3 Charlie Simmer 1.25 3.00
4 Chris Pronger 1.50 4.00
5 Guy Chouinard 1.50 4.00
6 Gary Bromley 2.50 6.00
7 Mike Modano 3.00 8.00
8 Nikolai Khabibulin 1.50 4.00
10 Gary Simmons 2.00 5.00

2011-12 Certified Throwback Threads Autographs

STATED PRINT RUN 50-100
1 Joel Quenneville/100 8.00 20.00
2 Randy Moller/100 5.00 12.00
3 Charlie Simmer/100 5.00 12.00
4 Chris Pronger/100 6.00 15.00
5 Guy Chouinard/100 6.00 15.00
6 Gary Bromley/50 10.00 25.00
7 Mike Modano/100 15.00 40.00
8 Nikolai Khabibulin/100 10.00 25.00
10 Gary Simmons/50 8.00 20.00

2012-13 Certified

COMP.SET w/o SPs (100) 15.00 40.00
101-140 MM/IMM PRINT RUN 999
141-152 ROOKIE PRINT RUN 999 1.00
153-176 RC AU PRINT RUN 999
177-188 JSY AU PRINT RUN 499
EXCH EXPIRATION: 5/7/2014
1 Jonas Hiller .30 .75
2 Brendan Smith .30 .75
3 Dion Phaneuf .40 1.00
4 Taylor Hall .75 2.00
5 Nicklas Lidstrom .40 1.00
6 Erik Johnson .25 .60
7 Jack Johnson .25 .60
8 Alex Ovechkin 1.50 4.00
9 Bobby Ryan .40 1.00
10 Marian Gaborik .40 1.00
11 Daniel Alfredsson .40 1.00
12 Jarome Iginla .40 1.00
13 Pavel Datsyuk .50 1.25
14 Jamie Benn .50 1.25
15 Dany Heatley .30 .75
16 Andrew Ladd .40 1.00
17 Ilya Kovalchuk .40 1.00
18 Marc Staal .30 .75
19 Shane Doan .30 .75
20 Chris Pronger .30 .75
21 Loui Eriksson .30 .75
22 Daniel Sedin .40 1.00
23 Dustin Brown .40 1.00
24 Ryan Callahan .40 1.00
25 Nick Johnson .30 .75
26 Patrik Elias .40 1.00
27 Rene Bourque .25 .60
28 Claude Giroux .40 1.00
29 Jason Pominville .30 .75
30 Scott Clemmensen .30 .75
31 Antti Niemi .30 .75
32 Kris Versteeg .30 .75
33 Henrik Sedin .40 1.00
34 James Reimer .40 1.00
35 Jean-Sebastien Giguere .30 .75
36 Patrick Kaleta .25 .60
37 Patrice Bergeron .50 1.25
38 Jonathan Toews .75 2.00
39 Logan Couture .40 1.00
40 Henrik Zetterberg .50 1.25
41 Craig Anderson .40 1.00
42 David Backes .40 1.00
43 Nazem Kadri .40 1.00
44 Jason Arnott .30 .75
45 Jonathan Bernier .40 1.00
46 Andrei Kostitsyn .30 .75
47 T.J. Oshie .60 1.50
48 Danny Briere .40 1.00
49 Ryan Ellis .25 .60
50 Antoine Vermette .25 .60
51 Ryan Getzlaf .60 1.50
52 Mike Green .40 1.00
53 Jeff Skinner .40 1.00
54 Vincent Lecavalier .30 .75
55 Sergei Gonchar .25 .60
56 Brian Boucher .30 .75
57 Tyler Myers .30 .75
58 Kris Letang .40 1.00
59 Steve Mason .30 .75
60 Shea Weber .30 .75
61 Rick Nash .40 1.00
62 Carl Hagelin .40 1.00
63 Brad Marchand .50 1.25
64 Zach Parise .40 1.00
65 Erik Karlsson .75 2.00
66 James Neal .40 1.00
67 Max Pacioretty .40 1.00
68 Jaromir Jagr 1.00 2.50
69 Zdeno Chara .40 1.00
70 Matt Martin .25 .60
71 Evgeni Malkin 1.25 3.00
72 Mikael Backlund .30 .75
73 Mikko Koivu .30 .75
74 John Carlson .50 1.25
75 Nicklas Backstrom .60 1.50
76 P.K. Subban .60 1.50
77 Jeff Carter .40 1.00
78 Martin St. Louis .40 1.00
79 Andrei Markov .40 1.00
80 Nik Antropov .30 .75
81 Marian Hossa .30 .75
82 Drew Doughty .40 1.00
83 Ales Hemsky .30 .75
84 Mikhail Grabovski .30 .75
85 Dustin Byfuglien .40 1.00
86 Wojtek Wolski .25 .60
87 Sidney Crosby 1.50 4.00
88 Patrick Kane .75 2.00
89 Sam Gagner .30 .75
90 John Tavares .75 2.00
91 Steven Stamkos .75 2.00
92 Gabriel Landeskog .40 1.00
93 Ryan Nugent-Hopkins .40 1.00
94 Michael Cammalleri .30 .75
95 Michael Grabner .30 .75
96 Eric Staal .50 1.25
97 Ryan Kesler .40 1.00
98 Mikkel Boedker .25 .60
99 Martin Havlat .30 .75
100 Brenden Morrow .30 .75
101 Henrik Lundqvist MM 2.00 5.00
102 Jonathan Quick MM 2.50 6.00
103 Pekka Rinne MM 2.00 5.00
104 Mike Smith MM 1.50 4.00
105 Braden Holtby MM 2.50 6.00
106 Ilya Bryzgalov MM 1.50 4.00
107 Kari Lehtonen MM 1.25 3.00
108 Marc-Andre Fleury MM 2.50 6.00
109 Brian Elliott MM 1.25 3.00
110 Cory Schneider MM 1.25 3.00
111 Ondrej Pavelec MM 1.50 4.00
112 Carey Price MM 4.00 10.00
113 Miikka Kiprusoff MM 1.25 3.00
114 Tim Thomas MM 1.50 4.00
115 Ryan Miller MM 1.50 4.00
116 Niklas Backstrom MM 1.25 3.00
117 Corey Crawford MM 2.00 5.00
118 Cam Ward MM 1.50 4.00
119 Martin Brodeur MM 3.00 8.00
120 Jimmy Howard MM 1.50 4.00
121 Gordie Howe IMM 4.00 10.00
122 Bobby Clarke IMM 2.00 5.00
123 Patrick Roy IMM 5.00 12.00
124 Ray Bourque IMM 3.00 8.00
125 Jean Beliveau IMM 2.00 5.00
126 Steve Yzerman IMM 4.00 10.00
127 Joe Sakic IMM 3.00 8.00
128 Johnny Bower IMM 2.00 5.00
129 Mike Bossy IMM 2.00 5.00
130 Phil Esposito IMM 3.00 8.00
131 Mario Lemieux IMM 6.00 15.00
132 Ron Francis IMM 2.50 6.00
133 Brendan Shanahan IMM 2.50 6.00
134 Doug Gilmour IMM 2.50 6.00
135 Bernie Parent IMM 2.00 5.00
136 Gilbert Perreault IMM 2.00 5.00
137 Brian Leetch IMM 2.00 5.00
138 Mike Modano IMM 3.00 8.00
139 Brett Hull IMM 2.00 5.00
140 Ed Belfour IMM 2.00 5.00
141 Andrew Joudrey RC 2.00 5.00
142 Travis Turnbull RC 2.00 5.00
143 Gabriel Dumont RC 2.00 5.00
144 Jason Zucker RC 2.50 6.00
145 Jeremy Welsh RC 2.00 5.00
146 Ryan Hamilton RC 2.00 5.00
147 Lane MacDermid RC 2.00 5.00
148 Matt Watkins RC 2.00 5.00
149 Akim Aliu RC 2.00 5.00
150 Shawn Hunwick RC 2.00 5.00
151 Riley Sheahan RC 2.00 5.00
152 Ryan Garbutt RC 2.00 5.00
153 Torey Krug AU RC 8.00 20.00
154 Tyler Cuma AU RC 3.00 8.00
155 Mark Stone AU RC 4.00 10.00
156 Aaron Ness AU RC 3.00 8.00
157 Tyson Sexsmith AU RC 3.00 8.00
158 Brandon Bollig AU RC 3.00 8.00
159 Brandon Manning AU RC 3.00 8.00
160 Brenden Dillon AU RC 3.00 8.00
161 Carter Camper AU RC 2.50 6.00
162 Casey Cizikas AU RC 3.00 8.00
163 Chay Genoway AU RC 3.00 8.00
164 Cody Goloubef AU RC 3.00 8.00
165 Colby Robak AU RC 3.00 8.00
166 Dalton Prout AU RC 3.00 8.00
167 Jordan Nolan AU RC 3.00 8.00
168 Kristopher Foucault AU RC 3.00 8.00
169 Mat Clark AU RC 3.00 8.00
170 Matt Donovan AU RC 3.00 8.00
171 Max Sauve AU RC 3.00 8.00
172 Michael Hutchinson AU RC 6.00 15.00
173 Michael Stone AU RC 3.00 8.00
174 Mike Connolly AU RC 3.00 8.00
175 Philippe Cornet AU RC 3.00 8.00
176 Robert Mayer AU RC 4.00 10.00
177 Sven Baertschi JSY AU RC 6.00 15.00
178 J.T. Brown JSY AU RC 5.00 12.00
179 Reilly Smith JSY AU RC 10.00 25.00
180 Tyson Barrie JSY AU RC 10.00 25.00
181 Carter Ashton JSY AU RC 4.00 10.00
182 Chet Pickard JSY AU RC 5.00 12.00
183 Chris Kreider JSY AU RC 10.00 25.00
184 J.Schwartz JSY AU RC 8.00 20.00
185 Jake Allen JSY AU RC 15.00 40.00
186 Silfverberg JSY AU RC 10.00 25.00
187 Jussi Rynnas JSY AU RC 5.00 12.00
188 S.Glennie JSY AU RC 5.00 12.00

2012-13 Certified Fabric of the Game

STATED PRINT RUN 100-299
*HOT BOX/50-75: .5X TO 1.2X JSY/150-299
*HOT BOX/25: .6X TO 1.5X JSY/199
*RED/150: .5X TO 1.2X BASIC JSY/150-299
*RED/50-75: .6X TO 1.5X BASIC JSY/150-299
*RED/25: .8X TO 2X BASIC JSY/199
*RED/25: .6X TO 1.5X BASIC JSY/100
*GOLD PRM/25: .8X TO 2X BASIC JSY/150-199
*GOLD PRIME/25: 1X TO 2.5X BASIC JSY/100
FOGAB Alexander Burmistrov/299 2.50 6.00
FOGABU Alexandre Burrows/299 3.00 8.00
FOGAE Alexander Edler/299 2.00 5.00
FOGALI Anders Lindback/299 2.00 5.00
FOGAO Alex Ovechkin/299 12.00 30.00
FOGAP Alex Pietrangelo/199 2.50 6.00
FOGBEL Ed Belfour/299 3.00 8.00
FOGBER Jonathan Bernier/299 3.00 8.00
FOGBET Brian Elliott/299 2.50 6.00
FOGBJC B.J. Crombeen/299 2.00 5.00
FOGBLI Bryan Little/299 3.00 8.00
FOGBOR Brooks Orpik/299 2.50 6.00
FOGBR Bobby Ryan/299 3.00 8.00
FOGBRO Dustin Brown/299 4.00 10.00
FOGBS2 Brendan Shanahan/299 4.00 10.00
FOGBSC Brayden Schenn/150 3.00 8.00
FOGBSU Brandon Sutter/100 3.00 8.00
FOGBUR Brent Burns/299 4.00 10.00
FOGCFO Cam Fowler/299 2.50 6.00
FOGCG Claude Giroux/299 3.00 8.00
FOGCKU Chris Kunitz/299 3.00 8.00
FOGCNE Chris Neil/299 2.00 5.00
FOGCPI Chet Pickard/299 2.50 6.00
FOGDB David Backes/299 3.00 8.00
FOGDD Drew Doughty/299 3.00 8.00
FOGDH Dany Heatley/299 2.50 6.00
FOGDSE Devin Setoguchi/299 2.50 6.00
FOGDSP Devante Smith-Pelly/299 2.50 6.00
FOGDWI Dennis Wideman/299 2.00 5.00
FOGEJ Erik Johnson/299 2.00 5.00
FOGEK Erik Karlsson/299 6.00 15.00
FOGEL Eric Lindros/299 5.00 12.00
FOGFN Frans Nielsen/299 2.00 5.00
FOGFP Felix Potvin/299 5.00 12.00
FOGGAB Marian Gaborik/299 3.00 8.00
FOGGLE Scott Glennie/299 2.50 6.00
FOGHAL Jaroslav Halak/299 3.00 8.00
FOGHEM Ales Hemsky/299 2.50 6.00
FOGHZ Henrik Zetterberg/299 4.00 10.00
FOGIB Ilya Bryzgalov/299 3.00 8.00
FOGIK Ilya Kovalchuk/299 3.00 8.00
FOGJA Jake Allen/299 8.00 20.00
FOGJAG Jaromir Jagr/299 8.00 20.00
FOGJC Jeff Carter/299 3.00 8.00
FOGJHE Jhonas Enroth/299 3.00 8.00
FOGJI Jarome Iginla/299 3.00 8.00
FOGJJ Jack Johnson/299 2.00 5.00
FOGJL Joffrey Lupul/299 2.50 6.00
FOGJPO Jason Pominville/299 2.50 6.00
FOGJS Joe Sakic/299 5.00 12.00
FOGJSG Jean-Sebastien Giguere/299 2.50 6.00
FOGJTO Jonathan Toews/299 6.00 15.00
FOGJVO Jakub Voracek/299 3.00 8.00
FOGKAN Patrick Kane/299 6.00 15.00
FOGKHA Nikolai Khabibulin/299 3.00 8.00
FOGKL Kari Lehtonen/299 2.50 6.00
FOGKS Kevin Shattenkirk/299 3.00 8.00
FOGKV Kris Versteeg/299 2.50 6.00
FOGLC Logan Couture/299 3.00 8.00
FOGLE Loui Eriksson/299 2.50 6.00
FOGLEM Mario Lemieux/299 10.00 25.00
FOGLET Kris Letang/299 4.00 10.00
FOGMAF Marc-Andre Fleury/299 5.00 12.00
FOGMAR Patrick Marleau/299 3.00 8.00
FOGMBA Mikael Backlund/299 2.50 6.00
FOGMBI Martin Biron/299 2.50 6.00
FOGMD Matt Duchene/299 3.00 8.00
FOGMGR Matt Greene/299 2.00 5.00
FOGMRI Mike Richards/299 3.00 8.00
FOGMRU Mike Rupp/299 2.00 5.00
FOGNF Nick Foligno/199 2.50 6.00
FOGNG Nathan Gerbe/299 2.00 5.00
FOGNLI Nicklas Lidstrom/299 3.00 8.00
FOGOP Ondrej Pavelec/299 3.00 8.00
FOGPBE Patrik Berglund/299 2.00 5.00
FOGPK Phil Kessel/299 4.00 10.00
FOGPRO Chris Pronger/299 2.50 6.00
FOGRDP Rick DiPietro/299 2.50 6.00
FOGRN Rick Nash/299 3.00 8.00
FOGRO Ryan O'Reilly/299 3.00 8.00
FOGSC2 Sidney Crosby/299 12.00 30.00
FOGSCL Scott Clemmensen/299 2.50 6.00
FOGSD Simon Despres/299 2.50 6.00
FOGSED Daniel Sedin/299 3.00 8.00
FOGSEM Alexander Semin/299 3.00 8.00
FOGSGA Simon Gagne/299 3.00 8.00
FOGSHA Scott Hartnell/299 3.00 8.00
FOGSM Steve Mason/199 2.50 6.00
FOGSTA Marc Staal/299 2.50 6.00
FOGSY Steve Yzerman/299 6.00 15.00
FOGTE Tyler Ennis/299 2.50 6.00
FOGTH Taylor Hall/299 6.00 15.00
FOGTM Tyler Myers/299 2.50 6.00
FOGTO T.J. Oshie/299 4.00 10.00
FOGTR Tuukka Rask/299 5.00 12.00
FOGTS Tyler Seguin/299 5.00 12.00
FOGTT Tim Thomas/299 3.00 8.00
FOGWIL Colin Wilson/299 2.50 6.00
FOGZB Zach Boychuk/299 2.00 5.00
FOGZP Zach Parise/299 3.00 8.00

2012-13 Certified Fabric of the Game Mirror Blue Jersey Autographs

STATED PRINT RUN 10-50
FOGAB Alexander Burmistrov/50 8.00 20.00
FOGABU Alexandre Burrows/50 8.00 20.00
FOGAO Alex Ovechkin/25 60.00 120.00
FOGAP Alex Pietrangelo/25 10.00 25.00
FOGBEL Ed Belfour/25 12.00 30.00
FOGBER Jonathan Bernier/50 10.00 25.00
FOGBET Brian Elliott/20
FOGBR Bobby Ryan/50 10.00 25.00
FOGBRO Dustin Brown/50 10.00 25.00
FOGBS2 Brendan Shanahan/25 40.00 80.00
FOGBUR Brent Burns/50 8.00 20.00
FOGCFO Cam Fowler/50 8.00 20.00
FOGCG Claude Giroux/50 12.00 30.00
FOGCNE Chris Neil/50 6.00 15.00
FOGCPI Chet Pickard/50 8.00 20.00
FOGDB David Backes/50 10.00 25.00
FOGDD Drew Doughty/50 15.00 30.00
FOGDH Dany Heatley/50 8.00 20.00
FOGDSE Devin Setoguchi/50 10.00 25.00
FOGDSP Devante Smith-Pelly/50 8.00 20.00
FOGEJ Erik Johnson/50 6.00 15.00
FOGEL Eric Lindros/25 25.00 50.00
FOGFN Frans Nielsen/50 6.00 15.00
FOGFP Felix Potvin/50 25.00 50.00
FOGGAB Marian Gaborik/50 12.00 30.00
FOGGLE Scott Glennie/50 8.00 20.00
FOGHAL Jaroslav Halak/50 10.00 25.00
FOGHEM Ales Hemsky/50 8.00 20.00
FOGIB Ilya Bryzgalov/20
FOGJA Jake Allen/50 25.00 60.00
FOGJAG Jaromir Jagr/25 30.00 60.00
FOGJC Jeff Carter/50
FOGJI Jarome Iginla/25 12.00 30.00
FOGJJ Jack Johnson/50 6.00 15.00
FOGJS Joe Sakic/25 20.00 50.00
FOGJSG Jean-Sebastien Giguere/50 15.00 40.00
FOGJTO Jonathan Toews/50 30.00 60.00
FOGKAN Patrick Kane/25 25.00 60.00
FOGKHA Nikolai Khabibulin/50 10.00 25.00
FOGKL Kari Lehtonen/50 8.00 20.00
FOGKS Kevin Shattenkirk/50 10.00 25.00
FOGLC Logan Couture/50 10.00 25.00
FOGLE Loui Eriksson/50 8.00 20.00
FOGLET Kris Letang/50 EXCH 25.00 50.00
FOGMAF Marc-Andre Fleury/50 15.00 40.00
FOGMAR Patrick Marleau/50 10.00 25.00
FOGMBA Mikael Backlund/24
FOGMD Matt Duchene/50 10.00 25.00
FOGNG Nathan Gerbe/50 6.00 15.00
FOGNLI Nicklas Lidstrom/25 12.00 30.00
FOGOP Ondrej Pavelec/50 6.00 15.00
FOGPK Phil Kessel/50 12.00 30.00
FOGPRO Chris Pronger/50 8.00 20.00
FOGRN Rick Nash/50 12.00 30.00
FOGRO Ryan O'Reilly/50 15.00 30.00
FOGSD Simon Despres/50 8.00 20.00
FOGSED Daniel Sedin/50 10.00 25.00
FOGSEM Alexander Semin/50 10.00 25.00
FOGSM Steve Mason/50 8.00 20.00
FOGSTA Marc Staal/50 8.00 20.00
FOGTE Tyler Ennis/25 12.00 30.00
FOGTH Taylor Hall/50 20.00 50.00
FOGTM Tyler Myers/50
FOGTO T.J. Oshie/50 15.00 40.00
FOGTR Tuukka Rask/50 10.00 25.00
FOGTS Tyler Seguin/50 25.00 50.00
FOGTT Tim Thomas/25
FOGWIL Colin Wilson/50 8.00 20.00
FOGZP Zach Parise/50 10.00 25.00

2012-13 Certified Face Off Dual Sticks

STATED PRINT RUN 20-50 SER.#'d SETS
1 A.Ovechkin/E.Malkin/50 30.00 80.00
2 B.Shanahan/P.Roy/50 25.00 60.00
3 C.Price/J.Halak/50 25.00 60.00
4 L.Robitaille/S.Yzerman/20 20.00 50.00
5 C.Neely/D.Gilmour/50 30.00 60.00
6 E.Lindros/M.Lemieux/50 30.00 80.00
7 H.Lundqvist/M.Streit/50 12.00 30.00
8 J.Sakic/L.Eriksson/20 20.00 50.00
9 R.McDonagh/Z.Parise/50 12.00 30.00
10 R.Kesler/V.Lecavalier/20

2012-13 Certified Goalie Pulls

*JERSEYS/25: 1X TO 2.5X BASIC INSERT
1 James Reimer 4.00 10.00
2 Jake Allen 10.00 25.00
3 Chet Pickard 3.00 8.00
4 Mike Smith 4.00 10.00
5 Kari Lehtonen 3.00 8.00
6 Brian Elliott 3.00 8.00
7 Curtis Joseph 4.00 10.00
8 Carey Price 12.00 30.00
9 Ed Belfour 4.00 10.00
10 Nikolai Khabibulin 4.00 10.00
11 Jaroslav Halak 4.00 10.00
12 Steve Mason 3.00 8.00
13 Brent Johnson 3.00 8.00
14 Ondrej Pavelec 4.00 10.00
15 Antti Niemi 3.00 8.00
16 Jonathan Quick 8.00 20.00
17 Tom Barrasso 4.00 10.00
18 Ron Hextall 8.00 20.00
19 Grant Fuhr 4.00 10.00
20 Marc-Andre Fleury 5.00 12.00
21 Jonas Hiller 6.00 15.00
22 Ilya Bryzgalov 6.00 15.00
23 Patrick Roy COL 15.00 30.00
24 Anders Lindback 2.50 6.00
25 Semyon Varlamov 4.00 10.00
26 Cam Ward 5.00 12.00
27 Roberto Luongo 4.00 10.00
28 Evgeni Nabokov 3.00 8.00
29 Niklas Backstrom 3.00 8.00
30 Tim Thomas 6.00 15.00
31 Tomas Vokoun 6.00 15.00
32 Craig Anderson 4.00 10.00
33 Jhonas Enroth 4.00 10.00
34 Patrick Roy MON 12.00 30.00
35 Rogie Vachon 5.00 12.00
36 Robin Lehner 3.00 8.00
37 Miikka Kiprusoff 3.00 8.00
38 Ryan Miller 4.00 10.00
39 Sergei Bobrovsky 4.00 10.00
40 Martin Brodeur 8.00 20.00
41 Jonathan Bernier 4.00 10.00
42 Scott Clemmensen 3.00 8.00
43 Jussi Rynnas 6.00 15.00
44 Tuukka Rask 4.00 10.00
45 Felix Potvin 12.00 30.00
46 Jimmy Howard 4.00 10.00
47 Henrik Lundqvist 8.00 20.00
48 Pekka Rinne 6.00 15.00
49 Braden Holtby 6.00 15.00
50 Cory Schneider 3.00 8.00

2012-13 Certified Icons

SEMISTARS/250 1.25 3.00
UNLISTED STARS/250 1.50 4.00
STATED PRINT RUN 250
1 Gordie Howe 3.00 8.00
2 Jean Beliveau 1.50 4.00
3 Alex Delvecchio 1.25 3.00
4 Stan Mikita 2.00 5.00
5 Johnny Bower 1.50 4.00
6 Bobby Clarke 1.50 4.00
7 Denis Potvin 1.50 4.00
8 Lanny McDonald 1.50 4.00
9 Bobby Hull 1.50 4.00
10 Johnny Bucyk 1.25 3.00
11 Gilbert Perreault 1.50 4.00
12 Bernie Parent 1.50 4.00

13 Marcel Dionne 2.00 5.00
14 Phil Esposito 2.50 6.00
15 Guy Lafleur 2.00 5.00

2012-13 Certified Icons Signatures

SEMISTARS 10.00 25.00
UNLISTED STARS 12.00 30.00
STATED PRINT RUN 5-25 SER.#'d SETS
1 Gordie Howe/5
2 Jean Beliveau/25 20.00 50.00
3 Alex Delvecchio/25 10.00 25.00
4 Stan Mikita/25 15.00 40.00
5 Johnny Bower/25 12.00 30.00
6 Bobby Clarke/25 30.00 60.00
7 Denis Potvin/25 12.00 30.00
8 Lanny McDonald/25 12.00 30.00
9 Bobby Hull/25 30.00 60.00
10 Johnny Bucyk/25 10.00 25.00
11 Gilbert Perreault/25 EXCH 12.00 30.00
12 Bernie Parent/25 12.00 30.00
13 Marcel Dionne/25 15.00 40.00
14 Phil Esposito/25 EXCH 15.00 40.00
15 Guy Lafleur/25 15.00 40.00

2012-13 Certified Junior Class Signatures

UNLISTED STARS /100 10.00 25.00
UNLISTED STARS /25-75 12.00 30.00
STATED PRINT RUN 10-100 SER.#'d SETS
1 C.Hodgson/M.Duchene/50 12.00 30.00
2 B.Shanahan/R.Nash/25 30.00 60.00
3 Landeskog/M.Boedker/75 10.00 25.00
4 Phaneuf/Nugent-Hpkns/100 15.00 40.00
5 C.Neely/S.Baertschi/100 10.00 25.00
7 A.Henrique/T.Hall/100 15.00 40.00
8 J.Staal/S.Yzerman/20 30.00 60.00
9 D.Doughty/D.Brown/100 10.00 25.00
10 C.Price/C.Pickard/50 15.00 40.00
11 E.Lindros/R.Middleton/100 20.00 40.00
12 D.Byfuglien/S.Glennie/100 10.00 25.00
13 Pietrangelo/Scheifele/100 20.00 40.00
14 D.Dubnyk/J.Iginla/50 12.00 30.00
15 T.Linden/T.Ennis/25 25.00 50.00
16 B.Trottier/J.Sakic/25 20.00 60.00
17 C.Perry/P.Kane/25 25.00 50.00
18 C.Simmer/J.Thornton/100 10.00 25.00
19 A.Shaw/B.Ryan/100 10.00 25.00
20 C.Giroux/L.Robitaille/50 12.00 30.00

2012-13 Certified Mirror Blue

*BLUE VETS/99: 2X TO 5X BASIC CARDS
*BLUE MM/IMM/50: .8X TO 2X BASIC CARDS
*BLUE ROOKIE/50: .6X TO 1.5X BASIC RC
*BLUE AU/99: .6X TO 1.5X BASIC AU RC
*BLUE JSY AU/50: .8X TO 2X JSY AU
MIRROR BLUE PRINT RUN 50-99

2012-13 Certified Mirror Gold

*GOLD VETS/25: 4X TO 10X BASIC CARDS
*GOLD MM/IMM/25: 1.2X TO 3X BASIC IMM
141-152 UNPRICED GOLD PRINT RUN 10
*GOLD AU/25: 1X TO 2.5X BASIC AU RC
*GOLD JSY AU/25: 1X TO 2.5X BASE JSY AU
GOLD PRINT RUN 10-25

2012-13 Certified Mirror Hot Box

*HB VETS(1-100): 1X TO 2.5X BASIC CARDS
*HB MM/IMM/75: .6X TO 1.5X BASIC MM/IMM
*HB ROOKIE/99: .5X TO 1.2X BASIC RC
*HB AU: .8X TO 2X BASIC AU RC /50
MIRROR HOT BOX PRINT RUN 10-99

2012-13 Certified Mirror Red

*RED VETS/199: 1.5X TO 4X BASIC CARDS
*RED MM/IMM/100: .6X TO 1.5X BASIC MM/IMM
*RED ROOKIE/100: .5X TO 1.2X BASIC RC
*RED AU/199: .5X TO 1.2X BASIC AU RC
*RED JSY AU/100: .6X TO 1.5X JSY AU RC
RED PRINT RUN 100-199

2012-13 Certified Path to the Cup Conference Finals

STATED PRINT RUN 199 SER.#'d SETS
1 D.Brown/S.Doan 2.00 5.00
2 J.Carter/K.Yandle 2.00 5.00
3 A.Martinez/P.Bissonnette 1.25 3.00
4 J.Quick/M.Smith 5.00 12.00
5 D.Doughty/M.Hanzal 2.00 5.00
6 C.Kreider/S.Bernier 2.00 5.00
7 H.Lundqvist/M.Brodeur 4.00 10.00
8 P.Elias/R.Callahan 2.00 5.00
9 R.Fedotenko/Z.Parise 2.00 5.00
10 I.Kovalchuk/M.Gaborik 2.00 5.00
11 B.Richards/M.Brodeur 4.00 10.00

2012-13 Certified Path to the Cup Conference Finals Dual Jerseys

STATED PRINT RUN 50 SER.#'d SETS
1 D.Brown/S.Doan 10.00 25.00
2 J.Carter/K.Yandle 10.00 25.00
3 A.Martinez/P.Bissonnette 8.00 20.00
4 J.Quick/M.Smith 15.00 40.00
5 D.Doughty/M.Hanzal 10.00 25.00
6 C.Kreider/S.Bernier 8.00 20.00
7 H.Lundqvist/M.Brodeur 20.00 50.00
8 P.Elias/R.Callahan 10.00 25.00
9 R.Fedotenko/Z.Parise 10.00 25.00
10 I.Kovalchuk/M.Gaborik 10.00 25.00
11 B.Richards/M.Brodeur 20.00 50.00

2012-13 Certified Path to the Cup Conference Trophy

STATED PRINT RUN 99 SER.#'d SETS
1 Zach Parise 10.00 25.00
2 Dustin Brown 12.00 30.00

2012-13 Certified Path to the Cup Conn Smythe

1 Jonathan Quick 60.00 120.00

2012-13 Certified Path to the Cup Quarter Finals

STATED PRINT RUN 399 SER.#'d SETS
1 D.Penner/R.Luongo 2.00 5.00
2 H.Sedin/T.Lewis 2.00 5.00
3 C.Schneider/J.Williams 1.50 4.00
4 R.Kesler/W.Mitchell 4.00 10.00
5 D.Sedin/J.Stoll 2.00 5.00
6 M.Havlat/P.Berglund 1.50 4.00
7 J.Halak/J.Thornton 2.00 5.00
8 J.Arnott/L.Couture 2.00 5.00
9 A.Niemi/B.Crombeen 1.50 4.00
10 J.Langenbrunner/P.Marleau 2.00 5.00
11 A.Vermette/J.Toews 4.00 10.00
12 K.Yandle/P.Sharp 2.00 5.00
13 M.Frolik/M.Boedker 1.25 3.00
14 D.Keith/M.Smith 2.00 5.00
15 P.Kane/S.Doan 4.00 10.00
16 B.Seabrook/M.Smith 2.00 5.00
17 B.Yip/H.Zetterberg 2.50 6.00
18 A.Kostitsyn/J.Howard 2.00 5.00
19 P.Hornqvist/P.Datsyuk 2.50 6.00
20 M.Erat/N.Lidstrom 3.00 8.00
21 D.Legwand/T.Holmstrom 1.50 4.00
22 A.Anisimov/D.Alfredsson 2.00 5.00
23 E.Karlsson/M.Del Zotto 4.00 10.00
24 B.Boyle/C.Anderson 2.00 5.00
25 M.Michalek/R.McDonagh 2.00 5.00
26 D.Girardi/J.Spezza 2.00 5.00
27 B.Prust/C.Neil 1.25 3.00
28 C.Kreider/N.Foligno 2.50 6.00
29 K.Alzner/T.Thomas 2.00 5.00
30 D.Krejci/N.Backstrom 3.00 8.00
31 M.Green/Z.Chara 2.00 5.00
32 D.Wideman/M.Lucic 2.00 5.00
33 M.Johansson/P.Bergeron 2.50 6.00
34 A.Ovechkin/T.Seguin 8.00 20.00
35 B.Marchand/J.Carlson 4.00 10.00
36 K.Versteeg/P.Elias 2.00 5.00
37 M.Samuelsson/T.Zajac 1.50 4.00
38 S.Clemmensen/Z.Parise 2.00 5.00
39 M.Brodeur/S.Weiss 4.00 10.00
40 B.Campbell/S.Bernier 1.25 3.00
41 D.Kulikov/I.Kovalchuk 2.00 5.00
42 J.Theodore/M.Brodeur 4.00 10.00
43 J.Voracek/K.Letang 4.00 10.00
44 E.Malkin/S.Couturier 6.00 15.00
45 D.Briere/J.Staal 2.00 5.00
46 K.Timonen/S.Despres 1.50 4.00
47 M.Fleury/S.Hartnell 3.00 8.00
48 I.Bryzgalov/J.Neal 2.50 6.00

2012-13 Certified Path to the Cup Quarter Finals Dual Jerseys

STATED PRINT RUN 250 SER.#'d SETS
1 D.Penner/R.Luongo 8.00 20.00
2 H.Sedin/T.Lewis 5.00 12.00
3 C.Schneider/J.Williams 6.00 15.00
4 R.Kesler/W.Mitchell 6.00 15.00
5 D.Sedin/J.Stoll 5.00 12.00
6 M.Havlat/P.Berglund 4.00 10.00
7 J.Halak/J.Thornton 5.00 12.00
8 J.Arnott/L.Couture 5.00 12.00
9 A.Niemi/B.Crombeen 4.00 10.00
10 J.Langenbrunner/P.Marleau 5.00 12.00
11 A.Vermette/J.Toews 5.00 12.00
12 K.Yandle/P.Sharp 5.00 12.00
13 M.Frolik/M.Boedker 3.00 8.00
14 D.Keith/M.Smith 5.00 12.00
15 P.Kane/S.Doan 10.00 25.00
16 B.Seabrook/M.Smith 5.00 12.00
17 B.Yip/H.Zetterberg 6.00 15.00
18 A.Kostitsyn/J.Howard 5.00 12.00
19 P.Hornqvist/P.Datsyuk 6.00 15.00
20 M.Erat/N.Lidstrom 5.00 12.00
21 D.Legwand/T.Holmstrom 4.00 10.00
22 A.Anisimov/D.Alfredsson 5.00 12.00
23 E.Karlsson/M.Del Zotto 10.00 25.00
24 B.Boyle/C.Anderson 5.00 12.00
25 M.Michalek/R.McDonagh 5.00 12.00
26 D.Girardi/J.Spezza 5.00 12.00
27 B.Prust/C.Neil 3.00 8.00
28 C.Kreider/N.Foligno 4.00 10.00
29 K.Alzner/T.Thomas 5.00 12.00
30 D.Krejci/N.Backstrom 6.00 15.00
31 M.Green/Z.Chara 5.00 12.00
32 D.Wideman/M.Lucic 5.00 12.00
33 M.Johansson/P.Bergeron 6.00 15.00
34 A.Ovechkin/T.Seguin 6.00 15.00
35 B.Marchand/J.Carlson 6.00 15.00
36 K.Versteeg/P.Elias 5.00 12.00
37 M.Samuelsson/T.Zajac 4.00 10.00
38 S.Clemmensen/Z.Parise 5.00 12.00
39 M.Brodeur/S.Weiss 8.00 20.00
40 B.Campbell/S.Bernier 3.00 8.00
41 D.Kulikov/I.Kovalchuk 5.00 12.00
42 J.Theodore/M.Brodeur 8.00 20.00
43 J.Voracek/K.Letang 6.00 15.00
44 E.Malkin/S.Couturier 15.00 40.00
45 D.Briere/J.Staal 5.00 12.00
46 K.Timonen/S.Despres 4.00 10.00
47 M.Fleury/S.Hartnell 8.00 20.00
48 I.Bryzgalov/J.Neal 5.00 12.00

2012-13 Certified Path to the Cup Semifinals

STATED PRINT RUN 299 SER.#'d SETS
1 D.Backes/M.Greene 2.50 6.00
2 J.Allen/M.Richards 6.00 15.00
3 A.Pietrangelo/A.Kopitar 4.00 10.00
4 J.Quick/T.Oshie 4.00 10.00
5 C.Wilson/M.Hanzal 2.00 5.00
6 A.Vermette/R.Suter 1.50 4.00
7 K.Yandle/P.Rinne 3.00 8.00
8 P.Hornqvist/S.Doan 2.00 5.00
9 M.Smith/S.Weber 2.50 6.00
10 A.Semin/B.Richards 2.50 6.00
11 A.Ovechkin/M.Del Zotto 10.00 25.00
12 J.Carlson/M.Gaborik 3.00 8.00
13 C.Hagelin/M.Green 2.50 6.00
14 D.Wideman/H.Lundqvist 3.00 8.00
15 B.Holtby/D.Stepan 4.00 10.00
16 M.Rupp/N.Backstrom 4.00 10.00
17 J.van Riemsdyk/Z.Parise 2.50 6.00
18 A.Larsson/B.Schenn 2.50 6.00
19 I.Kovalchuk/J.Jagr 6.00 15.00
20 C.Giroux/M.Brodeur 5.00 12.00
21 P.Elias/W.Simmonds 3.00 8.00

2012-13 Certified Path to the Cup Semifinals Dual Jerseys

STATED PRINT RUN 99 SER.#'d SETS
1 D.Backes/M.Greene 8.00 20.00
2 J.Allen/M.Richards 20.00 50.00
3 A.Pietrangelo/A.Kopitar 12.00 30.00
4 J.Quick/T.Oshie 12.00 30.00
5 C.Wilson/M.Hanzal 6.00 15.00
6 A.Vermette/R.Suter 5.00 12.00
7 K.Yandle/P.Rinne 10.00 25.00
8 P.Hornqvist/S.Doan 6.00 15.00
9 M.Smith/S.Weber 8.00 20.00
10 A.Semin/B.Richards 8.00 20.00
11 A.Ovechkin/M.Del Zotto 10.00 25.00
12 J.Carlson/M.Gaborik 10.00 25.00
13 C.Hagelin/M.Green 8.00 20.00
14 D.Wideman/H.Lundqvist 10.00 25.00
15 B.Holtby/D.Stepan 12.00 30.00
16 M.Rupp/N.Backstrom 12.00 30.00
17 J.van Riemsdyk/Z.Parise 8.00 20.00
18 A.Larsson/B.Schenn 8.00 20.00
19 I.Kovalchuk/J.Jagr 20.00 50.00
20 C.Giroux/M.Brodeur 10.00 25.00
21 P.Elias/W.Simmonds 10.00 25.00

2012-13 Certified Path to the Cup Stanley Cup Finals

STATED PRINT RUN 99 SER.#'d SETS
1 A.Kopitar/P.Elias 8.00 20.00
2 I.Kovalchuk/J.Carter 6.00 15.00
3 J.Quick/Z.Parise 12.50 30.00
4 D.Doughty/I.Kovalchuk 5.00 12.00
5 J.Williams/M.Brodeur 10.00 25.00
6 M.Richards/T.Zajac 5.00 12.00

2012-13 Certified Path to the Cup Stanley Cup Finals Dual Jerseys

STATED PRINT RUN 25 SER.#'d SETS
1 A.Kopitar/P.Elias
2 I.Kovalchuk/J.Carter 12.00 30.00
3 J.Quick/Z.Parise
4 D.Doughty/I.Kovalchuk 12.00 30.00
5 J.Williams/M.Brodeur 25.00 60.00
6 M.Richards/T.Zajac 12.00 30.00

2012-13 Certified Path to the Cup Stanley Cup Winner

STATED PRINT RUN 99 SER.#'d SETS
1 Dustin Brown 25.00 60.00
2 Jonathan Quick 25.00 60.00
3 Anze Kopitar 25.00 60.00
4 Willie Mitchell 12.00 30.00
5 Simon Gagne 20.00 50.00
6 Drew Doughty 12.00 30.00
7 Dustin Penner 12.00 30.00
8 Mike Richards 20.00 40.00
9 Matt Greene 10.00 25.00
10 Justin Williams 12.00 30.00
11 Jarret Stoll 12.00 30.00

2012-13 Certified Rookie Redemption

STATED PRINT RUN 99 SER.#'d SETS
1 Nail Yakupov 15.00 40.00
2 Alex Galchenyuk 12.00 30.00
3 Jonathan Huberdeau 10.00 25.00
4 Brendan Gallagher 12.00 30.00
5 Dougie Hamilton 10.00 25.00
6 Vladimir Tarasenko 12.00 30.00
7 Mikhail Grigorenko 10.00 25.00
8 Sean Monahan 12.00 30.00
9 Seth Jones 12.00 30.00
10 Morgan Rielly 8.00 20.00
11 Tomas Hertl 12.00 30.00
12 Jacob Trouba 8.00 20.00
13 Ryan Murray 6.00 15.00
14 Aleksander Barkov 12.00 30.00
15 Nathan MacKinnon 40.00 80.00

2012-13 Certified Signatures

COMMON CARD 5.00 12.00
SEMISTARS 6.00 15.00
UNLISTED STARS 8.00 20.00
1 Gabriel Landeskog 8.00 20.00
2 Colten Teubert 5.00 12.00
3 Dustin Byfuglien 5.00 12.00
4 Max Sauve
5 Brendan Shanahan 15.00 40.00
6 Brad Richards 8.00 20.00
7 Tuukka Rask 8.00 20.00
8 Keith Aulie 5.00 12.00
9 Allen York 5.00 12.00
10 Eddie Lack 8.00 20.00
11 Bryan Trottier
12 Tyler Seguin 12.00 30.00
13 Jaden Schwartz 12.00 30.00
14 Cody Eakin 6.00 15.00
15 Nick Palmieri 6.00 15.00
16 Roman Horak 6.00 15.00
17 Cam Neely 15.00 30.00
18 Pavel Datsyuk 10.00 25.00
19 Ryan Nugent-Hopkins 8.00 20.00
20 Peter Holland 5.00 12.00
21 Alexei Emelin 8.00 20.00
22 Stefan Elliott 6.00 15.00
23 Clarke MacArthur 5.00 12.00
24 Robert Bortuzzo 5.00 12.00
25 Tyler Bozak 6.00 15.00
26 Alex Ovechkin 25.00 60.00
27 Corey Tropp 6.00 15.00
28 Gustav Nyquist 8.00 20.00
29 Chris Kreider 15.00 40.00
30 Dmitry Orlov 8.00 20.00
31 Alexander Semin 8.00 20.00
32 David Savard 5.00 12.00
33 Harry Zolnierczyk 5.00 12.00
34 Anton Lander
35 Andy Miele 4.00 10.00
36 Anders Nilsson 5.00 12.00
37 Cody Almond 4.00 10.00
38 Dylan Olsen 5.00 12.00
39 Andrew Shaw 8.00 20.00
40 Brenden Dillon 6.00 15.00
41 Chris Vande Velde 5.00 12.00
42 Marcus Foligno 6.00 15.00
43 Cory Emmerton 5.00 12.00
44 Brendan Smith 6.00 15.00
45 Jimmy Hayes 6.00 15.00
46 Carl Hagelin 8.00 20.00
47 Carson McMillan 5.00 12.00
48 Matt Read 6.00 15.00
49 Harri Sateri 6.00 15.00
50 Brayden McNabb 8.00 20.00

2012-13 Certified Stars

STATED PRINT RUN 999 SER.#'d SETS
S1 Claude Giroux 1.50 4.00
S2 Evgeni Malkin 5.00 12.00
S3 Steven Stamkos 3.00 8.00
S4 Henrik Lundqvist 2.00 5.00
S5 Jonathan Quick 2.50 6.00
S6 Tyler Seguin 2.50 6.00
S7 Alex Ovechkin 6.00 15.00
S8 Jordan Eberle 1.50 4.00
S9 Jonathan Toews 3.00 8.00
S10 John Tavares 3.00 8.00
S11 Jarome Iginla 1.50 4.00
S12 Carey Price 5.00 12.00
S13 Sidney Crosby 6.00 15.00
S14 Rick Nash 1.50 4.00
S15 Ilya Kovalchuk 1.50 4.00
S16 Erik Karlsson 3.00 8.00
S17 Phil Kessel 2.00 5.00
S18 Henrik Sedin 1.50 4.00
S19 Joe Thornton 1.50 4.00
S20 Henrik Zetterberg 2.00 5.00

2012-13 Certified Stars Materials Mirror Red Jersey

STATED PRINT RUN 100 SER.#'d SETS
*BLUE/50: .6X TO 1.5X RED/100
*GOLD PATCH/25: 1.X TO 2.5X RED/100
S1 Claude Giroux 5.00 12.00
S2 Evgeni Malkin 15.00 40.00
S3 Steven Stamkos 10.00 25.00
S4 Henrik Lundqvist 6.00 15.00
S5 Jonathan Quick 8.00 20.00
S6 Tyler Seguin 8.00 20.00
S7 Alex Ovechkin 20.00 50.00
S8 Jordan Eberle 15.00 40.00
S9 Jonathan Toews 10.00 25.00
S10 John Tavares 10.00 25.00
S11 Jarome Iginla 6.00 15.00
S12 Carey Price 15.00 40.00
S13 Sidney Crosby 10.00 25.00
S14 Rick Nash 5.00 12.00
S15 Ilya Kovalchuk 5.00 12.00
S16 Erik Karlsson 10.00 25.00
S17 Phil Kessel 6.00 15.00
S18 Henrik Sedin 5.00 12.00
S19 Joe Thornton 5.00 12.00
S20 Henrik Zetterberg 6.00 15.00

1936 Champion Postcards

The set is in the same format as the 1936 Triumph set and was issued in the same manner as the Triumph set, except as an insert in "Boys" magazine published weekly in Great Britain. Three cards were issued in the first week of the promotion in "The Champion" and then one per week in "Boys" magazine. The cards are sepia toned and are postcard size, measuring approximately 3 1/2" by 5 1/2". The set is subtitled "Stars of the Ice Rinks". The cards are unnumbered and hence presented in alphabetical order. The date mentioned below is the issue date as noted on the card back in Canadian style, day/month/year.

COMPLETE SET (10) 875.00 1750.00
1 Marty Barry 40.00 80.00
Boston Bruins/18/1/36
2 Mush March 40.00 80.00
Chicago Blackhawks/8/2/36
3 Reg(Hooley) Smith 87.50 175.00
Montreal Canadiens/18/1/36
4 Sweeney Schriner/22/2/36 87.50 175.00
5 King Clancy 250.00 500.00
Toronto Maple Leafs/18/1/36
6 Bill Cook 100.00 200.00
New York Rangers/1/2/36
7 Pep Kelly 40.00 80.00
Toronto Maple Leafs/25/1/36
8 Aurel Joliat 225.00 450.00
Montreal Canadiens/15/2/36
9 Charles Conacher 200.00 400.00
Toronto Maple Leafs/29/2/36
10 Bun Cook 100.00 200.00
New York Rangers/7/3/36

1963-65 Chex Photos

The 1963-65 Chex Photos measure approximately 5" by 7". This unnumbered set depicts players from four NHL teams, Chicago Blackhawks, Detroit Red Wings, Toronto Maple Leafs, and Montreal Canadiens. These blank-backed, stiff-cardboard photos are thought to have been issued during the 1963-64 (Canadiens and Maple Leafs) and 1964-65 (Blackhawks, Red Wings, and Canadiens again) seasons. Since these photo cards are unnumbered, they are ordered and numbered below alphabetically according to the player's name. There is rumored to be a Denis DeJordy in this set. The complete set price below includes both varieties of Beliveau and Rousseau.

COMPLETE SET (60) 1000.00 2000.00
1 George Armstrong 20.00 40.00
2 Ralph Backstrom 10.00 20.00
3 Dave Balon 7.50 15.00
4 Bob Baun 12.50 25.00
5A Jean Beliveau 50.00 100.00
5B Jean Beliveau 50.00 100.00
6 Red Berenson 10.00 20.00
7 Toe Blake CO 15.00 30.00
8 Johnny Bower 25.00 50.00
9 Alex Delvecchio 20.00 40.00
10 Kent Douglas 7.50 15.00
11 Dick Duff 10.00 20.00
12 Phil Esposito 75.00 150.00
13 John Ferguson 12.50 25.00
14 Bill Gadsby 15.00 30.00
15 Jean Gauthier 7.50 15.00
16 BoomBoom Geoffrion 30.00 60.00
17 Glenn Hall 25.00 50.00
18 Terry Harper 10.00 20.00
19 Billy Harris 7.50 15.00
20 Bill Hay 7.50 15.00
21 Paul Henderson 20.00 40.00
22 Bill Hicke 7.50 15.00
23 Wayne Hillman 7.50 15.00
24 Charlie Hodge 12.50 25.00
25 Tim Horton 50.00 100.00
26 Gordie Howe 112.50 225.00
27 Bobby Hull 100.00 200.00
28 Punch Imlach CO 10.00 20.00
29 Red Kelly 20.00 40.00
30 Dave Keon 30.00 60.00
31 Jacques Laperriere 12.50 25.00
32 Ed Litzenberger 7.50 15.00
33 Parker MacDonald 7.50 15.00
34 Bruce MacGregor 7.50 15.00
35 Frank Mahovlich 30.00 60.00
36 Chico Maki 10.00 20.00
37 Pit Martin 10.00 20.00
38 John MacMillan 7.50 15.00
39 Stan Mikita 30.00 60.00
40 Bob Nevin 7.50 15.00
41 Pierre Pilote 12.50 25.00
42 Marcel Pronovost 15.00 30.00
43 Claude Provost 7.50 15.00
44 Bob Pulford 15.00 30.00
45 Marc Reaume 7.50 15.00
46 Henri Richard 30.00 60.00
47A Bobby Rousseau 10.00 20.00
47B Bob Rousseau 15.00 30.00
48 Eddie Shack 20.00 40.00
49 Don Simmons 10.00 20.00
50 Allan Stanley 15.00 30.00
51 Ron Stewart 7.50 15.00
52 Jean-Guy Talbot 10.00 20.00
53 Gilles Tremblay 7.50 15.00
54 J.C. Tremblay 10.00 20.00
55 Norm Ullman 20.00 40.00
56 Elmer Vasko 7.50 15.00
57 Ken Wharram 10.00 20.00
58 Gump Worsley 25.00 50.00

1992-93 Clark Candy Mario Lemieux

Issued by Clark Candy, this three-card set features three different color player photos of the Pittsburgh Penguins' Mario Lemieux. One card was inserted in each Bun candy bar pack. Each card measures approximately 3" by 3" and has a facsimile autograph in black inscribed across the picture. The pictures have black borders, and a gold stripe carrying the team logo cuts across the bottom of the card. The backs present biographical information, career summary, honors and awards, or career playing record. Only card number 3 listed below has a black-and-white close-up photo on its back. The cards are unnumbered and checklisted below in alphabetical order. There are reports that Lemieux may have signed some cards for insertion; to date, these rumors remain unsubstantiated.

COMPLETE SET (3) 2.50 6.00
COMMON CARD (1-3) 1.00 2.50

1995 Classic National

This 20-card multi-sport set was issued by Classic to commemorate the 16th National Sports Collectors Convention in St. Louis. The set included a certificate of limited edition, with the serial number out of 9,995 sets produced. One thousand Sprint 20-minute phone cards featuring Ki-Jana Carter and Nolan Ryan were also distributed.

COMPLETE SET (20) 8.00 20.00
NC15 Manon Rheaume .75 2.00

2012-13 Classics Signatures

1 Gordie Howe 2.00 5.00
2 Bobby Hull 1.00 2.50
3 Mike Bossy 1.00 2.50
4 Bill Barber .75 2.00
5 Dave Taylor .75 2.00
7 Gary Leeman .75 2.00
9 Bryan Trottier 1.25 3.00
10 Bobby Clarke 1.00 2.50
11 Marcel Dionne 1.25 3.00
12 Gilbert Perreault 1.00 2.50
13 Russ Courtnall .60 1.50
14 Eric Lindros 1.50 4.00
15 Clark Gillies 1.00 2.50
16 Reggie Leach .75 2.00
17 Charlie Simmer .60 1.50
19 Wendel Clark 1.00 2.50
20 John LeClair 1.00 2.50
22 Al Secord .75 2.00
23 Errol Thompson .60 1.50
25 Gordie Howe 2.00 5.00
26 Brian Mullen .60 1.50
27 Geoff Courtnall .60 1.50
28 Marian Stastny .60 1.50
31 Denis Savard 1.25 3.00
32 Darryl Sittler 1.00 2.50
35 Dale Hawerchuk 1.25 3.00
36 Cliff Ronning .60 1.50
37 Peter Stastny .75 2.00
38 Ron Francis 1.25 3.00
40 Steve Larmer .75 2.00
41 Lanny McDonald 1.00 2.50
43 Anders Hedberg .60 1.50
44 Paul MacLean .60 1.50
45 Trevor Linden 1.00 2.50
46 Anton Stastny .60 1.50
47 Kevin Dineen .60 1.50
48 Al Iafrate .75 2.00
49 Adam Foote .60 1.50
50 Johnny Bower 1.00 2.50
51 Stu Grimson .60 1.50
54 Valeri Bure .60 1.50
55 Richard Brodeur 1.00 2.50
57 Ray Ferraro .60 1.50
58 Bobby Hull 1.00 2.50
59 Nick Kypreos .60 1.50
60 Ron Hextall 1.00 2.50
61 Igor Larionov 1.00 2.50
62 Luc Robitaille 1.00 2.50
63 Tony Twist .60 1.50
64 Glenn Resch .75 2.00
65 Kirk Muller .75 2.00
66 Stan Mikita 1.25 3.00
67 Dave Schultz 1.00 2.50
68 Mario Lemieux 3.00 8.00
69 Brendan Shanahan 1.25 3.00
70 Joe Sakic 1.50 4.00
71 Steve Yzerman 2.00 5.00
73 Johnny Bucyk .75 2.00
74 Bernie Nicholls .75 2.00
75 Ed Belfour 1.00 2.50
76 Larry Robinson 1.00 2.50
77 Jim Craig 1.25 3.00
78 Rod Gilbert 1.00 2.50
79 Rick Tocchet .75 2.00
80 Kevin Weekes .75 2.00
81 Brian Leetch 1.00 2.50
82 Darren Pang .75 2.00
83 Marty McSorley .75 2.00
85 Craig Berube .60 1.50
86 Michel Goulet .75 2.00
87 Bruce Shoebottom .60 1.50
88 Bernie Federko .75 2.00
89 Andy Moog 1.00 2.50
90 Mark Messier 1.25 3.00
91 Neal Broten .75 2.00
92 Kris Draper .75 2.00
93 Doug Wilson .75 2.00
94 Reggie Lemelin 1.00 2.50
95 Jari Kurri 1.00 2.50
96 Darryl Sydor .60 1.50
97 Al MacInnis 1.00 2.50
98 Adam Graves .75 2.00
99 Denis Potvin 1.00 2.50
100 Guy Lafleur 1.25 3.00
101 Dave Tippett .60 1.50
102 Pat Verbeek .75 2.00
103 Guy Carbonneau 1.00 2.50
104 Tony Esposito 1.00 2.50
105 Dino Ciccarelli 1.00 2.50
106 John Vanbiesbrouck 1.00 2.50
107 Craig Patrick .60 1.50
108 Adam Oates 1.00 2.50
109 Phil Esposito 1.50 4.00
110 Brian Bellows .75 2.00
111 Dave Andreychuk 1.00 2.50
112 Serge Savard 1.00 2.50
113 Owen Nolan .75 2.00
114 Rick Middleton .75 2.00
115 Rod Brind'Amour .60 1.50
116 Curtis Joseph 1.00 2.50
118 Gerry Cheevers 1.00 2.50
119 Joe Mullen .75 2.00
120 Stephane Matteau .60 1.50
121 Craig Ramsay .75 2.00
122 Dirk Graham .60 1.50
123 Bill Clement .60 1.50
124 Jeff Hackett .75 2.00
125 Craig Hartsburg .60 1.50
126 Olaf Kolzig 1.00 2.50
127 Ken Morrow .75 2.00
128 Tim Kerr .75 2.00
130 Stu Barnes .60 1.50
131 Dennis Maruk .75 2.00
132 Grant Fuhr 1.00 2.50
133 Paul Coffey 1.00 2.50
134 Mike Richter 1.00 2.50
135 Billy Smith 1.00 2.50
136 Rod Langway .75 2.00
137 Pierre Pilote .75 2.00
138 Bob Baun .75 2.00
139 Sean Burke .60 1.50
140 Keith Primeau .75 2.00
141 Pierre Turgeon 1.00 2.50
142 Brad Park .75 2.00
144 Harry Howell .75 2.00
145 Ted Lindsay 1.00 2.50
146 Dave Babych .60 1.50
147 Dave Gagner .60 1.50
148 Bill Gadsby 1.00 2.50
149 Geoff Sanderson .60 1.50
151 Rich Sutter .60 1.50
152 Mike Gartner 1.00 2.50
154 Yvan Cournoyer 1.00 2.50
155 Duane Sutter .60 1.50
156 Milt Schmidt .75 2.00
157 Alex Delvecchio .75 2.00
158 Rogie Vachon 1.25 3.00
160 Andy Bathgate 1.00 2.50
161 Dan Cloutier .75 2.00
162 Ken Linseman .60 1.50
163 Jean Pronovost .60 1.50
164 Chris Chelios 1.00 2.50
165 John Ogrodnick .60 1.50
166 Mike Foligno .75 2.00
168 Bob Gainey 1.00 2.50
169 Dale Tallon .60 1.50
170 Orest Kindrachuk .60 1.50
171 Red Kelly .75 2.00
172 Pat Falloon .60 1.50
173 Dennis Hextall .60 1.50
175 Nick Fotiu .60 1.50
176 Guy Hebert .75 2.00
177 Mike Peca .60 1.50
179 Brent Sutter .60 1.50
180 Steve Shutt .75 2.00
181 Glenn Anderson 1.00 2.50
182 Darryl Sutter .60 1.50
183 Ron Sutter .60 1.50
184 Joe Juneau .60 1.50
185 Lou Fontinato .60 1.50
186 Terry O'Reilly .75 2.00
187 Mark Howe 1.00 2.50
188 Joe Nieuwendyk 1.00 2.50
189 Derian Hatcher .60 1.50
191 Bob Essensa 1.00 2.50
192 Norm Ullman 1.00 2.50
193 Rob Blake 1.00 2.50
194 Ulf Samuelsson 1.00 2.50
195 Kjell Samuelsson .60 1.50
196 Pat LaFontaine 1.00 2.50
198 Scott Mellanby .60 1.50
199 Ed Van Impe .60 1.50
200 Laurie Boschman .60 1.50

2012-13 Classics Signatures Autographs

ONE AUTO PER PACK
1 Gordie Howe SP 500.00 800.00
2 Bobby Hull SP 75.00 135.00
3 Mike Bossy SP 60.00 120.00
4 Bill Barber 6.00 15.00
5 Dave Taylor 6.00 15.00
7 Gary Leeman 6.00 15.00
9 Bryan Trottier SP 20.00 40.00
10 Bobby Clarke SP 40.00 80.00
11 Marcel Dionne 8.00 20.00
12 Gilbert Perreault 8.00 20.00
13 Russ Courtnall 6.00 15.00
14 Eric Lindros SP
15 Clark Gillies 6.00 15.00
16 Reggie Leach 6.00 15.00
17 Charlie Simmer 8.00 20.00
19 Wendel Clark 8.00 20.00
20 John LeClair 6.00 15.00
22 Al Secord 6.00 15.00
23 Errol Thompson 5.00 12.00
25 Gordie Howe SP
26 Brian Mullen 6.00 15.00
27 Geoff Courtnall 5.00 12.00
28 Marian Stastny 8.00 20.00
31 Denis Savard 6.00 15.00
32 Darryl Sittler SP 30.00 60.00
35 Dale Hawerchuk 10.00 25.00
36 Cliff Ronning 6.00 15.00
37 Peter Stastny SP 75.00 150.00
38 Ron Francis SP 75.00 150.00
40 Steve Larmer 6.00 15.00
41 Lanny McDonald SP 25.00 50.00
43 Anders Hedberg 6.00 15.00
44 Paul MacLean 6.00 15.00
45 Trevor Linden 10.00 25.00
46 Anton Stastny 8.00 20.00
47 Kevin Dineen 8.00 20.00
48 Al Iafrate 8.00 20.00
49 Adam Foote 6.00 15.00
50 Johnny Bower 8.00 20.00
51 Stu Grimson 5.00 12.00
54 Valeri Bure 5.00 12.00
55 Richard Brodeur 8.00 20.00
57 Ray Ferraro 6.00 15.00
58 Bobby Hull SP 40.00 80.00
59 Nick Kypreos 8.00 20.00
60 Ron Hextall SP 25.00 60.00
61 Igor Larionov SP 60.00 120.00
62 Luc Robitaille SP 30.00 60.00
63 Tony Twist 5.00 12.00
64 Glenn Resch 6.00 15.00
65 Kirk Muller 10.00 25.00
66 Stan Mikita SP 20.00 40.00
67 Dave Schultz 8.00 20.00
68 Mario Lemieux SP 200.00 350.00
69 Brendan Shanahan SP 125.00 200.00
70 Joe Sakic SP 60.00 120.00
71 Steve Yzerman SP 60.00 120.00
73 Johnny Bucyk SP 10.00 25.00
74 Bernie Nicholls 6.00 15.00
75 Ed Belfour SP 30.00 60.00
76 Larry Robinson 10.00 25.00
77 Jim Craig 8.00 20.00
78 Rod Gilbert SP 10.00 25.00
79 Rick Tocchet 6.00 15.00
80 Kevin Weekes 6.00 15.00
81 Brian Leetch SP 30.00 60.00
82 Darren Pang 6.00 15.00
83 Marty McSorley 6.00 15.00
85 Craig Berube 5.00 12.00
86 Michel Goulet 6.00 15.00
87 Bruce Shoebottom 6.00 15.00
88 Bernie Federko 6.00 15.00
89 Andy Moog 6.00 15.00
90 Mark Messier SP 100.00 200.00
91 Neal Broten 6.00 15.00
92 Kris Draper 5.00 12.00
93 Doug Wilson 6.00 15.00
94 Reggie Lemelin 8.00 20.00
95 Jari Kurri SP 15.00 30.00
96 Darryl Sydor 5.00 12.00
97 Al MacInnis SP 25.00 50.00
98 Adam Graves 6.00 15.00
99 Denis Potvin SP 20.00 50.00
100 Guy Lafleur SP 30.00 80.00
101 Dave Tippett 5.00 12.00
102 Pat Verbeek 6.00 15.00
103 Guy Carbonneau 6.00 15.00
104 Tony Esposito SP 40.00 80.00
106 John Vanbiesbrouck 6.00 15.00
107 Craig Patrick 5.00 12.00
108 Adam Oates 8.00 20.00
109 Phil Esposito SP
110 Brian Bellows 6.00 15.00
111 Dave Andreychuk 8.00 20.00
112 Serge Savard 12.00 30.00
113 Owen Nolan 6.00 15.00
114 Rick Middleton 8.00 20.00
115 Rod Brind'Amour 6.00 15.00
116 Curtis Joseph 15.00 40.00
118 Gerry Cheevers 8.00 20.00
119 Joe Mullen 6.00 15.00
120 Stephane Matteau 6.00 15.00
121 Craig Ramsay 5.00 12.00
122 Dirk Graham 5.00 12.00
123 Bill Clement 5.00 12.00
124 Jeff Hackett 6.00 15.00
125 Craig Hartsburg 5.00 12.00
126 Olaf Kolzig 6.00 15.00
127 Ken Morrow 6.00 15.00
128 Tim Kerr 6.00 15.00
130 Stu Barnes 5.00 12.00
131 Dennis Maruk 6.00 15.00
132 Grant Fuhr 20.00 50.00
133 Paul Coffey 30.00 80.00
134 Mike Richter 8.00 20.00
135 Billy Smith 8.00 20.00
136 Rod Langway 6.00 15.00
137 Pierre Pilote 8.00 20.00
138 Bob Baun 8.00 20.00
139 Sean Burke 5.00 12.00
140 Keith Primeau 10.00 25.00
141 Pierre Turgeon 8.00 20.00
142 Brad Park 8.00 20.00
144 Harry Howell 6.00 15.00
145 Ted Lindsay 8.00 20.00
146 Dave Babych 5.00 12.00
147 Dave Gagner 5.00 12.00
148 Bill Gadsby 8.00 20.00
149 Geoff Sanderson 6.00 15.00
151 Rich Sutter 5.00 12.00
152 Mike Gartner SP 75.00 150.00
154 Yvan Cournoyer SP 40.00 80.00
155 Duane Sutter 5.00 12.00
156 Milt Schmidt 6.00 15.00
157 Alex Delvecchio 8.00 20.00
158 Rogie Vachon 10.00 25.00
160 Andy Bathgate 8.00 20.00
161 Dan Cloutier 6.00 15.00
162 Ken Linseman 5.00 12.00
163 Jean Pronovost 6.00 15.00
164 Chris Chelios SP 2560.00 80.00
165 John Ogrodnick 5.00 12.00
166 Mike Foligno 6.00 15.00
168 Bob Gainey 10.00 25.00
169 Dale Tallon 5.00 12.00
170 Orest Kindrachuk 5.00 12.00
171 Red Kelly 10.00 25.00
173 Dennis Hextall 5.00 12.00
175 Nick Fotiu 5.00 12.00
176 Guy Hebert 6.00 15.00
177 Mike Peca 5.00 12.00
179 Brent Sutter 5.00 12.00
180 Steve Shutt 6.00 15.00
181 Glenn Anderson 50.00 100.00
182 Darryl Sutter 6.00 15.00
183 Ron Sutter 6.00 15.00
184 Joe Juneau 6.00 15.00
185 Lou Fontinato 6.00 15.00
186 Terry O'Reilly 8.00 20.00
187 Mark Howe SP 40.00 80.00
188 Joe Nieuwendyk SP 60.00 120.00
189 Derian Hatcher 6.00 15.00
191 Bob Essensa 6.00 15.00
192 Norm Ullman 8.00 20.00
193 Rob Blake 6.00 15.00
194 Ulf Samuelsson 6.00 15.00
195 Kjell Samuelsson 5.00 12.00
196 Pat LaFontaine 25.00 50.00
198 Scott Mellanby 5.00 12.00
199 Ed Van Impe 6.00 15.00
200 Laurie Boschman 6.00 15.00

2012-13 Classics Signatures Banner Numbers

ONE PER PACK
1 Lanny McDonald SP 3.00 8.00
2 Stan Mikita SP 4.00 10.00
3 Paul Coffey SP 3.00 8.00
4 Gordie Howe SP 6.00 15.00
5 Patrick Roy SP 8.00 20.00
6 Billy Smith SP 5.00 12.00
7 Mark Messier SP 4.00 10.00
8 Bernie Parent SP 3.00 8.00
9 Mario Lemieux SP 10.00 25.00
10 Bobby Hull SP 3.00 8.00
11 Ray Bourque 3.00 8.00
12 Johnny Bucyk 2.00 5.00
13 Phil Esposito 3.00 8.00
14 Cam Neely 5.00 12.00
15 Terry O'Reilly 1.50 4.00
16 Milt Schmidt 1.50 4.00
17 Pat LaFontaine 2.00 5.00
18 Rick Martin 2.00 5.00
19 Gilbert Perreault 3.00 8.00
20 Al MacInnis 2.00 5.00
21 Ron Francis 2.50 6.00
22 Tony Esposito 2.50 6.00
23 Bobby Hull 4.00 10.00
24 Denis Savard 2.50 6.00
25 Ray Bourque 4.00 10.00
26 Patrick Roy 5.00 12.00
27 Joe Sakic 3.00 8.00
28 Neal Broten 1.50 4.00
29 Alex Delvecchio 1.50 4.00
30 Gordie Howe 4.00 10.00
31 Steve Yzerman 6.00 15.00
32 Glenn Anderson 2.00 5.00
33 Grant Fuhr 2.00 5.00
34 Jari Kurri 2.50 6.00
35 Mark Messier 2.50 6.00
36 Marcel Dionne 2.50 6.00
37 Luc Robitaille 2.00 5.00
38 Dave Taylor 2.00 5.00
39 Rogie Vachon 3.00 8.00
40 Jean Beliveau 2.00 5.00
41 Yvan Cournoyer 2.00 5.00
42 Guy Lafleur 4.00 10.00
43 Henri Richard 2.00 5.00
44 Larry Robinson 2.00 5.00
45 Serge Savard 2.00 5.00
46 Scott Niedermayer 2.00 5.00
47 Mike Bossy 3.00 8.00
48 Clark Gillies 2.00 5.00
49 Denis Potvin 2.00 5.00
50 Bryan Trottier 2.00 5.00
51 Andy Bathgate 2.00 5.00
52 Ed Giacomin 2.00 5.00
53 Rod Gilbert 2.00 5.00
54 Adam Graves 1.50 4.00
55 Brian Leetch 2.50 6.00
56 Mike Richter 2.00 5.00
57 Bill Barber 1.50 4.00
58 Bobby Clarke 4.00 10.00
59 Mark Howe 2.00 5.00
60 Jeremy Roenick 2.00 5.00
61 Keith Tkachuk 2.00 5.00
62 Michel Goulet 1.50 4.00
63 Bernie Federko 1.50 4.00
64 Brett Hull 2.50 6.00

65 Al MacInnis 2.00 5.00
66 Trevor Linden 3.00 8.00
67 Markus Naslund 1.50 4.00
68 Mike Gartner 2.50 6.00
69 Dale Hunter 1.50 4.00
70 Dale Hawerchuk 2.50 6.00
71 Thomas Steen 1.25 3.00
72 Harry Howell 1.50 4.00
73 Ted Lindsay 2.50 6.00
74 Pierre Pilote 1.50 4.00
75 Marc Tardif 1.25 3.00

2012-13 Classics Signatures Classic Combos Dual Autographs

1 B.Hull/B.Hull/50 60.00 125.00
2 B.Clarke/R.Leach/100 60.00 120.00
3 B.Parent/B.Barber/100 30.00 60.00
5 P.Esposito/R.Bourque/50
8 Belfour/Roenick/50 50.00 100.00
9 Cheevers/M.Schmidt/100 30.00 60.00
10 G.Howe/M.Howe/25 60.00 125.00
12 D.Gilmour/W.Clark/100 25.00 60.00
13 E.Lindros/R.Hextall/50 60.00 120.00
17 B.Leetch/S.Matteau/100 20.00 40.00
18 D.Schultz/T.O'Reilly/100 25.00 60.00
20 M.Gartner/R.Langway/100 15.00 40.00
21 Vanbiesbrck/Mellanby/100 20.00 50.00
22 K.Samuels/U.Samuels/100 25.00 50.00
23 A.Moog/G.Fuhr/50 40.00 80.00
24 Hawerchuk/Babych/100 20.00 50.00
25 Bellows/Modano/100 25.00 60.00
27 R.Tocchet/T.Kerr/100 15.00 40.00
28 R.Sutter/R.Sutter/100 12.00 30.00

2012-13 Classics Signatures Classic Combos Triple Autographs

STATED PRINT RUN 25-50
EXCH EXPIRATION: 6/5/2014
2 Parent/Clarke/Schultz/50
4 Kurri/Robitaille/Dionne/50 50.00 100.00
6 Lafleur/Robinson/Cournoyer/50 60.00 100.00
7 Delvecchio/Howe/Kelly/25 125.00 200.00
8 Pang/Belfour/Esposito/25 100.00 200.00
9 Craig/Morrow/Broten/50 30.00 80.00
10 Andrsn/Fhr/Cffey/50 EXCH 15.00 40.00

2012-13 Classics Signatures Classic Lines Triple Autographs

STATED PRINT RUN 25 SER.#'d SETS
1 Trottier/Gillies/Bossy 60.00 120.00
2 Barber/Clarke/Leach 50.00 100.00
3 Simmer/Taylor/Dionne 60.00 120.00
8 Secord/Savard/Larmer 60.00 120.00
9 Sittler/Thompson/McDonald 30.00 80.00
12 Mullen/Hawerchuk/MacLean
14 Stastny/Stastny/Stastny 200.00 300.00

2012-13 Classics Signatures Inaugural INKS

STATED PRINT RUN 72-100
EXCH EXPIRATION: 6/5/2014
1 Gordie Howe/72 90.00 150.00
2 Bobby Hull/83 60.00 100.00
3 Mark Messier/100 40.00 80.00
4 Patrick Roy/100 50.00 120.00
5 Joe Nieuwendyk/100 15.00 40.00
6 Johnny Bower/76 25.00 50.00
7 Doug Gilmour/100 15.00 40.00
8 Jari Kurri/100 15.00 40.00
9 Adam Oates/100 12.00 30.00
10 Mario Lemieux/97 50.00 100.00
11 Gerry Cheevers/84 15.00 40.00
12 Brett Hull/100 30.00 60.00
13 Denis Potvin/91 15.00 40.00
14 Guy Lafleur/88 20.00 50.00
15 Ed Belfour/100 25.00 50.00
16 Tony Esposito/88 30.00 60.00
17 Bobby Clarke/87 25.00 60.00
18 Phil Esposito/84 EXCH 30.00 60.00
19 Dale Hawerchuk/100 15.00 40.00
20 Bernie Parent/84 25.00 60.00

2012-13 Classics Signatures Notable Nicknames

STATED PRINT RUN 50 SER.#'d SETS
1 Al Iafrate 15.00 40.00
2 Bobby Hull 50.00 100.00
3 Johnny Bower
4 Stu Grimson 10.00 25.00
5 Eddie Shack 15.00 30.00
8 Richard Brodeur 20.00 40.00
10 Ray Ferraro 10.00 25.00
11 Ron Francis 20.00 50.00
12 Gordie Howe 90.00 150.00
13 Ron Hextall 30.00 60.00
14 Igor Larionov 25.00 50.00
15 Luc Robitaille 20.00 40.00
16 Tony Twist 20.00 40.00
17 Glenn Resch
19 Stan Mikita 25.00 50.00
20 Dave Schultz 15.00 40.00
21 Mario Lemieux 100.00 175.00
22 Brendan Shanahan 30.00 60.00
23 Joe Sakic 30.00 60.00
24 Steve Yzerman 75.00 150.00
25 Reggie Leach 12.00 30.00
26 Johnny Bucyk 12.00 30.00
27 John Vanbiesbrouck 40.00 80.00
28 Ed Belfour 40.00 80.00

2012-13 Classics Signatures Social Signatures

ONE AUTO PER PACK OVERALL
EXCH EXPIRATION: 6/5/2014
SSBN Bernie Nicholls 6.00 15.00
SSBP Bernie Parent SP 30.00 60.00
SSBS Brendan Shanahan SP 30.00 60.00
SSDG Doug Gilmour SP 15.00 40.00
SSKH Kelly Hrudey EXCH 6.00 15.00
SSKW Kevin Weekes 6.00 15.00
SSMB Mike Bossy SP 25.00 50.00
SSMM Mike Modano SP 40.00 80.00
SSNK Nick Kypreos 6.00 15.00
SSRG Rod Gilbert 8.00 20.00
SSRT Rick Tocchet 5.00 12.00
SSTL Trevor Linden 15.00 40.00
SSVB Valeri Bure 5.00 12.00
SSFOX Jim Fox 6.00 15.00
SSJIM Jim Craig 10.00 25.00
SSPAN Darren Pang 6.00 15.00
SSREA Daryl Reaugh 6.00 15.00

2012-13 Classics Signatures The Expansion

STATED PRINT RUN 25-100
1 Gilbert Perreault/50 25.00 50.00
2 Craig Ramsay/100 8.00 20.00
5 Pat LaFontaine/50 20.00 40.00
6 Bobby Clarke/50 30.00 60.00
7 Bernie Parent/50 20.00 50.00
8 Reggie Leach/50 15.00 40.00
9 Bill Barber/50 15.00 40.00
10 Eric Lindros/50 30.00 60.00
11 Dave Taylor/50 15.00 40.00
12 Marcel Dionne/50 20.00 50.00
13 Charlie Simmer/50 12.00 30.00
14 Rogie Vachon/50 15.00 30.00
15 Luc Robitaille/50 15.00 40.00
16 Neal Broten/50 12.00 30.00
17 Brian Bellows/50 12.00 30.00
18 Dino Ciccarelli/50 12.00 30.00
19 Craig Hartsburg/50 10.00 25.00
20 Mike Modano/50 25.00 50.00
22 Orest Kindrachuk/100 8.00 20.00
23 Jean Pronovost/100 15.00 40.00
24 Ron Francis/50 30.00 60.00
25 Mario Lemieux/25 75.00 150.00
26 Dennis Maruk/100 10.00 25.00
27 Craig Patrick/100 8.00 20.00
28 Gary Simmons/100 12.00 30.00
29 Dennis Hextall/100 12.00 30.00
30 Bob Baun/100 15.00 40.00

2012-13 Classics Signatures The Originals

EXCH EXPIRATION: 6/5/2014
1 Jean Beliveau/50 EXCH 50.00 100.00
2 Larry Robinson/50 20.00 50.00
3 Guy Lafleur/50 30.00 60.00
4 Serge Savard/50 15.00 40.00
6 Yvan Cournoyer/50
7 Bob Gainey/50 15.00 40.00
8 Guy Carbonneau/100 12.00 30.00
9 Patrick Roy/25 100.00 200.00
11 Johnny Bower/100 25.00 50.00
13 Darryl Sittler/50 40.00 80.00
17 Doug Gilmour/50 25.00 50.00
18 Wendel Clark/50
19 Milt Schmidt/100 12.00 30.00
20 Bruce Shoebottom/100 6.00 15.00
21 Johnny Bucyk/50 15.00 40.00
22 Cam Neely/50 25.00 50.00
23 Gerry Cheevers/100 15.00 40.00
24 Adam Oates/50 15.00 40.00
25 Rick Middleton/50
26 Phil Esposito/25 EXCH
27 Ray Bourque/25 50.00 100.00
28 Stan Mikita/25
29 Tony Esposito/25
30 Pierre Pilote/100 10.00 25.00
31 Bill Gadsby/100 12.00 30.00
33 Denis Savard/50 20.00 50.00
34 Dirk Graham/100 12.00 30.00
35 Darryl Sutter/100 10.00 25.00
36 Chris Chelios/100 25.00 50.00
38 Lou Fontinato/100 12.00 30.00
39 Harry Howell/100 10.00 25.00
40 Andy Bathgate/100 12.00 30.00
41 Phil Esposito/25
42 Adam Graves/50 20.00 50.00
43 Brian Leetch/50 25.00 50.00
44 Mark Messier/25 30.00 60.00
45 Gordie Howe/25
46 Ted Lindsay/50 20.00 40.00
47 Red Kelly/100 20.00 40.00
48 Norm Ullman/50 20.00 40.00
49 Igor Larionov/50 25.00 50.00
50 Steve Yzerman/25

1972-73 Cleveland Crusaders WHA

This 15-card set measures 8 1/2" x 11" and features a black and white head shot on the front along with a facsimile autograph, and a Cleveland Crusaders color logo in the lower left corner. Featured portraits were done by Charles Linnett. The cards are unnumbered and checklisted below in alphabetical order.

COMPLETE SET (15) 25.00 50.00
1 Ron Buchanan 2.00 4.00
2 Ray Clearwater 2.00 4.00
3 Bob Dillabough 2.00 4.00
4 Grant Erickson 2.00 4.00
5 Ted Hodgson 2.00 4.00
6 Ralph Hopiavouri 2.00 4.00
7 Bill Horton 2.00 4.00
8 Gary Jarrett 2.00 4.00
9 Skip Krake 2.00 4.00
10 Wayne Muloin 2.00 4.00
11 Bill Needham CO 2.00 4.00
12 Rick Pumple 2.50 5.00
13 Paul Shmyr 2.00 4.00
14 Robert Whidden 2.00 4.00
15 Jim Wiste 2.50 5.00

1964-65 Coca-Cola Caps

The 1964-65 Coca-Cola Caps set contains 108 bottle caps measuring approximately 1 1/8" in diameter. The caps feature a black and white picture on the tops, and are unnumbered except for uniform numbers (which is listed to the right of the player's name in the checklist below). These caps were issued with both Coke and Sprite. Because Sprite was sold in lesser quantities than Coke, those caps tend to be harder to find. As such, some dealers charge a slight premium for those caps. There are also rumored to be French variations for both the Coke and the Sprite caps, making a total of four possible ways to put the set together. While no transactions have been reported for these French versions, it's fair to assume that their scarcity alone might earn them a slight premium over the prices listed below. The set numbering below is by teams and numerically within teams as follows: Boston Bruins (1-18), Chicago Blackhawks (19-36), Detroit Red Wings (37-54), Montreal Canadiens (55-72, New York Rangers (73-90), and Toronto Maple Leafs (91-108). A plastic holder (in the shape of a rink) was also available for holding and displaying the caps; the holder is not included in the complete set price below.

COMPLETE SET (108) 375.00 750.00
1 Ed Johnston 1 2.50 5.00
2 Bob McCord 4 1.50 3.00
3 Ted Green 6 2.00 4.00
4 Orland Kurtenbach 7 2.00 4.00
5 Gary Dornhoefer 8 2.00 4.00
6 Johnny Bucyk 9 5.00 10.00
7 Tom Johnson 10 2.00 4.00
8 Tom Williams 11 1.50 3.00
9 Murray Balfour 12 1.50 3.00
10 Forbes Kennedy 14 1.50 3.00
11 Murray Oliver 16 1.50 3.00
12 Dean Prentice 17 2.00 4.00
13 Ed Westfall 18 2.00 4.00
14 Reg Fleming 19 1.50 3.00
15 Leo Boivin 20 2.00 4.00
16 Ab McDonald 21 1.50 3.00
17 Ron Schock 23 1.50 3.00
18 Bob Leiter 24 1.50 3.00
19 Glenn Hall 1 6.00 12.00
20 Doug Mohns 2 2.00 4.00
21 Pierre Pilote 3 2.50 5.00
22 Elmer Vasko 4 1.50 3.00
23 Fred Stanfield 6 1.50 3.00
24 Phil Esposito 7 20.00 40.00
25 Bobby Hull 9 25.00 50.00
26 Bill Hay 11 1.25 2.50
27 John Brenneman 12 1.25 2.50
28 Doug Robinson 14 1.50 3.00
29 Eric Nesterenko 15 2.00 4.00
30 Chico Maki 16 2.00 4.00
31 Ken Wharram 17 1.50 3.00
32 John McKenzie 18 1.50 3.00
33 Al MacNeil 19 1.50 3.00
34 Wayne Hillman 20 1.50 3.00
35 Stan Mikita 21 7.50 15.00
36 Denis DeJordy 30 2.00 4.00
37 Roger Crozier 1 2.50 5.00
38 Albert Langlois 2 1.50 3.00
39 Marcel Pronovost 3 2.00 4.00
40 Bill Gadsby 4 2.00 4.00
41 Doug Barkley 5 1.50 3.00
42 Norm Ullman 7 4.00 8.00
43 Pit Martin 8 2.00 4.00
44 Gordie Howe 9 30.00 60.00
45A Gordie Howe 10 40.00 80.00
45B Alex Delvecchio 10 15.00 30.00
46 Ron Murphy 12 1.50 3.00
47 Larry Jeffrey 14 1.50 3.00
48 Ted Lindsay 15 5.00 10.00
49 Bruce MacGregor 16 1.50 3.00
50 Floyd Smith 17 1.50 3.00
51 Gary Bergman 18 1.50 3.00
52 Paul Henderson 19 3.00 6.00
53 Parker MacDonald 20 1.50 3.00
54 Eddie Joyal 21 1.50 3.00
55 Charlie Hodge 1 2.00 4.00
56 Jacques Laperriere 2 2.00 4.00
57 J.C. Tremblay 3 2.00 4.00
58 Jean Beliveau 4 10.00 20.00
59 Ralph Backstrom 6 2.00 4.00
60 Bill Hicke 8 1.50 3.00
61 Ted Harris 10 1.50 3.00
62 Claude Larose 11 1.50 3.00
63 Yvan Cournoyer 12 7.50 15.00
64 Claude Provost 14 1.50 3.00
65 Bobby Rousseau 15 2.00 4.00
66 Henri Richard 16 6.00 12.00
67 Jean-Guy Talbot 17 2.00 4.00
68 Terry Harper 19 2.00 4.00
69 Dave Balon 20 1.50 3.00
70 Gilles Tremblay 21 1.50 3.00
71 John Ferguson 22 2.50 5.00
72 Jim Roberts 26 1.50 3.00
73 Jacques Plante 1 10.00 20.00
74 Harry Howell 3 2.00 4.00
75 Arnie Brown 4 1.50 3.00
76 Don Johns 6 1.50 3.00
77 Rod Gilbert 7 4.00 8.00
78 Bob Nevin 8 1.50 3.00
79 Dick Duff 9 2.00 4.00
80 Earl Ingarfield 10 1.50 3.00
81 Vic Hadfield 11 2.00 4.00
82 Jim Mikol 12 1.50 3.00
83 Val Fonteyne 14 1.50 3.00
84 Jim Neilson 15 1.50 3.00
85 Rod Seiling 16 1.50 3.00
86 Lou Angotti 17 1.50 3.00
87 Phil Goyette 20 1.50 3.00
88 Camille Henry 21 2.00 4.00
89 Don Marshall 22 2.00 4.00
90 Marcel Paille 23 2.00 4.00
91 Johnny Bower 1 5.00 10.00
92 Carl Brewer 2 2.00 4.00
93 Red Kelly 4 5.00 10.00
94 Tim Horton 7 7.50 15.00
95 George Armstrong 9 4.00 8.00
96 Andy Bathgate 10 4.00 8.00
97 Ron Ellis 11 2.00 4.00
98 Ralph Stewart 12 1.50 3.00
99 Dave Keon 14 4.00 8.00
100 Dickie Moore 16 2.50 5.00
101 Don McKenney 17 1.50 3.00
102 Kent Douglas 19 1.50 3.00
103 Bob Pulford 20 2.50 5.00
104 Bob Baun 21 2.50 5.00
105 Eddie Shack 23 4.00 8.00
106 Terry Sawchuk 24 10.00 20.00
107 Allan Stanley 26 2.50 5.00
108 Frank Mahovlich 6.00 12.00
xx Cap Holder 50.00 100.00
(Plastic Rink

1965-66 Coca-Cola

This set contains 108 unnumbered black and white cards featuring 18 players from each of the six NHL teams. The cards were issued in perforated team panels of 18 cards. The cards are priced below as perforated cards; the value of unperforated strips is approximately 20-30 percent more than the sum of the individual prices. The cards are approximately 2 3/4" by 3 1/2" and have bi-lingual (French and English) write-ups on the card backs. An album to hold the cards was available from the company on a mail-order basis. It retails in the $50-$75 range in Near Mint. The set numbering below is by teams and numerically within teams as follows: Boston Bruins (1-18), Chicago Blackhawks (19-36), Detroit Red Wings (37-54), Montreal Canadiens (55-72, New York Rangers (73-90), and Toronto Maple Leafs (91-108).

COMPLETE SET (108) 250.00 500.00
1 Gerry Cheevers 15.00 30.00
2 Albert Langlois .75 1.50
3 Ted Green 1.00 2.00
4 Ron Stewart .75 1.50
5 Bob Woytowich .75 1.50
6 Johnny Bucyk 3.00 6.00
7 Tom Williams .75 1.50
8 Forbes Kennedy .75 1.50
9 Murray Oliver .75 1.50
10 Dean Prentice 1.00 2.00
11 Ed Westfall 1.00 2.00
12 Reg Fleming .75 1.50
13 Leo Boivin 1.50 3.00
14 Parker MacDonald .75 1.50
15 Bob Dillabough .75 1.50
16 Barry Ashbee 2.50 5.00
17 Don Awrey .75 1.50
18 Bernie Parent 15.00 30.00
19 Glenn Hall 5.00 10.00
20 Doug Mohns 1.00 2.00
21 Pierre Pilote 1.50 3.00
22 Elmer Vasko .75 1.50
23 Matt Ravlich .75 1.50
24 Fred Stanfield .75 1.50
25 Phil Esposito 20.00 40.00
26 Bobby Hull 20.00 40.00
27 Dennis Hull 2.50 5.00
28 Bill Hay 1.00 2.00
29 Ken Hodge 1.50 3.00
30 Eric Nesterenko 1.00 2.00
31 Chico Maki 1.00 2.00
32 Ken Wharram 1.00 2.00
33 Al MacNeil .75 1.50
34 Doug Jarrett .75 1.50
35 Stan Mikita 6.00 12.00
36 Dave Dryden 1.25 2.50
37 Roger Crozier 1.50 3.00
38 Warren Godfrey .75 1.50
39 Bert Marshall .75 1.50
40 Bill Gadsby 1.50 3.00
41 Doug Barkley .75 1.50
42 Norm Ullman 2.00 4.00
43 Gordie Howe 30.00 60.00
44 Alex Delvecchio 2.50 5.00
45 Val Fonteyne .75 1.50
46 Ron Murphy .75 1.50
47 Billy Harris .75 1.50
48 Bruce MacGregor .75 1.50
49 Floyd Smith .75 1.50
50 Paul Henderson 4.00 8.00
51 Andy Bathgate 1.75 3.50
52 Ab McDonald .75 1.50
53 Gary Bergman .75 1.50
54 Hank Bassen 1.25 2.50
55 Charlie Hodge 1.50 3.00
56 Jacques Laperriere 1.50 3.00
57 Jean-Claude Tremblay 1.00 2.00
58 Jean Beliveau 7.50 15.00
59 Ralph Backstrom 1.00 2.00
60 Dick Duff 1.25 2.50
61 Ted Harris 1.00 2.00
62 Claude Larose .75 1.50
63 Yvan Cournoyer 10.00 20.00
64 Claude Provost 1.00 2.00
65 Bobby Rousseau 1.00 2.00
66 Henri Richard 5.00 10.00
67 Jean-Guy Talbot 1.25 2.50
68 Terry Harper 1.00 2.00
69 Gilles Tremblay .75 1.50
70 John Ferguson 1.25 2.50
71 Jim Roberts 1.00 2.00
72 Gump Worsley 5.00 10.00
73 Ed Giacomin 12.50 25.00
74 Wayne Hillman .75 1.50
75 Harry Howell 2.00 4.00
76 Arnie Brown .75 1.50
77 Doug Robinson .75 1.50
78 Mike McMahon .75 1.50
79 Rod Gilbert 2.50 5.00
80 Bob Nevin .75 1.50
81 Earl Ingarfield .75 1.50
82 Vic Hadfield 1.25 2.50
83 Bill Hicke .75 1.50
84 John McKenzie 1.00 2.00
85 Jim Neilson .75 1.50
86 Jean Ratelle 2.50 5.00
87 Phil Goyette .75 1.50
88 Garry Peters .75 1.50
89 Don Marshall .75 1.50
90 Don Simmons 1.25 2.50
91 Johnny Bower 5.00 10.00
92 Marcel Pronovost 2.00 4.00
93 Red Kelly 2.50 5.00
94 Tim Horton 7.50 15.00
95 Ron Ellis 1.00 2.00
96 George Armstrong 2.00 4.00
97 Brit Selby .75 1.50
98 Pete Stemkowski .75 1.50
99 Dave Keon 5.00 10.00
100 Mike Walton 1.00 2.00
101 Kent Douglas .75 1.50
102 Bob Pulford 2.00 4.00
103 Bob Baun 2.00 4.00
104 Eddie Shack 2.50 5.00
105 Orland Kurtenbach 1.00 2.00
106 Allan Stanley 1.50 3.00
107 Frank Mahovlich 5.00 10.00
108 Terry Sawchuk 10.00 20.00
NNO Album 40.00 80.00

1965-66 Coca-Cola Booklets

These four "How To Play" booklets are illustrated with cartoon-like drawings, each measure approximately 4 7/8" by 3 1/2", and are printed on newsprint. Booklets A and B have yellow covers, while booklets C and D have blue covers. The 31-page booklets could be obtained through a mail-in offer. Under bottle caps of Coke or Sprite (marked with a hockey stick) were cork liners bearing the name of the player who wrote a booklet. To receive a booklet, the collector had to send in ten cork liners (with name of the player whose booklet was desired), ten cents, and the correct answer to a trivia question. Issued by Coca-Cola to promote hockey among the school-aged, they are designed in comic book fashion showing correct positions and moves for goalie, forward (both defensive and offensive), and defenseman. They are authored by the hockey players listed below. They are lettered rather than numbered and we have checklisted them below accordingly. The booklets were available in both English and French.

COMPLETE SET (4) 75.00 150.00
A Johnny Bower 25.00 50.00
How To Play
Goal
B Dave Keon 25.00 50.00
How To Play
Forward/Defense
C Jacques Laperriere 12.50 25.00
How to Play
Defense
D Henri Richard 25.00 50.00
How To Play
Forward/Offense

1977-78 Coca-Cola

Each of these mini-cards measures approximately 1 3/8" by 1 3/8". The fronts feature a color "mug shot" of the player, with his name given above the picture. Red and blue lines form the borders on the sides of the picture. The year 1978, the city from which the team hails, and the Coke logo appear below the picture. Inside a black border (with rounded corners) the back has basic biographical information. These unnumbered cards are listed alphabetically below.

COMPLETE SET (30) 62.50 300.00
1 Syl Apps .75 3.00
2 Dave Burrows .75 3.00
3 Bobby Clarke 6.00 25.00
4 Yvan Cournoyer 2.50 10.00
5 John Davidson 1.50 10.00
6 Marcel Dionne 4.00 15.00
7 Doug Favell 1.25 5.00
8 Rod Gilbert 1.50 10.00
9 Brian Glennie .75 3.00
10 Butch Goring .75 3.00
11 Lorne Henning .75 3.00
12 Cliff Koroll .75 3.00
13 Guy Lapointe 1.50 5.00
14 Dave Maloney .75 3.00
15 Pit Martin .75 3.00
16 Lou Nanne .75 3.00
17 Bobby Orr 30.00 125.00
18 Brad Park 2.50 10.00
19 Craig Ramsay .75 3.00
20 Larry Robinson 5.00 20.00
21 Jim Rutherford 1.25 5.00
22 Don Saleski .75 3.00
23 Steve Shutt 2.50 8.00
24 Darryl Sittler 4.00 20.00
25 Billy Smith 3.00 10.00
26 Bob Stewart .75 3.00
27 Rogatien Vachon 2.50 10.00
28 Jimmy Watson .75 3.00
29 Joe Watson .75 3.00
30 Ed Westfall .75 3.00

1994 Coca-Cola Wayne Gretzky Cups

Standing approximately 6" high, these full color cups featuring an image of Wayne along with a biographical fact from the appropriate year. Set may be incomplete and we welcome any additional information you may have.

COMPLETE SET (5) 8.00 20.00
COMMON CUP 1.50 4.00

1994 Coke/Mac's Milk Gretzky POGs

This 18-disc set features POGs measuring approximately 1 5/8" in diameter. These cards were offered through Mac's Milk stores in Canada (primarily Ontario); they were available at the store counter with the purchase of any Coke bottled product from May through middle of June of 1994. Inside a gold-foil holographic border, the fronts feature action color player photos with the words "The Great One" printed in black letters above the photo and a Coca-Cola Future Stars emblem at the bottom. The backs feature Gretzky's most prolific records and accomplishments.

COMPLETE SET (18) 6.00 15.00
COMMON POG (1-18) .40 1.00

1970-71 Colgate Stamps

The 1970-71 Colgate Stamps set includes 93 small color stamps measuring approximately 1" by 1 1/4". The set was distributed in three sheets of 31. Sheet one featured centers (numbered 1-31) and was available with the giant size of toothpaste, sheet two featured wings (numbered 32-62) and was available with the family size of toothpaste, and sheet three featured goalies and defensemen (numbered 63-93) and was available with king and super size toothpaste. The cards are priced below as individual stamps; the value of a complete sheet would be approximately 20 percent more than the sum of the individual stamp prices. Colgate also issued three calendars so that brushers could stick a stamp on each day for brushing regularly. These calendars retail in the $5-$10 range. The cards were numbered in a star in the upper left corner of the card face.

COMPLETE SET (93) 100.00 200.00
1 Walt McKechnie .50 1.00
2 Bob Pulford 1.50 3.00
3 Mike Walton .50 1.00
4 Alex Delvecchio 2.50 5.00
5 Tom Williams .50 1.00
6 Derek Sanderson 5.00 10.00
7 Garry Unger 1.00 2.00
8 Lou Angotti .50 1.00
9 Ted Hampson .50 1.00
10 Phil Goyette .50 1.00
11 Juha Widing .50 1.00
12 Norm Ullman 2.00 4.00
13 Garry Monahan .50 1.00
14 Henri Richard 2.50 5.00
15 Ray Cullen .50 1.00
16 Danny O'Shea .50 1.00
17 Marc Tardif .75 1.50
18 Jude Drouin .50 1.00
19 Charlie Burns .50 1.00
20 Gerry Meehan .75 1.50
21 Ralph Backstrom .75 1.50
22 Frank St.Marseille .50 1.00
23 Orland Kurtenbach .50 1.00
24 Red Berenson 1.00 2.00
25 Jean Ratelle 2.00 4.00
26 Syl Apps .75 1.50
27 Don Marshall .50 1.00
28 Gilbert Perreault 5.00 10.00
29 Andre Lacroix .75 1.50
30 Jacques Lemaire 1.50 3.00
31 Pit Martin .75 1.50
32 Dennis Hull .75 1.50
33 Dave Balon .50 1.00
34 Keith McCreary .50 1.00
35 Bobby Rousseau .75 1.50
36 Danny Grant .75 1.50
37 Brit Selby .50 1.00
38 Bob Nevin .50 1.00
39 Rosaire Paiement .50 1.00
40 Gary Dornhoefer 1.00 2.00
41 Eddie Shack 2.00 4.00
42 Ron Schock .50 1.00
43 Jim Pappin .50 1.00
44 Mickey Redmond 1.50 3.00
45 Vic Hadfield .75 1.50
46 Johnny Bucyk 2.00 4.00
47 Gordie Howe 12.00 30.00
48 Ron Anderson .50 1.00
49 Gary Jarrett .50 1.00
50 Jean Pronovost .75 1.50
51 Simon Nolet .50 1.00
52 Bill Goldsworthy .75 1.50
53 Rod Gilbert 2.00 4.00
54 Ron Ellis .75 1.50
55 Mike Byers .50 1.00
56 Norm Ferguson .50 1.00
57 Gary Sabourin .50 1.00
58 Tim Ecclestone .50 1.00
59 John McKenzie .50 1.00
60 Yvan Cournoyer 2.00 4.00
61 Ken Schinkel .50 1.00
62 Ken Hodge 1.00 2.00
63 Cesare Maniago 1.50 3.00
64 J.C. Tremblay .75 1.50
65 Gilles Marotte .50 1.00
66 Bob Baun 1.00 2.00
67 Gerry Desjardins 1.00 2.00
68 Charlie Hodge 1.50 3.00
69 Matt Ravlich .50 1.00
70 Ed Giacomin 3.00 6.00
71 Gerry Cheevers 4.00 8.00
72 Pat Quinn .75 1.50
73 Gary Bergman .50 1.00
74 Serge Savard 1.00 2.00
75 Les Binkley 1.00 2.00
76 Arnie Brown .50 1.00
77 Pat Stapleton .50 1.00
78 Ed Van Impe .50 1.00
79 Jim Dorey .50 1.00
80 Dave Dryden 1.50 3.00
81 Dale Tallon .75 1.50
82 Bruce Gamble 1.50 3.00
83 Roger Crozier 1.50 3.00
84 Denis DeJordy 1.50 3.00
85 Rogatien Vachon 2.00 4.00
86 Carol Vadnais .50 1.00
87 Bobby Orr 20.00 50.00
88 Noel Picard .50 1.00
89 Gilles Villemure 1.50 3.00
90 Gary Smith 1.50 3.00
91 Doug Favell 1.50 3.00
92 Ernie Wakely 1.50 3.00
93 Bernie Parent 5.00 10.00
NNO Stamp Calendar Sheet 5.00 10.00

1971-72 Colgate Heads

The 16 hockey collectibles in this set measure approximately 1 1/4" in height with a base of 7/8" and are made out of cream-colored or beige plastic. The promotion lasted approximately five months during the winter of 1972. The busts were issued in series of four in the various sizes of Colgate Toothpaste. The player's last name is found only on the back of the base of the head. The Ullmann error is not included in the complete set price below. The heads are unnumbered and checklisted below in alphabetical order.

COMPLETE SET (16) 100.00 200.00
1 Yvon Cournoyer 3.00 8.00
2 Marcel Dionne UER 6.00 15.00
3 Ken Dryden 8.00 20.00
4 Paul Henderson 2.50 6.00
5 Guy Lafleur 8.00 20.00
6 Frank Mahovlich 4.00 10.00
7 Richard Martin SP 15.00 30.00
8 Bobby Orr 20.00 40.00
9 Brad Park SP 20.00 40.00
10 Jacques Plante 6.00 15.00
11 Jean Ratelle 3.00 8.00
12 Derek Sanderson 6.00 15.00
13 Dale Tallon 2.00 5.00
14 Walt Tkaczuk 2.00 4.00
15A Norm Ullman ERR 5.00 12.00
(incorrectly spelled Ullmann
15B Norm Ullman COR 12.00 30.00
Spelled Ullman
16 Garry Unger 2.00 5.00

1995-96 Collector's Choice

This 396 card standard-size set was issued in 12-card packs with a suggested retail price of 99 cents per pack. The design is similar to the 1995 Collector Choice issues in baseball, basketball and football. Each card features a photo framed by white borders. The player's name and team is identified in the lower right-hand corner. The backs contain another photograph, biographical information and statistics. The last 70 cards of the set are dedicated to the following subsets: 1995 European Junior Championship (325-354), What's Your Game? (355-369), and Hardware Heroes (370-394). Rookie Cards in this set include Teemu Riihijarvi and Marcus Nilsson. In addition, a 15-card set was available only to collectors who redeemed through the mail a Young Guns Trade card, which was inserted at a rate of 1:34 packs. The cards were intended to "complete" the Collector's Choice set by including several of the top rookies of 1995-96, and thus bear the same design and continue the numbering from that set.

1 Wayne Gretzky .50 1.25
2 Darius Kasparaitis .05 .15
3 Scott Niedermayer .10 .25
4 Brendan Shanahan .12 .30
5 Doug Gilmour .12 .30
6 Lyle Odelein .05 .15
7 Dave Gagner .05 .15
8 Gary Suter .07 .20
9 Sandis Ozolinsh .07 .20
10 Sergei Zubov .07 .20
11 Don Beaupre .07 .20
12 Bill Lindsay .05 .15
13 David Oliver .05 .15
14 Bob Corkum .05 .15
15 German Titov .07 .20
16 Jari Kurri .10 .25
17 Cliff Ronning .05 .15
18 Paul Coffey .10 .25
19 Ian Laperriere .05 .15
20 Dave Andreychuk .10 .25
21 Andrei Nikolishin .05 .15
22 Blaine Lacher .07 .20
23 Yuri Khmylev .05 .15
24 Darren Turcotte .05 .15
25 Joe Mullen .07 .20
26 Peter Forsberg .25 .60
27 Paul Ysebaert .05 .15
28 Tommy Soderstrom .07 .20
29 Rod Brind'Amour .10 .25
30 Jim Carey .07 .20
31 Geoff Courtnall .05 .15
32 Slava Kozlov .07 .20
33 Ray Ferraro .05 .15
34 John MacLean .07 .20
35 Benoit Brunet .05 .15
36 Trent Klatt .05 .15
37 Chris Chelios .10 .25
38 Tom Pederson .10 .25
39 Pat Elynuik .07 .20
40 Rob Niedermayer .07 .20
41 Jason Arnott .07 .20
42 Patrik Carnback .05 .15
43 Steve Chiasson .05 .15
44 Marty McSorley .05 .15
45 Pavel Bure .12 .30
46 Glenn Anderson .10 .25
47 Doug Brown .05 .15
48 Mike Ridley .05 .15
49 Alexei Zhamnov .10 .25
50 Mariusz Czerkawski .05 .15
51 Derek Plante .05 .15
52 Andrew Cassels .05 .15
53 Tom Barrasso .07 .20
54 Andrei Kovalenko .05 .15
55 Pat Verbeek .07 .20
56 Alexander Semak .05 .15
57 Eric Lindros .15 .40
58 Peter Bondra .10 .25
59 Marty McInnis .05 .15
60 Bill Guerin .07 .20
61 Patrice Brisebois .05 .15
62 Andy Moog .10 .25
63 Eric Weinrich .05 .15
64 Arturs Irbe .07 .20
65 Sean Hill .05 .15
66 Jesse Belanger .05 .15
67 Bryan Marchment .05 .15
68 Joe Sacco .05 .15
69 Trevor Kidd .07 .20
70 Dan Quinn .07 .20
71 Kirk McLean .07 .20
72 Benoit Hogue .05 .15
73 Garry Galley .05 .15
74 Randy Wood .05 .15
75 Nikolai Khabibulin .07 .20
76 Ted Donato .05 .15
77 Doug Bodger .05 .15
78 Paul Ranheim .05 .15
79 Ulf Samuelsson .05 .15
80 Uwe Krupp .07 .20
81 Oleg Tverdovsky .10 .25
82 Kelly Miller .05 .15
83 Darryl Sydor .07 .20
84 Brian Bellows .07 .20
85 Jeremy Roenick .12 .30
86 Phil Bourque .07 .20
87 Louie DeBrusk .07 .20
88 Joel Otto .05 .15
89 Dino Ciccarelli .07 .20
90 Mats Sundin .10 .25
91 Don Sweeney .05 .15
92 Roman Hamrlik .05 .15
93 Petr Svoboda .05 .15
94 Zigmund Palffy .10 .25
95 Patrick Roy .25 .60
96 Sergei Krivokrasov .05 .15
97 Wade Flaherty RC .07 .20
98 Fredrik Olausson .07 .20
99 Sergio Momesso .05 .15
100 Mike Vernon .07 .20
101 Todd Gill .05 .15
102 Cam Neely .10 .25
103 Wendel Clark .10 .25
104 John Tucker .05 .15
105 Eric Desjardins .07 .20
106 Ed Olczyk .05 .15
107 Bob Beers .07 .20
108 Mark Recchi .12 .30
109 Ed Belfour .07 .20
110 Radek Bonk .05 .15
111 Cory Stillman .05 .15
112 Jeff Norton .05 .15
113 Terry Carkner .05 .15
114 Felix Potvin .10 .25
115 Alexei Kasatonov .05 .15
116 Brian Noonan .05 .15
117 Daren Puppa .07 .20
118 Joe Juneau .07 .20
119 Valeri Bure .05 .15
120 Murray Craven .05 .15
121 Marko Tuomainen .05 .15
122 Trevor Linden .10 .25
123 Zarley Zalapski .05 .15
124 Jeff Shantz .05 .15
125 Dmitri Mironov .05 .15
126 Jamie Huscroft .07 .20
127 Jaromir Jagr .25 .60
128 Brian Bradley .07 .20
129 Brett Lindros .05 .15
130 Calle Johansson .05 .15
131 Pierre Turgeon .10 .25
132 Denis Savard .12 .30
133 Joe Nieuwendyk .10 .25
134 Petr Klima .05 .15
135 John Druce .07 .20
136 Chris Osgood .07 .20
137 Kenny Jonsson .10 .25
138 Jocelyn Lemieux .07 .20
139 Tomas Sandstrom .07 .20
140 Chris Gratton .05 .15
141 Mark Tinordi .05 .15
142 Kirk Muller .07 .20
143 Vladimir Malakhov .05 .15
144 Jiri Slegr .05 .15
145 Shawn McEachern .05 .15
146 Shayne Corson .05 .15
147 Kelly Hrudey .07 .20
148 Sergei Fedorov .15 .40
149 Mike Gartner .10 .25
150 Stephane Fiset .07 .20
151 Larry Murphy .10 .25
152 Enrico Ciccone .05 .15
153 Mike Keane .05 .15
154 Steve Larmer .07 .20
155 Dale Hunter .07 .20
156 Joe Murphy .05 .15
157 Pat LaFontaine .10 .25
158 Rob Gaudreau .05 .15
159 Paul Kariya .12 .30
160 Rob Blake .07 .20
161 Keith Primeau .05 .15
162 Dave Ellett .05 .15
163 Alexander Mogilny .07 .20
164 Luc Robitaille .10 .25
165 Alexander Selivanov .07 .20
166 Keith Jones .07 .20
167 Turner Stevenson .05 .15
168 Keith Tkachuk .10 .25
169 Bernie Nicholls .05 .15
170 Stanislav Neckar .05 .15
171 Scott Mellanby .07 .20
172 Doug Weight .10 .25
173 Shaun Van Allen .05 .15
174 Gary Roberts .05 .15
175 Robert Lang .05 .15
176 Martin Gelinas .05 .15
177 Ray Sheppard .07 .20
178 Bryan Smolinski .05 .15
179 Wayne Presley .05 .15
180 Jimmy Carson .07 .20
181 John Cullen .05 .15
182 Mikael Andersson .07 .20
183 Dimitri Khristich .05 .15
184 Chris Therien .05 .15
185 Bobby Holik .05 .15
186 Kevin Hatcher .07 .20
187 Patrick Poulin .05 .15
188 Pat Falloon .05 .15
189 Alexei Yashin .07 .20
190 Gord Murphy .05 .15
191 Kirk Maltby .07 .20
192 Dave Karpa .05 .15
193 Kelly Kisio .07 .20
194 Tony Granato .05 .15
195 Al Iafrate .07 .20
196 Nelson Emerson .05 .15
197 Adam Oates .10 .25
198 Rob Ray .05 .15
199 Sean Burke .05 .15
200 Ron Francis .12 .30
201 Theo Fleury .12 .30
202 Patrick Flatley .05 .15
203 Ron Hextall .10 .25
204 Martin Brodeur .25 .60
205 Mike Kennedy .07 .20
206 Tony Amonte .07 .20
207 Sergei Makarov .05 .15
208 Alexandre Daigle .05 .15
209 Stu Barnes .05 .15
210 Todd Marchant .05 .15
211 Valeri Karpov .05 .15
212 Phil Housley .07 .20
213 Jamie Storr .07 .20
214 Brett Hull .12 .30
215 Kris King .05 .15
216 Ray Bourque .15 .40
217 Donald Audette .07 .20
218 Steven Rice .05 .15
219 Kevin Stevens .07 .20
220 Mark Messier .15 .40
221 Valeri Kamensky .07 .20
222 Mikael Renberg .07 .20

223 Scott Stevens .10 .25
224 Derian Hatcher .07 .20
225 Ray Whitney .07 .20
226 Bob Kudelski .05 .15
227 Mikhail Shtalenkov .05 .15
228 Nicklas Lidstrom .10 .25
229 Adam Creighton .05 .15
230 Dave Manson .05 .15
231 Craig Simpson .07 .20
232 Chris Pronger .10 .25
233 Adrien Plavsic .07 .20
234 Alexei Kovalev .05 .15
235 Tommy Salo RC .15 .40
236 Patrik Juhlin .05 .15
237 Tom Chorske .05 .15
238 Mike Modano .15 .40
239 Igor Larionov .05 .15
240 Johan Garpenlov .05 .15
241 Todd Krygier .05 .15
242 Tie Domi .07 .20
243 Bill Houlder .05 .15
244 Teemu Selanne .20 .50
245 Dale Hawerchuk .12 .30
246 Bill Ranford .07 .20
247 Brian Leetch .10 .25
248 Steve Thomas .07 .20
249 Dimitri Yushkevich .05 .15
250 Stephane Richer .07 .20
251 Todd Harvey .05 .15
252 Viktor Kozlov .07 .20
253 John Vanbiesbrouck .07 .20
254 Rick Tocchet .07 .20
255 Bret Hedican .05 .15
256 Mario Lemieux .30 .75
257 Igor Korolev .05 .15
258 Dominik Hasek .12 .30
259 Owen Nolan .10 .25
260 Michal Pivonka .05 .15
261 John LeClair .10 .25
262 Claude Lemieux .10 .25
263 Mike Donnelly .05 .15
264 Craig Janney .05 .15
265 Milos Holan .05 .15
266 Steve Yzerman .12 .30
267 Russ Courtnall .05 .15
268 Esa Tikkanen .05 .15
269 Dallas Drake .05 .15
270 Norm Maciver .07 .20
271 Scott Young .05 .15
272 Glenn Healy .07 .20
273 Brian Rolston .05 .15
274 Corey Millen .05 .15
275 Kevin Miller .07 .20
276 Eric LaCroix .05 .15
277 Adam Graves .07 .20
278 Christian Ruuttu .07 .20
279 Steve Duchesne .05 .15
280 Stephane Quintal .07 .20
281 Brent Gretzky .07 .20
282 Mike Ricci .07 .20
283 Sergei Nemchinov .05 .15
284 Sylvain Cote .05 .15
285 Neal Broten .07 .20
286 Greg Adams .05 .15
287 Guy Hebert .07 .20
288 Joe Sakic .15 .40
289 Bobby Dollas .05 .15
290 Gino Odjick .05 .15
291 Curtis Joseph .10 .25
292 Teppo Numminen .05 .15
293 Geoff Sanderson .05 .15
294 Adam Deadmarsh .05 .15
295 Kevin Haller .05 .15
296 Sergei Brylin .05 .15
297 Ulf Dahlen .05 .15
298 Robert Kron .05 .15
299 Dave Lowry .05 .15
300 Nikolai Borschevsky .05 .15
301 Jeff Brown .07 .20
302 Guy Carbonneau .10 .25
303 Alexei Zhitnik .05 .15
304 Frantisek Kucera .05 .15
305 Curtis Leschyshyn .05 .15
306 Mike Richter .10 .25
307 Dean Evason .05 .15
308 Jozef Stumpel .05 .15
309 Jeff Friesen .05 .15
310 Kelly Buchberger .05 .15
311 Michael Nylander .05 .15
312 Josef Beranek .05 .15
313 Al MacInnis .10 .25
314 Ken Wregget .07 .20
315 Glen Wesley .05 .15
316 Jocelyn Thibault .07 .20
317 Jeff Beukeboom .05 .15
318 Steve Konowalchuk .07 .20
319 Tim Cheveldae .07 .20
320 Vincent Damphousse .07 .20
321 Mats Naslund .07 .20
322 Mathieu Schneider .05 .15
323 Petr Nedved .07 .20
324 Brent Fedyk .05 .15
325 Jussi Tie RC .07 .20
326 Mikko Markkanen RC .07 .20
327 Timo Hakanen RC .07 .20
328 Sami Salonen RC .07 .20
329 Juha Viinikainen RC .07 .20
330 Jani Riihinen RC .07 .20
331 Teemu Riihijarvi RC .10 .25
332 Jaako Niskavaara RC .07 .20
333 Miika Elomo .10 .25
334 Tomi Kallio RC .25 .60
335 Vesa Toskala RC .10 .25
336 Tuomas Reijonen RC .10 .25
337 Aki Berg RC .10 .25
338 Tomi Hirvonen RC .10 .25
339 Jussi Salminen RC .10 .25
340 Andreas Sjolund RC .10 .25
341 Johan Ramstedt RC .10 .25
342 Bjorn Danielsson RC .10 .25
343 Per Gustavsson RC .10 .25
344 Niklas Anger RC .10 .25
345 Marcus Nilsson RC .20 .50
346 Per Anton Lundstrom RC .10 .25
347 Henrik Rehnberg RC .10 .25
348 Robert Borgqvist RC .10 .25
349 Ted Christensen RC .10 .25
350 Samuel Phalsson RC .10 .25
351 Fredrik Loven RC .10 .25
352 Patrik Wallenberg RC .10 .25
353 Jan Labraaten RC .10 .25
354 Peter Wallin RC .10 .25
355 Cam Neely WYG .10 .25
356 Keith Tkachuk WYG .10 .25
357 Chris Gratton WYG .05 .15
358 Adam Graves WYG .07 .20
359 Doug Gilmour WYG .12 .30
360 Adam Deadmarsh WYG .05 .15
361 Wayne Gretzky WYG .50 1.25
362 Joe Sakic WYG .15 .40
363 Paul Kariya WYG .12 .30
364 Brett Hull WYG .12 .30
365 Sergei Fedorov WYG .15 .40
366 Brian Rolston WYG .05 .15
367 Dominik Hasek WYG .12 .30
368 John Vanbiesbrouck WYG .07 .20
369 Jim Carey WYG .07 .20
370 Paul Kariya HH .12 .30
371 Peter Forsberg HH .25 .60
372 Jeff Friesen HH .05 .15
373 Kenny Jonsson HH .10 .25
374 Chris Therien HH .05 .15
375 Jim Carey HH .07 .20
376 John LeClair HH .10 .25
377 Eric Lindros HH .15 .40
378 Jaromir Jagr HH .25 .60
379 Paul Coffey HH .10 .25
380 Chris Chelios HH .10 .25
381 Dominik Hasek HH .12 .30
382 Keith Tkachuk HH .10 .25
383 Alexei Zhamnov HH .10 .25
384 Theo Fleury HH .12 .30
385 Ray Bourque HH .15 .40
386 Larry Murphy HH .10 .25
387 Ed Belfour HH .07 .20
388 Eric Lindros HH .15 .40
389 Jaromir Jagr HH .25 .60
390 Paul Coffey HH .10 .25
391 Peter Forsberg HH .25 .60
392 Claude Lemieux HH .10 .25
393 Ron Francis HH .12 .30
394 Dominik Hasek HH .12 .30
395 Checklist .50 1.25
Gretzky
396 Checklist .50 1.25
Gretzky
397 Saku Koivu YG 1.50 4.00
398 Radek Dvorak YG .60 1.50
399 Ed Jovanovski YG .50 1.25
400 Brendan Witt YG .50 1.25
401 Jeff O'Neill YG .50 1.25
402 Daymond Langkow YG .50 1.25
403 Shane Doan RC 1.50 4.00
404 Bryan McCabe YG .50 1.25
405 Marty Murray YG .50 1.25
406 Daniel Alfredsson YG 1.50 4.00
407 Jason Doig YG .50 1.25
408 Niklas Sundstrom YG .50 1.25
409 Vitali Yachmenev YG .50 1.25
410 Aki Berg YG .50 1.25
411 Eric Daze YG 1.00 2.50

1995-96 Collector's Choice Player's Club

Issued one per pack, this 396 card standard-size set is a parallel to the regular Collector's Choice issue. These cards have silver borders and the words "Players Club" are printed vertically on the left side of the card in silver-foil.

COMPLETE SET (396) 40.00 100.00
*SINGLES: 3X TO 8X BASIC CARDS

1995-96 Collector's Choice Player's Club Platinum

This 396-card standard size set is a parallel to the regular Collector's Choice set. Issued a rate of 1:34 packs, these cards are printed on silver-foil paper stock. Although difficult to pull from packs, many of the cards came over from Europe, where they were readily available from collectors clubs. This added supply dampened demand somewhat for these cards in North America.

*PLATINUM: 6X TO 15X BASIC CARDS

1995-96 Collector's Choice Crash the Game Silver

Consisting of 90 cards, this interactive set featured 30 players. Each player had three cards with different dates on the front. If the player scored a goal on either of the dates, the card with the corresponding date could be redeemed for a special 30-card set. Randomly inserted in packs, these cards came in silver (1:5 packs) and gold (1:34 packs) foil versions. The words "silver" or "gold" were in their respective color foil at bottom left and the date was also printed in foil. There are also several parallels of this set, including gold and silver redeemed winner sets, and gold and silver bonus cards awarded of the redeemed player along with the gold or silver set. Because not every player had a winning card, however, the gold and silver bonus sets are considered complete at 23 cards each. It should be noted however that a few copies of the bonus cards have been confirmed to exist of the seven players that did not have winning cards. Also, several erroneous variation cards have been reported featuring game dates on which that player's team did not play. These cards appear to be in short supply, but do not demand exorbitant premiums. To differentiate between each of the player's three insert cards, they are numbered here with A, B and C suffixes. The expiration date for redeeming cards was July 1st, 1996.

COMPLETE SET (90) 40.00 80.00
*GOLD STARS: 1.5X TO 4X BASIC CARDS
*EXCHANGE CARDS: .1X TO .25X BASIC CARDS
*GOLD EXCH.CARDS: .4X TO .8X BASIC CARDS
*BONUS CARDS: 1X TO 2X BASIC CARDS
*GOLD BONUS CARDS: 2.5X TO 5X BASIC CARDS
BONUS NOT PRICED: 3/4/17/18/20/22/27
C1A Pavel Bure 10/12/95 .30 .75
C1B Pavel Bure 12/17/95 .30 .75
C1C Pavel Bure 3/23/96 .30 .75
C2A Sergei Fedorov 10/19/95 .50 1.25
C2B Sergei Fedorov 12/31/95 .50 1.25
C2C Sergei Fedorov 3/12/96 .50 1.25
C3A Wayne Gretzky 10/7/95 2.00 5.00
C3B Wayne Gretzky 12/31/95 2.00 5.00
C3C Wayne Gretzky 2/10/96 2.00 5.00
C4A Eric Lindros 11/12/95 .30 .75
C4B Eric Lindros 1/3/96 .30 .75
C4C Eric Lindros 3/3/96 .30 .75
C5A Brett Hull 10/10/95 .50 1.25
C5B Brett Hull 12/9/95 .50 1.25
C5C Brett Hull 3/24/96 .50 1.25
C6A Mark Messier 11/8/95 .30 .75
C6B Mark Messier 1/22/96 .30 .75
C6C Mark Messier 3/31/96 .30 .75
C7A Jaromir Jagr 10/14/95 .50 1.25
C7B Jaromir Jagr 12/17/95 .50 1.25
C7C Jaromir Jagr 3/5/96 .50 1.25
C8A Alexei Zhamnov 10/9/95 .25 .60
C8B Alexei Zhamnov 12/28/95 .25 .60
C8C Alexei Zhamnov 2/21/96 .25 .60
C9A Joe Sakic 10/6/95 .60 1.50
C9B Joe Sakic 12/9/95 .60 1.50
C9C Joe Sakic 2/3/96 .60 1.50
C10A Paul Kariya 10/18/95 .30 .75
C10B Paul Kariya 12/19/95 .30 .75
C10C Paul Kariya 3/17/96 .30 .75
C11A Theo Fleury 10/27/95 .20 .50
C11B Theo Fleury 12/11/95 .20 .50
C11C Theo Fleury 2/6/96 .20 .50
C12A Owen Nolan 11/1/95 .25 .60
C12B Owen Nolan 1/4/96 .25 .60
C12C Owen Nolan 3/17/96 .25 .60
C13A Peter Bondra 10/13/95 .25 .60
C13B Peter Bondra 12/2/95 .25 .60
C13C Peter Bondra 3/12/96 .25 .60
C14A Cam Neely 11/7/95 .30 .75
C14B Cam Neely 1/11/96 .30 .75
C14C Cam Neely 3/23/96 .30 .75
C15A Pierre Turgeon 10/25/95 .25 .60
C15B Pierre Turgeon 12/23/95 .25 .60
C15C Pierre Turgeon 2/21/96 .25 .60
C16A Mike Modano 11/1/95 .60 1.50
C16B Mike Modano 1/5/96 .60 1.50
C16C Mike Modano 2/22/96 .60 1.50
C17A Bernie Nicholls 10/10/95 .20 .50
C17B Bernie Nicholls 12/15/95 .20 .50
C17C Bernie Nicholls 3/24/96 .20 .50
C18A Alexei Yashin 11/4/95 .20 .50
C18B Alexie Yashin 12/23/95 .20 .50
C18C Alexei Yashin 3/21/96 .20 .50
C19A Jason Arnott 10/27/95 .20 .50
C19B Jason Arnott 12/18/95 .20 .50
C19C Jason Arnott 2/28/96 .20 .50
C20A Peter Forsberg 11/22/95 .75 2.00
C20B Peter Forsberg 2/15/96 .75 2.00
C20C Peter Forsberg 3/27/96 .75 2.00
C21A Doug Gilmour 10/17/95 .25 .60
C21B Doug Gilmour 12/16/95 .25 .60
C21C Doug Gilmour 2/18/96 .25 .60
C22A Geoff Sanderson/ 10/11/95 .20 .50
C22B Geoff Sanderson/ 12/18/95 .20 .50
C22C Geoff Sanderson/ 3/6/96 .20 .50
C23A John LeClair 10/15/95 .30 .75
C23B John LeClair 12/16/95 .30 .75
C23C John LeClair 2/19/96 .30 .75
C24A Ray Bourque 10/11/95 .20 .50
C24B Ray Bourque 12/16/95 .20 .50
C24C Ray Bourque 2/6/96 .20 .50
C25A Mario Lemieux 11/1/95 1.50 4.00
C25B Mario Lemieux 12/1/95 1.50 4.00
C25C Mario Lemieux 2/6/96 1.50 4.00
C26A Steve Yzerman 11/7/95 1.50 4.00
C26B Steve Yzerman 1/24/96 1.50 4.00
C26C Steve Yzerman 2/27/96 1.50 4.00
C27A Pat LaFontaine 10/20/95 .30 .75
C27B Pat LaFontaine 12/27/95 .30 .75
C27C Pat LaFontaine 2/17/96 .30 .75
C28A Claude Lemieux 10/7/95 .20 .50
C28B Claude Lemieux 12/15/95 .20 .50
C28C Claude Lemieux 2/10/96 .20 .50
C29A Paul Coffey 10/15/95 .30 .75
C29B Paul Coffey 12/5/95 .30 .75
C29C Paul Coffey 2/13/96 .30 .75
C30A Mats Sundin 11/7/95 .30 .75
C30B Mats Sundin 1/3/96 .30 .75
C30C Mats Sundin 3/15/96 .30 .75

1996-97 Collector's Choice

The '96-97 Collector's Choice set was issued in one series totaling 348 cards. The 12-card packs retailed for $.99 each. The set contains three subsets: Scotty Bowman's Winning Formula (289-308), Three-Star Selection (309-336) and Captain Tomorrow (337-346). Fifteen additional Young Guns cards (numbered 349-363) were available via mail in exchange for the randomly inserted Young Guns Trade card (1:35 packs). They are not considered part of the complete set, but are listed below as they are numbered consecutively to the regular set. The Gretzky 4 X 6 cards were received when redeeming winning trivia cards from the Meet the Stars contest.

COMPLETE SET (348) 10.00 25.00
1 Paul Kariya .20 .50
2 Teemu Selanne .30 .75
3 Steve Rucchin .10 .25
4 Mikhail Shtalenkov .10 .25
5 Guy Hebert .12 .30
6 Shaun Van Allen .10 .25
7 Anatoli Semenov .10 .25
8 J.F. Jomphe RC .15 .40
9 Alex Hicks .15 .40
10 Roman Oksiuta .10 .25
11 Todd Ewen .10 .25
12 Adam Oates .15 .40
13 Ray Bourque .25 .60
14 Don Sweeney .10 .25
15 Kyle McLaren .10 .25
16 Cam Neely .15 .40
17 Bill Ranford .12 .30
18 Rick Tocchet .12 .30
19 Ted Donato .10 .25
20 Shawn McEachern .10 .25
21 Jon Rohloff .10 .25
22 Joe Mullen .12 .30
23 Pat LaFontaine .15 .40
24 Brian Holzinger .12 .30
25 Wayne Primeau .10 .25
26 Alexei Zhitnik .10 .25
27 Derek Plante .10 .25
28 Randy Burridge .10 .25
29 Brad May .10 .25
30 Dominik Hasek .25 .60
31 Jason Dawe .10 .25
32 Mike Peca .10 .25
33 Matthew Barnaby .10 .25
34 Trevor Kidd .10 .25
35 Theo Fleury .30 .75
36 Cale Hulse .10 .25
37 Bob Sweeney .10 .25
38 Michael Nylander .10 .25
39 German Titov .10 .25
40 Cory Stillman .10 .25
41 Zarley Zalapski .10 .25
42 Jocelyn Lemieux .10 .25
43 Sandy McCarthy .10 .25
44 Steve Chiasson .10 .25
45 Eric Daze .12 .30
46 Jeremy Roenick .25 .60
47 Chris Chelios .15 .40
48 Joe Murphy .10 .25
49 Tony Amonte .12 .30
50 Bernie Nicholls .10 .25
51 Eric Weinrich .10 .25
52 Gary Suter .10 .25
53 Jeff Shantz .10 .25
54 Jeff Hackett .12 .30
55 Ed Belfour .15 .40
56 Uwe Krupp .10 .25
57 Claude Lemieux .10 .25
58 Adam Deadmarsh .10 .25
59 Stephane Fiset .12 .30
60 Sandis Ozolinsh .10 .25
61 Stephane Yelle .10 .25
62 Valeri Kamensky .12 .30
63 Peter Forsberg .25 .60
64 Joe Sakic .25 .60
65 Patrick Roy .40 1.00
66 Chris Simon .10 .25
67 Todd Harvey .10 .25
68 Joe Nieuwendyk .15 .40
69 Mike Modano .25 .60
70 Derian Hatcher .10 .25
71 Kevin Hatcher .10 .25
72 Benoit Hogue .10 .25
73 Guy Carbonneau .15 .40
74 Jamie Langenbrunner .10 .25
75 Jere Lehtinen .10 .25
76 Craig Ludwig .10 .25
77 Grant Marshall .10 .25
78 Greg Johnson .10 .25
79 Steve Yzerman .40 1.00
80 Sergei Fedorov .25 .60
81 Vyacheslav Kozlov .10 .25
82 Vladimir Konstantinov .12 .30
83 Igor Larionov .15 .40
84 Chris Osgood .15 .40
85 Paul Coffey .15 .40
86 Nicklas Lidstrom .20 .50
87 Keith Primeau .10 .25
88 Dino Ciccarelli .15 .40
89 Darren McCarty .10 .25
90 Curtis Joseph .15 .40
91 Doug Weight .15 .40
92 Jason Arnott .12 .30
93 Mariusz Czerkawski .10 .25
94 Kelly Buchberger .10 .25
95 Zdeno Ciger .10 .25
96 David Oliver .10 .25
97 Todd Marchant .10 .25
98 Miroslav Satan .10 .25
99 Bryan Marchment .10 .25
100 Louie DeBrusk .10 .25
101 John Vanbiesbrouck .15 .40
102 Scott Mellanby .12 .30
103 Rob Niedermayer .12 .30
104 Robert Svehla .10 .25
105 Ed Jovanovski .12 .30
106 Johan Garpenlov .10 .25
107 Jody Hull .10 .25
108 Bill Lindsay .10 .25
109 Terry Carkner .10 .25
110 Stu Barnes .10 .25
111 Ray Sheppard .12 .30
112 Brendan Shanahan .20 .50
113 Geoff Sanderson .12 .30
114 Andrei Nikolishin .10 .25
115 Andrew Cassels .10 .25
116 Nelson Emerson .10 .25
117 Jason Muzzatti .12 .30
118 Marek Malik .10 .25
119 Sean Burke .10 .25
120 Jeff Brown .10 .25
121 Jeff O'Neill .10 .25
122 Kelly Chase .10 .25
123 Dimitri Khristich .10 .25
124 Kevin Stevens .10 .25
125 Vitali Yachmenev .10 .25
126 Yanic Perreault .10 .25
127 Kevin Todd .10 .25
128 Aki Berg .10 .25
129 Craig Johnson .10 .25
130 Mattias Norstrom .10 .25
131 Ray Ferraro .10 .25
132 Steven Finn .10 .25
133 Pierre Turgeon .15 .40
134 Saku Koivu .15 .40
135 Mark Recchi .20 .50
136 Jocelyn Thibault .15 .40
137 Andrei Kovalenko .10 .25
138 Vincent Damphousse .12 .30
139 Vladimir Malakhov .10 .25
140 Brian Savage .10 .25
141 Valeri Bure .10 .25
142 Patrice Brisebois .10 .25
143 Martin Rucinsky .10 .25
144 Martin Brodeur
145 Steve Thomas .10 .25
146 Bill Guerin .15 .40
147 Petr Sykora .10 .25
148 Scott Stevens .15 .40
149 Scott Niedermayer .15 .40
150 Phil Housley .12 .30
151 Brian Rolston .12 .30
152 Neal Broten .12 .30
153 Dave Andreychuk .15 .40
154 Randy McKay .10 .25
155 Eric Fichaud .12 .30
156 Zigmund Palffy .15 .40
157 Travis Green .12 .30
158 Darby Hendrickson .10 .25
159 Kenny Jonsson .10 .25
160 Marty McInnis .10 .25
161 Bryan McCabe .10 .25
162 Darius Kasparaitis .10 .25
163 Alexander Semak .10 .25
164 Todd Bertuzzi .15 .40
165 Niclas Andersson .10 .25
166 Mark Messier .25 .60
167 Mike Richter .15 .40
168 Niklas Sundstrom .10 .25
169 Brian Leetch .15 .40
170 Wayne Gretzky .10 .25
171 Luc Robitaille .15 .40
172 Marty McSorley .10 .25
173 Jari Kurri .15 .40
174 Adam Graves .10 .25
175 Sergei Nemchinov .10 .25
176 Alexei Kovalev .10 .25
177 Daniel Alfredsson .15 .40
178 Randy Cunneyworth .10 .25
179 Alexei Yashin .12 .30
180 Alexandre Daigle .10 .25
181 Radek Bonk .10 .25
182 Steve Duchesne .10 .25
183 Ted Drury .10 .25
184 Antti Tormanen .10 .25
185 Stan Neckar .10 .25
186 Damian Rhodes .12 .30
187 Janne Laukkanen .10 .25
188 Eric Lindros .25 .60
189 Mikael Renberg .12 .30
190 John LeClair .15 .40
191 Ron Hextall .12 .30
192 Rod Brind'Amour .15 .40
193 Joel Otto .10 .25
194 Pat Falloon .10 .25
195 Eric Desjardins .12 .30
196 Dale Hawerchuk .20 .50
197 Chris Therien .10 .25
198 Dan Quinn .10 .25
199 Oleg Tverdovsky .12 .30
200 Chad Kilger .10 .25
201 Keith Tkachuk .15 .40
202 Igor Korolev .10 .25
203 Alexei Zhamnov .12 .30
204 Nikolai Khabibulin .12 .30
205 Shane Doan .12 .30
206 Deron Quint .10 .25
207 Craig Janney .12 .30
208 Norm MacIver .10 .25
209 Teppo Numminen .10 .25
210 Mario Lemieux .50 1.25
211 Jaromir Jagr .40 1.00
212 Ron Francis .20 .50
213 Tom Barrasso .12 .30
214 Sergei Zubov .10 .25
215 Tomas Sandstrom .10 .25
216 Joe Dziedzic .10 .25
217 Richard Park .10 .25
218 Bryan Smolinski .10 .25
219 Petr Nedved .12 .30
220 Ken Wregget .12 .30
221 Dmitri Mironov .10 .25
222 Peter Zezel .75 2.00
223 Brett Hull .75 2.00
224 Grant Fuhr .15 .40
225 Shayne Corson .10 .25
226 Chris Pronger .12 .30
227 Craig MacTavish .10 .25
228 Al MacInnis .15 .40
229 Geoff Courtnall .10 .25
230 Stephane Matteau .10 .25
231 Tony Twist .10 .25
232 Brian Noonan .10 .25
233 Owen Nolan .15 .40
234 Shean Donovan .10 .25
235 Darren Turcotte .10 .25
236 Marcus Ragnarsson .10 .25
237 Viktor Kozlov .10 .25
238 Jeff Friesen .10 .25
239 Chris Terreri .12 .30
240 Ray Whitney .10 .25
241 Ville Peltonen .10 .25
242 Andrei Nazarov .10 .25
243 Ulf Dahlen .10 .25
244 Roman Hamrlik .12 .30
245 Chris Gratton .12 .30
246 Petr Klima .10 .25
247 Daren Puppa .12 .30
248 Rob Zamuner .10 .25
249 Aaron Gavey .10 .25
250 Brian Bradley .10 .25
251 Paul Ysebaert .10 .25
252 Igor Ulanov .10 .25
253 Alexander Selivanov .10 .25
254 Shawn Burr .10 .25
255 Mats Sundin .15 .40
256 Doug Gilmour .20 .50
257 Felix Potvin .15 .40
258 Wendel Clark .12 .30
259 Kirk Muller .10 .25
260 Dave Gagner .15 .40
261 Tie Domi .12 .30
262 Mathieu Schneider .10 .25
263 Dimitri Yushkevich .10 .25
264 Don Beaupre .12 .30
265 Larry Murphy .12 .30
266 Pavel Bure .20 .50
267 Alexander Mogilny .12 .30
268 Trevor Linden .12 .30
269 Jyrki Lumme .10 .25
270 Cliff Ronning .10 .25
271 Kirk McLean .12 .30
272 Corey Hirsch .12 .30
273 Esa Tikkanen .10 .25
274 Gino Odjick .10 .25
275 Markus Naslund .15 .40
276 Russ Courtnall .10 .25
277 Joe Juneau .10 .25
278 Jim Carey .15 .40
279 Peter Bondra .12 .30
280 Michal Pivonka .10 .25
281 Steve Konowalchuk .10 .25
282 Pat Peake .10 .25
283 Brendan Witt .10 .25
284 Stefan Ustorf .10 .25
285 Keith Jones .10 .25
286 Sergei Gonchar .10 .25
287 Sylvain Cote .10 .25
288 Dale Hunter .12 .30
289 Paul Kariya SB .20 .50
290 Wayne Gretzky SB .75 2.00
291 Eric Lindros SB .25 .60
292 Steve Yzerman SB .40 1.00
293 Mario Lemieux SB .50 1.25
294 Jaromir Jagr SB .40 1.00
295 Keith Tkachuk SB .15 .40
296 Mark Messier SB .25 .60
297 Jeremy Roenick SB .25 .60
298 Peter Forsberg SB .25 .60
299 Joe Sakic SB .25 .60
300 Theo Fleury SB .30 .75
301 Chris Chelios SB .15 .40
302 Vlad Konstantinov SB .12 .30
303 Brian Leetch SB .15 .40
304 Ray Bourque SB .25 .60
305 Scott Stevens SB .15 .40
306 Martin Brodeur SB .30 .75
307 Patrick Roy SB .40 1.00
308 Scotty Bowman .15 .40
309 Kariya .30 .75
Selanne
Hebert
310 Oates .25 .60
Bourque
Neely
311 LaFontaine .25 .60
Zhitnik
Hasek
312 Fleury .30 .75
Nylander
Kidd
313 Roenick .25 .60
Chelios
Daze
314 Sakic/Roy/Forsberg .40 1.00
315 Modano .25 .60
Nieuwendyk
Harvey
316 Fedorov .25 .60
Konstantinov
Coffey
317 Weight/Arnott/Joseph .15 .40
318 Jovan .15 .40
VBK
Nieder.
319 Shanahan .20 .50
Sanderson
Burke
320 Yachmenev .10 .25
Khristich
Ferraro
321 Thibault .15 .40
Turgeon
Koivu
322 Brodeur .30 .75
Thomas
Stevens
323 Bertuzzi .15 .40
Fichaud
Palffy
324 Leetch .15 .40
Graves
Richter
325 Daigle .12 .30
Yashin
Rhodes
326 Hextall .15 .40
LeClair
Renberg
327 Zhamnov .15 .40
Tkachuk
Tverdovsky
328 Jagr .40 1.00
Nedved
Francis
329 Gretzky/Hull/MacInnis .75 2.00
330 Nolan .15 .40
Turcotte
Terreri
331 Hamrlik .12 .30
Gratton
Puppa
332 Gilmour .20 .50
Potvin
Sundin
333 Mogilny .20 .50
Bure
Linden
334 Carey .15 .40
Juneau
Bondra
335 Lemieux .50 1.25
Messier
Lindros
336 Gretzky/Selanne/Sakic .75 2.00
337 Chad Kilger .10 .25
338 Todd Bertuzzi .15 .40
339 Petr Sykora .10 .25
340 Ed Jovanovski CT .12 .30
341 Kyle McLaren .10 .25
342 Brian Holzinger .12 .30
343 Jeff O'Neill .10 .25
344 Daniel Alfredsson .15 .40
345 Brendan Witt .10 .25
346 Daymond Langkow .12 .30
347 Checklist .10 .25
348 Checklist .10 .25
349 Jarome Iginla YG .60 1.50
350 Sergei Berezin YG .75 2.00
351 Jose Theodore YG .60 1.50
352 Rem Murray YG .50 1.25
353 Daniel Goneau YG .50 1.25
354 Ethan Moreau YG .50 1.25
355 Jonas Hoglund YG .30 .75
356 Anders Eriksson YG .30 .75
357 Christian Dube YG .30 .75
358 Roman Turek YG .50 1.25
359 Bryan Berard YG .50 1.25
360 Jim Campbell YG .30 .75
361 Janne Niinimaa YG .50 1.25
362 Wade Redden YG .30 .75
363 Marc Denis YG .50 1.25
P222 Wayne Gretzky PROMO .75 2.00
NNO1 Wayne Gretzky '79-80 .75 2.00
NNO2 Wayne Gretzky 802 .75 2.00

1996-97 Collector's Choice Jumbos 5x7

These 5 X 7 cards were inserted as box toppers.

COMPLETE SET (5) 3.00 8.00
1 Theo Fleury .75 2.00
2 Curtis Joseph 1.00 2.59
3 Jose Theodore 1.00 2.50
4 Wade Redden .40 1.00
5 Mats Sundin 1.00 2.50

1996-97 Collector's Choice MVP

This set consists of 45 of the NHL's top stars and rookies. Silver versions are found one per pack, while the tougher gold parallel version is found 1:35 packs. These cards can be differentiated by the color of the foil on the left-hand border. The card fronts feature a color action photo with abbreviation "MVP" appearing in either silver or gold (depending on the version) at the bottom of the card. Values for the gold cards can be determined by utilizing the multiplier below.

COMPLETE SET (45) 25.00 60.00
*GOLD: 2.5X TO 6X BASIC INSERTS
UD1 Wayne Gretzky 2.50 6.00
UD2 Ron Francis .60 1.50
UD3 Peter Forsberg .75 2.00
UD4 Alexander Mogilny .40 1.00
UD5 Joe Sakic .75 2.00
UD6 Claude Lemieux .30 .75
UD7 Teemu Selanne 1.00 2.50
UD8 John LeClair .50 1.25
UD9 Doug Weight .50 1.25
UD10 Paul Kariya .60 1.50
UD11 Theo Fleury 1.00 2.50
UD12 John Vanbiesbrouck .50 1.25
UD13 Sergei Fedorov .75 2.00
UD14 Steve Yzerman 1.25 3.00
UD15 Adam Oates .50 1.25
UD16 Keith Tkachuk .50 1.25
UD17 Mike Modano .75 2.00
UD18 Jeremy Roenick .75 2.00
UD19 Patrick Roy 1.25 3.00
UD20 Felix Potvin .50 1.25
UD21 Martin Brodeur 1.00 2.50
UD22 Pavel Bure .60 1.50
UD23 Peter Bondra .40 1.00
UD24 Zigmund Palffy .50 1.25
UD25 Roman Hamrlik .40 1.00
UD26 Brendan Shanahan .60 1.50
UD27 Ray Bourque .75 2.00
UD28 Paul Coffey .50 1.25
UD29 Brett Hull 2.50 6.00
UD30 Brian Leetch .50 1.25
UD31 Chris Chelios .50 1.25
UD32 Vitali Yachmenev .40 1.00
UD33 Nicklas Lidstrom .60 1.50
UD34 Ed Jovanovski .40 1.00
UD35 Sandis Ozolinsh .30 .75
UD36 Scott Stevens .50 1.25
UD37 Eric Daze .40 1.00
UD38 Saku Koivu .50 1.25
UD39 Daniel Alfredsson .50 1.25
UD40 Pat LaFontaine .50 1.25
UD41 Cam Neely .50 1.25
UD42 Owen Nolan .50 1.25
UD43 Jaromir Jagr 1.25 3.00
UD44 Mats Sundin .50 1.25
UD45 Doug Gilmour .60 1.50

1996-97 Collector's Choice Stick'Ums

This unusual set consists of 30 stickers, the first 25 of which feature the NHL's top players. The remaining stickers feature a variety of hockey-oriented doo-daddery. These stickers were randomly inserted at 1:3 packs.

COMPLETE SET (30) 10.00 20.00
S1 Wayne Gretzky 1.50 4.00
S2 Brett Hull 1.50 4.00
S3 Peter Forsberg .50 1.25
S4 Patrick Roy .75 2.00
S5 Cam Neely .30 .75
S6 Jeremy Roenick .50 1.25
S7 Mario Lemieux 1.00 2.50
S8 Jaromir Jagr .75 2.00
S9 Eric Lindros .50 1.25
S10 Mark Messier .50 1.25
S11 Felix Potvin .30 .75
S12 Brendan Shanahan .40 1.00
S13 Teemu Selanne .60 1.50
S14 Paul Kariya .40 1.00
S15 Mike Modano .50 1.25
S16 Pavel Bure .40 1.00
S17 Jim Carey .30 .75
S18 Roman Hamrlik .25 .60
S19 Pierre Turgeon .30 .75
S20 Theo Fleury .60 1.50
S21 Pat LaFontaine .30 .75
S22 Steve Yzerman .75 2.00
S23 Sergei Fedorov .50 1.25
S24 Martin Brodeur .60 1.50
S25 Owen Nolan .30 .75
S26 Ice Machine .20 .50
S27 Champions .20 .50
S28 Slap Shot .20 .50
S29 Stripes .20 .50
S30 Goal .20 .50

1996-97 Collector's Choice Crash the Game Silver

This interactive set features 30 NHL stars on a total of 88 cards. 28 players appear on 3 variations each, while two (Joe Sakic and Adam Oates) are featured on but two by virtue of an error by Upper Deck. Randomly inserted in packs, these cards come in silver (1:5 packs) and gold (1:44 packs) foil versions. If the player scored a goal against the team featured on his card, the winning card could be redeemed for a special exchange card. There are two versions of this set as well. Both versions feature the same design and photos, but they are different from the Crash cards for which they were redeemed. Furthermore, the gold versions of the exchange cards were die-cut. To differentiate between each of the player's three insert cards, they are numbered here with A, B and C suffixes. These suffixes do not appear on the cards themselves. The expiration date for these cards was July 1, 1997.

COMPLETE SET (88) 30.00 80.00
*GOLD: 1.25X TO 3X BASIC INSERTS
*EXCH.STARS: 1.25X TO 3X BASIC INSERTS
*GOLD EXCH: 4X TO 10X BASIC INSERTS
ONE EXCH.CARD VIA MAIL PER WINNER
EXCH.CARDS 20 AND 25 NOT ISSUED
C1A Wayne Gretzky 2.00 5.00
C1B Wayne Gretzky 2.00 5.00
C1C Wayne Gretzky 2.00 5.00
C2A Doug Gilmour .25 .60
C2B Doug Gilmour .25 .60
C2C Doug Gilmour .25 .60
C3A Alexander Mogilny .25 .60
C3B Alexander Mogilny .25 .60
C3C Alexander Mogilny .25 .60
C4A Peter Bondra .25 .60
C4B Peter Bondra .25 .60
C4C Peter Bondra .25 .60
C5A Mario Lemieux 1.50 4.00
C5B Mario Lemieux 1.50 4.00
C5C Mario Lemieux 1.50 4.00
C6A Jaromir Jagr .50 1.25
C6B Jaromir Jagr .50 1.25
C6C Jaromir Jagr .50 1.25
C7A Joe Sakic .60 1.50
C7B Joe Sakic .60 1.50
C8A Vitali Yachmenev .20 .50
C8B Vitali Yachmenev .20 .50
C8C Vitali Yachmenev .20 .50
C9A Doug Weight .25 .60
C9B Doug Weight .25 .60
C9C Doug Weight .25 .60
C10A Steve Yzerman 1.50 4.00
C10B Steve Yzerman 1.50 4.00
C10C Steve Yzerman 1.50 4.00
C11A Alexei Zhamnov .20 .50
C11B Alexei Zhamnov .20 .50
C11C Alexei Zhamnov .20 .50
C12A John LeClair .30 .75
C12B John LeClair .30 .75
C12C John LeClair .30 .75
C13A Daniel Alfredsson .25 .60
C13B Daniel Alfredsson .25 .60
C13C Daniel Alfredsson .25 .60
C14A Brendan Shanahan .30 .75
C14B Brendan Shanahan .50 1.25
C14C Brendan Shanahan .50 1.25
C15A Saku Koivu .30 .75
C15B Saku Koivu .30 .75
C15C Saku Koivu .30 .75
C16A Steve Thomas .20 .50
C16B Steve Thomas .20 .50
C16C Steve Thomas .20 .50
C17A Pavel Bure .30 .75
C17B Pavel Bure .50 1.25
C17C Pavel Bure .50 1.25
C18A Slava Kozlov .20 .50
C18B Slava Kozlov .20 .50
C18C Slava Kozlov .20 .50
C19A Teemu Selanne .30 .75
C19B Teemu Selanne .30 .75
C19C Teemu Selanne .30 .75
C20A Eric Daze .20 .50
C20B Eric Daze .20 .50
C20C Eric Daze .20 .50
C21A Adam Oates .25 .60
C21B Adam Oates .25 .60
C22A Ray Bourque .50 1.25
C22B Ray Bourque .50 1.25
C22C Ray Bourque .50 1.25
C23A Jason Arnott .20 .50
C23B Jason Arnott .20 .50
C23C Jason Arnott .20 .50
C24A Paul Kariya .30 .75
C24B Paul Kariya .30 .75
C24C Paul Kariya .30 .75
C25A Mikael Renberg .20 .50
C25B Mikael Renberg .20 .50
C25C Mikael Renberg .20 .50

C26A Keith Tkachuk .30 .75
C26B Keith Tkachuk .30 .75
C26C Keith Tkachuk .30 .75
C27A Brian Leetch .25 .60
C27B Brian Leetch .25 .60
C27C Brian Leetch .25 .60
C28A Eric Lindros .30 .75
C28B Eric Lindros .50 1.25
C28C Eric Lindros .50 1.25
C29A Mats Sundin .30 .75
C29B Mats Sundin .30 .75
C29C Mats Sundin .30 .75
C30A Mark Messier .40 1.00
C30B Mark Messier .40 1.00
C30C Mark Messier .40 1.00

1996-97 Collector's Choice Jumbos

The ten cards in this set were issued one per special retail box of Collector's Choice. The cards are identical in every way to their corresponding regular version, except for the size; these cards measure 4 X 6 inches.

COMPLETE SET (10) 10.00 25.00
13 Ray Bourque .75 2.00
23 Pat LaFontaine .50 1.25
35 Theo Fleury .60 1.50
62 Valeri Kamensky .50 1.25
69 Mike Modano .75 2.00
84 Chris Osgood .60 1.50
133 Pierre Turgeon .50 1.25
170 Wayne Gretzky 4.00 10.00
244 Roman Hamrlik .40 1.00
257 Felix Potvin .50 1.25

1996-97 Collector's Choice Jumbos Bi-Way

These eight oversized (4 by 6 inches) cards mirrored the regular edition Collector's Choice cards, save for the numbering on the back. The cards were inserted one per box sold through the Bi-Way discount chain in Canada.

COMPLETE SET (8) 6.00 15.00
1 Wayne Gretzky 4.00 10.00
2 Theo Fleury .60 1.50
3 Jason Arnott .50 1.25
4 Saku Koivu .60 1.50
5 Pierre Turgeon .50 1.25
6 Daniel Alfredsson .50 1.25
7 Felix Potvin .50 1.25
8 Alexander Mogilny .50 1.25

1997-98 Collector's Choice

This 320-card set features color photos of approximately ten players from each of the NHL's 26 teams and was distributed in 14-card packs with a suggested retail price of $1.29. The set contains 275 regular player cards and two subsets: National Heroes (36 cards) which includes some of the most talented junior players, and Chippy's Checklist (9 cards) which highlights nine of the mascot's favorite players on the set's checklist cards. The cards are dual numbered and are checklisted in team order alphabetized by city.

COMPLETE SET (320) 8.00 20.00
1 Guy Hebert .07 .20
2 Sean Pronger .05 .15
3 Dmitri Mironov .07 .20
4 Darren Van Impe .07 .20
5 Joe Sacco .07 .20
6 Ted Drury .07 .20
7 Steve Rucchin .07 .20
8 Teemu Selanne .20 .50
9 Paul Kariya .12 .30
10 Jari Kurri .10 .25
11 Kevin Todd .05 .15
12 Ray Bourque .15 .40
13 Anson Carter .05 .15
14 Ted Donato .05 .15
15 Kyle McLaren .05 .15
16 Jason Allison .07 .20
17 Jim Carey .05 .15
18 Jozef Stumpel .07 .20
19 Jean-Yves Roy .05 .15
20 Steve Heinze .05 .15
21 Sheldon Kennedy .05 .15
22 Dominik Hasek .15 .40
23 Rob Ray .05 .15
24 Derek Plante .07 .20
25 Brian Holzinger .07 .20
26 Mike Peca .07 .20
27 Matthew Barnaby .07 .20
28 Donald Audette .07 .20
29 Alexei Zhitnik .05 .15
30 Garry Galley .05 .15
31 Pat LaFontaine .10 .25
32 Jason Dawe .07 .20
33 Hnat Domenichelli .07 .20
34 Jarome Iginla .10 .25
35 Chris O'Sullivan .07 .20
36 Todd Simpson .07 .20
37 Trevor Kidd .05 .15
38 Dave Gagner .05 .15
39 German Titov .05 .15
40 Theo Fleury .12 .30
41 Dwayne Roloson .07 .20
42 Marty McInnis .05 .15
43 Jonas Hoglund .07 .20
44 Tony Amonte .07 .20
45 Gary Suter .05 .15
46 Chris Chelios .10 .25
47 Jeff Hackett .05 .15
48 Ulf Dahlen .05 .15
49 Bob Probert .05 .15
50 Kevin Miller .05 .15
51 Ethan Moreau .05 .15
52 Eric Weinrich .05 .15
53 Eric Daze .05 .15
54 Peter Forsberg .12 .30
55 Joe Sakic .15 .40
56 Patrick Roy .25 .60
57 Adam Deadmarsh .05 .15
58 Valeri Kamensky .07 .20
59 Keith Jones .05 .15
60 Sandis Ozolinsh .07 .20
61 Mike Ricci .07 .20
62 Claude Lemieux .07 .20
63 Mike Keane .05 .15
64 Adam Foote .05 .15
65 Mike Modano .15 .40
66 Pat Verbeek .07 .20
67 Andy Moog .10 .25
68 Joe Nieuwendyk .10 .25
69 Jamie Langenbrunner .07 .20
70 Derian Hatcher .07 .20
71 Greg Adams .07 .20
72 Darryl Sydor .05 .15
73 Dave Reid .05 .15
74 Jere Lehtinen .07 .20
75 Todd Harvey .07 .20
76 Brendan Shanahan .12 .30
77 Mike Vernon .07 .20
78 Steve Yzerman .20 .50
79 Sergei Fedorov .15 .40
80 Chris Osgood .10 .25
81 Nicklas Lidstrom .10 .25
82 Vladimir Konstantinov .05 .15
83 Darren McCarty .07 .20
84 Kirk Maltby .05 .15
85 Vyacheslav Kozlov .07 .20
86 Martin Lapointe .05 .15
87 Doug Weight .10 .25
88 Mike Grier .07 .20
89 Curtis Joseph .10 .25
90 Andrei Kovalenko .05 .15
91 Rem Murray .05 .15
92 Ryan Smyth .07 .20
93 Mariusz Czerkawski .05 .15
94 Drew Bannister .05 .15
95 Jason Arnott .07 .20
96 Luke Richardson .05 .15
97 Dean McAmmond .05 .15
98 Kirk Muller .05 .15
99 Ray Sheppard .07 .20
100 Scott Mellanby .07 .20
101 Ed Jovanovski .05 .15
102 John Vanbiesbrouck .10 .25
103 Radek Dvorak .07 .20
104 Robert Svehla .07 .20
105 Rob Niedermayer .05 .15
106 Dave Nemirovsky .05 .15
107 Steve Washburn .05 .15
108 Bill Lindsay .07 .20
109 Kevin Dineen .07 .20
110 Keith Primeau .07 .20
111 Sean Burke .05 .15
112 Derek King .07 .20
113 Andrew Cassels .05 .15
114 Glen Wesley .05 .15
115 Nelson Emerson .07 .20
116 Geoff Sanderson .07 .20
117 Jeff O'Neill .07 .20
118 Kent Manderville .05 .15
119 Dimitri Khristich .07 .20
120 Ian Laperriere .05 .15
121 Aki Berg .05 .15
122 Vladimir Tsyplakov .07 .20
123 Vitali Yachmenev .07 .20
124 Roman Vopat .07 .20
125 Rob Blake .10 .25
126 Jan Vopat .05 .15
127 Jeff Shevalier RC .05 .15
128 Byron Dafoe .05 .15
129 Saku Koivu .10 .25
130 Vincent Damphousse .07 .20
131 Brian Savage .05 .15
132 Valeri Bure .05 .15
133 Mark Recchi .12 .30
134 Jocelyn Thibault .05 .15
135 Jose Theodore .10 .25
136 Dave Manson .05 .15
137 Shayne Corson .05 .15
138 Stephane Richer .05 .15
139 Doug Gilmour .12 .30
140 Scott Stevens .10 .25
141 Martin Brodeur .20 .50
142 Dave Andreychuk .10 .25
143 Bobby Holik .05 .15
144 Brian Rolston .07 .20
145 Jay Pandolfo .07 .20
146 John MacLean .05 .15
147 Bill Guerin .10 .25
148 Scott Niedermayer .10 .25
149 Denis Pederson .05 .15
150 Zigmund Palffy .10 .25
151 Robert Reichel .07 .20
152 Bryan Smolinski .07 .20
153 Eric Fichaud .07 .20
154 Todd Bertuzzi .10 .25
155 Bryan Berard .05 .15
156 Niklas Anderson .05 .15
157 Bryan McCabe .05 .15
158 Tommy Salo .05 .15
159 Kenny Jonsson .07 .20
160 Travis Green .07 .20
161 Mike Richter .10 .25
162 Brian Leetch .10 .25
163 Adam Graves .05 .15
164 Vladimir Vorobiev RC .10 .25
165 Niklas Sundstrom .07 .20
166 Russ Courtnall .05 .15
167 Wayne Gretzky .50 1.25
168 Mark Messier .15 .40
169 Alexander Karpovtsev .05 .15
170 Luc Robitaille .10 .25
171 Ulf Samuelsson .10 .25
172 Daniel Alfredsson .10 .25
173 Alexei Yashin .07 .20
174 Alexandre Daigle .05 .15
175 Andreas Dackell .07 .20
176 Wade Redden .05 .15
177 Sergei Zholtok .07 .20
178 Damian Rhodes .07 .20
179 Steve Duchesne .05 .15
180 Shawn McEachern .05 .15
181 Ron Tugnutt .10 .25
182 John Leclair .10 .25
183 Janne Niinimaa .07 .20
184 Mikael Renberg .07 .20
185 Vaclav Prospal RC .07 .20
186 Eric Lindros .15 .40
187 Dainius Zubrus .07 .20
188 Ron Hextall .10 .25
189 Paul Coffey .10 .25
190 Dale Hawerchuk .12 .30
191 Trent Klatt .07 .20
192 Rod Brind'Amour .10 .25
193 Nikolai Khabibulin .10 .25
194 Keith Tkachuk .10 .25
195 Jeremy Roenick .12 .30
196 Mike Gartner .10 .25
197 Dallas Drake .07 .20
198 Oleg Tverdovsky .07 .20
199 Cliff Ronning .05 .15
200 Teppo Numminen .07 .20
201 Craig Janney .05 .15
202 Deron Quint .05 .15
203 Jason Wooley .07 .20
204 Ron Francis .12 .30
205 Jaromir Jagr .25 .60
206 Greg Johnson .05 .15
207 Kevin Hatcher .05 .15
200 Patrick Lalime .07 .20
209 Petr Nedved .10 .25
210 Ken Wregget .05 .15
211 Darius Kasparaitis .07 .20
212 Stu Barnes .05 .15
213 Joe Dziedzic .05 .15
214 Owen Nolan .10 .25
215 Jeff Friesen .07 .20
216 Ed Belfour .10 .25
217 Viktor Kozlov .07 .20
218 Tony Granato .07 .20
219 Darren Turcotte .07 .20
220 Stephen Guolla RC .05 .15
221 Marty McSorley .05 .15
222 Marcus Ragnarsson .05 .15
223 Al Iafrate .07 .20
224 Brett Hull .12 .30
225 Grant Fuhr .10 .25
226 Pierre Turgeon .10 .25
227 Geoff Courtnall .05 .15
228 Jim Campbell .05 .15
229 Harry York .07 .20
230 Tony Twist .07 .20
231 Joe Murphy .07 .20
232 Pavol Demitra .12 .30
233 Chris Pronger .07 .20
234 Al MacInnis .10 .25
235 Daren Puppa .07 .20
236 Chris Gratton .05 .15
237 Dino Ciccarelli .10 .25
238 Rob Zamuner .05 .15
239 Igor Ulanov .07 .20
240 Roman Hamrlik .07 .20
241 Alexander Selivanov .05 .15
242 Patrick Poulin .05 .15
243 Daymond Langkow .05 .15
244 Corey Schwab .07 .20
245 Mats Sundin .10 .25
246 Wendel Clark .10 .25
247 Sergei Berezin .07 .20
248 Steve Sullivan .07 .20
249 Fredrik Modin .07 .20
250 Darby Hendrickson .05 .15
251 Jason Podollan .07 .20
252 Felix Potvin .10 .25
253 Tie Domi .10 .25
254 Todd Warriner .07 .20
255 Pavel Bure .12 .30
256 Alexander Mogilny .07 .20
257 Martin Gelinas .05 .15
258 Corey Hirsch .07 .20
259 Trevor Linden .07 .20
260 Mike Sillinger .05 .15
261 Markus Naslund .07 .20
262 Jyrki Lumme .07 .20
263 Gino Odjick .07 .20
264 Mike Ridley .05 .15
265 Dave Roberts .05 .15
266 Adam Oates .10 .25
267 Bill Ranford .07 .20
268 Joe Juneau .07 .20
269 Chris Simon .07 .20
270 Peter Bondra .07 .20
271 Dale Hunter .07 .20
272 Jaroslav Svejkovski .07 .20
273 Sergei Gonchar .05 .15
274 Steve Konowalchuk .07 .20
275 Phil Housley .07 .20
276 Angela James RC .12 .30
277 Nancy Drolet RC .07 .20
278 Lesley Reddon RC .12 .30
279 Hayley Wickenheiser RC .12 .30
280 Vicky Sunohara RC .12 .30
281 Cassie Campbell RC .12 .30
282 Geraldine Heaney RC .07 .20
283 Judy Diduck RC .07 .20
284 France St. Louis RC .07 .20
285 Danielle Goyette RC .07 .20
286 Therese Brisson RC .07 .20
287 Stacey Wilson RC .07 .20
288 Danielle Dube RC .07 .20
289 Jayna Hefford RC .12 .30
290 Luce Letendre RC .07 .20
291 Lori Dupuis RC .07 .20
292 Rebecca Fahey RC .07 .20
293 Fiona Smith RC .07 .20
294 Laura Schuler RC .07 .20
295 Karen Nystrom RC .07 .20
296 Joe Thornton .10 .25
297 Peter Schaefer .07 .20
298 Daniel Tkaczuk .10 .25
299 Alyn McCauley .07 .20
300 Shane Willis .05 .15
301 Chris Phillips .07 .20
302 Marc Denis .10 .25
303 Jason Ward .05 .15
304 Patrick Marleau .12 .30
305 Brad Isbister .07 .20
306 Cameron Mann .07 .20
307 Daniel Cleary .07 .20
308 Brad Larsen .05 .15
309 Nick Boynton .05 .15
310 Scott Barney .05 .15
311 Boyd Devereaux .07 .20
312 Wayne Gretzky CL .50 1.25
313 Steve Yzerman CL .20 .50
314 Jaromir Jagr CL .25 .60
315 Jarome Iginla CL .10 .25
316 Patrick Roy CL .25 .60
317 John Vanbiesbrouck CL .10 .25
318 Paul Kariya CL .12 .30
319 Doug Weight CL .10 .25
320 Mats Sundin CL .10 .25

1997-98 Collector's Choice Blow-Ups

Very little is known about this oversized set that consisted of 5 cards other than the two mentioned below. Cards were numbered "X of 5" on the card backs.

1 Wayne Gretzky 4.00 10.00
2 Tony Amonte 1.00 2.50
3 Zigmund Palffy 1.00 2.50

1997-98 Collector's Choice Crash the Game

Randomly inserted in packs at the rate of 1:5, this 90-card set features color player photos. Each player had three cards featuring the same card number but a different opposing team listing on the front. If the pictured player scored against the designated team, that card could be redeemed for a special high quality redemption card of that player (expiration: 7/1/1998).

COMPLETE SET (90) 15.00 40.00
PLAYERS HAVE THREE CARDS OF EQUAL VALUE
COMP.PRIZE SET (30) 12.00 30.00
*PRIZE CARDS: 1.2X TO 3X BASIC INSERTS
C1A Wayne Gretzky COL W 1.25 3.00
C1B Wayne Gretzky DET L 1.25 3.00
C1C Wayne Gretzky EDM L 1.25 3.00
C2A Mike Modano FLO W .40 1.00
C2B Mike Modano NYI W .40 1.00
C2C Mike Modano NYR L .40 1.00
C3A Doug Weight BUF L .25 .60
C3B Doug Weight OTT W .25 .60
C3C Doug Weight NYR W .25 .60
C4A Brendan Shanahan MON W .30 .75
C4B Brendan Shanahan PIT W .30 .75
C4C Brendan Shanahan PHI W .30 .75
C5A Ray Sheppard ANA L .20 .50
C5B Ray Sheppard SET L .20 .50
C5C Ray Sheppard PHO W .20 .50
C6A Keith Primeau CAL W .20 .50
C6B Keith Primeau DET L .20 .50
C6C Keith Primeau TOR L .20 .50
C7A Ray Bourque DET L .40 1.00
C7B Ray Bourque LA L .40 1.00
C7C Ray Bourque VAN W .40 1.00
C8A Teemu Selanne NJ L .50 1.25
C8B Teemu Selanne NYI W .50 1.25
C8C Teemu Selanne WAS W .50 1.25
C9A Paul Kariya BOS L .30 .75
C9B Paul Kariya PIT L .30 .75
C9C Paul Kariya TB W .30 .75
C10A Tony Amonte MON L .20 .50
C10B Tony Amonte NYR W .20 .50
C10C Tony Amonte PHI L .20 .50
C11A Saku Koivu CAL L .25 .60
C11B Saku Koivu PHO L .25 .60
C11C Saku Koivu SJ W .25 .60
C12A Donald Audette ANA W .20 .50
C12B Donald Audette EDM L .20 .50
C12C Donald Audette STL L .20 .50
C13A Doug Gilmour CAL W .30 .75
C13B Doug Gilmour STL W .30 .75
C13C Doug Gilmour TOR W .30 .75
C14A Theo Fleury BUF L .30 .75
C14B Theo Fleury FLO L .30 .75
C14C Theo Fleury PHI W .30 .75
C15A Alexei Yashin COL W .20 .50
C15B Alexei Yashin LA L .20 .50
C15C Alexei Yashin TOR W .20 .50
C16A Zigmund Palffy CHI W .25 .60
C16B Zigmund Palffy DET W .25 .60
C16C Zigmund Palffy SJ W .25 .60
C17A Dimitri Khristich OTT W .20 .50
C17B Dimitri Khristich TB W .20 .50
C17C Dimitri Khristich WAS W .20 .50
C18A Joe Sakic NJ L .40 1.00
C18B Joe Sakic NYR L .40 1.00
C18C Joe Sakic PHI W .40 1.00
C19A Steve Yzerman BUF W .50 1.25
C19B Steve Yzerman MON L .50 1.25
C19C Steve Yzerman PHI W .50 1.25
C20A Eric Lindros ANA W .40 1.00
C20B Eric Lindros PHO W .40 1.00
C20C Eric Lindros TOR L .40 1.00
C21A Peter Forsberg FLO L .30 .75
C21B Peter Forsberg PHI L .30 .75
C21C Peter Forsberg WAS W .30 .75
C22A Dino Ciccarelli DAL W .25 .60
C22B Dino Ciccarelli DET L .25 .60
C22C Dino Ciccarelli EDM L .25 .60
C23A Mats Sundin BUF L .25 .60
C23B Mats Sundin MOT L .25 .60
C23C Mats Sundin OTT L .25 .60
C24A Pavel Bure NYI W .30 .75
C24B Pavel Bure NYR W .30 .75
C24C Pavel Bure PIT W .30 .75
C25A Peter Bondra CHI L .20 .50
C25B Peter Bondra LA W .20 .50
C25C Peter Bondra VAN W .20 .50
C26A Brett Hull BOS W .30 .75
C26B Brett Hull NYR L .30 .75
C26C Brett Hull WAS W .30 .75
C27A Keith Tkachuk BOS L .25 .60
C27B Keith Tkachuk NJ L .25 .60
C27C Keith Tkachuk TB W .25 .60
C28A Jaromir Jagr DET L .60 1.50
C28B Jaromir Jagr EDM W .60 1.50
C28C Jaromir Jagr STL L .60 1.50
C29A Jarome Iginla MON L .25 .60
C29B Jarome Iginla OTT L .25 .60
C29C Jarome Iginla WAS L .25 .60
C30A Owen Nolan BUF L .25 .60
C30B Owen Nolan FLO L .25 .60
C30C Owen Nolan NYI L .25 .60

1997-98 Collector's Choice Magic Men

Randomly inserted in Canadian packs at the rate of 1:32, this 10-card set features five color photos each of Wayne Gretzky and Patrick Roy.

COMMON GRETZKY (MM1-MM5) 5.00 10.00
COMMON ROY (MM6-MM10) 3.00 8.00

1997-98 Collector's Choice Star Quest

This 90-card, four-tier insert set features color photos of some of the top NHL Superstars printed using the hobby's top technology. The 45 cards in Tier One (SQ1-SQ45) were randomly inserted one in every pack; the 20 cards in Tier Two (SQ45-SQ65) were randomly inserted 1:21 packs; the 15 cards of Tier Three (SQ66-SQ80) were randomly inserted 1:71 packs; the 10 cards of Tier Four were randomly inserted 1:145 packs.

COMPLETE SET (90) 125.00 250.00
COMP.SERIES 1 (45) 3.00 8.00
SQ1 Bryan Berard .15 .40
SQ2 Robert Svehla .07 .20
SQ3 Petr Nedved .15 .40
SQ4 Steve Sullivan .07 .20
SQ5 Nicklas Lidstrom .20 .50
SQ6 Wade Redden .07 .20
SQ7 Jason Arnott .07 .20
SQ8 Martin Gelinas .07 .20
SQ9 Mikael Renberg .07 .20
SQ10 Jeff Friesen .07 .20
SQ11 Chris Chelios .20 .50
SQ12 Jarome Iginla .25 .60
SQ13 Vyacheslav Kozlov .07 .20
SQ14 Brian Holzinger .07 .20
SQ15 Eric Daze .15 .40
SQ16 Pat Verbeek .07 .20
SQ17 Jozef Stumpel .15 .40
SQ18 Rob Niedermayer .15 .40
SQ19 Sergei Fedorov .30 .75
SQ20 Brian Leetch .20 .50
SQ21 Bill Guerin .07 .20
SQ22 Dino Ciccarelli .07 .20
SQ23 Adam Oates .15 .40
SQ24 Mike Grier .07 .20
SQ25 Alexandre Daigle .07 .20
SQ26 Janne Niinimaa .15 .40
SQ27 Dimitri Khristich .07 .20
SQ28 Oleg Tverdovsky .07 .20
SQ29 Felix Potvin 1.00 2.50
SQ30 Mike Richter .20 .50
SQ31 Curtis Joseph .20 .50
SQ32 Vincent Damphousse .07 .20
SQ33 Vladimir Konstantinov .15 .40
SQ34 Andy Moog .15 .40
SQ35 Nikolai Khabibulin .15 .40
SQ36 Ed Belfour .20 .50
SQ37 Scott Mellanby .07 .20
SQ38 Sandis Ozolinsh .07 .20
SQ39 Travis Green .07 .20
SQ40 Patrick Lalime .15 .40
SQ41 Niklas Sundstrom .07 .20
SQ42 Guy Hebert .15 .40
SQ43 Vitali Yachmenev .07 .20
SQ44 Roman Hamrlik .07 .20
SQ45 Adam Deadmarsh .07 .20
SQ46 Alexei Zhamnov .60 1.50
SQ47 Saku Koivu 1.25 3.00
SQ48 Sergei Berezin 1.00 2.50
SQ49 Mark Messier 1.25 3.00
SQ50 Martin Brodeur 3.00 8.00
SQ51 Daniel Alfredsson 1.00 2.50
SQ52 John LeClair 1.25 3.00
SQ53 Mike Vernon 1.00 2.50
SQ54 Ron Francis 1.00 2.50
SQ55 Keith Primeau .60 1.50
SQ56 Pierre Turgeon 1.00 2.50
SQ57 Jim Carey 1.00 2.50
SQ58 Peter Bondra 1.00 2.50
SQ59 Pavel Bure 1.25 3.00
SQ60 Ray Sheppard .60 1.50
SQ61 Chris Gratton 1.00 2.50
SQ62 Derek Plante .60 1.50
SQ63 Joe Sakic 2.50 6.00
SQ64 Theo Fleury 1.00 2.50
SQ65 Tony Amonte 1.00 2.50
SQ66 Zigmund Palffy 1.50 4.00
SQ67 Steve Yzerman 10.00 25.00
SQ68 Doug Weight 2.00 5.00
SQ69 Alexander Mogilny 2.00 5.00
SQ70 Doug Gilmour 2.50 5.00
SQ71 Peter Forsberg 5.00 12.00
SQ72 Alexei Yashin 2.00 5.00
SQ73 Geoff Sanderson 2.00 5.00
SQ74 Brendan Shanahan 2.50 6.00
SQ75 Mark Recchi 2.00 5.00
SQ76 Brett Hull 3.00 8.00
SQ77 Ray Bourque 4.00 10.00
SQ78 Owen Nolan 2.00 5.00
SQ79 Jeremy Roenick 3.00 8.00
SQ80 Teemu Selanne 2.50 6.00
SQ81 Dominik Hasek 6.00 15.00
SQ82 Mike Modano 5.00 12.00
SQ83 Mats Sundin 4.00 10.00
SQ84 John Vanbiesbrouck 6.00 15.00
SQ85 Paul Kariya 3.00 8.00
SQ86 Patrick Roy 10.00 25.00
SQ87 Keith Tkachuk 4.00 10.00
SQ88 Eric Lindros 5.00 12.00
SQ89 Jaromir Jagr 6.00 15.00
SQ90 Wayne Gretzky 15.00 40.00

1997-98 Collector's Choice Stick 'Ums

Randomly inserted in packs at the rate of 1:3, this 30-card set features color action player photos printed on re-stickable stickers that stick anywhere.

COMPLETE SET (30) 15.00 30.00
S1 Wayne Gretzky 2.50 5.00
S2 John Vanbiesbrouck .25 .60
S3 Martin Brodeur .75 2.00
S4 Rob Blake .25 .60
S5 Saku Koivu .30 .75
S6 Curtis Joseph .30 .75
S7 Chris Chelios .30 .75
S8 Mike Modano .50 1.25
S9 Paul Kariya .30 .75
S10 Eric Lindros .30 .75
S11 Daniel Alfredsson .25 .60
S12 Jarome Iginla .40 1.00
S13 Jeremy Roenick .40 1.00
S14 Brendan Shanahan .30 .75
S15 Jaromir Jagr .50 1.25
S16 Zigmund Palffy .25 .60
S17 Mats Sundin .30 .75
S18 Teemu Selanne .30 .75
S19 Joe Sakic .60 1.50
S20 Ed Belfour .30 .75
S21 Peter Forsberg .75 2.00
S22 Dino Ciccarelli .25 .60
S23 Patrick Roy 1.50 4.00
S24 Doug Gilmour .25 .60
S25 Pavel Bure .30 .75
S26 Brett Hull .40 1.00
S27 Ray Bourque .50 1.25
S28 Adam Oates .25 .60
S29 Steve Yzerman 1.50 4.00
S30 Dominik Hasek .60 1.50

1997-98 Collector's Choice World Domination

Randomly inserted in Canadian packs at the rate of 1:4, this 20-card set features color photos of top players. The backs carry player information.

COMPLETE SET (20) 25.00 50.00
W1 Wayne Gretzky 5.00 12.00
W2 Mark Messier .75 2.00
W3 Steve Yzerman 4.00 10.00
W4 Brendan Shanahan .75 2.00
W5 Paul Kariya .75 2.00
W6 Joe Sakic 1.50 4.00
W7 Eric Lindros .75 2.00
W8 Rod Brind'Amour .60 1.50
W9 Keith Primeau .60 1.50
W10 Trevor Linden .60 1.50
W11 Theo Fleury .60 1.50
W12 Scott Niedermeyer .60 1.50
W13 Rob Blake .60 1.50
W14 Chris Pronger .60 1.50
W15 Eric Desjardins .60 1.50
W16 Adam Foote .60 1.50
W17 Scott Stevens .60 1.50
W18 Patrick Roy 4.00 10.00
W19 Curtis Joseph .75 2.00
W20 Martin Brodeur 2.00 5.00

2008-09 Collector's Choice

This set was released on February 24, 2009. The base set consists of 300 cards. Cards 201-250 consist of rookies.

COMPLETE SET (300) 30.00 60.00
COMP.SET w/o SPs (200) 12.00 30.00
RC STATED ODDS 1:2
3S STATED PRINT RUN 1:5
CC STATED ODDS 1:5
1 Ales Hemsky .15 .40
2 Ales Kulalik .12 .30
3 Alex Kovalev .15 .40
4 Alex Tanguay .12 .30
5 Alexander Edler .12 .30
6 Alexander Frolov .12 .30
7 Alexander Ovechkin .75 2.00
8 Alexander Semin .20 .50
9 Alexander Steen .20 .50
10 Andrei Kostitsyn .15 .40
11 Andrew Cogliano .15 .40
12 Anze Kopitar .30 .75
13 Bill Guerin .20 .50
14 Brad Boyes .12 .30
15 Brad Richards .20 .50
16 Brendan Morrison .12 .30
17 Aaron Voros .12 .30
18 Brenden Morrow .15 .40
19 Brian Campbell .15 .40
20 Brian Gionta .15 .40
21 Brian Rolston .15 .40
22 Cam Ward .20 .50
23 Carey Price .75 2.00
24 Chris Drury .15 .40
25 Chris Higgins .12 .30
26 Chris Kunitz .20 .50
27 Chris Osgood .20 .50
28 Chris Pronger .15 .40
29 Colby Armstrong .12 .30
30 Corey Perry .20 .50
31 Cristobal Huet .15 .40
32 Dan Boyle .15 .40
33 Dan Cleary .15 .40
34 Dan Ellis .12 .30
35 Daniel Alfredsson .20 .50
36 Daniel Briere .20 .50
37 Daniel Carcillo .12 .30
38 Daniel Sedin .20 .50
39 Dany Heatley .20 .50
40 Darcy Tucker .15 .40
41 David Booth .12 .30
42 David Clarkson .15 .40
43 David Legwand .15 .40
44 Daymond Langkow .12 .30
45 Derek Roy .12 .30
46 Dion Phaneuf .20 .50
47 Doug Weight .20 .50
48 Drew Stafford .15 .40
49 Duncan Keith .20 .50
50 Dustin Brown .20 .50
51 Dustin Penner .15 .40
52 Dwayne Roloson .15 .40
53 Ed Jovanovski .15 .40
54 Eric Staal .25 .60
55 Erik Cole .15 .40
56 Erik Johnson .15 .40
57 Evgeni Malkin .60 1.50
58 Evgeni Nabokov .15 .40
59 George Parros .12 .30
60 Gilbert Brule .12 .30
61 Chuck Kobasew .12 .30
62 Guillaume Latendresse .12 .30
63 Henrik Lundqvist .25 .60
64 Henrik Sedin .20 .50
65 Henrik Zetterberg .25 .60
66 Ilya Bryzgalov .15 .40
67 Ilya Kovalchuk .20 .50
68 J.P. Dumont .12 .30
69 Jack Johnson .12 .30
70 Jarome Iginla .20 .50
71 Jarret Stoll .15 .40
72 Jason Arnott .15 .40
73 Jason LaBarbera .15 .40
74 Jason Pominville .20 .50
75 Jason Spezza .20 .50
76 Jay Bouwmeester .20 .50
77 Jean-Sebastien Giguere .20 .50
78 Jeff Carter .20 .50
79 Jere Lehtinen .12 .30
80 Joe Sakic .30 .75
81 Joe Thornton .25 .60
82 Johan Franzen .20 .50
83 Johan Hedberg .15 .40
84 Jaroslav Halak .20 .50
85 Jonathan Cheechoo .20 .50
86 Jonathan Toews .50 1.25
87 Jordan Staal .20 .50
88 Josh Harding .20 .50
89 Jussi Jokinen .12 .30
90 Justin Williams .15 .40
91 Kari Lehtonen .15 .40
92 Keith Tkachuk .20 .50
93 Kristian Huselius .12 .30
94 Lee Stempniak .12 .30
95 Manny Legace .20 .50
96 Marc Savard .12 .30
97 Marc Staal .20 .50
98 Marc-Andre Fleury .30 .75
99 Marek Zidlicky .12 .30
100 Marian Gaborik .25 .60
101 Marian Hossa .15 .40
102 Markus Naslund .15 .40
103 Martin Biron .15 .40
104 Martin Brodeur .40 1.00
105 Martin Erat .12 .30
106 Martin Gerber .15 .40
107 Martin Hanzal .15 .40
108 Martin Havlat .20 .50
109 Martin St. Louis .20 .50
110 Marty Turco .20 .50
111 Mats Sundin .20 .50
112 Matt Stajan .15 .40
113 Matthew Lombardi .12 .30
114 Michael Peca .15 .40
115 Michael Ryder .12 .30
116 Michal Rozsival .12 .30
117 Miikka Kiprusoff .15 .40
118 Mike Cammalleri .15 .40
119 Mike Comrie .15 .40
120 Mike Knuble .12 .30
121 Mike Modano .30 .75
122 Mike Ribeiro .15 .40
123 Mike Richards .20 .50
124 Mike Smith .20 .50
125 Mikko Koivu .15 .40
126 Milan Hejduk .15 .40
127 Milan Lucic .30 .75
128 Milan Michalek .12 .30
129 Miroslav Satan .20 .50
130 Nathan Horton .15 .40
131 Nicklas Backstrom .30 .75
132 Nicklas Lidstrom .20 .50
133 Niklas Backstrom .20 .50
134 Nikolai Antropov .15 .40
135 Nikolai Khabibulin .20 .50
136 Nikolai Zherdev .12 .30
137 Olli Jokinen .15 .40
138 Pascal Leclaire .15 .40
139 Patrice Bergeron .25 .60
140 Patrick Kane .40 1.00
141 Patrick Marleau .20 .50
142 Patrick O'Sullivan .15 .40
143 Patrick Sharp .20 .50
144 Patrik Elias .20 .50
145 Paul Kariya .25 .60
146 Paul Ranger .12 .30
147 Paul Stastny .20 .50
148 Pavel Datsyuk .25 .60
149 Peter Budaj .15 .40
150 Peter Forsberg .25 .60
151 Peter Mueller .15 .40
152 Phil Kessel .25 .60
153 Pierre-Marc Bouchard .20 .50
154 R.J. Umberger .12 .30
155 Radim Vrbata .15 .40
156 Ray Whitney .15 .40
157 Rick DiPietro .15 .40
158 Rick Nash .20 .50
159 Robert Lang .12 .30
160 Roberto Luongo .25 .60
161 Rod Brind'Amour .20 .50
162 Ryan Getzlaf .30 .75
163 Ryan Kesler .25 .60
164 Ryan Malone .12 .30
165 Ryan Miller .20 .50
166 Ryan Smyth .15 .40
167 Ryan Suter .15 .40
168 Saku Koivu .20 .50
169 Sam Gagner .15 .40
170 Scott Gomez .15 .40
171 Scott Niedermayer .20 .50
172 Sergei Fedorov .30 .75
173 Sergei Zubov .15 .40
174 Shane Doan .15 .40
175 Shawn Horcoff .12 .30
176 Shea Weber .15 .40
177 Sidney Crosby .75 2.00
178 Simon Gagne .20 .50
179 Slava Kozlov .12 .30
180 Stephen Weiss .12 .30
181 Steve Bernier .12 .30
182 Teemu Selanne .40 1.00
183 Thomas Vanek .20 .50
184 Tim Thomas .20 .50
185 Tobias Enstrom .12 .30
186 Todd White .12 .30
187 Tomas Holmstrom .15 .40
188 Tomas Kaberle .12 .30
189 Tomas Vokoun .15 .40
190 Travis Zajac .15 .40
191 Trent Hunter .12 .30
192 Ty Conklin .15 .40
193 Vaclav Prospal .12 .30
194 Valtteri Filppula .20 .50
195 Vesa Toskala .15 .40
196 Vincent Lecavalier .15 .40
197 Wade Redden .12 .30
198 Wojtek Wolski .15 .40
199 Zach Parise .20 .50
200 Zdeno Chara .20 .50
201 Justin Abdelkader RC 1.00 2.50
202 Patrik Berglund RC .50 1.25
203 Mikkel Boedker RC .75 2.00
204 Zach Bogosian RC .60 1.50
205 Zach Boychuk RC .60 1.50
206 Derick Brassard RC .50 1.25
207 Fabian Brunnstrom RC .50 1.25
208 Matt D'Agostini RC .50 1.25
209 Drew Doughty RC 1.50 4.00
210 Robbie Earl RC .40 1.00
211 Andrew Ebbett RC .40 1.00
212 Jonathan Ericsson RC .60 1.50
213 Erik Ersberg RC .50 1.25
214 Nikita Filatov RC .60 1.50
215 Michael Frolik RC .60 1.50
216 Colton Gillies RC .50 1.25
217 Claude Giroux RC 1.25 3.00
218 Alex Goligoski RC .75 2.00
219 Darren Helm RC .60 1.50
220 Patric Hornqvist RC .60 1.50
221 Josh Bailey RC .75 2.00
222 Ryan Jones RC .60 1.50
223 Lauri Korpikoski RC .40 1.00
224 Nikolai Kulemin RC .60 1.50
225 Brian Lee RC .50 1.25
226 Shawn Matthias RC .60 1.50
227 Vladimir Mihalik RC .40 1.00
228 Oscar Moller RC .50 1.25
229 James Neal RC 1.25 3.00
230 Andreas Nodl RC .40 1.00
231 Kyle Okposo RC .60 1.50
232 T.J. Oshie RC 1.25 3.00
233 Nathan Oystrick RC .60 1.50
234 Alex Pietrangelo RC .75 2.00
235 Kevin Porter RC .50 1.25
236 Teddy Purcell RC .75 2.00
237 Tim Ramholt RC .50 1.25
238 Mattias Ritola RC .50 1.25
239 Luca Sbisa RC .40 1.00
240 Luke Schenn RC .75 2.00
241 Tom Sestito RC .60 1.50
242 Steven Stamkos RC 4.00 10.00
243 Brandon Sutter RC .60 1.50
244 Viktor Tikhonov RC .50 1.25
245 Kyle Turris RC 1.00 2.50
246 Boris Valabik RC .60 1.50
247 Jakub Voracek RC 1.25 3.00
248 Petr Vrana RC .40 1.00
249 Blake Wheeler RC 1.50 4.00
250 Ilya Zubov RC .50 1.25
251 Getzlaf/Giguere/Pronger 1.25 3.00
252 Kovalchuk/Lehtonen/Little .75 2.00
253 Savard/Thomas/Chara .75 2.00
254 Vanek/Miller/Roy .75 2.00
255 Iginla/Kiprusoff/Phaneuf .75 2.00
256 Staal/Ward/Whitney 1.00 2.50
257 Toews/Huet/Kane 2.00 5.00
258 Sakic/Budaj/Stastny 1.25 3.00
259 Nash/Leclaire/Huselius .75 2.00
260 Morrow/Turco/Richards .75 2.00
261 Zetterberg/Osgood/Datsyuk 1.00 2.50
262 Hemsky/Garon/Horcoff .60 1.50
263 Horton/Vokoun/Booth .60 1.50
264 Kopitar/LaBerbera/Frolov 1.25 3.00
265 Gaborik/Backstrom/Burns 1.00 2.50
266 Koivu/Price/Kovalev 3.00 8.00
267 Dumont/Ellis/Arnott .60 1.50
268 Parise/Brodeur/Elias 1.50 4.00
269 Comrie/DiPietro/Streit .60 1.50
270 Naslund/Lundqvist/Drury 1.00 2.50
271 Heatley/Gerber/Spezza .75 2.00
272 Richards/Biron/Carter .75 2.00
273 Doan/Bryzgalov/Jokinen .60 1.50
274 Crosby/Fleury/Malkin 3.00 8.00
275 Thornton/Nabokov/Cheechoo 1.00 2.50
276 Kariya/Legace/Boyes 1.00 2.50
277 Lecavalier/Smith/St. Louis .75 2.00
278 Antropov/Toskala/Kaberle .60 1.50
279 Sedin/Luongo/Sedsin 1.00 2.50
280 Ovechkin/Theodore/Green 3.00 8.00
281 Alexander Ovechkin 3.00 8.00
282 Brenden Morrow .60 1.50
283 Chris Pronger .60 1.50
284 Daniel Carcillo .50 1.25
285 Dion Phaneuf .75 2.00
286 Dustin Brown .75 2.00
287 Ed Jovanovski .60 1.50
288 Eric Staal 1.00 2.50
289 Henrik Lundqvist 1.00 2.50
290 Henrik Zetterberg 1.00 2.50
291 Ilya Kovalchuk .75 2.00
292 Jonathan Toews 2.00 5.00

293 Martin Brodeur	1.50	4.00
294 Rick Nash	.75	2.00
295 Roberto Luongo	1.00	2.50
296 Ryan Getzlaf	1.25	3.00
297 Sidney Crosby	3.00	8.00
298 Vincent Lecavalier	.60	1.50
299 Wade Redden	.50	1.25
300 Zdeno Chara	.75	2.00

2008-09 Collector's Choice Prime Reserve Gold

*GOLD (1-200): 5X TO 12X BASIC CARDS
*GOLD (201-250): 1.2X TO 3X BASIC CARDS
*GOLD (251-300): 1X TO 2.5X BASIC CARDS
STATED ODDS 1:24

131 Nicklas Backstrom	4.00	10.00

2008-09 Collector's Choice Reserve Silver

COMPLETE SET (300)	50.00	100.00

*SINGLES (1-200): .8X TO 2X BASIC CARDS
*SINGLES (201-250): 1X TO 2.5X BASIC CARDS
*SINGLES (251-300): .6X TO 1.5X BASIC CARDS
STATED ODDS 1 PER PACK

131 Nicklas Backstrom	.60	1.50

2008-09 Collector's Choice Cup Quest

COMPLETE SET (90)	50.00	100.00

FIRST ROUND STATED ODDS 1:10
SECOND ROUND STATED ODDS 1:14
SEMI-FINALS STATED ODDS 1:16
FINALS STATED ODDS 1:16
OVERALL STATED ODDS 1:6

CQ1 Ales Hemsky FR	.50	1.25
CQ2 Brian Rafalski FR	.50	1.25
CQ3 Brian Rolston FR	.50	1.25
CQ4 Corey Perry FR	.60	1.50
CQ5 Cristobal Huet FR	.50	1.25
CQ6 Daniel Sedin FR	.60	1.50
CQ7 David Booth FR	.40	1.00
CQ8 Derek Roy FR	.40	1.00
CQ9 Ed Jovanovski FR	.50	1.25
CQ10 J.P. Dumont FR	.40	1.00
CQ11 Jason Arnott FR	.50	1.25
CQ12 Jeff Carter FR	.60	1.50
CQ13 Jere Lehtinen FR	.40	1.00
CQ14 Jordan Staal FR	.60	1.50
CQ15 Kari Lehtonen FR	.50	1.25
CQ16 Manny Legace FR	.60	1.50
CQ17 Marian Hossa FR	.50	1.25
CQ18 Mark Streit FR	.40	1.00
CQ19 Martin Biron FR	.50	1.25
CQ20 Martin Gerber FR	.50	1.25
CQ21 Mike Green FR	.60	1.50
CQ22 Milan Hejduk FR	.50	1.25
CQ23 Nathan Horton FR	.50	1.25
CQ24 Niklas Backstrom FR	.60	1.50
CQ25 Pascal Leclaire FR	.50	1.25
CQ26 Pavol Demitra FR	.75	2.00
CQ27 Rob Blake FR	.60	1.50
CQ28 Rod Brind'Amour FR	.60	1.50
CQ29 Ryan Malone FR	.40	1.00
CQ30 Scott Gomez FR	.50	1.25
CQ31 Todd Bertuzzi FR	.60	1.50
CQ32 Tomas Holmstrom FR	.50	1.25
CQ33 Tomas Kaberle FR	.40	1.00
CQ34 Vesa Toskala FR	.50	1.25
CQ35 Zdeno Chara FR	.60	1.50
CQ36 Alex Kovalev SR	.60	1.50
CQ37 Andrew Cogliano SR	.60	1.50
CQ38 Anze Kopitar SR	1.25	3.00
CQ39 Brenden Morrow SR	.60	1.50
CQ40 Carey Price SR	3.00	8.00
CQ41 Chris Drury SR	.60	1.50
CQ42 Chris Osgood SR	.75	2.00
CQ43 Henrik Lundqvist SR	1.00	2.50
CQ44 Henrik Sedin SR	.75	2.00
CQ45 Jason Spezza SR	.75	2.00
CQ46 Joe Sakic SR	1.25	3.00
CQ47 Jonathan Toews SR	2.00	5.00
CQ48 Miikka Kiprusoff SR	.60	1.50
CQ49 Mike Ribeiro SR	.60	1.50
CQ50 Mikko Koivu SR	.60	1.50
CQ51 Nicklas Backstrom SR	1.25	3.00
CQ52 Olli Jokinen SR	.60	1.50
CQ53 Patrick Kane SR	1.50	4.00
CQ54 Peter Mueller SR	.60	1.50
CQ55 Ryan Miller SR	.75	2.00
CQ56 Sam Gagner SR	.60	1.50
CQ57 Shawn Horcoff SR	.50	1.25
CQ58 Thomas Vanek SR	.75	2.00
CQ59 Wade Redden SR	.50	1.25
CQ60 Zach Parise SR	.75	2.00
CQ61 Daniel Alfredsson SF	1.00	2.50
CQ62 Dany Heatley SF	1.00	2.50
CQ63 Dion Phaneuf SF	1.00	2.50
CQ64 Evgeni Nabokov SF	.75	2.00
CQ65 Jean-Sebastien Giguere SF	1.00	2.50
CQ66 Jonathan Cheechoo SF	1.00	2.50
CQ67 Marc-Andre Fleury SF	1.50	4.00
CQ68 Marian Gaborik SF	1.25	3.00
CQ69 Johan Franzen SF	1.00	2.50
CQ70 Markus Naslund SF	.75	2.00
CQ71 Martin St. Louis SF	1.00	2.50
CQ72 Mats Sundin SF	1.00	2.50
CQ73 Mike Modano SF	1.50	4.00
CQ74 Nicklas Lidstrom SF	1.00	2.50
CQ75 Paul Stastny SF	1.00	2.50
CQ76 Pavel Datsyuk SF	1.25	3.00
CQ77 Rick Nash SF	1.00	2.50
CQ78 Ryan Getzlaf SF	1.50	4.00
CQ79 Saku Koivu SF	1.00	2.50
CQ80 Shane Doan SF	.75	2.00
CQ81 Alexander Ovechkin F	6.00	15.00
CQ82 Sidney Crosby F	6.00	15.00
CQ83 Evgeni Malkin F	5.00	12.00
CQ84 Jarome Iginla F	1.50	4.00
CQ85 Vincent Lecavalier F	1.25	3.00
CQ86 Roberto Luongo F	2.00	5.00
CQ87 Henrik Zetterberg F	2.00	5.00
CQ88 Ilya Kovalchuk F	1.50	4.00
CQ89 Joe Thornton F	2.00	5.00
CQ90 Martin Brodeur F	3.00	8.00

2008-09 Collector's Choice Stick-Ums

COMPLETE SET (30)	25.00	60.00

STATED ODDS 1:18

UMS1 Alexander Ovechkin	2.50	6.00
UMS2 Anze Kopitar	1.00	2.50
UMS3 Carey Price	2.50	6.00
UMS4 Dany Heatley	.60	1.50
UMS5 Evgeni Malkin	2.00	5.00
UMS6 Henrik Lundqvist	.75	2.00
UMS7 Henrik Zetterberg	.75	2.00
UMS8 Ilya Kovalchuk	.60	1.50
UMS9 Jarome Iginla	.60	1.50
UMS10 Jean-Sebastien Giguere	.60	1.50
UMS11 Joe Sakic	1.00	2.50
UMS12 Joe Thornton	.75	2.00
UMS13 Jonathan Toews	1.50	4.00
UMS14 Marc-Andre Fleury	1.00	2.50
UMS15 Marian Gaborik	.75	2.00
UMS16 Martin Brodeur	1.25	3.00
UMS17 Martin St. Louis	.60	1.50
UMS18 Marty Turco	.60	1.50
UMS19 Mike Modano	1.00	2.50
UMS20 Mike Richards	.60	1.50
UMS21 Nicklas Backstrom	1.00	2.50
UMS22 Nicklas Lidstrom	.60	1.50
UMS23 Patrick Kane	1.25	3.00
UMS24 Paul Stastny	.60	1.50
UMS25 Pavel Datsyuk	.75	2.00
UMS26 Rick Nash	.60	1.50
UMS27 Roberto Luongo	.75	2.00
UMS28 Ryan Miller	.60	1.50
UMS29 Sidney Crosby	2.50	6.00
UMS30 Vincent Lecavalier	.50	1.25

2009-10 Collector's Choice

COMP.SET w/o SPS (200)	15.00	40.00
1 Rick DiPietro	.15	.40
2 Kyle Okposo	.20	.50
3 Josh Bailey	.15	.40
4 Mark Streit	.12	.30
5 Doug Weight	.20	.50
6 Trent Hunter	.12	.30
7 Vincent Lecavalier	.15	.40
8 Steven Stamkos	.40	1.00
9 Ryan Malone	.12	.30
10 Mike Smith	.20	.50
11 Vaclav Prospal	.12	.30
12 Martin St. Louis	.20	.50
13 Paul Stastny	.20	.50
14 Peter Budaj	.15	.40
15 John-Michael Liles	.12	.30
16 Milan Hejduk	.15	.40
17 Marek Svatos	.12	.30
18 Wojtek Wolski	.12	.30
19 Chris Stewart	.15	.40
20 Ilya Kovalchuk	.20	.50
21 Todd White	.12	.30
22 Bryan Little	.20	.50
23 Kari Lehtonen	.15	.40
24 Colby Armstrong	.12	.30
25 Zach Bogosian	.15	.40
26 Anze Kopitar	.30	.75
27 Dustin Brown	.15	.40
28 Jonathan Quick	.40	1.00
29 Alexander Frolov	.15	.40
30 Drew Doughty	.25	.60
31 Ryan Smyth	.15	.40
32 Peter Mueller	.15	.40
33 Shane Doan	.15	.40
34 Scottie Upshall	.12	.30
35 Ilya Bryzgalov	.15	.40
36 Keith Yandle	.20	.50
37 Matthew Lombardi	.12	.30
38 Nikolai Kulemin	.15	.40
39 Mike Komisarek	.15	.40
40 Vesa Toskala	.20	.50
41 Matt Stajan	.15	.40
42 Tomas Kaberle	.12	.30
43 Mikhail Grabovski	.20	.50
44 Luke Schenn	.15	.40
45 Marty Turco	.20	.50
46 James Neal	.20	.50
47 Mike Ribeiro	.15	.40
48 Steve Ott	.12	.30
49 Brad Richards	.20	.50
50 Loui Eriksson	.15	.40
51 Mike Modano	.30	.75
52 Jason Spezza	.20	.50
53 Jarkko Ruutu	.12	.30
54 Filip Kuba	.12	.30
55 Daniel Alfredsson	.20	.50
56 Alex Kovalev	.20	.50
57 Nick Foligno	.15	.40
58 Dany Heatley	.20	.50
59 Ales Hemsky	.15	.40
60 Patrick O'Sullivan	.15	.40
61 Nikolai Khabibulin	.20	.50
62 Sheldon Souray	.12	.30
63 Shawn Horcoff	.12	.30
64 Andrew Cogliano	.15	.40
65 Sam Gagner	.15	.40
66 Pekka Rinne	.25	.60
67 Jason Arnott	.15	.40
68 Shea Weber	.15	.40
69 Jordin Tootoo	.20	.50
70 Ryan Suter	.20	.50
71 J.P. Dumont	.12	.30
72 Mikko Koivu	.20	.50
73 Martin Havlat	.15	.40
74 Niklas Backstrom	.20	.50
75 Marek Zidlicky	.12	.30
76 Pierre-Marc Bouchard	.20	.50
77 Andrew Brunette	.12	.30
78 Thomas Vanek	.20	.50
79 Tim Connolly	.12	.30
80 Derek Roy	.15	.40
81 Ryan Miller	.20	.50
82 Jason Pominville	.20	.50
83 Drew Stafford	.20	.50
84 Clarke MacArthur	.12	.30
85 Stephen Weiss	.12	.30
86 Michael Frolik	.15	.40
87 Keith Ballard	.12	.30
88 David Booth	.12	.30
89 Nathan Horton	.20	.50
90 Tomas Vokoun	.15	.40
91 Ryan Getzlaf	.30	.75
92 Scott Niedermayer	.20	.50
93 Corey Perry	.20	.50
94 Saku Koivu	.20	.50
95 Teemu Selanne	.40	1.00
96 Bobby Ryan	.20	.50
97 Steve Mason	.15	.40
98 Rick Nash	.15	.40
99 Jakub Voracek	.20	.50
100 Kris Russell	.20	.50
101 R.J. Umberger	.15	.40
102 Derick Brassard	.20	.50
103 Paul Kariya	.25	.60
104 David Perron	.12	.30
105 T.J. Oshie	.30	.75
106 Brad Boyes	.12	.30
107 Andy McDonald	.15	.40
108 David Backes	.20	.50
109 Chris Mason	.15	.40
110 Carey Price	.75	2.00
111 Andrei Markov	.20	.50
112 Scott Gomez	.15	.40
113 Mike Cammalleri	.15	.40
114 Tomas Plekanec	.20	.50
115 Maxim Lapierre	.12	.30
116 Andrei Kostitsyn	.15	.40
117 Chris Drury	.15	.40
118 Brandon Dubinsky	.15	.40
119 Henrik Lundqvist	.30	.75
120 Marc Staal	.20	.50
121 Sean Avery	.15	.40
122 Chris Higgins	.12	.30
123 Marian Gaborik	.25	.60
124 Olli Jokinen	.15	.40
125 Dion Phaneuf	.25	.60
126 Jay Bouwmeester	.20	.50
127 Craig Conroy	.12	.30
128 Miikka Kiprusoff	.15	.40
129 Daymond Langkow	.12	.30
130 Jarome Iginla	.20	.50
131 Mike Richards	.20	.50
132 Claude Giroux	.20	.50
133 Braydon Coburn	.12	.30
134 Jeff Carter	.20	.50
135 Simon Gagne	.20	.50
136 Chris Pronger	.15	.40
137 Daniel Briere	.20	.50
138 Roberto Luongo	.25	.60
139 Henrik Sedin	.20	.50
140 Kyle Wellwood	.15	.40
141 Alexander Edler	.12	.30
142 Ryan Kesler	.20	.50
143 Daniel Sedin	.20	.50
144 Mason Raymond	.20	.50
145 Patrik Elias	.20	.50
146 Paul Martin	.12	.30
147 Martin Brodeur	.40	1.00
148 Zach Parise	.20	.50
149 Travis Zajac	.15	.40
150 Jamie Langenbrunner	.12	.30
151 David Clarkson	.15	.40
152 Alexander Ovechkin	.75	2.00
153 Semyon Varlamov	.20	.50
154 Tomas Fleischmann	.12	.30
155 Alexander Semin	.20	.50
156 Nicklas Backstrom	.30	.75
157 Brooks Laich	.20	.50
158 Mike Green	.20	.50
159 Tim Thomas	.20	.50
160 Michael Ryder	.12	.30
161 Marc Savard	.12	.30
162 David Krejci	.20	.50
163 Phil Kessel	.25	.60
164 Zdeno Chara	.20	.50
165 Patrice Bergeron	.25	.60
166 Joe Thornton	.20	.50
167 Ryane Clowe	.15	.40
168 Dan Boyle	.15	.40
169 Joe Pavelski	.20	.50
170 Patrick Marleau	.20	.50
171 Evgeni Nabokov	.15	.40
172 Devin Setoguchi	.15	.40
173 Eric Staal	.25	.60
174 Jussi Jokinen	.12	.30
175 Rod Brind'Amour	.20	.50
176 Tuomo Ruutu	.12	.30
177 Sergei Samsonov	.12	.30
178 Ray Whitney	.15	.40
179 Cam Ward	.20	.50
180 Patrick Kane	.40	1.00
181 Brian Campbell	.15	.40
182 Kris Versteeg	.20	.50
183 Marian Hossa	.15	.40
184 Cristobal Huet	.20	.50
185 Patrick Sharp	.20	.50
186 Jonathan Toews	.40	1.00
187 Sidney Crosby	.75	2.00
188 Maxime Talbot	.20	.50
189 Marc-Andre Fleury	.30	.75
190 Evgeni Malkin	.60	1.50
191 Sergei Gonchar	.12	.30
192 Kristopher Letang	.20	.50
193 Jordan Staal	.20	.50
194 Henrik Zetterberg	.25	.60
195 Dan Cleary	.20	.50
196 Chris Osgood	.20	.50
197 Pavel Datsyuk	.25	.60
198 Valtteri Filppula	.20	.50
199 Niklas Kronwall	.15	.40
200 Nicklas Lidstrom	.20	.50
201 Koivu/Ryan/Getzlaf	1.00	2.50
202 Little/Lehtonen/Kovalchuk	.60	1.50
203 Thomas/Savard/Chara	.60	1.50
204 Miller/Roy/Vanek	.60	1.50
205 Iginla/Kiprusoff/Phaneuf	.75	2.00
206 Staal/Ward/Whitney	.75	2.00
207 Sharp/Kane/Toews	1.25	3.00
208 Hejduk/Stastny/Wolski	.60	1.50
209 Brassard/Mason/Nash	.60	1.50
210 Turco/Eriksson/Ribeiro	.60	1.50
211 Zetterberg/Lidstrom/Datsyuk	.75	2.00
212 Gagner/Souray/Hemsky	.50	1.25
213 Booth/Vokoun/Weiss	.50	1.25
214 Frolov/Kopitar/Doughty	1.00	2.50
215 Koivu/Backstrom/Nolan	.60	1.50
216 Gomez/Markov/Price	2.50	6.00
217 Arnott/Weber/Rinne	.75	2.00
218 Brodeur/Parise/Elias	1.25	3.00
219 Streit/Okposo/Weight	.60	1.50
220 Gaborik/Lundqvist/Drury	1.00	2.50
221 Spezza/Kovalev/Alfredsson	.60	1.50
222 Pronger/Carter/Richards	.60	1.50
223 Doan/Bryzgalov/Mueller	.50	1.25
224 Crosby/Malkin/Fleury	2.50	6.00
225 Nabokov/Thornton/Marleau	.60	1.50
226 Boyes/Mason/Perron	.50	1.25
227 St. Louis/Lecavalier/Stamkos	1.25	3.00
228 Schenn/Kessel/Toskala	.75	2.00
229 Luongo/Sedin/Sedin	.75	2.00
230 Backstrom/Green/Ovechkin	2.50	6.00
231 Brian Salcido RC	.60	1.50
232 Matt Beleskey RC	.60	1.50
233 Spencer Machacek RC	.75	2.00
234 Evander Kane RC	1.50	4.00
235 Brad Marchand RC	2.00	5.00
236 Byron Bitz RC	.60	1.50
237 Jhonas Enroth RC	1.00	2.50
238 Tyler Myers RC	1.25	3.00
239 Chris Butler RC	.75	2.00
240 Riley Armstrong RC	.60	1.50
241 Mikael Backlund RC	.75	2.00
242 Kris Chucko RC	.60	1.50
243 Matt Pelech RC	.75	2.00
244 John Negrin RC	.75	2.00
245 Jakub Petruzalek RC	.75	2.00
246 Antti Niemi RC	1.25	3.00
247 Chris Durno RC	.60	1.50
248 T.J. Galiardi RC	.75	2.00
249 Ray Macias RC	.60	1.50
250 Matt Hendricks RC	.60	1.50
251 Matt Duchene RC	1.50	4.00
252 Ryan O'Reilly RC	1.25	3.00
253 Ivan Vishnevskiy RC	.60	1.50
254 Tom Wandell RC	.75	2.00
255 Jamie Benn RC	2.50	6.00
256 Ville Leino RC	.60	1.50
257 Taylor Chorney RC	.75	2.00
258 Dmitry Kulikov RC	.75	2.00
259 Davis Drewiske RC	.75	2.00
260 Alec Martinez RC	1.00	2.50
261 Jaime Sifers RC	.60	1.50
262 Mathieu Carle RC	.75	2.00
263 Yannick Weber RC	.75	2.00
264 Cal O'Reilly RC	.60	1.50
265 Alexander Sulzer RC	.50	1.25
266 Mike Santorelli RC	.75	2.00
267 Colin Wilson RC	.75	2.00
268 Teemu Laakso RC	.50	1.25
269 Cody Franson RC	.75	2.00
270 Jesse Joensuu RC	.60	1.50
271 Andrew MacDonald RC	.50	1.25
272 Joel Rechlicz RC	.50	1.25
273 John Tavares RC	6.00	15.00
274 Michael Sauer RC	.60	1.50
275 Artem Anisimov RC	.75	2.00
276 Matt Gilroy RC	.75	2.00
277 Michael Del Zotto RC	.75	2.00
278 Peter Regin RC	.60	1.50
279 Erik Karlsson RC	2.50	6.00
280 James van Riemsdyk RC	1.50	4.00
281 Mika Pyorala RC	.60	1.50
282 David Schlemko RC	.60	1.50
283 Luca Caputi RC	.75	2.00
284 Jason Demers RC	1.25	3.00
285 Benn Ferriero RC	.75	2.00
286 Frazer McLaren RC	.60	1.50
287 Steven Zalewski RC	.60	1.50
288 Logan Couture RC	1.50	4.00
289 Kevin Quick RC	.50	1.25
290 Riku Helenius RC	.75	2.00
291 James Wright RC	.75	2.00
292 Victor Hedman RC	1.50	4.00
293 Christian Hanson RC	.75	2.00
294 Viktor Stalberg RC	.75	2.00
295 Tyler Bozak RC	1.25	3.00
296 Jonas Gustavsson RC	5.00	12.00
297 Sergei Shirokov RC	.50	1.25
298 Guillaume Desbiens RC	.75	2.00
299 Michael Grabner RC	.75	2.00
300 Michal Neuvirth RC	1.25	3.00

2009-10 Collector's Choice Reserve

*SINGLES 1-200: .8X TO 2X BASIC
*SINGLES 201-230: .6X TO 1.5X BASIC
*ROOKIES 231-300: .6X TO 1.5X BASIC
OVERALL STATED ODDS 1 PER PACK

156 Nicklas Backstrom	.60	1.50

2009-10 Collector's Choice Reserve Prime

*SINGLES 1-200: 5X TO 12X BASIC
*SINGLES 201-230: 2X TO 5X BASIC
*SINGLES 231-300: 2X TO 5X BASIC
OVERALL ODDS 1:36

156 Nicklas Backstrom	4.00	10.00

2009-10 Collector's Choice Badge of Honor Tattoos

COMPLETE SET (30)	4.00	10.00

STATED ODDS 1:6

BH1 Anaheim Ducks	.20	.50
BH2 Atlanta Thrashers	.20	.50
BH3 Boston Bruins	.20	.50
BH4 Buffalo Sabres	.20	.50
BH5 Calgary Flames	.20	.50
BH6 Carolina Hurricanes	.20	.50
BH7 Chicago Blackhawks	.20	.50
BH8 Colorado Avalanche	.20	.50
BH9 Columbus Blue Jackets	.20	.50
BH10 Dallas Stars	.20	.50
BH11 Detroit Red Wings	.20	.50
BH12 Edmonton Oilers	.20	.50
BH13 Florida Panthers	.20	.50
BH14 Los Angeles Kings	.20	.50
BH15 Minnesota Wild	.20	.50
BH16 Montreal Canadiens	.20	.50
BH17 Nashville Predators	.20	.50
BH18 New Jersey Devils	.20	.50
BH19 New York Islanders	.20	.50
BH20 New York Rangers	.20	.50
BH21 Ottawa Senators	.20	.50
BH22 Philadelphia Flyers	.20	.50
BH23 Phoenix Coyotes	.20	.50
BH24 Pittsburgh Penguins	.20	.50
BH25 San Jose Sharks	.20	.50
BH26 St. Louis Blues	.20	.50
BH27 Tampa Bay Lightning	.20	.50
BH28 Toronto Maple Leafs	.20	.50
BH29 Vancouver Canucks	.20	.50
BH30 Washington Capitals	.20	.50

2009-10 Collector's Choice Cup Quest

COMPLETE SET (80)	150.00	300.00

F STATED PRINT RUN 100 SER.#'d SETS
OVERALL STATED ODDS 1:9

CQ1 Chris Pronger FR	.50	1.25
CQ2 Patrice Bergeron FR	.75	2.00
CQ3 Dion Phaneuf FR	.75	2.00
CQ4 Dany Heatley FR	.60	1.50
CQ5 Marty Turco FR	.60	1.50
CQ6 Nicklas Lidstrom FR	.60	1.50
CQ7 Ales Hemsky FR	.50	1.25
CQ8 Tomas Vokoun FR	.50	1.25
CQ9 Anze Kopitar FR	1.00	2.50
CQ10 Owen Nolan FR	.60	1.50
CQ11 Shea Weber FR	.50	1.25
CQ12 Doug Weight FR	.60	1.50
CQ13 Rick DiPietro FR	.50	1.25
CQ14 Chris Drury FR	.50	1.25
CQ15 Patrick Marleau FR	.60	1.50
CQ16 Simon Gagne FR	.60	1.50
CQ17 Shane Doan FR	.50	1.25
CQ18 Devin Setoguchi FR	.50	1.25
CQ19 David Perron FR	.40	1.00
CQ20 Matt Stajan FR	.50	1.25
CQ21 Mike Green FR	.60	1.50
CQ22 Zdeno Chara FR	.60	1.50
CQ23 Brian Campbell FR	.50	1.25
CQ24 Brad Richards FR	.60	1.50
CQ25 Andrew Cogliano FR	.50	1.25
CQ26 David Booth FR	.40	1.00
CQ27 Pekka Rinne FR	.75	2.00
CQ28 Peter Mueller FR	.50	1.25
CQ29 Paul Kariya FR	.75	2.00
CQ30 Ryan Kesler FR	.60	1.50
CQ31 Mikko Koivu SR	.75	2.00
CQ32 Jeff Carter SR	.75	2.00
CQ33 Jordan Staal SR	.75	2.00
CQ34 Jason Spezza SR	.75	2.00
CQ35 Nicklas Backstrom SR	1.25	3.00
CQ36 Marian Gaborik SR	1.00	2.50
CQ37 Bobby Ryan SR	.75	2.00
CQ38 Phil Kessel SR	1.00	2.50
CQ39 Ryan Miller SR	.75	2.00
CQ40 Miikka Kiprusoff SR	.60	1.50
CQ41 Eric Staal SR	1.00	2.50
CQ42 Rick Nash SR	.60	1.50
CQ43 Steve Mason SR	.60	1.50
CQ44 Mike Modano SR	1.25	3.00
CQ45 Pavel Datsyuk SR	1.00	2.50
CQ46 Sam Gagner SR	.60	1.50
CQ47 Drew Doughty SR	1.00	2.50
CQ48 Zach Parise SR	.75	2.00
CQ49 Henrik Lundqvist SR	1.25	3.00
CQ50 Paul Stastny SR	.75	2.00
CQ51 Mike Richards SR	.75	2.00
CQ52 Marc-Andre Fleury SR	1.25	3.00
CQ53 Teemu Selanne SR	1.50	4.00
CQ54 Martin St. Louis SR	.75	2.00
CQ55 Luke Schenn SR	.60	1.50
CQ56 Ryan Getzlaf SR	1.25	3.00
CQ57 Thomas Vanek SR	.75	2.00
CQ58 Cam Ward SR	.75	2.00
CQ59 Steven Stamkos SR	1.50	4.00
CQ60 Saku Koivu SR	.75	2.00
CQ61 Ilya Kovalchuk TR	1.00	2.50
CQ62 Jarome Iginla TR	1.25	3.00
CQ63 Jonathan Toews TR	2.50	6.00
CQ64 Joe Thornton TR	1.25	3.00
CQ65 Henrik Zetterberg TR	1.50	4.00
CQ66 Carey Price TR	5.00	12.00
CQ67 Evgeni Malkin TR	4.00	10.00
CQ68 Vincent Lecavalier TR	1.00	2.50
CQ69 Roberto Luongo TR	1.50	4.00
CQ70 Patrick Kane TR	2.50	6.00
CQ71 Martin Brodeur F/100	10.00	25.00
CQ72 Sidney Crosby F/100	20.00	50.00
CQ73 Alexander Ovechkin F/100	20.00	50.00
CQ74 Wayne Gretzky F/100	25.00	60.00
CQ75 Bobby Orr F/100	15.00	40.00
CQ76 Gordie Howe F/100	12.00	30.00
CQ77 Mario Lemieux F/100	15.00	40.00
CQ78 Steve Yzerman F/100	12.00	30.00
CQ79 Patrick Roy F/100	12.00	30.00
CQ80 Mark Messier F/100	6.00	15.00

2009-10 Collector's Choice Stick-Ums

COMPLETE SET (30)	12.00	30.00

STATED ODDS 1:4

SU1 Ilya Kovalchuk	.40	1.00
SU2 Phil Kessel	.50	1.25
SU3 Ryan Miller	.40	1.00
SU4 Jarome Iginla	.40	1.00
SU5 Eric Staal	.50	1.25
SU6 Patrick Kane	.75	2.00
SU7 Jonathan Toews	.75	2.00
SU8 Paul Stastny	.40	1.00
SU9 Rick Nash	.30	.75
SU10 Henrik Zetterberg	.50	1.25
SU11 Pavel Datsyuk	.50	1.25
SU12 Drew Doughty	.50	1.25
SU13 Carey Price	1.50	4.00
SU14 Shea Weber	.30	.75
SU15 Martin Brodeur	.75	2.00
SU16 Zach Parise	.40	1.00
SU17 Henrik Lundqvist	.60	1.50
SU18 Daniel Alfredsson	.40	1.00
SU19 Jason Spezza	.40	1.00
SU20 Jeff Carter	.40	1.00
SU21 Mike Richards	.40	1.00
SU22 Sidney Crosby	1.50	4.00
SU23 Evgeni Malkin	1.25	3.00
SU24 Marc-Andre Fleury	.60	1.50
SU25 Joe Thornton	.40	1.00
SU26 Vincent Lecavalier	.30	.75
SU27 Luke Schenn	.30	.75
SU28 Roberto Luongo	.50	1.25
SU29 Alexander Ovechkin	1.50	4.00
SU30 Mike Green	.40	1.00

2009-10 Collector's Choice Warriors of Ice

COMPLETE SET (6)	4.00	10.00

STATED ODDS 1:6

W1 Alexander Ovechkin	1.50	4.00
W2 Henrik Zetterberg	.50	1.25
W3 Jarome Iginla	.40	1.00
W4 Martin Brodeur	.75	2.00
W5 Sidney Crosby	1.50	4.00
W6 Zdeno Chara	.40	1.00

1959 Comet Sweets Olympic Achievements

Celebrating various Olympic events, ceremonies, and their history, this 25-card set was issued by Comet Sweets. The cards are printed on thin cardboard stock and measure 1 7/16" by 2 9/16". Inside white borders, the fronts display water color paintings of various Olympic events. Some cards are horizontally oriented; others are vertically oriented. The set title "Olympic Achievements" appears at the top on the backs, with a discussion of the event below. This set is the first series; the cards are numbered "X to 25."

COMPLETE SET (25)	30.00	60.00
20 Hockey	2.50	5.00

1993-94 Costacos Brothers Poster Cards

COMPLETE SET (18)	10.00	20.00
4 Ray Bourque Secretary of Defense	.20	.50
5 Theoren Fleury Fire on Ice	.20	.50
7 Brett Hull Top Gun	.40	1.00
9 Jaromir Jagr Czechmate	.60	1.50
10 Mario Lemieux Route 66	.75	2.00
11 Mark Messier Ice Warrior	.40	1.00
13 Alexander Mogilny Alexander the Great	.20	.50

1962-63 Cowan Ceramic Tiles

These unique collectibles featured artistic renditions (by H.M. Cowan) of top NHL players on smallish ceramic tiles. As they were unnumbered, the tiles were checklisted below by the number that appears on their original box.

1 Charlie Burns	75.00	150.00
2 Red Berenson	100.00	200.00
3 Ralph Backstrom	100.00	200.00
4 Larry Cahan	75.00	150.00
5 Bernie Geoffrion	250.00	500.00
6 Phil Goyette	75.00	150.00
7 Doug Harvey	150.00	300.00
8 Bronco Horvath	75.00	150.00
9 Harry Howell	125.00	250.00
10 Andy Hebenton	75.00	150.00
11 Jim Langlois	75.00	150.00
12 Bert Marshall	75.00	150.00
13 Marcel Pronovost	150.00	300.00
14 Henri Richard	350.00	600.00
15 Bobby Rousseau	75.00	150.00
16 Gilles Tremblay	100.00	200.00
17 Jerry Toppazzini	100.00	200.00
18 Gump Worsley	250.00	500.00
19 Dave Balon	75.00	150.00
20 Jean Beliveau	500.00	800.00
21 Claude Provost	125.00	250.00
22 Vic Hadfield	75.00	150.00
23 Jean-Guy Talbot	100.00	200.00
24 Dickie Moore	100.00	200.00
25 Jean Ratelle	75.00	150.00
26 Tom Johnson	100.00	200.00
27 Earl Ingarfield	75.00	150.00
28 Lou Fontinato	100.00	200.00
29 Cesare Maniago	100.00	200.00
30 Ted Hampson	75.00	150.00
31 Muzz Patrick	75.00	150.00
32 Andy Bathgate	100.00	200.00
33 Bill Hicke	75.00	150.00
34 J.C. Tremblay	100.00	200.00

1996-97 Coyotes Coca-Cola

This set features the Coyotes of the NHL. The postcard-sized set was issued for autograph sessions and other personal appearances by team players. There are multiple versions of the cards of some players. These cards features different front photos, but identical backs.

COMPLETE SET (37)	10.00	25.00
1 Bob Corkum	.20	.50
2 Shane Doan	.60	1.50
3 Dallas Drake	.20	.50
4 Dallas Eakins	.20	.50
5 Mike Eastwood	.20	.50
6 Jeff Finley	.20	.50
7 Mike Gartner	.30	.75
8 Mike Gartner	.30	.75
9 Mike Hudson	.20	.50
10 Craig Janney	.20	.50
11 Jim Johnson	.20	.50
12 Nikolai Khabibulin	.60	1.50
13 Nikolai Khabibulin	.60	1.50
14 Chad Kilger	.20	.50
15 Kris King	.20	.50
16 Kris King	.20	.50
17 Igor Korolev	.20	.50
18 Norm Maciver	.20	.50
19 Dave Manson	.20	.50
20 Brad McCrimmon	.20	.50
21 Jim McKenzie	.20	.50
22 Teppo Numminen	.30	.75
23 Deron Quint	.20	.50
24 Jeremy Roenick	.75	2.00
25 Jeremy Roenick	.75	2.00
26 Jeremy Roenick	.75	2.00
27 Cliff Ronning	.20	.50
28 Darrin Shannon	.20	.50
29 Mike Stapleton	.20	.50
30 Keith Tkachuk	.75	2.00
31 Keith Tkachuk	.75	2.00
32 Oleg Tverdovsky	.20	.50
33 Darcy Wakaluk	.25	.60
34 Zinetula Bilyaletinov CO	.08	.25
34 Don Hay CO	.08	.25
34 Paul MacLean CO	.08	.25
36 Team Photo	.20	.50

2001-02 Coyotes Team Issue

This set features the Phoenix Coyotes. This set was given away a few cards at a time at various home games, as well as at player autograph appearances. The oversized cards measure approximately 3 X 6. It is believed the checklist is complete, but due to the nature of the distribution, there may be other singles out there. If you discover one, please contact us at hockeymag@beckett.com.

COMPLETE SET (22)	10.00	25.00
1 Drake Berehowsky	.40	1.00
2 Sergei Berezin	.40	1.00
3 Daniel Briere	.75	2.00
4 Sean Burke	.75	2.00
5 Shane Doan	.75	2.00
6 Robert Esche	.75	2.00
7 Michal Handzus	.40	1.00
8 Mike Johnson	.40	1.00
9 Krys Kolanos	1.25	3.00
10 Daymond Langkow	.75	2.00
11 Claude Lemieux	.40	1.00
12 Paul Mara	.40	1.00
13 Daniil Markov	.40	1.00
14 Brad May	.40	1.00
15 Ladislav Nagy	.40	1.00
16 Teppo Numminen	.40	1.00
17 Denis Pederson	.40	1.00
18 Todd Simpson	.40	1.00
19 Radoslav Suchy	.40	1.00
20 Mike Sullivan	.40	1.00
21 Ossi Vaananen	.40	1.00
22 Landon Wilson	.40	1.00

2002-03 Coyotes Team Issue

Cards were issued by the team in an unknown fashion. Cards are oversized (3X6), unnumbered and are blank backed.

COMPLETE SET (25)	15.00	30.00
1 Header	.10	.25
2 Todd Simpson	.40	1.00
3 Ossi Vaananen	.40	1.00
4 Drake Berehowsky	.40	1.00
5 Deron Quint	.40	1.00
6 Daymond Langkow	.60	1.50
7 Mike Johnson	.40	1.00
8 Radoslav Suchy	.40	1.00
9 Kelly Buchberger	.40	1.00
10 Ladislav Nagy	.75	2.00
11 Shane Doan	.75	2.00
12 Paul Mara	.40	1.00
13 Teppo Numminen	.40	1.00
14 Landon Wilson	.40	1.00
15 Branko Radivojevic	.60	1.50
16 Brian Boucher	.60	1.50
17 Krys Kolanos	.40	1.00
18 Andrei Nazarov	.40	1.00
19 Brian Savage	.40	1.00
20 Danny Markov	.40	1.00
21 Sean Burke	.75	2.00
22 Benoit Allaire ACO	.10	.25
23 Pat Conacher ACO	.10	.25
24 Rick Bowness ACO	.10	.25
25 Bob Francis CO	.10	.25
26 Scott Pellerin	.40	1.00
27 Paul Ranheim	.40	1.00
28 Zac Bierk	.60	1.50
29 Tony Amonte	.75	2.00
30 Charlie Simmer ANN	.20	.50
31 Curt Keilback ANN	.10	.25
32 Ramzi Abid	.40	1.00
33 Dan Focht	.40	1.00
34 Daniel Briere	.75	2.00
35 Brad May	.40	1.00

2003-04 Coyotes Postcards

This checklist may be incomplete. Send additional info to hockeymag@beckett.com.

COMPLETE SET (27)	10.00	20.00
1 Zac Bierk	.40	1.00
2 Brian Boucher	.30	.75
3 Sean Burke	.40	1.00
4 Daniel Cleary	.20	.50
5 Shane Doan	1.00	2.50
6 Brad Ference	.20	.50
7 Dave Tanabe	.20	.50
8 Jan Hrdina	.20	.50
9 Cale Hulse	.20	.50
10 Mike Johnson	.20	.50
11 Krystofer Kolanos	.20	.50
12 Daymond Langkow	.30	.75
13 Paul Mara	.20	.50
14 Ladislav Nagy	.60	1.50
15 Tyson Nash	.40	1.00
16 Andrei Nazarov	.20	.50
17 Ivan Novoseltsev	.20	.50
18 Branko Radivojevic	.40	1.00
19 Brian Savage	.20	.50
20 Mike Sillinger	.20	.50
21 Fredrik Sjostrom	.30	.75
22 Matthew Spiller	.20	.50
23 Radoslav Suchy	.20	.50
24 Jeff Taffe	.20	.50
25 Dave Tanabe	.20	.50
26 Ossi Vaananen	.20	.50
27 Landon Wilson	.20	.50

1924-25 Crescent Falcon-Tigers

The 1924-25 Crescent Ice Cream Falcon-Tigers set contains 13 black and white cards measuring approximately 1 9/16" by 2 3/8". The back has the card number (at the top) and two offers: 1) a brick of ice cream to any person bringing to the Crescent Ice Cream plant any 14 Crescent Hockey Pictures bearing consecutive numbers; and 2) a hockey stick to anyone bringing to the ice cream plant three sets of Crescent Hockey Pictures bearing consecutive numbers from 1-14. The complete set price below does not include the unknown card 6, which is believed to have been short printed.

COMPLETE SET (13)	1200.00	2400.00
1 Bill Cockburn	112.50	225.00
2 Wally Byron	100.00	200.00
3 Wally Fridfinson	100.00	200.00
4 Murray Murdoch	125.00	250.00
5 Oliver Redpath	100.00	200.00
7 Ward McVey	100.00	200.00
8 Tote Mitchell	100.00	200.00
9 Lorne Carrol	100.00	200.00
10 Tony Wise	100.00	200.00
11 Johnny Myres	100.00	200.00
12 Gordon McKenzie	100.00	200.00
13 Harry Neal	112.50	225.00
14 Blake Watson	112.50	225.00

1923-24 Crescent Selkirks

The 1923-24 Crescent Ice Cream set contains 14 cards measuring approximately 1 9/16" by 2 3/8". The set features the Selkirks hockey club and was produced by Crescent Ice Cream of Winnipeg, Manitoba. The front shows a black and white head and shoulders shot of the player, with the team name written in a crescent over the player's head. At the bottom of the picture, the player's name and position appear in white lettering in a black stripe. The back has the card number (at the top) and two offers: 1) a brick of ice cream to any person bringing to the Crescent Ice Cream plant any 14 Crescent Hockey Pictures bearing consecutive numbers; and 2) a hockey stick to anyone bringing to the ice cream plant three sets of Crescent Hockey Pictures bearing consecutive numbers from 1-14. The complete set price below does not include the unknown card number 6.

COMPLETE SET (13)	600.00	1200.00
1 Cliff O'Meara	62.50	125.00
2 Leo Benard	50.00	100.00
3 Pete Speirs	50.00	100.00
4 Howard Brandon	50.00	100.00
5 George A. Clark	50.00	100.00
7 Cecil Browne	50.00	100.00
8 Jack Connelly	50.00	100.00
9 Charlie Gardner	100.00	200.00
10 Ward Turvey	50.00	100.00
11 Connie Johanneson	50.00	100.00
12 Frank Woodall	50.00	100.00
13 Harold McMunn	50.00	100.00
14 Connie Neil	62.50	125.00

1924-25 Crescent Selkirks

The 1924-25 Crescent Ice Cream Selkirks set contains 14 black and white cards measuring approximately 1 9/16" by 2 3/8". The back has the card number (at the top) and two offers: 1) a brick of ice cream to any person bringing to the Crescent Ice Cream plant any 14 Crescent Hockey Pictures bearing consecutive numbers; and 2) a hockey stick to anyone bringing to the ice cream plant three sets of Crescent Hockey Pictures bearing consecutive numbers from 1-14.

COMPLETE SET (14)	850.00	1700.00
1 Howard Brandon	50.00	100.00
2 Jack Hughes	50.00	100.00
3 Tony Baril	50.00	100.00
4 Bill Bowman	50.00	100.00
5 W. Roberts	50.00	100.00
6 Cecil Browne SP	375.00	750.00
7 Errol Gillis	50.00	100.00
8 Selkirks Team On The Ice	100.00	200.00
9 Fred Comfort	50.00	100.00
10 Cliff O'Meara	50.00	100.00
11 Leo Benard	50.00	100.00
12 Pete Speirs	50.00	100.00
13 Peter Meurer	50.00	100.00
14 Bill Borland	50.00	100.00

1935-40 Crown Brand Photos

49 Montreal Maroons 1936-37	30.00	60.00
50 Montreal Canadiens 1936-37	30.00	60.00
51 Baldy Northcott	12.50	25.00
52 Dave Trottier	12.50	25.00
53 Russ Blinco	12.50	25.00
54 Earl Robinson Maroons	12.50	25.00
55 Bob Gracie	12.50	25.00
56 Gus Marker	12.50	25.00
57 Howie Morenz	150.00	250.00
58 Johnny Gagnon	12.50	25.00
59 Wilfred Cude	60.00	100.00
60 Georges Mantha	12.50	25.00
61 Paul Haynes	12.50	25.00
62 Marty Barry	20.00	40.00
63 Peter Kelly	12.50	25.00
64 Dave Kerr	12.50	25.00
65 Roy Worters	12.50	25.00
66 Ace Bailey	20.00	40.00
67 Art Lesieur	15.00	30.00
68 Frank Boucher	15.00	30.00
69 Marty Burke	12.50	25.00
70 Alex Levinsky	12.50	25.00
71 Father Leveque's Maple Leafs	40.00	80.00
72 Father Leveque's Six Stars	40.00	80.00
76 Father Leveque's Canadiens	20.00	40.00
77 Stewart Evans	12.50	25.00
78 Herb Cain	12.50	25.00
79 Carl Voss	20.00	40.00
80 Roger Jenkins	12.50	25.00
81 Jack McGill	12.50	25.00
82 Mush March	15.00	30.00
106 Montreal Maroons 1937-38	40.00	80.00
107 Montreal Canadiens 1937-38	30.00	60.00

108 Toe Blake 40.00 80.00
109 Joffre Desilets 12.50 25.00
110 Babe Siebert 20.00 40.00
111 Frank Clancy 300.00 500.00
112 Aurel Joliat 50.00 100.00
113 Walter Buswell 12.50 25.00
114 Bill MacKenzie 12.50 25.00
115 Pit Lepine 12.50 25.00
116 Cliff Goupille 12.50 25.00
117 Rod Lorrain 12.50 25.00
118 Polly Drouin 12.50 25.00
119 Marvin Wentworth 12.50 25.00
120 Allan Shields 12.50 25.00
121 Jimmy Ward 12.50 25.00
122 Bill Beveridge 12.50 25.00
123 Gerry Shannon 12.50 25.00
124 Des Smith 12.50 25.00
125 Armand Mondou 15.00 30.00
151 Montreal Canadiens 1938-39 40.00 80.00
152 Herb Cain 12.50 25.00
153 Bob Gracie 12.50 25.00
154 Jimmy Ward 12.50 25.00
155 Stew Evans 12.50 25.00
156 Louis Trudel 12.50 25.00
157 Cy Wentworth 12.50 25.00
195 Marty Barry 12.50 25.00
196 Earl Robinson Canadiens 12.50 25.00
197 Ray Getliffe 12.50 25.00
198 Charlie Sands 12.50 25.00
199 Claude Bourque 12.50 25.00
200 Doug Young 12.50 25.00
NNO Montreal Canadiens (1935-36) 40.00 80.00
NNO Montreal Canadiens 1939-40 30.00 60.00
NNO Stanley Cup Champs 1934-35 25.00 50.00
NNO Team Canada 1936 20.00 40.00
NNO Album 25.00 50.00

1997-98 Crown Royale

The 1997-98 Pacific Crown Royale set was issued in one series totaling 144 cards and was distributed in four-card packs. The fronts features color player images printed on an all-die-cut crown format. The backs carry player information

1 Guy Hebert .25 .60
2 Paul Kariya .40 1.00
3 Steve Rucchin .25 .60
4 Tomas Sandstrom .20 .50
5 Teemu Selanne .60 1.50
6 Jason Allison .25 .60
7 Ray Bourque .50 1.25
8 Anson Carter .20 .50
9 Byron Dafoe .20 .50
10 Ted Donato .20 .50
11 Joe Thornton .30 .75
12 Jason Dawe .25 .60
13 Michal Grosek .20 .50
14 Dominik Hasek .50 1.25
15 Michael Peca .25 .60
16 Miroslav Satan .20 .50
17 Chris Dingman RC .30 .75
18 Theo Fleury .40 1.00
19 Jarome Iginla .30 .75
20 Tyler Moss RC .25 .60
21 Cory Stillman .25 .60
22 Kevin Dineen .25 .60
23 Nelson Emerson .25 .60
24 Trevor Kidd .20 .50
25 Keith Primeau .25 .60
26 Geoff Sanderson .25 .60
27 Tony Amonte .25 .60
28 Chris Chelios .30 .75
29 Eric Daze .20 .50
30 Jeff Hackett .20 .50
31 Chris Terreri .20 .50
32 Adam Deadmarsh .20 .50
33 Peter Forsberg .40 1.00
34 Valeri Kamesnky .25 .60
35 Jari Kurri .30 .75
36 Claude Lemieux .25 .60
37 Patrick Roy .75 2.00
38 Joe Sakic .50 1.25
39 Ed Belfour .30 .75
40 Derian Hatcher .25 .60
41 Mike Modano .50 1.25
42 Joe Nieuwendyk .30 .75
43 Pat Verbeek .25 .60
44 Sergei Zubov .25 .60
45 Sergei Fedorov .50 1.25
46 Vyacheslav Kozlov .25 .60
47 Nicklas Lidstrom .30 .75
48 Darren McCarty .25 .60
49 Chris Osgood .30 .75
50 Brendan Shanahan .40 1.00
51 Steve Yzerman .60 1.50
52 Jason Arnott .25 .60
53 Curtis Joseph .30 .75
54 Ryan Smyth .25 .60
55 Doug Weight .30 .75
56 Dave Gagner .20 .50
57 Ed Jovanovski .20 .50
58 Viktor Kozlov .25 .60
59 Scott Mellanby .25 .60
60 John Vanbiesbrouck .30 .75
61 Kevin Weekes RC .25 .60
62 Rob Blake .30 .75
63 Donald MacLean .30 .75
64 Yanic Perreault .25 .60
65 Luc Robitaille .30 .75
66 Jozef Stumpel .25 .60
67 Shayne Corson .20 .50
68 Vincent Damphousse .25 .60
69 Saku Koivu .30 .75
70 Andy Moog .30 .75
71 Mark Recchi .40 1.00
72 Stephane Richer .20 .50
73 Martin Brodeur .60 1.50
74 Patrik Elias RC .50 1.25
75 Doug Gilmour .40 1.00
76 Bobby Holik .20 .50
77 Scott Stevens .30 .75
78 Bryan Berard .20 .50
79 Zigmund Palffy .30 .75
80 Robert Reichel .25 .60
81 Tommy Salo .20 .50
82 Bryan Smolinski .25 .60
83 Adam Graves .20 .50
84 Wayne Gretzky 1.50 4.00
85 Pat LaFontaine .30 .75
86 Brian Leetch .30 .75
87 Mike Richter .30 .75
88 Niklas Sundstrom .25 .60
89 Daniel Alfredsson .30 .75
90 Alexandre Daigle .20 .50
91 Shawn McEachern .20 .50
92 Chris Phillips .25 .60
93 Ron Tugnutt .30 .75
94 Alexei Yashin .25 .60
95 Rod Brind'Amour .30 .75
96 Chris Gratton .20 .50
97 Ron Hextall .30 .75
98 John LeClair .30 .75
99 Eric Lindros .50 1.25
100 Vaclav Prospal RC .25 .60
101 Dainius Zubrus .25 .60
102 Mike Gartner .30 .75
103 Brad Isbister .25 .60
104 Nikolai Khabibulin .30 .75
105 Jeremy Roenick .40 1.00
106 Cliff Ronning .20 .50
107 Keith Tkachuk .30 .75
108 Tom Barrasso .25 .60
109 Ron Francis .40 1.00
110 Jaromir Jagr .75 2.00
111 Alexei Morozov .25 .60
112 Ed Olczyk .20 .50
113 Jim Campbell .20 .50
114 Pavol Demitra .40 1.00
115 Steve Duchesne .20 .50
116 Grant Fuhr .30 .75
117 Brett Hull .40 1.00
118 Pierre Turgeon .30 .75
119 Jeff Friesen .25 .60
120 Patrick Marleau .40 1.00
121 Owen Nolan .30 .75
122 Marco Sturm RC .75 2.00
123 Mike Vernon .25 .60
124 Dino Ciccarelli .30 .75
125 Roman Hamrlik .25 .60
126 Daren Puppa .25 .60
127 Paul Ysebaert .25 .60
128 Sergei Berezin .25 .60
129 Wendel Clark .30 .75
130 Alyn McCauley .25 .60
131 Felix Potvin .30 .75
132 Mats Sundin .30 .75
133 Pavel Bure .40 1.00
134 Martin Gelinas .20 .50
135 Trevor Linden .25 .60
136 Mark Messier .50 1.25
137 Alexander Mogilny .25 .60
138 Peter Bondra .25 .60
139 Dale Hunter .25 .60
140 Joe Juneau .25 .60
141 Olaf Kolzig .25 .60
142 Adam Oates .30 .75
143 Jaroslav Svejkovsky .25 .60
144 Richard Zednik .25 .60

1997-98 Crown Royale Emerald Green

Randomly inserted in Canadian packs only at the rate of 4:25, this 144-card set is a parallel version of the base set with green foil highlights.

1997-98 Crown Royale Ice Blue

Randomly inserted in packs at the rate of 1:25, this 144-card set is a parallel version of the base set with blue foil highlights.
*VETS: 2.5X TO 6X BSIC CARDS
*ROOKIES: 2X TO 5X BASIC CARDS

1997-98 Crown Royale Silver

Randomly inserted in U.S. packs only at the rate of 4:25, this 144-card set is a parallel version of the base set with silver foil highlights.
*VETS: 1.2X TO 3X BASIC CARDS
*ROOKIES: .8X TO 2X BASIC CARDS

1997-98 Crown Royale Blades of Steel Die-Cuts

Randomly inserted in packs at the rate of 1:49, this 20-card set features color images of top NHL players on a laser-cut and die-cut skate background.

COMPLETE SET (20) 50.00 125.00
1 Paul Kariya 2.00 5.00
2 Teemu Selanne 2.00 5.00
3 Joe Thornton 4.00 10.00
4 Chris Chelios 1.50 4.00
5 Peter Forsberg 4.00 10.00
6 Patrick Roy 10.00 25.00
7 Mike Modano 2.50 6.00
8 Sergei Fedorov 2.50 6.00
9 Brendan Shanahan 2.00 5.00
10 Steve Yzerman 8.00 20.00
11 Ryan Smyth 1.50 4.00
12 Saku Koivu 2.00 5.00
13 Bryan Berard .75 2.00
14 Wayne Gretzky 12.00 30.00
15 Brian Leetch 1.50 4.00
16 Eric Lindros 2.50 6.00
17 Jaromir Jagr 4.00 10.00
18 Brett Hull 2.50 6.00
19 Pavel Bure 2.00 5.00
20 Mark Messier 2.50 6.00

1997-98 Crown Royale Cramer's Choice Jumbos

Inserted one per box, this ten-card set features top NHL Hockey players as chosen by Pacific President and CEO, Michael Cramer. The fronts display a color action player cut-out on a pyramid die-cut shaped background printed on a premium-sized card.

COMPLETE SET (10) 15.00 40.00
*GOLD: 1.5X TO 4X BASIC CARDS
1 Paul Kariya 3.00 8.00
2 Teemu Selanne 2.50 6.00
3 Joe Thornton 5.00 12.00
4 Peter Forsberg 3.00 8.00
5 Patrick Roy 6.00 15.00
6 Steve Yzerman 5.00 12.00
7 Wayne Gretzky 8.00 20.00
8 Eric Lindros 3.00 8.00
9 Jaromir Jagr 3.00 8.00
10 Pavel Bure 2.50 6.00

1997-98 Crown Royale Freeze Out Die-Cuts

Randomly inserted in packs at the rate of 1:25, this 20-card set features color action photos of top goalies on a background of shattering ice and printed on a die-cut card.

COMPLETE SET (20) 30.00 80.00
1 Guy Hebert 1.00 2.50
2 Byron Dafoe 1.00 2.50
3 Dominik Hasek 4.00 10.00
4 Tyler Moss 1.00 2.50
5 Patrick Roy 10.00 25.00
6 Ed Belfour 2.00 5.00
7 Chris Osgood 1.00 2.50
8 Curtis Joseph 3.00 8.00
9 John Vanbiesbrouck 2.00 5.00
10 Andy Moog 2.00 5.00
11 Martin Brodeur 6.00 15.00
12 Mike Richter 2.00 5.00
13 Ron Hextall 2.00 5.00
14 Garth Snow 1.00 2.50
15 Nikolai Khabibulin 2.00 5.00
16 Tom Barrasso 1.00 2.50
17 Grant Fuhr 2.00 5.00
18 Mike Vernon 2.00 5.00
19 Felix Potvin 3.00 8.00
20 Olaf Kolzig 2.00 5.00

1997-98 Crown Royale Hat Tricks Die-Cuts

Randomly inserted in packs at the rate of 1:25, this 20-card set features color photos of top NHL scorers printed on a hat-shaped die-cut card.

COMPLETE SET (20) 40.00 100.00
1 Paul Kariya 2.50 6.00
2 Teemu Selanne 2.50 6.00
3 Joe Thornton 4.00 10.00
4 Peter Forsberg 4.00 10.00
5 Joe Sakic 5.00 12.00
6 Mike Modano 4.00 10.00
7 Brendan Shanahan 2.50 6.00
8 Steve Yzerman 6.00 15.00
9 Ryan Smyth 1.50 4.00
10 Zigmund Palffy 1.50 4.00
11 Wayne Gretzky 10.00 25.00
12 John LeClair 1.50 4.00
13 Eric Lindros 2.50 6.00
14 Keith Tkachuk 1.50 4.00
15 Jaromir Jagr 4.00 10.00
16 Brett Hull 3.00 8.00
17 Mats Sundin 2.00 5.00
18 Pavel Bure 2.00 5.00
19 Mark Messier 2.00 5.00
20 Peter Bondra 1.50 4.00

1997-98 Crown Royale Lamplighters Cel-Fusion Die-Cuts

Randomly inserted in packs at the rate of 1:73, this 20-card set features color photos of the NHL's top goal scorers with a net and goal light as background and printed on a die-cut cel-fusion card.

COMPLETE SET (20) 40.00 100.00
1 Paul Kariya 2.00 5.00
2 Teemu Selanne 2.00 5.00
3 Joe Thornton 6.00 15.00
4 Michael Peca 1.00 2.50
5 Peter Forsberg 6.00 15.00
6 Joe Sakic 8.00 20.00
7 Mike Modano 4.00 10.00
8 Brendan Shanahan 2.00 5.00
9 Steve Yzerman 12.00 30.00
10 Saku Koivu 2.00 5.00
11 Wayne Gretzky 20.00 50.00
12 Pat LaFontaine 1.00 2.50
13 John LeClair 1.00 2.50
14 Eric Lindros 4.00 10.00
15 Dainius Zubrus 1.00 2.50
16 Keith Tkachuk 2.00 5.00
17 Jaromir Jagr 6.00 15.00
18 Brett Hull 2.00 5.00
19 Pavel Bure 2.00 5.00
20 Mark Messier 4.00 10.00

1998-99 Crown Royale

The 1998-99 Pacific Crown Royale set was issued in one series totaling 144 cards and was distributed in six-card packs with a suggested retail price of $5.99. The set features color action player photos printed on cards with silver and gold foil highlights, dual etching and a die-cut crown as background

COMPLETE SET (144) 30.00 80.00
1 Travis Green .20 .50
2 Guy Hebert .30 .75
3 Paul Kariya .40 1.00
4 Tomas Sandstrom .20 .50
5 Teemu Selanne .40 1.00
6 Jason Allison .20 .50
7 Ray Bourque 1.00 2.50
8 Byron Dafoe .30 .75
9 Dimitri Khristich .20 .50
10 Sergei Samsonov .30 .75
11 Matthew Barnaby .20 .50
12 Michal Grosek .20 .50
13 Dominik Hasek 1.25 3.00
14 Michael Peca .20 .50
15 Miroslav Satan .20 .50
16 Andrew Cassels .20 .50
17 Rico Fata .20 .50
18 Theo Fleury .20 .50
19 Jarome Iginla .75 2.00
20 Martin St. Louis RC 4.00 10.00
21 Ken Wregget .30 .75
22 Ron Francis .30 .75
23 Arturs Irbe .30 .75
24 Sami Kapanen .20 .50
25 Trevor Kidd .30 .75
26 Keith Primeau .20 .50
27 Tony Amonte .30 .75
28 Chris Chelios .40 1.00
29 Eric Daze .20 .50
30 Doug Gilmour .30 .75
31 Jocelyn Thibault .30 .75
32 Chris Drury .30 .75
33 Peter Forsberg 1.25 3.00
34 Milan Hejduk RC 2.00 5.00
35 Patrick Roy 2.50 6.00
36 Joe Sakic 1.25 3.00
37 Ed Belfour .40 1.00
38 Brett Hull .40 1.00
39 Jamie Langenbrunner .20 .50
40 Jere Lehtinen .30 .75
41 Mike Modano 1.00 2.50
42 Joe Nieuwendyk .30 .75
43 Darryl Sydor .20 .50
44 Sergei Fedorov 1.00 2.50
45 Nicklas Lidstrom .40 1.00
46 Darren McCarty .20 .50
47 Chris Osgood .30 .75
48 Brendan Shanahan .40 1.00
49 Steve Yzerman 2.50 6.00
50 Bob Essensa .30 .75
51 Bill Guerin .30 .75
52 Janne Niinimaa .20 .50
53 Tom Poti .20 .50
54 Ryan Smyth .20 .50
55 Doug Weight .30 .75
56 Sean Burke .30 .75
57 Dino Ciccarelli .30 .75
58 Ed Jovanovski .20 .50
59 Viktor Kozlov .20 .50
60 Oleg Kvasha RC .40 1.00
61 Mark Parrish RC .75 2.00
62 Rob Blake .30 .75
63 Manny Legace .40 1.00
64 Yanic Perreault .20 .50
65 Luc Robitaille .30 .75
66 Jozef Stumpel .50 1.25
67 Shayne Corson .20 .50
68 Vincent Damphousse .20 .50
69 Jeff Hackett .30 .75
70 Saku Koivu .40 1.00
71 Mark Recchi .30 .75
72 Andrew Brunette .50 1.25
73 Mike Dunham .30 .75
74 Tom Fitzgerald .20 .50
75 Greg Johnson .20 .50
76 Sergei Krivokrasov .20 .50
77 Jason Arnott .20 .50
78 Martin Brodeur 1.50 4.00
79 Patrik Elias .30 .75
80 Bobby Holik .20 .50
81 Brendan Morrison .30 .75
82 Bryan Berard .20 .50
83 Trevor Linden .30 .75
84 Zigmund Palffy .30 .75
85 Robert Reichel .20 .50
86 Tommy Salo .30 .75
87 Adam Graves .20 .50
88 Wayne Gretzky 3.00 8.00
89 Brian Leetch .40 1.00
90 Manny Malhotra .20 .50
91 Mike Richter .40 1.00
92 Daniel Alfredsson .30 .75
93 Igor Kravchuk .20 .50
94 Shawn McEachern .20 .50
95 Damian Rhodes .30 .75
96 Alexei Yashin .20 .50
97 Rod Brind'Amour .30 .75
98 Ron Hextall .30 .75
99 John LeClair .40 1.00
100 Eric Lindros .40 1.00
101 John Vanbiesbrouck .30 .75
102 Dainius Zubrus .20 .50
103 Nikolai Khabibulin .30 .75
104 Jeremy Roenick .75 2.00
105 Keith Tkachuk .40 1.00
106 Rick Tocchet .30 .75
107 Oleg Tverdovsky .20 .50
108 Tom Barrasso .30 .75
109 Jan Hrdina RC .40 1.00
110 Jaromir Jagr 1.00 2.50
111 Alexei Morozov .20 .50
112 German Titov .20 .50
113 Jim Campbell .20 .50
114 Grant Fuhr .30 .75
115 Al MacInnis .30 .75
116 Chris Pronger .30 .75
117 Pierre Turgeon .30 .75
118 Jeff Friesen .20 .50
119 Patrick Marleau .20 .50
120 Owen Nolan .30 .75
121 Marco Sturm .20 .50
122 Mike Vernon .30 .75
123 Wendel Clark .30 .75
124 Vincent Lecavalier 1.25 3.00
125 Bill Ranford .30 .75
126 Stephane Richer .30 .75
127 Rob Zamuner .20 .50
128 Sergei Berezin .20 .50
129 Tie Domi .30 .75
130 Mike Johnson .20 .50
131 Curtis Joseph .40 1.00
132 Mats Sundin .40 1.00
133 Donald Brashear .20 .50
134 Pavel Bure .40 1.00
135 Mark Messier .40 1.00
136 Alexander Mogilny .30 .75
137 Bill Muckalt RC .20 .50
138 Mattias Ohlund .20 .50
139 Garth Snow .30 .75
140 Peter Bondra .30 .75
141 Matthew Herr RC .20 .50
142 Joe Juneau .30 .75
143 Olaf Kolzig .30 .75
144 Adam Oates .30 .75

1998-99 Crown Royale Limited Series

Randomly inserted into packs, this 144-card set is a limited parallel edition of the base set printed on 24-point card stock. Only 99 serial-numbered sets were produced.
*VETERANS: 3X TO 8X BASIC CARDS
*ROOKIES: 2.5X TO 6X BASIC CARDS
STATED PRINT RUN 99 SER.#'d SETS

1998-99 Crown Royale Cramer's Choice Jumbos

Inserted one per box, this 10-card set features color action cut-outs of top NHL players as chosen by Pacific President and CEO, Michael Cramer, printed on premium-sized, dual-foiled, die-cut pyramid-shaped cards. Six different serial-numbered parallel sets were also produced: 35 serial-numbered dark blue foil sets, 30 serial-numbered green foil sets, 25 serial-numbered red foil sets, 20 serial-numbered light blue foil sets, 10 serial-numbered gold foil sets, and 1 serial-numbered purple foil set.

COMPLETE SET (10) 12.00 30.00
*DARK BLUE/35: 10X TO 20X BASIC INSERTS
*GOLD/10: 20X TO 50X BASIC INSERTS
*GREEN/30: 10X TO 25X BASIC INSERTS
*LT.BLUE/20: 15X TO 40X BASIC INSERTS
*RED/25: 10X TO 25X BASIC INSERTS
1 Paul Kariya 1.25 3.00
2 Teemu Selanne 1.25 3.00
3 Dominik Hasek 2.00 5.00
4 Peter Forsberg 2.50 6.00
5 Patrick Roy 3.00 8.00
6 Steve Yzerman 3.00 8.00
7 Martin Brodeur 3.00 8.00
8 Wayne Gretzky 4.00 10.00
9 Eric Lindros 1.25 3.00
10 Jaromir Jagr 1.50 4.00

1998-99 Crown Royale Living Legends

Randomly inserted in hobby packs at the rate of 1:73, this 10-card set features color action photos of some of the NHL's all-time great players. Only 375 serial-numbered sets were produced.

COMPLETE SET (10) 75.00 150.00
LEGEND/375 STATED ODDS 1:73
1 Paul Kariya 5.00 12.00
2 Teemu Selanne 4.00 10.00
3 Dominik Hasek 8.00 20.00
4 Peter Forsberg 4.00 10.00
5 Patrick Roy 10.00 25.00
6 Steve Yzerman 10.00 25.00
7 Martin Brodeur 8.00 20.00
8 Wayne Gretzky 12.00 30.00
9 Eric Lindros 6.00 15.00
10 Jaromir Jagr 6.00 15.00

1998-99 Crown Royale Master Performers

Randomly inserted in hobby packs at the rate of 2:25, this 20-card set features color action photos of some of the most popular players printed on fully foiled, etched cards.

COMPLETE SET (20) 40.00 100.00
STATED ODDS 2:25
1 Paul Kariya 2.00 5.00
2 Teemu Selanne 2.00 5.00
3 Dominik Hasek 4.00 10.00
4 Peter Forsberg 3.00 8.00
5 Patrick Roy 6.00 15.00
6 Joe Sakic 4.00 10.00
7 Brett Hull 2.50 6.00
8 Mike Modano 3.00 8.00
9 Sergei Fedorov 2.50 6.00
10 Brendan Shanahan 2.00 5.00
11 Steve Yzerman 6.00 15.00
12 Saku Koivu 2.00 5.00
13 Martin Brodeur 5.00 12.00
14 Wayne Gretzky 8.00 20.00
15 John LeClair 1.50 4.00
16 Eric Lindros 2.00 5.00
17 Jaromir Jagr 3.00 8.00
18 Mats Sundin 2.00 5.00
19 Mark Messier 2.00 5.00
20 Peter Bondra 1.50 4.00

1998-99 Crown Royale Pillars of the Game

Inserted one at the bottom of every pack, this 25-card set features color action photos of popular players with a hockey puck in the background and printed on holographic gold foil cards.

COMPLETE SET (25) 10.00 20.00
STATED ODDS 1:1
1 Teemu Selanne .30 .75
2 Ray Bourque .50 1.25
3 Michael Peca .25 .60
4 Theo Fleury .25 .60
5 Chris Chelios .30 .75
6 Doug Gilmour .25 .60
7 Patrick Roy 1.50 4.00
8 Joe Sakic .60 1.50
9 Ed Belfour .30 .75
10 Brett Hull .40 1.00
11 Mike Modano .50 1.25
12 Sergei Fedorov .50 1.25
13 Brendan Shanahan .30 .75
14 Steve Yzerman 1.50 4.00
15 Saku Koivu .30 .75
16 Martin Brodeur .75 2.00
17 John LeClair .30 .75
18 Eric Lindros .30 .75
19 John Vanbiesbrouck .25 .60
20 Keith Tkachuk .30 .75
21 Jaromir Jagr .50 1.25
22 Curtis Joseph .30 .75
23 Mats Sundin .30 .75
24 Mark Messier .30 .75
25 Peter Bondra .25 .60

1998-99 Crown Royale Pivotal Players

Inserted one at the top of every pack, this 25-card set features color action photos of top stars and rookies printed on holographic silver foil cards.

COMPLETE SET (25) 10.00 20.00
STATED ODDS 1:1
1 Paul Kariya .30 .75
2 Dominik Hasek .60 1.50
3 Michael Peca .25 .60
4 Peter Forsberg .75 2.00
5 Joe Sakic .60 1.50
6 Brett Hull .40 1.00
7 Mike Modano .50 1.25
8 Sergei Fedorov .50 1.25
9 Chris Osgood .25 .60
10 Brendan Shanahan .30 .75
11 Ryan Smyth .25 .60
12 Mark Parrish .40 1.00
13 Saku Koivu .30 .75
14 Martin Brodeur .75 2.00
15 Trevor Linden .25 .60
16 Wayne Gretzky 2.00 5.00
17 Alexei Yashin .25 .60
18 John LeClair .30 .75
19 John Vanbiesbrouck .25 .60
20 Keith Tkachuk .30 .75
21 Vincent Lecavalier .75 2.00
22 Mats Sundin .30 .75
23 Mark Messier .30 .75
24 Peter Bondra .25 .60
25 Olaf Kolzig .25 .60

1998-99 Crown Royale Rookie Class

Randomly inserted in packs at the rate of 1:25, this 10-card set features color action photos of top rookies printed on full-foil designed cards.

COMPLETE SET (10) 15.00 40.00
1 Chris Drury 2.00 5.00
2 Milan Hejduk 2.00 5.00
3 Mark Parrish 1.25 3.00
4 Manny Legace 2.00 5.00
5 Brendan Morrison 1.25 3.00
6 Manny Malhotra 1.25 3.00
7 Daniel Briere 2.00 5.00
8 Vincent Lecavalier 4.00 10.00
9 Tomas Kaberle 1.25 3.00
10 Bill Muckalt 1.25 3.00

1999-00 Crown Royale

The 1999-00 Pacific Crown Royale set was issued in one series totaling 144 cards and was distributed in six-card packs with a suggested retail price of $5.99. The set features color action player photos printed on cards with silver and gold foil highlights, dual etching and a die-cut crown as background.

1 Guy Hebert .50 1.25
2 Paul Kariya .60 1.50
3 Steve Rucchin .30 .75
4 Teemu Selanne 1.00 2.50
5 Andrew Brunette .30 .75
6 Scott Fankhouser RC .30 .75
7 Andreas Karlsson SP RC .30 .75
8 Damian Rhodes .30 .75
9 Patrik Stefan SP RC .50 1.25
10 Jason Allison .40 1.00
11 Ray Bourque .75 2.00
12 Byron Dafoe .30 .75
13 Mikko Eloranta RC .40 1.00
14 Sergei Samsonov .40 1.00
15 Joe Thornton .75 2.00
16 Maxim Afinogenov SP .30 .75
17 Martin Biron SP .40 1.00
18 Dominik Hasek .75 2.00
19 Michael Peca .40 1.00
20 Miroslav Satan .40 1.00
21 Valeri Bure .30 .75
22 Grant Fuhr .50 1.25
23 Jarome Iginla .50 1.25
24 Robyn Regehr SP .30 .75
25 Oleg Saprykin SP RC .50 1.25
26 Ron Francis .60 1.50
27 Arturs Irbe .40 1.00
28 Sami Kapanen .30 .75
29 Jeff O'Neill .30 .75
30 Tony Amonte .40 1.00
31 Kyle Calder SP RC .40 1.00
32 Eric Daze .40 1.00
33 Doug Gilmour .60 1.50
34 Jocelyn Thibault .40 1.00
35 Marc Denis SP .40 1.00
36 Chris Drury .40 1.00
37 Peter Forsberg .50 1.25
38 Milan Hejduk .40 1.00
39 Patrick Roy 2.00 5.00
40 Joe Sakic .75 2.00
41 Alex Tanguay SP .40 1.00
42 Ed Belfour .50 1.25
43 Ryan Christie RC .30 .75
44 Brett Hull .75 2.00
45 Jere Lehtinen .40 1.00
46 Mike Modano .75 2.00
47 Joe Nieuwendyk .50 1.25
48 Chris Chelios .50 1.25
49 Sergei Fedorov .75 2.00
50 Nicklas Lidstrom .50 1.25
51 Chris Osgood .50 1.25
52 Brendan Shanahan .60 1.50
53 Steve Yzerman 1.50 4.00
54 Bill Guerin .50 1.25
55 Tommy Salo .40 1.00
56 Alexander Selivanov .30 .75
57 Ryan Smyth .40 1.00
58 Doug Weight .50 1.25
59 Pavel Bure .60 1.50
60 Trevor Kidd .30 .75
61 Ivan Novoseltsev SP RC .60 1.50
62 Ray Whitney .40 1.00
63 Mike Vernon .40 1.00
64 Rob Blake .50 1.25
65 Stephane Fiset .40 1.00
66 Zigmund Palffy .50 1.25
67 Luc Robitaille .50 1.25
68 Brian Smolinski .30 .75
69 Jeff Hackett .30 .75
70 Saku Koivu .50 1.25
71 Trevor Linden .50 1.25
72 Brian Savage .30 .75
73 Jose Theodore .50 1.25
74 Mike Dunham .30 .75
75 Sergei Krivokrasov .30 .75
76 David Legwand SP .30 .75
77 Cliff Ronning .30 .75
78 Martin Brodeur 1.00 2.50
79 Patrik Elias .50 1.25
80 Scott Gomez SP .40 1.00
81 Bobby Holik .30 .75
82 Claude Lemieux .40 1.00
83 Petr Sykora .40 1.00
84 Tim Connolly SP .30 .75
85 Mariusz Czerkawski .30 .75
86 Brad Isbister .30 .75
87 Kenny Jonsson .30 .75
88 Roberto Luongo SP .60 1.50
89 Theo Fleury .60 1.50
90 Milan Hnilicka RC .30 .75
91 Brian Leetch .50 1.25
92 Mike Richter .50 1.25
93 Michael York SP .30 .75
94 Daniel Alfredsson .50 1.25
95 Radek Bonk .30 .75
96 Mike Fisher SP RC .50 1.25
97 Marian Hossa .40 1.00
98 Joe Juneau .40 1.00
99 Ron Tugnutt .40 1.00
100 Alexei Yashin .40 1.00
101 Simon Gagne SP .50 1.25
102 John LeClair .50 1.25
103 Eric Lindros .75 2.00
104 Keith Primeau .30 .75
105 Mark Recchi .60 1.50
106 John Vanbiesbrouck .40 1.00
107 Travis Green .30 .75
108 Nikolai Khabibulin .40 1.00
109 Jeremy Roenick .50 1.25
110 Keith Tkachuk .50 1.25
111 Tom Barrasso .50 1.25
112 Jaromir Jagr 1.25 3.00
113 Alexei Kovalev .40 1.00
114 Robert Lang .30 .75
115 Pavol Demitra .60 1.50
116 Jochen Hecht SP RC .75 2.00
117 Al MacInnis .50 1.25
118 Ladislav Nagy SP RC .30 .75
119 Chris Pronger .40 1.00
120 Roman Turek .40 1.00
121 Pierre Turgeon .50 1.25
122 Vincent Damphousse .40 1.00
123 Jeff Friesen .40 1.00
124 Patrick Marleau .50 1.25
125 Owen Nolan .50 1.25
126 Steve Shields .40 1.00
127 Dan Cloutier .30 .75
128 Chris Gratton .30 .75
129 Vincent Lecavalier .40 1.00
130 Mike Sillinger .30 .75
131 Nikolai Antropov SP RC 1.25 3.00
132 Sergei Berezin .30 .75
133 Tie Domi .40 1.00
134 Curtis Joseph .50 1.25
135 Mats Sundin .50 1.25
136 Steve Kariya SP RC .50 1.25
137 Mark Messier .75 2.00
138 Markus Naslund .50 1.25
139 Peter Schaefer SP .30 .75
140 Garth Snow .40 1.00
141 Peter Bondra .40 1.00
142 Jan Bulis .30 .75
143 Olaf Kolzig .50 1.25
144 Adam Oates .50 1.25

1999-00 Crown Royale Limited Series

Randomly inserted in packs, This 144-card parallel set features the base card with a red foil Limited Series logo and box with the serial number in the lower front right corner. This set is serial numbered out of 99.
*LIMITED SER/99: 5X TO 12X BASIC CARDS
*LIMITED SER/99: 3X TO 8X BASIC SP

1999-00 Crown Royale Premiere Date

Randomly inserted in packs, This 144-card parallel set features the base card with a gold foil Premier Date logo and box with the serial number in the lower front right corner. This set is serial numbered out of 73.
*PREM.DATE/73: 6X TO 15X BASIC CARDS
*PREM.DATE/73: 4X TO 10X BASIC SP

1999-00 Crown Royale Prospects Parallel

Randomly inserted at 1:24 packs, this 23-card parallel set showcases the prospect cards with a gold foil box on the bottom right-front corner of the card. This set is skip-numbered. The cards are serial numbered out of 450.
*PROSPECT PAR: 1.2X TO 3X BASIC CARDS

1999-00 Crown Royale Card-Supials

Randomly inserted in packs at 2:25, this 25-card set was issued in two versions. The large version features player action-shots with a rainbow holo-foil border and a cut on the back where a Card-Supials Mini card is inserted. The Mini's may or may not match the large card.

COMP.LARGE SET (20) 20.00 50.00
1 Paul Kariya 1.00 2.50
2 Teemu Selanne 1.00 2.50
3 Patrik Stefan 1.50 4.00
4 Joe Thornton 1.25 3.00
5 Dominik Hasek 2.00 5.00
6 Peter Forsberg 1.50 4.00
7 Patrick Roy 4.00 10.00
8 Alex Tanguay 1.00 2.50
9 Mike Modano 1.50 4.00
10 Brendan Shanahan 1.00 2.50
11 Steve Yzerman 3.00 8.00
12 Pave Bure 1.00 2.50
13 Martin Brodeur 2.50 6.00
14 Scott Gomez 1.00 2.50
15 Roberto Luongo 1.50 4.00
16 Eric Lindros 1.00 2.50
17 John Vanbiesbrouck 1.00 2.50
18 Jaromir Jagr 1.50 4.00
19 Mats Sundin 1.00 2.50
20 Steve Kariya 1.50 4.00

1999-00 Crown Royale Century 21

Randomly inserted in packs, this 10-card set is out of this world. Player photos are set against an outer-space background and a rainbow foil "21." Each card is serial numbered out of 375.

COMPLETE SET (10) 30.00 60.00
1 Paul Kariya 3.00 8.00
2 Patrik Stefan .75 2.00
3 Chris Drury 2.00 5.00
4 Peter Forsberg 5.00 12.00
5 Pave Bure 3.00 8.00
6 Scott Gomez 1.25 3.00
7 Roberto Luongo 4.00 10.00
8 Marian Hossa 2.00 5.00
9 Jaromir Jagr 5.00 12.00
10 Vincent Lecavalier 3.00 8.00

1999-00 Crown Royale Cramer's Choice Jumbos

Inserted one per box, this 10-card set features color action cut-outs of top NHL players as chosen by Pacific President and CEO, Michael Cramer, printed on premium-sized, dual-foiled, die-cut pyramid-shaped cards. Six different serial-numbered parallel sets were also produced: 35 serial-numbered dark blue foil sets, 30 serial-numbered green foil sets, 25 serial-numbered red foil sets, 20 serial-numbered light blue foil sets, 10 serial-numbered gold foil sets, and 1 serial-numbered purple foil set. Purple and gold parallels are not priced due to scarcity.

COMPLETE SET (10) 15.00 30.00
*DARK BLUE/35: 5X TO 12X BASIC INSERTS
*GREEN/30: 5X TO 12X BASIC INSERTS
*LIGHT BLUE/20: 6X TO 15X BASIC INSERTS
*RED/25: 6X TO 15X BASIC CARDS
1 Paul Kariya 1.00 2.50
2 Teemu Selanne 1.00 2.50
3 Peter Forsberg 2.00 5.00
4 Patrick Roy 3.00 8.00
5 Mike Modano 1.25 3.00
6 Steve Yzerman 3.00 8.00
7 Pave Bure 1.00 2.50
8 Martin Brodeur 3.00 8.00
9 Eric Lindros 1.00 2.50
10 Jaromir Jagr 1.25 3.00

1999-00 Crown Royale Gold Crown Die-Cuts Jumbos

Inserted at six in 10 boxes, this 6-card jumbo set is an enhanced version of the base cards. The jumbos are vertical instead of horizontal, and feature rainbow foil on the die-cut crown background. Each card is serial numbered out of 960.

COMPLETE SET (6) 25.00 50.00
1 Teemu Selanne 3.00 8.00
2 Dominik Hasek 3.00 8.00
3 Patrick Roy 8.00 20.00
4 Steve Yzerman 8.00 20.00
5 Martin Brodeur 4.00 10.00
6 John LeClair 2.00 5.00

1999-00 Crown Royale Ice Elite

Inserted in packs at a rate of 1:1, this 25-card set silhouettes 25 of the NHL's most exciting players against a blue-ice background. A parallel of this set was also created and randomly inserted. The parallel was numbered to just 10.

COMPLETE SET (25) 10.00 20.00
1 Paul Kariya .30 .75
2 Teemu Selanne .30 .75
3 Joe Thornton .50 1.25
4 Dominik Hasek .60 1.50
5 Tony Amonte .25 .60
6 Milan Hejduk .30 .75
7 Patrick Roy 1.50 4.00
8 Joe Sakic .60 1.50
9 Ed Belfour .30 .75
10 Brett Hull .40 1.00
11 Brendan Shanahan .30 .75
12 Steve Yzerman 1.50 4.00
13 Luc Robitaille .25 .60
14 Trevor Linden .25 .60
15 David Legwand .25 .60
16 Martin Brodeur .75 2.00
17 Theo Fleury .25 .60
18 Marian Hossa .30 .75
19 John LeClair .30 .75
20 Mark Recchi .25 .60
21 Jeremy Roenick .40 1.00
22 Owen Nolan .25 .60
23 Vincent Lecavalier .30 .75
24 Curtis Joseph .30 .75
25 Steve Kariya .25 .60

1999-00 Crown Royale International Glory

Inserted in packs at a rate of one in one, this 25-card set places 25 of the NHL's top players in action to the background of their home country's flag. A parallel of this set was also created and randomly inserted in packs. The parallel was numbered to just 20.

COMPLETE SET (25) 10.00 20.00
*PASSPORT/20: 30X TO 80X BASIC INSERTS
1 Teemu Selanne .30 .75
2 Patrik Stefan .25 .60
3 Dominik Hasek .60 1.50

4 Arturs Irbe .25 .60
5 Chris Drury .25 .60
6 Peter Forsberg .75 2.00
7 Patrick Roy 1.25 3.00
8 Mike Modano .50 1.25
9 Sergei Fedorov .50 1.25
10 Brendan Shanahan .30 .75
11 Pave Bure .30 .75
12 Zigmund Palffy .25 .60
13 Saku Koivu .30 .75
14 Martin Brodeur .75 2.00
15 Scott Gomez .25 .60
16 Theo Fleury .25 .60
17 Simon Gagne .30 .75
18 Eric Lindros .30 .75
19 John Vanbiesbrouck .30 .75
20 Keith Tkachuk .30 .75
21 Jaromir Jagr .50 1.25
22 Pavol Demitra .25 .60
23 Jochen Hecht .25 .60
24 Jeff Friesen .25 .60
25 Mats Sundin .30 .75

1999-00 Crown Royale Team Captain Die-Cuts

Randomly inserted in packs at 1:25, this 10-card set showcases hockey's most respected team captains. Player action shots are set against a die-cut "C" background.

COMPLETE SET (10) 25.00 50.00
1 Paul Kariya 4.00 10.00
2 Ray Bourque 2.50 6.00
3 Joe Sakic 3.00 8.00
4 Steve Yzerman 8.00 20.00
5 Eric Lindros 2.50 6.00
6 Keith Tkachuk 1.50 4.00
7 Jaromir Jagr 2.50 6.00
8 Owen Nolan 1.25 3.00
9 Mats Sundin 1.50 4.00
10 Mark Messier 2.50 6.00

2000-01 Crown Royale

The 2000-01 Crown Royale set was issued in March 2001. The 6-card packs carried an SRP of $6.99. The set was issued as one series totaling 144 cards of which the last 35 were sequentially numbered to 400. The set features color action player photos printed on cards with silver and gold foil highlights, dual etching and a die-cut crown as background.

COMP.SET w/o SP's (108) 15.00 40.00
109-144 SP PRINT RUN 400
1 Guy Hebert .25 .60
2 Paul Kariya .40 1.00
3 Teemu Selanne .60 1.50
4 Donald Audette .25 .60
5 Andrew Brunette .20 .50
6 Damian Rhodes .20 .50
7 Patrik Stefan .25 .60
8 Jason Allison .25 .60
9 Byron Dafoe .25 .60
10 Bill Guerin .30 .75
11 Sergei Samsonov .25 .60
12 Joe Thornton .50 1.25
13 Doug Gilmour .40 1.00
14 Chris Gratton .20 .50
15 Dominik Hasek .50 1.25
16 Michael Peca .25 .60
17 Valeri Bure .25 .60
18 Jarome Iginla .30 .75
19 Marc Savard .25 .60
20 Ron Francis .40 1.00
21 Arturs Irbe .25 .60
22 Sami Kapanen .20 .50
23 Tony Amonte .25 .60
24 Jocelyn Thibault .25 .60
25 Alexei Zhamnov .25 .60
26 Ray Bourque .50 1.25
27 Chris Drury .25 .60
28 Peter Forsberg .40 1.00
29 Milan Hejduk .25 .60
30 Patrick Roy .75 2.00
31 Joe Sakic .50 1.25
32 Geoff Sanderson .25 .60
33 Ron Tugnutt .25 .60
34 Ed Belfour .30 .75
35 Brett Hull .50 1.25
36 Mike Modano .50 1.25
37 Joe Nieuwendyk .30 .75
38 Sergei Fedorov .50 1.25
39 Chris Osgood .30 .75
40 Brendan Shanahan .40 1.00
41 Steve Yzerman 1.00 2.50
42 Tommy Salo .25 .60
43 Ryan Smyth .25 .60
44 Doug Weight .30 .75
45 Pavel Bure .40 1.00
46 Rob Niedermayer .25 .60
47 Ray Whitney .25 .60
48 Stephane Fiset .20 .50
49 Zigmund Palffy .30 .75
50 Luc Robitaille .30 .75
51 Jamie Storr .25 .60
52 Jim Dowd .20 .50
53 Jamie McLennan .20 .50
54 Scott Pellerin .20 .50
55 Saku Koivu .30 .75
56 Martin Rucinsky .20 .50
57 Brian Savage .20 .50
58 Jose Theodore .40 1.00
59 Mike Dunham .20 .50
60 David Legwand .30 .75
61 Vitali Yachmenev .20 .50
62 Martin Brodeur .60 1.50
63 Patrik Elias .30 .75
64 Scott Gomez .25 .60
65 Alexander Mogilny .25 .60
66 Tim Connolly .20 .50
67 Brad Isbister .20 .50
68 John Vanbiesbrouck .25 .60
69 Theo Fleury .40 1.00
70 Brian Leetch .30 .75
71 Mark Messier .50 1.25
72 Mike Richter .30 .75
73 Daniel Alfredsson .30 .75
74 Radek Bonk .25 .60
75 Marian Hossa .25 .60
76 Patrick Lalime .25 .60
77 Alexei Yashin .25 .60
78 Brian Boucher .25 .60
79 Simon Gagne .30 .75
80 John LeClair .30 .75
81 Eric Lindros .50 1.25
82 Sean Burke .20 .50
83 Shane Doan .25 .60
84 Jeremy Roenick .30 .75
85 Keith Tkachuk .30 .75
86 Jaromir Jagr .75 2.00
87 Mario Lemieux 1.00 2.50
88 Martin Straka .25 .60
89 Chris Pronger .25 .60
90 Roman Turek .25 .60
91 Pierre Turgeon .30 .75
92 Scott Young .20 .50
93 Patrick Marleau .30 .75
94 Owen Nolan .30 .75
95 Steve Shields .20 .50
96 Vincent Lecavalier .25 .60
97 Fredrik Modin .20 .50
98 Kevin Weekes .20 .50
99 Sergei Berezin .20 .50
100 Curtis Joseph .40 1.00
101 Gary Roberts .20 .50
102 Mats Sundin .30 .75
103 Andrew Cassels .20 .50
104 Markus Naslund .25 .60
105 Felix Potvin .50 1.25
106 Peter Bondra .25 .60
107 Olaf Kolzig .30 .75
108 Adam Oates .30 .75
109 Samuel Pahlsson SP 1.50 4.00
110 Tomi Kallio SP 1.50 4.00
111 Andrew Raycroft RC 4.00 10.00
112 Eric Boulton RC 1.50 4.00
113 Dimitri Kalinin SP 1.50 4.00
114 Oleg Saprykin SP 1.50 4.00
115 Josef Vasicek RC 4.00 10.00
116 Shane Willis SP 1.50 4.00
117 Steven McCarthy SP 1.50 4.00
118 David Aebischer RC 3.00 8.00
119 Serge Aubin RC 2.00 5.00
120 Marc Denis SP 2.00 5.00
121 David Vyborny SP 1.50 4.00
122 Marty Turco RC 8.00 20.00
123 Roberto Luongo SP 6.00 15.00
124 Ivan Novoseltsev SP 1.50 4.00
125 Denis Shvidki SP 1.50 4.00
126 Steven Reinprecht RC 2.50 6.00
127 Marian Gaborik RC 8.00 20.00
128 Filip Kuba SP 1.50 4.00
129 Andrei Markov SP 3.00 8.00
130 Scott Hartnell RC 4.00 10.00
131 Colin White RC 1.50 4.00
132 Rick DiPietro RC 6.00 15.00
133 Taylor Pyatt SP 1.50 4.00
134 Martin Havlat RC 5.00 12.00
135 Jani Hurme RC 1.50 4.00
136 Justin Williams RC 4.00 10.00
137 Robert Esche SP 1.50 4.00
138 Milan Kraft SP 1.50 4.00
139 Brent Johnson SP 2.00 5.00
140 Evgeni Nabokov SP 2.00 5.00
141 Sheldon Keefe SP 1.50 4.00
142 Brad Richards SP 2.50 6.00
143 Daniel Sedin SP 5.00 12.00
144 Henrik Sedin SP 4.00 10.00
S1 Rick DiPietro Sample 3.00 8.00

2000-01 Crown Royale Ice Blue

This set paralleled the first 108 cards of the base set.
*1-108 BLUE/75: 6X TO 15X BASIC CARDS
STATED PRINT RUN 75 SER.#'d SETS

2000-01 Crown Royale Limited Series

This set paralleled the first 108 cards of the base set.The cards look the same as the base set except for silver foil in place of the gold and a serial number to 25 on the card front.
*1-108 LMTD/25: 15X TO 40X BASIC CARDS
STATED PRINT RUN 25 SER.#'d SETS

2000-01 Crown Royale Premiere Date

This set paralleled the first 108 cards of the base set.
*PREM.DATE/80: 6X TO 15X BASIC CARDS
PREM.DATE PRINT RUN 80 SER.#'d SETS

2000-01 Crown Royale Red

Randomly inserted in retail packs, this 108-card set parallels the base set with red foil highlights.
*1-108 RED: .8X TO 2X BASIC CARDS
RANDOM INSERTS IN RETAIL PACKS

2000-01 Crown Royale 21st Century Rookies

This 25-card set was inserted at the stated rate of 1:1. The set features color action photos of each player on a mostly green background accompanied by the players name, position, and team.

COMPLETE SET (25) 10.00 25.00
1 Tomi Kallio .20 .50
2 Andrew Raycroft 1.25 3.00
3 Eric Boulton .20 .50
4 Oleg Saprykin .20 .50
5 Shane Willis .20 .50
6 Steven McCarthy .20 .50
7 David Aebischer 1.25 3.00
8 Marc Denis .75 2.00
9 Marty Turco 1.25 3.00
10 Roberto Luongo 1.25 3.00
11 Steven Reinprecht .20 .50
12 Marian Gaborik 2.00 5.00
13 Andrei Markov .60 1.50
14 Colin White .20 .50
15 Rick DiPietro 1.25 3.00
16 Taylor Pyatt .20 .50
17 Martin Havlat 1.25 3.00
18 Jani Hurme .20 .50
19 Justin Williams 1.00 2.50
20 Milan Kraft .20 .50
21 Brent Johnson .20 .50
22 Evgeni Nabokov .75 2.00
23 Brad Richards .75 2.00
24 Daniel Sedin .20 .50
25 Henrik Sedin .20 .50

2000-01 Crown Royale Game-Worn Jerseys

Randomly inserted in packs, this 25-card set featured game-used jersey swatches and full-color player photographs on a mostly gray background. Please note that the cards have different print runs which are player specific. They are listed below, following the player's name.

STATED PRINT RUN 343-1157
1 Byron Dafoe/602 3.00 8.00
2 Valeri Bure/599 3.00 8.00
3 Rico Fata/596 2.50 6.00
4 Phil Housley/599 3.00 8.00
5 Marc Savard/597 3.00 8.00
6 Peter Forsberg/624 5.00 12.00
7 Ed Belfour/608 4.00 10.00
8 Brett Hull/591 6.00 15.00
9 Jamie Langenbrunner/599 3.00 8.00
10 Grant Marshall/593 3.00 8.00
11 Mike Modano/587 6.00 15.00
12 Joe Nieuwendyk/597 4.00 10.00
13 Chris Chelios/1157 4.00 10.00
14 Chris Osgood/592 4.00 10.00
15 Brendan Shanahan/781 5.00 12.00
16 Patric Kjellberg/594 2.50 6.00
17 Mike Richter/596 4.00 10.00
18 Alexei Yashin/946 3.00 8.00
19 Eric Desjardins/594 3.00 8.00
20 John LeClair/594 4.00 10.00
21 Jyrki Lumme/592 2.50 6.00
22 Michal Rozsival/591 2.50 6.00
23 Martin Straka/581 3.00 8.00
24 Mats Sundin/343 4.00 10.00
25 Felix Potvin/585 6.00 15.00

2000-01 Crown Royale Game-Worn Jersey Patches

This randomly inserted set paralleled the Crown Royale Game-Worn Jerseys set, but each card carries a swatch of jersey patch. Please note that the cards have different print runs which are player specific. They are listed below, following the player's name.

1 Byron Dafoe/141 10.00 25.00
2 Valeri Bure/145 10.00 25.00
3 Rico Fata/144 8.00 20.00
4 Phil Housley/144 10.00 25.00
5 Marc Savard/144 10.00 25.00
6 Peter Forsberg/141 15.00 40.00
7 Ed Belfour/145 12.00 30.00
8 Brett Hull/144 20.00 50.00
9 Jamie Langenbrunner/143 10.00 25.00
10 Grant Marshall/144 10.00 25.00
11 Mike Modano/143 20.00 50.00
12 Joe Nieuwendyk/142 12.00 30.00
13 Chris Chelios/192 12.00 30.00
14 Chris Osgood/143 12.00 30.00
15 Brendan Shanahan/163 15.00 40.00
16 Patric Kjellberg/136 8.00 20.00
17 Mike Richter/135 12.00 30.00
18 Alexei Yashin/283 10.00 25.00
19 Eric Desjardins/145 10.00 25.00
20 John LeClair/144 12.00 30.00
21 Jyrki Lumme/144 8.00 20.00
22 Michal Rozsival/144 8.00 20.00
23 Martin Straka/144 10.00 25.00
24 Mats Sundin/104 12.00 30.00
25 Felix Potvin/144 20.00 50.00

2000-01 Crown Royale Premium-Sized Game-Worn Jerseys

This 25-card set was inserted one per hobby box. Individual cards measured 3 1/2" x 5" and carry a premium-sized jersey swatch that measured 1 1/2" x 2". Each card also carried a color action photo of each player, and the back describes when the jersey was worn. Please note that the cards have different print runs which are player specific. They are listed below, following the player's name.

STATED PRINT RUN 94-357
1 Byron Dafoe/343 10.00 25.00
2 Valeri Bure/349 6.00 15.00
3 Rico Fata/343 6.00 15.00
4 Phil Housley/344 6.00 15.00
5 Marc Savard/343 6.00 15.00
6 Peter Forsberg/95 15.00 40.00
7 Ed Belfour/352 10.00 25.00
8 Brett Hull/317 15.00 40.00
9 Jamie Langenbrunner/338 6.00 15.00
10 Grant Marshall/342 6.00 15.00
11 Mike Modano/320 10.00 25.00
12 Joe Nieuwendyk/333 8.00 20.00
13 Chris Chelios/94 15.00 40.00
14 Chris Osgood/351 8.00 20.00
15 Brendan Shanahan/96 10.00 25.00
16 Patric Kjellberg/327 6.00 15.00
17 Mike Richter/346 10.00 25.00
18 Alexei Yashin/345 6.00 15.00
19 Eric Desjardins/349 6.00 15.00
20 John LeClair/330 6.00 15.00
21 Jyrki Lumme/336 6.00 15.00
22 Michal Rozsival/357 6.00 15.00
23 Martin Straka/334 6.00 15.00
25 Felix Potvin/345 10.00 25.00

2000-01 Crown Royale Game-Worn Jersey Redemptions

This 11-card set was inserted into random packs as redemption cards only. It was substituted into the product at the last minute in place of the Crown Royale Road To The Gold insert set. The cards are serial numbered between 100-475.

1 Stu Barnes/475 6.00 15.00
2 Jarome Iginla/475 6.00 15.00
3 Joe Sakic/475 6.00 12.00
4 David Legwand/475 6.00 15.00
5 Scott Niedermayer/475 8.00 20.00
6 Theo Fleury/475 8.00 20.00
7 Daniel Alfredsson/475 5.00 12.00
8 Jeremy Roenick/475 5.00 12.00
9 Jaromir Jagr/475 12.00 30.00
10 Curtis Joseph/475 6.00 12.00
11 Mario Lemieux/100 30.00 80.00

2000-01 Crown Royale Jewels of the Crown

Inserted at a rate of 1:1, this 25-card set features full-color action photos of top stars on front with computer-generated purple jewels in each corner.

COMPLETE SET (25) 15.00 40.00
1 Paul Kariya .60 1.50
2 Teemu Selanne .60 1.50
3 Patrik Stefan .40 1.00
4 Jason Allison .40 1.00
5 Joe Thornton 1.00 2.50
6 Dominik Hasek 1.25 3.00
7 Ray Bourque 1.25 3.00
8 Peter Forsberg 1.50 4.00
9 Patrick Roy 3.00 8.00
10 Joe Sakic 1.25 3.00
11 Brett Hull .75 2.00
12 Mike Modano 1.00 2.50
13 Brendan Shanahan 1.00 2.50
14 Steve Yzerman 3.00 8.00
15 Doug Weight .40 1.00
16 Pavel Bure .75 2.00
17 Martin Brodeur 1.50 4.00
18 Mark Messier .75 2.00
19 John LeClair .75 2.00
20 Eric Lindros 1.00 2.50
21 Jaromir Jagr 1.00 2.50
22 Mario Lemieux 4.00 10.00
23 Vincent Lecavalier .60 1.50
24 Curtis Joseph .60 1.50
25 Mats Sundin .60 1.50

2000-01 Crown Royale Landmarks

Randomly inserted in packs, this 10-card set features color action photos in the forefront and the skyline of the depicted player's team city in the background. Each card was serial numbered out of 102.

COMPLETE SET (10) 75.00 150.00
1 Paul Kariya 6.00 15.00
2 Dominik Hasek 10.00 25.00
3 Peter Forsberg 12.50 30.00
4 Patrick Roy 25.00 60.00
5 Steve Yzerman 25.00 60.00
6 Pavel Bure 6.00 15.00
7 Martin Brodeur 12.50 30.00
8 Jaromir Jagr 8.00 20.00
9 Mario Lemieux 30.00 80.00
10 Curtis Joseph 6.00 15.00

2000-01 Crown Royale Now Playing

Randomly inserted at a rate of 1:25, this 20-card set features a movie poster look, that carries a large color player photo over a small silhouette. The words "Now Playing" run diagonally in the left hand corner, and the player's name in bold is at the bottom above mock movie credits.

COMPLETE SET (20) 50.00 100.00
1 Paul Kariya 1.50 4.00
2 Teemu Selanne 1.50 4.00
3 Jason Allison 1.25 3.00
4 Ray Bourque 3.00 8.00
5 Peter Forsberg 3.00 8.00
6 Patrick Roy 8.00 20.00
7 Brett Hull 2.00 5.00
8 Steve Yzerman 6.00 15.00
9 Pavel Bure 2.00 5.00
10 Marian Gaborik 4.00 10.00
11 Martin Brodeur 4.00 10.00
12 Theo Fleury 1.25 3.00
13 John LeClair 1.50 4.00
14 Jaromir Jagr 2.50 6.00
15 Mario Lemieux 8.00 20.00
16 Vincent Lecavalier 1.50 4.00
17 Curtis Joseph 1.50 4.00
18 Mats Sundin 1.50 4.00
19 Daniel Sedin 1.25 3.00
20 Henrik Sedin 1.25 3.00

2001 Crown Royale Calder Collection All-Star Edition

This 8-card set was produced by Pacific as a wrapper redemption for the 2001 All-Star Fan Fest. Base cards feature full color player portrait photos on a silver and maroon crown die-cut card. Each card is sequentially numbered to 2001.

COMPLETE SET (8) 20.00 50.00
*GOLD/1000: .5X TO 1.2X SILVER/2001
C1 David Aebischer 3.00 8.00
C2 Marian Gaborik 4.00 10.00
C3 Rick DiPietro 3.00 8.00
C4 Martin Havlat 4.00 10.00
C5 Evgeni Nabokov 3.00 8.00
C6 Brad Richards 1.50 4.00
C7 Daniel Sedin 1.50 4.00
C8 Henrik Sedin 1.25 3.00

2001-02 Crown Royale

Released in both hobby and retail channels, this 180-card set featured die-cut base cards and 35 short printed rookies with a crown style die-cut. Rookies were serial-numbered out of 267. Hobby versions were enhanced with gold foil, retail versions with green foil. Hobby packs carried a SRP $5.99 for a 3-card pack. Retail packs included 5 cards.

1 Matt Cullen .20 .50
2 Jeff Friesen .20 .50
3 Jean-Sebastien Giguere .25 .60
4 Paul Kariya .40 1.00
5 Ray Ferraro .20 .50
6 Dany Heatley .30 .75
7 Milan Hnilicka .25 .60
8 Patrik Stefan .25 .60
9 Byron Dafoe .25 .60
10 Glen Murray .25 .60
11 Brian Rolston .25 .60
12 Sergei Samsonov .25 .60
13 Joe Thornton .40 1.00
14 Stu Barnes .25 .60
15 Martin Biron .25 .60
16 Tim Connolly .20 .50
17 J-P Dumont .20 .50
18 Miroslav Satan .25 .60
19 Craig Conroy .20 .50
20 Jarome Iginla .30 .75
21 Dean McAmmond .20 .50
22 Derek Morris .20 .50
23 Marc Savard .20 .50
24 Roman Turek .25 .60
25 Ron Francis .40 1.00
26 Arturs Irbe .25 .60
27 Sami Kapanen .20 .50
28 Jeff O'Neill .20 .50
29 Tony Amonte .25 .60
30 Mark Bell .20 .50
31 Kyle Calder .20 .50
32 Eric Daze .25 .60
33 Steve Sullivan .20 .50
34 Jocelyn Thibault .25 .60
35 Rob Blake .30 .75
36 Chris Drury .25 .60
37 Peter Forsberg .40 1.00
38 Milan Hejduk .25 .60
39 Patrick Roy .75 2.00
40 Joe Sakic .50 1.25
41 Alexei Tanguay .25 .60
42 Marc Denis .25 .60
43 Rostislav Klesla .20 .50
44 Geoff Sanderson .20 .50
45 Ron Tugnutt .25 .60
46 Ed Belfour .30 .75
47 Jere Lehtinen .25 .60
48 Mike Modano .50 1.25
49 Joe Nieuwendyk .30 .75
50 Pierre Turgeon .30 .75
51 Sergei Fedorov .50 1.25
52 Dominik Hasek .50 1.25
53 Brett Hull .40 1.00
54 Nicklas Lidstrom .30 .75
55 Luc Robitaille .30 .75
56 Brendan Shanahan .40 1.00
57 Steve Yzerman 1.00 2.50
58 Anson Carter .25 .60
59 Daniel Cleary .25 .60
60 Mike Comrie .25 .60
61 Tommy Salo .25 .60
62 Ryan Smyth .25 .60
63 Pavel Bure .40 1.00
64 Viktor Kozlov .20 .50
65 Roberto Luongo .50 1.25
66 Jason Allison .25 .60
67 Adam Deadmarsh .25 .60
68 Steve Heinze .20 .50
69 Zigmund Palffy .30 .75
70 Felix Potvin .50 1.25
71 Andrew Brunette .20 .50
72 Jim Dowd .20 .50
73 Manny Fernandez .25 .60
74 Marian Gaborik .50 1.25
75 Doug Gilmour .40 1.00
76 Jeff Hackett .25 .60
77 Yanic Perreault .20 .50
78 Brian Savage .20 .50
79 Jose Theodore .30 .75
80 Mike Dunham .25 .60
81 David Legwand .25 .60
82 Cliff Ronning .20 .50
83 Scott Walker .20 .50
84 Jason Arnott .25 .60
85 Martin Brodeur .60 1.50
86 Patrik Elias .30 .75
87 Scott Stevens .30 .75
88 Petr Sykora .20 .50
89 Rick DiPietro .25 .60
90 Chris Osgood .30 .75
91 Mark Parrish .20 .50
92 Mike Peca .25 .60
93 Alexei Yashin .25 .60
94 Theo Fleury .40 1.00
95 Brian Leetch .30 .75
96 Eric Lindros .50 1.25
97 Mark Messier .50 1.25
98 Mike Richter .30 .75
99 Daniel Alfredsson .30 .75
100 Martin Havlat .25 .60
101 Marian Hossa .25 .60
102 Patrick Lalime .25 .60
103 Todd White .20 .50
104 Brian Boucher .25 .60
105 Roman Cechmanek .25 .60
106 Simon Gagne .30 .75
107 John LeClair .30 .75
108 Mark Recchi .40 1.00
109 Jeremy Roenick .30 .75
110 Daniel Briere .25 .60
111 Sean Burke .20 .50
112 Shane Doan .25 .60
113 Claude Lemieux .25 .60
114 Johan Hedberg .25 .60
115 Alexei Kovalev .25 .60
116 Roberto Lang .20 .50
117 Mario Lemieux 1.00 2.50
118 Pavol Demitra .40 1.00
119 Brent Johnson .25 .60
120 Chris Pronger .25 .60
121 Keith Tkachuk .30 .75
122 Doug Weight .30 .75
123 Vincent Damphousse .25 .60
124 Evgeni Nabokov .25 .60
125 Owen Nolan .30 .75
126 Teemu Selanne .60 1.50
127 Nikolai Khabibulin .30 .75
128 Vincent Lecavalier .25 .60
129 Brad Richards .30 .75
130 Martin St. Louis .30 .75
131 Curtis Joseph .30 .75
132 Alexander Mogilny .25 .60
133 Gary Roberts .20 .50
134 Mats Sundin .30 .75
135 Darcy Tucker .20 .50
136 Dan Cloutier .25 .60
137 Brendan Morrison .25 .60
138 Markus Naslund .30 .75
139 Daniel Sedin .30 .75
140 Henrik Sedin .30 .75
141 Peter Bondra .30 .75
142 Jaromir Jagr .75 2.00
143 Olaf Kolzig .30 .75
144 Adam Oates .30 .75
145 Ilja Bryzgalov RC 6.00 15.00
146 Timo Parssinen RC 3.00 8.00
147 Ilya Kovalchuk RC 15.00 40.00
148 Brian Pothier RC 2.50 6.00
149 Jukka Hentunen RC 2.50 6.00
150 Erik Cole RC 5.00 12.00
151 Vaclav Nedorost RC 2.50 6.00
152 Brian Gionta 3.00 8.00
153 Mathieu Darche RC 4.00 10.00
154 Jody Shelley RC 3.00 8.00
155 Martin Spanhel RC 2.50 6.00
156 Niko Kapanen RC 4.00 10.00
157 Pavel Datsyuk RC 30.00 80.00
158 Jason Chimera RC 2.50 6.00
159 Ty Conklin RC 4.00 10.00
160 Jussi Markkanen 2.50 6.00
161 Niklas Hagman RC 3.00 8.00
162 Kristian Huselius RC 4.00 10.00
163 Jaroslav Bednar RC 2.50 6.00
164 David Cullen RC 2.50 6.00
165 Pascal Dupuis RC 4.00 10.00
166 Nick Schultz RC 2.50 6.00
167 Martin Erat RC 4.00 10.00
168 Andreas Salomonsson RC 2.50 6.00
169 Radek Martinek RC 2.50 6.00
170 Raffi Torres RC 4.00 10.00
171 Dan Blackburn RC 3.00 8.00
172 Chris Neil RC 3.00 8.00
173 Jiri Dopita RC 2.50 6.00
174 Krystofer Kolanos RC 2.50 6.00
175 Billy Tibbetts RC 2.50 6.00
176 Mark Rycroft RC 3.00 8.00
177 Jeff Jillson RC 2.50 6.00
178 Nikita Alexeev RC 2.50 6.00
179 Chris Corrinet RC 2.50 6.00
180 Brian Sutherby RC 2.50 6.00

2001-02 Crown Royale Blue

This 144-card set paralleled the base set not including the SP's, but carried blue foil in place of the green and were serial-numbered out of 89. These cards were found in retail packs only at a stated rate of 2:25.

2001-02 Crown Royale Premiere Date

This 144-card set paralleled the base set not including the SP's, but carried a premiere date stamp and were serial-numbered out of 60. These cards were found in hobby packs only at a stated rate of 1:25.
*PREM.DATE/60: 5X TO 12X BASIC CARDS
PREM.DATE/60 ODDS 1:25 HOBBY
97 Mark Messier 8.00 20.00

2001-02 Crown Royale Retail Green

*RETAIL: .5X TO 1.2X HOBBY
97 Mark Messier .75 2.00

2001-02 Crown Royale All-Star Honors

COMPLETE SET (1-20) 20.00 50.00
STATED ODDS 1:49 HOB, 1:97 RET
1 Paul Kariya 2.00 5.00
2 Roman Turek 1.50 4.00
3 Rob Blake 1.50 4.00
4 Patrick Roy 10.00 25.00
5 Joe Sakic 4.00 10.00
6 Mike Modano 3.00 8.00
7 Dominik Hasek 4.00 10.00
8 Brett Hull 2.50 6.00
9 Brendan Shanahan 3.00 8.00
10 Steve Yzerman 10.00 25.00
11 Pavel Bure 3.00 8.00
12 Martin Brodeur 5.00 12.00
13 Patrik Elias 1.50 4.00
14 Alexei Yashin 1.50 4.00
15 Eric Lindros 3.00 8.00
16 Mark Messier 2.50 6.00
17 Mario Lemieux 12.50 30.00
18 Doug Weight 1.50 4.00
19 Curtis Joseph 2.00 5.00
20 Mats Sundin 2.00 5.00

2001-02 Crown Royale Crowning Achievement

COMPLETE SET (20) 15.00 40.00
1-10 STATED ODDS 1:25 RET
11-20 STATED ODDS 1:25 HOB
1 Dany Heatley 2.00 5.00
2 Ilya Kovalchuk 8.00 10.00
3 Mark Bell .75 2.00
4 Rostislav Klesla .75 2.00
5 Kristian Huselius .75 2.00
6 Martin Erat .75 2.00
7 Rick Dipietro 1.25 3.00
8 Dan Blackburn .75 2.00
9 Krystofer Kolanos .75 2.00
10 Johan Hedberg .75 2.00
11 Jarome Iginla 2.50 6.00
12 Patrick Roy 6.00 15.00
13 Joe Sakic 2.00 5.00
14 Dominik Hasek 2.50 6.00
15 Steve Yzerman 4.00 10.00
16 Pavel Bure 1.25 3.00
17 Martin Brodeur 3.00 8.00
18 Eric Lindros 1.25 3.00
19 Mario Lemieux 6.00 15.00
20 Jaromir Jagr 2.00 5.00

2001-02 Crown Royale Jewels of the Crown

COMPLETE SET (1-30) 40.00 100.00
STATED ODDS 1:25 HOB/RET
1 Paul Kariya 1.00 2.50
2 Joe Thornton 2.00 5.00
3 Jarome Iginla 1.50 4.00
4 Roman Turek .75 2.00
5 Jeff O'Neill .75 2.00
6 Peter Forsberg 2.00 5.00
7 Patrick Roy 6.00 15.00
8 Joe Sakic 2.50 6.00
9 Mike Modano 1.50 4.00
10 Dominik Hasek 2.50 6.00
11 Brendan Shanahan 1.25 3.00
12 Steve Yzerman 4.00 10.00
13 Ryan Smyth .75 2.00
14 Pavel Bure 1.25 3.00
15 Jason Allison .75 2.00
16 Marian Gaborik 2.00 5.00
17 Saku Koivu 1.00 2.50
18 Martin Brodeur 3.00 8.00
19 Patrik Elias .75 2.00
20 Alexei Yashin .75 2.00
21 Eric Lindros 1.25 3.00
22 Mark Messier 1.50 4.00
23 Marian Hossa 1.00 2.50
24 Jeremy Roenick 1.25 3.00
25 Mario Lemieux 6.00 15.00
26 Keith Tkachuk 1.00 2.50
27 Teemu Selanne 1.00 2.50
28 Curtis Joseph 1.00 2.50
29 Mats Sundin 1.00 2.50
30 Jaromir Jagr 2.00 5.00

2001-02 Crown Royale Legendary Heroes

Inserted at a stated rate of 1:48 hobby boxes and 1:60 retail boxes, this 10-card set featured both a small full body photo on the left side of the card front and a larger head shot in the center under the players number. Each card was serial-numbered out of 31.

1 Paul Kariya 20.00 50.00
2 Patrick Roy 30.00 80.00
3 Dominik Hasek 12.50 30.00
4 Steve Yzerman 40.00 100.00
5 Martin Brodeur 20.00 50.00
6 Eric Lindros 12.50 30.00
7 Mark Messier 10.00 25.00
8 Mario Lemieux 50.00 125.00
9 Curtis Joseph 10.00 25.00
10 Jaromir Jagr 15.00 40.00

2001-02 Crown Royale Rookie Royalty

COMPLETE SET (1-20) 10.00 25.00
STATED ODDS 1:49 HOB/1:97 RET
1 Dany Heatley 4.00 10.00
2 Ilya Kovalchuk 8.00 20.00
3 Erik Cole 1.50 4.00
4 Mark Bell .75 2.00
5 Vaclav Nedorost .75 2.00
6 Brian Willsie .75 2.00
7 Rostislav Klesla .75 2.00
8 Pavel Datsyuk 8.00 20.00
9 Ty Conklin .75 2.00
10 Kristian Huselius .75 2.00
11 Jaroslav Bednar .75 2.00
12 Martin Erat .75 2.00
13 Rick Dipietro 2.00 5.00
14 Dan Blackburn .75 2.00
15 Krystofer Kolanos .75 2.00
16 Kris Beech .75 2.00
17 Johan Hedberg .75 2.00
18 Toby Petersen .75 2.00
19 Jeff Jillson .75 2.00
20 Nikita Alexeev .75 2.00

2001-02 Crown Royale Triple Threads

Inserted at a rate of 2:25 hobby and 1:97 retail, this 20-card set featured three swatches of game-used sweaters from the players featured. The swatches were affixed beside a small color photo of each player and arranged vertically.

1 Anaheim Mighty Ducks 4.00 10.00
2 Calgary Flames 2.50 6.00
3 Samsonov/V.Bure/Zubov 2.50 6.00
4 Giguere/Theodore/Roy 8.00 20.00
5 Buffalo Sabres 2.00 5.00
6 Calder/Dandenault/Daze 2.50 6.00
7 Colorado Avalanche 8.00 20.00
8 Dallas Stars 5.00 12.00
9 Iginla/Hecht/Cassels 3.00 8.00
10 Nashville Predators 2.00 5.00
11 Yzerman/Sakic/Lindros 10.00 25.00
12 Koivu/Sundin/Turek 3.00 8.00
13 Niedermayer/Terreri/Malholtra 3.00 8.00
14 Czerkawski/Lindgren/Alatalo 2.00 5.00
15 New York Rangers 4.00 10.00
16 Nashville Predators 2.50 6.00
17 Pittsburgh Penguins 10.00 25.00
18 Young/McLennan/Eastwood 2.00 5.00
19 St. Louis Blues 3.00 8.00
20 Bondra/Jagr/Straka 8.00 20.00

2001 Crown Royale Toronto Expo Rookie Collection

This set was issued by Pacific in a wrapper redemption program at the Toronto Spring Expo, May 4-6, 2001. The set features top rookies on the Crown Royale base card design with a blue background. Each card is serial numbered out of 499.

COMPLETE SET (8) 32.00 80.00
G1 Marty Turco 4.80 12.00
G2 Mike Comrie 10.00 25.00
G3 Rick DiPietro 6.00 15.00
G4 Martin Havlat 8.00 20.00
G5 Roman Cechmanek 4.00 10.00
G6 Brent Johnson 3.20 8.00
G7 Evgeni Nabokov 4.00 10.00
G8 Brad Richards 4.00 10.00

2002-03 Crown Royale

This 140-card set contained 100 veteran base cards and 40 shortprinted rookie cards that were inserted at 1:2 and serial-numbered to 2299 copies each.

1 Jean-Sebastien Giguere .40 1.00
2 Paul Kariya .50 1.25
3 Adam Oates .40 1.00
4 Dany Heatley .40 1.00
5 Ilya Kovalchuk .50 1.25
6 Glen Murray .30 .75
7 Sergei Samsonov .30 .75
8 Steve Shields .30 .75
9 Joe Thornton .50 1.25
10 Martin Biron .30 .75
11 Chris Gratton .25 .60
12 Miroslav Satan .40 1.00
13 Chris Drury .40 1.00
14 Jarome Iginla .40 1.00
15 Roman Turek .40 1.00
16 Rod Brind'Amour .40 1.00
17 Ron Francis .50 1.25
18 Arturs Irbe .30 .75
19 Jeff O'Neill .25 .60
20 Eric Daze .25 .60
21 Jocelyn Thibault .30 .75
22 Alexei Zhamnov .30 .75
23 Peter Forsberg .50 1.25
24 Milan Hejduk .30 .75
25 Patrick Roy 1.00 2.50
26 Joe Sakic .60 1.50
27 Andrew Cassels .25 .60
28 Marc Denis .30 .75
29 Bill Guerin .40 1.00
30 Mike Modano .60 1.50
31 Marty Turco .40 1.00
32 Sergei Fedorov .60 1.50
33 Brett Hull .50 1.25
34 Curtis Joseph .40 1.00
35 Nicklas Lidstrom .40 1.00
36 Brendan Shanahan .50 1.25
37 Steve Yzerman .75 2.00
38 Anson Carter .30 .75
39 Mike Comrie .40 1.00
40 Tommy Salo .30 .75
41 Ryan Smyth .30 .75
42 Kristian Huselius .25 .60
43 Roberto Luongo .60 1.50
44 Jason Allison .30 .75
45 Zigmund Palffy .40 1.00
46 Felix Potvin .60 1.50
47 Manny Fernandez .30 .75
48 Marian Gaborik .60 1.50
49 Bill Muckalt .25 .60
50 Jeff Hackett .30 .75
51 Saku Koivu .40 1.00
52 Jose Theodore .40 1.00
53 Richard Zednik .25 .60
54 David Legwand .30 .75
55 Tomas Vokoun .30 .75
56 Martin Brodeur .75 2.00
57 Patrik Elias .40 1.00
58 Scott Gomez .30 .75
59 Joe Nieuwendyk .40 1.00
60 Chris Osgood .40 1.00
61 Michael Peca .30 .75
62 Alexei Yashin .30 .75
63 Pavel Bure .50 1.25
64 Eric Lindros .60 1.50
65 Mike Richter .40 1.00
66 Daniel Alfredsson .40 1.00
67 Marian Hossa .30 .75
68 Patrick Lalime .30 .75
69 Roman Cechmanek .30 .75
70 Simon Gagne .40 1.00
71 John LeClair .40 1.00
72 Jeremy Roenick .40 1.00
73 Tony Amonte .30 .75
74 Daniel Briere .30 .75
75 Sean Burke .25 .60
76 Johan Hedberg .40 1.00
77 Alexei Kovalev .40 1.00
78 Mario Lemieux 1.25 3.00
79 Alexei Morozov .25 .60
80 Pavol Demitra .50 1.25
81 Brent Johnson .30 .75
82 Keith Tkachuk .40 1.00
83 Doug Weight .40 1.00
84 Vincent Damphousse .30 .75
85 Evgeni Nabokov .30 .75
86 Teemu Selanne .75 2.00
87 Nikolai Khabibulin .40 1.00
88 Vincent Lecavalier .30 .75
89 Martin St. Louis .40 1.00
90 Ed Belfour .40 1.00
91 Trevor Kidd .25 .60
92 Alexander Mogilny .30 .75
93 Mats Sundin .40 1.00
94 Todd Bertuzzi .40 1.00
95 Dan Cloutier .30 .75
96 Brendan Morrison .30 .75
97 Markus Naslund .30 .75
98 Peter Bondra .40 1.00
99 Jaromir Jagr 1.00 2.50
100 Olaf Kolzig .40 1.00
101 Stanislav Chistov RC .60 1.50
102 Martin Gerber RC 1.00 2.50
103 Alexei Smirnov RC .75 2.00
104 Tim Thomas RC 2.50 6.00
105 Ryan Miller RC 4.00 10.00
106 Chuck Kobasew RC .75 2.00
107 Jordan Leopold RC 1.00 2.50
108 Pascal Leclaire RC .75 2.00
109 Rick Nash RC 5.00 12.00
110 Lasse Pirjeta RC .60 1.50
111 Steve Ott RC 1.25 3.00
112 Dmitri Bykov RC .60 1.50

113 Henrik Zetterberg RC 6.00 15.00
114 Ales Hemsky RC 2.50 6.00
115 Jay Bouwmeester RC 2.00 5.00
116 Ivan Majesky RC .60 1.50
117 Mike Cammalleri RC 2.00 5.00
118 Alexander Frolov RC 1.25 3.00
119 P-M Bouchard RC 1.00 2.50
120 Stephane Veilleux RC .60 1.50
121 Kyle Wanvig SP .60 1.50
122 Sylvain Blouin RC .60 1.50
123 Ron Hainsey RC .60 1.50
124 Adam Hall RC .60 1.50
125 Scottie Upshall RC .75 2.00
126 Ray Schultz RC .60 1.50
127 Jason Spezza RC 4.00 10.00
128 Anton Volchenkov RC .60 1.50
129 Dennis Seidenberg RC 1.00 2.50
130 Patrick Sharp RC 2.00 5.00
131 Radovan Somik RC .60 1.50
132 Jeff Taffe RC .60 1.50
133 Dick Tarnstrom RC .60 1.50
134 Tom Koivisto RC .60 1.50
135 Curtis Sanford RC 1.00 2.50
136 Lynn Loyns RC .60 1.50
137 Alexander Svitov RC .60 1.50
138 Carlo Colaiacovo RC 1.00 2.50
139 Steve Eminger RC .60 1.50
140 Alex Henry RC .75 2.00

2002-03 Crown Royale Blue

*1-100 VETS: 1.2X TO 3X BASIC CARDS
BLUE VETERAN ODDS 1:2 RETAIL PACKS
*101-140 ROOKIES/350: .5X TO 1.2X
ROOKIE PRINT RUN 350 SER.#'d SETS

2002-03 Crown Royale Purple

This 40-card hobby only set paralleled the last 40 cards of the base set but carried purple foil highlights. These cards were inserted at 1:5 and were serial-numbered out of 799.
*101-140 PURPLE/799: .4X TO 1X BASIC CARDS

2002-03 Crown Royale Red

*1-100 VETS: .8X TO 2X BASIC CARDS
1-100 RED VET ODDS 1:4
*101-140 ROOKIES/350: .5X TO 1.2X
101-140 RED ROOKIE ODDS 1:12
101-140 RED ROOKIE PRINT RUN 350

2002-03 Crown Royale Retail

This 140-card set resembled the Hobby version but each card was highlighted with silver foil accents. Cards 101-140 were inserted at 1:7 packs.
*1-100 VETS: .4X TO 1X HOBBY
*101-140 ROKIE SP: .3X TO .8X HOB

2002-03 Crown Royale Jerseys

STATED ODDS 2:23 HOBBY, 1:25 RETAIL
STATED PRINT RUN 503-763
*GOLD/25: .8X TO 2X BASE JSY
1 Dany Heatley/755 5.00 12.00
2 Ilya Kovalchuk/762 8.00 20.00
3 Joe Sakic/513 6.00 15.00
4 Geoff Sanderson/758 4.00 10.00
5 Marty Turco/763 4.00 10.00
6 Mike Comrie/762 4.00 10.00
7 Valeri Bure/760 4.00 10.00
8 Zigmund Palffy/512 4.00 10.00
9 Jose Theodore/746 4.00 10.00
10 Martin Brodeur/511 10.00 25.00
11 Patrik Elias/503 4.00 10.00
12 Mike Peca/762 4.00 10.00
13 Brian Leetch/762 4.00 10.00
14 Martin Havlat/757 4.00 10.00
15 Jeremy Roenick/746 5.00 12.00
16 Mario Lemieux/752 10.00 25.00
17 Alexei Morozov/753 4.00 10.00
18 Chris Pronger/763 4.00 10.00
19 Sergei Varlamov/757 4.00 10.00
20 Owen Nolan/513 4.00 10.00
21 Fredrik Modin/759 4.00 10.00
22 Alexander Mogilny/762 4.00 10.00
23 Markus Naslund/754 4.00 10.00
24 Peter Bondra/761 4.00 10.00
25 Jaromir Jagr/763 8.00 20.00

2002-03 Crown Royale Dual Patches

Inserted as box toppers in hobby boxes, this 23-card set featured dual pieces of jersey patches. Print runs are listed below.
1 Heatley/I.Kovalchuk/63 25.00 60.00
2 M.Biron/J-P Dumont/273 10.00 25.00
3 R.Brind'Amour/E.Cole/203 12.50 30.00
4 Zhamnov/S.Sullivan/209 8.00 20.00
5 P.Roy/P.Forsberg SP 40.00 100.00
6 J.Sakic/A.Tanguay/228 15.00 40.00
7 Sanderson/R.Klesla/403 10.00 25.00
8 Modano/P.Turgeon/133 15.00 40.00
9 Fedorov/L.Robitaille/177 15.00 40.00
10 T.Salo/R.Smyth/188 10.00 25.00
11 V.Bure/K.Huselius/403 10.00 25.00
12 Deadmarsh/Smolinski/403 10.00 25.00
13 Gaborik/Fernandez/303 15.00 40.00
14 M.Brodeur/P.Elias/153 25.00 60.00
15 M.Peca/A.Yashin/253 10.00 25.00
16 B.Leetch/M.Richter/213 15.00 40.00
17 M.Lemieux/Morozov/203 25.00 60.00
18 A.Kovalev/M.Straka/403 20.00 50.00
19 E.Nabokov/P.Marleau/163 15.00 40.00
20 Khabibulin/B.Richards/303 15.00 40.00
21 A.Mogilny/D.Tucker/203 12.50 30.00
22 D.Sedin/H.Sedin/243 20.00 50.00
23 P.Bondra/O.Kolzig/347 10.00 25.00

2002-03 Crown Royale Coats of Armor

COMPLETE SET (10) 8.00 20.00
COMMON CARD (1-10) .60 1.50
STATED ODDS 1:8 HBBY/1:25 RETAIL
1 Patrick Roy 4.00 10.00
2 Marty Turco .60 1.50
3 Curtis Joseph .75 2.00
4 Roberto Luongo 1.50 3.50
5 Jose Theodore .60 1.50
6 Martin Brodeur 3.00 8.00
7 Mike Richter .75 2.00
8 Patrick Lalime .60 1.50
9 Nikolai Khabibulin .60 1.50
10 Ed Belfour .75 2.00

2002-03 Crown Royale Lords of the Rink

COMPLETE SET (20) 25.00 60.00
STATED ODDS 1:5
1 Paul Kariya .75 2.00
2 Dany Heatley .75 2.00
3 Ilya Kovalchuk 1.00 2.50
4 Joe Thornton 1.25 3.00
5 Jarome Iginla 1.00 2.50
6 Peter Forsberg 2.00 5.00
7 Joe Sakic 1.50 4.00
8 Mike Modano 1.25 3.00
9 Brendan Shanahan .75 2.00
10 Steve Yzerman 3.00 8.00
11 Zigmund Palffy .40 1.00
12 Marian Gaborik 1.50 4.00
13 Saku Koivu .75 2.00
14 Pavel Bure .75 2.00
15 Eric Lindros 1.00 2.50
16 Mario Lemieux 4.00 10.00
17 Teemu Selanne 1.00 2.50
18 Vincent Lecavalier .75 2.00
19 Mats Sundin .75 2.00
20 Jaromir Jagr 1.25 3.00

2002-03 Crown Royale Rookie Royalty

COMPLETE SET (20) 12.00 25.00
STATED ODDS 1:5 HBBY/1:13 RET
1 Stanislav Chistov .30 .75
2 Martin Gerber .50 1.25
3 Alexei Smirnov .40 1.00
4 Ivan Huml .30 .75
5 Chuck Kobasew .40 1.00
6 Tyler Arnason .50 1.25
7 Rick Nash 2.50 6.00
8 Dmitri Bykov .30 .75
9 Henrik Zetterberg 3.00 8.00
10 Ales Hemsky 1.25 3.00
11 Jay Bouwmeester 1.00 2.50
12 Stephen Weiss .50 1.25
13 Alexander Frolov .60 1.50
14 Scottie Upshall .40 1.00
15 Justin Mapletoft .30 .75
16 Jamie Lundmark .40 1.00
17 Jason Spezza 2.00 5.00
18 Petr Cajanek .30 .75
19 Jonathan Cheechoo .40 1.00
20 Alexander Svitov .30 .75

2002-03 Crown Royale Royal Portraits

STATED ODDS 1:45 HBBY/1:97 RETAIL
1 Paul Kariya 2.50 6.00
2 Ilya Kovalchuk 3.00 8.00
3 Patrick Roy 10.00 30.00
4 Joe Sakic 4.00 12.00
5 Rick Nash 12.50 40.00
6 Steve Yzerman 10.00 25.00
7 Martin Brodeur 10.00 25.00
8 Jason Spezza 12.50 30.00
9 Mario Lemieux 15.00 35.00
10 Jaromir Jagr 4.00 10.00

2003-04 Crown Royale

This 136-card die-cut set consisted of 100 veteran cards and 36 rookie cards short-printed to 575 serial-numbered copies each.
COMP.SET w/o SP's (100) 20.00 50.00
1 Sergei Fedorov .75 2.00
2 Martin Gerber .30 .75
3 Jean-Sebastien Giguere .50 1.25
4 Ilya Kovalchuk .50 1.25
5 Pasi Nurminen .40 1.00
6 Marc Savard .40 1.00
7 Glen Murray .40 1.00
8 Felix Potvin .75 2.00
9 Joe Thornton .60 1.50
10 Martin Biron .40 1.00
11 J-P Dumont .30 .75
12 Taylor Pyatt .30 .75
13 Jarome Iginla .50 1.25
14 Chuck Kobasew .30 .75
15 Roman Turek .40 1.00
16 Erik Cole .40 1.00
17 Jeff O'Neill .30 .75
18 Kevin Weekes .40 1.00
19 Tyler Arnason .30 .75
20 Brett McLean .30 .75
21 Jocelyn Thibault .40 1.00
22 David Aebischer .40 1.00
23 Peter Forsberg .60 1.50
24 Milan Hejduk .40 1.00
25 Paul Kariya .60 1.50
26 Joe Sakic .75 2.00
27 Philippe Sauve .40 1.00
28 Marc Denis .40 1.00
29 Todd Marchant .30 .75
30 Rick Nash .50 1.25
31 Jason Arnott .40 1.00
32 Bill Guerin .50 1.25
33 Mike Modano .75 2.00
34 Marty Turco .50 1.25
35 Dominik Hasek .75 2.00
36 Nicklas Lidstrom .50 1.25
37 Brendan Shanahan .60 1.50
38 Ray Whitney .40 1.00
39 Steve Yzerman 1.25 3.00
40 Georges Laraque .40 1.00
41 Tommy Salo .40 1.00
42 Ryan Smyth .40 1.00
43 Jay Bouwmeester .50 1.25
44 Olli Jokinen .50 1.25
45 Roberto Luongo .75 2.00
46 Jason Allison .40 1.00
47 Roman Cechmanek .40 1.00
48 Ziggy Palffy .50 1.25
49 Luc Robitaille .50 1.25
50 Pierre-Marc Bouchard .50 1.25
51 Marian Gaborik .75 2.00
52 Dwayne Roloson .40 1.00
53 Mathieu Garon .30 .75
54 Saku Koivu .50 1.25
55 Mike Ribeiro .40 1.00
56 Jose Theodore .50 1.25
57 Scottie Upshall .40 1.00
58 Tomas Vokoun .40 1.00
59 Martin Brodeur 1.00 2.50
60 Patrik Elias .50 1.25
61 Jeff Friesen .30 .75
62 Scott Gomez .40 1.00
63 Mariusz Czerkawski .30 .75
64 Jason Blake .30 .75
65 Rick DiPietro .40 1.00
66 Mike Dunham .40 1.00
67 Alex Kovalev .40 1.00
68 Mark Messier .75 2.00
69 Daniel Alfredsson .50 1.25
70 Marian Hossa .40 1.00
71 Patrick Lalime .40 1.00
72 Jason Spezza .50 1.25
73 Jeff Hackett .40 1.00
74 Mark Recchi .60 1.50
75 Jeremy Roenick .50 1.25
76 Justin Williams .40 1.00
77 Sean Burke .30 .75
78 Ladislav Nagy .30 .75
79 Rico Fata .30 .75
80 Mario Lemieux 1.50 4.00
81 Chris Osgood .50 1.25
82 Chris Pronger .40 1.00
83 Keith Tkachuk .50 1.25
84 Doug Weight .50 1.25
85 Jonathan Cheechoo .40 1.00
86 Alyn McCauley .30 .75
87 Evgeni Nabokov .40 1.00
88 Nikolai Khabibulin .50 1.25
89 Vincent Lecavalier .40 1.00
90 Brad Richards .50 1.25
91 Martin St. Louis .50 1.25
92 Ed Belfour .50 1.25
93 Alexander Mogilny .40 1.00
94 Owen Nolan .40 1.00
95 Mats Sundin .50 1.25
96 Todd Bertuzzi .50 1.25
97 Jason King .30 .75
98 Markus Naslund .50 1.25
99 Jaromir Jagr 1.25 3.00
100 Olaf Kolzig .50 1.25
101 Garrett Burnett RC 1.00 2.50
102 Joffrey Lupul RC 2.50 6.00
103 Patrice Bergeron RC 6.00 15.00
104 Sergei Zinovjev RC 1.00 2.50
105 Brent Krahn RC 1.00 2.50
106 Matthew Lombardi RC 1.25 3.00
107 Eric Staal RC 6.00 15.00
108 Tuomo Ruutu RC 1.50 4.00
109 Pavel Vorobiev RC 1.25 3.00
110 John-Michael Liles RC 1.25 3.00
111 Cody McCormick RC 1.25 3.00
112 Dan Fritsche RC 1.00 2.50
113 Nikolai Zherdev RC 2.00 5.00
114 Trevor Daley RC 1.50 4.00
115 Antti Miettinen RC 1.50 4.00
116 Jiri Hudler RC 2.50 6.00
117 Gregory Campbell RC 1.00 2.50
118 Nathan Horton RC 2.50 6.00
119 Dustin Brown RC 2.00 5.00
120 Tim Gleason RC 1.25 3.00
121 Brent Burns RC 2.50 6.00
122 Christopher Higgins RC 2.00 5.00
123 Dan Hamhuis RC 1.25 3.00
124 Jordin Tootoo RC 2.00 5.00
125 Marek Zidlicky RC 1.00 2.50
126 Paul Martin RC 1.25 3.00
127 Sean Bergenheim RC 1.25 3.00
128 Antoine Vermette RC 2.00 5.00
129 Joni Pilkanen RC 1.50 4.00
130 Matthew Spiller RC 1.25 3.00
131 Marc-Andre Fleury RC 8.00 20.00
132 Peter Sejna RC 1.25 3.00
133 Milan Michalek RC 2.00 5.00
134 Tom Preissing RC 1.25 3.00
135 Matt Stajan RC 1.50 4.00
136 Boyd Gordon RC 1.25 3.00

2003-04 Crown Royale Blue

*BLUE/850: 1.2X TO 3X BASIC CARDS
68 Mark Messier 2.50 6.00

2003-04 Crown Royale Retail

The retail version of this product carried silver foil highlights. Rookies in the retail set were serial-numbered out of 899.
*1-110 VETS: .4X TO 1X HOBBY
*111-136 ROOKIE/899: .3X TO .8X HOB.RC
68 Mark Messier .75 2.00

2003-04 Crown Royale Gauntlet of Glory

COMPLETE SET (20) 10.00 20.00
STATED ODDS 1:6
1 Jean-Sebastien Giguere .50 1.25
2 Pasi Nurminen .50 1.25
3 Felix Potvin .60 1.50
4 Martin Biron .50 1.25
5 Jocelyn Thibault .50 1.25
6 David Aebischer .50 1.25
7 Marc Denis .50 1.25
8 Marty Turco .50 1.25
9 Dominik Hasek 1.25 3.00
10 Roberto Luongo .75 2.00
11 Jose Theodore .75 2.00
12 Martin Brodeur 1.50 4.00
13 Rick DiPietro .50 1.25
14 Patrick Lalime .50 1.25
15 Sean Burke .50 1.25
16 Marc-Andre Fleury 1.50 4.00
17 Evgeni Nabokov .50 1.25
18 Nikolai Khabibulin .60 1.50
19 Ed Belfour .60 1.50
20 Dan Cloutier .50 1.25

2003-04 Crown Royale Global Conquest

STATED ODDS 1:11
1 M.Brodeur/M.Lemieux 2.00 5.00
2 D.Hasek/J.Jagr .75 2.00
3 T.Selanne/S.Koivu .60 1.50
4 O.Kolzig/M.Sturm .60 1.50
5 E.Nabokov/N.Antropov .60 1.50
6 S.Fedorov/I.Kovalchuk 1.25 3.00
7 M.Gaborik/M.Hossa 1.00 2.50
8 M.Naslund/P.Forsberg 1.25 3.00
9 D.Aebischer/M.Gerber .60 1.50
10 M.Modano/J.Roenick .60 1.50

2003-04 Crown Royale Jerseys

STATED ODDS 3:20
1 Sergei Fedorov 4.00 10.00
2 Ilya Kovalchuk 5.00 12.00
3 Joe Thornton 5.00 12.00
4 Ryan Miller 3.00 8.00
5 Matthew Lombardi 2.00 5.00
6 Peter Forsberg 6.00 15.00
7 Teemu Selanne 4.00 10.00
8 Mike Modano 4.00 10.00
9 Steve Yzerman 8.00 20.00
10 Ales Hemsky 2.50 6.00
11 Jay Bouwmeester 2.00 5.00
12 Nathan Horton 4.00 10.00
13 Saku Koivu 3.00 8.00
14 Martin Brodeur 8.00 20.00
15 Rick DiPietro 2.50 6.00
16 Eric Lindros 3.00 8.00
17 Jason Spezza 6.00 15.00
18 Antoine Vermette 2.00 5.00
19 Jeremy Roenick 4.00 10.00
20 Mario Lemieux 10.00 25.00
21 Barret Jackman 2.00 5.00
22 Vincent Lecavalier 3.00 8.00
23 Ed Belfour 3.00 8.00
24 Owen Nolan 2.50 6.00
25 Markus Naslund 3.00 8.00

2003-04 Crown Royale Patches

*PATCHES: .75X TO 2X JSY HI
STATED ODDS 1:20
20 Mario Lemieux/25 50.00 125.00

2003-04 Crown Royale Lords of the Rink

COMPLETE SET (24) 15.00 40.00
STATED ODDS 1:6
1 Sergei Fedorov .75 2.00
2 Ilya Kovalchuk .75 2.00
3 Joe Thornton .75 2.00
4 Eric Staal .50 1.25
5 Peter Forsberg 1.50 4.00
6 Milan Hejduk .60 1.50
7 Paul Kariya .60 1.50
8 Joe Sakic 1.25 3.00
9 Rick Nash .75 2.00
10 Mike Modano .75 2.00
11 Steve Yzerman 2.00 5.00
12 Henrik Zetterberg .75 2.00
13 Jay Bouwmeester .50 1.25
14 Ziggy Palffy .50 1.25
15 Marian Hossa .60 1.50
16 Jason Spezza .75 2.00
17 Jeremy Roenick .60 1.50
18 Mario Lemieux 2.50 6.00
19 Keith Tkachuk .60 1.50
20 Vincent Lecavalier .50 1.25
21 Mats Sundin .60 1.50
22 Todd Bertuzzi .60 1.50
23 Markus Naslund .60 1.50
24 Jaromir Jagr .75 2.00

2003-04 Crown Royale Royal Portraits

COMPLETE SET (10) 12.50 25.00
STATED ODDS 1:11
1 Joffrey Lupul 1.00 2.50
2 Patrice Bergeron 2.00 5.00
3 Eric Staal 1.50 4.00
4 Jiri Hudler 1.00 2.50
5 Nathan Horton 1.25 3.00
6 Jordin Tootoo 1.00 2.50
7 Joni Pitkanen 1.00 2.50
8 Marc-Andre Fleury 2.50 6.00
9 Milan Michalek 1.00 2.50
10 Matt Stajan 1.00 2.50

2010-11 Crown Royale

COMP.SET w/o SPs (100) 40.00 80.00
101-115 LEGEND PRINT RUN 499
116-129 ROOK.JSY AU PRINT RUN 99
130-173 ROOKIE AU PRINT RUN 99
1 Bobby Ryan .75 2.00
2 Ryan Getzlaf 1.25 3.00
3 Teemu Selanne 1.50 4.00
4 Corey Perry .75 2.00
5 Dustin Byfuglien .75 2.00
6 Nicklas Bergfors .60 1.50
7 Zach Bogosian .60 1.50
8 Nathan Horton .60 1.50
9 Tim Thomas .60 1.50
10 Zdeno Chara .60 1.50
11 Thomas Vanek .75 2.00
12 Tyler Myers .75 2.00
13 Tyler Ennis .60 1.50
14 Ryan Miller .75 2.00
15 Rene Bourque .50 1.25
16 Jarome Iginla .75 2.00
17 Jay Bouwmeester 1.00 2.50
18 Eric Staal 1.00 2.50
19 Cam Ward .75 2.00
20 Brandon Sutter .60 1.50
21 Jonathan Toews 1.50 4.00
22 Marty Turco .75 2.00
23 Patrick Kane 1.50 4.00
24 Marian Hossa .60 1.50
25 Paul Stastny .75 2.00
26 Matt Duchene .75 2.00
27 Craig Anderson .75 2.00
28 Rick Nash .75 2.00
29 Steve Mason .60 1.50
30 Jakub Voracek .75 2.00
31 Brenden Morrow .60 1.50
32 Brad Richards .75 2.00
33 Steve Ott .60 1.50
34 Mike Modano 1.25 3.00
35 Pavel Datsyuk 1.00 2.50
36 Jimmy Howard 1.00 2.50
37 Nicklas Lidstrom .75 2.00
38 Johan Franzen .75 2.00
39 Sam Gagner .60 1.50
40 Dustin Penner .50 1.25
41 Ales Hemsky .60 1.50
42 Tomas Vokoun .60 1.50
43 Shawn Matthias .50 1.25
44 David Booth .50 1.25
45 Drew Doughty .75 2.00
46 Jonathan Bernier .75 2.00
47 Anze Kopitar 1.25 3.00
48 Mikko Koivu .75 2.00
49 Niklas Backstrom .75 2.00
50 Matt Cullen .50 1.25
51 Carey Price 3.00 8.00
52 Tomas Plekanec .75 2.00
53 Michael Cammalleri .75 2.00
54 Brian Gionta .60 1.50
55 Pekka Rinne 1.00 2.50
56 Shea Weber .60 1.50
57 Colin Wilson .60 1.50
58 Ilya Kovalchuk .75 2.00
59 Martin Brodeur 1.50 4.00
60 Zach Parise .75 2.00
61 Dwayne Roloson .60 1.50
62 John Tavares 1.50 4.00
63 Josh Bailey .60 1.50
64 Marian Gaborik 1.00 2.50
65 Henrik Lundqvist 1.25 3.00
66 Brian Elliott .60 1.50
67 Jason Spezza .50 1.25
68 Daniel Alfredsson .75 2.00
69 Sergei Gonchar .50 1.25
70 Mike Richards .75 2.00
71 Jeff Carter .75 2.00
72 Chris Pronger .60 1.50
73 Claude Giroux .75 2.00
74 Wojtek Wolski .50 1.25
75 Ray Whitney .60 1.50
76 Ilya Bryzgalov .60 1.50
77 Evgeni Malkin 2.50 6.00
78 Marc-Andre Fleury 1.25 3.00
79 Sidney Crosby 3.00 8.00
80 Joe Pavelski .75 2.00
81 Joe Thornton .75 2.00
82 Antti Niemi .60 1.50
83 Dany Heatley .60 1.50
84 Alex Steen .75 2.00
85 Jaroslav Halak .75 2.00
86 Erik Johnson .50 1.25
87 Simon Gagne .75 2.00
88 Steven Stamkos 1.50 4.00
89 Vincent Lecavalier .60 1.50
90 Dion Phaneuf .75 2.00
91 Jonas Gustavsson 1.00 2.50
92 Phil Kessel 1.00 2.50
93 Tyler Bozak .75 2.00
94 Ryan Kesler .75 2.00
95 Henrik Sedin .75 2.00
96 Alexandre Burrows .75 2.00
97 Alex Ovechkin 3.00 8.00
98 Alexander Semin .75 2.00
99 Mike Green .75 2.00
100 Michal Neuvirth .60 1.50
101 Phil Esposito 2.50 6.00
102 Patrick Roy 4.00 10.00
103 Tony Esposito 1.50 4.00
104 Rogie Vachon 2.00 5.00
105 Rod Gilbert 1.50 4.00
106 Luc Robitaille 1.50 4.00
107 Lanny McDonald 1.50 4.00
108 Rick Middleton 2.00 5.00
109 Grant Fuhr 1.50 4.00
110 Johnny Bower 2.00 5.00
111 Mario Lemieux 5.00 12.00
112 Ken Hodge 1.25 3.00
113 Stan Mikita 2.00 5.00
114 Ed Belfour 1.50 4.00
115 Eric Lindros 2.50 6.00
116 Taylor Hall JSY AU RC 150.00 300.00
117 Tyler Seguin JSY AU RC 150.00 250.00
118 Jeff Skinner JSY AU RC 25.00 60.00
119 B.Schenn JSY AU RC 20.00 50.00
120 Jordan Eberle JSY AU RC 40.00 100.00
121 M.Paajarvi JSY AU RC 15.00 40.00
124 Derek Stepan JSY AU RC 40.00 100.00
125 Nazem Kadri JSY AU RC 40.00 80.00
126 M.Tedenby JSY AU RC 10.00 25.00
127 K.Shattenkirk JSY AU RC 25.00 60.00
128 Ekman-Larsson JSY AU RC 30.00 60.00
129 Zach Hamill JSY AU RC 12.00 30.00
130 Robin Lehner AU RC 8.00 20.00
131 A.Vasyunov AU RC 4.00 10.00
132 Jordan Caron AU RC 6.00 15.00
133 Sergei Bobrovsky AU RC 10.00 25.00
134 P.K. Subban AU RC 20.00 40.00
135 Eric Tangradi AU RC 4.00 10.00
136 Bobby Butler AU RC 4.00 10.00
137 Brandon Yip AU RC 4.00 10.00
138 Tommy Wingels AU RC 4.00 10.00
139 Kyle Clifford AU RC 4.00 10.00
140 Matt Taormina AU RC 4.00 10.00
141 Nick Bonino AU RC 5.00 12.00
142 Alexander Burmistrov AU RC 4.00 10.00
143 Nick Leddy AU RC 4.00 10.00
144 Zac Dalpe AU RC 4.00 10.00
145 Anders Lindback AU RC 4.00 10.00
146 Marcus Johansson AU RC 6.00 15.00
147 Jamie McBain AU RC 4.00 10.00
148 Brandon Pirri AU RC 4.00 10.00
149 Evgeny Grachev AU RC 4.00 10.00
150 Dana Tyrell AU RC 4.00 10.00
151 Jacob Josefson AU RC 4.00 10.00
152 Colby Cohen AU RC 4.00 10.00
153 Justin Falk AU RC 3.00 8.00
154 Mark Olver AU RC 4.00 10.00
155 Jake Muzzin AU RC 4.00 10.00
156 Henrik Karlsson AU RC 4.00 10.00
157 Ian Cole AU RC 4.00 10.00
158 John McCarthy AU RC 4.00 10.00
159 Ryan Reaves AU RC 5.00 12.00
160 Jeremy Morin AU RC 4.00 10.00
161 Eric Wellwood AU RC 5.00 12.00
162 Korbinian Holzer AU RC 4.00 10.00
163 Keith Aulie AU RC 4.00 10.00
164 Brandon McMillan AU RC 4.00 10.00
165 T.J. Brodie AU RC 4.00 10.00
166 Luke Adam AU RC 4.00 10.00
167 Nick Spaling AU RC 4.00 10.00
168 Dustin Tokarski AU RC 4.00 10.00
169 Maxim Noreau AU RC 3.00 8.00
170 Brayden Irwin AU RC 4.00 10.00
171 Nick Palmieri AU RC 4.00 10.00
172 Kyle Palmieri AU RC 8.00 20.00
173 Stephen Gionta AU RC 5.00 12.00
174 Brad Mills AU RC 4.00 10.00
175 Mike Moore AU RC 4.00 10.00

2010-11 Crown Royale Premiere Date

*PREMIERE DATE: 1.2X TO 3X BASE
STATED PRINT RUN 100 SER.#'d SETS

2010-11 Crown Royale Premiere Date Signatures

STATED PRINT RUN 5-100
1 Bobby Ryan/100 6.00 15.00
2 Ryan Getzlaf/50 8.00 20.00
3 Teemu Selanne/50 15.00 40.00
4 Corey Perry/50 6.00 15.00
5 Dustin Byfuglien/75 6.00 15.00
7 Zach Bogosian/50 5.00 12.00
8 Nathan Horton/100 5.00 12.00
9 Tim Thomas/100 12.00 30.00
10 Zdeno Chara/100 12.00 30.00
11 Thomas Vanek/100 6.00 15.00
12 Tyler Myers/100 6.00 15.00
13 Tyler Ennis/100 5.00 12.00
14 Ryan Miller/100 8.00 20.00
15 Rene Bourque/100 4.00 10.00
16 Jarome Iginla/25 8.00 20.00
17 Jay Bouwmeester/100 8.00 20.00
18 Eric Staal/75 8.00 20.00
19 Cam Ward/100 6.00 15.00
20 Brandon Sutter/100 5.00 12.00
21 Jonathan Toews/100 15.00 40.00
22 Marty Turco/100 12.00 30.00
23 Patrick Kane/75 15.00 40.00
24 Marian Hossa/100 12.00 30.00
25 Paul Stastny/50 6.00 15.00
26 Matt Duchene/100 6.00 15.00
28 Rick Nash/10
29 Steve Mason/100 5.00 12.00
30 Jakub Voracek/100 6.00 15.00
31 Brenden Morrow/100 5.00 12.00
32 Brad Richards/75 6.00 15.00
33 Steve Ott/100 5.00 12.00
34 Mike Modano/25 25.00 60.00
35 Pavel Datsyuk/25 15.00 40.00
36 Jimmy Howard/100 10.00 25.00
37 Nicklas Lidstrom/25 12.00 30.00
38 Johan Franzen/100 6.00 15.00
39 Sam Gagner/100 5.00 12.00
40 Dustin Penner/50 5.00 12.00
41 Ales Hemsky/100 6.00 15.00
42 Tomas Vokoun/100 5.00 12.00
45 Drew Doughty/100 6.00 15.00
46 Jonathan Bernier/50 6.00 15.00
47 Anze Kopitar/75 10.00 25.00
49 Niklas Backstrom/50 8.00 20.00
51 Carey Price/25 30.00 80.00
53 Michael Cammalleri/75 8.00 20.00
54 Brian Gionta/100 5.00 12.00
55 Pekka Rinne/100 8.00 20.00
56 Shea Weber/75 8.00 20.00
57 Colin Wilson/100 5.00 12.00
58 Ilya Kovalchuk/25 20.00 50.00
59 Martin Brodeur/5
60 Zach Parise/25 10.00 25.00
61 Dwayne Roloson/25 6.00 15.00
62 John Tavares/50 12.00 30.00
63 Josh Bailey/25 6.00 15.00
64 Marian Gaborik/10
65 Henrik Lundqvist/100 10.00 25.00
66 Brian Elliott/50 8.00 20.00
67 Jason Spezza/100 4.00 10.00
68 Daniel Alfredsson/100 10.00 25.00
70 Mike Richards/100 12.00 30.00
71 Jeff Carter/10
72 Chris Pronger/75 12.00 30.00
73 Claude Giroux/50 6.00 15.00
74 Wojtek Wolski/100 4.00 10.00
76 Ilya Bryzgalov/50 5.00 12.00
77 Evgeni Malkin/50 20.00 50.00
78 Marc-Andre Fleury/75 15.00 40.00
79 Sidney Crosby/25 75.00 135.00
80 Joe Pavelski/100 6.00 15.00
81 Joe Thornton/50 6.00 15.00
83 Dany Heatley/100 5.00 12.00
85 Jaroslav Halak/100 6.00 15.00
86 Erik Johnson/100 4.00 10.00
87 Simon Gagne/75 6.00 15.00
88 Steven Stamkos/10
89 Vincent Lecavalier/50 8.00 20.00
90 Dion Phaneuf/100 10.00 25.00
91 Jonas Gustavsson/100 8.00 20.00
92 Phil Kessel/50 8.00 20.00
93 Tyler Bozak/100 6.00 15.00
94 Ryan Kesler/25 12.00 30.00
95 Henrik Sedin/75 6.00 15.00
96 Alexandre Burrows/75 6.00 15.00
97 Alex Ovechkin/10
98 Alexander Semin/100 8.00 20.00
99 Mike Green/100 6.00 15.00

2010-11 Crown Royale Purple

*PURPLE: 2.5X TO 6X BASE
STATED PRINT RUN 25 SER.#'d SETS

2010-11 Crown Royale Rookie Silhouettes Patch Autographs

*PATCH/1525: .5X TO 1.2X JSY AU/99
STATED PRINT RUN 15-25
116 Taylor Hall/25 400.00 750.00
117 Tyler Seguin/25 150.00 300.00
118 Jeff Skinner/25 150.00 300.00
120 Jordan Eberle/25 40.00 100.00

2010-11 Crown Royale Calder Collection

STATED PRINT RUN 99 SER.#'d SETS
1 Tyler Ennis 3.00 8.00
2 Tyler Seguin 15.00 40.00
3 Jonathan Bernier 4.00 10.00
4 John Carlson 5.00 12.00
5 P.K. Subban 20.00 50.00
6 Taylor Hall 25.00 60.00
7 Magnus Paajarvi 4.00 10.00
8 Nikita Filatov 2.50 6.00
9 Jeff Skinner 6.00 15.00
10 Michal Neuvirth 3.00 8.00
11 Derek Stepan 4.00 10.00
12 Cam Fowler 6.00 20.00

2010-11 Crown Royale Coat of Arms Materials

STATED PRINT RUN 5-25
1 Alex Ovechkin/25 20.00 50.00
2 Zach Parise/10
3 Steve Ott/25 12.00 30.00
4 Milan Lucic/25 15.00 30.00
5 Miikka Kiprusoff/25 12.00 30.00
6 Roberto Luongo/25 10.00 25.00
7 Corey Perry/10
8 Nicklas Backstrom/10
9 Henrik Zetterberg/25 30.00 60.00
10 Mike Green/25 15.00 40.00
11 Travis Zajac/25 8.00 20.00
12 Tuukka Rask/25 10.00 25.00
14 Brad Richards/25 10.00 25.00
15 Shane Doan/25 15.00 40.00
16 John Tavares/25 20.00 50.00
17 Luke Schenn/25 8.00 20.00
18 Chris Pronger/25 8.00 20.00
19 Jay McClement/25 6.00 15.00
20 Brayden Schenn/25 12.00 30.00
21 Rick DiPietro/25 10.00 25.00
23 Jeff Skinner/25 15.00 40.00
24 Marian Gaborik/10
25 Taylor Hall/25 30.00 80.00
26 Sidney Crosby/25 40.00 100.00
27 Thomas Vanek/25 10.00 25.00
29 T.J. Galiardi/25 8.00 20.00
30 Jean-Sebastien Giguere/25 15.00 40.00
31 Jeff Carter/25 12.00 30.00
32 Mike Fisher/25 10.00 25.00
33 Niklas Backstrom/10
34 Steve Mason/25 15.00 40.00
35 Ryan Smyth/25 12.00 30.00
36 Eric Staal/5
37 Stephen Weiss/25 8.00 20.00
38 Bryan Little/25 10.00 25.00
39 Artem Anisimov/25 10.00 25.00
40 Shea Weber/25 10.00 25.00
41 Duncan Keith/25 12.00 30.00
42 Joe Thornton/25 10.00 25.00
44 Matt Duchene/25 10.00 25.00
45 Alexander Frolov/25 15.00 40.00
46 Andrei Kostitsyn/25 8.00 20.00
47 Derek Roy/25 10.00 25.00
48 Jordan Staal/25 10.00 25.00
49 Matt Moulson/25 8.00 20.00
50 Mike Smith/25 15.00 40.00

2010-11 Crown Royale Heirs to the Throne Materials

STATED PRINT RUN 25-250
*PRIME/30-50: .6X TO 1.5X BASIC JSY
AG Alex Goligoski 4.00 10.00
AR Andy Greene 3.00 8.00
BA Josh Bailey 4.00 10.00
BN Jamie Benn 6.00 15.00
RO Mikkel Roedker 3.00 8.00
BSC Brayden Schenn 4.00 10.00
CG Claude Giroux 5.00 12.00
CP Carey Price 20.00 50.00
CS Chris Stewart 4.00 10.00
CW Colin Wilson 4.00 10.00
DD Drew Doughty 5.00 12.00
DK David Krejci 5.00 12.00
EK Evander Kane 5.00 12.00
ER Erik Karlsson 10.00 25.00
FN Frans Nielsen 3.00 8.00
JB Jonathan Bernier 5.00 12.00
JE Jordan Eberle 6.00 15.00
JG Jonas Gustavsson 6.00 15.00
JN James Neal 5.00 12.00
JQ Jonathan Quick 8.00 20.00
JS Jordan Staal 5.00 12.00
JT John Tavares 8.00 20.00
JV Jakub Voracek 5.00 12.00
KL Kari Lehtonen 4.00 10.00
LE Loui Eriksson 4.00 10.00
MB Mikael Backlund 3.00 8.00
MD Matt Duchene/25 6.00 15.00
MF Marc-Andre Fleury 8.00 20.00
MP Magnus Paajarvi 3.00 8.00
MS Marc Staal 5.00 12.00
NB Nicklas Bergfors 4.00 10.00
NK Nazem Kadri 8.00 20.00
PH Patric Hornqvist 4.00 10.00
PR1 Peter Regin 4.00 10.00
PR2 Pekka Rinne 6.00 15.00
PS Paul Stastny 5.00 12.00
SG Sam Gagner 4.00 10.00
SK Jeff Skinner 5.00 12.00
TG T.J. Galiardi 4.00 10.00
TH Taylor Hall 12.00 30.00
TR Tuukka Rask 5.00 12.00
TS Tyler Seguin 10.00 25.00
ZB Zach Bogosian 4.00 10.00
ZH Zach Hamill 2.50 6.00
ZP Zach Parise/25 6.00 15.00

2010-11 Crown Royale Heirs to the Throne Materials Autographs

AG Alex Goligoski/25 5.00 12.00
AR Andy Greene 4.00 10.00
BA Josh Bailey 5.00 12.00
BN Jamie Benn 8.00 20.00
BO Mikkel Boedker 4.00 10.00
BS Brayden Schenn 8.00 20.00
CP Carey Price 30.00 80.00
CS Chris Stewart 5.00 12.00
CW Colin Wilson 5.00 12.00
DD Drew Doughty 6.00 15.00
EK Evander Kane 6.00 15.00
ER Erik Karlsson 30.00 80.00
FN Frans Nielsen 4.00 10.00
JB Jonathan Bernier 6.00 15.00
JE Jordan Eberle 12.00 30.00
JG Jonas Gustavsson 8.00 20.00
JN James Neal 6.00 15.00
JQ Jonathan Quick 10.00 25.00
JS Jordan Staal 6.00 15.00
JT John Tavares 12.00 30.00
KL Kari Lehtonen 5.00 12.00
LE Loui Eriksson 5.00 12.00
MB Mikael Backlund 4.00 10.00
MD Matt Duchene 6.00 15.00
MF Marc-Andre Fleury 10.00 25.00
MP Magnus Paajarvi 6.00 15.00
MS Marc Staal 6.00 15.00
NK Nazem Kadri 15.00 40.00
PH Patric Hornqvist 5.00 12.00
PR1 Peter Regin 5.00 12.00
PR2 Pekka Rinne 8.00 20.00
PS Paul Stastny 6.00 15.00
SG Sam Gagner 5.00 12.00
SK Jeff Skinner 10.00 25.00
TG T.J. Galiardi 5.00 12.00
TH Taylor Hall 20.00 50.00
TS Tyler Seguin 20.00 50.00
ZB Zach Bogosian 5.00 12.00
ZH Zach Hamill 5.00 12.00

2010-11 Crown Royale In Harm's Way

STATED PRINT RUN 299 SER.#'d SETS
1 Ryan Miller 1.50 4.00
2 Pekka Rinne 2.00 5.00
3 Roberto Luongo 1.50 4.00
4 Jimmy Howard 2.00 5.00
5 Jonas Hiller 1.25 3.00
6 Jonathan Bernier 1.50 4.00
7 Tim Thomas 1.25 3.00
8 Semyon Varlamov 1.50 4.00
9 Carey Price 6.00 15.00
10 Cam Ward 1.50 4.00
11 Tomas Vokoun 1.25 3.00
12 Henrik Lundqvist 2.50 6.00
13 Nikolai Khabibulin 1.25 3.00
14 Jean-Sebastien Giguere 1.25 3.00
15 Miikka Kiprusoff 1.25 3.00
16 Jaroslav Halak 1.50 4.00
17 Antti Niemi 1.25 3.00
18 Marty Turco 1.50 4.00
19 Rick DiPietro 1.25 3.00
20 Martin Brodeur 3.00 8.00

2010-11 Crown Royale Lancers

STATED PRINT RUN 250 SER.#'d SETS
1 Henrik Sedin 1.50 4.00
2 Steven Stamkos 3.00 8.00
3 Tomas Fleischmann 1.00 2.50
4 Alexandre Burrows 1.50 4.00
5 Patrick Marleau 1.50 4.00
6 Teemu Selanne 3.00 8.00
7 Mike Knuble 1.00 2.50
8 Dustin Penner 1.00 2.50
9 Jussi Jokinen 1.00 2.50
10 Ilya Kovalchuk 1.50 4.00
11 Alexander Semin 1.50 4.00
12 Dany Heatley 1.25 3.00
13 Zach Parise 1.50 4.00
14 Rick Nash 1.50 4.00
15 Bobby Ryan 1.50 4.00
16 Phil Kessel 2.00 5.00
17 Patrick Kane 3.00 8.00
18 Matt Moulson 1.25 3.00
19 Loui Eriksson 1.25 3.00
20 Eric Staal 2.00 5.00
21 Patric Hornqvist 1.25 3.00
22 Mike Richards 1.50 4.00
23 Anze Kopitar 2.50 6.00
24 Rene Bourque 1.00 2.50
25 James Neal 1.50 4.00

2010-11 Crown Royale Lancers Materials Prime

STATED PRINT RUN 50 SER.#'d SETS
*PATCH/25: .6X TO 1.5X PRIME
1 Henrik Sedin 6.00 15.00
2 Steven Stamkos 12.00 30.00
4 Alexandre Burrows 6.00 15.00
5 Patrick Marleau 6.00 15.00
6 Teemu Selanne 12.00 30.00
7 Mike Knuble 4.00 10.00
8 Dustin Penner 4.00 10.00
10 Ilya Kovalchuk 6.00 15.00
11 Alexander Semin 6.00 15.00
12 Dany Heatley 5.00 12.00
13 Zach Parise 6.00 15.00
15 Bobby Ryan 6.00 15.00
16 Phil Kessel 8.00 20.00

17 Patrick Kane 12.00 30.00
18 Matt Moulson 5.00 12.00
19 Loui Eriksson 5.00 12.00
20 Eric Staal 8.00 20.00
21 Patric Hornqvist 5.00 12.00
23 Anze Kopitar 10.00 25.00
24 Rene Bourque 4.00 10.00
25 James Neal 6.00 15.00

2010-11 Crown Royale Legends

COMPLETE SET (12) 20.00 50.00
1 Brian Leetch 1.50 4.00
2 Johnny Bucyk 1.50 4.00
3 Luc Robitaille 1.50 4.00
4 Mario Lemieux 5.00 12.00
5 Martin Brodeur 3.00 8.00
6 Patrick Roy 4.00 10.00
7 Teemu Selanne 3.00 8.00
8 Joe Sakic 2.50 6.00
9 Mike Modano 2.50 6.00
10 Marcel Dionne 2.00 5.00
11 Lanny McDonald 1.50 4.00
12 Mark Recchi 2.00 5.00

2010-11 Crown Royale Legends Memorabilia

STATED PRINT RUN 50-100
1 Brian Leetch 5.00 12.00
2 Johnny Bucyk 5.00 12.00
3 Luc Robitaille 5.00 12.00
4 Mario Lemieux 15.00 40.00
5 Martin Brodeur/50 10.00 25.00
6 Patrick Roy 12.00 30.00
8 Joe Sakic 8.00 20.00
9 Mike Modano 8.00 20.00
10 Marcel Dionne 6.00 15.00
11 Lanny McDonald 5.00 12.00
12 Mark Recchi 6.00 15.00

2010-11 Crown Royale Legends Signatures

STATED PRINT RUN 25 SER.#'d SETS
1 Brian Leetch 12.00 30.00
2 Johnny Bucyk 8.00 20.00
3 Luc Robitaille 15.00 40.00
4 Mario Lemieux 40.00 100.00
5 Martin Brodeur 40.00 80.00
6 Patrick Roy 50.00 100.00
7 Teemu Selanne 15.00 40.00
8 Joe Sakic 40.00 80.00
9 Mike Modano 12.00 30.00
10 Marcel Dionne 20.00 50.00
11 Lanny McDonald 8.00 20.00
12 Mark Recchi 15.00 40.00

2010-11 Crown Royale Lords of the NHL

STATED PRINT RUN 499 SER.#'d SETS
1 Alex Ovechkin 6.00 15.00
2 Henrik Sedin 1.50 4.00
3 Steven Stamkos 3.00 8.00
4 Sidney Crosby 6.00 15.00
5 Ryan Miller 1.50 4.00
6 Jonathan Toews 3.00 8.00
7 Evgeni Malkin 5.00 12.00
8 Pavel Datsyuk 2.00 5.00
9 Drew Doughty 1.50 4.00
10 Nicklas Lidstrom 1.50 4.00
11 Duncan Keith 1.50 4.00
12 Ilya Kovalchuk 1.50 4.00

2010-11 Crown Royale Lords of the NHL Memorabilia

STATED PRINT RUN 19-99
*PRIME/15: 1X TO 2.5X BASIC JSY/49-99
*PRIME/15: .6X TO 1.5X BASIC JSY/19
1 Alex Ovechkin/49 20.00 50.00
2 Henrik Sedin/99 5.00 12.00
3 Steven Stamkos/49 10.00 25.00
4 Sidney Crosby/99 20.00 50.00
5 Ryan Miller/19 8.00 20.00
7 Evgeni Malkin/99 15.00 40.00
8 Pavel Datsyuk/99 6.00 15.00
9 Drew Doughty/99 5.00 12.00
10 Nicklas Lidstrom/49 5.00 12.00
11 Duncan Keith/99 5.00 12.00
12 Ilya Kovalchuk/99 5.00 12.00

2010-11 Crown Royale Loyalty

STATED PRINT RUN 250 SER.#'d SETS
AH Ales Hemsky 1.25 3.00
AM Andrei Markov 1.50 4.00
BM Brenden Morrow 1.25 3.00
DA Daniel Alfredsson 1.50 4.00
DL David Legwand 1.25 3.00
DS Daniel Sedin 1.50 4.00
HS Henrik Sedin 1.50 4.00
HZ Henrik Zetterberg 2.00 5.00
JI Jarome Iginla 1.50 4.00
JS Jason Spezza 1.00 2.50
MB Martin Brodeur 3.00 8.00
NL Nicklas Lidstrom 1.50 4.00
PB Patrice Bergeron 2.00 5.00
PD Pavel Datsyuk 2.00 5.00
PE Patrik Elias 1.50 4.00
PM Patrick Marleau 1.50 4.00
RM Ryan Miller 1.50 4.00
RN Rick Nash 1.50 4.00
RR Robyn Regehr 1.00 2.50
SD Shane Doan 1.25 3.00
SW Stephen Weiss 1.25 3.00
TC Tim Connolly 1.00 2.50
TH Tomas Holmstrom 1.00 2.50
TK Tomas Kaberle 1.00 2.50
VL Vincent Lecavalier 1.25 3.00

2010-11 Crown Royale Loyalty Patches

STATED PRINT RUN 10-25
AH Ales Hemsky 6.00 15.00
BM Brenden Morrow 6.00 15.00
DA Daniel Alfredsson 8.00 20.00
DL David Legwand 6.00 15.00
DS Daniel Sedin 8.00 20.00
HS Henrik Sedin 8.00 20.00
HZ Henrik Zetterberg 10.00 25.00
JI Jarome Iginla 8.00 20.00
JS Jason Spezza
MB Martin Brodeur 15.00 40.00
NL Nicklas Lidstrom 8.00 20.00
PB Patrice Bergeron 10.00 25.00
PD Pavel Datsyuk 15.00 40.00
PE Patrik Elias 8.00 20.00
RM Ryan Miller 8.00 20.00
RR Robyn Regehr 5.00 12.00
SD Shane Doan 6.00 15.00
SW Stephen Weiss 6.00 15.00
TC Tim Connolly 5.00 12.00
TH Tomas Holmstrom 6.00 15.00
TK Tomas Kaberle 5.00 12.00
VL Vincent Lecavalier 6.00 15.00

2010-11 Crown Royale Razor's Choice

STATED PRINT RUN 99 SER.#'d SETS
1 Pavel Datsyuk 8.00 20.00
2 Chris Pronger 5.00 12.00
3 Mike Richards 6.00 15.00
4 Martin Brodeur 12.00 30.00
5 Tyler Myers 6.00 15.00
6 Martin St. Louis 6.00 15.00
7 Sidney Crosby 25.00 60.00
8 Jonathan Toews 12.00 30.00
9 Roberto Luongo 6.00 15.00
10 Mike Fisher 6.00 15.00
11 Ian Laperriere 8.00 20.00
12 Cal Clutterbuck 8.00 20.00

2010-11 Crown Royale Regal Achievements

STATED PRINT RUN 499 SER.#'d SETS
1 Patrick Kane 3.00 8.00
2 Martin Brodeur 3.00 8.00
3 Jonathan Toews 3.00 8.00
4 Ilya Bryzgalov 1.25 3.00
5 Steve Mason 1.25 3.00
6 Tyler Myers 1.50 4.00
7 Marian Hossa 1.25 3.00
8 Matt Carkner 1.25 3.00
9 Steven Stamkos 3.00 8.00
10 Sidney Crosby 6.00 15.00
11 Nicklas Backstrom 2.50 6.00
12 Mikko Koivu 1.50 4.00
13 Evgeni Malkin 5.00 12.00
14 Mike Modano 2.50 6.00
15 Pavel Datsyuk 2.00 5.00
16 Eric Staal 2.00 5.00
17 Daniel Alfredsson 1.50 4.00
18 Mark Recchi 2.00 5.00
19 Nicklas Lidstrom 1.50 4.00
20 Roberto Luongo 1.50 4.00

2010-11 Crown Royale Royal Lineage Materials

STATED PRINT RUN 25-100
*PRIME/50: .6X TO 1.5X MATRL/75-100
*PRIME/25: .8X TO 2X MATERIAL/100
*PATCH/15-25: .8X TO 2X MATERL/75-100
*PATCH/25: .6X TO 1.5X MATERIAL/25
ASE Alfredsson/Spezza/Elliott 6.00 15.00
BPK Brodeur/Parise/Kovalchuk 10.00 25.00
DKQ Doughty/Kopitar/Quick 12.00 30.00
GPR Getzlaf/Perry/Ryan 10.00 25.00
HEP Hall/Eberle/Paajarvi 15.00 40.00
HTS Hall/Tavares/Stamkos/25 20.00 50.00
IKT Iginla/Kiprusoff/Tanguay 6.00 15.00
KPG Kessel/Phaneuf/Giguere 8.00 20.00
KRB Kiprusoff/Rask/Backstrom 6.00 15.00
LGA Lundqvst/Gabork/Anismv 10.00 25.00
LMB Lucic/Morrow/Brown 6.00 15.00
MSC Malkin/Staal/Crosby 25.00 60.00
OKS Okposo/Kane/Simmonds 8.00 20.00
OSC Ovechkin/Stamkos/Crosby 25.00 60.00
PCG Price/Cammalleri/Gomez 25.00 60.00
SAD Stastny/Anderson/Duchene 6.00 15.00
SLS Sedin/Luongo/Sedin 6.00 15.00
SRM Selanne/Recchi/Modano 12.00 30.00
TMP Thrntn/Marlu/Pavlsk/75 6.00 15.00
TRS Thomas/Rask/Seguin 15.00 40.00
ZDL Zetterbr/Datsyuk/Lidstrm 8.00 20.00
SLSL Stamks/Lecavalr/St.Louis 12.00 30.00

2010-11 Crown Royale Royal Pains

STATED PRINT RUN 499 SER.#'d SETS
1 Milan Lucic 1.50 4.00
2 Dustin Byfuglien 1.50 4.00
3 Dion Phaneuf 1.50 4.00
4 Brenden Morrow 1.25 3.00
5 Alex Ovechkin 6.00 15.00
6 David Backes 1.50 4.00
7 Ryan Getzlaf 2.50 6.00
8 James Neal 1.50 4.00
9 Michael Del Zotto 1.25 3.00
10 Mike Richards 1.50 4.00
11 Rick Nash 1.50 4.00
12 Steve Downie 1.00 2.50

2010-11 Crown Royale Scratching the Surface Signatures

STATED PRINT RUN 10-100
1 Alex Ovechkin/10
2 Anze Kopitar 10.00 25.00
3 Bernie Parent/50 12.00 30.00
4 Bill Ranford/50 12.00 30.00
5 Bobby Clarke/50 12.00 30.00
6 Bobby Hull/50 25.00 60.00
7 Brandon Sutter 10.00 25.00
8 Brenden Morrow 6.00 15.00
9 Brian Gionta 12.00 30.00
10 Brian Leetch/25 15.00 40.00
11 Cam Fowler 6.00 15.00
12 Cam Neely/50 15.00 40.00
13 Cam Ward 10.00 25.00
14 Carey Price 25.00 60.00
15 Chris Neil 8.00 20.00
16 Chris Mason 5.00 12.00
17 Chris Pronger 12.00 30.00
18 Chris Stewart 5.00 12.00
19 Claude Giroux 12.00 30.00
20 Cody Almond 6.00 15.00
21 Colin Wilson 6.00 15.00
22 Corey Perry/50 8.00 20.00
23 Cory Schneider 8.00 20.00
24 Dale Tallon/50 12.00 30.00
25 Dan Hamhuis 12.00 30.00
26 Daniel Carcillo 8.00 20.00
27 David Backes 6.00 15.00
28 David Perron/99 4.00 10.00
29 Dany Heatley/25 6.00 15.00
30 Derek Dorsett/50 6.00 15.00
31 Dion Phaneuf 6.00 15.00
32 Drayson Bowman 8.00 20.00
33 Evander Kane 6.00 15.00
34 Evgeni Malkin/25 30.00 60.00
35 Guillaume Latendresse 6.00 15.00
36 Henrik Lundqvist/50 20.00 50.00
37 Henrik Sedin 12.00 30.00
38 Ilya Bryzgalov 10.00 25.00
39 Ilya Kovalchuk 8.00 20.00
40 Jakub Voracek 10.00 25.00
41 James Neal 6.00 15.00
42 James van Riemsdyk 10.00 25.00
43 Jamie Benn 8.00 20.00
44 Jarome Iginla 10.00 25.00
45 Jaroslav Halak 12.00 30.00
46 Jay Bouwmeester 8.00 20.00
47 Jeff Carter 12.00 30.00
48 Jimmy Howard 12.00 30.00
49 Joe Pavelski 6.00 15.00
50 Joe Thornton/25 20.00 50.00
51 Johan Franzen 10.00 25.00
25 John Carlson 10.00 25.00
53 John Tavares/50 20.00 40.00
54 Jonas Hiller/50 5.00 12.00
55 Jordan Staal 10.00 25.00
56 Jose Theodore 10.00 25.00
57 Josh Bailey 6.00 15.00
58 Justin Abdelkader 8.00 20.00
59 Kari Lehtonen 5.00 12.00
60 Keith Yandle 8.00 20.00
61 Luca Caputi 5.00 12.00
62 Marc Savard 4.00 10.00
63 Marc Staal 6.00 15.00
64 Marc-Andre Fleury 15.00 40.00
65 Marian Gaborik 8.00 20.00
66 Marian Hossa 12.00 30.00
67 Martin Brodeur/25 40.00 80.00
68 Matt Carkner 10.00 25.00
69 Mikael Samuelsson 6.00 15.00
70 Mike Brodeur 6.00 15.00
71 Mike Smith 8.00 20.00
72 Mikkel Boedker 6.00 15.00
73 Nathan Gerbe 6.00 15.00
74 Nicklas Lidstrom/25 15.00 40.00
75 Niklas Backstrom/50 6.00 15.00
76 Patric Hornqvist 5.00 12.00
77 Paul Stastny 10.00 25.00
78 Pekka Rinne 8.00 20.00
79 Phil Kessel 12.00 30.00
80 Rene Bourque 4.00 10.00
81 Rich Peverley/50 8.00 20.00
82 Rick Nash 10.00 25.00
83 Ryan Callahan 6.00 15.00
84 Ryan Getzlaf 10.00 25.00
85 Ryan Miller 12.00 30.00
86 Ryan Smyth 10.00 25.00
87 Ryan Stoa 4.00 10.00
88 Scott Gomez 8.00 20.00
89 Semyon Varlamov 6.00 15.00
90 Shea Weber 5.00 12.00
91 Sidney Crosby/10
92 Simon Gagne 10.00 25.00
93 Stephen Weiss 5.00 12.00
94 Steve Mason 5.00 12.00
95 Steve Ott 8.00 20.00
96 Steven Stamkos 20.00 50.00
97 Thomas Vanek 6.00 15.00
98 Tomas Holmstrom 10.00 25.00
99 Tyler Bozak 6.00 15.00
100 Viktor Stalberg 8.00 20.00

2010-11 Crown Royale Voices of the Game Signatures

1 Charlie Simmer 10.00 25.00
2 Daryl Reaugh 6.00 15.00
3 Jim Fox 6.00 15.00
4 Pete Weber 6.00 15.00
5 Joe Bowen 10.00 25.00
6 Bob Miller 25.00 60.00
7 Rick Jeanneret 20.00 50.00
8 Randy Moller 6.00 15.00
9 Denis Potvin 6.00 15.00
10 Darren Pang 6.00 15.00
11 Cassie Campbell 10.00 25.00
12 Mike Milbury 6.00 15.00
13 Kelly Hrudey 6.00 15.00
14 Mike Lange 25.00 60.00
15 Don Cherry 25.00 60.00

2011-12 Crown Royale

COMP.SET w/o SP's (100) 25.00 50.00
166-182 ROOKIE JSY AU PRINT RUN 49-99
142/152/154/162/186-235 INSERTS IN ANTHOL
1 Corey Perry .60 1.50
2 Ryan Getzlaf 1.00 2.50
3 Bobby Ryan .60 1.50
4 Saku Koivu .60 1.50
5 Tim Thomas .60 1.50
6 Brad Marchand .75 2.00
7 Tyler Seguin 1.25 3.00
8 Rich Peverley .60 1.50
9 Thomas Vanek .60 1.50
10 Ryan Miller .60 1.50
11 Tyler Ennis .50 1.25
12 Jarome Iginla .60 1.50
13 Miikka Kiprusoff .60 1.50
14 Curtis Glencross .40 1.00
15 Jeff Skinner .60 1.50
16 Eric Staal .75 2.00
17 Cam Ward .60 1.50
18 Patrick Kane 1.25 3.00
19 Jonathan Toews 1.25 3.00
20 Corey Crawford .75 2.00
21 Jean-Sebastien Giguere .50 1.25
22 Matt Duchene .60 1.50
23 Paul Stastny .60 1.50
24 Steve Mason .50 1.25
25 Rick Nash .60 1.50
26 Jeff Carter .60 1.50
27 Jamie Benn .75 2.00
28 Loui Eriksson .50 1.25
29 Kari Lehtonen .50 1.25
30 Henrik Zetterberg .75 2.00
31 Pavel Datsyuk .75 2.00
32 Jimmy Howard .60 1.50
33 Nicklas Lidstrom .60 1.50
34 Taylor Hall 1.25 3.00
35 Jordan Eberle .60 1.50
36 Nikolai Khabibulin .50 1.25
37 Jacob Markstrom .60 1.50
38 Mike Santorelli .40 1.00
39 Stephen Weiss .50 1.25
40 Mike Richards .60 1.50
41 Anze Kopitar 1.00 2.50
42 Drew Doughty .60 1.50
43 Jonathan Quick 1.00 2.50
44 Matt Kassian .40 1.00
45 Dany Heatley .50 1.25
46 Niklas Backstrom .60 1.50
47 Carey Price 2.00 5.00
48 P.K. Subban 1.25 3.00
49 David Desharnais .75 2.00
50 Lars Eller .50 1.25
51 Shea Weber .50 1.25
52 Pekka Rinne .75 2.00
53 Mike Fisher .60 1.50
54 Martin Brodeur 1.25 3.00
55 Zach Parise .60 1.50
56 Ilya Kovalchuk .60 1.50
57 Kyle Okposo .60 1.50
58 John Tavares 1.25 3.00
59 Michael Grabner .50 1.25
60 Brad Richards .60 1.50
61 Brandon Dubinsky .50 1.25
62 Henrik Lundqvist .75 2.00
63 Marian Gaborik .75 2.00
64 Jason Spezza .60 1.50
65 Erik Karlsson 1.25 3.00
66 Daniel Alfredsson .60 1.50
67 Brayden Schenn .60 1.50
68 Claude Giroux .60 1.50
69 Ilya Bryzgalov .60 1.50
70 James van Riemsdyk .60 1.50
71 Shane Doan .50 1.25
72 Ray Whitney .50 1.25
73 Paul Bissonnette .40 1.00
74 Evgeni Malkin 2.00 5.00
75 Marc-Andre Fleury 1.00 2.50
76 Sidney Crosby 2.50 6.00
77 Ryane Clowe .40 1.00
78 Logan Couture .60 1.50
79 Joe Thornton .60 1.50
80 Joe Pavelski .60 1.50
81 Alex Pietrangelo .50 1.25
82 Jaroslav Halak .60 1.50
83 T.J. Oshie 1.00 2.50
84 Steven Stamkos 1.25 3.00
85 Vincent Lecavalier .50 1.25
86 Martin St. Louis .60 1.50
87 James Reimer .60 1.50
88 Dion Phaneuf .60 1.50
89 Mikhail Grabovski .50 1.25
90 Roberto Luongo .60 1.50
91 Ryan Kesler .60 1.50
92 Henrik Sedin .60 1.50
93 Daniel Sedin .60 1.50
94 Alex Ovechkin 2.50 6.00
95 Tomas Vokoun .50 1.25
96 Nicklas Backstrom 1.00 2.50
97 Dustin Byfuglien .60 1.50
98 Andrew Ladd .60 1.50
99 Alexander Burmistrov .50 1.25
100 Ondrej Pavelec .60 1.50
101 Steve Yzerman 2.00 5.00
102 Patrick Roy 3.00 8.00
103 Mark Messier 1.50 4.00
104 Brett Hull 1.50 4.00
105 Cam Neely 1.25 3.00
106 Trevor Linden 1.25 3.00
107 Yvan Cournoyer 1.25 3.00
108 Tony Esposito 1.25 3.00
109 Stan Mikita 1.50 4.00
110 Ken Linseman 1.25 3.00
111 Don Cherry 1.25 3.00
112 Doug Gilmour 1.50 4.00
113 Ed Belfour 1.25 3.00
114 Doug Wilson 1.00 2.50
115 Brendan Shanahan 1.50 4.00
116 Bernie Parent 1.25 3.00
117 Phil Esposito 2.00 5.00
118 Manon Rheaume 3.00 8.00
119 Bobby Hull 1.50 4.00
120 Bobby Clarke 1.25 3.00
121 Thomas Steen .75 2.00
122 Luc Robitaille 1.25 3.00
123 Wendel Clark 1.25 3.00
124 Dale Hawerchuk 1.50 4.00
125 Dale Hunter 1.00 2.50
126 Bob McGill .75 2.00
126 Maxime Macenauer RC 1.50 4.00
127 Mikko Koskinen RC 2.00 5.00
128 Cam Talbot RC 4.00 10.00
129 Yann Sauve RC 1.50 4.00
130 Raphael Diaz RC 1.50 4.00
131 Erik Gustafsson RC 2.00 5.00
132 Colton Sceviour RC 1.50 4.00
133 Drew Bagnall RC 1.50 4.00
134 Brian Strait RC 2.00 5.00
135 Harri Sateri RC 1.50 4.00
136 Lance Bouma RC 1.50 4.00
137 T.Hartikainen RC 1.50 4.00
138 Brendon Nash RC 1.50 4.00
139 Mattias Ekholm RC 1.50 4.00
140 Lennart Petrell RC 2.00 5.00
141 Mark Scheifele AU RC 10.00 25.00
142 Tomas Kubalik AU RC 4.00 10.00
143 Anton Lander AU RC 4.00 10.00
144 Zac Rinaldo AU RC 4.00 10.00
145 Colin Greening AU SP RC 4.00 10.00
146 S.Da Costa AU RC 4.00 10.00
147 Erik Condra AU RC 4.00 10.00
148 Paul Postma AU RC 4.00 10.00
149 P.Wiercioch AU RC 4.00 10.00
150 Ben Scrivens AU RC 6.00 15.00
151 Greg Nemisz AU RC 4.00 10.00
152 Brett Bulmer AU RC 4.00 10.00
153 Cam Atkinson AU RC 10.00 25.00
154 Alexei Emelin AU RC 4.00 10.00
155 Roman Horak AU RC 4.00 10.00
156 Matt Frattin AU RC 4.00 10.00
157 D.Smith-Pelly AU RC 6.00 15.00
158 Justin Faulk AU SP RC 6.00 15.00
159 Craig Smith AU RC 5.00 12.00
160 Joe Vitale AU RC 4.00 10.00
161 David Savard AU RC 4.00 10.00
162 John Moore AU RC 4.00 10.00
163 Matt Read AU RC 8.00 20.00
164 Carl Klingberg AU RC 4.00 10.00
165 Tomas Vincour AU RC 4.00 10.00
166 J.Colborne JSY AU/99 RC 12.00 30.00
167 C.Hodgson JSY AU/49 RC 40.00 100.00
168 J.Blum JSY AU/99 RC 12.00 30.00
169 B.Geoffrion JSY AU/99 RC 12.00 30.00
170 Nugent-Hpk JSY AU/99 RC 150.00 300.00
171 A.Larsson JSY AU/99 RC 15.00 40.00
172 B.Saad JSY AU/99 RC 30.00 80.00
173 Landeskog JSY AU/99 RC 75.00 150.00
174 Johansen JSY AU/99 RC 25.00 60.00
175 J.Gardiner JSY AU/99 RC 20.00 50.00
176 Zibanejad JSY AU/99 RC 30.00 80.00
177 Gudbranson JSY AU/99 RC 15.00 40.00
178 S.Couturier JSY AU/99 RC 25.00 60.00
179 B.Connolly JSY AU/99 RC 12.00 30.00
180 Henrique JSY AU/99 RC 30.00 80.00
181 M.Kruger JSY AU/99 RC 20.00 50.00
182 Tim Erixon JSY AU/99 RC 12.00 30.00
183 Cody Eakin JSY AU/99 RC 15.00 40.00
184 A.Palushaj JSY AU/99 RC 12.00 30.00
185 Rundblad JSY AU/99 RC 12.00 30.00
186 Ryan Thang RC 1.00 2.50
187 Marc-Andre Bourdon RC 1.25 3.00
188 David Ullstrom RC 1.25 3.00
189 Jeremy Smith RC 1.50 4.00
190 Iiro Tarkki RC 1.50 4.00
191 Gabriel Bourque RC 1.25 3.00
192 Warren Peters RC 1.50 4.00
193 Patrick Maroon RC 1.25 3.00
194 Andrew Shaw RC 3.00 8.00
195 Mike Murphy RC 1.25 3.00
196 Milan Kytnar RC 1.50 4.00
197 Jarod Palmer RC 1.25 3.00
198 Stu Bickel RC 1.25 3.00
199 Cade Fairchild RC 1.00 2.50
200 Carl Sneep RC 1.25 3.00
201 Brian Foster RC 1.50 4.00
202 Mike Hoffman RC 5.00 12.00
203 Pierre-Cedric Labrie RC 1.25 3.00
204 Ryan Russell RC 1.50 4.00
205 Tomas Kundratek RC 1.50 4.00
206 Allen York AU RC 5.00 12.00
207 Colten Teubert AU RC 4.00 10.00
208 Keith Kinkaid AU RC 4.00 10.00
209 Harry Zolnierczyk AU RC 4.00 10.00
210 Jimmy Hayes AU RC 6.00 15.00
211 Marcus Foligno AU RC 6.00 15.00
212 Robert Bortuzzo AU RC 4.00 10.00
213 Slava Voynov AU RC 4.00 10.00
214 Corey Tropp AU RC 4.00 10.00
215 Roman Josi AU RC 6.00 15.00
216 Stefan Elliott AU RC 12.50 30.00
217 Anders Nilsson AU RC 4.00 10.00
218 Eddie Lack AU RC 4.00 10.00
219 Riley Nash AU RC 4.00 10.00
220 Dmitry Orlov AU RC 5.00 12.00
221 Dylan Olsen AU RC 5.00 12.00
222 Brayden McNabb AU RC 6.00 15.00
223 T.J. Brennan AU RC 4.00 10.00
224 Brad Malone AU RC 4.00 10.00
225 Andy Miele AU RC 4.00 10.00
226 Z.Kassian JSY AU/99 RC 15.00 40.00
227 Ryan Ellis JSY AU/99 RC 12.00 30.00
228 S.Despres JSY AU/99 RC 12.00 30.00
229 L.Leblanc JSY AU/99 RC 12.00 30.00
230 G.Nyquist JSY AU/99 RC 30.00 80.00
231 B.Smith JSY AU/99 RC 12.00 30.00
232 C.Hagelin JSY AU/99 RC 20.00 50.00
233 C.de Haan JSY AU/99 RC 12.00 30.00
234 P.Holland JSY AU/99 RC 12.00 30.00
235 C.Gaunce JSY AU/99 RC 10.00 25.00

2011-12 Crown Royale Red

*RED: 1.5X TO 4X BASIC CARDS
20 Corey Crawford 3.00 8.00
96 Nicklas Backstrom 4.00 10.00

2011-12 Crown Royale All The Kings Men Materials

*PATCH/25: 1X TO 2.5X BASIC JSY
*PRIME/50: .8X TO 2X BASIC JSY
*PRIME/25: 1X TO 2.5X BASIC JSY
1 Ales Hemsky 3.00 8.00
2 Alex Ovechkin 6.00 15.00
3 Antti Niemi 3.00 8.00
4 Anze Kopitar 6.00 15.00
5 Bobby Ryan 4.00 10.00
6 Joe Colborne 2.00 5.00
7 Cal Clutterbuck 4.00 10.00
8 Carey Price 12.00 30.00
9 Claude Giroux 4.00 10.00
10 Corey Perry 4.00 10.00
11 Curtis Glencross 2.50 6.00
12 Daniel Sedin 4.00 10.00
13 Danny Briere 4.00 10.00
14 David Rundblad 2.00 5.00
15 Derek Stepan 4.00 10.00
16 Charlie Simmer 2.50 6.00
17 Dion Phaneuf 4.00 10.00
18 Drew Doughty 4.00 10.00
19 Luc Robitaille 4.00 10.00
20 Dustin Brown 4.00 10.00
21 Dustin Byfuglien 4.00 10.00
22 Eric Staal 5.00 12.00
23 Evander Kane 4.00 10.00
24 Evgeni Malkin 6.00 15.00
25 George Parros 3.00 8.00
26 Henrik Lundqvist 5.00 12.00
27 Henrik Sedin 4.00 10.00
28 Marcel Dionne 5.00 12.00
29 Ilya Bryzgalov 4.00 10.00
30 Patrick Marleau 4.00 10.00
31 James Neal 4.00 10.00
32 Tyler Seguin 8.00 20.00
33 James van Riemsdyk 4.00 10.00
34 Jamie Benn 5.00 12.00
35 Jarome Iginla 4.00 10.00
36 Jaroslav Halak 4.00 10.00
37 Pat LaFontaine 4.00 10.00
38 Jeff Carter 4.00 10.00
39 Jeff Skinner 4.00 10.00
40 Joe Thornton 4.00 10.00
41 John Tavares 5.00 12.00
42 Jonathan Toews 8.00 20.00
43 Logan Couture 4.00 10.00
44 Marc-Andre Fleury 6.00 15.00
45 Dustin Penner 3.00 8.00
46 Ondrej Pavelec 4.00 10.00
47 P.K. Subban 8.00 20.00
48 Patrick Kane 8.00 20.00
49 Sidney Crosby 8.00 20.00
50 Taylor Hall 8.00 20.00

2011-12 Crown Royale All The Kings Men Materials Autographs

STATED PRINT RUN 10-100
*PRIME/25: .8X TO 2X JSY AU/70-100
*PRIME/25: .6X TO 1.5X JSY AU/40
*PRIME/25: .5X TO 1.2X JSY AU/25
1 Ales Hemsky/100 6.00 15.00
2 Alex Ovechkin/100 20.00 50.00
3 Antti Niemi/100 6.00 15.00
4 Anze Kopitar/100 10.00 25.00
5 Bobby Ryan/100 8.00 20.00
6 Joe Colborne/100 6.00 15.00
8 Carey Price/100 25.00 50.00
11 Curtis Glencross/75 6.00 15.00
12 Daniel Sedin/100 8.00 20.00
13 Danny Briere/100 8.00 20.00
14 David Rundblad/100 6.00 15.00
15 Derek Stepan/100 8.00 20.00
16 Charlie Simmer/100 6.00 15.00
20 Dustin Brown/100 8.00 20.00
22 Eric Staal/40
24 Evgeni Malkin/100 25.00 50.00
25 George Parros/100 6.00 15.00
26 Henrik Lundqvist/100 15.00 40.00
27 Henrik Sedin/100 10.00 25.00
29 Ilya Bryzgalov/100 8.00 20.00
30 Patrick Marleau/10
33 James van Riemsdyk/100 8.00 20.00
34 Jamie Benn/100 10.00 25.00
35 Jarome Iginla/100 8.00 20.00
36 Jaroslav Halak/70 8.00 20.00
37 Pat LaFontaine/100 12.00 30.00
38 Jeff Carter/100 8.00 20.00
39 Jeff Skinner/25 8.00 20.00
40 Joe Thornton/100 12.00 30.00
41 John Tavares/100 15.00 40.00
42 Jonathan Toews/100 20.00 40.00
43 Logan Couture/100 8.00 20.00
44 Marc-Andre Fleury/100 15.00 30.00
45 Dustin Penner/100 6.00 15.00
48 Patrick Kane/100 15.00 40.00
49 Sidney Crosby/25 75.00 150.00
50 Taylor Hall/10

2011-12 Crown Royale Calder Collection

1 Craig Smith 2.00 5.00
2 Ryan Nugent-Hopkins 6.00 15.00
3 Gabriel Landeskog 3.00 8.00
4 Brett Connolly 1.50 4.00
5 Mika Zibanejad 4.00 10.00
6 Luke Adam 1.50 4.00
7 Adam Larsson 2.00 5.00
8 Brayden Schenn 2.00 5.00
9 Sean Couturier 3.00 8.00
10 Mark Scheifele 4.00 10.00

2011-12 Crown Royale Calder Collection Autographs

STATED PRINT RUN 99 SER.#'d SETS
1 Craig Smith 6.00 15.00
2 Ryan Nugent-Hopkins 30.00 80.00
3 Gabriel Landeskog 12.00 30.00
4 Brett Connolly 5.00 12.00
6 Luke Adam 5.00 12.00
7 Adam Larsson 6.00 15.00
8 Brayden Schenn 10.00 25.00
9 Mark Scheifele 20.00 40.00
10 Sean Couturier 20.00 50.00

2011-12 Crown Royale Coat of Arms Patches

STATED PRINT RUN 5-25
1 Ryan Getzlaf/10
2 Tim Thomas/25 12.00 30.00
3 Brad Marchand/25 15.00 40.00
4 Ryan Miller/25 12.00 30.00
5 Tyler Ennis/25 10.00 25.00
6 Curtis Glencross/25 8.00 20.00
7 Jarome Iginla/25 12.00 30.00
8 Ryan Nugent-Hopkins/25 75.00 150.00
9 Marian Hossa/25 15.00 40.00
10 Matt Duchene/25 12.00 30.00
11 Gabriel Landeskog/25 10.00 25.00
12 Rick Nash/25 12.00 30.00
13 Loui Eriksson/25 12.00 30.00
14 Jamie Benn/25 10.00 25.00
15 Johan Franzen/25 12.00 30.00
16 Pavel Datsyuk/25 15.00 40.00
17 Nikolai Khabibulin/25 10.00 25.00
19 Stephen Weiss/25 10.00 25.00
20 Anze Kopitar/25 20.00 50.00
21 Dustin Brown/25 12.00 30.00
22 Niklas Backstrom/25 12.00 30.00
23 Carey Price/25 40.00 100.00
24 Jordan Eberle/25 12.00 30.00
25 Pekka Rinne/25 15.00 40.00
26 Martin Brodeur/25 25.00 60.00
27 Zach Parise/25 12.00 30.00
28 Brandon Dubinsky/25 10.00 25.00
29 Marian Gaborik/25 15.00 40.00
30 Erik Karlsson/25 25.00 60.00
31 James van Riemsdyk/25 12.00 30.00
32 Sergei Bobrovsky/25 12.00 30.00
33 Claude Giroux/25 12.00 30.00
34 Sidney Crosby/25 30.00 80.00
35 Marc-Andre Fleury/25 20.00 50.00
36 Jordan Staal/25 12.00 30.00
37 Joe Thornton/25 12.00 30.00
38 Patrick Marleau/25 12.00 30.00
39 David Rundblad/25 5.00 12.00
40 Vincent Lecavalier/25 10.00 25.00
41 Martin St. Louis/25 12.00 30.00
42 Nikolai Kulemin/25 12.00 30.00
43 Jonas Gustavsson/25 12.00 30.00
44 Roberto Luongo/25 12.00 30.00
45 Ryan Kesler/25 12.00 30.00
46 Alex Ovechkin/25 15.00 40.00
47 Alexander Semin/25 12.00 30.00
48 Alexander Burmistrov/25 10.00 25.00
49 Andrew Ladd/25 12.00 30.00
50 Shane Doan/25 10.00 25.00

2011-12 Crown Royale Crown Jewels

1 Alex Ovechkin 20.00 50.00
2 Martin Brodeur 10.00 25.00
3 Steven Stamkos 10.00 25.00
4 Carey Price 15.00 40.00
5 Sidney Crosby 20.00 50.00
6 Taylor Hall 10.00 25.00
7 Ryan Nugent-Hopkins 40.00 80.00
8 Tim Thomas 5.00 12.00
9 Corey Perry 5.00 12.00
10 Roberto Luongo 5.00 12.00

2011-12 Crown Royale Heirs To The Throne Materials

*PRIME/50: .8X TO 2X BASIC JSY
1 P.K. Subban 8.00 20.00
2 Jeff Skinner 4.00 10.00
3 Logan Couture 4.00 10.00
4 Derek Stepan 4.00 10.00
5 Tyler Ennis 3.00 8.00
6 Taylor Hall 8.00 20.00
7 John Carlson 5.00 12.00
8 Nazem Kadri 6.00 15.00
9 Blake Geoffrion 3.00 8.00
10 Jordan Eberle 5.00 12.00
11 Jamie Benn 5.00 12.00
12 Magnus Paajarvi 3.00 8.00
13 Jake Gardiner 4.00 10.00
14 Gabriel Landeskog 6.00 15.00
15 Devan Dubnyk 4.00 10.00
16 Tyler Seguin 8.00 20.00
17 James Reimer 4.00 10.00
18 Brayden Schenn 4.00 10.00
19 Joe Colborne 2.50 6.00
20 David Rundblad 2.50 6.00
21 Jonathon Blum 3.00 8.00
22 Aaron Palushaj 2.50 6.00
23 Ryan Nugent-Hopkins 8.00 20.00
24 Cody Hodgson 5.00 12.00
25 Greg Nemisz 3.00 8.00
26 James Neal 4.00 10.00
27 Erik Karlsson 8.00 20.00
28 Cody Eakin 3.00 8.00
29 Ryan Johansen 5.00 12.00
30 Erik Gudbranson 3.00 8.00

2011-12 Crown Royale Heirs To The Throne Materials Autographs

STATED PRINT RUN 15-100
3 Logan Couture/100 10.00 25.00
4 Derek Stepan/100 10.00 25.00
5 Tyler Ennis/100 6.00 15.00
6 Taylor Hall/25 30.00 60.00
7 John Carlson/100 10.00 25.00
8 Nazem Kadri/100 15.00 40.00
11 Jamie Benn/100 10.00 25.00
12 Magnus Paajarvi/100 10.00 25.00
13 Jake Gardiner/100 8.00 20.00
17 James Reimer/100 15.00 30.00
18 Brayden Schenn/75 8.00 20.00
19 Joe Colborne/75 12.00 30.00
20 David Rundblad/100 6.00 15.00
21 Jonathon Blum/100 6.00 15.00
22 Aaron Palushaj/100 6.00 15.00
23 Ryan Nugent-Hopkins/100 40.00 100.00
24 Cody Hodgson/15 60.00 120.00
25 Greg Nemisz/100 6.00 15.00
26 James Neal/100 8.00 20.00
28 Cody Eakin/100 10.00 25.00
29 Ryan Johansen/100 12.00 30.00
30 Erik Gudbranson/100 8.00 20.00

2011-12 Crown Royale Heirs To The Throne Materials Prime Autographs

*PRIME/25: .8X TO 2X JSY AU/75-100
PRIME STATED PRINT RUN 1-25
14 Gabriel Landeskog/25 20.00 50.00
16 Tyler Seguin/25 40.00 80.00
27 Erik Karlsson/25 30.00 60.00

2011-12 Crown Royale Ice Kings

1 Alex Ovechkin 10.00 25.00
2 Taylor Hall 5.00 12.00
3 Steven Stamkos 5.00 12.00
4 Daniel Sedin 2.50 6.00
5 Jeff Skinner 2.50 6.00
6 Sidney Crosby 10.00 25.00
7 Trevor Linden 2.50 6.00
8 Corey Perry 2.50 6.00
9 Ryan Nugent-Hopkins 5.00 12.00
10 Cam Ward 2.50 6.00
11 Nicklas Lidstrom 2.50 6.00
12 Tyler Seguin 5.00 12.00
13 Mario Lemieux 8.00 20.00
14 John Tavares 5.00 12.00
15 Gabriel Landeskog 2.50 6.00
16 Glenn Hall 2.50 6.00
17 Cody Hodgson 2.50 6.00
18 Gerry Cheevers 2.50 6.00
19 Henrik Lundqvist 3.00 8.00
20 Steve Yzerman 4.00 10.00

2011-12 Crown Royale Ice Kings Autographs

STATED PRINT RUN 25-99
10/15 INSERTED IN ANTHOLOGY
1 Alex Ovechkin/99 30.00 80.00
2 Taylor Hall/25 40.00 100.00
3 Steven Stamkos/99 20.00 50.00
4 Daniel Sedin/99 8.00 20.00
6 Sidney Crosby/25 60.00 120.00
7 Trevor Linden/99 20.00 40.00
9 Ryan Nugent-Hopkins/99 25.00 60.00
10 Cam Ward/99 8.00 20.00
11 Nicklas Lidstrom/99 15.00 40.00
12 Tyler Seguin/99 12.00 30.00
13 Mario Lemieux/25 60.00 120.00
14 John Tavares/99 15.00 40.00
15 Gabriel Landeskog/99 20.00 50.00
16 Glenn Hall/99 10.00 25.00
17 Cody Hodgson/99 10.00 25.00
19 Henrik Lundqvist/99 15.00 40.00
20 Steve Yzerman/25 40.00 100.00

2011-12 Crown Royale In Harms Way

1 Roberto Luongo 2.00 5.00
2 Carey Price 6.00 15.00
3 Cam Ward 2.00 5.00
4 Miikka Kiprusoff 2.00 5.00
5 Jimmy Howard 2.00 5.00
6 Henrik Lundqvist 2.50 6.00
7 Marc-Andre Fleury 3.00 8.00
8 Ilya Bryzgalov 2.00 5.00
9 Tim Thomas 2.00 5.00
10 Jonathan Quick 3.00 8.00
11 Antti Niemi 1.50 4.00
12 Ryan Miller 2.00 5.00
13 Martin Brodeur 4.00 10.00
14 Steve Mason 1.50 4.00
15 James Reimer 2.00 5.00
16 Tomas Vokoun 1.50 4.00
17 Undrej Pavelec 2.00 5.00
18 Jonas Hiller 1.50 4.00
19 Jaroslav Halak 2.00 5.00
20 Corey Crawford 2.50 6.00

2011-12 Crown Royale Lords of the NHL

1 Alex Ovechkin 8.00 20.00
2 Steven Stamkos 4.00 10.00
3 Anze Kopitar 3.00 8.00
4 Rick Nash 2.00 5.00
5 Henrik Lundqvist 2.50 6.00
6 Eric Staal 2.50 6.00
7 P.K. Subban 4.00 10.00
8 Evgeni Malkin 6.00 15.00
9 Tim Thomas 2.00 5.00
10 Brad Richards 2.00 5.00
11 Henrik Sedin 2.00 5.00
12 Sidney Crosby 8.00 20.00
13 Carey Price 6.00 15.00
14 Corey Perry 2.00 5.00
15 Pavel Datsyuk 2.50 6.00
16 Jonathan Toews 4.00 10.00
17 Claude Giroux 2.00 5.00
18 Daniel Sedin 2.00 5.00
19 Martin St. Louis 2.00 5.00
20 Patrick Kane 4.00 10.00
21 Roberto Luongo 2.00 5.00
22 Zach Parise 2.00 5.00
23 Patrice Bergeron 2.00 5.00
24 Jeff Skinner 2.00 5.00
25 Dustin Byfuglien 2.00 5.00

2011-12 Crown Royale Lords of the NHL Materials Patches

PATCH STATED PRINT RUN 25
*BASE JSY: .15X TO .4X PATCH/25
1 Alex Ovechkin 40.00 100.00
2 Steven Stamkos 15.00 40.00
3 Anze Kopitar 15.00 40.00
4 Rick Nash 10.00 25.00
5 Henrik Lundqvist 12.00 30.00
6 Eric Staal 12.00 30.00
7 P.K. Subban 20.00 50.00
8 Evgeni Malkin 15.00 40.00
9 Tim Thomas 10.00 25.00
10 Brad Richards 10.00 25.00
11 Henrik Sedin 10.00 25.00
12 Sidney Crosby 20.00 50.00
13 Carey Price 30.00 80.00
14 Corey Perry 10.00 25.00
15 Pavel Datsyuk 12.00 30.00
16 Jonathan Toews 20.00 50.00
17 Claude Giroux 12.00 30.00
18 Daniel Sedin 10.00 25.00
19 Martin St. Louis 10.00 25.00
20 Patrick Kane 20.00 50.00

21 Roberto Luongo 10.00 25.00
22 Zach Parise 12.00 30.00
23 Patrice Bergeron 12.00 30.00
24 Jeff Skinner 10.00 25.00
25 Dustin Byfuglien 10.00 25.00

2011-12 Crown Royale Mythology Materials

*PATCH/10: 1.5X TO 4X BASIC JSY
1 Steve Yzerman 6.00 15.00
2 Ron Francis 6.00 15.00
3 Curtis Joseph 4.00 10.00
4 Guy Lafleur 6.00 15.00
5 Brendan Shanahan 5.00 12.00
6 Eric Lindros 6.00 15.00
7 Patrick Roy 10.00 25.00
8 Grant Fuhr 4.00 10.00
9 Mario Lemieux 12.00 30.00
10 Charlie Simmer 3.00 8.00
11 Denis Savard 5.00 12.00
12 Wendel Clark 4.00 10.00
13 Joe Mullen 3.00 8.00
14 Ed Belfour 4.00 10.00
15 Joe Nieuwendyk 4.00 10.00
16 Cam Neely 4.00 10.00
17 Paul Coffey 4.00 10.00
18 Luc Robitaille 4.00 10.00
19 Adam Graves 3.00 8.00
20 Ray Bourque 6.00 15.00
21 Phil Esposito 5.00 12.00
22 Bryan Trottier 5.00 12.00
23 Ken Linseman 4.00 10.00
24 Joe Sakic 6.00 15.00
25 Jeremy Roenick 4.00 10.00

2011-12 Crown Royale Premiere Date Autographs

STATED PRINT RUN 5-99
2 Ryan Getzlaf/25 12.00 30.00
3 Bobby Ryan/99 6.00 15.00
4 Saku Koivu/99 6.00 15.00
5 Tim Thomas/99 15.00 40.00
6 Brad Marchand/99 10.00 25.00
8 Rich Peverley/99 6.00 15.00
9 Thomas Vanek/10
10 Ryan Miller/99 6.00 15.00
11 Tyler Ennis/99 5.00 12.00
12 Jarome Iginla/99 8.00 20.00
14 Curtis Glencross/99 6.00 15.00
15 Jeff Skinner/10
16 Eric Staal/99 10.00 25.00
17 Cam Ward/99 8.00 20.00
18 Patrick Kane/95 15.00 40.00
19 Jonathan Toews/99 20.00 40.00
21 Jean-Sebastien Giguere/88 15.00 40.00
22 Matt Duchene/99 6.00 15.00
23 Paul Stastny/5
24 Steve Mason/99 5.00 12.00
25 Rick Nash/99 6.00 15.00
26 Jeff Carter/99 6.00 15.00
27 Jamie Benn/99 8.00 20.00
28 Loui Eriksson/10
29 Kari Lehtonen/99 5.00 12.00
31 Pavel Datsyuk/99 20.00 40.00
32 Jimmy Howard/99 10.00 25.00
33 Nicklas Lidstrom/99 15.00 40.00
34 Taylor Hall/10
36 Nikolai Khabibulin/99 6.00 15.00
37 Jacob Markstrom/99 6.00 15.00
38 Mike Santorelli/99 4.00 10.00
39 Stephen Weiss/99 5.00 12.00
41 Anze Kopitar/99 8.00 20.00
44 Matt Kassian/99 4.00 10.00
45 Dany Heatley/99 5.00 12.00
47 Carey Price/99 15.00 40.00
50 Lars Eller/99 6.00 15.00
51 Shea Weber/99 5.00 12.00
52 Pekka Rinne/99 6.00 15.00
53 Mike Fisher/99 6.00 15.00
54 Martin Brodeur/25 40.00 80.00
55 Zach Parise/99 10.00 25.00
56 Ilya Kovalchuk/99 6.00 15.00
57 Kyle Okposo/99 6.00 15.00
58 John Tavares/99 15.00 40.00
59 Michael Grabner/99 12.00 30.00
60 Brad Richards/99 10.00 25.00
62 Henrik Lundqvist/99 10.00 25.00
65 Erik Karlsson/99 8.00 20.00
68 Claude Giroux/10
69 Ilya Bryzgalov/99 8.00 20.00
70 James van Riemsdyk/99 8.00 20.00
71 Shane Doan/99 5.00 12.00
73 Paul Bissonnette/99 5.00 12.00
74 Evgeni Malkin/99 20.00 40.00
75 Marc-Andre Fleury/99 12.00 30.00
78 Logan Couture/25 10.00 25.00
79 Joe Thornton/99 8.00 20.00
80 Joe Pavelski/99 8.00 20.00
81 Alex Pietrangelo/25 8.00 20.00
82 Jaroslav Halak/99 8.00 20.00
84 Steven Stamkos/99 15.00 40.00
85 Vincent Lecavalier/99 8.00 20.00
86 Martin St. Louis/99 6.00 15.00
87 James Reimer/25 15.00 40.00
90 Roberto Luongo/5
91 Ryan Kesler/99 6.00 15.00
92 Henrik Sedin/99 8.00 20.00
93 Daniel Sedin/99 10.00 25.00
94 Alex Ovechkin/49 25.00 60.00
95 Tomas Vokoun/25 8.00 20.00
97 Dustin Byfuglien/5
98 Andrew Ladd/99 8.00 20.00
99 Alexander Burmistrov/99 5.00 12.00

2011-12 Crown Royale Razor's Choice

STATED PRINT RUN 99 SER.#'d SETS
1 Ryan Kesler 8.00 20.00
2 Pekka Rinne 10.00 25.00
3 Sheldon Souray 5.00 12.00
4 Ryan Smyth 6.00 15.00
5 Brendan Morrison 5.00 12.00
6 Ryane Clowe 5.00 12.00
7 Shawn Thornton 8.00 20.00
8 Matt Moulson 6.00 15.00
9 Nathan Gerbe 5.00 12.00
10 Teemu Selanne 15.00 40.00

2011-12 Crown Royale Rookie Silhouette Patch Autographs

*PATCH/25: .6X TO 1.5X BASIC JSY AU
STATED PRINT RUN 25 SER.#'d SETS
226-235 INSERTED IN ANTHOLOGY
167 Cody Hodgson 200.00 400.00
170 Ryan Nugent-Hopkins 400.00 800.00
172 Brandon Saad 75.00 150.00
173 Gabriel Landeskog 150.00 300.00

2011-12 Crown Royale Royal Lineage Materials

*PATCH/25: .8X TO 2X BASIC JSY
*PRIME: .6X TO 1.5X BASIC JSY
1 Bartkow/Brque/Chara 10.00 25.00
2 Staal/Skinner/Francis 8.00 20.00
3 Landskg/Dchne/Hjduk 8.00 20.00
4 Morrow/Benn/Modano 5.00 12.00
5 Ovech/Maruk/Johansn 10.00 25.00
6 Malkin/Jagr/Letestu 20.00 50.00
7 Thorntn/Couture/Clowe 6.00 15.00
8 Backes/Mullen/Oshie 10.00 25.00
9 Stepan/Gaborik/Messier 8.00 20.00
10 Fuhr/Bernier/Quick 8.00 20.00
11 Colbrne/Grabvski/Clark 6.00 15.00
12 Yzerman/Hlmstrm/Tatar 10.00 25.00
14 Eberle/Coffey/Hall 12.00 30.00
15 Henriq/Kvlchk/Nieuwen 6.00 15.00
16 Palshaj/Kostsyn/Pleknec 6.00 15.00
17 Nemisz/Iginla/Nieuwen 6.00 15.00
18 Savard/Toews/Kane 12.00 30.00
19 Clutter/Maruk/Modano 10.00 25.00
20 Giroux/Briere/Roenick 6.00 15.00

2011-12 Crown Royale Scratching The Surface Signatures

1 Adam Graves 6.00 15.00
2 Ales Hemsky 6.00 15.00
5 Alexander Semin 6.00 15.00
6 Adam Henrique 12.00 30.00
7 David Rundblad 4.00 10.00
8 Antti Niemi 15.00 30.00
9 Tyler Bozak 8.00 20.00
10 Bill Ranford 10.00 25.00
11 Blake Geoffrion 6.00 15.00
12 Bobby Ryan 6.00 15.00
13 Tim Erixon 5.00 12.00
14 Brad Marchand 12.00 30.00
15 Brad Mills 4.00 10.00
16 Brandon McMillan 4.00 10.00
17 Brayden Schenn 10.00 25.00
18 Brian Elliott 10.00 25.00
20 Cam Atkinson 12.00 30.00
22 Cody Almond 4.00 10.00
23 Cody Hodgson SP 30.00 60.00
24 Colin Wilson 5.00 12.00
25 Craig Anderson 6.00 15.00
26 Curtis Joseph 10.00 25.00
27 Dan Bouchard 10.00 25.00
28 Felix Potvin 15.00 30.00
29 Tomas Tatar 10.00 25.00
30 Sean Couturier 12.00 30.00
32 Jonas Gustavsson 8.00 20.00
35 Mike Komisarek 8.00 20.00
37 Pavel Datsyuk 15.00 40.00
39 Ray Ferraro SP 6.00 15.00
41 Simon Nolet 8.00 20.00
42 Teemu Selanne 15.00 30.00
43 Tom Barrasso 12.50 25.00
45 Wojtek Wolski 5.00 12.00
46 Ben Scrivens 8.00 20.00
48 Jaromir Jagr SP 40.00 100.00
49 Jeff Carter 6.00 15.00
50 Mats Zuccarello 6.00 15.00
51 Nazem Kadri 10.00 25.00
58 Michael Ontkean SP 6.00 15.00
60 Roman Horak 5.00 12.00

2011-12 Crown Royale Veteran Silhouette Patch Autographs

STATED PRINT RUN 10-25
26-35 INSERTED IN ANTHOLOGY
1 Sidney Crosby/25 150.00 250.00
2 Carey Price/25 40.00 80.00
3 Roberto Luongo/15 40.00 80.00
4 Alex Ovechkin/25 60.00 120.00
5 Martin Brodeur/25 60.00 120.00
6 Steven Stamkos/25 40.00 80.00
7 Tim Thomas/25 30.00 60.00
8 Henrik Lundqvist/25 40.00 100.00
9 Corey Perry/25 25.00 60.00
10 Jarome Iginla/25 50.00 100.00
11 Joe Thornton/25 40.00 100.00
12 Matt Duchene/25 20.00 50.00
13 Pavel Datsyuk/25 50.00 100.00
14 Claude Giroux/25 30.00 80.00
15 Marc-Andre Fleury/25 50.00 100.00
16 Jimmy Howard/25 20.00 50.00
17 Ryan Miller/25 20.00 50.00
18 Rick Nash/25 60.00 120.00
19 Vincent Lecavalier/25 15.00 40.00
20 Marian Gaborik/25 30.00 80.00
21 James van Riemsdyk/25 50.00 100.00
22 Evgeni Malkin/25 75.00 150.00
23 Ryan Getzlaf/25 25.00 60.00
24 Patrick Kane/10
25 Eric Staal/10
26 Henrik Sedin/25 EXCH
27 Thomas Vanek/25 15.00 40.00
28 Anze Kopitar/25 EXCH 30.00 80.00
29 Zach Parise/25 30.00 80.00
30 Nicklas Lidstrom/25
31 Jordan Staal/25 15.00 40.00
32 Jonathan Quick/25 60.00 120.00
33 Tuukka Rask/25 EXCH 25.00 60.00
34 Nikolai Khabibulin/25
35 Phil Kessel/25 25.00 60.00

2011-12 Crown Royale Voices of the Game Signatures

Most subjects signed inscriptions, or Expression versions that were not certified in any way different than the basic autographs.
1 Mike Doc Emrick 20.00 50.00
2 Dick Irvin 6.00 15.00
3 Pierre McGuire 8.00 20.00
4 Bill Clement 6.00 15.00
5 Peter Maher 8.00 20.00
6 Pierre Houde 6.00 15.00
7 John Forslund 6.00 15.00
8 Joe Beninati 10.00 25.00
9 Dennis Beyak 6.00 15.00
10 John Shorthouse 8.00 20.00

2012-13 Crown Royale All the Kings Men Materials

*PRIME/50: .8X TO 2X BASIC JSY
INSERTS IN 2012-13 ROOKIE ANTHOLOGY
LAAK Anze Kopitar 8.00 20.00
LAAM Alec Martinez 3.00 8.00
LABR Brad Richardson 4.00 10.00
LADB Dustin Brown 5.00 12.00
LADD Drew Doughty 5.00 12.00
LADK Dwight King 3.00 8.00
LADP Dustin Penner 4.00 10.00
LAJB Jonathan Bernier 5.00 12.00
LAJC Jeff Carter 5.00 12.00
LAJQ Jonathan Quick 8.00 20.00
LAJS Jarret Stoll 3.00 8.00
LAJW Justin Williams 4.00 10.00
LAKC Kyle Clifford 3.00 8.00
LAMG Matt Greene 3.00 8.00
LAMR Mike Richards 5.00 12.00
LARS Rob Scuderi 3.00 8.00
LASG Simon Gagne 5.00 12.00
LASV Slava Voynov 5.00 12.00
LATL Trevor Lewis 5.00 12.00
LAWM Willie Mitchell 3.00 8.00

2012-13 Crown Royale Lords of the NHL Materials

*PRIME/25: 1X TO 2.5X BASIC JSY
INSERTS IN 2012-13 ROOKIE ANTHOLOGY
LNAO Alex Ovechkin SP 20.00 50.00
LNBD Brandon Dubinsky 3.00 8.00
LNBR Bobby Ryan 4.00 10.00
LNCG Claude Giroux 4.00 10.00
LNCP Carey Price 12.00 30.00
LNDB David Backes 4.00 10.00
LNDBY Dustin Byfuglien 4.00 10.00
LNEK Erik Karlsson 8.00 20.00
LNES Eric Staal 5.00 12.00
LNHL Henrik Lundqvist SP 6.00 15.00
LNHS Henrik Sedin 4.00 10.00
LNJI Jarome Iginla 4.00 10.00
LNJQ Jonathan Quick 6.00 15.00
LNJT John Tavares 8.00 20.00
LNJTH Joe Thornton 4.00 10.00
LNJTO Jonathan Toews 8.00 20.00
LNLE Loui Eriksson 3.00 8.00
LNMB Martin Brodeur 6.00 15.00
LNMD Matt Duchene 4.00 10.00
LNPD Pavel Datsyuk 5.00 12.00
LNPK Phil Kessel 5.00 12.00
LNPR Pekka Rinne 5.00 12.00
LNRM Ryan Miller 4.00 10.00
LNSC Sidney Crosby 8.00 20.00
LNSD Shane Doan 3.00 8.00
LNSS Steven Stamkos 5.00 12.00
LNSW Stephen Weiss 3.00 8.00
LNTH Taylor Hall 8.00 20.00
LNTS Tyler Seguin 6.00 15.00
LNZP Zach Parise 4.00 10.00

2012-13 Crown Royale Rookie Silhouette Prime Autographs

STATED PRINT RUN 99 SER.#'d SETS
*PATCH/25: .5X TO 1.2X BASIC JSY AU
EXCH EXPIRATION: 12/5/2014
41 Chris Kreider 30.00 80.00
42 J.T. Brown 15.00 40.00
43 Sven Baertschi 20.00 50.00
44 Jussi Rynnas 20.00 50.00
45 Tyson Barrie 30.00 80.00
46 Carter Ashton 15.00 40.00
47 Jaden Schwartz 30.00 80.00
48 Reilly Smith 25.00 60.00
49 Jake Allen 50.00 120.00
50 Jakob Silfverberg 20.00 50.00
51 Chet Pickard 12.00 30.00
52 Scott Glennie 12.00 30.00
53 Akim Aliu 15.00 40.00
54 Mat Clark 15.00 40.00
55 Michael Stone 15.00 40.00
56 Colby Robak 15.00 40.00
57 Brenden Dillon 12.00 30.00
58 Brandon Bollig 12.00 30.00
59 Robert Mayer 20.00 50.00
60 Ryan Hamilton 15.00 40.00
61 Matt Donovan 15.00 40.00
62 Kris Foucault 15.00 40.00
63 Jordan Nolan 12.00 30.00
64 Andrew Joudrey 15.00 40.00
65 Max Sauve 15.00 40.00
66 Jeremy Welsh 15.00 40.00
67 Jason Zucker 15.00 40.00
68 Brandon Manning 15.00 40.00
69 Aaron Ness 15.00 40.00
70 Dalton Prout 15.00 40.00
71 Michael Hutchinson 12.00 30.00
72 Philippe Cornet 15.00 40.00
73 Travis Turnbull 15.00 40.00
74 Gabriel Dumont 15.00 40.00
75 Chay Genoway 12.00 30.00
76 Casey Cizikas 15.00 40.00
77 Mark Stone 30.00 80.00
78 Ryan Garbutt 12.00 30.00
79 Riley Sheahan 15.00 40.00
80 Torey Krug 30.00 80.00
81 Cody Goloubef 15.00 40.00
82 Matt Watkins 12.00 30.00
83 Tyson Sexsmith 12.00 30.00
84 Shawn Hunwick 15.00 40.00
85 Mike Connolly 12.00 30.00
86 Carter Camper 12.00 30.00
87 Tyler Cuma 15.00 40.00
88 Lane MacDermid 15.00 40.00

2012-13 Crown Royale Royale Lineage Materials

*PRIME/50: .8X TO 2X BASIC INSERTS
*PRIME/25: 1X TO 2.5X BASIC INSERTS
INSERTS IN 2012-13 ROOKIE ANTHOLOGY
RLANA Perry/Bonino/Selnne SP 5.00 12.00
RLBOS Neely/Bergrn/Seguin SP 5.00 12.00
RLBUF Andrychk/Pomnvl/Vnek 5.00 12.00
RLCAR Staal/Staal/Francis SP 6.00 15.00
RLCBJ Anisimov/Dubinsky/Boll 3.00 8.00
RLCGY Tanguay/Iginla/Stajan 4.00 10.00
RLCHI Chelios/Toews/Hossa 8.00 20.00
RLCOL Johnson/Bourque/Barrie 6.00 15.00
RLCOL2 Landeskog/Sakic/Hejduk 6.00 15.00
RLDAL Morrow/Eriksson/Glennie 4.00 10.00
RLDET Howard/Datsyk/Yzermn 10.00 25.00
RLEDM Hemsky/Eberle/Gagner 4.00 10.00
RLFLA Kulikov/Parros/Weiss 3.00 8.00
RLHRT Shanhn/Hwe/Vrbek SP 12.00 30.00
RLLAK Taylor/Williams/Clifford 5.00 12.00
RLMON Price/Lafleur/Pacioretty 8.00 20.00
RLNJD Larsson/Kovalchuk/Elias 4.00 10.00
RLNSH Pickard/Legwand/Rinne 5.00 12.00
RLNYI Boyes/Trottier/Tavares 6.00 15.00
RLNYR Kreider/Messier/Nash SP 6.00 15.00
RLPHI Giroux/Lindros/Couturier 10.00 25.00
RLPHX Yandle/Hanzal/Doan 4.00 10.00
RLPIT Kunitz/Neal/Lemieux SP 10.00 25.00
RLSJS Pavelski/Thornton/Clowe 4.00 10.00
RLSTL MacInn/Bcks/Schwtz 6.00 15.00
RLTBL Brown/Stamkos/Lecav 8.00 20.00
RLTOR Joseph/Potvin/Rynnas 6.00 15.00
RLVAN Burrows/Sedin/Luongo 6.00 15.00
RLWAS Ovech/Holtby/Johansn 8.00 20.00
RLWIN Burmist/Byfglien/Bogsn 4.00 10.00

2012-13 Crown Royale Scratching the Surface Signatures

INSERTS IN 2012-13 ROOKIE ANTHOLOGY
1 Scott Glennie 3.00 8.00
2 Jake Allen 10.00 25.00
3 Chet Pickard 3.00 8.00
4 Jakob Silfverberg 8.00 20.00
5 Chris Kreider 10.00 25.00
6 Jussi Rynnas 6.00 15.00
7 Sven Baertschi 4.00 10.00
8 Carter Ashton 2.50 6.00
9 Jaden Schwartz 6.00 15.00
10 Brad Richards 6.00 15.00
11 Alex Urbom 15.00 40.00
12 Brett Hull 10.00 25.00
13 Cal Clutterbuck 6.00 15.00
14 Derek Stepan 8.00 20.00
15 Gabriel Landeskog 10.00 25.00
16 Jordan Eberle 12.00 30.00
17 Pat LaFontaine 15.00 30.00
18 Ryan Nugent-Hopkins 12.00 30.00
19 Steve Yzerman SP 50.00 100.00
21 Reilly Smith 6.00 15.00
22 Tyson Barrie 6.00 15.00

2012-13 Crown Royale Silhouette Materials

*PRIME/15-25: .8X TO 2X BASIC JSY
INSERTS IN 2012-13 ROOKIE ANTHOLOGY
1 Nick Fotiu 4.00 10.00
2 Mike Richards 6.00 15.00
3 Zdeno Chara 8.00 20.00
4 Jason Pominville 5.00 12.00
5 Jack Johnson 4.00 10.00
6 Kari Lehtonen 5.00 12.00
7 Henrik Zetterberg 10.00 25.00
8 Teemu Selanne SP 10.00 25.00
9 Pekka Rinne 8.00 20.00
10 P.K. Subban 10.00 25.00
11 Keith Primeau 5.00 12.00
12 John Vanbiesbrouck 25.00 60.00
13 Kris Letang 10.00 25.00
14 Daniel Sedin 6.00 15.00
15 Mike Gartner 6.00 15.00
16 Chris Chelios 6.00 15.00
17 Jaroslav Halak 6.00 15.00
18 Mikhail Grabovski 6.00 15.00
19 Patrick Sharp 6.00 15.00
20 Milan Lucic 6.00 15.00

2012-13 Crown Royale Silhouette Materials Signatures

INSERTS IN 2012-13 ROOKIE ANTHOLOGY
OVERALL ANNC'D PRINT RUN 99 OR LESS
SP A ANNC'D PRINT RUN 10
SP B ANNC'D PRINT RUN 25 OR LESS
22 Jarome Iginla 20.00 50.00
23 Loui Eriksson 10.00 25.00
24 Jeremy Roenick SP B 20.00 50.00
25 Jonathan Toews 40.00 80.00
26 Eric Lindros SP B 40.00 80.00
27 Matt Duchene 15.00 40.00
28 Steve Yzerman 40.00 80.00
29 Dustin Brown 15.00 40.00
30 John Tavares 40.00 100.00
31 Mario Lemieux SP B 75.00 150.00
32 Brett Hull 25.00 60.00
33 Martin St. Louis 20.00 50.00
34 Antti Niemi 15.00 40.00
35 Gordie Howe SP A
36 Sam Gagner 20.00 50.00
37 Cory Schneider 15.00 40.00
38 Jonas Hiller 10.00 25.00
39 Brad Richards 20.00 50.00
40 Joe Sakic SP B 15.00 40.00

2012-13 Crown Royale Towering Defenders Materials

*PRIME/25: 1X TO 2.5X BASIC JSY
INSERTS IN 2012-13 ROOKIE ANTHOLOGY
TDBB Brent Burns 5.00 12.00
TDCP Chris Pronger 3.00 8.00
TDDB Dustin Byfuglien 4.00 10.00
TDDP Dion Phaneuf 4.00 10.00
TDEJ Erik Johnson 2.50 6.00
TDHK Henrik Karlsson 3.00 8.00
TDIB Ilya Bryzgalov 4.00 10.00
TDJB Jay Bouwmeester 4.00 10.00
TDJC Jared Cowen 4.00 10.00
TDJG Jonas Gustavsson 4.00 10.00
TDJL Kari Lehtonen 3.00 8.00
TDJS Jeff Schultz 2.50 6.00
TDJSG Jean-Sebastien Giguere 3.00 8.00
TDMS Mike Smith 4.00 10.00
TDMST Marc Staal 3.00 8.00
TDPR Pekka Rinne 5.00 12.00
TDSW Shea Weber 3.00 8.00
TDTM Tyler Myers 3.00 8.00
TDTR Tuukka Rask 4.00 10.00
TDZC Zdeno Chara 4.00 10.00

2013-14 Crown Royale

EXCH EXPIRATION: 9/12/2015
1 Brian Gionta .50 1.25
2 Evander Kane .60 1.50
3 Jack Johnson .40 1.00
4 Mike Fisher .50 1.25
5 Evgeni Nabokov .50 1.25
6 Semyon Varlamov .60 1.50
7 Scott Hartnell .60 1.50
8 Teemu Selanne 1.25 3.00
9 Braden Holtby 1.00 2.50
10 Claude Giroux .60 1.50
11 Patrick Marleau .60 1.50
12 Marc-Andre Fleury 1.00 2.50
13 Pavel Datsyuk .75 2.00
14 Duncan Keith .60 1.50
15 Dany Heatley .50 1.25
16 Vincent Lecavalier .50 1.25
17 Thomas Vanek .60 1.50
18 Cory Schneider .50 1.25
19 Jonathan Toews 1.25 3.00
20 Alexander Steen .60 1.50
21 Curtis Glencross .40 1.00
22 Jacob Markstrom .50 1.25
23 Zdeno Chara .60 1.50
24 Shane Doan .50 1.25
25 Andrew Ladd .60 1.50
26 Martin St. Louis .60 1.50
27 Patrick Kane 1.25 3.00
28 Mark Giordano .50 1.25
29 Kari Lehtonen .50 1.25
30 Henrik Lundqvist .75 2.00
31 Cody Hodgson .60 1.50
32 Mike Smith .60 1.50
33 Kris Letang .60 1.50
34 Zach Parise .60 1.50
35 Eric Staal .75 2.00
36 Tyler Seguin 1.00 2.50
37 Mikko Koivu .50 1.25
38 Keith Yandle .60 1.50
39 Logan Couture .60 1.50
40 John Tavares 1.25 3.00
41 Niklas Kronwall .50 1.25
42 David Backes .60 1.50
43 Nazem Kadri .60 1.50
44 Henrik Zetterberg .75 2.00
45 Tuukka Rask .60 1.50
46 Alex Ovechkin 2.50 6.00
47 Matt Moulson .50 1.25
48 Pekka Rinne .75 2.00
49 Jay Bouwmeester .60 1.50
50 Joe Thornton .60 1.50
51 Ryan McDonagh .60 1.50
52 Matt Duchene .60 1.50
53 Evgeni Malkin 2.00 5.00
54 Jonathan Quick 1.00 2.50
55 Ryan Miller .60 1.50
56 Jason Spezza .60 1.50
57 Ben Bishop .60 1.50
58 Corey Perry .60 1.50
59 Joffrey Lupul .50 1.25
60 Jordan Eberle .60 1.50
61 Rick Nash .60 1.50
62 Martin Brodeur 1.25 3.00
63 Jordan Staal .60 1.50
64 Patrice Bergeron .75 2.00
65 Erik Karlsson 1.25 3.00
66 Daniel Sedin .60 1.50
67 Max Pacioretty .60 1.50
68 Shea Weber .50 1.25
69 Dustin Brown .60 1.50
70 Craig Anderson .60 1.50
71 Mike Cammalleri .50 1.25
72 Corey Crawford .75 2.00
73 Carey Price 2.00 5.00
74 Patrik Elias .60 1.50
75 Ryan Getzlaf 1.00 2.50
76 P.K. Subban 1.00 2.50
77 Taylor Hall 1.25 3.00
78 Ryan Kesler .60 1.50
79 Brian Campbell .40 1.00
80 Sergei Bobrovsky .60 1.50
81 Blake Wheeler .60 1.50
82 Ed Jovanovski .40 1.00
83 Henrik Sedin .60 1.50
84 Ryan Nugent-Hopkins .60 1.50
85 Jimmy Howard .60 1.50
86 Jamie Benn .75 2.00
87 Sidney Crosby 2.50 6.00
88 Phil Kessel .75 2.00
89 Sam Gagner .50 1.25
90 James Reimer .60 1.50
91 Steven Stamkos 1.25 3.00
92 Gabriel Landeskog .50 1.25
93 Milan Michalek .40 1.00
94 Mike Green .60 1.50
95 Roberto Luongo .60 1.50
96 Cam Ward .60 1.50
97 Anze Kopitar 1.00 2.50
98 Ryan Callahan .60 1.50
99 Marian Gaborik .60 1.50
100 Jarome Iginla .60 1.50
101 Sami Vatanen JSY AU RC 8.00 20.00
102 Carl Soderberg JSY AU RC 8.00 20.00
103 M.Grigorenko JSY AU RC 10.00 25.00
104 Max Reinhart JSY AU RC 8.00 20.00
105 Jared Staal JSY AU RC 8.00 20.00
106 Kuemper JSY AU RC EXCH 8.00 20.00
107 Antoine Roussel JSY AU RC 8.00 20.00
108 Alex Chiasson JSY AU RC 8.00 20.00
109 Brian Lashoff JSY AU RC 6.00 15.00
110 D.DeKeyser JSY AU RC 15.00 40.00
111 Petr Mrazek JSY AU RC 30.00 60.00
112 Nick Bjugstad JSY AU RC 12.00 30.00
113 Drew Shore JSY AU RC 6.00 15.00
114 Tanner Pearson JSY AU RC 8.00 20.00
115 R.Strome JSY AU RC 15.00 40.00
116 J.Brodin JSY AU RC EXCH 6.00 15.00
117 Mikael Granlund JSY AU RC 20.00 40.00
118 B.Gallagher JSY AU RC 25.00 60.00
119 Filip Forsberg JSY AU RC 30.00 60.00
120 Stefan Matteau JSY AU RC 6.00 15.00
121 Thomas Hickey JSY AU RC 6.00 15.00
122 J.T. Miller JSY AU RC 8.00 20.00
123 Matt Dumba JSY AU RC 10.00 25.00
124 Tarasenko JSY AU RC EXCH 75.00 150.00
125 Dmitrij Jaskin JSY AU RC 8.00 20.00
126 Alex Killorn JSY AU RC 8.00 20.00
127 Cory Conacher JSY AU RC 5.00 12.00
128 H.Lindholm JSY AU RC 12.00 30.00
129 Nicklas Jensen JSY AU RC 6.00 15.00
130 Tom Wilson JSY AU RC 12.00 30.00
131 Nail Yakupov JSY AU RC 30.00 60.00
132 D.Hamilton JSY AU RC 15.00 40.00
133 J.Huberdeau JSY AU RC 20.00 50.00
134 A.Galchenyuk JSY AU RC 40.00 100.00
135 Justin Schultz JSY AU RC 8.00 20.00
136 Q.Howden JSY AU RC 6.00 15.00
137 Tyler Toffoli JSY AU RC 25.00 50.00
138 Emerson Etem JSY AU RC 8.00 20.00
139 Scott Laughton JSY AU RC 10.00 25.00
140 Beau Bennett JSY AU RC 10.00 25.00
141 Viktor Fasth JSY AU RC 8.00 20.00
142 J.Schroeder JSY AU RC 8.00 20.00
143 Charlie Coyle JSY AU RC 8.00 20.00
144 Ryan Murphy JSY AU RC 8.00 20.00
145 Ryan Spooner JSY AU RC 8.00 20.00
146 Jarred Tinordi JSY AU RC 8.00 20.00
147 N.Beaulieu JSY AU RC 6.00 15.00
148 A.Watson JSY AU RC EXCH 6.00 15.00
149 Jack Campbell JSY AU RC 6.00 15.00
150 Igor Bobkov JSY AU RC 6.00 15.00
151 Tye McGinn JSY AU RC 8.00 20.00
152 Jamie Oleksiak JSY AU RC 6.00 15.00
153 F.Andersen JSY AU RC 20.00 50.00
154 Rickard Rakell JSY AU RC 8.00 20.00
155 Jamie Tardif JSY AU RC 5.00 12.00
156 Ben Street JSY AU RC 5.00 12.00
157 Brian Flynn JSY AU RC 6.00 15.00
158 Michal Jordan JSY AU RC 5.00 12.00
159 Calvin Pickard JSY AU RC 8.00 20.00
160 M.Sgarbossa JSY AU RC 6.00 15.00
161 Cristopher Nilstorp JSY AU RC 6.00 15.00
162 Mark Arcobello JSY AU RC 8.00 20.00
163 Brock Nelson JSY AU RC 8.00 20.00
164 Eric Hartzell JSY AU RC 8.00 20.00
165 Philipp Grubauer JSY AU RC 8.00 20.00
166 Michael Caruso JSY AU RC 5.00 12.00
167 Richard Panik JSY AU RC 8.00 20.00
168 Eric Gryba JSY AU RC 6.00 15.00
169 Matt Irwin JSY AU RC 6.00 15.00
170 Zach Redmond JSY AU RC 6.00 15.00
171 Johan Larsson JSY AU RC 6.00 15.00
172 Chris Brown JSY AU RC 5.00 12.00
173 Nick Petrecki JSY AU RC 5.00 12.00
174 Anthony Peluso JSY AU RC 5.00 12.00
175 Edward Pasquale JSY AU RC 5.00 12.00
176 Michael Kostka JSY AU RC EXCH 6.00 15.00
177 Christian Thomas JSY AU RC 6.00 15.00
178 Mark Pysyk JSY AU RC 8.00 20.00
179 Frank Corrado JSY AU RC 5.00 12.00
180 Jacob Trouba JSY AU RC EXCH 30.00 60.00
181 MacKinnon JSY AU RC EXCH 100.00 200.00
182 Girgensons JSY AU RC EXCH 15.00 40.00
183 J.Nordstrom JSY AU RC EXCH 6.00 15.00
184 Seth Jones JSY AU RC 25.00 50.00
185 Tomas Hertl JSY AU RC 40.00 80.00
186 Sean Monahan JSY AU RC 40.00 80.00
187 Nichushkin JSY AU RC EXCH 30.00 60.00
188 Olli Maatta JSY AU RC 30.00 60.00
189 Rasmus Ristolainen JSY AU RC 12.00 30.00
190 A.Barkov JSY AU RC 20.00 50.00
191 Boone Jenner JSY AU RC 8.00 20.00
192 R.Murray JSY AU RC EXCH 12.00 30.00
193 Morgan Rielly JSY AU RC 25.00 50.00
194 Matt Nieto JSY AU RC 6.00 15.00
195 Elias Lindholm JSY AU RC 12.00 30.00
196 Tomas Jurco JSY AU RC 12.00 30.00
197 J.Merrill JSY AU RC EXCH 8.00 20.00
198 Dylan McIlrath JSY AU RC 5.00 12.00
199 Cody Ceci JSY AU RC 6.00 15.00
200 Martin Jones JSY AU RC 20.00 50.00
201A Ben Hanowski RC 1.50 4.00
201B M.Mazanec JSY AU RC EXCH 8.00 20.00
202A Carter Bancks RC 1.50 4.00
202B M.Hellberg JSY AU RC EXCH 8.00 20.00
203A Brett Bellemore RC 1.50 4.00
203B Nikita Zadorov JSY AU RC 8.00 20.00
204A Nicolas Blanchard RC 1.50 4.00
204B Reto Berra JSY AU RC 8.00 20.00
205A Drew LeBlanc RC 1.25 3.00
205B J.Missiaen JSY AU RC EXCH 8.00 20.00
206A Sami Aittokallio RC 2.00 5.00
206B Jesper Fast JSY AU RC 6.00 15.00
207A Eric Selleck RC 1.50 4.00
207B J.Gustafsson JSY AU RC 10.00 25.00
208A Kevin Henderson RC 1.50 4.00
208B J.Gibson JSY AU RC EXCH 25.00 50.00
209A Matt Anderson RC 1.25 3.00
209B M.Bournival JSY AU RC 8.00 20.00
210A Eric Gelinas RC 2.00 5.00
210B Lucas Lessio JSY AU RC 5.00 12.00
211A Jean-Gabriel Pageau RC 1.50 4.00
211B C.Murphy JSY AU RC EXCH 6.00 15.00
212A Andrej Sustr RC 1.25 3.00
212B Jamie Devane JSY AU RC 6.00 15.00
213 Steven Pinizzotto RC 2.00 5.00
214 Damien Brunner RC 1.50 4.00
215 Connor Carrick RC 1.50 4.00
216 Mark Cundari AU/499 RC 2.00 5.00
217 Chris Terry AU/499 RC 2.00 5.00
218 Shawn Lalonde AU/499 RC 3.00 8.00
219 Ryan Stanton AU/499 RC 3.00 8.00
220 Greg Pateryn AU/499 RC 3.00 8.00
221 Jonathan Rheault AU/499 RC 2.00 5.00
222 Oliver Lauridsen AU/499 RC 2.50 6.00
223 Jeff Zatkoff AU/499 RC 3.00 8.00
224 Matt Tennyson AU/499 RC 2.00 5.00
225 Tyler Johnson AU/499 RC 8.00 20.00
226 Patrick Bordeleau AU/399 RC 3.00 8.00
227 Sean Collins AU/499 RC 2.50 6.00
228 Dave Dziurzynski AU/499 RC 2.50 6.00
229 Harri Pesonen AU/499 RC 2.50 6.00
230 Victor Bartley AU/499 RC 2.50 6.00
231 Derek Grant AU/499 RC 2.50 6.00
232 J.Marchessault AU/499 RC 6.00 15.00
233 Taylor Beck AU/399 RC 2.50 6.00
234 Ondrej Palat AU/499 RC 4.00 10.00
235 Radko Gudas AU/499 RC 3.00 8.00
236 John Muse AU/499 RC 3.00 8.00
237 Alex Petrovic AU/499 RC 2.50 6.00
238 Joonas Rask AU/499 RC 2.00 5.00
239 Steve Oleksy AU/499 RC 3.00 8.00
240 Matthew Konan AU/499 RC 3.00 8.00

2013-14 Crown Royale Red

*RED/99: 1.5X TO 4X BASIC CARDS
72 Corey Crawford 3.00 8.00

2013-14 Crown Royale Coat of Arms Materials

*PRIME/50: .6X TO 1.5X BASIC JSY
CAAR Antoine Roussel 2.50 6.00
CABG Brendan Gallagher 5.00 12.00
CABSC Brayden Schenn 2.50 6.00
CACC Cory Conacher 1.50 4.00
CACH Carl Hagelin 2.50 6.00
CACPE Corey Perry 3.00 8.00
CADBY Dustin Byfuglien 3.00 8.00
CADDK Danny DeKeyser 5.00 12.00
CADK Duncan Keith 3.00 8.00
CAGL Gabriel Landeskog 2.50 6.00
CAJFC Jeff Carter 3.00 8.00
CAJH Jonathan Huberdeau 4.00 10.00
CAMAF Marc-Andre Fleury 5.00 12.00
CAMGR Mikael Granlund 3.00 8.00
CAMIK Mikhail Grigorenko 3.00 8.00
CAMSL Martin St. Louis 3.00 8.00
CANCB Nicklas Backstrom 5.00 12.00
CANJ Nicklas Jensen 2.00 5.00
CANY Nail Yakupov 5.00 12.00
CAPM Patrick Marleau 3.00 8.00
CASJ Seth Jones 4.00 10.00
CATB Tyler Bozak 2.00 5.00
CATH Thomas Hickey 2.00 5.00
CAVT Vladimir Tarasenko 5.00 12.00
CAZC Zdeno Chara 3.00 8.00

2013-14 Crown Royale Fans of the Game Autographs

FGAP Audrina Patridge 8.00 20.00
FGCS Chantal Sutherland-Kruse 10.00 25.00
FGDO Dan O'Toole 15.00 40.00
FGGW Greg Wyshynski 12.00 30.00
FGJB John Buccigross 6.00 15.00
FGJBO Jennifer Botterill 10.00 25.00
FGJC Julie Chu 8.00 20.00
FGJM John C. McGinley 12.00 30.00
FGJO Jay Onrait 12.00 30.00
FGKB Katrina Bowden 15.00 40.00
FGMA Meghan Agosta 15.00 40.00
FGMC Melanie Collins 20.00 50.00
FGMD Meghan Duggan 12.00 30.00
FGSL Steve Levy 6.00 15.00
FGTB Tessa Bonhomme 15.00 40.00

2013-14 Crown Royale First Class Sigs

FCAG Alex Galchenyuk 15.00 40.00
FCCK Chris Kreider 6.00 15.00
FCDH Dougie Hamilton 12.00 30.00
FCEE Emerson Etem 6.00 15.00
FCJSC Jaden Schwartz 8.00 20.00
FCJUS Justin Schultz 6.00 15.00
FCNY Nail Yakupov 20.00 50.00
FCRMR Ryan Murray 10.00 25.00

2013-14 Crown Royale Heirs to the Throne Materials

*PRIME/50: .6X TO 1.5X BASIC JSY
HTAB Aleksander Barkov 6.00 15.00
HTAG Alex Galchenyuk 6.00 15.00
HTAK Alex Killorn 2.50 6.00
HTANP Anthony Peluso 1.50 4.00
HTAR Antoine Roussel 2.50 6.00
HTAW Austin Watson 2.00 5.00
HTBB Beau Bennett 3.00 8.00
HTBG Brendan Gallagher 6.00 15.00
HTCB Chris Brown 1.50 4.00
HTCC Cory Conacher 1.50 4.00
HTCOY Charlie Coyle 2.50 6.00
HTCSO Carl Soderberg 2.50 6.00
HTDDK Danny DeKeyser 3.00 8.00
HTDH Dougie Hamilton 5.00 12.00
HTEE Emerson Etem 2.50 6.00
HTFF Filip Forsberg 6.00 15.00
HTJAS Jared Staal 2.50 6.00
HTJB Jonas Brodin 2.00 5.00
HTJH Jonathan Huberdeau 5.00 12.00
HTJO Jamie Oleksiak 2.00 5.00
HTJSD Jordan Schroeder 2.50 6.00
HTJTM J.T. Miller 2.50 6.00
HTJTR Jacob Trouba 4.00 10.00
HTJUS Justin Schultz 2.50 6.00
HTMGR Mikael Granlund 4.00 10.00
HTMIK Mikhail Grigorenko 3.00 8.00
HTMXR Max Reinhart 2.50 6.00
HTNBJ Nick Bjugstad 3.00 8.00
HTNJ Nicklas Jensen 2.00 5.00
HTNMK Nathan MacKinnon 12.00 30.00
HTNP Nick Petrecki 1.50 4.00
HTNY Nail Yakupov 5.00 12.00
HTPMR Petr Mrazek 5.00 12.00
HTRLY Morgan Rielly 6.00 15.00
HTRMP Ryan Murphy 2.50 6.00
HTRMR Ryan Murray 4.00 10.00
HTRSP Ryan Spooner 2.50 6.00
HTSJ Seth Jones 2.50 6.00
HTSMA Stefan Matteau 2.00 5.00
HTSMO Sean Monahan 4.00 10.00
HTSV Sami Vatanen 2.50 6.00
HTTHE Tomas Hertl 3.00 8.00
HTTHI Thomas Hickey 2.00 5.00
HTTMG Tye McGinn 2.50 6.00
HTTP Tanner Pearson 2.50 6.00
HTTT Tyler Toffoli 5.00 12.00
HTTW Tom Wilson 4.00 10.00
HTVF Viktor Fasth 2.50 6.00
HTVT Vladimir Tarasenko 5.00 12.00
HTZG Zemgus Girgensons 5.00 12.00

2013-14 Crown Royale Heirs to the Throne Materials Patches

*PATCH/25: 1X TO 2.5X BASIC JSY
HTNMK Nathan MacKinnon 75.00 150.00

2013-14 Crown Royale Lords of the NHL Materials

*PRIME/25: .6X TO 1.5X BASIC JSY
*PRIME/25: .5X TO 1.2X BASIC JSY SP
LAH Adam Henrique SP 5.00 12.00
LCG Curtis Glencross 2.50 6.00
LCHO Cody Hodgson 4.00 10.00
LDS Daniel Sedin 4.00 10.00
LEK Erik Karlsson 8.00 20.00
LHL Henrik Lundqvist SP 6.00 15.00
LHZ Henrik Zetterberg 5.00 12.00
LJH Jonathan Huberdeau 4.00 10.00
LJQ Jonathan Quick 6.00 15.00
LJT John Tavares SP 5.00 12.00
LJTH Joe Thornton SP 5.00 12.00
LJTO Jonathan Toews SP 10.00 25.00
LKLE Kari Lehtonen 3.00 8.00
LMG Marian Gaborik 4.00 10.00
LNK Nazem Kadri 6.00 15.00
LNMK Nathan MacKinnon 8.00 20.00
LNY Nail Yakupov 5.00 12.00
LOVI Alex Ovechkin SP 20.00 50.00
LPKS P.K. Subban 6.00 15.00
LSC Sidney Crosby SP 20.00 50.00
LSCO Sean Couturier 4.00 10.00
LSJ Seth Jones 4.00 10.00
LSS Steven Stamkos SP 10.00 25.00
LTMU Teemu Selanne SP 10.00 25.00
LTR Tuukka Rask 5.00 12.00

2013-14 Crown Royale Majestic Marks

MJBPA Brad Park 5.00 12.00
MJBS Brendan Shanahan SP 15.00 40.00
MJGHA Glenn Hall SP 12.00 30.00
MJJE Jordan Eberle SP 12.00 30.00
MJJSK Jeff Skinner SP
MJML Mario Lemieux 40.00 80.00
MJMR Manon Rheaume 30.00 80.00
MJNK Nazem Kadri SP 8.00 20.00
MJOEL Oliver Ekman-Larsson SP 8.00 20.00
MJBOB Sergei Bobrovsky SP 10.00 25.00

2013-14 Crown Royale Mythology Materials

*PRIME/25: .5X TO 1.2X BASIC JSY
MYBH Brett Hull/100* 5.00 12.00
MYCN Cam Neely/100* 5.00 12.00
MYDG Doug Gilmour/100* 6.00 15.00
MYDSA Denis Savard/100* 6.00 15.00
MYEB Ed Belfour/100* 5.00 12.00
MYEL Eric Lindros/100* 8.00 20.00
MYGF Grant Fuhr/100* 5.00 12.00
MYGH Gordie Howe/25* 20.00 40.00
MYJN Joe Nieuwendyk/100* 5.00 12.00
MYJS Joe Sakic/100* 8.00 20.00
MYLM Lanny McDonald/100* 6.00 15.00
MYLUC Luc Robitaille/100* 5.00 12.00
MYML Mario Lemieux/100* 15.00 40.00
MYMM Mark Messier/50* 6.00 15.00
MYMO Mike Modano/100* 8.00 20.00
MYNL Nicklas Lidstrom/100* 5.00 12.00
MYPC Paul Coffey/100* 5.00 12.00
MYPE Phil Esposito/50* 6.00 15.00
MYPLF Pat LaFontaine/100* 5.00 12.00
MYPR Patrick Roy/100* 12.00 30.00
MYPT Pierre Turgeon/100* 5.00 12.00
MYRB Ray Bourque/50* 8.00 20.00
MYRBA Rod Brind'Amour/100* 5.00 12.00
MYRBL Rob Blake/100* 5.00 12.00
MYWC Wendel Clark/100* 5.00 12.00

2013-14 Crown Royale Pacific's Choice Autographs Bronze

EXCH EXPIRATION: 9/12/2015
PCCCH Chris Chelios 15.00 40.00
PCCGX Claude Giroux EXCH 15.00 40.00
PCCJ Curtis Joseph 15.00 40.00
PCDCI Dino Ciccarelli 10.00 25.00
PCDPH Dion Phaneuf EXCH 10.00 25.00
PCDPO Denis Potvin 10.00 25.00
PCDS Daniel Sedin 10.00 25.00
PCERS Eric Staal 12.00 30.00
PCGF Grant Fuhr 10.00 25.00
PCGL Gabriel Landeskog
PCGNY Bob Gainey 10.00 25.00
PCHS Henrik Sedin 10.00 25.00
PCJRE James Reimer 10.00 25.00
PCLR Larry Robinson 10.00 25.00
PCMDU Matt Duchene EXCH 10.00 25.00
PCMSL Martin St. Louis 10.00 25.00
PCPRI Pekka Rinne 12.00 30.00
PCTH Taylor Hall 15.00 40.00
PCYC Yvan Cournoyer 10.00 25.00
PCZP Zach Parise 10.00 25.00

2013-14 Crown Royale Pacific's Choice Autographs Ruby

EXCH EXPIRATION: 9/12/2015
*RUBY HOLO/25: .8X TO 2X BASIC AU/199
*RUBY HOLO/25: .6X TO 1.5X BASIC AU/99
PCAD Alex Delvecchio/99 10.00 25.00

Card	Low	High
PCAH Adam Henrique/199	5.00	12.00
PCBE Brian Elliott/199 EXCH	4.00	10.00
PCKT Kyle Turris/199	3.00	8.00
PCMP Max Pacioretty /199	5.00	12.00
PCRL Robin Lehner/199	4.00	10.00
PCTC Tyler Cuma/199	4.00	10.00
PCZK Zack Kassian/199	4.00	10.00
PCBCO Brett Connolly/199	3.00	8.00
PCBHY Braden Holtby/199	8.00	20.00
PCCDH Calvin de Haan/199	3.00	8.00
PCCHO Cody Hodgson/99	6.00	15.00
PCJEN Jhonas Enroth/199	5.00	12.00
PCJLC John LeClair/99	8.00	20.00
PCJZU Jason Zucker/199	4.00	10.00
PCMMO Matt Moulson/199	4.00	10.00
PCMXT Maxime Talbot/99	5.00	12.00
PCREL Ryan Ellis/199	3.00	8.00
PCRJU R.J. Umberger/199	3.00	8.00
PCTBA Tyson Barrie/199	5.00	12.00

2013-14 Crown Royale Pacific's Choice Autographs Sapphire

Card	Low	High
PCAL Andrew Ladd	8.00	20.00
PCAN Antti Niemi	6.00	15.00
PCBSC Brayden Schenn	8.00	20.00
PCBWR Johnny Bower	12.00	30.00
PCCGI Clark Gillies	8.00	20.00
PCCK Chris Kreider EXCH	8.00	20.00
PCDST Derek Stepan		
PCJHA Jaroslav Halak	8.00	20.00
PCJHO Jimmy Howard	8.00	20.00
PCJNE James Neal	8.00	20.00
PCJP Joe Pavelski	12.00	30.00
PCJVR James van Riemsdyk	8.00	20.00
PCMC Mike Cammalleri	6.00	15.00
PCMF Mike Fisher	6.00	15.00
PCMS Mike Smith	8.00	20.00
PCRFE Ray Ferraro	5.00	12.00
PCRNH Ryan Nugent-Hopkins	8.00	20.00
PCSSA Serge Savard	8.00	20.00
PCTL Trevor Linden	10.00	25.00
PCVH Victor Hedman	10.00	25.00

2013-14 Crown Royale Regal Achievements Materials

*PRIME/25: .6X TO 1.5X BASIC JSY
*PRIME/25: .5X TO 1.2X BASIC JSY SP

Card	Low	High
RABGI Brian Gionta	3.00	8.00
RABH Brett Hull	5.00	12.00
RABSY Mike Bossy SP	5.00	12.00
RACCH Chris Chelios	4.00	10.00
RADA Dave Andreychuk	4.00	10.00
RADSI Darryl Sittler	5.00	12.00
RAJH Jonathan Huberdeau	4.00	10.00
RAJJ Jaromir Jagr	8.00	20.00
RAJS Joe Sakic	6.00	15.00
RALUC Luc Robitaille	4.00	10.00
RAMB Martin Brodeur SP	10.00	25.00
RAMGO Michel Goulet	3.00	8.00
RAMO Mike Modano	6.00	15.00
RAMRI Mike Richards	4.00	10.00
RAPK Patrick Kane	8.00	20.00
RAPM Patrick Marleau	4.00	10.00
RAPR Patrick Roy	10.00	25.00
RARB Ray Bourque	6.00	15.00
RARF Ron Francis	5.00	12.00
RARLE Reggie Leach SP	4.00	10.00
RASG Sam Gagner	3.00	8.00
RASS Steven Stamkos SP	6.00	15.00
RASY Steve Yzerman	8.00	20.00
RATKE Tim Kerr SP	5.00	12.00
RATMU Teemu Selanne SP	10.00	25.00

2013-14 Crown Royale Rookie Royalty

*ROOKIES/99: .8X TO 2X BASIC RC

2013-14 Crown Royale Rookie Royalty Autographs Ruby

*RUBY/99: .6X TO 1.5X BASIC AU/399-499

2013-14 Crown Royale Rookie Silhouette Patch Autographs

*PATCH AU/25: 1X TO 2.5X JSY AU/99

Card	Low	High
124 Vladimir Tarasenko EXCH	90.00	150.00
181 Nathan MacKinnon EXCH	350.00	600.00

2013-14 Crown Royale Royal Lineage Materials

*PRIME/25: .6X TO 1.5X BASIC INSERTS

Card	Low	High
RLANA Kvu/Prry/Etem	5.00	12.00
RLBOS Brque/Chra/Hmltn	8.00	20.00
RLCA1 Blke/Wber/Schltz	2.50	6.00
RLCA2 Brdr/Prce/Roy	12.00	30.00
RLCA3 Yzrmn/Hbrdu/Toews	8.00	20.00
RLCOL Skic/Lndskg/McKnnon	12.00	30.00
RLCZE Vkn/Pvlc/Mrzek	10.00	25.00
RLDAL Nwndyk/Sguin/Rssel	10.00	25.00
RLDEN Jnsn/Nlsn/Ellr	4.00	10.00
RLFIN Slnne/Lhtnn/Grnlnd	8.00	20.00
RLLAK Kptr/Prsn/Rbtlle	8.00	20.00
RLMTL Gney/Gnta/Gllghr	8.00	20.00
RLNYR Mssr/Nsh/Mller	8.00	20.00
RLPHI Clrke/Grx/Lghtn	10.00	25.00
RLRU1 Lrnov/Ovchkn/Ykpv SP	10.00	25.00
RLRU2 Mlkn/Grgrnko/Bre	15.00	40.00
RLSLO Mkta/Gbrik/Pnk	6.00	15.00
RLSTL Elltt/Trsnko/Mclnns	10.00	25.00
RLSW1 Alfrdsn/Sdin/Frsbrg	10.00	30.00
RLSW2 Krlssn/Brdin/Ldstrm	10.00	25.00
RLTOR Slmng/Phnf/Rlly	6.00	15.00
RLUS1 Byfgln/Ltch/Jnes	2.50	6.00
RLUS2 Rnck/Brwn/Glchnyk	10.00	25.00
RLUS3 Vnbsbrk/Cmpbll/Qck	8.00	20.00
RLVAN Ksler/Schrder/Bre	6.00	15.00

2013-14 Crown Royale Scratching the Surface Signatures

Card	Low	High
SCAB Aleksander Barkov		
SCAG Alex Galchenyuk	15.00	40.00
SCAW Austin Watson	6.00	15.00
SCBB Beau Bennett	5.00	12.00
SCBG Brendan Gallagher	12.00	30.00
SCBJE Boone Jenner		
SCBNE Brock Nelson	4.00	10.00
SCCC Cory Conacher	5.00	12.00
SCCF Cam Fowler	3.00	8.00
SCCOY Charlie Coyle	4.00	10.00
SCDH Dougie Hamilton	12.00	30.00
SCEE Emerson Etem	4.00	10.00
SCJO Jamie Oleksiak	3.00	8.00
SCJTI Jarred Tinordi	4.00	10.00
SCJUS Justin Schultz	4.00	10.00
SCMDB Matt Dumba		
SCMGR Mikael Granlund	6.00	15.00
SCMIK Mikhail Grigorenko	5.00	12.00
SCNBE Nathan Beaulieu	3.00	8.00
SCNMK Nathan MacKinnon	30.00	80.00
SCNY Nail Yakupov	12.00	30.00
SCOM Olli Maatta		
SCQH Quinton Howden	5.00	12.00

Card	Low	High
SCRLY Morgan Rielly	10.00	25.00
SCRMP Ryan Murphy	4.00	10.00
SCRMR Ryan Murray	6.00	15.00
SCRSP Ryan Spooner	4.00	10.00
SCSL Scott Laughton	6.00	15.00
SCSMO Sean Monahan		
SCTT Tyler Toffoli	8.00	20.00

2013-14 Crown Royale Silhouette Materials

PRIME/15-25: .8X TO 2X BASIC JSY/100
PRIME/15-25: .6X TO 1.5X BASIC JSY/50

Card	Low	High
SAAN Artem Anisimov/100*	4.00	10.00
SAF Adam Foote/100*	5.00	12.00
SAKH Anton Khudobin/100*	4.00	10.00
SAMI Al MacInnis/100*	5.00	12.00
SBBE Brian Bellows/50*	5.00	12.00
SBEN Jamie Benn/100*	6.00	15.00
SBGI Brian Gionta/100*	4.00	10.00
SBHY Braden Holtby/100*	8.00	20.00
SBN Bernie Nicholls/50*	6.00	15.00
SBRM Brad Marchand/100*	6.00	15.00
SBRS Tom Barrasso/100*	5.00	12.00
SBSA Borje Salming/50*	6.00	15.00
SBYL Brian Boyle/100*	3.00	8.00
SCG Curtis Glencross/100*	5.00	12.00
SCTA Chris Tanev/100*	6.00	15.00
SDA Dave Andreychuk/100*	5.00	12.00
SDB David Backes/100*	5.00	12.00
SDBO Dan Boyle/100*	4.00	10.00
SDC Daniel Cleary/100*	5.00	12.00
SDJE Dustin Jeffrey/100*	3.00	8.00
SDK Duncan Keith/100*	6.00	15.00
SDKR David Krejci/100*	6.00	15.00
SDT Dave Taylor/50*	5.00	12.00
SET Eric Tangradi/100*	5.00	12.00
SGF Grant Fuhr/100*	5.00	12.00
SGUY Guy Lafleur/50*	8.00	20.00
SJE Jordan Eberle/50*	6.00	15.00
SJHI Jonas Hiller/100*	4.00	10.00
SJHO Jimmy Howard/50*	6.00	15.00
SJJ Jaromir Jagr/100*	10.00	25.00
SJLU Joffrey Lupul/100*	4.00	10.00
SJST Jarret Stoll/100*	4.00	10.00
SKO Kyle Okposo/100*	5.00	12.00
SKY Keith Yandle/100*	5.00	12.00
SLAI Brooks Laich/100*	3.00	8.00
SLS Luke Schenn/100*	3.00	8.00
SLSB Luca Sbisa/100*	4.00	10.00
SMBA Mikael Backlund/100*	4.00	10.00
SMBI Martin Biron/100*	4.00	10.00
SMDZ Michael Del Zotto/100*	3.00	8.00
SMG Marian Gaborik/50*	6.00	15.00
SMLO Matthew Lombardi/100*	3.00	8.00
SMMS Marty McSorley/100*	4.00	10.00
SMXT Maxime Talbot/100*	4.00	10.00
SNKB Niklas Backstrom/100*	4.00	10.00
SNS Nick Spaling/100*	3.00	8.00
SPAP P.A. Parenteau/100*	3.00	8.00
SPAS Paul Stastny/100*	5.00	12.00
SPB Pavel Bure/50*	8.00	20.00
SPLF Pat LaFontaine/50*	6.00	15.00
SPT Pierre Turgeon/100*	5.00	12.00
SPV Pat Verbeek/100*	3.00	8.00
SRB Ray Bourque/50*	10.00	25.00
SRBA Rod Brind'Amour/50*	6.00	15.00
SRBL Rob Blake/100*	5.00	12.00
SRBO Robert Bortuzzo/100*	3.00	8.00
SRF Ron Francis/100*	6.00	15.00
SRLE Reggie Leach/25*	6.00	15.00
SRPO Roman Polak/100*	3.00	8.00
SRRE Robyn Regehr/100*	3.00	8.00
SRSU Ryan Suter/100*	3.00	8.00
SRT Rick Tocchet/100*	5.00	12.00
SSBR Sheldon Brookbank/100*	3.00	8.00
SSC Sidney Crosby/50*	25.00	60.00
SSD Shane Doan/100*	4.00	10.00
SSGR Stu Grimson/100*	3.00	8.00
SSHA Scott Hartnell/100*	5.00	12.00
SSK Saku Koivu/100*	5.00	12.00
STPL Tomas Plekanec/100*	6.00	15.00
STR Tuukka Rask/100*	5.00	12.00

2013-14 Crown Royale Silhouette Materials Signatures

*PRIME/25: .6X TO 1.5X JSY AU/99

Card	Low	High
SSAL Andrew Ladd/99*	10.00	25.00
SSBE Brian Elliott/99*	8.00	20.00
SSBP Bernie Parent/25*	15.00	40.00
SSBS Brendan Shanahan/25*	25.00	50.00
SSCN Cam Neely/25*	15.00	40.00
SSCP Carey Price/25*	50.00	120.00
SSGH Gordie Howe/10*		
SSHL Henrik Lundqvist/25*	20.00	50.00
SSIL Igor Larionov/25*	15.00	40.00
SSJN Joe Nieuwendyk/99*	10.00	25.00
SSJP Joe Pavelski/99*	10.00	25.00
SSJQ Jonathan Quick/99*	25.00	50.00
SSMB Martin Brodeur/25*	40.00	80.00
SSMC Mike Cammalleri/99*	8.00	20.00
SSMM Mark Messier/25*		
SSNG Nathan Gerbe/99*	6.00	15.00
SSPR Patrick Roy/25*	50.00	100.00
SSRG Ryan Getzlaf/99*	15.00	40.00
SSRM Ryan Miller/99*	10.00	25.00
SSRV Rogie Vachon/25*	20.00	50.00
SSCGX Claude Giroux/99*	30.00	60.00
SSJTH Joe Thornton/99*	12.00	30.00
SSLUC Luc Robitaille/99*	10.00	25.00
SSMDU Matt Duchene/99*	10.00	25.00
SSMHE Milan Hejduk/99*	8.00	20.00
SSOVI Alex Ovechkin/25*	60.00	150.00
SSPKE Phil Kessel/99*	10.00	25.00
SSRJO Roman Josi/99*	10.00	25.00
SSRNH Ryan Nugent-Hopkins/99*	12.00	30.00

2013-14 Crown Royale Silver Chalice Materials

*PRIME/25: .8X TO 2X BASIC JSY
*PRIME/25: .6X TO 1.5X BASIC JSY SP

Card	Low	High
SIBC Bobby Clarke	6.00	15.00
SIBH Brett Hull	5.00	12.00
SIBS Brendan Shanahan	8.00	20.00
SIBSY Mike Bossy SP	6.00	15.00
SICCR Corey Crawford	6.00	15.00
SICPE Corey Perry	5.00	12.00
SIGH Gordie Howe SP		
SIHZ Henrik Zetterberg	6.00	15.00
SIJN Joe Nieuwendyk	5.00	12.00
SIJQ Jonathan Quick	8.00	20.00
SIJS Joe Sakic	8.00	20.00
SIMB Martin Brodeur SP	12.00	30.00
SIMHE Milan Hejduk	4.00	10.00
SIML Mario Lemieux SP	20.00	50.00
SIMM Mark Messier SP	8.00	20.00
SIMSL Martin St. Louis	5.00	12.00
SINL Nicklas Lidstrom	8.00	20.00
SIPC Paul Coffey	6.00	15.00
SIPEL Patrik Elias	5.00	12.00
SIPK Patrick Kane SP	12.00	30.00
SIPR Patrick Roy	12.00	30.00
SIRBA Rod Brind'Amour	4.00	10.00
SISC Sidney Crosby	15.00	40.00
SISY Steve Yzerman	8.00	20.00
SIZC Zdeno Chara	5.00	12.00

2013-14 Crown Royale Sovereign Sigs

*RUBY/25: .6X TO 1.5X BASIC AU

Card	Low	High
SOAA Akim Aliu	2.50	6.00
SOAJO Andrew Joudrey	2.50	6.00
SOANE Aaron Ness	2.50	6.00
SOANL Anton Lander	2.50	6.00
SOASH Carter Ashton	2.50	6.00
SOBDU Brandon Dubinsky	3.00	8.00
SOBRB Brent Burns	4.00	10.00
SOBRS Brian Strait	2.50	6.00
SOCA Craig Anderson	4.00	10.00
SOCCL Cal Clutterbuck	4.00	10.00
SOCCM Carter Camper	2.50	6.00
SOCHP Chet Pickard	2.50	6.00
SOCK Chris Kreider	4.00	10.00
SOCTR Corey Tropp	2.50	6.00
SODBO Dan Boyle	4.00	10.00
SODDU Devan Dubnyk	4.00	10.00
SODHA Dan Hamhuis	3.00	8.00
SODHT Derian Hatcher	2.50	6.00
SODRU David Rundblad	3.00	8.00
SODSA Denis Savard	5.00	12.00
SODW Doug Wilson	3.00	8.00
SOEF Eric Fehr	2.50	6.00
SOGB Gabriel Bourque	3.00	8.00
SOGD Gabriel Dumont	4.00	10.00
SOGNY Gustav Nyquist	8.00	20.00
SOJA Jake Allen	5.00	12.00
SOJCO Joe Colborne	4.00	10.00
SOJF Joe Finley	2.50	6.00
SOJGA Jake Gardiner	5.00	12.00
SOJM Jacob Markstrom	3.00	8.00
SOJSC Jaden Schwartz	5.00	12.00
SOJSI Jakob Silfverberg	3.00	8.00
SOJVI Joe Vitale	2.50	6.00
SOJZU Jason Zucker	3.00	8.00
SOKA Karl Alzner	2.50	6.00
SOKPO Kevin Poulin	3.00	8.00
SOLI Leland Irving	3.00	8.00
SOLMD Lane MacDermid	3.00	8.00
SOMDZ Michael Del Zotto	2.50	6.00
SOMHV Marty Havlat	5.00	12.00
SOMIS Michael Stone	3.00	8.00
SOMST Mark Stone	3.00	8.00
SONKU Nikolai Kulemin	3.00	8.00
SORJ Ryan Johansen	5.00	12.00
SORMA Robert Mayer	3.00	8.00
SORMI Rick Middleton	5.00	12.00
SORRA Rob Ray	4.00	10.00
SORSH Riley Sheahan	2.50	6.00
SOSB Sven Baertschi	5.00	12.00
SOSCH Shane Churla	2.50	6.00
SOSDE Simon Despres	3.00	8.00
SOSVA Semyon Varlamov	5.00	12.00
SOTBA Tyson Barrie	4.00	10.00
SOTER Tim Erixon	2.50	6.00
SOTK Torey Krug	6.00	15.00
SOTM Torrey Mitchell	2.50	6.00
SOTOR Terry O'Reilly	5.00	12.00

2013-14 Crown Royale Voices of the Game Autographs

Card	Low	High
VGBF Bernie Federko	5.00	12.00
VGCR Celena Rae	12.00	30.00
VGDD Darren Dreger	6.00	15.00
VGGR Glenn Resch	6.00	15.00
VGHR Howie Rose	8.00	20.00
VGJC Jim Cornelison	10.00	25.00
VGJJ Jeff Jimerson	10.00	25.00
VGJR Jeremy Roenick	8.00	20.00
VGKJ Keith Jones	6.00	15.00
VGKT Kathryn Tappen	50.00	100.00
VGKW Kevin Weekes	5.00	12.00
VGMD Mark Donnelly	5.00	12.00
VGPT Pia Toscano	10.00	25.00
VGRFE Ray Ferraro	5.00	12.00
VGTC Terry Crisp	8.00	20.00

1970-71 Dad's Cookies

The 1970-71 Dad's Cookies set contains 144 unnumbered color cards. Each card measures approximately 1 7/8" by 5 3/8". Each player is pictured on the front dressed in an "NHL Players" emblazoned jersey. The fronts contain player statistics for the 1969-70 season and for his career. The backs, in both English and French, are the same for all cards. The backs contain an ad for these cards and Dad's Cookies, a special offer for an NHL Players Association decal and a 1969 NHL Players Association copyright line.

Card	Low	High
COMPLETE SET (144)	100.00	200.00
1 Lou Angotti	.75	2.00
2 Don Awrey	.50	1.00
3 Bob Baun	1.25	3.00
4 Jean Beliveau	6.00	15.00
5 Red Berenson	.75	2.00
6 Gary Bergman	.50	1.00
7 Les Binkley	1.00	2.50
8 Andre Boudrias	.50	1.00
9 Wally Boyer	.50	1.00
10 Arnie Brown	.50	1.00
11 Johnny Bucyk	1.50	4.00
12 Charlie Burns	.50	1.00
13 Larry Cahan	.50	1.00
14 Gerry Cheevers	2.50	6.00
15 Bobby Clarke	5.00	12.00
16 Wayne Connelly	.50	1.00
17 Yvan Cournoyer	1.50	4.00
18 Roger Crozier	1.00	2.50
19 Ray Cullen	.50	1.00
20 Denis DeJordy	1.00	2.50
21 Alex Delvecchio	1.50	4.00
22 Bob Dillabough	.50	1.00
23 Gary Doak	.50	1.00
24 Gary Dornhoefer	1.00	2.50
25 Dick Duff	.75	2.00
26 Tim Ecclestone	.50	1.00
27 Roy Edwards	1.00	2.50
28 Gerry Ehman	.50	1.00
29 Ron Ellis	.75	2.00
30 Phil Esposito	5.00	12.00
31 Tony Esposito	5.00	12.00
32 Doug Favell	1.00	2.50
33 John Ferguson	.75	2.00
34 Norm Ferguson	.50	1.00
35 Reg Fleming	.50	1.00
36 Bill Flett	.50	1.00
37 Bruce Gamble	1.00	2.50
38 Jean-Guy Gendron	.50	1.00
39 Ed Giacomin	2.00	5.00
40 Rod Gilbert	1.50	4.00
41 Bill Goldsworthy	.75	2.00
42 Phil Goyette	.50	1.00
43 Danny Grant	.75	2.00
44 Ted Green	.75	2.00
45 Vic Hadfield	.75	2.00
46 Al Hamilton	.50	1.00
47 Ted Hampson	.50	1.00
48 Terry Harper	.75	2.00
49 Ted Harris	.50	1.00
50 Paul Henderson	2.50	6.00
51 Bryan Hextall	.50	1.00
52 Bill Hicke	.50	1.00
53 Larry Hillman	.50	1.00
54 Wayne Hillman	.50	1.00
55 Charlie Hodge	1.25	3.00
56 Ken Hodge	.75	2.00
57 Gordie Howe	10.00	25.00
58 Harry Howell	1.00	2.50
59 Bobby Hull	8.00	20.00
60 Dennis Hull	.75	2.00
61 Earl Ingarfield	.50	1.00
62 Doug Jarrett	.50	1.00
63 Gary Jarrett	.50	1.00
64 Ed Johnston	1.00	2.50
65 Dave Keon	1.50	4.00
66 Skip Krake	.50	1.00
67 Orland Kurtenbach	.75	2.00
68 Andre Lacroix	.75	2.00
69 Jacques Laperriere	1.25	3.00
70 Jacques Lemaire	1.50	4.00
71 Rick Ley	.50	1.00
72 Bruce MacGregor	.50	1.00
73 Keith Magnuson	.75	2.00
74 Frank Mahovlich	2.00	5.00
75 Chico Maki	.50	1.00
76 Gilles Marotte	.50	1.00
77 Bert Marshall	.50	1.00
78 Don Marshall	.50	1.00
79 Pit Martin	.75	2.00
80 Keith McCreary	.50	1.00
81 Ab McDonald	.50	1.00
82 Jim McKenny	.75	2.00
83 John McKenzie	.75	2.00
84 Mike McMahon	.50	1.00
85 Larry Mickey	.50	1.00
86 Stan Mikita	2.50	6.00
87 Doug Mohns	.50	1.00
88 Wayne Muloin	.50	1.00
89 Jim Neilson	.50	1.00
90 Bob Nevin	.50	1.00
91 Murray Oliver	.50	1.00
92 Bobby Orr	20.00	40.00
93 Danny O'Shea	.50	1.00
94 Rosaire Paiement	.50	1.00
95 Bernie Parent	2.50	6.00
96 Jean-Paul Parise	.50	1.00
97 Brad Park	4.00	10.00
98 Mike Pelyk	.50	1.00
99 Gilbert Perreault	2.00	5.00
100 Noel Picard	.50	1.00
101 Barclay Plager	.75	2.00
102 Jacques Plante	6.00	15.00
103 Tracy Pratt	.50	1.00
104 Dean Prentice	.50	1.00
105 Jean Pronovost	.75	2.00
106 Bob Pulford	.75	2.00
107 Pat Quinn	1.00	2.50
108 Jean Ratelle	1.00	2.50
109 Matt Ravlich	.50	1.00
110 Mickey Redmond	1.00	2.50
111 Henri Richard	2.50	6.00
112 Jim Roberts	.50	1.00
113 Dale Rolfe	.50	1.00
114 Bobby Rousseau	.50	1.00
115 Gary Sabourin	.50	1.00
116 Derek Sanderson	2.50	6.00
117 Glen Sather	1.50	4.00
118 Serge Savard	1.00	2.50
119 Ken Schinkel	.50	1.00
120 Rod Seiling	.50	1.00
121 Brit Selby	.50	1.00
122 Eddie Shack	1.50	4.00
123 Floyd Smith	.50	1.00
124 Fred Stanfield	.50	1.00
125 Pat Stapleton	.60	1.50
126 Frank St.Marseille	.50	1.00
127 Dale Tallon	.60	1.50
128 Walt Tkaczuk	.50	1.00
129 J.C. Tremblay	.50	1.00
130 Norm Ullman	.75	2.00
131 Garry Unger	.75	2.00
132 Rogatien Vachon	2.00	5.00
133 Carol Vadnais	.50	1.00
134 Ed Van Impe	.50	1.00
135 Bob Wall	.50	1.00
136 Mike Walton	.50	1.00
137 Bryan Watson	.50	1.00
138 Joe Watson	.50	1.00
139 Tom Webster	.50	1.00
140 Juha Widing	1.00	2.50
141 Tom Williams	.50	1.00
142 Jim Wiste	.50	1.00
143 Gump Worsley	2.50	6.00
144 Bob Woytowich	.75	2.00

2009-10 Danone Foods Pee-Wee Quebec World Cshampionships

Card	Low	High
COMPLETE SET (10)	4.00	10.00
1 Patrick Roy	1.00	2.50
2 Rick Nash	.30	.75
3 Vincent Lecavalier	.30	.75
4 Simon Gagne	.40	1.00
5 Patrice Bergeron	.50	1.25
6 Marc-Andre Fleury	.60	1.50
7 Mike Cammalleri	.30	.75
8 Mike Komisarek	.30	.75
9 Anze Kopitar	.60	1.50
10 Thomas Vanek	.40	1.00

1983-84 Devils Postcards

This set is the first confirmed to feature the franchise transferred from Colorado to New Jersey. The color postcards feature action photos and were issued by the team as promotional items at player appearances.

Card	Low	High
COMPLETE SET (25)	10.00	25.00
1 Mike Antonovich	.20	.50
2 Mel Bridgman	.30	.75
3 Aaron Broten	.20	.50
4 Murray Bromwell	.30	.75
5 Dave Cameron	.30	.75
6 Rich Chernomaz	.20	.50
7 Joe Cirella	.30	.75
8 Ken Daneyko	.60	1.50
9 Larry Floyd	.20	.50
10 Paul Gagne	.20	.50
11 Mike Kitchen	.30	.75
12 Jeff Larmer	.30	.75
13 Don Lever	.20	.50
14 Dave Lewis	.20	.50
15 Bob Lorimer	.20	.50
16 Ron Low	.30	.75
17 Jan Ludvig	.20	.50
18 John Maclean	2.50	6.00
19 Bob MacMillan	.30	.75
20 Hector Marini	.20	.50
21 Rick Meagher	.20	.50
22 Grant Mulvey	.30	.75
23 Glenn Resch	.60	1.50
24 Phil Russell	.20	.50
25 Pat Verbeek	2.50	6.00

1984-85 Devils Postcards

This 25-card set of New Jersey Devils features on the front borderless color photos of the players, with two team logos (in green and red) in the white stripe below the picture. The cards measure approximately 3 1/4" by 6 1/8" and are in the postcard type format. On the left half of the back appear a black and white head shot of the player, basic player information, and the Devils' team logo. The cards are checklisted below according to uniform number. The side panel of the package of Colgate Dental Cream listed the checklist of the complete set. The cards of John MacLean and Kirk Muller predate their Rookie Cards.

Card	Low	High
COMPLETE SET (25)	8.00	20.00
1 Chico Resch	.75	2.00
2 Joe Cirella	.30	.75
4 Bob Lorimer	.20	.50
5 Phil Russell	.20	.50
8 Dave Pichette	.20	.50
9 Don Lever	.30	.75
10 Aaron Broten	.20	.50
12 Pat Verbeek	2.00	5.00
14 Rich Chernomaz	.20	.50
15 John MacLean	1.50	4.00
16 Rick Meagher	.20	.50
17 Paul Gagne	.20	.50
18 Mel Bridgman	.30	.75
19 Rich Preston	.20	.50
20 Tim Higgins	.20	.50
21 Bob Hoffmeyer	.20	.50
22 Doug Sulliman	.20	.50
23 Bruce Driver	.40	1.00
25 Dave Lewis	.20	.50
27 Kirk Muller	2.00	5.00
28 Uli Hiemer	.20	.50
29 Jan Ludvig	.20	.50
30 Ron Low	.30	.75
33 Hannu Kamppurri	.30	.75
NNO Doug Carpenter CO	.20	.50

1985-86 Devils Postcards

This ten-card set of New Jersey Devils features on the front borderless color player photos. The cards measure approximately 3 5/8" by 5 1/2" and are in the postcard format. The horizontal backs are divided in half by a thin black line and have the year, biographical information, home town, and a career highlight at the upper left corner. The cards are unnumbered and checklisted below in alphabetical order. Key cards in the set are Kirk Muller in his Rookie Card year and Craig Billington prior to his Rookie Card year.

Card	Low	High
COMPLETE SET (10)	5.60	14.00
1 Greg Adams	.60	1.50
2 Perry Anderson	.40	1.00
3 Craig Billington	.75	2.00
4 Alain Chevrier	.60	1.50
5 Paul Gagne	.40	1.00
6 Mark Johnson	.40	1.00
7 Kirk Muller	1.50	4.00
8 Chico Resch	1.00	2.50
9 Randy Velischek	.40	1.00
10 Craig Wolanin	.40	1.00

1986-87 Devils Police

This 20-card set was jointly sponsored by the New Jersey Devils, S.O.B.E.R., Howard Bank, and Independent Insurance Agents of Bergen Country. Logos for these sponsors appear on the bottom of the card back. The front features a color action photo of the player, with the Devils' and NHL logos superimposed over the top corners of the picture. A thin black line and a green line serves as the inner and outer borders respectively; the area in between is yellow, with printing in the team's colors red and black. In addition to sponsors' logos, the back has biographical information, an anti-drug message, and career statistics. We have checklisted the cards below in alphabetical order, with uniform number to the right of the player's name.

Card	Low	High
COMPLETE SET (20)	12.00	30.00
1 Greg Adams 24	.60	1.50
2 Perry Anderson 25	.40	1.00
3 Timo Blomqvist 5	.40	1.00
4 Andy Brickley 26	.40	1.00
5 Mel Bridgman 18	.60	1.50
6 Aaron Broten 10	.40	1.00
7 Alain Chevrier 30	.60	1.50
8 Joe Cirella 2	.60	1.50
9 Ken Daneyko 3	.60	1.50
10 Bruce Driver 23	.75	2.00
11 Uli Hiemer 28	.40	1.00
12 Mark Johnson 12	.60	1.50
13 Jan Ludvig 29	.40	1.00
14 John MacLean 15	1.50	4.00
15 Peter McNab 7	.60	1.50
16 Kirk Muller 9	2.00	5.00
17 Doug Sulliman 22	.40	1.00
18 Randy Velischek 27	.40	1.00
19 Pat Verbeek	2.00	5.00
20 Craig Wolanin 6	.40	1.00

1988-89 Devils Carretta

This 30-card set has color action photos of the New Jersey Devils on the front, with a thin black border on white card stock. The cards measure approximately 2 7/8" by 4 1/4". The team name and logo on the top are printed in green and red; the text below the picture, giving player name, uniform number, and position, is printed in black. The horizontally oriented back has career statistics, a team logo, and a Carretta Trucking logo. We have checklisted the cards below in alphabetical order. Brendan Shanahan appears in his Rookie Card year.

Card	Low	High
COMPLETE SET (30)	10.00	25.00
1 Perry Anderson 25	.20	.50
2 Bob Bellemore CO	.20	.50
3 Aaron Broten 10	.20	.50
4 Doug Brown 24	.20	.50
5 Sean Burke 1	1.25	3.00
6 Anders Carlsson 20	.20	.50
7 Joe Cirella 2	.20	.50
8 Pat Conacher 32	.20	.50
9 Ken Daneyko 3	.30	.75
10 Bruce Driver 23	.30	.75
11 Bob Hoffmeyer CO	.20	.50
12 Jamie Huscroft 4	.20	.50
13 Mark Johnson 12	.30	.75
14 Jim Korn 14	.20	.50
15 Tom Kurvers 5	.20	.50
16 Lou Lamoriello P/GM	.08	.25
17 Claude Loiselle 19	.20	.50
18 John MacLean 15	.75	2.00
19 David Maley 8	.20	.50
20 Doug McKay CO	.08	.25
21 Kirk Muller 9	.75	2.00
22 Jack O'Callahan 7	.20	.50
23 Steve Rooney 18	.20	.50
24 Bob Sauve 28	.30	.75
25 Jim Schoenfeld CO	.40	1.00
26 Brendan Shanahan 11	6.00	15.00
27 Patrik Sundstrom 17	.30	.75
28 Randy Velischek 27	.20	.50
29 Pat Verbeek 16	.75	2.00
30 Craig Wolanin 6	.20	.50

1989-90 Devils Caretta

This 29-card set has color action photos of the New Jersey Devils on the front, with a thin red border on white card stock. The team name and logo on the top are printed in green and red; the text below the picture, giving player name, uniform number, and position, is printed in black. The horizontal back provides brief biographical information and career statistics, a black-and-white picture and a Caretta Trucking logo. (The set also was issued without the trucking logo.) The cards measure approximately 2 7/8" by 4 1/4". These unnumbered cards are checklisted below alphabetically with sweater number noted to the right.

Card	Low	High
COMPLETE SET (29)	8.00	20.00
1 Tommy Albelin 26	.20	.50
2 Bob Bellemore CO	.08	.25
3 Neil Brady 19	.20	.50
4 Aaron Broten 10	.20	.50
5 Doug Brown 24	.20	.50
6 Sean Burke 1	.75	2.00
7 Pat Conacher 32	.20	.50
8 John Cunniff CO	.08	.25
9 Ken Daneyko 3	.20	.50
10 Bruce Driver 23	.40	1.00
11 Slava Fetisov 2	.75	2.00
12 Mark Johnson 12	.20	.50
13 Jim Korn 14	.20	.50
14 Lou Lamoriello P/GM	.08	.25
15 John MacLean 15	.60	1.50
16 David Maley 8	.20	.50
17 Kirk Muller 9	.75	2.00
18 Janne Ojanen 22	.20	.50
19 Walt Poddubny 21	.20	.50
20 Reijo Ruotsalainen 29	.20	.50
21 Brendan Shanahan 11	2.00	5.00
22 Sergei Starikov 4	.20	.50
23 Patrik Sundstrom 17	.20	.50
24 Peter Sundstrom 20	.20	.50
25 Chris Terreri 31	.40	1.00
26 Sylvain Turgeon 16	.20	.50
27 Randy Velischek 27	.20	.50
28 Eric Weinrich 7	.20	.50
29 Craig Wolanin 6	.20	.50

1990-91 Devils Team Issue

This set contains 30 standard-size cards and features members of the New Jersey Devils. The front has a color photo of the player, with the team logo in the upper left corner. The back has statistical information. These cards are unnumbered and are checklisted below in alphabetical order.

Card	Low	High
COMPLETE SET (30)	6.00	15.00
1 Tommy Albelin	.15	.40
2 Laurie Boschman	.15	.40
3 Doug Brown	.20	.50
4 Sean Burke	.60	1.50
5 Tim Burke	.15	.40
6 Zdeno Ciger	.20	.50
7 Pat Conacher	.15	.40
8 Troy Crowder	.20	.50
9 John Cunniff CO	.08	.25
10 Ken Daneyko	.30	.75
11 Bruce Driver	.20	.50
12 Slava Fetisov	.30	.75
13 Alexei Kasatonov	.20	.50
14 Lou Lamoriello P/GM	.08	.25
15 Claude Lemieux	.40	1.00
16 David Maley	.15	.40
17 John MacLean	.40	1.00
18 Jon Morris	.15	.40
19 Kirk Muller	.60	1.50
20 Lee Norwood	.15	.40
21 Myles O'Connor	.15	.40
22 Walt Poddubny	.20	.50
23 Brendan Shanahan	2.00	5.00
24 Peter Stastny	.60	1.50
25 Alan Stewart	.15	.40
26 Warren Strelow	.15	.40
27 Doug Sulliman	.15	.40
28 Patrik Sundstrom	.20	.50
29 Chris Terreri	.20	.50
30 Eric Weinrich	.20	.50

1991-92 Devils Teams Carvel

This ten-card set features team photos of the ten Devils teams from 1982-83 through 1991-92. The cards have a coupon for Carvel Ice Cream with an entry form for the "Shoot to Win" contest. The backs list all the players who are pictured and the statistical leaders from that particular year. The cards are unnumbered and measure approximately 2 1/2" by 6" with coupon. One card was issued per spectator at certain home games during the 1991-92 season.

Card	Low	High
COMPLETE SET (10)	8.00	20.00
1 1982-83 Devils Team	1.25	3.00
2 1983-84 Devils Team	1.00	2.50
3 1984-85 Devils Team	1.00	2.50
4 1985-86 Devils Team	1.00	2.50
5 1986-87 Devils Team	1.00	2.50
6 1987-88 Devils Team	1.00	2.50
7 1988-89 Devils Team	1.00	2.50
8 1989-90 Devils Team	1.00	2.50
9 1990-91 Devils Team	1.00	2.50
10 1991-92 Devils Team	1.00	2.50

1996-97 Devils Team Issue

This attractive team-issued set is complete at 30-cards. It was apparently issued as a premium at a game sometime during the '96-97 season and was sponsored by Sharp Electronics. The fronts feature action color photos surrounded by a red border. The player's name and number appear at the top, while his position and team logo grace the bottom. The backs include a black and white head shot as well as comprehensive statistics.

Card	Low	High
COMPLETE SET (30)	12.00	30.00
1 Mike Dunham	.75	2.00
3 Ken Daneyko	.20	.50
4 Scott Stevens	.30	.75
10 Denis Pederson	.30	.75
11 Steve Sullivan	.40	1.00
12 Bill Guerin	.75	2.00
14 Brian Rolston	.30	.75
15 John MacLean	.30	.75
16 Bobby Holik	.30	.75
17 Petr Sykora	.75	2.00
18 Sergei Brylin	.20	.50
19 Bob Carpenter	.08	.25
20 Jay Pandolfo	.20	.50
21 Randy McKay	.30	.75
22 Patrik Elias	4.00	10.00
23 Dave Andreychuk	.20	.50
24 Lyle Odelein	.20	.50
25 Valeri Zelepukin	.08	.25
26 Jason Smith	.20	.50
27 Scott Niedermayer	.40	1.00
28 Kevin Dean	.08	.25
29 Shawn Chambers	.08	.25
30 Martin Brodeur	2.00	5.00
32 Steve Thomas	.20	.50
33 Reid Simpson	.08	.25
NNO John J. McMullen(Chairman)	.02	.10
NNO Jacques Lemaire CO	.20	.50
NNO Robbie Ftorek ASST CO	.08	.25
NNO Lou Lamoriello GM	.02	.10
NNO Jacques Caron ACO	.02	.10

1997-98 Devils Team Issue

This set features the Devils of the NHL. The cards were sponsored by Zebra Pens and were given away as a promotion at a single home game.

Card	Low	High
COMPLETE SET (32)	8.00	20.00
1 Mike Dunham	.40	1.00
2 Sheldon Souray	.15	.40
3 Ken Daneyko	.15	.40
4 Scott Stevens	.30	.75
5 Ken Sutton	.15	.40
6 Brad Bombardir	.15	.40
7 Vlastimil Kroupa	.15	.40
8 Denis Pederson	.15	.40
9 Bill Guerin	.40	1.00
10 John MacLean	.15	.40
11 Bobby Holik	.20	.50
12 Petr Sykora	.40	1.00
13 Sergei Brylin	.15	.40
14 Bobby Carpenter	.15	.40
15 Jay Pandolfo	.15	.40
16 Randy McKay	.20	.50
17 Scott Daniels	.15	.40
18 Dave Andreychuk	.20	.50
19 Lyle Odelein	.15	.40
20 Valeri Zelepukin	.15	.40
21 Patrik Elias	1.25	3.00
22 Kevin Dean	.15	.40
23 Krzysztof Oliwa	.30	.75
24 Martin Brodeur	1.25	3.00
25 Steve Thomas	.20	.50
26 Reid Simpson	.15	.40
27 Doug Gilmour	.40	1.00
28 Jacques Lemaire CO	.08	.25
29 Robbie Ftorek CO	.02	.10
30 Jacques Caron CO	.02	.10
31 Lou Lamoriello PRES	.02	.10
32 John McMullen CHAIR	.02	.10

1998-99 Devils Team Issue

Card	Low	High
COMPLETE SET (30)		20.00
1 Dave Andreychuk	.30	.75
2 Jason Arnott	.30	.75
3 Brad Bombardir	.20	.50
4 Martin Brodeur	2.00	5.00
5 Sergei Brylin	.20	.50
6 Jacques Caron ACO	.02	.10
7 Bob Carpenter ACO	.02	.10
8 Ken Daneyko	.20	.50
9 Kevin Dean	.20	.50
10 Patrik Elias	.40	1.00
11 Slava Fetisov CO	.08	.25
12 Robbie Ftorek HCO	.02	.10
13 Bobby Holik	.20	.50
14 Sasha Lakovic	.20	.50
15 Lou Lamoriello GM	.02	.10
16 John Madden	.40	1.00
17 Randy McKay	.20	.50
18 John McMullen OWN	.02	.10
19 Brendan Morrison	.40	1.00
20 Scott Niedermayer	.30	.75
21 Lyle Odelein	.20	.50
22 Krzysztof Oliwa	.40	1.00
23 Jay Pandolfo	.30	.75
24 Denis Pederson	.20	.50
25 Brian Rolston	.30	.75
26 Vadim Sharifijanov	.20	.50
27 Sheldon Souray	.20	.50
28 Scott Stevens	.40	1.00
29 Petr Sykora	.40	1.00
30 Chris Terreri	.30	.75

1999-00 Devils Team Issue

This set features the Devils of the NHL. The set is believed to have been issued as a promotional giveaway and was sponsored by PSEG Energy.

Card	Low	High
COMPLETE SET (31)	8.00	20.00
1 Scott Stevens	.30	.75
2 Sheldon Souray	.15	.40
3 Ken Daneyko	.15	.40
4 Brad Bombardir	.15	.40
5 Vadim Sharifijanov	.15	.40
6 Brendan Morrison	.40	1.00
7 John Madden	.40	1.00
8 Sergei Nemchinov	.15	.40
9 Bobby Holik	.20	.50
10 Petr Sykora	.40	1.00
11 Sergei Brylin	.15	.40
12 Denis Pederson	.15	.40
13 Jay Pandolfo	.15	.40
14 Randy McKay	.20	.50
15 Claude Lemieux	.30	.75
16 Scott Gomez	.40	1.00
17 Lyle Odelein	.15	.40
18 Jason Arnott	.30	.75
19 Patrik Elias	.60	1.50
20 Scott Niedermayer	.30	.75
21 Brian Rafalski	.20	.50
22 Krzysztof Oliwa	.40	1.00
23 Martin Brodeur	1.50	4.00
24 Chris Terreri	.20	.50
25 Robbie Ftorek CO	.15	.40
26 Slava Fetisov CO	.20	.50
27 Larry Robinson CO	.20	.50
28 Jacques Caron CO	.02	.10
29 Lou Lamoriello GM	.02	.10
30 Dr. John J. McMullen	.02	.10
31 PSEG Energy	.02	.10

2000-01 Devils Team Issue

This set was issued as a promotional giveaway at a single home game early in the season.

Card	Low	High
COMPLETE SET (30)	10.00	25.00
1 Jason Arnott	.40	1.00
2 Martin Brodeur	2.00	5.00
3 Sergei Brylin	.20	.50
4 Mike Commodore	.30	.75
5 Ken Daneyko	.20	.50
6 Patrik Elias	.80	2.00
7 Sascha Goc	.20	.50
8 Scott Gomez	.40	1.00
9 Bobby Holik	.30	.75
10 Steve Kelly	.20	.50
11 John Madden	.80	2.00
12 Randy McKay	.30	.75
13 Jim McKenzie	.20	.50
14 Alexander Mogilny	.30	.75
15 Sergei Nemchinov	.20	.50
16 Scott Niedermayer	.40	1.00
17 Jay Pandolfo	.20	.50
18 Brian Rafalski	.20	.50
19 Scott Stevens	.40	1.00
20 Turner Stevenson	.20	.50
21 Ken Sutton	.20	.50
22 Petr Sykora	.80	2.00

23 Chris Terreri .30 .75
24 Colin White .30 .75
25 Larry Robinson CO .20 .50
26 Slava Fetisov ACO .20 .50
27 Kurt Kleinendorst ACO .04 .10
28 Jacques Caron ACO .04 .10
29 Lou Lamoriello GM .04 .10
30 2000 Stanley Cup Champions .20 .50

2001-02 Devils Team Issue

This set features the Devils of the NHL. The set was sponsored by Model's and was issued as a promotional giveaway at a home game early in the 2001-02 season.

COMPLETE SET (25) 8.00 20.00
1 Jason Arnott .40 1.00
2 Martin Brodeur 2.00 5.00
3 Sergei Brylin .20 .50
4 Jacques Caron ACO .04 .10
5 Pierre Dagenais .20 .50
6 Patrik Elias .75 2.00
7 Slava Fetisov ACO .20 .50
8 Scott Gomez .40 1.00
9 Bobby Holik .30 .75
10 Lou Lamoriello GM .04 .10
11 Jay Leach ACO .04 .10
12 John Madden .40 1.00
13 Randy McKay .30 .75
14 Jim McKenzie .20 .50
15 Sergei Nemchinov .20 .50
16 Scott Niedermayer .40 1.00
17 Devil Mascot .04 .10
18 Jay Pandolfo .20 .50
19 Brian Rafalski .20 .50
20 Larry Robinson CO .20 .50
21 Andreas Salomonsson .75 2.00
22 Scott Stevens .40 1.00
23 Turner Stevenson .20 .50
24 Petr Sykora .75 2.00
NNO Title Card .04 .10

2002-03 Devils Team Issue

Issued by the team at a game late in 2002, this 30-card set featured color photos on the card fronts and blank backs. The cards were unnumbered and are listed below by jersey number.

COMPLETE SET (30)
1 Ken Daneyko .15 .40
2 Scott Stevens .40 1.00
3 Colin White .15 .40
4 Tommy Albelin .15 .40
5 Steve Guolla .15 .40
6 Jiri Bicek .20 .50
7 Craig Darby .15 .40
8 Oleg Tverdovsky .15 .40
9 John Madden .40 1.00
10 Jeff Friesen .30 .75
11 Brian Gionta .40 1.00
12 Jamie Langenbrunner .30 .75
13 Christian Berglund .15 .40
14 Sergei Brylin .15 .40
15 Jim McKenzie .15 .40
16 Jay Pandolfo .15 .40
17 Scott Gomez .30 .75
18 Turner Stevenson .15 .40
19 Joe Nieuwendyk .40 1.00
20 Patrik Elias .30 .75
21 Scott Niedermayer .40 1.00
22 Brian Rafalski .20 .50
23 Martin Brodeur 2.00 5.00
24 Corey Schwab .30 .75
25 Lou Lamoriello GM .04 .10
26 Pat Burns HCO .04 .10
27 Bobby Carpenter ACO .04 .10
28 John MacLean ACO .04 .10
29 Jacques Caron CO .04 .10
30 Mascot .04 .10

2003-04 Devils Team Issue

This team set was sponsored by Verizon and handed out at a home game during the 2003-04 season. They are listed below by player number.

2 Sean Brown .20 .50
4 Scott Stevens .30 .75
5 Colin White .20 .50
6 Tommy Albelin .20 .50
7 Paul Martin .40 1.00
8 Igor Larionov .30 .75
10 Erik Rasmussen .20 .50
11 John Madden .40 1.00
12 Jeff Friesen .30 .75
14 Brian Gionta .75 2.00
15 Jamie Langenbrunner .30 .75
16 Mike Rupp .20 .50
17 Christian Berglund .20 .50
18 Sergei Brylin .20 .50
20 Jay Pandolfo .20 .50
23 Scott Gomez .40 1.00
24 Turner Stevenson .20 .50
25 David Hale .20 .50
26 Patrik Elias .40 1.00
27 Scott Niedermayer .40 1.00
28 Brian Rafalski .20 .50
29 Grant Marshall .20 .50
30 Martin Brodeur 2.00 5.00
35 Corey Schwab .30 .75
40 Scott Clemmensen .30 .75
41 Lou Lamoriello GM .04 .10
42 Pat Burns HCO .04 .10
43 Bob Carpenter ACO .04 .10
44 John MacLean ACO .04 .10
45 Jacques Laperiere ACO .04 .10
46 Jacques Caron ACO .04 .10
47 Mascot .04 .10

2005-06 Devils Team Issue

COMPLETE SET (30) 10.00 20.00
1 N.J. Devil MASCOT .02 .10
2 Jacques Caron ACO .02 .10
3 John MacLean ACO .02 .10
4 Jacques Laperriere ACO .02 .10
5 Larry Robinson CO .02 .10
6 Lou Lamoriello GM .02 .10
7 Alexander Mogilny .30 .75
8 Scott Clemmensen .30 .75
9 Ari Ahonen .30 .75
10 Martin Brodeur 2.00 5.00
11 Grant Marshall .20 .50
12 Brian Rafalski .20 .50
13 Patrik Elias .30 .75
14 David Hale .20 .50
15 Richard Matvichuk .20 .50
16 Scott Gomez .30 .75
17 Viktor Kozlov .20 .50
18 Jay Pandolfo .20 .50
19 Sergei Brylin .20 .50
20 Darren Langdon .30 .75
21 Jamie Langenbrunner .20 .50
22 Brain Gionta .40 1.00
23 John Madden .20 .50
24 Erik Rasmussen .20 .50
25 Zach Parise 2.00 5.00
26 Sean Brown .20 .50
27 Paul Martin .20 .50
28 Dan McGillis .20 .50
29 Colin White .20 .50
30 Vladimir Malakhov .20 .50

2006-07 Devils Team Set

COMPLETE SET (41) 10.00 25.00
1 Martin Brodeur 2.00 5.00
2 Alex Brooks .20 .50
3 Sergei Brylin .20 .50
4 Scott Clemmensen .20 .50
5 Jim Dowd .20 .50
6 Patrik Elias .30 .75
7 Brian Gionta .40 1.00
8 Scott Gomez .40 1.00
9 David Hale .20 .50
10 Cam Janssen .40 1.00
11 Dan LaCouture .20 .50
12 Jamie Langenbrunner .20 .50
13 Brad Lukowich .20 .50
14 John Madden .20 .50
15 Paul Martin .20 .50
16 Richard Matvichuk .20 .50
17 Alexander Mogilny .30 .75
18 Johnny Oduya .20 .50
19 Jay Pandolfo .20 .50
20 Zach Parise .75 2.00
21 Brian Rafalski .20 .50
22 Erik Rasmussen .20 .50
23 Mike Rupp .20 .50
24 Barry Tallackson .20 .50
25 Colin White .20 .50
26 Jason Wiemer .20 .50
27 Travis Zajac .40 1.00
28 Lou Lamoriello GM .10 .25
29 Claude Julien CO .10 .25
30 Jacques Laperriere ACO .10 .25
31 John MacLean ACO .10 .25
32 Jacques Caron ACO .10 .25
33 Mel Bridgman .20 .50
34 Bruce Driver .20 .50
35 Patrik Elias .30 .75
36 Don Lever .20 .50
37 Kirk Muller .20 .50
38 Scott Niedermayer .30 .75
39 Scott Stevens .30 .75
40 Ken Daneyko .20 .50
41 Scott Stevens .30 .75

2013-14 Devils Score NHL Draft

COMPLETE SET (6) 4.00 8.00
1 Martin Brodeur
2 Patrik Elias
3 Adam Henrique
4 Ilya Kovalchuk
5 Bryce Salvador
6 David Clarkson

1934-35 Diamond Matchbooks Silver

Covers from this first hockey matchbook issue generally feature color action shots with a silver background and green and black vertical bars on the cover's left side. "The Diamond Match Co., NYC" imprint appears on a double line below the striker. These matchbooks usually were issued in twin-packs through cigar and drug stores of the day. Complete matchbooks carry a 50 percent premium over the prices listed below.

COMPLETE SET (60) 1500.00 2400.00
1 Taffy Abel 15.00 25.00
2 Marty Barry 15.00 25.00
3 Red Beattie 15.00 25.00
4 Frank Boucher 25.00 40.00
5 Doug Brennan 15.00 25.00
6 Bill Brydge 15.00 25.00
7 Eddie Burke 35.00 50.00
8 Marty Burke 15.00 25.00
9 Gerald Carson 15.00 25.00
10 Lorne Chabot 35.00 50.00
11 Art Chapman 15.00 25.00
12 Dit Clapper 50.00 80.00
13 Lionel Conacher 50.00 80.00
14 Red Conn 15.00 25.00
15 Bill Cook 35.00 50.00
16 Bun Cook 35.00 50.00
17 Thomas Cook 18.00 30.00
18 Rosario Lolo Couture 15.00 25.00
19 Bob Davie 15.00 25.00
20 Cecil Dillon 15.00 25.00
21 Duke Dutkowski 15.00 25.00
22 Red Dutton 25.00 40.00
23 Johnny Gagnon 15.00 25.00
24 Chuck Gardiner 35.00 50.00
25 Johnny Gottselig 15.00 25.00
26 Robert Gracie 15.00 25.00
27 Lloyd Gross 15.00 25.00
28 Ott Heller 15.00 25.00
29 Normie Himes 15.00 25.00
30 Lionel Hitchman 35.00 50.00
31 Red Jackson 15.00 25.00
32 Roger Jenkins 15.00 25.00
33 Aurel Joliat 50.00 80.00
34 Butch Keeling 15.00 25.00
35 William Kendall 15.00 25.00
36 Jim Klein 15.00 25.00
37 Joe Lamb 15.00 25.00
38 Wildor Larochelle 18.00 30.00
39 Pit Lepine 15.00 25.00
40 Jack Leswick 15.00 25.00
41 Georges Mantha 35.00 50.00
42 Sylvio Mantha 35.00 50.00
43 Mush March 18.00 30.00
44 Ronnie Martin 15.00 25.00
45 Rabbitt McVeigh 15.00 25.00
46 Howie Morenz 200.00 350.00
47 Murray Murdoch 15.00 25.00
48 Harold Oliver 25.00 40.00
49 George Patterson 15.00 25.00
50 Hal Picketts 15.00 25.00
51 Victor Ripley 15.00 25.00
52 Doc Romnes 15.00 25.00
53 Johnny Sheppard 15.00 25.00
54 Eddie Shore 75.00 125.00
55 Art Somers 15.00 25.00
56 Chris Speyers 15.00 25.00
57 Nelson Stewart 35.00 50.00
58 Tiny Thompson 50.00 80.00
59 Louis Trudel 15.00 25.00
60 Roy Worters 35.00 50.00

1935-36 Diamond Matchbooks Tan 1

The reverse of these tan-colored covers feature a brief player history with the player's name and team affiliation or position appearing at the top. "The Diamond Match Co., NYC" imprint appears below the striker on a single line. Complete matchbooks carry a 50 percent premium over the prices below. A matchbook of Joe Starke is reported to exist, but we cannot officially confirm that at this point in time.

COMPLETE SET (69) 1100.00 1800.00
1 Andy Aitkenhead 15.00 25.00
2 Vern Ayres 15.00 25.00
3 Bill Beveridge 18.00 30.00
4 Ralph Bowman 15.00 25.00
5 Bill Brydge 15.00 25.00
6 Glenn Brydson 15.00 25.00
7 Eddie Burke 18.00 30.00
8 Marty Burke 15.00 25.00
9 Lorne Carr 15.00 25.00
10 Gerald Carson 15.00 25.00
11 Lorne Chabot 25.00 40.00
12 Art Chapman 15.00 25.00
13 Red Conn 15.00 25.00
14 Bert Connoly 15.00 25.00
15 Bun Cook 25.00 40.00
16 Tommy Cook 15.00 25.00
17 Art Coulter 15.00 25.00
18 Lolo Couture 15.00 25.00
19 Bill Cowley 18.00 30.00
20 Wilf Cude 18.00 30.00
21 Red Dutton 18.00 30.00
22 Frank Finnigan 15.00 25.00
23 Irv Frew 15.00 25.00
24 LeRoy Goldsworthy 15.00 25.00
25 Johnny Gottselig 15.00 25.00
26 Bob Gracie 15.00 25.00
27 Ott Heller 15.00 25.00
28 Normie Himes 15.00 25.00
29 Syd Howe 25.00 40.00
30 Roger Jenkins 15.00 25.00
31 Ching Johnson 30.00 50.00
32 Aurel Joliat 35.00 60.00
33 Max Kaminsky 15.00 25.00
34 Butch Keeling 15.00 25.00
35 Bill Kendall 15.00 25.00
36 Lloyd Klein 15.00 25.00
37 Joe Lamb 15.00 25.00
38 Wildor Larochelle 15.00 25.00
39 Pit Lepine 15.00 25.00
40 Norman Locking 15.00 25.00
41 Georges Mantha 25.00 40.00
42 Sylvio Mantha 25.00 40.00
43 Mush March 15.00 25.00
44 Charlie Mason 15.00 25.00
45 Donnie McFadyen 15.00 25.00
46 Jack McGill 15.00 25.00
47 Rabbit McVeigh 15.00 25.00
48 Armand Mondou 15.00 25.00
49 Howie Morenz 180.00 300.00
50 Murray Murdoch 15.00 25.00
51 Al Murray 15.00 25.00
52 Harry Oliver 25.00 40.00
53 Jean Pusie 15.00 25.00
54 Paul Marcel Raymond 15.00 25.00
55 Jack Riley 15.00 25.00
56 Vic Ripley 15.00 25.00
57 Desse Roche 15.00 25.00
58 Earl Roche 15.00 25.00
59 Doc Romnes 15.00 25.00
60 Sweeney Schriner 30.00 50.00
61 Earl Seibert 25.00 40.00
62 Gerald Shannon 15.00 25.00
63 Alex Smith 15.00 25.00
64 Joe Starke 15.00 25.00
65 Nels Stewart 30.00 50.00
66 Paul Thompson 15.00 25.00
67 Louis Trudel 15.00 25.00
68 Carl Voss 15.00 25.00
69 Art Wiebe 15.00 25.00
70 Roy Worters 25.00 40.00

1935-36 Diamond Matchbooks Tan 2

The Type 2 covers are similar to the Type 1 tan-bordered set except that the player's position or team affiliation information has been omitted from the reverse side. "The Diamond Match Co., NYC" imprint appears in a single line. As complete matchbooks are fairly scarce, they carry a premium of 50 percent over the prices below.

COMPLETE SET (63) 1100.00 1800.00
1 Tommy Anderson 15.00 25.00
2 Vern Ayres 15.00 25.00
3 Frank Boucher 25.00 40.00
4 Frank Boucher 25.00 40.00
5 Bill Brydge 15.00 25.00
6 Marty Burke 15.00 25.00
7 Lorne Carr 15.00 25.00
8 Lorne Chabot 25.00 40.00
9 Art Chapman 15.00 25.00
10 Bert Connolly 15.00 25.00
11 Bill Cook 25.00 40.00
12 Bill Cook 25.00 40.00
13 Bun Cook 25.00 40.00
14 Tommy Cook 15.00 25.00
15 Art Coulter 15.00 25.00
16 Lolo Couture 15.00 25.00
17 Wilf Cude 25.00 40.00
18 Cecil Dillon 15.00 25.00
19 Cecil Dillon 15.00 25.00
20 Red Dutton 25.00 40.00
21 Happy Emms 25.00 40.00
22 Irv Frew 15.00 25.00
23 Johnny Gagnon 15.00 25.00
24 Leroy Goldsworthy 15.00 25.00
25 Johnny Gottselig 15.00 25.00
26 Paul Haynes 15.00 25.00
27 Ott Heller 15.00 25.00
28 Irving Jaffee 15.00 25.00
29 Joe Jerwa 15.00 25.00
30 Ching Johnson 25.00 40.00
31 Aurel Joliat 30.00 50.00
32 Butch Keeling 15.00 25.00
33 William Kendall 15.00 25.00
34 Davey Kerr 25.00 40.00
35 Lloyd Klein 15.00 25.00
36 Wildor Larochelle 15.00 25.00
37 Pit Lepine 15.00 25.00
38 Arthur Lesieur 15.00 25.00
39 Alex Levinsky 15.00 25.00
40 Alex Levinsky 15.00 25.00
41 Norm Locking 15.00 25.00
42 Georges Mantha 25.00 40.00
43 Sylvio Mantha 25.00 40.00
44 Mush Marsh 15.00 25.00
45 Charlie Mason 15.00 25.00
46 Donnie McFadyen 15.00 25.00
47 Jack McGill 15.00 25.00
48 Armand Mondou 15.00 25.00
49 Howie Morenz 180.00 300.00
50 Murray Murdoch 15.00 25.00
51 Al Murray 15.00 25.00
52 Harry Oliver 25.00 40.00
53 Eddie Ouellette 15.00 25.00
54 Lynn Patrick 25.00 40.00
55 Lynn Patrick 25.00 40.00
56 Paul Runge 15.00 25.00
57 Sweeney Schriner 25.00 40.00
58 Art Somers 15.00 25.00
59 Harold Starr 15.00 25.00
60 Nels Stewart 30.00 50.00
61 Paul Thompson 15.00 25.00
62 Louis Trudel 15.00 25.00
63 Carl Voss 15.00 25.00
64 Art Wiebe 25.00 40.00
65 Roy Worters 25.00 40.00

1935-36 Diamond Matchbooks Tan 3

The Type 3 matchbook covers are almost identical to the Type 2 covers except that the manufacturer's imprint "Made In The USA/The Diamond Match Co. NYC" is a double line designation. Complete matchbooks are rarely scarce and carry a 50 percent premium over the prices below.

COMPLETE SET (60) 950.00 1600.00
1 Tommy Anderson 15.00 25.00
2 Vern Ayres 15.00 25.00
3 Frank Boucher 18.00 30.00
4 Bill Brydge 15.00 25.00
5 Marty Burke 15.00 25.00
6 Walter Buswell 15.00 25.00
7 Lorne Carr 15.00 25.00
8 Lorne Chabot 25.00 40.00
9 Art Chapman 15.00 25.00
10 Bert Connolly 15.00 25.00
11 Bill Cook 25.00 40.00
12 Bun Cook 25.00 40.00
13 Tommy Cook 18.00 30.00
14 Art Coulter 15.00 25.00
15 Lolo Couture 15.00 25.00
16 Wilf Cude 18.00 30.00
17 Cecil Dillon 15.00 25.00
18 Red Dutton 18.00 30.00
19 Happy Emms 18.00 30.00
20 Irvin Frew 15.00 25.00
21 Johnny Gagnon 15.00 25.00
22 Leroy Goldsworthy 15.00 25.00
23 Johnny Gottselig 15.00 25.00
24 Paul Haynes 15.00 25.00
25 Ott Heller 15.00 25.00
26 Joe Jerwa 15.00 25.00
27 Ching Johnson 25.00 40.00
28 Aurel Joliat 30.00 50.00
29 Mike Karakas 18.00 30.00
30 Butch Keeling 15.00 25.00
31 Dave Kerr 18.00 30.00
32 Lloyd Klein 15.00 25.00
33 Wildor Larochelle 18.00 30.00
34 Pit Lepine 15.00 25.00
35 Arthur Lesieur 15.00 25.00
36 Alex Levinsky 18.00 30.00
37 Norman Locking 15.00 25.00
38 George Mantha 25.00 40.00
39 Sylvio Mantha 25.00 40.00
40 Mush March 18.00 30.00
41 Charlie Mason 15.00 25.00
42 Charlie Mason 15.00 25.00
43 Donnie McFadyen 15.00 25.00
44 Jack McGill 15.00 25.00
45 Armand Mondou 15.00 25.00
46 Howie Morenz 180.00 300.00
47 Murray Murdoch 15.00 25.00
48 Al Murray 15.00 25.00
49 Harry Oliver 25.00 40.00
50 Eddie Ouellette 15.00 25.00
51 Lynn Patrick 25.00 40.00
52 Paul Runge 15.00 25.00
53 Sweeney Schriner 25.00 40.00
54 Harold Starr 15.00 25.00
55 Nels Stewart 30.00 50.00
56 Paul Thompson 15.00 25.00
57 Louis Trudel 15.00 25.00
58 Carl Voss 18.00 30.00
59 Art Wiebe 18.00 30.00
60 Roy Worters 18.00 30.00

1935-36 Diamond Matchbooks Tan 4

This tan-bordered issue is comprised only of Chicago Blackhawks players. The set is similar to Type 1 in that the player's team name appears between the player's name and bio on the reverse. The "Made in USA/The Diamond Match Co., NYC" imprint appears on two lines. Complete matchbooks carry a 50 percent premium.

COMPLETE SET (15) 180.00 300.00
1 Andy Blair 15.00 25.00
2 Glenn Brydson 15.00 25.00
3 Marty Burke 15.00 25.00
4 Tommy Cook 18.00 30.00
5 Johnny Gottselig 15.00 25.00
6 Harold Jackson 15.00 25.00
7 Mike Karakas 18.00 30.00
8 Wildor Larochelle 18.00 30.00
9 Alex Levinsky 18.00 30.00
10 Clem Loughlin 15.00 25.00
11 Mush March 18.00 30.00
12 Earl Seibert 25.00 40.00
13 Paul Thompson 15.00 25.00
14 Louis Trudel 15.00 25.00
15 Art Wiebe 18.00 30.00

1935-36 Diamond Matchbooks Tan 5

This tan-bordered set features only players from the Chicago Blackhawks. This is the hardest match cover issue to distinguish. The difference is that the team name is not featured between the player's name and his bio on the reverse. Complete matchbooks carry a 50 percent premium over the prices below.

COMPLETE SET (14) 125.00 200.00
1 Glenn Brydson 15.00 25.00
2 Marty Burke 15.00 25.00
3 Tommy Cook 15.00 25.00
4 Cully Dahlstrom 15.00 25.00
5 Johnny Gottselig 15.00 25.00
6 Vic Heyliger 15.00 25.00
7 Mike Karakas 15.00 25.00
8 Alex Levinsky 15.00 25.00
9 Mush March 15.00 25.00
10 Earl Seibert 15.00 25.00
11 William J. Stewart 15.00 25.00
12 Paul Thompson 15.00 25.00
13 Louis Trudel 15.00 25.00
14 Art Wiebe 15.00 25.00

1937 Diamond Matchbooks Tan 6

This 14-matchbook set is actually a reissue of the Type 5 Blackhawks set, and was released one year later. The only difference between the two series is that the reissued matchbooks have black match tips while the Type 5 issue has tan match tips. Complete matchbooks carry a 50 percent premium over the prices listed below.

COMPLETE SET (14) 150.00 250.00
1 Glenn Brydson 15.00 25.00
2 Martin A. Burke 15.00 25.00
3 Tom Cook 15.00 25.00
4 Cully Dahlstrom 15.00 25.00
5 Johnny Gottselig 15.00 25.00
6 Vic Heyliger 15.00 25.00
7 Mike Karakas 15.00 25.00
8 Alex Levinsky 15.00 25.00
9 Mush March 15.00 25.00
10 Earl Seibert 18.00 30.00
11 William J. Stewart 15.00 25.00
12 Paul Thompson 15.00 25.00
13 Louis Trudel 15.00 25.00
14 Art Wiebe 15.00 25.00

1972-83 Dimanche/Derniere Heure

The blank-backed photo sheets in this multi-sport set measure approximately 8 1/2" by 11" and feature white-bordered color sports star photos from Dimanche Derniere Heure, a Montreal newspaper. The player's name, position and biographical information appear within the lower white margin. All text is in French. A white vinyl album was available for storing the photo sheets. Printed on the album's spine are the words, "Mes Vedettes du Sport" (My Stars of Sport).The photos are unnumbered and are checklisted below in alphabetical order according to sport or team as follows: Montreal Expos baseball players (1-117; National League baseball players (118-130); Montreal Canadiens hockey players (131-177); wrestlers (178-202); prize fighters (203-204); auto racing drivers (205-208); women's golf (209); Patof the circus clown (210); and CFL (211-278).

134 Chuck Arnason 1.25 2.50
135 Jean Beliveau VP 2.00 4.00
136 Pierre Bouchard (Action) 1.25 2.50
137 Pierre Bouchard (Posed) 1.25 2.50
138 Scotty Bowman CO 2.00 4.00
139 Yvan Cournoyer (Action) 2.00 4.00
140 Yvan Cournoyer (Posed) 2.00 4.00
141 Ken Dryden 5.00 10.00
142 Bob Gainey 2.00 4.00
143 Dale Hoganson 1.25 2.50
144 Rejean Houle 1.50 3.00
145 Guy Lafleur (Action) 5.00 10.00
146 Guy Lafleur (Posed) 5.00 10.00
147 Yvon Lambert 1.50 3.00
148 Jacques Laperriere (Action) 2.00 4.00
149 Jacques Laperriere (Posed) 2.00 4.00
150 Guy Lapointe (Action) 2.00 4.00
151 Guy Lapointe (Posed) 2.00 4.00
152 Michel Larocque 2.00 4.00
153 Claude Larose (Action) 1.50 3.00
154 Claude Larose (Posed) 1.50 3.00
155 Chuck Lefley (Action) 1.25 2.50
156 Chuck Lefley (Posed) 1.25 2.50
157 Jacques Lemaire (Action) 2.00 4.00
158 Jacques Lemaire (Posed) 2.00 4.00
159 Frank Mahovlich (Action) 3.00 6.00
160 Frank Mahovlich (Posed) 3.00 6.00
161 Pete Mahovlich (Action) 1.50 3.00
162 Pete Mahovlich (Posed) 1.50 3.00
163 Bob J. Murdoch 1.25 2.50
164 Michel Plasse (Action) 2.00 4.00
165 Michel Plasse (Posed) 2.00 4.00
166 Henri Richard (Action) 3.00 6.00
167 Henri Richard (Posed) 3.00 6.00
168 Jim Roberts (Action) 1.50 3.00
169 Jim Roberts (Posed) 1.50 3.00
170 Larry Robinson (Action) 3.00 6.00
171 Larry Robinson (Posed) 3.00 6.00
172 Serge Savard (Action) 2.00 4.00
173 Serge Savard (Posed) 2.00 4.00
174 Steve Shutt (Action) 2.00 4.00
175 Steve Shutt (Posed) 2.00 4.00
176 Marc Tardif 1.50 3.00
177 Wayne Thomas (Action) 1.50 3.00
178 Wayne Thomas (Posed) 1.50 3.00
179 Murray Wilson (Action) 1.25 2.50
180 Murray Wilson (Posed) 1.25 2.50

1992 Disney Mighty Ducks Movie

Issued to promote the Walt Disney movie "The Mighty Ducks", this eight-card set measures approximately 3 1/2" by 6" and is designed in the postcard format. Each card is perforated; the left portion, measuring the standard size, displays a full-bleed color photo, while the right portion is a solid neon color with a box for the stamp at the upper right. The back of the trading card portion has a brief player profile, while the other portion has an advertisement for the movie. The cards are unnumbered and checklisted below in alphabetical order. The character's name in the movie is given on the continuation line.

COMPLETE SET (8) 16.00 40.00
1 Brandon Adams Jesse 2.00 5.00
2 Emilio Estevez Coach Bombay 2.50 6.00
3 Joshua Jackson Charlie 3.00 8.00
4 Marguerite Moreau Connie 2.00 5.00
5 Elden Ratliff Fulton 2.00 5.00
6 Shaun Weiss Goldberg 2.00 5.00
7 Rollerblading in Shopping Mall 2.00 5.00
8 Team Photo 2.00 5.00

2010-11 Dominion

(1-100) PRINT RUN 249 SER.#'d SETS
(101-150) PRINT RUN 99 SER.#'d SETS
(151-230) PRINT RUN 199 SER.#'d SETS
(231-250) PRINT RUN 99 SER.#'d SETS

1 Corey Perry 3.00 8.00
2 Ryan Getzlaf 5.00 12.00
3 Saku Koivu 3.00 8.00
4 Bobby Ryan 3.00 8.00
5 Dustin Byfuglien 3.00 8.00
6 Andrew Ladd 3.00 8.00
7 Evander Kane 3.00 8.00
8 Milan Lucic 3.00 8.00
9 Patrice Bergeron 4.00 10.00
10 Tim Thomas 2.50 6.00
11 Ryan Miller 3.00 8.00
12 Thomas Vanek 3.00 8.00
13 Drew Stafford 3.00 8.00
14 Miikka Kiprusoff 2.50 6.00
15 Jarome Iginla 3.00 8.00
16 Alex Tanguay 2.00 5.00
17 Cam Ward 3.00 8.00
18 Eric Staal 4.00 10.00
19 Brandon Sutter 2.50 6.00
20 Jonathan Toews 6.00 15.00
21 Patrick Kane 6.00 15.00
22 Patrick Sharp 3.00 8.00
23 Corey Crawford 4.00 10.00
24 Duncan Keith 3.00 8.00
25 Erik Johnson 2.00 5.00
26 Brian Elliott 2.50 6.00
27 Matt Duchene 3.00 8.00
28 Rick Nash 3.00 8.00
29 Steve Mason 2.50 6.00
30 Antoine Vermette 2.00 5.00
31 Brad Richards 3.00 8.00
32 Loui Eriksson 2.50 6.00
33 Kari Lehtonen 2.50 6.00
34 Jimmy Howard 4.00 10.00
35 Pavel Datsyuk 4.00 10.00
36 Nicklas Lidstrom 3.00 8.00
37 Henrik Zetterberg 4.00 10.00
38 Ales Hemsky 2.50 6.00
39 Sam Gagner 2.50 6.00
40 Andrew Cogliano 2.00 5.00
41 Stephen Weiss 2.50 6.00
42 David Booth 2.00 5.00
43 Tomas Vokoun 2.50 6.00
44 Anze Kopitar 5.00 12.00
45 Drew Doughty 3.00 8.00
46 Jonathan Quick 5.00 12.00
47 Brent Burns 4.00 10.00
48 Cal Clutterbuck 3.00 8.00
49 Mikko Koivu 3.00 8.00
50 Andrei Kostitsyn 2.50 6.00
51 Carey Price 12.00 30.00
52 Brian Gionta 2.50 6.00
53 Tomas Plekanec 3.00 8.00
54 Shea Weber 2.50 6.00
55 Pekka Rinne 4.00 10.00
56 Sergei Kostitsyn 2.00 5.00
57 Martin Brodeur 6.00 15.00
58 Travis Zajac 2.50 6.00
59 Ilya Kovalchuk 3.00 8.00
60 John Tavares 6.00 15.00
61 Matt Moulson 2.50 6.00
62 Michael Grabner 2.50 6.00
63 Henrik Lundqvist 5.00 12.00
64 Marian Gaborik 4.00 10.00
65 Marc Staal 3.00 8.00
66 Craig Anderson 3.00 8.00
67 Jason Spezza 2.00 5.00
68 Daniel Alfredsson 3.00 8.00
69 Chris Pronger 2.50 6.00
70 Claude Giroux 3.00 8.00
71 Jeff Carter 3.00 8.00
72 Mike Richards 3.00 8.00
73 Mikkel Boedker 2.00 5.00
74 Ilya Bryzgalov 2.50 6.00
75 Keith Yandle 3.00 8.00
76 Kris Letang 3.00 8.00
77 Sidney Crosby 12.00 30.00
78 Marc-Andre Fleury 5.00 12.00
79 Jordan Staal 3.00 8.00
80 Evgeni Malkin 10.00 25.00
81 Joe Thornton 3.00 8.00
82 Ryane Clowe 2.00 5.00
83 Dany Heatley 2.50 6.00
84 Logan Couture 3.00 8.00
85 T.J. Oshie 5.00 12.00
86 David Backes 3.00 8.00
87 Jaroslav Halak 3.00 8.00
88 Steven Stamkos 6.00 15.00
89 Vincent Lecavalier 2.50 6.00
90 Martin St. Louis 3.00 8.00
91 Dion Phaneuf 3.00 8.00
92 James Reimer 3.00 8.00
93 Phil Kessel 4.00 10.00
94 Roberto Luongo 3.00 8.00
95 Henrik Sedin 3.00 8.00
96 Daniel Sedin 3.00 8.00
97 Ryan Kesler 3.00 8.00
98 Alex Ovechkin 12.00 30.00
99 Nicklas Backstrom 5.00 12.00
100 Semyon Varlamov 3.00 8.00
101 Cam Neely 4.00 10.00
102 Derek Sanderson 3.00 8.00
103 Felix Potvin 6.00 15.00
104 Milt Schmidt 3.00 8.00
105 Normand Leveille 5.00 12.00
106 Ray Bourque 6.00 15.00
107 Reggie Lemelin 5.00 12.00
108 Rick Middleton 5.00 12.00
109 Dale Hawerchuk 5.00 12.00
110 Gilbert Perreault 4.00 10.00
111 Tom Barrasso 4.00 10.00
112 Doug Gilmour 5.00 12.00
113 Bobby Hull 4.00 10.00
114 Denis Savard 5.00 12.00
115 Paul Coffey 4.00 10.00
116 Phil Esposito 6.00 15.00
117 Stan Mikita 5.00 12.00
118 Tony Esposito 4.00 10.00
119 Ed Belfour 4.00 10.00
120 Steve Yzerman 10.00 25.00
121 Grant Fuhr 4.00 10.00
122 Mark Messier 6.00 15.00
123 Kelly Hrudey 3.00 8.00
124 Guy Lafleur 5.00 12.00
125 Henri Richard 4.00 10.00
126 Jean Beliveau 4.00 10.00
127 Patrick Roy 10.00 25.00
128 Denis Potvin 4.00 10.00
129 Mike Bossy 4.00 10.00
130 Brad Park 3.00 8.00
131 Brian Leetch 4.00 10.00
132 Adam Graves 3.00 8.00
133 Ed Giacomin 6.00 15.00
134 Rod Gilbert 4.00 10.00
135 Bernie Parent 4.00 10.00
136 Bobby Clarke 4.00 10.00
137 Eric Lindros 6.00 15.00
138 Luc Robitaille 4.00 10.00
139 Mario Lemieux 12.00 30.00
140 Joe Sakic 6.00 15.00
141 Ron Hextall 5.00 12.00
142 Jeremy Roenick 4.00 10.00
143 Brendan Shanahan 5.00 12.00
144 Brett Hull 6.00 15.00
145 Glenn Hall 4.00 10.00
146 Manon Rheaume 8.00 20.00
147 Curtis Joseph 5.00 12.00
148 Darryl Sittler 3.00 8.00
149 Johnny Bower 5.00 12.00
150 Trevor Linden 4.00 10.00
151 Brandon McMillan AU RC 5.00 12.00
152 Kyle Palmieri AU RC 10.00 25.00
153 Nick Bonino AU RC 6.00 15.00
154 Alexander Burmistrov AU RC 5.00 12.00
155 Patrice Cormier AU RC 6.00 15.00
156 Jordan Caron AU RC 8.00 20.00
157 Jamie Arniel AU RC 5.00 12.00
158 Matt Bartkowski AU RC 8.00 20.00
159 Zach Hamill AU RC 5.00 12.00
160 Colby Cohen AU RC 5.00 12.00
161 Luke Adam AU RC 5.00 12.00
162 T.J. Brodie AU RC 5.00 12.00
163 Henrik Karlsson AU RC 5.00 12.00
164 Zac Dalpe AU RC 5.00 12.00
165 Jamie McBain AU RC 5.00 12.00
166 Nick Leddy AU RC 8.00 20.00
167 Brandon Pirri AU RC 5.00 12.00
168 Evan Brophey AU RC 5.00 12.00
169 Jeremy Morin AU RC 5.00 12.00
170 Ben Smith AU RC 15.00 30.00
171 Mark Olver AU RC 5.00 12.00
172 Jonas Holos AU RC 5.00 12.00
173 Brandon Yip AU RC 5.00 12.00
174 Matt Calvert AU RC 8.00 20.00
175 Grant Clitsome AU RC 5.00 12.00
176 Richard Bachman AU RC 8.00 20.00
177 Philip Larsen AU RC 5.00 12.00
178 Jan Mursak AU RC 10.00 25.00
179 Thomas McCollum AU RC 6.00 15.00
180 Jordan Pearce AU RC 8.00 20.00
181 Dave Hanson AU 10.00 25.00
182 Jeff Petry AU RC 6.00 15.00
183 Evgeny Dadonov AU RC 6.00 15.00
184 Jake Muzzin AU RC 5.00 12.00
185 Kyle Clifford AU RC 5.00 12.00
186 Steve Carlson AU 10.00 25.00
187 Cody Almond AU RC 5.00 12.00
188 Justin Falk AU RC 4.00 10.00
189 Matt Hackett AU RC 6.00 15.00
190 Andreas Engqvist AU RC 8.00 20.00
191 Anders Lindback AU RC 5.00 12.00
192 Mark Dekanich AU RC 5.00 12.00
193 Nick Spaling AU RC 5.00 12.00
194 Alex Urbom AU RC 5.00 12.00
195 Matt Taormina AU RC 5.00 12.00
196 Jeff Frazee AU RC 8.00 20.00
197 Jacob Josefson AU RC 5.00 12.00
198 Brad Mills AU RC 5.00 12.00
199 Stephen Gionta AU RC 6.00 15.00
200 Alexander Vasyunov AU RC 5.00 12.00
201 Travis Hamonic AU RC 6.00 15.00
202 Rhett Rakhshani AU RC 5.00 12.00
203 Nathan Lawson AU RC 5.00 12.00
204 Kevin Poulin AU RC 6.00 15.00
205 Trevor Gillies AU RC 5.00 12.00
206 Evgeny Grachev AU RC 5.00 12.00
207 Brodie Dupont AU RC 6.00 15.00
208 Jim O'Brien AU RC 6.00 15.00
209 Robin Lehner AU RC 10.00 25.00
210 Jared Cowen AU RC 5.00 12.00
211 Chris Summers AU RC 5.00 12.00
212 Eric Wellwood AU RC 6.00 15.00
213 Nick Johnson AU RC 4.00 10.00
214 Eric Tangradi AU RC 5.00 12.00
215 Alex Stalock AU RC 6.00 15.00
216 Andrew Desjardins AU RC 5.00 12.00
217 Justin Braun AU RC 5.00 12.00
218 Mike Moore AU RC 5.00 12.00
219 Ryan Reaves AU RC 6.00 15.00
220 S.Della Rovere AU RC 5.00 12.00
221 Philip McRae AU RC 5.00 12.00
222 Linus Omark AU RC 12.00 30.00
223 Ian Cole AU RC 5.00 12.00
224 Dustin Tokarski AU RC 5.00 12.00
225 Cedrick Desjardins AU RC 6.00 15.00
226 Brayden Irwin AU RC 5.00 12.00
227 Keith Aulie AU RC 5.00 12.00
228 Korbinian Holzer AU RC 5.00 12.00
229 Marcel Mueller AU RC 6.00 15.00
230 Marcus Johansson AU RC 8.00 20.00
231 Taylor Hall JSY AU RC 100.00 200.00
232 Tyler Seguin JSY AU RC 90.00 150.00
233 N.Niederreiter JSY AU RC 20.00 50.00
234 Cory Emmerton JSY AU RC 20.00 50.00
235 Jordan Eberle JSY AU RC 80.00 200.00
236 Tomas Tatar JSY AU RC 60.00 120.00
237 J.Markstrom JSY AU RC 60.00 150.00
238 Magnus Paajarvi JSY AU RC 20.00 50.00
239 B.Schenn JSY AU RC 100.00 200.00
240 Nazem Kadri JSY AU RC 90.00 150.00
241 Cam Fowler JSY AU RC 20.00 50.00
242 Derek Stepan JSY AU RC 25.00 60.00
243 P.K. Subban JSY AU RC 100.00 200.00
244 S.Bobrovsky JSY AU RC 50.00 100.00
245 Mats Zuccarello JSY AU RC 30.00 80.00
246 Jeff Skinner JSY AU RC 40.00 100.00
247 K.Shattenkirk JSY AU RC 30.00 80.00
248 M.Tedenby JSY AU RC 12.00 30.00
249 Dana Tyrell JSY AU RC 20.00 50.00
250 Ekman-Larsson JSY AU RC 50.00 100.00

2010-11 Dominion Gold

*GOLD/19-25: .6X TO 1.5X BASIC CARDS
STATED PRINT RUN 10-25

231 Taylor Hall JSY AU 200.00 400.00
232 Tyler Seguin JSY AU 200.00 350.00
233 N.Niederreiter JSY AU
234 Cory Emmerton JSY AU 30.00 80.00
235 Jordan Eberle JSY AU 100.00 250.00

236 Tomas Tatar JSY AU 40.00 100.00
237 J.Markstrom JSY AU 75.00 200.00
238 M.Paajarvi JSY AU/10
239 B.Schenn JSY AU 30.00 80.00
240 Nazem Kadri JSY AU 125.00 200.00
241 Cam Fowler JSY AU 25.00 60.00
242 Derek Stepan JSY AU 50.00 100.00
243 P.K. Subban JSY AU 75.00 150.00
244 S.Bobrovsky JSY AU 40.00 80.00
245 Mats Zuccarello JSY AU 30.00 80.00
246 Jeff Skinner JSY AU 125.00 250.00
247 K.Shattenkirk JSY AU 30.00 80.00
248 Mattias Tedenby JSY AU
250 OEkman-Larsson JSY AU 30.00 80.00

2010-11 Dominion All Decade Jerseys

STATED PRINT RUN 99 SER.#'d SETS
*PRIME/25: .6X TO 1.5X BASIC INSERTS
AO Alex Ovechkin 10.00 25.00
CP Chris Pronger 4.00 10.00
DA Daniel Alfredsson 5.00 12.00
DB Dan Boyle 4.00 10.00
DH Dany Heatley 4.00 10.00
EB Ed Belfour 5.00 12.00
EM Evgeni Malkin 15.00 40.00
ES Eric Staal
IK Ilya Kovalchuk 5.00 12.00
JI Jarome Iginla 5.00 12.00
JT Joe Thornton 5.00 12.00
MB Martin Brodeur 10.00 25.00
MH Marian Hossa 4.00 10.00
MK Miikka Kiprusoff
MS Martin St. Louis 5.00 12.00
NL Nicklas Lidstrom 5.00 12.00
PD Pavel Datsyuk 6.00 15.00
RM Ryan Miller 6.00 15.00
RN Rick Nash 5.00 12.00
SC Sidney Crosby 15.00 40.00
TV Tomas Vokoun 6.00 15.00
ZC Zdeno Chara 6.00 15.00

2010-11 Dominion All Decade Jerseys Autographs

STATED PRINT RUN 24-50
AO Alex Ovechkin/24 40.00 100.00
CP Chris Pronger 8.00 20.00
DA Daniel Alfredsson 20.00 50.00
DB Dan Boyle 8.00 20.00
DH Dany Heatley 8.00 20.00
EM Evgeni Malkin 20.00 50.00
IK Ilya Kovalchuk
JI Jarome Iginla 10.00 25.00
JT Joe Thornton 10.00 25.00
MB Martin Brodeur/24 20.00 50.00
MH Marian Hossa 8.00 20.00
MS Martin St. Louis 10.00 25.00
NL Nicklas Lidstrom 15.00 40.00
PD Pavel Datsyuk 20.00 50.00
RM Ryan Miller 10.00 25.00
RN Rick Nash 10.00 25.00
SC Sidney Crosby/24 75.00 150.00
TV Tomas Vokoun 8.00 20.00
ZC Zdeno Chara 15.00 30.00

2010-11 Dominion All Decade Autographs

STATED PRINT RUN 24-50
1 Martin Brodeur/24 30.00 60.00
3 Ryan Miller 10.00 25.00
4 Tomas Vokoun 10.00 25.00
5 Nicklas Lidstrom 12.00 30.00
6 Chris Pronger 6.00 15.00
7 Dan Boyle 6.00 15.00
8 Zdeno Chara 10.00 25.00
9 Pavel Datsyuk 15.00 40.00
10 Daniel Alfredsson 10.00 25.00
11 Jarome Iginla 8.00 20.00
12 Evgeni Malkin 20.00 40.00
13 Joe Thornton 8.00 20.00
14 Ilya Kovalchuk
15 Dany Heatley 6.00 15.00
16 Marian Hossa 6.00 15.00
17 Rick Nash 8.00 20.00
18 Martin St. Louis 8.00 20.00
19 Alex Ovechkin/24 30.00 80.00
20 Sidney Crosby/24 60.00 120.00

2010-11 Dominion All Decade Autographs Dual

STATED PRINT RUN 25 SER.#'d SETS
1 M.Brodeur/R.Miller 30.00 60.00
2 N.Lidstrom/Z.Chara
3 C.Pronger/D.Boyle 12.00 30.00
4 J.Iginla/R.Nash 20.00 50.00
5 J.Thornton/D.Heatley 25.00 60.00
6 A.Ovechkin/I.Kovalchuk
7 E.Malkin/D.Alfredsson
8 P.Datsyuk/M.Hossa
9 M.St. Louis/B.Richards 10.00 25.00
10 E.Belfour/T.Vokoun 10.00 25.00

2010-11 Dominion All Decade Autographs Quads

STATED PRINT RUN 25 SER.#'d SETS
1 Brodeur/Belfour/Miller/Vokoun
2 Lidstrom/Chara/Boyle/Pronger 30.00 60.00
3 Thornton/Heatley/Iginla/Nash 75.00 150.00
4 Datsyk/Koval/Malkn/Ovech 50.00 100.00
5 St.L/Alfredsn/Lecav/Richards

2010-11 Dominion All Decade Autographs Trios

STATED PRINT RUN 25 SER.#'d SETS
1 Brodeur/Vokoun/Miller 50.00 100.00
2 Lidstrom/Pronger/Chara
3 Ovech/Koval/Datsyuk 60.00 100.00
4 Iginla/Heatley/St. Louis 30.00 80.00
5 Thornton/Nash/Alfredsn 60.00 120.00

2010-11 Dominion Benchmark Sticks

STATED PRINT RUN 25-115
1 Brendan Shanahan 10.00 25.00
2 Brett Hull/25 12.00 30.00
3 Dale Hawerchuk/50 10.00 25.00
4 Dino Ciccarelli/50 8.00 20.00
5 Guy Lafleur/115 12.00 30.00
6 Joe Nieuwendyk 8.00 20.00
7 Lanny McDonald/50 8.00 20.00
8 Marcel Dionne/50 10.00 25.00
9 Mario Lemieux 12.00 30.00
10 Phil Esposito/25 12.00 30.00
11 Steve Yzerman/25 25.00 60.00
12 Stan Mikita/110 10.00 25.00
13 Joe Sakic 15.00 40.00

2010-11 Dominion Benchmark Sticks Autographs

STATED PRINT RUN 20-50
1 Brendan Shanahan/25 40.00 80.00
2 Brett Hull/20 75.00 150.00
3 Dale Hawerchuk/45 20.00 50.00
4 Dino Ciccarelli/50 15.00 40.00
5 Guy Lafleur/50 40.00 80.00
6 Joe Nieuwendyk/50 15.00 40.00
7 Lanny McDonald/50 20.00 50.00
8 Marcel Dionne/50 20.00 50.00
9 Mario Lemieux/25 200.00 300.00
10 Phil Esposito/20 20.00 50.00
11 Steve Yzerman/25 100.00 200.00
12 Stan Mikita/50 25.00 60.00
13 Joe Sakic/25 50.00 100.00

2010-11 Dominion Bonded in Silver Dual Autographs

STATED PRINT RUN 25 SER.#'d SETS
1 M.Lemieux/T.Barrasso 75.00 150.00
2 S.Yzerman/N.Lidstrom 75.00 150.00
3 B.Hull/E.Belfour 40.00 80.00
4 P.Roy/J.Sakic 75.00 150.00
5 E.Malkin/M.Fleury 50.00 125.00
6 J.Toews/P.Sharp
7 J.Beliveau/H.Richard 50.00 100.00
8 G.Lafleur/Y.Cournoyer 30.00 60.00
9 E.Staal/C.Ward 20.00 50.00
10 G.Cheevers/D.Sanderson 30.00 80.00
11 J.Bucyk/P.Esposito 25.00 60.00
12 J.Giguere/R.Getzlaf 20.00 50.00
13 M.Brodeur/S.Gomez 30.00 80.00
14 B.Hull/S.Mikita 25.00 60.00
15 M.Messier/B.Leetch 40.00 80.00
16 B.Parent/B.Clarke 40.00 80.00
17 D.Potvin/M.Bossy 15.00 40.00
18 V.Lecavalier/B.Richards 15.00 40.00
19 J.Nieuwendyk/D.Gilmour 40.00 80.00
20 G.Fuhr/P.Coffey 15.00 40.00

2010-11 Dominion Brass Bonanza Autographs

STATED PRINT RUN 24-50
1 Bobby Hull/24 50.00 100.00
2 Brendan Shanahan/24 30.00 80.00
3 Keith Primeau 12.00 30.00
4 Nick Fotiu 10.00 25.00
5 Paul Coffey 15.00 40.00
6 Ray Ferraro 15.00 40.00
7 Tiger Williams 20.00 50.00
8 Daryl Reaugh 12.00 30.00
9 Ron Francis 30.00 60.00
10 Pat Verbeek 15.00 40.00

2010-11 Dominion Championship Gear

STATED PRINT RUN 50 SER.#'d SETS
1 Patrick Kane 10.00 25.00
2 Sidney Crosby 20.00 50.00
3 Nicklas Lidstrom 10.00 25.00
4 Ryan Getzlaf 8.00 20.00
5 Eric Staal 6.00 15.00
6 Martin St. Louis 5.00 12.00
7 Vincent Lecavalier 4.00 10.00
8 Martin Brodeur 10.00 25.00
9 Patrick Sharp 6.00 15.00
10 Jonathan Toews 10.00 25.00
11 Jordan Staal 8.00 20.00
12 Max Talbot 10.00 25.00
13 Pavel Datsyuk 8.00 20.00
14 Jean-Sebastien Giguere 10.00 25.00
15 Cam Ward 5.00 12.00
16 Nikolai Khabibulin 4.00 10.00
17 Patrick Roy 12.00 30.00
18 Steve Yzerman 15.00 40.00
19 Joe Nieuwendyk 5.00 12.00
20 Yvan Cournoyer 5.00 12.00
21 Corey Perry 6.00 15.00
22 Marc-Andre Fleury 12.00 30.00
23 Mario Lemieux 15.00 40.00
24 Ed Belfour 5.00 12.00
25 Brian Leetch/25 8.00 20.00
26 Mike Modano 8.00 20.00
27 Evgeni Malkin 10.00 25.00
28 Brett Hull 8.00 20.00
29 Antti Niemi 10.00 25.00
30 Bryan Trottier 6.00 15.00
32 George Parros 6.00 15.00

2010-11 Dominion Eight Is Enough Jerseys

STATED PRINT RUN 25 SER.#'d SETS
1 GP/SD/ZK/MC/KB/BP/JB/ST 25.00 60.00
2 Goalies East 75.00 150.00
3 Goalies West 50.00 120.00
4 Superstars/Legends 75.00 150.00
5 CP/MR/RN/JT/ES/JI/RG/PB 50.00 100.00

2010-11 Dominion Franchise Legends Jerseys

STATED PRINT RUN 99 SER.#'d SETS
1 Yvan Cournoyer 5.00 12.00
2 Steve Yzerman 12.00 30.00
3 Charlie Simmer 3.00 8.00
4 Rick Middleton 6.00 15.00
5 Lanny McDonald 5.00 12.00
6 Johnny Bucyk 5.00 12.00
7 Guy Lafleur 6.00 15.00
8 Eric Lindros 8.00 20.00
9 Don Cherry 15.00 40.00
10 Brendan Shanahan 6.00 15.00
11 Mike Modano 8.00 20.00
12 Nicklas Lidstrom 5.00 12.00
13 Marcel Dionne 6.00 15.00
14 Martin Brodeur 10.00 25.00

2010-11 Dominion Franchise Legends Jerseys Autographs

STATED PRINT RUN 19-50
1 Yvan Cournoyer/50 10.00 25.00
2 Steve Yzerman/19 60.00 120.00
3 Charlie Simmer/50 6.00 15.00
4 Rick Middleton/50 12.00 30.00
5 Lanny McDonald/50 10.00 25.00
6 Johnny Bucyk/50 20.00 40.00
7 Guy Lafleur/50 30.00 60.00
8 Eric Lindros/50 40.00 80.00
9 Don Cherry/50 40.00 80.00
10 Brendan Shanahan/19 30.00 60.00
11 Mike Modano/50 20.00 50.00
12 Nicklas Lidstrom/25 30.00 60.00
13 Marcel Dionne/50 15.00 40.00
14 Martin Brodeur/25 40.00 80.00

2010-11 Dominion Got Your Number Dual Autographs

STATED PRINT RUN 10-50
1 J.Sakic/S.Yzerman/19
2 R.Vachon/M.Brodeur/30 50.00 100.00
3 D.Savard/M.Richards
4 H.Lundqvist/C.Ward 20.00 50.00
5 S.Stamkos/J.Tavares 40.00 80.00
6 Y.Cournoyer/J.Iginla 20.00 50.00
7 B.Shanahan/R.Smyth/10
8 B.Morrow/P.Sharp 10.00 25.00
9 D.Alfredsson/A.Kopitar 12.00 30.00
10 B.Trottier/J.Toews 25.00 60.00

2010-11 Dominion Got Your Number Dual Jerseys

STATED PRINT RUN 99 SER.#'d SETS
1 J.Sakic/S.Yzerman 15.00 40.00
2 R.Vachon/M.Brodeur 12.00 30.00
3 D.Savard/M.Richards 8.00 20.00
4 H.Lundqvist/C.Ward 10.00 25.00
5 S.Stamkos/J.Tavares 12.00 30.00
6 Y.Cournoyer/J.Iginla 6.00 15.00
7 B.Shanahan/R.Smyth 8.00 20.00
8 B.Morrow/P.Sharp 6.00 15.00
9 D.Alfredsson/A.Kopitar 8.00 20.00
10 B.Trottier/J.Toews 12.00 30.00

2010-11 Dominion Honoured Rivals Dual Jerseys

STATED PRINT RUN 49 SER.#'d SETS
1 E.Malkin/A.Ovechkin 25.00 60.00
2 D.Doughty/R.Getzlaf 10.00 25.00
3 M.Staal/J.Tavares 12.00 30.00
4 C.Pronger/J.Toews 12.00 30.00
5 H.Lundqvist/M.Brodeur 12.00 30.00
6 H.Sedin/D.Keith 6.00 15.00
7 N.Lidstrom/M.Fleury 12.00 30.00
8 T.Hall/T.Seguin 15.00 40.00
9 D.Sittler/G.Lafleur 15.00 40.00
10 J.Bucyk/R.Vachon 8.00 20.00

2010-11 Dominion Jerseys

STATED PRINT RUN 8-99
*PRIME/25: .6X TO 1.5X BASIC JSY
*PRIME PATCH/25: .8X TO 2X BASICJSY
*PRIME JSY #/23-25: .6X TO 1.5X BASIC JSY
*NAMEPLATE/15-25 .6X TO 1.5X BASIC JSY
1 Corey Perry 5.00 12.00
2 Ryan Getzlaf 8.00 20.00
3 Saku Koivu 5.00 12.00
4 Bobby Ryan 5.00 12.00
5 Dustin Byfuglien 5.00 12.00
6 Andrew Ladd 5.00 12.00
7 Evander Kane 5.00 12.00
8 Milan Lucic 5.00 12.00
9 Patrice Bergeron 6.00 15.00
10 Tim Thomas 6.00 15.00
11 Ryan Miller 5.00 12.00
12 Thomas Vanek 5.00 12.00
13 Drew Stafford 5.00 12.00
14 Miikka Kiprusoff 4.00 10.00
15 Jarome Iginla 5.00 12.00
16 Alex Tanguay 3.00 8.00
17 Cam Ward 5.00 12.00
18 Eric Staal 6.00 15.00
19 Brandon Sutter 4.00 10.00
20 Jonathan Toews 10.00 25.00
21 Patrick Kane 10.00 25.00
22 Patrick Sharp 5.00 12.00
23 Corey Crawford 6.00 15.00
24 Duncan Keith 5.00 12.00
25 Erik Johnson 3.00 8.00
26 Brian Elliott 4.00 10.00
27 Matt Duchene 5.00 12.00
28 Rick Nash 5.00 12.00
29 Steve Mason/8
30 Antoine Vermette 3.00 8.00
31 Brad Richards 5.00 12.00
32 Loui Eriksson 4.00 10.00
33 Kari Lehtonen 4.00 10.00
34 Jimmy Howard 6.00 15.00
35 Pavel Datsyuk 6.00 15.00
36 Nicklas Lidstrom 5.00 12.00
37 Henrik Zetterberg 6.00 15.00
38 Ales Hemsky 4.00 10.00
39 Sam Gagner 4.00 10.00
40 Andrew Cogliano 3.00 8.00
41 Stephen Weiss 4.00 10.00
42 David Booth 3.00 8.00
43 Tomas Vokoun 4.00 10.00
44 Anze Kopitar 8.00 20.00
45 Drew Doughty 5.00 12.00
46 Jonathan Quick 6.00 15.00
47 Brent Burns 6.00 15.00
48 Cal Clutterbuck 5.00 12.00
49 Mikko Koivu 5.00 12.00
50 Andrei Kostitsyn 4.00 10.00
51 Carey Price 20.00 50.00
52 Brian Gionta 4.00 10.00
53 Tomas Plekanec 5.00 12.00
54 Shea Weber 4.00 10.00
55 Pekka Rinne 6.00 15.00
57 Martin Brodeur 10.00 25.00
58 Travis Zajac 4.00 10.00
59 Ilya Kovalchuk 5.00 12.00
60 John Tavares 10.00 25.00
61 Matt Moulson 4.00 10.00
62 Michael Grabner 4.00 10.00
63 Henrik Lundqvist 8.00 20.00
64 Marian Gaborik 6.00 15.00
65 Marc Staal 5.00 12.00
66 Craig Anderson 5.00 12.00
67 Jason Spezza 3.00 8.00
68 Daniel Alfredsson 5.00 12.00
69 Chris Pronger 4.00 10.00
70 Claude Giroux 5.00 12.00
71 Jeff Carter 5.00 12.00
72 Mike Richards 5.00 12.00
74 Ilya Bryzgalov 4.00 10.00
75 Keith Yandle 5.00 12.00
76 Kris Letang 5.00 12.00
77 Sidney Crosby 20.00 50.00
78 Marc-Andre Fleury 6.00 15.00
79 Jordan Staal 5.00 12.00
80 Evgeni Malkin 15.00 40.00
81 Joe Thornton 5.00 12.00
83 Dany Heatley/25 4.00 10.00
85 T.J. Oshie 8.00 20.00
86 David Backes 5.00 12.00
87 Jaroslav Halak 5.00 12.00
88 Steven Stamkos 10.00 25.00
89 Vincent Lecavalier 4.00 10.00
90 Martin St. Louis 5.00 12.00
91 Dion Phaneuf 5.00 12.00
92 James Reimer 8.00 20.00
93 Phil Kessel 6.00 15.00
94 Roberto Luongo 5.00 12.00
95 Henrik Sedin 5.00 12.00
96 Daniel Sedin 5.00 12.00
97 Ryan Kesler 8.00 20.00
98 Alex Ovechkin 20.00 50.00
99 Nicklas Backstrom 8.00 20.00
100 Semyon Varlamov 5.00 12.00
105 Normand Leveille 5.00 12.00
106 Ray Bourque 6.00 15.00
108 Rick Middleton 5.00 12.00
111 Tom Barrasso 4.00 10.00
114 Denis Savard 5.00 12.00
115 Paul Coffey 4.00 10.00
119 Ed Belfour 4.00 10.00
120 Steve Yzerman 10.00 25.00
124 Guy Lafleur 8.00 20.00
127 Patrick Roy/33 15.00 40.00
131 Brian Leetch 4.00 10.00
132 Adam Graves 4.00 10.00
137 Eric Lindros 8.00 20.00
138 Luc Robitaille 4.00 10.00
139 Mario Lemieux 12.00 30.00
140 Joe Sakic 6.00 15.00
143 Brendan Shanahan 5.00 12.00
144 Brett Hull 6.00 15.00
147 Curtis Joseph 5.00 12.00
148 Darryl Sittler 3.00 8.00

2010-11 Dominion Mammoth

STATED PRINT RUN 10-25
1 Jacob Markstrom 60.00 120.00
2 Mattias Tedenby 8.00 20.00
3 Ryan McDonagh 25.00 60.00
4 Mats Zuccarello 15.00 40.00
5 Tyler Seguin/10
6 Taylor Hall/10
7 Nazem Kadri 30.00 80.00
8 Kevin Shattenkirk 20.00 50.00
9 Zach Hamill 25.00 60.00
10 Jeff Skinner 20.00 50.00

2010-11 Dominion NHL All-Star Memories Embroidered Patches Autographs

PATCH AU PRINT RUN 15
1 Nicklas Lidstrom 30.00 60.00
2 Patrick Kane 50.00 100.00
3 Martin St. Louis 15.00 40.00
4 Steven Stamkos 50.00 100.00
5 Henrik Sedin 12.00 30.00
6 Jonathan Toews 50.00 100.00
7 Brad Richards 12.00 30.00
8 Anze Kopitar 20.00 50.00
9 Matt Duchene 12.00 30.00
10 Loui Eriksson 10.00 25.00
11 Phil Kessel 25.00 50.00
13 Shea Weber 10.00 25.00
14 Dustin Byfuglien 12.00 30.00
15 Keith Yandle 10.00 25.00
16 Brent Burns 12.00 30.00
17 Tim Thomas 30.00 60.00
18 Marc-Andre Fleury 20.00 50.00
19 Jonas Hiller 10.00 25.00
20 Eric Staal 15.00 40.00
21 Ryan Kesler 15.00 30.00
22 Alex Ovechkin 60.00 120.00
23 Daniel Sedin 12.00 30.00
24 Rick Nash 25.00 60.00
25 Patrick Sharp 20.00 50.00
26 Jeff Skinner 20.00 50.00
27 Claude Giroux 50.00 100.00
28 Corey Perry
29 David Backes 12.00 30.00
30 Paul Stastny 12.00 30.00
31 Mike Green 12.00 30.00
32 Zdeno Chara 15.00 40.00
33 Marc Staal 15.00 40.00
34 Dan Boyle 15.00 40.00
35 Kris Letang 40.00 80.00
36 Erik Karlsson 20.00 50.00
37 Cam Ward 20.00 50.00
39 Carey Price 60.00 120.00
40 Taylor Hall 50.00 120.00
41 Tyler Seguin 30.00 80.00
42 P.K. Subban 75.00 150.00
43 Cam Fowler
44 Logan Couture 30.00 60.00
45 Derek Stepan 20.00 50.00

2010-11 Dominion NHL Heritage Classics Embroidered Patches Autographs

STATED PRINT RUN 25 SER.#'d SETS
1 Carey Price 25.00 60.00
2 Michael Cammalleri 20.00 50.00
3 P.K. Subban 80.00 200.00
5 Scott Gomez 10.00 25.00
6 Brian Gionta 12.00 30.00
8 Jarome Iginla 50.00 100.00
9 Jay Bouwmeester 15.00 40.00
10 Henrik Karlsson 12.00 30.00
11 Joe Nieuwendyk 15.00 40.00
12 Lanny McDonald 15.00 40.00

2010-11 Dominion Nifty 50 Autographs

STATED PRINT RUN 48-50
1 Joe Nieuwendyk 10.00 25.00
2 Johnny Bucyk 10.00 25.00
3 Dino Ciccarelli 10.00 25.00
4 Adam Graves 10.00 25.00
5 Dany Heatley 10.00 25.00
6 Steven Stamkos 20.00 50.00
7 Jarome Iginla 10.00 25.00
8 Cam Neely 10.00 25.00
9 Jeremy Roenick 20.00 50.00
10 Rick Middleton 12.00 30.00
11 Lanny McDonald 12.00 30.00
12 Dennis Maruk/48 8.00 20.00
13 Charlie Simmer 6.00 15.00
14 Phil Esposito 15.00 40.00
15 Bobby Hull 15.00 40.00
16 Brett Hull 20.00 50.00
17 Guy Lafleur 25.00 50.00
18 Mike Bossy 15.00 40.00
19 Marcel Dionne 12.00 30.00
20 Dale Hawerchuk 12.00 30.00

2010-11 Dominion Notable Nicknames Autographs

STATED PRINT RUN 50 SER.#'d SETS
1 Jean Beliveau 50.00 100.00
2 Mark Messier 30.00 60.00
3 Al Arbour 10.00 25.00
4 Dustin Byfuglien 25.00 50.00
5 Johan Franzen
6 Ken Linseman 12.00 30.00
7 Felix Potvin 25.00 60.00
8 Ed Belfour 12.00 30.00
9 Doug Gilmour 25.00 50.00
10 Jarome Iginla 30.00 80.00

2010-11 Dominion Peerless Patches

STATED PRINT RUN 10-25
1 Shea Weber 40.00 80.00
2 Pekka Rinne 25.00 60.00
3 Rick Nash 50.00 100.00
4 Jonathan Toews 50.00 100.00
5 Patrick Kane 60.00 120.00
6 Michael Del Zotto 50.00 100.00
7 Eric Staal 40.00 80.00
8 Marc-Andre Fleury 40.00 80.00
9 Kris Draper 25.00 60.00
10 Brett Hull/14
11 Dennis Maruk 15.00 40.00
12 Rogie Vachon 50.00 100.00
13 Alex Ovechkin 100.00 200.00
14 Milan Lucic 40.00 80.00
15 Jimmy Howard/19 40.00 80.00
16 Henrik Lundqvist 50.00 100.00
17 Dan Boyle 20.00 50.00
18 Cam Ward 25.00 60.00
19 Brent Burns 25.00 60.00
20 Ed Belfour 40.00 80.00
21 Evgeni Malkin 100.00 200.00
22 Mario Lemieux 125.00 250.00
23 Michael Grabner 50.00 100.00
24 Ryan Kesler 50.00 100.00
25 Sidney Crosby 125.00 250.00
26 Steven Stamkos 60.00 120.00
27 Ray Bourque 60.00 120.00
28 Miikka Kiprusoff 60.00 120.00
29 Bobby Ryan/10
30 Duncan Keith 25.00 60.00
31 Matt Duchene 30.00 80.00
32 Lanny McDonald 25.00 60.00
33 Roberto Luongo 25.00 60.00
34 Teddy Purcell 15.00 40.00
35 Jaroslav Halak 40.00 80.00
36 Mikko Koivu 25.00 60.00
37 Denis Savard 40.00 80.00

2010-11 Dominion Peerless Patches

38 Saku Koivu 30.00 80.00
39 Patrick Roy 75.00 150.00
40 Jason Pominville 20.00 50.00

2010-11 Dominion Peerless Patches Combos

STATED PRINT RUN 19-25
1 M.Dionne/A.Kopitar 100.00 175.00
2 R.Middleton/M.Recchi 50.00 120.00
3 E.Lindros/M.Richards 75.00 150.00
4 A.Graves/T.Hall 75.00 150.00
5 J.Nieuwendyk/J.Iginla 75.00 200.00

2010-11 Dominion Pen Pals

STATED PRINT RUN 19-50
1 M.Schmidt/J.Beliveau 40.00 80.00
2 R.Miller/J.Craig 25.00 60.00
3 C.Neely/E.Lindros 50.00 100.00
4 D.Hanson/C.Hanson 12.00 30.00
5 N.Leveille/R.Bourque 25.00 60.00
6 T.O'Reilly/D.Schultz 20.00 50.00
7 A.Graves/B.Leetch 15.00 40.00
8 M.Richards/C.Giroux
9 J.Halak/C.Price 40.00 80.00
10 L.McDonald/S.Nolet 10.00 25.00
11 A.Arbour/D.Cherry 20.00 50.00
12 R.Lemelin/D.Bouchard 15.00 40.00
13 D.Maruk/C.Simmer 12.00 30.00
14 D.Sanderson/G.Cheevers 10.00 25.00
15 K.Linseman/S.Ott 10.00 25.00
16 B.Shanahan/B.Hull
17 C.Joseph/F.Potvin 25.00 60.00
18 L.Schenn/B.Schenn 12.00 30.00
19 N.Lidstrom/Z.Chara
20 M.Duchene/P.Stastny
21 B.Ranford/G.Fuhr 20.00 50.00
22 P.Coffey/K.Letang 20.00 50.00
23 R.Francis/E.Staal 20.00 50.00
24 T.Kerr/C.Giroux 10.00 25.00
25 J.Nieuwendyk/J.Iginla 15.00 40.00

2010-11 Dominion Pen Pals Triples

STATED PRINT RUN 25 SER.#'d SETS
1 Hall/Fowler/Wellwood 75.00 150.00
2 Sanderson/Neely/Lucic 50.00 100.00
3 Linden/Brodeur/Williams 50.00 100.00
4 Park/Staal/Leetch 15.00 40.00
5 Parent/Bobrovsky/Hextall 30.00 80.00
6 Beliveau/Cournoyer/Savard 60.00 120.00
7 Hall/Eberle/Paajarvi 125.00 250.00
8 Hanson/Carlson/Carlson 50.00 100.00
9 Dionne/Robitaille/Doughty 75.00 150.00
10 Hull/Hawerchuk/Doan 60.00 120.00

2010-11 Dominion Rookie Dual Patches

STATED PRINT RUN 15 SER.#'d SETS
1 Bobby Butler 10.00 25.00
2 Travis Hamonic 12.00 30.00
3 Jamie McBain 10.00 25.00
4 Taylor Hall 60.00 120.00
5 Tyler Seguin 60.00 120.00
6 Henrik Karlsson 10.00 25.00
7 Jared Cowen 15.00 40.00
8 Philip Larsen 10.00 25.00
9 Jeff Skinner 15.00 40.00
10 Zach Hamill 15.00 40.00

2010-11 Dominion Rookie Showcase Showdown Colossal Jerseys

STATED PRINT RUN 50 SER.#'d SETS
*PRIME/75: .5X TO 1.2X BASIC JSY
*NAME-NMBR/25-50: .6X TO 1.5X BASIC JSY
*PATCH/19: 1X TO 2.5X BASIC JSY
1 Taylor Hall 15.00 40.00
2 Jeff Skinner 8.00 20.00
3 Tomas Tatar 8.00 20.00
4 Magnus Paajarvi 5.00 12.00
5 Ryan McDonagh 10.00 25.00
6 Mats Zuccarello 6.00 15.00
7 Mattias Tedenby 3.00 8.00

2010-11 Dominion Signatures Ruby

STATED PRINT RUN 25-50
1 Corey Perry 10.00 25.00
2 Ryan Getzlaf 10.00 25.00
3 Saku Koivu 6.00 15.00
4 Bobby Ryan 6.00 15.00
5 Dustin Byfuglien 6.00 15.00
7 Evander Kane 6.00 15.00
10 Tim Thomas 12.00 30.00
11 Ryan Miller 12.00 30.00
12 Thomas Vanek 8.00 20.00
13 Drew Stafford 8.00 20.00
15 Jarome Iginla 12.00 30.00
17 Cam Ward 6.00 15.00
18 Eric Staal 8.00 20.00
19 Brandon Sutter 5.00 12.00
20 Jonathan Toews 15.00 40.00
21 Patrick Kane 20.00 50.00
22 Patrick Sharp
23 Corey Crawford 12.00 30.00
25 Erik Johnson 4.00 10.00
26 Brian Elliott 5.00 12.00
27 Matt Duchene 12.00 30.00
28 Rick Nash 6.00 15.00
29 Steve Mason 5.00 12.00
30 Antoine Vermette 4.00 10.00
31 Brad Richards 6.00 15.00
32 Loui Eriksson 6.00 15.00
33 Kari Lehtonen 6.00 15.00
34 Jimmy Howard 10.00 25.00
35 Pavel Datsyuk 15.00 40.00
36 Nicklas Lidstrom 15.00 30.00
38 Ales Hemsky 8.00 20.00
39 Sam Gagner 5.00 12.00
41 Stephen Weiss 5.00 12.00
43 Tomas Vokoun 10.00 25.00
44 Anze Kopitar 10.00 25.00
45 Drew Doughty 10.00 25.00
46 Jonathan Quick 25.00 60.00
47 Brent Burns 8.00 20.00
48 Cal Clutterbuck 6.00 15.00
50 Andrei Kostitsyn
51 Carey Price 20.00 50.00
52 Brian Gionta 5.00 12.00
54 Shea Weber 6.00 15.00
55 Pekka Rinne 8.00 20.00
57 Martin Brodeur/25 25.00 50.00
58 Travis Zajac 5.00 12.00
60 John Tavares 15.00 40.00
61 Matt Moulson 5.00 12.00
62 Michael Grabner 5.00 12.00
63 Henrik Lundqvist 10.00 25.00
64 Marian Gaborik 8.00 20.00
65 Marc Staal 6.00 15.00
66 Craig Anderson 6.00 15.00
67 Jason Spezza
68 Daniel Alfredsson 6.00 15.00
69 Chris Pronger 8.00 20.00
70 Claude Giroux 15.00 30.00
71 Jeff Carter 6.00 15.00
72 Mike Richards 6.00 15.00
73 Mikkel Boedker 4.00 10.00
74 Ilya Bryzgalov 8.00 20.00
75 Keith Yandle 6.00 15.00
76 Kris Letang 15.00 40.00
77 Sidney Crosby/25 75.00 150.00
78 Marc-Andre Fleury 25.00 50.00
79 Jordan Staal 6.00 15.00
80 Evgeni Malkin 15.00 40.00
81 Joe Thornton 6.00 15.00
82 Ryane Clowe
83 Dany Heatley 5.00 12.00
84 Logan Couture 6.00 15.00
85 T.J. Oshie 10.00 25.00
86 David Backes 6.00 15.00
87 Jaroslav Halak 6.00 15.00
88 Steven Stamkos 20.00 50.00
89 Vincent Lecavalier 5.00 12.00
90 Martin St. Louis 6.00 15.00
91 Dion Phaneuf 6.00 15.00
93 Phil Kessel 8.00 20.00
94 Roberto Luongo 20.00 50.00
95 Henrik Sedin 6.00 15.00
96 Daniel Sedin 10.00 25.00
97 Ryan Kesler 15.00 40.00
98 Alex Ovechkin/25 60.00 120.00
100 Semyon Varlamov 6.00 15.00
101 Cam Neely/45 12.00 30.00
102 Derek Sanderson 5.00 12.00
103 Felix Potvin 15.00 30.00
104 Milt Schmidt 8.00 20.00
105 Normand Leveille 8.00 20.00
106 Ray Bourque 15.00 30.00
107 Reggie Lemelin 8.00 20.00
108 Rick Middleton 8.00 20.00
109 Dale Hawerchuk 8.00 20.00
110 Gilbert Perreault 6.00 15.00
111 Tom Barrasso 10.00 25.00
112 Doug Gilmour 12.00 30.00
113 Bobby Hull 12.00 30.00
114 Denis Savard 15.00 40.00
116 Phil Esposito 10.00 25.00
117 Stan Mikita 10.00 25.00
118 Tony Esposito 12.00 30.00
119 Ed Belfour 12.00 30.00
120 Steve Yzerman/25 40.00 80.00
121 Grant Fuhr 10.00 25.00
122 Mark Messier/25 25.00 60.00
123 Kelly Hrudey 5.00 12.00
124 Guy Lafleur 12.00 30.00
125 Henri Richard 12.00 30.00
126 Jean Beliveau 25.00 60.00
127 Patrick Roy/25 60.00 120.00
128 Denis Potvin 6.00 15.00
129 Mike Bossy 8.00 20.00
130 Brad Park 5.00 12.00
131 Brian Leetch 6.00 15.00
132 Adam Graves 12.00 30.00
133 Ed Giacomin 10.00 25.00
134 Rod Gilbert 8.00 20.00
135 Bernie Parent 15.00 40.00
136 Bobby Clarke 10.00 25.00
137 Eric Lindros/25 30.00 80.00
138 Luc Robitaille 10.00 25.00
139 Mario Lemieux 50.00 100.00
140 Joe Sakic/25 20.00 50.00
141 Ron Hextall 12.00 30.00
142 Jeremy Roenick 20.00 50.00
143 Brendan Shanahan/25 15.00 40.00
144 Brett Hull 15.00 40.00
145 Glenn Hall 12.00 30.00
146 Manon Rheaume 25.00 60.00
147 Curtis Joseph 8.00 20.00
148 Darryl Sittler 8.00 20.00
149 Johnny Bower 12.00 30.00
150 Trevor Linden 15.00 40.00

2010-11 Dominion Stickside Signatures

STATED PRINT RUN 49-50
1 Gerry Cheevers 12.00 30.00
2 Curtis Joseph 20.00 50.00
3 Ed Belfour 20.00 50.00
4 Johnny Bower 30.00 60.00
5 Patrick Roy 75.00 150.00
6 Jose Theodore 12.00 30.00
7 Marc-Andre Fleury 30.00 60.00
8 Martin Brodeur 60.00 120.00
9 Ilya Bryzgalov 15.00 40.00
10 Henrik Lundqvist 50.00 100.00
11 Jaroslav Halak 12.00 30.00
12 Tim Thomas 25.00 60.00
13 Carey Price/49 50.00 100.00
14 Marty Turco 12.00 30.00
15 Jonathan Bernier 15.00 40.00
16 Mike Smith 12.00 30.00
17 Tomas Vokoun 10.00 25.00
18 Rogie Vachon 15.00 40.00
19 Charlie Hodge 12.00 30.00
20 Grant Fuhr 25.00 60.00

2010-11 Dominion Strapping Lads

STATED PRINT RUN 25 SER.#'d SETS
1 Sidney Crosby 50.00 100.00
2 Alex Ovechkin 40.00 80.00
3 Carey Price 25.00 60.00
4 Tim Thomas 12.00 30.00
5 Milan Lucic 8.00 20.00
6 Dion Phaneuf 8.00 20.00
7 Mike Green 8.00 20.00
8 Jarome Iginla 8.00 20.00
9 Evander Kane 8.00 20.00
10 Ilya Kovalchuk 8.00 20.00

2010-11 Dominion Tape to Tape Autographs

STATED PRINT RUN 12-20
1 Marc-Andre Fleury 90.00 150.00
2 Johnny Bower 60.00 120.00
3 Alex Ovechkin 250.00 400.00
4 Gerry Cheevers 40.00 80.00
5 Henrik Lundqvist 100.00 200.00
6 Rogie Vachon 60.00 120.00
7 Steve Ott 20.00 50.00
8 Phil Kessel 50.00 100.00
9 Mario Lemieux 75.00 150.00
10 Brendan Shanahan 50.00 100.00
11 Tim Thomas/19 60.00 120.00
12 Patrick Roy 100.00 200.00
13 Marian Gaborik 40.00 80.00
14 Steve Yzerman/13
15 Scott Gomez 25.00 50.00
16 Rick Nash/12
17 Joe Nieuwendyk 40.00 80.00
18 Stan Mikita 40.00 80.00
19 Mark Messier/19 60.00 120.00

2011-12 Dominion

1-100 STATED PRINT RUN 199
101-130 ROOKIE AU PRINT RUN 99-199
131-182 ROOKIE JSY AU PRINT RUN 199
183-200 ROOKIE JSY AU PRINT RUN 99
1 Evgeni Malkin 5.00 12.00
2 Claude Giroux 6.00 15.00
3 Steven Stamkos 6.00 15.00
4 James Reimer 3.00 8.00
5 Phil Kessel 4.00 10.00
6 Dustin Byfuglien 3.00 8.00
7 Henrik Sedin 3.00 8.00
8 Pavel Datsyuk 4.00 10.00
9 Gordie Howe 6.00 15.00
10 Jordan Eberle 3.00 8.00
11 John Tavares 4.00 10.00
12 Jonathan Toews 6.00 15.00
13 Daniel Sedin 3.00 8.00
14 Ryan Miller 3.00 8.00
15 Shea Weber 2.50 6.00
16 Brett Hull 4.00 10.00
17 Erik Karlsson 6.00 15.00
18 Zach Parise 3.00 8.00
19 Steve Yzerman 5.00 12.00
20 Sidney Crosby 12.00 30.00
21 Alex Ovechkin 12.00 30.00
22 Jimmy Howard 3.00 8.00
23 Patrice Bergeron 4.00 10.00
24 Jamie Benn 4.00 10.00
25 Joe Thornton 3.00 8.00
26 Patrick Kane 6.00 15.00
27 Jonathan Quick 5.00 12.00
28 Loui Eriksson 2.50 6.00
29 Vincent Lecavalier 2.50 6.00
30 Marian Gaborik 4.00 10.00
31 Carey Price 10.00 25.00
32 Corey Perry 3.00 8.00
33 Patrick Roy 8.00 20.00
34 Taylor Hall 6.00 15.00
35 Tyler Seguin 6.00 15.00
36 Martin Brodeur 6.00 15.00
37 Eric Staal 4.00 10.00
38 Marc-Andre Fleury 5.00 12.00
39 Dany Heatley 2.50 6.00
40 David Backes 3.00 8.00
41 Jaromir Jagr 8.00 20.00
42 Ryan Getzlaf 5.00 12.00
43 Henrik Lundqvist 4.00 10.00
44 Rick Nash 3.00 8.00
45 Matt Duchene 3.00 8.00
46 Shane Doan 2.50 6.00
47 Evander Kane 3.00 8.00
48 Tim Thomas 3.00 8.00
49 Saku Koivu 3.00 8.00
50 Nicklas Lidstrom 3.00 8.00
51 P.K. Subban 6.00 15.00
52 Kris Letang 3.00 8.00
53 Pekka Rinne 4.00 10.00
54 Cam Ward 3.00 8.00
55 Marian Hossa 2.50 6.00
56 Logan Couture 3.00 8.00
57 Matt Moulson 2.50 6.00
58 Bobby Ryan 3.00 8.00
59 Dion Phaneuf 3.00 8.00
60 Jose Theodore 3.00 8.00
61 Patrick Sharp 3.00 8.00
62 Henrik Zetterberg 4.00 10.00
63 T.J. Oshie 5.00 12.00
64 Jarome Iginla 3.00 8.00
65 Mikko Koivu 2.50 6.00
66 Mario Lemieux 10.00 25.00
67 Scott Hartnell 3.00 8.00
68 Jean-Sebastien Giguere 2.50 6.00
69 Jonas Gustavsson 3.00 8.00
70 Ray Whitney 2.50 6.00
71 Ryan Kesler 4.00 10.00
72 Kari Lehtonen 2.50 6.00
73 Brian Elliott 2.50 6.00
74 Miikka Kiprusoff 3.00 8.00
75 Patrick Marleau 3.00 8.00
76 Ilya Kovalchuk 3.00 8.00
77 Michael Grabner 2.50 6.00
78 David Krejci 3.00 8.00
79 Max Pacioretty 3.00 8.00
80 Jason Spezza 3.00 8.00
81 Jeff Skinner 3.00 8.00
82 Paul Stastny 3.00 8.00
83 Alexander Semin 3.00 8.00
84 Jaroslav Halak 3.00 8.00
85 Braden Holtby 6.00 15.00
86 Daniel Alfredsson 3.00 8.00
87 Brad Richards 3.00 8.00
88 Eric Lindros 5.00 12.00
89 Bobby Hull 3.00 8.00
90 Martin St. Louis 3.00 8.00
91 Anze Kopitar 5.00 12.00
92 Curtis Joseph 3.00 8.00
93 Roberto Luongo 3.00 8.00
94 Guy Lafleur 5.00 12.00
95 Thomas Vanek 3.00 8.00
96 Cam Neely 3.00 8.00
97 Ron Hextall 4.00 10.00
98 Joe Sakic 5.00 12.00
99 Mike Modano 5.00 12.00
100 Phil Esposito 5.00 12.00
101 P.Maroon AU/199 RC EX 5.00 12.00
102 T.J. Brennan AU/199 RC 5.00 12.00
103 Joe Finley AU/199 RC 5.00 12.00
104 Marcus Foligno AU/199 RC 8.00 20.00
105 Brayden McNabb AU/199 RC 5.00 12.00
106 Corey Tropp AU/199 RC 5.00 12.00
107 Leland Irving AU/199 RC 5.00 12.00
108 Lance Bouma AU/99 RC 6.00 15.00
109 Riley Nash AU/199 RC 5.00 12.00
110 Jimmy Hayes AU/199 RC 6.00 15.00
111 Dylan Olsen AU/199 RC 5.00 12.00
112 Andrew Shaw AU/199 RC 15.00 40.00
113 Brad Malone AU/199 RC 5.00 12.00

14 Elliott AU/199 RC EX 5.00 12.00
15 Matt Fraser AU/199 RC 6.00 15.00
16 C.Vande Velde AU/199 RC 8.00 20.00
17 Colten Teubert AU/199 RC 5.00 12.00
18 Lennart Petrell AU/199 RC 6.00 15.00
19 Hugh Jessiman AU/199 RC 5.00 12.00
20 Scott Timmins AU/199 RC 5.00 12.00
21 Carson McMillan AU/199 RC 6.00 15.00
22 Bagnall AU/150 RC 5.00 12.00
23 Roman Josi AU/199 RC 8.00 20.00
24 G.Bourque AU/199 RC 5.00 12.00
25 Keith Kinkaid AU/199 RC 5.00 12.00
26 A.Nilsson AU/199 RC 5.00 12.00
27 Mark Katic AU/199 RC 5.00 12.00
28 Mikko Koskinen AU/199 RC 6.00 15.00
29 Ben Holmstrom AU/199 RC 5.00 12.00
30 Paul Postma AU/199 RC 5.00 12.00
31 Peter Holland JSY AU/199 RC 6.00 15.00
33 Greg Nemisz JSY AU/199 RC 6.00 15.00
34 Roman Horak JSY AU/199 RC 6.00 15.00
35 J.Faulk JSY AU/199 RC 12.00 30.00
36 Kruger JSY AU/199 RC EX 20.00 40.00
37 C.Gaunce JSY AU/199 RC 5.00 12.00
38 John Moore JSY AU/199 RC 8.00 20.00
39 C.Atkinson JSY AU/199 RC 15.00 40.00
40 Allen York JSY AU/199 RC 8.00 20.00
41 Tomas Kubalik JSY AU/199 RC 6.00 15.00
42 Da.Savard JSY AU/199 RC 12.00 30.00
43 T.Vincour JSY AU/199 RC 6.00 15.00
44 Sceviour JSY AU/199 RC 6.00 15.00
45 G.Nyquist JSY AU/199 RC 30.00 80.00
46 B.Smith JSY AU/199 RC 6.00 15.00
47 Hartikainn JSY AU/199 RC 6.00 15.00
48 Lander JSY AU/199 RC 6.00 15.00
49 S.Voynov JSY AU/199 RC 6.00 15.00
50 B.Bulmer JSY AU/199 RC 6.00 15.00
51 R.Diaz JSY AU/199 RC 6.00 15.00
52 A.Emelin JSY AU/199 RC 6.00 15.00
53 Palushaj JSY AU/199 RC 6.00 15.00
54 Geoffrion JSY AU/199 RC 12.00 30.00
55 J.Blum JSY AU/199 RC 6.00 15.00
56 Craig Smith JSY AU/199 RC 12.00 30.00
57 Ryan Ellis JSY AU/199 RC 6.00 15.00
58 Calvin de Haan JSY AU/199 RC 10.00 25.00
59 Cam Talbot JSY AU/199 RC 30.00 80.00
60 Tim Erixon JSY AU/199 RC 8.00 20.00
61 P.Wiercioch JSY AU/199 RC 6.00 15.00
62 Erik Condra JSY AU/199 RC 6.00 15.00
63 S.Da Costa JSY AU/199 RC 6.00 15.00
64 Colin Greening JSY AU/199 RC 8.00 20.00
65 Zac Rinaldo JSY AU/199 RC 10.00 25.00
66 H.Zolnierczyk JSY AU/199 RC 8.00 20.00
67 Gustafsson JSY AU/199 RC 12.00 30.00
68 Rundblad JSY AU/199 RC 10.00 25.00
69 Andy Miele JSY AU/199 RC 8.00 20.00
70 Despres JSY AU/199 RC 10.00 25.00
71 R.Bortuzzo JSY AU/199 RC 8.00 20.00
72 Joe Vitale JSY AU/199 RC 15.00 40.00
73 H.Sateri JSY AU/199 RC 12.00 30.00
74 B.Connolly JSY AU/199 RC 10.00 25.00
75 Matt Frattin JSY AU/199 RC 8.00 20.00
76 J.Gardiner JSY AU/199 RC 10.00 25.00
77 Scrivens JSY AU/199 RC 10.00 25.00
78 E.Lack JSY AU/199 RC 12.00 30.00
79 Yann Sauve JSY AU/199 RC 6.00 15.00
80 Cody Eakin JSY AU/199 RC 8.00 20.00
81 D.Orlov JSY AU/199 RC 8.00 20.00
82 Carl Klingberg JSY AU/199 RC 8.00 20.00
83 M.Macenauer JSY AU/99 RC 8.00 20.00
84 Hodgson JSY AU/99 RC 25.00 60.00
85 B.Saad JSY AU/99 RC 30.00 80.00
86 Landeskog JSY AU/99 RC 75.00 150.00
87 Johansen JSY AU/99 RC 50.00 100.00
88 RNH JSY AU/99 RC 100.00 200.00
89 Gudbranson JSY AU/99 RC 10.00 25.00
90 L.Leblanc JSY AU/99 RC 8.00 20.00
91 Henrique JSY AU/99 RC 30.00 80.00
92 Larsson JSY AU/99 RC 10.00 25.00
93 Hagelin JSY AU/99 RC 20.00 50.00
94 Zibanejad JSY AU/99 RC 20.00 50.00
95 Couturier JSY AU/99 RC 30.00 80.00
96 M.Read JSY AU/99 RC 15.00 40.00
97 Brian Strait JSY AU/99 RC 10.00 25.00
98 Colborne JSY AU/99 RC 25.00 60.00
99 Kassian JSY AU/99 RC 10.00 25.00
200 Scheifele JSY AU/99 RC 25.00 60.00

2011-12 Dominion Gold

*1-100 VETS/25: .6X TO 1.5X BASIC CARDS
*101-130 RK.AU/25: .6X TO 1.5X AU/99-199
*131-182 JSY AU/25: .6X TO 1.5X JSY AU/199
*183-200 JSY AU/25: .4X TO 1X JSY AU RC/99
STATED PRINT RUN 25 SER.#'d SETS
EXCH EXPIRATION: 3/28/2014
183 Patrick Roy 25.00 60.00
186 G.Landeskog JSY AU 100.00 200.00
188 R.Nugent-Hopkins JSY AU 300.00 600.00

2011-12 Dominion All-Star Embroidered Patches Autographs

STATED PRINT RUN 15 SER.#'d SETS
1 Corey Perry 15.00 40.00
2 Brian Elliott 15.00 40.00
3 Tim Thomas 12.00 30.00
4 Logan Couture 15.00 40.00
5 Tyler Seguin 50.00 120.00
6 Zdeno Chara 20.00 50.00
7 Jarome Iginla
8 Dion Phaneuf 15.00 40.00
9 Marian Hossa 12.00 30.00
10 Steven Stamkos 30.00 80.00
11 Patrick Kane 30.00 80.00
12 Jamie Benn 15.00 40.00
13 Pavel Datsyuk 20.00 50.00
14 Jimmy Howard
15 Henrik Lundqvist 50.00 100.00
16 Marian Gaborik 20.00 50.00
17 Carey Price 50.00 120.00
18 Shea Weber 12.00 30.00
19 Nick Johnson 12.00 30.00
20 Luke Adam 12.00 30.00
21 Gabriel Landeskog 50.00 100.00
22 Matt Read 25.00 60.00
23 Sean Couturier 30.00 60.00
24 Colin Greening
25 Cody Hodgson 30.00 60.00
26 Justin Faulk 20.00 50.00

2011-12 Dominion All-Star Skills Complete Sweaters

STATED PRINT RUN 15
1 Daniel Alfredsson 20.00 50.00
2 Keith Yandle 15.00 40.00
3 Shea Weber 12.00 30.00
4 Erik Karlsson 30.00 80.00
5 Jason Spezza 15.00 40.00
6 John Tavares
7 Claude Giroux 25.00 50.00
8 Daniel Sedin 15.00 40.00
9 Henrik Sedin 15.00 40.00
10 Scott Hartnell 15.00 40.00

11 Milan Michalek 10.00 25.00
12 Steven Stamkos 20.00 50.00
13 Henrik Lundqvist 20.00 50.00
14 Jonathan Quick 40.00 100.00
15 Brian Elliott 12.00 30.00
16 Zdeno Chara 30.00 60.00
17 Ryan Suter 10.00 25.00
18 Kimmo Timonen 12.00 30.00
19 Dion Phaneuf 15.00 40.00
20 Corey Perry 15.00 40.00
21 Marian Gaborik 20.00 50.00
22 Phil Kessel 20.00 50.00
23 Patrick Kane 30.00 80.00
24 Tyler Seguin 30.00 60.00
25 Jamie Benn 20.00 50.00
26 Marian Hossa 15.00 40.00
27 Joffrey Lupul 12.00 30.00
28 Jimmy Howard 15.00 40.00
29 Tim Thomas 15.00 40.00
30 Carey Price 50.00 120.00

2011-12 Dominion Autographed Rookie Patches Horizontal

STATED PRINT RUN 2-93
EXCH EXPIRATION: 3/28/2014
131 Peter Holland/74 8.00 20.00
133 Greg Nemisz/48 10.00 25.00
134 Roman Horak/51 10.00 25.00
135 Justin Faulk/28 15.00 40.00
136 Marcus Kruger/16 EXCH 20.00 50.00
137 Cameron Gaunce/43 8.00 20.00
140 Allen York/41 12.00 30.00
141 Tomas Kubalik/33 10.00 25.00
142 David Savard/58 10.00 25.00
143 Tomas Vincour/81 8.00 20.00
144 Colton Sceviour/22 12.00 30.00
147 Teemu Hartikainen/56 12.00 30.00
148 Anton Lander/57 10.00 25.00
149 Slava Voynov/26 10.00 25.00
150 Brett Bulmer/19 12.00 30.00
151 Raphael Diaz/61 8.00 20.00
152 Alexei Emelin/74 8.00 20.00
153 Aaron Palushaj/60 8.00 20.00
154 Blake Geoffrion/57 10.00 25.00
156 Craig Smith/15 25.00 50.00
157 Ryan Ellis/49 10.00 25.00
158 Calvin de Haan/44 15.00 40.00
159 Cam Talbot/81 30.00 80.00
160 Tim Erixon/53 10.00 25.00
161 Patrick Wiercioch/46 10.00 25.00
162 Erik Condra/22 10.00 25.00
163 Stephane Da Costa/24 10.00 25.00
165 Zac Rinaldo/36 10.00 25.00
166 Harry Zolnierczyk/29 10.00 25.00
167 Erik Gustafsson/26 12.00 30.00
169 Andy Miele/21 10.00 25.00
170 Simon Despres/47 15.00 40.00
171 Robert Bortuzzo/41 10.00 25.00
172 Joe Vitale/46 10.00 25.00
173 Harri Sateri/35 10.00 25.00
175 Matt Frattin/39 10.00 25.00
176 Jake Gardiner/51 15.00 40.00
177 Ben Scrivens/30 15.00 40.00
178 Eddie Lack/31 15.00 40.00
179 Yann Sauve/47 10.00 25.00
180 Cody Eakin/50 12.00 30.00
181 Dmitry Orlov/81 10.00 25.00
182 Carl Klingberg/48 15.00 40.00
183 Maxime Macenauer/49 10.00 25.00
184 Cody Hodgson/19 50.00 120.00
185 Brandon Saad/43 25.00 50.00
186 Gabriel Landeskog/92 15.00 40.00
187 Ryan Johansen/19
188 R.Nugent-Hopkins JSY 40.00 100.00
189 Erik Gudbranson/44 EXCH 12.00 30.00
190 Louis Leblanc/71 8.00 20.00
193 Carl Hagelin/62 15.00 40.00
194 Mika Zibanejad/93 15.00 40.00
196 Matt Read/24 25.00 60.00
197 Brian Strait/37 12.00 30.00
198 Joe Colborne/32 10.00 25.00
200 Mark Scheifele/55 20.00 50.00

2011-12 Dominion Benchmark Sticks

STATED PRINT RUN 10-99
1 Martin Brodeur/50 20.00 50.00
2 Ron Francis/50 12.00 30.00
3 Mark Messier/50 15.00 30.00
4 Steve Yzerman/50 15.00 40.00
5 Gordie Howe/25 40.00 80.00
6 Marcel Dionne/25 12.00 30.00
7 Mario Lemieux/50 30.00 80.00
8 Joe Sakic/25 15.00 40.00
9 Jaromir Jagr/25 30.00 60.00
10 Ed Belfour/99 12.00 25.00
11 Tony Esposito/50 15.00 40.00
12 Patrick Roy/99 15.00 40.00
13 Martin Brodeur/50 20.00 50.00
14 Gordie Howe/25 30.00 80.00
15 Mark Messier/50 15.00 40.00
16 Jaromir Jagr/50 15.00 40.00
17 Bobby Hull/25 30.00 60.00
18 Mike Modano/25 20.00 50.00
19 Gordie Howe/10
20 Mark Messier/10

2011-12 Dominion Complete Rookies Quad Jerseys

STATED PRINT RUN 25 SER.#'d SETS
1 Devante Smith-Pelly/25 12.00 30.00
2 Cody Hodgson/25 20.00 50.00
3 Greg Nemisz/25 12.00 30.00
4 Justin Faulk/25 15.00 40.00
5 Brandon Saad/25 25.00 60.00
6 Marcus Kruger/25 15.00 30.00
7 Gabriel Landeskog/25 30.00 60.00
8 Cam Atkinson/25 25.00 60.00
9 Ryan Johansen/25 20.00 50.00
10 Brendan Smith/25 10.00 25.00
11 Gustav Nyquist/25 15.00 40.00
12 Anton Lander/25 10.00 25.00
13 Ryan Nugent-Hopkins/25 50.00 100.00
14 Erik Gudbranson/25 12.00 30.00
15 Slava Voynov/25 10.00 25.00
16 Brett Bulmer/25 10.00 25.00
17 Blake Geoffrion/25 10.00 25.00
18 Louis Leblanc/25 15.00 40.00
19 Craig Smith/25 15.00 40.00
20 Ryan Ellis/25 10.00 25.00
21 Adam Henrique/25 30.00 80.00
22 Adam Larsson/25 20.00 50.00
23 Calvin de Haan/25 10.00 25.00
24 Carl Hagelin/25 15.00 40.00
25 Tim Erixon/25 10.00 25.00
26 Colin Greening/25 12.00 30.00
27 Mika Zibanejad/25 25.00 60.00
28 Matt Read/25 20.00 40.00
29 Sean Couturier/25 25.00 50.00
30 David Rundblad/25 10.00 25.00
31 Simon Despres/25 15.00 40.00
32 Brett Connolly/25 12.00 30.00
33 Ben Scrivens/25 15.00 40.00
34 Jake Gardiner/25 15.00 40.00
35 Joe Colborne/25 12.00 30.00
36 Eddie Lack/25 10.00 25.00
37 Zack Kassian/25 15.00 40.00
38 Cody Eakin/25 15.00 40.00
39 Dmitry Orlov/25 12.00 30.00
40 Mark Scheifele/15 40.00 80.00

2011-12 Dominion Crazy Eights Jerseys

STATED PRINT RUN 25 SER.#'d SETS
1 Ovechkin/RNH/Kane/MAF 60.00 100.00
2 Goalie Young Stars 40.00 80.00
3 Forward Young Stars 50.00 100.00
4 Defense Stars 40.00 80.00
5 Physical Leaders 40.00 80.00
6 Colorado Avalanche 50.00 100.00
7 Toronto Maple Leafs 25.00 60.00
8 Ovechkin/Kane/Lindros 50.00 100.00
9 LA Kings 60.00 100.00
10 Boston Bruins 40.00 80.00
11 Lemieux/Lindros/Roy/Messier 50.00 100.00
12 Philadelphia Flyers Vets 40.00 100.00
13 RNH/Landeskog Young Stars 50.00 120.00
14 Larsson/Gudbranson/Voynov 50.00 100.00
15 Scheifele/Connolly/Saad 40.00 100.00
16 Detroit Red Wings 60.00 120.00
17 Pittsburgh Penguins 25.00 60.00
18 Flyers Young Stars 60.00 100.00
19 Star Captains 50.00 100.00
20 Czech Stars 40.00 80.00
21 Finnish Stars 60.00 125.00
22 Canada Vets 30.00 80.00
23 Canada Young Stars 50.00 120.00
24 USA Stars 30.00 80.00
25 Russian Stars 50.00 100.00
26 Sweeden Stars 25.00 60.00
27 Retired Stars 100.00 200.00

2011-12 Dominion Engravatures Bruins 2011 Tribute

STATED PRINT RUN 15 SER.#'d SETS
1 Zdeno Chara 60.00 120.00
2 Tomas Kaberle 50.00 100.00
3 Andrew Ference 40.00 80.00
4 Dennis Seidenberg 50.00 100.00
5 Adam McQuaid 40.00 80.00
6 Johnny Boychuk 40.00 80.00
7 Nathan Horton 40.00 100.00
8 Daniel Paille 30.00 80.00
9 Shawn Thornton 40.00 80.00
10 Milan Lucic 60.00 120.00
11 Michael Ryder 50.00 100.00
12 Brad Marchand 60.00 120.00
13 Gregory Campbell 40.00 80.00
14 Tyler Seguin 100.00 175.00
15 Chris Kelly 40.00 80.00
16 Patrice Bergeron 60.00 120.00
17 Marc Savard 40.00 80.00
18 David Krejci 60.00 120.00
19 Rich Peverley 50.00 100.00
20 Tuukka Rask 75.00 150.00
21 Tim Thomas 75.00 150.00
22 Cam Neely 60.00 120.00
23 Johnny Bucyk 30.00 80.00
24 Claude Julien 40.00 80.00
25 Boston Bruins 2011 125.00 250.00

2011-12 Dominion Jerseys

COMMON CARD/50-100 2.50 6.00
SEMISTARS/50-100 3.00 8.00
UNL.STARS/50-100 4.00 10.00
STATED PRINT RUN 10-100
1 Cam Fowler/100 3.00 8.00
2 D.Smith-Pelly/100 5.00 12.00
3 Teemu Selanne/100 8.00 20.00
4 Milan Lucic/100 4.00 10.00
5 Tuukka Rask/100 4.00 10.00
6 Ray Bourque/50 8.00 20.00
7 Brad Boyes/100 2.50 6.00
8 Cody Hodgson/100 4.00 10.00
9 Tyler Myers/100 4.00 10.00
10 Mike Cammalleri/100 3.00 8.00
11 Greg Nemisz/100 3.00 8.00
12 Mikael Backlund/100 4.00 10.00
13 Justin Faulk/100 5.00 12.00
14 Zach Boychuk/100 2.50 6.00
15 Brandon Saad/100 6.00 15.00
16 Marcus Kruger/100 5.00 12.00
17 Stan Mikita/50 6.00 15.00
18 Gabriel Landeskog/100 6.00 15.00
19 Joe Sakic/100 6.00 15.00
20 Paul Stastny/100 4.00 10.00
21 Steve Downie/50 4.00 10.00
22 Cam Atkinson/100 8.00 20.00
23 Jack Johnson/100 2.50 6.00
24 Ryan Johansen/100 6.00 15.00
25 Colton Sceviour/100 3.00 8.00
26 Brenden Morrow/100 3.00 8.00
27 Loui Eriksson/100 3.00 8.00
28 Brendan Smith/100 3.00 8.00
29 Gordie Howe/10
30 Niklas Kronwall/100 3.00 8.00
31 Pavel Datsyuk/100 5.00 12.00
32 Jordan Eberle/100 5.00 12.00
33 R.Nugent-Hopkins/100 6.00 15.00
34 Sam Gagner/100 3.00 8.00
35 Teemu Hartikainen/100 3.00 8.00
36 Dmitry Kulikov/100 2.50 6.00
37 Erik Gudbranson/100 4.00 10.00
38 Wojtek Wolski/100 2.50 6.00
39 Kris Versteeg/100 3.00 8.00
40 Ron Francis/50 6.00 15.00
41 Jeff Carter/100 4.00 10.00
42 Luc Robitaille/100 4.00 10.00
43 Mike Richards/100 4.00 10.00
44 Cal Clutterbuck/50 5.00 12.00
45 Dany Heatley/100 3.00 8.00
46 Devin Setoguchi/100 3.00 8.00
47 Blake Geoffrion/100 4.00 10.00
48 Louis Leblanc/100 6.00 15.00
49 Patrick Roy/50 12.00 30.00
50 Raphael Diaz/100 3.00 8.00
51 Anders Lindback/100 3.00 8.00
52 Craig Smith/100 4.00 10.00
53 Patric Hornqvist/100 4.00 10.00
54 Adam Larsson/100 4.00 10.00
55 Joe Nieuwendyk/100 4.00 10.00
56 Martin Brodeur/100 6.00 15.00
57 Bryan Trottier/100 5.00 12.00
58 Frans Nielsen/100 2.50 6.00
59 Pat LaFontaine/100 5.00 12.00
60 Brandon Dubinsky/100 3.00 8.00
61 Carl Hagelin/100 4.00 10.00
62 Marian Gaborik/100 5.00 12.00
63 Ryan Callahan/100 4.00 10.00
64 Daniel Alfredsson/100 4.00 10.00
65 Erik Condra/100 3.00 8.00
66 Robin Lehner/100 5.00 12.00
67 Brayden Schenn/100 4.00 10.00
68 Matt Read/100 3.00 8.00
69 Scott Hartnell/100 4.00 10.00
70 Sean Couturier/100 5.00 12.00
71 David Rundblad/100 3.00 8.00
72 Mike Smith/100 4.00 10.00
73 Shane Doan/100 3.00 8.00
74 Chris Kunitz/100 4.00 10.00
75 Mario Lemieux/50 15.00 40.00
76 Sidney Crosby/50 20.00 50.00
77 Simon Despres/100 3.00 8.00
78 Dan Boyle/100 3.00 8.00
79 Joe Pavelski/100 4.00 10.00
80 Patrick Marleau/100 4.00 10.00
81 Brett Hull/100 5.00 12.00
82 David Perron/100 2.50 6.00
83 Patrik Berglund/100 3.00 8.00
84 Brett Connolly/100 3.00 8.00
85 Martin St. Louis/100 4.00 10.00
86 Ryan Malone/100 2.50 6.00
87 Steven Stamkos/50 6.00 15.00
88 Jake Gardiner/100 5.00 12.00
89 Joe Colborne/100 4.00 10.00
90 Mikhail Grabovski/100 3.00 8.00
91 Wendel Clark/100 5.00 12.00
92 Alexandre Burrows/100 4.00 10.00
93 Eddie Lack/100 3.00 8.00
94 Zack Kassian/100 4.00 10.00
95 Alex Ovechkin/100 6.00 15.00
96 Braden Holtby/100 8.00 20.00
97 Mike Green/100 4.00 10.00
98 Carl Klingberg/100 3.00 8.00
99 Mark Scheifele/100 8.00 20.00
100 Tobias Enstrom/100 2.50 6.00

2011-12 Dominion Jerseys Prime

*PRIME/25: 1X TO 2.5X BASIC JSY/100
*PRIME/25: .8X TO 2X BASIC JSY/50
STATED PRINT RUN 5-25
81 Brett Hull/25 15.00 40.00

2011-12 Dominion Mammoth Jerseys

1-50 STATED PRINT RUN 50
51-60 STATED PRINT RUN 25
*PRIME/25: .6X TO 1.5X MAMMOTH/50
1 D.Smith-Pelly/50 10.00 25.00
2 Cody Hodgson/50 12.00 30.00
3 Greg Nemisz/50 6.00 15.00
4 Justin Faulk/50 10.00 25.00
5 Brandon Saad/50 12.00 40.00
6 Marcus Kruger/50 10.00 25.00
7 Cameron Gaunce/50 5.00 12.00
8 Gabriel Landeskog/50 12.00 30.00
9 Cam Atkinson/50 15.00 40.00
10 David Savard/50 6.00 15.00
11 John Moore/50 6.00 15.00
12 Ryan Johansen/50 10.00 25.00
13 Tomas Vincour/50 6.00 15.00
14 Brendan Smith/50 6.00 15.00
15 Gustav Nyquist/50 10.00 25.00
16 Anton Lander/50 6.00 15.00
17 R.Nugent-Hopkins/50 12.00 30.00
18 Teemu Hartikainen/50 6.00 15.00
19 Erik Gudbranson/50 8.00 20.00
20 Slava Voynov/50 6.00 15.00
21 Brett Bulmer/50 6.00 15.00
22 Blake Geoffrion/50 6.00 15.00
23 Louis Leblanc/50 8.00 20.00
24 Raphael Diaz/50 6.00 15.00
25 Craig Smith/50 8.00 20.00
26 Ryan Ellis/50 6.00 15.00
27 Adam Henrique/50 10.00 25.00
28 Adam Larsson/50 6.00 15.00
29 Calvin de Haan/50 6.00 15.00
30 Carl Hagelin/50 8.00 20.00
31 Tim Erixon/50 6.00 15.00
32 Colin Greening/50 6.00 15.00
33 Erik Condra/50 6.00 15.00
34 Mika Zibanejad/50 8.00 20.00
35 Matt Read/50 8.00 20.00
36 Sean Couturier/50 6.00 15.00
37 Zac Rinaldo/50 6.00 15.00
38 David Rundblad/50 6.00 15.00
39 Joe Vitale/50 6.00 15.00
40 Simon Despres/50 6.00 15.00
41 Harri Sateri/50 6.00 15.00
42 Ben Scrivens/50 10.00 25.00
43 Jake Gardiner/50 12.00 30.00
44 Joe Colborne/50 8.00 20.00
45 Matt Frattin/50 10.00 25.00
46 Yann Sauve/50 6.00 15.00
47 Zack Kassian/50 8.00 20.00
48 Cody Eakin/50 6.00 15.00
49 Dmitry Orlov/50 8.00 20.00
50 Mark Scheifele/50 12.00 30.00
51 Ray Bourque/25 12.00 30.00
52 Joe Sakic/25 15.00 40.00
53 Steve Yzerman/25 15.00 40.00
54 Patrick Roy/25 25.00 60.00
55 Martin Brodeur/25 15.00 40.00
56 Mark Messier/25 12.00 30.00
57 Jaromir Jagr/25 25.00 60.00
58 Sidney Crosby/25 40.00 100.00
59 Steven Stamkos/25 15.00 40.00
60 Alex Ovechkin/25 40.00 100.00

2011-12 Dominion Patches Autographs

EXCH EXPIRATION: 3/28/2014
1 Corey Perry/60 12.00 30.00
3 Ryan Getzlaf/60 12.00 30.00
4 Brad Marchand/60 12.00 30.00
5 Patrice Bergeron/60 20.00 50.00
6 Ray Bourque/25 40.00 80.00
7 Tim Thomas/60 15.00 40.00
8 Cody Hodgson/60 15.00 40.00
9 Ryan Miller/60 20.00 50.00
10 Curtis Glencross/60 10.00 25.00
11 Greg Nemisz/60 10.00 25.00
12 Jarome Iginla/60 15.00 40.00
13 Mark Scheifele/25 25.00 60.00
14 Justin Faulk/60 12.00 30.00
15 Ron Francis/60 15.00 40.00
16 Brandon Saad/60 30.00 80.00
17 Jonathan Toews/60 30.00 60.00
18 Marcus Kruger/60 12.00 30.00
19 Patrick Kane/60 20.00 50.00
21 Joe Sakic/25 50.00 100.00
22 Matt Duchene/60 10.00 25.00
23 Lanny McDonald/10
24 Jack Johnson/60 10.00 25.00
25 Rick Nash/60 15.00 40.00
26 Ryan Johansen/60 15.00 40.00
27 Loui Eriksson/60 12.00 30.00
28 Mike Modano/25 30.00 60.00
29 Brendan Smith/60 15.00 40.00
30 Gordie Howe/5
31 Pavel Datsyuk/60 15.00 40.00
32 Steve Yzerman/25 60.00 120.00
33 Anton Lander/60 12.00 30.00
34 Jordan Eberle/60 40.00 80.00
35 Ryan Nugent-Hopkins/60 40.00 100.00
36 Taylor Hall/25 30.00 80.00
37 Ed Belfour/60 25.00 50.00
38 Erik Gudbranson/60 EXCH 12.00 30.00
39 Drew Doughty/60 EXCH 15.00 40.00
40 Dustin Brown/60 12.00 30.00
42 Jeremy Roenick/60 15.00 40.00
43 Luc Robitaille/60 12.00 30.00
44 Cal Clutterbuck/60 12.00 30.00
45 Niklas Backstrom/60 12.00 30.00
46 Brian Gionta/60 8.00 20.00
47 Carey Price/25 30.00 80.00
48 Louis Leblanc/60 8.00 20.00
49 Patrick Roy/25 60.00 120.00
50 Craig Smith/60 10.00 25.00
51 Pekka Rinne/60 15.00 40.00
52 Ryan Ellis/60 15.00 40.00
53 Adam Henrique/60 20.00 50.00
54 Adam Larsson/60 10.00 25.00
55 Joe Nieuwendyk/60 15.00 40.00
56 Martin Brodeur/25 90.00 150.00
57 Calvin de Haan/60 8.00 20.00
58 John Tavares/60 30.00 80.00
59 Pat LaFontaine/60 15.00 40.00
60 Carl Hagelin/60 12.00 30.00
61 Marc Staal/60 10.00 25.00
62 Marian Gaborik/60 12.00 30.00
63 Mark Messier/25 40.00 80.00
64 Colin Greening/60 8.00 20.00
65 Craig Anderson/60 10.00 25.00
66 Mika Zibanejad/60 20.00 50.00
67 Nick Foligno/60 8.00 20.00
68 Claude Giroux/60 EXCH 25.00 50.00
69 Eric Lindros/25 60.00 120.00
70 Jaromir Jagr/60 40.00 100.00
71 Matt Read/60 15.00 40.00
72 Sean Couturier/60 15.00 40.00
73 David Rundblad/60 12.00 30.00
74 Shane Doan/60 10.00 25.00
76 Joe Vitale/60 8.00 20.00
77 Mario Lemieux/25 100.00 175.00
78 Sidney Crosby/25 100.00 175.00
79 Dan Boyle/60 12.00 30.00
80 Joe Thornton/60 15.00 40.00
81 Patrick Marleau/60 12.00 30.00
82 Alex Pietrangelo/60 12.00 30.00
83 David Backes/60 12.00 30.00
84 Brett Connolly/60 8.00 20.00
85 Martin St. Louis/60 10.00 25.00
86 Steven Stamkos/25 30.00 80.00
87 Vincent Lecavalier/35 15.00 40.00
88 Curtis Joseph/60 15.00 40.00
89 Felix Potvin/60 15.00 40.00
90 Jake Gardiner/60 20.00 50.00
91 Joe Colborne/60 20.00 50.00
92 Phil Kessel/50 12.00 30.00
93 Cam Neely/25 30.00 60.00
94 Daniel Sedin/60 10.00 25.00
95 Henrik Sedin/60 15.00 40.00
96 Zack Kassian/60 10.00 25.00
97 Alex Ovechkin/25 60.00 120.00
98 Cody Eakin/60 10.00 25.00
99 Dustin Byfuglien/60 12.00 30.00

2011-12 Dominion Peerless Patches Autographs

EXCH EXPIRATION: 3/28/2014
1 Bobby Ryan/40 15.00 40.00
2 Corey Perry/40
3 D.Smith-Pelly/40
4 Tim Thomas/40 20.00 50.00
5 Tyler Seguin/40 30.00 80.00
6 Cam Neely/25 25.00 50.00
7 Ray Bourque/25 40.00 80.00
8 Ryan Miller/40 15.00 40.00
9 Henrik Sedin/40 25.00 50.00
10 Cody Hodgson/40 20.00 50.00
11 Jarome Iginla/40 25.00 50.00
12 Greg Nemisz/40 10.00 25.00
13 Ryan Kesler/40 15.00 40.00
14 Eric Staal/10
15 Patrick Kane/40 75.00 150.00
16 Jonathan Toews/40 40.00 100.00
17 Brandon Saad/40 30.00 60.00
18 Denis Savard/25 30.00 60.00
19 Matt Duchene/40 20.00 50.00
20 Patrick Roy/25 150.00 300.00
21 Gabriel Landeskog/40 40.00 80.00
22 Rick Nash/10
23 Ryan Johansen/40 20.00 50.00
24 Loui Eriksson/40 10.00 25.00
25 Jamie Benn/40 15.00 40.00
26 Ed Belfour/25 30.00 60.00
27 Mike Modano/40 30.00 80.00
28 Gordie Howe/5
30 Steve Yzerman/25 60.00 120.00
31 Brendan Smith/40 10.00 25.00
32 Brendan Shanahan/40 40.00 80.00
33 Nicklas Lidstrom/25 60.00 120.00
34 R.Nugent-Hopkins/40 50.00 100.00
35 Taylor Hall/40 60.00 120.00
37 Anton Lander/40 15.00 40.00
39 Stephen Weiss/40 10.00 25.00
40 Ron Francis/25 40.00 100.00
41 Anze Kopitar/40 25.00 50.00
43 Luc Robitaille/10
44 Bernie Nicholls/25 30.00 80.00
45 Alex Ovechkin/40 60.00 120.00
46 Niklas Backstrom/40 15.00 40.00
47 Cal Clutterbuck/40 12.00 30.00
48 Louis Leblanc/40 10.00 25.00
49 Carey Price/40 40.00 100.00
50 Patrick Roy/25 125.00 250.00
51 Guy Lafleur/25 90.00 150.00
52 Blake Geoffrion/40 10.00 25.00
53 Craig Smith/40 8.00 20.00
54 Pekka Rinne/40 25.00 60.00
55 Adam Larsson/40 12.00 30.00
56 Adam Henrique/40 20.00 50.00
57 Martin Brodeur/25 60.00 125.00
58 John Tavares/40 50.00 100.00
59 Pat LaFontaine/25 15.00 40.00
60 Marian Gaborik/40 15.00 40.00
61 Brad Richards/40 12.50 30.00
62 Carl Hagelin/40 15.00 40.00
63 Marc Staal/40 12.00 30.00
64 Cody Eakin/40 12.00 30.00
65 Mark Messier/25 40.00 80.00
66 Colin Greening/40 10.00 25.00
67 Mika Zibanejad/40 15.00 40.00
68 Erik Karlsson/40 EXCH 30.00 80.00
69 Claude Giroux/40 40.00 80.00
70 Sean Couturier/40 15.00 40.00
71 Matt Read/40 12.00 30.00
72 Jaromir Jagr/40 40.00 100.00
73 Ron Hextall/25 20.00 50.00
74 Eric Lindros/25 60.00 120.00
75 Shane Doan/10
76 Andy Miele/40 10.00 25.00
77 Mario Lemieux/25 150.00 300.00
79 Sidney Crosby/40 100.00 200.00
80 Marc-Andre Fleury/40 20.00 50.00
81 Joe Sakic/25 50.00 120.00
82 Joe Thornton/40 12.00 30.00
83 Patrick Marleau/40 15.00 40.00
84 Alex Pietrangelo/25 25.00 50.00
85 Jaroslav Halak/40 15.00 40.00
86 Brett Hull/25 50.00 100.00
87 Steven Stamkos/40 40.00 100.00
88 Brett Connolly/40 20.00 50.00
89 Martin St. Louis/40 12.00 30.00
90 Phil Kessel/40 15.00 40.00
91 Jake Gardiner/40 25.00 60.00
92 Joe Colborne/40 10.00 25.00
93 Curtis Joseph/10
94 Zack Kassian/40 20.00 50.00
95 Daniel Sedin/40 15.00 40.00

2011-12 Dominion Peerless Patches Combos

STATED PRINT RUN 5-15
1 J.Eberle/RNH/15 100.00 200.00
2 Alfredsson/Zetterberg/15 25.00 60.00
3 S.Koivu/T.Selanne/15 60.00 150.00
4 J.Carter/M.Richards/15 30.00 80.00
5 H.Lundqvist/M.Biron/15 60.00 125.00
6 Bryzgalov/Bobrovsky/15 50.00 100.00
7 A.Lindback/P.Rinne/15 60.00 150.00
8 J.Enroth/R.Miller/15 30.00 80.00
9 J.Bernier/J.Quick/15 50.00 120.00
10 S.Weber/Z.Chara/15
11 C.Hagelin/C.Greening/15 40.00 100.00
12 C.Perry/P.Kane/15 60.00 120.00
13 J.Benn/M.Read/15 20.00 50.00
14 S.Stamkos/T.Thomas/15 40.00 100.00
15 M.Brodeur/P.Roy/5
16 D.Phaneuf/RNH/15 75.00 150.00
17 Landeskog/Eriksson/15 60.00 150.00
18 M.Read/S.Couturier/15 40.00 100.00
19 B.Saad/M.Kruger/15 100.00 200.00
20 Sidney Crosby/5

2011-12 Dominion Pen Pals

STATED PRINT RUN 25-50
EXCH EXPIRATION: 3/28/2014
2 Bourque/Thomas/50 25.00 60.00
3 C.Hodgson/P.LaFontaine 15.00 40.00
4 A.Shaw/B.Saad/50 20.00 50.00
5 R.Nash/R.Johansen/50 15.00 40.00
6 B.Smith/G.Nyquist/50 20.00 50.00
7 B.Hull/B.Shanahan 20.00 50.00
8 Lander/RNH/50 20.00 50.00
10 Geoffrn/Leblnc/50 8.00 20.00
11 C.Smith/R.Ellis/50 10.00 25.00
12 Henrique/Larsson/50 15.00 40.00
13 C.Hagelin/G.Landeskog 10.00 25.00
14 Ovchkin/Malkin/25 EXCH 60.00 120.00
16 B.Schenn/S.Couturier 12.00 30.00
17 C.Giroux/M.Read 12.00 30.00
18 E.Lindros/J.Jagr/50 40.00 80.00
19 Vitale/Tocchet/50 EXCH 8.00 20.00
20 C.Joseph/J.Halak/50 25.00 60.00
21 B.Connolly/S.Stamkos 12.00 30.00
22 Gardiner/Colborne/50 20.00 50.00
23 B.Scrivens/F.Potvin/50 15.00 40.00
24 R.Kesler/Z.Kassian/50 20.00 50.00
25 Hawerchuk/Scheifele/50 20.00 50.00
26 Landeskog/Eriksson/50 20.00 50.00
27 Gudbranson/Despres/50 10.00 25.00
28 M.Modano/J.Iginla 15.00 40.00
29 M.Gaborik/S.Mikita 15.00 40.00

2011-12 Dominion Quad Jerseys

STATED PRINT RUN 5-25
1 Ducks/25 15.00 40.00
2 Bruins/25 12.00 30.00
3 Sabres/25 15.00 40.00
4 Flames/25 12.00 30.00
5 Blackhawks/25
6 Avalanche/25 15.00 40.00
7 Blue Jackets/25 15.00 40.00
8 Stars/25 12.00 30.00
9 Red Wings/25 20.00 50.00
10 Oilers/25 15.00 40.00
11 Panthers/25 20.00 50.00
12 Kings/25 25.00 60.00
13 Wild/25
14 Canadiens/25 15.00 40.00
15 Predators/25 15.00 40.00
16 Devils/25 25.00 60.00
17 Islanders/25 15.00 40.00
18 Rangers/25 15.00 40.00
19 Senators/25 20.00 50.00
20 Flyers/25 15.00 40.00
21 Coyotes/25 12.00 30.00
22 Penguins/25 10.00 25.00
23 Sharks/25 20.00 50.00
24 Blues/25 12.00 30.00
25 Lightning/25 15.00 40.00
26 Maple Leafs/25 15.00 40.00
27 Canucks/25 30.00 60.00
28 Capitals/25 30.00 80.00
29 Jets/25 20.00 50.00
30 Clarke/Howe/Espo/Mikta/5
31 Ovch/Giroux/Gabrk/Brodr/25 30.00 60.00
32 Backes/Brwn/Doan/Wber/25 15.00 40.00
33 Sedin/Lngo/Thms/Chra/25 20.00 50.00
34 Ebrle/Erksn/StLou/Moulsn/25 12.00 30.00
35 Backs/Bergrn/Dtsyk/Keslr/25
36 Lndqvst/Quick/Smth/Rnne/25 10.00 25.00
37 Karlssn/Lidst/Webr/Chara/25 15.00 40.00
38 Girx/Malkn/Lnqvst/Stmks/25 15.00 40.00
39 Henrq/Lndskg/Read/RNH/25 20.00 50.00
40 Joseph/Belfour/Roy/Hextll/25 30.00 60.00

2011-12 Dominion Rookie Showcase Autographed Pucks

STATED PRINT RUN 25 SER.#'d SETS
*PRIME JSY/25: .4X TO 1X DUAL PUCK/25
1 Landeskog/RNH 75.00 150.00
2 A.Palushaj/J.Colborne
3 D.Rundblad/M.Zibanejad
4 Gardiner/Colborne 15.00 40.00
6 B.Smith/R.Ellis 10.00 25.00
8 J.Faulk/T.Erixon 15.00 40.00
9 Klingbrg/Lndeskg 30.00 80.00
11 B.Connolly/C.Eakin 15.00 40.00
12 A.Henrique/S.Despres 25.00 60.00
13 Connolly/Nugent-Hopkins 15.00 40.00
14 A.Henrique/G.Nemisz 25.00 60.00
15 A.Palushaj/J.Moore 10.00 25.00
16 Lndeskg/Zibnejad 30.00 80.00
18 Landeskog/Kruger EXCH 30.00 80.00
19 Nugent-Hopkins/Kassian 50.00 120.00

2011-12 Dominion RPS Pen Pals

STATED PRINT RUN 25-99
1 Nugent-Hopkins/Hall/25 40.00 100.00
2 Landeskog/Duchene/99 12.00 30.00
3 R.Ellis/T.Hall/25 10.00 25.00
7 Landeskog/Zibanejad/99 12.00 30.00
9 Landeskog/RNH/25 50.00 120.00
10 B.Smith/N.Lidstrom/25 20.00 50.00
12 Eberle/RNH/25 40.00 100.00
13 Messier/RNH/25 40.00 100.00
14 RNH/Stamkos/25 75.00 150.00
15 Larsson/Lidstrom/25 30.00 60.00
16 Larsson/Niedermayer/25 20.00 50.00
17 Rundblad/Zibanejad/99 15.00 40.00
19 Geoffrion/Ellis/99 6.00 15.00

2011-12 Dominion RPS Pen Pals Triples

STATED PRINT RUN 25 SER.#'d SETS
1 Tavares/RNH/Hall 100.00 200.00
2 Larsson/Landeskog/RNH 75.00 150.00
4 Larsson/Landskg/Zibanjd 50.00 100.00
8 Park/Smith/Lidstrom 15.00 40.00
9 Miller/Vanek/Kassian 15.00 40.00

2011-12 Dominion Stanley Cup Championship Signatures

STATED PRINT RUN 25 SER.#'d SETS
1 Tim Thomas 30.00 60.00
2 Jonathan Toews 30.00 60.00
3 Sidney Crosby 100.00 175.00
6 Eric Staal 20.00 50.00
7 Martin St. Louis 25.00 50.00
9 Brendan Shanahan 40.00 80.00
10 Ray Bourque 40.00 80.00
11 Scott Niedermayer 15.00 40.00
12 Brett Hull 30.00 80.00
13 Steve Yzerman 60.00 120.00
14 Nicklas Lidstrom 40.00 80.00
15 Joe Sakic 50.00 100.00
16 Martin Brodeur 40.00 80.00
17 Mark Messier 30.00 60.00
18 Patrick Roy 75.00 150.00
19 Ron Francis 30.00 60.00
20 Mario Lemieux 60.00 120.00

2011-12 Dominion Stickside Signatures

STATED PRINT RUN 5-25
1 Cam Neely/25 50.00 100.00
2 Dale Hawerchuk/25 40.00 100.00
3 Tyler Seguin/25 50.00 120.00
4 Alex Ovechkin/15 150.00 300.00
5 Pat LaFontaine/25 25.00 60.00
6 Bobby Hull/25 50.00 100.00
7 Ryan Kesler/25 40.00 100.00
8 Joe Sakic/25 60.00 120.00
9 Loui Eriksson/25 15.00 40.00
10 Mike Modano/15 50.00 100.00
11 Gordie Howe/5
12 Steve Yzerman/15 75.00 150.00
13 Mark Messier/15
14 Ron Francis/25 30.00 80.00
15 Luc Robitaille/25 25.00 60.00
16 Marcel Dionne/25 30.00 80.00
17 Doug Gilmour/25 30.00 80.00
18 Vincent Lecavalier/25 15.00 40.00
19 Steven Stamkos/25 100.00 200.00
20 Denis Potvin/25 25.00 60.00
21 Brendan Shanahan/25
22 Marian Gaborik/25 30.00 80.00
23 Eric Lindros/25 40.00 100.00
24 Jaromir Jagr/10
25 Evgeni Malkin/25 EXCH 75.00 150.00
26 Jordan Staal/25 20.00 50.00
27 Mario Lemieux/15 150.00 300.00
28 Joe Thornton/25 40.00 80.00
29 Brett Hull/25 50.00 100.00

2011-12 Dominion Sweeter By The Dozen Jerseys

STATED PRINT RUN 25
1 Young Stars 60.00 120.00
2 Superstar Vets 150.00 300.00
3 Goalie Stars 125.00 250.00
4 Bruins/Canucks 60.00 150.00
5 Wings/Avalanche 60.00 120.00
6 Rangers/Flyers 60.00 120.00
7 Capitals/Penguins 60.00 120.00
8 Leafs/Canadiens 75.00 150.00
9 Oilers/Flames 60.00 150.00

2011-12 Dominion Tape to Tape Autographs

STATED PRINT RUN 5-20
3 Ed Belfour/16 30.00 80.00
4 Jonathan Toews/20 125.00 200.00
6 Brendan Shanahan/20
12 Carey Price/20 75.00 150.00
14 Martin Brodeur/18 75.00 150.00
18 Mike Smith/20 25.00 60.00
20 Sidney Crosby/15 150.00 300.00
21 Jaroslav Halak/20 25.00 60.00
25 Vincent Lecavalier/20 15.00 40.00
26 Curtis Joseph/20 30.00 80.00
29 Felix Potvin/20 60.00 120.00

2012-13 Dominion

101-148 ROOKIE JSY AU PRINT RUN 99
1 Teemu Selanne 6.00 15.00
2 Corey Perry 3.00 8.00
3 Cam Fowler 2.50 6.00
4 Jarome Iginla 3.00 8.00
5 Miikka Kiprusoff 2.50 6.00
6 Al MacInnis 3.00 8.00
7 Patrick Kane 6.00 15.00
8 Jonathan Toews 6.00 15.00
9 Ed Belfour 3.00 8.00
10 Gabriel Landeskog 3.00 8.00
11 Joe Sakic 5.00 12.00
12 Matt Duchene 3.00 8.00
13 Artem Anisimov 2.50 6.00
14 Sergei Bobrovsky 3.00 8.00
15 Jack Johnson 2.00 5.00
16 Jaromir Jagr 8.00 20.00
17 Loui Eriksson 2.50 6.00
18 Mike Modano 5.00 12.00
19 Henrik Zetterberg 4.00 10.00
20 Gordie Howe 6.00 15.00
21 Steve Yzerman 6.00 15.00
22 Pavel Datsyuk 4.00 10.00
23 Mark Messier 4.00 10.00
24 Ryan Nugent-Hopkins 6.00 15.00
25 Taylor Hall 6.00 15.00
26 Jordan Eberle 3.00 8.00
27 Jonathan Quick 5.00 12.00
28 Anze Kopitar 5.00 12.00
29 Luc Robitaille 3.00 8.00
30 Dustin Brown 3.00 8.00
31 Zach Parise 3.00 8.00
32 Niklas Backstrom 2.50 6.00
33 Ryan Suter 2.00 5.00
34 Pekka Rinne 4.00 10.00
35 Craig Smith 2.00 5.00
36 Shea Weber 2.50 6.00
37 Mike Smith 3.00 8.00
38 Oliver Ekman-Larsson 3.00 8.00
39 Mikkel Boedker 2.00 5.00
40 Joe Thornton 3.00 8.00
41 Logan Couture 3.00 8.00
42 Jeremy Roenick 3.00 8.00
43 Alex Pietrangelo 2.50 6.00
44 T.J. Oshie 5.00 12.00
45 Brett Hull 3.00 8.00

46 Pavel Bure 4.00 10.00
47 Daniel Sedin 3.00 8.00
48 Cory Schneider 2.50 6.00
49 Tyler Seguin 5.00 12.00
50 Tuukka Rask 3.00 8.00
51 Cam Neely 3.00 8.00
52 Ryan Miller 3.00 8.00
53 Thomas Vanek 3.00 8.00
54 Pierre Turgeon 3.00 8.00
55 Cody Hodgson 3.00 8.00
56 Jordan Staal 3.00 8.00
57 Eric Staal 4.00 10.00
58 Cam Ward 3.00 8.00
59 Scott Clemmensen 2.50 6.00
60 George Parros 2.50 6.00
61 John Vanbiesbrouck 3.00 8.00
62 Carey Price 10.00 25.00
63 Patrick Roy 8.00 20.00
64 Michael Ryder 2.00 5.00
65 Ilya Kovalchuk 3.00 8.00
66 Adam Henrique 3.00 8.00
67 Martin Brodeur 6.00 15.00
68 John Tavares 6.00 15.00
69 Pat LaFontaine 3.00 8.00
70 Matt Moulson 2.50 6.00
71 Rick Nash 3.00 8.00
72 Henrik Lundqvist 4.00 10.00
73 Mike Richter 3.00 8.00
74 Marian Gaborik 3.00 8.00
75 Daniel Alfredsson 3.00 8.00
76 Mika Zibanejad 3.00 8.00
77 Erik Karlsson 6.00 15.00
78 Claude Giroux 3.00 8.00
79 Simon Gagne 3.00 8.00
80 Eric Lindros 4.00 10.00
81 Sidney Crosby 12.00 30.00
82 Mario Lemieux 10.00 25.00
83 Marc-Andre Fleury 5.00 12.00
84 Evgeni Malkin 10.00 25.00
85 Vincent Lecavalier 2.50 6.00
86 Steven Stamkos 6.00 15.00
87 Anders Lindback 2.00 5.00
88 James van Riemsdyk 3.00 8.00
89 Felix Potvin 5.00 12.00
90 Phil Kessel 4.00 10.00
91 Nazem Kadri 3.00 8.00
92 Alex Ovechkin 6.00 15.00
93 Nicklas Backstrom 5.00 12.00
94 Braden Holtby 5.00 12.00
95 Mike Gartner 3.00 8.00
96 Andrew Ladd 3.00 8.00
97 Mark Scheifele 4.00 10.00
98 Ondrej Pavelec 3.00 8.00
99 Dustin Byfuglien 3.00 8.00
100 Dale Hawerchuk 4.00 10.00
101 Mat Clark JSY AU RC 10.00 25.00
102 Max Sauve JSY AU RC 10.00 25.00
103 Michael Hutchinson JSY AU RC 15.00 40.00
104 Torey Krug JSY AU RC 50.00 100.00
105 Carter Camper JSY AU RC 8.00 20.00
106 Lane MacDermid JSY AU RC 10.00 25.00
107 Travis Turnbull JSY AU RC 10.00 25.00
108 Akim Aliu JSY AU RC 10.00 25.00
109 Sven Baertschi JSY AU RC 12.00 30.00
110 Jeremy Welsh JSY AU RC 10.00 25.00
111 Brandon Bollig JSY AU RC 12.00 30.00
112 Mike Connolly JSY AU RC 10.00 25.00
113 Tyson Barrie JSY AU RC 20.00 50.00
114 Andrew Joudrey JSY AU RC 12.00 30.00
115 Cody Goloubef JSY AU RC 10.00 25.00
116 Dalton Prout JSY AU RC 12.00 30.00
117 Shawn Hunwick JSY AU RC 10.00 25.00
118 Brenden Dillon JSY AU RC 10.00 25.00
119 Reilly Smith JSY AU RC 20.00 50.00
120 Ryan Garbutt JSY AU RC 10.00 25.00
121 Scott Glennie JSY AU RC 10.00 25.00
122 Riley Sheahan JSY AU RC 10.00 25.00
123 Philippe Cornet JSY AU RC 10.00 25.00
124 Colby Robak JSY AU RC 10.00 25.00
125 Jordan Nolan JSY AU RC 10.00 25.00
126 Chay Genoway JSY AU RC 10.00 25.00
127 Jason Zucker JSY AU RC 12.00 30.00
128 Kris Foucault JSY AU RC 10.00 25.00
129 Tyler Cuma JSY AU RC 10.00 25.00
130 Gabriel Dumont JSY AU RC 10.00 25.00
131 Robert Mayer JSY AU RC 12.00 30.00
132 Chet Pickard JSY AU RC 10.00 25.00
133 Aaron Ness JSY AU RC 10.00 25.00
134 Casey Cizikas JSY AU RC 10.00 25.00
135 Matt Donovan JSY AU RC 10.00 25.00
136 Matt Watkins JSY AU RC 10.00 25.00
137 Chris Kreider JSY AU RC 25.00 60.00
138 Jakob Silfverberg JSY AU RC 20.00 50.00
139 Mark Stone JSY AU RC 20.00 50.00
140 Brandon Manning JSY AU RC 10.00 25.00
141 Michael Stone JSY AU RC 10.00 25.00
142 Tyson Sexsmith JSY AU RC 10.00 25.00
143 Jaden Schwartz JSY AU RC 25.00 60.00
144 Jake Allen JSY AU RC 30.00 80.00
145 J.T. Brown JSY AU RC 10.00 25.00
146 Carter Ashton JSY AU RC 8.00 20.00
147 Jussi Rynnas JSY AU RC 10.00 25.00
148 Ryan Hamilton JSY AU RC 10.00 25.00

2012-13 Dominion Gold

*1-100 VETS/25: .8X TO 2X BASIC CARDS
93 Nicklas Backstrom 10.00 25.00

2012-13 Dominion Autographed Rookie Patches Parallel

*PATCH/AU/31-74: .4X TO 1X JSY AU/99
*PATCH/AU/15-29: .5X TO 1.2X JSY AU/99

2012-13 Dominion Engravatures Kings

1 Dustin Brown 60.00 120.00
2 Anze Kopitar 100.00 200.00
3 Justin Williams 50.00 100.00
4 Dustin Penner 50.00 100.00
5 Mike Richards 60.00 120.00
6 Jeff Carter 50.00 100.00
7 Jarret Stoll 50.00 100.00
8 Simon Gagne 50.00 100.00
9 Jordan Nolan 40.00 80.00
10 Kyle Clifford 40.00 80.00
11 Rob Scuderi 40.00 80.00
12 Drew Doughty 75.00 135.00
13 Willie Mitchell 40.00 80.00
14 Slava Voynov 50.00 125.00
15 Alec Martinez 40.00 80.00
16 Matt Greene 40.00 80.00
17 Davis Drewiske 40.00 80.00
18 Jonathan Quick 75.00 150.00
19 Jonathan Bernier 50.00 100.00
20 Trevor Lewis 40.00 80.00
21 Dwight King 40.00 80.00
22 Darryl Sutter 40.00 80.00
23 Ron Hextall 60.00 120.00
24 Luc Robitaille 50.00 100.00
25 Los Angeles Kings 125.00 250.00

2012-13 Dominion Patches Autographs

1-29 ROOKIE PRINT RUN 60
31-100 VETERAN PRINT RUN 5-60
EXCH EXPIRATION: 2/28/2015
1 Chris Kreider/60 15.00 40.00
2 Jaden Schwartz/60 12.00 30.00
3 Jakob Silfverberg/60 12.00 30.00
4A Alex Ovechkin/25 40.00 80.00
4B Jake Allen/60 20.00 50.00
5 Reilly Smith/60 15.00 40.00
6 Jussi Rynnas/60 6.00 15.00
7 Sven Baertschi/60 8.00 20.00
8 Chet Pickard/60 6.00 15.00
9 J.T. Brown/60 10.00 25.00
10 Carter Ashton/60 5.00 12.00
11 Casey Cizikas/60 12.00 30.00
12 Jason Zucker/60 8.00 20.00
13 Michael Stone/60 6.00 15.00
14 Robert Mayer/60 8.00 20.00
15 Travis Turnbull/60 6.00 15.00
16 Tyler Cuma/60 6.00 15.00
17 Tyson Barrie/60 12.00 30.00
18 Andrew Joudrey/60 6.00 15.00
19 Ryan Hamilton/60 6.00 15.00
20 Brandon Manning/60 10.00 25.00
21 Matt Watkins/60 6.00 15.00
22 Matt Donovan/60 6.00 15.00
23 Mark Stone/60 12.00 30.00
24 Lane MacDermid/60 8.00 20.00
25 Kris Foucault/60 6.00 15.00
26 Jordan Nolan/60 6.00 15.00
27 Jeremy Welsh/60 6.00 15.00
28 Shawn Hunwick/60 6.00 15.00
29 Riley Sheahan/60 6.00 15.00
31 Joe Pavelski/60 10.00 25.00
32 Henrik Lundqvist/25 25.00 50.00
33 John Tavares/60 20.00 50.00
34 Gabriel Landeskog/60 8.00 20.00
35 Carl Hagelin/60 8.00 20.00
36 James Neal/60 10.00 25.00
37 Dustin Brown/60 10.00 25.00
39 Colin Wilson/60 8.00 20.00
40 Cory Schneider/60 8.00 20.00
41 Bobby Ryan/60 10.00 25.00
42 Patrick Kane/25 40.00 100.00
43 Milan Hejduk/60 8.00 20.00
44 Jonathan Quick/25 30.00 60.00
45 Marc-Andre Fleury/25 25.00 60.00
46 Loui Eriksson/60 8.00 20.00
48 Jay Bouwmeester/60 10.00 25.00
49 Stu Grimson/60 6.00 15.00
50 Richard Bachman/60 8.00 20.00
51 Stan Mikita/25 30.00 80.00
52 Cody Goloubef/60 8.00 20.00
53 Kevin Shattenkirk/60 10.00 25.00
54 Bernie Parent/25 40.00 80.00
55 Matt Duchene/60 12.00 30.00
56 Cody Hodgson/60 10.00 25.00
57 Patrik Elias/60 10.00 25.00
58 Pat LaFontaine/25 15.00 40.00
59 Phil Kessel/60 12.00 30.00
60 Ryan Nugent-Hopkins/60 20.00 50.00
61 Joe Thornton/25 15.00 40.00
62 Jamie Benn/40 12.00 30.00
63 Patrick Marleau/60 10.00 25.00
64 Nikolai Kulemin/60 8.00 20.00
65 Mason Raymond/60 8.00 20.00
66 Martin St. Louis/60 10.00 25.00
67 Devan Dubnyk/60 10.00 25.00
68 Semyon Varlamov/60 12.00 30.00
69 Ray Bourque/25 25.00 50.00
70 Reggie Leach/60 15.00 30.00
71 Logan Couture/60 10.00 25.00
72 Ryan Miller/25 15.00 40.00
73 Ryan Getzlaf/25 15.00 40.00
74 Pierre Turgeon/60 15.00 40.00
75 Pekka Rinne/60 12.00 30.00
76 Pavel Datsyuk/25
79 Keith Yandle/60 10.00 25.00
80 Jordan Eberle/60 15.00 40.00
82 Martin Brodeur/25 40.00 80.00
83 John Carlson/60 12.00 30.00
84 Claude Giroux/60 15.00 40.00
88 Luc Robitaille/25 20.00 50.00
89 Taylor Hall/60 20.00 50.00
90 Brett Hull/25 50.00 100.00
91 Ed Belfour/25 25.00 50.00
92 Rod Brind'Amour/60 10.00 25.00
93 Ron Francis/25 12.00 30.00
94 Joe Sakic/25 30.00 80.00
96 Igor Larionov/25 15.00 40.00

2012-13 Dominion Peerless Patches Autographs

*1-29 ROOKIE/40: .6X TO 1.5X PATCH AU/60
1-29 ROOKIE PRINT RUN 40
STATED PRINT RUN 5-40
1 Chris Kreider/40 20.00 50.00
2 Jaden Schwartz/40 20.00 50.00
3 Jakob Silfverberg/40 15.00 40.00
4B Jake Allen/40 30.00 80.00
5 Reilly Smith/40 15.00 40.00
6 Jussi Rynnas/40 10.00 25.00
7 Sven Baertschi/40 15.00 40.00
8 Chet Pickard/40 10.00 25.00
9 J.T. Brown/40 8.00 20.00
10 Carter Ashton/40 8.00 20.00
11 Casey Cizikas/40 15.00 40.00
12 Jason Zucker/40 12.00 30.00
13 Michael Stone/40 10.00 25.00
14 Robert Mayer/40 12.00 30.00
15 Travis Turnbull/40 8.00 20.00
16 Tyler Cuma/40 10.00 25.00
17 Tyson Barrie/40 20.00 50.00
18 Andrew Joudrey/40 10.00 25.00
19 Ryan Hamilton/40 10.00 25.00
20 Brandon Manning/40 15.00 40.00
21 Matt Watkins/40 10.00 25.00
22 Matt Donovan/40 15.00 40.00
23 Mark Stone/40 20.00 50.00
24 Lane MacDermid/40 12.00 30.00
25 Kris Foucault/40 10.00 25.00
26 Jordan Nolan/40 10.00 25.00
27 Jeremy Welsh/40 10.00 25.00
28 Shawn Hunwick/40 10.00 25.00
29 Riley Sheahan/40 15.00 40.00
31 Joe Pavelski/40 15.00 40.00
33 John Tavares/40 30.00 80.00
34 Gabriel Landeskog/40 15.00 40.00
35 Carl Hagelin/40 12.00 30.00
36 James Neal/40 15.00 40.00
37 Dustin Brown/40 15.00 40.00
39 Colin Wilson/40 12.00 30.00
40 Cory Schneider/40 12.00 30.00
41 Bobby Ryan/40 15.00 40.00
42 Patrick Kane/25 60.00 120.00
43 Milan Hejduk/40 12.00 30.00
44 Jonathan Quick/40 40.00 80.00
45 Marc-Andre Fleury/25 30.00 80.00
46 Loui Eriksson/40 10.00 25.00
47 Kevin Bieksa/40 12.00 30.00
48 Jay Bouwmeester/40 15.00 40.00
49 Sean Couturier/40 15.00 40.00
50 Richard Bachman/40 10.00 25.00
51 Jhonas Enroth/40 15.00 40.00
52 Henrik Lundqvist/25 25.00 60.00
53 Kevin Shattenkirk/40 15.00 40.00
54 Jonathan Bernier/40 15.00 40.00
55 Matt Duchene/40 10.00 25.00
56 Cody Hodgson/40 15.00 40.00
57 Stephen Weiss/30 15.00 40.00
58 David Backes/40 15.00 40.00
59 Phil Kessel/40 10.00 25.00
60 Ryan Nugent-Hopkins/40 40.00 100.00
61 Joe Thornton/25 20.00 50.00
62 Jamie Benn/40 20.00 50.00
63 Patrick Marleau/40 15.00 40.00
64 Nikolai Kulemin/40 12.00 30.00
65 Mason Raymond/40 12.00 30.00
66 Martin St. Louis/40 15.00 40.00
67 Devan Dubnyk/40 15.00 40.00
68 Semyon Varlamov/40 15.00 40.00
69 Matt Read/40 12.00 30.00
70 Kris Letang/40 20.00 50.00
71 Logan Couture/40 15.00 40.00
73 Ryan Getzlaf/40 25.00 60.00
74 Mikael Backlund/40 12.00 30.00
75 Pekka Rinne/40 20.00 50.00
76 Pavel Datsyuk/25 EXCH 40.00 80.00
79 Keith Yandle/40 15.00 40.00
80 Jordan Eberle/40 15.00 40.00
81 Evgeni Malkin/25 40.00 80.00
83 John Carlson/40 20.00 50.00
84 Claude Giroux/40 25.00 60.00
87 Felix Potvin/40 30.00 80.00
88 Luc Robitaille/25 25.00 60.00
89 John LeClair/40 12.00 30.00
90 Brett Hull/25 30.00 80.00
92 Keith Primeau/40 15.00 40.00
96 Ron Francis/25 25.00 60.00

2013-14 Dominion

1-100 VET STATED PRINT RUN 299
101-105 ROOKIE PRINT RUN 299
106-130 ROOKIE AU PRINT RUN 299
131-226 ROOK.JSY AU PRINT RUN 99-299
1 Bobby Ryan 2.00 5.00
2 Ryan Getzlaf 3.00 8.00
3 Corey Perry 2.00 5.00
4 Cam Fowler 1.50 4.00
5 Brad Marchand 2.50 6.00
6 Tuukka Rask 2.00 5.00
7 Tyler Seguin 3.00 8.00
8 Torey Krug 2.50 6.00
9 Ryan Miller 2.00 5.00
10 Cody Hodgson 2.00 5.00
11 Thomas Vanek 2.00 5.00
12 Mike Cammalleri 1.50 4.00
13 Curtis Glencross 1.25 3.00
14 Miikka Kiprusoff 1.50 4.00
15 Eric Staal 2.50 6.00
16 Jeff Skinner 1.50 4.00
17 Cam Ward 2.00 5.00
18 Patrick Kane 4.00 10.00
19 Jonathan Toews 4.00 10.00
20 Brandon Saad 2.00 5.00
21 Corey Crawford 2.50 6.00
22 Gabriel Landeskog 1.50 4.00
23 Matt Duchene 2.00 5.00
24 P.A. Parenteau 1.25 3.00
25 Tyson Barrie 2.00 5.00
26 Marian Gaborik 2.00 5.00
27 Brandon Dubinsky 1.50 4.00
28 Sergei Bobrovsky 2.00 5.00
29 Jamie Benn 2.50 6.00
30 Loui Eriksson 1.50 4.00
31 Kari Lehtonen 1.50 4.00
32 Pavel Datsyuk 2.50 6.00
33 Henrik Zetterberg 2.50 6.00
34 Brendan Smith 1.50 4.00
35 Jimmy Howard 2.00 5.00
36 Taylor Hall 4.00 10.00
37 Ryan Nugent-Hopkins 2.00 5.00
38 Jordan Eberle 1.50 4.00
39 Devan Dubnyk 2.00 5.00
40 Jacob Markstrom 1.50 4.00
41 Tomas Fleischmann 1.25 3.00
42 Brian Campbell 1.25 3.00
43 Jonathan Quick 3.00 8.00
44 Jeff Carter 2.00 5.00
45 Drew Doughty 2.00 5.00
46 Anze Kopitar 3.00 8.00
47 Zach Parise 2.00 5.00
48 Ryan Suter 1.25 3.00
49 Mikko Koivu 1.50 4.00
50 Carey Price 4.00 10.00
51 P.K. Subban 3.00 8.00
52 Max Pacioretty 2.00 5.00
53 Pekka Rinne 2.50 6.00
54 Shea Weber 1.50 4.00
55 Mike Fisher 1.50 4.00
56 Martin Brodeur 4.00 10.00
57 Patrik Elias 2.00 5.00
58 Adam Henrique 2.00 5.00
59 John Tavares 4.00 10.00
60 Matt Moulson 1.50 4.00
61 Kyle Okposo 2.00 5.00
62 Rick Nash 2.00 5.00
63 Henrik Lundqvist 2.50 6.00
64 Derek Stepan 2.00 5.00
65 Ryan Callahan 2.00 5.00
66 Erik Karlsson 4.00 10.00
67 Mika Zibanejad 2.00 5.00
68 Jakob Silfverberg 1.50 4.00
69 Claude Giroux 2.00 5.00
70 Jakub Voracek 2.00 5.00
71 Brayden Schenn 2.00 5.00
72 Mike Smith 2.00 5.00
73 Keith Yandle 2.00 5.00
74 Mikkel Boedker 1.25 3.00
75 Sidney Crosby 6.00 15.00
76 Marc-Andre Fleury 3.00 8.00
77 Evgeni Malkin 6.00 15.00
78 Kris Letang 2.00 5.00
79 Logan Couture 2.00 5.00
80 Patrick Marleau 2.00 5.00
81 Joe Pavelski 2.00 5.00
82 Chris Stewart 1.50 4.00
83 David Backes 2.00 5.00
84 Alex Pietrangelo 1.50 4.00
85 Martin St. Louis 2.00 5.00
86 Steven Stamkos 4.00 10.00
87 Ben Bishop 2.00 5.00
88 James Reimer 2.00 5.00
89 Nazem Kadri 2.00 5.00
90 Phil Kessel 2.50 6.00
91 Dion Phaneuf 2.00 5.00
92 Henrik Sedin 2.00 5.00
93 Cory Schneider 1.50 4.00
94 Ryan Kesler 2.00 5.00
95 Alex Ovechkin 8.00 20.00
96 Braden Holtby 3.00 8.00
97 Mike Ribeiro 1.50 4.00
98 Andrew Ladd 2.00 5.00
99 Dustin Byfuglien 2.00 5.00
100 Evander Kane 2.00 5.00
101 Matt Anderson RC 1.50 4.00
102 Anders Lee RC 3.00 8.00
103 Steven Pinizzotto RC 2.00 5.00
104 Brett Bellemore RC 1.50 4.00
105 Eric Selleck RC 1.50 4.00
106 Alex Petrovic AU RC 4.00 10.00
107 Mark Pysyk AU RC 5.00 12.00
108 Jonathan Marchessault AU RC 12.00 30.00
109 Zach Redmond AU RC 4.00 10.00
110 Radko Gudas AU RC 5.00 12.00
111 Mark Cundari AU RC 3.00 8.00
112 Chris Terry AU RC 3.00 8.00
113 Shawn Lalonde AU RC 5.00 12.00
114 Ryan Stanton AU RC 5.00 12.00
115 Jonathan Rheault AU RC 3.00 8.00
116 Greg Pateryn AU RC 5.00 12.00
117 Oliver Lauridsen AU RC 4.00 10.00
118 Jeff Zatkoff AU RC 5.00 12.00
119 Matt Tennyson AU RC 3.00 8.00
120 Tyler Johnson AU RC 12.00 30.00
121 Ben Street AU RC 3.00 8.00
123 Sean Collins AU RC 4.00 10.00
124 Michael Caruso AU RC 3.00 8.00
125 Victor Bartley AU RC 4.00 10.00
126 Harri Pesonen AU RC 4.00 10.00
127 Dave Dziurzynski AU RC 4.00 10.00
128 Derek Grant AU RC 4.00 10.00
129 Eric Gryba AU RC 4.00 10.00
130 Ondrej Palat AU RC 10.00 20.00
131 Emerson Etem JSY AU/299 RC 6.00 15.00
132 T.Pearson JSY AU/299 RC 10.00 25.00
133 I.Bobkov JSY AU/299 RC 5.00 12.00
134 Rickard Rakell JSY AU/299 RC 6.00 15.00
135 Sami Vatanen JSY AU/299 RC 6.00 15.00
136 Viktor Fasth JSY AU/299 RC 6.00 15.00
137 Jamie Tardif JSY AU/299 RC 4.00 10.00
138 R.Spooner JSY AU/299 RC 8.00 20.00
139 Brian Flynn JSY AU/299 RC 5.00 12.00
140 M.Grigorenko JSY AU/299 RC 8.00 20.00
141 Carl Soderberg JSY AU/299 RC 6.00 15.00
142 Brock Nelson JSY AU/199 RC 6.00 15.00
143 Michal Jordan JSY AU/299 RC 4.00 10.00
144 Ryan Murphy JSY AU/299 RC 6.00 15.00
145 A.Barkov JSY AU/99 RC 30.00 80.00
146 Calvin Pickard JSY AU/299 RC 6.00 15.00
147 M.Sgarbossa JSY AU/299 RC 5.00 12.00
148 Antoine Roussel JSY AU/299 RC 6.00 15.00
149 Alex Chiasson JSY AU/299 RC 6.00 15.00
150 Jack Campbell JSY AU/299 RC 5.00 12.00
151 Jamie Oleksiak JSY AU/299 RC 5.00 12.00
152 Brian Lashoff JSY AU/299 RC 5.00 12.00
153 F.Andersen JSY AU/199 RC 12.00 30.00
154 D.DeKeyser JSY AU/299 RC 8.00 20.00
155 Petr Mrazek JSY AU/299 RC 12.00 30.00
156 Justin Schultz JSY AU/299 RC 6.00 15.00
157 Mark Arcobello JSY AU/299 RC 6.00 15.00
158 Drew Shore JSY AU/299 RC 5.00 12.00
159 N.Bjugstad JSY AU/299 RC 8.00 20.00
160 Q.Howden JSY AU/299 RC 5.00 12.00
161 Tyler Toffoli JSY AU/299 RC 15.00 40.00
162 Charlie Coyle JSY AU/299 RC 6.00 15.00
163 Ryan Strome JSY AU/199 RC 8.00 20.00
164 Jonas Brodin JSY AU/299 RC 5.00 12.00
165 M.Granlund JSY AU/299 RC 10.00 25.00
166 B.Gallagher JSY AU/299 RC 25.00 60.00
167 Jarred Tinordi JSY AU/299 RC 6.00 15.00
168 N.Beaulieu JSY AU/299 RC 5.00 12.00
169 Austin Watson JSY AU/299 RC 5.00 12.00
170 Filip Forsberg JSY AU/299 RC 40.00 80.00
171 S.Matteau JSY AU/299 RC 5.00 12.00
172 T.Hickey JSY AU/299 RC 5.00 12.00
173 C.Thomas JSY AU/299 RC 5.00 12.00
174 J.T. Miller JSY AU/299 RC 6.00 15.00
175 Cory Conacher JSY AU/299 RC 4.00 10.00
176 Jared Staal JSY AU/299 RC 6.00 15.00
177 S.Laughton JSY AU/199 RC 12.00 30.00
178 Tye McGinn JSY AU/299 RC 6.00 15.00
179 Chris Brown JSY AU/299 RC 4.00 10.00
180 Beau Bennett JSY AU/299 RC 8.00 20.00
181 Matt Irwin JSY AU/299 RC 5.00 12.00
182 Dmitrij Jaskin JSY AU/299 RC 6.00 15.00
183 Alex Killorn JSY AU/299 RC 6.00 15.00
184 Richard Panik JSY AU/299 RC 6.00 15.00
185 H.Lindholm JSY AU/199 RC 10.00 25.00
186 M.Kostka JSY AU/299 RC 5.00 12.00
187 J.Schroeder JSY AU/299 RC 6.00 15.00
188 N.Jensen JSY AU/299 RC 5.00 12.00
189 P.Grubauer JSY AU/299 RC 6.00 15.00
190 A.Peluso JSY AU/299 RC 4.00 10.00
191 E.Pasquale JSY AU/299 RC 4.00 10.00
192 Tom Wilson JSY AU/299 RC 10.00 25.00
193 F.Corrado JSY AU/199 RC 4.00 10.00
195 M.Reinhart JSY AU/299 RC 6.00 15.00
196 D.Hamilton JSY AU/199 RC 12.00 30.00
197 J.Huberdeau JSY AU/199 RC 25.00 60.00
198 Tarasenko JSY AU/199 RC EX 40.00 100.00
199 Galchenyuk JSY AU/199 RC 60.00 120.00
200 N.Ykupov JSY AU/199 RC 30.00 80.00
201 N.MacKinnon JSY AU/99 RC 350.00 600.00
202 S.Monahan JSY AU/99 RC 75.00 150.00
203 V.Nichushkin JSY AU/99 RC 50.00 100.00
204 Seth Jones JSY AU/99 RC 50.00 120.00
205 Tomas Hertl JSY AU/99 RC 75.00 150.00
206 B.Jenner JSY AU/99 RC 20.00 50.00
207 Matt Dumba JSY AU/99 RC 20.00 50.00
208 J.Trouba JSY AU/99 RC 40.00 100.00
209 Elias Lindholm JSY AU/99 RC 40.00 80.00
211 J.Nordstrom JSY AU/199 RC 12.00 30.00
212 Jon Merrill JSY AU/199 RC 6.00 15.00
(inserted in 2013-14 Panini Prime)
213 Tomas Jurco JSY AU/199 RC 10.00 25.00
214 Marek Mazanec JSY AU/199 RC 6.00 15.00
(inserted in 2013-14 Panini Prime)
216 M.Bournival JSY AU/199 RC 6.00 15.00
217 M.Rielly JSY AU/199 RC 30.00 60.00
218 Martin Jones JSY AU/199 RC 10.00 25.00
219 Nikita Zadorov JSY AU/199 RC 6.00 15.00
(inserted in 2013-14 Panini Prime)
220 Magnus Hellberg JSY AU/199 RC 6.00 15.00
(inserted in 2013-14 Panini Prime)
222 Ryan Murray JSY AU/199 RC 10.00 25.00
223 Jamie Devane JSY AU/199 RC 5.00 12.00
224 D.McIlrath JSY AU/99 RC 12.00 30.00
225 John Gibson JSY AU/99 RC 100.00 200.00
226 Reto Berra JSY AU/199 RC 6.00 15.00

2013-14 Dominion Gold

*1-100 VETS/50: .8X TO 2X BASIC VET/299
*101-105 ROOKIE/50: .8X TO 2X RC/299
*106-130 ROOK.AU/50: .6X TO 1.5X AU RC/299
*131-192 JSY AU/50: .6X TO 1.5X JSY AU/199-299
*196-200 JSY AU/25: .6X TO 1.5X JSY AU/199
*201-209 JSY AU/25: .5X TO 1.2X JSY AU/99
21 Corey Crawford 5.00 12.00
197 Jonathan Huberdeau JSY AU 40.00 100.00
198 Vladimir Tarasenko JSY AU 60.00 150.00
199 Alex Galchenyuk JSY AU 90.00 150.00
200 Nail Yakupov JSY AU 75.00 150.00
201 Nathan MacKinnon JSY AU 400.00 700.00
202 Sean Monahan JSY AU 125.00 250.00
203 Valeri Nichushkin JSY AU 75.00 150.00
205 Tomas Hertl JSY AU 75.00 150.00
225 John Gibson JSY AU/25 125.00 200.00

2013-14 Dominion Back to Back Beginnings Autographs

BBBM R.Murphy/N.Beaulieu/149 5.00 12.00
BBCL C.Coyle/S.Laughton/149 5.00 12.00
BBEP E.Etem/T.Pearson/99 5.00 12.00
BBES E.Etem/J.Schultz/99 10.00 25.00
BBGB A.Glchnyk/N.Beaulieu/99 25.00 60.00
BBGG A.Galchenyuk/B.Gallagher/99 30.00 80.00
BBGH A.Glchnyk/J.Hbrdeau/49 30.00 60.00
BBHE Q.Howden/E.Etem/149 5.00 12.00
BBHG B.Gallagher/J.Huberdeau/99 12.00 30.00
BBHH J.Huberdeau/Q.Howden/99 10.00 25.00
BBHM D.Hamilton/R.Murphy/99 10.00 25.00
BBHS D.Hamilton/J.Schultz/49 12.00 30.00
BBHS D.Hamilton/R.Spooner/149 12.00 30.00
BBLG S.Lghton/M.Grgrenko/149 6.00 15.00
BBMC J.Campbell/P.Mrazek/149 10.00 25.00
BBRM M.Rielly/R.Murray/149 15.00 40.00
BBSG R.Spooner/M.Grigorenko/149 6.00 15.00
BBSM J.Schultz/R.Murphy/99 8.00 20.00
BBWR T.Wilson/M.Rielly/149 12.00 30.00
BBYG N.Ykpov/A.Glchnyk/99 25.00 60.00
BBYH N.Yakupov/D.Hamilton/49 20.00 50.00
BBYO M.Grigorenko/N.Yakupov/25 40.00 80.00
BBYS N.Yakupov/J.Schultz/99 20.00 50.00
BBYU N.Yakupov/J.Huberdeau/99 15.00 40.00

2013-14 Dominion Complete Rookie Jerseys

CRAB Aleksander Barkov 25.00 60.00
CRAG Alex Galchenyuk 25.00 60.00
CRAK Alex Killorn 10.00 25.00
CRAR Antoine Roussel 12.00 30.00
CRAW Austin Watson 8.00 20.00
CRBB Beau Bennett 15.00 40.00
CRBG Brendan Gallagher 20.00 50.00
CRBJ Nick Bjugstad 12.00 30.00
CRBJE Boone Jenner 10.00 25.00
CRBL Brian Lashoff 8.00 20.00
CRBN Brock Nelson 10.00 25.00
CRCC Cory Conacher 6.00 15.00
CRCC Cody Ceci 8.00 20.00
CRCM Connor Murphy 8.00 20.00
CRCS Carl Soderberg 15.00 40.00
CRCT Christian Thomas 8.00 20.00
CRDD Danny DeKeyser 12.00 30.00
CRDH Dougie Hamilton 20.00 50.00
CRDI Jarred Tinordi 10.00 25.00
CRED Jared Staal 10.00 25.00
CREE Emerson Etem 10.00 25.00
CRELI Elias Lindholm
CRFC Frank Corrado 8.00 20.00
CRFF Filip Forsberg 25.00 60.00
CRHI Thomas Hickey 8.00 20.00
CRHLI Hampus Lindholm 15.00 40.00
CRHY Ryan Murphy 10.00 25.00
CRJB Jonas Brodin 8.00 20.00
CRJC Jack Campbell 8.00 20.00
CRJH Jonathan Huberdeau 20.00 50.00
CRJM J.T. Miller 10.00 25.00
CRJME Jon Merrill 12.00 30.00
CRJTR Jacob Trouba 15.00 40.00
CRKO Mikhail Grigorenko 12.00 30.00
CRLK Leo Komarov 10.00 25.00
CRLV Calvin Pickard 10.00 25.00
CRMDB Matt Dumba 10.00 25.00
CRMG Mikael Granlund 15.00 40.00
CRMMZ Marek Mazanec 10.00 25.00
CRNMK Nathan MacKinnon
CRNU Nathan Beaulieu 8.00 20.00
CRNY Nail Yakupov 20.00 50.00
CRNZ Nikita Zadorov 10.00 25.00
CROE Jordan Schroeder 10.00 25.00
CROK Jamie Oleksiak 8.00 20.00
CROM Olli Maatta
CROY Charlie Coyle 10.00 25.00
CRPG Philipp Grubauer
CRQH Quinton Howden 8.00 20.00
CRRBE Reto Berra 10.00 25.00
CRRC Roman Cervenka 10.00 25.00
CRRLY Morgan Rielly 25.00 60.00
CRRMR Ryan Murray
CRRP Richard Panik 12.00 30.00
CRRR Rickard Rakell 10.00 25.00
CRRS Ryan Strome 20.00 50.00
CRRZ Petr Mrazek
CRSJ Seth Jones
CRSL Scott Laughton 15.00 40.00
CRSM Stefan Matteau 8.00 20.00
CRSMO Sean Monahan 15.00 40.00
CRSP Ryan Spooner 20.00 50.00
CRSZ Justin Schultz 10.00 25.00
CRTHE Tomas Hertl 25.00 60.00
CRTJU Tomas Jurco 15.00 40.00
CRTP Tanner Pearson 10.00 25.00
CRTT Tyler Toffoli 20.00 50.00
CRTW Tom Wilson 15.00 40.00
CRVF Viktor Fasth 10.00 25.00
CRVN Valeri Nichushkin 10.00 25.00
CRVT Vladimir Tarasenko 40.00 100.00
CRWE Drew Shore 8.00 20.00
CRYO Anthony Peluso 6.00 15.00

2013-14 Dominion Complete Sweaters

CSBC Bobby Clarke 30.00 60.00
CSBH Brett Hull 15.00 40.00
CSCP Carey Price 30.00 80.00
CSEL Eric Lindros
CSEM Evgeni Malkin 20.00 50.00
CSGH Gordie Howe 50.00 100.00
CSGL Gabriel Landeskog 12.00 30.00
CSGX Claude Giroux 15.00 40.00
CSHL Henrik Lundqvist 15.00 40.00
CSJQ Jonathan Quick 15.00 40.00
CSJR Jeremy Roenick 15.00 40.00
CSJS Joe Sakic 15.00 40.00
CSJT John Tavares 30.00 80.00
CSMB Martin Brodeur 30.00 80.00
CSML Mario Lemieux 50.00 120.00
CSMM Mark Messier 20.00 50.00
CSOV Alex Ovechkin 40.00 80.00
CSPB Pavel Bure 25.00 60.00
CSPR Patrick Roy 50.00 100.00
CSRB Ray Bourque 25.00 60.00
CSSC Sidney Crosby 40.00 80.00
CSSS Steven Stamkos 30.00 80.00
CSSY Steve Yzerman 30.00 60.00
CSTN Teemu Selanne 25.00 50.00
CSWS Jonathan Toews 30.00 80.00

2013-14 Dominion Engravatures Blackhawks

EC1 Chicago Blackhawks 200.00 350.00
EC2 Bryan Bickell 75.00 150.00
EC3 Dave Bolland 50.00 100.00
EC4 Brandon Bollig 50.00 100.00
EC5 Sheldon Brookbank 40.00 80.00
EC6 Corey Crawford 150.00 225.00
EC7 Ray Emery
EC8 Michael Frolik 75.00 150.00
EC9 Michal Handzus 125.00 200.00
EC10 Niklas Hjalmarsson 125.00 200.00
EC11 Marian Hossa 150.00 225.00
EC12 Patrick Kane 150.00 250.00
EC13 Duncan Keith 125.00 250.00
EC14 Marcus Kruger 100.00 200.00
EC15 Nick Leddy 150.00 250.00
EC16 Johnny Oduya 100.00 200.00
EC17 Michal Rozsival 75.00 150.00
EC18 Brandon Saad 175.00 300.00
EC19 Brent Seabrook 125.00 250.00
EC20 Patrick Sharp 150.00 250.00
EC21 Andrew Shaw 100.00 200.00
EC22 Ben Smith 75.00 150.00
EC23 Viktor Stalberg 75.00 150.00
EC24 Daniel Carcillo 40.00 80.00
EC25 Jonathan Toews 250.00 400.00

2013-14 Dominion Frozen Moments Autographs

EXCH EXPIRATION: 6/20/2015
FMBC Bobby Clarke/50 25.00 60.00
FMBH Brett Hull/50 30.00 80.00
FMHX Ron Hextall/50 40.00 80.00
FMJQ Jonathan Quick/50 50.00 100.00
FMKP Keith Primeau/99 15.00 40.00
FMMB Martin Brodeur/50 50.00 100.00
FMML Mario Lemieux/25 75.00 150.00
FMMM Mark Messier/99 40.00 100.00
FMNY Nail Yakupov/99 20.00 50.00
FMOV Alex Ovechkin/99 60.00 125.00
FMPD Pavel Datsyuk/50 40.00 80.00
FMPK Patrick Kane/99 50.00 100.00
FMPN Patrice Bergeron/99 30.00 80.00
FMRB Ray Bourque/50 40.00 80.00
FMRM Ryan Miller/99 EXCH 25.00 60.00
FMSY Steve Yzerman/25

2013-14 Dominion Hand Signed

HSBH Brett Hull 40.00 80.00
HSDX Derek Stepan 20.00 50.00
HSGX Claude Giroux 30.00 60.00
HSIC Brad Richards 20.00 50.00
HSIK Marian Gaborik 20.00 50.00
HSIL Igor Larionov 20.00 50.00
HSJO Joe Thornton 20.00 50.00
HSLR Luc Robitaille
HSOS Chris Chelios 30.00 60.00
HSOU Sean Couturier 20.00 50.00
HSPK Patrick Kane 50.00 100.00
HSPV Joe Pavelski 20.00 50.00
HSRE Matt Read 12.00 30.00
HSVR James van Riemsdyk 20.00 50.00
HSWC Matthew Carle 12.00 30.00

2013-14 Dominion Ice Level Jersey Autographs

EXCH EXPIRATION: 6/20/2015
ILAG Alex Galchenyuk 75.00 150.00
ILAW Austin Watson 12.00 30.00
ILBB Beau Bennett 20.00 50.00
ILCK Chris Kreider EXCH 15.00 40.00
ILDH Dougie Hamilton 30.00 80.00
ILDI Jarred Tinordi EXCH 15.00 40.00
ILEE Emerson Etem 15.00 40.00
ILHY Ryan Murphy 15.00 40.00
ILJC Jack Campbell 12.00 30.00
ILNB Nathan Beaulieu 12.00 30.00
ILNY Nail Yakupov 25.00 60.00
ILOK Jamie Oleksiak 12.00 30.00
ILOY Charlie Coyle EXCH 15.00 40.00
ILQH Quinton Howden 12.00 30.00
ILSL Scott Laughton 30.00 60.00
ILSP Ryan Spooner 15.00 40.00
ILSZ Justin Schultz 15.00 40.00
ILTT Tyler Toffoli 30.00 80.00
ILTZ Jaden Schwartz 20.00 50.00

2013-14 Dominion Jerseys

*PRIME/25: .8X TO 2X BASIC JSY/99
DAB Aleksander Barkov 6.00 15.00
DAC Alex Chiasson 2.50 6.00
DAG Alex Galchenyuk 10.00 25.00
DAS Alexander Semin 4.00 10.00
DAW Austin Watson 3.00 8.00
DAZ Anze Kopitar 6.00 15.00
DBB Beau Bennett 3.00 8.00
DBE Brian Elliott 3.00 8.00
DBG Brendan Gallagher 8.00 20.00
DBR Bobby Ryan 4.00 10.00
DBY Dustin Byfuglien 4.00 10.00
DCC Cory Conacher 5.00 12.00
DCC Cody Ceci 3.00 8.00
DCG Curtis Glencross 2.50 6.00
DCI David Krejci 4.00 10.00
DCL Scott Clemmensen 4.00 10.00
DCM Connor Murphy 2.50 6.00
DCN Cam Neely 4.00 10.00
DCP Carey Price 8.00 20.00
DDH Dougie Hamilton 5.00 12.00
DDI Jarred Tinordi 2.50 6.00
DDS Daniel Sedin 4.00 10.00
DDU Brandon Dubinsky 3.00 8.00
DDY Drew Doughty 4.00 10.00
DEE Emerson Etem 4.00 10.00
DEI James Reimer 4.00 10.00
DEK Erik Karlsson 8.00 20.00
DEV Evander Kane 4.00 10.00
DFC Frank Corrado 2.50 6.00
DFF Filip Forsberg 6.00 15.00
DFL Marc-Andre Fleury 8.00 20.00
DGL Gabriel Landeskog 3.00 8.00
DGX Claude Giroux 5.00 12.00
DHB Braden Holtby 5.00 12.00
DHL Henrik Lundqvist 5.00 12.00
DHW Jimmy Howard 4.00 10.00
DHY Ryan Murphy 4.00 10.00
DHZ Martin Hanzal 2.50 6.00
DIC Brad Richards 4.00 10.00
DIK Marian Gaborik 5.00 12.00
DJB Jonas Brodin 3.00 8.00
DJE Jordan Eberle 4.00 10.00
DJH Jonathan Huberdeau 6.00 15.00
DJM J.T. Miller 2.50 6.00
DJO Joe Thornton 4.00 10.00
DJQ Jonathan Quick 6.00 15.00
DJS Joe Sakic 8.00 20.00
DKO Mikhail Grigorenko 3.00 8.00
DKY Keith Yandle 4.00 10.00
DLA Adam Larsson 4.00 10.00
DLK Leo Komarov 5.00 12.00
DLS Luke Schenn 2.50 6.00
DLU Roberto Luongo 4.00 10.00
DLV Calvin Pickard 4.00 10.00
DMB Martin Brodeur 8.00 20.00
DMG Mikael Granlund 4.00 10.00
DML Mario Lemieux 12.00 30.00
DMM Mark Messier 5.00 12.00
DMR Mike Richards 5.00 12.00
DMV Marc-Edouard Vlasic 2.50 6.00
DNB Nathan Beaulieu 2.00 5.00
DNH Ryan Nugent-Hopkins 4.00 10.00
DNL Nicklas Lidstrom 5.00 12.00
DNN Jamie Benn 5.00 12.00
DNY Nail Yakupov 10.00 25.00
DNZ Nikita Zadorov 2.50 6.00
DOE Jordan Schroeder 4.00 10.00
DOK Jamie Oleksiak 3.00 8.00
DOM Olli Maatta 10.00 25.00
DOR Ryan O'Reilly 4.00 10.00
DOV Alex Ovechkin 15.00 40.00
DOY Charlie Coyle 2.50 6.00
DPB Pavel Bure 6.00 15.00
DPD Pavel Datsyuk 5.00 12.00
DPR Patrick Roy 10.00 25.00
DPS Patrick Sharp 4.00 10.00
DPU Patrick Marleau 4.00 10.00
DQH Quinton Howden 3.00 8.00
DRK Ryan Kesler 4.00 10.00
DRM Ryan Miller 4.00 10.00
DRP Richard Panik 6.00 15.00
DRS Ryan Strome 5.00 12.00
DRZ Petr Mrazek 5.00 12.00
DSC Sidney Crosby 12.00 30.00
DSD Shane Doan 3.00 8.00
DSJ Seth Jones 2.50 6.00
DSL Scott Laughton 4.00 10.00
DSM Stefan Matteau 3.00 8.00
DSP Ryan Spooner 6.00 15.00
DSV Sami Vatanen 4.00 10.00
DSZ Justin Schultz 2.50 6.00
DTH Taylor Hall 8.00 20.00
DTS Tyler Seguin 6.00 15.00
DTT Tyler Toffoli 6.00 15.00
DUC Milan Lucic 4.00 10.00
DUF Dion Phaneuf 4.00 10.00
DUU Tuukka Rask 4.00 10.00
DUW Jay Bouwmeester 4.00 10.00
DVA Semyon Varlamov 5.00 12.00
DVF Viktor Fasth 4.00 10.00
DVL Vincent Lecavalier 3.00 8.00
DVN Valeri Nichushkin 2.50 6.00
DVO Slava Voynov
DVT Vladimir Tarasenko 8.00 20.00
DWS Wayne Simmonds 5.00 12.00
DWS Jonathan Toews 8.00 20.00
DYR Ray Emery 3.00 8.00
DYR Cory Schneider 3.00 8.00
DYY Corey Perry 4.00 10.00
DBJE Boone Jenner 2.50 6.00
DELI Elias Lindholm 4.00 10.00
DHLI Hampus Lindholm 4.00 10.00
DJME Jon Merrill 5.00 12.00
DJTR Jacob Trouba 8.00 20.00
DMDB Matt Dumba 2.50 6.00
DMMZ Marek Mazanec 6.00 15.00
DNMK Nathan MacKinnon 20.00 50.00
DRBE Reto Berra 2.50 6.00
DRLY Morgan Rielly 6.00 15.00
DRMR Ryan Murray 4.00 10.00
DSMO Sean Monahan 6.00 15.00
DTHE Tomas Hertl 6.00 15.00
DTJU Tomas Jurco 8.00 20.00

2013-14 Dominion Mammoth Jerseys

*PRIME/15-25: .6X TO 1.5X BASIC JSY/50
MAB Aleksander Barkov/50 8.00 20.00
MAC Alex Chiasson/50 4.00 10.00
MAG Alex Galchenyuk/50 15.00 40.00
MAH Adam Henrique/50 6.00 15.00
MAK Alex Killorn/50 6.00 15.00
MAW Austin Watson/50 5.00 12.00
MBB Beau Bennett/50 5.00 12.00
MBG Brendan Gallagher/50 12.00 30.00
MBJE Boone Jenner/50 4.00 10.00
MBL Brian Lashoff/50 5.00 12.00
MBS Brendan Shanahan/50 8.00 20.00
MCC Cody Ceci/50 3.00 8.00
MCM Connor Murphy/50 3.00 8.00
MCS Cory Schneider/50 5.00 12.00
MDB David Backes/50 8.00 20.00
MDD Danny DeKeyser/50 5.00 12.00
MDH Dougie Hamilton/50 8.00 20.00
MDK Duncan Keith/50 8.00 20.00
MEE Emerson Etem/50 6.00 15.00
MEG Eric Gryba/50 5.00 12.00
MELI Elias Lindholm/50 6.00 15.00
MFC Frank Corrado/50 2.50 6.00
MFF Filip Forsberg/50 12.00 30.00
MGH Gordie Howe/25 25.00 50.00
MHL Henrik Lundqvist/50 8.00 20.00
MHLI Hampus Lindholm/50 6.00 15.00
MHX Ron Hextall/50 8.00 20.00
MHY Ryan Murphy/50 6.00 15.00
MJB Jonas Brodin/50 5.00 12.00
MJH Jonathan Huberdeau/50 10.00 25.00
MJM J.T. Miller/50 4.00 10.00
MJME Jon Merrill/50 6.00 15.00
MJN Joe Nieuwendyk/50 6.00 15.00
MJQ Jonathan Quick/50 10.00 25.00
MJTR Jacob Trouba/50 6.00 15.00
MKA Michael Kostka/50 5.00 12.00
MKL Kari Lehtonen/50 5.00 12.00
MKO Mikhail Grigorenko/50 5.00 12.00
MLR Luc Robitaille/50 6.00 15.00
MLV Calvin Pickard/50 6.00 15.00
MMDB Matt Dumba/50 4.00 10.00
MMG Mikael Granlund/50 6.00 15.00
MMH Milan Hejduk/50 5.00 12.00
MMK Miikka Kiprusoff/50 5.00 12.00
MMMZ Marek Mazanec/50 4.00 10.00
MNB Nicklas Backstrom/50 10.00 25.00
MNMK Nathan MacKinnon/50 15.00 40.00
MNY Nail Yakupov/50 12.00 30.00
MNZ Nikita Zadorov/50 4.00 10.00
MOM Olli Maatta/50 6.00 15.00
MOV Alex Ovechkin/50 25.00 60.00
MOY Charlie Coyle/50 4.00 10.00
MPG Philipp Grubauer/50 4.00 10.00
MPU Patrick Marleau/50 6.00 15.00
MQH Quinton Howden/50 5.00 12.00
MRBE Reto Berra/50 4.00 10.00
MRLY Morgan Rielly/50 10.00 25.00
MRMR Ryan Murray/50 6.00 15.00
MRS Ryan Strome/50 8.00 20.00
MSC Sidney Crosby/50 20.00 50.00
MSJ Seth Jones/50 4.00 10.00
MSM Stefan Matteau/50 5.00 12.00
MSMO Sean Monahan/50 6.00 15.00
MSZ Justin Schultz/50 4.00 10.00
MTHE Tomas Hertl/50 5.00 12.00
MTJU Tomas Jurco/50 6.00 15.00
MTM Tye McGinn/50 6.00 15.00
MTT Tyler Toffoli/50 8.00 20.00
MVF Viktor Fasth/50

N Valeri Nichushkin/50 4.00 10.00
T Vladimir Tarasenko/50 15.00 40.00
H Jonas Hiller/50 5.00 12.00
C Zdeno Chara/50 6.00 15.00
G Zemgus Girgensons/35 8.00 20.00

2013-14 Dominion Patches Autographs

AB Aleksander Barkov/99 15.00 40.00
AC Alex Chiasson/99 6.00 15.00
AG Alex Galchenyuk/99 25.00 60.00
AH Adam Henrique/99 10.00 25.00
AK Alex Killorn/99 8.00 20.00
AN Antti Niemi/99 12.00 30.00
AR Antoine Roussel/99 10.00 25.00
AW Austin Watson/99 8.00 20.00
BB Beau Bennett/99 8.00 20.00
BF Brian Flynn/99 8.00 20.00
BG Brendan Gallagher/99 15.00 40.00
BI Bill Barber/50 10.00 25.00
BJ Nick Bjugstad/99 12.00 30.00
BJE Boone Jenner/99 20.00 40.00
BNE Brock Nelson/99 6.00 15.00
BP Bernie Parent/50 20.00 50.00
BR Bobby Ryan/99 10.00 25.00
CC Cory Conacher/99 4.00 10.00
CG Curtis Glencross/99 6.00 15.00
CH Carl Hagelin/99 10.00 25.00
CN Cam Neely/50 15.00 40.00
CP Carey Price/50 30.00 60.00
CT Christian Thomas/99 8.00 20.00
DD Danny DeKeyser/99 12.00 30.00
DE Dan Boyle/99 8.00 20.00
DH Dougie Hamilton/99 15.00 40.00
DI Jarred Tinordi/99 6.00 15.00
DP David Perron/99 EXCH 6.00 15.00
DQ Daniel Briere/99 10.00 25.00
DS Daniel Sedin/99 10.00 25.00
DX Derek Stepan/99 10.00 25.00
ED Jared Staal/99 10.00 25.00
EE Emerson Etem/99 EXCH 10.00 25.00
EG Eric Gryba/99 8.00 20.00
EL Eric Lindros/50 20.00 50.00
ELI Elias Lindholm/99 15.00 40.00
EP Edward Pasquale/99 6.00 15.00
ER Jonathan Bernier/99 10.00 25.00
EY Bob Gainey/99 15.00 40.00
FA Frederik Andersen/99 10.00 25.00
FF Filip Forsberg/99 25.00 50.00
FL Marc-Andre Fleury/50 12.00 30.00
GF Grant Fuhr/99 15.00 40.00
GI Mikhail Grabovski/99 EXCH 10.00 25.00
GL Gabriel Landeskog/99 8.00 20.00
GU Jean-Sebastien Giguere/99 10.00 25.00
HI Thomas Hickey/99 8.00 20.00
HK Jaroslav Halak/99 10.00 25.00
HL Henrik Lundqvist/50 15.00 40.00
HO Cody Hodgson/50 10.00 25.00
HS Henrik Sedin/99 10.00 25.00
HY Ryan Murphy/99 10.00 25.00
IB Igor Bobkov/99 5.00 12.00
IF Jamie Tardif/99 6.00 15.00
IJ Dmitrij Jaskin/99 12.00 30.00
JB Jonas Brodin/99 EXCH 8.00 20.00
JC Jack Campbell/99 10.00 25.00
JGI John Gibson/99 20.00 50.00
JH Jonathan Huberdeau/99 15.00 40.00
JI Jarome Iginla/99 10.00 25.00
JJ Jaromir Jagr/50 50.00 100.00
JK Jack Johnson/99 6.00 15.00
JL Johan Larsson/99 8.00 20.00
JM Jon Merrill/99 8.00 20.00
JMI J.T. Miller/99 10.00 25.00
JN Joakim Nordstrom/99 5.00 12.00
JQ Jonathan Quick/99 25.00 50.00
JT John Tavares/50 25.00 60.00
JTR Jacob Trouba/99 10.00 25.00
JX John Carlson/99 12.00 30.00
KA Karl Alzner/99 6.00 15.00
KA Michael Kostka/99 5.00 12.00
KI Stan Mikita/25 20.00 40.00
KN Pekka Rinne/99 EXCH 12.00 30.00
KO Mikhail Grigorenko/99 8.00 20.00
KS Kevin Shattenkirk/99 10.00 25.00
LE Loui Eriksson/99 EXCH 8.00 20.00
LO Mark Arcobello/99 6.00 15.00
LV Calvin Pickard/99
MD Matt Duchene/99 12.00 30.00
MF Mike Fisher/99 8.00 20.00
MG Mikael Granlund/99 10.00 25.00
MJ Michal Jordan/99 6.00 15.00
MJO Martin Jones/99 15.00 40.00
MM Mark Messier/50 25.00 50.00
MP Max Pacioretty/99 EXCH 20.00 40.00
NH Nugent-Hopkins/99 EXCH 10.00 25.00
NJ Nicklas Jensen/99 8.00 20.00
NK Nazem Kadri/50 10.00 25.00
NL Nicklas Lidstrom/99 20.00 50.00
NM Nathan MacKinnon/99 50.00 120.00
NU Nathan Beaulieu/99 12.00 30.00
NY Nail Yakupov/99 25.00 60.00
OE Jordan Schroeder/99 8.00 20.00
OF Brian Lashoff/99 8.00 20.00
OK Jamie Oleksiak/99 8.00 20.00
OS Chris Chelios/99 12.00 30.00
OT Maxime Talbot/50 10.00 25.00
OV Alex Ovechkin/50 40.00 100.00
OW Brenden Morrow/99 8.00 20.00
OY Charlie Coyle/99 EXCH 8.00 20.00
PC Paul Coffey/99 15.00 40.00
PD Pavel Datsyuk/99 20.00 40.00
PE Phil Esposito/50 EXCH 15.00 40.00
PG Philipp Grubauer/99 10.00 25.00
PH Phil Kessel/99 10.00 25.00
PV Joe Pavelski/99 10.00 25.00
QD Simon Despres/99 8.00 20.00
QG Michael Sgarbossa/99 8.00 20.00
QH Quinton Howden/99 8.00 20.00
RE Matt Read/99 EXCH 6.00 15.00
RLY Morgan Rielly/99 15.00 40.00
RM Ryan Miller/99 12.00 30.00
RMR Ryan Murray/99 10.00 25.00
RP Richard Panik/99 12.00 30.00
RR Rickard Rakell/99 10.00 25.00
RS Ryan Strome/99 25.00 60.00
RZ Petr Mrazek/99 12.00 30.00
SC Sidney Crosby/25 90.00 150.00
SJ Seth Jones/99 6.00 15.00
SM Stefan Matteau/99 8.00 20.00
SMO Sean Monahan/99 50.00 100.00
SO Carl Soderberg/99 12.00 30.00
SP Ryan Spooner/99 12.00 30.00
SQ Craig Smith/99 6.00 15.00
SV Sami Vatanen/99 8.00 20.00
SZ Justin Schultz/99 12.00 30.00
TH Taylor Hall/99 15.00 40.00
THE Tomas Hertl/99 30.00 80.00
TJU Tomas Jurco/99 10.00 25.00
TM Tye McGinn/99 10.00 25.00
TP Tanner Pearson/99 10.00 25.00
TT Tyler Toffoli/99 8.00 20.00

APTW Tom Wilson/99 15.00 40.00
APVF Viktor Fasth/99 6.00 15.00
APVL Vincent Lecavalier/99 8.00 20.00
APVN V. Nichushkin/99 EXCH 15.00 40.00
APVO Slava Voynov/99 EXCH 8.00 20.00
APVT Vladimir Tarasenko/99 25.00 60.00
APWE Drew Shore/99 8.00 20.00
APWI Colin Wilson/99 8.00 20.00
APXA Alexander Semin/99 10.00 25.00
APXW Max Reinhart/99 6.00 15.00
APYO Anthony Peluso/99 10.00 25.00
APZL Ryan Getzlaf/99 15.00 40.00
APZR Zach Redmond/99 8.00 20.00

2013-14 Dominion Peerless Patches Autographs

PPAB Aleksander Barkov/50 25.00 60.00
PPAC Alex Chiasson/50 10.00 25.00
PPAG Alex Galchenyuk/50 60.00 120.00
PPAK Alex Killorn/50 15.00 40.00
PPAR Antoine Roussel/50 15.00 40.00
PPBB Beau Bennett/50 12.00 30.00
PPBG Brendan Gallagher/50 30.00 80.00
PPBH Brett Hull/50 30.00 60.00
PPBJ Nick Bjugstad/50 15.00 40.00
PPBJE Boone Jenner/50 10.00 25.00
PPBNE Brock Nelson/50 10.00 25.00
PPCC Cory Conacher/50 6.00 15.00
PPDD Danny DeKeyser/50 20.00 50.00
PPDH Dougie Hamilton/50 30.00 60.00
PPDS Drew Shore/50 12.00 30.00
PPED Jared Staal/50 15.00 40.00
PPEE Emerson Etem/50 15.00 40.00
PPELI E.Lindholm/50 EXCH 15.00 40.00
PPFA Frederik Andersen/50 15.00 40.00
PPFF Filip Forsberg/50 25.00 60.00
PPGL Gabriel Landeskog/50 20.00 50.00
PPHI Thomas Hickey/50 12.00 30.00
PPHL Henrik Lundqvist/50 20.00 50.00
PPHY Ryan Murphy/50 12.00 30.00
PPIJ Dmitrij Jaskin/50 10.00 25.00
PPJB Jonas Brodin/50 EXCH 12.00 30.00
PPJGI John Gibson/50 15.00 40.00
PPJH Jonathan Huberdeau/50 25.00 60.00
PPJM J.T. Miller/50 10.00 25.00
PPJN Joakim Nordstrom/50 20.00 50.00
PPJQ Jonathan Quick/50 30.00 60.00
PPJS Joe Sakic/50 30.00 80.00
PPJT John Tavares/50 30.00 80.00
PPJTR Jacob Trouba/50 15.00 40.00
PPKO Mikhail Grigorenko/50 12.00 30.00
PPMB Martin Brodeur/50 40.00 80.00
PPMG Mikael Granlund/50 20.00 50.00
PPMJO Martin Jones/50 25.00 60.00
PPML Mario Lemieux/50 60.00 120.00
PPMM Mark Messier/50 25.00 50.00
PPNJ Nicklas Jensen/50 12.00 30.00
PPNMK Nathan MacKinnon/50 125.00 250.00
PPNY Nail Yakupov/50 30.00 80.00
PPOE Jordan Schroeder/50 12.00 30.00
PPOV Alex Ovechkin/50 30.00 80.00
PPOY Charlie Coyle/50 EXCH 10.00 25.00
PPPR Patrick Roy/50 125.00 250.00
PPQH Quinton Howden/50 12.00 30.00
PPRLY Morgan Rielly/50 25.00 60.00
PPRMR Ryan Murray/50 15.00 40.00
PPRS Ryan Strome/50 20.00 50.00
PPRZ Petr Mrazek/50 20.00 50.00
PPSJ Seth Jones/50 60.00 120.00
PPSM Stefan Matteau/50 12.00 30.00
PPSMO Sean Monahan/50 15.00 40.00
PPSO Carl Soderberg/50 12.00 30.00
PPSP Ryan Spooner/50 20.00 50.00
PPSV Sami Vatanen/50 12.00 30.00
PPSY Steve Yzerman/50 50.00 100.00
PPSZ Justin Schultz/50 10.00 25.00
PPTHE Tomas Hertl/50 12.00 30.00
PPTJU Tomas Jurco/50 15.00 40.00
PPTP Tanner Pearson/50 12.00 30.00
PPTT Tyler Toffoli/50 20.00 50.00
PPTW Tom Wilson/50 25.00 60.00
PPVF Viktor Fasth/50 15.00 40.00
PPVN Valeri Nichushkin/50 30.00 80.00
PPVT Vladimir Tarasenko/50 30.00 80.00
PPWS Jonathan Toews/50 60.00 120.00
PPXW Max Reinhart/50 15.00 40.00

2013-14 Dominion Quad Jerseys

QALB Ykpv/Schltz/Strt/Crvnka/50 10.00 25.00
QANA Cglno/Bchmn/Hllr/Koivu/50 8.00 20.00
QARK Etem/Fsth/Rkll/Bbkv/50 8.00 20.00
QAVS Lnds/Skc/Jhnsn/Brq/50 12.00 30.00
QBGD Nwndyk/Olksk/Sydr/Benn/50 10.00 25.00
QBOS Mrch/Hmtn/Spnr/Chra/50 12.00 30.00
QBRU Lcic/Rask/Krjc/Sdrb/50 15.00 30.00
QBUF2 Hdgsn/Stffrd/Flynn/Mller/50 8.00 20.00
QBUF1 Grgn/Rstn/Pysk/Zdv/50 15.00 40.00
QCAR Mrphy/Jrdn/Staal/Smin/50 8.00 20.00
QCBJ1 Gbrik/Ltstu/Dbnsky/Ansmv/50 8.00 20.00
QCBJ2 Mrry/Jnnr/Jhnsn/Erxn/50 12.00 30.00
QCGY2 Mnh/Cmlr/Grdn/Wdm/50 12.00 30.00
QCGY1 Glncrss/Bcklnd/Stjn/Kprsoff/50 6.00 15.00
QCHI2 Shrp/Tws/Kth/Crwf/50 15.00 40.00
QCHI1 Nrdstm/Vrstg/Kne/Rnta/50 8.00 20.00
QCOL1 McKn/Tlbt/O'Re/Stst/50
QCOL2 Sgrb/Dchne/Pckrd/Vrlmv/50 8.00 20.00
QCZE Hrtl/Mzn/Jskn/Mrzk/50 25.00 60.00
QDAL2 Nchsh/Sgn/Cle/Glioki/50 15.00 40.00
QDAL1 Chsson/Rssel/Nlstrp/Cmpbll/50 10.00 25.00
QDET Krnwl/Lshf/Mrzk/DKy/50 12.00 30.00
QEDM Ykpv/RNH/Hll/Ebrle/50 12.00 30.00
QFIN Brkv/Mtta/Rstln/Grnl/50 12.00 30.00
QFLA Hbrdeau/Hwdn/Shre/Crso/50 8.00 20.00
QFLY Groux/Tlbt/Schnn/Smmnds/50 12.00 30.00
QHAB Eller/Armstrng/Mrkv/Sbbn/50 12.00 30.00
QHFD Hwe/Shn/Vrbk/Frnc/50 20.00 50.00
QKGR Rbte/Rnk/Nchls/Dne/50 20.00 50.00
QKNG Brwn/Rchr/Dght/Qck/50 15.00 30.00
QLAK Kptr/Tffli/Crtr/Prsn/50 10.00 25.00
QMIN Cyle/Brdn/Bckstrm/Htley/50 6.00 15.00
QMRK Glchnyk/Gllgh/Bli/Tnr/50 12.00 30.00
QMSG Byl/McDn/Grdi/Lndq/50 10.00 25.00
QMTL2 Gnta/Lflr/Prce/Roy/50 20.00 50.00
QMTL1 Brnvl/Brq/Plkn/Grges/50 8.00 20.00
QNJD Hnrque/Mttau/Lrssn/Zjac/50 8.00 20.00
QNSH1 Frsbrg/Smth/Wtsn/Lgwnd/50 20.00 50.00
QNSH2 Jns/Frsbrg/Mznc/Wtsn/50 12.00 30.00
QNYI1 Strm/Nlsn/Hcky/Vank/50 10.00 25.00
QNYI2 Tvres/Bley/Hmnc/Hcky/50 15.00 40.00
QNYR2 Nash/Mller/Brssrd/Staal/50 8.00 20.00
QNYR1 Fst/Stpn/Mcll/St.Lo/50 8.00 20.00
QOIL Ggnr/Schltz/Whtny/Dbnyk/50 10.00 25.00
QOTT Cncher/Spzza/Andrsn/Ryan/50 8.00 20.00
QPEN Neal/Mrrow/Ltng/Vitale/50 8.00 20.00
QPHI1 Ctrier/Lghton/Read/McGnn/50 8.00 20.00
QPHI2 Girx/Dwn/Msn/Tmnen/50 10.00 25.00
QPHX Doan/Hnzl/Brwn/Yndle/50 8.00 20.00
QPIT Mlkn/Bntt/Dsps/Flry/50 25.00 60.00
QRDW Hwe/Yzrmn/Shnhn/Lrnv/10
QRKD Mrphy/Brdin/Blu/Sch/50 12.00 30.00
QRKF Ykpv/Trsn/Hbrd/Gln/50 12.00 30.00

QRKG Mrzk/Cmp/Fsth/Psql/50 12.00 30.00
QRUS Ykpv/Nch/Trsn/Grig/50 15.00 40.00
QSC4 Sidney Crosby Quad/50 30.00 80.00
QSEN Mchlk/Neil/Gryba/Krlssn/50 15.00 40.00
QSJS Mrleau/Irwn/Thrntn/Ptrcki/50 8.00 20.00
QSJS Hrtl/Ptrcki/Irwn/Nieto/50 15.00 40.00
QSTL Trsn/Osh/Shttk/Elltt/50 12.00 30.00
QTBL Pnk/Kllrn/St.L/Stmk/50 15.00 40.00
QTOR Kssel/Kmrv/Phnf/Rmer/50 10.00 25.00
QUSA Glchn/Etm/Jns/Trba/50 15.00 40.00
QVAN1 Crrdo/Hgg/Hmhs/Tnv/50 6.00 15.00
QVAN2 Jnsn/Schrder/Sdin/Bksa/50 8.00 20.00
QWLD Pmnv/Prs/Grnln/Ster/50 12.00 30.00
QWPG1 Plso/Rdmnd/Pvlec/Psquale/50 8.00 20.00
QWPG2 Trba/Lttl/Whlr/Tngr/50 10.00 25.00
QWSH Ovch/Lch/Alzn/Grbr/50 30.00 80.00
QAMBH Andrs/Mzn/Brra/Hrtz/50 12.00 30.00
QJTLD Lndh/Jnes/Trba/Dmba/50 10.00 25.00
QLFLL Lndhm/Frsbrg/Lndh/Lrs/50 10.00 25.00
QMMHB McKin/Brkv/Hrtl/Mnh/50 25.00 60.00
QMSHJ McKn/Hbrd/Jnr/Strm/50 15.00 40.00
QRWML Jrco/Oullt/Rlly/Dvan/50 10.00 25.00

2013-14 Dominion Rookie Showcase Memorabilia

RSBE E.Etem/B.Nelson 5.00 12.00
RSBH B.Bennett/Q.Howden 6.00 15.00
RSBO T.Barrie/J.Oleksiak 5.00 12.00
RSBS T.Barrie/J.Schwartz 6.00 15.00
RSGB A.Glchnyk/N.Beaulieu 15.00 40.00
RSGY A.Glchnyk/N.Yakupov 15.00 40.00
RSHM D.Hamilton/R.Murphy 10.00 25.00
RSHO D.Hamilton/J.Oleksiak 10.00 25.00
RSLB S.Laughton/B.Bennett 8.00 20.00
RSLM S.Laughton/R.Murphy 5.00 12.00
RSMS R.Murphy/J.Schultz 8.00 20.00
RSNH R.Ngntl Ipkns/J.Hbrdeau 10.00 25.00
RSOC J.Oleksiak/J.Campbell 4.00 10.00
RSSC R.Smith/J.Campbell 5.00 12.00
RSSH R.Spooner/D.Hamilton 10.00 25.00
RSSK J.Schwartz/C.Kreider 6.00 15.00
RSSK R.Smith/C.Kreider 5.00 12.00
RSSL R.Spooner/S.Laughton 5.00 12.00
RSTB J.Tinordi/N.Beaulieu 5.00 12.00
RSTC T.Toffoli/B.Nelson
RSTE T.Toffoli/E.Etem
RSTG J.Tinordi/A.Galchenyuk 15.00 40.00
RSWH A.Watson/Q.Howden 6.00 15.00
RSYS N.Yakupov/J.Schultz 10.00 25.00
RSYW N.Yakupov/A.Watson 10.00 25.00

2013-14 Dominion Rookie Showcase Pen Pals

PPBC J.Brodin/C.Coyle 6.00 15.00
PPCK C.Conacher/A.Killorn 6.00 15.00
PPCO J.Campbell/J.Oleksiak 5.00 12.00
PPFW F.Forsberg/A.Watson 15.00 40.00
PPGG A.Galchenyuk/B.Gallagher 50.00 100.00
PPHH Q.Howden/J.Huberdeau 15.00 40.00
PPHS D.Hamilton/R.Spooner 12.00 30.00
PPJS N.Jensen/J.Schroeder 6.00 15.00
PPKM C.Kreider/J.Miller 6.00 15.00
PPMK P.Mrzaek/D.Kuemper 12.00 30.00
PPPT T.Pearson/T.Toffoli 12.00 30.00
PPRC A.Roussel/A.Chiasson 10.00 25.00
PPVE E.Etem/S.Vatanen 6.00 15.00
PPWM T.Wilson/S.Matteau 8.00 20.00

2013-14 Dominion Rookie Showcase Pen Pals Quad

PPCROC Chsn/Rssl/Olks/Cmpbl 40.00 100.00
PPSMHB Staal/Murphy/Huberdeau/Bjugstad

2013-14 Dominion Rookie Showcase Pen Pals Triple

PPCROC Chssn/Rssel/Cmpbll 15.00 40.00

2013-14 Dominion Stickside Signatures

EXCH EXPIRATION: 6/20/2015
SSBC Bobby Clarke/25 40.00 80.00
SSBH Brett Hull/25 40.00 80.00
SSBO Mike Bossy/25 30.00 80.00
SSBR Bobby Ryan/25 30.00 60.00
SSBT Bryan Trottier/25 25.00 60.00
SSCH Carl Hagelin/25 25.00 60.00
SSCJ Curtis Joseph/25 30.00 80.00
SSCN Cam Neely/25 30.00 80.00
SSCP Carey Price/25 40.00 80.00
SSDA Dave Andreychuk/25 20.00 50.00
SSDG Doug Gilmour/25 30.00 80.00
SSDS Daniel Sedin/25 20.00 50.00
SSDX Derek Stepan/25 20.00 50.00
SSEL Eric Lindros/25 30.00 80.00
SSES Eric Staal/25 25.00 60.00
SSGH Gordie Howe/25 100.00 200.00
SSHK Jaroslav Halak/25 20.00 50.00
SSHL Henrik Lundqvist/25 75.00 150.00
SSHS Henrik Sedin/25 20.00 50.00
SSHU Bobby Hull/25 30.00 60.00
SSHW Jimmy Howard/25 25.00 60.00
SSIC Brad Richards/25 20.00 50.00
SSJN Joe Nieuwendyk/25 20.00 50.00
SSJO Joe Thornton/25 30.00 60.00
SSJS Joe Sakic/25 30.00 80.00
SSJT John Tavares/25 50.00 100.00
SSKA Karl Alzner/25 12.00 30.00
SSLR Luc Robitaille/25 20.00 50.00
SSLX Adam Larsson/25 20.00 50.00
SSMB Martin Brodeur/25 40.00 80.00
SSML Mario Lemieux/25 90.00 200.00
SSMM Mark Messier/25 30.00 80.00
SSMO Mike Modano/25 40.00 80.00
SSMP Max Pacioretty/25 20.00 50.00
SSMR Mike Richter/25 50.00 100.00
SSOV Alex Ovechkin/25 100.00 175.00
SSOW Brenden Morrow/25 15.00 40.00
SSPC Paul Coffey/25 50.00 100.00
SSPE Phil Esposito/25 30.00 60.00
SSPL Pat LaFontaine/25 20.00 50.00
SSPR Patrick Roy/25 50.00 100.00
SSPT Pierre Turgeon/25 40.00 80.00
SSPU Patrick Marleau/25 20.00 50.00
SSPV Joe Pavelski/25 30.00 60.00
SSRB Ray Bourque/25 50.00 100.00
SSRE Matt Read/25 12.00 30.00
SSRF Ron Francis/25 25.00 60.00
SSRK Ryan Kesler/25 30.00 80.00
SSST Martin St. Louis/25 20.00 50.00
SSSY Steve Yzerman/25 50.00 100.00
SSTA Brian Gionta/25 15.00 40.00
SSTE Tony Esposito/25 30.00 60.00
SSUD Marcel Dionne/25 40.00 80.00
SSVR James van Riemsdyk/25 EXCH 20.00 50.00
SSXA Alexander Semin/25 12.00 30.00
SSYE Brad Boyes/25 12.00 30.00
SSZL Ryan Getzlaf/25 30.00 80.00
SSZP Zach Parise/25 20.00 50.00

2013-14 Dominion Tape to Tape Autographs

TTBS Brendan Shanahan/25 25.00 50.00
TTCJ Curtis Joseph/25 30.00 60.00
TTDX Derek Stepan/25 20.00 50.00
TTEL Eric Lindros/20 50.00 100.00
TTFP Felix Potvin/20 30.00 80.00
TTHK Jaroslav Halak/25 25.00 50.00
TTHL Henrik Lundqvist/20 40.00 80.00
TTJI Jarome Iginla/19 25.00 50.00
TTML Mario Lemieux/25 60.00 120.00
TTMM Mark Messier/25 40.00 80.00
TTOV Alex Ovechkin/16 150.00 250.00
TTPD Pavel Datsyuk/22 50.00 100.00
TTVL Vincent Lecavalier/25 25.00 50.00

2013-14 Dominion Time Warp Patches

TWBL B.Bennett/M.Lemieux 15.00 40.00
TWCB E.Belfour/J.Campbell 10.00 25.00
TWDL D.DeKeyser/N.Lidstrom 12.00 30.00
TWGA D.Andrychk/M.Grgrnko 10.00 25.00
TWGG A.Galchenyuk/B.Gainey 20.00 40.00
TWGR B.Gallagher/P.Roy 25.00 60.00
TWHB D.Hamilton/R.Bourque 15.00 40.00
TWLK S.Laughton/T.Kerr 10.00 25.00
TWMF R.Murphy/R.Francis 12.00 30.00
TWML T.McGinn/E.Lindros 12.00 30.00
TWMM J.Miller/M.Messier 15.00 40.00
TWMV I.Larionov/P.Mrazek 15.00 40.00
TWNB B.Bellows/V.Nichushkin 8.00 20.00
TWOS J.Oleksiak/D.Sydor 6.00 15.00
TWPF C.Pickard/A.Foote 10.00 25.00
TWPN T.Pearson/B.Nicholls 10.00 25.00
TWRM A.Roussel/M.Modano 25.00 60.00
TWRN J.Nieuwendyk/M.Reinhart 8.00 20.00
TWSB J.Staal/R.Brind'Amour 10.00 25.00
TWSC J.Schultz/P.Coffey 12.00 30.00
TWSN R.Spooner/C.Neely 10.00 25.00
TWTH V.Tarasenko/B.Hull 15.00 40.00
TWTR T.Toffoli/L.Robitaille 12.00 30.00
TWWG M.Gartner/T.Wilson 12.00 30.00
TWYG N.Yakupov/A.Graves 12.00 30.00

1925 Dominion Chocolates V31

13 Granite Club HK Olympic Champs 125.00 200.00
28 North Ontario Team HK 125.00 200.00
35 Peterborough Team HK 125.00 200.00
49 Owen Sound Jrs. HK 125.00 200.00
55 E.J. Collett HK 125.00 200.00
56 Hughie J. Fox HK 125.00 200.00
57 Dunc Munro HK 125.00 200.00
58 M.Rutherford HK 125.00 200.00
59 Beattie Ramsay HK 125.00 200.00
60 Bert McCaffrey HK 125.00 200.00
61 Soo Greyhounds HK 125.00 200.00
68 J.P. Aggatts HK 125.00 200.00
69 Hooley Smith HK 200.00 350.00
70 Jack Cameron HK 125.00 200.00
81 William Fraser HK 125.00 200.00
82 Vernon Forbes HK 125.00 200.00
83 Shorty Green HK 175.00 300.00
84 Red Green HK 125.00 200.00
86 Jack Langtry HK 125.00 200.00
89 Billy Coutu HK 125.00 200.00
92 Jack Hughes HK 125.00 200.00
95 Edouard Lalonde HK 250.00 500.00
101 Bill Brydge HK 125.00 200.00
103 Cecil Browne HK 125.00 200.00
106 Red Porter HK 125.00 200.00
112 North Bay Team HK 125.00 200.00
113 Ross Somerville HK 125.00 200.00
114 Harry Watson HK 175.00 300.00
117 Odie Cleghorn HK UER First Name Spelled Ogie 125.00 200.00
118 Lionel Conacher HK 250.00 500.00
119 Aurel Joliat HK 400.00 800.00
120 Georges Vezina HK 750.00 1500.00

1993-94 Donruss

These 510 standard-size cards feature borderless color player action shots on their fronts. The player's name appears in gold foil within a team-color-coded stripe near the bottom. His team logo rests in a lower corner. The backs, some of which are horizontal, carry another borderless color player action shot. The player's name, team, position, and biography are shown within a black rectangle on the left. His statistics appear in ghosted strips below or alongside. Production of the Update set (401-510) was limited to 4,000 cases. Rookie Cards include Jason Arnott, Chris Osgood, Jocelyn Thibault and German Titov.

1 Steven King .05 .15
2 Joe Sacco .05 .15
3 Anatoli Semenov .05 .15
4 Terry Yake .05 .15
5 Alexei Kasatonov .05 .15
6 Patrick Carnback RC .10 .25
7 Sean Hill .05 .15
8 Bill Houlder .05 .15
9 Todd Ewen .05 .15
10 Bob Corkum .05 .15
11 Tim Sweeney .05 .15
12 Ron Tugnutt .07 .20
13 Guy Hebert .07 .20
14 Shaun Van Allen .05 .15
15 Stu Grimson .05 .15
16 Jon Casey .07 .20
17 Dan Marois .05 .15
18 Adam Oates .10 .25
19 Glen Wesley .05 .15
20 Cam Stewart RC .10 .25
21 Don Sweeney .05 .15
22 Glen Murray .05 .15
23 Jozef Stumpel .05 .15
24 Ray Bourque .15 .40
25 Ted Donato .05 .15
26 Joe Juneau .07 .20
27 Dmitri Kvartalnov .05 .15
28 Steve Leach .05 .15
29 Cam Neely .10 .25
30 Bryan Smolinski .05 .15
31 Craig Simpson .05 .15
32 Donald Audette .05 .15
33 Doug Bodger .05 .15
34 Grant Fuhr .10 .25
35 Dale Hawerchuk .12 .30
36 Yuri Khmylev .05 .15
37 Pat LaFontaine .10 .25
38 Brad May .07 .20
39 Alexander Mogilny .07 .20
40 Richard Smehlik .05 .15
41 Petr Svoboda .05 .15
42 Matthew Barnaby .07 .20
43 Sergei Petrenko .05 .15
44 Mark Astley RC .10 .25
45 Derek Plante RC .10 .25
46 Theo Fleury .05 .15
47 Al MacInnis .07 .20
48 Joe Nieuwendyk .07 .20
49 Joel Otto .05 .15
50 Paul Ranheim .05 .15
51 Robert Reichel .05 .15
52 Gary Roberts .05 .15
53 Gary Suter .05 .15
54 Mike Vernon .07 .20
55 Kelly Kisio .05 .15
56 German Titov RC .10 .25
57 Wes Walz .05 .15
58 Ted Drury .05 .15
59 Sandy McCarthy .05 .15
60 Vesa Viitakoski RC .10 .25
61 Jeff Hackett .05 .15
62 Neil Wilkinson .05 .15
63 Dirk Graham .05 .15
64 Ed Belfour .10 .25
65 Chris Chelios .10 .25
66 Joe Murphy .05 .15
67 Jeremy Roenick .15 .40
68 Steve Smith .05 .15
69 Brent Sutter .05 .15
70 Steve Dubinsky RC .10 .25
71 Michel Goulet .05 .15
72 Christian Ruuttu .05 .15
73 Bryan Marchment .05 .15
74 Sergei Krivokrasov .05 .15
75 Jeff Shantz RC .05 .15
76 Mike Modano .15 .40
77 Derian Hatcher .05 .15
78 Ulf Dahlen .05 .15
79 Mark Tinordi .05 .15
80 Russ Courtnall .05 .15
81 Mike Craig .05 .15
82 Trent Klatt .05 .15
83 Dave Gagner .07 .20
84 Chris Tancill .05 .15
85 James Black .05 .15
86 Dean Evason .05 .15
87 Andy Moog .10 .25
88 Paul Cavallini .05 .15
89 Grant Ledyard .05 .15
90 Jarkko Varvio .05 .15
91 Slava Kozlov .07 .20
92 Mike Sillinger .05 .15
93 Aaron Ward RC .10 .25
94 Greg Johnson .05 .15
95 Steve Yzerman .25 .60
96 Tim Cheveldae .07 .20
97 Steve Chiasson .05 .15
98 Dino Ciccarelli .07 .20
99 Paul Coffey .10 .25
100 Dallas Drake RC .10 .25
101 Sergei Fedorov .15 .40
102 Nicklas Lidstrom .10 .25
103 Darren McCarty RC .15 .40
104 Bob Probert .07 .20
105 Ray Sheppard .07 .20
106 Scott Pearson .05 .15
107 Steven Rice .05 .15
108 Louie DeBrusk .05 .15
109 Dave Manson .05 .15
110 Dean McAmmond .05 .15
111 Roman Oksiuta RC .10 .25
112 Geoff Smith .05 .15
113 Zdeno Ciger .05 .15
114 Shayne Corson .05 .15
115 Luke Richardson .05 .15
116 Igor Kravchuk .05 .15
117 Bill Ranford .07 .20
118 Doug Weight .07 .20
119 Fred Brathwaite RC .10 .25
120 Jason Arnott RC .20 .50
121 Tom Fitzgerald .05 .15
122 Mike Hough .05 .15
123 Jesse Belanger .05 .15
124 Brian Skrudland .05 .15
125 Dave Lowry .05 .15
126 Scott Mellanby .07 .20
127 Evgeny Davydov .05 .15
128 Andrei Lomakin .05 .15
129 Brian Benning .05 .15
130 Scott Levins RC .10 .25
131 Gord Murphy .05 .15
132 John Vanbiesbrouck .07 .20
133 Mark Fitzpatrick .05 .15
134 Rob Niedermayer .07 .20
135 Alexander Godynyuk .05 .15
136 Eric Weinrich .05 .15
137 Mark Greig .05 .15
138 Jim Sandlak .05 .15
139 Adam Burt .05 .15
140 Nick Kypreos .05 .15
141 Sean Burke .05 .15
142 Andrew Cassels .05 .15
143 Robert Kron .05 .15
144 Michael Nylander .05 .15
145 Robert Petrovicky .05 .15
146 Patrick Poulin .05 .15
147 Geoff Sanderson .07 .20
148 Pat Verbeek .05 .15
149 Zarley Zalapski .05 .15
150 Chris Pronger .10 .25
151 Jari Kurri .10 .25
152 Wayne Gretzky .50 1.25
153 Pat Conacher .05 .15
154 Shawn McEachern .05 .15
155 Mike Donnelly .05 .15
156 Warren Rychel .05 .15
157 Gary Shuchuk .05 .15
158 Rob Blake .07 .20
159 Jimmy Carson .05 .15
160 Tony Granato .05 .15
161 Kelly Hrudey .07 .20
162 Luc Robitaille .07 .20
163 Tomas Sandstrom .05 .15
164 Darryl Sydor .05 .15
165 Alexei Zhitnik .05 .15
166 Benoit Brunet .05 .15
167 Lyle Odelein .05 .15
168 Kevin Haller .05 .15
169 Pierre Sevigny .05 .15
170 Brian Bellows .07 .20
171 Patrice Brisebois .05 .15
172 Vincent Damphousse .07 .20
173 Eric Desjardins .07 .20
174 Gilbert Dionne .05 .15
175 Stephan Lebeau .05 .15
176 John LeClair .10 .25
177 Kirk Muller .05 .15
178 Patrick Roy .25 .60
179 Mathieu Schneider .05 .15
180 Peter Popovic RC .10 .25
181 Corey Millen .05 .15
182 Jason Smith RC .05 .15
183 Bobby Holik .05 .15
184 John MacLean .07 .20
185 Bruce Driver .05 .15
186 Bill Guerin .05 .15
187 Claude Lemieux .05 .15
188 Bernie Nicholls .05 .15
189 Scott Niedermayer .10 .25
190 Stephane Richer .07 .20
191 Alexander Semak .05 .15
192 Scott Stevens .10 .25
193 Valeri Zelepukin .05 .15
194 Chris Terreri .07 .20
195 Martin Brodeur .25 .60
196 Ron Hextall .07 .20
197 Brad Dalgarno .05 .15
198 Ray Ferraro .05 .15
199 Patrick Flatley .05 .15
200 Travis Green .07 .20
201 Benoit Hogue .05 .15
202 Steve Junker RC .10 .25
203 Darius Kasparaitis .05 .15
204 Derek King .05 .15
205 Uwe Krupp .05 .15
206 Scott Lachance .05 .15
207 Vladimir Malakhov .05 .15
208 Steve Thomas .05 .15
209 Pierre Turgeon .07 .20
210 Scott Scissons .05 .15
211 Glenn Healy .07 .20
212 Alexander Karpovtsev .05 .15
213 James Patrick .05 .15
214 Sergei Nemchinov .05 .15
215 Esa Tikkanen .05 .15
216 Corey Hirsch .07 .20
217 Tony Amonte .07 .20
218 Mike Gartner .07 .20
219 Adam Graves .05 .15
220 Alexei Kovalev .07 .20
221 Brian Leetch .10 .25
222 Mark Messier .10 .25
223 Mike Richter .10 .25
224 Darren Turcotte .05 .15
225 Sergei Zubov .05 .15
226 Craig Billington .07 .20
227 Troy Mallette .05 .15
228 Vladimir Ruzicka .05 .15
229 Darrin Madeley RC .10 .25
230 Mark Lamb .05 .15
231 Dave Archibald .05 .15
232 Bob Kudelski .05 .15
233 Norm Maciver .05 .15
234 Brad Shaw .05 .15
235 Sylvain Turgeon .05 .15
236 Brian Glynn .05 .15
237 Alexandre Daigle .05 .15
238 Alexei Yashin .07 .20
239 Dimitri Filimonov .05 .15
240 Pavol Demitra .12 .30
241 Jason Bowen .10 .25
242 Eric Lindros .30 .75
243 Dominic Roussel .07 .20
244 Milos Holan RC .10 .25
245 Greg Hawgood .05 .15
246 Yves Racine .05 .15
247 Josef Beranek .05 .15
248 Rod Brind'Amour .07 .20
249 Kevin Dineen .05 .15
250 Pelle Eklund .05 .15
251 Garry Galley .05 .15
252 Mark Recchi .12 .30
253 Tommy Soderstrom .07 .20
254 Dimitri Yushkevich .05 .15
255 Mikael Renberg .10 .25
256 Marty McSorley .05 .15
257 Joe Mullen .07 .20
258 Doug Brown .05 .15
259 Kjell Samuelsson .05 .15
260 Tom Barrasso .07 .20
261 Ron Francis .12 .30
262 Mario Lemieux .40 1.00
263 Larry Murphy .07 .20
264 Ulf Samuelsson .05 .15
265 Kevin Stevens .05 .15
266 Martin Straka .05 .15
267 Rick Tocchet .07 .20
268 Bryan Trottier .12 .30
269 Markus Naslund .10 .25
270 Jaromir Jagr .25 .60
271 Martin Gelinas .05 .15
272 Adam Foote .05 .15
273 Curtis Leschyshyn .05 .15
274 Stephane Fiset .07 .20
275 Jocelyn Thibault RC .10 .25
276 Steve Duchesne .05 .15
277 Valeri Kamensky .07 .20
278 Andrei Kovalenko .05 .15
279 Owen Nolan .07 .20
280 Mike Ricci .05 .15
281 Martin Rucinsky .05 .15
282 Joe Sakic .25 .60
283 Mats Sundin .07 .20
284 Scott Young .05 .15
285 Claude Lapointe .05 .15
286 Brett Hull .15 .40
287 Vitali Karamnov .05 .15
288 Ron Sutter .05 .15
289 Garth Butcher .05 .15
290 Vitali Prokhorov .05 .15
291 Bret Hedican .05 .15
292 Tony Hrkac .05 .15
293 Jeff Brown .05 .15
294 Phil Housley .07 .20
295 Craig Janney .07 .20
296 Curtis Joseph .10 .25
297 Igor Korolev .05 .15
298 Kevin Miller .05 .15
299 Brendan Shanahan .12 .30
300 Jim Montgomery RC .10 .25
301 Gaetan Duchesne .05 .15
302 Jimmy Waite .07 .20
303 Jeff Norton .05 .15
304 Sergei Makarov .05 .15
305 Igor Larionov .05 .15
306 Mike Lalor .05 .15
307 Michal Sykora RC .10 .25
308 Pat Falloon .05 .15
309 Johan Garpenlov .05 .15
310 Rob Gaudreau RC .10 .25
311 Arturs Irbe .07 .20
312 Sandis Ozolinsh .05 .15
313 Doug Zmolek .05 .15
314 Mike Rathje .05 .15
315 Vlastimil Kroupa RC .10 .25
316 Daren Puppa .05 .15
317 Petr Klima .05 .15
318 Brent Gretzky RC .10 .25
319 Denis Savard .12 .30
320 Garard Gallant .05 .15
321 Joe Reekie .05 .15
322 Mikael Andersson .05 .15
323 Bill McDougall RC .10 .25
324 Brian Bradley .05 .15
325 Shawn Chambers .05 .15
326 Adam Creighton .05 .15
327 Roman Hamrlik .05 .15
328 John Tucker .05 .15
329 Rob Zamuner .05 .15
330 Chris Gratton .07 .20
331 Sylvain Lefebvre .05 .15
332 Nikolai Borschevsky .05 .15
333 Bob Rouse .05 .15
334 John Cullen .05 .15
335 Todd Gill .05 .15
336 Drake Berehowsky .05 .15
337 Wendel Clark .07 .20
338 Peter Zezel .05 .15
339 Rob Pearson .05 .15
340 Glenn Anderson .10 .25
341 Doug Gilmour .12 .30
342 Dave Andreychuk .10 .25
343 Felix Potvin .20 .50
344 David Ellett .05 .15
345 Alexei Kudashov RC .10 .25
346 Gino Odjick .05 .15
347 Jyrki Lumme .05 .15
348 Dana Murzyn .05 .15
349 Sergio Momesso .05 .15
350 Greg Adams .05 .15
351 Pavel Bure .10 .25
352 Geoff Courtnall .05 .15
353 Murray Craven .05 .15
354 Trevor Linden .07 .20
355 Kirk McLean .07 .20
356 Petr Nedved .05 .15
357 Cliff Ronning .05 .15
358 Jiri Slegr .05 .15
359 Kay Whitmore .05 .15
360 Gerald Diduck .05 .15
361 Pat Peake .05 .15
362 Dave Poulin .05 .15
363 Rick Tabaracci .05 .15
364 Jason Woolley .05 .15
365 Kelly Miller .05 .15
366 Peter Bondra .07 .20
367 Sylvain Cote .05 .15
368 Pat Elynuik .05 .15
369 Kevin Hatcher .05 .15
370 Dale Hunter .05 .15
371 Al Iafrate .05 .15
372 Calle Johansson .05 .15
373 Dimitri Khristich .05 .15
374 Michal Pivonka .05 .15
375 Mike Ridley .05 .15
376 Paul Ysebaert .05 .15
377 Stu Barnes .05 .15
378 Sergei Bautin .05 .15
379 Kris King .05 .15
380 Alexei Zhamnov .07 .20
381 Tie Domi .05 .15
382 Bob Essensa .07 .20
383 Nelson Emerson .05 .15
384 Boris Mironov .05 .15
385 Teppo Numminen .05 .15
386 Fredrik Olausson .05 .15
387 Teemu Selanne .20 .50
388 Darrin Shannon .05 .15
389 Thomas Steen .05 .15
390 Keith Tkachuk .10 .25
391 Panthers Opening Night .10 .25
392 Ducks Opening Night .10 .25
393 Daig Prong Gratton .10 .25
394 T.Selanne J.Juneau RB .20 .50
395 W.Gretzky L.Robitaille RB .50 1.25
396 Inserts Checklist .05 .15
397 Atlantic Div. Checklist .05 .15
398 Northeast Div. Checklist .05 .15
399 Central Div. Checklist .05 .15
400 Pacific Div. Checklist .05 .15
401 Garry Valk .05 .15
402 Al Iarante .05 .15
403 David Reid .05 .15
404 Jason Dawe .05 .15
405 Craig Muni .05 .15
406 Dan Keczmer RC .05 .15
407 Michael Nylander .05 .15
408 James Patrick .05 .15
409 Andrei Trefilov .05 .15
410 Zarley Zalapski .05 .15
411 Tony Amonte .07 .20
412 Keith Carney .05 .15
413 Randy Cunneyworth .05 .15
414 Ivan Droppa RC .05 .15
415 Gary Suter .05 .15
416 Eric Weinrich .05 .15
417 Paul Ysebaert .05 .15
418 Richard Matvichuk .05 .15
419 Alan May .05 .15
420 Darcy Wakaluk .05 .15
421 Micah Aivazoff RC .10 .25
422 Terry Carkner .05 .15
423 Kris Draper .05 .15
424 Chris Osgood RC .60 1.50
425 Keith Primeau .05 .15
426 Bob Beers .05 .15
427 Ilya Byakin RC .05 .15
428 Kirk Maltby RC .10 .25
429 Boris Mironov .05 .15
430 Fredrik Olausson .05 .15
431 Peter White RC .05 .15
432 Stu Barnes .05 .15
433 Mike Foligno .05 .15
434 Bob Kudelski .05 .15
435 Geoff Smith .05 .15
436 Igor Chibirev RC .05 .15
437 Ted Drury .05 .15
438 Alexander Godynyuk .05 .15
439 Frank Kucera .05 .15
440 Jocelyn Lemieux .05 .15
441 Brian Propp .05 .15
442 Paul Ranheim .05 .15
443 Jeff Reese .05 .15
444 Kevin Smyth RC .05 .15
445 Jim Storm RC .05 .15
446 Phil Crowe RC .05 .15
447 Marty McSorley .05 .15
448 Keith Redmond RC .05 .15
449 Dixon Ward .05 .15
450 Guy Carbonneau .05 .15
451 Mike Keane .05 .15
452 Oleg Petrov .05 .15
453 Ron Tugnutt .07 .20
454 Randy McKay .05 .15
455 Jaroslav Modry RC .10 .25
456 Yan Kaminsky .05 .15
457 Marty McInnis .05 .15

458 Jamie McLennan RC .05 .15
459 Zigmund Palffy .05 .15
460 Glenn Anderson .10 .25
461 Steve Larmer .07 .20
462 Craig MacTavish .05 .15
463 Stephane Matteau .05 .15
464 Brian Noonan .05 .15
465 Mattias Norstrom RC .10 .25
466 Scott Levins .10 .25
467 Derek Mayer RC .05 .15
468 Andy Schneider RC .05 .15
469 Todd Hlushko RC .07 .20
470 Stewart Malgunas RC .10 .25
471 Justin Duberman RC .05 .15
472 Ladislav Karabin RC .10 .25
473 Shawn McEachern .05 .15
474 Ed Patterson RC .05 .15
475 Tomas Sandstrom .05 .15
476 Bob Bassen .05 .15
477 Garth Butcher .05 .15
478 Iain Fraser RC .10 .25
479 Mike McKee RC .05 .15
480 Dwayne Norris RC .05 .15
481 Garth Snow RC .05 .15
482 Ron Sutter .05 .15
483 Kelly Chase .05 .15
484 Steve Duchesne .05 .15
485 Daniel Laperrire .05 .15
486 Petr Nedved .05 .15
487 Peter Stastny .05 .15
488 Ulf Dahlen .05 .15
489 Todd Elik .05 .15
490 Andrei Nazarov RC .05 .15
491 Danton Cole .05 .15
492 Chris Joseph .05 .15
493 Chris LiPuma RC .05 .15
494 Mike Gartner .07 .20
495 Mark Greig .05 .15
496 David Harlock .07 .20
497 Matt Martin RC .10 .25
498 Shawn Antoski .05 .15
499 Jeff Brown .05 .15
500 Jimmy Carson .05 .15
501 Martin Gelinas .05 .15
502 Yevgeny Namestnikov RC .05 .15
503 Randy Burridge .05 .15
504 Joe Juneau .07 .20
505 Kevin Kaminski RC .05 .15
506 Arto Blomsten .05 .15
507 Tim Cheveldae .07 .20
508 Dallas Drake .10 .25
509 Dave Manson .05 .15
510 Update Checklist .05 .15

1993-94 Donruss Elite Inserts

ese 15 cards feature on their fronts color player photos framed by diamond-shaped starburst designs set within dark marbleized inner borders and prismatic foil outer borders. The player's name appears within the lower prismatic foil margin. The back carries the player's name, career highlights, and a color head shot, all set on a dark marbleized background framed by a silver border. The 10 first-series Elite cards (1-10) were random inserts in '93-94 Donruss Series 1 packs. The five Elite Update cards (U1-U5) were randomly inserted in Donruss Update packs. All Elite cards are individually numbered on the back and have a production limited to 10,000 of each.

COMPLETE SET (10) 30.00 60.00
1 Mario Lemieux 5.00 12.00
2 Alexandre Daigle 1.25 3.00
3 Teemu Selanne 2.00 5.00
4 Eric Lindros 2.50 6.00
5 Brett Hull 2.00 5.00
6 Jeremy Roenick 2.00 5.00
7 Doug Gilmour 5.00 12.00
8 Alexander Mogilny 1.50 4.00
9 Patrick Roy 5.00 12.00
10 Wayne Gretzky 8.00 20.00
U1 Mikael Renberg 1.25 3.00
U2 Sergei Fedorov 2.50 6.00
U3 Felix Potvin 2.50 6.00
U4 Cam Neely 2.00 5.00
U5 Alexei Yashin 1.25 3.00

1993-94 Donruss Ice Kings

ndomly inserted in Series 1 packs, these 10 cards feature on their fronts borderless color player drawings by noted sports artist Dick Perez. The player's name, his team's logo, and the year, 1994, appear within a blue banner near the bottom. The blue-bordered back carries the player's career highlights on a ghosted representation of a hockey rink. The cards are numbered on the back as "X of 10."

COMPLETE SET (10) 10.00 25.00
1 Patrick Roy 1.50 4.00
2 Pat LaFontaine .60 1.50
3 Jaromir Jagr .75 2.00
4 Wayne Gretzky 2.00 5.00
5 Chris Chelios .60 1.50
6 Felix Potvin .75 2.00
7 Mario Lemieux 1.50 4.00
8 Pavel Bure .60 1.50
9 Eric Lindros .75 2.00
10 Teemu Selanne .60 1.50

1993-94 Donruss Rated Rookies

Randomly inserted in Series 1 packs, these 15 cards have borderless fronts that feature color player action shots on motion streaked backgrounds. The player's name appears at the top. On its right side, the black horizontal back carries a color player action cutout superposed upon his team's logo. Biography and career highlights are shown alongside on the left. The cards are numbered on the back as "X of 15."

COMPLETE SET (15) 6.00 15.00
1 Alexandre Daigle .20 .50
2 Chris Gratton .30 .75
3 Chris Pronger .75 2.00
4 Rob Niedermayer .30 .75
5 Mikael Renberg .30 .75
6 Jarkko Varvio .20 .50
7 Alexei Yashin .20 .50
8 Markus Naslund .60 1.50
9 Boris Mironov .20 .50
10 Martin Brodeur 2.00 5.00
11 Jocelyn Thibault .60 1.50
12 Jason Arnott .75 2.00
13 Jim Montgomery .20 .50
14 Ted Drury .20 .50
15 Roman Oksiuta .20 .50

1993-94 Donruss Special Print

Randomly inserted in Series 1 packs, these 26 cards feature on their fronts color player action shots that are borderless, except at the bottom, where the black edge carries the player's name in white cursive lettering. The prismatic foil set logo rests in a lower corner. The words "Special Print 1 of 20,000" appear in prismatic foil across the top. The cards are numbered, or rather lettered (A-Z), on the back. Two additional unnumbered special print cards (Robitaille WC and Lemieux EC) could be found at the rate of 1:360 packs.

COMPLETE SET (26) 25.00 60.00
A Ron Tugnutt 1.00 2.50
B Adam Oates 1.25 3.00
C Alexander Mogilny 1.00 2.50
D Theo Fleury 1.00 2.50
E Jeremy Roenick 1.50 4.00
F Mike Modano 1.50 4.00
G Steve Yzerman 2.50 6.00
H Jason Arnott 1.00 2.50
I Rob Niedermayer 1.00 2.50
J Chris Pronger 1.00 2.50
K Wayne Gretzky 5.00 12.00
L Patrick Roy 3.00 8.00
M Scott Niedermayer 1.00 2.50
N Pierre Turgeon 1.00 2.50
O Mark Messier 1.25 3.00
P Alexandre Daigle 1.00 2.50
Q Eric Lindros 1.50 4.00
R Mario Lemieux 4.00 10.00
S Mats Sundin 1.25 3.00
T Pat Falloon .75 2.00
U Brett Hull 1.50 4.00
V Chris Gratton .75 2.00
W Felix Potvin 1.50 4.00
X Pavel Bure 1.25 3.00
Y Al Iafrate 1.00 2.50
Z Teemu Selanne 1.25 3.00
NNO Luc Robitaille WC 1.50 4.00
NNO Mario Lemieux EC 5.00 12.00

1993-94 Donruss Team Canada

e of these 22 (or one of the 22 Team USA) cards were inserted in every 1993-94 Donruss Update pack. The front of each card features a player action cutout set on a red metallic background highlighted by a world map. The player's name appears at the upper left. The horizontal back carries a color player action shot on the right side. Below the photo are the player's statistics from his 1994 World Junior Championships play. On the left side are the player's name, position, biography, and NHL status. The cards are numbered on the back as "X of 22." The unnumbered checklist carries the 22 Team Canada cards, as well as the 22 Team USA cards.

COMPLETE SET (22) 5.00 10.00
1 Jason Allison .40 1.00
2 Chris Armstrong .30 .75
3 Drew Bannister .30 .75
4 Jason Botterill .30 .75
5 Joel Bouchard .30 .75
6 Curtis Bowen .30 .75
7 Anson Carter .50 1.25
8 Brandon Convery .30 .75
9 Yanick Dube .30 .75
10 Manny Fernandez .50 1.25
11 Jeff Friesen .30 .75
12 Aaron Gavey .30 .75
13 Martin Gendron .30 .75
14 Rick Girard .30 .75
15 Todd Harvey .40 1.00
16 Bryan McCabe .40 1.00
17 Marty Murray .30 .75
18 Mike Peca .50 1.25
19 Nick Stajduhar .30 .75
20 Jamie Storr .40 1.00
21 Brent Tully .30 .75
22 Brendan Witt .40 1.00
NNO WJC Checklist .30 .75

1993-94 Donruss Team USA

e of these 22 (or one of the 22 Team Canada) cards were inserted in every 1993-94 Donruss Update pack. The front of each card features a player action cutout set on a blue metallic background highlighted by a world map. The player's name appears at the upper left. The horizontal back carries a color player action shot on the right side. Below the photo are the player's statistics from his 1994 World Junior Championships play. On the left side are the player's name, position, biography, and NHL status. The cards are numbered on the back as "X of 22." The unnumbered checklist carries the 22 Team Canada cards, as well as the 22 Team USA cards.

COMPLETE SET (22) 3.00 8.00
1 Kevyn Adams .30 .75
2 Jason Bonsignore .30 .75
3 Andy Brink .30 .75
4 Jon Coleman .30 .75
5 Adam Deadmarsh .40 1.00
6 Aaron Ellis .30 .75
7 John Emmons .30 .75
8 Ashlin Halfnight .30 .75
9 Kevin Hilton .30 .75
10 Jason Karmanos .30 .75
11 Toby Kvalevog .30 .75
12 Bob Lachance .30 .75
13 Jamie Langenbrunner .40 1.00
14 Jason McBain .30 .75
15 Chris O'Sullivan .30 .75
16 Jay Pandolfo .30 .75
17 Richard Park .30 .75
18 Deron Quint .30 .75
19 Ryan Sittler .30 .75
20 Blake Sloan .30 .75
21 John Varga .30 .75
22 David Wilkie .30 .75
NNO WJC Checklist .30 .75

1994-95 Donruss

This 330-card standard-size set was issued in one series. Cards were issued in 12-card hobby packs and 18-card jumbo packs. Fronts feature a near full-bleed design, other than the bottom right corner which displays player name, set name, and position stamped in a silver foil sunburst design. This silver foil area is very difficult to read. Backs feature two additional photos, team logo, and single season stats. Rookie Cards in the set include Mariusz Czerkawski, Mikhail Shtalenkov and John Gruden.

1 Steve Yzerman .40 1.00
2 Paul Ysebaert .10 .25
3 Doug Weight .12 .30
4 Trevor Kidd .12 .30
5 Mario Lemieux .60 1.50
6 Andrei Kovalenko .10 .25
7 Arturs Irbe .12 .30
8 Doug Gilmour .20 .50
9 Mark Messier .15 .40
10 Milos Holan .10 .25
11 Kevin Miller .10 .25
12 Felix Potvin .15 .40
13 Josef Beranek .10 .25
14 Mikael Andersson .10 .25
15 Stephane Matteau .10 .25
16 Todd Simon RC .10 .25
17 Darcy Wakaluk .12 .30
18 Kelly Buchberger .10 .25
19 Pavel Bure .15 .40
20 Dave Lowry .10 .25
21 Bryan Smolinski .10 .25
22 Kirk McLean .12 .30
23 Pierre Turgeon .12 .30
24 Martin Brodeur .40 1.00
25 Jason Arnott .12 .30
26 Steve Dubinsky .10 .25
27 Larry Murphy .12 .30
28 Craig Janney .12 .30
29 Patrik Carnback .10 .25
30 Derek King .10 .25
31 Peter Bondra .12 .30
32 Jason Bowen .10 .25
33 Maxim Bets .10 .25
34 Matt Martin .10 .25
35 Jeff Hackett .10 .25
36 Kevin Dineen .10 .25
37 Trent Klatt .10 .25
38 Joe Murphy .10 .25
39 Sandy McCarthy .10 .25
40 Brian Bradley .10 .25
41 Scott Lachance .10 .25
42 Scott Mellanby .12 .30
43 Adam Graves .10 .25
44 Dale Hawerchuk .20 .50
45 Owen Nolan .15 .40
46 Keith Primeau .15 .40
47 Jim Dowd .10 .25
48 Dan Plante RC .10 .25
49 Rick Tabaracci .12 .30
50 Geoff Courtnall .10 .25
51 Markus Naslund .15 .40
52 Kelly Miller .10 .25
53 Kirk Maltby .10 .25
54 Paul Coffey .15 .40
55 Gord Murphy .10 .25
56 Joe Nieuwendyk .15 .40
57 Ulf Dahlen .10 .25
58 Dmitri Mironov .10 .25
59 Kevin Smyth .10 .25
60 Tie Domi .12 .30
61 Oleg Petrov .10 .25
62 Bill Guerin .12 .30
63 Alexei Yashin .15 .40
64 Joe Sacco .10 .25
65 Aris Brimanis RC .10 .25
66 Randy Burridge .10 .25
67 Neal Broten .12 .30
68 Ray Bourque .25 .60
69 Ron Tugnutt .12 .30
70 Darryl Sydor .10 .25
71 Jocelyn Thibault .15 .40
72 Shawn Chambers .10 .25
73 Alexei Zhamnov .12 .30
74 Michael Nylander .12 .30
75 Travis Green .12 .30
76 Brad May .10 .25
77 Geoff Sanderson .12 .30
78 Derek Plante .10 .25
79 Stephane Richer .12 .30
80 Rod Brind'Amour .12 .30
81 Guy Hebert .12 .30
82 Claude Lemieux .15 .40
83 Pat Falloon .10 .25
84 Alexei Kudashov .10 .25
85 Andrei Lomakin .10 .25
86 Dino Ciccarelli .12 .30
87 John Tucker .10 .25
88 Jamie McLennan .12 .30
89 Peter Taglianetti .10 .25
90 Bobby Holik .10 .25
91 Sergei Krivokrasov .10 .25
92 Alexander Mogilny .12 .30
93 Jari Kurri .12 .30
94 Dominik Hasek .30 .75
95 Shawn McEachern .10 .25
96 Bob Corkum .10 .25
97 Dimitri Filimonov .10 .25
98 John LeClair .15 .40
99 Theo Fleury .15 .40
100 Daren Puppa .12 .30
101 Greg Adams .10 .25
102 Joel Otto .10 .25
103 Sergei Makarov .10 .25
104 Mike Ricci .10 .25
105 Sylvain Turgeon .10 .25
106 Igor Larionov .10 .25
107 Tony Amonte .12 .30
108 Andy Moog .15 .40
109 Jeff Brown .10 .25
110 Checklist 1-83 .10 .25
111 Mike Gartner .15 .40
112 Craig Simpson .10 .25
113 Rob Niedermayer .12 .30
114 Robert Kron .10 .25
115 Jason York RC .10 .25
116 Valeri Kamensky .12 .30
117 Ray Whitney .10 .25
118 Chris Chelios .15 .40
119 Scott Levins .10 .25
120 Sandis Ozolinsh .10 .25
121 Mark Recchi .20 .50
122 Ron Francis .20 .50
123 Dean McAmmond .10 .25
124 Terry Yake .10 .25
125 Sergei Nemchinov .10 .25
126 Vitali Prokhorov .10 .25
127 Wayne Gretzky .75 2.00
128 Roman Hamrlik .12 .30
129 Jarkko Varvio .10 .25
130 Brian Skrudland .10 .25
131 Murray Craven .10 .25
132 Jeff Norton .10 .25
133 Pavol Demitra .20 .50
134 Mike Keane .10 .25
135 Paul Cavallini .10 .25
136 Richard Smehlik .10 .25
137 Eric Lindros .15 .40
138 Mariusz Czerkawski RC .15 .40
139 Darrin Shannon .10 .25
140 Brian Noonan .10 .25
141 Joe Sakic .30 .75
142 Steve Thomas .10 .25
143 Gary Roberts .10 .25
144 Patrick Poulin .10 .25
145 Tony Granato .10 .25
146 Donald Brashear RC .10 .25
147 Ron Hextall .12 .30
148 Corey Millen .10 .25
149 Dale Hunter .10 .25
150 Greg Johnson .10 .25
151 John MacLean .12 .30
152 Brian Leetch .15 .40
153 Sylvain Cote .10 .25
154 Thomas Steen .10 .25
155 Ted Donato .10 .25
156 Nathan Lafayette .10 .25
157 Kelly Chase .10 .25
158 Sean Burke .12 .30
159 Jaromir Jagr .40 1.00
160 Checklist 84-166 .10 .25
161 Scott Niedermayer .15 .40
162 Ray Ferraro .10 .25
163 Todd Elik .10 .25
164 Dave Gagner .12 .30
165 Mike Richter .15 .40
166 Garry Galley .10 .25
167 Russ Courtnall .10 .25
168 Marty McSorley .10 .25
169 Robert Reichel .10 .25
170 Mike Rathje .10 .25
171 Bill Ranford .12 .30
172 Danton Cole .10 .25
173 Sergei Fedorov .25 .60
174 Brendan Shanahan .20 .50
175 Byron Dafoe RC .50 1.25
176 John Vanbiesbrouck .12 .30
177 Eric Desjardins .12 .30
178 Andrew Cassels .10 .25
179 John Gruden RC .10 .25
180 Slava Kozlov .12 .30
181 Trevor Linden .12 .30
182 Kris Draper .10 .25
183 Steve Smith .10 .25
184 Andre Faust .10 .25
185 James Patrick .10 .25
186 Ted Drury .10 .25
187 Dan Laperriere .10 .25
188 Benoit Hogue .10 .25
189 Chris Gratton .10 .25
190 Jyrki Lumme .10 .25
191 Peter Stastny .12 .30
192 Keith Tkachuk .15 .40
193 Mike Modano .25 .60
194 Nicklas Lidstrom .15 .40
195 Pierre Sevigny .10 .25
196 Scott Pearson .10 .25
197 Jaroslav Modry .10 .25
198 Garry Valk .10 .25
199 Kevin Hatcher .10 .25
200 Denis Tsygurov RC .15 .40
201 Paul Laus .10 .25
202 Alexander Godynyuk .10 .25
203 Brian Bellows .12 .30
204 Michal Sykora .10 .25
205 Al Iafrate .10 .25
206 Mark Tinordi .10 .25
207 Kelly Hrudey .12 .30
208 Tom Barrasso .12 .30
209 Craig Billington .12 .30
210 Teemu Selanne .30 .75
211 Alexandre Daigle .10 .25
212 Grant Fuhr .15 .40
213 Doug Brown .10 .25
214 Tim Sweeney .10 .25
215 Chris Pronger .15 .40
216 Alexei Gusarov .12 .30
217 Gary Suter .10 .25
218 Boris Mironov .10 .25
219 Sergei Zubov .10 .25
220 Checklist 167-249 .10 .25
221 Shayne Corson .10 .25
222 Jeremy Roenick .30 .75
223 John Druce .12 .30
224 Martin Straka .10 .25
225 Stephane Fiset .12 .30
226 Vincent Damphousse .12 .30
227 Bob Kudelski .10 .25
228 German Titov .10 .25
229 Kevin Stevens .10 .25
230 Dave Ellett .10 .25
231 Steve Larmer .12 .30
232 Glen Wesley .10 .25
233 Mathieu Schneider .10 .25
234 Stephan Lebeau .10 .25
235 Mark Fitzpatrick .12 .30
236 Mikael Renberg .12 .30
237 Darren McCarty .10 .25
238 Todd Nelson .10 .25
239 Igor Korolev .10 .25
240 Warren Rychel .10 .25
241 Gino Odjick .10 .25
242 Dave Manson .10 .25
243 Calle Johansson .10 .25
244 Andrei Trefilov .10 .25
245 Jason Dawe .10 .25
246 Glen Murray .10 .25
247 Jeff Shantz .10 .25
248 Zarley Zalapski .10 .25
249 Petr Klima .10 .25
250 Patrice Brisebois .10 .25
251 Chris Osgood .25 .60
252 Darius Kasparaitis .10 .25
253 Chris Joseph .10 .25
254 Glenn Anderson .15 .40
255 Kirk Muller .10 .25
256 Jason Smith .12 .30
257 Bob Bassen .10 .25
258 Joe Juneau .12 .30
259 Igor Kravchuk .10 .25
260 John Lilley .10 .25
261 Philippe Bozon .12 .30
262 Scott Stevens .15 .40
263 Dominic Roussel .12 .30
264 Dimitri Khristich .10 .25
265 Ed Patterson .10 .25
266 Mike Peca .12 .30
267 Teppo Numminen .10 .25
268 Alexei Kovalev .10 .25
269 Cam Neely .15 .40
270 Iain Fraser .10 .25
271 Tomas Sandstrom .10 .25
272 Lyle Odelein .12 .30
273 Norm Maciver .10 .25
274 Zdeno Ciger .10 .25
275 Ed Belfour .15 .40
276 Brian Savage .10 .25
277 Vlastimil Kroupa .10 .25
278 Cliff Ronning .10 .25
279 Alexei Zhitnik .12 .30
280 Jim Storm .12 .30
281 Don Sweeney .10 .25
282 Mike Donnelly .10 .25
283 Glenn Healy .12 .30
284 Denis Savard .20 .50
285 Chris Terreri .12 .30
286 Darren Turcotte .10 .25
287 Curtis Joseph .25 .60
288 Ken Baumgartner .12 .30
289 Matthew Barnaby .12 .30
290 Brent Sutter .12 .30
291 Valeri Zelepukin .10 .25
292 Michal Pivonka .12 .30
293 Ray Sheppard .12 .30
294 Jiri Slegr .10 .25
295 Vesa Viitakoski .12 .30
296 Ulf Samuelsson .10 .25
297 Nelson Emerson .10 .25
298 John Slaney .10 .25
299 Pat Verbeek .12 .30
300 Pat LaFontaine .15 .40
301 Johan Garpenlov .10 .25
302 Eric Weinrich .10 .25
303 Richard Matvichuk .10 .25
304 Steve Duchesne .10 .25
305 Donald Audette .10 .25
306 Stu Barnes .10 .25
307 Vladimir Malakhov .10 .25
308 Dimitri Yushkevich .10 .25
309 David Sacco .10 .25
310 Scott Young .10 .25
311 Marty McInnis .10 .25
312 Grant Ledyard .10 .25
313 Peter Popovic .10 .25
314 Mikhail Shtalenkov RC .10 .25
315 Dave McLlwain .10 .25
316 Cam Stewart .10 .25
317 Derian Hatcher .10 .25
318 Pat Peake .10 .25
319 Wes Walz .10 .25
320 Fred Brathwaite .10 .25
321 Jesse Belanger .10 .25
322 Jozef Stumpel .10 .25
323 Dave Andreychuk .15 .40
324 Yuri Khmylev .10 .25
325 Tim Cheveldae .12 .30
326 Anatoli Semenov .10 .25
327 Alexander Karpovtsev .10 .25
328 Patrick Roy .40 1.00
329 Troy Mallette .10 .25
330 Checklist 250-330 .10 .25

1994-95 Donruss Dominators

e eight cards in this set were randomly inserted in Donruss product at the rate of 1:36 packs. Each card features head shots of three players, grouped by position and conference, over a silver foil set logo. Individual photos appear on the back with statistical information. Cards are numbered "X of 8."

COMPLETE SET (8) 15.00 40.00
1 Messier/Lemieux/Lindros 3.00 8.00
2 Leetch/Bourque/Stevens 4.00 10.00
3 Roy/Hasek/Vanbiesbrouck 6.00 15.00
4 Jagr/Renberg/Neely 2.00 5.00
5 Gretzky/Roenick/Fedorov 8.00 20.00
6 Chelios/Coffey/MacInnis 2.00 5.00
7 Potvin/Belfour/Irbe 2.00 5.00
8 Bure/Hull/Selanne 3.00 8.00

1994-95 Donruss Elite Inserts

is ten-card standard-size set was issued in Donruss product at the rate of 1:72 packs. The design features a silver border with a deckle edge cut and rounded corners surrounding an action player photo. The set title tops the photo, with team logo, player name and team name below it. Card backs feature a small photo and personal information. Each card is individually numbered out of 10,000 on the back.

COMPLETE SET (10) 30.00 60.00
1 Jason Arnott .60 1.50
2 Martin Brodeur 5.00 12.00
3 Pavel Bure 3.00 8.00
4 Sergei Fedorov 2.00 5.00
5 Wayne Gretzky 10.00 25.00
6 Mario Lemieux 6.00 15.00
7 Eric Lindros 3.00 8.00
8 Felix Potvin 4.00 10.00
9 Jeremy Roenick 2.50 6.00
10 Patrick Roy 6.00 15.00

1994-95 Donruss Ice Masters

This ten-card set was produced in the style of previous Diamond King sets in baseball, featuring the renderings of artist Dick Perez. The cards were randomly inserted at the rate of 1:18 packs A foil logo and player name are stamped in silver foil on the front. Backs are black and have a brief paragraph of information. Cards are numbered "X of 10."

COMPLETE SET (10) 8.00 15.00
1 Ed Belfour .50 1.25
2 Sergei Fedorov .75 2.00
3 Doug Gilmour .25 .60
4 Wayne Gretzky 3.00 8.00
5 Mario Lemieux 2.50 6.00
6 Eric Lindros .50 1.25
7 Mark Messier .50 1.25
8 Mike Modano .75 2.00
9 Luc Robitaille .25 .60
10 John Vanbiesbrouck .25 .60

1994-95 Donruss Masked Marvels

e ten cards in this set of NHL goalies were randomly inserted at a rate of 1:18 packs. The card fronts display a small action photo to the left and a holographic facial image printed in a silver foil disc at right. Cards are numbered X of 10 on the back. These cards feature a removable clear plastic coating on the front which is designed to protect the hologram from scratches. A white sticker reading "Remove Protective Coating" covers a small segment of each card front. Prices below reflect values for cards with the coating intact; collectors are free to preserve their cards with or without this coating.

COMPLETE SET (10) 15.00 30.00
1 Ed Belfour 1.00 2.50
2 Martin Brodeur 2.50 6.00
3 Dominik Hasek 2.00 5.00
4 Arturs Irbe .75 2.00
5 Curtis Joseph 1.25 3.00
6 Kirk McLean .75 2.00
7 Felix Potvin 1.00 2.50
8 Mike Richter 1.00 2.50
9 Patrick Roy 5.00 12.00
10 John Vanbiesbrouck 1.00 2.50

1995-96 Donruss

ese 390 standard-size cards represent the first and second series of the 1995-96 Donruss issue. The fronts feature borderless color action player photos. The player's name and team is identified on the bottom of the card. The borderless backs carry a color action photo with seasonal and career stats as an inset on the right side. Rookie Cards include Daniel Alfredsson and Daymond Langkow.

1 Eric Lindros .15 .40
2 Steve Larmer .07 .20
3 Oleg Tverdovsky .10 .25
4 Vladimir Malakhov .05 .15
5 Ian Laperriere .05 .15
6 Chris Marinucci RC .07 .20
7 Nelson Emerson .05 .15
8 David Oliver .05 .15
9 Felix Potvin .10 .25
10 Manny Fernandez .07 .20
11 Jason Wiemer .05 .15
12 Dale Hunter .07 .20
13 Wayne Gretzky .50 1.25
14 Todd Gill .05 .15
15 Radim Bicanek .07 .20
16 Kirk McLean .07 .20
17 Esa Tikkanen .05 .15
18 Yuri Khmylev .05 .15
19 Peter Bondra .10 .25
20 Brian Savage .05 .15
21 Mariusz Czerkawski .05 .15
22 Rob Blake .07 .20
23 Chris Osgood .07 .20
24 Bernie Nicholls .05 .15
25 Doug Weight .10 .25
26 Shaun Van Allen .05 .15
27 Jeremy Roenick .12 .30
28 Sean Burke .05 .15
29 Pat Verbeek .07 .20
30 Dino Ciccarelli .07 .20
31 Trevor Kidd .07 .20
32 Steve Thomas .07 .20
33 Dominik Hasek .12 .30
34 Sandis Ozolinsh .07 .20
35 Bill Guerin .07 .20
36 Scott Young .05 .15
37 Scott Mellanby .07 .20
38 Joe Mullen .07 .20
39 Steve Larouche RC .05 .15
40 Joe Nieuwendyk .10 .25
41 Rick Tocchet .07 .20
42 Keith Primeau .05 .15
43 Darren Turcotte .05 .15
44 Jason Arnott .07 .20
45 Brantt Myhres RC .05 .15
46 Murray Craven .05 .15
47 Martin Gendron .07 .20
48 Mark Recchi .12 .30
49 Uwe Krupp .07 .20
50 Alexei Zhitnik .05 .15
51 Rob Niedermayer .07 .20
52 Sergei Brylin .05 .15
53 Mats Naslund .07 .20
54 Glenn Healy .07 .20
55 Mathieu Schneider .05 .15
56 Marko Tuomainen .05 .15
57 Paul Kariya .12 .30
58 Dave Gagner .05 .15
59 Mike Richter .10 .25
60 Patrik Juhlin .05 .15
61 Pierre Turgeon .10 .25
62 Mike Modano .15 .40
63 Chris Pronger .10 .25
64 Chris Joseph .05 .15
65 Peter Forsberg .25 .60
66 Roman Oksiuta .05 .15
67 Jamie Storr .07 .20
68 Brett Hull .12 .30
69 Steve Chiasson .05 .15
70 Benoit Hogue .05 .15
71 Guy Hebert .07 .20
72 Chris Therien .05 .15
73 Darryl Sydor .07 .20
74 Phil Housley .07 .20
75 Jason Allison .07 .20
76 Richard Smehlik .07 .20
77 Shean Donovan .05 .15
78 Keith Tkachuk .10 .25
79 Cliff Ronning .05 .15
80 Mikael Renberg .07 .20
81 Steven Rice .05 .15
82 Adam Graves .07 .20
83 Nicklas Lidstrom .10 .25
84 Daren Puppa .07 .20
85 Todd Warriner .07 .20
86 Jon Rohloff .05 .15
87 Patrice Tardif .07 .20
88 John MacLean .07 .20
89 Ulf Samuelsson .05 .15
90 Alexander Selivanov .07 .20
91 Chris Chelios .10 .25
92 Ulf Dahlen .05 .15
93 Brad May .05 .15
94 Ron Francis .12 .30
95 Kevin Hatcher .07 .20
96 Steve Yzerman .12 .30
97 Jocelyn Thibault .07 .20
98 Dave Andreychuk .10 .25
99 Gary Suter .07 .20
100 Teemu Selanne .20 .50
101 Don Sweeney .05 .15
102 Valeri Bure .05 .15
103 Todd Harvey .05 .15
104 Luc Robitaille .10 .25
105 Scott Niedermayer .10 .25
106 John Vanbiesbrouck .07 .20
107 Alexei Yashin .07 .20
108 Ed Belfour .07 .20
109 Jyrki Lumme .05 .15
110 Petr Klima .05 .15
111 Tony Granato .05 .15
112 Bob Corkum .05 .15
113 Chris McAlpine RC .07 .20
114 John LeClair .10 .25
115 Kenny Jonsson .10 .25
116 Garry Galley .05 .15
117 Jeff Norton .05 .15
118 Tomas Sandstrom .07 .20
119 Paul Coffey .10 .25
120 Mike Ricci .07 .20
121 Tony Amonte .07 .20
122 Chris Gratton .05 .15
123 Blaine Lacher .07 .20
124 Andrei Nikolishin .05 .15
125 Michal Grosek .05 .15
126 Shawn Chambers .05 .15
127 Ray Bourque .15 .40
128 Jeff Nelson .07 .20
129 Kirk Muller .07 .20
130 Sergei Zubov .07 .20
131 Stanislav Neckar .05 .15
132 Stu Barnes .05 .15
133 Jari Kurri .10 .25
134 Slava Kozlov .07 .20
135 Curtis Joseph .10 .25
136 Joe Juneau .07 .20
137 Craig Janney .05 .15
138 Bryan Smolinski .05 .1
139 Brian Bradley .07 .2
140 Steve Rucchin .07 .2
141 Donald Audette .07 .2
142 Jaromir Jagr .25 .6
143 Mike Torchia RC .07 .2
144 Ray Ferraro .05 .1
145 Adam Deadmarsh .05 .1
146 Joe Murphy .05 .1
147 Ron Hextall .10 .2
148 Andrew Cassels .05 .1
149 Martin Brodeur .25 .6
150 Marek Malik .05 .1
151 Eric Desjardins .07 .2
152 Cory Stillman .05 .1
153 Owen Nolan .10 .2
154 Randy Wood .05 .1
155 Alexei Zhamnov .10 .2
156 John Cullen .05 .1
157 Zdenek Nedved .05 .1
158 Greg Adams .05 .1
159 Kelly Miller .05 .1
160 Alexandre Daigle .05 .1
161 Gord Murphy .05 .1
162 Jeff Friesen .05 .1
163 Scott Stevens .10 .2
164 Denis Chasse .05 .1
165 Cam Neely .10 .2
166 Magnus Svensson RC .07 .2
167 Joe Sakic .15 .4
168 Kevin Brown .07 .2
169 Craig Conroy RC .07 .2
170 Pavel Bure .12 .3
171 Viktor Kozlov .07 .2
172 Pat LaFontaine .10 .2
173 Sergei Gonchar .05 .1
174 Brett Lindros .05 .1
175 Jassen Cullimore .07 .2
176 Mats Sundin .10 .2
177 Zarley Zalapski .05 .1
178 Stephane Richer .07 .2
179 Steve Smith .05 .1
180 Brendan Shanahan .12 .3
181 Brian Leetch .10 .2
182 Ken Wregget .07 .2
183 Jeff Brown .07 .2
184 Darby Hendrickson .05 .1
185 Nikolai Khabibulin .07 .2
186 Glen Wesley .05 .1
187 Andrei Nazarov .07 .2
188 Rod Brind'Amour .10 .2
189 Jim Carey .07 .2
190 Derek Plante .05 .1
191 Valeri Karpov .05 .1
192 Mike Kennedy .07 .2
193 Wendel Clark .10 .2
194 Radek Bonk .05 .1
195 Jozef Stumpel .05 .1
196 Tommy Salo RC .15 .4
197 Michal Pivonka .05 .1
198 Ray Sheppard .07 .2
199 Russ Courtnall .05 .1
200 Todd Marchant .05 .1
201 Geoff Sanderson .05 .1
202 Vincent Damphousse .07 .2
203 Sergei Krivokrasov .05 .1
204 Jesse Belanger .05 .1
205 Al MacInnis .10 .2
206 Philippe DeRouville .07 .2
207 Mike Eastwood .05 .1
208 Travis Green .07 .2
209 Jeff Shantz .05 .1
210 Shane Doan RC .30 .7
211 Mike Sullivan .07 .2
212 Kevin Dineen .07 .2
213 Pat Falloon .05 .1
214 Rick Tabaracci .07 .2
215 Kelly Hrudey .07 .2
216 Alexei Kovalev .05 .1
217 Matt Johnson .07 .2
218 Turner Stevenson .05 .1
219 Mike Sillinger .05 .1
220 Bobby Holik .05 .1
221 Kevin Stevens .07 .2
222 Dave Lowry .05 .1
223 Martin Gelinas .05 .1
224 Darren Langdon RC .20 .5
225 Tie Domi .07 .2
226 Doug Bodger .05 .1
227 Patrick Flatley .05 .1
228 Anders Myrvold RC .07 .2
229 German Titov .07 .2
230 Pat Peake .05 .1
231 Robert Kron .05 .1
232 Mike Donnelly .05 .1
233 Denis Savard .12 .3
234 Mathieu Dandenault RC .20 .5
235 Joe Dziedzic .05 .1
236 Valeri Kamensky .07 .2
237 Joaquin Gage RC .07 .2
238 Geoff Courtnall .05 .1
239 Arturs Irbe .07 .2
240 Dan Quinn .07 .2
241 J.C. Bergeron .07 .2
242 Brian Noonan .05 .1
243 Ulf Samuelsson .05 .1
244 Jeff O'Neill .10 .2
245 Sandy Moger RC .05 .1
246 Don Beaupre .07 .2
247 Bob Probert .07 .2
248 Mattias Norstrom .07 .2
249 Jason Bonsignore .05 .1
250 Mike Ridley .05 .1
251 Joe Mullen .07 .2
252 Petr Nedved .07 .2
253 Jason Doig .10 .2
254 Olaf Kolzig .07 .2
255 Mark Tinordi .05 .1
256 Roman Hamrlik .05 .1
257 Denis Pederson .05 .1
258 Paul Ysebaert .05 .1
259 Neal Broten .07 .2
260 Jason Woolley .05 .1
261 Teppo Numminen .05 .1
262 Scott Thornton .07 .2
263 Ted Donato .05 .1
264 Marcus Ragnarsson RC .12 .3
265 Dimitri Khristich .05 .1
266 Mike Peca .07 .2
267 Dominic Roussel .05 .1
268 Owen Nolan .10 .2
269 Patrick Poulin .05 .1
270 Mario Lemieux .30 .7
271 Mark Messier .15 .4
272 Slava Fetisov .07 .2
273 Andrei Trefilov .05 .1
274 Damian Rhodes .07 .2
275 Alexander Mogilny .07 .2
276 Ray Sheppard .07 .2
277 Radek Dvorak RC .12 .3
278 Steve Duchesne .05 .1

279 Jason Smith .07 .20
280 Wade Flaherty RC .07 .20
281 Lyle Odelein .05 .15
282 Keith Jones .07 .20
283 Saku Koivu .10 .25
284 Marty Murray .10 .25
285 Sergei Fedorov .15 .40
286 Brian Rolston .05 .15
287 Dave Roche RC .07 .20
288 Sylvain Lefebvre .05 .15
289 Theo Fleury .12 .30
290 Andy Moog .10 .25
291 Tom Barrasso .07 .20
292 Craig Mills RC .05 .15
293 Mike Gartner .10 .25
294 Stefan Ustorf .05 .15
295 Darren Turcotte .05 .15
296 Steve Konowalchuk .07 .20
297 Ray Ferraro .05 .15
298 Brian Holzinger RC .20 .50
299 Daniel Alfredsson RC .50 1.25
300 Derek King .07 .20
301 Mark Fitzpatrick .07 .20
302 Joe Sacco .05 .15
303 Scott Walker RC .05 .15
304 Ricard Persson RC .07 .20
305 Mike Rathje .07 .20
306 Petr Svoboda .05 .15
307 Roman Vopat RC .05 .15
308 Ray Whitney .07 .20
309 Calle Johansson .05 .15
310 Grant Fuhr .10 .25
311 John Tucker .05 .15
312 Anatoli Semenov .07 .20
313 Darren McCarty .05 .15
314 Stephane Quintal .07 .20
315 Jason Dawe .05 .15
316 Zigmund Palffy .10 .25
317 Dave Manson .05 .15
318 Vitali Yachmenev .10 .25
319 Chris Pronger .10 .25
320 Valeri Zelepukin .05 .15
321 Ryan Smyth .07 .20
322 Johan Garpenlov .05 .15
323 Bill Ranford .07 .20
324 Daymond Langkow RC .10 .25
325 Aki Berg RC .10 .25
326 Derian Hatcher .07 .20
327 Bryan Smolinski .05 .15
328 Michel Picard .07 .20
329 Alek Stojanov .05 .15
330 Trent Klatt .05 .15
331 Richard Park .10 .25
332 Jere Lehtinen .07 .20
333 Bryan McCabe .10 .25
334 Kyle McLaren RC .05 .15
335 Todd Krygier .05 .15
336 Adam Creighton .05 .15
337 Jamie Pushor .07 .20
338 Patrick Roy .25 .60
339 Milos Holan .05 .15
340 Dave Ellett .05 .15
341 Brian Bellows .07 .20
342 Jamie Rivers .05 .15
343 Claude Lemieux .10 .25
344 Leif Rohlin RC .07 .20
345 Eric Daze .20 .50
346 Todd Bertuzzi RC .12 .30
347 Antti Tormanen RC .05 .15
348 Luc Robitaille .10 .25
349 Tim Taylor .05 .15
350 Stephane Yelle RC .07 .20
351 Marko Kiprusoff .07 .20
352 Igor Korolev .05 .15
353 Scott Lachance .05 .15
354 Marty McSorley .05 .15
355 Joel Otto .05 .15
356 Josef Beranek .05 .15
357 Sergei Zubov .07 .20
358 Rhett Warrener RC .05 .15
359 Jimmy Carson .07 .20
360 Zdeno Ciger .07 .20
361 Brendan Witt .10 .25
362 Byron Dafoe .07 .20
363 Steve Thomas .07 .20
364 Deron Quint .07 .20
365 Nelson Emerson .05 .15
366 Larry Murphy .10 .25
367 Benoit Brunet .05 .15
368 Kjell Samuelsson .05 .15
369 Aaron Gavey .05 .15
370 Robert Svehla RC .05 .15
371 Rene Corbet .05 .15
372 Gary Roberts .05 .15
373 Shawn McEachern .05 .15
374 Andrei Kovalenko .05 .15
375 Yanic Perreault .05 .15
376 Shayne Corson .05 .15
377 Brendan Shanahan .12 .30
378 Sergei Nemchinov .05 .15
379 Chad Kilger RC .10 .25
380 Sergio Momesso .05 .15
381 Craig Billington .07 .20
382 Niklas Sundstrom .10 .25
383 Matthew Barnaby .10 .25
384 Dale Hawerchuk .12 .30
385 Trevor Linden .10 .25
386 Adam Oates .10 .25
387 Dimitri Yushkevich .05 .15
388 Todd Elik .05 .15
389 Wendel Clark .10 .25
390 Stephane Fiset .07 .20
NNO Checklist Card 1 .05 .15
NNO Checklist Card 2 .05 .15
NNO Checklist Card 3 .05 .15
NNO Checklist Card 4 .05 .15
NNO Checklist Card 5 .05 .15
NNO Checklist Card 6 .05 .15
NNO Checklist Card 7 .05 .15
NNO Checklist Card 8 .05 .15

1995-96 Donruss Between the Pipes

aped like a goal and outlined in red foil, these ten cards were randomly inserted in series 1 (1-5) and 2 (6-10) packs at a rate of 1:36. The goaltender is pictured within the goal with a solid blue background. The backs feature a brief write-up and career statistics.

COMPLETE SET (10) 25.00 60.00
COMPLETE SERIES 1 (5) 12.00 30.00
COMPLETE SERIES 2 (5) 12.00 30.00
1 Blaine Lacher 2.00 5.00
2 Dominik Hasek 4.00 10.00
3 Mike Vernon 2.00 5.00
4 Trevor Kidd 2.00 5.00
5 Martin Brodeur 5.00 12.00
6 Jim Carey 2.00 5.00
7 Patrick Roy 10.00 25.00
8 Sean Burke 2.00 5.00
9 Felix Potvin 3.00 8.00
10 Ed Belfour 3.00 8.00

1995-96 Donruss Canadian World Junior Team

ese 22 standard-size cards were randomly inserted into series 1 (1-11) and series 2 (12-22) packs at a rate of 1:2. These cards honor players who represented Canada in the 1995 World Junior Championships. Large player photographs are superimposed on a maple leaf design. The backs feature two player photos. One is an inset photo in a maple leaf and the other on the left side is a black-and-white image. Information about the player is located in the upper left corner while his National Junior Team career stats are printed on the right side of the card. The cards are numbered "X of 22" in the upper right-hand corner.

COMPLETE SET (22) 5.00 12.00
COMP.SERIES 1 (11) 2.00 5.00
COMP.SERIES 2 (11) 3.00 8.00
1 Jamie Storr .60 1.50
2 Dan Cloutier .20 .50
3 Nolan Baumgartner .20 .50
4 Chad Allen .20 .50
5 Wade Redden .20 .50
6 Ed Jovanovski .60 1.50
7 Jamie Rivers .20 .50
8 Bryan McCabe .60 1.50
9 Lee Sorochan .20 .50
10 Marty Murray .20 .50
11 Larry Courville .20 .50
12 Jason Allison .20 .50
13 Darcy Tucker .20 .50
14 Jeff O'Neill .20 .50
15 Eric Daze .60 1.50
16 Alexandre Daigle .20 .50
17 Todd Harvey .60 1.50
18 Jason Botterill .20 .50
19 Shean Donovan .20 .50
20 Denis Pederson .20 .50
21 Jeff Friesen .20 .50
22 Ryan Smyth .40 1.00

1995-96 Donruss Dominators

e eight cards in this set were randomly inserted in series two hobby packs only at a rate of 1:35. Each features three of the top players at each position from each conference. The cards are individually numbered on the backs out of 5,000.

COMPLETE SET (8) 20.00 50.00
1 Forsberg/Lindros/Lemieux 6.00 15.00
2 LeClair/Renberg/Jagr 5.00 12.00
3 Zubov/Bourque/Leetch 2.00 5.00
4 Carey/Brodeur/Hasek 5.00 12.00
5 Gilmour/Gretzky/Fedorov 6.00 15.00
6 Hull/Kariya/Bure 2.50 6.00
7 Coffey/Chelios/MacInnis 2.00 5.00
8 Potvin/Belfour/Kidd 5.00 12.00

1995-96 Donruss Elite Inserts

ese ten standard-size cards were randomly inserted into first (1-5) and second series (6-10) Donruss at a rate of 1:116 and 1:47 packs respectively. Each card is sequentially numbered out of 10,000. The fronts feature blue holographic foil, layered with copper foil which emphasize the player's name and team logo. The word "Elite" is noted in the upper right-hand corner. The card backs are printed in metallic copper and metallic blue ink silhouetting the player's image. There is a brief blurb about the player on the left side of the card. The cards are numbered "X" of 10 in the upper right corner.

COMPLETE SET (10) 25.00 50.00
1 Alexei Zhamnov .60 1.50
2 Joe Sakic 2.50 6.00
3 Mikael Renberg .60 1.50
4 Sergei Fedorov 1.50 4.00
5 Paul Coffey 1.25 3.00
6 Paul Kariya 1.25 3.00
7 Wayne Gretzky 8.00 20.00
8 Eric Lindros 1.25 3.00
9 Mario Lemieux 6.00 15.00
10 Jaromir Jagr 2.00 5.00

1995-96 Donruss Igniters

ese 10 standard-size cards were randomly inserted in Series 1 hobby packs. The horizontally-oriented cards feature the player's photo superimposed against the word "Igniters". His name and team are identified on the bottom of the card. The backs are individually numbered out of 5,000.

COMPLETE SET (10) 15.00 30.00
1 Adam Oates 1.25 3.00
2 Paul Coffey 1.50 4.00
3 Doug Gilmour 1.25 3.00
4 Pierre Turgeon 1.25 3.00
5 Mark Messier 1.50 4.00
6 Alexei Zhamnov 1.25 3.00
7 Jeremy Roenick 2.00 5.00
8 Steve Yzerman 6.00 15.00
9 Joe Nieuwendyk 1.25 3.00
10 Ron Francis 1.25 3.00

1995-96 Donruss Marksmen

e eight cards in this set were randomly inserted into series one Donruss retail packs only at a rate of 1:24. The cards showcase the top eight goal scorers of the 1994-95 season.

COMPLETE SET (8) 6.00 12.00
1 Peter Bondra .75 2.00
2 Owen Nolan .75 2.00
3 Eric Lindros .75 2.00
4 Ray Sheppard .75 2.00
5 Jaromir Jagr 1.25 3.00
6 Theo Fleury .75 2.00
7 Brett Hull 1.00 2.50
8 Brendan Shanahan .75 2.00

1995-96 Donruss Pro Pointers

Inserted one per series two pack, these twenty cards feature hockey tips from top players born in the United States (1-10) and Canada (11-20).

COMPLETE SET (20) 3.00 6.00
1 Jeremy Roenick .20 .50
2 Pat LaFontaine .15 .40
3 Jason Bonsignore .02 .10
4 Chris Chelios .15 .40
5 Brian Leetch .07 .20
6 Brett Hull .20 .50
7 Keith Tkachuk .15 .40
8 Mike Modano .25 .60
9 Brian Rolston .02 .10
10 Darren Turcotte .02 .10
11 Jeff Friesen .02 .10
12 Theo Fleury .02 .10
13 Eric Lindros .15 .40
14 Mario Lemieux .75 2.00
15 Jamie Storr .07 .20
16 Trevor Kidd .07 .20
17 Chris Pronger .15 .40
18 Brendan Witt .02 .10
19 Paul Kariya .15 .40
20 Todd Harvey .07 .20

1995-96 Donruss Rated Rookies

ndomly inserted at a rate of 1:24 series two retail packs, this 16-card set features a plethora of players who made their NHL debuts in the 1995-96 season.

COMPLETE SET (16) 15.00 40.00
1 Saku Koivu 4.00 10.00
2 Todd Bertuzzi 2.00 5.00
3 Niklas Sundstrom .75 2.00
4 Jeff O'Neill .75 2.00
5 Zdenek Nedved .75 2.00
6 Eric Daze .75 2.00
7 Chad Kilger .75 2.00
8 Shane Doan .75 2.00
9 Vitali Yachmenev .75 2.00
10 Radek Dvorak .75 2.00
11 Marty Murray .75 2.00
12 Cory Stillman .75 2.00
13 Marcus Ragnarsson .75 2.00
14 Daniel Alfredsson 2.00 5.00
15 Antti Tormanen .75 2.00
16 Petr Sykora 1.50 4.00

1995-96 Donruss Rookie Team

ese nine standard-size cards featuring leading rookies from the 1994-95 season were issued in first series packs (1:12). The borderless fronts feature the player's photo blending into various colors which represent his team's color pattern. The player's name and team identification are located on the bottom. The horizontal back features a close-up player photo, along with a brief note. The cards are numbered on the upper right as "X" of 9.

COMPLETE SET (9) 3.00 6.00
1 Jim Carey .20 .50
2 Peter Forsberg 1.00 2.50
3 Paul Kariya .40 1.00
4 David Oliver .10 .30
5 Blaine Lacher .20 .50
6 Oleg Tverdovsky .10 .30
7 Jeff Friesen .10 .30
8 Todd Marchant .10 .30
9 Todd Harvey .20 .50

1996-97 Donruss

e 1996-97 Donruss set was issued in one series totaling 240 cards. The 10-card packs retailed for $1.89 each. Card fronts feature a borderless color action photo along with player name at the top and team name and logo at the bottom. Card backs feature another color action photo, along with stats and biographical information. Key Rookie Cards include Ethan Moreau and Kevin Hodson.

COMPLETE SET (240) 6.00 15.00
1 Joe Sakic .25 .60
2 Jeremy Roenick .25 .60
3 Kirk McLean .12 .30
4 Zarley Zalapski .10 .25
5 Jyrki Lumme .10 .25
6 Owen Nolan .15 .40
7 Luc Robitaille .15 .40
8 Bob Probert .12 .30
9 Ken Baumgartner .12 .30
10 Rick Tabaracci .12 .30
11 Alexei Zhitnik .10 .25
12 Al MacInnis .15 .40
13 Brian Leetch .15 .40
14 Valeri Kamensky .12 .30
15 Todd Gill .12 .30
16 Mark Messier .25 .60
17 Pierre Turgeon .15 .40
18 Mathieu Schneider .10 .25
19 Vyacheslav Kozlov .10 .25
20 Milos Holan .10 .25
21 Yanic Perreault .10 .25
22 Mike Modano .25 .60
23 Claude Lemieux .10 .25
24 Rob Niedermayer .12 .30
25 Eric Desjardins .12 .30
26 Alexander Semak .10 .25
27 Mark Recchi .20 .50
28 Slava Fetisov .10 .25
29 Kevin Hatcher .10 .25
30 Mats Sundin .15 .40
31 Jeff Reese .10 .25
32 Alexander Selivanov .10 .25
33 Jim Carey .15 .40
34 Daren Puppa .12 .30
35 Vincent Damphousse .12 .30
36 John LeClair .15 .40
37 Jon Casey .12 .30
38 Chris Terreri .12 .30
39 Larry Murphy .12 .30
40 Geoff Sanderson .12 .30
41 Adam Oates .15 .40
42 Sandy McCarthy .10 .25
43 Jaromir Jagr .40 1.00
44 Roman Oksiuta .10 .25
45 Zigmund Palffy .15 .40
46 Doug Gilmour .20 .50
47 Cliff Ronning .10 .25
48 Curtis Leschyshyn .10 .25
49 Scott Mellanby .12 .30
50 Sergei Fedorov .25 .60
51 Denis Savard .20 .50
52 Mike Vernon .12 .30
53 Todd Marchant .10 .25
54 Geoff Courtnall .10 .25
55 Shayne Corson .10 .25
56 Dimitri Khristich .10 .25
57 Scott Stevens .15 .40
58 German Titov .10 .25
59 Darren Turcotte .10 .25
60 Michal Pivonka .10 .25
61 Ron Hextall .12 .30
62 Ed Belfour .15 .40
63 Chris Pronger .12 .30
64 Brian Bellows .12 .30
65 Pavel Bure .20 .50
66 Adam Graves .10 .25
67 Tom Barrasso .12 .30
68 Stu Barnes .10 .25
69 Norm MacIver .10 .25
70 Jesse Belanger .10 .25
71 Chris Chelios .15 .40
72 Tommy Soderstrom .12 .30
73 Nelson Emerson .10 .25
74 Kenny Jonsson .10 .25
75 Bill Lindsay .10 .25
76 Petr Nedved .12 .30
77 Robert Svehla .10 .25
78 Tomas Sandstrom .10 .25
79 Jeff Friesen .10 .25
80 Tony Amonte .12 .30
81 Sylvain Lefebvre .10 .25
82 Greg Adams .10 .25
83 Vladimir Konstantinov .12 .30
84 Roman Hamrlik .12 .30
85 Doug Weight .15 .40
86 Shaun Van Allen .10 .25
87 Bill Ranford .12 .30
88 Jeff Hackett .12 .30
89 Alexei Zhamnov .12 .30
90 Dale Hawerchuk .20 .50
91 Sergei Zubov .10 .25
92 Dan Quinn .10 .25
93 Wayne Gretzky .75 2.00
94 Todd Harvey .10 .25
95 Chris Osgood .15 .40
96 Felix Potvin .15 .40
97 Richard Matvichuk .10 .25
98 Wendel Clark .12 .30
99 Bryan Smolinski .10 .25
100 Rob Blake .15 .40
101 Jocelyn Thibault .15 .40
102 Trevor Linden .12 .30
103 Craig MacTavish .10 .25
104 Sandis Ozolinsh .10 .25
105 Oleg Tverdovsky .12 .30
106 Garry Galley .10 .25
107 Derek Plante .10 .25
108 Stephane Richer .12 .30
109 Dave Andreychuk .15 .40
110 Curtis Joseph .15 .40
111 Greg Johnson .10 .25
112 Patrick Roy .40 1.00
113 Pat LaFontaine .15 .40
114 Uwe Krupp .10 .25
115 Ulf Dahlen .10 .25
116 Brian Bradley .10 .25
117 Grant Fuhr .15 .40
118 Brian Skrudland .10 .25
119 Nicklas Lidstrom .20 .50
120 Steve Chiasson .10 .25
121 Sean Burke .10 .25
122 Rick Tocchet .12 .30
123 Martin Rucinsky .10 .25
124 Alexei Yashin .12 .30
125 Mikael Renberg .12 .30
126 Teppo Numminen .10 .25
127 Randy Burridge .10 .25
128 Radek Bonk .10 .25
129 Scott Young .10 .25
130 Gary Suter .10 .25
131 Mario Lemieux .50 1.25
132 Ray Bourque .25 .60
133 Martin Gelinas .10 .25
134 Keith Tkachuk .15 .40
135 Benoit Hogue .10 .25
136 Ken Wregget .12 .30
137 Eric Lindros .25 .60
138 Keith Primeau .10 .25
139 Peter Forsberg .25 .60
140 Paul Coffey .15 .40
141 Mike Ridley .10 .25
142 Paul Kariya .20 .50
143 Jason Arnott .12 .30
144 Joe Murphy .10 .25
145 Adam Deadmarsh .10 .25
146 John MacLean .12 .30
147 Peter Bondra .12 .30
148 Martin Brodeur .30 .75
149 Ron Francis .20 .50
150 Dino Ciccarelli .15 .40
151 Joe Juneau .10 .25
152 Matthew Barnaby .10 .25
153 Mark Tinordi .10 .25
154 Craig Janney .12 .30
155 Rod Brind'Amour .15 .40
156 Damian Rhodes .12 .30
157 Teemu Selanne .30 .75
158 James Patrick .10 .25
159 Theo Fleury .30 .75
160 Trevor Kidd .10 .25
161 Kirk Muller .10 .25
162 Andrew Cassels .10 .25
163 Brent Fedyk .10 .25
164 Guy Hebert .12 .30
165 Jason Dawe .10 .25
166 Andy Moog .15 .40
167 Igor Larionov .15 .40
168 Brian Savage .10 .25
169 Kris Draper .10 .25
170 Dave Gagner .15 .40
171 Steve Yzerman .40 1.00
172 Nikolai Khabibulin .12 .30
173 Chris Gratton .12 .30
174 Dave Lowry .10 .25
175 Travis Green .12 .30
176 Alexei Kovalev .10 .25
177 Mike Ricci .10 .25
178 Brendan Shanahan .20 .50
179 Corey Hirsch .12 .30
180 Bill Guerin .15 .40
181 Alexander Mogilny .12 .30
182 Steve Duchesne .10 .25
183 Ray Ferraro .10 .25
184 Mike Richter .15 .40
185 Yuri Khmylev .10 .25
186 Stephane Fiset .12 .30
187 John Vanbiesbrouck .15 .40
188 Scott Niedermayer .15 .40
189 Brad May .10 .25
190 Shawn McEachern .10 .25
191 Joe Mullen .12 .30
192 Dominik Hasek .25 .60
193 Steve Thomas .10 .25
194 Russ Courtnall .10 .25
195 Joe Nieuwendyk .15 .40
196 Petr Klima .10 .25
197 Brett Hull .75 2.00
198 Bernie Nicholls .10 .25
199 Dale Hunter .12 .30
200 Pat Verbeek .10 .25
201 Phil Housley .12 .30
202 Todd Krygier .10 .25
203 Zdeno Ciger .10 .25
204 Alexandre Daigle .10 .25
205 Cam Neely .15 .40
206 Mike Gartner .15 .40
207 Garth Snow .12 .30
208 Pat Falloon .10 .25
209 Kelly Hrudey .12 .30
210 Ray Sheppard .12 .30
211 Ted Donato .10 .25
212 Glenn Healy .12 .30
213 Radek Dvorak .12 .30
214 Niclas Andersson .10 .25
215 Miroslav Satan .10 .25
216 Roman Vopat .10 .25
217 Bryan McCabe .10 .25
218 Jamie Langenbrunner .10 .25
219 Kyle McLaren .10 .25
220 Stephane Yelle .10 .25
221 Byron Dafoe .10 .25
222 Grant Marshall .10 .25
223 Ryan Smyth .12 .30
224 Ville Peltonen .10 .25
225 Deron Quint .10 .25
226 Brian Holzinger .12 .30
227 Jose Theodore .20 .50
228 Ethan Moreau RC .15 .40
229 Steve Sullivan RC .12 .30
230 Kevin Hodson RC .15 .40
231 Cory Stillman .10 .25
232 Ralph Intranuovo .10 .25
233 Vitali Yachmenev .10 .25
234 Marcus Ragnarsson .10 .25
235 Nolan Baumgartner .10 .25
236 Chad Kilger .10 .25
237 Niklas Sundstrom .10 .25
238 Paul Coffey CL (1-120) .15 .40
239 Doug Gilmour CL (121-240) .20 .50
240 Steve Yzerman CL .40 1.00

1996-97 Donruss Press Proofs

This 240-card standard size set is a parallel issue to the regular Donruss set. A cut-out star in the upper right-hand corner, along with the words "First 2,000 Printed, Press Proof" printed above the set logo, along the bottom distinguish these cards from their regular counterparts.

*SINGLES: 4X TO 10X BASIC CARDS

1996-97 Donruss Between the Pipes

is standard-size set features 10 of the NHL's top netminders. These cards are found only in retail packs and are serially numbered to 4,000.

COMPLETE SET (10) 20.00 50.00
1 Patrick Roy 6.00 15.00
2 Martin Brodeur 3.00 8.00
3 Jim Carey 1.50 4.00
4 John Vanbiesbrouck 2.00 5.00
5 Chris Osgood 2.50 6.00
6 Ed Belfour 2.50 6.00
7 Jocelyn Thibault 2.00 5.00
8 Curtis Joseph 2.50 6.00
9 Nikolai Khabibulin 2.00 5.00
10 Felix Potvin 4.00 10.00

1996-97 Donruss Dominators

e ten cards in this set were randomly inserted in hobby packs at indeterminate odds and feature three of the top players at each position. These cards are serially numbered to 5,000 and printed on laminated holographic foil stock.

COMPLETE SET (10) 20.00 40.00
1 Carey/Brodeur/Beezer 1.50 4.00
2 Khabib./Osgood/Thibault 1.50 4.00
3 Chelios/Coffey/Bourque 2.00 5.00
4 Lemieux/Jagr/Francis 4.00 10.00
5 Lindros/Gretzky/Arnott 4.00 10.00
6 Gilmour/Clark/Turgeon 1.50 4.00
7 Mogilny/Bure/Linden 1.50 4.00
8 Kariya/Selanne/Tkachuk 1.50 4.00
9 Modano/Roenick/Fedorov 1.50 4.00
10 Daze/Koivu/Jovanovski 1.50 4.00

1996-97 Donruss Elite Inserts

ese ten standard-size cards were randomly inserted into all varieties of packs. The basic version of the set has silver borders with cards serially numbered to 10,000. The tougher-to-find gold parallel version features, naturally enough, gold borders with serial numbering to 2,000.

COMPLETE SET (10) 15.00 40.00
*GOLD: 1.2X TO 3X BASIC INSERTS
1 Pavel Bure 1.25 3.00
2 Wayne Gretzky 8.00 20.00
3 Doug Weight 1.25 3.00
4 Brett Hull 2.00 5.00
5 Mark Messier 1.25 3.00
6 Brendan Shanahan 1.25 3.00
7 Joe Sakic 2.50 6.00
8 Sergei Fedorov 1.50 4.00
9 Eric Lindros 1.25 3.00
10 Patrick Roy 6.00 15.00

1996-97 Donruss Go Top Shelf

is 10-card set was distributed only through magazine packs, with each card numbered out of 2,000.

COMPLETE SET (10) 20.00 50.00
1 Mario Lemieux 8.00 20.00
2 Teemu Selanne 2.00 5.00
3 Joe Sakic 4.00 10.00
4 Alexander Mogilny 1.25 3.00
5 Jaromir Jagr 3.00 8.00
6 Brett Hull 2.50 6.00
7 Mike Modano 2.50 6.00
8 Paul Kariya 2.00 5.00
9 Eric Lindros 2.00 5.00
10 Peter Forsberg 3.00 8.00

1996-97 Donruss Hit List

is set features 20 of the NHL's top bangers and crashers. Individually numbered to 10,000, these cards feature an internal die-cut with a color photo, and the player's name and position in silver foil on the front.

COMPLETE SET (20) 10.00 25.00
1 Eric Lindros .75 2.00
2 Wendel Clark .40 1.00
3 Ed Jovanovski .20 .50
4 Jeremy Roenick 1.50 4.00
5 Doug Weight .40 1.00
6 Chris Chelios .75 2.00
7 Brendan Shanahan .75 2.00
8 Mark Messier 1.25 3.00
9 Scott Stevens .20 .50
10 Keith Tkachuk .60 1.50
11 Trevor Linden .60 1.50
12 Eric Daze .20 .50
13 John LeClair .60 1.50
14 Peter Forsberg 2.00 5.00
15 Doug Gilmour .60 1.50
16 Roman Hamrlik .20 .50
17 Owen Nolan .20 .50
18 Claude Lemieux .20 .50
19 Saku Koivu .75 2.00
20 Theo Fleury .20 .50
P1 Eric Lindros PROMO .40 1.00

1996-97 Donruss Rated Rookies

is set features ten top young superstars. A press proof version of these cards exists, though quantity of production is unknown. They are fairly easy to distinguish by virtue of their gold foil finish.

COMPLETE SET (10) 8.00 20.00
*PRESS PROOF: 4X TO 10X BASIC INSERTS
1 Eric Daze .75 2.00
2 Petr Sykora .75 2.00
3 Valeri Bure .75 2.00
4 Jere Lehtinen .75 2.00
5 Jeff O'Neill .75 2.00
6 Saku Koivu 1.50 4.00
7 Ed Jovanovski .75 2.00
8 Eric Fichaud .75 2.00
9 Todd Bertuzzi 1.50 4.00
10 Daniel Alfredsson 1.50 4.00

1997-98 Donruss

e 1997-98 Donruss set was issued in one series totaling 230 cards and distributed in 10-card packs. The fronts featured color action player photos. The backs carried player information.

COMPLETE SET (230) 10.00 25.00
1 Peter Forsberg .12 .30
2 Steve Yzerman .20 .50
3 Eric Lindros .15 .40
4 Mark Messier .15 .40
5 Patrick Roy .25 .60
6 Jeremy Roenick .12 .30
7 Paul Kariya .12 .30
8 Valeri Bure .05 .15
9 Dominik Hasek .15 .40
10 Doug Gilmour .12 .30
11 Garth Snow .07 .20
12 Todd Bertuzzi .10 .25
13 Chris Osgood .10 .25
14 Jarome Iginla .10 .25
15 Lonny Bohonos .07 .20
16 Jeff O'Neill .07 .20
17 Daniel Alfredsson .10 .25
18 Daymond Langkow .05 .15
19 Alexei Yashin .07 .20
20 Byron Dafoe .05 .15
21 Mike Peca .07 .20
22 Jim Carey .05 .15
23 Pat Verbeek .07 .20
24 Terry Ryan .05 .15
25 Adam Oates .10 .25
26 Kevin Hatcher .05 .15
27 Ken Wregget .05 .15
28 Pierre Turgeon .10 .25
29 John LeClair .10 .25
30 Jere Lehtinen .07 .20
31 Jamie Storr .07 .20
32 Doug Weight .10 .25
33 Tommy Salo .05 .15
34 Bernie Nicholls .07 .20
35 Jocelyn Thibault .05 .15
36 Dale Hawerchuk .12 .30
37 Chris Chelios .10 .25
38 Kirk Muller .05 .15
39 Steve Sullivan .07 .20
40 Andy Moog .10 .25
41 Martin Gelinas .05 .15
42 Shayne Corson .05 .15
43 Curtis Joseph .10 .25
44 Donald Audette .07 .20
45 Rick Tocchet .05 .15
46 Craig Janney .05 .15
47 Geoff Courtnall .05 .15
48 Wade Redden .05 .15
49 Steve Rucchin .07 .20
50 Ethan Moreau .05 .15
51 Steve Shields RC .10 .25
52 Jamie Pushor .05 .15
53 Saku Koivu .10 .25
54 Oleg Tverdovsky .07 .20
55 Jeff Friesen .07 .20
56 Chris Gratton .05 .15
57 Wendel Clark .10 .25
58 John Vanbiesbrouck .10 .25
59 Trevor Kidd .05 .15
60 Sandis Ozolinsh .07 .20
61 Dave Andreychuk .10 .25
62 Travis Green .07 .20
63 Paul Coffey .10 .25
64 Roman Turek .07 .20
65 Vladimir Konstantinov .05 .15
66 Ray Bourque .15 .40
67 Wayne Primeau .07 .20
68 Todd Harvey .07 .20
69 Derek King .07 .20
70 Adam Graves .05 .15
71 Brett Hull .12 .30
72 Scott Niedermayer .10 .25
73 Mike Vernon .07 .20
74 Brian Holzinger .07 .20
75 Dainius Zubrus .07 .20
76 Patrick Lalime .07 .20
77 Corey Schwab .07 .20
78 Alexandre Daigle .05 .15
79 Geoff Sanderson .07 .20
80 Dave Gagner .05 .15
81 Jose Theodore .10 .25
82 Sergei Fedorov .15 .40
83 Keith Tkachuk .10 .25
84 Owen Nolan .10 .25
85 Brandon Convery .05 .15
86 Trevor Linden .07 .20
87 Landon Wilson .05 .15
88 Claude Lemieux .07 .20
89 Dimitri Khristich .07 .20
90 Luc Robitaille .10 .25
91 Todd Warriner .07 .20
92 Kelly Hrudey .07 .20
93 Mike Dunham .07 .20
94 Mike Grier .07 .20
95 Joe Juneau .07 .20
96 Alexei Zhamnov .05 .15
97 Jamie Langenbrunner .07 .20
98 Sean Pronger .05 .15
99 Janne Niinimaa .07 .20
100 Chris Pronger .07 .20
101 Ray Sheppard .07 .20
102 Tony Amonte .07 .20
103 Ron Tugnutt .10 .25
104 Mike Modano .15 .40
105 Dan Trebil .05 .15
106 Alexander Mogilny .07 .20
107 Darren McCarty .07 .20
108 Ted Donato .05 .15
109 Brian Savage .05 .15
110 Mike Gartner .10 .25
111 Jim Campbell .05 .15
112 Roman Hamrlik .07 .20
113 Andreas Dackell .07 .20
114 Ron Hextall .10 .25
115 Steve Washburn .05 .15
116 Jeff Hackett .05 .15
117 Joe Sakic .15 .40
118 Anson Carter .05 .15
119 Vyacheslav Kozlov .07 .20
120 Nikolai Khabibulin .10 .25
121 Tony Granato .07 .20
122 Al MacInnis .10 .25
123 Daren Puppa .07 .20
124 Mike Richter .10 .25
125 Zigmund Palffy .10 .25
126 Martin Brodeur .20 .50
127 Rem Murray .05 .15
128 Sean Burke .05 .15
129 Aki Berg .05 .15
130 Dmitri Mironov .07 .20
131 Jamie Allison .07 .20
132 Valeri Kamensky .07 .20
133 Pat LaFontaine .10 .25
134 Jozef Stumpel .07 .20
135 Peter Bondra .07 .20
136 Mark Recchi .12 .30
137 Ron Francis .12 .30
138 Harry York .07 .20
139 Mats Sundin .10 .25
140 Bobby Holik .05 .15
141 Eric Desjardins .05 .15
142 Scott Lachance .07 .20
143 Wayne Gretzky .50 1.25
144 Ed Jovanovski .05 .15
145 Jason Arnott .07 .20
146 Andrew Cassels .05 .15
147 Roman Vopat .07 .20
148 Dwayne Roloson .07 .20
149 Derek Plante .07 .20
150 Phil Housley .07 .20
151 Mikael Renberg .07 .20
152 Petr Nedved .10 .25
153 Grant Fuhr .10 .25
154 Felix Potvin .10 .25
155 John MacLean .05 .15
156 Brian Leetch .10 .25
157 Rod Brind'Amour .10 .25
158 Ryan Smyth .07 .20
159 Teemu Selanne .20 .50
160 Theo Fleury .12 .30
161 Adam Deadmarsh .05 .15
162 Corey Hirsch .07 .20
163 Bryan Berard .05 .15
164 Ed Belfour .10 .25
165 Sergei Berezin .07 .20
166 Damian Rhodes .07 .20
167 Guy Hebert .07 .20
168 Derian Hatcher .07 .20
169 Jonas Hoglund .07 .20
170 Matthew Barnaby .07 .20
171 Scott Mellanby .07 .20
172 Bill Ranford .07 .20
173 Vincent Damphousse .07 .20
174 Anders Eriksson .07 .20
175 Chad Kilger .07 .20
176 Darren Turcotte .07 .20
177 Dino Ciccarelli .10 .25
178 Niklas Sundstrom .07 .20
179 Stephane Fiset .07 .20
180 Mike Ricci .07 .20
181 Brendan Shanahan .12 .30
182 Darcy Tucker .10 .25
183 Eric Fichaud .07 .20
184 Todd Marchant .07 .20
185 Keith Primeau .07 .20
186 Joe Nieuwendyk .10 .25
187 Pavel Bure .12 .30
188 Jaromir Jagr .25 .60
189 Kirk McLean .07 .20
190 Daniel Goneau .07 .20
191 Rob Niedermayer .05 .15
192 Eric Daze .05 .15
193 Richard Matvichuk .07 .20
194 Scott Stevens .10 .25
195 Dale Hunter .07 .20
196 Hnat Domenichelli .07 .20
197 Philippe DeRouville .07 .20
198 Marcel Cousineau .07 .20
199 Kevin Hodson .07 .20
200 Jean-Sebastien Giguere .10 .25
201 Paxton Schafer RC .05 .15
202 Marc Denis .10 .25
203 Frank Banham RC .07 .20
204 Vadim Sharifijanov .07 .20
205 Paul Healey RC .07 .20
206 D.J. Smith RC .10 .25
207 Christian Matte RC .10 .25
208 Sean Brown RC .10 .25
209 Tomas Vokoun RC .10 .25
210 Vladimir Vorobiev RC .10 .25
211 Jean-Yves Leroux RC .10 .25
212 Domenic Pittis RC .10 .25
213 Derek Wilkinson RC .10 .25
214 Jason Holland .10 .25
215 Pascal Rheaume RC .07 .20
216 Steve Kelly .07 .20
217 Vaclav Varada .05 .15
218 Mike Fountain .07 .20
219 Vaclav Prospal RC .07 .20
220 Jaroslav Svejkovsky .07 .20
221 Marty Murray .07 .20
222 Wade Belak RC .10 .25
223 Jamal Mayers RC .10 .25
224 Shayne Toporowski RC .10 .25
225 Mike Knuble RC .10 .25
226 Jarome Iginla CL (1-60) .10 .25
227 Keith Tkachuk CL (61-120) .10 .25
228 Adam Oates CL (121-180) .10 .25
229 John LeClair CL (181-230) .10 .25
230 Brian Leetch CL (inserts) .10 .25

1997-98 Donruss Press Proofs Silver

ndomly inserted in packs, this 230-card set was a parallel to the Donruss base set and featured a full foil card stock with silver foil accents. Only 2000 of this set were produced.

*VETS: 8X TO 20X BASIC CARDS
*ROOKIES: 4X TO 10X BASIC CARDS

1997-98 Donruss Press Proofs Gold

ndomly inserted in packs, this 230-card set was a parallel to the Donruss base set and featured a unique die cut design with gold foil stamping. Only 500 of this set were produced and were sequentially numbered.

*VETS: 15X TO 40X BASIC CARDS
*ROOKIES: 8X TO 20X BASIC CARDS

1997-98 Donruss Between the Pipes

Randomly inserted in hobby packs only, this 10-card set featured color photos of the league's top defensive players printed on an etched, full foil card stock with foil stamped accents. Only 3500 of this set were produced and were sequentially numbered.

COMPLETE SET (10) 50.00 125.00
1 Patrick Roy 12.00 30.00
2 Martin Brodeur 10.00 25.00
3 John Vanbiesbrouck 4.00 10.00
4 Dominik Hasek 10.00 20.00
5 Chris Osgood 4.00 10.00
6 Jose Theodore 5.00 12.00
7 Garth Snow 4.00 10.00
8 Curtis Joseph 6.00 15.00
9 Felix Potvin 6.00 15.00
10 Jocelyn Thibault 4.00 10.00

1997-98 Donruss Elite Inserts

ndomly inserted in packs, this 12-card set featured color photos of the league's most dominant superstars printed on card stock utilizing a double treatment of gold and holographic gold foils. Only 2500 of each card were produced and were sequentially numbered.

COMPLETE SET (12) 20.00 50.00
1 Wayne Gretzky 8.00 20.00
2 Jaromir Jagr 2.00 5.00
3 Eric Lindros 1.25 3.00
4 Paul Kariya 1.25 3.00
5 Patrick Roy 6.00 15.00
6 Steve Yzerman 5.00 12.00
7 Peter Forsberg 3.00 8.00
8 John Vanbiesbrouck .75 2.00
9 Brendan Shanahan 1.25 3.00
10 Martin Brodeur 3.00 8.00
11 Dominik Hasek 2.50 6.00

12 Teemu Selanne 1.25 3.00
13P Martin Brodeur PROMO 2.00 5.00

1997-98 Donruss Line 2 Line

Randomly inserted in packs, this 24-card fractured insert set contained three levels of scarcity with each level printed on foil card stocks. Level one was "Red Line" which featured color photos of 12 players with red foil enhancements and each card sequentially numbered to 4000; Level two was "Blue Line" which featured color photos of eight players with blue foil enhancements and each sequentially numbered to 2000; Level three was "Gold Line" which featured color photos of four players with each sequentially numbered to 1000. The first 250 of each Line two card featured a unique die-cut design.

COMPLETE SET (24) 100.00 200.00
*RED DIE CUT: 2X TO 5X BASIC RED
*BLUE DIE CUT: 1.2X TO 3X BASIC BLUE
*GOLD DIE CUT: 1X TO 2.5X BASIC GOLD
*PROMO: .2X TO 5X BASIC INSERTS
1 Wayne Gretzky G 12.00 30.00
2 Teemu Selanne R 2.00 5.00
3 Brian Leetch B 4.00 10.00
4 Peter Forsberg R 3.00 8.00
5 Steve Yzerman R 8.00 20.00
6 Oleg Tverdovsky B 1.25 3.00
7 Doug Gilmour R 1.50 4.00
8 Eric Lindros G 3.00 8.00
9 Bryan Berard B 2.50 6.00
10 Brendan Shanahan R 1.50 4.00
11 Pavel Bure R 3.00 8.00
12 Joe Sakic R 6.00 15.00
13 Chris Chelios B 3.00 8.00
14 Mike Modano R 5.00 12.00
15 Paul Coffey B 5.00 12.00
16 Jaromir Jagr G 8.00 20.00
17 Jarome Iginla R 4.00 10.00
18 Brett Hull R 4.00 10.00
19 Wade Redden B 2.50 6.00
20 Paul Kariya G 8.00 20.00
21 Ray Bourque B 7.50 15.00
22 Ryan Smyth R 1.50 4.00
23 Mark Messier R 3.00 8.00
24 Sandis Ozolinsh B 1.25 3.00

1997-98 Donruss Rated Rookies

ndomly inserted in packs, this 10-card set featured color action photos of the hottest young rookie prospects printed on a background with the letters "RR." A "Medalist" parallel was also created and printed on foil card stock accented with both gold foil and silver holographic foil treatments.

COMPLETE SET (10) 6.00 15.00
*MEDALIST: 1.5X TO 4X BASIC INSERTS
1 Tomas Vokoun 2.00 5.00
2 Paxton Schafer .40 1.00
3 Vaclav Prospal .75 2.00
4 Marc Denis .75 2.00
5 Domenic Pittis .40 1.00
6 Christian Matte .40 1.00
7 Marcel Cousineau .40 1.00
8 Steve Kelly .40 1.00
9 Jaroslav Svejkovsky .40 1.00
10 Jean-Sebastien Giguere 2.00 5.00

1997-98 Donruss Red Alert

ndomly inserted in retail packs only, this 10-card set featured color photos of the league's top goal scorers printed on thick plastic card stock, die cut in the shape of a goal light and highlighted with red holographic foil treatments. Only 5,000 of the set were produced and were sequentially numbered.

COMPLETE SET (10) 30.00 80.00
1 Adam Deadmarsh 2.00 5.00
2 Ryan Smyth 4.00 10.00
3 Sergei Fedorov 6.00 15.00
4 Keith Tkachuk 4.00 10.00
5 Brett Hull 6.00 15.00
6 Pavel Bure 6.00 15.00
7 John LeClair 2.00 5.00
8 Zigmund Palffy 4.00 10.00
9 Mats Sundin 4.00 10.00
10 Peter Bondra 4.00 10.00

2010-11 Donruss

COMP.SET w/o SPS (250) 15.00 40.00
*RR GHOSTED BOX: .4X TO 1X
1 Teemu Selanne .50 1.25
2 Milan Lucic .25 .60
3 Zach Boychuk .20 .50
4 Robyn Regehr .15 .40
5 Derick Brassard .25 .60
6 Craig Anderson .25 .60
7 Shawn Horcoff .15 .40
8 Wayne Simmonds .30 .75
9 Shea Weber .20 .50
10 Matt Moulson .20 .50
11 Mike Richards .25 .60
12 Mikkel Boedker .15 .40
13 Evgeni Malkin .75 2.00
14 Alex Steen .25 .60
15 Simon Gagne .25 .60
16 Henrik Sedin .25 .60
17 Jeff Schultz .15 .40
18 Ryan Kesler .25 .60
19 Tyler Bozak .25 .60
20 Joe Pavelski .25 .60
21 Daniel Alfredsson .25 .60
22 Dwayne Roloson .20 .50
23 Andrei Markov .25 .60
24 Stephen Weiss .20 .50
25 Jimmy Howard .30 .75
26 Jonathan Toews .50 1.25
27 Jamie Benn .30 .75
28 Martin Havlat .20 .50
29 Marian Gaborik .30 .75
30 Nikolai Zherdev .15 .40
31 Tim Connolly .15 .40
32 Corey Perry .25 .60
33 Rene Bourque .15 .40
34 Sean Avery .20 .50
35 Josh Bailey .20 .50
36 Wojtek Wolski .15 .40
37 Marc-Andre Fleury .40 1.00
38 Cam Janssen .15 .40
39 Dion Phaneuf .25 .60
40 Roberto Luongo .25 .60
41 Logan Couture .25 .60
42 Jonas Gustavsson .30 .75
43 Nicklas Lidstrom .25 .60
44 Miikka Kiprusoff .20 .50
45 Pavel Datsyuk .30 .75
46 Jarome Iginla .25 .60
47 Nathan Horton .20 .50
48 Zach Bogosian .20 .50
49 Rick Nash .25 .60
50 Matt Duchene .25 .60
51 Dan Boyle .20 .50
52 Colton Orr .15 .40
53 Alex Ovechkin 1.00 2.50
54 Brad Boyes .15 .40
55 Jordan Staal .25 .60
56 Victor Hedman .30 .75
57 Ilya Kovalchuk .25 .60
58 Michael Cammalleri .25 .60
59 Anze Kopitar .40 1.00
60 Ryan Suter .15 .40
61 James Neal .25 .60
62 Marian Hossa .20 .50
63 Henrik Zetterberg .30 .75
64 Kris Russell .15 .40
65 Dustin Penner .15 .40
66 Evander Kane .25 .60
67 Tuukka Rask .25 .60
68 Ryan Miller .25 .60
69 Mikael Backlund .15 .40
70 Cam Barker .15 .40
71 Cory Stillman .15 .40
72 Carey Price 1.00 2.50
73 Henrik Lundqvist .40 1.00
74 Keith Yandle .25 .60
75 Kyle Okposo .25 .60
76 Ilya Bryzgalov .20 .50
77 Martin Brodeur .50 1.25
78 Marc Staal .25 .60
79 Michael Leighton .20 .50
80 Joe Thornton .25 .60
81 Steven Stamkos .50 1.25
82 Tyler Kennedy .15 .40
83 Alexander Semin .25 .60
84 Dan Hamhuis .20 .50
85 Brian Gionta .20 .50
86 Colin Wilson .20 .50
87 Cal Clutterbuck .25 .60
88 Jonathan Quick .40 1.00
89 Matthew Lombardi .15 .40
90 Scott Gomez .20 .50
91 Steve Ott .20 .50
92 Paul Stastny .25 .60
93 Johan Franzen .25 .60
94 Duncan Keith .25 .60
95 Loui Eriksson .20 .50
96 Cam Ward .25 .60
97 Mark Recchi .30 .75
98 Dustin Byfuglien .25 .60
99 Brandon Sutter .20 .50
100 Saku Koivu .25 .60
101 Derek Roy .25 .60
102 Patrice Bergeron .30 .75
103 Luca Sbisa .20 .50
104 Daymond Langkow .15 .40
105 Chris Stewart .20 .50
106 Ales Hemsky .20 .50
107 Patrick Kane .50 1.25
108 Zack Stortini .15 .40
109 Mark Streit .15 .40
110 James van Riemsdyk .40 1.00
111 Peter Regin .20 .50
112 Jamie Langenbrunner .15 .40
113 Ed Jovanovski .15 .40
114 David Backes .25 .60
115 Martin St. Louis .25 .60
116 Alexandre Burrows .25 .60
117 Dany Heatley .20 .50
118 Phil Kessel .30 .75
119 Tomas Fleischmann .15 .40
120 Ryan Getzlaf .40 1.00
121 Thomas Vanek .25 .60
122 Joni Pitkanen .20 .50
123 Zdeno Chara .20 .50
124 Nicklas Bergfors .20 .50
125 T.J. Galiardi .20 .50
126 Kari Lehtonen .20 .50
127 Patrick Sharp .25 .60
128 Tomas Holmstrom .15 .40
129 R.J. Umberger .15 .40
130 Tom Gilbert .15 .40
131 Jordin Tootoo .20 .50
132 Travis Zajac .20 .50
133 Niklas Backstrom .25 .60
134 Drew Doughty .25 .60
135 Ryan Whitney .15 .40
136 Jean-Sebastien Giguere .20 .50
137 Vincent Lecavalier .20 .50
138 Max Talbot .25 .60
139 Jaroslav Halak .25 .60
140 Daniel Sedin .25 .60
141 Mike Green .25 .60
142 Chris Pronger .20 .50
143 Artem Anisimov .20 .50
144 Shane Doan .20 .50
145 Jason Spezza .15 .40
146 Pierre-Luc Leblond-Letourneau .15 .40
147 Mike Fisher .25 .60
148 Patric Hornqvist .20 .50
149 Zach Parise .25 .60
150 Guillaume Latendresse .20 .50
151 Steve Reinprecht .15 .40
152 Andrei Kostitsyn .20 .50
153 Sam Gagner .20 .50
154 Dave Bolland .20 .50
155 Mark Fistric .15 .40
156 Joffrey Lupul .20 .50
157 Ondrej Pavelec .25 .60
158 Matt Stajan .20 .50
159 Eric Staal .30 .75
160 David Krejci .25 .60
161 Josh Gorges .15 .40
162 Pekka Rinne .30 .75
163 Jonathan Bernier .25 .60
164 Chris Mason .20 .50
165 Dmitry Kulikov .20 .50
166 Alex Goligoski .20 .50
167 Patrick Marleau .25 .60
168 Luke Schenn .20 .50
169 Antero Niittymaki .20 .50
170 Semyon Varlamov .25 .60
171 Jeff Carter .25 .60
172 Andy Greene .15 .40
173 Chris Drury .20 .50
174 Brian Elliott .20 .50
175 Scottie Upshall .15 .40
176 Zenon Konopka .20 .50
177 Tomas Plekanec .25 .60
178 Ryan Smyth .20 .50
179 Jeff Deslauriers .15 .40
180 Mike Modano .40 1.00
181 Steve Mason .20 .50
182 Nathan Gerbe .15 .40
183 Tim Gleason .15 .40
184 Marc Savard .15 .40
185 Brenden Morrow .20 .50
186 Troy Brouwer .25 .60
187 Valtteri Filppula .25 .60
188 Brent Burns .30 .75
189 Michael Grabner .20 .50
190 Benoit Pouliot .15 .40
191 Ray Whitney .20 .50
192 Claude Giroux .25 .60
193 John Tavares .50 1.25
194 David Perron .15 .40
195 Colby Armstrong .15 .40
196 Mason Raymond .20 .50
197 Kristopher Letang .25 .60
198 Mike Komisarek .15 .40
199 Nicklas Backstrom .40 1.00
200 Rick Rypien .25 .60
201 Daniel Briere .25 .60
202 Milan Michalek .15 .40
203 Steve Sullivan .15 .40
204 Brad Richards .25 .60
205 Derek Dorsett .15 .40
206 Tuomo Ruutu .20 .50
207 Bobby Ryan .25 .60
208 Antti Niemi .20 .50
209 David Booth .15 .40
210 Frans Nielsen .15 .40
211 Ryane Clowe .15 .40
212 Eric Fehr .15 .40
213 Rich Peverley .25 .60
214 Adam Foote .15 .40
215 Andrew Brunette .15 .40
216 Erik Karlsson .50 1.25
217 Kris Versteeg .20 .50
218 Mike Knuble .15 .40
219 Jay Bouwmeester .30 .75
220 Milan Hejduk .20 .50
221 Mikko Koivu .25 .60
222 Sergei Gonchar .15 .40
223 Mike Smith .25 .60
224 Christian Ehrhoff .15 .40
225 Nik Antropov .20 .50
226 Antoine Vermette .15 .40
227 Jack Johnson .15 .40
228 Ryan Callahan .25 .60
229 Devin Setoguchi .20 .50
230 Michal Neuvirth .20 .50
231 Tyler Myers .25 .60
232 Jonas Hiller .20 .50
233 Jakub Voracek .25 .60
234 Michael Frolik .15 .40
235 Dustin Brown .25 .60
236 Tomas Vokoun .20 .50
237 Michael Del Zotto .20 .50
238 Dan Ellis .20 .50
239 Patrik Berglund .15 .40
240 Ryan Malone .15 .40
241 Tyler Ennis .20 .50
242 Tobias Enstrom .15 .40
243 Patrik Elias .25 .60
244 Erik Johnson .15 .40
245 Peter Mueller .20 .50
246 Jason Pominville .25 .60
247 Patrick Dwyer .15 .40
248 Jiri Hudler .20 .50
249 Andrei Loktionov .20 .50
250 Ville Leino .20 .50
251 Eric Tangradi RC 1.25 3.00
252 P.K. Subban RC 4.00 10.00
253 Brandon Yip RC 1.25 3.00
254 Jamie McBain RC 1.25 3.00
255 Bobby Butler RC 1.25 3.00
256 Nazem Kadri RC 4.00 10.00
257 Brayden Irwin RC 1.25 3.00
258 Nick Palmieri RC 1.25 3.00
259 Zach Hamill RC 1.25 3.00
260 Nick Bonino RC 1.50 4.00
261 Dustin Tokarski RC 1.25 3.00
262 Jared Cowen RC 1.25 3.00
263 Philip Larsen RC 1.25 3.00
264 Justin Mercier RC 1.25 3.00
265 Kyle Wilson RC 1.50 4.00
266 Nick Johnson RC 1.00 2.50
267 James Wyman RC 1.25 3.00
268 Nick Spaling RC 1.25 3.00
269 Maxim Noreau RC 1.00 2.50
270 Cody Almond RC 1.25 3.00
271 Casey Wellman RC 1.25 3.00
272 Evgeny Dadonov RC 1.50 4.00
273 Jerome Samson RC 1.25 3.00
274 Arturs Kulda RC 1.25 3.00
275 Jean Philippe Levasseur RC 1.25 3.00
276 Bryan Pitton RC 1.50 4.00
277 Alexander Pechurskiy RC 1.50 4.00
278 Carter Hutton RC 2.50 6.00
279 Matt Zaba RC 1.50 4.00
280 Brock Trotter RC 2.50 6.00
281 Jeff Skinner RC 2.50 6.00
282 Evan Oberg RC 1.50 4.00
283 Grant Clitsome RC 1.25 3.00
284 Derek Smith RC 1.25 3.00
285 Justin Falk RC 1.00 2.50
286 Marc-Andre Cliche RC 1.00 2.50
287 Jeff Penner RC 2.00 5.00
288 Taylor Hall RC 5.00 12.00
289 Trevor Frischmon RC 1.25 3.00
290 Oliver Ekman-Larsson RC 2.00 5.00
291 Corey Elkins RC 1.00 2.50
292 Adam McQuaid RC 1.50 4.00
293 Andrew Bodnarchuk RC 1.25 3.00
294 Magnus Paajarvi RC 1.50 4.00
295 Brayden Schenn RC 2.00 5.00
296 John McCarthy RC 1.25 3.00
297 Nino Niederreiter RC 1.50 4.00
298 Jordan Eberle RC 3.00 8.00
299 Tyler Seguin RC 5.00 12.00
300 Anton Klementyev RC 1.25 3.00

2010-11 Donruss Die-Cut Gems

*SINGLES: 6X TO 15X BASE
STATED PRINT RUN 30 SER.#'d SETS
199 Nicklas Backstrom 6.00 15.00

2010-11 Donruss Die-Cut Gems Autographs

STATED PRINT RUN 10-25
1 Teemu Selanne 12.00 30.00
3 Zach Boychuk
6 Craig Anderson 8.00 20.00
9 Shea Weber 4.00 10.00
10 Matt Moulson
11 Mike Richards 25.00 60.00
12 Mikkel Boedker 3.00 8.00
13 Evgeni Malkin
15 Simon Gagne 5.00 12.00
16 Henrik Sedin 8.00 20.00
18 Ryan Kesler 12.00 30.00
19 Tyler Bozak 8.00 20.00
20 Joe Pavelski
22 Dwayne Roloson
24 Stephen Weiss
25 Jimmy Howard
26 Jonathan Toews 25.00 60.00
27 Jamie Benn 8.00 20.00
29 Marian Gaborik 12.00 30.00
32 Corey Perry 5.00 12.00
33 Rene Bourque 8.00 20.00
35 Josh Bailey 4.00 10.00
36 Wojtek Wolski
37 Marc-Andre Fleury 15.00 40.00
38 Cam Janssen 12.00 30.00
42 Jonas Gustavsson 10.00 25.00
43 Nicklas Lidstrom 30.00 80.00
45 Pavel Datsyuk 10.00 25.00
46 Jarome Iginla 8.00 20.00
48 Zach Bogosian
49 Rick Nash 20.00 50.00
50 Matt Duchene 10.00 25.00
51 Dan Boyle
52 Colton Orr 20.00 50.00
53 Alex Ovechkin 60.00 120.00
55 Jordan Staal 10.00 25.00
57 Ilya Kovalchuk 5.00 20.00
58 Michael Cammalleri
59 Anze Kopitar 10.00 25.00
61 James Neal 6.00 15.00
62 Marian Hossa
64 Kris Russell
65 Dustin Penner 6.00 15.00
66 Evander Kane
68 Ryan Miller 8.00 20.00
69 Mikael Backlund
72 Carey Price 20.00 40.00
73 Henrik Lundqvist 15.00 40.00
74 Keith Yandle
76 Ilya Bryzgalov 4.00 10.00
77 Martin Brodeur
78 Marc Staal/10
79 Michael Leighton 15.00 40.00
80 Joe Thornton
81 Steven Stamkos 25.00 60.00
84 Dan Hamhuis 15.00 40.00
85 Brian Gionta/10
86 Colin Wilson 4.00 10.00
87 Cal Clutterbuck 8.00 20.00
90 Scott Gomez 10.00 25.00
91 Steve Ott 10.00 25.00
92 Paul Stastny
93 Johan Franzen
96 Cam Ward 5.00 12.00
98 Dustin Byfuglien 8.00 20.00
99 Brandon Sutter 12.00 30.00
101 Derek Roy
106 Ales Hemsky 6.00 15.00
107 Patrick Kane 20.00 50.00
108 Zack Stortini
110 James van Riemsdyk
114 David Backes 10.00 25.00
115 Martin St. Louis
116 Alexandre Burrows 10.00 25.00
117 Dany Heatley 4.00 10.00
118 Phil Kessel 10.00 25.00
120 Ryan Getzlaf 8.00 20.00
121 Thomas Vanek
125 T.J. Galiardi 8.00 20.00
126 Kari Lehtonen 4.00 10.00
128 Tomas Holmstrom
131 Jordin Tootoo 8.00 20.00
132 Travis Zajac
133 Niklas Backstrom 12.00 30.00
134 Drew Doughty
137 Vincent Lecavalier
138 Max Talbot 6.00 15.00
139 Jaroslav Halak
140 Daniel Sedin
142 Chris Pronger 12.00 30.00
143 Artem Anisimov
144 Shane Doan 5.00 12.00
146 Pierre-Luc Leblond-Letourneau
147 Mike Fisher
148 Patric Hornqvist 4.00 10.00
149 Zach Parise 12.00 30.00
150 Guillaume Latendresse
153 Sam Gagner 10.00 25.00
157 Ondrej Pavelec
159 Eric Staal 8.00 20.00
162 Pekka Rinne 8.00 20.00
163 Jonathan Bernier 8.00 20.00
166 Alex Goligoski 12.00 30.00
167 Patrick Marleau
170 Semyon Varlamov 15.00 40.00
171 Jeff Carter 15.00 40.00
172 Andy Greene 3.00 8.00
174 Brian Elliott 8.00 20.00
178 Ryan Smyth 10.00 25.00
179 Jeff Deslauriers 3.00 8.00
180 Mike Modano 15.00 40.00
181 Steve Mason
182 Nathan Gerbe
185 Brenden Morrow
192 Claude Giroux 12.00 30.00
193 John Tavares 40.00 80.00
194 David Perron 8.00 20.00
204 Brad Richards
205 Derek Dorsett 8.00 20.00
207 Bobby Ryan 8.00 20.00
210 Frans Nielsen
213 Rich Peverley 5.00 12.00
219 Jay Bouwmeester 12.00 30.00
223 Mike Smith 8.00 20.00
226 Antoine Vermette 10.00 25.00
228 Ryan Callahan 5.00 12.00
231 Tyler Myers 5.00 12.00
232 Jonas Hiller
234 Michael Frolik
235 Dustin Brown
236 Tomas Vokoun
241 Tyler Ennis 4.00 10.00
245 Peter Mueller

2010-11 Donruss Press Proofs

*SINGLES: 5X TO 12X BASE
STATED PRINT RUN 100 SER.#'d SETS
199 Nicklas Backstrom 5.00 12.00

2010-11 Donruss Rated Rookies Autographs

STATED PRINT RUN 20-100
251 Eric Tangradi/75 5.00 12.00
252 P.K. Subban/25 30.00 80.00
253 Brandon Yip 5.00 12.00
255 Bobby Butler 5.00 12.00
256 Nazem Kadri 15.00 40.00
257 Brayden Irwin 5.00 12.00
258 Nick Palmieri 5.00 12.00
259 Zach Hamill 5.00 12.00
260 Nick Bonino 6.00 15.00
262 Jared Cowen 8.00 20.00
263 Philip Larsen 5.00 12.00
264 Justin Mercier 5.00 12.00
273 Jerome Samson/50 5.00 12.00
276 Bryan Pitton/20 10.00 25.00
278 Carter Hutton/50 10.00 25.00
281 Jeff Skinner 20.00 50.00
284 Derek Smith/50 5.00 12.00
288 Taylor Hall 30.00 80.00
290 Oliver Ekman-Larsson 8.00 20.00
291 Corey Elkins/20 6.00 15.00
292 Adam McQuaid/75 6.00 15.00
294 Magnus Paajarvi 6.00 15.00
295 Brayden Schenn 15.00 40.00
297 Nino Niederreiter 6.00 15.00
298 Jordan Eberle 40.00 80.00
299 Tyler Seguin 40.00 80.00

2010-11 Donruss Boys of Winter

MPLETE SET (80) 75.00 150.00
1 Alexandre Burrows 1.50 4.00
2 Sidney Crosby 6.00 15.00
3 Evander Kane 1.50 4.00
4 Daniel Carcillo 1.00 2.50
5 Niklas Backstrom 1.50 4.00
6 Tyler Bozak 1.50 4.00
7 Patric Hornqvist 1.25 3.00
8 Steve Downie 1.00 2.50
9 Zenon Konopka 1.25 3.00
10 Cory Schneider 1.25 3.00
11 Scott Hartnell 1.50 4.00
12 Scott Gomez 1.25 3.00
13 Craig Anderson 1.50 4.00
14 Mike Fisher 1.50 4.00
15 Steve Valiquette 1.25 3.00
16 Erik Karlsson 3.00 8.00
17 Jeff Carter 1.50 4.00
18 Anze Kopitar 2.50 6.00
19 James Neal 1.50 4.00
20 Mason Raymond 1.25 3.00
21 Mark Flood 1.00 2.50
22 Ales Hemsky 1.25 3.00
23 Evgeni Malkin 5.00 12.00
24 Jonas Gustavsson 2.00 5.00
25 Jose Theodore 1.50 4.00
26 Roberto Luongo 1.50 4.00
27 Marty Turco 1.50 4.00
28 Dan Hamhuis 1.25 3.00
29 Mikael Backlund 1.00 2.50
30 Daniel Sedin 1.50 4.00
31 Anton Klementyev 1.25 3.00
32 Rene Bourque 1.00 2.50
33 Johan Backlund 1.25 3.00
34 Mike Modano 2.50 6.00
35 Teddy Purcell 1.50 4.00
36 Matt Martin 2.00 5.00
37 Rich Peverley 1.50 4.00
38 Jonathan Toews 3.00 8.00
39 Mikael Samuelsson 1.00 2.50
40 Luke Schenn 1.25 3.00
41 Wade Redden 1.00 2.50
42 Shea Weber 1.25 3.00
43 Colton Orr 1.00 2.50
44 Corey Perry 1.50 4.00
45 Max Pacioretty 1.50 4.00
46 Zach Bogosian 1.25 3.00
47 Brian Elliott 1.25 3.00
48 Patrice Bergeron 2.00 5.00
49 Matt Carkner 1.25 3.00
50 Peter Budaj 1.25 3.00
51 Brian Boucher 1.25 3.00
52 Josh Gorges 1.00 2.50
53 Steve Ott 1.25 3.00
54 Jonas Hiller 1.25 3.00
55 Dustin Penner 1.00 2.50
56 Maxim Lapierre 1.00 2.50
57 Brenden Morrow 1.25 3.00
58 Dylan Reese 1.25 3.00
59 Tim Thomas 1.25 3.00
60 Tomas Plekanec 1.50 4.00
61 T.J. Galiardi 1.25 3.00
62 Michael Frolik 1.00 2.50
63 Carey Price 6.00 15.00
64 Travis Zajac 1.25 3.00
65 Kari Lehtonen 1.25 3.00
66 Alex Ovechkin 6.00 15.00
67 Colin Wilson 1.25 3.00
68 Ryan Smyth 1.25 3.00
69 Jordin Tootoo 1.25 3.00
70 Jay Rosehill 1.00 2.50
71 Martin Brodeur 3.00 8.00
72 Pavel Datsyuk 2.00 5.00
73 Zach Parise 1.50 4.00
74 Matt Moulson 1.25 3.00
75 Henrik Lundqvist 2.50 6.00
76 Daniel Briere 1.50 4.00
77 Jamie Benn 2.00 5.00
78 Jeremy Duchesne 1.50 4.00
79 Phil Kessel 2.00 5.00
80 Nathan Horton 1.25 3.00

2010-11 Donruss Boys of Winter Autographs

STATED PRINT RUN 10-25
1 Alexandre Burrows 40.00 80.00
2 Sidney Crosby 75.00 150.00
3 Evander Kane 5.00 12.00
4 Daniel Carcillo
5 Niklas Backstrom
6 Tyler Bozak 5.00 12.00
7 Patric Hornqvist 4.00 10.00
8 Steve Downie 3.00 8.00
10 Cory Schneider
12 Scott Gomez 8.00 20.00
13 Craig Anderson
14 Mike Fisher
17 Jeff Carter 15.00 40.00
18 Anze Kopitar 10.00 25.00
19 James Neal 5.00 12.00
22 Ales Hemsky 4.00 10.00
23 Evgeni Malkin 20.00 40.00
24 Jonas Gustavsson
25 Jose Theodore 12.00 30.00
28 Dan Hamhuis 4.00 10.00
29 Mikael Backlund 3.00 8.00
30 Daniel Sedin 15.00 40.00
32 Rene Bourque 6.00 15.00
34 Mike Modano
36 Matt Martin/20
37 Rich Peverley 12.00 30.00
38 Jonathan Toews 10.00 25.00
42 Shea Weber 4.00 10.00
43 Colton Orr 30.00 80.00
44 Corey Perry 6.00 15.00
45 Max Pacioretty 5.00 12.00
46 Zach Bogosian 8.00 20.00
47 Brian Elliott 10.00 25.00
49 Matt Carkner 4.00 10.00
51 Brian Boucher 4.00 10.00
53 Steve Ott
54 Jonas Hiller 4.00 10.00
55 Dustin Penner 12.00 30.00
57 Brenden Morrow
59 Tim Thomas 12.00 30.00
61 T.J. Galiardi 12.00 30.00
62 Michael Frolik 3.00 8.00
63 Carey Price 40.00 80.00
64 Travis Zajac/10
65 Kari Lehtonen 4.00 10.00
66 Alex Ovechkin 25.00 60.00
67 Colin Wilson 4.00 10.00
68 Ryan Smyth 10.00 25.00
69 Jordin Tootoo 10.00 25.00
71 Martin Brodeur 30.00 60.00
72 Pavel Datsyuk 12.00 30.00
73 Zach Parise 8.00 20.00
74 Matt Moulson 4.00 10.00
75 Henrik Lundqvist 12.00 30.00
77 Jamie Benn 6.00 15.00
78 Jeremy Duchesne/10
79 Phil Kessel 10.00 25.00

2010-11 Donruss Boys of Winter Threads

RIME/50-100: .6X TO 1.5X THREADS
*PRIME/25: .8X TO 2X THREADS
1 Alexandre Burrows 4.00 10.00
2 Sidney Crosby 12.00 30.00
3 Evander Kane 4.00 10.00
4 Daniel Carcillo 2.50 6.00
5 Niklas Backstrom 4.00 10.00
6 Tyler Bozak 4.00 10.00
7 Patric Hornqvist 3.00 8.00
8 Steve Downie 2.50 6.00
9 Zenon Konopka 3.00 8.00
10 Cory Schneider 3.00 8.00
11 Scott Hartnell 4.00 10.00
12 Scott Gomez 3.00 8.00
13 Craig Anderson 5.00 12.00
14 Mike Fisher 4.00 10.00
15 Steve Valiquette 3.00 8.00
16 Erik Karlsson 8.00 20.00
17 Jeff Carter 4.00 10.00
18 Anze Kopitar 6.00 15.00
19 James Neal 4.00 10.00
20 Mason Raymond 3.00 8.00
21 Mark Flood 2.50 6.00
22 Ales Hemsky 3.00 8.00
23 Evgeni Malkin 6.00 15.00
24 Jonas Gustavsson 5.00 12.00
25 Jose Theodore 4.00 10.00
26 Roberto Luongo 4.00 10.00
27 Marty Turco 4.00 10.00
28 Dan Hamhuis 3.00 8.00
29 Mikael Backlund 2.50 6.00
30 Daniel Sedin 4.00 10.00
31 Anton Klementyev 3.00 8.00
32 Rene Bourque 2.50 6.00
33 Johan Backlund 3.00 8.00
34 Mike Modano 6.00 15.00
35 Teddy Purcell 4.00 10.00
36 Matt Martin 5.00 12.00
37 Rich Peverley 4.00 10.00
38 Jonathan Toews 8.00 20.00
39 Mikael Samuelsson 2.50 6.00
40 Luke Schenn 3.00 8.00
41 Wade Redden 2.50 6.00
42 Shea Weber 3.00 8.00
43 Colton Orr 2.50 6.00
44 Corey Perry 4.00 10.00
45 Max Pacioretty 4.00 10.00
46 Zach Bogosian 3.00 8.00
47 Brian Elliott 3.00 8.00
48 Patrice Bergeron 5.00 12.00
49 Matt Carkner 3.00 8.00
50 Peter Budaj 3.00 8.00
51 Brian Boucher 3.00 8.00
52 Josh Gorges 2.50 6.00
53 Steve Ott 3.00 8.00
54 Jonas Hiller 3.00 8.00
55 Dustin Penner 2.50 6.00
56 Maxim Lapierre 2.50 6.00
57 Brenden Morrow 3.00 8.00
58 Dylan Reese 3.00 8.00
59 Tim Thomas 5.00 12.00
60 Tomas Plekanec 4.00 10.00
61 T.J. Galiardi 3.00 8.00
62 Michael Frolik 2.50 6.00
63 Carey Price 15.00 40.00
64 Travis Zajac 3.00 8.00
65 Kari Lehtonen 3.00 8.00
66 Alex Ovechkin 15.00 40.00
67 Colin Wilson 3.00 8.00
68 Ryan Smyth 3.00 8.00
69 Jordin Tootoo 3.00 8.00
70 Jay Rosehill 2.50 6.00
71 Martin Brodeur 8.00 20.00
72 Pavel Datsyuk 5.00 12.00
73 Zach Parise 4.00 10.00
74 Matt Moulson 3.00 8.00
75 Henrik Lundqvist 8.00 20.00
76 Daniel Briere 4.00 10.00
77 Jamie Benn 5.00 12.00
78 Jeremy Duchesne 4.00 10.00
79 Phil Kessel 5.00 12.00
80 Nathan Horton 3.00 8.00

2010-11 Donruss Elite

STATED PRINT RUN 100 SER.#'d SETS
1 Sidney Crosby 20.00 50.00
2 Alex Ovechkin 20.00 50.00
3 Steven Stamkos 10.00 25.00
4 Jonathan Toews 10.00 25.00
5 Henrik Sedin 5.00 12.00
6 Ryan Miller 5.00 12.00
7 Martin Brodeur 10.00 25.00
8 Zach Parise 5.00 12.00
9 Patrick Kane 10.00 25.00
10 Nicklas Backstrom 8.00 20.00
11 Drew Doughty 5.00 12.00
12 Tuukka Rask 5.00 12.00
13 Marian Gaborik 6.00 15.00
14 Daniel Alfredsson 5.00 12.00
15 Pavel Datsyuk 6.00 15.00

2010-11 Donruss Fans of the Game

MPLETE SET (4) 5.00 12.00
2 Pamela Anderson 2.00 5.00
3 Justin Bieber 1.50 4.00
4 Michael Ontkean 1.50 4.00
5 Willa Ford 1.50 4.00

2010-11 Donruss Fans of the Game Autographs

2 Pamela Anderson 100.00 175.00
3 Justin Bieber 100.00 200.00
4 Michael Ontkean 8.00 20.00
5 Willa Ford 6.00 15.00

2010-11 Donruss Ice Kings

COMPLETE SET (15) 15.00 40.00
1 Ray Bourque 2.50 6.00
2 Darryl Sittler 1.25 3.00
3 Patrick Roy 4.00 10.00
4 Cam Neely 1.50 4.00
5 Joe Sakic 2.50 6.00
6 Glenn Hall 1.50 4.00
7 Brett Hull 2.50 6.00
8 Jim Craig 1.25 3.00
9 Bobby Hull 1.50 4.00
10 Mike Bossy 1.50 4.00
11 Bobby Clarke 1.50 4.00
12 Mario Lemieux 5.00 12.00
13 Johnny Bucyk 1.50 4.00
14 Jean Beliveau 1.50 4.00
15 Gerry Cheevers 1.50 4.00

2010-11 Donruss Les Gardiens

COMPLETE SET (15) 15.00 40.00
1 Martin Brodeur 3.00 8.00
2 Roberto Luongo 1.50 4.00
3 Patrick Roy 4.00 10.00
4 Felix Potvin 2.50 6.00
5 Marc-Andre Fleury 2.50 6.00
6 Ryan Miller 1.50 4.00
7 Jonathan Quick 2.50 6.00
8 Craig Anderson 1.50 4.00
9 Jimmy Howard 2.00 5.00
10 Curtis Joseph 2.00 5.00
11 Tuukka Rask 1.50 4.00
12 Miikka Kiprusoff 1.25 3.00
13 Antti Niemi 1.25 3.00
14 Jonas Gustavsson 2.00 5.00
15 Jaroslav Halak 1.50 4.00

2010-11 Donruss Line of the Times

1 Toews/Kane/Hossa 8.00 20.00
2 Sedin/Sedin/Burrows 8.00 20.00
3 Richards/Neal/Eriksson 5.00 12.00
6 Cammalleri/Gomez/Gionta 8.00 20.00
7 Thornton/Heatley/Marleau 5.00 12.00
8 Ovechkin/Backstrom/Knuble 20.00 50.00
9 Stamkos/St. Louis/Malone 8.00 20.00
10 Tavares/Okposo/Moulson 10.00 25.00

2010-11 Donruss Rookie Showcase Threads

STATED PRINT RUN 250 SER.#'d SETS
*PRIME/25: .8X TO 2X BASIC JSY
BS Brayden Schenn 4.00 10.00
JC Joe Colborne 3.00 8.00
JE Jordan Eberle 12.00 30.00
JS Jeff Skinner 10.00 25.00
MP Magnus Paajarvi 3.00 8.00
NK Nazem Kadri 8.00 20.00
TH Taylor Hall 25.00 60.00
TS Tyler Seguin 12.00 30.00
ZH Zach Hamill 2.50 6.00

2010-11 Donruss Rookie Showcase Threads Autographs

STATED PRINT RUN 100 SER.#'d SETS
BS Brayden Schenn 8.00 20.00
JE Jordan Eberle 30.00 80.00
JS Jeff Skinner 10.00 25.00
MP Magnus Paajarvi 6.00 15.00
NK Nazem Kadri 15.00 40.00
TH Taylor Hall 40.00 100.00
TS Tyler Seguin 30.00 60.00
ZH Zach Hamill 10.00 25.00

2010-11 Donruss The Ultimate Draft

COMPLETE SET (30) 15.00 40.00
1 Marc-Andre Fleury 2.50 6.00
2 Eric Staal 2.00 5.00
3 Nathan Horton 1.25 3.00
4 Thomas Vanek 1.50 4.00
5 Milan Michalek 1.00 2.50
6 Ryan Suter 1.00 2.50
7 Braydon Coburn 1.00 2.50
8 Dion Phaneuf 1.50 4.00
9 Andrei Kostitsyn 1.25 3.00
10 Jeff Carter 1.50 4.00
11 Dustin Brown 1.50 4.00
12 Brent Seabrook 1.50 4.00
13 Zach Parise 1.50 4.00
14 Eric Fehr 1.00 2.50
15 Ryan Getzlaf 2.50 6.00
16 Brent Burns 2.00 5.00
17 Ryan Kesler 1.50 4.00
18 Mike Richards 1.50 4.00
19 Corey Perry 1.50 4.00
20 Loui Eriksson 1.25 3.00
21 Patrice Bergeron 2.00 5.00
22 David Backes 1.50 4.00
23 Jimmy Howard 2.00 5.00
24 Daniel Carcillo 1.00 2.50
25 Joe Pavelski 1.50 4.00
26 Tobias Enstrom 1.00 2.50
27 Dustin Byfuglien 1.50 4.00
28 Matt Moulson 1.25 3.00
29 Jaroslav Halak 1.50 4.00
30 Brian Elliott 1.25 3.00

2010-11 Donruss Tough Times

COMPLETE SET (9) 10.00 25.00
1 Lyndon Byers 1.50 4.00
2 Ron Hextall 2.00 5.00
3 Joey Kocur 1.50 4.00
4 Dave Brown 2.00 5.00
5 Basil McRae 1.25 3.00
6 Torrie Robertson 1.25 3.00
7 Paul Baxter 1.25 3.00
8 Jay Miller 1.50 4.00
9 Tim Hunter 1.50 4.00

2010-11 Donruss Tough Times Autographs

STATED PRINT RUN 250 SER.#'d SETS
1 Lyndon Byers 10.00 25.00
2 Ron Hextall 12.00 30.00
3 Joey Kocur 10.00 25.00
4 Dave Brown 12.00 30.00
5 Basil McRae 8.00 20.00
6 Torrie Robertson 8.00 20.00
7 Paul Baxter 8.00 20.00

Jay Miller 10.00 25.00
Tim Hunter 10.00 25.00
0 Bob McGill 6.00 15.00

2010-11 Donruss Toronto Fall Expo

Alexander Ovechkin 5.00 12.00
Sidney Crosby 5.00 12.00
Ryan Miller 1.25 3.00
Nazem Kadri 3.00 8.00
Jonas Gustavsson 1.50 4.00
Henrik Sedin 1.25 3.00
H Taylor Hall RR 5.00 12.00
S Tyler Seguin RR 5.00 12.00

2010-11 Donruss Ice Kings Toronto Fall Expo

STATED PRINT RUN 250 SER.#'d SETS
ML Mario Lemieux 6.00 15.00
RB Ray Bourque 3.00 8.00

1996-97 Donruss Canadian Ice

his 150-card set was issued eight cards per pack with suggested retail price of $2.99. While these sets were initially made for distribution to Canada, a large mount of the product was shipped to the United States. Card fronts featured a full color action photo with the player's name and team appearing near the bottom of the card. Key rookies in this set included Mike Grier, Kevin Hodson, Ethan Moreau, and Dainius Zubrus.

COMPLETE SET (150) 10.00 25.00
Jaromir Jagr .50 1.25
Jocelyn Thibault .20 .50
Paul Kariya .25 .60
Derian Hatcher .12 .30
Wayne Gretzky 1.00 2.50
Peter Forsberg .30 .75
Eric Lindros .30 .75
Adam Oates .20 .50
Paul Coffey .20 .50
0 Chris Osgood .20 .50
1 Pat LaFontaine .20 .50
2 Mats Sundin .20 .50
3 Rob Niedermayer .15 .40
4 Doug Weight .20 .50
5 Al MacInnis .20 .50
6 Damian Rhodes .15 .40
7 Stephane Fiset .15 .40
8 Mike Gartner .20 .50
9 Patrick Roy .50 1.25
0 Eric Daze .15 .40
1 Ray Bourque .30 .75
2 Keith Tkachuk .20 .50
3 Mark Recchi .25 .60
4 Peter Bondra .15 .40
5 Mike Modano .30 .75
6 Mike Richter .20 .50
7 Keith Primeau .12 .30
8 Todd Bertuzzi .20 .50
9 Wendel Clark .15 .40
0 Scott Young .12 .30
1 Mario Lemieux .60 1.50
2 Valeri Kamensky .15 .40
3 Kirk McLean .15 .40
4 Daniel Alfredsson .20 .50
5 Ed Jovanovski .15 .40
6 Kelly Hrudey .15 .40
7 Trevor Kidd .12 .30
8 Joe Juneau .12 .30
9 Steve Yzerman .50 1.25
0 Saku Koivu .20 .50
1 Alexei Kovalev .12 .30
2 Rob Blake .20 .50
3 Shayne Corson .12 .30
4 Roman Hamrlik .15 .40
5 Stephane Yelle .12 .30
6 Martin Brodeur .40 1.00
7 Kirk Muller .12 .30
8 Pat Verbeek .12 .30
9 Jari Kurri .20 .50
0 Michal Pivonka .12 .30
1 Ron Hextall .15 .40
2 Trevor Linden .15 .40
3 Vincent Damphousse .15 .40
4 Owen Nolan .20 .50
5 Sergei Fedorov .30 .75
6 Chris Chelios .20 .50
7 Jeremy Roenick .30 .75
8 Zigmund Palffy .20 .50
9 Pavel Bure .25 .60
0 Dominik Hasek .30 .75
1 Alexei Yashin .15 .40
2 Chris Gratton .15 .40
3 Joe Nieuwendyk .20 .50
4 Luc Robitaille .20 .50
5 Brett Hull 1.00 2.50
6 Sean Burke .12 .30
7 Felix Potvin .20 .50
8 Jason Arnott .15 .40
9 Valeri Bure .12 .30
0 Tom Barrasso .15 .40
1 Vyacheslav Kozlov .12 .30
2 Petr Sykora .12 .30
3 Corey Hirsch .15 .40
4 Joe Sakic .30 .75
5 Bill Ranford .15 .40
6 Yanic Perreault .12 .30
7 Mikael Renberg .15 .40
8 Theo Fleury .40 1.00
9 Jim Carey .20 .50
0 Vitali Yachmenev .12 .30
1 Martin Rucinsky .12 .30
2 Jeff O'Neill .12 .30
3 Marcus Ragnarsson .12 .30
4 John Vanbiesbrouck .20 .50
5 Teemu Selanne .40 1.00
6 Larry Murphy .15 .40
7 Mark Messier .30 .75
8 Alexei Zhamnov .15 .40
9 Ryan Smyth .15 .40
0 Andy Moog .20 .50
1 Alexander Mogilny .15 .40
2 Kris Draper .12 .30
3 Ron Francis .25 .60
4 Mike Vernon .15 .40
5 Nikolai Khabibulin .15 .40
6 Mariusz Czerkawski .12 .30
7 Mathieu Schneider .12 .30
8 Stephane Richer .15 .40
9 Mike Ricci .12 .30
00 John LeClair .20 .50
01 Brendan Shanahan .25 .60
02 Daren Puppa .15 .40
03 Scott Stevens .20 .50
04 Alexandre Daigle .12 .30
05 Dimitri Khristich .12 .30
06 Bernie Nicholls .12 .30
07 Scott Mellanby .15 .40
08 Brian Leetch .20 .50
09 Grant Fuhr .20 .50
10 Pierre Turgeon .20 .50
111 Jere Lehtinen .12 .30
112 Doug Gilmour .25 .60
113 Ed Belfour .20 .50
114 Geoff Sanderson .15 .40
115 Claude Lemieux .12 .30
116 Curtis Joseph .20 .50
117 Igor Larionov .20 .50
118 Jamie Pushor .12 .30
119 Sergei Berezin RC .30 .75
120 Eric Fichaud .15 .40
121 Wade Redden .12 .30
122 Hnat Domenichelli .12 .30
123 Rem Murray RC .20 .50
124 Jarome Iginla .25 .60
125 Richard Zednik RC .25 .60
126 Daniel Goneau RC .20 .50
127 Ethan Moreau RC .20 .50
128 Janne Niinimaa .20 .50
129 Tomas Holmstrom RC .60 1.50
130 Fredrik Modin RC .50 1.25
131 Bryan Berard .20 .50
132 Jim Campbell .12 .30
133 Chris O'Sullivan .12 .30
134 Andreas Dackell RC .20 .50
135 Daymond Langkow .15 .40
136 Kevin Hodson RC .20 .50
137 Jamie Langenbrunner .12 .30
138 Mattias Timander RC .20 .50
139 Tuomas Gronman .12 .30
140 Jonas Hoglund .12 .30
141 Mike Grier RC .25 .60
142 Terry Ryan RC .20 .50
143 Darcy Tucker .12 .30
144 Brandon Convery .12 .30
145 Anders Eriksson .12 .30
146 Christian Dube .12 .30
147 Dainius Zubrus RC .25 .60
148 Grant Fuhr CL .20 .50
149 Paul Coffey CL .20 .50
150 Ray Bourque CL .30 .75

1996-97 Donruss Canadian Ice Gold Press Proofs

is 150-card set was the tougher of two parallels to the base set. Production of these cards were limited to 150 sets, a fact which is noted on the card. The words Canadian Gold appeared on the top of the card, and a gold foil treatment was used to enhance the appearance.
*VETS: 12X TO 30X BASIC CARDS
*ROOKIES: 6X TO 15X BASIC CARDS

1996-97 Donruss Canadian Ice Red Press Proofs

is 150-card set was the easier of two parallels to the base set. Production of these cards was limited to 750 sets, a fact noted on the card. The fronts featured silver and red foil enhancements, along with the words Canadian Red.
*VETS: 6X TO 15X BASIC CARDS
*ROOKIES: 3X TO 8X

1996-97 Donruss Canadian Ice Les Gardiens

is bronze foil set featured 10 of the NHL's top netminders, each of whom were born in Quebec. A full-color portrait of each player adorned the card fronts, along with the skyline of Montreal in the background. The player's name and team were printed in gold foil along the bottom of these cards. Each card was serially numbered out of 1,500.

COMPLETE SET (10) 25.00 60.00
1 Patrick Roy 10.00 25.00
2 Jocelyn Thibault 2.00 5.00
3 Felix Potvin 3.00 8.00
4 Martin Brodeur 6.00 15.00
5 Stephane Fiset 2.00 5.00
6 Eric Fichaud 2.00 5.00
7 Dominic Roussel 2.00 5.00
8 Emmanuel Fernandez 2.00 5.00
9 Martin Biron 2.00 5.00
10 Jose Theodore 4.00 10.00

1996-97 Donruss Canadian Ice Mario Lemieux Scrapbook

This 25-card set was made as a tribute to Mario Lemieux. Each card depicted a different highlight from the storied career of the Penguins' great. Only 1,966 individually numbered copies of each card were produced. Mario also hand signed a number of these cards, and there were two distinct versions of this card. The first, numbered out of 1200, was randomly inserted into packs. The second, numbered out of 500, was available in a framed version of the set available directly through an in-pack offer from Donruss.

COMPLETE SET (25) 30.00 80.00
COMMON CARD (1-25) 4.00 10.00
NNO1 M.Lemieux AU/500 100.00 250.00
NNO2 M.Lemieux AU/1200 30.00 80.00

1996-97 Donruss Canadian Ice O Canada

This 16-card set featured some of the top players born in Canada. Card fronts contained a color action photo, with the Canadian flag in the background. Each card had die-cut corners and featured gold and red foil printing. Just 2,000 individually numbered copies of each of these cards were produced.

COMPLETE SET (16) 40.00 100.00
1 Joe Sakic 6.00 15.00
2 Paul Kariya 2.50 6.00
3 Mark Messier 2.50 6.00
4 Jarome Iginla 3.00 8.00
5 Theo Fleury .75 2.00
6 Ed Belfour 2.50 6.00
7 Wayne Gretzky 10.00 25.00
8 Chris Gratton .75 2.00
9 Doug Gilmour 2.00 5.00
10 Kirk Muller .75 2.00
11 Eric Lindros 2.50 6.00
12 Brendan Shanahan 2.50 6.00
13 Mario Lemieux 10.00 25.00
14 Eric Daze .75 2.00
15 Geoff Sanderson .75 2.00
16 Terry Ryan .75 2.00

1997-98 Donruss Canadian Ice

e 1997-98 Donruss Canadian Ice set was issued in one series totaling 150 cards and distributed in eight-card packs. The fronts featured color action player photos. The backs carryed player information.

COMPLETE SET (150) 15.00 30.00
1 Patrick Roy 1.00 2.50
2 Paul Kariya .20 .50
3 Eric Lindros .20 .50
4 Steve Yzerman 1.00 2.50
5 Wayne Gretzky 1.25 3.00
6 Peter Forsberg .50 1.25
7 John Vanbiesbrouck .08 .25
8 Jaromir Jagr .30 .75
9 Jim Campbell .02 .10
10 Dominik Hasek .40 1.00
11 Ray Bourque .30 .75
12 Jarome Iginla .25 .60
13 Mike Modano .30 .75
14 Ed Jovanovski .08 .25
15 Jocelyn Thibault .08 .25
16 Keith Tkachuk .20 .50
17 Brett Hull .25 .60
18 Pavel Bure .20 .50
19 Saku Koivu .20 .50
20 Curtis Joseph .20 .50
21 Eric Daze .08 .25
22 Keith Primeau .02 .10
23 Theo Fleury .02 .10
24 Pierre Turgeon .08 .25
25 Peter Bondra .08 .25
26 Ed Belfour .20 .50
27 Pat Verbeek .02 .10
28 Chris Osgood .08 .25
29 Ray Sheppard .02 .10
30 Stephane Fiset .08 .25
31 Wade Redden .02 .10
32 Trevor Linden .08 .25
33 Zigmund Palffy .08 .25
34 Tony Amonte .08 .25
35 Derek Plante .02 .10
36 Jonas Hoglund .02 .10
37 Guy Hebert .08 .25
38 Garth Snow .08 .25
39 Chris Gratton .08 .25
40 Mats Sundin .20 .50
41 Geoff Sanderson .08 .25
42 Martin Brodeur .50 1.25
43 Jozef Stumpel .08 .25
44 Ron Francis .08 .25
45 Alexander Mogilny .08 .25
46 Bill Ranford .08 .25
47 Kirk Muller .02 .10
48 Ron Hextall .08 .25
49 Doug Gilmour .08 .25
50 Mark Messier .20 .50
51 Joe Nieuwendyk .08 .25
52 Ryan Smyth .08 .25
53 Mark Recchi .08 .25
54 Mike Gartner .08 .25
55 Al MacInnis .08 .25
56 Felix Potvin .20 .50
57 Rob Blake .08 .25
58 Dimitri Khristich .02 .10
59 Jim Carey .08 .25
60 Trevor Kidd .08 .25
61 Martin Gelinas .02 .10
62 Oleg Tverdovsky .02 .10
63 Ron Tugnutt .08 .25
64 Paul Coffey .20 .50
65 Travis Green .02 .10
66 Andrew Cassels .02 .10
67 Brendan Shanahan .20 .50
68 Luc Robitaille .08 .25
69 Pat LaFontaine .20 .50
70 Daymond Langkow .08 .25
71 Petr Nedved .08 .25
72 Sergei Fedorov .30 .75
73 Anson Carter .08 .25
74 Teemu Selanne .20 .50
75 Nikolai Khabibulin .08 .25
76 Ken Wregget .08 .25
77 Dino Ciccarelli .02 .10
78 Adam Oates .08 .25
79 Kirk McLean .08 .25
80 Wendel Clark .08 .25
81 Jeff Friesen .02 .10
82 Valeri Kamensky .08 .25
83 Ethan Moreau .02 .10
84 Matthew Barnaby .02 .10
85 Andy Moog .08 .25
86 Doug Weight .08 .25
87 Mike Dunham .08 .25
88 Brian Leetch .20 .50
89 Mike Peca .02 .10
90 Chris Pronger .08 .25
91 Alexei Zhamnov .02 .10
92 Bryan Berard .08 .25
93 John LeClair .20 .50
94 Steve Sullivan .02 .10
95 Grant Fuhr .08 .25
96 Mikael Renberg .08 .25
97 Adam Graves .02 .10
98 Ray Ferraro .02 .10
99 Sean Burke .08 .25
100 Jeremy Roenick .25 .60
101 Jeff Hackett .08 .25
102 Joe Sakic .40 1.00
103 Jamie Langenbrunner .02 .10
104 Stephane Richer .02 .10
105 Dave Andreychuk .02 .10
106 Tommy Salo .08 .25
107 Mike Richter .20 .50
108 Owen Nolan .08 .25
109 Corey Hirsch .08 .25
110 Daren Puppa .08 .25
111 Darcy Tucker .02 .10
112 Daniel Alfredsson .08 .25
113 Rod Brind'Amour .08 .25
114 Scott Stevens .08 .25
115 Vincent Damphousse .02 .10
116 Mathieu Schneider .02 .10
117 Jason Arnott .02 .10
118 Mike Vernon .08 .25
119 Sandis Ozolinsh .02 .10
120 Chris Chelios .20 .50
121 Mike Grier .02 .10
122 Alexandre Daigle .02 .10
123 Roman Hamrlik .02 .10
124 Derian Hatcher .02 .10
125 Damian Rhodes .08 .25
126 Adam Deadmarsh .02 .10
127 Alexei Yashin .02 .10
128 Terry Ryan .02 .10
129 Jeff Ware .02 .10
130 Steve Kelly .02 .10
131 Hnat Domenichelli .02 .10
132 Steve Shields RC .30 .75
133 Paxton Schafer RC .08 .25
134 Vadim Sharifijanov .02 .10
135 Vaclav Prospal RC .20 .50
136 Mike Fountain .02 .10
137 Christian Matte RC .02 .10
138 Tomas Vokoun RC .60 1.50
139 Vladimir Vorobiev RC .02 .10
140 Domenic Pittis RC .02 .10
141 Vaclav Varada .02 .10
142 D.J. Smith RC .02 .10
143 Jaroslav Svejkovsky .08 .25
144 Jason Holland .02 .10
145 Marc Denis .08 .25
146 Jean-Sebastien Giguere .08 .25
147 Marcel Cousineau .08 .25
148 Dave Andreychuk CL (1-75) .02 .10
149 Mike Gartner CL (76-150) .02 .10
150 Stanley Cup Team Picture CL (inserts) .02 .10

1997-98 Donruss Canadian Ice Dominion Series

This 150-card set was a parallel to the base set and was similar in design. Only 150 of each card were produced. Serial numbered and non-serial numbered cards carry the same value.
*VETS: 8X TO 20X BASIC CARDS
*ROOKIES: 4X TO 10X BASIC CARDS

1997-98 Donruss Canadian Ice Provincial Series

is 150-card set was a parallel to the base set and was similar in design. Only 750 of each card were produced, and were sequentially numbered.
*VETS: 5X TO 12X BASIC CARDS
*ROOKIES: 1X TO 2.5X BASIC CARDS

1997-98 Donruss Canadian Ice Les Gardiens

ndomly inserted in packs, this 12-card set featured color photos honoring great goaltenders from Quebec printed on micro-etched foil board. Only 1500 of each card were produced and were sequentially numbered.

COMPLETE SET (12) 30.00 80.00
*PROMOS: .4X TO 1X BASIC INSERTS
1 Patrick Roy 12.00 30.00
2 Felix Potvin 6.00 15.00
3 Martin Brodeur 8.00 20.00
4 Jean-Sebastien Giguere 4.00 10.00
5 Stephane Fiset 2.00 5.00
6 Jose Theodore 4.00 10.00
7 Jocelyn Thibault 2.00 5.00
8 Eric Fichaud 2.00 5.00
9 Patrick Lalime 2.00 5.00
10 Marcel Cousineau 2.00 5.00
11 Philippe DeRouville 2.00 5.00
12 Marc Denis 2.00 5.00

1997-98 Donruss Canadian Ice National Pride

ndomly inserted in packs, this 30-card set featured color photos of the most prominent native Canadian players printed on a die cut plastic card in the shape of a maple leaf and with gold foil highlights.

COMPLETE SET (30) 75.00 175.00
1 Wayne Gretzky 12.00 30.00
2 Mark Messier 3.00 8.00
3 Paul Kariya 3.00 8.00
4 Steve Yzerman 8.00 20.00
5 Brendan Shanahan 4.00 10.00
6 Chris Osgood 2.50 6.00
7 Adam Oates 2.50 6.00
8 Eric Lindros 4.00 10.00
9 Doug Gilmour 3.00 8.00
10 Ryan Smyth 2.50 6.00
11 Ray Bourque 5.00 12.00
12 Jason Arnott 2.00 5.00
13 Jarome Iginla 3.00 8.00
14 Geoff Sanderson 2.00 5.00
15 Alexandre Daigle 2.00 5.00
16 Trevor Linden 3.00 8.00
17 Joe Sakic 6.00 15.00
18 Mark Recchi 2.50 6.00
19 Theo Fleury 3.00 8.00
20 Ron Francis 2.50 6.00
21 Daymond Langkow 2.00 5.00
22 Ed Belfour 3.00 8.00
23 Paul Coffey 3.00 8.00
24 Pierre Turgeon 2.50 6.00
25 Claude Lemieux 2.00 5.00
26 Ron Hextall 3.00 8.00
27 Curtis Joseph 3.00 8.00
28 Mike Vernon 2.50 6.00
29 Vincent Damphousse 3.00 8.00
30 Owen Nolan 2.50 6.00

1997-98 Donruss Canadian Ice Stanley Cup Scrapbook

ndomly inserted in packs, this 33-card set was a fractured chase set which features color photos of players from each round of the 1997 Stanley Cup Playoffs. Only 2000 of the 16 Quarterfinals cards were produced and were sequentially numbered; 1500 of the eight sequentially numbered Conference Semifinals cards were produced; 1000 of the six sequentially numbered Conference Finals cards were produced; 750 of the two sequentially numbered Stanley Cup Finals cards were produced; only 250 of the one Stanley Cup Champions cards were produced and were sequentially numbered. Mike Vernon and Eric Lindros each autographed 750 of the Stanley Cup Finals cards, and Brendan Shanahan autographed 250 of the Stanley Cup Champions cards. A framed version of this set serial numbered to 500 was also available through a mail-in offer in packs. The cards were a parallel to the base set except that the words "Canadian Collectors Set" appeared at the top of the card. Sets were available intially for $500 through this offer.
*FRAMED/500: .5X TO 1.2X BASIC INSERTS
FRAMED/500 ISSUED VIA MAIL REDEMPTION

1 Mike Modano Q 4.00 10.00
2 Curtis Joseph Q 4.00 10.00
3 Joe Sakic Q 8.00 20.00
4 Chris Chelios Q 2.50 6.00
5 Chris Osgood Q 2.50 6.00
6 Brett Hull Q 4.00 10.00
7 Jeremy Roenick Q 4.00 10.00
8 Teemu Selanne Q 4.00 10.00
9 Jaromir Jagr Q 6.00 15.00
10 Garth Snow Q 2.00 5.00
11 Alexei Yashin Q 2.00 5.00
12 Steve Shields Q 2.00 5.00
13 Doug Gilmour Q 3.00 8.00
14 Jose Theodore Q 4.00 10.00
15 Mike Richter Q 2.50 6.00
16 John Vanbiesbrouck Q 2.50 6.00
17 Ryan Smyth CS 2.50 6.00
18 Peter Forsberg CS 8.00 20.00
19 Steve Yzerman CS 12.00 30.00
20 Paul Kariya CS 4.00 10.00
21 Janne Niinimaa CS 2.00 5.00
22 Dominik Hasek CS 8.00 20.00
23 Mark Messier CS 4.00 10.00
24 Martin Brodeur CS 12.50 30.00
25 Slava Kozlov CF 2.50 6.00
26 Sergei Fedorov CF 8.00 20.00
27 Patrick Roy CF 15.00 40.00
28 Wayne Gretzky CF 25.00 60.00
29 John LeClair CF 2.50 6.00
30 Paul Coffey CF 4.00 10.00
31 Mike Vernon AU/750 10.00 25.00
32 Eric Lindros AU/750 20.00 40.00
33 B.Shanahan AU/250 40.00 80.00

1995-96 Donruss Elite

is 110-card super premium set was the last mainstream release of the 1995-96 card season. The product was distributed by Pinnacle Brands, which purchased Donruss and all of its sports licenses just prior to the set's debut. The eight-card packs had a suggested retail of $2.99. The Cool Trade Exchange card was randomly inserted 1:48 packs, although there were numerous reports of collectors finding up to eight copies per box. When found, it could be redeemed for parallel versions of the four Donruss Elite cards found in the NHL Cool Trade wrapper redemption set. This offer expired on September 30, 1996. Rookie Cards include Daniel Alfredsson, Todd Bertuzzi, Radek Dvorak, Chad Kilger and Shane Doan.

COMPLETE SET (110) 12.00 30.00
1 Jocelyn Thibault .12 .30
2 Nicklas Lidstrom .15 .40
3 Brendan Shanahan .20 .50
4 Kenny Jonsson .15 .40
5 Doug Weight .15 .40
6 Oleg Tverdovsky .15 .40
7 Brett Hull .20 .50
8 Larry Murphy .15 .40
9 Ray Bourque .15 .40
10 Adam Graves .12 .30
11 Gary Suter .12 .30
12 Bill Ranford .12 .30
13 Zigmund Palffy .15 .40
14 Cam Neely .15 .40
15 Al MacInnis .15 .40
16 Joe Sakic .25 .60
17 Kevin Hatcher .12 .30
18 Alexander Mogilny .12 .30
19 Radek Dvorak RC .20 .50
20 Ed Belfour .12 .30
21 Jeff O'Neill .15 .40
22 Valeri Kamensky .12 .30
23 John MacLean .12 .30
24 Zdeno Ciger .12 .30
25 Daniel Alfredsson RC .75 2.00
26 Owen Nolan .15 .40
27 Wendel Clark .15 .40
28 Brian Savage .10 .25
29 Alexei Zhamnov .15 .40
30 Dominik Hasek .20 .50
31 Paul Kariya .20 .50
32 Mike Modano .25 .60
33 Craig Janney .10 .25
34 Todd Harvey .10 .25
35 Jaromir Jagr .40 1.00
36 Roman Hamrlik .10 .25
37 Sergei Zubov .12 .30
38 Marcus Ragnarsson RC .20 .50
39 Peter Forsberg .40 1.00
40 Ron Francis .20 .50
41 German Titov .12 .30
42 Grant Fuhr .15 .40
43 Martin Brodeur .40 1.00
44 Claude Lemieux .10 .25
45 Trevor Linden .15 .40
46 Mark Messier .25 .60
47 Jeremy Roenick .20 .50
48 Peter Bondra .15 .40
49 Donald Audette .12 .30
50 Joe Nieuwendyk .10 .25
51 Mario Lemieux CL .50 1.25
52 Vitali Yachmenev .15 .40
53 Sergei Fedorov .25 .60
54 Kirk Muller .12 .30
55 Chad Kilger RC .15 .40
56 John LeClair .15 .40
57 Todd Bertuzzi RC .20 .50
58 Wayne Gretzky .50 1.25
59 Curtis Joseph .15 .40
60 Niklas Sundstrom .15 .40
61 Chris Chelios .15 .40
62 Radek Bonk .10 .25
63 Eric Daze .30 .75
64 Patrick Roy .40 1.00
65 Rob Niedermayer .12 .30
66 Mario Lemieux .50 1.25
67 Saku Koivu .15 .40
68 Ed Jovanovski .15 .40
69 Jim Carey .12 .30
70 Scott Stevens .15 .40
71 Steve Thomas .12 .30
72 Mats Sundin .15 .40
73 Teemu Selanne .30 .75
74 Tomas Sandstrom .12 .30
75 Pat LaFontaine .15 .40
76 Pat Verbeek .12 .30
77 Pavel Bure .20 .50
78 Jeff Brown .12 .30
79 Alexei Yashin .12 .30
80 Adam Oates .15 .40
81 Keith Tkachuk .15 .40
82 Brian Bradley .12 .30
83 John Vanbiesbrouck .12 .30
84 Alexander Selivanov .12 .30
85 Paul Coffey .15 .40
86 Scott Mellanby .12 .30
87 Slava Kozlov .12 .30
88 Eric Lindros .25 .60
89 Deron Quint .12 .30
90 Pierre Turgeon .15 .40
91 Rod Brind'Amour .15 .40
92 Doug Gilmour .20 .50
93 Sandis Ozolinsh .12 .30
94 Mikael Renberg .12 .30
95 Kevin Stevens .12 .30
96 Vincent Damphousse .12 .30
97 Felix Potvin .15 .40
98 Brian Leetch .15 .40
99 Steve Yzerman .20 .50
100 Dale Hawerchuk .20 .50
101 Jason Arnott .12 .30
102 Ray Sheppard .12 .30
103 Mark Recchi .20 .50
104 Joe Juneau .12 .30
105 Luc Robitaille .10 .25
106 Theo Fleury .20 .50
107 Sean Burke .10 .25
108 Ron Hextall .15 .40
109 Shane Doan RC .50 1.25
110 Eric Lindros CL .25 .60
NNO Cool Trade Exch. EXP. .05 .15

1995-96 Donruss Elite Die Cuts

is die-cut set paralleled the main Donruss Elite set. The first 500 cards off the press had the die-cut pattern. Interestingly, boxes from early in the production run contained cards intended to be die-cut which weren't. These cards are differentiated from regular issue cards by a curved pattern which runs across the top of the cards just above the photo. Although some collectors speculated that these cards were in shorter supply than the regular die-cuts, that was not verified by the company, and unsubstantiated by market evidence.
*DIE CUT VETS: 12X TO 30X BASIC CARDS
*DIE CUT ROOKIES: 4X TO 10X

1995-96 Donruss Elite Die Cuts Uncut

ese cards are discernible from regular issue cards by a curved pattern which runs across the top of the cards just above the photo. Although some collectors speculate that these cards are in shorter supply than the regular die-cuts, that was not verified by the company, and unsubstantiated by market evidence.
*UNCUT VETS: 10X TO 25X BASIC CARDS
*UNCUT ROOKIES: 5X TO 12X

1995-96 Donruss Elite Cutting Edge

This 15-card insert set celebrated the top performers of the 1995-96 season. The cards were printed and embossed on laminated polycarbonate material that simulated brushed steel. Each card was serially numbered out of 2,500. The cards were randomly inserted at a rate of 1:32 packs.

COMPLETE SET (15) 25.00 60.00
1 Eric Lindros 2.00 5.00
2 Mario Lemieux 5.00 12.00
3 Wayne Gretzky 8.00 20.00
4 Peter Forsberg 3.00 8.00
5 Paul Kariya 2.00 5.00
6 Jaromir Jagr 3.00 8.00
7 Alexander Mogilny 1.00 2.50
8 Mark Messier 2.00 5.00
9 Sergei Fedorov 2.00 5.00
10 Pierre Turgeon 1.00 2.50
11 Mats Sundin 2.00 5.00
12 Brett Hull 2.00 5.00
13 Paul Coffey 1.00 2.50
14 Jeremy Roenick 2.00 5.00
15 Teemu Selanne 2.00 5.00

1995-96 Donruss Elite Lemieux/Lindros Series

These two seven-card sets recognized two of the most dominating players in the game, Eric Lindros and Mario Lemieux, who also happened to be Donruss spokesmen. The cards were printed on gold holographic foil, with the Lindros cards serially numbered up to 1,088 and the Lemieux cards to 1,066. The seventh card in each series was autographed, giving it a considerably higher value. The seven cards were inserted at a rate of 1:160. There also was a card signed by both Lindros and Lemieux, which was not considered part of either complete set. Both this card and the Lemieux autograph were available only through redemption cards; Lemieux was unable to sign them in time for random insertion. The dual signed card was limited to 500 copies and was inserted in 1:2400 packs. The Lindros cards were assigned an E suffix for cataloguing purposes only.

COMP.LEMIEUX SET (7) 125.00 300.00
COMMON LEMIEUX (1-6) 8.00 20.00
COMP.LINDROS SET (7) 75.00 200.00
COMMON LINDROS (1-6) 6.00 15.00
7 Mario Lemieux AU 30.00 80.00
7E Eric Lindros AU 10.00 25.00
NNO Lemieux/Lindros AU/500 50.00 120.00

1995-96 Donruss Elite Painted Warriors

This ten card insert set focused on top goalies and their brightly painted headgear. Each card was printed on clear plastic and then die-cut around the face mask. The cards were individually numbered out of 2,500. The cards were inserted at a rate of 1:48 packs.

COMPLETE SET (10) 25.00 60.00
1 Patrick Roy 6.00 15.00
2 Felix Potvin 4.00 10.00
3 Martin Brodeur 6.00 15.00
4 Ed Belfour 2.00 5.00
5 Guy Hebert 2.00 5.00
6 John Vanbiesbrouck 2.50 6.00
7 Jocelyn Thibault 2.00 5.00
8 Ron Hextall 3.00 8.00
9 Grant Fuhr 2.50 6.00
10 Jim Carey 2.00 5.00
P3 Martin Brodeur PROMO 2.50 6.00
P4 Ed Belfour PROMO 2.50 6.00
P9 Grant Fuhr PROMO 2.50 6.00
P10 Jim Carey PROMO 1.50 4.00

1995-96 Donruss Elite Rookies

e fifteen cards in this set -- inserted 1:16 packs -- highlighted the top rookies of the 1995-96 season. The cards were printed on an icy silver foil background and detailed with gold trim. The cards were individually numbered out of 5,000.

COMPLETE SET (15) 15.00 40.00
1 Eric Daze 1.00 2.50
2 Vitali Yachmenev 1.00 2.50
3 Daniel Alfredsson 2.00 5.00
4 Todd Bertuzzi 2.00 5.00
5 Byron Dafoe 1.00 2.50
6 Eric Fichaud 1.00 2.50
7 Marcus Ragnarsson 1.00 2.50
8 Saku Koivu 3.00 8.00
9 Chad Kilger 1.00 2.50
10 Radek Dvorak 1.00 2.50
11 Ed Jovanovski 2.00 5.00
12 Jeff O'Neill 2.00 5.00
13 Shane Doan 2.00 5.00
14 Niklas Sundstrom 1.00 2.50
15 Kyle McLaren 1.00 2.50

1995-96 Donruss Elite World Juniors

is 44-card insert set featured the top Canadian and US players from the 1996 World Junior Championships. The cards were printed on canvas stock that simulated the flag of the player's home country. Each card was individually numbered out of 1,000. The cards were inserted 1:30 packs.

COMPLETE SET (44) 125.00 200.00
1 Marc Denis 3.00 8.00
2 Jose Theodore 5.00 12.00
3 Chad Allan 2.00 5.00
4 Nolan Baumgartner 2.00 5.00
5 Denis Gauthier 2.00 5.00
6 Jason Holland 2.00 5.00
7 Chris Phillips 3.00 8.00
8 Wade Redden 4.00 10.00
9 Rhett Warrener 2.00 5.00
10 Jason Botterill 2.00 5.00
11 Curtis Brown 2.00 5.00
12 Hnat Domenichelli 2.00 5.00
13 Christian Dube 2.00 5.00
14 Robb Gordon 2.00 5.00
15 Jarome Iginla 10.00 25.00
16 Daymond Langkow 3.00 8.00
17 Brad Larsen 2.00 5.00
18 Alyn McCauley 2.00 5.00
19 Craig Mills 2.00 5.00
20 Jason Podollan 2.00 5.00
21 Mike Watt 2.00 5.00
22 Jamie Wright 2.00 5.00
23 Brian Boucher 3.00 8.00
24 Marc Magliarditi 2.00 5.00
25 Bryan Berard 2.00 5.00
26 Chris Bogas 2.00 5.00
27 Ben Clymer 2.00 5.00
28 Jeff Kealty 2.00 5.00
29 Mike McBain 2.00 5.00
30 Jeremiah McCarthy 2.00 5.00
31 Tom Poti 2.00 5.00
32 Reg Berg 2.00 5.00
33 Matt Cullen 3.00 8.00
34 Chris Drury 6.00 15.00
35 Jeff Farkas 2.00 5.00
36 Casey Hankinson 2.00 5.00
37 Matt Herr 2.00 5.00
38 Mark Parrish 3.00 8.00
39 Erik Rasmussen 2.00 5.00
40 Marty Reasoner 2.00 5.00
41 Wyatt Smith 2.00 5.00
42 Brian Swanson 2.00 5.00
43 Mike Sylvia 2.00 5.00
44 Mike York 3.00 8.00

1996-97 Donruss Elite

The 1996-97 Donruss Elite set was issued in one series totaling 150 cards. Packs contained eight cards for a suggested retail price of $3.99, and were distributed as a hobby-only product. Card fronts featured a color action photo with a foil background. A 20-card rookie subset was found at the end of the set (#128-147). Key rookies included Sergei Berezin, Patrick Lalime, Ethan Moreau, and Dainius Zubrus.

COMPLETE SET (150) 12.50 25.00
1 Paul Kariya .60 1.50
2 Ron Hextall .40 1.00
3 Andy Moog .50 1.25
4 Brett Hull 2.50 6.00
5 Felix Potvin .50 1.25
6 Jocelyn Thibault .50 1.25
7 Eric Lindros .75 2.00
8 Jaromir Jagr 1.25 3.00
9 Sergei Fedorov .75 2.00
10 Wayne Gretzky 2.50 6.00
11 Peter Bondra .40 1.00
12 Peter Forsberg .75 2.00
13 Stephane Fiset .40 1.00
14 Owen Nolan .50 1.25
15 Rob Niedermayer .40 1.00
16 Martin Brodeur 1.00 2.50
17 Ray Bourque .75 2.00
18 Todd Bertuzzi .50 1.25
19 Jim Carey .50 1.25
20 Chris Chelios .50 1.25
21 Chris Osgood .50 1.25
22 Mark Messier .75 2.00
23 Roman Hamrlik .40 1.00
24 Kevin Hatcher .30 .75
25 Doug Weight .50 1.25
26 Mark Recchi .60 1.50
27 Jeremy Roenick .75 2.00
28 Derian Hatcher .30 .75
29 Grant Fuhr .50 1.25
30 Scott Stevens .50 1.25
31 Adam Oates .50 1.25
32 Scott Mellanby .40 1.00
33 Mikael Renberg .40 1.00
34 Corey Hirsch .40 1.00
35 Michal Pivonka .30 .75
36 Stephane Richer .40 1.00
37 Dominik Hasek .75 2.00
38 Steve Yzerman 1.25 3.00
39 Jeff O'Neill .30 .75
40 Ron Francis .60 1.50
41 Alexei Yashin .40 1.00
42 Pat Verbeek .30 .75
43 Geoff Courtnall .30 .75
44 Doug Gilmour .60 1.50
45 Trevor Kidd .30 .75
46 Jason Arnott .40 1.00
47 Niklas Sundstrom .30 .75
48 Rob Blake .50 1.25
49 Nikolai Khabibulin .40 1.00
50 Igor Larionov .50 1.25
51 Sean Burke .30 .75
52 Zigmund Palffy .50 1.25
53 Jeff Friesen .30 .75
54 Theo Fleury 1.00 2.50
55 Mats Sundin .50 1.25
56 Alexander Mogilny .40 1.00
57 John LeClair .50 1.25
58 Shayne Corson .30 .75
59 Teemu Selanne 1.00 2.50
60 Kelly Hrudey .40 1.00
61 Keith Tkachuk .50 1.25
62 Joe Nieuwendyk .50 1.25
63 Tom Barrasso .40 1.00
64 Aaron Gavey .30 .75
65 Alexei Zhamnov .40 1.00
66 Patrick Roy 1.25 3.00
67 Al MacInnis .50 1.25
68 Trevor Linden .40 1.00
69 Bill Guerin .50 1.25
70 Dimitri Khristich .30 .75
71 Eric Daze .40 1.00
72 Paul Coffey .50 1.25
73 Keith Primeau .30 .75
74 John Vanbiesbrouck .50 1.25
75 Bernie Nicholls .30 .75
76 Yanic Perreault .30 .75
77 Jere Lehtinen .30 .75
78 Luc Robitaille .50 1.25
79 Todd Gill .40 1.00
80 Saku Koivu .50 1.25
81 Vyacheslav Kozlov .30 .75
82 Ed Jovanovski .40 1.00
83 Brendan Witt .30 .75
84 Alexandre Daigle .30 .75
85 Jari Kurri .50 1.25
86 Mike Vernon .40 1.00
87 Jeff Beukeboom .30 .75
88 Mathieu Schneider .30 .75
89 Niklas Andersson .30 .75
90 Joe Juneau .30 .75
91 Ed Belfour .50 1.25
92 Curtis Joseph .50 1.25
93 Rod Brind'Amour .50 1.25
94 Vitali Yachmenev .30 .75
95 Alexander Selivanov .30 .75
96 Mike Richter .50 1.25
97 Bill Ranford .40 1.00
98 Wendel Clark .40 1.00
99 Slava Fetisov .30 .75
100 Daniel Alfredsson .50 1.25
101 Pat LaFontaine .50 1.25
102 Joe Murphy .30 .75
103 Pavel Bure .60 1.50
104 Craig Janney .40 1.00
105 Radek Dvorak .40 1.00
106 Cory Stillman .30 .75
107 Adam Graves .30 .75
108 Aki Berg .30 .75
109 Mario Lemieux 1.50 4.00
110 Claude Lemieux .30 .75
111 Sergei Zubov .30 .75
112 Pierre Turgeon .50 1.25
113 Damian Rhodes .40 1.00
114 Daren Puppa .40 1.00
115 Alexei Zhitnik .30 .75
116 Mike Modano .75 2.00
117 Kenny Jonsson .30 .75

118 Valeri Kamensky .40 1.00
119 Valeri Bure .30 .75
120 Joe Sakic .75 2.00
121 Kirk McLean .40 1.00
122 Petr Sykora .30 .75
123 Mike Gartner .50 1.25
124 Ryan Smyth .40 1.00
125 Brian Leetch .50 1.25
126 Brendan Shanahan .60 1.50
127 Geoff Sanderson .40 1.00
128 Corey Schwab .40 1.00
129 Anders Eriksson .30 .75
130 Harry York RC .50 1.25
131 Jarome Iginla .60 1.50
132 Eric Fichaud .40 1.00
133 Patrick Lalime RC .60 1.50
134 Daymond Langkow .40 1.00
135 Mattias Timander RC .50 1.25
136 Ethan Moreau RC .50 1.25
137 Christian Dube .30 .75
138 Sergei Berezin RC .75 2.00
139 Jose Theodore .60 1.50
140 Wade Redden .30 .75
141 Dainius Zubrus RC .60 1.50
142 Jim Campbell .30 .75
143 Daniel Goneau RC .50 1.25
144 Jamie Langenbrunner .30 .75
145 Rem Murray RC .50 1.25
146 Jonas Hoglund .30 .75
147 Bryan Berard .50 1.25
148 Chris Osgood CL (1-75) .50 1.25
149 Eric Lindros CL .75 2.00
150 Jason Arnott CL (inserts) .40 1.00

1996-97 Donruss Elite Die Cut Stars

This die-cut set paralleled the main Donruss Elite set. Card fronts featured a die-cut, silver-poly laminate foil to distinguish them from their base counterparts.
*VETS: 4X TO 10X BASIC CARDS
*ROOKIES: 2X TO 5X

1996-97 Donruss Elite Aspirations

is set featured twenty-five of the NHL's top rookies and young superstars. Each card was serially numbered out of 3,000. Card fronts featured a color action photo with blue and silver foil surrounding the photo.

COMPLETE SET (25) 12.00 30.00
1 Eric Daze .40 1.00
2 Daniel Alfredsson 2.00 5.00
3 Petr Sykora .40 1.00
4 Todd Bertuzzi .75 2.00
5 Saku Koivu 2.00 5.00
6 Ed Jovanovski .75 2.00
7 Jim Campbell .40 1.00
8 Valeri Bure .40 1.00
9 Jeff O'Neill .40 1.00
10 Jere Lehtinen .75 2.00
11 Terry Ryan .40 1.00
12 Jonas Hoglund .40 1.00
13 Daymond Langkow .40 1.00
14 Eric Fichaud .40 1.00
15 Dainius Zubrus .40 1.00
16 Janne Niinimaa .40 1.00
17 Sergei Berezin .40 1.00
18 Daniel Goneau .40 1.00
19 Jarome Iginla 4.00 10.00
20 Ethan Moreau .40 1.00
21 Jamie Langenbrunner .40 1.00
22 Rem Murray .40 1.00
23 Bryan Berard .40 1.00
24 Wade Redden .40 1.00
25 Christian Dube .40 1.00

1996-97 Donruss Elite Hart to Hart

This special insert set was issued in two parts, one featuring Eric Lindros and the other featuring Mario Lemieux. Each set contained six cards. The Lindros set was serial numbered to 1,996 sets, with the first 188 signed by Lindros. The Lemieux set was serial numbered to 1,995 sets, with the first 166 signed by Lemieux. In addition, Donruss also included a dual autograph of Lemieux and Lindros, serial numbered to just 500. The prefixes listed below for the autographs are for checklisting purposes only.

COMPLETE LEMIEUX SET (6) 40.00 100.00
COMMON LEMIEUX 8.00 20.00
COMMON LEMIEUX AU 25.00 60.00
LEMIEUX PRINT RUN 1995 SER.#'d SETS
COMPLETE LINDROS SET (6) 30.00 80.00
COMMON LINDROS 6.00 15.00
COMMON LINDROS AU 20.00 50.00
LINDROS PRINT RUN 1996 SER.#'d SETS
ELML Lindros/Lemieux AU/500 50.00 125.00

1996-97 Donruss Elite Painted Warriors

This 10-card insert set focusesd on top goalies and their brightly painted headgear. Each card was printed on clear plastic and then die-cut around the mask. The cards were individually numbered out of 2,500.

COMPLETE SET (10) 30.00 80.00
1 Patrick Roy 8.00 20.00
2 Mike Richter 4.00 10.00
3 Jim Carey 2.00 5.00
4 John Vanbiesbrouck 4.00 10.00
5 Jocelyn Thibault 2.00 5.00
6 Felix Potvin 5.00 12.00
7 Ed Belfour 4.00 10.00
8 Martin Brodeur 6.00 15.00
9 Nikolai Khabibulin 4.00 10.00
10 Stephane Fiset 2.00 5.00

1996-97 Donruss Elite Painted Warriors Promos

These cards mirrored the regular versions except in the serial number box on the back, where the number read PROMO/2500. The Brodeur was the most readily available of these cards.

COMPLETE SET (10) 30.00 75.00
P1 Patrick Roy 6.00 12.00
P2 Mike Richter 6.00 12.00
P3 Jim Carey 6.00 12.00
P4 John Vanbiesbrouck 6.00 12.00
P5 Jocelyn Thibault 6.00 12.00
P6 Felix Potvin 6.00 12.00
P7 Ed Belfour 6.00 12.00
P8 Martin Brodeur 6.00 12.00
P9 Nikolai Khabibulin 6.00 12.00
P10 Stephane Fiset 6.00 12.00

1996-97 Donruss Elite Perspective

This 12-card set focused on the NHL's veteran stars. Card fronts featured a die-cut, micro-etched, foil design. Each card was individually numbered out of 500.

COMPLETE SET (12) 40.00 100.00
1 Wayne Gretzky 15.00 40.00
2 Mark Messier 3.00 8.00
3 Steve Yzerman 10.00 25.00
4 Mario Lemieux 12.00 30.00
5 Paul Coffey 2.00 5.00
6 Doug Gilmour 2.00 5.00
7 Brendan Shanahan 3.00 8.00
8 Jaromir Jagr 5.00 12.00
9 Brett Hull 4.00 10.00
10 Pat LaFontaine 2.00 5.00
11 Chris Chelios 2.00 5.00
12 Grant Fuhr 2.00 5.00

1996-97 Donruss Elite Status

This 12-card set took an up-close look at some of the NHL's top players who were in the prime of their careers. Card fronts were foil laminate and featured a full-color photo. Each card was serially numbered out of 750.

COMPLETE SET (12) 20.00 50.00
1 Pavel Bure 2.50 6.00
2 Keith Tkachuk 2.50 6.00
3 Sergei Fedorov 3.00 8.00
4 Doug Weight 1.25 3.00
5 Paul Kariya 2.50 6.00
6 Owen Nolan 1.25 3.00
7 Peter Forsberg 6.00 15.00
8 Eric Lindros 2.50 6.00
9 Alexander Mogilny 1.25 3.00
10 Teemu Selanne 2.50 6.00
11 Joe Sakic 5.00 12.00
12 Jeremy Roenick 3.00 8.00

1997-98 Donruss Elite

The 1997-98 Donruss Elite hobby exclusive set was issued in one series totaling 150 cards and was distributed in five-card packs with a suggested retail price of $3.99. The fronts featured color player photos printed on thick foil card stock. The backs carried player information. The set contained the topical subset: Elite Generations (115-144).

COMPLETE SET (150) 15.00 40.00
1 Peter Forsberg .25 .60
2 Mike Modano .30 .75
3 John Vanbiesbrouck .20 .50
4 Pavel Bure .25 .60
5 Mark Messier .30 .75
6 Joe Thornton .20 .50
7 Paul Kariya .25 .60
8 Martin Brodeur .40 1.00
9 Wayne Gretzky 1.00 2.50
10 Eric Lindros .30 .75
11 Jaromir Jagr .50 1.25
12 Brett Hull .25 .60
13 Jarome Iginla .20 .50
14 Patrick Roy .50 1.25
15 Steve Yzerman .40 1.00
16 Sergei Samsonov .12 .30
17 Teemu Selanne .40 1.00
18 Brendan Shanahan .25 .60
19 Curtis Joseph .20 .50
20 Saku Koivu .20 .50
21 Ray Bourque .30 .75
22 Jaroslav Svejkovsky .15 .40
23 Keith Primeau .15 .40
24 Alexandre Daigle .12 .30
25 Vyacheslav Kozlov .15 .40
26 Jozef Stumpel .15 .40
27 Alexei Yashin .15 .40
28 Marian Hossa RC .25 .60
29 Bryan Berard .12 .30
30 Dominik Hasek .30 .75
31 Chris Chelios .20 .50
32 Derian Hatcher .15 .40
33 Ed Jovanovski .12 .30
34 Zigmund Palffy .20 .50
35 Ron Hextall .20 .50
36 Daymond Langkow .12 .30
37 Daniel Cleary .15 .40
38 Alyn McCauley .15 .40
39 Sean Burke .12 .30
40 Brian Leetch .20 .50
41 Joe Juneau .15 .40
42 Damian Rhodes .15 .40
43 Dino Ciccarelli .20 .50
44 Valeri Kamensky .15 .40
45 Guy Hebert .15 .40
46 Brad Isbister .15 .40
47 Adam Graves .12 .30
48 Andrew Cassels .12 .30
49 Joe Sakic .30 .75
50 Dainius Zubrus .15 .40
51 Roberto Luongo RC 3.00 8.00
52 Ethan Moreau .12 .30
53 Chris Osgood .20 .50
54 Stephane Fiset .15 .40
55 Sergei Berezin .15 .40
56 Mike Richter .20 .50
57 Valeri Bure .12 .30
58 Mats Sundin .20 .50
59 Mike Dunham .15 .40
60 Byron Dafoe .12 .30
61 Joe Nieuwendyk .20 .50
62 Mike Grier .15 .40
63 Paul Coffey .20 .50
64 Chris Phillips .15 .40
65 Patrik Elias RC .30 .75
66 Andy Moog .20 .50
67 Geoff Sanderson .15 .40
68 Jere Lehtinen .15 .40
69 Alexander Mogilny .15 .40
70 Ryan Smyth .15 .40
71 John LeClair .20 .50
72 Olli Jokinen RC .25 .60
73 Doug Gilmour .25 .60
74 Theo Fleury .25 .60
75 Adam Deadmarsh .12 .30
76 Scott Mellanby .15 .40
77 Jeremy Roenick .25 .60
78 Jim Campbell .12 .30
79 Daren Puppa .15 .40
80 Vaclav Prospal RC .15 .40
81 Vincent Damphousse .15 .40
82 Derek Plante .15 .40
83 Sandis Ozolinsh .15 .40
84 Darren McCarty .15 .40
85 Luc Robitaille .20 .50
86 Wade Redden .12 .30
87 Eric Fichaud .15 .40
88 Jocelyn Thibault .12 .30
89 Trevor Linden .15 .40
90 Boyd Devereaux .15 .40
91 Chris Gratton .12 .30
92 Janne Niinimaa .15 .40
93 Jeff Friesen .15 .40
94 Roman Hamrlik .15 .40
95 Jason Arnott .15 .40
96 Sergei Fedorov .30 .75
97 Tony Amonte .15 .40
98 Mattias Ohlund .15 .40
99 Patrick Marleau .25 .60
100 Felix Potvin .20 .50
101 Tommy Salo .12 .30
102 Ed Belfour .20 .50
103 Doug Weight .20 .50
104 Daniel Alfredsson .20 .50
105 Pierre Turgeon .20 .50
106 Espen Knutsen RC .20 .50
107 Trevor Kidd .12 .30
108 Alexei Morozov .15 .40
109 Oleg Tverdovsky .15 .40
110 Grant Fuhr .20 .50
111 Pat LaFontaine .20 .50
112 Keith Tkachuk .20 .50
113 Ron Francis .25 .60
114 Derek Morris RC .20 .50
115 Joe Sakic G .30 .75
116 Brian Leetch G .20 .50
117 Alyn McCauley G .15 .40
118 Pavel Bure G .25 .60
119 Eric Lindros G .30 .75
120 Teemu Selanne G .40 1.00
121 Jarome Iginla G .20 .50
122 Steve Yzerman G .40 1.00
123 Daniel Cleary G .15 .40
124 Bryan Berard G .12 .30
125 Jaromir Jagr G .50 1.25
126 John Vanbiesbrouck G .20 .50
127 Mark Messier G .30 .75
128 Patrick Marleau G .25 .60
129 Mike Modano G .30 .75
130 Zigmund Palffy G .20 .50
131 Felix Potvin G .20 .50
132 Derek Morris G .20 .50
133 Brendan Shanahan G .25 .60
134 Sergei Samsonov G .12 .30
135 Dainius Zubrus G .15 .40
136 Paul Kariya G .25 .60
137 Martin Brodeur G .40 1.00
138 Joe Thornton G .20 .50
139 Mattias Ohlund G .15 .40
140 Ryan Smyth G .15 .40
141 Jaroslav Svejkovsky G .15 .40
142 Patrick Roy G .50 1.25
143 Wayne Gretzky G 1.00 2.50
144 Espen Knutsen G .20 .50
145 Patrick Marleau CL .25 .60
146 Pat Lafontaine CL .20 .50
147 Mike Gartner CL .20 .50
148 Joe Thornton CL .20 .50
149 Teemu Selanne CL .40 1.00
150 Mark Messier CL .30 .75

1997-98 Donruss Elite Aspirations

Randomly inserted in packs, this 150-card set was a die-cut parallel version of the base set printed on foil board. Each card was numbered 1 of 750.
*VETS: 4X TO 10X BASIC CARDS
*ROOKIE STAR: 2.5X TO 6X BASIC RC

1997-98 Donruss Elite Status

Randomly inserted in packs, this 150-card set was a die-cut parallel version of the base set printed on holofoil board. Each card was sequentially numbered to 100.
*VETS: 10X TO 25X BASIC CARDS
*ROOKIES: 6X TO 15X BASIC CARDS

1997-98 Donruss Elite Back to the Future

Randomly inserted in packs, this eight-card set featured color player photos printed on double-sided cards. One side displayed a veteran star or Hockey HOF member while the other side highlighted a younger talent. The first 100 of each card was autographed by both of the featured players.

COMPLETE SET (8) 30.00 60.00
1 E.Lindros/J.Thornton 3.00 8.00
2 J.Thibault/M.Denis 3.00 8.00
3 T.Selanne/P.Marleau 3.00 8.00
4 J.Jagr/D.Cleary 4.00 10.00
5 S.Fedorov/P.Forsberg 5.00 12.00
6 B.Hull/B.Hull 4.00 10.00
7 M.Brodeur/R.Luongo 5.00 12.00
8 G.Howe/S.Yzerman 6.00 15.00

1997-98 Donruss Elite Back to the Future Autographs

Randomly inserted in packs, this eight-card set was a parallel to the regular Back to the Future insert set and consisted of the first 100 cards of the regular set autographed by both players.

1 E.Lindros/J.Thornton 60.00 150.00
2 J.Thibault/M.Denis 30.00 80.00
3 T.Selanne/P.Marleau 50.00 120.00
4 J.Jagr/D.Cleary 80.00 150.00
5 S.Fedorov/P.Forsberg 80.00 150.00
6 B.Hull/B.Hull 75.00 150.00
7 M.Brodeur/R.Luongo 150.00 300.00
8 G.Howe/S.Yzerman 200.00 400.00

1997-98 Donruss Elite Craftsmen

Randomly inserted in packs, this 30-card set featured color photos of top players printed on full foil board and micro-etched. The cards were sequentially numbered to 2,500.

COMPLETE SET (30) 75.00 150.00
*MASTER/100: 2X TO 5X BASIC INSERTS
1 John Vanbiesbrouck 1.00 2.50
2 Eric Lindros 1.50 4.00
3 Joe Sakic 2.50 6.00
4 Mark Messier 2.00 5.00
5 Jaroslav Svejkovsky 1.00 2.50
6 Dominik Hasek 3.00 8.00
7 Chris Osgood 1.00 2.50
8 Martin Brodeur 4.00 10.00
9 Sergei Fedorov 2.00 5.00
10 Daniel Cleary 1.00 2.50
11 Patrick Marleau 1.50 4.00
12 Sergei Samsonov 1.25 3.00
13 Felix Potvin 1.50 4.00
14 Patrick Roy 8.00 20.00
15 Teemu Selanne 1.50 4.00
16 Steve Yzerman 8.00 20.00
17 Jarome Iginla 2.00 5.00
18 Mike Modano 2.50 6.00
19 Wayne Gretzky 6.00 15.00
20 Pavel Bure 1.50 4.00
21 Ryan Smyth 1.25 3.00
22 Paul Kariya 1.50 4.00
23 Peter Forsberg 4.00 10.00
24 Joe Thornton 2.50 6.00
25 Jaromir Jagr 2.50 6.00
26 Bryan Berard 1.00 2.50
27 Brendan Shanahan 1.50 4.00
28 Keith Tkachuk 1.50 4.00
29 Curtis Joseph 1.50 4.00
30 Brian Leetch 1.00 2.50

1997-98 Donruss Elite Prime Numbers

Randomly inserted in packs, this 36-card set featured color photos of 12 top stars with a number in the background. Each star appeared on three cards which, when linked together in the right order, displayed a significant career statistic. Each card in the set could be combined with its die cut counterpart to total a career statistic for that player. Announced print runs are listed below for the non die cut version of each card.

SERIAL #'d UNDER 20 NOT PRICED
1A Peter Forsberg 2/54* 30.00 80.00
1B Peter Forsberg 5/204* 8.00 20.00
1C Peter Forsberg 4/250* 8.00 20.00
2A Patrick Roy 3/49* 40.00 100.00
2B Patrick Roy 4/309* 15.00 40.00
2C Patrick Roy 9/340* 15.00 40.00
3A Mark Messier 2/95* 8.00 20.00
3B Mark Messier 9/205* 4.00 10.00
3C Mark Messier 5/290* 4.00 10.00
4A Eric Lindros 4/36* 15.00 40.00
4B Eric Lindros 3/406* 4.00 10.00
4C Eric Lindros 6/430* 5.00 12.00
5A Paul Kariya 2/46* 30.00 80.00
5B Paul Kariya 4/206* 8.00 20.00
5C Paul Kariya 6/240* 4.00 10.00
6A Jaromir Jagr 2/66* 20.00 50.00
6B Jaromir Jagr 6/206* 10.00 25.00
6C Jaromir Jagr 6/260* 10.00 25.00
7A Teemu Selanne 2/37* 15.00 40.00
7B Teemu Selanne 3/207* 4.00 10.00
7C Teemu Selanne 7/230* 6.00 15.00
8A John Vanbiesbrouck 2/88* 6.00 15.00
8B John Vanbiesbrouck 8/208* 4.00 10.00
8C John Vanbiesbrouck 8/280* 4.00 10.00
9A Brendan Shanahan 3/35* 12.50 30.00
9B Brendan Shanahan 3/305* 4.00 10.00
9C Brendan Shanahan 5/330* 4.00 10.00
10A Steve Yzerman 5/39* 60.00 150.00
10B Steve Yzerman 3/509* 12.50 30.00
10C Steve Yzerman 9/530* 12.50 30.00
11A Joe Sakic 3/7*
11B Joe Sakic 0/307* 6.00 15.00
11C Joe Sakic 7/300* 6.00 15.00
12A Pavel Bure 3/88* 8.00 20.00
12B Pavel Bure 8/308* 4.00 10.00
12C Pavel Bure 8/380* 4.00 10.00

1997-98 Donruss Elite Prime Numbers Die-Cuts

Randomly inserted in packs, this 36-card set was a die-cut parallel version of the regular Prime Numbers set. Each card was serial numbered to the sum of the print run of the basic insert plus the die cut version. Announced production runs are listed below and print runs of less than 10 not priced due to scarcity.

1A Peter Forsberg 2/200* 12.50 30.00
1B Peter Forsberg 5/50* 50.00 125.00
1C Peter Forsberg 4/4*
2A Patrick Roy 3/300* 15.00 40.00
2B Patrick Roy 4/40* 60.00 150.00
2C Patrick Roy 9/9*
3A Mark Messier 2/200* 8.00 20.00
3B Mark Messier 9/90* 12.50 30.00
3C Mark Messier 5/5*
4A Eric Lindros 4/400* 8.00 20.00
4B Eric Lindros 3/30* 20.00 50.00
4C Eric Lindros 6/6*
5A Paul Kariya 2/200* 12.50 30.00
5B Paul Kariya 4/40* 50.00 125.00
5C Paul Kariya 6/6*
6A Jaromir Jagr 2/200* 10.00 25.00
6B Jaromir Jagr 6/60* 30.00 80.00
6C Jaromir Jagr 6/6*
7A Teemu Selanne 2/200* 8.00 20.00
7B Teemu Selanne 3/30* 15.00 40.00
7C Teemu Selanne 7/7*
8A John Vanbiesbrouck 2/200* 8.00 20.00
8B John Vanbiesbrouck 8/80* 12.50 30.00
8C John Vanbiesbrouck 8/8*
9A Brendan Shanahan 3/300* 8.00 20.00
9B Brendan Shanahan 3/30* 20.00 50.00
9C Brendan Shanahan 5/5*
10A Steve Yzerman 5/500* 15.00 40.00
10B Steve Yzerman 3/30* 60.00 150.00
10C Steve Yzerman 9/9*
11A Joe Sakic 3/300* 10.00 25.00
11C Joe Sakic 7/7*
12A Pavel Bure 3/300* 8.00 20.00
12B Pavel Bure 8/80* 12.50 30.00
12C Pavel Bure 8/8*

1998-99 Donruss Elite Promos

ese cards were issued in the summer of 1998 in anticipation of an upcoming Donruss Elite hockey product. Prior to the release of the full set, Donruss went out of business. No regular cards from this set exist. Each card is marked PROMO/2500 on the back, although it is believed that far fewer than 2,500 copies were produced of each, with some probably limited to 100 or less. Some were believed to be easier to acquire than others, including the Sergei Samsonov and Dominik Hasek issue.

1 John LeClair 10.00 25.00
2 Brett Hull 6.00 15.00
3 Saku Koivu 4.00 10.00
4 Mark Messier 10.00 25.00
5 Keith Tkachuk 6.00 15.00
6 Teemu Selanne 15.00 40.00
7 Sergei Samsonov 2.00 5.00
8 Pavel Bure 15.00 40.00
9 Brendan Shanahan 10.00 25.00
10 Dominik Hasek 2.00 5.00
11 Joe Thornton 20.00 50.00
12 Joe Sakic 20.00 50.00
13 Martin Brodeur 10.00 25.00
14 Peter Forsberg 20.00 50.00
15 Steve Yzerman 40.00 100.00
16 Patrick Roy 40.00 100.00
17 Jaromir Jagr 10.00 25.00
18 Paul Kariya 20.00 50.00
19 Eric Lindros 15.00 40.00
20 Wayne Gretzky 40.00 125.00

2010 Donruss Elite National Convention

ANNOUNCED PRINT RUN 499 SETS
41 Alex Ovechkin 1.50 4.00
42 Henrik Sedin 1.25 3.00
43 Jonathan Toews 1.25 3.00
44 Mike Green 1.25 3.00
45 Ryan Miller 1.25 3.00
46 Sidney Crosby 5.00 12.00
47 P.K. Subban 6.00 15.00
48 Nazem Kadri 8.00 20.00

2010 Donruss Elite National Convention Aspirations

*ASPIRATIONS: .8X TO 2X BASIC CARDS
ANNOUNCED PRINT RUN 50

2010 Donruss Elite National Convention Status

*STATUS: .8X TO 2X BASIC CARDS
ANNOUNCED PRINT RUN 25

2011 Donruss Elite National Convention

ANNOUNCED PRINT RUN 500 SETS
*BLUE/10: 2X TO 5X BASIC CARDS
*RED/25: 1.5X TO 4X BASIC CARDS
13 Alex Ovechkin 1.50 3.50
14 Dustin Byfuglien 1.25 3.00
15 Martin Brodeur 1.50 4.00
16 Sidney Crosby 2.00 5.00
17 Steve Stamkos 1.50 4.00
18 Tim Thomas 1.25 3.00

2011 Donruss Rated Rookies National Convention

COMPLETE SET (10)
*RED/25: 1.5X TO 4X BASIC CARDS
RR6 Cam Fowler 1.25 3.00
RR7 Taylor Hall 2.50 6.00
RR8 Tyler Seguin 2.00 5.00
RR9 P.K. Subban 1.50 4.00
RR10 Jeff Skinner 1.50 4.00

1997-98 Donruss Limited

This 200-card set was distributed in five-card packs with a suggested retail price of $4.99 and featured full-bleed player photographs printed on double-sided cards. The set contained the following subsets: Counterparts, which displayed photos of two superstar players connected by their positions utilizing a Poly-Chromium print technology; Double Team, which featured two formidable teammates back-to-back; Star Factor, which highlighted the top stars using a different photo of the same star on each side; and Unlimited Potential/Talent, which combineed a photo of a young rookie on one side and a veteran star's photo on the other.

COMPLETE SET (200) 150.00 400.00
COMP.COUNTERPART.SET (100) 10.00 25.00
1 Brendan Shanahan .25 .60
Harry York C
2 P.Forsberg/M.Knuble RC C .60 1.50
3 Chris Osgood .25 .60
Kirk McLean C
4 Wayne Gretzky S 20.00 50.00
5 John Vanbiesbrouck 1.00 2.50
Ed Jovanovski D
6 Paul Coffey .25 .60
Darryl Sydor C
7 Pavel Bure .25 .60
Valeri Bure C
8 Sergei Berezin 2.00 5.00
Jaromir Jagr U
9 Saku Koivu .15 .40
Mats Sundin C
10 Trevor Kidd .08 .25
Corey Hirsch C
11 Teemu Selanne S 2.50 6.00
12 Zigmund Palffy .08 .25
Radek Bonk C
13 Mats Sundin 1.00 2.50
Sergei Berezin D
14 Jim Carey .08 .25
Bill Ranford C
15 John LeClair .08 .25
Claude Lemieux C
16 Janne Niinimaa 1.50 4.00
Chris Chelios U
17 Kevin Hodson 1.00 2.50
Michael Knuble D
18 Adam Graves .08 .25
Keith Jones C
19 M.Modano/T.Linden C .40 1.00
20 Brett Hull S 4.00 10.00
21 Derian Hatcher .08 .25
Kevin Hatcher C
22 Daniel Alfredsson .08 .25
Dave Andreychuk C
23 Steve Shields 1.00 2.50
Vaclav Varada D
24 Theo Fleury .08 .25
Geoff Courtnall C
25 Mark Messier .25 .60
Dino Ciccarelli C
26 Ryan Smyth S 2.00 5.00
27 Mike Grier 1.00 2.50
Jason Arnott D
28 Ed Belfour .25 .60
Andy Moog C
29 Jarome Iginla 2.00 5.00
Ed Belfour
Martin St. Louis
Jean-Sebastien Giguere
Jose Theodore
Manny Legace
30 Eric Lindros .25 .60
Todd Bertuzzi C
31 Daymond Langkow .08 .25
David Roberts C
32 Mike Richter .15 .40
Grant Fuhr C
33 Adam Oates 1.00 2.50
Jaroslav Svejkovsky D
34 Saku Koivu 1.00 2.50
Darcy Tucker D
35 Paul Kariya S 2.50 6.00
36 J.Sakic/B.Nicholls C .50 1.25
37 Ed Jovanovski .08 .25
D.J. Smith C RC
38 Vaclav Prospal 1.50 4.00
Brendan Shanahan U
39 Mike Peca .08 .25
Marty Murray C
40 Mike Gartner .08 .25
Wendel Clark C
41 Steve Yzerman S 12.00 30.00
42 M.Modano/R.Turek D 1.50 4.00
43 Joe Nieuwendyk .08 .25
Jarome Iginla C
44 P.Roy/J.Thibault C 1.25 3.00
45 Hnat Domenichelli .08 .25
Andrew Cassels C
46 Christian Dube .08 .25
Steve Sullivan C
47 Marc Denis 1.00 2.50
Valeri Kamensky D
48 Peter Forsberg S 6.00 15.00
49 Derek Plante .08 .25
Todd Harvey C
50 Mike Grier 2.50 6.00
Eric Lindros U
51 B.Hull/J.Campbell D 1.25 3.00
52 Mark Recchi .08 .25
Landon Wilson C
53 Darcy Tucker .08 .25
Pascal Rheaume C RC
54 Chris O'Sullivan .08 .25
Anders Eriksson C
55 Jaromir Jagr S 6.00 15.00
56 Paul Kariya 1.00 2.50
Teemu Selanne D
57 Felix Potvin .25 .60
Damian Rhodes C
58 Brian Holzinger .08 .25
Mike Ricci C
59 Eric Fichaud 1.00 2.50
Travis Green D
60 Ethan Moreau .08 .25
John MacLean C
61 Joe Juneau .08 .25
Jeff O'Neill C
62 John Vanbiesbrouck S 2.00 5.00
63 Byron Dafoe .08 .25
Steve Shields C RC
64 Mikael Renberg .08 .25
Niklas Sundstrom C
65 Ryan Smyth .08 .25
Eric Daze C
66 Doug Gilmour 1.00 2.50
Pascal Rheaume D
67 Jim Campbell .08 .25
Craig Janney C
68 Alexander Mogilny .08 .25
Mathew Barnaby C
69 Alexei Yashin S 2.00 5.00
70 Bryan Berard 1.50 4.00
Brian Leetch U
71 Alexei Yashin .08 .25
Brain Savage C
72 Jeff Friesen .08 .25
Darren McCarty C
73 Dimitri Khristich .08 .25
Chad Kilger C
74 M.Brodeur/D.Andreychuk D 2.50 6.00
75 Luc Robitaille .08 .25
Pat Verbeek C
76 D.Hasek/J.Storr C .50 1.25
77 Felix Potvin S 2.50 6.00
78 Mike Dunham 1.00 2.50
Vadim Sharifijanov D
79 Jason Arnott .08 .25
Rob Niedermayer C
80 Eric Desjardins .08 .25
Chris Phillips C
81 Curtis Joseph .25 .60
Jose Theodore C
82 Doug Gilmour .08 .25
Rod Brind'Amour C
83 Keith Tkachuk .25 .60
Rick Tocchet C
84 Mark Messier S 2.50 6.00
85 Chris Pronger .08 .25
Aki Berg C
86 Marcel Cousineau 2.50 6.00
Dominik Hasek U
87 Ethan Moreau 1.00 2.50
Chris Chelios D
88 Jonas Hoglund .08 .25
Rob Zamuner C
89 Ron Hextall .08 .25
Kevin Hodson C
90 John LeClair S 2.50 6.00
91 Vaclav Prospal RC .25 .60
Viktor Kozlov C
92 R.Bourque/J.Thornton D 2.50 6.00
93 Oleg Tverdovsky .08 .25
Sergei Zubov C
94 Ethan Moreau 1.50 4.00
John LeClair U
95 Adam Deadmarsh S 2.00 5.00
96 Jaroslav Svejkovsky .08 .25
Jozef Stumpel C
97 W.Gretzky/V.Vorobiev D 6.00 15.00
98 Sergei Fedorov S 3.00 8.00
99 Jim Campbell 1.50 4.00
Ryan Smyth U
100 Vaclav Prospal 1.00 2.50
Paul Coffey D
101 Wayne Primeau .08 .25
Sean Pronger C
102 Jean Giguere .08 .25
Felix Potvin U
103 Curtis Joseph S 2.50 6.00
104 Pavel Bure 1.00 2.50
Alexander Mogilny D
105 Jeremy Roenick .25 .60
Tony Amonte C
106 Sandis Ozolinsh .08 .25
Kirk McLaren C
107 Anson Carter .08 .25
Steve Kelly C
108 Paul Coffey S 2.00 5.00
109 Dainius Zubrus 2.50 6.00
Peter Forsberg U
110 Travis Green .08 .25
Scott Mellanby C
111 Pat LaFontaine .08 .25
Valeri Kamensky C
112 Adam Oates S 2.00 5.00
113 John Vanbiesbrouck .08 .25
Roman Turek C
114 J.Iginla/P.Kariya U 4.00 10.00
115 S.Yzerman/C.Osgood D 4.00 10.00
116 Marcel Cousineau .60 1.50
Steve Sullivan D
117 Owen Nolan .08 .25
Steve Rucchin C
118 Donald Audette .08 .25
Ted Donato C
119 Geoff Sanderson .75 2.00
Sean Burke D
120 Jeremy Roenick S 4.00 10.00
121 Vladimir Vorobiev RC .08 .25
Andreas Johansson
122 Alexander Mogilny S 2.00 5.00
123 Jocelyn Thibault 1.00 2.50
Terry Ryan D
124 Eric Fichaud .08 .25
Nikolai Khabibulin C
125 R.Bourque/E.Messier RC C .50 1.25
126 S.Fedorov/K.Primeau C .30 .75
127 M.Denis/M.Brodeur U 4.00 10.00
128 Mats Sundin S 2.50 6.00
129 Peter Bondra .08 .25
Roman Vopat C
130 Tommy Salo .08 .25
Corey Schwab C
131 Sergei Samsonov 1.00 2.50
Jim Carey D
132 A.Deadmarsh/J.Sakic D 2.00 5.00
133 Daymond Langkow 1.50 4.00
Keith Tkachuk U
134 Mike Richter S 2.50 6.00
135 Geoff Sanderson .08 .25
Jere Lehtinen C
136 Janne Niinimaa .08 .25
Jamie Pushor C
137 Andreas Dackell .08 .25
Vincent Damphousse C
138 Keith Tkachuk S 2.00 5.00
139 Ray Bourque S 4.00 10.00
140 K.Tkachuk/J.Roenick D 1.25 3.00
141 Rem Murray .08 .25
Ray Sheppard C
142 Peter Schafer .08 .25
Patrick Lalime C
143 Jaroslav Svejkovsky 2.00 5.00
Teemu Selanne U
144 Todd Marchant .08 .25
Tony Granato C
145 Sandis Ozolinsh S 1.50 4.00
146 Roman Hamrlik .25 .60
Nicklas Lidstrom C
147 Dominik Hasek S 6.00 15.00
148 Chris Gratton .08 .25
Daniel Goneau C
149 Martin Brodeur S 8.00 20.00
150 M.Brodeur/S.Fiset C .60 1.50
151 J.Theodore/P.Roy U 8.00 20.00
152 Jose Theodore 1.00 2.50
Mark Recchi D
153 Pavel Bure S 2.50 6.00
154 Sergei Berezin .08 .25
Denis Pederson C
155 Doug Gilmour S 2.00 5.00
156 Peter Nedved .08 .25
Kirk Muller C
157 Theo Fleury S 2.00 5.00
158 Harry York 1.00 2.50
Pierre Turgeon D
159 Andreas Johansson 1.00 2.50
Patrick Lalime D
160 Marcel Cousineau .08 .25
Jeff Hackett C
161 Adam Deadmarsh .08 .25
Alexandre Daigle C
162 Adam Oates .08 .25
Todd Warriner C
163 Zigmund Palffy S 1.50 4.00
164 Ed Belfour S 2.50 6.00
165 S.Koivu/S.Yzerman U 6.00 15.00
166 Chris Chelios .25 .60
Scott Lachance C
167 Jamie Langenbrunner .08 .25
Brandon Convery C
168 Janne Niinimaa .75 2.00
John LeClair D
169 Brendan Shanahan S 2.50 6.00
170 Darren Puppa .08 .25
Garth Snow C
171 Chris Osgood S 2.00 5.00
172 Pierre Turgeon .08 .25
Shane Corson C
173 Doug Weight .75 2.00
Rem Murray D
174 Eric Fichaud 1.50 4.00
Curtis Joseph U
175 Chris Chelios S 2.00 5.00
176 Wade Redden .08 .25
Scott Stevens C
177 Jarome Iginla 1.00 2.50
Theo Fleury D
178 Vaclav Varada .08 .25
Igor Larionov C
179 Brian Leetch S 2.00 5.00
180 Stephane Fiset 1.00 2.50
Roman Vopat D
181 Zigmund Palffy 1.00 2.50
Bryan Berard D
182 Bryan Berard 1.00 2.50
Brian Leetch C
183 Eric Lindros S 2.50 6.00
184 Derek Plante .60 1.50
Brian Holzinger D
185 B.Hull/M.Gelinas C .30 .75
186 Daniel Alfredsson 1.00 2.50
Damian Rhodes D
187 J.Thornton/M.Messier U 4.00 10.00
188 Mike Vernon .08 .25
Ken Wregget C
189 Alexei Yashin .60 1.50
Wade Redden D
190 Joe Sakic S 8.00 20.00
191 Doug Weight .08 .25
Darren Turcotte C
192 Daymond Langkow .08 .25
Darren Puppa C
193 Mike Modano S 4.00 10.00
194 Sean Burke .08 .25
Mike Dunham C
195 Dainius Zubrus .08 .25
Sebastien Bordeleau C
196 Owen Nolan .75 2.00
Jeff Friesen D
197 Vladimir Vorobiev 2.00 5.00
Sergei Fedorov U
198 Patrick Roy S 15.00 40.00
199 Mike Grier .08 .25
Ron Francis C
200 P.Marleau/W.Gretzky U 12.00 30.00
P183 Eric Lindros PROMO .40 1.00

1997-98 Donruss Limited Exposure

ndomly inserted in packs, this 200-card set was a parallel to the base set and featured holographic poly-chromium technology on both sides. The set was designated by an exclusive "Limited Exposure" stamp. Donruss announced that 25 or fewer sets of the Star Factor cards and 40 or less Unlimited cards were produced.
*COUNTERPARTS: 5X TO 10X BASIC CARDS
*DOUBLE TEAM: 5X TO 10X BASIC CARDS
*STAR FACTOR: 2.5X TO 6X BASIC CARDS
*UNLIMITED: 2X TO 5X BASIC CARDS

1997-98 Donruss Limited Fabric of the Game

ndomly inserted in packs, this 72-card partial multi-fractured set featured color player photos distinguished by using three different technologies, each of which represented a different statistical category: Embossed Canvas (Wins), Leather (Goals), and Wood (Assists). Five more levels crossed the sections and were sequentially numbered: Legendary Material (numbered to 100), Hall of Fame Material (numbered to 250), Superstar Material (numbered to 500), Star Material (numbered to 750), and Major Material (numbered to 1000)

ALL MATERIAL TYPES EQUAL VALUE
1 Wayne Gretzky HF 40.00 100.00
2 Martin Brodeur S 6.00 15.00

3 Dainius Zubrus M	1.00	2.50
4 Joe Sakic SS	8.00	20.00
5 Joe Sakic HF	12.00	30.00
6 Sergei Fedorov S	3.00	8.00
7 John Vanbiesbrouck HF	8.00	20.00
8 Saku Koivu M	2.50	6.00
9 Jean-Sebastien Giguere M	2.50	6.00
10 Paul Kariya S	3.00	8.00
11 Mike Richter SS	4.00	10.00
12 Paul Coffey L	10.00	25.00
13 Brendan Shanahan L	20.00	50.00
14 Jaromir Jagr SS	6.00	15.00
15 Felix Potvin SS	6.00	15.00
16 Mats Sundin SS	4.00	10.00
17 Mike Vernon HF	6.00	15.00
18 Keith Tkachuk S	2.00	5.00
19 Doug Gilmour HF	6.00	15.00
20 Patrick Roy L	40.00	100.00
21 Sergei Samsonov M	2.50	6.00
22 Mike Grier M	1.00	2.50
23 Curtis Joseph SS	3.00	8.00
24 Zigmund Palffy S	2.00	5.00
25 Chris Osgood S	2.00	5.00
26 Mats Sundin S	3.00	8.00
27 Kelly Hrudey HF	6.00	15.00
28 Brett Hull L	25.00	60.00
29 Ray Bourque HF	10.00	25.00
30 Nikolai Khabibulin S	2.00	5.00
31 Bryan Berard M	1.00	2.50
32 Jaroslav Svejkovsky M	1.00	2.50
33 Ed Belfour SS	4.00	10.00
34 Wayne Gretzky I	75.00	200.00
35 Jeremy Roenick SS	5.00	12.00
36 Andy Moog L	10.00	25.00
37 Eric Lindros S	3.00	8.00
38 Brett Hull SS	5.00	12.00
39 Marcel Cousineau M	1.00	2.50
40 Paul Kariya M	2.50	6.00
41 Mike Dunham M	1.00	2.50
42 Chris Phillips M	1.00	2.50
43 Teemu Selanne SS	6.00	15.00
44 Mark Messier L	15.00	40.00
45 Grant Fuhr L	15.00	40.00
46 Daniel Alfredsson M	1.50	4.00
47 Marc Denis M	1.00	2.50
48 Daymond Langkow M	1.00	2.50
49 Steve Yzerman HF	20.00	50.00
50 Ryan Smyth S	2.00	5.00
51 Alexander Mogilny HF	6.00	15.00
52 Ron Hextall HF	8.00	20.00
53 Brendan Shanahan S	3.00	8.00
54 Jim Carey S	2.00	5.00
55 Eric Lindros S	3.00	8.00
56 Eric Fichaud M	1.00	2.50
57 Sergei Berezin M	1.00	2.50
58 Chris Chelios HF	6.00	15.00
59 Mark Messier HF	10.00	25.00
60 Damian Rhodes M	2.50	6.00
61 Jarome Iginla M	3.00	8.00
62 Jocelyn Thibault S	2.00	5.00
63 John LeClair S	2.00	5.00
64 Brian Leetch SS	4.00	10.00
65 Dominik Hasek S	6.00	15.00
66 Pavel Bure SS	4.00	10.00
67 Mike Modano S	4.00	10.00
68 Daniel Cleary M	1.00	2.50
69 Janne Niinimaa M	1.00	2.50
70 Steve Yzerman L	40.00	100.00
71 Jose Theodore M	3.00	6.00
72 Peter Forsberg S	5.00	12.00

1997-98 Donruss Preferred

The 1997-98 Donruss Preferred set was issued in one series totaling 200 cards and distributed in five-card packs inside collectible tins. The set featured color player photos on an all micro-etched foil board card with bronze, silver, gold, and platinum finishes.

COMPLETE SET (200)	200.00	400.00
COMP.BRONZE SET (100)	12.50	30.00
1 Dominik Hasek G	8.00	20.00
2 Peter Forsberg G	10.00	25.00
3 Brendan Shanahan P	8.00	20.00
4 Wayne Gretzky P	20.00	50.00
5 Eric Lindros P	8.00	20.00
6 Keith Tkachuk G	4.00	10.00
7 Mark Messier P	8.00	20.00
8 Mike Modano G	6.00	15.00
9 John Vanbiesbrouck P	8.00	20.00
10 Paul Kariya P	8.00	20.00
11 Saku Koivu G	4.00	10.00
12 Paul Coffey B	.25	.60
13 Joe Juneau B	.20	.50
14 Jeff Friesen S	.75	2.00
15 Brett Hull G	5.00	12.00
16 Martin Brodeur G	10.00	25.00
17 Jarome Iginla G	5.00	12.00
18 Keith Primeau S	.75	2.00
19 Ed Jovanovski B	.20	.50
20 Jamie Langenbrunner B	.08	.25
21 Derian Hatcher S	.75	2.00
22 Brian Leetch G	4.00	10.00
23 Daymond Langkow S	1.50	4.00
24 Ray Bourque S	3.00	8.00
25 Pavel Bure G	2.50	6.00
26 Janne Niinimaa S	1.50	4.00
27 Jamie Storr S	1.50	4.00
28 Darcy Tucker B	.08	.25
29 Anson Carter B	.20	.50
30 Jeff O'Neill B	.08	.25
31 Jason Arnott G	1.50	4.00
32 Tommy Salo B	.20	.50
33 Petr Nedved B	.20	.50
34 Mike Peca B	.20	.50
35 Ethan Moreau S	.75	2.00
36 Ray Sheppard B	.20	.50
37 Damian Rhodes B	.20	.50
38 Mats Sundin S	2.00	5.00
39 Alexander Mogilny G	3.00	8.00
40 Mike Dunham S	1.50	4.00
41 Steve Yzerman P	15.00	40.00
42 Alexei Yashin S	.75	2.00
43 Jim Carey S	1.50	4.00
44 Mike Grier S	.75	2.00
45 Steve Rucchin B	.08	.25
46 Mark Recchi S	.75	2.00
47 Mike Gartner B	.20	.50
48 Alexandre Daigle S	1.50	4.00
49 Eric Fichaud G	3.00	8.00
50 Harry York B	.08	.25
51 Dino Ciccarelli B	.20	.50
52 Bill Ranford B	.20	.50
53 Adam Deadmarsh G	1.50	4.00
54 Ed Belfour B	.25	.60
55 Jozef Stumpel S	1.50	4.00
56 Rem Murray B	.08	.25
57 Pat Verbeek B	.08	.25
58 Pat LaFontaine S	1.50	4.00
59 Dainius Zubrus S	1.50	4.00
60 Grant Fuhr B	.20	.50
61 Rob Niedermayer B	.20	.50
62 Brian Savage B	.08	.25
63 Gary Roberts B	.08	.25
64 Tony Amonte B	.20	.50
65 Jere Lehtinen B	.20	.50
66 Dave Andreychuk B	.20	.50
67 Rod Brind'Amour B	.20	.50
68 Mikael Renberg B	.20	.50
69 Doug Gilmour S	1.50	4.00
70 Kevin Hatcher B	.08	.25
71 Byron Dafoe B	.20	.50
72 Derek Plante S	.75	2.00
73 Trevor Kidd B	.20	.50
74 Doug Weight S	1.50	4.00
75 Valeri Bure B	.08	.25
76 John LeClair G	4.00	10.00
77 Sergei Berezin B	.20	.50
78 Peter Bondra S	1.50	4.00
79 Bryan Berard G	3.00	8.00
80 Steve Shields B RC	.25	.60
81 Chris Osgood G	3.00	8.00
82 Mike Vernon B	.20	.50
83 Martin Gelinas B	.20	.50
84 Curtis Joseph S	2.00	5.00
85 Geoff Sanderson S	1.50	4.00
86 Patrick Roy P	15.00	40.00
87 Jocelyn Thibault G	3.00	8.00
88 Jeremy Roenick S	2.50	6.00
89 Trevor Linden B	.20	.50
90 Daniel Alfredsson S	1.50	4.00
91 Sergei Zubov B	.08	.25
92 Dimitri Khristich S	.75	2.00
93 Brian Holzinger B	.08	.25
94 Andrew Cassels B	.08	.25
95 Teemu Selanne G	4.00	10.00
96 Ron Hextall B	.20	.50
97 Wade Redden B	.08	.25
98 Jim Campbell B	.08	.25
99 Felix Potvin G	5.00	12.00
100 Adam Oates S	1.50	4.00
101 Nikolai Khabibulin B	.20	.50
102 Jose Theodore S	2.50	6.00
103 Sandis Ozolinsh S	.75	2.00
104 Sean Burke B	.20	.50
105 Vaclav Prospal G RC	3.00	8.00
106 Zigmund Palffy G	3.00	8.00
107 Kyle McLaren B	.08	.25
108 Owen Nolan S	1.50	4.00
109 Chris Pronger S	1.50	4.00
110 Daren Puppa B	.20	.50
111 Garth Snow B	.20	.50
112 Aki Berg B	.08	.25
113 Andy Moog B	.20	.50
114 Darren McCarty B	.08	.25
115 Joe Nieuwendyk B	.20	.50
116 Eric Daze S	1.50	4.00
117 Pierre Turgeon S	1.50	4.00
118 Ken Wregget B	.20	.50
119 Ryan Smyth G	3.00	8.00
120 Kirk Muller B	.08	.25
121 Luc Robitaille B	.20	.50
122 Sergei Fedorov G	6.00	15.00
123 Sean Pronger B	.08	.25
124 Mike Richter S	2.00	5.00
125 Jaromir Jagr P	8.00	20.00
126 Claude Lemieux B	.08	.25
127 Chris Chelios S	2.00	5.00
128 Joe Sakic P	12.50	30.00
129 Guy Hebert S	1.50	4.00
130 Chris Gratton S	1.50	4.00
131 Steve Sullivan B	.08	.25
132 Al MacInnis B	.20	.50
133 Adam Graves S	.75	2.00
134 Vyacheslav Kozlov B	.08	.25
135 Scott Mellanby S	.75	2.00
136 Stephane Fiset B	.20	.50
137 Oleg Tverdovsky S	.75	2.00
138 Theo Fleury S	.75	2.00
139 Jeff Hackett B	.20	.50
140 Vincent Damphousse B	.08	.25
141 Roman Hamrlik S	.75	2.00
142 Ron Francis S	1.50	4.00
143 Scott Lachance B	.08	.25
144 Todd Harvey B	.08	.25
145 Marc Denis S	1.50	4.00
146 Jaroslav Svejkovsky G	3.00	8.00
147 Olli Jokinen S RC	6.00	15.00
148 Sergei Samsonov G	3.00	8.00
149 Chris Phillips G	1.50	4.00
150 Patrick Marleau G	8.00	20.00
151 Joe Thornton G	10.00	25.00
152 Daniel Cleary S	1.50	4.00
153 Alyn McCauley G	3.00	8.00
154 Brad Isbister S	.75	2.00
155 Alexei Morozov S	2.00	5.00
156 Shawn Bates B RC	.08	.25
157 Jean-Yves Leroux B RC	.08	.25
158 Marcel Cousineau B	.20	.50
159 Vaclav Varada B	.08	.25
160 Jean-Sebastien Giguere S	1.50	4.00
161 Espen Knutsen B RC	.75	2.00
162 Marian Hossa S RC	15.00	30.00
163 Robert Dome B RC	.08	.25
164 Juha Lind B RC	.08	.25
165 Sergei Fedorov NT B	.40	1.00
166 Jarome Iginla NT B	.30	.75
167 Jaroslav Svejkovsky NT B	.20	.50
168 Patrick Roy NT S	10.00	25.00
169 Dominik Hasek NT B	.50	1.25
170 Alexander Mogilny NT B	.20	.50
171 Chris Chelios NT B	.25	.60
172 Wayne Gretzky NT S	12.50	30.00
173 Peter Forsberg NT B	.60	1.50
174 Ray Bourque NT B	.40	1.00
175 Joe Sakic NT S	4.00	10.00
176 Mike Modano NT B	.25	.60
177 Mark Messier NT B	.25	.60
178 Teemu Selanne NT B	.25	.60
179 Steve Yzerman NT S	10.00	25.00
180 Eric Lindros NT S	2.00	5.00
181 Doug Weight NT B	.20	.50
182 John Vanbiesbrouck NT B	.20	.50
183 Paul Kariya NT S	2.00	5.00
184 Brendan Shanahan NT S	2.00	5.00
185 Martin Brodeur NT B	.60	1.50
186 Bryan Berard NT B	.20	.50
187 Marc Denis NT B	.20	.50
188 Brian Leetch NT B	.25	.60
109 Ryan Smyth NT S	2.00	5.00
190 Dainius Zubrus NT B	.20	.50
191 Keith Tkachuk NT B	.25	.60
192 Jaromir Jagr NT S	3.00	8.00
193 Brett Hull NT B	.30	.75
194 Pavel Bure NT B	.25	.60
195 Sergei Samsonov B	.20	.50
196 Olli Jokinen B	.40	1.00
197 Chris Phillips B	.20	.50
198 Patrick Marleau B	.60	1.50
199 Daniel Cleary B	.20	.50
200 Joe Thornton B	.75	2.00

1997-98 Donruss Preferred Cut to the Chase

Randomly inserted in packs, this 200-card set was a die-cut parallel version of the base set. Each card featured a background of bronze, silver gold, or platinum.

*BRONZE VETS: 4X TO 10X BASIC CARDS
*BRONZE ROOKIES: 2X TO 5X
*SILVER VETS: 1.5X TO 4X BASIC CARDS
*SILVER ROOKIES: 1X TO 2.5X
*GOLD: 1.2X TO 3X BASIC CARDS
*PLATINUM: 1X TO 2.5X BASIC CARDS

162 Marian Hossa S	60.00	100.00

1997-98 Donruss Preferred Color Guard

ndomly inserted in packs, this 18-card set featured color images of top puckstoppers printed on die-cut plastic cards with the player's team colors in the background. The set was sequentially numbered to 1500.

*PROMOS: .6X TO 1.5X BASIC INSERTS

1 Patrick Roy	15.00	40.00
2 Martin Brodeur	10.00	25.00
3 Curtis Joseph	5.00	12.00
4 John Vanbiesbrouck	3.00	8.00
5 Felix Potvin	5.00	12.00
6 Dominik Hasek	6.00	15.00
7 Chris Osgood	4.00	10.00
8 Eric Fichaud	3.00	8.00
9 Jocelyn Thibault	2.00	5.00
10 Marc Denis	3.00	8.00
11 Jose Theodore	5.00	12.00
12 Mike Vernon	3.00	8.00
13 Jim Carey	2.50	6.00
14 Ron Hextall	3.00	8.00
15 Mike Richter	4.00	10.00
16 Ed Belfour	4.00	10.00
17 Mike Dunham	2.50	6.00
18 Damian Rhodes	3.00	8.00

1997-98 Donruss Preferred Line of the Times

ndomly inserted in packs, this 24-card set featured color photos of star players printed on die-cut cards and utilizing micro-etching technology. Three cards were made to be placed side by side to form one interactive card which spelled out a particular word in the background. The set was sequentially numbered to 2500.

COMPLETE SET (24)	125.00	250.00
*PROMO: .3X TO .8X BASIC INSERTS		
1A Ryan Smyth	2.50	6.00
1B Sergei Fedorov	5.00	12.00
1C Jaromir Jagr	5.00	12.00
2A Eric Lindros	4.00	10.00
2B Joe Thornton	4.00	10.00
2C Brendan Shanahan	4.00	10.00
3A John LeClair	3.00	8.00
3B Keith Tkachuk	3.00	8.00
3C Brett Hull	4.00	10.00
4A Pavel Bure	4.00	10.00
4B Sergei Samsonov	2.50	6.00
4C Paul Kariya	3.00	8.00
5A Mike Modano	4.00	10.00
5B Teemu Selanne	3.00	8.00
5C Patrick Marleau	2.50	6.00
6A Wayne Gretzky	12.00	30.00
6B Steve Yzerman	8.00	20.00
6C Daniel Cleary	2.50	6.00
7A Jarome Iginla	4.00	10.00
7B Peter Forsberg	3.00	8.00
7C Mark Messier	3.00	8.00
8A Joe Sakic	6.00	15.00
8B Jaroslav Svejkovsky	2.00	5.00
8C Dainius Zubrus	2.00	5.00

1997-98 Donruss Preferred Precious Metals

is 15-card set is a partial parallel version of the base set. The player photos are printed on cards that contain one gram (roughly .032 troy ounce) of actual .999 silver, gold, or platinum. It was announced that no more than 100 of each card was produced.

1 Brendan Shanahan P	50.00	100.00
2 Joe Thornton G	60.00	150.00
3 Wayne Gretzky P	200.00	400.00
4 Mark Messier P	75.00	150.00
5 Patrick Roy P	100.00	200.00
6 Martin Brodeur G	75.00	150.00
7 Eric Lindros P	60.00	120.00
8 Paul Kariya P	40.00	100.00
9 Teemu Selanne G	60.00	120.00
10 Jaromir Jagr P	75.00	150.00
11 Joe Sakic P	60.00	150.00
12 Peter Forsberg G	100.00	200.00
13 John Vanbiesbrouck P	60.00	120.00
14 Steve Yzerman P	125.00	250.00
15 Sergei Samsonov G	40.00	80.00

1997-98 Donruss Preferred Tin Packs

This 24-tin set features color images printed on special tin containers of the NHL players who played in the 1998 Winter Olympic Games on either the Canadian or United States teams. The larger US tin outer boxes are highlighted in blue and limited to 499 serial numbered sets, and the Canadian version is highlighted in red and also limited to 499 sets. There was also a gold version of these tin packs which were originally slated to be included in boxes, but was later available only through the manufacturer. Golds were limited to 499 serial numbered sets. Prices below refer to opened packs.

COMPLETE SET (24)	8.00	20.00
*GOLD PACK/499: 4X TO 10X BASIC TIN		
*BLUE BOX/499: 2.5X TO 6X BASIC TIN		
*RED PACK: .4X TO 1X BASIC TIN		
*RED BOX/499: 2.5X TO 6X BASIC TIN		
1 Eric Lindros	.25	.60
2 Paul Kariya	.50	1.25
3 Wayne Gretzky	1.00	2.50
4 Teemu Selanne	.30	.75
5 Patrick Roy	.75	2.00
6 John Vanbiesbrouck	.25	.60
7 Mike Modano	.25	.60
8 Joe Sakic	.30	.75
9 Peter Forsberg	.40	1.00
10 Martin Brodeur	.40	1.00
11 Sergei Samsonov	.40	1.00
12 Brendan Shanahan	.25	.60
13 Steve Yzerman	.60	1.50
14 Jaromir Jagr	.40	1.00
15 Mark Messier	.20	.50
16 Joe Thornton	.40	1.00
17 Pavel Bure	.40	1.00
18 Brett Hull	.20	.50
19 Brendan Shanahan MC	.25	.60
20 Jaromir Jagr MC	.40	1.00
21 Eric Lindros MC	.25	.60
22 Paul Kariya MC	.50	1.25
23 Wayne Gretzky MC	1.00	2.50
24 Patrick Roy MC	.75	2.00

1997-98 Donruss Preferred Tin Packs Double Wide

These packages contained five Donruss Preferred cards, but are considered collectibles themselves by virture of the pair of players pictured on the front.

COMPLETE SET (12)	10.00	25.00
1 W.Gretzky/J.Thornton	1.25	3.00
2 P.Kariya/B.Hull	.50	1.25
3 E.Lindros/J.Sakic	.50	1.25
4 T.Selanne/P.Forsberg	.60	1.50
5 P.Bure/M.Modano	.60	1.50
6 S.Samsonov/S.Yzerman	1.50	4.00
7 J.Jagr/B.Shanahan	.50	1.25
8 M.Messier/J.Vanbiesbrouck	.40	1.00
9 P.Roy/M.Brodeur	1.25	3.00
10 B.Shanahan/E.Lindros	.40	1.00
11 J.Jagr/P.Kariya	1.00	2.50
12 W.Gretzky/P.Roy	1.50	4.00

1997-98 Donruss Priority

The 1997-98 Donruss Priority hobby only set was issued in one series totaling 220 cards and was distributed in two-types of five-card packs, postcard and stamp packs, with a suggested retail price of $4.99. Postcard packs had a 5" by 7" horizontal format and contained only even numbered cards from the set. The odd numbered cards were twice as scarce and could be found only in the stamp packs. The fronts featured color action player photos printed with foil treatments, while the backs carried player information. The set contained the topical subset: 1st Class Package (185-214). The set was released towards the end of the 97-98 NHL season.

COMPLETE SET (220)	25.00	50.00
1 Patrick Roy SP	1.25	3.00
2 Eric Lindros	.20	.50
3 Keith Tkachuk SP	.15	.40
4 Steve Yzerman	.75	2.00
5 John Vanbiesbrouck SP	.25	.60
6 Teemu Selanne	.20	.50
7 Martin Brodeur SP	.60	1.50
8 Peter Forsberg	.40	1.00
9 Brett Hull SP	.30	.75
10 Wayne Gretzky	1.00	2.50
11 Mike Modano SP	.40	1.00
12 Sergei Fedorov	.25	.60
13 Paul Kariya SP	.60	1.50
14 Saku Koivu	.20	.50
15 Pavel Bure SP	.25	.60
16 Mark Messier	.20	.50
17 Joe Sakic SP	.50	1.25
18 Jaromir Jagr	.25	.60
19 Brendan Shanahan SP	.25	.60
20 Ray Bourque	.25	.60
21 Daymond Langkow SP	.10	.30
22 Alexandre Daigle	.07	.20
23 Dainius Zubrus SP	.10	.30
24 Ryan Smyth	.10	.30
25 Derek Plante SP	.10	.30
26 Eric Daze	.10	.30
27 Ed Jovanovski SP	.10	.30
28 Sergei Berezin	.07	.20
29 Roman Turek SP	.15	.40
30 Derian Hatcher	.07	.20
31 Jarome Iginla SP	.25	.60
32 Luc Robitaille	.10	.30
33 Rod Brind'Amour SP	.15	.40
34 Mathieu Schneider	.07	.20
35 Olaf Kolzig SP	.15	.40
36 Nikolai Khabibulin	.10	.30
37 Scott Niedermayer SP	.10	.30
38 Keith Primeau	.07	.20
39 Dimitri Khristich SP	.10	.30
40 Eric Fichaud	.10	.30
41 Pierre Turgeon SP	.15	.40
42 Kevin Stevens	.07	.20
43 Nicklas Lidstrom SP	.10	.30
44 Sean Burke	.10	.30
45 Sandis Ozolinsh SP	.10	.30
46 Owen Nolan	.10	.30
47 Peter Bondra SP	.25	.60
48 Ron Hextall	.10	.30
49 Rob Blake SP	.10	.30
50 Geoff Sanderson	.10	.30
51 Sergei Zubov SP	.10	.30
52 Doug Gilmour	.10	.30
53 Oleg Tverdovsky SP	.10	.30
54 Bryan Berard	.07	.20
55 Bill Ranford SP	.15	.40
56 Mats Sundin	.20	.50
57 Damian Rhodes SP	.15	.40
58 Zigmund Palffy	.10	.30
59 Mike Grier SP	.10	.30
60 Jozef Stumpel	.10	.30
61 Mark Recchi SP	.10	.30
62 Alexei Zhamnov	.07	.20
63 Jere Lehtinen SP	.10	.30
64 Andrew Cassels	.07	.20
65 Kevin Hodson SP	.15	.40
66 Dino Ciccarelli	.10	.30
67 Niklas Sundstrom SP	.10	.30
68 Jeff Hackett	.10	.30
69 Brian Holzinger SP	.15	.40
70 Jeff Friesen	.07	.20
71 Ed Belfour SP	.25	.60
72 Wayne Primeau	.07	.20
73 Sami Kapanen SP	.10	.30
74 Brian Leetch	.10	.30
75 Mikael Renberg SP	.15	.40
76 Ron Tugnutt	.10	.30
77 Ron Francis SP	.15	.40
78 Jocelyn Thibault	.10	.30
79 Jamie Langenbrunner SP	.10	.30
80 Dominik Hasek	.30	.75
81 Chris Osgood SP	.15	.40
82 Grant Fuhr	.10	.30
83 Adam Graves SP	.10	.30
84 Janne Niinimaa	.10	.30
85 Kelly Hrudey SP	.15	.40
86 Mike Dunham	.10	.30
87 Valeri Kamensky SP	.15	.40
88 Cory Stillman	.07	.20
89 Anson Carter SP	.10	.30
90 Igor Larionov	.07	.20
91 Chris Pronger SP	.15	.40
92 Steve Sullivan	.07	.20
93 Mike Gartner SP	.15	.40
94 Jim Campbell	.10	.30
95 Valeri Bure SP	.10	.30
96 Stephane Fiset	.10	.30
97 Jason Arnott SP	.10	.30
98 Trevor Kidd	.10	.30
99 Chris Chelios SP	.25	.60
100 Kevin Hatcher	.07	.20
101 Felix Potvin SP	.30	.75
102 Travis Green	.07	.20
103 Dave Gagner SP	.10	.30
104 Byron Dafoe	.10	.30
105 Rick Tabaracci SP	.15	.40
106 Gary Roberts	.07	.20
107 Mike Ricci SP	.10	.30
108 Andy Moog	.10	.30
109 Sean Pronger SP	.10	.30
110 Paul Coffey	.10	.30
111 Trevor Linden SP	.15	.40
112 Rob Zamuner	.07	.20
113 Daniel Alfredsson SP	.15	.40
114 Ray Sheppard	.10	.30
115 Steve Shields SP RC	.40	1.00
116 Ethan Moreau	.07	.20
117 Tomas Sandstrom SP	.10	.30
118 Chris Gratton	.10	.30
119 Alexander Mogilny SP	.15	.40
120 Roman Hamrlik	.07	.20
121 Tommy Salo SP	.15	.40
122 Jason Allison	.07	.20
123 Curtis Joseph SP	.25	.60
124 Guy Hebert	.10	.30
125 Jeff O'Neill SP	.10	.30
126 Donald Audette	.07	.20
127 Claude Lemieux SP	.10	.30
128 Brian Savage	.07	.20
129 Scott Mellanby SP	.10	.30
130 Vyacheslav Kozlov	.10	.30
131 Wade Redden SP	.10	.30
132 John LeClair	.20	.50
133 Jeremy Roenick SP	.25	.60
134 Andreas Johansson	.07	.20
135 Nelson Emerson SP	.10	.30
136 Daren Puppa	.10	.30
137 Joe Juneau SP	.15	.40
138 Garth Snow	.10	.30
139 Tom Barrasso SP	.15	.40
140 Joe Nieuwendyk	.10	.30
141 Theo Fleury SP	.10	.30
142 Yanic Perreault	.07	.20
143 Mike Richter SP	.25	.60
144 Al MacInnis	.10	.30
145 Mike Peca SP	.15	.40
146 Darren McCarty	.07	.20
147 Alexei Yashin SP	.10	.30
148 Rick Tocchet	.10	.30
149 Adam Oates SP	.15	.40
150 Wendel Clark	.07	.20
151 Tony Amonte SP	.15	.40
152 Dave Andreychuk	.07	.20
153 Jamie Storr SP	.15	.40
154 Craig Janney	.10	.30
155 Todd Bertuzzi SP	.10	.30
156 Harry York	.07	.20
157 Todd Harvey SP	.10	.30
158 Bobby Holik	.07	.20
159 Mike Vernon SP	.15	.40
160 Pat LaFontaine	.10	.30
161 Doug Weight SP	.15	.40
162 Kirk McLean	.10	.30
163 Adam Deadmarsh SP	.10	.30
164 Vincent Damphousse	.07	.20
165 Vaclav Prospal SP RC	.15	.40
166 Daniel Cleary	.10	.30
167 Jaroslav Svejkovsky SP	.15	.40
168 Marco Sturm RC	.20	.50
169 Robert Dome SP RC	.10	.30
170 Patrik Elias RC	.50	1.25
171 Mattias Ohlund SP	.15	.40
172 Espen Knutsen RC	.20	.50
173 Joe Thornton SP	.60	1.50
174 Jan Bulis RC	.07	.20
175 Patrick Marleau SP	.40	1.00
176 Brad Isbister	.07	.20
177 Kevin Weekes SP RC	1.00	2.50
178 Sergei Samsonov	.10	.30
179 Tyler Moss RC SP	.10	.30
180 Chris Phillips	.07	.20
181 Alyn McCauley SP	.10	.30
182 Derek Morris RC	.10	.30
183 Alexei Morozov SP	.15	.40
184 Boyd Devereaux	.07	.20
185 Peter Forsberg SP	.15	.40
186 Brendan Shanahan	.10	.30
187 Teemu Selanne SP	.15	.40
188 Eric Lindros	.10	.30
189 Mark Messier SP	.15	.40
190 Vaclav Prospal	.10	.30
191 Jarome Iginla SP	.25	.60
192 Mike Modano	.10	.30
193 John Vanbiesbrouck SP	.15	.40
194 Bryan Berard	.07	.20
195 Patrick Marleau SP	.15	.40
196 Martin Brodeur	.10	.30
197 Patrick Roy SP	1.25	3.00
198 Felix Potvin	.25	.60
199 Wayne Gretzky SP	1.50	4.00
200 Sergei Samsonov	.10	.30
201 Ryan Smyth SP	.15	.40
202 Keith Tkachuk	.20	.50
203 Chris Osgood SP	.15	.40
204 Paul Kariya	.10	.30
205 John LeClair SP	.25	.60
206 Alyn McCauley	.10	.30
207 Joe Thornton SP	.40	1.00
208 Joe Sakic	.10	.30
209 Steve Yzerman SP	1.25	3.00
210 Saku Koivu	.20	.50
211 Pavel Bure SP	.15	.40
212 Zigmund Palffy	.10	.30
213 Alexei Yashin SP	.10	.30
214 Sergei Fedorov	.10	.30
215 Joe Thornton CL SP	.40	1.00
216 Patrick Marleau CL	.10	.30
217 Daniel Cleary CL SP	.10	.30
218 Sergei Samsonov CL	.10	.30
219 Jaroslav Svejkovsky CL SP	.10	.30
220 Alyn McCauley CL	.07	.20

1997-98 Donruss Priority Stamp of Approval

is 220-card set was a parallel to the base set. Each card was randomly inserted into packs and was serial numbered out of 100. Card design featured a deckle edge similar to a postage stamp, and design front was different from that of the base set.

*EVEN CARD #: 20X TO 50X BASIC CARDS
*ODD CARD #: 15X TO 40X BASIC CARDS

1997-98 Donruss Priority Direct Deposit

ndomly inserted in packs, this 30-card set featured color action photos of top goal scorers printed on swirled-look foil board with micro etching. The cards were sequentially numbered to just 3,000.

COMPLETE SET (30)	100.00	200.00
*PROMOS: .3X TO .8X BASIC INSERTS		
1 Brendan Shanahan	2.50	6.00
2 Steve Yzerman	8.00	20.00
3 Pavel Bure	2.50	6.00
4 Jaromir Jagr	4.00	10.00
5 Ryan Smyth	1.50	4.00
6 Sergei Samsonov	1.50	4.00
7 Mark Messier	2.50	6.00
8 Wayne Gretzky	10.00	25.00
9 Jarome Iginla	3.00	8.00
10 Peter Forsberg	6.00	15.00
11 Joe Sakic	5.00	12.00
12 Sergei Fedorov	4.00	10.00
13 Mike Modano	4.00	10.00
14 Paul Kariya	2.50	6.00
15 Teemu Selanne	2.50	6.00
16 Eric Lindros	2.50	6.00
17 Keith Tkachuk	2.50	6.00
18 Patrick Marleau	1.50	4.00
19 Jaroslav Svejkovsky	1.50	4.00
20 Alyn McCauley	1.50	4.00
21 Saku Koivu	2.50	6.00
22 Zigmund Palffy	1.50	4.00
23 Brett Hull	3.00	8.00
24 Patrik Elias	2.50	6.00
25 Joe Thornton	6.00	15.00
26 Espen Knutsen	1.50	4.00
27 Daniel Alfredsson	2.00	5.00
28 John LeClair	2.50	6.00
29 Dainius Zubrus	1.50	4.00
30 Jason Arnott	1.50	4.00

1997-98 Donruss Priority Postcards

serted one per large pack, this 36-card set featured standard postcard sized cards.

COMPLETE SET (36)	20.00	50.00
*OPEN.DAY/1000: 2X TO 5X BASIC INSERTS		
1 Patrick Roy	2.50	6.00
2 Brendan Shanahan	.50	1.25
3 Steve Yzerman	2.50	6.00
4 Jaromir Jagr	.75	2.00
5 Pavel Bure	.60	1.50
6 Mark Messier	.50	1.25
7 Wayne Gretzky	3.00	8.00
8 Eric Lindros	.60	1.50
9 Joe Sakic	1.00	2.50
10 Peter Forsberg	1.25	3.00
11 John Vanbiesbrouck	.50	1.25
12 Mike Modano	.75	2.00
13 Paul Kariya	.50	1.25
14 Teemu Selanne	.50	1.25
15 Sergei Fedorov	.75	2.00
16 Joe Thornton	1.25	3.00
17 Sergei Samsonov	.40	1.00
18 Patrick Marleau	.75	2.00
19 Ryan Smyth	.40	1.00
20 Jarome Iginla	.60	1.50
21 John LeClair	.50	1.25
22 Brian Leetch	.50	1.25
23 Chris Chelios	.50	1.25
24 Martin Brodeur	1.25	3.00
25 Bryan Berard	.40	1.00
26 Keith Tkachuk	.50	1.25
27 Saku Koivu	.50	1.25
28 Brett Hull	.60	1.50
29 Felix Potvin	1.00	2.50
30 Chris Osgood	.40	1.00
31 Dominik Hasek	1.00	2.50
32 Zigmund Palffy	.40	1.00
33 Jeremy Roenick	.60	1.50
34 Dainius Zubrus	.40	1.00
35 Ray Bourque	.75	2.00
36 Jocelyn Thibault	.40	1.00

1997-98 Donruss Priority Postmaster Generals

ndomly inserted in packs, this 20-card set featured color photos of top goalies printed on all-foil board with foil stamping. Only 1,500 of each card were produced and sequentially numbered.

COMPLETE SET (20)	40.00	80.00
*PROMO: .3X TO .8X BASIC INSERTS		
1 Patrick Roy	12.00	30.00
2 John Vanbiesbrouck	2.00	5.00
3 Felix Potvin	3.00	8.00
4 Curtis Joseph	3.00	8.00
5 Mike Richter	2.00	5.00
6 Jocelyn Thibault	1.00	2.50
7 Ed Belfour	2.00	5.00
8 Chris Osgood	2.00	5.00
9 Ron Hextall	2.00	5.00
10 Martin Brodeur	8.00	20.00
11 Mike Vernon	2.00	5.00
12 Eric Fichaud	1.00	2.50
13 Dominik Hasek	6.00	15.00
14 Byron Dafoe	1.00	2.50
15 Tommy Salo	1.00	2.50
16 Garth Snow	1.00	2.50
17 Tom Barrasso	1.00	2.50
18 Marc Denis	1.00	2.50
19 Grant Fuhr	2.00	5.00
20 Guy Hebert	1.00	2.50

1997-98 Donruss Priority Stamps

Randomly inserted one per small pack, this 36-card set featured color photos of top NHL players printed on real currency stamps. Printed in the country of Grenada, each stamp came protected in a stamp holder card. Bronze, silver, and gold parallel versions of this set were also produced with an insertion rate of 1:6.

COMPLETE SET (36)	20.00	40.00
*BRONZE: .8X TO 2X BASIC INSERTS		
*SILVER: 1.5X TO 4X BASIC INSERTS		
*GOLD: 3X TO 8X BASIC INSERTS		
1 Patrick Roy	2.50	6.00
2 Brendan Shanahan	.50	1.25
3 Steve Yzerman	2.50	6.00
4 Jaromir Jagr	.75	2.00
5 Pavel Bure	.50	1.25
6 Mark Messier	.50	1.25
7 Wayne Gretzky	3.00	8.00
8 Eric LIndros	.50	1.25
9 Joe Sakic	1.00	2.50
10 Peter Forsberg	1.25	3.00
11 John Vanbiesbrouck	.40	1.00
12 Mike Modano	.75	2.00
13 Paul Kariya	.50	1.25
14 Teemu Selanne	.50	1.25
15 Sergei Fedorov	.75	2.00
16 Joe Thornton	1.25	3.00
17 Sergei Samsonov	.40	1.00
18 Patrick Marleau	1.00	2.50
19 Ryan Smyth	.40	1.00
20 Jarome Iginla	.60	1.50
21 John LeClair	.50	1.25
22 Brian Leetch	.40	1.00
23 Chris Chelios	.40	1.00
24 Martin Brodeur	1.25	3.00
25 Bryan Berard	.40	1.00
26 Keith Tkachuk	.50	1.25
27 Saku Koivu	.50	1.25
28 Brett Hull	.60	1.50
29 Felix Potvin	.50	1.25
30 Chris Osgood	.40	1.00
31 Dominik Hasek	1.00	2.50
32 Zigmund Palffy	.40	1.00
33 Jeremy Roenick	.60	1.50
34 Dainius Zubrus	.40	1.00
35 Ray Bourque	.75	2.00
36 Jocelyn Thibault	.40	1.00

2008 Donruss Sports Legends

This set was released on December 10, 2008. The base set consists of 144 cards and features cards of players from various sports.

COMPLETE SET (144)	40.00	100.00
11 Patrick Roy	1.00	2.50
17 Ray Bourque	.75	2.00
24 Norm Ullman	.50	1.25
34 Bill Gadsby	.50	1.25
54 Gerry Cheevers	.40	1.00
58 Pierre Pilote	.60	1.50
66 Brad Park	.60	1.50
84 Alex Delvecchio	.60	1.50
91 Phil Esposito	.60	1.50
103 Mike Bossy	.60	1.50
111 Paul Coffey	.60	1.50
126 Tony Esposito	.50	1.25
132 Pat LaFontaine	.60	1.50

2008 Donruss Sports Legends Mirror Red

*RED/250: 1.5X TO 4X BASIC CARDS
STATED PRINT RUN 250 SER.#'d SETS

2008 Donruss Sports Legends Mirror Blue

*BLUE/100: 2X TO 5X BASIC CARDS
STATED PRINT RUN 100 SER.#'d SETS

2008 Donruss Sports Legends Mirror Gold

*GOLD/25: 3X TO 8X BASIC CARDS
STATED PRINT RUN 25 SER.#'d SETS

2008 Donruss Sports Legends Certified Cuts

STATED PRINT RUN 1-100
SERIAL #'d TO 1 NOT PRICED

5 Alex Delvecchio/100	10.00	25.00

2008 Donruss Sports Legends Museum Collection

LVER PRINT RUN 1000 SER.#'d SETS
*GOLD/100: .6X TO 1.5X SILVER/1000
GOLD PRINT RUN 100 SER.#'d SETS

3 Ray Bourque	2.00	5.00
35 Mike Bossy	1.50	4.00

2008 Donruss Sports Legends Museum Collection Signatures

STATED PRINT RUN 1-250
SERIAL #'d UNDER 25 NOT PRICED

3 Ray Bourque/50	20.00	40.00
35 Mike Bossy/100	6.00	15.00

2008 Donruss Sports Legends Signature Connection Combos

STATED PRINT RUN 25-100

13 B.Gadsby/P.Pilote/100	20.00	40.00
15 P.Esposito/Chvers/100	20.00	40.00

2008 Donruss Sports Legends Signatures Mirror Red

*MIRROR RED: .3X TO .8X MIRROR BLUE
MIRROR RED PRINT RUN 25-1370

17 Ray Bourque/25	20.00	50.00
24 Norm Ullman/714	4.00	10.00
34 Bill Gadsby/564	4.00	10.00
54 Gerry Cheevers/568	4.00	10.00
58 Pierre Pilote/539	4.00	10.00
66 Brad Park/269	3.00	8.00
84 Alex Delvecchio/563	4.00	10.00
91 Phil Esposito/109	10.00	25.00
103 Mike Bossy/269	8.00	20.00
111 Paul Coffey/25	10.00	25.00
126 Tony Esposito/93	10.00	25.00
132 Pat LaFontaine/290	6.00	15.00

2008 Donruss Sports Legends Signatures Mirror Blue

MIRROR BLUE PRINT RUN 2-250
SERIAL #'d UNDER 10 NOT PRICED
UNPRICED MIRROR EMERALD PRINT RUN 1-5
UNPRICED MIRROR BLACK PRINT RUN 1

17 Ray Bourque/25	20.00	50.00
24 Norm Ullman/250	5.00	12.00
34 Bill Gadsby/250	5.00	12.00
54 Gerry Cheevers/250	5.00	12.00
58 Pierre Pilote/250	5.00	12.00
66 Brad Park/50	4.00	10.00
84 Alex Delvecchio/250	5.00	12.00
91 Phil Esposito/25	12.00	30.00
103 Mike Bossy/50	10.00	25.00
111 Paul Coffey/25	10.00	25.00
126 Tony Esposito/25	12.00	30.00
132 Pat LaFontaine/100	8.00	20.00

2008 Donruss Sports Legends Signatures Mirror Gold

MIRROR GOLD PRINT RUN 4-25
SERIAL #'d UNDER 10 NOT PRICED

11 Patrick Roy/5		
17 Ray Bourque/10	25.00	60.00
24 Norm Ullman/25	8.00	20.00
34 Bill Gadsby/25	8.00	20.00
54 Gerry Cheevers/25	8.00	20.00
58 Pierre Pilote/25	8.00	20.00
66 Brad Park/25	5.00	12.00
84 Alex Delvecchio/25	6.00	15.00
91 Phil Esposito/10	15.00	40.00
103 Mike Bossy/25	12.00	30.00
111 Paul Coffey/10	12.00	30.00
126 Tony Esposito/15	15.00	40.00
132 Pat LaFontaine/25	10.00	25.00

2008 Donruss Sports Legends Materials Mirror Red

MIRROR RED PRINT RUN 10-500
SERIAL #'d UNDER 25 NOT PRICED
*GOLD/25: .8X TO 2X MIRROR RED
UNPRICED MIRROR EMERALD PRINT RUN 1-5
UNPRICED MIRROR BLACK PRINT RUN 1

11 Patrick Roy Jsy/500	6.00	15.00
24 Norm Ullman Jsy/250	4.00	10.00
34 Bill Gadsby Jsy/500	3.00	8.00
58 Pierre Pilote Jsy/500	4.00	10.00
126 Tony Esposito Jsy/250	4.00	10.00

2008 Donruss Sports Legends Materials Mirror Blue

*MIRROR BLUE: .5X TO 1.2X MIRROR RED
MIRROR BLUE PRINT RUN 5-250
SERIAL #'d UNDER 15 NOT PRICED

2008 Donruss Sports Legends Materials Mirror Gold

*GOLD/25: .8X TO 2X MIRROR RED
GOLD PRINT RUN 1-25 SER.#'d SETS
SERIAL #'d UNDER 20 NOT PRICED

1993-94 Ducks Milk Caps

This set of six milk caps measured approximately 1 1/2" in diameter and featuresdthe Mighty Ducks of Anaheim. The fronts showed a color player headshot set against a teal green background with a neon yellow stripe. The player's name appeared at the bottom, along with the production figures "One of 15,000". The backs were solid white. The milk caps were numbered on the front.

COMPLETE SET (6) 2.00 5.00
1 Tim Sweeney .40 1.00
2 Bobby Dollas .40 1.00
3 Stu Grimson .60 1.50
4 Terry Yake .40 1.00
5 Bob Corkum .40 1.00
NNO Inaugural Season First Win .40 1.00

1994-95 Ducks Carl's Jr.

The 28-card standard-size set was sponsored by Carl's Jr. The fronts featured a color action player photo on a back ground with a purple border. The player's name and team logo was at the left. The backs carried a head shot of the player, biographical information, statistics, and jersey number. The sponsor name and logo was at the bottom with a saying against drug use.

COMPLETE SET (28) 6.00 15.00
1 Patrik Carnback .08 .25
2 Bob Corkum .08 .25
3 Robert Dirk .08 .25
4 Bobby Dollas .08 .25
5 Peter Douris .08 .25
6 Todd Ewen .20 .50
7 Shaun Van Allen .08 .25
8 Garry Valk .08 .25
9 Guy Hebert .60 1.50
10 Paul Kariya 3.00 8.00
11 Valeri Karpov .08 .25
12 Steven King .08 .25
13 Todd Krygier .08 .25
14 Tom Kurvers .08 .25
15 Randy Ladouceur .08 .25
16 Stephan Lebeau .20 .50
17 John Lilley .08 .25
18 Don McSween .08 .25
19 Steve Rucchin .30 .75
20 David Sacco .08 .25
21 Joe Sacco .08 .25
22 Mikhail Shtalenkov .30 .75
23 Jim Thomson .08 .25
24 Oleg Tverdovsky .30 .75
25 David Williams .08 .25
26 Wild Wing (Mascot) .08 .25
27 Carl Karcher (Sponsor Owner) .01 .05
28 Happy Star (Sponsor Logo) .01 .05

1995-96 Ducks Team Issue

These five oversized (5" X 7") black and white photos pictured members of the '95-96 Mighty Ducks of Anaheim. The cards featured a posed head shot, with the player's name and a pair of team logos along the bottom. The backs were blank. The photos were unnumbered, and were listed below alphabetically. It's highly unlikely that the checklist was complete as listed below. Additional information would be appreciated and can be forwarded to Beckett Publications.

COMPLETE SET (5) 1.25 3.00
1 Bobby Dollas .20 .50
2 David Karpa .20 .50
3 Steve Rucchin .30 .75
4 Mikhail Shtalenkov .30 .75
5 Garry Valk .20 .50

1996-97 Ducks Team Issue

This unique 26-card set was produced by Up Front Sports and sponsored by Southland Micro Systems. The first twenty cards in the set followed the standard design of action photo on the front and stats on the back. Cards 21-24, however, were die-cut pop-up cards. Reports indicated that the Garry Valk destroyed or pulled since he was traded before the set's release. It's non known how many copies may still exist, but the card has been confirmed.

COMPLETE SET (26) 8.00 20.00
1 Mikhail Shtalenkov .20 .50
2 Bobby Dollas .15 .40
3 Roman Oksiuta .15 .40
4 Kevin Todd .15 .40
5 Ted Drury .15 .40
6 Joe Sacco .15 .40
7 Dmitri Mironov .20 .50
8 Warren Rychel .20 .50
10 Shawn Antoski .15 .40
11 Steve Rucchin .20 .50
12 Ken Baumgartner .15 .40
13 Brian Bellows .15 .40
14 Nikolai Tsulygin .15 .40
15 Jason Marshall .15 .40
16 Darren Van Impe .15 .40
17 David Karpa .15 .40
18 Wild Wing .15 .40
19 J.F. Jomphe .15 .40
20 Sean Pronger .15 .40
21 Guy Hebert .60 1.50
22 Paul Kariya 2.50 6.00
23 Jari Kurri 1.00 2.50
24 Teemu Selanne 1.50 4.00
25 Southland .01 .05
26 Southland .01 .05
27 Ron Wilson CO .08 .25
28 Garry Valk .02 .10

2002-03 Ducks Team Issue

The singles in this odd size set were distributed at promotional events. The set listing below is not complete. If you can confirm others, please contact us at hockeymag@beckett.com.

COMPLETE SET
1 Dan Bylsma .20 .50
1 Adam Oates .40 1.00
2 Jean-Sebastien Giguere 1.25 3.00
3 Paul Kariya 1.25 3.00
4 Ruslan Salei .20 .50
5 Petr Sykora .20 .50
6 Vitaly Vishnevski .20 .50

2005-06 Ducks Team Issue

COMPLETE SET (22) 6.00 15.00
1 Kip Brennan .20 .50
2 Ilya Bryzgalov .30 .75
3 Keith Carney .20 .50
4 Joe DiPenta .30 .75
5 Todd Fedoruk .20 .50
6 Ryan Getzlaf .75 2.00
7 Jean-Sebastien Giguere .40 1.00
8 Jonathan Hedstrom .20 .50
9 Joffrey Lupul .40 1.00
10 Jason Marshall .20 .50
11 Andy McDonald .20 .50
12 Travis Moen .20 .50
13 Rob Niedermayer .20 .50
14 Scott Niedermayer .20 .50
15 Sandis Ozolinsh .20 .50
16 Samuel Pahlsson .20 .50
17 Corey Perry .75 2.00
18 Ruslan Salei .20 .50
19 Teemu Selanne .75 2.00
20 Petr Sykora .20 .50
21 Vitali Vishnevsky .20 .50
22 Randy Carlyle HC .02 .10

1992-93 Durivage Panini

is 50-card standard-size set showcased hockey stars who were born in Quebec. The cards, which were inserted in loaves of bread, featured color, action player photos set on a gold plaque design. The player's name appeared below the photo on the plaque. The words "Les Grands Hockeyeurs Quebecois" were printed in red at the top of the card. The backs had a ghosted black-and-white player photo with biography and career summary printed in French over the picture. The Patrick Roy signed card was randomly inserted. It is believed he signed 500 copies, although that has not been confirmed.

COMPLETE SET (50) 8.00 20.00
1 Guy Carbonneau .08 .25
2 Lucien Deblois .07 .20
3 Benoit Hogue .07 .20
4 Steve Kasper .07 .20
5 Mike Krushelnyski Toron .07 .20
6 Claude Lapointe Quebec .07 .20
7 Stephan Lebeau Montreal .07 .20
8 Mario Lemieux 1.50 4.00
9 Stephane Morin .07 .20
10 Denis Savard .08 .25
11 Pierre Turgeon .08 .25
12 Kevin Dineen .07 .20
13 Gord Donnelly .07 .20
14 Claude Lemieux .08 .25
15 Jocelyn Lemieux .07 .20
16 Daniel Marois .07 .20
17 Scott Mellanby .07 .20
18 Stephane Richer .08 .25
19 Benoit Brunet Montreal .08 .25
20 Vincent Damphousse .08 .25
21 Gilbert Dionne Montreal .08 .25
22 Gaetan Duchesne .07 .20
23 Bob Errey .07 .20
24 Michel Goulet .08 .25
25 Mike Hough .07 .20
26 Sergio Momesso .07 .20
27 Mario Roberge .07 .20
28 Luc Robitaille Los Ange .10 .30
29 Sylvain Turgeon .07 .20
30 Marc Bergevin .07 .20
31 Ray Bourque .50 1.25
32 Patrice Brisebois .07 .20
33 Jeff Chychrun .07 .20
34 Sylvain Cote .07 .20
35 J.J. Daigneault .07 .20
36 Eric Desjardins .08 .25
37 Gord Dineen .07 .20
38 Steve Duchesne .07 .20
39 Donald Dufresne .07 .20
40 Steven Finn .07 .20
41 Garry Galley .07 .20
42 Kevin Lowe .08 .25
43 Michel Petit .07 .20
44 Normand Rochefort .07 .20
45 Randy Velischek .07 .20
46 Jacques Cloutier Quebec .08 .25
47 Stephane Fiset Quebec N .10 .30
48 Rejean Lemelin Boston B .08 .25
49 Andre Racicot Montreal .08 .25
50 Patrick Roy Montreal Ca 3.00 8.00
NNO Patrick Roy AU 50.00 125.00

1993-94 Durivage Score

ese 50 standard-size white-bordered cards featured color player action shots "mounted" on golden plaque designs. The player's name and hometown appeared within a black stripe below the photo. All the players in the set were from the province of Quebec. His team's logo appeared further below. The white-bordered back carried a color player action photo on the right and, on the left, bilingual biography and statistics. Cards 1-6 belonged to a "Special Edition" subset and had gold-foil highlights on their fronts. The cards were numbered on the back as "X of 50."

COMPLETE SET (50) 12.00 30.00
1 Alexandre Daigle .30 .75
2 Pierre Sevigny .10 .30
3 Jocelyn Thibault .50 1.25
4 Philippe Boucher .10 .30
5 Martin Brodeur New Jers 1.50 4.00
6 Martin Lapointe Detroit .40 1.00
7 Patrice Brisebois Montr .40 1.00
8 Benoit Brunet .10 .30
9 Guy Carbonneau Montreal .40 1.00
10 Jean-Jacques Daigneault .10 .30
11 Vincent Damphousse .40 1.00
12 Eric Desjardins .40 1.00
13 Gilbert Dionne Montreal .10 .30
14 Stephan Lebeau Montreal .40 1.00
15 Andre Racicot Montreal .40 1.00
16 Mario Roberge .10 .30
17 Patrick Roy Montreal Ca 3.00 8.00
18 Jacques Cloutier Quebec .40 1.00
19 Alain Cote .10 .30
20 Steven Finn .10 .30
21 Stephane Fiset .30 .75
22 Martin Gelinas .10 .30
23 Reggie Savage .10 .30
24 Claude Lapointe .10 .30
25 Denis Savard .50 1.25
26 Ray Bourque Boston Brui .75 2.00
27 Joe Juneau Boston Bruin .30 .75
28 Ron Stern .10 .30
29 Benoit Hogue New York I .40 1.00
30 Pierre Turgeon .50 1.25
31 Mike Krushelnyski .10 .30
32 Felix Potvin .50 1.25
33 Sergio Momesso .10 .30
34 Yves Racine .10 .30
35 Sylvain Cote .10 .30
36 Sylvain Turgeon .10 .30
37 Kevin Dineen Philadelph .40 1.00
38 Garry Galley Philadelph .40 1.00
39 Dominic Roussel .40 1.00
40 Gaetan Duchesne .10 .30
41 Luc Robitaille .50 1.25
42 Michel Goulet .50 1.25
43 Jocelyn Lemieux .10 .30
44 Stephane Matteau .10 .30
45 Mike Hough .10 .30
46 Scott Mellanby .50 1.25
47 Claude Lemieux .30 .75
48 Stephane Richer .50 1.25
49 Jimmy Waite San Jose Sh .10 .30
50 Patrick Poulin .40 1.00
NNO Patrick Roy AU 75.00 200.00
NNO Jocelyn Thibault AU 40.00 100.00

1996-97 Duracell All-Cherry Team

This 22-card set was available in three-card packs with the purchase of specially-marked packages of Duracell batteries in English-speaking Canada and was produced by Pinnacle Brands. The players featured in the set were chosen by CBC commentator and fashion doyenne Don Cherry. The card fronts featured a color action photo, along with manufacturer logos. The backs included a brief resume. Interestingly, the player's stats could only be revealed by pressing a trio of heat-sensitive strips. There were rumored to be short printed cards in the set, but no confirmation of this has become available.

COMPLETE SET (22) 8.00 20.00
DC1 Paul Coffey .30 .75
DC2 Lyle Odelein .08 .25
DC3 Joe Sakic .50 1.25
DC4 Curtis Joseph .40 1.00
DC5 Brett Hull .40 1.00
DC6 Eric Lindros .60 1.50
DC7 Doug Gilmour .30 .75
DC8 Chris Chelios .30 .75
DC9 Marty McSorley .08 .25
DC10 Kirk Muller .08 .25
DC11 Trevor Linden .08 .25
DC12 Brendan Shanahan .60 1.50
DC13 Tie Domi .20 .50
DC14 Rick Tocchet .08 .25
DC15 Steve Yzerman 1.25 3.00
DC16 Scott Stevens .08 .25
DC17 Patrick Roy 1.50 4.00
DC18 Keith Tkachuk .30 .75
DC19 Owen Nolan .20 .50
DC20 Dale Hunter .08 .25
DC21 Don Cherry .40 1.00
DC22 Don Cherry .40 1.00

1996-97 Duracell L'Equipe Beliveau

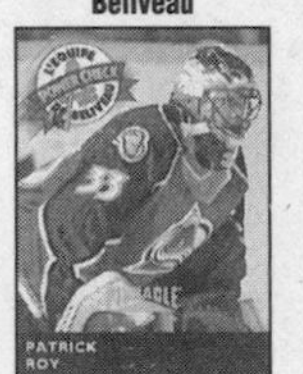

This 22-card set was available in 3-card packs with specially marked packages of Duracell batteries in French-speaking Canada. The set was produced by Pinnacle. The design was the same as that of the All-Cherry team cards, save for the different logo in the upper left corner of the front; also the text on the back of these cards is French. As the team was selected by former Habs great Jean Beliveau, the player composition was slightly different, with a notable increase in the francophone content. As this series was produced in more limited quantities than the Cherry set, the French version of the singles which appear in both sets carry a slight premium.

COMPLETE SET (22) 14.00 35.00
JB1 Paul Coffey .40 1.00
JB2 Lyle Odelein .08 .25
JB3 Joe Sakic 1.00 2.50
JB4 Eric Daze .30 .75
JB5 Brett Hull .75 2.00
JB6 Martin Brodeur 1.25 3.00
JB7 Doug Gilmour .60 1.50
JB8 Peter Forsberg 1.25 3.00
JB9 Mike Gartner .20 .50
JB10 Saku Koivu .60 1.50
JB11 Trevor Linden .08 .25
JB12 Felix Potvin .40 1.00
JB13 Mats Sundin .40 1.00
JB14 Pierre Turgeon .20 .50
JB15 Vincent Damphousse .08 .25
JB16 Scott Stevens .08 .25
JB17 Patrick Roy 2.00 5.00
JB18 Keith Tkachuk .60 1.50
JB19 Ray Bourque .75 2.00
JB20 Paul Kariya 1.25 3.00
JB21 Jean Beliveau .40 1.00
JB22 Jean Beliveau .40 1.00

2003-04 Duracell

These cards were issued as a mail-in premium with the purchase of Duracell batteries in Canada.

COMPLETE SET (15) 20.00
1 Jean-Sebastien Giguere .40 1.00
2 Patrick Lalime .20 .50
3 Curtis Joseph .75 2.00
4 Marty Turco .40 1.00
5 Ed Belfour .75 2.00
6 Sean Burke .20 .50
7 Roberto Luongo .75 2.00
8 Jose Theodore .75 2.00
9 Olaf Kolzig .20 .50
10 Martin Brodeur 1.25 3.00
11 Mike Richter .20 .50
12 Dan Blackburn .20 .50
13 Patrick Roy 1.50 4.00
14 Dwayne Roloson .20 .50
15 Dan Cloutier .20 .50

1994 EA Sports

This 225-card boxed set was issued by Electronic Arts Sports as a premium within packages of its NHLPA '94 video game. Two cards were included with each game. In addition, an order form for a complete set was found inside the game box; the original price was 24.95 direct. The fronts were white with action player photos that had airbrushed edges. The team logo appeard in the upper left corner with the player's name printed on a black bar across the bottom edge. The player's position was on a team color-coded stripe above the player's name. The borderless backs displayed a head shot in the upper left corner with player performance rating below. A brief biography and career summary appeared to the right.

COMPLETE SET (225) 30.00 75.00
1 Alexei Kasatonov .01 .05
2 Randy Ladouceur .01 .05
3 Terry Yake .01 .05
4 Troy Loney .01 .05
5 Anatoli Semenov .01 .05
6 Guy Hebert .05 .15
7 Ray Bourque 1.25 3.00
8 Don Sweeney .01 .05
9 Adam Oates .20 .50
10 Joe Juneau .15 .40
11 Cam Neely .40 1.00
12 Andy Moog .08 .25
13 Doug Bodger .01 .05
14 Petr Svoboda .01 .05
15 Pat LaFontaine .20 .50
16 Dale Hawerchuk .08 .25
17 Alexander Mogilny .20 .50
18 Grant Fuhr .08 .25
19 Gary Suter .01 .05
20 Al MacInnis .05 .15
21 Joe Nieuwendyk .05 .15
22 Gary Roberts .05 .15
23 Theo Fleury .08 .25
24 Mike Vernon .05 .15
25 Chris Chelios .40 1.00
26 Steve Smith .01 .05
27 Jeremy Roenick .60 1.50
28 Michel Goulet .05 .15
29 Steve Larmer .05 .15
30 Ed Belfour .60 1.50
31 Mark Tinordi .01 .05
32 Tommy Sjodin .01 .05
33 Mike Modano .75 2.00
34 Dave Gagner .05 .15
35 Russ Courtnall .05 .15
36 Jon Casey .05 .15
37 Paul Coffey .40 1.00
38 Steve Chiasson .01 .05
39 Steve Yzerman 2.50 6.00
40 Sergei Fedorov 1.25 3.00
41 Dino Ciccarelli .05 .15
42 Tim Cheveldae .05 .15
43 Dave Manson .01 .05
44 Igor Kravchuk .01 .05
45 Doug Weight .08 .25
46 Shayne Corson .05 .15
47 Petr Klima .01 .05
48 Bill Ranford .05 .15
49 Joe Cirella .01 .05
50 Gord Murphy .01 .05
51 Brian Skrudland .01 .05
52 Andrei Lomakin .01 .05
53 Scott Mellanby .01 .05
54 John Vanbiesbrouck .40 1.00
55 Zarley Zalapski .01 .05
56 Eric Weinrich .01 .05
57 Andrew Cassels .01 .05
58 Geoff Sanderson .05 .15
59 Pat Verbeek .05 .15
60 Sean Burke .05 .15
61 Rob Blake .05 .15
62 Marty McSorley .05 .15
63 Wayne Gretzky 4.00 10.00
64 Luc Robitaille .20 .50
65 Tomas Sandstrom .05 .15
66 Kelly Hrudey .05 .15
67 Eric Desjardins .05 .15
68 Mathieu Schneider .05 .15
69 Kirk Muller .05 .15
70 Vincent Damphousse .08 .25
71 Brian Bellows .01 .05
72 Patrick Roy 3.00 8.00
73 Scott Stevens .05 .15
74 Slava Fetisov .05 .15
75 Alexander Semak .01 .05
76 Stephane Richer .05 .15
77 Claude Lemieux .08 .25
78 Chris Terreri .05 .15
79 Vladimir Malakhov .01 .05
80 Darius Kasparaitis .01 .05
81 Pierre Turgeon .20 .50
82 Steve Thomas .05 .15
83 Benoit Hogue .01 .05
84 Glenn Healy .05 .15
85 Brian Leetch .40 1.00
86 James Patrick .01 .05
87 Mark Messier .75 2.00
88 Designer Tip The Wong One-Timer From Boards To .01 .05
89 Mike Gartner .05 .15
90 Mike Richter .40 1.00
91 Norm Maciver .01 .05
92 Brad Shaw .01 .05
93 Jamie Baker .01 .05
94 Sylvain Turgeon .01 .05
95 Bob Kudelski .01 .05
96 Peter Sidorkiewicz .01 .05
97 Garry Galley .01 .05
98 Dimitri Yushkevich .01 .05
99 Eric Lindros 1.50 4.00
100 Rod Brind'Amour .05 .15
101 Mark Recchi .20 .50
102 Tommy Soderstrom .01 .05
103 Larry Murphy .08 .25
104 Ulf Samuelsson .05 .15
105 Mario Lemieux 3.00 8.00
106 Kevin Stevens .05 .15
107 Jaromir Jagr 2.00 5.00
108 Tom Barrasso .08 .25
109 Steve Duchesne .05 .15
110 Curtis Leschyshyn .01 .05
111 Mats Sundin .40 1.00
112 Joe Sakic 1.25 3.00
113 Owen Nolan .20 .50
114 Ron Hextall .08 .25
115 Doug Wilson .05 .15
116 Neil Wilkinson .01 .05
117 Kelly Kisio .01 .05
118 Johan Garpenlov .01 .05
119 Pat Falloon .05 .15
120 Arturs Irbe .15 .40
121 Jeff Brown .05 .15
122 Garth Butcher .05 .15
123 Craig Janney .05 .15
124 Brendan Shanahan .75 2.00
125 Brett Hull .75 2.00
126 Curtis Joseph .75 2.00
127 Bob Beers .01 .05
128 Roman Hamrlik .08 .25
129 Brian Bradley .05 .15
130 Mikael Andersson .01 .05
131 Chris Kontos .01 .05
132 Wendell Young .01 .05
133 Todd Gill .01 .05
134 Dave Ellett .01 .05
135 Doug Gilmour .40 1.00
136 Dave Andreychuk .05 .15
137 Nikolai Borschevsky .01 .05
138 Felix Potvin .40 1.00
139 Jyrki Lumme .01 .05
140 Doug Lidster .01 .05
141 Cliff Ronning .05 .15
142 Geoff Courtnall .01 .05
143 Pavel Bure 1.50 4.00
144 Kirk McLean .05 .15
145 Phil Housley .05 .15
146 Teppo Numminen .01 .05
147 Alexei Zhamnov .05 .15
148 Thomas Steen .01 .05
149 Teemu Selanne 1.25 3.00
150 Bob Essensa .05 .15
151 Kevin Hatcher .01 .05
152 Al Iafrate .05 .15
153 Mike Ridley .01 .05
154 Dimitri Khristich .01 .05
155 Peter Bondra .08 .25
156 Don Beaupre .01 .05
157 All Stars East CL .05 .15
158 All Stars West CL .05 .15
159 Mighty Ducks Team CL .08 .25
160 Bruins Team CL .08 .25
161 Sabres Team CL .05 .15
162 Flames Team CL .05 .15
163 Blackhawks Team CL .08 .25
164 Red Wings Team CL .08 .25
165 Oilers Team CL .05 .15
166 Panthers Team CL .05 .15
167 Whalers Team CL .05 .15
168 Kings Team CL .08 .25
169 Stars Team CL .05 .15
170 Canadiens Team CL .08 .25
171 Devils Team CL .05 .15
172 Islanders Team CL .05 .15
173 Rangers Team CL .08 .25
174 Senators Team CL .05 .15
175 Flyers Team CL .05 .15
176 Penguins Team CL .05 .15
177 Nordiques Team CL .05 .15
178 Sharks Team CL .08 .25
179 Blues Team CL .05 .15
180 Lightning Team CL .05 .15
181 Leafs Team CL .08 .25
182 Canucks Team CL .05 .15
183 Capitals Team CL .05 .15
184 Jets Team CL .05 .15
185 Skill Leaders Checking# .08 .25
186 Skill Leaders Defense/ .08 .25
187 Skill Leaders Goaltendi .40 1.00
188 Skill Leaders Passing/ .08 .25
189 Skill Leaders Shot Accu 1.50 4.00
190 Al Iafrate SL .05 .15
191 Skill Leaders Skating/ .20 .50
192 Skill Leaders Stickhand 2.00 5.00
193 New Feature .01 .05
194 Derian Hatcher .01 .05
195 Dmitri Kvartalnov .01 .05
196 Randy Wood .01 .05
197 Gord Murphy .01 .05
198 New Feature .01 .05
199 New Feature Expansion T .08 .25
200 New Feature Goalie Cont .08 .25
201 Terry Yake .01 .05
202 Mark Fitzpatrick .01 .05
203 Brad Shaw .01 .05
204 NHL Logos .01 .05
205 Jyrki Lumme .01 .05
206 New Feature Penalty Sho .01 .05
207 Gord Murphy .01 .05
208 Slava Fetisov .01 .05
209 Stephan LeBeau .01 .05
210 Gord Murphy .01 .05
211 New Feature Shootout Ga 1.25 3.00
212 New Feature User Record .40 1.00
213 Designer Tips .01 .05
214 Designer Tips .01 .05
215 Designer Tips .01 .05
216 Designer Tips The Lange Use Goalie To Take Out .01 .05
217 Designer Tips The Lesser Create A Screen With D .01 .05
218 Designer Tips The Matulac Fake Outside& Shoot I .01 .05
219 Designer Tips The Scott Fake Inside& Shoot Outs .01 .05
220 Designer Tips The Probin Set Up One-Timer In Th .01 .05
221 Designer Tips The Rogers Set Up One-Sider Acros .01 .05
222 Designer Tips The Rubinelli Fake Outside& Fake .01 .05
223 Designer Tips The Shin Wrap Around Goal& Shoot .01 .05
224 Designer Tips The White Deflection At Goal Mout .01 .05
225 Designer Tips The Wike Set Up One-Timer From Be .01 .05

1964-67 Eaton's Sports Adviser

Issued between 1964 and 1967, these cards were used as promotional material by Eaton's of Canada.

NNO Gordie Howe action 10.00 25.00
NNO Gordie Howe All-Star uniform 10.00 25.00
NNO Gordie Howe standing 10.00 25.00

1935 Edwards, Ringer and Bigg Sports Games in Many Lands

Made as a multi-sport set in Britain, these cards measure approximately 1 1/2 x 2 1/2. Cards are black and white with text on back.

3 Ice Hockey-Canada 30.00 60.00
3 Ice Hockey-Canada same as above, but with Imperial Tobacco 22.50 45.00

2011-12 Elite

COMP.SET w/o RC's (200) 15.00 40.00
201-260 ROOKIE PRINT RUN 999
261-280 ROOKIE PRINT RUN 99
1 Teemu Selanne .60 1.50
2 Evgeni Malkin 1.00 2.50
3 Jimmy Howard .30 .75
4 Patrick Sharp .30 .75
5 Keith Yandle .30 .75
6 Michael Grabner .25 .60
7 Pascal Dupuis .20 .50
8 Ryan Getzlaf .50 1.25
9 Steven Stamkos .60 1.50
10 Aaron Johnson .20 .50
11 Brian Gionta .25 .60
12 Dany Heatley .25 .60
13 Evander Kane .30 .75
14 Joe Pavelski .30 .75
15 Kevin Shattenkirk .25 .60
16 Michal Neuvirth .25 .60
17 Patrice Bergeron .40 1.00
18 Ryan Kesler .30 .75
19 Taylor Hall .60 1.50
20 Al Montoya .20 .50
21 Cal Clutterbuck .30 .75
22 David Backes .30 .75
23 Henrik Lundqvist .40 1.00
24 Joe Thornton .30 .75
25 Kris Letang .30 .75
26 Michael Ryder .20 .50
27 Patrick Kane .60 1.50
28 Ryan Miller .30 .75
29 Thomas Greiss .25 .60
30 Alexander Burmistrov .25 .60
31 Cam Fowler .25 .60
32 David Clarkson .20 .50
33 Henrik Sedin .30 .75
34 Joel Ward .20 .50
35 Kris Versteeg .25 .60
36 Miikka Kiprusoff .30 .75
37 Patrick Marleau .30 .75
38 Ryan O'Reilly .30 .75
39 Thomas Vanek .30 .75
40 Alexandre Burrows .30 .75
41 Cam Ward .30 .75
42 David Desharnais .40 1.00
43 Henrik Zetterberg .40 1.00
44 Joffrey Lupul .25 .60
45 Kyle Wellwood .25 .60
46 Mikhail Grabovski .25 .60
47 Patrik Elias .30 .75
48 Ryan Smyth .25 .60
49 Tim Connolly .20 .50
50 Alexander Edler .20 .50
51 Carey Price 1.00 2.50
52 David Legwand .25 .60
53 Ilya Bryzgalov .30 .75
54 Johan Franzen .30 .75
55 Loui Eriksson .25 .60
56 Mike Ribeiro .25 .60
57 Paul Bissonnette .20 .50
58 Ryan Suter .20 .50
59 Tim Thomas .30 .75
60 Alex Ovechkin 1.25 3.00
61 Chad LaRose .20 .50
62 Derek Stepan .30 .75
63 Ilya Kovalchuk .30 .75
64 Johan Hedberg .25 .60
65 Luke Adam .25 .60
66 Mike Richards .30 .75
67 Paul Stastny .30 .75
68 Ryan Wilson .25 .60
69 T.J. Oshie .50 1.25
70 Alex Pietrangelo .25 .60
71 Chris Neil .20 .50
72 Devan Dubnyk .30 .75
73 James Neal .30 .75
74 John Tavares .60 1.50
75 Marc-Andre Bergeron .20 .50
76 Mike Smith .30 .75
77 Pavel Datsyuk .40 1.00
78 Ryane Clowe .20 .50
79 Tomas Fleischmann .20 .50
80 Alexander Semin .30 .75
81 Chris Pronger .25 .60
82 Devin Setoguchi .25 .60
83 James Reimer .30 .75
84 John-Michael Liles .20 .50
85 Marc-Andre Fleury .50 1.25
86 Mikko Koivu .25 .60
87 Pekka Rinne .40 1.00
88 Saku Koivu .30 .75
89 Tomas Plekanec .30 .75
90 Alex Tanguay .20 .50
91 Clarke MacArthur .20 .50
92 Dion Phaneuf .30 .75
93 James van Riemsdyk .30 .75
94 Jonas Hiller .25 .60
95 Marian Gaborik .40 1.00
96 Milan Lucic .30 .75
97 Phil Kessel .40 1.00
98 Scott Hartnell .30 .75
99 Tomas Vokoun .25 .60
100 Alexander Steen .30 .75
101 Claude Giroux .30 .75
102 Drew Doughty .30 .75
103 Jonathan Quick .50 1.25
104 James Wisniewski .20 .50
105 Marian Hossa .25 .60
106 Milan Michalek .20 .50
107 P.K. Subban .60 1.50
108 Semyon Varlamov .30 .75
109 Tuomo Ruutu .25 .60
110 Andrew Ladd .30 .75
111 Corey Crawford .40 1.00
112 Duncan Keith .30 .75
113 Jamie Benn .40 1.00
114 Jonathan Toews .60 1.50
115 Mark Giordano .25 .60
116 Nathan Gerbe .20 .50
117 Pierre-Marc Bouchard .30 .75
118 Sergei Kostitsyn .20 .50
119 Ty Conklin .25 .60
120 Antti Niemi .25 .60
121 Corey Perry .30 .75
122 Jarome Iginla .30 .75
123 Jordan Eberle .30 .75
124 Mark Streit .20 .50
125 Nathan Horton .30 .75
126 Radim Vrbata .25 .60
127 Shane Doan .25 .60
128 Tyler Myers .30 .75
129 Anze Kopitar .50 1.25
130 Corey Potter .25 .60
131 Dustin Brown .30 .75
132 Jaromir Jagr .75 2.00
133 Jordan Staal .30 .75
134 Martin Brodeur .60 1.50
135 Nicklas Backstrom .50 1.25
136 Ray Emery .25 .60
137 Shawn Horcoff .20 .50
138 Tyler Seguin .60 1.50
139 Bobby Ryan .30 .75
140 Cory Schneider .25 .60
141 Dustin Byfuglien .30 .75
142 Jaroslav Halak .30 .75
143 Jordin Tootoo .25 .60
144 Martin Havlat .25 .60
145 Nicklas Lidstrom .30 .75
146 Ray Whitney .25 .60
147 Shea Weber .25 .60
148 Valtteri Filppula .30 .75
149 Brad Marchand .40 1.00
150 Craig Anderson .30 .75
151 Dwayne Roloson .25 .60
152 Jason Pominville .25 .60
153 Jose Theodore .30 .75
154 Martin St. Louis .30 .75
155 Nik Antropov .25 .60
156 Sheldon Souray .20 .50
157 Victor Hedman .40 1.00
158 Brad Richards .30 .75
159 Curtis Glencross .20 .50
160 Ed Jovanovski .20 .50
161 Jason Spezza .30 .75
162 Josh Harding .30 .75
163 Matt Cullen .20 .50
164 Niklas Backstrom .30 .75
165 Rene Bourque .20 .50
166 Rich Peverley .30 .75
167 Sidney Crosby 1.25 3.00
168 Vincent Lecavalier .25 .60
169 Brandon Dubinsky .25 .60
170 Daniel Alfredsson .30 .75
171 Eric Staal .40 1.00
172 Jeff Carter .30 .75
173 Jean-Sebastien Giguere .25 .60
174 Matt Duchene .30 .75
175 Nikolai Khabibulin .25 .60
176 Rick Nash .30 .75
177 Simon Gagne .30 .75
178 Vinny Prospal .20 .50
179 Brenden Morrow .25 .60
180 Daniel Sedin .30 .75
181 Erik Johnson .20 .50
182 Jeff Skinner .30 .75
183 Jussi Jokinen .20 .50
184 Matt Moulson .25 .60
185 Ondrej Pavelec .30 .75
186 Roberto Luongo .30 .75
187 Stephen Weiss .25 .60
188 Wayne Simmonds .40 1.00
189 Brian Campbell .20 .50
190 Danny Briere .30 .75
191 Erik Karlsson .60 1.50
192 Jhonas Enroth .30 .75
193 Kari Lehtonen .25 .60
194 Max Pacioretty .30 .75
195 P.A. Parenteau .20 .50
196 Ryan Callahan .30 .75
197 Steve Mason .25 .60
198 Zach Parise .30 .75
199 Brian Elliott .25 .60
200 Zdeno Chara .30 .75
201 Allen York RC 3.00 8.00
202 Brett Bulmer RC 2.50 6.00
203 Carl Hagelin RC 4.00 10.00
204 T.J. Brennan RC 2.50 6.00
205 Brayden McNabb RC 2.50 6.00
206 Roman Horak RC 2.50 6.00
207 Aaron Palushaj RC 2.50 6.00
208 Anton Lander RC 2.50 6.00
209 Cam Atkinson RC 6.00 15.00
210 Erik Condra RC 2.50 6.00
211 Joe Vitale RC 2.50 6.00
212 Marcus Kruger RC 4.00 10.00
213 Tomas Kubalik RC 2.50 6.00
214 Robert Bortuzzo RC 2.50 6.00
215 Bracken Kearns RC 2.50 6.00
216 Lance Bouma RC 2.50 6.00
217 David Rundblad RC 2.50 6.00
218 Yann Sauve RC 2.50 6.00
219 Adam Henrique RC 6.00 15.00
220 Carl Klingberg RC 2.50 6.00
221 Greg Nemisz RC 2.50 6.00
222 John Moore RC 2.50 6.00
223 Matt Read RC 5.00 12.00
224 Teemu Hartikainen RC 2.50 6.00
225 Tomas Vincour RC 2.50 6.00
226 Corey Tropp RC 2.50 6.00
227 Cam Talbot RC 6.00 15.00
228 Maxime Macenauer RC 2.50 6.00
229 Paul Postma RC 2.50 6.00
230 Marcus Foligno RC 6.00 15.00
231 Alexei Emelin RC 2.50 6.00
232 Ben Scrivens RC 4.00 10.00
233 Colin Greening RC 2.50 6.00
234 Harri Sateri RC 2.50 6.00
235 Jonathon Blum RC 2.50 6.00
236 Keith Kinkaid RC 2.50 6.00
237 Raphael Diaz RC 2.50 6.00
238 Zac Rinaldo RC 2.50 6.00
239 Peter Holland RC 2.50 6.00
240 Erik Gustafsson RC 3.00 8.00
241 Mikko Koskinen RC 3.00 8.00
242 Ryan Thang RC 2.00 5.00
243 Scott Timmins RC 2.50 6.00
244 Colten Teubert RC 2.50 6.00
245 Andy Miele RC 2.50 6.00
246 Brendon Nash RC 2.50 6.00
247 Brian Strait RC 3.00 8.00
248 David Savard RC 2.50 6.00

249 Erik Gudbranson RC 3.00 8.00
250 Harry Zolnierczyk RC 2.50 6.00
251 Justin Faulk RC 4.00 10.00
252 Slava Voynov RC 2.50 6.00
253 Stephane Da Costa RC 2.50 6.00
254 Mattias Ekholm RC 2.50 6.00
255 Tim Erixon RC 2.50 6.00
256 Drew Bagnall RC 2.50 6.00
257 Zack Kassian RC 3.00 8.00
258 Eddie Lack RC 2.50 6.00
259 Calvin de Haan RC 2.50 6.00
260 Kris Fredheim RC 2.50 6.00
261 Adam Larsson/99 RC 12.00 30.00
262 Cody Eakin/99 RC 15.00 40.00
263 Gustav Nyquist/99 RC 15.00 40.00
264 Mika Zibanejad/99 RC 25.00 60.00
265 Brendan Smith/99 RC 10.00 25.00
266 Brandon Saad/99 RC 15.00 40.00
267 Cody Hodgson/99 RC 20.00 50.00
268 Jake Gardiner/99 RC 15.00 40.00
269 R.Nugent-Hopkins/99 RC 40.00 100.00
270 Craig Smith/99 RC 12.00 30.00
271 Blake Geoffrion/99 RC 10.00 25.00
272 Louis Leblanc/99 RC 20.00 50.00
273 Joe Colborne/99 RC 12.00 30.00
274 Ryan Johansen/99 RC 20.00 50.00
275 Brett Connolly/99 RC 10.00 25.00
276 D.Smith-Pelly/99 RC 15.00 40.00
277 Mark Scheifele/99 RC 20.00 50.00
278 Sean Couturier/99 RC 25.00 50.00
279 Gabriel Landeskog/99 RC 15.00 40.00
280 Matt Frattin/99 RC 10.00 25.00

2011-12 Elite Aspirations

1-200 VETS: 2X TO 5X BASIC CARDS
201-260 ROOKIES: .8X TO 2X BASIC RC
201-260 ROOKIE PRINT RUN 99
201-260 ROOKIES: .6X TO 1.5X BASIC RC
261-280 ROOKIE PRINT RUN 25
11 Corey Crawford 2.00 5.00
35 Nicklas Backstrom 2.50 6.00
75 Brett Connolly 12.00 30.00

2011-12 Elite Status Gold

1-200 VETS: 6X TO 15X BASIC CARDS
-200 VETERAN STATED PRINT RUN 99
201-280 UNPRICED ROOKIE PRINT RUN 10
11 Corey Crawford 6.00 15.00
35 Nicklas Backstrom 8.00 20.00

2011-12 Elite Materials

PATCH/15: 1X TO 2.5X BASIC JSY
PATCH/15: .8X TO 2X BASIC JSY SP
Ales Hemsky 3.00 8.00
Alex Ovechkin 15.00 40.00
Antoine Vermette 2.50 6.00
Antti Niemi 3.00 8.00
Anze Kopitar 6.00 15.00
Brad Marchand 5.00 12.00
Brenden Morrow 3.00 8.00
Chris Pronger 3.00 8.00
0 Corey Perry 4.00 10.00
1 Dan Boyle 3.00 8.00
2 Sean Couturier 6.00 15.00
3 Derek Roy 3.00 8.00
4 Derek Stepan 5.00 12.00
5 Dion Phaneuf 4.00 10.00
6 Dustin Brown 4.00 10.00
7 Erik Johnson 2.50 6.00
9 Henrik Lundqvist 6.00 15.00
20 Ilya Kovalchuk SP 5.00 12.00
21 James Neal 5.00 12.00
2 James van Riemsdyk 4.00 10.00
23 Jarome Iginla SP 5.00 12.00
24 Joe Pavelski 4.00 10.00
25 Joe Thornton SP 5.00 12.00
26 Johan Franzen 4.00 10.00
27 John Carlson 5.00 12.00
29 Jonathan Toews SP 10.00 25.00
1 Zdeno Chara 4.00 10.00
2 Marian Gaborik 5.00 12.00
3 Gabriel Landeskog 4.00 10.00
4 Martin Brodeur SP 10.00 25.00
5 Matt Duchene 4.00 10.00
6 Mike Fisher 4.00 10.00
7 Nikolai Khabibulin 5.00 12.00
8 Pavel Datsyuk 5.00 12.00
9 Rick Nash 4.00 10.00
0 Robin Lehner 3.00 8.00
1 Ryan Getzlaf 6.00 15.00
2 Ryan Nugent-Hopkins 8.00 20.00
3 Ryan O'Reilly 4.00 10.00
4 Scott Gomez 3.00 8.00
5 Sidney Crosby SP 12.00 30.00
6 Steve Ott 3.00 8.00
7 Shane Doan 3.00 8.00
8 Victor Hedman 5.00 12.00
9 Zach Parise SP 5.00 12.00
0 Ryan Kesler 5.00 12.00

2011-12 Elite Materials Autographs

STATED PRINT RUN 13-25
Ales Hemsky/25 10.00 25.00
Alex Ovechkin/25 40.00 80.00
Antoine Vermette/25
Antti Niemi/25 10.00 25.00
Anze Kopitar/25 20.00 50.00
Brad Marchand/25 15.00 40.00
Brenden Morrow/25
Chris Pronger/25 10.00 25.00
Craig Anderson/25 12.00 30.00
0 Corey Perry/25 10.00 25.00
1 Dan Boyle/25 10.00 25.00
2 Sean Couturier/25 20.00 50.00
3 Derek Roy/25
4 Derek Stepan/25 12.00 30.00
5 Dion Phaneuf/25 12.00 30.00
6 Dustin Brown/25 12.00 30.00
7 Erik Johnson/25
8 Evgeni Malkin/25 30.00 60.00
9 Henrik Lundqvist/25 25.00 50.00
0 Ilya Kovalchuk/25 12.00 30.00
1 James Neal/25 10.00 25.00
2 James van Riemsdyk/25 12.00 30.00
3 Jarome Iginla/25 15.00 40.00
4 Joe Pavelski/25 12.00 30.00
5 Joe Thornton/25 12.00 30.00
6 Johan Franzen/25
7 John Carlson/25 15.00 40.00
8 Jonas Gustavsson/25 12.00 30.00
9 Jonathan Toews/25 25.00 50.00
0 Loui Eriksson/25 10.00 25.00
1 Zdeno Chara/25 12.00 30.00
2 Marian Gaborik/25 15.00 40.00
3 Gabriel Landeskog/25 25.00 50.00
4 Martin Brodeur/25 40.00 80.00
5 Matt Duchene/20 12.00 30.00
6 Mike Fisher/13
7 Nikolai Khabibulin/25 12.00 30.00
8 Pavel Datsyuk/25 30.00 60.00
9 Rick Nash/25 10.00 25.00
40 Robin Lehner/25 10.00 25.00
41 Ryan Getzlaf/25 20.00 50.00
42 Ryan Nugent-Hopkins/25 60.00 125.00
43 Ryan O'Reilly/25 12.00 30.00
44 Scott Gomez/25 10.00 25.00
45 Sidney Crosby/25 75.00 150.00
46 Steve Ott/25 12.00 30.00
47 Shane Doan/25 10.00 25.00
48 Victor Hedman/25 20.00 40.00
49 Zach Parise/25 12.00 30.00
50 Ryan Kesler/25 20.00 40.00

2011-12 Elite New Breed Materials

*PATCH/25: 1.2X TO 3X BASIC INSERTS
*PRIME/25: 1.2X TO 3X BASIC INSERTS
1 Adam Larsson 2.50 6.00
2 Adam Henrique 5.00 12.00
3 Blake Geoffrion 2.00 5.00
4 Brandon Saad 3.00 8.00
5 Brett Connolly 2.00 5.00
6 Cody Eakin 3.00 8.00
7 Cody Hodgson 5.00 12.00
8 David Rundblad 2.00 5.00
9 Devante Smith-Pelly 3.00 8.00
10 Gabriel Landeskog 6.00 15.00
11 Gustav Nyquist 6.00 15.00
12 Jake Gardiner 3.00 8.00
13 Joe Colborne 2.50 6.00
14 Mark Scheifele 6.00 15.00
15 Matt Frattin 5.00 12.00
16 Mika Zibanejad 5.00 12.00
17 Ryan Johansen 4.00 10.00
18 Ryan Nugent-Hopkins 10.00 25.00
19 Sean Couturier 5.00 12.00
20 Tim Erixon 2.00 5.00
21 Aaron Palushaj 2.00 5.00
22 Greg Nemisz 2.00 5.00
23 Erik Gudbranson 2.50 6.00
24 John Moore 2.00 5.00
25 Jonathon Blum 2.00 5.00
26 Justin Faulk 3.00 8.00
27 Marcus Kruger 3.00 8.00
28 Simon Despres 2.00 5.00
29 Zack Kassian 2.50 6.00
30 Calvin de Haan 2.00 5.00
32 Tyler Seguin 6.00 15.00
33 Raphael Diaz 2.00 5.00
34 Tomas Vincour 2.00 5.00
35 Harri Sateri 2.00 5.00
36 Derek Stepan 2.50 6.00
38 Stephane Da Costa 2.00 5.00
39 Tomas Kubalik 2.00 5.00
40 Slava Voynov 2.00 5.00
41 Cam Atkinson 5.00 12.00
42 Patrick Wiercioch 2.00 5.00
43 Brendan Smith 2.00 5.00
45 Colin Greening 2.00 5.00
46 Zac Dalpe 2.00 5.00
48 Victor Hedman 4.00 10.00
49 Matt Read 4.00 10.00
50 Ben Scrivens 3.00 8.00

2011-12 Elite New Breed Materials Autographs

STATED PRINT RUN 10-50
1 Adam Larsson/50 8.00 20.00
2 Adam Henrique/50 15.00 40.00
3 Blake Geoffrion/50 6.00 15.00
4 Brandon Saad/50 10.00 25.00
5 Brett Connolly/50 6.00 15.00
6 Cody Eakin/50 8.00 20.00
7 Cody Hodgson/50 12.00 30.00
8 David Rundblad/50 6.00 15.00
9 Devante Smith-Pelly/50 10.00 25.00
10 Gabriel Landeskog/50 12.00 30.00
11 Gustav Nyquist/50 15.00 40.00
12 Jake Gardiner/50 10.00 25.00
13 Joe Colborne/50 6.00 15.00
14 Mark Scheifele/50 15.00 40.00
15 Matt Frattin/50 6.00 15.00
16 Mika Zibanejad/50 15.00 40.00
17 Ryan Johansen/50 12.00 30.00
18 Ryan Nugent-Hopkins/50 25.00 60.00
19 Sean Couturier/50 12.00 30.00
20 Tim Erixon/50 6.00 15.00
21 Aaron Palushaj/50 6.00 15.00
22 Greg Nemisz/50 6.00 15.00
23 Erik Gudbranson/50 8.00 20.00
24 John Moore/50 6.00 15.00
25 Jonathon Blum /50 6.00 15.00
26 Justin Faulk/50 10.00 25.00
27 Marcus Kruger/50 10.00 25.00
28 Simon Despres/50 6.00 15.00
29 Zack Kassian/50 8.00 20.00
30 Calvin de Haan/50 6.00 15.00
32 Tyler Seguin/10
33 Raphael Diaz/50 6.00 15.00
34 Tomas Vincour/50 6.00 15.00
35 Harri Sateri/50 6.00 15.00
36 Derek Stepan/50 8.00 20.00
38 Stephane Da Costa/50 6.00 15.00
39 Tomas Kubalik/50 6.00 15.00
40 Slava Voynov/50 6.00 15.00
41 Cam Atkinson/50 15.00 40.00
42 Patrick Wiercioch/50 6.00 15.00
43 Brendan Smith/50 6.00 15.00
45 Colin Greening/50 6.00 15.00
46 Zac Dalpe/50 5.00 12.00
48 Victor Hedman/50 10.00 25.00
49 Matt Read/50 12.00 30.00
50 Ben Scrivens/50 10.00 25.00

2011-12 Elite Passing the Torch Autographs

STATED PRINT RUN 100 SER.#'d SETS
1 M.St. Louis/N.Gerbe 10.00 25.00
2 Gudbranson/Pronger 10.00 25.00
3 B.Smith/N.Lidstrom 20.00 50.00
4 H.Lundqvist/R.Lehner 20.00 50.00
5 D.Dubnyk/B.Ranford 15.00 40.00
6 S.Doan/A.Miele 12.00 30.00
7 C.Eakin/A.Semin 12.00 30.00
8 D.Graham/B.Saad 15.00 40.00
9 J.Anderson/A.Niemi 15.00 40.00
10 J.Howard/T.McCollum 12.00 30.00
11 S.Weber/J.Blum 12.00 30.00
12 C.Hodgson/R.Kesler 15.00 40.00
13 J.Shelley/Z.Rinaldo 12.00 30.00
14 J.Davidson/J.Halak 12.00 30.00
15 Belfour/Lehtonen 20.00 40.00
16 R.Clowe/D.Cleary 10.00 25.00
17 Scheifele/Hawerchuk 25.00 50.00
18 D.Gilmour/A.Henrique 15.00 40.00
19 B.Scrivens/C.Joseph 12.00 30.00
20 B.Clarke/S.Couturier 30.00 60.00

2011-12 Elite Passing the Torch Autographs SP

STATED PRINT RUN 25 SER.#'d SETS
1 P.Roy/C.Price 75.00 150.00
2 Messier/Nugent-Hopkins 100.00 200.00
3 M.Lemieux/E.Malkin 100.00 200.00
4 V.Lecavalier/B.Connolly 25.00 50.00
5 S.Niedermayer/A.Larsson 25.00 50.00
6 M.Duchene/J.Sakic 50.00 100.00
7 F.Potvin/J.Reimer 60.00 120.00
8 B.Trottier/J.Tavares 50.00 120.00
9 S.Mikita/J.Toews 75.00 125.00
10 C.Neely/T.Seguin 60.00 120.00

2011-12 Elite Prime Number Autographs

ANNOUNCED PRINT RUN 10-90
1 Joe Sakic/20* 50.00 100.00
2 Steve Yzerman/90* 40.00 100.00
3 Ray Bourque/90* 30.00 60.00
4 Patrick Roy/50* 50.00 100.00
5 Ron Francis/40* 20.00 50.00
6 Mario Lemieux/70* 60.00 120.00
7 Bernie Nicholls/70* 15.00 40.00
8 Curtis Joseph/50* 15.00 40.00
9 Scott Niedermayer/70* 12.00 30.00
10 Luc Robitaille/50* 15.00 40.00
11 Ed Belfour/80* 15.00 40.00
12 Bryan Trottier/20*
13 Wendel Clark/30* 15.00 40.00
14 Alex Ovechkin/10*
15 Zach Parise/40* 12.00 30.00
16 Tim Thomas/90* 15.00 40.00
17 Nikolai Khabibulin/10*
18 Joe Thornton/10*
19 Jarome Iginla/80* 15.00 40.00
20 Henrik Sedin/60* 15.00 40.00
21 Henrik Lundqvist/10*
22 Rick Nash/50* 15.00 40.00
23 Ilya Kovalchuk/60* EXCH 15.00 40.00
24 Marc-Andre Fleury/80* 25.00 60.00
25 Marian Gaborik/80* 12.00 30.00
26 Thomas Vanek/80* 15.00 40.00
27 Evgeni Malkin/10*
28 Ryan Miller/50* 15.00 40.00
29 Anze Kopitar/50* 25.00 60.00
30 Patrick Marleau/50* 15.00 40.00
31 Nicklas Lidstrom/50* 40.00 80.00
32 Sidney Crosby/10*
33 Martin Brodeur/10*

2011-12 Elite Prime Number Jerseys

STATED PRINT RUN 100-666
1 Joe Sakic/600* 8.00 20.00
2 Steve Yzerman/600* 8.00 20.00
3 Ray Bourque/300* 8.00 20.00
4 Patrick Roy/500* 12.00 30.00
5 Ron Francis/500* 6.00 15.00
6 Mario Lemieux/100* 15.00 40.00
7 Bernie Nicholls/400* 5.00 12.00
8 Curtis Joseph/400* 5.00 12.00
9 Scott Niedermayer/100* 5.00 12.00
10 Luc Robitaille/500* 5.00 12.00
11 Ed Belfour/400* 6.00 15.00
12 Bryan Trottier/500* 5.00 12.00
13 Wendel Clark/290* 5.00 12.00
14 Alex Ovechkin/290* 15.00 40.00
15 Zach Parise/300* 4.00 10.00
16 Tim Thomas/100* 5.00 12.00
17 Nikolai Khabibulin/300* 3.00 8.00
18 Joe Thornton/290* 4.00 10.00
19 Jarome Iginla/400* 5.00 12.00
20 Henrik Sedin/600* 5.00 12.00
21 Henrik Lundqvist/200* 5.00 12.00
22 Rick Nash/200* 4.00 10.00
23 Ilya Kovalchuk/300* 4.00 10.00
24 Marc-Andre Fleury/100* 8.00 20.00
25 Marian Gaborik/200* 5.00 12.00
26 Thomas Vanek/300* 4.00 10.00
27 Evgeni Malkin/400* 6.00 15.00
28 Ryan Miller/200* 6.00 15.00
29 Anze Kopitar/300* 6.00 15.00
30 Patrick Marleau/300* 4.00 10.00
31 Nicklas Lidstrom/200* 5.00 12.00
32 Sidney Crosby/200* 15.00 40.00
33 Martin Brodeur/100* 10.00 25.00

2011-12 Elite Rookie Autographs

202 Brett Bulmer 4.00 10.00
206 Roman Horak 4.00 10.00
207 Aaron Palushaj 4.00 10.00
209 Cam Atkinson 10.00 25.00
210 Erik Condra 4.00 10.00
212 Marcus Kruger 6.00 15.00
219 Adam Henrique 6.00 15.00
220 Carl Klingberg 4.00 10.00
221 Greg Nemisz 4.00 10.00
223 Matt Read 4.00 10.00
225 Tomas Vincour 4.00 10.00
229 Paul Postma 4.00 10.00
231 Alexei Emelin 4.00 10.00
232 Ben Scrivens 6.00 15.00
233 Colin Greening 4.00 10.00
235 Jonathon Blum 4.00 10.00
236 Keith Kinkaid 4.00 10.00
238 Zac Rinaldo 4.00 10.00
239 Peter Holland 4.00 10.00
241 Mikko Koskinen 5.00 12.00
245 Andy Miele 4.00 10.00
248 David Savard 4.00 10.00
249 Erik Gudbranson 5.00 12.00
251 Justin Faulk 6.00 15.00
252 Slava Voynov 4.00 10.00
253 Stephane Da Costa 4.00 10.00
255 Tim Erixon 4.00 10.00
258 Eddie Lack 4.00 10.00
259 Calvin de Haan 4.00 10.00
261 Adam Larsson SP 15.00 40.00
262 Cody Eakin SP 15.00 40.00
263 Gustav Nyquist SP 25.00 50.00
264 Mika Zibanejad SP 25.00 50.00
265 Brendan Smith SP 12.00 30.00
266 Brandon Saad SP 20.00 50.00
267 Cody Hodgson SP 30.00 60.00
268 Jake Gardiner SP 25.00 50.00
269 Nugent-Hopkins SP 250.00 400.00
270 Craig Smith SP 15.00 40.00
271 Blake Geoffrion SP 12.00 30.00
272 Louis Leblanc SP 8.00 20.00
273 Joe Colborne SP 15.00 40.00
274 Ryan Johansen SP 25.00 60.00
275 Brett Connolly SP 12.00 30.00
276 Devante Smith-Pelly SP 20.00 50.00
277 Mark Scheifele SP 12.00 30.00
278 Sean Couturier SP 15.00 40.00
279 Gabriel Landeskog SP 20.00 50.00
280 Matt Frattin SP 15.00 40.00

2011-12 Elite Rookie Stars

1 Ryan Nugent-Hopkins 4.00 10.00
2 Gabriel Landeskog 2.00 5.00
3 Brett Connolly 1.00 2.50
4 Sean Couturier 2.00 5.00
5 Craig Smith 1.25 3.00
6 Devante Smith Pelly 1.50 4.00
7 Cody Hodgson 2.00 5.00
8 Adam Larsson 1.25 3.00
9 Matt Read 2.00 5.00
10 Ryan Johansen 2.00 5.00

2011-12 Elite Series Alexander Ovechkin

COMMON OVECHKIN (1-6) 2.00 5.00

2011-12 Elite Series Autographs

STATED PRINT RUN 29-50
1 Joe Sakic/50 30.00 80.00
2 Alex Ovechkin/50 30.00 80.00
4 Sidney Crosby/50 75.00 150.00
5 Steven Stamkos/50 25.00 60.00
6 Steve Yzerman/50 40.00 80.00
7 Mark Messier/29 30.00 60.00

2011-12 Elite Series Dual

COMMON HALL/RYAN N-H 4.00 10.00

2011-12 Elite Series Dual Autographs

5 T.Hall/R.Nugent-Hopkins 100.00 200.00

2011-12 Elite Series Joe Sakic

COMMON SAKIC (1-6) 1.50 4.00

2011-12 Elite Series Mark Messier

COMMON MESSIER (1-6) 1.50 4.00

2011-12 Elite Series Sidney Crosby

COMMON CROSBY (1-6) 2.50 6.00

2011-12 Elite Series Steve Yzerman

COMMON YZERMAN (1-6) 2.00 5.00

2011-12 Elite Series Steven Stamkos

COMMON STAMKOS (1-6) 2.00 5.00

2011-12 Elite Signings

1 Zenon Konopka 4.00 10.00
2 Zach Boychuk 3.00 8.00
4 Wojtek Wolski SP
5 Vincent Lecavalier SP 15.00 30.00
6 Viktor Stalberg 3.00 8.00
7 Valtteri Filppula SP
8 Tyler Seguin 25.00 50.00
9 Tyler Myers
10 Tyler Bozak SP 10.00 25.00
11 Tuukka Rask SP 20.00 40.00
12 Trevor Linden 12.00 30.00
13 Trevor Gillies 4.00 10.00
14 Tony Esposito SP 12.00 30.00
15 Tomas Tatar 5.00 12.00
16 Taylor Hall 10.00 25.00
17 Teemu Selanne SP 25.00 50.00
18 Thomas Vanek SP 8.00 20.00
19 T.J. Galiardi 4.00 10.00
20 Steven Stamkos SP 25.00 50.00
21 Steven Kampfer EXCH 4.00 10.00
22 Steve Yzerman SP 50.00 100.00
23 Simon Gagne 8.00 20.00
24 Scott Gomez 6.00 15.00
25 Ryan Nugent-Hopkins SP 50.00 100.00
26 Ryan Miller SP 8.00 20.00
27 Ryan McDonagh 5.00 12.00
28 Rick Nash SP 8.00 20.00
29 Rhett Rakhshani 4.00 10.00
30 Ray Ferraro 5.00 12.00
31 Phil Esposito SP 12.00 30.00
32 Peter Regin SP
33 Patrik Elias 5.00 12.00
34 Patrick Marleau SP 8.00 20.00
35 Patrick Kane 15.00 30.00
36 Patric Hornqvist 5.00 12.00
37 Ryan Johansen 8.00 20.00
38 Ondrej Pavelec 15.00 30.00
39 Patrick Roy SP 40.00 80.00
40 Nicklas Lidstrom SP 20.00 40.00
41 Nick Palmieri 4.00 10.00
42 Nick Johnson 4.00 10.00
43 Nazem Kadri 8.00 20.00
44 Nathan Horton 25.00 50.00
45 Mikkel Boedker SP
46 Mike Santorelli 3.00 8.00
47 Kris Letang 10.00 25.00
48 Michael Frolik 6.00 15.00
49 Max Pacioretty 6.00 15.00
50 Matt Duchene 8.00 20.00
51 Mats Zuccarello EXCH 5.00 12.00
52 Mark Scheifele SP 10.00 25.00
53 Mario Lemieux SP 50.00 100.00
54 David Rundblad 6.00 15.00
55 Magnus Paajarvi 8.00 20.00
56 Luke Adam 4.00 10.00
58 Lee Stempniak 3.00 8.00
59 Krys Barch 4.00 10.00
60 Kevin Shattenkirk 4.00 10.00
61 Kelly Hrudey SP 6.00 15.00
62 Kari Lehtonen 8.00 20.00
63 Jordan Eberle SP 10.00 25.00
64 Justin Abdelkader 5.00 12.00
65 Jonathan Quick 15.00 40.00
66 Jonas Gustavsson 5.00 12.00
67 John Tavares SP 15.00 30.00
68 John McCarthy 3.00 8.00
69 Joe Thornton SP 20.00 40.00
70 Joe Nieuwendyk SP 20.00 40.00
71 Brendan Smith 15.00 30.00
72 Jack Johnson 3.00 8.00
73 Ilya Bryzgalov SP 15.00 30.00
74 Stephane Da Costa SP 6.00 15.00
75 George Parros SP 6.00 15.00
76 Gabriel Landeskog SP 20.00 50.00
77 Evander Kane 6.00 15.00
78 Eric Staal
80 Don Cherry SP 15.00 30.00
81 Adam Henrique 8.00 20.00
82 Dany Heatley SP 6.00 15.00
83 Dan Boyle SP 6.00 15.00
84 Colin Wilson 4.00 10.00
85 Chris Neil 4.00 10.00
86 Charlie Hodge SP 8.00 20.00
87 Carey Price SP 15.00 40.00
88 Cam Ward SP 8.00 20.00
89 Cal Clutterbuck
90 Bryan Trottier SP 15.00 40.00
91 Bobby Hull SP 20.00 40.00
92 Bernie Parent SP 20.00 40.00
93 Andrew Ladd 5.00 12.00
94 Alex Urbom 4.00 10.00
95 Alexander Semin
96 Andre Dupont SP 30.00 60.00
97 Zack Kassian 5.00 12.00
98 Simon Despres 10.00 25.00
99 Jonathan Toews SP 25.00 50.00
100 Ed Belfour SP 20.00 40.00

2011-12 Elite Social Signatures

1 Paul Bissonnette 10.00 25.00
2 Bobby Ryan 12.00 30.00
3 Matt Duchene 10.00 25.00
4 Michael Grabner 12.00 30.00
5 Dustin Brown 12.00 30.00
6 James van Riemsdyk 10.00 25.00
7 Steven Stamkos SP 40.00 80.00
8 Nazem Kadri 8.00 20.00
9 Daniel Carcillo 10.00 25.00
10 Evander Kane 12.00 30.00

2011-12 Elite Stars

1 Alex Ovechkin 6.00 15.00
2 Martin Brodeur 3.00 8.00
3 Steven Stamkos 3.00 8.00
4 Tim Thomas 1.50 4.00
5 Tyler Seguin 3.00 8.00
6 Patrick Kane 3.00 8.00
7 Matt Duchene 1.50 4.00
8 Jaromir Jagr 4.00 10.00
9 Carey Price 5.00 12.00
10 Sidney Crosby 4.00 10.00

2012-13 Elite Inscriptions

INSERTS IN 2012-13 ROOKIE ANTHOLOGY
OVERALL ANNC'D PRINT RUN 99 OR LESS
SP A ANNC'D PRINT RUN 10 OR LESS
SP B ANNC'D PRINT RUN 25 OR LESS
EIAH Adam Henrique 8.00 20.00
EICH Carl Hagelin 8.00 20.00
EICO Sean Couturier 8.00 20.00
EICS Cory Schneider 6.00 15.00
EIDB Dustin Brown 8.00 20.00
EIDP Dion Phaneuf
EIEM Evgeni Malkin SP B
EIES Eric Staal 10.00 25.00
EIGH Gordie Howe SP A
EIJB Jamie Benn 6.00 15.00
EIJH Jonas Hiller 6.00 15.00
EIJQ Jonathan Quick 20.00 40.00
EIJS Joe Sakic SP B
EIJT John Tavares SP B 15.00 40.00
EIMD Matt Duchene 8.00 20.00
EIMF Marcus Foligno 6.00 15.00
EIMM Mark Messier SP A
EIMS Mike Smith 8.00 20.00
EIMSL Martin St. Louis 8.00 20.00
EIPD Pavel Datsyuk 10.00 25.00
EIPR Patrick Roy SP A
EIRG Ryan Getzlaf 12.00 30.00
EIRM Ryan Miller 8.00 20.00
EIRN Ryan Nugent-Hopkins 50.00 100.00
EISC Sidney Crosby SP A
EISW Stephen Weiss 5.00 12.00
EISY Steve Yzerman SP A
EIZP Zach Parise 12.00 30.00

2012-13 Elite Intensity

INSERTS IN 2012-13 ROOKIE ANTHOLOGY
STATED PRINT RUN 500 SER.#'d SETS
1 Jarome Iginla 2.50 6.00
2 Mark Messier 3.00 8.00
3 Martin Brodeur 5.00 12.00
4 Claude Giroux 2.50 6.00
5 Chris Kreider 2.50 6.00
6 Nicklas Lidstrom 3.00 8.00
7 Jonathan Quick 4.00 10.00
8 Patrick Roy 6.00 15.00
9 Henrik Lundqvist 3.00 8.00
10 Sidney Crosby 10.00 25.00
11 Bobby Clarke 2.50 6.00
12 Wendel Clark 2.50 6.00
13 Cam Neely 2.50 6.00
14 Teemu Selanne 5.00 12.00
15 Gordie Howe 5.00 12.00
16 Alex Ovechkin 10.00 25.00
17 Zdeno Chara 2.50 6.00
18 Steven Stamkos 5.00 12.00
19 Ryan Miller 2.50 6.00
20 Jonathan Toews 5.00 12.00
21 Doug Gilmour 3.00 8.00
22 Shea Weber 2.00 5.00
23 Carey Price 8.00 20.00
24 Eric Staal 3.00 8.00
25 Gabriel Landeskog 2.50 6.00
26 Chris Chelios 2.50 6.00
27 Steve Yzerman 5.00 12.00
28 Daniel Alfredsson 2.50 6.00
29 Brett Hull 2.50 6.00
30 Luc Robitaille 2.50 6.00

2012-13 Elite Rookies

INSERTS IN 2012-13 ROOKIE ANTHOLOGY
STATED PRINT RUN 999 SER.#'d SETS
1 Andrew Joudrey 1.50 4.00
2 Mike Connolly 1.50 4.00
3 Jordan Nolan 1.50 4.00
4 Ryan Garbutt 1.50 4.00
5 Casey Cizikas 1.50 4.00
6 Max Sauve 1.50 4.00
7 Jaden Schwartz 3.00 8.00
8 Travis Turnbull 1.50 4.00
9 Gabriel Dumont 1.50 4.00
10 Riley Sheahan 1.50 4.00
11 Tyson Barrie 3.00 8.00
12 Aaron Ness 1.50 4.00
13 Colby Robak 1.50 4.00
14 Michael Stone 1.50 4.00
15 Brandon Manning 1.50 4.00
16 Cody Goloubef 1.50 4.00
17 Mat Clark 1.50 4.00
18 Dalton Prout 1.50 4.00
19 Torey Krug 6.00 15.00
20 Matt Donovan 1.50 4.00
21 Tyler Cuma 1.50 4.00
22 Chay Genoway 1.50 4.00
23 Brenden Dillon 1.50 4.00
24 Tyson Sexsmith 1.50 4.00
25 Jussi Rynnas 1.50 4.00
26 Shawn Hunwick 1.50 4.00
27 Robert Mayer 2.00 5.00
28 Chet Pickard 1.50 4.00
29 Jake Allen 5.00 12.00
30 Michael Hutchinson 3.00 8.00
31 Philippe Cornet 1.50 4.00
32 Kris Foucault 1.50 4.00
33 Brandon Bollig 1.50 4.00
34 Lane MacDermid 1.50 4.00
35 Sven Baertschi 2.00 5.00
36 Ryan Hamilton 1.50 4.00
37 Jeremy Welsh 1.50 4.00
38 Chris Kreider 3.00 8.00
39 Jason Zucker 2.00 5.00
40 Jakob Silfverberg 3.00 8.00
41 Carter Camper 1.25 3.00
42 Carter Ashton 1.25 3.00
43 Reilly Smith 5.00 12.00
44 J.T. Brown 1.50 4.00
45 Akim Aliu 1.50 4.00
46 Scott Glennie 1.50 4.00
47 Matt Watkins 1.50 4.00
48 Mark Stone 3.00 8.00

2012-13 Elite Rookies Aspirations

ASPIR/50-96: .6X TO 1.5X BASIC INSERTS
ASPIR/30-49: .8X TO 2X BASIC INSERTS
ASPIR/26-29: 1X TO 2.5X BASIC INSERTS
INSERTS IN 2012-13 ROOKIE ANTHOLOGY

2012-13 Elite Rookies Status

STATUS/50-74: .6X TO 1.5X BASIC INSERTS
STATUS/31-48: .8X TO 2X BASIC INSERTS
STATUS/15-29: 1X TO 2.5X BASIC INSERTS
INSERTS IN 2012-13 ROOKIE ANTHOLOGY
ANNOUNCED PRINT RUN 1-74

2012-13 Elite The Great Outdoors

INSERTS IN 2012-13 ROOKIE ANTHOLOGY
STATED PRINT RUN 500 SER.#'d SETS
1 Sidney Crosby 10.00 25.00
2 Kris Letang 2.50 6.00
3 Jordan Staal 2.50 6.00
4 Ryan Miller 2.50 6.00
5 Thomas Vanek 2.50 6.00
6 Pavel Datsyuk 3.00 8.00
7 Henrik Zetterberg 3.00 8.00
8 Nicklas Lidstrom 3.00 8.00
9 Patrick Kane 5.00 12.00
10 Jonathan Toews 5.00 12.00
11 Mike Richards 2.50 6.00
12 Claude Giroux 2.50 6.00
13 Tim Thomas 2.50 6.00
14 Patrice Bergeron 3.00 8.00
15 Zdeno Chara 2.50 6.00
16 Alex Ovechkin 10.00 25.00
17 Nicklas Backstrom 4.00 10.00
18 Mike Green 2.50 6.00
19 Evgeni Malkin 8.00 20.00
20 Marc-Andre Fleury 4.00 10.00
21 Carl Hagelin 2.50 6.00
22 Henrik Lundqvist 3.00 8.00
23 Marian Gaborik 2.50 6.00
24 Brayden Schenn 2.50 6.00
25 Danny Briere 2.50 6.00
26 Scott Hartnell 2.50 6.00
27 Carey Price 6.00 15.00
28 P.K. Subban 4.00 10.00
29 Jarome Iginla 2.50 6.00
30 Miikka Kiprusoff 2.00 5.00
31 Ales Hemsky 2.00 5.00
32 Ryan Smyth 2.00 5.00
33 Jose Theodore 2.50 6.00
34 Saku Koivu 2.50 6.00
35 Guy Carbonneau 2.50 6.00
36 Guy Lafleur 3.00 8.00
37 Kirk Muller 2.00 5.00
38 Grant Fuhr 2.50 6.00
39 Mark Messier 3.00 8.00
40 Jari Kurri 3.00 8.00

1962-63 El Producto Discs

The six discs in this set measured approximately 3" in diameter. They were issued as a strip of six connected in a fragile manner and were in full color. The discs were unnumbered and checklisted below in alphabetical order. The set in unperforated form is valued 25 percent greater than the value below.

COMPLETE SET (6) 150.00 300.00
1 Jean Beliveau 30.00 60.00
2 Glenn Hall 25.00 50.00
3 Gordie Howe 75.00 150.00
4 Dave Keon 30.00 60.00
5 Frank Mahovlich 25.00 50.00
6 Henri Richard 25.00 50.00

1995-96 Emotion Promo Strip

This 6" by 3" strip was distributed by Skybox to introduce its Emotion line of cards. The front featured two cards of Jeremy Roenick of the Chicago Blackhawks: his basic Emotion issue and his X-Cited insert. They were identical to the regularly issued cards, save for the word sample found in the back upper right corner. They were separated by a white bar with the sponsor logo horizontally printed in gold and date cards premier in black.

1 Jeremy Roenick .40 1.00

1995-96 Emotion

This 200-card high end set was released in 8-card packs with an SRP of $4.99. The set was distinguished by its use of an "emotional" term to describe the action on the card face. The Jeremy Roenick SkyMotion card was obtainable in exchange for three wrappers and $25. The unique card featured three seconds of actual game footage. The offer for this card expired on June 30, 1996.

1 Bobby Dollas .10 .25
2 Guy Hebert .12 .30
3 Paul Kariya .20 .50
4 Oleg Tverdovsky .15 .40
5 Shaun Van Allen .10 .25
6 Ray Bourque .25 .60
7 Al Iafrate .12 .30
8 Blaine Lacher .12 .30
9 Joe Mullen .12 .30
10 Cam Neely .15 .40
11 Adam Oates .15 .40
12 Kevin Stevens .12 .30
13 Don Sweeney .10 .25
14 Donald Audette .12 .30
15 Garry Galley .10 .25
16 Dominik Hasek .20 .50
17 Brian Holzinger RC .30 .75
18 Pat LaFontaine .15 .40
19 Alexei Zhitnik .10 .25
20 Steve Chiasson .10 .25
21 Theo Fleury .20 .50
22 Phil Housley .12 .30
23 Trevor Kidd .12 .30
24 Joe Nieuwendyk .15 .40
25 Gary Roberts .10 .25
26 Zarley Zalapski .10 .25
27 Ed Belfour .12 .30
28 Chris Chelios .15 .40
29 Sergei Krivokrasov .10 .25
30 Joe Murphy .10 .25
31 Bernie Nicholls .10 .25
32 Patrick Poulin .10 .25
33 Jeremy Roenick .20 .50
34 Gary Suter .12 .30
35 Rene Corbet .10 .25
36 Peter Forsberg .40 1.00
37 Valeri Kamensky .12 .30
38 Uwe Krupp .12 .30
39 Curtis Leschyshyn .10 .25
40 Owen Nolan .15 .40
41 Mike Ricci .12 .30
42 Joe Sakic .25 .60
43 Jocelyn Thibault .12 .30
44 Bob Bassen .10 .25
45 Dave Gagner .10 .25
46 Todd Harvey .10 .25
47 Derian Hatcher .12 .30
48 Kevin Hatcher .12 .30
49 Mike Modano .25 .60
50 Andy Moog .15 .40
51 Dino Ciccarelli .12 .30
52 Paul Coffey .15 .40
53 Sergei Fedorov .25 .60
54 Vladimir Konstantinov .12 .30
55 Slava Kozlov .12 .30
56 Nicklas Lidstrom .15 .40
57 Keith Primeau .10 .25
58 Ray Sheppard .12 .30
59 Mike Vernon .12 .30
60 Steve Yzerman .20 .50
61 Jason Arnott .12 .30
62 Curtis Joseph .15 .40
63 Igor Kravchuk .10 .25
64 Todd Marchant .10 .25
65 David Oliver .10 .25
66 Bill Ranford .12 .30
67 Doug Weight .15 .40
68 Stu Barnes .10 .25
69 Jesse Belanger .10 .25
70 Gord Murphy .10 .25
71 Magnus Svensson RC .12 .30
72 John Vanbiesbrouck .12 .30
73 Sean Burke .10 .25
74 Andrew Cassels .10 .25
75 Frantisek Kucera .10 .25
76 Andrei Nikolishin .10 .25
77 Geoff Sanderson .10 .25
78 Brendan Shanahan .20 .50
79 Darren Turcotte .10 .25
80 Rob Blake .12 .30
81 Wayne Gretzky .75 2.00
82 Dimitri Khristich .10 .25
83 Jari Kurri .15 .40
84 Jamie Storr .12 .30
85 Darryl Sydor .12 .30
86 Rick Tocchet .12 .30
87 Vincent Damphousse .12 .30
88 Vladimir Malakhov .10 .25
89 Stephane Quintal .12 .30
90 Mark Recchi .20 .50
91 Patrick Roy .40 1.00
92 Brian Savage .10 .25
93 Pierre Turgeon .15 .40
94 Martin Brodeur .40 1.00
95 Neal Broten .12 .30
96 Shawn Chambers .10 .25
97 Claude Lemieux .15 .40
98 John MacLean .12 .30
99 Randy McKay .10 .25
100 Scott Niedermayer .15 .40
101 Stephane Richer .12 .30
102 Scott Stevens .15 .40
103 Todd Bertuzzi RC .20 .50
104 Patrick Flatley .10 .25
105 Brett Lindros .10 .25
106 Kirk Muller .12 .30
107 Tommy Salo RC .25 .60
108 Mathieu Schneider .10 .25
109 Alexander Semak .10 .25
110 Dennis Vaske .10 .25
111 Ray Ferraro .10 .25
112 Adam Graves .12 .30
113 Alexei Kovalev .10 .25
114 Steve Larmer .12 .30
115 Brian Leetch .15 .40
116 Mark Messier .25 .60
117 Mike Richter .15 .40
118 Luc Robitaille .15 .40
119 Ulf Samuelsson .10 .25
120 Pat Verbeek .12 .30
121 Don Beaupre .12 .30
122 Radek Bonk .10 .25
123 Alexandre Daigle .10 .25
124 Steve Duchesne .10 .25
125 Steve Larouche .10 .25
126 Dan Quinn .12 .30
127 Martin Straka .10 .25
128 Alexei Yashin .12 .30
129 Rod Brind'Amour .15 .40
130 Eric Desjardins .12 .30
131 Ron Hextall .15 .40
132 John LeClair .15 .40
133 Eric Lindros .25 .60
134 Mikael Renberg .12 .30
135 Chris Therien .10 .25
136 Ron Francis .20 .50
137 Jaromir Jagr .40 1.00
138 Mario Lemieux .50 1.25
139 Dmitri Mironov .10 .25
140 Petr Nedved .12 .30
141 Tomas Sandstrom .12 .30
142 Bryan Smolinski .10 .25
143 Ken Wregget .12 .30
144 Sergei Zubov .12 .30
145 Shayne Corson .10 .25
146 Geoff Courtnall .10 .25
147 Dale Hawerchuk .20 .50
148 Brett Hull .20 .50
149 Ian Laperriere .10 .25
150 Al MacInnis .15 .40
151 Chris Pronger .15 .40
152 David Roberts .10 .25
153 Esa Tikkanen .10 .25
154 Ulf Dahlen .10 .25
155 Jeff Friesen .10 .25
156 Arturs Irbe .12 .30
157 Craig Janney .10 .25
158 Sergei Makarov .10 .25
159 Sandis Ozolinsh .12 .30
160 Mike Rathje .12 .30
161 Ray Whitney .12 .30
162 Brian Bradley .12 .30
163 Chris Gratton .10 .25
164 Roman Hamrlik .10 .25
165 Petr Klima .10 .25
166 Daren Puppa .12 .30
167 Paul Ysebaert .10 .25
168 Dave Andreychuk .15 .40
169 Mike Gartner .15 .40
170 Todd Gill .10 .25
171 Doug Gilmour .20 .50
172 Kenny Jonsson .15 .40
173 Larry Murphy .15 .40
174 Felix Potvin .15 .40

Card	Low	High
175 Mats Sundin	.15	.40
176 Josef Beranek	.10	.25
177 Jeff Brown	.12	.30
178 Pavel Bure	.20	.50
179 Russ Courtnall	.10	.25
180 Trevor Linden	.15	.40
181 Kirk McLean	.12	.30
182 Alexander Mogilny	.12	.30
183 Roman Oksiuta	.10	.25
184 Mike Ridley	.10	.25
185 Jason Allison	.12	.30
186 Jim Carey	.12	.30
187 Sergei Gonchar	.10	.25
188 Dale Hunter	.12	.30
189 Calle Johansson	.10	.25
190 Joe Juneau	.12	.30
191 Joe Reekie	.10	.25
192 Nelson Emerson	.10	.25
193 Nikolai Khabibulin	.12	.30
194 Dave Manson	.10	.25
195 Teppo Numminen	.10	.25
196 Teemu Selanne	.30	.75
197 Keith Tkachuk	.15	.40
198 Alexei Zhamnov	.15	.40
199 Checklist #1	.05	.15
200 Checklist #2	.05	.15
NNO Roenick Exch. EXPIRED	2.50	5.00
NNO J.Roenick SkyMotion	15.00	30.00

1995-96 Emotion generatioNext

This ten-card set took a look at those players thought to be the stars of tomorrow. The cards, which featured a player bust over a fiery metallic foil background were inserted at a rate of 1:10 packs. The cards were numbered "X of 10" on the back.

Card	Low	High
COMPLETE SET (10)	8.00	15.00
1 Brian Holzinger	1.00	2.50
2 Eric Daze	.60	1.50
3 Jason Bonsignore	.30	.75
4 Jamie Storr	.60	1.50
5 Tommy Salo	2.00	5.00
6 Brendan Witt	.30	.75
7 Saku Koivu	1.00	2.50
8 Todd Bertuzzi	3.00	8.00
9 Ed Jovanovski	.30	.75
10 Chad Kilger	.30	.75

1995-96 Emotion Ntense Power

This ten-card set highlighted the game's top power forwards. Utilizing a design element similar to the previous set using this name, the cards featured a cut-out player photo over a swirling foil background. The cards were randomly inserted 1:30 packs, and were numbered "X of 10" on the back.

Card	Low	High
COMPLETE SET (10)	10.00	20.00
1 Cam Neely	1.50	4.00
2 Keith Primeau	.50	1.25
3 Mark Messier	1.50	4.00
4 Eric Lindros	1.50	4.00
5 Mikael Renberg	1.00	2.50
6 Owen Nolan	1.00	2.50
7 Brendan Shanahan	1.50	4.00
8 Kevin Stevens	.50	1.25
9 Keith Tkachuk	1.50	4.00
10 Rick Tocchet	1.00	2.50

1995-96 Emotion Xcel

This ten-card set featured the top ten players in the league as chosen by the Fleer staff. The cards were issued randomly in packs at the rate of 1:72 packs. It was apparent, however, that a significant quantity of these cards entered the market through non-pack distribution, making them significantly easier to acquire than the long pack odds would suggest.

Card	Low	High
COMPLETE SET (10)	30.00	60.00
1 Adam Oates	.75	2.00
2 Jeremy Roenick	2.00	5.00
3 Sergei Fedorov	2.00	5.00
4 Wayne Gretzky	10.00	25.00
5 Alexei Yashin	.60	1.50
6 Eric Lindros	1.25	3.00
7 Ron Francis	.75	2.00
8 Mario Lemieux	8.00	20.00
9 Joe Sakic	3.00	8.00
10 Alexei Zhamnov	.60	1.50

1995-96 Emotion Xcited

This twenty-card set was the easiest pull from this issue, randomly inserted 1:3 packs. The set included many of the top offensive players in the game.

Card	Low	High
COMPLETE SET (20)	15.00	30.00
1 Theo Fleury	.20	.50
2 Jeremy Roenick	.75	2.00
3 Mike Modano	1.00	2.50
4 Sergei Fedorov	1.00	2.50
5 Wayne Gretzky	5.00	12.00
6 Brian Leetch	.40	1.00
7 Alexei Yashin	.20	.50
8 Brett Hull	.75	2.00
9 Jaromir Jagr	1.00	2.50
10 Mario Lemieux	3.00	8.00
11 Ron Francis	.40	1.00
12 Keith Primeau	.20	.50
13 Joe Sakic	1.25	3.00
14 Peter Forsberg	1.50	4.00
15 Paul Kariya	.60	1.50
16 Pavel Bure	.60	1.50
17 Alexei Zhamnov	.40	1.00
18 Martin Brodeur	1.50	4.00
19 Jim Carey	.40	1.00
20 Chris Chelios	.60	1.50

1992-93 Enor Mark Messier

One card from this ten-card standard-size set was included in each specially marked package of Enor Progard Plus sports card pages. The cards featured color player photos with silver borders. A red stripe that ran along the right edge and top of the photo accented the card face and provided a backdrop for the player's name, which was printed in white and blue. The horizontal back showed a close-up player photo that overlaped a red border stripe similar to the one on the front and a pale blue panel. The red stripe contained the player's name. The blue panel containsedplayer information. A black vertical bar ran along the left edge of the panel and contained biographical information.

Card	Low	High
COMPLETE SET (10)	2.00	5.00
COMMON MESSIER (1-10)	.20	.50

1967-73 Equitable Sports Hall of Fame

This set consists of copies of art work found over a number of years in many national magazines, especially "Sports Illustrated," honoring sports heroes that Equitable Life Assurance Society selected to be in its very own Sports Hall of Fame. The cards consists of charcoal-type drawings on white backgrounds by artists, George Loh and Robert Riger, and measure approximately 11" by 7 3/4". The unnumbered cards have been assigned numbers below using a sport prefix (BB- baseball, BK- basketball, FB- football, HK-hockey, OT-other).

Card	Low	High
COMPLETE SET (95)	250.00	500.00
HK1 Phil Esposito	3.00	6.00
HK2 Bernie Geoffrion	3.00	6.00
HK3 Gordie Howe	5.00	10.00
HK4 Ching Johnson	2.00	4.00
HK5 Stan Mikita	3.00	6.00
HK6 Maurice Richard	4.00	8.00

1969-73 Equitable Sports Hall of Fame

Little is known about these miniature prints beyond the confirmed checklist. Additional information can be forwarded to hockeymag@beckett.com.

Card	Low	High
COMPLETE SET (6)	62.50	125.00
1 Phil Esposito	10.00	20.00
2 Bernie Geoffrion	10.00	20.00
3 Gordie Howe	25.00	50.00
4 Ching Johnson	7.50	15.00
5 Stan Mikita	10.00	20.00
6 Maurice Richard	12.50	25.00

1970-71 Esso Power Players

The 1970-71 Esso Power Players set included 252 color stamps measuring approximately 1 1/2" by 2". The stamps were issued in six-stamp sheets and given away free with a minimum purchase of $3 of Esso gasoline. There were 18 stamps for each of the 14 teams then in the NHL. The stamps were unnumbered except for jersey (uniform) number. The set was issued with an album, which could be found in either a soft or hard bound version. The hard cover album supposedly had extra pages with additional players. The stamps and albums were available in both French and English language versions. The set was numbered below numerically within each team as follows: Montreal Canadiens (1-18), Toronto Maple Leafs (19-36), Vancouver Canucks (37-54), Boston Bruins (55-72), Buffalo Sabres (73-90), California Golden Seals (91-108), Chicago Blackhawks (109-126), Detroit Red Wings (127-144), Los Angeles Kings (145-162), Minnesota North Stars (163-180), New York Rangers (181-198), Philadelphia Flyers (199-216), Pittsburgh Penguins (217-234), and St. Louis Blues (235-252). Supposedly there were 59 stamps which are tougher to find than the others. The short-printed stamps were apparently those players who were pre-printed into the soft-cover album and hence not included in the first stamp printing.

Card	Low	High
COMPLETE SET (252)	125.00	250.00
1 Rogatien Vachon 1	1.50	3.00
2 Jacques Laperriere 2	.38	.75
3 J.C. Tremblay 3	.25	.50
4 Jean Beliveau 4	4.00	8.00
5 Guy Lapointe 5	.50	1.00
6 Fran Huck 6	.20	.40
7 Bill Collins 10	.20	.40
8 Marc Tardif 11	.25	.50
9 Yvan Cournoyer 12	.75	1.50
10 Claude Larose 15	.20	.40
11 Henri Richard 16	2.00	4.00
12 Serge Savard 18	.38	.75
13 Terry Harper 19	.25	.50
14 Pete Mahovlich 20	.38	.75
15 John Ferguson 22	.50	1.00
16 Mickey Redmond 24	.63	1.25
17 Jacques Lemaire 25	.63	1.25
18 Phil Myre 30	.38	.75
19 Jacques Plante 1	4.00	8.00
20 Rick Ley 2	.25	.50
21 Mike Pelyk 4	.20	.40
22 Ron Ellis 6	.25	.50
23 Jim Dorey 8	.20	.40
24 Norm Ullman 9	1.00	2.00
25 Guy Trottier 11	.20	.40
26 Jim Harrison 12	.20	.40
27 Dave Keon 14	1.00	2.00
28 Mike Walton 16	.25	.50
29 Jim McKenny 18	.20	.40
30 Paul Henderson 19	.50	1.00
31 Garry Monahan 20 SP	.50	1.00
32 Bob Baun 21	.38	.75
33 Bill MacMillan 23	.20	.40
34 Brian Glennie 24	.20	.40
35 Darryl Sittler 27	5.00	10.00
36 Bruce Gamble 30	.50	1.00
37 Charlie Hodge 1	.63	1.25
38 Gary Doak 2	.20	.40
39 Pat Quinn 3	.38	.75
40 Barry Wilkins 4	.20	.40
41 Darryl Sly 5 SP	.50	1.00
42 Marc Reaume 6	.20	.40
43 Andre Boudrias 7	.20	.40
44 Danny Johnson 8	.20	.40
45 Ray Cullen 10 SP	.50	1.00
46 Wayne Maki 11	.20	.40
47 Mike Corrigan 12	.20	.40
48 Rosaire Paiement 15	.20	.40
49 Paul Popiel 18 SP	.38	.75
50 Dale Tallon 19	.25	.50
51 Murray Hall 23 SP	.50	1.00
52 Len Lunde 24	.20	.40
53 Orland Kurtenbach 25	.25	.50
54 Dunc Wilson 30 SP	.50	1.00
55 Ed Johnston 1	.50	1.00
56 Bobby Orr 4	12.50	25.00
57 Ted Green 6	.25	.50
58 Phil Esposito 7	2.50	5.00
59 Ken Hodge 8	.38	.75
60 Johnny Bucyk 9	1.00	2.00
61 Rick Smith 10 SP	.50	1.00
62 Wayne Carleton 11 SP	.50	1.00
63 Wayne Cashman 12 SP	.75	1.50
64 Garnet Bailey 14	.20	.40
65 Derek Sanderson 16	2.00	4.00
66 Fred Stanfield 17 SP	.50	1.00
67 Ed Westfall 18	.25	.50
68 John McKenzie 19	.20	.40
69 Dallas Smith 20	.20	.40
70 Don Marcotte 21	.20	.40
71 Don Awrey 26 SP	.50	1.00
72 Gerry Cheevers 30	1.50	3.00
73 Roger Crozier 1	.75	1.50
74 Jim Watson 2	.25	.50
75 Tracy Pratt 3	.20	.40
76 Doug Barrie 5 SP	.50	1.00
77 Al Hamilton 6	.25	.50
78 Cliff Schmautz 7 SP	.50	1.00
79 Reg Fleming 9	.20	.40
80 Phil Goyette 10	.20	.40
81 Gilbert Perreault 11	2.50	5.00
82 Skip Krake 12	.20	.40
83 Gerry Meehan 15	.25	.50
84 Ron Anderson 16	.20	.40
85 Floyd Smith 17 SP	.50	1.00
86 Steve Atkinson 19	.20	.40
87 Paul Andrea 21 SP	.50	1.00
88 Don Marshall 22	.20	.40
89 Eddie Shack 23 SP	1.50	3.00
90 Larry Keenan 26	.20	.40
91 Gary Smith 1	.50	1.00
92 Doug Roberts 2	.20	.40
93 Harry Howell 3	.63	1.25
94 Wayne Muloin 4	.20	.40
95 Carol Vadnais 5	.20	.40
96 Dick Mattiussi 6	.20	.40
97 Earl Ingarfield 7	.20	.40
98 Gerry Ehman 8	.20	.40
99 Bill Hicke 9	.20	.40
100 Ted Hampson 10	.20	.40
101 Gary Jarrett 12	.20	.40
102 Joe Hardy 14 SP	.50	1.00
103 Tony Featherstone 16 SP	.50	1.00
104 Gary Croteau 18	.20	.40
105 Ernie Hicke 20 SP	.50	1.00
106 Ron Stackhouse 21	.20	.40
107 Dennis Hextall 22 SP	.75	1.50
108 Bob Sneddon 30 SP	.50	1.00
109 Gerry Desjardins 1 SP	.75	1.50
110 Bill White 2	.25	.50
111 Keith Magnuson 3	.25	.50
112 Doug Jarrett 4 SP	.50	1.00
113 Lou Angotti 6	.20	.40
114 Pit Martin 7	.25	.50
115 Jim Pappin 8	.20	.40
116 Bobby Hull 9	5.00	10.00
117 Dennis Hull 10 SP	1.00	2.00
118 Doug Mohns 11	.25	.50
119 Pat Stapleton 12	.25	.50
120 Bryan Campbell 14 SP	.50	1.00
121 Eric Nesterenko 15	.25	.50
122 Chico Maki 16	.25	.50
123 Gerry Pinder 18	.25	.50
124 Cliff Koroll 20	.20	.40
125 Stan Mikita 21	3.00	6.00
126 Tony Esposito 35	3.00	6.00
127 Jim Rutherford 1 SP	1.00	2.00
128 Gary Bergman 2	.25	.50
129 Dale Rolfe 3	.20	.40
130 Larry Brown 4 SP	.50	1.00
131 Serge Lajeunesse 5	.20	.40
132 Garry Unger 7	.38	.75
133 Tom Webster 8	.25	.50
134 Gordie Howe 9	7.50	15.00
135 Alex Delvecchio 10	1.00	2.00
136 Don Luce 11 SP	.50	1.00
137 Bruce MacGregor 12	.20	.40
138 Nick Libett 14	.25	.50
139 Al Karlander 15	.20	.40
140 Ron Harris 16	.20	.40
141 Wayne Connelly 17 SP	.50	1.00
142 Billy Dea 21 SP	.50	1.00
143 Frank Mahovlich 27	2.00	4.00
144 Roy Edwards 30	.38	.75
145 Jack Norris 1	.20	.40
146 Dale Hoganson 2	.20	.40
147 Larry Cahan 3	.20	.40
148 Gilles Marotte 4 SP	.50	1.00
149 Noel Price 5 SP	.50	1.00
150 Paul Curtis 6 SP	.50	1.00
151 Ross Lonsberry 8	.20	.40
152 Gord Labossiere 9	.20	.40
153 Doug Robinson 11 SP	.50	1.00
154 Larry Mickey 12	.20	.40
155 Juha Widing 15	.20	.40
156 Eddie Joyal 16	.20	.40
157 Bill Flett 17	.20	.40
158 Bob Berry 18	.25	.50
159 Bob Pulford 20	.38	.75
160 Matt Ravlich 21	.20	.40
161 Mike Byers 24 SP	.50	1.00
162 Denis DeJordy 30	.50	1.00
163 Gump Worsley 1	2.00	4.00
164 Barry Gibbs 2 SP	.50	1.00
165 Fred Barrett 3	.20	.40
166 Ted Harris 4	.20	.40
167 Danny O'Shea 7	.20	.40
168 Bill Goldsworthy 8	.25	.50
169 Charlie Burns 9	.20	.40
170 Murray Oliver 10	.20	.40
171 Jean-Paul Parise 11	.25	.50
172 Tom Williams 12 SP	.50	1.00
173 Bobby Rousseau 15	.25	.50
174 Buster Harvey 18 SP	.50	1.00
175 Tom Reid 20 SP	.50	1.00
176 Danny Grant 21	.25	.50
177 Walt McKechnie 22	.20	.40
178 Lou Nanne 23	.25	.50
179 Danny Lawson 24 SP	.50	1.00
180 Cesare Maniago 30	.50	1.00
181 Ed Giacomin 1	1.50	3.00
182 Brad Park 2	3.00	8.00
183 Tim Horton 3	2.50	5.00
184 Arnie Brown 4	.20	.40
185 Rod Gilbert 7	.75	1.50
186 Bob Nevin 8	.20	.40
187 Bill Fairbairn 10 SP	.50	1.00
188 Vic Hadfield 11	.25	.50
189 Ron Stewart 12	.20	.40
190 Jim Neilson 15	.25	.50
191 Rod Seiling 16 SP	.50	1.00
192 Dave Balon 17 SP	.50	1.00
193 Walt Tkaczuk 18	.25	.50
194 Jean Ratelle 19	.75	1.50
195 Jack Egers 20	.20	.40
196 Pete Stemkowski 21 SP	.50	1.00
197 Ted Irvine 27	.20	.40
198 Gilles Villemure 30	.50	1.00
199 Doug Favell 1	.75	1.50
200 Ed Van Impe 2	.20	.40
201 Larry Hillman 3	.20	.40
202 Barry Ashbee 4	.38	.75
203 Wayne Hillman 6 SP	.50	1.00
204 Andre Lacroix 7	.25	.50
205 Lew Morrison 8	.20	.40
206 Bob Kelly 9 SP	.50	1.00
207 Jean-Guy Gendron 11	.20	.40
208 Gary Dornhoefer 12	.38	.75
209 Joe Watson 14	.20	.40
210 Garry Peters 15 SP	.50	1.00
211 Bobby Clarke 16	5.00	10.00
212 Earl Heiskala 19 SP	.50	1.00
213 Jim Johnson 20	.20	.40
214 Serge Bernier 21	.20	.40
215 Larry Hale 23 SP	.50	1.00
216 Bernie Parent 30	2.50	5.00
217 Al Smith 1	.38	.75
218 Duane Rupp 2	.20	.40
219 Bob Woytowich 3	.20	.40
220 Bob Blackburn 4	.20	.40
221 Bryan Watson 5 SP	.50	1.00
222 Dunc McCallum 6	.25	.50
223 Bryan Hextall 7	.25	.50
224 Andy Bathgate 9 SP	1.25	2.50
225 Keith McCreary 10 SP	.50	1.00
226 Nick Harbaruk 11	.20	.40
227 Ken Schinkel 12	.20	.40
228 Glen Sather 16 SP	1.25	2.50
229 Ron Schock 17	.20	.40
230 Wally Boyer 18	.20	.40
231 Jean Pronovost 19	.25	.50
232 Dean Prentice 20	.25	.50
233 Jim Morrison 27	.20	.40
234 Les Binkley 30 SP	.75	1.50
235 Glenn Hall 1	2.00	4.00
236 Bob Wall 2	.20	.40
237 Noel Picard 4	.20	.40
238 Bob Plager 5	.25	.50
239 Jim Roberts 6	.25	.50
240 Red Berenson 7	.25	.50
241 Barclay Plager 8	.25	.50
242 Frank St.Marseille 9	.20	.40
243 George Morrison 10 SP	.50	1.00
244 Gary Sabourin 11	.20	.40
245 Terry Crisp 12 SP	1.00	2.00
246 Tim Ecclestone 14	.20	.40
247 Bill McCreary 15	.20	.40
248 Brit Selby 18 SP	.50	1.00
249 Jim Lorentz 19 SP	.50	1.00
250 Ab McDonald 20	.20	.40
251 Chris Bordeleau 21 SP	.50	1.00
252 Ernie Wakely 31	.50	1.00
xx Soft Cover Album	7.50	15.00
xx Hard Cover Album	25.00	50.00

1983-84 Esso

The 1983-84 Esso set contained 21 color cards measuring approximately 4 1/2" by 3" although the player photo portion of the card was only 2" by 3". There were actually two different sets, one in French and one in English. The cards were actually part of a lottery-type game where 5000.00 cash could be won instantly via a scratch-off. The card backs contained information about the contest on the back of the contest portion and player statistics on the back of the player photo portion of the card. The cards were numbered and hence they are checklisted below alphabetically.

Card	Low	High
COMPLETE SET (21)	6.00	15.00
*FRENCH: .5X TO 1.2X ENGLISH		
1 Glenn Anderson	.40	1.00
2 John Anderson	.20	.50
3 Dave Babych	.20	.50
4 Richard Brodeur	.40	1.00
5 Paul Coffey	1.50	4.00
6 Bill Derlago	.20	.50
7 Bob Gainey	.60	1.50
8 Michel Goulet	.40	1.00
9 Dale Hawerchuk	.75	2.00
10 Dale Hunter	.30	.75
11 Morris Lukowich	.20	.50
12 Lanny McDonald	.60	1.50
13 Mark Messier	2.00	5.00
14 Jim Peplinski	.20	.50
15 Paul Reinhart	.20	.50
16 Larry Robinson	.50	1.25
17 Stan Smyl	.30	.75
18 Harold Snepsts	.30	.75
19 Marc Tardif	.20	.50
20 Mario Tremblay	.20	.50
21 Rick Vaive	.30	.75

1988-89 Esso All-Stars

e 1988-89 Esso All-Stars set contained 48 color cards (actually adhesive-backed "stickers") measuring approximately 2 1/8" by 3 1/4". The fronts featured borderless color action photos with facsimile autographs. The backs had complete checklists for the whole set. The players depicted included hockey greats from the past and present. The cards (stickers) were unnumbered and hence are checklisted below in alphabetical order. There was a 32-page album (8 1/2" by 11") available in either English or French, which was intended to hold the stickers. In fact each album already contained five pasted-in cards, Ed Giacomin, Al MacInnis, Rick Middleton, Bernie Parent, and Pierre Pilote. The cards were distributed in Canada in packs of six with a purchase of gasoline at participating Esso service stations. The complete set price below includes the album.

Card	Low	High
COMPLETE SET (48)	6.00	15.00
1 Jean Beliveau	.30	.75
2 Mike Bossy	.30	.75
3 Ray Bourque	.30	.75
4 Johnny Bower	.15	.40
5 Bobby Clarke	.20	.50
6 Paul Coffey	.30	.75
7 Yvan Cournoyer	.08	.25
8 Marcel Dionne	.15	.40
9 Ken Dryden	.40	1.00
10 Phil Esposito	.30	.75
11 Tony Esposito	.20	.50
12 Grant Fuhr	.15	.40
13 Clark Gillies	.07	.20
14 Michel Goulet	.08	.25
15 Wayne Gretzky	1.50	4.00
16 Dale Hawerchuk	.08	.25
17 Ron Hextall	.15	.40
18 Gordie Howe	.60	1.50
19 Mark Howe	.07	.20
20 Bobby Hull	.30	.75
21 Tim Kerr	.07	.20
22 Jari Kurri	.08	.25
23 Guy Lafleur	.30	.75
24 Rod Langway	.07	.20
25 Jacques Laperriere	.07	.20
26 Guy Lapointe	.08	.25
27 Mario Lemieux	1.00	2.50
28 Frank Mahovlich	.20	.50
29 Lanny McDonald	.08	.25
30 Mark Messier	.40	1.00
31 Stan Mikita	.20	.50
32 Mats Naslund	.07	.20
33 Bobby Orr	.75	2.00
34 Brad Park	.08	.25
35 Gilbert Perreault	.08	.25
36 Denis Potvin	.08	.25
37 Larry Robinson	.08	.25
38 Luc Robitaille	.20	.50
39 Borje Salming	.07	.20
40 Denis Savard	.08	.25
41 Serge Savard	.08	.25
42 Steve Shutt	.08	.25
43 Darryl Sittler	.08	.25
44 Billy Smith	.08	.25
45 John Tonelli	.07	.20
46 Bryan Trottier	.08	.25
47 Norm Ullman	.08	.25
48 Gump Worsley	.20	.50
xx Album	1.25	3.00

1997-98 Esso Olympic Hockey Heroes

These oversized cards featured color action photos on the front, along with biographical information on the back. Each player was pictured in his or her respective Olympic uniform. The set was available in six series from Esso gas stations and comes complete with a black binder.

Card	Low	High
COMPLETE SET (60)	12.00	30.00
*FRENCH: .5X TO 1.2X ENGLISH		
1 Header Card	.02	.10
2 Olympic Hockey History	.02	.10
3 CBC Broadcast Guide	.02	.10
4 Olympic Hockey Bracket	.02	.10
5 Team Canada	.02	.10
6 Eric Lindros	.75	2.00
7 Joe Sakic	.60	1.50
8 Trevor Linden	.15	.40
9 Paul Kariya	.75	2.00
10 Brendan Shanahan	.40	1.00
11 Rod Brind'Amour	.15	.40
12 Theo Fleury	.15	.40
13 Eric Desjardins	.08	.25
14 Scott Niedermayer	.08	.25
15 Chris Pronger	.15	.40
16 Rob Blake	.08	.25
17 Patrick Roy	1.00	2.50
18 Curtis Joseph	.20	.50
19 Keith Primeau	.15	.40
20 Mark Messier	.30	.75
21 Adam Foote	.08	.25
22 Team USA	.02	.10
23 Keith Tkachuk	.25	.60
24 Mike Modano	.20	.50
25 John LeClair	.30	.75
26 Doug Weight	.15	.40
27 Brett Hull	.25	.60
28 Jeremy Roenick	.20	.50
29 Brian Leetch	.20	.50
30 Chris Chelios	.20	.50
31 Kevin Hatcher	.08	.25
32 Derian Hatcher	.08	.25
33 Mike Richter	.20	.50
34 John Vanbiesbrouck	.40	1.00
35 Team Russia	.02	.10
36 Sergei Fedorov	.40	1.00
37 Alexei Yashin	.15	.40
38 Pavel Bure	.40	1.00
39 Alexander Mogilny	.15	.40
40 Nikolai Khabibulin	.15	.40
41 Team Sweden	.02	.10
42 Mats Sundin	.20	.50
43 Peter Forsberg	.60	1.50
44 Daniel Alfredsson	.15	.40
45 Nicklas Lidstrom	.15	.40
46 Kenny Jonsson	.08	.25
47 Team Finland	.02	.10
48 Saku Koivu	.40	1.00
49 Esa Tikkanen	.15	.40
50 Teemu Selanne	.40	1.00
51 Team Czech Republic	.02	.10
52 Jaromir Jagr	.60	1.50
53 Roman Hamrlik	.15	.40
54 Dominik Hasek	.40	1.00
55 Women's Team Canada	.02	.10
56 Nancy Drolet	.20	.50
57 Geraldine Heaney	.20	.50
58 Hayley Wickenheiser	.20	.50
59 Cassie Campbell	.20	.50
60 Stacy Wilson	.20	.50
NNO Eric Lindros AU	40.00	100.00

2001-02 eTopps

The 2001-02 eTopps cards were issued via Topps' website and initially sold exclusively on eBay's eTopps Trade Floor. Owner's of the cards could hold the cards on account with Topps and freely trade those cards similar to shares of stock. They also could pay a fee to take actual delivery of their cards, but most are still held on account with Topps. The production quantity of each card is listed beside the player's name. Prices below are derived from sales on the eTopps trading floor on ebay.

Card	Low	High
COMMON CARD	.75	2.00
SEMISTARS	1.00	2.50
UNLISTED STARS	1.25	3.00
1 Joe Sakic/782	2.00	5.00
2 Paul Kariya/1032	1.50	4.00
3 Curtis Joseph/714	1.25	3.00
4 Brendan Shanahan/2000	1.50	4.00
5 Patrik Elias/859	1.25	3.00
6 Evgeni Nabokov/549	1.00	2.50
7 Johan Hedberg/574	1.00	2.50
8 Patrick Roy/938	3.00	8.00
9 John LeClair/494	1.25	3.00
10 Martin Brodeur/663	2.50	6.00
11 Teemu Selanne/784	2.50	6.00
12 Mike Modano/559	2.00	5.00
13 Martin Havlat/510	1.00	2.50
14 Roberto Luongo/747	2.00	5.00
15 Peter Forsberg/598	1.50	4.00
16 Steve Yzerman/796	4.00	10.00
17 Pavel Bure/896	1.50	4.00
18 Mark Messier/618	2.00	5.00
19 Mike Comrie/809	1.00	2.50
20 Mats Sundin/717	1.25	3.00
21 Owen Nolan/457	1.25	3.00
22 Ed Belfour/730	1.25	3.00
23 Mario Lemieux/1116	4.00	10.00
24 Keith Tkachuk/751	1.25	3.00
25 Milan Hejduk/532	1.00	2.50
26 Rick Dipietro/579	1.00	2.50
27 Roman Cechmanek/511	1.00	2.50
28 Sergei Fedorov/710	2.00	5.00
29 Vincent Lecavalier/550	1.00	2.50
30 Eric Lindros/634	2.00	5.00
31 Ilya Kovalchuk/2513	4.00	10.00
32 Zigmund Palffy/550	1.25	3.00
33 Dominik Hasek/753	2.00	5.00
34 Jaromir Jagr/569	3.00	8.00
35 Doug Weight/521	1.25	3.00

2002-03 eTopps

The 2002-03 eTopps cards were issued via Topps' website and initially sold exclusively on eBay's eTopps Trade Floor. Owner's of the cards could hold the cards on account with Topps and freely trade those cards similar to shares of stock. They also could pay a fee to take actual delivery of their cards, but most are still held on account with Topps. Prices below are derived from sales on the eTopps trading floor on ebay. Production numbers are listed below.

Card
1 Jarome Iginla/1668
2 Pavel Bure/1475
3 Patrick Roy/1500
4 Mats Sundin/1320
5 Jaromir Jagr/1500
6 Martin Brodeur/1459
7 Jose Theodore/1181
8 Nicklas Lidstrom/1551
9 Joe Sakic/1162
10 Ilya Kovalchuk/1500
11 Mike Modano/922
12 Sergei Fedorov/1583
13 Pavel Datsyuk/1500
14 Saku Koivu/1276
15 Peter Forsberg/1240
16 Dany Heatley/2580
17 Erik Cole/1952
18 Mario Lemieux/2000
19 Eric Lindros/1243
20 Patrik Elias/1500
21 Steve Yzerman/1000
22 Michael Peca/837
23 Todd Bertuzzi/2000
24 Evgeni Nabokov/925
25 Paul Kariya/971
26 Peter Bondra/1102
27 Chris Pronger/1147
28 Alexei Yashin/1133
29 Daniel Alfredsson/840
30 Teemu Selanne/949
31 Brendan Shanahan/1078
32 Brett Hull/1739
33 Ron Francis/1063
34 Simon Gagne/1500
35 Marty Turco/1500
36 Roberto Luongo/918
37 Joe Thornton/1500
38 Mike Comrie/1196
39 Rick Nash/3000
40 Stanislav Chistov/2000
41 Henrik Zetterberg/3000
42 Ales Hemsky/2000
43 Jay Bouwmeester/3000
44 Alexei Smirnov/2000
45 Chuck Kobasew/2000
46 P-M Bouchard/2000
47 Jason Spezza/2000
48 Alexander Svitov/2000
49 Marian Gaborik/2000
50 Jeremy Roenick/1145
51 Olli Jokinen/1260
52 Marian Hossa/1500
53 Markus Naslund/2000
54 Ryan Miller/2000
55 Martin St. Louis/1489
56 Jocelyn Thibault/930

2003-04 eTopps

e 2003-04 eTopps cards were issued via Topps' website and initially sold exclusively on eBay's eTopps Trade Floor. Owner's of the cards could hold the cards on account with Topps and freely trade those cards similar to shares of stock. They also could pay a fee to take actual delivery of their cards, but most are still held on account with Topps. Since most do not trade hands as physical cards, we've simply listed the checkliProduction numbers are listed below. Prices below are derived from sales on the eTopps trading floor on ebay.

Card
1 Pasi Nurminen/757
2 Al MacInnis/871
3 Daniel Briere/743
4 Jordan Leopold/861
5 Tyler Arnason/920
6 Niko Kapanen/780
7 Kristian Huselius/797
8 Jamie Langenbrunner/756
10 Jean-Sebastien Giguere/693
11 Mario Lemieux/1000
12 Patrick Lalime/832
13 Milan Hejduk/817
14 Rick DiPietro/749
15 Owen Nolan/839
16 Dany Heatley/698
17 Mattias Weinhandl/774
18 Brendan Morrison/687
19 Paul Kariya/767
20 Zigmund Palffy/636
21 Marian Gaborik/872
22 Sergei Fedorov/706
23 Tony Amonte/558
24 Roberto Luongo/674
26 Saku Koivu/651
27 Todd Bertuzzi/868
28 Patrik Elias/804
29 Jeremy Roenick/1000
30 Marian Hossa/839
31 Brad Richards/1000
32 Joe Thornton/1123
33 Peter Forsberg/1000
34 Daymond Langkow/644
35 Ed Jovanovski/873
36 Martin Brodeur/1000
37 Jarome Iginla/913
38 Jaromir Jagr/792
39 Rick Nash/1035
40 Teemu Selanne/769
41 Patrice Bergeron/1500
42 Peter Sejna/838
43 Matthew Stajan/1000
44 Eric Staal/1500
45 Nathan Horton/1000
46 Joffrey Lupul/886
47 Tuomo Ruutu/1462
48 Jordin Tootoo/990
49 Dustin Brown/918
50 Marc-Andre Fleury/2000
51 Patrick Marleau/932
52 Joni Pitkanen/1000
53 Pavel Datsyuk/1000
54 Brian Leetch/1000
55 Chris Chelios/896
56 Andrew Raycroft/1500

1948-52 Exhibits Canadian

These cards measured approximately 3 1/4" by 5 1/4" and were issued on heavy cardboard stock. The cards showed full-bleed photos with the player's name burned in toward the bottom. The hockey exhibit cards were generally considered more scarce than their baseball exhibit counterparts. Since the cards were unnumbered, the set is arranged below alphabetically within teams as follows: Montreal (1-27), Toronto (28-42), Detroit (43-46), Boston (47-48), Chicago (49-50), and New York (51). The set closes with an Action subset (52-65).

Card	Low	High
COMPLETE SET (65)	750.00	1500.00
1 Reggie Abbott	6.00	12.00
2 Jean Beliveau	37.50	75.00
3 Jean Beliveau	50.00	100.00
4 Toe Blake	20.00	40.00
5 Butch Bouchard	10.00	20.00
6 Bob Fillion	6.00	12.00
7 Dick Gamble	7.50	15.00
8 Bernie Geoffrion	25.00	50.00
9 Doug Harvey	20.00	40.00
10 Tom Johnson	10.00	20.00
11 Elmer Lach	20.00	40.00
12 Hal Laycoe	6.00	12.00
13 Jacques Locas	6.00	12.00
14 Bud McPherson	6.00	12.00
15 Paul Maznick	6.00	12.00
16 Gerry McNeil	20.00	40.00
17 Paul Meger	6.00	12.00
18 Dickie Moore	20.00	40.00
19 Ken Mosdell	6.00	12.00
20 Bert Olmstead	10.00	20.00
21 Ken Reardon	12.50	25.00
22 Billy Reay	7.50	15.00
23 Maurice Richard	50.00	100.00
24 Maurice Richard	50.00	100.00
25 Dollard St.Laurent	7.50	15.00
26 Grant Warwick	6.00	12.00
27 Floyd Curry	7.50	15.00
28 Bill Barilko	20.00	40.00
29 Turk Broda	20.00	40.00
30 Cal Gardner	10.00	20.00
31 Bill Juzda	6.00	12.00
32 Ted Kennedy	20.00	40.00
33 Joe Klukay	6.00	12.00
34 Fleming Mackell	6.00	12.00
35 Howie Meeker	15.00	30.00
36 Gus Mortson	6.00	12.00
37 Al Rollins	12.50	25.00
38 Sid Smith	7.50	15.00
39 Tod Sloan	6.00	12.00
40 Ray Timgren	6.00	12.00
41 Jim Thomson	6.00	12.00
42 Max Bentley	12.50	25.00
43 Sid Abel	10.00	20.00
44 Gordie Howe	62.50	125.00
45 Ted Lindsay	25.00	50.00
46 Harry Lumley	20.00	40.00
47 Jack Gelineau	6.00	12.00
48 Paul Ronty	6.00	12.00
49 Doug Bentley	12.50	25.00
50 Roy Conacher	7.50	15.00
51 Chuck Rayner	12.50	25.00
52 Boston vs. Montreal	10.00	20.00
53 Detroit vs. New York	30.00	60.00
54 Montreal vs. Toronto	30.00	60.00
55 New York vs. Montreal	30.00	60.00
56 New York vs. Montreal	10.00	20.00
57 Montreal vs. Boston	10.00	20.00
58 Detroit vs. Montreal	10.00	20.00
59 Chicago vs. Montreal	10.00	20.00
60 New York vs. Montreal	25.00	50.00
61 Chicago vs. Montreal	15.00	30.00
62 Detroit vs. Montreal	20.00	40.00
63 Detroit vs. Montreal	10.00	20.00
64 Toronto vs. Montreal	10.00	20.00
65 Chicago vs. Montreal	10.00	20.00

2009-10 Exquisite Collection Rookie Patch Flashback

STATED PRINT RUN 25 SER.#'d SETS

Card	Low	High
78P Wayne Gretzky/25	750.00	1500.00
78Q Mario Lemieux/25	400.00	800.00
78R Steve Yzerman/25	200.00	400.00
78S Sidney Crosby/25	1200.00	2000.00
78T Patrick Roy/25	250.00	600.00
78U Gordie Howe/25	250.00	500.00

2014-15 Exquisite Collection Signature Patches

Card	Low	High
SP-BG Brendan Gallagher/99 (inserted in 2015-16 The Cup)	15.00	40.00
SP-JN James Neal/99 (inserted in 2015-16 The Cup)	15.00	40.00
SP-KR Chris Kreider/99 (inserted in 2015-16 The Cup)	15.00	40.00
SP-LC Logan Couture/99 (inserted in 2015-16 The Cup)	15.00	40.00
SP-NY Nail Yakupov/99 (inserted in 2015-16 The Cup)	12.00	30.00
SP-OM Olli Maatta/99 (inserted in 2015-16 The Cup)	15.00	40.00
SP-PF Peter Forsberg/25 (inserted in 2015-16 The Cup)	15.00	40.00

2015-16 Exquisite Collection

1-45 STATED PRINT RUN 149-499
ROOKIE PRINT RUN 299-399
ROOKIE JERSEY PRINT RUN 199-299
EXQUISITE INSERTED IN '15-16 BLACK DIAMOND
EXQUISITE INSERTED IN '15-16 UPPER DECK ICE

Card	Low	High
1 Ryan Getzlaf	5.00	12.00
2 Shane Doan	2.50	6.00
3 Zdeno Chara	3.00	8.00
4 Tyler Ennis	2.50	6.00
5 Johnny Gaudreau	5.00	12.00
6 Eric Staal	4.00	10.00
7 Jonathan Toews	6.00	15.00
8 Nathan MacKinnon	6.00	15.00
9 Ryan Johansen	4.00	10.00
10 Tyler Seguin	5.00	12.00
11 Henrik Zetterberg	4.00	10.00
12 Taylor Hall	6.00	15.00
13 Aaron Ekblad	3.00	8.00
14 Anze Kopitar	5.00	12.00
15 Zach Parise	3.00	8.00
16 Carey Price	10.00	25.00
17 Shea Weber	2.50	6.00
18 Cory Schneider	2.50	6.00
19 John Tavares	6.00	15.00
20 Henrik Lundqvist	4.00	10.00
21 Erik Karlsson	6.00	15.00
22 Claude Giroux	3.00	8.00
23 Sidney Crosby	12.00	30.00
24 Joe Pavelski	3.00	8.00
25 Vladimir Tarasenko	5.00	12.00
26 Steven Stamkos	6.00	15.00
27 Jonathan Bernier	3.00	8.00
28 Ryan Miller	3.00	8.00
29 Alexander Ovechkin	12.00	30.00
30 Blake Wheeler	3.00	8.00
31 Bobby Orr	10.00	25.00
32 Bobby Hull	3.00	8.00
33 Mario Lemieux	10.00	25.00
34 Patrick Roy	8.00	20.00
35 Mark Messier	5.00	12.00
36 Doug Gilmour	4.00	10.00
37 Terry Sawchuk	3.00	8.00
38 Wayne Gretzky	15.00	40.00
39 Joe Sakic	5.00	12.00
40 Doug Harvey	3.00	8.00
41 Phil Esposito	5.00	12.00
42 Peter Forsberg	3.00	8.00
43 Ray Bourque	5.00	12.00

Mike Bossy 3.00 8.00
Guy Lafleur 4.00 10.00
Artemi Panarin RC 12.00 30.00
Kevin Fiala RC 4.00 10.00
Andrew Copp RC 4.00 10.00
Emile Poirier RC 4.00 10.00
Mikko Rantanen RC 8.00 20.00
Noah Hanifin RC 5.00 12.00
Oscar Lindberg RC 4.00 10.00
Brock McGinn RC 4.00 10.00
Robby Fabbri RC 5.00 12.00
Jared McCann RC 4.00 10.00
Viktor Arvidsson RC 5.00 12.00
Sergei Plotnikov RC 3.00 8.00
Jake Virtanen RC 5.00 12.00
Ronalds Kenins RC 4.00 10.00
Ryan Hartman RC 5.00 12.00
Nikolay Goldobin RC 4.00 10.00
Radek Faksa RC 4.00 10.00
Joonas Donskoi RC 4.00 10.00
Colton Parayko RC 5.00 12.00
Daniel Sprong RC 8.00 20.00
Jordan Weal RC 4.00 10.00
Mattias Janmark RC 4.00 10.00
Nick Shore RC 4.00 10.00
Nicolas Petan RC 4.00 10.00
Jack Eichel RC 20.00 60.00
Dylan Larkin RC 12.00 30.00
Nikolaj Ehlers RC 8.00 20.00
Max Domi RC 8.00 20.00
Sam Bennett RC 5.00 12.00
Connor McDavid RC 80.00 150.00
H Connor Hellebuyck JSY/299 15.00 40.00
M Connor McDavid JSY/199 125.00 250.00
Dylan Larkin JSY/299 60.00 100.00
P Emile Poirier JSY/299 5.00 12.00
S Henrik Samuelsson JSY/299 3.00 8.00
Jacob de la Rose JSY/299 4.00 10.00
Jack Eichel JSY/199 40.00 80.00
Jake Virtanen JSY/299 5.00 12.00
Kevin Fiala JSY/299 4.00 10.00
D Max Domi JSY/299 8.00 20.00
P Matt Puempel JSY/299 3.00 8.00
E Nikolaj Ehlers JSY/299 8.00 20.00
H Noah Hanifin JSY/299 5.00 12.00
Ryan Hartman JSY/299 5.00 12.00
Sam Bennett JSY/199 10.00 25.00
Slater Koekkoek JSY/299 3.00 8.00
Shane Prince JSY/299 3.00 8.00

2015-16 Exquisite Collection Materials

AK Anze Kopitar Glove 20.00 50.00
BL Rob Blake Socks 12.00 30.00
BR Martin Brodeur Patch
BS Brayden Schenn Skates 12.00 30.00
CP Carey Price Pants 50.00 100.00
DA Pavel Datsyuk Pad 15.00 40.00
DD Drew Doughty Glove 12.00 30.00
DG Doug Gilmour Patch
DP Denis Potvin Stick 12.00 30.00
EM Evgeni Malkin Skates 30.00 60.00
HS Henrik Sedin Stick 12.00 30.00
HZ Henrik Zetterberg Patch 15.00 40.00
JP Jason Spezza Stick 10.00 25.00
JQ Jonathan Quick Blocker 20.00 50.00
JT John Tavares Patch 25.00 60.00
KA Patrick Kane Patch 25.00 60.00
MB Martin Brodeur Blocker 50.00 100.00
MD Marcel Dionne Skates 60.00 100.00
MF Marc-Andre Fleury Pads 25.00 50.00
MG Marian Gaborik Patch 25.00 50.00
MH Marian Hossa Patch 10.00 25.00
MK Mike Keane Stick 10.00 25.00
MT Marty Turco Pads 12.00 30.00
NK Niklas Kronwall Patch 10.00 25.00
ON Owen Nolan Patch 10.00 25.00
PD Pascal Dupuis Glove 12.00 30.00
PF Peter Forsberg Patch 25.00 50.00
PR Patrick Roy Pads 60.00 100.00
RA Bill Ranford Pads 12.00 30.00
RB Rob Blake Pants 12.00 30.00
RG Ryan Getzlaf Patch 20.00 50.00
RN Ryan Nugent-Hopkins Patch 25.00 50.00
RO Rob Blake Stick 12.00 30.00
SH Scott Hartnell Glove 12.00 30.00
TR Tuukka Rask Patch 12.00 30.00
TS Teemu Selanne Glove 15.00 40.00
WG Wayne Gretzky Glove 50.00 100.00
ZP Zach Parise Skates 12.00 30.00

2015-16 Exquisite Collection Materials Combos

2BB N.Bjugstad/A.Barkov 8.00 20.00
2DE S.Doan/Ekman-Lrsn 6.00 15.00
2EG T.Ennis/Girgensons 6.00 15.00
2FK C.Kunitz/M.Fleury 8.00 20.00
2GA J.Gibson/F.Andersen 8.00 20.00
2HD S.Hartnell/B.Dubinsky 8.00 20.00
2IL J.Iginla/G.Landeskog 8.00 20.00
2JK J.Spezza/K.Lehtonen 6.00 15.00
2MB Marchand/P.Bergeron 12.00 30.00
2OS K.Okposo/R.Strome 8.00 20.00
2PG Pacioretty/Galchenyuk 12.00 30.00
2SK D.Keith/B.Seabrook 12.00 30.00
2SL E.Lindholm/J.Skinner 6.00 15.00
2SN T.Seguin/Nichushkin 12.00 30.00
2SP O.Palat/S.Stamkos 15.00 40.00
2TP T.Toffoli/T.Pearson 8.00 20.00
2ZN Zetterberg/G.Nyquist 10.00 25.00

2015-16 Exquisite Collection Material Signatures

SBR Bill Ranford/135 12.00 30.00
SCP Carey Price/135 40.00 100.00
SDG Doug Gilmour/25 25.00 60.00
SEM Evgeni Malkin/99 40.00 100.00
SGF Grant Fuhr/99 12.00 30.00
SGL Guy Lafleur/25 30.00 80.00
SGR Wayne Gretzky/10
SJP Joe Pavelski/135 12.00 30.00
SJS Jason Spezza/135 10.00 25.00
SMF Marc-Andre Fleury/99 20.00 50.00
SMG Guy Carbonneau/135 10.00 25.00
SMK Mike Keane/135 10.00 25.00
SML Mario Lemieux/10
SMM Mark Messier/10
SRB Rod Brind'Amour/135 10.00 25.00
SSC Sidney Crosby/10
SSE Tyler Seguin/99 20.00 50.00
STS Teemu Selanne/25 25.00 60.00
SWG Wayne Gretzky/10

2015-16 Exquisite Collection Materials Quads

4CGY Gdru/Mnhn/Hillr/Hdlr 20.00 50.00
4EDM RNH/Ebrle/Drstl/Ykpv 30.00 60.00
4FLY Schn/Ctrier/Vrck/Msn 12.00 30.00
4NYR Nsh/Krdr/St.Ls/Zcrlo 25.00 50.00
4OTT Andn/Krlsn/Trs/Ryn 25.00 60.00
4STL Bcks/Ststny/Trsn/Aln 25.00 50.00
4TML Bzk/Brnr/vn Rms/Kdr 12.00 30.00
EM4VAN Mlr/Brws/Sdin/Sdin 30.00 60.00
EM4WAS Hltby/Bksm/Crln/Kznt 40.00 80.00
EM4JETS Whlr/Schf/Pvlc/Trba 15.00 40.00
EM4PRED Jrnk/Nl/Webr/Jnes 12.00 30.00
EM4WILD Prse/Cyl/Pmnvl/Grnl 12.00 30.00

2015-16 Exquisite Collection Rookie Dual Jerseys

*DUAL SPECTRUM/25: .6X TO 1.5X DUAL/149
*QUAD/99: .5X TO 1.2X DUAL/149
R2CM Connor McDavid 100.00 200.00
R2EP Emile Poirier 5.00 12.00
R2JE Jack Eichel 40.00 80.00
R2JR Jacob de la Rose 5.00 12.00
R2KF Kevin Fiala 5.00 12.00
R2MD Max Domi 10.00 25.00
R2NE Nikolaj Ehlers 10.00 25.00
R2NH Noah Hanifin 6.00 15.00

2015-16 Exquisite Collection Endorsements Relics

ER-AO Alexander Ovechkin 60.00 150.00
ER-CO Chris Osgood 12.00 30.00
ER-CP Carey Price 60.00 150.00
ER-DH Dale Hawerchuk 15.00 40.00
ER-EM Evgeni Malkin 40.00 100.00
ER-JB Jamie Benn 15.00 40.00
ER-JG Johnny Gaudreau 20.00 50.00
ER-JI Jarome Iginla 12.00 30.00
ER-JR Jeremy Roenick 12.00 30.00
ER-JT Jonathan Toews 30.00 80.00
ER-MB Martin Brodeur 60.00 150.00
ER-ML Mario Lemieux
ER-MM Mike Modano 20.00 50.00
ER-PB Pavel Bure
ER-PC Paul Coffey 25.00 60.00
ER-PD Pavel Datsyuk 30.00 80.00
ER-PF Peter Forsberg 60.00 150.00
ER-PR Patrick Roy
ER-RB Rob Blake 12.00 30.00
ER-SC Sidney Crosby 150.00 300.00
ER-TS Teemu Selanne 25.00 60.00
ER-WG Wayne Gretzky

2015-16 Exquisite Collection Endorsements Rookie Relics

ERCH Charles Hudon 15.00 40.00
ERCM Connor McDavid 400.00 800.00
ERDL Dylan Larkin 50.00 125.00
ERJM Jared McCann 15.00 40.00
ERJV Jake Virtanen 20.00 50.00
ERKF Kevin Fiala 15.00 40.00
ERMD Max Domi 30.00 80.00
ERMR Mikko Rantanen 30.00 80.00
ERNE Nikolaj Ehlers 30.00 80.00
ERNH Noah Hanifin 20.00 50.00
ERNR Nick Ritchie 15.00 40.00
ERRF Robby Fabbri 20.00 50.00
ERSB Sam Bennett 20.00 50.00
ERZF Zachary Fucale 15.00 40.00

2015-16 Exquisite Collection Rookie Jumbo Patches

RJCH Connor Hellebuyck/35 25.00 50.00
RJCM Connor McDavid/35 150.00 300.00
RJEP Emile Poirier/35 12.00 30.00
RJJR Jacob de la Rose/35 12.00 30.00
RJKF Kevin Fiala/35 12.00 30.00
RJMD Max Domi/35 25.00 60.00
RJNE Nikolaj Ehlers/35 25.00 60.00
RJNH Noah Hanifin/35 15.00 40.00
RJSB Sam Bennett/35 15.00 40.00
RJSP Shane Prince/35 10.00 25.00

2015-16 Exquisite Collection Rookie Signatures

ERSBM Brock McGinn/399 6.00 15.00
ERSCH Connor Hellebuyck/399 15.00 40.00
ERSCM Connor McDavid/149 300.00 500.00
ERSCS Chandler Stephenson/399 6.00 15.00
ERSDL Dylan Larkin/399 25.00 60.00
ERSDS Daniel Sprong/399 12.00 30.00
ERSEP Emile Poirier/399 6.00 15.00
ERSFA Radek Faksa/399 6.00 15.00
ERSJD Joonas Donskoi/399 6.00 15.00
ERSJM Jared McCann/399 6.00 15.00
ERSJV Jake Virtanen/199 8.00 20.00
ERSJW Jordan Weal/399 6.00 15.00
ERSKF Kevin Fiala/399 6.00 15.00
ERSMJ Mattias Janmark/399 6.00 15.00
ERSMR Mikko Rantanen/199 12.00 30.00
ERSNE Nikolaj Ehlers/199 12.00 30.00
ERSNG Nikolay Goldobin/399 6.00 15.00
ERSNH Noah Hanifin/399 8.00 20.00
ERSNP Nicolas Petan/399 6.00 15.00
ERSOL Oscar Lindberg/399 6.00 15.00
ERSRH Ryan Hartman/399 8.00 20.00
ERSSB Sam Bennett/199 8.00 20.00
ERSSP Sergei Plotnikov/399 5.00 12.00
ERSVA Viktor Arvidsson/399 8.00 20.00
ERSVH Vincent Hinostroza/399 4.00 10.00

2015-16 Exquisite Collection Rookie Signatures Gold Spectrum

*GOLD/35: .6X TO 1.5X BASIC INSERTS
STATED PRINT RUN 35 SER.#'d SETS
ERSCM Connor McDavid 400.00 500.00
ERSDL Dylan Larkin 90.00 150.00
ERSRH Ryan Hartman 12.00 30.00

2015-16 Exquisite Collection '03-04 Rookie Tribute Patch Autographs

03TAP Artemi Panarin 300.00 600.00
03TCM Connor McDavid 3000.00 5000.00
03TDL Dylan Larkin 400.00 600.00
03TJV Jake Virtanen 75.00 150.00
03TMD Max Domi 150.00 300.00
03TMR Mikko Rantanen 150.00 250.00
03TNE Nikolaj Ehlers 150.00 250.00
03TNH Noah Hanifin 100.00 200.00
03TRF Robby Fabbri 150.00 250.00
03TSB Sam Bennett 150.00 250.00

2015-16 Exquisite Collection Signatures

ESAE Aaron Ekblad/125 12.00 30.00
ESAG Alex Galchenyuk/125 15.00 40.00
ESAI Arturs Irbe 10.00 25.00
ESAO Alexander Ovechkin/15 90.00 150.00
ESBC Bobby Clarke 15.00 40.00
ESBH Bobby Hull 20.00 50.00
ESCP Corey Perry/125 12.00 30.00
ESDK David Krejci 10.00 25.00
ESEM Evgeni Malkin/35 60.00 150.00
ESFP Felix Potvin/125 20.00 50.00
ESGA Glenn Anderson/35 20.00 50.00
ESGL Guy Lafleur/35 25.00 60.00
ESJB Jonathan Bernier/125 12.00 30.00
ESJF Justin Faulk/125 15.00 40.00
ESJG Johnny Gaudreau 20.00 50.00
ESJP Joe Pavelski/125 12.00 30.00
ESJS Joe Sakic/35 30.00 80.00
ESJT Jonathan Toews/35 40.00 100.00
ESLA Gabriel Landeskog 12.00 30.00
ESLR Larry Robinson/99 15.00 40.00
ESMB Martin Brodeur/15 70.00 150.00
ESML Mario Lemieux/15 70.00 150.00
ESMM Mark Messier/15 40.00 100.00
ESNL Nicklas Lidstrom/125 12.00 30.00
ESPB Pavel Bure/35 30.00 80.00
ESPD Pavel Datsyuk/35 25.00 60.00
ESRM Ryan Miller/99 15.00 40.00
ESSC Sidney Crosby/15
ESSJ Seth Jones/125 10.00 25.00
ESSM Sean Monahan 12.00 30.00
ESSY Steve Yzerman/15 70.00 150.00
ESTH Taylor Hall/125 25.00 60.00
ESTJ Tyler Johnson/125 10.00 25.00
ESTS Teemu Selanne/35 40.00 100.00
ESWG Wayne Gretzky/15 300.00 400.00
ESZP Zach Parise/125 12.00 30.00

2015-16 Exquisite Collection Signatures Rookie Previews

STATED PRINT RUN 99-249 SER.#'d SETS
ESRPCM Connor McDavid/99 450.00 600.00
ESRPDL Dylan Larkin/149 30.00 80.00
ESRPDS Daniel Sprong/249
ESRPJM Jared McCann/249 10.00 25.00
ESRPJV Jake Virtanen/249 12.00 30.00
ESRPKF Kevin Fiala/249 10.00 25.00
ESRPMR Mikko Rantanen/249 20.00 50.00
ESRPNE Nikolaj Ehlers/149 20.00 50.00
ESRPNH Noah Hanifin/249 12.00 30.00
ESRPOL Oscar Lindberg/249 10.00 25.00
ESRPRF Robby Fabbri/249 12.00 30.00
ESRPSB Sam Bennett/149 12.00 30.00

2015-16 Exquisite Collection Rookie Spectrum

RCH Connor Hellebuyck/30 20.00 50.00
RCM Connor McDavid/97 500.00 800.00
RDL Dylan Larkin/71 200.00 350.00
REP Emile Poirier/57 10.00 25.00
RHS Henrik Samuelsson/55 8.00 20.00
RJD Jacob de la Rose/25 15.00 40.00
RJE Jack Eichel/15 350.00 550.00
RJV Jake Virtanen/18 90.00 150.00
RKF Kevin Fiala/56 10.00 25.00
RMD Max Domi/16 100.00 200.00
RMP Matt Puempel/26 12.00 30.00
RNE Nikolaj Ehlers/27 30.00 80.00
RNH Noah Hanifin/5
RRH Ryan Hartman/38 15.00 40.00
RSB Sam Bennett/93 40.00 80.00
RSK Slater Koekkoek/29 12.00 30.00
RSP Shane Prince/10

2016-17 Exquisite Collection

1 Ryan Getzlaf 5.00 12.00
2 Max Domi 4.00 10.00
3 Patrice Bergeron 4.00 10.00
4 Jack Eichel 6.00 15.00
5 Sean Monahan 3.00 8.00
6 Justin Faulk 2.50 6.00
7 Patrick Kane 6.00 15.00
8 Matt Duchene 3.00 8.00
9 Brandon Saad 3.00 8.00
10 Jamie Benn 4.00 10.00
11 Dylan Larkin 5.00 12.00
12 Connor McDavid 15.00 40.00
13 Aleksander Barkov 3.00 8.00
14 Drew Doughty 3.00 8.00
15 Ryan Suter 2.50 6.00
16 Carey Price 10.00 25.00
17 Ryan Johansen 4.00 10.00
18 Cory Schneider 2.50 6.00
19 John Tavares 6.00 15.00
20 Henrik Lundqvist 3.00 8.00
21 Erik Karlsson 6.00 15.00
22 Shayne Gostisbehere 4.00 10.00
23 Sidney Crosby 12.00 30.00
24 Brent Burns 4.00 10.00
25 Vladimir Tarasenko 5.00 12.00
26 Steven Stamkos 6.00 15.00
27 Morgan Rielly 2.50 6.00
28 Daniel Sedin 3.00 8.00
29 Alexander Ovechkin 12.00 30.00
30 Dustin Byfuglien 3.00 8.00
31 Wayne Gretzky 15.00 40.00
32 Martin Brodeur 6.00 15.00
33 Milt Schmidt 3.00 8.00
34 Mike Bossy 3.00 8.00
35 Bobby Orr 10.00 25.00
36 Pavel Bure 3.00 8.00
37 Paul Coffey 3.00 8.00
38 Red Kelly 3.00 8.00
39 Mike Modano 5.00 12.00
40 Mario Lemieux 10.00 25.00
41 Dominik Hasek 3.00 8.00
42 Steve Yzerman 4.00 10.00
43 Mark Messier 4.00 10.00
44 Luc Robitaille 3.00 8.00
45 Patrick Roy 8.00 20.00
46 Zach Werenski JSY AU/8 RC
47 Mathew Barzal JSY AU/13 RC
48 Jakob Chychrun JSY AU/6 RC
49 Dylan Strome JSY AU/20 RC
50 Anthony Mantha JSY AU/39 RC
51 Ivan Provorov JSY AU/9 RC
52 Thomas Chabot JSY AU/72 RC 50.00 120.00
53 Sonny Milano JSY AU/22 RC 80.00 150.00
54 Artturi Lehkonen JSY AU/62 RC 30.00 80.00
55 Michael Matheson JSY AU/19 RC
56 Jake Guentzel JSY AU/59 RC 150.00 300.00
57 Hudson Fasching JSY AU/52 RC 100.00 200.00
58 Pavel Buchnevich JSY AU/89 RC 80.00 200.00
59 Matthew Tkachuk JSY AU/16 RC 300.00 400.00
60 Kasperi Kapanen JSY AU/37 RC 300.00 400.00
61 Brendan Perlini JSY AU/29 RC 30.00 80.00
62 Brendan Leipsic JSY AU/49 RC 60.00 150.00
63 Travis Konecny JSY AU/11 RC
64 Anthony DeAngelo JSY AU/77 RC 50.00 120.00
65 Julius Honka JSY AU/6 RC
67 Patrik Laine JSY AU/29 RC 2000.00 2500.00
68 Sebastian Aho JSY AU/20 RC
69 Ryan Pulock JSY AU/6 RC
70 John Quenneville JSY AU/47 RC 25.00 60.00
71 Jimmy Vesey JSY AU/26 RC 600.00 700.00
72 Brandon Montour JSY AU/71 RC 30.00 80.00
73 Brandon Carlo JSY AU/25 RC
74 William Nylander JSY AU/29 RC
75 Connor Brown JSY AU/12 RC
76 Mikhail Sergachev JSY AU/22 RC 200.00 500.00
77 Nick Schmaltz JSY AU/8 RC
78 Kevin Labanc JSY AU/62 RC 30.00 80.00
79 Brayden Point JSY AU/21 RC 250.00 350.00
80 Auston Matthews JSY AU/34 RC 2500.00 3500.00
81 Oliver Bjorkstrand JSY AU/28 RC 80.00 200.00
82 Josh Morrissey JSY AU/44 RC 40.00 100.00
83 Esa Lindell JSY AU/23 RC 40.00 100.00
04 Anthony Beauvillier JSY AU/72 RC 50.00 120.00
85 Jesse Puljujarvi JSY AU/98 RC 80.00 200.00
86 Tyler Motte JSY AU/64 RC 80.00 200.00
87 Christian Dvorak JSY AU/18 RC
88 Kyle Connor JSY AU/81 RC 50.00 125.00
89 Timo Meier JSY AU/28 RC 100.00 200.00
90 Joel Eriksson Ek JSY AU/14 RC
91 Mitch Marner JSY AU/16 RC
92 Thatcher Demko JSY AU/35 RC 100.00 250.00
93 Jakub Vrana JSY AU/13 RC
94 Pavel Zacha JSY AU/37 RC 80.00 200.00
95 Miles Wood JSY AU/44 RC 30.00 80.00

2016-17 Exquisite Collection '09-10 Rookie Auto Tribute

09TAM Auston Matthews 800.00 1000.00
09TDS Dylan Strome 80.00 150.00
09TJP Jesse Puljujarvi 60.00 150.00
09TJV Jimmy Vesey 50.00 120.00
09TMA Anthony Mantha 80.00 200.00
09TMM Mitch Marner 150.00 400.00
09TMT Matthew Tkachuk 150.00 250.00
09TPL Patrik Laine 250.00 500.00
09TWN William Nylander 350.00 500.00

2016-17 Exquisite Collection Gold Rookies

R1 Anthony Mantha/299 6.00 15.00
R2 Oliver Bjorkstrand/299 2.00 5.00
R3 Dominik Simon/299 2.50 6.00
R4 Kyle Connor/299 6.00 15.00
R5 Brendan Leipsic/299 2.50 6.00
R6 Ivan Provorov/299 5.00 12.00
R7 Matthew Tkachuk/299 8.00 20.00
R8 Josh Morrissey/299 3.00 8.00
R9 Joel Eriksson Ek/299 4.00 10.00
R10 Connor Brown/299 4.00 10.00
R11 Sonny Milano/299 3.00 8.00
R12 Esa Lindell/299 2.50 6.00
R13 Travis Konecny/299 5.00 12.00
R14 Pavel Zacha/299 3.00 8.00
R15 Hudson Fasching/299 2.50 6.00
R16 Charlie Lindgren/299 5.00 12.00
R17 William Nylander/299 10.00 25.00
R18 Mikhail Sergachev/299 5.00 12.00
R19 Chris Bigras/299 2.00 5.00
R20 Jason Dickinson/299 2.00 5.00
R21 Ryan Pulock/299 2.50 6.00
R22 Kasperi Kapanen/299 5.00 12.00
R23 Steven Santini/299 2.00 5.00
R24 Michael Matheson/299 2.50 6.00
R25 Patrik Laine/199 25.00 60.00
R26 Mitch Marner/199 20.00 50.00
R27 Jesse Puljujarvi/199 6.00 15.00
R28 Jimmy Vesey/199 5.00 12.00
R29 Dylan Strome/199 5.00 12.00
R30 Auston Matthews/199 60.00 150.00

2016-17 Exquisite Collection Gold Rookies Spectrum

COMMON CARD 3.00 8.00
SEMISTARS 4.00 10.00
UNLISTED STARS 5.00 12.00
R1 Anthony Mantha 40.00 100.00
R2 Oliver Bjorkstrand 20.00 50.00
R4 Kyle Connor 12.00 30.00
R7 Matthew Tkachuk 50.00 120.00
R8 Josh Morrissey 12.00 30.00
R9 Joel Eriksson Ek 40.00 100.00
R10 Connor Brown 25.00 60.00
R11 Sonny Milano 20.00 50.00
R12 Esa Lindell 15.00 40.00
R13 Travis Konecny 40.00 100.00
R16 Charlie Lindgren 20.00 50.00
R17 William Nylander 50.00 120.00
R18 Mikhail Sergachev 40.00 100.00
R20 Jason Dickinson 12.00 30.00
R22 Kasperi Kapanen 15.00 40.00
R24 Michael Matheson 25.00 60.00
R25 Patrik Laine 150.00 300.00
R26 Mitch Marner 150.00 400.00
R27 Jesse Puljujarvi 15.00 40.00
R28 Jimmy Vesey 25.00 60.00
R29 Dylan Strome 20.00 50.00
R30 Auston Matthews 200.00 500.00

2016-17 Exquisite Collection Material Combos

ECCE C.Crawford/T.Esposito 15.00 40.00
ECDB D.Doughty/R.Blake 12.00 30.00
ECED O.Ekman-Larsson/M.Domi 15.00 40.00
ECEO J.Eichel/R.O'Reilly 25.00 60.00
ECFR G.Fuhr/B.Ranford 12.00 30.00
ECKH E.Karlsson/M.Hoffman 10.00 25.00
ECKZ N.Kronwall/H.Zetterberg 15.00 40.00
ECLN H.Lundqvist/R.Nash 12.00 30.00
ECMG C.McDavid/W.Gretzky 60.00 150.00
ECOK A.Ovechkin/E.Kuznetsov 50.00 125.00
ECPG C.Price/A.Galchenyuk 40.00 100.00
ECRC T.Rask/G.Cheevers 12.00 30.00
ECSL H.Sedin/T.Linden 15.00 40.00
ECSM B.Salming/M.Rielly 12.00 30.00
ECWB B.Wheeler/D.Byfuglien 12.00 30.00

2016-17 Exquisite Collection Material Quads

EQBB Bergeron/Bourque/Rask/Cheevers 25.00 60.00
EQCA MacKinnon/Sakic/Duchene/Roy 40.00 100.00
EQFP Barkov/Bure/Ekblad/Luongo 15.00 40.00
EQLA Doughty/Quick/Kopitar/Carter 25.00 60.00
EQRW Kronwall/Zetterberg/Mrazek/Hasek 20.00 50.00
EQST Tarasenko/Steen/Pietrangelo/Allen 25.00 60.00

2016-17 Exquisite Collection Materials

EMAK Anze Kopitar 15.00 40.00
EMBB Brent Burns 12.00 30.00
EMBH Braden Holtby 15.00 40.00
EMCA John Carlson 12.00 30.00
EMCG Claude Giroux 10.00 25.00
EMCM Connor McDavid 80.00 200.00
EMCP Carey Price 30.00 80.00
EMDB Dustin Byfuglien 10.00 25.00
EMDK Duncan Keith 10.00 25.00
EMEK Erik Karlsson 20.00 50.00
EMEM Evgeni Malkin 30.00 80.00
EMGL Gabriel Landeskog 8.00 20.00
EMHL Henrik Lundqvist 10.00 25.00
EMJB Jamie Benn 12.00 30.00
EMJC Jeff Carter 10.00 25.00
EMJE Jack Eichel 20.00 50.00
EMJL John LeClair 10.00 25.00
EMJS Jeff Skinner 10.00 25.00
EMJV Jakub Voracek 10.00 25.00
EMKE Phil Kessel 12.00 30.00
EMMB Martin Brodeur 20.00 50.00
EMNK Nazem Kadri 8.00 20.00
EMNM Nathan MacKinnon 20.00 50.00
EMOE Oliver Ekman-Larsson 8.00 20.00
EMPR Patrick Roy 25.00 60.00
EMRB Rob Blake 10.00 25.00
EMRG Ryan Getzlaf 15.00 40.00
EMRI Pekka Rinne 12.00 30.00
EMRL Roberto Luongo 10.00 25.00
EMRN Rick Nash 10.00 25.00
EMSC Sidney Crosby 40.00 100.00
EMTA John Tavares 20.00 50.00
EMTR Tuukka Rask 10.00 25.00
EMVH Victor Hedman 12.00 30.00
EMVT Vladimir Tarasenko 15.00 40.00

2016-17 Exquisite Collection Material Signatures

EMSAK Anze Kopitar 20.00 50.00
EMSBB Brent Burns 25.00 60.00
EMSCA Carey Price
EMSCM Connor McDavid
EMSCP Corey Perry 12.00 30.00
EMSCS Cory Schneider 10.00 25.00
EMSDH Dale Hawerchuk 15.00 40.00
EMSFP Felix Potvin 30.00 80.00
EMSGL Guy Lafleur 40.00 100.00
EMSHL Henrik Lundqvist
EMSHZ Henrik Zetterberg 40.00 100.00
EMSIL Igor Larionov 25.00 60.00
EMSJJ Jaromir Jagr 80.00 150.00
EMSJS Joe Sakic 30.00 80.00
EMSJT John Tavares 25.00 60.00
EMSLD Leon Draisaitl 60.00 150.00
EMSMB Martin Brodeur
EMSML Mario Lemieux
EMSMP Max Pacioretty 12.00 30.00
EMSPB Pavel Bure 12.00 30.00
EMSPR Patrick Roy
FMSRJ Roman Josi 12.00 30.00
EMSSY Steve Yzerman
EMSTJ Tyler Johnson 10.00 25.00
EMSTL Trevor Linden 25.00 60.00
EMSWG Wayne Gretzky

2016-17 Exquisite Collection Rookie Draft Day

RDDAM Auston Matthews 80.00 150.00
RDDDS Dylan Strome 8.00 20.00
RDDIP Ivan Provorov 8.00 20.00
RDDMA Anthony Mantha 10.00 25.00
RDDMM Mitch Marner 30.00 80.00
RDDPL Patrik Laine 15.00 40.00
RDDPZ Pavel Zacha 5.00 12.00
RDDSM Sonny Milano 5.00 12.00
RDDWN William Nylander 15.00 40.00

2016-17 Exquisite Collection Rookie Draft Day Spectrum

RDDMA Anthony Mantha/20 20.00 50.00
RDDSM Sonny Milano/16 10.00 25.00

2016-17 Exquisite Collection Rookie Dual Materials

RDAM Auston Matthews/25 150.00 300.00
RDDS Dylan Strome/99 12.00 30.00
RDHF Hudson Fasching/99 6.00 15.00
RDIP Ivan Provorov/99 12.00 30.00
RDJM Josh Morrissey/99 8.00 20.00
RDJP Jesse Puljujarvi/99 15.00 40.00
RDJV Jimmy Vesey/99 12.00 30.00
RDKC Kyle Connor/99 15.00 40.00
RDKK Kasperi Kapanen/99 15.00 40.00
RDMA Anthony Mantha/99 15.00 40.00
RDMM Mitch Marner/99 30.00 80.00
RDOB Oliver Bjorkstrand/99 5.00 12.00
RDPL Patrik Laine/99 25.00 60.00
RDPZ Pavel Zacha/99 8.00 20.00
RDSM Sonny Milano/99 8.00 20.00
RDWN William Nylander/99 25.00 60.00

2016-17 Exquisite Collection Rookie Patches

RPAM Auston Matthews/99 80.00 150.00
RPDS Dylan Strome/299 12.00 30.00
RPHF Hudson Fasching/299 6.00 15.00
RPIP Ivan Provorov/299 12.00 30.00
RPJD Jason Dickinson/299 5.00 12.00
RPJM Josh Morrissey/299 8.00 20.00
RPJP Jesse Puljujarvi/299 15.00 40.00
RPKC Kyle Connor/299 15.00 40.00
RPKK Kasperi Kapanen/299 12.00 30.00
RPLC Lawson Crouse/299 5.00 12.00
RPMA Anthony Mantha/299 15.00 40.00
RPMM Mitch Marner/299 30.00 80.00
RPMT Matthew Tkachuk/299 20.00 50.00
RPPL Patrik Laine/199 25.00 60.00
RPPZ Pavel Zacha/299 8.00 20.00
RPSM Sonny Milano/299 8.00 20.00
RPWN William Nylander/199 20.00 50.00

2016-17 Exquisite Collection Rookie Quad Materials

RQCD Christian Dvorak/49 12.00 30.00
RQCL Charlie Lindgren/49 25.00 60.00
RQHF Hudson Fasching/49 12.00 30.00
RQIP Ivan Provorov/49 25.00 60.00
RQJP Jesse Puljujarvi/49 30.00 80.00
RQKC Kyle Connor/49 30.00 80.00
RQKK Kasperi Kapanen/49 25.00 60.00
RQLC Lawson Crouse/49 10.00 25.00
RQMA Anthony Mantha/49 30.00 80.00
RQMI Michael Matheson/49 12.00 30.00
RQMM Mitch Marner/49 60.00 150.00
RQPL Patrik Laine/49 50.00 120.00
RQPZ Pavel Zacha/49 15.00 40.00
RQSM Sonny Milano/49 15.00 40.00
RQWN William Nylander/49 50.00 125.00

2016-17 Exquisite Collection Rookie Signatures

ERSAM Auston Matthews 500.00 900.00
ERSBL Brendan Leipsic 5.00 12.00
ERSCB Connor Brown 8.00 20.00
ERSCL Charlie Lindgren 10.00 25.00
ERSDS Dylan Strome 15.00 40.00
ERSHF Hudson Fasching 5.00 12.00
ERSIP Ivan Provorov 10.00 25.00
ERSJD Jason Dickinson 4.00 10.00
ERSJM Josh Morrissey 6.00 15.00
ERSJP Jesse Puljujarvi 15.00 40.00
ERSJV Jimmy Vesey 20.00 50.00
ERSKC Kyle Connor 12.00 30.00
ERSKK Kasperi Kapanen 10.00 25.00
ERSMA Anthony Mantha 12.00 30.00
ERSMB Mathew Barzal 15.00 40.00
ERSMI Michael Matheson 5.00 12.00
ERSMM Mitch Marner 100.00 250.00
ERSMT Matthew Tkachuk 15.00 40.00
ERSMW Miles Wood 4.00 10.00
ERSNI Nikita Soshnikov 3.00 8.00
ERSOK Oliver Kylington 4.00 10.00
ERSOS Oskar Sundqvist 5.00 12.00
ERSPL Patrik Laine 150.00 250.00
ERSPZ Pavel Zacha/225
ERSRP Ryan Pulock 5.00 12.00
ERSSA Sebastian Aho/225
ERSSM Sonny Milano/225
ERSTK Travis Konecny 10.00 25.00
ERSWN William Nylander 40.00 100.00
ERSZW Zach Werenski 25.00 60.00

2016-17 Exquisite Collection Signatures

ESBG Brendan Gallagher/99
ESBH Brett Hull/25
ESBO Bobby Orr/49 80.00 150.00
ESBS Borje Salming/49 15.00 40.00
ESBU Johnny Bucyk/99 10.00 25.00
ESCG Clark Gillies/49 15.00 40.00
ESCH Carl Hagelin/125 10.00 25.00
ESDH Dominik Hasek/49 15.00 40.00
ESDK David Krejci/125 10.00 25.00
ESJB Jamie Benn/49 20.00 50.00
ESJH Jonathan Huberdeau/125 10.00 25.00
ESJI Jarome Iginla/99 10.00 25.00
ESJK Jari Kurri/125 10.00 25.00
ESJP Joe Pavelski/99 10.00 25.00
ESJR Jeremy Roenick/99 10.00 25.00
ESKP Kyle Palmieri/125 8.00 20.00
ESLR Luc Robitaille/25 20.00 50.00
ESMB Mike Bossy/25 20.00 50.00
ESMM Mark Messier/15
ESMO Mike Modano/49 25.00 60.00
ESMU Matt Murray/99 15.00 40.00
ESNL Nicklas Lidstrom/25 20.00 50.00
ESRL Roberto Luongo/99 10.00 25.00
ESRN Rick Nash/99 10.00 25.00
ESTH Taylor Hall/49 30.00 80.00
ESTS Teemu Selanne/49 30.00 80.00
ESWG Wayne Gretzky/15
ESZP Zach Parise/99 10.00 25.00

2017-18 Exquisite Collection

1 Nicklas Backstrom 2.00 5.00
2 Carey Price 4.00 10.00
3 Jack Eichel 2.00 5.00
4 Aleksander Barkov 1.25 3.00
5 John Tavares 2.50 6.00
6 Brent Burns 1.50 4.00
7 Artemi Panarin 1.25 3.00
8 Ryan Getzlaf 1.25 3.00
9 Nikita Kucherov 2.00 5.00
10 Connor McDavid 8.00 20.00
11 Patrick Kane 2.50 6.00
12 Erik Karlsson 1.50 4.00
13 Vladimir Tarasenko 2.00 5.00
14 P.K. Subban 1.25 3.00
15 Jamie Benn 1.50 4.00
16 Patrice Bergeron 1.50 4.00
17 Sidney Crosby 10.00 25.00
18 Anze Kopitar 2.00 5.00
19 Marc-Andre Fleury 10.00 25.00
20 Johnny Gaudreau 2.00 5.00
21 Claude Giroux 1.25 3.00
22 Steven Stamkos 2.50 6.00
23 Patrik Laine 2.00 5.00
24 Kevin Shattenkirk 1.25 3.00
25 Auston Matthews 5.00 12.00
26 Pat LaFontaine 1.25 3.00
27 Frank Mahovlich 1.25 3.00
28 Jean Beliveau 1.25 3.00
29 Phil Esposito 2.00 5.00
30 Wayne Gretzky 12.00 30.00

2017-18 Exquisite Collection '07-08 Rookie Tribute

07TCM Connor McDavid PATCH AU 450.00 500.00
07TCP Carey Price PATCH AU 80.00 150.00
07TJT Jonathan Toews PATCH AU
07TNH Nico Hischier 40.00 100.00
07TNP Nolan Patrick 40.00 100.00
07TSS Steven Stamkos PATCH AU
08TAD Alex DeBrincat PATCH AU 150.00 250.00
08TBB Brock Boeser PATCH AU
08TCK Clayton Keller PATCH AU
08TCM Charlie McAvoy PATCH AU 200.00 300.00
08TJH Josh Ho-Sang PATCH AU 80.00 150.00
08TNH Nico Hischier 40.00 100.00
08TNP Nolan Patrick 40.00 100.00
08TOT Owen Tippett PATCH AU
08TPD Pierre-Luc Dubois PATCH AU
08TTJ Tyson Jost PATCH AU
08TTT Tage Thompson PATCH AU 80.00 150.00

2017-18 Exquisite Collection Material Signatures

EMSAK Anze Kopitar/25 20.00 50.00
EMSBH Bo Horvat/49 12.00 30.00
EMSBP Brian Propp/25 10.00 25.00
EMSCM Connor McDavid/15
EMSCP Colton Parayko/49 12.00 30.00
EMSGN Gustav Nyquist/49 12.00 30.00
EMSHL Henrik Lundqvist/15
EMSJC John Carlson/49 15.00 40.00
EMSJI Jarome Iginla/49 12.00 30.00
EMSJP Joe Pavelski/25 12.00 30.00
EMSMB Martin Brodeur/15
EMSPL Patrik Laine/25 20.00 50.00
EMSPR Patrick Roy/15
EMSRL Rod Langway/49 12.00 30.00

2017-18 Exquisite Collection Material Quads

EQBJ Wennberg/Jenner/Jones/Bobrovsky 10.00 25.00
EQMC Pacioretty/Galchenyuk 30.00 80.00
Price/Weber
EQML Marner/Kadri/Rielly/Andersen 10.00 25.00
EQNP Johansen/Forsberg/Subban/Rinne 25.00 60.00
EQPP Lemieux/Barrasso/Malkin/Murray 30.00 80.00
EQWC Ovechkin/Backstrom/Oshie/Holtby 40.00 100.00

2017-18 Exquisite Collection Materials

EMAO Alexander Ovechkin 30.00 80.00
EMBB Brent Burns 15.00 40.00
EMBH Brett Hull 25.00 60.00
EMCP Carey Price 25.00 60.00
EMDH Dominik Hasek 8.00 20.00
EMEK Erik Karlsson 10.00 25.00
EMHL Henrik Lundqvist 12.00 30.00
EMJB Jamie Benn 10.00 25.00
EMKL Kris Letang 8.00 20.00
EMNB Nicklas Backstrom 12.00 30.00
EMPK Patrick Kane 15.00 40.00
EMSS Steven Stamkos 15.00 40.00

2017-18 Exquisite Collection Rookie Dual Materials

RDBB Brock Boeser 30.00 80.00
RDCK Clayton Keller 15.00 40.00
RDCM Charlie McAvoy 15.00 40.00
RDHF Haydn Fleury 5.00 12.00
RDJG Jon Gillies 5.00 12.00
RDJR Jack Roslovic 6.00 15.00
RDLK Luke Kunin 5.00 12.00
RDOT Owen Tippett 15.00 40.00
RDPD Pierre-Luc Dubois 10.00 25.00
RDTJ Tyson Jost 10.00 25.00
RDTT Tage Thompson 8.00 20.00

2017-18 Exquisite Collection Rookie Patches

RPAR Anders Bjork/299 10.00 25.00
RPAD Alex DeBrincat/299 20.00 50.00
RPAN Alexander Nylander/299 12.00 30.00
RPBB Brock Boeser/99 40.00 100.00
RPCK Clayton Keller/99 20.00 50.00
RPCM Charlie McAvoy/299 25.00 60.00
RPCW Colin White/299 8.00 20.00
RPES Evgeny Svechnikov/299 15.00 40.00
RPHF Haydn Fleury/299 8.00 20.00
RPIB Ivan Barbashev/299 8.00 20.00
RPLK Luke Kunin/299 8.00 20.00
RPMB Madison Bowey/299 6.00 15.00
RPPD Pierre-Luc Dubois/299 15.00 40.00
RPTJ Tyson Jost/299 15.00 40.00
RPVS Vadim Shipachyov/99 25.00 60.00

2017-18 Exquisite Collection Rookie Signatures

ERSAD Alex DeBrincat/199 30.00 80.00
ERSAK Adrian Kempe/199 12.00 30.00
ERSAN Alexander Nylander/99 25.00 60.00
ERSAT Alex Tuch/199 30.00 80.00
ERSBB Brock Boeser/99 150.00 250.00
ERSCF Christian Fischer/199 12.00 30.00
ERSCH Filip Chlapik/199 10.00 25.00
ERSCK Clayton Keller/99 25.00 60.00
ERSCM Charlie McAvoy/99 30.00 80.00
ERSCW Colin White/199 10.00 25.00
ERSDG Denis Gurianov/199 10.00 25.00
ERSES Evgeny Svechnikov/199 20.00 50.00
ERSFC Filip Chytil/199 10.00 25.00
ERSHF Haydn Fleury/199 10.00 25.00
ERSJD Jake DeBrusk/199 15.00 40.00
ERSJH Josh Ho-Sang/199 12.00 30.00
ERSKY Kailer Yamamoto/199 25.00 60.00
ERSLK Luke Kunin/199 10.00 25.00
ERSOT Owen Tippett/199 20.00 50.00
ERSPD Pierre-Luc Dubois/99 20.00 50.00
ERSRH Robert Hagg/99 10.00 25.00
ERSSM Samuel Morin/199 10.00 25.00
ERSTJ Tyson Jost/199 20.00 50.00
ERSTT Tage Thompson/199 15.00 40.00
ERSVH Ville Husso/199 10.00 25.00
ERSVM Victor Mete/199 10.00 25.00
ERSWB Will Butcher/199 12.00 30.00

2017-18 Exquisite Collection Rookie Quad Materials

RQBB Brock Boeser 50.00 125.00
RQCK Clayton Keller 25.00 60.00
RQCM Charlie McAvoy 30.00 80.00
RQCW Colin White 10.00 25.00
RQIB Ivan Barbashev 10.00 25.00
RQJH Josh Ho-Sang 12.00 30.00
RQMB Madison Bowey 8.00 20.00
RQPD Pierre-Luc Dubois 20.00 50.00
RQTJ Tyson Jost 20.00 50.00
RQVS Vadim Shipachyov 30.00 80.00

2017-18 Exquisite Collection Rookies

R1 Tyson Jost 10.00 25.00
Issued in ICE
R2 Colin White 5.00 12.00
Issued in ICE
R3 Josh Ho-Sang 6.00 15.00
Issued in ICE
R4 Christian Fischer 6.00 15.00
Issued in ICE
R5 Alexander Nylander 8.00 20.00
Issued in ICE
R6 Adrian Kempe 6.00 15.00
Issued in ICE
R7 Evgeny Svechnikov 10.00 25.00
Issued in ICE
R8 Jack Roslovic 6.00 15.00
Issued in ICE
R9 Will Butcher 6.00 15.00
Issued in ICE
R10 Victor Mete 5.00 12.00
Issued in ICE
R11 Kailer Yamamoto 12.00 30.00
Issued in ICE
R12 Tage Thompson 8.00 20.00
Issued in ICE
R13 Jake DeBrusk 8.00 20.00
Issued in ICE
R14 Filip Chytil 5.00 12.00
Issued in ICE
R15 Travis Sanheim 5.00 12.00
Issued in ICE
R16 Logan Brown 5.00 12.00
Issued in ICE
R17 Alex DeBrincat 12.00 30.00
Issued in ICE
R18 Anders Bjork 6.00 15.00
Issued in ICE
R19 Haydn Fleury 5.00 12.00
Issued in ICE
R20 Nikita Scherbak 10.00 25.00
Issued in ICE
R21 Luke Kunin 5.00 12.00
Issued in ICE
R22 Alex Kerfoot 5.00 12.00
Issued in ICE
R23 Owen Tippett 10.00 25.00
Issued in ICE
R24 Alex Tuch 12.00 30.00
Issued in ICE
R25 Brock Boeser 25.00 60.00
Issued in ICE
R26 Clayton Keller 12.00 30.00
Issued in ICE
R27 Charlie McAvoy 15.00 40.00
Issued in ICE
R28 Pierre-Luc Dubois 10.00 25.00
Issued in ICE
R29 Nolan Patrick 10.00 25.00
Issued in ICE
R30 Nico Hischier 15.00 40.00
Issued in ICE
RAD Alex DeBrincat/299 12.00 30.00
Issued in Black Diamond
RAN Alexander Nylander/299 8.00 20.00
Issued in Black Diamond
RBB Brock Boeser/299 25.00 60.00
Issued in Black Diamond
RCK Clayton Keller/199 12.00 30.00
Issued in Black Diamond
RCM Charlie McAvoy/199 15.00 40.00
Issued in Black Diamond
RCW Colin White/299 5.00 12.00
Issued in Black Diamond
RES Evgeny Svechnikov/299 10.00 25.00
Issued in Black Diamond
RJD Jake DeBrusk/299 8.00 20.00
Issued in Black Diamond
RJH Josh Ho-Sang/299 6.00 15.00
Issued in Black Diamond
RMB Madison Bowey/299 4.00 10.00
Issued in Black Diamond
RNH Nico Hischier/199 15.00 40.00
Issued in Black Diamond

RNP Nolan Patrick/199	10.00	25.00
Issued in Black Diamond		
RPD Pierre-Luc Dubois/299	10.00	25.00
Issued in Black Diamond		
RTJ Tyson Jost/299	10.00	25.00
Issued in Black Diamond		
RTT Tage Thompson/299	8.00	20.00
Issued in Black Diamond		
RVS Vadim Shipachyov/199	15.00	40.00
Issued in Black Diamond		

2017-18 Exquisite Collection Rookies Draft Day

RDDAN Alexander Nylander	8.00	20.00
RDDCK Clayton Keller	12.00	30.00
RDDCM Charlie McAvoy	15.00	40.00
RDDES Evgeny Svechnikov	10.00	25.00
RDDLK Luke Kunin	5.00	12.00
RDDNH Nico Hischier	15.00	40.00
RDDNP Nolan Patrick	10.00	25.00
RDDPD Pierre-Luc Dubois	10.00	25.00
RDDTJ Tyson Jost	10.00	25.00

2017-18 Exquisite Collection Rookies Spectrum

RAD Alex DeBrincat/12	150.00	225.00
RAN Alexander Nylander/70	25.00	60.00
RCK Clayton Keller/14	125.00	250.00
RCM Charlie McAvoy/73	50.00	125.00
RCW Colin White/82	12.00	30.00
RES Evgeny Svechnikov/37	15.00	40.00
RJD Jake DeBrusk/74	15.00	40.00
RJH Josh Ho-Sang/66	15.00	40.00
RMB Madison Bowey/22	12.00	30.00
RNH Nico Hischier/13	250.00	325.00
RNP Nolan Patrick/64	40.00	100.00
RTJ Tyson Jost/27	30.00	80.00
RTT Tage Thompson/32	30.00	80.00
RVS Vadim Shipachyov/87	12.00	30.00

1995-96 Fanfest Phil Esposito

This five-card set was sponsored by the five licensed card companies (Donruss, Fleer/Skybox, Pinnacle, Topps, and Upper Deck) who each produced one card for distribution at the 1996 All-Star Game Fanfest, which was held in Boston. The fronts featured color action photos of Phil Esposito in designs unique to each manufacturer. The backs carried information about the legendary Bruin great.

COMPLETE SET (5)	8.00	20.00
COMMON ESPO (1-5)	2.50	6.00

2008-09 Fathead Tradeables

COMPLETE SET (30)	40.00	100.00
1 Ales Hemsky	.75	2.00
2 Alexander Ovechkin	4.00	10.00
3 Anze Kopitar	1.50	4.00
4 Carey Price	4.00	10.00
5 Daniel Alfredsson	1.00	2.50
6 Eric Staal	1.25	3.00
7 Henrik Lundqvist	1.25	3.00
8 Henrik Zetterberg	1.25	3.00
9 Ilya Kovalchuk	1.00	2.50
10 Jarome Iginla	1.00	2.50
11 Jason Arnott	.75	2.00
12 Joe Sakic	1.50	4.00
13 Joe Thornton	1.25	3.00
14 Jonathan Toews	2.50	6.00
15 Luke Schenn	1.25	3.00
16 Martin Brodeur	2.00	5.00
17 Mike Modano	1.50	4.00
18 Mike Richards	1.00	2.50
19 Mikko Koivu	.75	2.00
20 Nathan Horton	.75	2.00
21 Paul Kariya	1.25	3.00
22 Rick DiPietro	.75	2.00
23 Rick Nash	1.00	2.50
24 Roberto Luongo	1.25	3.00
25 Ryan Getzlaf	1.50	4.00
26 Ryan Miller	1.00	2.50
27 Shane Doan	.75	2.00
28 Sidney Crosby	4.00	10.00
29 Vincent Lecavalier	.75	2.00
30 Zdeno Chara	1.00	2.50

2009-10 Fathead Tradeables

1 Sidney Crosby	4.00	10.00
2 Nicklas Lidstrom	1.00	2.50
3 Alex Ovechkin	4.00	10.00
4 John Tavares	5.00	12.00
5 Henrik Lundqvist	1.50	4.00
6 Jarome Iginla	1.00	2.50
7 Ilya Kovalchuk	1.00	2.50
8 Henrik Sedin	1.00	2.50
9 Martin Brodeur	2.00	5.00
10 Corey Perry	1.00	2.50
11 Patrick Marleau	1.00	2.50
12 Steven Stamkos	2.00	5.00
13 Sam Gagner	.75	2.00
14 Jonas Gustavsson	1.25	3.00
15 Shea Weber	.75	2.00
16 Jeff Carter	1.00	2.50
17 Steve Mason	.75	2.00
18 Scott Gomez	.75	2.00
19 Martin Havlat	.75	2.00
20 Roberto Luongo	1.25	3.00
21 Jason Spezza	1.00	2.50
22 Dion Phaneuf	1.25	3.00
23 Evgeni Malkin	3.00	8.00
24 Marian Hossa	.75	2.00
25 Martin St. Louis	1.00	2.50
26 Milan Lucic	.75	2.00
27 Zach Parise	1.00	2.50
28 Thomas Vanek	1.00	2.50
29 Marian Gaborik	1.25	3.00
30 Nathan Horton	1.00	2.50
31 Phil Kessel	1.25	3.00
32 Shane Doan	.75	2.00
33 Niklas Backstrom	1.00	2.50
34 Mike Cammalleri	.75	2.00
35 Rick Nash	.75	2.00
36 Tim Thomas	1.00	2.50
37 Teemu Selanne	2.00	5.00
38 Patrick Kane	2.00	5.00
39 Dustin Penner	.60	1.50
40 Erik Johnson	.75	2.00
41 Matt Duchene	2.00	5.00
42 Cam Ward	1.00	2.50
43 Drew Doughty	1.25	3.00
44 Mike Green	1.00	2.50
45 Mike Fisher	.60	1.50
46 Mike Richards	1.00	2.50
47 Derek Roy	.75	2.00
48 Dany Heatley	1.00	2.50
49 Pavel Datsyuk	1.25	3.00
50 Brenden Morrow	.75	2.00

2010-11 Fathead Tradeables

1 Jonathan Toews	2.00	5.00
2 Sidney Crosby	4.00	10.00
3 Alex Ovechkin	4.00	10.00
4 Ilya Kovalchuk	1.00	2.50
5 John Tavares	2.00	5.00
6 Miikka Kiprusoff	.75	2.00
7 Milan Lucic	1.00	2.50
8 Dion Phaneuf	1.00	2.50
9 Shea Weber	.75	2.00
10 Ryan Getzlaf	1.50	4.00
11 Joe Thornton	1.00	2.50
12 Phil Kessel	1.25	3.00
13 Henrik Zetterberg	1.25	3.00
14 Roberto Luongo	1.00	2.50
15 Brian Gionta	.75	2.00
16 Mike Richards	1.00	2.50
17 Brad Richards	1.00	2.50
18 Pavel Datsyuk	1.25	3.00
19 Mikko Koivu	1.00	2.50
20 Henrik Sedin	1.00	2.50
21 Henrik Lundqvist	1.50	4.00
22 Jarome Iginla	1.00	2.50
23 Evgeni Malkin	3.00	8.00
24 Patrick Kane	2.00	5.00
25 Steven Stamkos	2.00	5.00
26 Zdeno Chara	.75	2.00
27 Martin Brodeur	2.00	5.00
28 Thomas Vanek	1.00	2.50
29 Marian Gaborik	1.25	3.00
30 Stephen Weiss	.75	2.00
31 Jonas Gustavsson	1.25	3.00
32 Shane Doan	.75	2.00
33 Niklas Backstrom	1.00	2.50
34 Michael Cammalleri	1.00	2.50
35 Rick Nash	1.00	2.50
36 Patrice Bergeron	1.25	3.00
37 Evander Kane	1.00	2.50
38 Duncan Keith	1.00	2.50
39 Ales Hemsky	.75	2.00
40 T.J. Oshie	1.50	4.00
41 Paul Stastny	1.00	2.50
42 Eric Staal	1.25	3.00
43 Drew Doughty	1.00	2.50
44 Nicklas Backstrom	1.50	4.00
45 Daniel Alfredsson	1.00	2.50
46 Jeff Carter	1.00	2.50
47 Ryan Miller	1.00	2.50
48 Marc-Andre Fleury	1.50	4.00
49 Taylor Hall	3.00	8.00
50 Winter Classic Logo	.75	2.00

2013-14 Fathead Tradeables

COMPLETE SET (50)	20.00	50.00
3 Steven Stamkos	1.25	3.00
4 Henrik Sedin	.60	1.50
5 Patrice Bergeron	.75	2.00
6 Pekka Rinne	.75	2.00
10 Ilya Kovalchuk	.60	1.50
11 Jimmy Howard	.60	1.50
12 Jarome Iginla	.60	1.50
14 David Backes	.60	1.50
15 Taylor Hall	1.25	3.00
17 Corey Perry	.60	1.50
23 Dion Phaneuf	.60	1.50
25 Zdeno Chara	.60	1.50
27 Daniel Sedin	.60	1.50
28 Brad Richards	.60	1.50
29 Loui Eriksson	.50	1.25
32 Andrew Ladd	.60	1.50
34 Eric Staal	.75	2.00
35 Jordan Eberle	.60	1.50
38 Shane Doan	.50	1.25
40 Tomas Fleischmann	.40	1.00
42 Shea Weber	.50	1.25
43 Pavel Datsyuk	.75	2.00
48 Phil Kessel	.75	2.00
AK Anze Kopitar	1.00	2.50
AO Alex Ovechkin	2.50	6.00
CG Claude Giroux	.60	1.50
CP Carey Price	2.00	5.00
DB Danny Briere	.60	1.50
DB Dustin Brown	.60	1.50
EK Erik Karlsson	1.25	3.00
EM Evgeni Malkin	2.00	5.00
GL Gabriel Landeskog	.50	1.25
HL Henrik Lundqvist	.75	2.00
HZ Henrik Zetterberg	.75	2.00
JJ Jack Johnson	.40	1.00
JN James Neal	.60	1.50
JQ Jonathan Quick	1.00	2.50
JT John Tavares	1.25	3.00
LC Logan Couture	.60	1.50
MB Martin Brodeur	1.25	3.00
MK Mikko Koivu	.50	1.25
PK Patrick Kane	1.25	3.00
PS Patrick Sharp	.60	1.50
RM Ryan Miller	.60	1.50
SC Sidney Crosby	2.50	6.00
TO T.J. Oshie	1.00	2.50
TS Tyler Seguin	1.00	2.50
JTO Johnathan Toews	1.25	3.00
MSL Martin St. Louis	.60	1.50
PKS P.K. Subban	1.00	2.50

2014-15 Fathead Tradeables

1 Patrick Kane	1.25	3.00
2 Alex Ovechkin	2.50	6.00
3 Sergei Bobrovsky	.60	1.50
4 P.K. Subban	1.00	2.50
5 Sidney Crosby	2.50	6.00
6 Jonathan Toews	1.25	3.00
7 Martin St. Louis	.60	1.50
8 Patrice Bergeron	.75	2.00
9 John tavares	1.25	3.00
10 Henrik Lundqvist	.75	2.00
11 Ryan Suter	.60	1.50
12 Pavel Datsyuk	.75	2.00
13 Scott Hartnell	.60	1.50
14 Corey Perry	.60	1.50
15 Marian Gaborik	.60	1.50
16 Erik Karlsson	1.25	3.00
17 Joffrey Lupul	.50	1.25
18 Shea Weber	.50	1.25
19 Eric Staal	.75	2.00
20 Jonathan Huberdeau	.60	1.50
21 Claude Giroux	.60	1.50
22 Logan Couture	.60	1.50
23 Henrik Sedin	.60	1.50
24 Dustin Brown	.50	1.25
25 Patrick Sharp	.60	1.50
26 Evgeni Malkin	2.00	5.00
27 Taylor Hall	1.25	3.00
28 Martin Brodeur	1.25	3.00
29 James Neal	.60	1.50
30 Steven Stamkos	1.25	3.00
31 Daniel Sedin	.60	1.50
32 Zdeno Chara	.60	1.50
33 Joe Thornton	.60	1.50
34 Henrik Zetterberg	.75	2.00
35 Carey Price	2.00	5.00
36 Thomas Vanek	.60	1.50
37 Andrew Ladd	.60	1.50
38 Jamie Benn	.75	2.00
39 Ryan Getzlaf	1.00	2.50
40 Jordan Staal	.60	1.50
41 Zach Parise	.60	1.50
42 Rick Nash	.60	1.50
43 David Backes	.60	1.50
44 Phil Kessel	.75	2.00
45 Nicklas Backstrom	1.00	2.50
46 Matt Duchene	.60	1.50
47 Mike Cammalleri	.50	1.25
48 Jonathan Quick	1.00	2.50
49 Jordan Eberle	.60	1.50
50 Shane Doan	.50	1.25

1993 Fax Pax World of Sport

The 1993 Fax Pax World of Sport set was issued in Great Britain and contains 40 standard size cards. This multisport set spotlights notable sports figures from around the world, who are the best in their respective sports. An Olympic subset of seven cards (28-34) is included. The full-bleed fronts feature color action and posed photos with a red-edged white stripe intersecting the photo across the bottom. Within the white stripe is displayed the athlete's name and his country's flag. The horizontal, white backs carry the athlete's name and sport at the top followed by biographical information. Career summary and statistics are printed within a gray box, edged in red.

COMPLETE SET (40)	6.00	15.00
25 Wayne Gretzky	1.25	3.00
26 Brett Hull	.10	.30
27 Eric Lindros	.30	.75

1993 FCA 50

This 50-card standard-size set was sponsored by Fellowship of Christian Athletes. The color player photos on the fronts are accented on three sides by a thin pink stripe; the card face itself shades from blue to white as one moves toward the bottom. The FCA logo, featuring a cross with two olive branches, is superimposed in the upper left corner, while the player's name is printed beneath the picture and his sport in the pink stripe on the left. On a blue background, the backs carry a close-up photo, biography, and the player's testimony.

COMPLETE SET (50)	10.00	20.00
17 Mike Gartner HK	.30	.75

1994-95 Finest

This 165-card super-premium set was issued in seven-card packs, in 24-pack boxes. The cards featured a blue marbleized foil border with a centered player photo. The player's last name only, along with the Finest logo, dominated the top of the front. The card fronts also featured a clear protective peel-off coating which was designed to prevent scratches and other damage to the card. Values below reflect unpeeled cards, although hobby opinions on whether to leave the coating intact or remove it vary. Collectors are advised to make a decision based on their own preference. Card backs had player photos, brief stats, and a recap of that player's finest moment. Card numbers 5, 56, 68, and 99 had wrong photos and player names on the back. These were corrected only in the '94-95 Finest Super Team Stanley Cup Winner Redemption set. A World Junior players subset was included (112-165). Rookie cards in the set included Bryan Berard, Radek Bonk, Eric Daze, Miikka Elomo, Eric Fichaud, Sean Haggerty, Ed Jovanovski, Ryan Smyth, Jeff O'Neill and Wade Redden.

1 Peter Forsberg	1.00	2.50
2 Oleg Tverdovsky	.30	.75
3 Radek Bonk RC	.25	.60
4 Brian Rolston	.25	.60
5 Kenny Jonsson UER	.40	1.00
6 Patrik Juhlin RC	.25	.60
7 Paul Kariya	.50	1.25
8 Janne Laukkanen	.30	.75
9 Brett Lindros	.25	.60
10 Andrei Nikolishin	.25	.60
11 Jeff Friesen	.25	.60
12 Jamie Storr	.30	.75
13 Chris Therien	.25	.60
14 Alexander Cherbayev	.25	.60
15 Kevin Brown RC	.40	1.00
16 Mark Messier	.40	1.00
17 Kevin Hatcher	.25	.60
18 Scott Stevens	.40	1.00
19 Keith Tkachuk	.40	1.00
20 Guy Hebert	.30	.75
21 Jason Arnott	.30	.75
22 Cam Neely	.40	1.00
23 Adam Graves	.25	.60
24 Pavel Bure	.40	1.00
25 Mark Tinordi	.25	.60
26 Felix Potvin	.40	1.00
27 Nikolai Khabibulin	.30	.75
28 Theo Fleury	.40	1.00
29 Curtis Joseph	.60	1.50
30 Patrick Roy	1.00	2.50
31 Adam Deadmarsh	.25	.60
32 Pat Falloon	.25	.60
33 Jaromir Jagr	1.00	2.50
34 Chris Chelios	.40	1.00
35 Ray Bourque	.60	1.50
36 Mike Vernon	.30	.75
37 Steve Thomas	.25	.60
38 Eric Lindros	.40	1.00
39 Dave Andreychuk	.40	1.00
40 John Vanbiesbrouck	.30	.75
41 Wayne Gretzky	2.00	5.00
42 Brett Hull	.75	2.00
43 Dominik Hasek	.75	2.00
44 Kirk Muller	.25	.60
45 Rob Blake	.40	1.00
46 Viktor Kozlov	.25	.60
47 Todd Harvey	.25	.60
48 Valeri Bure	.25	.60
49 Brian Leetch	.40	1.00
50 Ray Sheppard	.30	.75
51 Ed Belfour	.40	1.00
52 Rick Tocchet	.30	.75
53 Daren Puppa	.30	.75
54 Russ Courtnall	.25	.60
55 Jason Allison	.30	.75
56 Alexei Yashin UER	.40	1.00
57 Sandis Ozolinsh	.25	.60
58 Chris Gratton	.25	.60
59 Mike Peca	.30	.75
60 Glen Wesley	.25	.60
61 Kirk McLean	.30	.75
62 Chris Pronger	.40	1.00
63 Steve Larmer	.30	.75
64 Michal Grosek RC	.25	.60
65 Sergei Fedorov	.60	1.50
66 Stu Barnes	.25	.60
67 Adam Oates	.40	1.00
68 Paul Coffey UER	.40	1.00
69 Joe Sakic	.75	2.00
70 Pat LaFontaine	.40	1.00
71 Martin Brodeur	1.00	2.50
72 Bob Corkum	.25	.60
73 Jeremy Roenick	.75	2.00
74 Shayne Corson	.25	.60
75 German Titov	.25	.60
76 Teemu Selanne	.75	2.00
77 Eric Fichaud RC	.40	1.00
78 Pierre Turgeon	.30	.75
79 Alexander Selivanov RC	.30	.75
80 Kevin Stevens	.25	.60
81 Jari Kurri	.30	.75
82 Gary Roberts	.25	.60
83 Geoff Courtnall	.25	.60
84 Steve Yzerman	1.00	2.50
85 Rod Brind'Amour	.30	.75
86 Mike Richter	.40	1.00
87 Bernie Nicholls	.30	.75
88 Alexandre Daigle	.25	.60
89 Luc Robitaille	.40	1.00
90 John MacLean	.30	.75
91 Phil Housley	.30	.75
92 Brendan Shanahan	.50	1.25
93 Joe Juneau	.30	.75
94 Stephane Richer	.30	.75
95 Blaine Lacher RC	.30	.75
96 Mike Gartner	.40	1.00
97 Rene Corbet	.25	.60
98 Vincent Damphousse	.30	.75
99 Alexander Mogilny UER	.30	.75
100 Doug Gilmour	.50	1.25
101 Petr Nedved	.30	.75
102 Alexei Zhamnov	.30	.75
103 Wendel Clark	.30	.75
104 Arturs Irbe	.30	.75
105 Brian Bellows	.30	.75
106 Mike Modano	.60	1.50
107 Ravil Gusmanov RC	.25	.60
108 Geoff Sanderson	.30	.75
109 Mark Recchi	.50	1.25
110 Mats Sundin	.30	.75
111 Pavol Demitra	.50	1.25
112 Richard Park	.25	.60
113 Doug Bonner RC	.40	1.00
114 Bryan Berard RC	.60	1.50
115 Rory Fitzpatrick RC	.40	1.00
116 Deron Quint	.25	.60
117 Jason Bonsignore	.40	1.00
118 Adam Deadmarsh	.25	.60
119 Sean Haggerty RC	.40	1.00
120 Jamie Langenbrunner	.30	.75
121 Jeff Mitchell RC	.30	.75
122 Antti Aalto RC	.30	.75
123 Tommi Rajamaki RC	.30	.75
124 J. Markkanen RC UER	1.25	3.00
125 Miikka Kiprusoff RC	6.00	15.00
126 Jere Karalahti RC	.40	1.00
127 Petri Kokko RC	.40	1.00
128 Janne Niinimaa	.40	1.00
129 Kimmo Timonen	.30	.75
130 Martti Jarventie RC	.40	1.00
131 Mikko Helisten RC	.40	1.00
132 Niko Halttunen RC	.40	1.00
133 Tommi Miettinen	.30	.75
134 Miska Kangasniemi RC	.40	1.00
135 Veli-Pekka Nutikka RC	.40	1.00
136 Jani Hassinen RC	.40	1.00
137 Timo Salonen RC	.40	1.00
138 Tommi Sova RC	.40	1.00
139 Toni Makiaho RC	.40	1.00
140 Tommi Hamalainen RC	.40	1.00
141 Juha Vuorivirta RC	.40	1.00
142 Jussi Tarvainen RC	.40	1.00
143 Miikka Elomo RC	.40	1.00
144 Jason Botterill	.30	.75
145 Dan Cloutier RC	.60	1.50
146 Jamie Storr	.30	.75
147 Chad Allan RC	.40	1.00
148 Nolan Baumgartner RC	.40	1.00
149 Ed Jovanovski RC	.60	1.50
150 Bryan McCabe	.25	.60
151 Wade Redden RC	.60	1.50
152 Jamie Rivers RC	.40	1.00
153 Lee Sorochan RC	.40	1.00
154 Jason Allison	.30	.75
155 Alexandre Daigle	.25	.60
156 Larry Courville RC	.40	1.00
157 Eric Daze RC	.60	1.50
158 Shean Donovan RC	.40	1.00
159 Jeff Friesen	.25	.60
160 Todd Harvey	.25	.60
161 Marty Murray	.30	.75
162 Jeff O'Neill RC	.30	.75
163 Denis Pederson RC	.30	.75
164 Darcy Tucker RC	.60	1.50
165 Ryan Smyth RC	1.25	3.00

1994-95 Finest Super Team Winners

is 165-card set was awarded to collectors who redeemed the winning New Jersey Devils team card. The cards were the same as the regular Finest cards save for the Super Team Winner embossed logo.

COMPLETE SET (165)	50.00	100.00
*SUPER TEAM: 1.2X TO 3X BASIC CARDS		
125 Miikka Kiprusoff WJC	15.00	40.00

1994-95 Finest Refractors

The cards in this set were parallel to the Finest set. They were randomly inserted at the rate of 1:12 packs. These cards appeared identical to the regular issue; careful examination in the proper light revealed a reflective, rainbow-like sheen to the foil on the front. If in doubt, we recommend comparing to other cards from the set; in this setting, a refractor truly stands out. These cards also came with the clear protective peel-off coating. Multipliers can be found in the header below to determine value for these.

*VETS: 4X TO 10X BASIC CARDS		
*ROOKIES: 2.5X TO 6X BASIC CARDS		
125 Miikka Kiprusoff WJC	30.00	60.00

1994-95 Finest Bowman's Best

is 45-card set was randomly inserted in Finest packs at the rate of 1:4. Card fronts featured a cut-out player photo over a blue or red hi-tech half moon background utilizing the Finest printing technology. The first twenty cards in the set feature NHL veterans. The second twenty consists of NHL rookies. The last five cards pair a star veteran and a top rookie in a horizontal format. The card fronts have the clear protective peel-off coating. The backs of the first forty cards have brief text information outlining the player's strong points, and a small portrait photo. The final five cards simply feature text comparing the two players. Cards are numbered with a B (1-20) prefix for veterans, R (1-20) for rookies, and X (21-25) for dual player cards.

COMPLETE SET (45)	40.00	100.00
*B1-B20 REF: 3X TO 8X BASIC INSERTS		
*R1-R20 REF: 2X TO 5X BASIC INSERTS		
*X21-X25 REF: 1.5X TO 4X BASIC INSERTS		
B1 Ray Bourque	2.00	5.00
B2 Mark Messier	1.50	4.00
B3 Cam Neely	1.50	4.00
B4 Theo Fleury	1.25	3.00
B5 Jeremy Roenick	2.00	5.00
B6 Mike Modano	2.00	5.00
B7 Sergei Fedorov	2.00	5.00
B8 John Vanbiesbrouck	1.25	3.00
B9 Pierre Turgeon	.40	1.00
B10 Kirk Muller	.40	1.00
B11 Pavel Bure	2.00	5.00
B12 Brian Leetch	1.25	3.00
B13 Mike Richter	1.25	3.00
B14 Teemu Selanne	1.25	3.00
B15 Brett Hull	1.50	4.00
B16 Eric Lindros	1.25	3.00
B17 Keith Tkachuk	1.25	3.00
B18 Joe Sakic	3.00	8.00
B19 Doug Gilmour	1.25	3.00
B20 Jaromir Jagr	2.00	5.00
R1 Paul Kariya	1.25	3.00
R2 Oleg Tverdovsky	.40	1.00
R3 Blaine Lacher	.40	1.00
R4 Todd Harvey	.40	1.00
R5 Roman Oksiuta	.40	1.00
R6 David Oliver	.40	1.00
R7 Jamie Storr	.40	1.00
R8 Brian Savage	.40	1.00
R9 Brian Rolston	.40	1.00
R10 Brett Lindros	.40	1.00
R11 Radek Bonk	.40	1.00
R12 Peter Forsberg	2.00	5.00
R13 Adam Deadmarsh	.40	1.00
R14 Jeff Friesen	.40	1.00
R15 Denis Chasse	.40	1.00
R16 Jason Wiemer	.40	1.00
R17 Alexander Selivanov	.40	1.00
R18 Kenny Jonsson	.40	1.00
R19 Todd Marchant	.40	1.00
R20 Mariusz Czerkawski	.40	1.00
X21 T.Fleury/P.Kariya	1.25	3.00
X22 D.Gilmour/P.Forsberg	2.00	5.00
X23 J.Sakic/R.Bonk	1.25	3.00
X24 B.Leetch/O.Tverdovsky	1.25	3.00
X25 C.Neely/J.Weimer	1.25	3.00

1994-95 Finest Division's Finest Clear Cut

e 20 cards in this set were randomly inserted in Finest packs at the rate of 1:12.

COMPLETE SET (20)	25.00	60.00
1 Patrick Roy	5.00	12.00
2 Ray Bourque	2.00	5.00
3 Adam Oates	.60	1.50
4 Luc Robitaille	.60	1.50
5 Mark Recchi	.60	1.50
6 Mike Richter	1.25	3.00
7 Scott Stevens	.60	1.50
8 Eric Lindros	1.50	4.00
9 Adam Graves	.40	1.00
10 Stephane Richer	.60	1.50
11 Ed Belfour	1.25	3.00
12 Al MacInnis	.60	1.50
13 Sergei Fedorov	2.00	5.00
14 Brendan Shanahan	1.25	3.00
15 Brett Hull	2.00	5.00
16 Arturs Irbe	.60	1.50
17 Sandis Ozolinsh	.40	1.00
18 Wayne Gretzky	8.00	20.00
19 Gary Roberts	.40	1.00
20 Pavel Bure	1.50	4.00

1994-95 Finest Ring Leaders

is 20-card set was comprised of players who have earned at least two Stanley Cup rings. Unlike other Finest cards, these did not come with a peel-off coating.

COMPLETE SET (20)	30.00	80.00
1 Mark Messier	3.00	8.00
2 Kevin Lowe	2.00	5.00
3 Jari Kurri	3.00	8.00
4 Grant Fuhr	3.00	8.00
5 Wayne Gretzky	12.00	30.00
6 Paul Coffey	3.00	8.00
7 Craig Simpson	2.00	5.00
8 Craig MacTavish	2.00	5.00
9 Jeff Beukeboom	2.00	5.00
10 Joe Mullen	2.50	6.00
11 Marty McSorley	2.50	6.00
12 Steve Smith	2.50	6.00
13 Kevin Stevens	2.50	6.00
14 Patrick Roy	6.00	15.00
15 Jaromir Jagr	4.00	10.00
16 Ron Francis	3.00	8.00
17 Bill Ranford	2.50	6.00
18 Larry Murphy	2.50	6.00
19 Tom Barrasso	2.50	6.00
20 Adam Graves	2.50	6.00

1995-96 Finest

The 1995-96 Finest set was issued in one series totaling 191 cards. The 6-card hobby packs had an SRP of $5.00 each. The players were featured across three themes: Finest Rookies, Finest Performers and Finest Defenders. Within those themes, cards were produced in different quantities: some players were common, some uncommon and some rare. The breakdown for the player selection of common (bronze), uncommon (silver) and rare (gold) cards was supposedly random with no consideration given to the status of each player in the set, although many of the gold cards did feature upper-echelon stars. Odds of finding an uncommon silver card were 1:4 packs, while golds were found 1:24 packs.

1 Eric Lindros B	.75	2.00
2 Ray Bourque G	8.00	20.00
3 Eric Daze B	1.00	2.50
4 Craig Janney S	.30	.75
5 Wayne Gretzky B	4.00	10.00
6 Dave Andreychuk B	.50	1.25
7 Phil Housley B	.40	1.00
8 Mike Gartner B	.50	1.25
9 Cam Neely B	.50	1.25
10 Brett Hull B	.60	1.50
11 Daren Puppa S	.40	1.00
12 Tomas Sandstrom S	.40	1.00
13 Patrick Roy G	12.00	30.00
14 Steve Thomas B	.40	1.00
15 Joe Sakic B	.75	2.00
16 Ray Sheppard S	.40	1.00
17 Steve Duchesne B	.30	.75
18 Shayne Corson S	.30	.75
19 Chris Chelios G	3.00	8.00
20 John Vanbiesbrouck B	.40	1.00
21 Randy Burridge B	.30	.75
22 Shane Doan B RC	1.50	4.00
23 Brian Savage B	.30	.75
24 Luc Robitaille B	.50	1.25
25 Jeremy Roenick G	8.00	20.00
26 Peter Forsberg B	1.25	3.00
27 Jeff Friesen S	.30	.75
28 Aaron Gavey S	.30	.75
29 Kenny Jonsson S	.50	1.25
30 Theo Fleury G	6.00	15.00
31 Dave Gagner S	.30	.75
32 Alexander Selivanov S	.40	1.00
33 Scott Stevens B	.50	1.25
34 Valeri Bure B	.30	.75
35 Teemu Selanne G	5.00	12.00
36 Ray Ferraro S	.30	.75
37 Sylvain Cote S	.30	.75
38 John MacLean B	.40	1.00
39 Brendan Shanahan B	.60	1.50
40 Pat LaFontaine B	.50	1.25
41 Brian Leetch G	4.00	10.00
42 Larry Murphy B	.50	1.25
43 Adam Oates B	.50	1.25
44 Rod Brind'Amour B	.50	1.25
45 Martin Brodeur G	8.00	20.00
46 Pierre Turgeon B	.50	1.25
47 Claude Lemieux B	.50	1.25
48 Al MacInnis S	.50	1.25
49 Geoff Courtnall S	.30	.75
50 Mark Messier B	.75	2.00
51 Bill Ranford B	.40	1.00
52 Vincent Damphousse S	.40	1.00
53 Jere Lehtinen B	.40	1.00
54 Bryan McCabe S	.50	1.25
55 Doug Gilmour G	4.00	10.00
56 Mathieu Schneider S	.30	.75
57 Igor Larionov S	.30	.75
58 Joe Murphy S	.30	.75
59 Niklas Sundstrom B	.50	1.25
60 John LeClair B	.50	1.25
61 Cory Stillman B	.30	.75
62 David Oliver B	.30	.75
63 Nikolai Khabibulin B	.40	1.00
64 Steve Rucchin B	.40	1.00
65 Brendan Shanahan S	.60	1.50
66 Jim Carey B	.40	1.00
67 Brian Holzinger S RC	1.00	2.50
68 Stu Barnes S	.30	.75
69 Nicklas Lidstrom B	.50	1.25
70 Jaromir Jagr B	1.25	3.00
71 Donald Audette S	.40	1.00
72 Dominik Hasek B	.60	1.50
73 Peter Bondra S	.50	1.25
74 Andrew Cassels B	.30	.75
75 Pavel Bure B	.60	1.50
76 Marcus Ragnarsson B RC	.60	1.50
77 Ray Bourque S	5.00	12.00
78 Alexei Zhamnov B	.50	1.25
79 Travis Green S	.40	1.00
80 Joe Sakic B	.75	2.00
81 Chad Kilger B RC	.50	1.25
82 Bill Guerin S	.40	1.00
83 Vyacheslav Kozlov B	.40	1.00
84 Igor Korolev S	.30	.75
85 Saku Koivu G	4.00	10.00
86 Ron Hextall B	.50	1.25
87 Wendel Clark S	.50	1.25
88 Eric Lindros G	5.00	12.00
89 Richard Park B	.50	1.25
90 Dominik Hasek S	5.00	12.00
91 Shawn McEachern B	.30	.75
92 Martin Straka S	.30	.75
93 Roman Hamrlik B	.30	.75
94 Roman Oksiuta S	.30	.75
95 Sergei Fedorov B	.75	2.00
96 Jeff O'Neill S	.50	1.25
97 Todd Harvey S	.30	.75
98 Rob Niedermayer B	.40	1.00
99 Mark Messier G	5.00	12.00
100 Peter Forsberg G	8.00	20.00
101 Deron Quint B	.40	1.00
102 Nelson Emerson S	.30	.75
103 Scott Niedermayer B	.50	1.25
104 Doug Weight S	.50	1.25
105 Felix Potvin B	.50	1.25
106 Brendan Witt B	.50	1.25
107 Zdeno Ciger B	.40	1.00
108 Ed Belfour S	.40	1.00
109 Jody Hull B	.30	.75
110 Cam Neely S	.50	1.25
111 Kyle McLaren B RC	.30	.75
112 Petr Klima S	.30	.75
113 Grant Fuhr B	.50	1.25
114 Todd Krygier B	.30	.75
115 Brian Leetch B	.50	1.25
116 Daniel Alfredsson S RC	6.00	15.00
117 Zigmund Palffy B	.50	1.25
118 Antti Tormanen B	.30	.75
119 Mark Recchi B	.60	1.50
120 Mikael Renberg B	.40	1.00
121 Chris Chelios B	.50	1.25
122 Guy Hebert B	.40	1.00
123 Keith Tkachuk G	5.00	12.00
124 Joe Juneau S	.40	1.00
125 Radek Dvorak S RC	.60	1.50
126 Gary Suter B	.40	1.00
127 Ron Francis B	.60	1.50
128 Mike Modano G	8.00	20.00
129 Tom Barrasso B	.40	1.00
130 Pat LaFontaine B	.50	1.25
131 Pat Verbeek B	.40	1.00
132 Sean Burke S	.30	.75
133 Rick Tocchet B	.40	1.00
134 Petr Sykora B RC	1.25	3.00
135 Felix Potvin B	.50	1.25
136 Scott Mellanby B	.40	1.00
137 Paul Coffey B	.50	1.25
138 Aki Berg G RC	.50	1.25
139 Jason Arnott B	.40	1.00
140 Alexander Mogilny G	6.00	15.00
141 Sandis Ozolinsh B	.40	1.00
142 Owen Nolan S	.50	1.25
143 Brian Bradley B	.40	1.00
144 Trevor Linden B	.50	1.25
145 Patrick Roy B	2.50	6.00
146 Todd Bertuzzi B RC	1.50	4.00
147 Michal Pivonka B	.30	.75
148 Kevin Hatcher S	.40	1.00
149 Chris Terreri B	.40	1.00
150 Mario Lemieux B	1.50	4.00
151 Alexei Yashin S	.40	1.00
152 Scott Stevens S	.50	1.25
153 Dale Hawerchuk B	.60	1.50
154 Markus Naslund B	.50	1.25
155 Teemu Selanne B	1.00	2.50
156 Darcy Wakaluk S	.30	.75
157 Vitali Yachmenev B	.50	1.25
158 Jason Dawe B	.30	.75
159 Chris Osgood B	.40	-1.00
160 Alexander Mogilny B	.40	1.00
161 Kirk McLean S	.40	1.00
162 Steve Yzerman G	8.00	20.00
163 Shean Donovan B	.30	.75
164 Valeri Kamensky S	.40	1.00
165 Paul Kariya B	.60	1.50
166 Dimitri Khristich S	.30	.75
167 Teppo Numminen B	.30	.75
168 Joe Nieuwendyk S	.50	1.25
169 Mike Richter S	.50	1.25
170 Doug Gilmour B	.60	1.50
171 Sergei Zubov B	.40	1.00
172 Michael Nylander B	.30	.75
173 Geoff Sanderson B	.30	.75
174 Eric Desjardins S	.40	1.00
175 Jeremy Roenick B	.60	1.50
176 Ed Jovanovski G	5.00	12.00
177 Mats Sundin B	.50	1.25
178 Martin Brodeur B	1.25	3.
179 John LeClair G	4.00	10.
180 Wayne Gretzky G	15.00	40.
181 Theo Fleury B	.60	1.
182 Pierre Turgeon S	.50	1.
183 Robert Svehla B RC	.30	
184 Brett Hull G	5.00	12.
185 Jaromir Jagr G	8.00	20.
186 Sergei Fedorov B	.75	2.
187 Pavel Bure G	5.00	12.
188 John Vanbiesbrouck B	.40	1.
189 Paul Kariya B	.60	1.
190 Mario Lemieux G	10.00	25.
191 Checklist UER G	5.00	12.

1995-96 Finest Refractors

The 1995-96 Finest Refractors set was issued as a parallel to the Finest set. Mirroring it's three levels o difficulty, the cards were inserted at varying rates. Common refractors could be found 1:12 packs. Uncommon refractors were 1:48, while the rare refractors were hidden 1:288 packs. It is believed th were less than 150 rare refractors, less than 450 uncommon and less than 1,000 common refractors available.

1 Eric Lindros B	5.00	12.
2 Ray Bourque G	20.00	50.
3 Eric Daze B	2.50	6.
4 Craig Janney S	5.00	12.
5 Wayne Gretzky B	25.00	60.
6 Dave Andreychuk B	2.50	6.
7 Phil Housley B	2.00	5.
8 Mike Gartner B	2.00	5.
9 Cam Neely B	5.00	12.
10 Brett Hull B	8.00	20.
11 Daren Puppa S	8.00	20.
12 Tomas Sandstrom S	5.00	12.
13 Patrick Roy G	25.00	60.
14 Steve Thomas B	2.00	5.
15 Joe Sakic B	8.00	20.
16 Ray Sheppard S	5.00	12.
17 Steve Duchesne B	2.00	5.
18 Shayne Corson S	5.00	12.
19 Chris Chelios G	12.00	30.
20 John Vanbiesbrouck B	2.50	6.
21 Randy Burridge B	1.50	4.
22 Shane Doan B	6.00	15.
23 Brian Savage B	2.00	5.
24 Luc Robitaille B	2.50	6.
25 Jeremy Roenick G	12.00	30.
26 Peter Forsberg B	6.00	15.
27 Jeff Friesen S	5.00	12.
28 Aaron Gavey S	4.00	10.
29 Kenny Jonsson S	5.00	12.
30 Theo Fleury G	12.00	30.
31 Dave Gagner S	5.00	12.
32 Alexander Selivanov S	5.00	12.
33 Scott Stevens B	3.00	8.
34 Valeri Bure B	3.00	8.
35 Teemu Selanne G	20.00	50.
36 Ray Ferraro S	4.00	10.
37 Sylvain Cote S	5.00	12.
38 John MacLean B	1.50	4.
39 Brendan Shanahan B	3.00	8.
40 Pat LaFontaine B	1.50	4.
41 Brian Leetch G	10.00	25.
42 Larry Murphy B	3.00	8.
43 Adam Oates B	3.00	8.
44 Rod Brind'Amour B	3.00	8.
45 Martin Brodeur G	25.00	60.
46 Pierre Turgeon B	1.50	4.
47 Claude Lemieux B	2.50	6.
48 Al MacInnis S	5.00	12.
49 Geoff Courtnall S	5.00	12.
50 Mark Messier B	5.00	12.
51 Bill Ranford B	3.00	8.
52 Vincent Damphousse S	5.00	12.
53 Jere Lehtinen B	1.50	4.
54 Bryan McCabe S	5.00	12.
55 Doug Gilmour G	8.00	20.
56 Mathieu Schneider S	5.00	12.
57 Igor Larionov S	5.00	12.
58 Joe Murphy S	6.00	12.
59 Niklas Sundstrom B	1.25	3.
60 John LeClair B	8.00	20.
61 Cory Stillman B	2.00	5.
62 David Oliver B	2.00	5.
63 Nikolai Khabibulin B	5.00	12.
64 Steve Rucchin B	2.50	6.
65 Brendan Shanahan S	5.00	12.
66 Jim Carey B	3.00	8.
67 Brian Holzinger S	3.00	8.
68 Stu Barnes S	4.00	10.
69 Nicklas Lidstrom B	5.00	12.
70 Jaromir Jagr B	8.00	20.
71 Donald Audette S	5.00	12.
72 Dominik Hasek B	10.00	25.
73 Peter Bondra S	6.00	15.
74 Andrew Cassels B	2.50	6.
75 Pavel Bure B	12.00	30.
76 Marcus Ragnarsson B	1.50	4.
77 Ray Bourque S	8.00	20.
78 Alexei Zhamnov B	1.50	4.
79 Travis Green S	5.00	12.
80 Joe Sakic B	12.00	30.
81 Chad Kilger B	1.25	3.
82 Bill Guerin S	5.00	12.
83 Vyacheslav Kozlov B	2.50	6
84 Igor Korolev S	8.00	20.
85 Saku Koivu G	12.00	30.
86 Ron Hextall B	3.00	8.
87 Wendel Clark S	6.00	15.
88 Eric Lindros G	20.00	50.
89 Richard Park B	2.50	6.
90 Dominik Hasek S	12.00	30.
91 Shawn McEachern B	1.50	4.
92 Martin Straka S	6.00	15.
93 Roman Hamrlik B	1.50	4.
94 Roman Oksiuta S	5.00	12.
95 Sergei Fedorov B	8.00	20.
96 Jeff O'Neill S	5.00	12.
97 Todd Harvey S	5.00	12.
98 Rob Niedermayer B	2.50	6.
99 Mark Messier G	15.00	40.
100 Peter Forsberg G	20.00	50.
101 Deron Quint B	1.25	3.
102 Nelson Emerson S	5.00	12.
103 Scott Niedermayer B	2.50	6.
104 Doug Weight S	6.00	15.
105 Felix Potvin B	6.00	15.
106 Brendan Witt B	1.25	3.
107 Zdeno Ciger B	2.50	6.
108 Ed Belfour S	6.00	15.
109 Jody Hull B	2.50	6.
110 Cam Neely S	6.00	15
111 Kyle McLaren B	1.25	3
112 Petr Klima S	5.00	12
113 Grant Fuhr B	3.00	8
114 Todd Krygier B	1.50	4
115 Brian Leetch B	4.00	10
116 Daniel Alfredsson S	8.00	20

17 Zigmund Palffy B 2.00 5.00
18 Antti Tormanen B 2.00 5.00
19 Mark Recchi B 3.00 8.00
20 Mikael Renberg B 2.00 5.00
21 Chris Chelios B 5.00 12.00
22 Guy Hebert B 3.00 8.00
23 Keith Tkachuk G 10.00 25.00
24 Joe Juneau S 5.00 12.00
25 Radek Dvorak S 15.00 40.00
26 Gary Suter B 1.25 3.00
27 Ron Francis B 2.50 6.00
28 Mike Modano G 10.00 25.00
29 Tom Barrasso B 3.00 8.00
30 Pat LaFontaine B 2.00 5.00
31 Pat Verbeek B 2.00 5.00
32 Sean Burke S 8.00 20.00
33 Rick Tocchet B 1.50 4.00
34 Petr Sykora B 5.00 12.00
35 Felix Potvin B 6.00 15.00
36 Scott Mellanby B 2.50 6.00
37 Paul Coffey B 5.00 12.00
38 Aki Berg G 8.00 20.00
39 Jason Arnott B 1.25 3.00
40 Alexander Mogilny G 8.00 20.00
41 Sandis Ozolinsh B 1.50 4.00
42 Owen Nolan S 8.00 20.00
43 Brian Bradley B 1.25 3.00
44 Trevor Linden B 3.00 8.00
45 Patrick Roy B 12.00 30.00
46 Todd Bertuzzi B 10.00 25.00
47 Michal Pivonka B 2.00 5.00
48 Kevin Hatcher S 5.00 12.00
49 Chris Terreri B 3.00 8.00
50 Mario Lemieux B 12.00 30.00
51 Alexei Yashin S 4.00 10.00
52 Scott Stevens S 5.00 12.00
53 Dale Hawerchuk B 1.50 4.00
54 Markus Naslund B 5.00 12.00
55 Teemu Selanne B 6.00 15.00
56 Darcy Wakaluk S 5.00 12.00
57 Vitali Yachmenev B 1.25 3.00
58 Jason Dawe B 2.50 6.00
59 Chris Osgood B 5.00 12.00
60 Alexander Mogilny B 3.00 8.00
61 Kirk McLean S 5.00 12.00
62 Steve Yzerman G 30.00 80.00
63 Shean Donovan B 2.00 5.00
64 Valeri Kamensky S 5.00 12.00
65 Paul Kariya B 5.00 12.00
66 Dimitri Khristich S 5.00 12.00
67 Teppo Numminen B 1.25 3.00
68 Joe Nieuwendyk S 8.00 20.00
69 Mike Richter S 8.00 20.00
70 Doug Gilmour B 2.00 5.00
71 Sergei Zubov B 1.50 4.00
72 Michael Nylander B 2.00 5.00
73 Geoff Sanderson B 1.25 3.00
74 Eric Desjardins S 4.00 10.00
75 Jeremy Roenick B 6.00 15.00
76 Ed Jovanovski G 8.00 20.00
77 Mats Sundin B 5.00 12.00
78 Martin Brodeur B 10.00 25.00
79 John LeClair G 8.00 20.00
80 Wayne Gretzky G 50.00 125.00
81 Theo Fleury B 3.00 8.00
82 Pierre Turgeon S 5.00 12.00
83 Robert Svehla B 1.25 3.00
84 Brett Hull G 12.00 30.00
85 Jaromir Jagr G 30.00 80.00
86 Sergei Fedorov B 8.00 20.00
87 Pavel Bure G 12.00 30.00
88 John Vanbiesbrouck B 3.00 8.00
89 Paul Kariya B 5.00 12.00
90 Mario Lemieux G 25.00 60.00
91 Checklist G 6.00 15.00

1998-99 Finest

The 1998-99 Finest set was issued in one series totaling 150 cards and was distributed in six-card packs with a suggested retail price of $5. The fronts featured color action player photos printed on 29-pt. stock and identified by a different graphic according to the player's position. The backs carried player information and career statistics.

COMPLETE SET (150) 30.00 60.00
Teemu Selanne .30 .75
Theo Fleury .10 .30
Ed Belfour .30 .75
Dominik Hasek .60 1.50
Dino Ciccarelli .25 .60
Peter Forsberg .75 2.00
Rob Blake .25 .60
Martin Gelinas .10 .30
Vincent Damphousse .10 .30
Doug Brown .10 .30
Dave Andreychuk .25 .60
Bill Guerin .25 .60
Daniel Alfredsson .25 .60
Dainius Zubrus .10 .30
Nikolai Khabibulin .25 .60
Sergei Nemchinov .10 .30
Rod Brind'Amour .25 .60
Patrick Marleau .20 .50
Brett Hull .40 1.00
Rob Zamuner .10 .30
Anson Carter .25 .60
Chris Pronger .25 .60
Owen Nolan .25 .60
Alexandre Daigle .10 .30
Darius Kasparaitis .10 .30
Steve Rucchin .10 .30
Grant Fuhr .25 .60
Mike Sillinger .10 .30
Tony Amonte .25 .60
Jeremy Roenick .40 1.00
Garry Galley .10 .30
Jeff Friesen .10 .30
Alexei Zhitnik .10 .30
Sergei Fedorov .50 1.25
Martin Brodeur .75 2.00
Curtis Joseph .30 .75
Mike Johnson .10 .30
Mattias Ohlund .25 .60
Derian Hatcher .10 .30
Zigmund Palffy .25 .60
Rob Niedermayer .10 .30
Keith Primeau .10 .30
Valeri Kamensky .10 .30
Cliff Ronning .10 .30
Saku Koivu .30 .75
Jiri Slegr .10 .30
Igor Korolev .10 .30
Sergei Samsonov .25 .60
Vaclav Prospal .10 .30
Ron Francis .25 .60
John LeClair .30 .75
Peter Bondra .25 .60
Matt Cullen .10 .30
Doug Gilmour .25 .60
John Vanbiesbrouck .25 .60
Kevin Stevens .25 .60
57 Vladimir Malakhov .10 .30
58 Guy Hebert .25 .60
59 Patrik Elias .25 .60
60 Boris Mironov .10 .30
61 Rob DiMaio .10 .30
62 Pavol Demitra .25 .60
63 Michael Nylander .10 .30
64 Wayne Gretzky 2.00 5.00
65 Miroslav Satan .10 .30
66 Eric Daze .25 .60
67 Jozef Stumpel .25 .60
68 Mark Messier .30 .75
69 Pat Verbeek .10 .30
70 Felix Potvin .30 .75
71 Ethan Moreau .10 .30
72 Steve Yzerman 1.50 4.00
73 Paul Ysebaert .10 .30
74 Jaromir Jagr .50 1.25
75 Mike Modano .50 1.25
76 Chris Osgood .25 .60
77 Robert Svehla .10 .30
78 Joe Juneau .25 .60
79 Adam Deadmarsh .10 .30
80 Keith Tkachuk .30 .75
81 Mark Recchi .25 .60
82 Andrew Cassels .10 .30
83 Mike Hough .10 .30
84 Rem Murray .10 .30
85 Trevor Kidd .25 .60
86 Jeff Hackett .25 .60
87 Mikael Renberg .25 .60
88 Al MacInnis .25 .60
89 Mike Richter .30 .75
90 Markus Naslund .30 .75
91 Joe Sakic .60 1.50
92 Michael Peca .10 .30
93 Scott Thornton .10 .30
94 Vyacheslav Kozlov .25 .60
95 Bobby Holik .10 .30
96 Alexei Yashin .10 .30
97 Robert Kron .10 .30
98 Adam Oates .25 .60
99 Chris Simon .10 .30
100 Paul Kariya .30 .75
101 Ray Bourque .50 1.25
102 Eric Desjardins .25 .60
103 Glen Murray .10 .30
104 Oleg Tverdovsky .10 .30
105 Pavel Bure .30 .75
106 Mats Sundin .30 .75
107 Bryan Berard .25 .60
108 Janne Niinimaa .10 .30
109 Wade Redden .10 .30
110 Trevor Linden .25 .60
111 Jarome Iginla .40 1.00
112 Joe Nieuwendyk .25 .60
113 Alexei Kovalev .10 .30
114 Dave Gagner .10 .30
115 Dimitri Yushkevich .10 .30
116 Sandis Ozolinsh .10 .30
117 Dimitri Khristich .10 .30
118 Jim Campbell .10 .30
119 Nicklas Lidstrom .30 .75
120 Scott Niedermayer .10 .30
121 Niklas Sundstrom .10 .30
122 Karl Dykhuis .10 .30
123 Brendan Shanahan .30 .75
124 Sandy McCarthy .10 .30
125 Pierre Turgeon .25 .60
126 Olaf Kolzig .25 .60
127 Chris Chelios .30 .75
128 Luc Robitaille .25 .60
129 Alexander Mogilny .25 .60
130 Sami Kapanen .10 .30
131 Stu Barnes .10 .30
132 Scott Stevens .25 .60
133 Doug Weight .25 .60
134 Alexei Zhamnov .10 .30
135 Mike Vernon .25 .60
136 Derek Morris .10 .30
137 Brian Leetch .30 .75
138 Ray Whitney .10 .30
139 Chris Gratton .25 .60
140 Patrick Roy 1.50 4.00
141 Jason Allison .10 .30
142 Tom Barrasso .25 .60
143 Derek Plante .10 .30
144 Denis Pederson .10 .30
145 Mike Ricci .10 .30
146 Damian Rhodes .25 .60
147 Marco Sturm .10 .30
148 Darryl Sydor .10 .30
149 Eric Lindros .30 .75
150 Checklist .10 .30

1998-99 Finest No Protectors

Randomly inserted into packs at the rate of 1:4, this 150-card set was a parallel to the base set without the Finest Protector.
*NO PROTECTOR: 1.2X TO 3X BASIC CARDS

1998-99 Finest No Protectors Refractors

Randomly inserted into packs at the rate of 1:24, this 150-card set was a parallel to the regular refractor set without the Finest protector.
*NO PROT REF: 4X TO 10X BASIC CARDS
STATED ODDS 1:24

1998-99 Finest Refractors

Randomly inserted into packs at the rate of 1:12, this 150-card set was a parallel to the base set and was distinguished by the refractive quality of the card.
COMPLETE SET (150) 120.00 300.00
*REFRACTORS: 2X TO 5X BASIC CARDS

1998-99 Finest Centurion

Randomly inserted into packs at the rate of 1:72, this 20-card set featured color action photos of rising NHL stars. Only 500 serial-numbered sets were produced. A refractor parallel was also produced and inserted at a rate of 1:477. Each refractor was serial numbered out of 75.
COMPLETE SET (20) 75.00 150.00
STATED PRINT RUN 500 SER.#'d SETS
*REFRACTOR/75: 2X TO 4X BASIC INSERTS
REFRACTOR/75 STATED ODDS 1:477
REFRACTOR PRINT RUN 75 SER.#'d SETS
C1 Patrik Elias 5.00 12.00
C2 Bryan Berard 5.00 12.00
C3 Chris Osgood 3.00 8.00
C4 Saku Koivu 6.00 15.00
C5 Alexei Yashin 3.00 8.00
C6 Zigmund Palffy 3.00 8.00
C7 Peter Forsberg 12.00 30.00
C8 Jason Allison 3.00 8.00
C9 Wade Redden 3.00 8.00
C10 Paul Kariya 6.00 15.00
C11 Martin Brodeur 15.00 40.00
C12 Patrick Marleau 3.00 8.00
C13 Jaromir Jagr 10.00 25.00
C14 Mattias Ohlund 5.00 12.00
C15 Teemu Selanne 6.00 15.00
C16 Mike Johnson 5.00 12.00
C17 Joe Thornton 8.00 20.00
C18 Jocelyn Thibault 5.00 12.00
C19 Daniel Alfredsson 5.00 12.00
C20 Sergei Samsonov 5.00 12.00

1998-99 Finest Double Sided Mystery Finest

Randomly inserted into packs at the rate of 1:36, this 50-card set featured color action photos of 20 players printed on double-sided cards with one of three other players on the back or the same player on both sides. The opaque Finest Protector had to be peeled off in order to view the card. A refractor parallel was also produced and randomly inserted at a rate of 1:144.
COMPLETE SET (50) 250.00 500.00
*REFRACTORS: .8X TO 2X BASIC INSERTS
REFRACTOR STATED ODDS 1:144
M1 J.Jagr/W.Gretzky 10.00 25.00
M2 J.Jagr/D.Hasek 5.00 12.00
M3 J.Jagr/E.Lindros 6.00 15.00
M4 J.Jagr/J.Jagr 5.00 12.00
M5 D.Hasek/W.Gretzky 10.00 25.00
M6 D.Hasek/E.Lindros 5.00 12.00
M7 D.Hasek/D.Hasek 5.00 12.00
M8 W.Gretzky/E.Lindros 12.50 30.00
M9 W.Gretzky/W.Gretzky 20.00 50.00
M10 E.Lindros/E.Lindros 6.00 15.00
M11 P.Kariya/T.Selanne 5.00 12.00
M12 P.Kariya/R.Bourque 5.00 12.00
M13 P.Kariya/S.Samsonov 5.00 12.00
M14 P.Kariya/P.Kariya 5.00 12.00
M15 T.Selanne/R.Bourque 5.00 12.00
M16 T.Selanne/S.Samsonov 5.00 12.00
M17 T.Selanne/T.Selanne 5.00 12.00
M18 R.Bourque/S.Samsonov 5.00 12.00
M19 R.Bourque/R.Bourque 5.00 12.00
M20 S.Samsonov/S.Samsonov 5.00 12.00
M21 M.Brodeur/P.Forsberg 10.00 25.00
M22 M.Brodeur/P.Roy 10.00 25.00
M23 M.Brodeur/J.Sakic 10.00 25.00
M24 M.Brodeur/M.Brodeur 10.00 25.00
M25 P.Forsberg/P.Roy 12.50 30.00
M26 P.Forsberg/J.Sakic 10.00 25.00
M27 P.Forsberg/P.Forsberg 10.00 25.00
M28 P.Roy/J.Sakic 8.00 20.00
M29 P.Roy/P.Roy 15.00 40.00
M30 J.Sakic/J.Sakic 5.00 12.00
M31 M.Modano/S.Yzerman 12.50 30.00
M32 M.Modano/S.Fedorov 8.00 20.00
M33 M.Modano/B.Shanahan 8.00 20.00
M34 M.Modano/M.Modano 5.00 12.00
M35 S.Yzerman/S.Fedorov 8.00 20.00
M36 S.Yzerman/B.Shanahan 8.00 20.00
M37 S.Yzerman/S.Yzerman 15.00 40.00
M38 S.Fedorov/B.Shanahan 5.00 12.00
M39 S.Fedorov/S.Fedorov 5.00 12.00
M40 B.Shanahan/B.Shanahan 5.00 12.00
M41 M.Messier/J.Leclair 5.00 12.00
M42 M.Messier/K.Tkachuk 5.00 12.00
M43 M.Messier/P.Bure 5.00 12.00
M44 M.Messier/M.Messier 5.00 12.00
M45 J.Leclair/K.Tkachuk 5.00 12.00
M46 J.Leclair/P.Bure 5.00 12.00
M47 J.Leclair/J.Leclair 5.00 12.00
M48 P.Bure/K.Tkachuk 5.00 12.00
M49 P.Bure/P.Bure 5.00 10.00
M50 K.Tkachuk/K.Tkachuk 5.00 12.00

1998-99 Finest Futures Finest

Randomly inserted into packs at the rate of 1:72, this 20-card set featured color action photos of hard-charging NHL prospects and CHL players. Only 500 serial-numbered sets were produced. A refractor parallel was also produced and randomly inserted at a rate of 1:238. Refractors were serial numbered to 150.
COMPLETE SET (20) 40.00 80.00
*REFRACTOR/150: .6X TO 1.5X BASIC INSERTS
REFRACTOR/150 ODDS 1:238
REFRACTOR PRINT RUN 150 SER.#'d SETS
F1 David Legwand 2.00 5.00
F2 Manny Malhotra 2.00 5.00
F3 Vincent Lecavalier 6.00 15.00
F4 Brad Stuart 2.00 5.00
F5 Bryan Allen 2.00 5.00
F6 Rico Fata 2.00 5.00
F7 Mark Bell 2.00 5.00
F8 Michael Rupp 2.00 5.00
F9 Jeff Heerema 2.00 5.00
F10 Alex Tanguay 5.00 10.00
F11 Patrick Desrochers 2.00 5.00
F12 Mathieu Chouinard 2.00 5.00
F13 Eric Chouinard 2.00 5.00
F14 Martin Skoula 2.00 5.00
F15 Robyn Regehr 2.00 5.00
F16 Marian Hossa 6.00 15.00
F17 Daniel Cleary 2.00 5.00
F18 Olli Jokinen 2.00 5.00
F19 Brendan Morrison 2.00 5.00
F20 Erik Rasmussen 2.00 5.00

1998-99 Finest Futures Finest Refractors

Randomly inserted into packs at the rate of 1:238, this 20-card set was a refractive version of the regular insert set. Only 150 of each card were produced and sequentially numbered.
*REFRACTOR/150: .6X TO 1.5X BASIC INSERTS
REFRACTOR/150 ODDS 1:238

1998-99 Finest Oversize

serted one per hobby box, this seven-card set featured color action photos of top NHL players printed on oversized cards measuring approximately 3 1/4" by 4 9/16". A refractor parallel was also produced and inserted at a rate of 1 in 6 boxes.
COMPLETE SET (7) 15.00 30.00
*REFRACTORS: 1.2X TO 3X BASIC INSERTS
REFRACTOR ODDS ONE PER 6 BOXES
1 Teemu Selanne 1.50 4.00
2 Dominik Hasek 1.50 4.00
3 Martin Brodeur 2.00 5.00
4 Wayne Gretzky 5.00 12.00
5 Steve Yzerman 4.00 10.00
6 Jaromir Jagr 1.25 3.00
7 Eric Lindros 1.50 4.00

1998-99 Finest Promos

This six-card set featured color action player photos printed on an embossed card with faint skating marks in the background. The fronts were covered with the Finest Protector film. The backs carried another player photos, biographical information, and season and career statistics. The cards were numbered with a "PP" prefix on the backs.
COMPLETE SET (6) 2.00 5.00
PP1 Scott Stevens .20 .50
PP2 Michael Nylander .20 .50
PP3 Brendan Shanahan .60 1.50
PP4 Trevor Kidd .30 .75
PP5 Bill Guerin .40 1.00
PP6 Brian Leetch .40 1.00

1998-99 Finest Red Lighters

Randomly inserted in packs at the rate of 1:24, this 20-card set featured color action photos of top NHL scorers printed on die-cut chromium cards. A refractor parallel was also created and inserted at 1:72.
COMPLETE SET (20) 40.00 80.00
*REFRACTORS: 1X TO 2.5X BASIC INSERTS
REFRACTOR STATED ODDS 1:72
R1 Jaromir Jagr 2.50 6.00
R2 Mike Modano 2.50 6.00
R3 Paul Kariya 1.25 3.00
R4 Pavel Bure 1.25 3.00
R5 Peter Bondra 1.50 4.00
R6 Sergei Fedorov 2.00 5.00
R7 Steve Yzerman 6.00 15.00
R8 Teemu Selanne 1.25 3.00
R9 Wayne Gretzky 8.00 20.00
R10 Brendan Shanahan 1.25 3.00
R11 Eric Lindros 1.25 3.00
R12 Alexei Yashin 1.25 3.00
R13 Jason Allison 1.25 3.00
R14 Joe Nieuwendyk 1.50 4.00
R15 Joe Sakic 3.00 8.00
R16 John Leclair 1.25 3.00
R17 Keith Tkachuk 1.25 3.00
R18 Mark Messier 1.25 3.00
R19 Mats Sundin 1.25 3.00
R20 Zigmund Palffy 1.50 4.00

1994-95 Flair

This 225-card super premium set was issued in 10-card packs with a suggested retail price of $3.99. The cards featured a full-bleed design with dual action photos on the front and gold foil printing. The card stock was thicker than any basic issue. Yearly stats appeared on back in silver, printed over one more photo. The cards were arranged alphabetically within teams. Rookie cards in this set included Mariusz Czerkawski, David Oliver, Eric Fichaud and Jason Wiemer. To prevent tampering or searching, Fleer employed an innovative packaging design: the packs are actually a cello-wrapped, two-piece silver foil box, with the cards inside wrapped again in a sealed cello pouch.
1 Bob Corkum .10 .25
2 Bobby Dollas .10 .25
3 Guy Hebert .12 .30
4 Paul Kariya .20 .50
5 Anatoli Semenov .10 .25
6 Tim Sweeney .10 .25
7 Garry Valk .10 .25
8 Ray Bourque .25 .60
9 Mariusz Czerkawski RC .15 .40
10 Al Iafrate .10 .25
11 Cam Neely .15 .40
12 Adam Oates .15 .40
13 Vincent Riendeau .10 .25
14 Don Sweeney .10 .25
15 Donald Audette .10 .25
16 Doug Bodger .10 .25
17 Dominik Hasek .30 .75
18 Dale Hawerchuk .20 .50
19 Pat LaFontaine .15 .40
20 Alexander Mogilny .12 .30
21 Craig Muni .10 .25
22 Richard Smehlik .10 .25
23 Denis Tsygurov RC .15 .40
24 Theo Fleury .15 .40
25 Trevor Kidd .12 .30
26 James Patrick .10 .25
27 Robert Reichel .10 .25
28 Gary Roberts .10 .25
29 German Titov .10 .25
30 Zarley Zalapski .10 .25
31 Ed Belfour .15 .40
32 Chris Chelios .15 .40
33 Dirk Graham .10 .25
34 Joe Murphy .10 .25
35 Bernie Nicholls .12 .30
36 Jeremy Roenick .30 .75
37 Steve Smith .10 .25
38 Gary Suter .10 .25
39 Neal Broten .12 .30
40 Russ Courtnall .10 .25
41 Todd Harvey .10 .25
42 Grant Ledyard .10 .25
43 Mike Modano .25 .60
44 Andy Moog .15 .40
45 Mark Tinordi .10 .25
46 Dino Ciccarelli .12 .30
47 Paul Coffey .15 .40
48 Sergei Fedorov .25 .60
49 Vladimir Konstantinov .12 .30
50 Slava Kozlov .12 .30
51 Keith Primeau .15 .40
52 Ray Sheppard .12 .30
53 Mike Vernon .12 .30
54 Jason York RC .10 .25
55 Steve Yzerman .40 1.00
56 Jason Arnott .12 .30
57 Shayne Corson .10 .25
58 Igor Kravchuk .10 .25
59 Dean McAmmond .10 .25
60 David Oliver RC .10 .25
61 Bill Ranford .12 .30
62 Doug Weight .12 .30
63 Jesse Belanger .10 .25
64 Bob Kudelski .10 .25
65 Scott Mellanby .12 .30
66 Gord Murphy .10 .25
67 Rob Niedermayer .12 .30
68 Brian Skrudland .10 .25
69 John Vanbiesbrouck .12 .30
70 Sean Burke .12 .30
71 Andrew Cassels .10 .25
72 Alexander Godynyuk .10 .25
73 Chris Pronger .15 .40
74 Geoff Sanderson .12 .30
75 Darren Turcotte .10 .25
76 Pat Verbeek .12 .30
77 Rob Blake .15 .40
78 Mike Donnelly .10 .25
79 Wayne Gretzky .75 2.00
80 Kelly Hrudey .12 .30
81 Jari Kurri .12 .30
82 Marty McSorley .10 .25
83 Rick Tocchet .12 .30
84 Brian Bellows .12 .30
85 Patrice Brisebois .10 .25
86 Valeri Bure .10 .25
87 Vincent Damphousse .12 .30
88 Eric Desjardins .12 .30
89 Kirk Muller .10 .25
90 Oleg Petrov .10 .25
91 Patrick Roy .40 1.00
92 Martin Brodeur .40 1.00
93 David Emma .10 .25
94 Bill Guerin .12 .30
95 John MacLean .12 .30
96 Scott Niedermayer .15 .40
97 Stephane Richer .12 .30
98 Brian Rolston .10 .25
99 Alexander Semak .10 .25
100 Scott Stevens .15 .40
101 Valeri Zelepukin .10 .25
102 Patrick Flatley .10 .25
103 Derek King .10 .25
104 Brett Lindros .10 .25
105 Vladimir Malakhov .10 .25
106 Marty McInnis .10 .25
107 Jamie McLennan .12 .30
108 Steve Thomas .10 .25
109 Pierre Turgeon .12 .30
110 Jeff Beukeboom .10 .25
111 Adam Graves .10 .25
112 Alexei Kovalev .10 .25
113 Steve Larmer .12 .30
114 Brian Leetch .15 .40
115 Mark Messier .15 .40
116 Sergei Nemchinov .10 .25
117 Mike Richter .15 .40
118 Sergei Zubov .10 .25
119 Craig Billington .12 .30
120 Alexandre Daigle .10 .25
121 Sean Hill .10 .25
122 Norm Maciver .10 .25
123 Dave McLlwain .10 .25
124 Alexei Yashin .15 .40
125 Vladislav Boulin RC .15 .40
126 Rod Brind'Amour .12 .30
127 Ron Hextall .12 .30
128 Patrik Juhlin RC .10 .25
129 Eric Lindros .15 .40
130 Mark Recchi .20 .50
131 Mikael Renberg .12 .30
132 Chris Therien .10 .25
133 Tom Barrasso .12 .30
134 Ron Francis .20 .50
135 Mario Lemieux .60 1.50
136 Shawn McEachern .10 .25
137 Larry Murphy .12 .30
138 Luc Robitaille .15 .40
139 Ulf Samuelsson .10 .25
140 Kevin Stevens .10 .25
141 Martin Straka .10 .25
142 Wendel Clark .12 .30
143 Rene Corbet .10 .25
144 Adam Deadmarsh .10 .25
145 Stephane Fiset .12 .30
146 Peter Forsberg .40 1.00
147 Valeri Kamensky .12 .30
148 Janne Laukkanen .12 .30
149 Sylvain Lefebvre .10 .25
150 Mike Ricci .10 .25
151 Joe Sakic .30 .75
152 Steve Duchesne .10 .25
153 Brett Hull .30 .75
154 Craig Janney .12 .30
155 Craig Johnson .10 .25
156 Curtis Joseph .25 .60
157 Al MacInnis .12 .30
158 Brendan Shanahan .20 .50
159 Peter Stastny .12 .30
160 Esa Tikkanen .10 .25
161 Ulf Dahlen .10 .25
162 Todd Elik .10 .25
163 Pat Falloon .10 .25
164 Jeff Friesen .10 .25
165 Johan Garpenlov .10 .25
166 Arturs Irbe .12 .30
167 Sergei Makarov .12 .30
168 Jeff Norton .10 .25
169 Sandis Ozolinsh .10 .25
170 Brian Bradley .10 .25
171 Shawn Chambers .10 .25
172 Aaron Gavey .10 .25
173 Chris Gratton .10 .25
174 Petr Klima .10 .25
175 Daren Puppa .12 .30
176 Jason Wiemer RC .12 .30
177 Dave Andreychuk .15 .40
178 Dave Ellett .10 .25
179 Eric Fichaud RC .15 .40
180 Mike Gartner .15 .40
181 Doug Gilmour .20 .50
182 Kenny Jonsson .10 .25
183 Dmitri Mironov .10 .25
184 Felix Potvin .15 .40
185 Mike Ridley .10 .25
186 Mats Sundin .12 .30
187 Greg Adams .10 .25
188 Jeff Brown .10 .25
189 Pavel Bure .15 .40
190 Nathan Lafayette .10 .25
191 Trevor Linden .12 .30
192 Jyrki Lumme .10 .25
193 Kirk McLean .12 .30
194 Cliff Ronning .10 .25
195 Jason Allison .12 .30
196 Peter Bondra .12 .30
197 Randy Burridge .10 .25
198 Sylvain Cote .10 .25
199 Dale Hunter .10 .25
200 Joe Juneau .10 .25
201 Dimitri Khristich .10 .25
202 Todd Nelson .10 .25
203 Pat Peake .10 .25
204 Rick Tabaracci .12 .30
205 Tim Cheveldae .12 .30
206 Dallas Drake .10 .25
207 Dave Manson .10 .25
208 Teppo Numminen .10 .25
209 Teemu Selanne .30 .75
210 Darrin Shannon .10 .25
211 Keith Tkachuk .15 .40
212 Alexei Zhamnov .12 .30
213 Sergei Fedorov .25 .60
214 Sergei Fedorov .25 .60
215 Sergei Fedorov .25 .60
216 Sergei Fedorov .25 .60
217 Sergei Fedorov .25 .60
218 Sergei Fedorov .25 .60
219 Sergei Fedorov .25 .60
220 Sergei Fedorov .25 .60
221 Sergei Fedorov .25 .60
222 Sergei Fedorov .25 .60
223 Checklist .10 .25
224 Checklist .10 .25
225 Checklist .10 .25

1994-95 Flair Center Spotlight

The 10 cards in this set, which highlighted some of the league's top centers, were randomly inserted in Flair product at the rate of 1:4 packs. The cards featured an action shot with two spotlights defining the background. Backs featured another action photo, along with a player profile. The cards were numbered on the back as "X of 10".
COMPLETE SET (10) 10.00 20.00
1 Jason Arnott .15 .40
2 Sergei Fedorov 1.00 2.50
3 Doug Gilmour .30 .75
4 Wayne Gretzky 4.00 10.00
5 Pat LaFontaine .60 1.50
6 Mario Lemieux 3.00 8.00
7 Eric Lindros .60 1.50
8 Mark Messier .60 1.50
9 Mike Modano 1.00 2.50
10 Jeremy Roenick .75 2.00

1994-95 Flair Hot Numbers

e ten cards in this set, which highlight some of the game's deadliest snipers, were randomly inserted in Flair product at the rate of 1:16 packs. The cards featured an action shot over a black background featuring a scribble of neon colors. The player, team, and set name appeared vertically along the left border of the card. Card backs had a similar style as the front and are numbered as "X of 10".
COMPLETE SET (10) 20.00 40.00
1 Pavel Bure .75 2.00
2 Wayne Gretzky 5.00 12.00
3 Dominik Hasek 2.00 5.00
4 Brett Hull 1.00 2.50
5 Mario Lemieux 4.00 10.00
6 Adam Oates .40 1.00
7 Luc Robitaille .40 1.00
8 Patrick Roy 4.00 10.00
9 Brendan Shanahan .75 2.00
10 Steve Yzerman 4.00 10.00

1994-95 Flair Scoring Power

is 10-card standard-size set was inserted in packs at a rate of 1:8. The fronts had a color action photo on the right side and the player's name and the word "Power" going down the left side in silver-foil. The background consisted of many multi-color lines scrawled about. The backs has a color photo with player information and the player's name and "Scoring Power" in silver-foil at the top. The background was similar to the front and they are numbered "X of 10" at the bottom.
COMPLETE SET (10) 6.00 12.00
1 Pavel Bure .75 2.00
2 Alexandre Daigle .20 .50
3 Sergei Fedorov 1.25 3.00
4 Alexei Kovalev .40 1.00
5 Brian Leetch .75 2.00
6 Eric Lindros .75 2.00
7 Mike Modano 1.25 3.00
8 Alexander Mogilny .40 1.00
9 Jeremy Roenick 1.00 2.50
10 Alexei Yashin .20 .50

1996-97 Flair

The 1996-97 Flair set was issued in one series totaling 125 cards. The set contained the Wave of the Future subset (101-125). Although numbered as part of the set, these cards were short printed and inserted at a rate of 1:4 packs. Card fronts featured a color action photo, and a background portrait of the player. Card backs contained a color action photo and statistics. Cards were distributed in four-card packs and carried a suggested retail price of $3.99. Key rookies include Sergei Berezin, Mike Grier, Patrick Lalime, Ethan Moreau and Dainius Zubrus.
COMPLETE SET (125) 30.00 80.00
COMP.BASE SET (100) 20.00 40.00
1 Guy Hebert .30 .75
2 Paul Kariya .50 1.25
3 Teemu Selanne .75 2.00
4 Ray Bourque .60 1.50
5 Adam Oates .40 1.00
6 Bill Ranford .30 .75
7 Jozef Stumpel .25 .60
8 Dominik Hasek .60 1.50
9 Pat LaFontaine .40 1.00
10 Alexei Zhitnik .25 .60
11 Theo Fleury .75 2.00
12 Dave Gagner .40 1.00
13 Trevor Kidd .25 .60
14 Tony Amonte .30 .75
15 Chris Chelios .40 1.00
16 Eric Daze .30 .75
17 Alexei Zhamnov .30 .75
18 Peter Forsberg .60 1.50
19 Sandis Ozolinsh .25 .60
20 Patrick Roy 1.00 2.50
21 Joe Sakic .60 1.50
22 Derian Hatcher .25 .60
23 Mike Modano .60 1.50
24 Andy Moog .40 1.00
25 Pat Verbeek .25 .60
26 Sergei Fedorov .60 1.50
27 Slava Fetisov .25 .60
28 Nicklas Lidstrom .50 1.25
29 Chris Osgood .40 1.00
30 Brendan Shanahan .50 1.25
31 Steve Yzerman 1.00 2.50
32 Jason Arnott .30 .75
33 Curtis Joseph .40 1.00
34 Boris Mironov .25 .60
35 Ryan Smyth .30 .75
36 Doug Weight .40 1.00
37 Ed Jovanovski .30 .75
38 Ray Sheppard .30 .75
39 Robert Svehla .25 .60
40 John Vanbiesbrouck .40 1.00
41 Andrew Cassels .25 .60
42 Jason Muzzatti .30 .75
43 Keith Primeau .25 .60
44 Geoff Sanderson .30 .75
45 Rob Blake .40 1.00
46 Dimitri Khristich .25 .60
47 Vincent Damphousse .30 .75
48 Saku Koivu .40 1.00
49 Mark Recchi .50 1.25
50 Martin Rucinsky .25 .60
51 Jocelyn Thibault .40 1.00
52 Martin Brodeur .75 2.00
53 Bill Guerin .40 1.00
54 Scott Stevens .40 1.00
55 Scott Lachance .25 .60
56 Zigmund Palffy .40 1.00
57 Tommy Salo .30 .75
58 Bryan Smolinski .25 .60
59 Wayne Gretzky 2.00 5.00
60 Brian Leetch .40 1.00
61 Mark Messier .60 1.50
62 Mike Richter .40 1.00
63 Daniel Alfredsson .40 1.00
64 Damian Rhodes .30 .75
65 Alexei Yashin .30 .75
66 Paul Coffey .40 1.00
67 Dale Hawerchuk .50 1.25
68 Ron Hextall .30 .75
69 John LeClair .40 1.00
70 Eric Lindros .60 1.50
71 Nikolai Khabibulin .30 .75
72 Jeremy Roenick .60 1.50
73 Keith Tkachuk .40 1.00
74 Oleg Tverdovsky .30 .75
75 Ron Francis .50 1.25
76 Kevin Hatcher .25 .60
77 Jaromir Jagr 1.00 2.50
78 Mario Lemieux 1.25 3.00
79 Petr Nedved .30 .75
80 Grant Fuhr .40 1.00
81 Brett Hull 2.00 5.00
82 Al MacInnis .40 1.00
83 Ed Belfour .40 1.00
84 Tony Granato .25 .60
85 Owen Nolan .40 1.00
86 Dino Ciccarelli .40 1.00
87 John Cullen .30 .75
88 Roman Hamrlik .30 .75
89 Wendel Clark .30 .75
90 Doug Gilmour .50 1.25
91 Felix Potvin .40 1.00
92 Mats Sundin .40 1.00
93 Pavel Bure .50 1.25
94 Corey Hirsch .30 .75
95 Trevor Linden .30 .75
96 Alexander Mogilny .30 .75
97 Peter Bondra .30 .75
98 Jim Carey .40 1.00
99 Dale Hunter .30 .75
100 Chris Simon .25 .60
101 Mattias Timander RC .60 1.50
102 Vaclav Varada RC .60 1.50
103 Jarome Iginla SP .75 2.00
104 Ethan Moreau RC .60 1.50
105 Jamie Langenbrunner SP .40 1.00
106 Roman Turek RC .60 1.50
107 Tomas Holmstrom RC 2.00 5.00
108 Kevin Hodson RC .60 1.50
109 Mats Lindgren SP .75 2.00
110 Mike Grier SP RC .75 2.00
111 Rem Murray RC .60 1.50
112 Jose Theodore SP .75 2.00
113 David Wilkie SP .40 1.00
114 Bryan Berard SP .60 1.50
115 Eric Fichaud SP .50 1.25
116 Daniel Goneau RC .60 1.50
117 Andreas Dackell RC .60 1.50
118 Wade Redden SP .40 1.00
119 Dainius Zubrus RC .75 2.00
120 Janne Niinimaa SP .60 1.50
121 Patrick Lalime RC .75 2.00
122 Harry York RC SP .60 1.50
123 Jim Campbell SP .40 1.00
124 Sergei Berezin RC 1.00 2.50
125 Jaro. Svejkovsky RC .75 2.00

1996-97 Flair Blue Ice

This 125-card set paralleled the basic Flair set. The cards were randomly inserted in packs at a rate of 1:20, though many dealers suggested they were harder to obtain than the odds suggest. Each card was serial numbered to 250, and card fronts carried a blue foil background along with the words BLUE ICE. No complete set price is listed below due to the extremely short print run of the set, and the lack of market activity in complete set form. Values can be determined by applying the multipliers below to the prices for the corresponding regular card.
*VETS: 8X TO 20X BASIC CARDS
*SPs: 1.5X TO 3X

1996-97 Flair Center Ice Spotlight

This set featured ten of the NHL's top players. Card fronts featured a color action photo, with purple, red and yellow spotlights highlighting the background. The cards were randomly inserted in packs at a rate of 1:30.
COMPLETE SET (10) 15.00 40.00
1 Pavel Bure 1.50 4.00
2 Sergei Fedorov 2.00 5.00
3 Peter Forsberg 2.00 5.00
4 Brett Hull 2.00 5.00
5 Jaromir Jagr 2.50 6.00
6 Paul Kariya 1.50 4.00
7 Joe Sakic 3.00 8.00
8 Teemu Selanne 1.50 4.00
9 Mats Sundin 1.50 4.00
10 Steve Yzerman 6.00 15.00

1996-97 Flair Hot Gloves

is insert set focused on twelve of the NHL's best netminders. Card fronts featured a color action photo with the mesh of a goalie glove in the background. Card backs contained a player photo and biographical information. Each card was die-cut and randomly inserted in packs at a rate of 1:40.
COMPLETE SET (12) 15.00 40.00
1 Ed Belfour 2.00 5.00
2 Martin Brodeur 6.00 15.00
3 Jim Carey 1.50 4.00
4 Dominik Hasek 4.00 10.00
5 Curtis Joseph 2.00 5.00
6 Patrick Lalime 1.50 4.00
7 Chris Osgood 2.00 5.00
8 Felix Potvin 4.00 10.00
9 Mike Richter 2.00 5.00
10 Patrick Roy 8.00 20.00
11 Jocelyn Thibault 1.50 4.00
12 John Vanbiesbrouck 2.00 5.00

1996-97 Flair Hot Numbers

This 10-card insert set featured NHL superstars who wear double numbers on their jerseys. Card fronts featured a color photo with an orange/red background and their jersey number along the top of the card. The cards were randomly inserted in packs at a rate of 1:72.
COMPLETE SET (10) 25.00 50.00
1 Ray Bourque 2.50 6.00
2 Paul Coffey 1.50 4.00
3 Eric Daze 1.00 2.50

4 Wayne Gretzky 10.00 25.00
5 Ed Jovanovski 1.00 2.50
6 Saku Koivu 1.50 4.00
7 Mario Lemieux 8.00 20.00
8 Eric Lindros 1.50 4.00
9 Mark Messier 1.50 4.00
10 Owen Nolan 1.00 2.50

1996-97 Flair Now And Then

ch card in this set featured three players who share a common bond. They are pictured in their rookie seasons on the front, while the back gave an up-to-date look. The cards were randomly inserted in packs at a rate of 1:400.

COMPLETE SET (3) 40.00 100.00
1 Gretzky/Messier/Gartner 15.00 40.00
2 Lemieux/Roy/Muller 15.00 40.00
3 Lindros/Forsberg/Nieder. 10.00 25.00

2006-07 Flair Showcase

is 300-card set was issued to the hobby in five-card packs, with an $4.99 SRP, which came 18 packs to a box and 16 boxes to a case. This set was broken into several levels with cards from what was called the press and lower level being inserted into packs at a stated rate of one in six and cards from the private box and executive level being inserted at a stated rate of one in 18. A cards of Evgeni Malkin was issued as a redemption at the Toronto Sportscard and Memorabilia Expo. Cards numbered 301-330 were inserted into update dealer packs available through hobby dealers.

COMP.SET w/o SPs (100) 12.00 30.00
101-200 STATED ODDS 1:6
200-300 STATED ODDS 1:18
UPD. RCs AVAIL IN UPDATE DEALER PACKS
FE301 MALKIN ISSUED AS EXPO EXCH
1 Jean-Sebastien Giguere .50 1.25
2 Teemu Selanne 1.00 2.50
3 Corey Perry .50 1.25
4 Scott Niedermayer .50 1.25
5 Joffrey Lupul .40 1.00
6 Ilya Kovalchuk .50 1.25
7 Marian Hossa .40 1.00
8 Kari Lehtonen .40 1.00
9 Patrice Bergeron .60 1.50
10 Marc Savard .30 .75
11 Brad Boyes .30 .75
12 Mark Stuart RC .30 .75
13 Chris Drury .40 1.00
14 Ryan Miller .50 1.25
15 Thomas Vanek .60 1.50
16 Jarome Iginla .50 1.25
17 Miikka Kiprusoff .40 1.00
18 Dion Phaneuf .50 1.25
19 Eric Staal .60 1.50
20 Cam Ward .50 1.25
21 Justin Williams .40 1.00
22 Erik Cole .40 1.00
23 Doug Weight .50 1.25
24 Nikolai Khabibulin .50 1.25
25 Tuomo Ruutu .50 1.25
26 Dustin Byfuglien RC .75 2.00
27 Milan Hejduk .40 1.00
28 Alex Tanguay .30 .75
29 Jose Theodore .50 1.25
30 Marek Svatos .30 .75
31 Rob Blake .50 1.25
32 Rick Nash .50 1.25
33 Sergei Fedorov .75 2.00
34 Mike Modano .75 2.00
35 Marty Turco .50 1.25
36 Brenden Morrow .40 1.00
37 Jere Lehtinen .30 .75
38 Steve Yzerman 1.25 3.00
39 Tomas Kopecky RC .40 1.00
40 Henrik Zetterberg .60 1.50
41 Pavel Datsyuk .60 1.50
42 Tomas Holmstrom .40 1.00
43 Kris Draper .30 .75
44 M-A Pouliot RC .30 .75
45 Ales Hemsky .40 1.00
46 Roberto Luongo .75 2.00
47 Olli Jokinen .50 1.25
48 K. Pushkarev RC .40 1.00
49 Jeremy Roenick .50 1.25
50 Alexander Frolov .30 .75
51 Marian Gaborik .60 1.50
52 Manny Fernandez .40 1.00
53 Saku Koivu .50 1.25
54 Michael Ryder .30 .75
55 Mike Ribeiro .40 1.00
56 Cristobal Huet .40 1.00
57 Paul Kariya .60 1.50
58 Tomas Vokoun .40 1.00
59 Shea Weber RC .75 2.00
60 Patrik Elias .50 1.25
61 Masi Marjamaki RC .30 .75
62 Alexei Yashin .40 1.00
63 Rick DiPietro .40 1.00
64 Miroslav Satan .40 1.00
65 Henrik Lundqvist 1.00 2.50
66 Jarkko Immonen RC .30 .75
67 Daniel Alfredsson .50 1.25
68 Martin Gerber .40 1.00
69 Jason Spezza .50 1.25
70 Dany Heatley .50 1.25
71 Martin Havlat .30 .75
72 Zdeno Chara .50 1.25
73 Simon Gagne .50 1.25
74 Ryan Potulny RC .30 .75
75 Jeff Carter .50 1.25
76 Peter Forsberg .60 1.50
77 Shane Doan .40 1.00
78 Ladislav Nagy .30 .75
79 Curtis Joseph .50 1.25
80 Marc-Andre Fleury .75 2.00
81 Noah Welch RC .30 .75
82 Matt Carle RC .30 .75
83 Evgeni Nabokov .40 1.00
84 Jonathan Cheechoo .50 1.25
85 Patrick Marleau .50 1.25
86 Keith Tkachuk .50 1.25
87 Vincent Lecavalier .40 1.00
88 Martin St. Louis .50 1.25
89 Brad Richards .50 1.25
90 Ian White RC .40 1.00
91 Ben Ondrus RC .30 .75
92 Eric Lindros .75 2.00
93 Alexander Steen .50 1.25
94 Jeremy Williams RC .30 .75
95 Todd Bertuzzi .50 1.25
96 Markus Naslund .40 1.00
97 Ed Jovanovski .40 1.00
98 Eric Fehr RC .50 1.25
99 Alexander Ovechkin 2.00 5.00
100 Olaf Kolzig .50 1.25
101 Teemu Selanne 1.50 4.00
102 Scott Niedermayer .75 2.00
103 Corey Perry .75 2.00
104 Marian Hossa .60 1.50
105 Kari Lehtonen .60 1.50
106 Yan Stastny RC .50 1.25
107 Glen Murray .60 1.50
108 Brian Leetch .75 2.00
109 Brad Boyes .50 1.25
110 Chris Drury .60 1.50
111 Ryan Miller .75 2.00
112 Thomas Vanek 1.00 2.50
113 Dion Phaneuf .75 2.00
114 Erik Cole .60 1.50
115 Cam Ward .75 2.00
116 Mark Recchi 1.00 2.50
117 Nikolai Khabibulin .75 2.00
118 Tuomo Ruutu .75 2.00
119 Rob Blake .75 2.00
120 Milan Hejduk .60 1.50
121 Marek Svatos .50 1.25
122 Sergei Fedorov 1.25 3.00
123 Brenden Morrow .60 1.50
124 Marty Turco .75 2.00
125 Tomas Kopecky .60 1.50
126 Pavel Datsyuk 1.00 2.50
127 Henrik Zetterberg 1.00 2.50
128 M-A Pouliot RC .50 1.25
129 Ales Hemsky .60 1.50
130 Olli Jokinen .75 2.00
131 K. Pushkarev RC .60 1.50
132 Luc Robitaille .75 2.00
133 Jeremy Roenick .75 2.00
134 Alexander Frolov .50 1.25
135 Marian Gaborik 1.00 2.50
136 Michael Ryder .50 1.25
137 Shea Weber 1.25 3.00
138 Paul Kariya 1.00 2.50
139 Tomas Vokoun .60 1.50
140 Patrik Elias .75 2.00
141 Alexei Yashin .60 1.50
142 Rick DiPietro .60 1.50
143 Miroslav Satan .60 1.50
144 Henrik Lundqvist 1.50 4.00
145 Billy Thompson RC .50 1.25
146 Filip Novak RC .50 1.25
147 Daniel Alfredsson .75 2.00
148 Zdeno Chara .75 2.00
149 Martin Havlat .50 1.25
150 Simon Gagne .75 2.00
151 Keith Primeau .75 2.00
152 Jeff Carter .75 2.00
153 Shane Doan .60 1.50
154 Ladislav Nagy .50 1.25
155 Curtis Joseph .75 2.00
156 Noah Welch .50 1.25
157 Marc-Andre Fleury 1.25 3.00
158 Evgeni Nabokov .60 1.50
159 Jonathan Cheechoo .75 2.00
160 Patrick Marleau .75 2.00
161 Keith Tkachuk .75 2.00
162 Brad Richards .75 2.00
163 Ben Ondrus .50 1.25
164 Brendan Bell RC .50 1.25
165 Ian White .60 1.50
166 Eric Lindros 1.25 3.00
167 Todd Bertuzzi .75 2.00
168 Ed Jovanovski .60 1.50
169 Eric Fehr .75 2.00
170 Olaf Kolzig .75 2.00
171 Jean-Sebastien Giguere .75 2.00
172 Ilya Kovalchuk .75 2.00
173 Patrice Bergeron 1.00 2.50
174 Jarome Iginla .75 2.00
175 Miikka Kiprusoff .60 1.50
176 Eric Staal 1.00 2.50
177 Joe Sakic 1.25 3.00
178 Jose Theodore .75 2.00
179 Alex Tanguay .50 1.25
180 Rick Nash .75 2.00
181 Mike Modano 1.25 3.00
182 Steve Yzerman 2.00 5.00
183 Brendan Shanahan 1.00 2.50
184 Chris Pronger .60 1.50
185 Roberto Luongo 1.25 3.00
186 Saku Koivu .75 2.00
187 Martin Brodeur 1.50 4.00
188 Jaromir Jagr 2.00 5.00
189 Jason Spezza .75 2.00
190 Dany Heatley .75 2.00
191 Martin Gerber .60 1.50
192 Peter Forsberg 1.00 2.50
193 Sidney Crosby 3.00 8.00
194 Joe Thornton 1.00 2.50
195 Vincent Lecavalier .60 1.50
196 Martin St. Louis .75 2.00
197 Mats Sundin .75 2.00
198 Andrew Raycroft .60 1.50
199 Markus Naslund .60 1.50
200 Alexander Ovechkin 3.00 8.00
201 Jean-Sebastien Giguere 2.50 6.00
202 Teemu Selanne 5.00 12.00
203 Kari Lehtonen 2.00 5.00
204 Marian Hossa 2.00 5.00
205 Ilya Kovalchuk 2.50 6.00
206 Ray Bourque 4.00 10.00
207 Patrice Bergeron 3.00 8.00
208 Brian Leetch 2.50 6.00
209 Chris Drury 2.00 5.00
210 Ryan Miller 2.50 6.00
211 Jarome Iginla 2.50 6.00
212 Miikka Kiprusoff 2.00 5.00
213 Dion Phaneuf 2.50 6.00
214 Eric Staal 3.00 8.00
215 Cam Ward 2.50 6.00
216 Rod Brind`Amour 2.50 6.00
217 Nikolai Khabibulin 2.50 6.00
218 Joe Sakic 4.00 10.00
219 Alex Tanguay 1.50 4.00
220 Milan Hejduk 2.00 5.00
221 Jose Theodore 2.50 6.00
222 Marek Svatos 1.50 4.00
223 Rick Nash 2.50 6.00
224 Sergei Fedorov 4.00 10.00
225 Mike Modano 4.00 10.00
226 Marty Turco 2.50 6.00
227 Brenden Morrow 2.00 5.00
228 Steve Yzerman 6.00 15.00
229 Gordie Howe 8.00 20.00
230 Brendan Shanahan 3.00 8.00
231 Henrik Zetterberg 3.00 8.00
232 Pavel Datsyuk 3.00 8.00
233 Chris Pronger 2.00 5.00
234 Roberto Luongo 4.00 10.00
235 Olli Jokinen 2.50 6.00
236 Luc Robitaille 2.50 6.00
237 Jeremy Roenick 2.50 6.00
238 Marian Gaborik 3.00 8.00
239 Saku Koivu 2.50 6.00
240 Patrick Roy 6.00 15.00
241 Michael Ryder 1.50 4.00
242 Paul Kariya 3.00 8.00
243 Martin Brodeur 5.00 12.00
244 Patrik Elias 2.50 6.00
245 Alexei Yashin 2.00 5.00
246 Rick DiPietro 2.00 5.00
247 Jaromir Jagr 6.00 15.00
248 Henrik Lundqvist 5.00 12.00
249 Martin Gerber 2.00 5.00
250 Dany Heatley 2.50 6.00
251 Jason Spezza 2.50 6.00
252 Daniel Alfredsson 2.50 6.00
253 Peter Forsberg 3.00 8.00
254 Simon Gagne 2.50 6.00
255 Shane Doan 2.00 5.00
256 Mario Lemieux 8.00 20.00
257 Sidney Crosby 10.00 25.00
258 Marc-Andre Fleury 4.00 10.00
259 Evgeni Nabokov 2.00 5.00
260 Joe Thornton 3.00 8.00
261 Jonathan Cheechoo 2.50 6.00
262 Vincent Lecavalier 2.00 5.00
263 Martin St. Louis 2.50 6.00
264 Brad Richards 2.50 6.00
265 Andrew Raycroft 2.00 5.00
266 Mats Sundin 2.50 6.00
267 Markus Naslund 2.00 5.00
268 Todd Bertuzzi 2.50 6.00
269 Alexander Ovechkin 10.00 25.00
270 Olaf Kolzig 2.50 6.00
271 Jean-Sebastien Giguere 2.50 6.00
272 Ilya Kovalchuk 2.50 6.00
273 Ray Bourque 4.00 10.00
274 Jarome Iginla 2.50 6.00
275 Miikka Kiprusoff 2.00 5.00
276 Eric Staal 3.00 8.00
277 Joe Sakic 4.00 10.00
278 Rick Nash 2.50 6.00
279 Mike Modano 4.00 10.00
280 Steve Yzerman 6.00 15.00
281 Gordie Howe 8.00 20.00
282 Henrik Zetterberg 3.00 8.00
283 Roberto Luongo 4.00 10.00
284 Saku Koivu 2.50 6.00
285 Patrick Roy 6.00 15.00
286 Paul Kariya 3.00 8.00
287 Martin Brodeur 5.00 12.00
288 Jaromir Jagr 6.00 15.00
289 Daniel Alfredsson 2.50 6.00
290 Dany Heatley 2.50 6.00
291 Jason Spezza 2.50 6.00
292 Peter Forsberg 3.00 8.00
293 Mario Lemieux 8.00 20.00
294 Sidney Crosby 10.00 25.00
295 Joe Thornton 3.00 8.00
296 Vincent Lecavalier 2.00 5.00
297 Andrew Raycroft 2.00 5.00
298 Mats Sundin 2.50 6.00
299 Markus Naslund 2.00 5.00
300 Alexander Ovechkin 10.00 25.00
301 Ryan Shannon RC 2.50 6.00
302 David McKee RC 2.50 6.00
303 Phil Kessel RC 6.00 15.00
304 Matt Lashoff RC 2.50 6.00
305 Drew Stafford RC 4.00 10.00
306 Clarke MacArthur RC 3.00 8.00
307 Dustin Boyd RC 2.50 6.00
308 Brandon Prust RC 2.50 6.00
309 Dave Bolland RC 4.00 10.00
310 Paul Stastny RC 6.00 15.00
311 Loui Eriksson RC 4.00 10.00
312 Ladislav Smid RC 2.50 6.00
313 Patrick O'Sullivan RC 4.00 10.00
314 Anze Kopitar RC 10.00 25.00
315 Benoit Pouliot RC 3.00 8.00
316 G. Latendresse RC 4.00 10.00
317 Alexander Radulov RC 5.00 12.00
318 Travis Zajac RC 5.00 12.00
319 Nigel Dawes RC 2.50 6.00
320 Josh Hennessy RC 2.50 6.00
321 Enver Lisin RC 2.50 6.00
322 Evgeni Malkin RC 15.00 40.00
323 Jordan Staal RC 6.00 15.00
324 Kristopher Letang RC 8.00 20.00
325 Marc-Edouard Vlasic RC 2.50 6.00
326 Joe Pavelski RC 12.00 30.00
327 Marek Schwarz RC 4.00 10.00
328 Karri Ramo RC 2.50 6.00
329 Luc Bourdon RC 4.00 10.00
330 Jesse Schultz RC 2.50 6.00
FE301 Evgeni Malkin 15.00 40.00

2006-07 Flair Showcase Parallel

*PARALLEL 1-100: 3X TO 8X BASE
*PARALLEL 101-200: 2X TO 5X BASE
(1-200) PRINT RUN 100 SER.#'d SETS
*PARALLEL 201-270: .8X TO 2X BASE
(201-270) PRINT RUN 50 SER.#'d SETS
*PARALLEL 271-300: 1X TO 2.5X BASE
(271-300) PRINT RUN 35 SER.#'d SETS

2006-07 Flair Showcase Hot Gloves

STATED ODDS 1:72
HG1 Jean-Sebastien Giguere 5.00 12.00
HG2 Kari Lehtonen 4.00 10.00
HG3 Hannu Toivonen 4.00 10.00
HG4 Ryan Miller 5.00 12.00
HG5 Miikka Kiprusoff 4.00 10.00
HG6 Martin Gerber 4.00 10.00
HG7 Nikolai Khabibulin 5.00 12.00
HG8 Jose Theodore 5.00 12.00
HG9 Marc Denis 4.00 10.00
HG10 Marty Turco 5.00 12.00
HG11 Cam Ward 5.00 12.00
HG12 Dwayne Roloson 4.00 10.00
HG13 Roberto Luongo 8.00 20.00
HG14 Mathieu Garon 4.00 10.00
HG15 Manny Fernandez 4.00 10.00
HG16 Cristobal Huet 4.00 10.00
HG17 Tomas Vokoun 4.00 10.00
HG18 Martin Brodeur 10.00 25.00
HG19 Rick DiPietro 4.00 10.00
HG20 Henrik Lundqvist 10.00 25.00
HG21 Pascal Leclaire 4.00 10.00
HG22 Antero Niittymaki 4.00 10.00
HG23 Curtis Joseph 5.00 12.00
HG24 Marc-Andre Fleury 8.00 20.00
HG25 Evgeni Nabokov 4.00 10.00
HG26 Curtis Sanford 4.00 10.00
HG27 Vesa Toskala 4.00 10.00
HG28 Andrew Raycroft 4.00 10.00
HG29 Alex Auld 3.00 8.00
HG30 Olaf Kolzig 5.00 12.00

2006-07 Flair Showcase Hot Numbers

STATED ODDS 1:180
HN1 Teemu Selanne 12.00 30.00
HN2 Kari Lehtonen 5.00 12.00
HN3 Ray Bourque 10.00 25.00
HN4 Miikka Kiprusoff 5.00 12.00
HN5 Jarome Iginla 6.00 15.00
HN6 Martin Gerber 5.00 12.00
HN7 Eric Staal 8.00 20.00
HN8 Nikolai Khabibulin 6.00 15.00
HN9 Alex Tanguay 4.00 10.00
HN10 Jose Theodore 6.00 15.00
HN11 Joe Sakic 10.00 25.00
HN12 Milan Hejduk 5.00 12.00
HN13 Rick Nash 6.00 15.00
HN14 Sergei Fedorov 10.00 25.00
HN15 Mike Modano 10.00 25.00
HN16 Henrik Zetterberg 8.00 20.00
HN17 Gordie Howe 20.00 50.00
HN18 Brendan Shanahan 8.00 20.00
HN19 Steve Yzerman 15.00 40.00
HN20 Ales Hemsky 5.00 12.00
HN21 Jeremy Roenick 6.00 15.00
HN22 Luc Robitaille 6.00 15.00
HN23 Marian Gaborik 8.00 20.00
HN24 Patrick Roy 15.00 40.00
HN25 Michael Ryder 4.00 10.00
HN26 Saku Koivu 6.00 15.00
HN27 Martin Brodeur 12.00 30.00
HN28 Alexei Yashin 5.00 12.00
HN29 Jaromir Jagr 15.00 40.00
HN30 Dominik Hasek 8.00 20.00
HN31 Dany Heatley 6.00 15.00
HN32 Peter Forsberg 8.00 20.00
HN33 Sidney Crosby 25.00 60.00
HN34 Mario Lemieux 20.00 50.00
HN35 Joe Thornton 8.00 20.00
HN36 Vincent Lecavalier 5.00 12.00
HN37 Martin St. Louis 6.00 15.00
HN38 Mats Sundin 6.00 15.00
HN39 Eric Lindros 10.00 25.00
HN40 Todd Bertuzzi 6.00 15.00
HN41 Markus Naslund 5.00 12.00
HN42 Alexander Ovechkin 25.00 60.00

2006-07 Flair Showcase Hot Numbers Parallel

*PARALLEL/60-97: .5X TO 1.2X BASIC
*PARALLEL/30-50: .6X TO 1.5X BASIC
*PARALLEL/20-29: .8X TO 2X BASIC
SER.#'d TO JERSEY NUMBER

2006-07 Flair Showcase Inks

ATED ODDS 1:18
IAF Alexander Frolov 4.00 10.00
IAH Ales Hemsky 5.00 12.00
IAL Andrew Ladd 6.00 15.00
IAM Andy McDonald 5.00 12.00
IAN Antero Niittymaki 5.00 12.00
IAO Alexander Ovechkin SP 50.00 120.00
IBB Brad Boyes 4.00 10.00
IBE Ben Eager 5.00 12.00
IBG Brian Gionta 5.00 12.00
IBI Martin Biron 5.00 12.00
IBL Brian Leetch 6.00 15.00
IBR Brenden Morrow 5.00 12.00
ICD Chris Drury 5.00 12.00
ICH Cristobal Huet 5.00 12.00
ICK Chris Kunitz 6.00 15.00
IDA David Aebischer 5.00 12.00
IDB Daniel Briere 6.00 15.00
IDC Dan Cloutier 5.00 12.00
IDK Duncan Keith 8.00 20.00
IDL David Leneveu 5.00 12.00
IDP Dion Phaneuf 6.00 15.00
IDR Dwayne Roloson 5.00 12.00
IDU Dustin Brown 6.00 15.00
IED Eric Daze 4.00 10.00
IEN Evgeni Nabokov 5.00 12.00
IFP Fernando Pisani 4.00 10.00
IHA Michal Handzus 5.00 12.00
IHE Dany Heatley 6.00 15.00
IHJ Milan Hejduk 5.00 12.00
IHO Marcel Hossa 4.00 10.00
IHZ Henrik Zetterberg 15.00 40.00
IIK Ilya Kovalchuk SP 15.00 40.00
IJC Jonathan Cheechoo 6.00 15.00
IJI Jarome Iginla 6.00 15.00
IJL Joffrey Lupul 5.00 12.00
IJO Jeff O'Neill 4.00 10.00
IJP Joni Pitkanen 4.00 10.00
IJR Jeremy Roenick SP 15.00 40.00
IJT Jose Theodore 6.00 15.00
IKD Kris Draper 4.00 10.00
IKE Ryan Kesler 8.00 20.00
IKI Miikka Kiprusoff 5.00 12.00
IKL Kari Lehtonen 5.00 12.00
IKO Chuck Kobasew 4.00 10.00
ILR Luc Robitaille 6.00 15.00
ILX Mario Lemieux SP 75.00 150.00
IMA Maxim Afinogenov 4.00 10.00
IMB Martin Brodeur SP 50.00 100.00
IMC Mike Cammalleri 4.00 10.00
IMF Marc-Andre Fleury 10.00 25.00
IMG Marian Gaborik 8.00 20.00
IMH Martin Havlat 4.00 10.00
IMI Ryan Miller 6.00 15.00
IML Manny Legace 5.00 12.00
IMM Milan Michalek 4.00 10.00
IMN Markus Naslund 5.00 12.00
IMO Brendan Morrison 4.00 10.00
IMP Mark Parrish 4.00 10.00
IMR Mike Richards 6.00 15.00
IMS Marc Savard 4.00 10.00
IMT Marty Turco SP 6.00 15.00
INA Nikolai Antropov 5.00 12.00
IOJ Olli Jokinen 6.00 15.00
IOK Olaf Kolzig 6.00 15.00
IPA Jay McClement 4.00 10.00
IPB Pierre-Marc Bouchard 6.00 15.00
IPM Patrick Marleau SP 6.00 15.00
IRB Rob Blake 6.00 15.00
IRF Ruslan Fedotenko 4.00 10.00
IRI Mike Ribeiro 5.00 12.00
IRM Ryan Malone 4.00 10.00
IRS Ryan Smyth 5.00 12.00
IRY Michael Ryder 4.00 10.00
ISA Miroslav Satan 5.00 12.00
ISC Sidney Crosby SP 100.00 200.00
ISG Scott Gomez 5.00 12.00
ISH Shawn Horcoff 4.00 10.00
ISS Sergei Samsonov SP 5.00 12.00
ISV Marek Svatos SP 12.00 30.00
ITB Todd Bertuzzi SP 10.00 25.00
ITC Ty Conklin 5.00 12.00
ITE Mikael Tellqvist 6.00 15.00
ITH Joe Thornton SP 20.00 50.00
ITV Tomas Vokoun 5.00 12.00
IVL Vincent Lecavalier 5.00 12.00
IWR Wade Redden 4.00 10.00

2006-07 Flair Showcase Stitches

STATED ODDS 1:9
SSAH Ales Hemsky 4.00 10.00
SSAK Alex Kovalev 4.00 10.00
SSAO Alexander Ovechkin 12.00 30.00
SSAT Alex Tanguay 3.00 8.00
SSBG Bill Guerin 5.00 12.00
SSBL Rob Blake 5.00 12.00
SSBM Brenden Morrow 4.00 10.00
SSBO Radek Bonk 3.00 8.00
SSBR Martin Brodeur 10.00 25.00
SSBS Brad Stuart 3.00 8.00
SSCA Carlo Colaiacovo 3.00 8.00
SSCC Chris Chelios 5.00 12.00
SSCD Chris Drury 4.00 10.00
SSCO Chris Osgood 5.00 12.00
SSCP Chris Pronger 4.00 10.00
SSDA Daniel Alfredsson 5.00 12.00
SSDB Donald Brashear 3.00 8.00
SSDC Dan Cloutier 4.00 10.00
SSDE Pavol Demitra 6.00 15.00
SSDH Dan Hamhuis 4.00 10.00
SSDL David Legwand 4.00 10.00
SSDM Darren McCarty 3.00 8.00
SSDR Dwayne Roloson 4.00 10.00
SSEB Ed Belfour 8.00 20.00
SSED Eric Daze 3.00 8.00
SSEL Eric Lindros 8.00 20.00
SSEN Evgeni Nabokov 4.00 10.00
SSES Eric Staal 6.00 15.00
SSFP Fernando Pisani 3.00 8.00
SSGA Mathieu Garon 4.00 10.00
SSGM Glen Murray 4.00 10.00
SSGR Gary Roberts 3.00 8.00
SSHO Marcel Hossa 3.00 8.00
SSJA Jason Arnott 4.00 10.00
SSJB Jay Bouwmeester 5.00 12.00
SSJC Jonathan Cheechoo 5.00 12.00
SSJG Jean-Sebastien Giguere 5.00 12.00
SSJI Jarome Iginla 5.00 12.00
SSJJ Jaromir Jagr 12.00 30.00
SSJL Joffrey Lupul 4.00 10.00
SSJO Joe Thornton 6.00 15.00
SSJR Jeremy Roenick 5.00 12.00
SSJS Jason Spezza 5.00 12.00
SSJT Jose Theodore 5.00 12.00
SSJW Justin Williams 4.00 10.00
SSKP Keith Primeau 5.00 12.00
SSKT Keith Tkachuk 5.00 12.00
SSLE Jere Lehtinen 3.00 8.00
SSLM Mario Lemieux 12.00 30.00
SSLN Ladislav Nagy 3.00 8.00
SSLU Jamie Lundmark 3.00 8.00
SSMA Marian Gaborik 6.00 15.00
SSMB Martin Biron 4.00 10.00
SSMC Bryan McCabe 3.00 8.00
SSMG Martin Gerber 4.00 10.00
SSMH Marian Hossa 4.00 10.00
SSMK Miikka Kiprusoff 4.00 10.00
SSML Manny Legace 4.00 10.00
SSMM Mike Modano 8.00 20.00
SSMN Markus Naslund 4.00 10.00
SSMO Brendan Morrison 3.00 8.00
SSMP Michael Peca 4.00 10.00
SSMR Mike Ribeiro 4.00 10.00
SSMS Marek Svatos 3.00 8.00
SSNA Nikolai Antropov 4.00 10.00
SSOH Mattias Ohlund 3.00 8.00
SSOJ Olli Jokinen 5.00 12.00
SSPA Mark Parrish 3.00 8.00
SSPB Pierre-Marc Bouchard 5.00 12.00
SSPD Pavel Datsyuk 6.00 15.00
SSPE Patrik Elias 5.00 12.00
SSPF Peter Forsberg 6.00 15.00
SSRA Brian Rafalski 4.00 10.00
SSRB Rod Brind`Amour 5.00 12.00
SSRE Robert Esche 4.00 10.00
SSRL Robert Lang 3.00 8.00
SSRM Ryan Miller 5.00 12.00
SSRR Robyn Regehr 3.00 8.00
SSRT Raffi Torres 3.00 8.00
SSRY Michael Ryder 3.00 8.00
SSRZ Richard Zednik 3.00 8.00
SSSA Miroslav Satan 4.00 10.00
SSSC Sidney Crosby 15.00 40.00
SSSG Simon Gagne 5.00 12.00
SSSK Sami Kapanen 3.00 8.00
SSSM Matt Stajan 4.00 10.00
SSSN Scott Niedermayer 5.00 12.00
SSST Martin Straka 3.00 8.00
SSSU Mats Sundin 5.00 12.00
SSSW Stephen Weiss 3.00 8.00
SSSY Steve Yzerman 12.00 30.00
SSTA Tony Amonte 4.00 10.00
SSTC Ty Conklin 4.00 10.00
SSTH Tomas Holmstrom 4.00 10.00
SSTL Trevor Linden 5.00 12.00
SSTR Tuomo Ruutu 5.00 12.00
SSTS Teemu Selanne 10.00 25.00
SSWI Jason Williams 3.00 8.00
SSWR Wade Redden 3.00 8.00
SSZC Zdeno Chara 5.00 12.00

2006-07 Flair Showcase Wave of the Future

STATED ODDS 1:6
WF1 Joffrey Lupul 1.25 3.00
WF2 Kari Lehtonen 1.25 3.00
WF3 Ilya Kovalchuk 1.50 4.00
WF4 Patrice Bergeron 2.00 5.00
WF5 Brad Boyes 1.00 2.50
WF6 Ryan Miller 1.50 4.00
WF7 Dion Phaneuf 1.50 4.00
WF8 Eric Staal 2.00 5.00
WF9 Tuomo Ruutu 1.50 4.00
WF10 Marek Svatos 1.00 2.50
WF11 Rick Nash 1.50 4.00
WF12 Jussi Jokinen 1.25 3.00
WF13 Henrik Zetterberg 2.00 5.00
WF14 Ales Hemsky 1.25 3.00
WF15 Jarret Stoll 1.25 3.00
WF16 Nathan Horton 1.50 4.00
WF17 Dustin Brown 1.50 4.00
WF18 Alexander Frolov 1.00 2.50
WF19 Marian Gaborik 2.00 5.00
WF20 Mikko Koivu 1.25 3.00
WF21 Corey Perry 1.50 4.00
WF22 Thomas Vanek 2.00 5.00
WF23 Michael Ryder 1.00 2.50
WF24 Chris Higgins 1.00 2.50
WF25 Zach Parise 2.00 5.00
WF26 Rick DiPietro 1.25 3.00
WF27 Henrik Lundqvist 3.00 8.00
WF28 Petr Prucha 1.25 3.00
WF29 Jason Spezza 1.50 4.00
WF30 Dany Heatley 1.50 4.00
WF31 Martin Havlat 1.00 2.50
WF32 Jeff Carter 1.50 4.00
WF33 Joni Pitkanen 1.00 2.50
WF34 Mike Richards 1.50 4.00
WF35 Sidney Crosby 6.00 15.00
WF36 Marc-Andre Fleury 2.50 6.00
WF37 Steve Bernier 1.00 2.50
WF38 Alexander Steen 1.50 4.00
WF39 Kyle Wellwood 1.25 3.00
WF40 Andrew Raycroft 1.25 3.00
WF41 Ryan Kesler 2.00 5.00
WF42 Alexander Ovechkin 6.00 15.00

1972-73 Flames Postcards

This 20-card set of the Atlanta Flames measured 3 1/2" by 5 1/2". The fronts featured color action player photos with a white border. The player's autograph was across the bottom of the photo. The backs were blank. The cards were unnumbered and checklisted below in alphabetical order.

COMPLETE SET (20) 30.00 60.00
1 Curt Bennett 1.00 2.00
2 Dan Bouchard 2.50 5.00
3 Rey Comeau 1.00 2.00
4 BoomBoom Geoffrion CO 5.00 10.00
5 Bob Leiter 1.00 2.00
6 Kerry Ketter 1.00 2.00
7 Billy MacMillan 1.00 2.00
8 Randy Manery 1.00 2.00
9 Keith McCreary 1.00 2.00
10 Lew Morrison 1.00 2.00
11 Phil Myre 3.00 6.00
12 Bob Paradise 1.00 2.00
13 Noel Picard 1.00 2.00
14 Bill Plager 1.50 3.00
15 Noel Price 1.50 3.00
16 Pat Quinn 2.50 5.00
17 Jacques Richard 1.50 3.00
18 Leon Rochefort 1.00 2.00
19 Larry Romanchych 1.00 2.00
20 John Stewart 1.00 2.00

1978-79 Flames Majik Market

This 20 card set was issued during the 1978-79 season and features members of the Atlanta Flames. The front had an action shot as well as a facsimile autograph. The back had the player's name, uniform number and some personal statistics. At the bottom, sponsors "Coca-Cola Bottling" and radio station WTLA are credited. Pat Ribble, who was traded during the season, was the most difficult card to obtain and is listed as an SP. We have checklisted this set by the uniform number.

COMPLETE SET (20) 15.00 30.00
1 Rejean Lemelin 1.50 3.00
2 Greg Fox .50 1.00
3 Pat Ribble SP 5.00 10.00
5 Brad Marsh 2.00 4.00
6 Ken Houston .50 1.00
7 Bobby LaLonde .50 1.00
8 David Shand .50 1.00
9 Jean Pronovost .75 1.50
10 Bill Clement 1.50 3.00
11 Bob MacMillan .50 1.00
12 Tom Lysiak 1.00 2.00
15 Rod Seiling .50 1.00
16 Guy Chouinard 1.00 2.00
17 Don Red Laurence .50 1.00
19 Ed Kea .50 1.00
20 Bob Murdoch .75 1.50
24 Harold Phillipoff .50 1.00
25 Willi Plett 1.00 2.00
27 Eric Vail 1.00 2.00
30 Daniel Bouchard 1.50 3.00

1979-80 Flames Postcards

This 20-card set was sponsored by the Atlanta Coca-Cola Bottling Company, Winn Dixie, and radio station WLTA-100. The set was in the postcard format, with each card measuring approximately 3 1/2" by 5 1/2". The fronts featured full-bleed color action shots; a facsimile autograph was inscribed across the lower portion of the pictures. The backs carried the player's name, uniform number, biography, and sponsor logos. The cards were unnumbered and checklisted below according to jersey number.

COMPLETE SET (20) 15.00 30.00
1 Jim Craig 2.50 5.00
2 Curt Bennett .50 1.00
3 Phil Russell .50 1.00
4 Pekka Rautakallio .50 1.00
5 Brad Marsh 2.50 5.00
6 Ken Houston .50 1.00
7 Garry Unger 1.50 3.00
8 David Shand .50 1.00
9 Jean Pronovost .75 1.50
10 Bill Clement 2.00 4.00
11 Bob MacMillan .50 1.00
12 Don Lever .50 1.00
14 Kent Nilsson 2.50 5.00
16 Guy Chouinard 1.00 2.00
20 Bob Murdoch .75 1.50
23 Paul Reinhardt .75 1.50
25 Willi Plett 1.25 2.50
27 Eric Vail .75 1.50
30 Dan Bouchard 1.50 3.00
31 Pat Riggin 1.25 2.50

1979-80 Flames Team Issue

Cards measured 3 3/4 x 5 1/4 and featured black and white action photos on the front along with a facsimile signature. Backs were blank. Cards were unnumbered and checklisted below in alphabetical order.

COMPLETE SET (22) 20.00 40.00
1 Curt Bennett .50 1.00
2 Ivan Boldirev .50 1.00
3 Dan Bouchard 1.50 3.00
4 Guy Chouinard 1.00 2.00
5 Bill Clement 1.50 3.00
6 Jim Craig 2.00 4.00
7 Ken Houston .50 1.00
8 Brad Marsh 1.50 3.00
9 Bob MacMillan .50 1.00
10 Al MacNeil .50 1.00
11 Bob Murdoch .75 1.50
12 Kent Nilsson 2.00 4.00
13 Willi Plett 1.00 2.00
14 Jean Pronovost .75 1.50
15 Pekka Rautakallio .50 1.00
16 Paul Reinhart .75 1.50
17 Pat Riggin 1.00 2.00
18 Darcy Rota .50 1.00
19 Phil Russell .50 1.00
20 David Shand .50 1.00
21 Garry Unger 1.25 2.50
22 Eric Vail 1.00 2.00

1980-81 Flames Postcards

This 24-postcard set measured approximately 3 3/4" by 5". The fronts featured borderless posed color player photos. The backs were blank. The cards were unnumbered and checklisted below in alphabetical order.

COMPLETE SET (24) 20.00 40.00
1 Daniel Bouchard 1.25 3.00
2 Guy Chouinard .75 2.00
3 Bill Clement .75 2.00
4 Denis Cyr .40 1.00
5 Randy Holt .40 1.0
6 Ken Houston .40 1.0
7 Rejean Lemelin 2.50 5.0
8 Kevin Lavallee .40 1.0
9 Don Lever .40 1.0
10 Bob MacMillan .40 1.0
11 Bob Murdoch .40 1.0
12 Brad Marsh 1.00 2.5
13 Kent Nilsson 1.50 4.0
14 Willi Plett .60 1.5
15 Jim Peplinski 1.00 2.5
16 Pekka Rautakallio .75 2.0
17 Paul Reinhart 1.00 2.5
18 Pat Riggin .75 2.0
19 Phil Russell .40 1.0
20 Brad Smith .40 1.0
21 Jay Soleway .40 1.0
22 Eric Vail .60 1.5
23 Bert Wilson .40 1.0
24 Team Photo .60 1.5

1981-82 Flames Postcards

This 20-postcard set measured approximately 3 3/4" by 5". The fronts featured borderless posed color player photos. The backs were blank. The cards are unnumbered and checklisted below in alphabetical order.

COMPLETE SET (20) 10.00 25.0
1 Charlie Bourgeois .30 .7
2 Mel Bridgman .40 1.0
3 Guy Chouinard .60 1.5
4 Bill Clement .60 1.5
5 Denis Cyr .30 .7
6 Jamie Hislop .30 .7
7 Ken Houston .30 .7
8 Steve Konroyd .30 .7
9 Dan Labraaten .30 .7
10 Kevin Lavallee .30 .7
11 Rejean Lemelin 1.25 3.0
12 Lanny McDonald 1.25 3.0
13 Gary McAdam .30 .7
14 Bob Murdoch .40 1.0
15 Jim Peplinski .75 2.0
16 Willi Plett .60 1.5
17 Pekka Rautakallio .40 1.0
18 Paul Reinhart .60 1.5
19 Pat Riggin .60 1.5
20 Phil Russell .30 .7

1982-83 Flames Dollars

These six cards, measuring approximately 3" by 5" ar perforated on each end, were issued with "Hockey Dollars" or what may be better described as silver-colored coins. Each coin (measuring approximately 1/4" in diameter) displayed an engraving of the player face on the obverse and the team logo on the reverse. The card fronts were gray with tan lettering. They had the player's name, number, year, team logo, and a picture of the coin. In a horizontal format, the backs carried biography, career highlights, and career statistics. The cards were numbered on the back in th upper right corner. The prices below refer to the coin-card combination intact.

COMPLETE SET (6) 10.00 25.0
1 Mel Bridgman 1.50 4.0
2 Don Edwards 1.50 4.0
3 Lanny McDonald DP 3.00 8.0
4 Kent Nilsson 2.50 6.0
5 Jim Peplinski 1.50 4.0
6 Paul Reinhart 2.00 5.0

1985-86 Flames Red Rooster

This 30-card set of Calgary Flames was sponsored b Red Rooster Food Stores, Old Dutch Potato Chips, a Post Cereals. The player cards could be collected fro any Red Rooster Food Stores. The cards measured approximately 2 3/4" by 3 5/8" and featured on the front a color posed head shot (with rounded corners) the player, with a facsimile autograph in white ink in the lower right-hand corner of the picture. The player name, uniform number, the Calgary Flames' logo, an a hockey tip appeared below the picture. The back ha biographical and statistical information on the top portion, while the bottom has sponsor advertisement and the anti-crime slogan "Support Crime Stoppers." The set included two different cards of Lanny McDonald and Doug Risebrough. Al MacInnis appea in his Rookie Card year whereas Mike Vernon's appearance predated his Rookie Card by two years.

COMPLETE SET (30) 10.00 25.0
1 Paul Baxter .15
2 Ed Beers .15
3 Perry Berezan .15
4 Charlie Bourgeois .15
5 Steve Bozek .15
6 Gino Cavallini .15
7 Marc D'Amour .20
8 Tim Hunter .40 1.0
9 Bob Johnson CO 1.00 2.5
10 Steve Konroyd .15
11 Richard Kromm .15
12 Rejean Lemelin .40 1.0
13 Hakan Loob .40 1.0
14 Lanny McDonald .75 2.0
15 Lanny McDonald .75 2.0
16 Al MacInnis 2.50 6.0
17 Jamie Macoun .20
18 Bob Murdoch CO .15
19 Joel Otto .60 1.5
20 Pierre Page CO .20
21 Colin Patterson .15
22 Jim Peplinski .30
23 Dan Quinn .20
24 Paul Reinhart .30
25 Doug Risebrough .15
26 Doug Risebrough .15
27 Neil Sheehy .15
28 Gary Suter .40 1.0
29 Mike Vernon 2.50 6.0
(No facsimile autograph
30 Carey Wilson .15

1986-87 Flames Red Rooster

This 30-card set of Calgary Flames was sponsored b Red Rooster Food Stores in conjunction with Old Dutch Potato Chips. The player cards could be collected from any Red Rooster Food Stores. The ca measured approximately 2 3/4" by 3 5/8" and featur a color posed photo (with rounded corners) of the player, with a facsimile autograph in blue ink across the bottom of the picture. The player's name, unifor number, the Calgary Flames' logo, and a hockey tip appeared below the picture. The back had biograph and statistical information on the top portion, while bottom has sponsor advertisements and the anti-cri slogan "Support Crime Stoppers." The set included different cards of Lanny McDonald, Joe Mullen, and Paul Reinhart. Gary Roberts' card predated his Rook Card year by three years.

COMPLETE SET (30) 8.00 20.
1 Paul Baxter .20
2 Perry Berezan .20
3 Steve Bozek .20

1996-97 Flair Now And Then

Brian Bradley .40 1.00
Brian Engblom .20 .50
Nick Fotiu .20 .50
Tim Hunter .30 .75
Bob Johnson CO .75 2.00
Rejean Lemelin .40 1.00
0 Hakan Loob .40 1.00
1 Al MacInnis 1.25 3.00
2 Jamie Macoun .20 .50
3 Lanny McDonald .60 1.50
4 Lanny McDonald .60 1.50
5 Joe Mullen .60 1.50
6 Joe Mullen .60 1.50
7 Bob Murdoch CO .20 .50
8 Joel Otto .40 1.00
9 Pierre Page CO .20 .50
0 Colin Patterson .20 .50
1 Jim Peplinski .20 .50
2 Paul Reinhart .20 .50
3 Paul Reinhart .20 .50
4 Doug Risebrough .20 .50
5 Gary Roberts 1.50 4.00
6 Neil Sheehy .20 .50
7 Gary Suter .30 .75
8 John Tonelli .30 .75
9 Mike Vernon 1.25 3.00
0 Carey Wilson .20 .50

1987-88 Flames Red Rooster

his 30-card set of Calgary Flames was sponsored by ed Rooster Food Stores, and the player cards could e collected from any of these stores. The cards neasured 2 11/16" by 3 9/16" and featured on the front color posed head-and-shoulders shot (with rounded orners) of the player, with a facsimile autograph in lue ink across the bottom of the picture. The player's ame, uniform number, the Calgary Flames' logo, and hockey tip appeared below the picture. The back had iographical and statistical information on the top ortion, while the bottom had a sponsor advertisement nd the anti-crime slogan "Support Crime Stoppers." he set included two different cards of Hakan Loob, anny McDonald, and Joe Nieuwendyk. The Brett Hull nd Joe Nieuwendyk cards were the key cards in the et since they pre-dated their O-Pee-Chee and Topps ookie Cards by one year.

OMPLETE SET (30) 20.00 50.00
Perry Berezan .15 .40
Steve Bozek .15 .40
Mike Bullard .20 .50
Shane Churla .30 .75
Terry Crisp CO .15 .40
Doug Dadswell .20 .50
Brian Glynn .15 .40
Brett Hull 12.00 30.00
Tim Hunter .20 .50
0 Hakan Loob .30 .75
1 Hakan Loob .30 .75
2 Al MacInnis .75 2.00
3 Brad McCrimmon .20 .50
4 Lanny McDonald .40 1.00
5 Lanny McDonald .40 1.00
6 Joe Mullen .40 1.00
7 Dana Murzyn .15 .40
8 Ric Nattress .15 .40
9 Joe Nieuwendyk 2.50 6.00
0 Joe Nieuwendyk 2.50 6.00
1 Joel Otto .30 .75
2 Pierre Page CO .15 .40
3 Colin Patterson .15 .40
4 Jim Peplinski .20 .50
5 Paul Reinhart .20 .50
6 Doug Risebrough CO .15 .40
7 Gary Roberts .75 2.00
8 Gary Suter .30 .75
9 John Tonelli .20 .50
0 Mike Vernon .75 2.00

1990-91 Flames IGA/McGavin's

his 30-card standard-size set was sponsored by IGA od stores in conjunction with McGavin's, a stributor of bread and other products in Alberta. rotected by a cello pack, one card was inserted in read loaves distributed by McGavin's to IGA stores in algary and Edmonton. Calgary consumers received a ames' card, while Edmonton consumers received an ilers' card. Checklist and coaches cards were not serted in the loaves but were included on five undred individually numbered and uncut sheets not fered to the general public. The cards were printed on in card stock. The fronts had posed color player hotos, with a border that shaded from red to orange d back to red. The player's name was printed in the ttom border, and his uniform number was printed in circle in the upper left corner of each picture. The rizontally oriented backs featured biographical formation, with year-by-year statistics presented in a nk rectangle. Sponsor logos at the bottom round ed t the back. The cards were unnumbered and ecklisted below in alphabetical order.

OMPLETE SET (30) 14.00 35.00
Paul Baxter CO SP 1.25 3.00
Guy Charron CO SP 1.50 4.00
Theo Fleury 2.00 5.00
Doug Gilmour 2.00 5.00
Jiri Hrdina .20 .50
Mark Hunter .20 .50
Tim Hunter .40 1.00
Roger Johansson .20 .50
Al MacInnis .75 2.00
Brian MacLellan .20 .50
Jamie Macoun .30 .75
Sergei Makarov .60 1.50
Sergei Makarov .60 1.50
Al MacInnis
Stephane Matteau .30 .75
Dana Murzyn .20 .50
Frantisek Musil .20 .50
Ric Nattress .20 .50
Joe Nieuwendyk 1.25 3.00
Joel Otto .40 1.00
Colin Patterson .20 .50
Sergei Priakin .20 .50
Paul Ranheim .30 .75
Robert Reichel .60 1.50
Doug Risebrough CO/GM SP 1.25 3.00
Gary Roberts .75 2.00
Gary Suter .40 1.00
Tim Sweeney .20 .50
Mike Vernon .75 2.00
Rick Wamsley .40 1.00
Checklist Card SP 1.25 3.00

1991 Flames Panini Team Stickers

is 32-sticker set was issued in a plastic bag that ntained two 16-sticker sheets (approximately 9" by ") and a foldout poster, "Super Poster - Hockey 91", which the stickers could be affixed. The players' mes appeared only on the poster, not on the stickers. ch sticker measured about 2 1/8" by 2 7/8" and tured a color player action shot on its white bordered front. The back of the white sticker sheet was lined off into 16 panels, each carried the logos for Panini, the NHL, and the NHLPA, as well as the same number that appears on the front of the sticker. Every Canadian NHL team was featured in this promotion. Each team set was available by mail-order from Panini Canada Ltd. for 2.99 plus 50 cents for shipping and handling.

COMPLETE SET (32) 1.50 4.00
1 Theo Fleury .30 .75
2 Doug Gilmour .30 .75
3 Jiri Hrdina .01 .05
4 Mark Hunter .01 .05
5 Tim Hunter .02 .10
6 Roger Johansson .01 .05
7 Al MacInnis .15 .40
8 Brian MacLellan .01 .05
9 Jamie Macoun .01 .05
10 Sergei Makarov .08 .25
11 Stephane Matteau .01 .05
12 Dana Murzyn .01 .05
13 Ric Nattress .01 .05
14 Joe Nieuwendyk .15 .40
15 Joel Otto .05 .15
16 Colin Patterson .01 .05
17 Sergei Priakin .01 .05
18 Paul Ranheim .02 .10
19 Gary Roberts .15 .40
20 Ken Sabourin .01 .05
21 Gary Suter .02 .10
22 Tim Sweeney .01 .05
23 Mike Vernon .15 .40
24 Rick Wamsley .02 .10
A Team Logo .01 .05
Left Side
B Team Logo .01 .05
Right Side
C Flames' Time Out .01 .05
Upper Left Corner
D Flames' Time Out .01 .05
Lower Left Corner
E Flames' Time Out .01 .05
Upper Right Corner
F Flames' Time Out .01 .05
Lower Right Corner
G Joel Otto .02 .10
Roger Johansson
H Gary Suter .02 .10

1991-92 Flames IGA

This 30-card standard-size set of Calgary Flames was sponsored by IGA food stores and included manufacturers' discount coupons. One pack of cards was distributed in Calgary and Edmonton IGA stores with any grocery purchase of 10.00 or more. The cards were printed on thin card stock. The fronts had posed color action photos bordered in red. The player's name was printed vertically in the wider left border, and his uniform number and the team name appeared at the bottom of the picture. In black print on a white background, the backs presented biography and statistics (regular season and playoff). Packs were kept under the cash drawer, and therefore many of the cards were creased. Each pack contained three Oilers and two Flames cards. The checklist and coaches cards for both teams were not included in the packs but were available on a very limited basis through an uncut team sheet offer. Also the Osiecki card seemed to be in short supply, either because of short printing or short distribution. The cards were unnumbered and checklisted below in alphabetical order, with the coaches cards listed after the players.

COMPLETE SET (30) 10.00 25.00
1 Theo Fleury 1.00 2.50
2 Tomas Forslund .15 .40
3 Doug Gilmour 1.00 2.50
4 Marc Habscheid .15 .40
5 Tim Hunter .25 .60
6 Jim Kyte .15 .40
7 Al MacInnis .40 1.00
8 Jamie Macoun .15 .40
9 Sergei Makarov .40 1.00
10 Stephane Matteau .15 .40
11 Frantisek Musil .15 .40
12 Ric Nattress .15 .40
13 Joe Nieuwendyk .50 1.25
14 Mark Osiecki .75 2.00
15 Joel Otto .25 .60
16 Paul Ranheim .15 .40
17 Robert Reichel .30 .75
18 Gary Roberts .40 1.00
19 Neil Sheehy .15 .40
20 Martin Simard .15 .40
21 Ronnie Stern .15 .40
22 Gary Suter .30 .75
23 Tim Sweeney .15 .40
24 Mike Vernon .40 1.00
25 Rick Wamsley .30 .75
26 Carey Wilson .15 .40
27 Paul Baxter CO SP 1.00 2.50
28 Guy Charron CO SP 1.00 2.50
29 Doug Risebrough CO SP 1.00 2.50
30 Checklist Card SP 1.00 2.50

1992-93 Flames IGA

Sponsored by IGA food stores, the 30 standard-size cards comprising this Special Edition Collector Series set featured color player action shots on their fronts. Each photo was trimmed with a black line and offset flush with the thin white border on the right, which surrounds the card. On the remaining three sides, the picture was edged with a gray and white netlike pattern. The player's name appeard in the upper right and the Flames logo rested in the lower left. The back carried the player's name at the top, with his position, uniform number, biography, and stat table set within a reddish-gray screened background. The Flames logo in the upper right rounded out the card.

COMPLETE SET (30) 8.00 20.00
1 Checklist .02 .10
2 Craig Berube .20 .50
3 Gary Leeman .15 .40
4 Joel Otto .30 .75
5 Robert Reichel .40 1.00
6 Gary Roberts .40 1.00
7 Greg Smyth .15 .40
8 Gary Suter .30 .75
9 Jeff Reese .25 .60
10 Mike Vernon .40 1.00
11 Carey Wilson .15 .40
12 Trent Yawney .15 .40
13 Michel Petit .15 .40
14 Paul Ranheim .15 .40
15 Sergei Makarov .40 1.00
16 Frantisek Musil .15 .40
17 Joe Nieuwendyk .75 2.00
18 Alexander Godynyuk .15 .40
19 Roger Johansson .15 .40
20 Theo Fleury 1.00 2.50
21 Chris Lindberg .15 .40
22 Al MacInnis .60 1.50
23 Kevin Dahl .15 .40
24 Chris Dahlquist .15 .40
25 Ronnie Stern .20 .50
26 Dave King CO .15 .40
27 Guy Charron CO .02 .10
28 Slavomir Lener CO .02 .10
29 Jamie Hislop CO .02 .10
30 Franchise History .02 .10

1994-95 Fleer

This set was issued in a single 250-card series. Cards were issued in 12-card hobby and 18-card jumbo packs. There were four different card front designs, one unique to each of the NHL's divisions. Each card front had personal information in varying positions on the card. The card backs were all similar as they featured two photos, the player's name and expanded statistics. Rookie Cards included Mariusz Czerkawski, Blaine Lacher, David Oliver, Radek Bonk and Jim Carey.

1 Patrik Carnback .05 .15
2 Bob Corkum .05 .15
3 Paul Kariya .12 .30
4 Valeri Karpov RC .05 .15
5 Tom Kurvers .05 .15
6 John Lilley .05 .15
7 Mikhail Shtalenkov RC .05 .15
8 Oleg Tverdovsky .07 .20
9 Ray Bourque .15 .40
10 Mariusz Czerkawski RC .10 .25
11 John Gruden RC .05 .15
12 Al Iafrate .05 .15
13 Blaine Lacher RC .07 .20
14 Mats Naslund .05 .15
15 Cam Neely .10 .25
16 Adam Oates .10 .25
17 Bryan Smolinski .05 .15
18 Don Sweeney .05 .15
19 Donald Audette .05 .15
20 Dominik Hasek .20 .50
21 Dale Hawerchuk .12 .30
22 Yuri Khmylev .05 .15
23 Pat LaFontaine .10 .25
24 Brad May .05 .15
25 Alexander Mogilny .07 .20
26 Derek Plante .05 .15
27 Richard Smehlik .05 .15
28 Steve Chiasson .05 .15
29 Theo Fleury .10 .25
30 Phil Housley .07 .20
31 Trevor Kidd .07 .20
32 Joe Nieuwendyk .10 .25
33 James Patrick .05 .15
34 Robert Reichel .05 .15
35 Gary Roberts .05 .15
36 German Titov .05 .15
37 Tony Amonte .07 .20
38 Ed Belfour .10 .25
39 Chris Chelios .10 .25
40 Dirk Graham .05 .15
41 Sergei Krivokrasov .05 .15
42 Joe Murphy .05 .15
43 Bernie Nicholls .07 .20
44 Patrick Poulin .05 .15
45 Jeremy Roenick .20 .50
46 Steve Smith .05 .15
47 Gary Suter .05 .15
48 Russ Courtnall .05 .15
49 Dave Gagner .07 .20
50 Brent Gilchrist .05 .15
51 Todd Harvey .05 .15
52 Derian Hatcher .05 .15
53 Kevin Hatcher .05 .15
54 Mike Kennedy RC .10 .25
55 Mike Modano .15 .40
56 Andy Moog .10 .25
57 Dino Ciccarelli .07 .20
58 Paul Coffey .10 .25
59 Sergei Fedorov .15 .40
60 Vladimir Konstantinov .07 .20
61 Slava Kozlov .07 .20
62 Nicklas Lidstrom .10 .25
63 Chris Osgood .15 .40
64 Keith Primeau .10 .25
65 Ray Sheppard .07 .20
66 Mike Vernon .07 .20
67 Steve Yzerman .25 .60
68 Jason Arnott .07 .20
69 Shayne Corson .05 .15
70 Igor Kravchuk .05 .15
71 Todd Marchant .05 .15
72 Roman Oksiuta .05 .15
73 Fredrik Olausson .05 .15
74 David Oliver RC .05 .15
75 Bill Ranford .07 .20
76 Stu Barnes .05 .15
77 Jesse Belanger .05 .15
78 Keith Brown .05 .15
79 Bob Kudelski .05 .15
80 Scott Mellanby .07 .20
81 Gord Murphy .05 .15
82 Rob Niedermayer .07 .20
83 John Vanbiesbrouck .07 .20
84 Sean Burke .07 .20
85 Jimmy Carson .05 .15
86 Andrew Cassels .05 .15
87 Andrei Nikolishin .05 .15
88 Chris Pronger .10 .25
89 Geoff Sanderson .07 .20
90 Darren Turcotte .05 .15
91 Pat Verbeek .07 .20
92 Glen Wesley .05 .15
93 Rob Blake .10 .25
94 Wayne Gretzky .50 1.25
95 Kelly Hrudey .07 .20
96 Jari Kurri .07 .20
97 Eric Lacroix .10 .25
98 Marty McSorley .05 .15
99 Jamie Storr .07 .20
100 Rick Tocchet .07 .20
101 Brian Bellows .07 .20
102 Patrice Brisebois .05 .15
103 Vincent Damphousse .07 .20
104 Kirk Muller .05 .15
105 Lyle Odelein .07 .20
106 Mark Recchi .12 .30
107 Patrick Roy .25 .60
108 Brian Savage .05 .15
109 Mathieu Schneider .05 .15
110 Turner Stevenson .05 .15
111 Martin Brodeur .25 .60
112 Bill Guerin .07 .20
113 Claude Lemieux .10 .25
114 John MacLean .07 .20
115 Scott Niedermayer .10 .25
116 Stephane Richer .07 .20
117 Brian Rolston .05 .15
118 Alexander Semak .05 .15
119 Scott Stevens .10 .25
120 Ray Ferraro .05 .15
121 Patrick Flatley .05 .15
122 Darius Kasparaitis .05 .15
123 Derek King .05 .15
124 Scott Lachance .05 .15
125 Brett Lindros .05 .15
126 Vladimir Malakhov .05 .15
127 Jamie McLennan .07 .20
128 Zigmund Palffy .07 .20
129 Steve Thomas .05 .15
130 Pierre Turgeon .07 .20
131 Jeff Beukeboom .05 .15
132 Adam Graves .05 .15
133 Alexei Kovalev .05 .15
134 Steve Larmer .07 .20
135 Brian Leetch .10 .25
136 Mark Messier .10 .25
137 Petr Nedved .07 .20
138 Sergei Nemchinov .05 .15
139 Mike Richter .10 .25
140 Sergei Zubov .05 .15
141 Don Beaupre .07 .20
142 Radek Bonk RC .05 .15
143 Alexandre Daigle .05 .15
144 Pavol Demitra .12 .30
145 Pat Elynuik .05 .15
146 Rob Gaudreau .05 .15
147 Sean Hill .05 .15
148 Sylvain Turgeon .05 .15
149 Alexei Yashin .10 .25
150 Rod Brind'Amour .07 .20
151 Eric Desjardins .07 .20
152 Gilbert Dionne .05 .15
153 Garry Galley .05 .15
154 Ron Hextall .07 .20
155 Patrik Juhlin RC .05 .15
156 John LeClair .10 .25
157 Eric Lindros .10 .25
158 Mikael Renberg .07 .20
159 Chris Therien .05 .15
160 Dimitri Yushkevich .05 .15
161 Len Barrie .05 .15
162 Ron Francis .12 .30
163 Jaromir Jagr .25 .60
164 Shawn McEachern .05 .15
165 Joe Mullen .07 .20
166 Larry Murphy .07 .20
167 Luc Robitaille .10 .25
168 Ulf Samuelsson .05 .15
169 Tomas Sandstrom .05 .15
170 Kevin Stevens .05 .15
171 Martin Straka .05 .15
172 Ken Wregget .07 .20
173 Wendel Clark .07 .20
174 Adam Deadmarsh .05 .15
175 Stephane Fiset .07 .20
176 Peter Forsberg .25 .60
177 Valeri Kamensky .07 .20
178 Andrei Kovalenko .05 .15
179 Uwe Krupp .05 .15
180 Sylvain Lefebvre .05 .15
181 Owen Nolan .10 .25
182 Mike Ricci .05 .15
183 Joe Sakic .20 .50
184 Denis Chasse RC .10 .25
185 Adam Creighton .05 .15
186 Steve Duchesne .05 .15
187 Brett Hull .20 .50
188 Curtis Joseph .15 .40
189 Ian Laperriere RC .10 .25
190 Al MacInnis .07 .20
191 Brendan Shanahan .12 .30
192 Patrice Tardif RC .10 .25
193 Esa Tikkanen .05 .15
194 Ulf Dahlen .05 .15
195 Pat Falloon .05 .15
196 Jeff Friesen .05 .15
197 Arturs Irbe .07 .20
198 Sergei Makarov .05 .15
199 Andrei Nazarov .05 .15
200 Sandis Ozolinsh .05 .15
201 Michal Sykora .05 .15
202 Ray Whitney .05 .15
203 Brian Bradley .05 .15
204 Shawn Chambers .05 .15
205 Eric Charron .10 .25
206 Chris Gratton .05 .15
207 Roman Hamrlik .07 .20
208 Petr Klima .05 .15
209 Daren Puppa .07 .20
210 Alexander Selivanov RC .07 .20
211 Jason Wiemer RC .05 .15
212 Dave Andreychuk .10 .25
213 Dave Ellett .05 .15
214 Mike Gartner .10 .25
215 Doug Gilmour .12 .30
216 Kenny Jonsson .05 .15
217 Dmitri Mironov .05 .15
218 Felix Potvin .10 .25
219 Mike Ridley .05 .15
220 Mats Sundin .07 .20
221 Josef Beranek .05 .15
222 Jeff Brown .05 .15
223 Pavel Bure .10 .25
224 Geoff Courtnall .05 .15
225 Trevor Linden .07 .20
226 Jyrki Lumme .05 .15
227 Kirk McLean .07 .20
228 Gino Odjick .05 .15
229 Mike Peca .07 .20
230 Cliff Ronning .05 .15
231 Jason Allison .07 .20
232 Peter Bondra .07 .20
233 Jim Carey RC .10 .25
234 Sylvain Cote .05 .15
235 Dale Hunter .05 .15
236 Joe Juneau .07 .20
237 Dimitri Khristich .05 .15
238 Pat Peake .05 .15
239 Mark Tinordi .05 .15
240 Nelson Emerson .05 .15
241 Michal Grosek .05 .15
242 Nikolai Khabibulin .07 .20
243 Dave Manson .05 .15
244 Stephane Quintal .05 .15
245 Teemu Selanne .20 .50
246 Keith Tkachuk .10 .25
247 Alexei Zhamnov .07 .20
248 Checklist .02 .10
249 Checklist .02 .10
250 Checklist .02 .10

1994-95 Fleer Franchise Futures

The 10-card set was randomly inserted at a rate of 1:7 12-card hobby packs. The set featured young stars of the NHL in action photos positioned over the card title. The background was in the color of the team. The back had a photo and player information.

COMPLETE SET (10) 5.00 10.00
1 Jason Arnott .40 1.00
2 Rob Blake .60 1.50
3 Adam Graves .40 1.00
4 Arturs Irbe .60 1.50
5 Joe Juneau .60 1.50
6 Sandis Ozolinsh .40 1.00
7 Mikael Renberg .60 1.50
8 Keith Tkachuk 1.25 3.00
9 Alexei Yashin .40 1.00
10 Sergei Zubov .40 1.00

1994-95 Fleer Headliners

is 10-card set was randomly inserted in packs at the rate of 1:4. The set featured the superstars of the league in a borderless design. The word "Headliner", the player's name and team were printed in silver foil on the lower portion of the card front. A photo and informative text were on the back.

COMPLETE SET (10) 8.00 15.00
1 Pavel Bure .60 1.50
2 Sergei Fedorov .75 2.00
3 Doug Gilmour .30 .75
4 Wayne Gretzky 3.00 8.00
5 Brian Leetch .60 1.50
6 Eric Lindros .60 1.50
7 Mark Messier .60 1.50
8 Cam Neely .60 1.50
9 Mark Recchi .30 .75
10 Brendan Shanahan .60 1.50

1994-95 Fleer Netminders

e easiest of the Fleer insert sets, this 10-card set was found at the rate of 1:2 packs. The set featured the top goalies in the league in a silhouetted design. The word "Netminder" and the player's name were printed in gold foil on the front side portion of the card front. A portrait photo and player information were on the back.

COMPLETE SET (10) 3.00 8.00
1 Ed Belfour .30 .75
2 Martin Brodeur .75 2.00
3 Dominik Hasek .60 1.50
4 Arturs Irbe .15 .40
5 Curtis Joseph .30 .75
6 Kirk McLean .15 .40
7 Felix Potvin .30 .75
8 Mike Richter .30 .75
9 Patrick Roy 1.50 4.00
10 John Vanbiesbrouck .15 .40

1994-95 Fleer Rookie Sensations

is 10-card set was randomly inserted at a rate of 1:7 jumbo retail packs. The set featured the top first-year stars of the league over a water-splashed design. The phrase "Rookie Sensation" along with the player's name were printed in silver foil in the center portion of the card front. A photo and text information were on the back.

COMPLETE SET (10) 10.00 25.00
1 Radek Bonk .75 2.00
2 Peter Forsberg 4.00 10.00
3 Jeff Friesen .75 2.00
4 Todd Harvey .75 2.00
5 Paul Kariya 2.50 6.00
6 Blaine Lacher .75 2.00
7 Brett Lindros .75 2.00
8 Mike Peca .75 2.00
9 Jamie Storr .75 2.00
10 Oleg Tverdovsky .75 2.00

1994-95 Fleer Slapshot Artists

e most difficult of the Fleer inserts, the ten cards in this set were inserted at the rate of 1:12 packs. The cards featured a silhouetted player photo surrounded by three smaller cut-out versions of the same photo. The background was in the team's color. The back had the player's photo and career information.

COMPLETE SET (10) 10.00 20.00
1 Wendel Clark .75 2.00
2 Brett Hull 2.00 5.00
3 Al Iafrate .50 1.25
4 Jaromir Jagr 2.50 6.00
5 Al MacInnis .75 2.00
6 Mike Modano .75 2.00
7 Stephane Richer .75 2.00
8 Jeremy Roenick 2.00 5.00
9 Geoff Sanderson .75 2.00
10 Steve Thomas .50 1.25

1996-97 Fleer Promo Sheet

This sheet, which featured samples of John LeClair and Peter Ferraro regular cards, as well as a John LeClair Art Ross insert card, contained product and release date information for '96-97 Fleer. The cards were unnumbered, and would bear perforation marks if removed, distinguishing them from their regular counterparts. They are listed below as they appear on the sheet.

COMPLETE SET (3) .40 1.00
1 John LeClair .20 .50
2 John LeClair .20 .50
Art Ross insert
3 Peter Ferraro .08 .25

1996-97 Fleer

is 150-card set was released in one series in 10-card packs for both the hobby and retail markets with an SRP of $1.49. Although rarely delving past first-line players, the set boasted a strong player selection. All major stars were represented, among them Wayne Gretzky's first card in a New York Rangers sweater. The only Rookie Card of note was Martin Biron.

COMPLETE SET (150) 7.50 15.00
1 Guy Hebert .07 .20
2 Paul Kariya .12 .30
3 Teemu Selanne .20 .50
4 Ray Bourque .15 .40
5 Kyle McLaren .05 .15
6 Adam Oates .10 .25
7 Bill Ranford .07 .20
8 Rick Tocchet .07 .20
9 Jason Dawe .05 .15
10 Dominik Hasek .15 .40
11 Pat LaFontaine .10 .25
12 Theo Fleury .20 .50
13 Trevor Kidd .05 .15
14 German Titov .05 .15
15 Ed Belfour .10 .25
16 Chris Chelios .10 .25
17 Eric Daze .07 .20
18 Jeremy Roenick .15 .40
19 Gary Suter .05 .15
20 Peter Forsberg .15 .40
21 Valeri Kamensky .07 .20
22 Claude Lemieux .05 .15
23 Sandis Ozolinsh .05 .15
24 Patrick Roy .25 .60
25 Joe Sakic .15 .40
26 Derian Hatcher .05 .15
27 Mike Modano .15 .40
28 Sergei Zubov .05 .15
29 Paul Coffey .10 .25
30 Sergei Fedorov .15 .40
31 Vladimir Konstantinov .07 .20
32 Slava Kozlov .05 .15
33 Chris Osgood .10 .25
34 Keith Primeau .05 .15
35 Steve Yzerman .25 .60
36 Jason Arnott .07 .20
37 Curtis Joseph .10 .25
38 Doug Weight .10 .25
39 Ed Jovanovski .07 .20
40 Scott Mellanby .07 .20
41 Rob Niedermayer .07 .20
42 Ray Sheppard .07 .20
43 Robert Svehla .05 .15
44 John Vanbiesbrouck .10 .25
45 Sean Burke .05 .15
46 Andrew Cassels .05 .15
47 Geoff Sanderson .07 .20
48 Brendan Shanahan .12 .30
49 Ray Ferraro .05 .15
50 Dimitri Khristich .05 .15
51 Vitali Yachmenev .05 .15
52 Valeri Bure .05 .15
53 Vincent Damphousse .07 .20
54 Saku Koivu .10 .25
55 Mark Recchi .12 .30
56 Jocelyn Thibault .10 .25
57 Pierre Turgeon .10 .25
58 Martin Brodeur .20 .50
59 Phil Housley .07 .20
60 Scott Niedermayer .10 .25
61 Scott Stevens .10 .25
62 Steve Thomas .05 .15
63 Todd Bertuzzi .10 .25
64 Travis Green .07 .20
65 Kenny Jonsson .05 .15
66 Zigmund Palffy .10 .25
67 Adam Graves .05 .15
68 Wayne Gretzky .50 1.25
69 Alexei Kovalev .05 .15
70 Brian Leetch .10 .25
71 Mark Messier .15 .40
72 Niklas Sundstrom .05 .15
73 Daniel Alfredsson .10 .25
74 Radek Bonk .05 ..15
75 Steve Duchesne .05 .15
76 Damian Rhodes .07 .20
77 Alexei Yashin .07 .20
78 Rod Brind'Amour .10 .25
79 Eric Desjardins .07 .20
80 Ron Hextall .07 .20
81 John LeClair .10 .25
82 Eric Lindros .15 .40
83 Mikael Renberg .07 .20
84 Tom Barrasso .07 .20
85 Ron Francis .12 .30
86 Jaromir Jagr .25 .60
87 Mario Lemieux .30 .75
88 Petr Nedved .07 .20
89 Bryan Smolinski .05 .15
90 Nikolai Khabibulin .07 .20
91 Teppo Numminen .05 .15
92 Keith Tkachuk .10 .25
93 Oleg Tverdovsky .07 .20
94 Alexei Zhamnov .07 .20
95 Shayne Corson .05 .15
96 Grant Fuhr .10 .25
97 Brett Hull .50 1.25
98 Al MacInnis .10 .25
99 Chris Pronger .07 .20
100 Owen Nolan .10 .25
101 Marcus Ragnarsson .05 .15
102 Chris Terreri .07 .20
103 Brian Bradley .05 .15
104 Roman Hamrlik .07 .20
105 Daren Puppa .07 .20
106 Alexander Selivanov .05 .15
107 Doug Gilmour UER .12 .30
108 Larry Murphy .07 .20
109 Felix Potvin .10 .25
110 Mats Sundin .10 .25
111 Pavel Bure .12 .30
112 Trevor Linden .07 .20
113 Kirk McLean .07 .20
114 Alexander Mogilny .07 .20
115 Peter Bondra .07 .20
116 Jim Carey .10 .25
117 Sergei Gonchar .05 .15
118 Joe Juneau .05 .15
119 Michal Pivonka .05 .15
120 Brendan Witt .05 .15
121 Nolan Baumgartner .05 .15
122 Martin Biron RC .12 .30
123 Jason Bonsignore .05 .15
124 Andrew Brunette RC .12 .30
125 Jason Doig .05 .15
126 Peter Ferraro .05 .15
127 Eric Fichaud .07 .20
128 Ladislav Kohn RC .05 .15
129 Jamie Langenbrunner .05 .15
130 Daymond Langkow .07 .20
131 Jay McKee RC .05 .15
132 Wayne Primeau RC .05 .15
133 Jamie Storr RC .05 .15
134 Jose Theodore .12 .30
135 Roman Vopat .05 .15
136 Rookie Scor.Ldrs .05 .15
137 Points Ldrs. .10 .30
138 Goals Ldrs. .05 .15
139 Assists Ldrs. .10 .30
140 Def.Pts.Ldrs .10 .30
141 Pow.Play.Goal Ldrs .10 .30
142 Game.Winning.Goal Ldrs. .02 .10
143 Plus .02 .10
Minus Ldrs.
144 G.A.A. Ldrs. .05 .15
145 Games Won Ldrs. .05 .15
146 Shutouts Ldrs. .05 .15
147 Save Percentage Ldrs. .05 .15
148 Checklist (1-72) .02 .10
149 Checklist (73-150) .02 .10
150 Checklist (Inserts) .02 .10

1996-97 Fleer Art Ross

ndomly inserted in packs at a rate of 1:6, this 25-card set featured players in contention for the Art Ross trophy as the league's leading scorer.

COMPLETE SET (25) 20.00 50.00
1 Pavel Bure .60 1.50
2 Sergei Fedorov .75 2.00
3 Theo Fleury .30 .75
4 Peter Forsberg 1.50 4.00
5 Ron Francis .30 .75
6 Wayne Gretzky 5.00 10.00
7 Brett Hull .75 2.00
8 Jaromir Jagr 1.00 2.50
9 Valeri Kamensky .30 .75
10 Paul Kariya .60 1.50
11 Pat LaFontaine .60 1.50
12 John LeClair .60 1.50
13 Mario Lemieux 4.00 8.00
14 Eric Lindros .60 1.50
15 Mark Messier .60 1.50
16 Alexander Mogilny .30 .75
17 Petr Nedved .30 .75
18 Adam Oates .30 .75
19 Jeremy Roenick .75 2.00
20 Joe Sakic 1.25 3.00
21 Teemu Selanne .60 1.50
22 Keith Tkachuk .60 1.50
23 Pierre Turgeon .30 .75
24 Doug Weight .30 .75
25 Steve Yzerman 4.00 8.00

1996-97 Fleer Calder Candidates

ndomly inserted in packs at a rate of 1:96, this 10-card set featured up-and-comers poised to make a run at the Calder trophy, which is awarded to the NHL's rookie of the year.

COMPLETE SET (10) 8.00 20.00
1 Andrew Brunette .75 2.00
2 Jason Doig .75 2.00
3 Peter Ferraro .75 2.00
4 Eric Fichaud .75 2.00
5 Ladislav Kohn .75 2.00
6 Jamie Langenbrunner 1.25 3.00
7 Daymond Langkow 1.25 3.00
8 Jamie Storr .75 2.00
9 Jose Theodore 3.00 8.00
10 Roman Vopat .75 2.00

1996-97 Fleer Norris

ndomly inserted in retail packs only at a rate of 1:36, this 10-card set featured veteran rearguards in contention for recognition as the game's top blueliner.

COMPLETE SET (10) 15.00 40.00
1 Ray Bourque 6.00 15.00
2 Chris Chelios 4.00 10.00
3 Paul Coffey 4.00 10.00
4 Eric Desjardins 1.25 3.00
5 Phil Housley 1.25 3.00
6 Vladimir Konstantinov 2.50 6.00
7 Brian Leetch 4.00 10.00
8 Teppo Numminen 1.25 3.00
9 Larry Murphy 1.25 3.00
10 Sandis Ozolinsh 1.25 3.00

1996-97 Fleer Pearson

Randomly inserted in packs at a rate of 1:144, this 10-card set was the most difficult to come by of this year's Fleer offering, and also the most star-studded. Gracing this set were ten top stars worthy of consideration for the NHLPA MVP award.

COMPLETE SET (10) 50.00 125.00
1 Pavel Bure 3.00 8.00
2 Sergei Fedorov 3.00 8.00
3 Peter Forsberg 5.00 12.00
4 Wayne Gretzky 15.00 40.00
5 Jaromir Jagr 5.00 12.00
6 Paul Kariya 3.00 8.00
7 Mario Lemieux 10.00 25.00
8 Eric Lindros 3.00 8.00
9 Patrick Roy 10.00 25.00
10 Joe Sakic 6.00 15.00

1996-97 Fleer Rookie Sensations

Randomly inserted in hobby packs only at a rate of 1:20, this 10-card set featured some of the top rookie attractions of the '95-96 campaign.

COMPLETE SET (10) 6.00 15.00
1 Daniel Alfredsson .75 2.00
2 Todd Bertuzzi .75 2.00
3 Valeri Bure .40 1.00
4 Eric Daze .40 1.00
5 Sergei Gonchar .40 1.00
6 Ed Jovanovski .40 1.00
7 Saku Koivu .75 2.00
8 Marcus Ragnarsson .40 1.00
9 Petr Sykora .40 1.00
10 Vitali Yachmenev .40 1.00

1996-97 Fleer Vezina

ndomly inserted in packs at a rate of 1:60, this set featured ten netminders who are perennial favorites to win the Vezina award.

COMPLETE SET (10) 30.00 80.00
1 Ed Belfour 3.00 8.00
2 Sean Burke 2.50 6.00
3 Jim Carey 3.00 8.00
4 Dominik Hasek 6.00 15.00
5 Ron Hextall 3.00 8.00
6 Chris Osgood 3.00 8.00
7 Felix Potvin 4.00 10.00
8 Daren Puppa 3.00 8.00
9 Patrick Roy 12.00 30.00
10 John Vanbiesbrouck 3.00 8.00

1996-97 Fleer Picks

is 90-card set was a joint venture with Topps and was skip-numbered. All cards in this set had even numbers, while the Topps Picks set had the odds. The cards were issued in seven-card packs with a suggested retail price of $.99. The two card companies held a fantasy-style draft with each picking 56 forwards, 28 defensemen and six goaltenders to be included in their half of the set. The fronts featured color action player photos in a bordered design with the backs displaying projected stats for the 1996-97 season.

COMPLETE SET (92) 4.00 10.00
2 Joe Sakic .20 .50
4 Eric Lindros .08 .25
6 Paul Kariya .08 .25
8 Wayne Gretzky 1.50 4.00
10 Chris Osgood .02 .10
12 Brian Leetch .08 .25
14 Ray Bourque .15 .40
16 Ron Francis .02 .10
18 Keith Tkachuk .08 .25
20 Paul Coffey .08 .25
22 Phil Housley .02 .10
24 Theo Fleury .01 .05
26 Sergei Zubov .01 .05
28 Adam Oates .02 .10
30 John LeClair .08 .25
32 Pierre Turgeon .02 .10
34 Nicklas Lidstrom .08 .25
36 Vincent Damphousse .01 .05
38 Pat LaFontaine .08 .25
40 Brendan Shanahan .08 .25
42 Robert Svehla .01 .05
44 Peter Bondra .02 .10
46 Mikael Renberg .02 .10
48 Alexei Yashin .01 .05
50 Zigmund Palffy .02 .10
52 Larry Murphy .02 .10
54 Rod Brind'Amour .02 .10
56 Alexei Zhamnov .02 .10

1996-97 Fleer Picks

58 Jason Arnott .01 .05
60 Craig Janney .02 .10
62 Jason Woolley .01 .05
64 Jeff Brown .01 .05
66 Tomas Sandstrom .01 .05
68 Doug Gilmour .02 .10
70 Travis Green .02 .10
72 Teppo Numminen .01 .05
74 Petr Sykora .01 .05
76 Saku Koivu .08 .25
78 Daniel Alfredsson .02 .10
80 Ron Hextall .02 .10
82 Jocelyn Thibault .08 .25
84 Mike Richter .08 .25
86 Nikolai Khabibulin .02 .10
88 John Vanbiesbrouck .02 .10
90 Adam Graves .01 .05
92 Kenny Jonsson .01 .05
94 Jyrki Lumme .01 .05
96 Zdeno Ciger .01 .05
98 Ed Jovanovski .02 .10
100 Greg Johnson .01 .05
102 Pat Falloon .01 .05
104 Andrew Cassels .01 .05
106 German Titov .01 .05
108 Joe Juneau .01 .05
110 Igor Larionov .01 .05
112 Norm Maciver .01 .05
114 Chris Pronger .02 .10
116 Scott Niedermayer .01 .05
118 Vladimir Malakhov .01 .05
120 Dale Hawerchuk .02 .10
122 Jason Dawe .01 .05
124 Valeri Bure .01 .05
126 Marcus Ragnarsson .01 .05
128 Stephane Richer .02 .10
130 Wendel Clark .02 .10
132 Bryan Smolinski .01 .05
134 Dimitri Khristich .01 .05
136 Benoit Hogue .01 .05
138 Kirk Muller .01 .05
140 Peter Ferraro .01 .05
142 Vitali Yachmenev .01 .05
144 Jere Lehtinen .01 .05
146 Brandon Convery .01 .05
148 Darcy Tucker .01 .05
150 Curtis Brown .01 .05
152 Alexei Zhitnik .01 .05
154 John Slaney .01 .05
156 Bruce Driver .01 .05
158 Jeff O'Neill .01 .05
160 Patrice Brisebois .01 .05
162 Gord Murphy .01 .05
164 Doug Bodger .01 .05
166 Marty McSorley .01 .05
168 Nolan Baumgartner .01 .05
170 Mike Gartner .02 .10
172 Andrei Nikolishin .01 .05
174 Alexei Yegorov RC .01 .05
176 Dave Reid .01 .05
178 Marty Murray .01 .05
180 Anders Eriksson .01 .05
182 Checklist (2-180) .01 .05
184 Checklist (inserts) .01 .05

1996-97 Fleer Picks Captain's Choice

ndomly inserted in packs at a rate of 1:360, this set featured ten top team captains. The fronts carried borderless color action player photos while the backs displayed player information.

COMPLETE SET (10) 50.00 100.00
1 Eric Lindros 2.00 5.00
2 Steve Yzerman 10.00 25.00
3 Mario Lemieux 15.00 40.00
4 Wayne Gretzky 20.00 50.00
5 Mark Messier 3.00 8.00
6 Joe Sakic 6.00 15.00
7 Keith Tkachuk 2.00 5.00
8 Doug Gilmour 2.50 6.00
9 Trevor Linden 2.00 5.00
10 Brendan Shanahan 2.50 6.00

1996-97 Fleer Picks Dream Lines

Randomly inserted in packs at a rate of 1:70, this 10-card set featured three star players sharing some connection on each card.

COMPLETE SET (10) 40.00 80.00
1 Gretzky/Lemieux/Lindros 15.00 40.00
2 Roenick/Chelios/Richt. 3.00 8.00
3 Alfred./Forsberg/Brodeur 4.00 10.00
4 Fedorov/Mogilny/Bure 6.00 15.00
5 Selanne/Kariya/Tkachuk 5.00 12.00
6 Jagr/Hasek/Hamrlik 5.00 12.00
7 LeClair/Shan./Modano 4.00 10.00
8 Roy/Belfour/Beezer 10.00 25.00
9 Sakic/Kamensky/Ozol. 4.00 10.00
10 Hull/Verbeek/LaFont. 3.00 8.00

1996-97 Fleer Picks Fabulous 50

serted one in every pack, this 50-card set featured color action photos of the best players in the NHL. The nature of this set allowed Fleer to include players they were unable to select in the draft, thus giving a more complete feel to the entire product.

COMPLETE SET (50) 12.50 30.00
1 Daniel Alfredsson .20 .50
2 Peter Bondra .20 .50
3 Ray Bourque .50 1.25
4 Martin Brodeur .75 2.00
5 Pavel Bure .30 .75
6 Jim Carey .30 .75
7 Chris Chelios .30 .75
8 Paul Coffey .30 .75
9 Eric Daze .20 .50
10 Sergei Fedorov .40 1.00
11 Theo Fleury .07 .20
12 Peter Forsberg .75 2.00
13 Ron Francis .20 .50
14 Sergei Gonchar .07 .20
15 Wayne Gretzky 2.00 5.00
16 Roman Hamrlik .20 .50
17 Kevin Hatcher .07 .20
18 Ron Hextall .07 .20
19 Brett Hull .40 1.00
20 Jaromir Jagr .50 1.25
21 Ed Jovanovski .20 .50
22 Valeri Kamensky .07 .20
23 Paul Kariya .30 .75
24 John LeClair .30 .75
25 Brian Leetch .30 .75
26 Mario Lemieux 1.50 4.00
27 Trevor Linden .07 .20
28 Eric Lindros .30 .75
29 Mark Messier .30 .75
30 Mike Modano .50 1.25
31 Alexander Mogilny .20 .50
32 Petr Nedved .07 .20
33 Joe Nieuwendyk .07 .20
34 Owen Nolan .20 .50
35 Adam Oates .07 .20
36 Chris Osgood .20 .50
37 Sandis Ozolinsh .07 .20
38 Zigmund Palffy .20 .50
39 Jeremy Roenick .40 1.00
40 Patrick Roy 1.50 4.00
41 Joe Sakic .60 1.50
42 Teemu Selanne .30 .75
43 Brendan Shanahan .30 .75
44 Keith Tkachuk .30 .75
45 Pierre Turgeon .07 .20
46 John Vanbiesbrouck .20 .50
47 Doug Weight .07 .20
48 Alexei Yashin .07 .20
49 Steve Yzerman 1.50 4.00
50 Alexei Zhamnov .20 .50

1996-97 Fleer Picks Fantasy Force

ndomly inserted in packs at a rate of 1:50, this 10-card set featured color action photos of ten of the league's most valuable assets to fantasy league owners.

COMPLETE SET (10) 25.00 60.00
1 John LeClair 1.25 3.00
2 Chris Osgood 1.25 3.00
3 Ron Hextall 1.25 3.00
4 Eric Daze .75 2.00
5 Jaromir Jagr 4.00 10.00
6 Brett Hull 2.00 5.00
7 Ron Francis 1.25 3.00
8 Martin Brodeur 6.00 15.00
9 Sergei Fedorov 3.00 8.00
10 Petr Nedved .75 2.00

1996-97 Fleer Picks Jagged Edge

ndomly inserted in packs at a rate of 1:18, this 20-card set featured color action photos of players with a propensity for the dramatic.

COMPLETE SET (20) 10.00 25.00
1 Daniel Alfredsson 1.25 3.00
2 Theo Fleury 1.00 2.50
3 Alexander Mogilny 1.25 3.00
4 Doug Weight .75 2.00
5 Alexei Yashin .75 2.00
6 Paul Kariya 1.25 3.00
7 Saku Koivu 1.25 3.00
8 Sandis Ozolinsh .40 1.00
9 Petr Nedved .40 1.00
10 Jeremy Roenick 2.00 5.00
11 Mike Modano 2.00 5.00
12 Jim Carey .40 1.00
13 Ed Jovanovski .40 1.00
14 Alexei Zhamnov .40 1.00
15 Adam Oates .75 2.00
16 Ron Francis .75 2.00
17 Brian Leetch 1.25 3.00
18 Paul Coffey 1.25 3.00
19 Eric Daze .40 1.00
20 Zigmund Palffy .60 1.50

2006-07 Fleer

is 230-card set was released into the hobby in 10-card packs, with a $1.59 SRP, which came 36 packs to a box. Cards numbered 1-200 feature veterans in team alphabetical order while cards 201-230 feature NHL rookies.

COMPLETE SET w/o SPs (200) 6.00 15.00
COMPLETE SET (230) 40.00 80.00
1 Jean-Sebastien Giguere .25 .60
2 Andy McDonald .20 .50
3 Teemu Selanne .50 1.25
4 Scott Niedermayer .25 .60
5 Chris Pronger .20 .50
6 Ilya Bryzgalov .25 .60
7 Ryan Getzlaf .40 1.00
8 Corey Perry .25 .60
9 Jim Slater .15 .40
10 Ilya Kovalchuk .25 .60
11 Kari Lehtonen .20 .50
12 Marian Hossa .20 .50
13 Bobby Holik .15 .40
14 Slava Kozlov .15 .40
15 Patrice Bergeron .30 .75
16 Hannu Toivonen .20 .50
17 Brad Boyes .15 .40
18 Zdeno Chara .25 .60
19 Marco Sturm .15 .40
20 Glen Murray .20 .50
21 Marc Savard .15 .40
22 Maxim Afinogenov .15 .40
23 Chris Drury .20 .50
24 Ryan Miller .25 .60
25 Ales Kotalik .15 .40
26 Thomas Vanek .30 .75
27 Daniel Briere .25 .60
28 Jaroslav Spacek .15 .40
29 Jarome Iginla .25 .60
30 Miikka Kiprusoff .20 .50
31 Daymond Langkow .15 .40
32 Dion Phaneuf .25 .60
33 Chuck Kobasew .15 .40
34 Alex Tanguay .15 .40
35 Eric Staal .30 .75
36 Justin Williams .20 .50
37 Cam Ward .25 .60
38 Cory Stillman .15 .40
39 Rod Brind'Amour .25 .60
40 Mike Commodore .15 .40
41 Erik Cole .20 .50
42 Andrew Ladd .25 .60
43 Michal Handzus .20 .50
44 Tuomo Ruutu .25 .60
45 Nikolai Khabibulin .25 .60
46 Martin Havlat .15 .40
47 Rene Bourque .15 .40
48 Brent Seabrook .25 .60
49 Joe Sakic .40 1.00
50 Wojtek Wolski .20 .50
51 Milan Hejduk .20 .50
52 Marek Svatos .15 .40
53 Jose Theodore .25 .60
54 Pierre Turgeon .25 .60
55 Peter Budaj .20 .50
56 Sergei Fedorov .40 1.00
57 Fredrik Modin .15 .40
58 Rick Nash .25 .60
59 Pascal Leclaire .20 .50
60 Bryan Berard .15 .40
61 David Vyborny .15 .40
62 Mike Modano .40 1.00
63 Marty Turco .25 .60
64 Brenden Morrow .20 .50
65 Eric Lindros .40 1.00
66 Jussi Jokinen .20 .50
67 Jere Lehtinen .15 .40
68 Sergei Zubov .20 .50
69 Pavel Datsyuk .30 .75
70 Tomas Holmstrom .20 .50
71 Henrik Zetterberg .30 .75
72 Nicklas Lidstrom .25 .60
73 Dominik Hasek .30 .75
74 Robert Lang .15 .40
75 Kris Draper .15 .40
76 Ales Hemsky .20 .50
77 Joffrey Lupul .20 .50
78 Dwayne Roloson .20 .50
79 Ryan Smyth .20 .50
80 Jarret Stoll .20 .50
81 Shawn Horcoff .15 .40
82 Fernando Pisani .15 .40
83 Todd Bertuzzi .25 .60
84 Nathan Horton .25 .60
85 Jay Bouwmeester .25 .60
86 Olli Jokinen .25 .60
87 Joe Nieuwendyk .25 .60
88 Jozef Stumpel .15 .40
89 Alexander Frolov .15 .40
90 Mike Cammalleri .15 .40
91 Mathieu Garon .20 .50
92 Lubomir Visnovsky .15 .40
93 Craig Conroy .15 .40
94 Rob Blake .25 .60
95 Pavol Demitra .30 .75
96 Brian Rolston .20 .50
97 Manny Fernandez .20 .50
98 Marian Gaborik .30 .75
99 Pierre-Marc Bouchard .25 .60
100 Mikko Koivu .20 .50
101 Mark Parrish .15 .40
102 Cristobal Huet .20 .50
103 Saku Koivu .25 .60
104 Alex Kovalev .20 .50
105 Michael Ryder .15 .40
106 Mike Ribeiro .20 .50
107 Chris Higgins .15 .40
108 David Aebischer .20 .50
109 Paul Kariya .30 .75
110 Steve Sullivan .15 .40
111 Tomas Vokoun .20 .50
112 David Legwand .20 .50
113 Jason Arnott .20 .50
114 Scott Hartnell .25 .60
115 Martin Brodeur .50 1.25
116 Patrik Elias .25 .60
117 Brian Gionta .20 .50
118 Brian Rafalski .20 .50
119 Scott Gomez .20 .50
120 Zach Parise .30 .75
121 Alexei Yashin .20 .50
122 Jason Blake .15 .40
123 Rick DiPietro .20 .50
124 Miroslav Satan .20 .50
125 Trent Hunter .15 .40
126 Mike Sillinger .15 .40
127 Jaromir Jagr .60 1.50
128 Henrik Lundqvist .50 1.25
129 Martin Straka .15 .40
130 Brendan Shanahan .30 .75
131 Petr Prucha .20 .50
132 Matt Cullen .15 .40
133 Martin Gerber .20 .50
134 Antoine Vermette .20 .50
135 Daniel Alfredsson .25 .60
136 Jason Spezza .25 .60
137 Dany Heatley .25 .60
138 Wade Redden .15 .40
139 Patrick Eaves .15 .40
140 Ray Emery .20 .50
141 Simon Gagne .25 .60
142 Antero Niittymaki .20 .50
143 Peter Forsberg .30 .75
144 Keith Primeau .25 .60
145 Jeff Carter .25 .60
146 Joni Pitkanen .15 .40
147 R.J. Umberger .15 .40
148 Shane Doan .20 .50
149 Curtis Joseph .25 .60
150 Ladislav Nagy .15 .40
151 Mike Comrie .20 .50
152 Jeremy Roenick .25 .60
153 Ed Jovanovski .20 .50
154 Sidney Crosby 1.00 2.50
155 Ryan Malone .15 .40
156 Colby Armstrong .20 .50
157 Marc-Andre Fleury .40 1.00
158 Sergei Gonchar .15 .40
159 John LeClair .25 .60
160 Patrick Marleau .25 .60
161 Jonathan Cheechoo .25 .60
162 Vesa Toskala .20 .50
163 Joe Thornton .30 .75
164 Evgeni Nabokov .20 .50
165 Steve Bernier .15 .40
166 Keith Tkachuk .25 .60
167 Manny Legace .20 .50
168 Doug Weight .25 .60
169 Petr Cajanek .15 .40
170 Lee Stempniak .15 .40
171 Bill Guerin .25 .60
172 Vincent Lecavalier .20 .50
173 Martin St. Louis .25 .60
174 Marc Denis .20 .50
175 Brad Richards .25 .60
176 Vaclav Prospal .15 .40
177 Ryan Craig .15 .40
178 Ruslan Fedotenko .15 .40
179 Mats Sundin .25 .60
180 Michael Peca .20 .50
181 Kyle Wellwood .20 .50
182 Bryan McCabe .15 .40
183 Alexander Steen .25 .60
184 Andrew Raycroft .20 .50
185 Darcy Tucker .20 .50
186 Tomas Kaberle .15 .40
187 Roberto Luongo .40 1.00
188 Markus Naslund .20 .50
189 Daniel Sedin .25 .60
190 Henrik Sedin .25 .60
191 Mattias Ohlund .15 .40
192 Brendan Morrison .15 .40
193 Willie Mitchell .15 .40
194 Ryan Kesler .30 .75
195 Alexander Ovechkin 1.00 2.50
196 Olaf Kolzig .25 .60
197 Dainius Zubrus .15 .40
198 Brent Johnson .20 .50
199 Chris Clark .15 .40
200 Richard Zednik .15 .40
201 Shea Weber RC 2.00 5.00
202 Noah Welch RC .75 2.00
203 Eric Fehr RC 1.25 3.00
204 Mark Stuart RC .75 2.00
205 Matt Carle RC .75 2.00
206 Jarkko Immonen RC .75 2.00
207 Michel Ouellet RC 1.00 2.50
208 Konstantin Pushkarev RC 1.00 2.50
209 Marc-Antoine Pouliot RC .75 2.00
210 Ian White RC 1.00 2.50
211 Filip Novak RC .75 2.00
212 Tomas Kopecky RC 1.00 2.50
213 Billy Thompson RC .75 2.00
214 Dustin Byfuglien RC 2.00 5.00
215 Yan Stastny RC .75 2.00
216 Ben Ondrus RC .75 2.00
217 Brendan Bell RC .75 2.00
218 Steve Regier RC .75 2.00
219 Erik Reitz RC .75 2.00
220 Joel Perrault RC .75 2.00
221 Bill Thomas RC .75 2.00
222 Carsen Germyn RC .75 2.00
223 Rob Collins RC .75 2.00
224 Frank Doyle RC 1.00 2.50
225 Dan Jancevski RC .75 2.00
226 David Liffiton RC .75 2.00
227 Matt Koalska RC .75 2.00
228 Ryan Potulny RC .75 2.00
229 Ryan Caldwell RC .75 2.00
230 David Printz RC .75 2.00

2006-07 Fleer Oversized

COMPLETE SET (14) 12.00 30.00
15 Patrice Bergeron 1.50 4.00
30 Miikka Kiprusoff 1.00 2.50
35 Eric Staal 1.50 4.00
49 Joe Sakic 2.00 5.00
71 Henrik Zetterberg 1.50 4.00
103 Saku Koivu 1.25 3.00
115 Martin Brodeur 2.50 6.00
127 Jaromir Jagr 3.00 8.00
137 Dany Heatley 1.25 3.00
143 Peter Forsberg 1.50 4.00
154 Sidney Crosby 4.00 10.00
163 Joe Thornton 1.50 4.00
179 Mats Sundin 1.25 3.00
195 Alexander Ovechkin 3.00 8.00

2006-07 Fleer Tiffany

-200 VETS: 5X TO 12X BASIC CARDS
1-200 STATED ODDS 1:36
*201-300 ROOKIES: 1.5X TO 4X BASIC RC
201-300 ROOKIE ODDS 1:360

2006-07 Fleer Fabricology

ATED ODDS 1:40
FAA Ari Ahonen 2.50 6.00
FAF Alexander Frolov 2.50 6.00
FAH Adam Hall 2.50 6.00
FAK Alex Kovalev 2.50 6.00
FAM Andrej Meszaros 2.50 6.00
FAO Alexander Ovechkin SP 15.00 40.00
FAR Andrew Raycroft 3.00 8.00
FAU Alex Auld 3.00 8.00
FBG Bill Guerin 2.50 6.00
FBJ Barret Jackman 2.50 6.00
FBM Brendan Morrison 2.50 6.00
FBO Jay Bouwmeester 2.50 6.00
FBR Brian Rolston 2.50 6.00
FBS Brad Stuart 2.50 6.00
FBT Barry Tallackson 2.50 6.00
FCC Chris Chelios 3.00 8.00
FCD Chris Drury 3.00 8.00
FCO Chris Osgood 4.00 10.00
FCP Chris Pronger 3.00 8.00
FDB Donald Brashear 2.50 6.00
FDE Pavol Demitra 2.50 6.00
FDH Dan Hamhuis 2.50 6.00
FDL David Legwand 2.50 6.00
FDM Dominic Moore 2.50 6.00
FDS Daniel Sedin 2.50 6.00
FDW Doug Weight 2.50 6.00
FEB Ed Belfour SP 8.00 20.00
FED Eric Daze 2.50 6.00
FEL Eric Lindros 4.00 10.00
FEP Patrik Elias 2.50 6.00
FGA Mathieu Garon 3.00 8.00
FGR Gary Roberts 2.50 6.00
FHO Marian Hossa 3.00 8.00
FIK Ilya Kovalchuk 6.00 15.00
FJA Jason Arnott 2.50 6.00
FJB Jason Bacashihua 3.00 8.00
FJG Jean-Sebastien Giguere 3.00 8.00
FJJ Jaromir Jagr 6.00 15.00
FJL Jamie Lundmark 2.50 6.00
FJR Jeremy Roenick 4.00 10.00
FJS Jason Spezza 4.00 10.00
FJT Joe Thornton 6.00 15.00
FJW Justin Williams 2.50 6.00
FKL Kari Lehtonen 4.00 10.00
FKO Mike Komisarek 2.50 6.00
FKP Keith Primeau 2.50 6.00
FKT Keith Tkachuk 3.00 8.00
FLE Jere Lehtinen 3.00 8.00
FMA Martin Brodeur 8.00 20.00
FMB Martin Biron 3.00 8.00
FMC Bryan McCabe 2.50 6.00
FMG Marian Gaborik 5.00 12.00
FMH Marcel Hossa 2.50 6.00
FMK Miikka Kiprusoff 4.00 10.00
FMM Mike Modano 5.00 12.00
FMN Markus Naslund 3.00 8.00
FMO Mattias Ohlund 2.50 6.00
FMP Mark Parrish 2.50 6.00
FMS Martin Straka 2.50 6.00
FMT Marty Turco 3.00 8.00
FNA Nikolai Antropov 2.50 6.00
FNO Mika Noronen 3.00 8.00
FOJ Olli Jokinen 2.50 6.00
FOK Olaf Kolzig 4.00 10.00
FPA Patrik Stefan 2.50 6.00
FPB Peter Bondra 3.00 8.00
FPD Pavel Datsyuk 4.00 10.00
FPE Michael Peca 2.50 6.00
FPF Peter Forsberg 6.00 15.00
FPL Patrick Lalime 3.00 8.00
FPM Patrick Marleau 3.00 8.00
FPS Patrick Sharp 3.00 8.00
FPT Pierre Turgeon 2.50 6.00
FRB Rob Blake 2.50 6.00
FRE Robert Esche 3.00 8.00
FRF Ruslan Fedotenko 2.50 6.00
FRH Ryan Hollweg 2.50 6.00
FRK Rostislav Klesla 2.50 6.00
FRL Robert Lang 2.50 6.00
FRM Ryan Miller 4.00 10.00
FRN Rob Niedermayer 2.50 6.00
FRO Rod Brind'Amour 2.50 6.00
FRT Raffi Torres 3.00 8.00
FSA Philippe Sauve 3.00 8.00
FSC Sidney Crosby SP 25.00 60.00
FSF Sergei Fedorov 6.00 15.00
FSG Simon Gagne 3.00 8.00
FSK Sami Kapanen 2.50 6.00
FSN Scott Niedermayer 2.50 6.00
FSS Sergei Samsonov 3.00 8.00
FST Matt Stajan 2.50 6.00
FSW Stephen Weiss 2.50 6.00
FTC Tim Connolly 2.50 6.00
FTH Tomas Holmstrom 3.00 8.00
FTO Jordin Tootoo 4.00 10.00
FTP Tom Poti 2.50 6.00
FTR Tuomo Ruutu 3.00 8.00
FTS Teemu Selanne 4.00 10.00
FTY Ty Conklin 3.00 8.00
FZC Zdeno Chara 2.50 6.00

2006-07 Fleer Hockey Headliners

MPLETE SET (25) 10.00 25.00
STATED ODDS 1:4
HL1 Sidney Crosby 2.50 6.00
HL2 Alexander Ovechkin 1.00 2.50
HL3 Teemu Selanne .30 .75
HL4 Cam Ward .30 .75
HL5 Luc Robitaille .25 .60
HL6 Mario Lemieux 1.50 4.00
HL7 Joe Thornton .50 1.25
HL8 Ilya Kovalchuk .40 1.00
HL9 Daniel Alfredsson .25 .60
HL10 Henrik Lundqvist .40 1.00
HL11 Brian Leetch .30 .75
HL12 Pierre Turgeon .15 .40
HL13 Fernando Pisani .15 .40
HL14 Alexander Ovechkin 1.00 2.50
HL15 Sidney Crosby 2.50 6.00
HL16 Alexander Ovechkin 1.00 2.50
HL17 Dany Heatley .40 1.00
HL18 Martin Havlat .25 .60
HL19 Dion Phaneuf .40 1.00
HL20 Miikka Kiprusoff .30 .75
HL21 Jaromir Jagr .50 1.25
HL22 Jonathan Cheechoo .30 .75
HL23 Martin Brodeur 1.00 2.50
HL24 Ilya Bryzgalov .25 .60
HL25 Marek Svatos .15 .40

2006-07 Fleer Netminders

MPLETE SET (25) 8.00 20.00
STATED ODDS 1:4
N1 Ilya Bryzgalov .75 2.00
N2 Kari Lehtonen .60 1.50
N3 Ryan Miller .75 2.00
N4 Dominik Hasek 1.00 2.50
N5 Miikka Kiprusoff .60 1.50
N6 Cam Ward .75 2.00
N7 Nikolai Khabibulin .75 2.00
N8 Jose Theodore .75 2.00
N9 Marty Turco 1.00 2.50
N10 Dwayne Roloson .60 1.50
N11 Roberto Luongo 1.25 3.00
N12 Manny Fernandez .60 1.50
N13 Cristobal Huet .75 2.00
N14 Tomas Vokoun .75 2.00
N15 Martin Brodeur 1.25 3.00
N16 Rick DiPietro .60 1.50
N17 Henrik Lundqvist 1.50 4.00
N18 Martin Gerber .60 1.50
N19 Antero Niittymaki .60 1.50
N20 Curtis Joseph .75 2.00
N21 Marc-Andre Fleury 1.50 4.00
N22 Andrew Raycroft .60 1.50
N23 Vesa Toskala .60 1.50
N24 Olaf Kolzig .75 2.00
N25 Marc Denis .60 1.50

2006-07 Fleer Signing Day

STATED ODDS 1:432
SDAA Adrian Aucoin 6.00 15.00
SDAF Alexander Frolov 6.00 15.00
SDAH Ales Hemsky 10.00 25.00
SDAO Alexander Ovechkin SP 250.00 350.00
SDBA Matthew Barnaby 6.00 15.00
SDBB Brad Boyes 6.00 15.00
SDBI Martin Biron 8.00 20.00
SDBL Brian Leetch 20.00 50.00
SDBR Dustin Brown 6.00 15.00
SDBS Brent Seabrook 8.00 20.00
SDCD Chris Drury 6.00 15.00
SDCK Chuck Kobasew 6.00 15.00
SDCP Chris Phillips 6.00 15.00
SDCW Cam Ward 12.00 30.00
SDDA David Aebischer 8.00 20.00
SDDB Daniel Briere 15.00 40.00
SDDP Dion Phaneuf 15.00 40.00
SDDR Dwayne Roloson 8.00 20.00
SDEA Evgeni Artyukhin 6.00 15.00
SDGL Georges Laraque 12.00 30.00
SDHO Marcel Hossa 6.00 15.00
SDJC Jonathan Cheechoo 10.00 25.00
SDJF Johan Franzen 6.00 15.00
SDJH Jeff Halpern 8.00 20.00
SDJI Jarome Iginla SP 15.00 40.00
SDJT Jose Theodore 12.00 30.00
SDKC Kyle Calder 6.00 15.00
SDKD Kris Draper 6.00 15.00
SDKI Miikka Kiprusoff SP
SDMB Martin Brodeur SP 20.00 50.00
SDMG Marian Gaborik SP
SDMH Milan Hejduk 8.00 20.00
SDMJ Milan Jurcina 6.00 15.00
SDMK Mikko Koivu 10.00 25.00
SDMR Mike Ribeiro 6.00 15.00
SDMS Marc Savard 6.00 15.00
SDMT Mikael Tellqvist 10.00 25.00
SDPB Peter Budaj 10.00 25.00
SDPN Petteri Nokelainen 6.00 15.00
SDRB Rob Blake 8.00 20.00
SDRF Ruslan Fedotenko 6.00 15.00
SDRG Ryan Getzlaf 12.00 30.00
SDRI Raitis Ivanans 6.00 15.00
SDRO Rostislav Olesz 6.00 15.00
SDRS Ryan Suter 6.00 15.00
SDRY Michael Ryder 8.00 20.00
SDSC Sidney Crosby 125.00 250.00
SDSG Scott Gomez 6.00 15.00
SDSH Scott Hartnell 6.00 15.00
SDTA Jeff Tambellini 6.00 15.00
SDTC Ty Conklin 8.00 20.00
SDTH Joe Thornton SP
SDTV Thomas Vanek 12.00 30.00
SDVL Vincent Lecavalier SP

2006-07 Fleer Speed Machines

COMPLETE SET (25) 6.00 15.00
STATED ODDS 1:4
SM1 Scott Niedermayer .50 1.25
SM2 Teemu Selanne 1.00 2.50
SM3 Ilya Kovalchuk .50 1.25
SM4 Marian Hossa .40 1.00
SM5 Erik Cole .40 1.00
SM6 Chris Drury .40 1.00
SM7 Alex Tanguay .30 .75
SM8 Joe Sakic .75 2.00
SM9 Sergei Fedorov .75 2.00
SM10 Bill Guerin .50 1.25
SM11 Mike Modano .75 2.00
SM12 Pavel Datsyuk .60 1.50
SM13 Jay Bouwmeester .50 1.25
SM14 Marian Gaborik .60 1.50
SM15 Alex Kovalev .40 1.00
SM16 Paul Kariya .60 1.50
SM17 Miroslav Satan .40 1.00
SM18 Dany Heatley .50 1.25
SM19 Sami Kapanen .30 .75
SM20 Simon Gagne .50 1.25
SM21 Patrick Marleau .50 1.25
SM22 Martin St. Louis .50 1.25
SM23 Mats Sundin .50 1.25
SM24 Markus Naslund .40 1.00
SM25 Alexander Ovechkin 2.00 5.00

2006-07 Fleer Total O

MPLETE SET (25) 8.00 20.00
STATED ODDS 1:4
O1 Ilya Kovalchuk .50 1.25
O2 Patrice Bergeron .60 1.50
O3 Jarome Iginla .50 1.25
O4 Eric Staal .60 1.50
O5 Joe Sakic .75 2.00
O6 Rick Nash .50 1.25
O7 Mike Modano .75 2.00
O8 Pavel Datsyuk .60 1.50
O9 Henrik Zetterberg .60 1.50
O10 Ales Hemsky .40 1.00
O11 Olli Jokinen .50 1.25
O12 Saku Koivu .50 1.25
O13 Paul Kariya .60 1.50
O14 Patrik Elias .50 1.25
O15 Jaromir Jagr 1.25 3.00
O16 Dany Heatley .50 1.25
O17 Daniel Alfredsson .50 1.25
O18 Jason Spezza .50 1.25
O19 Peter Forsberg .60 1.50
O20 Sidney Crosby 2.00 5.00
O21 Joe Thornton .60 1.50
O22 Jonathan Cheechoo .50 1.25
O23 Mats Sundin .50 1.25
O24 Markus Naslund .40 1.00
O25 Alexander Ovechkin 2.00 5.00

2001-02 Fleer Legacy

leased in mid-March 2002, this 64-card set was carried an SRP of $4.99 for a 4 card pack. Cards 1-8 resembled the design of Ultra and were short printed to 2002 copies each. Cards 9-64 were a horizontal design featuring color photos on a white card front.

COMPLETE SET (64) 40.00 80.00
1 Mario Lemieux SP 5.00 12.00
2 Bobby Hull SP 2.50 6.00
3 Guy Lafleur SP 2.00 5.00
4 Phil Esposito SP 2.50 6.00
5 Cam Neely SP 2.00 5.00
6 Jean Beliveau SP 1.50 4.00
7 Bryan Trottier SP 1.50 4.00
8 Jari Kurri SP 2.00 5.00
9 Jean Beliveau .30 .75
10 Bob Nystrom .12 .30
11 Phil Esposito .50 1.25
12 Bobby Hull .50 1.25
13 Guy Lafleur .40 1.00
14 Gilbert Perreault .12 .30
15 Henri Richard .30 .75
16 Marcel Dionne .30 .75
17 Tony Esposito .40 1.00
18 Clark Gillies .12 .30
19 Grant Fuhr .25 .60
20 Brad Park .25 .60
21 Frank Mahovlich .30 .75
22 John Bucyk .12 .30
23 Billy Smith .25 .60
24 Ulf Samuelsson .12 .30
25 Mario Lemieux 1.25 3.00
26 Rod Gilbert .30 .75
27 Basil McRae .12 .30
28 Dave Semenko .12 .30
29 Neal Broten .12 .30
30 Terry Sawchuk .50 1.25
31 Dino Ciccarelli .12 .30
32 Mike Bossy .30 .75
33 Borje Salming .25 .60
34 Stan Mikita .40 1.00
35 Ted Lindsay .30 .75
36 Gerry Cheevers .40 1.00
37 Michel Goulet .12 .30
38 Red Kelly .30 .75
39 Bobby Clarke .30 .75
40 Todd Ewen .12 .30
41 Denis Potvin .25 .60
42 Paul Henderson .12 .30
43 Butch Goring .25 .60
44 Nick Fotiu .12 .30
45 Denis Savard .25 .60
46 Larry Robinson .25 .60
47 Joe Kocur .40 1.00
48 Bernie Parent .30 .75
49 Mike Liut .25 .60
50 Bernie Geoffrion .30 .75
51 Tony Twist .12 .30
52 Bryan Trottier .25 .60
53 Cam Neely .30 .75
54 Brent Sutter .12 .30
55 Dave Schultz .25 .60
56 Terry O'Reilly .12 .30
57 Jari Kurri .25 .60
58 Lanny McDonald .12 .30
59 Mike Gartner .12 .30
60 Alex Delvecchio .30 .75
61 Ron Hextall .40 1.00
62 Darryl Sittler .30 .75
63 Dale Hunter .12 .30
64 John Vanbiesbrouck .25 .60

2001-02 Fleer Legacy Ultimate

is set paralleled the entire base set and carried a serial-numbering to 202. Gold replaced the white on the card front backgrounds.

*ULT 9-64: 4X TO 10X BASIC CARDS
*ULT 1-8: 1.2X TO 3X BASIC SP

2001-02 Fleer Legacy Autographed Puck Redemptions

Inserted a stated odds of 1:48 hobby and 1:360 retail, this 22-card redemption set entitled the owner to an autographed puck of the featured player. Exchange cards have expired.

COMMON EXPIRED CARD .30 .75

2001-02 Fleer Legacy In the Corners

serted at stated rates of 1:24 hobby and 1:36 retail, this 12-card set features pieces of dasher boards from Joe Louis Arena. Card fronts carry a color photo of the featured player on the left, the player's name vertically on the right and a postage stamp-sized board piece in the center. Card backs carry a congratulatory message. Cards are unnumbered and are listed below in alphabetical order.

1 Dino Ciccarelli 5.00 12.00
2 Jari Kurri 6.00 15.00
3 Guy Lafleur 6.00 15.00
4 Mario Lemieux 10.00 25.00
5 Lanny McDonald 5.00 12.00
6 Cam Neely 5.00 12.00
7 Denis Potvin 5.00 12.00
8 Larry Robinson 5.00 12.00
9 Borje Salming 5.00 12.00
10 Darryl Sittler 5.00 12.00
11 Billy Smith 5.00 12.00
12 Tony Twist 5.00 12.00

2001-02 Fleer Legacy Memorabilia

serted at stated odds of 1:24 hobby and 1:36 retail, this 25-card set featured game-used swatches of jersey or sticks. Card fronts carry a color photo on the left side and the memorabilia piece on the left. Jersey cards had the words "Tailor Made" printed under the jersey swatch and the swatch was postage stamp-sized. Stick cards had the words "Hockey Kings" above the dime-sized stick piece. Card backs carried a congratulatory message and they were unnumbered.

1 Dino Ciccarelli JSY 6.00 15.00
2 Tony Esposito JSY 8.00 20.00
3 Michel Goulet JSY 6.00 15.00
4 Guy Lafleur JSY 8.00 20.00
5 Mario Lemieux JSY 10.00 25.00
6 Larry Robinson JSY 6.00 15.00
7 Borje Salming JSY 6.00 15.00
8 Denis Savard JSY 6.00 15.00
9 Jean Beliveau STK 8.00 20.00
10 Marcel Dionne STK 5.00 12.00
11 Tony Esposito STK 6.00 15.00
12 Phil Esposito STK 10.00 25.00
13 Mike Gartner STK 6.00 15.00
14 Bobby Hull STK 10.00 25.00
15 Guy Lafleur STK 6.00 15.00
16 Mario Lemieux STK 12.50 30.00
17 Stan Mikita STK 10.00 25.00
18 Cam Neely STK 10.00 25.00
19 Brad Park STK 6.00 15.00
20 Gilbert Perreault STK 6.00 15.00
21 Henri Richard STK 6.00 15.00
22 Terry Sawchuk STK 20.00 50.00
23 Darryl Sittler STK 8.00 20.00
24 Bryan Trottier STK 6.00 15.00
25 John Vanbiesbrouck STK 6.00 15.00

2001-02 Fleer Legacy Memorabilia Autographs

This 9-card set paralleled the stick cards in the memorabilia set but also carried the player's autograph under the stick piece. All cards in the checklist were only available as redemption cards out of packs. Cards were serial-numbered out of 100 each. Redemption cards expired March 2003.

1 Jean Beliveau 40.00 80.00
2 Phil Esposito 25.00 60.00
3 Bobby Hull 30.00 80.00
4 Guy Lafleur 20.00 50.00
5 Mario Lemieux 50.00 125.00
6 Stan Mikita 20.00 50.00
7 Darryl Sittler 20.00 50.00
8 Bryan Trottier 15.00 40.00

2002 Fleer Lemieux All-Star Fantasy

Available as a wrapper redemption from the Fleer booth at the NHL All-Star Game in LA, this special Mario Lemieux card was limited to 10,000 copies.

1 Mario Lemieux 2.00 5.00

2012-13 Fleer Retro

COMPLETE SET (100) 12.00 30.00
1 Dale Hawerchuk .50 1.25
2 Evander Kane .40 1.00
3 Alexander Burmistrov .30 .75
4 Alexander Ovechkin 1.50 4.00
5 Braden Holtby .60 1.50
6 Nicklas Backstrom .60 1.50
7 Pavel Bure .50 1.25
8 Alexandre Burrows .40 1.00
9 Markus Naslund .30 .75
10 Ryan Kesler .40 1.00
11 Trevor Linden .40 1.00
12 Doug Gilmour .50 1.25
13 Dion Phaneuf .40 1.00
14 Phil Kessel .50 1.25
15 Mats Sundin .40 1.00
16 Steven Stamkos .75 2.00
17 Curtis Joseph .40 1.00
18 Brett Hull .40 1.00
19 David Backes .40 1.00
20 Chris Stewart .30 .75
21 Alex Pietrangelo .30 .75
22 Joe Pavelski .40 1.00
23 Antti Niemi .30 .75
24 Logan Couture .40 1.00
25 Evgeni Malkin 1.25 3.00
26 Marc-Andre Fleury .60 1.50
27 Mario Lemieux 1.25 3.00
28 Sidney Crosby 1.50 4.00
29 Shane Doan .30 .75
30 Dave Schultz .40 1.00
31 Eric Lindros .60 1.50
32 Brayden Schenn .40 1.00
33 Bobby Clarke .40 1.00
34 Erik Karlsson .75 2.00
35 Jason Spezza .40 1.00
36 Rick Nash .40 1.00
37 Brad Richards .40 1.00
38 Theoren Fleury .50 1.25
39 Marian Gaborik .40 1.00
40 Mark Messier .50 1.25
41 Henrik Lundqvist .50 1.25
42 Clark Gillies .40 1.00
43 John Tavares .75 2.00
44 Bryan Trottier .50 1.25
45 Ilya Kovalchuk .40 1.00
46 Martin Brodeur .75 2.00
47 Pekka Rinne .50 1.25
48 Jean Beliveau .40 1.00
49 Lars Eller .30 .75
50 P.K. Subban .60 1.50
51 Carey Price 1.25 3.00
52 Dany Heatley .30 .75
53 Mike Modano .60 1.50
54 Anze Kopitar .60 1.50
55 Drew Doughty .40 1.00
56 Dustin Brown .40 1.00
57 Luc Robitaille .40 1.00
58 Jonathan Quick .60 1.50
59 Ron Francis .50 1.25
60 Stephen Weiss .30 .75
61 Grant Fuhr .40 1.00
62 Ryan Smyth .30 .75
63 Jordan Eberle .40 1.00
64 Jari Kurri .40 1.00

5 Paul Coffey .40 1.00
6 Ryan Nugent-Hopkins .40 1.00
7 Taylor Hall .75 2.00
8 Wayne Gretzky 2.00 5.00
9 Johan Franzen .40 1.00
0 Nicklas Lidstrom .40 1.00
1 Pavel Datsyuk .50 1.25
2 Derek Roy .30 .75
3 Jamie Benn .50 1.25
4 Jaromir Jagr 1.00 2.50
5 Joe Sakic .60 1.50
Matt Duchene .40 1.00
7 Gabriel Landeskog .40 1.00
8 Bobby Hull .40 1.00
9 Doug Wilson .30 .75
Ed Belfour .40 1.00
Jonathan Toews .75 2.00
2 Marian Hossa .30 .75
3 Patrick Kane .75 2.00
Jeff Skinner .40 1.00
Eric Staal .50 1.25
Jarome Iginla .40 1.00
7 Thomas Vanek .40 1.00
8 Dominik Hasek .50 1.25
9 Bobby Orr 1.25 3.00
Cam Neely .40 1.00
Brad Marchand .50 1.25
2 Tuukka Rask .40 1.00
3 Patrice Bergeron .50 1.25
Ray Bourque .60 1.50
Terry O'Reilly .30 .75
5 Adam Oates .40 1.00
7 Bobby Ryan .40 1.00
3 Ryan Getzlaf .60 1.50
9 Jonas Hiller .30 .75
00 Teemu Selanne .75 2.00

2012-13 Fleer Retro 1992-93 Ultra

TATED ODDS 1:8
21 Ryan Getzlaf 1.50 4.00
2 Patrice Bergeron 1.25 3.00
3 Tyler Seguin 1.50 4.00
4 Jeff Skinner 1.00 2.50
5 Jonathan Toews 2.00 5.00
6 Patrick Kane 2.00 5.00
7 Gabriel Landeskog 1.00 2.50
8 Pavel Datsyuk 1.25 3.00
9 Jordan Eberle 1.00 2.50
10 Ryan Nugent-Hopkins 1.00 2.50
11 Taylor Hall 2.00 5.00
12 Jonathan Quick 1.50 4.00
13 Carey Price 3.00 8.00
14 Adam Larsson 1.00 2.50
15 John Tavares 2.00 5.00
16 Pekka Rinne 1.25 3.00
17 Erik Karlsson 2.00 5.00
18 Zach Parise 1.00 2.50
19 Claude Giroux 1.00 2.50
20 Evgeni Malkin 3.00 8.00
21 Marc-Andre Fleury 1.50 4.00
22 Sidney Crosby 4.00 10.00
23 Steven Stamkos 2.00 5.00
24 Dion Phaneuf 1.00 2.50
25 Alexander Ovechkin 4.00 10.00

2012-13 Fleer Retro 1992-93 Ultra Autographs

VERALL STATED ODDS 1:360
ROUP B ODDS 1:1158
ROUP C ODDS 1:579
1 Ryan Getzlaf B 20.00 50.00
2 Patrice Bergeron B 15.00 40.00
3 Tyler Seguin A
4 Jeff Skinner B
5 Jonathan Toews B 25.00 50.00
6 Patrick Kane C 25.00 50.00
7 Gabriel Landeskog B
8 Pavel Datsyuk B 20.00 40.00
9 Jordan Eberle A
10 Ryan Nugent-Hopkins B 30.00 60.00
11 Taylor Hall C 20.00 50.00
12 Jonathan Quick A 20.00 50.00
13 Carey Price B 30.00 80.00
14 Adam Larsson C 10.00 25.00
15 John Tavares C 20.00 40.00
16 Pekka Rinne A
17 Erik Karlsson C 12.00 30.00
19 Claude Giroux A 12.00 30.00
20 Evgeni Malkin A
21 Marc-Andre Fleury B 20.00 50.00
22 Sidney Crosby A
23 Steven Stamkos C 20.00 40.00
24 Dion Phaneuf C 10.00 25.00
25 Alexander Ovechkin C 30.00 80.00

2012-13 Fleer Retro 1993-94 Ultra

TATED ODDS 1:6
1 Zdeno Chara 1.00 2.50
2 Patrice Bergeron 1.25 3.00
3 Marcus Foligno .75 2.00
4 Theoren Fleury 1.25 3.00
5 Jonathan Toews 2.00 5.00
6 Patrick Kane 2.00 5.00
7 Matt Duchene 1.00 2.50
8 Jamie Benn 1.25 3.00
9 Pavel Datsyuk 1.25 3.00
10 Jordan Eberle 1.00 2.50
11 Ryan Nugent-Hopkins 1.00 2.50
12 Taylor Hall 2.00 5.00
13 Carey Price 3.00 8.00
14 P.K. Subban 1.50 4.00
15 Martin Brodeur 2.00 5.00
16 Adam Henrique 1.00 2.50
17 John Tavares 2.00 5.00
18 Marian Gaborik 1.00 2.50
19 Chris Kreider 1.25 3.00
20 Erik Karlsson 2.00 5.00
21 Claude Giroux 1.00 2.50
22 Evgeni Malkin 3.00 8.00
23 Sidney Crosby 4.00 10.00
24 Joe Pavelski 1.00 2.50
25 Antti Niemi .75 2.00
26 Alex Pietrangelo .75 2.00
27 Steven Stamkos 2.00 5.00
28 Mats Sundin 1.00 2.50
29 Pavel Bure 1.25 3.00
30 Alexandre Burrows 1.00 2.50
31 Cory Schneider .75 2.00
32 Ryan Kesler 1.00 2.50
33 Alexander Ovechkin 4.00 10.00
34 Alexander Burmistrov .75 2.00
35 Evander Kane 1.00 2.50

2012-13 Fleer Retro 1993-94 Ultra Autographs

ERALL ODDS 1:240
OUP A ODDS 1:1714
OUP B ODDS 1:1245
OUP C ODDS 1:306
CH EXPIRATION: 3/26/2015

932 Patrice Bergeron C 15.00 30.00
933 Marcus Foligno C 8.00 20.00
934 Theoren Fleury B
935 Jonathan Toews A 30.00 60.00
936 Patrick Kane C 25.00 50.00
937 Matt Duchene B 10.00 25.00
938 Jamie Benn C 12.00 30.00
939 Pavel Datsyuk B 15.00 30.00
9310 Jordan Eberle A 25.00 60.00
9311 Ryan Nugent-Hopkins A 15.00 40.00
9312 Taylor Hall C 20.00 50.00
9313 Carey Price C 30.00 80.00
9314 P.K. Subban C 15.00 40.00
9315 Martin Brodeur A
9316 Adam Henrique C 10.00 25.00
9317 John Tavares C 20.00 50.00
9318 Marian Gaborik B EXCH 12.00 30.00
9319 Chris Kreider C 25.00 50.00
9320 Erik Karlsson C 20.00 50.00
9321 Claude Giroux B 15.00 40.00
9322 Evgeni Malkin B 20.00 40.00
9323 Sidney Crosby A 75.00 125.00
9324 Joe Pavelski C 10.00 25.00
9325 Antti Niemi A 12.00 30.00
9326 Alex Pietrangelo C 8.00 20.00
9327 Steven Stamkos C 20.00 40.00
9328 Mats Sundin A 30.00 80.00
9329 Pavel Bure B 30.00 60.00
9331 Cory Schneider C 12.00 30.00
9332 Ryan Kesler A 25.00 60.00
9333 Alexander Ovechkin C 25.00 60.00
9334 Alexander Burmistrov A
9335 Evander Kane C 8.00 20.00

2012-13 Fleer Retro 1994-95 Ultra

STATED ODDS 1:5
941 Corey Perry 1.00 2.50
942 Bobby Ryan 1.00 2.50
943 Zdeno Chara 1.00 2.50
944 Patrice Bergeron 1.25 3.00
945 Ryan Miller 1.00 2.50
946 Theoren Fleury 1.25 3.00
947 Sven Baertschi .75 2.00
948 Eric Staal 1.25 3.00
949 Jonathan Toews 2.00 5.00
9410 Patrick Kane 2.00 5.00
9411 Marian Hossa .75 2.00
9412 Johan Franzen 1.00 2.50
9413 Jordan Eberle 1.00 2.50
9414 Ryan Nugent-Hopkins 1.00 2.50
9415 Taylor Hall 2.00 5.00
9416 Jonathan Quick 1.50 4.00
9417 Anze Kopitar 1.50 4.00
9418 Zach Parise 1.00 2.50
9419 Josh Gorges .75 2.00
9420 Carey Price 3.00 8.00
9421 John Tavares 2.00 5.00
9422 Rick Nash 1.00 2.50
9423 Erik Karlsson 2.00 5.00
9424 Pekka Rinne 1.25 3.00
9425 Claude Giroux 1.00 2.50
9426 Shane Doan .75 2.00
9427 Evgeni Malkin 3.00 8.00
9428 Sidney Crosby 4.00 10.00
9429 Kris Letang 1.00 2.50
9430 Patrick Marleau 1.00 2.50
9431 Joe Pavelski 1.00 2.50
9432 Logan Couture 1.00 2.50
9433 Arturs Irbe .75 2.00
9434 Jaden Schwartz 1.25 3.00
9435 Steven Stamkos 2.00 5.00
9436 Martin St. Louis 1.00 2.50
9437 Jake Gardiner 1.00 2.50
9438 Dion Phaneuf 1.00 2.50
9439 Alexander Ovechkin 4.00 10.00
9440 Evander Kane 1.00 2.50

2012-13 Fleer Retro 1994-95 Ultra Autographs

OVERALL ODDS 1:180
GROUP B ODDS 1:500
GROUP C ODDS 1:337
GROUP D ODDS 1:364
941 Corey Perry B 10.00 25.00
942 Bobby Ryan B 10.00 25.00
944 Patrice Bergeron B 10.00 25.00
945 Ryan Miller B 8.00 20.00
946 Theoren Fleury C EXCH 15.00 30.00
947 Sven Baertschi D 6.00 15.00
948 Eric Staal B 12.00 30.00
949 Jonathan Toews B 25.00 50.00
9410 Patrick Kane D 20.00 40.00
9411 Marian Hossa B
9412 Johan Franzen C 10.00 25.00
9413 Jordan Eberle A
9414 Ryan Nugent-Hopkins B 15.00 40.00
9415 Taylor Hall B 20.00 50.00
9416 Jonathan Quick B 25.00 50.00
9417 Anze Kopitar C 15.00 40.00
9419 Josh Gorges B 8.00 20.00
9420 Carey Price C 25.00 50.00
9421 John Tavares D 15.00 30.00
9422 Rick Nash C 15.00 30.00
9423 Erik Karlsson D 15.00 40.00
9424 Pekka Rinne B 12.00 30.00
9425 Claude Giroux C 10.00 25.00
9426 Shane Doan B 8.00 20.00
9427 Evgeni Malkin C 15.00 40.00
9428 Sidney Crosby B 75.00 125.00
9429 Kris Letang C EXCH 10.00 25.00
9430 Patrick Marleau B 15.00 40.00
9431 Joe Pavelski D 8.00 20.00
9432 Logan Couture C 10.00 25.00
9433 Arturs Irbe B 25.00 50.00
9434 Jaden Schwartz C 6.00 15.00
9435 Steven Stamkos C 20.00 40.00
9436 Martin St. Louis D 8.00 20.00
9437 Jake Gardiner B 10.00 25.00
9438 Dion Phaneuf D 8.00 20.00
9439 Alexander Ovechkin C 25.00 60.00
9440 Evander Kane C 6.00 15.00

2012-13 Fleer Retro Autographics 1996-97

OVERALL ODDS 1:8
GROUP A ODDS 1:1224
GROUP B ODDS 1:536
GROUP C ODDS 1:129
GROUP D ODDS 1:17
GROUP E ODDS 1:10
96AL Adam Larsson B 6.00 15.00
96AO Alexander Ovechkin A 20.00 50.00
96BB Brett Bulmer E 2.50 6.00
96BF Benn Ferriero E 2.50 6.00
96BG Blake Geoffrion C 4.00 10.00
96BL Jonathon Blum E 3.00 8.00
96BM Brendan Mikkelson E 2.50 6.00
96BR Bobby Ryan D 4.00 10.00
96BS Brendan Smith D 5.00 12.00
96CA Cam Atkinson D 4.00 10.00
96CD Calvin de Haan E 3.00 8.00
96CK Chris Kunitz D 5.00 12.00
96CO Cal O'Reilly E 2.50 6.00
96DB Drayson Bowman E 2.50 6.00
96DH Dany Heatley C 3.00 8.00
96DP Daniel Paille D 6.00 15.00
96DS David Savard D 2.50 6.00
96JA Jason Arnott D 4.00 10.00
96JB Josh Bailey E 3.00 8.00
96JF Justin Falk D 2.50 6.00
96JG Jake Gardiner D 4.00 10.00
96JS James Sheppard E 2.50 6.00
96KA Keith Aulie E 2.50 6.00
96KL Carl Klingberg E 2.50 6.00
96KS Kevin Shattenkirk D 4.00 10.00
96LK Lauri Korpikoski D 2.50 6.00
96MH Matthew Halischuk E 2.50 6.00
96ML Maxim Lapierre D 3.00 8.00
96MM Matt Martin D 2.50 6.00
96MP Michael Peca E 3.00 8.00
96MS Michael Sauer E 2.50 6.00
96NG Nicklas Grossman E 2.50 6.00
96PH Dion Phaneuf B 10.00 25.00
96PL Pascal Leclaire D 3.00 8.00
96PM Peter Mueller C 3.00 8.00
96PO Patrick O'Sullivan E 2.50 6.00
96RE Ryan Ellis E 2.50 6.00
96RJ Ryan Jones D 3.00 8.00
96RO Ryan O'Marra D 2.50 6.00
96RW Roman Wick E 3.00 8.00
96SC Brayden Schenn C 4.00 10.00
96SD Simon Despres D 3.00 8.00
96SM Shawn Matthias D 2.50 6.00
96SS Steven Stamkos A 15.00 40.00
96TL Trevor Lewis E 4.00 10.00
96TW Tommy Wingels E 2.50 6.00
96VF Valtteri Filppula E 4.00 10.00
96VH Victor Hedman E 5.00 12.00
96WC Wendel Clark D 6.00 15.00

2012-13 Fleer Retro Autographics 1999

OVERALL ODDS 1:16
GROUP A ODDS 1:2142
GROUP B ODDS 1:1071
GROUP C ODDS 1:214
GROUP D ODDS 1:20
99AM Andrei Markov D 4.00 10.00
99AO Alexander Ovechkin C 25.00 60.00
99BH Ben Holmstrom D 3.00 8.00
99BS Ben Scrivens D 4.00 10.00
99CK Chris Kreider B 15.00 40.00
99CS Craig Smith D 2.50 6.00
99DB Dustin Byfuglien D 4.00 10.00
99EG Erik Gustafsson D 2.50 6.00
99EL Eric Lindros A 40.00 80.00
99GN Greg Nemisz D 2.50 6.00
99JB Josh Bailey C 4.00 10.00
99JC John Carlson D 5.00 12.00
99JS Jaden Schwartz C 8.00 20.00
99JV Joe Vitale D 4.00 10.00
99MF Michael Frolik D 4.00 10.00
99ML Mario Lemieux A 60.00 120.00
99MR Mike Ribeiro D 4.00 10.00
99MS Matt Stajan D 3.00 8.00
99NK Nikolai Kulemin D 3.00 8.00
99PB Pavel Bure A
99PE Patrik Elias D 4.00 10.00
99PW Patrick Wiercioch D 2.50 6.00
99RH Roman Horak D 3.00 8.00
99RJ Ryan Johansen D 5.00 12.00
99SA Jerome Samson D 2.50 6.00
99SB Sven Baertschi C 5.00 12.00
99SM Steve Mason D 3.00 8.00
99SS Steven Stamkos B 12.00 30.00
99TH Teemu Hartikainen D 3.00 8.00
99VS Viktor Stalberg D 2.50 6.00
99WG Wayne Gretzky A 200.00 350.00

2012-13 Fleer Retro Autographs

OVERALL STATED ODDS 1:40
GROUP B ODDS 1:1190
GROUP C ODDS 1:424
GROUP D ODDS 1:136
GROUP E ODDS 1:62
1 Dale Hawerchuk D 10.00 25.00
2 Evander Kane D 8.00 20.00
3 Alexander Burmistrov E 5.00 12.00
4 Alexander Ovechkin B 15.00 40.00
5 Braden Holtby D 12.00 30.00
6 Nicklas Backstrom E 8.00 20.00
7 Pavel Bure B 30.00 60.00
8 Alexandre Burrows D 8.00 20.00
9 Markus Naslund E 5.00 12.00
10 Ryan Kesler D 8.00 20.00
11 Trevor Linden D 15.00 30.00
12 Doug Gilmour C 25.00 60.00
13 Dion Phaneuf E 6.00 15.00
14 Phil Kessel D 10.00 25.00
15 Mats Sundin C 15.00 30.00
16 Steven Stamkos E 15.00 40.00
17 Curtis Joseph B
18 Brett Hull C 30.00 60.00
19 David Backes D 8.00 20.00
20 Chris Stewart E 5.00 12.00
21 Alex Pietrangelo D 6.00 15.00
22 Joe Pavelski E 6.00 15.00
23 Antti Niemi D 6.00 15.00
24 Logan Couture D 10.00 25.00
25 Evgeni Malkin E 20.00 50.00
26 Marc-Andre Fleury D 10.00 25.00
27 Mario Lemieux B 50.00 100.00
28 Sidney Crosby B 50.00 100.00
29 Shane Doan E 5.00 12.00
30 Dave Schultz D 6.00 15.00
31 Eric Lindros C 40.00 80.00
32 Brayden Schenn E 6.00 15.00
33 Bobby Clarke D 12.00 30.00
34 Erik Karlsson E 8.00 20.00
36 Rick Nash E 12.00 30.00
37 Brad Richards D 8.00 20.00
38 Theoren Fleury E 8.00 20.00
39 Marian Gaborik C 10.00 25.00
40 Mark Messier B 40.00 80.00
41 Henrik Lundqvist C 15.00 40.00
42 Clark Gillies C 8.00 20.00
43 John Tavares E 15.00 30.00
44 Bryan Trottier E 8.00 20.00
45 Ilya Kovalchuk C 10.00 25.00
46 Martin Brodeur A
47 Pekka Rinne C 8.00 20.00
48 Jean Deliveau C 30.00 60.00
49 Lars Eller E 5.00 12.00
50 P.K. Subban D 12.00 30.00
51 Carey Price D 15.00 40.00
52 Dany Heatley E 5.00 12.00
53 Mike Modano C 25.00 50.00
54 Anze Kopitar D 12.00 30.00
55 Drew Doughty C 20.00 40.00
56 Dustin Brown C 15.00 30.00
57 Luc Robitaille E 8.00 20.00
58 Jonathan Quick E 15.00 30.00
59 Ron Francis B 15.00 40.00
60 Stephen Weiss E 5.00 12.00
61 Grant Fuhr D 10.00 25.00
62 Ryan Smyth E 5.00 12.00
63 Jordan Eberle A
64 Jari Kurri D 8.00 20.00
65 Paul Coffey A 20.00 40.00
66 Ryan Nugent-Hopkins B
67 Taylor Hall E 10.00 25.00
68 Wayne Gretzky B 175.00 300.00
69 Johan Franzen D 8.00 20.00
70 Nicklas Lidstrom E 15.00 40.00
71 Pavel Datsyuk C 15.00 40.00
72 Derek Roy E 5.00 12.00
73 Jamie Benn E 8.00 20.00
74 Jaromir Jagr B 30.00 60.00
75 Joe Sakic B 20.00 40.00
76 Matt Duchene E 8.00 20.00
77 Gabriel Landeskog D 8.00 20.00
78 Bobby Hull E 15.00 30.00
79 Doug Wilson E 8.00 20.00
80 Ed Belfour D 15.00 30.00
81 Jonathan Toews C 20.00 40.00
82 Marian Hossa C 8.00 20.00
83 Patrick Kane E 15.00 40.00
84 Jeff Skinner D 8.00 20.00
85 Eric Staal C
86 Jarome Iginla C 10.00 25.00
87 Thomas Vanek E 6.00 15.00
88 Dominik Hasek C 20.00 40.00
89 Bobby Orr B 100.00 175.00
90 Cam Neely E 8.00 20.00
91 Brad Marchand D 10.00 25.00
92 Tuukka Rask E 8.00 20.00
93 Patrice Bergeron E 12.50 25.00
94 Ray Bourque D 12.00 30.00
96 Adam Oates E 8.00 20.00
97 Bobby Ryan E 6.00 15.00
98 Ryan Getzlaf D 12.00 30.00
99 Jonas Hiller E 5.00 12.00

2012-13 Fleer Retro Diamond Tribute

STATED ODDS 1:40
1 Bobby Orr 8.00 20.00
2 Sven Baertschi 2.00 5.00
3 Jonathan Toews 5.00 12.00
4 Joe Sakic 4.00 10.00
5 Ryan Nugent-Hopkins 2.50 6.00
6 Mark Messier 3.00 8.00
7 Jordan Eberle 2.50 6.00
8 Taylor Hall 5.00 12.00
9 Wayne Gretzky 12.00 30.00
10 Patrick Roy 6.00 15.00
11 Ilya Kovalchuk 2.50 6.00
12 Chris Kreider 4.00 10.00
13 Eric Lindros 4.00 10.00
14 Sidney Crosby 10.00 25.00
15 Mario Lemieux 8.00 20.00
16 Jaden Schwartz 3.00 8.00
17 Steven Stamkos 5.00 12.00
18 Mats Sundin 2.50 6.00
19 Pavel Bure 3.00 8.00
20 Alexander Ovechkin 5.00 12.00

2012-13 Fleer Retro E-X 2001

STATED ODDS 1:12
1 Sidney Crosby 12.00 30.00
2 Alexander Ovechkin 4.00 10.00
3 Ryan Nugent-Hopkins 2.00 5.00
4 Bobby Orr 6.00 15.00
5 Teemu Selanne 4.00 10.00
6 Mario Lemieux 6.00 15.00
7 Pavel Bure 2.50 6.00
8 Eric Lindros 3.00 8.00
9 Wayne Gretzky 10.00 25.00
10 Tyler Seguin 3.00 8.00
11 Mark Messier 2.50 6.00
12 Henrik Lundqvist 2.50 6.00
13 Mats Sundin 2.00 5.00
14 Jordan Eberle 2.00 5.00
15 Jason Spezza 2.00 5.00
16 Brett Hull 4.00 10.00
17 Gabriel Landeskog 2.00 5.00
18 Evgeni Malkin 6.00 15.00
19 Jonathan Toews 4.00 10.00
20 Jonathan Quick 3.00 8.00
21 John Tavares 4.00 10.00
22 Erik Karlsson 4.00 10.00
23 Ondrej Pavelec 2.00 5.00
24 Trevor Linden 2.00 5.00
25 Jeff Skinner 2.00 5.00
26 Pekka Rinne 2.50 6.00
27 Cory Schneider 1.50 4.00
28 Dominik Hasek 3.00 8.00
29 Mikko Koivu 1.50 4.00
30 Martin Brodeur 4.00 10.00
31 Carey Price 6.00 15.00
32 Pavel Datsyuk 2.50 6.00
33 Patrick Roy 6.00 15.00
34 Taylor Hall 4.00 10.00
35 Jaromir Jagr 5.00 12.00
36 Steven Stamkos 4.00 10.00
37 Patrice Bergeron 2.50 6.00
38 Joe Sakic 3.00 8.00
39 Jussi Rynnas 1.25 3.00
40 Jaden Schwartz 2.50 6.00
41 Sven Baertschi 1.50 4.00
42 Chris Kreider 5.00 12.00

2012-13 Fleer Retro E-X 2001 Essential Credentials Future

*FUTURE/30-42: 2X TO 5X BASIC INSERTS
*FUTURE/20-29: 3X TO 8X BASIC INSERTS
*FUTURE/15-19: 4X TO 10X BASIC INSERTS
1 Sidney Crosby/42 40.00 100.00
9 Wayne Gretzky/34 75.00 150.00

2012-13 Fleer Retro E-X 2001 Essential Credentials Now

*NOW/30-42: 2.5X TO 5X BASIC INSERTS
*NOW/20-29: 3X TO 8X BASIC INSERTS
*NOW/15-19: 4X TO 10X BASIC INSERTS
33 Patrick Roy/33 40.00 100.00

2012-13 Fleer Retro E-X 2001 Jambalaya

STATED ODDS 1:360
1JB Teemu Selanne 50.00 100.00
2JB Bobby Orr 60.00 120.00
3JB Jonathan Toews 40.00 100.00
4JB Joe Sakic 40.00 100.00
5JB Patrick Roy 50.00 120.00
6JB Evgeni Malkin 30.00 80.00
7JB Taylor Hall 60.00 120.00
8JB Jordan Eberle 30.00 80.00
9JB Ryan Nugent-Hopkins 20.00 50.00
10JB Wayne Gretzky 150.00 300.00
11JB Carey Price 60.00 120.00
12JB Martin Brodeur 60.00 120.00
13JB Jonathan Quick 25.00 60.00
14JB Eric Lindros 40.00 100.00
15JB Mario Lemieux 60.00 120.00
16JB Sidney Crosby 75.00 150.00
17JB Brett Hull 40.00 100.00
18JB Pelle Lindbergh 50.00 100.00
19JB Mats Sundin 40.00 100.00
20JB Pavel Bure 30.00 80.00
21JB Alexander Ovechkin 40.00 100.00

2012-13 Fleer Retro Tradition Electrifying

STATED ODDS 1:70
1 Bobby Orr 10.00 25.00
2 Sven Baertschi 2.00 5.00
3 Ryan Nugent-Hopkins 3.00 8.00
4 Wayne Gretzky 15.00 40.00
5 Anze Kopitar 5.00 12.00
6 Patrick Roy 6.00 15.00
7 Martin Brodeur 6.00 15.00
8 Chris Kreider 3.00 8.00
9 Eric Lindros 5.00 12.00
10 Sidney Crosby 10.00 25.00
11 Mario Lemieux 10.00 25.00
12 Evgeni Malkin 10.00 25.00
13 Jaromir Jagr 8.00 20.00
14 Mats Sundin 3.00 8.00
15 Joe Sakic 5.00 12.00
16 Brett Hull 3.00 8.00
17 Jaden Schwartz 3.00 8.00
18 Steven Stamkos 6.00 15.00
19 Pavel Bure 4.00 10.00
20 Alexander Ovechkin 6.00 15.00

2012-13 Fleer Retro Flair Showcase Hot Shots

STATED ODDS 1:60
1 Ray Bourque 5.00 12.00
2 Bobby Orr 10.00 25.00
3 Zdeno Chara 3.00 8.00
4 Theoren Fleury 4.00 10.00
5 Bobby Hull 3.00 8.00
6 Nicklas Lidstrom 3.00 8.00
7 Paul Coffey 3.00 8.00
8 Wayne Gretzky 15.00 40.00
9 Mark Messier 4.00 10.00
10 Shea Weber 2.50 6.00
11 Ilya Kovalchuk 3.00 8.00
12 John Tavares 6.00 15.00
13 Teemu Selanne 6.00 15.00
14 Evgeni Malkin 10.00 25.00
15 Mario Lemieux 10.00 25.00
16 Sidney Crosby 10.00 25.00
17 Kris Letang 3.00 8.00
18 Brett Hull 3.00 8.00
19 Al MacInnis 3.00 8.00
20 Steven Stamkos 6.00 15.00
21 Phil Kessel 4.00 10.00
22 Dion Phaneuf 3.00 8.00
23 Trevor Linden 3.00 8.00
24 Pavel Bure 4.00 10.00
25 Alexander Ovechkin 6.00 15.00

2012-13 Fleer Retro Flair Showcase Row 2

STATED ODDS 1:6
*LEGACY/150: 1.2X TO 3X BASIC INSERTS
1 Steven Stamkos 2.50 6.00
2 Mats Sundin 1.25 3.00
3 Pavel Bure 1.50 4.00
4 Alexander Ovechkin 5.00 12.00
5 Brett Hull 1.25 3.00
6 Joe Sakic 2.00 5.00
7 Jaromir Jagr 3.00 8.00
8 Taylor Hall 2.50 6.00
9 Jordan Eberle 1.25 3.00
10 Ryan Nugent-Hopkins 1.25 3.00
11 Mario Lemieux 4.00 10.00
12 Carey Price 4.00 10.00
13 Martin Brodeur 2.50 6.00
14 Sidney Crosby 5.00 12.00
15 Henrik Lundqvist 1.50 4.00
16 Mark Messier 1.50 4.00
17 Eric Lindros 2.00 5.00
18 Bobby Orr 4.00 10.00
19 Wayne Gretzky 4.00 10.00
20 Patrick Roy 3.00 8.00
21 Erik Karlsson 2.50 6.00
22 Jake Allen 2.50 6.00
23 Claude Giroux 1.25 3.00
24 Marc-Andre Fleury 2.00 5.00
25 Jeff Skinner 1.25 3.00
26 Ondrej Pavelec 1.25 3.00
27 Trevor Linden 1.25 3.00
28 Nicklas Lidstrom 1.25 3.00
29 Pekka Rinne 1.50 4.00
30 Jaden Schwartz 1.50 4.00
31 Sven Baertschi 1.00 2.50
32 Chris Kreider 1.50 4.00
33 Cory Schneider 1.00 2.50
34 Jussi Rynnas .75 2.00
35 Antti Niemi 1.00 2.50
36 Dominik Hasek 1.50 4.00
37 Mikko Koivu 1.00 2.50
38 Zdeno Chara 1.25 3.00
39 Milan Lucic 1.25 3.00
40 Pavel Datsyuk 1.50 4.00
41 Anze Kopitar 2.00 5.00
42 Teemu Selanne 2.50 6.00
43 Patrice Bergeron 1.50 4.00
44 Tyler Seguin 2.00 5.00
45 Jonathan Toews 2.50 6.00
46 Gabriel Landeskog 1.25 3.00
47 Jonathan Quick 2.00 5.00
48 John Tavares 2.50 6.00
49 Jason Spezza 1.25 3.00
50 Evgeni Malkin 4.00 10.00

2012-13 Fleer Retro Premium Golden Touch

STATED ODDS 1:120
1GT Teemu Selanne 6.00 15.00
2GT Tyler Seguin 10.00 25.00
3GT Chris Kreider 5.00 12.00
4GT Jeff Skinner 6.00 15.00
5GT Jonathan Toews 12.00 30.00
6GT Matt Duchene 6.00 15.00
7GT Pavel Datsyuk 8.00 20.00
8GT Henrik Zetterberg 8.00 20.00
9GT Taylor Hall 12.00 30.00
10GT Jordan Eberle 6.00 15.00
11GT Ryan Nugent-Hopkins 10.00 25.00
12GT Mike Richards 6.00 15.00
13GT Wayne Gretzky 15.00 40.00
14GT John Tavares 5.00 12.00
15GT Marian Gaborik 6.00 15.00
16GT Jason Spezza 6.00 15.00
17GT Claude Giroux 6.00 15.00
18GT Evgeni Malkin 20.00 50.00
19GT Mario Lemieux 20.00 50.00
20GT Sidney Crosby 10.00 25.00
21GT James Neal 6.00 15.00
22GT Logan Couture 6.00 15.00
23GT Steven Stamkos 12.00 30.00
24GT Pavel Bure 6.00 15.00
25GT Alexander Ovechkin 25.00 60.00

2012-13 Fleer Retro Metal Universe

STATED ODDS 1:4
1 Bobby Orr 2.00 5.00
2 Teemu Selanne 1.50 4.00
3 Ryan Nugent-Hopkins 1.25 3.00
4 Eric Lindros 2.00 5.00
5 Tie Domi 1.25 3.00
6 Marc-Andre Fleury 1.50 4.00
7 Jaden Schwartz 1.50 4.00
8 Antti Niemi 1.00 2.50
9 Wayne Gretzky 4.00 10.00
10 Dominik Hasek 1.50 4.00
11 Chris Kreider 1.50 4.00
12 Arturs Irbe 1.00 2.50
13 Jeff Skinner 1.50 4.00
14 Pelle Lindbergh 1.50 4.00
15 Doug Gilmour 1.50 4.00
16 Alexander Ovechkin 5.00 12.00
17 Steven Stamkos 2.50 6.00
18 Jarome Iginla 1.25 3.00
19 Pavel Datsyuk 1.50 4.00
20 Saku Koivu 1.25 3.00
21 Zdeno Chara 1.25 3.00
22 Mikko Koivu 1.00 2.50
23 Jussi Rynnas .75 2.00
24 Sven Baertschi 1.00 2.50
25 Nicklas Lidstrom 1.25 3.00
26 Ondrej Pavelec 1.25 3.00
27 Ilya Kovalchuk 1.25 3.00
28 Erik Karlsson 2.50 6.00
29 P.K. Subban 2.00 5.00
30 Mats Sundin 1.25 3.00
31 Patrice Bergeron 1.50 4.00
32 Gabriel Landeskog 1.25 3.00
33 Patrick Roy 3.00 8.00
34 Henrik Lundqvist 1.50 4.00
35 Jason Spezza 1.25 3.00
36 Evgeni Malkin 4.00 10.00
37 Pavel Bure 1.50 4.00
38 Claude Giroux 1.25 3.00
39 Tyler Seguin 2.00 5.00
40 Mark Messier 1.50 4.00
41 Patrick Kane 2.50 6.00
42 Pekka Rinne 1.50 4.00
43 Cory Schneider 1.00 2.50
44 Daniel Sedin 1.25 3.00
45 Ray Bourque 2.00 5.00
46 Milan Lucic 1.25 3.00
47 Drew Doughty 1.25 3.00
48 Jonathan Toews 2.50 6.00
49 Jaromir Jagr 3.00 8.00
50 Mario Lemieux 4.00 10.00
51 Carey Price 4.00 10.00
52 Martin Brodeur 2.50 6.00
53 John Tavares 2.50 6.00
54 Jordan Eberle 1.25 3.00
55 Joe Sakic 2.00 5.00
56 Taylor Hall 2.50 6.00
57 Brett Hull 1.25 3.00
58 Jonathan Quick 2.00 5.00
59 Henrik Sedin 1.25 3.00
60 Sidney Crosby 2.00 5.00

2012-13 Fleer Retro Metal Universe Precious Metal Gems Blue

*BLUE/50: 2.5X TO 6X BASIC INSERTS
9 Wayne Gretzky 60.00 120.00
16 Alexander Ovechkin 15.00 40.00
33 Patrick Roy 25.00 60.00
60 Sidney Crosby 25.00 60.00

2012-13 Fleer Retro Metal Universe Precious Metal Gems Red

*RED/100: 1.5X TO 4X BASIC INSERTS
9 Wayne Gretzky 25.00 60.00
16 Alexander Ovechkin 12.00 30.00
60 Sidney Crosby 15.00 40.00

2012-13 Fleer Retro Metal Universe Championship Hardware

STATED ODDS 1:108
1CH Bobby Orr 12.00 30.00
2CH Tyler Seguin 6.00 15.00
3CH Sven Baertschi 3.00 8.00
4CH Patrick Kane 8.00 20.00
5CH Patrick Roy 10.00 25.00
6CH Ryan Nugent-Hopkins 4.00 10.00
7CH Jordan Eberle 4.00 10.00
8CH Taylor Hall 8.00 20.00
9CH Wayne Gretzky 20.00 50.00
10CH Henrik Lundqvist 5.00 12.00
11CH Chris Kreider 5.00 12.00
12CH Erik Karlsson 8.00 20.00
13CH Sidney Crosby 12.00 30.00
14CH Mario Lemieux 12.00 30.00
15CH Jaden Schwartz 5.00 12.00
16CH Steven Stamkos 8.00 20.00
17CH Henrik Sedin 4.00 10.00
18CH Daniel Sedin 4.00 10.00
19CH Alexander Ovechkin 8.00 20.00
20CH Ondrej Pavelec 4.00 10.00

2012-13 Fleer Retro Playmaker's Theatre

STATED PRINT RUN 100 SER.#'d SETS
1 Bobby Orr 20.00 50.00
2 Tyler Seguin 10.00 25.00
3 Sven Baertschi 4.00 10.00
4 Jonathan Toews 12.00 30.00
5 Ryan Nugent-Hopkins 8.00 20.00
6 Mark Messier 8.00 20.00
7 Jordan Eberle 6.00 15.00
8 Taylor Hall 12.00 30.00
9 Wayne Gretzky 15.00 40.00
10 Jonathan Quick 10.00 25.00
11 Patrick Roy 15.00 40.00
12 Martin Brodeur 12.00 30.00
13 Chris Kreider 6.00 15.00
14 Eric Lindros 8.00 20.00
15 Sidney Crosby 20.00 40.00
16 Mario Lemieux 20.00 50.00
17 Evgeni Malkin 8.00 20.00
18 Carey Price 8.00 20.00
19 Mats Sundin 6.00 15.00
20 Joe Sakic 10.00 25.00
21 Brett Hull 6.00 15.00
22 Jaden Schwartz 5.00 12.00
23 Steven Stamkos 8.00 20.00
24 Pavel Bure 8.00 20.00
25 Alexander Ovechkin 8.00 20.00

2012-13 Fleer Retro Premium Intimidation Nation

STATED ODDS 1:160
1IN Alexander Ovechkin 20.00 50.00
2IN Pavel Bure 6.00 15.00
3IN Alexandre Burrows 5.00 12.00
4IN Tie Domi 5.00 12.00
5IN Steven Stamkos 10.00 25.00
6IN Jaden Schwartz 5.00 12.00
7IN Sidney Crosby 20.00 50.00
8IN Mario Lemieux 15.00 40.00
9IN Eric Lindros 8.00 20.00
10IN Dave Schultz 5.00 12.00
11IN Chris Kreider 5.00 12.00
12IN Patrick Roy 12.00 30.00
13IN Claude Lemieux 4.00 10.00
14IN Wayne Gretzky 25.00 60.00
15IN Ryan Nugent-Hopkins 5.00 12.00
16IN Jordan Eberle 5.00 12.00
17IN Taylor Hall 10.00 25.00
18IN Jeff Skinner 5.00 12.00
19IN Sven Baertschi 3.00 8.00
20IN Terry O'Reilly 4.00 10.00

2012-13 Fleer Retro Rookie Sensations Autographs

OVERALL ODDS 1:25
GROUP A ODDS 1:2142
GROUP B ODDS 1:857
GROUP C ODDS 1:28
1 Akim Aliu C 3.00 8.00
2 Carter Ashton C 2.50 6.00
3 Casey Cizikas C 8.00 20.00
4 Chet Pickard C 3.00 8.00
5 Chris Kreider B 10.00 25.00
6 Cody Goloubef A 10.00 25.00
7 J.T. Brown C 3.00 8.00
8 Jaden Schwartz C 6.00 15.00
9 Jake Allen C 10.00 25.00
10 Jakob Silfverberg C 10.00 25.00
11 Jason Zucker C 4.00 10.00
12 Jussi Rynnas C 3.00 8.00
13 Mark Stone C 6.00 15.00
14 Reilly Smith C 6.00 15.00
15 Riley Sheahan C 6.00 15.00
16 Scott Glennie C 3.00 8.00
17 Sven Baertschi C 4.00 10.00
18 Tyson Barrie C 6.00 15.00

2012-13 Fleer Retro Thunder Noyz Boyz

STATED ODDS 1:132
1NB Evander Kane 5.00 12.00
2NB Alexander Ovechkin 10.00 25.00
3NB Tie Domi 5.00 12.00
4NB Steven Stamkos 10.00 25.00
5NB Joe Sakic 8.00 20.00
6NB Mats Sundin 5.00 12.00
7NB Evgeni Malkin 15.00 40.00
8NB Mario Lemieux 15.00 40.00
9NB Sidney Crosby 15.00 40.00
10NB Jaromir Jagr 12.00 30.00
11NB Claude Giroux 5.00 12.00
12NB Erik Karlsson 10.00 25.00
13NB Chris Kreider 6.00 15.00
14NB Henrik Lundqvist 6.00 15.00
15NB John Tavares 10.00 25.00
16NB Drew Doughty 5.00 12.00
17NB Jonathan Quick 8.00 20.00
18NB Pavel Bure 6.00 15.00
19NB Taylor Hall 10.00 25.00
20NB Jordan Eberle 5.00 12.00
21NB Ryan Nugent-Hopkins 5.00 12.00
22NB Wayne Gretzky 25.00 60.00
23NB P.K. Subban 8.00 20.00
24NB Theoren Fleury 6.00 15.00
25NB Milan Lucic 5.00 12.00

2012-13 Fleer Retro Ultra Stars Gold

STATED ODDS 1:96
1US Bobby Orr 10.00 25.00
2US Sven Baertschi 2.00 5.00
3US Jeff Skinner 3.00 8.00
4US Ryan Nugent-Hopkins 3.00 8.00
5US Jordan Eberle 3.00 8.00
6US Taylor Hall 6.00 15.00
7US Wayne Gretzky 15.00 40.00
8US Patrick Roy 8.00 20.00
9US Pekka Rinne 4.00 10.00
10US John Tavares 6.00 15.00
11US Chris Kreider 3.00 8.00
12US Erik Karlsson 6.00 15.00
13US Sidney Crosby 12.00 30.00
14US Mario Lemieux 10.00 25.00
15US Jaden Schwartz 3.00 8.00
16US Steven Stamkos 6.00 15.00
17US Pavel Bure 4.00 10.00
18US Cory Schneider 2.50 6.00
19US Alexander Ovechkin 6.00 15.00
20US Teemu Selanne 4.00 10.00

2013-14 Fleer Showcase

COMP.SET w/o RC's (100) 10.00 25.00
EXCH EXPIRATION: 3/20/2016
1 Evgeni Malkin AS 1.25 3.00
2 Jeremy Roenick AS .40 1.00
3 Ryan Getzlaf .60 1.50
4 Corey Perry .40 1.00
5 Jonas Hiller .30 .75
6 Milan Lucic .40 1.00
7 Tuukka Rask .40 1.00
8 Zdeno Chara .40 1.00
9 Glen Murray .30 .75
10 Ryan Miller .40 1.00
11 Dominik Hasek .50 1.25
12 Matt Stajan .30 .75
13 Eric Staal .50 1.25
14 Cam Ward .40 1.00
15 Jonathan Toews .75 2.00
16 Patrick Kane .75 2.00
17 Duncan Keith .40 1.00
18 Corey Crawford .50 1.25
19 Bryan Bickell .25 .60
20 Matt Duchene .40 1.00
21 Milan Hejduk .30 .75
22 Paul Stastny .40 1.00
23 Patrick Roy 1.00 2.50
24 Peter Forsberg .40 1.00
25 Henrik Zetterberg .50 1.25
26 Jim Howard .40 1.00
27 Johan Franzen .40 1.00
28 Pavel Datsyuk .50 1.25
29 Steve Yzerman .75 2.00
30 Ryan Nugent-Hopkins .40 1.00
31 Wayne Gretzky 2.00 5.00
32 Taylor Hall .75 2.00
33 Jordan Eberle .40 1.00
34 David Perron .25 .60
35 Ales Hemsky .25 .60
36 Sam Gagner .30 .75
37 Pavel Bure .50 1.25
38 Ed Belfour .40 1.00
39 Jonathan Quick .60 1.50
40 Mike Richards .40 1.00
41 Anze Kopitar .60 1.50

42 Dustin Brown .40 1.00
43 Slava Voynov .30 .75
44 Zach Parise .40 1.00
45 Mikko Koivu .30 .75
46 Tomas Plekanec .40 1.00
47 P.K. Subban .60 1.50
48 Max Pacioretty .40 1.00
49 Larry Robinson .40 1.00
50 Carey Price 1.25 3.00
51 David Desharnais .40 1.00
52 David Legwand .30 .75
53 Pekka Rinne .50 1.25
54 Patrik Elias .40 1.00
55 Martin Brodeur .75 2.00
56 Travis Zajac .30 .75
57 Mike Bossy .40 1.00
58 Kyle Okposo .40 1.00
59 John Tavares .75 2.00
60 Rick Nash .40 1.00
61 Mike Gartner .40 1.00
62 Derek Stepan .40 1.00
63 Chris Kreider .40 1.00
64 Theoren Fleury .50 1.25
65 Carl Hagelin .40 1.00
66 Bobby Ryan .40 1.00
67 Robin Lehner .30 .75
68 Jason Spezza .40 1.00
69 Erik Karlsson .75 2.00
70 Simon Gagne .40 1.00
71 Claude Giroux .40 1.00
72 Bill Barber .40 1.00
73 Scott Hartnell .40 1.00
74 Steve Mason .30 .75
75 Shane Doan .30 .75
76 Mario Lemieux 1.25 3.00
77 Kris Letang .40 1.00
78 Marc-Andre Fleury .60 1.50
79 Sidney Crosby 1.50 4.00
80 Logan Couture .40 1.00
81 Patrick Marleau .40 1.00
82 Antti Niemi .30 .75
83 Alexander Steen .40 1.00
84 Patrik Berglund .25 .60
85 Brett Hull .40 1.00
86 Martin St. Louis .40 1.00
87 Steven Stamkos .75 2.00
88 Mats Sundin .40 1.00
89 Grant Fuhr .40 1.00
90 Eric Lindros .60 1.50
91 Phil Kessel .50 1.25
92 Nazem Kadri .40 1.00
93 Daniel Sedin .40 1.00
94 Henrik Sedin .40 1.00
95 Ryan Kesler .40 1.00
96 Alexandre Burrows .40 1.00
97 Roberto Luongo .40 1.00
98 Braden Holtby .60 1.50
99 Nicklas Backstrom .60 1.50
100 Alexander Ovechkin 1.50 4.00
101 Trtmn/Flrk/Cnnghm RC 5.00 12.00
102 Bncks/Cndri/Brn RC 1.50 4.00
103 Sstr/Mgna/Hys RC 2.00 5.00
104 Rnhrt/Jhnsn/Ptrvc RC 3.00 8.00
105 Jnes/Brra/Rnta RC 3.00 8.00
106 Hnwski/LBlnc/Lrdsn RC 1.50 4.00
107 Rsk/Brtly/Hndrsn RC 1.50 4.00
108 Grba/Grnt/Dzzynski RC 1.50 4.00
109 Grbr/Crrck/Olksy RC 2.50 6.00
110 Dmln/Wey/Smlssn RC 3.00 8.00
111 Gds/Plt/Krbv RC 2.50 6.00
112 Chpt/Ady-Mrchsslt/Rssl RC 4.00 10.00
113 Ptryn/Glndning/Bllns RC 3.00 8.00
114 Vtnn/Lndhlm/Grnt RC 3.00 8.00
115 Albrt/Mlchri/O'Dll RC 2.00 5.00
116 Mllr/Gbbns/Wrsfsky RC 2.50 6.00
117 Cnntn/Olksk/Nlstrp RC 1.50 4.00
118 Llnde/Aksn/Cci RC 3.00 8.00
119 Jskn/Brbrio/Sll RC 2.00 5.00
120 Crrdo/Cnnta/Archbld RC 1.50 4.00
121 Irwn/Alln/Kstka RC 1.50 4.00
122 Stl/Sgrbssa/Chrt RC 2.00 5.00
123 Actn/Ptlck/Gzdc RC 2.00 5.00
124 Mrncn/Fdn/Hnt RC 2.50 6.00
125 Mse/Psqle/Bbkv RC 2.00 5.00
126 S.Abbott/J.D'Amigo RC 2.00 5.00
127 Bournival/P.Holland RC 3.00 8.00
128 N.Schmidt/E.Haula RC 6.00 15.00
129 C.Pickard/K.Simpson RC 2.50 6.00
130 R.Boucher/C.Murphy RC 2.50 6.00
131 J.Leivo/D.Broll RC 2.00 5.00
132 M.Raffl/M.Konan RC 2.50 6.00
133 J.Eriksson/N.Svedberg RC 4.00 10.00
134 Almqvist/Marchenko RC 2.50 6.00
135 E.Hartzell/J.Zatkoff RC 2.00 5.00
136 M.Mazanec/M.Hellberg RC 2.00 5.00
137 E.Gelinas/M.Sislo RC 2.00 5.00
138 O.Maatta/N.Zadorov RC 5.00 12.00
139 Frederik Andersen AU RC 8.00 20.00
140 Freddie Hamilton AU RC 4.00 10.00
141 John Gibson AU RC 25.00 50.00
142 Linden Vey AU RC 2.50 6.00
143 Rickard Rakell AU RC 4.00 10.00
144 Mathew Dumba AU RC 5.00 12.00
145 Zemgus Girgensons AU RC 8.00 20.00
146 Justin Fontaine AU RC 4.00 10.00
147 Jon Merrill AU RC 4.00 10.00
148 Matt Nieto AU RC 3.00 8.00
149 Alex Killorn AU RC 4.00 10.00
150 Tomas Jurco AU RC 8.00 20.00
151 Ryan Murphy JSY AU/375 RC 6.00 15.00
152 Mark Arcobello JSY AU/375 RC 6.00 15.00
153 T.Hickey JSY AU/375 RC 8.00 20.00
154 Tom Wilson JSY AU/375 RC 8.00 20.00
155 Brock Nelson JSY AU/375 RC 6.00 15.00
156 R.Ristolainen JSY AU/375 RC 10.00 25.00
157 J.G.Pageau JSY AU/175 RC 6.00 15.00
158 Nichushkin JSY AU/175 RC 15.00 40.00
159 Johan Larsson JSY AU/375 RC 5.00 12.00
160 M.Rielly JSY AU/175 RC 20.00 50.00
161 D.DeKeyser JSY AU/375 RC 8.00 20.00
162 Jacob Trouba JSY AU/375 RC 10.00 25.00
163 C.Thomas JSY AU/375 RC 5.00 12.00
164 Chris Brown JSY AU/375 RC 4.00 10.00
165 Richard Panik JSY AU/375 RC 6.00 15.00
166 J.Schroeder JSY AU/375 RC 6.00 15.00
167 Zach Redmond JSY AU/375 RC 5.00 12.00
168 Ryan Strome JSY AU/375 RC 8.00 20.00
169 C.Soderberg JSY AU/375 RC 6.00 15.00
170 Drew Shore JSY AU/175 RC 6.00 15.00
171 Dylan McIlrath JSY AU/375 RC 4.00 10.00
172 Maatta JSY AU/175 RC EXCH 20.00 50.00
173 M.Granlund JSY AU/375 RC 8.00 20.00
174 Grigorenko JSY AU/375 RC 8.00 20.00
175 N.Beaulieu JSY AU/375 RC 10.00 25.00
176 Charlie Coyle JSY AU/375 RC 6.00 15.00
177 D.Hamilton JSY AU/175 RC 15.00 40.00
178 E.Lindholm JSY AU/375 RC 10.00 25.00
179 Beau Bennett JSY AU/375 RC 10.00 25.00
180 Austin Watson JSY AU/375 RC 5.00 12.00
181 Ryan Murray JSY AU/375 RC 10.00 25.00
182 Emerson Etem JSY AU/375 RC 6.00 15.00
183 Jonas Brodin JSY AU/175 RC 6.00 15.00
184 Jack Campbell JSY AU/375 RC 5.00 12.00
185 Petr Mrazek JSY AU/375 RC 12.00 30.00
186 Q.Howden JSY AU/375 RC 5.00 12.00
187 Ryan Spooner JSY AU/175 RC 8.00 20.00
188 Scott Laughton JSY AU/375 RC 6.00 15.00
189 D.Brunner JSY AU/375 RC 5.00 12.00
190 Viktor Fasth JSY AU/375 RC 6.00 15.00
191 Jarred Tinordi JSY AU/375 RC 6.00 15.00
192 Cory Conacher JSY AU/375 RC 4.00 10.00
193 Nicklas Jensen JSY AU/375 RC 5.00 12.00
194 F.Forsberg JSY AU/375 RC 15.00 40.00
195 Boone Jenner JSY AU/175 RC 8.00 20.00
196 T.Pearson JSY AU/375 RC 6.00 15.00
197 Alex Chiasson JSY AU/375 RC 6.00 15.00
198 N.Bjugstad JSY AU/375 RC 8.00 20.00
199 N.Yakupov JSY AU/175 RC 25.00 60.00
200 Galchenyuk JSY AU/175 RC 40.00 100.00
201 J.Huberdeau JSY AU/175 RC 15.00 40.00
202 B.Gallagher JSY AU/175 RC 25.00 60.00
203 Tomas Hertl JSY AU/175 RC 10.00 25.00
204 S.Monahan JSY AU/175 RC 30.00 80.00
205 Justin Schultz JSY AU/175 RC 8.00 20.00
206 Tyler Toffoli JSY AU/175 RC 20.00 50.00
207 MacKinnon JSY AU/175 RC 100.00 200.00
208 Seth Jones JSY AU/175 RC 8.00 20.00
209 A.Barkov JSY AU/175 RC 20.00 50.00
210 V.Tarasenko JSY AU/175 RC 50.00 100.00

2013-14 Fleer Showcase Jambalaya

STATED ODDS 1:180
1JB Tony Esposito 15.00 40.00
2JB Mario Lemieux 25.00 60.00
3JB Ron Hextall 20.00 50.00
4JB Peter Forsberg 15.00 40.00
5JB Tuukka Rask 15.00 40.00
6JB Marcel Dionne 20.00 50.00
7JB Wayne Gretzky 60.00 120.00
8JB Pavel Bure 20.00 50.00
9JB Ray Bourque 15.00 40.00
10JB Ryan Nugent-Hopkins 15.00 40.00
11JB Steve Yzerman 20.00 50.00
12JB Nazem Kadri 15.00 40.00
13JB Corey Crawford 20.00 50.00
14JB Taylor Hall 12.00 30.00
15JB Zdeno Chara 15.00 40.00
16JB Jonathan Toews 25.00 60.00
17JB Zach Parise 12.00 30.00
18JB Carey Price 20.00 50.00
19JB P.K. Subban 15.00 40.00
20JB Evander Kane 12.00 30.00
21JB Sidney Crosby 60.00 120.00
22JB Jonathan Quick 12.00 30.00
23JB Antti Niemi 12.00 30.00
24JB James van Riemsdyk 12.00 30.00
25JB Anze Kopitar 12.00 30.00
26JB Patrick Roy 25.00 60.00
27JB Nathan MacKinnon 30.00 80.00
28JB Marc-Andre Fleury 12.00 30.00
29JB Henrik Lundqvist 20.00 50.00
30JB Sean Monahan 25.00 60.00
31JB Ryan Miller 15.00 40.00
32JB Doug Gilmour 20.00 50.00
33JB Teemu Selanne 30.00 80.00
34JB Evgeni Malkin 15.00 40.00
35JB Tomas Hertl 20.00 50.00
36JB Bobby Orr 30.00 60.00
37JB Alexander Ovechkin 30.00 80.00
38JB Alex Galchenyuk 40.00 80.00
39JB Brendan Gallagher 30.00 60.00
40JB Henrik Zetterberg 15.00 40.00
41JB Jonathan Huberdeau 15.00 40.00
42JB Nail Yakupov 15.00 40.00

2013-14 Fleer Showcase Metal Universe

STATED ODDS 1:3
MU1 Bobby Orr 1.50 4.00
MU2 Alex Galchenyuk 2.50 6.00
MU3 Claude Giroux .75 2.00
MU4 Zach Parise .75 2.00
MU5 Wayne Gretzky 4.00 10.00
MU6 Jonas Brodin .50 1.25
MU7 Brad Marchand 1.00 2.50
MU8 Nail Yakupov 2.00 5.00
MU9 Corey Crawford 1.00 2.50
MU10 Brendan Gallagher 2.00 5.00
MU11 Felix Potvin 1.25 3.00
MU12 Vladimir Tarasenko 2.50 6.00
MU13 Peter Forsberg .75 2.00
MU14 Aleksander Barkov 2.00 5.00
MU15 Tyler Seguin 1.25 3.00
MU16 Elias Lindholm 1.00 2.50
MU17 John Tavares 1.50 4.00
MU18 Dino Ciccarelli .75 2.00
MU19 Patrick Kane 1.50 4.00
MU20 Teemu Selanne 1.00 2.50
MU21 Paul Coffey .75 2.00
MU22 Sean Monahan 1.00 2.50
MU23 Nazem Kadri .75 2.00
MU24 Tomas Hertl .75 2.00
MU25 Matt Duchene .75 2.00
MU26 Mikhail Grigorenko .75 2.00
MU27 Brett Hull .75 2.00
MU28 Bobby Ryan .75 2.00
MU29 Guy Lafleur 1.00 2.50
MU30 Nathan MacKinnon 5.00 12.00
MU31 Doug Gilmour 1.00 2.50
MU32 Valeri Nichushkin .60 1.50
MU33 Tyler Toffoli 1.25 3.00
MU34 Beau Bennett .75 2.00
MU35 Sidney Crosby 3.00 8.00
MU36 Seth Jones .60 1.50
MU37 Patrick Roy 2.00 5.00
MU38 Ryan Strome .75 2.00
MU39 Cam Neely .75 2.00
MU40 Morgan Rielly 1.50 4.00
MU41 Nicklas Lidstrom .75 2.00
MU42 Justin Schultz .60 1.50

2013-14 Fleer Showcase Metal Universe Precious Metal Gems Blue

*BLUE/25: 3X TO 8X BASIC INSERTS
MU1 Bobby Orr 15.00 40.00
MU5 Wayne Gretzky 50.00 100.00
MU9 Corey Crawford 8.00 20.00
MU30 Nathan MacKinnon 50.00 120.00
MU33 Tyler Toffoli 20.00 50.00
MU35 Sidney Crosby 15.00 40.00

2013-14 Fleer Showcase Metal Universe Precious Metal Gems Red

MU1 Bobby Orr 12.00 30.00
MU5 Wayne Gretzky 15.00 40.00
MU9 Corey Crawford 3.00 8.00
MU30 Nathan MacKinnon 20.00 50.00
MU33 Tyler Toffoli 8.00 20.00
MU35 Sidney Crosby 15.00 40.00

2013-14 Fleer Showcase Red Glow

*101-138 ROOK/27: 1X TO 2.5X RC/299-399
*139-150 ROOK.AU/27: .6X TO 1.5X RC/149
*151-210 ROOK.JSY AU/18-27: .6X TO 1.5X
*1-100 WHITE/18: .8X TO 2X RED/36
1 Evgeni Malkin AS JSY 15.00 40.00
2 Jeremy Roenick AS JSY 5.00 12.00
3 Ryan Getzlaf JSY 8.00 20.00
4 Corey Perry JSY 5.00 12.00
5 Jonas Hiller JSY 4.00 10.00
6 Milan Lucic JSY 5.00 12.00
7 Tuukka Rask JSY 5.00 12.00
8 Zdeno Chara JSY 5.00 12.00
9 Glen Murray JSY 4.00 10.00
10 Ryan Miller JSY 5.00 12.00
11 Dominik Hasek JSY 6.00 15.00
12 Matt Stajan JSY 4.00 10.00
13 Eric Staal JSY 6.00 15.00
14 Cam Ward JSY 5.00 12.00
15 Jonathan Toews JSY 10.00 25.00
17 Duncan Keith JSY 5.00 12.00
18 Corey Crawford JSY 6.00 15.00
19 Bryan Bickell JSY 3.00 8.00
20 Matt Duchene JSY 5.00 12.00
21 Milan Hejduk JSY 4.00 10.00
22 Paul Stastny JSY 5.00 12.00
23 Patrick Roy JSY 12.00 30.00
24 Peter Forsberg JSY 5.00 12.00
25 Henrik Zetterberg JSY 6.00 15.00
26 Jim Howard JSY 5.00 12.00
27 Johan Franzen JSY 5.00 12.00
28 Pavel Datsyuk JSY 6.00 15.00
29 Steve Yzerman JSY 10.00 25.00
30 Ryan Nugent-Hopkins JSY 5.00 12.00
31 Wayne Gretzky JSY 25.00 60.00
32 Taylor Hall JSY 10.00 25.00
33 Jordan Eberle JSY 5.00 12.00
34 David Perron JSY 3.00 8.00
35 Ales Hemsky JSY 3.00 8.00
36 Sam Gagner JSY 4.00 10.00
37 Pavel Bure JSY 8.00 20.00
38 Ed Belfour JSY 5.00 12.00
39 Jonathan Quick JSY 8.00 20.00
40 Mike Richards JSY 5.00 12.00
41 Anze Kopitar JSY 8.00 20.00
42 Dustin Brown JSY 6.00 15.00
43 Slava Voynov JSY 4.00 10.00
45 Mikko Koivu JSY 4.00 10.00
46 Tomas Plekanec JSY 6.00 15.00
47 P.K. Subban JSY 8.00 20.00
48 Max Pacioretty JSY 5.00 12.00
50 Carey Price JSY 15.00 40.00
52 David Legwand JSY 4.00 10.00
53 Pekka Rinne JSY 6.00 15.00
54 Patrik Elias JSY 5.00 12.00
55 Martin Brodeur JSY 12.50 25.00
56 Travis Zajac JSY 4.00 10.00
58 Kyle Okposo JSY 5.00 12.00
59 John Tavares JSY 10.00 25.00
60 Rick Nash JSY 5.00 12.00
61 Mike Gartner JSY 5.00 12.00
62 Derek Stepan JSY 5.00 12.00
63 Chris Kreider JSY 5.00 12.00
64 Theoren Fleury JSY 6.00 15.00
65 Carl Hagelin JSY 5.00 12.00
67 Robin Lehner JSY 4.00 10.00
68 Jason Spezza JSY 5.00 12.00
69 Erik Karlsson JSY 10.00 25.00
70 Simon Gagne JSY 5.00 12.00
72 Bill Barber JSY 5.00 12.00
73 Scott Hartnell JSY 5.00 12.00
74 Steve Mason JSY 4.00 10.00
75 Shane Doan JSY 4.00 10.00
76 Mario Lemieux JSY 15.00 40.00
78 Marc-Andre Fleury JSY 8.00 20.00
79 Sidney Crosby JSY 15.00 40.00
80 Logan Couture JSY 5.00 12.00
81 Patrick Marleau JSY 5.00 12.00
82 Antti Niemi JSY 4.00 10.00
84 Patrik Berglund JSY 3.00 8.00
85 Brett Hull JSY 8.00 20.00
86 Martin St. Louis JSY 5.00 12.00
87 Steven Stamkos JSY 12.00 30.00
88 Mats Sundin JSY 5.00 12.00
89 Grant Fuhr JSY 5.00 12.00
90 Eric Lindros JSY 10.00 20.00
91 Phil Kessel JSY 6.00 15.00
92 Nazem Kadri JSY 5.00 12.00
93 Daniel Sedin JSY 5.00 12.00
95 Ryan Kesler JSY 5.00 12.00
97 Roberto Luongo JSY 5.00 12.00
98 Braden Holtby JSY 8.00 20.00
99 Nicklas Backstrom JSY 8.00 20.00
100 Alexander Ovechkin JSY 20.00 50.00
145 Zemgus Girgensons AU 30.00 60.00
207 N.MacKinnon GLV AU/18 400.00 600.00

2013-14 Fleer Showcase SkyBox Premium

1-15 STATED ODDS 1:17
16-25 STATED ODDS 1:50
26-45 STATED PRINT RUN 299
*1-15 RUBY/50: 1.2X TO 3X BASIC INSERTS
*16-25 RUBY/50: .8X TO 2X BASIC INSERTS
*26-45 RBY/50: .8X TO 2X BAS.INSERT/299
1 Wayne Gretzky 6.00 15.00
2 Bobby Orr 2.50 6.00
3 Mario Lemieux 4.00 10.00
4 Eric Lindros 2.00 5.00
5 Steve Yzerman 2.50 6.00
6 Sidney Crosby 5.00 12.00
7 Alexander Ovechkin 5.00 12.00
8 Martin St. Louis 1.25 3.00
9 Jonathan Toews 2.50 6.00
10 Henrik Lundqvist 1.50 4.00
11 John Tavares 2.50 6.00
12 Steven Stamkos 2.50 6.00
13 Carey Price 4.00 10.00
14 P.K. Subban 2.00 5.00
15 Evgeni Malkin 4.00 10.00
16 Rick Nash SP 2.00 5.00
17 Ryan Getzlaf SP 3.00 8.00
18 Phil Kessel SP 2.50 6.00
19 Jordan Eberle SP 2.00 5.00
20 Anze Kopitar SP 3.00 8.00
21 Logan Couture SP 2.00 5.00
22 Henrik Zetterberg SP 2.50 6.00
23 Eric Staal SP 2.50 6.00
24 Patrice Bergeron SP 2.50 6.00
25 Martin Brodeur SP 4.00 10.00
26 Nail Yakupov/299 4.00 10.00
27 Alex Galchenyuk/299 6.00 15.00
28 Aleksander Barkov/299 4.00 10.00
29 Morgan Rielly/299 4.00 10.00
30 Nikita Kucherov/299 4.00 10.00
31 Sean Monahan/299 2.50 6.00
32 Justin Schultz/299 1.50 4.00
33 Taylor Beck/299 1.25 3.00
34 Seth Jones/299 1.50 4.00
35 Mikhail Grigorenko/299 2.00 5.00
36 Ryan Murray/299 2.50 6.00
37 Tomas Hertl/299 2.00 5.00
38 Dougie Hamilton/299 3.00 8.00
39 Philipp Grubauer/299 1.50 4.00
40 Valeri Nichushkin/299 1.50 4.00
41 Zemgus Girgensons/299 3.00 8.00
42 Nathan MacKinnon/299 6.00 15.00
43 Olli Maatta/299 2.50 6.00
44 Jonathan Huberdeau/299 4.00 10.00
45 Brendan Gallagher/299 5.00 12.00

2013-14 Fleer Showcase Stitches

STATED ODDS 1:30
SAG Alex Galchenyuk 5.00 12.00
SAK Anze Kopitar 3.00 8.00
SAN Antti Niemi 1.50 4.00
SBB Beau Bennett 2.00 5.00
SCA Carey Price 6.00 15.00
SDD Devan Dubnyk 2.00 5.00
SDK Duncan Keith 2.00 5.00
SDS Drew Stafford 1.50 4.00
SEM Evgeni Malkin 6.00 15.00
SHE Tomas Hertl 4.00 10.00
SJC Jack Campbell 1.25 3.00
SJE Jordan Eberle 2.00 5.00
SJM J.T. Miller 1.50 4.00
SMD Matt Duchene 2.00 5.00
SMS Martin St. Louis 2.00 5.00
SNB Nicklas Backstrom 3.00 8.00
SNM Nathan MacKinnon 6.00 15.00
SPK Phil Kessel 2.50 6.00
SPR Pekka Rinne 2.50 6.00
SPS P.K. Subban 3.00 8.00
SRG Ryan Getzlaf 3.00 8.00
SSJ Seth Jones 1.50 4.00
SSV Slava Voynov 1.50 4.00
STH Taylor Hall 4.00 10.00

2013-14 Fleer Showcase Ultra

1-25 STATED ODDS 1:10
26-35 STATED ODDS 1:50
36-65 ROOKIE PRINT RUN 499
*1-25 VETS/99: 1X TO 2.5X BASIC INSERTS
*26-35 VETS/99: .6X TO 1.5X BASIC INSERT
*36-65 ROOKIES/99: .8X TO 2X ROOKIE/499
1 Wayne Gretzky 6.00 15.00
2 Bobby Orr 2.50 6.00
3 Mario Lemieux 4.00 10.00
4 Peter Forsberg 1.25 3.00
5 Steve Yzerman 2.50 6.00
6 Patrick Roy 3.00 8.00
7 Bobby Clarke 1.25 3.00
8 Bobby Hull 1.25 3.00
9 Mike Bossy 1.25 3.00
10 Grant Fuhr 1.50 4.00
11 Sidney Crosby 5.00 12.00
12 Alexander Ovechkin 5.00 12.00
13 Ryan Nugent-Hopkins 1.25 3.00
14 Jonathan Toews 2.50 6.00
15 Henrik Lundqvist 1.50 4.00
16 John Tavares 2.50 6.00
17 Steven Stamkos 2.50 6.00
18 Carey Price 4.00 10.00
19 P.K. Subban 2.00 5.00
20 Evgeni Malkin 4.00 10.00
21 Rick Nash 1.25 3.00
22 Teemu Selanne 2.50 6.00
23 Phil Kessel 1.50 4.00
24 Jordan Eberle 1.25 3.00
25 Anze Kopitar 2.00 5.00
26 Logan Couture SP 2.00 5.00
27 Henrik Zetterberg SP 2.50 6.00
28 Eric Staal SP 2.50 6.00
29 Patrice Bergeron SP 2.50 6.00
30 Martin Brodeur SP 4.00 10.00
31 Drew Doughty SP 2.00 5.00
32 Claude Giroux SP 2.00 5.00
33 Tuukka Rask SP 2.00 5.00
34 Marian Gaborik SP 2.00 5.00
35 Pavel Datsyuk SP 2.50 6.00
36 Nail Yakupov/499 3.00 8.00
37 Alex Galchenyuk/499 5.00 12.00
38 Jonathan Huberdeau/499 3.00 8.00
39 Brendan Gallagher/499 4.00 10.00
40 Cory Conacher/499 .75 2.00
41 Aleksander Barkov/499 4.00 10.00
42 Justin Schultz/499 1.25 3.00
43 Vladimir Tarasenko/499 4.00 10.00
44 Mikael Granlund/499 2.00 5.00
45 John Gibson/499 6.00 15.00
46 Elias Lindholm/499 2.00 5.00
47 Charlie Coyle/499 1.25 3.00
48 Dougie Hamilton/499 2.50 6.00
49 Linden Vey/499 .75 2.00
50 Jon Merrill/499 1.25 3.00
51 Tyler Toffoli/499 2.50 6.00
52 Sean Monahan/499 2.00 5.00
53 Ryan Murray/499 2.00 5.00
54 Tomas Hertl/499 1.50 4.00
55 Valeri Nichushkin/499 1.25 3.00
56 J.T. Miller/499 1.25 3.00
57 Nikita Zadorov/499 1.25 3.00
58 Jonas Brodin/499 1.00 2.50
59 Filip Forsberg/499 3.00 8.00
60 Ryan Strome/499 1.50 4.00
61 Martin Jones/499 3.00 8.00
62 Seth Jones/499 1.25 3.00
63 Nathan MacKinnon/499 10.00 25.00
64 Jacob Trouba/499 3.00 8.00
65 Morgan Rielly/499 3.00 8.00

2013-14 Fleer Showcase Ultra Platinum Medallion

*1-25 VETS/25: 2X TO 5X BASIC INSERTS
*26-35 VETS/25: 1.2X TO 3X BASIC INSERT
*36-65 ROOKIE/25: 1.5X TO 4X ROOKIE/499
45 John Gibson 40.00 80.00
63 Nathan MacKinnon 125.00 200.00

2013-14 Fleer Showcase Uniformity

STATED ODDS 1:45
UBN N.Bckstrm/M.Nvirth 3.00 8.00
UCN J.Cmpbll/V.Nchshkn 2.00 5.00
UDE D.Dubnyk/J.Eberle 2.00 5.00
UDM M.Dchne/N.McKnnon 8.00 20.00
UEH J.Eberle/T.Hall 4.00 10.00
UER E.Etem/R.Rakell 2.00 5.00
UGF R.Getzlaf/V.Fasth 3.00 8.00
UHB J.Huberdeau/A.Barkov 6.00 15.00
UHM C.Hagelin/J.Miller 2.00 5.00
UJF S.Jones/F.Forsberg 5.00 12.00
UKC D.Keith/C.Crawford 2.50 6.00
UKQ A.Kopitar/J.Quick 3.00 8.00
UMR R.Miller/R.Ristolainen 3.00 8.00
UNH R.Ngnt-Hpkns/T.Hall 4.00 10.00
UPJ P.Subban/J.Tinordi 3.00 8.00
USN R.Strome/B.Nelson 2.50 6.00
UST R.Strome/J.Tavares 4.00 10.00
UWJ A.Watson/S.Jones 2.00 5.00

2014-15 Fleer Showcase

EXCH EXPIRATION 2/16/2017
1 Cam Ward .40 1.00
2 Andy Greene .25 .60
3 Jari Kurri .40 1.00
4 Adam Henrique .40 1.00
5 Sean Couturier .40 1.00
6 Jonathan Toews .75 2.00
7 Cory Schneider .30 .75
8 Darcy Kuemper .30 .75
9 Gabriel Landeskog .30 .75
10 Max Pacioretty .40 1.00
11 Ondrej Pavelec .40 1.00
12 Ryan Miller .40 1.00
13 Taylor Hall .75 2.00
14 Matt Duchene .40 1.00
15 Tuukka Rask .40 1.00
16 T.J. Oshie .60 1.50
17 Dustin Brown .30 .75
18 Chris Osgood .40 1.00
19 Ryan Johansen .50 1.25
20 Brendan Gallagher .40 1.00
21 Pavel Datsyuk .50 1.25
22 Brett Hull .40 1.00
23 Steven Stamkos .75 2.00
24 Shea Weber .30 .75
25 Glen Murray .30 .75
26 Braden Holtby .60 1.50
27 Lars Eller .30 .75
28 Filip Forsberg .50 1.25
29 Curtis Joseph .40 1.00
30 Doug Weight .40 1.00
31 P.K. Subban .60 1.50
32 Patrick Marleau .40 1.00
33 Nail Yakupov .30 .75
34 Patrick Sharp .40 1.00
35 Zdeno Chara .40 1.00
36 John Tavares .75 2.00
37 Ed Belfour .40 1.00
38 Bobby Hull .40 1.00
39 Wayne Simmonds .50 1.25
40 Semyon Varlamov .40 1.00
41 Nathan MacKinnon .75 2.00
42 Roberto Luongo .40 1.00
43 Dale Hawerchuk .50 1.25
44 Dominik Hasek .50 1.25
45 Tyler Seguin .60 1.50
46 Steve Mason .30 .75
47 Antti Niemi .30 .75
48 Ryan Getzlaf .60 1.50
49 Jaromir Jagr 1.00 2.50
50 Zack Kassian .30 .75
51 Evander Kane .40 1.00
52 Karri Ramo .30 .75
53 Claude Giroux .40 1.00
54 Carey Price 1.25 3.00
55 Eric Staal .50 1.25
56 Johan Franzen .40 1.00
57 Kris Letang .40 1.00
58 Alexandre Burrows .40 1.00
59 Phil Kessel .50 1.25
60 Jonathan Bernier .40 1.00
61 Jake Muzzin .25 .60
62 Jonathan Quick .60 1.50
63 Mark Messier .40 1.00
64 Matt Moulson .30 .75
65 Corey Crawford .50 1.25
66 Jeremy Roenick .40 1.00
67 Henrik Zetterberg .50 1.25
68 Mats Zuccarello .40 1.00
69 Duncan Keith .40 1.00
70 Sean Monahan .40 1.00
71 Pete Peeters .30 .75
72 Cam Fowler .30 .75
73 Marc-Andre Fleury .60 1.50
74 R.J. Umberger .25 .60
75 Ryan Nugent-Hopkins .40 1.00
76 Shane Doan .30 .75
77 Joe Thornton .40 1.00
78 Alexander Ovechkin 1.50 4.00
79 Steve Yzerman .75 2.00
80 Anze Kopitar .60 1.50
81 David Backes .40 1.00
82 Brian Bellows .30 .75
83 Dominic Moore .25 .60
84 Sidney Crosby 1.50 4.00
85 Zach Parise .40 1.00
86 Chris Chelios .40 1.00
87 Adam Oates .40 1.00
88 Brett Hull .40 1.00
89 Wayne Gretzky 2.00 5.00
90 Milan Hejduk .30 .75
91 Drew Doughty .40 1.00
92 Denis Savard .50 1.25
93 Andrei Markov .40 1.00
94 Alex Galchenyuk .60 1.50
95 Pekka Rinne .50 1.25
96 Derek Stepan .40 1.00
97 Alex Tanguay .25 .60
98 Kyle Clifford .25 .60
99 Mike Smith .40 1.00
100 Mike Richards .40 1.00
101 Halmo/Persson/Gallant RC 1.50 4.00
102 A.Frsbrg/Hmnd/Grsnck RC 6.00 15.00
103 Lindbhm/Davdsn/Jokpka RC 2.00 5.00
104 Everberg/Agozzino/Carey RC 2.00 5.00
105 Uher/Rust/Farnham RC 1.50 4.00
106 Makarov/Knapp/Lieuwen RC 2.00 5.00
107 Paqtte/Gudlvsk/Kunyk RC 2.00 5.00
108 Sutter/Shinnimin/Varone RC 1.50 4.00
109 Payrl/Whtny/Pkarin RC 1.50 4.00
110 Agsti/Ferland/Van Brbt RC 2.50 6.00
111 B.Robins/M.Lindblad RC 1.50 4.00
112 S.Darling/M.Carey RC 5.00 12.00
113 S.Moser/M.Van Guilder RC 1.25 3.00
114 C.Wagner/J.Manson RC 2.00 5.00
115 M.Friberg/J.Armia RC 2.00 5.00
116 T.Graovac/T.Gaudet RC 1.50 4.00
117 S.Mayfield/K.Czuczman RC 1.50 4.00
118 B.Woods/J.Shugg RC 1.25 3.00
119 L.Ferraro/M.Callahan RC 1.25 3.00
120 J.Racine/G.Wilson RC 2.00 5.00
121 J.Johnson/J.Sundstrom RC 2.00 5.00
122 B.Rendulic/C.Smith RC 2.00 5.00
123 C.Gibson/R.Zepp RC 3.00 8.00
124 M.Zalewski/B.Defazio RC 1.50 4.00
125 P.Granberg/S.Carrick RC 2.00 5.00
126 Justin Hodgman AU/149 RC 3.00 8.00
127 S.Harrington AU/149 RC 4.00 10.00
128 Phillip Danault AU/149 RC 4.00 10.00
129 B.Goodrow AU/149 RC 4.00 10.00
130 Seth Helgeson AU/149 RC 3.00 8.00
131 John Klingberg AU/149 RC 12.00 30.00
132 Melker Karlsson AU/149 RC 4.00 10.00
133 Josh Jooris AU/149 RC 4.00 10.00
134 Joe Morrow AU/149 RC 5.00 12.00
135 Brett Ritchie AU/149 RC 4.00 10.00
136 Rocco Grimaldi AU/149 RC 4.00 10.00
137 T.van Riemsdyk AU/149 RC 6.00 15.00
138 Tobias Rieder AU/149 RC 4.00 10.00
139 S.Andrighetto AU/149 RC 5.00 12.00
140 Andrej Nestrasil AU/149 RC 4.00 10.00
151 K.Rychel JSY AU/375 RC 4.00 10.00
152 D.Severson JSY AU/375 RC 5.00 12.00
153 N.Deslauriers JSY AU/175 RC 6.00 15.00
154 C.Knight JSY AU/175 RC 6.00 15.00
155 Patrick Brown JSY AU/175 RC 6.00 15.00
156 Marko Dano JSY AU/375 RC 5.00 12.00
157 A.Vasilevskiy JSY AU/375 RC 15.00 40.00
158 Brandon Gormley JSY AU/375 RC 5.00 12.00
159 V.Trocheck JSY AU/175 RC 8.00 20.00
160 William Karlsson JSY AU/375 RC 20.00 50.00
161 Joonas Nattinen JSY AU/175 RC 6.00 15.00
162 J.Binnington JSY AU/375 RC 5.00 12.00
163 Greg McKegg JSY AU/175 RC 5.00 12.00
164 Curtis McKenzie JSY AU/175 RC 5.00 12.00
165 G.Reinhart JSY AU/175 RC 8.00 20.00
166 M.Granlund JSY AU/175 RC 10.00 25.00
167 Adam Lowry JSY AU/375 RC 6.00 15.00
168 A.Clendening JSY AU/375 RC 5.00 12.00
169 Dennis Everberg JSY AU/375 RC 5.00 12.00
170 K.Hayes JSY AU/175 RC 20.00 50.00
171 V.Namestnikov JSY AU/375 RC 8.00 20.00
172 M.Mueller JSY AU/375 RC 5.00 12.00
173 Ty Rattie JSY AU/175 RC 8.00 20.00
174 Wotherspoon JSY AU/175 RC 6.00 15.00
175 L.Brossoit JSY AU/175 RC 6.00 15.00
176 A.Andreoff JSY AU/175 RC EX 6.00 15.00
177 C.Sissons JSY AU/175 RC 8.00 20.00
178 Joey Hishon JSY AU/375 RC 6.00 15.00
179 D.Nurse JSY AU/375 RC 15.00 40.00
180 Jiri Sekac JSY AU/375 RC 5.00 12.00
181 S.Gostisbehere JSY AU/375 RC 20.00 50.00
182 Jake McCabe JSY AU/175 RC 6.00 15.00
183 B.Yakimov JSY AU/175 RC 6.00 15.00
184 Ryan Sproul JSY AU/375 RC 5.00 12.00
185 Derrick Pouliot JSY AU/375 RC 6.00 15.00
186 Oscar Klefbom JSY AU/175 RC 12.00 30.00
187 D.Pastrnak JSY AU/175 RC EX 50.00 125.00
188 Khokhlachev JSY AU/375 RC 5.00 12.00
189 T.Teravainen JSY AU/375 RC 8.00 20.00
190 T.Pulkkinen JSY AU/375 RC 6.00 15.00
191 Liam O'Brien JSY AU/375 RC 6.00 15.00
192 P.Nemeth JSY AU/375 RC 5.00 12.00
193 C.Tierney JSY AU/375 RC 5.00 12.00
194 A.Wennberg JSY AU/175 RC 12.00 30.00
195 Curtis Lazar JSY AU/375 RC 6.00 15.00
196 Victor Rask JSY AU/175 RC 6.00 15.00
197 M.Visentin JSY AU/375 RC 5.00 12.00
198 Stuart Percy JSY AU/375 RC 5.00 12.00
199 C.Jarnkrok JSY AU/175 RC 6.00 15.00
200 Seth Griffith JSY AU/375 RC 6.00 15.00
201 S.Reinhart JSY AU/175 RC 20.00 50.00
202 J.Gaudreau JSY AU/175 RC 40.00 100.00
203 L.Draisaitl JSY AU/175 RC 60.00 150.00
204 A.Ekblad JSY AU/175 RC 25.00 60.00
205 Jori Lehtera JSY AU/375 RC 8.00 20.00
206 A.Burakovsky JSY AU/175 RC 15.00 40.00
207 Bo Horvat JSY AU/175 RC 20.00 50.00
208 E.Kuznetsov JSY AU/175 RC 25.00 60.00
209 A.Duclair JSY AU/175 RC EX 10.00 25.00
210 Drouin JSY AU/175 RC EXCH 25.00 60.00

2014-15 Fleer Showcase Red Glow

*101-125 ROOK/27: 1X TO 2.5X RC/299-399
*126-140 ROOK.AU/27: .6X TO 1.5X RC/149
*151-210 ROOK.JSY AU/18-27: .8X TO 2X
1 Cam Ward JSY 5.00 12.00
3 Jari Kurri JSY 5.00 12.00
4 Adam Henrique JSY 5.00 12.00
5 Sean Couturier JSY 5.00 12.00
6 Jonathan Toews JSY 10.00 25.00
7 Cory Schneider JSY 4.00 10.00
8 Darcy Kuemper JSY 4.00 10.00
9 Gabriel Landeskog JSY 4.00 10.00
10 Max Pacioretty JSY 5.00 12.00
11 Ondrej Pavelec JSY 5.00 12.00
12 Ryan Miller JSY 5.00 12.00
13 Taylor Hall JSY 10.00 25.00
14 Matt Duchene JSY 5.00 12.00
15 Tuukka Rask JSY 5.00 12.00
16 T.J. Oshie JSY 8.00 20.00
17 Dustin Brown JSY 4.00 10.00
18 Chris Osgood JSY 5.00 12.00
19 Ryan Johansen JSY 6.00 15.00
20 Brendan Gallagher JSY 5.00 12.00
21 Pavel Datsyuk JSY 6.00 15.00
22 Brett Hull JSY 5.00 12.00
23 Steven Stamkos JSY 10.00 25.00
24 Shea Weber JSY 4.00 10.00
25 Glen Murray JSY 4.00 10.00
26 Braden Holtby JSY 8.00 20.00
27 Lars Eller JSY 4.00 10.00
29 Curtis Joseph JSY 5.00 12.00
31 P.K. Subban JSY 8.00 20.00
32 Patrick Marleau JSY 5.00 12.00
33 Nail Yakupov JSY 4.00 10.00
34 Patrick Sharp JSY 5.00 12.00
35 Zdeno Chara JSY 5.00 12.00
36 John Tavares JSY 10.00 25.00
37 Ed Belfour JSY 5.00 12.00
38 Bobby Hull JSY 5.00 12.00
39 Wayne Simmonds JSY 6.00 15.00
40 Semyon Varlamov JSY 5.00 12.00
41 Nathan MacKinnon JSY 10.00 25.00
42 Roberto Luongo JSY 5.00 12.00
43 Dale Hawerchuk JSY 6.00 15.00
44 Dominik Hasek JSY 6.00 15.00
45 Tyler Seguin JSY 8.00 20.00
46 Steve Mason JSY 4.00 10.00
47 Antti Niemi JSY 4.00 10.00
48 Ryan Getzlaf JSY 8.00 20.00
49 Jaromir Jagr JSY 12.00 30.00
50 Zack Kassian JSY 4.00 10.00
51 Evander Kane JSY 5.00 12.00
52 Karri Ramo JSY 4.00 10.00
53 Claude Giroux JSY 5.00 12.00
54 Carey Price JSY 15.00 30.00
55 Eric Staal JSY 6.00 15.00
56 Johan Franzen JSY 5.00 12.00
57 Kris Letang JSY 5.00 12.00
58 Alexandre Burrows JSY 5.00 12.00
59 Phil Kessel JSY 6.00 15.00
60 Jonathan Bernier JSY 5.00 12.00
61 Jake Muzzin JSY 3.00 8.00
62 Jonathan Quick JSY 8.00 20.00
63 Mark Messier JSY 5.00 12.00
64 Matt Moulson JSY 4.00 10.00
65 Corey Crawford JSY 6.00 15.00
66 Jeremy Roenick JSY 5.00 12.00
67 Henrik Zetterberg JSY 6.00 15.00
68 Mats Zuccarello JSY 5.00 12.00
69 Duncan Keith JSY 5.00 12.00
70 Sean Monahan JSY 5.00 12.00
71 Pete Peeters JSY 4.00 10.00
72 Cam Fowler JSY 4.00 10.00
73 Marc-Andre Fleury JSY 8.00 20.00
74 R.J. Umberger JSY 3.00 8.00
75 Ryan Nugent-Hopkins JSY 5.00 12.00
76 Shane Doan JSY 4.00 10.00
77 Joe Thornton JSY 5.00 12.0
78 Alexander Ovechkin JSY 20.00 50.0
79 Steve Yzerman JSY 15.00 30.0
80 Anze Kopitar JSY 8.00 20.0
81 David Backes JSY 5.00 12.0
82 Brian Bellows JSY 4.00 10.0
83 Dominic Moore JSY 3.00 8.0
84 Sidney Crosby JSY 20.00 50.0
86 Chris Chelios JSY 5.00 12.0
87 Adam Oates JSY 8.00 20.0
88 Brett Hull JSY 5.00 12.0
89 Wayne Gretzky JSY 20.00 40.0
90 Milan Hejduk JSY 4.00 10.0
91 Drew Doughty JSY 5.00 12.0
92 Denis Savard JSY 6.00 15.0
94 Alex Galchenyuk JSY 8.00 20.0
95 Pekka Rinne JSY 6.00 15.0
96 Derek Stepan JSY 5.00 12.0
99 Mike Smith JSY 5.00 12.0
100 Mike Richards JSY 5.00 12.0
187 David Pastrnak FS AU/18
202 Johnny Gaudreau GLV AU/18 100.00 175.0
204 Aaron Ekblad GLV AU/18 75.00 150.0
210 Jonathan Drouin GLV AU/18 40.00 100.0

2014-15 Fleer Showcase Flair

ROW 2 STATED ODDS 1:8 HOBBY
ROW 1 STATED ODDS 1:25 HOBBY
ROW 0 STATED ODDS 1:25 HOBBY
*BLUE ICE/99: 1X TO 2.5X FLAIR R2
*BLUE ICE/99: .6X TO 1.5X FLAIR R1-R0
1 Marian Hossa R2 1.00 2.5
2 Braden Holtby R2 2.00 5.0
3 Alex Pietrangelo R2 1.00 2.5
4 Alex Galchenyuk R2 2.00 5.0
5 David Clarkson R2 .75 2.0
6 Corey Perry R2 1.25 3.0
7 Shane Doan R2 1.00 2.5
8 Nail Yakupov R2 1.00 2.5
9 Mats Zuccarello R2 1.25 3.0
10 David Backes R2 1.25 3.0
11 Kris Letang R2 1.25 3.0
12 Dougie Hamilton R2 1.25 3.0
13 Derek Stepan R2 1.25 3.0
14 Dany Heatley R2 1.00 2.5
15 Darcy Kuemper R2 1.00 2.5
16 Drew Doughty R2 1.25 3.0
17 Brendan Gallagher R2 1.25 3.0
18 Karri Ramo R2 1.00 2.5
19 Patrick Marleau R2 1.25 3.0
20 R.J. Umberger R2 .75 2.0
21 Matt Moulson R2 1.00 2.5
22 Milan Hejduk R2 1.00 2.5
23 Matt Duchene R2 1.25 3.0
24 Lars Eller R2 1.00 2.5
25 Max Pacioretty R2 1.25 3.0
26 Mike Richards R2 1.25 3.0
27 Ryan McDonagh R2 1.25 3.0
28 Marc-Andre Fleury R2 2.00 5.0
29 Semyon Varlamov R2 1.25 3.0
30 Cory Schneider R2 1.00 2.5
31 Anze Kopitar R1 3.00 8.0
32 Jonathan Quick R1 3.00 8.0
33 Joe Thornton R1 2.00 5.0
34 Phil Kessel R1 2.50 6.0
35 Evgeni Malkin R1 6.00 15.0
36 Jamie Benn R1 2.50 6.0
37 P.K. Subban R1 3.00 8.0
38 Sidney Crosby R1 8.00 20.0
39 Henrik Zetterberg R1 2.50 6.0
40 John Tavares R1 4.00 10.0
41 Teemu Selanne R1 4.00 10.0
42 Brett Hull R1 2.00 5.0
43 Jean Beliveau R1 2.00 5.0
44 Mark Messier R1 2.00 5.0
45 Nicklas Lidstrom R1 2.00 5.0
46 Mats Sundin R1 2.00 5.0
47 Joe Sakic R1 3.00 8.0
48 Rob Blake R1 2.00 5.0
49 Patrick Roy R1 5.00 12.0
50 Steve Yzerman R1 4.00 10.0
51 Victor Rask R0 2.00 5.0
52 Evgeny Kuznetsov R0 8.00 20.0
53 Teuvo Teravainen R0 3.00 8.0
54 Aaron Ekblad R0 8.00 20.0
55 Jiri Sekac R0 2.00 5.0
56 Andrei Vasilevskiy R0 6.00 15.0
57 Jonathan Drouin R0 5.00 12.0
58 Curtis Lazar R0 2.50 6.0
59 Darnell Nurse R0 6.00 15.0
60 Andre Burakovsky R0 3.00 8.0
61 Kevin Hayes R0 6.00 15.0
62 Anthony Duclair R0 3.00 8.0
63 David Pastrnak R0 8.00 20.0
64 Griffin Reinhart R0 2.50 6.0
65 Jori Lehtera R0 2.50 6.0
66 Sam Reinhart R0 6.00 15.0
67 Johnny Gaudreau R0 6.00 15.0
68 Alexander Wennberg R0 4.00 10.0
69 Leon Draisaitl R0 10.00 25.0
70 Damon Severson R0 2.00 5.0

2014-15 Fleer Showcase Flair Hot Gloves

STATED ODDS 1:240 HOBBY
1 Ben Bishop 12.00 30.0
2 Corey Crawford 15.00 40.0
3 Tuukka Rask 12.00 30.0
4 Cory Schneider 10.00 25.0
5 Curtis Joseph 12.00 30.0
6 Ed Belfour 12.00 30.0
7 Jonathan Bernier
8 Kari Lehtonen 10.00 25.0
9 Dominik Hasek 15.00 40.0
10 Patrick Roy 40.00 80.0
11 Steve Mason 10.00 25.0
12 Pekka Rinne 15.00 40.0
13 Sergei Bobrovsky 12.00 30.0
14 Marc-Andre Fleury 20.00 50.0
15 Carey Price 25.00 50.0
16 Tony Esposito 12.00 30.0
17 Semyon Varlamov 12.00 30.0
18 Henrik Lundqvist 15.00 40.0
19 Antti Niemi
20 Jonathan Quick 20.00 50.0

2014-15 Fleer Showcase Flair Jerseys

1 Marian Hossa R2 2.00 5.
2 Braden Holtby R2 4.00 10.
3 Alex Pietrangelo R2 2.00 5.
4 Alex Galchenyuk R2 4.00 10.
5 David Clarkson R2 1.50 4.
6 Corey Perry R2 2.50 6.
7 Shane Doan R2 2.00 5.
8 Nail Yakupov R2 2.00 5.
9 Mats Zuccarello R2 2.50 6.
10 David Backes R2 2.50 6.
12 Dougie Hamilton R2 2.50 6.
13 Derek Stepan R2 2.50 6.
14 Dany Heatley R2 2.00 5.
15 Darcy Kuemper R2 2.00 5.

Drew Doughty R2 2.50 6.00
Brendan Gallagher R2 2.50 6.00
Karri Ramo R2 2.00 5.00
Patrick Marleau R2 2.50 6.00
R.J. Umberger R2 1.50 4.00
Matt Moulson R2 2.00 5.00
Milan Hejduk R2 2.00 5.00
Matt Duchene R2 2.50 6.00
Lars Eller R2 2.00 5.00
Max Pacioretty R2 2.50 6.00
Mike Richards R2 2.50 6.00
Ryan McDonagh R2 2.50 6.00
Marc-Andre Fleury R2 4.00 10.00
Semyon Varlamov R2 2.50 6.00
Anze Kopitar R1 6.00 15.00
Jonathan Quick R1 6.00 15.00
Joe Thornton R1 4.00 10.00
Phil Kessel R1 5.00 12.00
Evgeni Malkin R1 12.00 30.00
Jamie Benn R1 5.00 12.00
P.K. Subban R1 6.00 15.00
Sidney Crosby R1 15.00 40.00
Henrik Zetterberg R1 5.00 12.00
John Tavares R1 8.00 20.00
Teemu Selanne R1 8.00 20.00
Brett Hull R1 4.00 10.00
Mark Messier R1 4.00 10.00
Nicklas Lidstrom R1 4.00 10.00
Joe Sakic R1 6.00 15.00
Rob Blake R1 4.00 10.00
Patrick Roy R1 10.00 25.00
Steve Yzerman R1 8.00 20.00
Evgeny Kuznetsov R0 10.00 25.00
Teuvo Teravainen R0 4.00 10.00
Aaron Ekblad R1 4.00 10.00
Jiri Sekac R1 2.50 6.00
Andrei Vasilevskiy R0 8.00 20.00
Jonathan Drouin R0 6.00 15.00
Curtis Lazar R0 3.00 8.00
Darnell Nurse R0 8.00 20.00
Andre Burakovsky R0 4.00 10.00
Griffin Reinhart R0 3.00 8.00
Jori Lehtera R0 3.00 8.00
Sam Reinhart R0 8.00 20.00
Johnny Gaudreau R0 8.00 20.00
Alexander Wennberg R0 5.00 12.00
Leon Draisaitl R0 12.00 30.00
Damon Severson R0 2.50 6.00

2014-15 Fleer Showcase Flair Memorabilia Prime

50 UNPRICED VET PRINT RUN 10
-70 ROOKIE PRINT RUN 49
CH EXPIRATION: 2/16/2017
Teuvo Teravainen AU R0 25.00 60.00
Aaron Ekblad AU R0 30.00 60.00
Jiri Sekac AU R0 10.00 25.00
Andrei Vasilevskiy AU R0 30.00 80.00
Jonathan Drouin AU R0 EXCH 40.00 80.00
Curtis Lazar AU R0 12.00 30.00
Darnell Nurse AU R0 30.00 80.00
Andre Burakovsky AU R0 15.00 40.00
Griffin Reinhart AU R0 10.00 25.00
Jori Lehtera AU R0 12.00 30.00
Sam Reinhart AU R0 30.00 60.00
Johnny Gaudreau AU R0 60.00 120.00
Leon Draisaitl AU R0 50.00 120.00
Damon Severson AU R0 10.00 25.00

2014-15 Fleer Showcase Flair Wave of the Future

aron Ekblad 25.00 50.00
am Reinhart 12.00 30.00
riffin Reinhart 5.00 12.00
arnell Nurse 12.00 30.00
dam Lowry 4.00 10.00
hris Tierney 4.00 10.00
urtis Lazar 5.00 12.00
amon Severson 4.00 10.00
ohnny Gaudreau 20.00 40.00
William Karlsson 15.00 40.00
Jiri Sekac 4.00 10.00
Victor Rask 4.00 10.00
Calle Jarnkrok 4.00 10.00
Andre Burakovsky 6.00 15.00
Anthony Duclair 6.00 15.00
Evgeny Kuznetsov 15.00 40.00
Teuvo Teravainen 20.00 40.00
Stuart Percy 4.00 10.00
Leon Draisaitl 20.00 50.00
Alexander Wennberg 8.00 20.00

2014-15 Fleer Showcase Metal Universe

ATED ODDS 1:3 HOBBY
teven Stamkos 1.25 3.00
lexander Ovechkin 2.50 6.00
Vayne Gretzky 2.50 6.00
laude Giroux .60 1.50
ohn Tavares 1.25 3.00
Mario Lemieux 2.50 6.00
yan Getzlaf 1.00 2.50
idney Crosby 2.50 6.00
teve Yzerman 2.50 6.00
Evgeni Malkin 2.00 5.00
Jonathan Toews 1.25 3.00
Tuukka Rask .60 1.50
Patrick Roy 2.00 5.00
Pavel Datsyuk .75 2.00
Tyler Seguin 1.00 2.50
P.K. Subban 1.00 2.50
Anze Kopitar 1.00 2.50
Patrick Kane 1.25 3.00
Phil Kessel 1.00 2.50
Bobby Hull .75 2.00
Taylor Hall 1.25 3.00
Teuvo Teravainen 1.00 2.50
Anthony Duclair 1.00 2.50
Jori Lehtera .75 2.00
David Pastrnak 2.50 6.00
Aaron Ekblad 2.50 6.00
Andre Burakovsky 1.00 2.50
Bo Horvat 2.00 5.00
Damon Severson .60 1.50
Evgeny Kuznetsov 2.50 6.00
Leon Draisaitl 3.00 8.00
Jiri Sekac .60 1.50
Sam Reinhart 2.00 5.00
Vladislav Namestnikov 1.00 2.50
Stuart Percy .60 1.50
Sven Andrighetto .75 2.00
Griffin Reinhart .75 2.00
Curtis Lazar .75 2.00
Alexander Wennberg 1.25 3.00
Ryan Sproul .60 1.50
Johnny Gaudreau 2.00 5.00
Jonathan Drouin 1.50 4.00

2014-15 Fleer Showcase Metal Universe Precious Metal Gems Blue

UE/25*: 3X TO 8X BASIC INSERTS
3 Wayne Gretzky 40.00 80.00
8 Sidney Crosby 12.00 30.00

2014-15 Fleer Showcase Metal Universe Precious Metal Gems Red

RED/65: 1.2X TO 3X BASIC INSERTS
3 Wayne Gretzky 25.00 50.00
8 Sidney Crosby 12.00 30.00
25 David Pastrnak 12.00 30.00
26 Aaron Ekblad 10.00 25.00
41 Johnny Gaudreau 10.00 25.00

2014-15 Fleer Showcase SkyBox Premium

1 Patrice Bergeron 2.00 5.00
2 Anze Kopitar 2.50 6.00
3 Jonathan Bernier 1.50 4.00
4 Brett Hull 1.50 4.00
5 Alexander Ovechkin 6.00 15.00
6 Evgeni Malkin 5.00 12.00
7 Pekka Rinne 2.00 5.00
8 Jordan Eberle 1.50 4.00
9 Ryan Getzlaf 2.50 6.00
10 Vladimir Tarasenko 2.50 6.00
11 Tyler Seguin 2.50 6.00
12 Henrik Sedin 1.50 4.00
13 P.K. Subban 2.50 6.00
14 Nathan MacKinnon 3.00 8.00
15 Thomas Vanek 1.50 4.00
16 Jamie Benn 2.00 5.00
17 Steven Stamkos 3.00 8.00
18 Filip Forsberg 2.00 5.00
19 Sergei Bobrovsky 1.50 4.00
20 John Tavares 3.00 8.00
21 Chris Chelios 1.50 4.00
22 Felix Potvin 2.50 6.00
23 Patrick Kane 3.00 8.00
24 Rick Nash 1.50 4.00
25 Claude Giroux 1.50 4.00
26 Henrik Zetterberg 2.00 5.00
27 Sidney Crosby 6.00 15.00
28 Wayne Gretzky 8.00 20.00
29 Jonathan Toews 3.00 8.00
30 Jaromir Jagr 4.00 10.00
31 Martin Brodeur 3.00 8.00
32 Tuukka Rask 1.50 4.00
33 Taylor Hall 3.00 8.00
34 Ryan Miller 1.50 4.00
35 Jakub Voracek 1.50 4.00
36 Damon Severson 1.50 4.00
37 Andre Burakovsky 2.50 6.00
38 Stuart Percy 1.50 4.00
39 Sam Reinhart 5.00 12.00
40 Curtis Lazar 2.00 5.00
41 Bo Horvat 5.00 12.00
42 Teuvo Teravainen 2.50 6.00
43 David Pastrnak 6.00 15.00
44 Leon Draisaitl 8.00 20.00
45 Aaron Ekblad 6.00 15.00
46 Shayne Gostisbehere 6.00 15.00
47 Anthony Duclair 2.50 6.00
48 Adam Clendening 1.50 4.00
49 Victor Rask 1.50 4.00
50 Evgeny Kuznetsov 6.00 15.00
51 Griffin Reinhart 2.00 5.00
52 Jonathan Drouin 4.00 10.00
53 Jiri Sekac 1.50 4.00
54 Johnny Gaudreau 5.00 12.00
55 Alexander Wennberg 3.00 8.00
56 Kerby Rychel 1.25 3.00
57 Josh Jooris 1.50 4.00
58 Jori Lehtera 2.00 5.00
59 Tobias Rieder 1.50 4.00
60 Colin Smith 1.50 4.00

2014-15 Fleer Showcase SkyBox Premium Star Rubies

*RUBIES: .8X TO 2X BASIC INSERTS
22 Felix Potvin 8.00 20.00
28 Wayne Gretzky 25.00 50.00
31 Martin Brodeur 15.00 30.00

2015-16 Fleer Showcase

EXCH EXPIRATION 3/14/2018
1 Steven Stamkos .75 2.00
2 P.K. Subban .60 1.50
3 Ryan Getzlaf .60 1.50
4 Daniel Sedin .40 1.00
5 Alexander Ovechkin 1.50 4.00
6 Sam Gagner .30 .75
7 Henrik Zetterberg .50 1.25
8 Jonathan Bernier .40 1.00
9 Anze Kopitar .60 1.50
10 Rick Nash .40 1.00
11 Jordan Eberle .40 1.00
12 Evgeni Malkin 1.25 3.00
13 Corey Crawford .50 1.25
14 Jiri Hudler .30 .75
15 John Tavares .75 2.00
16 Joe Thornton .40 1.00
17 Patrice Bergeron .50 1.25
18 Bobby Ryan .30 .75
19 Claude Giroux .40 1.00
20 Vladimir Tarasenko .60 1.50
21 Tyler Ennis .30 .75
22 Andrew Ladd .40 1.00
23 Tyler Johnson .30 .75
24 Eric Staal .50 1.25
25 Tyler Seguin .60 1.50
26 Gabriel Landeskog .40 1.00
27 Filip Forsberg .50 1.25
28 Kris Letang .40 1.00
29 John Carlson .50 1.25
30 Max Pacioretty .40 1.00
31 Jonathan Quick .60 1.50
32 Nick Foligno .30 .75
33 Nazem Kadri .30 .75
34 Johnny Gaudreau .60 1.50
35 Joe Pavelski .40 1.00
36 Justin Faulk .40 1.00
37 Jonathan Toews .75 2.00
38 Oliver Ekman-Larsson .30 .75
39 Brock Nelson .30 .75
40 Derek Stepan .40 1.00
41 Logan Couture .40 1.00
42 Henrik Sedin .40 1.00
43 Zemgus Girgensons .30 .75
44 Jaromir Jagr 1.00 2.50
45 Ryan Kesler .40 1.00
46 Jarome Iginla .40 1.00
47 Loui Eriksson .30 .75
48 Braden Holtby .60 1.50
49 Taylor Hall .75 2.00
50 Sidney Crosby 1.50 4.00
51 Carey Price 1.25 3.00
52 Ondrej Palat .30 .75
53 Marian Hossa .30 .75
54 Jeff Skinner .30 .75
55 Jakub Voracek .40 1.00
56 Mark Stone .30 .75
57 Alexander Steen .40 1.00
58 Pavel Datsyuk .50 1.25
59 Ryan Suter .25 .60
60 Sean Monahan .40 1.00
61 Brendan Gallagher .50 1.25
62 Jeff Carter .40 1.00
63 Jaroslav Halak .30 .75
64 Patrick Kane .75 2.00
65 Corey Perry .40 1.00
66 Patrik Elias .40 1.00
67 James van Riemsdyk .40 1.00
68 David Backes .40 1.00
69 Ben Bishop .40 1.00
70 Matt Duchene .40 1.00
71 Henrik Lundqvist .50 1.25
72 Matt Moulson .30 .75
73 Pekka Rinne .50 1.25
74 Ryan Johansen .50 1.25
75 Shane Doan .30 .75
76 Zach Parise .40 1.00
77 Patric Hornqvist .30 .75
78 Erik Karlsson .75 2.00
79 Kyle Okposo .40 1.00
80 Brad Marchand .50 1.25
81 Jamie Benn .50 1.25
82 Mark Giordano .40 1.00
83 Ryan Nugent-Hopkins .40 1.00
84 Shea Weber .30 .75
85 Nikita Kucherov .60 1.50
86 Gustav Nyquist .40 1.00
87 Nathan MacKinnon .75 2.00
88 Jonathan Huberdeau .40 1.00
89 Adam Henrique .40 1.00
90 Dustin Byfuglien .40 1.00
91 Peter Forsberg .40 1.00
92 Bobby Hull .40 1.00
93 Ray Bourque .60 1.50
94 Mark Messier .60 1.50
95 Theoren Fleury .50 1.25
96 Steve Yzerman .60 1.50
97 Bobby Clarke .40 1.00
98 Guy Lafleur .50 1.25
99 Wayne Gretzky 2.00 5.00
100 Johnny Bucyk .30 .75
101 Korpisalo RC/Dansk RC 4.00 10.00
Hannikainen RC
102 O'Neill RC/Blandisi RC 3.00 8.00
Hrabarenka RC
103 Biega RC/Rissanen RC/Slavin RC 2.50 6.00
104 Mersch RC/Skjei RC/Shore RC 3.00 8.00
105 Alt RC/Straka RC/Medvedev RC 2.50 6.00
106 Biega RC/Grenier RC/Pedan RC 4.00 10.00
107 Pesce RC/Olofsson RC/Carr RC 3.00 8.00
108 Musil RC/Kulak RC/Oesterle RC 2.50 6.00
109 Murray RC/Hellebuyck RC/Berube RC 15.0040.00
110 Carpenter RC/Dzingel RC 3.00 8.00
Di Giuseppe RC
111 Ranford RC/Holloway RC 3.00 8.00
Mouillierat RC
112 Martinsen RC/Thompson RC 4.00 10.00
Nosek RC
113 Hamilton RC/Khaira RC/Miller RC 3.00 8.00
114 Ferlin RC/Randell RC/Cross RC 3.00 8.00
115 Domingue RC/Dauphin RC 4.00 10.00
Langhamer RC
116 A.Bitetto RC/J.Saros RC 4.00 10.00
117 T.Kero RC/E.Gustafsson RC 5.00 12.00
118 R.Bourque RC/C.Sheary RC 10.00 25.00
119 B.Lerg RC/D.Tarasov RC 2.50 6.00
120 B.Froese RC/C.Bailey RC 3.00 8.00
121 L.Shaw RC/Y.Gourde RC 6.00 15.00
122 K.Gabriel RC/M.Keranen RC 2.50 6.00
123 C.Wideman RC/M.McCormick RC 3.00 8.00
124 D.Rasmussen RC/F.Claesson RC 4.00 10.00
125 J.Vermin RC/L.Witkowski RC 2.50 6.00
126 Adam Pelech AU RC 5.00 12.00
127 Linus Ullmark AU RC 8.00 20.00
128 Frank Vatrano AU RC 12.00 30.00
129 Garret Sparks AU RC 8.00 20.00
130 Joel Edmundson AU RC 5.00 12.00
131 Shea Theodore AU RC 6.00 15.00
132 Charles Hudon AU RC 6.00 15.00
133 Keegan Lowe AU RC 6.00 15.00
134 Devin Shore AU RC 6.00 15.00
135 Taylor Leier AU RC 6.00 15.00
136 Mike McCarron AU RC 8.00 20.00
137 Christoph Bertschy AU RC 5.00 12.00
138 Chris Driedger AU RC 5.00 12.00
139 Anton Slepyshev AU RC 5.00 12.00
140 Dylan DeMelo AU RC 5.00 12.00
141 Viktor Arvidsson JSY AU/499 RC 8.00 20.00
142 Colton Parayko JSY AU/499 RC 8.00 20.00
143 Matt O'Connor JSY AU/499 RC 5.00 12.00
144 Nikolay Goldobin JSY AU/499 RC 6.00 15.00
145 Mattias Janmark JSY AU/499 RC 6.00 15.00
146 Oscar Lindberg JSY AU/499 RC 6.00 15.00
147 Sergei Kalinin JSY AU/499 RC 5.00 12.00
148 Jordan Weal JSY AU/499 RC 6.00 15.00
149 Daniel Sprong JSY AU/499 RC 12.00 30.00
150 Stefan Noesen JSY AU/499 RC 5.00 12.00
151 Joonas Donskoi JSY AU/499 RC 6.00 15.00
152 Malcolm Subban JSY AU/499 RC 15.00 40.00
153 Kevin Fiala JSY AU/499 RC 6.00 15.00
154 Shane Prince JSY AU/499 RC 5.00 12.00
155 Andrew Copp JSY AU/499 RC 6.00 15.00
156 Emile Poirier JSY AU/499 RC 6.00 15.00
157 Jared McCann JSY AU/499 RC 6.00 15.00
158 Ben Hutton JSY AU/499 RC 6.00 15.00
159 Mike Condon JSY AU/499 RC 6.00 15.00
160 Colin Miller JSY AU/499 RC 5.00 12.00
161 Henrik Samuelsson JSY AU/499 RC 5.00 12.00
162 Anthony Stolarz JSY AU/499 RC 6.00 15.00
163 Jacob de la Rose JSY AU/499 RC 6.00 15.00
164 Ronalds Kenins JSY AU/499 RC 6.00 15.00
165 Antoine Bibeau JSY AU/499 RC 6.00 15.00
166 Slater Koekkoek JSY AU/499 RC 5.00 12.00
167 Matt Puempel JSY AU/499 RC 5.00 12.00
168 Nick Cousins JSY AU/499 RC 6.00 15.00
169 Brock McGinn JSY AU/499 RC 6.00 15.00
170 Derek Forbort JSY AU/499 RC 5.00 12.00
171 Mackenzie Skapski JSY AU/499 RC 6.00 15.00
172 Ryan Hartman JSY AU/499 RC 8.00 20.00
173 Radek Faksa JSY AU/499 RC 6.00 15.00
174 Kyle Baun JSY AU/499 RC 6.00 15.00
175 Brendan Gaunce JSY AU/499 RC 8.00 20.00
176 Joonas Kemppainen JSY AU/499 RC 5.00 12.00
177 Josh Anderson JSY AU/499 RC 6.00 15.00
178 Hunter Shinkaruk JSY AU/499 RC 6.00 15.00
179 Sam Brittain JSY AU/499 RC 6.00 15.00
180 Sergei Plotnikov JSY AU/499 RC 5.00 12.00
181 Stanislav Galiev JSY AU/499 RC 6.00 15.00
182 Viktor Svedberg JSY AU/499 RC 5.00 12.00
183 Vincent Hinostroza JSY AU/499 RC 4.00 10.00
184 Chandler Stephenson JSY AU 6.00 15.00
499 RC
185 Connor Brickley JSY AU/499 RC 5.00 12.00
186 Zachary Fucale JSY AU/499 RC 6.00 15.00
187 Mikko Rantanen JSY AU/499 RC 12.00 30.00
188 Andreas Athanasiou JSY AU/499 RC 15.00 40.00
189 Connor McDavid JSY AU/299 RC 250.00 400.00
190 Dylan Larkin JSY AU/299 RC 60.00 120.00
191 Noah Hanifin JSY AU/299 RC 12.00 30.00
192 Artemi Panarin JSY AU/299 RC 60.00 120.00
193 Jake Virtanen JSY AU/299 RC 12.00 30.00
194 Robby Fabbri JSY AU/299 RC 12.00 30.00
195 Nikolaj Ehlers JSY AU/299 RC 20.00 50.00
196 Max Domi JSY AU/299 RC 20.00 50.00
197 Nicolas Petan JSY AU/299 RC 10.00 25.00
198 Sam Bennett JSY AU/299 RC 12.00 30.00
199 Nick Ritchie JSY AU/299 RC 10.00 25.00
200 Jack Eichel JSY RC 40.00 100.00

2015-16 Fleer Showcase Red Glow

109 Matt Murray 60.00 120.00
Connor Hellebuyck
Jean-Francois Berube
172 Ryan Hartman GLV AU 12.00 30.00

2015-16 Fleer Showcase Flair

ROW 1 STATED ODDS 1:6 HOBBY
ROW 0 STATED ODDS 1:13 HOBBY
*BLUE ICE/99: 1X TO 2.5X FLAIR R1
*BIUE ICE/199: .75X TO 2X FLAIR R0
1 Sidney Crosby R1 6.00 15.00
2 Corey Perry R1 1.50 4.00
3 Pekka Rinne R1 2.00 5.00
4 Blake Wheeler R1 1.50 4.00
5 Alexander Ovechkin R1 6.00 15.00
6 Erik Karlsson R1 3.00 8.00
7 Ryan Johansen R1 2.00 5.00
8 Oliver Ekman-Larsson R1 1.25 3.00
9 Steven Stamkos R1 3.00 8.00
10 Vladimir Tarasenko R1 2.50 6.00
11 Anze Kopitar R1 2.50 6.00
12 Eric Staal R1 2.00 5.00
13 Jamie Benn R1 2.00 5.00
14 Henrik Lundqvist R1 2.00 5.00
15 P.K. Subban R1 2.50 6.00
16 Tuukka Rask R1 1.50 4.00
17 John Tavares R1 3.00 8.00
18 Joe Pavelski R1 1.50 4.00
19 Pavel Datsyuk R1 2.00 5.00
20 Jordan Eberle R1 1.50 4.00
21 James van Riemsdyk R1 1.50 4.00
22 Jonathan Toews R1 3.00 8.00
23 Gabriel Landeskog R1 1.50 4.00
24 Zach Parise R1 1.50 4.00
25 Claude Giroux R1 1.50 4.00
26 Patrick Roy R1 4.00 10.00
27 Doug Gilmour R1 2.00 5.00
28 Larry Robinson R1 1.50 4.00
29 Mark Messier R1 2.50 6.00
30 Jeremy Roenick R1 1.50 4.00
31 Mike Bossy R1 1.50 4.00
32 Denis Savard R1 2.00 5.00
33 Guy Carbonneau R1 1.25 3.00
34 Paul Coffey R1 1.50 4.00
35 Wayne Gretzky R1 8.00 20.00
36 Connor McDavid R0 15.00 40.00
37 Noah Hanifin R0 2.50 6.00
38 Dylan Larkin R0 6.00 15.00
39 Sam Bennett R0 2.50 6.00
40 Max Domi R0 4.00 10.00
41 Nikolaj Ehlers R0 4.00 10.00
42 Jake Virtanen R0 2.50 6.00
43 Malcolm Subban R0 5.00 12.00
44 Artemi Panarin R0 6.00 15.00
45 Daniel Sprong R0 4.00 10.00
46 Oscar Lindberg R0 2.00 5.00
47 Nick Cousins R0 2.00 5.00
48 Mattias Janmark R0 2.00 5.00
49 Jordan Weal R0 2.00 5.00
50 Jared McCann R0 2.00 5.00
51 Robby Fabbri R0 2.50 6.00
52 Stefan Noesen R0 1.50 4.00
53 Nick Ritchie R0 2.00 5.00
54 Mikko Rantanen R0 4.00 10.00
55 Nicolas Petan R0 2.00 5.00
56 Kevin Fiala R0 2.00 5.00
57 Henrik Samuelsson R0 1.50 4.00
58 Nikolay Goldobin R0 2.00 5.00
59 Slater Koekkoek R0 1.50 4.00
60 Emile Poirier R0 2.00 5.00
61 Antoine Bibeau R0 2.00 5.00
62 Zachary Fucale R0 2.00 5.00
63 Matt Puempel R0 1.50 4.00
64 Jacob de la Rose R0 2.00 5.00
65 Jack Eichel R0 8.00 20.00

2015-16 Fleer Showcase Metal Universe

STATED ODDS 1:4 HOBBY
RANDOM INSERTS IN PACKS
MU1 Connor McDavid 8.00 20.00
MU2 Max Domi 2.00 5.00
MU3 Joonas Donskoi 1.00 2.50
MU4 Robby Fabbri 1.25 3.00
MU5 Sam Bennett 1.25 3.00
MU6 Nikolaj Ehlers 2.00 5.00
MU7 Noah Hanifin 1.25 3.00
MU8 Dylan Larkin 3.00 8.00
MU9 Artemi Panarin 3.00 8.00
MU10 Jared McCann 1.00 2.50
MU11 Oscar Lindberg 1.00 2.50
MU12 Mikko Rantanen 2.00 5.00
MU13 Nicolas Petan 1.00 2.50
MU14 Mattias Janmark 1.00 2.50
MU15 Daniel Sprong 2.00 5.00
MU16 Nikolay Goldobin 1.00 2.50
MU17 Nick Shore 1.00 2.50
MU18 Zachary Fucale 1.00 2.50
MU19 Radek Faksa 1.00 2.50
MU20 Jack Eichel 4.00 10.00
MU21 Nick Ritchie 1.00 2.50
MU22 Colin Miller .75 2.00
MU23 Sergei Plotnikov .75 2.00
MU24 Chandler Stephenson 1.00 2.50
MU25 Colton Parayko 1.25 3.00
MU26 Sergei Kalinin .75 2.00
MU27 Hunter Shinkaruk 1.00 2.50
MU28 Connor Brickley .75 2.00
MU29 Brock McGinn 1.00 2.50
MU30 Jake Virtanen 1.25 3.00

2015-16 Fleer Showcase Metal Universe Precious Metal Gems Blue

*BLUE/50 1.5X TO 3 X BASIC INSERTS
MU1 Connor McDavid 125.00 200.00
MU8 Dylan Larkin 30.00 80.00
MU9 Artemi Panarin 30.00 80.00

2015-16 Fleer Showcase Metal Universe Precious Metal Gems Red

MU1 Connor McDavid 100.00 200.00
MU8 Dylan Larkin 25.00 50.00

2015-16 Fleer Showcase SkyBox Premium Prospects

STATED PRINT RUN 499 SER.#'d SETS
S1 Jack Eichel 8.00 20.00
S2 Joonas Donskoi 2.00 5.00
S3 Noah Hanifin 2.50 6.00
S4 Malcolm Subban 5.00 12.00
S5 Max Domi 4.00 10.00
S6 Nikolaj Ehlers 4.00 10.00
S7 Mikko Rantanen 4.00 10.00
S8 Artemi Panarin 6.00 15.00
S9 Dylan Larkin 6.00 15.00
S10 Nicolas Petan 2.00 5.00
S11 Daniel Sprong 4.00 10.00
S12 Jared McCann 2.00 5.00
S13 Mattias Janmark 2.00 5.00
S14 Jake Virtanen 2.50 6.00
S15 Nikolay Goldobin 2.00 5.00
S16 Juuse Saros 2.50 6.00
S17 Linus Ullmark 2.50 6.00
S18 Connor Hellebuyck 5.00 12.00
S19 Robby Fabbri 2.50 6.00
S20 Connor McDavid 15.00 40.00
S21 Sam Bennett 2.50 6.00
S22 Colton Parayko 2.50 6.00
S23 Kevin Fiala 2.00 5.00
S24 Hunter Shinkaruk 2.00 5.00
S25 Garret Sparks 2.50 6.00
S26 Mike Condon 2.00 5.00
S27 Frank Vatrano 4.00 10.00
S28 Oscar Lindberg 2.00 5.00
S29 Colin Miller 1.50 4.00
S30 Nick Ritchie 2.00 5.00

2015-16 Fleer Showcase SkyBox Premium Prospects Star Rubies

*RUBIES: 1.5X TO 4X BASIC INSERTS
S1 Jack Eichel 30.00 80.00
S20 Connor McDavid 90.00 150.00

2015-16 Fleer Showcase Ultra Rookies

STATED PRINT RUN 499 SER.#'d SETS
U1 Connor McDavid 15.00 40.00
U2 Jack Eichel 8.00 20.00
U3 Noah Hanifin 2.50 6.00
U4 Dylan Larkin 6.00 15.00
U5 Artemi Panarin 6.00 15.00
U6 Max Domi 4.00 10.00
U7 Nikolaj Ehlers 4.00 10.00
U8 Mattias Janmark 2.00 5.00
U9 Robby Fabbri 2.50 6.00
U10 Joonas Donskoi 2.00 5.00
U11 Nicolas Petan 2.00 5.00
U12 Mike Condon 2.00 5.00
U13 Daniel Sprong 4.00 10.00
U14 Jared McCann 2.00 5.00
U15 Juuse Saros 2.50 6.00
U16 Ben Hutton 2.00 5.00
U17 Jake Virtanen 2.50 6.00
U18 Jaccob Slavin 1.50 4.00
U19 Colton Parayko 2.50 6.00
U20 Sam Bennett 2.50 6.00
U21 Oscar Lindberg 2.00 5.00
U22 Connor Brickley 1.50 4.00
U23 Frank Vatrano 4.00 10.00
U24 Sergei Plotnikov 1.50 4.00
U25 Nick Ritchie 2.00 5.00
U26 Mikko Rantanen 4.00 10.00
U27 Nick Cousins 2.00 5.00
U28 Hunter Shinkaruk 2.00 5.00
U29 Garret Sparks 2.50 6.00
U30 Gustav Olofsson 2.00 5.00

2015-16 Fleer Showcase Ultra Rookies Violet Medallion

*VIOLET/25: .8X TO 5X BASIC INSERTS
U1 Connor McDavid 250.00 400.00
U2 Jack Eichel 100.00 200.00
U4 Dylan Larkin 60.00 150.00
U5 Artemi Panarin 50.00 125.00
U23 Frank Vatrano 20.00 50.00

2016-17 Fleer Showcase

1 Sidney Crosby 1.50 4.00
2 Anze Kopitar .60 1.50
3 Ryan Getzlaf .60 1.50
4 Daniel Sedin .40 1.00
5 Alexander Ovechkin 1.50 4.00
6 Shayne Gostisbehere .50 1.25
7 Henrik Zetterberg .50 1.25
8 Frederik Andersen .30 .75
9 P.K. Subban .60 1.50
10 Rick Nash .40 1.00
11 Jordan Eberle .40 1.00
12 Frans Nielsen .30 .75
13 Corey Crawford .50 1.25
14 Shea Weber .30 .75
15 John Tavares .75 2.00
16 Joe Thornton .40 1.00
17 Patrice Bergeron .50 1.25
18 Evgeni Malkin 1.25 3.00
19 Claude Giroux .40 1.00
20 Vladimir Tarasenko .60 1.50
21 Ryan O'Reilly .40 1.00
22 Seth Jones .30 .75
23 Jonathan Drouin .50 1.25
24 Loui Eriksson .40 1.00
25 Tyler Seguin .60 1.50
26 Gabriel Landeskog .30 .75
27 Roman Josi .40 1.00
28 Kris Letang .40 1.00
29 T.J. Oshie .60 1.50
30 Max Pacioretty .40 1.00
31 Jonathan Quick .60 1.50
32 Brandon Saad .40 1.00
33 Nazem Kadri .30 .75
34 Johnny Gaudreau .60 1.50
35 Joe Pavelski .40 1.00
36 Teuvo Teravainen .40 1.00
37 Jonathan Toews .75 2.00
38 Oliver Ekman-Larsson .30 .75
39 Andrew Ladd .40 1.00
40 Derek Stepan .30 .75
41 Logan Couture .40 1.00
42 Henrik Sedin .40 1.00
43 Zemgus Girgensons .30 .75
44 Jaromir Jagr 1.00 2.50
45 John Gibson .40 1.00
46 Jarome Iginla .40 1.00
47 David Backes .40 1.00
48 Braden Holtby .60 1.50
49 Connor McDavid 2.00 5.00
50 Steven Stamkos .75 2.00
51 Carey Price 1.25 3.00
52 Ondrej Palat .30 .75
53 Marian Hossa .30 .75
54 Jeff Skinner .40 1.00
55 Jakub Voracek .40 1.00
56 Mark Stone .40 1.00
57 Robby Fabbri .40 1.00
58 Aaron Ekblad .40 1.00
59 Ryan Suter .30 .75
60 Sean Monahan .40 1.00
61 Brendan Gallagher .50 1.25
62 Drew Doughty .40 1.00
63 Jaroslav Halak .40 1.00
64 Patrick Kane .75 2.00
65 Corey Perry .40 1.00
66 Cory Schneider .30 .75
67 James van Riemsdyk .40 1.00
68 Kevin Shattenkirk .30 .75
69 Andrei Vasilevskiy .50 1.25
70 Matt Duchene .40 1.00
71 Henrik Lundqvist .40 1.00
72 Jack Eichel .75 2.00
73 Pekka Rinne .50 1.25
74 Ryan Johansen .50 1.25
75 Max Domi .50 1.25
76 Zach Parise .40 1.00
77 Patric Hornqvist .30 .75
78 Erik Karlsson .75 2.00
79 Nicklas Backstrom .60 1.50
80 Brad Marchand .50 1.25
81 Jamie Benn .50 1.25
82 Mark Giordano .30 .75
83 Leon Draisaitl .50 1.25
84 Taylor Hall .75 2.00
85 Nikita Kucherov .60 1.50
86 Gustav Nyquist .40 1.00
87 Nathan MacKinnon .75 2.00
88 Jonathan Marchessault .40 1.00
89 Kyle Palmieri .30 .75
90 Dustin Byfuglien .40 1.00
91 Phil Kessel .50 1.25
92 Mike Hoffman .30 .75
93 Patrick Sharp .30 .75
94 Aleksander Barkov .40 1.00
95 Mats Zuccarello .40 1.00
96 Blake Wheeler .40 1.00
97 Artemi Panarin .50 1.25
98 Evgeny Kuznetsov .60 1.50
99 Martin Jones .40 1.00
100 Brent Burns .50 1.25
101 Mozik RC/Pietila RC 3.00 8.00
Auvitu RC/Lappin RC
102 Kase RC/Cramarossa RC 3.00 8.00
Dowling RC/Smith RC
103 Kuraly RC/Lyubimov RC 10.00 25.00
Archibald RC/Hrivik RC
104 Tanev RC/Nelson RC 3.00 8.00
Benning RC/Johnston RC
105 Coreau RC/Dell RC 5.00 12.00
Mcintyre RC/Wedgewood RC
106 Johnston RC/Hyman RC 15.00 40.00
Stecher RC/Robinson RC
107 Lernout RC/Hanley RC 5.00 12.00
Czarnik RC/Acciari RC
108 McFarland RC/Malgin RC 5.00 12.00
Regner RC/Harper RC
109 Carrier RC/Catenacci RC 3.00 8.00
Nutivaara RC/Sedlak RC
110 Gravel RC/O'Gara RC 4.00 10.00
Hathaway RC/Kosmachuk RC
111 Brandon Carlo RC 3.00 8.00
112 A.J. Greer RC 3.00 8.00
113 Michal Kempny RC 3.00 8.00
114 Martin Frk RC 4.00 10.00
115 Gustav Forsling RC 3.00 8.00
116 Zach Sanford RC 3.00 8.00
117 Tyler Bertuzzi RC 4.00 10.00
118 Tobias Lindberg RC 5.00 12.00
119 Nick Baptiste RC 3.00 8.00
120 Jacob Larsson RC 5.00 12.00
121 Frederick Gaudreau RC 4.00 10.00
122 Joseph LaBate RC 4.00 10.00
123 Jake Guentzel RC 30.00 80.00
124 Drake Caggiula RC 3.00 8.00
125 Cristoval Nieves RC 4.00 10.00
126 Steven Santini RC 2.50 6.00
127 Tristan Jarry AU/499 RC 12.00 30.00
128 Spencer Martin RC 4.00 10.00
129 Zack Mitchell RC 3.00 8.00
130 Cole Schneider RC 3.00 8.00
131 Nick Paul RC 4.00 10.00
132 Nic Dowd RC 3.00 8.00
133 Frederik Gauthier RC 2.50 6.00
134 Stephen Johns RC 2.50 6.00
135 Mark Jankowski RC 2.50 6.00
136 Nick Sorensen RC 3.00 8.00
137 Daniel O' Regan RC 3.00 8.00
138 Alan Quine RC 3.00 8.00
139 Blake Speers RC 3.00 8.00
140 Nikita Zaitsev RC 3.00 8.00
141 Sonny Milano AU/499 RC 5.00 12.00
142 Justin Bailey AU/499 RC 4.00 10.00
143 Ryan Pulock AU/499 RC 4.00 10.00
144 Charlie Lindgren AU/499 RC 8.00 20.00
145 Brendan Leipsic AU/499 RC 4.00 10.00
146 Nikita Soshnikov AU/499 RC 2.50 6.00
147 Kasperi Kapanen AU/499 RC 8.00 20.00
148 Oliver Kylington AU/499 RC 3.00 8.00
149 Connor Brown AU/499 RC 6.00 15.00
150 Oskar Sundqvist AU/499 RC 4.00 10.00
151 Jason Dickinson AU/499 RC 3.00 8.00
152 Hudson Fasching AU/499 RC 4.00 10.00
153 Michael Matheson AU/499 RC 4.00 10.00
154 Miles Wood AU/499 RC 3.00 8.00
155 Daniel Altshuller AU/499 RC 3.00 8.00
156 Oliver Bjorkstrand AU/499 RC 3.00 8.00
157 Josh Morrissey AU/499 RC 5.00 12.00
158 Pontus Aberg AU/499 RC 5.00 12.00
159 Ivan Provorov AU/499 RC 8.00 20.00
160 Jimmy Vesey AU/499 RC 8.00 20.00
161 Kyle Connor AU/499 RC 10.00 25.00
162 Christian Dvorak AU/499 RC 4.00 10.00
163 Sebastian Aho AU/499 RC 8.00 20.00
164 Nick Schmaltz AU/499 RC 4.00 10.00
165 Zach Werenski AU/499 RC 8.00 20.00
166 Mathew Barzal AU/499 RC 12.00 30.00
167 Thomas Chabot AU/499 RC 8.00 20.00
168 Jakob Chychrun AU/499 RC 4.00 10.00
169 Joel Eriksson Ek AU/499 RC 4.00 10.00
170 Brayden Point AU/499 RC 10.00 25.00
171 Tyler Motte AU/499 RC 4.00 10.00
172 Pavel Buchnevich AU/499 RC 6.00 15.00
173 Anthony Beauvillier AU/499 RC 4.00 10.00
174 Lawson Crouse AU/499 RC 3.00 8.00
175 Kevin Labanc AU/499 RC 4.00 10.00
176 Anthony DeAngelo AU/499 RC 4.00 10.00
177 Mikhail Sergachev AU/499 RC 8.00 20.00
178 Danton Heinen AU/499 RC 6.00 15.00
179 Julius Honka AU/499 RC 4.00 10.00
180 Artturi Lehkonen AU/499 RC 4.00 10.00
181 Patrik Laine AU/299 RC 30.00 80.00
182 Matthew Tkachuk AU/299 RC 12.00 30.00
183 Jesse Puljujarvi AU/299 RC 10.00 25.00
184 Travis Konecny AU/299 RC 8.00 20.00
185 William Nylander AU/299 RC 25.00 60.00
186 Anthony Mantha AU/299 RC 10.00 25.00
187 Mitch Marner AU/99 RC 60.00 150.00
188 Pavel Zacha AU/299 RC 5.00 12.00
189 Dylan Strome AU/299 RC 8.00 20.00
190 Auston Matthews AU/99 RC 200.00 350.00
191 Brendan Perlini AU/499 RC 4.00 10.00
192 Brendan Guhle AU/499 RC 4.00 10.00
193 John Quenneville AU/499 RC 4.00 10.00
194 Timo Meier AU/499 RC 4.00 10.00
195 Nikita Tryamkin AU/499 RC 3.00 8.00
196 Thatcher Demko AU/499 RC 8.00 20.00
197 Jakub Vrana AU/499 RC 4.00 10.00
198 Brandon Montour AU/499 RC 4.00 10.00
199 Sergey Tolchinsky AU/499 RC 3.00 8.00
200 Bliidh RC/Grzelcyk RC 6.00 15.00
Burgdoerfer RC/Kasdorf RC
201 Alves RC/Ryan RC 3.00 8.00
Nakladal RC/Carrick RC
202 Henley RC/Elson RC 6.00 15.00
Kukan RC/Jensen RC
203 Simpson RC/Ellis RC 3.00 8.00
Cannone RC/Liambas RC
204 Englund RC/Harpur RC 3.00 8.00
Sieloff RC/De Leo RC
205 Friesen RC/Megan RC 4.00 10.00
Rodin RC/Garteig RC
206 Erne RC/Wilcox RC 5.00 12.00
Peca RC/Richard RC
207 Johansson RC/Will RC 3.00 8.00
Halverson RC/Treutle RC

2016-17 Fleer Showcase Red Glow

*VETS: 1.25X TO 3X BASIC CARDS
*ROOKIES/25-49: .6X TO 1.5X BASIC CARDS
79 Nicklas Backstrom 2.00 5.00
98 Evgeny Kuznetsov 2.00 5.00
183 Jesse Puljujarvi AU/25 80.00 150.00
184 Travis Konecny AU/25 25.00 60.00
186 Anthony Mantha AU/25 30.00 80.00
190 Auston Matthews AU/15

2016-17 Fleer Showcase White Hot

*VETS/25: 2.5X TO 6X BASIC CARDS
*ROOKIES/15: .75X TO 2X BASIC CARDS
79 Nicklas Backstrom 4.00 10.00
98 Evgeny Kuznetsov 4.00 10.00
159 Ivan Provorov AU/15 60.00 120.00

2016-17 Fleer Showcase E-X2017

1 Connor McDavid 5.00 12.00
2 Sidney Crosby 4.00 10.00
3 Wayne Gretzky 5.00 12.00
4 Bobby Orr 3.00 8.00
5 Steven Stamkos 2.00 5.00
6 Patrick Kane 2.00 5.00
7 Henrik Lundqvist 1.00 2.50
8 Alexander Ovechkin 4.00 10.00
9 Matt Duchene 1.00 2.50
10 Carey Price 3.00 8.00
11 Anze Kopitar 1.50 4.00
12 John Tavares 2.00 5.00
13 Johnny Gaudreau 1.50 4.00
14 Jamie Benn 1.25 3.00
15 Ryan Getzlaf 1.50 4.00
16 Joe Pavelski 1.00 2.50
17 Dylan Larkin 1.50 4.00
18 Brad Marchand 1.25 3.00
19 Jonathan Toews 2.00 5.00
20 Vladimir Tarasenko 1.50 4.00
21 Patrick Roy 2.50 6.00
22 Tyler Motte 1.00 2.50
23 Sebastian Aho 2.00 5.00
24 Nick Schmaltz 1.00 2.50
25 Zach Werenski 2.00 5.00
26 Anthony Mantha 2.50 6.00
27 Pavel Zacha 1.25 3.00
28 Artturi Lehkonen 1.00 2.50
29 Ivan Provorov 2.00 5.00
30 Mathew Barzal 3.00 8.00
31 Travis Konecny 2.00 5.00
32 Christian Dvorak 1.00 2.50
33 Mikhail Sergachev 2.00 5.00
34 Matthew Tkachuk 3.00 8.00
35 Kyle Connor 2.50 6.00
36 Jimmy Vesey 2.00 5.00
37 Jesse Puljujarvi 2.50 6.00
38 Dylan Strome 2.00 5.00
39 Mitch Marner 5.00 12.00
40 William Nylander 4.00 10.00
41 Patrik Laine 8.00 20.00
42 Auston Matthews 12.00 30.00

2016-17 Fleer Showcase Flair

1 Sidney Crosby R1 6.00 15.00
2 Carey Price R1 5.00 12.00
3 Patrick Kane R1 3.00 8.00
4 Joe Pavelski R1 1.50 4.00
5 Mario Lemieux R1 5.00 12.00
6 Jonathan Quick R1 2.50 6.00
7 Alexander Ovechkin R1 6.00 15.00
8 Jamie Benn R1 2.00 5.00
9 Claude Giroux R1 1.50 4.00
10 Patrick Roy R1 4.00 10.00
11 Connor McDavid R1 8.00 20.00
12 Mark Messier R1 2.00 5.00
13 Henrik Lundqvist R1 1.50 4.00
14 Jack Eichel R1 3.00 8.00
15 Bobby Orr R1 5.00 12.00
16 Dylan Larkin R1 2.50 6.00
17 Vladimir Tarasenko R1 2.50 6.00
18 John Tavares R1 3.00 8.00
19 Johnny Gaudreau R1 2.50 6.00
20 Wayne Gretzky R1 8.00 20.00
21 Auston Matthews R0 10.00 25.00
22 Kyle Connor R0 4.00 10.00
23 Mikhail Sergachev R0 3.00 8.00
24 Travis Konecny R0 3.00 8.00
25 William Nylander R0 6.00 15.00
26 Christian Dvorak R0 1.50 4.00
27 Joel Eriksson Ek R0 1.50 4.00
28 Artturi Lehkonen R0 1.50 4.00
29 Pavel Buchnevich R0 2.50 6.00
30 Jesse Puljujarvi R0 5.00 12.00
31 Zach Werenski R0 3.00 8.00
32 Tyler Motte R0 1.50 4.00
33 Pavel Zacha R0 2.00 5.00
34 Anthony Mantha R0 4.00 10.00
35 Mathew Barzal R0 6.00 15.00
36 Nick Schmaltz R0 1.50 4.00
37 Ivan Provorov R0 3.00 8.00
38 Brayden Point R0 4.00 10.00
39 Jakob Chychrun R0 1.50 4.00
40 Jimmy Vesey R0 3.00 8.00
41 Sebastian Aho R0 3.00 8.00
42 Matthew Tkachuk R0 5.00 12.00
43 Lawson Crouse R0 1.25 3.00
44 Anthony Beauvillier R0 1.50 4.00
45 Mitch Marner R0 8.00 20.00
46 Thomas Chabot R0 3.00 8.00
47 Brandon Carlo R0 1.50 4.00
48 Dylan Strome R0 3.00 8.00
49 Connor Brown R0 2.50 6.00
50 Patrik Laine R0 6.00 15.00

2016-17 Fleer Showcase Flair Blue Ice

*R1/99: .75X TO 2X BASIC INSERTS
*R0/199: .75X TO 2X BASIC INSERTS

21 Auston Matthews RO 30.00 80.00
50 Patrik Laine RO 20.00 50.00

2016-17 Fleer Showcase Flair Hot Gloves

HG1 Patrick Roy 4.00 10.00
HG2 Henrik Lundqvist 1.25 3.00
HG3 Jonathan Quick 2.00 5.00
HG4 Pekka Rinne 1.50 4.00
HG5 Martin Brodeur 4.00 10.00
HG6 Cory Schneider 1.00 2.50
HG7 Corey Crawford 1.50 4.00
HG8 Braden Holtby 2.00 5.00
HG9 Matt Murray 5.00 12.00
HG10 Carey Price 8.00 20.00

2016-17 Fleer Showcase Hot Prospects Autograph Patches

141 Sonny Milano/135 10.00 25.00
142 Justin Bailey/135 8.00 20.00
143 Ryan Pulock/135 8.00 20.00
144 Charlie Lindgren/135 15.00 40.00
145 Brendan Leipsic/135 8.00 20.00
146 Nikita Soshnikov/135 5.00 12.00
147 Kasperi Kapanen/135 15.00 40.00
148 Oliver Kylington/135 6.00 15.00
149 Connor Brown/135 12.00 30.00
150 Oskar Sundqvist/135 8.00 20.00
151 Jason Dickinson/135 6.00 15.00
152 Hudson Fasching/135 8.00 20.00
153 Michael Matheson/135 8.00 20.00
154 Miles Wood/135 6.00 15.00
155 Daniel Altshuller/135 6.00 15.00
156 Oliver Bjorkstrand/135 6.00 15.00
157 Josh Morrissey/135 10.00 25.00
158 Pontus Aberg/135 10.00 25.00
159 Ivan Provorov/135 15.00 40.00
160 Jimmy Vesey/135 15.00 40.00
161 Kyle Connor/135 20.00 50.00
162 Christian Dvorak/135 8.00 20.00
163 Sebastian Aho/135 15.00 40.00
164 Nick Schmaltz/135 8.00 20.00
165 Zach Werenski/135 15.00 40.00
166 Mathew Barzal/135 25.00 60.00
167 Thomas Chabot/135 15.00 40.00
168 Jakob Chychrun/135 8.00 20.00
169 Joel Eriksson Ek/135 8.00 20.00
170 Brayden Point/135 20.00 50.00
171 Tyler Motte/135 8.00 20.00
172 Pavel Buchnevich/135 12.00 30.00
173 Anthony Beauvillier/135 8.00 20.00
174 Lawson Crouse/135 6.00 15.00
175 Kevin Labanc/135 8.00 20.00
176 Anthony DeAngelo/135 8.00 20.00
177 Mikhail Sergachev/135 15.00 40.00
179 Julius Honka/135 8.00 20.00
181 Patrik Laine/85 150.00 250.00
182 Matthew Tkachuk/85 40.00 100.00
183 Jesse Puljujarvi/85 30.00 80.00
184 Travis Konecny/85 25.00 60.00
185 William Nylander/85 60.00 150.00
186 Anthony Mantha/85 30.00 80.00
188 Pavel Zacha/85 15.00 40.00
189 Dylan Strome/85 25.00 60.00
190 Auston Matthews/35 300.00 500.00

2016-17 Fleer Showcase Metal Universe

MU1 Connor McDavid 5.00 12.00
MU2 Sidney Crosby 4.00 10.00
MU3 Carey Price 3.00 8.00
MU4 Steven Stamkos 2.00 5.00
MU5 P.K. Subban 1.50 4.00
MU6 Shea Weber .75 2.00
MU7 Taylor Hall 2.00 5.00
MU8 Henrik Lundqvist 1.00 2.50
MU9 Dylan Larkin 1.50 4.00
MU10 Patrick Kane 2.00 5.00
MU11 John Tavares 2.00 5.00
MU12 Brent Burns 1.25 3.00
MU13 Jack Eichel 2.00 5.00
MU14 Jamie Benn 1.25 3.00
MU15 Drew Doughty 1.00 2.50
MU16 Patrice Bergeron 1.25 3.00
MU17 Johnny Gaudreau 1.50 4.00
MU18 Vladimir Tarasenko 1.50 4.00
MU19 Jaromir Jagr 2.50 6.00
MU20 Alexander Ovechkin 4.00 10.00
MU21 Matthew Tkachuk 3.00 8.00
MU22 Anthony Mantha 2.50 6.00
MU23 Christian Dvorak 1.00 2.50
MU24 Mathew Barzal 3.00 8.00
MU25 Mitch Marner 5.00 12.00
MU26 Kyle Connor 2.50 6.00
MU27 Mikhail Sergachev 2.00 5.00
MU28 Pavel Buchnevich 1.50 4.00
MU29 Artturi Lehkonen 1.00 2.50
MU30 William Nylander 4.00 10.00
MU31 Travis Konecny 2.00 5.00
MU32 Jesse Puljujarvi 2.50 6.00
MU33 Sebastian Aho 2.00 5.00
MU34 Anthony Beauvillier 1.00 2.50
MU35 Dylan Strome 2.00 5.00
MU36 Tyler Motte 1.00 2.50
MU37 Pavel Zacha 1.25 3.00
MU38 Connor Brown 1.50 4.00
MU39 Lawson Crouse .75 2.00
MU40 Patrik Laine 4.00 10.00
MU41 Ivan Provorov 2.00 5.00
MU42 Nick Schmaltz 1.00 2.50
MU43 Brayden Point 2.50 6.00
MU44 Zach Werenski 2.00 5.00
MU45 Jimmy Vesey 2.00 5.00
MU46 Jakob Chychrun 1.00 2.50
MU47 Joel Eriksson Ek 1.00 2.50
MU48 Brandon Carlo 1.00 2.50
MU49 Thomas Chabot 2.00 5.00
MU50 Auston Matthews 6.00 15.00

2016-17 Fleer Showcase Metal Universe Planet Metal

PM1 Alexander Ovechkin 5.00 12.00
PM2 Steven Stamkos 2.50 6.00
PM3 P.K. Subban 2.00 5.00
PM4 Jaromir Jagr 3.00 8.00
PM5 Jonathan Toews 2.50 6.00
PM6 Wayne Simmonds 1.50 4.00
PM7 Erik Karlsson 2.50 6.00
PM8 Artemi Panarin 1.50 4.00
PM9 Drew Doughty 1.25 3.00
PM10 Jamie Benn 1.50 4.00
PM11 Patrice Bergeron 1.50 4.00
PM12 Brent Burns 1.50 4.00
PM13 John Tavares 2.50 6.00
PM14 Shea Weber 1.00 2.50
PM15 Sidney Crosby 5.00 12.00

2016-17 Fleer Showcase Metal Universe Precious Metal Gems Blue

*BLUE/50: 2X TO 5X BASIC INSERTS
MU1 Connor McDavid 20.00 50.00
MU50 Auston Matthews 60.00 150.00

2016-17 Fleer Showcase Metal Universe Precious Metal Gems Red

*RED/150: 1X TO 2.5X BASIC INSERTS
MU1 Connor McDavid 15.00 40.00
MU40 Patrik Laine 30.00 80.00
MU50 Auston Matthews 30.00 80.00

2016-17 Fleer Showcase SkyBox Premium Prospects

S1 Patrik Laine 8.00 20.00
S2 Travis Konecny 4.00 10.00
S3 Matthew Tkachuk 6.00 15.00
S4 Jimmy Vesey 4.00 10.00
S5 Jesse Puljujarvi 5.00 12.00
S6 Christian Dvorak 2.00 5.00
S7 Sebastian Aho 4.00 10.00
S8 Zach Werenski 4.00 10.00
S9 Mathew Barzal 6.00 15.00
S10 Dylan Strome 4.00 10.00
S11 Kyle Connor 5.00 12.00
S12 Anthony Mantha 5.00 12.00
S13 Nick Schmaltz 2.00 5.00
S14 Ivan Provorov 4.00 10.00
S15 Pavel Zacha 2.50 6.00
S16 Tyler Motte 2.00 5.00
S17 Artturi Lehkonen 2.00 5.00
S18 Mikhail Sergachev 4.00 10.00
S19 Lawson Crouse 1.50 4.00
S20 William Nylander 8.00 20.00
S21 Brandon Carlo 2.00 5.00
S22 Jake Guentzel 15.00 40.00
S23 Pavel Buchnevich 3.00 8.00
S24 Julius Honka 2.00 5.00
S25 Mitch Marner 10.00 25.00
S26 Anthony DeAngelo 2.00 5.00
S27 Jakob Chychrun 2.00 5.00
S28 Denis Malgin 2.00 5.00
S29 Connor Brown 3.00 8.00
S30 Auston Matthews 12.00 30.00

2016-17 Fleer Showcase Ultra Rookies Platinum Medallion

*PLATINUM/99: .6X TO 1.5X BASIC INSERTS
U1 Auston Matthews 40.00 100.00
U30 Patrik Laine 25.00 60.00

2016-17 Fleer Showcase Ultra Rookies Violet Medallion

U1 Auston Matthews
U25 Mitch Marner 60.00 150.00
U30 Patrik Laine 90.00 150.00

2002-03 Fleer Throwbacks

is 91-card set featured players from the past and featured a few former players first main stream card. Card #92 was not available in packs, and was only available via redemption at the 2003 NHL All-Star Block Party.

1 Terry O'Reilly .25 .60
2 Barry Beck .15 .40
3 Bobby Clarke .25 .60
4 Mike Foligno .15 .40
5 Danny Gare .15 .40
6 Clark Gillies .25 .60
7 Bernie Federko .20 .50
8 Dale Hunter .20 .50
9 Kris King .15 .40
10 Ted Lindsay .30 .75
11 Tie Domi .20 .50
12 Rob Ramage .15 .40
13 Jim Schoenfeld .15 .40
14 Steve Smith .15 .40
15 Harold Snepsts .15 .40
16 Rod Langway .20 .50
17 Denis Potvin .25 .60
18 John Bucyk .20 .50
19 Dirk Graham .15 .40
20 Lanny McDonald .20 .50
21 Stan Smyl .15 .40
22 Andre Dupont .15 .40
23 Todd Ewen .15 .40
24 George McPhee .15 .40
25 Paul Baxter .15 .40
26 Keith Magnuson .15 .40
27 Kevin Kaminski .15 .40
28 Mike Peluso .15 .40
29 Dave Semenko .20 .50
30 David Maley .15 .40
31 Jeff Beukeboom .15 .40
32 Dave Brown .15 .40
33 Troy Crowder .15 .40
34 Bobby Hull .40 1.00
35 Dan Maloney .15 .40
36 Jimmy Mann .15 .40
37 Rudy Poeschek .15 .40
38 John Wensink .15 .40
39 Kim Clackson .15 .40
40 Jay Wells .15 .40
41 Glen Cochrane RC .25 .60
42 Alan May .15 .40
43 Willi Plett .15 .40
44 Kevin McClelland .15 .40
45 Jim Cummins .15 .40
46 Basil McRae .15 .40
47 Ron Delorme .15 .40
48 John Ferguson .15 .40
49 Gord Donnelly .15 .40
50 Nick Kypreos .20 .50
51 Larry Playfair .15 .40
52 Marty McSorley .20 .50
53 Tim Hunter .15 .40
54 Billy Smith .25 .60
55 Laurie Boschman .15 .40
56 Wayne Cashman .20 .50
57 Link Gaetz .15 .40
58 Darin Kimble .15 .40
59 Bob Nystrom .20 .50
60 Ronnie Stern .15 .40
61 Ken Baumgartner .15 .40
62 Ken Linseman .20 .50
63 Kelly Chase .15 .40
64 Bob Gassoff .15 .40
65 Joey Kocur .15 .40
66 Chris Nilan .15 .40
67 Dave Schultz .25 .60
68 Tony Twist .20 .50
69 Enrico Ciccone .15 .40
70 Jay Miller .15 .40
71 Phil Russell .15 .40
72 Bryan Watson .15 .40
73 Paul Holmgren .15 .40
74 Garth Butcher .15 .40
75 Al Iafrate .20 .50
76 Barclay Plager .15 .40
77 Brent Severyn .15 .40
78 Ron Hextall .25 .60
79 Shane Churla .15 .40
80 Dino Ciccarelli .25 .60
81 Cam Neely .25 .60
82 Ulf Samuelsson .15 .40
83 Mick Vukota .15 .40
84 Garry Howatt .15 .40
85 Gary Rissling RC .25 .60
86 Behn Wilson .15 .40
87 Jack Carlson RC .30 .75
88 Bob Bassen .15 .40
89 Curt Brackenbury .15 .40
90 Mario Roberge .15 .40
91 Serge Roberge RC .25 .60
92 Bob Probert 3.00 8.00

2002-03 Fleer Throwbacks Gold

*GOLD: 2X TO 5X BASIC CARDS
STATED ODDS 1:1

2002-03 Fleer Throwbacks Platinum

*PLATINUM/50: 6X TO 15X BASE HI
STAT.PRINT RUN 50 SER.#' d SETS

2002-03 Fleer Throwbacks Autographs

is 23-card set featured certified player autographs and was inserted at a rate of 1:144.

1 Terry O'Reilly 15.00 40.00
2 Bobby Clarke 15.00 40.00
3 Clark Gillies 8.00 20.00
4 Dale Hunter 8.00 20.00
5 Ted Lindsay 25.00 60.00
6 Tie Domi 15.00 40.00
7 Jim Schoenfeld 15.00 40.00
8 Denis Potvin 8.00 20.00
9 Todd Ewen 10.00 25.00
10 Kevin Kaminski 8.00 20.00
11 Bob Probert 100.00 250.00
12 Dave Brown 12.50 30.00
13 Bobby Hull 35.00 80.00
14 Basil McRae 15.00 40.00
15 Larry Playfair 8.00 20.00
16 Marty McSorley 20.00 50.00
17 Billy Smith 40.00 100.00
18 Bob Nystrom 8.00 20.00
19 Ken Baumgartner 8.00 20.00
20 Kelly Chase 8.00 20.00
21 Joey Kocur 15.00 40.00
22 Dave Schultz 15.00 30.00
23 Tony Twist 25.00 60.00

2002-03 Fleer Throwbacks Drop the Gloves

rial-numbered to 200 copies each, this 5-card set featured pieces of game-used gloves. Cards were not numbered and are listed below in checklist order.

1 Bob Probert 30.00 80.00
2 Ron Hextall 20.00 50.00
3 Tony Twist 8.00 20.00
4 Marty McSorley 8.00 20.00
5 Jim Cummins 8.00 20.00

2002-03 Fleer Throwbacks Scraps

serted at 1:25, this 8-card set featured pieces of game jerseys. Cards were not numbered and are listed below in checklist order.

1 Basil McRae 5.00 12.00
2 Enrico Ciccone 5.00 12.00
3 Bob Bassen 6.00 15.00
4 Joey Kocur 6.00 15.00
5 Clark Gillies 5.00 12.00
6 Marty McSorley 5.00 12.00
7 Tony Twist 5.00 12.00
8 Dale Hunter 5.00 12.00

2002-03 Fleer Throwbacks Tie Downs

is 8-card set paralleled the basic jersey set but featured swatches of jersey tie-downs. Each card was serial-numbered out of 50.

1 Basil McRae 15.00 40.00
2 Enrico Ciccone 15.00 40.00
3 Bob Bassen 20.00 50.00
4 Joey Kocur 20.00 50.00
5 Clark Gillies 15.00 40.00
6 Marty McSorley 15.00 40.00
7 Tony Twist 15.00 40.00
8 Dale Hunter 15.00 40.00

2002-03 Fleer Throwbacks Squaring Off

MPLETE SET (9) 15.00 30.00
STATED ODDS 1:24
1 B.Probert/J.Kocur 2.50 6.00
2 D.Schultz/C.Gillies 2.00 5.00
3 C.Neely/U.Samuelsson 2.00 5.00
4 T.O'Reilly/J.Schoenfeld 1.50 4.00
5 B.Beck/D.Potvin 1.50 4.00
6 B.Clarke/D.Hunter 1.50 4.00
7 T.Twist/M.McSorley 2.50 6.00
8 D.Brown/D.Schultz 2.50 6.00
9 R.Hextall/B.Smith 2.00 5.00

2002-03 Fleer Throwbacks Squaring Off Memorabilia

is 8-card set was inserted at 1:48 and paralleled the basic insert set but carried dual memorabilia swatches.

1 B.Probert J/J.Kocur S 8.00 20.00
2 D.Schultz J/C.Gillies J 6.00 15.00
3 C.Neely J/U.Samuelsson J 8.00 20.00
4 T.O'Reilly J/J.Schoenfeld J 6.00 15.00
5 B.Beck J/D.Potvin J 6.00 15.00
6 B.Clarke S/D.Hunter J 6.00 15.00
7 T.Twist J/M.McSorley J 8.00 20.00
8 D.Brown J/D.Schultz J 8.00 20.00

2002-03 Fleer Throwbacks Stickwork

rds are not numbered and are listed below in checklist order.

1 Kelly Chase 8.00 20.00
2 Dale Hunter 5.00 12.00
3 Curt Brackenbury 5.00 12.00
4 Todd Ewen 5.00 12.00
5 Jim Cummins 6.00 15.00
6 Rudy Poeschek 5.00 12.00
7 Jay Wells 5.00 12.00
8 Enrico Ciccone 5.00 12.00
9 Marty McSorley 12.50 35.00
10 Bobby Hull 8.00 20.00
11 Cam Neely 6.00 15.00
12 Bobby Clarke 8.00 20.00
13 Bob Probert 10.00 25.00

1994 Fleury Hockey Tips

Titled "Theoren Fleury Hockey School Tip of the Week," this 14-card set measuresd the standard size. The lavender-bordered fronts had color action photos illustrating each hockey tip. The backs carried the "Tip of the Week" in black lettering followed by discussion. The cards were numbered on both sides.

COMPLETE SET (14) 2.00 5.00
COMMON CARD (1-14) .20 .50

1970-71 Flyers Postcards

This 12-card, team-issued set measured 3 1/2" by 5 1/2" and was in the postcard format. The fronts featured full-bleed color photos, with the players posed on ice at the skating rink. A facsimile autograph was inscribed across the bottom. The white backs carried player information and team logo across the top. The cards were unnumbered and checklisted below in alphabetical order.

COMPLETE SET (12) 20.00 40.00
1 Barry Ashbee 3.00 6.00
2 Gary Dornhoefer 3.00 6.00
3 Warren Elliott 1.00 2.00
Frank Leurs
4 Doug Favell 3.00 6.00
5 Earl Heiskala 1.50 3.00
6 Larry Hillman 2.50 5.00
7 Andre Lacroix 2.50 5.00
8 Lew Morrison 1.50 3.00
9 Simon Nolet 2.00 4.00
10 Garry Peters 1.50 3.00
11 Vic Stasiuk CO 1.50 3.00
12 George Swarbrick 1.50 3.00

1972 Flyers Mighty Milk

These seven panels, which were issued on the sides of half gallon cartons of Mighty Milk, featured members of the Philadelphia Flyers. After cutting, the panels measured approximately 3 5/8" by 7 1/2". All lettering and the portrait itself were in blue. Inside a frame with rounded corners, each panel displayed a portrait of the player and a player profile. The words "Philadelphia Hockey Star" and the player's name appeared above the frame, while an advertisement for Mighty Milk and another for TV Channel 29 appeared immediately below. The backs were blank. The panels were unnumbered and checklisted below in alphabetical order.

COMPLETE SET (8) 87.50 175.00
1 Serge Bernier 7.50 15.00
2 Bobby Clarke 40.00 80.00
3 Gary Dornhoefer 10.00 20.00
4 Doug Favell 15.00 30.00
5 Jean-Guy Gendron 7.50 15.00
6 Bob Kelly
7 Bill Lesuk 7.50 15.00
8 Ed Van Impe 10.00 20.00

1973-74 Flyers Linnett

These oversize cards were produce by Charles Linnett Studios. Cards were done in black and white and featured a facsimile signature. Original price per piece was only 50 cents. Cards measure 8 1/2 x 11. They were unnumbered and checklisted below in alphabetical order.

COMPLETE SET (1-18) 40.00 80.00
1 Barry Ashbee 1.50 3.00
2 Bill Barber 5.00 10.00
3 Tom Bladon 1.50 3.00
4 Bob Clarke 5.00 10.00
5 Bill Clement 3.00 6.00
6 Terry Crisp 2.50 5.00
7 Bill Flett 2.00 4.00
8 Bob Kelly 1.50 3.00
9 Orest Kindrachuk 1.50 3.00
10 Ross Lonsberry 1.50 3.00
11 Rick Macleish 2.00 4.00
12 Simon Nolet 2.00 4.00
13 Bernard Parent 5.00 10.00
14 Don Saleski 1.50 3.00
15 Dave Schultz 3.00 6.00
16 Ed Van Impe 1.50 3.00
17 Jimmy Watson 2.00 4.00
18 Joe Watson 2.00 4.00

1983-84 Flyers J.C. Penney

Sponsored by J.C. Penney, this 22-card set measured approximately 4" by 6". The fronts featured color posed action shots of the players on ice. Beneath the picture were the team name, logo, player's name, and the phrase "Compliments of J.C. Penney Stores in the Delaware Valley." The backs were blank. The cards were unnumbered and checklisted below in alphabetical order.

COMPLETE SET (22) 14.00 35.00
1 Ray Allison .40 1.00
2 Bill Barber .75 2.00
3 Frank Bathe .40 1.00
4 Lindsay Carson .40 1.00
5 Bobby Clarke 2.00 5.00
6 Glen Cochrane .40 1.00
7 Doug Crossman .60 1.50
8 Miroslav Dvorak .40 1.00
9 Thomas Eriksson .40 1.00
10 Bob Froese .60 1.50
11 Randy Holt .40 1.00
12 Mark Howe .75 2.00
13 Tim Kerr .75 2.00
14 Pelle Lindbergh 6.00 15.00
15 Brad Marsh .60 1.50
16 Brad McCrimmon .60 1.50
17 Dave Poulin .60 1.50
18 Brian Propp .75 2.00
19 Ilkka Sinisalo .60 1.50
20 Darryl Sittler 1.50 4.00
21 Rich Sutter .40 1.00
22 Ron Sutter .40 1.00

1985-86 Flyers Postcards

This 31 card set featured action photos on the front, and came complete with player name, number and statistics.

COMPLETE SET (31) 15.00 30.00
1 Bill Barber .40 1.00
2 Dave Brown .30 .75
3 Lindsay Carson .20 .50
4 Bob Clarke .75 2.00
5 Murray Craven .20 .50
6 Pat Croce .08 .25
7 Doug Crossman .20 .50
8 Per-Erik Eklund .20 .50
9 Thomas Eriksson .20 .50
10 Bob Froese .30 .75
11 Len Hachborn .08 .25
12 Paul Holmgren .20 .50
13 Ed Hospodar .20 .50
14 Mark Howe .30 .75
15 Mike Keenan .40 1.00
16 Tim Kerr .30 .75
17 Pelle Lindbergh 6.00 15.00
18 Brad Marsh .20 .50
19 Brad McCrimmon .30 .75
20 E.J. McGuire CO .08 .25
21 Bernie Parent CO .40 1.00
22 Joe Paterson .08 .25
23 Dave Poulin .20 .50
24 Brian Propp .40 1.00
25 Ilkka Sinisalo .20 .50
26 Derrick Smith .20 .50
27 Rich Sutter .20 .50
28 Ron Sutter .20 .50
29 Rick Tocchet 2.50 6.00
30 Peter Zezel 1.00 2.50
31 Team Photo .75 2.00

1986-87 Flyers Postcards

This 29-card set of Philadelphia Flyers featured full-bleed, color action and posed photos. The cards measured approximately 4 1/8" by 6" and were in a postcard format. A player's autograph facsimile was printed on the front. A diagonal black stripe cut across the lower portion of the picture. Within the black stripe appeared narrow orange stripes, the Flyers logo, and player information. The horizontal white backs carryed career statistics and biography on the left, and the postcard format mailing address space on the right. The cards were unnumbered and checklisted below in alphabetical order.

COMPLETE SET (29) 10.00 25.00
1 Bill Barber CO .40 1.00
2 Dave Brown .30 .75
3 Lindsay Carson .20 .50
4 Murray Craven .20 .50
5 Pat Croce TR .08 .25
6 Doug Crossman .20 .50
7 Jean-Jacques Daigneault .20 .50
8 Pelle Eklund .30 .75
9 Ron Hextall 1.50 4.00
10 Paul Holmgren CO .20 .50
11 Ed Hospodar .20 .50
12 Mark Howe .60 1.50
13 Mike Keenan CO .40 1.00
14 Tim Kerr .60 1.50
15 Brad Marsh .20 .50
16 Brad McCrimmon .30 .75
17 E.J. McGuire CO .30 .75
18 Scott Mellanby .60 1.50
19 Bernie Parent CO .40 1.00
20 Dave Poulin .30 .75
21 Brian Propp .40 1.00
22 Glenn Resch .40 1.00
23 Ilkka Sinisalo .20 .50
24 Derrick Smith .20 .50
25 Daryl Stanley .20 .50
26 Ron Sutter .20 .50
27 Rick Tocchet 2.00 5.00
28 Peter Zezel .60 1.50
29 Team Photo .75 2.00

1989-90 Flyers Postcards

This 29-card set measured 4 1/8" by 6" and was in the postcard format. The fronts featured full-bleed color action player photos. A team color-coded (black with thin orange stripes) diagonal stripe cut across the bottom portion and carried the team logo, biographical information, and jersey number. The white horizontal backs carried the team logo, biography, and career summary. The cards were unnumbered and checklisted below in alphabetical order.

COMPLETE SET (29) 8.00 20.00
1 Keith Acton .20 .50
2 Craig Berube .20 .50
3 Mike Bullard .20 .50
4 Terry Carkner .20 .50
5 Jeff Chychrun .20 .50
6 Bob Clarke VP/GM .75 2.00
7 Murray Craven .20 .50
8 Mike Eaves ACO .08 .25
9 Pelle Eklund .30 .75
10 Ron Hextall .75 2.00
11 Paul Holmgren CO .20 .50
12 Mark Howe .40 1.00
13 Kerry Huffman .20 .50
14 Tim Kerr .40 1.00
15 Scott Mellanby .40 1.00
16 Gord Murphy .20 .50
17 Andy Murray ACO .08 .25
18 Pete Peeters .40 1.00
19 Dave Poulin .40 1.00
20 Brian Propp .40 1.00
21 Kjell Samuelsson .40 1.00
22 Ilkka Sinisalo .20 .50
23 Derrick Smith .20 .50
24 Doug Sulliman .20 .50
25 Ron Sutter .20 .50
26 Rick Tocchet .75 2.00
27 Jay Wells .20 .50
28 Ken Wregget .75 2.00
29 Team Photo .75 2.00

1990-91 Flyers Postcards

This 26-card set was issued by the Philadelphia Flyers. Each card measured approximately 4 1/8" by 6". The fronts displayed full-bleed color action photos. A team color-coded (black with thin orange stripes) diagonal stripe cut across the bottom portion and carried the team logo, biographical information, and jersey number. The horizontal backs were postcard design and, on the left, presented biography, statistics, and notes. The cards were unnumbered and checklisted below in alphabetical order.

COMPLETE SET (26) 6.00 15.00
1 Keith Acton .30 .75
2 Murray Baron .20 .50
3 Craig Berube .20 .50
4 Terry Carkner .20 .50
5 Jeff Chychrun .20 .50
6 Murray Craven .30 .75
7 Pelle Eklund .30 .75
8 Ron Hextall .60 1.50
9 Tony Horacek .20 .50
10 Martin Hostak .20 .50
11 Mark Howe .40 1.00
12 Kerry Huffman .20 .50
13 Tim Kerr .40 1.00
14 Dale Kushner .20 .50
15 Norman Lacombe .20 .50
16 Jiri Latal .20 .50
17 Scott Mellanby .40 1.00
18 Gord Murphy .20 .50
19 Pete Peeters .30 .75
20 Mike Ricci .60 1.50
21 Kjell Samuelsson .30 .75
22 Derrick Smith .20 .50
23 Ron Sutter .20 .50
24 Rick Tocchet .75 2.00
25 Ken Wregget .40 1.00
26 Team Photo .75 2.00

1991-92 Flyers J.C. Penney

This 26-card set was issued by the Flyers in conjunction with J.C. Penney Stores and Lee. Each card measured approximately 4 1/8" by 6", The fronts displayed full-bleed color action photos. A team color-coded (black with thin orange stripes) diagonal stripe cut across the bottom portion and carried the team logo, biographical information, and jersey number. The horizontal backs were postcard design and, on the left, presented biography, statistics, and notes. The cards were unnumbered and checklisted below in alphabetical order.

COMPLETE SET (26) 6.00 15.00
1 Keith Acton .30 .75
2 Rod Brind'Amour .60 1.50
3 Dave Brown .30 .75
4 Terry Carkner .20 .50
5 Kimbi Daniels .20 .50
6 Kevin Dineen .40 1.00
7 Steve Duchesne .30 .75
8 Pelle Eklund .20 .50
9 Corey Foster .20 .50
10 Ron Hextall .60 1.50
11 Tony Horacek .20 .50
12 Mark Howe .40 1.00
13 Kerry Huffman .20 .50
14 Brad Jones .20 .50
15 Steve Kasper UER .20 .50
(Misspelled Kaspar on front)
16 Dan Kordic .20 .50
17 Jiri Latal .20 .50
18 Andrei Lomakin .20 .50
19 Gord Murphy .20 .50
20 Mark Pederson .20 .50
21 Dan Quinn .20 .50
22 Mike Ricci .40 1.00
23 Kjell Samuelsson .25 .60
24 Rick Tocchet .60 1.50
25 Ken Wregget .40 1.00
26 Team Photo .60 1.50

1992-93 Flyers J.C. Penney

This 23-card set was sponsored by J.C. Penney Stores and Lee in the Delaware Valley. The cards measured approximately 4 1/8" by 6" and featured color, action player photos with facsimile autographs near the bottom of each picture. A gray border stripe across the bottom carried the team logo, player's name, position, and jersey number. The horizontal backs displayed biographical information, statistics, and career notes within a postcard-type format. The cards were unnumbered and checklisted below in alphabetical order.

COMPLETE SET (23) 8.00 20.00
1 Keith Acton .25 .60
2 Stephane Beauregard .25 .60
3 Brian Benning .20 .50
4 Rod Brind'Amour .60 1.50
5 Claude Boivin .20 .50
6 Dave Brown .30 .75
7 Terry Carkner .20 .50
8 Shawn Cronin .20 .50
9 Kevin Dineen .30 .75
10 Pelle Eklund .20 .50
11 Doug Evans .20 .50
12 Brent Fedyk .20 .50
13 Garry Galley .30 .75
14 Gord Hynes .20 .50
15 Eric Lindros 4.00 10.00
16 Andrei Lomakin .20 .50
17 Ryan McGill .20 .50
18 Ric Nattress .20 .50
19 Greg Paslawski .20 .50
20 Mark Recchi .75 2.00
21 Dominic Roussel .30 .75
22 Dimitri Yushkevich .20 .50
23 Team Photo .60 1.50

1992-93 Flyers Upper Deck Sheets

The 44 commemorative sheets in this set were distributed individually in game programs at Philadelphia Flyers home games during the 1992-93 season in Flyer magazine. The sheets measured approximately 8 1/2" by 11" and featured color, posed and action, player photos with orange and white borders. A black bar with an orange accent stripe above it carried either the player's name or a picture title. On sheets with a title, the player's name was printed on the photo in either orange or white lettering. A black diamond design was printed with the individual sheet number and the production run. The backs displayed the game date and teams playing. All sheets were the Flyers versus another NHL team. The roster and management of each team was also given. The sheets are unnumbered and checklisted below in chronological order. There was a second team photo issued March 13th. Due to a violent winter storm, only a few thousand spectators made it to the Spectrum. Play was halted when a severe wind blew out a few windows in the concourse area causing debris to scatter out into the seats. The sheets were distributed again during the make-up game on April 1.

COMPLETE SET (44) 100.00 250.00
1 Quebec Nordiques 2.00 5.00
Sept. 19& 1992 (4&500)
Kevin Di
2 New Jersey Devils 1.25 3.00
Sept. 24& 1992 (4&500)
Brian B
3 Washington Capitals 3.00 8.00
Oct. 3& 1992 (4&500)
Mark Re
4 New Jersey Devils 1.50 4.00
Oct. 9& 1992 (7&500)
Keith Act
5 New York Islanders 3.00 8.00
Oct. 15& 1992 (4&500)
Rod Bri
6 Winnipeg Jets 1.50 4.00
Oct. 18& 1992 (4&500)
Dave Brown
7 Vancouver Canucks 2.00 5.00
Oct. 22& 1992 (4&500)
Dominic
8 Montreal Canadiens 1.25 3.00
Oct. 24& 1992 (4&500)
Gord Hy
9 St. Louis Blues 1.25 3.00
Nov. 7& 1992 (4&500)
Claude Boiv
10 New York Islanders 1.25 3.00
Nov. 12& 1992 (4&500)
Dimitri
11 Ottawa Senators 15.00 40.00
Nov. 15& 1992 (5&500)
Eric Lindr
12 New York Rangers 1.50 4.00
Nov. 19& 1992 (4&500)
Steve Kas
13A Buffalo Sabres 5.00 12.00
Nov. 22& 1992 (4&500)/1992-93 Tea
13B Buffalo Sabres 4.00 10.0
Nov. 22& 1992/1992-93 Team Pictur
14 New York Islanders 1.25 3.
Nov. 27& 1992 (5&500)
Greg Pa
15 Quebec Nordiques 1.50 4.
Dec. 3& 1992 (4&500)
Terry Cark
16 Boston Bruins 1.25 3.
Dec. 6& 1992 (4&500)
Shawn Cronin
17 Washington Capitals 1.25 3.
Dec. 12& 1992 (4&500)
Brent
18 Pittsburgh Penguins 1.50 4.
Dec. 17& 1992 (4&500)
Garry
19 Chicago Blackhawks 1.25 3.
Dec. 19& 1992 (5&000)
Andrei
20 Pittsburgh Penguins 2.00 5.
Dec. 23& 1992 (5&500)
Bill a
21 Washington Capitals 1.50 4.
Jan. 7& 1993 (4&500)
Stephan
22 New York Rangers 3.00 8.
Jan. 9& 1993 (6&000)
Mark Recch
23 Edmonton Oilers 1.25 3.
Jan. 10& 1993 (5&000)
Ryan McGil
24 Calgary Flames 1.25 3.
Jan. 14& 1993 (6&500)
Doug Evans
25 Detroit Red Wings 2.00 5.
Jan. 17& 1993 (5&000)
The Capt
26 Boston Bruins 1.25 3.
Jan. 21& 1993 (5&000)
Ric Nattress
27 Hartford Whalers 3.00 8.
Jan. 24& 1993 (5&000)
Rod Brind
28 Buffalo Sabres 2.00 5.
Jan. 26& 1993 (5&000)
Tommy Soder
29 Quebec Nordiques 1.50 4.
Jan. 28& 1993 (5&000)
Pelle Ekl
30 Ottawa Senators 1.50 4.
Feb. 9& 1993 (5&000)
Dave Brown
31 Montreal Canadiens 10.00 25.
Feb. 11& 1993 (5&500)
The Roo
32 New Jersey Devils 1.25 3.
Feb. 14& 1993 (5&000)
Josef Be
33 New Jersey Devils 1.25 3.
Feb. 25& 1993 (6&000)
Greg Pas
34 New York Islanders 1.50 4.
Feb. 27& 1993 (5&000)
The Coa
35 Pittsburgh Penguins 1.50 4.
Mar. 2& 1993 (5&000)
Keith A
36 Washington Capitals 3.00 8.
Mar. 11& 1993 (5&500)
NHL Al
37A Los Angeles Kings 1.50 4.
Mar. 13& 1993 (5&500)
Garry Ga
37B Los Angeles Kings 3.00 8.
Make-up Game/1992-93 Team Pict
38 Minnesota North Stars 1.50 4.
Mar. 16& 1993 (5&000)
Terr
39 New Jersey Devils 2.00 5.
Mar. 21& 1993 (5&000)
Dominic
40 San Jose Sharks 1.25 3.
Mar. 25& 1993 (5&000)
Greg Hawgo
41 Tampa Bay Lightning 1.25 3.
Apr. 3& 1993 (5&500)
Viaches
42 Toronto Maple Leafs 10.00 25.
Apr. 4& 1993 (6&000)
Crazy 8
43 Washington Capitals 2.00 5.
Apr. 8& 1993 (5&500)
Europea
44 New York Rangers 4.00 10.
Apr. 12& 1993 (5&500)
Hockey Ha

1993-94 Flyers J.C. Penney

This 24-card set was issued by the Flyers as a promotional item at a home game, and was sponsor by JC Penney. These collectibles were postcard size featured full color action photos on the front, and player data on the back. The cards were unnumbere and were checklisted below in alphabetical order.

COMPLETE SET (24) 8.00 20.
1 Josef Beranek .30
2 Claude Boivin .20
3 Jason Bowen .20
4 Rod Brind'Amour .60 1.
5 Slava Butsayev .20
6 Dave Brown .30
7 Al Conroy .20
8 Kevin Dineen .30
9 Pelle Eklund .20
10 Brent Fedyk .20
11 Jeff Finley .20
12 Garry Galley .30
13 Eric Lindros 3.00 8.
14 Stewart Malgunas .20
15 Ryan McGill .20
16 Rob Ramage .20
17 Mark Recchi .75 2.
18 Mikael Renberg .60 1.
19 Dominic Roussel .30
20 Yves Racine .20
21 Tommy Soderstrom .30
22 Dave Tippett .20
23 Dimitri Yuskevich .20
NNO Team Photo .40 1

1993-94 Flyers Lineup Sheets

The 44 commemorative sheets in this set were distributed individually in game programs at Philadelphia Flyers home games during the 1993-9 season in Flyer magazine. The sheets measured approximately 8 1/2" by 11" and featured color, pos and action, player photos with orange and white borders. The sheets are listed below by player in alphabetical order.

COMPLETE SET (43) 50.00 125
1 Josef Beranek 1.00 2

laude Boivin 1.00 2.50
son Bowen 1.00 2.50
od Brind'Amour 2.00 5.00
od Brind'Amour 2.00 5.00
ave Brown 2.00 5.00
ava Butsayev 1.00 2.50
rry Carkner 1.00 2.50
Conroy 1.00 2.50
Kevin Dineen 1.00 2.50
Kevin Dineen 1.00 2.50
Pelle Eklund 1.00 2.50
Andre Faust 1.00 2.50
Brent Fedyk 1.00 2.50
Brent Fedyk 1.00 2.50
Jeff Finley 1.00 2.50
Garry Galley 1.00 2.50
Greg Hawgood 1.00 2.50
Tim Kerr 2.00 5.00
Mark Lamb 1.00 2.50
Eric Lindros 4.00 10.00
Eric Lindros 4.00 10.00
Eric Lindros 4.00 10.00
Stewart Malgunas 1.00 2.50
Ryan McGill 1.00 2.50
Yves Racine 1.00 2.50
Rob Ramage 1.00 2.50
Mark Recchi 2.00 5.00
Mark Recchi 2.00 5.00
Mikael Renberg 1.00 2.50
Dominic Roussel 1.50 4.00
Dominic Roussel 1.50 4.00
Dave Tippett 1.00 2.50
Dmitri Yushkevich 1.00 2.50
Dmitri Yushkevich 1.00 2.50
Rob Zettler 1.00 2.50
The Coaches 1.00 2.50
Team Photo 1.00 2.50
Team Photo 1.00 2.50
Renberg, Bowen, Malgunas 1.00 2.50
The Captains 2.00 5.00
Recchi, Lindros, Galley 2.00 5.00
Flyers and their Fans 1.00 2.50

1996-97 Flyers Postcards

attractive 24-card set was produced late in the 97 season by the club. The standard-sized cards featured an action photo on the front, along the player's name, position and jersey number. back contained a remarkably thorough stats age, including career numbers, awards and action info. Unnumbered, the cards are listed w in alphabetical order.

MPLETE SET (24) 6.00 15.00
am Photo .20 .50
d Brind'Amour .30 .75
ul Coffey .40 1.00
ott Daniels .08 .25
c Desjardins .15 .40
hn Druce .08 .25
rl Dykhuis .08 .25
t Falloon .08 .25
le Hawerchuk .30 .75
on Hextall .30 .75
rent Klatt .08 .25
an Kordic .08 .25
aniel Lacroix .08 .25
ohn LeClair .75 2.00
ric Lindros 2.00 5.00
anne Niinimaa .60 1.50
oel Otto .08 .25
hjon Podein .08 .25
Mikael Renberg .30 .75
jell Samuelsson .08 .25
arth Snow .20 .50
etr Svoboda .08 .25
hris Therien .08 .25
ainius Zubrus .75 2.00

1997 Flyers Phone Cards

e phone cards produced by Comcast, were able only in the Philadelphia area. Each card was h 15-minutes of long distance.

MPLETE SET (4) 3.00 8.00
exandre Daigle .40 1.00
ris Gratton .40 1.00
hn LeClair 1.25 3.00
c Lindros 2.00 5.00

1998-99 Flyers Postcards

MPLETE SET (24) 5.00 12.00
ve Babych .20 .50
d Brind'Amour .30 .75
rc Bureau .20 .50
exandre Daigle .20 .50
c Desjardins .20 .50
lin Forbes .20 .50
n Hextall .30 .75
dy Hull .20 .50
th Jones .20 .50
ohn LeClair .60 1.50
ric Lindros 1.25 3.00
an McGillis .20 .50
ke Richardson .20 .50
mitri Tertyshny .20 .50
hris Therien .20 .50
ohn Vanbiesbrouck .30 .75
oman Vopat .20 .50
aleri Zelepukin .20 .50
ainius Zubrus .40 1.00
ll Barber .20 .50
roadcasters .08 .25
oaches .08 .25
hiladelphia Flyers .08 .25
hiladelphia Phantoms .08 .25

2001-02 Flyers Postcards

-card set featured full-color action photos ered by team colors and logos. Each card ured approximately 4" X 6". The set was mbered and is listed below in alphabetical order.

PLETE SET (30) 10.00 25.00
an Boucher 1.00 2.50
nald Brashear .30 .75
man Cechmanek .40 1.00
: Desjardins .20 .50
Dopita .40 1.00
d Fedoruk .30 .75
lan Fedotenko .30 .75
mon Gagne 1.25 3.00
Johnsson .20 .50
nt Manderville .20 .50
hn LeClair .75 2.00
ris McAllister .20 .50
m McGillis .20 .50
arty Murray .20 .50
ith Primeau .40 1.00
ul Ranheim .20 .50
ark Recchi .40 1.00
ke Richardson .20 .50
remy Roenick .75 2.00
ris Therien .20 .50
k Tocchet .30 .75
c Weinrich .20 .50

23 Justin Williams .40 1.00
24 Flyers Team Photo .40 1.00
25 Bill Barber .10 .25
Mike Stothers
E.J. McGuire
26 Broadcasters .04 .10
27 Bob Clarke GM .30 .75
28 Ron Hextall ACO .30 .75
29 Phantoms Team Photo .20 .50
30 Phlex MASCOT .10 .25

2002-03 Flyers Postcards

MPLETE SET (24) 8.00 20.00
1 Eric Weinrich .30 .75
2 Kim Johnsson .30 .75
3 Mark Recchi .40 1.00
4 John LeClair .40 1.00
5 Simon Gagne .60 1.50
6 Justin Williams .30 .75
7 Paul Ranheim .30 .75
8 Radovan Somik .30 .75
9 Chris McAllister .30 .75
10 Keith Primeau .40 1.00
11 Chris Therien .30 .75
12 Michal Handzus .30 .75
13 Todd Fedoruk .40 1.00
14 Roman Cechmanek .40 1.00
15 Dennis Seidenberg .30 .75
16 Eric Desjardins .30 .75
17 Marty Murray .30 .75
18 Robert Esche .40 1.00
19 Pavel Brendl .30 .75
20 Donald Brashear .30 .75
21 Jeremy Roenick .75 2.00
22 The Coaches .10 .25
23 Team Card .20 .50
24 Philadelphia Phantoms .20 .50

2003-04 Flyers Program Inserts

Inserted into individual game programs, these sheets measure approximately 8 1/2" x 11" and each sheet was individually serial-numbered at the top. The checklist below is incomplete. If you have any further info on this set, please forward it to hockeymag@beckett.com.

1 Jeremy Roenick 2.00 5.00
2 Joni Pitkanen 1.25 3.00
3 Tony Amonte 1.50 4.00
4 Robert Esche 1.50 4.00
5 Danny Markov 1.25 3.00
6 Keith Primeau 1.50 4.00

2003-04 Flyers Postcards

is 24-card set was produced by the team and available through the team website and appearances.

COMPLETE SET (24) 8.00 20.00
1 Tony Amonte .40 1.00
2 Donald Brashear .40 1.00
3 Mike Comrie .40 1.00
4 Eric Desjardins .20 .50
5 Robert Esche .40 1.00
6 Todd Fedoruk .40 1.00
7 Simon Gagne .40 1.00
8 Jeff Hackett .30 .75
9 Michal Handzus .20 .50
10 Kim Johnsson .20 .50
11 Sami Kapanen .20 .50
12 Claude Lapointe .20 .50
13 John LeClair .40 1.00
14 Danny Markov .20 .50
15 Joni Pitkanen .40 1.00
16 Keith Primeau .40 1.00
17 Marcus Ragnarsson .20 .50
18 Mark Recchi .40 1.00
19 Jeremy Roenick .75 2.00
20 Radovan Somik .20 .50
21 Chris Therien .20 .50
22 Jim Vandermeer .20 .50
23 Eric Weinrich .20 .50
24 Coaches .10 .25

2005-06 Flyers Team Issue

COMPLETE SET (25) 8.00 15.00
1 Philadelphia Flyers CL .01 .01
2 Donald Brashear .30 .75
3 Jeff Carter 2.00 5.00
4 Eric Desjardins .20 .50
5 Robert Esche .30 .75
6 Peter Forsberg .75 2.00
7 Simon Gagne .40 1.00
8 Michal Handzus .20 .50
9 Derian Hatcher .20 .50
10 Kim Johnsson .20 .50
11 Sami Kapanen .20 .50
12 Mike Knuble .20 .50
13 Antero Niittymaki .75 2.00
14 Joni Pitkanen .40 1.00
15 Keith Primeau .20 .50
16 Branko Radivojevic .20 .50
17 Mike Rathje .20 .50
18 Mike Richards .40 1.00
19 Brian Savage .20 .50
20 Dennis Seidenberg .20 .50
21 Patrick Sharp .20 .50
22 Jonathan Sim .20 .50
23 Turner Stevenson .20 .50
24 Chris Therien .20 .50
25 R.J. Umberger .40 1.00

2006-07 Flyers Postcards

COMPLETE SET (23) 10.00 25.00
1 Derian Hatcher .40 1.00
2 Mike Rathje .40 1.00
3 Randy Jones .40 1.00
4 Geoff Sanderson .40 1.00
5 Scottie Upshall .40 1.00
6 Simon Gagne .75 2.00
7 Jeff Carter .75 2.00
8 Mike Richards .75 2.00
9 Kyle Calder .40 1.00
10 R.J. Umberger .40 1.00
11 Mike Knuble .40 1.00
12 Denis Gauthier .40 1.00
13 Sami Kapanen .40 1.00
14 Dmitry Afanasenkov .40 1.00
15 Todd Fedoruk .75 2.00
16 Antero Niittymaki .60 1.50
17 Robert Esche .60 1.50
18 Joni Pitkanen .40 1.00

19 Alexandre Picard .40 1.00
20 Michael Leighton .60 1.50
21 Ben Eager .40 1.00
22 Mike York .40 1.00
23 Alexei Zhitnik .40 1.00

1936 Frank Coffey Olympics

Produced for the 1936 Berlin Olympics, each card features a full color front along with biographical information on the back.

NNO Ice Hockey 15.00 30.00
NNO Field Hockey 15.00 30.00

1971-72 Frito-Lay

This ten-card set featured members of the Toronto Maple Leafs and Montreal Canadiens. Since the cards were unnumbered, they had been listed below in alphabetical order within team, Montreal (1-5) and Toronto (6-10). The cards were paper thin, each measuring approximately 1 1/2" by 2".

COMPLETE SET (10) 50.00 100.00
1 Yvan Cournoyer 4.00 8.00
2 Ken Dryden 25.00 50.00
3 Frank Mahovlich 5.00 10.00
4 Henri Richard 5.00 10.00
5 J.C. Tremblay 2.00 4.00
6 Bobby Baun 2.00 4.00
7 Ron Ellis 2.00 4.00
8 Paul Henderson 3.00 6.00
9 Jacques Plante 10.00 20.00
10 Norm Ullman 3.00 6.00

1988-89 Frito-Lay Stickers

The 1988-89 Frito-Lay Hockey Stickers set included 42 small (1 3/8" by 1 3/4") stickers. The fronts were dominated by color photos, but also had each player's name and uniform number. The stickers were distributed in sealed plastic, and packaged one per special Frito-Lay snack bag. Reportedly distribution was via 35 million bags of Ruffles, O'Gradys, Dulac, Lays, Doritos, Fritos, Tostitos, Cheetos, and Chester Popcorn -- each containing one of the 42 players in the set. Since they were actually stickers, there was very little information on the backing. The checklist below also gave the player's uniform number as listed on each card. A poster was also available from the company by sending in 2.00 and one UPC symbol from any Frito-Lay product.

COMPLETE SET (42) 12.00 30.00
1 Mario Lemieux 66 2.50 6.00
2 Bryan Trottier 19 .20 .50
3 Steve Yzerman 19 1.50 4.00
4 Bernie Federko 24 .15 .40
5 Brian Bellows 23 .15 .40
6 Denis Savard 18 .20 .50
7 Neal Broten 7 .15 .40
8 Doug Gilmour 9 .60 1.50
9 Dale Hawerchuk 10 .20 .50
10 Luc Robitaille 20 .60 1.50
11 Ed Olczyk 16 .08 .25
12 Andrew McBain 20 .08 .25
13 Mike Gartner 11 .20 .50
14 Pat LaFontaine 16 .40 1.00
15 Scott Stevens 3 .20 .50
16 Ray Bourque 77 .75 2.00
17 Cam Neely 8 .60 1.50
18 Mike Foligno 17 .08 .25
19 Tom Barrasso 30 .20 .50
20 Ron Francis 10 .30 .75
21 Peter Stastny 26 .20 .50
22 Michel Goulet 16 .20 .50
23 Bernie Nicholls 9 .20 .50
24 Paul Coffey 77 .60 1.50
25 Mats Naslund 26 .15 .40
26 Glenn Anderson 9 .20 .50
27 Dave Poulin 20 .08 .25
28 Kevin Dineen 11 .08 .25
29 Wendel Clark 17 .30 .75
30 James Patrick 3 .08 .25
31 Al MacInnis 2 .30 .75
32 Troy Murray 19 .08 .25
33 Kirk Muller 9 .20 .50
34 Marcel Dionne 16 .20 .50
35 Mark Messier 11 .75 2.00
36 Joe Nieuwendyk 25 .60 1.50
37 Ron Hextall 27 .30 .75
38 Sean Burke 1 .20 .50
39 Barry Pederson 7 .08 .25
40 Stephane Richer 44 .20 .50
41 Bob Probert 24 .75 2.00
42 Tony Tanti 9 .08 .25
NNO Set Poster 1.25 3.00

1996-97 Frosted Flakes Masks

One of these 7 cards was inserted into specially marked boxes of Frosted Flakes in Canada early in the season. These unique die-cut cards featured a net design and a goalie mask, which could be popped up on display in front of the net. Just two of the cards featured the actual faces and mask designs of individual goalies (#1-2). Cards 3-6 featured generic masks with the design of the team logo, while the seventh featured a Tony the Tiger mask. The complete set was available by mail for $2.50 plus three proofs of purchase.

COMPLETE SET (7) 8.00 20.00
1 Felix Potvin 1.25 3.00
2 Curtis Joseph 2.00 5.00
3 Montreal Canadiens 1.25 3.00
4 Ottawa Senators 1.25 3.00
5 Calgary Flames 1.25 3.00
6 Vancouver Canucks 1.25 3.00
7 Tony the Tiger 1.25 3.00

1991-92 Future Trends Canada '72 Promos

This standard-size three-card set was issued to promote the release of Future Trends' Team Canada '72 set. To commemorate Team Canada of 1972, 7200 of each promotional card were offered for sale at Canada's Hudson Bay Stores. The fronts featured full-bleed black-and-white action shots from a game between Team Canada and the Soviet team. The card title appeared in white lettering within a red stripe across the bottom of the picture. The '72 Hockey Canada logo appeared in the lower right. Except for their horizontal orientation, the backs were similar to the fronts, with full-bleed black-and-white photos, white lettering within a red stripe at the bottom, and logo in the lower right. The cards were unnumbered and checklisted below in alphabetical order by title. These promos were issued in English and French versions.

COMPLETE SET (3) 8.00 20.00
1 The Goal 3.00 8.00
The Scoreboard
Paul Henderson
2 The Leader 4.00 10.00
Phil Esposito
3 The Challenge/The Kid 3.00 8.00
Vladislav Tretiak

1991-92 Future Trends Canada '72

ture Trends Experience Ltd. produced this 101-card standard-size set to celebrate the 20th anniversary of the 1972 Summit Series between the Soviets and the Canadians. The cards were available initially only at the Bay and were sold in ten-card foil packs with no factory sets. The 70 players of the Canadian and Russian teams were represented, and 30 additional special cards captured unforgettable moments from the series. Between one and two special cards, signed in gold paint pen by living Canadian players, were randomly inserted into each foil case. Only one non-Canadian, Vladislav Tretiak, signed cards. Supposedly each of the signers signed only 750 cards for insertion and distribution within the packs. These cards were specially coated with a swirl pattern over the autograph. Reportedly, The Bay also issued 2500 autographed sets without the special coating, but we have no confirmation of this at this time. The cards featured on the fronts borderless black-and-white, action or posed pictures. A white, red, and gold stripe cut across the bottom of the card face and intersected the '72 Hockey Canada logo at the lower right corner. The backs carried additional photos, biographical information, series statistics, sportswriters' editorial comments, and/or player quotes. Card number 40 featured Phil Esposito's September 8, 1972, address to the nation. The card number appeared in a blue oblong design within the bottom red stripe on both sides. The '72 Hockey Canada logo also appeared in the lower right corner of the back. The set was issued in both an English and a French version. The production quantities were reportedly 9,000 English and 1,000 French 12-box cases. Also released were 1972 uncut sheet sets.

COMPLETE SET (101) 10.00 25.00
1 In The Beginning .15 .40
2 The Backyard Rink .08 .20
3 It Didn't Take Long .08 .20
4 The Patriarch .15 .40
Anatoli Tarasov
5 More Hours a Day .75 2.00
Vladislav Tretiak
6 Coming Out Party .15 .40
7 Never In Doubt .08 .20
8 Team Canada .30 .75
9 Pat Stapleton .08 .20
10 Vsevolod Bobrov .08 .20
11 Vladislav Tretiak .75 2.00
12 Faceoff .08 .20
Game 1, Montreal (9/2/72)
13 30 Seconds .15 .40
Game 1, Montreal (9/2/72)
14 Yevgeny Zimin .08 .20
15 Bill White .08 .20
16 7-3, Game 1 Statistics .08 .20
17 Don Awrey .08 .20
18 Mickey Redmond .15 .40
19 Alexander Gusev .15 .40
20 Alexander Maltsev .30 .75
21 Rod Seiling .08 .20
22 Dale Tallon .08 .20
23 Coming Back .08 .20
Game 2, Toronto (9/4/72)
24 Unforgettable .08 .20
Game 2 Statistics
25 Wayne Cashman .15 .40
26 Frank Mahovlich .30 .75
27 Peter Mahovlich .08 .20
28 Vyacheslav Solodukhin .15 .40
Alexander Sidelnikov
29 Yuri Shatalov .15 .40
30 Brothers .15 .40
Frank Mahovlich
Peter Mahovlich
31 The Goalies .75 2.00
32 Alexander Bodunov .08 .20
33 All Even .08 .20
Game 3 Statistics
34 Yuri Blinov .08 .20
35 Jocelyn Guevremont .08 .20
36 Vic Hadfield .08 .20
37 Yuri Lebedev .08 .20
38 Yevgeny Poladiev .15 .40
Vyacheslav Starshinov
39 Disaster .08 .20
Game 4 Statistics
40 Address to The Nation .30 .75
Phil Esposito
41 Victor Kuzkin .08 .20
42 Vladimir Lutchenko .30 .75
43 Boris Mikhailov .40 1.00
44 Grace Under Pressure .08 .20
Game 5, Moscow (9/22/72)
45 Afraid to Lose .08 .20
46 Ready To Win .08 .20
Game 5 Statistics
47 Vladimir Vikulov .08 .20
48 Red Berenson .08 .20
49 Richard Martin .08 .20
50 Alexander Martynyuk .08 .20
51 Gilbert Perreault .30 .75
52 Vladimir Petrov .40 1.00
53 Serge Savard .15 .40
54 Vladimir Shadrin .08 .20
55 Ready To Win .08 .20
Game 5 Statistics
56 One Step Back .08 .20
Game 6 Statistics
57 Bobby Clarke .40 1.00
58 Valeri Kharlamov .75 2.00
59 Alexander Volchkov .15 .40
60 Standing Guard .15 .40
61 Stan Mikita .40 1.00
62 One More To Go .08 .20
Game 7 Statistics
Moscow (9/26/72)
63 The Winner .08 .20
64 The Fans Go Wild .08 .20
65 Alexander Ragulin .15 .40
66 Jean Ratelle .15 .40
67 Gennady Tsygankov .15 .40
68 Valeri Vasiliev .40 1.00
69 International Dialogue .08 .20
70 Series Stars .40 1.00
Phil Esposito
Alexander Yakushev
71 Series Stars .40 1.00
Paul Henderson
Vladislav Tretiak
72 No Solitudes .08 .20
Game 8& Moscow (9/28/72)
The Telegrams
73 2-2, Game 8, Moscow (9/28/72) .08 .20
74 Rod Gilbert .15 .40
75 Yevgeny Mishokov .15 .40
76 Ron Ellis .08 .20
77 5-4 score .08 .20
78 Different Games .08 .20
Game 8, Moscow (9/28/72)
Interlude
79 Bill Goldsworthy .08 .20
80 The Huddle .08 .20
81 The Moment 1.00 2.50
82 Yvan Cournoyer .30 .75
83 Yuri Liapkin .08 .20
84 Phil Esposito .40 1.00
85 Ken Dryden .75 2.00
86 Peace .08 .20
Game 8 Statistics
87 Gary Bergman .08 .20
88 Brian Glennie .08 .20
89 Dennis Hull .08 .20
90 Vyacheslav Anisin .08 .20
91 Marcel Dionne .30 .75
92 Guy Lapointe .15 .40
93 Ed Johnston .15 .40
94 Harry Sinden GM .08 .20
95 Brad Park .30 .75
96 Tony Esposito .40 1.00
97 Alexander Yakushev .60 1.50
98 Paul Henderson .75 2.00
99 J.P. Parise .08 .20
100 Valeri Kharlamov .75 2.00
Alex Kharlamov on back
101 Checklist .15 .40

1992 Future Trends '76 Canada Cup

This 100-card, standard-size set was produced by The Future Trends Experience Ltd. And licensed by Hockey Canada. Commemorating the 1976 Canada Cup, the card numbering picked up where the '72 Team Canada set left off by tracing the growth of international hockey. According to the company the production run was 50,000 numbered display boxes. Randomly inserted in the packs were gold-foil stamped signature cards. Bobby Orr, Bobby Hull, Rogatien Vachon, Darryl Sittler, and Bobby Clarke each signed 750 cards. The cards are not serial numbered. A Vladislav Tretiak card serial-numbered out of 1976 is also known to exist. The cards featured vertical and horizontal color action and posed player and team photos. Some shots were of game action with several players pictured. The bottom of each was accented by red and gold border stripes with a red Canada Cup logo in the right corner. Most cards were bordered in white, but some were bordered on the top by the national flags of the various teams in the set. The horizontal backs carried the same flag pattern ghosted behind information about the pictured player or team. A color photo of the players or player was displayed to the right of the copy. Red and gold border stripes similar to the front appeared below. Topical subsets featured are '72 Retrospective (102-106), 1974 Russian team vs. WHA (107-110), a 6-card training camp subset (111-116), MVPs (184-190), and the first ever Canada Cup All-Star team (195-200). The cards were numbered on the back. An 8 1/2" by 11" sheet was also issued; it has an artist's color painting of the players on the front and a checklist on its back.

COMPLETE SET (100) 8.00 20.00
102 Phil Esposito .20 .50
Sergeant
103 Vladislav Tretiak .30 .75
Soviet Ambassador
Retrospective
104 Bobby Orr .40 1.00
Impossible
105 Paul Henderson .05 .15
The Goal
106 Alexander Yakushev .15 .40
107 Bobby Hull .30 .75
108 Valeri Kharlamov .40 1.00
Soviet
109 Gerry Cheevers .20 .50
Vladislav Tretiak
110 Bobby Hull .30 .75
Vladislav Tretiak
What If Series
111 Soviet on-ice workout .02 .10
112 Czech on-ice workout .01 .05
113 Finn on-ice workout .01 .05
114 Swedes take the ice .01 .05
115 USA on-ice workout .02 .10
116 Darryl Sittler .08 .25
117 Serge Savard .05 .15
118 Team Finland .01 .05
119 Team Sweden .01 .05
120 Team Czechoslavakia .01 .05
121 Soviets .05 .15
122 Team USA .05 .15
123 Team Canada .05 .15
124 The Opening Barrage .01 .05
125 Richard Martin .01 .05
Canada Cup
126 Bobby Orr .40 1.00
127 Sweden vs. USA .01 .05
Power Play
128 Ivan Hlinka .01 .05
129 CSSR 5 - CCCP 3 .01 .05
Canada Cup
130 Helmut Balderis .05 .15
Canada Cup
131 Peter Stastny .07 .20
Canada Cu
132 Valeri Vasiliev .10 .25
Canada Cup
133 Out of Contention .01 .05
Canada Cup
134 Standing Alone .01 .05
Canada Cup
135 The Miracle On Ice .01 .05
136 Josef Augusta .01 .05
Canada Cup
137 A Soviet Rout .01 .05
Canada Cup
138 Vicktor Zhluktov .02 .10
Canada Cup
139 Bobby Hull .20 .50
Phil Esposito
Marcel Dionne
140 Bob Gainey .05 .15
141 Anders Hedberg .05 .15
Canada Cup
142 Bobby Hull .30 .75
143 Ulf Nilsson .05 .15
144 Sergei Kapustin .05 .15
Canada Cup
145 Borje Salming .05 .15
Canada Cup
146 Well Enough To Win .01 .05
Canada Cup
147 Biggest Upset .01 .05
Canada Cup
148 Matti Hagman .01 .05
149 Unbeatable .01 .05
150 Boris Alexandrov .05 .15
Canada
151 A Goal Tending Duel .02 .10
Can
152 Vladimir Dzurilla .02 .10
Canad
153 Phil Esposito .20 .50
Canada Cup
154 Rogatien Vachon .05 .15
Canada Cup
155 Milan Novy .01 .05
156 Vladimir Martinec .02 .10
Canada Cup
157 Good For Hockey .01 .05
Canada Cup
158 Bill Nyrop .01 .05
159 Pride .01 .05
160 Another Summit .01 .05
Canada Cup
161 Alexander Maltsev .15 .40
Canada Cup
162 Gilbert Perreault .08 .25
Canada Cup
163 Vladislav Tretiak .40 1.00
163A Vladislav Tretiak AU
164 Vladimir Vikulov .02 .10
Canada Cup
165 Canada Cup Final .01 .05
Game 1
166 Not There Yet .01 .05
Canada Cup
167 Fast and Furious .01 .05
Canada Cup
168 4 - 3/Canada Cup/4 - 4 .01 .05
169 Bill Barber .05 .15
170 The Grapevine .02 .10
Canada Cup
171 Guy Lapointe .05 .15
172 Reggie Leach .01 .05
173 Sittler's Goal .08 .25
Canada Cup
174 Lanny McDonald .08 .25
Canada Cup
175 Darryl Sittler .08 .25
Canada Cup
176 The Canada Cup .05 .15
Canada Cup
177 Bobby Clarke .08 .25
178 Last Time for No. 9 .08 .25
Canada Cup
179 Marcel Dionne .08 .25
Canada Cup
180 Peter Mahovlich .01 .05
Canada Cup
181 Denis Potvin .08 .25
182 Larry Robinson .08 .25
Canada Cup
183 Steve Shutt .05 .15
184 Bobby Orr .40 1.00
Tournament MVP
185 Rogatien Vachon .05 .15
MVP
186 Milan Novy .02 .10
MVP -- CSSR
187 Matti Hagman .01 .05
MVP -- Finland
188 Borje Salming .05 .15
MVP -- Sweden
189 Robbie Ftorek .01 .05
MVP -- US
190 Alexander Maltsev .15 .40
MVP
191 Canada Final Series .01 .05
192 Canada Series Totals .01 .05
Canada Cup
193 CSSR Final Series .01 .05
Total
194 CSSR Series Totals .01 .05
Canada Cup
195 Rogatien Vachon AS .05 .15
Canada Cup
196 Bobby Orr AS .40 1.00
197 Borje Salming AS .05 .15
Canada
198 Milan Novy AS .01 .05
Canada Cup
199 Darryl Sittler AS .05 .15
Canada Cup
200 Alexander Maltsev AS .15 .40
Canada Cup
201 Canada Cup Checklist .02 .10
NNO Checklist Sheet 8-1/2x11 .75 2.00
artist rendition

1992 Future Trends Promo Sheet

Produced by The Future Trends Experience Ltd., this limited edition sample sheet commemorated the 1976 U.S. Olympic Team. The front of this 11" by 8 1/2" sheet featured a full-bleed ghosted team photo as the background for six Canada Cup cards. The cards were placed in two rows diagonally across the sheet. Red and gold stripes formed a border surrounding the cards and intersecting a white panel on the left side of the sheet. The panel had a thin red, gold, and blue border and contained an American flag icon, the Team USA emblem, text about the team, and a gold limited edition stamp with the production run total (10,000). The back was blank. The cards were unnumbered and checklisted below as they appear from left to right starting with the first row.

1 Team USA Sheet 1.50 4.00

1997 Gatorade Stickers

This set was issued as a promotional giveaway with the purchase of a Gatorade beverage in Canada. The stickers featured head shots and a brief note of interest about the player. They were distributed in six sheets, with four players appearing on each sheet.

COMPLETE SET (6) 8.00 20.00
PAN1 Daniel Alfredsson .40 1.00
Vincent Damphousse
Bill Guerin
Jarome Iginla
PAN2 Saku Koivu
Eric Lindros
Mark Messier
Mike Modano
PAN3 Alexander Mogilny .60 1.50
Jose Theodore
Ron Tugnutt
Doug Weight
PAN4 Joe Nieuwendyk .60 1.50
Chris Pronger
Mark Recchi
Luc Robitaille
PAN5 Tie Domi 2.00 5.00
Grant Fuhr
Jaromir Jagr
Paul Kariya
PAN6 Patrick Roy 4.00 10.00
Joe Sakic
Teemu Selanne
Mats Sundin

2006-07 Gatorade

MPLETE SET (91) 60.00 100.00
1 Miikka Kiprusoff 1.50 4.00
2 Dion Phaneuf 2.00 5.00
3 Jarome Iginla 2.00 5.00
4 Alex Tanguay 1.25 3.00
5 Daymond Langkow .75 2.00
6 Matthew Lombardi .75 2.00
7 Chuck Kobasew .40 1.00
8 Kristian Huselius .40 1.00
9 Roman Hamrlik .40 1.00
10 Stephane Yelle .40 1.00
11 Tony Amonte .40 1.00
12 Robyn Regehr .40 1.00
13 Jeff Friesen .40 1.00
14 Marcus Nilson .40 1.00
15 Andrew Ference .40 1.00
16 Petr Sykora .40 1.00
17 Ales Hemsky 1.25 3.00
18 Joffrey Lupul .75 2.00
19 Dwayne Roloson .75 2.00
20 Ryan Smyth 1.25 3.00
21 Jarret Stoll .75 2.00
22 Patrick Thoresen .75 2.00
23 Raffi Torres .75 2.00
24 Fernando Pisani .75 2.00
25 Shawn Horcoff .75 2.00
26 Marc-Andre Bergeron .40 1.00
27 Jason Smith .40 1.00
28 Ladislav Smid .40 1.00
29 Steve Staios .40 1.00
30 Jussi Markkanen .60 1.50
31 Saku Koivu 2.00 5.00
32 Chris Higgins .75 2.00
33 Sheldon Souray .40 1.00
34 Andrei Markov .40 1.00
35 Michael Ryder .75 2.00
36 Cristobal Huet 1.50 4.00
37 David Aebischer .75 2.00
38 Alex Kovalev .40 1.00
39 Mike Johnson .40 1.00
40 Alexander Perezhogin .40 1.00
41 Guillaume Latendresse 2.00 5.00
42 Radek Bonk .40 1.00
43 Sergei Samsonov .75 2.00
44 Tomas Plekanec .75 2.00
45 Michael Komisarek .75 2.00
46 Jason Spezza 1.25 3.00
47 Dany Heatley 1.50 4.00
48 Joe Corvo .40 1.00
49 Daniel Alfredsson 1.25 3.00
50 Martin Gerber .75 2.00
51 Ray Emery 1.25 3.00
52 Antoine Vermette .40 1.00
53 Patrick Eaves .75 2.00
54 Dean McAmmond .40 1.00
55 Mike Fisher .75 2.00
56 Chris Neil .75 2.00
57 Wade Redden .75 2.00
58 Chris Phillips .75 2.00
59 Andrej Meszaros .75 2.00
60 Chris Kelly .40 1.00
61 Mats Sundin 1.25 3.00
62 Alexander Steen 1.25 3.00
63 Darcy Tucker 1.25 3.00
64 Kyle Wellwood .75 2.00
65 Andrew Raycroft .75 2.00
66 Bryan McCabe .75 2.00
67 Tomas Kaberle .75 2.00
68 Jeff O'Neill .40 1.00
69 Alexei Ponikarovsky .40 1.00
70 Ian White .40 1.00
71 Michael Peca .75 2.00
72 Chad Kilger .40 1.00
73 Hal Gill .40 1.00
74 Matt Stajan .75 2.00
75 Pavel Kubina .40 1.00
76 Markus Naslund .75 2.00
77 Roberto Luongo 2.00 5.00
78 Daniel Sedin .75 2.00
79 Henrik Sedin .75 2.00
80 Brendan Morrison .40 1.00
81 Sami Salo .40 1.00
82 Jan Bulis .40 1.00
83 Taylor Pyatt .40 1.00
84 Mattias Ohlund .40 1.00
85 Lukas Krajicek .40 1.00
86 Trevor Linden 1.25 3.00
87 Ryan Kesler .40 1.00
88 Matt Cooke .40 1.00
89 Willie Mitchell .40 1.00
90 Kevin Bieksa .75 2.00
91 Sidney Crosby SP 25.00 60.00

1967-68 General Mills

Little is known about this recently catalogued five-card set, save for it measured approximately 2 5/16" by 2 13/16" and featured color player photos in a white border. It appeared the cards were cut-outs from boxes of General Mills cereal, as a full box back picturing Harry Howell with a checklist listing these cards was known to exist. Further information would be appreciated. The backs are blank. The cards are unnumbered and checklisted below in alphabetical order.

COMPLETE SET (5) 500.00 1000.00
1 Jean Beliveau 75.00 150.00
2 Gordie Howe 150.00 300.00
3 Harry Howell 40.00 80.00
4 Stan Mikita 62.50 125.00
5 Bobby Orr 250.00 500.00

1991-92 Gillette

is 48-card standard-size set, sponsored by Gillette, featured players from the old four divisions of the NHL: Smythe (1-10), Norris (11-20), Adams (21-30), and Patrick (31-40). Each ten-card pack came with a trivia card and a checklist card. To receive one ten-card pack, collectors were required to send to Gillette of Canada one UPC symbol from any Canadian Gillette product, the dated receipt with purchase price circled, and 2.00 for shipping and handling. The entire set could be obtained by sending in three UPC symbols plus 5.00. Reportedly just 30,000 sets were produced, and the offer expired on August 28, 1992. On a black card face, the fronts carried a color action photo enclosed by a gold border. The title "Gillette Series" appear in gold lettering at the top, while the player's name appear at the bottom between the 75th NHL Anniversary logo and the team logo. Some of the cards had the words "Rookie Card" in the bottom gold border (numbers 3, 10, 20, 30, 40). In a horizontal format, the backs had biography and statistics (1987-91) in English and French, as well as a color head shot. The player cards were numbered on the back. Although the backs of the four unnumbered checklist cards were identical (each one lists all 40 cards), a different division name appear on the front of each checklist card: Smythe, Norris, Adams, and Patrick. The fronts of each of the four unnumbered trivia card were identical, while their backs featured two different questions and answers.

COMPLETE SET (48) 10.00 25.00
1 Luc Robitaille .20 .50

2 Esa Tikkanen .08 .25
3 Pat Falloon .05 .15
4 Theo Fleury .30 .75
5 Trevor Linden .20 .50
6 Rob Blake .20 .50
7 Al MacInnis .20 .50
8 Bob Essensa .20 .50
9 Bill Ranford .20 .50
10 Pavel Bure .75 2.00
11 Wendel Clark .20 .50
12 Sergei Fedorov .60 1.50
13 Jeremy Roenick .30 .75
14 Brett Hull .40 1.00
15 Mike Modano .40 1.00
16 Chris Chelios .30 .75
17 Dave Ellett .05 .15
18 Ed Belfour .30 .75
19 Grant Fuhr .20 .50
20 Martin Lapointe .05 .15
21 Kirk Muller .08 .25
22 Joe Sakic .60 1.50
23 Pat LaFontaine .20 .50
24 Pat Verbeek .20 .50
25 Owen Nolan .20 .50
26 Ray Bourque .40 1.00
27 Eric Desjardins .08 .25
28 Patrick Roy 1.50 4.00
29 Andy Moog .20 .50
30 Valeri Kamensky .20 .50
31 Mark Messier .40 1.00
32 Mike Ricci .20 .50
33 Mario Lemieux 1.50 4.00
34 Jaromir Jagr 1.00 2.50
35 Pierre Turgeon .20 .50
36 Kevin Hatcher .05 .15
37 Paul Coffey .30 .75
38 Chris Terreri .08 .25
39 Mike Richter .30 .75
40 Kevin Todd .05 .15
NNO Patrick Checklist .02 .10
NNO Norris Checklist .02 .10
NNO Adams Trivia .02 .10
NNO Patrick Trivia .02 .10
NNO Smythe Checklist .02 .10
NNO Adams Checklist .02 .10
NNO Smythe Trivia .02 .10
NNO Norris Trivia .02 .10

2001-02 Greats of the Game

leased in mid-October 2001, this set carried an SRP of $5.99 for a 5-card pack. The 89-card set featured past greats of the NHL with color and black-and-white photos on white background card fronts.

COMPLETE SET (89) 15.00 30.00
1 Gordie Howe .75 2.00
2 Glenn Hall .30 .75
3 Jean Beliveau .30 .75
4 Bob Nystrom .20 .50
5 Phil Esposito .40 1.00
6 Dennis Maruk .20 .50
7 Bobby Hull .40 1.00
8 Guy Lafleur .30 .75
9 Gilbert Perreault .25 .60
10 John Davidson .25 .60
11 Peter Stastny .25 .60
12 Steve Shutt .25 .60
13 Henri Richard .30 .75
14 Johnny Bower .25 .60
15 Barry Beck .20 .50
16 Marcel Dionne .30 .75
17 Billy Smith .25 .60
18 Dale Hunter .20 .50
19 Tony Esposito .40 1.00
20 Guy Lapointe .20 .50
21 Ed Giacomin .25 .60
22 Denis Savard .30 .75
23 Rod Gilbert .30 .75
24 Steve Larmer .20 .50
25 Yvan Cournoyer .25 .60
26 Ulf Nilsson .20 .50
27 Jean Ratelle .20 .50
28 Dino Ciccarelli .25 .60
29 Bryan Trottier .30 .75
30 Tim Horton .25 .60
31 Stan Mikita .40 1.00
32 Glenn Anderson .25 .60
33 Bobby Clarke .25 .60
34 Wendel Clark .25 .60
35 Reggie Leach .20 .50
36 Terry Sawchuk .40 1.00
37 Bernie Geoffrion .30 .75
38 Bill Barber .20 .50
39 Tiger Williams .25 .60
40 Alex Delvecchio .30 .75
41 Bernie Parent .25 .60
42 Paul Henderson .20 .50
43 Norm Ullman .25 .60
44 Larry Robinson .25 .60
45 Dave Schultz .25 .60
46 John Ogrodnick .20 .50
47 Rick MacLeish .20 .50
48 Richard Brodeur .25 .60
49 Rick Martin .20 .50
50 Bobby Smith .20 .50
51 Denis Potvin .25 .60
52 Darryl Sittler .30 .75
53 Lanny McDonald .20 .50
54 Brian Bellows .20 .50
55 Frank Mahovlich .25 .60
56 Cam Neely .25 .60
57 Grant Fuhr .25 .60
58 Harry Howell .20 .50
59 Michel Goulet .20 .50
60 Gerry Cheevers .40 1.00
61 Dave Taylor .20 .50
62 Clark Gillies .25 .60
63 Bernie Federko .20 .50
64 Chico Resch .25 .60
65 Andy Bathgate .30 .75
66 Jacques Lemaire .25 .60
67 Ken Hodge .20 .50
68 Rogie Vachon .25 .60
69 Brian Sutter .25 .60
70 Rick Middleton .20 .50
71 Neal Broten .20 .50
72 Mike Bossy .25 .60
73 Borje Salming .25 .60
74 Ted Lindsay .25 .60
75 Mike Gartner .25 .60
76 John Bucyk .20 .50
77 Brad Park .20 .50
78 Red Kelly .30 .75
79 Joe Mullen .20 .50
80 Terry O'Reilly .20 .50
81 Mario Lemieux .75 2.00
82 Butch Goring .25 .60
83 Mike Liut .25 .60
84 Marcel Pronovost .20 .50
85 Serge Savard .25 .60
86 Jari Kurri .25 .60
87 Rick Kehoe .20 .50
88 Gump Worsley .30 .75
89 Kent Nilsson .20 .50

2001-02 Greats of the Game Retro Collection

This 13-card set featured both color and vintage black-and-white action photos on the card fronts with colored foil at each top corner and along the card bottom. The players name was printed on the bottom of the card front, and the card backs carried a player bio and league stats.

COMPLETE SET (13) 15.00 30.00
1 Gordie Howe 2.50 6.00
2 Jean Beliveau 1.00 2.50
3 Phil Esposito 1.25 3.00
4 Bobby Hull 1.25 3.00
5 Guy LaFleur 1.00 2.50
6 Peter Stastny .60 1.50
7 Henri Richard .60 1.50
8 Marcel Dionne .75 2.00
9 Bryan Trottier .60 1.50
10 Bobby Clarke .75 2.00
11 Terry Sawchuk 1.25 3.00
12 Mario Lemieux 3.00 8.00
13 Tony Esposito 1.00 2.50

2001-02 Greats of the Game Autographs

Inserted at a rate of 1:12 hobby and 1:120 retail, this set paralleled the base set but the featured player's autograph on the front bottom of the card. Card backs carried a congratulatory message and a statement of authenticity. Cards #30, 36, and 88 were not produced. Most players signed between 400-475 cards except those marked as SP below. Short prints were reported to be less than 200 copies each.

1 Gordie Howe SP 150.00 300.00
2 Glenn Hall SP 25.00 60.00
3 Jean Beliveau SP 60.00 125.00
4 Bob Nystrom 8.00 20.00
5 Phil Esposito SP 25.00 60.00
6 Dennis Maruk 8.00 20.00
7 Bobby Hull SP 30.00 80.00
8 Guy Lafleur SP 40.00 80.00
9 Gilbert Perreault 8.00 20.00
10 John Davidson 8.00 20.00
11 Peter Stastny SP 40.00 80.00
12 Steve Shutt 8.00 20.00
13 Henri Richard SP 40.00 80.00
14 Johnny Bower 15.00 40.00
15 Barry Beck 8.00 20.00
16 Marcel Dionne SP 20.00 50.00
17 Billy Smith 8.00 20.00
18 Dale Hunter 8.00 20.00
19 Tony Esposito 12.00 30.00
20 Guy LaPointe 12.00 30.00
21 Ed Giacomin 10.00 25.00
22 Denis Savard 8.00 20.00
23 Rod Gilbert 25.00 60.00
24 Steve Larmer 10.00 25.00
25 Yvan Cournoyer 10.00 25.00
26 Ulf Nilsson 8.00 20.00
27 Jean Ratelle 15.00 40.00
28 Dino Ciccarelli 10.00 25.00
29 Bryan Trottier SP 15.00 40.00
31 Stan Mikita SP 25.00 60.00
32 Glenn Anderson 10.00 25.00
33 Bobby Clarke SP 30.00 60.00
34 Wendel Clark 15.00 40.00
35 Reggie Leach 8.00 20.00
37 Bernie Geoffrion 15.00 40.00
38 Bill Barber 8.00 20.00
39 Tiger Williams 10.00 25.00
40 Alex Delvecchio SP 15.00 40.00
41 Bernie Parent 10.00 25.00
42 Paul Henderson SP 100.00 200.00
43 Norm Ullman 8.00 20.00
44 Larry Robinson 8.00 20.00
45 Dave Schultz 8.00 20.00
46 John Ogrodnick 8.00 20.00
47 Rick MacLeish 8.00 20.00
48 Richard Brodeur 8.00 20.00
49 Rick Martin 10.00 25.00
50 Bobby Smith 8.00 20.00
51 Denis Potvin 10.00 25.00
52 Darryl Sittler 8.00 20.00
53 Lanny McDonald 8.00 20.00
54 Brian Bellows 10.00 25.00
55 Frank Mahovlich 8.00 20.00
56 Cam Neely SP 25.00 60.00
57 Grant Fuhr 10.00 25.00
58 Harry Howell 10.00 25.00
59 Michel Goulet 8.00 20.00
60 Gerry Cheevers 10.00 25.00
61 Dave Taylor 8.00 20.00
62 Clark Gillies 8.00 20.00
63 Bernie Federko 8.00 20.00
64 Chico Resch 15.00 30.00
65 Andy Bathgate 8.00 20.00
66 Jacques Lemaire 8.00 20.00
67 Ken Hodge 8.00 20.00
68 Rogie Vachon 8.00 20.00
69 Brian Sutter 8.00 20.00
70 Rick Middleton 8.00 20.00
71 Neal Broten 8.00 20.00
72 Mike Bossy SP 20.00 50.00
73 Borje Salming 8.00 20.00
74 Ted Lindsay SP 25.00 60.00
75 Mike Gartner SP 15.00 40.00
76 John Bucyk 12.00 30.00
77 Brad Park 8.00 20.00
78 Red Kelly 8.00 20.00
79 Joe Mullen 8.00 20.00
80 Terry O'Reilly 8.00 20.00
81 Mario Lemieux 40.00 100.00
82 Butch Goring 8.00 20.00
83 Mike Liut 8.00 20.00
84 Marcel Pronovost 8.00 20.00
85 Serge Savard 8.00 20.00
86 Jari Kurri 8.00 20.00
87 Rick Kehoe 8.00 20.00
89 Kent Nilsson 8.00 20.00
NNO Rod Langway 8.00 20.00

2001-02 Greats of the Game Board Certified

Inserted at a rate of 1:24 hobby and 1:17 retail packs, this 5-card set featured a swatch of the boards from Joe Louis Arena in Detroit. The card fronts carried a full color photo of the featured player and the board swatch. The card backs carried a congratulatory message and authenticity statement. Cards were not numbered and are listed below in alphabetical order.

1 Mike Bossy 5.00 12.00
2 Guy LaFleur 4.00 10.00
3 Mario Lemieux 8.00 20.00
4 Cam Neely 4.00 10.00
5 Peter Stastny 3.00 8.00

2001-02 Greats of the Game Jerseys

Inserted at a rate of 1:30 hobby packs, this 8-card set featured a swatch of game-worn jersey from the featured player on the card front accompanied by a full color photo of the player trimmed in the team's colors. Card backs carried a congratulatory message and a statement of authenticity. Cards were not numbered and are listed below in alphabetical order. The Patrick Roy, long believed to have been pulled from circulation, has shown up in large numbers recently as a result of the Fleer inventory liquidation. The prices are reflective of this widespread availability.

1 Dino Ciccarelli 6.00 15.00
2 Tony Esposito 6.00 15.00
3 Michel Goulet 6.00 15.00
4 Guy Lafleur 10.00 25.00
5 Larry Robinson 8.00 20.00
6 Borje Salming 6.00 15.00
7 Glen Sather 6.00 15.00
8 Denis Savard 6.00 15.00
9 Patrick Roy 15.00 40.00

2001-02 Greats of the Game Sticks

Inserted at a rate of 1:84 hobby and 1:400 retail, this 11-card set featured pieces of game-used sticks of the featured players on the card fronts. The card backs carried a congratulatory message and authenticity statement.

1 Marcel Dionne 10.00 25.00
2 Phil Esposito 12.50 30.00
3 Tony Esposito 10.00 25.00
4 Gordie Howe 12.50 30.00
5 Bobby Hull 12.50 30.00
6 Cam Neely 10.00 25.00
7 Willie O'Ree 8.00 20.00
8 Brad Park 10.00 25.00
9 Henri Richard 10.00 25.00
10 Terry Sawchuk 20.00 50.00
11 Darryl Sittler 10.00 25.00
12 Patrick Roy 12.50 30.00

1983 Hall of Fame Postcards

These postcard-sized (approximately 4" by 6") cards were distributed by complete sub-series. The set was complete at 15 series totaling 240 members of the Hockey Hall of Fame. Cards were listed alphabetically within each sub-series in the checklist below. The cards in this imperial postcard-sized set featured full-color art work by Carlton McDiarmid. The set was produced by the Hockey Hall of Fame, McDiarmid, and Cartophilium. The postcard backs contained the player's name and the year he was elected to the Hockey Hall of Fame. Career milestones or significant accomplishments of the player were listed in both French and English.

COMPLETE SET (240) 140.00 350.00
A1 Sid Abel .75 2.00
A2 Punch Broadbent .40 1.00
A3 Clarence Campbell .40 1.00
A4 Neil Colville .40 1.00
A5 Charlie Conacher 1.25 3.00
A6 Red Dutton .40 1.00
A7 Foster Hewitt 1.25 3.00
A8 Fred Hume .40 1.00
A9 Mickey Ion .40 1.00
A10 Ernest Johnson .40 1.00
A11 Bill Mosienko .40 1.00
A12 Maurice Richard 6.00 15.00
A13 Barney Stanley .40 1.00
A14 Lord Stanley .75 2.00
A15 Cyclone Taylor 1.00 2.50
A16 Tiny Thompson 1.25 3.00
B1 Dan Bain .40 1.00
B2 Hobey Baker .75 2.00
B3 Frank Calder .40 1.00
B4 Frank Foyston .40 1.00
B5 James Hendy .40 1.00
B6 Gordie Howe 6.00 15.00
B7 Harry Lumley 1.25 3.00
B8 Reg Noble .40 1.00
B9 Frank Patrick .40 1.00
B10 Harvey Pulford .40 1.00
B11 Ken Reardon .60 1.50
B12 Bullet Joe Simpson .60 1.50
B13 Conn Smythe .75 2.00
B14 Red Storey .40 1.00
B15 Lloyd Turner .40 1.00
B16 Georges Vezina 3.00 8.00
C1 Jean Beliveau 3.00 8.00
C2 Max Bentley .60 1.50
C3 King Clancy 1.25 3.00
C4 Babe Dye .40 1.00
C5 Ebbie Goodfellow .40 1.00
C6 Charles Hay .40 1.00
C7 Percy Lesueur .60 1.50
C8 Tommy Lockhart .40 1.00
C9 Jack Marshall .40 1.00
C10 Lester Patrick .75 2.00
C11 Bill Quackenbush .60 1.50
C12 Frank Selke .60 1.50
C13 Cooper Smeaton .40 1.00
C14 Hooley Smith .40 1.00
C15 Capt.J.T.Sutherland .40 1.00
C16 Fred Whitcroft .40 1.00
D1 Charles F. Adams .40 1.00
D2 Russell Bowie .40 1.00
D3 Frank Frederickson .40 1.00
D4 H.L. Gilmour .40 1.00
D5 Ching Johnson .60 1.50
D6 Tom Johnson .60 1.50
D7 Aurel Joliat 1.50 4.00
D8 Duke Keats .40 1.00
D9 Red Kelly 1.25 3.00
D10 Frank McGee .40 1.00
D11 James D. Norris .60 1.50
D12 Philip D. Ross .40 1.00
D13 Terry Sawchuk 3.00 8.00
D14 Babe Siebert .60 1.50
D15 Anatoli V. Tarasov .60 1.50
D16 Roy Worters .75 2.00
E1 T. Franklin Ahearn .40 1.00
E2 Harold E. Ballard .75 2.00
E3 Billy Burch .40 1.00
E4 Bill Chadwick .40 1.00
E5 Sprague Cleghorn .75 2.00
E6 Rusty Crawford .40 1.00
E7 Alex Delvecchio 1.25 3.00
E8 George S. Dudley .40 1.00
E9 Ted Kennedy .75 2.00
E10 Newsy Lalonde 1.00 2.50
E11 Billy McGimsie .40 1.00
E12 Frank Nighbor .60 1.50
E13 Bobby Orr 6.00 15.00
E14 Sen. Donat Raymond .40 1.00
E15 Art Ross 1.00 2.50
E16 Jack Walker .40 1.00
F1 Doug Bentley .60 1.50
F2 Walter A. Brown .40 1.00
F3 Dit Clapper 1.00 2.50
F4 Hap Day .40 1.00
F5 Frank Dilio .40 1.00
F6 Bobby Hewitson .40 1.00
F7 Harry Howell .40 1.00
F8 Paul Loicq .40 1.00
F9 Sylvio Mantha .60 1.50
F10 Jacques Plante 3.00 8.00
F11 George Richardson .40 1.00
F12 Nels Stewart .75 2.00
F13 Hod Stuart .40 1.00
F14 Harry Trihey .40 1.00
F15 Marty Walsh .40 1.00
F16 Arthur M. Wirtz .40 1.00
G1 Toe Blake 1.25 3.00
G2 Frank Boucher .60 1.50
G3 Turk Broda 1.50 4.00
G4 Harry Cameron .40 1.00
G5 Leo Dandurand .40 1.00
G6 Joe Hall .40 1.00
G7 George Hay .40 1.00
G8 William A. Hewitt .40 1.00
G9 Bouse Hutton .40 1.00
G10 Dick Irvin .75 2.00
G11 Henri Richard 1.25 3.00
G12 John Ross Robertson .40 1.00
G13 Frank D. Smith .40 1.00
G14 Allan Stanley .40 1.00
G15 Norm Ullman .40 1.00
G16 Harry Watson .40 1.00
H1 Clint Benedict 1.25 3.00
H2 Dickie Boon .40 1.00
H3 Gordie Drillon .60 1.50
H4 Bill Gadsby .40 1.00
H5 Rod Gilbert .40 1.00
H6 Moose Goheen .40 1.00
H7 Tommy Gorman .40 1.00
H8 Glenn Hall 1.25 3.00
H9 Red Horner .40 1.00
H10 Gen.J.R.Kilpatrick .40 1.00
H11 Robert Lebel .40 1.00
H12 Howie Morenz 3.00 8.00
H13 Fred Scanlan .40 1.00
H14 Tommy Smith .40 1.00
H15 Fred C. Waghorne .40 1.00
H16 Cooney Weiland .75 2.00
I1 Weston Adams .40 1.00
I2 Sir Montagu Allan .40 1.00
I3 Frank Brimsek 1.25 3.00
I4 Angus Campbell .40 1.00
I5 Bill Cook .75 2.00
I6 Tom Dunderdale .40 1.00
I7 Emile Francis .40 1.00
I8 Charlie Gardiner .60 1.50
I9 Elmer Lach .60 1.50
I10 Frank Mahovlich 1.25 3.00
I11 Didier Pitre .40 1.00
I12 Joe Primeau 1.25 3.00
I13 Frank Rankin .40 1.00
I14 Ernie Russell .40 1.00
I15 Thayer Tutt .40 1.00
I16 Harry Westwick .40 1.00
J1 Jack Adams .40 1.00
J2 Bunny Ahearne .40 1.00
J3 J.P. Bickell .40 1.00
J4 Johnny Bucyk .60 1.50
J5 Art Coulter .40 1.00
J6 C.G. Drinkwater .40 1.00
J7 George Hainsworth 1.25 3.00
J8 Tim Horton 2.00 5.00
J9 Maj. F. McLaughlin .40 1.00
J10 Dickie Moore .75 2.00
J11 Pierre Pilote .40 1.00
J12 Claude C. Robinson .40 1.00
J13 Sweeney Schriner .40 1.00
J14 Oliver Seibert .40 1.00
J15 Alfred Smith .40 1.00
J16 Phat Wilson .60 1.50
K1 Yvan Cournoyer .60 1.50
K2 Scotty Davidson .40 1.00
K3 Cy Denneny .60 1.50
K4 Bill Durnan 1.00 2.50
K5 Shorty Green .40 1.00
K6 Riley Hern .40 1.00
K7 Bryan Hextall Sr. .40 1.00
K8 Bill Jennings .40 1.00
K9 Gordon W. Juckes .40 1.00
K10 Paddy Moran .60 1.50
K11 James Norris .40 1.00
K12 Harry Oliver .40 1.00
K13 Sam Pollock .40 1.00
K14 Marcel Pronovost .40 1.00
K15 Jack Ruttan .40 1.00
K16 Earl Seibert .40 1.00
L1 Buck Boucher .40 1.00
L2 George V. Brown .40 1.00
L3 Arthur F. Farrell .40 1.00
L4 Herb Gardiner .40 1.00
L5 Si Griffis .40 1.00
L6 Hap Holmes .40 1.00
L7 Harry Hyland .40 1.00
L8 Tommy Ivan .40 1.00
L9 Jack Laviolette .40 1.00
L10 Ted Lindsay 1.25 3.00
L11 Francis Nelson .40 1.00
L12 William M. Northey .40 1.00
L13 Babe Pratt .40 1.00
L14 Chuck Rayner .75 2.00
L15 Milt Rodden .40 1.00
L16 Milt Schmidt 1.00 2.50
M1 Butch Bouchard .60 1.50
M2 Jack Butterfield .40 1.00
M3 Joseph Cattarinich .40 1.00
M4 Alex Connell .75 2.00
M5 Bill Cowley .60 1.50
M6 Chaucer Elliott .40 1.00
M7 James Gardner .40 1.00
M8 Boom Boom Geoffrion 1.50 4.00
M9 Tom Hooper .40 1.00
M10 Syd Howe .40 1.00
M11 Harvey(Busher)Jackson .60 1.50
M12 Al Leader .40 1.00
M13 Steamer Maxwell .40 1.00
M14 Blair Russell .40 1.00
M15 William W. Wirtz .40 1.00
M16 Gump Worsley 1.25 3.00
N1 George Armstrong .75 2.00
N2 Ace Bailey 1.25 3.00
N3 Jack Darragh .40 1.00
N4 Ken Dryden 3.00 8.00
N5 Eddie Gerard .40 1.00
N6 Jack Gibson .40 1.00
N7 Hugh Lehman .40 1.00
N8 Mickey MacKay .40 1.00
N9 Joe Malone 1.25 3.00
N10 Bruce A. Norris .40 1.00
N11 J. Ambrose O'Brien .40 1.00
N12 Lynn Patrick .60 1.50
N13 Tommy Phillips .40 1.00
N14 Allan W. Pickard .40 1.00
N15 Jack Stewart .40 1.00
N16 Frank Udvari .40 1.00
O1 Syl Apps .75 2.00
O2 John G. Ashley .40 1.00
O3 Marty Barry .40 1.00
O4 Andy Bathgate .60 1.50
O5 Johnny Bower 1.25 3.00
O6 Frank Buckland .40 1.00
O7 Jimmy Dunn .40 1.00
O8 Michael Grant .40 1.00
O9 Doug Harvey 1.25 3.00
O10 George McNamara .40 1.00
O11 Stan Mikita 1.25 3.00
O12 Sen.H.de M. Molson .40 1.00
O13 Gordon Roberts .40 1.00
O14 Eddie Shore 3.00 8.00
O15 Bruce Stuart .40 1.00
O16 Carl P. Voss .40 1.00
NNO Binder .40 1.00

1985-87 Hall of Fame

This 261-card standard-size set was basically two different sets but the second set was merely a reissue of the first Hall of Fame set done two years before, adding the new inductees since that time. The only difference in the first 240 cards in this later 1987 set and the prior set was the different copyright year at the bottom of each reverse in this set. Note however that the copyright line for the 1985 set confusingly showed a 1983 copyright date (apparently referring back to the post card set) vertically printed on the card back. One exception was Gordie Howe; his career was so long that his season-by-season statistics filled up the entire card back leaving no room for a copyright line. The set featured members of the Hockey Hall of Fame portrayed by the artwork of Carlton McDiarmid. Backs were written in both French and English. The set was originally sold in the Canadian Sears 1985 Christmas Catalog.

COMPLETE SET (261) 40.00 100.00
1 Maurice Richard 3.00 8.00
2 Sid Abel .30 .75
3 Punch Broadbent .15 .40
4 Clarence S. Campbell .15 .40
5 Neil Colville .15 .40
6 Charlie Conacher .40 1.00
7 Red Dutton .15 .40
8 Foster W. Hewitt .40 1.00
9 Mickey Ion .15 .40
10 Ernest Johnson .15 .40
11 Bill Mosienko .15 .40
12 Russell Stanley .15 .40
13 Lord Stanley .30 .75
14 Cyclone Taylor .30 .75
15 Tiny Thompson .30 .75
16 Gordie Howe 3.00 8.00
17 Hobey Baker .30 .75
18 Frank Calder .15 .40
19 Jim Hendy .15 .40
20 Frank Foyston .15 .40
21 Harry Lumley .40 1.00
22 Reg Noble .15 .40
23 Frank A. Patrick .15 .40
24 Harvey Pulford .15 .40
25 Ken Reardon .20 .50
26 Bullet Joe Simpson .20 .50
27 Conn Smythe .30 .75
28 Red Storey .15 .40
29 Lloyd Turner .15 .40
30 Georges Vezina 1.00 2.50
31 Jean Beliveau 1.00 2.50
32 Max Bentley .20 .50
33 King Clancy .40 1.00
34 Babe Dye .15 .40
35 Ebbie Goodfellow .15 .40
36 Charles Hay .15 .40
37 Percy Lesueur .20 .50
38 Tommy Lockhart .15 .40
39 Jack Marshall .15 .40
40 Lester Patrick .30 .75
41 Frank Selke .20 .50
42 J. Cooper Smeaton .15 .40
43 Hooley Smith .15 .40
44 Capt.J.T. Sutherland .15 .40
45 Fred Whitcroft .15 .40
46 Terry Sawchuk 1.50 4.00
47 Charles F. Adams .15 .40
48 Russell Bowie .15 .40
49 Frank Fredrickson .15 .40
50 Billy Gilmour .15 .40
51 Ching Johnson .20 .50
52 Tom Johnson .30 .75
53 Aurel Joliat .60 1.50
54 Duke Keats .15 .40
55 Red Kelly .40 1.00
56 Frank McGee .15 .40
57 James D. Norris .15 .40
58 Philip D. Ross .15 .40
59 Babe Siebert .20 .50
60 Roy Worters .30 .75
61 Bobby Orr 3.00 8.00
62 T. Franklin Ahearn .15 .40
63 Harold E. Ballard .30 .75
64 Billy Burch .15 .40
65 Bill Chadwick .15 .40
66 Sprague Cleghorn .30 .75
67 Rusty Crawford .15 .40
68 George S. Dudley .15 .40
69 Teeder Kennedy .30 .75
70 Newsy Lalonde .40 1.00
71 Billy McGimsie .15 .40
72 Frank Nighbor .20 .50
73 Sen. Donat Raymond .15 .40
74 Art Ross .40 1.00
75 Jack Walker .15 .40
76 Jacques Plante 1.50 4.00
77 Doug Bentley .20 .50
78 Walter A. Brown .15 .40
79 Dit Clapper .40 1.00
80 Hap Day .15 .40
81 Frank Dilio .15 .40
82 Bobby Hewitson .15 .40
83 Harry Howell .15 .40
84 Sylvio Mantha .20 .50
85 George Richardson .15 .40
86 Nels Stewart .30 .75
87 Hod Stuart .15 .40
88 Harry Trihey .15 .40
89 Marty Walsh .15 .40
90 Arthur M. Wirtz .15 .40
91 Henri Richard .60 1.50
92 Toe Blake .40 1.00
93 Frank Boucher .20 .50
94 Turk Broda .60 1.50
95 Harry Cameron .15 .40
96 Leo J.V. Dandurand .15 .40
97 Joe Hall .15 .40
98 George W. Hay .15 .40
99 William A. Hewitt .15 .40
100 Bouse Hutton .15 .40
101 Dick Irvin .20 .50
102 John Ross Robertson .15 .40
103 Frank D. Smith .15 .40
104 Norm Ullman .15 .40
105 Moose Watson .15 .40
106 Howie Morenz 1.00 2.50
107 Clint Benedict .40 1.00
108 Dickie Boon .15 .40
109 Gordon Drillon .20 .50
110 Bill Gadsby .15 .40
111 Rod Gilbert .15 .40
112 Moose Goheen .15 .40
113 Tommy Gorman .15 .40
114 Glenn Hall .40 1.00
115 Red Horner .15 .40
116 Gen.J.R. Kilpatrick .15 .40
117 Robert Lebel .15 .40
118 Fred Scanlan .15 .40
119 Fred C. Waghorne .15 .40
120 Cooney Weiland .30 .75
121 Frank Mahovlich .40 1.00
122 Weston Adams Sr. .15 .40
123 Sir Montagu Allan .15 .40
124 Frank Brimsek .40 1.00
125 Angus D. Campbell .15 .40
126 Bill Cook .30 .75
127 Tom Dunderdale .15 .40
128 Chuck Gardiner .15 .40
129 Elmer Lach .20 .50
130 Didier Pitre .15 .40
131 Joe Primeau .40 1.00
132 Frank Rankin .15 .40
133 Ernie Russell .15 .40
134 W. Thayer Tutt .15 .40
135 Harry Westwick .15 .40
136 Yvan Cournoyer .20 .50
137 Scotty Davidson .15 .40
138 Cy Denneny .20 .50
139 Bill Durnan .40 1.00
140 Shorty Green .15 .40
141 Bryan Hextall Sr. .15 .40
142 Bill Jennings .15 .40
143 Gordon W. Juckes .15 .40
144 Paddy Moran .20 .50
145 James Norris .15 .40
146 Harold Oliver .15 .40
147 Sam Pollock .15 .40
148 Marcel Pronovost .15 .40
149 Jack Ruttan .15 .40
150 Earl W. Seibert .15 .40
151 Ted Lindsay .40 1.00
152 George V. Brown .15 .40
153 Arthur F. Farrell .15 .40
154 Herb Gardiner .15 .40
155 Si Griffis .15 .40
156 Hap Holmes .15 .40
157 Harry Hyland .15 .40
158 Tommy Ivan .15 .40
159 Jack Laviolette .15 .40
160 Francis Nelson .15 .40
161 William M. Northey .15 .40
162 Babe Pratt .15 .40
163 Chuck Rayner .30 .75
164 Mike Rodden .15 .40
165 Milt Schmidt .40 1.00
166 Boom Boom Geoffrion .60 1.50
167 Jack Butterfield .15 .40
168 Joseph Cattarinich .15 .40
169 Alex Connell .30 .75
170 Bill Cowley .20 .50
171 Chaucer Eliott .15 .40
172 James Gardner .15 .40
173 Tom Hooper .15 .40
174 Syd Howe .15 .40
175 Harvey(Busher) Jackson .20 .50
176 Al Leader .15 .40
177 Steamer Maxwell .15 .40
178 Blair Russell .15 .40
179 William W. Wirtz .15 .40
180 Gump Worsley .40 1.00
181 Johnny Bucyk .20 .50
182 Jack Adams .15 .40
183 Bunny Ahearne .15 .40
184 J.P. Bickell .15 .40
185 Art Coulter .15 .40
186 C.G. Drinkwater .15 .40
187 George Hainsworth .40 1.00
188 Tim Horton 1.00 2.50
189 Maj.F. McLaughlin .15 .40
190 Dickie Moore .30 .75
191 Pierre Pilote .15 .40
192 Claude C. Robinson .15 .40
193 Oliver L. Seibert .15 .40
194 Alfred E. Smith .15 .40
195 Phat Wilson .15 .40
196 Ken Dryden 1.50 4.00
197 George Armstrong .30 .75
198 Ace Bailey .40 1.00
199 Jack Darragh .15 .40
200 Eddie Gerard .15 .40
201 Jack Gibson .15 .40
202 Hugh Lehman .15 .40
203 Mickey MacKay .15 .40
204 Joe Malone .30 .75
205 Bruce A. Norris .15 .40
206 J.Ambrose O'Brien .15 .40
207 Lynn Patrick .20 .50
208 Tommy Phillips .15 .40
209 Allan W. Pickard .15 .40
210 Jack Stewart .15 .40
211 Johnny Bower .40 1.00
212 Syl Apps .30 .75
213 John G. Ashley .15 .40
214 Marty Barry .15 .40
215 Andy Bathgate .20 .50
216 Frank Buckland .15 .40
217 Jimmy Dunn .15 .40
218 Michael Grant .15 .40
219 Doug Harvey .40 1.00
220 George McNamara .15 .40
221 Sen.H.deM. Molson .15 .40
222 Gordon Roberts .15 .40
223 Eddie Shore 1.00 2.50
224 Bruce Stuart .15 .40
225 Carl P. Voss .15 .40
226 Stan Mikita .40 1.00
227 Dan Bain .15 .40
228 Butch Bouchard .20 .50
229 Buck Boucher .15 .40
230 Alex Delvecchio .40 1.00
231 Emile P. Francis .15 .40
232 Riley Hern .15 .40
233 Fred J. Hume .15 .40
234 Paul Loicq .15 .40
235 Bill Quackenbush .20
236 Sweeney Schriner .15
237 Tommy Smith .15
238 Allan Stanley .15
239 Anatoli V. Tarasov .20
240 Frank Udvari .15
241 Harry Sinden .30
242 Bobby Hull 1.50 4
243 Punch Imlach .25
244 Phil Esposito .75 2
245 Jacques Lemaire .30
246 Bernie Parent .40 1
247 Rudy Pilous .25
248 Bert Olmstead .25
249 Jean Ratelle .40 1.
250 Gerry Cheevers .40 1.
251 William Hanley .25
252 Leo Boivin .25
253 Jake Milford .25
254 John Mariucci .25
255 Dave Keon .40 1
256 Serge Savard .25
257 John A. Ziegler Jr. .25
258 Bobby Clarke .60 1
259 Ed Giacomin .40 1.
260 Jacques Laperriere .25
261 Matt Pavelich .25

1992-93 Hall of Fame Legend

The Hockey Hall of Fame in association with the Diamond Connection and the Sports Gallery of Art produced this 18-card set as the first of three series be released each year. Over a four year period, all members and builders of Hockey's Hall of Fame wil have been featured. Production was limited to 10,0 numbered sets, and buyers retained exclusive right their assigned number throughout the duration of th project. Issued in a cardboard box, the cards measu approximately 3 1/2" by 5 1/2" and featured the wo noted sports artist Doug West. The front displayed color reproduction of the artist's original painting. T back had a parchment background with navy blue borders and included biographical information, a player profile, career statistics, each team played fo and the years played. A registration form and an ownership transfer form were included with each se The card number and set serial number are in the lo right corner.

COMPLETE SET (36) 60.00 150
1 Harry Lumley 2.00 5
2 Conn Smythe CO 1.50 4
3 Maurice Richard 6.00 15
4 Bobby Orr 8.00 20
5 Bernie Geoffrion 2.50 6
6 Hobey Baker 2.00 5
7 Phil Esposito 2.50 6
8 King Clancy 2.50 6
9 Gordie Howe 6.00 15
10 Emile Francis 1.50 4
11 Jacques Plante 3.00 8
12 Sid Abel 1.50 4
13 Foster Hewitt 2.00 5
14 Charlie Conacher 2.00 5
15 Stan Mikita 2.50 6
16 Bobby Clarke 2.00 5
17 Norm Ullman 1.50 4
18 Lord Stanley of Preston 2.00 5
19 Ted Lindsay 2.00 5
20 Duke Keats 1.50 4
21 Jack Adams 1.50 4
22 Bill Mosienko 1.50 4
23 Johnny Bower 2.00 5
24 Tim Horton 3.00 8
25 Punch Imlach 1.50 4
26 Georges Vezina 4.00 10
27 Earl Seibert 1.50 4
28 Bryan Hextall Sr. 1.50 4
29 Babe Pratt 1.50 4
30 Gump Worsley 2.00 5
31 Ed Giacomin 2.00 5
32 Ace Bailey 2.00 5
33 Harry Sinden 1.50 4
34 Lanny McDonald 2.00 5
35 Tommy Ivan 1.50 4
36 Frank Calder 1.50 4

1994 Hall of Fame Tickets

Measuring approximately 2 5/16" by 3 1/2", each o these tickets admitted one to the Hockey Hall of Fa in Toronto. Each ticket was printed on thin cardboa stock and featured a full-bleed photo on its front. O background that shades from blue to white, the horizontal backs carried the Hall of Fame's street address, a description of the front picture, founding sponsors' logos, and a barcode. The tickets were numbered on the back.

COMPLETE SET (12) 18.00 45
1 Stanley Cup 1.50 4
2 O'Brien Trophy 1.25 3
3 Dan Bain Artifacts 1.25 3
4 Art Ross Artifacts 1.50 4
5 Artifacts of Irvine (Ac 1.50 4
6 Artifacts of Clint Bene 2.00 5
7 Artifacts of Howie More 3.00 8
8 Artifacts of Roy (Shrim 1.50 4
9 Artifacts of Andy Bathg 1.25 3
10 Artifacts of Jacques Pl 3.00 8
11 Artifacts of Terry Sawc 3.00 8
12 Artifacts of Milt Schmi 1.50 4

1998 Hall of Fame Medallion

Issued only in Canada, these medallions were mou on a clear plastic holder and featured statistical an biographical information on the back.

COMPLETE SET (2) 6.00 15
1 Michel Goulet 3.00 8
2 Peter Stastny 4.00 8

1914 Happy Christmas Postca

Full color postcard that measures 3 1/2 x 5 1/2. Fr featured a young lady with a hockey stick and the words Happy Christmas in the lower right-hand co Small print on card back said Series 259 F.

NNO Happy Christmas 10.00 20

1999 Hasbro Starting Lineup Cards

These cards were packaged along with plastic figur in the Hasbro Starting Lineup product. Because th packages often were left intact, it could be difficult obtain these singles. This set was produced by Up Deck.

COMPLETE SET (17) 10.00 25
1 Mike Dunham .40 1

2 Peter Forsberg .60 1.50
3 Wayne Gretzky 2.00 5.00
Jeff Hackett .60 1.50
5 Dominik Hasek .60 1.50
5 Jaromir Jagr .60 1.50
7 Curtis Joseph .75 2.00
3 Paul Kariya .60 1.50
9 Nikolai Khabibulin .40 1.00
0 Olaf Kolzig .40 1.00
1 Nicklas Lidstrom .75 2.00
2 Eric Lindros .60 1.50
3 Mike Modano .40 1.00
4 Keith Primeau .40 1.00
5 Chris Pronger .40 1.00
6 Sergei Samsonov .75 2.00
7 Steve Yzerman 1.25 3.00

1975-76 HCA Steel City Vacuum

.ittle is known about this set beyond the checklist. The set has the same look as the Hamilton Fincups set produced that same season.

COMPLETE SET (22) 5.00 10.00
Mike Buchko .25 .50
2 Pino Caterini .25 .50
3 Rich Chittley .25 .50
S. Hutchings .25 .50
5 Jim Italiano .25 .50
5 Scott Kyle .25 .50
7 Stan Malecki .25 .50
3 Mike McHugh .25 .50
9 Jeff Ninham .25 .50
0 Brad Roberts .25 .50
1 Chris Roberts .25 .50
2 Bruce Shipley .25 .50
3 G. Stevenson .25 .50
4 Keith Taylor .25 .50
5 Mark Tonaj .25 .50
6 F. Warwick .25 .50
7 Pat Windsor .25 .50
8 Bill Zenette .25 .50
9 Fred LeBlanc PR .13 .25
0 John Taylor VP .13 .25
1 Management .13 .25
2 Ange Savelli CO .50 1.00

1975-76 Heroes Stand-Ups

These 31 "Hockey Heroes Autographed Pin-up/Stand-Up Sportrophies" featured NHL players from five different teams. The stand-ups came in two different sizes. The Bruins and Flyers stand-ups were approximately 15 1/2" by 8/3/4", while the Islanders stand-ups were approximately 13 1/2" by 7 1/2" and were issued three to a strip. The stand-ups were made of laminated cardboard, and the yellow frame is decorated with red stars. Each stand-up featured a color action shot of the player. A facsimile autograph was inscribed across the bottom of the stand-up. The stand-ups were unnumbered and checklisted below alphabetically according to and within teams as follows: Boston Bruins (1-7), Montreal Canadiens (8-13), New York Islanders (14-19), Philadelphia Flyers (20-25), and Toronto Maple Leafs (26-31).

COMPLETE SET (31) 125.00 250.00
Gerry Cheevers 6.00 12.00
Terry O'Reilly 3.00 6.00
Bobby Orr 25.00 50.00
Brad Park 4.00 8.00
Jean Ratelle 4.00 8.00
Andre Savard 2.50 5.00
Gregg Sheppard 2.50 5.00
Yvan Cournoyer 4.00 8.00
Guy Lafleur 10.00 20.00
0 Jacques Lemaire 4.00 8.00
1 Peter Mahovlich 2.50 5.00
2 Doug Risebrough 2.50 5.00
3 Larry Robinson 6.00 12.00
4 Billy Harris 2.50 5.00
5 Gerry Hart 2.50 5.00
6 Denis Potvin 6.00 12.00
7 Glenn Resch 4.00 8.00
8 Bryan Trottier 6.00 12.00
9 Ed Westfall 2.50 5.00
0 Bill Barber 4.00 8.00
1 Bobby Clarke 6.00 12.00
2 Reggie Leach 2.50 5.00
3 Rick MacLeish 2.50 5.00
4 Bernie Parent 6.00 12.00
5 Dave Schultz 4.00 8.00
6 Lanny McDonald 4.00 8.00
7 Borje Salming 3.00 6.00
8 Darryl Sittler 4.00 8.00
9 Wayne Thomas 3.00 6.00
0 Errol Thompson 2.50 5.00
1 Tiger Williams 4.00 8.00

1992-93 High Liner Stanley Cup

National Sea Products Ltd., producer and manufacturer of High Liner brand fish products, produced a 28-card, standard-size set to celebrate the Centennial of the Stanley Cup (1893-1993). Specially marked packages of High Liner frozen fish products contained two cards. Collectors could also order additional cards by clipping the order form from the box, checking the cards desired, and sending it in with six UPC symbols from any High Liner brand product plus 3.99. The form limited requests to one card request per card number. The fronts featured full-bleed black-and-white and color team pictures of Stanley Cup champions. The pale blue, horizontal backs presented a French and English summary of the championship season and a list of the players pictured. A darker blue stripe across the top displayed the Stanley Cup logo and the set name in French and English. The team name and the year they won the Stanley Cup appeared in the lower left corner.

COMPLETE SET (28) 16.00 40.00
Montreal AAA .40 1.00
Winnipeg Victorias .40 1.00
Montreal Victorias .40 1.00
Montreal Shamrocks .40 1.00
Ottawa Silver Seven .40 1.00
Kenora Thistles .40 1.00
Montreal Wanderers 1.00 2.50
Quebec Bulldogs .40 1.00
Toronto Blueshirts 1.00 2.50
0 Vancouver Millionaires 1.00 2.50
1 Seattle Metropolitans 1.00 2.50
2 Toronto Arenas 1.00 2.50
3 Toronto St. Patricks 1.00 2.50
4 Victoria Cougars .40 1.00
5 Ottawa Senators .40 1.00
5 Montreal Maroons 1.00 2.50
7 New York Rangers .40 1.00
3 Detroit Red Wings 1.25 3.00
9 Montreal Canadiens 1.50 4.00
0 Chicago Blackhawks .40 1.00
1 Toronto Maple Leafs 1.25 3.00
2 Boston Bruins 1.25 3.00
3 Philadelphia Flyers .40 1.00
4 New York Islanders .40 1.00
5 Edmonton Oilers 2.00 5.00
6 Calgary Flames .40 1.00
27 Pittsburgh Penguins 1.00 2.50
28 Checklist Card .40 1.00

1993-94 High Liner Greatest Goalies

National Sea Products Ltd., producer and manufacturer of High Liner brand fish products, produced a 15-card, standard-size set of the Greatest Goalies of the NHL, a follow-up to High Liner's 28-card 1992-93 Stanley Cup Centennial set. Specially marked packages of High Liner frozen fish products contained one card. Collectors could also order the complete set through a mail-in offer as outlined on the inside of the specially marked High Liner packages. The set was made from white card stock and was primarily devoted to goalies that have won the Vezina Trophy, the NHL's top annual award for goaltenders. The fronts featured white-bordered color player action shots, with the player's name, team and, season printed in white within a blue band at the bottom. The logo, with Greatest Goalies printed in French and English, appeared in the lower left. The white back had a color posed player head shot in the upper left, with the player's name in orange lettering alongside to the right. A biography, stat table, and career highlights were printed in English and French. The High Liner, NHLPA, and NHL logos on the bottom rounded out the card.

COMPLETE SET (15) 8.00 20.00
1 Patrick Roy 3.00 8.00
2 Ed Belfour .60 1.50
3 Grant Fuhr .40 1.00
4 Ron Hextall .40 1.00
5 John Vanbiesbrouck New .40 1.00
6 Tom Barrasso .40 1.00
7 Bernie Parent .40 1.00
8 Tony Esposito .60 1.50
9 Johnny Bower .60 1.50
10 Jacques Plante 1.00 2.50
11 Terry Sawchuk 1.00 2.50
12 Bill Durnan .40 1.00
13 Felix Potvin Toronto Ma .75 2.00
14 The Evolution of the Goalie Mask 1.00 2.50
15 Vezina Trophy Checklist .40 1.00

1992 High-5 Previews

These six cards featured color action player photos with the player's name and position printed above the photo. The backs carried another color player photo, with the player's name and career highlights on a white panel. The words "Preview Sample" appeared in the top left corner. The cards were numbered on the back with a "P" prefix. Bourque and Belfour were produced in larger quantities. The cards were originally distributed as promo items at the 1992 National which led to extremely high values. In 1996, an additional supply of these cards was inserted into boxes of Collector's Edge Future Legends product in three-card sleeves. The additional quantities severely dampened demand. A signed version of the Belfour card also was included as a random insert in these packs, and as a promotional giveaway direct from Collector's Edge. This card was serially numbered out of 1500.

COMPLETE SET (6) 50.00 120.00
P1 Brett Hull 15.00 40.00
P2 Mario Lemieux 4.00 10.00
P3 Wayne Gretzky 3.00 8.00
P4 Mark Messier 4.00 10.00
P5 Ray Bourque DP 12.00 30.00
P6 Ed Belfour DP 1.50 4.00
P6A Ed Belfour AU/1500 20.00 50.00

1997 Highland Mint Legends Mint-Cards

The Highland Mint Legends Collection featured NHL greats in a Highland Mint designed Mint-Card and were produced in the same way as the regular Highland Mint series with 4.25 Troy Ounces of actual metal. These standard-sized bronze ingots were enclosed in a plastic display holder case. The Silver versions of the cards were produced with 4.25 Troy Ounces of .999 silver metal. Since these cards are unnumbered, they are listed below in alphabetical order.

1 Gordie Howe 95 S/1000 175.00 250.00
2 Gordie Howe 95 B/5000 20.00 50.00
3 Bobby Orr 95 S/1000 150.00 225.00
4 Bobby Orr 95 B/5000 20.00 50.00

1997 Highland Mint Magnum Series Medallions

Measuring 2 1/2" in diameter and encased in a 6" by 5" velvet box, these larger medallions feature star major leaguers. The relief on these medallions are 10 times greater than the regular medallions. The silver version included 4 Troy Ounces of .999 silver.

1 Colorado Avalanche S/250 150.00 200.00
2 Colorado Avalanche B/1000 25.00 50.00

1997 Highland Mint Mint-Cards Pinnacle/Score

These Highland Mint cards were exact replicas of Pinnacle or Score brand cards. The silver (.999 silver) and bronze cards contained 4.25 Troy Ounces of metal; the gold cards were 24-karat gold-plated on 4.25 ounces of .999 silver. Each card was individually numbered, packaged in a Lucite display holder and accompanied by a certificate of authenticity. The production mintage according to Highland Mint is listed below.

1 Martin Brodeur 95 S/250 150.00 225.00
2 Martin Brodeur 95 B/1500 25.00 60.00
3 Alexandre Daigle 94 S/250 150.00 200.00
4 Alexandre Daigle 94 B/1500 20.00 50.00
5 Jaromir Jagr 94 S/500 150.00 200.00
6 Jaromir Jagr 94 B/2500 25.00 60.00
7 Paul Kariya 94 S/250 150.00 225.00
8 Paul Kariya 94 B/1500 25.00 60.00
9 Pat LaFontaine 93 S/250 150.00 225.00
10 Pat LaFontaine 93 B/1500 20.00 50.00
11 Cam Neely 95 S/250 150.00 225.00
12 Cam Neely 95 B/1500 20.00 50.00
13 Jeremy Roenick 94 S/500 150.00 225.00
14 Jeremy Roenick 94 B/2500 20.00 50.00

1997 Highland Mint Mint-Cards Topps

These cards, from the Highland Mint, measured 2 1/2" by 3 1/2", and were exact reproductions of Topps hockey cards. The cards were packaged in a Lucite display case within a numbered album. Each card came with a sequentially numbered Certificate of Authenticity. The cards featured future heroes, current, and past stars and were produced with 4.25 Troy Ounces of .999 silver or bronze. When the Highland Mint/Topps relationship ended in 1994, the remaining unsold stock was destroyed; the final available mintage according to Highland Mint is listed below. The cards are checklisted below alphabetically.

1 Ray Bourque 80 S/128 150.00 250.00
2 Ray Bourque 80 B/634 25.00 60.00
3 Pavel Bure 92 S/414 150.00 225.00
4 Pavel Bure 92 B/1519 20.00 50.00
5 Sergei Fedorov 91 S/208 150.00 250.00
6 Sergei Fedorov 91 B/914 25.00 60.00
7 Doug Gilmour 85 S/101 150.00 250.00
8 Doug Gilmour 85 R/461 20.00 50.00
9 Wayne Gretzky 79 S/1000 200.00 350.00
10 Wayne Gretzky 79 B/5000 40.00 100.00
11 Bobby Hull 95 S/500 150.00 225.00
12 Bobby Hull 95 B/2500 20.00 50.00
13 Brett Hull 88 S/500 150.00 225.00
14 Brett Hull 88 B/1202 20.00 50.00
15 Mario Lemieux 85 S/999 200.00 350.00
16 Mario Lemieux 85 B/3557 25.00 60.00
17 Eric Lindros 92 S/694 150.00 250.00
18 Eric Lindros 92 B/2668 25.00 60.00
19 Mark Messier 84 S/280 150.00 225.00
20 Mark Messier 84 B/1034 20.00 50.00
21 Felix Potvin 92 S/210 150.00 225.00
22 Felix Potvin 92 B/902 20.00 50.00
23 Patrick Roy 86 S/500 150.00 250.00
24 Patrick Roy 86 B/1986 25.00 60.00
25 Teemu Selanne 92 S/131 150.00 225.00
26 Teemu Selanne 92 B/537 20.00 50.00
27 Steve Yzerman 84 S/233 150.00 225.00
28 Steve Yzerman 84 B/926 30.00 60.00

1997 Highland Mint Mint-Coins

Each medallion weighed one-troy ounce (.999 silver) and was individually numbered. The fronts featured a player likeness as well as name, uniform number, and signature. The backs displayed the team logo and statistics. The suggested retail prices for silver ranged from $19.95 to $24.95. The medallions were packaged in a hard plastic capsule and a velvet jewelry box. The Gold-Signature series medallions were two-tone silver medallions (one troy ounce .999 silver) with gold plating in selected areas. Packaged in a box with a special foil certificate of authenticity, the front featured the player's likeness, name, uniform number and signatures, while the back carried the NHLPA logo. The suggested retail price was $49.95.

1 Ray Bourque S/5000 35.00 50.00
2 Pavel Bure S/5000 35.00 50.00
3 Sergei Fedorov S/5000 35.00 50.00
4 Brett Hull S/5000 35.00 50.00
5 Jaromir Jagr S/5000 35.00 50.00
6 Mario Lemieux Gold Sig./1000 35.00 60.00
7 Mario Lemieux S/5000 35.00 50.00
8 Mario Lemieux B/25000 5.00 12.00
9 Eric Lindros Gold Sig./1000 35.00 60.00
10 Eric Lindros S/5000 35.00 50.00
11 Bobby Orr S/5000 35.00 50.00
12 B.Orr R.Bourque S/500 35.00 50.00
13 Chris Osgood S/5000 35.00 50.00
14 Patrick Roy S/5000 35.00 50.00
15 Teemu Selanne S/5000 35.00 50.00
16 John Vanbiesbrouck S/5000 35.00 50.00
17 Steve Yzerman S/5000 35.00 50.00

1997 Highland Mint Sandblast Mint-Cards

These Highland Mint cards were metal replicas of already issued Pinnacle cards. All these standard size replicas contained approximately 4.25 Troy Ounces of .999 silver or bonrze metal and featured a "sandblast" background that accents the shiny surface of the player's likeness. Suggested retail was 60.00 for bronze and 250.00 for silver. Each card included a certificate of authenticity, and was packaged in a numbered album and a three-piece Lucite display. The cards were checklisted below alphabetically; the final mintage figures for each card are also listed.

1 Mario Lemieux 96 S/250 175.00 250.00
2 Mario Lemieux 96 B/1500 25.00 60.00

1994 Hockey Wit

Seventh in a series of "WIT" trivia games, this Hockey Wit card set featured 108 standard-size cards and included hockey players of the past and present. The fronts featured full-bleed color action player photos, with the player's name inside a blue box with a gold-foil border and the words "Hockey Wit". On a white background, the backs carried a small color headshot, player biography and trivia questions and answers. Inserted in each master case of 72 games was a bonus card which collectors could redeem for one of 500 limited edition sets of uncut flat sheets. The production run was reportedly limited to 30,000 sets, and a portion of the proceeds from the sale benefited amateur hockey in Canada and the United States. The set included 21 Hall of Famers. The collector who answers all the questions on the backs achieved a perfect score of 801, the total number of goals scored in the NHL by Gordie Howe. The cards were numbered on the back at the lower right corner.

COMPLETE SET (108) 8.00 20.00
1 Mike Richter New York R .07 .20
2 Tony Amonte .07 .20
3 Patrick Roy Montreal Ca 1.25 3.00
4 Craig Janney .02 .10
5 Adam Oates Boston Bruin .07 .20
6 Geoff Sanderson .07 .20
7 Pavel Bure .60 1.50
8 Steve Duchesne .02 .10
9 Gordie Howe .75 2.00
10 Brad Park .07 .20
11 Brian Bellows .02 .10
12 Chris Chelios Chicago B .20 .50
13 Bill Barber .07 .20
14 Gump Worsley .07 .20
15 The Stanley Cup .07 .20
16 Maurice Richard .20 .50
17 Kevin Hatcher .02 .10
18 Ed Belfour Chicago Blac .20 .50
19 Kirk Muller .07 .20
20 Kevin Stevens Pittsburg .07 .20
21 Dave Taylor .02 .10
22 Dale Hawerchuk .08 .25
23 Jean Beliveau .08 .25
24 Rogatien Vachon .07 .20
25 Tom Barrasso .07 .20
26 Rod Langway .02 .10
27 Pierre Turgeon .08 .25
28 Derek King .02 .10
29 Brendan Shanahan St. Lo .40 1.00
30 Darren Turcotte .02 .10
31 Chris Terreri .02 .10
32 Tony Granato .02 .10
33 Michel Goulet .02 .10
34 Felix Potvin .15 .40
35 Curtis Joseph St. Louis .30 .75
36 Cam Neely .08 .25
37 Borje Salming .07 .20
38 Denis Savard .07 .20
39 Stan Mikita Chicago Bla .08 .25
40 Grant Fuhr .07 .20
41 Gary Suter .02 .10
42 Serge Savard .02 .10
43 Steve Larmer .07 .20
44 Bryan Trottier .08 .25
45 Mike Vernon Calgary Fla .07 .20
46 Paul Coffey Detroit Red .08 .25
47 Bernie Federko .02 .10
48 Larry Murphy .07 .20
49 Scotty Bowman CO .08 .25
50 Glenn Anderson .02 .10
51 Mats Sundin Quebec Nord .20 .50
52 Henri Richard .08 .25
53 Ron Francis Pittsburgh .08 .25
54 Scott Niedermayer .07 .20
55 Teemu Selanne Winnipeg .40 1.00
56 Frank Mahovlich .08 .25
57 Owen Nolan Quebec Nordi .07 .20
58 Rick Tocchet Pittsburgh .07 .20
59 Rod Brind'Amour Philade .07 .20
60 Mike Modano .08 .25
61 Doug Gilmour Toronto Ma .08 .25
62 Jimmy Carson .02 .10
63 Mike Keane .02 .10
64 Bernie Nicholls .07 .20
65 Scott Stevens .07 .20
66 Mario Lemieux Pittsburg 1.25 3.00
67 Keith Primeau Detroit R .08 .25
68 Bobby Carpenter .02 .10
69 Sergei Fedorov Detroit .40 1.00
70 Peter Stastny .07 .20
71 Brian Leetch New York R .08 .25
72 Vincent Damphousse .07 .20
73 Darryl Sitter .07 .20
74 Al Iafrate .07 .20
75 Alexander Mogilny .07 .20
76 Bill Ranford Edmonton O .08 .25
77 Ray Bourque Boston .30 .75
78 Joey Mullen Pittsburgh .02 .10
79 Mike Ricci .07 .20
80 Bobby Clarke .08 .25
81 Gerry Cheevers .07 .20
82 Joe Nieuwendyk .07 .20
83 Terry Sawchuk Detroit R .08 .25
84 Ray Ferraro .02 .10
85 Lanny McDonald .07 .20
86 Adam Graves .07 .20
87 Tomas Sandstrom Los Ang .02 .10
88 Eric Lindros Philadelph .60 1.50
89 Jari Kurri .08 .25
90 Al MacInnis .07 .20
91 Alexandre Daigle Ottawa .02 .10
92 Larry Robinson .08 .25
93 Kelly Hrudey .07 .20
94 Theo Fleury Calgary .08 .25
95 Billy Smith .07 .20
96 Luc Robitaille Los Ange .08 .25
97 Brett Hull St. Louis Bl .30 .75
98 Pat Falloon .07 .20
99 Wayne Gretzky Los Angel 1.50 4.00
100 Joe Sakic Quebec Nordiq .40 1.00
101 Phil Housley .07 .20
102 Mark Messier .20 .50
103 Jeremy Roenick .08 .25
104 Mark Recchi Philadelphi .08 .25
105 Pat LaFontaine Buffalo .08 .25
106 Trevor Linden Vancouver .07 .20
107 Jaromir Jagr Pittsburgh .75 2.00
108 Steve Yzerman Detroit R .75 2.00

1996-97 Hockey Greats Coins

This 25-coin set featured one coin and checklist card per pack. Each box, with a suggested retail price of $149.95, contained 80 packs. The coins were silver in color, about the size of a half dollar and featured a bust of the player on the obverse. A Collectors Album also was available for $5.49. The Chris Chelios coin (#4) was believed to be short printed. A gold colored parallel version of the set existed as well and were inserted at a rate of 1:150 packs.

COMPLETE SET (25) 30.00 75.00
*GOLD PLATED: 6X TO 15X SILVER
*GOLD CHELIOS: 1.5X TO 4X SILVER
1 Ed Belfour .40 1.00
2 Ray Bourque .50 1.25
3 Pavel Bure .60 1.50
4 Chris Chelios 5.00 12.00
5 Vincent Damphousse .30 .75
6 Sergei Fedorov .75 2.00
7 Theo Fleury .40 1.00
8 Doug Gilmour .40 1.00
9 Wayne Gretzky 2.50 6.00
10 Brett Hull .50 1.25
11 Jaromir Jagr .75 2.00
12 Paul Kariya .60 1.50
13 Mario Lemieux 1.50 4.00
14 Eric Lindros .75 2.00
15 Mark Messier .50 1.25
16 Alexander Mogilny .30 .75
17 Jeremy Roenick .40 1.00
18 Patrick Roy 1.50 4.00
19 Joe Sakic .60 1.50
20 Steve Yzerman 1.00 2.50
21 Sergei Berezin .20 .50
22 Jim Campbell .20 .50
23 Jarome Iginla .40 1.00
24 Rem Murray .20 .50
25 David Wilkie .20 .50
NNO Album 1.50 4.00

1924-25 Holland Creameries

The 1924-25 Holland Creameries set contained ten black and white cards measuring approximately 1 1/2" by 3". The front had a black and white head and shoulders shot of the player, in an oval-shaped black frame on white card stock. The words Holland Hockey Competition~ appeared above the picture, with the player's name and position below. The cards were numbered in the lower left corner on the front. The horizontally formatted card back had an offer to exchange one complete collection of ten players for either a brick of ice cream or three Holland Banquets. Supposedly the difficult card in the set was Connie Neil, marked as SP in the checklist below.

COMPLETE SET (10) 1000.00 1500.00
1 Wally Fridfinson 60.00 150.00
2 Harold McMunn 60.00 150.00
3 Art Somers 60.00 150.00
4 Frank Woodall 60.00 150.00
5 Frank Frederickson 125.00 300.00
6 Bobby Benson 60.00 150.00
7 Harry Neal 60.00 150.00
8 Wally Byron 60.00 150.00
9 Connie Neil SP 300.00 500.00
10 J. Austman 60.00 150.00

2005-06 Hot Prospects

This 276-card set was released in the hobby in five-card packs which came 15 packs to a box and 12 boxes to a case. Cards numbered 1-100 feature veterans in team alphabetical order while cards 101-276 are all Rookie Cards. The Rookie Cards were issued in several groupings: Cards 101-186; Cards 187-216 were signed and cards 217-276 included both a signature and a player-worn jersey swatch. The cards numbeed 101-186 were issued to a stated print run of 1999 serial numbered sets, cards 187-216 were issued to a stated print run of 999 serial numbered sets and 217-276 were issued to a stated print run of 199 to 349 serial numbered sets.

COMPLETE SET w/o SPs (100) 8.00 20.00
1 Joffrey Lupul .25 .60
2 Jean-Sebastien Giguere .30 .75
3 Teemu Selanne .60 1.50
4 Marian Hossa .25 .60
5 Ilya Kovalchuk .30 .75
6 Kari Lehtonen .25 .60
7 Patrice Bergeron .40 1.00
8 Brian Leetch .30 .75
9 Andrew Raycroft .25 .60
10 Glen Murray .25 .60
11 Ryan Miller .30 .75
12 Chris Drury .25 .60
13 Tim Connolly .20 .50
14 Jarome Iginla .30 .75
15 Miikka Kiprusoff .25 .60
16 Mark Recchi .40 1.00
17 Eric Staal .40 1.00
18 Martin Gerber .25 .60
19 Doug Weight .30 .75
20 Erik Cole .25 .60
21 Nikolai Khabibulin .30 .75
22 Tuomo Ruutu .30 .75
23 Joe Sakic .50 1.25
24 Marek Svatos .25 .60
25 Milan Hejduk .25 .60
26 Alex Tanguay .30 .75
27 Jose Theodore .30 .75
28 Sergei Fedorov .50 1.25
29 Rick Nash .30 .75
30 Mike Modano .50 1.25
31 Marty Turco .30 .75
32 Brenden Morrow .25 .60
33 Steve Yzerman .75 2.00
34 Brendan Shanahan .40 1.00
35 Pavel Datsyuk .40 1.00
36 Henrik Zetterberg .40 1.00
37 Nicklas Lidstrom .30 .75
38 Chris Pronger .25 .60
39 Shawn Horcoff .20 .50
40 Ryan Smyth .25 .60
41 Ales Hemsky .25 .60
42 Olli Jokinen .30 .75
43 Roberto Luongo .50 1.25
44 Nathan Horton .30 .75
45 Alexander Frolov .20 .50
46 Luc Robitaille .30 .75
47 Pavol Demitra .40 1.00
48 Jeremy Roenick .30 .75
49 Marian Gaborik .50 1.25
50 Manny Fernandez .25 .60
51 David Aebischer .25 .60
52 Saku Koivu .30 .75
53 Michael Ryder .25 .60
54 Mike Ribeiro .25 .60
55 Paul Kariya .40 1.00
56 Tomas Vokoun .25 .60
57 Steve Sullivan .20 .50
58 Martin Brodeur .60 1.50
59 Patrik Elias .30 .75
60 Brian Gionta .25 .60
61 Scott Gomez .25 .60
62 Alexei Yashin .25 .60
63 Rick DiPietro .25 .60
64 Miroslav Satan .25 .60
65 Jaromir Jagr .75 2.00
66 Martin Straka .20 .50
67 Jason Spezza .30 .75
68 Dominik Hasek .50 1.25
69 Daniel Alfredsson .30 .75
70 Dany Heatley .30 .75
71 Peter Forsberg .40 1.00
72 Simon Gagne .30 .75
73 Keith Primeau .30 .75
74 Antero Niittymaki .25 .60
75 Curtis Joseph .30 .75
76 Shane Doan .25 .60
77 Ladislav Nagy .20 .50
78 Mario Lemieux 1.00 2.50
79 Marc-Andre Fleury .50 1.25
80 Sergei Gonchar .20 .50
81 Ryan Malone .20 .50
82 Joe Thornton .40 1.00
83 Patrick Marleau .30 .75
84 Evgeni Nabokov .25 .60
85 Jonathan Cheechoo .30 .75
86 Barret Jackman .20 .50
87 Keith Tkachuk .30 .75
88 Vincent Lecavalier .25 .60
89 Brad Richards .30 .75
90 Vaclav Prospal .20 .50
91 Martin St. Louis .30 .75
92 Mats Sundin .30 .75
93 Ed Belfour .30 .75
94 Bryan McCabe .20 .50
95 Eric Lindros .50 1.25
96 Markus Naslund .30 .75
97 Alexander Auld .20 .50
98 Todd Bertuzzi .30 .75
99 Brendan Morrison .20 .50
100 Olaf Kolzig .30 .75
101 Dustin Penner RC 3.00 8.00
102 Zenon Konopka RC 2.00 5.00
103 Michael Wall RC 2.50 6.00
104 Brian Eklund RC 2.50 6.00
105 Jay Leach RC 2.50 6.00
106 Eric Healey RC 2.50 6.00
107 Ben Guite RC 2.50 6.00
108 Nathan Paetsch RC 2.50 6.00
109 Jiri Novotny RC 2.50 6.00
110 Richie Regehr RC 2.00 5.00
111 Mark Giordano RC 3.00 8.00
112 Chad Larose RC 2.00 5.00
113 Keith Aucoin RC 2.00 5.00
114 David Gove RC 2.50 6.00
115 Cam Barker RC 2.50 6.00
116 Corey Crawford RC 10.00 20.00
117 Martin St. Pierre RC 2.00 5.00
118 Mark Cullen RC 2.50 6.00
119 James Wisniewski RC 2.50 6.00
120 Vitaly Kolesnik RC 2.50 6.00
121 Steven Goertzen RC 2.00 5.00
122 Joakim Lindstrom RC 2.00 5.00
123 Andrew Penner RC 2.50 6.00
124 Geoff Platt RC 2.50 6.00
125 Junior Lessard RC 2.00 5.00
126 Vojtech Polak RC 2.00 5.00
127 Kyle Brodziak RC 2.00 5.00
128 Matt Greene RC 2.00 5.00
129 Danny Syvret RC 2.00 5.00
130 Adam Hauser RC 2.50 6.00
131 J-F Jacques RC 2.00 5.00
132 Mathieu Roy RC 3.00 8.00
133 Petr Taticek RC 2.50 6.00
134 Greg Jacina RC 2.00 5.00
135 Rob Globke RC 2.00 5.00
136 Yanick Lehoux RC 3.00 8.00
137 Petr Kanko RC 2.50 6.00
138 Jeff Giuliano RC 2.50 6.00
139 Matt Ryan RC 2.50 6.00
140 Connor James RC 2.50 6.00
141 Richard Petiot RC 2.50 6.00
142 J-P Cote RC 2.00 5.00
143 Mark Streit RC 2.00 5.00
144 Jonathan Ferland RC 2.50 6.00
145 Kevin Klein RC 2.00 5.00
146 Pekka Rinne RC 5.00 12.00
147 Greg Zanon RC 2.50 6.00
148 Jason Ryznar RC 2.00 5.00
149 Cam Janssen RC 2.50 6.00
150 Bruno Gervais RC 2.00 5.00
151 Kevin Colley RC 2.50 6.00
152 Petr Prucha RC 3.00 8.00
153 Brandon Bochenski RC 3.00 8.00
154 Brian McGrattan RC 2.00 5.00
155 Stefan Ruzicka RC 2.00 5.00
156 Wade Skolney RC 2.00 5.00
157 Ryan Ready RC 2.50 6.00
158 Josh Gratton RC 2.50 6.00
159 Alexandre Picard RC 2.00 5.00
160 Matt Jones RC 2.00 5.00
161 Colby Armstrong RC 3.00 8.00
162 Doug Murray RC 2.00 5.00
163 Grant Stevenson RC 2.00 5.00
164 Dennis Wideman RC 2.00 5.00
165 Andy Roach RC 2.00 5.00
166 Colin Hemingway RC 2.00 5.00
167 Chris Beckford-Tseu RC 2.50 6.00
168 Jon DiSalvatore RC 2.50 6.00
169 Mike Glumac RC 2.50 6.00
170 Gerald Coleman RC 2.00 5.00
171 Nick Tarnasky RC 2.00 5.00
172 Paul Ranger RC 2.00 5.00
173 Darren Reid RC 2.00 5.00
174 Doug O'Brien RC 2.00 5.00
175 Chris Holt RC 2.00 5.00
176 Jay Harrison RC 2.50 6.00
177 Staffan Kronwall RC 2.00 5.00
178 Tomas Mojzis RC 2.00 5.00
179 Rob McVicar RC 2.50 6.00
180 Rick Rypien RC 4.00 10.00
181 Alexandre Burrows RC 4.00 10.00
182 Prestin Ryan RC 1.50 4.00
183 Mike Green RC 4.00 10.00
184 David Steckel RC 2.50 6.00
185 Joey Tenute RC 2.50 6.00
186 Louis Robitaille RC 2.00 5.00
187 Jim Slater AU RC 4.00 10.00
188 Adam Berkhoel AU RC 4.00 10.00
189 Jordan Sigalet AU RC 3.00 8.00
190 Ben Walter AU RC 3.00 8.00
191 Chris Thorburn AU RC 4.00 10.00
192 Niklas Nordgren AU RC 5.00 12.00
193 Danny Richmond AU RC 3.00 8.00
194 Rene Bourque AU RC 5.00 12.00
195 Duncan Keith AU RC 15.00 30.00
196 Jaroslav Balastik AU RC 3.00 8.00
197 Ole-Kristian Tollefsen AU RC 4.00 10.00
198 Alexandre Picard AU RC 3.00 8.00
199 Brett Lebda AU RC 3.00 8.00
200 Kyle Quincey AU RC 4.00 10.00
201 George Parros AU RC 3.00 8.00
202 Matt Foy AU RC 3.00 8.00
203 Derek Boogaard AU RC 6.00 15.00
204 Maxim Lapierre AU RC 5.00 12.00
205 Chris Campoli AU RC 3.00 8.00
206 Ryan Hollweg AU RC 3.00 8.00
207 Patrick Eaves AU RC 5.00 12.00
208 Christoph Schubert AU RC 3.00 8.00
209 Erik Christensen AU RC 3.00 8.00
210 Dimitri Patzold AU RC 3.00 8.00
211 Josh Gorges AU RC 4.00 10.00
212 Ryane Clowe AU RC 6.00 15.00
213 Jay McClement AU RC 3.00 8.00
214 Lee Stempniak AU RC 5.00 12.00
215 Kevin Dallman AU RC 4.00 10.00
216 Andrew Wozniewski AU RC 4.00 10.00
217 C.Perry JSY AU RC 25.00 60.00
218 R.Getzlaf JSY AU RC 15.00 40.00
219 B.Coburn JSY AU RC 8.00 20.00
220 Andrew Alberts JSY AU RC 5.00 12.00
221 H.Toivonen JSY AU RC 8.00 20.00
222 Milan Jurcina JSY AU RC 6.00 15.00
223 Daniel Paille JSY AU RC 8.00 20.00
224 T.Vanek JSY AU RC 15.00 40.00
225 Eric Nystrom JSY AU RC 6.00 15.00
226 A.Ladd JSY AU RC 10.00 25.00
227 Cam Ward JSY AU RC 12.00 30.00
228 K.Nastiuk JSY AU RC 5.00 12.00
229 B.Seabrook JSY AU RC 15.00 40.00
230 Brad Richardson JSY AU RC 8.00 20.00
231 P.Budaj JSY AU RC 10.00 25.00
232 W.Wolski JSY AU RC 6.00 15.00
233 G.Brule JSY AU RC 12.00 30.00
234 J.Jokinen JSY AU RC 8.00 20.00
235 J.Howard JSY AU RC 20.00 50.00
236 Johan Franzen JSY AU RC 12.00 30.00
238 Brad Winchester JSY AU RC 8.00 20.00
239 A.Stewart JSY AU RC 6.00 15.00
240 R.Olesz JSY AU RC 6.00 15.00
241 Jeff Tambellini JSY AU RC 5.00 12.00
242 M.Koivu JSY AU RC 10.00 25.00
243 A.Perezhogin JSY AU RC 6.00 15.00
244 A.Kostitsyn JSY AU RC 15.00 40.00
245 Y.Danis JSY AU RC 6.00 15.00
246 Raitis Ivanans JSY AU RC 5.00 12.00
247 Ryan Suter JSY AU RC 10.00 25.00
248 Barry Tallackson JSY AU RC 6.00 15.00
249 Z.Parise JSY AU RC 25.00 50.00
250 Jeremy Colliton JSY AU RC 5.00 12.00
251 Petteri Nokelainen JSY AU RC 5.00 12.00
252 Robert Nilsson JSY AU RC 8.00 20.00
253 A.Montoya JSY AU RC 8.00 20.00
254 H.Lundqvist JSY AU RC 60.00 150.00
255 A.Meszaros JSY AU RC 6.00 15.00
256 Ben Eager JSY AU RC 6.00 15.00
257 Jeff Carter JSY AU RC 25.00 60.00
258 M.Richards JSY AU RC 15.00 40.00
259 R.J. Umberger JSY AU RC 8.00 20.00
260 D.LeNeveu JSY AU RC 10.00 25.00
261 Keith Ballard JSY AU RC 6.00 15.00
262 Maxime Talbot JSY AU RC 8.00 20.00
263 Ryan Whitney JSY AU RC 8.00 20.00
264 Steve Bernier AU RC 8.00 20.00
265 Jeff Hoggan JSY AU RC 5.00 12.00
266 Jeff Woywitka JSY AU RC 5.00 12.00
267 Timo Helbling JSY AU RC 5.00 12.00
268 E.Artyukhin JSY AU RC 6.00 15.00
269 Ryan Craig JSY AU RC 5.00 12.00
270 A.Steen JSY AU RC 15.00 40.00
271 Kevin Bieksa JSY AU RC 10.00 25.00
272 Jakub Klepis JSY AU RC 5.00 12.00
273 T.Fleischmann JSY AU RC 8.00 20.00
274 D.Phaneuf JSY AU RC 25.00 60.00
275 A. Ovechkin JSY AU RC 250.00 400.00
276 S. Crosby JSY AU RC 350.00 600.00

2005-06 Hot Prospects Hot Materials

STATED ODDS 1:8
HMAA Andrew Alberts 1.50 4.00
HMAH Adam Hall 1.50 4.00
HMAK Andrei Kostitsyn 3.00 8.00
HMAL Andrew Ladd 3.00 8.00
HMAM Andrej Meszaros 2.00 5.00
HMAO Alexander Ovechkin 12.00 30.00
HMAP Alexander Perezhogin 2.00 5.00
HMAS Anthony Stewart 2.00 5.00
HMBC Braydon Coburn 2.50 6.00
HMBE Ben Eager 2.00 5.00
HMBG Bill Guerin 2.50 6.00
HMBI Kevin Bieksa 3.00 8.00
HMBR Brad Richardson 2.50 6.00
HMBS Brent Seabrook 5.00 12.00
HMBT Barry Tallackson 2.00 5.00
HMBW Brad Winchester 2.50 6.00
HMCA Carlo Colaiacovo 1.50 4.00
HMCC Chris Campoli 1.50 4.00
HMCO Jeremy Colliton 1.50 4.00
HMCP Corey Perry 10.00 25.00
HMCS Christoph Schubert 1.50 4.00
HMCT Chris Thorburn 2.00 5.00
HMCW Cam Ward 4.00 10.00
HMDB Derek Boogaard 3.00 8.00
HMDH Dan Hamhuis 2.00 5.00
HMDK Duncan Keith 5.00 12.00
HMDL David Legwand 2.00 5.00
HMDP Dimitri Patzold 1.50 4.00
HMDR Danny Richmond 1.50 4.00
HMEA Evgeny Artyukhin 2.00 5.00
HMEC Erik Christensen 1.50 4.00
HMEN Eric Nystrom 2.00 5.00
HMFP Fernando Pisani 1.50 4.00
HMGB Gilbert Brule 2.50 6.00
HMGP George Parros 1.50 4.00
HMHL Henrik Lundqvist 10.00 25.00
HMHT Hannu Toivonen 2.50 6.00
HMJB Jaroslav Balastik 1.50 4.00

HMJC Jeff Carter 4.00 10.00
HMJF Johan Franzen 4.00 10.00
HMJH Jim Howard 6.00 15.00
HMJJ Jussi Jokinen 2.50 6.00
HMJK Jakub Klepis 1.50 4.00
HMJS Jim Slater 2.00 5.00
HMJT Jeff Tambellini 1.50 4.00
HMJW Jeff Woywitka 1.50 4.00
HMKB Keith Ballard 2.00 5.00
HMKD Kevin Dallman 2.00 5.00
HMKI Jason King 1.50 4.00
HMKN Kevin Nastiuk 1.50 4.00
HMKQ Kyle Quincey 2.00 5.00
HMLE David Leneveu 2.00 5.00
HMLS Lee Stempniak 2.50 6.00
HMMC Mike Cammalleri 2.50 6.00
HMMF Matt Foy 1.50 4.00
HMMG Martin Gerber 2.00 5.00
HMMJ Milan Jurcina 2.00 5.00
HMMK Mikko Koivu 3.00 8.00
HMML Maxim Lapierre 2.50 6.00
HMMO Al Montoya 2.50 6.00
HMMR Mike Richards 5.00 12.00
HMMT Maxime Talbot 2.50 6.00
HMNN Niklas Nordgren 2.50 6.00
HMOT Ole-Kristian Tollefsen 2.00 5.00
HMPA Daniel Paille 2.50 6.00
HMPB Peter Budaj 3.00 8.00
HMPH Dion Phaneuf 4.00 10.00
HMPN Petteri Nokelainen 1.50 4.00
HMPS Patrik Stefan 1.50 4.00
HMRC Ryan Craig 1.50 4.00
HMRG Ryan Getzlaf 6.00 15.00
HMRI Raitis Ivanans 1.50 4.00
HMRN Robert Nilsson 2.50 6.00
HMRO Rostislav Olesz 2.00 5.00
HMRS Ryan Suter 3.00 8.00
HMRU R.J. Umberger 2.50 6.00
HMRW Ryan Whitney 2.50 6.00
HMSA Philippe Sauve 2.00 5.00
HMSB Steve Bernier 2.50 6.00
HMSC Sidney Crosby 15.00 40.00
HMSI Jordan Sigalet 1.50 4.00
HMST Alexander Steen 5.00 12.00
HMTF Tomas Fleischmann 2.50 6.00
HMTH Timo Helbling 1.50 4.00
HMTV Thomas Vanek 5.00 12.00
HMVF Valtteri Filppula 3.00 8.00
HMWI Brendan Witt 1.50 4.00
HMWW Wojtek Wolski 2.00 5.00
HMYD Yann Danis 2.00 5.00
HMZP Zach Parise 6.00 15.00

2005-06 Hot Prospects Red Hot

*VETS 1-100: 5X TO 12X BASIC CARDS
*ROOKIES 101-186: .8X TO 2X RC/1999
1-186 STATED PRINT RUN 100
*ROOKIE AU 187-216: .8X TO 2X AU RC
*RK.JSY AU: .6X TO 1.5X JSY AU/349
*RK.JSY AU: .5X TO 1.2X JSY AU/199
217-276 STATED PRINT RUN 50
275 A. Ovechkin JSY AU 150.00 300.00
276 Sidney Crosby JSY AU 350.00 500.00

2006-07 Hot Prospects

This 202-card set was released in March, 2007. The set was issued into the hobby in five-card packs with a $6.99 SRP which came 15 packs to a box and 12 boxes to a case. Cards numbered 1-100 feature veterans while the rest of the set are all Rookie Cards. Cards numbered 101-139 feature both a player-worn swatch and an autograph and were issued to a stated print run of 599 serial numbered sets while cards numbered 140-142 also have player-worn swatches and an autograph and were issued to a stated print run of 199 serial numbered sets. Cards numbered 143-202 were issued to a stated print run of 1999 serial numbered sets

COMP.SET w/o SPs (100) 12.00 30.00
1 Chris Pronger .25 .60
2 Jean-Sebastien Giguere .30 .75
3 Teemu Selanne .60 1.50
4 Ilya Kovalchuk .30 .75
5 Marian Hossa .25 .60
6 Kari Lehtonen .25 .60
7 Patrice Bergeron .40 1.00
8 Hannu Toivonen .25 .60
9 Zdeno Chara .30 .75
10 Brad Boyes .20 .50
11 Ryan Miller .30 .75
12 Thomas Vanek .40 1.00
13 Daniel Briere .30 .75
14 Maxim Afinogenov .20 .50
15 Jarome Iginla .30 .75
16 Dion Phaneuf .30 .75
17 Alex Tanguay .20 .50
18 Miikka Kiprusoff .25 .60
19 Eric Staal .40 1.00
20 Cam Ward .30 .75
21 Rod Brind`Amour .30 .75
22 Tuomo Ruutu .30 .75
23 Nikolai Khabibulin .30 .75
24 Martin Havlat .20 .50
25 Joe Sakic .50 1.25
26 Jose Theodore .30 .75
27 Milan Hejduk .25 .60
28 Marek Svatos .20 .50
29 Rick Nash .30 .75
30 Sergei Fedorov .50 1.25
31 Pascal LeClaire .25 .60
32 Nikolai Zherdev .20 .50
33 Mike Modano .50 1.25
34 Eric Lindros .50 1.25
35 Marty Turco .30 .75
36 Pavel Datsyuk .40 1.00
37 Dominik Hasek .40 1.00
38 Nicklas Lidstrom .30 .75
39 Henrik Zetterberg .40 1.00
40 Ryan Smyth .25 .60
41 Ales Hemsky .25 .60
42 Dwayne Roloson .25 .60
43 Ed Belfour .30 .75
44 Todd Bertuzzi .30 .75
45 Olli Jokinen .30 .75
46 Rob Blake .30 .75
47 Alexander Frolov .20 .50
48 Marian Gaborik .40 1.00
49 Manny Fernandez .25 .60
50 Pavol Demitra .40 1.00
51 Saku Koivu .30 .75
52 Cristobal Huet .25 .60
53 Michael Ryder .20 .50
54 David Aebischer .25 .60
55 Paul Kariya .40 1.00
56 Tomas Vokoun .25 .60
57 Martin Brodeur .60 1.50
58 Patrik Elias .30 .75
59 Brian Gionta .25 .60
60 Rick DiPietro .25 .60
61 Alexei Yashin .25 .60
62 Miroslav Satan .25 .60
63 Jaromir Jagr .75 2.00
64 Brendan Shanahan .40 1.00
65 Henrik Lundqvist .60 1.50
66 Daniel Alfredsson .30 .75
67 Jason Spezza .30 .75
68 Dany Heatley .30 .75
69 Martin Gerber .25 .60
70 Peter Forsberg .40 1.00
71 Simon Gagne .30 .75
72 Jeff Carter .30 .75
73 Antero Niittymaki .25 .60
74 Shane Doan .25 .60
75 Jeremy Roenick .30 .75
76 Curtis Joseph .30 .75
77 Sidney Crosby 1.25 3.00
78 Marc-Andre Fleury .50 1.25
79 Mark Recchi .40 1.00
80 Doug Weight .30 .75
81 Manny Legace .25 .60
82 Keith Tkachuk .30 .75
83 Joe Thornton .40 1.00
84 Jonathan Cheechoo .30 .75
85 Patrick Marleau .30 .75
86 Vesa Toskala .25 .60
87 Vincent Lecavalier .25 .60
88 Brad Richards .30 .75
89 Martin St. Louis .30 .75
90 Mats Sundin .30 .75
91 Andrew Raycroft .25 .60
92 Alexander Steen .30 .75
93 Darcy Tucker .25 .60
94 Roberto Luongo .50 1.25
95 Markus Naslund .25 .60
96 Daniel Sedin .30 .75
97 Henrik Sedin .30 .75
98 Alexander Ovechkin 1.25 3.00
99 Olaf Kolzig .30 .75
100 Alexander Semin .30 .75
101 Ryan Shannon JSY AU RC 6.00 15.00
102 Shane O'Brien JSY AU RC 6.00 15.00
103 Yan Stastny JSY AU RC 6.00 15.00
104 Mark Stuart JSY AU RC 6.00 15.00
105 D.Stafford JSY AU RC/199 12.50 30.00
106 Dustin Boyd JSY AU RC 6.00 15.00
107 Dustin Byfuglien JSY AU RC 15.00 40.00
108 Paul Stastny JSY AU RC 10.00 25.00
109 Fredrik Norrena JSY AU RC 6.00 15.00
110 Filip Novak JSY AU RC 6.00 15.00
111 Loui Eriksson JSY AU RC 10.00 25.00
112 Tomas Kopecky JSY AU RC 8.00 20.00
113 M-A Pouliot JSY AU RC 6.00 15.00
114 Ladislav Smid JSY AU RC 6.00 15.00
115 Patrick Thoresen JSY AU RC 6.00 15.00
116 Patrick O'Sullivan JSY AU RC 10.00 25.00
117 Anze Kopitar JSY AU RC 15.00 40.00
118 Pushkarev JSY AU RC 8.00 20.00
119 G. Latendresse JSY AU RC 10.00 25.00
120 Shea Weber JSY AU RC 15.00 40.00
121 A. Radulov JSY AU RC 12.00 30.00
122 Travis Zajac JSY AU RC 12.00 30.00
123 Jarkko Immonen JSY AU RC 6.00 15.00
124 Nigel Dawes JSY AU RC 6.00 15.00
125 Ryan Potulny JSY AU RC 6.00 15.00
126 Benoit Pouliot JSY AU RC 8.00 20.00
127 Keith Yandle JSY AU RC 12.00 30.00
128 Noah Welch JSY AU RC 6.00 15.00
129 Kristopher Letang JSY AU RC 20.00 50.00
130 Michel Ouellet JSY AU RC 8.00 20.00
131 Matt Carle JSY AU RC 6.00 15.00
132 M-E Vlasic JSY AU RC 6.00 15.00
133 Marek Schwarz JSY AU RC 10.00 25.00
134 Roman Polak JSY AU RC 8.00 20.00
135 Ben Ondrus JSY AU RC 6.00 15.00
136 Brendan Bell JSY AU RC 6.00 15.00
137 Ian White JSY AU RC 8.00 20.00
138 Jeremy Williams JSY AU RC 6.00 15.00
139 Eric Fehr JSY AU RC 10.00 25.00
140 J. Staal JSY AU RC/199 12.00 30.00
141 P. Kessel JSY AU RC/199 25.00 60.00
142 E. Malkin JSY AU RC/199 100.00 200.00
143 David McKee RC 2.50 6.00
144 Mike Brown RC 2.50 6.00
145 Matt Lashoff RC 2.50 6.00
146 Nate Thompson RC 2.50 6.00
147 Mike Card RC 2.50 6.00
148 Adam Dennis RC 2.50 6.00
149 Michael Funk RC 2.50 6.00
150 Michael Ryan RC 2.50 6.00
151 Brandon Prust RC 2.50 6.00
152 Adam Burish RC 4.00 10.00
153 Michael Blunden RC 2.50 6.00
154 Dave Bolland RC 4.00 10.00
155 Stefan Liv RC 2.50 6.00
156 Alexei Mikhnov RC 2.50 6.00
157 Jan Hejda RC 2.50 6.00
158 Jeff Drouin-Deslauriers RC 2.50 6.00
159 Drew Larman RC 2.50 6.00
160 Janis Sprukts RC 2.50 6.00
161 David Booth RC 3.00 8.00
162 Peter Harrold RC 2.50 6.00
163 Benoit Pouliot RC 3.00 8.00
164 Niklas Backstrom RC 5.00 12.00
165 Miroslav Kopriva RC 2.50 6.00
166 Mikko Lehtonen RC 3.00 8.00
167 John Oduya RC 4.00 10.00
168 Alex Brooks RC 2.50 6.00
169 Kelly Guard RC 3.00 8.00
170 Martin Houle RC 3.00 8.00
171 Jussi Timonen RC 3.00 8.00
172 Lars Jonsson RC 2.50 6.00
173 Triston Grant RC 2.50 6.00
174 Bill Thomas RC 2.50 6.00
175 Patrick Fischer RC 2.50 6.00
176 Joe Pavelski RC 12.00 30.00
177 D.J. King RC 2.50 6.00
178 Blair Jones RC 2.50 6.00
179 Jean-Francois Racine RC 3.00 8.00
180 Nathan McIver RC 2.50 6.00
181 Alexander Edler RC 4.00 10.00
182 Luc Bourdon RC 4.00 10.00
183 Patrick Coulombe RC 2.50 6.00
184 Jesse Schultz RC 2.50 6.00
185 Kyle Cumiskey RC 3.00 8.00
186 David Backes RC 10.00 25.00
187 Mikhail Grabovski RC 5.00 12.00
188 Daren Machesney RC 2.50 6.00
189 Enver Lisin RC 2.50 6.00
190 Tim Brent RC 3.00 8.00
191 Blake Comeau RC 4.00 10.00
192 Barry Brust RC 3.00 8.00
193 Karri Ramo RC 2.50 6.00
194 Kris Newbury RC 2.50 6.00
195 Kamil Kreps RC 2.50 6.00
196 Derek Meech RC 2.50 6.00
197 Andrej Sekera RC 3.00 8.00
198 Clarke MacArthur RC 3.00 8.00
199 Josh Hennessy RC 2.50 6.00
200 Niklas Grossman RC 4.00 10.00
201 Joel Perrault RC 2.50 6.00
202 Troy Brouwer RC 3.00 8.00

2006-07 Hot Prospects Red Hot

*1-100: 8X TO 20X BASE
(1-100) PRINT RUN 100 SER.#'d SETS
*101-142: .5X TO 1.2X BASE
(101-142) PRINT RUN 25 SER.#'d SETS
*143-184 NON-AU: .6X TO 1.5X BASE
*143-184 AU: .8X TO 2X BASE
(143-184) PRINT RUN 100 SER.#'d SETS

2006-07 Hot Prospects Hot Materials

STATED ODDS 1:8
*RED HOT/100: .6X TO 1.5X BASIC JSY
*RED HOT/100: .5X TO 1.2X BASIC JSY SP
HMAE David Aebischer 2.50 6.00
HMAK Anze Kopitar 6.00 15.00
HMAO Alexander Ovechkin SP 10.00 25.00
HMAS Alexander Steen SP 4.00 10.00
HMBB Brandon Bochenski 2.00 5.00
HMBE Brendan Bell 2.00 5.00
HMBM Brenden Morrow 2.50 6.00
HMBO Ben Ondrus 2.00 5.00
HMBR Brad Boyes 2.00 5.00
HMBS Brendan Shanahan 5.00 12.00
HMBT Billy Thompson 2.00 5.00
HMCD Chris Drury 2.50 6.00
HMCJ Curtis Joseph 3.00 8.00
HMCP Corey Perry 3.00 8.00
HMCS Curtis Sanford 2.50 6.00
HMCW Cam Ward 3.00 8.00
HMDA Daniel Alfredsson 3.00 8.00
HMDH Dominik Hasek SP 5.00 12.00
HMDP Dion Phaneuf 3.00 8.00
HMDS Drew Stafford 2.50 6.00
HMEB Ed Belfour 3.00 8.00
HMEF Eric Fehr 2.50 6.00
HMEM Evgeni Malkin 8.00 20.00
HMES Eric Staal 4.00 10.00
HMGL Guillaume Latendresse 2.50 6.00
HMGM Glen Murray 2.50 6.00
HMGR Gary Roberts 2.00 5.00
HMHA Martin Havlat 2.00 5.00
HMHE Dany Heatley SP 4.00 10.00
HMHJ Milan Hejduk 2.50 6.00
HMHS Henrik Sedin 3.00 8.00
HMHT Hannu Toivonen 2.50 6.00
HMIG Jarome Iginla 3.00 8.00
HMIK Ilya Kovalchuk 3.00 8.00
HMIW Ian White 2.50 6.00
HMJB Jay Bouwmeester 3.00 8.00
HMJC Jeff Carter 3.00 8.00
HMJD J.P. Dumont 2.00 5.00
HMJI Jarkko Immonen 2.00 5.00
HMJJ Jaromir Jagr 8.00 20.00
HMJL Jere Lehtinen 2.00 5.00
HMJP Joni Pitkanen 2.00 5.00
HMJS Jarret Stoll 2.50 6.00
HMJT Joe Thornton 4.00 10.00
HMKL Kristopher Letang 5.00 12.00
HMKP Konstantin Pushkarev 2.50 6.00
HMKY Keith Yandle 3.00 8.00
HMLB Luc Bourdon 2.50 6.00
HMLE Loui Eriksson 2.50 6.00
HMLS Ladislav Smid 2.00 5.00
HMLU Joffrey Lupul 2.50 6.00
HMMB Martin Brodeur 6.00 15.00
HMMC Matt Carle 2.00 5.00
HMMG Marian Gaborik 4.00 10.00
HMMH Marian Hossa 2.50 6.00
HMMI Mike Grier 2.00 5.00
HMML Mario Lemieux 10.00 25.00
HMMM Mike Modano 5.00 12.00
HMMN Markus Naslund 2.50 6.00
HMMP Marc-Antoine Pouliot 2.00 5.00
HMMR Mark Recchi 4.00 10.00
HMMS Mark Stuart 2.00 5.00
HMMV Marc-Edouard Vlasic 2.00 5.00
HMND Nigel Dawes 2.00 5.00
HMNL Nicklas Lidstrom 3.00 8.00
HMNW Noah Welch 2.00 5.00
HMOK Olaf Kolzig 3.00 8.00
HMOS Patrick O'Sullivan 3.00 8.00
HMPA Patrick Thoresen 2.00 5.00
HMPB Patrice Bergeron 4.00 10.00
HMPE Michael Peca 2.50 6.00
HMPF Peter Forsberg 4.00 10.00
HMPK Phil Kessel 4.00 10.00
HMPM Patrick Marleau 3.00 8.00
HMPR Patrick Roy 8.00 20.00
HMPS Paul Stastny 4.00 10.00
HMPT Pierre Turgeon 3.00 8.00
HMRE Robert Esche 2.50 6.00
HMRI Brad Richards 3.00 8.00
HMRL Roberto Luongo 5.00 12.00
HMRN Rick Nash 3.00 8.00
HMRY Michael Ryder 2.00 5.00
HMSA Joe Sakic 5.00 12.00
HMSC Sidney Crosby SP 15.00 40.00
HMSD Shane Doan 2.50 6.00
HMSK Saku Koivu 3.00 8.00
HMSO Shane O'Brien 2.00 5.00
HMSP Jason Spezza 3.00 8.00
HMSS Sergei Samsonov 2.50 6.00
HMST Jordan Staal 4.00 10.00
HMSU Mats Sundin 3.00 8.00
HMSW Shea Weber 4.00 10.00
HMTH Tomas Holmstrom 2.50 6.00
HMTP Tom Poti 2.00 5.00
HMTS Teemu Selanne 6.00 15.00
HMTT Tim Thomas 4.00 10.00
HMTV Tomas Vokoun 2.50 6.00
HMTZ Travis Zajac 4.00 10.00
HMZC Zdeno Chara 3.00 8.00

2006-07 Hot Prospects Hotagraphs

1 HOT PACK PER 180 PACKS
5 HOTAGRAPHS PER HOT PACK
HAF Alexander Frolov 5.00 12.00
HAK Anze Kopitar 20.00 50.00
HAR Andrew Raycroft 6.00 15.00
HBB Brendan Bell 5.00 12.00
HBE Patrice Bergeron 10.00 25.00
HBI Martin Biron 6.00 15.00
HBM Brenden Morrow 6.00 15.00
HBO Ben Ondrus 5.00 12.00
HBP Benoit Pouliot 6.00 15.00
HBR Brad Boyes 5.00 12.00
HBT Barry Tallackson 5.00 12.00
HCA Mike Cammalleri 5.00 12.00
HCH Chris Higgins 5.00 12.00
HCK Chris Kunitz 8.00 20.00
HCP Chris Phillips 5.00 12.00
HDA David Aebischer 6.00 15.00
HDK Duncan Keith 10.00 25.00
HDL David Leneveu 6.00 15.00
HDR Dwayne Roloson 6.00 15.00
HEF Eric Fehr 8.00 20.00
HEM Evgeni Malkin 30.00 60.00
HES Eric Staal 10.00 25.00
HFL Marc-Andre Fleury 12.00 30.00
HFN Filip Novak 5.00 12.00
HFP Fernando Pisani 5.00 12.00
HGB Gilbert Brule 6.00 15.00
HGL Guillaume Latendresse 8.00 20.00
HHA Martin Havlat 5.00 12.00
HHO Tomas Holmstrom 6.00 15.00
HHU Cristobal Huet 6.00 15.00
HIG Jarome Iginla 8.00 20.00
HIK Ilya Kovalchuk 8.00 20.00
HIW Ian White 6.00 15.00
HJB Jaroslav Balastik 5.00 12.00
HJC Jeff Carter 8.00 20.00
HJI Jarkko Immonen 5.00 12.00
HJL John-Michael Liles 5.00 12.00
HJO Jonathan Cheechoo 8.00 20.00
HJP Joni Pitkanen 5.00 12.00
HJS Jarret Stoll 6.00 15.00
HJT Joe Thornton 10.00 25.00
HJW Jeremy Williams 5.00 12.00
HKB Keith Ballard 5.00 12.00
HKC Kyle Calder 5.00 12.00
HKE Kevin Bieksa 6.00 15.00
HKL Kari Lehtonen 6.00 15.00
HKO Chuck Kobasew 5.00 12.00
HLE Loui Eriksson 8.00 20.00
HLN Ladislav Nagy 5.00 12.00
HLS Ladislav Smid 5.00 12.00
HMA Mark Stuart 5.00 12.00
HMB Martin Brodeur EXCH 15.00 40.00
HMC Matt Carle 5.00 12.00
HMF Matt Foy 5.00 12.00
HMH Marcel Hossa 5.00 12.00
HMI Michal Handzus 6.00 15.00
HML Mario Lemieux SP
HMM Masi Marjamaki 5.00 12.00
HMO Michel Ouellet 6.00 15.00
HMP Marc-Antoine Pouliot 5.00 12.00
HMR Michael Ryder 5.00 12.00
HMS Marek Svatos 5.00 12.00
HMV Mike Van Ryn 5.00 12.00
HND Nigel Dawes 5.00 12.00
HNW Noah Welch 5.00 12.00
HNZ Nikolai Zherdev 5.00 12.00
HOT Ole-Kristian Tollefsen 5.00 12.00
HPA Patrik Elias 8.00 20.00
HPB Pierre-Marc Bouchard 8.00 20.00
HPE Michael Peca 6.00 15.00
HPK Phil Kessel EXCH 12.00 30.00
HPM Paul Mara 5.00 12.00
HPO Patrick O'Sullivan 8.00 20.00
HPP Petr Prucha 6.00 15.00
HPR Paul Ranger 5.00 12.00
HPS Paul Stastny 12.00 30.00
HRA Alexander Radulov 10.00 25.00
HRB Keith Yandle 10.00 25.00
HRE Robert Esche 6.00 15.00
HRK Rostislav Klesla 5.00 12.00
HRL Roberto Luongo 12.00 30.00
HRM Ryan Malone 5.00 12.00
HRP Roman Polak 6.00 15.00
HRS Ryan Shannon 5.00 12.00
HRY Ryan Potulny 5.00 12.00
HSC Sidney Crosby 75.00 150.00
HSG Scott Gomez 6.00 15.00
HSO Shane O'Brien 5.00 12.00
HST Jordan Staal 12.00 30.00
HSW Shea Weber 12.00 30.00
HTH Trent Hunter 5.00 12.00
HTK Tomas Kopecky 6.00 15.00
HTZ Travis Zajac 10.00 25.00
HVF Valtteri Filppula 8.00 20.00
HVL Vincent Lecavalier 6.00 15.00
HYS Yan Stastny 5.00 12.00
HZC Zdeno Chara 8.00 20.00

2007-08 Hot Prospects

COMP.SET w/o SP's (100) 15.00 40.00
HC STATED PRINT RUN 999
PP RC STATED PRINT RUNS 999
PP JSY AU RC PRINT RUN 399
PP JSY AU RC SP STATED PRINT RUN 199
1 Ales Hemsky .25 .60
2 Alex Tanguay .20 .50
3 Alexander Frolov .20 .50
4 Alexander Ovechkin 1.25 3.00
5 Alexander Radulov .30 .75
6 Alexander Semin .30 .75
7 Alexander Steen .30 .75
8 Anze Kopitar .50 1.25
9 Bill Guerin .30 .75
10 Brad Richards .30 .75
11 Brendan Shanahan .40 1.00
12 Brian Gionta .25 .60
13 Cam Ward .30 .75
14 Chris Drury .25 .60
15 Chris Mason .25 .60
16 Corey Perry .30 .75
17 Cristobal Huet .25 .60
18 Daniel Alfredsson .30 .75
19 Daniel Briere .30 .75
20 Daniel Sedin .30 .75
21 Dany Heatley .30 .75
22 Darcy Tucker .25 .60
23 David Vyborny .20 .50
24 Dion Phaneuf .30 .75
25 Dominik Hasek .40 1.00
26 Doug Weight .30 .75
27 Drew Stafford .25 .60
28 Dwayne Roloson .25 .60
29 Eric Staal .40 1.00
30 Evgeni Malkin 1.00 2.50
31 Guillaume Latendresse .25 .60
32 Henrik Lundqvist .40 1.00
33 Henrik Sedin .30 .75
34 Henrik Zetterberg .40 1.00
35 Ilya Kovalchuk .30 .75
36 Jarome Iginla .30 .75
37 Jaromir Jagr .75 2.00
38 Jason Spezza .30 .75
39 Jean-Sebastien Giguere .30 .75
40 Jeff Carter .30 .75
41 Joe Sakic .50 1.25
42 Joe Thornton .40 1.00
43 Jonathan Cheechoo .30 .75
44 Joni Pitkanen .20 .50
45 Jordan Staal .30 .75
46 Justin Williams .25 .60
47 Kari Lehtonen .25 .60
48 Keith Tkachuk .30 .75
49 Marc Savard .20 .50
50 Marc-Andre Fleury .50 1.25
51 Marian Gaborik .40 1.00
52 Marian Hossa .25 .60
53 Markus Naslund .30 .75
54 Martin Brodeur .60 1.50
55 Tuomo Ruutu .30 .75
56 Martin St. Louis .30 .75
57 Marty Turco .30 .75
58 Mats Sundin .30 .75
59 Michael Ryder .20 .50
60 Miikka Kiprusoff .25 .60
61 Mike Modano .50 1.25
62 Mike Ribeiro .25 .60
63 Mikko Koivu .25 .60
64 Milan Hejduk .25 .60
65 Miroslav Satan .25 .60
66 Nathan Horton .30 .75
67 Nicklas Lidstrom .30 .75
68 Niklas Backstrom .30 .75
69 Nikolai Khabibulin .30 .75
70 Olaf Kolzig .30 .75
71 Olli Jokinen .25 .60
72 Patrice Bergeron .40 1.00
73 Patrick Marleau .30 .75
74 Patrik Elias .30 .75
75 Paul Kariya .40 1.00
76 Paul Stastny .30 .75
77 Pavel Datsyuk .40 1.00
78 Phil Kessel .40 1.00
79 Ray Emery .25 .60
80 Rick DiPietro .25 .60
81 Rick Nash .30 .75
82 Rob Blake .30 .75
83 Roberto Luongo .40 1.00
84 Ryan Getzlaf .50 1.25
85 Ryan Miller .30 .75
86 Ryan Smyth .25 .60
87 Saku Koivu .30 .75
88 Chris Pronger .25 .60
89 Sergei Fedorov .50 1.25
90 Sergei Samsonov .25 .60
91 Shane Doan .25 .60
92 Sidney Crosby 1.25 3.00
93 Simon Gagne .30 .75
94 Steve Bernier .20 .50
95 Jason Arnott .25 .60
96 Thomas Vanek .40 1.00
97 Tomas Vokoun .25 .60
98 Vesa Toskala .25 .60
99 Vincent Lecavalier .25 .60
100 Zach Parise .40 1.00
101 Alexander Ovechkin HC 6.00 15.00
102 Alexander Radulov HC 1.50 4.00
103 Alexander Semin HC 1.50 4.00
104 Anze Kopitar HC 2.50 6.00
105 Bobby Orr HC 5.00 12.00
106 Brendan Shanahan HC 2.00 5.00
107 Cam Ward HC 1.50 4.00
108 Daniel Briere HC 1.50 4.00
109 Dany Heatley HC 1.50 4.00
110 Dominik Hasek HC 2.00 5.00
111 Dwayne Roloson HC 1.25 3.00
112 Eric Staal HC 2.00 5.00
113 Evgeni Malkin HC 5.00 12.00
114 Gordie Howe HC 4.00 10.00
115 Henrik Lundqvist HC 2.00 5.00
116 Henrik Zetterberg HC 2.00 5.00
117 Ilya Kovalchuk HC 1.50 4.00
118 Jarome Iginla HC 1.50 4.00
119 Jaromir Jagr HC 4.00 10.00
120 Jason Spezza HC 1.50 4.00
121 Jean-Sebastien Giguere HC 1.50 4.00
122 Joe Sakic HC 2.50 6.00
123 Joe Thornton HC 2.00 5.00
124 Jonathan Cheechoo HC 1.50 4.00
125 Kari Lehtonen HC 1.25 3.00
126 Marc-Andre Fleury HC 2.50 6.00
127 Marian Gaborik HC 2.00 5.00
128 Marian Hossa HC 1.25 3.00
129 Mario Lemieux HC 5.00 12.00
130 Mark Messier HC 2.50 6.00
131 Markus Naslund HC 1.50 4.00
132 Martin Brodeur HC 3.00 8.00
133 Martin Havlat HC 1.50 4.00
134 Martin St. Louis HC 1.50 4.00
135 Marty Turco HC 1.50 4.00
136 Mats Sundin HC 1.50 4.00
137 Michael Ryder HC 1.00 2.50
138 Miikka Kiprusoff HC 1.25 3.00
139 Mike Modano HC 2.50 6.00
140 Nicklas Lidstrom HC 1.50 4.00
141 Patrice Bergeron HC 2.00 5.00
142 Patrick Marleau HC 1.50 4.00
143 Paul Kariya HC 2.00 5.00
144 Paul Stastny HC 1.50 4.00
145 Phil Kessel HC 2.00 5.00
146 Rick DiPietro HC 1.25 3.00
147 Rick Nash HC 1.50 4.00
148 Roberto Luongo HC 2.00 5.00
149 Ryan Getzlaf HC 2.50 6.00
150 Ryan Miller HC 1.50 4.00
151 Saku Koivu HC 1.50 4.00
152 Scott Niedermayer HC 1.50 4.00
153 Shane Doan HC 1.25 3.00
154 Sidney Crosby HC 6.00 15.00
155 Simon Gagne HC 1.50 4.00
156 Thomas Vanek HC 2.00 5.00
157 Tomas Vokoun HC 1.25 3.00
158 Vincent Lecavalier HC 1.25 3.00
159 Mark Recchi HC 2.00 5.00
160 Zach Parise HC 2.00 5.00
161 Mike Weber RC 2.50 6.00
162 Tyler Kennedy RC 4.00 10.00
163 Bryan Young RC 2.50 6.00
164 Cal Clutterbuck RC 4.00 10.00
165 Curtis Glencross RC 4.00 10.00
166 Daniel Carcillo RC 3.00 8.00
167 Magnus Johansson RC 2.50 6.00
168 Marc Methot RC 2.50 6.00
169 David Clarkson RC 4.00 10.00
170 Drew Fata RC 2.50 6.00
171 Duncan Milroy RC 2.50 6.00
172 Tobias Enstrom RC 4.00 10.00
173 Chris Bourque RC 3.00 8.00
174 Jeff Finger RC 2.50 6.00
175 Jeff Schultz RC 3.00 8.00
176 Joel Lundqvist RC 2.50 6.00
177 John Zeiler RC 2.50 6.00
178 Cory Murphy RC 2.50 6.00
179 Kent Huskins RC 2.50 6.00
180 Mark Fraser RC 2.50 6.00
181 Mark Mancari RC 3.00 8.00
182 Martin Lojek RC 2.50 6.00
183 Matt Keetley RC 3.00 8.00
184 Steve Wagner RC 2.50 6.00
185 Nathan Guenin RC 3.00 8.00
186 Ryan Carter RC 2.50 6.00
187 Petteri Wirtanen RC 2.50 6.00
188 Rod Pelley RC 2.50 6.00
189 David Moss RC 4.00 10.00
190 Matt Ellis RC 3.00 8.00
191 Sebastien Bisaillon RC 2.50 6.00
192 Daniel Winnik RC 3.00 8.00
193 Craig Weller RC 2.50 6.00
194 Tomas Plihal RC 3.00 8.00
195 Riley Cote RC 3.00 8.00
196 Brady Murray RC 2.50 6.00
197 Tomas Popperle RC 3.00 8.00
198 Tom Gilbert RC 3.00 8.00
199 Denis Tolpeko RC 2.50 6.00
200 Zach Stortini RC 2.50 6.00
201 B Ryan JSY AU RC 25.00 50.00
202 S Gagner JSY AU RC 6.00 15.00
203 N Bergfors JSY AU RC 6.00 15.00
204 J Bernier JSY AU RC 12.00 30.00
205 Bryan Little JSY AU RC 10.00 25.00
206 Kris Russell JSY AU RC 8.00 20.00
207 M Niskanen JSY AU RC 10.00 25.00
208 A Cogliano JSY AU RC 10.00 25.00
209 Nick Foligno JSY AU RC 12.00 30.00
210 B Sterling JSY AU RC 6.00 15.00
211 M Hanzal JSY AU RC 8.00 20.00
212 J Hlinka JSY AU RC 8.00 20.00
213 Matt Smaby JSY AU RC 6.00 15.00
214 Petr Kalus JSY AU RC 6.00 15.00
215 A Greene JSY AU RC 8.00 20.00
216 Frans Nielsen JSY AU RC 10.00 25.00
217 R Schremp JSY AU RC 8.00 20.00
218 J Sheppard JSY AU RC 6.00 15.00
219 K Chipchura JSY AU RC 8.00 20.00
220 R Parent JSY AU RC 6.00 15.00
221 D Krejci JSY AU RC 20.00 40.00
222 L Tukonen JSY AU RC 6.00 15.00
223 T Rask JSY AU RC 20.00 50.00
224 M Raymond JSY AU RC 10.00 25.00
225 B Dubinsky JSY AU RC 12.00 30.00
226 C McElhinney JSY AU RC 10.00 25.00
227 B Elliott JSY AU RC 12.00 30.00
228 Drew Miller JSY AU RC 8.00 20.00
229 R Callahan JSY AU RC 15.00 30.00
230 O Pavelec JSY AU RC 12.00 30.00
231 V Koistinen JSY AU RC 6.00 15.00
232 T Mitchell JSY AU RC 8.00 20.00
233 D Perron JSY AU RC 10.00 25.00
234 J Sigalet JSY AU RC 6.00 15.00
235 J Hansen JSY AU RC 8.00 20.00
236 J Halak JSY AU RC 15.00 40.00
237 D Setoguchi JSY AU RC 10.00 25.00
238 Milan Lucic JSY AU RC 30.00 80.00
239 L Kaspar JSY AU RC 6.00 15.00
240 T Weiman JSY AU RC 8.00 20.00
241 T Stephan JSY AU RC 8.00 20.00
242 D Girardi JSY AU RC 8.00 20.00
243 S Meyer JSY AU RC 8.00 20.00
244 Jared Boll JSY AU RC 8.00 20.00
245 Jiri Tlusty JSY AU RC 10.00 25.00
246 J Hiller JSY AU RC 12.00 30.00
247 T.J. Hensick JSY AU RC 8.00 20.00
248 A Stralman JSY AU RC 6.00 15.00
249 J Toews JSY AU/199 RC 80.00 200.00
250 C Price JSY AU/199 RC 100.00 250.00
251 P Mueller JSY AU/199 RC 12.00 30.00
252 P Kane JSY AU/199 RC 80.00 200.00
253 M Staal JSY AU/199 RC 15.00 40.00
254 N Backstrom JSY AU/199 RC 30.00 80.00
255 E Johnson JSY AU/199 RC 12.00 30.00
256 J Johnson JSY AU/199 RC 12.00 30.00

2007-08 Hot Prospects Red Hot

COMMON CARD (1-100) 4.00 10.00
SEMISTARS JSY 5.00 12.00
UNL.STARS JSY 6.00 15.00
*101-160 HC/100: .5X TO 1.2X BASIC HC
*161-200 PP/100: .5X TO 1.2X BASIC PP
1-200 STATED PRINT RUN 100
*201-248 PP JSY AU/25: .5X TO 1.2X
*249-256 PP JSY AU/25: .6X TO 1.5X
201-256 STATED PRINT RUN 25
4 Alexander Ovechkin JSY 25.00 60.00
8 Anze Kopitar JSY 10.00 25.00
21 Dany Heatley JSY 6.00 15.00
25 Dominik Hasek JSY 8.00 20.00
30 Evgeni Malkin JSY 15.00 40.00
32 Henrik Lundqvist JSY 8.00 20.00
34 Henrik Zetterberg JSY 8.00 20.00
36 Jarome Iginla JSY 6.00 15.00
37 Jaromir Jagr JSY 15.00 40.00
41 Joe Sakic JSY 10.00 25.00
42 Joe Thornton JSY 8.00 20.00
51 Marian Gaborik JSY 8.00 20.00
54 Martin Brodeur JSY 12.00 30.00
67 Nicklas Lidstrom JSY 6.00 15.00
83 Roberto Luongo JSY 8.00 20.00
84 Ryan Getzlaf JSY 10.00 25.00
92 Sidney Crosby JSY 25.00 60.00
96 Thomas Vanek JSY 8.00 20.00
100 Zach Parise JSY 8.00 20.00
249 Jonathan Toews JSY AU 125.00 250.00
250 Carey Price JSY AU 150.00 250.00
252 Patrick Kane JSY AU 150.00 300.00

2007-08 Hot Prospects Hot Materials

STATED ODDS 1:8
HMAG Andy Greene 4.00 10.00
HMAK Alex Kovalev 4.00 10.00
HMAM Andrej Meszaros 3.00 8.00
HMAO Alexander Ovechkin 20.00 50.00
HMAR Alexander Radulov 5.00 12.00
HMAS Alexander Steen 5.00 12.00
HMBB Brad Boyes 3.00 8.00
HMBD Brandon Dubinsky 6.00 15.00
HMBE Bryan Berard 3.00 8.00
HMBG Bill Guerin 5.00 12.00
HMBJ Barret Jackman 3.00 8.00
HMBL Brendan Bell 3.00 8.00
HMBM Brendan Morrison 3.00 8.00
HMBO Brandon Bochenski 3.00 8.00
HMBR Brenden Morrow 4.00 10.00
HMBS Brad Stuart 3.00 8.00
HMCA Matt Carle 3.00 8.00
HMCH Jonathan Cheechoo 5.00 12.00
HMCK Chuck Kobasew 3.00 8.00
HMCM Mike Cammalleri 4.00 10.00
HMCS Curtis Sanford 4.00 10.00
HMCW Cam Ward 5.00 12.00
HMDA David Aebischer 4.00 10.00
HMDB Dustin Brown 5.00 12.00
HMDH Dany Heatley 5.00 12.00
HMDK David Krejci 10.00 25.00
HMDL David Legwand 4.00 10.00
HMDM Drew Miller 4.00 10.00
HMDO Dominik Hasek 6.00 15.00
HMDP Daniel Paille 3.00 8.00
HMDR Dwayne Roloson 4.00 10.00
HMDU Duncan Keith 5.00 12.00
HMDW Doug Weight 5.00 12.00
HMEC Erik Cole 4.00 10.00
HMES Eric Staal 6.00 15.00
HMFN Frans Nielsen 5.00 12.00
HMGB Gilbert Brule 4.00 10.00
HMGE Martin Gerber 4.00 10.00
HMGI Brian Gionta 4.00 10.00
HMHA Jannik Hansen 4.00 10.00
HMHS Henrik Sedin 5.00 12.00
HMIK Ilya Kovalchuk 5.00 12.00
HMIW Ian White 3.00 8.00
HMJA Jaromir Jagr 12.00 30.00
HMJB Jay Bouwmeester 5.00 12.00
HMJC Jeff Carter 5.00 12.00
HMJH Jaroslav Halak 8.00 20.00
HMJI Jarome Iginla 5.00 12.00
HMJJ Jack Johnson 4.00 10.00
HMJL Jere Lehtinen 3.00 8.00
HMJO Jussi Jokinen 3.00 8.00
HMJP Joni Pitkanen 3.00 8.00
HMJS Jonathan Sigalet 3.00 8.00
HMJT Joe Thornton 6.00 15.00
HMJW Justin Williams 4.00 10.00
HMKE Phil Kessel 6.00 15.00
HMKL Kari Lehtonen 4.00 10.00
HMKT Keith Tkachuk 5.00 12.00
HMLE Jordan Leopold 3.00 8.00
HMLT Lauri Tukonen 3.00 8.00
HMLU Joffrey Lupul 4.00 10.00
HMMA Marc Savard 3.00 8.00
HMMB Martin Brodeur 10.00 25.00
HMMC Bryan McCabe 3.00 8.00
HMMF Manny Fernandez 4.00 10.00
HMMG Marian Gaborik 6.00 15.00
HMMH Marian Hossa 4.00 10.00
HMMI Milan Michalek 3.00 8.00
HMMK Mikko Koivu 4.00 10.00
HMMM Marc Methot 3.00 8.00
HMMN Markus Naslund 5.00 12.00
HMMO Mike Modano 8.00 20.00
HMMR Mike Richards 5.00 12.00
HMMS Matt Stajan 4.00 10.00
HMMT Marty Turco 5.00 12.00
HMNH Nathan Horton 5.00 12.00
HMNL Nicklas Lidstrom 5.00 12.00
HMPB Patrice Bergeron 6.00 15.00
HMPF Peter Forsberg 6.00 15.00
HMPK Petr Kalus 3.00 8.00
HMPL Pascal Leclaire 4.00 10.00
HMRA Andrew Raycroft 4.00 10.00
HMRC Ryan Callahan 6.00 15.00
HMRE Mark Recchi 6.00 15.00
HMRP Ryan Parent 3.00 8.00
HMRS Rob Schremp 4.00 10.00
HMRY Michael Ryder 3.00 8.00
HMSA Joe Sakic 8.00 20.00
HMSB Steve Bernier 3.00 8.00
HMSC Sidney Crosby 12.00 30.00
HMSE Brent Seabrook 5.00 12.00
HMSH Brendan Shanahan 6.00 15.00
HMSL Martin St. Louis 5.00 12.00
HMSM Ryan Smyth 4.00 10.00
HMSP Jason Spezza 5.00 12.00
HMST Jarret Stoll 4.00 10.00
HMSV Marek Svatos 3.00 8.00
HMTR Tuomo Ruutu 5.00 12.00
HMVL Vincent Lecavalier 4.00 10.00

2007-08 Hot Prospects Hot Materials Red Hot

*RED HOT: .5X TO 1.2X HOT MATERIALS
STATED PRINT RUN 100 SER.#'d SETS

1995-96 Hoyle Eastern Playing Cards

COMPLETE SET (54) 8.00 20.00
1 Eric Lindros .20 .50
2 Peter Bondra .20 .50
3 Radek Bonk .08 .25
4 Ray Bourque .40 1.00
5 Brian Bradley .08 .25
6 Rod Brind'Amour .20 .50
7 Martin Brodeur .75 2.00
8 Wendel Clark .40 1.00
9 Alexandre Daigle .08 .25
10 Vincent Damphousse .08 .25
11 Ray Ferraro .08 .25
12 Stephane Fiset .20 .50
13 Peter Forsberg .60 1.50
14 Joe Sakic .75 2.00
15 Mikael Renberg .08 .25
16 Stephane Richer .08 .25
17 Mike Richter .40 1.00
18 Luc Robitaille .40 1.00
19 Geoff Sanderson .08 .25
20 Bryan Smolinski .08 .25
21 Kevin Stevens .08 .25
22 Scott Stevens .08 .25
23 Steve Thomas .08 .25
24 Darren Turcotte .08 .25
25 John Vanbiesbrouck .20 .50
26 New Jersey Devils Cup Winners .08 .25
27 Patrick Roy 1.25 3.00
28 Chris Gratton .08 .25
29 Adam Graves .08 .25
30 Dominik Hasek .60 1.50
31 Ron Hextall .40 1.00
32 Jaromir Jagr .60 1.50
33 Joe Juneau .08 .25
34 Dimitri Khristich .08 .25
35 Petr Klima .08 .25
36 Bob Kudelski .08 .25
37 Scott Lachance .08 .25
38 Pat Lafontaine .08 .25
39 John Leclair .08 .25
40 Mark Messier .40 1.00
41 Brian Leetch .20 .50
42 Alexander Mogilny .20 .50
43 Kirk Muller .08 .25
44 Cam Neely .40 1.00
45 Rob Niedermayer .08 .25
46 Scott Niedermayer .20 .50
47 Owen Nolan .08 .25
48 Adam Oates .08 .25
49 Michal Pivonka .08 .25
50 Derek Plante .08 .25
51 Chris Pronger .20 .50
52 Mark Recchi .20 .50
53 Sergei Zubov .08 .25
54 Alexei Yashin .08 .25

1995-96 Hoyle Western Playing Cards

COMPLETE SET (54) 8.00 20.00
1 Jeremy Roenick .40 1.00
2 Dave Andreychuk .08 .25
3 Jason Arnott .08 .25
4 Ed Belfour .40 1.00
5 Rob Blake .20 .50
6 Jeff Brown .08 .25
7 Patrick Carnback .08 .25
8 Chris Chelois .30 .75
9 Tim Cheveldae .20 .50
10 Paul Coffey .30 .75
11 Shayne Corson .08 .25

2 Geoff Courtnall .08 .25
3 Russ Courtnall .08 .25
4 Wayne Gretzky 2.00 5.00
5 Joe Sacco .08 .25
6 Denis Savard .20 .50
7 Teemu Selanne .40 1.00
8 Brendan Shanahan .40 1.00
9 Ray Sheppard .08 .25
0 Mats Sundin .40 1.00
1 Esa Tikkanen .08 .25
2 German Titov .08 .25
3 Keith Tkachuk .20 .50
4 Rick Tocchet .08 .25
5 Doug Weight .08 .25
6 Detroit Red Wings Team Photo .08 .25
7 Sergei Fedorov .40 1.00
8 Ulf Dahlen .08 .25
9 Pat Falloon .08 .25
0 Theoren Fleury .20 .50
1 Doug Gilmour .40 1.00
2 Todd Harvey .08 .25
3 Kevin Hatcher .08 .25
4 Guy Hebert .20 .50
5 Phil Housley .08 .25
6 Brett Hull .60 1.50
7 Arturs Irbe .20 .50
8 Curtis Joseph .40 1.00
9 Paul Kariya .40 1.00
0 Pavel Bure .30 .75
1 Jari Kurri .30 .75
2 Igor Larionov .08 .25
3 Nicklas Lidstrom .20 .50
4 Trevor Linden .40 1.00
5 Marty McSorley .08 .25
6 Mike Modano .40 1.00
7 Bernie Nicholls .08 .25
8 Joe Nieuwendyk .20 .50
9 David Oliver .08 .25
0 Felix Potvin .40 1.00
1 Bill Ranford .20 .50
2 Gary Roberts .08 .25
3 Steve Yzerman 1.25 3.00
4 Alexei Zhamnov .08 .25

1975-76 Houston Aeros WHA

ittle was known about this rare WHA issue. The heckList was confirmed and as the cards are nnumbered, they are listed below in alphabetical rder. Any additional information can be forwarded to ockeymag@beckett.com.

OMPLETE SET (19) 40.00 80.00
Ron Grahame 2.00 4.00
Larry Hale 1.00 2.00
Murray Hall 1.50 3.00
Gordie Howe 15.00 30.00
Mark Howe 5.00 10.00
Marty Howe 4.00 8.00
Andre Hinse 1.00 2.00
Frank Hughes 1.00 2.00
Glen Irwin 1.00 2.00
0 Gord Labossiere 1.50 3.00
1 Don Larway 1.00 2.00
2 Larry Lund 1.50 3.00
3 Paul Popeil 1.50 3.00
4 Rich Preston 1.50 3.00
5 Terry Ruskowski 1.50 3.00
6 Wayne Rutledge 2.00 4.00
7 John Schella 1.00 2.00
8 Ted Taylor 1.00 2.00
9 John Tonelli 5.00 10.00

1992-93 Humpty Dumpty I

his 26-card set was sponsored by Humpty Dumpty oods Ltd., a snack food company located in Eastern anada and owned by Borden Inc. This promotion onsisted of one cello-wrapped (approximately) 1 /16" by 1 15/16" mini-hockey card, which was nserted into specially marked bags of Humpty Dumpty hips and Snacks. Two series of cards were produced, nd complete sets could be obtained only by collecting e cards through the promotion. The promotion lasted om October 1992 to March 1993. A total of 1,000,000 series I cards were produced, or 423,077 f each card, and they were evenly distributed between ntario, Quebec, and the Atlantic provinces. The fronts isplayed glossy color action photos, with the team ogo superimposed toward the bottom of the picture. n a white panel framed by gray, the back presented 991-92 season statistics and biography in French and nglish. The cards were unnumbered and checklisted elow in alphabetical order.

OMPLETE SET (26) 8.00 20.00
Ray Bourque .40 1.00
Rod Brind'Amour .20 .50
Chris Chelios .30 .75
Wendel Clark .20 .50
Toronto Ma
Gilbert Dionne .08 .25
Pat Falloon .15 .40
San Jose Sh
Ray Ferraro .15 .40
Theo Fleury .30 .75
Grant Fuhr .20 .50
0 Wayne Gretzky 2.00 5.00
Los Angel
1 Kevin Hatcher .08 .25
2 Valeri Kamensky .20 .50
3 Mike Keane .08 .25
4 Brian Leetch .30 .75
New York R
5 Kirk McLean .20 .50
Vancouver C
6 Alexander Mogilny .25 .60
Buffa
7 Troy Murray .08 .25
8 Patrick Roy 1.50 4.00
Montreal Ca
9 Joe Sakic .60 1.50
Quebec Nordiq
0 Brendan Shanahan .60 1.50
1 Kevin Stevens .15 .40
2 Scott Stevens .20 .50
3 Mark Tinordi .08 .25
4 Steve Yzerman 1.00 2.50
5 Zarley Zalapski .08 .25
6 Checklist .20 .50

1992-93 Humpty Dumpty II

his 26-card set was sponsored by Humpty Dumpty oods Ltd., a snack food company located in Eastern anada and owned by Borden Inc. This promotion onsisted of one cello-wrapped approximately 1 7/16" 1 15/16" mini-hockey card randomly inserted into pecially marked bags of Humpty Dumpty Chips and nacks. Two series of cards were produced, and omplete sets could be obtained only by collecting the rds through the promotion. The promotion lasted om October 1992 to March 1993. A total of 3,000,000 series II cards were produced, or 692,307 each card, and they were evenly distributed between ntario, Quebec, and the Atlantic provinces. The fronts splayed glossy color action photos, with the team logo superimposed toward the bottom of the picture. On a white panel framed by beige, the back presented 1991-92 season statistics and biography in French and English. The cards were unnumbered and checklisted below in alphabetical order.

COMPLETE SET (26) 8.00 20.00
1 Drake Berehowsky .08 .25
2 Shayne Corson .15 .40
Edmonton
3 Russ Courtnall .15 .40
4 Dave Ellett .08 .25
5 Sergei Fedorov .60 1.50
Detroit
6 Dave Gagner .15 .40
7 Doug Gilmour .30 .75
Toronto Ma
8 Phil Housley .15 .40
9 Brett Hull .40 1.00
St. Louis Bl
10 Jaromir Jagr 1.00 2.50
Pittsburgh
11 Pat LaFontaine .20 .50
Buffalo
12 Mario Lemieux 1.50 4.00
13 Trevor Linden .15 .40
Vancouver
14 Al MacInnis .20 .50
15 Mark Messier .40 1.00
New York R
16 Cam Neely .30 .75
17 Owen Nolan .20 .50
Quebec Nordi
18 Bill Ranford .20 .50
19 Luc Robitaille .25 .60
20 Jeremy Roenick .30 .75
21 Mats Sundin .30 .75
22 Chris Terreri .15 .40
23 Steve Thomas .15 .40
24 Pat Verbeek .15 .40
25 Neil Wilkinson .08 .25
26 Checklist .20 .50

1997-98 Hurricanes Team Issue

The set was issued by the team as a promotional giveaway. The cards were unnumbered and checklisted below in alphabetical order.

COMPLETE SET (28) 4.80 12.00
1 Jeff Brown .08 .25
2 Sean Burke .40 1.00
3 Adam Burt .08 .25
4 Steve Chiasson .08 .25
5 Enrico Ciccone .08 .25
6 Kevin Dineen .10 .30
7 Nelson Emerson .10 .30
8 Martin Gelinas .10 .30
9 Stu Grimson .10 .30
10 Steve Halko .08 .25
11 Kevin Haller .08 .25
12 Sean Hill .08 .25
13 Sami Kapanen 1.25 3.00
14 Trevor Kidd .40 1.00
15 Robert Kron .10 .30
16 Steve Leach .08 .25
17 Curtis Leschyshyn .08 .25
18 Kent Manderville .08 .25
19 Jeff O'Neill .08 .25
20 Nolan Pratt .08 .25
21 Keith Primeau .60 1.50
22 Paul Ranheim .08 .25
23 Steven Rice .10 .30
24 Gary Roberts .10 .30
25 Geoff Sanderson .20 .50
26 Glen Wesley .10 .30
27 Paul Maurice .07 .20
Tom Webster
Randy Ladouceur CO
28 Stormy the Mascot .02 .10

1998-99 Hurricanes Team Issue

This set featured the Hurricanes of the NHL. The postcard-sized singles were issued at autograph signings and other promotional ventures.

COMPLETE SET (25) 12.00 30.00
1 Arturs Irbe .75 2.00
2 Glen Wesley .40 1.00
3 Steve Chiasson .40 1.00
4 Nolan Pratt .40 1.00
5 Marek Malik .40 1.00
6 Adam Burt .40 1.00
7 Curtis Leschyshyn .40 1.00
8 Gary Roberts .40 1.00
9 Kevin Dineen .40 1.00
10 Bates Battaglia .60 1.50
11 Steven Halko .40 1.00
12 Byron Ritchie .40 1.00
13 Ron Francis 1.25 3.00
14 Sean Hill .40 1.00
15 Martin Gelinas .40 1.00
16 Sami Kapanen .75 2.00
17 Ray Sheppard .40 1.00
18 Paul Ranheim .40 1.00
19 Dave Karpa .40 1.00
20 Trevor Kidd .60 1.50
21 Kent Manderville .40 1.00
22 Mike Rucinski .40 1.00
23 Keith Primeau .60 1.50
24 Jeff O'Neill .75 2.00
25 Stormy MASCOT .08 .25

1999-00 Hurricanes Team Issue

COMPLETE SET (21) 6.00 15.00
1 Arturs Irbe .60 1.50
2 Glen Wesley .40 1.00
3 Nolan Pratt .40 1.00
4 Marek Malik .40 1.00
5 Curtis Leschyshyn .40 1.00
6 Gary Roberts .40 1.00
7 Bates Battaglia .40 1.00
8 Steve Halko .40 1.00
9 Tommy Westlund .40 1.00
10 Jeff Daniels .40 1.00
11 Robert Kron .40 1.00
12 Ron Francis .60 1.50
13 Sean Hill .40 1.00
14 Martin Gelinas .40 1.00
15 Sami Kapanen .40 1.00
16 Rod Brind'Amour .60 1.50
17 Dave Karpa .40 1.00
18 Andrei Kovalenko .40 1.00
19 Paul Coffey .60 1.50
20 Jeff O'Neill .40 1.00
21 Randy Ladouceur .40 1.00
Kevin McCarthy
Paul Maurice

2002-03 Hurricanes Postcards

These 3X5 blank backed cards feature a photo, stats and player ID on the front. They were issued as promotional items at team events. The checklist is not complete -- if you can confirm others, please write us at hockeymag@beckett.com.

COMPLETE SET
1 Rod Brind'Amour .60 1.50
2 Erik Cole .60 1.50
3 Ron Francis .60 1.50
4 Arturs Irbe .75 2.00
5 Jeff O'Neill .40 1.00
6 Kevin Weekes .60 1.50
7 Glen Wesley .40 1.00

2003-04 Hurricanes Postcards

These oversized cards were issued by the team and sponsored by Pepsi.

COMPLETE SET (24) 10.00 25.00
1 Craig Adams .30 .75
2 Kevyn Adams .30 .75
3 Ryan Bayda .30 .75
4 Bob Boughner .30 .75
5 Jesse Boulerice .30 .75
6 Pavel Brendl .30 .75
7 Rod Brind'Amour .60 1.50
8 Erik Cole .40 1.00
9 Ron Francis .60 1.50
10 Bret Hedican .30 .75
11 Sean Hill .30 .75
12 Kevin McCarthy .30 .75
13 Marty Murray .30 .75
14 Jeff O'Neill .40 1.00
15 Eric Staal 2.00 5.00
16 Bruno St. Jacques .30 .75
17 Jamie Storr .40 1.00
18 Jaroslav Svoboda .30 .75
19 Josef Vasicek .30 .75
20 Radim Vrbata .30 .75
21 Niclas Wallin .30 .75
22 Aaron Ward .30 .75
23 Kevin Weekes .40 1.00
24 Glen Wesley .30 .75

2006-07 Hurricanes Postcards

COMPLETE SET (28) 15.00 25.00
1 Logo Card .10 .25
2 Craig Adams .40 1.00
3 Kevyn Adams .40 1.00
4 Anton Babchuk .40 1.00
5 Eric Belanger .40 1.00
6 Rod Brind'Amour .75 2.00
7 Erik Cole 1.00 2.50
8 Mike Commodore .40 1.00
9 Jeff Daniels ACO .10 .25
10 Tim Gleason .40 1.00
11 John Grahame .60 1.50
12 Bret Hedican .40 1.00
13 Andrew Hutchinson .40 1.00
14 Frantisek Kaberle .40 1.00
15 Andrew Ladd .40 1.00
16 Chad Larose .40 1.00
17 Peter Laviolette CO .20 .50
18 Trevor Letowski .40 1.00
19 Kevin McCarthy ACO .10 .25
20 Eric Staal 1.25 3.00
21 Cory Stillman .40 1.00
22 David Tanabe .40 1.00
23 Scott Walker .40 1.00
24 Niclas Wallin .40 1.00
25 Cam Ward .75 2.00
26 Glen Wesley .40 1.00
27 Ray Whitney .40 1.00
28 Justin Williams .75 2.00

1991 Impel U.S. Olympic Hall of Fame

Produced by Impel Marketing Inc., this 90-card set salutes members of the U.S. Olympic Hall of Fame. A portion of the proceeds from the sale of these cards supported the 1992 U.S. Olympic team. The cards were available in 15-card packs, and collectors could obtain a collector's album to display the set for $12.99 plus $3.00 postage and handling. Also the cards were packaged in sets of three, along with a "Medals and Millions" game piece, inside specially-marked multi-packs of Coca-Cola products in a promotion cosponsored by Coca-Cola U.S.A. and CBS. Six cards from the set (Beamon, Fleming, Jenner, Owens, Rudolph, and Spitz) were issued as prototypes in a cello pack; they are unnumbered and clearly marked as such on the backs in the upper right corner. The fronts display a mix of color and black-and-white photos inside a gold inner border. The outer border is light gray, and a red, white, and blue ribbon cuts across the middle of the card. The backs carry a closeup photo, career summary, and career highlights.

COMPLETE SET (90) 6.00 15.00
66 1980 U.S. Hockey Team .20 .50
Moment of Victory
67 1980 U.S. Hockey Team .12 .30
Aggressive blocking
68 Dave Christian .12 .30
Buzz Schneider
69 1980 U.S. Hockey Team .20 .50
Victory Celebration
71 1980 U.S. Hockey Team .20 .50
Gold-medal victory
72 Herb Brooks CO .12 .30

1927 Imperial Tobacco

This card was black and white and measured approximately 1 1/2 x 2 1/2.

NNO Montreal Victorias 25.00 50.00

1929 Imperial Tobacco

This card is black and white and measures approximately 2 1/2 x 3.

NNO Ice Hockey 20.00 40.00

2010-11 ITG 100 Years of Card Collecting

HP ISSUED IN HEROES AND PROSPECTS
BTP ISSUED IN BETWEEN THE PIPES
D ISSUED IN ITG DECADES 1980s
CW ISSUED IN 11-12 CANADA VS WORLD

1 Georges Vezina BTP 3.00 8.00
2 Eddie Shore HP 2.00 5.00
3 Charlie Conacher HP 2.00 5.00
4 Ron Francis D 3.00 8.00
5 Bill Barilko HP 1.50 4.00
6 Doug Harvey CW 2.50 6.00
7 Howie Morenz HP 2.00 5.00
8 Luc Robitaille D 2.50 6.00
9 Bobby Hull CW 2.50 6.00
10 Daniel Sedin CW 2.50 6.00
11 Peter Forsberg CW 3.00 8.00
12 Borje Salming CW 2.50 6.00
13 Teemu Selanne CW 5.00 12.00
14 Dave Keon HP 2.50 6.00
15 Cyclone Taylor HP 2.50 6.00
16 Brett Hull CW 4.00 10.00
17 Valeri Kharlamov CW 1.50 4.00
18 Hobey Baker HP 2.00 5.00
19 Ted Lindsay HP 2.50 6.00
20 Vladislav Tretiak BTP 3.00 8.00
21 Mario Lemieux D 8.00 20.00
22 Mike Bossy D 2.50 6.00
23 Red Kelly HP 2.50 6.00
24 Steven Stamkos CW 5.00 12.00
25 Felix Potvin BTP 4.00 10.00
26 Lester Patrick HP 2.50 6.00
27 Darryl Sittler CW 2.00 5.00
28 Gump Worsley BTP 2.50 6.00
29 George Hainsworth BTP 2.50 6.00
30 Martin Brodeur BTP 5.00 12.00
31 Pelle Lindbergh D 4.00 10.00
32 Denis Potvin D 2.50 6.00
33 Patrick Roy BTP 6.00 15.00
34 Charlie Gardiner BTP 2.00 5.00
35 Tony Esposito BTP 2.50 6.00
36 Newsy Lalonde HP 2.00 5.00
37 Turk Broda BTP 2.50 6.00
38 Aurel Joliat HP 2.50 6.00
39 Sid Abel HP 2.00 5.00
40 Sid Abel CW 2.00 5.00
41 Igor Larionov CW 2.50 6.00
42 Maurice Richard HP 4.00 10.00
43 Bobby Bauer HP 2.50 6.00
44 Teeder Kennedy HP 2.50 6.00
45 Woody Dumart HP 1.50 4.00
46 Carey Price BTP 10.00 25.00
47 Chris Chelios D 2.50 6.00
48 Paul Coffey D 2.50 6.00
49 Syl Apps HP 3.00 8.00
50 Bill Durnan BTP 2.50 6.00
51 Terry Sawchuk BTP 3.00 8.00
52 Milt Schmidt HP 2.00 5.00
53 Elmer Lach HP 2.00 5.00
54 Marcel Dionne D 3.00 8.00
55 Johnny Bucyk D 2.50 6.00
56 Henri Richard HP 2.50 6.00
57 Miikka Kiprusoff BTP 2.00 5.00
58 Frank Mahovlich CW 2.50 6.00
59 Stan Mikita D 3.00 8.00
60 Jean Beliveau D 2.50 6.00
61 Glenn Hall BTP 2.50 6.00
62 Vincent Lecavalier CW 2.00 5.00
63 Phil Esposito D 4.00 10.00
64 Ron Hextall BTP 3.00 8.00
65 Gerry Cheevers BTP 2.50 6.00
66 Bernie Parent BTP 2.50 6.00
67 Johnny Bower BTP 3.00 8.00
68 Jaromir Jagr CW 6.00 15.00
69 Toe Blake HP 1.50 4.00
70 Gilbert Perreault D 2.50 6.00
71 Ilya Kovalchuk CW 2.50 6.00
72 Guy Lafleur D 3.00 8.00
73 Larry Robinson D 2.50 6.00
74 Tim Horton HP 2.50 6.00
75 Bobby Clarke CW 2.50 6.00
76 Bryan Trottier D 3.00 8.00
77 Raymond Bourque D 4.00 10.00
78 Ed Giacomin BTP 4.00 10.00
79 Bernie Geoffrion HP 2.00 5.00
80 Peter Stastny D 2.00 5.00
81 Grant Fuhr BTP 2.50 6.00
82 Marian Gaborik CW 3.00 8.00
83 Jacques Plante BTP 3.00 8.00
84 Pat LaFontaine D 2.50 6.00
85 Patrick Roy BTP 6.00 15.00
86 Jari Kurri D 2.50 6.00
87 Joe Sakic CW 4.00 10.00
88 Mike Modano CW 5.00 12.00
89 Lanny McDonald D 2.50 6.00
90 Henrik Sedin CW 2.50 6.00
91 Sergei Fedorov CW 4.00 10.00
92 Nicklas Lidstrom CW 2.50 6.00
93 Doug Gilmour D 3.00 8.00
94 Cam Neely D 2.50 6.00
95 Pavel Bure CW 3.00 8.00
96 Roberto Luongo BTP 2.50 6.00
97 Joe Thornton CW 2.50 6.00
98 Wendel Clark D 2.50 6.00
99 Tim Thomas BTP 2.00 5.00
100A Steve Yzerman BTP 6.00 15.00
100B Steve Yzerman D 6.00 15.00

2003-04 ITG Action

ITG Action was the largest set of the year consisiting of 600 veteran cards found in packs and 74 update cards available via various redemptions. Cards 601-616 were initially available via redemption cards found in hobby boxes. Each card was serial numbered to 750 but ITG announced much lower actual print runs after the EXCH cards had expired. Cards 617-624 were available only in factory sets as EXCH cards also with announced lower actual print runs. Finally, cards 625-674 were available via an online only purchase.

COMP.SET w/o SP's (600) 30.00 80.00
1 Joe Thornton .30 .75
2 Dany Heatley .25 .60
3 Ales Kotalik .15 .40
4 Steve Montador .15 .40
5 Dan Bylsma .15 .40
6 Andrew Ference .15 .40
7 Andy Hilbert .15 .40
8 Andy McDonald .20 .50
9 Bob Boughner .15 .40
10 Brad Tapper .15 .40
11 Brian Campbell .20 .50
12 Brian Rolston .20 .50
13 Daniel Tjarnqvist .15 .40
14 Glen Murray .20 .50
15 Byron Dafoe .20 .50
16 Bryan Berard .20 .50
17 Alexei Zhitnik .20 .50
18 Craig Conroy .15 .40
19 Curtis Brown .15 .40
20 Dan McGillis .15 .40
21 Dan Snyder .15 .40
22 Daniel Briere .25 .60
23 Chris Clark .15 .40
24 Frantisek Kaberle .15 .40
25 Adam Oates .25 .60
26 Denis Gauthier .15 .40
27 Dimitri Kalinin .15 .40
28 Martin Lapointe .20 .50
29 Keith Carney .15 .40
30 Garnet Exelby .15 .40
31 Dean McAmmond .15 .40
32 Hal Gill .15 .40
33 Henrik Tallinder .15 .40
34 Ilya Kovalchuk .25 .60
35 Ivan Huml .15 .40
36 J-P Dumont .15 .40
37 Alexei Smirnov .15 .40
38 Jarome Iginla .25 .60
39 Jason Krog .15 .40
40 Jay McKee .15 .40
41 Jean-Sebastien Giguere .25 .60
42 Krzysztof Oliwa .15 .40
43 Jeff Odgers .15 .40
44 Jochen Hecht .15 .40
45 Joe DiPenta RC .20 .50
46 Adam Mair .15 .40
47 Jonathan Girard .15 .40
48 Jordan Leopold .15 .40
49 Andrew Raycroft .20 .50
50 Kamil Piros .15 .40
51 Eric Boulton .15 .40
52 Kurt Sauer .15 .40
53 Lubos Bartecko .15 .40
54 Marc Chouinard .15 .40
55 Marc Savard .20 .50
56 Martin Biron .20 .50
57 Martin Gelinas .15 .40
58 Martin Gerber .15 .40
59 Chuck Kobasew .15 .40
60 Martin Samuelsson .20 .50
61 Jamie McLennan .15 .40
62 Mika Noronen .15 .40
63 Mike Knuble .15 .40
64 Mike Leclerc .15 .40
65 Pasi Nurminen .20 .50
66 Miroslav Satan .20 .50
67 Nick Boynton .15 .40
68 Niclas Havelid .15 .40
69 Oleg Saprykin .15 .40
70 Milan Bartovic RC .20 .50
71 P.J. Stock .15 .40
72 Roman Turek .20 .50
73 Patrik Stefan .15 .40
74 Maxim Afinogenov .15 .40
75 Petr Sykora .20 .50
76 Rick Mrozik RC .15 .40
77 Rob Niedermayer .20 .50
78 Robyn Regehr .15 .40
79 P.J. Axelsson .15 .40
80 Ruslan Salei .15 .40
81 Ryan Miller .25 .60
82 Sandis Ozolinsh .15 .40
83 Blake Sloan .20 .50
84 Tim Connolly .15 .40
85 Shaone Morrisonn .15 .40
86 Shawn McEachern .15 .40
87 Shean Donovan .15 .40
88 Simon Gamache .15 .40
89 Stanislav Chistov .15 .40
90 Stephane Yelle .15 .40
91 Steve Rucchin .15 .40
92 Steve Shields .20 .50
93 Steve Thomas .15 .40
94 Taylor Pyatt .15 .40
95 Yannick Tremblay .15 .40
96 Toni Lydman .15 .40
97 Tony Hrkac .15 .40
98 Vitali Vishnevsky .15 .40
99 Slava Kozlov .20 .50
100 Sergei Samsonov .20 .50
101 Riku Hahl .15 .40
102 Tyler Wright .15 .40
103 Tyler Arnason .15 .40
104 Tomas Kurka .15 .40
105 Theo Fleury .30 .75
106 Stu Barnes .15 .40
107 Steve Sullivan .15 .40
108 Paul Kariya .30 .75
109 Steve Poapst .15 .40
110 Steve Ott .20 .50
111 Steve McCarthy .15 .40
112 Sergei Zubov .20 .50
113 Serge Aubin .15 .40
114 Niko Kapanen .15 .40
115 Pascal Leclaire .15 .40
116 Patrick Roy .60 1.50
117 Pavel Brendl .15 .40
118 Peter Forsberg .30 .75
119 Philippe Boucher .15 .40
120 Radim Vrbata .20 .50
121 Ray Whitney .20 .50
122 Richard Matvichuk .15 .40
123 Rick Nash .25 .60
124 Sami Helenius .15 .40
125 Rob Blake .25 .60
126 Rob DiMaio .15 .40
127 Rod Brind'Amour .25 .60
128 Chris McAllister .15 .40
129 Ron Tugnutt .20 .50
130 Rostislav Klesla .15 .40
131 Ryan Bayda .15 .40
132 Ryan VandenBussche .15 .40
133 Ron Francis .30 .75
134 Charlie Stephens .15 .40
135 Scott Young .15 .40
136 Sean Hill .15 .40
137 Sean Pronger .15 .40
138 Nathan Dempsey .15 .40
139 Jason Bacashihua .15 .40
140 Jason Strudwick .15 .40
141 Jeff O'Neill .15 .40
142 Jere Lehtinen .20 .50
143 Alexander Karpovtsev .15 .40
144 Jody Shelley .15 .40
145 Alex Tanguay .20 .50
146 John Erskine .15 .40
147 Jon Klemm .15 .40
148 Josef Vasicek .15 .40
149 Kent McDonell RC .20 .50
150 Kevyn Adams .15 .40
151 Kyle Calder .15 .40
152 Lasse Pirjeta .15 .40
153 Manny Malhotra .15 .40
154 Marc Denis .20 .50
155 Mark Bell .15 .40
156 Martin Skoula .15 .40
157 Marty Turco .25 .60
158 Matt Davidson .15 .40
159 Michael Leighton .15 .40
160 Kevin Weekes .20 .50
161 Luke Richardson .15 .40
162 Mike Keane .20 .50
163 Mike Modano .40 1.00
164 Scott Lachance .15 .40
165 Mike Zigomanis .15 .40
166 Milan Hejduk .20 .50
167 Jason Arnott .20 .50
168 Jaroslav Svoboda .15 .40
169 Jaroslav Spacek .15 .40
170 Aaron Ward .15 .40
171 Alexei Zhamnov .20 .50
172 Teemu Selanne .50 1.25
173 Jan Hlavac .15 .40
174 Duvie Westcott .15 .40
175 Erik Cole .20 .50
176 Philippe Sauve .20 .50
177 Eric Daze .20 .50
178 Derrick Walser .15 .40
179 Aaron Downey .15 .40
180 Derek Morris .15 .40
181 David Vyborny .15 .40
182 Craig Andersson .25 .60
183 Patrick DesRochers .15 .40
184 David Aebischer .20 .50
185 Stephane Robidas .20 .50
186 Dan Hinote .15 .40
187 Craig Adams .15 .40
188 Burke Henry .15 .40
189 Bret Hedican .15 .40
190 Brenden Morrow .20 .50
191 Brad DeFauw .15 .40
192 Bill Guerin .25 .60
193 Bates Battaglia .15 .40
194 Andrew Cassels .15 .40
195 Adam Foote .15 .40
196 Geoff Sanderson .15 .40
197 Jocelyn Thibault .20 .50
198 Joe Sakic .40 1.00
199 Espen Knutsen .15 .40
200 Igor Radulov .15 .40
201 Jason Smith .15 .40
202 Dominik Hasek .40 1.00
203 Sean Avery .15 .40
204 Steve Staios .15 .40
205 Kirk Maltby .15 .40
206 Denis Shvidki .15 .40
207 Sergei Fedorov .40 1.00
208 Sergei Zholtok .15 .40
209 Shawn Horcoff .15 .40
210 Stephen Weiss .15 .40
211 Steve Yzerman .60 1.50
212 Brad Chartrand .15 .40
213 Brad Isbister .15 .40
214 Valeri Bure .15 .40
215 Brendan Shanahan .30 .75
216 Ryan Smyth .20 .50
217 Chris Chelios .25 .60
218 Cliff Ronning .15 .40
219 Curtis Joseph .25 .60
220 Darcy Hordichuk .15 .40
221 Darren McCarty .15 .40
222 Eric Brewer .15 .40
223 Derek Armstrong .15 .40
224 Dwayne Roloson .20 .50
225 Eric Belanger .15 .40
226 Brett Hull .30 .75
227 Joe Corvo .15 .40
228 Ethan Moreau .15 .40
229 Felix Potvin .40 1.00
230 Fernando Pisani .15 .40
231 Filip Kuba .15 .40
232 Georges Laraque .20 .50
233 Henrik Zetterberg .30 .75
234 Ian Laperriere .15 .40
235 Igor Larionov .25 .60
236 Mattias Norstrom .15 .40
237 Ivan Novoseltsev .15 .40
238 Jamie Storr .20 .50
239 Jani Hurme .15 .40
240 Jani Rita .15 .40
241 Willie Mitchell .15 .40
242 Jaroslav Bednar .15 .40
243 Jaroslav Modry .15 .40
244 Lubomir Sekeras .15 .40
245 Lubomir Visnovsky .15 .40
246 Manny Fernandez .20 .50
247 Jared Aulin .15 .40
248 Marcus Nilson .15 .40
249 Ales Hemsky .25 .60
250 Igor Ulanov .15 .40
251 Alexei Semenov .15 .40
252 Mathieu Schneider .15 .40
253 Matt Cullen .15 .40
254 Andrew Brunette .15 .40
255 Viktor Kozlov .15 .40
256 Mike Comrie .20 .50
257 Brad Bombardir .15 .40
258 Scott Ferguson .15 .40
259 Tomas Holmstrom .20 .50
260 Tomas Zizka .15 .40
261 Manny Legace .15 .40
262 Jon Sim .15 .40
263 Wes Walz .15 .40
264 Jay Bouwmeester .25 .60
265 Zigmund Palffy .25 .60
266 Andreas Lilja .15 .40
267 Pascal Dupuis .15 .40
268 Alexander Frolov .20 .50
269 Tommy Salo .20 .50
270 Antti Laaksonen .15 .40
271 Mike Cammalleri .25 .60
272 Bill Muckalt .15 .40
273 Mike York .15 .40
274 Nick Schultz .15 .40
275 Nicklas Lidstrom .25 .60
276 Andrei Zyuzin .15 .40
277 Adam Deadmarsh .20 .50
278 Olli Jokinen .25 .60
279 Pavel Datsyuk .30 .75
280 Jason Chimera .15 .40
281 Kristian Huselius .15 .40
282 Jarret Stoll .15 .40
283 Jason Allison .20 .50
284 Richard Park .15 .40
285 Marty Reasoner .15 .40
286 Mathieu Biron .20 .50
287 Jason Woolley .15 .40
288 Pavel Trnka .15 .40
289 Jim Dowd .15 .40
290 Kris Draper .15 .40
291 Peter Worrell .15 .40
292 P-M Bouchard .25 .60
293 Radek Dvorak .20 .50
294 Matt Johnson .15 .40
295 Aaron Miller .15 .40
296 Mathieu Dandenault .15 .40
297 Marian Gaborik .40 1.00
298 Roberto Luongo .40 1.00
299 Jason Williams .15 .40
300 Niklas Hagman .15 .40
301 Jamie Langenbrunner .20 .50
302 Greg Johnson .15 .40
303 Alexei Kovalev .20 .50
304 Ron Hainsey .15 .40
305 Ari Ahonen .15 .40
306 Mark Parrish .15 .40
307 Andrei Markov .25 .60
308 Jason York .15 .40
309 Jason Wiemer .15 .40
310 Mark Messier .40 1.00
311 Joe Juneau .20 .50
312 Colin White .15 .40
313 Mike Dunham .20 .50
314 Brian Finley .15 .40
315 Jeff Friesen .15 .40
316 Boris Mironov .15 .40
317 Brian Rafalski .20 .50
318 Chad Kilger .15 .40
319 Arron Asham .15 .40
320 Corey Schwab .20 .50
321 Craig Rivet .15 .40
322 Dale Purinton .15 .40
323 John Madden .15 .40
324 Bill Houlder .15 .40
325 Denis Arkhipov .15 .40
326 Bobby Holik .15 .40
327 Jay Pandolfo .15 .40
328 Adam Hall .15 .40
329 Adrian Aucoin .15 .40
330 Michael Rupp .15 .40
331 Donald Audette .15 .40
332 Brian Gionta .20 .50
333 Jan Bulis .15 .40
334 Jamie Lundmark .15 .40
335 Jason Ward .15 .40
336 Anson Carter .20 .50
337 Grant Marshall .15 .40
338 Garth Snow .20 .50
339 Eric Lindros .40 1.00
340 Dusan Salficky RC .20 .50
341 Darius Kasparaitis .15 .40
342 Patrik Elias .25 .60
343 David Legwand .20 .50
344 Brian Leetch .25 .60
345 Jason Blake .15 .40
346 Kimmo Timonen .15 .40
347 Dan Blackburn .20 .50
348 Jose Theodore .25 .60
349 Justin Mapletoft .15 .40
350 Vernon Fiddler .15 .40
351 Ken Daneyko .15 .40
352 Martin Erat .15 .40
353 Janne Niinimaa .15 .40
354 Marcel Hossa .15 .40
355 Scott Niedermayer .25 .60
356 Petr Nedved .15 .40
357 Martin Brodeur .50 1.25
358 Rick DiPietro .20 .50
359 Mathieu Garon .15 .40
360 Vladimir Malakhov .15 .40
361 Mike Ribeiro .20 .50
362 Michael Peca .20 .50
363 Andreas Dackell .15 .40
364 Scott Stevens .25 .60
365 Dave Scatchard .15 .40
366 Mike Richter .25 .60
367 Niklas Sundstrom .15 .40
368 Oleg Petrov .15 .40
369 Alexei Yashin .20 .50
370 Darren Haydar .15 .40
371 Patrice Brisebois .15 .40
372 Scott Walker .15 .40
373 Pavel Bure .30 .75
374 Yanic Perreault .15 .40
375 Vladimir Orszagh .15 .40
376 Kenny Jonsson .15 .40
377 Vitali Yachmenev .15 .40
378 Turner Stevenson .15 .40
379 Trent Hunter .15 .40
380 Tomas Vokoun .20 .50
381 Tom Poti .15 .40
382 Shawn Bates .15 .40
383 Sergei Brylin .15 .40
384 Scottie Upshall .20 .50
385 Mattias Weinhandl .15 .40
386 Joe Nieuwendyk .25 .60
387 Mike Komisarek .15 .40
388 Matthew Barnaby .20 .50
389 Scott Gomez .20 .50
390 Sandy McCarthy .15 .40
391 Saku Koivu .25 .60
392 Ronald Petrovicky .15 .40
393 Scott Hartnell .25 .60
394 Roman Hamrlik .20 .50
395 Andreas Johansson .15 .40
396 Richard Zednik .15 .40
397 Rem Murray .15 .40
398 Randy Robitaille .15 .40
399 Randy McKay .15 .40
400 Oleg Kvasha .15 .40
401 Steve McKenna .15 .40
402 Radoslav Suchy .15 .40
403 Wayne Primeau .15 .40
404 Wade Redden .15 .40
405 Vincent Damphousse .20 .50
406 Sebastien Caron .20 .50
407 Vaclav Varada .15 .40
408 Tony Amonte .20 .50
409 Tomas Surovy .15 .40
410 Sami Kapanen .15 .40
411 Mike Ricci .20 .50
412 Alexei Morozov .15 .40
413 Miroslav Zalesak .15 .40
414 Mark Recchi .30 .75
415 Patrick Marleau .25 .60
416 Robert Esche .15 .40
417 Brooks Orpik .20 .50
418 Ville Nieminen .15 .40
419 Mike Rathje .15 .40
420 Michal Rozsival .15 .40
421 Todd Harvey .15 .40
422 Zdeno Chara .25 .60
423 Scott Hannan .15 .40
424 Rob Ray .15 .40
425 Zac Bierk .15 .40
426 Vesa Toskala .15 .40
427 Todd White .15 .40
428 Eric Meloche .15 .40
429 Niko Dimitrakos .15 .40
430 Patrick Lalime .20 .50
431 Simon Gagne .25 .60
432 Sean Burke .15 .40
433 John LeClair .25 .60
434 Petr Schastlivy .15 .40
435 Scott Thornton .20 .50
436 Radek Bonk .20 .50
437 Rico Fata .15 .40
438 Mike Johnson .15 .40
439 Mike Fisher .15 .40
440 Radovan Somik .15 .40
441 Peter Schaefer .15 .40
442 Michal Handzus .20 .50
443 Landon Wilson .15 .40
444 Jonathan Cheechoo .20 .50
445 Mario Lemieux .75 2.00
446 Martin Havlat .25 .60
447 Mark Smith .15 .40
448 Kris Beech .15 .40
449 Keith Primeau .25 .60
450 Marian Hossa .20 .50
451 Marcus Ragnarsson .15 .40
452 Martin Straka .15 .40
453 Kim Johnsson .15 .40
454 Milan Kraft .15 .40
455 Martin Prusek .15 .40
456 Krys Kolanos .15 .40
457 Kyle McLaren .15 .40
458 Ladislav Nagy .15 .40
459 Claude Lapointe .15 .40
460 Magnus Arvedson .15 .40
461 Marco Sturm .15 .40

462 Karel Rachunek .15 .40
463 Justin Williams .20 .50
464 Evgeni Nabokov .20 .50
465 Mathias Johansson .15 .40
466 Eric Desjardins .20 .50
467 Daniel Alfredsson .25 .60
468 Chris Therien .15 .40
469 Jeremy Roenick .25 .60
470 Jeff Taffe .15 .40
471 Johan Hedberg .20 .50
472 Dimitri Yushkevich .15 .40
473 Shane Doan .20 .50
474 Paul Mara .15 .40
475 Eric Weinrich .15 .40
476 Jim Fahey .15 .40
477 Konstantin Koltsov .15 .40
478 Jason Jaspers .15 .40
479 Jason Spezza .25 .60
480 J-S Aubin .15 .40
481 Deron Quint .15 .40
482 Dennis Seidenberg .25 .60
483 Daymond Langkow .15 .40
484 Kelly Buchberger .20 .50
485 Michal Sivek .15 .40
486 Donald Brashear .15 .40
487 Chris Phillips .15 .40
488 Chris Gratton .15 .40
489 Bryan Smolinski .15 .40
490 Guillaume Lefebvre .15 .40
491 Brian Savage .15 .40
492 Alyn McCauley .15 .40
493 Andrei Nazarov .15 .40
494 Anton Volchenkov .15 .40
495 Brad Ference .15 .40
496 Brad Stuart .15 .40
497 Branko Radivojevic .15 .40
498 Brian Boucher .20 .50
499 Dick Tarnstrom .15 .40
500 Adam Graves .20 .50
501 Al MacInnis .25 .60
502 Scott Mellanby .15 .40
503 Matt Stajan RC .25 .60
504 Andre Roy .15 .40
505 Alexander Mogilny .20 .50
506 Barret Jackman .15 .40
507 Nik Antropov .20 .50
508 Ben Clymer .15 .40
509 Maxime Ouellet .20 .50
510 Trevor Kidd .15 .40
511 Brad Richards .25 .60
512 Todd Bertuzzi .25 .60
513 Wade Belak .15 .40
514 Brian Sutherby .15 .40
515 Fedor Fedorov .15 .40
516 Cory Sarich .15 .40
517 Brent Sopel .15 .40
518 Chris Pronger .20 .50
519 Brendan Morrison .20 .50
520 Sebastien Charpentier .15 .40
521 Alexander Svitov .15 .40
522 Calle Johansson .15 .40
523 Bryan McCabe .15 .40
524 Bryan Allen .15 .40
525 Bryce Salvador .15 .40
526 Dainius Zubrus .15 .40
527 Dallas Drake .15 .40
528 Dan Boyle .20 .50
529 Dan Cloutier .20 .50
530 Ken Klee .15 .40
531 Keith Tkachuk .25 .60
532 Brandon Reid .15 .40
533 Sergei Berezin .15 .40
534 Alex Auld .15 .40
535 Jaromir Jagr .60 1.50
536 Markus Naslund .25 .60
537 Jamal Mayers .15 .40
538 Ivan Ciernik .15 .40
539 Marek Malik .15 .40
540 Karel Pilar .15 .40
541 Fredrik Modin .15 .40
542 Gary Roberts .15 .40
543 Eric Boguniecki .15 .40
544 Henrik Sedin .25 .60
545 Ed Belfour .25 .60
546 Doug Weight .25 .60
547 Carlo Colaiacovo .15 .40
548 Peter Sejna RC .20 .50
549 Michael Nylander .15 .40
550 Daniel Sedin .25 .60
551 Kip Miller .15 .40
552 Robert Reichel .15 .40
553 Olaf Kolzig .25 .60
554 Reed Low .15 .40
555 Mikael Renberg .15 .40
556 Mike Grier .15 .40
557 Owen Nolan .20 .50
558 Nikolai Khabibulin .25 .60
559 Brad May .15 .40
560 Nikita Alexeev .15 .40
561 Sami Salo .15 .40
562 Martin St. Louis .25 .60
563 Brendan Witt .15 .40
564 Martin Rucinsky .15 .40
565 Mattias Ohlund .15 .40
566 Doug Gilmour .30 .75
567 Matt Cooke .15 .40
568 Dave Andreychuk .25 .60
569 Robert Lang .15 .40
570 Alexander Khavanov .15 .40
571 Tie Domi .20 .50
572 Ruslan Fedotenko .15 .40
573 Robert Svehla .15 .40
574 Tim Taylor .15 .40
575 Brent Johnson .20 .50
576 Brad Lukowich .15 .40
577 Sergei Gonchar .15 .40
578 Sheldon Keefe .15 .40
579 Steve Eminger .15 .40
580 Tomas Kaberle .15 .40
581 Steve Konowalchuk .15 .40
582 Chris Osgood .25 .60
583 Trevor Linden .25 .60
584 Travis Green .15 .40
585 Steve Martins .15 .40
586 John Grahame .15 .40
587 Darcy Tucker .20 .50
588 Jassen Cullimore .15 .40
589 Peter Bondra .20 .50
590 Pavol Demitra .30 .75
591 Nolan Pratt .15 .40
592 Jeff Halpern .15 .40
593 Vincent Lecavalier .20 .50
594 Petr Cajanek .15 .40
595 Chris Dingman .15 .40
596 Artem Chubarov .15 .40
597 Curtis Sanford .15 .40
598 Ed Jovanovski .20 .50
599 Mats Sundin .25 .60
600 Jarkko Ruutu .15 .40
601 Marc-Andre Fleury RC/321 20.00 50.00
602 Eric Staal RC/340 15.00 40.00
603 Tuomo Ruutu RC/299 5.00 12.00
604 Joni Pitkanen RC/316 5.00 12.00
605 Dustin Brown RC/287 6.00 15.00
606 Alexander Semin RC/291 10.00 25.00
607 Boyd Gordon RC/268 4.00 10.00
608 Pavel Vorobiev RC/203 4.00 10.00
609 Dan Hamhuis RC/286 4.00 10.00
610 Marek Zidlicky RC/308 3.00 8.00
611 Brent Burns RC/270 8.00 20.00
612 Cody McCormick RC/271 4.00 10.00
613 Antoine Vermette RC/280 6.00 15.00
614 Sean Bergenheim RC/291 4.00 10.00
615 Ryan Malone RC/310 6.00 15.00
616 Peter Sarno RC/284 3.00 8.00
617 Nathan Horton XRC/301 8.00 20.00
618 Joffrey Lupul XRC/306 8.00 20.00
619 Jordin Tootoo XRC/302 6.00 15.00
620 Patrice Bergeron XRC/299 15.00 40.00
621 Jiri Hudler XRC/291 8.00 20.00
622 Chris Higgins XRC/297 6.00 15.00
623 Maxim Kondratiev XRC/293 3.00 8.00
624 Brent Krahn XRC/283 3.00 8.00
625 Cover Card Checklist .15 .40
626 Kari Lehtonen XRC 2.50 6.00
627 Dan Fritsche XRC .50 1.25
628 Tim Gleason XRC .60 1.50
629 Derek Roy XRC .75 2.00
630 Matthew Lombardi XRC .60 1.50
631 John-Michael Liles XRC .60 1.50
632 Brian Leetch .50 1.25
633 Michael Ryder .40 1.00
634 Karl Stewart XRC .50 1.25
635 Jed Ortmeyer XRC .50 1.25
636 Dominic Moore XRC .50 1.25
637 Andrew Allen XRC .50 1.25
638 Ryan Kesler XRC 2.50 6.00
639 Tony Salmelainen XRC .50 1.25
640 Mikhail Yakubov XRC .50 1.25
641 Nathan Robinson XRC .50 1.25
642 Chris Simon .30 .75
643 Jeff Hamilton XRC .50 1.25
644 Nikolai Zherdev XRC 1.00 2.50
645 Steve Sullivan .30 .75
646 Niklas Kronwall XRC 1.00 2.50
647 Joey MacDonald XRC .60 1.50
648 Antero Niittymaki XRC 1.25 3.00
649 Noah Clarke XRC .50 1.25
650 Tim Jackman XRC .60 1.50
651 Timofei Shishkanov XRC .50 1.25
652 Marek Svatos XRC 1.00 2.50
653 Sergei Fedorov .75 2.00
654 Aleksander Suglobov XRC .50 1.25
655 Darryl Bootland XRC .60 1.50
656 Andrew Peters XRC .60 1.50
657 Anton Babchuk XRC .50 1.25
658 Kyle Wellwood XRC .75 2.00
659 Chris Kunitz XRC 1.00 2.50
660 Jozef Balej XRC .50 1.25
661 Christian Ehrhoff XRC .60 1.50
662 Dan Ellis XRC .60 1.50
663 Robert Lang .30 .75
664 Thomas Pihlman XRC .60 1.50
665 Andy Chiodo XRC .50 1.25
666 Adam Munro XRC .50 1.25
667 Denis Grebeshkov XRC .50 1.25
668 Matt Underhill XRC .50 1.25
669 Brad Boyes XRC .75 2.00
670 Paul Martin XRC .60 1.50
671 Matthew Yeats XRC .50 1.25
672 Alexei Zhamnov .40 1.00
673 Wade Dubielewicz XRC .50 1.25
674 Miikka Kiprusoff .40 1.00

2003-04 ITG Action Center of Attention

COMPLETE SET (10) 20.00 40.00
STATED ODDS 1:46
CA1 Mario Lemieux 4.00 10.00
CA2 Steve Yzerman 6.00 15.00
CA3 Joe Sakic 2.50 6.00
CA4 Peter Forsberg 2.50 6.00
CA5 Todd Bertuzzi 1.25 3.00
CA6 Joe Thornton 1.50 4.00
CA7 Sergei Fedorov 1.50 4.00
CA8 Mike Modano 1.50 4.00
CA9 Jason Spezza 2.00 5.00
CA10 Mats Sundin 1.25 3.00

2003-04 ITG Action First Time All-Star

COMPLETE SET (10) 8.00 15.00
STATED ODDS 1:38
FT1 Marian Gaborik 2.00 5.00
FT2 Dany Heatley 1.25 3.00
FT3 Marty Turco .75 2.00
FT4 Todd Bertuzzi .75 2.00
FT5 Olli Jokinen .75 2.00
FT6 Vincent Lecavalier .75 2.00
FT7 Patrick Lalime .75 2.00
FT8 Glen Murray .75 2.00
FT9 Martin St-Louis .75 2.00
FT10 Jocelyn Thibault .75 2.00

2003-04 ITG Action Highlight Reel

COMPLETE SET (12) 20.00 40.00
STATED ODDS 1:38
HR1 Jean-Sebastien Giguere .75 2.00
HR2 Patrick Roy 2.50 6.00
HR3 Martin Brodeur 2.50 6.00
HR4 Mario Lemieux 4.00 10.00
HR5 Dany Heatley .75 2.00
HR6 Joe Sakic 1.50 4.00
HR7 Joe Nieuwendyk .75 2.00
HR8 Jaromir Jagr 1.25 3.00
HR9 Brett Hull .75 2.00
HR10 Rick Nash 1.00 2.50
HR11 Marty Turco .75 2.00
HR12 Marian Gaborik 1.25 3.00

2003-04 ITG Action Homeboys

COMPLETE SET (14) 15.00 30.00
STATED ODDS 1:24
HB1 M.Naslund/P.Forsberg 1.25 3.00
HB2 R.Francis/M.Turco .75 2.00
HB3 Z.Chara/M.Gaborik .75 2.00
HB4 M.Comrie/S.Niedermayer .75 2.00
HB5 M.Messier/J.Iginla .75 2.00
HB6 D.Gilmour/K.Muller .75 2.00
HB7 E.Lindros/J.Thornton 1.00 2.50
HB8 N.Khabibulin/A.Yashin .75 2.00
HB9 J.Hurme/S.Koivu .75 2.00
HB10 M.Brodeur/M.Lemieux 4.00 10.00
HB11 B.Battaglia/C.Chelios .75 2.00
HB12 S.Weiss/A.Carter .75 2.00
HB13 J-S Giguere/R.Luongo 1.00 2.50
HB14 P.Bure/S.Samsonov .75 2.00

2003-04 ITG Action Jerseys

This 270-card memorabilia set was tiered by color. Ruby cards (M1-M90) were serial-numbered to 500 each. Sapphire (M91-M120) were serial-numbered to 300 each. Emerald cards (M121-150) were serial-numbered to 200 sets. Bronze (M151-M180) were serial-numbered to 100. Silver (M181-M200) were serial-numbered to 50 each. Gold cards (M201-M220) were 1/1's and are not priced due to scarcity. Quad jerseys (M221-M240) were serial-numbered to 50 each. Cards M240-M270 were only available in factory sets and were limited to 100 each.

M1-M90 RUBY PRINT RUN 500
M91-M120 SAPPHIRE PRINT RUN 300
M121-M150 EMERALD PRINT RUN 200
BRONZE PRINT RUN 100
M181-M200 SILVER PRINT RUN 50
M221-M240 QUAD JSY PRINT RUN 50
M1 Nik Antropov 4.00 10.00
M2 Jason Arnott 4.00 10.00
M3 Jared Aulin 4.00 10.00
M4 Mark Bell 4.00 10.00
M5 Bryan Berard 4.00 10.00
M6 Martin Biron 4.00 10.00
M7 Radek Bonk 4.00 10.00
M8 Nick Boynton 4.00 10.00
M9 Donald Brashear 6.00 15.00
M10 Eric Brewer 4.00 10.00
M11 Sergei Brylin 4.00 10.00
M12 Mike Cammalleri 4.00 10.00
M13 Dan Cloutier 4.00 10.00
M14 Carlo Colaiacovo 4.00 10.00
M15 Tim Connolly 4.00 10.00
M16 Byron Dafoe 4.00 10.00
M17 Adam Deadmarsh 4.00 10.00
M18 Shane Doan 4.00 10.00
M19 Tie Domi 4.00 10.00
M20 J-P Dumont 4.00 10.00
M21 Robert Esche 4.00 10.00
M22 Mike Fisher 4.00 10.00
M23 Adam Foote 4.00 10.00
M24 Martin Gerber 6.00 15.00
M25 Scott Gomez 4.00 10.00
M26 John Grahame 6.00 15.00
M27 Jeff Hackett 6.00 15.00
M28 Ron Hainsey 4.00 10.00
M29 Scott Hartnell 4.00 10.00
M30 Derian Hatcher 4.00 10.00
M31 Bobby Holik 4.00 10.00
M32 Marcel Hossa 4.00 10.00
M33 Ivan Huml 4.00 10.00
M34 Barret Jackman 6.00 15.00
M35 Brent Johnson 6.00 15.00
M36 Ed Jovanovski 6.00 15.00
M37 Tomas Kaberle 4.00 10.00
M38 Niko Kapanen 4.00 10.00
M39 Sami Kapanen 4.00 10.00
M40 Darius Kasparaitis 4.00 10.00
M41 Rostislav Klesla 4.00 10.00
M42 Chuck Kobasew 4.00 10.00
M43 Vyacheslav Kozlov 4.00 10.00
M44 Georges Laraque 6.00 15.00
M45 Igor Larionov 6.00 15.00
M46 Manny Legace 4.00 10.00
M47 David Legwand 4.00 10.00
M48 Jordan Leopold 4.00 10.00
M49 Trevor Linden 4.00 10.00
M50 John Madden 4.00 10.00
M51 Patrick Marleau 6.00 15.00
M52 Aleksey Morozov 4.00 10.00
M53 Derek Morris 4.00 10.00
M54 Brendan Morrison 6.00 15.00
M55 Brenden Morrow 6.00 15.00
M56 Rob Niedermayer 4.00 10.00
M57 Scott Niedermayer 4.00 10.00
M58 Joe Nieuwendyk 6.00 15.00
M59 Mika Noronen 4.00 10.00
M60 Pasi Nurminen 4.00 10.00
M61 Sandis Ozolinsh 4.00 10.00
M62 Yanic Perreault 4.00 10.00
M63 Chris Phillips 4.00 10.00
M64 Tom Poti 4.00 10.00
M65 Keith Primeau 4.00 10.00
M66 Branko Radivojevic 4.00 10.00
M67 Brian Rafalski 4.00 10.00
M68 Wade Redden 4.00 10.00
M69 Brandon Reid 4.00 10.00
M70 Steven Reinprecht 4.00 10.00
M71 Mike Richter 8.00 20.00
M72 Brian Rolston 4.00 10.00
M73 Miroslav Satan 4.00 10.00
M74 Kevin Sawyer 4.00 10.00
M75 Nick Schultz 4.00 10.00
M76 Daniel Sedin 6.00 15.00
M77 Henrik Sedin 6.00 15.00
M78 Alexei Smirnov 4.00 10.00
M79 Ryan Smyth 4.00 10.00
M80 Garth Snow 4.00 10.00
M81 Radovan Somik 4.00 10.00
M82 Martin Straka 4.00 10.00
M83 Alexander Svitov 4.00 10.00
M84 Darryl Sydor 4.00 10.00
M85 Roman Turek 6.00 15.00
M86 Pierre Turgeon 4.00 10.00
M87 Scottie Upshall 4.00 10.00
M88 Anton Volchenkov 4.00 10.00
M89 Peter Worrell 4.00 10.00
M90 Scott Young 5.00 10.00
M91 David Aebischer 6.00 15.00
M92 Jason Allison 6.00 15.00
M93 Tyler Arnason 6.00 15.00
M94 Dan Blackburn 6.00 15.00
M95 Daniel Briere 6.00 15.00
M96 Sean Burke 6.00 15.00
M97 Roman Cechmanek 6.00 15.00
M98 Erik Cole 6.00 15.00
M99 Vincent Damphousse 6.00 15.00
M100 Pavol Demitra 6.00 15.00
M101 Marc Denis 6.00 15.00
M102 Chris Drury 6.00 15.00
M103 Mike Dunham 6.00 15.00
M104 Manny Fernandez 6.00 15.00
M105 Simon Gagne 10.00 25.00
M106 Mathieu Garon 6.00 15.00
M107 Sergei Gonchar 6.00 15.00
M108 Johan Hedberg 6.00 15.00
M109 Ales Hemsky 6.00 15.00
M110 Kristian Huselius 6.00 15.00
M111 Jamie Langenbrunner 6.00 15.00
M112 Felix Potvin 12.00 30.00
M113 Brad Richards 6.00 15.00
M114 Dwayne Roloson 10.00 25.00
M115 Patrik Stefan 6.00 15.00
M116 Scott Stevens 6.00 15.00
M117 Alex Tanguay 6.00 15.00
M118 Kevin Weekes 6.00 15.00
M119 Stephen Weiss 6.00 15.00
M120 Sergei Zubov 6.00 15.00
M121 Daniel Alfredsson 8.00 20.00
M122 Tony Amonte 8.00 20.00
M123 Peter Bondra 8.00 20.00
M124 Chris Chelios 10.00 25.00
M125 Stanislav Chistov 8.00 20.00
M126 Pavel Datsyuk 12.00 30.00
M127 Eric Daze 8.00 20.00
M128 Patrik Elias 8.00 20.00
M129 Alexander Frolov 8.00 20.00
M130 Doug Gilmour 8.00 20.00
M131 Martin Havlat 8.00 20.00
M132 Olli Jokinen 8.00 20.00
M133 Nikolai Khabibulin 10.00 25.00
M134 Olaf Kolzig 8.00 20.00
M135 Patrick Lalime 8.00 20.00
M136 Vincent Lecavalier 10.00 25.00
M137 Ryan Miller 8.00 20.00
M138 Glen Murray 8.00 20.00
M139 Evgeni Nabokov 8.00 20.00
M140 Adam Oates 8.00 20.00
M141 Zigmund Palffy 8.00 20.00
M142 Mike Peca 8.00 20.00
M143 Chris Pronger 8.00 20.00
M144 Mark Recchi 8.00 20.00
M145 Gary Roberts 8.00 20.00
M146 Tommy Salo 8.00 20.00
M147 Martin St-Louis 8.00 20.00
M148 Keith Tkachuk 10.00 25.00
M149 Doug Weight 8.00 20.00
M150 Alexei Yashin 8.00 20.00
M151 Ed Belfour 12.00 30.00
M152 Todd Bertuzzi 12.00 30.00
M153 Rob Blake 10.00 25.00
M154 Jay Bouwmeester 10.00 25.00
M155 Mike Comrie 10.00 25.00
M156 Rick DiPietro 10.00 25.00
M157 Ron Francis 10.00 25.00
M158 Bill Guerin 10.00 25.00
M159 Milan Hejduk 12.00 30.00
M160 Marian Hossa 12.00 30.00
M161 Jarome Iginla 15.00 40.00
M162 Saku Koivu 12.00 30.00
M163 John LeClair 12.00 30.00
M164 Brian Leetch 10.00 25.00
M165 Eric Lindros 12.00 30.00
M166 Roberto Luongo 12.00 30.00
M167 Al MacInnis 10.00 25.00
M168 Mark Messier 15.00 40.00
M169 Alexander Mogilny 10.00 25.00
M170 Rick Nash 12.00 30.00
M171 Markus Naslund 12.00 30.00
M172 Owen Nolan 10.00 25.00
M173 Luc Robitaille 10.00 25.00
M174 Jeremy Roenick 15.00 40.00
M175 Sergei Samsonov 12.00 30.00
M176 Brendan Shanahan 12.00 30.00
M177 Jason Spezza 12.00 30.00
M178 Mats Sundin 12.00 30.00
M179 Jocelyn Thibault 10.00 25.00
M180 Marty Turco 10.00 20.00
M181 Martin Brodeur 30.00 80.00
M182 Pavel Bure 12.50 30.00
M183 Sergei Fedorov 20.00 50.00
M184 Peter Forsberg 15.00 40.00
M185 Marian Gaborik 15.00 40.00
M186 Jean-Sebastien Giguere 12.50 30.00
M187 Dany Heatley 12.50 30.00
M188 Brett Hull 20.00 50.00
M189 Jaromir Jagr 20.00 50.00
M190 Paul Kariya 12.50 30.00
M191 Ilya Kovalchuk 20.00 50.00
M192 Mario Lemieux 30.00 80.00
M193 Nicklas Lidstrom 12.50 30.00
M194 Mike Modano 15.00 40.00
M195 Patrick Roy 25.00 60.00
M196 Joe Sakic 25.00 60.00
M197 Dominik Hasek 15.00 40.00
M198 Jose Theodore 15.00 40.00
M199 Joe Thornton 15.00 40.00
M200 Steve Yzerman 30.00 80.00
M221 Gig/Chistv/Kriya/Sykra 15.00 40.00
M222 Brdur/Elias/Stens/Maddn 15.00 40.00
M223 Belfr/Sndin/Mgilny/Noln 25.00 50.00
M224 LeClr/Rnick/Amnte/Ggne 30.00 80.00
M225 Berrd/Smsnv/Thrntn/Mrry 20.00 50.00
M226 Hull/Yze/Hasek/Fedrv 40.00 80.00
M227 Roy/Frsbrg/Sakic/Hduk 40.00 100.00
M228 Turco/Mdno/Guerin/Mrrow 20.00 50.00
M229 Blckbrn/Bure/Mess/Lndros 25.00 60.00
M230 Lalime/Hssa/Spzza/Hvlat 25.00 60.00
M231 Thiblt/Daze/Sllivn/Arnson 15.00 40.00
M232 Miller/Satn/Afingnv/Briere 20.00 50.00
M233 Salo/Comrie/Smith/Laraque 20.00 50.00
M234 Heat/Kvlchuk/Dfoe/Stfan 20.00 50.00
M235 Osgd/Jkmn/Prngr/McInns 20.00 50.00
M236 Klzig/Jagr/Bndra/Emnger 15.00 40.00
M237 Lmieux/Hdbrg/Strka/Mrzv 30.00 80.00
M238 Clotier/Brtzzi/Nslnd/Jovo 15.00 40.00
M239 Vkun/Hartnll/Lgwnd/Upshll 20.00 50.00
M240 Theodre/Koivu/Garn/Hnsy 25.00 60.00
M241 J-S Giguere 10.00 25.00
M242 Dany Heatley 12.00 30.00
M243 Joe Thornton 12.00 30.00
M244 Miroslav Satan 10.00 25.00
M245 Jarome Iginla 15.00 40.00
M246 Ron Francis 10.00 25.00
M247 Jocelyn Thibault 10.00 25.00
M248 Patrick Roy 20.00 50.00
M249 Rick Nash 12.00 30.00
M250 Mike Modano 12.00 30.00
M251 Steve Yzerman 40.00 80.00
M252 Mike Comrie 10.00 25.00
M253 Roberto Luongo 15.00 40.00
M254 Zigmund Palffy 10.00 25.00
M255 Marian Gaborik 15.00 40.00
M256 Jose Theodore 15.00 40.00
M257 David Legwand 10.00 25.00
M258 Martin Brodeur 20.00 50.00
M259 Alexei Yashin 10.00 25.00
M260 Pavel Bure 12.00 30.00
M261 Marian Hossa 12.00 30.00
M262 Jeremy Roenick 12.00 30.00
M263 Sean Burke 10.00 25.00
M264 Mario Lemieux 30.00 80.00
M265 Chris Pronger 10.00 25.00
M266 Evgeni Nabokov 10.00 25.00
M267 Vincent Lecavalier 12.00 30.00
M268 Mats Sundin 12.00 30.00
M269 Markus Naslund 10.00 25.00
M270 Jaromir Jagr 12.00 30.00

2003-04 ITG Action League Leaders

COMPLETE SET (10) 12.50 25.00
STATED ODDS 1:29
L1 P.Forsberg/M.Hejduk 2.50 5.00
L2 Milan Hejduk .60 1.50
L3 Peter Forsberg 1.50 4.00
L4 Peter Forsberg 1.50 4.00
L5 Marty Turco .60 1.50
L6 Henrik Zetterberg .75 2.00
L7 Martin Brodeur 1.50 4.00
L8 Martin Brodeur 1.50 4.00
L9 Markus Naslund .60 1.50
L10 Dany Heatley .75 2.00

2003-04 ITG Action Oh Canada

COMPLETE SET 25.00 50.00
STATED ODDS 1:21
OC1 Mario Lemieux 4.00 10.00
OC2 Patrick Roy 3.00 8.00
OC3 Steve Yzerman 3.00 8.00
OC4 Martin Brodeur 2.50 6.00
OC5 Paul Kariya .75 2.00
OC6 Joe Sakic 2.00 5.00
OC7 Mark Messier .75 2.00
OC8 Jean-Sebastien Giguere .75 2.00
OC9 Jason Spezza 1.25 3.00
OC10 Dany Heatley 1.00 2.50
OC11 Curtis Joseph .75 2.00
OC12 Ed Belfour .75 2.00
OC13 Brendan Shanahan .75 2.00
OC14 Joe Thornton 1.00 2.50

2003-04 ITG Action Trophy Winners

STATED ODDS 1:64
TW1 Peter Forsberg 2.50 6.00
TW2 Martin Brodeur 3.00 8.00
TW3 Nicklas Lidstrom 1.50 4.00
TW4 Barret Jackman 1.50 4.00
TW5 Markus Naslund 1.50 4.00
TW6 Peter Forsberg 2.50 6.00

2004 ITG NHL All-Star FANtasy All-Star History Jerseys

Available only in "Super Boxes" produced by ITG for the 2004 NHL All-Star FANtasy, this 54-card set featured jerseys of players who represented the All-Star game from 1947 to the present. Cards SB1-SB21 were limited to 10 copies each; cards SB22-SB41 were limited to 20 copies each and cards SB42-SB54 were limited to 30 copies each. Cards under 30 were not priced due to scarcity.

SB1 Turk Broda
SB2 Frank Brimsek
SB3 Ted Kennedy
SB4 Maurice Richard
SB5 Chuck Rayner
SB6 Bill Mosienko
SB7 Jean Beliveau
SB8 Doug Harvey
SB9 Ted Lindsay
SB10 Henri Richard
SB11 Jacques Plante
SB12 Glenn Hall
SB13 Terry Sawchuk
SB14 Bobby Hull
SB15 Johnny Bower
SB16 Tim Horton
SB17 John Bucyk
SB18 Stan Mikita
SB19 Bill Gadsby
SB20 Ed Giacomin
SB21 Bobby Orr
SB22 Bernie Parent
SB23 Bobby Clarke
SB24 Gilbert Perreault
SB25 Frank Mahovlich
SB26 Tony Esposito
SB27 Denis Potvin
SB28 Guy Lafleur
SB29 Bryan Trottier
SB30 Lanny McDonald
SB31 Marcel Dionne
SB32 Bill Barber
SB33 Mike Bossy
SB34 Mark Messier
SB35 Ray Bourque
SB36 Steve Yzerman
SB37 Mario Lemieux
SB38 Grant Fuhr
SB39 Patrick Roy
SB40 Brett Hull
SB41 Brian Leetch
SB42 Jeremy Roenick 12.50 30.00
SB43 Jaromir Jagr 12.50 30.00
SB44 Luc Robitaille 12.50 30.00
SB45 Joe Sakic 15.00 40.00
SB46 Eric Lindros 12.50 30.00
SB47 Paul Kariya 15.00 40.00
SB48 Mike Modano 12.50 30.00
SB49 Peter Forsberg 20.00 50.00
SB50 Pavel Bure 12.50 30.00
SB51 Milan Hejduk 12.50 30.00
SB52 Mats Sundin 12.50 30.00
SB53 Marian Gaborik 15.00 40.00
SB54 Ilya Kovalchuk 12.50 30.00

2004 ITG All-Star FANtasy Hail Minnesota

This 10-card set was only available in "Super Boxes" produced by ITG booth for the 2004 NHL All-Star Fantasy. Each card was limited to 100 copies each.

COMPLETE SET (10) 75.00 125.00
1 Mike Gartner 4.00 10.00
2 Derian Hatcher 4.00 10.00
3 Mike Modano 12.00 30.00
4 Jordan Leopold 4.00 10.00
5 Manny Fernandez 6.00 15.00
6 Dwayne Roloson 6.00 15.00
7 Marian Gaborik 20.00 50.00
8 Pierre-Marc Bouchard 6.00 15.00
9 Gump Worsley 12.00 30.00
10 Dino Ciccarelli 4.00 10.00

2008-09 ITG Bleu Blanc et Rouge

This set was released on January 23, 2009. The base set consists of 40 cards.

STATED PRINT RUN 20
1 Alex Tanguay 6.00 15.00
2 Bernie Geoffrion 6.00 15.00
3 Bobby Rousseau 8.00 20.00
4 Bobby Smith 6.00 15.00
5 Carey Price 40.00 100.00
6 Charlie Hodge 8.00 20.00
7 Chris Chelios 10.00 25.00
8 Denis Savard 12.00 30.00
9 Dick Duff 8.00 20.00
10 Dickie Moore 8.00 20.00
11 Dollard St. Laurent 6.00 15.00
12 Doug Gilmour 15.00 40.00
13 Doug Harvey 10.00 25.00
14 Frank Mahovlich 10.00 25.00
15 Guillaume Latendresse 6.00 15.00
16 Gump Worsley 8.00 20.00
17 Guy Carbonneau 10.00 25.00
18 Guy Lafleur 12.00 30.00
19 Guy Lapointe 8.00 20.00
20 Henri Richard 12.00 30.00
21 J.C. Tremblay 6.00 15.00
22 Jacques Laperriere 12.00 30.00
23 Jacques Lemaire 8.00 20.00
24 Jacques Plante 15.00 40.00
25 Jean Beliveau 10.00 25.00
26 Jean Guy Talbot 8.00 20.00
27 Cristobal Huet 8.00 20.00
28 Larry Robinson 10.00 25.00
29 Mats Naslund 8.00 20.00
30 Patrick Roy 25.00 60.00
31 Pete Mahovlich 12.00 30.00
32 Phil Goyette 6.00 15.00
33 Ralph Backstrom 6.00 15.00
34 Rogie Vachon 12.00 30.00
35 Saku Koivu 10.00 25.00
36 Serge Savard 15.00 40.00
37 Stephane Richer 8.00 20.00
38 Steve Shutt 12.00 30.00
39 Terry Harper 6.00 15.00
40 Yvan Cournoyer 10.00 25.00

2008-09 ITG Bleu Blanc et Rouge Autographs

ANNOUNCED PRINT RUN 19-40
AAT Alex Tanguay/19 12.00 30.00
ABR Bobby Rousseau/40 10.00 25.00
ABS Bobby Smith/40 8.00 20.00
ABSA Brian Savage/25 12.00 30.00
ACC Chris Chelios/25 20.00 50.00
ACH Charlie Hodge/40 10.00 25.00
ACHU Cristobal Huet/25 15.00 40.00
ACP1 Carey Price/25 30.00 80.00
ACP2 Carey Price/25 30.00 80.00
ADD Dick Duff/40 10.00 25.00
ADG Doug Gilmour/40 15.00 40.00
ADM1 Dickie Moore/40 10.00 25.00
ADM2 Dickie Moore/25 15.00 40.00
AEB Emile Bouchard/40 15.00 40.00
AEL1 Elmer Lach/40 20.00 50.00
AEL2 Elmer Lach/40 20.00 50.00
AGC Guy Carbonneau/40 12.00 30.00
AGL1 Guy Lafleur/19 20.00 50.00
AGL2 Guy Lafleur/19 20.00 50.00
AGLA Guy Lapointe/40 10.00 25.00
AGLAT G.Latendresse/25 12.00 30.00
AHR1 Henri Richard/19 25.00 60.00
AHR2 Henri Richard/19 25.00 60.00
AJB1 Jean Beliveau/19 25.00 60.00
AJB2 Jean Beliveau/19 25.00 60.00
AJGT1 Jean Guy Talbot/25 15.00 40.00
AJGT2 Jean Guy Talbot/25 15.00 40.00
AJL1 Jacques Laperriere/40 25.00 60.00
AJL2 Jacques Laperriere/25 30.00 80.00
AJLE Jacques Lemaire/40 10.00 25.00
ALR1 Larry Robinson/25 20.00 50.00
ALR2 Larry Robinson/25 20.00 50.00
AMD Mathieu Dandenault/40 12.00 30.00
AMN Mats Naslund/40 10.00 25.00
AMT Marc Tardif/40 10.00 25.00
AMTR Mario Tremblay/40 15.00 40.00
APG1 Phil Goyette/25 15.00 40.00
APG2 Phil Goyette/25 15.00 40.00
APM Pete Mahovlich/40 15.00 40.00
APR1 Patrick Roy/19 50.00 120.00
APR2 Patrick Roy/19 50.00 120.00
ARV Rogie Vachon/25 25.00 60.00
ARW Ryan Walter/40 8.00 20.00
ASD Denis Savard/40 15.00 40.00
ASK1 Saku Koivu/19 20.00 50.00
ASK2 Saku Koivu/19 20.00 50.00
ASQ Stephane Quintal/25 12.00 30.00
ASR Stephane Richer/40 10.00 25.00
ASS1 Serge Savard/25 25.00 60.00
ASS2 Serge Savard/25 25.00 60.00
ASSH1 Steve Shutt/25 20.00 50.00
ASSH2 Steve Shutt/25 20.00 50.00
AYC1 Yvan Cournoyer/40 12.00 30.00
AYC2 Yvan Cournoyer/25 20.00 50.00
AYL Yvon Lambert/40 12.00 30.00

2008-09 ITG Bleu Blanc et Rouge Vintage

STATED PRINT RUN 35 SERIAL #'d SETS
1 Armand Mondou 6.00 15.00
2 Aurel Joliat 10.00 25.00
3 Babe Siebert 8.00 20.00
4 Albert Leduc 8.00 20.00
5 Bill Boucher 6.00 15.00
6 Bill Durnan 10.00 25.00
7 Cecil Hart 6.00 15.00
8 Didier Pitre 6.00 15.00
9 Elmer Lach 15.00 40.00
10 Pit Lepine 12.00 30.00
11 George Hainsworth 12.00 30.00
12 Georges Vezina 15.00 40.00
13 Herb Gardiner 6.00 15.00
14 Howie Morenz 6.00 15.00
15 Jack Laviolette 8.00 20.00
16 Joe Malone 8.00 20.00
17 Johnny Gagnon 6.00 15.00
18 Lorne Chabot 8.00 20.00
19 Maurice Richard 25.00 60.00
20 Newsy Lalonde 8.00 20.00
21 Paul Haynes 6.00 15.00
22 Sprague Cleghorn 15.00 40.00
23 Sylvio Mantha 8.00 20.00
24 Toe Blake 6.00 15.00
25 Wilf Cude 12.00 30.00

2011-12 ITG Broad Street Boys

1 Andre Lacroix EY .75 2.00
2 Bernie Parent EY 1.25 3.00
3 Bill Sutherland EY .75 2.00
4 Brit Selby EY .75 2.00
5 Doug Favell EY 1.25 3.00
6 Ed Van Impe EY 1.00 2.50
7 Forbes Kennedy EY .75 2.00
8 Gary Dornhoefer EY .75 2.00
9 Joe Watson EY 1.00 2.50
10 Larry Zeidel EY .75 2.00
11 Leon Rochefort EY .75 2.00
12 Lou Angotti EY .75 2.00
13 Pat Hannigan EY .75 2.00
14 Simon Nolet EY 1.00 2.50
15 Andre Dupont BSB .75 2.00
16 Bernie Parent BSB 1.25 3.00
17 Bill Barber BSB 1.25 3.00
18 Bill Clement BSB 1.00 2.50
19 Bob Dailey BSB .75 2.00
20 Bob Kelly BSB 1.00 2.50
21 Bobby Clarke BSB 1.25 3.00
22 Bobby Taylor BSB 1.00 2.50
23 Dave Schultz BSB 1.25 3.00
24 Don Saleski BSB .75 2.00
25 Jack McIlhargey BSB 1.00 2.50
26 Jim Watson BSB 1.00 2.50
27 Larry Goodenough BSB .75 2.00
28 Orest Kindrachuk BSB .75 2.00
29 Paul Holmgren BSB 1.25 3.00
30 Reggie Leach BSB 1.00 2.50
31 Rick MacLeish BSB 1.00 2.50
32 Ross Lonsberry BSB .75 2.00
33 Simon Nolet BSB 1.00 2.50
34 Terry Crisp BSB .75 2.00
35 Tom Bladon BSB .75 2.00
36 Wayne Stephenson BSB .75 2.00
37 Dave Brown TT 1.25 3.00
38 Brad Marsh TT .75 2.00
39 Brian Propp TT 1.00 2.50
40 Darryl Sittler TT 1.25 3.00
41 Dave Poulin TT .75 2.00
42 Ken Linseman TT 1.25 3.00
43 Mark Howe TT 1.25 3.00
44 Mel Bridgman TT .75 2.00
45 Mike Keenan TT 1.00 2.50
46 Murray Craven TT .75 2.00
47 Pelle Lindbergh TT 2.00 5.00
48 Phil Myre TT 1.00 2.50
49 Rich Sutter TT 1.00 2.50
50 Ron Hextall TT 1.50 4.00
51 Ron Sutter TT 1.00 2.50
52 Tim Kerr TT 1.00 2.50
53 Bob Froese TT 1.00 2.50
54 Pete Peeters TT 1.25 3.00
55 Chico Resch TT 1.25 3.00
56 Craig Berube C90 .75 2.00
57 Dale Hawerchuk C90 1.50 4.00
58 Eric Desjardins C90 1.00 2.50
59 Eric Lindros C90 2.00 5.00
60 John LeClair C90 1.25 3.00
61 John Vanbiesbrouck C90 1.25 3.00
62 Chris Therien C90 1.00 2.50
63 Kjell Samuelsson C90 .75 2.00
64 Mark Recchi C90 1.50 4.00
65 Paul Coffey C90 1.25 3.00
66 Rod Brind'Amour C90 1.00 2.50
67 Sandy McCarthy C90 1.00 2.50
68 Scott Mellanby C90 1.00 2.50
69 Antero Niittymaki NM 1.00 2.50
70 Brian Boucher NM 1.00 2.50
71 Dan Carcillo NM .75 2.00
72 Donald Brashear NM 1.00 2.50
73 Jeff Carter NM 1.25 3.00
74 Jeremy Roenick NM 1.25 3.00
75 Joffrey Lupul NM 1.00 2.50
76 Keith Primeau NM 1.25 3.00
77 Mike Richards NM 1.25 3.00
78 Peter Forsberg NM 1.25 3.00
79 Ray Emery NM 1.00 2.50
80 Roman Cechmanek NM 1.25 3.00
81 Tony Amonte NM 1.00 2.50
82 Erik Gustafsson TC 1.25 3.00
83 Matt Carle TC 1.00 2.50
84 Braydon Coburn TC .75 2.00
85 Sean Couturier TC 2.00 5.00
86 Maxime Talbot TC 1.00 2.50
87 Brayden Schenn TC 1.25 3.00
88 Chris Pronger TC 1.00 2.50
89 Claude Giroux TC 1.25 3.00
90 Daniel Briere TC 1.25 3.00
91 Ilya Bryzgalov TC 1.25 3.00
92 James van Riemsdyk TC 1.25 3.00
93 Jaromir Jagr TC 3.00 8.00
94 Matt Read TC 2.00 5.00
95 Sergei Bobrovsky TC 1.25 3.00
96 Tom Sestito TC .75 2.00
97 Zac Rinaldo TC 1.00 2.50
98 First Cup GM/B.Clarke/B.Parent 1.25 3.00
99 Second Cup GM/Clarke/Parent 1.25 3.00
100 1976 Red Army Game GM 2.00 5.00

2011-12 ITG Broad Street Boys Gold

GOLD/50: 1.5X TO 4X BASIC CARDS
GOLD ANNOUNCED PRINT RUN 50

2011-12 ITG Broad Street Boys Autographs

FIVE AUTO AND MEM PER BOX
AAD Andre Dupont 5.00 12.00
AAL Andre Lacroix 5.00 12.00
AAN Antero Niittymaki 6.00 15.00
ABB Bill Barber 8.00 20.00
ABC Bill Clement 6.00 15.00
ABCL Bobby Clarke SP 40.00 80.00
ABCO Braydon Coburn SP 40.00 80.00
ABD Bob Dailey 5.00 12.00
ABF Bob Froese 6.00 15.00
ABK Bob Kelly 6.00 15.00
ABM Brad Marsh 5.00 12.00
ABP Bernie Parent SP 40.00 80.00
ABPR Brian Propp 8.00 20.00
ABS Brit Selby 5.00 12.00
ABSU Bill Sutherland 6.00 15.00
ABT Bobby Taylor 8.00 20.00
ACB Craig Berube 5.00 12.00
ACG Claude Giroux SP 30.00 60.00
ACP Chris Pronger SP 30.00 60.00
ACT Chris Therien 6.00 15.00
ADB Daniel Briere SP 20.00 50.00
ADBR Dave Brown 8.00 20.00
ADC Dan Carcillo 5.00 12.00
ADF Doug Favell SP 30.00 80.00
ADH Dale Hawerchuk SP 25.00 50.00
ADL1 Dave Leonardi 5.00 12.00
ADL2 Dave Leonardi 5.00 12.00
ADL3 Dave Leonardi 6.00 15.00
ADP Dave Poulin 5.00 12.00
ADS Dave Schultz 6.00 15.00
ADSA Don Saleski 6.00 15.00
ADSI Darryl Sittler SP 75.00 150.00
AED Eric Desjardins 6.00 15.00
AEL Eric Lindros SP 60.00 100.00
AEVA Ed Van Impe 6.00 15.00
AFK Forbes Kennedy 6.00 15.00
AGD Gary Dornhoefer 5.00 12.00
AGR Glenn Resch 8.00 20.00
AIB Ilya Bryzgalov SP 25.00 50.00
AJJ Jaromir Jagr SP 40.00 80.00
AJL Joffrey Lupul 6.00 15.00
AJLE John LeClair SP 25.00 60.00
AJM Jack McIlhargey 6.00 15.00
AJR Jeremy Roenick SP 40.00 80.00
AJV John Vanbiesbrouck 15.00 30.00
AJW Joe Watson 6.00 15.00
AJWA Jim Watson 6.00 15.00
AKL Ken Linseman 8.00 20.00
AKP Keith Primeau 6.00 15.00
AKS Kjell Samuelsson 6.00 15.00
ALA Lou Angotti 5.00 12.00
ALG Larry Goodenough 5.00 12.00
ALR Leon Rochefort 5.00 12.00
ALZ Larry Zeidel 6.00 15.00
AMB Mel Bridgman 5.00 12.00
AMC Murray Craven 5.00 12.00
AMH Mark Howe SP 20.00 40.00
AMK Mike Keenan 8.00 20.00
AML Michael Leighton 6.00 15.00
AMLA Mark Laforest 5.00 12.00

AMR Mark Recchi 15.00 30.00
AMRE Matt Read SP 20.00 50.00
AOK Orest Kindrachuk 6.00 15.00
APC Paul Coffey SP 60.00 120.00
APF Peter Forsberg SP 75.00 125.00
APH Paul Holmgren 8.00 20.00
APM Phil Myre 6.00 15.00
APP Pete Peeters 8.00 20.00
ARB Rod Brind'Amour 12.50 25.00
ARH Ron Hextall SP 25.00 50.00
ARL Reggie Leach 6.00 15.00
ARLO Ross Lonsberry 5.00 12.00
ARM Rick MacLeish 8.00 20.00
ARS Rich Sutter 6.00 15.00
ARST Rick St. Croix 5.00 12.00
ARSU Ron Sutter 6.00 15.00
ASB Sean Burke SP 75.00 135.00
ASBO Sergei Bobrovsky 8.00 20.00
ASC Sean Couturier SP 60.00 100.00
ASD Steve Downie 6.00 15.00
ASM Sandy McCarthy 6.00 15.00
ASME Scott Mellanby 6.00 15.00
ASN Simon Nolet 6.00 15.00
ASP Shjon Podein 5.00 12.00
ATA Tony Amonte 6.00 15.00
ATC Terry Crisp 5.00 12.00
ATK Tim Kerr 8.00 20.00
AUS Ulf Samuelsson 8.00 20.00

2011-12 ITG Broad Street Boys Brotherly Love Dual Jerseys

ANNOUNCED PRINT RUN 40
CBL01 J.Watson/J.Watson 15.00 40.00
CBL02 R.Sutter/R.Sutter 10.00 25.00

2011-12 ITG Broad Street Boys Game-Used Jerseys

ANNOUNCED PRINT RUN 15-120
M01 Tony Amonte/120* 5.00 12.00
M02 Blair Betts/120* 5.00 12.00
M03 Sergei Bobrovsky/120* 6.00 15.00
M04 Brian Boucher/120* 5.00 12.00
M05 Donald Brashear/120* 5.00 12.00
M06 Mel Bridgman/120* 5.00 12.00
M07 Daniel Briere/120* 6.00 15.00
M08 Rod Brind'Amour/120* 6.00 15.00
M09 Dave Brown/120* 6.00 15.00
M10 Ilya Bryzgalov/120* 6.00 15.00
M11 Dan Carcillo/120* 4.00 10.00
M12 Jeff Carter/120* 6.00 15.00
M13 Braydon Coburn/120* 4.00 10.00
M14 Eric Desjardins/120* 6.00 15.00
M15 Ray Emery/120* 5.00 12.00
M16 Peter Forsberg/120* 6.00 15.00
M17 Nicklas Grossman/120* 6.00 15.00
M18 Ron Hextall/120* 8.00 20.00
M19 Mark Howe/120* 6.00 15.00
M20 Pavel Kubina/120* 5.00 12.00
M21 Mark LaForest/120* 4.00 10.00
M22 Reggie Leach/120* 5.00 12.00
M23 John LeClair/120* 8.00 20.00
M24 Andreas Lilja/120* 4.00 10.00
M25 Eric Lindros/120* 6.00 15.00
M26 Phil Myre/120* 5.00 12.00
M27 Keith Primeau/120* 6.00 15.00
M28 Brian Propp/120* 6.00 15.00
M29 Mark Recchi/120* 6.00 15.00
M30 Chico Resch/120* 6.00 15.00
M31 Zac Rinaldo/120* 5.00 12.00
M32 Jeremy Roenick/120* 6.00 15.00
M33 Jody Shelley/120* 6.00 15.00
M34 Darryl Sittler/120* 6.00 15.00
M35 P.J. Stock/120* 5.00 12.00
M36 Rich Sutter/120* 5.00 12.00
M37 Ron Sutter/120* 5.00 12.00
M38 John Vanbiesbrouck/120* 10.00 25.00
M39 Bill Barber/40* 10.00 25.00
M40 Bobby Clarke/40* 20.00 50.00
M41 Rick MacLeish/40* 10.00 25.00
M42 Claude Giroux/40* 10.00 25.00
M43 Bernie Parent/15* 40.00 80.00
M44 Dave Schultz/15* 100.00 200.00

2011-12 ITG Broad Street Boys Goaltenders Jerseys

ANNOUNCED PRINT RUN 9-50
G01 Sergei Bobrovsky/50* 8.00 20.00
G02 Brian Boucher/50* 6.00 15.00
G03 Ilya Bryzgalov/50* 8.00 20.00
G04 Roman Cechmanek/50* 10.00 25.00
G05 Ray Emery/50* 6.00 15.00
G06 Robert Esche/50* 6.00 15.00
G07 Ron Hextall/50* 10.00 25.00
G08 Chico Resch/50* 8.00 20.00
G09 Michael Leighton/50* 6.00 15.00
G10 Phil Myre/50* 6.00 15.00
G11 Antero Niittymaki/50* 6.00 15.00
G12 John Vanbiesbrouck/50* 10.00 25.00
G13 Pelle Lindbergh/9*
G14 Bernie Parent/9*

2011-12 ITG Broad Street Boys Quad Memorabilia

ANNOUNCED PRINT RUN 30
QM01 Rnick/Amnte/Lndrs/Leclr 25.00 60.00
QM02 Briere/Bryzg/Girx/Coburn 15.00 40.00
QM03 Brshr/Brwn/Brb/McCrth 15.00 40.00
QM04 Saleski/Dmh/Lch/Brdg 15.00 40.00
QM05 Clrke/Barbr/McLsh/Lch 15.00 40.00
QM06 Hextll/Prnt/Bryzg/Vanbs 20.00 50.00

2011-12 ITG Broad Street Boys Raised To The Rafters Jerseys

ANNOUNCED PRINT RUN 19
RTR01 Bernie Parent 40.00 80.00
RTR02 Bill Barber 20.00 50.00
RTR03 Bobby Clarke 20.00 50.00
RTR04 Mark Howe 20.00 50.00

2011-12 ITG Broad Street Boys Starting Line-Up Six Jerseys

ANNOUNCED PRINT RUN 20
SL01 Prn/Wts/Wts/Clk/Brb/McLs 60.00 120.00
SL02 Vnb/Dsj/Sml/Lnd/Lclr/Rec 50.00 100.00

2011-12 ITG Broad Street Boys Tough Materials Triples

ANNOUNCED PRINT RUN 19-120
TM01 Brash/Brube/Brwn/120* 10.00 25.00
TM02 Carcillo/Kane/Shlly/120* 8.00 20.00
TM03 Hxtll/Lndrs/McCrthy/120* 15.00 40.00
TM04 Clrko/Salski/Schultz/19* 60.00 120.00

2011-12 ITG Canada vs The World Autographs

TWO AUTOGRAPHS PER PACK OVERALL
AAH Anders Hedberg 5.00 12.00
AAI Arturs Irbe 8.00 20.00
AAJ Angela James 5.00 12.00
AAL Adam Larsson 6.00 15.00
AAM Al MacInnis 6.00 15.00
AAMA Alexander Maltsev 10.00 25.00
AAN Antti Niemi 5.00 12.00
AAO Alexander Ovechkin 40.00 100.00
AAS Alexander Semin 6.00 15.00
AAY Alexander Yakushev SP 20.00 50.00
ABBA Bill Barber 6.00 15.00
ABC Bobby Clarke SP 20.00 50.00
ABH Bobby Hull 12.00 30.00
ABHU Brett Hull SP 20.00 50.00
ABL Brian Leetch 6.00 15.00
ABM Boris Mikhailov 30.00 60.00
ABMO Brendan Morrow SP 8.00 20.00
ABP Brad Park 5.00 12.00
ABPR Brian Propp 5.00 12.00
ABR Bobby Ryan 6.00 15.00
ABRA Bill Ranford 6.00 15.00
ABS Borje Salming 6.00 15.00
ABSM Billy Smith 8.00 20.00
ABSMI Bobby Smith 5.00 12.00
ABT Bryan Trottier SP
ACC Chris Chelios 6.00 15.00
ACG Clark Gillies SP 8.00 20.00
ACH Craig Hartsburg 4.00 10.00
ACHO Cody Hodgson 12.50 30.00
ACJ Curtis Joseph 8.00 20.00
ACL Charline Labonte SP 15.00 40.00
ACN Chris Nilan 4.00 10.00
ACP Carey Price 20.00 50.00
ADG Doug Gilmour 12.00 30.00
ADGA Danny Gare 5.00 12.00
ADH Dominik Hasek 12.00 30.00
ADHA Dale Hawerchuk 8.00 20.00
ADHE Darren Helm 5.00 12.00
ADK Duncan Keith 8.00 20.00
ADP Denis Potvin 6.00 15.00
ADS Darryl Sittler 8.00 20.00
ADSE Daniel Sedin SP 25.00 60.00
ADW Doug Wilson 5.00 12.00
AEL Eric Lindros 40.00 80.00
AES Eric Staal 8.00 20.00
AET Esa Tikkanen 5.00 12.00
AGA Glenn Anderson 6.00 15.00
AGC Gerry Cheevers 6.00 15.00
AGF Grant Fuhr SP 25.00 60.00
AGL Guy Lafleur 12.00 30.00
AGLA Guy Lapointe 5.00 12.00
AGP Gilbert Perreault 6.00 15.00
AHS Henrik Sedin SP 30.00 60.00
AIK Ilya Kovalchuk 8.00 20.00
AIL Igor Larionov SP 15.00 40.00
AJA Jake Allen 10.00 25.00
AJC Jim Craig 15.00 40.00
AJH Jaroslav Halak SP 12.00 30.00
AJHI Jonas Hiller SP 12.00 30.00
AJJ Jaromir Jagr 40.00 80.00
AJK Jari Kurri 6.00 15.00
AJL John LeClair 6.00 15.00
AJM Jacob Markstrom 6.00 15.00
AJMU Joe Mullen 5.00 12.00
AJN Joe Nieuwendyk SP 8.00 20.00
AJPP J-P Parise 4.00 10.00
AJR Jeremy Roenick 12.00 30.00
AJS Joe Sakic 20.00 50.00
AJT Joe Thornton SP 10.00 25.00
AJV John Vanbiesbrouck 6.00 15.00
AKD Kevin Dineen 5.00 12.00
AKN Kent Nilsson SP 6.00 15.00
AKT Keith Tkachuk 6.00 15.00
AKTU Kyle Turris 4.00 10.00
ALC Logan Couture 6.00 15.00
ALM Lanny McDonald SP
ALMU Larry Murphy 5.00 12.00
ALR Luc Robitaille 10.00 25.00
ALRO Larry Robinson 6.00 15.00
AMB Mike Bossy 8.00 20.00
AMBR Martin Brodeur SP 15.00 40.00
AMD Marcel Dionne SP 15.00 40.00
AMF Marc-Andre Fleury SP 12.00 30.00
AMG Michel Goulet 5.00 12.00
AMGA Marian Gaborik 8.00 20.00
AMGAR Mike Gartner 12.00 30.00
AMGR Mike Green 6.00 15.00
AMH Matt Halischuk 4.00 10.00
AMH Mark Howe 6.00 15.00
AMK Mikko Koivu 5.00 12.00
AML Mario Lemieux SP 50.00 100.00
AMLI Mike Liut SP 15.00 40.00
AMLU Milan Lucic 6.00 15.00
AMM Mark Messier SP 40.00 80.00
AMM Mike Modano 10.00 25.00
AMN Mats Naslund 6.00 15.00
AMR Manon Rheaume 15.00 40.00
AMRI Mike Richter SP 25.00 60.00
AMS Marian Stastny 6.00 15.00
AMSL Martin St. Louis 6.00 15.00
AMW Mark Wells 4.00 10.00
ANB Niklas Backstrom 8.00 20.00
ANBR Neal Broten SP 6.00 15.00
ANL Nicklas Lidstrom 8.00 20.00
AOE Oliver Ekman-Larsson 6.00 15.00
APB Pavel Bure SP 15.00 40.00
APC Paul Coffey 8.00 20.00
APE Phil Esposito 10.00 25.00
APF Peter Forsberg 20.00 50.00
APH Phil Housley 5.00 12.00
APHE Paul Henderson 12.00 30.00
APL Pat LaFontaine 6.00 15.00
APM Patrick Marleau 8.00 20.00
APR Patrick Roy SP 60.00 120.00
APS Pat Stapleton 4.00 10.00
APST Peter Stastny 10.00 25.00
ARB Raymond Bourque SP 15.00 40.00
ARG Ryan Getzlaf 10.00 25.00
ARH Ron Hextall 8.00 20.00
ARL Rod Langway SP 6.00 15.00
ARLU Roberto Luongo 6.00 15.00
ARM Rick Middleton 10.00 25.00
ARN Rick Nash SP 20.00 50.00
ARV Rogie Vachon 8.00 20.00
ASB Sean Burke 6.00 15.00
ASK Saku Koivu SP 40.00 80.00
ASL Steve Larmer 5.00 12.00
ASM Stan Mikita 10.00 25.00
ASN Scott Niedermayer 6.00 15.00
ASS Steve Shutt 10.00 25.00
ASSA Serge Savard 6.00 15.00
ASSM Sami Jo Small 5.00 12.00
ASST Steven Stamkos 15.00 40.00
ASV Semyon Varlamov 12.00 30.00
ASW Shea Weber SP 12.00 30.00
ASY Steve Yzerman SP 50.00 100.00
ATA Tony Amonte 5.00 12.00
ATB Tom Barrasso 6.00 15.00
ATE Tony Esposito SP 10.00 25.00
ATE2 Tony Esposito SP 10.00 25.00
ATF Theoren Fleury 15.00 40.00
ATG Tony Granato 4.00 10.00
ATH Thomas Hickey 5.00 12.00
ATL Trevor Linden 15.00 40.00
ATR Tuukka Rask SP 15.00 30.00
ATS Teemu Selanne 12.00 30.00
ATST Thomas Steen 4.00 10.00
ATT Tim Thomas 10.00 25.00
ATV Tomas Vokoun 8.00 20.00
AUN Ulf Nilsson 5.00 12.00
AUS Ulf Samuelsson 6.00 15.00
AVK Vladimir Krutov 12.00 30.00
AVL Vincent Lecavalier SP 10.00 25.00
AVT Vladislav Tretiak SP 50.00 100.00
AVTA Vladimir Tarasenko 50.00 100.00
AVV Valeri Vasiliev 10.00 25.00
AYC Yvan Cournoyer 6.00 15.00
AZB Zach Boychuk 4.00 10.00
AZC Zdeno Chara 8.00 20.00
AZP Zigmund Palffy 6.00 15.00

2011-12 ITG Canada vs The World Canada's Best Silver

ANNCD PRINT RUN 40 SER.#'d SETS
CB01 Lngo/Brodr/Roy/Joseph 30.00 60.00
CB02 Price/Ward/Fleury/Pogge 30.00 60.00
CB03 Stmk/Lecv/Thrntn/St.Lou 30.00 60.00
CB04 Sakic/Yzer/Blke/Nieuw 25.00 50.00
CB05 Lind/Flry/Hwrchk/MacInn 30.00 60.00
CB06 Sittlr/Espos/Perrlt/Bossy 25.00 50.00

2011-12 ITG Canada vs The World Canadian Cloth Black

BLACK ANNCD PRINT RUN 19-120
*SILVER/30: .6X TO 1.5X BLACK/120
CCM01 Alex Auld 3.00 8.00
CCM02 Jonathan Bernier 4.00 10.00
CCM03 Dino Ciccarelli 4.00 10.00
CCM04 Martin Brodeur 8.00 20.00
CCM05 Angela James 3.00 8.00
CCM06 Devan Dubnyk 4.00 10.00
CCM07 Theoren Fleury 12.00 30.00
CCM08 Sami Jo Small 3.00 8.00
CCM09 Danny Gare 3.00 8.00
CCM10 Michel Goulet 3.00 8.00
CCM11 Dale Hawerchuk 5.00 12.00
CCM12 Curtis Joseph 4.00 10.00
CCM13 Vincent Lecavalier 3.00 8.00
CCM14 Kristopher Letang 12.00 30.00
CCM15 Eric Lindros 6.00 15.00
CCM16 Roberto Luongo 4.00 10.00
CCM17 Al MacInnis 4.00 10.00
CCM18 Patrick Marleau 4.00 10.00
CCM19 Joe Nieuwendyk 4.00 10.00
CCM20 Ron Francis 5.00 12.00
CCM21 Joe Sakic 6.00 15.00
CCM22 Darryl Sittler 4.00 10.00
CCM23 Steve Shutt 4.00 10.00
CCM24 Martin St. Louis 4.00 10.00
CCM25 Eric Staal 5.00 12.00
CCM26 Garry Unger 5.00 12.00
CCM27 Joe Thornton 4.00 10.00
CCM28 Kim St-Pierre 4.00 10.00
CCM29 Cam Ward 4.00 10.00
CCM30 Darren Helm 3.00 8.00
CCM31 Kyle Turris 2.50 6.00
CCM32 Patrice Bergeron 5.00 12.00
CCM33 Logan Couture 4.00 10.00
CCM34 Zach Boychuk 2.50 6.00
CCM35 Marcel Dionne 5.00 12.00
CCM36 Phil Esposito
CCM37 Gilbert Perreault
CCM38 Steve Yzerman
CCM39 Mike Bossy
CCM40 Jason Spezza
CCM41 Carey Price
CCM42 Patrick Roy
CCM43 Mario Lemieux
CCM44 Bobby Clarke
CCM45 Steven Stamkos

2011-12 ITG Canada vs The World Global Greats Silver

ANNCD PRINT RUN 50 SER.#'d SETS
GG01 Mark Messier 5.00 12.00
GG02 Raymond Bourque 6.00 15.00
GG03 Steve Yzerman 6.00 15.00
GG04 Paul Coffey 4.00 10.00
GG05 Theoren Fleury 15.00 40.00
GG06 Mario Lemieux 12.00 30.00
GG07 Joe Sakic 6.00 15.00
GG08 Rick Nash 4.00 10.00
GG09 Scott Niedermayer 4.00 10.00
GG10 Jaromir Jagr 8.00 20.00
GG11 Dominik Hasek 6.00 15.00
GG12 Teemu Selanne 8.00 20.00
GG13 Jari Kurri 4.00 10.00
GG14 Saku Koivu 4.00 10.00
GG15 Mike Richter 4.00 10.00
GG16 Brett Hull 5.00 12.00
GG17 Keith Tkachuk 4.00 10.00
GG18 Jeremy Roenick 8.00 20.00
GG19 Ryan Miller 4.00 10.00
GG20 Tim Thomas 5.00 12.00
GG21 Henrik Sedin 4.00 10.00
GG22 Daniel Sedin 4.00 10.00
GG23 Borje Salming 4.00 10.00
GG24 Henrik Lundqvist 5.00 12.00
GG25 Peter Forsberg 4.00 10.00
GG26 Alexander Ovechkin 15.00 40.00
GG27 Ilya Kovalchuk 4.00 10.00
GG28 Pavel Bure 5.00 12.00
GG29 Vladislav Tretiak 12.00 30.00
GG30 Marian Gaborik 5.00 12.00

2011-12 ITG Canada vs The World Great Moments

COMPLETE SET (15) 15.00 40.00
GM01 Phil Esposito 1.50 4.00
GM02 Paul Henderson .75 2.00
GM03 Darryl Sittler 1.00 2.50
GM04 Jim Craig 1.50 4.00
GM05 Vladislav Tretiak 1.50 4.00
GM06 Larry Robinson 1.00 2.50
GM07 Mario Lemieux 3.00 8.00
GM08 Bill Ranford 1.00 2.50
GM09 Peter Forsberg 1.00 2.50
GM10 Mike Richter 1.00 2.50
GM11 Dominik Hasek 1.25 3.00
GM12 Martin Brodeur 2.00 5.00
GM13 Joe Sakic 1.50 4.00
GM14 Henrik Lundqvist 1.25 3.00
GM15 Roberto Luongo 1.00 2.50

2011-12 ITG Canada vs The World International Goalies Silver

ANNCD PRINT RUN 50 SER.#'d SETS
IG01 Niklas Backstrom 8.00 20.00
IG02 Robin Lehner 4.00 10.00
IG03 Ilya Bryzgalov 5.00 12.00
IG04 Tim Thomas 10.00 25.00
IG05 Philipp Grubauer 5.00 12.00
IG06 Mikael Tellqvist 4.00 10.00
IG07 Nikolai Khabibulin 4.00 10.00
IG08 Olaf Kolzig 5.00 12.00
IG09 Roman Turek 4.00 10.00
IG10 Tommy Salo 4.00 10.00
IG11 Roman Cechmanek 5.00 12.00
IG12 Jacob Markstrom 5.00 12.00
IG13 Jonas Gustavsson 5.00 12.00
IG14 Tuukka Rask 5.00 12.00
IG15 Mike Richter 8.00 20.00
IG16 Vladimir Myshkin 5.00 12.00
IG17 Sergei Mylnikov 5.00 12.00
IG18 Vladimir Dzurilla 5.00 12.00
IG19 Pelle Lindbergh 30.00 80.00
IG20 Vladislav Tretiak 25.00 50.00

2011-12 ITG Canada vs The World International Materials Black

BLACK ANNCD PRINT RUN 19-120
*SILVER/30: .6X TO 1.5X BLACK/120
IM01 Adam Larsson 4.00 10.00
IM02 Philipp Grubauer 4.00 10.00
IM03 Alexander Maltsev 5.00 12.00
IM04 Vladimir Myshkin 4.00 10.00
IM05 Sergei Mylnikov 5.00 12.00
IM06 Ulf Nilsson 3.00 8.00
IM07 Pavel Bure 12.00 30.00
IM08 Peter Forsberg 4.00 10.00
IM09 Tony Amonte 3.00 8.00
IM10 Nicklas Lidstrom 4.00 10.00
IM11 Mike Modano 6.00 15.00
IM12 Alexander Semin 4.00 10.00
IM13 Nikolai Khabibulin 3.00 8.00
IM14 Alexander Mogilny 3.00 8.00
IM15 Chris Chelios 4.00 10.00
IM16 Niklas Backstrom 6.00 15.00
IM17 Kyle Okposo 4.00 10.00
IM18 Oliver Ekman-Larsson 4.00 10.00
IM19 Brian Leetch 4.00 10.00
IM20 Teemu Selanne 6.00 15.00
IM21 Mikko Koivu 3.00 8.00
IM22 Saku Koivu 4.00 10.00
IM23 Ulf Samuelsson 4.00 10.00
IM24 Ilya Bryzgalov 4.00 10.00
IM25 Jaromir Jagr 10.00 25.00
IM26 Mats Sundin 4.00 10.00
IM27 Zigmund Palffy 4.00 10.00
IM28 Pat LaFontaine 4.00 10.00
IM29 Tuukka Rask 4.00 10.00
IM30 Jacob Markstrom 4.00 10.00
IM31 Robin Lehner 3.00 8.00
IM32 Keith Tkachuk 4.00 10.00
IM33 Olaf Kolzig 4.00 10.00
IM34 Mats Naslund 4.00 10.00
IM35 Brett Hull 5.00 12.00
IM36 Vladislav Tretiak
IM37 Alexander Ovechkin 60.00 120.00
IM38 Peter Stastny
IM39 Jari Kurri 20.00 50.00
IM40 Vladimir Krutov
IM41 Mike Richter 20.00 50.00
IM42 Borje Salming
IM43 Boris Mikhailov 30.00 60.00
IM44 Valeri Kharlamov
IM45 Pelle Lindbergh 25.00 60.00

2011-12 ITG Canada vs The World International Showdown Rivals Silver

ANNCD PRINT RUN 50 SER.#'d SETS
ISR01 Hndr/Dryd/Khrlv/Trtk 60.00 120.00
ISR02 Hull/Hwe/Yaksh/Mikhv 25.00 60.00
ISR03 Sittlr/Orr/Ststny/Dzurilla 25.00 60.00
ISR04 Laflr/Gret/Krutov/Tretiak 40.00 100.00
ISR05 Mess/Bossy/Nslnd/Loob 25.00 60.00
ISR06 Lem/Gret/Mylnikv/Larnv 40.00 100.00
ISR07 Ranfrd/Lind/Hull/Rnick 30.00 80.00
ISR08 Gret/Josph/Rich/Leetch 40.00 100.00
ISR09 Bourque/Roy/Hasek/Jagr 30.00 80.00
ISR10 Lem/Brodr/Rchtr/Chelios 25.00 60.00
ISR11 Sak/Brodr/Kiprsf/Koivu 25.00 60.00
ISR12 Weber/Lngo/Miller/Kane 20.00 50.00

2011-12 ITG Canada vs The World International Showdown Teammates Silver

ANNCD PRINT RUN 50 SER.#'d SETS
IST01 Hend/Crnyer/Clrke/Dryden 50.00 100.00
IST02 Chvrs/Bo.Hul/Mahov/Hwe
IST03 Sittlr/Bo.Hull/Vachon/Orr 25.00 60.00
IST04 Lafleur/Bossy/Trott/Grtzky 30.00 80.00
IST05 Mess/Yzrman/Robin/Bssy 30.00 80.00
IST06 Lemx/Fuhr/Hawer/Gretz 30.00 80.00
IST07 Rnfrd/Mess/Fleury/Lindrs 25.00 60.00
IST08 Shan/Coffy/Lindrs/Josph 25.00 60.00
IST09 Bourq/Lindrs/Gretz/Roy 50.00 100.00
IST10 Lem/Sakc/Yzrmn/Brodr 25.00 60.00
IST11 Sakc/Lecav/Lem/Brodr 25.00 60.00
IST12 Webr/Ignla/Toews/Lngo 20.00 50.00

2011-12 ITG Canada vs The World My Country My Team Silver

ANNCD PRINT RUN 50 SER.#'d SETS
MCMT01 Peter Stastny 6.00 15.00
MCMT02 Teemu Selanne 15.00 40.00
MCMT03 Borje Salming 6.00 15.00
MCMT04 Nicklas Lidstrom 6.00 15.00
MCMT05 Mike Richter 6.00 15.00
MCMT06 Pavel Bure 8.00 20.00
MCMT07 Brian Leetch 6.00 15.00
MCMT08 Jaromir Jagr 10.00 25.00
MCMT09 Alexander Ovechkin 10.00 25.00
MCMT10 Mats Sundin 6.00 15.00
MCMT11 Theoren Fleury 10.00 25.00
MCMT12 Eric Lindros 10.00 25.00
MCMT13 Joe Sakic 10.00 25.00
MCMT14 Carey Price 20.00 50.00
MCMT15 Phil Esposito 10.00 25.00
MCMT16 Mario Lemieux 20.00 50.00
MCMT17 Joe Thornton 8.00 20.00
MCMT18 Martin Brodeur 12.00 30.00
MCMT19 Roberto Luongo 6.00 15.00
MCMT20 Marc-Andre Fleury 10.00 25.00
MCMT21 Martin St. Louis 6.00 15.00

2011-12 ITG Canada vs The World Protecting Canada's Crease

COMPLETE SET (10) 12.00 30.00
PCC01 M.Liut/B.Smith 1.00 2.50
PCC02 G.Fuhr/R.Hextall 1.25 3.00
PCC03 B.Ranford/E.Belfour 1.00 2.50
PCC04 P.Roy/C.Joseph 2.50 6.00
PCC05 M.Brodeur/C.Joseph 2.00 5.00
PCC06 C.Labonte/K.St-Pierre 2.00 5.00
PCC07 C.Price/L.Irving 3.00 8.00
PCC08 C.Ward/D.Roloson 1.00 2.50
PCC09 R.Luongo/M.Brodeur 2.00 5.00
PCC10 J.Reimer/J.Bernier 1.00 2.50

2011-12 ITG Canada vs The World Roots of International Hockey

COMPLETE SET (10) 8.00 20.00
RIH01 Frank Frederickson .75 2.00
RIH02 Harry Watson .75 2.00
RIH03 Anatoli Tarasov 1.00 2.50
RIH04 Harry Sinden .75 2.00
RIH05 Bunny Ahearne 1.00 2.50
RIH06 Jack McCartan 1.00 2.50
RIH07 Tumba Johansson 1.00 2.50
RIH08 Valeri Kharlamov .75 2.00
RIH09 Alexander Ragulin 1.00 2.50
RIH10 Borje Salming 1.00 2.50

2011-12 ITG Canada vs The World Summit Series

COMPLETE SET (10) 10.00 25.00
SS01 Paul Henderson .75 2.00
SS02 Bobby Clarke 1.00 2.50
SS03 Phil Esposito 1.50 4.00
SS04 Yvan Cournoyer 1.00 2.50
SS05 Frank Mahovlich 1.00 2.50
SS06 Brad Park .75 2.00
SS07 Valeri Kharlamov .75 2.00
SS08 Boris Mikhailov 1.50 4.00
SS09 Alexander Yakushev 2.00 5.00
SS10 Vladislav Tretiak 1.50 4.00

2011-12 ITG Canada vs The World Triple Gold Silver

ANNCD PRINT RUN 50 SER.#'d SETS
TG01 Peter Forsberg 5.00 12.00
TG02 Igor Larionov 8.00 20.00
TG03 Joe Sakic 8.00 20.00
TG04 Eric Staal 6.00 15.00
TG05 Nicklas Lidstrom 5.00 12.00
TG06 Scott Niedermayer 5.00 12.00
TG07 Mats Naslund 5.00 12.00
TG08 Hakan Loob 6.00 15.00
TG09 Patrice Bergeron 6.00 15.00
TG10 Jaromir Jagr 10.00 25.00

2011-12 ITG Canada vs The World World Junior Grads Silver

ANNCD PRINT RUN 90 SER.#'d SETS
WJG01 Joe Sakic 6.00 15.00
WJG02 Eric Lindros 6.00 15.00
WJG03 Mario Lemieux 12.00 30.00
WJG04 Joe Thornton 4.00 10.00
WJG05 Roberto Luongo 4.00 10.00
WJG06 Marc-Andre Fleury 6.00 15.00
WJG07 Carey Price 12.00 30.00
WJG08 Vincent Lecavalier 3.00 8.00
WJG09 Jason Spezza 4.00 10.00
WJG10 Brad Marchand 5.00 12.00
WJG11 Kyle Turris 2.50 6.00
WJG12 Eric Staal 5.00 12.00
WJG13 Justin Pogge 2.50 6.00
WJG14 Kristopher Letang 5.00 12.00
WJG15 Patrice Bergeron 5.00 12.00
WJG16 Jay Bouwmeester 4.00 10.00
WJG17 Esa Tikkanen 6.00 15.00
WJG18 Saku Koivu 4.00 10.00
WJG19 Oliver Ekman-Larsson 4.00 10.00
WJG20 Peter Forsberg 4.00 10.00
WJG21 Nicklas Lidstrom 4.00 10.00
WJG22 Jaromir Jagr 10.00 25.00
WJG23 Keith Tkachuk 4.00 10.00
WJG24 Chris Chelios 4.00 10.00
WJG25 Mike Modano 6.00 15.00
WJG26 Brian Leetch 4.00 10.00
WJG27 Alexander Semin 4.00 10.00
WJG28 Alexander Ovechkin 15.00 40.00
WJG29 Nikolai Khabibulin 3.00 8.00
WJG30 Pavel Bure 12.00 30.00

2011-12 ITG Canada vs The World World's Best Silver

ANNCD PRINT RUN 40 SER.#'d SETS
WB01 Rchtr/Mlr/Brrso/Vanbies 20.00 50.00
WB02 Lids/Frsbrg/Nslnd/Slmg 20.00 50.00
WB03 Koiv/Slne/Kurri/Tikk 30.00 80.00
WB04 Ovech/Bre/Fdrv/Mlkn 40.00 100.00
WB05 Khrlmv/Trtk/Mikh/Yak 25.00 60.00
WB06 Hull/LaFont/Mod/Ltch 20.00 50.00

2011 In The Game Canadiana Authentic Patch Silver

ANNOUNCED PRINT RUN 30
AP1 Angela James 30.00 60.00
AP6 Jean Beliveau L
AP8 Phil Esposito L 15.00 30.00
AP9 Phil Esposito L 15.00 30.00
AP10 Scott Niedermayer 10.00 20.00
AP11 Scott Niedermayer 10.00 20.00
AP12 Steve Yzerman L
AP13 Steve Yzerman L
AP15 Manon Rheaume 30.00 60.00
AP16 Patrick Roy L

2011 In The Game Canadiana Autographs

OVERALL AUTO/MEM ODDS THREE PER BOX
ALK Kwong, Larry 10.00 20.00
AAJ1 Angela James 15.00 30.00
AAJ2 Angela James 15.00 30.00
ADC1 Don Cherry 25.00 50.00
ADC2 Don Cherry 25.00 50.00
AJB1 Jean Beliveau 30.00 60.00
AJB2 Jean Beliveau 30.00 60.00
AMR1 Manon Rheaume 40.00 80.00
AMR2 Manon Rheaume 40.00 80.00
APE1 Phil Esposito 20.00 40.00
APE2 Phil Esposito 20.00 40.00
APH1 Paul Henderson 10.00 20.00
APH2 Paul Henderson 10.00 20.00
ASN1 Scott Niedermayer 10.00 20.00
ASN2 Scott Niedermayer 10.00 20.00
ASY1 Steve Yzerman 30.00 60.00
ASY2 Steve Yzerman

2011 In The Game Canadiana Autographs Blue

*BLUE: .75X TO 1.5X BLACK AUTOS
OVERALL AUTO ODDS ONE PER BOX

2011 In The Game Canadiana Double Memorabilia Silver

ANNOUNCED PRINT RUN 90
DM1 Steve Yzerman 15.00 30.00
DM2 Scott Niedermayer 10.00 20.00
DM4 Patrick Roy 15.00 30.00
DM6 S.Yzerman/S.Niedermayer 10.00 20.00
DM9 A.James/M.Rheaume 30.00 60.00
DM10 E.Stojko/M.Lemieux 10.00 20.00
DM12 S.Yzerman/M.Lemieux 15.00 30.00
DM13 M.Lemieux/P.Roy 15.00 30.00

2011 In The Game Canadiana Mega Memorabilia Silver

MM1 Angela James L 10.00 20.00
MM6 Jean Beliveau EL
MM8 Phil Esposito EL 10.00 20.00
MM9 Phil Esposito EL 10.00 20.00
MM10 Scott Niedermayer EL 10.00 20.00
MM11 Scott Niedermayer EL 10.00 20.00
MM12 Steve Yzerman EL
MM13 Steve Yzerman L 20.00 40.00
MM15 Manon Rheaume L 25.00 50.00
MM17 Patrick Roy EL
MM39 Wayne Gretzky EL

2011 In The Game Canadiana Red

BLUE/50: .75X TO 2X BASIC RED
UNPRICED ONYX ANNOUNCED RUN 5
ANNOUNCED PRINT RUN 180 SETS
5 Angela James .60 1.50
8 Bobby Hull 1.00 2.50
14 Conn Smythe .60 1.50
16 Danny Gallivan .60 1.50
19 Georges Vezina .60 1.50
22 Larry Kwong .60 1.50
28 Foster Hewitt .60 1.50
42 Jean Beliveau .75 2.00
48 Johnny Bower .75 2.00
61 Manon Rheaume 1.00 2.50
64 Maurice Richard .60 1.50
65 Patrick Roy 1.25 3.00
71 Paul Henderson .60 1.50
72 Phil Esposito .75 2.00
74 Raymond Bourque .75 2.00
80 Scott Niedermayer .60 1.50
85 Steve Yzerman .75 2.00
90 Terry Sawchuk .75 2.00

2011-12 ITG Captain-C

COMPLETE SET (100) 100.00 175.00
ANNOUNCED PRINT RUN 150
1 Al MacInnis 1.50 4.00
2 Alex Delvecchio 1.25 3.00
3 Alexander Ovechkin 6.00 15.00
4 Andrew Ladd 1.50 4.00
5 Andy Bathgate 1.50 4.00
6 Bill Durnan 1.50 4.00
7 Bob Baun 1.00 2.50
8 Bobby Clarke 1.50 4.00
9 Brad Park 1.25 3.00
10 Brenden Morrow 1.25 3.00
11 Brett Hull 2.00 5.00
12 Brian Leetch 1.50 4.00
13 Butch Bouchard 1.25 3.00
14 Charlie Conacher 1.25 3.00
15 Chris Chelios 1.50 4.00
16 Clark Gillies 1.50 4.00
17 Dale Hawerchuk 2.00 5.00
18 Dale Hunter 1.25 3.00
19 Danny Gare 1.25 3.00
20 Darryl Sittler 1.50 4.00
21 Dave Keon 1.50 4.00
22 David Backes 1.50 4.00
23 Denis Potvin 1.50 4.00
24 Denis Savard 2.00 5.00
25 Dit Clapper 1.00 2.50
26 Doug Gilmour 2.00 5.00
27 Doug Harvey 1.50 4.00
28 Mats Sundin 1.50 4.00
29 Eric Lindros 2.50 6.00
30 Eric Staal 2.00 5.00
31 Fern Flaman 1.00 2.50
32 Garry Unger 2.00 5.00
33 George Hainsworth 1.50 4.00
34 Gilbert Perreault 1.50 4.00
35 Guy Carbonneau 1.50 4.00
36 Dion Phaneuf 1.50 4.00
37 Henri Richard 1.50 4.00
38 Henrik Sedin 1.50 4.00
39 Jaromir Jagr 4.00 10.00
40 Jean Beliveau 1.50 4.00
41 Joe Nieuwendyk 1.50 4.00
42 Joe Sakic 2.50 6.00
43 Joe Thornton 1.50 4.00
44 Johnny Bucyk 1.50 4.00
45 Keith Tkachuk 1.50 4.00
46 King Clancy 1.50 4.00
47 Kirk Muller 1.25 3.00
48 Lanny McDonald 1.50 4.00
49 Luc Robitaille 1.50 4.00
50 Mario Lemieux 5.00 12.00
51 Mark Messier 2.00 5.00
52 Maurice Richard 1.50 4.00
53 Mikko Koivu 1.25 3.00
54 Milt Schmidt 1.25 3.00
55 Gordie Howe 3.00 8.00
56 Newsy Lalonde 1.25 3.00
57 Nicklas Lidstrom 1.50 4.00
58 Pat LaFontaine 1.50 4.00
59 Pat Verbeek 1.00 2.50
60 Patrick Marleau 1.50 4.00
61 Pavel Bure 2.00 5.00
62 Peter Stastny 1.50 4.00
63 Phil Esposito 2.50 6.00
64 Pierre Pilote 1.00 2.50
65 Ray Bourque 2.50 6.00
66 Red Dutton 1.00 2.50
67 Red Kelly 1.25 3.00
68 Rick Nash 1.50 4.00
69 Rick Vaive 1.25 3.00
70 Mike Modano 2.50 6.00
71 Roberto Luongo 1.50 4.00
72 Rod Langway 1.25 3.00
73 Ron Francis 2.00 5.00
74 Ron Greschner 1.25 3.00
75 Ryan Getzlaf 2.50 6.00
76 Saku Koivu 1.50 4.00
77 Scott Niedermayer 1.50 4.00
78 Serge Savard 1.50 4.00
79 Shea Weber 1.25 3.00
80 Sid Abel 1.25 3.00
81 Sprague Cleghorn 1.25 3.00
82 Stan Mikita 2.00 5.00
83 Steve Yzerman 2.50 6.00
84 Sweeney Schriner 1.00 2.50
85 Syl Apps 1.25 3.00
86 Ted Kennedy 1.25 3.00
87 Ted Lindsay 1.50 4.00
88 Teemu Selanne 3.00 8.00
89 Terry O'Reilly 1.25 3.00
90 Terry Ruskowski 1.25 3.00
91 Theoren Fleury 2.50 6.00
92 Toe Blake 1.00 2.50
93 Tony Amonte 1.25 3.00
94 Trevor Linden 1.50 4.00
95 Vincent Lecavalier 1.25 3.00
96 Wayne Cashman 1.00 2.50
97 Wendel Clark 1.50 4.00
98 Yvan Cournoyer 1.50 4.00
99 Zach Parise 1.50 4.00
100 Zdeno Chara 1.50 4.00

2011-12 ITG Captain-C Gold

*GOLD/50: .6X TO 1.5X BASIC CARDS
GOLD ANNOUNCED PRINT RUN 50

2011-12 ITG Captain-C Autographs Silver

FIVE AUTO OR MEM CARDS PER BOX
AAA Al Arbour 5.00 12.00
AAB Andy Bathgate 5.00 12.00
AAD Alex Delvecchio 6.00 15.00
AAM Al MacInnis SP 15.00 30.00
AAO Alexander Ovechkin SP 40.00 80.00
ABB Bill Barber 6.00 15.00
ABBA Bob Baun 4.00 10.00
ABBE Brian Bellows 4.00 10.00
ABBK Barry Beck 3.00 8.00
ABC Bobby Clarke SP 20.00 40.00
ABF Bernie Federko 4.00 10.00
ABG Bill Gadsby 8.00 20.00
ABH Brett Hull SP 30.00 60.00
ABL Brian Leetch 8.00 20.00
ABM Brad Marsh 3.00 8.00
ABMO Brenden Morrow 4.00 10.00
ABP Brad Park 6.00 15.00
ACC Chris Chelios SP 8.00 20.00
ACG Clark Gillies 5.00 12.00
ACH Craig Hartsburg 3.00 8.00
ACP Chris Pronger SP 8.00 20.00
ADG Danny Gare 4.00 10.00
ADGI Doug Gilmour 10.00 25.00
ADH Dale Hawerchuk 6.00 15.00
ADHU Dale Hunter 4.00 10.00
ADK Dave Keon SP 20.00 50.00
ADL Don Lever 8.00 20.00
ADP Denis Potvin 5.00 12.00
ADPH Dion Phaneuf 8.00 20.00
ADS Denis Savard 6.00 15.00
ADSI Darryl Sittler 8.00 20.00
ADT Dave Taylor 4.00 10.00
AEL Eric Lindros SP 40.00 100.00
AES Eric Staal 6.00 15.00
AEV Ed Van Impe 4.00 10.00
AFF Fern Flaman 8.00 20.00
AGB Garth Butcher 3.00 8.00
AGC Guy Carbonneau 6.00 15.00
AGH Gordie Howe SP 50.00 100.00
AGP Gilbert Perreault 8.00 20.00
AGU Garry Unger 6.00 15.00
AHH Harry Howell 4.00 10.00
AHR Henri Richard 10.00 25.00
AHS Henrik Sedin SP 15.00 30.00
AJB Jean Beliveau SP 40.00 80.00
AJBU Johnny Bucyk 6.00 15.00
AJJ Jaromir Jagr SP 30.00 60.00
AJN Joe Nieuwendyk SP 8.00 20.00
AJS Joe Sakic SP 25.00 50.00
AJT Joe Thornton SP 10.00 25.00
AKM Kirk Muller 4.00 10.00
AKT Keith Tkachuk 5.00 12.00
ALM Lanny McDonald 6.00 15.00
ALR Luc Robitaille SP 15.00 30.00
AMD Marcel Dionne 6.00 15.00
AMK Mikko Koivu SP 8.00 20.00
AML Mario Lemieux SP 40.00 80.00
AMM Mark Messier SP 40.00 80.00
AMMO Mike Modano 8.00 20.00
AMR Maurice Richard SP 150.00 300.00
AMS Milt Schmidt SP 6.00 15.00
AMS Mats Sundin SP 50.00 100.00
ANL Nicklas Lidstrom SP 25.00 50.00
APB Pavel Bure SP 25.00 50.00
APE Phil Esposito 10.00 25.00
APL Pat Lafontaine 12.50 25.00
APM Patrick Marleau 6.00 15.00
APP Pierre Pilote 6.00 15.00
APS Peter Stastny 8.00 20.00
ARB Ray Bourque SP 20.00 40.00
ARBL Rob Blake 5.00 12.00
ARF Ron Francis SP
ARK Red Kelly SP 12.00 30.00
ARL Rod Langway 4.00 10.00
ARLA Reed Larson 3.00 8.00
ARLU Roberto Luongo 10.00 25.00
ARM Rick Middleton 8.00 20.00
ARN Rick Nash SP 8.00 20.00
ARV Rick Vaive 10.00 25.00
ASK Saku Koivu SP 20.00 40.00
ASM Stan Mikita SP 10.00 25.00
ASN Scott Niedermayer 5.00 12.00
ASS Serge Savard 6.00 15.00
ASW Shea Weber SP 10.00 25.00
ASY Steve Yzerman SP 40.00 80.00
ATA Tony Amonte 6.00 15.00
ATF Theoren Fleury SP 20.00 40.00
ATK Ted Kennedy SP 30.00 60.00
ATL Trevor Linden 10.00 25.00
ATLI Ted Lindsay 8.00 20.00
ATLY Tom Lysiak 3.00 8.00
ATO Terry O'Reilly 6.00 15.00
ATR Terry Ruskowski 4.00 10.00
ATS Teemu Selanne SP 20.00 40.00
ATST Thomas Steen 3.00 8.00
AVH Vic Hadfield 4.00 10.00
AVL Vincent Lecavalier SP 10.00 25.00
AWC Wayne Cashman 5.00 12.00
AWCL Wendel Clark 12.50 25.00
AYC Yvan Cournoyer 6.00 15.00
AZC Zdeno Chara SP 10.00 25.00

2011-12 ITG Captain-C Franchise Captains Jerseys Silver

SILVER ANNOUNCED PRINT RUN 1-30
FC01 Bucyk/Schmdt/O'Rlly 25.00 50.00
FC02 Chara/Thrntn/Brque 15.00 30.00
FC03 Fleury/Nieuw/McDnld 15.00 40.00
FC04 Mikita/Chelios/Amonte 15.00 30.00
FC05 Lindsay/Delvec/Howe 20.00 40.00
FC06 Lidstrm/Dnne/Yzerman 20.00 40.00
FC07 Hwrchk/Steen/Tkchk 12.00 30.00
FC08 Taylor/Robitlle/Brown 6.00 15.00
FC09 Durnan/Lalnde/Richrd
FC10 Koivu/Keane/Muller 20.00 40.00
FC11 Carbon/Savrd/Crnyr 15.00 30.00
FC12 Richrd/Beliv/Harvy 60.00 120.00
FC13 Leetch/Messier/Jagr 15.00 30.00
FC14 P.Espo/Park/Hadfield 8.00 20.00
FC15 Frsbrg/Primeau/Lindrs 20.00 40.00
FC16 Barber/Clarke/Toccht 25.00 50.00
FC17 Lemieux/Jagr/Francis 20.00 40.00
FC18 MacInns/Ungr/Arbour 25.00 50.00
FC19 Sundin/Gilmour/Clark/9* 20.00 40.00
FC20 Sittler/Keon/Kennedy/9*
FC21 Gare/Perreault/LaFontaine/9*
FC22 Selanne/Niedermayer/Getzlaf/9*
FC23 Linden/Luongo/Sedin/9*
FC24 Langway/Hunter/Ovechkin/9*

2011-12 ITG Captain-C Jerseys Silver

SILVER ANNOUNCED PRINT RUN 90
MU1 Al MacInnis 4.00 10.00
M02 Alexander Ovechkin 20.00 50.00
M03 Brenden Morrow 4.00 10.00
M04 Brett Hull 6.00 15.00
M05 Brian Bellows 4.00 10.00
M06 Brian Leetch 5.00 12.00
M07 Chris Chelios 5.00 12.00
M08 Chris Pronger 4.00 10.00
M09 Craig Hartsburg 3.00 8.00
M10 Dale Hawerchuk 5.00 12.00

M11 Dale Hunter 4.00 10.00
M12 Dave Taylor 4.00 10.00
M13 Denis Savard 6.00 15.00
M14 Dion Phaneuf 5.00 12.00
M15 Mats Sundin 5.00 12.00
M16 Dustin Brown 5.00 12.00
M17 Eric Lindros 6.00 15.00
M18 Eric Staal 6.00 15.00
M19 Gilbert Perreault 5.00 12.00
M20 Guy Carbonneau 5.00 12.00
M21 Henrik Sedin 5.00 12.00
M22 Jaromir Jagr 6.00 15.00
M23 Jaromir Jagr 6.00 15.00
M24 Joe Nieuwendyk 5.00 12.00
M25 Joe Sakic 8.00 20.00
M26 Joe Sakic 8.00 20.00
M27 Joe Thornton 5.00 12.00
M28 Joe Thornton 5.00 12.00
M29 Keith Tkachuk 5.00 12.00
M30 Kirk Muller 5.00 12.00
M31 Lanny McDonald 5.00 12.00
M32 Luc Robitaille 5.00 12.00
M33 Mario Lemieux 15.00 40.00
M34 Mark Messier 6.00 15.00
M35 Mark Messier 6.00 15.00
M36 Mark Messier 6.00 15.00
M37 Mike Modano 8.00 20.00
M38 Mikko Koivu 4.00 10.00
M39 Nicklas Lidstrom 5.00 12.00
M40 Pat LaFontaine 5.00 12.00
M41 Patrick Marleau 5.00 12.00
M42 Pavel Bure 6.00 15.00
M43 Peter Stastny 5.00 12.00
M44 Ray Bourque 8.00 20.00
M45 Rick Nash 5.00 12.00
M46 Roberto Luongo 5.00 12.00
M47 Rod Langway 4.00 10.00
M48 Ryan Getzlaf 8.00 20.00
M49 Saku Koivu 5.00 12.00
M50 Scott Niedermayer 5.00 12.00
M51 Shea Weber 5.00 12.00
M52 Steve Yzerman 8.00 20.00
M53 Teemu Selanne 10.00 25.00
M54 Theoren Fleury 6.00 15.00
M55 Tony Amonte 4.00 10.00
M56 Trevor Linden 6.00 15.00
M57 Vincent Lecavalier 4.00 10.00
M58 Wendel Clark 5.00 12.00
M59 Zach Parise 5.00 12.00
M60 Zdeno Chara 5.00 12.00

2011-12 ITG Captain-C Junior Captains Jerseys Silver

SILVER ANNOUNCED PRINT RUN 50
JC01 Karl Alzner 4.00 10.00
JC02 Tyson Barrie 6.00 15.00
JC03 Jonathon Blum 5.00 12.00
JC04 Ryan Callahan 6.00 15.00
JC05 Landon Ferraro 4.00 10.00
JC06 Cody Eakin 6.00 15.00
JC07 Ryan Ellis 5.00 12.00
JC08 Cory Emmerton 5.00 12.00
JC09 Colton Sissons 4.00 10.00
JC10 Thomas Hickey 4.00 10.00
JC11 Cody Hodgson 6.00 15.00
JC12 Boone Jenner 5.00 12.00
JC13 Zack Kassian 6.00 15.00
JC14 Bryan Little 6.00 15.00
JC15 Greg McKegg 5.00 12.00
JC16 Mark Pysyk 4.00 10.00
JC17 Ryan Murray 8.00 20.00
JC18 Ryan O'Marra 4.00 10.00
JC19 Patrick O'Sullivan 4.00 10.00
JC20 Marc-Antoine Pouliot 5.00 12.00
JC21 Brayden Schenn 5.00 12.00
JC22 Duncan Siemens 5.00 12.00
JC23 Chris Stewart 4.00 10.00
JC24 Chris Terry 5.00 12.00

2011-12 ITG Captain-C Stick and Jersey Silver

SILVER ANNOUNCED PRINT RUN 40
SJ01 Alexander Ovechkin 20.00 50.00
SJ02 Al MacInnis 10.00 25.00
SJ03 Chris Chelios 8.00 20.00
SJ04 Mike Modano 12.00 30.00
SJ05 Denis Potvin 8.00 20.00
SJ06 Dale Hawerchuk 10.00 25.00
SJ07 Doug Gilmour 12.00 30.00
SJ08 Eric Lindros 12.00 30.00
SJ09 Gilbert Perreault 8.00 20.00
SJ10 Jaromir Jagr 15.00 40.00
SJ11 Joe Sakic 15.00 40.00
SJ12 Joe Thornton 8.00 20.00
SJ13 Keith Tkachuk 8.00 20.00
SJ14 Mario Lemieux 25.00 50.00
SJ15 Mark Messier 20.00 40.00
SJ16 Nicklas Lidstrom 10.00 25.00
SJ17 Dale Hunter 6.00 15.00
SJ18 Pavel Bure 12.00 30.00
SJ19 Ray Bourque 12.00 30.00
SJ20 Eric Staal 10.00 25.00
SJ21 Ryan Getzlaf 12.00 30.00
SJ22 Luc Robitaille 12.00 30.00
SJ23 Pat LaFontaine 10.00 25.00
SJ24 Steve Yzerman 12.00 30.00
SJ25 Teemu Selanne 12.00 30.00
SJ26 Theoren Fleury 15.00 40.00
SJ27 Tony Amonte 6.00 15.00
SJ28 Trevor Linden 12.00 30.00
SJ29 Vincent Lecavalier 6.00 15.00
SJ30 Mats Sundin 10.00 25.00

2010-11 ITG Decades 1980s All-Stars Jerseys Silver

ANNCD PRINT RUN 40 SETS
AS01 Dion/Laflr/Robnsn/Espo 10.00 25.00
AS02 Liut/Simmer/Bossy/Potvin 20.00 50.00
AS03 Smith/Bourq/Bossy/Mess 12.00 30.00
AS04 Lang/Bourq/Mess/Peetrs 12.00 30.00
AS05 Barras/Goult/Bourq/Bossy 20.00 50.00
AS06 Lindbrg/Bourq/Coffy/Kurri 12.00 30.00
AS07 Vanbies/Goult/Bossy/Coffy 15.00 40.00
AS08 Hextall/Bourq/Kurri/Goult 12.00 30.00
AS09 Fuhr/Robit/Mario/Bourq 25.00 60.00
AS10 Roy/Mario/Coffy/Robit 25.00 60.00

2010-11 ITG Decades 1980s Autographs

STATED ODDS 3 PER PACK
AAA Al Arbour 5.00 12.00
AAB Allan Bester 5.00 12.00
AAH Anders Hedberg 5.00 12.00
AAM Andy Moog 6.00 15.00
AAMA Al MacInnis 6.00 15.00
AAS Anton Stastny 6.00 15.00
ABA Brent Ashton 4.00 10.00
ABB Bill Barber 5.00 12.00
ABBA Bill Baker USA 12.00 30.00
ABBA2 Bill Baker MTL 8.00 20.00
ABBE Brian Bellows 5.00 12.00
ABBK Barry Beck 4.00 10.00
ABD Bill Derlago 5.00 12.00
ABF Bernie Federko 5.00 12.00
ABH Bobby Hull 15.00 40.00
ABM Brad Marsh 5.00 12.00
ABN Bernie Nicholls 6.00 15.00
ABNY Bob Nystrom 4.00 10.00
ABOS Bobby Smith 5.00 12.00
ABP Brad Park 5.00 12.00
ABPE Barry Pederson 4.00 10.00
ABPR Brian Propp 6.00 15.00
ABS Buzz Schneider USA 15.00 30.00
ABSA Borje Salming 8.00 20.00
ABSK Brian Skrudland 6.00 15.00
ABSM Billy Smith 6.00 15.00
ABST Blaine Stoughton 5.00 12.00
ABSU Bob Suter 8.00 20.00
ABSV Bob Sauve 6.00 15.00
ABT Bryan Trottier 8.00 20.00
ACC Chris Chelios 8.00 20.00
ACGA Guy Carbonneau 6.00 15.00
ACH Craig Hartsburg 4.00 10.00
ACN Cam Neely 6.00 15.00
ACR Chico Resch 6.00 15.00
ACS Charlie Simmer 4.00 10.00
ADB Don Beaupre 5.00 12.00
ADBA Dave Babych 6.00 15.00
ADBO Dan Bouchard 8.00 20.00
ADC Dave Christian USA 12.00 30.00
ADC Dino Ciccarelli 8.00 20.00
ADC2 Dave Christian WIN 8.00 20.00
ADG Doug Gilmour 15.00 40.00
ADGA Danny Gare 6.00 15.00
ADH Dale Hawerchuk 10.00 25.00
ADHU Dale Hunter 5.00 12.00
ADK Dave Keon SP 20.00 50.00
ADL Don Lever 8.00 20.00
ADM Dennis Maruk 5.00 12.00
ADP Denis Potvin 6.00 15.00
ADPA Darren Pang 8.00 20.00
ADS Dave Silk USA 25.00 50.00
ADS2 Dave Silk NYR 6.00 15.00
ADSA Denis Savard 8.00 20.00
ADSE Dave Semenko 6.00 15.00
ADSI Darryl Sittler 12.00 30.00
ADT Dave Taylor 6.00 15.00
ADW Doug Wilson 5.00 12.00
AES Eric Strobel 8.00 20.00
AET Esa Tikkanen 6.00 15.00
AGA Glenn Anderson 6.00 15.00
AGC Gerry Cheevers 8.00 20.00
AGF Grant Fuhr 6.00 15.00
AGL Guy Lafleur 20.00 50.00
AGLE Gary Leeman 5.00 12.00
AGM Greg Millen 5.00 12.00
AGP Gilbert Perreault 6.00 15.00
AGS Gary Suter 4.00 10.00
AHS Harold Snepsts 6.00 15.00
AIL Igor Larionov 15.00 30.00
AJC Jim Craig USA 15.00 40.00
AJC2 Jim Craig BOS 10.00 25.00
AJG John Garrett 6.00 15.00
AJH John Harrington USA 10.00 25.00
AJK Jari Kurri 10.00 25.00
AJM Joe Mullen CAL 5.00 12.00
AJM2 Joe Mullen USA 6.00 15.00
AJO Jack O'Callahan USA 20.00 40.00
AJO2 Jack O'Callahan CHI 10.00 25.00
AJOG John Ogrodnick 5.00 12.00
AJR Jeremy Roenick SP 15.00 40.00
AJS Joe Sakic 40.00 80.00
AJV John Vanbiesbrouck 12.00 30.00
AKB Kelly Buchberger 4.00 10.00
AKD Kevin Dineen 6.00 15.00
AKH Kelly Hrudey 5.00 12.00
AKM Ken Morrow USA 25.00 50.00
AKM2 Ken Morrow NYI 6.00 15.00
AKMC Kirk McLean 8.00 20.00
AKMU Kirk Muller 4.00 10.00
AKN Kent Nilsson 4.00 10.00
ALM Lanny McDonald 6.00 15.00
ALMU Larry Murphy 6.00 15.00
ALR Larry Robinson 6.00 15.00
ALRO Luc Robitaille 8.00 20.00
AMB Mike Bossy 10.00 25.00
AMBA Murray Bannerman 6.00 15.00
AMBU Mike Bullard 5.00 12.00
AMD Marcel Dionne 8.00 20.00
AME Mike Eruzione 25.00 50.00
AMG Michel Goulet QUE 8.00 20.00
AMG2 Michel Goulet CAN 8.00 20.00
AMGA Mike Gartner 6.00 15.00
AMH Mark Hunter 5.00 12.00
AMHO Mark Howe 6.00 15.00
AMJ Mark Johnson USA 30.00 60.00
AMJ2 Mark Johnson HART 5.00 12.00
AML Mario Lemieux SP 75.00 150.00
AMLI Mike Liut 5.00 12.00
AMLU Morris Lukowich 4.00 10.00
AMM Mark Messier EDM SP 40.00 80.00
AMM2 Mark Messier CAN SP 90.00 150.00
AMN Mats Naslund 8.00 20.00
AMP Mark Pavelich USA 25.00 50.00
AMP2 Mark Pavelich NYR 8.00 20.00
AMR Mike Ramsey BUF 6.00 15.00
AMR2 Mike Ramsey USA 40.00 80.00
AMRO Mike Rogers 4.00 10.00
AMST Marian Stastny 8.00 20.00
AMV Mike Vernon 5.00 12.00
AMW Mark Wells 10.00 25.00
ANB Neal Broten USA 30.00 60.00
ANB2 Neal Broten MIN 8.00 20.00
APC Paul Coffey SP 15.00 30.00
APE Phil Esposito SP 8.00 20.00
APH Phil Housley 6.00 15.00
APL Pat LaFontaine 10.00 25.00
APP Pete Peeters 6.00 15.00
APR Patrick Roy SP 50.00 100.00
APRE Pokey Reddick 5.00 12.00
APRH Paul Reinhart 4.00 10.00
APRI Pat Riggin 4.00 10.00
APS Peter Stastny 10.00 25.00
APV Phil Verchota 12.00 30.00
APVE Pat Verbeek 5.00 12.00
ARB Raymond Bourque SP 30.00 60.00
ARBR Richard Brodeur 6.00 15.00
ARC Randy Carlyle 5.00 12.00
ARF Ron Francis 12.00 30.00
ARG Ron Greschner 4.00 10.00
ARH Ron Hextall 8.00 20.00
ARK Rick Kehoe 5.00 12.00
ARL Rod Langway 5.00 12.00
ARLA Reed Larson 4.00 10.00
ARLO Ron Low 6.00 15.00
ARM Rob McClanahan USA 15.00 30.00
ARM2 Rob McClanahan BUF 6.00 15.00
ARMI Rick Middleton 8.00 20.00
ARV Rick Vaive 5.00 12.00
ARW Rick Wamsley 8.00 20.00
ASC Steve Christoff 10.00 25.00
ASJ Steve Janaszak 10.00 25.00
ASK Steve Kasper 4.00 10.00
ASP Steve Payne 5.00 12.00
ASPE Steve Penney 8.00 20.00
ASS Steve Shutt 10.00 25.00
ASY Steve Yzerman SP 25.00 60.00
ATB Tom Barrasso 8.00 20.00
ATE Tony Esposito SP 20.00 50.00
ATK Tim Kerr 6.00 15.00
ATL Tom Lysiak 4.00 10.00
ATLI Trevor Linden 12.00 30.00
ATS Thomas Steen 4.00 10.00
ATT Tony Tanti 5.00 12.00
ATW Tiger Williams 5.00 12.00
AVK Vladimir Krutov 20.00 50.00
AVT Vladislav Tretiak SP 75.00 135.00
AWC Wendel Clark 10.00 25.00
AWP Willi Plett 5.00 12.00
AWW Wally Weir 5.00 12.00

2010-11 ITG Decades 1980s Battle of Alberta

COMPLETE SET (5) 8.00 20.00
BA01 M.Vernon/G.Fuhr 2.00 5.00
BA02 L.McDonald/M.Messier 3.00 8.00
BA03 H.Loob/J.Kurri 2.00 5.00
BA04 P.Reinhart/P.Coffey 2.00 5.00
BA05 J.Mullen/G.Anderson 2.00 5.00

2010-11 ITG Decades 1980s Battle of New York

COMPLETE SET (5) 8.00 20.00
BNY01 D.Potvin/B.Beck 2.00 5.00
BNY02 B.Smith/J.Vanbiesbrouck 2.50 6.00
BNY03 M.Bossy/A.Hedberg 2.00 5.00
BNY04 K.Morrow/R.Greschner 1.50 4.00
BNY05 B.Trottier/P.Esposito 3.00 8.00

2010-11 ITG Decades 1980s Battle of Quebec

COMPLETE SET (5) 10.00 25.00
BQ01 P.Stastny/G.Lafleur 2.50 6.00
BQ02 M.Goulet/S.Shutt 2.00 5.00
BQ03 D.Bouchard/P.Roy 5.00 12.00
BQ04 D.Hunter/L.Robinson 2.00 5.00
BQ05 J.Sakic/C.Chelios 3.00 8.00

2010-11 ITG Decades 1980s Between The Pipes Jerseys Black

BLACK ANNCD PRINT RUN 29-100
SILVER/30: .5X TO 1.2X BLACK/100*
BTPJ01 Patrick Roy 12.00 30.00
BTPJ02 Billy Smith 5.00 12.00
BTPJ03 Tony Esposito 6.00 15.00
BTPJ04 Grant Fuhr 8.00 20.00
BTPJ05 Tom Barrasso 8.00 20.00
BTPJ06 John Vanbiesbrouck 6.00 15.00
BTPJ07 Allan Bester 4.00 10.00
BTPJ08 Richard Brodeur 5.00 12.00
BTPJ09 Darren Pang 5.00 12.00
BTPJ10 Pokey Reddick 10.00 25.00
BTPJ11 Ron Hextall 6.00 15.00
BTPJ12 Pelle Lindbergh/29* 15.00 40.00
BTPJ13 Mike Palmateer 5.00 12.00
BTPJ14 Don Beaupre 4.00 10.00
BTPJ15 Andy Moog 6.00 15.00
BTPJ16 Pat Riggin 3.00 8.00
BTPJ17 Ed Belfour 6.00 15.00
BTPJ18 Mike Vernon 6.00 15.00
BTPJ19 Dan Bouchard 8.00 20.00
BTPJ20 Bill Ranford 5.00 12.00

2010-11 ITG Decades 1980s Canada's Best

COMPLETE SET (5) 10.00 25.00
CB01 Mark Messier 3.00 8.00
CB02 Paul Coffey 2.00 5.00
CB03 Guy Lafleur 2.50 6.00
CB04 Grant Fuhr 2.00 5.00
CB05 Mario Lemieux 6.00 15.00

2010-11 ITG Decades 1980s Decades Rookies

DR01 Andy Moog 2.00 5.00
DR02 Bernie Nicholls 2.50 6.00
DR03 Brian Bellows 2.00 5.00
DR04 Brian Propp 2.50 6.00
DR05 Cam Neely 2.50 6.00
DR06 Dale Hawerchuk 2.50 6.00
DR07 Darren Pang 2.50 6.00
DR08 Denis Savard 2.50 6.00
DR09 Dino Ciccarelli 2.50 6.00
DR10 Don Beaupre 2.00 5.00
DR11 Doug Gilmour 3.00 8.00
DR12 Gary Suter 1.50 4.00
DR13 Glenn Anderson 2.50 6.00
DR14 Grant Fuhr 2.50 6.00
DR15 Guy Carbonneau 2.50 6.00
DR16 Jari Kurri 2.00 5.00
DR17 Jeremy Roenick 2.50 6.00
DR18 Joe Mullen 2.00 5.00
DR19 Joe Nieuwendyk 2.00 5.00
DR20 Joe Sakic 4.00 10.00
DR21 John Vanbiesbrouck 3.00 8.00
DR22 Kelly Hrudey 2.00 5.00
DR23 Kirk McLean 2.50 6.00
DR24 Kirk Muller 1.50 4.00
DR25 Larry Murphy 2.00 5.00
DR26 Luc Robitaille 2.00 5.00
DR27 Mario Lemieux 6.00 15.00
DR28 Mats Naslund 2.50 6.00
DR29 Mike Vernon 2.00 5.00
DR30 Neal Broten 2.00 5.00
DR31 Pat LaFontaine 2.50 6.00
DR32 Pat Verbeek 1.50 4.00
DR33 Patrick Roy 6.00 15.00
DR34 Paul Coffey 2.00 5.00
DR35 Pelle Lindbergh 4.00 10.00
DR36 Peter Stastny 1.50 4.00
DR37 Phil Housley 2.50 6.00
DR38 Raymond Bourque 4.00 10.00
DR39 Ron Francis 2.50 6.00
DR40 Ron Hextall 2.50 6.00
DR41 Steve Penney 2.50 6.00
DR42 Steve Yzerman 6.00 15.00
DR43 Thomas Steen 1.50 4.00
DR44 Tom Barrasso 2.00 5.00
DR45 Wendel Clark 2.50 6.00

2010-11 ITG Decades 1980s Edmonton Dynasty

COMPLETE SET (5) 8.00 20.00
ED01 Mark Messier 3.00 8.00
ED02 Grant Fuhr 2.00 5.00
ED03 Glenn Anderson 2.00 5.00
ED04 Paul Coffey 2.00 5.00
ED05 Jari Kurri 2.00 5.00

2010-11 ITG Decades 1980s For Your Country Jerseys Black

ANNCD PRINT RUN 90 SETS
SILVER/30: .5X TO 1.2X BLACK/90*
CARDS HAVE FYCJ PREFIX
01 Bossy/Perr/Bourq/Goulet 10.00 25.00
02 Laflr/Yzer/Hawer/Robnsn 15.00 40.00
03 Dion/Ststny/Coffy/Mario 15.00 40.00
04 Messr/Gilmr/Potvin/Fuhr 10.00 25.00
05 Mullen/Espo/Chelios/Brrs 12.00 30.00
06 Housley/Vnbs/LaFnt/Lang 12.00 30.00
07 Slmng/Nslnd/Lndbrg/Loob 15.00 40.00
08 Tretk/Krutv/Larnv/Mshkn 25.00 60.00

2010-11 ITG Decades 1980s Franchise Jerseys Silver

ANNCD PRINT RUN 40 SETS
F01 Bourq/Neely/Moog/Mddltn 20.00 50.00
F02 Perrlt/Barrso/Hsley/Gare 15.00 40.00
F03 MacInn/Loob/Vern/McDnld 8.00 20.00
F04 T.Espo/Savard/Belfr/Rnick 25.00 60.00
F05 Yzerman/Sittlr/Gilbrt/Larsn 15.00 40.00
F06 Fuhr/Messier/Coffey/Kurri 25.00 60.00
F07 Keon/Francis/Howe/Babych 15.00 40.00
F08 Dionne/Robit/Hrudey/Nichls 15.00 40.00
F09 Bellws/Harts/Ciccr/Payne 15.00 40.00
F10 Carbn/Rbnsn/Lafleur/Roy 20.00 50.00
F11 Smith/Trottier/Bossy/Potvin 15.00 40.00
F12 P.Espo/Vanbs/Dione/Ltch 12.00 30.00
F13 Lindb/Clarke/Propp/Hextall 15.00 40.00
F14 Lemieux/Coffy/Barrso/Carly 25.00 60.00
F15 Ststny/Bchrd/Sakic/Goulet 15.00 40.00
F16 Fedrko/Gilmr/Mullen/Liut 25.00 60.00
F17 Vaive/Salming/Bestr/Sittl 15.00 40.00
F18 Brodr/Willms/Snpsts/Tanti 12.00 30.00
F19 Riggin/Hntr/Grtnr/Lngwy 12.00 30.00
F20 Hwrchk/Hull/Redd/Carly 20.00 50.00

2010-11 ITG Decades 1980s Game Used Jerseys Black

ANNCD PRINT RUN 120 SETS
SILVER/30: .5X TO 1.2X BLACK/120*
M01 Al MacInnis 5.00 12.00
M02 Allan Bester 4.00 10.00
M03 Bernie Federko 4.00 10.00
M04 Bernie Nicholls 5.00 12.00
M05 Bill Barber 4.00 10.00
M06 Billy Smith 5.00 12.00
M07 Bob Nystrom 3.00 8.00
M08 Tony Tanti 4.00 10.00
M09 Bobby Clarke 5.00 12.00
M10 Borje Salming 5.00 12.00
M11 Brian Bellows 4.00 10.00
M12 Brian Propp 5.00 12.00
M13 Brian Skrudland 5.00 12.00
M14 Bryan Trottier 6.00 15.00
M15 Cam Neely 5.00 12.00
M16 Chris Chelios 5.00 12.00
M17 Craig Hartsburg 3.00 8.00
M18 Dale Hunter 6.00 15.00
M19 Dan Bouchard 6.00 15.00
M20 Dave Babych 5.00 12.00
M21 Darryl Sittler 4.00 10.00
M22 Dale Hawerchuk 6.00 15.00
M23 Denis Potvin 5.00 12.00
M24 Denis Savard 6.00 15.00
M25 Dino Ciccarelli 5.00 12.00
M26 Wendel Clark 5.00 12.00
M27 Gary Leeman 4.00 10.00
M28 Gary Suter 3.00 8.00
M29 Gilbert Perreault/30* 5.00 12.00
M30 Glenn Anderson 5.00 12.00
M31 Grant Fuhr/30* 5.00 12.00
M32 Guy Carbonneau 5.00 12.00
M33 Harold Snepsts 5.00 12.00
M34 Jari Kurri/30* 6.00 15.00
M35 Jeremy Roenick 8.00 20.00
M36 Joe Mullen 8.00 20.00
M37 John Vanbiesbrouck 8.00 20.00
M38 Lanny McDonald 5.00 12.00
M39 Larry Robinson 5.00 12.00
M40 Luc Robitaille 5.00 12.00
M41 Marcel Dionne 8.00 20.00
M42 Mats Naslund 8.00 20.00
M43 Mike Bossy 5.00 12.00
M44 Mike Gartner 10.00 25.00
M45 Mike Modano 8.00 20.00
M46 Neal Broten 4.00 10.00
M47 Pat LaFontaine 5.00 12.00
M48 Pat Riggin 3.00 8.00
M49 Paul Reinhart 3.00 8.00
M50 Peter Stastny 4.00 10.00
M51 Anders Hedberg 4.00 10.00
M52 Randy Carlyle 4.00 10.00
M53 Raymond Bourque 8.00 20.00
M54 Richard Brodeur 5.00 12.00
M55 Rick Middleton 6.00 15.00
M56 Rick Vaive 4.00 10.00
M57 Rod Langway 4.00 10.00
M58 Ron Hextall 6.00 15.00
M59 Steve Payne 4.00 10.00
M60 Steve Shutt 5.00 12.00
M61 Tiger Williams 4.00 10.00
M62 Trevor Linden 10.00 25.00
M63 Doug Gilmour/30* 12.00 30.00
M64 Brad Park/30* 4.00 10.00
M65 Reed Larson 3.00 8.00
M66 Guy Lafleur 10.00 25.00
M67 Joe Sakic 8.00 20.00
M68 Mario Lemieux 15.00 40.00
M69 Mark Messier/30* 8.00 20.00
M70 Patrick Roy/30* 12.00 30.00
M71 Phil Esposito/30* 8.00 20.00
M72 Paul Coffey 8.00 20.00
M73 Steve Yzerman 12.00 30.00
M74 Tony Esposito/30* 6.00 15.00
M75 Dave Keon/30* 5.00 12.00

2010-11 ITG Decades 1980s Great Moments

COMPLETE SET (5) 10.00 25.00
GM01 Mike Bossy 2.00 5.00
GM02 Jim Craig 1.50 4.00
GM03 Mark Messier 3.00 8.00
GM04 Bob Nystrom 1.25 3.00
GM05 Mario Lemieux 6.00 15.00

2010-11 ITG Decades 1980s Long Island Dynasty

COMPLETE SET (5) 6.00 15.00
LID01 Denis Potvin 2.00 5.00
LID02 Mike Bossy 2.00 5.00
LID03 Bryan Trottier 2.50 6.00
LID04 Billy Smith 2.00 5.00
LID05 Clark Gillies 2.00 5.00

2010-11 ITG Decades 1980s Memorable Masks

COMPLETE SET (10) 20.00 50.00
MM01 Grant Fuhr 2.50 6.00
MM02 Andy Moog 2.50 6.00
MM03 Mike Liut 2.00 5.00
MM04 Tom Barrasso 2.50 6.00
MM05 Bunny Larocque 2.00 5.00
MM06 Pelle Lindbergh 4.00 10.00
MM07 Michel Dion 2.00 5.00
MM08 Allan Bester 2.00 5.00
MM09 Patrick Roy 6.00 15.00
MM10 Murray Bannerman 2.50 6.00

2010-11 ITG Decades 1980s Rivalries Jerseys Silver

ANNCD PRINT RUN 40 SETS
R01 Fuhr/Messr/McDon/Nieu 12.00 30.00
R02 Kurri/Coffey/Trottier/Gillies 25.00 60.00
R03 Chelios/Roy/McIn/Vernon 20.00 50.00
R04 Vanbies/Dnne/Ptvin/Smith 20.00 50.00
R05 Naslnd/Carbon/Bchrd/Stst 15.00 40.00
R06 Laflr/Robn/Middle/Brque 15.00 40.00
R07 Vaive/Slmng/T.Esp/Svrd 20.00 50.00
R08 Clark/Bester/Fedrko/Gilm 20.00 50.00
R09 Andrsn/Fuhr/Hext/Propp 10.00 25.00
R10 Langwy/Riggn/Sittlr/Clrke 12.00 30.00
R11 Perrlt/Gare/Shutt/Lafleur 15.00 40.00
R12 Bossy/Mess/Tretk/Krutv 12.00 30.00

2010-11 ITG Decades 1980s Rookie Game Used Jerseys Silver

ANNCD PRINT RUN 40 SETS
RJ01 Raymond Bourque 10.00 25.00
RJ02 Paul Coffey 10.00 25.00
RJ03 Denis Savard 8.00 20.00
RJ04 Jari Kurri 8.00 20.00
RJ05 Ron Francis 15.00 40.00
RJ06 Dale Hawerchuk 8.00 20.00
RJ07 Grant Fuhr 6.00 15.00
RJ08 Doug Gilmour 12.00 30.00
RJ09 Tom Barrasso 6.00 15.00
RJ10 Steve Yzerman 15.00 40.00
RJ11 Chris Chelios 6.00 15.00
RJ12 Pat LaFontaine 8.00 20.00
RJ13 Mario Lemieux 20.00 50.00
RJ14 Patrick Roy 15.00 40.00
RJ15 Wendel Clark 6.00 15.00
RJ16 Ron Hextall 8.00 20.00
RJ17 Luc Robitaille 10.00 25.00
RJ18 Joe Nieuwendyk 6.00 15.00
RJ19 Brian Leetch 10.00 25.00
RJ20 Joe Sakic 15.00 40.00

2010-11 ITG Decades 1980s Stanley Cup Clashes Jerseys Silver

ANNCD PRINT RUN 40 SETS
CC01 Nystrom/Trottier/Clrke/Barbr 15.00 40.00
CC02 Potvin/Bossy/Cicc/Hartsbrg
CC03 Bossy/Trottier/Brodeur/Will 25.00 60.00
CC04 Smith/Potvin/Andrsn/Kurri 15.00 40.00
CC05 Fuhr/Messier/Gillies/LaFont 12.00 30.00
CC06 Kurri/Coffey/Propp/Lind 20.00 50.00
CC07 Roy/Naslnd/Mulln/Vern 20.00 50.00
CC08 Messier/Andrsn/Hext/Propp 12.00 30.00
CC09 Tikkan/Fuhr/Moog/Brque 60.00 120.00
CC10 MacIn/McDon/Rbinsn/Roy 20.00 50.00

2010-11 ITG Decades 1980s Trophy Winners Jerseys Black

ANNCD PRINT RUN 50-100
SILVER/20-30: .5X TO 1.2X BLACK/50-100*
TWJ01 Raymond Bourque 8.00 20.00
TWJ02 Bryan Trottier 6.00 15.00
TWJ03 Larry Robinson 5.00 12.00
TWJ04 Peter Stastny 4.00 10.00
TWJ05 Dale Hawerchuk 8.00 20.00
TWJ06 Billy Smith 5.00 12.00
TWJ07 Mike Bossy 5.00 12.00
TWJ08 Mike Bossy 5.00 12.00
TWJ09 Mario Lemieux 15.00 40.00
TWJ10 Billy Smith 5.00 12.00
TWJ11 Rod Langway 4.00 10.00
TWJ12 Tom Barrasso 5.00 12.00
TWJ13 Tom Barrasso 5.00 12.00
TWJ14 Mark Messier 8.00 20.00
TWJ15 Mario Lemieux 15.00 40.00
TWJ16 Pelle Lindbergh/50* 12.00 30.00
TWJ17 Paul Coffey 5.00 12.00
TWJ18 Gary Suter 3.00 8.00
TWJ19 John Vanbiesbrouck 8.00 20.00
TWJ20 Patrick Roy 12.00 30.00
TWJ21 Paul Coffey 5.00 12.00
TWJ22 Luc Robitaille 6.00 15.00
TWJ23 Ron Hextall 6.00 15.00
TWJ24 Ron Hextall 6.00 15.00
TWJ25 Joe Nieuwendyk 5.00 12.00
TWJ26 Grant Fuhr/50* 5.00 12.00
TWJ27 Raymond Bourque 8.00 20.00
TWJ28 Brian Leetch 5.00 12.00
TWJ29 Patrick Roy 12.50 30.00
TWJ30 Al MacInnis/50* 8.00 20.00

2013-14 ITG Decades 1990s

1 Brett Hull INTL 1.50 4.00
2 Al MacInnis INTL 1.50 4.00
3 Bill Ranford INTL 1.50 4.00
4 Borje Salming INTL 1.50 4.00
5 Pat LaFontaine INTL 1.50 4.00
6 Dale Hawerchuk INTL 2.00 5.00
7 Dominik Hasek INTL 2.00 5.00
8 Ed Belfour INTL 1.50 4.00
9 Eric Lindros INTL 2.50 6.00
10 Jari Kurri INTL 1.50 4.00
11 Jaromir Jagr INTL 4.00 10.00
12 Paul Coffey INTL 1.50 4.00
13 Luc Robitaille INTL 1.50 4.00
14 Mark Messier INTL 2.00 5.00
15 Mats Naslund INTL 1.50 4.00
16 Mats Sundin INTL 1.50 4.00
17 Mike Modano INTL 2.50 6.00
18 Mike Richter INTL 1.50 4.00
19 Nicklas Lidstrom INTL 1.50 4.00
20 Sergei Fedorov INTL 2.50 6.00
21 Teemu Selanne INTL 3.00 8.00
22 Teppo Numminen INTL 1.50 4.00
23 Theoren Fleury INTL 2.00 5.00
24 Tony Granato INTL 1.00 2.50
25 Adam Oates 1.50 4.00
26 Al Iafrate 1.25 3.00
27 Al MacInnis 1.50 4.00
28 Andy Moog 1.50 4.00
29 Arturs Irbe 1.25 3.00
30 Bernie Nicholls 1.25 3.00
31 Bill Ranford 1.50 4.00
32 Bob Boughner 1.00 2.50
33 Bob Essensa 1.50 4.00
34 Bob Sweeney 1.00 2.50
35 Bobby Holik 1.00 2.50
36 Brad May 1.00 2.50
37 Brian Skrudland 1.00 2.50
38 Byron Dafoe 1.50 4.00
39 Cam Neely 1.50 4.00
40 Chris Chelios 1.50 4.00
41 Chris Terreri 1.00 2.50
42 Claude Lemieux 1.25 3.00
43 Craig Billington 1.00 2.50
44 Curtis Joseph 1.50 4.00
45 Damian Rhodes 1.00 2.50
46 Dan Cloutier 1.25 3.00
47 Dave Andreychuk 1.50 4.00
48 Dave Ellett 1.00 2.50
49 Denis Savard 2.00 5.00
50 Dominik Hasek 2.00 5.00
51 Don Beaupre 1.00 2.50
52 Doug Gilmour 2.00 5.00
53 Doug Weight 1.50 4.00
54 Ed Belfour 1.50 4.00
55 Eric Lindros 2.50 6.00
56 Felix Potvin 2.50 6.00
57 Garth Snow 1.25 3.00
58 Gary Roberts 1.00 2.50
59 Gary Suter 1.00 2.50
60 Gilbert Dionne 1.25 3.00
61 Gino Odjick 1.00 2.50
62 Gordie Howe 3.00 8.00
63 Grant Fuhr 1.50 4.00
64 Greg Johnson 1.00 2.50
65 Guy Carbonneau 1.50 4.00
66 Guy Hebert 1.25 3.00
67 Igor Larionov 1.50 4.00
68 Jaromir Jagr 4.00 10.00
69 Jason Woolley 1.00 2.50
70 Jeff Odgers 1.00 2.50
71 Jeremy Roenick 1.50 4.00
72 Jim Carey 1.25 3.00
73 Jim Cummins 1.00 2.50
74 Joe Mullen 1.25 3.00
75 Joe Nieuwendyk 1.50 4.00
76 Joe Sakic 2.50 6.00
77 Joe Thornton 1.50 4.00
78 Joel Otto 1.00 2.50
79 John Cullen 1.00 2.50
80 John Druce 1.00 2.50
81 John LeClair 1.50 4.00
82 John Vanbiesbrouck 1.50 4.00
83 Keith Tkachuk 1.50 4.00
84 Kelly Buchberger 1.00 2.50
85 Kelly Chase 1.00 2.50
86 Kelly Hrudey 1.25 3.00
87 Ken Hodge, Jr. 1.00 2.50
88 Kevin Stevens 1.00 2.50
89 Kirk McLean 1.25 3.00
90 Kirk Muller 1.25 3.00
91 Kris Draper 1.25 3.00
92 Kris King 1.00 2.50
93 Kyle McLaren 1.00 2.50
94 Larry Murphy 1.50 4.00
95 Louie DeBrusk 1.00 2.50
96 Luc Robitaille 1.50 4.00
97 Lyle Odelein 1.00 2.50
98 Mario Lemieux 5.00 12.00
99 Mariusz Czerkawski 1.00 2.50
100 Mark Howe 1.50 4.00
101 Mark Messier 2.00 5.00
102 Marty McSorley 1.25 3.00
103 Mats Sundin 1.50 4.00
104 Brett Hull 1.50 4.00
105 Michael Peca 1.25 3.00
106 Mike Gartner 1.50 4.00
107 Mike Modano 2.50 6.00
108 Mike Richter 1.50 4.00
109 Nicklas Lidstrom 1.50 4.00
110 Nikolai Borschevsky 1.00 2.50
111 Nikolai Khabibulin 1.50 4.00
112 Olaf Kolzig 1.50 4.00
113 Owen Nolan 1.25 3.00
114 Pat Elynuik 1.00 2.50
115 Patrick Marleau 1.50 4.00
116 Patrick Roy 4.00 10.00
117 Paul Laus 1.00 2.50
118 Pavel Bure 2.00 5.00
119 Peter Bondra 1.50 4.00
120 Peter Forsberg 1.50 4.00
121 Peter Sidorkiewicz 1.00 2.50
122 Phil Housley 1.25 3.00
123 Ray Ferraro 1.00 2.50
124 Raymond Bourque 2.50 6.00
125 Rob Ray 1.00 2.50
126 Ron Francis 2.00 5.00
127 Ron Hextall 1.50 4.00
128 Ron Tugnutt 1.25 3.00
129 Russ Courtnall 1.25 3.00
130 Ryan VandenBussche 1.25 3.00
131 Sean Burke 1.00 2.50
132 Sergei Fedorov 2.50 6.00
133 Sergei Samsonov 1.25 3.00
134 Shayne Corson 1.00 2.50
135 Stephane Richer 1.00 2.50
136 Steve Smith 1.00 2.50
137 Steve Thomas 1.00 2.50
138 Steve Yzerman 3.00 8.00
139 Stu Grimson 1.00 2.50
140 Teemu Selanne 3.00 8.00
141 Teppo Numminen 1.50 4.00
142 Theoren Fleury 2.00 5.00
143 Tie Domi 1.50 4.00
144 Tim Cheveldae 1.50 4.00
145 Tony Amonte 1.25 3.00
146 Tony Granato 1.00 2.50
147 Trevor Linden 1.50 4.00
148 Vincent Damphousse 1.25 3.00
149 Mark Recchi 2.00 5.00
150 Warren Rychel 1.00 2.50
151 Wendel Clark 1.50 4.00
152 Wendell Young 1.00 2.50
153 Adam Graves 1.25 3.00
154 Geoff Courtnall 1.00 2.50
155 Guy Lafleur 2.00 5.00
156 Doug MacLean DC 1.00 2.50
157 Jacques Lemaire DC 1.50 4.00
158 Mike Keenan DC 1.25 3.00
159 Pat Quinn DC 1.50 4.00
160 Scotty Bowman DC 1.50 4.00
161 Ted Nolan DC 1.25 3.00
162 Mario Lemieux DYN 5.00 12.00
163 Jaromir Jagr DYN 4.00 10.00
164 Bryan Trottier DYN 2.00 5.00
165 Kevin Stevens DYN 1.00 2.50
166 Joe Mullen DYN 1.25 3.00
167 Steve Yzerman DYN 3.00 8.00
168 Nicklas Lidstrom DYN 1.50 4.00
169 Igor Larionov DYN 1.50 4.00
170 Darren McCarty DYN 1.25 3.00
171 Sergei Fedorov DYN 2.50 6.00
172 Eric Lindros FRP 2.50 6.00
173 Jaromir Jagr FRP 4.00 10.00
174 Joe Thornton FRP 1.50 4.00
175 Keith Tkachuk FRP 1.50 4.00
176 Owen Nolan FRP 1.25 3.00
177 Patrick Marleau FRP 1.50 4.00
178 Peter Forsberg FRP 1.50 4.00
179 Roberto Luongo FRP 1.50 4.00
180 Scott Niedermayer FRP 1.50 4.00
181 B.Probert/T.Domi ENF 1.50 4.00
182 P.Roy/C.Osgood ENF 4.00 10.00
183 J.Kocur/K.Bchbrgr ENF 1.00 2.50
184 K.Chase/C.Berube ENF 1.00 2.50
185 J.Odgers/G.Odjick ENF 1.00 2.50
186 C.Lemieux/D.McCarty ENF 1.25 3.00
187 F.Potvin/R.Hextall ENF 2.50 6.00
188 S.Grimson/B.Probert ENF 1.50 4.00
189 R.Ray/T.Domi ENF 1.50 4.00
190 M.McSorley/W.Clark ENF 1.50 4.00
191 B.Ranford/R.Bourque CC 2.50 6.00
192 M.Lemieux/M.Modano CC 5.00 12.00
193 R.Francis/J.Roenick CC 2.00 5.00
194 P.Roy/L.Robitaille CC 4.00 10.00
195 P.Bure/M.Richter CC 2.00 5.00
196 C.Lemieux/N.Lidstrom CC 1.50 4.00
197 J.Sakic/J.Vnbsbrck CC 2.50 6.00
198 M.Vernon/E.Lindros CC 2.50 6.00
199 S.Yzrmn/A.Oates CC 3.00 8.00
200 B.Hull/D.Hasek CC 2.00 5.00

2013-14 ITG Decades 1990s Gold

GOLD/30: .6X TO 1.5X BASIC CARDS

2013-14 ITG Decades 1990s All Stars Quad Jerseys Black

SILVER/30: .5X TO 1.2X BLACK/95*
AS01 McInns/Jsph/Rnck/Brque 15.00 40.00
AS02 Fdrv/Lmeux/Ptvn/Chlios 12.00 30.00
AS03 Hsek/Nlan/Flry/Yzrmn 15.00 40.00
AS04 Lndrs/Skic/Khbbln/Jagr 25.00 60.00
AS05 Ldstrm/Sndin/Tkchk/Mdno 12.00 30.00
AS06 Slnne/Irbe/Rcchi/Roy 15.00 40.00
AS07 Hull/Mssier/Blfr/Osgd 12.00 30.00
AS08 Bure/LeClr/Ndrmyr/Frsbrg 12.00 30.00

2013-14 ITG Decades 1990s Autographs

THREE AUTOS PER PACK
AAI Al Iafrate 5.00 12.00
AAI Arturs Irbe 8.00 20.00
AAM Al MacInnis 12.00 30.00
AAMO Andy Moog 6.00 15.00
AAO Adam Oates 6.00 15.00
ABB Bob Boughner 4.00 10.00
ABD Byron Dafoe 6.00 15.00
ABE Bob Essensa 6.00 15.00
ABH Brett Hull SP 30.00 80.00
ABHAO B.Hull/A.Oates SP 175.00 300.00
ABHO Bobby Holik 4.00 10.00
ABL Brian Leetch SP 25.00 60.00
ABM Brad May 4.00 10.00
ABN Bernie Nicholls 5.00 12.00
ABR Bill Ranford 6.00 15.00
ABS Brian Skrudland 4.00 10.00
ABS Bob Sweeney 4.00 10.00
ACB Craig Billington 4.00 10.00
ACC Chris Chelios SP 25.00 50.00
ACJ Curtis Joseph 12.00 30.00
ACL Claude Lemieux 5.00 12.00
ACN Cam Neely SP 15.00 40.00
ACT Chris Terreri 4.00 10.00
ADA Dave Andreychuk 6.00 15.00
ADB Don Beaupre 4.00 10.00
ADC Dan Cloutier 5.00 12.00
ADE Dave Ellett 4.00 10.00
ADG Doug Gilmour 12.00 30.00
ADGWC D.Gilmour/W.Clark SP
ADH Dominik Hasek SP 40.00 80.00
ADM Doug MacLean 4.00 10.00
ADR Damian Rhodes 4.00 10.00
ADS Denis Savard 8.00 20.00
ADW Doug Weight 6.00 15.00
AEB Ed Belfour SP 15.00 40.00
AED Eric Desjardins 5.00 12.00
AFP Felix Potvin 15.00 40.00
AGC Guy Carbonneau 6.00 15.00
AGCO Geoff Courtnall 4.00 10.00
AGD Gilbert Dionne 5.00 12.00
AGF Grant Fuhr 20.00 40.00
AGH Gordie Howe SP 175.00 300.00
AGHE Guy Hebert 5.00 12.00
AGJ Greg Johnson 4.00 10.00
AGO Gino Odjick 6.00 15.00
AGR Gary Roberts 8.00 20.00
AGS Garth Snow 5.00 12.00
AGSU Gary Suter 4.00 10.00
AIL Igor Larionov 10.00 25.00
AJC Jim Carey 5.00 12.00
AJCU John Cullen 4.00 10.00
AJCUM Jim Cummins 4.00 10.00
AJD John Druce 4.00 10.00
AJD Jacques Demers 6.00 15.00
AJJ Jaromir Jagr SP 60.00 120.00
AJL Jacques Lemaire 6.00 15.00
AJL John LeClair 6.00 15.00
AJM Joe Mullen 5.00 12.00
AJN Joe Nieuwendyk 12.00 30.00
AJO Jeff Odgers 4.00 10.00
AJOT Joel Otto 4.00 10.00
AJR Jeremy Roenick 12.00 30.00
AJS Joe Sakic SP 40.00 100.00
AJSPF J.Sakic/P.Forsberg SP 30.00 60.00
AJT Joe Thornton SP 25.00 50.00
AJV John Vanbiesbrouck 15.00 30.00
AJW Jason Woolley 4.00 10.00
AKB Kelly Buchberger 4.00 10.00
AKC Kelly Chase 4.00 10.00
AKD Kris Draper 5.00 12.00
AKH Kelly Hrudey 5.00 12.00
AKHJR Ken Hodge, Jr. 4.00 10.00
AKK Kris King 4.00 10.00
AKM Kyle McLaren 4.00 10.00
AKM Kirk Muller 5.00 12.00
AKS Kevin Stevens 4.00 10.00
AKT Keith Tkachuk 8.00 20.00
ALD Louis DeBrusk
ALM Larry Murphy 6.00 15.00
ALO Lyle Odelein 4.00 10.00
ALR Luc Robitaille 10.00 25.00
AMC Mariusz Czerkawski 4.00 10.00
AMG Mike Gartner 10.00 25.00
AMH Mark Howe 6.00 15.00
AMK Mike Keenan 8.00 20.00
AML Mario Lemieux SP
AMM Mike Modano SP 25.00 50.00
AMMC Marty McSorley 5.00 12.00
AMMC Kirk McLean 5.00 12.00
AMME Mark Messier SP 40.00 80.00
AMP Michael Peca 5.00 12.00
AMR Mike Richter 15.00 40.00
AMRE Mark Recchi SP 15.00 40.00
AMS1 Mats Sundin SP 40.00 100.00
AMS2 Mats Sundin SP 40.00 100.00
ANB Nikolai Borschevsky 4.00 10.00
ANK Nikolai Khabibulin 6.00 15.00

NL Nicklas Lidstrom SP 30.00 60.00
OK Olaf Kolzig 6.00 15.00
ON Owen Nolan 5.00 12.00
PB Pavel Bure SP 40.00 80.00
PBO Peter Bondra 6.00 15.00
PE Pat Elynuik 4.00 10.00
PF Peter Forsberg SP 40.00 80.00
PH Phil Housley 5.00 12.00
PLA Paul Laus 4.00 10.00
PM Patrick Marleau 6.00 15.00
PQ Pat Quinn 6.00 15.00
PR Patrick Roy SP 60.00 100.00
PS Peter Sidorkiewicz 4.00 10.00
RB Raymond Bourque SP 40.00 80.00
RC Russ Courtnall 8.00 20.00
RF Ron Francis 12.00 30.00
RFE Ray Ferraro 4.00 10.00
RH Ron Hextall 12.00 30.00
RR Rob Ray 4.00 10.00
RT Ron Tugnutt 5.00 12.00
RV Ryan VandenBussche 5.00 12.00
SB Scotty Bowman 6.00 15.00
SB Sean Burke 4.00 10.00
SC Shayne Corson 5.00 12.00
SF Sergei Fedorov SP 60.00 120.00
SG Stu Grimson 4.00 10.00
SR Stephane Richer 8.00 20.00
SS Sergei Samsonov 5.00 12.00
SSM Steve Smith 4.00 10.00
ST Steve Thomas 4.00 10.00
SY Steve Yzerman 40.00 100.00
TA Tony Amonte 5.00 12.00
TB Tom Barrasso SP 30.00 60.00
TC Tim Cheveldae 6.00 15.00
TD Tie Domi 8.00 20.00
TF Theoren Fleury 8.00 20.00
TG Tony Granato 4.00 10.00
TL Trevor Linden 15.00 30.00
TN Ted Nolan 5.00 12.00
TNU Teppo Numminen 6.00 15.00
TS Teemu Selanne 25.00 50.00
VD Vincent Damphousse 8.00 20.00
VL Vincent Lecavalier SP 15.00 40.00
WC Wendel Clark SP 25.00 50.00
WR Warren Rychel 4.00 10.00
WY Wendell Young 4.00 10.00
EL Eric Lindros SP 30.00 60.00

2013-14 ITG Decades 1990s Between the Pipes Jerseys Black

SILVER/30: .6X TO 1.5X BLACK/80*
BTPJ01 Arturs Irbe 6.00 15.00
BTPJ02 Chris Osgood 4.00 10.00
BTPJ03 Curtis Joseph 4.00 10.00
BTPJ04 Dominik Hasek 5.00 12.00
BTPJ05 Felix Potvin 6.00 15.00
BTPJ06 John Vanbiesbrouck 6.00 15.00
BTPJ07 Mike Richter 4.00 10.00
BTPJ08 Nikolai Khabibulin 4.00 10.00
BTPJ09 Olaf Kolzig 4.00 10.00
BTPJ10 Patrick Roy 10.00 25.00
BTPJ11 Ron Hextall 4.00 10.00
BTPJ12 Tom Barrasso 5.00 12.00

2013-14 ITG Decades 1990s Cup Clashes Quad Jerseys Black

SILVER/30: .5X TO 1.2X BLACK/80*
CC01 Msser/Fhr/Neely/Brque 15.00 40.00
CC02 Lmeux/Brrsso/Mdno/Bllws 12.00 30.00
CC03 Lmeux/Frncs /Rnck/Blfr 15.00 40.00
CC04 Roy/Mller/Rbtlle/Kurri 10.00 25.00
CC05 Rchtr/Msser/Bure/Lnden 12.00 30.00
CC06 Hlik/Ndrmyr/Cccrlli/Fdrv 15.00 40.00
CC07 Roy/Skic/Vnbsbrck/Laus 15.00 40.00
CC08 Yzrmn/Vrnon/LeClr/Lndrs 15.00 40.00
CC09 Yzrmn/Ldstrm/Klzg/Bndra 15.00 40.00
CC10 Hull/Blfr/Hsek/Peca 12.00 30.00

2013-14 ITG Decades 1990s Entire Decade Jerseys Black

SILVER/30: .6X TO 1.5X BLACK JSY/87*
ED01 Olaf Kolzig 4.00 10.00
ED02 Steve Yzerman 10.00 25.00
ED03 Tom Barrasso 4.00 10.00
ED04 Rob Ray 2.50 6.00
ED05 Mike Richter 4.00 10.00
ED06 Raymond Bourque 6.00 15.00
ED07 Mike Modano 6.00 15.00
ED08 Joe Sakic 6.00 15.00

2013-14 ITG Decades 1990s European Influence Dual Jerseys Black

SILVER/30: .6X TO 1.5X BLACK.80*
EI01 J.Jagr/N.Khabibulin 8.00 20.00
EI02 D.Hasek/A.Irbe 10.00 25.00
EI03 M.Sundin/S.Fedorov 12.00 30.00
EI04 O.Kolzig/T.Selanne 15.00 40.00
EI05 T.Holmstrom/P.Bure 10.00 25.00
EI06 N.Lidstrom/P.Forsberg 8.00 20.00

2013-14 ITG Decades 1990s For Your Country Quad Jerseys Black

SILVER/30: .5X TO 1.2X BLACK/85*
FYCJ01 Lndrs/Skic/Cffy/Yzrmn 20.00 50.00
FYCJ02 Roy/Brque/Mssr/Flry 12.00 30.00
FYCJ03 Rchtr/Rnck/Hull/Mdno 12.00 30.00
FYCJ04 Fdrv/Lrnov/Bure/Khbbln 15.00 40.00
FYCJ05 Ldstrm/Frsbrg/Sndn/Nslnd 12.00 30.00
FYCJ06 Nmmnen/Slnne/Krri/Tkknn 15.00 40.00

2013-14 ITG Decades 1990s Franchises Quad Jerseys Black

SILVER/30: .5X TO 1.2X BLACK/95*
F01 Brque/Neely/Thrntn/Oates 15.00 40.00
F02 Flry/Vrnon/McInns/Nwndk 10.00 25.00
F03 Blfr/Rnck/Glet/Chlios 10.00 25.00
F04 Yzrmn/Ldstrm/Osgd/Vrnon 12.00 30.00
F05 Mssr/Jsph/Wght/Rnfrd 12.00 30.00
F06 Rbtlle/Hrdy/Krri/McSrly 10.00 25.00
F07 Mdno/Blfr/Nuwndk/Hull 15.00 40.00
F08 Roy/Mller/Crbnnu/Crsn 12.00 30.00
F09 Lmeux/Brrsso/Frncs/Jagr 15.00 40.00
F10 Roy/Frsbrg/Skic/Odgrs 12.00 30.00
F11 Hull/Jsph/Chse/McInns 10.00 25.00
F12 Ptvn/Glmr/Clrk/Sndn 12.00 30.00
F13 Bure/Lndn/Mssr/Odjck 10.00 25.00
F14 Slnne/Tkchk/Khbbln/Chvlde 20.00 50.00

2013-14 ITG Decades 1990s Game Used Jerseys Black

SILVER/30: .6X TO 1.5X BLACK/84*
M01 Adam Oates 4.00 10.00
M02 Bernie Nicholls 3.00 8.00
M03 Brett Hull 6.00 15.00
M04 Cam Neely 5.00 12.00
M05 Chris Chelios 4.00 10.00
M06 Curtis Joseph 4.00 10.00
M07 Dominik Hasek 5.00 12.00
M08 Doug Gilmour 5.00 12.00
M09 Ed Belfour 4.00 10.00
M10 Eric Lindros 6.00 15.00
M11 Felix Potvin 6.00 15.00
M12 Jaromir Jagr 10.00 25.00
M13 Jeremy Roenick 4.00 10.00
M14 Joe Nieuwendyk 4.00 10.00
M15 Joe Sakic 6.00 15.00
M16 Joe Thornton 4.00 10.00
M17 John LeClair 4.00 10.00
M18 John Vanbiesbrouck 6.00 15.00
M19 Keith Tkachuk 4.00 10.00
M20 Larry Murphy 4.00 10.00
M21 Luc Robitaille 4.00 10.00
M22 Mario Lemieux 12.00 30.00
M23 Mark Messier 5.00 12.00
M24 Mats Sundin 4.00 10.00
M25 Michael Peca 3.00 8.00
M26 Mike Modano 6.00 15.00
M27 Mike Richter 4.00 10.00
M28 Nicklas Lidstrom 5.00 12.00
M29 Olaf Kolzig 4.00 10.00
M30 Patrick Roy 10.00 25.00
M31 Pavel Bure 5.00 12.00
M32 Peter Bondra 5.00 12.00
M33 Peter Forsberg 4.00 10.00
M34 Raymond Bourque 6.00 15.00
M35 Ron Francis 5.00 12.00
M36 Ron Hextall 4.00 10.00
M37 Sergei Fedorov 5.00 12.00
M38 Sergei Samsonov 3.00 8.00
M39 Steve Yzerman 8.00 20.00
M40 Teemu Selanne 8.00 20.00
M41 Teppo Numminen 5.00 12.00
M42 Theoren Fleury 5.00 12.00
M43 Tie Domi 4.00 10.00
M44 Trevor Linden 5.00 12.00
M45 Wendel Clark 4.00 10.00

2013-14 ITG Decades 1990s Masks

DM01 Andy Moog 2.50 6.00
DM02 Arturs Irbe 2.00 5.00
DM03 Bill Ranford 2.50 6.00
DM04 Bob Essensa 2.50 6.00
DM05 Brian Hayward 2.00 5.00
DM06 Curtis Joseph 2.50 6.00
DM07 Ed Belfour 2.50 6.00
DM08 Felix Potvin 4.00 10.00
DM09 Grant Fuhr 2.50 6.00
DM10 Guy Hebert 2.00 5.00
DM11 Jim Carey 2.00 5.00
DM12 John Vanbiesbrouck 2.50 6.00
DM13 Kelly Hrudey 2.00 5.00
DM14 Kirk McLean 2.00 5.00
DM15 Mike Richter 2.50 6.00
DM16 Mike Vernon 2.00 5.00
DM17 Patrick Roy 6.00 15.00
DM18 Patrick Roy 6.00 15.00
DM19 Ron Hextall 2.50 6.00
DM20 Ron Tugnutt 2.00 5.00
DM21 Sean Burke 1.50 4.00
DM22 Tom Barrasso 2.50 6.00

2013-14 ITG Decades 1990s Rivalries Quad Jerseys Black

SILVER/30: .5X TO 1.2X BLACK/95*
R1 Rnfrd/Mssr/Flry/McInns 12.00 30.00
R2 Skc/Roy/Yzrmn/Osgd 15.00 40.00
R3 Skrdlnd/Crbnnau/Nly/Brque 10.00 25.00
R4 Hsek/Ray/Domi/Jsph 10.00 25.00
R5 Chlos/Rnck/Ldstrm/Yzrmn 15.00 40.00
R6 Hull/Jsph/Glmr/Ptvn 15.00 40.00
R7 Mller/Roy/Skic/Nlan 10.00 25.00
R8 Lmeux/Jagr/Mssr/Rchtr 12.00 30.00

2013-14 ITG Decades 1990s Rookie and Retired Dual Jerseys Black

SILVER/30: .5X TO 1.2X BLACK/80*
RRDM01 M.Sundin/G.Lafleur 6.00 15.00
RRDM02 E.Lindros/R.Langway 8.00 20.00
RRDM03 C.Osgood/M.Goulet 5.00 12.00
RRDM04 D.McCarty/D.Taylor 5.00 12.00
RRDM05 N.Khabibulin/T.Steen 5.00 12.00
RRDM06 T.Holmstrom/D.Savard 6.00 15.00

2013-14 ITG Decades 1990s Rookies

DR01 Curtis Joseph 1.50 4.00
DR02 Mats Sundin 1.50 4.00
DR03 Owen Nolan 1.25 3.00
DR04 Sergei Fedorov 2.50 6.00
DR05 Jaromir Jagr 4.00 10.00
DR06 Peter Bondra 1.50 4.00
DR07 Dominik Hasek 2.00 5.00
DR08 John LeClair 1.50 4.00
DR09 Tony Amonte 1.25 3.00
DR10 Nicklas Lidstrom 1.50 4.00
DR11 Scott Niedermayer 1.50 4.00
DR12 Pavel Bure 2.00 5.00
DR13 Arturs Irbe 1.25 3.00
DR14 Felix Potvin 2.50 6.00
DR15 Keith Tkachuk 1.50 4.00
DR16 Eric Lindros 2.50 6.00
DR17 Teemu Selanne 3.00 8.00
DR18 Chris Osgood 1.50 4.00
DR19 Peter Forsberg 1.50 4.00
DR20 Tomas Holmstrom 1.00 2.50
DR21 Sergei Samsonov 1.25 3.00
DR22 Joe Thornton 1.50 4.00
DR23 Roberto Luongo 1.50 4.00

2013-14 ITG Decades 1990s Trophy Winners Jerseys Black

SILVER/30: .6X TO 1.5X BLACK/80*
TW01 Dominik Hasek 5.00 12.00
TW02 Ed Belfour 4.00 10.00
TW03 Steve Yzerman 8.00 20.00
TW04 Jaromir Jagr 10.00 25.00
TW05 Joe Sakic 6.00 15.00
TW06 Mario Lemieux 12.00 30.00
TW07 Mark Messier 5.00 12.00
TW08 Patrick Roy 10.00 25.00
TW09 Pavel Bure 8.00 20.00
TW10 Eric Lindros 6.00 15.00
TW11 Teemu Selanne 5.00 12.00
TW12 Sergei Fedorov 8.00 20.00

2012-13 ITG Draft Prospects

1 Adam Erne 1.25 3.00
2 Aleksander Barkov 3.00 8.00
3 Alexander Wennberg 1.25 3.00
4 Anthony Duclair 2.00 5.00
5 Anthony Mantha 2.00 5.00
6 Bo Horvat 2.50 6.00
7 Brody Silk .75 2.00
8 Connor Rankin .75 2.00
9 Curtis Lazar 1.50 4.00
10 Darnell Nurse 1.50 4.00
11 Dillon Heatherington 1.25 3.00
12 Elias Lindholm 2.00 5.00
13 Eric ComrieÂ• 1.25 3.00
14 Eric Roy 1.25 3.00
15 Frederik Gauthier 2.00 5.00
16 Hunter Shinkaruk 2.00 5.00
17 Jackson Whistle .75 2.00
18 Jacob de la Rose 1.50 4.00
19 Jason Dickinson 1.00 2.50
20 Jonathan Drouin 4.00 10.00
21 Jordan Subban 1.50 4.00
22 Josh Morrissey 1.25 3.00
23 Justin Bailey 1.00 2.50
24 Kerby Rychel 1.25 3.00
25 Madison Bowey 1.25 3.00
26 Max Domi 2.50 6.00
27 Morgan Klimchuk 1.25 3.00
28 Nathan MacKinnon 4.00 10.00
29 Nicolas Petan 1.25 3.00
30 Nicholas Baptiste 1.00 2.50
31 Nick Sorensen 1.25 3.00
32 Nikita Zadorov 1.25 3.00
33 Rasmus Ristolainen 2.00 5.00
34 Robert Hagg 2.00 5.00
35 Ryan Hartman 1.25 3.00
36 Ryan Kujawinski 1.00 2.50
37 Ryan Pulock 1.50 4.00
38 Samuel Morin 1.50 4.00
39 Sean Monahan 3.00 8.00
40 Sergey Tolchinsky .75 2.00
41 Seth Jones 3.00 8.00
42 Shea Theodore 1.25 3.00
43 Spencer MartinÂ• 1.00 2.50
44 Stephen Harper 1.50 4.00
45 Tristan Jarry 1.25 3.00
46 Valentin Zykov 1.50 4.00
47 William Carrier 1.25 3.00
48 Zachary FucaleÂ• 2.50 6.00
49 Mirco Mueller 1.50 4.00
50 Chris Bigras 1.00 2.50
51 Marc-Olivier Roy 1.25 3.00
52 Mitchell Wheaton 1.00 2.50
53 Zach Nastasiuk 1.25 3.00
54 Gabryel Paquin-Boudreau 1.00 2.50
55 Philippe Desrosiers 1.00 2.50
56 Jimmy Lodge 1.25 3.00
57 Oliver Bjorkstrand .75 2.00
58 Laurent Dauphin .75 2.00
59 Michael Giugovaz .75 2.00
60 Aaron Ekblad FDP 4.00 10.00
61 Alexis Pepin FDP 1.00 2.50
62 Anthony DeAngelo FDP .75 2.00
63 Blake Clarke FDP 1.25 3.00
64 Brandon Robinson FDP 1.00 2.50
65 Brayden Point FDP 1.25 3.00
66 Brycen Martin FDP 1.25 3.00
67 Daniel Audette FDP 1.50 4.00
68 Eric Cornel FDP 1.00 2.50
69 Haydn Fleury FDP 1.25 3.00
70 Ivan Barbashev FDP 1.25 3.00
71 Jake Virtanen FDP 1.50 4.00
72 Jared McCann FDP 1.25 3.00
73 Jordan Thomson FDP 1.00 2.50
74 Josh Ho-Sang FDP 1.50 4.00
75 Leon Draisaitl FDP 2.50 6.00
76 Matt Mistele FDP 1.00 2.50
77 Michael Dal Colle FDP 1.00 2.50
78 Nick Ritchie FDP 1.25 3.00
79 Nikolay Goldobin FDP 1.25 3.00
80 Robby Fabbri FDP 1.00 2.50
81 Roland McKeown FDP 1.00 2.50
82 Sam Bennett FDP 2.00 5.00
83 Sam Reinhart FDP 4.00 10.00
84 Connor McDavid FDP 12.50 25.00
85 Travis Konecny FDP 2.50 6.00
86 Dylan Strome FDP 3.00 8.00
87 Sean Day FDP 2.50 6.00
88 Tyler Benson FDP 3.00 8.00
89 Sam Steel FDP 2.50 6.00
90 Alexander Ovechkin FRP 5.00 12.00
91 Bobby Smith FRP 1.00 2.50
92 Brad Park FRP 1.00 2.50
93 Brian Bellows FRP 1.00 2.50
94 Cam Neely FRP 1.25 3.00
95 Carey Price FRP 4.00 10.00
96 Al MacInnis FRP 1.25 3.00
97 Dale Hawerchuk FRP 1.50 4.00
98 Daniel Sedin FRP 1.25 3.00
99 Darryl Sittler FRP 1.25 3.00
100 Denis Savard FRP 1.50 4.00
101 Eric Lindros FRP 2.00 5.00
102 Evgeni Malkin FRP 4.00 10.00
103 Gary Roberts FRP .75 2.00
104 Gilbert Perreault FRP 1.25 3.00
105 Grant Fuhr FRP 1.25 3.00
106 Guy Lafleur FRP 1.50 4.00
107 Henrik Sedin FRP 1.25 3.00
108 Jaromir Jagr FRP 3.00 8.00
109 Jeremy Roenick FRP 1.25 3.00
111 Joe Sakic FRP 2.00 5.00
112 Joe Thornton FRP 1.25 3.00
113 Kari Lehtonen FRP 1.00 2.50
114 Keith Primeau FRP 1.00 2.50
116 Kirk Muller FRP 1.00 2.50
117 Lanny McDonald FRP 1.25 3.00
118 Larry Murphy FRP 1.25 3.00
119 Marc-Andre Fleury FRP 2.00 5.00
120 Marcel Dionne FRP 1.50 4.00
121 Marian Gaborik FRP 1.25 3.00
122 Mario Lemieux FRP 4.00 10.00
123 Mats Sundin FRP 1.25 3.00
124 Mike Bossy FRP 1.25 3.00
125 Mike Gartner FRP 1.25 3.00
126 Mike Modano FRP 2.00 5.00
127 Niklas Kronwall FRP 1.00 2.50
128 Olaf Kolzig FRP 1.25 3.00
129 Owen Nolan FRP 1.00 2.50
130 Pat LaFontaine FRP 1.25 3.00
131 Patrick Marleau FRP 1.25 3.00
132 Paul Coffey FRP 1.25 3.00
133 Peter Forsberg FRP 1.25 3.00
134 Raymond Bourque FRP 2.00 5.00
136 Roberto Luongo FRP 1.25 3.00
138 Ron Francis FRP 1.50 4.00
139 Scott Niedermayer FRP 1.25 3.00
140 Semyon Varlamov FRP 1.25 3.00
141 Steve Yzerman FRP 2.50 6.00
142 Teemu Selanne FRP 2.50 6.00
143 Trevor Linden FRP 1.25 3.00
144 Vincent Damphousse FRP 1.00 2.50
145 Wendel Clark FRP 1.25 3.00
146 Mark Scheifele FRP 1.50 4.00
147 Ryan Strome FRP 1.50 4.00
148 Ryan Murphy FRP 1.25 3.00
149 Phillip Danault FRP 1.00 2.50
150 Malcolm Subban FRP 1.50 4.00
151 Morgan Rielly FRP 1.50 4.00
152 Ryan Murray FRP 1.50 4.00
153 Griffin Reinhart FRP 1.25 3.00
154 Mathew Dumba FRP 1.25 3.00
155 Derrick Pouliot FRP 1.50 4.00
156 Peter Bondra DS 1.25 3.00
157 Jari Kurri DS 1.25 3.00
158 Sergei Fedorov DS 2.00 5.00
159 Jonathan Quick DS 2.00 5.00
160 Nicklas Lidstrom DS 1.25 3.00
161 Mark Messier DS 1.50 4.00
162 Mark Recchi DS 1.50 4.00
163 Theoren Fleury DS 1.50 4.00
164 Patrick Roy DS 3.00 8.00
165 Henrik Lundqvist DS 1.50 4.00
166 Luc Robitaille DS 1.25 3.00
167 Doug Gilmour DS 1.50 4.00
168 Brett Hull DS 1.25 3.00
169 Dominik Hasek DS 1.50 4.00
170 Pavel Bure DS 1.50 4.00
171 Ilya Bryzgalov DS 1.25 3.00
172 Bernie Nicholls DS 1.00 2.50
173 Shea Weber DS 1.00 2.50
174 Tony Amonte DS 1.00 2.50
175 Ron Hextall DS 1.25 3.00
176 Evgeni Nabokov DS 1.00 2.50
177 Glenn Anderson DS 1.25 3.00
178 Igor Larionov DS 1.25 3.00
179 Tomas Holmstrom DS .75 2.00
180 Joe Nieuwendyk DS 1.25 3.00

2012-13 ITG Draft Prospects Emerald

EMERALD/50: .5X TO 1.2X BASIC CARDS

2012-13 ITG Draft Prospects Autographs

THREE AUTOS PER BOX OVERALL
EACH HAS TWO CARDS OF EQUAL VALUE
GOLD/20: .6X TO 1.5X BASIC AU
GOLD/20: .5X TO 1.2X BASIC AU SP
AAB Aleksander Barkov 20.00 40.00
AAB2 Aleksander Barkov 20.00 40.00
AAD Anthony Duclair 8.00 20.00
AAD2 Anthony Duclair 8.00 20.00
AAE Aaron Ekblad 10.00 25.00
AAE2 Aaron Ekblad 10.00 25.00
AAER Adam Erne 5.00 12.00
AAER2 Adam Erne 5.00 12.00
AAM Anthony Mantha 8.00 20.00
AAM2 Anthony Mantha 8.00 20.00
AAW Alexander Wennberg 5.00 12.00
AAW2 Alexander Wennberg 5.00 12.00
ABH Bo Horvat 10.00 25.00
ABH2 Bo Horvat 10.00 25.00
ABS Brody Silk 3.00 8.00
ABS2 Brody Silk 3.00 8.00
ACL Curtis Lazar 6.00 15.00
ACL2 Curtis Lazar 6.00 15.00
ACM Connor McDavid 100.00 175.00
ACM2 Connor McDavid 100.00 175.00
ACR Connor Rankin 3.00 8.00
ACR2 Connor Rankin 3.00 8.00
ADH Dillon Heatherington 5.00 12.00
ADH2 Dillon Heatherington 5.00 12.00
ADN Darnell Nurse 6.00 15.00
ADN2 Darnell Nurse 6.00 15.00
ADS Dylan Strome 10.00 25.00
ADS2 Dylan Strome 10.00 25.00
AEC Eric Comrie 5.00 12.00
AEC2 Eric Comrie 5.00 12.00
AEL Elias Lindholm 6.00 15.00
AEL2 Elias Lindholm 6.00 15.00
AER Eric Roy 5.00 12.00
AER2 Eric Roy 5.00 12.00
AFG Frederik Gauthier 8.00 20.00
AFG2 Frederik Gauthier 8.00 20.00
AHS Hunter Shinkaruk 6.00 15.00
AHS2 Hunter Shinkaruk 6.00 15.00
AJB Justin Bailey 4.00 10.00
AJB2 Justin Bailey 4.00 10.00
AJD Jonathan Drouin SP 30.00 80.00
AJD2 Jonathan Drouin SP 30.00 80.00
AJDI Jason Dickinson 4.00 10.00
AJDI2 Jason Dickinson 4.00 10.00
AJDLR Jacob de la Rose 8.00 20.00
AJDLR2 Jacob de la Rose 8.00 20.00
AJG Jeremy Gregoire 4.00 10.00
AJG2 Jeremy Gregoire 4.00 10.00
AJM Josh Morrissey 5.00 12.00
AJM2 Josh Morrissey 5.00 12.00
AJS Jordan Subban 6.00 15.00
AJS2 Jordan Subban 5.00 12.00
AJW Jackson Whistle 3.00 8.00
AJW2 Jackson Whistle 3.00 8.00
AKR Kerby Rychel 5.00 12.00
AKR2 Kerby Rychel 5.00 12.00
AMB Madison Bowey 5.00 12.00
AMB2 Madison Bowey 5.00 12.00
AMD Max Domi 10.00 25.00
AMD2 Max Domi 10.00 25.00
AMG Morgan Klimchuk 5.00 12.00
AMG2 Morgan Klimchuk 5.00 12.00
AMM Mirco Mueller 6.00 15.00
AMM2 Mirco Mueller 6.00 15.00
ANB Nicholas Baptiste 4.00 10.00
ANB2 Nicholas Baptiste 4.00 10.00
ANM Nathan MacKinnon SP 30.00 80.00
ANM2 Nathan MacKinnon SP 30.00 80.00
ANP Nicolas Petan 5.00 12.00
ANP2 Nicolas Petan 5.00 12.00
ANS Nick Sorensen 5.00 12.00
ANS2 Nick Sorensen 5.00 12.00
ANZ Nikita Zadorov 5.00 12.00
ANZ2 Nikita Zadorov 5.00 12.00
ARH Robert Hagg 8.00 20.00
ARH2 Robert Hagg 8.00 20.00
ARHA Ryan Hartman 5.00 12.00
ARHA2 Ryan Hartman 5.00 12.00
ARK Ryan Kujawinski 4.00 10.00
ARK2 Ryan Kujawinski 4.00 10.00
ARP Ryan Pulock 6.00 15.00
ARP2 Ryan Pulock 5.00 12.00
ARR Rasmus Ristolainen 8.00 20.00
ARR2 Rasmus Ristolainen 8.00 20.00
ASD Sean Day 12.00 30.00
ASD2 Sean Day 12.00 30.00
ASH Stephen Harper 6.00 15.00
ASH2 Stephen Harper 6.00 15.00
ASJ Seth Jones SP 30.00 60.00
ASJ2 Seth Jones SP 30.00 60.00
ASM Spencer Martin 4.00 10.00
ASM2 Spencer Martin 4.00 10.00
ASMO Samuel Morin 6.00 15.00
ASMO2 Samuel Morin 6.00 15.00
ASMON Sean Monahan 8.00 20.00
ASMON2 Sean Monahan 8.00 20.00
ASS Sam Steel 10.00 25.00
ASS2 Sam Steel 10.00 25.00
AST Shea Theodore 5.00 12.00
AST2 Shea Theodore 5.00 12.00
ATB Tyler Benson 12.00 30.00
ATB2 Tyler Benson 12.00 30.00
ATJ Tristan Jarry 5.00 12.00
ATJ2 Tristan Jarry 5.00 12.00
ATK Travis Konecny 10.00 25.00
ATK2 Travis Konecny 10.00 25.00
AVZ Valentin Zykov 8.00 20.00
AVZ2 Valentin Zykov 8.00 20.00
AWC William Carrier 5.00 12.00
AWC2 William Carrier 5.00 12.00
AZF Zachary Fucale 15.00 40.00
AZF2 Zachary Fucale 15.00 40.00

2012-13 ITG Draft Prospects Country of Origin Jerseys

ANNOUNCED PRINT RUN 90
CO001 Seth Jones 8.00 20.00
CO002 Nathan MacKinnon 10.00 25.00
CO003 Jonathan Drouin 8.00 20.00
CO004 Robert Hagg 5.00 12.00
CO005 Valentin Zykov 4.00 10.00
CO006 Nikita Zadorov 3.00 8.00
CO007 Sergey Tolchinsky 3.00 8.00
CO008 Aleksander Barkov 8.00 20.00

2012-13 ITG Draft Prospects Draft Year Jerseys

ANNOUNCED PRINT RUN 100
DY01 Connor McDavid 15.00 40.00
DY02 Jake Virtanen 6.00 15.00
DY03 Robert Hagg 6.00 15.00
DY04 Hunter Shinkaruk 8.00 20.00
DY05 Curtis Lazar 6.00 15.00
DY06 Morgan Klimchuk 5.00 12.00
DY07 Nikita Zadorov 5.00 12.00
DY08 Darnell Nurse 6.00 15.00
DY09 Justin Bailey 4.00 10.00
DY10 Seth Jones 12.00 30.00
DY11 Nathan MacKinnon 12.00 30.00
DY12 Jonathan Drouin 12.00 30.00
DY13 Jacob de la Rose 6.00 15.00
DY14 Aleksander Barkov 10.00 25.00
DY15 Carey Price 15.00 40.00
DY16 Jonathan Quick 8.00 20.00
DY17 Alexander Ovechkin 20.00 50.00
DY18 Evgeni Malkin 15.00 40.00
DY19 Marc-Andre Fleury 8.00 20.00
DY20 Jimmy Howard 5.00 12.00
DY21 Daniel Sedin 5.00 12.00
DY22 Henrik Sedin 5.00 12.00
DY23 Joe Thornton 5.00 12.00
DY24 Roberto Luongo 5.00 12.00
DY25 Peter Forsberg 6.00 15.00
DY26 Eric Lindros 8.00 20.00
DY27 Felix Potvin 8.00 20.00
DY28 Jaromir Jagr 12.00 30.00
DY29 Jeremy Roenick 6.00 15.00
DY30 Mike Modano 8.00 20.00
DY31 Mario Lemieux 15.00 40.00
DY32 Patrick Roy 12.00 30.00
DY33 Steve Yzerman 15.00 40.00
DY34 Cam Neely 6.00 15.00

2012-13 ITG Draft Prospects Future Prospects Jerseys

ANNOUNCED PRINT RUN 100
FPM01 Jake Virtanen 5.00 12.00
FPM02 Connor McDavid 15.00 40.00
FPM03 Dylan Strome 8.00 20.00
FPM04 Travis Konecny 8.00 20.00
FPM05 Nick Ritchie 4.00 10.00
FPM06 Josh Ho-Sang 5.00 12.00
FPM07 Daniel Audette 5.00 12.00
FPM08 Sam Reinhart 10.00 25.00
FPM09 Roland McKeown 3.00 8.00
FPM10 Storm Phaneuf 3.00 8.00

2012-13 ITG Draft Prospects Jerseys

ANNOUNCED PRINT RUN 110
M01 Adam Erne 4.00 10.00
M02 Anthony Duclair 6.00 15.00
M03 Anthony Mantha 8.00 20.00
M04 Bo Horvat 8.00 20.00
M05 Curtis Lazar 5.00 12.00
M06 Darnell Nurse 5.00 12.00
M07 Eric ComrieÂ• 4.00 10.00
M08 Frederik Gauthier 6.00 15.00
M09 Hunter Shinkaruk 6.00 15.00
M10 Jacob de la Rose 5.00 12.00
M11 Philippe Desrosiers 3.00 8.00
M12 Jason Dickinson 3.00 8.00
M13 Aleksander Barkov 10.00 25.00
M14 Jonathan Drouin 10.00 25.00
M15 Jordan Subban 5.00 12.00
M16 Josh Morrissey 4.00 10.00
M17 Justin Bailey 3.00 8.00
M18 Kerby Rychel 4.00 10.00
M19 Max Domi 8.00 20.00
M20 Morgan Klimchuk 4.00 10.00
M21 Nathan MacKinnon 12.00 30.00
M22 Nicolas Petan 4.00 10.00
M23 Nikita Zadorov 4.00 10.00
M24 Robert Hagg 6.00 15.00
M25 Ryan Kujawinski 3.00 8.00
M26 Ryan Pulock 5.00 12.00
M27 Samuel Morin 5.00 12.00
M28 Sean Monahan 10.00 25.00
M29 Seth Jones 10.00 25.00
M30 Spencer Martin 3.00 8.00
M31 Stephen Harper 5.00 12.00
M32 Tristan Jarry 4.00 10.00
M33 Valentin Zykov 5.00 12.00
M34 William Carrier 4.00 10.00
M35 Zachary Fucale 8.00 20.00

2012-13 ITG Draft Prospects Past and Future Jerseys

ANNOUNCED PRINT RUN 90
PF01 Lindros/MacKinnon 12.00 30.00
PF02 Kurri/Barkov 10.00 25.00
PF03 Roenick/Jones 8.00 20.00
PF04 Joseph/Desrosiers 5.00 12.00
PF05 Lemieux/MacKinnon 15.00 40.00
PF06 Bossy/McDavid 15.00 40.00
PF07 Modano/Erne 5.00 12.00
PF08 Nolan/Shinkaruk 6.00 15.00
PF09 Forsberg/Hagg 6.00 15.00
PF10 Niedermayer/Jones 10.00 25.00
PF11 Yzerman/Drouin 12.00 30.00
PF12 Roy/Fucale 12.00 30.00

2012-13 ITG Draft Prospects Past Present and Future Jerseys

ANNOUNCED PRINT RUN 90
PPF01 Bure/Ovechkin/Tolchinsky 12.00 30.00
PPF02 Forsberg/Sedin/de la Rose 10.00 25.00
PPF03 Larionov/Malkin/Zadorov 20.00 50.00
PPF04 Hasek/Lundqvist/Comrie 10.00 25.00
PPF05 Kurri/Lehtonen/Barkov 15.00 40.00
PPF06 Fedorov/Malkin/Zykov 15.00 40.00
PPF07 Roenick/Kesler/Jones 12.00 30.00
PPF08 Yzerman/Giroux/McDavid 20.00 50.00
PPF09 Lemieux/Thornton/MacKin 15.00 40.00
PPF10 Sundin/Sedin/Hagg 10.00 25.00
PPF11 Roy/Price/Fucale 15.00 40.00
PPF12 Messier/Thornton/Drouin 12.00 30.00

2012-13 ITG Draft Prospects Present and Future Jerseys

ANNOUNCED PRINT RUN 90
PAF01 Ovechkin/Zykov 8.00 20.00
PAF02 Price/Fucale 10.00 25.00
PAF03 Sedin/Hagg 6.00 15.00
PAF04 Malkin/Zadorov 8.00 20.00
PAF05 H.Sedin/J.de la Rs 12.00 30.00
PAF06 Lehtonen/Barkov 10.00 25.00
PAF07 Fleury/Comrie 6.00 10.00
PAF08 Thornton/MacKinnon 12.00 30.00
PAF09 Jagr/Gauthier 10.00 25.00
PAF10 Marleau/Monahan 10.00 25.00
PAF11 Giroux/Drouin 10.00 25.00
PAF12 Luongo/Martin 4.00 10.00

2012-13 ITG Draft Prospects Teammates Jerseys

ANNOUNCED PRINT RUN 90
TM01 Roy/Pulock 6.00 15.00
TM02 MacKinnon/Drouin 15.00 40.00
TM03 Fucale/Drouin 10.00 25.00
TM04 MacKinnon/Fucale 12.00 30.00
TM05 Horvat/Zadorov 8.00 20.00
TM06 Domi/Horvat 8.00 20.00
TM07 Zadorov/Domi 8.00 20.00
TM08 Jones/Petan 10.00 25.00
TM09 Duclair/Erne 6.00 15.00
TM10 Lazar/Jarry 5.00 12.00
TM11 Nurse/Tolchinsky 6.00 15.00
TM12 Morin/Gauthier 6.00 15.00

2014-15 ITG Draft Prospects

1 Sam Bennett 2.00 5.00
2 Leon Draisaitl 6.00 15.00
3 Aaron Ekblad 2.50 6.00
4 Sam Reinhart 4.00 10.00
5 Michael Dal Colle 1.50 4.00
6 Haydn Fleury 1.25 3.00
7 Nick Ritchie 1.25 3.00
8 Brendan Perlini 2.00 5.00
9 Jake Virtanen 1.50 4.00
10 Anthony DeAngelo 1.00 2.50
11 Jared McCann 1.25 3.00
12 Ivan Barbashev 1.25 3.00
13 Julius Honka 1.00 2.50
14 Nikolay Goldobin 1.25 3.00
15 Roland McKeown 1.25 3.00
16 Josh Ho-Sang 1.50 4.00
17 Brycen Martin 1.25 3.00
18 Nikolaj Ehlers 2.50 6.00
19 Eric Cornel 1.00 2.50
20 Nikita Scherbak 1.25 3.00
21 Robby Fabbri 1.00 2.50
22 Chase De Leo 1.00 2.50
23 Aaron Haydon 1.00 2.50
24 Connor Chatham 1.25 3.00
25 Conner Bleackley 1.25 3.00
26 Ryan MacInnis 1.00 2.50
27 John Quenneville 1.00 2.50
28 Vaclav Karabacek .75 2.00
29 Alex Peters .75 2.00
30 Michael Bunting 1.50 4.00
31 Brendan Lemieux 1.25 3.00
32 Reid Gardiner .75 2.00
33 Jayce Hawryluk .75 2.00
34 Spencer Watson 1.25 3.00
35 Dylan Sadowy .75 2.00
36 Nicolas Aube-Kubel .75 2.00
37 Brett Pollock 1.25 3.00
38 Blake Siebenaler 1.00 2.50
39 Hunter Smith .75 2.00
40 Julien Nantel .75 2.00
41 Richard Nejezchleb .75 2.00
42 Nick Magyar .75 2.00
43 Brayden Point 1.25 3.00
44 Brett Lernout .75 2.00
45 Travis Sanheim 1.50 4.00
46 Jaden Lindo .75 2.00
47 Brandon Robinson 1.00 2.50
48 Alexis Pepin 1.00 2.50
49 Clark Bishop .75 2.00
50 Matt Mistele 1.00 2.50
51 Reid Duke .75 2.00
52 Brandon Prophet .75 2.00
53 Olivier LeBlanc 1.00 2.50
54 Blake Clarke 1.00 2.50
55 Matthew Mancina .75 2.00
56 Alex Nedeljkovic 1.25 3.00
57 Brent Moran 1.00 2.50
58 Mason McDonald 1.25 3.00
59 Ty Edmonds 1.25 3.00
60 Julio Billia 1.00 2.50
61 Brandon Halverson 1.25 3.00
62 Kasperi Kapanen 2.00 5.00
63 William Nylander 3.00 8.00
64 Adrian Kempe 1.25 3.00
65 David Pastrnak 8.00 20.00
66 Jakub Vrana 1.50 4.00
67 Anton Karlsson .75 2.00
68 Marcus Pettersson 1.00 2.50
69 Adam Ollas Mattsson 1.00 2.50
70 Julius Bergman 1.00 2.50
71 Connor McDavid 6.00 15.00
72 Mathew Barzal 2.50 6.00
73 Dylan Strome 2.50 6.00
74 Jeremy Roy 1.25 3.00
75 Travis Konecny 2.00 5.00
76 Nicolas Roy 1.25 3.00
77 Ryan Pilon .75 2.00
78 Nathan Noel 1.50 4.00
79 Mitchell Marner 4.00 10.00
80 Daniel Sprong 2.00 5.00
81 Bobby Clarke 1.25 3.00
82 Gilbert Perreault 1.25 3.00
83 Guy Lafleur 1.50 4.00
84 Denis Potvin 1.25 3.00
85 Mike Bossy 1.25 3.00
86 Raymond Bourque 2.00 5.00
87 Mark Messier 1.25 3.00
88 Steve Yzerman 3.00 8.00
89 Vladislav Tretiak 1.50 4.00
90 Mario Lemieux 4.00 10.00
91 Patrick Roy 3.00 8.00
92 Joe Sakic 2.00 5.00
93 Teemu Selanne 2.50 6.00
94 Pavel Bure 1.50 4.00
95 Nicklas Lidstrom 1.25 3.00
96 Jaromir Jagr 3.00 8.00
97 Eric Lindros 2.00 5.00
98 Joe Thornton 1.25 3.00
99 Marc-Andre Fleury 2.00 5.00
100 Carey Price 4.00 10.00

2014-15 ITG Draft Prospects Bronze

*BRONZE/25: .6X TO 1.5X BASIC CARDS
88 Steve Yzerman 8.00 20.00

2014-15 ITG Draft Prospects Autographs

PLAYERS WITH TWO CARDS ARE EQUAL VALUE
GOLD/20: .6X TO 1.5X BASIC AUTO
AAD1 Anthony DeAngelo 4.00 10.00
AAD2 Anthony DeAngelo 4.00 10.00
AAE1 Aaron Ekblad 10.00 25.00
AAE2 Aaron Ekblad 10.00 25.00
AAK1 Adrian Kempe 5.00 12.00
AAK2 Adrian Kempe 5.00 12.00
AAKA1 Anton Karlsson 3.00 8.00
AAKA2 Anton Karlsson 3.00 8.00
AAM1 Aleksandar Mikulovich 5.00 12.00
AAM2 Aleksandar Mikulovich 5.00 12.00
AAO1 Adam Ollas Mattsson 4.00 10.00
AAO2 Adam Ollas Mattsson 4.00 10.00
AAP1 Alexis Pepin 4.00 10.00
AAP2 Alexis Pepin 4.00 10.00
AAPR1 Alexander Protapovich 3.00 8.00
AAPR2 Alexander Protapovich 3.00 8.00
ABC1 Blake Clarke 4.00 10.00
ABC2 Blake Clarke 4.00 10.00
ABM1 Brent Moran 4.00 10.00
ABM2 Brent Moran 4.00 10.00
ABMA1 Brycen Martin 5.00 12.00
ABMA2 Brycen Martin 5.00 12.00
ABP1 Brandon Prophet 3.00 8.00
ABP2 Brandon Prophet 3.00 8.00
ABPE1 Brendan Perlini 8.00 20.00
ABPE2 Brendan Perlini 8.00 20.00
ABPO1 Brayden Point 5.00 12.00
ABPO2 Brayden Point 5.00 12.00
ABR1 Brandon Robinson 4.00 10.00
ABR2 Brandon Robinson 4.00 10.00
ACB1 Clark Bishop 3.00 8.00
ACB2 Clark Bishop 3.00 8.00
ADP1 David Pastrnak 50.00 100.00
ADP2 David Pastrnak 50.00 100.00
AEC1 Eric Cornel 4.00 10.00
AEC2 Eric Cornel 4.00 10.00
AHF1 Haydn Fleury 5.00 12.00
AHF2 Haydn Fleury 5.00 12.00
AIB1 Ivan Barbashev 5.00 12.00
AIB2 Ivan Barbashev 5.00 12.00
AJB1 Julius Bergman 4.00 10.00
AJB2 Julius Bergman 4.00 10.00
AJL1 Jaden Lindo 3.00 8.00
AJL2 Jaden Lindo 3.00 8.00
AJM1 Jared McCann 5.00 12.00
AJM2 Jared McCann 5.00 12.00
AJV1 Jake Virtanen 6.00 15.00
AJV2 Jake Virtanen 6.00 15.00
AJVR1 Jakub Vrana 6.00 15.00
AJVR2 Jakub Vrana 6.00 15.00
AKK1 Kasperi Kapanen 8.00 20.00
AKK2 Kasperi Kapanen 8.00 20.00
ALD1 Leon Draisaitl 25.00 60.00
ALD2 Leon Draisaitl 25.00 60.00
AMD1 Michael Dal Colle 6.00 15.00
AMD2 Michael Dal Colle 6.00 15.00
AML1 Maxim Lazarev 3.00 8.00
AML2 Maxim Lazarev 3.00 8.00
AMM1 Matt Mistele 4.00 10.00
AMM2 Matt Mistele 4.00 10.00
AMP1 Marcus Pettersson 4.00 10.00
AMP2 Marcus Pettersson 4.00 10.00
ANA1 Nicolas Aube-Kubel 3.00 8.00
ANA2 Nicolas Aube-Kubel 3.00 8.00
ANE1 Nikolaj Ehlers 10.00 25.00
ANE2 Nikolaj Ehlers 10.00 25.00
ANG1 Nikolay Goldobin 5.00 12.00
ANG2 Nikolay Goldobin 5.00 12.00
ANR1 Nick Ritchie 5.00 12.00
ANR2 Nick Ritchie 5.00 12.00
AOL1 Olivier LeBlanc 4.00 10.00
AOL2 Olivier LeBlanc 4.00 10.00
ARD1 Reid Duke 3.00 8.00
ARD2 Reid Duke 3.00 8.00
ARF1 Robby Fabbri 4.00 10.00
ARF2 Robby Fabbri 4.00 10.00
ARM1 Ryan MacInnis 4.00 10.00
ARM2 Ryan MacInnis 4.00 10.00
ARMC1 Roland McKeown 5.00 12.00
ARMC2 Roland McKeown 5.00 12.00
ASB1 Sam Bennett 8.00 20.00
ASB2 Sam Bennett 8.00 20.00
ASR1 Sam Reinhart 15.00 40.00
ASR2 Sam Reinhart 15.00 40.00
ASW1 Spencer Watson 5.00 12.00
ASW2 Spencer Watson 5.00 12.00
AWN1 William Nylander 12.00 30.00
AWN2 William Nylander 12.00 30.00
DPACM1 Connor McDavid/50 90.00 150.00
DPACM2 Connor McDavid/50 90.00 150.00
PA9 Dylan Strome 10.00 25.00
PA31 Travis Konecny 8.00 20.00

2014-15 ITG Draft Prospects Draft Class Dual Jerseys Blue

STATED PRINT RUN 50 SER.#'d SETS
DC21 C.Neely/S.Yzerman 10.00 25.00
DC22 P.Roy/M.Lemieux 15.00 40.00
DC23 O.Nolan/J.Jagr 12.00 30.00
DC24 J.Howard/M.Fleury 8.00 20.00
DC25 J.Drouin/N.Zadorov 8.00 20.00
DC26 J.Roenick/M.Modano 8.00 20.00
DC27 S.Bennett/S.Reinhart 8.00 20.00
DC28 F.Gauthier/B.Horvat 15.00 40.00

2014-15 ITG Draft Prospects Draft Class Dual Jerseys Bronze

*BRONZE/20: .5X TO 1.2X BLUE/50
STATED PRINT RUN 20 SER.#'d SETS
DC22 P.Roy/M.Lemieux 20.00 50.00
DC24 J.Howard/M.Fleury
DC26 J.Roenick/M.Modano

2014-15 ITG Draft Prospects Draft Dream Team Jerseys Blue

STATED PRINT RUN 15-55
UNPRICED PRINT RUN 15
*BRONZE/30: .5X TO 1.2X BLUE/55
DT1 Carey Price 12.00 30.00
DT2 Claude Giroux 4.00 10.00
DT3 Corey Crawford 5.00 12.00
DT4 Dominik Hasek 5.00 12.00
DT5 Eric Lindros 6.00 15.00
DT6 Igor Larionov 4.00 10.00
DT7 Jari Kurri 4.00 10.00
DT8 Jeremy Roenick 4.00 10.00
DT9 Jimmy Howard 4.00 10.00
DT10 Joe Sakic 6.00 15.00
DT11 Joe Thornton 4.00 10.00
DT12 Mario Lemieux 12.00 30.00
DT13 Mark Messier 4.00 10.00
DT14 Mats Sundin 4.00 10.00
DT15 Mike Bossy 4.00 10.00
DT16 Mike Modano/15
DT17 Patrick Marleau 4.00 10.00
DT18 Patrick Roy 10.00 25.00
DT19 Pavel Bure 5.00 12.00
DT20 Peter Forsberg 4.00 10.00
DT21 Sergei Fedorov 8.00 20.00
DT22 Steve Yzerman 8.00 20.00

2014-15 ITG Draft Prospects Dream Trios Jerseys Blue

STATED PRINT RUN 15-25

D31 Roy/Howard/Crawford 12.00 30.00
D32 Larionov/Fedorov/Bure 25.00 60.00
D33 Modano/Roenick/Howard
D34 Price/Roy/Hasek
D35 Thornton/Giroux/Lemieux
D36 Marleau/Messier/Sakic 8.00 20.00
D37 Forsberg/Sundin/Lidstrom
D38 Yzerman/Lemieux/Messier 15.00 40.00

2014-15 ITG Draft Prospects Future Prospects Jerseys Blue

STATED PRINT RUN 75 SER.#'d SETS
FP1 Connor McDavid 12.00 30.00
FP2 Dylan Strome 5.00 12.00
FP3 Mathew Barzal 5.00 12.00
FP4 Travis Konecny 4.00 10.00

2014-15 ITG Draft Prospects Future Prospects Jerseys Bronze

*BRONZE/45: .5X TO 1.2X BLUE
FP1 Connor McDavid 20.00 40.00

2014-15 ITG Draft Prospects Go Big Or Go Home Jerseys Blue

STATED PRINT RUN 15-25
UNPRICED PRINT RUN 15
BIG1 Aaron Ekblad 6.00 15.00
BIG2 Brendan Perlini
BIG4 Leon Draisaitl 25.00 60.00
BIG5 Mario Lemieux 15.00 40.00
BIG6 Mark Messier
BIG7 Patrick Roy 12.00 30.00
BIG9 Sam Reinhart 10.00 25.00
BIG10 Steve Yzerman 8.00 20.00

2014-15 ITG Draft Prospects Jerseys Blue

STATED PRINT RUN 75 SER.#'d SETS
*BRONZE/45: .5X TO 1.2X BLUE/75
PGU1 Aaron Ekblad 6.00 15.00
PGU2 Alex Nedeljkovic 3.00 8.00
PGU3 Anthony DeAngelo 2.50 6.00
PGU4 Blake Clarke 2.50 6.00
PGU5 Brendan Perlini 4.00 10.00
PGU6 Brycen Martin 3.00 8.00
PGU7 Chase De Leo 2.50 6.00
PGU8 Daniel Audette 3.00 8.00
PGU9 Dominic Turgeon 3.00 8.00
PGU10 Eric Cornel 2.50 6.00
PGU11 Haydn Fleury 3.00 8.00
PGU12 Ivan Barbashev 3.00 8.00
PGU13 Jaden Lindo 2.00 5.00
PGU14 Jared McCann 3.00 8.00
PGU15 Josh Ho-Sang 4.00 10.00
PGU16 Julius Bergman 2.50 6.00
PGU17 Leon Draisaitl 15.00 40.00
PGU18 Marcus Pettersson 2.50 6.00
PGU19 Matt Mistele 2.50 6.00
PGU20 Michael Dal Colle 4.00 10.00
PGU21 Nick Ritchie 3.00 8.00
PGU22 Nikolay Goldobin 3.00 8.00
PGU23 Nikolaj Ehlers 6.00 15.00
PGU24 Olivier LeBlanc 2.50 6.00
PGU25 Robby Fabbri 2.50 6.00
PGU26 Roland McKeown 3.00 8.00
PGU27 Sam Bennett 5.00 12.00
PGU28 Sam Reinhart 10.00 25.00
PGU29 Tyson Baillie 2.50 6.00
PGU30 William Nylander 8.00 20.00

2014-15 ITG Draft Prospects Pride of a Nation Jerseys Blue

STATED PRINT RUN 70 SER.#'d SETS
*BRONZE/40: .5X TO 1.2X BLUE/70
PN1 Ivan Barbashev 3.00 8.00
PN2 Jack Glover 2.00 5.00
PN3 Julius Bergman 2.50 6.00
PN4 Julius Honka 4.00 10.00
PN5 Leon Draisaitl 15.00 40.00
PN6 Marcus Pettersson 2.50 6.00
PN7 Nikolay Goldobin 3.00 8.00
PN8 Dylan Larkin 20.00 40.00
PN9 Sam Bennett 5.00 12.00
PN10 Sam Reinhart 10.00 25.00

2011-12 ITG Enforcers

1 Wens/Millr/O'Rlly/Jnthn 2.00 5.00
2 Will/McGill/Clark/Domi 2.00 5.00
3 Kord/Niln/Odel/Crsn 1.25 3.00
4 Fotiu/Beck/King/Domi 2.00 5.00
5 Lind/Gall/Prbrt/Kocr 2.00 5.00
6 Cicc/Mnsn/Grim/Prbrt 2.00 5.00
7 Rychl/Wlls/McSrl/Mil 2.00 5.00
8 Schltz/Klly/Brbe/Brsh 2.00 5.00
9 Ray/May/Barn/Petrs 1.50 4.00
10 Snep/Will/Butch/Odjick 1.50 4.00
11 Sem/McSr/Buch/Lara 2.00 5.00
12 Paie/Hntr/Weir/Twist 1.50 4.00
13 Gtz/Odgrs/Mrch/McSr 2.00 5.00
14 Nystrm/Gill/Piln/Knpka 2.00 5.00
15 Ewn/Grim/Pros/Knpka 1.50 4.00
16 McCrt/Brbe/Olwa/Phnf 2.00 5.00
17 Laus/Wor/Thmp/Belak 1.50 4.00
18 Twst/McR/Chase/Low 1.50 4.00
19 Dave Schultz RH 2.00 5.00
20 Tiger Williams RH 1.50 4.00
21 Brad MayÂ•RH 1.25 3.00
22 D.Brashear RH/Z.Chara 2.00 5.00
23 Kelly Buchberger RH 1.25 3.00
24 Steve PayneÂ•RH 1.25 3.00
25 Chris Nilan RH 1.25 3.00
26 Chris Nilan RH 1.25 3.00
27 Dale Hunter RH 1.50 4.00
28 Dave Schultz RH 2.00 5.00
29 Brashear/Laraque TOTT 1.50 4.00
30 Z.Chara/D.Koci TOTT 2.00 5.00
31 R.Cote/S.Thornton TOTT 1.50 4.00
32 D.Schultz/T.Williams TOTT 2.00 5.00
33 R.Horner/E.Shore TOTT 1.50 4.00
34 W.Clark/M.McSorley TOTT 2.00 5.00
35 M.Richard/H.Laycoe TOTT 2.00 5.00
36 Watson/V.Hadfield TOTT 1.50 4.00
37 T.Domi/B.Probert TOTT 2.00 5.00
38 B.May/J.Wells TOTT 1.25 3.00
39 J.Miller/C.Nilan TOTT 2.00 5.00
40 McSorley/Probert TOTT 2.00 5.00
41 D.Brashear/R.Ray TOTT 1.50 4.00
42 Mirasty/J.Yablonski TOTT 2.00 5.00
43 T.Ewen/S.Churla TOTT 1.25 3.00
44 D.Schultz/C.Gillies TOTT 2.00 5.00
45 D.Hunter/M.Hunter TOTT 1.50 4.00
46 L.Gaetz/G.Odjick TOTT 1.50 4.00
47 Kocur/Buchberger TOTT 1.25 3.00
48 J.Kordic/B.McRae TOTT 1.50 4.00
49 T.Williams/T.O'Reilly TOTT 1.50 4.00
50 Odelein/M.Barnaby TOTT 1.25 3.00
51 Grimson/B.Probert TOTT 2.00 5.00
52 R.Ray/T.Domi TOTT 2.00 5.00
53 G.Laraque/B.Probert BB 2.00 5.00
54 C.Berube/C.Tamer BB 1.25 3.00
55 C.Berube/J.Cummins BB 1.25 3.00
56 D.Kordic/C.Berube BB 1.25 3.00
57 T.Domi/B.Probert BB 2.00 5.00
58 Brashear/McSorley BB 2.00 5.00
59 Brashear/Z.Chara BB 2.00 5.00
60 D.Brashear/C.Orr BB 2.00 5.00
61 D.Brashear/G.Parros BB 1.50 4.00
62 B.Probert/McSorley BB 2.00 5.00
63 W.Clark/M.McSorley BB 2.00 5.00
64 Brashear/B.Probert BB 2.00 5.00
65 L.Odelein/T.Domi BB 2.00 5.00
66 Gillies/S.Brookbank BB 1.25 3.00
67 Grimson/M.Barnaby BB 1.25 3.00
68 K.King/L.Odelein BB 1.25 3.00
69 K.King/W.Rychel BB 1.25 3.00
70 D.Koci/W.Belak BB 1.50 4.00
71 J.Kocur/S.Grimson BB 1.25 3.00
72 D.Lambert/C.Berube BB 1.25 3.00
73 Laraque/Brashear BB 1.50 4.00
74 G.Laraque/R.Ray BB 1.50 4.00
75 McCarthy/Probert BB 2.00 5.00
76 T.Domi/B.McRae BB 2.00 5.00
77 B.McRae/G.Odjick BB 1.50 4.00
78 J.Mirasty/R.Hand BB 2.00 5.00
79 G.Odjick/L.Gaetz BB 1.50 4.00
80 B.Probert/W.Clark BB 2.00 5.00
81 A.Peters/R.Emery BB 1.50 4.00
82 B.Probert/T.Domi BB 2.00 5.00
83 R.Ray/J.Odgers BB 1.50 4.00
84 D.Manson/W.Rychel BB 1.25 3.00
85 D.Schultz/D.Rolfe BB 2.00 5.00
86 Semenko/L.Playfair BB 1.25 3.00
87 W.Rychel/T.Twist BB 1.25 3.00
88 P.Worrell/E.Lindros BB 4.00 10.00
89 T.Twist/B.Probert BB 2.00 5.00
90 J.Cummins/T.Twist BB 1.25 3.00

2011-12 ITG Enforcers Autographs

FIVE AUTOS PER BOX
AAD Andre Dupont 4.00 10.00
AAP Andrew Peters 5.00 12.00
ABB Barry Beck 4.00 10.00
ABBO Bob Boughner 4.00 10.00
ABG Bill Goldthorpe 6.00 15.00
ABK Bob Kelly 6.00 15.00
ABMAR Bryan Marchment 5.00 12.00
ABMAY Brad May 4.00 10.00
ABMCG Bob McGill 4.00 10.00
ABMCR Basil McRae 5.00 12.00
ABN Bob Nystrom 8.00 12.00
ABP Bob Probert 200.00 400.00
ABW Bryan Watson 5.00 12.00
ACB Craig Berube 4.00 10.00
ACBR Curt Brackenbury 4.00 10.00
ACG Clark Gillies 40.00 100.00
ACN Chris Nilan 5.00 12.00
ADB Dave Brown 8.00 20.00
ADBRA Donald Brashear 40.00 100.00
ADC Dan Carcillo 6.00 15.00
ADL Denny Lambert 4.00 10.00
ADM Dan Maloney 4.00 10.00
ADMAN Dave Manson 5.00 12.00
ADS Dave Schultz 8.00 20.00
ADSE Dave Semenko 12.00 30.00
ADT Darcy Tucker 5.00 12.00
AEC Enrico Ciccone 4.00 10.00
AEV Ed Van Impe 5.00 12.00
AFB Frank Bialowas 6.00 15.00
AGB Garth Butcher 4.00 10.00
AGG Gerard Gallant 5.00 12.00
AGL Georges Laraque 6.00 15.00
AGO Gino Odjick 5.00 12.00
AHS Harold Snepsts 4.00 10.00
AJC Jim Cummins 5.00 12.00
AJK Joey Kocur 5.00 12.00
AJKY Jim Kyte 4.00 10.00
AJM Jon Mirasty 6.00 15.00
AJMA Jimmy Mann 4.00 10.00
AJMC Jim McKenzie 4.00 10.00
AJMCI Jack McIlhargey 6.00 15.00
AJMI Jay Miller 6.00 15.00
AJO Jeff Odgers 4.00 10.00
AJT Jordin Tootoo 6.00 15.00
AJW John Wensink 5.00 12.00
AJWA Joe Watson 5.00 12.00
AJWE Jay Wells 4.00 10.00
AKB Kelly Buchberger 4.00 10.00
AKC Kelly Chase 4.00 10.00
AKK Kris King 4.00 10.00
ALB Laurie Boschman 4.00 10.00
ALF Lou Fontinato 5.00 12.00
ALG Link Gaetz 6.00 15.00
ALO Lyle Odelein 4.00 10.00
AMB Matthew Barnaby 6.00 12.00
AMM Marty McSorley 6.00 15.00
ANF Nick Fotiu 6.00 15.00
APH Paul Holmgren 6.00 15.00
APL Paul Laus 4.00 10.00
APR Phil Russell 4.00 10.00
APW Peter Worrell 4.00 10.00
ARL Reed Low 4.00 10.00
ARP Rich Pilon 4.00 10.00
ARR Rob Ray 6.00 15.00
ASC Shayne Corson 6.00 15.00
ASCH Shane Churla 4.00 10.00
ASG Stu Grimson 4.00 10.00
ASJ Stan Jonathan 5.00 12.00
ASM Sandy McCarthy 5.00 12.00
ATD Tie Domi 15.00 40.00
ATE Todd Ewen 4.00 10.00
ATG Trevor Gillies 5.00 12.00
ATL Tom Lysiak 4.00 10.00
ATO Terry O'Reilly 8.00 20.00
ATP Theo Peckham 4.00 10.00
ATR Terry Ruskowski 5.00 12.00
ATT Tony Twist 5.00 12.00
ATW Tiger Williams 8.00 20.00
AWB Wade Belak 30.00 60.00
AWC Wendel Clark 125.00 250.00
AWP Wilf Paiement 8.00 20.00
AWPL Willi Plett 5.00 12.00
AWR Warren Rychel 4.00 10.00
AWW Wally Weir 4.00 10.00
AZK Zenon Konopka 5.00 12.00

2011-12 ITG Enforcers Combatants Jersey Duals

TWO GAME USED CARDS PER BOX
ANNOUNCED PRINT RUN 120
C01 W.Clark/M.McSorley 10.00 25.00
C02 D.Schultz/T.O'Reilly 10.00 25.00
C03 J.Odgers/D.Manson 6.00 15.00
C04 J.Miller/J.Kocur 10.00 25.00
C05 T.Domi/M.Barnaby 10.00 25.00
C06 W.Belak/D.Brashear 8.00 20.00
C07 P.Laus/C.Berube 6.00 15.00
C08 J.Kocur/D.Manson 8.00 20.00
C09 D.Maloney/T.Williams 8.00 20.00
C10 M.Barnaby/L.Odelein 6.00 15.00
C11 A.Peters/W.Belak 8.00 20.00
C12 Z.Chara/P.Worrell 10.00 25.00
C13 B.Probert/W.Clark 12.00 30.00
C14 C.Berube/T.Domi 10.00 25.00
C15 T.Ewen/S.Churla 6.00 15.00
C16 R.Ray/T.Domi 8.00 20.00
C17 T.Twist/B.Probert 10.00 25.00
C18 B.May/G.Laraque 8.00 20.00
C19 D.Brashear/C.Orr 8.00 20.00
C20 G.Laraque/W.Belak 8.00 20.00
C21 S.Grimson/J.Cummins 10.00 25.00
C22 T.Williams/T.O'Reilly 8.00 20.00
C23 L.Odelein/D.Lambert 6.00 15.00
C24 C.Gillies/D.Schultz 10.00 25.00
C25 J.Odgers/T.Domi 10.00 25.00
C27 H.Snepsts/D.Schultz 8.00 20.00
C28 S.Grimson/B.Probert 12.00 30.00
C29 B.McRae/D.Manson 8.00 20.00
C30 D.Brashear/M.McSorley 10.00 25.00
C31 S.Grimson/E.Ciccone 8.00 20.00
C32 B.McRae/T.Ewen 8.00 20.00
C33 P.Laus/R.Ray 8.00 20.00
C34 D.Hunter/T.O'Reilly 8.00 20.00
C35 K.Oliwa/T.Domi 10.00 25.00
C36 C.Orr/A.Peters 8.00 20.00
C37 G.Odjick/S.Grimson 8.00 20.00
C38 P.Worrell/D.Bonvie 6.00 15.00
C39 K.Chase/C.Berube 6.00 15.00
C40 F.Bialowas/T.Twist 8.00 20.00

2011-12 ITG Enforcers Instigator Jerseys

TWO GAME USED CARDS PER BOX
ANNOUNCED PRINT RUN 120
I01 Matthew Barnaby 5.00 12.00
I02 Barry Beck 6.00 15.00
I03 Wade Belak 8.00 20.00
I04 Craig BerubeÂ• 5.00 12.00
I05 Frank Bialowas 8.00 20.00
I06 Dennis Bonvie 6.00 15.00
I07 Donald Brashear 6.00 15.00
I08 Sheldon Brookbank 5.00 12.00
I09 Dan Carcillo 5.00 12.00
I10 Matt Carkner 8.00 20.00
I11 Zdeno Chara 10.00 25.00
I12 Kelly Chase 6.00 15.00
I13 Shane Churla 5.00 12.00
I14 Enrico Ciccone 6.00 15.00
I15 Wendel Clark 8.00 20.00
I16 Shayne Corson 5.00 12.00
I17 Jim Cummins 5.00 12.00
I18 Tie Domi 8.00 20.00
I19 Steve Downie 6.00 15.00
I20 Todd Ewen 5.00 12.00
I21 Gerard Gallant 6.00 15.00
I22 Clark Gillies 6.00 15.00
I23 Bill Goldthorpe 8.00 20.00
I24 Stu Grimson 6.00 15.00
I25 Dale Hunter 6.00 15.00
I26 Boyd Kane 6.00 15.00
I27 Darius Kasparaitis 8.00 20.00
I28 Joey Kocur 8.00 20.00
I29 Jim Kyte 5.00 12.00
I30 Denny Lambert 5.00 12.00
I31 Georges Laraque 6.00 15.00
I32 Paul Laus 5.00 12.00
I33 Dan Maloney 8.00 20.00
I34 Dave Manson 6.00 15.00
I35 Brad May 6.00 15.00
I36 Cody McCormick 5.00 12.00
I37 Basil McRae 6.00 15.00
I38 Marty McSorley 8.00 20.00
I39 Jay Miller 8.00 20.00
I40 Tyson Nash 8.00 20.00
I41 Bob Nystrom 5.00 12.00
I42 Terry O'Reilly 8.00 20.00
I43 Lyle Odelein 6.00 15.00
I44 Jeff Odgers 8.00 20.00
I45 Gino Odjick 6.00 15.00
I46 Krzysztof Oliwa 6.00 15.00
I47 Colton Orr 5.00 12.00
I48 Theo Peckham 8.00 20.00
I49 Andrew Peters 6.00 15.00
I50 Dion Phaneuf 8.00 20.00
I51 Bob Probert 12.00 25.00
I52 Rob Ray 8.00 20.00
I53 Dave Schultz 8.00 20.00
I54 Harold Snepsts 5.00 12.00
I55 Jordin Tootoo 6.00 15.00
I56 Darcy Tucker 6.00 15.00
I57 Tony Twist 6.00 15.00
I58 Pat Verbeek 6.00 15.00
I59 Tiger Williams 8.00 20.00
I60 Peter Worrell 5.00 15.00

2011-12 ITG Enforcers Tough Franchise Jersey Quads

TWO GAME USED CARDS PER BOX
ANNOUNCED PRINT RUN 40
TF01 Snps/Will/Odjick/Brshr 20.00 50.00
TF02 Will/Clark/Belk/Phnf 25.00 60.00
TF04 Ray/Brnby/May/Ptrs 20.00 50.00
TF05 Lndsy/Prbrt/Gllnt/Kcur 25.00 60.00
TF06 Chse/McR/Twst/Nsh 40.00 80.00
TF07 Mik/Mnsn/Grmsn/Prbrt 25.00 60.00
TF08 Cshm/O'Rlly/Jnth/Chra 20.00 50.00
TF09 Hdfld/Beck/Domi/Orr
TF10 Schltz/Brbe/Brshr/Crclo 12.00 30.00
TF11 Mssr/Crsn/Lrque/Pckhm 25.00 60.00
TF12 Hntr/Odgrs/Cmns/McCrm 15.00 40.00

2013-14 ITG Enforcers

91 F.Potvin/R.Hextall CC 4.00 10.00
92 P.Myre/G.Hanlon CC 1.50 4.00
93 C.Joseph/T.Cheveldae CC 2.00 5.00
94 O.Kolzig/B.Dafoe CC 2.00 5.00
95 T.Salo/D.Cloutier CC 1.50 4.00
96 P.Roy/M.Vernon CC 5.00 12.00
97 C.Osgood/P.Roy CC 5.00 12.00
98 S.Burke/M.LaForest CC 1.25 3.00
99 B.Parent/E.Giacomin CC 2.00 5.00
100 Tiger Williams PIM 1.50 4.00
101 Dale Hunter PIM 1.50 4.00
102 Tie Domi PIM 2.00 5.00
103 Marty McSorley PIM 1.50 4.00
104 Bob Probert PIM 2.00 5.00
105 Rob Ray PIM 1.25 3.00
106 Craig Berube PIM 1.25 3.00
107 Tim Hunter PIM 1.50 4.00
108 Chris Nilan PIM 1.25 3.00
109 Dave Schultz LL 2.00 5.00
110 Paul Baxter LL 1.50 4.00
111 Mike Peluso LL 1.25 3.00
112 Marty McSorley LL 1.50 4.00
113 Bob Probert LL 2.00 5.00
114 Joe Kocur LL 1.25 3.00
115 Tim Hunter LL 1.50 4.00
116 Gino Odjick LL 1.25 3.00
117 Maurice Richard LL 2.00 5.00
118 B.Probert/J.Kocur TT 2.00 5.00
119 R.Ray/M.Hartman TT 1.25 3.00
120 L.DeBrusk/D.Bonvie TT 1.25 3.00
121 T.Williams/C.Fraser TT 1.50 4.00
122 G.Howatt/B.Nystrom TT 1.25 3.00
123 T.Hunter/J.Otto TT 1.50 4.00
124 M.Peluso/C.Russell TT 1.25 3.00
125 J.Dorey/F.Kennedy TT 1.25 3.00
126 K.McClelland/M.McSorley TT 1.50 4.00
127 B.Witt/K.Kaminski TT 1.50 4.00
128 D.Schultz/D.Saleski TT 2.00 5.00
129 T.Horton/B.Baun TT 2.00 5.00
130 E.Shore/L.Hitchman TT 1.50 4.00
131 S.Cleghorn/O.Cleghorn TT 1.50 4.00
132 G.Howe/T.Lindsay TT 4.00 10.00
133 D.Vial/P.Laus TOTT 1.25 3.00
134 Dingman/VandnBshe TOTT 1.50 4.00
135 B.May/D.McCarty TOTT 1.50 4.00
136 B.Probert/C.Coxe TOTT 2.00 5.00
137 M.McSorley/M.Messier TOTT 2.50 6.00
138 T.Domi/C.Russell TOTT 2.00 5.00
139 G.Odjick/K.Buchberger TOTT 1.25 3.00
140 G.Howe/L.Fontinato TOTT 4.00 10.00
141 M.Vukota/M.Peluso TOTT 1.25 3.00
142 J.Caufield/J.Chychrun TOTT 1.25 3.00
143 T.Mallette/K.Chase TOTT 1.25 3.00
144 A.Roy/T.Domi TOTT 2.00 5.00
145 S.Brown/J.Cummins TOTT 1.25 3.00
146 D.Bonvie/R.Ray TOTT 1.25 3.00
147 L.McDonald/D.Polonich TOTT 2.00 5.00
148 G.Howatt/D.Schultz TOTT 2.00 5.00
149 C.Fraser/T.O'Reilly TOTT 1.50 4.00
150 J.McIlhargey/K.Walker TOTT 1.25 3.00
151 T.Williams/M.Bridgman TOTT 1.50 4.00
152 C.Neely/D.Semenko TOTT 2.00 5.00
153 J.Shelley/S.Parker TOTT 1.25 3.00
154 T.Hunter/M.McSorley TOTT 1.50 4.00
155 R.Stern/S.Corson TOTT 1.25 3.00
156 K.Daneyko/C.Berube TOTT 1.25 3.00
157 M.Peluso/T.Domi BB 2.00 5.00
158 K.Belanger/S.Brown BB 1.25 3.00
159 D.Bonvie/D.Langdon BB 1.25 3.00
160 J.Chychrun/B.Probert BB 2.00 5.00
161 L.DeBrusk/G.Odjick BB 1.25 3.00
162 J.Cummins/P.Kruse BB 1.25 3.00
163 D.McCarty/C.Lemieux BB 1.50 4.00
164 A.Downey/T.Fedoruk BB 1.25 3.00
165 D.Kimble/J.Kordic BB 1.25 3.00
166 T.Hunter/J.Kordic BB 1.50 4.00
167 M.McSorley/S.Grimson BB 1.50 4.00
168 P.Kruse/D.McCarty BB 1.50 4.00
169 G.Odjick/D.Langdon BB 1.25 3.00
170 B.Probert/K.Chase BB 2.00 5.00
171 R.Ray/G.Dwyer BB 1.25 3.00
172 T.Ewen/P.Kruse BB 1.25 3.00
173 K.Daneyko/R.Ray BB 1.25 3.00
174 R.VndnBssche/J.Shelley BB 1.50 4.00
175 D.Vial/M.Vukota BB 1.25 3.00
176 B.Witt/I.Laperriere BB 1.25 3.00
177 L.DeBrusk/T.Ewen BB 1.25 3.00
178 P.Kruse/D.Langdon BB 1.25 3.00
179 T.Domi/R.Stern BB 2.00 5.00
180 B.Probert/S.Grimson BB 2.00 5.00

2013-14 ITG Enforcers Autographs

FOUR AUTOs PER BOX OVERALL
AAD Aaron Downey 3.00 8.00
AAN Andrei Nazarov 3.00 8.00
AAR Andre Roy 3.00 8.00
ABH Bob Halkidis 3.00 8.00
ABM Brantt Myhres 3.00 8.00
ABS Brent Severyn 3.00 8.00
ABW Brendan Witt 3.00 8.00
ACC Cam Connor 3.00 8.00
ACCO Craig Coxe 3.00 8.00
ACD Chris Dingman 3.00 8.00
ACF Curt Fraser 3.00 8.00
ACN Cam Neely 15.00 40.00
ACR Cam Russell 3.00 8.00
ACS Chris Simon 3.00 8.00
ADB Dennis Bonvie 4.00 10.00
ADH Dave Hanson 6.00 15.00
ADK Darin Kimble 3.00 8.00
ADL Darren Langdon 3.00 8.00
ADM Darren McCarty 5.00 12.00
ADP Dennis Polonich 3.00 8.00
ADV Dennis Vial 3.00 8.00
AFK Forbes Kennedy 3.00 8.00
AGC Glen Cochrane 3.00 8.00
AGD Gordie Dwyer 3.00 8.00
AGH Garry Howatt 3.00 8.00
AGHO Gordie Howe 150.00 225.00
AIL Ian Laperriere 3.00 8.00
AJC Jay Caufield 3.00 8.00
AJCA Jeff Carlson
AJCH Jeff Chychrun 3.00 8.00
AJD Jim Dorey 3.00 8.00
AJN Jim Nill 3.00 8.00
AJR Jeremy Roenick 50.00 100.00
AJS Jim Sandlak 3.00 8.00
AJSH Jody Shelley 3.00 8.00
AKB Ken Belanger 3.00 8.00
AKC Kim Clackson 3.00 8.00
AKD Ken Daneyko 3.00 8.00
AKK Kevin Kaminski 4.00 10.00
AKM Kevin McClelland 3.00 8.00
AKW Kurt Walker 3.00 8.00
ALB Lyndon Byers 3.00 8.00
ALD Louie DeBrusk 3.00 8.00
ALP Larry Playfair 3.00 8.00
AMH Mike Hartman 3.00 8.00
AMP Mike Peluso 3.00 8.00
AMV Mick Vukota 3.00 8.00
APB Paul Baxter 4.00 10.00
APK Paul Kruse 3.00 8.00
ARS Ron Stern 3.00 8.00
ART Rocky Thompson 3.00 8.00
ARV Ryan VandenBussche 4.00 10.00
ASB Sean Brown 4.00 10.00
ASC Steve Carlson 5.00 12.00
ASH Sami Helenius 3.00 8.00
ASP Scott Parker 3.00 8.00
AST Scott Thornton 3.00 8.00
ATF Todd Fedoruk 3.00 8.00
ATH Tim Hunter 4.00 10.00
ATL Ted Lindsay 8.00 20.00
ATM Troy Mallette 3.00 8.00

2013-14 ITG Enforcers Between the Pipes Battles Jersey Duals

ANNOUNCED PRINT RUN 150
BTPB01 C.Joseph/T.Cheveldae 6.00 15.00
BTPB02 P.Roy/C.Osgood 10.00 25.00
BTPB03 P.Roy/M.Vernon 10.00 25.00
BTPB04 O.Kolzig/B.Dafoe 6.00 15.00
BTPB05 F.Potvin/R.Hextall 10.00 25.00
BTPB06 D.Cloutier/T.Salo 8.00 20.00

2013-14 ITG Enforcers Combatants Jersey Duals

ANNOUNCED PRINT RUN 150
C01 K.Belanger/B.May 4.00 10.00
C02 D.Bonvie/R.VndnBssche 5.00 12.00
C03 J.Caufield/G.Odjick 4.00 10.00
C04 J.Chychrun/W.Clark 6.00 15.00
C05 G.Cochrane/R.Larson 4.00 10.00
C06 C.Coxe/B.Probert 8.00 20.00
C07 C.Dingman/R.VndnBssche 5.00 12.00
C08 A.Downey/P.Worrell 4.00 10.00
C09 T.Hunter/M.McSorley 6.00 15.00
C10 D.Langdon/S.McCarthy 4.00 10.00
C11 I.Laperriere/K.Tkachuk 6.00 15.00
C12 T.Mallette/P.Laus 4.00 10.00
C13 D.McCarty/C.Lemieux 8.00 20.00
C14 S.Parker/B.Probert 8.00 20.00
C15 C.Simon/R.Ray 4.00 10.00
C16 A.Roy/T.Domi 6.00 15.00
C17 B.Severyn/M.Vukota 4.00 10.00
C18 C.Simon/D.McCarty 5.00 12.00
C19 S.Thornton/P.Laus 5.00 12.00
C20 R.VndnBssche/S.Brown 5.00 12.00
C21 R.Ray/M.Vukota 4.00 10.00
C22 K.Walker/S.Jonathan 4.00 10.00
C23 B.Witt/J.Thornton 6.00 15.00
C24 B.Probert/C.Dingman 6.00 15.00
C25 S.Brown/B.May 4.00 10.00
C26 T.Fedoruk/A.Downey 4.00 10.00
C27 D.Brown/T.Hunter 6.00 15.00
C28 B.Nystrom/M.Bridgman 4.00 10.00
C29 D.Langdon/C.Simon 5.00 12.00
C30 T.O'Reilly/D.Maloney 5.00 12.00
C31 K.Daneyko/C.Berube 4.00 10.00
C32 J.Chychrun/G.Odjick 4.00 10.00
C33 M.McSorley/M.Messier 8.00 20.00
C34 K.Daneyko/K.Primeau 5.00 12.00
C35 S.Brown/K.Belanger 4.00 10.00
C36 M.Vukota/K.Daneyko 4.00 10.00
C37 M.Bridgman/T.Williams 5.00 12.00
C38 A.Roy/C.Simon 4.00 10.00

2013-14 ITG Enforcers Instigator Jerseys

ANNOUNCED PRINT RUN 150
PATCH/20: 1X TO 2.5X BASIC JSY/150*
IM01 Ken Belanger 3.00 8.00
IM02 Dennis Bonvie 4.00 10.00
IM03 Jay Caufield 4.00 10.00
IM04 Jeff Chychrun 3.00 8.00
IM05 Glen Cochrane 3.00 8.00
IM06 Chris Simon 5.00 12.00
IM07 Chris Dingman 4.00 10.00
IM08 Aaron Downey 3.00 8.00
IM09 Todd Fedoruk 3.00 8.00
IM10 Tim Hunter 4.00 10.00
IM11 Darren Langdon 3.00 8.00
IM12 Ian Laperriere 4.00 10.00
IM13 Troy Mallette 3.00 8.00
IM14 Darren McCarty 5.00 12.00
IM15 Scott Parker 3.00 8.00
IM16 Brantt Myhres 3.00 8.00
IM17 Andre Roy 3.00 8.00
IM18 Brent Severyn 3.00 8.00
IM19 Scott Thornton 4.00 10.00
IM20 Rocky Thompson 3.00 8.00
IM21 Ryan VandenBussche 4.00 10.00
IM22 Mick Vukota 3.00 8.00
IM23 Kurt Walker 3.00 8.00
IM24 Brendan Witt 3.00 8.00

2013-14 ITG Enforcers Pugilistic Puck Stoppers Jerseys

PATCH/20: 1.5X TO 4X BASIC JSY/150*
PPSM01 Tom Barrasso 5.00 12.00
PPSM02 Dan Cloutier 4.00 10.00
PPSM03 Byron Dafoe 5.00 12.00
PPSM04 Ray Emery 5.00 12.00
PPSM05 Ron Hextall 8.00 20.00
PPSM06 Curtis Joseph 5.00 12.00
PPSM07 Olaf Kolzig 5.00 12.00
PPSM08 Chris Osgood 5.00 12.00
PPSM09 Felix Potvin 8.00 20.00
PPSM10 Patrick Roy 8.00 20.00
PPSM11 Garth Snow 4.00 10.00
PPSM12 Mike Vernon 4.00 10.00

2013-14 ITG Enforcers Tough Franchise Jerseys Quad

ANNOUNCED PRINT RUN 50
TF01 Cshm/O'Rly/Nly/Blngr 20.00 50.00
TF02 Gare/Wlley/Ray/May 12.00 30.00
TF03 Brdgm/Brwn/Shlly/Fdrk 15.00 40.00
TF04 Hnter/Rbrts/Fleury/Phnf 20.00 50.00
TF05 Prbrt/Rnck/Rsll/VndBs 25.00 60.00
TF06 Chls/Prbrt/Kcur/McCrty 25.00 60.00
TF07 Dngm/Odgr/Cmins/Prkr 12.00 30.00
TF08 Smth/Gllies/Nystrm/Vkta 15.00 40.00
TF09 Chych/McSrl/Bck/Mlny 25.00 60.00
TF10 Svryn/Wrll/Laus/Thmps 20.00 50.00

2010-11 ITG Enshrined

ANNOUNCED PRINT RUN 175
1 Ace Bailey 2.00 5.00
2 Al Arbour 2.50 6.00
3 Al MacInnis 3.00 8.00
4 Alex Connell 2.50 6.00
5 Alex Delvecchio 2.50 6.00
6 Allan Stanley 3.00 8.00
7 Andy Bathgate 3.00 8.00
8 Angela James 3.00 8.00
9 Art Ross 2.00 5.00
10 Aurel Joliat 3.00 8.00
11 Babe Dye 2.00 5.00
12 Babe Pratt 2.00 5.00
13 Babe Siebert 2.50 6.00
14 Bernie Federko 2.50 6.00
15 Bernie Geoffrion 2.50 6.00
16 Bernie Parent 3.00 8.00
17 Bert Olmstead 2.50 6.00
18 Bill Barber 2.50 6.00
19 Bill Cook 2.00 5.00
20 Bill Cowley 2.00 5.00
21 Bill Durnan 3.00 8.00
22 Bill Gadsby 3.00 8.00
23 Bill Mosienko 2.50 6.00
24 Bill Quackenbush 2.50 6.00
25 Billy Burch 2.00 5.00
26 Billy Smith 3.00 8.00
27 Bob Johnson 2.00 5.00
28 Bob Pulford 2.50 6.00
29 Bobby Bauer 3.00 8.00
30 Bobby Clarke 3.00 8.00
31 Bobby Hull 3.00 8.00
32 Borje Salming 3.00 8.00
33 Brad Park 2.50 6.00
34 Brian Leetch 3.00 8.00
35 Bryan Hextall 2.50 6.00
36 Bryan Trottier 4.00 10.00
37 Bun Cook 3.00 8.00
38 Busher Jackson 2.50 6.00
39 Cam Neely 3.00 8.00
40 Cammi Granato 2.50 6.00
41 Carl Voss 3.00 8.00
42 Charlie Conacher 2.50 6.00
43 Charlie Gardiner 2.50 6.00
44 Ching Johnson 2.00 5.00
45 Chuck Rayner 2.50 6.00
46 Clarence Campbell 2.00 5.00
47 Clark Gillies 3.00 8.00
48 Clint Benedict 2.50 6.00
49 Clint Smith 2.00 5.00
50 Conn Smythe 2.50 6.00
51 Cooney Weiland 2.00 5.00
52 Cy Denneny 2.00 5.00
53 Cyclone Taylor 3.00 8.00
54 Dale Hawerchuk 4.00 10.00
55 Darryl Sittler 2.50 6.00
56 Dave Keon 3.00 8.00
57 Denis Potvin 3.00 8.00
58 Denis Savard 4.00 10.00
59 Dick Duff 2.50 6.00
60 Dick Irvin 2.50 6.00
61 Dickie Moore 2.50 6.00
62 Didier Pitre 2.00 5.00
63 Dino Ciccarelli 3.00 8.00
64 Dit Clapper 2.00 5.00
65 Doug Bentley 2.00 5.00
66 Doug Harvey 3.00 8.00
67 Earl Seibert 2.50 6.00
68 Ebbie Goodfellow 2.50 6.00
69 Ed Giacomin 5.00 12.00
70 Eddie Shore 2.50 6.00
71 Edgar Laprade 2.50 6.00
72 Elmer Lach 2.50 6.00
73 Emile Bouchard 3.00 8.00
74 Emile Francis 2.00 5.00
75 Fern Flaman 4.00 10.00
76 Foster Hewitt 2.50 6.00
77 Frank Boucher 2.00 5.00
78 Frank Brimsek 2.50 6.00
79 Frank Calder 2.00 5.00
80 Frank Frederickson 2.00 5.00
81 Frank Mahovlich 3.00 8.00
82 Frank McGee 3.00 8.00
83 Frank Nighbor 3.00 8.00
84 Frank Patrick 2.00 5.00
85 Frank Selke 2.50 6.00
86 George Hainsworth 3.00 8.00
87 Georges Vezina 4.00 10.00
88 Gerry Cheevers 3.00 8.00
89 Gilbert Perreault 3.00 8.00
90 Glenn Anderson 3.00 8.00
91 Glenn Hall 3.00 8.00
92 Gordie Drillon 2.50 6.00
93 Grant Fuhr 3.00 8.00
94 Gump Worsley 3.00 8.00
95 Guy Lafleur 4.00 10.00
96 Guy Lapointe 2.50 6.00
97 Hap Day 2.50 6.00
98 Hap Holmes 2.50 6.00
99 Harold Ballard 2.00 5.00
100 Harry Howell 2.50 6.00
101 Harry Lumley 3.00 8.00
102 Harry Oliver 2.50 6.00
103 Harry Sinden 3.00 8.00
104 Harry Watson 2.50 6.00
105 Henri Richard 3.00 8.00
106 Herb Brooks 2.50 6.00
107 Hobey Baker 2.50 6.00
108 Hooley Smith 2.00 5.00
109 Howie Morenz 2.50 6.00
110 Igor Larionov 3.00 8.00
111 Jack Adams 3.00 8.00
112 Jack Darragh 2.00 5.00
113 Jack Stewart 2.00 5.00
114 Jacques Laperriere 3.00 8.00
115 Jacques Lemaire 3.00 8.00
116 Jacques Plante 4.00 10.00
117 Jari Kurri 3.00 8.00
118 Jean Beliveau 3.00 8.00
119 Jean Ratelle 2.50 6.00
120 Joe Hall 2.00 5.00
121 Joe Malone 2.00 5.00
122 Joe Mullen 2.50 6.00
123 Joe Primeau 2.00 5.00
124 Joe Simpson 2.00 5.00
125 Johnny Bower 4.00 10.00
126 Johnny Bucyk 3.00 8.00
127 Ken Reardon 2.50 6.00
128 King Clancy 3.00 8.00
129 Lanny McDonald 3.00 8.00
130 Larry Murphy 2.50 6.00
131 Larry Robinson 3.00 8.00
132 Lester Patrick 3.00 8.00
133 Lionel Conacher 2.00 5.00
134 Lord Stanley 3.00 8.00
135 Luc Robitaille 3.00 8.00
136 Lynn Patrick 2.00 5.00
137 Marcel Dionne 4.00 10.00
138 Marcel Pronovost 3.00 8.00
139 Mario Lemieux 10.00 25.00
140 Mark Messier 5.00 12.00
141 Maurice Richard 5.00 12.00
142 Max Bentley 2.00 5.00
143 Michel Goulet 2.50 6.00
144 Mike Bossy 3.00 8.00
145 Mike Gartner 3.00 8.00
146 Milt Schmidt 2.50 6.00
147 Moose Goheen 2.00 5.00
148 Neil Colville 2.00 5.00
149 Nels Stewart 2.00 5.00
150 Newsy Lalonde 2.50 6.00
151 Norm Ullman 3.00 8.00
152 Paddy Moran 2.50 6.00
153 Pat LaFontaine 3.00 8.00
154 Patrick Roy 8.00 20.00
155 Paul Coffey 3.00 8.00
156 Percy LeSueur 2.50 6.00
157 Peter Stastny 2.50 6.00
158 Phil Esposito 5.00 12.00
159 Pierre Pilote 2.50 6.00
160 Punch Broadbent 2.00 5.00
161 Punch Imlach 2.00 5.00
162 Raymond Bourque 5.00 12.00
163 Red Dutton 2.00 5.00
164 Red Horner 2.50 6.00
165 Red Kelly 3.00 8.00
166 Red Storey 2.00 5.00
167 Rod Gilbert 3.00 8.00
168 Rod Langway 2.50 6.00
169 Roger Neilson 2.00 5.00
170 Ron Francis 4.00 10.00
171 Roy Conacher 3.00 8.00
172 Roy Worters 3.00 8.00
173 Rudy Pilous 3.00 8.00
174 Sam Pollock 2.00 5.00
175 Scotty Bowman 2.50 6.00
176 Serge Savard 3.00 8.00
177 Sid Abel 2.50 6.00
178 Sprague Cleghorn 2.50 6.00
179 Stan Mikita 4.00 10.00
180 Steve Shutt 3.00 8.00
181 Steve Yzerman 8.00 20.00
182 Sweeney Schriner 2.00 5.00
183 Syd Howe 2.50 6.00
184 Syl Apps 4.00 10.00
185 Sylvio Mantha 2.00 5.00
186 Ted Kennedy 3.00 8.00
187 Ted Lindsay 3.00 8.00
188 Terry Sawchuk 4.00 10.00
189 Tim Horton 3.00 8.00
190 Tiny Thompson 3.00 8.00
191 Toe Blake 2.00 5.00
192 Tom Johnson 2.50 6.00
193 Tommy Ivan 2.50 6.00
194 Tony Esposito 3.00 8.00
195 Turk Broda 3.00 8.00
196 Valeri Kharlamov 2.00 5.00
197 Vladislav Tretiak 4.00 10.00
198 Wilfred Green 2.00 5.00
199 Woody Dumart 2.00 5.00
200 Yvan Cournoyer 3.00 8.00

2010-11 ITG Enshrined Autographs Silver

ANNCD PRINT RUN 49 SETS
AAA Al Arbour 10.00 25.00
AAB Andy Bathgate 12.00 30.00
AAD Alex Delvecchio 10.00 25.00
AAJ Angela James 12.00 30.00
AAM Al MacInnis 12.00 30.00
AAS Allan Stanley 12.00 30.00
ABB Bill Barber 10.00 25.00
ABF Bernie Federko 10.00 25.00
ABG Bill Gadsby 12.00 30.00
ABH Bobby Hull 15.00 40.00
ABL Brian Leetch 12.00 30.00
ABO Bert Olmstead 15.00 40.00
ABP Bernie Parent 12.00 30.00
ABPA Brad Park/48* 10.00 25.00
ABPU Bob Pulford/48* 10.00 25.00
ABS Billy Smith 8.00 20.00
ABSA Borje Salming 12.00 30.00
ABT Bryan Trottier 15.00 40.00
ACG Clark Gillies 12.00 30.00
ACGR Cammi Granato 10.00 25.00
ACN Cam Neely 12.00 30.00
ADC Dino Ciccarelli 12.00 30.00
ADD Dick Duff 10.00 25.00
ADH Dale Hawerchuk 15.00 40.00
ADK Dave Keon 12.00 30.00
ADM Dickie Moore 12.50 30.00
ADP Denis Potvin 12.00 30.00
ADS Darryl Sittler 10.00 25.00
ADSA Denis Savard 15.00 40.00
AEB Emile Bouchard 12.00 30.00
AEF Emile Francis 15.00 40.00
AEG Ed Giacomin 12.00 30.00
AEL Elmer Lach 15.00 40.00
AELA Edgar Laprade 10.00 25.00
AFF Fern Flaman/48* 15.00 40.00
AFM Frank Mahovlich 12.00 30.00
AGA Glenn Anderson 12.00 30.00
AGC Gerry Cheevers 15.00 40.00
AGF Grant Fuhr 12.00 30.00
AGH Glenn Hall 12.00 30.00
AGL Guy Lafleur 15.00 40.00
AGLA Guy Lapointe 10.00 25.00
AGP Gilbert Perreault 15.00 40.00
AHH Harry Howell 10.00 25.00
AHR Henri Richard 12.00 30.00
AHS Harry Sinden 12.00 30.00
AIL Igor Larionov 25.00 60.00
AJB Jean Beliveau 40.00 80.00
AJBO Johnny Bower 15.00 40.00
AJBU John Bucyk 8.00 20.00
AJK Jari Kurri 12.00 30.00
AJL Jacques Laperriere 15.00 40.00
AJLE Jacques Lemaire 12.00 30.00
AJM Joe Mullen 10.00 25.00
ALM Lanny McDonald 12.00 30.00
ALMU Larry Murphy 10.00 25.00
ALR Larry Robinson 12.00 30.00
ALRO Luc Robitaille 15.00 40.00
AMB Mike Bossy 15.00 40.00
AMD Marcel Dionne 15.00 40.00
AMG Michel Goulet 10.00 25.00
AMGA Mike Gartner 12.00 30.00
AML Mario Lemieux 60.00 120.00
AMM Mark Messier 40.00 80.00
AMP Marcel Pronovost 12.00 30.00
AMS Milt Schmidt 10.00 25.00
ANU Norm Ullman 12.00 30.00
APC Paul Coffey 12.00 30.00
APE Phil Esposito 20.00 50.00
APL Pat Lafontaine 12.00 30.00
APP Pierre Pilote 10.00 25.00
APR Patrick Roy 30.00 80.00
APS Peter Stastny 10.00 25.00
ARB Raymond Bourque 20.00 50.00
ARF Ron Francis 12.00 30.00
ARG Rod Gilbert/48* 12.00 30.00
ARK Red Kelly 12.00 30.00
ARL Rod Langway/48* 10.00 25.00
ASB Scotty Bowman 12.00 30.00
ASM Stan Mikita 15.00 40.00
ASS Steve Shutt 15.00 40.00
ASSA Serge Savard 12.00 30.00
ASY Steve Yzerman 25.00 60.00
ATE Tony Esposito 15.00 40.00
ATL Ted Lindsay 12.00 30.00
AVT Vladislav Tretiak 15.00 40.00
AYC Yvan Cournoyer 12.00 30.00

2015-16 ITG Enshrined

C001 A.Delvecchio/T.Horton 12.00 30.00
C002 B.Parent/P.Esposito
C003 B.Barber/G.Perreault 12.00 30.00
C004 B.Hull/S.Mikita
C005 B.Jackson/T.Sawchuk
C006 C.Chelios/B.Shanahan
C007 D.Hasek/P.Forsberg
C008 D.Gilmour/E.Belfour
C009 E.Giacomin/B.Clarke 6.00 15.00
C010 F.Brimsek/T.Kennedy
C011 F.Nighbor/E.Shore
C012 G.Howe/J.Beliveau
C013 G.Fuhr/P.LaFontaine
C014 J.Ratelle/G.Cheevers 5.00 12.00
C015 J.Sakic/P.Bure 12.00 30.00
C016 L.Robitaille/B.Leetch
C017 M.Dionne/L.McDonald 12.00 30.00
C018 M.Messier/S.Stevens
C019 M.Richard/H.Day
C020 M.Bossy/D.Potvin
C021 R.Bourque/P.Coffey
C022 R.Blake/M.Modano
C023 R.Langway/C.Gillies
C024 S.Yzerman/B.Hull 12.00 30.00
C025 T.Esposito/G.Lafleur

2015-16 ITG Enshrined Eight All Star Seasons Silver

E8S01 Bure/Roy/Sakic/Fedorov/Lemieux
Bourque/Blake/Forsberg
E8S02 Fedorov/Lemieux/Lidstrom
Hasek/Shanahan/Blake/Roy/Chelios
E8S03 Gretzky/Chelios/Forsberg/Hasek
Modano/Roy/Sakic/Bure
E8S04 Gretzky/Hull/Roy/Fedorov/Bourque
Bure/Messier/Blake
E8S05 Housley/Messier/Yzerman/Stevens 3.00 8.00
Modano/Bure/Sundin/Shanahan

8S06 Lemieux/Fedorov/Belfour/Hull20.00 50.00
Messier/Forsberg/Chelios/Shanahan
8S07 Modano/Pronger/Sundin 15.00 40.00
Robitaille/Lidstrom/MacInnis/Hasek/Shanahan

2015-16 ITG Enshrined Exhibits Silver

E01 Bobby Clarke/20 20.00 50.00
E02 Brett Hull/25
E03 Doug Gilmour/25 20.00 50.00
E04 Gordie Howe/15
E05 Grant Fuhr/20
E06 Marcel Dionne/20 20.00 50.00
E07 Mats Sundin/25
E08 Maurice Richard/15
E09 Pavel Bure/25
E10 Bobby Orr/10
E11 Jacques Plante/10
E12 Mario Lemieux/25
E13 Patrick Roy/25
E14 Stan Mikita/15
E15 Wayne Gretzky/20

2015-16 ITG Enshrined Hall Patch Silver

HP01 Adam Oates/20 20.00 40.00
HP02 Bobby Orr/5
HP03 Brendan Shanahan/20
HP04 Brett Hull/20
HP05 Brian Leetch/20
HP06 Cam Neely/15
HP07 Chris Chelios/15
HP08 Chris Pronger/15
HP09 Clark Gillies/10
HP10 Dale Hawerchuk/10
HP11 Dominik Hasek/20
HP12 Doug Gilmour/15
HP13 Doug Harvey/5
HP14 Ed Belfour/15
HP15 Gordie Howe/5
HP16 Guy Lafleur/15
HP17 Igor Larionov/15
HP18 Joe Sakic/15
HP19 Luc Robitaille/20
HP20 Marcel Dionne/15
HP21 Mario Lemieux/20
HP22 Mats Sundin/15
HP23 Mike Bossy/20
HP24 Mike Modano/20
HP25 Nicklas Lidstrom/20
HP26 Pat LaFontaine/10
HP27 Patrick Roy/20
HP28 Pavel Bure/20
HP29 Peter Forsberg/15
HP30 Phil Esposito/10
HP31 Raymond Bourque/20
HP32 Rob Blake/20 12.00 30.00
HP33 Scott Stevens/15
HP34 Sergei Fedorov/20 20.00 50.00
HP35 Stan Mikita/5
HP36 Steve Yzerman/20 12.00 30.00
HP37 Wayne Gretzky/10

2015-16 ITG Enshrined Mount Rushmore Silver

MR04 Gretzky/Fuhr/Coffey/Messier/20
MR05 Gretzky/Roy/Lemieux/Bourque/30
MR06 Howe/Yzerman/Sawchuk 20.00 50.00
Lidstrom/25
MR08 Mikita/Howe/Horton/Hull/15
MR09 Niedermayer/Lidstrom 15.00 40.00
Sakic/Pronger/35
MR10 Orr/Dionne/Lafleur/Hull/25
MR12 Orr/Neely/Esposito/Bourque/15
MR13 Parent/Clarke/Barber/Lindbergh/25 40.0080.00
MR14 Plante/Richard/Beliveau/Lafleur/15
MR17 Roy/Hasek/Sawchuk/Plante/15
MR18 Sundin/Kennedy/Horton/Salming/20
MR19 Lemieux/Gretzky/Yzerman/Roy/30 40.00 80.00

2015-16 ITG Enshrined Signature Showcase Silver

SSBH1 Bobby Hull/35 12.00 30.00
SSBH2 Brett Hull/35
SSCG1 Clark Gillies/35
SSDG1 Doug Gilmour/35
SSEB1 Ed Belfour/35 12.00 30.00
SSEG1 Ed Giacomin/35 12.00 30.00
SSGC1 Gerry Cheevers/35
SSGL1 Guy Lafleur/35
SSIL1 Igor Larionov/35
SSMD1 Marcel Dionne/35
SSML1 Mario Lemieux/25
SSNL1 Nicklas Lidstrom/35 12.00 30.00
SSPB1 Pavel Bure/35 15.00 40.00
SSPH1 Phil Housley/35 12.00 30.00
SSPR1 Patrick Roy/25
SSRB1 Raymond Bourque/35
SSSY1 Steve Yzerman/15

2010-11 ITG Fall Expo Team ITG VIP

ITG1 Antti Niemi 1.25 3.00
ITG2 Bobby Clarke 1.50 4.00
ITG3 Bobby Hull 1.50 4.00
ITG4 Borje Salming 1.50 4.00
ITG5 Cam Neely 1.50 4.00
ITG6 Daniel Sedin 1.50 4.00
ITG7 Darryl Sittler 1.25 3.00
ITG8 Dave Keon 1.50 4.00
ITG9 Denis Potvin 1.50 4.00
ITG10 Doug Gilmour 2.00 5.00
ITG11 Doug Harvey 1.50 4.00
ITG12 Guy LaFleur 2.00 5.00
ITG13 Henrik Sedin 1.50 4.00
ITG14 Jacques Plante 2.00 5.00
ITG15 Jari Kurri 1.50 4.00
ITG16 Jaromir Jagr 4.00 10.00
ITG17 Jean Beliveau 1.50 4.00
ITG18 Joe Sakic 2.50 6.00
ITG19 Joe Thornton 1.50 4.00
ITG20 Mario Lemieux 5.00 12.00
ITG21 Mark Messier 2.50 6.00
ITG22 Martin Brodeur 3.00 8.00
ITG23 Martin St. Louis 1.50 4.00
ITG24 Maurice Richard 2.50 6.00
ITG25 Mike Bossy 1.50 4.00
ITG26 Mike Modano 2.50 6.00
ITG27 Nicklas Lidstrom 1.50 4.00
ITG28 Patrick Roy 4.00 10.00
ITG29 Paul Coffey 1.50 4.00
ITG30 Pavel Bure 2.00 5.00
ITG31 Phil Esposito 2.50 6.00
ITG32 Raymond Bourque 2.50 6.00
ITG33 Rick Nash 1.50 4.00
ITG34 Roberto Luongo 1.50 4.00
ITG35 Scott Niedermayer 1.50 4.00
ITG36 Steve Yzerman 4.00 10.00
ITG37 Steven Stamkos 3.00 8.00
ITG38 Ted Lindsay 1.50 4.00
ITG39 Teemu Selanne 3.00 8.00
ITG40 Terry Sawchuk 2.00 5.00
ITG41 Tim Horton 1.50 4.00
ITG42 Tyler Seguin 5.00 12.00
ITG43 Valeri Kharlamov 1.00 2.50
ITG44 Vincent Lecavalier 1.25 3.00
ITG45 Vladislav Tretiak 2.00 5.00

2012-13 ITG Forever Rivals

1 Georges Vezina 2.00 5.00
2 Joe Malone 1.25 3.00
3 Newsy Lalonde 1.50 4.00
4 Aurel Joliat 2.00 5.00
5 George Hainsworth 2.00 5.00
6 Howie Morenz 1.50 4.00
7 Bill Durnan 2.00 5.00
8 Elmer Lach 1.50 4.00
9 Maurice Richard 2.00 5.00
10 Toe Blake 1.25 3.00
11 Bernie Geoffrion 1.50 4.00
12 Butch Bouchard 1.50 4.00
13 Dickie Moore 1.50 4.00
14 Doug Harvey 2.00 5.00
15 Jacques Plante 2.50 6.00
16 Jean Beliveau 2.00 5.00
17 Jean-Guy Talbot 1.50 4.00
18 Tom Johnson 1.50 4.00
19 Bobby Rousseau 1.50 4.00
20 Charlie Hodge 1.50 4.00
21 Claude Provost 1.25 3.00
22 Gump Worsley 2.00 5.00
23 Henri Richard 2.00 5.00
24 J.C. Tremblay 1.25 3.00
25 Jacques Laperriere 2.00 5.00
26 Ralph Backstrom 1.25 3.00
27 Rogie Vachon 2.50 6.00
28 Bunny Larocque 1.50 4.00
29 Guy Lafleur 2.50 6.00
30 Guy Lapointe 1.50 4.00
31 Jacques Lemaire 2.00 5.00
32 Larry Robinson 2.00 5.00
33 Serge Savard 2.00 5.00
34 Steve Shutt 1.50 4.00
35 Bobby Smith 1.50 4.00
36 Chris Chelios 2.00 5.00
37 Guy Carbonneau 2.00 5.00
38 Mats Naslund 2.00 5.00
39 Patrick Roy 5.00 12.00
40 Denis Savard 2.50 6.00
41 John LeClair 2.00 5.00
42 Kirk Muller 1.50 4.00
43 Mark Recchi 2.50 6.00
44 Jose Theodore 2.00 5.00
45 Saku Koivu 2.00 5.00
46 Brian Gionta 1.50 4.00
47 Josh Gorges 1.50 4.00
48 Lars Eller 1.50 4.00
49 Carey Price 6.00 15.00
50 P.K. Subban 3.00 8.00
51 Hap Day 1.50 4.00
52 Ace Bailey 1.25 3.00
53 Busher Jackson 1.50 4.00
54 Charlie Conacher 1.50 4.00
55 Joe Primeau 1.25 3.00
56 King Clancy 2.00 5.00
57 Wally Stanowski 1.50 4.00
58 Red Horner 1.50 4.00
59 Bill Barilko 1.50 4.00
60 Bob Davidson 1.50 4.00
61 Howie Meeker 2.00 5.00
62 Max Bentley 1.25 3.00
63 Syl Apps 1.50 4.00
64 Ted Kennedy 1.50 4.00
65 Turk Broda 2.00 5.00
66 Bob Pulford 1.50 4.00
67 Dick Duff 1.50 4.00
68 Harry Lumley 2.00 5.00
69 Tim Horton 2.00 5.00
70 Bob Baun 1.50 4.00
71 Dave Keon 2.00 5.00
72 Bob Nevin 1.25 3.00
73 Frank Mahovlich 2.00 5.00
74 Johnny Bower 2.00 5.00
75 Red Kelly 1.50 4.00
76 Terry Sawchuk 2.00 5.00
77 Borje Salming 2.00 5.00
78 Darryl Sittler 2.00 5.00
79 Lanny McDonald 2.00 5.00
80 Mike Palmateer 2.00 5.00
81 Paul Henderson 1.50 4.00
82 Ron Ellis 1.25 3.00
83 Tiger Williams 1.50 4.00
84 Gary Leeman 1.50 4.00
85 Rick Vaive 1.50 4.00
86 Dave Andreychuk 2.00 5.00
87 Doug Gilmour 2.50 6.00
88 Felix Potvin 4.00 10.00
89 Glenn Anderson 2.00 5.00
90 Mats Sundin 2.00 5.00
91 Wendel Clark 2.00 5.00
92 Curtis Joseph 2.00 5.00
93 Darcy Tucker 1.50 4.00
94 Ed Belfour 2.00 5.00
95 Tie Domi 2.00 5.00
96 Joffrey Lupul 1.50 4.00
97 Jake Gardiner 2.00 5.00
98 Dion Phaneuf 2.00 5.00
99 James Reimer 2.00 5.00
100 Mikhail Grabovski 1.50 4.00

2012-13 ITG Forever Rivals Gold

GOLD/30: 1X TO 2.5X BASIC CARDS

2012-13 ITG Forever Rivals Autographs

AAB Andy Bathgate 8.00 20.00
AABE Allan Bester 6.00 15.00
AAM Ab McDonald 6.00 15.00
ABB Butch Bouchard 20.00 40.00
ABBA Bob Baun 6.00 15.00
ABD Bill Derlago 5.00 12.00
ABE Brian Engblom 8.00 20.00
ABG Brian Glennie 6.00 15.00
ABN Bob Nevin 5.00 12.00
ABO Bert Olmstead 8.00 20.00
ABP Bernie Parent 12.00 30.00
ABPU Bob Pulford SP 30.00 60.00
ABR Bobby Rousseau 6.00 15.00
ABS Bobby Smith 6.00 15.00
ABSA Borje Salming 8.00 20.00
ABSE Brit Selby 6.00 15.00
ABSK Brian Skrudland 8.00 20.00
ACC Chris Chelios SP 20.00 50.00
ACH Charlie Hodge 6.00 15.00
ACJ Curtis Joseph 10.00 25.00
ACL Claude Lemieux 6.00 15.00
ACN Chris Nilan 6.00 15.00
ACP Carey Price SP 25.00 60.00
ADA Dave Andreychuk 8.00 20.00
ADD Dick Duff SP 12.00 30.00
ADD2 Dick Duff SP 12.00 30.00
ADDA Dan Daoust 6.00 15.00
ADE Dave Ellett 5.00 12.00
ADG Doug Gilmour SP 60.00 125.00
ADJ Doug Jarvis 6.00 15.00
ADK Dave Keon SP 40.00 80.00
ADM Dickie Moore 8.00 20.00
ADMA Don Marshall 5.00 12.00
ADMAL Dan Maloney 6.00 15.00
ADP Dion Phaneuf 8.00 20.00
ADSA Denis Savard 10.00 25.00
ADSI Darryl Sittler 12.00 30.00
ADT1 Darcy Tucker 6.00 15.00
ADT2 Darcy Tucker 6.00 15.00
AEB Ed Belfour 10.00 25.00
AEC Ed Chadwick 6.00 15.00
AED Eric Desjardins 6.00 15.00
AEL Elmer Lach 15.00 30.00
AES Eddie Shack 8.00 20.00
AET Errol Thompson 5.00 12.00
AFM Fleming MacKell 6.00 15.00
AFMA Frank Mahovlich SP 30.00 60.00
AFP Felix Potvin 15.00 40.00
AGC Guy Carbonneau 8.00 20.00
AGD Gilbert Dionne 8.00 20.00
AGL Guy Lafleur SP 100.00 200.00
AGLA Guy Lapointe 6.00 15.00
AGLE Gary Leeman 6.00 15.00
AGR Gary Roberts SP 20.00 40.00
AGT Greg Terrion 5.00 12.00
AHM Howie Meeker 8.00 20.00
AHR Henri Richard 15.00 30.00
AIT Ian Turnbull 6.00 15.00
AJA John Anderson 5.00 12.00
AJB Jean Beliveau SP 100.00 175.00
AJBO Johnny Bower SP 30.00 60.00
AJC Jiri Crha 8.00 20.00
AJD Jim Dorey 5.00 12.00
AJGT Jean-Guy Talbot 8.00 20.00
AJL Jacques Lemaire 8.00 20.00
AJLA Jacques Laperriere 8.00 20.00
AJLE John LeClair 8.00 20.00
AJM Jim McKenny 5.00 12.00
AJP Jim Pappin 5.00 12.00
AJR Jim Roberts 6.00 15.00
AKK Kris King 5.00 12.00
AKM Kirk Muller 6.00 15.00
ALB Laurie Boschman 5.00 12.00
ALM Lanny McDonald SP 30.00 60.00
ALO Lyle Odelein 6.00 15.00
ALR Larry Robinson 8.00 20.00
AMF Miroslav Frycer 5.00 12.00
AMG Mike Gartner SP 20.00 40.00
AMK Mike Keane 6.00 15.00
AMM Mike McPhee 5.00 12.00
AMN Mats Naslund 6.00 15.00
AMP Marcel Pronovost 8.00 20.00
AMPA Mike Palmateer SP 15.00 40.00
AMS Mats Sundin SP 40.00 80.00
ANB Nikolai Borschevsky 8.00 20.00
ANU Norm Ullman 8.00 20.00
APG Phil Goyette 6.00 15.00
APH Paul Henderson 8.00 20.00
APM Pete Mahovlich 8.00 20.00
APR Patrick Roy SP 100.00 200.00
ARB Ralph Backstrom 8.00 20.00
ARC Russ Courtnall 6.00 15.00
ARC2 Russ Courtnall 6.00 15.00
ARE Ron Ellis 6.00 15.00
ARK Red Kelly SP 25.00 50.00
ARL Rod Langway 6.00 15.00
ARS Richard Sevigny 8.00 20.00
ARST Rick St. Croix 6.00 15.00
ARV Rogie Vachon 10.00 25.00
ARVA Rick Vaive 6.00 15.00
ARW Ryan Walter 5.00 12.00
ARWA Rick Wamsley 8.00 20.00
ASB Scotty Bowman 12.00 30.00
ASC1 Shayne Corson 5.00 12.00
ASC2 Shayne Corson 5.00 12.00
ASP Steve Penney 8.00 20.00
ASR Stephane Richer 6.00 15.00
ASS Serge Savard 8.00 20.00
ASSH Steve Shutt 6.00 15.00
AST Steve Thomas 5.00 12.00
ATD Tie Domi 10.00 25.00
ATE Tony Esposito SP 40.00 80.00
ATG Todd Gill 5.00 12.00
ATL Trevor Linden 8.00 20.00
ATS Tod Sloan 8.00 20.00
ATW Tiger Williams 6.00 15.00
AVD1 Vincent Damphousse SP 30.00 60.00
AVD2 Vincent Damphousse SP 30.00 60.00
AWC Wendel Clark SP 30.00 60.00
AWP Wilf Paiement 6.00 15.00
AWS Wally Stanowski 8.00 20.00
AYC Yvan Cournoyer 8.00 20.00
AYL Yvon Lambert 8.00 20.00

2012-13 ITG Forever Rivals Autographs Dual

DABSLR B.Salming/L.Robinson 50.00 100.00
DADGKM D.Gilmour/K.Muller 100.00 200.00
DADKJB D.Keon/J.Beliveau 100.00 200.00
DAFPPR F.Potvin /P.Roy

2012-13 ITG Forever Rivals Between The Pipes Jerseys Dual

STATED PRINT RUN 9-85
BTPD01 F.Potvin/P.Roy/85 15.00 30.00
BTPD02 C.Joseph/J.Theodore/85 8.00 20.00
BTPD03 V.Toskala/J.Halak/85 6.00 15.00
BTPD04 A.Bester/P.Roy/85 15.00 40.00
BTPD05 J.Reimer/C.Price/85 20.00 50.00
BTPD06 A.Raycroft/C.Huet/85 5.00 12.00
BTPD07 E.Belfour/J.Hackett/85 6.00 15.00
BTPD08 T.Sawchuk/R.Vachon/9
BTPD09 J.Bower/J.Plante/9

2012-13 ITG Forever Rivals Between The Pipes Memorabilia Blue/Red

STATED PRINT RUN 6-130
SILVER/30: .5X TO 1.2X BLUE-RED/130*
BTP01 Felix Potvin/130* 8.00 20.00
BTP02 James Reimer/130* 5.00 12.00
BTP03 Curtis Joseph/130* 5.00 12.00
BTP04 Ed Belfour/130* 5.00 12.00
BTP05 Grant Fuhr/130* 5.00 12.00
BTP06 Mike Palmateer/130* 5.00 12.00
BTP07 Vesa Toskala/130* 5.00 12.00
BTP08 Patrick Roy/130* 12.00 30.00
BTP09 Carey Price/130* 15.00 40.00
BTP10 Jaroslav Halak/130* 5.00 12.00
BTP11 Cristobal Huet/130* 4.00 10.00
BTP12 Jose Theodore/130* 5.00 12.00
BTP13 Jeff Hackett/130* 4.00 10.00
BTP14 Doug Soetaert/130* 4.00 10.00

2012-13 ITG Forever Rivals Cup Winners Jerseys Silver

SILVER ANNOUNCED PRINT RUN 9-85
CW01 Patrick Roy/85* 10.00 25.00
CW02 Guy Lafleur/85* 10.00 25.00
CW03 Kirk Muller/85* 5.00 12.00
CW04 Mike Keane/85* 5.00 12.00
CW05 Guy Carbonneau/85* 6.00 15.00
CW06 Guy Lapointe/85* 8.00 20.00
CW07 Bob Baun/85* 8.00 20.00
CW08 Mats Naslund/85* 6.00 15.00
CW09 Larry Robinson/85* 6.00 15.00
CW10 Yvan Cournoyer/85* 6.00 15.00
CW11 Denis Savard/85* 8.00 20.00
CW12 Harry Watson/85* 8.00 20.00

2012-13 ITG Forever Rivals Double Agents

DAG01 Darcy Tucker 1.50 4.00
DAG02 Dick Duff 1.50 4.00
DAG03 Shayne Corson 1.25 3.00
DAG04 Doug Gilmour 2.50 6.00
DAG05 Frank Mahovlich 2.00 5.00
DAG06 Jacques Plante 2.50 6.00
DAG07 Kirk Muller 1.50 4.00
DAG08 Lorne Chabot 1.50 4.00

2012-13 ITG Forever Rivals Dual Rivals Jerseys Silver

STATED PRINT RUN 9-85
R01 D.Gilmour/K.Muller/85 8.00 20.00
R02 B.Salming/L.Robinson/85 6.00 15.00
R03 L.McDonald/S.Shutt/85 6.00 15.00
R04 R.Vaive/B.Smith/85 6.00 15.00
R05 F.Potvin/P.Roy/85 15.00 40.00
R06 J.Gustavsson/C.Price/85 20.00 50.00
R07 W.Clark/G.Carbonneau/85 8.00 20.00
R08 M.Sundin/S.Koivu/85 8.00 20.00
R09 D.Phaneuf/P.Subban/85 10.00 25.00
R10 T.Domi/S.Corson/85 6.00 15.00
R11 G.Leeman/M.Naslund/85 6.00 15.00
R12 M.Gartner/M.Recchi/85 8.00 20.00

2012-13 ITG Forever Rivals Game Used Jerseys Blue/Red

M01-M50 STATED PRINT RUN 130
M51-M60 ANNOUNCED PRINT RUN 20
SILVER/30: .6X TO 1.5X BLUE-RED/130*
M01 Ed Belfour/130* 5.00 12.00
M02 Wendel Clark/130* 5.00 12.00
M03 Dion Phaneuf/130* 5.00 12.00
M04 Tie Domi/130* 5.00 12.00
M05 Mike Gartner/130* 5.00 12.00
M06 Doug Gilmour/130* 6.00 15.00
M07 Curtis Joseph/130* 5.00 12.00
M08 Nikolai Kulemin/130* 4.00 10.00
M09 Gary Leeman/130* 4.00 10.00
M10 Brian Leetch/130* 5.00 12.00
M11 Mikhail Grabovski/130* 4.00 10.00
M12 Larry Murphy/130* 5.00 12.00
M13 Clarke MacArthur/130* 3.00 8.00
M14 Mike Palmateer/130* 5.00 12.00
M15 Felix Potvin/130* 8.00 20.00
M16 James Reimer/130* 5.00 12.00
M17 Grant Fuhr/130* 5.00 12.00
M18 Borje Salming/130* 5.00 12.00
M19 Alexander Mogilny/130* 5.00 12.00
M20 Matt Stajan/130* 4.00 10.00
M21 Mats Sundin/130* 5.00 12.00
M22 Steve Thomas/130* 3.00 8.00
M23 Darcy Tucker/130* 4.00 10.00
M24 Rick Vaive/130* 4.00 10.00
M25 Nik Antropov/130* 4.00 10.00
M26 Brian Bellows/130* 4.00 10.00
M27 Guy Carbonneau/130* 5.00 12.00
M28 Chris Chelios/130* 5.00 12.00
M29 Shayne Corson/130* 3.00 8.00
M30 Patrick Roy/130* 12.00 30.00
M31 Gilbert Dionne/130* 5.00 12.00
M32 Lars Eller/130* 4.00 10.00
M33 Doug Gilmour/130* 6.00 15.00
M34 Jeff Hackett/130* 4.00 10.00
M35 Brian Savage/130* 4.00 10.00
M36 Saku Koivu/130* 5.00 12.00
M37 Guy Lafleur/130* 6.00 15.00
M38 Claude Lemieux/130* 4.00 10.00
M39 Patrick Poulin/130* 3.00 8.00
M40 Michael Ryder/130* 3.00 8.00
M41 Trevor Linden/130* 5.00 12.00
M42 Mats Naslund/130* 5.00 12.00
M43 Mark Recchi/130* 5.00 12.00
M44 Larry Robinson/130* 5.00 12.00
M45 Jose Theodore/130* 5.00 12.00
M46 Carey Price/130* 15.00 40.00
M47 Chris Higgins/130* 3.00 8.00
M48 Bobby Smith/130* 4.00 10.00
M49 P.K. Subban/130* 8.00 20.00
M50 Denis Savard/130* 6.00 15.00
M51 Darryl Sittler/20* 8.00 20.00
M52 Tiger Williams/20* 8.00 20.00
M53 Lanny McDonald/20* 10.00 25.00
M54 Bob Baun/20* 8.00 20.00
M55 Terry Sawchuk/20* 12.00 30.00
M56 Steve Shutt/20* 6.00 15.00
M57 Serge Savard/20* 8.00 20.00
M58 Jacques Laperriere/20* 8.00 20.00
M59 Henri Richard/20* 10.00 25.00
M60 Jean Beliveau/20* 15.00 40.00

2012-13 ITG Forever Rivals Greatest Moments

GM01 Maurice Richard 2.00 5.00
GM02 Turk Broda 2.00 5.00
GM03 Bill Barilko 1.50 4.00
GM04 Bernie Geoffrion 1.50 4.00
GM05 Rogie Vachon 2.50 6.00
GM06 Curtis Joseph 2.00 5.00

2012-13 ITG Forever Rivals Immortals

I01 Georges Vezina 2.00 5.00
I02 Howie Morenz 1.50 4.00
I03 Aurel Joliat 2.00 5.00
I04 Newsy Lalonde 1.50 4.00
I05 King Clancy 2.00 5.00
I06 Joe Primeau 1.25 3.00
I07 Busher Jackson 1.50 4.00
I08 Charlie Conacher 1.50 4.00

2012-13 ITG Forever Rivals Net Rivals

NR01 J.Bower/J.Plante 2.50 6.00
NR02 M.Palmateer/B.Larocque 2.00 5.00
NR03 T.Broda/B.Durnan 2.00 5.00
NR04 J.Reimer/C.Price 6.00 15.00
NR05 E.Belfour/C.Huet 2.00 5.00
NR06 C.Joseph/J.Theodore 2.00 5.00
NR07 H.Lumley/G.McNeil 2.00 5.00
NR08 F.Potvin/P.Roy 5.00 12.00

2012-13 ITG Forever Rivals Playoff Matchups

PM01 D.Keon/R.Vachon 2.50 6.00
PM02 J.Beliveau/R.Kelly 2.00 5.00
PM03 F.Mahovlich/C.Hodge 2.00 5.00
PM04 J.Plante/T.Horton 2.50 6.00
PM05 D.Moore/J.Bower 2.00 5.00
PM06 B.Barilko/G.McNeil 1.50 4.00
PM07 T.Kennedy/B.Durnan 2.00 5.00
PM08 F.McCool/M.Richard 2.00 5.00

2012-13 ITG Forever Rivals Post Season Battles Quad Jerseys Silver

STATED PRINT RUN 9-85
PSB01 Lemre/Shtt/Slmng/Sittlr/85 8.00 20.00
PSB02 Lafl/Rbn/McDn/Plmtr/85 12.00 30.00
PSB03 Vchn/Blv/Swchk/Keon/85 15.00 40.00

2012-13 ITG Forever Rivals Quad Memorabilia Silver

ANNOUNCED PRINT RUN 85
QM01 Grbvsk/Phnf/Plek/Sbbn 15.00 40.00
QM02 Reimer/Gustv/Prce/Hlk 12.00 30.00
QM03 Josph/Belfr/Hcktt/Thdre 12.00 30.00
QM04 Gilmour/Potvn/Roy/Mull 25.00 60.00
QM05 Sundn/Grtnr/Rcchi/Kvu 12.00 30.00
QM06 Lmn/Bstr/Corsn/Chelios 12.00 30.00
QM07 Vaive/Clrk/Rbin/Nslnd 12.00 30.00
QM08 Palmtr/Will/Lemre/Crnyr 12.00 30.00
QM09 Sittlr/Slmng/Laflr/Shutt 15.00 40.00

2012-13 ITG Forever Rivals Rivalry

RI01 Fleming Mackell 1.25 3.00
RI02 Johnny Bower 2.00 5.00
RI03 Frank Mahovlich 2.00 5.00
RI04 Dave Keon 2.00 5.00
RI05 Gerry McNeil 1.25 3.00
RI06 Yvan Cournoyer 2.00 5.00
RI07 Jean Beliveau 2.00 5.00

2012-13 ITG Forever Rivals Trophy Winners Memorabilia Silver

ANNOUNCED PRINT RUN 9-85
TW01 Patrick Roy/85* 15.00 40.00
TW02 Chris Chelios/85* 6.00 15.00
TW03 Doug Gilmour/85* 8.00 20.00
TW04 Guy Lafleur/85* 8.00 20.00
TW05 Mats Naslund/85* 6.00 15.00
TW06 Saku Koivu/85* 6.00 15.00
TW07 Larry Robinson/85* 6.00 15.00
TW08 Jose Theodore/85* 6.00 15.00

2004-05 ITG Franchises Canadian

This 150-card set was the first release in the Franchise trio produced by In the Game. The set focused on vintage players from Canadian clubs.

COMPLETE SET (150) 25.00 60.00
1 Dan Bouchard .30 .75
2 Phil Housley .20 .50
3 Reggie Lemelin .30 .75
4 Hakan Loob .20 .50
5 Jamie Macoun .20 .50
6 Kent Nilsson .20 .50
7 Joel Otto .20 .50
8 Jim Peplinski .20 .50
9 Paul Ranheim .20 .50
10 Mark Hunter .20 .50
11 Doug Gilmour .30 .75
12 Joe Mullen .30 .75
13 Lanny McDonald .30 .75
14 Paul Reinhart .20 .50
15 Gary Suter .20 .50
16 Guy Chouinard .20 .50
17 Grant Fuhr .40 1.00
18 Bernie Nicholls .20 .50
19 Andy Moog .30 .75
20 Esa Tikkanen .20 .50
21 Dave Semenko .20 .50
22 Mark Napier .20 .50
23 Bill Ranford .30 .75
24 Paul Coffey .40 1.00
25 Glenn Anderson .20 .50
26 Kent Nilsson .20 .50
27 Jari Kurri .50 1.25
28 Randy Gregg .20 .50
29 Charlie Huddy .20 .50
30 Dave Hunter .20 .50
31 Mike Krushelnyski .20 .50
32 Ed Mio .30 .75
33 Garry Unger .20 .50
34 Lee Fogolin .20 .50
35 Billy Burch .20 .50
36 Goldie Prodgers .20 .50
37 Rocket Richard .75 2.00
38 Henri Richard .40 1.00
39 Jean Beliveau .50 1.25
40 Jacques Plante .60 1.50
41 Doug Harvey .30 .75
42 Howie Morenz .30 .75
43 Bernie Geoffrion .40 1.00
44 Georges Vezina .60 1.50
45 Gump Worsley .40 1.00
46 Rogie Vachon .40 1.00
47 John Ferguson .20 .50
48 Guy Lafleur .50 1.25
49 Dickie Moore .40 1.00
50 Larry Robinson .30 .75
51 Serge Savard .40 1.00
52 Yvan Cournoyer .40 1.00
53 Toe Blake .40 1.00
54 Butch Bouchard .30 .75
55 Steve Shutt .40 1.00
56 Jacques Lemaire .40 1.00
57 Frank Mahovlich .40 1.00
58 Georges Hainsworth .30 .75
59 Patrick Roy .75 2.00
60 Guy Lapointe .30 .75
61 Elmer Lach .20 .50
62 Jacques Laperriere .30 .75
63 Aurel Joliat .40 1.00
64 Bill Durnan .20 .50
65 Nels Stewart .20 .50
66 Clint Benedict .30 .75
67 Hooley Smith .20 .50
68 Art Ross .30 .75
69 Cy Denneny .20 .50
70 Frank Finnigan .20 .50
71 Joe Malone .30 .75
72 Harry Mummery RC .60 1.50
73 Andre Savard .20 .50
74 Marian Stastny .20 .50
75 Marc Tardif .20 .50
76 Peter Stastny .30 .75
77 Dan Bouchard .30 .75
78 Michel Goulet .30 .75
79 Dale Hunter .20 .50
80 Real Cloutier .20 .50
81 Robbie Ftorek .20 .50
82 Mike Hough .20 .50
83 Anton Stastny .20 .50
84 Jack Adams .30 .75
85 Reg Noble .20 .50
86 Ken Randall .20 .50
87 Red Kelly .40 1.00
88 Teeder Kennedy .20 .50
89 Frank Mahovlich .40 1.00
90 Dick Duff .30 .75
91 Bob Pulford .30 .75
92 Ace Bailey .30 .75
93 Sid Smith .20 .50
94 Johnny Bower .40 1.00
95 Bob Nevin .20 .50
96 Bob Baun .30 .75
97 Jim McKenny .20 .50
98 Mike Palmateer .30 .75
99 Frank McCool RC .60 1.50
100 Lanny McDonald .30 .75
101 Tiger Williams .30 .75
102 Darryl Sittler .40 1.00
103 Borje Salming .30 .75
104 Ian Turnbull .20 .50
105 King Clancy .30 .75
106 Joe Primeau .20 .50
107 Turk Broda .40 1.00
108 Howie Meeker .30 .75
109 Rick Vaive .20 .50
110 Tim Horton .40 1.00
111 Wendel Clark .30 .75
112 Doug Gilmour .30 .75
113 Bill Barilko 1.25 3.00
114 Red Horner .20 .50
115 Babe Dye .20 .50
116 Hap Day .30 .75
117 Tiger Williams .30 .75
118 Harold Snepsts .20 .50
119 Richard Brodeur .30 .75
120 Stan Smyl .20 .50
121 Cam Neely .40 1.00
122 Dennis Kearns .20 .50
123 Brian Bradley .20 .50
124 Jack McIlhargey .20 .50
125 Andre Boudrias .20 .50
126 Gary Smith .30 .75
127 Gino Odjick .20 .50
128 Kirk McLean .20 .50
129 Darcy Rota .20 .50
130 Garth Butcher .20 .50
131 Ron Delorme .20 .50
132 Thomas Gradin .20 .50
133 Dale Tallon .20 .50
134 Don Lever .20 .50
135 Bobby Hull .60 1.50
136 Laurie Boschman .20 .50
137 Bob Essensa .30 .75
138 Jimmy Mann .20 .50
139 Randy Carlyle .20 .50
140 Dale Hawerchuck .20 .50
141 Thomas Steen .20 .50
142 Darrin Shannon .20 .50
143 Doug Smail .20 .50
144 Mario Marois .20 .50
145 Morris Lukowich .20 .50
146 Jim Kyte .20 .50
147 Dave Ellet .20 .50
148 Dave Babych .20 .50
149 Tim Watters .20 .50
150 Paul MacLean .20 .50

2004-05 ITG Franchises Canadian Autographs

STATED ODDS 1:16
AM2 Andy Moog 8.00 20.00
AS2 Allan Stanley 15.00 40.00
BB2 Bobby Baun 15.00 40.00
BG Bernie Geoffrion 25.00 60.00
BH2 Bobby Hull SP 40.00 80.00
BN2 Bob Nevin 10.00 25.00
BR Bill Ranford 5.00 12.00
BS Borje Salming SP 20.00 50.00
CN2 Cam Neely SP 20.00 50.00
DB2 Dan Bouchard 8.00 20.00
DB3 Dan Bouchard 8.00 20.00
DD Dick Duff 15.00 40.00
DG2 Doug Gilmour 20.00 50.00
DK Dennis Kearns 5.00 12.00
DM2 Dickie Moore 15.00 40.00
DS2 Darryl Sittler SP 20.00 50.00
EL Elmer Lach SP 20.00 50.00
EM Ed Mio 5.00 12.00
FM2 Frank Mahovlich SP 25.00 50.00
FM3 Frank Mahovlich SP 25.00 50.00
GA Glenn Anderson 5.00 12.00
GB Garth Butcher 5.00 12.00
GF Grant Fuhr SP 20.00 50.00
GL Guy Lafleur SP 30.00 80.00
GO Gino Odjick 6.00 15.00
GS Gary Suter 5.00 12.00
GU2 Garry Unger 5.00 12.00
GW3 Gump Worsley 25.00 50.00
HM Howie Meeker 20.00 50.00
HR Henri Richard SP 12.00 30.00
HS Harold Snepsts 6.00 15.00
IT Ian Turnbull 5.00 12.00
JB Johnny Bower 20.00 50.00
JF John Ferguson 10.00 25.00
JK Jari Kurri SP 12.50 30.00
JL Jacques Laperriere 10.00 25.00
KN Kent Nilsson 5.00 12.00
LF Lee Fogolin 8.00 20.00
LM2 Lanny McDonald SP 25.00 60.00
LM3 Lanny McDonald SP 20.00 50.00
MG2 Michel Goulet 12.00 30.00
MM Mario Marois 5.00 12.00
MN Mark Napier 5.00 12.00
MP Mike Palmateer 25.00 60.00
MT Marc Tardiff 5.00 12.00
PC1 Paul Coffey SP 25.00 60.00
PH2 Phil Housley 6.00 15.00
PR2 Patrick Roy 100.00 200.00
RC2 Randy Carlyle 8.00 20.00
RD Ron Delorme 5.00 12.00
RV2 Rogie Vachon 12.00 30.00
TG Thomas Gradin 5.00 12.00
TK Teeder Kennedy 20.00 50.00
TW1 Tiger Williams 15.00 40.00
TW2 Tiger Williams SP 12.00 30.00
YC Yvan Cournoyer 12.00 30.00
ABO Andre Boudrias 5.00 12.00
ASV Andre Savard 5.00 12.00
BBO Butch Bouchard 15.00 40.00
BES Bob Essensa 6.00 15.00
BPL Bob Pulford 8.00 20.00
CHU Charlie Huddy 5.00 12.00
DBB Dave Babych 5.00 12.00
DEL Dave Ellett 5.00 12.00
DHA Dale Hawerchuk 15.00 40.00
DHU2 Dale Hunter 6.00 15.00
DLV Don Lever 12.50 30.00
DRO Darcy Rota 5.00 12.00
DSE Dave Semenko 8.00 20.00
DSH Darrin Shannon 5.00 12.00
DSM Doug Smail 5.00 12.00
DTL Dale Tallon 6.00 15.00
DVH Dave Hunter 5.00 12.00
GCH Guy Chouinard 5.00 12.00
GLP Guy Lapointe 12.00 30.00
JBE Jean Beliveau SP 30.00 60.00
JKY Jim Kyte 8.00 20.00
JLE Jacques Lemaire 12.00 30.00
JMC Jamie Macoun 5.00 12.00
JMI0 Jack McIlhargey 5.00 12.00
JMK Jim McKenny 5.00 12.00
JMN Jimmy Mann 5.00 12.00
JOT Joel Otto 5.00 12.00
JPE Jim Peplinski 5.00 12.00
KML Kirk McLean 6.00 15.00
LBH Laurie Boschman 5.00 12.00
MKR Mike Krushelnyski 5.00 12.00
MLU Morris Lukowich 5.00 12.00
MST Marian Stastny 5.00 12.00
PML Paul MacLean 5.00 12.00
PRA Paul Ranheim 5.00 12.00
PRE Paul Reinhart 5.00 12.00
RBR Richard Brodeur 8.00 20.00
RCL Real Cloutier 5.00 12.00
RFT Robbie Ftorek 5.00 12.00
RGR Randy Gregg 5.00 12.00
RHU Red Horner SP 75.00 150.00
RLM Reggie Lemelin 5.00 12.00
RVA Rick Vaive 12.50 30.00
SSH Steve Shutt 10.00 25.00
SSM Stan Smyl 5.00 12.00
SSV Serge Savard 8.00 20.00
TWA Tim Watters 5.00 12.00
WCL2 Wendel Clark 20.00 50.00

2004-05 ITG Franchises Canadian Barn Burners

NOUNCED PRINT RUN 50
GOLD/20: .5X TO 1.2X MEM/50*
BB1 Lanny McDonald 12.50 30.00
BB2 Darryl Sittler 12.50 30.00
BB3 Jean Beliveau 15.00 40.00
BB4 Rick Vaive 12.50 30.00
BB5 Paul Coffey 12.50 30.00
BB6 Henri Richard 12.50 30.00
BB7 Jacques Plante 25.00 60.00
BB8 Rocket Richard 50.00 125.00

2004-05 ITG Franchises Canadian Boxtoppers

is 25-card set of jumbo boxtoppers were inserted at 1 per box and depicted the various Canadian clubs' logos through the years.

TH1 Calgary Flames Original 2.00 5.00
TH2 Calgary Flames Horse 2.00 5.00
TH3 Calgary Flames 2.00 5.00
TH4 Edmonton Oilers Original 2.00 5.00
TH5 Edmonton Oilers 2.00 5.00
TH6 Edmonton Oilers 25th Ann. 2.00 5.00
TH7 Hamilton Tigers 2.00 5.00
TH8 Montreal Canadiens 2.00 5.00
TH9 Montreal Maroons 2.00 5.00
TH10 Montreal Wanderers 2.00 5.00
TH11 Ottawa Senators Original 2.00 5.00
TH12 Ottawa Senators 2.00 5.00
TH13 Quebec Bulldogs 2.00 5.00
TH14 Quebec Nordiques 2.00 5.00
TH15 Toronto Arenas 2.00 5.00
TH16 Toronto Maple Leafs Original 2.00 5.00
TH17 Toronto Maple Leafs 1950s 2.00 5.00
TH18 Toronto Maple Leafs 1960s 2.00 5.00
TH19 Toronto Maple Leafs 2.00 5.00
TH20 Toronto St. Patricks 2.00 5.00
TH21 Vancouver Canucks original 2.00 5.00
TH22 Vancouver Canucks 1980s 2.00 5.00
TH23 Vancouver Canucks 2.00 5.00
TH24 Winnipeg Jets 1980s 2.00 5.00
TH25 Winnipeg Jets 1990s 2.00 5.00

2004-05 ITG Franchises Canadian Double Memorabilia

ANNOUNCED PRINT RUN 60
GOLD/20: .5X TO 1.2X DUAL/60*
DM1 George Hainsworth 25.00 60.00
DM2 Jean Beliveau 25.00 60.00
DM3 Johnny Bower 25.00 60.00
DM4 Georges Vezina 100.00 175.00
DM5 Patrick Roy 30.00 80.00
DM6 Aurel Joliat 25.00 60.00
DM7 Jacques Plante 30.00 80.00
DM8 Howie Morenz 75.00 150.00
DM9 Gump Worsley 15.00 40.00
DM10 Guy Lafleur 25.00 60.00
DM11 Wendel Clark 20.00 50.00
DM12 Grant Fuhr 15.00 40.00
DM13 Bernie Geoffrion 15.00 40.00
DM14 Tim Horton 40.00 80.00
DM15 Frank Mahovlich 15.00 40.00
DM16 Joe Mullen 15.00 40.00
DM17 Henri Richard 15.00 40.00
DM18 Jari Kurri 15.00 40.00
DM19 Glenn Anderson 12.00 30.00
DM20 Paul Coffey 12.00 30.00
DM21 Phil Housley 10.00 25.00
DM22 Doug Gilmour 15.00 40.00

2004-05 ITG Franchises Canadian Forever Rivals

ANNOUNCED PRINT RUN 50
FR1 J.Bower/J.Plante 75.00 150.00
FR2 R.Kelly/J.Beliveau 30.00 80.00
FR3 G.Fuhr/M.Vernon 20.00 50.00
FR4 B.Salming/G.Lafleur 25.00 60.00
FR5 P.Coffey/J.Mullen 15.00 40.00
FR6 J.Kurri/H.Loob 25.00 60.00
FR7 D.Sittler/L.Robinson 15.00 40.00
FR8 W.Clark/P.Roy 50.00 100.00
FR9 T.Horton/H.Richard 40.00 100.00
FR10 L.McDonald/S.Shutt 15.00 40.00

2004-05 ITG Franchises Canadian Goalie Gear

ANNOUNCED PRINT RUN 70
GOLD/20: .5X TO 1.2X GEAR/70*
GG1 Bill Durnan 15.00 40.00
GG2 Johnny Bower 15.00 40.00
GG3 Patrick Roy 25.00 60.00
GG4 Grant Fuhr 15.00 40.00
GG5 Jacques Plante 25.00 60.00
GG6 Gump Worsley 15.00 40.00
GG7 Mike Vernon 15.00 40.00
GG8 Dan Bouchard 10.00 25.00
GG9 Bill Ranford 10.00 25.00
GG10 Richard Brodeur 10.00 25.00

2004-05 ITG Franchises Canadian Memorabilia
ANNOUNCED PRINT RUN 70
GOLD/20: .5X TO 1.2X BASIC MEM/70*
SM1 Jacques Plante 20.00 50.00
SM2 Henri Richard 10.00 25.00
SM3 Jean Beliveau 15.00 40.00
SM4 Larry Robinson 8.00 20.00
SM5 Patrick Roy 15.00 40.00
SM6 Paul Coffey 10.00 25.00
SM7 Grant Fuhr 10.00 25.00
SM8 Yvan Cournoyer 8.00 20.00
SM9 Lanny McDonald 8.00 20.00
SM10 Guy Lapointe 8.00 20.00
SM11 Serge Savard 8.00 20.00
SM12 Gump Worsley 10.00 25.00
SM13 Guy Lafleur 12.00 30.00
SM14 Borje Salming 10.00 25.00
SM15 Joe Mullen 8.00 20.00
SM17 Steve Shutt 8.00 20.00
SM18 Wendel Clark 10.00 25.00
SM19 Frank Mahovlich 10.00 25.00
SM20 Glenn Anderson
SM21 John Ferguson 8.00 20.00
SM22 Richard Brodeur 8.00 20.00
SM23 Tim Horton 20.00 50.00
SM24 Jari Kurri 10.00 25.00
SM25 Jacques Laperriere 8.00 20.00
SM26 Newsy Lalonde 25.00 60.00
SM27 Phil Housley 8.00 20.00
SM28 Bernie Geoffrion 10.00 25.00
SM29 Aurel Joliat 20.00 50.00
SM30 Doug Gilmour 10.00 25.00
SM31 Rick Vaive 8.00 20.00
SM32 Hakan Loob 8.00 20.00

2004-05 ITG Franchises Canadian Original Sticks
ANNOUNCED PRINT RUN 70
GOLD/20: .6X TO 1.5X STICK/70*
OS1 Jean Beliveau 15.00 40.00
OS2 Paul Coffey 8.00 20.00
OS3 Guy Lafleur 12.50 30.00
OS4 Lanny McDonald 10.00 25.00
OS5 Guy Lapointe 6.00 15.00
OS6 Larry Robinson 6.00 15.00
OS7 Steve Shutt 6.00 15.00
OS8 Patrick Roy 15.00 40.00
OS9 Rogie Vachon 12.00 30.00
OS10 Denis Savard 10.00 25.00
OS11 Jacques Plante 15.00 40.00
OS12 Dale Hawerchuk 8.00 20.00
OS13 Phil Housley 6.00 15.00
OS14 Doug Gilmour 12.00 30.00
OS15 Jari Kurri 10.00 25.00
OS16 Glenn Anderson 6.00 15.00

2004-05 ITG Franchises Canadian Teammates
ANNOUNCED PRINT RUN 60
GOLD/20: .5X TO 1.2X TEAMMATE/60*
TM1 G.Hainsworth/A.Joliat 25.00 60.00
TM2 G.Anderson/J.Kurri 15.00 40.00
TM3 M.Vernon/P.Housley 12.50 30.00
TM4 J.Beliveau/J.Plante 20.00 50.00
TM5 L.McDonald/D.Sittler 12.50 30.00
TM6 G.Fuhr/P.Coffey 15.00 40.00
TM7 G.Lapointe/L.Robinson 12.50 30.00
TM8 P.Roy/D.Savard 25.00 60.00
TM9 H.Richard/G.Worsley 20.00 50.00
TM10 D.Gilmour/W.Clark 12.50 30.00

2004-05 ITG Franchises Canadian Triple Memorabilia
ANNOUNCED PRINT RUN 20
TM1 Patrick Roy 75.00 135.00
TM2 Maurice Richard 75.00 150.00
TM3 Guy Lafleur 50.00 100.00
TM4 Jacques Plante 40.00 80.00
TM5 Aurel Joliat 90.00 150.00
TM6 Tim Horton
TM7 Jean Beliveau
TM8 Grant Fuhr
TM9 Johnny Bower 30.00 80.00
TM10 Wendel Clark 25.00 60.00

2004-05 ITG Franchises Canadian Trophy Winners
ANNOUNCED PRINT RUN 70
GOLD/20: .5X TO 1.2X BASIC MEM/70*
TW1 Guy Lafleur 12.50 30.00
TW2 Jacques Plante 25.00 50.00
TW3 Gump Worsley 12.50 30.00
TW4 Patrick Roy 20.00 50.00
TW5 Larry Robinson 8.00 20.00
TW6 Paul Coffey 12.50 30.00
TW7 Bill Ranford 8.00 20.00
TW8 Jean Beliveau 15.00 40.00
TW9 Doug Gilmour 12.50 30.00
TW10 Henri Richard 12.50 30.00

2004-05 ITG Franchises Update
Available only online, this 50-card set rounded out the Franchises product run. Each update set contained included a memorabilia card or autograph card also.
COMPLETE SET (50) 20.00 40.00
451 Jari Kurri .40 1.00
452 Bill Quackenbush .20 .50
453 Jean Ratelle .40 1.00
454 Lionel Hitchman .20 .50
455 Terry Sawchuk .60 1.50
456 Grant Fuhr .40 1.00
457 Bill Clement .20 .50
458 Paul Coffey .40 1.00
459 Dick Irvin .20 .50
460 Pierre Pilote .40 1.00
461 Mike Karakas .20 .50
462 Tom Lysiak .20 .50
463 Andy Moog .30 .75
464 Marcel Dionne .40 1.00
465 Borje Salming .30 .75
466 Johnny Bucyk .40 1.00
467 Norm Smith .20 .50
468 Marty McSorley .20 .50
469 Dave Keon .20 .50
470 Rick MacLeish .20 .50
471 Steve Shutt .20 .50
472 Billy Smith .30 .75
473 Neal Broten .20 .50
474 Guy Carbonneau .30 .75
475 Peter Mahovlich .20 .50
476 Tony Esposito .40 1.00
477 Rod Langway .20 .50
478 Newsy Lalonde .50 1.25
479 Pat Verbeek .20 .50
480 Joe Simpson .20 .50
481 Wendel Clark .30 .75
482 Marcel Dionne .40 1.00
483 Frank Boucher .20 .50
484 Johnny Bower .40 1.00
485 Don Beaupre .20 .50
486 Brad Marsh .20 .50
487 Darryl Sittler .40 1.00
488 Barry Ashbee .20 .50
489 Michel Briere 8.00 20.00
490 Guy Lafleur .50 1.25
491 Brian Sutter .20 .50
492 Denis Savard .40 1.00
493 Terry Sawchuk .60 1.50
494 Syl Apps .20 .50
495 Marcel Pronovost .30 .75
496 Dave Keon .20 .50
497 Garth Boesch .20 .50
498 Rick Vaive .20 .50
499 Dino Ciccarelli .20 .50
500 Serge Savard .40 1.00

2004-05 ITG Franchises Update Autographs
ONE AUTO OR MEM.CARD PER SET
AA Al Arbour 8.00 20.00
CK Cliff Koroll 6.00 15.00
DC2 Dino Ciccarelli 12.50 30.00
ET Esa Tikkanen 8.00 20.00
HL Hakan Loob 6.00 15.00
JG John Garrett 6.00 15.00
KW Ken Wregget 6.00 15.00
PF Pat Falloon 6.00 15.00
PV1 Pat Verbeek SP 8.00 20.00
TR Tom Reid 6.00 15.00
TS Thomas Steen 6.00 15.00
ALX Andre Lacroix 6.00 15.00
DKN1 Dave Keon Har. SP 30.00 80.00
DKN2 Dave Keon TML SP 50.00 125.00
JPA Jim Pappin 10.00 25.00
MBU Mike Bullard 6.00 15.00
PBR Pat Price 6.00 15.00
RBA Ralph Backstrom 6.00 15.00
RLY Rick Ley 6.00 15.00

2004-05 ITG Franchises Update Double Memorabilia
ANNOUNCED PRINT RUN 60
GOLD/20: .5X TO 1.2X BASIC MEM/60*
UDM1 Pat Lafontaine 15.00 40.00
UDM2 Bill Durnan 20.00 50.00
UDM3 Frank Brimsek 15.00 40.00
UDM4 Billy Smith 12.50 30.00

2004-05 ITG Franchises Update Goalie Gear
ANNOUNCED PRINT RUN 60
GOLD/20: .5X TO 1.2X MEM/60*
UGG1 Jacques Plante 25.00 50.00
UGG2 Terry Sawchuk 25.00 50.00
UGG3 Mike Richter 12.50 30.00
UGG4 John Vanbiesbrouck 12.50 30.00

2004-05 ITG Franchises Update Memorabilia
ANNOUNCED PRINT RUN 70
GOLD/20: .6X TO 1.5X BASIC MEM/70*
USM1 Patrick Roy 15.00 40.00
USM2 Mario Lemieux 12.00 30.00
USM3 Steve Yzerman 12.00 30.00
USM4 Frank Brimsek 10.00 25.00
USM5 Gary Dornhoefer 8.00 20.00
USM6 Rick MacLeish 8.00 20.00
USM7 Pelle Lindbergh 15.00 40.00
USM8 Marcel Dionne 8.00 20.00

2004-05 ITG Franchises Update Original Sticks
ANNOUNCED PRINT RUN 70
GOLD/20: .5X TO 1.2X BASIC MEM/70*
UOS1 Doug Harvey 20.00 50.00
UOS2 Dave Keon 12.00 30.00
UOS3 Bill Durnan 10.00 25.00
UOS4 Terry Sawchuk 25.00 60.00
UOS5 Wayne Cashman 8.00 20.00
UOS6 Phil Esposito 15.00 40.00
UOS7 Mark Howe 10.00 25.00
UOS8 Clark Gillies 8.00 20.00
UOS9 Howie Morenz 25.00 60.00
UOS10 Bob Davidson 8.00 20.00

2004-05 ITG Franchises Update Teammates
ANNOUNCED PRINT RUN 60
GOLD/20: .5X TO 1.2X TEAMMATE/60*
UTM1 G.Gilbert/G.Cheevers 12.00 30.00
UTM2 M.Dionne/C.Simmer 10.00 25.00
UTM3 D.Keon/R.Kelly 12.00 30.00

2004-05 ITG Franchises Update Trophy Winners
COMPLETE SET (4)
ANNOUNCED PRINT RUN 70
GOLD/20: .5X TO 1.2X BASIC MEM/70*
UTW1 Mario Lemieux 15.00 40.00
UTW2 Steve Yzerman 12.50 30.00
UTW3 Dave Keon 10.00 25.00
UTW4 John Vanbiesbrouck 8.00 20.00

2004-05 ITG Franchises US East
The last in the series issued in pack form, Franchises US East focused on the history of clubs from the eastern United States. Numbering picked up where US West left ended.
COMPLETE SET (150) 25.00 50.00
301 Tom Lysiak .20 .50
302 Bob MacMillan .20 .50
303 Guy Chouinard .20 .50
304 Pat Quinn .50 1.25
305 Eric Vail .20 .50
306 Dan Bouchard .30 .75
307 Curt Bennett .20 .50
308 Phil Myre .30 .75
309 Milt Schmidt .50 1.25
310 Woody Dumart .30 .75
311 Gerry Cheevers .60 1.50
312 Brad Park .30 .75
313 Jacques Plante .60 1.50
314 Johnny Bucyk .40 1.00
315 Terry O'Reilly .20 .50
316 Derek Sanderson .20 .50
317 Phil Esposito .75 2.00
318 Wayne Cashman .20 .50
319 Frank Brimsek .30 .75
320 Wayne Carleton .20 .50
321 Gilles Gilbert .30 .75
322 Bronco Horvath .20 .50
323 Eddie Shore .40 1.00
324 Bill Cowley .20 .50
325 Don Marcotte .20 .50
326 Cam Neely .40 1.00
327 Ray Bourque .75 2.00
328 Andy Moog .30 .75
329 Pete Peeters .20 .50
330 Bobby Bauer .20 .50
331 Tiny Thompson .30 .75
332 Don Awrey .20 .50
333 Rogie Vachon .40 1.00
334 Dit Clapper .30 .75
335 Rick Middleton .30 .75
336 Chuck Rayner .30 .75
337 Mel Hill .20 .50
338 Rick Martin .20 .50
339 Pat LaFontaine .20 .50
340 Sean McKenna RC .20 .50
341 Gilbert Perreault .40 1.00
342 Mike Foligno .20 .50
343 Don Edwards .30 .75
344 Danny Gare .20 .50
345 Phil Housley .20 .50
346 Larry Playfair .20 .50
347 Don Luce .20 .50
348 Tim Horton .40 1.00
349 Roger Crozier .30 .75
350 John Vanbiesbrouck .30 .75
351 Mike Hough .20 .50
352 Bobby Hull .75 2.00
353 Dave Babych .20 .50
354 Tiger Williams .30 .75
355 Mark Howe .20 .50
356 Mike Liut .20 .50
357 Chico Resch .30 .75
358 Bob Carpenter .20 .50
359 Doug Gilmour .40 1.00
360 Chris Terreri .30 .75
361 Kirk Muller .20 .50
362 John MacLean .20 .50
363 Don Lever .20 .50
364 Bruce Driver .20 .50
365 Red Dutton .20 .50
366 Ching Johnson .20 .50
367 Roy Worters .30 .75
368 Sweeney Schriner .20 .50
369 Mike Bossy .40 1.00
370 Billy Smith .30 .75
371 Denis Potvin .30 .75
372 Butch Goring .30 .75
373 Clark Gillies .20 .50
374 Bryan Trottier .30 .75
375 Chico Resch .30 .75
376 Pat LaFontaine .20 .50
377 Garry Howatt .20 .50
378 Bob Bourne .20 .50
379 Bob Nystrom .20 .50
380 J.P. Parise .20 .50
381 Edgar Laprade .20 .50
382 Nick Fotiu .20 .50
383 Rod Gilbert .40 1.00
384 Ed Giacomin .40 1.00
385 Brad Park .30 .75
386 Jean Ratelle .40 1.00
387 John Davidson .30 .75
388 Barry Beck .20 .50
389 Gump Worsley .40 1.00
390 Ron Duguay .20 .50
391 Andy Bathgate .40 1.00
392 Harry Howell .30 .75
393 Phil Esposito .75 2.00
394 Bob Nevin .20 .50
395 Bill Cook .20 .50
396 Allan Stanley .40 1.00
397 Bernie Geoffrion .40 1.00
398 Red Garrett RC .20 .50
399 Don Marshall .20 .50
400 Ron Greschner .20 .50
401 Mike Richter .40 1.00
402 Doug Harvey .20 .50
403 Don Murdoch .20 .50
404 Red Sullivan .20 .50
405 Camille Henry .20 .50
406 Terry Sawchuk .60 1.50
407 Fred Shero .20 .50
408 Red Berenson .20 .50
409 Jim Neilson .20 .50
410 Vic Hadfield .20 .50
411 Bobby Clarke .40 1.00
412 Dave Schultz .30 .75
413 Joe Watson .20 .50
414 Bernie Parent .40 1.00
415 Ron Hextall .30 .75
416 Reggie Leach .20 .50
417 Bill Barber .20 .50
418 Gary Dornhoefer .20 .50
419 Don Saleski .20 .50
420 Bill Clement .20 .50
421 Orest Kindrachuk .20 .50
422 Pelle Lindbergh .30 .75
423 Bobby Taylor .20 .50
424 Mark Howe .20 .50
425 Tom Bladon .20 .50
426 Doug Favell .30 .75
427 Mel Bridgman .20 .50
428 Andre Dupont .20 .50
429 Bob Kelly .20 .50
430 Tim Kerr .20 .50
431 Brad Marsh .20 .50
432 Brian Propp .20 .50
433 Rick MacLeish .20 .50
434 Paul Holmgren .20 .50
435 Keith Acton .20 .50
436 Syd Howe .20 .50
437 Brian Bradley .20 .50
438 Wendel Clark .30 .75
439 Dino Ciccarelli .20 .50
440 Daren Puppa .30 .75
441 Larry Murphy .20 .50
442 Bob Mason RC .30 .75
443 Yvon Labre .20 .50
444 Dennis Maruk .20 .50
445 Dale Hunter .20 .50
446 Al Iafrate .20 .50
447 Rod Langway .20 .50
448 Ryan Walter .20 .50
449 Mike Palmateer .20 .50
450 Don Beaupre .30 .75

2004-05 ITG Franchises US East Autographs
STATED ODDS 1:16
AIA Al Iafrate 5.00 12.00
AADU Andre Dupont 6.00 15.00
AAB Andy Bathgate 8.00 20.00
AAM1 Andy Moog 10.00 25.00
ABBK1 Barry Beck 5.00 12.00
ABPA Bernie Parent 20.00 50.00
ABBA Bill Barber 10.00 25.00
ABCL Bill Clement 8.00 20.00
ABSM Billy Smith 12.00 30.00
ABBN Bob Bourne 5.00 12.00
ABK Bob Kelly 8.00 20.00
ABMM Bob MacMillan 5.00 12.00
ABMS Bob Mason 5.00 12.00
ABN1 Bob Nevin 10.00 25.00
ABNY Bob Nystrom 6.00 15.00
ABCA Bobby Carpenter 5.00 12.00
ABC Bobby Clarke 15.00 40.00
ABTA Bobby Taylor 6.00 15.00
ABM Brad Marsh 5.00 12.00
ABP1 Brad Park BOS SP 20.00 50.00
ABP2 Brad Park NYR SP 15.00 40.00
ABBR Brian Bradley 5.00 12.00
ABPR Brian Propp 8.00 20.00
ABHV Bronco Horvath 10.00 25.00
ABDR Bruce Driver 5.00 12.00
ABT Bryan Trottier 12.00 30.00
ABGO2 Butch Goring 5.00 12.00
ACN1 Cam Neely SP 25.00 60.00
ACR2 Chico Resch 10.00 25.00
ACR3 Chico Resch 10.00 25.00
ACT Chris Terreri 5.00 12.00
ACG Clark Gillies 8.00 20.00
ACBN Curt Bennett 5.00 12.00
ADHU1 Dale Hunter 5.00 12.00
ADB1 Dan Bouchard 10.00 25.00
ADGA Danny Gare 8.00 20.00
ADPU Daren Puppa 5.00 12.00
ADSC1 Dave Schultz 10.00 25.00
ADP Denis Potvin 8.00 20.00
ADMK1 Dennis Maruk 6.00 15.00
ADSA1 Derek Sanderson 10.00 25.00
ADC1 Dino Ciccarelli SP 10.00 25.00
ADA Don Awrey 6.00 15.00
ADBR Don Beaupre 5.00 12.00
ADE Don Edwards 8.00 20.00
ADLU Don Luce 8.00 20.00
ADMA Don Marcotte 5.00 12.00
ADMR Don Marshall 5.00 12.00
ADMU Don Murdoch 8.00 20.00
ADOS Don Saleski 6.00 15.00
ADF1 Doug Favell 6.00 15.00
AEG1 Ed Giacomin 15.00 40.00
AEV Eric Vail 5.00 12.00
AGHO Garry Howatt 5.00 12.00
AGD Gary Dornhoefer 6.00 15.00
AGC Gerry Cheevers SP 15.00 40.00
AGP Gilbert Perreault 12.00 30.00
AGG Gilles Gilbert 10.00 25.00
AGW1 Gump Worsley
AHH Harry Howell 5.00 12.00
AJR Jean Ratelle 8.00 20.00
AJN Jim Neilson 5.00 12.00
AJW1 Joe Watson 5.00 12.00
AJD John Davidson 8.00 20.00
AJMA John MacLean 5.00 12.00
AJV John Vanbiesbrouck 8.00 20.00
AJBU Johnny Bucyk 8.00 20.00
AKM2 Kirk Muller 6.00 15.00
ALMU2 Larry Murphy 10.00 25.00
ALP Larry Playfair 5.00 12.00
ALA Lou Angotti 8.00 20.00
AMH Mark Howe 6.00 15.00
AMBO Mike Bossy 10.00 25.00
AMF Mike Foligno 8.00 20.00
AMHO Mike Hough 5.00 12.00
ANF Nick Fotiu 6.00 15.00
AOK Orest Kindrachuk 6.00 15.00
APL1 Pat LaFontaine BUF SP 40.00 80.00
APL2 Pat LaFontaine NYI SP 40.00 80.00
APQ Pat Quinn 8.00 20.00
APV2 Pat Verbeek 6.00 15.00
APC2 Paul Coffey SP 25.00 60.00
APHO Paul Holmgren 5.00 12.00
APPE1 Pete Peeters 8.00 20.00
APPE2 Pete Peeters 8.00 20.00
APE1 Phil Esposito BOS SP 25.00 60.00
APE2 Phil Esposito NYR SP 20.00 50.00
APH1 Phil Housley 20.00 40.00
APMY Phil Myre 8.00 20.00
ARB1 Ray Bourque SP 75.00 125.00
ARSU Red Sullivan 6.00 15.00
ARL Reggie Leach 10.00 25.00
ARM Rick MacLeish 8.00 20.00
ARMA Rick Martin 8.00 20.00
ARMI Rick Middleton 8.00 20.00
ARGI Rod Gilbert 12.00 30.00
ARLN Rod Langway 6.00 15.00
ARDU Ron Duguay 6.00 15.00
ARG Ron Greschner 5.00 12.00
ARH Ron Hextall 12.50 30.00
ARW Ryan Walter 6.00 15.00
ASMK Sean McKenna 5.00 12.00
ATO Terry O'Reilly 8.00 20.00
ATKR Tim Kerr 5.00 12.00
ATBL Tom Bladon 8.00 20.00
ATLY Tom Lysiak 5.00 12.00
AWCA Wayne Carleton 6.00 15.00
AWC Wayne Cashman 6.00 15.00
AWCL Wendel Clark SP 20.00 50.00
AYL Yvon Labre 5.00 12.00

2004-05 ITG Franchises US East Barn Burners
ANNOUNCED PRINT RUN 50
GOLD/20: .6X TO 1.5X BASIC JSY/50*
EBB1 Jean Ratelle 8.00 20.00
EBB2 Mike Bossy 10.00 25.00
EBB3 Denis Potvin 8.00 20.00
EBB4 Gerry Cheevers 12.50 30.00
EBB5 Reggie Leach 8.00 20.00
EBB6 Ray Bourque 15.00 40.00
EBB7 Billy Smith 8.00 20.00
EBB8 Cam Neely 20.00 50.00
EBB9 Pat LaFontaine 15.00 40.00
EBB10 Mike Richter 10.00 25.00

2004-05 ITG Franchises US East Boxtoppers
COMPLETE SET (25) 60.00 150.00
ONE PER BOX
TH51 Atlanta Flames 4.00 10.00
TH52 Atlanta Thrashers 3.00 8.00
TH53 Atlanta Thrashers Alt 3.00 8.00
TH54 Boston Bruins Orig 4.00 10.00
TH55 Boston Bruins 3.00 8.00
TH56 Boston Bruins Alt 3.00 8.00
TH57 Brooklyn Americans 6.00 15.00
TH58 Buffalo Sabres Orig 3.00 8.00
TH59 Buffalo Sabres 3.00 8.00
TH60 Carolina Hurricanes 3.00 8.00
TH61 Florida Panthers 3.00 8.00
TH62 Hartford Whalers 4.00 10.00
TH63 Nashville Predators 3.00 8.00
TH64 Nashville Predators Alt 3.00 8.00
TH65 New Jersey Devils 3.00 8.00
TH66 New York Americans 6.00 15.00
TH67 New York Islanders 3.00 8.00
TH68 New York Islanders Fish 3.00 8.00
TH69 New York Rangers 3.00 8.00
TH70 New York Rangers Liberty 4.00 10.00
TH71 Philadelphia Flyers 3.00 8.00
TH72 Philadelphia Quakers 6.00 15.00
TH73 Tampa Bay Lightning 3.00 8.00
TH74 Washington Capitals Orig 3.00 8.00
TH75 Washington Capitals 3.00 8.00

2004-05 ITG Franchises US East Double Memorabilia
ANNOUNCED PRINT RUN 60
GOLD/20: .6X TO 1.5X MEM/60*
EDM1 Eddie Shore 12.00 30.00
EDM2 Bobby Clarke 12.50 30.00
EDM3 Gerry Cheevers 15.00 40.00
EDM4 Cam Neely 25.00 60.00
EDM5 Bernie Parent 20.00 50.00
EDM6 Tiny Thompson 20.00 50.00
EDM7 Ray Bourque 15.00 40.00
EDM8 Ron Hextall 30.00 80.00
EDM9 Ed Giacomin 15.00 40.00
EDM10 Gilles Gilbert 10.00 25.00
EDM11 Bryan Trottier 10.00 25.00
EDM12 Mike Bossy 10.00 25.00
EDM13 Gilbert Perreault 15.00 40.00
EDM14 Denis Potvin 10.00 25.00
EDM15 Bill Barber 10.00 25.00
EDM16 Terry O'Reilly 8.00 20.00
EDM17 Reggie Leach 10.00 25.00
EDM18 Bob Nystrom 10.00 25.00
EDM19 Pelle Lindbergh 25.00 60.00
EDM20 Phil Esposito 20.00 50.00
EDM21 Rick Middleton 10.00 25.00
EDM22 Mike Richter 12.50 30.00

2004-05 ITG Franchises US East Forever Rivals
ANNOUNCED PRINT RUN 50
GOLD/20: .5X TO 1.2X MEM/50*
EFR1 P.Esposito/B.Park 15.00 40.00
EFR2 M.Bossy/R.Middleton 12.50 30.00
EFR3 G.Perreault/B. Clarke 12.50 30.00
EFR4 C.Neely/P.LaFontaine 12.50 20.00
EFR5 G.Cheevers/B.Parent 30.00 60.00
EFR6 R.Bourque/D.Potvin 15.00 40.00

2004-05 ITG Franchises US East Goalie Gear
ANNOUNCED PRINT RUN 60
GOLD/20: .5X TO 1.2X GEAR/60*
EGG1 Gerry Cheevers 12.50 30.00
EGG2 Billy Smith 12.50 30.00
EGG3 Tiny Thompson 15.00 40.00
EGG4 Bernie Parent 15.00 40.00
EGG5 Pelle Lindbergh 20.00 50.00
EGG6 Ed Giacomin 20.00 50.00
EGG7 Andy Moog 12.50 30.00
EGG8 Gilles Gilbert 12.50 30.00

2004-05 ITG Franchises US East Memorabilia
ANNOUNCED PRINT RUN 70
GOLD/20: .5X TO 1.2X BASIC MEM/70*
ESM1 Eddie Shore 12.50 30.00
ESM2 Bobby Clarke 8.00 20.00
ESM3 Ray Bourque 12.50 30.00
ESM4 Reggie Leach 8.00 20.00
ESM5 Gerry Cheevers 12.50 30.00
ESM6 Ron Hextall 15.00 40.00
ESM7 Paul Coffey 10.00 25.00
ESM8 Cam Neely 15.00 40.00
ESM9 Gilbert Perreault 10.00 25.00
ESM10 Brad Park 8.00 20.00
ESM11 Billy Smith 8.00 20.00
ESM12 Dave Schultz 12.50 30.00
ESM13 Denis Potvin 8.00 20.00
ESM14 Bill Barber 6.00 15.00
ESM15 Tiny Thompson 12.50 30.00
ESM16 Mike Bossy 8.00 20.00
ESM17 Bryan Trottier 8.00 20.00
ESM18 Gilles Gilbert 10.00 25.00
ESM19 Phil Esposito 15.00 40.00
ESM20 Roy Worters 12.50 30.00
ESM21 Ed Giacomin 15.00 40.00
ESM22 Terry O'Reilly 8.00 20.00
ESM23 Rick Middleton 8.00 20.00
ESM24 Doug Gilmour 8.00 20.00
ESM25 Dale Hawerchuk 12.50 30.00
ESM26 Kirk McLean 8.00 20.00
ESM27 Andy Moog 10.00 25.00
ESM28 Bob Nystrom 6.00 15.00
ESM29 Bernie Parent 12.00 30.00
ESM30 Jean Ratelle 8.00 20.00
ESM31 Pat Verbeek 6.00 15.00
ESM32 John Vanbiesbrouck 10.00 25.00
ESM33 Pat LaFontaine 12.00 30.00
ESM34 Mike Richter 10.00 25.00

2004-05 ITG Franchises US East Original Sticks
ANNOUNCED PRINT RUN 70
GOLD/20: .6X TO 1.5X STICK/70*
EOS1 Cam Neely 10.00 25.00
EOS2 Larry Murphy 8.00 20.00
EOS3 Bobby Clarke 8.00 20.00
EOS4 Ron Duguay 6.00 15.00
EOS5 Phil Esposito 12.50 30.00
EOS6 Vic Hadfield 6.00 15.00
EOS7 Reggie Leach 6.00 15.00
EOS8 Pelle Lindbergh 20.00 50.00
EOS9 Ray Bourque 12.50 30.00
EOS10 Bob Nystrom 6.00 15.00
EOS11 Terry O'Reilly 6.00 15.00
EOS12 Denis Potvin 6.00 15.00
EOS13 Bill Barber 8.00 20.00
EOS14 Ed Giacomin 15.00 40.00
EOS15 Ron Hextall 15.00 40.00
EOS16 Bernie Parent 12.50 30.00
EOS17 Gerry Cheevers 10.00 25.00
EOS18 Johnny Bucyk 8.00 20.00
EOS19 Rick Middleton 8.00 20.00
EOS20 John Davidson 6.00 15.00

2004-05 ITG Franchises US East Teammates
ANNOUNCED PRINT RUN 60
GOLD/20: .6X TO 1.5X BASIC JSY/60
ETM1 E.Shore/T.Thompson 25.00 60.00
ETM2 M.Bossy/B.Trottier 15.00 40.00
ETM3 B.Clarke/B.Barber 12.50 30.00
ETM4 R.Bourque/C.Neely 20.00 50.00
ETM5 B.Park/R.Middleton 12.50 30.00
ETM6 R.Leach/D.Schultz 15.00 40.00
ETM7 B.Nystrom/D.Potvin 12.50 30.00
ETM8 G.Cheevers/T.O'Reilly 12.50 30.00

2004-05 ITG Franchises US East Triple Memorabilia
ANNOUNCED PRINT RUN 20
ETM1 Gerry Cheevers 30.00 80.00
ETM2 Bernie Parent
ETM3 Eddie Shore 40.00 80.00
ETM4 Ray Bourque 40.00 100.00
ETM5 Cam Neely 40.00 100.00
ETM6 Ron Hextall 40.00 80.00
ETM7 Ed Giacomin 40.00 80.00

2004-05 ITG Franchises US East Trophy Winners
ANNOUNCED PRINT RUN 70
ETW1 Eddie Shore 15.00 40.00
ETW2 Bobby Clarke 8.00 20.00
ETW3 Mike Bossy 8.00 20.00
ETW4 Bryan Trottier 8.00 20.00
ETW5 Ray Bourque 15.00 40.00
ETW6 Reggie Leach 8.00 20.00
ETW7 Ron Hextall 20.00 50.00
ETW8 Denis Potvin 8.00 20.00
ETW9 Bernie Parent 12.00 30.00
ETW10 Pelle Lindbergh 15.00 40.00

2004-05 ITG Franchises US West
The second product of the series, Franchises US West focused on the history of clubs in the western United States. Numbering picked up where Franchises Canadian ended.
COMPLETE SET (150) 20.00 40.00
151 Guy Hebert .30 .75
152 Wayne Carleton .20 .50
153 Gary Sabourin .20 .50
154 Gilles Meloche .30 .75
155 Gary Smith .30 .75
156 Bob Stewart .20 .50
157 Reggie Leach .20 .50
158 Glenn Hall .40 1.00
159 Bobby Hull .60 1.50
160 Dennis Hull .30 .75
161 Stan Mikita .50 1.25
162 Bill White .20 .50
163 Tony Esposito .50 1.25
164 Pat Stapleton .20 .50
165 Elmer Vasko .20 .50
166 Bill Mosienko .40 1.00
167 Michel Goulet .30 .75
168 Dirk Graham .20 .50
169 Doug Bentley .20 .50
170 Max Bentley .20 .50
171 Phil Esposito .75 2.00
172 Charlie Gardiner .30 .75
173 Lou Angotti .20 .50
174 Denis Savard .40 1.00
175 Murray Bannerman .30 .75
176 Cliff Koroll .20 .50
177 Johnny Gottselig .20 .50
178 Al MacAdam .20 .50
179 Dennis Maruk .20 .50
180 Greg Smith .20 .50
181 Dave Gardner .20 .50
182 Gilles Meloche .20 .50
183 Patrick Roy .75 2.00
184 Ray Bourque .60 1.50
185 Barry Beck .20 .50
186 Chico Resch .30 .75
187 Joe Watson .20 .50
188 Wilf Paiement .20 .50
189 Doug Favell .20 .50
190 Lanny McDonald .30 .75
191 Bob MacMillan .20 .50
192 Jack Valiquette .20 .50
193 Guy Carbonneau .30 .75
194 Kirk Muller .20 .50
195 Neal Broten .20 .50
196 Craig Ludwig .20 .50
197 Frank Foyston RC .50 1.25
198 Carson Cooper .20 .50
199 Ebbie Goodfellow .30 .75
200 Herb Lewis .20 .50
201 Frank Mahovlich .40 1.00
202 Peter Mahovlich .20 .50
203 Ted Lindsay .40 1.00
204 Red Kelly .40 1.00
205 Ed Giacomin .30 .75
206 Roger Crozier .30 .75
207 Henry Boucha .20 .50
208 Reed Larson .20 .50
209 Vladimir Konstantinov .20 .50
210 Steve Yzerman .75 2.00
211 Glenn Hall .40 1.00
212 Sid Abel .40 1.00
213 Terry Sawchuk .50 1.25
214 Alex Delvecchio .40 1.00
215 Mud Bruneteau .20 .50
216 Mark Howe .20 .50
217 Harry Lumley .30 .75
218 Bruce MacGregor .20 .50
219 Jack Stewart .20 .50
220 Darryl Sittler .40 1.00
221 John Ogrodnick .20 .50
222 Norm Ullman .20 .50
223 Alex Faulkner .20 .50
224 Marcel Pronovost .30 .75
225 Joe Kocur .20 .50
226 Wilf Paiement .20 .50
227 Denis Herron .30 .75
228 Henry Boucha .20 .50
229 Gary Croteau .20 .50
230 Marcel Dionne .40 1.00
231 Charlie Simmer .20 .50
232 Dave Taylor .20 .50
233 Terry Sawchuk .50 1.25
234 Grant Fuhr .40 1.00
235 Rogie Vachon .40 1.00
236 Mike Murphy .20 .50
237 Bob Pulford .30 .75
238 Butch Goring .30 .75
239 Larry Robinson .30 .75
240 Jari Kurri .40 1.00
241 Bernie Nicholls .20 .50
242 Larry Murphy .20 .50
243 Bill Masterton RC 1.25 3.00
244 Bobby Smith .20 .50
245 J.P. Parise .20 .50
246 Gump Worsley .40 1.00
247 Cesare Maniago .30 .75
248 Keith Acton .20 .50
249 Fred Barrett .20 .50
250 Brian Bellows .20 .50
251 Don Beaupre .20 .50
252 Dino Ciccarelli .30 .75
253 Lou Nanne .20 .50
254 Dave Gagner .20 .50
255 Bill Goldsworthy .20 .50
256 Danny Grant .20 .50
257 Craig Hartsburg .20 .50
258 Basil McRae .20 .50
259 Bob Baun .30 .75
260 Bill Hicke .20 .50
261 Carol Vadnais .20 .50
262 Ted Hampson .20 .50
263 Charlie Hodge .20 .50
264 Kent Dougs .20 .50
265 Harry Howell .20 .50
266 Darrin Shannon .20 .50
267 Mario Lemieux 1.00 2.50
268 Greg Malone .20 .50
269 Rick Kehoe .20 .50
270 Les Binkley .30 .75
271 Randy Carlyle .20 .50
272 Lowell MacDonald .20 .50
273 Paul Coffey .40 1.00
274 Kevin Stevens .20 .50
275 Syl Apps Jr. .20 .50
276 Dave Schultz .20 .50
277 Pierre Larouche .20 .50
278 Tim Horton .40 1.00
279 Mike Bullard .20 .50
280 Lionel Conacher .20 .50
281 Odie Cleghorn .20 .50
282 Roy Worters .30 .75
283 Red Berenson .20 .50
284 Mark Hunter .20 .50
285 Glenn Hall .40 1.00
286 Dickie Moore .40 1.00
287 Derek Sanderson .20 .50
288 Wayne Babych .20 .50
289 Bernie Federko .30 .75
290 Doug Harvey .30 .75
291 Jacques Plante .50 1.25
292 Garry Unger .20 .50
293 Doug Gilmour .30 .75
294 Joe Mullen .30 .75
295 Mike Liut .30 .75
296 Frank Finnigan .20 .50
297 Syd Howe .20 .50
298 Brian Hayward .20 .50
299 Kelly Kisio .20 .50
300 Pat Falloon .20 .50

2004-05 ITG Franchises US West Autographs
STATED ODDS 1:16
AAMA Al MacAdam 8.00 20.00
AAD Alex Delvecchio SP 20.00 50.00
AAF Alex Faulkner 15.00 40.00
ABBK2 Barry Beck 5.00 12.00
ABMC Basil McRae 5.00 12.00
ABF Bernie Federko 8.00 20.00
ABNI Bernie Nicholls 5.00 12.00
ABHI Bill Hicke 5.00 12.00
ABW Bill White 5.00 12.00
ABST Bob Stewart 5.00 12.00
ABB1 Bobby Baun 12.00 30.00
ABH1 Bobby Hull SP 40.00 80.00
ABSH Bobby Smith 6.00 15.00
ABBE Brian Bellows 5.00 12.00
ABHA Brian Hayward 6.00 15.00
ABMG Bruce MacGregor 5.00 12.00
ABGO1 Butch Goring 6.00 15.00
ACV Carol Vadnais 8.00 20.00
ACM Cesare Maniago 8.00 20.00
ACH Charlie Hodge 8.00 20.00
ACS Charlie Simmer 5.00 12.00
ACR1 Chico Resch 8.00 20.00
ACHA Craig Hartsburg 5.00 12.00
ACLU Craig Ludwig 5.00 12.00
ADGR Danny Grant 5.00 12.00
ADS1 Darryl Sittler 20.00 50.00
ADGG Dave Gagner 5.00 12.00
ADVG Dave Gardner 6.00 15.00
ADTA Dave Taylor 6.00 15.00
ADHE Denis Herron 5.00 12.00
ADSV Denis Savard 15.00 40.00
ADH Dennis Hull 10.00 25.00
ADMK2 Dennis Maruk 8.00 20.00
ADM1 Dickie Moore 15.00 40.00
ADGH Dirk Graham 5.00 12.00
ADF1 Doug Favell 5.00 12.00
ADG1 Doug Gilmour SP 20.00 50.00
AEG2 Ed Giacomin SP 30.00 80.00
AFM1 Frank Mahovlich SP 30.00 80.00
AFB Fred Barrett 5.00 12.00
AGU Garry Unger 5.00 12.00
AGCR Gary Croteau 5.00 12.00
AGSB Gary Sabourin 5.00 12.00
AGAS Gary Smith 12.00 30.00
AGME1 Gilles Meloche 8.00 20.00
AGME2 Gilles Meloche 8.00 20.00
AGH3 Glenn Hall SP 15.00 40.00
AGH2 Glenn Hall SP 20.00 50.00
AGH1 Glenn Hall SP 20.00 50.00
AGMA Greg Malone 5.00 12.00
AGRS Greg Smith 5.00 12.00
AGW2 Gump Worsley SP
AGCA Guy Carbonneau 5.00 12.00
AGHE Guy Hebert 10.00 25.00
AHB Henry Boucha 8.00 20.00
AJPP J.P. Parise 6.00 15.00
AJVA Jack Valiquette 5.00 12.00
AJM2 Joe Mullen 10.00 25.00
AJKO Joey Kocur 6.00 15.00
AJOG John Ogrodnick 5.00 12.00
AKA Keith Acton 5.00 12.00
AKK Kelly Kisio 5.00 12.00
AKD Kent Douglas 5.00 12.00
AKS Kevin Stevens 8.00 20.00
AKM1 Kirk Muller 8.00 20.00
ALM1 Lanny McDonald SP 20.00 50.00
ALMU1 Larry Murphy 8.00 20.00
ALR1 Larry Robinson 12.00 30.00
ALB Les Binkley 10.00 25.00
ALN Lou Nanne 5.00 12.00
ALMD Lowell MacDonald 8.00 20.00
AMD Marcel Dionne SP 15.00 40.00
AMPR Marcel Pronovost 10.00 25.00
AMLE Mario Lemieux 75.00 150.00
AMHU Mark Hunter 8.00 20.00
AMG1 Michel Goulet 8.00 20.00
AML Mike Liut 8.00 20.00
AMIM Mike Murphy 5.00 12.00
AMBN Murray Bannerman 10.00 25.00
ANB Neal Broten 5.00 12.00
ANU Norm Ullman 6.00 15.00
APS Pat Stapleton 10.00 25.00
APR1 Patrick Roy SP 100.00 200.00
APC3 Paul Coffey SP 40.00 100.00
APE3 Phil Esposito SP 30.00 80.00
APLA Pierre Larouche 5.00 12.00
ARC1 Randy Carlyle 8.00 20.00
ARB2 Ray Bourque SP 40.00 80.00
ARBE Red Berenson 6.00 15.00
ARK Red Kelly 15.00 40.00
ARLA Reed Larson 5.00 12.00
ARKE Rick Kehoe 5.00 12.00
ARV1 Rogie Vachon 15.00 30.00
ASM Stan Mikita SP 15.00 40.00
ASY Steve Yzerman SP 75.00 150.00
ASA Syl Apps Jr 6.00 15.00
ATHA Ted Hampson 5.00 12.00
ATL Ted Lindsay SP 20.00 40.00
ATE Tony Esposito SP 25.00 50.00
AWB Wayne Babych 8.00 20.00
AWP1 Wilf Paiement 5.00 12.00
AWP2 Wilf Paiement 8.00 20.00

2004-05 ITG Franchises US West Barn Burners

ANNOUNCED PRINT RUN 50
GOLD/20: .5X TO 1.2X BASIC JSY/70*
WBB1 Mario Lemieux 20.00 50.00
WBB2 Bill Mosienko 10.00 25.00
WBB3 Ray Bourque 15.00 40.00
WBB4 Garry Unger 10.00 25.00
WBB5 Patrick Roy 15.00 40.00
WBB6 Marcel Dionne 10.00 25.00
WBB7 Ted Lindsay 12.50 30.00
WBB8 Bobby Hull 12.50 30.00
WBB9 Steve Yzerman 15.00 40.00
WBB10 Glenn Hall 12.50 30.00

2004-05 ITG Franchises US West Boxtoppers

COMPLETE SET (25) 60.00 150.00
ONE PER BOX
TH26 Mighty Ducks of Anaheim 3.00 8.00
TH27 California Golden Seals 4.00 10.00
TH28 Chicago Blackhawks/1930's 4.00 10.00
TH29 Chicago Blackhawks 3.00 8.00
TH30 Cleveland Barons 4.00 10.00
TH31 Colorado Avalanche 3.00 8.00
TH32 Colorado Rockies 6.00 15.00
TH33 Columbus Blue Jackets 3.00 8.00
TH34 Dallas Stars 3.00 8.00
TH35 Detroit Cougars 5.00 12.00
TH36 Detroit Falcons 6.00 15.00
TH37 Detroit Red Wings 3.00 8.00
TH38 Kansas City Scouts 4.00 10.00
TH39 LA Kings 3.00 8.00
Original
TH40 Los Angeles Kings 3.00 8.00
TH41 Minnesota North Stars 3.00 8.00
TH42 Minnesota Wild 3.00 8.00
TH43 Oakland Seals 4.00 10.00
TH44 Phoenix Coyotes 3.00 8.00
TH45 Pittsburgh Penguins 3.00 8.00
Original
TH46 Pittsburgh Penguins 3.00 8.00
TH47 Pittsburgh Pirates 3.00 8.00
TH48 St. Louis Blues 3.00 8.00
TH49 St. Louis Eagles 5.00 12.00
TH50 San Jose Sharks 3.00 8.00

2004-05 ITG Franchises US West Double Memorabilia

ANNOUNCED PRINT RUN 60
GOLD/20: .5X TO 1.2X BASIC JSY/60*
WDM1 Bill Mosienko 15.00 40.00
WDM2 Harry Lumley 15.00 40.00
WDM3 Dino Ciccarelli 12.50 30.00
WDM4 Marcel Dionne 12.50 30.00
WDM5 Frank Brimsek 10.00 25.00
WDM6 Patrick Roy 20.00 50.00
WDM7 Ray Bourque 12.50 30.00
WDM8 Glenn Hall 15.00 40.00
WDM9 Jari Kurri 12.50 30.00
WDM10 Mario Lemieux 25.00 60.00
WDM11 Stan Mikita 12.50 30.00
WDM12 Bobby Hull 12.50 30.00
WDM13 Steve Yzerman 20.00 50.00
WDM14 Tony Esposito 12.50 30.00
WDM15 Terry Sawchuk 25.00 60.00
WDM16 Norm Ullman 12.50 30.00
WDM17 Garry Unger 12.50 30.00
WDM18 Michel Goulet 10.00 25.00
WDM19 Roger Crozier 10.00 25.00

2004-05 ITG Franchises US West Forever Rivals

ANNOUNCED PRINT RUN 50
GOLD/20: .5X TO 1.2X DUAL/50*
WFR1 P.Roy/S.Yzerman 25.00 60.00
WFR2 B.Mosienko/S.Abel 12.50 30.00
WFR3 T.Lindsay/H.Lumley 15.00 40.00
WFR4 A.Delvecchio/S.Mikita 20.00 50.00
WFR5 B.Hull/T.Sawchuk 25.00 60.00

2004-05 ITG Franchises US West Goalie Gear

ANNOUNCED PRINT RUN 60
GOLD/20: .5X TO 1.2X GEAR/60*
WGG1 Roger Crozier 10.00 25.00
WGG2 Tony Esposito 12.50 30.00
WGG3 Charlie Gardiner 10.00 25.00
WGG4 Patrick Roy 15.00 40.00
WGG5 Frank Brimsek 12.50 30.00
WGG6 Glenn Hall 12.50 30.00

2004-05 ITG Franchises US West Memorabilia

ANNOUNCED PRINT RUN 70
WSM1 Bill Mosienko 10.00 25.00
WSM2 Roger Crozier 8.00 20.00
WSM3 Ted Lindsay 12.00 30.00
WSM4 Harry Lumley 10.00 25.00
WSM5 Dino Ciccarelli 8.00 20.00
WSM6 Alex Delvecchio 8.00 20.00
WSM7 Marcel Dionne 8.00 20.00
WSM8 Frank Brimsek 10.00 25.00
WSM9 Patrick Roy 15.00 40.00
WSM10 Ray Bourque 12.50 30.00
WSM11 Charlie Gardiner 12.00 30.00
WSM12 Glenn Hall 10.00 25.00
WSM13 Jari Kurri 12.50 30.00
WSM14 Mario Lemieux 12.50 30.00
WSM15 Stan Mikita 8.00 20.00
WSM16 Sid Abel 8.00 20.00
WSM17 Bobby Hull 12.50 30.00
WSM18 Craig Hartsburg 8.00 20.00
WSM19 Paul Coffey 12.50 30.00
WSM20 Grant Fuhr 10.00 25.00
WSM21 Steve Yzerman 12.50 30.00
WSM22 Tony Esposito 10.00 25.00
WSM23 Bill Gadsby 8.00 20.00
WSM24 Michel Goulet 8.00 20.00
WSM25 Dennis Hull 8.00 20.00
WSM26 Terry Sawchuk 15.00 40.00
WSM27 Norm Ullman 8.00 20.00
WSM28 Steve Yzerman 12.50 30.00
WSM29 Patrick Roy 12.00 30.00
WSM30 Mario Lemieux 15.00 40.00
WSM31 Garry Unger 8.00 20.00
WSM32 Larry Murphy 8.00 20.00
WSM33 Mike Vernon 12.50 30.00

2004-05 ITG Franchises US West Original Sticks

ANNOUNCED PRINT RUN 70
GOLD/20: .5X TO 1.2X STICK/70*
WOS1 Patrick Roy 15.00 40.00
WOS2 Harry Lumley 10.00 25.00
WOS3 Steve Yzerman 12.50 30.00
WOS4 Glenn Hall 8.00 20.00
WOS5 Jari Kurri 10.00 25.00
WOS6 Garry Unger 6.00 15.00
WOS7 Stan Mikita 6.00 15.00
WOS8 Ray Bourque 12.50 30.00
WOS9 Roger Crozier 6.00 15.00
WOS10 Marcel Dionne 6.00 15.00
WOS11 Tony Esposito 8.00 20.00
WOS12 Denis Savard 6.00 15.00
WOS13 Mario Lemieux 15.00 40.00
WOS14 Cesare Maniago 6.00 15.00
WOS15 Charlie Simmer 6.00 15.00

2004-05 ITG Franchises US West Teammates

ANNOUNCED PRINT RUN 60
GOLD/20: .5X TO 1.2X TEAMMATE/60*
WTM1 S.Abel/T.Lindsay 20.00 50.00
WTM2 S.Mikita/B.Hull 15.00 40.00
WTM3 G.Unger/G.Hall 12.50 30.00
WTM4 P.Roy/R.Bourque 20.00 50.00
WTM5 M.Lemieux/P.Coffey 20.00 50.00
WTM6 B.Gadsby/N.Ullman 12.50 30.00
WTM7 M.Goulet/D.Savard 12.50 30.00
WTM8 S.Yzerman/D.Ciccarelli 20.00 50.00
WTM9 T.Esposito/D.Hull 12.50 30.00
WTM10 T.Sawchuk/A.Delvecchio 20.00 50.00

2004-05 ITG Franchises US West Triple Memorabilia

ANNOUNCED PRINT RUN 20
WTM1 Roger Crozier 25.00 50.00
WTM2 Harry Lumley
WTM3 Marcel Dionne 30.00 60.00
WTM4 Patrick Roy 60.00 120.00
WTM5 Ray Bourque 30.00 60.00
WTM6 Glenn Hall 40.00 80.00
WTM7 Steve Yzerman 50.00 100.00
WTM8 Mario Lemieux 60.00 120.00
WTM9 Stan Mikita 40.00 80.00
WTM10 Tony Esposito 30.00 60.00

2004-05 ITG Franchises US West Trophy Winners

ANNOUNCED PRINT RUN 70
GOLD/20: .5X TO 1.2X JSY/70*
WTW1 Stan Mikita 8.00 20.00
WTW2 Mario Lemieux 12.50 30.00
WTW3 Bobby Hull 10.00 25.00
WTW4 Ted Lindsay 10.00 25.00
WTW5 Marcel Dionne 8.00 20.00
WTW6 Roger Crozier 8.00 20.00
WTW7 Glenn Hall 10.00 25.00
WTW8 Patrick Roy 15.00 40.00
WTW9 Steve Yzerman 12.50 30.00
WTW10 Charlie Gardiner 8.00 20.00

2006 ITG Going For Gold Women's National Team

COMPLETE SET (25) 4.00 10.00
1 Charline Labonte .40 1.00
2 Kim St. Pierre .40 1.00
3 Gillian Ferrari .20 .50
4 Becky Kellar .20 .50
5 Carla MacLeod .20 .50
6 Caroline Ouellette .20 .50
7 Cheryl Pounder .20 .50
8 Colleen Sostorics .20 .50
9 Meghan Agosta .20 .50
10 Gillian Apps .20 .50
11 Jennifer Botterill .20 .50
12 Cassie Campbell .40 1.00
13 Danielle Goyette .20 .50
14 Jayna Hefford .40 1.00
15 Gina Kingsbury .20 .50
16 Cherie Piper .20 .50
17 Vicky Sunohara .20 .50
18 Sarah Vaillancourt .20 .50
19 Katie Weatherston .20 .50
20 Hayley Wickenheiser .75 2.00
21 Sami Jo Small .40 1.00
22 Delaney Collins .20 .50
23 France St. Louis .20 .50
24 Stacy Wilson .20 .50
25 Checklist .02 .10

2006 ITG Going For Gold Women's National Team Autographs

ONE AU OR GJ PER BOX SET
AA Meghan Agosta 10.00 25.00
AAP Gillian Apps 15.00 40.00
AB Jennifer Botterill 10.00 25.00
AC Cassie Campbell 25.00 60.00
ACO Delaney Collins 10.00 25.00
AF Gillian Ferrari 10.00 25.00
AG Danielle Goyette 10.00 25.00
AH Jayna Hefford 15.00 40.00
AK Becky Kellar 10.00 25.00
AKI Gina Kingsbury 10.00 25.00
AL Charline Labonte 15.00 40.00
AM Carla MacLeod 10.00 25.00
AO Caroline Ouellette 10.00 25.00
AP Cherie Piper 10.00 25.00
APO Cheryl Pounder 10.00 25.00
AS Colleen Sostorics 10.00 25.00
ASM Sami Jo Small 15.00 40.00
AST Kim St. Pierre 15.00 40.00
ASTL France St. Louis 10.00 25.00
ASU Vicky Sunohara 10.00 25.00
AV Sarah Vaillancourt 10.00 25.00
AW Katie Weatherston 10.00 25.00
AWI Hayley Wickenheiser 25.00 60.00
AWIL Stacy Wilson 10.00 25.00

2006 ITG Going For Gold Women's National Team Jerseys

ONE GJ OR AU PER BOXED SET
GUJ01 Charline Labonte 15.00 40.00
GUJ02 Kim St. Pierre 12.00 30.00
GUJ03 Gillian Ferrari 10.00 25.00
GUJ04 Becky Kellar 10.00 25.00
GUJ05 Carla MacLeod 10.00 25.00
GUJ06 Caroline Ouellette 10.00 25.00
GUJ07 Cheryl Pounder 10.00 25.00
GUJ08 Colleen Sostorics 10.00 25.00
GUJ09 Meghan Agosta 10.00 25.00
GUJ10 Gillian Apps 10.00 25.00
GUJ11 Jennifer Botterill 10.00 25.00
GUJ12 Cassie Campbell 20.00 50.00
GUJ13 Danielle Goyette 10.00 25.00
GUJ14 Jayna Hefford 15.00 40.00
GUJ15 Gina Kingsbury 10.00 25.00
GUJ16 Cherie Piper 10.00 25.00
GUJ17 Vicky Sunohara 10.00 25.00
GUJ18 Sarah Vaillancourt 10.00 25.00
GUJ19 Katie Weatherston 10.00 25.00
GUJ20 Hayley Wickenheiser 15.00 40.00
GUJ21 Sami Jo Small 15.00 40.00
GUJ22 Delaney Collins 10.00 25.00

2007 ITG Going For Gold World Juniors

COMPLETE SET (30) 10.00 25.00
1 Carey Price 2.00 5.00
2 Leland Irving .40 1.00
3 Karl Alzner .30 .75
4 Ryan Parent .20 .50
5 Kristopher Letang .30 .75
6 Luc Bourdon .30 .75
7 Kris Russell .20 .50
8 Marc Staal .30 .75
9 Cody Franson .20 .50
10 Steve Downie .40 1.00
11 Andrew Cogliano .30 .75
12 Marc-Andre ClichÃ© .20 .50
13 Kenndal McArdle .20 .50
14 Darren Helm .30 .75
15 Brad Marchand .20 .50
16 James Neal .30 .75
17 Bryan Little .30 .75
18 Daniel Bertram .20 .50
19 Ryan O'Marra .20 .50
20 Tom Pyatt .20 .50
21 Jonathan Toews 1.25 3.00
22 Sam Gagner .75 2.00
23 Eric Lindros .40 1.00
24 Roberto Luongo .60 1.50
25 Jason Spezza .40 1.00
26 Dion Phaneuf .40 1.00
27 Marc-Andre Fleury .60 1.50
28 Joe Thornton .60 1.50
29 Justin Pogge .40 1.00
30 Checklist .02 .10

2007 ITG Going For Gold World Juniors Autographs

1 Carey Price 40.00 80.00
2 Leland Irving 15.00 40.00
3 Karl Alzner 10.00 25.00
4 Ryan Parent 10.00 25.00
5 Kristopher Letang 10.00 25.00
6 Luc Bourdon 10.00 25.00
7 Kris Russell 8.00 20.00
8 Marc Staal 8.00 20.00
9 Cody Franson 6.00 15.00
10 Steve Downie 12.00 30.00
11 Andrew Cogliano 8.00 20.00
12 Marc-Andre Cliche 6.00 15.00
13 Kenndal McArdle 8.00 20.00
14 Darren Helm 8.00 20.00
15 Brad Marchand 6.00 15.00
16 James Neal 8.00 20.00
17 Bryan Little 8.00 20.00
18 Daniel Bertram 6.00 15.00
19 Ryan O'Marra 6.00 15.00
20 Tom Pyatt 6.00 15.00
21 Jonathan Toews 20.00 50.00
22 Sam Gagner 20.00 50.00
23 Eric Lindros 10.00 25.00
24 Roberto Luongo 15.00 40.00
25 Jason Spezza 10.00 25.00
26 Dion Phaneuf 10.00 25.00
27 Marc-Andre Fleury 15.00 40.00
28 Joe Thornton 12.00 30.00
29 Justin Pogge 12.00 30.00

2007 ITG Going For Gold World Juniors Emblems

GUE1-GUE22 ANNOUNCED PRINT RUN 20
GUE23-GUE28 ANNOUNCED PRINT RUN 10
GUE1 Carey Price 30.00 80.00
GUE2 Leland Irving 25.00 60.00
GUE3 Karl Alzner 20.00 50.00
GUE4 Ryan Parent 20.00 50.00
GUE5 Kristopher Letang 15.00 40.00
GUE6 Luc Bourdon 20.00 50.00
GUE7 Kris Russell 20.00 50.00
GUE8 Marc Staal 15.00 40.00
GUE9 Cody Franson 15.00 40.00
GUE10 Steve Downie 25.00 60.00
GUE11 Andrew Cogliano 25.00 60.00
GUE12 Marc-Andre Cliche 15.00 40.00
GUE13 Kenndal McArdle 15.00 40.00
GUE14 Darren Helm 15.00 40.00
GUE15 Brad Marchand 15.00 40.00
GUE16 James Neal 25.00 50.00
GUE17 Bryan Little 15.00 40.00
GUE18 Daniel Bertram 15.00 40.00
GUE19 Ryan O'Marra 15.00 40.00
GUE20 Tom Pyatt 15.00 40.00
GUE21 Jonathan Toews 30.00 80.00
GUE22 Sam Gagner 25.00 60.00
GUE23 Dion Phaneuf
GUE24 Roberto Luongo
GUE25 Jason Spezza
GUE26 Justin Pogge
GUE27 Marc-Andre Fleury
GUE28 Dany Heatley

2007 ITG Going For Gold World Juniors Jerseys

GUJ1 Carey Price 20.00 50.00
GUJ2 Leland Irving 12.00 30.00
GUJ3 Karl Alzner 10.00 25.00
GUJ4 Ryan Parent 8.00 20.00
GUJ5 Kristopher Letang 8.00 20.00
GUJ6 Luc Bourdon 10.00 25.00
GUJ7 Kris Russell 8.00 20.00
GUJ8 Marc Staal 8.00 20.00
GUJ9 Cody Franson 8.00 20.00
GUJ10 Steve Downie 10.00 25.00
GUJ11 Andrew Cogliano 10.00 25.00
GUJ12 Marc-Andre Cliche 8.00 20.00
GUJ13 Kenndal McArdle 8.00 20.00
GUJ14 Darren Helm 8.00 20.00
GUJ15 Brad Marchand 8.00 20.00
GUJ16 James Neal 10.00 25.00
GUJ17 Bryan Little 10.00 25.00
GUJ18 Daniel Bertram 8.00 20.00
GUJ19 Ryan O'Marra 8.00 20.00
GUJ20 Tom Pyatt 8.00 20.00
GUJ21 Jonathan Toews 12.00 30.00
GUJ22 Sam Gagner 12.00 30.00
GUJ23 Dion Phaneuf
GUJ24 Roberto Luongo
GUJ25 Jason Spezza
GUJ26 Justin Pogge
GUJ27 Marc-Andre Fleury
GUJ28 Dany Heatley

2007 ITG Going For Gold World Juniors Numbers

ANNOUNCED PRINT RUN 20
GUN1 Carey Price 30.00 80.00
GUN2 Leland Irving 25.00 60.00
GUN3 Karl Alzner 20.00 50.00
GUN4 Ryan Parent 20.00 50.00
GUN5 Kristopher Letang 15.00 40.00
GUN6 Luc Bourdon 20.00 50.00
GUN7 Kris Russell 20.00 50.00
GUN8 Marc Staal 15.00 40.00
GUN9 Cody Franson 15.00 40.00
GUN10 Steve Downie 25.00 60.00
GUN11 Andrew Cogliano 20.00 50.00
GUN12 Marc-Andre Cliche 15.00 40.00
GUN13 Kenndal McArdle 15.00 40.00
GUN14 Darren Helm 15.00 40.00
GUN15 Brad Marchand 15.00 40.00
GUN16 James Neal 25.00 50.00
GUN17 Bryan Little 15.00 40.00
GUN18 Daniel Bertram 15.00 40.00
GUN19 Ryan O'Marra 15.00 40.00
GUN20 Tom Pyatt 15.00 40.00
GUN21 Jonathan Toews 30.00 80.00
GUN22 Sam Gagner 25.00 60.00

2004-05 ITG Heroes and Prospects

Released in Novemeber 2004 in the wake of the NHL lockout, this 180-card set focused on top minor league prospects, top juniors and retired greats as well as Russian star Alexander Ovechkin. Heroes and Prospects was available as a hobby product that featured 2 autographs and 1 memorabilia card per box (on average) and also as an arena reatail version with no memorabilia and tougher odds on autographs.

COMPLETE SET (230) 35.00 80.00
COMP.SET w/o UPDATE (180) 25.00 50.00
COMP. UPDATE SET (50) 10.00 30.00
1 Cory Pecker .20 .50
2 Hannu Toivonen .30 .75
3 Duncan Keith .30 .75
4 Jiri Novotny .20 .50
5 Carlo Colaiacovo .20 .50
6 Igor Knyazev .20 .50
7 Pascal Leclaire .25 .60
8 Brad Boyes .30 .75
9 Duncan Milroy .20 .50
10 Jeff Woywitka .20 .50
11 Peter Budaj .30 .75
12 Timofei Shishkanov .20 .50
13 Brandon Nolan .20 .50
14 Denis Grebeshkov .20 .50
15 Danny Groulx .20 .50
16 Martin Kariya .30 .75
17 Greg Watson .20 .50
18 Tomas Kopecky .20 .50
19 Petr Taticek .20 .50
20 Filip Novak .20 .50
21 Matt Foy .20 .50
22 Adam Hauser .20 .50
23 Yanick Lehoux .20 .50
24 Kari Lehtonen .40 1.00
25 Marcel Goc .30 .75
26 Scottie Upshall .20 .50
27 David LeNeveu .25 .60
28 Kiel McLeod .20 .50
29 Jean-Marc Pelletier .25 .60
30 Colby Armstrong .25 .60
31 Adrian Foster .20 .50
32 Victor Uchevatov .20 .50
33 Jay McClement .20 .50
34 Marc-Andre Fleury .75 2.00
35 Kirill Koltsov .20 .50
36 Alexandre Giroux .20 .50
37 Rastislav Stana .20 .50
38 Ryan Miller .30 .75
39 Mike Glumac .20 .50
40 Chris Kunitz .40 1.00
41 Martin Podlesak .20 .50
42 Michel Ouellet .30 .75
43 Ryan Kesler .20 .50
44 Garrett Stafford .20 .50
45 Ray Emery .30 .75
46 Fedor Tyutin .20 .50
47 Jozef Balej .20 .50
48 Antero Niittymaki .20 .50
49 Tom Lawson .20 .50
50 Grant Stevenson .20 .50
51 Adam Berti .20 .50
52 Alexandre Picard .30 .75
53 Andrew Ladd .30 .75
54 Anthony Stewart .25 .60
55 Bobby Ryan .40 1.00
56 Boris Valabik .20 .50
57 Braydon Coburn .25 .60
58 Brent Seabrook .25 .60
59 Bryan Bickell .25 .60
60 Bryan Little .30 .75
61 Cam Barker .30 .75
62 Cam Ward .30 .75
63 Chris Campoli .20 .50
64 Corey Locke .20 .50
65 Corey Perry .60 1.50
66 Andy Rogers .20 .50
67 Daniel Paille .25 .60
68 David Bolland .25 .60
69 David Shantz .25 .60
70 Dennis Wideman .20 .50
71 Devan Dubnyk .50 1.25
72 Dion Phaneuf .75 2.00
73 Doug O'Brien .20 .50
74 Eric Fehr .25 .60
75 Eric Himelfarb .20 .50
76 Gilbert Brule .30 .75
77 James Wisniewski .20 .50
78 Jeff Carter .60 1.50
79 Jeff Drouin-Deslauriers .25 .60
80 Jeff Glass .25 .60
81 Jeff Schultz .20 .50
82 Josh Gorges .20 .50
83 Julien Ellis-Plante .25 .60
84 Justin Peters .20 .50
85 Kelly Guard .25 .60
86 Kevin Klein .20 .50
87 Kyle Chipchura .30 .75
88 Liam Reddox .20 .50
89 Marc Staal .30 .75
90 Marc-Antoine Pouliot .25 .60
91 Martin Houle .25 .60
92 Martin St. Pierre .20 .50
93 Matt Lashoff .25 .60
94 Maxime Daigneault .25 .60
95 Mike Green .20 .50
96 Mike Richards .30 .75
97 Paulo Colaiacovo .25 .60
98 Patrick O'Sullivan .30 .75
99 Philippe Roberge .20 .50
100 Robbie Schremp .30 .75
101 Ryan Garlock .20 .50
102 Ryan Getzlaf .50 1.25
103 Shawn Belle .25 .60
104 Sidney Crosby 5.00 12.00
105 Stefan Ruzicka .25 .60
106 Steve Bernier .25 .60
107 Tim Brent .20 .50
108 Tomas Fleischmann .20 .50
109 Vaclav Meidl .20 .50
110 Wojtek Wolski .30 .75
111 Stephen Weiss .20 .50
112 Fredrik Sjostrom .20 .50
113 Alexander Svitov .20 .50
114 Anton Babchuk .20 .50
115 Jason Spezza .30 .75
116 Alexander Ovechkin 3.00 8.00
117 Alexander Ovechkin 3.00 8.00
118 Alexander Ovechkin 3.00 8.00
119 Alexander Ovechkin 3.00 8.00
120 Marc-Andre Fleury .75 2.00
121 Marc-Andre Fleury .75 2.00
122 Marc-Andre Fleury .75 2.00
123 Tim Horton .30 .75
124 Frank Mahovlich .30 .75
125 Gilbert Perreault .30 .75
126 Ed Giacomin .30 .75
127 Jean Ratelle .25 .60
128 Marcel Dionne .40 1.00
129 Milt Schmidt .20 .50
130 Phil Esposito .50 1.25
131 Bernie Parent .30 .75
132 Serge Savard .30 .75
133 Stan Mikita .40 1.00
134 Tony Esposito .30 .75
135 Vic Hadfield .20 .50
136 Wayne Cashman .20 .50
137 Yvan Cournoyer .30 .75
138 Johnny Bower .30 .75
139 Bill Barber .25 .60
140 Bobby Hull .50 1.25
141 Denis Potvin .30 .75
142 Gerry Cheevers .30 .75
143 Guy Lafleur .40 1.00
144 Larry Robinson .30 .75
145 Rogie Vachon .30 .75
146 Steve Shutt .25 .60
147 Ted Lindsay .30 .75
148 Red Kelly .30 .75
149 Wendel Clark .30 .75
150 Ray Bourque .40 1.00
151 Cam Neely .30 .75
152 Glenn Hall .30 .75
153 Jean Beliveau .40 1.00
154 Grant Fuhr .30 .75
155 Andy Bathgate .30 .75
156 Gump Worsley .30 .75
157 Henri Richard .30 .75
158 Mike Bossy .30 .75
159 Johnny Bucyk .30 .75
160 Elmer Lach .25 .60
161 Vladislav Tretiak .30 .75
162 Lanny McDonald .25 .60
163 Guy Lapointe .25 .60
164 Jacques Plante .40 1.00
165 Terry Sawchuk .40 1.00
166 Rocket Richard .60 1.50
167 Doug Harvey .30 .75
168 Howie Morenz .25 .60
169 Bill Barilko .25 .60
170 Brad Park .25 .60
171 Bobby Orr 1.00 2.50
172 Mario Lemieux 1.00 2.50
173 Paul Coffey .30 .75
174 Patrick Roy .75 2.00
175 Bobby Clarke .25 .60
176 Georges Vezina .40 1.00
177 Alex Delvecchio .30 .75
178 Toe Blake .30 .75
179 Sid Abel .30 .75
180 Woody Dumart .25 .60
181 Jason King .20 .50
182 Yann Danis .25 .60
183 Zach Parise .50 1.25
184 Dan Hamhuis .25 .60
185 Thomas Vanek .75 2.00
186 Mikko Koivu .30 .75
187 Ryan Whitney .25 .60
188 Jakub Klepis .20 .50
189 Ben Eager .20 .50
190 Kyle Wellwood .25 .60
191 Jiri Hudler .30 .75
192 Aaron Voros .20 .50
193 Eric Staal .40 1.00
194 Jay Bouwmeester .30 .75
195 Patrice Bergeron .40 1.00
196 Peter Sarno .20 .50
197 Mike Cammalleri .25 .60
198 Derek Roy .20 .50
199 R.J. Umberger .25 .60
200 Junior Lessard .20 .50
201 Rene Vydareny .20 .50
202 Alexander Ovechkin 3.00 8.00
203 Dylan Hunter .20 .50
204 Alexandre Vincent .25 .60
205 Kevin Nastiuk .25 .60
206 Evan McGrath .20 .50
207 Alex Bourret .20 .50
208 Andrej Meszaros .20 .50
209 Benoit Pouliot .20 .50
210 Dany Roussin .20 .50
211 Jeremy Colliton .20 .50
212 Danny Syvret .20 .50
213 Jonathan Boutin .25 .60
214 Ryan Stone .25 .60
215 Jordan Staal 1.00 2.50
216 Marek Zagrapan .20 .50
217 Clarke MacArthur .25 .60
218 John Hughes .20 .50
219 Alexander Radulov .50 1.25
220 Colin Fraser .20 .50
221 Jakub Petruzalek .20 .50
222 Sidney Crosby 8.00 20.00
223 Nigel Dawes .25 .60
224 Luc Bourdon .40 1.00
225 Devin Setoguchi .25 .60
226 Carey Price 5.00 12.00
227 Daren Machesney .25 .60
228 Corey Crawford .75 2.00
229 Marek Schwarz .25 .60
230 Gerald Coleman .25 .60
NNO Roy/AO/Sid/Fleury CL 2.00 5.00

2004-05 ITG Heroes and Prospects Aspiring

ANNOUNCED PRINT RUN 50
1 M. Lemieux/S.Crosby 30.00 80.00
2 M.Lemieux/A.Ovechkin 30.00 80.00
3 P.Roy/M.Fleury 25.00 60.00
4 P.Roy/K.Lehtonen 25.00 60.00
5 R.Bourque/D.Phaneuf 15.00 40.00
6 C.Neely/A.Ovechkin 15.00 40.00
7 M.Bossy/M.Richards 12.00 30.00
8 F.Mahovlich/O'Sullivan 15.00 40.00
9 P.Esposito/B.Boyes 12.00 30.00
10 G.Fuhr/D.Dubnyk 15.00 40.00
11 B.Clarke/J.Carter 12.00 30.00
12 J.Plante/J.Ellis-Plante 12.00 30.00
13 G.Perreault/S.Crosby 25.00 60.00
14 S.Mikita/C.Perry 10.00 25.00
15 J.Beliveau/C.Locke 12.00 30.00
16 Cheevers/D.LeNeveu 12.00 30.00

2004-05 ITG Heroes and Prospects Autographs

Inserted on an average of 2 per hobby box, this 160-card set featured certified autographs of young prospects and retired greats. Odds for retail arena boxes were not given. Cards with "U" prefix available in Update sets only, please note that card backs do not carry the "U" prefix, they are for checklisting only.

STATED ODDS 2 PER HOBBY BOX
U PREFIX IN H&P UPDATE SETS ONLY
AB Adam Berti 4.00 10.00
AD Alex Delvecchio 10.00 25.00
AF Adrian Foster 4.00 10.00
AG Alexandre Giroux 4.00 10.00
AH Adam Hauser 4.00 10.00
AL Andrew Ladd 8.00 20.00
AO1 Alexander Ovechkin 60.00 120.00
AO2 Alexander Ovechkin 60.00 120.00
AO3 Alexander Ovechkin 60.00 120.00
AO4 Alexander Ovechkin 60.00 120.00
AP Alexandre Picard 8.00 20.00
AR Andy Rogers 4.00 10.00
AS Anthony Stewart 8.00 20.00
BB Brad Boyes 4.00 10.00
BC Braydon Coburn 8.00 20.00
BH Bobby Hull 25.00 60.00
BL Bryan Little 6.00 15.00
BN Brandon Nolan 4.00 10.00
BO Bobby Orr 60.00 120.00
BP Bernie Parent 10.00 25.00
BR Bobby Ryan 10.00 25.00
BS Brent Seabrook 6.00 15.00
BV Boris Valabik 4.00 10.00
CA Colby Armstrong 8.00 20.00
CB Cam Barker 8.00 20.00
CC Carlo Colaiacovo 4.00 10.00
CK Chris Kunitz 8.00 20.00
CL Corey Locke 4.00 10.00
CN Cam Neely 12.00 30.00
CP Cory Pecker 4.00 10.00
CW Cam Ward 10.00 25.00
DB David Bolland 8.00 20.00
DD Devan Dubnyk 6.00 15.00
DG Denis Grebeshkov 4.00 10.00
DK Duncan Keith 6.00 15.00
DL David LeNeveu 4.00 10.00
DM Duncan Milroy 4.00 10.00
DO Doug O'Brien 4.00 10.00
DP Daniel Paille 4.00 10.00
DS David Shantz 4.00 10.00
DW Dennis Wideman 4.00 10.00
EF Eric Fehr 8.00 20.00
EG Ed Giacomin 15.00 40.00
EH Eric Himelfarb 6.00 15.00
EL Elmer Lach 10.00 25.00
FM Frank Mahovlich 8.00 20.00
FN Filip Novak 4.00 10.00
FS Fredrik Sjostrom 4.00 10.00
FT Fedor Tyutin 6.00 15.00
GB Gilbert Brule 10.00 25.00
GC Gerry Cheevers 8.00 20.00
GF Grant Fuhr 10.00 25.00
GH Glenn Hall 10.00 25.00
GL Guy Lafleur 10.00 25.00
GP Gilbert Perreault 10.00 25.00
GS Garrett Stafford 6.00 15.00
GW Greg Watson 4.00 10.00
HR Henri Richard 10.00 25.00
HT Hannu Toivonen 6.00 15.00
JB Jozef Balej 6.00 15.00
JC Jeff Carter 20.00 50.00
JD Jeff Drouin-Deslauriers 6.00 15.00
JE Julien Ellis-Plante 6.00 15.00
JG Jeff Glass 8.00 20.00
JM Jay McClement 4.00 10.00
JN Jiri Novotny 4.00 10.00
JP Jean-Marc Pelletier 4.00 10.00
JR Jean Ratelle 8.00 20.00
JS Jeff Schultz 4.00 10.00
JW Jeff Woywitka 6.00 15.00
KC Kyle Chipchura 8.00 20.00
KG Kelly Guard 4.00 10.00
KM Kiel McLeod 4.00 10.00
LM Lanny McDonald 8.00 20.00
LR Liam Reddox 4.00 10.00
LW Lorne Worsley 10.00 25.00
MC Marcel Goc 8.00 20.00
MF1 Marc-Andre Fleury 12.00 30.00
MF2 Marc-Andre Fleury 12.00 30.00
MF3 Marc-Andre Fleury 12.00 30.00
MF4 Marc-Andre Fleury 12.00 30.00
MH Martin Houle 6.00 15.00
MK Martin Kariya 8.00 20.00
ML Matt Lashoff 4.00 10.00
MO Michel Ouellet 6.00 15.00
MP Martin Podlesak 4.00 10.00
MR Mike Richards 15.00 40.00
MS Marc Staal 12.00 30.00
PB Peter Budaj 4.00 10.00
PC Paulo Colaiacovo 4.00 10.00
PE Phil Esposito 12.50 30.00
PL Pascal Leclaire 4.00 10.00
PO Patrick O'Sullivan 10.00 25.00
PR Philippe Roberge 4.00 10.00
PT Petr Taticek 4.00 10.00
RB Ray Bourque 15.00 40.00
RE Ray Emery 5.00 12.00
RG Ryan Garlock 4.00 10.00
RK Ryan Kesler 4.00 10.00
RM Ryan Miller 10.00 25.00
RV Rogie Vachon 8.00 20.00
SB Shawn Belle 6.00 15.00
SC Sidney Crosby 150.00 300.00
SM Stan Mikita 12.00 30.00
SR Stefan Ruzicka 4.00 10.00
SS Serge Savard 10.00 25.00
SU Scottie Upshall 4.00 10.00
TB Tim Brent 4.00 10.00
TE Tony Esposito 15.00 40.00
TF Tomas Fleischmann 4.00 10.00
TK Tomas Kopecky 4.00 10.00
TL Tom Lawson 4.00 10.00
TS Timofei Shishkanov 4.00 10.00
VH Vic Hadfield 8.00 20.00
VM Vaclav Meidl 4.00 10.00
VT Vladislav Tretiak 15.00 40.00
VU Victor Uchevatov 4.00 10.00
WC Wayne Cashman 8.00 20.00
WW Wojtek Wolski 12.00 30.00
YC Yvan Cournoyer 10.00 25.00
YL Yanick Lehoux 4.00 10.00
ABA Andy Bathgate 8.00 20.00
BBA Bill Barber 6.00 15.00
BBI Bryan Bickell 6.00 15.00
BCL Bobby Clarke 12.00 30.00
BPA Brad Park 6.00 15.00
CCA Chris Campoli 4.00 10.00
CPE Corey Perry 15.00 40.00
DGR Danny Groulx 4.00 10.00
DPH Dion Phaneuf 20.00 50.00
DPO Denis Potvin 10.00 25.00
GLA Guy Lapointe 8.00 20.00
GST Grant Stevenson 4.00 10.00
JBE Jean Beliveau 25.00 50.00
JBO Johnny Bower 10.00 25.00
JBU Johnny Bucyk 6.00 15.00
JGO Josh Gorges 4.00 10.00
JPE Justin Peters 6.00 15.00
JWI James Wisniewski 4.00 10.00
KKL Kevin Klein 4.00 10.00
LRO Larry Robinson 8.00 20.00
MBO Mike Bossy 6.00 15.00
MDI Marcel Dionne 10.00 25.00
MFO Matt Foy 4.00 10.00
MGL Mike Glumac 4.00 10.00
MGR Mike Green 4.00 10.00
MLE Mario Lemieux 30.00 80.00
MPO Marc-Antoine Pouliot 8.00 20.00
MSC Milt Schmidt 8.00 20.00
MSP Martin St. Pierre 4.00 10.00
PCO Paul Coffey 10.00 25.00
PRO Patrick Roy 30.00 80.00
RGE Ryan Getzlaf 20.00 50.00
RKE Red Kelly 6.00 15.00
RSC Robbie Schremp 10.00 25.00
SBE Steve Bernier 8.00 20.00
SSH Steve Shutt 8.00 20.00
TLI Ted Lindsay 8.00 20.00
WCL Wendel Clark 10.00 25.00
UJBW Jay Bouwmeester 6.00 15.00
UPBE Patrice Bergeron 10.00 25.00
UPSR Peter Sarno 6.00 15.00
UMCA Mike Cammalleri 4.00 10.00
UMKO Mikko Koivu 6.00 15.00
UAN Antero Niittymaki 10.00 25.00
UDH Dan Hamhuis 4.00 10.00
UDR Derek Roy 6.00 15.00
UES Eric Staal 10.00 25.00
UJH Jiri Hudler 8.00 20.00
UKW Kyle Wellwood 10.00 25.00
UMD Maxime Daigneault 4.00 10.00
URS Rastislav Stana 6.00 15.00
URV Rene Vydareny 4.00 10.00
URW Ryan Whitney 4.00 10.00
SC2 Sidney Crosby 150.00 350.00
USW Stephen Weiss 4.00 10.00
UTV Thomas Vanek 15.00 40.00
UZP Zach Parise 15.00 40.00
ABAB Anton Babchuk 4.00 10.00

2004-05 ITG Heroes and Prospects Combos

Cards 15-18 only available randomly in sets of ITG Heroes and Prospects Update.

COMMON CARD (1-14) 6.00 15.00
CARDS 15-18 AVAIL. H&P UPDATE ONLY
CARDS 1-14 PRINT RUN 50 SETS
1 M.Fleury/K.Lehtonen 25.00 60.00
2 S.Crosby/M.Ouellet 75.00 200.00
3 D.Dubnyk/R.Miller 10.00 25.00
4 R.Getzlaf/B.Boyes 25.00 60.00
5 B.Seabrook/G.Stafford 6.00 15.00
6 D.Bolland/K.McLeod 6.00 15.00
7 M.Pouliot/T.Kopecky 8.00 20.00
8 C.Perry/S.Upshall 15.00 40.00
9 J.Ellis-Plante/P.Leclaire 12.50 30.00
10 J.Carter/R.Emery 12.50 30.00
11 P.O'Sullivan/R.Kesler 12.50 30.00
12 M.Richards/M.Green 15.00 40.00
13 K.Chipchura/D.Phaneuf 12.50 30.00
14 B.Coburn/C.Colaiacovo 15.00 40.00
15 S.Crosby/A.Ovechkin Jsys/90 150.00 300.00
16 S.Crosby/A.Ovechkin Emblms/20
17 S.Crosby/A.Ovechkin Nmbrs/20
18 S.Crosby/A.Ovechkin Gloves/20

2004-05 ITG Heroes and Prospects Gloves

Available only in random sets of ITG Heroes and Prospects Update.

AVAIL. IN UPD.PACKS ONLY
PRINT RUN 50 SETS
1 Sidney Crosby 60.00 150.00
SC Sidney Crosby AU

2004-05 ITG Heroes and Prospects Hero Memorabilia

STATED PRINT RUN 30 SETS
1 Tony Esposito 8.00 20.00
2 Stan Mikita 8.00 20.00
3 Gump Worsley 10.00 25.00
4 Ray Bourque 12.50 30.00
5 Phil Esposito 15.00 40.00
6 Patrick Roy 40.00 100.00
7 Mike Bossy 15.00 40.00
8 Marcel Dionne 8.00 20.00
9 Larry Robinson 8.00 20.00
10 Johnny Bower 12.50 30.00
11 Jean Beliveau 25.00 60.00
12 Jacques Plante 25.00 60.00
13 Henri Richard 8.00 20.00
14 Mario Lemieux 25.00 60.00
15 Gilbert Perreault 12.50 30.00
16 Gerry Cheevers 12.00 30.00
17 Ed Giacomin 15.00 40.00
18 Denis Potvin 8.00 20.00
19 Cam Neely 30.00 80.00
20 Frank Mahovlich/10
21 Alex Delvecchio 15.00 40.00
22 Rogie Vachon 15.00 40.00
23 Serge Savard 15.00 40.00
24 Guy Lapointe 12.50 30.00
25 Bill Barber 12.50 30.00
26 Grant Fuhr
27 Ted Lindsay 25.00 60.00
28 Paul Coffey 15.00 40.00
29 Doug Harvey/10
30 Bobby Orr 40.00 100.00

2004-05 ITG Heroes and Prospects Jerseys

Cards 59-66 were only available randomly in the ITG Heroes and Prospects Update sets.

CARDS 59-66 AVAIL. H&P UPDATE ONLY
ANNOUNCED PRINT RUN 90
1-58 EMBLEM/30: .6X TO 1.5X JSY/90*
59-66 EMBLEM/20: .8X TO 2X JSY
1-58 NUMBERS/25: .8X TO 2X JSY/90*
1 Jiri Novotny 4.00 10.00
2 Marc-Andre Fleury 15.00 40.00
3 Corey Perry 15.00 40.00
4 Jeff Carter 15.00 40.00
5 Kari Lehtonen 15.00 40.00
6 David LeNeveu 5.00 12.00
7 Colby Armstrong 5.00 12.00
8 Adrian Foster 4.00 10.00
9 Ryan Miller 10.00 25.00
10 Grant Stevenson 4.00 10.00
11 Garrett Stafford 4.00 10.00

12 Michel Ouellet 6.00 15.00
13 Ray Emery 6.00 15.00
14 Fedor Tyutin 4.00 10.00
15 Brad Boyes 6.00 15.00
16 Marc-Andre Fleury 15.00 40.00
17 Eric Healey 6.00 15.00
18 Devan Dubnyk 6.00 15.00
19 Alexandre Picard 6.00 15.00
20 Patrick O'Sullivan 6.00 15.00
21 Corey Locke 5.00 12.00
22 Kyle Chipchura 6.00 15.00
23 Jean-Marc Pelletier 5.00 12.00
24 Mike Richards 12.00 30.00
25 Michael Ryder 6.00 15.00
26 Carlo Colaiacovo 4.00 10.00
27 Garth Murray 4.00 10.00
28 John Pohl 4.00 10.00
29 Mark Popovic 4.00 10.00
30 Trent Hunter 5.00 12.00
31 Ron Hainsey 4.00 10.00
32 Tony Salmelainen 4.00 10.00
33 Jason Spezza 10.00 25.00
34 Fedor Fedorov 6.00 15.00
35 Denis Shvidki 4.00 10.00
36 Andrew Hutchinson 4.00 10.00
37 Denis Grebeshkov 4.00 10.00
38 Julien Vauclair 5.00 12.00
39 Brandon Reid 4.00 10.00
40 Kiel McLeod 4.00 10.00
41 Chris Kunitz 6.00 15.00
42 Timofei Shishkanov 4.00 10.00
43 Peter Budaj 6.00 15.00
44 Danny Groulx 4.00 10.00
45 Brent Seabrook 12.50 30.00
46 Dion Phaneuf 15.00 40.00
47 Eric Fehr 6.00 15.00
48 Yanick Lehoux 4.00 10.00
49 Ryan Getzlaf 15.00 40.00
50 Matt Foy 4.00 10.00
51 Marc-Antoine Pouliot 6.00 15.00
52 Tomas Kopecky 5.00 12.00
53 David Bolland 6.00 15.00
54 Wojtek Wolski 6.00 15.00
55 Sidney Crosby 50.00 100.00
56 Anthony Stewart 6.00 15.00
57 Alexander Ovechkin 25.00 60.00
58 Scottie Upshall 6.00 15.00
59 Alexander Ovechkin 25.00 60.00
60 Sidney Crosby 40.00 80.00
61 Patrice Bergeron 8.00 20.00
62 Robbie Schremp 6.00 15.00
63 Ryan Whitney 5.00 12.00
64 Danny Syvret 5.00 12.00
65 Dany Roussin 4.00 10.00
66 Wojtek Wolski 6.00 15.00

2004-05 ITG Heroes and Prospects National Pride

STATED PRINT RUN 50 SETS
1 Sidney Crosby 100.00 200.00
2 Jeff Carter 20.00 50.00
3 Jason Spezza 15.00 40.00
4 Alexander Ovechkin 40.00 100.00
5 Marc-Andre Fleury 25.00 60.00
6 Mike Richards 15.00 40.00
7 Kari Lehtonen 25.00 60.00
8 Patrick O'Sullivan 15.00 40.00

2004-05 ITG Heroes and Prospects Net Prospects

STATED PRINT RUN 60 SETS
GOLD PRINT RUN 20 SETS
1 Kari Lehtonen 15.00 40.00
2 Marc-Andre Fleury 15.00 40.00
3 Andrew Raycroft 12.00 30.00
4 Rick DiPietro 6.00 15.00
5 Ilja Bryzgalov 6.00 15.00
6 Antero Niittymaki 12.00 30.00
7 Ryan Miller 12.00 30.00
8 Jason Bacashihua 10.00 25.00
9 Rastislav Stana 6.00 15.00
10 Philippe Sauve 6.00 15.00
11 Ray Emery 10.00 25.00
12 Ari Ahonen 6.00 15.00
13 Alex Auld 10.00 25.00
14 David LeNeveu 10.00 25.00
15 Neil Little 6.00 15.00
16 Tim Thomas 8.00 20.00
17 Devan Dubnyk 10.00 25.00
18 Jean-Marc Pelletier 6.00 15.00
19 Mathieu Garon 10.00 25.00
20 Marc-Andre Fleury 15.00 40.00
21 Michael Garnett 6.00 15.00
22 Sebastien Centomo 6.00 15.00
23 Peter Budaj 8.00 20.00
24 Sebastien Charpentier 6.00 15.00
25 Martin Prusek 6.00 15.00
26 Pascal Leclaire 10.00 25.00
27 Mikael Tellqvist 10.00 25.00
28 Reinhard Divis 6.00 15.00
29 Phil Osaer 6.00 15.00
30 Maxime Ouellet 6.00 15.00
31 Mika Noronen 6.00 15.00
32 Julien Ellis-Plante 10.00 25.00

2004-05 ITG Heroes and Prospects Top Prospects

1 Wojtek Wolski 1.25 3.00
2 David Shantz .75 2.00
3 Adam Berti .75 2.00
4 Cam Barker 1.25 3.00
5 Dave Bolland .75 2.00
6 Jeff Schultz .75 2.00
7 Alexandre Picard 1.25 3.00
8 Julien Ellis-Plante .75 2.00
9 Vaclav Meidl .75 2.00
10 Eric Fehr .75 2.00
11 Robbie Schremp 1.25 3.00
12 Andrew Ladd 1.25 3.00
13 Devan Dubnyk .75 2.00
14 Boris Valabik .75 2.00
15 Justin Peters .75 2.00
16 Mike Green .75 2.00
17 Bryan Bickell 1.25 3.00
18 Marc-Andre Fleury 2.00 5.00
19 Anthony Stewart 1.25 3.00
20 Ryan Getzlaf 1.25 3.00

2005-06 ITG Heroes and Prospects

This 430-card set was released in two series. Each series had five-card packs which came 24 packs to a box and 24 boxes to a case. This set features a mix of retired greats and players yet to make their NHL debut.

COMPLETE SET (430) 40.00 100.00
COMP.SERIES 1 SET (180) 15.00 40.00
COMP.SERIES 2 SET (200) 15.00 40.00
COMP. UPDATE SET (50) 10.00 20.00
1 Martin Brodeur .60 1.50
2 Bobby Hull .40 1.00
3 Glenn Hall .40 1.00
4 Harry Howell .30 .75
5 Doug Gilmour .30 .75
6 Phil Esposito .40 1.00
7 Red Kelly .40 1.00
8 Cam Neely .40 1.00
9 Jean Beliveau .40 1.00
10 Johnny Bower .40 1.00
11 Milt Schmidt .20 .50
12 Jose Theodore .40 1.00
13 Ray Bourque .40 1.00
14 Dave Keon .40 1.00
15 Henri Richard .30 .75
16 Marcel Dionne .30 .75
17 Paul Henderson .30 .75
18 Wendel Clark .30 .75
19 Steve Yzerman .75 2.00
20 Vladislav Tretiak .30 .75
21 Brett Hull .40 1.00
22 Mike Bossy .30 .75
23 Tony Esposito .40 1.00
24 Bobby Clarke .40 1.00
25 Brian Leetch .40 1.00
26 Guy Lafleur .40 1.00
27 Grant Fuhr .40 1.00
28 Pat LaFontaine .20 .50
29 Jean Ratelle .20 .50
30 Bernie Parent .40 1.00
31 Ed Giacomin .30 .75
32 Darryl Sittler .40 1.00
33 Patrick Roy .75 2.00
34 Dino Ciccarelli .20 .50
35 Frank Mahovlich .40 1.00
36 Stan Mikita .30 .75
37 Neal Broten .20 .50
38 Ted Lindsay .30 .75
39 Derek Sanderson .20 .50
40 Mario Lemieux .75 2.00
41 Cam Ward .40 1.00
42 Brandon Bochenski .20 .50
43 Steve Ott .20 .50
44 Kevin Bieksa .20 .50
45 Ryane Clowe .40 1.00
46 Jason Spezza .40 1.00
47 Adam Hauser .20 .50
48 Derek Roy .30 .75
49 R.J. Umberger .30 .75
50 Alex Auld .30 .75
51 Joey MacDonald .40 1.00
52 Denis Hamel .20 .50
53 Yann Danis .30 .75
54 Brent Burns .20 .50
55 Josh Harding .30 .75
56 Jason LaBarbera .30 .75
57 Antero Niittymaki .40 1.00
58 Mike Egener .20 .50
59 Thomas Vanek .40 1.00
60 Rene Bourque .30 .75
61 Brad Boyes .30 .75
62 Kari Lehtonen .40 1.00
63 Jeff Carter .60 1.50
64 Ryan Kesler .40 1.00
65 Cam Barker .30 .75
66 Ray Emery .30 .75
67 Michel Ouellet .20 .50
68 Andrew Hutchinson .20 .50
69 Mike Richards .40 1.00
70 Yanick Lehoux .20 .50
71 Lawrence Nycholat .20 .50
72 Jay Bouwmeester .20 .50
73 Ryan Whitney .30 .75
74 Zach Parise .40 1.00
75 Jordin Tootoo .40 1.00
76 Joni Pitkanen .30 .75
77 Chris Bourque .30 .75
78 Mikko Koivu .40 1.00
79 Eric Nystrom .20 .50
80 Mathieu Garon .30 .75
81 Patrice Bergeron .40 1.00
82 Eric Staal .60 1.50
83 Dustin Brown .30 .75
84 Marc-Andre Fleury .60 1.50
85 Marek Svatos .30 .75
86 Steve Eminger .20 .50
87 Andy Hilbert .20 .50
88 Chris Campoli .20 .50
89 Pascal Leclaire .30 .75
90 Anton Volchenkov .20 .50
91 Corey Locke .20 .50
92 Ryan Miller .40 1.00
93 Mike Cammalleri .20 .50
94 Simon Gamache .20 .50
95 Chuck Kobasew .30 .75
96 Christian Ehrhoff .20 .50
97 Hannu Toivonen .40 1.00
98 Mike Zigomanis .20 .50
99 Niklas Kronwall .20 .50
100 Patrick Sharp .20 .50
101 Ryan Suter .30 .75
102 Michael Leighton .30 .75
103 Denis Grebeshkov .20 .50
104 Dan Hamhuis .20 .50
105 Sidney Crosby 3.00 8.00
106 Alexander Svitov .20 .50
107 Al Montoya .40 1.00
108 Carlo Colaiacovo .20 .50
109 Alexander Ovechkin 1.50 4.00
110 Evgeni Malkin 2.00 5.00
111 John Tavares 6.00 15.00
112 Bobby Ryan .40 1.00
113 Steve Downie .60 1.50
114 Adam McQuaid .20 .50
115 Robbie Schremp .40 1.00
116 Jordan Staal .75 2.00
117 Matt Lashoff .30 .75
118 Ryan O'Marra .40 1.00
119 James Neal .30 .75
120 Bryan Little .30 .75
121 David Bolland .30 .75
122 Evan McGrath .30 .75
123 Kevin Lalande .20 .50
124 Radek Smolenak .40 1.00
125 Marc Staal .60 1.50
126 Michael Blunden .20 .50
127 Tom Pyatt .20 .50
128 Daren Machesney .30 .75
129 Evan Brophey .20 .50
130 Jakub Kindl .20 .50
131 Ryan Parent .30 .75
132 Daniel Ryder .20 .50
133 Matt Pelech .20 .50
134 Benoit Pouliot .40 1.00
135 Derick Brassard .60 1.50
136 Brad Marchand .20 .50
137 Alexander Radulov .75 2.00
138 Marc-Andre Cliche .30 .75
139 Luc Bourdon .40 1.00
140 David Krejci .40 1.00
141 Marek Zagrapan .20 .50
142 Chad Denny .20 .50
143 James Sheppard .30 .75
144 Jean-Philippe Levasseur .30 .75
145 Alex Bourret .20 .50
146 Kristopher Letang .40 1.00
147 Pier-Olivier Pelletier .30 .75
148 Jean-Philippe Paquet .20 .50
149 Marc-Edouard Vlasic .40 1.00
150 Nicolas Blanchard .20 .50
151 Guillaume Latendresse .50 1.25
152 Jonathan Bernier .75 2.00
153 Oskars Bartulis .20 .50
154 Corey Perry .40 1.00
155 Alexandre Vincent .20 .50
156 Marc-Andre Gragnani .20 .50
157 Carey Price 1.25 3.00
158 Brett Sutter .20 .50
159 Angelo Esposito 2.00 5.00
160 Devin Setoguchi .30 .75
161 Shea Weber .20 .50
162 Tyler Plante .20 .50
163 Kris Russell .20 .50
164 Gilbert Brule .50 1.25
165 Brendan Mikkelson .20 .50
166 Dustin Kohn .20 .50
167 Chris Durand .20 .50
168 Kristofer Westblom .20 .50
169 Blair Jones .20 .50
170 Raymond Macias .20 .50
171 Michael Sauer .20 .50
172 Brodie Dupont .20 .50
173 Ben Maxwell .20 .50
174 Kenndal McArdle .20 .50
175 Matt Kassian .20 .50
176 J.D. Watt .20 .50
177 Scott Jackson .20 .50
178 Devan Dubnyk .30 .75
179 Tyler Mosienko .20 .50
180 Cody Bass .20 .50
181 Martin Brodeur .50 1.25
182 Ray Bourque .40 1.00
183 Steve Yzerman .50 1.25
184 Dany Heatley .40 1.00
185 Herb Carnegie .75 2.00
186 Jim Craig .50 1.25
187 Gilbert Perreault .30 .75
188 Ron Hextall .30 .75
189 Gerry Cheevers 1.25 3.00
190 Yvan Cournoyer .30 .75
191 Larry Robinson .30 .75
192 Borje Salming .30 .75
193 Ted Kennedy .20 .50
194 Rod Gilbert .50 1.25
195 Patrick Roy .75 2.00
196 Mario Lemieux .50 1.25
197 Eric Lindros .50 1.25
198 Ilya Kovalchuk .40 1.00
199 Tod Sloan .20 .50
200 Mark Howe .20 .50
201 Erik Westrum .20 .50
202 Chris Madden .20 .50
203 Alexandre Picard .40 1.00
204 Jeff Tambellini .20 .50
205 Marc-Antoine Pouliot .30 .75
206 Brian Finley .20 .50
207 Sean Bergenheim .20 .50
208 Ryan Shannon .20 .50
209 Clarke MacArthur .20 .50
210 Nicklas Bergfors .30 .75
211 Noah Welch .20 .50
212 Mark Hartigan .20 .50
213 Dan DaSilva .20 .50
214 Eric Fehr .20 .50
215 Shawn Belle .30 .75
216 Joey Tenute .20 .50
217 Maxime Ouellet .20 .50
218 Yan Stastny .20 .50
219 Petr Taticek .20 .50
220 Ladislav Smid .20 .50
221 Curtis Sanford .30 .75
222 Erik Christensen .20 .50
223 Tyler Redenbach .20 .50
224 Roman Voloshenko .20 .50
225 Dustin Penner .40 1.00
226 Rejean Beauchemin .20 .50
227 Martin St. Pierre .20 .50
228 Tim Gleason .20 .50
229 Brent Krahn .20 .50
230 Jason Pominville .30 .75
231 Andrei Kostitsyn .20 .50
232 Steve Gainey .20 .50
233 Pekka Rinne .50 1.25
234 Nigel Dawes .20 .50
235 Braydon Coburn .30 .75
236 Corey Crawford .50 1.25
237 Ryan Stone .40 1.00
238 Jeremy Colliton .20 .50
239 Ron Hainsey .20 .50
240 Nolan Schaefer .20 .50
241 Jason Bacashihua .30 .75
242 Geoff Platt .20 .50
243 Chad Larose .20 .50
244 Drew MacIntyre .20 .50
245 Peter Sejna .20 .50
246 Ryan Vesce .20 .50
247 Brian Pothier .20 .50
248 Colin Murphy .20 .50
249 Curtis McElhinney .20 .50
250 Mike Glumac .20 .50
251 Lauri Tukonen .20 .50
252 Nathan Marsters .20 .50
253 Matt Ellison .20 .50
254 Kurtis Foster .20 .50
255 Jean-Francois Jacques .20 .50
256 Dmitri Patzold .30 .75
257 John Pohl .20 .50
258 Alexander Perezhogin .20 .50
259 Nathan Paetsch .20 .50
260 Kelly Guard .30 .75
261 Andrew Wozniewski .20 .50
262 Tomi Maki .20 .50
263 Tomas Plekanec .20 .50
264 Noah Clarke .20 .50
265 Steve Bernier .40 1.00
266 Gerald Coleman .30 .75
267 Jiri Hudler .40 1.00
268 Daniel Carcillo .20 .50
269 Bruno Gervais .20 .50
270 Dany Sabourin .20 .50
271 Junior Lessard .20 .50
272 Thomas Pock .20 .50
273 Andy Chiodo .30 .75
274 Vitaly Kolesnik .20 .50
275 Patrick Eaves .20 .50
276 Petr Prucha .40 1.00
277 Henrik Lundqvist .75 2.00
278 Evgeni Malkin 2.00 5.00
279 Alexander Ovechkin 1.50 4.00
280 Nick Foligno .20 .50
281 Chris Stewart .20 .50
282 Ryan MacDonald .20 .50
283 Liam Reddox .20 .50
284 Tyler Kennedy .20 .50
285 Dylan Hunter .20 .50
286 Bob Sanguinetti .20 .50
287 Dan LaCosta .30 .75
288 Derek Joslin .20 .50
289 Ryan Daniels .20 .50
290 Sergei Kostitsyn .20 .50
291 Jonathan D'Aversa .20 .50
292 Cory Emmerton .20 .50
293 Dan Turple .20 .50
294 John de Gray .20 .50
295 Bobby Hughes .20 .50
296 Rafael Rotter .20 .50
297 Justin Garay .20 .50
298 Marek Horsky .20 .50
299 Joe Ryan .20 .50
300 Ondrej Pavelec .40 1.00
301 Olivier Latendresse .20 .50
302 Maxime Boisclair .20 .50
303 Mathieu Roy .40 1.00
304 Ryan Hillier .20 .50
305 Stanislav Lascek .20 .50
306 Julien Ellis .40 1.00
307 Mathiew Carle .20 .50
308 Alex Grant .20 .50
309 David Desharnais .40 1.00
310 Bryce Swan .20 .50
311 Jeff Schultz .20 .50
312 Zach Hamill .20 .50
313 A.J. Thelen .20 .50
314 Brandon Sutter .75 2.00
315 Brady Calla .20 .50
316 Troy Brouwer .20 .50
317 Mark Fistric .20 .50
318 Codey Burki .20 .50
319 Kevin Armstrong .20 .50
320 Michael Funk .20 .50
321 Ty Wishart .20 .50
322 Dustin Boyd .20 .50
323 Peter Mueller .60 1.50
324 Wacey Rabbit .20 .75
325 Andy Rogers .20 .50
326 Leland Irving .60 1.50
327 Logan Stephenson .20 .50
328 Kyle Chipchura .40 1.00
329 Ryan White .20 .50
330 Blake Comeau .20 .50
331 Justin Pogge .40 1.00
332 Corey Perry .40 1.00
333 Ryan Getzlaf .50 1.25
334 Dion Phaneuf .75 2.00
335 Cam Ward .40 1.00
336 Mike Richards .40 1.00
337 Sidney Crosby 3.00 8.00
338 Mario Lemieux .50 1.25
339 Guy Lafleur .50 1.25
340 Jeff Carter .60 1.50
341 Eric Lindros .50 1.25
342 Jose Theodore .50 1.25
343 Mike Cammalleri .20 .50
344 Jason Spezza .60 1.50
345 Patrick Roy .75 2.00
346 Brett Hull .60 1.50
347 Ron Hextall .30 .75
348 Kari Lehtonen .60 1.50
349 Keith Ballard .20 .50
350 Greg Hogeboom .20 .50
351 Hugh Jessiman .20 .50
352 Chris Beckford-Tseu .40 1.00
353 Mike Brodeur .20 .50
354 Andy Franck .20 .50
355 Brett Jaeger .20 .50
356 D'Arcy McConvey .20 .50
357 Chris Durno .20 .50
358 Rosario Ruggeri .20 .50
359 Garett Bembridge .20 .50
360 Mike Morrison .20 .50
361 Sidney Crosby 3.00 8.00
362 Alexander Ovechkin 1.50 4.00
363 Marek Svatos .60 1.50
364 Mike Richards .40 1.00
365 Jeff Carter 1.25 3.00
366 Eric Nystrom .40 1.00
367 Evgeni Malkin 2.00 5.00
368 Ray Emery .30 .75
369 Thomas Vanek 1.25 3.00
370 Eric Staal .30 .75
371 John Tavares 2.00 5.00
372 Bobby Ryan .60 1.50
373 Angelo Esposito 1.50 4.00
374 Al Montoya .50 1.25
375 Patrick O'Sullivan .30 .75
376 Dion Phaneuf 1.50 4.00
377 Corey Perry .40 1.00
378 Henrik Lundqvist 1.50 4.00
379 Andrew Ladd .30 .75
380 Wojtek Wolski .60 1.50
381 Staffan Kronwall .20 .50
382 Ben Walter .30 .75
383 Jamie Holden .20 .50
384 Danny Richmond .20 .50
385 Tomas Fleischmann .20 .50
386 Alexandre Picard .30 .75
387 Jeff Glass .40 1.00
388 Josh Hennessy .20 .50
389 Brad Winchester .30 .75
390 Richie Regehr .20 .50
391 Alexandre Burrows .40 1.00
392 Robert Nilsson .30 .75
393 Mark Stuart .30 .75
394 Filip Novak .20 .50
395 Stefan Ruzicka .20 .50
396 Loui Eriksson .50 1.25
397 Jay McClement .20 .50
398 Ryan Callahan .20 .50
399 Ben Shutron .20 .50
400 Logan Couture .60 1.50
401 Adam Dennis .20 .50
402 Justin Donati .20 .50
403 Luch Aquino .20 .50
404 John Armstrong .20 .50
405 Matt Beleskey .20 .50
406 Jamie McGinn .20 .50
407 Matthew Corrente .20 .50
408 Theo Peckham .20 .50
409 Mike Weber .20 .50
410 Cal Clutterbuck .30 .75
411 Jean-Christophe Blanchard .20 .50
412 Francois Bouchard .20 .50
413 Claude Giroux .75 2.00
414 Ilya Ejov .20 .50
415 Benjamin Breault .20 .50
416 Keith Yandle .20 .50
417 Ivan Vishnevskiy .20 .50
418 Ondrej Fiala .20 .50
419 Michael Grabner .40 1.00
420 Riley Holzapfel .20 .50
421 Lukas Bohunicky .20 .50
422 Tysen Dowzak .20 .50
423 Colton Yellow Horn .40 1.00
424 Dustin Slade .20 .50
425 Bud Holloway .20 .50
426 David Ruzicka .20 .50
427 Marek Schwarz .30 .75
428 Michael Frolik .60 1.50
429 Cristobal Huet .40 1.00
430 Ray Emery .30 .75

2005-06 ITG Heroes and Prospects AHL Grads

PRINT RUN 70 SETS
AG1 Jason Spezza 6.00 15.00
AG2 Brett Hull 6.00 15.00
AG3 Patrick Roy 15.00 40.00
AG4 Kari Lehtonen 8.00 20.00
AG5 Keith Ballard 3.00 8.00
AG6 Jose Theodore 6.00 15.00
AG7 Ron Hextall 6.00 15.00
AG8 Mike Cammalleri 4.00 10.00
AG9 Cam Ward 8.00 20.00

2005-06 ITG Heroes and Prospects Aspiring

PRINT RUN 50 SETS
ASP1 P.Roy/C.Price 40.00 80.00
ASP2 M.Lemieux/E.Malkin 40.00 100.00
ASP3 D.Keon/P.O'Sullivan 15.00 40.00
ASP4 B.Mosienko/T.Mosienko 10.00 25.00
ASP5 P.Coffey/J.Pitkanen 10.00 25.00
ASP6 C.Neely/P.Bergeron 15.00 40.00
ASP7 M.Bossy/R.Schremp 10.00 25.00
ASP8 P.LaFontaine/B.Ryan 10.00 25.00
ASP9 R.Bourque/S.Weber 15.00 40.00
ASP10 B.Parent/A.Niittymaki 15.00 40.00
ASP11 M.Dionne/D.Brown 10.00 25.00
ASP12 B.Clarke/J.Carter 20.00 50.00
ASP13 G.Lafleur/G.Latendresse 15.00 40.00
ASP14 J.Beliveau/P.Bouchard 15.00 40.00
ASP15 D.Sittler/E.Staal 15.00 40.00
ASP16 B.Hull/J.Spezza 20.00 50.00
ASP17 S.Yzerman/B.Pouliot 20.00 50.00
ASP18 M.Brodeur/M.Fleury 25.00 60.00
ASP19 M.Lemieux/S.Crosby 100.00 200.00
ASP20 M.Lemieux/A.Ovechkin 40.00 100.00

2005-06 ITG Heroes and Prospects Autographs

AAA Alex Auld 6.00 15.00
AAB Alex Bourret 5.00 12.00
AAH Adam Hauser 5.00 12.00
AAHI Andy Hilbert 4.00 10.00
AAHU Andrew Hutchinson 4.00 10.00
AAM Al Montoya 10.00 25.00
AAMQ Adam McQuaid 4.00 10.00
AAN Antero Niittymaki 8.00 20.00
AAO Alexander Ovechkin SP 50.00 100.00
AAR Alexander Radulov 12.00 30.00
AAS Alexander Svitov 4.00 10.00
AAV Anton Volchenkov 4.00 10.00
AAVI Alexandre Vincent 4.00 10.00
ABB Brad Boyes 4.00 10.00
ABBO Brandon Bochenski 5.00 12.00
ABBU Brent Burns 5.00 12.00
ABCL Bobby Clarke SP 12.50 30.00
ABD Brodie Dupont 4.00 10.00
ABJ Blair Jones 4.00 10.00
ABL Brian Leetch SP 10.00 25.00
ABLI Bryan Little 8.00 20.00
ABMA Brad Marchand 6.00 15.00
ABMI Brendan Mikkelson 4.00 10.00
ABMX Ben Maxwell 4.00 10.00
ABOH Bobby Hull SP 15.00 40.00
ABP Benoit Pouliot 6.00 15.00
ABPA Bernie Parent 12.50 30.00
ABR Bobby Ryan SP 12.00 30.00
ABRH Brett Hull SP 15.00 40.00
ABS Brett Sutter 5.00 12.00
ACB Cam Barker 6.00 15.00
ACBA Cody Bass 6.00 15.00
ACBQ Chris Bourque SP 8.00 20.00
ACC Chris Campoli 4.00 10.00
ACCO Carlo Colaiacovo 4.00 10.00
ACD Chad Denny 4.00 10.00
ACDU Chris Durand 4.00 10.00
ACE0 Christian Ehrhoff 4.00 10.00
ACK Chuck Kobasew 4.00 10.00
ACL Corey Locke 4.00 10.00
ACN Cam Neely SP 10.00 25.00
ACP Carey Price 40.00 80.00
ACPE Corey Perry 10.00 25.00
ACW Cam Ward 15.00 40.00
ADB David Bolland 6.00 15.00
ADBN Dustin Brown 8.00 20.00
ADBR Derick Brassard 8.00 20.00
ADC Dino Ciccarelli 4.00 10.00
ADD Devan Dubnyk 8.00 20.00
ADG Denis Grebeshkov 4.00 10.00
ADGI Doug Gilmour 6.00 15.00
ADH Denis Hamel 4.00 10.00
ADHA Dan Hamhuis 5.00 12.00
ADK Dave Keon SP 20.00 50.00
ADKO Dustin Kohn 5.00 12.00
ADKR David Krejci 8.00 20.00
ADMA Daren Machesney 4.00 10.00
ADR Daniel Ryder 4.00 10.00
ADRY Derek Roy 6.00 15.00
ADS Darryl Sittler SP 8.00 20.00
ADSA Derek Sanderson 6.00 15.00
ADSE Devin Setoguchi 6.00 15.00
AEB Evan Brophey 4.00 10.00
AEG Ed Giacomin 12.00 30.00
AEM Evan McGrath 4.00 10.00
AEMA Evgeni Malkin SP 60.00 120.00
AEN Eric Nystrom 4.00 10.00
AES Eric Staal 12.00 30.00
AFM Frank Mahovlich 8.00 20.00
AGB Gilbert Brule 10.00 25.00
AGF Grant Fuhr 8.00 20.00
AGH Glenn Hall 10.00 25.00
AGL Guillaume Latendresse 8.00 20.00
AGLF Guy Lafleur 8.00 20.00
AHH Harry Howell 5.00 12.00
AHR Henri Richard 10.00 25.00
AHT Hannu Toivonen 8.00 20.00
AJB Jean Beliveau 25.00 50.00
AJBE Jonathan Bernier 10.00 25.00
AJBO Jay Bouwmeester SP 8.00 20.00
AJBW Johnny Bower 8.00 20.00
AJC Jeff Carter 15.00 40.00
AJDW J.D. Watt 4.00 10.00
AJH Josh Harding 8.00 20.00
AJK Jakub Kindl 4.00 10.00
AJLB Jason LaBarbera 4.00 10.00
AJM Joey MacDonald 12.50 25.00
AJN James Neal 10.00 25.00
AJPI Joni Pitkanen 4.00 10.00
AJPL Jean-Philippe Levasseur 4.00 10.00
AJPP Jean-Philippe Paquet 4.00 10.00
AJR Jean Ratelle 8.00 20.00
AJSH James Sheppard 6.00 15.00
AJST Jordan Staal 30.00 80.00
AJT John Tavares SP 60.00 120.00
AJTH Jose Theodore SP 20.00 40.00
AJTO Jordin Tootoo 8.00 20.00
AKBI Kevin Bieksa 6.00 15.00
AKLA Kevin Lalande 4.00 10.00
AKLT Kristopher Letang 8.00 20.00
AKMC Kenndal McArdle 5.00 12.00
AKR Kris Russell 5.00 12.00
AKW Kristofer Westblom 4.00 10.00
ALB Luc Bourdon 8.00 20.00
ALN Lawrence Nycholat 4.00 10.00
AMAC Marc-Andre Cliche 4.00 10.00
AMAF Marc-Andre Fleury 10.00 25.00
AMAG Marc-Andre Gragnani 4.00 10.00
AMB Martin Brodeur SP 15.00 40.00
AMBL Michael Blunden 5.00 12.00
AMBO Mike Bossy 6.00 15.00
AMC Mike Cammalleri 5.00 12.00
AMD Marcel Dionne 6.00 15.00
AME Mike Egener 4.00 10.00
AMEV Marc-Edouard Vlasic 8.00 20.00
AMG Mathieu Garon 6.00 15.00
AMK Mikko Koivu 8.00 20.00
AMKA Matt Kassian 4.00 10.00
AML Mario Lemieux SP 30.00 80.00
AMLF Matt Lashoff 5.00 12.00
AMLN Michael Leighton 5.00 12.00
AMO Michel Ouellet 6.00 15.00
AMP Matt Pelech 4.00 10.00
AMR Mike Richards 10.00 25.00
AMSH Milt Schmidt 6.00 15.00
AMSR Michael Sauer 4.00 10.00
AMST Marc Staal 10.00 25.00
AMSV Marek Svatos 8.00 20.00
AMZ Marek Zagrapan 4.00 10.00
AMZI Mike Zigomanis 4.00 10.00
ANB Neal Broten 8.00 20.00
ANBL Nicolas Blanchard 4.00 10.00
AOB Oksars Bartulis 4.00 10.00
APBR Patrice Bergeron 10.00 25.00
APE Phil Esposito SP 10.00 25.00
APH Paul Henderson 6.00 15.00
APL Pascal Leclaire 5.00 12.00
APLF Pat LaFontaine 8.00 20.00
APOP Pier-Olivier Pelletier 4.00 10.00
APR Patrick Roy SP 30.00 80.00
APS Patrick Sharp 10.00 25.00
ARB Ray Bourque SP 15.00 40.00
ARBQ Rene Bourque 4.00 10.00
ARC Ryane Clowe 8.00 20.00
ARE Ray Emery 6.00 15.00
ARJU R.J. Umberger 5.00 12.00
ARK Red Kelly 6.00 15.00
ARKS Ryan Kesler 6.00 15.00
ARM Raymond Macias 4.00 10.00
ARMI Ryan Miller 12.50 30.00
ARO Ryan O'Marra 5.00 12.00
ARP Ryan Parent 5.00 12.00
ARS Radek Smolenak 6.00 15.00
ARSC Robbie Schremp 8.00 20.00
ARSU Ryan Suter 8.00 20.00
ASC Sidney Crosby SP 75.00 200.00
ASD Steve Downie 10.00 25.00
ASE Steve Eminger 6.00 15.00
ASG Simon Gamache 4.00 10.00
ASJ Scott Jackson 4.00 10.00
ASM Stan Mikita 10.00 25.00
ASO Steve Ott 5.00 12.00
ASW Shea Weber 6.00 15.00
ASY Steve Yzerman SP 30.00 80.00
ATE Tony Esposito 8.00 20.00
ATL Ted Lindsay 6.00 15.00
ATM Tyler Mosienko 4.00 10.00
ATP Tom Pyatt 4.00 10.00
ATPL Tyler Plante 4.00 10.00
ATV Thomas Vanek 15.00 30.00
AVT Vladislav Tretiak SP 15.00 40.00
AWC Wendel Clark 10.00 25.00
AYD Yann Danis 6.00 15.00
AYL Yanick Lehoux 4.00 10.00
AZP Zach Parise 8.00 20.00
DABB Chris Bourque
Ray Bourque
DABC Gilbert Brule
Bobby Clarke
DABF Martin Brodeur
Marc-Andre Fleury
DABL Jay Bouwmeester
Brian Leetch
DABO Patrice Bergeron
Alexander Ovechkin
DACR Jeff Carter 15.00 30.00
Mike Richards
DADF Devan Dubnyk
Grant Fuhr
DADT Yann Danis
Jose Theodore
DAHH Brett Hull
Bobby Hull
DALL Guillaume Latendresse
Guy Lafleur
DAML Evgeni Malkin
Mario Lemieux
DAMO Evgeni Malkin
Alexander Ovechkin
DAPM Zach Parise
Frank Mahovlich
DAPR Carey Price
Patrick Roy
DARL Bobby Ryan
Pat LaFontaine
DASY Eric Staal 40.00 80.00
Steve Yzerman

2005-06 ITG Heroes and Prospects Autographs Series II

UNPRICED DUAL AUTO PRINT RUN 15
AAC Andy Chiodo 6.00 15.00
AAE2 Angelo Esposito SP 60.00 150.00
AAF Andy Franck 4.00 10.00
AAG Alex Grant 6.00 15.00
AAJT A.J. Thelen 4.00 10.00
AAK Andrei Kostitsyn 8.00 20.00
AAL Andrew Ladd SP 8.00 20.00
AAM2 Al Montoya SP 6.00 15.00
AAO2 Alexander Ovechkin SP 50.00 125.00
AAO3 Alexander Ovechkin SP 50.00 125.00
AAP Alexandre Picard 6.00 15.00
AAPR Alexander Perezhogin 8.00 20.00
AARG Andy Rogers 4.00 10.00
AAW Andrew Wozniewski 4.00 10.00
ABC Braydon Coburn 6.00 15.00
ABCA Brady Calla 4.00 10.00
ABCO Blake Comeau 5.00 12.00
ABF Brian Finley 4.00 10.00
ABG Bruno Gervais 4.00 10.00
ABH Bobby Hughes 4.00 10.00
ABJG Brett Jaeger 4.00 10.00
ABJS Borje Salming 10.00 25.00
ABK Brent Krahn 6.00 15.00
ABPO Brian Pothier 4.00 10.00
ABR2 Bobby Ryan SP 12.00 30.00
ABRH2 Brett Hull SP 12.00 30.00
ABSG Bob Sanguinetti 10.00 25.00
ABSU Brandon Sutter 8.00 20.00
ABSW Bryce Swan 4.00 10.00
ACBK Codey Burki 4.00 10.00
ACCR Corey Crawford 8.00 20.00
ACDR Chris Durno 4.00 10.00
ACEM Cory Emmerton 4.00 10.00
ACLR Chad Larose 4.00 10.00
ACM Clarke MacArthur 4.00 10.00
ACMD Chris Madden 4.00 10.00
ACME Curtis McElhinney 4.00 10.00
ACMU Colin Murphy 4.00 10.00
ACP2 Corey Perry SP 8.00 20.00
ACP3 Corey Perry SP 10.00 25.00
ACS Chris Stewart 5.00 12.00
ACSA Curtis Sanford 6.00 15.00
ACW2 Cam Ward SP 10.00 25.00
ADBO Dustin Boyd 6.00 15.00
ADCA Daniel Carcillo 4.00 10.00
ADDE David Desharnais 6.00 15.00
ADDS Dan DaSilva 4.00 10.00
ADHE Dany Heatley SP 10.00 25.00
ADHU Dylan Hunter 5.00 12.00
ADJ Derek Joslin 4.00 10.00
ADL Dan LaCosta 4.00 10.00
ADMC D'Arcy McConvey 4.00 10.00
ADMI Drew MacIntyre 4.00 10.00
ADP Dion Phaneuf SP 20.00 40.00
ADP2 Dion Phaneuf SP 20.00 50.00
ADPE Dustin Penner 6.00 15.00
ADPZ Dmitri Patzold 5.00 12.00
ADSB Dany Sabourin 4.00 10.00
ADT Dan Turple 4.00 10.00
AEF Eric Fehr 6.00 15.00
AEL Eric Lindros SP 15.00 40.00
AEL2 Eric Lindros SP 12.00 30.00
AEMA2 Evgeni Malkin SP 40.00 100.00
AEMA3 Evgeni Malkin SP 40.00 100.00
AEN2 Eric Nystrom SP 5.00 12.00
AES2 Eric Staal SP 15.00 40.00
AEW Erik Westrum 4.00 10.00
AGBE Garrett Bembridge 4.00 10.00
AGC Gerry Cheevers 10.00 25.00
AGCL Gerald Coleman 5.00 12.00
AGHO Greg Hogeboom 4.00 10.00
AGLF2 Guy Lafleur SP 10.00 25.00
AGP Gilbert Perreault 10.00 25.00
AGPL Geoff Platt 4.00 10.00
AHC Herb Carnegie 20.00 50.00
AHJ Hugh Jessiman 4.00 10.00
AHL Henrik Lundqvist SP 25.00 60.00
AHL2 Henrik Lundqvist SP 30.00 80.00
AIK Ilya Kovalchuk SP 12.00 30.00
AJBC Jason Bacashihua 6.00 15.00
AJC2 Jeff Carter SP 12.00 30.00
AJC3 Jeff Carter SP 12.00 30.00
AJCO Jeremy Colliton 6.00 15.00
AJCR Jim Craig 8.00 20.00
AJD John de Gray 4.00 10.00
AJDA Jonathan D'Aversa 4.00 10.00
AJE Julien Ellis-Plante 6.00 15.00
AJFJ Jean-Francois Jacques 4.00 10.00
AJG Justin Garay 6.00 15.00
AJHU Jiri Hudler 6.00 15.00
AJL Junior Lessard 6.00 15.00
AJOP John Pohl 6.00 15.00
AJPG Justin Pogge 20.00 50.00
AJPO Jason Pominville 8.00 20.00
AJRY Joe Ryan 4.00 10.00
AJSC Jeff Schultz 4.00 10.00
AJT2 John Tavares SP 90.00 150.00
AJTA Jeff Tambellini 6.00 15.00
AJTE Joey Tenute 4.00 10.00
AJTH2 Jose Theodore SP 8.00 20.00
AKA Kevin Armstrong 4.00 10.00
AKB Keith Ballard SP 5.00 12.00
AKC Kyle Chipchura 6.00 15.00
AKF Kurtis Foster 4.00 10.00
AKG Kelly Guard 5.00 12.00
AKL2 Kari Lehtonen SP 12.00 30.00
ALI Leland Irving 8.00 20.00
ALR Larry Robinson 6.00 15.00
ALRD Liam Reddox 4.00 10.00
ALS Ladislav Smid 4.00 10.00
ALST Logan Stephenson 4.00 10.00
ALT Lauri Tukonen 4.00 10.00
AMAP Marc-Antoine Pouliot 6.00 15.00
AMB2 Martin Brodeur 40.00 80.00
AMBR Mike Brodeur SP 6.00 15.00
AMC2 Mike Cammalleri SP 5.00 12.00
AMCL Mathieu Carle 4.00 10.00
AMEL Matt Ellison 4.00 10.00
AMFI Mark Fistric 4.00 10.00
AMFU Michael Funk 4.00 10.00
AMGL Mike Glumac 4.00 10.00
AMH Mark Howe 10.00 25.00
AMHA Mark Hartigan 6.00 15.00
AMHO Marek Horsky 4.00 10.00
AML2 Mario Lemieux SP 40.00 80.00
AML3 Mario Lemieux SP 40.00 80.00
AMM Mike Morrison 6.00 15.00
AMR2 Mike Richards SP 10.00 25.00
AMR3 Mike Richards SP 10.00 25.00
AMRY Mathieu Roy 6.00 15.00
AMSP Martin St. Pierre 4.00 10.00
AMSV2 Marek Svatos SP 5.00 12.00
AMXB Maxime Boisclair 6.00 15.00
AMXO Maxime Ouellet 4.00 10.00
ANBG Nicklas Bergfors 6.00 15.00
ANC Noah Clarke 4.00 10.00
AND Nigel Dawes 5.00 12.00
ANF Nick Foligno 5.00 12.00
ANM Nathan Marsters 4.00 10.00
ANP Nathan Paetsch 4.00 10.00
ANS Nolan Schaefer 4.00 10.00

ANW Noah Welch 6.00 15.00
AOL Olivier Latendresse 6.00 15.00
AOP Ondrej Pavelec 6.00 15.00
APM Peter Mueller 10.00 25.00
APOS Patrick O'Sullivan SP 8.00 20.00
APP Petr Prucha SP 10.00 25.00
APR2 Patrick Roy SP 40.00 100.00
APR3 Patrick Roy SP 40.00 80.00
APRI Pekka Rinne 8.00 20.00
APSJ Peter Sejna 4.00 10.00
APT Petr Taticek 4.00 10.00
ARB2 Ray Bourque SP 25.00 60.00
ARBE Rejean Beauchemin 5.00 12.00
ARD Ryan Daniels 4.00 10.00
ARE2 Ray Emery SP 6.00 15.00
ARG Ryan Getzlaf SP 10.00 25.00
ARGI Rod Gilbert 6.00 15.00
ARH Ron Hextall 20.00 50.00
ARH2 Ron Hextall SP 10.00 25.00
ARHA Ron Hainsey 6.00 15.00
ARHI Ryan Hillier 4.00 10.00
ARMC Ryan MacDonald 5.00 12.00
ARR Rosario Ruggeri 4.00 10.00
ARRO Rafael Rotter 4.00 10.00
ARSH Ryan Shannon 4.00 10.00
ARST Ryan Stone 4.00 10.00
ARV Roman Voloshenko 6.00 15.00
ARVE Ryan Vesce 4.00 10.00
ARWH Ryan White 4.00 10.00
ASB Sean Bergenheim 4.00 10.00
ASBE Shawn Belle 4.00 10.00
ASBR Steve Bernier 8.00 20.00
ASC2 Sidney Crosby SP 75.00 150.00
ASC3 Sidney Crosby SP 75.00 150.00
ASGA Steve Gainey 4.00 10.00
ASKO Sergei Kostitsyn 6.00 15.00
ASL Stanislav Lascek 4.00 10.00
ASY2 Steve Yzerman SP 40.00 80.00
ATB Troy Brouwer 4.00 10.00
ATG Tim Gleason 4.00 10.00
ATK Tyler Kennedy 4.00 10.00
ATKE Ted Kennedy 8.00 20.00
ATMK Tomi Maki 4.00 10.00
ATPC Tomas Plekanec 4.00 10.00
ATPK Thomas Pock 4.00 10.00
ATR Tyler Redenbach 4.00 10.00
ATS Tod Sloan 4.00 10.00
ATV2 Thomas Vanek SP 12.00 30.00
ATW Ty Wishart 4.00 10.00
AVK Vitaly Kolesnik 5.00 12.00
AWR Wacey Rabbit 6.00 15.00
AYC Yvan Cournoyer 8.00 20.00
AYS Yan Stastny 4.00 10.00
AZH Zach Hamill 6.00 15.00
BP Martin Brodeur
Justin Pogge
CM2 Jim Craig
Al Montoya
HK Dany Heatley
Ilya Kovalchuk
LN Henrik Lundqvist
Antero Niittymaki
LT2 Eric Lindros
John Tavares
PL Petr Prucha
Henrik Lundqvist
RP Larry Robinson
Dion Phaneuf
RT Patrick Roy
Jose Theodore
YC2 Jim Craig
Vladislav Tretiak

2005-06 ITG Heroes and Prospects Autographs Update

ONE PER UPDATE BOX
AAE Angelo Esposito SP 75.00 150.00
AFB Francois Bouchard 3.00 8.00
AFN Filip Novak 3.00 8.00
AMF Michael Frolik SP 20.00 50.00
AOF Ondrej Fiala 3.00 8.00
ARN Robert Nilsson 4.00 10.00
ASK Staffan Kronwall 3.00 8.00
ATD Tysen Dowzak 3.00 8.00
ATF Tomas Fleischmann 4.00 10.00
ABSH Ben Shutron 3.00 8.00
ACBT Chris Beckford-Tseu 12.00 30.00
ACHT Cristobal Huet SP 15.00 40.00
ADRI Danny Richmond 3.00 8.00
ADRU David Ruzicka SP
AJGL Jeff Glass 5.00 12.00
AJHO Jamie Holden 3.00 8.00
AMCO Matthew Corrente 4.00 10.00
AMKS Mark Stuart 4.00 10.00
AMSZ Marek Schwarz SP 15.00 30.00
ARE3 Ray Emery SP 6.00 15.00
ARRG Richie Regehr 3.00 8.00
DAET J.Tavares/A.Esposito 125.00 250.00

2005-06 ITG Heroes and Prospects CHL Grads

PRINT RUN 70 SETS
CG1 Marc Antoine Pouliot 6.00 15.00
CG2 Gilbert Brule 10.00 25.00
CG3 Jeff Carter 12.00 30.00
CG4 Mike Richards 6.00 15.00
CG5 Mario Lemieux 15.00 40.00
CG6 Patrick Roy 15.00 40.00
CG7 Steve Yzerman 15.00 40.00
CG8 Guy Lafleur 10.00 25.00
CG9 Dion Phaneuf 15.00 40.00
CG10 Ryan Getzlaf 10.00 25.00
CG11 Corey Perry 8.00 20.00
CG12 Ray Bourque 10.00 25.00
CG13 Grant Fuhr 10.00 25.00
CG14 Martin Brodeur 12.00 30.00
CG15 Eric Fehr 6.00 15.00
CG16 Sidney Crosby 25.00 60.00

2005-06 ITG Heroes and Prospects Future Teammates

PRINT RUN 30 SETS
FT1 P.Bouchard/M.Koivu 10.00 25.00
FT2 J.Pitkanen/A.Niittymaki 10.00 25.00
FT3 C.Perry/R.Getzlaf 15.00 40.00
FT4 M.Fleury/M.Lemieux 50.00 125.00
FT5 J.Spezza/B.Bochenski 20.00 50.00
FT6 C.Ward/E.Staal 20.00 50.00
FT7 D.Keon/F.Mahovlich 20.00 50.00
FT8 P.Roy/R.Bourque 25.00 60.00
FT9 P.LaFontaine/G.Fuhr 15.00 40.00
FT10 P.Bergeron/B.Boyes 15.00 40.00
FT11 R.Bourque/C.Neely 20.00 50.00
FT12 B.Hull/G.Hall 20.00 50.00
FT13 S.Crosby/E.Malkin 40.00 100.00
FT14 A.Ovechkin/E.Fehr 50.00 100.00

2005-06 ITG Heroes and Prospects He Shoots He Scores Prizes

STATED PRINT RUN 20 SER.#'d SETS
1 S.Crosby/M.Lemieux 60.00 120.00
2 G.Latendresse/G.Lafleur 8.00 20.00
3 K.Lehtonen/M.Brodeur 12.00 30.00
4 D.Phaneuf/R.Bourque 10.00 25.00
5 J.Theodore/P.Roy 15.00 40.00
6 E.Malkin/A.Ovechkin 40.00 80.00
7 B.Pouliot/S.Yzerman 15.00 40.00
8 A.Ovechkin/M.Lemieux 30.00 80.00
9 J.Bouwmeester/B.Leetch 8.00 20.00
10 C.Price/J.Theodore 20.00 50.00
11 E.Malkin/M.Lemieux 25.00 60.00
12 T.Mosienko/B.Mosienko 5.00 12.00
13 E.Staal/M.Staal 12.00 30.00
14 Br.Hull/Bo.Hull 15.00 40.00
15 D.Syvret/D.Fritsche 5.00 12.00
16 C.Perry/D.Bolland 25.00 60.00
17 K.Westblom/B.Comeau 8.00 20.00
18 B.Ryan/R.Getzlaf 15.00 40.00
19 K.Lehtonen/A.Ovechkin 30.00 80.00
20 P.Bergeron/B.Boyes 8.00 20.00
21 D.Roy/R.Miller 8.00 20.00
22 B.Krahn/D.Phaneuf 10.00 25.00
23 C.Ward/E.Staal 10.00 25.00
24 B.Seabrook/P.Vorobiev 12.00 30.00
25 W.Wolski/M.Svatos 5.00 12.00
26 P.Leclaire/D.Fritsche 6.00 15.00
27 M.Pouliot/R.Schremp 8.00 20.00
28 J.Bouwmeester/A.Stewart 6.00 15.00
29 J.LaBarbera/M.Cammalleri 8.00 20.00
30 M.Koivu/P.O'Sullivan 8.00 20.00
31 K.Chipchura/G.Latendresse 5.00 12.00
32 S.Upshall/D.Hamhuis 6.00 15.00
33 B.Bochenski/J.Spezza 8.00 20.00
34 A.Niittymaki/J.Pitkanen 6.00 15.00
35 J.Carter/M.Richards 12.00 30.00
36 S.Crosby/E.Malkin 75.00 150.00
37 M.Fleury/R.Whitney 10.00 25.00
38 S.Crosby/C.Colaiacovo 30.00 80.00
39 R.Kesler/A.Auld 8.00 20.00
40 A.Ovechkin/E.Fehr 30.00 80.00
41 A.Ovechkin/A.Radulov 30.00 80.00
42 M.Lemieux/E.Malkin 25.00 60.00
43 S.Yzerman/J.Tavares 15.00 40.00
44 P.Roy/A.Esposito 15.00 40.00
45 M.Messier/S.Downie 10.00 25.00
46 F.Mahovlich/B.Pouliot 8.00 20.00
47 M.Brodeur/C.Price 20.00 50.00
48 J.Jagr/M.Frolik 15.00 40.00
49 T.Sawchuk/L.Irving 10.00 25.00
50 M.Richard/J.Tavares 12.00 30.00
51 A.Ovechkin/D.Phaneuf 30.00 80.00
52 M.Lemieux/J.Staal 20.00 50.00
53 S.Yzerman/P.O'Sullivan 15.00 40.00
54 P.Roy/C.Crawford 20.00 50.00
55 M.Messier/P.Mueller 10.00 25.00
56 T.Horton/M.Staal 8.00 20.00
57 M.Brodeur/M.Schwarz 12.00 30.00
58 J.Jagr/J.Tlusty 12.00 30.00
59 B.Hull/R.Getzlaf 15.00 40.00
60 J.Bower/J.Pogge 8.00 20.00

2005-06 ITG Heroes and Prospects Hero Memorabilia

HM1-HM20 PRINT RUN 50 SETS
HM21-HM41 PRINT RUN 30 SETS
HM42-56 PRINT RUN 60 SETS
HM1 Mario Lemieux 20.00 50.00
HM2 Ray Bourque 10.00 25.00
HM3 Cam Neely 6.00 15.00
HM4 Doug Gilmour 6.00 15.00
HM5 Wendel Clark 6.00 15.00
HM6 Stan Mikita 6.00 15.00
HM7 Pat LaFontaine 6.00 15.00
HM8 Patrick Roy 20.00 50.00
HM9 Dino Ciccarelli 6.00 15.00
HM10 Ed Giacomin 12.50 30.00
HM11 Vladislav Tretiak 15.00 40.00
HM12 Brad Park 6.00 15.00
HM13 Brett Hull 8.00 20.00
HM14 Brian Leetch 6.00 15.00
HM15 Martin Brodeur 20.00 50.00
HM16 Steve Yzerman 12.50 30.00
HM17 Jose Theodore 8.00 20.00
HM18 Bobby Hull 10.00 25.00
HM19 Jean Beliveau 15.00 40.00
HM20 Guy Lafleur 10.00 25.00
HM21 Frank Mahovlich 8.00 20.00
HM22 Grant Fuhr 12.00 30.00
HM23 Glenn Hall 6.00 15.00
HM24 Gerry Cheevers 15.00 40.00
HM25 Marcel Dionne 6.00 15.00
HM26 Phil Esposito 12.50 30.00
HM27 Valeri Kharlamov 15.00 40.00
HM28 Tony Esposito 8.00 20.00
HM29 Bobby Clarke 10.00 25.00
HM30 Eddie Shore 8.00 20.00
HM31 Bernie Parent 10.00 25.00
HM32 Mike Bossy 12.50 30.00
HM33 Jean Ratelle 15.00 40.00
HM34 Gump Worsley 12.00 30.00
HM35 Darryl Sittler 8.00 20.00
HM36 Jacques Plante 20.00 50.00
HM37 Steve Shutt 8.00 20.00
HM38 Ted Lindsay 8.00 20.00
HM39 Red Kelly 8.00 20.00
HM40 Johnny Bower 12.50 30.00
HM41 Dave Keon 15.00 40.00
HM42 Borje Salming 15.00 40.00
HM43 Lanny McDonald 6.00 15.00
HM44 Rod Gilbert 6.00 15.00
HM45 Eric Lindros 6.00 15.00
HM46 Ilya Kovalchuk 10.00 25.00
HM47 Dany Heatley 10.00 25.00
HM48 George Hainsworth 25.00 60.00
HM49 Bill Barber 6.00 15.00
HM50 Serge Savard 6.00 15.00
HM51 Guy Lapointe 6.00 15.00
HM52 Yvan Cournoyer 6.00 15.00
HM53 Denis Potvin 10.00 25.00
HM54 Larry Robinson 6.00 15.00
HM55 Rogie Vachon 6.00 15.00
HM56 Mark Howe 6.00 15.00

2005-06 ITG Heroes and Prospects Hero Memorabilia Dual

ANNOUNCED PRINT RUN 30 SETS
HDM1 Bill Mosienko 8.00 20.00
HDM2 Brett Hull 15.00 40.00
HDM3 Wendel Clark 12.50 30.00
HDM4 Patrick Roy 20.00 50.00
HDM5 Ray Bourque 15.00 40.00
HDM6 Cam Neely 10.00 25.00
HDM7 Doug Gilmour 8.00 20.00
HDM8 Steve Yzerman 25.00 60.00
HDM9 Brian Leetch 10.00 25.00
HDM10 Grant Fuhr 15.00 40.00
HDM11 Jose Theodore 10.00 25.00
HDM12 Guy Lafleur 10.00 25.00
HDM13 Dave Keon 8.00 20.00
HDM14 Mario Lemieux 25.00 60.00
HDM15 Bobby Hull 12.50 30.00
HDM16 Stan Mikita 8.00 20.00
HDM17 Ron Hextall 12.50 30.00

2005-06 ITG Heroes and Prospects Jerseys

ANNOUNCED PRINT RUN 100
EMBLEMS/30: .8X TO 2X JSY/100*
NUMBERS/30: .8X TO 2X JSY/100*
NUMBERS/15: 1X TO 2.5X JSY/100*
GUJ1 Bobby Ryan 6.00 15.00
GUJ2 Brian Sutherby 4.00 10.00
GUJ3 Jay Bouwmeester 6.00 15.00
GUJ4 Denis Hamel 5.00 12.00
GUJ5 Andy Hilbert 5.00 12.00
GUJ6 Mike Cammalleri 6.00 15.00
GUJ7 Mikko Koivu 8.00 20.00
GUJ8 Boyd Gordon 4.00 10.00
GUJ9 Brad Boyes 5.00 12.00
GUJ10 Ryan Kesler 8.00 20.00
GUJ11 Joni Pitkanen 4.00 10.00
GUJ12 Pascal Leclaire 5.00 12.00
GUJ13 Derek Roy 4.00 10.00
GUJ14 Ryan Whitney 6.00 15.00
GUJ15 Jason Spezza 6.00 15.00
GUJ16 Eric Staal 8.00 20.00
GUJ17 Dustin Brown 6.00 15.00
GUJ18 Chuck Kobasew 4.00 10.00
GUJ19 Ray Emery 6.00 15.00
GUJ20 Jason LaBarbera 5.00 12.00
GUJ21 Michel Ouellet 5.00 12.00
GUJ22 Antero Niittymaki 5.00 12.00
GUJ23 Cam Ward 10.00 25.00
GUJ24 Marc-Andre Fleury 10.00 25.00
GUJ25 Devin Setoguchi 6.00 15.00
GUJ26 Shea Weber 6.00 15.00
GUJ27 Chris Durand 4.00 10.00
GUJ28 Guillaume Latendresse 6.00 15.00
GUJ29 Brandon Bochenski 6.00 15.00
GUJ30 Pavel Vorobiev 4.00 10.00
GUJ31 P-M Bouchard 6.00 15.00
GUJ32 Patrice Bergeron 8.00 20.00
GUJ33 Kenndal McArdle 4.00 10.00
GUJ34 Patrick O'Sullivan 6.00 15.00
GUJ35 Marek Zagrapan 5.00 12.00
GUJ36 Carey Price 20.00 50.00
GUJ37 Corey Crawford 8.00 20.00
GUJ38 Rob Schremp 6.00 15.00
GUJ39 Lee Goren 4.00 10.00
GUJ40 Tyler Mosienko 4.00 10.00
GUJ41 Brent Burns 8.00 20.00
GUJ42 Travis Roche 4.00 10.00
GUJ43 Kristofer Westblom 4.00 10.00
GUJ44 Lawrence Nycholat 4.00 10.00
GUJ45 Wojtek Wolski 5.00 12.00
GUJ46 Mathieu Garon 5.00 12.00
GUJ47 Adam Munro 4.00 10.00
GUJ48 Blake Comeau 6.00 15.00
GUJ49 Evgeni Malkin 25.00 60.00
GUJ50 Benoit Pouliot 4.00 10.00
GUJ51 Gerald Coleman 4.00 10.00
GUJ52 Marc Staal 8.00 20.00
GUJ53 Sidney Crosby 50.00 80.00
GUJ54 Alexander Ovechkin 25.00 60.00
GUJ55 Al Montoya 6.00 15.00
GUJ56 Gilbert Brule 6.00 15.00
GUJ57 David Bolland 6.00 15.00
GUJ58 Zach Parise 15.00 40.00
GUJ59 Mike Richards 12.00 30.00
GUJ60 Jeff Carter 12.00 30.00
GUJ61 Jeff Tambellini 4.00 10.00
GUJ62 Chris Campoli 4.00 10.00
GUJ63 Shawn Belle 4.00 10.00
GUJ64 Chris Bourque 10.00 25.00
GUJ65 John Tavares 25.00 50.00
GUJ66 Tim Thomas 6.00 15.00
GUJ67 Justin Pogge 6.00 15.00
GUJ68 Bryan Little 6.00 15.00
GUJ69 Patrick Eaves 6.00 15.00
GUJ70 Brett Sutter 4.00 10.00
GUJ71 Yan Stastny 5.00 12.00
GUJ72 Gerald Coleman 4.00 10.00
GUJ73 Rejean Beauchemin 5.00 12.00
GUJ74 Chris Beckford-Tseu 5.00 12.00
GUJ75 Luc Bourdon 10.00 25.00
GUJ76 Matt Ellison 4.00 10.00
GUJ77 Brian Pothier 4.00 10.00
GUJ78 Alexandre Vincent 4.00 10.00
GUJ79 Corey Perry 25.00 60.00
GUJ80 Anthony Stewart 5.00 12.00
GUJ81 Ryan Getzlaf 15.00 40.00
GUJ82 Eric Fehr 5.00 12.00
GUJ83 Keith Ballard 5.00 12.00
GUJ84 Marc-Antoine Pouliot 5.00 12.00
GUJ85 Julien Ellis 10.00 25.00
GUJ86 Dany Roussin 4.00 10.00
GUJ87 Eric Nystrom 5.00 12.00
GUJ88 Brent Krahn 5.00 12.00
GUJ89 Evgeni Malkin 25.00 60.00
GUJ90 Sidney Crosby 50.00 80.00
GUJ91 Alexander Ovechkin 25.00 60.00
GUJ92 Maxime Ouellet 12.00 30.00
GUJ93 Carlo Colaiacovo 4.00 10.00
GUJ94 Henrik Lundqvist 12.00 30.00
GUJ95 Alexander Perezhogin 5.00 12.00
GUJ96 Sean Bergenheim 4.00 10.00
GUJ97 Kari Lehtonen 5.00 12.00
GUJ98 Jason Bacashihua 8.00 20.00
GUJ99 Jordin Tootoo 6.00 15.00
GUJ100 Marek Svatos 5.00 12.00
GUJ101 Dennis Wideman 4.00 10.00
GUJ102 Colby Armstrong 6.00 15.00
GUJ103 Mike Brodeur 4.00 10.00
GUJ104 Matt Foy 4.00 10.00
GUJ105 Grant Stevenson 4.00 10.00
GUJ106 Ari Ahonen 5.00 12.00
GUJ107 Andrew Ladd 8.00 20.00
GUJ108 Adam Hauser 5.00 12.00
GUJ109 Dion Phaneuf 12.00 30.00
GUJ110 Jeff Schultz 4.00 10.00
GUJ111 Petr Prucha 6.00 15.00
GUJ112 Alexander Mogilny 5.00 12.00
GUJ113 Devan Dubnyk 8.00 20.00
GUJ114 Thomas Vanek 12.00 30.00
GUJ115 Carey Price 20.00 50.00
GUJ116 Tom Pyatt 4.00 10.00

2005-06 ITG Heroes and Prospects Making the Bigs

PRINT RUN 40
MTB1 Jose Theodore 8.00 20.00
MTB2 Jason Spezza 10.00 25.00
MTB3 P-M Bouchard 5.00 12.00
MTB4 Brian Sutherby 4.00 10.00
MTB5 Eric Staal 10.00 25.00
MTB6 Boyd Gordon 4.00 10.00
MTB7 Alexander Ovechkin 25.00 60.00
MTB8 Ray Emery 6.00 15.00
MTB9 Derek Roy 8.00 20.00
MTB10 Maxime Ouellet 5.00 12.00
MTB11 Dustin Brown 5.00 12.00
MTB12 Scottie Upshall 4.00 10.00
MTB13 Guillaume Latendresse 6.00 15.00
MTB14 Mike Richards 6.00 15.00
MTB15 Jeff Carter 12.00 30.00
MTB16 Gerald Coleman 4.00 10.00

2005-06 ITG Heroes and Prospects Measuring Up

COMMON CARD (MU1-MU20) 15.00 30.00
PRINT RUN 60 SETS
MU1 C.Ward/P.Roy 15.00 30.00
MU2 J.LaBarbera/P.Roy 15.00 30.00
MU3 J.Ellis-Plante/P.Roy 15.00 30.00
MU4 J.Bacashihua/P.Roy 15.00 30.00
MU5 A.Auld/P.Roy 15.00 30.00
MU6 S.Clemmensen/P.Roy 15.00 30.00
MU7 M.Ouellet/P.Roy 20.00 40.00
MU8 B.Krahn/P.Roy 15.00 30.00
MU9 H.Lundqvist/P.Roy 20.00 50.00
MU10 R.Miller/P.Roy 20.00 50.00
MU11 A.Niittymaki/P.Roy 20.00 40.00
MU12 M.Fleury/P.Roy 20.00 40.00
MU13 G.Coleman/P.Roy 15.00 30.00
MU14 D.Dubnyk/P.Roy 15.00 30.00
MU15 R.Beauchemin/P.Roy 15.00 30.00
MU16 K.Guard/P.Roy 15.00 30.00
MU17 C.Price/P.Roy 25.00 50.00
MU18 A.Montoya/P.Roy 20.00 40.00
MU19 J.Pogge/P.Roy 20.00 40.00
MU20 K.Lehtonen/P.Roy 20.00 40.00

2005-06 ITG Heroes and Prospects Memorial Cup

COMPLETE SET (13) 8.00 20.00
COMMON CARD (MC1-MC13) 1.00 2.50
MC1 Danny Syvret 1.00 2.50
MC2 Robbie Schremp 2.00 5.00
MC3 Dylan Hunter 1.00 2.50
MC4 Corey Perry 2.00 5.00
MC5 Dan Fritsche 1.00 2.50
MC6 David Bolland 1.00 2.50
MC7 Adam Dennis 1.00 2.50
MC8 Gerald Coleman 1.00 2.50
MC9 Brandon Prust 1.00 2.50
MC10 Bryan Rodney 1.00 2.50
MC11 Drew Larman 1.00 2.50
MC12 Josh Beaulieu 1.00 2.50
MC13 Marc Methot 1.00 2.50

2005-06 ITG Heroes and Prospects National Pride

NPR1-12/22-41 PRINT RUN 60 SETS
NPR13-21 PRINT RUN 20 SETS
NPR1 Kari Lehtonen 6.00 15.00
NPR2 Marc-Andre Fleury 8.00 20.00
NPR3 Dany Roussin 4.00 10.00
NPR4 Jason Spezza 8.00 20.00
NPR5 Jay Bouwmeester 4.00 10.00
NPR6 Dion Phaneuf 15.00 40.00
NPR7 P-M Bouchard 4.00 10.00
NPR8 Mikko Koivu 4.00 10.00
NPR9 Mike Cammalleri 4.00 10.00
NPR10 Evgeni Malkin 25.00 60.00
NPR11 Sidney Crosby 40.00 100.00
NPR12 Alexander Ovechkin 25.00 60.00
NPR13 Tony Esposito
NPR14 Darryl Sittler
NPR15 Patrick Roy
NPR16 Bobby Clarke
NPR17 Martin Brodeur 15.00 40.00
NPR18 Brett Hull
NPR19 Steve Yzerman
NPR20 Brian Leetch
NPR21 Pat LaFontaine
NPR22 Pelle Lindbergh 15.00 40.00
NPR23 Phil Esposito 8.00 20.00
NPR24 Lanny McDonald 4.00 10.00
NPR25 Dany Heatley 8.00 20.00
NPR26 Borje Salming 6.00 15.00
NPR27 Eric Lindros 8.00 20.00
NPR28 Gilbert Perreault 6.00 15.00
NPR29 Gerry Cheevers 8.00 20.00
NPR30 Larry Robinson 6.00 15.00
NPR31 Ilya Kovalchuk 12.00 30.00
NPR32 Justin Pogge 15.00 40.00
NPR33 Alexander Ovechkin 20.00 50.00
NPR34 Bobby Ryan 8.00 20.00
NPR35 Evgeni Malkin 20.00 50.00
NPR36 Sidney Crosby 40.00 100.00
NPR37 Corey Perry 8.00 20.00
NPR38 Jeff Carter 10.00 25.00
NPR39 Mike Richards 6.00 15.00
NPR40 Al Montoya 6.00 15.00
NPR41 Anthony Stewart 4.00 10.00

2005-06 ITG Heroes and Prospects Net Prospects

COMMON CARD (NP1-NP21) 4.00 10.00
SEMISTARS 6.00 15.00
PRINT RUN 80 SETS
NP1 Kari Lehtonen 6.00 15.00
NP2 Marc-Andre Fleury 8.00 20.00
NP3 Antero Niittymaki 6.00 15.00
NP4 Adam Hauser 4.00 10.00
NP5 Mathieu Garon 4.00 10.00
NP6 Pascal Leclaire 4.00 10.00
NP7 Ray Emery 6.00 15.00
NP8 Adam Munro 4.00 10.00
NP9 Cam Ward 8.00 20.00
NP10 Jason LaBarbera 4.00 10.00
NP11 Ryan Miller 8.00 20.00
NP12 Brent Krahn 4.00 10.00
NP13 Alex Auld 5.00 12.00
NP14 Devan Dubnyk 4.00 10.00
NP15 Carey Price 12.00 30.00
NP16 Kyle Moir 4.00 10.00
NP17 Corey Crawford 8.00 20.00
NP18 Kevin Nastiuk 4.00 10.00
NP19 Jonathan Boutin 4.00 10.00
NP20 Gerald Coleman 4.00 10.00
NP21 Kristofer Westblom 4.00 10.00

2005-06 ITG Heroes and Prospects Net Prospects Dual

COMMON CARD (NPD1-NPD10) 6.00 15.00
PRINT RUN 80 SETS
NPD1 M.Ouellet/A.Auld 8.00 20.00
NPD2 A.Hauser/J.LaBarbera 6.00 15.00
NPD3 A.Niittymaki/R.Beauchemin 8.00 20.00
NPD4 K.Westblom/G.Coleman 6.00 15.00
NPD5 A.Montoya/P.Leclaire 12.00 30.00
NPD6 B.Krahn/C.Ward 6.00 15.00
NPD7 K.Lehtonen/M.Fleury 20.00 50.00
NPD8 D.Dubnyk/J.Pogge 15.00 40.00
NPD9 C.Beckford-Tseu/Mi.Brodeur 6.00 15.00
NPD10 C.Price/J.Ellis-Plante 10.00 25.00

2005-06 ITG Heroes and Prospects Oh Canada

ANNOUNCED PRINT RUN 50
OC1 Liam Reddox 8.00 20.00
OC2 Julien Ellis-Plante 8.00 20.00
OC3 Cody Bass 8.00 20.00
OC4 Derick Brassard 8.00 20.00
OC5 Ryan O'Marra 8.00 20.00
OC6 Kristopher Letang 10.00 25.00
OC7 David Bolland 8.00 20.00
OC8 Benoit Pouliot 10.00 25.00
OC9 Blake Comeau 8.00 20.00
OC10 Ryan Parent 8.00 20.00
OC11 Dustin Boyd 8.00 20.00
OC12 Steve Downie 8.00 20.00
OC13 Kyle Chipchura 8.00 20.00
OC14 Justin Peters 8.00 20.00
OC15 Dustin Kohn 8.00 20.00
OC16 Justin Keller 8.00 20.00
OC17 Dan LaCosta 8.00 20.00

2005-06 ITG Heroes and Prospects Shooting Stars

COMPLETE SET (12) 8.00 15.00
AS1 Jason LaBarbera .60 1.50
AS2 Lawrence Nycholat .40 1.00
AS3 Dennis Wideman .40 1.00
AS4 Jason Spezza .75 2.00
AS5 Mike Cammalleri .75 2.00
AS6 Michel Ouellet .60 1.50
AS7 Kari Lehtonen 2.00 5.00
AS8 Niklas Kronwall .75 2.00
AS9 Joni Pitkanen .60 1.50
AS10 Zach Parise 1.00 2.50
AS11 Andy Hilbert .40 1.00
AS12 Dustin Brown 1.00 2.50

2005-06 ITG Heroes and Prospects Team Cherry

TC1 Ty Wishart 2.00 5.00
TC2 Mike Weber 2.00 5.00
TC3 Chris Stewart 2.00 5.00
TC4 Joe Ryan 2.00 5.00
TC5 Theo Peckham 2.00 5.00
TC6 Peter Mueller 2.50 6.00
TC7 Jamie McGinn 2.00 5.00
TC8 Ben Maxwell 2.00 5.00
TC9 Bobby Hughes 2.00 5.00
TC10 Ryan Hillier 2.00 5.00
TC11 Nick Foligno 2.00 5.00
TC12 John de Gray 2.00 5.00
TC13 Cal Clutterbuck 2.50 6.00
TC14 Mathieu Carle 2.00 5.00
TC15 Brady Calla 2.00 5.00
TC16 Derick Brassard 2.50 6.00
TC17 Francois Bouchard 2.00 5.00
TC18 Jonathan Bernier 4.00 10.00
TC19 Matt Beleskey 2.00 5.00
TC20 Kevin Armstrong 2.00 5.00

2005-06 ITG Heroes and Prospects Team Orr

TO1 John Armstrong 2.00 5.00
TO2 Lukas Bohunicky 2.00 5.00
TO3 Benjamin Breault 2.00 5.00
TO4 Codey Burki 2.00 5.00
TO5 Matthew Corrente 2.00 5.00
TO6 Ryan Daniels 2.00 5.00
TO7 Tysen Dowzak 2.00 5.00
TO8 Cory Emmerton 2.00 5.00
TO9 Ondrej Fiala 2.00 5.00
TO10 Claude Giroux 4.00 10.00
TO11 Michael Grabner 3.00 8.00
TO12 Riley Holzapfel 2.00 5.00
TO13 Leland Irving 2.50 6.00
TO14 Bryan Little 3.00 8.00
TO15 Bob Sanguinetti 2.00 5.00
TO16 James Sheppard 2.00 5.00
TO17 Ben Shutron 2.00 5.00
TO18 Jordan Staal 3.00 8.00
TO19 Ivan Vishnevskiy 2.00 5.00
TO20 Ryan White 2.00 5.00

2006-07 ITG Heroes and Prospects

The final 50-cards in this set were issued as a factory set by ITG. Those factory sets included either an autograph or a game-used memorabilia card.

COMPLETE SET (200) 25.00 60.00
COMP.SET (150) 12.50 30.00
COMP.UPDATE SET (50) 12.50 30.00
1 Elmer Lach .25 .60
2 Milt Schmidt .25 .60
3 Brian Leetch .25 .60
4 Peter Stastny .25 .60
5 Mark Messier .40 1.00
6 Willie O'Ree .25 .60
7 Bryan Trottier .30 .75
8 Jaromir Jagr .60 1.50
9 Mario Lemieux .75 2.00
10 Luc Robitaille .25 .60
11 Dick Duff .20 .50
12 Ron Francis .30 .75
13 Guy Lafleur .30 .75
14 Patrick Roy .60 1.50
15 Martin Brodeur .50 1.25
16 Tim Thomas .30 .75
17 Cristobal Huet .20 .50
18 Jeff Carter .25 .60
19 Marc-Andre Fleury .40 1.00
20 Billy Smith .25 .60
21 Johnny Bower .40 1.00
22 Antero Niittymaki .20 .50
23 Brad Boyes .15 .40
24 Sidney Crosby 1.00 2.50
25 Cam Ward .25 .60
26 Kyle Wellwood .20 .50
27 Jason Spezza .25 .60
28 Wendel Clark .25 .60
29 Denis Potvin .25 .60
30 Bobby Clarke .25 .60
31 Tony Voce .15 .40
32 Martin Houle .20 .50
33 Brendan Bell .15 .40
34 Eric Fehr .25 .60
35 Carsen Germyn .15 .40
36 Yann Danis .20 .50
37 Roman Voloshenko .15 .40
38 Tomas Kopecky .20 .50
39 Ben Ondrus .15 .40
40 Nathan Marsters .15 .40
41 Marc-Antoine Pouliot .15 .40
42 Konstantin Pushkarev .20 .50
43 Ian White .20 .50
44 Jeremy Williams .15 .40
45 Noah Welch .15 .40
46 Rick Rypien .40 1.00
47 Lauri Tukonen .15 .40
48 Danny Syvret .15 .40
49 Mark Giordano .20 .50
50 Andrew Penner .20 .50
51 Aleksander Suglobov .15 .40
52 David LeNeveu .20 .50
53 Doug O'Brien .15 .40
54 Martin St. Pierre .15 .40
55 Dan Fritsche .15 .40
56 Connor James .15 .40
57 Dustin Penner .20 .50
58 Ryan Vesce .15 .40
59 Colby Genoway .15 .40
60 Ben Walter .15 .40
61 Richie Regehr .15 .40
62 Trevor Gillies .15 .40
63 Mark Hartigan .15 .40
64 Garett Bembridge .15 .40
65 Ladislav Smid .15 .40
66 Braydon Coburn .15 .40
67 Jeremy Colliton .15 .40
68 Nathan Paetsch .15 .40
69 Pavel Vorobiev .15 .40
70 Matt Jones .15 .40
71 Corey Locke .15 .40
72 Corey Crawford .25 .60
73 Erik Westrum .15 .40
74 Patrick O'Sullivan .25 .60
75 Jeff Tambellini .15 .40
76 Al Montoya .25 .60
77 Matthew Spiller .15 .40
78 Nigel Dawes .15 .40
79 Ryan Shannon .15 .40
80 Steven Stamkos 2.00 5.00
81 Angelo Esposito .30 .75
82 John Tavares 2.00 5.00
83 Jordan Staal .40 1.00
84 Derick Brassard .25 .60
85 Peter Mueller .25 .60
86 Bryan Little .15 .40
87 James Sheppard .15 .40
88 Cory Emmerton .20 .50
89 Bob Sanguinetti .20 .50
90 Ondrej Fiala .15 .40
91 Logan Couture .40 1.00
92 Ty Wishart .15 .40
93 Ryan Hillier .15 .40
94 Jared Staal .25 .60
95 Bobby Hughes .15 .40
96 Brady Calla .15 .40
97 Joe Ryan .15 .40
98 Ivan Vishnevskiy .20 .50
99 Gilbert Brule .20 .50
100 Bud Holloway .15 .40
101 Ben Maxwell .25 .60
102 Matt Beleskey .25 .60
103 John Armstrong .15 .40
104 Michael Grabner .25 .60
105 Oskar Osala .15 .40
106 Jamie McGinn .20 .50
107 Luke Lynes .15 .40
108 Drew Doughty .50 1.25
109 Alex Bourret .15 .40
110 Chris Stewart .20 .50
111 Jonathan Bernier .50 1.25
112 Leland Irving .30 .75
113 Claude Giroux .75 2.00
114 Ryan Daniels .20 .50
115 Nick Foligno .20 .50
116 Matthew Corrente .15 .40
117 Francois Bouchard .20 .50
118 Brandon Sutter .20 .50
119 Michael Del Zotto .25 .60
120 Sergei Kostitsyn .20 .50
121 Corey Syvret .15 .40
122 Steve Downie .15 .40
123 Brett Sutter .20 .50
124 Shawn Matthias .20 .50
125 Alexander Radulov .30 .75
126 Guillaume Latendresse .25 .60
127 Ryan White .20 .50
128 Luc Bourdon .25 .60
129 Colton Gillies .20 .50
130 Marc Staal .25 .60
131 Anze Kopitar .60 1.50
132 Jiri Tlusty .25 .60
133 Yuri Alexandrov .15 .40
134 Tuukka Rask .60 1.50
135 Evgeni Malkin 1.00 2.50
136 Phil Kessel .40 1.00
137 Alexander Vasyunov .15 .40
138 Michael Frolik .20 .50
139 John Tavares 1.25 3.00
140 Justin Pogge .25 .60
141 Jonathan Bernier .50 1.25
142 Brandon Sutter .20 .50
143 Luc Bourdon .40 1.00
144 Steve Downie .15 .40
145 Kristopher Letang .50 1.25
146 Ryan Parent .25 .60
147 Sidney Crosby 1.00 2.50
148 Marc Staal .25 .60
149 Guillaume Latendresse .25 .60
150 Tom Pyatt .15 .40
151 Joe Pavelski .75 2.00
152 Chris Harrington .15 .40
153 Bill Thomas .15 .40
154 Loui Eriksson .25 .60
155 Benoit Pouliot .20 .50
156 Eric Nystrom .15 .40
157 Bryan Bickell .30 .75
158 Nicklas Bergfors .25 .60
159 Hugh Jessiman .15 .40
160 Jiri Hudler .25 .60
161 Alexander Radulov .30 .75
162 Mike Green .25 .60
163 Staffan Kronwall .15 .40
164 Drew Miller .20 .50
165 Brett Sterling .15 .40
166 Jeff Taffe .15 .40
167 Geoff Platt .15 .40
168 Blake Comeau .25 .60
169 Ryan Carter .15 .40
170 Drew Stafford .25 .60
171 Petr Kalus .15 .40
172 Josh Hennessy .15 .40
173 Rob Schremp .20 .50
174 Janis Sprukts .15 .40
175 Patrick Kane 4.00 10.00
176 Bobby Ryan .25 .60
177 Devin Setoguchi .25 .60
178 Michael Frolik .20 .50
179 Brodie Dupont .15 .40
180 Tom Pyatt .15 .40
181 Kenndal McArdle .15 .40
182 Michael Caruso .15 .40
183 James Neal .40 1.00
184 Ben Shutron .15 .40
185 Marc-Andre Cliche .15 .40
186 Felix Schutz .15 .40
187 Cody Bass .15 .40
188 Dustin Kohn .15 .40
189 Marc-Edouard Vlasic .15 .40
190 Dan Ryder .15 .40
191 Mathieu Carle .15 .40
192 Justin Azevedo .15 .40
193 Kristopher Letang .50 1.25
194 Kris Russell .15 .40
195 Patrick McNeill .15 .40
196 Marc-Andre Gragnani .15 .40
197 Cody Franson .20 .50
198 Cal Clutterbuck .20 .50
199 Jakub Voracek .60 1.50
200 Sam Gagner .30 .75

2006-07 ITG Heroes and Prospects AHL All-Star Emblems

*EMBLEMS: 1X TO 2.5X JERSEY HI
STATED PRINT RUN 30 SER.#'d SETS

2006-07 ITG Heroes and Prospects AHL All-Star Jerseys

COMMON CARD 4.00 10.00
STATED PRINT RUN 80 SER.#'d SETS
AJ01 Jeff Tambellini 4.00 10.00
AJ02 Martin St. Pierre 4.00 10.00
AJ03 Jiri Hudler 4.00 10.00
AJ04 John Pohl 4.00 10.00
AJ05 Yann Danis 4.00 10.00
AJ06 Patrick O'Sullivan 4.00 10.00
AJ07 Denis Hamel 4.00 10.00
AJ08 Keith Ballard 4.00 10.00
AJ09 Denis Shvidki 4.00 10.00
AJ10 Rick DiPietro 4.00 10.00
AJ11 Phillipe Sauve 4.00 10.00
AJ12 Kyle Wellwood 4.00 10.00

2006-07 ITG Heroes and Prospects AHL All-Star Numbers

*NUMBERS: 1X TO 2.5X JERSEY HI
STATED PRINT RUN 30 SER.#'d SETS

2006-07 ITG Heroes and Prospects AHL Shooting Stars

COMPLETE SET (12) 6.00 15.00
AS01 Pekka Rinne .75 2.00
AS02 Sven Butenschon .40 1.00
AS03 Noah Welch .75 2.00
AS04 Jiri Hudler .75 2.00
AS05 John Pohl .75 2.00
AS06 Erik Westrum .75 2.00
AS07 Wade Flaherty .75 2.00
AS08 Nathan Paetsch .40 1.00
AS09 John Slaney .40 1.00
AS10 Jimmy Roy .40 1.00
AS11 Kirby Law .40 1.00
AS12 Eric Fehr .75 2.00

2006-07 ITG Heroes and Prospects Autographs

STATED ODDS 1:14
AAB Alex Bourret 3.00 8.00
AAE Angelo Esposito 15.00 40.00
AAK Anze Kopitar 12.00 30.00
AAN Antero Niittymaki 4.00 10.00
AAP Andrew Penner 4.00 10.00
AAR Alexander Radulov 6.00 15.00
AAS Aleksander Suglobov 3.00 8.00
AAV Alexander Vasyunov 3.00 8.00
ABB Brendan Bell 3.00 8.00
ABC Bobby Clarke 5.00 12.00
ABD Brodie Dupont 3.00 8.00
ABH Bobby Hughes 3.00 8.00
ABL Brian Leetch 15.00 40.00
ABM Ben Maxwell 5.00 12.00
ABO Ben Ondrus 3.00 8.00
ABP Benoit Pouliot 4.00 10.00
ABR Bobby Ryan 6.00 15.00
ABT Bill Thomas 3.00 8.00
ABW Ben Walter 3.00 8.00
ACB Cody Bass 3.00 8.00
ACC Corey Crawford 10.00 25.00
ACE Cory Emmerton 4.00 10.00
ACF Cody Franson 4.00 10.00
ACG Carsen Germyn 3.00 8.00
ACH Cristobal Huet 6.00 15.00
ACJ Connor James 3.00 8.00
ACL Corey Locke 3.00 8.00
ACS Chris Stewart 4.00 10.00
ACW Cam Ward 5.00 12.00
ADB Derick Brassard 5.00 12.00
ADD Dick Duff 4.00 10.00
ADF Dan Fritsche 3.00 8.00
ADK Dustin Kohn 3.00 8.00
ADL David LeNeveu 4.00 10.00
ADM Drew Miller 4.00 10.00
ADO Doug O'Brien 3.00 8.00
ADP Denis Potvin 5.00 12.00
ADR Dan Ryder 3.00 8.00
ADS Drew Stafford 5.00 12.00
AEF Eric Fehr 5.00 12.00
AEL Elmer Lach 5.00 12.00
AEM Evgeni Malkin 30.00 80.00
AEN Eric Nystrom 3.00 8.00
AEW Erik Westrum 3.00 8.00
AFB Francois Bouchard 4.00 10.00
AFS Felix Schutz 3.00 8.00
AGB Garett Bembridge 3.00 8.00
AGP Geoff Platt 3.00 8.00
AHJ Hugh Jessiman 3.00 8.00
AIV Ivan Vishnevskiy 4.00 10.00
AIW Ian White 4.00 10.00
AJA John Armstrong 3.00 8.00
AJC Jeremy Colliton 3.00 8.00
AJH Jiri Hudler 5.00 12.00
AJJ Jaromir Jagr 20.00 40.00
AJM Jamie McGinn 4.00 10.00
AJN James Neal 8.00 20.00
AJP Justin Pogge 5.00 12.00
AJR Joe Ryan 3.00 8.00
AJS Jason Spezza 5.00 12.00
AJV Jakub Voracek
AJW Jeremy Williams 3.00 8.00
AKL Kristopher Letang 10.00 25.00
AKM Kenndal McArdle 3.00 8.00
AKP Konstantin Pushkarev 4.00 10.00

AKR Kris Russell 3.00 8.00
AKW Kyle Wellwood 4.00 10.00
ALC Logan Couture 8.00 20.00
ALE Loui Eriksson 5.00 12.00
ALI Leland Irving 6.00 15.00
ALL Luke Lynes 3.00 8.00
ALR Luc Robitaille 5.00 12.00
ALS Ladislav Smid 3.00 8.00
ALT Lauri Tukonen 3.00 8.00
AMB Martin Brodeur 30.00 60.00
AMC Matthew Corrente 3.00 8.00
AMF Michael Frolik 4.00 10.00
AMG Mike Green 5.00 12.00
AMH Martin Houle 4.00 10.00
AMJ Matt Jones 3.00 8.00
AML Mario Lemieux 25.00 60.00
AMM Mark Messier 25.00 60.00
ANB Nicklas Bergfors 5.00 12.00
AND Nigel Dawes 3.00 8.00
ANF Nick Foligno 4.00 10.00
ANM Nathan Marsters 3.00 8.00
ANP Nathan Paetsch 3.00 8.00
ANW Noah Welch 3.00 8.00
AOF Ondrej Fiala 3.00 8.00
AOO Oskar Osala 3.00 8.00
APK Phil Kessel 8.00 20.00
APM Peter Mueller 5.00 12.00
APR Patrick Roy 30.00 60.00
APS Peter Stastny 6.00 15.00
APV Pavel Vorobiev 3.00 8.00
ARC Ryan Carter 3.00 8.00
ARF Ron Francis 15.00 40.00
ARH Ryan Hillier 3.00 8.00
ARP Ryan Parent 5.00 12.00
ARR Rick Rypien 15.00 40.00
ARS Ryan Shannon 3.00 8.00
ARV Roman Voloshenko 3.00 8.00
ARW Ryan White 4.00 10.00
ASG Sam Gagner 20.00 50.00
ASK Sergei Kostitsyn 4.00 10.00
ASM Shawn Matthias 4.00 10.00
ASS Steven Stamkos 50.00 100.00
ATG Trevor Gillies 3.00 8.00
ATK Tomas Kopecky 4.00 10.00
ATP Tom Pyatt 3.00 8.00
ATR Tuukka Rask 15.00 30.00
ATT Tim Thomas 10.00 25.00
ATV Tony Voce 3.00 8.00
ATW Ty Wishart 3.00 8.00
AWC Wendel Clark 6.00 15.00
AWO Willie O'Ree 10.00 25.00
AYA Yuri Alexandrov 3.00 8.00
AYD Yann Danis 4.00 10.00
AAMO Al Montoya 5.00 12.00
AAR2 Alexander Radulov 6.00 15.00
ABBI Bryan Bickell 6.00 15.00
ABBO Brad Boyes 3.00 8.00
ABCA Brady Calla 3.00 8.00
ABCM Blake Comeau 5.00 12.00
ABCO Braydon Coburn 3.00 8.00
ABHO Bud Holloway 3.00 8.00
ABLI Bryan Little 3.00 8.00
ABRS Brett Sutter 4.00 10.00
ABS1 Brandon Sutter 4.00 10.00
ABS2 Brandon Sutter 4.00 10.00
ABSA Bob Sanguinetti 4.00 10.00
ABSH Ben Shutron 3.00 8.00
ABSM Billy Smith 5.00 12.00
ABST Brett Sterling 3.00 8.00
ABTR Bryan Trottier 6.00 15.00
ACCL Cal Clutterbuck 4.00 10.00
ACGE Colby Genoway 3.00 8.00
ACGI Colton Gillies 4.00 10.00
ACGR Claude Giroux 15.00 40.00
ACHA Chris Harrington 3.00 8.00
ACSV Corey Syvret 3.00 8.00
ADDO Drew Doughty 10.00 25.00
ADPE Dustin Penner 4.00 10.00
ADSE Devin Setoguchi 5.00 12.00
ADSV Danny Syvret 3.00 8.00
AGBR Gilbert Brule 4.00 10.00
AGLF Guy Lafleur 10.00 25.00
AJAS Jared Staal 6.00 15.00
AJAZ Justin Azevedo 3.00 8.00
AJB1 Jonathan Bernier 10.00 25.00
AJB2 Jonathan Bernier 10.00 25.00
AJBO Johnny Bower 8.00 20.00
AJCA Jeff Carter 5.00 12.00
AJHE Josh Hennessy 3.00 8.00
AJPV Joe Pavelski 15.00 40.00
AJSH James Sheppard 3.00 8.00
AJSP Janis Sprukts 3.00 8.00
AJST Jordan Staal 8.00 20.00
AJT1 John Tavares 25.00 60.00
AJT2 John Tavares 25.00 60.00
AJTA Jeff Tambellini 3.00 8.00
AJTF Jeff Taffe 3.00 8.00
AJTL Jiri Tlusty 5.00 12.00
AKL2 Kristopher Letang 10.00 25.00
ALB1 Luc Bourdon 8.00 20.00
ALB2 Luc Bourdon 8.00 20.00
AMAC Marc-Andre Cliche 3.00 8.00
AMAF Marc-Andre Fleury 8.00 20.00
AMAG Marc-Andre Gragnani 3.00 8.00
AMAP Marc-Antoine Pouliot 3.00 8.00
AMBL Matt Beleskey 5.00 12.00
AMCA Michael Caruso 3.00 8.00
AMCR Mathieu Carle 3.00 8.00
AMDZ Michael Del Zotto 5.00 12.00
AMEV Marc-Edouard Vlasic 3.00 8.00
AMF2 Michael Frolik 4.00 10.00
AMGI Mark Giordano 4.00 10.00
AMGR Michael Grabner 5.00 12.00
AMHA Mark Hartigan 3.00 8.00
AMS1 Marc Staal 5.00 12.00
AMS2 Marc Staal 5.00 12.00
AMSC Milt Schmidt 5.00 12.00
AMSP Matthew Spiller 3.00 8.00
AMST Martin St. Pierre 3.00 8.00
APKA Petr Kalus 3.00 8.00
APKN Patrick Kane 40.00 100.00
APMC Patrick McNeill 3.00 8.00
APOS Patrick O'Sullivan 5.00 12.00
ARDA Ryan Daniels 4.00 10.00
ARRG Richie Regehr 3.00 8.00
ARSC Rob Schremp
ARVE Ryan Vesce 3.00 8.00
ASC1 Sidney Crosby 60.00 120.00
ASC2 Sidney Crosby 75.00 135.00
ASD1 Steve Downie 3.00 8.00
ASD2 Steve Downie 3.00 8.00
ASKR Staffan Kronwall 3.00 8.00
ATP2 Tom Pyatt 3.00 8.00

2006-07 ITG Heroes and Prospects Calder Cup Champions

COMPLETE SET (13) 20.00 50.00
CC01 Frederic Cassivi 2.50 6.00
CC02 Tomas Fleischmann 2.00 5.00
CC03 Mike Green 2.00 5.00
CC04 Kris Beech 2.00 5.00
CC05 Brooks Laich 2.00 5.00
CC06 Graham Mink 2.50 6.00
CC07 Boyd Gordon 2.00 5.00
CC08 Dave Steckel 2.00 5.00
CC09 Lawrence Nycholat 2.00 5.00
CC10 Boyd Kane 2.00 5.00
CC11 Joey Tenute 2.00 5.00
CC12 Jeff Schultz 2.00 5.00
CC13 Eric Fehr 2.00 5.00

2006-07 ITG Heroes and Prospects CHL Top Prospects

ANNOUNCED PRINT RUN 100
TP01 Ben Shutron 2.50 6.00
TP02 Claude Giroux 10.00 25.00
TP03 Francois Bouchard 3.00 8.00
TP04 Ivan Visnevskiy 3.00 8.00
TP05 Corey Perry 4.00 10.00
TP06 Mike Richards 4.00 10.00
TP07 Bob Sanguinetti 3.00 8.00
TP08 Derick Brassard 4.00 10.00
TP09 James Sheppard 2.50 6.00
TP10 Jonathan Bernier 8.00 20.00
TP11 Jordan Staal 6.00 15.00
TP12 Matthew Corrente 2.50 6.00
TP13 Ryan Daniels 3.00 8.00
TP14 Tysen Dowzak 2.50 6.00
TP15 Ben Maxwell 4.00 10.00
TP16 Carey Price 15.00 40.00
TP17 Eric Fehr 4.00 10.00
TP18 Julien Elllis 3.00 8.00
TP19 Eric Staal 5.00 12.00

2006-07 ITG Heroes and Prospects Class of 2006

COMPLETE SET (13) 10.00 25.00
COMMON CARD .75 2.00
SEMISTARS 1.00 2.50
UNLISTED STARS 1.25 3.00
STATED ODDS 1:24
CL01 Jordan Staal 2.00 5.00
CL02 Phil Kessel 1.50 4.00
CL03 Derick Brassard 1.25 3.00
CL04 Peter Mueller 1.25 3.00
CL05 James Sheppard 1.25 3.00
CL06 Michael Frolik 1.25 3.00
CL07 Jonathan Bernier 1.25 3.00
CL08 Bryan Little 1.25 3.00
CL09 Michael Grabner .75 2.00
CL10 Ty Wishart .75 2.00
CL11 Chris Stewart .75 2.00
CL12 Bob Sanguinetti .75 2.00
CL13 Claude Giroux 1.50 4.00

2006-07 ITG Heroes and Prospects Double Memorabilia

STATED PRINT RUN 30 SER.#'d SETS
DM01 Jordan Staal 15.00 40.00
DM02 Mario Lemieux 30.00 60.00
DM03 Sidney Crosby 30.00 80.00
DM04 Martin Brodeur 20.00 50.00
DM05 Patrick Roy 30.00 60.00
DM06 Mark Messier 20.00 40.00
DM07 Joe Sakic 12.00 30.00
DM08 John Tavares 25.00 60.00
DM09 Roberto Luongo 15.00 40.00
DM10 Sam Gagner 15.00 40.00

2006-07 ITG Heroes and Prospects Emblems

*EMBLEMS: 1X TO 2.5X JERSEY HI
STATED PRINT RUN 30 SER.#'d SETS

2006-07 ITG Heroes and Prospects He Shoots He Scores Points

1 Acadie-Bathurst Titan .40 1.00
2 Albany River Rats .40 1.00
3 Baie-Comeau Drakkar .40 1.00
4 Barrie Colts .40 1.00
5 Belleville Bulls .40 1.00
6 Binghamton Senators .40 1.00
7 Brampton Battalion .40 1.00
8 Brandon Wheat Kings .40 1.00
9 Bridgeport Sound Tigers .40 1.00
10 Calgary Hitmen .40 1.00
11 Cape Breton Screaming Eagles .40 1.00
12 Chicago Wolves .40 1.00
13 Chicoutimi Sagueneens .40 1.00
14 Cleveland Barons .40 1.00
15 Drummondville Voltigeurs .40 1.00
16 Erie Otters .40 1.00
17 Everett Silvertips .40 1.00
18 Gatineau Olympiques .40 1.00
19 Grand Rapids Griffins .40 1.00
20 Guelph Storm .40 1.00
21 Halifax Mooseheads .40 1.00
22 Hamilton Bulldogs .40 1.00
23 Hartford Wolf Pack .40 1.00
24 Hershey Bears .40 1.00
25 Houston Aeros .40 1.00
26 Iowa Stars .40 1.00
27 Kamloops Blazers .40 1.00
28 Kelowna Rockets .40 1.00
29 Kingston Frontenacs .40 1.00
30 Kitchener Rangers .40 1.00
31 Kootenay Ice .40 1.00
32 Lethbridge Hurricanes .40 1.00
33 Lewiston Maineiacs .40 1.00
34 London Knights .40 1.00
35 Lowell Lock Monsters .40 1.00
36 Manchester Monarchs .40 1.00
37 Manitoba Moose .40 1.00
38 Medicine Hat Tigers .40 1.00
39 Milwaukee Admirals .40 1.00
40 Mississauga Icedogs .40 1.00
41 Moncton Wildcats .40 1.00
42 Moose Jaw Warriors .40 1.00
43 Norfolk Admirals .40 1.00
44 Omaha Ak-Sar-Ben Knights .40 1.00
45 Oshawa Generals .40 1.00
46 Ottawa 67s .40 1.00
47 Owen Sound Attack .40 1.00
48 Pei Rocket .40 1.00
49 Peoria Reivermen .40 1.00
50 Peterborough Petes .40 1.00
51 Philadelphia Phantoms .40 1.00
52 Plymouth Whalers .40 1.00
53 Portland Pirates .40 1.00
54 Portland Winterhawks .40 1.00
55 Prince Albert Raiders .40 1.00
56 Prince George Cougars .40 1.00
57 Providence Bruins .40 1.00
58 Quebec Remparts .40 1.00
59 Red Deer Rebels .40 1.00
60 Regina Pats .40 1.00
61 Rimouski Oceanic .40 1.00
62 Rochester Americans .40 1.00
63 Rouyn-Noranda Huskies .40 1.00
64 Saginaw Spirit .40 1.00
65 San Antonio Rampage .40 1.00
66 Sarnia Sting .40 1.00
67 Saskatoon Blades .40 1.00
68 Sault Ste. Marie Greyhounds .40 1.00
69 Seattle Thunderbirds .40 1.00
70 Shawinigan Cataractes .40 1.00
71 Spokane Chiefs .40 1.00
72 Springfield Falcons .40 1.00
73 St. Michael's Majors .40 1.00
74 Sudbury Wolves .40 1.00
75 Swift Current Broncos .40 1.00
76 Syracuse Crunch .40 1.00
77 Toronto Marlies .40 1.00
78 Tri-City Americans .40 1.00
79 Val-D'or Foreurs .40 1.00
80 Vancouver Giants .40 1.00
81 Victoriaville Tigres .40 1.00
82 Wilkes-Barre/Scranton Penguins .40 1.00
83 Windsor Spitfires .40 1.00
84 In The Game Logo .40 1.00
85 AHL Logo .40 1.00
86 CHL Logo .40 1.00
87 LHJMQ Logo .40 1.00
88 OHL Logo .40 1.00
89 PHPA Logo .40 1.00
90 WHL Logo .40 1.00

2006-07 ITG Heroes and Prospects Heroes Memorabilia

HM01 Luc Robitaille 10.00 25.00
HM02 Billy Smith 10.00 25.00
HM03 Steve Yzerman 25.00 60.00
HM04 Ron Francis 10.00 25.00
HM05 Martin Brodeur 20.00 50.00
HM06 Patrick Roy 12.00 30.00
HM07 Jaromir Jagr 12.00 30.00
HM08 Mark Messier 12.00 30.00
HM09 Brian Leetch 10.00 25.00
HM10 Dave Keon 10.00 25.00
HM11 Milt Schmidt 12.00 30.00
HM12 Jacques Plante 20.00 50.00
HM13 Bobby Hull 15.00 40.00
HM14 Frank Mahovlich 12.00 30.00
HM15 Jean Beliveau 15.00 40.00
HM16 Red Kelly 12.00 30.00
HM17 Stan Mikita 15.00 40.00
HM18 Tim Horton 20.00 50.00
HM19 Terry Sawchuk 15.00 40.00
HM20 Johnny Bower 12.00 30.00
HM21 Joe Sakic 12.50 30.00
HM22 Ed Belfour 10.00 25.00
HM23 Joe Thornton 12.00 30.00
HM24 Roberto Luongo 12.00 30.00
HM25 Nicklas Lidstrom 12.00 30.00
HM26 Manny Fernandez 10.00 25.00

2006-07 ITG Heroes and Prospects Jerseys

STATED PRINT RUN 100 SER.#'d SETS
GUJ01 Marek Schwarz 5.00 12.00
GUJ02 David Ruzicka 4.00 10.00
GUJ03 Jimmy Howard 8.00 20.00
GUJ04 Daniel Girardi 4.00 10.00
GUJ05 Mike Green 4.00 10.00
GUJ06 Nigel Dawes 4.00 10.00
GUJ07 Curtis McElhinney 6.00 15.00
GUJ08 Mike Smith 8.00 20.00
GUJ09 Corey Locke 4.00 10.00
GUJ10 Yann Danis 6.00 15.00
GUJ11 Tomi Maki 4.00 10.00
GUJ12 Erik Christensen 6.00 15.00
GUJ13 Maxime Talbot 6.00 15.00
GUJ14 Tony Voce 4.00 10.00
GUJ15 Josh Harding 6.00 15.00
GUJ16 Ian White 4.00 10.00
GUJ17 Jarkko Immonen 4.00 10.00
GUJ18 Ryan Getzlaf 8.00 20.00
GUJ19 Jeremy Colliton 4.00 10.00
GUJ20 Fernando Pisani 6.00 15.00
GUJ21 Noah Welch 4.00 10.00
GUJ22 Billy Thompson 6.00 15.00
GUJ23 Staffan Kronwall 4.00 10.00
GUJ24 Darryl Bootland 4.00 10.00
GUJ25 Dustin Penner 6.00 15.00
GUJ26 Paul Ranger 4.00 10.00
GUJ27 Alexandre Picard 6.00 15.00
GUJ28 Daniel Paille 4.00 10.00
GUJ29 Andy Rogers 4.00 10.00
GUJ30 Tysen Dowzak 4.00 10.00
GUJ31 Jamie McGinn 4.00 10.00
GUJ32 Ryan Callahan 6.00 15.00
GUJ33 Angelo Esposito 15.00 30.00
GUJ34 John Tavares 12.00 30.00
GUJ35 Tim Thomas 8.00 20.00
GUJ36 Bud Holloway 4.00 10.00
GUJ37 Kevin Lalande 4.00 10.00
GUJ38 Leland Irving 6.00 15.00
GUJ39 Peter Mueller 6.00 15.00
GUJ40 Marc Staal 6.00 15.00
GUJ41 Benoit Pouliot 6.00 15.00
GUJ42 Wojtek Wolski 8.00 20.00
GUJ43 Bryan Little 8.00 20.00
GUJ44 Ben Shutron 4.00 10.00
GUJ45 Ryan O'Marra 4.00 10.00
GUJ46 Adam Perry 4.00 10.00
GUJ47 James Sheppard 6.00 15.00
GUJ48 Nicholas Drazenovic 4.00 10.00
GUJ49 Bobby Ryan 8.00 20.00
GUJ50 Tyler Plante 4.00 10.00
GUJ51 Matt Corrente 4.00 10.00
GUJ52 Ondrej Fiala 6.00 15.00
GUJ53 J-S Aubin 6.00 15.00
GUJ54 Ryan Vesce 4.00 10.00
GUJ55 Petr Taticek 4.00 10.00
GUJ56 Ben Walter 4.00 10.00
GUJ57 Andrew Penner 6.00 15.00
GUJ58 Francois Beauchemin 6.00 15.00
GUJ59 Cristobal Huet 6.00 15.00
GUJ60 Jay Bouwmeester 6.00 15.00
GUJ61 Phil Kessel 10.00 25.00
GUJ62 Petr Kalus 6.00 15.00
GUJ63 Drew Stafford 5.00 12.00
GUJ64 Alexander Radulov 12.00 30.00
GUJ65 Jiri Hudler 6.00 15.00
GUJ66 Cory Emmerton 4.00 10.00
GUJ67 Loui Eriksson 5.00 12.00
GUJ68 Bobby Ryan 6.00 15.00
GUJ69 Jakub Voracek 12.00 30.00
GUJ70 Sam Gagner 12.00 30.00
GUJ71 Michael Grabner 6.00 15.00
GUJ72 Rob Schremp 10.00 25.00
GUJ73 Cal Clutterbuck 4.00 10.00

2006-07 ITG Heroes and Prospects Making The Bigs

STATED PRINT RUN 70 SER.#'d SETS
MTB01 Wojtek Wolski 6.00 15.00
MTB02 Tim Gleason 5.00 12.00
MTB03 Cam Ward 12.00 30.00
MTB04 Ryan Miller 10.00 25.00
MTB05 Mike Glumac 6.00 15.00
MTB06 Pascal Leclaire 6.00 15.00
MTB07 Ryan Getzlaf 10.00 25.00
MTB08 Eric Nystrom 5.00 12.00
MTB09 Ray Emery 5.00 12.00
MTB10 Eric Staal 10.00 25.00
MTB11 Marc-Antoine Pouliot 6.00 15.00
MTB12 Alexander Ovechkin 12.00 30.00

2006-07 ITG Heroes and Prospects Memorial Cup Champions

COMPLETE SET (12) 8.00 20.00
MC01 Cedrick Desjardins .75 2.00
MC02 Joe Ryan .60 1.50
MC03 Brent Aubin .60 1.50
MC04 Jordan LaVallee .60 1.50
MC05 Andrew Andricopoulos .60 1.50
MC06 Marc-Edouard Vlasic 1.25 3.00
MC07 Mathieu Melanson .60 1.50
MC08 Michal Sersen .60 1.50
MC09 Angelo Esposito 2.50 6.00
MC10 Maxime Lacroix .60 1.50
MC11 Alexander Radulov 2.00 5.00
MC12 Patrick Roy 4.00 10.00

2006-07 ITG Heroes and Prospects National Pride

STATED PRINT RUN 80 SER.#'d SETS
NP01 Logan Stephenson 4.00 10.00
NP02 Sidney Crosby 20.00 50.00
NP03 Frederik Cabana 4.00 10.00
NP04 Alex Bourret 4.00 10.00
NP05 Tom Pyatt 4.00 10.00
NP06 Marc-Andre Gragnani 4.00 10.00
NP07 Olivier Latendresse 4.00 10.00
NP08 Marc Staal 8.00 20.00
NP09 Tyler Kennedy 4.00 10.00
NP10 Stephane Goulet 4.00 10.00
NP11 Devin Setoguchi 8.00 20.00
NP12 Benoit Pouliot 8.00 20.00
NP13 Jeff Schultz 4.00 10.00
NP14 Wacey Rabbit 6.00 15.00
NP15 Patrick McNeill 4.00 10.00
NP16 Steve Downie 10.00 25.00
NP17 Blake Comeau 6.00 15.00
NP18 Dustin Boyd 6.00 15.00
NP19 Kyle Chipchura 6.00 15.00
NP20 Carey Price 12.00 30.00
NP21 Marc Staal 8.00 20.00
NP22 Sam Gagner 10.00 25.00
NP23 Steve Downie 10.00 25.00

2006-07 ITG Heroes and Prospects Net Prospects

STATED PRINT RUN 70 SER.#'d SETS
NPR01 Leland Irving 8.00 20.00
NPR02 Marek Schwarz 6.00 15.00
NPR03 Jimmy Howard 8.00 20.00
NPR04 Cam Ward 12.00 30.00
NPR05 Cristobal Huet 8.00 25.00
NPR06 Ryan Miller 6.00 15.00
NPR07 Ray Emery 6.00 15.00
NPR08 Justin Pogge 10.00 25.00
NPR09 Carey Price 12.00 30.00
NPR10 Jonathan Bernier 8.00 20.00
NPR11 Hannu Toivonen 8.00 20.00
NPR12 Thomas McCollum 6.00 15.00
NPR13 Justin Pogge 12.00 30.00
NPR14 Mike Smith 6.00 15.00

2006-07 ITG Heroes and Prospects Numbers

*NUMBERS: 1X TO 2.5X JERSEY HI
STATED PRINT RUN 30 SER.#'d SETS

2006-07 ITG Heroes and Prospects Sticks and Jerseys

STATED PRINT RUN 100 SER.#'d SETS
SJ01 Eric Staal 12.00 30.00
SJ02 John Tavares
SJ03 Patrice Bergeron 10.00 25.00
SJ04 Alexander Ovechkin 20.00 50.00
SJ05 Peter Mueller 12.00 30.00
SJ06 Brady Calla 20.00
SJ07 Leland Irving 12.00 30.00
SJ08 Ondrej Fiala 8.00 20.00
SJ09 Ryan Miller 15.00 40.00
SJ10 Sidney Crosby 40.00 80.00
SJ11 Antero Niittymaki 12.00 30.00
SJ12 Jason Spezza 10.00 25.00
SJ13 Petr Prucha 20.00
SJ14 Henrik Lundqvist 12.00 40.00
SJ15 Al Montoya 10.00 25.00
SJ16 Dion Phaneuf 12.00 40.00
SJ17 Marek Svatos 8.00 20.00
SJ18 Hannu Toivonen 12.00 30.00
SJ19 Ray Emery 8.00 20.00
SJ20 Brad Boyes 8.00 20.00

2006-07 ITG Heroes and Prospects Triple Memorabilia

STATED PRINT RUN 50 SER.#'d SETS
TM01 Messier/Fuhr/Kurri 20.00 50.00
TM02 Roy/Brodeur/Parent 30.00 80.00
TM03 Ovech/Malkin/Koval 30.00 80.00
TM04 Crosby/Malkin/Lemieux 75.00 150.00
TM05 Irving/Price/Pogge 25.00 60.00
TM06 Latend/Radulov/Bourdon 20.00 50.00
TM07 Perry/Ryan/Getzlaf 25.00 60.00
TM08 Staal/Staal/Staal 25.00 60.00
TM09 Radulov/Stafford/Pouliot 20.00 50.00
TM10 Sakic/Thornton/Jagr 25.00 60.00
TM11 Esposito/Gagner/Alzner 15.00 40.00
TM12 Belfour/Luongo/Fernandez 15.00 40.00

2007-08 ITG Heroes and Prospects

COMP.SET w/o SP's (100) 10.00 25.00
COMP.UPDATE SET (50) 10.00 25.00
1 Joe Sakic .40 1.00
2 Ed Belfour .25 .60
3 Mike Modano .40 1.00
4 Vincent Lecavalier .20 .50
5 Chris Pronger .20 .50
6 Jean-Sebastien Giguere .25 .60
7 Dominik Hasek .30 .75
8 Roberto Luongo .30 .75
9 Joe Thornton .30 .75
10 Keith Tkachuk .25 .60
11 Dave Keon .25 .60
12 Alexei Cherepanov .30 .75
13 Tuukka Rask .60 1.50
14 Ilya Zubov .20 .50
15 Simeon Varlamov .50 1.25
16 Jack Skille .20 .50
17 Adam Dennis .20 .50
18 Ryan Callahan .30 .75
19 Justin Pogge .25 .60
20 Nathan Oystrick .15 .40
21 Benoit Pouliot .15 .40
22 Andrew Ebbett .15 .40
23 Matt Moulson .25 .60
24 Bobby Ryan .40 1.00
25 Cal Clutterbuck .25 .60
26 Matt D'Agostini .15 .40
27 Kyle Wilson .15 .40
28 Keith Yandle .25 .60
29 Bob Sanguinetti .15 .40
30 T.J. Kemp .15 .40
31 Cal O'Reilly .30 .75
32 Marek Zagrapan .15 .40
33 Jannik Hansen .20 .50
34 Danny Irmen .15 .40
35 Marek Schwarz .25 .60
36 Alex Bourret .20 .50
37 David Krejci .50 1.25
38 Brett Sterling .15 .40
39 Tobias Stephan .20 .50
40 Mikhail Grabovski .25 .60
41 Carey Price 1.50 4.00
42 Tyler Weiman .20 .50
43 Rich Peverley .25 .60
44 Jordan Caron .15 .40
45 Claude Giroux .75 2.00
46 T.J. Brennan .20 .50
47 Francois Bouchard .15 .40
48 Maxime Tanguay .15 .40
49 Antoine Lafleur .20 .50
50 Yann Sauve .25 .60
51 Jonathan Bernier .40 1.00
52 Olivier Fortier .15 .40
53 Jean-Simon Allard .15 .40
54 Brad Marchand .60 1.50
55 Alex Grant .15 .40
56 Kevin Armstrong .15 .40
57 Colten Teubert .25 .60
58 Jusso Puustinen .20 .50
59 Riley Holzapfel .20 .50
60 Codey Burki .15 .40
61 Milan Lucic .75 2.00
62 Luke Schenn .30 .75
63 Dana Tyrell .20 .50
64 Kyle Beach .25 .60
65 Zach Boychuk .25 .60
66 Mark Santorelli .15 .40
67 Justin McCrae .15 .40
68 Ryan White .20 .50
69 Cass Mappin .15 .40
70 Leland Irving .25 .60
71 Scott Jackson .15 .40
72 Jesse Dudas .15 .40
73 Graham Potuer .15 .40
74 John Tavares 1.00 2.50
75 Matt Caria .15 .40
76 Josh Godfrey .15 .40
77 P.K. Subban 1.25 3.00
78 Jamie McGinn .20 .50
79 Cody Hodgson .60 1.50
80 Steve Mason .50 1.25
81 Drew Doughty .50 1.25
82 Cory Emmerton .20 .50
83 Ryan O'Reilly .40 1.00
84 Dale Mitchell .15 .40
85 Steven Stamkos .75 2.00
86 Thomas McCollum .25 .60
87 Matt Duchene .40 1.00
88 Michael Del Zotto .25 .60
89 Alex Pietrangelo .40 1.00
90 Zack Torquato .15 .40
91 J.Staal/T.Cann .25 .60
92 D.Sittler/S.Gagner .30 .75
93 A.Delvecchio/J.Tavares 1.00 2.50
94 G.Lafleur/A.Esposito .30 .75
95 D.Potvin/L.Couture .25 .60
96 J.Thornton/J.Tlusty .30 .75
97 J.Sakic/K.Moir .40 1.00
98 W.Clark/C.Gillies .25 .60
99 R.Luongo/B.Marchand .60 1.50
100 V.Lecavalier/J.Caron .20 .50
101 Thomas Hickey TP JSY 10.00 25.00
102 Logan MacMillan TP JSY 5.00 12.00
103 Akim Aliu TP JSY 10.00 25.00
104 Linden Rowat TP JSY 8.00 20.00
105 Zach Hamill TP JSY 6.00 15.00
106 Nick Ross TP JSY 5.00 12.00
107 Jakub Voracek TP JSY 8.00 20.00
108 Ruslan Bashkirov TP JSY 5.00 12.00
109 John Negrin TP JSY 6.00 15.00
110 Sam Gagner TP JSY 10.00 25.00
111 Stefan Legein TP JSY 5.00 12.00
112 Jeremy Smith TP JSY 8.00 20.00
113 Nick Palmieri TP JSY 5.00 12.00
114 David Skokan TP JSY 5.00 12.00
115 Logan Couture TP JSY 8.00 20.00
116 Drayson Bowman TP JSY 5.00 12.00
117 Alex Plante TP JSY 5.00 12.00
118 Eric Doyle TP JSY 5.00 12.00
119 Keaton Ellerby TP JSY 6.00 15.00
120 Brandon Sutter TP JSY 8.00 20.00
121 Trevor Cann TP JSY 6.00 15.00
122 Keven Veilleux TP JSY 6.00 15.00
123 Karl Alzner TP JSY 5.00 12.00
124 Michal Repik TP JSY 10.00 25.00
125 Angelo Esposito TP JSY 10.00 25.00
126 Taylor Ellington TP JSY 5.00 12.00
127 Brett MacLean TP JSY 5.00 12.00
128 Tyson Sexsmith TP JSY 6.00 15.00
129 Mark Katic TP JSY 5.00 12.00
130 Jonathon Blum TP JSY 8.00 20.00
131 Bryan Cameron TP JSY 5.00 12.00
132 Colton Gillies TP JSY 8.00 20.00
133 Brett Sonne TP JSY 5.00 12.00
134 David Stich TP JSY 5.00 12.00
135 Patrick Kane TP JSY 12.00 30.00
136 Kevin Marshall TP JSY 5.00 12.00
137 Oscar Moller TP JSY 6.00 15.00
138 Maxim Gratchev TP JSY 5.00 12.00
139 Carey Price TP JSY 12.00 30.00
140 Jordan Staal TP JSY 8.00 20.00
141 Kyle Okposo .50 1.25
142 Teddy Purcell .50 1.25
143 Alex Goligoski .50 1.25
144 T.J. Hensick .30 .75
145 Brian Lee .50 1.25
146 Derick Brassard .30 .75
147 Darryl Boyce .40 1.00
148 Jonathan Matsumoto .25 .60
149 John Curry .40 1.00
150 Alexander Nikulin .30 .75
151 Cody Franson .50 1.25
152 Chris Stewart .30 .75
153 Jaroslav Halak .60 1.50
154 Kyle Greentree .25 .60
155 Jerome Samson .30 .75
156 Brian Boyle .50 1.25
157 Julian Talbot .25 .60
158 Devin Setoguchi .40 1.00
159 Michael Grabner .30 .75
160 Steve Downie .30 .75
161 Chris Doyle .40 1.00
162 Mikhail Stefanovich .25 .60
163 Joel Champagne .40 1.00
164 Maxime Sauve .40 1.00
165 Kelsey Tessier .30 .75
166 Philippe Cornet .25 .60
167 Tomas Knotek .25 .60
168 Nicolas Deschamps .40 1.00
169 Jordan Eberle .60 1.50
170 Chet Pickard .30 .75
171 Mitch Wahl .40 1.00
172 Colby Robak .25 .60
173 James Wright .40 1.00
174 Tyler Ennis .50 1.25
175 Geordie Wudrick .25 .60
176 Kruise Reddick .25 .60
177 Mitch Fadden .40 1.00
178 Tyler Myers .40 1.00
179 Luca Sbisa .25 .60
180 Shawn Matthias .25 .60
181 Patrick Maroon .40 1.00
182 Zach Bogosian .60 1.50
183 Mikkel Boedker .50 1.25
184 Jared Staal .40 1.00
185 Luca Caputi .40 1.00
186 Jamie Arniel .30 .75
187 Taylor Hall 2.00 5.00
188 Josh Bailey .25 .60
189 Tyler Cuma .25 .60
190 Philip McRae .30 .75

2007-08 ITG Heroes and Prospects Autographs

STATED ODDS 1:24
AAA Akim Aliu 6.00 15.00
AAC Alexei Cherepanov 15.00 30.00
AAD Adam Dennis 4.00 10.00
AAE Angelo Esposito 6.00 15.00
AAEB Andrew Ebbett 3.00 8.00
AAG Alex Grant 3.00 8.00
AAL Antoine Lafleur 4.00 10.00
AAO Alexander Ovechkin 30.00 80.00
AAP Alex Pietrangelo 8.00 20.00
ABB Brian Boyle 6.00 15.00
ABC Blake Comeau 3.00 8.00
ABLI Bryan Little 4.00 10.00
ABM Brad Marchand 12.00 30.00
ABP Benoit Pouliot 3.00 8.00
ABR Bobby Ryan 8.00 20.00
ABS Brandon Sutter 5.00 12.00
ABST Brett Sterling 3.00 8.00
ACB Codey Burki 3.00 8.00
ACC Cal Clutterbuck 5.00 12.00
ACD Chris Doyle 5.00 12.00
ACE Cory Emmerton 4.00 10.00
ACF Cody Franson 6.00 15.00
ACG Claude Giroux 15.00 40.00
ACH Cody Hodgson 12.00 30.00
ACM Curtis McElhinney 5.00 12.00
ACMA Cass Mappin 3.00 8.00
ACO Cal O'Reilly 6.00 15.00
ACP Chris Pronger 8.00 20.00
ACP Chet Pickard
ACPR Carey Price 40.00 80.00
ACS Chris Stewart 10.00 25.00
ACT Colten Teubert 5.00 12.00
ADB Derick Brassard 4.00 10.00
ADB Darryl Boyce 5.00 12.00
ADD Drew Doughty 10.00 25.00
ADH Dominik Hasek
ADI Danny Irmen 3.00 8.00
ADK Dave Keon 10.00 25.00
ADM Dale Mitchell 3.00 8.00
ADS Drew Stafford 4.00 10.00
ADS Devin Setoguchi 5.00 12.00
ADT Dana Tyrell 4.00 10.00
AEB Ed Belfour
AFB Francois Bouchard 3.00 8.00
AGP Graham Potuer 3.00 8.00
AGW Geordie Wudrick 3.00 8.00
AJB Josh Bailey 15.00 40.00
AJB Jonathan Bernier 15.00 40.00
AJC Jordan Caron 3.00 8.00
AJC Joel Champagne 5.00 12.00
AJD Jeff Deslauriers 4.00 10.00
AJDU Jesse Dudas 3.00 8.00
AJE Jordan Eberle 30.00 60.00
AJG Josh Godfrey 3.00 8.00
AJH Jaroslav Halak 8.00 20.00
AJHA Jannik Hansen 4.00 10.00
AJM Jamie McGinn 4.00 10.00
AJM Jonathan Matsumoto 3.00 8.00
AJMC Justin McCrae 3.00 8.00
AJOS Joe Sakic 40.00 80.00
AJP Justin Pogge 5.00 12.00
AJPU Jusso Puustinen 4.00 10.00
AJPV Joe Pavelski 5.00 12.00
AJS Jordan Sigalet 4.00 10.00
AJS Jerome Samson 4.00 10.00
AJSA Jean-Simon Allard 3.00 8.00
AJSG Jean-Sebastien Giguere
AJSH James Sheppard 3.00 8.00
AJSK Jack Skille 4.00 10.00
AJSM Jeremy Smith 5.00 12.00
AJST Jordan Staal 5.00 12.00
AJT John Tavares 20.00 50.00
AJTH Joe Thornton 6.00 15.00
AKA Kevin Armstrong 3.00 8.00
AKAL Karl Alzner 3.00 8.00
AKB Kyle Beach 5.00 12.00
AKO Kyle Okposo 15.00 40.00
AKT Kelsey Tessier 4.00 10.00
AKT Keith Tkachuk 5.00 12.00
AKW Kyle Wilson 3.00 8.00
AKY Keith Yandle 5.00 12.00
ALC Luca Caputi
ALI Leland Irving 5.00 12.00
ALR Linden Rowat 5.00 12.00
ALS Luke Schenn 6.00 15.00
AMB Mikael Boedker 6.00 15.00
AMC Matt Caria 3.00 8.00
AMD Matt Duchene 10.00 25.00
AMDA Matt D'Agostini 3.00 8.00
AMDZ Michael Del Zotto 10.00 25.00
AMF Mitch Fadden 5.00 12.00
AMG Michael Grabner
AMG Mikhail Grabovski 5.00 12.00
AMM Matt Moulson 5.00 12.00
AMMO Mike Modano 8.00 20.00
AMN Michal Neuvirth 6.00 15.00
AMS Marek Schwarz 5.00 12.00
AMT Maxime Tanguay 3.00 8.00
AMW Mitch Wahl 5.00 12.00
AMZ Marek Zagrapan 3.00 8.00
AND Nicolas Deschamps 5.00 12.00
AOF Olivier Fortier 3.00 8.00
APD Peter Delmas 3.00 8.00
APK Patrick Kane 25.00 60.00
APKS P.K. Subban 12.50 30.00
APMU Peter Mueller 4.00 10.00
APO Patrick O'Sullivan 4.00 10.00
ARC Ryan Callahan 8.00 20.00
ARH Riley Holzapfel 4.00 10.00
ARL Roberto Luongo 15.00 40.00
ARO Ryan O'Reilly 8.00 20.00
ARP Rich Peverley 5.00 12.00
ARS Rob Schremp 4.00 10.00
ARW Ryan White 4.00 10.00
ASD Steve Downie 4.00 10.00
ASG Sam Gagner 6.00 15.00
ASJ Scott Jackson 3.00 8.00
ASM Shawn Matthias 3.00 8.00
ASM Shawn Matthias 3.00 8.00
ASMA Steve Mason 10.00 25.00
ASMU Scott Munroe 3.00 8.00
ASS Steven Stamkos 20.00 50.00
ATC Trevor Cann 4.00 10.00
ATH Thomas Hickey 6.00 15.00
ATJB T.J. Brennan 4.00 10.00
ATJK T.J. Kemp 3.00 8.00
ATK Tomas Knotek 3.00 8.00
ATM Thomas McCollum 5.00 12.00
ATP Teddy Purcell 5.00 12.00
ATR Tuukka Rask 12.00 30.00
ATS Tobias Stephan 4.00 10.00
ATSE Tyson Sexsmith 4.00 10.00
AVL Vincent Lecavalier 4.00 10.00
AYS Yann Sauve 5.00 12.00
AZB Zach Boychuk 5.00 12.00
AZB Zach Bogosian 15.00 40.00
AZT Zack Torquato 3.00 8.00

2007-08 ITG Heroes and Prospects Calder Cup Champions

COMPLETE SET (9) 5.00 12.00
STATED ODDS 1:12
CC01 Corey Locke .60 1.50
CC02 Kyle Chipchura 1.00 2.50
CC03 Dan Jancevski .60 1.50
CC04 Matt D'Agostini .60 1.50
CC05 Maxime Lapierre .60 1.50
CC06 Mikhail Grabovski 1.00 2.50
CC07 Ajay Baines .60 1.50
CC08 Andre Benoit 1.00 2.50
CC09 Carey Price 6.00 15.00

2007-08 ITG Heroes and Prospects Canada and Russia Challenge

STATED PRINT RUN 50 SETS
CR01 Logan Couture 6.00 15.00
CR02 John Tavares 25.00 60.00
CR03 Drew Doughty 12.00 30.00
CR04 Sam Gagner 8.00 20.00
CR05 Bryan Little 5.00 12.00
CR06 Steve Mason 12.00 30.00
CR07 Chris Stewart 5.00 12.00
CR08 Francois Bouchard 4.00 10.00
CR09 Jean-Philippe Levasseur 4.00 10.00
CR10 Angelo Esposito 8.00 20.00
CR11 Claude Giroux 20.00 50.00
CR12 Yann Sauve 6.00 15.00
CR13 Brad Marchand 15.00 40.00
CR14 Karl Alzner 4.00 10.00
CR15 Keaton Ellerby 5.00 12.00
CR16 Colton Gillies 6.00 15.00
CR17 Zach Hamill 5.00 12.00
CR18 Carey Price 40.00 100.00
CR19 Kris Russell 5.00 12.00
CR20 Brandon Sutter 6.00 15.00

2007-08 ITG Heroes and Prospects Double Memorabilia

STATED PRINT RUN 20 SER.#'d SETS
DM01 P.Kane/S.Gagner 20.00 50.00
DM02 B.Sutter/B.Sutter 15.00 30.00
DM03 J.Tavares/S.Stamkos 25.00 60.00
DM04 A.Esposito/C.Giroux 15.00 40.00
DM05 B.Ryan/B.Pouliot 20.00 40.00
DM06 J.Pogge/C.Price 20.00 50.00

2007-08 ITG Heroes and Prospects Gloves Are Off

STATED PRINT RUN 70 SERIAL #'d SETS
GO01 Patrick Kane 20.00 50.00
GO02 Angelo Esposito 12.00 30.00
GO03 Keaton Ellerby 8.00 20.00
GO04 Drew Doughty 20.00 50.00
GO05 Luc Bourdon 10.00 25.00
GO06 Marc Staal 10.00 25.00
GO07 Karl Alzner 6.00 15.00
GO08 Jordan Staal 10.00 25.00
GO09 James Sheppard 6.00 15.00
GO10 Sam Gagner 12.00 30.00
GO11 Bryan Little 8.00 20.00
GO12 Peter Mueller 8.00 20.00
GO13 Devin Setoguchi 10.00 25.00
GO14 Zach Hamill 8.00 20.00
GO15 Benoit Pouliot 6.00 15.00
GO16 Steve Downie 8.00 20.00

2007-08 ITG Heroes and Prospects Heroes Memorabilia

STATED PRINT RUN 30 SETS
HM01 Chris Pronger 6.00 15.00
HM02 Vincent Lecavalier 6.00 15.00
HM03 Roberto Luongo 10.00 25.00
HM04 Dominik Hasek 10.00 25.00
HM05 Joe Thornton 10.00 25.00
HM06 Dany Heatley 8.00 20.00
HM07 Joe Sakic 12.00 30.00
HM08 Mike Modano 12.00 30.00
HM09 Ilya Kovalchuk 8.00 20.00
HM10 Dave Keon 8.00 20.00
HM11 Peter Forsberg 10.00 25.00
HM12 Mats Sundin 8.00 20.00

2007-08 ITG Heroes and Prospects Jerseys

STATED PRINT RUN 130 SER.#'d SETS
*EMBLEMS/30: .8X TO 2X JERSEY/130
GUJ01 Alexei Cherepanov 6.00 15.00
GUJ02 Tuukka Rask 8.00 20.00
GUJ03 Jack Skille 4.00 10.00
GUJ04 John Tavares 15.00 40.00
GUJ05 Karl Alzner 3.00 8.00
GUJ06 Brandon Sutter 5.00 12.00
GUJ07 Angelo Esposito 6.00 15.00
GUJ08 Zach Hamill 4.00 10.00
GUJ09 Marc Staal 5.00 12.00
GUJ10 Sam Gagner 6.00 15.00
GUJ11 Leland Irving 5.00 12.00
GUJ12 Steve Downie 4.00 10.00
GUJ13 Peter Mueller 4.00 10.00

GUJ14 Thomas McCollum 5.00 12.00
GUJ15 Luc Bourdon 5.00 12.00
GUJ16 Cal Clutterbuck 5.00 12.00
GUJ17 Keaton Ellerby 4.00 10.00
GUJ18 Patrick Kane 20.00 50.00
GUJ19 Bryan Cameron 3.00 8.00
GUJ20 Claude Giroux 10.00 25.00
GUJ21 Drew Doughty 10.00 25.00
GUJ22 Michael Del Zotto 5.00 12.00
GUJ23 Trevor Cann 4.00 10.00
GUJ24 Michael Frolik 4.00 10.00
GUJ25 Trevor Lewis 5.00 12.00
GUJ26 James Sheppard 3.00 8.00
GUJ27 Steven Stamkos 10.00 25.00
GUJ28 Alexander Radulov 5.00 12.00
GUJ29 Marc-Antoine Pouliot 3.00 8.00
GUJ30 Ryan Callahan 6.00 15.00
GUJ31 Cody Bass 4.00 10.00
GUJ32 Benoit Pouliot 3.00 8.00
GUJ33 Rob Schremp 4.00 10.00
GUJ34 Marek Schwarz 5.00 12.00
GUJ35 Andrew Ebbett 3.00 8.00
GUJ36 Justin Pogge 5.00 12.00
GUJ37 Drew Stafford 4.00 10.00
GUJ38 Carey Price 12.00 30.00
GUJ39 Jiri Tlusty 5.00 12.00
GUJ40 Jeff Glass 4.00 10.00
GUJ41 Adam Dennis 4.00 10.00
GUJ42 Tobias Stephan 4.00 10.00
GUJ43 Josh Hennessy 3.00 8.00
GUJ44 Nigel Dawes 3.00 8.00
GUJ45 Loui Eriksson 5.00 12.00
GUJ46 Martin Houle 3.00 8.00
GUJ47 Jon Filewich 3.00 8.00
GUJ48 Jimmy Howard 8.00 20.00
GUJ49 Keith Aucoin 3.00 8.00
GUJ50 Bryan Little 4.00 10.00
GUJ51 Kevin Klein 3.00 8.00
GUJ52 Tyler Weiman 4.00 10.00
GUJ53 Stefan Legein 3.00 8.00
GUJ54 Michael Grabner 4.00 10.00
GUJ55 Thomas Hickey 6.00 15.00
GUJ56 David LeNeveu 4.00 10.00
GUJ57 Keith Yandle 5.00 12.00
GUJ58 Mikhail Grabovski 5.00 12.00
GUJ59 David Krejci 10.00 25.00
GUJ60 Jonathan Bernier 8.00 20.00
GUJ61 Kyle Okposo 8.00 20.00
GUJ62 Alex Pietrangelo 10.00 25.00
GUJ63 Luke Schenn 8.00 20.00
GUJ64 Jonas Hiller 8.00 20.00
GUJ65 Steve Mason 12.00 30.00
GUJ66 Devin Setoguchi 6.00 15.00
GUJ67 Brett MacLean 4.00 10.00
GUJ68 Zach Bogosian 10.00 25.00
GUJ69 Cody Hodgson 15.00 40.00

2007-08 ITG Heroes and Prospects John Tavares Firsts

COMPLETE SET (9) 25.00 60.00
COMMON CARD 4.00 10.00
STATED ODDS 1:14
JT01 John Tavares First Overall 4.00 10.00
JT02 John Tavares First Game 4.00 10.00
JT03 John Tavares First Goal 4.00 10.00
JT04 John Tavares First Multi-Point Game 4.00 10.00
JT05 John Tavares First Assist 4.00 10.00
JT06 John Tavares First Hat Trick 4.00 10.00
JT07 John Tavares First ADT Canada Russia Challenge 4.00 10.00
JT08 John Tavares First OHL All-Star Classic 4.00 10.00
JT09 John Tavares First Playoff Game 4.00 10.00

2007-08 ITG Heroes and Prospects Memorial Cup Champions

COMPLETE SET (9) 8.00 20.00
STATED ODDS 1:14 ARENA PACKS
MC01 Spencer Machacek 1.50 4.00
MC02 Kenndal McArdle 1.50 4.00
MC03 Michal Repik 3.00 8.00
MC04 Milan Lucic 8.00 20.00
MC05 Brendan Mikkelson 1.50 4.00
MC06 Cody Franson 3.00 8.00
MC07 Jonathon Blum 2.50 6.00
MC08 A.J. Thelen 2.00 5.00
MC09 Tyson Sexsmith 2.00 5.00

2007-08 ITG Heroes and Prospects My Country My Team

STATED PRINT RUN 50 SETS
MCT01 John Tavares 15.00 40.00
MCT02 Marc Staal 6.00 15.00
MCT03 Ty Wishart 4.00 10.00
MCT04 Ryan O'Marra 4.00 10.00
MCT05 Angelo Esposito 8.00 20.00
MCT06 Bryan Little 5.00 12.00
MCT07 Leland Irving
MCT08 Carey Price 40.00 100.00
MCT09 Joe Sakic 10.00 25.00
MCT10 Martin Brodeur 12.00 30.00

2007-08 ITG Heroes and Prospects Net Prospects

STATED PRINT RUN 90 SETS
NP01 Carey Price 40.00 100.00
NP02 Adam Dennis 5.00 12.00
NP03 Justin Pogge 6.00 15.00
NP04 Tobias Stephan 5.00 12.00
NP05 Jeremy Smith 6.00 15.00
NP06 Thomas McCollum 6.00 15.00
NP07 Steve Mason 12.00 30.00
NP08 Trevor Cann 5.00 12.00
NP09 Tyson Sexsmith 5.00 12.00
NP10 Jonathan Bernier 10.00 25.00
NP11 Leland Irving 6.00 15.00
NP12 Tuukka Rask 15.00 40.00
NP13 Jonas Hiller
NP14 Chet Pickard 6.00 15.00

2007-08 ITG Heroes and Prospects Numbers

STATED PRINT RUN 20 SETS
GUN01 Alexei Cherepanov 20.00 50.00
GUN02 Tuukka Rask 40.00 100.00
GUN03 Jack Skille 12.00 30.00
GUN04 John Tavares 50.00 120.00
GUN05 Karl Alzner 10.00 25.00
GUN06 Brandon Sutter 15.00 40.00
GUN07 Angelo Esposito 20.00 50.00
GUN08 Zach Hamill 12.00 30.00
GUN09 Marc Staal 15.00 40.00
GUN10 Sam Gagner 20.00 50.00
GUN11 Leland Irving 15.00 40.00
GUN12 Steve Downie 12.00 30.00
GUN13 Peter Mueller 12.00 30.00
GUN14 Thomas McCollum 12.00 30.00
GUN15 Luc Bourdon 15.00 40.00
GUN16 Cal Clutterbuck 15.00 40.00
GUN17 Keaton Ellerby 12.00 30.00
GUN18 Patrick Kane 60.00 150.00
GUN19 Bryan Cameron 10.00 25.00
GUN20 Claude Giroux 40.00 100.00
GUN21 Drew Doughty 15.00 40.00
GUN22 Michael Del Zotto 15.00 40.00
GUN23 Trevor Cann 12.00 30.00
GUN24 Michael Frolik 12.00 30.00
GUN25 Trevor Lewis 15.00 40.00
GUN26 James Sheppard 10.00 25.00
GUN27 Steven Stamkos 50.00 125.00
GUN28 Alexander Radulov 15.00 40.00
GUN29 Marc-Antoine Pouliot 10.00 25.00
GUN30 Ryan Callahan 15.00 40.00
GUN31 Cody Bass 12.00 30.00
GUN32 Benoit Pouliot 10.00 25.00
GUN33 Rob Schremp 12.00 30.00
GUN34 Marek Schwarz 15.00 40.00
GUN35 Andrew Ebbett 10.00 25.00
GUN36 Justin Pogge 15.00 40.00
GUN37 Drew Stafford 12.00 30.00
GUN38 Carey Price 100.00 250.00
GUN39 Jiri Tlusty 15.00 40.00
GUN40 Jeff Glass 12.00 30.00
GUN41 Adam Dennis 12.00 30.00
GUN42 Tobias Stephan 12.00 30.00
GUN43 Josh Hennessy 10.00 25.00
GUN44 Nigel Dawes 10.00 25.00
GUN45 Loui Eriksson 15.00 40.00
GUN46 Martin Houle 10.00 25.00
GUN47 Jon Filewich 10.00 25.00
GUN48 Jimmy Howard 25.00 60.00
GUN49 Keith Aucoin 10.00 25.00
GUN50 Bryan Little 12.00 30.00
GUN51 Kevin Klein 10.00 25.00
GUN52 Tyler Weiman 12.00 30.00
GUN53 Stefan Legein 10.00 25.00
GUN54 Michael Grabner 12.00 30.00
GUN55 Thomas Hickey 20.00 50.00
GUN56 David LeNeveu 12.00 30.00
GUN57 Keith Yandle 15.00 40.00
GUN58 Mikhail Grabovski 15.00 40.00
GUN59 David Krejci 30.00 80.00
GUN60 Jonathan Bernier 15.00 40.00
GUN61 Kyle Okposo
GUN62 Alex Pietrangelo 15.00 40.00
GUN63 Luke Schenn
GUN64 Jonas Hiller 20.00 50.00
GUN65 Steve Mason
GUN66 Devin Setoguchi 15.00 40.00
GUN67 Brett MacLean 10.00 25.00
GUN68 Zach Bogosian 25.00 60.00
GUN69 Cody Hodgson

2007-08 ITG Heroes and Prospects Triple Memorabilia

STATED PRINT RUN 20 SERIAL #'d SETS
TM01 Montoya/Pogge/Price 30.00 80.00
TM02 Alzner/Sutter/Gillies 15.00 30.00
TM03 Tavar/Dougty/Stamk 50.00 80.00
TM04 Vorack/Espo/Shep 25.00 50.00
TM05 Staffd/O'Sulli/Radulv 25.00 50.00
TM06 Staal/Staal/Staal 30.00 60.00

2008-09 ITG Heroes and Prospects

This set was released on December 17, 2008. The base set consists of 100 cards.
COMPLETE SET (100) 15.00 40.00
COMP.UPD.SET (50) 12.00 30.00
1 Mats Sundin .25 .60
2 Peter Forsberg .30 .75
3 Pavel Datsyuk .30 .75
4 Ryan Getzlaf .40 1.00
5 Alexander Ovechkin 1.00 2.50
6 Teemu Selanne .50 1.25
7 Chris Osgood .25 .60
8 Fabian Brunnstrom .20 .50
9 Ville Leino .30 .75
10 Victor Hedman .50 1.25
11 Alex Goligoski .30 .75
12 Alexander Nikulin .15 .40
13 Benoit Pouliot .15 .40
14 Blake Comeau .15 .40
15 Brendan Mikkelson .15 .40
16 Brian Boyle .20 .50
17 Brian Lee .20 .50
18 Bryan Little .20 .50
19 Chris Collins .15 .40
20 Chris Stewart .25 .60
21 Cody Franson .20 .50
22 Darren Helm .25 .60
23 Derick Brassard .20 .50
24 Devin Setoguchi .20 .50
25 Jack Skille .20 .50
26 Max Pacioretty 1.00 2.50
27 Jiri Tlusty .20 .50
28 Julian Talbot .15 .40
29 Kyle Greentree .25 .60
30 Kyle Okposo .25 .60
31 Marc-Andre Gragnani .20 .50
32 Michael Grabner .25 .60
33 Mike Santorelli .20 .50
34 Nick Foligno .25 .60
35 Rob Schremp .20 .50
36 Ryan Parent .15 .40
37 Sergei Kostitsyn .15 .40
38 Justin Pogge .25 .60
39 Teddy Purcell .30 .75
40 Vladimir Mihalik .15 .40
41 Alex Pietrangelo .30 .75
42 Brett MacLean .15 .40
43 Cody Hodgson .60 1.50
44 Drew Doughty .60 1.50
45 Greg Nemisz .15 .40
46 Jamie Arniel .20 .50
47 Jared Staal .40 1.00
48 John Tavares .75 2.00
49 Joshua Bailey .30 .75
50 Justin Azevedo .15 .40
51 Matt Duchene .50 1.25
52 John McFarland .15 .40
53 Michael Del Zotto .20 .50
54 Mikkel Boedker .30 .75
55 P.K. Subban .50 1.25
56 John Carlson .15 .40
57 Ryan O'Reilly .30 .75
58 Taylor Hall 1.25 3.00
59 Steven Stamkos 1.50 4.00
60 Tyler Cuma .15 .40
61 Zach Bogosian .25 .60
62 Brandon Sutter .25 .60
63 Brayden Schenn .50 1.25
64 Colton Gillies .20 .50
65 Drayson Bowman .30 .75
66 Geordie Wudrick .15 .40
67 Jared Cowen .25 .60
68 Jonathon Blum .25 .60
69 Jordan Eberle .40 1.00
70 Jyri Niemi .15 .40
71 Karl Alzner .15 .40
72 Keaton Ellerby .20 .50
73 Kyle Beach .25 .60
74 Luke Schenn .30 .75
75 Landon Ferraro .15 .40
76 Mitch Wahl .15 .40
77 Nick Ross .15 .40
78 Oscar Moller .20 .50
79 T.J. Galiardi .20 .50
80 Thomas Hickey .30 .75
81 Tyler Ennis .30 .75
82 Zach Hamill .15 .40
83 Zach Boychuk .25 .60
84 Angelo Esposito .40 1.00
85 Claude Giroux .50 1.25
86 Danick Paquette .15 .40
87 Francois Bouchard .15 .40
88 Philippe Cornet .15 .40
89 Jakub Voracek .50 1.25
90 Joel Champagne .15 .40
91 Kelsey Tessier .15 .40
92 Keven Veilleux .15 .40
93 Logan MacMillan .15 .40
94 Marco Scandella .15 .40
95 Mathieu Perreault .30 .75
96 Mikhail Stefanovich .15 .40
97 Nicolas Deschamps .25 .60
98 Patrice Cormier .20 .50
99 Stefan Chaput .15 .40
100 Yann Sauve .25 .60
101 Nikita Filatov .25 .60
102 Chris Minard .25 .60
103 Justin Abdelkader .40 1.00
104 Oskar Osala .25 .60
105 David Desharnais .50 1.25
106 Mattias Karlsson .15 .40
107 Brad Marchand .60 1.50
108 Bob Sanguinetti .20 .50
109 Chad Kolarik .15 .40
110 Simeon Varlamov .50 1.25
111 Luca Caputi .25 .60
112 Michal Repik .25 .60
113 Mark Dekanich .15 .40
114 Zack Smith .20 .50
115 Jeff Frazee .20 .50
116 Tim Kennedy .25 .60
117 Patrick Maroon .25 .60
118 Ben Maxwell .25 .60
119 Viatcheslav Voynov .25 .60
120 Nathan Gerbe .25 .60
121 Simon Despres .25 .60
122 Andrej Nestrasil .25 .60
123 Charles-Olivier Roussel .25 .60
124 Christopher DiDomenico .25 .60
125 David Gilbert .15 .40
126 Dmitry Kulikov .25 .60
127 Jordan Caron .25 .60
128 Olivier Roy .25 .60
129 Keith Aulie .15 .40
130 Colten Teubert .25 .60
131 Carter Ashton .25 .60
132 Brett Sonne .15 .40
133 Tyler Myers .25 .60
134 Scott Glennie .25 .60
135 Levko Koper .25 .60
136 Cody Eakin .25 .60
137 Jamie Benn .50 1.25
138 Stefan Elliott .25 .60
139 Jimmy Bubnick .15 .40
140 Evander Kane .40 1.00
141 Peter Holland .20 .50
142 Evgeny Grachev .25 .60
143 Edward Pasquale .25 .60
144 Stefan Della Rovere .25 .60
145 Nazem Kadri .50 1.25
146 Zack Kassian .25 .60
147 Calvin de Haan .20 .50
148 Michael Latta .25 .60
149 Ryan Ellis .25 .60
150 John Tavares .75 2.00

2008-09 ITG Heroes and Prospects ADT Canada/Russia Challenge Emblems

STATED PRINT RUN 19 SERIAL #'d SETS

2008-09 ITG Heroes and Prospects ADT Canada/Russia Challenge Jerseys

STATED PRINT RUN 29 SERIAL #'d SETS
CRJ01 John Tavares 15.00 40.00
CRJ02 Alex Pietrangelo 6.00 15.00
CRJ03 Karl Alzner
CRJ04 Steven Stamkos
CRJ05 Luke Schenn 6.00 15.00
CRJ06 Shawn Matthias
CRJ07 Steve Mason 8.00 20.00
CRJ08 Brett MacLean
CRJ09 Thomas Hickey 6.00 15.00
CRJ10 Michael Del Zotto

2008-09 ITG Heroes and Prospects ADT Canada/Russia Challenge Numbers

STATED PRINT RUN 19 SERIAL #'d SETS

2008-09 ITG Heroes and Prospects Autographs

AAE Angelo Esposito 10.00 25.00
AAN Alexander Nikulin 4.00 10.00
AANE Andrej Nestrasil 6.00 15.00
AAO Alexander Ovechkin SP 40.00 80.00
AAP Alex Pietrangelo 8.00 20.00
ABB Brian Boyle 5.00 12.00
ABLE Brian Lee 5.00 12.00
ABLI Bryan Little 5.00 12.00
ABMA Brett MacLean 4.00 10.00
ABMAR Brad Marchand 15.00 40.00
ABMAR2 Brad Marchand 15.00 40.00
ABMAX Ben Maxwell 6.00 15.00
ABMI Brendan Mikkelson 4.00 10.00
ABP Benoit Pouliot 4.00 10.00
ABR Bobby Ryan 6.00 15.00
ABS Bob Sanguinetti 5.00 12.00
ABSC Brayden Schenn 12.00 30.00
ABSU Brandon Sutter 6.00 15.00
ACA Carter Ashton 6.00 15.00
ACD Chris Doyle 5.00 12.00
ACDH Calvin de Haan 5.00 12.00
ACE Cody Eakin 6.00 15.00
ACF Cody Franson 5.00 12.00
ACG Claude Giroux 20.00 50.00
ACH Cody Hodgson 12.00 30.00
ACO Chris Osgood SP 12.00 30.00
ACR Charles-Olivier Roussel 6.00 15.00
ACS Chris Stewart 6.00 15.00
ADB Derick Brassard 5.00 12.00
ADD Drew Doughty 10.00 25.00
ADG David Gilbert 4.00 10.00
ADH Darren Helm 6.00 15.00
ADK Dmitry Kulikov 6.00 15.00
ADS Devin Setoguchi 5.00 12.00
AEK Evander Kane 10.00 25.00
AEP Edward Pasquale 6.00 15.00
AFB Fabian Brunnstrom SP 5.00 12.00
AGB Gilbert Brule 4.00 10.00
AGW Geordie Wudrick 4.00 10.00
AIV Ivan Vishnevskiy 4.00 10.00
AJAR Jamie Arniel 5.00 12.00
AJAZ Justin Azevedo 4.00 10.00
AJBA Joshua Bailey 8.00 20.00
AJBL Jonathon Blum 6.00 15.00
AJBU Jimmy Bubnick 4.00 10.00
AJCA Jordan Caron 6.00 15.00
AJCH Joel Champagne 4.00 10.00
AJCO Jared Cowen 6.00 15.00
AJE Jordan Eberle 20.00 50.00
AJM Jonathan Matsumoto 4.00 10.00
AJN James Neal 8.00 20.00
AJN Jyri Niemi 4.00 10.00
AJSA Jerome Samson 4.00 10.00
AJST Jared Staal 10.00 25.00
AJT Jiri Tlusty 5.00 12.00
AJTAV John Tavares 30.00 60.00
AJTAV2 John Tavares 30.00 60.00
AJTAV3 John Tavares 25.00 60.00
AJV Jakub Voracek 8.00 20.00
AKA Karl Alzner 4.00 10.00
AKE Keaton Ellerby 5.00 12.00
AKL Kristopher Letang 6.00 15.00
AKO Kyle Okposo 6.00 15.00
AKT Kelsey Tessier 4.00 10.00
AKV Keven Veilleux 4.00 10.00
ALC Logan Couture 12.00 30.00
ALC Luca Caputi 6.00 15.00
ALC2 Luca Caputi 6.00 15.00
ALK Levko Koper 6.00 15.00
ALM Logan MacMillan 4.00 10.00
AMAG Marc-Andre Gragnani 5.00 12.00
AMB Mikkel Boedker 8.00 20.00
AMD Matt Duchene 12.00 30.00
AMDZ Michael Del Zotto 5.00 12.00
AMFA Mitch Fadden 4.00 10.00
AMFR Michael Frolik 6.00 15.00
AMG Michael Grabner 6.00 15.00
AML Matt Lashoff 4.00 10.00
AMLA Michael Latta 6.00 15.00
AMO Oscar Moller 5.00 12.00
AMR Michal Repik 6.00 15.00
AMSA Mark Santorelli 4.00 10.00
AMSU Mats Sundin SP 20.00 50.00
AMW Mitch Wahl 4.00 10.00
AND Nicolas Deschamps 6.00 15.00
ANK Nazem Kadri 15.00 30.00
ANR Nick Ross 4.00 10.00
AOO Oskar Osala
AOR Olivier Roy 6.00 15.00
APD Pavel Datsyuk SP 15.00 40.00
APF Peter Forsberg SP 25.00 60.00
APH Peter Holland 5.00 12.00
APKS P.K. Subban 12.00 30.00
ARE Ryan Ellis 6.00 15.00
ARG Ryan Getzlaf SP 15.00 40.00
ARP Ryan Parent 4.00 10.00
ARS Rob Schremp 5.00 12.00
ASD Simon Despres 6.00 15.00
ASE Stefan Elliott 6.00 15.00
ASG Scott Glennie 6.00 15.00
ASMA Spencer Machacek 4.00 10.00
ASMAT Shawn Matthias 6.00 15.00
ASST Steven Stamkos 25.00 60.00
ASV Simeon Varlamov 12.00 30.00
ATE Tyler Ennis 8.00 20.00
ATH Taylor Hall 40.00 80.00
ATH Thomas Hickey 8.00 20.00
ATP Teddy Purcell 8.00 20.00
ATS Teemu Selanne SP 25.00 50.00
ATW Ty Wishart 5.00 12.00
AVH Victor Hedman 30.00 80.00
AVL Ville Leino 8.00 20.00
AYS Yann Sauve 6.00 15.00
AZBOG Zach Bogosian 6.00 15.00
AZBOY Zack Boychuk 6.00 15.00
AZH Zach Hamill 4.00 10.00
AZK Zack Kassian 15.00 30.00

2008-09 ITG Heroes and Prospects Autographs Team Canada

4 P.K. Subban 15.00 30.00
9 Cody Hodgson 20.00 40.00

2008-09 ITG Heroes and Prospects Calder Cup Winners

COMPLETE SET (13) 20.00 50.00
1 Jason Krog 5.00 12.00
2 Darren Haydar 2.50 6.00
3 Joel Kwiatkowski 2.50 6.00
4 Brian Fahey 2.50 6.00
5 Steve Martins 2.50 6.00
6 Brett Sterling 3.00 8.00
7 Jesse Shultz 2.50 6.00
8 Joe Motzko 2.50 6.00
9 Nathan Oystrick 4.00 10.00
10 Jordan LaVallee 4.00 10.00
11 Boris Valabik 4.00 10.00
12 Bryan Little 3.00 8.00
13 Ondrej Pavelec 5.00 12.00

2008-09 ITG Heroes and Prospects Draft Picks

COMPLETE SET (20) 15.00 40.00
DP1 Steven Stamkos 6.00 15.00
DP2 Drew Doughty 2.50 6.00
DP3 Zach Bogosian 1.00 2.50
DP4 Alex Pietrangelo 1.25 3.00
DP5 Luke Schenn 1.25 3.00
DP6 Mikkel Boedker 1.25 3.00
DP7 Joshua Bailey 1.25 3.00
DP8 Cody Hodgson 2.50 6.00
DP9 Kyle Beach 1.00 2.50
DP10 Tyler Myers 1.00 2.50
DP11 Zach Boychuk 1.00 2.50
DP12 Chet Pickard 1.00 2.50
DP13 Michael Del Zotto .75 2.00
DP14 Jordan Eberle 1.50 4.00
DP15 Tyler Ennis 1.25 3.00
DP16 Thomas McCollum 1.00 2.50
DP17 Philip McRae .75 2.00
DP18 Nicolas Deschamps 1.00 2.50
DP19 Mitch Wahl .60 1.50
DP20 Jared Staal 1.50 4.00

2008-09 ITG Heroes and Prospects Gloves Are Off Memorabilia Autographs

STATED PRINT RUN 19 SERIAL #'d SETS

2008-09 ITG Heroes and Prospects Hero and Prospect Memorabilia

STATED PRINT RUN 50 SERIAL #'d SETS
HP01 P.Roy/C.Price 60.00 120.00
HP02 A.Ovechkin/S.Kostitsyn 15.00 40.00
HP03 M.Brodeur/J.Bernier 15.00 40.00
HP04 J.Jagr/J.Tlusty 12.00 30.00
HP05 M.Lemieux/M.Gragnani 50.00 100.00
HP06 C.Neely/J.Tavares 20.00 50.00
HP07 V.Lecavalier/S.Stamkos 20.00 50.00
HP08 M.Gaborik/J.Voracek 25.00 60.00
HP09 B.Clarke/S.Downie 12.00 30.00
HP10 J.Sakic/K.Alzner 20.00 50.00

2008-09 ITG Heroes and Prospects Heroes Memorabilia

STATED PRINT RUN 60 SERIAL #'d SETS
HM01 Mats Sundin 8.00 20.00
HM02 Peter Forsberg 10.00 25.00
HM03 Pavel Datsyuk 10.00 25.00
HM04 Ryan Getzlaf 12.00 30.00
HM05 Alexander Ovechkin 30.00 80.00
HM06 Teemu Selanne 15.00 40.00
HM07 Chris Osgood 8.00 20.00

2008-09 ITG Heroes and Prospects Jerseys

STATED PRINT RUN 100 SERIAL #'d SETS
GUJ01 Bryan Little 4.00 10.00
GUJ02 Blake Comeau 3.00 8.00
GUJ03 Benoit Pouliot 3.00 8.00
GUJ04 Matt Duchene 10.00 25.00
GUJ05 Chris Collins 3.00 8.00
GUJ06 Chris Stewart 5.00 12.00
GUJ07 Nick Foligno 5.00 12.00
GUJ08 Brian Lee 4.00 10.00
GUJ09 Stephen Dixon 4.00 10.00
GUJ10 Cody Hodgson 12.00 30.00
GUJ11 Joshua Bailey 6.00 15.00
GUJ12 Michael Del Zotto 4.00 10.00
GUJ13 Steven Stamkos 15.00 40.00
GUJ14 Brandon Sutter 5.00 12.00
GUJ15 Colton Gillies 4.00 10.00
GUJ16 Keaton Ellerby 4.00 10.00
GUJ17 Karl Alzner 3.00 8.00
GUJ18 Jakub Voracek 8.00 20.00
GUJ19 Logan MacMillan 3.00 8.00
GUJ20 Carey Price 20.00 50.00
GUJ21 P.K. Subban 10.00 25.00
GUJ22 Patrick Maroon 5.00 12.00
GUJ23 Keven Veilleux 3.00 8.00
GUJ24 Mark Katic 3.00 8.00
GUJ25 Kyle DeCoste 4.00 10.00
GUJ26 John Tavares 15.00 40.00
GUJ27 Mikhail Grabovski 8.00 20.00
GUJ28 Marc Staal 5.00 12.00
GUJ29 Marc-Andre Gragnani 4.00 10.00
GUJ30 Bobby Hughes 3.00 8.00
GUJ31 Alexander Nikulin 3.00 8.00
GUJ32 Brendan Mikkelson 3.00 8.00
GUJ33 Cody Franson 4.00 10.00
GUJ34 Devin Setoguchi 4.00 10.00
GUJ35 Gilbert Brule 3.00 8.00
GUJ36 James Neal 10.00 25.00
GUJ37 Jerome Samson 3.00 8.00
GUJ38 Jiri Tlusty 4.00 10.00
GUJ39 Julian Talbot 3.00 8.00
GUJ40 Kristopher Letang 5.00 12.00
GUJ41 Kyle Greentree 5.00 12.00
GUJ42 Matt Lashoff 3.00 8.00
GUJ43 Mike Santorelli 4.00 10.00
GUJ44 Sergei Kostitsyn 3.00 8.00
GUJ45 Vladimir Mihalik 3.00 8.00

2008-09 ITG Heroes and Prospects Jerseys Autographs

ANNOUNCED PRINT RUN 19
JAAN Alexander Nikulin 6.00 15.00
JABB Brian Boyle 8.00 20.00
JABC Blake Comeau 6.00 15.00
JABL Brian Lee 8.00 20.00
JABS Brandon Sutter
JACC Chris Collins 6.00 15.00
JACF Cody Franson 8.00 20.00
JACS Chris Stewart 10.00 25.00
JADD Drew Doughty 25.00 60.00
JADP Dustin Penner 8.00 20.00
JADS Devin Setoguchi 8.00 20.00
JAGB Gilbert Brule 6.00 15.00
JAJH Jonas Hiller 8.00 20.00
JAJN James Neal 20.00 50.00
JAJP Justin Pogge 10.00 25.00
JAJS Jack Skille 8.00 20.00
JAJSA Jerome Samson 6.00 15.00
JAJT John Tavares 40.00 80.00
JAJTL Jiri Tlusty 8.00 20.00
JAJV Jakub Voracek 20.00 50.00
JAKA Karl Alzner 6.00 15.00
JAKE Keaton Ellerby 8.00 20.00
JAKL Kristopher Letang 30.00 60.00
JAKO Kyle Okposo 10.00 25.00
JALM Logan MacMillan 6.00 15.00
JAMD Michael Del Zotto 8.00 20.00
JAMG Marc-Andre Gragnani 8.00 20.00
JAML Matt Lashoff 6.00 15.00
JAMS Marc Staal 10.00 25.00
JANF Nick Foligno
JAPO Patrick O'Sullivan
JAPS P.K. Subban 25.00 50.00
JASG Sam Gagner 8.00 20.00
JASK Sergei Kostitsyn 6.00 15.00
JASS Steven Stamkos 60.00 120.00

2008-09 ITG Heroes and Prospects Memorial Cup Winners

COMPLETE SET (12) 15.00 40.00
1 Mitch Wahl 2.50 6.00
2 Chris Bruton 2.50 6.00
3 Jared Cowen 4.00 10.00
4 Levko Koper 4.00 10.00
5 Dustin Tokarski 4.00 10.00
6 Drayson Bowman 5.00 12.00
7 Justin Falk 4.00 10.00
8 Trevor Glass 2.50 6.00
9 Ondrej Roman 2.50 6.00
10 Judd Blackwater 2.50 6.00
11 Justin McCrae 2.50 6.00
12 Jared Spurgeon 3.00 8.00

2008-09 ITG Heroes and Prospects Prospect Combos Memorabilia

STATED PRINT RUN 60 SERIAL #'d SETS
PC01 K.Letang/J.Tavares 15.00 40.00
PC02 J.Neal/S.Stamkos 15.00 40.00
PC03 M.Lashoff/D.Doughty 12.00 30.00
PC04 J.Pogge/S.Mason 12.00 30.00
PC05 M.Gragnani/M.Del Zotto 10.00 25.00
PC06 G.Brule/B.Sutter 6.00 15.00
PC07 C.Franson/P.Subban 12.00 30.00
PC08 J.Tlusty/L.Schenn 10.00 25.00
PC09 S.Kostitsyn/A.Plante 6.00 15.00
PC10 A.Nikulin/M.Boedker 6.00 15.00

2008-09 ITG Heroes and Prospects Top Prospects Jerseys

TPJ01 Akim Aliu 4.00 10.00
TPJ02 Trevor Cann 5.00 12.00
TPJ03 Keaton Ellerby 5.00 12.00
TPJ04 Angelo Esposito 10.00 25.00
TPJ05 Sam Gagner 5.00 12.00
TPJ06 Zach Hamill 4.00 10.00
TPJ07 Thomas Hickey
TPJ08 Patrick Kane
TPJ09 Brandon Sutter 6.00 15.00
TPJ10 Jakub Voracek 10.00 25.00
TPJ11 Jonathon Blum 6.00 15.00
TPJ12 Alex Pietrangelo 8.00 20.00
TPJ13 Jared Staal 10.00 25.00
TPJ14 Joshua Bailey 8.00 20.00
TPJ15 Michael Del Zotto 5.00 12.00
TPJ16 Drew Doughty
TPJ17 Logan MacMillan 4.00 10.00
TPJ18 Colton Gillies 5.00 12.00
TPJ19 Zach Boychuk 6.00 15.00
TPJ20 Zach Bogosian 6.00 15.00

2009-10 ITG Heroes and Prospects

COMPLETE SET (200) 20.00 50.00
COMP.SERIES 1 (150) 15.00 40.00
COMP.UPDATE SET (52) 12.00 30.00
1 Elmer Lach .50 1.25
2 Ted Lindsay .20 .50
3 Larry Kwong .60 1.50
4 Ted Kennedy .40 1.00
5 Oliver Ekman-Larsson .30 .75
6 Jacob Josefson .20 .50
7 Dmitry Kulikov .25 .60
8 Mikkel Boedker .15 .40
9 Kevin Bieksa .20 .50
10 Jay Bouwmeester .25 .60
11 Mike Cammalleri .20 .50
12 David Backes .25 .60
13 Kyle Okposo .25 .60
14 Kristopher Letang .25 .60
15 Ryan Getzlaf .40 1.00
16 Eric Staal .30 .75
17 Jason Spezza .25 .60
18 Maxime Talbot .25 .60
19 Devin Setoguchi .20 .50
20 Jason Pominville .25 .60
21 Zach Parise .25 .60
22 Matt Stajan .20 .50
23 Shea Weber .20 .50
24 Jhonas Enroth .30 .75
25 Mattias Karlsson .15 .40
26 Yannick Weber .25 .60
27 Justin Abdelkader .20 .50
28 Ben Maxwell .20 .50
29 Shawn Matthias .25 .60
30 Bobby Sanguinetti .15 .40
31 Michal Neuvirth .40 1.00
32 Brad Marchand .60 1.50
33 Brandon Sutter .20 .50
34 Maxsim Mayorov .20 .50
35 Nathan Gerbe .20 .50
36 Karl Alzner .15 .40
37 Artem Anisimov .25 .60
38 Justin Azevedo .15 .40
39 Nathan Lawson .20 .50
40 Matt Beaudoin .15 .40
41 Jonathan Bernier .25 .60
42 Kevin Porter .15 .40
43 David Desharnais .50 1.25
44 Zack Smith .15 .40
45 Chad Kolarik .15 .40
46 Cory Schneider .30 .75
47 Byron Bitz .20 .50
48 Tim Kennedy .20 .50
49 Tuukka Rask .25 .60
50 Patrick Maroon .15 .40
51 Kyle Turris .25 .60
52 Cody Franson .25 .60
53 Luca Caputi .25 .60
54 Mikko Lehtonen .40 1.00
55 Nikita Filatov .20 .50
56 Max Pacioretty .30 .75
57 Michal Repik .20 .50
58 Spencer Machacek .25 .60
59 Angelo Esposito .20 .50
60 Andrei Loktionov .30 .75
61 Jonathon Blum .25 .60
62 Christian Hanson .25 .60
63 Viktor Stalberg .25 .60
64 P.K. Subban .75 2.00
65 Thomas Hickey .15 .40
66 Tyler Ennis .30 .75
67 Zach Boychuk .20 .50
68 Lars Eller .25 .60
69 Brayden Schenn .50 1.25
70 Scott Glennie .20 .50
71 Jared Cowen .25 .60
72 Evander Kane .50 1.25
73 Matt Duchene .50 1.25
74 Peter Holland .20 .50
75 Zack Kassian .25 .60
76 Calvin de Haan .20 .50
77 Ryan Ellis .25 .60
78 Nazem Kadri .50 1.25
79 Ryan O'Reilly .40 1.00
80 Matthew Hackett .30 .75
81 Tyler Seguin 1.00 2.50
82 Shawn Lalonde .20 .50
83 Taylor Beck .20 .50
84 Michael Latta .25 .60
85 Taylor Doherty .15 .40
86 John McFarland .25 .60
87 Ryan Spooner .25 .60
88 Tyler Toffoli .40 1.00
89 Erik Gudbranson .25 .60
90 Cody Hodgson .75 2.00
91 Jesse Blacker .20 .50
92 Ethan Werek .15 .40
93 Edward Pasquale .25 .60
94 Joey Hishon .25 .60
95 Taylor Hall .75 2.00
96 Cam Fowler .25 .60
97 Cameron Gaunce .20 .50
98 Ryan Bourque .25 .60
99 Jake Allen .40 1.00
100 Simon Despres .25 .60
101 Brandon Gormley .30 .75
102 Nicolas Deschamps .25 .60
103 Marco Scandella .15 .40
104 Benjamin Casavant .15 .40
105 Charles-Olivier Roussel .25 .60
106 Luke Adam .25 .60
107 Kirill Kabanov .30 .75
108 Peter Delmas .20 .50
109 Mathieu Brodeur .20 .50
110 Jordan Caron .25 .60
111 Dave Labrecque .15 .40
112 Olivier Roy .25 .60
113 Eric Gelinas .30 .75
114 Chris Doyle .15 .40
115 Kelsey Tessier .15 .40
116 Philippe Paradis .25 .60
117 Nicolas Deslauriers .15 .40
118 Gleason Fournier .15 .40
119 Andrej Nestrasil .20 .50
120 Louis Domingue .30 .75
121 Ryan Howse .15 .40
122 Brayden McNabb .25 .60
123 Quinton Howden .25 .60
124 Carter Ashton .25 .60
125 Jimmy Bubnick .15 .40
126 Stefan Elliott .25 .60
127 Nathan Lieuwen .30 .75
128 Tyson Barrie .25 .60
129 Landon Ferraro .20 .50
130 Jordan Eberle .40 1.00
131 Travis Hamonic .15 .40
132 Martin Jones .40 1.00
133 Calvin Pickard .40 1.00
134 Adam Morrison .20 .50
135 Brandon McMillan .15 .40
136 Brandon Kozun .25 .60
137 Brett Ponich .15 .40
138 Colby Robak .15 .40
139 Brett Connolly .25 .60
140 Cody Eakin .25 .60
141 Stanislav Galiev .30 .75
142 Daniel Catenacci .20 .50
143 Brandon Maxwell .20 .50
144 Matt Puempel .25 .60
145 Ivan Telegin .15 .40
146 Olivier Archambault .20 .50
147 Brent Andrews .15 .40
148 Alexander Burmistrov .25 .60
149 Ryan Nugent-Hopkins .75 2.00
150 Shane McColgan .25 .60
151 Logan Couture .50 1.25
152 Jamie McBain .25 .60
153 Sergei Shirokov .15 .40
154 Evgeny Dadonov .25 .60
155 John Carlson .40 1.00
156 Brad Thiessen .25 .60
157 Tyler Bozak .40 1.00
158 Anton Khudobin .25 .60
159 Mikael Backlund .25 .60
160 Chris Terry .25 .60
161 Tomas Tatar .60 1.50
162 Dustin Tokarski .25 .60
163 Ryan Stoa .20 .50
164 Nick Palmieri .25 .60
165 Travis Moran .25 .60
166 Benn Ferriero .25 .60
167 Corey Elkins .25 .60
168 Matt Taormina .25 .60
169 Philipp Grubauer .30 .75
170 Ryan Martindale .25 .60
171 Jeff Skinner .40 1.00
172 Jacob Muzzin .25 .60
173 Austin Watson .40 1.00
174 Adam Henrique .50 1.25
175 Brock Beukeboom .25 .60
176 Devante Smith-Pelly .30 .75
177 Alex Pietrangelo .20 .50
178 Boone Jenner .25 .60
179 Stephen Silas .25 .60
180 Greg Nemisz .20 .50
181 Sean Couturier .50 1.25
182 Gabriel Bourque .25 .60
183 Michael Bournival .25 .60
184 Jakub Culek .25 .60
185 Gabriel Levesque .25 .60
186 Michael Kirkpatrick .15 .40
187 Maxime Clermont .20 .50
188 Jerome Gauthier-Leduc .25 .60
189 Petr Straka .25 .60
190 Nino Niederreiter .25 .60
191 Dylan McIlrath .20 .50
192 Ryan Johansen .40 1.00
193 Alexander Petrovic .25 .60
194 Emerson Etem .25 .60
195 Troy Rutkowski .25 .60
196 Jordan Weal .25 .60
197 Luca Sbisa .25 .60
198 Mark Pysyk .20 .50
199 Vladimir Tarasenko .60 1.50
200 Jacob Markstrom .40 1.00

2009-10 ITG Heroes and Prospects AHL All Star Legends

COMPLETE SET (20) 40.00 100.00
AS01 Tuukka Rask 2.50 6.00
AS02 Bobby Ryan 2.50 6.00
AS03 Drew Stafford 2.50 6.00
AS04 Dustin Byfuglien 2.50 6.00
AS05 Jaroslav Halak 2.50 6.00
AS06 Pekka Rinne 3.00 8.00
AS07 Mike Keane 2.00 5.00
AS08 Patrick O'Sullivan 2.00 5.00
AS09 Zach Parise 2.50 6.00
AS10 Jason Spezza 2.50 6.00
AS11 Mikko Koivu 2.50 6.00
AS12 Ryan Miller 2.50 6.00
AS13 Jay Bouwmeester 2.50 6.00
AS14 Mike Cammalleri 2.00 5.00
AS15 Eric Staal 3.00 8.00
AS16 Patrice Bergeron 3.00 8.00
AS17 Brad Boyes 1.50 4.00
AS18 Miikka Kiprusoff 2.00 5.00
AS19 Kari Lehtonen 2.00 5.00
AS20 Jason LaBarbera 2.00 5.00

2009-10 ITG Heroes and Prospects AHL Grad Jerseys

SILVER ANNC'D PRINT RUN 30
AG01 Blake Comeau 4.00 10.00
AG02 Corey Perry
AG03 David Krejci
AG04 Devin Setoguchi 5.00 12.00
AG05 Jay Bouwmeester 6.00 15.00
AG06 Jeff Carter 6.00 15.00
AG07 Kari Lehtonen
AG08 Kyle Okposo 6.00 15.00
AG09 Carey Price 8.00 20.00
AG10 Marc-Andre Fleury 15.00 40.00
AG11 Mike Green
AG12 Pascal Leclaire 6.00 15.00
AG13 Ryan Callahan
AG14 Ryan Getzlaf 10.00 25.00
AG15 Ryan Miller 8.00 20.00
AG16 Tim Thomas 6.00 15.00
AG17 Jaroslav Halak 12.00 30.00
AG18 Claude Giroux 6.00 15.00
AG19 Loui Eriksson 5.00 12.00
AG20 Bobby Ryan 6.00 15.00
AG21 Tuuka Rask 12.00 30.00

2009-10 ITG Heroes and Prospects Autographs

AAB Alex Bourret 4.00 10.00
AAE Angelo Esposito 5.00 12.00
AAL Andrei Loktionov 8.00 20.00
AAN Andrej Nestrasil 5.00 12.00
ABA Brent Andrews 4.00 10.00
ABB Byron Bitz 5.00 12.00

ABC Brett Connolly 6.00 15.00
ABC2 Brett Connolly 6.00 15.00
ABG Brandon Gormley 8.00 20.00
ABG2 Brandon Gomley 8.00 20.00
ABH Bobby Hull 8.00 20.00
ABK Brandon Kozun 6.00 15.00
ABM Brad Marchand 15.00 40.00
ABMA Brandon Maxwell 5.00 12.00
ABMC Brandon McMillan 4.00 10.00
ABP Benoit Pouliot 4.00 10.00
ABR2 Bobby Ryan 6.00 15.00
ABS Bobby Sanguinetti 4.00 10.00
ABSC Brayden Schenn 12.00 30.00
ABSU Brandon Sutter 5.00 12.00
ACA Carter Ashton 6.00 15.00
ACC Cal Clutterbuck 4.00 10.00
ACDH Calvin de Haan 5.00 12.00
ACF Cody Franson 6.00 15.00
ACF2 Cam Fowler 6.00 15.00
ACFO Cam Fowler 20.00 40.00
ACG Claude Giroux 6.00 15.00
ACG2 Colton Gillies 6.00 15.00
ACGA Cameron Gaunce 5.00 12.00
ACH Christian Hanson 6.00 15.00
ACK Chuck Kobasew 4.00 10.00
ACR Charles-Olivier Roussel 6.00 15.00
ACRO Colby Robak 4.00 10.00
ACS Cory Schneider 8.00 20.00
ADB2 Derick Brassard 6.00 15.00
ADC Daniel Catenacci 5.00 12.00
ADK Dmitry Kulikov 6.00 15.00
ADP2 Dustin Penner 4.00 10.00
ADS Devin Setoguchi 5.00 12.00
ADS2 Drew Stafford 6.00 15.00
AEG Erik Gudbranson 6.00 15.00
AEG2 Erik Gudbranson 6.00 15.00
AEK Evander Kane 12.00 30.00
AEL Elmer Lach 12.00 30.00
AES Eric Staal 6.00 15.00
AEW Ethan Werek 4.00 10.00
AGB Gilbert Brule 8.00 20.00
AIL Igor Larionov 8.00 20.00
AIT Ivan Telegin 4.00 10.00
AJA Justin Azevedo 4.00 10.00
AJAL Jake Allen 10.00 25.00
AJB Jonathan Bernier 6.00 15.00
AJBE Jean Beliveau 40.00 80.00
AJBL Jonathon Blum 6.00 15.00
AJBU Jimmy Bubnick 4.00 10.00
AJC Jeff Carter 6.00 15.00
AJCA Jordan Caron 6.00 15.00
AJCO Jared Cowen 20.00 40.00
AJD2 Jacob DeSerres 12.00 30.00
AJE Jordan Eberle 30.00 60.00
AJH Joey Hishon 6.00 15.00
AJJ Jacob Josefson 5.00 12.00
AJM John McFarland 6.00 15.00
AJM2 Jacob Markstrom 8.00 20.00
AJS2 Jared Staal 6.00 15.00
AKA Karl Alzner 4.00 10.00
AKM Kenndal McArdle 5.00 12.00
AKO Kyle Okposo 6.00 15.00
AKT Kyle Turris 6.00 15.00
AKV Keven Veilleux 4.00 10.00
ALA Luke Adam 6.00 15.00
ALC Luca Caputi 6.00 15.00
ALCO Logan Couture 10.00 25.00
ALD Louis Domingue 8.00 20.00
ALE Lars Eller 6.00 15.00
ALE2 Loui Eriksson 5.00 12.00
ALF Landon Ferraro 5.00 12.00
ALK Larry Kwong 15.00 40.00
AMB Mikkel Boedker 4.00 10.00
AMBE Matt Beaudoin 4.00 10.00
AMC Mike Cammalleri 5.00 12.00
AMD Matt Duchene 12.00 30.00
AMF2 Marcus Foligno 8.00 20.00
AMH Matthew Hackett 8.00 20.00
AMH2 Matt Halischuk 5.00 12.00
AMJ Martin Jones 10.00 25.00
AML Michael Latta 6.00 15.00
AMM Maxsim Mayorov 5.00 12.00
AMN Michal Neuvirth 10.00 25.00
AMP Max Pacioretty 8.00 20.00
AMPU Matt Puempel 6.00 15.00
AMR Michal Repik 5.00 12.00
AMS Marco Scandella 4.00 10.00
AMW Mike Weber 4.00 10.00
ANB2 Nicklas Bergfors 6.00 15.00
AND Nicolas Deschamps 6.00 15.00
ANK Nazem Kadri 15.00 40.00
ANL Nathan Lawson 5.00 12.00
ANP Nick Petrecki 5.00 12.00
AOA Olivier Archambault 5.00 12.00
AOEL Oliver Ekman-Larsson 8.00 20.00
AOM2 Oscar Moller 4.00 10.00
AOR Olivier Roy 6.00 15.00
APH Peter Holland 5.00 12.00
APO2 Patrick O'Sullivan 5.00 12.00
APP Philippe Paradis 6.00 15.00
APS2 P.K. Subban 20.00 50.00
AQH Quinton Howden 6.00 15.00
AQH2 Quinton Howden 6.00 15.00
ARB Raphael Bussieres 4.00 10.00
ARG Ryan Getzlaf 10.00 25.00
ARNH Ryan Nugent-Hopkins 20.00 50.00
ARO Ryan O'Reilly 6.00 15.00
ARS Ryan Spooner 6.00 15.00
ASD Simon Despres 6.00 15.00
ASE Stefan Elliott 6.00 15.00
ASG Scott Glennie 5.00 12.00
ASGA Stanislav Galiev 8.00 20.00
ASL Shawn Lalonde 5.00 12.00
ASM Spencer Machacek 6.00 15.00
ASMA Shawn Matthias 6.00 15.00
ASMC Shane McColgan 6.00 15.00
ASV2 Simeon Varlamov 6.00 15.00
ATB Tyler Bozak 12.00 30.00
ATBA Tyson Barrie 6.00 15.00
ATBE Taylor Beck 5.00 12.00
ATD Taylor Doherty 4.00 10.00
ATE Tyler Ennis 8.00 20.00
ATH Thomas Hickey 4.00 10.00
ATH2 Taylor Hall 20.00 50.00
ATHA Taylor Hall 20.00 50.00
ATHS2 T.Hall/T.Seguin 125.00 200.00
ATK Ted Kennedy 40.00 80.00
ATL Ted Lindsay 5.00 12.00
ATP Tom Pyatt 6.00 15.00
ATS Tyler Seguin 20.00 50.00
ATS2 Tyler Seguin 25.00 60.00
ATT Tyler Toffoli 10.00 25.00
ATW Tyler Weiman 6.00 15.00
AVS Viktor Stalberg 6.00 15.00
AVT2 Vladimir Tarasenko 60.00 125.00
AYW Yannick Weber 6.00 15.00
AZK Zack Kassian 6.00 15.00
AZP Zach Parise 6.00 15.00

2009-10 ITG Heroes and Prospects Calder Cup Winners

COMPLETE SET (18) 50.00 100.00
CC01 Michal Neuvirth 5.00 12.00
CC02 Alexandre Giroux 4.00 10.00
CC03 Keith Aucoin 4.00 10.00
CC04 Chris Bourque 3.00 8.00
CC05 Graham Mink 3.00 8.00
CC06 Staffan Kronwall 2.50 6.00
CC07 Andrew Gordon 2.50 6.00
CC08 Oskar Osala 3.00 8.00
CC09 Mathieu Perreault 5.00 12.00
CC10 Karl Alzner 2.00 5.00
CC11 Francois Bouchard 3.00 8.00
CC12 John Carlson 5.00 12.00
CC13 Tyler Sloan 3.00 8.00
CC14 Kyle Wilson 2.00 5.00
CC15 Bryan Helmer 4.00 10.00
CC16 Steve Pinizzotto 2.50 6.00
CC17 Quintin Lang 2.50 6.00
CC18 Jay Beagle 4.00 10.00

2009-10 ITG Heroes and Prospects Class of 2010

COMPLETE SET (15)
C01A Taylor Hall 10.00 25.00
C01B T.Hall WINNER 1
C02 Kirill Kabanov 4.00 10.00
C03 John McFarland 3.00 8.00
C04A Cam Fowler 3.00 8.00
C04B C.Fowler WINNER 12
C05A Tyler Seguin 12.00 30.00
C05B T.Seguin WINNER 2
C06A Joey Hishon 3.00 8.00
C06B J.Hison WINNER 17
C07A Erik Gudbranson 3.00 8.00
C07B E.Gudbranson WINNER 3
C08A Brett Connolly 3.00 8.00
C08B B.Connolly WINNER 6
C09A Brandon Gormley 4.00 10.00
C09B B.Gormley WINNER 13
C10 Stanislav Galiev 5.00 12.00
C11A Quinton Howden 3.00 8.00
C11B Q.Howden WINNER 25
C12A Jeffery Skinner 5.00 12.00
C12B J.Skinner WINNER 7
C13A Mark Pysyk 2.50 6.00
C13B M.Pysyk WINNER 23
C14A Alexander Burmistrov 3.00 8.00
C14B A.Burmistrov WINNER 8
C15A Vladimir Tarasenko 12.00 30.00
C15B V.Tarasenko WINNER 16

2009-10 ITG Heroes and Prospects Enforcers

COMPLETE SET (10) 30.00 60.00
E01 Matt Clackson 4.00 10.00
E02 Jeremy Yablonski 5.00 12.00
E03 Justin Soryal 4.00 10.00
E04 Trevor Gillies 4.00 10.00
E05 Kip Brennan 4.00 10.00
E06 Wade Brookbank 3.00 8.00
E07 Tim Spencer 3.00 8.00
E08 Brodie Dupont 3.00 8.00
E09 Jesse Boulerice 5.00 12.00
E10 Brett Henley 4.00 10.00

2009-10 ITG Heroes and Prospects Game Used Jerseys

ANNCD PRINT RUN 100 SETS
M01 Leland Irving 6.00 15.00
M02 Brandon Sutter 5.00 12.00
M03 Brian Lee 6.00 15.00
M04 Cody Hodgson 20.00 50.00
M05 Matt Duchene 20.00 50.00
M06 Brayden Schenn 12.00 30.00
M07 Scott Glennie 5.00 12.00
M08 Mark Katic 4.00 10.00
M09 Michael Latta 6.00 15.00
M10 Peter Holland 5.00 12.00
M11 Sergei Kostitsyn 4.00 10.00
M12 Karl Alzner 4.00 10.00
M13 Tyler Myers 10.00 25.00
M14 Tyson Barrie 6.00 15.00
M15 Phillippe Paradis 6.00 15.00
M16 Chris Stewart 5.00 12.00
M17 Jonathan Bernier
M18 James Neal 6.00 15.00
M19 Chet Pickard 8.00 20.00
M20 Jonathon Blum 6.00 15.00
M21 Calvin de Haan 5.00 12.00
M22 Joey Hishon 6.00 15.00
M23 Ben Duffy
M24 Zack Kassian 6.00 15.00
M25 Tyler Seguin 15.00 40.00
M26 Riley Boychuk 6.00 15.00
M27 Brett Connolly 6.00 15.00
M28 Mikhail Stefanovich 4.00 10.00
M29 Alex Petrovic 4.00 10.00
M30 Landon Ferraro 5.00 12.00
M31 Jordan Weal 6.00 15.00
M32 Partrice Cormier
M33 Carter Ashton 6.00 15.00
M34 Michal Repik 5.00 12.00
M35 Andrej Nestrasil
M36 Stefan Elliott 6.00 15.00
M37 Jared Cowen 6.00 15.00
M38 Jared Staal 5.00 12.00
M39 Cody Eakin 6.00 15.00
M40 Brandon Gormley
M41 Evander Kane 12.00 30.00
M42 Keven Veilleux 4.00 10.00
M43 Ryan Ellis 6.00 15.00
M44 Taylor Hall 20.00 50.00
M45 Erik Gudbranson
M46 P.K. Subban 12.00 30.00
M47 Mikkel Boedker 8.00 20.00
M48 Jeff Skinner 10.00 25.00
M49 Cam Fowler 6.00 15.00
M50 Ryan Nugent-Hopkins 20.00 50.00
M51 Vladimir Tarasenko 12.00 30.00
M52 Jacob Markstrom 6.00 15.00
M53 Alexander Burmistrov 6.00 15.00

2009-10 ITG Heroes and Prospects Game Used Jerseys Silver

*SINGLES: .5X TO 1.2X BASIC INSERTS
ANNCD PRINT RUN 40 SETS
M27 Brett Connolly 8.00 20.00

2009-10 ITG Heroes and Prospects Gloves Are Off

ANNCD PRINT RUN 40 SETS
GA001 Angelo Esposito 8.00 20.00
GA002 Bob Sanguinetti 6.00 15.00
GA003 Cody Hodgson 20.00 50.00
GA004 Bryan Little
GA005 Devin Setoguchi 8.00 20.00
GA006 Karl Alzner 6.00 15.00
GA007 Zach Hamill
GA008 Marc-Andre Gragnani 8.00 20.00

2009-10 ITG Heroes and Prospects Hero and Prospect Jerseys

ANNCD PRINT RUN 30 SETS
HP01 Roy/Price
HP02 Brodeur/Bernier 20.00 50.00
HP03 Kovalchuk/Esposito 10.00 25.00
HP04 Lemieux/Hall 25.00 60.00
HP05 Neely/Lucic 10.00 25.00
HP06 Kiprusoff/Irving 10.00 25.00
HP07 Sakic/Duchene 25.00 60.00
HP08 Robinson/Subban 20.00 50.00
HP09 Hall/Messier 15.00 40.00
HP10 Seguin/Yzerman 25.00 60.00

2009-10 ITG Heroes and Prospects Memorial Cup Winners

COMPLETE SET (18) 50.00 100.00
MC01 Taylor Hall 8.00 20.00
MC02 Greg Nemisz 2.00 5.00
MC03 Scott Timmins 4.00 10.00
MC04 Dale Mitchell 4.00 10.00
MC05 Ryan Ellis 2.50 6.00
MC06 Jesse Blacker 2.00 5.00
MC07 Andrei Loktionov 3.00 8.00
MC08 Rob Kwiet 1.50 4.00
MC09 Eric Wellwood 3.00 8.00
MC10 Ben Shutron 2.00 5.00
MC11 Lane MacDermid 2.50 6.00
MC12 Adam Henrique 5.00 12.00
MC13 Justin Shugg 1.50 4.00
MC14 Mark Cundari 4.00 10.00
MC15 Andrew Engelage 5.00 12.00
MC16 Harry Young 4.00 10.00
MC17 Conor O'Donnell 2.00 5.00
MC18 Austin Watson 4.00 10.00

2009-10 ITG Heroes and Prospects Prospect Combos Jerseys

ANNCD PRINT RUN 40 SETS
PC01 Ellis/Subban 10.00 25.00
PC02 Kane/Esposito 15.00 40.00
PC03 Hodgson/Couture 20.00 50.00
PC04 Schenn/Boychuk
PC05 Hall/Marchand 15.00 40.00
PC06 Roy/Bernier 8.00 20.00
PC07 de Haan/Hickey
PC08 Allen/McCollum 12.00 30.00
PC09 Nugent-Hopkins/Sutter 20.00 50.00
PC10 Kadri/Stewart 15.00 40.00
PC11 Gudbranson/Alzner 8.00 20.00
PC12 Skinner/Boychuk 12.00 30.00

2009-10 ITG Heroes and Prospects Real Heroes

COMPLETE SET (24) 75.00 150.00
RH01 Woody Dumart 2.50 6.00
RH02 Milt Schmidt 3.00 8.00
RH03 Gordie Drillon 4.00 10.00
RH04 Ken Reardon 4.00 10.00
RH05 Sid Abel 4.00 10.00
RH06 Turk Broda 4.00 10.00
RH07 Hobey Baker 3.00 8.00
RH08 Frank Brimsek 3.00 8.00
RH09 Syl Apps 4.00 10.00
RH10 Conn Smythe 4.00 10.00
RH11 Red Garrett 2.50 6.00
RH12 Joe Turner 2.50 6.00
RH13 Bobby Bauer 5.00 12.00
RH14 Frank McGee 4.00 10.00
RH15 Howie Meeker 4.00 10.00
RH16 Johnny Bower 5.00 12.00
RH17 Frank Frederickson 2.50 6.00
RH18 Bob Carse 3.00 8.00
RH19 Alex Shibicky 4.00 10.00
RH20 Lynn Patrick 6.00 15.00
RH21 Max Bentley 2.50 6.00
RH22 Neil Colville 2.50 6.00
RH23 Chuck Rayner 3.00 8.00
RH24 Roy Conacher 4.00 10.00

2009-10 ITG Heroes and Prospects Selects Jerseys

ANNCD PRINT RUN 19 SETS

2009-10 ITG Heroes and Prospects Subway Series Jerseys

ANNCD PRINT RUN 60 SETS
*SILVER/30: .5X TO 1.2X BASIC JSY
CRM34 Karl Alzner 4.00 10.00
CRM35 P.K. Subban
CRM36 Brandon Sutter
SSM01 Jake Allen 10.00 25.00
SSM02 Maxime Clermont 5.00 12.00
SSM03 Louis Domingue 8.00 20.00
SSM04 Olivier Roy 6.00 15.00
SSM05 Simon Despres 6.00 15.00
SSM06 Brandon Gormley 8.00 20.00
SSM07 Charles-Olivier Roussel 6.00 15.00
SSM08 Yann Sauve
SSM09 Jordan Caron
SSM10 Patrice Cormier 6.00 15.00
SSM11 Michael Kirkpatrick 4.00 10.00
SSM12 Philippe Paradis 6.00 15.00
SSM13 Taylor Hall 20.00 50.00
SSM14 Nazem Kadri 12.00 30.00
SSM15 Peter Holland
SSM16 Jeff Skinner
SSM17 Michael Hutchinson 8.00 20.00
SSM18 Erik Gudbranson 6.00 15.00
SSM19 Stefan Della Rovere 6.00 15.00
SSM20 Tyler Toffoli 10.00 25.00
SSM21 Colten Teubert 6.00 15.00
SSM22 Zack Kassian
SSM23 Scott Glennie 5.00 12.00
SSM24 Brayden Schenn 12.00 30.00
SSM25 Brent Raedeke
SSM26 Linden Vey 5.00 12.00
SSM27 Jordan Eberle 10.00 25.00
SSM28 Brendan Shinnimin
SSM29 Mark Pysyk
SSM30 Jared Cowen 6.00 15.00
SSM31 Martin Jones
SSM32 Calvin Pickard
SSM33 Brett Ponich

2009-10 ITG Heroes and Prospects Subway Series Jerseys Silver

*SILVER/30: .5X TO 1.2X BASIC JSY
ANNCD PRINT RUN 30 SETS

2009-10 ITG Heroes and Prospects Top Prospects Game Used Jerseys

ANNCD PRINT RUN 60 SETS
JM01 Bobby Hughes 4.00 10.00
JM02 Brayden Schenn 10.00 25.00
JM03 Calvin de Haan 5.00 12.00
JM04 Carter Ashton 6.00 15.00
JM05 Chet Pickard 8.00 20.00
JM06 Chris Stewart 5.00 12.00
JM07 Colten Teubert 6.00 15.00
JM08 Corey Perry 6.00 15.00
JM09 Dmitry Kulikov 6.00 15.00
JM10 Ethan Werek 4.00 10.00
JM11 Evander Kane 12.00 30.00
JM12 Greg Nemisz 5.00 12.00
JM13 Jamie Arniel 5.00 12.00
JM14 Jared Cowen 6.00 15.00
JM15 Jared Staal 5.00 12.00
JM16 Jimmy Bubnick 4.00 10.00
JM17 Jordan Caron 6.00 15.00
JM18 Jordan Eberle 10.00 25.00
JM19 Landon Ferraro 5.00 12.00
JM20 Luca Sbisa 6.00 15.00
JM21 Marcus Foligno 8.00 20.00
JM22 Matt Duchene 20.00 50.00
JM23 Maxime Sauve 6.00 15.00
JM24 Nazem Kadri 12.00 30.00
JM25 Nicholas Deschamps 6.00 15.00
JM26 Olivier Roy 6.00 15.00
JM27 Peter Delmas 5.00 12.00
JM28 Ryan Ellis 6.00 15.00
JM29 Ryan Getzlaf 10.00 25.00
JM30 Scott Glennie 5.00 12.00
JM31 Simon Despres 6.00 15.00
JM32 Stefan Elliott 6.00 15.00
JM33 Thomas McCollum 6.00 15.00
JM34 Tyler Cuma 4.00 10.00
JM35 Zach Boychuk 5.00 12.00
JM36 Zack Kassian 6.00 15.00

2009-10 ITG Heroes and Prospects Top Prospects Game Used Jerseys Silver

*SINGLES: .5X TO 1.2X BASIC INSERTS
ANNCD PRINT RUN 30 SETS
JM09 Dmitry Kulikov 8.00 20.00

2010-11 ITG Heroes and Prospects

COMPLETE SET (200) 20.00 50.00
COMP.SERIES 1 (150) 15.00 40.00
COMP.UPDATE (50) 10.00 25.00
1 D.Sedin/H.Sedin HH .25 .60
2 Pavel Bure HH .30 .75
3 Steve Yzerman HH .60 1.50
4 Roberto Luongo HH .25 .60
5 Steven Stamkos HH .50 1.25
6 Pelle Lindbergh HH .40 1.00
7 Rick Nash HH .25 .60
8 Adam Larsson .40 1.00
9 Victor Rask .15 .40
10 Sergei Bobrovsky .50 1.25
11 Tyler Seguin .75 2.00
12 J.P. Anderson .25 .60
13 Greg McKegg .25 .60
14 Ryan Murphy .30 .75
15 Richard Panik .15 .40
16 Tyler Toffoli .30 .75
17 Freddie Hamilton .25 .60
18 Erik Gudbranson .25 .60
19 Michael Curtis .15 .40
20 Matt Puempel .25 .60
21 Boone Jenner .20 .50
22 Taylor Beck .20 .50
23 Jack Campbell .25 .60
24 Austin Watson .25 .60
25 Jarred Tinordi .25 .60
26 Joey Hishon .25 .60
27 Philipp Grubauer .30 .75
28 Ryan Spooner .25 .60
29 Christian Thomas .20 .50
30 Taylor Doherty .15 .40
31 Brock Beukeboom .15 .40
32 Mark Visentin .25 .60
33 Devante Smith-Pelly .30 .75
34 John McFarland .20 .50
35 Ryan Ellis .25 .60
36 Gabriel Landeskog .60 1.50
37 Peter Holland .20 .50
38 Philip Danault .15 .40
39 Tomas Jurco .40 1.00
40 Kirill Kabanov .20 .50
41 Maxime Clermont .20 .50
42 Gabriel Beaupre .15 .40
43 Jerome Gauthier-Leduc .15 .40
44 Michael Bournival .20 .50
45 Ryan Bourque .25 .60
46 Nathan Beaulieu .25 .60
47 Jakub Culek .15 .40
48 Brandon Gormley .25 .60
49 Robin Gusse .25 .60
50 Louis-Marc Aubry .15 .40
51 Stanislav Galiev .25 .60
52 Michael Chaput .15 .40
53 Jonathan Huberdeau .50 1.25
54 Gleason Fournier .15 .40
55 Olivier Archambault .20 .50
56 Louis Domingue .25 .60
57 Louis Leblanc .30 .75
58 Zack Phillips .25 .60
59 Petr Straka .25 .60
60 Olivier Roy .25 .60
61 Sean Couturier .50 1.25
62 Ryan Johansen .40 1.00
63 Michael St. Croix .15 .40
64 Curtis Hamilton .20 .50
65 Brett Connolly .25 .60
66 Calvin Pickard .25 .60
67 Joey Leach .15 .40
68 Jordan Weal .20 .50
69 Dylan McIlrath .20 .50
70 Alexander Petrovic .15 .40
71 Quinton Howden .20 .50
72 Emerson Etem .25 .60
73 Brendan Shinnimin .15 .40
74 Ryan Nugent-Hopkins .75 2.00
75 Brad Ross .20 .50
76 Kevin Sundher .15 .40
77 Matt MacKenzie .15 .40
78 Tyler Bunz .20 .50
79 Shane McColgan .20 .50
80 Taylor Aronson .15 .40
81 Mark Pysyk .15 .40
82 Kent Simpson .20 .50
83 Nino Niederreiter .25 .60
84 Scott Glennie .20 .50
85 Craig Cunningham .15 .40
86 Brendan Ranford .25 .60
87 David Musil .20 .50
88 Ryan Murray .30 .75
89 Tobias Rieder .25 .60
90 Brandon Saad .30 .75
91 Alex Galchenyuk .75 2.00
92 Brendan Gaunce .25 .60
93 Max Iafrate .25 .60
94 Nail Yakupov 1.00 2.50
95 Nick Ebert .20 .50
96 Luca Ciampini .25 .60
97 Martin Frk .20 .50
98 Tomas Filippi .15 .40
99 Derrick Pouliot .40 1.00
100 David Toews .20 .50
101 P.K. Subban .60 1.50
102 Andrei Loktionov .20 .50
103 Tomas Tatar .40 1.00
104 Chris Terry .20 .50
105 Anton Khudobin .20 .50
106 Jonathon Blum .25 .60
107 Dana Tyrell .20 .50
108 Ryan Stoa .15 .40
109 Thomas Hickey .15 .40
110 Mikael Backlund .15 .40
111 Evgeny Grachev .20 .50
112 Kyle Turris .20 .50
113 Braden Holtby .50 1.25
114 Erik Karlsson .50 1.25
115 Tyler Ennis .20 .50
116 Tyler Bozak .25 .60
117 Travis Morin .15 .40
118 John Carlson .30 .75
119 Alex Stalock .25 .60
120 Brett Sonne .15 .40
121 Dustin Tokarski .20 .50
122 Sergei Shirokov .20 .50
123 Corey Elkins .15 .40
124 Evgeny Dadonov .25 .60
125 Christian Hanson .15 .40
126 Brad Thiessen .25 .60
127 Logan Couture .25 .60
128 Chet Pickard .20 .50
129 Nick Palmieri .20 .50
130 Benn Ferriero .15 .40
131 Chad Johnson .20 .50
132 Zach Boychuk .20 .50
133 Colton Sceviour .15 .40
134 Jamie Arniel .20 .50
135 Lars Eller .20 .50
136 Eric Tangradi .20 .50
137 John Moore .20 .50
138 Ryan McDonagh .50 1.25
139 Jordan Schroeder .25 .60
140 Blake Geoffrion .25 .60
141 Jussi Rynnas .25 .60
142 Kevin Shattenkirk .40 1.00
143 Luke Adam .20 .50
144 Jared Staal .15 .40
145 Joe Colborne .25 .60
146 Cody Hodgson .75 2.00
147 Linus Omark .50 1.25
148 Kyle Beach .25 .60
149 Nazem Kadri .60 1.50
150 Mattias Tedenby .15 .40
151 Mark Olver .20 .50
152 Zac Dalpe .20 .50
153 Bill Sweatt .20 .50
154 Tomas Kubalik .20 .50
155 Colin Greening .30 .75
156 Rhett Rakhshani .20 .50
157 Bobby Butler .20 .50
158 Teemu Hartikainen .25 .60
159 Erik Gustafsson .25 .60
160 Adam Henrique .50 1.25
161 Mats Zuccarello .30 .75
162 Kyle Palmieri .40 1.00
163 Brandon Kozun .25 .60
164 Nick Leddy .20 .50
165 Gabriel Bourque .25 .60
166 Jake Allen .40 1.00
167 Linus Klasen .20 .50
168 Jacob Markstrom .30 .75
169 Ryan Strome .30 .75
170 Shane Prince .20 .50
171 Garrett Wilson .20 .50
172 Ryan Martindale .20 .50
173 Maxim Kitsyn .20 .50
174 Nicklas Jensen .25 .60
175 Jordan Binnington .20 .50
176 Richard Rakell .25 .60
177 Mark Scheifele .50 1.25
178 Vladislav Namestnikov .40 1.00
179 Dougie Hamilton .60 1.50
180 Alexander Khokhlachev .30 .75
181 Christopher Gibson .30 .75
182 David Honzik .20 .50
183 Xavier Ouellet .15 .40
184 Maximilien Le Sieur .20 .50
185 Ryan Tesink .25 .60
186 Logan Shaw .20 .50
187 Scott Oke .20 .50
188 Linden Vey .20 .50
189 Ty Rattie .40 1.00
190 Sven Bartschi .25 .60
191 Joel Edmundson .20 .50
192 Griffin Reinhart .25 .60
193 Mark McNeill .20 .50
194 Joe Morrow .40 1.00
195 Duncan Siemens .25 .60
196 Colin Jacobs .20 .50
197 Reece Scarlett .20 .50
198 Morgan Rielly .30 .75
199 Eric Lindros .40 1.00
200 Theoren Fleury .40 1.00

2010-11 ITG Heroes and Prospects AHL 75th Anniversary

AHLA01 Bill Sweeney 2.00 5.00
AHLA02 Billy Smith 2.50 6.00
AHLA03 Brett Hull 4.00 10.00
AHLA04 Bruce Boudreau 2.00 5.00
AHLA05 Carey Price 10.00 25.00
AHLA06 Doug Harvey 2.50 6.00
AHLA07 Eddie Shore 2.00 5.00
AHLA08 Emile Francis 1.50 4.00
AHLA09 Frank Mathers 2.00 5.00
AHLA10 Fred Glover 2.00 5.00
AHLA11 Gerry Cheevers 4.00 10.00
AHLA12 Gil Mayer 2.00 5.00
AHLA13 Jason Spezza 1.50 4.00
AHLA14 Jim Anderson 2.00 5.00
AHLA15 Jody Gage 2.00 5.00
AHLA16 John Paddock 2.00 5.00
AHLA17 John Slaney 2.00 5.00
AHLA18 Johnny Bower 3.00 8.00
AHLA19 Kent Douglas 2.00 5.00
AHLA20 Larry Robinson 2.50 6.00
AHLA21 Les Cunningham 2.00 5.00
AHLA22 Lou Trudel 2.00 5.00
AHLA23 Marcel Paille 2.00 5.00
AHLA24 Martin Brodeur 5.00 12.00
AHLA25 Mike Nykoluk 2.00 5.00
AHLA26 Milt Schmidt 2.00 5.00
AHLA27 Noel Price 2.00 5.00
AHLA28 Patrick Roy 6.00 15.00
AHLA29 Paul Gardner 2.00 5.00
AHLA30 Pelle Lindbergh 4.00 10.00
AHLA31 Steve Kraftcheck 2.00 5.00
AHLA32 Terry Sawchuk 3.00 8.00
AHLA33 Mitch Lamoureux 2.00 5.00
AHLA34 Willie Marshall 2.00 5.00
AHLA35 Zdeno Chara 2.00 5.00

2010-11 ITG Heroes and Prospects AHL 75th Anniversary Autographs

OVERALL AU ODDS 1:8
AHLAABB Bruce Boudreau 10.00 25.00
AHLAAEF Emile Francis
AHLAAGC Gerry Cheevers 5.00 12.00
AHLAAGM Gil Mayer 8.00 20.00
AHLAAJB Johnny Bower
AHLAAJP John Paddock 8.00 20.00
AHLAAJS Jason Spezza 10.00 25.00
AHLAAMK Mike Nykoluk 10.00 25.00
AHLAAML Mitch Lamoureux 12.00 30.00
AHLAAMS Milt Schmidt 6.00 15.00
AHLAANP Noel Price 12.00 30.00
AHLAAPG Paul Gardner 6.00 15.00
AHLAAWM Willie Marshall 6.00 15.00

2010-11 ITG Heroes and Prospects Autographs

OVERALL AUTO ODDS 1:8
AAA Akim Aliu 6.00 15.00
AAK Anton Khudobin 4.00 10.00
AAL Andrei Loktionov SP 6.00 15.00
AALA Adam Larsson SP 20.00 40.00
AALA2 Adam Larsson SP 20.00 40.00
AALD Andrew Ladd 5.00 12.00
AAN Andrej Nestrasil 5.00 12.00
AAS Alex Stalock 5.00 12.00
AAW Austin Watson 5.00 12.00
ABA Brent Andrews SP 8.00 20.00
ABB Brock Beukeboom 3.00 8.00
ABC Brett Connolly 5.00 12.00
ABF Benn Ferriero 5.00 12.00
ABG Brendan Gaunce 5.00 12.00
ABGE Blake Geoffrion 5.00 12.00
ABGO Brandon Gormley 5.00 12.00
ABH Braden Holtby 8.00 20.00
ABJ Boone Jenner 5.00 12.00
ABK Brandon Kozun SP 8.00 20.00
ABM Brayden McNabb 8.00 20.00
ABR Bobby Ryan 5.00 12.00
ABS Brett Sonne 3.00 8.00
ABSC Brayden Schenn SP 10.00 25.00
ABT Brad Thiessen 5.00 12.00
ACB Cody Bass 4.00 10.00
ACD Cedrick Desjardins 5.00 12.00
ACDO Chris Doyle 4.00 10.00
ACE Corey Elkins 3.00 8.00
ACEA Cody Eakin 5.00 12.00
ACH Christian Hanson 3.00 8.00
ACHO Cody Hodgson 15.00 40.00
ACJ Chad Johnson 4.00 10.00
ACOR Charles-Olivier Roussel 3.00 8.00
ACP Calvin Pickard 5.00 12.00
ACPR Carey Price SP 30.00 80.00
ACR Chad Rau 3.00 8.00
ACS Colton Sceviour 3.00 8.00
ACT Chris Terry 4.00 10.00
ADC Daniel Catenacci 5.00 12.00
ADD David Desharnais 10.00 25.00
ADG David Gilbert 4.00 10.00
ADM David Musil 4.00 10.00
ADO Dylan Olsen 6.00 15.00
ADP Derrick Pouliot 8.00 20.00
ADT David Toews 6.00 15.00
ADTO Dustin Tokarski 4.00 10.00
ADTY Dana Tyrell 4.00 10.00
AED Evgeny Dadonov 5.00 12.00
AEE Emerson Etem 8.00 20.00
AEG Evgeny Grachev 4.00 10.00
AEGE Eric Gelinas 6.00 15.00
AEGU Erik Gudbranson 5.00 12.00
AET Eric Tangradi 4.00 10.00
AGL Gabriel Landeskog 15.00 40.00
AGL2 Gabriel Landeskog SP 30.00 60.00
AIB Igor Bobkov 10.00 25.00
AIT Ivan Telegin SP 6.00 15.00
AJA J.P. Anderson 5.00 12.00
AJAR Jamie Arniel 4.00 10.00
AJB Jonathon Blum 5.00 12.00
AJBA Johan Backlund 4.00 10.00
AJBE Jonathan Bernier 5.00 12.00
AJBU Jimmy Bubnick 3.00 8.00
AJC Jack Campbell 15.00 40.00
AJCA Jordan Caron SP 10.00 25.00
AJCH Joel Champagne 5.00 12.00
AJCO Joe Colborne 6.00 15.00
AJCU Jakub Culek 3.00 8.00
AJE Jhonas Enroth 5.00 12.00
AJF Jeff Frazee 6.00 15.00
AJH Jonathan Huberdeau 20.00 40.00
AJL Jacob Lagace 5.00 12.00
AJMA Jacob Markstrom SP 10.00 25.00
AJMF John McFarland SP 6.00 15.00
AJS Jared Staal SP 5.00 12.00
AJSC Jordan Schroeder 5.00 12.00
AJT Jarred Tinordi 5.00 12.00
AJZ Jeff Zatkoff 5.00 12.00
AKB Kyle Beach 5.00 12.00
AKE Keaton Ellerby 3.00 8.00
AKS Kent Simpson 4.00 10.00
AKSE Keith Seabrook 3.00 8.00
AKT Kyle Turris 4.00 10.00
ALA Luke Adam SP 6.00 15.00
ALC Luca Ciampini 8.00 20.00
ALCA Luca Caputi 4.00 10.00
ALCO Logan Couture 8.00 20.00
ALCO2 Logan Couture 5.00 12.00
ALD Louis Domingue 5.00 12.00
ALE Lars Eller 4.00 10.00
ALER Loui Eriksson 5.00 12.00
ALF Landon Ferraro 3.00 8.00
ALI Leland Irving 5.00 12.00
ALK Levko Koper 3.00 8.00
ALL Louis Leblanc 12.00 30.00
AMBE Matt Beleskey 4.00 10.00
AMBO Mikkel Boedker SP
AMC Matt Climie 4.00 10.00
AMCL Maxime Clermont 4.00 10.00
AMDZ Michael Del Zotto 5.00 12.00
AMF Martin Frk 10.00 25.00
AMFO Marcus Foligno SP 10.00 25.00
AMH Matt Halischuk 4.00 10.00
AMI Max Iafrate 5.00 12.00
AMK Mark Katic 3.00 8.00
AMKO Mikko Koivu SP 8.00 20.00
AMLA Michael Latta 5.00 12.00
AMM Mike Murphy 5.00 12.00
AMP Mark Pysyk 3.00 8.00
AMPU Matt Puempel 10.00 25.00
AMV Mark Visentin 5.00 12.00
ANE Nick Ebert 4.00 10.00
ANK Nazem Kadri 12.00 30.00
ANN Nino Niederreiter 5.00 12.00
AOA Olivier Archambault SP 6.00 15.00
AOEL Oliver Ekman-Larsson 6.00 15.00
AOR Olivier Roy 5.00 12.00
APB Pavel Bure SP 25.00 50.00
APBE Patrice Bergeron 6.00 15.00
APP Philippe Paradis 3.00 8.00
APS Petr Straka 5.00 12.00
AQH Quinton Howden 4.00 10.00
ARG Robin Gusse 5.00 12.00
ARJ Ryan Johansen 8.00 20.00
ARLU Roberto Luongo SP 25.00 50.00
ARM Ryan Murray 10.00 25.00
ARMC Ryan McDonagh 6.00 15.00
ARN Ryan Nugent-Hopkins 15.00 40.00
ARN2 Ryan Nugent-Hopkins SP 30.00 60.00
ARNA Rick Nash SP 15.00 40.00
ARO Ryan O'Marra 3.00 8.00
ARS Ryan Stoa 3.00 8.00
ASB Sergei Bobrovsky 6.00 15.00
ASC Sean Couturier 15.00 40.00
ASC2 Sean Couturier SP 20.00 50.00
ASD Simon Despres 5.00 12.00
ASG Stanislav Galiev 10.00 25.00
ASM Shane McColgan 4.00 10.00
ASS Steven Stamkos SP 15.00 40.00
ATB Tyler Bunz 5.00 12.00
ATBA Tyson Barrie 5.00 12.00
ATBE Taylor Beck 4.00 10.00
ATBO Tyler Bozak SP 8.00 20.00
ATBR T.J. Brennan 4.00 10.00
ATD Taylor Doherty 3.00 8.00
ATF Theoren Fleury SP 40.00 80.00
ATH Thomas Hickey 3.00 8.00
ATJ Tomas Jurco 8.00 20.00
ATM Travis Morin 3.00 8.00
ATMC Thomas McCollum 5.00 12.00
ATT Tyson Teichmann 4.00 10.00
ATTA Tomas Tatar 10.00 25.00
ATTH Tim Thomas SP 25.00 50.00
ATTO Tyler Toffoli 6.00 15.00
AVR Victor Rask 4.00 10.00
AVT Vladimir Tarasenko 50.00 100.00
AYA Yuri Alexandrov 4.00 10.00
AZB Zach Boychuk 4.00 10.00
AZC Zdeno Chara SP 15.00 30.00
AZH Zach Hamill SP 6.00 15.00
AZP Zack Phillips 5.00 12.00

2010-11 ITG Heroes and Prospects Calder Cup Champions

CC01 Alexandre Giroux 6.00 15.00
CC02 Chris Bourque 3.00 8.00
CC03 Keith Aucoin 4.00 10.00
CC04 Andrew Gordon 6.00 15.00
CC05 Mathieu Perreault 2.50 6.00
CC06 Kyle Wilson 3.00 8.00
CC07 Francois Bouchard 3.00 8.00
CC08 Karl Alzner 2.00 5.00
CC09 John Carlson 4.00 10.00
CC10 Patrick McNeill 2.50 6.00
CC11 Bryan Helmer 5.00 12.00
CC12 Jay Beagle 6.00 15.00
CC13 Steve Pinizzotto 4.00 10.00
CC14 Braden Holtby 6.00 15.00
CC15 Michal Neuvirth 2.50 6.00

2010-11 ITG Heroes and Prospects Draft Star Jerseys Black

ANNCD PRINT RUN 40 SER.#'d SETS
SILVER/19: .5X TO 1.2X BLACK/40*
DS01 Ryan Nugent-Hopkins 20.00 50.00
DS02 Gabriel Landeskog 15.00 40.00
DS03 Jonathan Huberdeau 12.00 30.00
DS04 Sean Couturier 12.00 30.00
DS05 Dougie Hamilton 15.00 40.00
DS06 Nathan Beaulieu 6.00 15.00
DS07 Sven Bartschi 6.00 15.00
DS08 Ryan Murphy 8.00 20.00

2010-11 ITG Heroes and Prospects Game Used Jerseys Black

ANNOUNCED PRINT RUN 100-120
SILVER/30-40: .5X TO 1.2X BLACK
M01 Blake Geoffrion 5.00 12.00
M02 Brandon Gormley 5.00 12.00
M03 Brayden Schenn 10.00 25.00
M04 Brendan Shinnimin 3.00 8.00
M05 Brett Connolly 5.00 12.00
M06 Brock Beukeboom 3.00 8.00
M07 Chet Pickard 4.00 10.00
M08 Chris Terry 4.00 10.00
M09 Cody Eakin 5.00 12.00
M10 Cody Hodgson 10.00 25.00
M11 Cory Schneider 8.00 20.00
M12 Drayson Bowman 4.00 10.00
M13 Ethan Werek 5.00 12.00
M14 Greg McKegg 5.00 12.00
M15 Jake Allen 8.00 20.00
M16 Jamie Arniel 4.00 10.00
M17 Jared Cowen 4.00 10.00
M18 Jean-Francois Berube 5.00 12.00
M19 Joe Colborne 6.00 15.00
M20 Joey Hishon 5.00 12.00
M21 John Carlson 10.00 25.00
M22 John McFarland 4.00 10.00
M23 Jordan Binnington 4.00 10.00
M24 Jordan Weal 4.00 10.00
M25 Kevin Shattenkirk 8.00 20.00
M26 Kyle Turris 4.00 10.00
M27 Landon Ferraro 3.00 8.00
M28 Lars Eller 4.00 10.00
M29 Logan Couture 8.00 20.00
M30 Matt Puempel 5.00 12.00
M31 Michael St. Croix 3.00 8.00
M32 Nathan Beaulieu 5.00 12.00
M33 Nazem Kadri 10.00 25.00
M34 Oliver Ekman-Larsson 6.00 15.00
M35 Oscar Moller 4.00 10.00
M36 P.K. Subban 12.00 30.00
M37 Petr Straka 5.00 12.00
M38 Philipp Grubauer 6.00 15.00
M39 Riley Boychuk 3.00 8.00
M40 Ryan Ellis 5.00 12.00
M41 Ryan Nugent-Hopkins 12.00 30.00

42 Ryan Stoa 3.00 8.00
43 Scott Glennie 4.00 10.00
44 Sean Couturier 12.00 30.00
45 Stanislav Galiev 5.00 12.00
46 Taylor Doherty 3.00 8.00
47 Thomas Hickey 3.00 8.00
48 Tomas Jurco 6.00 15.00
49 Tyler Ennis 4.00 10.00
50 Tyler Seguin 12.00 30.00
51 Vladimir Tarasenko 15.00 40.00
52 Zach Boychuk 4.00 10.00
53 Zach Hamill 4.00 10.00
54 Zack Kassian 5.00 12.00
55 Robin Lehner/100 8.00 20.00
56 Boone Jenner/100 4.00 10.00
57 Luke Adam/100 4.00 10.00
58 Louis Leblanc/100 6.00 15.00
59 Nathan Lieuwen/100 4.00 10.00
60 Ryan Murray/100 6.00 15.00
61 Matt Calvert/100 6.00 15.00
62 Sergei Bobrovsky/100 10.00 25.00
63 Michael Del Zotto/100 4.00 10.00
64 Jordan Caron/100 6.00 15.00

2010-11 ITG Heroes and Prospects He Shoots He Scores Prizes

SHS01 Brodeur/Luongo/Roy 15.00 40.00
SHS02 Dionne/Schenn/Robitle 8.00 20.00
SHS03 Couture/Ennis/Eller 6.00 15.00
SHS04 Gilmour/Kadri/Sittler 15.00 40.00
SHS05 Bure/Tarsnko/Fedorov 12.00 30.00
SHS06 Jurco/Huberd/Beaulieu 12.00 30.00
SHS07 Sedin/Landeskog/Sedin 15.00 40.00
SHS08 Lecvlr/Yzerman/Stamkos 15.00 40.00
SHS09 Subban/LeBlanc/Eller 15.00 40.00
SHS10 Roy/Roy/Domingue 15.00 40.00
SHS11 Saad/Bourque/Hamilton 15.00 40.00
SHS12 Kadri/Reimer/Colborne 15.00 40.00
SHS13 Lapointe/Subban/Robnsn 15.00 40.00
SHS14 RNH/Stamkos/Couturier 20.00 50.00
SHS15 Ennis/Kassian/Adam 6.00 15.00
SHS16 Kurri/Messier/Fuhr 10.00 25.00
SHS17 Johansen/Neely/Niedrtr 10.00 25.00
SHS18 Geoffrion/Pickard/Ellis 6.00 15.00
SHS19 Bure/Hodgson/Sedin 15.00 40.00
SHS20 Lndbrgh/Bobrvsky/Prent 12.00 30.00
SHS21 Markstrom/Holtby/Allen 12.00 30.00
SHS22 Rask/Esposito/Caron 10.00 25.00
SHS23 Lemieux/Lafleur/Beliveau 20.00 50.00
SHS24 Couturier/RNH/Landeskog 20.00 50.00
SHS25 Nash/Kadri/Ciccarelli 15.00 40.00
SHS26 Murphy/Coffey/Landeskog 15.00 40.00
SHS27 Ellis/Connolly/Schenn 8.00 20.00
SHS28 Hishon/Sakic/Shattenkirk 10.00 25.00
SHS29 Selanne/Etem/Getzlaf 12.00 30.00
SHS30 Gormley/Chara/Gudbrnsn 6.00 15.00

2010-11 ITG Heroes and Prospects Hero and Prospect Jerseys Silver

ANNOUNCED PRINT RUN 50
HP01 V.Tarasenko/P.Bure 15.00 40.00
HP02 T.Seguin/M.Lemieux 20.00 50.00
HP03 P.Subban/S.Savard 15.00 40.00
HP04 N.Kadri/S.Stamkos 15.00 40.00
HP05 O.Roy/R.Luongo 6.00 15.00
HP06 J.Bernier/M.Brodeur 12.00 30.00
HP07 B.Connolly/S.Yzerman 15.00 40.00
HP08 L.Couture/J.Thornton 6.00 15.00
HP09 J.Allen/P.Roy 15.00 40.00
HP10 B.Schenn/L.Robitaille 8.00 20.00
HP11 G.Landeskog/P.Forsberg 15.00 40.00
HP12 R.Nugent-Hopkins/M.Messier 25.00 50.00
HP13 D.Hamilton/Z.Chara 15.00 40.00
HP14 S.Couturier/E.Lindros 10.00 25.00
HP15 R.Murphy/P.Coffey 8.00 20.00

2010-11 ITG Heroes and Prospects Heroes Game Used Jerseys Silver

ANNOUNCED PRINT RUN 30
HM01 Daniel Sedin 15.00 40.00
HM02 Patrick Roy 15.00 40.00
HM03 Rick Nash 10.00 25.00
HM04 Steven Stamkos 12.00 30.00
HM05 Henrik Sedin 15.00 40.00
HM06 Mark Messier
HM07 Pavel Bure 12.50 30.00
HM08 Steve Yzerman 15.00 40.00
HM09 Roberto Luongo 6.00 15.00
HM10 Vladislav Tretiak 20.00 50.00
HM11 Eric Lindros
HM12 Theoren Fleury 25.00 50.00
HM13 Tim Thomas 5.00 12.00
HM14 Shea Weber

2010-11 ITG Heroes and Prospects Memorial Cup Champions

MC01 Taylor Hall 10.00 25.00
MC02 Adam Henrique 6.00 15.00
MC03 Justin Shugg 4.00 10.00
MC04 Dale Mitchell 3.00 8.00
MC05 Cam Fowler 4.00 10.00
MC06 Eric Wellwood 3.00 8.00
MC07 Zack Kassian 5.00 12.00
MC08 Scott Timmins 3.00 8.00
MC09 Greg Nemisz 2.50 6.00
MC10 Ryan Ellis 3.00 8.00
MC11 Kenny Ryan 2.50 6.00
MC12 Mark Cundari 2.50 6.00
MC13 Marc Cantin 2.50 6.00
MC14 Stephen Johnston 2.50 6.00
MC15 Philipp Grubauer 4.00 10.00

2010-11 ITG Heroes and Prospects National Pride Jerseys Black

ANNOUNCED PRINT RUN 80
SILVER/30: .5X TO 1.2X JSY BLK/80*
NATP01 Andrej Nestrasil 5.00 12.00
NATP02 Anton Khudobin
NATP03 Lars Eller 4.00 10.00
NATP04 Jacob Markstrom 6.00 15.00
NATP05 John Carlson 10.00 25.00
NATP06 Nazem Kadri 8.00 20.00
NATP07 Nino Niederreiter 5.00 12.00
NATP08 P.K. Subban 12.00 30.00
NATP09 Philipp Grubauer 6.00 15.00
NATP10 Vladimir Tarasenko 15.00 40.00

2010-11 ITG Heroes and Prospects Net Prospects Jerseys Black

ANNOUNCED PRINT RUN 80
SILVER/20: .6X TO 1.5X BLACK/80*
NPM01 Jake Allen 8.00 20.00
NPM02 Calvin Pickard 5.00 12.00
NPM03 Olivier Roy 5.00 12.00
NPM04 Louis Domingue 6.00 15.00
NPM05 Mark Visentin 5.00 12.00
NPM06 Chet Pickard 4.00 10.00
NPM07 Cory Schneider 8.00 20.00
NPM08 Braden Holtby 8.00 20.00
NPM09 Philipp Grubauer 6.00 15.00
NPM10 Jacob Markstrom 6.00 15.00

2010-11 ITG Heroes and Prospects Prospect Trios Silver

ANNOUNCED PRINT RUN 30
PT1 Subban/LeBlanc/Eller 25.00 60.00
PT2 Hopkins/Couturier/Puempel 15.00 40.00
PT3 Kadri/Cowen/Glennie 12.00 30.00
PT4 Markstrm/Ellerby/Gudbrans 12.00 30.00
PT5 Seguin/Hamill/Colbourne 30.00 80.00

2010-11 ITG Heroes and Prospects Subway Series Jumbo Jerseys Black

ANNOUNCED PRINT RUN 100
*SILVER/30: .5X TO 1.2X JUMBO JSY BLK
CRM31 Chris Stewart 4.00 10.00
CRM32 Steven Stamkos 8.00 20.00
CRM33 P.K. Subban
CRM35 Logan Couture 5.00 12.00
SSM01 Scott Stajcer 4.00 10.00
SSM02 Scott Wedgewood 4.00 10.00
SSM03 J.P. Anderson 5.00 12.00
SSM04 Mark Visentin 5.00 12.00
SSM05 Christian Thomas 4.00 10.00
SSM06 Boone Jenner 4.00 10.00
SSM07 Matt Puempel 5.00 12.00
SSM08 Taylor Doherty 3.00 8.00
SSM09 Devante Smith-Pelly 6.00 15.00
SSM10 Greg McKegg 5.00 12.00
SSM11 Jean-Francois Berube 5.00 12.00
SSM12 Brandon Gormley 5.00 12.00
SSM13 Jonathan Huberdeau 10.00 25.00
SSM14 Sean Couturier 12.00 30.00
SSM15 Louis Leblanc 8.00 20.00
SSM16 Zack Phillips 5.00 12.00
SSM17 Michael Bournival 4.00 10.00
SSM18 Xavier Ouellet 3.00 8.00
SSM19 Nathan Beaulieu 5.00 12.00
SSM20 Olivier Roy 5.00 12.00
SSM21 Quinton Howden 4.00 10.00
SSM22 Ryan Murray 8.00 20.00
SSM23 Kent Simpson 4.00 10.00
SSM24 Calvin Pickard 5.00 12.00
SSM25 Ty Rattie 8.00 20.00
SSM26 Ryan Nugent-Hopkins 6.00 15.00
SSM27 Curtis Hamilton 4.00 10.00
SSM28 Ryan Johansen 6.00 15.00
SSM29 Brad Ross 4.00 10.00
SSM30 Dougie Hamilton 12.00 30.00
SSM34 Tyler Seguin 10.00 25.00

2010-11 ITG Heroes and Prospects Top Prospects Game Used Jerseys Black

ANNOUNCED PRINT RUN 100
SILVER/30: .5X TO 1.2X JSY BLK/100*
JM01 Alexander Petrovic 3.00 8.00
JM02 Brock Beukeboom 3.00 8.00
JM03 Alex Hutchings 3.00 8.00
JM04 Cody Eakin 5.00 12.00
JM05 Michael Latta 5.00 12.00
JM06 Philippe Paradis 3.00 8.00
JM07 Emerson Etem 5.00 12.00
JM08 Levko Koper 3.00 8.00
JM09 John McFarland 4.00 10.00
JM10 Louis Domingue 5.00 12.00
JM11 Mark Pysyk 3.00 8.00
JM12 Mark Visentin 5.00 12.00
JM13 Maxime Clermont 4.00 10.00
JM14 Nino Niederreiter 5.00 12.00
JM15 Michael Bournival 4.00 10.00
JM16 Peter Holland 4.00 10.00
JM17 Taylor Beck 4.00 10.00
JM18 Quinton Howden 4.00 10.00
JM19 Ryan Spooner 5.00 12.00
JM20 Scott Stajcer 4.00 10.00
JM21 Stanislav Galiev 5.00 12.00
JM22 Stephen Silas 4.00 10.00
JM23 Taylor Doherty 3.00 8.00
JM24 Troy Rutkowski 3.00 8.00
JM25 Tyler Seguin 15.00 40.00
JM26 Tyler Toffoli 6.00 15.00

2011-12 ITG Heroes and Prospects

COMP.SERIES 1 (200) 20.00 50.00
1 Brad Park HH .20 .50
2 Cam Neely HH .25 .60
3 Henri Richard HH .25 .60
4 Mike Gartner HH .25 .60
5 Red Kelly HH .20 .50
6 Teemu Selanne HH .50 1.25
7 Tony Amonte HH .20 .50
8 Adam Larsson INT .25 .60
9 Mika Zibanejad INT .50 1.25
10 Vladimir Tarasenko INT .60 1.50
11 Alex Galchenyuk CP .75 2.00
12 Alexander Khokhlachev CP .30 .75
13 Boone Jenner CP .20 .50
14 Brandon Saad CP .40 1.00
15 Brendan Gaunce CP .20 .50
16 Brett Ritchie CP .20 .50
17 Dougie Hamilton CP .50 1.25
18 Jarrod Maidens CP .25 .60
19 Jordan Binnington CP .20 .50
20 Malcolm Subban CP .40 1.00
21 Mark Scheifele CP .50 1.25
22 Matia Marcantuoni CP .20 .50
23 Matt Murray CP .30 .75
24 Matt Puempel CP .25 .60
25 Mathew Campagna CP .20 .50
26 Max Iafrate CP .25 .60
27 Nail Yakupov CP .75 2.00
28 Nick Cousins CP .20 .50
29 Nick Ebert CP .15 .40
30 Nicklas Jensen CP .25 .60
31 Rickard Rakell CP .25 .60
32 Ryan Murphy CP .25 .60
33 Ryan Spooner CP .25 .60
34 Ryan Strome CP .30 .75
35 Shane Prince CP .20 .50
36 Scott Harrington CP .25 .60
37 Scott Laughton CP .25 .60
38 Slater Koekkoek CP .25 .60
39 Stefan Noesen CP .20 .50
40 Stuart Percy CP .25 .60
41 Vladislav Namestnikov CP .40 1.00
42 Alexandre Grenier CP .20 .50
43 Andrew Ryan CP .20 .50
44 Charles Hudon CP .25 .60
45 Christopher Gibson CP .25 .60
46 David Honzik CP .25 .60
47 Domenic Graham CP .20 .50
48 Dominic Poulin CP .20 .50
49 Jean-Gabriel Pageau CP .20 .50
50 Jeremie Fraser CP .15 .40
51 Jonathan Huberdeau CP .50 1.25
52 Jonathan Racine CP .20 .50
53 Logan Shaw CP .20 .50
54 Luca Ciampini CP .25 .60
55 Martin Frk CP .25 .60
56 Nathan Beaulieu CP .25 .60
57 Olivier Archambault CP .20 .50
58 Phillip Danault CP .25 .60
59 Ryan Tesink CP .25 .60
60 Scott Oke CP .20 .50
61 Sean Couturier CP .40 1.00
62 Tomas Jurco CP .30 .75
63 Xavier Ouellet CP .25 .60
64 Zach O'Brien CP .20 .50
65 Zack Phillips CP .25 .60
66 Adam Lowry CP .25 .60
67 Brendan Ranford CP .20 .50
68 Colin Jacobs CP .20 .50
69 Colton Sissons CP .25 .60
70 David Musil CP .20 .50
71 Derrick Pouliot CP .40 1.00
72 Duncan Siemens CP .25 .60
73 Griffin Reinhart CP .25 .60
74 Joe Morrow CP .30 .75
75 Joel Edmundson CP .20 .50
76 Kale Kessy CP .20 .50
77 Keegan Lowe CP .20 .50
78 Keith Hamilton CP .20 .50
79 Laurent Brossoit CP .25 .60
80 Mark McNeill CP .20 .50
81 Mathew Dumba CP .25 .60
82 Morgan Rielly CP .30 .75
83 Ryan Murray CP .30 .75
84 Sven Baertschi CP .25 .60
85 Troy Bourke CP .15 .40
86 Ty Rattie CP .30 .75
87 Ty Rimmer CP .20 .50
88 Tyler Wotherspoon CP .25 .60
89 Zachary Yuen CP .20 .50
90 Aaron Ekblad CR .60 1.50
91 Alex Forsberg CR .30 .75
92 Curtis Lazar CR .40 1.00
93 Daniel Altshuller CR .25 .60
94 Denis Kamaev CR .25 .60
95 Dominik Volek CR .25 .60
96 Eric Comrie CR .20 .50
97 Jamie Oleksiak CR .20 .50
98 Jordan Subban CR .40 1.00
99 Max Domi CR .50 1.25
100 Mikhail Grigorenko CR .60 1.50
101 Nathan MacKinnon CR 3.00 8.00
102 Olli Maatta CR .50 1.25
103 Adam Henrique AP .40 1.00
104 Ben Scrivens AP .30 .75
105 Bill Sweatt AP .20 .50
106 Blake Geoffrion AP .20 .50
107 Brandon Kozun AP .20 .50
108 Brandon Pirri AP .20 .50
109 Brendan Smith AP .20 .50
110 Casey Wellman AP .20 .50
111 Colin Greening AP .20 .50
112 David Savard AP .20 .50
113 Erik Gustafsson AP .25 .60
114 Gabriel Bourque AP .20 .50
115 Gabriel Dumont AP .20 .50
116 Greg Nemisz AP .20 .50
117 Jake Allen AP .40 1.00
118 Joe Colborne AP .20 .50
119 John Moore AP .20 .50
120 Jordan Caron AP .25 .60
121 Keven Veilleux AP .15 .40
122 Kyle Palmieri AP .20 .50
123 Luke Adam AP .20 .50
124 Mark Olver AP .15 .40
125 Martin Jones AP .40 1.00
126 Maxime Sauve AP .25 .60
127 Mike Murphy AP .20 .50
128 Nazem Kadri AP .40 1.00
129 Rhett Rakhshani AP .20 .50
130 Richard Bachman AP .20 .50
131 Robin Lehner AP .20 .50
132 Ryan Thang AP .15 .40
133 Tomas Kubalik AP .20 .50
134 Zac Dalpe AP .15 .40
135 Andy Miele AR .20 .50
136 Blake Kessel AR .20 .50
137 Brayden Schenn AR .25 .60
138 Calvin de Haan AR .20 .50
139 Cam Atkinson AR .50 1.25
140 Carl Klingberg AR .20 .50
141 Carter Ashton AR .25 .60
142 Cody Eakin AR .25 .60
143 Harri Sateri AR .20 .50
144 Justin Faulk AR .30 .75
145 Landon Ferraro AR .15 .40
146 Nathan Moon AR .15 .40
147 Ryan Ellis AR .20 .50
148 Stefan Elliott AR .20 .50
149 Taylor Beck AR .15 .40
150 Zack Kassian AR .25 .60
151 David Backes AG .25 .60
152 Patrice Bergeron AG .30 .75
153 Jay Bouwmeester AG .25 .60
154 Dustin Brown AG .25 .60
155 Mike Cammalleri AG .20 .50
156 Loui Eriksson AG .20 .50
157 Claude Giroux AG .25 .60
158 Michael Grabner AG .20 .50
159 Mikhail Grabovski AG .20 .50
160 Jaroslav Halak AG .25 .60
161 Jimmy Howard AG .25 .60
162 Ryan Kesler AG .25 .60
163 Mikko Koivu AG .20 .50
164 Kari Lehtonen AG .20 .50
165 Ryan Miller AG .25 .60
166 Kyle Okposo AG .25 .60
167 Zach Parise AG .25 .60
168 Jason Pominville AG .20 .50
169 Tuukka Rask AG .25 .60
170 Chris Stewart AG .20 .50
171 Cory Schneider AG .20 .50
172 Eric Staal AG .30 .75
173 Joey Crabb AG .15 .40
174 Thomas Vanek AG .25 .60
175 Semyon Varlamov AG .25 .60
176 Pekka Rinne AG .30 .75
177 Ryan Callahan CG .25 .60
178 Corey Crawford CG .30 .75
179 Logan Couture CG .25 .60
180 Tyler Ennis CG .20 .50
181 Marc-Andre Fleury CG .40 1.00
182 Ryan Getzlaf CG .40 1.00
183 Cody Hodgson CG .75 2.00
184 David Krejci CG .25 .60
185 Bryan Little CG .25 .60
186 Brad Marchand CG .30 .75
187 Corey Perry CG .25 .60
188 Carey Price CG .75 2.00
189 Bobby Ryan CG .25 .60
190 Devin Setoguchi CG .20 .50
191 Jason Spezza CG .25 .60
192 Dion Phaneuf CG .25 .60
193 P.K. Subban CG .50 1.25
194 Cam Ward CG .25 .60
195 Shea Weber CG .20 .50
196 Jonathan Bernier CG .25 .60
197 Luc Bourdon TRIB .50 1.25
198 Rick Rypien TRIB .40 1.00
199 Derek Boogaard TRIB .30 .75
200 Wade Belak TRIB .40 1.00
201 Jason Akeson .40 1.00
202 Matt Donovan .30 .75
203 Jonathan Audy-Marchessault
204 Gustav Nyquist 1.00 2.50
205 Louis Leblanc .40 1.00
206 Justin Fontaine .30 .75
207 Linden Vey .40 1.00
208 Cory Conacher .60 1.50
209 Tyler Johnson 1.00 2.50
210 Cade Fairchild .30 .75
211 Carter Camper .30 .75
212 Andrew Shaw 1.00 2.50
213 Edward Pasquale .40 1.00
214 Peter Holland .40 1.00
215 Matt Fraser .50 1.25
216 Tanner Pearson .50 1.25
217 Daniil Zharkov .30 .75
218 Matt Finn .30 .75
219 Scott Kosmachuk .30 .75
220 Radek Faksa .75 2.00
221 Cody Ceci .50 1.25
222 Sean Monahan 1.25 3.00
223 Gemel Smith .60 1.50
224 Tom Wilson .75 2.00
225 J.T. Miller .50 1.25
226 Kerby Rychel .30 .75
227 Brady Vail .30 .75
228 Mark Stone 1.00 2.50
229 Henrik Samuelsson .30 .75
230 Tim Bozon .30 .75
231 Damon Severson .50 1.25
232 Sam Reinhart 1.50 4.00
233 Emerson Etem .40 1.00
234 Hunter Shinkaruk .60 1.50
235 Mike Winther .30 .75
236 Chandler Stephenson .30 .75
237 Lukas Sutter .60 1.50
238 Dalton Thrower .30 .75
239 Branden Troock .30 .75
240 Raphael Bussieres .50 1.25
241 Christopher Clapperton .30 .75
242 Jeremy Gregoire .30 .75
243 Tomas Hyka .60 1.50
244 Zachary Fucale 1.00 2.50
245 Anthony Duclair .75 2.00
246 Adam Erne .60 1.50
247 Francis Beauvillier .30 .75
248 Dillon Fournier .30 .75
249 Charlie Coyle .30 .75
250 Brandon Whitney .75 2.00

2011-12 ITG Heroes and Prospects Autographs

OVERALL AUTO STATED ODDS 1:8
UDP INSERTED IN UPDATE SETS
AAE Aaron Ekblad 20.00 40.00
AAEN Andreas Engqvist 4.00 10.00
AAG Alex Galchenyuk 25.00 50.00
AAH Adam Henrique 8.00 20.00
AAK Alexander Khokhlachev 8.00 20.00
AAL Adam Larsson 10.00 25.00
AALO Adam Lowry 5.00 12.00
AAM Andy Miele 4.00 10.00
AAR Andrew Ryan 4.00 10.00
ABF Brian Foster UPD 5.00 12.00
ABG Brendan Gaunce 4.00 10.00
ABGE Blake Geoffrion 4.00 10.00
ABJ Boone Jenner 4.00 10.00
ABK Brandon Kozun 4.00 10.00
ABKE Blake Kessel 4.00 10.00
ABM Brad Marchand SP 8.00 20.00
ABP Brad Park SP 8.00 20.00
ABR Brett Ritchie 4.00 10.00
ABRA Brendan Ranford SP 10.00 25.00
ABRY Bobby Ryan SP 6.00 15.00
ABS Brandon Saad 8.00 20.00
ABSC Ben Scrivens 6.00 15.00
ABSW Bill Sweatt 4.00 10.00
ACA Cam Atkinson 10.00 25.00
ACB Chris Bourque UPD SP 6.00 15.00
ACD Calvin de Haan 4.00 10.00
ACG Colin Greening 4.00 10.00
ACGI Christopher Gibson 5.00 12.00
ACGIR Claude Giroux SP 5.00 30.00
ACH Charles Hudon 5.00 12.00
ACHO Cody Hodgson SP 25.00 50.00
ACK Carl Klingberg 4.00 10.00
ACN Cam Neely SP 10.00 25.00
ACPR Carey Price SP 12.00 30.00
ACS Colton Sissons 5.00 12.00
ACW Casey Wellman 4.00 10.00
ADG Domenic Graham 4.00 10.00
ADH Dougie Hamilton 12.00 30.00
ADHO David Honzik 5.00 12.00
ADM David Musil 4.00 10.00
ADP Dominic Poulin 4.00 10.00
ADPH Dion Phaneuf SP 8.00 20.00
ADPO Derrick Pouliot 8.00 20.00
ADS David Savard 4.00 10.00
ADSI Duncan Siemens SP 6.00 15.00
AEP Edward Pasquale UPD SP 5.00 12.00
AES Eric Staal SP
AGB Gabriel Bourque 4.00 10.00
AGD Gabriel Dumont 4.00 10.00
AGH Gordie Howe 60.00 100.00
AGN Greg Nemisz 4.00 10.00
AGR Griffin Reinhart SP 6.00 15.00
AHR Henri Richard SP 10.00 25.00
AHS Harri Sateri UPD 4.00 10.00
AIB Igor Bobkov UPD SP 6.00 15.00
AJA J.P. Anderson UPD SP 5.00 12.00
AJB Jordan Binnington 4.00 10.00
AJC Joey Crabb 3.00 8.00
AJE Joel Edmundson 4.00 10.00
AJF Jeremie Fraser 3.00 8.00
AJH Jonathan Huberdeau 12.00 30.00
AJHO Jimmy Howard SP 12.50 25.00
AJL Jacob Lagace UPD 4.00 10.00
AJM John Moore 4.00 10.00
AJMA Jarrod Maidens 5.00 12.00
AJMO Joe Morrow 6.00 15.00
AJP Jean-Gabriel Pageau 4.00 10.00
AJR Jonathan Racine SP 5.00 12.00
AJS Jordan Schroeder UPD SP 6.00 15.00
AJT Jarred Tinordi UPD SP
AKH Keith Hamilton SP 6.00 15.00
AKL Keegan Lowe 4.00 10.00
ALB Laurent Brossoit 5.00 12.00
ALBO Luc Bourdon TRIB 25.00 60.00
ALC Luca Ciampini 5.00 12.00
ALCO Logan Couture SP
ALE Loui Eriksson SP 6.00 15.00
ALF Landon Ferraro 3.00 8.00
ALL Louis Leblanc UPD 8.00 20.00
ALS Logan Shaw 4.00 10.00
AMC Mathew Campagna 4.00 10.00
AMCA Mike Cammalleri SP 5.00 12.00
AMD Mathew Dumba SP 6.00 15.00
AMDO Max Domi 12.00 30.00
AMF Martin Frk 5.00 12.00
AMG Mike Gartner SP 25.00 50.00
AMGR Mikhail Grigorenko 25.00 50.00
AMGRA Michael Grabner SP 8.00 20.00
AMGRAB Mikhail Grabovski SP 12.50 30.00
AMH Michael Houser UPD SP 5.00 12.00
AMI Max Iafrate 5.00 12.00
AMJ Martin Jones SP 10.00 25.00
AMK Mikko Koivu SP
AMM Matia Marcantuoni 4.00 10.00
AMMC Mark McNeill 4.00 10.00
AMMU Matt Murray SP 8.00 20.00
AMMUR Mike Murphy SP 5.00 12.00
AMO Mark Olver 3.00 8.00
AMP Matt Puempel 5.00 12.00
AMR Morgan Rielly 8.00 20.00
AMS Malcolm Subban SP 10.00 25.00
AMSC Mark Scheifele 8.00 20.00
AMZ Mika Zibanejad SP 8.00 20.00
ANB Nathan Beaulieu 5.00 12.00
ANE Nick Ebert 3.00 8.00
ANJ Nicklas Jensen 5.00 12.00
ANM Nathan MacKinnon 25.00 60.00
ANMO Nathan Moon 3.00 8.00
ANN Nino Niederreiter UPD 3.00 8.00
ANY Nail Yakupov 20.00 50.00
AOM Olli Maatta 15.00 30.00
APB Patrice Bergeron SP 20.00 40.00
APD Phillip Danault 5.00 12.00
APM Patrick Maroon UPD 4.00 10.00
ARB Richard Bachman SP
ARC Ryan Callahan SP 8.00 20.00
ARE Ryan Ellis SP 8.00 20.00
ARK Red Kelly SP 8.00 20.00
ARKE Ryan Kesler SP 20.00 40.00
ARM Ryan Murphy 5.00 12.00
ARMU Ryan Murray SP 8.00 20.00
ARR Rickard Rakell 5.00 12.00
ARS Ryan Spooner SP
ARST Ryan Strome 8.00 20.00
ART Ryan Tesink 5.00 12.00
ASB Sven Baertschi 10.00 25.00
ASC Sean Couturier 8.00 20.00
ASD Simon Despres UPD SP 8.00 20.00
ASG Scott Glennie UPD SP
ASK Slater Koekkoek 5.00 12.00
ASL Scott Laughton 5.00 12.00
ASM Shane McColgan UPD 5.00 12.00
ASN Stefan Noesen 5.00 12.00
ASO Scott Oke 4.00 10.00
ASP Stuart Percy 5.00 12.00
ASV Semyon Varlamov SP 12.00 30.00
ASW Shea Weber SP
ATA Tony Amonte SP 8.00 20.00
ATB Troy Bourke 3.00 8.00
ATJ Tomas Jurco 6.00 15.00
ATK Tomas Kubalik 4.00 10.00
ATR Ty Rattie 6.00 15.00
ATRI Ty Rimmer SP 5.00 12.00
ATS Teemu Selanne SP 20.00 40.00
ATV Thomas Vanek SP 10.00 25.00
ATW Tyler Wotherspoon 5.00 12.00
AVN Vladislav Namestnikov 8.00 20.00
AVR Victor Rask UPD 5.00 12.00
AVT Vladimir Tarasenko 40.00 100.00
AWB Wade Belak TRIB 15.00 40.00
AXO Xavier Ouellet 5.00 12.00
AZB Zach Boychuk UPD 3.00 8.00
AZD Zac Dalpe 3.00 8.00
AZK Zack Kassian 10.00 25.00
AZO Zach O'Brien 4.00 10.00
AZP Zack Phillips UPD 5.00 12.00
AAG2 Alex Galchenyuk UPD 25.00 50.00
ABG2 Brendan Gaunce UPD 4.00 10.00
ABMC Brayden McNabb UPD 4.00 10.00
ACS2 Colton Sissons UPD 5.00 12.00
AGR2 Griffin Reinhart UPD SP 6.00 15.00
AJCA Jack Campbell UPD SP 6.00 15.00
AMD2 Mathew Dumba UPD 5.00 12.00
AMF2 Martin Frk UPD SP 6.00 15.00
AMR2 Morgan Rielly UPD SP 10.00 25.00
AMS2 Malcolm Subban UPD 10.00 25.00
ANY2 Nail Yakupov UPD 40.00 80.00
AOM2 Olli Maatta UPD SP 15.00 30.00
ARBU Raphael Bussieres UPD SP 6.00 15.00
ASK2 Slater Koekkoek UPD SP 6.00 15.00
ATBE Tyler Beskorowany UPD SP 4.00 10.00
ATBR T.J. Brennan UPD SP 5.00 12.00
ATSE Tyson Sexsmith UPD SP 5.00 12.00
AALOK Andrei Loktionov UPD 4.00 10.00
ADPO2 Derrick Pouliot UPD 8.00 20.00
AMGR2 Mikhail Grigorenko UPD 15.00 40.00
ARMU2 Ryan Murray UPD 6.00 15.00

2011-12 ITG Heroes and Prospects Calder Cup Champions

COMPLETE SET (10) 15.00 30.00
OVERALL INSERT ODDS 1:8
CC01 Robin Lehner 1.50 4.00
CC02 Colin Greening 1.50 4.00
CC03 Ryan Potulny 1.25 3.00
CC04 Ryan Keller 1.25 3.00
CC05 Kaspars Daugavins 1.25 3.00
CC06 Zack Smith 1.25 3.00
CC07 Erik Condra 1.50 4.00
CC08 Bobby Butler 1.50 4.00
CC09 Andre Benoit 2.00 5.00
CC10 Corey Locke 1.50 4.00

2011-12 ITG Heroes and Prospects Class of 2012

OVERALL INSERT ODDS 1:8
C01 Nail Yakupov 8.00 20.00
C02 Mathew Dumba 12.00 30.00
C03 Morgan Rielly 6.00 15.00
C04 Alex Galchenyuk 10.00 25.00
C05 Mikhail Grigorenko 6.00 15.00
C06 Griffin Reinhart 6.00 15.00
C07 Ryan Murray 6.00 15.00
C08 Radek Faksa 5.00 12.00
C09 Martin Frk 4.00 10.00
C10 Derrick Pouliot 5.00 12.00

2011-12 ITG Heroes and Prospects Draft Day Stars Memorabilia Black

ANNOUNCED PRINT RUN 60 SETS
SILVER/20: .6X TO 1.5X BLACK/60*
DDSJ01 Nail Yakupov 10.00 25.00
DDSJ02 Ryan Murray 6.00 15.00
DDSJ03 Alex Galchenyuk 15.00 40.00
DDSJ04 Griffin Reinhart 5.00 12.00
DDSJ05 Morgan Rielly 6.00 15.00
DDSJ06 Mathew Dumba 5.00 12.00
DDSJ07 Derrick Pouliot 8.00 20.00
DDSJ08 Slater Koekkoek 5.00 12.00

2011-12 ITG Heroes and Prospects Dual Jerseys Silver

DJ01-DJ15 SLVR ANNOUNCED PRINT RUN 80
DJ16-DJ17 UPDATE ANNOUNCED PRINT RUN 50
OVERALL MEM INSERT ODDS 1:8
DJ01 N.Kadri/J.Colborne 12.00 30.00
DJ02 G.Reinhart/R.Murray 12.00 30.00
DJ03 N.MacKinnon/L.Ciampini 20.00 40.00
DJ04 S.Wedgewood/M.Visentin 5.00 12.00
DJ05 R.Murphy/M.Marcantuoni 5.00 12.00
DJ06 T.Rattie/S.Bartschi 10.00 25.00
DJ07 F.Hamilton/D.Hamilton 8.00 20.00
DJ08 L.Leblanc/P.Subban 15.00 40.00
DJ09 R.Ellis/B.Geoffrion 12.00 30.00
DJ10 J.Allen/J.Markstrom 8.00 20.00
DJ11 S.Couturier/B.Schenn 12.00 30.00
DJ12 S.Percy/J.Anderson 5.00 12.00
DJ13 J.Huberdeau/N.Beaulieu 15.00 30.00
DJ14 B.Jenner/N.Jensen 5.00 12.00
DJ15 A.Galchenyuk/N.Yakupov 20.00 50.00
DJ16 L.Brossoit/G.Reinhart 6.00 15.00
DJ17 Z.Kassian/C.Hodgson 10.00 25.00

2011-12 ITG Heroes and Prospects Family Ties

OVERALL INSERT ODDS 1:8
FT01 Reinhart/Reinhart/Reinhart/Reinhart 6.00 15.00
FT02 Geoffrion/Geoffrion/Morenz 2.50 6.00
FT03 Subban/Subban/Subban 3.00 8.00
FT04 Bourque/Bourque/Bourque 2.00 5.00
FT05 T.Domi/M.Domi 4.00 10.00
FT06 B.Ashton/C.Ashton 2.00 5.00
FT07 S.Burke/B.Burke 1.25 3.00
FT08 P.Roy/F.Roy 3.00 8.00

2011-12 ITG Heroes and Prospects Game Used Jerseys Black

BLACK ANNOUNCED PRINT RUN 100
*GOLD/10: .8X TO 2X BASIC JSY
*SILVER/30: .5X TO 1.2X BASIC JSY
M01-M50 OVERALL MEM ODDS 1:8
M51-M56 ISSUED IN UPDATE SET
M01 Zach Boychuk 3.00 8.00
M02 Matt Kassian 3.00 8.00
M03 Aaron Boogaard 4.00 10.00
M04 Dustin Boyd 4.00 10.00
M05 Alex Bourret 4.00 10.00
M06 Alexander Vasyunov 5.00 12.00
M07 Teddy Purcell 5.00 12.00
M08 Devan Dubnyk 5.00 12.00
M09 Ben Bishop 5.00 12.00
M10 Kyle Chipchura 3.00 8.00
M11 Mike MooreÂ• 3.00 8.00
M12 Joe Colborne 6.00 15.00
M13 Cal O'Reilly 3.00 8.00
M14 Kevin Shattenkirk 4.00 10.00
M15 Jeremie Fraser 3.00 8.00
M16 Logan Shaw 4.00 10.00
M17 Charles Hudon 5.00 12.00
M18 Dominic Poulin 4.00 10.00
M19 Sean Couturier 8.00 20.00
M20 Griffin Reinhart 5.00 12.00
M21 Keegan Lowe 4.00 10.00
M22 Laurent Brossoit 5.00 12.00
M23 Michael St. Croix 4.00 10.00
M24 Ryan Murray 6.00 15.00
M25 Richard Panik 5.00 12.00
M26 Anthony Terenzio 3.00 8.00
M27 Luca Ciampini 5.00 12.00
M28 Brendan Ranford 4.00 10.00
M29 Colton Sissons 5.00 12.00
M30 Matia Marcantuoni 4.00 10.00
M31 Scott Harrington 5.00 12.00
M32 Max Domi 8.00 20.00
M33 Stuart Percy 5.00 12.00
M34 Morgan Rielly 6.00 15.00
M35 Sean Aschim 3.00 8.00
M36 Boone Jenner 4.00 10.00
M37 Nicklas Jensen 5.00 12.00
M38 Slater Koekkoek 5.00 12.00
M39 Mark McNeill 4.00 10.00
M40 Troy Bourke 3.00 8.00
M41 Ty Rimmer 4.00 10.00
M42 Alex Galchenyuk 8.00 20.00
M43 Scott Oke 4.00 10.00
M44 Ryan Tesink 5.00 12.00
M45 Zack Phillips 5.00 12.00
M46 Zack Kassian 6.00 15.00
M47 Mac Engel 3.00 8.00
M48 Adam Lowry 5.00 12.00
M49 David Musil 4.00 10.00
M50 Nail Yakupov 12.00 30.00
M51 Ryan Kujawinski 4.00 10.00
M52 Scott Glennie 4.00 10.00
M53 Brody Silk 4.00 10.00
M54 Cody Ceci 4.00 10.00
M55 Mikhail Grigorenko 10.00 25.00
M56 Radek Faksa 6.00 15.00

2011-12 ITG Heroes and Prospects He Shoots He Scores Prizes

HSHS01 Nail Yakupov 25.00 60.00
HSHS02 R.Strome/Niederreiter 10.00 25.00
HSHS03 Sean Couturier 12.00 30.00
HSHS04 J.Blum/R.Ellis 6.00 15.00
HSHS05 Jonathan Huberdeau 15.00 40.00
HSHS06 R.Lehner/B.Bishop 8.00 20.00
HSHS07 Dougie Hamilton 15.00 40.00
HSHS08 B.Schenn/S.Couturier 12.00 30.00
HSHS09 Charles Hudon 8.00 20.00
HSHS10 N.Yakupov/Galchenyuk 25.00 60.00
HSHS11 Louis Leblanc 6.00 15.00
HSHS12 D.Hamilton/F.Hamilton 15.00 40.00
HSHS13 Ryan Murray 10.00 25.00
HSHS14 M.Domi/N.MacKinnon 30.00 60.00
HSHS15 Sven Baertschi 8.00 20.00
HSHS16 R.Faksa/R.Murphy 12.00 30.00
HSHS17 Mikhail Grigorenko 20.00 50.00
HSHS18 N.Kadri/J.Reimer 12.00 30.00
HSHS19 Matt Dumba 8.00 20.00
HSHS20 M.Visentin/Wedgewood 8.00 20.00
HSHS21 Nathan MacKinnon 30.00 60.00
HSHS22 Grigorenko/N.Yakupov 25.00 60.00
HSHS23 Max Domi 15.00 40.00
HSHS24 M.Dumba/R.Murray 10.00 25.00
HSHS25 Griffin Reinhart 8.00 20.00
HSHS26 S.Bartschi/G.Nemisz 8.00 20.00
HSHS27 Robin Lehner 6.00 15.00
HSHS28 L.Leblanc/N.Beaulieu 8.00 20.00
HSHS29 Alex Galchenyuk 25.00 60.00
HSHS30 J.Binnington/S.Stajcer 6.00 15.00

2011-12 ITG Heroes and Prospects Hero and Prospect Jerseys Silver

SILVER ANNOUNCED PRINT RUN 50
OVERALL MEM INSERT ODDS 1:8
HP01 S.Weber/R.Ellis 20.00 50.00
HP02 B.Clarke/S.Couturier 8.00 20.00
HP03 R.Bourque/D.Hamilton 12.00 30.00
HP04 G.Hall/J.Allen 10.00 25.00
HP05 G.Lafleur/L.Leblanc 15.00 40.00
HP06 E.Lindros/B.Schenn 12.00 30.00
HP07 T.Domi/M.Domi 12.00 30.00
HP08 P.Coffey/G.Reinhart 6.00 15.00
HP09 N.Lidstrom/A.Larsson 8.00 20.00
HP10 A.Ovechkin/N.Yakupov 15.00 40.00

2011-12 ITG Heroes and Prospects Heroes Memorabilia Silver

H01-H10 SLVR ANNOUNCED PRINT RUN 9-60
H11-H14 SLVR/20 INSERTED IN UPDATE SET
OVERALL MEM INSERT ODDS 1:8
HM01 Brett Hull 6.00 15.00
HM02 Cam Neely 5.00 12.00
HM03 Eric Lindros 8.00 20.00
HM04 Mike Gartner 6.00 15.00
HM05 Pavel Bure 10.00 25.00
HM06 Shea Weber 6.00 15.00
HM07 Teemu Selanne 8.00 20.00
HM08 Theoren Fleury 12.00 30.00
HM10 Trevor Linden 10.00 25.00
HM11 Mats Sundin 10.00 25.00
HM12 Joe Sakic 15.00 40.00
HM13 Pavel Bure 12.00 30.00
HM14 Adam Oates 10.00 25.00

2011-12 ITG Heroes and Prospects Memorial Cup Champions

COMPLETE SET (10) 20.00 40.00
OVERALL INSERT ODDS 1:8
MC01 Jonathan Huberdeau 4.00 10.00
MC02 Michael Kirkpatrick 2.00 5.00
MC03 Stanislav Galiev 2.00 5.00
MC04 Tomas Jurco 2.50 6.00
MC05 Ryan Tesink 2.00 5.00
MC06 Simon Despres 1.50 4.00
MC07 Zack Phillips 2.00 5.00
MC08 Kevin Gagne 1.50 4.00
MC09 Jacob DeSerres 2.00 5.00
MC10 Nathan Beaulieu 2.00 5.00

2011-12 ITG Heroes and Prospects Moving All the Way Up Dual Jerseys Silver

SILVER ANNOUNCED PRINT RUN 50
OVERALL MEM INSERT ODDS 1:8
MAU01 Marc-Andre Fleury 8.00 20.00
MAU02 Ryan Getzlaf 6.00 15.00
MAU03 Mikko Koivu 4.00 10.00
MAU04 Ryan Miller 5.00 12.00
MAU05 Rick Nash 10.00 25.00
MAU06 Corey Perry 5.00 12.00
MAU07 Carey Price 15.00 40.00
MAU08 Jason Spezza 5.00 12.00
MAU09 Shea Weber 6.00 15.00
MAU10 Alexander Ovechkin 20.00 50.00

2011-12 ITG Heroes and Prospects Moving Up Dual Jerseys Silver

SILVER ANNOUNCED PRINT RUN 50
OVERALL MEM INSERT ODDS 1:8
MU01 Robin Lehner 5.00 12.00
MU02 Devan Dubnyk 6.00 15.00
MU03 Zach Boychuk 4.00 10.00
MU04 Thomas Hickey 5.00 12.00
MU05 Patrick O'Sullivan 4.00 10.00

2011-12 ITG Heroes and Prospects National Pride Jerseys Silver

SILVER ANNOUNCED PRINT RUN 40
OVERALL MEM INSERT ODDS 1:8
NAT01 Adam Larsson
NAT02 Tomas Jurco
NAT03 Sven Bartschi 8.00 20.00
NAT04 Alex Galchenyuk 10.00 25.00
NAT05 Emerson Etem 10.00 25.00
NAT06 Christopher Gibson 6.00 15.00
NAT07 Nicklas Jensen 6.00 15.00
NAT08 David Musil 5.00 12.00
NAT09 Jonathan Huberdeau 12.00 30.00
NAT10 Brendan Gallagher 15.00 40.00

2011-12 ITG Heroes and Prospects Net Prospects Jerseys Silver

SILVER ANNOUNCED PRINT RUN 40
OVERALL MEM INSERT ODDS 1:8
NP01 Kevin Bailie 6.00 15.00
NP02 Jacob Markstrom 6.00 15.00
NP03 Martin Jones 8.00 20.00
NP04 Mike Murphy
NP05 Christopher Gibson 6.00 15.00
NP06 Scott Wedgewood 6.00 15.00
NP07 Mark Visentin 5.00 12.00
NP08 Louis Domingue 4.00 10.00
NP09 Olivier Roy
NP10 Calvin Pickard 6.00 15.00

2011-12 ITG Heroes and Prospects Prospect Trios Jerseys Silver

SILVER ANNOUNCED PRINT RUN 50
OVERALL MEM INSERT ODDS 1:8
PT01 Machck/Holzpfel/Cormier 8.00 20.00
PT02 Tarasenko/Rattie/Allen 20.00 50.00
PT03 Larssn/Clermnt/Wedgewd 8.00 20.00
PT04 Colborne/Kadri/Percy 10.00 25.00
PT05 Hamilton/Caron/Spooner 8.00 20.00
PT06 Lehner/Pageau/Puempel 12.00 30.00
PT07 Huber/Markstrom/Howden 12.00 30.00
PT08 Jones/Hickey/Toffoli 6.00 15.00
PT09 Ellis/Geoffrio/Pickard 10.00 25.00
PT10 Adam/Kassian/EnrothÂ• 8.00 20.00

2011-12 ITG Heroes and Prospects Quad Jerseys Silver

SILVER ANNOUNCED PRINT RUN 80
*PATCH SILVER/19: 1X TO 2.5X SLVR JSY/80
QJ01 Rnhrt/Lwe/St.Crx/Brss 12.00 30.00

QJ02 Mrph/Mrks/Allen/Jnes 12.00 30.00
QJ03 Strme/Hmiltn's/Visnt 12.00 30.00
QJ04 Huber/Phill/Beaul/Jrco 12.00 30.00
QJ05 Kadri/Adm/Carn/Geof 10.00 25.00
QJ06 Schn/Ashtn/Kassn/Vey 8.00 20.00
QJ07 Mrry/Rielly/Dmba/Rein 12.00 30.00
QJ08 Hmltn/Mrphy/Lrsn/Smns 12.00 30.00
QJ09 Rattie/Brts/Mrrw/Wthr 15.00 40.00
QJ10 Listn/Hnzik/Gbsn/Binn 10.00 25.00

2011-12 ITG Heroes and Prospects Subway Series Jerseys Black

BLACK ANNOUNCED PRINT RUN 100
*GOLD/10: .8X TO 2X BASIC JSY
*SILVER/30: .5X TO 1.2X BASIC JSY
OVERALL MEM ODDS 1:8
SSM01 Matthew Bissonnette 3.00 8.00
SSM02 Daniel Catenacci 4.00 10.00
SSM03 Andrew D'Agostini 4.00 10.00
SSM04 Yannick Dube 5.00 12.00
SSM05 Mathew Dumba 5.00 12.00
SSM06 Brendan Gallagher 12.00 30.00
SSM07 Tyler Graovac 5.00 12.00
SSM08 Philippe Halley 4.00 10.00
SSM09 Freddie Hamilton 5.00 12.00
SSM10 Quinton Howden 4.00 10.00
SSM11 Charles Hudon 5.00 12.00
SSM12 Maxime Lagace 5.00 12.00
SSM13 Lucas Lessio 4.00 10.00
SSM14 Adam Lowry 5.00 12.00
SSM15 Nathan MacKinnon 20.00 40.00
SSM16 Joe Morrow 6.00 15.00
SSM17 Zach O'Brien 4.00 10.00
SSM18 Jean-Gabriel Pageau 4.00 10.00
SSM19 Tanner Pearson 5.00 12.00
SSM20 Stuart Percy 4.00 10.00
SSM21 Brett Ritchie 4.00 10.00
SSM22 Ryan Spooner 5.00 12.00
SSM23 Ryan Strome 5.00 12.00
SSM24 Kevin Sundher 4.00 10.00
SSM25 Sean Couturier 6.00 15.00

2011-12 ITG Heroes and Prospects Subway Series Trios Jerseys Silver

SILVER ANNOUNCED PRINT RUN 70
OVERALL MEM ODDS 1:8
SST01 Dumba/Gallagher/Morrow 8.00 20.00
SST02 MacKin/Hudon/Pagu 10.00 25.00
SST03 Pearson/Strome/Catenci 8.00 20.00
SST04 Wdgewd/Andrsn/Visentin 6.00 15.00
SST05 Roy/Stajcer/Pickard 5.00 12.00
SST06 Coutur/Grmly/Beaul 10.00 25.00
SST07 Bourn/Hubr/Leblanc 15.00 40.00
SST08 Dohrty/Hamilt/Pmpl 15.00 40.00
SST09 Howdn/Murry/Ratt 15.00 40.00
SST10 Jenner/McKg/Thoms 6.00 15.00
SST11 Allen/Domingue/Jones 10.00 25.00
SST12 Vey/Glennie/Pysyk 8.00 20.00
SST13 Kadri/Kassn/Schenn 12.00 30.00
SST14 Cormier/Carn/Desprs 12.00 30.00
SST15 Ennis/Hdgsn/Coutre
SST16 Ellis/Subban/Matthias 12.00 30.00
SST17 Sexsmith/Irving/Hickey 8.00 20.00
SST18 Alzner/Mrchnd/Del Zot 10.00 25.00
SST19 Stewart/Setoguchi/Little 6.00 15.00
SST20 Price/Giroux/Helm 10.00 25.00

2011-12 ITG Heroes and Prospects Top Prospects Jerseys Black

BLACK ANNOUNCED PRINT RUN 100
*GOLD/10: .8X TO 2X BASIC JSY
*SILVER/30: .5X TO 1.2X BASIC JSY
OVERALL MEM ODDS 1:8
TPM01 Sven Bartschi 5.00 12.00
TPM02 Myles Bell 4.00 10.00
TPM03 Jordan Binnington 4.00 10.00
TPM04 Sean Couturier 6.00 15.00
TPM05 Christopher Gibson 5.00 12.00
TPM06 Dougie Hamilton 10.00 25.00
TPM07 David Honzik 5.00 12.00
TPM08 Colin Jacobs 4.00 10.00
TPM09 Tomas Jurco 6.00 15.00
TPM10 Lucas Lessio 4.00 10.00
TPM11 Liam Liston 3.00 8.00
TPM12 Shane McColgan 5.00 12.00
TPM13 Ryan Murphy 5.00 12.00
TPM14 David Musil 4.00 10.00
TPM15 Vladislav Namestnikov 8.00 20.00
TPM16 Matt Puempel 5.00 12.00
TPM17 Ty Rattie 6.00 15.00
TPM18 Brandon Saad 6.00 15.00
TPM19 Duncan Siemens 5.00 12.00
TPM20 Ryan Strome 6.00 15.00

2011-12 ITG Heroes and Prospects Tough Customers

OVERALL INSERT ODDS 1:8
TC01 Joel Rechlicz 1.50 4.00
TC02 Zack FitzGerald 1.25 3.00
TC03 Garnet Exelby 1.25 3.00
TC04 Matt Clackson 1.50 4.00
TC05 Pierre-Luc Letourneau-Leblond 1.50 4.00
TC06 Zac Rinaldo 1.50 4.00
TC07 Francis Lessard 1.25 3.00

2012-13 ITG Heroes and Prospects

COMP.SET w/o SPs (150) 15.00 40.00
1 Adam Oates H .25 .60
2 Al MacInnis H .25 .60
3 Chris Chelios H .25 .60
4 Doug Gilmour H .30 .75
5 Eric Lindros H .40 1.00
6 Evgeni Malkin H .75 2.00
7 Gilbert Perreault H .25 .60
8 Gordie Howe H .50 1.25
9 Grant Fuhr H .25 .60
10 Guy Lafleur H .30 .75
11 Henri Richard H .25 .60
12 Jari Kurri H .25 .60
13 Jean Beliveau H .25 .60
14 Jeremy Roenick H .25 .60
15 Joe Sakic H .40 1.00
16 Keith Tkachuk H .25 .60
17 Mario Lemieux H .75 2.00
18 Mark Recchi H .30 .75
19 Mats Sundin H .25 .60
20 Nicklas Lidstrom H .25 .60
21 Patrick Roy H .60 1.50
22 Pavel Bure H .30 .75
23 Peter Forsberg H .25 .60
24 Phil Esposito H .40 1.00
25 Scott Niedermayer H .25 .60
26 Sergei Fedorov H .40 1.00
27 Steve Yzerman H .50 1.25
28 Theoren Fleury H .30 .75
29 Tony Esposito H .25 .60
30 Trevor Linden H .25 .60
31 Connor McDavid CHL 4.00 10.00
32 Roland McKeown CHL .20 .50
33 Sam Bennett CHL .40 1.00
34 Michael Dal Colle CHL .20 .50
35 Dominik Kubalik CHL .15 .40
36 Josh Ho-Sang CHL .30 .75
37 Stefan Matteau CHL .25 .60
38 Laurent Dauphin CHL .15 .40
39 Ivan Barbashev CHL .25 .60
40 Alexis Pepin CHL .20 .50
41 Anthony DeLuca CHL .25 .60
42 Frederik Gauthier CHL .40 1.00
43 Dylan Labbe CHL .15 .40
44 Daniel Audette CHL .30 .75
45 Jake Virtanen CHL .30 .75
46 Miles Koules CHL .15 .40
47 Brayden Point CHL .25 .60
48 Oliver Bjorkstrand CHL .15 .40
49 Eetu Laurikainen CHL .25 .60
50 Patrik Polivka CHL .25 .60
51 Aaron Ekblad OHL .50 1.25
52 Mark Scheifele OHL .30 .75
53 Brendan Gaunce OHL .20 .50
54 Daniil Zharkov OHL .15 .40
55 Malcolm Subban OHL .30 .75
56 Dylan Blujus OHL .15 .40
57 Oscar Dansk OHL .40 1.00
58 Garret Sparks OHL .30 .75
59 Matt Finn OHL .25 .60
60 Scott Kosmachuk OHL .15 .40
61 Matt Puempel OHL .25 .60
62 Radek Faksa OHL .30 .75
63 Ryan Murphy OHL .25 .60
64 Olli Maatta OHL .05 .15
65 Seth Griffith OHL .40 1.00
66 Stuart Percy OHL .25 .60
67 Brett Ritchie OHL .20 .50
68 Dougie Hamilton OHL .75 2.00
69 Ryan Strome OHL .30 .75
70 Boone Jenner OHL .20 .50
71 Scott Laughton OHL .25 .60
72 Cody Ceci OHL .20 .50
73 Tyler Graovac OHL .15 .40
74 Gemel Smith OHL .25 .60
75 Nick Ritchie OHL .25 .60
76 Slater Koekkoek OHL .20 .50
77 Rickard Rakell OHL .25 .60
78 Stefan Noesen OHL .20 .50
79 Tom Wilson OHL .40 1.00
80 Vincent Trocheck OHL .30 .75
81 Alex Galchenyuk OHL 1.00 2.50
82 Anthony DeAngelo OHL .15 .40
83 Matt Murray OHL .25 .60
84 Ryan Sproul OHL .25 .60
85 Joshua Leivo OHL .20 .50
86 Brady Vail OHL .15 .40
87 Zach Oâ•™Brien QMJHL .20 .50
88 Christophe Lalancette QMJHL .15 .40
89 Raphael Bussieres QMJHL .25 .60
90 Christopher Clapperton QMJHL .15 .40
91 Xavier Ouellet QMJHL .25 .60
92 Charles Hudon QMJHL .25 .60
93 Olivier Archambault QMJHL .20 .50
94 Tomas Hyka QMJHL .25 .60
95 Konrad Abeltshauser QMJHL .15 .40
96 Luca Ciampini QMJHL .25 .60
97 Martin Frk QMJHL .25 .60
98 James Melindy QMJHL .15 .40
99 Jonathan Racine QMJHL .20 .50
100 Mikhail Grigorenko QMJHL .75 2.00
101 Logan Shaw QMJHL .20 .50
102 Ryan Culkin QMJHL .20 .50
103 Francois Brassard QMJHL .15 .40
104 Scott Oke QMJHL .20 .50
105 Francis Beauvillier QMJHL .15 .40
106 Jean-Sebastien Dea QMJHL .20 .50
107 Dillon Fournier QMJHL .15 .40
108 Jonathan Huberdeau QMJHL .60 1.50
109 Ryan Tesink QMJHL .25 .60
110 Stephen MacAulay QMJHL .20 .50
111 Anton Zlobin QMJHL .20 .50
112 Francois Tremblay QMJHL .20 .50
113 Phillip Danault QMJHL .20 .50
114 Brandon Whitney QMJHL .25 .60
115 Chris Driedger WHL .20 .50
116 Griffin Reinhart WHL .25 .60
117 Henrik Samuelsson WHL .20 .50
118 Laurent Brossoit WHL .25 .60
119 Michael St. Croix WHL .15 .40
120 Mitchell Moroz WHL .20 .50
121 Ryan Murray WHL .30 .75
122 Brendan Ranford WHL .20 .50
123 Tim Bozon WHL .40 1.00
124 Colton Sissons WHL .25 .60
125 Damon Severson WHL .20 .50
126 Myles Bell WHL .15 .40
127 Sam Reinhart WHL .60 1.50
128 Jayden Hart WHL .15 .40
129 Morgan Rielly WHL .30 .75
130 Derrick Pouliot WHL .30 .75
131 Nicolas Petan WHL .25 .60
132 Troy Rutkowski WHL .15 .40
133 Ty Rattie WHL .25 .60
134 Mark McNeill WHL .25 .60
135 Colin Jacobs WHL .15 .40
136 Troy Bourke WHL .15 .40
137 Mathew Dumba WHL .25 .60
138 Chandler Stephenson WHL .15 .40
139 Andrey Makarov WHL .25 .60
140 Dalton Thrower WHL .15 .40
141 Lukas Sutter WHL .25 .60
142 Shane McColgan WHL .15 .40
143 Branden Troock WHL .15 .40
144 Liam Stewart WHL .20 .50
145 Adam Lowry WHL .25 .60
146 Coda Gordon WHL .15 .40
147 Zachary Yuen WHL .20 .50
148 David Musil WHL .20 .50
149 Marek Tvrdon WHL .15 .40
150 Keegan Kanzig WHL .15 .40
151 Nathan MacKinnon C13 10.00 25.00
152 Sean Monahan C13 8.00 20.00
153 Seth Jones C13 8.00 20.00
154 Ryan Kujawinski C13 2.50 6.00
155 Kerby Rychel C13 3.00 8.00
156 Eric Roy C13 3.00 8.00
157 Darnell Nurse C13 4.00 10.00
158 Morgan Klimchuk C13 3.00 8.00
159 Nick Baptiste C13 2.50 6.00
160 Jeremy Gregoire C13 2.50 6.00
161 Ryan Pulock C13 4.00 10.00
162 Zachary Fucale C13 6.00 15.00
163 Adam Erne C13 3.00 8.00
164 Curtis Lazar C13 4.00 10.00
165 Hunter Shinkaruk C13 5.00 12.00
166 Anthony Duclair C13 5.00 12.00
167 Jonathan Drouin C13 8.00 20.00
168 Nick Sorensen C13 3.00 8.00
169 Josh Morrissey C13 3.00 8.00
170 Eric Comrie C13 3.00 8.00
171 Bo Horvat C13 6.00 15.00
172 Madison Bowey C13 3.00 8.00
173 Alex Forsberg C13 3.00 8.00
174 Max Domi C13 6.00 15.00
175 William Carrier C13 3.00 8.00
176 Jordan Subban C13 4.00 10.00
177 Anthony Mantha C13 5.00 12.00
178 Connor Rankin C13 2.50 6.00
179 Shea Theodore C13 3.00 8.00
180 Jason Dickinson C13 2.50 6.00
181 Spencer Martin C13 2.50 6.00
182 Greg Chase C13 2.50 6.00
183 Jamal Watson C13 2.50 6.00
184 Stephen Harper C13 4.00 10.00
185 Zach Nastasiuk C13 3.00 8.00
186 Nikita Zadorov C13 3.00 8.00
187 Brody Silk C13 2.50 6.00
188 Carter Hansen C13 2.50 6.00
189 Brian Williams C13 2.50 6.00
190 Chris Bigras C13 2.50 6.00
191 Matt Murphy C13 3.00 8.00
192 Nikolas Brouillard C13 4.00 10.00
193 Ryan Hartman C13 3.00 8.00
194 Matt Needham C13 4.00 10.00
195 Samuel Morin C13 4.00 10.00
196 Jay Merkley C13 2.50 6.00
197 Justin Bailey C13 2.50 6.00
198 Martin Reway C13 2.50 6.00
199 Sergey Tolchinsky C13 2.50 6.00

2012-13 ITG Heroes and Prospects Autographs

AAD Anthony DeLuca 5.00 12.00
AADU Anthony Duclair 8.00 20.00
AAE Aaron Ekblad 10.00 25.00
AAER Adam Erne 5.00 12.00
AAF Alex Forsberg SP 6.00 15.00
AAG Alex Galchenyuk 25.00 50.00
AAL Adam Lowry 5.00 12.00
AAM Anthony Mantha SP 10.00 25.00
AAMA Andrey Makarov SP 6.00 15.00
AAO Adam Oates Hero SP 15.00 30.00
AAP Alexis Pepin 4.00 10.00
AAZ Anton Zlobin 4.00 10.00
ABG Brendan Gaunce 4.00 10.00
ABH Bo Horvat 8.00 20.00
ABW Brandon Whitney SP 6.00 15.00
ACB Clark Bishop 3.00 8.00
ACC Cody Ceci 4.00 10.00
ACCH Chris Chelios Hero SP 8.00 20.00
ACD Chris Driedger SP 5.00 12.00
ACG Christopher Gibson SP 6.00 15.00
ACH Charles Hudon 5.00 12.00
ACJ Colin Jacobs 3.00 8.00
ACL Curtis Lazar SP 8.00 20.00
ACM Connor McDavid SP 100.00 175.00
ACR Connor Rankin 3.00 8.00
ACS Chandler Stephenson 3.00 8.00
ACSI Colton Sissons 5.00 12.00
ADA Daniel Audette 6.00 15.00
ADAL Daniel Altshuller SP 5.00 12.00
ADB Dakota Odgers 4.00 10.00
ADG Doug Gilmour Hero SP 20.00 40.00
ADH Dougie Hamilton 8.00 20.00
ADN Darnell Nurse 10.00 25.00
ADP Derrick Pouliot 6.00 15.00
AEC Eric Comrie SP 6.00 15.00
AEL Eetu Laurikainen SP 6.00 15.00
AER Eric Roy 8.00 20.00
AFG Frederik Gauthier 12.00 30.00
AFT Francois Tremblay SP 5.00 12.00
AGH Gordie Howe Hero SP 60.00 120.00
AGL Guy Lafleur Hero SP 20.00 40.00
AGP Gilbert Perreault Hero SP 20.00 40.00
AGR Griffin Reinhart 5.00 12.00
AHR Henri Richard Hero SP 15.00 30.00
AHS Henrik Samuelsson 4.00 10.00
AHSH Hunter Shinkaruk 10.00 25.00
AJA J.P. Anderson SP 5.00 12.00
AJB Justin Bailey 4.00 10.00
AJBE Jean Beliveau Hero SP 20.00 50.00
AJBI Jordan Binnington SP 6.00 15.00
AJD Jason Dickinson SP 5.00 12.00
AJDR Jonathan Drouin SP 25.00 60.00
AJG Jeremy Gregoire 4.00 10.00
AJGI John Gibson SP 12.50 25.00
AJH Josh Ho-Sang 6.00 15.00
AJHU Jonathan Huberdeau 12.00 30.00
AJK Jari Kurri Hero SP 15.00 30.00
AJM Josh Morrissey 5.00 12.00
AJP Jake Paterson SP 8.00 20.00
AJR Jeremy Roenick Hero SP 15.00 40.00
AJS Jordan Subban 6.00 15.00
AJSA Joe Sakic Hero SP 25.00 50.00
AJV Jake Virtanen 6.00 15.00
AKA Konrad Abeltshauser 3.00 8.00
AKB Kevin Bailie SP 6.00 15.00
AKK Kale Kessy 3.00 8.00
AKR Kerby Rychel 5.00 12.00
AKT Keith Tkachuk Hero SP 10.00 25.00
ALB Laurent Brossoit SP 6.00 15.00
ALS Liam Stewart 4.00 10.00
AMB Madison Bowey 5.00 12.00
AMD Mathew Dumba 5.00 12.00
AMDO Max Domi 10.00 25.00
AMF Martin Frk 5.00 12.00
AMFI Matt Finn 5.00 12.00
AMG Mikhail Grigorenko 10.00 25.00
AMK Morgan Klimchuk 5.00 12.00
AMM Mitchell Moroz 4.00 10.00
AMMU Matt Murray 5.00 12.00
AMR Morgan Reilly 6.00 15.00
AMRE Mark Recchi Hero SP 15.00 30.00
AMS Mark Scheifele 6.00 15.00
AMST Michael St. Croix 3.00 8.00
AMSU Malcolm Subban SP 10.00 25.00
ANB Nick Baptiste 4.00 10.00
ANL Nicklas Lidstrom Hero SP 25.00 50.00
ANM Nathan MacKinnon SP 40.00 80.00
ANP Nicolas Petan 5.00 12.00
ANR Nick Ritchie 5.00 12.00
ANS Nick Sorensen 5.00 12.00
ANY Nail Yakupov 15.00 40.00
ANZ Nikita Zadorov 5.00 12.00
AOD Oscar Dansk SP 10.00 25.00
AOM Olli Maatta 20.00 40.00
APB Pavel Bure Hero SP 25.00 50.00
APD Phillip Danault 4.00 10.00
APE Phil Esposito Hero SP 20.00 40.00
APF Peter Forsberg Hero SP 25.00 50.00
APP Patrik Polivka SP 6.00 15.00
ARB Raphael Bussieres 5.00 12.00
ARC Ryan Culkin 4.00 10.00
ARF Radek Faksa 6.00 15.00
ARG Robin Gusse SP 5.00 12.00
ARH Ryan Hartman 5.00 12.00
ARK Ryan Kujawinski 4.00 10.00
ARM Roland McKeown 4.00 10.00
ARM Ryan Murray 6.00 15.00
ARMU Ryan Murphy SP 6.00 15.00
ARP Ryan Pulock 6.00 15.00
ARS Ryan Strome 6.00 15.00
ASG Seth Griffith 8.00 20.00
ASJ Seth Jones SP 15.00 40.00
ASK Slater Koekkoek 4.00 10.00
ASL Scott Laughton 5.00 12.00
ASM Sean Monahan 12.00 30.00
ASMA Stefan Matteau 5.00 12.00
ASMAR Spencer Martin SP 5.00 12.00
ASN Scott Niedermayer Hero SP 20.00 40.00
ASR Sam Reinhart SP 25.00 50.00
AST Shea Theodore 5.00 12.00
ASTO Sergey Tolchinsky 3.00 8.00
ASY Steve Yzerman Hero SP 30.00 60.00
ATB Tim Bozon 8.00 20.00
ATF Theoren Fleury Hero SP 20.00 40.00
ATW Tom Wilson 8.00 20.00
AVT Vincent Trocheck 6.00 15.00
AWC William Carrier 5.00 12.00
AZF Zachary Fucale SP 20.00 40.00
AZO Zach O'Brien 4.00 10.00

2012-13 ITG Heroes and Prospects Dual Jerseys

ANNOUNCED PRINT RUN 40
DJ01 Subban/Gaunce 8.00 20.00
DJ02 Galchenyk/Yakupov 30.00 60.00
DJ03 Strome/D.Hamilton 12.00 30.00
DJ04 R.Faksa/R.Murphy 8.00 20.00
DJ05 McKeown/Kujawnsk 5.00 12.00
DJ06 Jenner/Altshuller 5.00 12.00
DJ07 Ranford/Bozon 10.00 25.00
DJ08 Reinhart/Brossoit 6.00 15.00
DJ09 McDavid/Reinhart 15.00 40.00
DJ10 Bourke/Forsberg 6.00 15.00
DJ11 Huberdeau/Tesink 15.00 40.00
DJ12 Murphy/Mantha 10.00 25.00
DJ13 DeLuca/Gauthier 10.00 25.00
DJ14 Shaw/Grigorenko 12.00 30.00
DJ15 MacKinnon/Drouin 20.00 50.00

2012-13 ITG Heroes and Prospects Hero and Prospect Jerseys

ANNOUNCED PRINT RUN 40
HP01 D.Potvin/Reinhart 8.00 20.00
HP02 B.Salming/M.Rielly 10.00 25.00
HP03 E.Lindros/B.Jenner 12.00 30.00
HP04 Lemieux/MacKinn 25.00 50.00
HP05 C.Price/E.Comrie 25.00 60.00
HP06 P.Bure/Yakupov 20.00 50.00
HP07 J.Jagr/R.Faksa 12.00 30.00
HP08 Bourque/Hamilton 12.00 30.00
HP09 Perreault/Grigornk 15.00 40.00

2012-13 ITG Heroes and Prospects Heroes Memorabilia

HM01 Al MacInnis 12.00 30.00
HM02 Patrick Roy 20.00 50.00
HM03 Jari Kurri
HM04 Theoren Fleury 15.00 40.00
HM05 Sergei Fedorov 15.00 40.00
HM06 Pavel Bure 15.00 40.00
HM07 Joe Sakic 15.00 40.00
HM08 Mario Lemieux 20.00 50.00
HM09 Scott Niedermayer 12.00 30.00

2012-13 ITG Heroes and Prospects Net Prospects Memorabilia

N01 Laurent Brossoit 5.00 12.00
N02 Ty Rimmer 4.00 10.00
N03 Cole Cheveldave 6.00 15.00
N04 Jordan Binnington 5.00 12.00
N05 Kevin Bailie 5.00 12.00
N06 J.P. Anderson 4.00 10.00
N07 Robin Gusse 4.00 10.00
N08 Malcolm Subban 6.00 15.00
N09 Zach Fucale 10.00 25.00

2012-13 ITG Heroes and Prospects Prospects Trios Jerseys

PT01 Fucal/MacKin/Drn 25.00 60.00
PT02 Koekko/Ritch/Giogvz 8.00 20.00
PT03 Ranford/Bozn/Chevldv 12.00 30.00
PT04 Cooke/Baillie/Sissons 8.00 20.00
PT05 Huberd/Shaw/Hodgs 20.00 50.00
PT06 Poult/Murry/Marcantni 10.00 25.00
PT07 Galchenyk/Hudn/Bozn 25.00 60.00
PT08 Scheifl/Suttr/Lowry 10.00 25.00
PT09 Rielly/Finn/Percy 10.00 25.00

2012-13 ITG Heroes and Prospects He Shoots He Scores Points

EACH HAS NINE CARDS OF EQUAL VALUE
AG1 Alex Galchenyuk 1.00 2.50
AM1 Anthony Mantha .50 1.25
CM1 Connor McDavid 1.25 3.00
HS1 Hunter Shinkaruk .50 1.25
MG1 Mikhail Grigorenko .60 1.50
MS1 Malcolm Subban .40 1.00
NM1 Nathan MacKinnon 1.00 2.50
RM1 Ryan Murray .40 1.00
SJ1 Seth Jones .75 2.00
MSC1 Mark Scheifele .40 1.00

2012-13 ITG Heroes and Prostpects He Shoots He Scores Prizes

ISSUED VIA MAIL REDEMPTION
ANNOUNCED PRINT RUN 20
HSHS01 Nathan MacKinnon 25.00 60.00
HSHS02 Stefan Matteau AU 15.00 40.00
HSHS03 Griffin Reinhart 8.00 20.00
HSHS04 Connor McDavid AU 175.00 300.00
HSHS05 Jonathan Drouin 20.00 50.00
HSHS06 Sam Reinhart AU 30.00 80.00
HSHS07 Adam Erne 8.00 20.00
HSHS08 Hunter Shinkaruk AU 20.00 50.00
HSHS-09 Morgan Rielly 10.00 25.00
HSHS10 Sean Monahan AU 30.00 60.00
HSHS11 Malcolm Subban 10.00 25.00
HSHS12 Ryan Murphy AU 12.00 30.00
HSHS13 Mark Scheifele 10.00 25.00
HSHS14 Seth Jones AU 30.00 80.00
HSHS15 Mathew Dumba 8.00 20.00
HSHS16 Nathan MacKinnon AU 60.00 120.00
HSHS17 Stefan Matteau 8.00 20.00
HSHS18 Griffin Reinhart AU 12.00 30.00
HSHS19 Connor McDavid 30.00 60.00
HSHS20 Jonathan Drouin AU 60.00 120.00
HSHS21 Sam Reinhart 20.00 50.00
HSHS22 Adam Erne AU 12.00 30.00
HSHS23 Hunter Shinkaruk 12.00 30.00
HSHS24 Morgan Rielly AU 15.00 40.00
HSHS25 Sean Monahan 20.00 40.00
HSHS26 Malcolm Subban AU 15.00 40.00
HSHS27 Ryan Murphy 8.00 20.00
HSHS28 Mark Scheifele AU 25.00 50.00
HSHS29 Seth Jones 20.00 50.00
HSHS30 Mathew Dumba AU 12.00 30.00

2012-13 ITG Heroes and Prospects Jersey

ANNOUNCED PRINT RUN 120
*PATCH/25: .8X TO 2X JERSEY/120
*SILVER/30: .5X TO 1.2X JERSEY/120
M01 Daniel Altshuller 4.00 10.00
M02 Daniel Audette 6.00 15.00
M03 Justin Bailey 4.00 10.00
M04 Tyson Baillie 4.00 10.00
M05 Tim Bozon 8.00 20.00
M06 William Carrier 6.00 15.00
M07 Cole Cheveldave 5.00 12.00
M08 Jordon Cooke 4.00 10.00
M09 Anthony DeLuca 5.00 12.00
M10 Jason Dickinson 4.00 10.00
M11 Radek Faksa 8.00 20.00
M12 Alex Forsberg 5.00 12.00
M13 Frederik Gauthier 8.00 20.00
M14 John Gibson 8.00 20.00
M15 Sam Reinhart 12.00 30.00
M16 Jeremy Gregoire 4.00 10.00
M17 Stefan Matteau 5.00 12.00
M18 Ryan Hartman 5.00 12.00
M19 Josh Ho-Sang 6.00 15.00
M20 Anthony Mantha 8.00 20.00
M21 Roland McKeown 4.00 10.00
M22 Samuel Morin 6.00 15.00
M23 Xavier Ouellet 5.00 12.00
M24 Nick Ritchie 5.00 12.00
M25 Kerby Rychel 5.00 12.00
M26 Hunter Shinkaruk 6.00 15.00
M27 Garret Sparks 6.00 15.00
M28 Lukas Sutter 5.00 12.00
M29 Sergey Tolchinsky 3.00 8.00
M30 Jake Virtanen 6.00 15.00
M31 Matt Murray 5.00 12.00
M32 Stuart Percy 5.00 12.00
M33 Nick Baptiste 4.00 10.00
M34 Max Domi 6.00 15.00
M35 Scott Harrington 3.00 8.00
M36 Adam Lowry 5.00 12.00
M37 Matia Marcantuoni 3.00 8.00
M38 Mark McNeill 5.00 12.00
M39 Brendan Ranford 4.00 10.00
M40 Morgan Rielly 5.00 12.00
M41 Colton Sissons 5.00 12.00
M42 Tyler Wotherspoon 4.00 10.00
M43 Michael Gioguvaz 3.00 8.00
M44 Robin Gusse 4.00 10.00
M45 Connor McDavid 20.00 50.00

2012-13 ITG Heroes and Prospects Jersey Autographs

MAAF Alex Forsberg 12.00 30.00
MAAG Alex Galchenyuk 50.00 80.00
MAAL Adam Lowry 12.00 30.00
MABG Brendan Gaunce 10.00 25.00
MACC Cody Ceci 10.00 25.00
MACH Charles Hudon 12.00 30.00
MACM Connor McDavid 125.00 200.00
MACS Colton Sissons 12.00 30.00
MADH Dougie Hamilton 20.00 50.00
MAJD Jason Dickinson 10.00 25.00
MAJH Josh Ho-Sang 15.00 40.00
MAJV Jake Virtanen 15.00 40.00
MAMD Max Domi 15.00 40.00
MAMF Martin Frk 15.00 40.00
MAMG Mikhail Grigorenko 20.00 50.00
MAMR Morgan Rielly 12.00 30.00
MANM Nathan MacKinnon 40.00 100.00
MANY Nail Yakupov 25.00 60.00
MARF Radek Faksa 15.00 40.00
MARK Ryan Kujawinski 8.00 20.00
MARMU Ryan Murphy 15.00 40.00
MARS Ryan Strome 12.00 30.00
MASK Slater Koekkoek 10.00 25.00
MATB Tim Bozon 30.00 60.00

2012-13 ITG Heroes and Prospects Jersey Quads Silver

QJ01 MacKinn/Drn/Fucl/Frk 25.00 60.00
QJ02 Puempl/Faks/Murph/Bail 10.00 25.00
QJ03 Low/Brosst/St.Crx/Rein 8.00 20.00
QJ04 Lazr/Domi/Shinkrk/Mon 15.00 40.00
QJ05 Lipn/Chevld/Bozn/Rnfrd 12.00 30.00
QJ06 Subbn/Binnt/Sprk/Andrs 10.00 25.00
QJ07 Galchyk/Yaku/Murry/Rein 25.00 60.00
QJ08 Manth/MacKin/DeLc/Gth 25.00 60.00
QJ09 Reinhrt/Murry/Riel/Dumb 10.00 25.00

2012-13 ITG Heroes and Prospects Memorial Cup

COMPLETE SET (15) 10.00 25.00
MC01 Brossoir/Poudrier 1.00 2.50
MC02Â•R.Tesink/S.Griffith 1.50 4.00
MC03Â•Girard/Athanas 1.25 3.00
MC04Â•Huberdeau/Samuels 2.50 6.00
MC05Â•B.Horvat/K.Lowe 2.00 5.00
MC06Â•Arseneau/MacAuly 1.25 3.00
MC07Â•Veilleux/Reinhart 1.00 2.50
MC08Â•Le Sieur/Gagne .75 2.00
MC09 A.Zlobin/M.Domi 2.00 5.00
MC10 Vincent Arseneau 1.25 3.00
MC11 Yannick Veilleux .75 2.00
MC12 Maximilien Le Sieur .75 2.00
MC13 Anton Zlobin .75 2.00
MC14 Loik Poudrier .75 2.00
MC15 Gabriel Girard 1.00 2.50

2012-13 ITG Heroes and Prospects Subway Series

COMPLETE SET (15) 15.00 40.00
SSS01 Zachary Fucale 2.00 5.00
SSS02 Anthony Mantha 1.50 4.00
SSS03 Jonathan Huberdeau 2.50 6.00
SSS04 Nathan MacKinnon 3.00 8.00
SSS05 Jean-Sebastien Dea .75 2.00
SSS06 Jordan Binnington 1.00 2.50
SSS07 Connor McDavid 6.00 15.00
SSS08 Ryan Strome 1.25 3.00
SSS09 Dougie Hamilton 2.00 5.00
SSS10 Mark Scheifele 1.25 3.00
SSS11 Morgan Rielly 1.25 3.00
SSS12 Sam Reinhart 2.50 6.00
SSS13 Hunter Shinkaruk 1.50 4.00
SSS14 Mark McNeill 1.00 2.50
SSS15 Nail Yakupov 3.00 8.00

2012-13 ITG Heroes and Prospects Subway Super Series Jersey

*PATCH/25: .8X TO 2X BASIC JSY/120
*SILVER/30: .5X TO 1.2X BASIC JSY/120
SSM01 Cody Ceci 4.00 10.00
SSM02 Dougie Hamilton 10.00 25.00
SSM03 Jake Paterson 6.00 15.00
SSM04 Joshua Leivo 4.00 10.00
SSM05 Kerby Rychel 5.00 12.00
SSM06 Malcolm Subban 6.00 15.00
SSM07 Mark Scheifele 6.00 15.00
SSM08 Matt Finn 5.00 12.00
SSM09 Max Domi 6.00 15.00
SSM10 Ryan Murphy 5.00 12.00
SSM11 Scott Harrington 3.00 8.00
SSM12 Scott Laughton 5.00 12.00
SSM13 Sean Monahan 12.00 30.00
SSM14 Seth Griffith 8.00 20.00
SSM15 Slater Koekkoek 4.00 10.00
SSM16 Tom Wilson 8.00 20.00
SSM17 Anthony Mantha 8.00 20.00
SSM18 Christopher Clapperton 3.00 8.00
SSM19 James Melindy 3.00 8.00
SSM20 Jean-Sebastien Dea 4.00 10.00
SSM21 Jonathan Drouin 12.00 30.00
SSM22 Jonathan Huberdeau 12.00 30.00
SSM23 Matt Murphy 5.00 12.00
SSM24 Nathan MacKinnon 15.00 40.00
SSM25 Stephen Hodges 4.00 10.00
SSM26 Phillip Danault 4.00 10.00
SSM27 William Carrier 6.00 15.00
SSM28 Zachary Fucale 6.00 15.00
SSM29 Graham Black 3.00 8.00
SSM30 Ty Rattie 5.00 12.00
SSM31 Derrick Pouliot 6.00 15.00
SSM32 J.C. Lipon 4.00 10.00
SSM33 Sam Reinhart 6.00 15.00
SSM34 Michael St. Croix 3.00 8.00
SSM35 Mathew Dumba 5.00 12.00
SSM36 Griffin Reinhart 5.00 12.00
SSM37 Morgan Rielly 5.00 12.00
SSM38 Duncan Siemens 3.00 8.00
SSM39 Ryan Pulock 6.00 15.00
SSM40 Curtis Lazar 6.00 15.00
SSM41 Eric Comrie 5.00 12.00
SSM42 Ryan Murray 6.00 15.00
SSM43 Hunter Shinkaruk 6.00 15.00
SSM44 Mark McNeill 5.00 12.00
SSM45 Laurent Brossoit 5.00 12.00

2012-13 ITG Heroes and Prospects Subway Super Series Jersey Autographs

SSMAAM A.Mantha QMJHL 20.00 50.00
SSMACC Cody Ceci OHL 10.00 25.00
SSMACL Curtis Lazar WHL 15.00 40.00
SSMADH Dougie Hamilton OHL 15.00 40.00
SSMADP Derrick Pouliot WHL 15.00 40.00
SSMAGR Griffin Reinhart WHL 12.00 30.00
SSMAHS Hunter Shinkaruk WHL 15.00 40.00
SSMAJD J.Drouin QMJHL 60.00 125.00
SSMAJH J.Huberdeau QMJHL 15.00 40.00
SSMAMD Max Domi OHL 15.00 40.00
SSMAMDU Mathew Dumba WHL 10.00 25.00
SSMAMF Matt Finn OHL 10.00 25.00
SSMAMR Morgan Rielly WHL 15.00 40.00
SSMAMS Mark Scheifele OHL 12.00 30.00
SSMANM N.MacKinnon QMJHL 50.00 100.00
SSMAPD Phillip Danault QMJHL 10.00 25.00
SSMARM Ryan Murphy OHL 15.00 40.00
SSMARP Ryan Pulock WHL 15.00 40.00
SSMASG Seth Griffith OHL 15.00 40.00
SSMASK Slater Koekkoek OHL 10.00 25.00
SSMASL Scott Laughton OHL 12.00 30.00
SSMASM Sean Monahan OHL 25.00 50.00
SSMASR Sam Reinhart WHL 15.00 40.00
SSMATW Tom Wilson OHL 20.00 50.00

2012-13 ITG Heroes and Prospects Subway Super Series Trios Jerseys

SST01 Ceci/Hamilton/Finn 15.00 40.00
SST02 Subban/Percy/Patrsn 10.00 25.00
SST03 Rychel/Domi/Monahn 20.00 50.00
SST04 Carrier/Murph/Fucal 15.00 40.00
SST05 Drouin/Manth/MacKinn 25.00 50.00
SST06 DanaultÂ•Dea/Huberd 12.00 30.00
SST07 Reinhart/Shinkrk/Lazr 20.00 50.00
SST08 Dumba/Rielly/Murray 10.00 25.00
SST09 Brosst/St.Croix/Reinhrt 8.00 20.00
SST10 Murph/Harrngtn/Koek 8.00 20.00
SST11 Rattie/Pouliot/McNeill 10.00 25.00
SST12 Strom/Ritchie/Graovc 10.00 25.00

2012-13 ITG Heroes and Prospects Top Prospects

COMPLETE SET (15) 10.00 25.00
TOP01 Tom Wilson 2.00 5.00
TOP02 Brendan Gaunce 1.00 2.50
TOP03 Tim Bozon 2.00 5.00
TOP04 Scott Laughton 1.25 3.00
TOP05 Mathew Dumba 1.25 3.00
TOP06 Ryan Murray 1.50 4.00
TOP07 Matt Murray .75 2.00
TOP08 Griffin Reinhart 1.25 3.00
TOP09 Branden Troock .75 2.00
TOP10 Colton Sissons 1.25 3.00
TOP11 Mikhail Grigorenko 2.50 6.00
TOP12 Derrick Pouliot 1.50 4.00
TOP13 Tomas Hyka 1.25 3.00
TOP14 Radek Faksa 1.50 4.00
TOP15 Chris Driedger 1.00 2.50

2012-13 ITG Heroes and Prospects Top Prospects Jerseys

TP01 Mathew Dumba 6.00 15.00
TP02 Radek Faksa 8.00 20.00
TP03 Martin Frk 6.00 15.00
TP04 Brendan Gaunce 5.00 12.00
TP05 Mikhail Grigorenko 15.00 40.00
TP06 Ryan Murray 8.00 20.00
TP07 Derrick Pouliot 8.00 20.00
TP08 Griffin Reinhart 6.00 15.00
TP09 Gemel Smith 6.00 15.00
TP10 Jordan Binnington 6.00 15.00
TP11 Dougie Hamilton 15.00 40.00
TP12 Ryan Murphy 6.00 15.00
TP13 Matt Puempel 6.00 15.00
TP14 Ty Rattie 6.00 15.00
TP15 Ryan Strome 8.00 20.00

2013-14 ITG Heroes and Prospects

COMP.SET w/o SP's (150) 15.00 40.00
C14 ANNOUNCED ODDS 1:9
1 Zach Hall OHL .15 .40
2 Brendan Gaunce OHL .20 .50
3 Jordan Subban OHL .25 .60
4 Remi Elie OHL .15 .40
5 Connor McDavid OHL 3.00 8.00
6 Jason Dickinson OHL .20 .50
7 Matt Finn OHL .25 .60
8 Scott Kosmachuk OHL .15 .40
9 Tyler Bertuzzi OHL .15 .40
10 Justin Bailey OHL .20 .50
11 Radek Faksa OHL .25 .60
12 Anthony Stolarz OHL .15 .40
13 Bo Horvat OHL .50 1.25
14 Max Domi OHL .50 1.25
15 Michael McCarron OHL .25 .60
16 Ryan Rupert OHL .15 .40
17 Spencer Martin OHL .25 .60
18 Trevor Carrick OHL .15 .40
19 Cole Cassels OHL .15 .40
20 Scott Laughton OHL .25 .60
21 Sean Monahan OHL .40 1.00
22 Chris Bigras OHL .20 .50
23 Gemel Smith OHL .25 .60
24 Zach Nastasiuk OHL .25 .60
25 Ryan Hartman OHL .25 .60
26 Jake Paterson OHL .25 .60
27 Jimmy Lodge OHL .25 .60
28 Darnell Nurse OHL .25 .60
29 Connor Crisp OHL .15 .40
30 Nicholas Baptiste OHL .20 .50
31 Kerby Rychel OHL .25 .60
32 Slater Koekkoek OHL .20 .50
33 Eric Roy WHL .25 .60
34 Ryan Pulock WHL .25 .60
35 Greg Chase WHL .20 .50
36 Curtis Lazar WHL .30 .75
37 Griffin Reinhart WHL .25 .60
38 Henrik Samuelsson WHL .20 .50
39 Tristan Jarry WHL .20 .50
40 Mirco Mueller WHL .25 .60
41 Tim Bozon WHL .30 .75
42 Jordon Cooke WHL .15 .40
43 Madison Bowey WHL .25 .60
44 Mitchell Wheaton WHL .20 .50
45 Curtis Valk WHL .15 .40
46 Hunter Shinkaruk WHL .30 .75
47 Brendan Burke WHL .15 .40
48 Brendan Leipsic WHL .20 .50
49 Derrick Pouliot WHL .30 .75
50 Nicolas Petan WHL .25 .60
51 Oliver Bjorkstrand WHL .15 .40
52 Cole Cheveldave WHL .25 .60
53 Josh Morrissey WHL .20 .50
54 Patrik Bartosak WHL .15 .40
55 Morgan Klimchuk WHL .20 .50
56 Shea Theodore WHL .25 .60
57 Mitch Holmberg WHL .15 .40
58 Dillon Heatherington WHL .25 .60
59 Eetu Laurikainen WHL .25 .60
60 Eric Comrie WHL .20 .50
61 Keegan Kanzig WHL .15 .40
62 Ryan Pilon WHL .15 .40
63 G.Paquin-Boudreau QMJHL .20 .50
64 Jeremy Gregoire QMJHL .25 .60
65 Valentin Zykov QMJHL .25 .60
66 C.Clapperton QMJHL .15 .40
67 Etienne Marcoux QMJHL .15 .40
68 Marc-Olivier Roy QMJHL .25 .60
69 William Carrier QMJHL .20 .50
70 Yan Pavel Laplante QMJHL .15 .40
71 Charles Hudon QMJHL .25 .60
72 Laurent Dauphin QMJHL .15 .40
73 C.Lalancette QMJHL .15 .40
74 Nikolas Brouillard QMJHL .25 .60
75 Emile Poirier QMJHL .25 .60
76 Martin Reway QMJHL .50 1.25
77 Jonathan Drouin QMJHL .50 1.25
78 MacKenzie Weegar QMJHL .15 .40
79 Zachary Fucale QMJHL .30 .75
80 Adam Erne QMJHL .25 .60
81 Anthony Duclair QMJHL .40 1.00
82 Francois Brassard QMJHL .15 .40
83 Nick Sorensen QMJHL .20 .50
84 Frederik Gauthier QMJHL .25 .60
85 Philippe Desrosiers QMJHL .20 .50
86 Samuel Morin QMJHL .25 .60
87 Alexandre Belanger QMJHL .20 .50
88 Jean-Sebastien Dea QMJHL .20 .50
89 Anthony Mantha QMJHL .30 .75
90 Brandon Whitney QMJHL .25 .60
91 Rihards Bukarts WHL .15 .40
92 Daniel Sprong QMJHL .30 .75
93 Nicolas Roy QMJHL .20 .50
94 Sergei Boikov QMJHL .15 .40
95 Andre Burakovsky OHL .60 1.50
96 Dylan Strome OHL .50 1.25
97 Ivan Nikolishin WHL .15 .40
98 Anthony Brodeur QMJHL .40 1.00
99 Ty Edmonds WHL .25 .60
100 Mitchell Marner OHL .75 2.00
101 Sean Day OHL .40 1.00
102 Alex Lintuniemi OHL .15 .40
103 Travis Konecny OHL .40 1.00
104 Matt Spencer OHL .15 .40
105 Adam Musil WHL .20 .50
106 Mathew Barzal WHL .50 1.25
107 Anthony Beauvillier QMJHL .20 .50
108 Nikita Yazkov OHL .15 .40
109 Dmitri Osipov WHL .15 .40
110 Ty Ronning WHL .15 .40
111 Marcus Pettersson IP .20 .50
112 Adam Ollas Mattsson IP .20 .50
113 Aleksandar Mikulovich IP .25 .60
114 Alexander Protapovich IP .25 .60
115 Alexander Wennberg IP .25 .60
116 Elias Lindholm IP .40 1.00
117 Jacob de la Rose IP .25 .60
118 Aleksander Barkov IP .60 1.50
119 Rasmus Ristolainen IP .40 1.00
120 Robert Hagg IP .30 .75
121 Tomas Hertl IP .30 .75
122 Borje Salming H .25 .60
123 Brett Hull H .25 .60
124 Brian Leetch H .25 .60
125 Carey Price H .75 2.00
126 Claude Giroux H .25 .60
127 Darryl Sittler H .25 .60
128 Dave Andreychuk H .25 .60
129 Dave Keon H .25 .60
130 Denis Savard H .30 .75
131 Dominik Hasek H .30 .75
132 Felix Potvin H .40 1.00
133 Frank Mahovlich H .25 .60
134 Georges Vezina H .25 .60
135 Igor Larionov H .25 .60
136 Joe Nieuwendyk H .25 .60
137 John LeClair H .25 .60
138 Kelly Hrudey H .20 .50
139 Luc Robitaille H .25 .60
140 Marian Gaborik H .25 .60
141 Mike Modano H .40 1.00
142 Mike Richter H .25 .60
143 Owen Nolan H .20 .50
144 Pat LaFontaine H .25 .60
145 Peter Bondra H .25 .60
146 Ron Francis H .30 .75
147 Ron Hextall H .25 .60
148 Sergei Samsonov H .20 .50
149 Tom Barrasso H .25 .60
150 Vladislav Tretiak H .30 .75
151 Mason McDonald C14 2.00 5.00
152 Aaron Ekblad C14 4.00 10.00
153 Brendan Lemieux C14 2.00 5.00
154 Nikita Scherbak C14 2.00 5.00
155 Jayce Hawryluk C14 1.25 3.00
156 Jake Virtanen C14 2.50 6.00
157 Alex Bureau C14 1.50 4.00
158 Alexis Pepin C14 1.50 4.00
159 Tyler Sandhu C14 2.00 5.00

160 Robby Fabbri C14 1.50 4.00
161 Nikolaj Ehlers C14 4.00 10.00
162 Ryan Falkenham C14 2.00 5.00
163 Rourke Chartier C14 1.50 4.00
164 Tyson Baillie C14 1.50 4.00
165 Roland McKeown C14 2.00 5.00
166 Sam Bennett C14 3.00 8.00
167 Spencer Watson C14 2.00 5.00
168 Ryan MacInnis C14 1.50 4.00
169 Luke Philp C14 1.50 4.00
170 Sam Reinhart C14 3.00 8.00
171 Ivan Barbashev C14 2.00 5.00
172 Brayden Point C14 2.00 5.00
173 Justin Paulic C14 2.00 5.00
174 Aaron Haydon C14 1.50 4.00
175 Brendan Perlini C14 3.00 8.00
176 Blake Clarke C14 1.50 4.00
177 Brandon Robinson C14 1.50 4.00
178 Michael Dal Colle C14 2.50 6.00
179 Jacob Middleton C14 1.50 4.00
180 Nick Ritchie C14 2.00 5.00
181 Alex Nedeljkovic C14 2.00 5.00
182 Matt Mistele C14 1.50 4.00
183 Chase De Leo C14 1.50 4.00
184 Dominic Turgeon C14 2.00 5.00
185 Leon Draisaitl C14 4.00 10.00
186 Duncan MacIntyre C14 1.50 4.00
187 Conner Bleackley C14 2.00 5.00
188 Haydn Fleury C14 2.00 5.00
189 Nikita Serebryakov C14 2.00 5.00
190 Anthony DeAngelo C14 1.50 4.00
191 Nikolay Goldobin C14 2.00 5.00
192 Jared McCann C14 2.00 5.00
193 Daniel Audette C14 2.00 5.00
194 Brycen Martin C14 2.00 5.00
195 Nicolas Aube-Kubel C14 1.25 3.00
196 Josh Ho-Sang C14 2.50 6.00
197 Julius Honka C14 1.50 4.00
198 Julius Bergman C14 1.50 4.00
199 William Nylander C14 5.00 12.00

2013-14 ITG Heroes and Prospects Autographs

OVERALL AUTO ANNC'D ODDS 1:7
AAB Anthony Brodeur 15.00 30.00
AABI Antoine Bibeau 2.50 6.00
AAD Anthony DeAngelo 3.00 8.00
AAE Aaron Ekblad 8.00 20.00
AAER Adam Erne 4.00 10.00
AAF Alex Forsberg 4.00 10.00
AAM Anthony Mantha 10.00 25.00
AAMI Aleksandar Mikulovich 4.00 10.00
AAO Adam Ollas Mattsson 3.00 8.00
AAP Alexis Pepin 3.00 8.00
AAPR Alexander Protapovich 4.00 10.00
ABC Blake Clarke 3.00 8.00
ABG Brendan Gaunce 3.00 8.00
ABH Bo Horvat 8.00 20.00
ABHU Brett Hull SP 15.00 30.00
ABL Brian Leetch SP 10.00 25.00
ABM Brent Moran 3.00 8.00
ABMA Brycen Martin 4.00 10.00
ABP Brayden Point 4.00 10.00
ABPR Brandon Prophet 2.50 6.00
ABR Brandon Robinson 3.00 8.00
ABS Brody Silk 2.50 6.00
ACB Clark Bishop 2.50 6.00
ACG Claude Giroux SP 8.00 20.00
ACL Curtis Lazar 6.00 15.00
ACM Connor McDavid 90.00 150.00
ACR Connor Rankin 3.00 8.00
ADA Daniel Audette 4.00 10.00
ADAN Dave Andreychuk SP 10.00 25.00
ADM Duncan MacIntyre 3.00 8.00
ADN Darnell Nurse 4.00 10.00
ADO Dakota Odgers 3.00 8.00
ADS Dylan Strome 8.00 20.00
ADT Dominic Turgeon 4.00 10.00
AEC Eric Comrie 3.00 8.00
AEP Emile Poirier 4.00 10.00
AER Eric Roy 4.00 10.00
AFG Frederik Gauthier 4.00 10.00
AFM Frank Mahovlich SP 10.00 25.00
AHF Haydn Fleury 4.00 10.00
AHS Hunter Shinkaruk 5.00 12.00
AIB Ivan Barbashev 4.00 10.00
AIL Igor Larionov SP 10.00 25.00
AJB Julius Bergman 3.00 8.00
AJBA Justin Bailey 3.00 8.00
AJD Jonathan Drouin 15.00 30.00
AJG Jeremy Gregoire 4.00 10.00
AJH Jayce Hawryluk 2.50 6.00
AJHS Josh Ho-Sang 8.00 20.00
AJL Jaden Lindo 2.50 6.00
AJM Josh Morrissey 3.00 8.00
AJMC Jared McCann 4.00 10.00
AJN Joe Nieuwendyk SP 10.00 25.00
AJS Jordan Subban SP 5.00 12.00
AJV Jake Virtanen 5.00 12.00
AKR Kerby Rychel 4.00 10.00
ALD Leon Draisaitl 15.00 40.00
ALS Liam Stewart 2.50 6.00
AMB Mathew Barzal 20.00 50.00
AMBO Madison Bowey 4.00 10.00
AMD Mathew Dumba 4.00 10.00
AMDC Michael Dal Colle 5.00 12.00
AMG Marian Gaborik 6.00 15.00
AMGI Michael Giugovaz SP 5.00 12.00
AMI Max Iafrate 3.00 8.00
AMK Morgan Klimchuk 3.00 8.00
AML Maxim Lazarev 2.50 6.00
AMM Matt Mistele 3.00 8.00
AMMO Mike Modano SP 15.00 40.00
AMMU Mirco Mueller 4.00 10.00
AMP Marcus Pettersson 3.00 8.00
ANA Nicolas Aube-Kubel 2.50 6.00
ANB Nicholas Baptiste 3.00 8.00
ANE Nikolaj Ehlers 8.00 20.00
ANG Nikolay Goldobin 4.00 10.00
ANR Nicolas Roy 3.00 8.00
ANRI Nick Ritchie 4.00 10.00
ANS Nick Sorensen 3.00 8.00
AOL Olivier Leblanc 3.00 8.00
APB Peter Bondra SP 15.00 40.00
APL Payton Lee 3.00 8.00
ARC Rourke Chartier 3.00 8.00
ARD Reid Duke 2.50 6.00
ARF Robby Fabbri 3.00 8.00
ARFR Ron Francis SP 12.00 30.00
ARH Ryan Hartman 4.00 10.00
ARK Ryan Kujawinski 3.00 8.00
ARM Roland McKeown 4.00 10.00
ARMA Ryan MacInnis 3.00 8.00
ARP Ryan Pulock 4.00 10.00
ARR Rasmus Ristolainen 6.00 15.00
ASB Sam Bennett 10.00 25.00
ASD Sean Day 6.00 15.00
ASM Samuel Morin 4.00 10.00
ASMA Spencer Martin 4.00 10.00
ASMO Sean Monahan 6.00 15.00
ASP Storm Phaneuf 2.50 6.00
ASR Sam Reinhart 10.00 25.00
AST Shea Theodore 4.00 10.00
ASTO Sergey Tolchinsky 3.00 8.00
ASW Spencer Watson 4.00 10.00
ATB Tim Bozon 5.00 12.00
ATH Tomas Hertl 12.50 25.00
ATJ Tristan Jarry 3.00 8.00
ATK Travis Konecny 6.00 15.00
ATW Tom Wilson
AWC William Carrier 5.00 12.00
AWN William Nylander 10.00 25.00

2013-14 ITG Heroes and Prospects AutoThreads

ATEK Evander Kane/25
ATJC Jared Cowen/25 8.00 20.00
ATMD Matt Duchene/25 12.00 30.00
ATTS Tyler Seguin/25 12.00 30.00
ATJT1 John Tavares/15 25.00 60.00
ATJT2 John Tavares/25 25.00 60.00

2013-14 ITG Heroes and Prospects Canadiana

CAE Aaron Ekblad 10.00 25.00
CAM Anthony Mantha 6.00 15.00
CAP Adam Pelech 5.00 12.00
CBH Bo Horvat 10.00 25.00
CCB Chris Bigras 4.00 10.00
CCH Charles Hudon 5.00 12.00
CCL Curtis Lazar 6.00 15.00
CCM Connor McDavid
CDP Derrick Pouliot 6.00 15.00
CFGA Frederik Gauthier 5.00 12.00
CGR Griffin Reinhart 5.00 12.00
CJA Josh Anderson 6.00 15.00
CJD Jonathan Drouin 10.00 25.00
CJM Josh Morrissey 4.00 10.00
CJP Jake Paterson 5.00 12.00
CKR Kerby Rychel 5.00 12.00
CMD Mathew Dumba 5.00 12.00
CNP Nicolas Petan 5.00 12.00
CSL Scott Laughton 5.00 12.00
CSR Sam Reinhart 8.00 20.00
CTL Taylor Leier 8.00 20.00
CZF Zachary Fucale 6.00 15.00

2013-14 ITG Heroes and Prospects Dual Autographs

FSDABBSB B.Burke/S.Burke 10.00 25.00
FSDAGRPR G.Reinhart/P.Reinhrt 12.00 30.00
FSDASRPR S.Reinhart/P.Reinhrt 12.00 30.00
FSDAWNMN W.Nylander/M.Nylndr 15.00 40.00

2013-14 ITG Heroes and Prospects Dual Jerseys Silver

DJ01 Aaron Ekblad 10.00 25.00
DJ02 Bo Horvat 10.00 25.00
DJ03 Connor McDavid 15.00 40.00
DJ04 Curtis Lazar 6.00 15.00
DJ05 Frederik Gauthier 5.00 12.00
DJ06 Jonathan Drouin 10.00 25.00
DJ07 Max Domi 10.00 25.00
DJ08 Sam Reinhart 8.00 20.00
DJ09 Sean Monahan 10.00 25.00

2013-14 ITG Heroes and Prospects He Shoots He Scores Points

EACH HAS NINE CARDS OF EQUAL VALUE
AM1 Anthony Mantha C .40 1.00
CM1 Connor McDavid C 1.00 2.50
DN1 Darnell Nurse C .30 .75
FG1 Frederik Gauthier C .30 .75
HF1 Haydn Fleury C .30 .75
JD1 Jonathan Drouin C .60 1.50
LD1 Leon Draisaitl C .60 1.50
MB1 Matthew Barzal C .60 1.50
NP1 Nicolas Petan C .30 .75
SR1 Sam Reinhart C .50 1.25
WN1 William Nylander C .75 2.00

2013-14 ITG Heroes and Prospects Hero and Prospect Jerseys Silver

SILVER ANNOUNCED PRINT RUN 40
HP01 B.Leetch/G.Reinhart 5.00 12.00
HP02 C.Price/E.Comrie 15.00 40.00
HP03 J.Kurri/A.Barkov 10.00 25.00
HP04 C.Giroux/S.Laughton
HP05 B.Salming/R.Hagg 5.00 12.00
HP06 P.Roy/Z.Fucale 12.00 30.00
HP07 M.Lemieux/C.McDavid 25.00 60.00
HP08 T.Barrasso/M.Murray 6.00 15.00
HP09 B.Hull/S.Monahan 10.00 25.00

2013-14 ITG Heroes and Prospects Jersey Autographs Silver

ANNOUNCED PRINT RUN 19
MAAE Aaron Ekblad 25.00 60.00
MAAM Anthony Mantha 15.00 40.00
MAAP Alexis Pepin 8.00 20.00
MACL Curtis Lazar 12.00 30.00
MACM Connor McDavid 125.00 200.00
MADA Daniel Audette 10.00 25.00
MAEC Eric Comrie 8.00 20.00
MAEP Emile Poirier 10.00 25.00
MAFG Frederik Gauthier 10.00 25.00
MAHS Hunter Shinkaruk 12.00 30.00
MAIB Ivan Barbashev 10.00 25.00
MAJB Justin Bailey 8.00 20.00
MAJG Jeremy Gregoire 10.00 25.00
MAJH Josh Ho-Sang 12.00 30.00
MAJM Jared McCann 10.00 25.00
MAKR Kerby Rychel 10.00 25.00
MAMD Max Domi 20.00 50.00
MANB Nicholas Baptiste 8.00 20.00
MANR Nick Ritchie 10.00 25.00
MAOL Olivier Leblanc 8.00 20.00
MAPD Philippe Desrosiers 8.00 20.00
MASM Samuel Morin 10.00 25.00
MATJ Tristan Jarry 8.00 20.00
MAWC William Carrier 8.00 20.00

2013-14 ITG Heroes and Prospects Jersey Quads Silver

ANNOUNCED PRINT RUN 40
QJ01 McDvd/Rnhrt/Lmeux/Lflr 25.00 50.00
QJ02 Rose/Brkv/Krri/Sndin 12.00 30.00
QJ03 Pliot/Mrry/Mlkn/Fleury 20.00 50.00
QJ04 Shnkrk/Hrvt/Sdin/Sdin 12.00 30.00
QJ05 Mnhn/Prier/McInns/Fleury 12.00 30.00
QJ06 Mntha/Ptrsn/Yzrmn/Osgd 12.00 30.00
QJ07 Mrin/Hagg/Clrke/Lndros 10.00 25.00
QJ08 Mrtn/Brke/Roy/Sakic 15.00 40.00
QJ09 Rose/Fcle/Nslnd/Roy 15.00 40.00

2013-14 ITG Heroes and Prospects Jersey

PATCH/30: .8X TO 2X BASIC JSY
SILVER/30: .5X TO 1.2X BASIC JSY
M01 Aaron Ekblad 8.00 20.00
M02 Frederik Gauthier 4.00 10.00
M03 Jared McCann 4.00 10.00
M04 Emile Poirier 4.00 10.00
M05 Curtis Lazar 5.00 12.00
M06 Daniel Audette 4.00 10.00
M07 Leon Draisaitl 8.00 20.00
M08 Jake Virtanen 5.00 12.00
M09 Sam Reinhart 6.00 15.00
M10 Rourke Chartier 4.00 10.00
M11 Niki Petti 3.00 8.00
M12 Alexis Pepin 3.00 8.00
M13 Matt Mistele 3.00 8.00
M14 Connor McDavid 12.00 30.00
M15 Olivier Leblanc 3.00 8.00
M16 Ivan Barbashev 4.00 10.00
M17 Conor Garland 3.00 8.00
M18 Sam Bennett 6.00 15.00
M19 Sean Day 6.00 15.00
M20 Nikolay Goldobin 4.00 10.00
M21 Matt Fonteyne 3.00 8.00
M22 Colby Cave 4.00 10.00
M23 Noah Juulesen 3.00 8.00
M24 Bo Horvat 8.00 20.00
M25 Mathew Barzal 8.00 20.00
M26 Anthony Duclair 6.00 15.00
M27 Nick Sorensen 3.00 8.00
M28 Robby Fabbri 3.00 8.00
M29 Ryan Hartman 4.00 10.00
M30 Eric Cornel 3.00 8.00

2013-14 ITG Heroes and Prospects Prospects Trios Jerseys Silver

ANNOUNCED PRINT RUN 40
PT01 McDvd/Rnhrt/Ekbld 25.00 60.00
PT02 Audtte/Ppin/Brbshv 6.00 15.00
PT03 Chvldve/Jarry/Cmrie 6.00 15.00
PT04 Prier/Grgre/Crrier 6.00 15.00
PT05 Altshllr/Mrry/Ggvaz 6.00 15.00
PT06 Shnkrk/Vrtnen/Lazar 8.00 20.00
PT07 Mntha/Gthier/Drouin 12.00 30.00
PT08 Domi/Rychl/Hrtman 12.00 30.00
PT09 Rnhart/Ekbld/Adette 12.00 30.00

2013-14 ITG Heroes and Prospects Subway Series Jersey Autographs Silver

SSMAAD Anthony Duclair 15.00 40.00
SSMAAE Aaron Ekblad 20.00 50.00
SSMAAM Anthony Mantha 15.00 40.00
SSMABG Brendan Gaunce 8.00 20.00
SSMABH Bo Horvat 20.00 50.00
SSMACM Connor McDavid 125.00 200.00
SSMADA Daniel Audette 10.00 25.00
SSMADN Darnell Nurse 10.00 25.00
SSMAEC Eric Comrie 8.00 20.00
SSMAEP Emile Poirier 10.00 25.00
SSMAFG Frederik Gauthier 10.00 25.00
SSMAJD Jonathan Drouin 40.00 80.00
SSMAJG Jeremy Gregoire 10.00 25.00
SSMAJM Josh Morrissey 8.00 20.00
SSMAMB Madison Bowey 10.00 25.00
SSMAMD Max Domi 20.00 50.00
SSMAMK Morgan Klimchuk 8.00 20.00
SSMANP Nicolas Petan 10.00 25.00
SSMASB Sam Bennett
SSMASL Scott Laughton 10.00 25.00
SSMASM Samuel Morin 10.00 25.00
SSMASR Sam Reinhart
SSMAWC William Carrier 8.00 20.00
SSMAZF Zachary Fucale 12.00 30.00

2013-14 ITG Heroes and Prospects Subway Series Jersey

ANNOUNCED PRINT RUN 160
PATCH/30: .8X TO 2X BASIC JSY
SILVER/30: .5X TO 1.2X BASIC JSY
SSM01 Anthony DeLuca 3.00 8.00
SSM02 Jonathan Drouin 5.00 12.00
SSM03 Anthony Duclair 6.00 15.00
SSM04 Dillon Fournier 3.00 8.00
SSM05 Frederik Gauthier 4.00 10.00
SSM06 Samuel Morin 4.00 10.00
SSM07 Emile Poirier 4.00 10.00
SSM08 Chris Bigras 3.00 8.00
SSM09 Aaron Ekblad 8.00 20.00
SSM10 Brendan Gaunce 3.00 8.00
SSM11 Bo Horvat 8.00 20.00
SSM12 Connor McDavid 12.00 30.00
SSM13 Matt Murray 4.00 10.00
SSM14 Darnell Nurse 4.00 10.00
SSM15 Sam Bennett 6.00 15.00
SSM16 Sam Reinhart 6.00 15.00
SSM17 Nicolas Petan 4.00 10.00
SSM18 Eric Comrie 3.00 8.00
SSM19 Morgan Klimchuk 3.00 8.00
SSM20 Josh Morrissey 3.00 8.00
SSM21 Madison Bowey 4.00 10.00
SSM22 Brendan Leipsic 3.00 8.00
SSM23 Jaedon Descheneau 2.50 6.00
SSM24 Jujhar Khaira 3.00 8.00
SSM25 Tristan Jarry 3.00 8.00
SSM26 Carter Verhaeghe 2.50 6.00
SSM27 Nicholas Baptiste 3.00 8.00
SSM28 Sebastien Auger 3.00 8.00
SSM29 Jeremy Gregoire 4.00 10.00
SSM30 Daniel Audette 4.00 10.00

2013-14 ITG Heroes and Prospects Tenth Anniversary Jersey

AP11 Carey Price/20* 20.00 50.00
AP12 Eric Staal/20* 8.00 20.00
AP13 Claude Giroux/20* 6.00 15.00
AP14 Taylor Hall/20* 6.00 15.00
AP15 Marc-Andre Fleury/20* 10.00 25.00
AP16 Tuukka Rask/20* 8.00 20.00
AP17 Phil Kessel/20* 8.00 20.00
AP18 Kari Lehtonen/20* 5.00 12.00
AP19 Shea Weber/20* 5.00 12.00
AP20 Alex Galchenyuk/20* 15.00 40.00
AP21 Alex Pietrangelo/30* 4.00 10.00
AP22 Ryan Miller/30* 5.00 12.00
AP23 Anze Kopitar/30* 8.00 20.00
AP24 Sean Monahan/30* 5.00 12.00
AP25 Dion Phaneuf/30* 5.00 12.00
AP26 Patrice Bergeron/30* 6.00 15.00
AP27 Ryan Nugent-Hopkins/30* 6.00 15.00
AP28 Nail Yakupov/30* 8.00 20.00
AP29 Nathan MacKinnon/30* 12.00 30.00
AP30 Seth Jones/30* 5.00 12.00
AP31 Pekka Rinne/40* 6.00 15.00
AP32 Connor McDavid/40* 25.00 50.00
AP33 Aleksander Barkov/40* 6.00 15.00
AP34 Malcolm Subban/40* 5.00 12.00
AP35 Hunter Shinkaruk/40* 6.00 15.00
AP36 Brendan Gallagher/40* 8.00 20.00
AP37 Matt Duchene/40* 5.00 12.00
AP38 Jimmy Howard/40* 5.00 12.00
AP39 Sergei Bobrovsky/40* 5.00 12.00
AP40 Thomas Vanek/40* 5.00 12.00
AP41 Loui Eriksson/50* 4.00 10.00
AP42 Mike Richards/50* 6.00 15.00
AP43 Jonathan Huberdeau/50* 5.00 12.00
AP44 Mikko Koivu/50* 4.00 10.00
AP45 Jaroslav Halak/50* 5.00 12.00
AP46 Jason Spezza/50* 5.00 12.00
AP47 Tyler Seguin/50* 8.00 20.00
AP48 Ryan Kesler/50* 5.00 12.00
AP49 Sam Reinhart/50* 8.00 20.00
AP50 Lars Eller/50* 4.00 10.00
AP51 Mark Scheifele/60* 5.00 12.00
AP52 Cody Hodgson/60* 4.00 10.00
AP53 Jonathan Drouin/60* 8.00 20.00
AP54 Drew Doughty/60* 4.00 10.00
AP55 Morgan Rielly/60* 5.00 12.00
AP56 Darnell Nurse/60* 4.00 10.00
AP57 Sam Gagner/60* 3.00 8.00
AP58 Jeff Carter/60* 4.00 10.00
AP59 Dougie Hamilton/60* 6.00 15.00
AP60 Ondrej Pavelec/60* 4.00 10.00
AP61 Vladimir Tarasenko/70* 6.00 15.00
AP62 Bobby Ryan/70* 4.00 10.00
AP63 Logan Couture/70* 4.00 10.00
AP64 James Neal/70* 4.00 10.00
AP65 Ryan Getzlaf/70* 6.00 15.00
AP66 Nazem Kadri/70* 4.00 10.00
AP67 Brent Seabrook/70* 4.00 10.00
AP68 Jordan Staal/70* 4.00 10.00
AP69 Aaron Ekblad/70* 8.00 20.00
AP70 Mikhail Grigorenko/70* 5.00 12.00
AP71 Sean Couturier/80* 4.00 10.00
AP72 Corey Crawford/80* 5.00 12.00
AP73 Gabriel Landeskog/80* 3.00 8.00
AP74 Max Domi/80* 8.00 20.00
AP75 Braden Holtby/80* 6.00 15.00
AP76 Evander Kane/80* 4.00 10.00
AP77 Jakub Voracek/80* 4.00 10.00
AP78 Chris Kunitz/80* 4.00 10.00
AP79 David Bolland/80* 2.50 6.00
AP80 Dustin Brown/80* 4.00 10.00
AP81 Oliver Ekman-Larsson/90* 3.00 8.00
AP82 Milan Lucic/90* 4.00 10.00
AP83 Jordan Eberle/90* 4.00 10.00
AP84 Zachary Fucale/90* 5.00 12.00
AP85 Ryan Strome/90* 5.00 12.00
AP86 Boone Jenner/90* 4.00 10.00
AP87 Brandon Saad/90* 4.00 10.00
AP88 Kris Letang/90* 4.00 10.00
AP89 Brad Marchand/90* 5.00 12.00
AP90 Jonathan Bernier/90* 4.00 10.00
AP91 Jeff Skinner/100* 3.00 8.00
AP92 David Krejci/100* 4.00 10.00
AP93 Mathew Dumba/100* 4.00 10.00
AP94 Cam Ward/100* 4.00 10.00
AP95 Semyon Varlamov/100* 4.00 10.00
AP96 Mikhail Grabovski/100* 3.00 8.00
AP97 Mike Green/100* 4.00 10.00
AP98 Ryan Murray/100* 6.00 15.00
AP99 Cory Schneider/100* 3.00 8.00
AP100 Ryan Callahan/100* 4.00 10.00

2013-14 ITG Heroes and Prospects Tenth Anniversary Tribute

T01 Valentin Zykov 2.00 5.00
T02 Aaron Ekblad 4.00 10.00
T03 Brendan Gaunce 1.50 4.00
T04 Marc-Olivier Roy 2.00 5.00
T05 Jake Virtanen 2.50 6.00
T06 Alexis Pepin 1.50 4.00
T07 Laurent Dauphin 1.25 3.00
T08 Nicolas Roy 1.50 4.00
T09 Curtis Lazar 2.50 6.00
T10 Griffin Reinhart 2.00 5.00
T11 Tristan Jarry 1.50 4.00
T12 Connor McDavid 6.00 15.00
T13 Andre Burakovsky 5.00 12.00
T14 Aleksander Barkov 5.00 12.00
T15 Emile Poirier 2.00 5.00
T16 Jonathan Drouin 4.00 10.00
T17 Nikolaj Ehlers 4.00 10.00
T18 Madison Bowey 2.00 5.00
T19 Spencer Watson 2.00 5.00
T20 Radek Faksa 2.00 5.00
T21 Sam Reinhart 3.00 8.00
T22 Max Domi 4.00 10.00
T23 Bo Horvat 4.00 10.00
T24 Hunter Shinkaruk 2.50 6.00
T25 Spencer Martin 2.00 5.00
T26 Sean Day 3.00 8.00
T27 Ivan Barbashev 2.00 5.00
T28 Scott Laughton 2.00 5.00
T29 Michael Dal Colle 2.50 6.00
T30 Sean Monahan 3.00 8.00
T31 Travis Konecny 3.00 8.00
T32 Ryan Hartman 2.00 5.00
T33 Nicolas Petan 2.00 5.00
T34 Josh Morrissey 1.50 4.00
T35 Haydn Fleury 2.00 5.00
T36 Morgan Klimchuk 1.50 4.00
T37 Frederik Gauthier 2.00 5.00
T38 Darnell Nurse 2.00 5.00
T39 Shea Theodore 2.00 5.00
T40 Mathew Barzal 4.00 10.00
T41 Daniel Audette 2.00 5.00
T42 William Nylander 5.00 12.00
T43 Eric Comrie 1.50 4.00
T44 Anthony Mantha 2.50 6.00
T45 Kerby Rychel 2.00 5.00

2013-14 ITG Heroes and Prospects Top Prospects Jersey Autographs Silver

TPMAAD Anthony Duclair 15.00 40.00
TPMABG Brendan Gaunce 8.00 20.00
TPMABH Bo Horvat 20.00 50.00
TPMACL Curtis Lazar 12.00 30.00
TPMADN Darnell Nurse 8.00 20.00
TPMADP Derrick Pouliot 12.00 30.00
TPMAER Eric Roy 10.00 25.00
TPMAFG Frederik Gauthier 10.00 25.00
TPMAJD Jonathan Drouin 40.00 80.00
TPMAJM Josh Morrissey 8.00 20.00
TPMAJS Jordan Subban 10.00 25.00
TPMAMD Max Domi 20.00 40.00
TPMAMK Morgan Klimchuk 8.00 20.00
TPMANP Nicolas Petan 10.00 25.00
TPMANS Nick Sorensen 8.00 20.00
TPMARF Radek Faksa 10.00 25.00
TPMARH Ryan Hartman 10.00 25.00
TPMASM Sean Monahan 12.00 30.00
TPMAST Shea Theodore 10.00 25.00
TPMATJ Tristan Jarry 8.00 20.00
TPMAZF Zachary Fucale 12.00 30.00
TPMASMA Spencer Martin 10.00 25.00

2013-14 ITG Heroes and Prospects Top Prospects Jersey

PATCH/30: .8X TO 2X BASIC JSY
SILVER/30: .5X TO 1.2X BASIC JSY
TPM01 Oliver Bjorkstrand 2.50 6.00
TPM02 Laurent Dauphin 2.50 6.00
TPM03 Max Domi 8.00 20.00
TPM04 Jonathan Drouin 8.00 20.00
TPM05 Anthony Duclair 6.00 15.00
TPM06 Adam Erne 4.00 10.00
TPM07 Radek Faksa 4.00 10.00
TPM08 Zachary Fucale 5.00 12.00
TPM09 Brendan Gaunce 3.00 8.00
TPM10 Frederik Gauthier 4.00 10.00
TPM11 Stephen Harper 2.50 6.00
TPM12 Ryan Hartman 4.00 10.00
TPM13 Bo Horvat 8.00 20.00
TPM14 Tristan Jarry 3.00 8.00
TPM15 Morgan Klimchuk 3.00 8.00
TPM16 Curtis Lazar 5.00 12.00
TPM17 Spencer Martin 4.00 10.00
TPM18 Sean Monahan 6.00 15.00
TPM19 Josh Morrissey 3.00 8.00
TPM20 Darnell Nurse 4.00 10.00
TPM21 Nicolas Petan 4.00 10.00
TPM22 Derrick Pouliot 5.00 12.00
TPM23 Griffin Reinhart 4.00 10.00
TPM24 Eric Roy 4.00 10.00
TPM25 Gemel Smith 4.00 10.00
TPM26 Nick Sorensen 3.00 8.00
TPM27 Jordan Subban 4.00 10.00
TPM28 Shea Theodore 4.00 10.00
TPM29 Nikita Zadorov 4.00 10.00
TPM30 Valentin Zykov 4.00 10.00

2013-14 ITG Heroes and Prospects Top Prospects Trios Jerseys Silver

TPT01 Domi/Hrpr/Hrvat 8.00 20.00
TPT02 Dphin/Drouin/Erne 6.00 15.00
TPT03 Bjrkst/Klmchk/Lzar 6.00 15.00
TPT04 Hrtmn/Ptan/Mnhn 15.00 40.00
TPT05 Dclair/Gthier/Zykv 10.00 25.00
TPT06 Thdore/Sbban/Pliot 8.00 20.00
TPT07 Rnhart/Nrse/Mrrssy 6.00 15.00
TPT08 Mrtn/Jrry/Fcale 8.00 20.00
TPT09 Fksa/Gnce/Smith 6.00 15.00

2014-15 ITG Heroes and Prospects Prospect Autographs

*GOLD/30: .6X TO 1.5X BASIC AU/80
1 Adam Mascherin/50 5.00 12.00
2 Adam Musil/80 4.00 10.00
3 Alex Forsberg/80 3.00 8.00
4 Alexandre Carrier/50 5.00 12.00
5 Andrew Picco/80 3.00 8.00
6 Anthony Beauvillier/80 4.00 10.00
7 Beck Malenstyn/50 4.00 10.00
8 Blake Speers/80 4.00 10.00
9 Brandon Saigeon/50 5.00 12.00
10 Brendan Guhle/80 3.00 8.00
11 Brett Howden/50 5.00 12.00
12 Brett McKenzie/50 5.00 12.00
13 Cameron Askew/80 4.00 10.00
14 Chaz Reddekopp/80 3.00 8.00
15 Cliff Pu/80 3.00 8.00
16 Cole Johnson/80 4.00 10.00
17 Connor Hobbs/80 4.00 10.00
18 Connor Ingram/80 3.00 8.00
19 Connor McDavid/50 150.00 225.00
20 Daniel Sprong/50 10.00 25.00
21 Dante Salituro/50 6.00 15.00
22 Davis Koch/80 6.00 15.00
23 Dylan Strome/50 12.00 30.00
24 Evan Fitzpatrick/80 6.00 15.00
25 Evan Sarthou/80 3.00 8.00
26 Evgeny Svechnikov/50 8.00 20.00
27 Frederic Allard/80 3.00 8.00
28 Gabriel Gagne/80 4.00 10.00
29 Giorgio Estephan/80 3.00 8.00
30 Glenn Gawdin/80 3.00 8.00
31 Graham Knott/80 4.00 10.00
32 Ivan Provorov/50 10.00 25.00
33 Jaeger White/80 3.00 8.00
34 Jakob Chychrun/50 12.00 30.00
35 Jakub Zboril/50 5.00 12.00
36 Jansen Harkins/50 6.00 15.00
37 Jason Bell/80 6.00 15.00
38 Jeremiah Addison/80 3.00 8.00
39 Jeremy Roy/50 6.00 15.00
40 Jonathan Ang/80 4.00 10.00
41 Jordan Hollett/80 6.00 15.00
42 Josh Anderson/80 4.00 10.00
43 Julien Gauthier/50 4.00 10.00
44 Justin Almeida/80 5.00 12.00
45 Kaden Elder/80 3.00 8.00
46 Kale Clague/50 12.00 30.00
47 Keoni Texeira/80 3.00 8.00
48 Kody McDonald/80 3.00 8.00
49 Kyle Capobianco/80 3.00 8.00
50 Lawson Crouse/50 6.00 15.00
51 Logan Brown/80 4.00 10.00
52 Loik Leveille/80 4.00 10.00
53 Luke Green/80 3.00 8.00
54 Mackenzie Blackwood/50 8.00 20.00
55 Mathew Barzal/50 12.00 30.00
56 Matt Spencer/50 6.00 15.00
57 Matteo Gennaro/80 3.00 8.00
58 Matthew Kreis/80 4.00 10.00
59 Maxime Fortier/80 3.00 8.00
60 Medric Mercier/80 3.00 8.00
61 Michael McLeod/50 5.00 12.00
62 Mitchell Marner/50 20.00 50.00
63 Mitchell Stephens/80 3.00 8.00
64 Nathan Noel/50 8.00 20.00
65 Nick Merkley/50 15.00 40.00
66 Nicolas Meloche/50 5.00 12.00
67 Nicolas Roy/50 6.00 15.00
68 Nikita Korostelev/50 8.00 20.00
69 Nolan Kneen/80 4.00 10.00
70 Nolan Patrick/80 20.00 40.00
71 Parker Wotherspoon/80 5.00 12.00
72 Pascal Laberge/80 5.00 12.00
73 Paul Bittner/50 8.00 20.00
74 Pavel Karnaukhov/80 5.00 12.00
75 Pavel Zacha/50 10.00 25.00
76 Pierre-Luc Dubois/80 8.00 20.00
77 Quinn Benjafield/80 4.00 10.00
78 Ryan Gropp/80 5.00 12.00
79 Ryan Kubic/80 5.00 12.00
80 Ryan Pilon/80 3.00 8.00
81 Sam Steel/50 8.00 20.00
82 Samuel Girard/80 4.00 10.00
83 Simon Stransky/80 3.00 8.00
84 Tanner Kaspick/80 3.00 8.00
85 Thomas Schemitsch/80 4.00 10.00
86 Timo Meier/80 10.00 25.00
87 Travis Barron/80 5.00 12.00
88 Travis Konecny/50 10.00 25.00
89 Ty Ronning/50 5.00 12.00
90 Tyler Benson/50 12.00 30.00
91 Tyler Soy/80 4.00 10.00
92 Vince Dunn/50 6.00 15.00
93 Will Bitten/50 6.00 15.00

2014-15 ITG Heroes and Prospects All-Star Heroes Jerseys

ASH01 Jaromir Jagr 15.00 40.00
ASH02 Mario Lemieux 20.00 50.00
ASH03 Nicklas Lidstrom 6.00 15.00
ASH04 Patrick Roy 15.00 40.00
ASH05 Sergei Fedorov 12.00 30.00
ASH06 Steve Yzerman 12.00 30.00
ASH07 Wayne Gretzky 30.00 80.00

2014-15 ITG Heroes and Prospects Between the Pipes Glovemen Memorabilia

GMCP1 Carey Price 20.00 40.00
GMDH1 Dominik Hasek 10.00 25.00
GMGW1 Gump Worsley 20.00 50.00
GMJP1 Jacques Plante 10.00 25.00
GMMAF Marc-Andre Fleury 12.00 30.00
GMPR1 Patrick Roy
GMTE1 Tony Esposito 25.00 50.00
GMTS1 Terry Sawchuk 25.00 50.00

2014-15 ITG Heroes and Prospects Between the Pipes Padmen Memorabilia

PMCG1 Charlie Gardiner
PMCP1 Carey Price 20.00 40.00
PMGC1 Gerry Cheevers 10.00 25.00
PMJB1 Johnny Bower 20.00 40.00
PMPL2 Pelle Lindbergh 8.00 20.00
PMPR1 Patrick Roy
PMTS1 Terry Sawchuk 25.00 50.00
PMVT1 Vladislav Tretiak 25.00 50.00

2014-15 ITG Heroes and Prospects Draft Prospect Autographs

DPACMD Connor McDavid 250.00 400.00
DPADS1 Daniel Sprong 20.00 50.00
DPADS2 Dylan Strome 25.00 60.00
DPAIP1 Ivan Provorov 20.00 50.00
DPAJH1 Jansen Harkins 12.00 30.00
DPAJR1 Jeremy Roy 12.00 30.00
DPALC1 Lawson Crouse 12.00 30.00
DPAMB1 Mackenzie Blackwood
DPAMB3 Mathew Barzal
DPAMM3 Mitchell Marner 15.00 40.00
DPANM1 Nick Merkley 20.00 50.00
DPANR1 Nicolas Roy 12.00 30.00
DPAPB1 Paul Bittner 20.00 50.00
DPAPZ1 Pavel Zacha 20.00 50.00
DPATK2 Travis Konecny 15.00 40.00

2014-15 ITG Heroes and Prospects Hero and Prospect Jerseys

HPJ01 C.McDavid/W.Gretzky 75.00 150.00
HPJ02 J.Roy/R.Bourque 8.00 20.00
HPJ03 L.Crouse/M.Lemieux 25.00 60.00
HPJ04 M.Barzal/S.Yzerman 10.00 25.00
HPJ05 P.Roy/M.Blackwood 10.00 25.00
HPJ06 P.Bittner/M.Modano 12.00 30.00
HPJ07 P.Zacha/J.Jagr 20.00 50.00
HPJ08 P.Zacha/S.Fedorov 12.00 30.00
HPJ09 T.Konecny/J.Sakic 12.00 30.00

2014-15 ITG Heroes and Prospects Hero Autographs

1 Bill Gadsby
2 Bobby Hull 8.00 20.00
3 Brett Hull 10.00 25.00
4 Gerry Cheevers 8.00 20.00
5 Grant Fuhr 12.00 30.00
6 Harry Howell 6.00 15.00
7 Henri Richard 8.00 20.00
8 Jacques Lemaire 8.00 20.00
9 Jaromir Jagr 20.00 50.00
10 Joe Thornton 12.00 30.00
11 Johnny Bucyk 12.00 30.00
12 Paul Coffey 8.00 20.00
13 Raymond Bourque 12.00 30.00
14 Sergei Fedorov 15.00 30.00
15 Vladislav Tretiak 10.00 25.00
16 Wendel Clark 8.00 20.00

2014-15 ITG Heroes and Prospects Jersey

*GOLD/15: .6X TO 1.5X JSY/60
*PATCH/20: .6X TO 1.5X JSY/60
AM1 Adam Mascherin 4.00 10.00
CMD Connor McDavid 25.00 60.00
DS1 Daniel Sprong 8.00 20.00
DS2 Dylan Strome 10.00 25.00
GG1 Glenn Gawdin 3.00 8.00
JC1 Jakob Chychrun 10.00 25.00
JH1 Jansen Harkins 5.00 12.00
JR1 Jeremy Roy 5.00 12.00
LC1 Lawson Crouse 5.00 12.00
MB1 Mackenzie Blackwood 6.00 15.00
MB3 Mathew Barzal 10.00 25.00
MM3 Mitchell Marner 15.00 40.00
MS1 Matt Spencer 6.00 15.00
NM1 Nick Merkley 8.00 20.00
NM2 Nicolas Meloche 4.00 10.00
NR1 Nicolas Roy 5.00 12.00
SS1 Sam Steel 5.00 12.00
TB3 Tyler Benson 10.00 25.00
TK2 Travis Konecny 8.00 20.00

2014-15 ITG Heroes and Prospects Prospect Trio Jerseys

P301 Benson/Day/Chychrun 12.00 30.00
P302 Bittner/Barzal/Harkins 12.00 30.00
P303 Blackwood/Zacha/McDavid 30.00 80.00
P304 Domi/McDavid/Crouse 30.00 80.00
P305 McDavid/Barzal/Marner 30.00 80.00
P306 McDavid/Strome/Crouse 30.00 80.00
P307 McDavid/Virtanen/Comrie 30.00 80.00
P308 Meloche/Roy/McDavid 30.00 80.00
P309 Merkley/Konecny/Bittner 10.00 25.00
P310 Trenin/Svechnikov/McDavid 30.00 80.00

2014-15 ITG Heroes and Prospects Subway Series Jerseys

*GOLD/15: .6X TO 1.5X JSY/60
*PATCH/20: .6X TO 1.5X JSY/60
SSJ01 Alexandre Alain 4.00 10.00
SSJ02 Alexandre Carrier 4.00 10.00
SSJ03 Anthony Beauvillier 4.00 10.00
SSJ04 Brayden Point 5.00 12.00
SSJ05 Brendan Lemieux 5.00 12.00
SSJ06 Carter Verhaeghe 3.00 8.00
SSJ07 Conner Bleackley 5.00 12.00
SSJ09 Eric Comrie 5.00 12.00
SSJ10 Greg Chase 3.00 8.00
SSJ11 Guillaume Brisebois 5.00 12.00
SSJ12 Haydn Fleury 5.00 12.00
SSJ13 Jake Virtanen 6.00 15.00
SSJ14 Jason Dickinson 5.00 12.00
SSJ15 Jayce Hawryluk 3.00 8.00
SSJ17 John Quenneville 4.00 10.00
SSJ18 Josh Ho-Sang 6.00 15.00
SSJ19 Julien Pelletier 4.00 10.00
SSJ20 Mackenzie Blackwood 6.00 15.00
SSJ21 Max Domi 8.00 20.00
SSJ22 Nicolas Aube-Kubel 3.00 8.00
SSJ23 Nicolas Meloche 4.00 10.00
SSJ24 Nicolas Roy 5.00 12.00
SSJ25 Philippe Desrosiers 4.00 10.00
SSJ26 Spencer Martin 6.00 15.00
SSJ27 Travis Sanheim 6.00 15.00
SSJ28 Tristan Jarry 4.00 10.00
SSJ29 Tyler Bertuzzi 5.00 12.00
SSJ30 Zach Nastasiuk 4.00 10.00

2014-15 ITG Heroes and Prospects Top Prospects Jersey

*GOLD/15: .6X TO 1.5X JSY/60
*PATCH/20: .6X TO 1.5X JSY/60
TPJ01 Adam Musil 4.00 10.00
TPJ02 Connor McDavid 25.00 60.00
TPJ03 Daniel Sprong 8.00 20.00
TPJ04 Dennis Yan 4.00 10.00
TPJ05 Dylan Strome 12.00 30.00
TPJ06 Evgeny Svechnikov 6.00 15.00
TPJ07 Filip Chlapik 4.00 10.00
TPJ08 Jeremy Roy 5.00 12.00
TPJ09 Lawson Crouse 5.00 12.00
TPJ10 Matt Spencer 6.00 15.00
TPJ11 Mitchell Marner 10.00 25.00
TPJ12 Nick Merkley 8.00 20.00
TPJ13 Paul Bittner 6.00 15.00
TPJ14 Travis Konecny 8.00 20.00
TPJ15 Yakov Trenin 4.00 10.00

2015-16 ITG Heroes and Prospects Prospect Autographs

PSAC1 Alexander Chmelevski 5.00 12.00
PSAD1 Alex DeBrincat 6.00 15.00
PSAD2 Arnaud Durandeau 4.00 10.00
PSAM1 Antoine Morand 4.00 10.00
PSAP1 Austin Pratt 4.00 10.00
PSAR1 Anthony Richard 5.00 12.00
PSBC1 Brett Crossley 4.00 10.00
PSBD1 Brett Davis 6.00 15.00
PSBG1 Brady Gilmour 6.00 15.00
PSBH1 Brett Howden 5.00 12.00
PSBJ1 Ben Jones 4.00 10.00
PSBM1 Beck Malenstyn 6.00 15.00
PSCB2 Connor Bunnaman 4.00 10.00
PSCG1 Conor Garland 4.00 10.00
PSCH1 Carter Hart 6.00 15.00
PSCH2 Cameron Hebig 5.00 12.00
PSCP1 Christopher Paquette 4.00 10.00
PSDB1 Dereck Baribeau 4.00 10.00
PSDD1 Dillon Dube 6.00 15.00
PSDL1 David Levin 6.00 15.00
PSDS1 Dmitry Sokolov 6.00 15.00
PSDS1 Dylan Sadowy 6.00 15.00
PSDT1 Dmytro Timashov 6.00 15.00
PSDW1 Dylan Wells 4.00 10.00
PSDZ1 Dmitry Zhukenov 4.00 10.00
PSEB1 Egor Babenko 4.00 10.00
PSEC2 Evan Cormier 5.00 12.00
PSGS1 Gabriel Sylvestre 4.00 10.00
PSGS2 Givani Smith 4.00 10.00
PSGV1 Gabriel Vilardi 6.00 15.00
PSHD1 Hayden Davis 4.00 10.00
PSJA1 Josh Anderson 6.00 15.00
PSJB1 Jake Bean 6.00 15.00
PSJB2 Jordy Bellerive 4.00 10.00
PSJC1 Jakob Chychrun 8.00 20.00
PSJD1 Jared Dmytriw 4.00 10.00
PSJE1 Jack Eichel 25.00 60.00
PSJG1 Julien Gauthier 8.00 20.00
PSJK1 Jake Kryski 4.00 10.00
PSJK2 Jordan Kyrou 6.00 15.00
PSJM1 Josh Mahura 4.00 10.00
PSJP1 Jesse Puljujarvi 25.00 60.00
PSJV1 Joe Veleno 6.00 15.00
PSJV2 Juuso Valimaki 4.00 10.00
PSJW1 Jaeger White 4.00 10.00
PSJW2 Jeff De Wit 4.00 10.00
PSKA1 Kristian Afanasyev 4.00 10.00
PSKC1 Kale Clague 6.00 15.00
PSKM2 Keaton Middleton 4.00 10.00
PSKY2 Keanu Yamamoto 5.00 12.00
PSLB1 Logan Brown 10.00 25.00
PSLC1 Louis-Filip Cote 4.00 10.00
PSLJ1 Lucas Johansen 4.00 10.00
PSLM1 Liam Murphy 4.00 10.00
PSLT1 Lucas Thierus 4.00 10.00
PSMB1 Matt Barberis 5.00 12.00
PSMB1 Mitchell Balmas 4.00 10.00
PSMC1 Maxime Comtois 6.00 15.00
PSMD1 Martins Dzierkals 4.00 10.00
PSMJ1 Max Jones 10.00 25.00
PSML1 Max Lajoie 6.00 15.00
PSMM1 Michael McLeod 6.00 15.00
PSMS1 Mathieu Sevigny 4.00 10.00
PSMS2 Michael Spacek 4.00 10.00
PSMS3 Mikhail Sergachev 10.00 25.00
PSMT1 Matthew Tkachuk 20.00 50.00
PSNB1 Nathan Bastian 6.00 15.00
PSNC1 Noah Carroll 5.00 12.00
PSNK1 Nolan Kneen 4.00 10.00
PSNP1 Nolan Patrick 12.00 30.00
PSNV1 Nolan Volcan 4.00 10.00
PSOT1 Owen Tippett 4.00 10.00
PSPB1 Patrick Bajkov 4.00 10.00
PSPD1 Pierre-Luc Dubois 10.00 25.00
PSPH1 Peyton Hoyt 4.00 10.00
PSPL1 Pascal Laberge 5.00 12.00
PSRB1 Radovan Bondra 4.00 10.00
PSRK1 Ryan Kubic 4.00 10.00
PSSB1 Shawn Boudrias 4.00 10.00
PSSG1 Samuel Girard 4.00 10.00
PSSM1 Stelio Mattheos 6.00 15.00
PSSS1 Sam Steel 8.00 20.00
PSSS2 Simon Stransky 6.00 15.00
PSSS3 Stuart Skinner 4.00 10.00
PSTB1 Travis Barron 5.00 12.00
PSTB2 Tyler Benson 8.00 20.00
PSTF1 Tye Felhaber 4.00 10.00
PSTK1 Tanner Kaspick 4.00 10.00
PSTP1 Tyler Parsons 4.00 10.00
PSTR1 Taylor Raddysh 6.00 15.00
PSTR2 Ty Ronning 4.00 10.00
PSTT1 Troy Timpano 4.00 10.00
PSVK1 Vladimir Kuznetsov 4.00 10.00
PSVM1 Victor Mete 4.00 10.00
PSVS1 Vili Saarijarvi 4.00 10.00
PSWB1 Will Bitten 4.00 10.00
PSZG1 Zach Gallant 4.00 10.00
PSZS1 Zach Sawchenko 4.00 10.00
PSZS2 Zachary Senyshyn 4.00 10.00
PSAN1

Alexander Nylander
10.00

2015-16 ITG Heroes and Prospects Canada Russia Series Jerseys
CR01 Anthony Beauvillier 5.00 12.00
CR02 Brendan Guhle 3.00 8.00
CR03 Carter Hart 5.00 12.00
CR04 Clark Bishop 5.00 12.00
CR05 Dylan Strome 10.00 25.00
CR06 Jansen Harkins 5.00 12.00
CR07 Julien Gauthier 6.00 15.00
CR08 Julien Nantel 5.00 12.00
CR09 Kale Clague 5.00 12.00
CR10 Lawson Crouse 5.00 12.00
CR11 Mathew Barzal 15.00 40.00
CR12 Maxime Fortier 3.00 8.00
CR13 Michael McLeod 5.00 12.00
CR14 Michael McNiven 5.00 12.00
CR15 Mitchell Marner 15.00 40.00
CR16 Nathan Bastian 5.00 12.00
CR17 Nick Merkley 6.00 15.00
CR18 Noah Juulsen 5.00 12.00
CR19 Nolan Patrick 10.00 25.00
CR20 Pierre-Luc Dubois 8.00 20.00
CR21 Ryan Gropp 5.00 12.00
CR22 Samuel Girard 3.00 8.00
CR23 Samuel Montembeault 5.00 12.00
CR24 Thomas Chabot 5.00 12.00
CR25 Victor Mete 3.00 8.00
CR26 Will Bitten 3.00 8.00

2015-16 ITG Heroes and Prospects Canada Russia Series Patches
CRP01 Anthony Beauvillier 6.00 15.00
CRP02 Brendan Guhle 4.00 10.00
CRP03 Carter Hart 6.00 15.00
CRP04 Clark Bishop 6.00 15.00
CRP05 Dylan Strome 12.00 30.00
CRP06 Jansen Harkins 6.00 15.00
CRP07 Julien Gauthier 8.00 20.00
CRP08 Julien Nantel 6.00 15.00
CRP09 Kale Clague 6.00 15.00
CRP10 Lawson Crouse 6.00 15.00
CRP11 Mathew Barzal 20.00 50.00
CRP12 Maxime Fortier 4.00 10.00
CRP13 Michael McLeod 6.00 15.00
CRP14 Michael McNiven 6.00 15.00
CRP15 Mitchell Marner 15.00 40.00
CRP16 Nathan Bastian 6.00 15.00
CRP17 Nick Merkley 8.00 20.00
CRP18 Noah Juulsen 6.00 15.00
CRP19 Nolan Patrick 20.00 50.00
CRP20 Pierre-Luc Dubois 10.00 25.00
CRP21 Ryan Gropp 6.00 15.00
CRP22 Samuel Girard 4.00 10.00
CRP23 Samuel Montembeault 6.00 15.00
CRP24 Thomas Chabot 6.00 15.00
CRP25 Victor Mete 4.00 10.00
CRP26 Will Bitten 4.00 10.00

2015-16 ITG Heroes and Prospects Draft Prospect Autographs
DPAD1 Alex DeBrincat 10.00 25.00
DPJB1 Jake Bean 10.00 25.00
DPJC1 Jakob Chychrun 12.00 30.00
DPJG1 Julien Gauthier 12.00 30.00
DPJP1 Jesse Puljujarvi 40.00 100.00
DPMJ1 Max Jones 15.00 40.00
DPMS1 Mikhail Sergachev 15.00 40.00
DPMT1 Matthew Tkachuk 30.00 80.00
DPPD1 Pierre-Luc Dubois 15.00 40.00
DPVA1 Vitalii Abramov 12.00 30.00

2015-16 ITG Heroes and Prospects Hero and Prospect Jerseys
HPJ01 D.Gilmour/B.Gilmour/30 5.00 12.00
HPJ02 J.Brodeur/M.Brodeur/30 8.00 20.00
HPJ03 J.Veleno/W.Gretzky/20 20.00 50.00
HPJ04 K.Tkachuk/M.Tkachuk/30 12.00 30.00
HPJ05 N.Patrick/E.Lindros/30 8.00 20.00
HPJ06 V.Abramov/P.Bure/30 6.00 15.00
HPJ07 X.Potvin/F.Potvin/30 6.00 15.00

2015-16 ITG Heroes and Prospects Hero Autographs
HABB1 Bill Barber/30 12.00 30.00
HABS1 Billy Smith/20 15.00 40.00
HAGL1 Guy Lafleur/25 20.00 50.00
HAIL1 Igor Larionov/25 15.00 40.00
HAMB1 Martin Brodeur/20 30.00 80.00
HAMD1 Marcel Dionne/30 20.00 50.00
HAME1 Mike Eruzione/30 12.00 30.00
HAOK1 Olaf Kolzig/30 15.00 40.00
HAPB1 Pavel Bure/25 25.00 60.00
HAPS1 Peter Stastny/30 12.00 30.00
HATE1 Tony Esposito/20 15.00 40.00

2015-16 ITG Heroes and Prospects Hero Eight Jerseys
H801 Larkin/Eichel/McDavid/Domi 30.00 80.00
Bennett/Reinhart/Duclair/Ehlers
H802 Roy/Gretzky/Lemieux/Messier 30.00 80.00
Bourque/Fedorov/Hull/Yzerman
H803 Selanne/Kariya/Fedorov 30.00 80.00
Getzlaf/Niedermayer/Niedermayer/Oates/Pronger

2015-16 ITG Heroes and Prospects Jersey Autographs
AGBD1 Brett Davis/20 10.00 25.00
AGDT1 Dmytro Timashov/20 10.00 25.00
AGJB1 Jake Bean/20 10.00 25.00
AGJE1 Jack Eichel/25 40.00 100.00
AGJE2 Jack Eichel/20 40.00 100.00
AGJV1 Joe Veleno/25 10.00 25.00
AGMJ1 Max Jones/15 15.00 40.00
AGSM1 Stelio Mattheos/15 10.00 25.00
AGVA1 Vitalii Abramov/15 12.00 30.00

2015-16 ITG Heroes and Prospects Jerseys
GU01 Alex DeBrincat 5.00 12.00
GU02 Alexander Chmelevski 4.00 10.00
GU03 Alexander Nylander 8.00 20.00
GU04 Beck Malenstyn 5.00 12.00
GU05 Brady Gilmour 5.00 12.00
GU06 David Levin 5.00 12.00
GU07 Dillon Dube 5.00 12.00
GU08 Dmitry Sokolov 5.00 12.00
GU09 Dmytro Timashov 5.00 12.00
GU10 Dylan Sadowy 5.00 12.00
GU11 Dylan Strome 10.00 25.00
GU12 Gabriel Vilardi 5.00 12.00
GU13 Jack Eichel 20.00 50.00
GU14 Jakob Chychrun 6.00 15.00
GU15 Joe Veleno 5.00 12.00
GU16 Jordan Kyrou 5.00 12.00
GU17 Julien Gauthier 6.00 15.00
GU18 Juuso Valimaki 3.00 8.00
GU19 Matthew Tkachuk 15.00 40.00
GU20 Max Jones 8.00 20.00
GU21 Max Lajoie 5.00 12.00
GU22 Maxime Comtois 5.00 12.00
GU23 Nolan Patrick 10.00 25.00
GU24 Sam Steel 6.00 15.00
GU25 Simon Stransky 5.00 12.00
GU26 Stelio Mattheos 5.00 12.00
GU27 Taylor Raddysh 5.00 12.00
GU28 Vitalii Abramov 6.00 15.00

2015-16 ITG Heroes and Prospects Metal Autographs
BMJE1 Jack Eichel 25.00 60.00
BMJP1 Jesse Puljujarvi 25.00 60.00
BMJV1 Joe Veleno 20.00 50.00

2015-16 ITG Heroes and Prospects Patches
GUP01 Alex DeBrincat 8.00 20.00
GUP02 Alexander Chmelevski 6.00 15.00
GUP03 Alexander Nylander 12.00 30.00
GUP04 Beck Malenstyn 8.00 20.00
GUP05 Brady Gilmour 8.00 20.00
GUP06 David Levin 8.00 20.00
GUP07 Dillon Dube 8.00 20.00
GUP08 Dmitry Sokolov 8.00 20.00
GUP09 Dmytro Timashov 8.00 20.00
GUP10 Dylan Sadowy 8.00 20.00
GUP11 Dylan Strome 15.00 40.00
GUP12 Gabriel Vilardi 8.00 20.00
GUP13 Jack Eichel 30.00 80.00
GUP14 Jakob Chychrun 10.00 25.00
GUP15 Joe Veleno 8.00 20.00
GUP16 Jordan Kyrou 8.00 20.00
GUP17 Julien Gauthier 10.00 25.00
GUP18 Juuso Valimaki 5.00 12.00
GUP19 Matthew Tkachuk 25.00 60.00
GUP20 Max Jones 12.00 30.00
GUP21 Max Lajoie 8.00 20.00
GUP22 Maxime Comtois 8.00 20.00
GUP23 Nolan Patrick 15.00 40.00
GUP24 Sam Steel 10.00 25.00
GUP25 Simon Stransky 8.00 20.00
GUP26 Stelio Mattheos 8.00 20.00
GUP27 Taylor Raddysh 8.00 20.00
GUP28 Vitalii Abramov 10.00 25.00

2015-16 ITG Heroes and Prospects Prospect Eight Jerseys
P801 DeBrincat/Strome/Raddysh 15.00 40.00
Vilardi/McLeod/Nylander/Gilmour/Chychrun
P802 Patrick/Malenstyn/Bean/Steel 15.00 40.00
Benson/Stransky/Valimaki/Mahura
P803 Abramov/Veleno/Comtois 10.00 25.00
Timashov/Gauthier/Morand/Girard/Sylvestre
P804 Blackwood/Cormier/Papirny 6.00 15.00
McDonald/Potvin/Brodeur/Dumont-Bouchard/Smith
P805 Patrick/DeBrincat/Levin 25.00 60.00
Abramov/Benson/Tkachuk/Bean/Gauthier

2015-16 ITG Heroes and Prospects Rare Materials Signatures
RMBS1 Borje Salming/15 10.00 25.00
RMGL1 Guy Lafleur/15 12.00 30.00
RMJE1 Jack Eichel/15 40.00 100.00
RMJT1 Jose Theodore/15 10.00 25.00
RMJV1 Joe Veleno/20 10.00 25.00
RMMC1 Maxime Comtois/15 10.00 25.00
RMPB1 Pavel Bure/15 15.00 40.00
RMTS1 Teemu Selanne/15 20.00 50.00

2015-16 ITG Heroes and Prospects Top Prospects Jerseys
TP01 Alex DeBrincat 5.00 12.00
TP02 Alexander Nylander 8.00 20.00
TP03 Brett Howden 4.00 10.00
TP04 Carter Hart 5.00 12.00
TP05 Evan Fitzpatrick 6.00 15.00
TP06 Jake Bean 5.00 12.00
TP07 Jordan Kyrou 5.00 12.00
TP08 Julien Gauthier 6.00 15.00
TP09 Logan Brown 8.00 20.00
TP10 Matthew Tkachuk 15.00 40.00
TP11 Max Jones 8.00 20.00
TP12 Michael McLeod 5.00 12.00
TP13 Mikhail Sergachev 8.00 20.00
TP14 Olli Juolevi 5.00 12.00
TP15 Pierre-Luc Dubois 8.00 20.00
TP16 Simon Stransky 5.00 12.00
TP17 Taylor Raddysh 5.00 12.00
TP18 Vitalii Abramov 6.00 15.00

2015-16 ITG Heroes and Prospects Top Prospects Patches
TPP01 Alex DeBrincat 8.00 20.00
TPP02 Alexander Nylander 12.00 30.00
TPP03 Brett Howden 6.00 15.00
TPP04 Carter Hart 8.00 20.00
TPP05 Evan Fitzpatrick 10.00 25.00
TPP06 Jake Bean 8.00 20.00
TPP07 Jordan Kyrou 8.00 20.00
TPP08 Julien Gauthier 10.00 25.00
TPP09 Logan Brown 12.00 30.00
TPP10 Matthew Tkachuk 25.00 60.00
TPP11 Max Jones 12.00 30.00
TPP12 Michael McLeod 8.00 20.00
TPP13 Mikhail Sergachev 12.00 30.00
TPP14 Olli Juolevi 8.00 20.00
TPP15 Pierre-Luc Dubois 12.00 30.00
TPP16 Simon Stransky 8.00 20.00
TPP17 Taylor Raddysh 8.00 20.00
TPP18 Vitalii Abramov 10.00 25.00

2015-16 ITG Heroes and Prospects Trinity Signatures
JE Jack Eichel 30.00 80.00

2016-17 ITG Heroes and Prospects Prospect Autographs
PAAC1 Alexander Chmelevski 4.00 10.00
PAAD1 Alex DeBrincat 8.00 20.00
PAAH1 Aleksi Heponiemi 6.00 15.00
PAAM1 Adam McMaster 5.00 12.00
PAAM2 Antoine Morand 4.00 10.00
PAAMD Anderson MacDonald 4.00 10.00
PAAR1 Adam Ruzicka 6.00 15.00
PABG1 Benoit-Olivier Groulx 4.00 10.00
PABG2 Brady Gilmour 4.00 10.00
PABK1 Boris Katchouk 8.00 20.00
PABM1 Beck Malenstyn SP 4.00 10.00
PACB1 Connor Bunnaman SP 4.00 10.00
PACF1 Cal Foote 8.00 20.00
PACG1 Cody Glass 10.00 25.00
PACH1 Carter Hart 6.00 15.00
PACR1 Connor Roberts 4.00 10.00
PADA1 Danil Antropov 6.00 15.00
PADB1 Dennis Busby 6.00 15.00
PADG1 Damien Giroux 4.00 10.00
PADS1 Dylan Strome 8.00 20.00
PADV1 Daniil Vertiy 8.00 20.00
PAGF1 Gabriel Fortier 8.00 20.00
PAGS1 Givani Smith SP 4.00 10.00
PAGV1 Gabriel Vilardi 4.00 10.00
PAHD1 Hayden Davis 4.00 10.00
PAIL1 Ivan Lodnia 10.00 25.00
PAIS1 Ian Scott 8.00 20.00
PAJAD Jaret Anderson-Dolan 8.00 20.00
PAJB1 Jordy Bellerive 4.00 10.00
PAJD1 Jared Dmytriw 4.00 10.00
PAJDW Jeff De Wit 4.00 10.00
PAJK1 Jordan Kyrou 3.00 8.00
PAJL1 Jake Leschyshyn SP 4.00 10.00
PAJM1 Josh Mahura SP 3.00 8.00
PAJP1 Jacob Paquette 4.00 10.00
PAJR1 Jason Robertson 4.00 10.00
PAJV1 Joe Veleno 12.00 30.00
PAJV2 Juuso Valimaki 4.00 10.00
PAJW1 Jaeger White 4.00 10.00
PAKC1 Kale Clague 4.00 10.00
PAKK1 Klim Kostin SP 8.00 20.00
PAKV1 Kristian Vesalainen 10.00 25.00
PAKY1 Kailer Yamamoto 6.00 15.00
PAKY2 Keanu Yamamoto SP 8.00 20.00
PALJ1 Lucas Johansen 4.00 10.00
PALM1 Liam Murphy 4.00 10.00
PALT1 Lucas Thierus 4.00 10.00
PAMB1 Mitchell Balmas SP 4.00 10.00
PAMC1 Maxime Comtois 4.00 10.00
PAMD1 Michael DiPietro 8.00 20.00
PAML1 Max Lajoie SP 4.00 10.00
PAMM1 Michael McLeod 4.00 10.00
PAMR1 Michael Rasmussen 8.00 20.00
PAMS1 Mathieu Sevigny SP 4.00 10.00
PAMS2 Matthew Strome 4.00 10.00
PAMS3 Michael Spacek 4.00 10.00
PANB1 Nathan Bastian SP 4.00 10.00
PAND1 Nathan Dunkley 5.00 12.00
PANH1 Nick Henry 4.00 10.00
PANH2 Nicolas Hague 3.00 8.00
PANH3 Nico Hischier 30.00 80.00
PANJ1 Noah Juulsen 4.00 10.00
PANM1 Nick Merkley 8.00 20.00
PANP1 Nikita Popugaev 4.00 10.00
PANP2 Nolan Patrick 25.00 60.00
PANS1 Nick Suzuki 8.00 20.00
PANV1 Nolan Volcan 4.00 10.00
PAOR1 Olivier Rodrigue 4.00 10.00
PAOT1 Owen Tippett 4.00 10.00
PAPB1 Patrick Bajkov SP 4.00 10.00
PAPL1 Pascal Laberge SP 3.00 8.00
PARM1 Ryan McLeod 4.00 10.00
PARM2 Ryan Merkley 8.00 20.00
PASE1 Shawn Element 4.00 10.00
PASG1 Samuel Girard SP 3.00 8.00
PASS1 Stuart Skinner 4.00 10.00
PATB1 Travis Barron SP 4.00 10.00
PATD1 Ty Dellandrea 4.00 10.00
PATF1 Tye Felhaber SP 4.00 10.00
PATK1 Tanner Kaspick SP 4.00 10.00
PATP1 Tyler Parsons SP 4.00 10.00
PATR1 Taylor Raddysh SP 4.00 10.00
PATR2 Ty Ronning SP 4.00 10.00
PATS1 Ty Smith 5.00 12.00
PATT1 Troy Timpano SP 4.00 10.00
PAVA1 Vitalii Abramov SP 4.00 10.00
PAVM1 Victor Mete 3.00 8.00
PAVS1 Vili Saarijarvi SP 4.00 10.00
PAWB1 Will Bitten SP 3.00 8.00
PAZS1 Zach Sawchenko SP 4.00 10.00
PAZS2 Zachary Senyshyn 4.00 10.00

2016-17 ITG Heroes and Prospects Heroes Eight Memorabilia
H801 Gretzky/Lemieux/Bourque 50.00 120.00
Hull/Messier/Yzerman/Roy/Fedorov
H802 Hall/Kane/Burns/Draisaitl 20.00 50.00
Subban/Tavares/MacKinnon/Stamkos
H803 Brodeur/Nabokov/Luongo 20.00 50.00
Turco/Kolzig/Khabibulin/Theodore/Vokoun
H804 Thornton/Iginla/Lecavalier/St. Louis 10.0025.00
Kovalchuk/Kovalev/Hossa/Alfredsson
H805 Belfour/Vanbiesbrouck 15.00 40.00
Richter/Joseph/Hasek/Vernon/Potvin/Burke
H806 Coffey/Bourque/Murphy 10.00 25.00
Housley/Reinhart/MacInnis/Potvin/Babych
H807 Fuhr/Beaupre/Smith/Riggin 10.00 25.00
Moog/Barrasso/Resch/Meloche
H808 Orr/Sittler/Unger/Lafleur 30.00 80.00
Esposito/Dionne/Cashman/Redmond

2016-17 ITG Heroes and Prospects Heroes Memorabilia
HM01 Adam Oates 3.00 8.00
HM02 Alexander Mogilny 3.00 8.00
HM03 Alexander Ovechkin 12.00 30.00
HM04 Arturs Irbe 2.50 6.00
HM05 Brian Leetch 3.00 8.00
HM06 Bryan Berard 3.00 8.00
HM07 Carey Price 10.00 25.00
HM08 Chris Chelios 3.00 8.00
HM09 Chris Osgood 3.00 8.00
HM10 Chris Pronger 2.50 6.00
HM11 Curtis Joseph 3.00 8.00
HM12 Daniel Alfredsson 3.00 8.00
HM13 Dany Heatley 3.00 8.00
HM14 Darryl Sydor 3.00 8.00
HM15 Doug Weight 3.00 8.00
HM16 Gary Sargent 3.00 8.00
HM17 Guy Lafleur 4.00 10.00
HM18 Henrik Lundqvist 3.00 8.00
HM19 Jack Eichel 6.00 15.00
HM20 Jaromir Jagr 10.00 25.00
HM21 Jason Arnott 3.00 8.00
HM22 Jeremy Roenick 3.00 8.00
HM23 Joe Nieuwendyk 3.00 8.00
HM24 Joe Sakic 5.00 12.00
HM25 Joe Thornton 3.00 8.00
HM26 John LeClair 3.00 8.00
HM27 Markus Naslund 3.00 8.00
HM28 Martin Brodeur 6.00 15.00
HM29 Mats Sundin 3.00 8.00
HM30 Mike Modano 5.00 12.00
HM31 Milan Hejduk 3.00 8.00
HM32 Nicklas Lidstrom 3.00 8.00
HM33 Owen Nolan 3.00 8.00
HM34 Patrick Roy 8.00 20.00
HM35 Paul Kariya 4.00 10.00
HM36 Pavel Bure 3.00 8.00
HM37 Peter Forsberg 3.00 8.00
HM38 Pierre Turgeon 3.00 8.00
HM39 Raymond Bourque 5.00 12.00
HM40 Rick Nash 3.00 8.00
HM41 Scott Niedermayer 3.00 8.00
HM42 Sergei Fedorov 5.00 12.00
HM43 Steve Larmer 3.00 8.00
HM44 Steve Shutt 3.00 8.00
HM45 Teemu Selanne 6.00 15.00
HM46 Trevor Linden 4.00 10.00
HM47 Vincent Damphousse 2.50 6.00
HM48 Wayne Gretzky SP 20.00 50.00
HM49 Zdeno Chara 3.00 8.00

2016-17 ITG Heroes and Prospects International Ice Autographs
IIAD1 Alex DeBrincat 10.00 25.00
IIAH1 Aleksi Heponiemi 8.00 20.00
IIAR1 Adam Ruzicka 8.00 20.00
IIBG1 Brady Gilmour 5.00 12.00
IIBK1 Boris Katchouk 10.00 25.00
IIBOG Benoit-Olivier Groulx 5.00 12.00
IICH1 Carter Hart 8.00 20.00
IIDS1 Dylan Strome SP 10.00 25.00
IIDV1 Daniil Vertiy 10.00 25.00
IIJB1 Jordy Bellerive 5.00 12.00
IIJE1 Jack Eichel 15.00 40.00
IIJV1 Joe Veleno 15.00 40.00
IIJV2 Juuso Valimaki 5.00 12.00
IIKC1 Kale Clague 5.00 12.00
IIKK1 Klim Kostin SP 10.00 25.00
IIKV1 Kristian Vesalainen 12.00 30.00
IINH1 Nico Hischier SP 20.00 50.00
IINP1 Nikita Popugaev 5.00 12.00
IINP2 Nolan Patrick 30.00 80.00
IISS1 Stuart Skinner 5.00 12.00

2016-17 ITG Heroes and Prospects Reflections Memorabilia
R01 W.Gretzky/C.McDavid 25.00 60.00
R02 G.Howe/M.Howe 12.00 30.00
R03 J.Eichel/M.Modano 10.00 25.00
R04 P.Roy/C.Price 15.00 40.00
R05 J.Kurri/T.Selanne 10.00 25.00
R06 P.Esposito/M.Lemieux 15.00 40.00
R07 S.Fedorov/A.Ovechkin 20.00 50.00
R08 G.Lafleur/S.Crosby 20.00 50.00
R09 D.Doughty/S.Stevens 5.00 12.00
R10 P.Kane/P.LaFontaine 10.00 25.00
R11 P.Bure/E.Malkin 15.00 40.00
R12 P.Turgeon/T.Seguin 8.00 20.00
R13 S.Patrick/N.Patrick 30.00 80.00
R14 B.Burns/K.Hatcher 6.00 15.00
R15 P.Kane/M.Marner 25.00 60.00
R16 T.Sawchuk/P.Roy 12.00 30.00

2012-13 ITG History Of Hockey Great Moments Memorabilia Silver
STATED PRINT RUN 40
81 Roy breaks Sawchuk Mark 30.00 60.00
82 Finally Sakic/Bourque 40.00 100.00
83 Esposito Shatters Record 30.00 80.00
84 Ovechkin scores on back 30.00 60.00
85 First Rookie to Score 50 40.00 100.00
86 Canada Wins 2002 Games 30.00 60.00
87 Ten Point Game 30.00 60.00
88 Esposito First To 100 Points 30.00 60.00
89 Flyers win 35 straight-Parent 30.00 60.00
90 Esposito's 1972 Speech 40.00 80.00
91 Captain Returns-Koivu 30.00 60.00
92 Hextall scores a goal 30.00 60.00
93 Controverisal Cup Winner 40.00 80.00
94 The Fog Game-Parent 25.00 60.00
95 First Cup Since 55 Yzerman 25.00 60.00
96 Eddie Returns to MSG 20.00 50.00
97 Lafleur's Comeback 15.00 40.00
98 US Wins First World Cup 20.00 50.00
99 Rookie Scoring T.Selanne 40.00 80.00
100 The China Wall-Bower 15.00 40.00
101 Clarke Wins First Hart 25.00 60.00
102 Lemieux Scores Five Ways 50.00 100.00
103 Lindros Plays Canada Cup 40.00 100.00
104 Clarke's Big Break 25.00 60.00
105 Longest Undefeated Streak 20.00 50.00
106 Baun Scores on Broken leg 12.00 30.00
107 Nolan Calls Shot AS Game 15.00 40.00
108 Hasek Lead Czech Gold 30.00 80.00
109 Lemieux Returns 40.00 80.00
110 Pelle Lindbergh Death 30.00 80.00
111 Roy's Last Game 40.00 80.00
112 Canada Cup Winner-Sittler 25.00 60.00
113 First Heritage Classic-Messier 30.00 80.00
114 Greatest Tie 30.00 60.00
115 Passing The Torch 30.00 60.00
116 Four Straight Cups-Bossy 25.00 60.00
117 Lemieux leads Pens Cup 40.00 80.00
118 LaFontaine overtime winner 25.00 60.00
119 Hull signs contract with Jets 15.00 40.00
120 Russian Invasion 30.00 80.00
121 48 Goals by Defenseman 25.00 60.00
122 Richter beats Bure 15.00 40.00
123 Rangers End 54-Year Drought 20.00 50.00
124 Gold Medal Save-Salo 20.00 50.00
125 Gold Medal Goal-Forsberg 25.00 60.00
126 Saying Goodbye-Tkachuk 15.00 40.00
127 The Save-McLean 20.00 50.00
128 50 Goals in 49 Games-Neely 15.00 40.00
129 Howe Family In Houston 25.00 60.00
130 Final Game Maple Leaf Gardens 30.00 80.00
131 87 Canada Cup-Gretzky 40.00 80.00
132 Canada Wins 04 World Cup 40.00 80.00
133 First Goalie to Score 25.00 60.00
134 Roy wins cup rookie year 50.00 100.00
135 Thomas Bruins to Cup 15.00 40.00
136 McDonald Scores Winner 25.00 60.00
137 Oilers Win Cup-Messier 30.00 80.00
138 First Overall-M.Lemieux 25.00 60.00
139 Neilson Surrenders 15.00 40.00
140 Calgary's First Stanley Cup 25.00 60.00
141 Back-To-Back Playoff MVP 25.00 60.00
142 Dionne Scores 40, 10X 15.00 40.00
143 Esposito Sets Rookie Record 20.00 50.00
144 Miracle on Ice-Jim Craig 40.00 100.00

2006-07 ITG International Ice
1 Vladislav Tretiak 2.00 5.00
2 Bobby Hull 2.00 5.00
3 Bobby Clarke 1.25 3.00
4 Raymond Bourque 2.00 5.00
5 Paul Coffey 1.25 3.00
6 Pat LaFontaine 1.25 3.00
7 Brett Hull 1.00 2.50
8 Steve Yzerman 3.00 8.00
9 Marek Schwarz 1.25 3.00
10 Sidney Crosby 5.00 12.00
11 Gerry Cheevers 1.25 3.00
12 Phil Esposito 2.00 5.00
13 Marcel Dionne 1.50 4.00
14 Grant Fuhr 1.25 3.00
15 Jaromir Jagr 3.00 8.00
16 Antero Niittymaki 1.00 2.50
17 Mario Lemieux 4.00 10.00
18 Henrik Lundqvist 2.50 6.00
19 Alexander Yakushev 1.00 2.50
20 Michel Goulet 1.00 2.50
21 Paul Coffey 1.25 3.00
22 Darryl Sittler 1.25 3.00
23 Stan Mikita 1.50 4.00
24 Borje Salming 1.25 3.00
25 Vladislav Tretiak 2.00 5.00
26 Steve Yzerman 3.00 8.00
27 Dale Hawerchuk 1.50 4.00
28 Martin Brodeur 2.50 6.00
29 Ilya Bryzgalov 1.25 3.00
30 Bobby Ryan 1.25 3.00
31 Tony Esposito 1.25 3.00
32 Jari Kurri 1.25 3.00
33 Larry Robinson 1.25 3.00
34 Doug Gilmour 1.50 4.00
35 Mike Richter 1.25 3.00
36 Brett Hull 1.00 2.50
37 Michael Frolik 1.00 2.50
38 Cristobal Huet 1.00 2.50
39 Phil Esposito 2.00 5.00
40 Valeri Vasilyev .75 2.00
41 Borje Salming 1.25 3.00
42 Glenn Anderson 1.25 3.00
43 Raymond Bourque 2.00 5.00
44 Luc Robitaille 1.25 3.00
45 Pat LaFontaine 1.25 3.00
46 Petr Prucha 1.00 2.50
47 Steve Shutt 1.25 3.00
48 Larry Robinson 1.25 3.00
49 Mats Naslund .75 2.00
50 Dale Hawerchuk 1.50 4.00
51 Pat LaFontaine 1.25 3.00
52 Jaromir Jagr 3.00 8.00
53 John Tavares 6.00 15.00
54 Tuukka Rask 3.00 8.00
55 Anders Hedberg .75 2.00
56 John Vanbiesbrouck 2.00 5.00
57 Larry Murphy 1.00 2.50
58 Jari Kurri 1.25 3.00
59 Alexander Ovechkin 5.00 12.00
60 Mike Bossy 1.25 3.00
61 Valeri Kharlamov 1.25 3.00
62 Rick Ley .75 2.00
63 Guy Lafleur 1.50 4.00
64 Tony Esposito 1.25 3.00
65 Kent Nilsson .75 2.00
66 Paul Coffey 1.25 3.00
67 Bill Ranford 1.25 3.00
68 Nicklas Lidstrom 1.25 3.00
69 Evgeni Malkin 5.00 12.00
70 Alexander Radulov 1.50 4.00
71 Borje Salming 1.25 3.00
72 Michel Goulet 1.00 2.50
73 Thomas Steen .75 2.00
74 Denis Potvin 1.25 3.00
75 Larry Robinson 1.25 3.00
76 Mark Howe 1.25 3.00
77 Wayne Cashman .75 2.00
78 Marcel Dionne 1.50 4.00
79 Neal Broten .75 2.00
80 Grant Fuhr 1.25 3.00
81 Jari Kurri 1.25 3.00
82 Brian Leetch 1.25 3.00
83 Jim Craig .75 2.00
84 Al Montoya 1.25 3.00
85 Mark Messier 2.00 5.00
86 Esa Tikkanen .75 2.00
87 Glenn Anderson 1.25 3.00
88 Brian Bellows 1.00 2.50
89 Ulf Nilsson .75 2.00
90 Gilbert Perreault 1.25 3.00
91 Peter Mahovlich 1.50 4.00
92 Peter Stastny 1.25 3.00
93 Igor Larionov 1.25 3.00
94 Mark Messier 2.00 5.00
95 Vladimir Krutov .75 2.00
96 Mats Naslund .75 2.00
97 Mike Richter 1.25 3.00
98 Martin Brodeur 2.50 6.00
99 Justin Pogge 1.25 3.00
100 Paul Coffey 1.25 3.00
101 Paul Henderson 1.00 2.50
102 Mark Messier 2.00 5.00
103 Gilbert Perreault 1.25 3.00
104 Pelle Lindbergh 1.50 4.00
105 Bill Barber .75 2.00
106 Andre Lacroix .75 2.00
107 J.P. Parise .75 2.00
108 Brad Park 1.00 2.50
109 Alex Auld .75 2.00
110 Phil Kessel 2.00 5.00
111 Yan Stastny .75 2.00
112 Steve Larmer .75 2.00
113 Mats Naslund .75 2.00
114 Rod Langway 1.00 2.50
115 Peter Stastny 1.25 3.00
116 Bryan Trottier 1.50 4.00
117 Bobby Hull 2.00 5.00
118 Frank Mahovlich 1.00 2.50
119 Guy Lapointe 1.00 2.50
120 Danny Gare .75 2.00
121 Guy Lafleur 1.50 4.00
122 Rick Middleton 1.00 2.50
123 Larry Murphy 1.00 2.50
124 Jeff Glass 1.00 2.50
125 Chris Chelios 1.25 3.00
126 Ryan Malone .75 2.00
127 Marc-Andre Fleury 2.00 5.00
128 Patrick Roy 3.00 8.00
129 Paul Henderson 1.00 2.50
130 Marcel Dionne 1.50 4.00
131 Serge Savard 1.25 3.00
132 Gilbert Perreault 1.25 3.00
133 Raymond Bourque 2.00 5.00
134 Phil Housley 1.00 2.50
135 Rogie Vachon 1.50 4.00
136 Vladimir Myshkin .75 2.00
137 Bobby Clarke 1.25 3.00
138 Robbie Schremp 1.00 2.50
139 Peter Mahovlich 1.50 4.00
140 Mike Bossy 1.25 3.00
141 Esa Tikkanen .75 2.00
142 Chris Chelios 1.25 3.00
143 Serge Savard 1.25 3.00
144 Lanny McDonald 1.25 3.00
145 Ilya Kovalchuk 1.25 3.00
146 Jason Spezza 1.25 3.00
147 Ryan Miller 1.25 3.00
148 Denis Potvin 1.25 3.00
149 Peter Mueller 1.25 3.00
150 Yvan Cournoyer 1.25 3.00
151 Ladislav Smid .75 2.00
152 Chris Bourque .75 2.00
153 Ralph Backstrom .75 2.00
154 Henrik Zetterberg 1.50 4.00
155 Angelo Esposito 1.50 4.00
156 Alexei Kasatonov .75 2.00
157 Ed Olczyk .75 2.00
158 Mark Messier 2.00 5.00
159 Andrei Markov 1.25 3.00
160 A.Ovechkin/E.Malkin 3.00 8.00

2006-07 ITG International Ice Autographs
ATED ODDS 1:1
AAA Alex Auld 4.00 10.00
AAE Angelo Esposito SP 25.00 50.00
AAH Anders Hedberg 4.00 10.00
AAK Alexei Kasatonov 10.00 25.00
AAL Andre Lacroix 4.00 10.00
AAM Al Montoya 6.00 15.00
AAMK Andrei Markov 4.00 10.00
AAN Antero Niittymaki 6.00 15.00
AAO Alexander Ovechkin SP 50.00 100.00
AAR Alexander Radulov SP 15.00 40.00
AAY Alexander Yakushev 20.00 50.00
ABB Brian Bellows 4.00 10.00
ABBR Bill Barber 8.00 20.00
ABC Bobby Clarke 12.50 30.00
ABC2 Bobby Clarke 15.00 40.00
ABH Bobby Hull SP 15.00 40.00
ABH2 Bobby Hull SP 20.00 50.00
ABHU Brett Hull SP 40.00 80.00
ABHU2 Brett Hull SP 40.00 80.00
ABL Brian Leetch SP 15.00 40.00
ABP Brad Park 8.00 20.00
ABR Bill Ranford 6.00 15.00
ABRY Bobby Ryan 8.00 20.00
ABS Borje Salming 8.00 20.00
ABS2 Borje Salming 8.00 20.00
ABS3 Borje Salming 8.00 20.00
ABT Bryan Trottier 15.00 40.00
ACB Chris Bourque 6.00 15.00
ACC Chris Chelios 10.00 25.00
ACC2 Chris Chelios 10.00 25.00
ACH Cristobal Huet 8.00 20.00
ADG Doug Gilmour 12.00 30.00
ADGR Danny Gare 6.00 15.00
ADH Dale Hawerchuk 12.00 30.00
ADH2 Dale Hawerchuk 12.00 30.00
ADP Denis Potvin 6.00 15.00
ADP2 Denis Potvin 10.00 25.00
ADS Darryl Sittler 10.00 25.00
AEM Evgeni Malkin SP 100.00 200.00
AEO Ed Olczyk 4.00 10.00
AET Esa Tikkanen 8.00 20.00
AET2 Esa Tikkanen 8.00 20.00
AFM Frank Mahovlich SP 30.00 60.00
AGA Glenn Anderson 6.00 15.00
AGA2 Glenn Anderson 6.00 15.00
AGC Gerry Cheevers 10.00 25.00
AGF Grant Fuhr 10.00 25.00
AGF2 Grant Fuhr 12.00 30.00
AGL Guy Lafleur 15.00 40.00
AGL2 Guy Lafleur 15.00 40.00
AGLP Guy Lapointe 10.00 25.00
AGP Gilbert Perreault 10.00 25.00
AGP2 Gilbert Perreault 10.00 25.00
AGP3 Gilbert Perreault 10.00 25.00
AHL Henrik Lundqvist 20.00 40.00
AHZ Henrik Zetterberg SP 30.00 80.00
AIB Ilya Bryzgalov 10.00 25.00
AIK Ilya Kovalchuk SP 25.00 50.00
AIL Igor Larionov 12.00 30.00
AJC Jim Craig 15.00 40.00
AJG Jeff Glass 6.00 15.00
AJJ Jaromir Jagr SP 30.00 60.00
AJJ2 Jaromir Jagr SP 40.00 80.00
AJK Jari Kurri 10.00 25.00
AJK2 Jari Kurri 8.00 20.00
AJK3 Jari Kurri 8.00 20.00
AJP Justin Pogge 15.00 40.00
AJPP J.P. Parise 5.00 12.00
AJS Jason Spezza SP 15.00 40.00
AJT John Tavares SP 50.00 100.00
AJV John Vanbiesbrouck 8.00 20.00
AKN Kent Nilsson 4.00 10.00
ALM Larry Murphy 8.00 20.00
ALM2 Larry Murphy 8.00 20.00
ALMC Lanny McDonald 6.00 15.00
ALR Larry Robinson 8.00 20.00
ALR2 Larry Robinson 8.00 20.00
ALR3 Larry Robinson 10.00 25.00
ALRO Luc Robitaille SP 15.00 40.00
ALS Ladislav Smid 4.00 10.00
AMAF Marc-Andre Fleury 20.00 40.00
AMB Martin Brodeur SP 60.00 100.00
AMB2 Martin Brodeur SP 60.00 120.00
AMBO Mike Bossy 12.00 30.00
AMBO2 Mike Bossy 12.00 30.00
AMD Marcel Dionne 10.00 25.00
AMD2 Marcel Dionne 10.00 25.00
AMD3 Marcel Dionne 12.00 30.00
AMF Michael Frolik 8.00 20.00
AMG Michel Goulet 5.00 12.00
AMG2 Michel Goulet 5.00 12.00
AMH Mark Howe 4.00 10.00
AML Mario Lemieux SP 100.00 175.00
AMM Mark Messier SP 50.00 100.00
AMM2 Mark Messier SP 40.00 80.00
AMM3 Mark Messier SP 40.00 80.00
AMM4 Mark Messier SP 50.00 100.00
AMN Mats Naslund 10.00 25.00
AMN2 Mats Naslund 10.00 25.00
AMN3 Mats Naslund 10.00 25.00
AMS Marek Schwarz 6.00 15.00
ANB Neal Broten 8.00 20.00
ANL Nicklas Lidstrom SP 15.00 40.00
AOM Ovechkin/Malkin/10 300.00 450.00
APC Paul Coffey SP 30.00 60.00
APC2 Paul Coffey SP 20.00 50.00
APC3 Paul Coffey SP 20.00 50.00
APC4 Paul Coffey SP 20.00 50.00
APE Phil Esposito SP 25.00 50.00
APE2 Phil Esposito SP 30.00 60.00
APH Paul Henderson 12.00 30.00
APH2 Paul Henderson 12.00 30.00
APHO Phil Housley 4.00 10.00
APK Phil Kessel 12.50 30.00
APL Pat LaFontaine SP 15.00 40.00
APL2 Pat LaFontaine SP 15.00 40.00
APL3 Pat LaFontaine SP 15.00 40.00
APM Peter Mahovlich 8.00 20.00
APM2 Peter Mahovlich 8.00 20.00
APMU Peter Mueller 8.00 20.00
APP Petr Prucha 8.00 20.00
APR Patrick Roy 40.00 100.00
APS Peter Stastny 12.00 30.00
APS2 Peter Stastny 8.00 20.00
ARB Raymond Bourque SP 30.00 80.00
ARB2 Raymond Bourque SP 30.00 80.00
ARB3 Raymond Bourque SP 30.00 80.00
ARBA Ralph Backstrom 4.00 10.00
ARL Rick Ley 4.00 10.00
ARLW Rod Langway 6.00 15.00
ARM Rick Middleton 6.00 15.00
ARMI Ryan Miller 12.00 30.00
ARML Ryan Malone 4.00 10.00
ARS Robbie Schremp 6.00 15.00
ARV Rogie Vachon 8.00 20.00
ASC Sidney Crosby SP 100.00 200.00
ASL Steve Larmer 8.00 20.00
ASM Stan Mikita 12.00 30.00
ASS Steve Shutt 12.00 30.00
ASSV Serge Savard 4.00 10.00
ASSV2 Serge Savard 6.00 15.00
ASY Steve Yzerman SP 40.00 100.00
ASY2 Steve Yzerman SP 40.00 100.00
ATE Tony Esposito SP 25.00 60.00
ATE2 Tony Esposito SP 30.00 80.00
ATR Tuukka Rask 25.00 50.00
ATS Thomas Steen 4.00 10.00
AUN Ulf Nilsson 4.00 10.00
AVK Vladimir Krutov 10.00 25.00
AVM Vladimir Myshkin 30.00 60.00
AVT Vladislav Tretiak 30.00 60.00
AVT2 Vladislav Tretiak 50.00 100.00
AVV Valeri Vasilyev 15.00 30.00
AWC Wayne Cashman 4.00 10.00
AYC Yvan Cournoyer 12.00 30.00
AYS Yan Stastny 4.00 10.00

2006-07 ITG International Ice Best of the Best
STATED PRINT RUN 60 SER.#'d SETS
BB01 Vladislav Tretiak 25.00 50.00
BB02 Brian Leetch 6.00 15.00
BB03 Paul Coffey 6.00 15.00
BB04 Mark Messier 10.00 25.00
BB05 Valeri Kharlamov 20.00 50.00
BB06 Mario Lemieux 20.00 50.00
BB07 Martin Brodeur 12.00 30.00
BB08 Raymond Bourque 8.00 20.00
BB09 Nicklas Lidstrom 6.00 15.00
BB10 Phil Esposito 8.00 20.00
BB11 Jaromir Jagr 15.00 40.00
BB12 Bobby Hull 10.00 25.00

2006-07 ITG International Ice Canadian Dream Team
STATED PRINT RUN 60 SER.#'d SETS
DT01 Bobby Hull 10.00 25.00
DT02 Mark Messier 10.00 25.00
DT03 Martin Brodeur 12.00 30.00
DT04 Bobby Clarke 10.00 25.00
DT05 Phil Esposito 8.00 20.00
DT06 Darryl Sittler 8.00 20.00
DT07 Raymond Bourque 10.00 25.00
DT08 Mario Lemieux 15.00 40.00
DT09 Grant Fuhr 10.00 25.00
DT10 Paul Coffey 10.00 25.00
DT11 Sidney Crosby 25.00 60.00
DT12 John Tavares 12.00 30.00

2006-07 ITG International Ice Double Memorabilia
STATED PRINT RUN 20
UNLISTED GOLD VERSION 1/1
DM01 Eric Lindros 10.00 25.00
DM02 Patrick Roy 30.00 80.00
DM03 Martin Brodeur 25.00 50.00
DM04 Alexander Ovechkin 40.00 100.00
DM05 Sidney Crosby 40.00 100.00
DM06 Mario Lemieux 30.00 80.00

2006-07 ITG International Ice Goaltending Glory
ATED PRINT RUN 60
GG01 Tony Esposito 10.00 25.00
GG02 Grant Fuhr 12.00 30.00
GG03 Martin Brodeur 15.00 40.00
GG04 Justin Pogge 8.00 20.00
GG05 Henrik Lundqvist 15.00 40.00
GG06 Mike Richter 8.00 20.00
GG07 Pelle Lindbergh 15.00 60.00
GG08 Vladimir Dzurilla 8.00 20.00
GG09 Jonathan Bernier 8.00 20.00
GG10 Rogie Vachon 15.00 40.00
GG11 Bill Ranford 12.00 30.00
GG12 Antero Niittymaki 12.00 30.00
GG13 Cristobal Huet 12.00 30.00
GG14 John Vanbiesbrouck 12.00 30.00
GG15 Vladislav Tretiak 30.00 80.00
GG16 Vladimir Myshkin 10.00 25.00
GG17 Ilya Bryzgalov 12.00 30.00
GG18 Al Montoya 6.00 15.00
GG19 Gerry Cheevers 10.00 25.00
GG20 Sergei Mylnikov 15.00 40.00
GG21 Patrick Roy 20.00 50.00
GG22 Miikka Kiprusoff 10.00 25.00

2006-07 ITG International Ice Greatest Moments
STATED PRINT RUN 50
GM01 Russian Upset 12.00 30.00
GM02 Esposito's Speech 8.00 20.00
GM03 Cournoyer's Assist 20.00 50.00
GM04 Hull Gets His Chance 10.00 25.00
GM05 Sittler's Goal 8.00 20.00
GM06 Swapping Sweaters 12.00 30.00
GM07 1984 Comeback 12.00 30.00
GM08 Lemieux's Big Moment 15.00 40.00
GM09 American Victory 10.00 25.00
GM10 WJC Gold/Crosby 30.00 80.00

2006-07 ITG International Ice Hockey Passport
UNLISTED STARS 10.00 25.00
STATED PRINT RUN 60
HP01 Jaromir Jagr 10.00 25.00
HP02 Vladislav Tretiak 12.00 30.00
HP03 Valeri Kharlamov 12.00 30.00
HP04 Bobby Hull 10.00 25.00
HP05 Martin Brodeur 12.00 30.00
HP06 Borje Salming 8.00 20.00
HP07 Jari Kurri 10.00 25.00
HP08 Mark Messier 10.00 25.00
HP09 Brett Hull 10.00 25.00
HP10 Mario Lemieux 15.00 40.00

HP11 Henrik Lundqvist 8.00 20.00
HP12 Sidney Crosby 25.00 60.00

2006-07 ITG International Ice International Rivals

UNLISTED STARS 8.00 20.00
STATED PRINT RUN 50 SER.#'d SETS
UNLISTED GOLD VERSION /10
IR01 T.Esposito/V.Tretiak 20.00 40.00
IR02 A.Maltsev/P.Esposito 12.00 30.00
IR03 F.Mahovlich/A.Yakushev 12.00 30.00
IR04 V.Kharlamov/G.Cheevers 15.00 40.00
IR05 D.Sittler/V.Dzurilla 25.00 50.00
IR06 P.Stastny/B.Hull 10.00 25.00
IR07 G.Fuhr/S.Mylnikov 10.00 25.00
IR08 R.Bourque/M.Naslund 8.00 20.00
IR09 M.Bossy/J.Kurri 8.00 20.00
IR10 G.LaFleur/B.Salming 10.00 25.00
IR11 V.Krutov/M.Lemieux 15.00 40.00
IR12 S.Yzerman/P.LaFontaine 15.00 40.00
IR13 M.Goulet/V.Myshkin 6.00 15.00
IR14 P.LaFontaine/B.Ranford 8.00 20.00
IR15 J.Jagr/I.Larionov 25.00 50.00
IR16 M.Messier/B.Hull 15.00 40.00
IR17 M.Brodeur/M.Richter 12.00 30.00
IR18 S.Crosby/A.Montoya 15.00 40.00
IR19 E.Malkin/J.Pogge 20.00 50.00
IR20 P.Coffey/C.Chelios 6.00 15.00

2006-07 ITG International Ice Jerseys

STATED PRINT RUN 100
GUJ01 Brett Hull 6.00 15.00
GUJ02 Alexander Yakushev 25.00 50.00
GUJ03 Vladimir Krutov 12.00 30.00
GUJ04 Vladislav Tretiak 12.00 30.00
GUJ05 Valeri Kharlamov 12.00 30.00
GUJ06 Nicklas Lidstrom 5.00 12.00
GUJ07 Vladimir Myshkin 8.00 20.00
GUJ08 Michel Goulet 5.00 12.00
GUJ09 Jason Spezza 8.00 20.00
GUJ10 Jay Bouwmeester 5.00 12.00
GUJ11 John Tavares 15.00 40.00
GUJ12 Martin Brodeur 10.00 25.00
GUJ13 Sidney Crosby 25.00 60.00
GUJ14 Dale Hawerchuk 5.00 12.00
GUJ15 Steve Yzerman 10.00 25.00
GUJ16 Mike Bossy 5.00 12.00
GUJ17 Patrice Bergeron 5.00 12.00
GUJ18 Sergei Mylnikov 8.00 20.00
GUJ19 Mario Lemieux 15.00 40.00
GUJ20 Gilbert Perreault 8.00 20.00
GUJ21 Phil Esposito 8.00 20.00
GUJ22 Ilya Bryzgalov 8.00 20.00
GUJ23 Jaromir Jagr 15.00 40.00
GUJ24 Vladimir Dzurilla 25.00 60.00
GUJ25 Borje Salming 5.00 12.00
GUJ26 Mats Naslund 5.00 12.00
GUJ27 Brian Leetch 5.00 12.00
GUJ28 Pat LaFontaine 5.00 12.00
GUJ29 Jari Kurri 8.00 20.00
GUJ30 Peter Stastny 5.00 12.00
GUJ31 Danny Gare 5.00 12.00
GUJ33 Bobby Clarke 12.00 30.00
GUJ34 Marcel Dionne 5.00 12.00
GUJ35 Darryl Sittler 6.00 15.00
GUJ36 Eric Lindros 6.00 15.00
GUJ37 Boris Mikhailov 15.00 40.00
GUJ38 Patrick Roy 15.00 40.00
GUJ39 Chris Chelios 5.00 12.00
GUJ40 Ilya Kovalchuk 8.00 20.00

2006-07 ITG International Ice My Country My Team

ATED PRINT RUN 60
MC1 Chris Chelios 6.00 15.00
MC2 Jaromir Jagr 10.00 25.00
MC3 Steve Yzerman 15.00 40.00
MC4 Brett Hull 10.00 25.00
MC5 Pat LaFontaine 4.00 10.00
MC7 Steve Shutt 4.00 10.00
MC8 Gilbert Perreault 6.00 15.00
MC9 Michel Goulet 4.00 10.00
MC10 Patrick Roy 15.00 40.00
MC11 Jason Spezza 6.00 15.00
MC12 Jay Bouwmeester 4.00 10.00
MC13 Mike Bossy 6.00 15.00
MC14 Phil Esposito 10.00 25.00
MC15 Mario Lemieux 20.00 50.00
MC16 Mats Naslund 4.00 10.00
MC17 Borje Salming 6.00 15.00
MC18 Jari Kurri 6.00 15.00
MC19 Dale Hawerchuk 4.00 10.00
MC20 Bobby Clarke 8.00 20.00
MC21 Eric Lindros 8.00 20.00
MC22 Ilya Bryzgalov 6.00 15.00
MC23 Marcel Dionne 6.00 15.00
MC24 Darryl Sittler 6.00 15.00
MC25 John Tavares 15.00 40.00
MC26 Martin Brodeur 12.00 30.00

2006-07 ITG International Ice Passing The Torch

STATED PRINT RUN 60 SER.#'d SETS
PTT1 T.Esposito/G.Fuhr 12.00 30.00
PTT2 G.Fuhr/M.Brodeur 15.00 40.00
PTT3 M.Brodeur/J.Pogge 15.00 30.00
PTT4 M.Richter/A.Montoya 8.00 20.00
PTT5 S.Mylnikov/I.Bryzgalov 10.00 25.00
PTT6 M.Kiprusoff/A.Niittymaki 12.00 30.00
PTT7 V.Dzurilla/M.Schwarz 10.00 25.00
PTT8 V.Tretiak/V.Myshkin 15.00 40.00
PTT9 P.Esposito/M.Messier 12.00 30.00
PTT10 M.Lemieux/S.Crosby 30.00 80.00
PTT11 P.Statsny/J.Jagr 12.00 30.00
PTT12 V.Kharlamov/I.Kovalchuk 10.00 25.00
PTT13 A.Yakushev/E.Malkin 12.00 30.00
PTT14 B.Salming/N.Lidstrom 8.00 20.00
PTT15 I.Larionov/A.Ovechkin 20.00 50.00
PTT16 J.Jagr/M.Frolik 10.00 25.00

2006-07 ITG International Ice Stick and Jersey

STATED PRINT RUN 90
SJ01 Mario Lemieux 15.00 40.00
SJ02 Mark Messier 10.00 25.00
SJ03 Raymond Bourque 10.00 25.00
SJ04 Steve Yzerman 15.00 40.00
SJ05 Brian Leetch 8.00 20.00
SJ06 Sidney Crosby 20.00 50.00
SJ07 Alexander Ovechkin 20.00 50.00
SJ08 Patrick Roy 25.00 60.00
SJ09 Henrik Lundqvist 12.50 30.00
SJ10 Eric Lindros 12.50 30.00
SJ11 Peter Stastny 10.00 25.00
SJ12 Mike Richter 10.00 25.00
SJ13 Bobby Clarke 10.00 25.00
SJ14 Phil Esposito 10.00 25.00
SJ15 Brett Hull 12.50 30.00
SJ16 Jaromir Jagr 12.00 30.00
SJ17 Jason Spezza 8.00 20.00
SJ18 Jari Kurri 10.00 25.00
SJ19 Martin Brodeur 15.00 40.00
SJ20 Guy Lafleur 20.00 50.00
SJ21 Gilbert Perreault 8.00 20.00
SJ22 Igor Larionov 20.00 50.00
SJ23 Vladimir Krutov 15.00 40.00
SJ24 Chris Chelios 8.00 20.00
SJ25 Henrik Zetterberg 10.00 25.00
SJ26 Nicklas Lidstrom 10.00 25.00
SJ27 Marcel Dionne 8.00 20.00
SJ28 Cristobal Huet 8.00 20.00

2006-07 ITG International Ice Teammates

STATED PRINT RUN 70
IT01 P.Esposito/T.Esposito 15.00 40.00
IT02 M.Lemieux/M.Messier 15.00 40.00
IT03 D.Sittler/L.McDonald 8.00 20.00
IT04 M.Dionne/G.Perreault 12.00 30.00
IT05 M.Bossy/G.Lafleur 10.00 25.00
IT06 R.Bourque/R.Middleton 10.00 25.00
IT07 S.Yzerman/P.Coffey 12.00 30.00
IT08 E.Lindros/M.Messier 10.00 25.00
IT09 M.Lemieux/M.Brodeur 20.00 50.00
IT10 S.Crosby/D.Phaneuf 25.00 60.00
IT11 G.Cheevers/B.Hull 10.00 25.00
IT12 M.Richter/B.Leetch 8.00 20.00
IT13 B.Hull/C.Chelios 10.00 25.00
IT14 J.Vanbiesbrouck/P.LaFontaine 8.00 20.00
IT15 M.Naslund/B.Salming 8.00 20.00
IT16 N.Lidstrom/H.Lundqvist 10.00 25.00
IT17 I.Larionov/V.Krutov 12.00 30.00
IT18 V.Tretiak/A.Yakushev 25.00 60.00
IT19 V.Kharlamov/A.Maltsev 20.00 50.00
IT20 P.Stastny/V.Dzurilla 10.00 25.00
IT21 A.Ovechkin/E.Malkin 25.00 60.00
IT22 F.Mahovlich/P.Mahovlich 8.00 20.00

2014-15 ITG Leaf Metal

HB1 Hanson Brothers 30.00 60.00
BAAB1 Anthony Beauvillier 3.00 8.00
BAAC1 Alexandre Carrier 3.00 8.00
BAAF1 Alex Forsberg 2.50 6.00
BAAM1 Adam Mascherin 3.00 8.00
BAAM2 Adam Musil 3.00 8.00
BAAP1 Andrew Picco 2.50 6.00
BABG2 Brendan Guhle 2.50 6.00
BABH3 Brett Howden 3.00 8.00
BABM1 Beck Malenstyn 2.50 6.00
BABM2 Brett McKenzie 3.00 8.00
BABS1 Blake Speers 3.00 8.00
BABS2 Brandon Saigeon 3.00 8.00
BACA1 Cameron Askew 3.00 8.00
BACH1 Connor Hobbs 3.00 8.00
BACI1 Connor Ingram 2.50 6.00
BACJ1 Cole Johnson 3.00 8.00
BACMD Connor McDavid 125.00 200.00
BACP1 Cliff Pu 2.50 6.00
BACR1 Chaz Reddekopp 2.50 6.00
BADK1 Davis Koch 6.00 15.00
BADS1 Daniel Sprong 6.00 15.00
BADS2 Dante Salituro 4.00 10.00
BADS3 Dylan Strome 10.00 25.00
BAEF1 Evan Fitzpatrick 5.00 12.00
BAES1 Evan Sarthou 2.50 6.00
BAES2 Evgeny Svechnikov 5.00 12.00
BAFA1 Frederic Allard 2.50 6.00
BAGE1 Giorgio Estephan 2.50 6.00
BAGG1 Gabriel Gagne 3.00 8.00
BAGG2 Glenn Gawdin 2.50 6.00
BAGK1 Graham Knott 3.00 8.00
BAIP1 Ivan Provorov 6.00 15.00
BAJA1 Jeremiah Addison 2.50 6.00
BAJA2 Jonathan Ang
BAJA3 Josh Anderson 3.00 8.00
BAJB3 Jason Bell 8.00 20.00
BAJC1 Jakob Chychrun 8.00 20.00
BAJG1 Julien Gauthier 2.50 6.00
BAJH1 Jansen Harkins 4.00 10.00
BAJH2 Jordan Hollett 5.00 12.00
BAJR1 Jeremy Roy 4.00 10.00
BAJW1 Jaeger White 2.50 6.00
BAJZ1 Jakub Zboril 3.00 8.00
BAKC1 Kale Clague 4.00 10.00
BAKC2 Kyle Capobianco 2.50 6.00
BAKE1 Kaden Elder 2.50 6.00
BAKM1 Kody McDonald 2.50 6.00
BAKT1 Keoni Texeira 2.50 6.00
BALB1 Logan Brown 3.00 8.00
BALC1 Lawson Crouse 4.00 10.00
BALG1 Luke Green 2.50 6.00
BALL1 Loik Leveille 3.00 8.00
BAMB1 Mackenzie Blackwood 5.00 12.00
BAMB2 Mathew Barzal 8.00 20.00
BAMF1 Maxime Fortier 2.50 6.00
BAMG1 Matteo Gennaro 2.50 6.00
BAMK1 Matthew Kreis 3.00 8.00
BAMM2 Medric Mercier 2.50 6.00
BAMM3 Michael McLeod 3.00 8.00
BAMM4 Mitchell Marner 15.00 40.00
BAMS1 Matt Spencer 5.00 12.00
BAMS2 Mitchell Stephens 2.50 6.00
BANK1 Nikita Korostelev 5.00 12.00
BANK2 Nolan Kneen 3.00 8.00
BANM1 Nick Merkley 6.00 15.00
BANM2 Nicolas Meloche 3.00 8.00
BANN1 Nathan Noel 5.00 12.00
BANP1 Nolan Patrick 6.00 15.00
BANR2 Nicolas Roy 4.00 10.00
BAPB1 Paul Bittner 5.00 12.00
BAPD1 Pierre-Luc Dubois 6.00 15.00
BAPK1 Pavel Karnaukhov 4.00 10.00
BAPL1 Pascal Laberge 4.00 10.00
BAPW1 Parker Wotherspoon 4.00 10.00
BAPZ1 Pavel Zacha 6.00 15.00
BAQB1 Quinn Benjafield 3.00 8.00
BARG2 Ryan Gropp 4.00 10.00
BARK2 Ryan Kubic 4.00 10.00
BARP1 Ryan Pilon 2.50 6.00
BASG1 Samuel Girard 3.00 8.00
BASS1 Simon Stransky 2.50 6.00
BASS2 Sam Steel
BATB1 Travis Barron 4.00 10.00
BATB2 Tyler Benson 8.00 20.00
BATK1 Tanner Kaspick 2.50 6.00
BATK2 Travis Konecny 6.00 15.00
BATM1 Timo Meier 8.00 20.00
BATR1 Ty Ronning 3.00 8.00
BATS1 Thomas Schemitsch 3.00 8.00
BATS2 Tyler Soy 3.00 8.00
BAVD1 Vince Dunn 4.00 10.00
BAWB1 Will Bitten 4.00 10.00

2014-15 ITG Leaf Metal Prismatic Canada Leaf

*CANADA/10: .8X TO 2X BASIC CARDS
BACMD Connor McDavid 175.00 300.00

2014-15 ITG Leaf Metal Prismatic Blue

*BLUE: .5X TO 1.2X BASIC CARDS
BACMD Connor McDavid/15 200.00 300.00

2014-15 ITG Leaf Metal Prismatic Green

*GREEN/10: .8X TO 2X BASIC CARDS

2014-15 ITG Leaf Metal Prismatic Purple

*PURPLE/15: .6X TO 1.5X BASIC CARDS
BACMD Connor McDavid/10 175.00 300.00

2014-15 ITG Leaf Metal Prismatic USA Star

*USA/10: .8X TO 2X BASIC CARDS
BACMD Connor McDavid 175.00 300.00

2014-15 ITG Leaf Metal Canadian Pride

*BLUE/10: .6X TO 1.5X BASIC AU/25
*BLUE/10: .5X TO 1.2X BASIC AU/15
CPBP1 Brad Park 8.00 20.00
CPCMD Connor McDavid/15 150.00 250.00
CPEG1 Ed Giacomin 12.00 30.00
CPJB2 Johnny Bucyk 8.00 20.00
CPJS1 Joe Sakic
CPMAF Marc-Andre Fleury 20.00 40.00
CPPC1 Paul Coffey 10.00 25.00
CPPE1 Phil Esposito 15.00 40.00
CPRB1 Raymond Bourque 15.00 40.00
CPWC1 Wendel Clark 10.00 25.00

2014-15 ITG Leaf Metal ETA 2015 Die Cut

*BLUE/10: .6X TO 1.5X BASIC AUTO/25
*BLUE/10: .6X TO 1.2X BASIC AUTO/15
ETABM2 Brett McKenzie 4.00 10.00
ETACH1 Connor Hobbs 4.00 10.00
ETACMD Connor McDavid/15 150.00 250.00
ETADS1 Daniel Sprong 10.00 25.00
ETADS3 Dylan Strome 10.00 25.00
ETAGG1 Gabriel Gagne 4.00 10.00
ETAGK1 Graham Knott 4.00 10.00
ETAJR1 Jeremy Roy 5.00 12.00
ETALC1 Lawson Crouse 5.00 12.00
ETAMB1 Mackenzie Blackwood 6.00 15.00
ETAMB2 Mathew Barzal 8.00 20.00
ETAMM4 Mitchell Marner 15.00 40.00
ETAMS1 Matt Spencer 6.00 15.00
ETANM1 Nick Merkley 8.00 20.00
ETANM2 Nicolas Meloche 4.00 10.00
ETANR2 Nicolas Roy 5.00 12.00
ETAPB1 Paul Bittner 6.00 15.00
ETARG2 Ryan Gropp 5.00 12.00
ETATK2 Travis Konecny 8.00 20.00
ETATS1 Thomas Schemitsch 4.00 10.00

2014-15 ITG Leaf Metal Heroes

*BLUE/10: .6X TO 1.5X BASIC AU/25
MHAD1 Alex Delvecchio 8.00 20.00
MHBG1 Bill Gadsby 10.00 25.00
MHBH1 Bobby Hull 10.00 25.00
MHBH2 Brett Hull 20.00 40.00
MHBP1 Brad Park 8.00 20.00
MHBT1 Bryan Trottier 12.00 30.00
MHCC1 Chris Chelios 10.00 25.00
MHEG1 Ed Giacomin 12.00 30.00
MHGC1 Gerry Cheevers 8.00 20.00
MHGF1 Grant Fuhr 15.00 30.00
MHHH1 Harry Howell 8.00 20.00
MHHR1 Henri Richard 10.00 25.00
MHJB1 Johnny Bower 8.00 20.00
MHJB2 Johnny Bucyk 8.00 20.00
MHJJ1 Jaromir Jagr 30.00 60.00
MHJL1 Jacques Lemaire 10.00 25.00
MHJS1 Joe Sakic 15.00 40.00
MHML1 Mario Lemieux 40.00 80.00
MHMM1 Mike Modano
MHNU1 Norm Ullman 10.00 25.00
MHPC1 Paul Coffey 10.00 25.00
MHPE1 Phil Esposito 15.00 40.00
MHPR1 Patrick Roy 30.00 60.00
MHRB1 Raymond Bourque 15.00 40.00
MHRK1 Red Kelly 8.00 20.00
MHSS1 Serge Savard 10.00 25.00
MHSY1 Steve Yzerman
MHTL1 Ted Lindsay 10.00 25.00
MHVT1 Vladislav Tretiak 12.00 30.00
MHWC1 Wendel Clark 10.00 25.00
MHYC1 Yvan Cournoyer 12.00 30.00

2014-15 ITG Leaf Metal Star is Born Die Cut

*BLUE/10: .6X TO 1.5X BASIC AUTO/25
*BLUE/10: .6X TO 1.2X BASIC AUTO/15
SIBCMD Connor McDavid/15 200.00 300.00
SIBDS1 Daniel Sprong 8.00 20.00
SIBDS3 Dylan Strome 10.00 25.00
SIBJR1 Jeremy Roy 5.00 12.00
SIBLC1 Lawson Crouse 5.00 12.00
SIBMB2 Mathew Barzal 8.00 20.00
SIBMM4 Mitchell Marner 15.00 40.00
SIBMS1 Matt Spencer 6.00 15.00
SIBNR2 Nicolas Roy 5.00 12.00
SIBTK2 Travis Konecny 8.00 20.00

2014-15 ITG Leaf Metal Team Effort Dual

TE1 M.Blackwood/M.Kreis 6.00 15.00
TE2 K.Clague/R.Pilon 5.00 12.00
TE3 J.Bell/P.L.Dubois 15.00 40.00
TE4 C.Reddekopp/T.Soy 4.00 10.00
TE5 P.Wotherspoon/E.Sarthou 5.00 12.00
TE6 G.Gawdin/C.Johnson 4.00 10.00
TE7 A.Beauvillier/S.Girard 4.00 10.00
TE8 B.Speers/M.Mercier 4.00 10.00
TE9 J.Chychrun/N.Korostelev 10.00 25.00
TE10 L.Green/N.Noel 15.00 40.00
TE11 J.Addison/M.Stephens 3.00 8.00
TE12 J.Hollett/S.Steel 6.00 15.00
TE13 J.Harkins/A.Forsberg 5.00 12.00
TE14 K.McDonald/J.Anderson 4.00 10.00
TE16 D.Salituro/T.Barron 5.00 12.00
TE18 G.Estephan/J.White 3.00 8.00
TE19 M.Fortier/T.Meier 10.00 25.00
TE20 A.Carrier/P.Laberge 4.00 10.00
TE21 N.Kneen/Q.Benjafield 4.00 10.00
TE22 L.Leveille/E.Svechnikov 15.00 40.00

2015-16 Leaf Metal

BAAC1 Alexander Chmelevski 3.00 8.00
BAAD1 Alex DeBrincat 4.00 10.00
BAAD2 Arnaud Durandeau 2.50 6.00
BAAM1 Antoine Morand 2.50 6.00
BAAN1 Alexander Nylander 6.00 15.00
BAAP1 Austin Pratt 2.50 6.00
BAAR1 Anthony Richard 3.00 8.00
BABC1 Brett Crossley 2.50 6.00
BABD1 Brett Davis 4.00 10.00
BABG1 Brady Gilmour 4.00 10.00
BABH1 Brett Howden 3.00 8.00
BABJ1 Ben Jones 2.50 6.00
BABM1 Beck Malenstyn 4.00 10.00
BACB1 Connor Bunnaman 2.50 6.00
BACG1 Conor Garland 2.50 6.00
BACH1 Carter Hart 4.00 10.00
BACP1 Christopher Paquette 2.50 6.00
BADB1 Dereck Baribeau 2.50 6.00
BADD1 Dillon Dube 4.00 10.00
BADL1 David Levin 4.00 10.00
BADS1 Dmitry Sokolov 4.00 10.00
BADS2 Dylan Sadowy 4.00 10.00
BADT1 Dmytro Timashov 4.00 10.00
BADW1 Dylan Wells 2.50 6.00
BADZ1 Dmitry Zhukenov 2.50 6.00
BAEB1 Egor Babenko 2.50 6.00
BAEC2 Evan Cormier 3.00 8.00
BAGS1 Gabriel Sylvestre 2.50 6.00
BAGS2 Givani Smith 2.50 6.00
BAGV1 Gabriel Vilardi 4.00 10.00
BAHD1 Hayden Davis 2.50 6.00
BAJA1 Josh Anderson 4.00 10.00
BAJB1 Jake Bean 4.00 10.00
BAJB2 Jordy Bellerive 2.50 6.00
BAJC1 Jakob Chychrun 5.00 12.00
BAJD1 Jared Dmytriw 2.50 6.00
BAJD2 Jeff De Wit 2.50 6.00
BAJE1 Jack Eichel 15.00 40.00
BAJG1 Julien Gauthier 5.00 12.00
BAJK1 Jordan Kyrou 4.00 10.00
BAJK2 Jake Kryski 2.50 6.00
BAJM1 Josh Mahura 2.50 6.00
BAJP1 Jesse Puljujarvi 15.00 40.00
BAJV1 Joe Veleno 4.00 10.00
BAJV2 Juuso Valimaki 2.50 6.00
BAJW1 Jaeger White 2.50 6.00
BAKA1 Kristian Afanasyev 2.50 6.00
BAKC1 Kale Clague 4.00 10.00
BAKM1 Keaton Middleton 2.50 6.00
BALB1 Logan Brown 6.00 15.00
BALC1 Louis-Filip Cole 2.50 6.00
BALJ1 Lucas Johansen 2.50 6.00
BALM1 Liam Murphy 2.50 6.00
BALT1 Lucas Thierus 2.50 6.00
BAMB1 Mitchell Balmas 2.50 6.00
BAMC1 Maxime Comtois 4.00 10.00
BAMD1 Martins Dzierkals 2.50 6.00
BAMJ1 Max Jones 6.00 15.00
BAML1 Max Lajoie 4.00 10.00
BAMM1 Michael McLeod 4.00 10.00
BAMS1 Mikhail Sergachev 6.00 15.00
BAMS2 Mathieu Sevigny 2.50 6.00
BAMS3 Michael Spacek 2.50 6.00
BAMT1 Matthew Tkachuk 12.00 30.00
BANB1 Nathan Bastien 2.50 6.00
BANC1 Noah Carroll 2.50 6.00
BANK1 Nolan Kneen 2.50 6.00
BANP1 Nolan Patrick 8.00 20.00
BANV1 Nolan Volcan 2.50 6.00
BAOT1 Owen Tippett 2.50 6.00
BAPB1 Patrick Bajkov 2.50 6.00
BAPD1 Pierre-Luc Dubois 6.00 15.00
BAPH1 Peyton Hoyt 2.50 6.00
BAPL1 Pascal Laberge 3.00 8.00
BARB1 Radovan Bondra 2.50 6.00
BARK1 Ryan Kubic 2.50 6.00
BASB1 Shawn Boudrias 2.50 6.00
BASG1 Samuel Girard 2.50 6.00
BASM1 Stelio Mattheos 4.00 10.00
BASS1 Stuart Skinner 2.50 6.00
BASS2 Sam Steel 5.00 12.00
BASS3 Simon Stransky 4.00 10.00
BATB1 Travis Barron 3.00 8.00
BATB2 Tyler Benson 5.00 12.00
BATF1 Tye Felhaber 2.50 6.00
BATK1 Tanner Kaspick 2.50 6.00
BATP1 Tyler Parsons 2.50 6.00
BATR1 Taylor Raddysh 4.00 10.00
BATR2 Ty Ronning 2.50 6.00
BATT1 Troy Timpano 2.50 6.00
BAVA1 Vitalii Abramov 5.00 12.00
BAVK1 Vladimir Kuznetsov 2.50 6.00
BAVM1 Victor Mete 2.50 6.00
BAVS1 Vili Saarijarvi 2.50 6.00
BAWB1 Will Bitten 2.50 6.00
BAZG1 Zach Gallant 2.50 6.00
BAZS1 Zachary Senyshyn 2.50 6.00
BAZS2 Zach Sawchenko 2.50 6.00

2015-16 Leaf Metal ETA The Show

STATED PRINT RUN 25 SER.#'d SETS
TSAD1 Alex DeBrincat 8.00 15.00
TSGV1 Gabriel Vilardi 5.00 12.00
TSJC1 Jakob Chychrun
TSJP1 Jesse Puljujarvi
TSJV1 Juuso Valimaki 8.00 15.00
TSJV2 Joe Veleno
TSKT1 Matthew Tkachuk
TSKY1 Brady Gilmour
TSLB1 Logan Brown 10.00 25.00
TSMM1 Michael McLeod
TSMS1 Mikhail Sergachev 8.00 20.00
TSNP1 Nolan Patrick 25.00 60.00
TSOT1 Owen Tippett
TSTB1 Tyler Benson 12.00 30.00
TSVA1 Vitalii Abramov 6.00 15.00

2015-16 Leaf Metal Immortals

MIBS1 Borje Salming 8.00 20.00
MIDM1 Dickie Moore 6.00 15.00
MIEF1 Emile Francis 6.00 15.00
MIGF1 Grant Fuhr 12.00 30.00
MIGH1 Glenn Hall 6.00 15.00
MIJB1 Johnny Bower 10.00 25.00
MIMB1 Martin Brodeur 25.00 60.00
MIMS1 Milt Schmidt 8.00 20.00
MIPH1 Phil Housley 8.00 20.00
MIPR1 Patrick Roy 25.00 60.00

2015-16 Leaf Metal Light the Lamp

LTLAD1 Alex DeBrincat 12.00 30.00
LTLAN1 Alexander Nylander 25.00 60.00
LTLJE1 Jack Eichel 40.00 100.00
LTLJG1 Julien Gauthier 8.00 20.00
LTLJP1 Jesse Puljujarvi 15.00 40.00
LTLNP1 Nolan Patrick 25.00 60.00

2015-16 Leaf Metal Pride of a Nation

STATED PRINT RUN 25 SER.#'d SETS
PNBS1 Borje Salming 10.00 25.00
PNEL1 Eric Lindros 15.00 40.00
PNGL1 Guy Lafleur 12.00 30.00
PNIL1 Igor Larionov 10.00 25.00
PNJE1 Jack Eichel 75.00 150.00
PNJP1 Jesse Puljujarvi 40.00 100.00
PNJV1 Joe Veleno 10.00 25.00
PNMB1 Martin Brodeur 20.00 50.00
PNME1 Mike Eruzione 8.00 20.00
PNOK1 Olaf Kolzig 10.00 25.00
PNPB1 Pavel Bure 15.00 40.00
PNPH1 Paul Henderson 10.00 25.00
PNPS1 Peter Stastny 8.00 20.00
PNTB1 Tom Barrasso 10.00 25.00
PNTS1 Teemu Selanne 20.00 50.00
PNVT1 Vladislav Tretiak 12.00 30.00

2015-16 Leaf Metal Team Miracle

TMBS1 Buzz Schneider 15.00 40.00
TMCP1 Craig Patrick 15.00 40.00
TMDC1 Dave Christian 15.00 40.00
TMDS1 Dave Silk 15.00 40.00
TMES1 Eric Strobel 25.00 60.00
TMJC1 Jim Craig 40.00 100.00
TMJH1 John Harrington 20.00 50.00
TMJO1 Jack Oâ•™Callahan 20.00 50.00
TMKM1 Ken Morrow 20.00 50.00
TMME1 Mike Eruzione 30.00 80.00
TMMJ1 Mark Johnson 40.00 100.00
TMMR1 Mike Ramsey 20.00 50.00
TMMW1 Mark Wells 15.00 40.00
TMNB1 Neal Broten 25.00 60.00
TMPV1 Phil Verchota 20.00 50.00
TMRM1 Rob McClanahan 15.00 40.00
TMSJ1 Steve Janaszak 20.00 50.00

2015-16 Leaf Metal The Naturals

TNAD1 Alex DeBrincat 10.00 25.00
TNAN1 Alexander Nylander 15.00 40.00
TNBG1 Brady Gilmour 10.00 25.00
TNDL1 David Levin 10.00 25.00
TNEB1 Egor Babenko 6.00 15.00
TNGV1 Gabriel Vilardi 10.00 25.00
TNJB1 Jake Bean 10.00 25.00
TNJC1 Jakob Chychrun 12.00 30.00
TNJE1 Jack Eichel 40.00 100.00
TNJP1 Jesse Puljujarvi 40.00 100.00
TNJV1 Joe Veleno 10.00 25.00
TNMC1 Maxime Comtois 10.00 25.00
TNMJ1 Max Jones 15.00 40.00
TNMT1 Matthew Tkachuk 30.00 80.00
TNNP1 Nolan Patrick 20.00 50.00
TNSM1 Stelio Mattheos 10.00 25.00

2016-17 Leaf Metal

BAAD1 Alex DeBrincat 8.00 20.00
BAAD2 Arnaud Durandeau 4.00 10.00
BAAH1 Aleksi Heponiemi 6.00 15.00
BAAM1 Adam McMaster 5.00 12.00
BAAM2 Anderson MacDonald 4.00 10.00
BAAM3 Antoine Morand 4.00 10.00
BAAP1 Austin Pratt 4.00 10.00
BAAR1 Adam Ruzicka 6.00 15.00
BABC1 Brett Crossley 5.00 12.00
BABD2 Brett Davis 4.00 10.00
BABG1 Benoit-Olivier Groulx 4.00 10.00
BABG2 Brady Gilmour 4.00 10.00
BABH1 Brett Howden 4.00 10.00
BABJ1 Ben Jones 4.00 10.00
BABK1 Boris Katchouk 8.00 20.00
BACF1 Cal Foote 8.00 20.00
BACG1 Cody Glass 10.00 25.00
BACH1 Cameron Hebig 4.00 10.00
BACH2 Carter Hart 6.00 15.00
BACP1 Christopher Paquette 4.00 10.00
BACR1 Connor Roberts 10.00 25.00
BADA1 Danil Antropov 6.00 15.00
BADB1 Dennis Busby 6.00 15.00
BADB2 Dereck Baribeau 4.00 10.00
BADD1 Dillon Dube 4.00 10.00
BADG1 Damien Giroux 4.00 10.00
BADS1 Dmitry Sokolov 10.00 25.00
BADS3 Dylan Strome 8.00 20.00
BADV1 Daniil Vertiy 8.00 20.00
BADW1 Dylan Wells 4.00 10.00
BADZ1 Dmitry Zhukenov 4.00 10.00
BAEB1 Egor Babenko 4.00 10.00
BAGF1 Gabriel Fortier 8.00 20.00
BAGS1 Gabriel Sylvestre 4.00 10.00
BAGV1 Gabriel Vilardi 4.00 10.00
BAIL1 Ivan Lodnia 10.00 25.00
BAIS1 Ian Scott 8.00 20.00
BAJAD Jaret Anderson-Dolan 8.00 20.00
BAJB1 Jordy Bellerive 4.00 10.00
BAJE1 Jack Eichel 8.00 20.00
BAJE2 Jack Eichel 8.00 20.00
BAJE3 Jack Eichel 8.00 20.00
BAJK1 Jake Kryski 3.00 8.00
BAJL1 Jake Leschyshyn 4.00 10.00
BAJP1 Jacob Paquette 4.00 10.00
BAJR1 Jason Robertson 4.00 10.00
BAJV1 Joe Veleno 12.00 30.00
BAJV2 Joe Veleno 12.00 30.00
BAJV3 Juuso Valimaki 4.00 10.00
BAKK1 Klim Kostin 8.00 20.00
BAKM1 Keaton Middleton 4.00 10.00
BAKV1 Kristian Vesalainen 10.00 25.00
BAKY1 Kailer Yamamoto 6.00 15.00
BAKY2 Keanu Yamamoto 8.00 20.00
BALC1 Louis-Filip Cote 4.00 10.00
BAMB1 Matt Barberis 4.00 10.00
BAMC1 Maxime Comtois 4.00 10.00
BAMD1 Michael DiPietro 8.00 20.00
BAMM1 Michael McLeod 4.00 10.00
BAMR1 Michael Rasmussen 8.00 20.00
BAMS1 Matthew Strome 4.00 10.00
BANC1 Noah Carroll 4.00 10.00
BAND1 Nathan Dunkley 5.00 12.00
BANH1 Nico Hischier 30.00 80.00
BANH2 Nicolas Hague 3.00 8.00
BANH3 Nick Henry 4.00 10.00
BANJ1 Noah Juulsen 4.00 10.00
BANK1 Nolan Kneen 4.00 10.00
BANM1 Nick Merkley 8.00 20.00
BANP1 Nikita Popugaev 4.00 10.00
BANP2 Nolan Patrick 25.00 60.00
BANP4 Nolan Patrick 25.00 60.00
BANS1 Nick Suzuki 8.00 20.00
BAOR1 Olivier Rodrigue 4.00 10.00
BAOT1 Owen Tippett 4.00 10.00
BAPH1 Peyton Hoyt 4.00 10.00
BARK1 Ryan Kubic 4.00 10.00
BARM1 Ryan McLeod 4.00 10.00
BARM2 Ryan Merkley 8.00 20.00
BASB1 Shawn Boudrias 4.00 10.00
BASE1 Shawn Element 4.00 10.00
BASM1 Stelio Mattheos 4.00 10.00
BASS1 Stuart Skinner 4.00 10.00
BATD1 Ty Dellandrea 4.00 10.00
BATS1 Ty Smith 5.00 12.00
BAVK1 Vladimir Kuznetsov 4.00 10.00
BAZG1 Zach Gallant 4.00 10.00

2016-17 Leaf Metal CHL Award Winners

AWNP3 Nolan Patrick/12 30.00 80.00

2016-17 Leaf Metal Draft Class

DCBG1 Benoit-Olivier Groulx 5.00 12.00
DCCG1 Cody Glass 12.00 30.00
DCDB1 Dennis Busby 8.00 20.00
DCGV1 Gabriel Vilardi 5.00 12.00
DCJR1 Jason Robertson 5.00 12.00
DCJV1 Joe Veleno 15.00 40.00
DCMC2 Maxime Comtois 5.00 12.00
DCNH1 Nico Hischier 20.00 50.00
DCNP2 Nolan Patrick 30.00 80.00
DCRM1 Ryan Merkley 10.00 25.00

2016-17 Leaf Metal National Pride

NPAK1 Alexei Kasatonov 12.00 30.00
NPAO1 Adam Oates 12.00 30.00
NPCC2 Chris Chelios 12.00 30.00
NPGF1 Grant Fuhr 12.00 30.00
NPJE1 Jack Eichel 25.00 60.00
NPJLC John LeClair 12.00 30.00
NPJR3 Jeremy Roenick 12.00 30.00
NPMN1 Mats Naslund 12.00 30.00
NPNL1 Nicklas Lidstrom 12.00 30.00
NPNP3 Nolan Patrick 40.00 100.00

2016-17 Leaf Metal Vision Quest

VQAM1 Antoine Morand 5.00 12.00
VQCF1 Cal Foote 10.00 25.00
VQGV2 Gabriel Vilardi 5.00 12.00
VQJE2 Jack Eichel 10.00 25.00
VQJL1 Jake Leschyshyn 5.00 12.00
VQJV2 Joe Veleno 15.00 40.00
VQJV3 Juuso Valimaki 5.00 12.00
VQKK1 Klim Kostin 10.00 25.00
VQKY1 Kailer Yamamoto 8.00 20.00
VQMC1 Maxime Comtois 5.00 12.00
VQMR1 Michael Rasmussen 10.00 25.00
VQMS1 Matthew Strome 5.00 12.00
VQNP4 Nolan Patrick 30.00 80.00
VQOT1 Owen Tippett 5.00 12.00
VQRB1 Radovan Bondra 5.00 12.00
VQSS1 Stuart Skinner 5.00 12.00

2016-17 Leaf Metal Winters Future

WFAM2 Antoine Morand 5.00 12.00
WFCF2 Cal Foote 10.00 25.00
WFCG2 Cody Glass 12.00 30.00
WFDV1 Daniil Vertiy 10.00 25.00
WFIL1 Ivan Lodnia 12.00 30.00
WFIS1 Ian Scott 10.00 25.00
WFJE3 Jack Eichel 10.00 25.00
WFJR2 Jason Robertson 5.00 12.00
WFJV4 Joe Veleno 15.00 40.00
WFKK2 Klim Kostin 10.00 25.00
WFKV1 Kristian Vesalainen 12.00 30.00
WFKY2 Kailer Yamamoto 8.00 20.00
WFMR2 Michael Rasmussen 10.00 25.00
WFMS2 Matthew Strome 5.00 12.00
WFNH2 Nico Hischier 20.00 50.00
WFNP1 Nikita Popugaev 5.00 12.00
WFNP5 Nolan Patrick 30.00 80.00
WFNS1 Nick Suzuki 10.00 25.00
WFOT2 Owen Tippett 5.00 12.00
WFRM1 Ryan McLeod 5.00 12.00
WFSS2 Stuart Skinner 5.00 12.00

2013-14 ITG Lord Stanley's Mug

COMPLETE SET (100) 75.00 150.00
1 Sid Abel 1.25 3.00
2 Glenn Anderson 1.50 4.00
3 Syl Apps 1.25 3.00
4 Bill Barber 1.50 4.00
5 Bill Barilko 1.25 3.00
6 Tom Barrasso 1.50 4.00
7 Bob Baun 1.25 3.00
8 Ed Belfour 1.50 4.00
9 Jean Beliveau 2.50 6.00
10 Clint Benedict 1.25 3.00
11 Toe Blake 1.00 2.50
12 Mike Bossy 1.50 4.00
13 Frank Boucher 1.00 2.50
14 Raymond Bourque 2.50 6.00
15 Johnny Bower 2.00 5.00
16 Frank Brimsek 1.25 3.00
17 Turk Broda 1.50 4.00
18 Guy Carbonneau 1.50 4.00
19 Gerry Cheevers 1.50 4.00
20 Chris Chelios 1.50 4.00
21 King Clancy 1.50 4.00
22 Dit Clapper 1.00 2.50
23 Bobby Clarke 1.50 4.00
24 Paul Coffey 1.50 4.00
25 Charlie Conacher 1.25 3.00
26 Yvan Cournoyer 1.50 4.00
27 Corey Crawford 2.00 5.00
28 Alex Delvecchio 1.25 3.00
29 Cy Denneny 1.00 2.50
30 Bill Durnan 1.50 4.00
31 Phil Esposito 2.50 6.00
32 Peter Forsberg 1.50 4.00
33 Grant Fuhr 1.50 4.00
34 Charlie Gardiner 1.25 3.00
35 Bernie Geoffrion 1.25 3.00
36 Glenn Hall 1.50 4.00
37 Doug Harvey 1.25 3.00
38 Dominik Hasek 2.00 5.00
39 Tim Horton 1.50 4.00
40 Gordie Howe 3.00 8.00
41 Bobby Hull 1.50 4.00
42 Brett Hull 1.50 4.00
43 Jaromir Jagr 3.00 8.00
44 Aurel Joliat 1.50 4.00
45 Red Kelly 1.25 3.00
46 Ted Kennedy 1.25 3.00
47 Dave Keon 1.50 4.00
48 Jari Kurri 1.50 4.00
49 Elmer Lach 1.25 3.00
50 Guy Lafleur 2.00 5.00
51 Newsy Lalonde 1.25 3.00
52 Guy Lapointe 1.25 3.00
53 Igor Larionov 1.50 4.00
54 Jacques Lemaire 1.50 4.00
55 Mario Lemieux 5.00 12.00
56 Nicklas Lidstrom 2.00 5.00
57 Ted Lindsay 1.50 4.00
58 Al MacInnis 1.50 4.00
59 Rick MacLeish 1.25 3.00
60 Frank Mahovlich 1.50 4.00
61 Lanny McDonald 1.50 4.00
62 Howie Meeker 1.50 4.00
63 Mark Messier 2.00 5.00
64 Stan Mikita 2.00 5.00
65 Mike Modano 2.50 6.00
66 Dickie Moore 1.25 3.00
67 Howie Morenz 1.25 3.00
68 Antti Niemi 1.25 3.00
69 Joe Nieuwendyk 1.50 4.00
70 Frank Nighbor 1.25 3.00
71 Bob Nystrom 1.00 2.50
72 Chris Osgood 1.50 4.00
73 Bernie Parent 2.00 5.00
74 Lester Patrick 1.50 4.00
75 Jacques Plante 2.00 5.00
76 Denis Potvin 1.50 4.00
77 Mark Recchi 2.00 5.00
78 Henri Richard 1.50 4.00
79 Maurice Richard 1.50 4.00
80 Larry Robinson 1.50 4.00
81 Art Ross 1.00 2.50
82 Patrick Roy 5.00 12.00
83 Joe Sakic 2.50 6.00
84 Serge Savard 1.50 4.00
85 Terry Sawchuk 1.50 4.00
86 Milt Schmidt 1.25 3.00
87 Dave Schultz 1.50 4.00
88 Teemu Selanne 2.50 6.00
89 Eddie Shore 1.25 3.00
90 Billy Smith 1.50 4.00
91 Martin St. Louis 1.50 4.00
92 Nels Stewart 1.00 2.50
93 Cyclone Taylor 1.50 4.00
94 Tiny Thompson 1.50 4.00
95 J.C. Tremblay 1.00 2.50
96 Bryan Trottier 2.00 5.00
97 Rogie Vachon 2.00 5.00
98 Georges Vezina 1.50 4.00
99 Gump Worsley 1.50 4.00
100 Steve Yzerman 3.00 8.00

2013-14 ITG Lord Stanley's Mug Autographs

AAM Al MacInnis 8.00 20.00
ABH Bobby Hull 15.00 30.00
AEB Ed Belfour
AMF Marc-Andre Fleury 12.00 30.00
ARL Reggie Leach 6.00 15.00
ASM Stan Mikita 12.00 30.00
AAD1 Alex Delvecchio 10.00 25.00
AAD2 Alex Delvecchio 10.00 25.00
AAD3 Alex Delvecchio 10.00 25.00
ABB1 Bob Baun 6.00 15.00
ABB2 Bob Baun 6.00 15.00
ABB3 Bob Baun 6.00 15.00
ABB4 Bob Baun 6.00 15.00
ABBA1 Bill Barber 8.00 20.00
ABBA2 Bill Barber 8.00 20.00
ABC1 Bobby Clarke 12.00 30.00
ABC2 Bobby Clarke 12.00 30.00
ABN1 Bob Nystrom 6.00 15.00
ABN2 Bob Nystrom 6.00 15.00
ABN3 Bob Nystrom 6.00 15.00
ABN4 Bob Nystrom 6.00 15.00
ABP1 Bernie Parent 10.00 25.00
ABP2 Bernie Parent 10.00 25.00
ABS1 Billy Smith 8.00 20.00
ABS2 Billy Smith 8.00 20.00
ABS3 Billy Smith 8.00 20.00
ABS4 Billy Smith 8.00 20.00
ABT1 Bryan Trottier 8.00 20.00
ABT2 Bryan Trottier 8.00 20.00
ABT3 Bryan Trottier 8.00 20.00
ABT4 Bryan Trottier 8.00 20.00
ABT5 Bryan Trottier 8.00 20.00
ABT6 Bryan Trottier 8.00 20.00
ACC1 Chris Chelios 10.00 25.00
ACC2 Chris Chelios 10.00 25.00
ACC3 Chris Chelios 10.00 25.00
ACCR Corey Crawford 10.00 25.00
ACH1 Charlie Hodge 10.00 25.00
ACH2 Charlie Hodge 10.00 25.00
ACH3 Charlie Hodge 10.00 25.00
ACH4 Charlie Hodge 10.00 25.00
ACH5 Charlie Hodge 10.00 25.00
ACH6 Charlie Hodge 10.00 25.00
ACO1 Chris Osgood 8.00 20.00
ACO2 Chris Osgood 8.00 20.00
ACO3 Chris Osgood 8.00 20.00
ADD1 Dick Duff 8.00 20.00
ADD2 Dick Duff 8.00 20.00
ADD3 Dick Duff 8.00 20.00
ADD4 Dick Duff 8.00 20.00
ADD5 Dick Duff 8.00 20.00
ADD6 Dick Duff 8.00 20.00
ADH1 Dominik Hasek 20.00 50.00
ADH2 Dominik Hasek 20.00 50.00
ADK1 Dave Keon 12.00 30.00
ADK2 Dave Keon 12.00 30.00
ADK3 Dave Keon 12.00 30.00
ADK4 Dave Keon 12.00 30.00
ADM1 Dickie Moore 6.00 15.00
ADM2 Dickie Moore 6.00 15.00
ADM3 Dickie Moore 6.00 15.00
ADM4 Dickie Moore 6.00 15.00
ADM5 Dickie Moore 6.00 15.00
ADM6 Dickie Moore 6.00 15.00
ADMC1 Darren McCarty 6.00 15.00
ADMC2 Darren McCarty 6.00 15.00
ADMC3 Darren McCarty 6.00 15.00
ADMC4 Darren McCarty 6.00 15.00
ADP1 Denis Potvin 8.00 20.00
ADP2 Denis Potvin 8.00 20.00
ADP3 Denis Potvin 8.00 20.00
ADP4 Denis Potvin 8.00 20.00
ADS1 Dave Schultz 8.00 20.00
ADS2 Dave Schultz 8.00 20.00
ADSA1 Derek Sanderson 8.00 20.00
ADSA2 Derek Sanderson 8.00 20.00
AEL1 Elmer Lach 12.00 30.00
AEL2 Elmer Lach 12.00 30.00
AEL3 Elmer Lach 12.00 30.00
AFM1 Frank Mahovlich 12.00 30.00
AFM2 Frank Mahovlich 12.00 30.00
AFM3 Frank Mahovlich 12.00 30.00
AFM4 Frank Mahovlich 12.00 30.00
AFM5 Frank Mahovlich 12.00 30.00
AFM6 Frank Mahovlich 12.00 30.00
AGA1 Glenn Anderson 8.00 20.00
AGA2 Glenn Anderson 8.00 20.00
AGA3 Glenn Anderson 8.00 20.00
AGA4 Glenn Anderson 8.00 20.00
AGA5 Glenn Anderson 8.00 20.00
AGA6 Glenn Anderson 8.00 20.00
AGC1 Gerry Cheevers 10.00 25.00
AGC2 Gerry Cheevers 10.00 25.00
AGCA1 Guy Carbonneau 8.00 20.00
AGCA2 Guy Carbonneau 8.00 20.00
AGCA3 Guy Carbonneau 8.00 20.00
AGF1 Grant Fuhr 12.00 30.00
AGF2 Grant Fuhr 12.00 30.00
AGF3 Grant Fuhr 12.00 30.00
AGF4 Grant Fuhr 12.00 30.00
AGF5 Grant Fuhr 12.00 30.00
AGH1 Gordie Howe 50.00 120.00
AGH2 Gordie Howe 50.00 120.00
AGH3 Gordie Howe 50.00 120.00
AGH4 Gordie Howe 50.00 120.00
AGHA Glenn Hall 10.00 25.00
AGL1 Guy Lafleur 10.00 25.00
AGL2 Guy Lafleur 10.00 25.00
AGL3 Guy Lafleur 10.00 25.00
AGL4 Guy Lafleur 10.00 25.00
AGL5 Guy Lafleur 10.00 25.00
AGLA1 Guy Lapointe 6.00 15.00
AGLA2 Guy Lapointe 6.00 15.00
AGLA3 Guy Lapointe 6.00 15.00
AGLA4 Guy Lapointe 6.00 15.00
AGLA5 Guy Lapointe 6.00 15.00
AGLA6 Guy Lapointe 6.00 15.00
AHM1 Howie Meeker 6.00 15.00
AHM2 Howie Meeker 6.00 15.00
AHM3 Howie Meeker 6.00 15.00
AHM4 Howie Meeker 6.00 15.00
AHR1 Henri Richard 12.00 30.00

AHR2 Henri Richard 12.00 30.00
AHR3 Henri Richard 12.00 30.00
AHR4 Henri Richard 12.00 30.00
AHR5 Henri Richard 12.00 30.00
AHR6 Henri Richard 12.00 30.00
AHR7 Henri Richard 12.00 30.00
AHR8 Henri Richard 12.00 30.00
AHR9 Henri Richard 12.00 30.00
AHR10 Henri Richard 12.00 30.00
AHR11 Henri Richard 12.00 30.00
AIL1 Igor Larionov 8.00 20.00
AIL2 Igor Larionov 8.00 20.00
AIL3 Igor Larionov 8.00 20.00
AJB1 Jean Beliveau 30.00 80.00
AJB2 Jean Beliveau 30.00 80.00
AJB3 Jean Beliveau 30.00 80.00
AJB4 Jean Beliveau 30.00 80.00
AJB5 Jean Beliveau 30.00 80.00
AJB6 Jean Beliveau 30.00 80.00
AJB7 Jean Beliveau 30.00 80.00
AJB8 Jean Beliveau 30.00 80.00
AJB9 Jean Beliveau 30.00 80.00
AJB10 Jean Beliveau 30.00 80.00
AJBO1 Johnny Bower 10.00 25.00
AJBO2 Johnny Bower 10.00 25.00
AJBO3 Johnny Bower 10.00 25.00
AJBO4 Johnny Bower 10.00 25.00
AJBU1 Johnny Bucyk 6.00 15.00
AJBU2 Johnny Bucyk 6.00 15.00
AJJ1 Jaromir Jagr 30.00 80.00
AJJ2 Jaromir Jagr 30.00 80.00
AJK1 Jari Kurri 8.00 20.00
AJK2 Jari Kurri 8.00 20.00
AJK3 Jari Kurri 8.00 20.00
AJK4 Jari Kurri 8.00 20.00
AJK5 Jari Kurri 8.00 20.00
AJKO1 Joe Kocur 6.00 15.00
AJKO2 Joe Kocur 6.00 15.00
AJKO3 Joe Kocur 6.00 15.00
AJL1 Jacques Lemaire 8.00 20.00
AJL2 Jacques Lemaire 8.00 20.00
AJL3 Jacques Lemaire 8.00 20.00
AJL4 Jacques Lemaire 8.00 20.00
AJL5 Jacques Lemaire 8.00 20.00
AJL6 Jacques Lemaire 8.00 20.00
AJL7 Jacques Lemaire 8.00 20.00
AJL8 Jacques Lemaire 8.00 20.00
AJLA1 Jacques Laperriere 8.00 20.00
AJLA2 Jacques Laperriere 8.00 20.00
AJLA3 Jacques Laperriere 8.00 20.00
AJLA4 Jacques Laperriere 8.00 20.00
AJLA5 Jacques Laperriere 8.00 20.00
AJLA6 Jacques Laperriere 8.00 20.00
AJN1 Joe Nieuwendyk 8.00 20.00
AJN2 Joe Nieuwendyk 8.00 20.00
AJN3 Joe Nieuwendyk 8.00 20.00
AJS1 Joe Sakic 15.00 40.00
AJS2 Joe Sakic 15.00 40.00
AJW1 Joe Watson 6.00 15.00
AJW1 Joe Watson 6.00 15.00
AJW2 Joe Watson 6.00 15.00
AJWA1 Jim Watson 6.00 15.00
AJWA2 Jim Watson 6.00 15.00
ALM1 Larry Murphy 8.00 20.00
ALM2 Larry Murphy 8.00 20.00
ALM3 Larry Murphy 8.00 20.00
ALM4 Larry Murphy 8.00 20.00
ALMC Lanny McDonald 8.00 20.00
ALRO1 Larry Robinson 8.00 20.00
ALRO2 Larry Robinson 8.00 20.00
ALRO3 Larry Robinson 8.00 20.00
ALRO4 Larry Robinson 8.00 20.00
ALRO5 Larry Robinson 8.00 20.00
ALRO6 Larry Robinson 8.00 20.00
AMB1 Mike Bossy 12.00 30.00
AMB2 Mike Bossy 12.00 30.00
AMB3 Mike Bossy 12.00 30.00
AMB4 Mike Bossy 12.00 30.00
AML1 Mario Lemieux 60.00 100.00
AML2 Mario Lemieux 60.00 100.00
AMM1 Mark Messier 20.00 50.00
AMM2 Mark Messier 20.00 50.00
AMM3 Mark Messier 20.00 50.00
AMM4 Mark Messier 20.00 50.00
AMM5 Mark Messier 20.00 50.00
AMM6 Mark Messier 20.00 50.00
AMMC1 Marty McSorley 6.00 15.00
AMMC2 Marty McSorley 6.00 15.00
AMR1 Mark Recchi 12.00 30.00
AMR2 Mark Recchi 12.00 30.00
AMR3 Mark Recchi 12.00 30.00
AMS1 Milt Schmidt 8.00 20.00
AMS2 Milt Schmidt 8.00 20.00
AMST Martin St. Louis 8.00 20.00
ANL1 Nicklas Lidstrom 12.00 30.00
ANL2 Nicklas Lidstrom 12.00 30.00
ANL3 Nicklas Lidstrom 12.00 30.00
ANL4 Nicklas Lidstrom 12.00 30.00
APC1 Paul Coffey 8.00 20.00
APC2 Paul Coffey 8.00 20.00
APC3 Paul Coffey 8.00 20.00
APC4 Paul Coffey 8.00 20.00
APE1 Phil Esposito 10.00 25.00
APE2 Phil Esposito 10.00 25.00
APF1 Peter Forsberg 15.00 40.00
APF2 Peter Forsberg 15.00 40.00
APR1 Patrick Roy 25.00 50.00
APR2 Patrick Roy 25.00 50.00
APR3 Patrick Roy 25.00 50.00
APR4 Patrick Roy 25.00 50.00
ARB1 Ralph Backstrom 5.00 12.00
ARB2 Ralph Backstrom 5.00 12.00
ARB3 Ralph Backstrom 5.00 12.00
ARB4 Ralph Backstrom 5.00 12.00
ARB5 Ralph Backstrom 5.00 12.00
ARB6 Ralph Backstrom 5.00 12.00
ARBO Raymond Bourque 12.00 30.00
ARK1 Red Kelly 8.00 20.00
ARK2 Red Kelly 8.00 20.00
ARK3 Red Kelly 8.00 20.00
ARK4 Red Kelly 8.00 20.00
ARK5 Red Kelly 8.00 20.00
ARK6 Red Kelly 8.00 20.00
ARK7 Red Kelly 8.00 20.00
ARK8 Red Kelly 8.00 20.00
ARM1 Rick MacLeish 8.00 20.00
ARM2 Rick MacLeish 8.00 20.00
ARV1 Rogie Vachon 10.00 25.00
ARV2 Rogie Vachon 10.00 25.00
ARV3 Rogie Vachon 10.00 25.00
ASN1 Scott Niedermayer 8.00 20.00
ASN2 Scott Niedermayer 8.00 20.00
ASN3 Scott Niedermayer 8.00 20.00
ASN4 Scott Niedermayer 8.00 20.00
ASS1 Steve Shutt 6.00 15.00
ASS2 Steve Shutt 6.00 15.00
ASS3 Steve Shutt 6.00 15.00
ASS4 Steve Shutt 6.00 15.00
ASS5 Steve Shutt 6.00 15.00
ASY1 Steve Yzerman 40.00 80.00
ASY2 Steve Yzerman 40.00 80.00
ASY3 Steve Yzerman 40.00 80.00
ATB1 Tom Barrasso 8.00 20.00
ATB2 Tom Barrasso 8.00 20.00
ATL1 Ted Lindsay 8.00 20.00
ATL2 Ted Lindsay 8.00 20.00
ATL3 Ted Lindsay 8.00 20.00
ATL4 Ted Lindsay 8.00 20.00
AWC1 Wayne Cashman 6.00 15.00
AWC2 Wayne Cashman 6.00 15.00
AYC1 Yvan Cournoyer 8.00 20.00
AYC2 Yvan Cournoyer 8.00 20.00
AYC3 Yvan Cournoyer 8.00 20.00
AYC4 Yvan Cournoyer 8.00 20.00
AYC5 Yvan Cournoyer 8.00 20.00
AYC6 Yvan Cournoyer 8.00 20.00
AYC7 Yvan Cournoyer 8.00 20.00
AYC8 Yvan Cournoyer 8.00 20.00
AYC9 Yvan Cournoyer 8.00 20.00
AYC10 Yvan Cournoyer 8.00 20.00

2013-14 ITG Lord Stanley's Mug Back to Back Cup Jerseys

BBC1-BBC20 ANNC'D PRINT RUN 20
BBC21-BBC32 UNPRICED ANNC'D PRINT RUN 9
BBC01 Johnny Bower/20*
BBC02 Bob Baun/20* 4.00 10.00
BBC03 Serge Savard/20* 6.00 15.00
BBC04 Jacques Lemaire/20*
BBC05 Bobby Clarke/20* 5.00 12.00
BBC06 Bernie Parent/20* 5.00 12.00
BBC07 Rick MacLeish/20* 4.00 10.00
BBC08 Guy Lafleur/20* 8.00 20.00
BBC09 Steve Shutt/20*
BBC10 Larry Robinson/20* 6.00 15.00
BBC11 Mike Bossy/20*
BBC12 Denis Potvin/20* 5.00 12.00
BBC13 Mark Messier/20* 6.00 15.00
BBC14 Grant Fuhr/20*
BBC15 Glenn Anderson/20* 5.00 12.00
BBC16 Mario Lemieux/20* 15.00 40.00
BBC17 Jaromir Jagr/20*
BBC18 Steve Yzerman/20* 10.00 25.00
BBC19 Nicklas Lidstrom/20* 6.00 15.00
BBC20 Sergei Fedorov/20* 10.00 25.00

2013-14 ITG Lord Stanley's Mug Cup Holders Jerseys

CH1-CH26 ANNOUNCED PRINT RUN 80
CH33-CH52 ANNC'D PRINT RUN 50
CH01 C.Osgood/N.Lidstrom/80* 5.00 12.00
CH02 T.Selanne/S.Ndrmyer/80* 8.00 20.00
CH03 N.Khbbln/M.St.Louis/80* 5.00 12.00
CH04 C.Chelios/D.Hasek/80* 6.00 15.00
CH05 J.Sakic/P.Roy/80* 12.00 30.00
CH06 B.Hull/M.Modano/80* 8.00 20.00
CH07 S.Yzerman/N.Lidstrom/80*
CH08 S.Fedorov/I.Larionov/80* 8.00 20.00
CH09 P.Forsberg/P.Roy/80* 12.00 30.00
CH10 M.Richter/M.Messier/80* 6.00 15.00
CH11 K.Muller/P.Roy/80* 6.00 15.00
CH12 M.Lemieux/T.Brrsso/80* 15.00 40.00
CH13 P.Coffey/J.Jagr/80* 12.00 30.00
CH14 M.Messier/J.Kurri/80* 8.00 20.00
CH15 M.Vernon/J.Nwndyk/80* 6.00 15.00
CH16 M.Messier/G.Anderson/80* 8.00 20.00
CH17 C.Chelios/G.Crbnneau/80* 5.00 12.00
CH18 D.Potvin/B.Smith/80* 5.00 12.00
CH19 B.Nystrom/B.Trttier/80* 6.00 15.00
CH20 G.Lafleur/S.Shutt/80* 6.00 15.00
CH21 S.Savard/L.Robinson/80* 5.00 12.00
CH22 B.Clarke/R.MacLeish/80* 8.00 20.00
CH23 G.Drnhfer/B.Barber/80* 5.00 12.00
CH24 P.Esposito/W.Cashman/80* 8.00 20.00
CH25 J.Lprrere/J.Beliveau/80* 8.00 20.00
CH26 J.Bucyk/G.Cheevers/80* 5.00 12.00
CH33 Osgd/Ldstrm/Chlios/50* 8.00 20.00
CH34 Nwndyk/Dnkyo/Brdeur/50* 6.00 15.00
CH35 Hsek/Fdrv/Rbtlle/50* 10.00 25.00
CH36 Yzrmn/Ldstrm/Hull/50* 12.00 30.00
CH37 Skic/Roy/Brque/50* 8.00 20.00
CH38 Hull/Mdno/Blfr/50* 8.00 20.00
CH39 Yzrmn/Ldstrm/Fdrv/50* 12.00 30.00
CH40 Yzrmn/Lmv/McCrty/50* 12.00 30.00
CH41 Frsbrg/Ry/Skic/50* 8.00 20.00
CH42 Svrd/Roy/Mller/50* 10.00 25.00
CH43 Lmux/Brrsso/Frncs/50* 12.00 30.00
CH44 Lmx/Jagr/Cffy/50* 10.00 25.00
CH45 Mssr/Krri/Rnfrd/50* 10.00 25.00
CH46 Flry/McInns/Nwndyk/50*
CH47 Andrsn/Fhr/Grtzky/50* 20.00 40.00
CH48 Roy/Crbnnu/Nslnd/50* 8.00 20.00
CH49 Ptvn/Smth/Nystrm/50* 6.00 15.00
CH50 Lflr/Svrd/Shtt/50* 8.00 20.00
CH51 Clrke/Prnt/Brbr/50*
CH52 Mhvlch/Crnyer/Lflr/50* 8.00 20.00

2013-14 ITG Lord Stanley's Mug Cup Records Jerseys

CR01 Jean Beliveau/80* 6.00 15.00
CR02 Mike Bossy/80* 4.00 10.00
CR03 Chris Chelios/80* 4.00 10.00
CR04 Dino Ciccarelli/80* 4.00 10.00
CR05 Paul Coffey/80* 4.00 10.00
CR06 Wayne Gretzky/80* 20.00 40.00
CR07 Brett Hull/80* 4.00 10.00
CR08 Bryan Trottier/80* 5.00 12.00
CR09 Reggie Leach/80* 5.00 12.00
CR10 Mario Lemieux/80* 6.00 15.00
CR11 Mark Messier/80* 8.00 20.00
CR13 Larry Robinson/80* 4.00 10.00
CR15 Patrick Roy/80* 6.00 15.00
CR16 Joe Sakic/80* 5.00 12.00

2013-14 ITG Lord Stanley's Mug Cup Rivals Jerseys

CRI1-CRI18 ANNC'D PRINT RUN 80
CRI25-CRI32 ANNC'D PRINT RUN 40
CRI01 C.Crawford/T.Rask/80* 8.00 20.00
CRI02 M.A.Fleury/C.Osgood/80* 8.00 20.00
CRI03 N.Lidstrom/R.Francis/80* 6.00 15.00
CRI04 B.Hull/D.Hasek/80* 6.00 15.00
CRI05 S.Fedorov/P.Bondra/80* 10.00 25.00
CRI06 S.Yzerman/E.Lindros/80* 8.00 20.00
CRI07 P.Roy/J.Vnbsbrck/80* 8.00 20.00
CRI08 M.Messier/T.Linden/80* 8.00 20.00
CRI09 D.Savard/L.Robitaille/80* 6.00 15.00
CRI10 J.Jagr/J.Roenick/80* 12.00 30.00
CRI11 M.Lemieux/M.Modano/80* 8.00 20.00
CRI12 B.Ranford/A.Moog/80* 5.00 12.00
CRI13 L.McDonald/P.Roy/80* 6.00 15.00
CRI14 G.Fuhr/R.Hextall/80* 6.00 15.00
CRI15 M.Messier/D.Potvin/80* 6.00 15.00
CRI16 B.Smith/T.Williams/80* 6.00 15.00
CRI17 J.Lemaire/P.Esposito/80* 8.00 20.00
CRI18 G.Lafleur/T.O'Reilly/80* 6.00 15.00
CRI25 Ldstrm/Lmv/Frncs/Irbe/40* 15.00 30.00
CRI26 Hll/Nwndyk/Hsk/Pca/40* 15.00 30.00
CRI27 Yzrmn/Osgd/Bndra/Klzg/40* 10.00 25.00
CRI28 Vrnn/McCrty/Lndrs/LClr/40* 10.00 25.00
CRI29 Mssr/Rchtr/Lndn/Bure/40* 8.00 20.00
CRI30 Lmx/Brrsso/Rnck/Blfr/40* 15.00 40.00
CRI31 Rnfrd/Krri/Brque/Nly/40* 8.00 20.00
CRI32 McDnld/Vrnn/Roy/Nslnd/40* 8.00 20.00

2013-14 ITG Lord Stanley's Mug Cup Winning Goals Jerseys

GWG1-GWG20 ANNC'D PRINT RUN 80
CWG01 Patrice Bergeron/80* 8.00 20.00
CWG02 Henrik Zetterberg/80* 6.00 15.00
CWG03 Brendan Shanahan/80* 6.00 15.00
CWG04 Jason Arnott/80* 4.00 10.00
CWG05 Brett Hull/80* 5.00 12.00
CWG06 Darren McCarty/80* 4.00 10.00
CWG07 Mark Messier/80* 6.00 15.00
CWG08 Kirk Muller/80* 4.00 10.00
CWG09 Ron Francis/80* 6.00 15.00
CWG10 Ulf Samuelsson/80* 5.00 12.00
CWG11 Wayne Gretzky/80* 25.00 50.00
CWG12 Jari Kurri/80* 6.00 15.00
CWG13 Bobby Smith/80* 4.00 10.00
CWG14 Paul Coffey/80* 5.00 12.00
CWG15 Mike Bossy/80* 6.00 15.00
CWG16 Bob Nystrom/80* 3.00 8.00
CWG17 Jacques Lemaire/80* 5.00 12.00
CWG18 Guy Lafleur/80* 6.00 15.00
CWG19 Rick MacLeish/80* 4.00 10.00
CWG20 Yvan Cournoyer/80* 6.00 15.00

2013-14 ITG Lord Stanley's Mug History

HLSM01 Lord Stanley 2.00 5.00
HLSM02 Dan Bain 2.00 5.00
HLSM03 Frank McGee 2.00 5.00
HLSM04 Art Ross 1.25 3.00
HLSM05 Joe Malone 1.25 3.00
HLSM06 Cyclone Taylor 5.00 12.00
HLSM07 Georges Vezina 2.00 5.00
HLSM08 Hap Holmes 1.50 4.00
HLSM09 Frank Nighbor 1.50 4.00
HLSM10 Aurel Joliat 2.00 5.00
HLSM11 Clint Benedict 1.50 4.00
HLSM12 Lester Patrick 2.00 5.00
HLSM13 Eddie Shore 1.50 4.00
HLSM14 Howie Morenz 1.50 4.00
HLSM15 Charlie Conacher 1.50 4.00
HLSM16 Charlie Gardiner 1.50 4.00
HLSM17 Syd Howe 2.00 5.00
HLSM18 Frank Brimsek 1.50 4.00
HLSM19 Turk Broda 2.00 5.00
HLSM20 Toe Blake 1.25 3.00
HLSM21 Ted Kennedy 1.50 4.00
HLSM22 Bill Barilko 1.50 4.00
HLSM23 Terry Sawchuk 2.00 5.00
HLSM24 Gordie Howe 3.00 8.00
HLSM25 Maurice Richard 2.00 5.00
HLSM26 Glenn Hall 2.00 5.00
HLSM27 Dave Keon 2.00 5.00
HLSM28 Jean Beliveau 2.00 5.00
HLSM29 Yvan Cournoyer 2.00 5.00
HLSM30 Phil Esposito 3.00 8.00
HLSM31 Bobby Clarke 2.50 6.00
HLSM32 Guy Lafleur 2.50 6.00
HLSM33 Billy Smith 2.00 5.00
HLSM34 Jari Kurri 3.00 8.00
HLSM35 Patrick Roy 5.00 12.00
HLSM36 Lanny McDonald 2.00 5.00
HLSM37 Mario Lemieux 3.00 8.00
HLSM38 Mark Messier 2.50 6.00
HLSM39 Steve Yzerman 3.00 8.00
HLSM40 Joe Sakic 2.50 6.00
HLSM41 Brett Hull 2.00 5.00
HLSM42 Teemu Selanne 4.00 10.00
HLSM43 Nicklas Lidstrom 2.00 5.00
HLSM44 Marc-Andre Fleury 3.00 8.00
HLSM45 Corey Crawford 2.50 6.00

2013-14 ITG Lord Stanley's Mug Hoisting the Cup Jerseys

HTC01 Mario Lemieux/60* 15.00 40.00
HTC02 Nicklas Lidstrom/60* 5.00 12.00
HTC03 Martin St. Louis/60* 5.00 12.00
HTC04 Corey Crawford/60* 6.00 15.00
HTC05 Joe Sakic/60* 8.00 20.00
HTC06 Bob Nystrom/60* 3.00 8.00
HTC08 Bryan Trottier/60* 5.00 12.00
HTC09 Peter Forsberg/60* 5.00 12.00
HTC10 Raymond Bourque/60* 8.00 20.00
HTC11 Al MacInnis/60* 5.00 12.00
HTC12 Tom Barrasso/60* 5.00 12.00
HTC13 Mark Messier/60* 6.00 15.00
HTC14 Mark Messier/60* 6.00 15.00
HTC15 Jimmy Howard/60* 5.00 12.00
HTC16 Mike Modano/60* 8.00 20.00
HTC17 Bill Ranford/60* 6.00 15.00
HTC18 Mike Richter/60* 5.00 12.00
HTC19 Ed Belfour/60* 5.00 12.00
HTC20 Lanny McDonald/60* 5.00 12.00
HTC21 Jean Beliveau/60* 10.00 25.00
HTC22 Mike Bossy/60* 4.00 10.00
HTC23 Teemu Selanne/60* 8.00 20.00
HTC24 Chris Chelios/60* 4.00 10.00
HTC25 Antti Niemi/60* 4.00 10.00
HTC26 Steve Yzerman/60* 10.00 25.00
HTC27 Patrick Roy/60* 12.00 30.00
HTC28 Patrick Roy/60* 12.00 30.00
HTC29 Chris Osgood/60* 5.00 12.00
HTC30 Dominik Hasek/60* 6.00 15.00

2013-14 ITG Lord Stanley's Mug Mug Shots Jerseys

ANNOUNCED PRINT RUN 60
MS01 Mario Lemieux 6.00 15.00
MS02 Mark Messier 5.00 12.00
MS03 Steve Yzerman 8.00 20.00
MS04 Nicklas Lidstrom 4.00 10.00
MS05 Patrick Roy 10.00 25.00
MS06 Patrick Roy 10.00 25.00
MS07 Grant Fuhr 4.00 10.00
MS08 Mike Bossy 4.00 10.00
MS09 Chris Osgood 4.00 10.00
MS10 Bryan Trottier 5.00 12.00
MS11 Jaromir Jagr 8.00 20.00
MS12 Marc-Andre Fleury 6.00 15.00
MS13 Corey Crawford 5.00 12.00
MS14 Peter Forsberg 4.00 10.00
MS15 Brett Hull 4.00 10.00
MS16 Mike Modano 3.00 8.00
MS17 Ed Belfour 4.00 10.00
MS18 Joe Sakic 6.00 15.00
MS19 Larry Robinson 4.00 10.00
MS20 Mike Richter 4.00 10.00

2012-13 ITG Motown Madness

1 Sid Abel 1.25 3.00
2 Jack Adams 1.00 2.50
3 Larry Aurie 1.25 3.00
4 Doug Barkley 1.00 2.50
5 John Barrett 1.00 2.50
6 Hank Bassen 1.25 3.00
7 Andy Bathgate 1.50 4.00
8 Bobby Baun 1.25 3.00
9 Red Berenson 1.25 3.00
10 Gary Bergman 1.00 2.50
11 Henry Boucha 1.00 2.50
12 Scotty Bowman 1.50 4.00
13 Rick Bowness 1.00 2.50
14 Mud Bruneteau 1.00 2.50
15 Johnny Bucyk 1.25 3.00
16 Shawn Burr 1.25 3.00
17 Jimmy Carson 1.00 2.50
18 Joe Carveth 1.00 2.50
19 Chris Chelios 1.50 4.00
20 Tim Cheveldae 1.50 4.00
21 Dino Ciccarelli 1.50 4.00
22 Wendel Clark 1.50 4.00
23 Paul Coffey 1.50 4.00
24 Carson Cooper 1.00 2.50
25 Roger Crozier 1.25 3.00
26 Billy Dea 1.00 2.50
27 Alex Delvecchio 1.25 3.00
28 Bill Dineen 1.00 2.50
29 Connie Dion 1.25 3.00
30 Marcel Dionne 2.00 5.00
31 Kris Draper 1.25 3.00
32 Ron Duguay 1.25 3.00
33 Art Duncan 1.00 2.50
34 Hap Emms 1.25 3.00
35 Bob Essensa 1.50 4.00
36 Bernie Federko 1.25 3.00
37 Sergei Fedorov 2.50 6.00
38 Guyle Fielder 1.00 2.50
39 Mike Foligno 1.25 3.00
40 Val Fonteyne 1.00 2.50
41 Frank Foyston 1.00 2.50
42 Frank Fredrickson 1.00 2.50
43 Bill Gadsby 1.50 4.00
44 Gerard Gallant 1.00 2.50
45 Danny Gare 1.00 2.50
46 Ed Giacomin 1.50 4.00
47 Gilles Gilbert 1.25 3.00
48 Warren Godfrey 1.00 2.50
49 Pete Goegan 1.00 2.50
50 Bob Goldham 1.00 2.50
51 Ebbie Goodfellow 1.00 2.50
52 Danny Grant 1.00 2.50
53 Don Grosso 1.00 2.50
54 Glenn Hall 1.50 4.00
55 Glen Hanlon 1.25 3.00
56 Ron Harris 1.00 2.50
57 Dominik Hasek 2.50 6.00
58 George Hay 1.25 3.00
59 Darren Helm 1.25 3.00
60 Paul Henderson 1.25 3.00
61 Dennis Hextall 1.00 2.50
62 Flash Hollett 1.00 2.50
63 Hap Holmes 1.00 2.50
64 Jimmy Howard 1.50 4.00
65 Gordie Howe 3.00 8.00
66 Mark Howe 1.50 4.00
67 Syd Howe 1.00 2.50
68 Stu Grimson 1.00 2.50
69 Brett Hull 2.00 5.00
70 Larry Jeffrey 1.00 2.50
71 Greg Johnson 1.00 2.50
72 Curtis Joseph 2.00 5.00
73 Duke Keats 1.00 2.50
74 Red Kelly 1.25 3.00
75 Forbes Kennedy 1.25 3.00
76 Kelly Kisio 1.00 2.50
77 Joe Kocur 1.50 4.00
78 Niklas Kronwall 1.25 3.00
79 Martin Lapointe 1.00 2.50
80 Igor Larionov 1.50 4.00
81 Reed Larson 1.00 2.50
82 Reggie Leach 1.25 3.00
83 Manny Legace 1.25 3.00
84 Tony Leswick 1.00 2.50
85 Herbie Lewis 1.00 2.50
86 Nick Libett 1.00 2.50
87 Nicklas Lidstrom 2.00 5.00
88 Ted Lindsay 2.00 5.00
89 Harry Lumley 1.50 4.00
90 Len Lunde 1.00 2.50
91 Parker MacDonald 1.00 2.50
92 Bruce MacGregor 1.00 2.50
93 Rick MacLeish 2.50 6.00
94 Frank Mahovlich 1.50 4.00
95 Peter Mahovlich 1.50 4.00
96 Dan Maloney 1.25 3.00
97 Darren McCarty 1.50 4.00
98 Dale McCourt 1.25 3.00
99 Corrado Micalef 1.00 2.50
100 Mike Modano 2.50 6.00
101 Johnny Mowers 1.00 2.50
102 Joe Murphy 1.00 2.50
103 Larry Murphy 2.00 5.00
104 Jim Nill 1.00 2.50
105 Ted Nolan 1.50 4.00
106 Adam Oates 1.50 4.00
107 Gerry Odrowski 1.00 2.50
108 John Ogrodnick 1.00 2.50
109 Jimmy Orlando 1.00 2.50
110 Chris Osgood 2.00 5.00
111 Brad Park 1.25 3.00
112 Bud Poile 1.00 2.50
113 Dennis Polonich 1.00 2.50
114 Dean Prentice 1.00 2.50
115 Keith Primeau 1.25 3.00
116 Bob Probert 2.50 6.00
117 Marcel Pronovost 1.50 4.00
118 Metro Prystai 1.25 3.00
119 Bill Quackenbush 1.25 3.00
120 Dutch Reibel 1.00 2.50
121 Leo Reise 1.25 3.00
122 Dennis Riggin 2.00 5.00
123 Luc Robitaille 1.50 4.00
124 Borje Salming 1.50 4.00
125 Terry Sawchuk 2.00 5.00
126 Ray Sheppard 1.00 2.50
127 Darryl Sittler 1.50 4.00
128 Brad Smith 1.00 2.50
129 Floyd Smith 1.25 3.00
130 Greg Smith 1.00 2.50
131 Harold Snepsts 1.00 2.50
132 Vic Stasiuk 1.00 2.50
133 Greg Stefan 1.25 3.00
134 Jack Stewart 1.25 3.00
135 Errol Thompson 1.00 2.50
136 Tiny Thompson 1.50 4.00
137 Norm Ullman 1.50 4.00
138 Garry Unger 1.00 2.50
139 Rogie Vachon 2.00 5.00
140 Mike Vernon 1.25 3.00
141 Carl Voss 1.00 2.50
142 Bryan Watson 1.00 2.50
143 Harry Watson 1.25 3.00
144 Tiger Williams 1.50 4.00
145 Paul Woods 1.00 2.50
146 Jason Woolley 1.00 2.50
147 Howie Young 1.25 3.00
148 Warren Young 1.00 2.50
149 Steve Yzerman 4.00 10.00
150 Rick Zombo 1.00 2.50

2012-13 ITG Motown Madness Autographs

OVERALL FOUR AUTOS PER BOX
AAB Andy Bathgate 5.00 12.00
AAO Adam Oates 6.00 15.00
ABB Bobby Baun 5.00 12.00
ABD Bill Dineen 4.00 10.00
ABDE Billy Dea 4.00 10.00
ABE Bob Essensa 6.00 15.00
ABF Bernie Federko 5.00 12.00
ABG Bill Gadsby SP 15.00 30.00
ABH Brett Hull SP 30.00 60.00
ABM Bruce MacGregor 4.00 10.00
ABP Brad Park SP 15.00 30.00
ABPR Bob Probert SP 100.00 200.00
ABR Bill Ranford SP 15.00 40.00
ABS Brad Smith 4.00 10.00
ABSA Borje Salming SP 25.00 50.00
ABW Bryan Watson 4.00 10.00
ACC Chris Chelios 12.50 25.00
ACD Connie Dion 5.00 12.00
ACJ Curtis Joseph SP 20.00 40.00
ACM Corrado Micalef 4.00 10.00
ACO Chris Osgood SP 20.00 40.00
ADB Doug Barkley 4.00 10.00
ADBR Damien Brunner 60.00 120.00
ADC Dino Ciccarelli SP 15.00 40.00
ADG Danny Gare 4.00 10.00
ADGR Danny Grant 4.00 10.00
ADH Dennis Hextall 4.00 10.00
ADHA Dominik Hasek SP 30.00 60.00
ADHE Darren Helm 5.00 12.00
ADM Dale McCourt 5.00 12.00
ADMA Dan Maloney 5.00 12.00
ADMC Darren McCarty 6.00 15.00
ADP Dean Prentice 4.00 10.00
ADPO Dennis Polonich 4.00 10.00
ADR Dennis Riggin 8.00 20.00
AEG Ed Giacomin 8.00 20.00
AEM Ed Mio 6.00 15.00
AET Errol Thompson 4.00 10.00
AFK Forbes Kennedy 5.00 12.00
AFM Frank Mahovlich SP 15.00 40.00
AFS Floyd Smith 5.00 12.00
AGF Guyle Fielder 4.00 10.00
AGG Gilles Gilbert 8.00 20.00
AGGA Gerard Gallant 4.00 10.00
AGH Glen Hanlon 5.00 12.00
AGHA Glenn Hall SP 20.00 40.00
AGHO Gordie Howe SP 75.00 135.00
AGJ Greg Johnson 4.00 10.00
AGO Gerry Odrowski 4.00 10.00
AGS Greg Stefan 5.00 12.00
AGSM Greg Smith 4.00 10.00
AGU Garry Unger 4.00 10.00
AHB Henry Boucha 4.00 10.00
AHS Harold Snepsts 5.00 12.00
AIL Igor Larionov 12.50 25.00
AJA Joakim Andersson 5.00 12.00
AJB John Barrett 4.00 10.00
AJBU Johnny Bucyk SP 12.00 30.00
AJC Jimmy Carson 4.00 10.00
AJH Jimmy Howard 8.00 20.00
AJK Joe Kocur 6.00 15.00
AJM Joe Murphy 4.00 10.00
AJN Jim Nill 4.00 10.00
AJO John Ogrodnick 4.00 10.00
AJT Jordin Tootoo 8.00 20.00
AJW Jason Woolley 4.00 10.00
AKD Kris Draper 6.00 15.00
AKK Kelly Kisio 4.00 10.00
AKP Keith Primeau 5.00 12.00
ALJ Larry Jeffrey 4.00 10.00
ALM Larry Murphy 6.00 15.00
ALR Leo Reise 5.00 12.00
ALRO Luc Robitaille SP 15.00 40.00
AMD Marcel Dionne SP 20.00 50.00
AMF Mike Foligno 5.00 12.00
AMH Mark Howe 8.00 20.00
AML Manny Legace 5.00 12.00
AMLA Martin Lapointe 4.00 10.00
AMM Mike Modano SP 25.00 50.00
AMP Metro Prystai 5.00 12.00
AMPR Marcel Pronovost 6.00 15.00
AMV Mike Vernon SP 60.00 100.00
ANK Niklas Kronwall 5.00 12.00
ANL Nick Libett 4.00 10.00
ANLI Nicklas Lidstrom SP 50.00 100.00
ANU Norm Ullman 6.00 15.00
APC Paul Coffey SP 25.00 50.00
APH Paul Henderson SP 25.00 50.00
APM Parker MacDonald 4.00 10.00
APMA Peter Mahovlich SP 12.00 30.00
APW Paul Woods 4.00 10.00
ARB Red Berenson 5.00 12.00
ARBO Rick Bowness 4.00 10.00
ARD Ron Duguay 5.00 12.00
ARH Ron Harris 4.00 10.00
ARK Red Kelly SP 20.00 40.00
ARL Reed Larson 4.00 10.00
ARLE Reggie Leach 5.00 12.00
ARLO Ron Low 5.00 12.00
ARM Rick MacLeish SP 25.00 50.00
ARS Ray Sheppard 4.00 10.00
ARV Rogie Vachon SP 30.00 60.00
ARZ Rick Zombo 4.00 10.00
ASB Scotty Bowman 15.00 30.00
ASBU Shawn Burr 5.00 12.00
ASF Sergei Fedorov SP 90.00 150.00
ASG Stu Grimson 4.00 10.00
ASY Steve Yzerman SP 90.00 150.00
ATC Tim Cheveldae 6.00 15.00
ATH Tomas Holmstrom 6.00 15.00
ATL Ted Lindsay 8.00 20.00
ATN Ted Nolan 6.00 15.00
ATW Tiger Williams 6.00 15.00
AVF Val Fonteyne 4.00 10.00
AVS Vic Stasiuk 4.00 10.00
AWY Warren Young 4.00 10.00

2012-13 ITG Motown Madness Battle For The Cup Jerseys

BC1 Osgd/Lids/Fleury/Malkn/30* 25.00 60.00
BC2 Hsk/Yzr/Lds/Irb/Brn/Frns/30* 50.00 100.00
BC3 Hask/Yzer/Irbe/Brind/30 25.00 60.00
BC4 Yzr/Lar/Lds/Hnt/Klz/Ots/30* 25.00 60.00
BC5 Yzer/Lids/Ots/Kolzg/30* 25.00 60.00
BC6 Yzr/Vrn/Kcr/Lnd/Lclr/Hx/30* 20.00 50.00
BC7 Yzer/Vern/Lindrs//Hex/30* 25.00 60.00

2012-13 ITG Motown Madness Equipment Room Memorabilia

EQ1 Sergei Fedorov/60* 12.00 30.00
EQ2 Chris Osgood/60* 8.00 20.00
EQ3 Steve Yzerman/60* 12.00 30.00
EQ4 Manny Legace/60* 5.00 12.00
EQ5 Nicklas Lidstrom/60* 8.00 20.00
EQ6 Chris Chelios/60* 6.00 15.00

2012-13 ITG Motown Madness Game Used Jersey

M1 Steve Yzerman/140* 10.00 25.00
M2 Sergei Fedorov/140* 10.00 25.00
M3 Shawn Burr/140* 4.00 10.00
M4 Mike Foligno/140* 4.00 10.00
M5 Bob Probert/140* 8.00 20.00
M6 Jimmy Carson/140* 3.00 8.00
M7 Brad Marsh/140* 4.00 10.00
M8 Jim Nill/140* 3.00 8.00
M9 Bill Ranford/140* 5.00 12.00
M10 Dominik Hasek/140* 8.00 20.00
M11 Martin Lapointe/140* 3.00 8.00
M12 Manny Legace/140* 4.00 10.00
M13 Nicklas Lidstrom/140* 5.00 12.00
M14 Chris Osgood/140* 5.00 12.00
M15 Joe Kocur/140* 5.00 12.00
M16 Dino Ciccarelli/140* 5.00 12.00
M17 Darren Helm/140* 4.00 10.00
M18 Curtis Joseph/140* 5.00 12.00
M19 Igor Larionov/140* 6.00 15.00
M20 Reed Larson/140* 3.00 8.00
M21 Darren McCarty/140* 5.00 12.00
M22 Larry Murphy/140* 5.00 12.00
M23 Keith Primeau/140* 4.00 10.00
M24 Greg Stefan/140* 4.00 10.00
M25 Mike Vernon/140* 4.00 10.00
M26 Jason Woolley/140* 3.00 8.00
M27 Chris Chelios/140* 5.00 12.00
M28 Darryl Sittler/140* 5.00 12.00
M29 Kris Draper/140* 4.00 10.00
M30 Tomas Holmstrom/140* 4.00 10.00
M31 Danny Gare/140* 3.00 8.00
M32 Niklas Kronwall/140* 4.00 10.00
M33 Dennis Hextall/140* 4.00 10.00
M34 Gerard Gallant/140* 3.00 8.00
M35 Tim Cheveldae/140* 5.00 12.00
M36 Brett Hull/140* 5.00 12.00

2012-13 ITG Motown Madness Games To Remember Jerseys

GTR1 Yzer/Fed/Sakic/Roy/19* 60.00 120.00
GTR2 Lids/Yzer/Francs/Brind/19* 60.00 120.00
GTR3 Vern/Fed/Roy/Sakic/19* 60.00 120.00
GTR4 Howe/Sawc/Beliv/Rich/19* 30.00 80.00
GTR6 Yzer/Vern/Lindrs/Hxtl/19* 60.00 120.00
GTR7 Yzer/Os/Fed/Kolz/Huntr/19* 60.00 120.00
GTR8 Hull/Robit/Roy/Sakic/19* 50.00 100.00

2012-13 ITG Motown Madness Goaltenders Memorabilia

G1 Jimmy Howard/60* 6.00 15.00
G2 Curtis Joseph/60* 6.00 15.00
G3 Chris Osgood/60* 6.00 15.00
G4 Greg Stefan/60* 5.00 12.00
G5 Mike Vernon/60* 6.00 15.00
G6 Dominik Hasek/60* 8.00 20.00
G7 Manny Legace/60* 5.00 12.00
G8 Tim Cheveldae/60* 8.00 20.00

2012-13 ITG Motown Madness Jersey Quads

MQ1 Howrd/Hsk/Vern/Jsph 12.00 30.00
MQ2 Lids/Cheli/Murph/Osgd 15.00 40.00
MQ3 Prob/Kocr/McCrt/Drapr 20.00 50.00
MQ4 Yzer/Delvc/Howe/Lids 30.00 80.00
MQ5 Larion/Fedr/Hull/Robt 25.00 50.00
MQ6 Lrsn/Yzer/Stefn/Gare 15.00 40.00

2012-13 ITG Motown Madness Patch of Honor

ONE PER BOX
PH1 Sergei Fedorov 10.00 25.00
PH2 Chris Osgood 6.00 15.00
PH3 Mike Vernon 8.00 20.00
PH4 Steve Yzerman 12.00 30.00
PH5 Joe Kocur 6.00 15.00
PH6 Darren McCarty 6.00 15.00
PH7 Larry Murphy 6.00 15.00
PH8 Chris Chelios 6.00 15.00
PH9 Dominik Hasek 8.00 20.00
PH10 Brett Hull 8.00 20.00
PH11 Luc Robitaille 6.00 15.00
PH12 Kris Draper 5.00 12.00
PH13 Ed Giacomin 5.00 12.00
PH14 Dennis Hextall 4.00 10.00
PH15 Nick Libett 4.00 10.00
PH16 Bryan Watson 4.00 10.00
PH17 Danny Gare 4.00 10.00
PH18 Frank Mahovlich 6.00 15.00
PH19 Alex Delvecchio 5.00 12.00
PH20 Marcel Dionne 5.00 12.00
PH21 Bill Gadsby 6.00 15.00
PH22 Glenn Hall 5.00 12.00
PH23 Red Kelly 5.00 12.00
PH24 Reed Larson 4.00 10.00
PH25 John Ogrodnick 4.00 10.00
PH26 Marcel Pronovost 6.00 15.00
PH27 Terry Sawchuk 8.00 20.00
PH28 Dale McCourt 5.00 12.00
PH29 Norm Ullman 6.00 15.00
PH30 Jimmy Howard 6.00 15.00
PH31 Igor Larionov 6.00 15.00
PH32 Nicklas Lidstrom 8.00 20.00
PH33 Sid Abel 5.00 12.00
PH34 Jack Adams 4.00 10.00
PH35 Gordie Howe 10.00 25.00
PH36 Syd Howe 4.00 10.00
PH37 Ted Lindsay 6.00 15.00
PH38 Harry Lumley 6.00 15.00
PH39 Jack Stewart 5.00 12.00
PH40 Tiny Thompson 6.00 15.00
PH41 Gerard Gallant 4.00 10.00
PH42 Dino Ciccarelli 6.00 15.00
PH43 Adam Oates 5.00 12.00
PH44 Keith Primeau 5.00 12.00
PH45 Bob Probert 8.00 20.00

2012-13 ITG Motown Madness Starting Lineup Jerseys

SL1 Os/Lds/Chl/Hl/Fd/Yz/19* 60.00 120.00

2012-13 ITG Motown Madness Teammates Jerseys

TM1 Yzerman/Lidstrom/110* 12.00 30.00
TM2 Osgood/Hasek/110* 8.00 20.00
TM3 Hull/Larionov/110* 8.00 20.00
TM4 Draper/McCarty/110* 6.00 15.00
TM5 Joseph/Legacy/110* 6.00 15.00
TM6 Robitaille/Fedorov/110* 10.00 25.00
TM7 Chelios/Lidstrom/110* 6.00 15.00
TM8 Lapointe/Primeau/110* 5.00 12.00
TM9 Vernon/Osgood/110* 6.00 15.00
TM10 Draper/Kocur/110* 8.00 20.00
TM11 Fedorov/Larionov/110* 8.00 20.00
TM12 Hull/Robitaille/110* 8.00 20.00
TM13 Murphy/Lidstrom/110* 6.00 15.00
TM14 Yzerman/Gallant/110* 10.00 25.00
TM15 Ciccarelli/Premeau/110* 6.00 15.00
TM16 Probert/Kocur/110* 10.00 25.00
TM17 Sittler/Yzerman/110* 10.00 25.00
TM18 Larson/Stefan/110* 5.00 12.00
TM19 Gare/Sittler/110* 6.00 15.00
TM20 Maloney/Giacomin/110* 5.00 12.00

2012-13 ITG Motown Madness Tough Materials

TM1 Bob Probert/140* 8.00 20.00
TM2 Chris Chelios/140* 5.00 12.00
TM3 Darren McCarty/140* 5.00 12.00
TM4 Reed Larson/140* 3.00 8.00
TM5 Dan Maloney/140* 4.00 10.00
TM6 Joe Kocur/140* 5.00 12.00
TM7 Shawn Burr/140* 4.00 10.00
TM8 Gerard Gallant/140* 3.00 8.00

2011 In the Game National Convention VIP

1 Mario Lemieux 3.00 8.00
2 Patrick Roy 2.50 6.00
3 Steve Yzerman 2.50 6.00
4 Mark Messier 2.50 6.00
5 Tim Thomas 2.00 5.00
6 Steve Stamkos 2.50 6.00

2007-08 ITG O Canada

This 100 card set was issued into the hobby in five-card packs which came 24 packs to a box and 24 boxes to a case.This set honored players who participated in series in which any version of a Canadian National Team (Senior, Junior or Women) competed.

COMPLETE SET (100) 10.00 25.00
1 Alex Grant .12 .30
2 Angelo Esposito .25 .60
3 Braden Holtby .50 1.25
4 Brandon Sutter .20 .50
5 Colton Gillies .20 .50
6 Dion Knelsen .12 .30
7 Drew Doughty .40 1.00
8 Eric Doyle .12 .30
9 Jamie Arniel .15 .40
10 John Negrin .15 .40
11 Kyle Turris .60 1.50
12 Logan Couture .20 .50
13 Luke Schenn .25 .60
14 Mark Katic .12 .30
15 Olivier Fortier .12 .30
16 Steven Stamkos .60 1.50
17 Trevor Cann .15 .40
18 Yann Sauve .20 .50
19 Yves Bastien .12 .30
20 Zachary Boychuk .20 .50
21 Zack Torquato .12 .30
22 Carla MacLeod .20 .50
23 Caroline Ouellette .20 .50
24 Charline Labonte .30 .75
25 Cheryl Pounder .20 .50
26 Colleen Sostorics .20 .50
27 Danielle Goyette .25 .60
28 Delaney Collins .20 .50
29 Gillian Apps .25 .60
30 Gillian Ferrari .20 .50
31 Gina Kingsbury .20 .50
32 Hayley Wickenheiser .50 1.25
33 Jayna Hefford .25 .60
34 Jennifer Botterill .20 .50
35 Katie Weatherston .20 .50
36 Kelly Bechard .20 .50
37 Kim St. Pierre .60 1.50
38 Meghan Agosta .25 .60
39 Sarah Vaillancourt .20 .50
40 Tessa Bonhomme .20 .50
41 Vicky Sunohara .25 .60
42 Karl Alzner .12 .30
43 Daniel Bertram .12 .30
44 Luc Bourdon .20 .50
45 Marc-Andre ClichÃ© .12 .30
46 Andrew Cogliano .20 .50
47 Steve Downie .15 .40
48 Cody Franson .25 .60
49 Sam Gagner .25 .60
50 Darren Helm .20 .50
51 Leland Irving .20 .50
52 Kristopher Letang .30 .75
53 Bryan Little .15 .40
54 Brad Marchand .50 1.25
55 Kenndal McArdle .12 .30
56 James Neal .30 .75
57 Ryan O'Marra .12 .30
58 Ryan Parent .12 .30
59 Carey Price 1.25 3.00
60 Tom Pyatt .25 .60
61 Kris Russell .15 .40
62 Marc Staal .20 .50
63 Jonathan Toews .75 2.00
64 Martin Brodeur .40 1.00
65 Marc-Andre Fleury .30 .75
66 Vincent Lecavalier .15 .40
67 Chris Pronger .15 .40
68 Eric Lindros .30 .75
69 Roberto Luongo .25 .60
70 Dion Phaneuf .20 .50
71 Justin Pogge .20 .50
72 Joe Sakic .30 .75
73 Jason Spezza .20 .50
74 Patrick Roy .50 1.25
75 Jordan Staal .20 .50
76 Joe Thornton .25 .60
77 Dany Heatley .20 .50
78 Steve Yzerman .60 1.50
79 Cassie Campbell .50 1.25
80 Manon Rheaume .50 1.25
81 A.Esposito/S.Stamkos .60 1.50
82 D.Goyette/V.Sunohara .25 .60
83 H.Wickenheiser/J.Botterill .50 1.25
84 K.Alzner/M.Staal .12 .30
85 S.Downie/J.Toews .75 2.00
86 C.Price/L.Irving 1.25 3.00
87 K.Letang/L.Bourdon .30 .75
88 S.Gagner/B.Little .25 .60
89 C.Labonte/K.St. Pierre .60 1.50
90 C.Campbell/M.Rheaume .50 1.25
91 Jaromir Jagr .50 1.25
92 Henrik Zetterberg .25 .60
93 Alexei Cherepanov .25 .60
94 Dominik Hasek .25 .60
95 Mike Modano .30 .75
96 Bill Guerin .20 .50
97 Alexander Ovechkin .75 2.00

98 Vladislav Tretiak .20 .50
99 Chris Chelios .20 .50
100 Jari Kurri .20 .50

2007-08 ITG O Canada Autographs

AAC Andrew Cogliano 5.00 12.00
AACH Alexei Cherepanov SP 20.00 50.00
AAE Angelo Esposito 6.00 15.00
AAG Alex Grant 3.00 8.00
AAO Alexander Ovechkin SP 40.00 100.00
ABG Bill Guerin SP 12.00 30.00
ABH Braden Holtby 12.00 30.00
ABL Bryan Little 4.00 10.00
ABM Brad Marchand 12.00 30.00
ABS Brandon Sutter 5.00 12.00
ACC Cassie Campbell 12.00 30.00
ACF Cody Franson 6.00 15.00
ACG Colton Gillies 5.00 12.00
ACL Charline Labonte 8.00 20.00
ACM Carla MacLeod 5.00 12.00
ACO Caroline Ouellette 5.00 12.00
ACP Carey Price 40.00 80.00
ACPD Cheryl Pounder 5.00 12.00
ACPR Chris Pronger SP 10.00 25.00
ACS Colleen Sostorics 5.00 12.00
ADB Daniel Bertram 3.00 8.00
ADC Delaney Collins 5.00 12.00
ADD Drew Doughty 10.00 25.00
ADG Danielle Goyette 6.00 15.00
ADH Darren Helm 5.00 12.00
ADHA Dominik Hasek SP 15.00 40.00
ADK Dion Knelsen 3.00 8.00
ADP Dion Phaneuf SP 15.00 30.00
AED Eric Doyle 3.00 8.00
AGA Gillian Apps 6.00 15.00
AGF Gillian Ferrari 5.00 12.00
AGK Gina Kingsbury 5.00 12.00
AHW Hayley Wickenheiser 12.00 30.00
AJA Jamie Arniel 4.00 10.00
AJB Jennifer Botterill 5.00 12.00
AJH Jayna Hefford 6.00 15.00
AJJ Jaromir Jagr SP 30.00 80.00
AJK Jari Kurri SP 12.00 30.00
AJN James Neal 8.00 20.00
AJNE John Negrin 4.00 10.00
AJP Justin Pogge SP
AJS Joe Sakic SP 40.00 80.00
AJSP Jason Spezza SP
AJST Jordan Staal SP 12.00 30.00
AJT Jonathan Toews 60.00 120.00
AJTA John Tavares SP 50.00 125.00
AJTH Joe Thornton SP 15.00 40.00
AKA Karl Alzner 3.00 8.00
AKB Kelly Bechard 5.00 12.00
AKL Kristopher Letang 15.00 30.00
AKMA Kenndal McArdle 3.00 8.00
AKR Kris Russell 4.00 10.00
AKS Kim St. Pierre 12.00 30.00
AKT Kyle Turris 15.00 40.00
AKW Katie Weatherston 5.00 12.00
ALB Luc Bourdon 8.00 20.00
ALC Logan Couture 6.00 15.00
ALI Leland Irving 5.00 12.00
ALS Luke Schenn 6.00 15.00
AMAC Meghan Agosta 8.00 20.00
AMAC Marc-Andre Cliche 3.00 8.00
AMAF Marc-Andre Fleury SP 20.00 50.00
AMB Martin Brodeur SP 50.00 100.00
AMK Mark Katic 3.00 8.00
AMM Mike Modano SP 20.00 50.00
AMR Manon Rheaume 20.00 40.00
AMS Marc Staal 5.00 12.00
AOF Olivier Fortier 3.00 8.00
ARL Roberto Luongo SP 60.00 120.00
ARO Ryan O'Marra 3.00 8.00
ARP Ryan Parent 3.00 8.00
ASD Steve Downie 4.00 10.00
ASG Sam Gagner 6.00 15.00
ASS Steven Stamkos 40.00 80.00
ASV Sarah Vaillancourt 5.00 12.00
ASY Steve Yzerman SP 40.00 100.00
ATB Tessa Bonhomme 5.00 12.00
ATC Trevor Cann 4.00 10.00
ATP Tom Pyatt 6.00 15.00
AVL Vincent Lecavalier SP 10.00 25.00
AVS Vicky Sunohara 6.00 15.00
AVT Vladislav Tretiak SP 60.00 120.00
AYB Yves Bastien 3.00 8.00
AYS Yann Sauve 5.00 12.00
AZB Zachary Boychuk 5.00 12.00
AZT Zack Torquato 3.00 8.00

2007-08 ITG O Canada Dual Jerseys

STATED PRINT RUN 50 SETS
DJ01 C.Labonte/K.St. Pierre 25.00 60.00
DJ02 V.Sunohara/D.Goyette 10.00 25.00
DJ03 Wickenheiser/Botterill 20.00 50.00
DJ04 J.Hefford/C.Ouellette 10.00 25.00
DJ05 C.Labonte/C.Price 50.00 120.00
DJ06 K.Turris/C.Gillies 25.00 60.00
DJ07 A.Esposito/L.Couture 10.00 25.00
DJ08 S.Stamkos/B.Sutter 25.00 60.00
DJ09 D.Doughty/Y.Sauve 15.00 40.00
DJ10 T.Cann/B.Holtby 20.00 50.00
DJ11 J.Toews/D.Bertram 30.00 80.00
DJ12 S.Gagner/S.Downie 10.00 25.00
DJ13 K.Alzner/L.Bourdon 5.00 12.00
DJ14 K.Letang/K.Russell 12.00 30.00
DJ15 C.Price/L.Irving 50.00 120.00
DJ16 D.Goyette/S.Downie 10.00 25.00
DJ17 V.Sunohara/S.Stamkos 25.00 60.00
DJ18 J.Botterill/J.Toews 30.00 80.00
DJ19 Wickenheiser/Turris 25.00 60.00

2007-08 ITG O Canada Formidable Foes Jerseys

STATED PRINT RUN 50 SETS
FF01 D.Hasek/P.Roy 15.00 40.00
FF02 J.Jagr/J.Sakic 15.00 40.00
FF03 K.Lehtonen/D.Roloson 5.00 12.00
FF04 K.Tkachuk/E.Lindros 10.00 25.00
FF05 Modano/Lecavalier 10.00 25.00
FF06 C.Chelios/C.Pronger 6.00 15.00
FF07 H.Zetterberg/J.Thornton 8.00 20.00
FF08 M.Richter/M.Brodeur 12.00 30.00
FF09 A.Ovechkin/D.Phaneuf 25.00 60.00
FF10 V.Tretiak/P.Henderson 20.00 50.00
FF11 V.Kharlamov/B.Clarke 10.00 25.00
FF12 B.Salming/L.Robinson 6.00 15.00
FF13 J.Kurri/M.Bossy 6.00 15.00
FF14 B.Hull/S.Yzerman 20.00 50.00
FF15 P.Housley/R.Bourque 10.00 25.00
FF16 P.Stastny/G.Lafleur 8.00 20.00
FF17 B.Leetch/P.Coffey 6.00 15.00
FF18 LaFontaine/Robitaille 8.00 20.00
FF19 A.Yakushev/P.Esposito 10.00 25.00
FF20 M.Naslund/M.Goulet 6.00 15.00

2007-08 ITG O Canada International Goalies Jerseys

STATED PRINT RUN 50 SETS
IG01 Mike Richter 12.00 30.00
IG02 Vladislav Tretiak 12.00 30.00
IG03 Cristobal Huet 5.00 12.00
IG04 Dominik Hasek 8.00 20.00
IG05 Tom Barrasso 6.00 15.00
IG06 Tony Esposito 6.00 15.00
IG07 John Vanbiesbrouck 8.00 20.00
IG08 Vladimir Dzurilla 6.00 15.00
IG09 Tuukka Rask 15.00 40.00
IG10 Kari Lehtonen 5.00 12.00

2007-08 ITG O Canada Jerseys

ANNOUNCED PRINT RUN 100
EMBLEMS/20: .8X TO 2X JSY/100*
GUJ01 Alex Grant 2.50 6.00
GUJ02 Angelo Esposito 5.00 12.00
GUJ03 Braden Holtby 10.00 25.00
GUJ04 Brandon Sutter 4.00 10.00
GUJ05 Colton Gillies 4.00 10.00
GUJ06 Dion Knelsen 2.50 6.00
GUJ07 Drew Doughty 8.00 20.00
GUJ08 Eric Doyle 2.50 6.00
GUJ09 Jamie Arniel 3.00 8.00
GUJ10 John Negrin 3.00 8.00
GUJ11 Keven Veilleux 3.00 8.00
GUJ12 Kyle Turris 12.00 30.00
GUJ13 Logan Couture 4.00 10.00
GUJ14 Luke Schenn 5.00 12.00
GUJ15 Mark Katic 2.50 6.00
GUJ16 Olivier Fortier 2.50 6.00
GUJ17 Steven Stamkos 12.00 30.00
GUJ18 Trevor Cann 3.00 8.00
GUJ19 Yann Sauve 4.00 10.00
GUJ20 Yves Bastien 2.50 6.00
GUJ21 Zachary Boychuk 4.00 10.00
GUJ22 Zack Torquato 2.50 6.00
GUJ23 Carla MacLeod 4.00 10.00
GUJ24 Caroline Ouellette 4.00 10.00
GUJ25 Charline Labonte 6.00 15.00
GUJ26 Cheryl Pounder 4.00 10.00
GUJ27 Colleen Sostorics 4.00 10.00
GUJ28 Danielle Goyette 5.00 12.00
GUJ29 Delaney Collins 4.00 10.00
GUJ30 Gillian Apps 5.00 12.00
GUJ31 Gillian Ferrari 4.00 10.00
GUJ32 Gina Kingsbury 4.00 10.00
GUJ33 Hayley Wickenheiser 10.00 25.00
GUJ34 Jayna Hefford 5.00 12.00
GUJ35 Jennifer Botterill 4.00 10.00
GUJ36 Katie Weatherston 4.00 10.00
GUJ37 Kelly Bechard 4.00 10.00
GUJ38 Kim St. Pierre 12.00 30.00
GUJ39 Meghan Agosta 5.00 12.00
GUJ40 Sarah Vaillancourt 4.00 10.00
GUJ41 Tessa Bonhomme 4.00 10.00
GUJ42 Vicky Sunohara 5.00 12.00
GUJ43 Karl Alzner 2.50 6.00
GUJ44 Daniel Bertram 2.50 6.00
GUJ45 Luc Bourdon 4.00 10.00
GUJ46 Marc-Andre ClichÃ© 2.50 6.00
GUJ47 Andrew Cogliano 4.00 10.00
GUJ48 Steve Downie 3.00 8.00
GUJ49 Cody Franson 5.00 12.00
GUJ50 Sam Gagner 5.00 12.00
GUJ51 Darren Helm 4.00 10.00
GUJ52 Leland Irving 4.00 10.00
GUJ53 Kristopher Letang 6.00 15.00
GUJ54 Bryan Little 3.00 8.00
GUJ55 Brad Marchand 10.00 25.00
GUJ56 Kenndal McArdle 2.50 6.00
GUJ57 James Neal 6.00 15.00
GUJ58 Ryan O'Marra 2.50 6.00
GUJ59 Ryan Parent 2.50 6.00
GUJ60 Carey Price 25.00 60.00
GUJ61 Tom Pyatt 5.00 12.00
GUJ62 Kris Russell 3.00 8.00
GUJ63 Marc Staal 4.00 10.00
GUJ64 Jonathan Toews 12.00 30.00
GUJ65 Cassie Campbell 10.00 25.00
GUJ66 Vincent Lecavalier 6.00 15.00
GUJ67 Roberto Luongo 5.00 12.00
GUJ68 John Tavares 10.00 25.00
GUJ69 Joe Thornton 5.00 12.00
GUJ70 Jason Spezza 4.00 10.00
GUJ71 Joe Sakic 6.00 15.00
GUJ73 Dany Heatley 4.00 10.00
GUJ74 Eric Lindros 6.00 15.00
GUJ75 Chris Pronger 3.00 8.00
GUJ77 Steve Yzerman 12.00 30.00
GUJ78 Martin Brodeur 8.00 20.00
GUJ79 Marc-Andre Fleury 6.00 15.00
GUJ80 Dion Phaneuf 4.00 10.00

2005 ITG Passing the Torch

Available only in ITG Super Boxes available for the 2005 Chicago Sportsfest, this 30-card set honored the two greatest goalies in recent history. Each box contained one set and two memorabilia cards or one memorabilia card and one dual signed card.
COMPLETE SET (25) 8.00 20.00
1 Checklist .40 1.00
2 Martin Brodeur .40 1.00
Rookie Season
3 Martin Brodeur .40 1.00
Calder Trophy
4 Martin Brodeur .40 1.00
First Stanley Cup
5 Martin Brodeur .40 1.00
First Vezina Trophy
6 Martin Brodeur .40 1.00
First NHL All-Star Game
7 Martin Brodeur/400th Career Win .40 1.00
8 Martin Brodeur/50th Career Shutout .40 1.00
9 Martin Brodeur .40 1.00
Winning Streak
10 Martin Brodeur .40 1.00
International Experience
11 Martin Brodeur .40 1.00
Patrick Roy NHL Dreams
12 Martin Brodeur .40 1.00
Patrick Roy Immediate Impact
13 Martin Brodeur .40 1.00
Patrick Roy First Cup
14 Martin Brodeur .40 1.00
Patrick Roy Best of the Best
15 Martin Brodeur .40 1.00
Patrick Roy Among the Stars
16 Martin Brodeur .40 1.00
Patrick Roy Passing the Torch
17 Patrick Roy .40 1.00
Rookie Season
18 Patrick Roy .40 1.00
First Stanley Cup and Conn Smythe Trophy
19 Patrick Roy .40 1.00
First NHL All-Star Game
20 Patrick Roy .40 1.00
First Vezina Trophy
21 Patrick Roy .40 1.00
Traded to Colorado
22 Patrick Roy .40 1.00
First Stanley Cup in Colorado
23 Patrick Roy .40 1.00
Most Career Playoff Wins
24 Patrick Roy .40 1.00
Most Career Wins
25 Patrick Roy .40 1.00
Retirement

2005 ITG Passing the Torch Memorabilia

Available only in ITG Super Boxes during the 2005 National Convention, this 31 -card set featured game-used memorabilia of Patrick Roy and Martin Brodeur. Cards were limited to just 100 copies each unless marked differently below.
UNDER 25 NOT PRICED DUE TO SCARCITY
PTT1 Martin Brodeur NJ 12.00 30.00
PTT2 Martin Brodeur AS 12.00 30.00
PTT3 Martin Brodeur AS 12.00 30.00
PTT4 Martin Brodeur AS 12.00 30.00
PTT5 Martin Brodeur Pad 12.00 30.00
PTT6 Martin Brodeur Stk 12.00 30.00
PTT7 Patrick Roy MTL 12.00 30.00
PTT8 Patrick Roy COL 12.00 30.00
PTT9 Patrick Roy AS 12.00 30.00
PTT10 Patrick Roy AS 12.00 30.00
PTT11 Patrick Roy AS 12.00 30.00
PTT12 Patrick Roy Glove 12.00 30.00
PTT13 Patrick Roy Pad 12.00 30.00
PTT14 Patrick Roy Stk 12.00 30.00
PTT15 M.Brodeur 15.00 40.00
P.Roy MTL J/J
PTT16 M.Brodeur 15.00 40.00
P.Roy AVS J/J
PTT17 M.Brodeur 15.00 40.00
P.Roy AS J/J
PTT18 M.Brodeur 15.00 40.00
P.Roy Dual Pad
PTT19 M.Brodeur 15.00 40.00
P.Roy S/S
PTT20 Martin Brodeur Jsy/Stk 15.00 40.00
PTT21 Patrick Roy Jsy/Stk MTL 15.00 40.00
PTT22 Patrick Roy Jsy/Stk COL 15.00 40.00
PTT23 Brod/Roy MTL EMB/20
PTT24 Brod/Roy COL EMB/20
PTT25 M.Brodeur NUM/30 40.00 100.00
PTT26 M.Brodeur EMB/30
PTT27 P.Roy NUM MTL/33 50.00 125.00
PTT28 P.Roy EMB MTL/30 50.00 125.00
PTT29 P.Roy NUM COL/33 40.00 100.00
PTT30 P.Roy EMB COL/30 40.00 100.00
NNO Checklist

2005-06 ITG Sidney Crosby Series

COMPLETE SET (25) 15.00 40.00
COMMON CARD (1-25) 1.00 2.50
COMMON GOLD/87* 8.00 20.00

2005-06 ITG Sidney Crosby Series Autographs

COMMON AUTO/35* 75.00 150.00
ANNOUNCED PRINT RUN 35
ONE PER BOX SET

2005-06 ITG Sidney Crosby Series Memorabilia

ANNOUNCED PRINT RUN 25-87
SCM1 S.Crosby/M.Lemieux Jsys/87* 75.00 200.00
SCM2 S.Crosby/M.Lemieux Emblms/10*
SCM3 S.Crosby/M.Lemieux Nmbrs/10 *
SCM4 S.Crosby/M.Lemieux Gloves/10*
SCM5 S.Crosby/M.Fleury Jsys/87* 60.00 150.00
SCM6 S.Crosby/M.Fleury Emblms/15*
SCM7 S.Crosby/M.Fleury Nmbrs/15*
SCM8 S.Crosby/E.Malkin Nmbrs/15*
SCM9 S.Crosby/E.Malkin Jsys/87* 75.00 200.00
SCM10 S.Crosby/E.Malkin Emblms/15*
SCM11 Sidney Crosby Jsy/87* 40.00 100.00
SCM12 Sidney Crosby Jsy/87* 40.00 100.00
SCM13 Sidney Crosby Jsy/Stk/87* 50.00 125.00
SCM14 Sidney Crosby Jsy/Stk/87* 50.00 125.00
SCM15 Sidney Crosby Glove/15*
SCM16 Sidney Crosby Emblm/15*
SCM17 Sidney Crosby Emblm/10*
SCM18 Sidney Crosby Triple Mem/87* 100.00200.00
SCM19 Sidney Crosby Jsy/Glve/87* 60.00 150.00
SCM20 Sidney Crosby Dual Jsy/87* 50.00 125.00

2005-06 ITG Sidney Crosby Series Signed Memorabilia

ANNOUNCED PRINT RUN 25
CAM1 Sidney Crosby Jsy 200.00 400.00
CAM2 Sidney Crosby Jsy 200.00 400.00
CAM3 Sidney Crosby Glove 200.00 400.00
CAM4 Sidney Crosby Stk 200.00 400.00

2013-14 ITG Stickwork Game Used Sticks Silver

GUS01 Al MacInnis 12.00 30.00
GUS02 Alexander Ovechkin 25.00 60.00
GUS03 Aleksander Barkov 12.00 30.00
GUS04 Anders Hedberg 8.00 20.00
GUS05 Andrew Ladd 12.00 30.00
GUS06 Bernie Nicholls 10.00 25.00
GUS07 Bob Gainey 12.00 30.00
GUS08 Bob Probert 15.00 40.00
GUS09 Bobby Orr 100.00 200.00
GUS10 Brad Richards 12.00 30.00
GUS11 Brayden Schenn 12.00 30.00
GUS12 Brendan Gallagher 15.00 40.00
GUS13 Brian Bellows 10.00 25.00
GUS14 Brian Leetch 12.00 30.00
GUS15 Bryan Trottier 15.00 40.00
GUS16 Chris Chelios 12.00 30.00
GUS17 Chris Pronger 10.00 25.00
GUS18 Dale Hawerchuk 15.00 40.00
GUS19 David Clarkson 8.00 20.00
GUS20 David Krejci 12.00 30.00
GUS21 Denis Savard 15.00 40.00
GUS22 Denis Potvin
GUS23 Zach Parise 12.00 30.00
GUS24 Dion Phaneuf 12.00 30.00
GUS25 Doug Gilmour
GUS26 Dougie Hamilton 15.00 40.00
GUS27 Drew Doughty 12.00 30.00
GUS28 Dustin Brown 12.00 30.00
GUS29 Dustin Byfuglien 12.00 30.00
GUS30 Evgeni Malkin 40.00 100.00
GUS31 Gabriel Landeskog 10.00 25.00
GUS32 George Armstrong 30.00 80.00
GUS33 Gilbert Perreault 12.00 30.00
GUS34 Guy Carbonneau 12.00 30.00
GUS35 Guy Lafleur 25.00 50.00
GUS36 Ilya Kovalchuk 12.00 30.00
GUS37 James Van Riemsdyk 12.00 30.00
GUS38 Jari Kurri 15.00 40.00
GUS39 Jason Pominville 10.00 25.00
GUS40 Jason Spezza 12.00 30.00
GUS41 Jeff Carter 12.00 30.00
GUS42 Jeff Skinner 10.00 25.00
GUS43 Jeremy Roenick 15.00 40.00
GUS44 Joe Mullen 10.00 25.00
GUS45 Joe Sakic
GUS46 Joffrey Lupul 10.00 25.00
GUS47 John LeClair 12.00 30.00
GUS48 Jonathan Huberdeau 12.00 30.00
GUS49 Kyle Turris 10.00 25.00
GUS50 Larry Robinson 12.00 30.00
GUS51 Lars Eller 10.00 25.00
GUS52 Luc Robitaille 12.00 30.00
GUS53 Marc Staal 10.00 25.00
GUS54 Marcel Dionne 15.00 40.00
GUS55 Marian Gaborik 12.00 30.00
GUS56 Marian Hossa 15.00 40.00
GUS57 Mario Lemieux 40.00 100.00
GUS58 Mark Messier 30.00 60.00
GUS59 Mark Recchi 12.00 30.00
GUS60 Mark Scheifele 15.00 40.00
GUS61 Mathew Dumba 12.00 30.00
GUS62 Mats Sundin 12.00 30.00
GUS63 Sidney Crosby 75.00 135.00
GUS64 Mike Bossy 25.00 50.00
GUS65 Mike Gartner 12.00 30.00
GUS66 Mike Modano
GUS67 Mike Richards 12.00 30.00
GUS68 Mikko Koivu 10.00 25.00
GUS69 Nazem Kadri 12.00 30.00
GUS70 Niklas Kronwall 10.00 25.00
GUS71 Patrice Bergeron 15.00 40.00
GUS72 Paul Coffey 12.00 30.00
GUS73 Peter Stastny 15.00 40.00
GUS74 Phil Kessel 25.00 50.00
GUS75 Raymond Bourque 25.00 50.00
GUS76 Rick Nash 12.00 30.00
GUS77 Rob Blake 12.00 30.00
GUS78 Rod Langway 10.00 25.00
GUS79 Ron Francis 15.00 40.00
GUS80 Ryan Callahan 12.00 30.00
GUS81 Ryan O'Reilly 12.00 30.00
GUS82 Ryan Suter 10.00 25.00
GUS83 Saku Koivu 12.00 30.00
GUS84 Sean Couturier 12.00 30.00
GUS85 Sergei Fedorov 25.00 60.00
GUS86 Sergei Samsonov 10.00 25.00
GUS87 Steve Yzerman 25.00 60.00
GUS88 Steven Stamkos 30.00 60.00
GUS89 Teemu Selanne
GUS90 Terry O'Reilly 10.00 25.00
GUS91 Theoren Fleury 15.00 40.00
GUS92 Tony Amonte 10.00 25.00
GUS93 Trevor Linden 12.00 30.00
GUS94 Tyler Bozak 10.00 25.00
GUS95 Vincent Damphousse 10.00 25.00
GUS96 Wayne Gretzky 90.00 150.00

2015-16 ITG Stickwork Complete Stick Silver

CS02 Curtis Joseph/25 10.00 25.00
CS03 Gordie Howe/15 20.00 50.00
CS05 Marcel Dionne/30 10.00 25.00
CS06 Mario Lemieux/40 20.00 50.00
CS07 Maurice Richard/35 30.00 60.00
CS08 Patrick Roy/40 15.00 40.00
CS09 Paul Coffey/25 10.00 25.00
CS10 Phil Esposito/25 15.00 40.00
CS11 Raymond Bourque/25 15.00 40.00
CS12 Sergei Fedorov/25 12.00 30.00
CS13 Wayne Gretzky/35 20.00 80.00
CS14 Yvan Cournoyer/20 10.00 25.00

2015-16 ITG Stickwork Face Off Silver

FO01 J.Roenick/S.Fedorov/30 12.00 30.00
FO04 N.Ullman/Y.Cournoyer/40 8.00 20.00
FO05 P.Mahovlich/G.Howe/40 15.00 40.00
FO06 S.Fedorov/M.Modano/25 12.00 30.00
FO07 W.Gretzky/M.Lemieux/40 30.00 80.00
FO08 W.Gretzky/R.Francis/15 40.00 80.00
FO09 W.Gretzky/S.Fedorov/40 30.00 80.00

2015-16 ITG Stickwork Game Used Goalie Paddles Silver

GGP01 Andy Moog/25 12.00 30.00
GGP02 Ben Bishop/30 10.00 25.00
GGP03 Bernie Parent/40 12.00 30.00
GGP04 Carey Price/25 40.00 100.00
GGP05 Charlie Hodge/25 10.00 25.00
GGP06 Chris Osgood/25 12.00 30.00
GGP07 Curtis Joseph/40 10.00 25.00
GGP08 Ed Giacomin/15 12.00 30.00
GGP09 Felix Potvin/40 15.00 40.00
GGP10 Grant Fuhr/30 10.00 25.00
GGP11 Gump Worsley/24 12.00 30.00
GGP12 Harry Lumley/15 15.00 40.00
GGP13 Henrik Lundqvist/30 12.00 30.00
GGP14 Jacques Plante/15 15.00 40.00
GGP15 Jim Carey/30 8.00 20.00
GGP16 Jim Rutherford/20 10.00 25.00
GGP17 Jimmy Howard/30 10.00 25.00
GGP18 John Vanbiesbrouck/30 10.00 25.00
GGP20 Marc-Andre Fleury/20 20.00 50.00
GGP21 Miikka Kiprusoff/30 8.00 20.00
GGP22 Mike Richter/18 12.00 30.00
GGP23 Niklas Backstrom/26 10.00 25.00
GGP24 Nikolai Khabibulin/30 10.00 25.00
GGP25 Olaf Kolzig/30 10.00 25.00
GGP26 Patrick Roy/40 30.00 60.00
GGP27 Sean Burke/30 12.00 30.00
GGP28 Terry Sawchuk/18 15.00 40.00
GGP29 Tom Barrasso/25 12.00 30.00
GGP30 Tuukka Rask/30 10.00 25.00
GGP31 Vladislav Tretiak/40 12.00 30.00

2015-16 ITG Stickwork Game Used Goalie Sticks Silver

GGS01 Andy Moog/5
GGS02 Ben Bishop/4
GGS03 Bernie Parent/25 10.00 25.00
GGS04 Carey Price/20 30.00 80.00
GGS05 Charlie Hodge/30 6.00 15.00
GGS06 Chris Osgood/11
GGS07 Curtis Joseph/35 8.00 20.00
GGS08 Ed Giacomin/19 10.00 25.00
GGS09 Felix Potvin/30 12.00 30.00
GGS10 Grant Fuhr/35 8.00 20.00
GGS11 Gump Worsley/15 10.00 25.00
GGS12 Harry Lumley/12
GGS13 Henrik Lundqvist/20 12.00 30.00
GGS14 Jacques Plante/5
GGS15 Jim Carey/8
GGS16 Jim Rutherford/4
GGS17 Jimmy Howard/15 10.00 25.00
GGS18 John Vanbiesbrouck/8
GGS20 Marc-Andre Fleury/5
GGS22 Mike Richter/5
GGS23 Niklas Backstrom/14 8.00 20.00
GGS24 Nikolai Khabibulin/11
GGS25 Olaf Kolzig/7
GGS26 Patrick Roy/25 25.00 60.00
GGS27 Sean Burke/14 6.00 15.00
GGS29 Tom Barrasso/14 10.00 25.00
GGS30 Tuukka Rask/9
GGS31 Vladislav Tretiak/18 12.00 30.00

2015-16 ITG Stickwork Game Used Sticks Silver

GUS01 Adam Oates/19 15.00 40.00
GUS02 Al MacInnis/40 8.00 20.00
GUS03 Alexander Mogilny/25 12.00 30.00
GUS04 Alexander Ovechkin/30 15.00 40.00
GUS05 Andy Bathgate/7
GUS06 Bernie Geoffrion/5
GUS07 Bill Barber/12
GUS08 Bill Mosienko/3
GUS09 Bob Probert/11
GUS11 Brayden Schenn/5
GUS12 Brett Hull/40 8.00 20.00
GUS13 Brian Bellows/40 6.00 15.00
GUS14 Bryan Trottier/1
GUS15 Chris Chelios/26 10.00 25.00
GUS16 Chris Pronger/40 6.00 15.00
GUS17 Claude Lemieux/40 6.00 15.00
GUS18 Daniel Alfredsson/25 10.00 25.00
GUS19 Dave Andreychuk/40 8.00 20.00
GUS20 Denis Savard/6
GUS21 Dion Phaneuf/11
GUS23 Eric Lindros/30 15.00 40.00
GUS24 Evgeni Malkin/6
GUS25 Gabriel Landeskog/8
GUS26 George Armstrong/7
GUS27 Glenn Anderson/13
GUS28 Gordie Howe/40 40.00 80.00
GUS29 Guy Lafleur/5
GUS30 Henrik Zetterberg/11
GUS31 Jari Kurri/23 10.00 25.00
GUS33 Jeremy Roenick/39 8.00 20.00
GUS34 Joe Kocur/25 12.00 30.00
GUS35 Joe Thornton/28 10.00 25.00
GUS36 Keith Tkachuk/25 10.00 25.00
GUS38 King Clancy/6
GUS39 Larry Murphy/4
GUS40 Larry Robinson/5
GUS41 Luc Robitaille/38 8.00 20.00
GUS42 Luke Schenn/30 5.00 12.00
GUS43 Marcel Dionne/40 12.00 30.00
GUS44 Marian Gaborik/13
GUS45 Mario Lemieux/40 20.00 50.00
GUS46 Mark Messier/40 10.00 25.00
GUS47 Mark Recchi/7
GUS48 Mats Naslund/25 10.00 25.00
GUS50 Maurice Richard/40 30.00 60.00
GUS52 Mike Gartner/17 10.00 25.00
GUS54 Mike Ricci/27 8.00 20.00
GUS55 Norm Ullman/35 8.00 20.00
GUS56 Paul Coffey/29 10.00 25.00
GUS58 Phil Housley/18 10.00 25.00
GUS59 Pierre Pilote/3
GUS60 Pierre Turgeon/10
GUS61 Raymond Bourque/35 12.00 30.00
GUS62 Red Kelly/8
GUS63 Rick Nash/34 8.00 20.00
GUS64 Rod Langway/5
GUS65 Rod Langway/5
GUS66 Ron Duguay/23 12.00 30.00
GUS67 Serge Savard/40 8.00 20.00
GUS68 Sergei Fedorov/40 12.00 30.00
GUS69 Stan Mikita/4
GUS70 Steve Shutt/12
GUS71 Steve Yzerman/27 25.00 50.00
GUS72 Ted Kennedy/5
GUS73 Terry O'Reilly/7
GUS74 Tie Domi/11
GUS76 Tony Amonte/12
GUS77 Trevor Linden/11
GUS78 Wayne Gretzky/40 30.00 80.00
GUS79 Yvan Cournoyer/40 8.00 20.00

2015-16 ITG Stickwork Hockey History Assist Leaders Silver

HHA02 Al MacInnis/40 8.00 20.00
HHA03 Doug Gilmour/11
HHA04 Gordie Howe/40 15.00 40.00
HHA06 Joe Thornton/30 8.00 20.00
HHA07 Larry Murphy/40 8.00 20.00
HHA08 Marcel Dionne/40 10.00 25.00
HHA09 Mario Lemieux/40 20.00 50.00
HHA10 Mark Messier/15 12.00 30.00
HHA11 Mark Recchi/25 12.00 30.00
HHA12 Nicklas Lidstrom/5
HHA13 Paul Coffey/40 8.00 20.00
HHA14 Phil Esposito/40 12.00 30.00
HHA15 Phil Housley/40 8.00 20.00
HHA16 Raymond Bourque/40 12.00 30.00
HHA17 Ron Francis/5
HHA18 Stan Mikita/5
HHA19 Steve Yzerman/5
HHA20 Wayne Gretzky/40 30.00 80.00

2015-16 ITG Stickwork Hockey History Goal Leaders Silver

HHG02 Brendan Shanahan/16 12.00 30.00
HHG04 Dave Andreychuk/40 8.00 20.00
HHG06 Gordie Howe/40 15.00 40.00
HHG11 Luc Robitaille/40 8.00 20.00
HHG12 Marcel Dionne/40 10.00 25.00
HHG13 Mario Lemieux/40 20.00 50.00
HHG14 Mark Messier/25 12.00 30.00
HHG15 Maurice Richard/35 30.00 60.00
HHG16 Mike Gartner/35 8.00 20.00
HHG17 Phil Esposito/40 12.00 30.00
HHG20 Wayne Gretzky/40 30.00 80.00

2015-16 ITG Stickwork Stick Rack Dual Silver

SR201 A.Mogilny/T.Linden/25 12.00 30.00
SR202 A.Ovechkin/S.Fedorov/35 15.00 40.00
SR204 B.Bishop/T.Rask/17 10.00 25.00
SR206 B.Mosienko/S.Mikita/30 10.00 25.00
SR207 Bob Gainey
Guy Lafleur/5
SR209 Bobby Hull
Stan Mikita/5
SR210 B.Orr/W.Gretzky/40 40.00 80.00
SR211 B.Shanahan/H.Zetterberg/19 12.00 30.00
SR212 C.Neely/R.Bourque/35 12.00 30.00
SR213 C.Chelios/A.MacInnis/40 8.00 20.00
SR214 C.Chelios/S.Savard/40 8.00 20.00
SR215 C.Pronger/A.MacInnis/35 8.00 20.00
SR216 C.Gillies/B.Trottier/13
SR217 C.Joseph/F.Potvin/40 12.00 30.00
SR218 C.Joseph/G.Fuhr/40 8.00 20.00
SR219 D.Savard/C.Chelios/30 10.00 25.00
SR220 D.Doughty/R.Blake/30 8.00 20.00
SR221 E.Malkin/A.Ovechkin/30 30.00 80.00
SR222 Frank Brimsek
Johnny Bower/9
SR223 George Armstrong
Ted Kennedy/5
SR224 J.Kurri/G.Anderson/30 8.00 20.00
SR225 J.Spezza/I.Kovalchuk/30 8.00 20.00
SR226 J.Skinner/S.Stamkos/30 15.00 40.00
SR227 Jeremy Roenick
Luc Robitaille/9
SR228 J.Kocur/M.Messier/35 15.00 30.00
SR229 K.Tkachuk/J.Roenick/30 8.00 20.00
SR230 K.Hodge/P.Esposito/40 12.00 30.00
SR231 M.Dionne/S.Fedorov/40 12.00 30.00
SR232 M.Gaborik/D.Ciccarelli/30 8.00 20.00
SR233 M.Scheifele/G.Landeskog/25 8.00 20.00
SR234 M.Naslund/B.Bellows/40 8.00 20.00
SR235 Maurice Richard
Guy Lafleur/5
SR237 Mike Gartner
Adam Oates/5
SR238 Mike Modano
Brett Hull/5
SR239 N.Ullman/R.Kelly/40 10.00 25.00
SR240 Patrick Roy
Ken Dryden/3
SR241 P.Stastny/P.Stastny/30 8.00 20.00
SR242 P.Turgeon/D.Andreychuk/25 10.00 25.00
SR243 Red Kelly
Ted Kennedy/9
SR244 R.Langway/L.Robinson/30 8.00 20.00
SR245 S.Savard/Y.Cournoyer/40 8.00 20.00
SR246 S.Gagne/R.Nash/35 8.00 20.00
SR247 W.Gretzky/G.Howe/35 40.00 80.00
SR248 W.Gretzky/M.Richard/35 30.00 80.00

2015-16 ITG Stickwork Stick Rack Quad Silver

SR401 Brimsek/Hodge/Bower/Worsley/10
SR403 Dionne/Robitaille 40.00 100.00
Coffey/Gretzky/40
SR404 Dionne/Trottier 15.00 40.00
Esposito/Lafleur/15
SR405 Esposito/Mikita 15.00 40.00
Richard/Geoffrion/15
SR406 Fedorov/Yzerman/Hull 25.00 50.00
Lidstrom/20
SR407 Gainey/Shutt/Lafleur/Savard/15 12.00 30.00
SR409 Gretzky/Lemieux/Fedorov 40.00 100.00
Roenick/25
SR410 Housley/MacInnis/Bourque 15.00 40.00
Potvin/15
SR411 Housley/MacInnis/Murphy 12.00 30.00
Bourque/40
SR412 Kelly/Kennedy/Horton/Bower/3
SR413 Kurri/Gretzky/Messier/Fuhr/35 40.00 100.00
SR414 Lindros/Fedorov/Messier 15.00 40.00
Roenick/35
SR416 Mullen/Mogilny/Bellows/Fleury/20 12.0030.00
SR417 Oates/Linden/Roenick/Naslund/15 15.0040.00
SR418 Ovechkin/Stamkos/Nash 25.00 50.00
Kovalchuk/15
SR419 Parent/Potvin/Joseph/Tretiak/40 12.00 30.00
SR420 Pilote/Hull/Mikita/Savard/5
SR421 Pronger/MacInnis/Chelios 8.00 20.00
Housley/35
SR423 Roy/Fuhr/Potvin/Joseph/40 20.00 50.00
SR424 Roy/Tretiak/Parent/Fuhr/40 20.00 50.00
SR425 Savard/Chelios/Naslund 8.00 20.00
Bellows/40
SR426 Savard/Shutt/Cournoyer 12.00 30.00
Lafleur/15
SR427 Stastny/Stastny/Hull/Hull/5

2015-16 ITG Stickwork Stick Rack Triple Silver

SR301 Anderson/Kurri/Coffey/25 10.00 25.00
SR303 Byfuglien/Bergeron/Suter/30 10.00 25.00
SR305 Carter/Parise/Phaneuf/30 8.00 20.00
SR306 Chelios/MacInnis/Coffey/40 8.00 20.00
SR307 Chelios/Pronger/Housley/35 8.00 20.00
SR308 Dionne/Esposito/Mikita/30 12.00 30.00
SR309 Gretzky/Esposito/Cournoyer/40 30.00 80.00
SR310 Gretzky/Howe/Richard/40 40.00 80.00
SR311 Gretzky/Messier/Lindros/30 30.00 80.00
SR312 Horton/Robinson/Bourque/5
SR313 Housley/MacInnis/Bourque/40 12.00 30.00
SR314 Howe/Kelly/Ullman/40 15.00 40.00
SR315 Joseph/Potvin/Parent/40 12.00 30.00
SR316 Kurri/Gretzky/Dionne/40 30.00 80.00
SR317 Lafleur/Savard/Cournoyer/13
SR318 Lafleur/Shutt/Savard/5
SR319 Langway/Potvin/Savard/25 15.00 40.00
SR320 Lemieux/Gretzky/Richard/40 40.00 80.00
SR321 Lidstrom/Fedorov/Yzerman/25 15.00 40.00
SR322 Linden/Oates/Gilmour/5
SR323 Mikita/Hull/Pilote/5
SR324 Murphy/MacInnis/Housley/40 8.00 20.00
SR325 Orr/Hodge/Esposito/40 25.00 60.00
SR326 Parise/Skinner/Spezza/25 10.00 25.00
SR327 Potvin/Barrasso/Khabibulin/13
SR329 Savard/Naslund/Cournoyer/40 8.00 20.00
SR330 Ullman/Richard/Howe/40 25.00 50.00
SR331 Worsley/Giacomin/Hodge/11
SR332 Zetterberg/Nash/Malkin/25 30.00 80.00

2015-16 ITG Stickwork Tape Job Silver

TJ03 Guy Lafleur/30 10.00 25.00
TJ05 Marcel Dionne/20 12.00 30.00
TJ06 Mario Lemieux/40 20.00 50.00
TJ07 Mark Messier/40 10.00 25.00
TJ08 Patrick Roy/40 20.00 50.00
TJ09 Saku Koivu/15 20.00 40.00
TJ10 Trevor Linden/30 8.00 20.00
TJ11 Wayne Gretzky/20 50.00 100.00

2015-16 ITG Stickwork Tape to Tape Silver

TT01 E.Lindros/J.Roenick/12
TT02 E.Lindros/M.Lemieux/12
TT03 M.Messier/W.Gretzky/15 30.00 80.00
TT04 N.Lidstrom/S.Fedorov/25 15.00 40.00
TT05 P.Roy/G.Fuhr/30 15.00 40.00
TT06 S.Yzerman/S.Fedorov/35 20.00 40.00
TT07 Ted Kennedy
Frank Brimsek/5
TT08 W.Gretzky/M.Lemieux/20 40.00 100.00
TT09 Y.Cournoyer/G.Lafleur/18 12.00 30.00

2016-17 ITG Stickwork 100 Greatest of All Time

GAT01 Adam Oates/25 10.00 25.00
GAT02 Al MacInnis/25 10.00 25.00
GAT03 Alex Delvecchio/25 10.00 25.00
GAT04 Alexander Ovechkin/25 40.00 100.00
GAT05 Andy Bathgate/25 10.00 25.00
GAT06 Bob Gainey/25 10.00 25.00
GAT07 Bobby Clarke/25 10.00 25.00
GAT08 Bobby Hull/25 15.00 40.00
GAT09 Bobby Orr/25 30.00 80.00
GAT10 Borje Salming/25 10.00 25.00
GAT11 Brad Park/25 10.00 25.00
GAT12 Brendan Shanahan/25 12.00 30.00
GAT13 Chris Chelios/25 10.00 25.00
GAT14 Darryl Sittler/25 10.00 25.00
GAT15 Dave Keon/25 10.00 25.00
GAT16 Denis Potvin/25 10.00 25.00
GAT17 Denis Savard/25 12.00 30.00
GAT18 Eddie Shore/25 10.00 25.00
GAT19 Eric Lindros/25 10.00 25.00
GAT20 Frank Mahovlich/25 10.00 25.00
GAT21 Gilbert Perreault/25 10.00 25.00
GAT22 Gordie Howe/25 25.00 60.00
GAT23 Grant Fuhr/25 10.00 25.00
GAT24 Guy Lafleur/25 12.00 30.00
GAT25 Henri Richard/25 10.00 25.00
GAT26 Jacques Plante/25 15.00 40.00
GAT27 Jari Kurri/25 10.00 25.00
GAT28 Jaromir Jagr/25 25.00 60.00
GAT29 Jean Beliveau/25 10.00 25.00
GAT30 Jean Ratelle/25 10.00 25.00
GAT31 Joe Nieuwendyk/25 10.00 25.00
GAT32 Joe Sakic/25 15.00 40.00
GAT33 Johnny Bower/20 10.00 25.00
GAT34 Johnny Bucyk/25 10.00 25.00
GAT35 Ken Dryden/25 20.00 50.00
GAT36 King Clancy/20 10.00 25.00
GAT37 Larry Robinson/25 10.00 25.00
GAT38 Luc Robitaille/25 10.00 25.00
GAT39 Marcel Dionne/25 12.00 30.00
GAT40 Mario Lemieux/25 30.00 80.00
GAT41 Mark Messier/25 12.00 30.00
GAT42 Martin Brodeur/25 20.00 50.00
GAT43 Mats Sundin/25 10.00 25.00
GAT44 Maurice Richard/25 10.00 25.00
GAT45 Mike Bossy/25 10.00 25.00
GAT46 Mike Gartner/25 10.00 25.00
GAT47 Mike Modano/25 15.00 40.00
GAT48 Milt Schmidt/25 10.00 25.00
GAT49 Pat LaFontaine/25 10.00 25.00
GAT50 Patrick Roy/25 25.00 60.00
GAT51 Paul Coffey/25 10.00 25.00
GAT52 Peter Forsberg/25 10.00 25.00
GAT53 Peter Stastny/25 10.00 25.00
GAT54 Phil Esposito/25 15.00 40.00
GAT55 Raymond Bourque/25 15.00 40.00
GAT56 Red Kelly/25 10.00 25.00
GAT57 Ron Francis/25 12.00 30.00
GAT58 Scott Stevens/25 8.00 20.00
GAT59 Serge Savard/25 10.00 25.00
GAT60 Sergei Fedorov/25 15.00 40.00
GAT61 Sid Abel/25 10.00 25.00
GAT62 Sidney Crosby/25 40.00 100.00
GAT63 Stan Mikita/25 12.00 30.00
GAT64 Steve Yzerman/25 12.00 30.00
GAT65 Ted Kennedy/20 10.00 25.00
GAT66 Ted Lindsay/20 10.00 25.00
GAT67 Teemu Selanne/25 20.00 50.00
GAT68 Tim Horton/25 20.00 50.00
GAT69 Wayne Gretzky/25 50.00 120.00
GAT70 Yvan Cournoyer/25 10.00 25.00

2016-17 ITG Stickwork Award Season

AS01 Shore/Abel/Richard/Howe 25.00 60.00
Kennedy/Beliveau/Bathgate/Geoffrion
AS02 Hull/Esposito/Orr/Mikita 50.00 125.00
Clarke/Lafleur/Trottier/Gretzky
AS03 Keon/Hull/Mikita/Bucyk 15.00 40.00
Ratelle/Perreault/Goring/Dionne
AS04 Lumley/Plante/Worsley 25.00 60.00
Barrasso/Vanbiesbrouck/Hextall/Fuhr/Roy
AS05 Stewart/Worsley/Mahovlich 30.00 80.00
Keon/Rousseau/Laperriere/Orr/Sanderson
AS06 Perreault/Potvin/Trottier 12.00 30.00
Bossy/Smith/Bourque/Hawerchuk/Stastny
AS07 Larmer/Lemieux/Robitaille 30.00 80.00
Nieuwendyk/Makarov/Selanne/Brodeur/Forsberg
AS08 Lindsay/Howe/Beliveau/Hull 30.00 80.00
Mikita/Esposito/Orr/Lafleur
AS09 Beliveau/Keon/Orr/Cournoyer 30.00 80.00
Leach/Lafleur/Robinson/Gainey
AS10 Trottier/Goring/Bossy 50.00 125.00
Messier/Gretzky/Lemieux/Sakic/Yzerman
AS11 Laperriere/Orr/Potvin/Robinson 30.00 80.00
Carlyle/Langway/Coffey/Bourque
AS12 Ratelle/Clarke/Richard/Gilbert 30.00 80.00
Goring/McDonald/Park/Lemieux

2016-17 ITG Stickwork Decade Leaders

DL01 Mikita/Howe/Hull/Ullman 15.00 40.00
DL02 Mikita/Howe/Beliveau/Richard 15.00 40.00
DL03 Hull/Mahovlich/Howe/Mikita 15.00 40.00
DL04 Howe/Lindsay/Richard/Beliveau 15.00 40.00
DL05 Howe/Lindsay/Beliveau/Bathgate 15.00 40.00

2016-17 ITG Stickwork Enshrined Eight

EE01 Hull/Beliveau/Richard/Howe 20.00 50.00
Orr/Keon/Ullman/Abel
EE02 Bower/Plante/Lumley 15.00 40.00
Worsley/Dryden/Cheevers/Roy/Fuhr
EE03 Horton/Pronovost/Orr 20.00 50.00
Lapointe/Savard/Salming/Stanley/Bourque

2016-17 ITG Stickwork Enshrined Eight Franchise

E8F01 Bower/Stanley/Salming 20.00 50.00
Sittler/McDonald/Keon/Horton/Kennedy
E8F02 Beliveau/Dryden 20.00 50.00
Cournoyer/Laperriere/Plante/Richard/Robinson/Shutt
E8F03 Gainey/Lafleur/Chelios 25.00 60.00
Lapointe/Roy/Langway/Savard/Mahovlich
E8F04 Abel/Hull/Mikita/Esposito 30.00 80.00
Orr/Goulet/Savard/Chelios
E8F05 Bucyk/Cheevers/Esposito 30.00 80.00
Neely/Oates/Orr/Park/Bourque
E8F06 Howe/Lindsay/Yzerman 25.00 60.00
Abel/Pronovost/Ullman/Shanahan/Larionov
E8F07 Gretzky/Coffey/Messier/Fuhr 50.00 120.00
Anderson/Kurri/Oates/Ullman
E8F08 Gretzky/Dionne/Kurri 50.00 125.00
Coffey/Robinson/Robitaille/Fuhr/Murphy
E8F09 Lemieux/Murphy/Francis 30.00 80.00
Coffey/Horton/Mullen/Robitaille/Bathgate
E8F10 Messier/Gartner/Esposito 15.00 40.00
Stanley/Bathgate/Ratelle/Park/Lafleur

2016-17 ITG Stickwork Enshrined Goalie Sticks

EGS01 Dominik Hasek/19 10.00 25.00
EGS02 Gerry Cheevers/22 10.00 25.00
EGS03 Grant Fuhr/22 10.00 25.00
EGS04 Harry Lumley/15 10.00 25.00
EGS05 Jacques Plante/15 15.00 40.00
EGS06 Johnny Bower/15 10.00 25.00
EGS07 Patrick Roy/25 25.00 60.00
EGS08 Vladislav Tretiak/22 10.00 25.00

2016-17 ITG Stickwork Enshrined Sticks

ES01 Adam Oates/19 12.00 30.00
ES02 Bernie Federko/10
ES03 Bobby Hull/25 20.00 50.00
ES04 Bobby Orr/17 40.00 100.00
ES05 Cam Neely/22 12.00 30.00
ES06 Chris Pronger/19 10.00 25.00
ES07 Denis Savard/17 15.00 40.00
ES08 Gordie Howe/17 30.00 80.00
ES09 Guy Lafleur/25 15.00 40.00
ES10 Henri Richard/17 12.00 30.00
ES11 Jacques Laperriere/17 12.00 30.00

ES12 Jean Beliveau/17 12.00 30.00
ES13 Joe Nieuwendyk/15 12.00 30.00
ES14 Mario Lemieux/25 40.00 100.00
ES15 Maurice Richard/22 12.00 30.00
ES16 Phil Esposito/22 20.00 50.00
ES18 Serge Savard/14 12.00 30.00
ES19 Sergei Fedorov/25 20.00 50.00
ES20 Stan Mikita/22 15.00 40.00
ES21 Tim Horton/17 25.00 60.00
ES22 Wayne Gretzky/22 60.00 150.00

2016-17 ITG Stickwork Game Used Goalie Sticks

GGS01 Andy Moog/25 12.00 30.00
GGS02 Bruce Gamble/22 12.00 30.00
GGS03 Charlie Hodge/22 12.00 30.00
GGS04 Curtis Joseph/17 12.00 30.00
GGS05 Dan Bouchard/22 12.00 30.00
GGS06 Eddie Johnston/25 12.00 30.00
GGS07 John Vanbiesbrouck/25 12.00 30.00
GGS08 Kirk McLean/22 12.00 30.00
GGS09 Manon Rheaume/22 12.00 30.00
GGS10 Martin Brodeur/25 25.00 60.00
GGS11 Mike Richter/14 12.00 30.00
GGS12 Mike Vernon/22 12.00 30.00
GGS13 Ron Hextall/14 12.00 30.00

2016-17 ITG Stickwork Game Used Sticks

GS01 Al Iafrate/19 8.00 20.00
GS02 Alexander Ovechkin/17 30.00 80.00
GS03 Brent Sutter/17 8.00 20.00
GS04 Brian Sutter/17 8.00 20.00
GS05 Claude Lemieux/19 8.00 20.00
GS06 Claude Provost/17 8.00 20.00
GS07 Craig Hartsburg/19 8.00 20.00
GS08 Dave Andreychuk/14 8.00 20.00
GS09 Doug Weight/10 8.00 20.00
GS10 Garry Unger/17 8.00 20.00
GS11 Gary Leeman/17 8.00 20.00
GS12 Jeremy Roenick/22 8.00 20.00
GS13 Ken Linseman/20 8.00 20.00
GS14 Kirk Muller/18 8.00 20.00
GS15 Marc Tardif/19 8.00 20.00
GS16 Mark Messier/17 10.00 25.00
GS17 Owen Nolan/17 8.00 20.00
GS18 Paul Kariya/17 10.00 25.00
GS19 Pete Mahovlich/22 8.00 20.00
GS20 Peter Forsberg/22 8.00 20.00
GS21 Petr Nedved/21 8.00 20.00
GS22 Rod Brind'Amour/19 8.00 20.00
GS23 Sidney Crosby/25 30.00 80.00
GS24 Stephane Richer/15 8.00 20.00
GS25 Steve Larmer/16 8.00 20.00
GS26 Tiger Williams/15 8.00 20.00
GS27 Vincent Damphousse/19

2016-17 ITG Stickwork Stick Rack 4

SR01 Hull/Esposito/Dionne/Lafleur 20.00 50.00
SR02 Orr/Shore/Bourque/Park 40.00 100.00
SR03 Salming/Sittler/Keon/Horton 25.00 60.00
SR04 Larionov/Fedorov/Makarov/Krutov 20.00 50.00
SR05 Richard/Richard Mahovlich/Mahovlich 12.00 30.00
SR06 Roy/Richter/Joseph/Vanbiesbrouck 30.00 80.00
SR07 Lindros/Lemieux/Jagr/Messier 40.00 100.00
SR08 Mikita/Hull/Bucyk/Orr 40.00 100.00

2016-17 ITG Stickwork Stick Save

SS01 Curtis Joseph 10.00 25.00
SS02 Grant Fuhr 10.00 25.00
SS03 Harry Lumley 10.00 25.00
SS04 Jacques Plante 15.00 40.00
SS05 John Vanbiesbrouck 10.00 25.00
SS06 Johnny Bower 10.00 25.00
SS07 Manon Rheaume 10.00 25.00
SS08 Martin Brodeur 20.00 50.00
SS09 Mike Richter 10.00 25.00
SS10 Patrick Roy 25.00 60.00
SS11 Tom Barrasso 10.00 25.00
SS12 Vladislav Tretiak 10.00 25.00

2016-17 ITG Stickwork Tape to Twine

TT01 Howe/Mahovlich/Richard Lindsay/Mikita/Hull/Horton/Beliveau/25 30.00 80.00
TT02 Messier/Kurri/Hull/Yzerman Robitaille/Hawerchuk/Modano/Oates/25 20.00 50.00
TT03 Savard/Lafleur/Gainey Bucyk/Trottier/Richard/Hull/Park/25 20.00 50.00
TT04 Bathgate/Richard/Beliveau Stewart/Howe/Lindsay/Delvecchio/Keon/20 30.00 80.00

2016-17 ITG Stickwork Vintage Stick Rack 4

VSR01 Howe/Beliveau/Mahovlich Richard/25 30.00 80.00
VSR02 Plante/Bower/Lumley/Worsley/25 20.00 50.00
VSR03 Stewart/Clancy/Shore/Abel/15 12.00 30.00
VSR04 Howe/Lindsay/Pronovost Delvecchio/25 30.00 80.00
VSR05 Barilko/Stanley/Kennedy Armstrong/25 12.00 30.00
VSR06 Ullman/Keon/Horton/Baun/25 25.00 60.00

2007-08 ITG Superlative Autographs Silver

OVERALL AU ODDS 3 PER PACK
AAO Alexander Ovechkin 40.00 80.00
ABC Bobby Clarke 20.00 40.00
ABH Brett Hull 15.00 40.00
ABL Brian Leetch 10.00 25.00
ABOH Bobby Hull 15.00 40.00
ABP Bernie Parent 10.00 25.00
ACC Chris Chelios 20.00 40.00
ACN Cam Neely 10.00 25.00
ACO Chris Osgood 12.50 30.00
ACP Chris Pronger 8.00 20.00
ADH Dominik Hasek 20.00 40.00
ADH Dany Heatley 10.00 25.00
ADK Dave Keon 15.00 30.00
ADP Denis Potvin 10.00 25.00
AEG Ed Giacomin 10.00 25.00
AFM Frank Mahovlich 15.00 40.00
AGF Grant Fuhr 10.00 25.00
AGH Glenn Hall 12.00 30.00
AGL Guy Lafleur 20.00 40.00
AHR Henri Richard 15.00 40.00
AIK Ilya Kovalchuk 10.00 25.00
AJB Jean Beliveau 25.00 50.00
AJBO Johnny Bower 10.00 25.00
AJJ Jaromir Jagr 25.00 50.00
AJSG Jean-Sebastien Giguere 8.00 20.00
AJSK Joe Sakic 25.00 60.00
AJT Joe Thornton 10.00 25.00
AMB Martin Brodeur 30.00 80.00
AMD Marcel Dionne 8.00 20.00
AMG Marian Gaborik 12.00 30.00
AML Mario Lemieux 50.00 100.00
AMM Mike Modano 15.00 40.00
AMS Milt Schmidt 10.00 25.00
AMSL Martin St-Louis 10.00 25.00
AMT Marty Turco 10.00 25.00
ANL Nicklas Lidstrom 15.00 30.00
APC Paul Coffey 10.00 25.00
APD Pavel Datsyuk 20.00 40.00
APE Phil Esposito 20.00 40.00
APR Patrick Roy 50.00 100.00
ARB Raymond Bourque 30.00 60.00
ARE Ray Emery 8.00 20.00
ARK Red Kelly 10.00 25.00
ARL Roberto Luongo 15.00 40.00
ASM Stan Mikita 15.00 40.00
ATE Tony Esposito 10.00 25.00
ATL Ted Lindsay 12.50 30.00
AVL Vincent Lecavalier 12.50 30.00
AVT Vladislav Tretiak 20.00 40.00
AJSN Scott Niedermayer 10.00 25.00

2007-08 ITG Superlative Jerseys Autographs Silver

STATED PRINT RUN 50 SERIAL #'d SETS
AJAO Alexander Ovechkin 30.00 80.00
AJBC Bobby Clarke 12.00 30.00
AJBH Brett Hull 20.00 50.00
AJBL Brian Leetch 12.00 30.00
AJBOH Bobby Hull 15.00 40.00
AJBP Bernie Parent 12.00 30.00
AJCC Chris Chelios 12.50 30.00
AJCN Cam Neely 12.00 30.00
AJCO Chris Osgood 12.50 30.00
AJCP Chris Pronger 10.00 25.00
AJDH Dominik Hasek 15.00 40.00
AJDH Dany Heatley 12.50 30.00
AJDK Dave Keon 15.00 40.00
AJDP Denis Potvin 12.00 30.00
AJEG Ed Giacomin 12.00 30.00
AJFM Frank Mahovlich 15.00 40.00
AJGF Grant Fuhr 12.50 30.00
AJGH Glenn Hall 15.00 40.00
AJGL Guy Lafleur 25.00 50.00
AJHR Henri Richard 20.00 50.00
AJIK Ilya Kovalchuk 10.00 25.00
AJJB Jean Beliveau 25.00 50.00
AJJBO Johnny Bower 15.00 40.00
AJJJ Jaromir Jagr 25.00 60.00
AJJSG Jean-Sebastien Giguere 15.00 40.00
AJJSK Joe Sakic 20.00 50.00
AJJT Joe Thornton 15.00 40.00
AJMB Martin Brodeur 30.00 80.00
AJMD Marcel Dionne 15.00 40.00
AJMG Marian Gaborik 15.00 40.00
AJML Mario Lemieux 60.00 120.00
AJMM Mike Modano 20.00 50.00
AJMS Milt Schmidt 15.00 40.00
AJMSL Martin St-Louis 12.00 30.00
AJMT Marty Turco 12.00 30.00
AJNL Nicklas Lidstrom 15.00 40.00
AJPC Paul Coffey 12.00 30.00
AJPD Pavel Datsyuk 15.00 40.00
AJPE Phil Esposito 15.00 40.00
AJPR Patrick Roy 30.00 80.00
AJRB Raymond Bourque 25.00 50.00
AJRE Ray Emery 10.00 25.00
AJRK Red Kelly 10.00 25.00
AJRL Roberto Luongo 15.00 40.00
AJSM Stan Mikita 12.50 30.00
AJSN Scott Niedermayer 10.00 25.00
AJTE Tony Esposito 12.00 30.00
AJTL Ted Lindsay 12.50 30.00
AJVL Vincent Lecavalier 10.00 25.00
AJVT Vladislav Tretiak 25.00 60.00

2007-08 ITG Superlative Jerseys Silver

ANNOUNCED PRINT RUN 30
GUJ01 Jean Beliveau 12.00 30.00
GUJ02 Raymond Bourque BOS 15.00 40.00
GUJ03 Raymond Bourque COL 15.00 40.00
GUJ04 Martin Brodeur 25.00 50.00
GUJ05 Gerry Cheevers 10.00 25.00
GUJ06 Chris Chelios 10.00 25.00
GUJ07 Alexei Cherepanov 15.00 40.00
GUJ08 Bobby Clarke 15.00 40.00
GUJ09 Paul Coffey 10.00 25.00
GUJ10 Marcel Dionne 10.00 25.00
GUJ11 Ray Emery 8.00 20.00
GUJ12 Angelo Esposito 12.00 30.00
GUJ13 Phil Esposito 15.00 40.00
GUJ14 Tony Esposito 10.00 25.00
GUJ15 Grant Fuhr 12.50 30.00
GUJ16 Jaromir Jagr Pittsburgh 25.00 60.00
GUJ17 Ed Giacomin 10.00 25.00
GUJ18 Glenn Hall 12.00 30.00
GUJ19 Dominik Hasek 10.00 25.00
GUJ20 Dany Heatley
GUJ21 Bobby Hull 15.00 40.00
GUJ22 Brett Hull Dallas 15.00 40.00
GUJ23 Brett Hull Detroit 15.00 40.00
GUJ24 Jaromir Jagr New York 25.00 60.00
GUJ25 Dave Keon 10.00 25.00
GUJ26 Ilya Kovalchuk 10.00 25.00
GUJ27 Guy Lafleur 12.00 30.00
GUJ28 Pat LaFontaine 8.00 20.00
GUJ29 Vincent Lecavalier 8.00 20.00
GUJ30 Brian Leetch 10.00 25.00
GUJ31 Joe Thornton San Jose 12.00 30.00
GUJ32 Ted Lindsay 10.00 25.00
GUJ33 Roberto Luongo Vancouver 12.00 30.00
GUJ34 Roberto Luongo Florida 12.00 30.00
GUJ35 Frank Mahovlich 12.00 30.00
GUJ36 Stan Mikita 12.00 30.00
GUJ37 Mike Modano 15.00 40.00
GUJ38 Cam Neely 10.00 25.00
GUJ39 Alexander Ovechkin 30.00 60.00
GUJ40 Denis Potvin 10.00 25.00
GUJ41 Felix Potvin 20.00 50.00
GUJ42 Carey Price 30.00 60.00
GUJ43 Chris Pronger 8.00 20.00
GUJ44 Tuukka Rask 25.00 50.00
GUJ45 Henri Richard 12.00 30.00
GUJ46 Maurice Richard 50.00 100.00
GUJ47 Patrick Roy Montreal 25.00 50.00
GUJ48 Patrick Roy Colorado 25.00 50.00
GUJ49 Joe Sakic 15.00 40.00
GUJ50 Milt Schmidt 8.00 20.00
GUJ51 Jari Kurri 20.00 40.00
GUJ52 John Tavares 30.00 60.00
GUJ53 Joe Thornton Boston 10.00 25.00
GUJ54 Vladislav Tretiak 25.00 50.00
GUJ55 Marty Turco 10.00 25.00
GUJ56 Mario Lemieux 25.00 50.00
GUJ57 Pavel Datsyuk 12.00 30.00
GUJ58 Mats Sundin 10.00 25.00
GUJ59 Steven Stamkos 25.00 50.00
GUJ60 Ed Belfour 12.00 30.00
GUJ61 Markus Naslund 10.00 25.00
GUJ62 Paul Stastny 10.00 25.00
GUJ63 Doug Gilmour 12.00 30.00
GUJ64 Marc Staal 10.00 25.00
GUJ65 Sam Gagner 12.00 30.00
GUJ66 Jordan Staal 10.00 25.00
GUJ67 Bill Barber 6.00 15.00
GUJ68 Martin St. Louis 10.00 25.00
GUJ69 Scott Niedermayer 10.00 25.00
GUJ70 Lanny McDonald 12.00 30.00
GUJ71 Borje Salming 10.00 25.00
GUJ72 Darryl Sittler 8.00 20.00
GUJ73 Marian Gaborik 12.00 30.00
GUJ74 Jean-Sebastien Giguere 10.00 25.00
GUJ75 Paul Kariya 12.00 30.00

2007-08 ITG Superlative Patches Silver

STATED PRINT RUN 30 SERIAL #'d SETS
SP01 Alexander Ovechkin 30.00 60.00
SP02 Alexei Cherepanov 15.00 40.00
SP03 Angelo Esposito 15.00 40.00
SP04 Bobby Clarke 15.00 40.00
SP05 Bobby Hull 20.00 50.00
SP06 Borje Salming 15.00 40.00
SP07 Brett Hull Dallas 15.00 40.00
SP08 Brett Hull Detroit 15.00 40.00
SP09 Brian Leetch 12.00 30.00
SP10 Cam Neely 12.00 30.00
SP11 Carey Price 25.00 50.00
SP12 Chris Chelios 12.00 30.00
SP13 Chris Osgood 15.00 40.00
SP14 Chris Pronger 10.00 25.00
SP15 Dany Heatley 12.00 30.00
SP16 Darryl Sittler 10.00 25.00
SP17 Dave Keon 12.00 30.00
SP18 Denis Potvin 15.00 40.00
SP19 Dominik Hasek 12.00 30.00
SP20 Doug Gilmour 10.00 25.00
SP21 Ed Belfour 12.00 30.00
SP22 Felix Potvin 20.00 50.00
SP23 Frank Mahovlich 15.00 40.00
SP24 Glenn Hall
SP25 Guy Lafleur 20.00 50.00
SP26 Henri Richard 20.00 50.00
SP27 Ilya Kovalchuk 12.00 30.00
SP28 Jari Kurri 30.00 60.00
SP29 Jaromir Jagr Pittsburgh 30.00 60.00
SP30 Jaromir Jagr New York 30.00 60.00
SP31 Jean Beliveau 15.00 40.00
SP32 Joe Sakic 20.00 50.00
SP33 Joe Thornton San Jose 15.00 40.00
SP34 Joe Thornton Boston 15.00 40.00
SP35 John Tavares 20.00 50.00
SP36 Jordan Staal 12.00 30.00
SP37 Jean-Sebastien Giguere 15.00 40.00
SP38 Lanny McDonald 10.00 25.00
SP39 Marc Staal 12.00 30.00
SP40 Marcel Dionne 10.00 25.00
SP41 Marian Gaborik 15.00 40.00
SP42 Mario Lemieux 30.00 60.00
SP43 Markus Naslund 12.00 30.00
SP44 Martin Brodeur 30.00 60.00
SP45 Martin St. Louis 12.00 30.00
SP46 Marty Turco 12.00 30.00
SP47 Mats Sundin 20.00 50.00
SP48 Mike Modano 20.00 50.00
SP49 Milt Schmidt 15.00 40.00
SP50 Pat LaFontaine 20.00 50.00
SP51 Patrick Roy MONT 40.00 80.00
SP52 Patrick Roy COL 40.00 80.00
SP53 Paul Coffey 12.00 30.00
SP54 Paul Stastny 10.00 25.00
SP55 Pavel Datsyuk 15.00 40.00
SP56 Phil Esposito 20.00 50.00
SP57 Ray Emery 10.00 25.00
SP58 Ray Bourque BOS 15.00 40.00
SP59 Ray Bourque COL 15.00 40.00
SP60 R. Luongo VAN 15.00 40.00
SP61 R. Luongo FLA 15.00 40.00
SP62 Sam Gagner 12.00 30.00
SP63 Scott Niedermayer 10.00 25.00
SP64 Stan Mikita 12.00 30.00
SP65 Vladislav Tretiak 30.00 60.00
SP66 Steven Stamkos 40.00 80.00
SP67 Tony Esposito 25.00 60.00
SP68 Tuukka Rask 40.00 80.00
SP69 Vincent Lecavalier 10.00 25.00
SP70 Larry Robinson 12.00 30.00
SP71 Grant Fuhr Edmonton 20.00 50.00
SP72 Gilbert Perreault 12.00 30.00
SP73 Jean Ratelle 15.00 40.00
SP74 Peter Forsberg 15.00 40.00
SP75 Paul Kariya 15.00 40.00

2007-08 ITG Superlative Prospects Jerseys Autographs Silver

STATED PRINT RUN 50 SERIAL #'d SETS
SPAB Alex Bourret 8.00 20.00
SPACO Andrew Cogliano 15.00 40.00
SPAE Angelo Esposito 15.00 40.00
SPAP Alex Pietrangelo 15.00 40.00
SPAS Alexander Semin 15.00 40.00
SPBB Brian Boyle 12.00 30.00
SPBL Bryan Little 12.00 30.00
SPBLE Brian Lee 10.00 25.00
SPBM Brett MacLean 10.00 25.00
SPBS Brandon Sutter 12.00 30.00
SPCF Cody Franson 10.00 25.00
SPCG Colton Gillies 10.00 25.00
SPCGI Claude Giroux 25.00 50.00
SPCPR Carey Price 50.00 100.00
SPDD Drew Doughty 20.00 50.00
SPDP Dustin Penner 12.00 30.00
SPDS Devin Setoguchi 12.00 30.00
SPGB Gilbert Brule 15.00 40.00
SPJBL Jonathon Blum 12.00 30.00
SPJH Jonas Hiller 10.00 25.00
SPJS Jordan Staal 20.00 40.00
SPJSK Jack Skille 12.00 30.00
SPJT John Tavares 60.00 120.00
SPJTL Jiri Tlusty 15.00 40.00
SPKA Karl Alzner 15.00 40.00
SPKE Keaton Ellerby 12.00 30.00
SPKM Kenndal McArdle 8.00 20.00
SPKR Kris Russell 10.00 25.00
SPLB Luc Bourdon 12.00 30.00
SPLC Logan Couture 10.00 25.00
SPLI Leland Irving 10.00 25.00
SPMC Matthew Corrente 8.00 20.00
SPMDZ Michael Del Zotto 10.00 25.00
SPMF Michael Frolik 8.00 20.00
SPMG Michael Grabner 10.00 25.00
SPML Matt Lashoff 8.00 20.00
SPMS Marc Staal 15.00 40.00
SPOM Oscar Moller 15.00 40.00
SPPM Peter Mueller 12.00 30.00
SPPS Paul Stastny 15.00 40.00
SPRP Ryan Parent 15.00 40.00
SPSD Steve Downie 12.00 30.00
SPSG Sam Gagner 15.00 40.00
SPSM Steve Mason 15.00 40.00
SPSS Steven Stamkos 40.00 100.00
SPTH Thomas Hickey 12.00 30.00
SPTM Thomas McCollum 10.00 25.00
SPTP Tom Pyatt 8.00 20.00
SPTR Tuukka Rask 15.00 40.00
SPTW Ty Wishart 8.00 20.00

2009-10 ITG Superlative Autographs

STATED PRINT RUN 50 SER.#'d SETS
AAK Anze Kopitar 15.00 40.00
AAO Alexander Ovechkin 40.00 100.00
AAS Alexander Semin 10.00 25.00
ACC Chris Chelios 10.00 25.00
ACP Carey Price 40.00 100.00
ADB Daniel Briere 10.00 25.00
ADG Doug Gilmour 12.00 30.00
ADH Dominik Hasek 12.00 30.00
AEN Evgeni Nabokov 8.00 20.00
AGL Guy Lafleur 12.00 30.00
AIK Ilya Kovalchuk 10.00 25.00
AJB Jean Beliveau 25.00 50.00
AJJ Jaromir Jagr 25.00 60.00
AJS Joe Sakic 15.00 40.00
AJT Joe Thornton 10.00 25.00
ALR Larry Robinson 10.00 25.00
AMB Martin Brodeur 30.00 60.00
AMG Mike Green 10.00 25.00
AMGA Marian Gaborik 10.00 25.00
AMK Mikko Koivu 10.00 25.00
AML Mario Lemieux 40.00 80.00
AMM Mike Modano 15.00 40.00
AMS Martin St. Louis 10.00 25.00
ANL Nicklas Lidstrom 10.00 25.00
APM Patrick Marleau 10.00 25.00
APR Patrick Roy 40.00 100.00
APRO Patrick Roy 40.00 80.00
ARB Rob Blake 10.00 25.00
ARBO Ray Bourque 15.00 40.00
ARG Ryan Getzlaf 15.00 40.00
ARL Roberto Luongo 12.00 30.00
ASF Sergei Fedorov 15.00 40.00
ASK Saku Koivu 10.00 25.00
ASN Scott Niedermayer 10.00 25.00
ATS Teemu Selanne 20.00 50.00
ATT Tim Thomas 12.00 30.00

2009-10 ITG Superlative Game Used Jerseys Silver

STATED PRINT RUN 15-40
*PATCH SLVR/30: .5X TO 1.2X BASIC JSY
GUJ01 Alexander Ovechkin/40 15.00 40.00
GUJ02 John Tavares 20.00 50.00
GUJ03 Corey Perry 8.00 20.00
GUJ04 Jean-Sebastien Giguere 15.00 40.00
GUJ05 Ryan Getzlaf 12.00 30.00
GUJ06 Scott Niedermayer 8.00 20.00
GUJ07 Teemu Selanne 15.00 40.00
GUJ08 Ilya Kovalchuk 8.00 20.00
GUJ09 Kari Lehtonen 6.00 15.00
GUJ10 Ray Bourque 10.00 25.00
GUJ11 Milan Lucic 6.00 15.00
GUJ12 Tim Thomas 8.00 20.00
GUJ13 Gilbert Perreault 8.00 20.00
GUJ14 Ryan Miller 15.00 40.00
GUJ15 Miikka Kiprusoff 6.00 15.00
GUJ16 Cam Ward 8.00 20.00
GUJ17 Chris Chelios 8.00 20.00
GUJ18 Denis Savard 10.00 25.00
GUJ19 Ray Bourque 12.00 30.00
GUJ20 Joe Sakic 12.00 30.00
GUJ21 Patrick Roy 15.00 40.00
GUJ22 Rob Blake 8.00 20.00
GUJ23 Brenden Morrow 6.00 15.00
GUJ24 Brett Hull 12.00 30.00
GUJ25 Ed Belfour 8.00 20.00
GUJ26 Marty Turco 8.00 20.00
GUJ27 Mike Modano 12.00 30.00
GUJ28 Dominik Hasek 10.00 25.00
GUJ29 Nicklas Lidstrom 8.00 20.00
GUJ30 Sergei Fedorov 12.00 30.00
GUJ31 Nazem Kadri 15.00 40.00
GUJ32 Anze Kopitar 12.00 30.00
GUJ33 Luc Robitaille 8.00 20.00
GUJ34 Marcel Dionne 10.00 25.00
GUJ35 Rob Blake 8.00 20.00
GUJ36 Marian Gaborik 10.00 25.00
GUJ37 Carey Price 30.00 80.00
GUJ38 Eric Staal 10.00 25.00
GUJ39 Mats Sundin 8.00 20.00
GUJ40 Patrick Roy 15.00 40.00
GUJ41 Saku Koivu 8.00 20.00
GUJ42 Martin Brodeur 15.00 40.00
GUJ43 Scott Niedermayer 8.00 20.00
GUJ44 Ilya Kovalchuk 8.00 20.00
GUJ45 Marian Gaborik 10.00 25.00
GUJ46 Dominik Hasek 10.00 25.00
GUJ47 Dale Hawerchuk 10.00 25.00
GUJ48 Daniel Briere 8.00 20.00
GUJ49 Jaromir Jagr 20.00 50.00
GUJ50 Marc-Andre Fleury 12.00 30.00
GUJ51 Mario Lemieux 15.00 40.00
GUJ52 Tyler Seguin 15.00 40.00
GUJ53 Patrick Marleau 8.00 20.00
GUJ54 Doug Gilmour 10.00 25.00
GUJ55 Martin St. Louis 8.00 20.00
GUJ56 Mike Green 8.00 20.00
GUJ57 Alexander Semin 8.00 20.00
GUJ58 Jaromir Jagr 20.00 50.00
GUJ59 Taylor Hall 15.00 40.00
GUJ60 Teemu Selanne 15.00 40.00
GUJ61 Dave Keon SP/15
GUJ62 Larry Robinson SP/15
GUJ63 Milt Schmidt SP/15
GUJ64 Stan Mikita SP/15
GUJ65 Tony Esposito SP/15

2009-10 ITG Superlative Game Used Patches Silver

*PATCH SLVR/30: .5X TO 1.2X BASIC JSY
SILVER STATED PRINT RUN 30
SP02 John Tavares 30.00 80.00

2009-10 ITG Superlative Jerseys Autographs Silver

SILVER PRINT RUN 50 SER.#'d SETS
AJAK Anze Kopitar 12.00 30.00
AJAO Alexander Ovechkin 40.00 80.00
AJAS Alexander Semin 12.00 30.00
AJCC Chris Chelios 15.00 40.00
AJCP Carey Price 20.00 50.00
AJDB Daniel Briere 12.00 30.00
AJDG Doug Gilmour 12.00 30.00
AJDH Dominik Hasek 15.00 40.00
AJEN Evgeni Nabokov 10.00 25.00
AJGL Guy Lafleur 20.00 50.00
AJIK Ilya Kovalchuk 15.00 40.00
AJJB Jean Beliveau 20.00 50.00
AJJJ Jaromir Jagr 25.00 60.00
AJJS Joe Sakic 25.00 60.00
AJJT Joe Thornton 15.00 40.00
AJLR Larry Robinson 10.00 25.00
AJMB Martin Brodeur 25.00 60.00
AJMG Mike Green 10.00 25.00
AJMGA Marian Gaborik 15.00 40.00
AJMGA2 Marian Gaborik 12.00 30.00
AJMK Mikko Koivu 12.00 30.00
AJML Mario Lemieux 40.00 80.00
AJMM Mike Modano 15.00 40.00
AJMS Martin St. Louis 10.00 25.00
AJNL Nicklas Lidstrom 15.00 40.00
AJPM Patrick Marleau 12.00 30.00
AJPR Patrick Roy 30.00 80.00
AJPRO Patrick Roy 30.00 80.00
AJRBO Ray Bourque 20.00 50.00
AJRG Ryan Getzlaf 10.00 25.00
AJRL Roberto Luongo 20.00 50.00
AJSF Sergei Fedorov 15.00 40.00
AJSK Saku Koivu 15.00 40.00
AJSN Scott Niedermayer 10.00 25.00
AJTS Teemu Selanne 15.00 40.00
AJTT Tim Thomas 15.00 40.00

2009-10 ITG Superlative Prospect Autographs Silver

ANNOUNCED PRINT RUN 40
PABS Brayden Schenn 12.00 30.00
PACH Cody Hodgson 20.00 50.00
PACP Chet Pickard 8.00 20.00
PADH Darren Helm 6.00 15.00
PADT Dana Tyrell 6.00 15.00
PAEK Evander Kane 12.00 30.00
PAFB Fabian Brunnstrom 5.00 12.00
PAJC Jared Cowen 6.00 15.00
PAJE Jordan Eberle 25.00 60.00
PAJT John Tavares 25.00 60.00
PAKA Karl Alzner 4.00 10.00
PAMB Mikkel Boedker 4.00 10.00
PAMD Matt Duchene 12.00 30.00
PANK Nazem Kadri 15.00 40.00
PARN Ryan Nugent-Hopkins 30.00 80.00
PASV Semyon Varlamov 6.00 15.00
PATH Taylor Hall 25.00 60.00
PATS Tyler Seguiin 40.00 80.00
PAVH Victor Hedman 12.00 30.00
PAZB Zach Boychuk 5.00 12.00
PATHI Thomas Hickey 4.00 10.00

2009-10 ITG Superlative Prospect Jerseys Autographs Silver

SILVER PRINT RUN 40 SER.#'d SETS
PAJBS Brayden Schenn 20.00 50.00
PAJCH Cody Hodgson 30.00 60.00
PAJCP Chet Pickard 12.00 30.00
PAJDH Darren Helm 12.00 30.00
PAJDT Dana Tyrell 10.00 25.00
PAJEK Evander Kane 15.00 40.00
PAJFB Fabian Brunnstrom 10.00 25.00
PAJJC Jared Cowen 10.00 25.00
PAJJE Jordan Eberle 40.00 80.00
PAJJT John Tavares 60.00 120.00
PAJKA Karl Alzner 10.00 25.00
PAJMB Mikkel Boedker 10.00 25.00
PAJMD Matt Duchene 30.00 60.00
PAJNK Nazem Kadri 30.00 60.00
PAJSV Semyon Varlamov 25.00 60.00
PAJTH Taylor Hall 40.00 100.00
PAJTS Tyler Seguin 30.00 80.00
PAJVH Victor Hedman 12.00 30.00
PAJZB Zach Boychuk 12.00 30.00
PAJRNH Ryan Nugent-Hopkins 50.00 100.00
PAJTHI Thomas Hickey 20.00 50.00

2008-09 ITG Superlative Franchise Vintage Blue

ANNOUNCED PRINT RUN 40
1 Syl Apps 12.00 30.00
2 Ace Bailey 6.00 15.00
3 Bill Barilko 5.00 12.00
4 Max Bentley 5.00 12.00
5 Hugh Bolton 6.00 15.00
6 Turk Broda 8.00 20.00
7 Lorne Chabot 6.00 15.00
8 King Clancy 8.00 20.00
9 Charlie Conacher 6.00 15.00
10 Baldy Cotton 5.00 12.00
11 Bob Davidson 6.00 15.00
12 Hap Day 8.00 20.00
13 Gordie Drillon 5.00 12.00
14 Bob Goldham 5.00 12.00
15 George Hainsworth 10.00 25.00
16 Reg Hamilton 5.00 12.00
17 Red Horner 5.00 12.00
18 Busher Jackson 6.00 15.00
19 Ted Kennedy 8.00 20.00
20 Harry Lumley 5.00 12.00
21 Frank McCool 6.00 15.00
22 Howie Meeker 8.00 20.00
23 Nick Metz 5.00 12.00
24 Babe Pratt 5.00 12.00
25 Joe Primeau 6.00 15.00
26 Al Rollins 5.00 12.00
27 Sweeney Schriner 5.00 12.00
28 Tod Sloan 8.00 20.00
29 Sid Smith 5.00 12.00
30 Conn Smythe 6.00 15.00
31 Gaye Stewart 5.00 12.00
32 Harry Watson 5.00 12.00

2008-09 ITG Superlative Franchise Autograph Plus Jersey

ANNOUNCED PRINT RUN 30
APAB Allan Bester 10.00 25.00
APBB Bob Baun 12.00 30.00
APBS Borje Salming 12.00 30.00
APDG Doug Gilmour 15.00 40.00
APDK Dave Keon 12.00 30.00
APDS Darryl Sittler 12.00 30.00
APDT Darcy Tucker 10.00 25.00
APDW Dave Williams 10.00 25.00
APEB Ed Belfour 15.00 40.00
APFM Frank Mahovlich 15.00 40.00
APFP Felix Potvin 30.00 60.00
APGF Grant Fuhr 12.00 30.00
APGL Gary Leeman 10.00 25.00
APGR Gary Roberts 10.00 25.00
APJB Johnny Bower
APJN Joe Nieuwendyk
APLM Lanny McDonald 12.00 30.00
APMG Mikael Grabovski 20.00 50.00
APMP Mike Palmateer 12.00 30.00
APNK Nikoalai Kulemin 12.00 30.00
APRK Red Kelly 12.00 30.00
APRV Rick Vaive 8.00 20.00
APSC Shayne Corson 10.00 25.00
APST Steve Thomas 10.00 25.00
APTD Tie Domi 10.00 25.00
APTG Todd Gill 8.00 20.00
APWC Wendel Clark 12.00 30.00

2008-09 ITG Superlative Franchise Autographs

ANNOUNCED PRINT RUN 19-40
AAB Allan Bester/40* 8.00 20.00
ABP Bernie Parent/40* 10.00 25.00
ADD Dick Duff/40* 8.00 20.00
AEB Ed Belfour/19* 25.00 50.00
AGG Gerry Cheevers/40* 10.00 25.00
AJN Joe Nieuwendyk/40* 10.00 25.00
AMG Mikhail Grabovski/40* 10.00 25.00
ANK Nikolai Kulemin/40* 10.00 25.00
APH Paul Henderson/40* 8.00 20.00
ARC Russ Courtnall/19* 25.00 50.00
ARK Red Kelly/40* 12.00 30.00
ARV Rick Vaive/40* 8.00 20.00
ATS Tod Sloan/40* 10.00 25.00
AAA1 Al Arbour/40* 8.00 20.00
AAA2 Al Arbour/40* 8.00 20.00
AAS1 Allan Stanley/40* 10.00 25.00
AAS2 Allan Stanley/40* 10.00 25.00
ABB1 Bob Baun/40* 10.00 25.00
ABB2 Bob Baun/40* 10.00 25.00
ABO1 Bert Olmstead/19* 25.00 50.00
ABO2 Bert Olmstead/19* 25.00 50.00
ABPU Bob Pulford/40* 8.00 20.00
ABS1 Borje Salming/19* 15.00 40.00
ABS2 Borje Salming/19* 15.00 40.00
ADG1 Doug Gilmour/19* 15.00 40.00
ADG2 Doug Gilmour/19* 15.00 40.00
ADK1 Dave Keon/19* 12.00 30.00
ADK2 Dave Keon/19* 12.00 30.00
ADS1 Darryl Sittler/19* 12.00 30.00
ADS2 Darryl Sittler/19* 12.00 30.00
ADT1 Darcy Tucker/19*
ADT2 Darcy Tucker/19*
ADW1 Dave Williams/40* 8.00 20.00
ADW2 Dave Williams/40* 8.00 20.00
AES1 Eddie Shack/40* 10.00 25.00
AES2 Eddie Shack/40* 10.00 25.00
AFM1 Frank Mahovlich/19* 25.00 50.00
AFM2 Frank Mahovlich/19* 25.00 50.00
AFP1 Felix Potvin/19* 30.00 60.00
AFP2 Felix Potvin/19* 30.00 60.00
AGF1 Grant Fuhr/19* 12.00 30.00
AGF2 Grant Fuhr/19* 12.00 30.00
AGR1 Gary Roberts/40* 6.00 15.00
AGR2 Gary Roberts/40* 6.00 15.00
AHM1 Howie Meeker/19* 12.00 30.00
AHM2 Howie Meeker/19* 12.00 30.00
AIT1 Ian Turnbull/40* 8.00 20.00
AIT2 Ian Turnbull/40* 8.00 20.00
AJB1 Johnny Bower/19*
AJB2 Johnny Bower/19*
ALM1 Lanny McDonald/19* 12.00 30.00
ALM2 Lanny McDonald/19* 12.00 30.00
AMPA Mike Palmateer/40* 10.00 25.00
ANU1 Norm Ullman/19* 12.00 30.00
ANU2 Norm Ullman/19* 12.00 30.00
APQ1 Pat Quinn/40* 10.00 25.00
ARE1 Ron Ellis/40* 6.00 15.00
ARE2 Ron Ellis/40* 6.00 15.00
ASC1 Shayne Corson/40* 6.00 15.00
ASC2 Shayne Corson/40* 6.00 15.00
ATD1 Tie Domi/35* 8.00 20.00
ATD2 Tie Domi/35* 8.00 20.00
AWC1 Wendel Clark/19* 15.00 40.00
AWC2 Wendel Clark/19* 15.00 40.00
AABA1 Andy Bathgate/40* 10.00 25.00
AABA2 Andy Bathgate/40* 10.00 25.00

2008-09 ITG Superlative Franchise Double Autographs

ANNOUNCED PRINT RUN 25
DABB J.Bower/E.Belfour 15.00 40.00
DAEH R.Ellis/P.Henderson 12.00 30.00
DAGC D.Gilmour/W.Clark 15.00 40.00
DAMK F.Mahovlich/R.Kelly 15.00 40.00
DAMS H.Meeker/T.Sloan 12.00 30.00
DASB A.Stanley/B.Baun 12.00 30.00
DASC D.Sittler/W.Clark 15.00 40.00
DASM D.Sittler/L.McDonald 15.00 40.00
DAST B.Salming/I.Turnbull 12.00 30.00
DAWD D.Williams/T.Domi 10.00 25.00

2008-09 ITG Superlative Franchise Famous Fabrics 500 Goal Scorers

GS01 Frank Mahovlich
GS02 Dave Andreychuk
GS03 Lanny McDonald 6.00 15.00
GS04 Mike Gartner 6.00 15.00
GS05 Joe Nieuwendyk
GS06 Mats Sundin
GS07 Ron Francis

2008-09 ITG Superlative Franchise Patch Blue

ANNOUNCED PRINT RUN 25-30
1 Allan Bester/25* 8.00 20.00
2 Allan Stanley/25* 10.00 25.00
3 Andy Bathgate/25* 10.00 25.00
4 Bob Baun/25* 10.00 25.00
5 Bob Pulford/25* 8.00 20.00
6 Borje Salming/25* 10.00 25.00
7 Brian Glennie/25* 10.00 25.00
8 Darcy Tucker/25* 8.00 20.00
9 Darryl Sittler/25* 10.00 25.00
10 Dave Tiger Williams/25* 8.00 20.00
11 Dave Keon/25* 10.00 25.00
12 Dick Duff/25* 8.00 20.00
13 Doug Gilmour/25* 12.00 30.00
14 Ed Belfour/25* 10.00 25.00
15 Eddie Shack/25* 10.00 25.00
16 Errol Thompson/25* 6.00 15.00
17 Felix Potvin/25* 15.00 40.00
18 Frank Mahovlich/25* 10.00 25.00
19 Gary Leeman/25* 8.00 20.00
20 Gary Roberts/25* 6.00 15.00
21 Grant Fuhr/25* 10.00 25.00
22 Ian Turnbull/25* 8.00 20.00
23 Jacques Plante/25* 15.00 40.00
24 Johnny Bower/25* 12.00 30.00
25 Lanny McDonald/25* 10.00 25.00
26 Marcel Pronovost/25* 10.00 25.00
27 Mats Sundin/25* 10.00 25.00
28 Mikhail Grabovski/25* 10.00 25.00
29 Mike Palmateer/25* 10.00 25.00
30 Joe Nieuwendyk/25* 10.00 25.00
31 Nikolai Kulemin/25* 10.00 25.00
32 Norm Ullman/25* 10.00 25.00
33 Paul Henderson/25* 8.00 20.00
34 Red Kelly/25* 12.00 30.00
35 Rick Vaive/25* 6.00 15.00
36 Ron Ellis/25* 6.00 15.00
37 Bert Olmstead/25* 8.00 20.00
38 Russ Courtnall/25* 6.00 15.00
39 Shayne Corson/25* 6.00 15.00
40 Steve Thomas/25* 6.00 15.00
41 Terry Sawchuk/30* 12.00 30.00
42 Tie Domi/30* 8.00 20.00
43 Tim Horton/30* 20.00 50.00
44 Vesa Toskala/30* 8.00 20.00
45 Wendel Clark/30* 10.00 25.00

2008-09 ITG Superlative Franchise Triple Autographs

ANNOUNCED PRINT RUN 25
TABFF Bester/Favell/Fuhr
TABPP Bower/Palmateer/Potvin 40.00 80.00
TABUP Baun/Ullman/Pronovost 15.00 40.00
TACLC Clark/Leeman/Courtnall 15.00 40.00
TADMK Duff/Mahovlich/Kelly 15.00 40.00
TAEGH Ellis/Glennie/Henderson 15.00 40.00
TALDH Ley/Dorey/Henderson 12.00 30.00
TALTG Leeman/Thomas/Gill 15.00 40.00
TAMPS Meeker/Pulford/Sloan
TAOSM Olmstead/Sloan/Mahovlich 25.00 50.00
TAOUP Olmstead/Ullman/Pulford 30.00 60.00
TAPGC Potvin/Gilmour/Clark 30.00 60.00
TAQAK Quinn/Arbour/Kelly 12.00 30.00
TASBQ Stanley/Baun/Quinn 15.00 40.00
TASMW Sittler/McDonald/Williams 15.00 40.00
TASTM Salming/Turnbull/McKenny 12.00 30.00
TAVSC Vaive/Sittler/Clark 25.00 50.00
TAWDS Williams/Domi/Shack 15.00 40.00

2012-13 ITG Superlative Autographs Silver

ANNOUNCED PRINT RUN 15-40
AAM Al MacInnis/40 10.00 25.00
ADK Dave Keon/30 10.00 25.00
AJQ Jonathan Quick/40 15.00 40.00
AJR Jeremy Roenick/40 10.00 25.00
AJS Joe Sakic/20 25.00 60.00
AML Mario Lemieux/20 50.00 120.00
AMM Mark Messier/20 20.00 50.00
APB Pavel Bure/20 20.00 50.00
APR Patrick Roy MON/20 40.00 100.00
ARB Raymond Bourque/30 15.00 40.00
ARL Roberto Luongo/20
ASN Scott Niedermayer/20 15.00 40.00
ASW Shea Weber/40 8.00 20.00
ASY Steve Yzerman/30 40.00 80.00
ATF Theoren Fleury/40 12.00 30.00
ATL Trevor Linden/40 12.50 30.00
AVT Vladislav Tretiak/20 20.00 50.00
AAO1 Alexander Ovechkin/20
AAO2 A.Ovechkin WAS/20 25.00 50.00
AAO3 A.Ovechkin KHL/20 30.00 60.00
ABH1 Brett Hull DAL/40 12.50 30.00
ABH2 Brett Hull/40 12.50 30.00
ABHU Bobby Hull/30 15.00 40.00
AGH1 Gordie Howe D/15 40.00 100.00
AGH2 Gordie Howe H/15 40.00 100.00
AGH3 Gordie Howe/15 40.00 100.00
AGHA Glenn Hall/30 10.00 25.00
AJJ1 Jaromir Jagr PHI/20 30.00 60.00
AJJ2 Jaromir Jagr WAS/20 30.00 60.00
AJJ3 Jaromir Jagr PIT/20 30.00 60.00
AMME Mark Messier/20 20.00 50.00
AMSL Martin St. Louis/40 10.00 25.00
APRO Patrick Roy COL/20 30.00 60.00

2012-13 ITG Superlative Jerseys Autographs Silver

ANNOUNCED PRINT RUN 15-40
AJAM Al MacInnis 12.00 30.00
AJAO Alexander Ovechkin 30.00 80.00
AJDK Dave Keon 12.00 30.00
AJJQ Jonathan Quick 25.00 60.00
AJJR Jeremy Roenick 15.00 40.00
AJJS Joe Sakic 30.00 80.00
AJLR Luc Robitaille 12.00 30.00
AJML Mario Lemieux 40.00 80.00
AJMM Mark Messier 25.00 60.00
AJRB Raymond Bourque 20.00 50.00
AJRK Ryan Kesler 20.00 50.00
AJRL Roberto Luongo
AJSN Scott Niedermayer
AJSW Shea Weber 15.00 40.00
AJSY Steve Yzerman 40.00 80.00
AJTF Theoren Fleury 15.00 40.00
AJTL Trevor Linden 20.00 50.00
AJVT Vladislav Tretiak 25.00 60.00
AJBH1 Brett Hull 25.00 50.00
AJBH2 Brett Hull 25.00 50.00
AJBHU Bobby Hull 12.00 30.00
AJGH1 Gordie Howe 60.00 120.00
AJGH2 Gordie Howe 60.00 120.00
AJGH3 Gordie Howe 60.00 120.00
AJGHA Glenn Hall 12.00 30.00
AJJJ1 Jaromir Jagr 15.00 40.00
AJJJ2 Jaromir Jagr 15.00 40.00
AJJJ3 Jaromir Jagr 15.00 40.00
AJMME Mark Messier 25.00 60.00
AJMSL Martin St. Louis 12.00 30.00
AJPB1 Pavel Bure 25.00 60.00
AJPB2 Pavel Bure 25.00 60.00
AJPR1 Patrick Roy 30.00 80.00
AJPR2 Patrick Roy 50.00 100.00

2012-13 ITG Superlative Jerseys Silver

STATED PRINT RUN 6-30
GUJ01 Adam Oates/30 8.00 20.00
GUJ02 Alexander Ovechkin/30 30.00 80.00
GUJ03 Brett Hull/30 8.00 20.00
GUJ04 Carey Price/30 25.00 60.00
GUJ05 Claude Giroux/30 8.00 20.00
GUJ06 Corey Perry/30 8.00 20.00
GUJ07 Curtis Joseph/30 8.00 20.00
GUJ08 Daniel Sedin/30 8.00 20.00
GUJ09 Denis Potvin/30 8.00 20.00
GUJ10 Doug Gilmour/30 10.00 25.00
GUJ11 Ed Belfour/30 8.00 20.00
GUJ12 Eric Lindros/30 12.00 30.00
GUJ13 Henrik Lundqvist/30 8.00 20.00
GUJ14 Henrik Sedin/30 8.00 20.00
GUJ15 Jaromir Jagr/30 20.00 50.00
GUJ16 Jeremy Roenick/30 8.00 20.00
GUJ17 Joe Sakic/30 12.00 30.00
GUJ18 Joe Thornton/30 8.00 20.00
GUJ19 Mario Lemieux/30 12.00 30.00
GUJ20 Mats Sundin/30 8.00 20.00
GUJ21 Mike Bossy/30 8.00 20.00
GUJ22 Nicklas Lidstrom/30 8.00 20.00
GUJ23 Patrick Roy/30 20.00 50.00
GUJ24 Patrick Roy/30 20.00 50.00
GUJ25 Pavel Bure/30 12.00 30.00
GUJ26 Peter Forsberg/30 8.00 20.00
GUJ27 Raymond Bourque/30 12.00 30.00
GUJ28 Roberto Luongo/30 8.00 20.00
GUJ29 Theoren Fleury/30 10.00 25.00
GUJ30 Trevor Linden/30 8.00 20.00

2012-13 ITG Superlative Prospect Autographs Silver

STATED PRINT RUN 30
PAAG Alex Galchenyuk 60.00 100.00
PABD Brenden Dillon 5.00 12.00
PABS Brody Silk
PACC Cody Ceci 5.00 12.00
PADT Dana Tyrell
PAIS Ian Schultz 5.00 12.00
PAMC Matt Calvert 4.00 10.00
PAMM Matt Murray 6.00 15.00
PANB Nick Baptiste 5.00 12.00
PANY Nail Yakupov 30.00 60.00
PARK Ryan Kujawinski 5.00 12.00
PARM Ryan Murphy
PASC Sean Couturier 8.00 20.00

SG Scott Glennie
TH Thomas Hickey 12.00 30.00

2012-13 ITG Superlative Prospect Jerseys Autographs Silver

ATED PRINT RUN 30
JAG Alex Galchenyuk 80.00 150.00
JBD Brenden Dillon
JBS Brody Silk
JCC Cody Ceci 6.00 15.00
JDT Dana Tyrell 5.00 12.00
JIS Ian Schultz 6.00 15.00
JMC Matt Calvert 5.00 12.00
JMM Matt Murray 8.00 20.00
JNB Nick Baptiste 6.00 15.00
JNY Nail Yakupov 30.00 80.00
JRK Ryan Kujawinski
JRM Ryan Murphy 15.00 40.00
JSC Sean Couturier 8.00 20.00
JSG Scott Glennie 6.00 15.00
JTH Thomas Hickey 5.00 12.00

2013-14 ITG Superlative The First Six Jerseys

JJ01 Borje Salming/20* 8.00 20.00
JJ02 Mats Sundin/20* 8.00 20.00
JJ03 Doug Gilmour/20* 10.00 25.00
JJ04 Wendel Clark/20* 8.00 20.00
JJ05 Curtis Joseph/20* 8.00 20.00
JJ06 Felix Potvin/20* 12.00 30.00
JJ07 Darryl Sittler/20* 12.00 30.00
JJ08 Bob Baun/20* 6.00 15.00
JJ09 Pavel Bure/20* 15.00 30.00
JJ10 Marian Gaborik/20* 8.00 20.00
JJ11 Henrik Lundqvist/20* 8.00 20.00
JJ12 Brian Leetch/20* 6.00 15.00
JJ13 Mike Richter/20* 8.00 20.00
JJ14 John Vanbiesbrouck/20* 12.00 30.00
JJ15 Carey Price/20* 10.00 25.00
JJ16 Guy Lafleur/20* 10.00 25.00
JJ17 Patrick Roy/20* 20.00 50.00
JJ18 Guy Lapointe/20* 6.00 15.00
JJ19 Mark Recchi/20* 10.00 25.00
JJ20 Jacques Lemaire/20* 8.00 20.00
JJ21 Larry Robinson/20* 8.00 20.00
JJ22 Steve Yzerman/20* 25.00 50.00
JJ23 Dominik Hasek/20* 10.00 25.00
JJ24 Jimmy Howard/20* 8.00 20.00
JJ25 Niklas Kronwall/20* 8.00 20.00
JJ26 Chris Osgood/20* 8.00 20.00
JJ27 Bob Probert/20* 8.00 20.00
JJ28 Nicklas Lidstrom/20* 10.00 25.00
JJ29 Tony Amonte/20* 6.00 15.00
JJ30 Jeremy Roenick/20* 8.00 20.00
JJ31 Corey Crawford/20* 10.00 25.00
JJ32 Denis Savard/20* 10.00 25.00
JJ33 Ed Belfour/20* 8.00 20.00
JJ34 Chris Chelios/20* 8.00 20.00
JJ35 Cam Neely/20* 8.00 20.00
JJ36 Joe Thornton/20* 8.00 20.00
JJ37 Raymond Bourque/20* 12.00 30.00
JJ38 Tuukka Rask/20* 8.00 20.00
JJ39 Sergei Samsonov/20* 8.00 20.00
JJ40 Andy Moog/20* 8.00 20.00

2013-14 ITG Superlative The First Six Autographs

U+MEM/20*: .5X TO 1.2X AU/20*
SY AU/20*: .5X TO 1.2X AU/20*
AD Alex Delvecchio 10.00 25.00
AO Adam Oates 20.00 40.00
BB Bob Baun 10.00 25.00
BH Brett Hull 20.00 40.00
BHU Bobby Hull 20.00 50.00
BL Brian Leetch 12.00 30.00
BP Brad Park 10.00 25.00
BS Borje Salming 20.00 40.00
CC1 Chris Chelios 12.00 30.00
CCR Corey Crawford 15.00 40.00
CJ Curtis Joseph 12.00 30.00
CN Cam Neely 12.00 30.00
CO Chris Osgood 12.00 30.00
CP Carey Price 12.00 30.00
DG Doug Gilmour 15.00 40.00
DH Dominik Hasek 15.00 40.00
DK Dave Keon 12.00 30.00
DP Dion Phaneuf 12.00 30.00
DS Darryl Sittler 12.00 30.00
EB Ed Belfour 12.00 30.00
EG Ed Giacomin 12.00 30.00
EL Elmer Lach 12.00 30.00
FM Frank Mahovlich 12.00 30.00
FP Felix Potvin 15.00 40.00
GC Gerry Cheevers 12.00 30.00
GH Glenn Hall 12.00 30.00
GH Gordie Howe 50.00 100.00
GL Guy Lafleur 15.00 40.00
GLA Guy Lapointe 10.00 25.00
HR Henri Richard 12.00 30.00
JB Jean Beliveau 15.00 40.00
JBO Johnny Bower 25.00 50.00
JBU Johnny Bucyk 12.00 30.00
JH Jimmy Howard 12.00 30.00
JR Jeremy Roenick 12.00 30.00
JV John Vanbiesbrouck 12.00 30.00
LM Lanny McDonald 12.00 30.00
LR Larry Robinson 12.00 30.00
MM Mark Messier 15.00 40.00
MR Mike Richter 12.00 30.00
MS Milt Schmidt 10.00 25.00
NL Nicklas Lidstrom 20.00 40.00
PE1 Phil Esposito 20.00 50.00
PE2 Phil Esposito 20.00 50.00
PR Patrick Roy
RB Raymond Bourque 20.00 50.00
RG Rod Gilbert 12.00 30.00
RK Red Kelly 12.00 30.00
RV Rogie Vachon 15.00 40.00
SM Stan Mikita 15.00 40.00
SS Serge Savard 12.00 30.00
SSA Sergei Samsonov 10.00 25.00
SY Steve Yzerman 30.00 60.00
TA Tony Amonte 10.00 25.00
TE Tony Esposito 12.00 30.00
TL Ted Lindsay 12.00 30.00
TO Terry O'Reilly 10.00 25.00
TR Tuukka Rask 12.00 30.00
VH Vic Hadfield 10.00 25.00
WC Wendel Clark 12.00 30.00
WCA Wayne Cashman 10.00 25.00

2013-14 ITG Superlative The First Six Captain C

CC01 Dvdsn/Keon/Phneuf
CC02 Cnchr/Sttlr/Sndin 25.00 50.00
CC03 Hdfld/Park/Mssier 20.00 50.00
CC04 Espsto/Ltch/Jagr 25.00 50.00
CC05 Llnde/Hnswrth/Crnneau 40.00 80.00
CC06 Rchrd/Blveau/Rchrd 60.00 120.00
CC07 Lndsy/Yzrmn/Ldstrm 30.00 80.00
CC08 Howe/Dlvcchio/Dnne 30.00 80.00
CC09 Grdner/Stpltn/Svrd 20.00 50.00
CC10 Mkta/Chlios/Amnte 20.00 50.00
CC11 Schmdt/Bcyk/Cshmn 12.00 30.00
CC12 O'Rlly/Brque/Thrntn 25.00 60.00

2013-14 ITG Superlative The First Six Cup Final Jerseys Six

FL01 Bqe/Mta/Hw/Lfr/Gbt/Sdn 40.00 80.00
FL02 Esp/Hll/Yzm/Lfr/Jgr/Vve 30.00 80.00
FL03 Esp/Svd/Yzn/Lf/Jgr/Glmr 40.00 80.00
FL04 Byk/Hl/Hwe/Rc/Glb/Sdn 50.00 100.00
FL05 Bqe/Lmr/Yz/Cny/Glr/Sdn 40.00 80.00
FL06 Esp/Mkt/Yzm/Lfr/Glrt/Sdn 40.00 80.00
FL07 Chv/Esp/Osg/Ry/Vbk/Plt 40.00 80.00
FL08 Bqe/Mkt/Yzm/Lfr/Lch/Sg 40.00 100.00
FL09 Thm/Esp/Sch/Hns/Gn/Bd 50.00 100.00
FL10 Thm/Esp/Sch/Pln/Rct/Bd 40.00 80.00
FL11 Esp/Hl/Yzm/Lfr/Jgr/Sttlr 50.00 100.00
FL12 Esp/Rnk/Fdv/Lfr/Msr/Sn 40.00 80.00

2013-14 ITG Superlative The First Six Cup Final Quad Jerseys

1-18 ANNOUNCED PRINT RUN 19
19-32 UNPRICED ANNC'D PRINT RUN 9
1 Lfr/Lmre/Epsto/Hbrg/19* 25.00 60.00
2 Rbsn/Svrd/Mdltn/Byk/19* 15.00 40.00
3 Shtt/Lfr/Prk/O'Rly/19* 20.00 50.00
4 Svrd/Lpte/Prk/Mdltn/19* 15.00 40.00
5 Rbsn/Lfr/O'Rly/Gbrt/19* 20.00 50.00
6 Lpte/Lre/Epsto/Wte/19* 15.00 40.00
7 Crnr/Mhvch/Hll/Mkta/19* 20.00 50.00
8 Epsto/Chvrs/Gbrt/Gmn/19* 25.00 60.00
9 Cshmn/Bck/Prk/Hfld/19* 12.00 30.00
10 Mvlch/Blvau/Mkta/Sttn/19* 25.00 60.00
11 Rcrd/Crnr/Epsto/Hll/19* 20.00 50.00
12 Hrtn/Bwr/Blvau/Rhrd/19* 25.00 60.00
13 Keon/Swck/Vchn/Cnyr/19* 20.00 50.00
14 Rchrd/Lprre/Ulmn/Czr/19* 15.00 40.00
15 Blvau/Wsly/Hll/Mkta/19* 40.00 80.00
16 Baun/Hrtn/Hwe/Ulmn/19* 30.00 80.00
17 Bwr/Mvlh/Swck/Dvco/19* 25.00 50.00
18 Keon/Klly/Hall/Mkta/19* 20.00 50.00

2013-14 ITG Superlative The First Six Draft Highlights Triple Jerseys

DH01 Sttlr/McDnld/Plmteer 15.00 40.00
DH02 Bstr/Clrk/Ptvn 25.00 60.00
DH03 Park/Vnbsbrck/Rchtr 15.00 40.00
DH04 Ltch/Cltier/Lndqvst 20.00 50.00
DH05 Lflr/Rbnsn/Shutt 20.00 50.00
DH06 Nslnd/Chlios/Roy 20.00 50.00
DH07 Dnne/Fdrov/Ldstrm 25.00 60.00
DH08 Yzrmn/Osgd/Hwrd 30.00 60.00
DH09 Lrmr/Svrd/Rnick 25.00 50.00
DH10 Hsek/Mnsn/Crwfrd 15.00 40.00
DH11 O'Rlly/Jnthn/Brque 25.00 60.00
DH12 Leach/Smsnv/Thrntn 15.00 40.00

2013-14 ITG Superlative The First Six Enshrined Triple Jerseys

E01 Wtsn/Keon/Sndin 15.00 40.00
E02 Hrtn/Sttlr/Glmour 20.00 50.00
E03 Gcmn/Park/Dnne 30.00 80.00
E04 Glbrt/Mssier/Bure 20.00 50.00
E05 Rchrd/Lfleur/Roy 40.00 80.00
E06 Jliat/Plnte/Blveau 60.00 120.00
E07 Lndsy/Ullmn/Yzrmn 25.00 60.00
E08 Howe/Dlvcchio/Hull 40.00 80.00
E09 Hall/Espsto/Blfour 15.00 40.00
E10 Msnko/Hull/Mkita 25.00 60.00
E11 Schmdt/Espsto/Neely 25.00 60.00
E12 Shre/Chvers/Brque 25.00 60.00

2013-14 ITG Superlative The First Six Franchises Jerseys Six

ANNOUNCED PRINT RUN 14
F01 Crfd/Hrd/Phn/Lng/Rsk/Prc 30.00 60.00
F02 Ant/Hsk/Sdn/Ldrs/Thrt/Rch 40.00 80.00
F03 Rnk/Lstm/Glmr/Msr/Brq/Ry 40.00 80.00
F04 Svd/Yzm/Pvn/Rch/Nly/Nlnd
F05 Blfr/Prbrt/Clrk/Lflr/Moog/Rbn 30.00 60.00
F06 Mta/Dlc/McDd/Esp/Byk/Lflr 40.00 80.00
F07 Esp/Dne/Stlr/Glbt/Esp/Lmre 30.00 80.00
F08 Hll/Hwe/Bwr/Hfld/Chvr/Blv 40.00 80.00
F09 Hll/Ullm/Keon/Gcm/Prnt/Plnt 40.00 80.00
F10 Mko/Sch/Mlc/Rynr/Sch/Rcrd 40.00 80.00
F11 Lmly/Ldsy/Knd/Wrl/Clpr/Hrv 50.00 100.00
F12 Bmsk/Thp/Cnch/Frn/Shr/Jlt 40.00 80.00

2013-14 ITG Superlative The First Six Lord Stanley's Mug Triple Jerseys

LSM01 Yzrmn/Hsek/Hull 30.00 60.00
LSM02 Ldstrm/Fdrov/Osgd 25.00 60.00
LSM03 Mssr/Ltch/Rchtr 20.00 50.00
LSM04 Roy/Svrd/Mller 20.00 50.00
LSM05 Chlos/Nslnd/Roy 20.00 50.00
LSM06 Lflr/Shutt/Lmaire 20.00 50.00
LSM07 Rbnsn/Svrd/Lpnte 15.00 40.00
LSM08 Espsto/Cshmn/Chvers 25.00 60.00
LSM09 Blveau/Crnyer/Mhvlch 40.00 80.00
LSM10 Keon/Hrton/Mhvlch 20.00 50.00
LSM11 Hull/Mkta/Hall 20.00 50.00
LSM12 Rchrd/Rchrd/Plnte 50.00 100.00
LSM13 Howe/Lndsy/Swchk 40.00 80.00
LSM14 Krndy/Brda/Wtson 25.00 60.00
LSM15 Schmdt/Bauer/Brmsk 25.00 60.00
LSM16 Clncy/Cnchr/Bailey 50.00 100.00
LSM17 Mrnz/Jliat/Hnswrth 100.00 175.00
LSM18 Shore/Clppr/Thmpsn 15.00 40.00

2013-14 ITG Superlative The First Six Memorable Moments Jerseys

MM01 King Clancy 40.00 80.00
MM02 Johnny Bower 12.00 30.00
MM03 Darryl Sittler 20.00 50.00
MM04 Ed Giacomin 12.00 30.00
MM05 Mike Richter 10.00 25.00
MM06 Mark Messier 10.00 25.00
MM07 Maurice Richard 30.00 60.00
MM08 Jacques Plante 12.00 30.00
MM09 Jean Beliveau 20.00 50.00
MM10 Ted Lindsay 12.00 30.00
MM11 Gordie Howe 20.00 50.00
MM12 Steve Yzerman 12.00 30.00
MM13 Bill Mosienko 12.00 30.00
MM14 Stan Mikita 10.00 25.00
MM15 Tony Esposito 8.00 20.00
MM16 Eddie Shore 15.00 40.00
MM17 Phil Esposito 12.00 30.00
MM18 Cam Neely 8.00 20.00

2013-14 ITG Superlative The First Six Raised to the Rafters Triple Jerseys

RTR01 Bwer/Clncy/Glmour 50.00 120.00
RTR02 Cnchr/Hrtn/Sttler 25.00 60.00
RTR03 Mhvlch/Slmng/Sndin 20.00 50.00
RTR04 Gcmin/Mssr/Rchtr 20.00 50.00
RTR05 Blveau/Lflr/Rbnsn 40.00 80.00
RTR06 Plnte/Rchrd/Roy 60.00 120.00
RTR07 Hrvy/Rchrd/Svrd 15.00 40.00
RTR08 Howe/Lndsy/Yzrmn 30.00 60.00
RTR09 Hull/Mkta/Svrd 20.00 50.00
RTR10 Hall/Espsto/Hull 25.00 60.00
RTR11 Brque/Espsto/Neely 25.00 60.00
RTR12 Shre/O'Rlly/Bcyk 20.00 50.00

2013-14 ITG Superlative The First Six Rivalry Quad Jerseys

R01 Roy/Mllr/Ptvn/Glmr/19* 25.00 60.00
R02 Clk/Lmn/Prbt/Yzmn/19* 30.00 80.00
R03 Rbsn/Crnu/Lflr/Dne/19* 20.00 50.00
R04 Chs/Bfr/Chde/Lstm/19* 15.00 40.00
R05 Jsph/Sdn/Rctr/Bre/19* 20.00 50.00
R06 Ltch/Mssr/Nly/Otes/19* 20.00 50.00
R07 Clk/Ptn/McCty/Osgd/19* 25.00 60.00
R08 Roy/Chls/Brqe/Moog/19* 20.00 50.00
R09 Svrd/Epsto/Bstr/Slng/19* 20.00 50.00
R10 Prk/Brqe/Rbsn/Svrd/19* 12.00 30.00
R11 Shtt/Lflr/McDnld/Sttlr/19* 20.00 50.00
R12 Yzmn/Fdrv/Msr/Ldrs/19* 30.00 60.00
R13 Epsto/Chvs/Gcmn/Hfld/19* 25.00 60.00
R14 Lprre/Blvau/Hrtn/Keon/19* 30.00 60.00
R15 Chmn/Bcyk/Rcrd/Crnyr/19* 25.00 50.00
R16 Dnne/Dlvcio/Epsto/Mkta/19* 20.00 50.00
R17 Vchn/Hdge/Swck/Bwr/19* 20.00 50.00
R18 Hull/Hull/Mhvlch/Mhvlch/19*
R19 Espsto/Glbrt/Lflr/Rbnsn/19* 25.00 60.00
R20 Hwe/Lndsy/Rcrd/Blvau/19* 60.00 120.00
R21 Hull/Hall/Plnte/Moore/19* 25.00 60.00
R22 Dlvcio/Ulmn/Kon/Kly/19* 15.00 40.00

2013-14 ITG Superlative The First Six Trophy Case Jerseys

TC49-TC72 UNPRICED ANNC'D PRINT RUN 9
TC01 Frank Mahovlich/19* 10.00 25.00
TC02 Dave Keon/19* 8.00 20.00
TC03 Doug Gilmour/19* 10.00 25.00
TC04 Red Kelly/19* 8.00 20.00
TC05 Dave Keon/19* 8.00 20.00
TC06 Ted Kennedy/19* 8.00 20.00
TC07 Johnny Bower/19* 10.00 25.00
TC08 Terry Sawchuk/19* 12.00 30.00
TC09 Mark Messier/19* 10.00 25.00
TC10 Brian Leetch/19* 6.00 15.00
TC11 Rod Gilbert/19* 12.00 30.00
TC12 John Vanbiesbrouck/19* 15.00 40.00
TC13 Jaromir Jagr/19* 20.00 50.00
TC14 Mark Messier/19* 12.00 30.00
TC15 Phil Esposito/19* 12.00 30.00
TC16 Henrik Lundqvist/19* 8.00 20.00
TC17 Guy Lafleur/19* 10.00 25.00
TC18 Larry Robinson/19* 8.00 20.00
TC19 Patrick Roy/19* 20.00 50.00
TC20 Chris Chelios/19* 8.00 20.00
TC21 Mats Naslund/19* 8.00 20.00
TC22 Jacques Plante/19* 12.00 30.00
TC23 Jean Beliveau/19* 15.00 40.00
TC24 Maurice Richard/19* 30.00 80.00
TC25 Steve Yzerman/19* 20.00 50.00
TC26 Sergei Fedorov/19* 10.00 25.00
TC27 Roger Crozier/19* 10.00 25.00
TC28 Nicklas Lidstrom/19* 10.00 25.00
TC29 Alex Delvecchio/19* 10.00 25.00
TC30 Marcel Dionne/19* 10.00 25.00
TC31 Steve Yzerman/19* 20.00 50.00
TC32 Dominik Hasek/19* 10.00 25.00
TC33 Bobby Hull/19* 8.00 20.00
TC34 Stan Mikita/19* 10.00 25.00
TC35 Tony Esposito/19* 8.00 20.00
TC36 Ed Belfour/19* 8.00 20.00
TC37 Steve Larmer/19* 10.00 25.00
TC38 Chris Chelios/19* 8.00 20.00
TC39 Corey Crawford/19* 10.00 25.00
TC40 Stan Mikita/19* 10.00 25.00
TC41 Joe Thornton/19* 8.00 20.00
TC42 Cam Neely/19* 8.00 20.00
TC43 Phil Esposito/19* 12.00 30.00
TC44 Raymond Bourque/19* 12.00 30.00
TC45 Phil Esposito/19* 12.00 30.00
TC46 Johnny Bucyk/19* 8.00 20.00
TC47 Andy Moog/19* 8.00 20.00
TC48 Sergei Samsonov/19* 6.00 15.00

2015-16 ITG Superlative Famous Fabrics 1000 Point Club Silver

TPC01 Adam Oates/25 12.00 30.00
TPC02 Alexander Mogilny/25 10.00 25.00
TPC03 Bobby Clarke/25 10.00 25.00
TPC04 Bobby Hull/25 6.00 15.00
TPC05 Bobby Smith/25 5.00 12.00
TPC06 Brendan Shanahan/25 8.00 20.00
TPC07 Darryl Sittler/25
TPC08 Denis Potvin/25 6.00 15.00
TPC09 Dino Ciccarelli/25 6.00 15.00
TPC10 Gilbert Perreault/25 10.00 25.00
TPC11 Gordie Howe/12
TPC12 Guy Lafleur/25 8.00 20.00
TPC13 Jaromir Jagr/25 15.00 40.00
TPC14 Jean Ratelle/25 5.00 12.00
TPC15 Jeremy Roenick/25 6.00 15.00
TPC16 Joe Mullen/25 5.00 12.00
TPC17 Joe Nieuwendyk/25
TPC18 Joe Sakic/25 10.00 25.00
TPC19 Marcel Dionne/25 12.00 30.00
TPC20 Michel Goulet/25 5.00 12.00
TPC21 Mike Modano/25 10.00 25.00
TPC22 Paul Coffey/25 6.00 15.00
TPC23 Peter Stastny/25 5.00 12.00
TPC24 Rod Gilbert/5
TPC25 Ron Francis/25 8.00 20.00
TPC26 Sergei Fedorov/25 10.00 25.00
TPC27 Stan Mikita/25 8.00 20.00
TPC28 Teemu Selanne/25 12.00 30.00
TPC29 Theoren Fleury/25 8.00 20.00
TPC30 Wayne Gretzky/12

2015-16 ITG Superlative Famous Fabrics 300 Win Club Silver

3WC01 Andy Moog 8.00 20.00
3WC02 Billy Smith 8.00 20.00
3WC03 Chris Osgood 8.00 20.00
3WC04 Curtis Joseph 8.00 20.00
3WC05 Dominik Hasek 10.00 25.00
3WC06 Ed Belfour 8.00 20.00
3WC07 Evgeni Nabokov 6.00 15.00
3WC08 Glenn Hall 8.00 20.00
3WC09 Grant Fuhr 8.00 20.00
3WC10 Gump Worsley Pads 20.00 40.00
3WC11 Harry Lumley 20.00 40.00
3WC12 Henrik Lundqvist 10.00 25.00
3WC13 Jacques Plante 12.00 30.00
3WC14 John Vanbiesbrouck 8.00 20.00
3WC15 Marc-Andre Fleury 12.00 30.00
3WC16 Martin Brodeur 10.00 25.00
3WC17 Miikka Kiprusoff
3WC18 Mike Richter 8.00 20.00
3WC19 Mike Vernon 6.00 15.00
3WC20 Nikolai Khabibulin 8.00 20.00
3WC21 Olaf Kolzig 12.00 30.00
3WC22 Patrick Roy 20.00 50.00
3WC23 Roberto Luongo 8.00 20.00
3WC24 Rogie Vachon 10.00 25.00
3WC25 Ryan Miller
3WC26 Sean Burke 12.00 30.00
3WC27 Terry Sawchuk 12.00 30.00
3WC28 Tom Barrasso 8.00 20.00
3WC29 Tomas Vokoun 10.00 25.00
3WC30 Tony Esposito 8.00 20.00
3WC31 Turk Broda/5

2015-16 ITG Superlative Famous Fabrics Four Silver

F401 Grtz/Lemx/Roy/Yzrn/15 25.00 50.00
F402 Rchrd/Roy/Bliveau/Plnte/5
F403 Roy/Josph/Blfr/Hask/20 15.00 40.00
F404 Salmng/Sndin/Hortn/Sittlr/8
F405 Lindrs/Clrke/LeClr/Parnt/10
F406 Grtzky/Mesr/Coffy/Fuhr/5
F407 Morn/Mornz/Clncy/Taylr/3
F408 Brque/Orr/Neely/P.Espo/10
F409 Hull/Mikt/Chls/T.Esp/15 12.00 30.00
F411 Hwrc/Slnn/Tkch/Hull/15 12.00 30.00
F412 Hull/Hull/Domi/Domi/15 15.00 40.00

2015-16 ITG Superlative Famous Fabrics Record Book Silver

RB01 Bobby Orr/8
RB02 Bryan Trottier/3
RB03 Darryl Sittler/15
RB04 Gerry Cheevers/15 15.00 40.00
RB05 Gordie Howe/9
RB07 Mario Lemieux/25 20.00 50.00
RB08 Maurice Richard/5
RB09 Patrick Roy/25 15.00 40.00
RB10 Raymond Bourque/25 10.00 25.00
RB11 Teemu Selanne/25 8.00 20.00
RB12 Wayne Gretzky/12

2015-16 ITG Superlative Immortals Autographs Silver

TIAD1 Alex Delvecchio/25 8.00 20.00
TIBG1 Bill Gadsby/25 10.00 25.00
TIBH1 Bobby Hull/20 10.00 25.00
TIBH2 Brett Hull/20 20.00 40.00
TIGH1 Glenn Hall/20 8.00 20.00
TIJB1 Johnny Bower/25 12.00 30.00
TIJB2 Johnny Bucyk/25 8.00 20.00
TIML1 Mario Lemieux/20 30.00 60.00
TIMM1 Mike Modano/25 20.00 40.00
TINL1 Nicklas Lidstrom/25 20.00 40.00
TINU1 Norm Ullman/25 10.00 25.00
TIPE1 Phil Esposito/20 EXCH 15.00 40.00
TIPR1 Patrick Roy/20 30.00 60.00
TIRB1 Raymond Bourque/25 20.00 40.00
TISF1 Sergei Fedorov/25 EXCH
TISY1 Steve Yzerman/20 15.00 40.00
TITE1 Tony Esposito/20 10.00 25.00
TITL1 Ted Lindsay/25 10.00 25.00
TIVT1 Vladislav Tretiak/20 20.00 40.00

2015-16 ITG Superlative International Ice Autographs

ANNOUNCED PRINT RUN 60
EXCH EXPIRATION: 10/17/2017
IIBH1 Bobby Hull 12.00 30.00
IIBH2 Brett Hull 15.00 40.00
IIEL1 Eric Lindros 15.00 40.00
IIJS1 Joe Sakic 25.00 50.00
IIML1 Mario Lemieux 30.00 60.00
IIMM1 Mike Modano 20.00 50.00
IINL1 Nicklas Lidstrom 20.00 40.00
IIPR1 Patrick Roy 50.00 100.00
IISF1 Sergei Fedorov EXCH 30.00 60.00
IISY1 Steve Yzerman 30.00 60.00
IITS1 Teemu Selanne EXCH 20.00 40.00
IIVT1 Vladislav Tretiak 15.00 40.00

2015-16 ITG Superlative International Ice Jerseys Silver

IIJ01 Alexander Yakushev/15 10.00 25.00
IIJ02 Bobby Clarke/15 10.00 25.00
IIJ03 Boris Mikhailov/15 8.00 20.00
IIJ04 Brett Hull/15 8.00 20.00
IIJ05 Chris Chelios/15 8.00 20.00
IIJ06 Eric Lindros/15 10.00 25.00
IIJ07 Keith Tkachuk/15 8.00 20.00
IIJ08 Mario Lemieux/15 25.00 60.00
IIJ09 Mats Sundin/15 10.00 25.00
IIJ10 Mike Bossy/15 8.00 20.00
IIJ11 Mike Modano/15 12.00 30.00
IIJ12 Nicklas Lidstrom/15 12.00 30.00
IIJ13 Peter Forsberg/15 8.00 20.00
IIJ14 Phil Esposito/15 12.00 30.00
IIJ15 Steve Yzerman/15
IIJ16 Valeri Kharlamov/15 25.00 50.00
IIJ17 Vladimir Krutov/15 6.00 15.00
IIJ18 Vladislav Tretiak/10

2015-16 ITG Superlative Jumbo Numbers Silver

SN01 Bobby Orr/4
SN02 Brett Hull/25 10.00 25.00
SN03 Eddie Shore/5
SN04 Eric Lindros/25 15.00 40.00
SN05 Georges Vezina/3
SN06 Gordie Howe/9
SN07 Ken Dryden/10
SN08 Mario Lemieux/25 20.00 50.00
SN09 Martin Brodeur/25 15.00 40.00
SN10 Maurice Richard/5
SN11 Patrick Roy/25 20.00 50.00
SN12 Phil Esposito/15
SN13 Raymond Bourque/25 20.00 40.00
SN14 Steve Yzerman/25 12.00 30.00
SN15 Terry Sawchuk/15 15.00 40.00
SN16 Wayne Gretzky/12

2015-16 ITG Superlative Signature Memorabilia Silver

SSMBB1 Brian Bellows/30 10.00 25.00
SSMBH1 Brett Hull/20 20.00 40.00
SSMBP1 Bernie Parent/20 12.00 30.00
SSMCJ1 Curtis Joseph/30 12.00 30.00
SSMDG1 Doug Gilmour/20 15.00 40.00
SSMEL1 Eric Lindros/30 20.00 40.00
SSMFP1 Felix Potvin/20 20.00 40.00
SSMGC1 Gerry Cheevers/20 12.00 30.00
SSMGF1 Grant Fuhr/20
SSMGH1 Glenn Hall/25 10.00 25.00
SSMJLC John LeClair/25 12.00 30.00
SSMJS1 Joe Sakic/20 20.00 50.00
SSMJV1 John Vanbiesbrouck/20 15.00 40.00
SSMML1 Mario Lemieux/20 40.00 80.00
SSMMM1 Mike Modano/30 20.00 50.00
SSMNL1 Nicklas Lidstrom/20 12.00 30.00
SSMPE1 Phil Esposito/25 20.00 50.00
SSMPLF Pat LaFontaine/25 12.00 30.00
SSMPR1 Patrick Roy/25 40.00 80.00
SSMRB1 Raymond Bourque/30 20.00 50.00
SSMRL1 Reggie Leach/25 10.00 25.00
SSMSF1 Sergei Fedorov/30 EXCH 40.00 80.00
SSMSY1 Steve Yzerman/20 30.00 60.00
SSMTE1 Tony Esposito/20 12.00 30.00
SSMTL1 Ted Lindsay/30 15.00 40.00
SSMTL2 Trevor Linden/20 12.00 30.00
SSMVT1 Vladislav Tretiak Pads/20 30.00 60.00

2015-16 ITG Superlative Signatures Silver

SIGBB1 Brian Bellows/35 8.00 20.00
SIGBG1 Bill Gadsby/35 10.00 25.00
SIGBH1 Bobby Hull/30 15.00 30.00
SIGBH2 Brett Hull/30 15.00 30.00
SIGBP1 Bernie Parent/35 10.00 25.00
SIGBT1 Bryan Trottier/30 12.00 30.00
SIGCJ1 Curtis Joseph/35 10.00 25.00
SIGDM1 Dickie Moore/30 10.00 25.00
SIGEL1 Eric Lindros/35 15.00 40.00
SIGFP1 Felix Potvin/25 15.00 40.00
SIGGC1 Gerry Cheevers/30 10.00 25.00
SIGGF1 Grant Fuhr/30 EXCH 20.00 40.00
SIGGH1 Glenn Hall/25 10.00 25.00
SIGJB1 Johnny Bower/35 EXCH 12.00 30.00
SIGJB2 Johnny Bucyk/35 8.00 20.00
SIGJE1 Jack Eichel/25 175.00 350.00
SIGJLC John LeClair/35 10.00 25.00
SIGJS1 Joe Sakic/25 8.00 20.00
SIGKH1 Ken Hodge/35 8.00 20.00
SIGML1 Mario Lemieux/25 30.00 60.00
SIGMM1 Mike Modano/35 12.00 30.00
SIGMN1 Mats Naslund/35 10.00 25.00
SIGNL1 Nicklas Lidstrom/30 15.00 30.00
SIGNU1 Norm Ullman/35 10.00 25.00
SIGPE1 Phil Esposito/30 EXCH 15.00 40.00
SIGPF1 Peter Forsberg/20 EXCH 12.00 30.00
SIGPL1 Pat LaFontaine/30 10.00 25.00
SIGPR1 Patrick Roy/25 25.00 50.00
SIGRB1 Raymond Bourque/30 15.00 40.00
SIGRL1 Reggie Leach/35 8.00 20.00
SIGSF1 Sergei Fedorov/30 EXCH
SIGSY1 Steve Yzerman/15 30.00 60.00
SIGTE1 Tony Esposito/30 10.00 25.00
SIGTL1 Trevor Linden/35 10.00 25.00
SIGTS1 Teemu Selanne/30 EXCH 20.00 40.00
SIGVT1 Vladislav Tretiak/25 20.00 40.00

2015-16 ITG Superlative Sticks Silver

SS03 Gordie Howe/15
SS05 Jean Beliveau/15 25.00 60.00
SS06 Johnny Bucyk/15 12.00 30.00
SS07 Keith Tkachuk/15 10.00 25.00
SS08 Maurice Richard/15
SS09 Phil Esposito/15 15.00 40.00
SS10 Raymond Bourque/20
SS11 Steve Yzerman/15
SS12 Ted Kennedy/15 10.00 25.00
SS13 Tim Horton/15 15.00 30.00
SS14 Wayne Gretzky/15 40.00 80.00

2015-16 ITG Superlative Swatch Jerseys Silver

*SLVR PTCH/15-18: .5X TO 1.2X SLVR/25-30
*SLVR PTCH/15-18: .4X TO 1X SILVER/15
SSP01 Wayne Gretzky/15 40.00 80.00
SSP02 Theoren Fleury/30 8.00 20.00
SSP03 Teemu Selanne/30 8.00 20.00
SSP04 Ted Lindsay/25 8.00 20.00
SSP05 Ron Francis/25 8.00 20.00
SSP06 Phil Esposito/25 10.00 25.00
SSP07 Patrick Roy/30 15.00 40.00
SSP08 Maurice Richard/10
SSP09 Mario Lemieux/30 20.00 50.00
SSP10 Marc-Andre Fleury/30
SSP11 John LeClair/25 6.00 15.00
SSP12 Joe Sakic/30 8.00 20.00
SSP13 Jean Beliveau/15 15.00 40.00
SSP14 Jaromir Jagr/30
SSP15 Grant Fuhr/25 10.00 25.00
SSP16 Eddie Shore/10
SSP17 Ed Giacomin/25 6.00 15.00
SSP18 Doug Gilmour/25 8.00 20.00
SSP19 Bobby Hull/25 6.00 15.00

2017-18 ITG Superlative Signatures Spectrum Magenta

SSAD1 Alex Delvecchio 10.00 25.00
SSBH1 Bobby Hull 10.00 25.00
SSBP1 Bernie Parent 10.00 25.00
SSBS1 Billy Smith 10.00 25.00
SSDH1 Dale Hawerchuk 12.00 30.00
SSJB1 Johnny Bower 10.00 25.00
SSJE1 Jack Eichel
SSJS1 Joe Sakic 12.00 30.00
SSJV1 Joe Veleno 10.00 25.00
SSLM1 Larry Murphy 8.00 20.00
SSLMD Lanny McDonald 10.00 25.00
SSMG1 Mike Gartner 10.00 25.00
SSML1 Mario Lemieux 40.00 100.00
SSMR1 Manon Rheaume 10.00 25.00
SSNH1 Nico Hischier 30.00 80.00
SSNP1 Nolan Patrick EXCH 20.00 50.00
SSPB1 Pavel Bure 10.00 25.00
SSPE1 Phil Esposito 15.00 40.00
SSPS1 Peter Stastny 10.00 25.00
SSPT1 Pierre Turgeon 10.00 25.00
SSRB1 Raymond Bourque 15.00 40.00
SSSS1 Serge Savard 10.00 25.00
SSSS2 Steve Shutt 10.00 25.00
SSTE1 Tony Esposito 10.00 25.00
SSTL1 Ted Lindsay 10.00 25.00
SSYC1 Yvan Cournoyer 10.00 25.00

2017-18 ITG Superlative Blades of Steel Spectrum Magenta

BS01 Al MacInnis/25 5.00 12.00
BS02 Alexander Ovechkin/19 20.00 50.00
BS03 Brendan Shanahan/25 6.00 15.00
BS04 Dany Heatley/25 5.00 12.00
BS05 Darryl Sittler/19 5.00 12.00
BS06 Dave Keon/19 5.00 12.00
BS07 Denis Potvin/25 5.00 12.00
BS08 Doug Gilmour/19 6.00 15.00
BS09 Gilbert Perreault/19 5.00 12.00
BS10 Henrik Zetterberg/19 5.00 12.00
BS11 Jarome Iginla/25 5.00 12.00
BS12 John LeClair/25 5.00 12.00
BS13 Johnny Bucyk/19 5.00 12.00
BS14 Keith Tkachuk/25 5.00 12.00
BS15 Luc Robitaille/19 5.00 12.00
BS16 Mario Lemieux/25 15.00 40.00
BS17 Pavel Datsyuk/25 8.00 20.00
BS18 Rick Nash/25 5.00 12.00
BS19 Scott Gomez/19 5.00 12.00
BS20 Stan Mikita/19 6.00 15.00
BS21 Tim Horton/25 5.00 12.00
BS22 Vincent Lecavalier/25 4.00 10.00
BS23 Willie Oâ•™Ree/25 5.00 12.00

2017-18 ITG Superlative Careers Spectrum Magenta

C01 Bobby Orr 15.00 40.00
C02 Brendan Shanahan 6.00 15.00
C03 Brett Hull 5.00 12.00
C04 Brian Leetch 5.00 12.00
C05 Carey Price 15.00 40.00
C06 Chris Chelios 5.00 12.00
C07 Darryl Sittler 5.00 12.00
C08 Gordie Howe 12.00 30.00
C09 Guy Lafleur 6.00 15.00
C10 Jaromir Jagr 12.00 30.00
C11 Joe Sakic 6.00 15.00
C12 Larry Murphy 4.00 10.00
C13 Mario Lemieux 15.00 40.00
C14 Martin Brodeur 10.00 25.00
C15 Mats Sundin 5.00 12.00
C16 Mike Modano 8.00 20.00
C17 Nikolai Khabibulin 5.00 12.00
C18 Patrick Roy 12.00 30.00
C19 Pavel Bure 5.00 12.00
C20 Phil Esposito 8.00 20.00
C21 Pierre Turgeon 5.00 12.00
C22 Raymond Bourque 8.00 20.00
C23 Sergei Fedorov 8.00 20.00
C24 Teemu Selanne 6.00 15.00
C25 Wayne Gretzky 25.00 60.00

2017-18 ITG Superlative Debut Spectrum Magenta

SD01 Dave Andreychuk 5.00 12.00
Phil Housley
Brian Bellows
Scott Stevens
SD02 Martin Brodeur 10.00 25.00
Pavel Bure
Nicklas Lidstrom
Scott Niedermayer
SD03 Phil Esposito 8.00 20.00
Yvan Cournoyer
John Ferguson
Roger Crozier
SD04 Doug Gilmour 6.00 15.00
Kelly Hrudey
Chris Chelios
Claude Lemieux
SD05 Wayne Gretzky 25.00 60.00
Mark Messier
Raymond Bourque
Mike Gartner
SD06 Brett Hull 6.00 15.00
Adam Oates
Wendel Clark
Gary Suter
SD07 Jaromir Jagr 12.00 30.00
Sergei Fedorov
Dominik Hasek
Mats Sundin
SD08 Curtis Joseph 5.00 12.00
Rob Blake
Alexander Mogilny
Igor Larionov
SD09 Paul Kariya 8.00 20.00
Peter Forsberg
Tommy Salo
Nikolai Khabibulin
SD10 Guy Lafleur 6.00 15.00
Billy Smith
Marcel Dionne
Rick Martin
SD11 Mario Lemieux 15.00 40.00
Patrick Roy
Ulf Samuelsson
Kevin Hatcher
SD12 Pelle Lindbergh 6.00 15.00
Dale Hawerchuk
Ron Francis
Grant Fuhr
SD13 Eric Lindros 8.00 20.00
Teemu Selanne
Sandis Ozolinsh
Alexei Zhamnov
SD14 Mike Modano 8.00 20.00
Joe Sakic
Jeremy Roenick
Mike Richter
SD15 Larry Murphy 5.00 12.00
Paul Coffey
Peter Stastny
Denis Savard
SD16 Bobby Orr 15.00 40.00
Carol Vadnais
Serge Savard
Rogie Vachon
SD17 Gilbert Perreault 5.00 12.00
Gilles Meloche
Darryl Sittler
Reggie Leach
SD18 Denis Potvin 5.00 12.00
John Davidson
Borje Salming
Lanny McDonald
SD19 Larry Robinson 5.00 12.00
Steve Shutt
Bob Nystrom
Bill Barber
SD20 Bobby Rousseau 5.00 12.00
Rod Gilbert
Jean Ratelle
Dave Keon
SD21 Derek Sanderson 5.00 12.00
Ed Giacomin
Bernie Parent
Pete Mahovlich
SD22 Brendan Shanahan 6.00 15.00
Brian Leetch
Pierre Turgeon
Kevin Stevens
SD23 Steve Yzerman 6.00 15.00
Tom Barrasso
Cam Neely
Pat LaFontaine

2017-18 ITG Superlative League Leaders Spectrum Magenta

LL01 Peter Bondra 8.00 20.00
Ron Francis
Eric Lindros/25
LL02 Pavel Bure
Wayne Gretzky
Mike Richter/25
LL03 Pavel Bure 12.00 30.00
Mark Recchi
Jaromir Jagr/25
LL04 Crosby/McDavid/Holtby/25 20.00 50.00
LL05 Phil Esposito 15.00 40.00
Bobby Orr
Bernie Parent/20
LL06 Wayne Gretzky 25.00 60.00
Mario Lemieux
Grant Fuhr/25
LL07 Wayne Gretzky 25.00 60.00
Mario Lemieux
Brett Hull/25
LL08 Gordie Howe
Henri Richard
Glenn Hall/15
LL09 Bobby Hull
Stan Mikita
Glenn Hall/15
LL10 Iginla/Oates/Hasek/25
LL11 Reggie Leach 8.00 20.00
Bobby Clarke
Phil Esposito/25
LL12 Teemu Selanne 12.00 30.00
Jaromir Jagr
Martin Brodeur/25
LL13 Steve Shutt 6.00 15.00
Guy Lafleur
Ken Dryden/20
LL14 Keith Tkachuk 15.00 40.00
Mario Lemieux
Patrick Roy/25

2017-18 ITG Superlative Retired Numbers Multi Spectrum Magenta

RNM01 Bill Barber 8.00 20.00
Paul Coffey
Tim Horton
Ted Lindsay
Phil Esposito
RNM02 Andy Bathgate 12.00 30.00
Gordie Howe
Mike Modano
Lanny McDonald
Bobby Hull
RNM03 Pavel Bure 6.00 15.00
Guy Lafleur
George Armstrong
Alex Delvecchio
Ron Francis
RNM04 Bobby Clarke 6.00 15.00
Marcel Dionne
Pat LaFontaine
Trevor Linden
Brett Hull
RNM05 Tim Horton
Mark Howe
Al MacInnis
Brian Leetch
Doug Harvey
RNM06 Rod Langway
Nicklas Lidstrom
Denis Potvin
Bill Barilko
Bernie Geoffrion
RNM07 Markus Naslund 6.00 15.00
Larry Robinson
Joe Sakic
Bryan Trottier
Steve Yzerman
RNM08 Maurice Richard
Bobby Hull
Gordie Howe
Johnny Bucyk
Charlie Conacher
RNM09 Terry Sawchuk
Jacques Plante
Glenn Hall
Bernie Parent
Turk Broda
RNM10 Brian Sutter 8.00 20.00
Daniel Alfredsson
Mark Messier
Mike Gartner
Gilbert Perreault

2017-18 ITG Superlative Rookie Spectrum Magenta

SRNH1 Nico Hischier 25.00 60.00
SRNP1 Nolan Patrick EXCH 15.00 20.00

2017-18 ITG Superlative Seasons Spectrum Magenta

SE01 Jean Beliveau 5.00 12.00
Alex Delvecchio
Andy Bathgate
Tom Johnson
Jacques Plante
Doug Harvey
SE02 Phil Esposito 15.00 40.00
Bobby Orr
Gordie Howe
Stan Mikita
Gump Worsley
Derek Sanderson
SE03 Wayne Gretzky 25.00 60.00
Mike Bossy
Marcel Dionne
Randy Carlyle
Butch Goring
Peter Stastny
SE04 Gordie Howe 12.00 30.00
Doug Harvey
Jean Beliveau
Jacques Plante
Ted Lindsay
Glenn Hall
SE05 Gordie Howe 12.00 30.00
Stan Mikita
Tim Horton
Phil Goyette
Dave Keon
Glenn Hall
SE06 Jaromir Jagr 12.00 30.00
Teemu Selanne
Paul Kariya
Joe Sakic
Nicklas Lidstrom
Dominik Hasek
SE07 Hakan Loob 25.00 60.00
Patrick Roy
Wayne Gretzky
Grant Fuhr
Mario Lemieux
Raymond Bourque
SE08 McDavid/Crosby/Kane 20.00 50.00
Holtby/Burns/Draisaitl
SE09 Stan Mikita 6.00 15.00
Jean Beliveau
Bobby Hull
Terry Sawchuk
Norm Ullman
Roger Crozier
SE10 Bill Mosienko
Toe Blake
Maurice Richard
Elmer Lach
Ted Kennedy
Harry Lumley
SE11 Bobby Orr 15.00 40.00
Phil Esposito
Bill White
Vic Hadfield
Jean Ratelle
Rod Gilbert

SE12 Bobby Orr 15.00 40.00
Denis Potvin
Bernie Parent
Guy Lafleur
Bobby Clarke
Marcel Dionne
SE13 Thornton/Jagr/Ovechkin 20.00 50.00
Alfredsson/Chara/Kiprusoff

2017-18 ITG Superlative Super Teams Spectrum Magenta

ST01 Wayne Gretzky 25.00 60.00
Mark Messier
Jari Kurri
Grant Fuhr
Paul Coffey
Glenn Anderson/25
ST02 Mario Lemieux 15.00 40.00
Jaromir Jagr
Larry Murphy
Ron Francis
Joe Mullen
Tom Barrasso/25
ST03 Guy Lafleur 6.00 15.00
Steve Shutt
Serge Savard
Larry Robinson
Ken Dryden
Guy Lapointe/20
ST04 Sergei Fedorov 8.00 20.00
Steve Yzerman
Nicklas Lidstrom
Igor Larionov
Chris Osgood
Larry Murphy/25
ST05 Bryan Trottier 8.00 20.00
Denis Potvin
Mike Bossy
Billy Smith
Clark Gillies
Butch Goring/25
ST06 Bobby Orr 15.00 40.00
Phil Esposito
Wayne Cashman
Gerry Cheevers
Johnny Bucyk
Ken Hodge/20
ST07 Jean Beliveau
Maurice Richard
Jacques Plante
Doug Harvey
Henri Richard
Tom Johnson/9
ST08 Gordie Howe
Alex Delvecchio
Ted Lindsay
Terry Sawchuk
Sid Abel
Marcel Pronovost/12
ST09 Adam Graves 8.00 20.00
Mark Messier
Alexei Kovalev
Brian Leetch
Sergei Zubov
Mike Richter/25
ST10 Hakan Loob 6.00 15.00
Joe Mullen
Doug Gilmour
Al MacInnis
Joe Nieuwendyk
Mike Vernon/25
ST11 Patrick Roy 12.00 30.00
Joe Sakic
Rob Blake
Peter Forsberg
Milan Hejduk
Raymond Bourque/25
ST12 Brett Hull 8.00 20.00
Mike Modano
Joe Nieuwendyk
Sergei Zubov
Darryl Sydor
Ed Belfour/25
ST13 Rick MacLeish 5.00 12.00
Bobby Clarke
Bill Barber
Reggie Leach
Joe Watson
Bernie Parent/25
ST14 Dave Keon
George Armstrong
Frank Mahovlich
Johnny Bower
Bobby Baun
Tim Horton/15
ST15 Kane/Toews/Crawford 10.00 25.00
Hossa/Saad/Seabrook

2003-04 ITG Toronto Fall Expo Forever Rivals

This 10-card set was a bonus available in "Super Boxes" available from In the Game, Inc. during the 2003 Toronto Fall Expo. Cards were limited to 100 copies each.

FR1 M.Sundin 6.00 15.00
S.Koivu
FR2 D.Gilmour 8.00 20.00
P.Roy
FR3 W.Clark 6.00 15.00
C.Chelios
FR4 R.Vaive 8.00 20.00
G.Lafleur
FR5 L.McDonald 6.00 15.00
L.Robinson
FR6 D.Sittler 6.00 15.00
Y.Cournoyer
FR7 J.Bower 8.00 20.00
J.Plante
FR8 T.Horton 6.00 15.00
D.Harvey
FR9 T.Kennedy 6.00 15.00
M.Richard
FR10 G.Hainsworth 6.00 15.00
H.Morenz

2003-04 ITG Toronto Fall Expo Jerseys

This 30-card set was a bonus inside "Super Boxes" available from In the Game, Inc. during the 2003 Toronto Fall Expo. Cards FE1-FE20 were limited to 40 copies while cards FE21-FE30 were limited to 20 copies and are unpriced due to scarcity.

FE1 Pavel Datsyuk 12.00 30.00
FE2 Vincent Lecavalier 12.00 30.00
FE3 Jay Bouwmeester 10.00 25.00
FE4 Saku Koivu 12.00 30.00
FE5 Roberto Luongo 12.00 30.00
FE6 Rick Nash 12.00 30.00
FE7 Owen Nolan 10.00 25.00
FE8 Brendan Shanahan 12.00 30.00
FE9 Jason Spezza 10.00 25.00
FE10 Mats Sundin 12.00 30.00
FE11 Marty Turco 10.00 25.00
FE12 Henrik Zetterberg 12.00 30.00
FE13 Nicklas Lidstrom 12.00 30.00
FE14 Pavel Bure 12.00 30.00
FE15 Jose Theodore 12.00 30.00
FE16 Joe Thornton 15.00 40.00
FE17 Jaromir Jagr 15.00 40.00
FE18 Ilya Kovalchuk 15.00 40.00
FE19 Mike Modano 15.00 40.00
FE20 Brett Hull 15.00 40.00
FE21 Ed Belfour
FE22 Jean-Sebastien Giguere
FE23 Dany Heatley
FE24 Mario Lemieux
FE25 Patrick Roy
FE26 Joe Sakic
FE27 Peter Forsberg
FE28 Marian Gaborik
FE29 Martin Brodeur
FE30 Steve Yzerman

2003-04 ITG Toronto Spring Expo Class of 2004

Inserted one in each "Super Box" available at the Toronto Spring Expo, this 10 -card set featured promising prospects. Each card was limited to 100 copies each.

1 E.Staal 6.00 15.00
T.Ruutu
2 M.Fleury 8.00 20.00
M.Lombardi
3 R.Malone 6.00 15.00
J.Lupul
4 M.Stajan 6.00 15.00
D.Brown
5 P.Bergeron 6.00 15.00
J.Hudler
6 F.Tyutin 6.00 15.00
A.Babchuk
7 D.Roy 8.00 20.00
N.Zherdev
8 N.Horton 6.00 15.00
J.Tootoo
9 J.Pitkanen 6.00 15.00
D.Hamhuis
10 K.Lehtonen 10.00 25.00
A.Munro

2006-07 ITG Toronto Spring Expo Maple Leafs Forever

1 Charlie Conacher
2 Hap Day
3 Joe Primeau
4 Johnny Bower
5 Tim Horton
6 Dave Keon
7 Dave Keon
8 Terry Sawchuk
9 Red Kelly
10 Frank Mahovlich
11 Lanny McDonald
12 Darryl Sittler
13 Borje Salming
14 Borje Salming
15 Tiger Williams
16 Darryl Sittler
17 Wendel Clark
18 Wendel Clark
19 Rick Vaive
20 Doug Gilmour
21 Felix Potvin
22 Felix Potvin
23 Ed Belfour
24 Ed Belfour
25 Brian Leetch

2014-15 ITG Toronto Spring Expo Beliveau Tribute

JB Jean Beliveau 3.00 8.00

2005-06 ITG Tough Customers

COMPLETE SET (25) 6.00 15.00
BG Bill Goldthorpe .40 1.00
BM Basil McRae .20 .50
BP Bob Probert .40 1.00
CN Cam Neely .75 2.00
DB Donald Brashear .20 .50
DH Dale Hunter .20 .50
DM Dan Maloney .20 .50
DS Dave Schultz .40 1.00
ES Eddie Shack .40 1.00
FB Frank Bialowas .40 1.00
GO Gino Odjick .20 .50
JF John Ferguson .20 .50
JK Joey Kocur .20 .50
JM Jimmy Mann .20 .50
KC Kelly Chase .20 .50
LF Lou Fontinato .20 .50
LG Link Gaetz .20 .50
SG Stu Grimson .20 .50
SJ Stan Jonathan .40 1.00
TL Ted Lindsay .40 1.00
TO Terry O'Reilly .40 1.00
TW Tiger Williams .40 1.00
WC Wendel Clark .40 1.00
CNI Chris Nilan .20 .50
DSE Dave Semenko .20 .50

2005-06 ITG Tough Customers Autographs

Bill Goldthorpe 4.00 10.00
BM Basil McRae 4.00 10.00
BP Bob Probert 10.00 25.00
CN Chris Nilan 4.00 10.00
DB Donald Brashear 4.00 10.00
DH Dale Hunter 4.00 10.00
DM Dan Maloney 4.00 10.00
DS Dave Schultz 8.00 20.00
ES Eddie Shack 8.00 20.00
FB Frank Bialowas 8.00 20.00
GO Gino Odjick 4.00 10.00
JK Joey Kocur 4.00 10.00
JM Jimmy Mann 4.00 10.00
KC Kelly Chase 6.00 15.00
LF Lou Fontinato 6.00 15.00
LG Link Gaetz 4.00 10.00
SG Stu Grimson 4.00 10.00
SJ Stan Jonathan 8.00 20.00
TL Ted Lindsay 6.00 15.00
TO Terry O'Reilly 10.00 25.00
TW Tiger Williams 8.00 20.00
WC Wendel Clark 10.00 25.00

2005-06 ITG Tough Customers Double Memorabilia

BP Bob Probert 10.00 25.00
CN Cam Neely 12.00 30.00
DB Donald Brashear 8.00 20.00
SG Stu Grimson 8.00 20.00
TO Terry O'Reilly 12.00 30.00
WC Wendel Clark 12.00 30.00

2005-06 ITG Tough Customers Famous Battles Autographs

BB Donald Brashear 12.00 30.00
Frank Bialowas
GP Stu Grimson 15.00 40.00
Bob Probert
HN Dale Hunter 12.00 30.00
Chris Nilan
PC Bob Probert 20.00 50.00
Wendel Clark
SO Dave Schultz 15.00 40.00
Terry O'Reilly
WS Tiger Williams 12.00 30.00
Dave Schultz

2005-06 ITG Tough Customers Jerseys

BG Bill Goldthorpe 3.00 8.00
BP Bob Probert 6.00 15.00
DB Donald Brashear 3.00 8.00
DM Dan Maloney 3.00 8.00
DS Dave Schultz 5.00 12.00
FB Frank Bialowas 4.00 10.00
GO Gino Odjick 3.00 8.00
JF John Ferguson 5.00 12.00
KC Kelly Chase 3.00 8.00
SG Stu Grimson 3.00 8.00
SJ Stan Jonathan 4.00 10.00
TO Terry O'Reilly 5.00 12.00
TW Tiger Williams 5.00 12.00
WC Wendel Clark 5.00 12.00

2005-06 ITG Tough Customers Signed Memorabilia

BG Bill Goldthorpe 10.00 25.00
BP Bob Probert 15.00 40.00
CN Cam Neely 15.00 40.00
DB Donald Brashear 10.00 25.00
DM Dan Maloney 10.00 25.00
DS Dave Schultz 12.00 30.00
FB Frank Bialowas 10.00 25.00
GO Gino Odjick 10.00 25.00
KC Kelly Chase 10.00 25.00
SG Stu Grimson 10.00 25.00
TW Tiger Williams 12.00 30.00
WC Wendel Clark 15.00 40.00

2005-06 ITG Tough Customers Stickwork

Bob Probert 10.00 25.00
CN Cam Neely 10.00 25.00
DH Dale Hunter 6.00 15.00
DS Dave Semenko 6.00 15.00
SG Stu Grimson 6.00 15.00
SJ Stan Jonathan 8.00 20.00
CNI Chris Nilan 6.00 15.00

2004-05 ITG Ultimate Memorabilia

ITG's fifth installment of Ultimate Memorabilia contained one autograph card, one memorabilia card and one base card or "Archives" 1/1 card per pack. Base cards were limited to 45 copies each. Every card was encased in a Beckett slab.

PRINT RUN 45 SER.#'d SETS
1 Bun Cook 6.00 15.00
2 Doug Harvey 6.00 15.00
3 Butch Bouchard 6.00 15.00
4 Bill Barilko 20.00 50.00
5 Jean Ratelle 10.00 25.00
6 Phil Esposito 12.00 30.00
7 Ted Lindsay 10.00 25.00
8 Gordie Drillon 6.00 15.00
9 Johnny Bucyk 6.00 15.00
10 Bobby Hull 12.00 30.00
11 Ted Lindsay 10.00 25.00
12 Bill Gadsby 6.00 15.00
13 Busher Jackson 6.00 15.00
14 Aurel Joliat 12.00 30.00
15 John Davidson 12.00 30.00
16 Billy Smith 10.00 25.00
17 Bill Cook 12.00 30.00
18 Bill Cowley 10.00 25.00
19 Babe Pratt 10.00 25.00
20 Ed Giacomin 10.00 25.00
21 Neil Colville 6.00 15.00
22 Foster Hewitt 10.00 25.00
23 Georges Vezina 20.00 50.00
24 King Clancy 10.00 25.00
25 Red Dutton 6.00 15.00
26 Cyclone Taylor 30.00 80.00
27 Dale Hawerchuk 6.00 15.00
28 Norm Ullman 10.00 25.00
29 Harry Howell 12.00 30.00
30 Stan Mikita 12.00 30.00
31 Borje Salming 10.00 25.00
32 Ching Johnson 12.00 30.00
33 Harry Lumley 12.00 30.00
34 Bernie Geoffrion 12.00 30.00
35 Ted Kennedy 12.00 30.00
36 Howie Morenz 12.00 30.00
37 Ace Bailey 12.00 30.00
38 Bill Ranford 6.00 15.00
39 Charlie Gardiner 10.00 25.00
40 Rod Gilbert 10.00 25.00
41 Syl Apps 10.00 25.00
42 Ed Giacomin 10.00 25.00
43 Norm Ullman 10.00 25.00
44 Guy Lafleur 12.00 30.00
45 Andy Bathgate 10.00 25.00
46 Max Bentley 10.00 25.00
47 Steve Shutt 10.00 25.00
48 Bobby Hull 12.00 30.00
49 Denis Potvin 10.00 25.00
50 Dit Clapper 10.00 25.00
51 Phil Esposito 12.00 30.00
52 Hap Day 10.00 25.00
53 Henri Richard 12.00 30.00
54 Bernie Geoffrion 12.00 30.00
55 Marcel Pronovost 10.00 25.00
56 Bill Gadsby 6.00 15.00
57 Jean-Guy Talbot 6.00 15.00
58 Pelle Lindbergh 12.00 30.00
59 Marcel Dionne 10.00 25.00
60 Allan Stanley 10.00 25.00
61 Frank Brimsek 12.00 30.00
62 Alex Delvecchio 12.00 30.00
63 Chuck Rayner 10.00 25.00
64 Frank Brimsek 12.00 30.00
65 Ebbie Goodfellow 10.00 25.00
66 Newsy Lalonde 12.00 30.00
67 Jean Ratelle 10.00 25.00
68 Bryan Hextall 6.00 15.00
69 Bobby Bauer 6.00 15.00
70 Red Horner 12.00 30.00
71 Lord Stanley 6.00 15.00
72 Phil Esposito 12.00 30.00
73 Jacques Laperriere 10.00 25.00
74 Ken Wharram 6.00 15.00
75 Dickie Moore 10.00 25.00
76 Harry Lumley 12.00 30.00
77 Charlie Conacher 10.00 25.00
78 Elmer Lach 10.00 25.00
79 Terry Sawchuk 12.00 30.00
80 George Hainsworth 12.00 30.00
81 Red Kelly 12.00 30.00
82 Joe Primeau 12.00 30.00
83 Eddie Shore 12.00 30.00
84 Pierre Pilote 10.00 25.00
85 Lester Patrick 10.00 25.00
86 Ken Reardon 10.00 25.00
87 Bobby Baun 10.00 25.00
88 Jack Stewart 10.00 25.00
89 Doug Gilmour 12.00 30.00
90 Frank Boucher 6.00 15.00
91 Red Kelly 12.00 30.00
92 Joe Mullen 6.00 15.00
93 John Ferguson 12.00 30.00
94 Allan Stanley 10.00 25.00
95 Bill Mosienko 10.00 25.00
96 Milt Schmidt 12.00 30.00
97 Sweeney Schriner 10.00 25.00
98 Marcel Dionne 10.00 25.00
99 Bill Durnan 12.00 30.00
100 Babe Siebert 10.00 25.00
101 Brad Park 10.00 25.00
102 Cam Neely 12.00 30.00
103 Derek Sanderson 12.00 30.00
104 Gerry Cheevers 12.00 30.00
105 Milt Schmidt 12.00 30.00
106 Ray Bourque 12.00 30.00
107 Terry O'Reilly 10.00 25.00
108 Tiny Thompson 12.00 30.00
109 Wayne Cashman 10.00 25.00
110 Woody Dumart 10.00 25.00
111 Terry Sawchuk 12.00 30.00
112 Gilbert Perreault 12.00 30.00
113 Grant Fuhr 12.00 30.00
114 Pat LaFontaine 6.00 15.00
115 Rick Martin 6.00 15.00
116 Roger Crozier 12.00 30.00
117 Lanny McDonald 12.00 30.00
118 Denis Savard 12.00 30.00
119 Doug Bentley 10.00 25.00
120 Glenn Hall 12.00 30.00
121 Roy Conacher 10.00 25.00
122 Tony Esposito 12.00 30.00
123 Howie Morenz 12.00 30.00
124 Patrick Roy 30.00 80.00
125 Ray Bourque 12.00 30.00
126 Brad Park 10.00 25.00
127 Darryl Sittler 12.00 30.00
128 Dino Ciccarelli 6.00 15.00
129 Glenn Hall 12.00 30.00
130 Paul Coffey 10.00 25.00
131 Roger Crozier 12.00 30.00
132 Tiny Thompson 12.00 30.00
133 Sid Abel 10.00 25.00
134 Steve Yzerman 20.00 50.00
135 Syd Howe 10.00 25.00
136 Frank Mahovlich 12.00 30.00
137 Vladimir Konstantinov 12.00 30.00
138 Sid Abel 10.00 25.00
139 Grant Fuhr 12.00 30.00
140 Jari Kurri 10.00 25.00
141 Paul Coffey 10.00 25.00
142 Jari Kurri 10.00 25.00
143 Larry Robinson 10.00 25.00
144 Rogie Vachon 10.00 25.00
145 Dino Ciccarelli 6.00 15.00
146 Gump Worsley 12.00 30.00
147 Denis Savard 12.00 30.00
148 Frank Mahovlich 12.00 30.00
149 Gump Worsley 12.00 30.00
150 Guy Lapointe 6.00 15.00
151 Jacques Lemaire 10.00 25.00
152 Jacques Plante 12.00 30.00
153 Jean Beliveau 12.00 30.00
154 Larry Robinson 10.00 25.00
155 Maurice Richard 25.00 60.00
156 Patrick Roy 30.00 80.00
157 Rogie Vachon 10.00 25.00
158 Serge Savard 10.00 25.00
159 Toe Blake 10.00 25.00
160 Toe Blake 10.00 25.00
161 Lionel Conacher 10.00 25.00
162 Art Ross 10.00 25.00
163 Lady Byng 10.00 25.00
164 Roy Worters 10.00 25.00
165 Al Arbour 6.00 15.00
166 Bryan Trottier 10.00 25.00
167 Clark Gillies 10.00 25.00
168 Mike Bossy 12.00 30.00
169 Brad Park 10.00 25.00
170 Gump Worsley 12.00 30.00
171 Guy Lafleur 12.00 30.00
172 Vic Hadfield 10.00 25.00
173 Jacques Plante 12.00 30.00
174 Bernie Parent 12.00 30.00
175 Bill Barber 6.00 15.00
176 Bobby Clarke 12.00 30.00
177 Fred Shero 6.00 15.00
178 Bryan Trottier 10.00 25.00
179 Larry Murphy 6.00 15.00
180 Mario Lemieux 30.00 80.00
181 Paul Coffey 10.00 25.00
182 Hobey Baker 6.00 15.00
183 Guy Lafleur 12.00 30.00
184 Michel Goulet 6.00 15.00
185 Glenn Hall 12.00 30.00
186 Jack Adams 10.00 25.00
187 Al Arbour 6.00 15.00
188 Andy Bathgate 10.00 25.00
189 Darryl Sittler 12.00 30.00
190 Frank Mahovlich 12.00 30.00
191 Jacques Plante 12.00 30.00
192 Johnny Bower 10.00 25.00
193 Lanny McDonald 12.00 30.00
194 Terry Sawchuk 12.00 30.00
195 Tim Horton 12.00 30.00
196 Turk Broda 6.00 15.00
197 Wendel Clark 12.00 30.00
198 Valeri Kharlamov 12.00 30.00
199 Cam Neely 12.00 30.00
200 Roger Neilson 6.00 15.00

2004-05 ITG Ultimate Memorabilia Art Ross Trophy

PRINT RUN 25 SER.#'d SETS
1 Mario Lemieux 25.00 60.00
2 Jean Beliveau 15.00 40.00
3 Bobby Hull 15.00 40.00
4 Stan Mikita 12.50 30.00
5 Bryan Trottier 12.50 30.00
6 Phil Esposito 12.50 30.00
7 Ted Lindsay 12.50 30.00
8 Guy Lafleur 20.00 50.00

2004-05 ITG Ultimate Memorabilia Autographs

ANNOUNCED PRINT RUN 60
1 Henri Richard 20.00 50.00
2 Larry Robinson 20.00 50.00
3 Marcel Dionne 20.00 50.00
4 Ray Bourque COL 20.00 50.00
5 Guy Lapointe 15.00 40.00
6 Cam Neely 20.00 50.00
7 Patrick Roy COL 50.00 125.00
8 Ray Bourque BOS 25.00 60.00
9 Ed Giacomin 20.00 50.00
10 Wendel Clark 25.00 60.00
11 Stan Mikita 20.00 50.00
12 Alex Delvecchio 20.00 50.00
13 Marcel Pronovost 15.00 40.00
14 Paul Coffey 15.00 40.00
15 Patrick Roy MTL 60.00 150.00
16 Glenn Hall 20.00 50.00
17 Cam Neely 15.00 40.00
18 Marcel Dionne 15.00 40.00
19 Joe Mullen 15.00 40.00
20 Phil Esposito 25.00 60.00
21 Denis Savard 15.00 40.00
22 Glenn Hall 15.00 40.00
23 Tony Esposito 25.00 60.00
24 Bobby Hull 30.00 80.00
25 Phil Esposito 20.00 50.00
26 Jean Beliveau 40.00 80.00
27 Bobby Hull 25.00 60.00
28 Steve Yzerman 50.00 100.00
29 Terry O'Reilly 15.00 40.00
30 Denis Potvin 20.00 50.00
31 Harry Howell 20.00 50.00
32 Dino Ciccarelli 15.00 40.00
33 Gilbert Perreault 20.00 50.00
34 Mark Howe 15.00 40.00
35 Bobby Clarke 20.00 50.00
36 Brad Park NYR 20.00 50.00
37 Ron Hextall 30.00 80.00
38 Jean Ratelle 15.00 40.00
39 John Bucyk 15.00 40.00
40 Bernie Parent 25.00 60.00
41 Billy Smith 15.00 40.00
42 Brad Park BOS 20.00 50.00
43 Bryan Trottier 15.00 40.00
44 Mike Bossy 25.00 60.00
45 Bill Barber 15.00 40.00
46 Gerry Cheevers 25.00 60.00
47 Pat LaFontaine 15.00 40.00
48 Johnny Bower 20.00 50.00
49 Doug Gilmour 25.00 60.00
50 Glenn Anderson 20.00 50.00
51 Bill Gadsby 15.00 40.00
52 Pierre Pilote 20.00 50.00
53 Grant Fuhr 20.00 50.00
54 Mario Lemieux 60.00 125.00
55 Butch Bouchard 15.00 40.00
56 Chuck Rayner 25.00 60.00
57 Elmer Lach 20.00 50.00
58 Frank Brimsek 50.00 100.00
59 Harry Lumley 25.00 60.00
60 Harry Watson 50.00 100.00
61 Howie Meeker 15.00 40.00
62 Rocket Richard 150.00 300.00
63 Milt Schmidt 15.00 40.00
64 Red Horner 75.00 150.00
65 Red Kelly 20.00 50.00
66 Sid Abel 30.00 80.00
67 Ted Kennedy 30.00 80.00
68 Ted Lindsay 20.00 50.00
69 Woody Dumart 25.00 60.00

2004-05 ITG Ultimate Memorabilia Blades of Steel

STATED PRINT RUN 25 SETS
CARDS UNDER 25 NOT PRICED
1 Bill Barilko 60.00 150.00
2 Rocket Richard 75.00 200.00
3 Cyclone Taylor 100.00 250.00
4 Jacques Plante 40.00 100.00
5 Hap Day 30.00 80.00
6 Elmer Lach 25.00 60.00
7 Eddie Shore 50.00 125.00
8 Nels Stewart 25.00 60.00
9 Tim Horton 30.00 80.00
10 Toe Blake 30.00 80.00
11 Busher Jackson 30.00 80.00
12 Jean Beliveau 40.00 100.00
13 Mario Lemieux 30.00 80.00
14 Clint Benedict 30.00 80.00
15 Joe Primeau 25.00 60.00
16 Paddy Moran 30.00 80.00
17 Dit Clapper 40.00 100.00
18 Georges Vezina/10
19 Frank Patrick/10
20 Frank Nighbor/10
21 Aurel Joliat/10

2004-05 ITG Ultimate Memorabilia Broad Street Bullies Jerseys

PRINT RUN 25 SER.#'d SETS
AUTO PRINT RUN 10 SER.#'d SETS
AUTOS NOT PRICED DUE TO SCARCITY
1 Bobby Clarke 25.00 60.00
2 Bill Barber 15.00 40.00
3 Bernie Parent 20.00 50.00
4 Dave Schultz 25.00 60.00
5 Rick MacLeish 15.00 40.00
6 Reggie Leach 15.00 40.00
7 Gary Dornhoefer 15.00 40.00
8 Joe Watson 15.00 40.00

2004-05 ITG Ultimate Memorabilia Calder Trophy

PRINT RUN 25 SER.#'d SETS
1 Mario Lemieux 30.00 80.00
2 Mike Bossy 15.00 40.00
3 Bryan Trottier 12.50 30.00
4 Gilbert Perreault 20.00 50.00
5 Terry Sawchuk 25.00 60.00
6 Glenn Hall 12.50 30.00
7 Ray Bourque 15.00 40.00
8 Denis Potvin 10.00 25.00

2004-05 ITG Ultimate Memorabilia Changing the Game

INT RUN 25 SER.#'d SETS
1 Phil Esposito 12.50 30.00
2 Patrick Roy 40.00 100.00
3 Mario Lemieux 40.00 100.00
4 Ted Lindsay 12.50 30.00
5 Bobby Hull 15.00 40.00
6 Jacques Plante 30.00 80.00
7 Rocket Richard 40.00 100.00
8 Borje Salming 15.00 40.00
9 Steve Yzerman 25.00 60.00
10 Howie Morenz 30.00 80.00
11 Eddie Shore 30.00 80.00
12 Doug Harvey 15.00 40.00

2004-05 ITG Ultimate Memorabilia Conn Smythe Trophy

PRINT RUN 25 SER.#'d SETS
1 Jean Beliveau 15.00 40.00
2 Patrick Roy 40.00 100.00
3 Steve Yzerman 30.00 80.00
4 Mario Lemieux 40.00 100.00
5 Mike Bossy 12.50 30.00
6 Bryan Trottier 12.50 30.00
7 Glenn Hall 12.50 30.00
8 Guy Lafleur 20.00 50.00

2004-05 ITG Ultimate Memorabilia Country of Origin

PRINT RUN 25 SER.#'d SETS
1 Pelle Lindbergh 40.00 80.00
2 Gilbert Perreault 20.00 50.00
3 Bobby Hull 20.00 50.00
4 Mario Lemieux 60.00 120.00
5 Jari Kurri 20.00 50.00
6 Valeri Kharlamov 25.00 60.00
7 Steve Yzerman 40.00 100.00
8 Patrick Roy 40.00 100.00
9 Mike Bossy 15.00 40.00
10 Phil Esposito 20.00 50.00
11 Joe Mullen 15.00 40.00
12 Lanny McDonald 15.00 40.00
13 Ray Bourque 20.00 50.00
14 Tony Esposito 20.00 50.00
15 Yvan Cournoyer 15.00 40.00
16 Denis Potvin 15.00 40.00
17 Bobby Clarke 15.00 40.00
18 Paul Coffey 15.00 40.00
19 Larry Robinson 15.00 40.00
20 Guy Lafleur 25.00 60.00

2004-05 ITG Ultimate Memorabilia Gloves are Off

PRINT RUN 25 SER.#'d SETS
CARDS UNDER 25 NOT PRICED
1 Ray Bourque 15.00 40.00
2 Cam Neely 25.00 60.00
3 Steve Yzerman 30.00 80.00
4 Mario Lemieux 40.00 100.00
5 Patrick Roy 40.00 100.00
6 Dale Hawerchuk 25.00 60.00
7 Pelle Lindbergh 30.00 80.00
8 Charlie Conacher 25.00 60.00
9 Bill Durnan/10
10 Rocket Richard/10
11 Doug Harvey/10
12 King Clancy/10
13 George Hainsworth/10
14 Ace Bailey/10

2004-05 ITG Ultimate Memorabilia Hart Trophy

PRINT RUN 25 SER.#'d SETS
1 Mario Lemieux 40.00 100.00
2 Rocket Richard 40.00 100.00
3 Jacques Plante 20.00 50.00
4 Stan Mikita 12.50 30.00
5 Guy Lafleur 15.00 40.00
6 Bobby Hull 20.00 50.00
7 Phil Esposito 12.50 30.00
8 Howie Morenz 30.00 80.00

2004-05 ITG Ultimate Memorabilia Heroes Mario Lemieux

PRINT RUN 25 SER.#'d SETS
1 Rookie Season 30.00 80.00
2 Five Goals, Five Ways 30.00 80.00
3 First Cup 30.00 80.00
4 M.Lemieux 25.00 60.00
P.Coffey
5 M.Lemieux 25.00 60.00
L.Murphy
6 M.Lemieux 30.00 80.00
B.Trottier
7 All-Star Career 30.00 80.00
8 International Play AU 75.00 150.00
9 Short-Handed Goals AU 75.00 150.00
10 Points in Playoff Game AU 75.00 150.00

2004-05 ITG Ultimate Memorabilia Heroes Patrick Roy

1-7 PRINT RUN 25
1 Rookie Season 30.00 80.00
2 First Conn Smythe Trophy 30.00 80.00
3 First Cup 30.00 80.00
4 P.Roy/L.Robinson 30.00 80.00
5 P.Roy/R.Bourque 30.00 80.00
6 All-Star Career 30.00 80.00
7 International Play 30.00 80.00
8 Most Career Playoff Wins AU
9 Most Career Wins AU
10 Most Career Games AU

2004-05 ITG Ultimate Memorabilia Heroes Steve Yzerman

PRINT RUN 25 SER.#'d SETS
1 Rookie Season 25.00 60.00
2 First Cup 25.00 60.00
3 Team Points Record 25.00 60.00
4 S.Yzerman/D.Sittler 25.00 60.00
5 S.Yzerman/P.Coffey 25.00 60.00
6 S.Yzerman/D.Ciccarelli 25.00 60.00
7 All-Star Career 25.00 60.00
8 International Play 25.00 60.00
9 Youngest All-Star AU 75.00 150.00
10 Longest Captaincy AU 75.00 150.00

2004-05 ITG Ultimate Memorabilia Jerseys

PRINT RUN 25 SER.#'d SETS
1 Ray Bourque 15.00 40.00
2 Patrick Roy 40.00 100.00
3 Aurel Joliat 30.00 80.00
4 Paul Coffey 15.00 40.00
5 George Hainsworth 20.00 50.00
6 Mario Lemieux 30.00 80.00
7 Red Kelly 15.00 40.00
8 Terry Sawchuk 25.00 60.00
9 Jean Beliveau 20.00 50.00
10 Rocket Richard 50.00 100.00
11 Steve Yzerman 25.00 60.00
12 Roy Worters 20.00 50.00
13 Frank Brimsek 12.50 30.00
14 Phil Esposito 12.50 30.00
15 Norm Ullman 12.50 30.00
16 Sid Abel 12.50 30.00
17 Ted Lindsay 12.50 30.00

2004-05 ITG Ultimate Memorabilia Jersey Autographs

ANNOUNCED PRINT RUN 40
1 Larry Robinson 12.00 30.00
2 Steve Yzerman 50.00 120.00
3 Jean Beliveau 50.00 100.00
4 Bill Barber 12.00 30.00
5 Paul Coffey 15.00 40.00
6 Guy Lapointe 15.00 40.00
7 Pat LaFontaine 15.00 40.00
8 Guy Lafleur 30.00 80.00
9 Dino Ciccarelli 15.00 40.00
10 Jari Kurri 25.00 60.00
11 Bobby Hull 40.00 80.00
12 Dale Hawerchuk 12.00 30.00
13 Bernie Parent 25.00 60.00
14 Patrick Roy COL 75.00 150.00
15 Gerry Cheevers 15.00 40.00
16 Brad Park 20.00 50.00
17 Gilbert Perreault 15.00 40.00
18 Joe Mullen 12.00 30.00
19 Terry O'Reilly 15.00 40.00
20 Cam Neely 25.00 60.00
21 Patrick Roy MTL 100.00 200.00
22 Mike Bossy 12.00 30.00
23 Jacques Laperriere 12.00 30.00
24 Marcel Dionne 12.00 30.00
25 Yvan Cournoyer 12.00 30.00
26 Grant Fuhr 25.00 60.00
27 Ed Giacomin 20.00 50.00
28 Johnny Bower 25.00 60.00
29 Jean Ratelle 12.00 30.00
30 Ted Lindsay 20.00 50.00
31 Mario Lemieux 75.00 150.00
32 Frank Mahovlich 25.00 60.00
33 Denis Potvin 20.00 50.00
34 Stan Mikita 20.00 50.00
35 Billy Smith 12.00 30.00
36 Red Kelly 20.00 50.00
37 Lanny McDonald 15.00 40.00
38 Phil Esposito 25.00 60.00
39 Darryl Sittler 25.00 60.00
40 Denis Savard 20.00 50.00
41 John Ferguson 12.00 30.00
42 Tony Esposito 25.00 60.00
43 Wendel Clark 25.00 60.00
44 Doug Gilmour 25.00 60.00
45 Glenn Anderson/33 12.00 30.00
46 Bobby Clarke 20.00 50.00
47 Henri Richard 15.00 40.00
48 Johnny Bucyk 15.00 40.00
49 Michel Goulet 12.00 30.00
50 Ray Bourque 40.00 80.00
51 Alex Delvecchio 15.00 40.00
52 Gump Worsley 20.00 50.00
53 Bryan Trottier 12.00 30.00

2004-05 ITG Ultimate Memorabilia Jersey and Sticks

PRINT RUN 25 SER.#'d SETS
1 Doug Harvey 15.00 40.00
2 Denis Potvin 12.50 30.00
3 Ray Bourque 20.00 50.00
4 Paul Coffey 20.00 50.00
5 Brad Park 12.50 30.00
6 Mike Bossy 15.00 40.00
7 Jean Beliveau 20.00 50.00
8 Steve Yzerman 30.00 80.00
9 Phil Esposito 20.00 50.00
10 Marcel Dionne 12.50 30.00
11 Bobby Hull 20.00 50.00
12 Doug Gilmour 25.00 60.00
13 Mario Lemieux 40.00 100.00
14 Guy Lafleur 25.00 60.00
15 Cam Neely 25.00 60.00
16 Patrick Roy 40.00 100.00
17 Grant Fuhr 20.00 50.00
18 Johnny Bower 20.00 50.00
19 Jacques Plante 30.00 80.00
20 Harry Lumley 12.50 30.00

2004-05 ITG Ultimate Memorabilia Nicknames

PRINT RUN 25 SER.#'d SETS
1 Stan Mikita 25.00 60.00
2 Rocket Richard 60.00 120.00
3 Toe Blake 30.00 80.00
4 Jacques Plante 25.00 60.00
5 Mario Lemieux 60.00 120.00
6 Terry Sawchuk 30.00 80.00
7 Steve Yzerman 25.00 60.00
8 Glenn Hall 15.00 40.00
9 Larry Robinson 15.00 40.00
10 Bernie Geoffrion Glv 20.00 40.00
11 Henri Richard 15.00 40.00
12 Jean Beliveau 20.00 50.00
13 Johnny Bower 25.00 60.00
14 Ted Kennedy
15 Doug Gilmour 25.00 60.00
16 Ace Bailey 30.00 80.00
17 Nels Stewart 30.00 80.00
18 Tony Esposito 20.00 50.00
19 Frank Mahovlich 15.00 40.00
20 Gump Worsley 25.00 60.00
21 Marcel Dionne
22 Frank Brimsek 25.00 60.00
23 Ted Lindsay 15.00 40.00
24 Gerry Cheevers 50.00 100.00
25 Patrick Roy 50.00 100.00
26 Cyclone Taylor 250.00 350.00
27 Howie Morenz 50.00 100.00
28 Bobby Hull 20.00 50.00
29 Guy Lafleur 25.00 60.00
30 Georges Vezina 125.00 200.00

2004-05 ITG Ultimate Memorabilia Norris Trophy

INT RUN 25 SER.#'d SETS
1 Ray Bourque 25.00 60.00
2 Larry Robinson 15.00 40.00
3 Doug Harvey 15.00 40.00
4 Jacques Laperriere 10.00 25.00
5 Paul Coffey 15.00 40.00
6 Denis Potvin 10.00 25.00

2004-05 ITG Ultimate Memorabilia Raised to the Rafters

PRINT RUN 25 SER.#'d SETS
1 Patrick Roy 40.00 100.00
2 Jacques Plante 30.00 80.00
3 Ray Bourque 20.00 50.00
4 Johnny Bower 20.00 50.00
5 Doug Harvey 20.00 50.00
6 Stan Mikita 20.00 50.00
7 Bobby Hull 20.00 50.00
8 Jean Beliveau 25.00 60.00
9 Bobby Clarke 25.00 60.00
10 Jari Kurri 25.00 60.00

2004-05 ITG Ultimate Memorabilia Retro Teammates

PRINT RUN 25 SER.#'d SETS
1 Bourq/Neely/Middle/Moog 50.00 100.00
2 Rich/Rich/Harvey/Plante 100.00 200.00
3 Mik/Hull/Hall/Hull 60.00 120.00
4 Sittler/McD/Salm/Williams 40.00 100.00
5 Trott/Boss/Pot/Smith 25.00 60.00
6 Abel/Delv/Lndsy/Sawchuk 60.00 120.00
7 Shore/Thomp/Stewrt/Clap 75.00 150.00
8 Coffey/Fuhr/Ander/Kurri 60.00 120.00
9 Lafleur/Shutt/Robin/Savrd 100.00 200.00
10 Bailey/Day/Clancy/Prim 100.00 200.00

Barb/Parent/Clarke/Leach 75.00 150.00
Ratelle/Giac/Park/Gilbert 40.00 100.00
Bucyk/Espo/Cheev/Cash 40.00 100.00
O'Reilly/Park/Bourq/Gilb 60.00 120.00
Beliveau/Worsly/Courn/Lap 60.00 120.00

2004-05 ITG Ultimate Memorabilia Seams Unbelievable

RINT RUN 25 SER.#'d SETS
Mario Lemieux 40.00 100.00
Steve Yzerman 25.00 60.00
Patrick Roy 50.00 125.00
Mike Bossy 15.00 40.00
Bryan Trottier 15.00 40.00
Charlie Gardiner 25.00 60.00
Rocket Richard 75.00 200.00
Darryl Sittler 20.00 50.00
Ray Bourque 25.00 60.00
Roy Worters 25.00 60.00

2004-05 ITG Ultimate Memorabilia Stick Autographs

RINT RUN 40 SER.#'d SETS
Michel Goulet 12.50 30.00
Mike Bossy 12.50 30.00
Cam Neely 25.00 60.00
Phil Esposito 25.00 60.00
Ray Bourque 25.00 60.00
Dale Hawerchuk 12.50 30.00
Tony Esposito 20.00 50.00
Mario Lemieux 60.00 150.00
Guy Lapointe 12.50 30.00
Marcel Dionne 12.50 30.00
Henri Richard 15.00 40.00
Larry Robinson 12.50 30.00
Gerry Cheevers 20.00 50.00
Bobby Hull 30.00 80.00
Bryan Trottier 12.50 30.00
Dino Ciccarelli 12.50 30.00
Gump Worsley 30.00 80.00
Guy Lafleur 25.00 60.00
Johnny Bower 25.00 60.00
Pat LaFontaine 12.50 30.00
Steve Yzerman 50.00 125.00
Terry O'Reilly 12.50 30.00
Bernie Geoffrion/30 30.00 80.00
Bill Barber/30 12.50 30.00
Bobby Clarke/30 25.00 60.00
Frank Mahovlich/30 25.00 60.00
Gilbert Perreault/30 25.00 60.00
Johnny Bucyk/30 20.00 50.00
Paul Coffey/30 25.00 60.00
Stan Mikita/30 25.00 60.00
Jean Beliveau/30 50.00 100.00
Jari Kurri 20.00 50.00
Bernie Parent 20.00 50.00
Alex Delvecchio 20.00 50.00
John Ferguson 12.50 30.00
Joe Mullen 12.50 30.00
Brad Park 20.00 50.00
Wendel Clark 20.00 50.00
Doug Gilmour 20.00 50.00
Yvan Cournoyer 12.50 30.00
Billy Smith 12.50 30.00
Ed Giacomin 12.50 30.00
Denis Savard/30 20.00 50.00
Grant Fuhr/30 30.00 80.00
Darryl Sittler/30 25.00 60.00

2004-05 ITG Ultimate Memorabilia Triple Threads

RINT RUN 25 SER.#'d SETS
Savard/Lapointe/Laperriere 20.00 50.00
Park/Potvin/Robinson 20.00 50.00
Worsley/Bower/Lumley 25.00 60.00
Brimsek/Hains/Worters 30.00 80.00
Crozier/Cheevers/T.Esposito 25.00 60.00
Bourque/Coffey/Housley 30.00 80.00
R.Brodeur/B.Smith/Parent 20.00 50.00
P.Esposito/Dionne/Clarke 30.00 80.00
Kurri/Bossy/Neely 30.00 80.00
Williams/Schultz/Ferguson 25.00 50.00
Lemieux/Yzer/Gilmour 50.00 125.00
Sittler/Trottier/Lafleur 25.00 60.00
Beliv/Richard/Mahov 30.00 80.00

2004-05 ITG Ultimate Memorabilia Vezina Trophy

RINT RUN 25 SER.#'d SETS
Jacques Plante 25.00 60.00
Terry Sawchuk 25.00 60.00
Pelle Lindbergh 40.00 100.00
George Hainsworth 25.00 60.00
Bernie Parent 30.00 80.00
Patrick Roy 40.00 100.00
Grant Fuhr 25.00 60.00
Tony Esposito 25.00 60.00

2005-06 ITG Ultimate Memorabilia Level 2

NNOUNCED PRINT RUN 45
Alex Delvecchio 6.00 15.00
Alexander Ovechkin 20.00 50.00
Alexander Yakushev 6.00 15.00
Antero Niittymaki 6.00 15.00
Aurel Joliat 6.00 15.00
Bernie Geoffrion 8.00 20.00
Bernie Parent 6.00 15.00
Bill Barilko 12.00 30.00
Bill Durnan 6.00 15.00
Billy Smith 6.00 15.00
Bobby Clarke 8.00 20.00
Bobby Hull 10.00 25.00
Borje Salming 6.00 15.00
Brett Hull 8.00 20.00
Brian Leetch 5.00 12.00
Cam Neely 6.00 15.00
Charlie Conacher 6.00 15.00
Charlie Gardiner 5.00 12.00
Corey Perry 6.00 15.00
Cyclone Taylor 20.00 50.00
Dany Heatley 6.00 15.00
Darryl Sittler 5.00 12.00
Dave Keon 8.00 20.00
Denis Potvin 6.00 15.00
Dion Phaneuf 8.00 20.00
Dit Clapper 6.00 15.00
Doug Gilmour 6.00 15.00
Doug Harvey 6.00 15.00
Ed Giacomin 6.00 15.00
Eddie Shack 6.00 15.00
Eddie Shore 6.00 15.00
Elmer Lach 6.00 15.00
Eric Lindros 10.00 25.00
Evgeni Malkin 20.00 50.00
Frank Brimsek 6.00 15.00
Frank Mahovlich 6.00 15.00
Frank McGee 6.00 15.00
Frank Nighbor 6.00 15.00
George Hainsworth 6.00 15.00
Georges Vezina 12.00 30.00

41 Gerry Cheevers 6.00 15.00
42 Gilbert Perreault 6.00 15.00
43 Glenn Hall 6.00 15.00
44 Grant Fuhr 6.00 15.00
45 Gump Worsley 6.00 15.00
46 Guy Lafleur 6.00 15.00
47 Henri Richard 6.00 15.00
48 Henrik Lundqvist 8.00 20.00
49 Howie Meeker 5.00 12.00
50 Howie Morenz 8.00 20.00
51 Ilya Kovalchuk 6.00 15.00
52 Jacques Plante 8.00 20.00
53 Jari Kurri 8.00 20.00
54 Jean Beliveau 6.00 15.00
55 Jim Craig 6.00 15.00
56 Joe Malone 6.00 15.00
57 Johnny Bower 4.00 10.00
58 Johnny Bucyk 4.00 10.00
59 Jose Theodore 6.00 15.00
60 King Clancy 6.00 15.00
61 Lanny McDonald 6.00 15.00
62 Larry Robinson 6.00 15.00
63 Lester Patrick 4.00 10.00
64 Lionel Conacher 6.00 15.00
65 Lord Stanley 5.00 12.00
66 Marcel Dionne 5.00 12.00
67 Mario Lemieux 12.00 30.00
68 Martin Brodeur 10.00 25.00
69 Maurice Richard 8.00 20.00
70 Mike Bossy 6.00 15.00
71 Mike Richards 6.00 15.00
72 Milt Schmidt 4.00 10.00
73 Nels Stewart 6.00 15.00
74 Newsy Lalonde 6.00 15.00
75 Pat LaFontaine 5.00 12.00
76 Patrick Roy 12.00 30.00
77 Paul Coffey 6.00 15.00
78 Paul Henderson 5.00 12.00
79 Pelle Lindbergh 8.00 20.00
80 Petr Prucha 6.00 15.00
81 Phil Esposito 6.00 15.00
82 Raymond Bourque 8.00 20.00
83 Red Kelly 4.00 10.00
84 Rogie Vachon 4.00 10.00
85 Ron Hextall 6.00 15.00
86 Sid Abel 6.00 15.00
87 Sidney Crosby 40.00 100.00
88 Stan Mikita 6.00 15.00
89 Steve Yzerman 10.00 25.00
90 Ted Kennedy 6.00 15.00
91 Ted Lindsay 6.00 15.00
92 Terry Sawchuk 8.00 20.00
93 Tim Horton 8.00 20.00
94 Tiny Thompson 6.00 15.00
95 Toe Blake 6.00 15.00
96 Tony Esposito 6.00 15.00
97 Turk Broda 6.00 15.00
98 Valeri Kharlamov 6.00 15.00
99 Vladislav Tretiak 8.00 20.00
100 Yvan Cournoyer 5.00 12.00

2005-06 ITG Ultimate Memorabilia Level 3

ANNOUNCED PRINT RUN 40
*LEVEL 3/40: .4X TO 1X LEVEL 2/45

2005-06 ITG Ultimate Memorabilia Level 4

*LEVEL 2/30: .5X TO 1.2X LEVEL 2/45
ANNOUNCED PRINT RUN 30

2005-06 ITG Ultimate Memorabilia Blades of Steel

PRINT RUN 25 SER.#'d SETS
1 Alexander Ovechkin 60.00 125.00
2 Mario Lemieux 30.00 80.00
3 Ray Bourque 20.00 50.00
4 Joe Primeau 25.00 50.00
5 Elmer Lach 15.00 40.00
6 Jack Adams 30.00 80.00
7 Nels Stewart 20.00 50.00
8 Tim Horton 25.00 60.00
9 Toe Blake 20.00 50.00
10 Frank Nighbor 20.00 50.00
11 Aurel Joliat 40.00 100.00
12 Dit Clapper 20.00 50.00
13 Eddie Shore 20.00 50.00
14 Jean Beliveau 40.00 80.00
15 Georges Vezina 90.00 150.00
16 Jacques Plante 20.00 50.00
17 Cyclone Taylor 450.00 600.00
18 Clint Benedict 25.00 60.00
19 Maurice Richard 30.00 80.00
20 Bill Barilko 40.00 80.00

2005-06 ITG Ultimate Memorabilia Double Autos

PRINT RUN 34 SER.#'d SETS
1 D.Phaneuf/B.Leetch 30.00 60.00
2 P.Roy/A.Esposito 50.00 125.00
3 P.Esposito/G.Cheevers 25.00 50.00
4 P.Henderson/V.Tretiak 30.00 60.00
5 A.Niittymaki/B.Parent 15.00 40.00
6 M.Brodeur/P.Roy 75.00 200.00
7 D.Keon/T.Kennedy 30.00 60.00
8 M.Lemieux/J.Beliveau 75.00 125.00
9 Lundqvist/Giacomin 30.00 60.00
10 S.Yzerman/T.Lindsay 40.00 80.00
11 B.Salming/L.Robinson 20.00 40.00
12 A.Ovechkin/E.Malkin 75.00 150.00
13 G.Hall/T.Esposito 25.00 50.00
14 M.Lemieux/R.Francis 75.00 125.00
15 T.Esposito/P.Esposito 25.00 50.00
16 M.Schmidt/E.Lach 20.00 40.00
17 C.Huet/P.Roy 50.00 125.00
18 P.Coffey/G.Fuhr 25.00 50.00
19 D.Heatley/I.Kovalchuk 20.00 40.00
20 Cournoyer/Henderson 30.00 60.00

2005-06 ITG Ultimate Memorabilia Double Memorabilia

ANNOUNCED PRINT RUN 25
1 Martin Brodeur
2 Eric Lindros 20.00 50.00
3 Vladislav Tretiak 25.00 50.00
4 Patrick Roy 30.00 60.00
5 Guy Lafleur 12.00 30.00
6 Stan Mikita
7 Brett Hull 12.00 30.00
8 Cam Neely
9 Marcel Dionne 12.00 30.00
10 Bernie Parent 15.00 40.00
11 Borje Salming
12 Jose Theodore 10.00 25.00
13 Dave Keon 15.00 40.00
14 Paul Coffey 12.00 30.00
15 Raymond Bourque
16 Steve Yzerman 30.00 60.00
17 Mario Lemieux 40.00 80.00
18 Jacques Plante 15.00 40.00
19 Eddie Shore 12.00 30.00
20 Bobby Hull 12.00 30.00
21 Bobby Clarke 15.00 40.00
22 Grant Fuhr 12.00 30.00
23 Sidney Crosby 40.00 80.00
24 Alexander Ovechkin 25.00 60.00
25 Tony Esposito 10.00 25.00

2005-06 ITG Ultimate Memorabilia Double Memorabilia Autos

PRINT RUN 34 SER.#'d SETS
1 Ovechkin/Malkin 100.00 200.00
2 Brodeur/Roy 125.00 250.00
3 P. Esposito/Cheevers 40.00 80.00
4 Phaneuf/Leetch 30.00 75.00
5 Lundqvist/Giacomin 30.00 75.00
6 Yzerman/Lindsay 40.00 100.00
7 Keon/Kennedy 25.00 60.00
8 Lemieux/Beliveau 50.00 125.00
9 Niittymaki/Parent 25.00 60.00
10 Esposito/Esposito 40.00 80.00
11 Coffey/Fuhr 20.00 50.00
12 Hall/T.Esposito 25.00 60.00
13 LaFontaine/Perreault 25.00 60.00
14 Sittler/McDonald 25.00 50.00
15 Mahovlich/Richard 40.00 80.00
16 Hextall/Parent
17 Hull/Mikita 30.00 75.00
18 Tretiak/Cournoyer 50.00 100.00
19 Gilmour/Clark 25.00 60.00
20 Bossy/Lafleur 25.00 60.00

2005-06 ITG Ultimate Memorabilia First Overall Jerseys

PRINT RUN 25 SER.#'d SETS
1 Gilbert Perreault 20.00 40.00
2 Guy Lafleur 20.00 40.00
3 Denis Potvin 20.00 40.00
4 Dale Hawerchuk 20.00 40.00
5 Mario Lemieux 40.00 80.00
6 Wendel Clark 20.00 40.00
7 Marc-Andre Fleury 20.00 50.00
8 Alexander Ovechkin 40.00 80.00
9 Sidney Crosby 75.00 150.00

2005-06 ITG Ultimate Memorabilia First Rounders Jerseys

PRINT RUN 25 SER.#'d SETS
1 Mario/Perr/Guy/Hawer 50.00 100.00
2 Fleury/Mario/Crosby/Malk 100.00 200.00
3 Fuhr/Leetch/Yzerm/Savard 40.00 80.00
4 Dionne/Lafleur/Bossy/Sittler 40.00 80.00
5 Brodr/Lehtn/Montya/Fleury 40.00 80.00
6 Mario/Crosby/Malkin/AO 75.00 150.00
7 Neely/Phaneuf/Getzlaf/Ward 40.00 80.00
8 Brque/Leetch/Phnf/Pitkanen 40.00 80.00
9 Bourq/Goul/Hawer/Mario 40.00 80.00
10 Yzer/AO/Perry/Rich 50.00 100.00

2005-06 ITG Ultimate Memorabilia Future Stars Autographs

PRINT RUN 40 SER.#'d SETS
1 Marc-Andre Fleury 15.00 40.00
2 Henrik Lundqvist 20.00 50.00
3 Marek Svatos 8.00 20.00
4 Ray Emery 10.00 25.00
5 Cam Ward 15.00 40.00
6 Sidney Crosby 100.00 175.00
7 Alexander Ovechkin 50.00 100.00
8 Evgeni Malkin 60.00 125.00
9 Cristobal Huet 12.00 30.00
10 Thomas Vanek 15.00 40.00
11 Al Montoya 8.00 20.00
12 Dion Phaneuf 20.00 50.00
13 Ryan Getzlaf 12.00 30.00
14 Marek Schwarz 8.00 20.00
15 David Ruzicka 8.00 20.00
16 Jason LaBarbera 8.00 20.00
17 Mike Richards 15.00 40.00
18 Petr Prucha 12.00 30.00
19 Angelo Esposito 20.00 50.00
20 Michael Frolik 12.00 30.00
21 Eric Nystrom 8.00 20.00
22 Antero Niittymaki 12.00 30.00

2005-06 ITG Ultimate Memorabilia Future Stars Jerseys

PRINT RUN 25 SER.#'d SETS
1 Marc-Andre Fleury 30.00 60.00
2 Henrik Lundqvist 20.00 50.00
3 Marek Svatos 20.00 40.00
4 Ray Emery 20.00 40.00
5 Cam Ward 25.00 50.00
6 Sidney Crosby 60.00 150.00
7 Alexander Ovechkin 25.00 60.00
8 Evgeni Malkin 30.00 80.00
9 Antero Niittymaki 20.00 40.00
10 Thomas Vanek 20.00 40.00
11 Al Montoya
12 Dion Phaneuf 30.00 60.00
13 Ryan Getzlaf 20.00 40.00
14 Corey Perry 20.00 40.00
15 Marek Schwarz 10.00 25.00
16 David Ruzicka 10.00 25.00
17 Jason LaBarbera 10.00 25.00
18 Mike Richards 20.00 40.00
19 Petr Prucha 25.00 50.00

2005-06 ITG Ultimate Memorabilia Future Stars Memorabilia Autographs

ANNOUNCED PRINT RUN 40
1 Marc-Andre Fleury 15.00 40.00
2 Henrik Lundqvist 30.00 60.00
3 Marek Svatos 10.00 25.00
4 Ray Emery 10.00 25.00
5 Cam Ward 12.00 30.00
6 Sidney Crosby 125.00 200.00
7 Alexander Ovechkin 75.00 125.00
8 Evgeni Malkin 75.00 200.00
9 Antero Niittymaki 12.00 30.00
10 Thomas Vanek 25.00 50.00
11 Al Montoya 10.00 25.00
12 Dion Phaneuf 20.00 50.00
13 Ryan Getzlaf 12.00 30.00
14 Marek Schwarz 10.00 25.00
15 David Ruzicka 10.00 25.00
16 Jason LaBarbera 10.00 25.00
17 Mike Richards 12.00 30.00
18 Petr Prucha 12.00 30.00

2005-06 ITG Ultimate Memorabilia Gloves Are Off

PRINT RUN 25 SER.#'d SETS
1 Sidney Crosby 60.00 125.00
2 Alexander Ovechkin 40.00 80.00
3 Mario Lemieux 40.00 80.00
4 Paul Coffey 20.00 40.00
5 Maurice Richard 50.00 100.00
6 Steve Yzerman 30.00 60.00
7 Raymond Bourque 25.00 50.00
8 Patrick Roy 40.00 80.00
9 Cam Neely 25.00 50.00
10 Brett Hull 25.00 50.00
11 King Clancy 20.00 40.00
12 Glenn Hall 20.00 40.00
13 Jacques Plante 30.00 60.00
14 Ace Bailey 20.00 40.00
15 Charlie Conacher 20.00 40.00
16 Bill Durnan 20.00 40.00
17 Stan Mikita 20.00 40.00
18 Eddie Shore 25.00 50.00
19 Howie Morenz 40.00 80.00
20 Aurel Joliat 20.00 40.00

2005-06 ITG Ultimate Memorabilia Goalie Gear

PRINT RUN 25 SER.#'d SETS
1 Bernie Parent 20.00 50.00
2 Bill Durnan 20.00 50.00
3 Billy Smith 20.00 50.00
4 Ed Giacomin 20.00 50.00
5 Frank Brimsek 20.00 50.00
6 George Hainsworth 25.00 60.00
7 Gerry Cheevers 20.00 50.00
8 Glenn Hall 15.00 40.00
9 Gump Worsley 20.00 50.00
10 Harry Lumley 15.00 50.00
11 Jacques Plante 40.00 80.00
12 Johnny Bower 20.00 50.00
13 Martin Brodeur 25.00 60.00
14 Patrick Roy MON 50.00 100.00
15 Patrick Roy COL 30.00 80.00
16 Pelle Lindbergh 25.00 60.00
17 Jose Theodore 15.00 40.00
18 Ron Hextall 15.00 40.00
19 Tiny Thompson 20.00 50.00
20 Tony Esposito 20.00 50.00

2005-06 ITG Ultimate Memorabilia Jersey Autos

PRINT RUN 50 SER.#'d SETS
1 Martin Brodeur 40.00 80.00
2 Marcel Dionne 12.00 30.00
3 Bobby Clarke 20.00 40.00
4 Phil Esposito 20.00 40.00
5 Tony Esposito 20.00 40.00
6 Ed Giacomin 20.00 40.00
7 Rod Gilbert 12.00 30.00
8 Doug Gilmour 12.00 30.00
9 Glenn Hall 15.00 40.00
10 Dany Heatley 20.00 40.00
11 Bobby Hull 25.00 50.00
12 Brett Hull
13 Dave Keon 25.00 50.00
14 Ilya Kovalchuk 20.00 50.00
15 Guy Lafleur 20.00 40.00
16 Brian Leetch 12.00 30.00
17 Mario Lemieux 50.00 100.00
18 Eric Lindros 20.00 40.00
19 Frank Mahovlich 20.00 40.00
20 Stan Mikita 20.00 40.00
21 Jean Beliveau 25.00 50.00
22 Gilbert Perreault 20.00 40.00
23 Henri Richard 20.00 40.00
24 Larry Robinson 12.00 30.00
25 Patrick Roy 50.00 100.00
26 Borje Salming 20.00 40.00
27 Jose Theodore 25.00 50.00
28 Vladislav Tretiak 40.00 80.00
29 Gump Worsley 20.00 40.00
30 Steve Yzerman 40.00 100.00
31 Wendel Clark 20.00 40.00
32 Brad Park 12.00 30.00
33 Denis Potvin 12.00 30.00
34 Lanny McDonald 12.00 30.00
35 Terry O'Reilly 12.00 30.00
36 Alexander Ovechkin 75.00 125.00
37 Sidney Crosby 125.00 200.00
38 Henrik Lundqvist 25.00 60.00
39 Marek Svatos 20.00 40.00
40 Antero Niittymaki 20.00 40.00

2005-06 ITG Ultimate Memorabilia Jerseys

ANNOUNCED PRINT RUN 25
1 Alexander Ovechkin 40.00 80.00
2 Bernie Parent 15.00 30.00
3 Bobby Clarke 20.00 40.00
4 Bobby Hull 15.00 30.00
5 Brett Hull 15.00 30.00
6 Brian Leetch 15.00 30.00
7 Bryan Trottier 15.00 30.00
8 Cam Neely 15.00 30.00
9 Darryl Sittler 15.00 30.00
10 Dave Keon 20.00 40.00
11 Denis Potvin 15.00 30.00
12 Doug Gilmour 15.00 30.00
13 Evgeni Malkin 30.00 80.00
14 Frank Mahovlich 15.00 30.00
15 Gilbert Perreault 20.00 40.00
16 Guy Lafleur 20.00 40.00
17 Henri Richard 15.00 30.00
18 Jacques Plante 25.00 50.00
19 Jari Kurri 25.00 50.00
20 Jean Beliveau 20.00 40.00
21 Jose Theodore 20.00 40.00
22 Lanny McDonald 20.00 40.00
23 Marcel Dionne 15.00 30.00
24 Mario Lemieux 40.00 80.00
25 Martin Brodeur 25.00 50.00
26 Mike Bossy 15.00 30.00
27 Pat LaFontaine 15.00 30.00
28 Patrick Roy
29 Paul Coffey 15.00 30.00
30 Phil Esposito 15.00 30.00
31 Raymond Bourque 20.00 40.00
32 Rod Gilbert 15.00 30.00
33 Ron Hextall 20.00 50.00
34 Sidney Crosby 60.00 125.00
35 Stan Mikita 20.00 40.00
36 Steve Yzerman 30.00 60.00
37 Terry Sawchuk
38 Tony Esposito 15.00 30.00
39 Wendel Clark 15.00 30.00

2005-06 ITG Ultimate Memorabilia Passing the Torch Jerseys

COMMON CARD 30.00 60.00
PRINT RUN 25 SER.#'d SETS
1 Rocket/Mario/Sid 150.00 250.00
2 Plante/Roy/Theo 90.00 150.00
3 Kharlamov/Krutov/AO 40.00 80.00
4 Sawchuk/Fuhr/Brod 60.00 100.00
5 Tiny/Cheesy/Gilbert 40.00 80.00
6 Shore/Park/Bourque 60.00 100.00
7 Bower/Cheesy/Roy 75.00 125.00
8 Harvey/Savard/Robin 30.00 60.00
9 Worters/Giaco/Richt 30.00 60.00
10 Lindsay/Delv/Yzer 60.00 100.00
11 Mosien/Mikita/Sav 30.00 80.00
12 Hull/Hull/Hull 40.00 80.00
13 Joliat/Beliveau/Guy 60.00 100.00
14 Gardiner/Hall/TonyO 40.00 80.00
15 Parent/Pelle/Hexy 50.00 100.00
16 Horton/Borje/Leetch 20.00 50.00
17 Fergie/Schultz/Probt 40.00 80.00
18 Roy/Brodeur/Fleury 50.00 125.00
19 Keon/Trots/Gilmour 30.00 60.00
20 Perreault/LaF/ Vanek 30.00 60.00

2005-06 ITG Ultimate Memorabilia R.O.Y. Autos

PRINT RUN 39 SER.#'d SETS
1 Brian Leetch 20.00 40.00
2 Denis Potvin 15.00 30.00
3 Thomas Vanek 20.00 40.00
4 Cam Ward 20.00 40.00
5 Dion Phaneuf 30.00 60.00
6 Sidney Crosby 125.00 250.00
7 Mike Richards 15.00 30.00
8 Henrik Lundqvist 25.00 50.00
9 Petr Prucha 10.00 25.00
10 Jason LaBarbera 10.00 25.00
11 Dany Heatley 20.00 40.00
12 Dave Keon 25.00 50.00
13 Tony Esposito 20.00 40.00
14 Martin Brodeur 40.00 80.00
15 Marek Svatos 10.00 25.00
16 Gilbert Perreault 15.00 30.00
17 Raymond Bourque 25.00 50.00
18 Mario Lemieux 60.00 125.00
19 Antero Niittymaki 15.00 30.00
20 Alexander Ovechkin 60.00 120.00

2005-06 ITG Ultimate Memorabilia R.O.Y. Jerseys

ANNOUNCED PRINT RUN 25
1 Dave Keon 6.00 15.00
2 Tony Esposito 6.00 15.00
3 Gilbert Perreault 6.00 15.00
4 Raymond Bourque 10.00 25.00
5 Mario Lemieux 20.00 50.00
6 Brian Leetch 6.00 15.00
7 Martin Brodeur 12.00 30.00
8 Dany Heatley 6.00 15.00
9 Alexander Ovechkin 25.00 60.00
10 Sidney Crosby 25.00 60.00
11 Henrik Lundqvist 25.00 60.00
12 Dion Phaneuf 10.00 25.00
13 Petr Prucha 6.00 15.00
14 Marek Svatos 5.00 12.00
15 Thomas Vanek 12.00 30.00

2005-06 ITG Ultimate Memorabilia Raised to the Rafters

PRINT RUN 25 SER.#'d SETS
1 Mario Lemieux 50.00 125.00
2 Henri Richard 12.00 30.00
3 Grant Fuhr 15.00 40.00
4 Bobby Clarke 15.00 40.00
5 Darryl Sittler 12.00 30.00
6 Mike Bossy 12.00 30.00
7 Pat LaFontaine 15.00 40.00
8 Gilbert Perreault 15.00 40.00
9 Bernie Parent 15.00 40.00
10 Denis Potvin 15.00 40.00
11 Alex Delvecchio 15.00 40.00
12 Yvan Cournoyer 15.00 40.00
13 Lanny McDonald 15.00 40.00
14 Tim Horton 20.00 50.00
15 Patrick Roy 40.00 100.00
16 Raymond Bourque 25.00 60.00
17 Cam Neely 15.00 40.00
18 Stan Mikita 20.00 50.00
19 Bobby Hull 25.00 60.00
20 Jean Beliveau 15.00 40.00

2005-06 ITG Ultimate Memorabilia Record Breakers Jerseys

PRINT RUN 25 SER.#'d SETS
1 Newsy Lalonde
Reggie Leach
2 Bobby Hull 12.00 30.00
Phil Esposito
3 Elmer Lach
Ted Lindsay
4 Jean Beliveau
Stan Mikita
5 Bill Mosienko
Dale Hawerchuk
6 Patrick Roy 20.00 50.00
Martin Brodeur
7 Bobby Hull
Steve Shutt
8 Guy Lafleur
Mike Bossy
9 Jari Kurri 15.00 40.00
Brett Hull
10 Darryl Sittler
Bryan Trottier
11 George Hainsworth
Terry Sawchuk
12 Terry Sawchuk
Patrick Roy
13 Grant Fuhr 20.00 50.00
Patrick Roy
14 Terry Sawchuk
Bernie Parent
15 Tony Esposito
Patrick Roy
16 Stan Mikita
Phil Esposito
17 Nels Stewart 30.00 60.00
Maurice Richard
18 Paul Coffey
Raymond Bourque
19 Dave Schultz 20.00 50.00
Tiger Williams
20 Denis Potvin
Paul Coffey

2005-06 ITG Ultimate Memorabilia Retro Teammates Jerseys

COMPLETE SET (30)
PRINT RUN 25 SER.#'d SETS
1 Bossy/Trottier 15.00 30.00
2 Shore/Thompson 20.00 40.00
3 Smith/Potvin 20.00 40.00
4 Lindsay/Abel 15.00 30.00
5 Coffey/Lemieux 30.00 75.00
6 Kurri/Fuhr 25.00 50.00
7 Hainsworth/Joliat 25.00 50.00
8 Clarke/Parent 20.00 40.00
9 Sittler/Salming 15.00 30.00
10 Beliveau/Mahovlich 20.00 40.00
11 Gilmour/Clark 20.00 40.00
12 H.Richard/F.Mahovlich 20.00 40.00
13 Lafleur/Cournoyer 20.00 40.00
14 Roy/Robinson 30.00 60.00
15 Beliveau/Harvey 20.00 50.00
16 Shutt/Lafleur 20.00 40.00
17 Cheevers/O'Reilly 15.00 30.00
18 Roy/Bourque 30.00 60.00
19 Neely/Bourque 20.00 50.00
20 Horton/Kelly
21 Ratelle/Giacomin 15.00 30.00
22 Esposito/Gilbert
23 Esposito/Savard 15.00 30.00
24 Delvecchio/Ullman 15.00 30.00
25 Ciccarelli/Yzerman 20.00 50.00
26 Goulet/Savard 15.00 30.00
27 Mikita/Hull
28 Mosienko/Lumley 15.00 30.00
29 Richter/Leetch 15.00 30.00
30 Kharlamov/Tretiak 15.00 40.00

2005-06 ITG Ultimate Memorabilia Stick Autographs

ANNOUNCED PRINT RUN 50
1 Jean Beliveau 25.00 50.00
2 Raymond Bourque 15.00 40.00
3 Martin Brodeur 40.00 80.00
4 Marcel Dionne 15.00 30.00
5 Phil Esposito 20.00 40.00
6 Grant Fuhr 15.00 40.00
7 Gerry Cheevers 15.00 40.00
8 Glenn Hall 20.00 40.00
9 Dany Heatley 20.00 40.00
10 Ron Francis 25.00 50.00
11 Red Kelly 25.00 50.00
12 Dave Keon 20.00 40.00
13 Ilya Kovalchuk 25.00 50.00
14 Vladimir Krutov 20.00 40.00
15 Guy Lafleur 15.00 40.00
16 Brian Leetch 15.00 30.00
17 Mario Lemieux 50.00 100.00
18 Eric Lindros 20.00 40.00
19 Petr Prucha 20.00 40.00
20 Cam Neely 15.00 40.00
21 Bernie Parent 15.00 30.00
22 Gilbert Perreault 20.00 40.00
23 Jose Theodore 15.00 40.00
24 Gump Worsley 20.00 40.00
25 Steve Yzerman 40.00 80.00
26 Marek Svatos 20.00 40.00
27 Paul Coffey 15.00 30.00
28 Bill Barber 15.00 30.00
29 Marc-Andre Fleury 25.00 50.00
30 Alexander Ovechkin 75.00 125.00
31 Sidney Crosby 125.00 250.00
32 Ed Giacomin 20.00 40.00
33 Antero Niittymaki 20.00 40.00
34 Frank Mahovlich 20.00 40.00
35 Patrick Roy 50.00 100.00
36 Wendel Clark 15.00 30.00
37 Denis Potvin 15.00 30.00
38 Doug Gilmour 20.00 40.00
39 Lanny McDonald 20.00 40.00
40 Stan Mikita 15.00 30.00

2005-06 ITG Ultimate Memorabilia Sticks and Jerseys

PRINT RUN 25 SER.#'d SETS
1 Mario Lemieux 30.00 60.00
2 Steve Yzerman 30.00 60.00
3 Ilya Kovalchuk 12.00 30.00
4 Phil Esposito 12.00 30.00
5 Eric Lindros 12.00 30.00
6 Alexander Ovechkin 30.00 60.00
7 Sidney Crosby 60.00 100.00
8 Doug Harvey 15.00 40.00
9 Dany Heatley 12.00 30.00
10 Jean Beliveau 15.00 40.00
11 Guy Lafleur 12.00 30.00
12 Pat LaFontaine 12.00 30.00
13 Jari Kurri 12.00 30.00
14 Red Kelly 12.00 30.00
15 Lanny McDonald 12.00 30.00
16 Cam Neely 12.00 30.00
17 Mark Howe 12.00 30.00
18 Paul Coffey 12.00 30.00
19 Denis Potvin 12.00 30.00
20 Steve Shutt 12.00 30.00
21 Gump Worsley 12.00 30.00
22 Roger Crozier 12.00 30.00
23 Ed Giacomin 12.00 30.00
24 Grant Fuhr 12.00 30.00
25 Marc-Andre Fleury 15.00 40.00
26 Tony Esposito 15.00 40.00
27 Patrick Roy
28 Martin Brodeur 20.00 50.00
29 Ron Hextall 12.00 30.00
30 Jacques Plante 15.00 40.00

2005-06 ITG Ultimate Memorabilia Three Stars of the Game Jerseys

PRINT RUN 25 SER.#'d SETS
1 Shore/Tiny/ Joliat 25.00 60.00
2 Harvey/Kennedy/Durnan 20.00 50.00
3 Brimsek/Mosienko/Abel 20.00 50.00
4 Plante/Lind/H.Richard
5 Geoff/Moore/Horton 20.00 50.00
6 Big M/Bob. Hull/Kelly 20.00 50.00
7 Delvec/Keon/Ullman 20.00 50.00
8 Gump/Beliveau/Bower 30.00 60.00
9 Crozier/Hall/Mikita 20.00 50.00
10 Ratelle/Giaco/Bucyk 20.00 50.00
11 Lafleur/Shutt/Cheev 20.00 50.00
12 Terry O/Tony O/Park 20.00 50.00
13 Sittler/Savard/Courn 20.00 50.00
14 Espo/Nystrom/Gilbert 20.00 50.00
15 Perreault/Clarke/Leach 20.00 50.00
16 Smith/Anderson/Trottier 20.00 50.00
17 Kurri/Lanny/Fuhr 50.00
18 Roy/Robinson/Middle. 30.00 60.00
19 Tiger/Dionne/R. Brod 20.00 50.00
20 Potvin/Verbeek/Bossy 20.00 50.00
21 Salming/Savard/Vaive 20.00 50.00
22 Yzer./Gilmour/Clark 30.00 60.00
23 Richter/McL./Leetch 20.00 50.00
24 Bourque/Brodeur/Roy 75.00 125.00
25 Dion/Sid/Ovechkin 40.00 100.00

2005-06 ITG Ultimate Memorabilia Triple Threads Jerseys

PRINT RUN 25 SER.#'d SETS
1 A.O./Crosby/Malkin 50.00 120.00
2 Brodeur/Roy/Fleury 60.00 100.00
3 Yzerman/Mario/Cam 50.00 100.00
4 Smith/Hextall/Fuhr 25.00 60.00
5 Bourque/Robin/Potvin 25.00 60.00
6 Bob Hull/Big M/Ullman 25.00 60.00
7 H.Richard/Keon/Mikita 20.00 50.00
8 Bower/Hall/Plante 40.00 80.00
9 Parent/Cheev/T.Espo 40.00 80.00
10 Lafleur/Dionne/Perr 25.00 60.00

2005-06 ITG Ultimate Memorabilia Ultimate Autos

ANNOUNCED PRINT RUN 50
1 Steve Yzerman 25.00 60.00
2 Gump Worsley 20.00 40.00
3 Valeri Vasilyev 15.00 30.00
4 Vladislav Tretiak 25.00 50.00
5 Darryl Sittler 15.00 30.00
6 Tod Sloan 10.00 25.00
7 Milt Schmidt 15.00 30.00
8 Borje Salming 20.00 40.00
9 Patrick Roy 40.00 100.00
10 Larry Robinson 10.00 25.00
11 Henri Richard 15.00 30.00
12 Jean Ratelle 10.00 25.00
13 Gilbert Perreault 15.00 30.00
14 Bernie Parent 20.00 40.00
15 Cam Neely 20.00 40.00
16 Stan Mikita 15.00 30.00
17 Frank Mahovlich 15.00 30.00
18 Ted Lindsay
19 Eric Lindros 20.00 40.00
20 Mario Lemieux 40.00 100.00
21 Brian Leetch 10.00 25.00
22 Pat LaFontaine 15.00 30.00
23 Guy Lafleur 20.00 40.00
24 Elmer Lach 20.00 40.00
25 Vladimir Krutov 12.50 30.00
26 Alexander Yakushev 20.00 40.00
27 Dave Keon 20.00 40.00
28 Ted Kennedy 10.00 25.00
29 Red Kelly 10.00 25.00
30 Brett Hull 10.00 25.00
31 Bobby Hull 12.00 30.00
32 Paul Henderson 10.00 25.00
33 Dany Heatley 15.00 30.00
34 Glenn Hall 15.00 30.00
35 Doug Gilmour 20.00 40.00
36 Rod Gilbert 10.00 25.00
37 Ed Giacomin 10.00 25.00
38 Grant Fuhr 25.00 50.00
39 Tony Esposito 15.00 30.00
40 Phil Esposito 15.00 30.00
41 Bobby Clarke 15.00 30.00
42 Marcel Dionne 10.00 25.00
43 Paul Coffey 20.00 40.00
44 Jim Craig 15.00 40.00
45 Yvan Cournoyer 15.00 30.00
46 Gerry Cheevers 20.00 40.00
47 Martin Brodeur 30.00 80.00
48 Raymond Bourque 20.00 40.00
49 Mike Bossy 15.00 30.00
50 Jean Beliveau 20.00 50.00

2005-06 ITG Ultimate Memorabilia Ultimate Hero Double Jerseys

ANNOUNCED PRINT RUN 20
1 Terry Sawchuk 25.00 50.00
2 Maurice Richard
3 Jacques Plante
4 Dave Keon 12.00 30.00
5 Mario Lemieux 20.00 50.00
6 Patrick Roy 15.00 40.00
7 Martin Brodeur 12.00 30.00
8 Steve Yzerman 15.00 40.00

2005-06 ITG Ultimate Memorabilia Ultimate Hero Single Jerseys

ANNOUNCED PRINT RUN 20
1 Terry Sawchuk
2 Maurice Richard 20.00 40.00
3 Jacques Plante 25.00 50.00
4 Dave Keon 6.00 15.00
5 Mario Lemieux 20.00 50.00
6 Patrick Roy 15.00 40.00
7 Martin Brodeur 12.00 30.00
8 Steve Yzerman 15.00 40.00

2005-06 ITG Ultimate Memorabilia Ultimate Hero Triple Jerseys

ANNOUNCED PRINT RUN 25
1 Terry Sawchuk
2 Maurice Richard
3 Jacques Plante 25.00 60.00
4 Dave Keon
5 Mario Lemieux
6 Patrick Roy
7 Martin Brodeur
8 Steve Yzerman 30.00 80.00

2005-06 ITG Ultimate Memorabilia Vintage Lumber

ANNOUNCED PRINT RUN 25
1 Howie Morenz 50.00 100.00
2 Georges Vezina 60.00 125.00
3 Jacques Plante 30.00 80.00
4 Henri Richard 15.00 40.00
5 Maurice Richard 50.00 100.00
6 Terry Sawchuk 60.00 120.00
7 Bernie Geoffrion 15.00 40.00
8 Joe Primeau 15.00 40.00
9 Red Kelly 15.00 40.00
10 Doug Harvey 15.00 40.00
11 Stan Mikita 20.00 50.00
12 Johnny Bucyk 15.00 40.00
13 Glenn Hall 20.00 50.00
14 Bill Durnan 15.00 40.00
15 Jean Beliveau 20.00 50.00
16 Bobby Hull 40.00 100.00
17 Harry Lumley 20.00 50.00
18 Ed Giacomin 15.00 40.00
19 Dave Keon 25.00 60.00
20 Alex Delvecchio 15.00 40.00
21 Turk Broda 15.00 40.00
22 Tim Horton 25.00 60.00
23 Bob Davidson 12.00 30.00
24 Frank Mahovlich 15.00 40.00
25 Phil Esposito 15.00 40.00
26 Emile Francis 15.00 40.00
27 King Clancy 25.00 60.00
28 Bill Barilko 40.00 80.00

29 Gump Worsley 15.00 40.00
30 Roger Crozier 12.00 30.00

2006-07 ITG Ultimate Memorabilia

1 Ace Bailey 3.00 8.00
2 Al Montoya 4.00 10.00
3 Alex Connell 3.00 8.00
4 Alex Delvecchio 4.00 10.00
5 Alexander Ovechkin 8.00 20.00
6 Anders Hedberg 3.00 8.00
7 Angelo Esposito 8.00 20.00
8 Antero Niittymaki 3.00 8.00
9 Art Ross 4.00 10.00
10 Aurel Joliat 5.00 12.00
11 Babe Pratt 4.00 10.00
12 Bernie Geoffrion 5.00 12.00
13 Bernie Parent 4.00 10.00
14 Bill Barber 3.00 8.00
15 Bill Barilko 4.00 10.00
16 Bill Durnan 4.00 10.00
17 Bobby Clarke 4.00 10.00
18 Bobby Hull 5.00 12.00
19 Borje Salming 4.00 10.00
20 Brad Park 3.00 8.00
21 Brett Hull 5.00 12.00
22 Brian Leetch 4.00 10.00
23 Bryan Trottier 4.00 10.00
24 Butch Bouchard 3.00 8.00
25 Cam Neely 5.00 12.00
26 Cam Ward 5.00 12.00
27 Charlie Conacher 4.00 10.00
28 Charlie Gardiner 3.00 8.00
29 Ching Johnson 3.00 8.00
30 Chris Chelios 5.00 12.00
31 Clarence Campbell 3.00 8.00
32 Conn Smythe 3.00 8.00
33 Cristobal Huet 5.00 12.00
34 Cyclone Taylor 12.00 30.00
35 Dany Heatley 6.00 15.00
36 Darryl Sittler 5.00 12.00
37 Dave Keon 6.00 15.00
38 Dave Schultz 3.00 8.00
39 Denis Potvin 4.00 10.00
40 Dion Phaneuf 6.00 15.00
41 Dominik Hasek 6.00 15.00
42 Doug Gilmour 5.00 12.00
43 Ed Belfour 4.00 10.00
44 Ed Giacomin 4.00 10.00
45 Ed Olczyk 3.00 8.00
46 Eddie Shore 4.00 10.00
47 Eric Staal 3.00 8.00
48 Evgeni Malkin 8.00 20.00
49 Foster Hewitt 3.00 8.00
50 Frank Calder 3.00 8.00
51 Frank Mahovlich 4.00 10.00
52 George Hainsworth 6.00 15.00
53 Georges Vezina 6.00 15.00
54 Gerry Cheevers 5.00 12.00
55 Gilbert Brule 3.00 8.00
56 Gilbert Perreault 5.00 12.00
57 Glenn Hall 5.00 12.00
58 Grant Fuhr 6.00 15.00
59 Gump Worsley 4.00 10.00
60 Guy Lafleur 5.00 12.00
61 Guy Lapointe 3.00 8.00
62 Hap Day 3.00 8.00
63 Henri Richard 4.00 10.00
64 Henrik Lundqvist 6.00 15.00
65 Henrik Zetterberg 8.00 20.00
66 Herb Carnegie 15.00 40.00
67 Hobey Baker 4.00 10.00
68 Howie Morenz 6.00 15.00
69 Igor Larionov 3.00 8.00
70 Jack Adams 3.00 8.00
71 Jacques Plante 6.00 15.00
72 Jari Kurri 5.00 12.00
73 Jaromir Jagr 6.00 15.00
74 Jason Spezza 5.00 12.00
75 Jean Beliveau 5.00 12.00
76 Jean Ratelle 3.00 8.00
77 Joe Malone 4.00 10.00
78 Joe Sakic 8.00 20.00
79 Joe Thornton 8.00 20.00
80 John Bucyk 4.00 10.00
81 John Tavares 10.00 25.00
82 Johnny Bower 5.00 12.00
83 Jordan Staal 6.00 15.00
84 Kari Lehtonen 4.00 10.00
85 Lady Byng 3.00 8.00
86 Lanny McDonald 4.00 10.00
87 Larry Robinson 4.00 10.00
88 Lester Patrick 3.00 8.00
89 Lionel Conacher 3.00 8.00
90 Ilya Kovalchuk 6.00 15.00
91 Lord Stanley 4.00 10.00
92 Luc Robitaille 5.00 12.00
93 Lynn Patrick 3.00 8.00
94 Marc-Andre Fleury 6.00 15.00
95 Marcel Dionne 4.00 10.00
96 Mario Lemieux 10.00 25.00
97 Mark Messier 5.00 12.00
98 Martin Brodeur 8.00 20.00
99 Marty Turco 3.00 8.00
100 Mats Naslund 4.00 10.00
101 Maurice Richard 6.00 15.00
102 Max Bentley 4.00 10.00
103 Michel Goulet 3.00 8.00
104 Mike Bossy 5.00 12.00
105 Mike Modano 5.00 12.00
106 Milt Schmidt 4.00 10.00
107 Newsy Lalonde 5.00 12.00
108 Nicklas Lidstrom 4.00 10.00
109 Pat LaFontaine 4.00 10.00
110 Patrick Roy Colorado 10.00 25.00
111 Patrick Roy Montreal 12.00 30.00
112 Paul Coffey 4.00 10.00
113 Paul Henderson 3.00 8.00
114 Pelle Lindbergh 5.00 12.00
115 Peter Stastny 3.00 8.00
116 Phil Esposito 5.00 12.00
117 Phil Kessel 5.00 12.00
118 Punch Imlach 3.00 8.00
119 Raymond Bourque 6.00 15.00
120 Red Kelly 3.00 8.00
121 Roberto Luongo 6.00 15.00
122 Rod Gilbert 3.00 8.00
123 Rogie Vachon 4.00 10.00
124 Ron Francis 4.00 10.00
125 Ron Hextall 4.00 10.00
126 Ryan Miller 4.00 10.00
127 Scotty Bowman 5.00 12.00
128 Serge Savard 4.00 10.00
129 Sid Abel 3.00 8.00
130 Stan Mikita 5.00 12.00
131 Steve Shutt 3.00 8.00
132 Steve Yzerman 10.00 25.00
133 Syl Apps 4.00 10.00
134 Ted Kennedy 4.00 10.00
135 Ted Lindsay 4.00 10.00
136 Terry Sawchuk 6.00 15.00
137 Tiger Williams 5.00 12.00
138 Tim Horton 5.00 12.00
139 Tiny Thompson 5.00 12.00
140 Toe Blake 3.00 8.00
141 Tom Barrasso 4.00 10.00
142 Tommy Ivan 3.00 8.00
143 Tony Esposito 5.00 12.00
144 Turk Broda 4.00 10.00
145 Ulf Nilsson 3.00 8.00
146 Valeri Kharlamov 5.00 12.00
147 Vladislav Tretiak 6.00 15.00
148 Wendel Clark 4.00 10.00
149 Willie O'Ree 3.00 8.00
150 Yvan Cournoyer 4.00 10.00

2006-07 ITG Ultimate Memorabilia Autographs

STATED PRINT RUN 50
1 Bill Barber 10.00 25.00
2 Jean Beliveau 20.00 50.00
3 Martin Brodeur 20.00 50.00
4 Chris Chelios 10.00 25.00
5 Wendel Clark 12.00 30.00
6 Paul Coffey 12.00 30.00
7 Bobby Clarke 12.00 30.00
8 Alex Delvecchio 10.00 25.00
9 Marcel Dionne 10.00 25.00
10 Angelo Esposito 30.00 60.00
11 Phil Esposito 15.00 40.00
12 Tony Esposito 15.00 40.00
13 Doug Gilmour 12.00 30.00
14 Michel Goulet 12.00 30.00
15 Glenn Hall 12.00 30.00
16 Bobby Hull 15.00 40.00
17 Brett Hull 15.00 40.00
18 Jaromir Jagr 20.00 50.00
19 Dave Keon 15.00 40.00
20 Jari Kurri 20.00 50.00
21 Guy Lafleur 15.00 40.00
22 Pat LaFontaine 12.00 30.00
23 Lanny McDonald 10.00 25.00
24 Ted Lindsay 10.00 25.00
25 Mark Messier 30.00 80.00
26 Stan Mikita 15.00 40.00
27 Cam Neely 12.00 30.00
28 Brad Park 10.00 25.00
29 Gilbert Perreault 12.00 30.00
30 Larry Robinson 10.00 25.00
31 Darryl Sittler 15.00 40.00
32 Vladislav Tretiak 25.00 60.00
33 Bryan Trottier 10.00 25.00
34 Rogie Vachon 12.00 30.00
35 Gump Worsley 15.00 40.00
36 Denis Potvin 12.00 30.00
37 Ray Emery 10.00 25.00
38 Marc-Andre Fleury 12.00 30.00
39 Dominik Hasek 15.00 40.00
40 Dany Heatley 15.00 40.00
41 Cristobal Huet 10.00 25.00
42 Ilya Kovalchuk 12.00 30.00
43 Brian Leetch 12.00 30.00
44 Kari Lehtonen 12.00 30.00
45 Nicklas Lidstrom 12.00 30.00
46 Henrik Lundqvist 20.00 50.00
47 Roberto Luongo 20.00 50.00
48 Frank Mahovlich 15.00 40.00
49 Mike Modano 15.00 40.00
50 Alexander Ovechkin 20.00 50.00
51 Dion Phaneuf 15.00 40.00
52 Petr Prucha 10.00 25.00
53 Henri Richard 10.00 25.00
54 Patrick Roy 50.00 100.00
55 Joe Sakic 20.00 50.00
56 Eric Staal 12.00 30.00
57 John Tavares 30.00 80.00
58 Joe Thornton 20.00 50.00
59 Marty Turco 12.00 30.00
60 Cam Ward 10.00 25.00
61 Steve Yzerman 40.00 80.00
62 Henrik Zetterberg 25.00 50.00
63 Ed Belfour 15.00 40.00
64 Ryan Miller 15.00 40.00
65 Boris Mikhailov 10.00 25.00
66 Bernie Parent 15.00 40.00
67 Paul Henderson 10.00 25.00
68 Felix Potvin 20.00 50.00
69 Jason Spezza 12.00 30.00
70 Vincent Lecavalier 15.00 40.00
71 Thomas Vanek 15.00 40.00
72 Maurice Richard/30 250.00 400.00

2006-07 ITG Ultimate Memorabilia Autographs Dual

STATED PRINT RUN 40
UNPRICED GOLD PRINT RUN 1
1 J.Jagr/M.Lemieux 60.00 150.00
2 S.Yzerman/T.Lindsay 30.00 60.00
3 M.Brodeur/P.Roy 50.00 100.00
4 E.Staal/J.Staal 20.00 50.00
5 P.Kessel/P.Esposito 20.00 50.00
6 N.Lidstrom/H.Zetterberg 30.00 60.00
7 A.Ovechkin/J.Thornton 25.00 60.00
8 M.Messier/J.Tavares 60.00 120.00
9 V.Tretiak/P.Henderson 30.00 80.00
10 M.Modano/D.Gilmour 25.00 60.00
11 I.Kovalchuk/K.Lehtonen 15.00 40.00
12 R.Luongo/D.Hasek 25.00 60.00

2006-07 ITG Ultimate Memorabilia Blades of Steel

STATED PRINT RUN 25
1 Elmer Lach 20.00 50.00
2 Aurel Joliat 20.00 50.00
3 Busher Jackson 25.00 60.00
4 Clint Benedict 25.00 60.00
5 Darryl Sittler 15.00 40.00
6 Dave Keon 15.00 40.00
7 Dit Clapper 20.00 50.00
8 Doug Gilmour 12.00 30.00
9 Eddie Shore 20.00 50.00
10 Jaromir Jagr 15.00 40.00
11 Frank Nighbor 15.00 40.00
12 Frank Patrick 30.00 80.00
13 Gilbert Perreault 12.00 30.00
14 Hap Day 20.00 50.00
15 Henrik Zetterberg 12.00 30.00
16 Jack Adams 15.00 40.00
17 Jacques Plante 25.00 50.00
18 Jean Beliveau 20.00 50.00
19 Joe Thornton 15.00 40.00
20 Johnny Bucyk 12.00 30.00
21 Keith Tkachuk 10.00 25.00
22 King Clancy 20.00 50.00
23 Luc Robitaille 12.00 30.00
24 Mario Lemieux 25.00 60.00
25 Nels Stewart 15.00 40.00
26 Paddy Moran 25.00 60.00
27 Paul Coffey 10.00 25.00
28 Phil Esposito 12.00 30.00
29 Stan Mikita 10.00 25.00
30 Tim Horton 25.00 60.00

2006-07 ITG Ultimate Memorabilia Bloodlines

STATED PRINT RUN 25
1 Stastny/Stastny/Stastny 25.00 60.00
2 Staal/Staal/Staal 20.00 50.00
3 R.Bourque/C.Bourque 20.00 50.00
4 F.Mahovlich/P.Mahovlich 15.00 40.00
5 M.Richard/H.Richard 30.00 80.00
6 P.Esposito/T.Esposito 20.00 50.00
7 Hull/Hull/Hull 25.00 60.00

2006-07 ITG Ultimate Memorabilia Bowman Factor

STATED PRINT RUN 25
1 Glenn Hall 10.00 25.00
2 Frank Mahovlich 10.00 25.00
3 Yvan Cournoyer 10.00 25.00
4 Guy Lafleur 12.00 30.00
5 Steve Shutt 10.00 25.00
6 Larry Robinson 10.00 25.00
7 Henri Richard 10.00 25.00
8 Serge Savard 10.00 25.00
9 Gilbert Perreault 10.00 25.00
10 Danny Gare 10.00 25.00
11 Ron Francis 10.00 25.00
12 Paul Coffey 10.00 25.00
13 Jaromir Jagr 20.00 50.00
14 Mario Lemieux 30.00 60.00
15 Brett Hull 15.00 40.00
16 Steve Yzerman 30.00 60.00

2006-07 ITG Ultimate Memorabilia Boys Will Be Boys

STATED PRINT RUN 25
1 Brett Hull 15.00 40.00
2 Frank Mahovlich 12.00 30.00
3 Guy Lafleur 15.00 40.00
4 Howie Morenz 20.00 50.00
5 Jean Beliveau 15.00 40.00
6 Larry Robinson 10.00 25.00
7 Mario Lemieux 25.00 60.00
8 Glenn Hall 12.00 30.00
9 Norm Ullman 10.00 25.00
10 Dave Keon 15.00 40.00
11 Alex Delvecchio 10.00 25.00
12 Ed Giacomin 15.00 40.00
13 Rod Gilbert 10.00 25.00
14 Steve Shutt 10.00 25.00
15 Guy Lapointe 10.00 25.00
16 Serge Savard 10.00 25.00
17 Billy Smith 12.00 30.00
18 Denis Potvin 12.00 30.00
19 Mike Bossy 15.00 40.00
20 Bryan Trottier 12.00 30.00
21 Peter Stastny 12.00 30.00
22 Red Kelly 12.00 30.00
23 Bobby Hull 15.00 40.00
24 Brad Park 10.00 25.00
25 Bobby Clarke 10.00 25.00
26 Marcel Dionne 12.00 30.00
27 Vladislav Tretiak 20.00 50.00
28 Ed Belfour 12.00 30.00

2006-07 ITG Ultimate Memorabilia Double Memorabilia

STATED PRINT RUN 25
1 Mark Messier 15.00 40.00
2 Patrick Roy 30.00 80.00
3 Martin Brodeur 15.00 40.00
4 Mike Modano 12.00 30.00
5 Steve Yzerman 30.00 60.00
6 John Tavares 40.00 80.00
7 Joe Thornton 15.00 40.00
8 Bobby Hull 20.00 50.00
9 Alexander Ovechkin 25.00 60.00
10 Jean Beliveau 15.00 40.00
11 Tim Horton 25.00 60.00
12 Dave Keon 15.00 40.00
13 Aurel Joliat 20.00 50.00
14 Brett Hull 15.00 40.00
15 Chris Chelios 12.00 30.00
16 Dominik Hasek 20.00 50.00
17 Borje Salming 12.00 30.00
18 Cam Neely 12.00 30.00
19 Joe Sakic 25.00 60.00
20 Ed Belfour 15.00 40.00
21 Raymond Bourque 15.00 40.00
22 Vladislav Tretiak
23 Guy Lafleur 15.00 40.00
24 Mario Lemieux 30.00 60.00
25 Henrik Zetterberg 20.00 50.00
26 Jacques Plante 20.00 50.00
27 Doug Harvey 15.00 40.00
28 Jordan Staal 20.00 50.00
29 Eddie Shore 15.00 40.00
30 Stan Mikita 12.00 30.00

2006-07 ITG Ultimate Memorabilia Double Memorabilia Autographs

STATED PRINT RUN 50
1 E.Staal/J.Staal 20.00 40.00
2 R.Emery/D.Heatley 12.00 30.00
3 G.Lafleur/M.Dionne 25.00 50.00
4 J.Jagr/M.Lemieux 75.00 150.00
5 M.Brodeur/P.Roy 75.00 150.00
6 S.Yzerman/D.Gilmour 40.00 80.00
7 J.Thornton/P.Esposito 25.00 60.00
8 A.Ovechkin/I.Kovalchuk 40.00 80.00
9 J.Tavares/M.Messier 60.00 125.00
10 D.Phaneuf/N.Lidstrom 20.00 40.00
11 B.Hull/M.Modano 25.00 60.00
12 R.Luongo/C.Price 50.00 100.00

2006-07 ITG Ultimate Memorabilia First Round Picks

STATED PRINT RUN 25
1 Evgeni Malkin 20.00 50.00
2 Alexander Ovechkin 20.00 50.00
3 Ilya Kovalchuk 10.00 25.00
4 Jaromir Jagr 15.00 40.00
5 Joe Thornton 12.00 30.00
6 Carey Price 20.00 50.00
7 Marc-Andre Fleury 12.00 30.00
8 Eric Staal 10.00 25.00
9 Kari Lehtonen 10.00 25.00
10 Anze Kopitar 12.00 30.00
11 Guy Lafleur 12.00 30.00
12 Marcel Dionne 10.00 25.00
13 Mike Bossy 10.00 25.00
14 Paul Coffey 12.00 30.00
15 Ron Francis 12.00 30.00
16 Pat LaFontaine 12.00 30.00
17 Steve Yzerman 20.00 50.00
18 Wendel Clark 12.00 30.00
19 Martin Brodeur 15.00 40.00
20 Joe Sakic 15.00 40.00
21 Mike Modano 12.00 30.00
22 Marc Staal 10.00 25.00
23 Vincent Lecavalier 12.00 30.00
24 Gilbert Perreault 12.00 30.00
25 Jordan Staal 12.00 30.00
26 Jason Spezza 10.00 25.00
27 Roberto Luongo 12.00 30.00
28 Brian Leetch 10.00 25.00
29 Mario Lemieux 20.00 60.00
30 Raymond Bourque 15.00 40.00

2006-07 ITG Ultimate Memorabilia Future Star

STATED PRINT RUN 25
1 Angelo Esposito 12.00 30.00
2 John Tavares 20.00 50.00
3 Evgeni Malkin 20.00 50.00
4 Wojtek Wolski 8.00 20.00
5 Marek Schwarz 10.00 25.00
6 Carey Price 25.00 60.00
7 Anze Kopitar 25.00 60.00
8 Jordan Staal 15.00 40.00
9 Gilbert Brule 8.00 20.00
10 Phil Kessel 15.00 40.00
11 Peter Mueller 10.00 25.00
12 Bobby Ryan 10.00 25.00
13 Rob Schremp 8.00 20.00
14 Paul Stastny 15.00 40.00
15 Dustin Penner 8.00 20.00
16 Bryan Little 6.00 15.00
17 Derick Brassard 10.00 25.00
18 Justin Pogge 10.00 25.00
19 Alexander Radulov 12.00 30.00
20 Al Montoya 10.00 25.00
21 Ryan Getzlaf 15.00 40.00
22 Marc Staal 10.00 25.00
23 Alexei Cherepanov 8.00 20.00
24 Ryan Callahan 10.00 25.00
25 Jack Skille 8.00 20.00

2006-07 ITG Ultimate Memorabilia Future Star Autographs

PRINT RUN 40 UNLESS NOTED
1 Phil Kessel/40* 12.00 30.00
2 Peter Mueller/40* 10.00 25.00
3 Bobby Ryan/40* 12.00 30.00
4 Rob Schremp/40* 8.00 20.00
5 Paul Stastny/40* 15.00 30.00
6 Dustin Penner/40* 8.00 20.00
7 Bryan Little/40* 10.00 25.00
8 Derick Brassard/40* 15.00 30.00
9 Justin Pogge/40* 12.00 30.00
10 Jeff Glass/40* 8.00 20.00
11 Ryan Getzlaf/40* 15.00 40.00
12 Jack Skille/40* 8.00 20.00
13 Ryan Callahan/40* 8.00 20.00
14 Alexei Cherepanov/40* 40.00 80.00
15 Angelo Esposito/30* 30.00 60.00
16 John Tavares/30* 60.00 120.00
17 Alexander Radulov/30* 12.00 30.00
18 Wojtek Wolski/30* 10.00 25.00
19 Marek Schwarz/30* 8.00 20.00
20 Carey Price/30* 50.00 100.00
21 Anze Kopitar/30* 20.00 40.00
22 Jordan Staal/30* 30.00 60.00
23 Gilbert Brule/30* 15.00 30.00
24 Michael Frolik/30* 8.00 20.00
25 Jonathan Toews/40* 50.00 100.00

2006-07 ITG Ultimate Memorabilia Future Star Patches Autographs

STATED PRINT RUN 40
1 Phil Kessel 30.00 60.00
2 Peter Mueller 25.00 60.00
3 Bobby Ryan 20.00 50.00
4 Rob Schremp 15.00 40.00
5 Paul Stastny 20.00 50.00
6 Dustin Penner 15.00 40.00
7 Bryan Little 12.00 30.00
8 Derick Brassard 15.00 40.00
9 Justin Pogge 15.00 40.00
10 Jeff Glass 12.00 30.00
11 Al Montoya 12.00 30.00
12 Jack Skille 12.00 30.00
13 Ryan Callahan 15.00 40.00
14 Alexei Cherepanov 40.00 80.00
15 Angelo Esposito 20.00 50.00
16 John Tavares 60.00 120.00
17 Hannu Toivonen 15.00 40.00
18 Wojtek Wolski 12.00 30.00
19 Marek Schwarz 12.00 30.00
20 Carey Price 40.00 80.00
21 Anze Kopitar 30.00 80.00
22 Jordan Staal 30.00 60.00
23 Gilbert Brule 15.00 40.00
24 Michael Frolik 15.00 40.00
25 Benoit Pouliot 15.00 40.00
26 Jonathan Toews 60.00 120.00

2006-07 ITG Ultimate Memorabilia Gloves Are Off

STATED PRINT RUN 25
1 Alexander Ovechkin 30.00 60.00
2 Bobby Clarke 20.00 40.00
3 Brett Hull 15.00 40.00
4 Bryan Trottier 12.00 30.00
5 Cam Neely 15.00 40.00
6 Charlie Conacher 20.00 50.00
7 Dale Hawerchuk 12.00 30.00
8 Dominik Hasek 20.00 40.00
9 Eddie Shore 20.00 50.00
10 Eric Lindros 15.00 40.00
11 Jacques Plante 20.00 50.00
12 Joe Sakic 25.00 50.00
13 Joe Thornton 15.00 40.00
14 Mario Lemieux 30.00 80.00
15 Martin Brodeur 20.00 50.00
16 Pat LaFontaine 10.00 25.00
17 Patrick Roy 30.00 80.00
18 Raymond Bourque 15.00 40.00
19 Stan Mikita 10.00 25.00
20 Steve Yzerman 25.00 60.00

2006-07 ITG Ultimate Memorabilia Going For Gold

STATED PRINT RUN 25
1 Alexander Ovechkin 15.00 40.00
2 Mike Modano 10.00 25.00
3 Bobby Clarke 10.00 25.00
4 Brett Hull 12.00 30.00
5 Brian Leetch 8.00 20.00
6 Cristobal Huet 10.00 25.00
7 Eric Staal 10.00 25.00
8 Evgeni Malkin 20.00 50.00
9 Henrik Lundqvist 15.00 30.00
10 Henrik Zetterberg 12.00 30.00
11 Ilya Kovalchuk 12.00 30.00
12 Jari Kurri 20.00 40.00
13 Jaromir Jagr 20.00 40.00
14 Jason Spezza 10.00 25.00
15 Joe Thornton 15.00 30.00
16 Alexei Cherepanov 12.00 30.00
17 Mario Lemieux 20.00 50.00
18 Mark Messier 20.00 40.00
19 Martin Brodeur 20.00 40.00
20 Nicklas Lidstrom 12.00 30.00
21 Phil Esposito 12.00 30.00
22 Raymond Bourque 15.00 30.00
23 Steve Yzerman 15.00 40.00
24 Valeri Kharlamov 15.00 40.00
25 Vladislav Tretiak 20.00 40.00
26 Dominik Hasek 12.00 30.00
27 Keith Tkachuk 8.00 20.00
28 Vincent Lecavalier 12.00 30.00
29 Joe Sakic 15.00 40.00
30 John Tavares 20.00 50.00

2006-07 ITG Ultimate Memorabilia Jerseys

STATED PRINT RUN 25
1 Evgeni Malkin 20.00 50.00
2 Joe Thornton 10.00 25.00
3 Brett Hull 15.00 40.00
4 Chris Chelios 10.00 25.00
5 Patrick Roy 20.00 50.00
6 Alexander Ovechkin 15.00 40.00
7 Dominik Hasek 10.00 25.00
8 Joe Sakic 15.00 40.00
9 Mark Messier 15.00 40.00
10 Steve Yzerman 15.00 40.00
11 Jean Beliveau 12.00 30.00
12 Milt Schmidt 10.00 25.00
13 Martin Brodeur 15.00 40.00
14 Jaromir Jagr 15.00 40.00
15 Ed Belfour 10.00 25.00
16 Mario Lemieux 20.00 50.00
17 Borje Salming 10.00 25.00
18 Bobby Hull 10.00 25.00
19 Doug Gilmour 10.00 25.00
20 Guy Lafleur 10.00 25.00
21 Dave Keon 10.00 25.00
22 Jason Spezza 10.00 25.00
23 Nicklas Lidstrom 10.00 25.00
24 Eric Staal 10.00 25.00
25 Luc Robitaille 10.00 25.00
26 John Tavares 25.00 60.00
27 Vincent Lecavalier 10.00 25.00

2006-07 ITG Ultimate Memorabilia Jerseys and Emblems

STATED PRINT RUN 25
1 Evgeni Malkin 40.00 80.00
2 Joe Thornton 30.00 60.00
3 Patrick Roy 50.00 100.00
5 Martin Brodeur 30.00 60.00
6 Alexander Ovechkin 25.00 60.00
7 Mark Messier 30.00 60.00
8 Joe Sakic 30.00 60.00
9 Brian Leetch 30.00 60.00
10 Jean Beliveau 30.00 60.00
11 Mario Lemieux 50.00 100.00
12 Dominik Hasek 25.00 50.00
13 Dave Keon 25.00 50.00
14 Ilya Kovalchuk 25.00 50.00
15 Bobby Hull 30.00 60.00
16 Steve Yzerman 40.00 80.00
17 Jaromir Jagr 30.00 60.00
18 Nicklas Lidstrom 25.00 50.00
19 John Tavares 75.00 125.00
20 Jordan Staal 30.00 60.00
21 Vincent Lecavalier 15.00 40.00

2006-07 ITG Ultimate Memorabilia Jerseys Autographs

STATED PRINT RUN 50
1 Tom Barrasso 12.00 30.00
2 Glenn Hall 15.00 40.00
3 Chris Chelios 15.00 40.00
4 Martin Brodeur 40.00 80.00
5 Gerry Cheevers 15.00 40.00
6 Dominik Hasek 25.00 60.00
7 Bobby Clarke 15.00 40.00
8 Paul Coffey 15.00 40.00
9 Yvan Cournoyer 12.00 30.00
10 Ron Hextall 12.00 30.00
11 Marcel Dionne 12.00 30.00
12 Ray Emery 10.00 25.00
13 Angelo Esposito 25.00 50.00
14 Phil Esposito 15.00 40.00
15 Cristobal Huet 10.00 25.00
16 Manny Fernandez 8.00 20.00
17 Ron Francis 12.00 30.00
18 Grant Fuhr 12.00 30.00
19 Ed Giacomin 12.00 30.00
20 Doug Gilmour 12.00 30.00
21 Jean Beliveau 20.00 50.00
22 Wendel Clark 15.00 40.00
23 Alex Delvecchio 10.00 30.00
24 Brett Hull 12.00 30.00
25 Jaromir Jagr 25.00 60.00
26 Dave Keon 15.00 40.00
27 Ilya Kovalchuk 15.00 40.00
28 Jari Kurri 15.00 40.00
29 Guy Lafleur 25.00 60.00
30 Pat LaFontaine 12.00 30.00
31 Brian Leetch 12.00 30.00
32 Kari Lehtonen 12.00 30.00
33 Nicklas Lidstrom 15.00 40.00
34 Henrik Lundqvist 15.00 40.00
35 Roberto Luongo 15.00 40.00
36 Frank Mahovlich 12.00 30.00
37 Lanny McDonald 8.00 20.00
38 Mark Messier 50.00 100.00
39 Stan Mikita 20.00 50.00
40 Mike Modano 15.00 40.00
41 Cam Neely 15.00 40.00
42 Alexander Ovechkin 40.00 100.00
43 Brad Park 12.00 30.00
44 Gilbert Perreault 12.00 30.00
45 Dion Phaneuf 15.00 40.00
46 Denis Potvin 12.00 30.00
47 Petr Prucha 8.00 20.00
48 Jean Ratelle 15.00 40.00
49 Larry Robinson 12.00 30.00
50 Luc Robitaille 25.00 60.00
51 Patrick Roy 40.00 100.00
52 Joe Sakic 30.00 80.00
53 Darryl Sittler 12.00 30.00
54 Jason Spezza 12.00 30.00
55 Eric Staal 12.00 30.00
56 Marek Svatos 8.00 20.00
57 John Tavares 25.00 60.00
58 Joe Thornton 20.00 50.00
59 Vladislav Tretiak 25.00 60.00
60 Bryan Trottier 12.00 30.00
61 Marty Turco 12.00 30.00
62 Rogie Vachon 12.00 30.00
63 Cam Ward 12.00 30.00
64 Steve Yzerman 40.00 80.00
65 Henrik Zetterberg 20.00 40.00
66 Felix Potvin 20.00 50.00
67 Vincent Lecavalier 15.00 40.00
68 Keith Tkachuk 12.00 30.00
69 Thomas Vanek 15.00 40.00

2006-07 ITG Ultimate Memorabilia Journey Jersey

STATED PRINT RUN 25
1 Raymond Bourque 15.00 40.00
2 Patrick Roy 25.00 60.00
3 Dave Keon 12.00 30.00
4 Dany Heatley 12.00 30.00
5 Joe Sakic 15.00 40.00
6 Ed Giacomin 12.00 30.00
7 Eric Lindros 12.00 30.00
8 Brian Leetch 12.00 30.00
9 Jaromir Jagr 15.00 40.00
10 Ron Francis 12.00 30.00
11 Ed Belfour 12.00 30.00
12 Doug Gilmour 12.00 30.00
13 Mark Messier 15.00 40.00
14 Brett Hull 12.00 30.00
15 Luc Robitaille 12.00 30.00
16 Dominik Hasek 15.00 40.00
17 Paul Coffey 12.00 30.00
18 Felix Potvin 20.00 50.00

2006-07 ITG Ultimate Memorabilia Legendary Captains

STATED PRINT RUN 25
1 Maurice Richard/10
2 Dave Keon 12.00 30.00
3 Jean Beliveau 15.00 40.00
4 Steve Yzerman 15.00 40.00
5 Mario Lemieux 15.00 40.00
6 Mark Messier 15.00 40.00
7 Bobby Clarke 12.00 30.00
8 Raymond Bourque 12.00 30.00
9 Darryl Sittler 12.00 30.00
10 Phil Esposito 12.00 30.00
11 Henri Richard 12.00 30.00
12 Gilbert Perreault 12.00 30.00
13 Joe Sakic 15.00 40.00
14 Mike Modano 12.00 30.00
15 Bill Durnan/10
16 Milt Schmidt 12.00 30.00

2006-07 ITG Ultimate Memorabilia Passing The Torch

STATED PRINT RUN 25
1 J.Beliveau/G.Lafleur 20.00 50.00
2 D.Keon/D.Sittler 20.00 50.00
3 M.Dionne/L.Robitaille 20.00 50.00
4 J.Plante/P.Roy 20.00 50.00
5 S.Yzerman/N.Lidstrom 20.00 50.00
6 E.Shore/R.Bourque 12.00 30.00
7 T.Horton/B.Salming 25.00 60.00
8 B.Parent/R.Hextall 15.00 40.00
9 B.Clarke/M.Messier 12.00 30.00
10 M.Schmidt/J.Thornton 12.00 30.00
11 T.Sawchuk/M.Brodeur
12 B.Hull/B.Hull 15.00 40.00
13 E.Belfour/M.Turco 12.00 30.00
14 M.Lemieux/J.Jagr 30.00 60.00
15 D.Hasek/R.Miller 20.00 50.00
16 G.Hall/T.Esposito 15.00 40.00
17 V.Kharlamov/A.Ovechkin 15.00 40.00
18 I.Kovalchuk/E.Malkin 20.00 50.00
19 E.Lindros/J.Tavares 20.00 50.00
20 E.Giacomin/M.Richter 12.00 30.00

2006-07 ITG Ultimate Memorabilia R.O.Y. Autographs

COMMON CARDS 10.00 25.00
SEMISTARS 12.00 30.00
UNLISTED STARS 15.00 40.00
STATED PRINT RUN 19 SER.#'d SETS
1 Anze Kopitar 30.00 60.00
2 Gilbert Brule 20.00 40.00
3 Phil Kessel 25.00 50.00
4 Alexander Radulov 25.00 50.00
5 Wojtek Wolski 20.00 40.00
6 Jordan Staal 10.00 25.00
7 Dustin Penner 10.00 25.00
8 Paul Stastny 30.00 60.00
9 Evgeni Malkin 50.00 100.00
10 Alexander Ovechkin 40.00 80.00
11 Dany Heatley 12.00 30.00
12 Martin Brodeur
13 Ed Belfour 15.00 40.00
14 Brian Leetch
15 Luc Robitaille 20.00 40.00
16 Mario Lemieux 40.00 80.00
17 Tony Esposito 20.00 40.00
18 Dave Keon 20.00 40.00
19 Glenn Hall 20.00 40.00
20 Gump Worsley 25.00 50.00

2006-07 ITG Ultimate Memorabilia R.O.Y. Jerseys

COMMON CARDS 10.00 25.00
SEMISTARS 12.00 30.00
UNLISTED STARS 15.00 40.00
STATED PRINT RUN 25
1 Anze Kopitar 20.00 40.00
2 Gilbert Brule 10.00 25.00
3 Phil Kessel 12.00 30.00
4 Alexander Radulov 12.00 30.00
5 Wojtek Wolski 12.00 30.00
6 Jordan Staal
7 Dustin Penner 10.00 25.00
8 Paul Stastny 15.00 40.00
9 Evgeni Malkin 25.00 60.00
10 Alexander Ovechkin 20.00 50.00
11 Dany Heatley 10.00 25.00
12 Martin Brodeur 15.00 40.00
13 Ed Belfour 10.00 25.00
14 Brian Leetch 10.00 25.00
15 Luc Robitaille 10.00 25.00
16 Mario Lemieux 25.00 60.00
17 Tony Esposito 15.00 30.00
18 Dave Keon 15.00 40.00
19 Glenn Hall 12.00 30.00
20 Gump Worsley 15.00 40.00

2006-07 ITG Ultimate Memorabilia Raised to the Rafters

STATED PRINT RUN 25
1 Pat LaFontaine 20.00 40.00
2 Mark Messier 25.00 50.00
3 Yvan Cournoyer 20.00 40.00
4 Bernie Geoffrion 25.00 50.00
5 Paul Coffey 20.00 40.00
6 Luc Robitaille 20.00 40.00
7 Ron Francis 20.00 40.00
8 Milt Schmidt 20.00 40.00
9 Brett Hull 20.00 50.00
10 Steve Yzerman 30.00 60.00
11 Mario Lemieux 30.00 80.00
12 Bobby Hull

2006-07 ITG Ultimate Memorabilia Retro Teammates

STATED PRINT RUN 25 SER.#'d SETS
1 Morenz/Joliat/Hains 50.00 100.00
2 Thomp/Schmidt/Shore 30.00 60.00
3 Sawchuk/Abel/Lindsay
4 Plante/Richard/Harvey 50.00 100.00
5 Bower/Keon/Horton 50.00 100.00
6 Beliv/Gump/Richard 40.00 80.00
7 Mikita/Hall/Hull 20.00 50.00
8 Delv/Crozier/Ullman 15.00 40.00
9 Gilbert/Ratelle/Giac 30.00 60.00
10 Cheev/Bucyk/Espo 25.00 60.00
11 Kharla/Tretiak/Yakus 50.00 100.00
12 Lafleur/Courn/Shutt 20.00 50.00
13 Clarke/Parent/Barber 30.00 80.00
14 Sittler/Salm/Lanny 20.00 50.00
15 Bossy/Trot/Potvin 30.00 60.00
16 Mess/Coffey/Kurri 50.00 100.00
17 Richard/Lach/Blake 75.00 150.00
18 Roy/Chelios/Robin 40.00 80.00
19 Bourq/Moog/Neely 30.00 60.00
20 Messier/Fuhr/Ander 40.00 80.00
21 Mario/Francis/Jagr 50.00 100.00
22 Gilm/Clark/Potvin 30.00 60.00
23 Mess/Leetch/Richt 30.00 80.00
24 Yzer/Hasek/Larion 40.00 80.00
25 Hull/Yzer/Lidstrom 40.00 80.00

2006-07 ITG Ultimate Memorabilia Ring Leaders

STATED PRINT RUN 25
1 Henri Richard 15.00 40.00
2 Jean Beliveau 12.00 30.00
3 Steve Yzerman 20.00 50.00
4 Jaromir Jagr 15.00 40.00
5 Mario Lemieux 20.00 50.00
6 Mark Messier 12.00 30.00
7 Martin Brodeur 15.00 40.00
8 Larry Robinson 10.00 25.00
9 Dave Keon 12.00 30.00
10 Guy Lafleur 12.00 30.00
11 Jari Kurri 10.00 25.00
12 Red Kelly 12.00 30.00
13 Frank Mahovlich 10.00 25.00
14 Johnny Bower 12.00 30.00
15 Serge Savard 10.00 25.00
16 Patrick Roy 20.00 50.00
17 Paul Coffey 10.00 25.00
18 Yvan Cournoyer 12.00 30.00

2006-07 ITG Ultimate Memorabilia Sensational Season

UNLISTED STARS 12.00 30.00
STATED PRINT RUN 25
1 Phil Esposito 12.00 30.00
2 Mario Lemieux 20.00 50.00
3 Stan Mikita 12.00 30.00
4 George Hainsworth 15.00 40.00
5 Maurice Richard 30.00 80.00
6 Paul Coffey 12.00 30.00
7 John Tavares 30.00 80.00
8 Tony Esposito 12.00 30.00
9 Martin Brodeur 15.00 40.00
10 Mike Bossy 12.00 30.00
11 Brett Hull 15.00 40.00

2006-07 ITG Ultimate Memorabilia Stick Rack

ANNOUNCED PRINT RUN 9-25
1 Lafleur/Beliv/Courn 60.00 125.00
2 Harv/Richard/Plante 60.00 125.00
3 Big M/Keon/Bower 50.00 100.00
4 Roy/Plante/Huet 50.00 100.00
5 Hull/Yzerm/Ciccar 50.00 100.00
6 Bucyk/Espo/Cheev 30.00 80.00
7 Harvey/Kelly/Horton 30.00 80.00
8 Mario/Francis/Trots 60.00 125.00
9 Keon/Sitt/Gilmour 60.00 125.00
10 Robin/Savard/Lap 30.00 80.00
11 Sawchuk/Kelly/Delv 30.00 80.00
12 Hull/Mikita/Hall 30.00 80.00
13 Roy/Bourque/Svatos 30.00 80.00
14 Gump/Giaco/Lundq 60.00 125.00
15 Clarke/Barber/Leach 30.00 80.00
16 Mario/Beliv/Richard 90.00 150.00
17 Staal/Ovech/Dion 50.00 100.00
18 Stastny Brothers 25.00 60.00
19 Durnan/Broda/Lum 30.00 80.00
22 Sittler/Lanny/Williams 30.00 80.00
23 Parent/Hextall/Niitty 30.00 80.00
24 Bossy/Trottier/Potvin 60.00 100.00
25 Gump/Giac/Richter 30.00 80.00
26 Kurri/Anderson/Fuhr 40.00 100.00
27 Bourque/Leetch/Coff 30.00 80.00
28 Clancy/Prim/Barilko 75.00 125.00

2006-07 ITG Ultimate Memorabilia Sticks and Jerseys

COMMON CARDS 10.00 25.00
UNLISTED STARS 12.00 30.00
SEMISTARS 10.00 25.00
STATED PRINT RUN 25
1 Patrick Roy 30.00 60.00
2 Dave Keon 12.50 30.00
3 Steve Yzerman 25.00 50.00
4 Martin Brodeur 15.00 40.00
5 Ray Emery 10.00 25.00
6 Ron Francis 10.00 25.00
7 Dominik Hasek 15.00 40.00
8 Eric Staal 10.00 25.00
9 Peter Stastny 12.50 30.00
10 Roberto Luongo 20.00 50.00
11 Bernie Parent 12.50 30.00
12 Vincent Lecavalier 12.50 30.00
13 Rogie Vachon 15.00 40.00
14 Gilbert Perreault 12.50 30.00
15 Mario Lemieux 30.00 60.00

2006-07 ITG Ultimate Memorabilia Sticks Autographs

TATED PRINT RUN 50
Marcel Dionne 15.00 40.00
Manny Fernandez 8.00 20.00
Bobby Clarke 12.00 30.00
Ed Belfour 10.00 25.00
Guy Lafleur 25.00 60.00
Jari Kurri 15.00 40.00
Cam Neely 12.00 30.00
Mark Messier 40.00 80.00
Roberto Luongo 20.00 50.00
Henrik Lundqvist 15.00 40.00
Nicklas Lidstrom 15.00 40.00
Pat LaFontaine 12.00 30.00
Dave Keon 12.00 30.00
Paul Coffey 12.00 30.00
Petr Prucha 8.00 20.00
Luc Robitaille 25.00 60.00
Phil Esposito 12.00 30.00
Doug Gilmour 12.00 30.00
Glenn Hall 12.00 30.00
Brett Hull 15.00 40.00
Mike Modano 12.00 30.00
Alexander Ovechkin 40.00 100.00
Brad Park 8.00 20.00
Dion Phaneuf 15.00 40.00
Patrick Roy 60.00 125.00
Joe Sakic 30.00 60.00
Darryl Sittler 10.00 25.00
Eric Staal 10.00 25.00
John Tavares 75.00 150.00
Steve Yzerman 40.00 100.00
Felix Potvin
Vincent Lecavalier 15.00 40.00

2006-07 ITG Ultimate Memorabilia Triple Thread Jerseys

TATED PRINT RUN 25
Malkin/Kovalchuk/Ovechkin 30.00 80.00
Perreault/Clarke/Lafleur 25.00 50.00
Yzerman/Lemieux/Messier
Luongo/Brodeur/Hasek 30.00 80.00
Roy/Potvin/Belfour 40.00 100.00
Chelios/Leetch/Lidstrom 25.00 60.00
Keon/Beliveau/Hull 20.00 50.00
Lindsay/Richard/Schmidt 40.00 100.00
Gilmour/Neely/Tkachuk 20.00 50.00
Sawchuk/Plante/Bower 40.00 80.00
Giacomin/Cheevers/Parent 40.00 80.00
Tavares/Esposito/Mueller 50.00 125.00
Staal/Spezza/Phaneuf 15.00 40.00
Radulov/Kopitar/Staal 30.00 80.00
Robitaille/Hull/Lindros 30.00 80.00
Sakic/Thornton/Jagr 30.00 80.00

2006-07 ITG Ultimate Memorabilia Ultimate Hero Single Jerseys

TATED PRINT RUN 25
Maurice Richard 30.00 80.00
Terry Sawchuk 15.00 40.00
Patrick Roy 25.00 60.00
Steve Yzerman 20.00 50.00
Mark Messier 15.00 40.00
Mario Lemieux 20.00 50.00

2006-07 ITG Ultimate Memorabilia Ultimate Hero Double Jerseys

TATED PRINT RUN 25
Maurice Richard 30.00 80.00
Terry Sawchuk 15.00 40.00
Patrick Roy 25.00 60.00
Steve Yzerman 20.00 50.00
Mark Messier 15.00 40.00
Mario Lemieux 25.00 60.00

2006-07 ITG Ultimate Memorabilia Ultimate Hero Triple Jerseys

TATED PRINT RUN 25
Maurice Richard 40.00 100.00
Terry Sawchuk 25.00 50.00
Patrick Roy 30.00 80.00
Steve Yzerman 30.00 60.00
Mark Messier 25.00 50.00
Mario Lemieux 40.00 80.00

2007-08 ITG Ultimate Memorabilia

his set was released on November 12, 2008. The
ase set consists of 100 cards.
TATED PRINT RUN 90 SERIAL #'d SETS
Alexander Ovechkin 15.00 40.00
Gilbert Perreault 4.00 10.00
Martin Brodeur 8.00 20.00
Dave Keon 4.00 10.00
Joe Sakic 6.00 15.00
Patrick Roy 10.00 25.00
Eddie Shore 4.00 10.00
Ilya Kovalchuk 4.00 10.00
Luc Robitaille 4.00 10.00
Bernie Parent 4.00 10.00
Glenn Hall 5.00 12.00
Maurice Richard 6.00 15.00
Cyclone Taylor 4.00 10.00
Bobby Hull 6.00 15.00
Dany Heatley 4.00 10.00
Georges Vezina 4.00 10.00
Dominik Hasek 5.00 12.00
Brett Hull 6.00 15.00
Phil Esposito 6.00 15.00
Guy Lafleur 5.00 12.00
Brian Leetch 4.00 10.00
Ted Lindsay 4.00 10.00
Frank Mahovlich 5.00 12.00
Johnny Bower 4.00 10.00
Larry Robinson 4.00 10.00
Jaromir Jagr 10.00 25.00
Jean Beliveau 5.00 12.00
Turk Broda 4.00 10.00
Tony Esposito 4.00 10.00
Markus Naslund 4.00 10.00
Henri Richard 6.00 15.00
Terry Sawchuk 5.00 12.00
Howie Morenz 3.00 8.00
Patrick Roy 10.00 25.00
Marian Gaborik 5.00 12.00
Chris Osgood 4.00 10.00
Jacques Plante 6.00 15.00
Pelle Lindbergh 5.00 12.00
Red Kelly 3.00 8.00
Peter Forsberg 5.00 12.00
Mike Modano 6.00 15.00
Pat LaFontaine 4.00 10.00
Syl Apps 3.00 8.00
Ron Hextall 6.00 15.00
Stan Mikita 5.00 12.00
Tim Horton 4.00 10.00
47 Roberto Luongo 5.00 12.00
48 Pavel Datsyuk 5.00 12.00
49 Mats Sundin 4.00 10.00
50 Nicklas Lidstrom 4.00 10.00
51 Alex Delvecchio 2.50 6.00
52 Bill Durnan 4.00 10.00
53 Bobby Clarke 4.00 10.00
54 Borje Salming 4.00 10.00
55 Brad Park 2.50 6.00
56 Cam Neely 4.00 10.00
57 Chris Chelios 4.00 10.00
58 Darryl Sittler 3.00 8.00
59 Denis Potvin 4.00 10.00
60 Doug Gilmour 5.00 12.00
61 Drew Doughty 10.00 25.00
62 Ed Belfour 4.00 10.00
63 Ed Giacomin 4.00 10.00
64 George Hainsworth 4.00 10.00
65 Gerry Cheevers 4.00 10.00
66 Grant Fuhr 4.00 10.00
67 Gump Worsley 5.00 12.00
68 Guy Lapointe 3.00 8.00
69 Jari Kurri 4.00 10.00
70 Jean Ratelle 3.00 8.00
71 Joe Thornton 5.00 12.00
72 John Tavares 10.00 25.00
73 Lanny McDonald 4.00 10.00
74 Lord Stanley 4.00 10.00
75 Mario Lemieux 12.00 30.00
76 Marcel Dionne 5.00 12.00
77 Marty Turco 4.00 10.00
78 Michel Goulet 3.00 8.00
79 Mike Bossy 4.00 10.00
80 Milt Schmidt 3.00 8.00
81 Paul Coffey 4.00 10.00
82 Paul Stastny 4.00 10.00
83 Peter Stastny 3.00 8.00
84 Raymond Bourque 6.00 15.00
85 Elmer Lach 4.00 10.00
86 Rogie Vachon 5.00 12.00
87 Ron Francis 5.00 12.00
88 Sam Gagner 5.00 12.00
89 Scott Niedermayer 4.00 10.00
90 Sid Abel 2.50 6.00
91 Steven Stamkos 12.00 30.00
92 Ted Kennedy 2.50 6.00
93 Roy Worters 4.00 10.00
94 Toe Blake 2.50 6.00
95 Valeri Kharlamov 4.00 10.00
96 Victor Hedman 8.00 20.00
97 Vincent Lecavalier 3.00 8.00
98 Vladislav Tretiak 4.00 10.00
99 Wendel Clark 4.00 10.00
100 Yvan Cournoyer 4.00 10.00

2007-08 ITG Ultimate Memorabilia Autographs

STATED PRINT RUN 30 SERIAL #'d SETS
1 Alexander Ovechkin 40.00 80.00
2 Bobby Clarke 8.00 20.00
3 Bobby Hull 12.00 30.00
4 Brett Hull
5 Cam Neely 8.00 20.00
6 Chris Chelios 8.00 20.00
7 Chris Osgood 8.00 20.00
8 Dominik Hasek 10.00 25.00
9 Glenn Hall 10.00 25.00
10 Gump Worsley 10.00 25.00
11 Guy Lafleur 10.00 25.00
12 Henri Richard 12.00 30.00
13 Ilya Kovalchuk 8.00 20.00
14 Jaromir Jagr 20.00 50.00
15 Jean Beliveau 25.00 50.00
16 Joe Sakic 12.00 30.00
17 Joe Thornton 10.00 25.00
18 John Tavares 20.00 50.00
19 Johnny Bower 8.00 20.00
20 Jean-Sebastien Giguere 12.00 30.00
21 Luc Robitaille 8.00 20.00
22 Marian Gaborik 10.00 25.00
23 Marcel Dionne 10.00 25.00
24 Mario Lemieux 25.00 60.00
25 Martin Brodeur 25.00 60.00
26 Martin St. Louis 8.00 20.00
27 Marty Turco 8.00 20.00
28 Mats Sundin 8.00 20.00
29 Mike Modano 12.00 30.00
30 Nicklas Lidstrom 12.00 30.00
31 Patrick Roy 40.00 80.00
32 Pavel Datsyuk 10.00 25.00
33 Peter Forsberg 10.00 25.00
34 Phil Esposito 12.00 30.00
35 Roberto Luongo 10.00 25.00
36 Ron Francis 10.00 25.00
37 Scott Niedermayer 8.00 20.00
38 Stan Mikita 10.00 25.00
39 Steven Stamkos 15.00 30.00
40 Ted Lindsay 8.00 20.00
41 Tony Esposito 12.00 30.00
42 Vincent Lecavalier 6.00 15.00
43 Vladislav Tretiak 15.00 40.00
44 Elmer Lach 8.00 20.00
45 Dave Keon 8.00 20.00
46 Milt Schmidt 6.00 15.00
47 Ted Kennedy 8.00 20.00
48 Joe Nieuwendyk/11*
49 Red Kelly/11*
50 Paul Coffey/11*

2007-08 ITG Ultimate Memorabilia Autos Dual

STATED PRINT RUN 24 SERIAL #'d SETS
1 Ovechkin/Kovalchuk 75.00 150.00
2 D.Keon/D.Sittler 12.00 30.00
3 B.Hull/B.Hull
4 S.Niedermayer/C.Pronger 12.00 30.00
5 T.Esposito/P.Esposito 20.00 50.00
6 M.Lemieux/J.Jagr
7 J.Tavares/S.Stamkos 75.00 125.00
8 J.Thornton/M.Schmidt 15.00 40.00
9 M.Brodeur/P.Roy 30.00 80.00
10 Lecavalier/M.St. Louis 12.00 30.00
11 R.Luongo/J.Giguere 15.00 40.00
12 D.Hasek/C.Osgood 15.00 40.00
13 J.Beliveau/G.Lafleur 30.00 80.00
14 B.Leetch/R.Bourque 20.00 50.00
15 M.Sundin/M.Naslund 15.00 40.00
16 E.Giacomin/G.Cheevers 12.00 30.00
17 P.Forsberg/J.Sakic 20.00 50.00
18 C.Chelios/N.Lidstrom 25.00 50.00
19 B.Clarke/B.Parent 20.00 50.00
20 M.Gaborik/P.Datsyuk 15.00 40.00
21 R.Francis/L.Robitaille 15.00 40.00
22 F.Mahovlich/J.Bower 15.00 40.00
23 P.Stastny/P.Stastny 12.00 30.00

2007-08 ITG Ultimate Memorabilia Battle of Alberta

STATED PRINT RUN 24 SERIAL #'d SETS
1 McDonald/Kurri 15.00 40.00
2 B.Hull/G.Anderson 25.00 60.00
3 M.Vernon/G.Fuhr 15.00 40.00
4 Nieuwendyk/Coffey 15.00 40.00
5 P.Housley/B.Ranford 15.00 40.00

2007-08 ITG Ultimate Memorabilia Battle of Quebec

STATED PRINT RUN 24 SERIAL #'d SETS
1 M.Sundin/P.Roy 30.00 80.00
2 D.Bouchard/G.Lafleur 25.00 60.00
3 M.Goulet/L.Robinson 12.00 30.00
4 P.Stastny/S.Shutt 12.00 30.00
5 J.Sakic/P.Roy 30.00 80.00

2007-08 ITG Ultimate Memorabilia Blades of Steel

STATED PRINT RUN 24 SERIAL #'d SETS
1 Dave Keon 12.00 30.00
2 Jaromir Jagr 30.00 80.00
3 Dany Heatley 12.00 30.00
4 Gerry Cheevers 12.00 30.00
5 Doug Gilmour 15.00 40.00
6 Phil Esposito 20.00 50.00
7 Pavel Datsyuk 15.00 40.00
8 Gilbert Perreault 12.00 30.00
9 Luc Robitaille 12.00 30.00
10 Mario Lemieux 40.00 100.00
11 Paul Coffey 12.00 30.00
12 Alexander Ovechkin 50.00 125.00
13 Darryl Sittler 10.00 25.00
14 Marcel Dionne 15.00 40.00
15 Joe Thornton 15.00 40.00
16 Jacques Plante 20.00 50.00
17 Jean Beliveau 15.00 40.00
18 Maurice Richard 20.00 50.00
19 Tim Horton 12.00 30.00
20 Stan Mikita 15.00 40.00

2007-08 ITG Ultimate Memorabilia Cityscapes

STATED PRINT RUN 24 SERIAL #'d SETS
1 B.Hull/E.Banks 15.00 40.00
2 I.Kovalchuk/D.Wilkins 10.00 25.00
3 D.Hasek/D.Flutie 10.00 25.00
4 M.Turco/D.Sanders 10.00 25.00
5 P.Esposito/Pele 15.00 40.00
6 T.Esposito/A.Dawson 10.00 25.00
7 G.Hall/B.Gibson 10.00 25.00
8 P.Roy/G.Carter 20.00 50.00
9 P.Roy/J.Elway 20.00 50.00
10 Datsyuk/Sanders 10.00 25.00
11 Leetch/Jackson 10.00 25.00
12 M.Gaborik/J.Morneau 10.00 25.00
13 M.Lemieux/J.Bay 30.00 80.00
14 J.Beliveau/T.Perez 10.00 25.00
15 M.Modano/M.Irvin 15.00 40.00
16 B.Hull/L.Brock 15.00 40.00
17 J.Jagr/R.Clemente 20.00 50.00

2007-08 ITG Ultimate Memorabilia Country Wide

STATED PRINT RUN 24 SERIAL #'d SETS
1 Jaromir Jagr 15.00 40.00
2 Jari Kurri 6.00 15.00
3 Roberto Luongo 8.00 20.00
4 Vincent Lecavalier 5.00 12.00
5 Brett Hull 10.00 25.00
6 Michel Goulet 5.00 12.00
7 Marcel Dionne 8.00 20.00
8 Bobby Clarke 6.00 15.00
9 Chris Chelios 6.00 15.00
10 Gilbert Perreault 6.00 15.00
11 Chris Pronger 5.00 12.00
12 Mats Naslund 6.00 15.00
13 Mike Richter 12.00 30.00
14 Joe Sakic
15 Borje Salming 6.00 15.00
16 Mats Sundin 6.00 15.00
17 Joe Thornton 8.00 20.00
18 Brian Leetch 6.00 15.00
19 Mike Modano 10.00 25.00
20 Nicklas Lidstrom
21 Mario Lemieux
22 Alexander Ovechkin 25.00 60.00
23 Patrick Roy 15.00 40.00
24 Kyle Okposo 8.00 20.00
25 John Tavares 25.00 60.00
26 Steven Stamkos 15.00 40.00
27 Sam Gagner 8.00 20.00
28 Martin Brodeur 12.00 30.00
29 Dany Heatley 6.00 15.00
30 Peter Forsberg 10.00 25.00
31 Pelle Lindbergh 8.00 20.00

2007-08 ITG Ultimate Memorabilia Double Memorabilia Autos

STATED PRINT RUN 24 SER.#'d SETS
1 Ovechkin/Kovalchuk 50.00 100.00
2 D.Keon/D.Sittler 25.00 60.00
3 B.Hull/B.Hull 40.00 80.00
4 Niedermayer/Pronger 10.00 25.00
5 T.Esposito/P.Esposito 40.00 80.00
6 M.Lemieux/J.Jagr 60.00 120.00
7 J.Tavares/S.Stamkos 40.00 80.00
8 J.Thornton/M.Schmidt 15.00 40.00
9 M.Brodeur/P.Roy 75.00 150.00
10 Lecavalier/M.St. Louis 20.00 50.00
11 R.Luongo/J.Giguere 30.00 60.00
12 D.Hasek/C.Osgood 15.00 40.00
13 J.Beliveau/G.Lafleur 25.00 60.00
14 B.Leetch/R.Bourque 25.00 60.00
15 M.Sundin/M.Naslund 25.00 60.00
16 E.Giacomin/G.Cheevers 20.00 50.00
17 P.Forsberg/J.Sakic 20.00 50.00
18 C.Chelios/N.Lidstrom 25.00 60.00
19 B.Clarke/B.Parent 25.00 60.00
20 M.Gaborik/P.Datsyuk
21 R.Francis/L.Robitaille
22 F.Mahovlich/J.Bower 30.00 80.00
23 P.Stastny/P.Stastny 20.00 50.00

2007-08 ITG Ultimate Memorabilia First Rounders

STATED PRINT RUN 24 SERIAL #'d SETS
1 John Tavares 25.00 60.00
2 Victor Hedman 12.00 30.00
3 Steven Stamkos 15.00 40.00
4 Drew Doughty
5 Alex Pietrangelo
6 Luke Schenn 25.00 60.00
7 Karl Alzner 10.00 25.00
8 Sam Gagner 15.00 40.00
9 Peter Mueller 15.00 40.00
10 Kyle Okposo 12.00 30.00
11 Bryan Little 12.00 30.00
12 Carey Price 30.00 60.00
13 Alexander Ovechkin 15.00 40.00
14 Alexander Semin 15.00 40.00
15 Ilya Kovalchuk 8.00 20.00
16 Dany Heatley 8.00 20.00
17 Marian Gaborik 12.00 30.00
18 Vincent Lecavalier 12.00 30.00
19 Joe Thornton
20 Roberto Luongo 12.00 30.00
21 Scott Niedermayer 10.00 25.00
22 Peter Forsberg 15.00 40.00
23 Jaromir Jagr 20.00 50.00
24 Martin Brodeur 20.00 50.00
25 Mats Sundin 12.00 30.00
26 Mike Modano 12.00 30.00
27 Joe Sakic
28 Brian Leetch 8.00 20.00
29 Wendel Clark 15.00 40.00
30 Mario Lemieux 20.00 50.00
31 Raymond Bourque 15.00 40.00
32 Denis Potvin 8.00 20.00
33 Guy Lafleur 12.00 30.00
34 Gilbert Perreault 10.00 25.00
35 Darryl Sittler

2007-08 ITG Ultimate Memorabilia Franchises

STATED PRINT RUN 24 SERIAL #'d SETS
1 Sundin/Gilmour/Potvin 20.00 50.00
2 Keon/Mahov/Horton 15.00 40.00
3 Beliveau/Harvey/Plante 20.00 50.00
4 Lafleur/Robinsn/Savard 15.00 40.00
5 Delvecchio/Abel/Lindsay 12.00 30.00
6 Datsyk/Lidstrm/Osgd 15.00 40.00
7 Lumley/Mosienko/Gadsby 12.00 30.00
8 Chelios/Belfour/Goulet 12.00 30.00
9 Giacomin/Park/Ratelle 12.00 30.00
10 Richter/Leetch/Vanbies 25.00 60.00
11 Shore/Thompson/Brimsk 12.00 30.00
12 Neely/Moog/Bourque 20.00 50.00
13 Forsberg/Roy/Sakic 30.00 80.00
14 Fuhr/Kurri/Anderson 12.00 30.00
15 Modano/Hull/Turco 20.00 50.00
16 Potvin/Smith/Bossy 12.00 30.00
17 Parent/Barber/Clarke 12.00 30.00
18 Lemieux/Jagr/Francis 40.00 100.00
19 Giguere/Hiller/Nieder 15.00 40.00
20 Lecav/St.L/Stamks 40.00 100.00
21 Sittler/McDonald/Salming 12.00 30.00

2007-08 ITG Ultimate Memorabilia Future Star Autos

STATED PRINT RUN 40 SERIAL #'d SETS
1 John Tavares 40.00 100.00
2 Ryan Parent 15.00 40.00
3 Ryan O'Marra 6.00 15.00
4 Logan Couture 10.00 25.00
5 Jonas Hiller 12.00 30.00
6 Alex Pietrangelo 15.00 40.00
7 Steve Mason 20.00 50.00
8 Andrew Cogliano 10.00 25.00
9 Leland Irving 15.00 40.00
10 Tuukka Rask 25.00 60.00
11 Kyle Okposo 8.00 20.00
12 Karl Alzner 6.00 15.00
13 Steven Stamkos 30.00 80.00
14 Steve Downie 8.00 20.00
15 Sam Gagner 12.00 30.00
16 Peter Mueller 8.00 20.00
17 Paul Stastny 10.00 25.00
18 Michael Frolik 8.00 20.00
19 Michael Del Zotto 10.00 25.00
20 Marc Staal 10.00 25.00
21 Jordan Staal 10.00 25.00
22 Jiri Tlusty 10.00 25.00
23 Jack Skille 8.00 20.00
24 Drew Doughty 20.00 50.00
25 Devin Setoguchi 10.00 25.00
26 Carey Price 60.00 120.00
27 Bryan Little 8.00 20.00
28 Angelo Esposito 12.00 30.00
29 Alexei Cherepanov 12.00 30.00
30 Brandon Sutter 10.00 25.00
31 Victor Hedman 15.00 40.00

2007-08 ITG Ultimate Memorabilia Gloves Are Off

STATED PRINT RUN 24 SERIAL #'d SETS
1 Joe Sakic 20.00 50.00
2 Joe Thornton 15.00 40.00
3 Alexander Ovechkin 25.00 60.00
4 Stan Mikita 15.00 40.00
5 Raymond Bourque 20.00 50.00
6 Pat LaFontaine 12.00 30.00
7 Martin Brodeur 25.00 60.00
8 Mario Lemieux 40.00 100.00
9 Eddie Shore 12.00 30.00
10 Dominik Hasek 15.00 40.00
11 Cam Neely 12.00 30.00
12 Brett Hull 20.00 50.00
13 Bobby Clarke 12.00 30.00
14 Patrick Roy 30.00 80.00
15 Sam Gagner 15.00 40.00
16 Bill Durnan 12.00 30.00
17 Paul Coffey 12.00 30.00
18 Mats Sundin
19 Drew Doughty 25.00 60.00
20 Charlie Conacher 10.00 25.00

2007-08 ITG Ultimate Memorabilia Jerseys

STATED PRINT RUN 24 SERIAL #'d SETS
1 Alexander Ovechkin 20.00 50.00
2 Bobby Hull 15.00 40.00
3 Borje Salming 10.00 25.00
4 Brett Hull 10.00 25.00
5 Carey Price 12.00 30.00
6 Chris Osgood 10.00 25.00
7 Dave Keon 20.00 50.00
8 Dominik Hasek 12.00 30.00
9 Glenn Hall 10.00 25.00
10 Guy Lafleur 12.00 30.00
11 Ilya Kovalchuk 10.00 25.00
12 Jean Beliveau 12.00 30.00
13 Joe Sakic 15.00 40.00
14 Joe Thornton 10.00 25.00
15 John Tavares 40.00 100.00
16 Marian Gaborik 12.00 30.00
17 Mario Lemieux 30.00 80.00
18 Martin Brodeur 20.00 50.00
19 Marty Turco 10.00 25.00
20 Mats Sundin 10.00 25.00
21 Maurice Richard 25.00 60.00
22 Mike Modano 15.00 40.00
23 Patrick Roy 25.00 60.00
24 Pavel Datsyuk 12.00 30.00
25 Peter Forsberg 12.00 30.00
26 Roberto Luongo 12.00 30.00
27 Scott Niedermayer 8.00 20.00
28 Steven Stamkos 30.00 80.00
29 Vincent Lecavalier 8.00 20.00
30 Vladislav Tretiak 15.00 30.00
31 Victor Hedman 20.00 50.00
32 Joe Nieuwendyk 10.00 25.00

2007-08 ITG Ultimate Memorabilia Jerseys Autographs

STATED PRINT RUN 30 SERIAL #'d SETS
1 Alexander Ovechkin 60.00 150.00
2 Bobby Clarke 15.00 40.00
3 Bobby Hull 25.00 60.00
4 Brett Hull 25.00 60.00
5 Cam Neely 15.00 40.00
6 Chris Chelios 15.00 40.00
7 Chris Osgood 15.00 40.00
8 Dominik Hasek 20.00 50.00
9 Ed Giacomin 15.00 40.00
10 Glenn Hall 20.00 50.00
11 Guy Lafleur 25.00 60.00
12 Ilya Kovalchuk 15.00 40.00
13 Jaromir Jagr 40.00 100.00
14 Jean Beliveau 20.00 50.00
15 Joe Sakic 25.00 60.00
16 Joe Thornton 20.00 50.00
17 John Tavares 25.00 60.00
18 Jean-Sebastien Giguere 15.00 40.00
19 Luc Robitaille 15.00 40.00
20 Marian Gaborik 15.00 40.00
21 Marcel Dionne 20.00 50.00
22 Mario Lemieux 60.00 120.00
23 Martin Brodeur 40.00 80.00
24 Martin St. Louis 15.00 40.00
25 Marty Turco 15.00 40.00
26 Mats Sundin 15.00 40.00
27 Mike Modano 25.00 60.00
28 Nicklas Lidstrom 15.00 40.00
29 Patrick Roy 40.00 100.00
30 Paul Stastny 15.00 40.00
31 Pavel Datsyuk 20.00 50.00
32 Peter Forsberg 20.00 50.00
33 Phil Esposito 25.00 60.00
34 Roberto Luongo 20.00 50.00
35 Ron Francis 20.00 50.00
36 Scott Niedermayer 15.00 40.00
37 Stan Mikita 15.00 40.00
38 Steven Stamkos 50.00 125.00
39 Tony Esposito 15.00 30.00
40 Vincent Lecavalier 12.00 30.00
41 Vladislav Tretiak 20.00 50.00
42 Joe Nieuwendyk 15.00 40.00
43 Victor Hedman 30.00 80.00
44 Brian Leetch 15.00 40.00
45 Bernie Parent 15.00 40.00
46 Frank Mahovlich 20.00 50.00
47 Pat LaFontaine 15.00 40.00
48 Red Kelly 12.00 30.00
49 Doug Gilmour 20.00 50.00
50 Alex Delvecchio 10.00 25.00

2007-08 ITG Ultimate Memorabilia Journey Jersey

STATED PRINT RUN 24 SERIAL #'d SETS
1 Mats Sundin 20.00 50.00
2 Ed Belfour 20.00 50.00
3 Raymond Bourque 30.00 80.00
4 Martin Brodeur 30.00 80.00
5 Chris Chelios 20.00 50.00
6 Paul Coffey 20.00 50.00
7 Peter Forsberg 25.00 60.00
8 Domink Hasek
9 Brett Hull 30.00 80.00
10 Jaromir Jagr 50.00 120.00
11 Brian Leetch 20.00 50.00
12 Mario Lemieux 60.00 150.00
13 Nicklas Lidstrom 20.00 50.00
14 Felix Potvin 30.00 80.00
15 Luc Robitaille 20.00 50.00
16 Patrick Roy 50.00 120.00
17 Dany Heatley 20.00 50.00
18 Joe Thornton 25.00 60.00
19 Mike Modano 30.00 80.00
20 Joe Sakic 30.00 80.00

2007-08 ITG Ultimate Memorabilia Net Average

STATED PRINT RUN 24 SERIAL #'d SETS
1 R.Worters/T.Thompson 20.00 50.00
2 E.Belfour/M.Brodeur
3 Marty Turco 10.00 25.00
4 Patrick Roy 25.00 60.00
5 Dominik Hasek 12.00 30.00
6 Bernie Parent 10.00 25.00
7 Tony Esposito 10.00 25.00
8 Frank Brimsek 10.00 25.00

2007-08 ITG Ultimate Memorabilia Net Wins

STATED PRINT RUN 24 SERIAL #'d SETS
1 P.Roy/M.Brodeur 40.00 100.00
2 Richter/Vanbiesbrouck 30.00 80.00
3 B.Parent/R.Hextall 25.00 60.00
4 Ed Belfour 10.00 25.00
6 Jacques Plante 15.00 40.00
7 Tony Esposito 10.00 25.00
8 Glenn Hall 10.00 25.00
9 Grant Fuhr 10.00 25.00
10 Dominik Hasek 12.00 30.00
12 Billy Smith 10.00 25.00

2007-08 ITG Ultimate Memorabilia Net Zero

STATED PRINT RUN 24 SERIAL #'d SETS
1 Sawchuk/Brodeur
2 G.Hall/T.Esposito 15.00 40.00
3 J.Plante/P.Roy 30.00 80.00
4 George Hainsworth 15.00 40.00
5 Tiny Thompson 20.00 50.00
6 Dominik Hasek 15.00 40.00
7 Ed Belfour 12.00 30.00
8 Harry Lumley 12.00 30.00
9 Roy Worters 15.00 40.00
10 Bernie Parent 12.00 30.00
11 Ed Giacomin 12.00 30.00
12 Rogie Vachon 15.00 40.00

2007-08 ITG Ultimate Memorabilia New Millennium First Rounders Autographs

STATED PRINT RUN 40 SERIAL #'d SETS
1 Alexei Cherepanov 25.00 50.00
2 Angelo Esposito 15.00 40.00
3 Bryan Little 10.00 25.00
4 Carey Price 40.00 80.00
5 Devin Setoguchi 12.00 30.00
6 Jack Skille 10.00 25.00
7 Jiri Tlusty 12.00 30.00
8 Jordan Staal 12.00 30.00
9 Marc Staal 12.00 30.00
10 Michael Del Zotto 10.00 25.00
11 Michael Frolik 10.00 25.00
12 Peter Mueller 10.00 25.00
13 Sam Gagner 15.00 40.00
14 Steve Downie 10.00 25.00
15 Karl Alzner 8.00 20.00
16 Kyle Okposo 15.00 40.00
17 Tuukka Rask 30.00 80.00
18 Leland Irving 12.00 30.00
19 Andrew Cogliano 12.00 30.00
20 Logan Couture 12.00 30.00
21 Ryan O'Marra 8.00 20.00
22 Ryan Parent 8.00 20.00
23 Brandon Sutter 12.00 30.00
24 Thomas Hickey 15.00 40.00
25 Benoit Pouliot 8.00 20.00
26 Jonathon Blum 12.00 30.00
27 Alex Pietrangelo 20.00 50.00
28 Steven Stamkos 40.00 80.00
29 Drew Doughty 25.00 60.00
30 John Tavares 40.00 80.00
31 Victor Hedman 25.00 60.00

2007-08 ITG Ultimate Memorabilia Past Present and Future

STATED PRINT RUN 24 SERIAL #'d SETS
1 Keon/Sundin/Schenn 20.00 50.00
2 Harvey/Nieder/Doughty 20.00 50.00
3 Beliveau/Lecav/Giroux 60.00 150.00
4 Hall/Luongo/Mason 40.00 100.00
5 Lafleur/Gaborik/Tavares 80.00 200.00
6 Lemieux/Thorntn/Gagner 25.00 60.00
7 Richard/St. Louis/Brule 30.00 80.00
8 Fuhr/Brodeur/Irving 40.00 100.00
9 Clarke/Heatley/Cogliano 20.00 50.00
10 Larionov/Ovech/Chere 25.00 60.00
11 Roy/Sakic/Budaj 40.00 108.00
12 Potvin/Pronger/Del Zotto 20.00 50.00
13 Salming/Chelios/Hickey 20.00 50.00
14 Richter/Modano/Okposo 40.00 100.00
15 Lindsay/Datsyuk/McCollum
16 Sawchuk/Turco/Hiller 20.00 50.00
17 Lindbergh/Giguere/Rask 40.00 100.00
18 Stastny/Jagr/Tlusty 40.00 108.00
19 Horton/Lidstrom/Pietrangelo 30.00 80.00
20 Naslund/Forsberg/Hedmn 40.00 100.00
21 Tretiak/Osgood/Price 60.00 120.00

2007-08 ITG Ultimate Memorabilia Raised to the Rafters

STATED PRINT RUN 24 SERIAL #'d SETS
1 Glenn Hall 12.00 30.00
2 Brian Leetch 10.00 25.00
3 Tony Esposito 10.00 25.00
4 Guy Lafleur 12.00 30.00
5 Larry Robinson 10.00 25.00
6 Johnny Bucyk 8.00 20.00

2007-08 ITG Ultimate Memorabilia Retro Teammates

STATED PRINT RUN 24 SERIAL #'d SETS
1 T.Thompson/E.Shore 12.00 30.00
2 S.Abel/A.Delvecchio 8.00 20.00
3 R.Bourque/C.Neely 20.00 50.00
4 P.Coffey/R.Francis 15.00 40.00
5 J.Sakic/M.Sundin 20.00 50.00
6 Hasek/LaFontaine 12.00 30.00
7 Anderson/Fuhr 12.00 30.00
8 E.Belfour/C.Chelios 12.00 30.00
9 Beliveau/J.Plante 15.00 40.00
10 M.Bossy/D.Potvin 12.00 30.00
11 B.Clarke/P.Lindbergh 15.00 40.00
12 B.Barber/B.Parent 12.00 30.00
13 D.Keon/Mahovlich 15.00 40.00
14 G.Lafleur/Cournoyer 15.00 40.00
15 R.Gilbert/E.Giacomin 12.00 30.00
16 T.Esposito/S.Mikita 15.00 40.00
17 G.Hall/B.Hull 20.00 50.00
18 G.Hainsworth/A.Joliat 20.00 50.00
19 T.Horton/J.Bower 12.00 30.00
20 B.Hull/L.McDonald 20.00 50.00
21 M.Lemieux/J.Jagr 40.00 100.00
22 Richter/Vanbiesbrouck 25.00 60.00
23 B.Mosienko/H.Lumley 12.00 30.00
24 B.Park/J.Ratelle 10.00 25.00
25 P.Roy/P.Forsberg 30.00 80.00
26 Lapointe/Robinson 12.00 30.00
27 B.Leetch/L.Robitaille 12.00 30.00
28 D.Gilmour/F.Potvin 20.00 50.00
29 B.Salming/D.Sittler 12.00 30.00
30 V.Tretiak/V.Kharlamov 12.00 30.00

2007-08 ITG Ultimate Memorabilia St. Patrick's Legacy

1 Patrick Roy Montreal Jersey 10.00 25.00
2 Patrick Roy Colorado Jersey 10.00 25.00
3 Patrick Roy Dual Jersey 12.00 30.00
4 Patrick Roy Montreal Pad 15.00 40.00
5 Patrick Roy Colorado Pad 15.00 40.00
6 Patrick Roy Dual Pad 20.00 50.00
7 Patrick Roy Montreal Glove 15.00 40.00
8 Patrick Roy Colorado Glove 15.00 40.00
9 Patrick Roy Dual Glove 20.00 50.00

2007-08 ITG Ultimate Memorabilia Stick Rack

ANNOUNCED PRINT RUN 24
1 Martin Brodeur 30.00 80.00
2 Felix Potvin 25.00 60.00
3 Pat LaFontaine 15.00 40.00
4 Mike Richter 20.00 50.00
5 Cam Neely 15.00 40.00
6 Joe Sakic 25.00 60.00
7 Jaromir Jagr 40.00 100.00
8 Vincent Lecavalier 12.00 30.00
9 Rogie Vachon 20.00 50.00
10 Grant Fuhr 15.00 40.00
11 Mario Lemieux 50.00 125.00
12 Alexander Ovechkin 40.00 100.00
13 Peter Stastny 15.00 40.00
14 Peter Forsberg 20.00 50.00
15 Martin St. Louis 15.00 40.00
16 Joe Thornton 20.00 50.00
17 Tony Esposito 15.00 40.00
18 Dominik Hasek 20.00 50.00
19 Chris Osgood 15.00 40.00
20 Luc Robitaille 15.00 40.00
21 Guy Lafleur 30.00 80.00
22 Phil Housley 12.00 30.00
23 Dale Hawerchuk 20.00 50.00
24 Michel Goulet 12.00 30.00
25 Ron Francis 20.00 50.00

2007-08 ITG Ultimate Memorabilia Sticks Autos

STATED PRINT RUN 30 SERIAL #'d SETS
1 Alexander Ovechkin 30.00 80.00
2 Marcel Dionne
3 Cam Neely 15.00 40.00
4 Chris Chelios 15.00 40.00
5 Dominik Hasek 20.00 50.00
6 Guy Lafleur 20.00 50.00
7 Jaromir Jagr 40.00 100.00
8 Joe Sakic 25.00 60.00
9 Joe Thornton 20.00 50.00
10 Jean-Sebastien Giguere 15.00 40.00
11 Luc Robitaille 15.00 40.00
12 Mario Lemieux 50.00 125.00
13 Martin Brodeur 30.00 80.00
14 Martin St. Louis 15.00 40.00
15 Marty Turco 15.00 40.00
16 Mike Modano 25.00 60.00
17 Tony Esposito 25.00 60.00
18 Mats Sundin 15.00 40.00
19 Pavel Datsyuk 20.00 50.00
20 Peter Forsberg 20.00 50.00
21 Roberto Luongo 20.00 50.00
22 Ron Francis 20.00 50.00
23 Scott Niedermayer 15.00 40.00
24 Stan Mikita 20.00 50.00
25 Vincent Lecavalier 12.00 30.00

2007-08 ITG Ultimate Memorabilia Vintage Lumber

STATED PRINT RUN 24 SERIAL #'d SETS
13 Chuck Rayner 12.00 30.00
14 Ed Giacomin 12.00 30.00
15 Stan Mikita 12.00 30.00
16 Joe Primeau 30.00 60.00
17 Johnny Bucyk 12.00 30.00
18 Roger Crozier 12.00 30.00
19 Norm Ullman 12.00 30.00
20 Harry Lumley 12.00 30.00

2008-09 ITG Ultimate Memorabilia

(1-15) PRINT RUN 30
(16-30) PRINT RUN 50
(31-90) PRINT RUN 90
1 Alex Delvecchio/30* 10.00 25.00
2 Alexander Ovechkin/30* 30.00 80.00
3 Denis Potvin/30* 8.00 20.00
4 Dominik Hasek/30* 10.00 25.00
5 Georges Vezina/30* 12.00 30.00
6 Gump Worsley/30* 6.00 15.00
7 Howie Morenz/30* 5.00 12.00
8 Joe Thornton/30* 10.00 25.00
9 Mario Lemieux/30* 25.00 60.00
10 Mario Lemieux/30* 25.00 60.00
11 Marty Turco/30* 8.00 20.00
12 Mike Modano/30* 12.00 30.00
13 Raymond Bourque/30* 12.00 30.00
14 Ted Lindsay/30* 8.00 20.00
15 Terry Sawchuk/30* 12.00 30.00
16 Brett Hull/50* 15.00 40.00
17 Chris Osgood/50* 6.00 15.00
18 Henri Richard/50* 8.00 20.00
19 Martin Brodeur/50* 12.00 30.00
20 Maurice Richard/50* 15.00 40.00
21 Maurice Richard/50* 15.00 40.00
22 Maurice Richard/50* 15.00 40.00
23 Maurice Richard/50* 15.00 40.00
24 Maurice Richard/50* 15.00 40.00
25 Maurice Richard/50* 15.00 40.00
26 Maurice Richard/50* 15.00 40.00
27 Maurice Richard/50* 15.00 40.00
28 Maurice Richard/50* 15.00 40.00
29 Maurice Richard/50* 15.00 40.00
30 Mikko Koivu/50* 5.00 12.00
31 Alexander Ovechkin/90* 25.00 60.00
32 Bill Barilko/90* 4.00 10.00
33 Borje Salming/90* 6.00 15.00
34 Cam Neely/90* 6.00 15.00
35 Carey Price/90* 25.00 60.00
36 Chris Chelios/90* 10.00 25.00
37 Chris Chelios/90* 12.00 30.00
38 Chris Osgood/90* 6.00 15.00
39 Darryl Sittler/90* 8.00 20.00
40 Dave Keon/90* 6.00 15.00
41 Dominik Hasek/90* 8.00 20.00
42 Doug Gilmour/90* 8.00 20.00
43 Ed Belfour/90* 6.00 15.00
44 Elmer Lach/90* 10.00 25.00
45 Evgeni Nabokov/90* 5.00 12.00
46 Frank Mahovlich/90* 6.00 15.00
47 Grant Fuhr/90* 6.00 15.00
48 Grant Fuhr/90* 6.00 15.00
49 Guy Lafleur/90* 8.00 20.00
50 Jacques Plante 10.00 25.00
51 Jari Kurri/90* 6.00 15.00
52 Jaromir Jagr/90* 10.00 25.00
53 Jaromir Jagr/90* 10.00 25.00
54 Jean Beliveau/90* 6.00 15.00
55 Joe Sakic/90* 12.00 30.00
56 Joe Sakic/90* 12.00 30.00
57 Joe Sakic/90* 12.00 30.00
58 Joe Thornton/90* 8.00 20.00
59 Johnny Bower/90* 8.00 20.00
60 John Tavares/90* 20.00 50.00
61 Lanny McDonald/90* 8.00 20.00
62 Larry Robinson/90* 6.00 15.00
63 Mario Lemieux/90* 20.00 50.00
64 Martin Brodeur/90* 12.00 30.00
65 Martin Brodeur/90* 12.00 30.00
66 Martin St. Louis/90* 6.00 15.00
67 Mats Sundin/90* 6.00 15.00
68 Mike Modano/90* 10.00 25.00
69 Nicklas Lidstrom/90* 12.50 30.00
70 Nicklas Lidstrom/90* 12.50 30.00
71 Pat LaFontaine/90* 6.00 15.00
72 Pat LaFontaine/90* 6.00 15.00
73 Patrick Roy/90* 15.00 40.00
74 Patrick Roy/90* 15.00 40.00
75 Patrick Roy/90* 15.00 40.00
76 Patrick Roy/90* 15.00 40.00
77 Phil Esposito/90* 10.00 25.00
78 Red Kelly/90* 8.00 20.00
79 Rob Blake/90* 6.00 15.00
80 Roberto Luongo/90* 8.00 20.00
81 Saku Koivu/90* 6.00 15.00
82 Scott Niedermayer/90* 6.00 15.00
83 Sergei Fedorov/90* 10.00 25.00
84 Syl Apps/90* 10.00 25.00
85 Ted Kennedy/90* 6.00 15.00
86 Tim Horton/90* 12.00 30.00
87 Tim Horton/90* 12.00 30.00
88 Tim Thomas/90* 6.00 15.00
89 Tony Esposito/90* 6.00 15.00
90 Turk Broda/90* 6.00 15.00

2008-09 ITG Ultimate Memorabilia Autographs

COMMON CARD/24* 8.00 20.00
UNLISTED STARS/24* 10.00 25.00
ANNOUNCED PRINT RUN 24
1 Alexander Ovechkin 40.00 80.00
2 Alexander Semin 10.00 25.00
3 Anze Kopitar 15.00 40.00
4 Carey Price 25.00 50.00
5 Chris Chelios 10.00 25.00
6 Miikka Kiprusoff 8.00 20.00
7 Evgeni Nabokov 8.00 20.00
8 Joe Thornton 12.00 30.00
9 Martin St. Louis 10.00 25.00
10 Marty Turco 8.00 20.00
11 Mike Green 10.00 25.00
12 Mike Modano
13 Mikko Koivu 8.00 20.00
14 Niklas Backstrom 10.00 25.00
15 Nicklas Lidstrom 10.00 25.00
16 Pavel Datsyuk 12.00 30.00
17 Roberto Luongo 12.00 30.00
18 Ryan Getzlaf 15.00 40.00
19 Scott Niedermayer 8.00 20.00
20 Sergei Fedorov 15.00 40.00

21 Teemu Selanne 15.00 40.00
22 Rob Blake 10.00 25.00
23 Saku Koivu 15.00 40.00
24 Jaromir Jagr 20.00 40.00
25 Marian Gaborik 12.00 30.00
26 Martin Brodeur 30.00 60.00
27 Daniel Briere 10.00 25.00
28 Ilya Kovalchuk 10.00 25.00
29 Patrick Marleau 10.00 25.00
30 Mats Sundin 10.00 25.00

2008-09 ITG Ultimate Memorabilia AutoMates

ANNOUNCED PRINT RUN 24
1 Ovechkin/Semin
2 Niedermayer/Selanne 25.00 50.00
3 Ovechkin/Green 40.00 100.00
4 Tavares/Kadri 40.00 100.00
5 Nabokov/Marleau 12.00 30.00
6 Datsyuk/Helm 15.00 40.00
7 Alzner/Varlamov 15.00 40.00
8 Koivu/Backstrom 12.00 30.00
9 Blake/Thornton 15.00 40.00
10 Price/Koivu 50.00 120.00
11 Turco/Modano 20.00 50.00
12 Chelios/Lidstrom 12.00 30.00
13 Stastny/Sakic 20.00 50.00
14 Luongo/Sundin 15.00 40.00
15 Giguere/Getzlaf 20.00 50.00
16 Thomas/Fernandez 12.00 30.00
17 Fedorov/Lidstrom 20.00 50.00
18 Henderson/Esposito 20.00 50.00
19 Yakushev/Mikhailov 15.00 40.00
20 Parent/Sanderson 20.00 50.00
21 Kane/Boychuk 20.00 50.00
22 Hickey/Eberle 30.00 60.00
23 Jagr/Lemieux 60.00 120.00
24 Duchene/Hodgson 30.00 80.00
25 Brodeur/Luongo 40.00 80.00
26 Esposito/Cheevers 20.00 50.00
27 Hasek/Hull 30.00 80.00
28 Richard/Lafleur 60.00 120.00
29 Hull/Mikita 40.00 100.00
30 Sittler/Salming 15.00 40.00

2008-09 ITG Ultimate Memorabilia Blades of Steel

ANNOUNCED PRINT RUN 19
1 Alexander Ovechkin 20.00 50.00
2 Ryan Getzlaf 8.00 20.00
3 Gilbert Perreault 6.00 15.00
4 Phil Esposito 15.00 40.00
5 Marcel Dionne 8.00 20.00
6 Joe Thornton 8.00 20.00
7 Jacques Plante 12.00 30.00
8 Stan Mikita 8.00 20.00
9 Johnny Bucyk 6.00 15.00
10 Mario Lemieux 20.00 50.00
11 Pavel Datsyuk 12.00 30.00
12 Jaromir Jagr 12.00 30.00

2008-09 ITG Ultimate Memorabilia Cityscapes

ANNOUNCED PRINT RUN 24
1 Clarke/Schmidt 30.00 80.00
2 Gilbert/Namath
3 Br.Hull/Warner
4 Sakic/Roy 15.00 40.00
5 Lemieux/Jagr 20.00 50.00
6 P.Esposito/Jackson
7 Hull/Rodman 10.00 25.00
8 Park/Pele 15.00 40.00
9 Beliveau/Carter 25.00 50.00
10 St. Louis/Sapp

2008-09 ITG Ultimate Memorabilia Cornerstones

STATED PRINT RUN 24 SER.#'d SETS
1 Kharl/Tretiak/Datsyuk/Ovech 60.00 120.00
2 Thmp/Brimse/Cheev/Thmas 30.00 60.00
3 Hainsworth/Plante/Roy/Price 50.00 100.00
4 Broda/Bower/Potvin/Toskala 30.00 60.00
5 Clarke/Parent/Lindbgh/Briere 50.00 100.00
6 Morenz/Richard/Lafleur/Koivu
7 Esposito/Sittler/Lemieux/Sakic 40.00 100.00
8 Salm/Naslnd/Lidstrm/Hedman 25.00 50.00
9 Esposito/Vachon/Fuhr/Brodeur 30.00 60.00
10 Lindsy/Delvch/Dionne/Datsyk 25.00 50.00
11 Luong/Thrnton/Price/Tavares 20.00 50.00
12 Sawchk/Dionne/Blake/Kopitr 25.00 60.00

2008-09 ITG Ultimate Memorabilia Decade Dominance

ANNOUNCED PRINT RUN 19
1 Gbk/Thn/Dts/Lds/Lng/Ovi 40.00 80.00
2 Brd/Lmx/Jgr/Ry/Snd/Skc 30.00 80.00
3 Ry/Smt/Nly/Clk/Brg/Lmx 30.00 80.00
4 Lfl/Str/Esp/Clk/Trk/Slm 30.00 60.00
5 Rch/Kn/Glb/Bwr/Hll/Mkt
6 Rch/Lnd/Blv/Plt/Swc/Abl 50.00 100.00

2008-09 ITG Ultimate Memorabilia Franchises

STATED PRINT RUN 24 SER.#'d SETS
1 Ovechkin/Semin/Varlamov 20.00 50.00
2 Clarke/MacLeish/Parent 15.00 30.00
3 Hull/Mikita/White 15.00 30.00
4 Park/Hadfield/Tkaczuk 15.00 30.00
5 Hull/Nieuwendyk/McDonald 15.00 30.00
6 Sittler/McDonald/Salming 15.00 30.00
7 Mahovlich/Kelly/Sawchuk 25.00 50.00
8 Thornton/Marleau/Nabokov
9 Bucyk/Cheevers/Esposito 15.00 30.00
10 L.Robinson/S.Savard/Lapointe 15.00 30.00
11 Brodeur/Nieuwndyk/S.Niedrmyr 15.00 30.00
12 Sundin/W.Clark/Gilmour 20.00 40.00
13 M.Richard/Beliveau/H.Richard 20.00 50.00
14 Modano/Turco/Brunnstrom 10.00 25.00
15 Roy/Chelios/Naslund 20.00 40.00
16 Datsyuk/Lidstrom/Osgood
17 Selanne/S.Niedermayer/Hiller 20.00 40.00
18 Thomas/Lucic/Fernandez 12.00 30.00

2008-09 ITG Ultimate Memorabilia From Russia with Love

STATED PRINT RUN 24 SER.#'d SETS
1 Alexander Ovechkin 15.00 40.00
2 Vladislav Tretiak 20.00 50.00
3 Pavel Datsyuk
4 Evgeni Nabokov 15.00 40.00
5 Valeri Kharlamov 20.00 50.00
6 Alexander Semin 15.00 40.00
7 Alexander Yakushev 15.00 40.00
8 Boris Mikhailov
9 Sergei Fedorov 15.00 40.00
10 Nikolai Kulemin 15.00 40.00
11 Simeon Varlamov 15.00 40.00
12 Ilya Kovalchuk 15.00 40.00

2008-09 ITG Ultimate Memorabilia Future Stars Autographs

STATED PRINT RUN 30 SER.#'d SETS
1 Simeon Varlamov 25.00 50.00
2 Nikolai Kulemin
3 Chet Pickard
4 Zach Boychuk
5 Dana Tyrell 6.00 15.00
6 Darren Helm 6.00 15.00
7 Scott Glennie 12.00 30.00
8 Evander Kane 12.00 30.00
9 Fabian Brunnstrom 6.00 15.00
10 Thomas Hickey 6.00 15.00
11 John Tavares 50.00 100.00
12 Taylor Hall 30.00 80.00
13 Jordan Eberle 25.00 50.00
14 Guillaume Latendresse
15 Jacob Josefson
16 Matt Duchene 15.00 40.00
17 Mikkel Boedker 6.00 15.00
18 Milan Lucic 15.00 40.00
19 Nazem Kadri 15.00 40.00
20 Oliver Ekman-Larsson 15.00 40.00
21 Ryan Ellis 15.00 40.00
22 Dustin Tokarski 12.00 30.00
23 Jonas Hiller 10.00 25.00
24 Jared Cowen 5.00 12.00
25 Victor Hedman 12.00 30.00
26 Carter Ashton
27 Mikhail Grabovski 15.00 40.00
28 Brayden Schenn 12.00 30.00
29 Paul Stastny 10.00 25.00
30 Cody Hodgson 25.00 50.00

2008-09 ITG Ultimate Memorabilia Future Stars Jerseys Autographs

ANNOUNCED PRINT RUN 15-19
1 Simeon Varlamov 20.00 50.00
2 Nikolai Kulemin 10.00 25.00
3 Chet Pickard 10.00 25.00
4 Zach Boychuk 10.00 25.00
5 Dana Tyrell 10.00 25.00
6 Darren Helm 10.00 25.00
7 Scott Glennie 10.00 25.00
8 Evander Kane 15.00 40.00
9 Fabian Brunnstrom 8.00 20.00
10 Thomas Hickey 12.00 30.00
11 John Tavares 75.00 125.00
12 Taylor Hall 20.00 50.00
13 Jordan Eberle 15.00 40.00
14 Azne Kopitar 15.00 40.00
15 Guillaume Latendresse 6.00 15.00
16 Matt Duchene 20.00 50.00
17 Mikkel Boedker 12.00 30.00
18 Milan Lucic 15.00 40.00
19 Nazem Kadri 20.00 50.00
20 Ryan Ellis 10.00 25.00
21 Dustin Tokarski 10.00 25.00
22 Jonas Hiller 8.00 20.00
23 Jared Cowen 10.00 25.00
24 Victor Hedman 20.00 50.00
25 Carter Ashton 10.00 25.00
26 Mikhail Grabovski 10.00 25.00
27 Brayden Schenn 20.00 50.00
28 Paul Stastny 10.00 25.00
29 Cody Hodgson 25.00 60.00
30 Karl Alzner/15 6.00 15.00

2008-09 ITG Ultimate Memorabilia Future Stars Patches Autographs

ANNOUNCED PRINT RUN 19
1 Oliver Ekman-Larsson 12.00 30.00
2 Simeon Varlamov 30.00 60.00
3 Nikolai Kulemin 10.00 25.00
4 Chet Pickard 10.00 25.00
5 Zach Boychuk 10.00 25.00
6 Dana Tyrell 10.00 25.00
7 Darren Helm 10.00 25.00
8 Scott Glennie 10.00 25.00
9 Evander Kane 20.00 50.00
10 Fabian Brunnstrom 8.00 20.00
11 Thomas Hickey 12.00 30.00
12 John Tavares 30.00 60.00
13 Taylor Hall 40.00 80.00
14 Jordan Eberle
15 Karl Alzner 6.00 15.00
16 Guillaume Latendresse 6.00 15.00
17 Matt Duchene 25.00 60.00
18 Mikkel Boedker 12.00 30.00
19 Milan Lucic 20.00 40.00
20 Nazem Kadri 30.00 60.00
21 Ryan Ellis 10.00 25.00
22 Dustin Tokarski 10.00 25.00
23 Jonas Hiller 8.00 20.00
24 Jared Cowen 10.00 25.00
25 Victor Hedman 20.00 50.00
26 Carter Ashton 10.00 25.00
27 Mikhail Grabovski 10.00 25.00
28 Brayden Schenn 20.00 50.00
29 Paul Stastny 10.00 25.00
30 Cody Hodgson 25.00 60.00
31 Anze Kopitar 15.00 40.00

2008-09 ITG Ultimate Memorabilia Gloves are Off

COMMON CARD/24* 8.00 20.00
UNL.STARS/24* 10.00 25.00
ANNOUNCED PRINT RUN 24
1 Alexander Ovechkin 20.00 50.00
2 Bobby Clarke
3 Ryan Getzlaf 10.00 25.00
4 Dominik Hasek 15.00 40.00
5 Ed Belfour 10.00 25.00
6 Evgeni Nabokov 10.00 25.00
7 Joe Sakic 12.00 30.00
8 Joe Thornton
9 John Tavares 15.00 40.00
10 Marian Gaborik 10.00 25.00
11 Mario Lemieux
12 Martin Brodeur 15.00 40.00
13 Patrick Roy Canadiens 20.00 50.00
14 Patrick Roy Avs 20.00 50.00
15 Raymond Bourque 10.00 25.00
16 Rob Blake 8.00 20.00
17 Chris Chelios 10.00 25.00
18 Scott Niedermayer
19 Sergei Fedorov
20 Stan Mikita 10.00 25.00

2008-09 ITG Ultimate Memorabilia Hometown Heroes

ANNOUNCED PRINT RUN 24
1 Alexander Ovechkin 25.00 60.00
2 Joe Sakic 10.00 25.00
3 Joe Thornton 8.00 20.00
4 John Tavares 20.00 50.00
5 Martin Brodeur 12.00 30.00
6 Patrick Roy 15.00 40.00
7 Bobby Clarke 10.00 25.00
8 Borje Salming 6.00 15.00
9 Mario Lemieux 20.00 50.00
10 Guy Lafleur 8.00 20.00
11 Teemu Selanne 10.00 25.00
12 Jaromir Jagr 12.00 30.00
13 Miikka Kiprusoff 5.00 12.00
14 Raymond Bourque 10.00 25.00
15 Roberto Luongo 8.00 20.00
16 Dominik Hasek 8.00 20.00
17 Ryan Getzlaf 10.00 25.00
18 Mike Modano 10.00 25.00

2008-09 ITG Ultimate Memorabilia Journey Jersey

ANNOUNCED PRINT RUN 24
1 Mats Sundin 10.00 25.00
2 Joe Sakic 10.00 25.00
3 Raymond Bourque 10.00 25.00
4 Patrick Roy 15.00 40.00
5 Joe Thornton 8.00 20.00
6 Roberto Luongo 8.00 20.00

2008-09 ITG Ultimate Memorabilia Legends Autographs

ANNOUNCED PRINT RUN 24
1 Jean Beliveau 25.00 50.00
2 Raymond Bourque 15.00 40.00
3 Johnny Bower 10.00 25.00
4 Gerry Cheevers 8.00 20.00
5 Wendel Clark 8.00 20.00
6 Bobby Clarke 12.00 30.00
7 Yvan Cournoyer 8.00 20.00
8 Marcel Dionne 10.00 25.00
9 Phil Esposito 12.00 30.00
10 Tony Esposito 8.00 20.00
11 Grant Fuhr 8.00 20.00
12 Glenn Hall 12.00 30.00
13 Dominik Hasek 10.00 25.00
14 Bobby Hull 12.00 30.00
15 Doug Gilmour 10.00 25.00
16 Brett Hull 15.00 40.00
17 Dave Keon 8.00 20.00
18 Derek Sanderson 10.00 25.00
19 Elmer Lach 12.00 30.00
20 Guy Lafleur 10.00 25.00
21 Ted Lindsay 15.00 30.00
22 Lanny McDonald 8.00 20.00
23 Stan Mikita 10.00 25.00
24 Boris Mikhailov 10.00 25.00
25 Alexander Yakushev 25.00 50.00
26 Joe Sakic 25.00 50.00
27 Henri Richard 25.00 50.00
28 Vladislav Tretiak 20.00 40.00
29 Mario Lemieux 40.00 80.00
30 Joe Nieuwendyk 8.00 20.00

2008-09 ITG Ultimate Memorabilia Numerology

ANNOUNCED PRINT RUN 24
1 Alexander Ovechkin 30.00 80.00
2 Mario Lemieux 25.00 60.00
3 Joe Sakic 12.00 30.00
4 Martin Brodeur 15.00 40.00
5 Patrick Roy 20.00 50.00
6 Pavel Datsyuk 10.00 25.00
7 Nicklas Lidstrom 10.00 25.00
8 John Tavares 20.00 50.00
9 Mats Sundin 8.00 20.00
10 Raymond Bourque 12.00 30.00
11 Jaromir Jagr 20.00 50.00
12 Frank Brimsek 6.00 15.00
13 Mike Modano 12.00 30.00
14 Carey Price 30.00 80.00
15 Vladislav Tretiak 6.00 15.00
16 Bobby Hull 12.00 30.00
17 Stan Mikita
18 Dominik Hasek 10.00 25.00
19 Ed Belfour 8.00 20.00
20 Brett Hull 20.00 50.00
21 Doug Harvey 8.00 20.00
22 Miikka Kiprusoff 6.00 15.00
23 Ilya Kovalchuk 8.00 20.00
24 Ryan Getzlaf 12.00 30.00

2008-09 ITG Ultimate Memorabilia Past Present and Future

ANNOUNCED PRINT RUN 24
1 Slmng/Ldstrm/Hedmn 12.00 30.00
2 Hull/Turco/Glennie 12.00 30.00
3 Neely/Thomas/Lucic 12.00 30.00
4 Sittler/Grabovski/Kadri 25.00 50.00
5 Gilmour/Tskla/Kulemin 8.00 20.00
6 Fuhr/Luongo/Price 25.00 60.00
7 Nwndyk/Modno/Brnstrm 10.00 25.00
8 Sakic/Stastny/Duchene 12.00 30.00
9 Dionne/Kopitar/Schenn 12.00 30.00
10 Dionne/Datsyuk/Helm 8.00 20.00
11 Lemx/Thorntn/Tavars 20.00 50.00
12 Kolzig/Ovech/Varlamov 25.00 60.00
13 Roy/Brodeur/Pickard 15.00 40.00
14 Brque/Ndrmayer/Cowen 12.00 30.00
15 Blake/Kopitar/Hickey 10.00 25.00
16 Vachon/Brdeur/Tokrski 25.00 50.00
17 Fedorov/Getzlaf/Hiller 10.00 25.00
18 Tretiak/Nabkv/Varlamv 15.00 40.00

2008-09 ITG Ultimate Memorabilia Retro Teammates

STATED PRINT RUN 24 SER.#'d SETS
1 Bernie Parent 10.00 25.00
Bobby Clarke
2 Bobby Hull 15.00 40.00
Glenn Hall
3 Brad Park 8.00 20.00
Rod Gilbert
4 Darryl Sittler 10.00 25.00
Lanny McDonald
5 Dave Keon 10.00 25.00
Frank Mahovlich
6 Felix Potvin 15.00 40.00
Wendel Clark
7 Gilbert Perreault 10.00 25.00
Rick Martin
8 Guy Lafleur 12.00 30.00
Steve Shutt
9 Jacques Plante 15.00 40.00
Henri Richard
10 Jean Beliveau 25.00 60.00
Maurice Richard
11 Joe Sakic 20.00 50.00
Patrick Roy
12 Mario Lemieux 30.00 80.00
Jaromir Jagr
13 Phil Esposito 15.00 40.00
Johnny Bucyk
14 Stan Mikita 12.00 30.00
Tony Esposito
15 Ted Lindsay 12.00 30.00
Alex Delvecchio
16 Terry Sawchuk 20.00 40.00
Johnny Bower
17 Tim Horton 12.00 30.00
Red Kelly
18 Valeri Kharlamov 10.00 25.00
Vladislav Tretiak

2008-09 ITG Ultimate Memorabilia Stick Autographs

ANNOUNCED PRINT RUN 24
1 Mike Modano 20.00 50.00
2 Pavel Datsyuk 15.00 40.00
3 Jean-Sebastien Giguere 12.00 30.00
4 Alexander Ovechkin 75.00 150.00
5 John Tavares 25.00 60.00
6 Ryan Getzlaf 20.00 50.00
7 Doug Gilmour 15.00 40.00
8 Brett Hull
9 Jaromir Jagr 30.00 60.00
10 Guy Lafleur 25.00 50.00
11 Chris Chelios 12.00 30.00
12 Nicklas Lidstrom 20.00 40.00
13 Joe Nieuwendyk 12.00 30.00
14 Joe Sakic 15.00 40.00
15 Borje Salming 12.00 30.00
16 Derek Sanderson 12.00 30.00
17 Teemu Selanne 25.00 60.00
18 Alexander Semin 10.00 25.00
19 Darryl Sittler 12.00 30.00
20 Mats Sundin 12.00 30.00
21 Marian Gaborik 15.00 40.00
22 Joe Thornton 15.00 40.00
23 Dominik Hasek 15.00 40.00
24 Evgeni Nabokov 10.00 25.00
25 Sergei Fedorov 25.00 50.00
26 Patrick Roy 50.00 100.00
27 Martin Brodeur 30.00 60.00
28 Daniel Briere 12.00 30.00
29 Roberto Luongo 15.00 40.00
30 Carey Price 40.00 80.00

2008-09 ITG Ultimate Memorabilia Stick Rack

ANNOUNCED PRINT RUN 24
1 Alexander Ovechkin 50.00 125.00
2 Chris Chelios 12.00 30.00
3 Marian Gaborik 15.00 40.00
4 Nicklas Lidstrom 15.00 40.00
5 Joe Thornton 15.00 40.00
6 Pavel Datsyuk 15.00 40.00
7 Dominik Hasek 15.00 40.00
8 Ryan Getzlaf 15.00 40.00
9 John Tavares 20.00 50.00
10 Evegeni Nabokov 10.00 25.00
11 Joe Sakic 20.00 50.00
12 Teemu Selanne 30.00 60.00
13 Jaromir Jagr 30.00 60.00
14 Martin Brodeur 40.00 80.00
15 Patrick Roy 30.00 60.00
16 Roberto Luongo 15.00 40.00
17 Mike Modano 25.00 50.00
18 Milan Lucic 20.00 50.00

2008-09 ITG Ultimate Memorabilia Trophy Winners

ANNOUNCED PRINT RUN 24
1 Alexander Ovechkin 25.00 60.00
2 Alexander Ovechkin 25.00 60.00
3 Mario Lemieux 20.00 50.00
4 Sergei Fedorov 10.00 25.00
5 Alexander Ovechkin 25.00 60.00
6 Pavel Datsyuk 8.00 20.00
7 Nicklas Lidstrom 6.00 15.00
8 Alexander Ovechkin 25.00 60.00
9 Alexander Ovechkin 25.00 60.00
10 Martin Brodeur 12.00 30.00
11 Jaromir Jagr 12.00 30.00
12 Martin Brodeur 12.00 30.00
13 Patrick Roy 15.00 40.00
14 Doug Gilmour 8.00 20.00
15 Joe Sakic 12.00 30.00
16 Joe Sakic 12.00 30.00
17 Raymond Bourque 10.00 25.00
18 Mario Lemieux 20.00 50.00
19 Ilya Kovalchuk 6.00 15.00
20 Patrick Roy 15.00 40.00

2008-09 ITG Ultimate Memorabilia Ultimate Defensemen

ANNOUNCED PRINT RUN 24
1 Scott Niedermayer/Nicklas LidstromChris Chelios/Borje SalmingLarry Robinson 15.00 40.00

2008-09 ITG Ultimate Memorabilia Ultimate Draft Pick Autographs

COMMON TAVARES/19* 30.00 60.00
COMMON TVRES/OVECH/19* 100.00 200.00
ANNOUNCED PRINT RUN 19

2008-09 ITG Ultimate Memorabilia Ultimate Forwards

ANNOUNCED PRINT RUN 24
1 Ovn/Thn/Skc/Hll/Abl/Jol 25.00 60.00
2 Tvr/Snd/Dne/Kn/Rch/Sch 40.00 80.00
3 Dat/Lmx/Esp/Lfl/Blv/Mrn 12.00 30.00

2008-09 ITG Ultimate Memorabilia Ultimate Goalies

STATED PRINT RUN 24 SER.#'d SETS
1 Plnt/Prc/Roy/Lng/Thm/Brd
2 Nbv/Hsk/Roy/Prt/Esp/Saw 30.00 80.00

2008-09 ITG Ultimate Memorabilia Ultimate Players Dual Swatch

ANNOUNCED PRINT RUN 19
TRIPLE/19: .4X TO 1X DUAL/19*
QUAD/19: .5X TO 1.2X DUAL/19*
FIVE/19: .6X TO 1.5X DUAL/19*
1 Alexander Ovechkin 20.00 50.00
2 John Tavares 10.00 25.00
3 Roberto Luongo 8.00 20.00
4 Nicklas Lidstrom 8.00 20.00
5 Mario Lemieux 20.00 50.00
6 Martin Brodeur 12.00 30.00
7 Patrick Roy 15.00 40.00
8 Joe Sakic 10.00 25.00
9 Jaromir Jagr 12.00 30.00

2008-09 ITG Ultimate Memorabilia Jerseys

ANNOUNCED PRINT RUN 24
1 Alexander Ovechkin 25.00 60.00
2 Joe Sakic 10.00 25.00
3 John Tavares 10.00 25.00
4 Ryan Getzlaf 10.00 25.00
5 Martin Brodeur 12.00 30.00
6 Patrick Roy 15.00 40.00
7 Mario Lemieux 20.00 50.00
8 Raymond Bourque 10.00 25.00
9 Mike Modano 10.00 25.00
10 Miikka Kiprusoff 5.00 12.00
11 Milan Lucic 10.00 25.00
12 Pavel Datsyuk 8.00 20.00

2010-11 ITG Ultimate Memorabilia

ANNOUNCED PRINT RUN 54
1 Georges Vezina 8.00 20.00
2 Eddie Shore 5.00 12.00
3 Charlie Conacher 5.00 12.00
4 Ron Francis 8.00 20.00
5 Bill Barilko 4.00 10.00
6 Doug Harvey 6.00 15.00
7 Howie Morenz 5.00 12.00
8 Luc Robitaille 6.00 15.00
9 Bobby Hull 6.00 15.00
10 Daniel Sedin 8.00 20.00
11 Peter Forsberg 8.00 20.00
12 Borje Salming 6.00 15.00
13 Teemu Selanne 15.00 40.00
14 Dave Keon 6.00 15.00
15 Cyclone Taylor 6.00 15.00
16 Brett Hull 10.00 25.00
17 Valeri Kharlamov 4.00 10.00
18 Hobey Baker 5.00 12.00
19 Ted Lindsay 6.00 15.00
20 Vladislav Tretiak 8.00 20.00
21 Mario Lemieux 20.00 50.00
22 Mike Bossy 6.00 15.00
23 Red Kelly 6.00 15.00
24 Steven Stamkos 10.00 25.00
25 Felix Potvin 10.00 25.00
26 Lester Patrick 6.00 15.00
27 Darryl Sittler 5.00 12.00
28 Gump Worsley 6.00 15.00
29 George Hainsworth 6.00 15.00
30 Martin Brodeur 12.00 30.00
31 Pelle Lindbergh 10.00 25.00
32 Denis Potvin 6.00 15.00
33 Patrick Roy COL 12.00 30.00
34 Charlie Gardiner 5.00 12.00
35 Tony Esposito 6.00 15.00
36 Newsy Lalonde 5.00 12.00
37 Turk Broda 6.00 15.00
38 Aurel Joliat 6.00 15.00
39 Dominik Hasek 10.00 25.00
40 Sid Abel 5.00 12.00
41 Igor Larionov 6.00 15.00
42 Maurice Richard 10.00 25.00
43 Bobby Bauer 6.00 15.00
44 Ted Kennedy 6.00 15.00
45 Woody Dumart 4.00 10.00
46 Carey Price 10.00 25.00
47 Chris Chelios 6.00 15.00
48 Paul Coffey 6.00 15.00
49 Syl Apps 8.00 20.00
50 Bill Durnan 6.00 15.00
51 Terry Sawchuk 8.00 20.00
52 Milt Schmidt 5.00 12.00
53 Elmer Lach 5.00 12.00
54 Marcel Dionne 8.00 20.00
55 Johnny Bucyk 6.00 15.00
56 Henri Richard 6.00 15.00
57 Miikka Kiprusoff 6.00 15.00
58 Frank Mahovlich 6.00 15.00
59 Stan Mikita 8.00 20.00
60 Jean Beliveau 6.00 15.00
61 Glenn Hall 6.00 15.00
62 Vincent Lecavalier 6.00 15.00
63 Phil Esposito 10.00 25.00
64 Ron Hextall 8.00 20.00
65 Gerry Cheevers 6.00 15.00
66 Bernie Parent 6.00 15.00
67 Johnny Bower 8.00 20.00
68 Jaromir Jagr 15.00 40.00
69 Toe Blake 4.00 10.00
70 Gilbert Perreault 6.00 15.00
71 Ilya Kovalchuk 8.00 20.00
72 Guy Lafleur 8.00 20.00
73 Larry Robinson 6.00 15.00
74 Tim Horton 6.00 15.00
75 Bobby Clarke 6.00 15.00
76 Bryan Trottier 8.00 20.00
77 Raymond Bourque 10.00 25.00
78 Ed Giacomin 10.00 25.00
79 Bernie Geoffrion 5.00 12.00
80 Peter Stastny 5.00 12.00
81 Grant Fuhr 6.00 15.00
82 Marian Gaborik 8.00 20.00
83 Jacques Plante 8.00 20.00
84 Pat LaFontaine 6.00 15.00
85 Patrick Roy MTL 12.00 30.00
86 Jari Kurri 6.00 15.00
87 Joe Sakic 10.00 25.00
88 Mike Modano 12.00 30.00
89 Lanny McDonald 6.00 15.00
90 Henrik Sedin 8.00 20.00
91 Sergei Fedorov 10.00 25.00
92 Nicklas Lidstrom 8.00 20.00
93 Doug Gilmour 8.00 20.00
94 Cam Neely 6.00 15.00
95 Tyler Seguin 10.00 25.00
96 Roberto Luongo 8.00 20.00
97 Joe Thornton 8.00 20.00
98 Wendel Clark 6.00 15.00
99 Tim Thomas 6.00 15.00
100 Steve Yzerman 20.00 50.00

2010-11 ITG Ultimate Memorabilia 500 Goal Combos

ANNOUNCED PRINT RUN 24
1 M.Richard/G.Hall 15.00 40.00
2 G.Howe/G.Worsley 25.00 60.00
3 B.Hull/E.Giacomin 25.00 50.00
4 J.Beliveau/G.Gilbert 15.00 30.00
5 S.Mikita/C.Maniago 12.00 30.00
6 G.Lafleur/C.Resch 12.00 30.00
7 D.Ciccarelli/K.Hrudy 10.00 25.00
8 M.Lemieux/T.Soderstrom 30.00 80.00
9 M.Messier/R.Tabaracci 20.00 30.00
10 S.Yzerman/P.Roy 25.00 60.00
11 D.Hawerchuk/F.Potvin 15.00 40.00
12 B.Hull/S.Fiset 15.00 40.00
13 J.Mullen/P.Roy 20.00 50.00
14 D.Andreychuk/B.Ranford 10.00 25.00
15 L.Robitaille/D.Roloson 10.00 25.00
16 P.Verbeek/F.Brathwaite 8.00 20.00
17 R.Francis/B.Dafoe 15.00 40.00
18 B.Shanahan/P.Roy 25.00 60.00
19 J.Sakic/D.Cloutier 15.00 40.00
20 J.Nieuwendyk/K.Weekes 10.00 25.00
21 J.Jagr/J.Grahame 15.00 40.00
22 P.Turgeon/V.Toskala 10.00 25.00
23 M.Sundin/M.Kiprusoff 25.00 50.00
24 T.Selanne/J.Theodore 15.00 40.00
25 P.Bondra/J.Aubin 8.00 20.00
26 M.Recchi/M.Turco 12.00 30.00
27 M.Modano/A.Niittymaki 15.00 40.00
28 J.Roenick/A.Auld 15.00 40.00

2010-11 ITG Ultimate Memorabilia Autographs

ANNOUNCED PRINT RUN 24
1 Rick Nash 12.00 30.00
2 Carey Price 20.00 50.00
3 Martin Brodeur 20.00 50.00
4 Marian Gaborik
5 Ryan Getzlaf
6 Niklas Backstrom 12.00 30.00
7 Nicklas Lidstrom
8 Roberto Luongo 12.00 30.00
9 Patrick Marleau
10 Teemu Selanne 12.00 30.00
11 Vincent Lecavalier
12 Joe Thornton
13 Martin St. Louis 10.00 25.00
14 Miikka Kiprusoff 8.00 20.00
15 Alexander Semin
16 Duncan Keith
17 Jimmy Howard 12.00 30.00
18 Zdeno Chara 12.00 30.00
19 Steven Stamkos 20.00 40.00
20 Daniel Sedin 12.00 30.00
21 Henrik Sedin
22 Ilya Kovalchuk 8.00 20.00
23 Brenden Morrow 10.00 25.00
24 Eric Staal
25 Milan Lucic
26 Mike Modano 12.00 30.00
27 Marty Turco 10.00 25.00

2010-11 ITG Ultimate Memorabilia Autographs Duals

ANNOUNCED PRINT RUN 19
1 Mahovlich/Kelly 40.00 80.00
2 Salming/Clark 15.00 40.00
3 R.Brodeur/Luongo 20.00 40.00
4 Stamkos/Nash 40.00 80.00
5 Beliveau/Lafleur 30.00 60.00
6 Yzerman/Hull 40.00 80.00
7 Fuhr/Messier 30.00 60.00
8 Lidstrom/Niedermayer
9 Thornton/Nabokov
10 P.Esposito/Bucyk 20.00 50.00
11 Lecavalier/St. Louis 12.00 30.00
12 Giguere/Bower
13 Bure/Neely 15.00 40.00
14 Hull/Mikita 25.00 50.00
15 M.Brodeur/Kovalchuk 40.00 80.00
16 Clark/Sittler 20.00 40.00
17 Gaborik/Jagr 30.00 60.00
18 Price/Roy 50.00 100.00
19 Niedermayer/Selanne 20.00 50.00
20 D.Sedin/H.Sedin 20.00 40.00
21 Bure/Larionov 20.00 50.00
22 Lindsay/Lach 15.00 40.00
23 Niemi/Keith 15.00 40.00
24 Hull/Hall 25.00 50.00

2010-11 ITG Ultimate Memorabilia AutoMates

ANNOUNCED PRINT RUN 19
1 Lach/Beliveau 40.00 80.00
2 Keon/Bower 20.00 40.00
3 Sittler/McDonald 20.00 40.00
4 Thornton/Marleau
5 M.Koivu/Gaborik 20.00 40.00
6 Yzerman/Robitaille 40.00 80.00
7 Kurri/Messier
8 Lidstrom/Salming 30.00 60.00
9 Tretiak/Yakushev
10 P.Esposito/T.Esposito 25.00 50.00
11 Lecavalier/St. Louis
12 Keith/Niedermayer 20.00 40.00
13 Trottier/Smith 25.00 50.00
14 Hull/Hall 25.00 50.00
15 Brodeur/Kovalchuk
16 Clarke/Schultz 25.00 50.00
17 Gilmour/Clark 30.00 60.00
18 Neely/Bourque 30.00 60.00
19 Lafleur/Richard 30.00 60.00
20 Mahovlich/Olmstead 25.00 50.00

2010-11 ITG Ultimate Memorabilia Brotherly Love

ANNOUNCED PRINT RUN 24
1 P.Bure/V.Bure 12.00 30.00
2 M.Dionne/G.Dionne 12.00 30.00
3 P.Esposito/T.Esposito 15.00 40.00
4 M.Hossa/M.Hossa 8.00 20.00
5 B.Hull/D.Hull 12.00 30.00
6 S.Koivu/M.Koivu 10.00 25.00
7 F.Mahovlich/P.Mahovlich 10.00 25.00
8 S.Niedermayer/R.Niedermayer 10.00 25.00
9 R.Sutter/R.Sutter 8.00 20.00
10 K.Primeau/W.Primeau 10.00 25.00
11 M.Richard/H.Richard 15.00 40.00
12 S.Fedorov/F.Fedorov 15.00 40.00
13 H.Sedin/D.Sedin 10.00 25.00
14 E.Staal/M.Staal 12.00 30.00
15 J.Staal/J.Staal 10.00 25.00
16 P.Stastny/A.Stastny 10.00 25.00

2010-11 ITG Ultimate Memorabilia Country of Origin

ANNOUNCED PRINT RUN 24
1 P.Esposito/B.Clarke
2 M.Messier/S.Yzerman 20.00 50.00
3 M.Lemieux/J.Sakic
4 M.Brodeur/J.Thornton 15.00 40.00
5 J.Jagr/D.Hasek 20.00 40.00
6 P.Stastny/M.Gaborik 15.00 40.00
7 M.Modano/B.Hull 15.00 40.00
8 P.LaFontaine/C.Chelios 12.00 30.00
9 R.Miller/Z.Parise 15.00 30.00
10 J.Kurri/T.Selanne
11 M.Kiprusoff/S.Koivu 20.00 40.00
12 I.Kovalchuk/E.Malkin 15.00 40.00
13 P.Bure/S.Fedorov 20.00 50.00
14 V.Tretiak/V.Kharlamov 30.00 80.00
15 N.Lidstrom/P.Forsberg 20.00 40.00
16 P.Lindbergh/M.Naslund 20.00 50.00

2010-11 ITG Ultimate Memorabilia Days Gone By

ANNOUNCED PRINT RUN 24
1 Lanny McDonald 10.00 25.00
2 Roy Worters 15.00 40.00
3 Keith Tkachuk 10.00 25.00
4 Dave Keon 10.00 25.00
5 Mike Modano 15.00 40.00
6 Mats Sundin 10.00 25.00
7 Joe Sakic 15.00 40.00
8 Michel Goulet 8.00 20.00
9 Bobby Hull 10.00 25.00
10 Teemu Selanne 20.00 50.00

2010-11 ITG Ultimate Memorabilia Decades

ANNOUNCED PRINT RUN 24
1 Lalonde/Tylr/Nighbor/Morn
2 Shore/Joliat/Mornz/Hnswrth 75.00 135.00
3 Wortrs/Clncy/Cnchr/Baily 60.00 120.00
4 Richrd/Schmdt/Abel/Durnn 60.00 120.00
5 Mosnko/Hrvy/Swchk/Plante 40.00 80.00
6 Hull/Beliveau/Mahovlich/Hall 40.00 80.00
7 Esposito/Sittler/Laflr/Clrk 25.00 60.00
8 Messr/Bossy/Dionne/Mario 40.00 80.00
9 Fuhr/Roy/Bourque/Potvin 40.00 80.00
10 Brodeur/Hasek/Belfour/Roy 40.00 80.00
11 Yzerman/Sakic/Jagr/Mario 40.00 80.00
12 Brodeur/Thrntn/Lecavl/Kvlchk 25.00 60.00

2010-11 ITG Ultimate Memorabilia European Influence

ANNOUNCED PRINT RUN 24
1 Evgeni Malkin 25.00 60.00
2 Ilya Kovalchuk 8.00 20.00
3 Igor Larionov 8.00 20.00
4 Sergei Fedorov 12.00 30.00
5 Peter Forsberg 10.00 25.00
6 Borje Salming 8.00 20.00
7 Mats Naslund 8.00 20.00
8 Pelle Lindbergh 12.00 30.00
9 Nicklas Lidstrom 8.00 20.00
10 Jari Kurri 8.00 20.00
11 Esa Tikkanen 8.00 20.00
12 Teemu Selanne 15.00 40.00
13 Saku Koivu 8.00 20.00
14 Miikka Kiprusoff 6.00 15.00
15 Peter Stastny 6.00 15.00
16 Jaromir Jagr 20.00 50.00
17 Dominik Hasek 12.00 30.00
18 Marian Gaborik 6.00 15.00

2010-11 ITG Ultimate Memorabilia Father's Day

ANNOUNCED PRINT RUN 24
1 T.Lindsay/B.Lindsay 10.00 25.00
2 J.Grahame/R.Grahame 10.00 25.00
3 R.Hextall/B.Hextall Jr. 12.00 30.00
4 B.Hull/B.Hull 15.00 40.00
5 E.Nystrom/B.Nystrom 8.00 20.00
6 Z.Parise/J.Parise 10.00 25.00
7 C.Bourque/R.Bourque 10.00 25.00
8 Y.Stastny/P.Stastny 8.00 20.00

2010-11 ITG Ultimate Memorabilia Future Stars Autographs

ANNOUNCED PRINT RUN 24
1 Tyler Seguin
2 Jacob Markstrom 12.00 30.00
3 Oliver Ekman-Larsson 12.00 30.00
4 Zach Boychuk
5 Mikkel Boedker 6.00 15.00
6 Colton Gillies 6.00 15.00
7 Cody Hodgson 30.00 60.00
8 Brayden Schenn 20.00 40.00
9 Ryan Nugent-Hopkins 30.00 80.00
10 Kyle Turris 8.00 20.00
11 Scott Glennie
12 Thomas Hickey
13 Jared Cowen 8.00 20.00
14 Lars Eller 8.00 20.00
15 Oscar Moller 8.00 20.00
16 Dana Tyrell 8.00 20.00
17 Karl Alzner 6.00 15.00
18 Tyler Bozak 10.00 25.00
19 Michal Neuvirth 8.00 20.00
20 P.K. Subban 25.00 60.00
21 Vladimir Tarasenko 40.00 80.00
22 Ryan Murray 12.00 30.00
23 Antti Niemi 8.00 20.00

2010-11 ITG Ultimate Memorabilia Future Stars Jerseys Autographs

ANNOUNCED PRINT RUN 24
PATCH/19: .4X TO 1X JSY/24*
1 Tyler Seguin
2 Nazem Kadri 25.00 60.00
3 Vladimir Tarasenko 75.00 150.00
4 Jacob Markstrom 12.00 30.00
5 Oliver Ekman-Larsson
6 Zach Boychuk 8.00 20.00
7 Mikkel Boedker 6.00 15.00
8 Colton Gillies 6.00 15.00
9 Cody Hodgson 30.00 60.00
10 Brayden Schenn 12.00 30.00
11 Ryan Nugent-Hopkins 30.00 80.00
12 Kyle Turris 10.00 25.00
13 Scott Glennie 8.00 20.00
14 Thomas Hickey
15 Jared Cowen 8.00 20.00
16 Lars Eller
17 Oscar Moller 10.00 25.00
18 Dana Tyrell 8.00 20.00
19 Ryan Murray 12.00 30.00
20 Antti Niemi 8.00 20.00

2010-11 ITG Ultimate Memorabilia Goalies Autographs

ANNOUNCED PRINT RUN 24
1 Martin Brodeur 40.00 80.00
2 Jean-Sebastien Giguere 12.00 30.00
3 Roberto Luongo 15.00 40.00
4 Evgeni Nabokov
5 Carey Price
6 Jonathan Quick 30.00 60.00
7 Tim Thomas
8 Semyon Varlamov 20.00 40.00
9 Niklas Backstrom 15.00 40.00
10 Jonas Hiller 10.00 25.00

2010-11 ITG Ultimate Memorabilia Goalies Legends Autographs

ANNOUNCED PRINT RUN 19
1 Patrick Roy 50.00 100.00
2 Glenn Hall 12.00 30.00
3 Billy Smith
4 Tony Esposito 12.00 30.00
5 Gump Worsley 15.00 40.00
6 Bernie Parent 12.00 30.00
7 Ed Giacomin 12.00 30.00
8 Gerry Cheevers 20.00 40.00
9 Vladislav Tretiak 15.00 40.00
10 Dominik Hasek 15.00 40.00

2010-11 ITG Ultimate Memorabilia Goalies Legends Memorabilia Autographs

ANNOUNCED PRINT RUN 19
1 Patrick Roy
2 Glenn Hall 12.00 30.00
3 Billy Smith 12.00 30.00
4 Tony Esposito
5 Gump Worsley 15.00 40.00
6 Bernie Parent 12.00 30.00
7 Ed Giacomin 25.00 50.00
8 Gerry Cheevers 15.00 40.00
9 Vladislav Tretiak 30.00 60.00
10 Dominik Hasek 25.00 50.00

2010-11 ITG Ultimate Memorabilia Goalies Memorabilia Autographs
NNOUNCED PRINT RUN 19
Martin Brodeur 30.00 60.00
Jean-Sebastien Giguere 8.00 20.00
Roberto Luongo 40.00 80.00
Evgeni Nabokov 8.00 20.00
Carey Price 25.00 50.00
Jonathan Quick 30.00 60.00
Tim Thomas 15.00 40.00
Semyon Varlamov 10.00 25.00
Niklas Backstrom
Jonas Hiller

2010-11 ITG Ultimate Memorabilia Hall of Famer Autographs
NNOUNCED PRINT RUN 24
Mario Lemieux 50.00 100.00
Stan Mikita
Mark Messier
Johnny Bucyk 25.00 50.00
Raymond Bourque
Dickie Moore
Frank Mahovlich
Patrick Roy
Bernie Parent 25.00 50.00
Bobby Clarke
Gump Worsley
Borje Salming 15.00 40.00
Glenn Anderson 15.00 40.00
Milt Schmidt 15.00 40.00
Vladislav Tretiak
Henri Richard 15.00 40.00
Denis Potvin 12.00 30.00
Dino Ciccarelli
Cam Neely 15.00 40.00
Ted Lindsay 15.00 40.00
Bill Barber
Pat Lafontaine 15.00 40.00
Guy Lafleur 20.00 50.00
Elmer Lach 12.00 30.00
Jari Kurri 15.00 40.00
Dave Keon 15.00 40.00
Phil Esposito 25.00 60.00
Marcel Dionne 20.00 50.00
Alex Delvecchio 12.00 30.00
Paul Coffey 15.00 40.00
Ron Francis 12.00 30.00
Grant Fuhr 15.00 40.00
Jean Beliveau 25.00 50.00
Gilbert Perreault 15.00 40.00
Luc Robitaille 15.00 40.00
Yvan Cournoyer 15.00 40.00
Scotty Bowman 15.00 40.00
Bert Olmstead 15.00 40.00
Brett Hull 25.00 60.00
Brad Park 12.00 30.00
Jacques Laperriere
Rod Langway
Igor Larionov 12.00 30.00
Serge Savard 15.00 40.00
Norm Ullman
Dick Duff 12.00 30.00
Lanny McDonald 10.00 25.00
Steve Yzerman 30.00 60.00
Bobby Hull
Red Kelly

2010-11 ITG Ultimate Memorabilia Legends Autographs
NNOUNCED PRINT RUN 24
Doug Gilmour 15.00 40.00
Sergei Fedorov 12.00 30.00
Jaromir Jagr 25.00 50.00
Joe Sakic 20.00 50.00
Mats Sundin 25.00 50.00
Rogie Vachon
Dominik Hasek 30.00 60.00
Joe Nieuwendyk 10.00 25.00
Rob Blake 12.00 30.00
Chris Chelios 10.00 25.00
Scott Niedermayer 12.00 30.00
Keith Tkachuk 12.00 30.00
Wendel Clark 15.00 40.00
Alexander Yakushev
Richard Brodeur 12.00 30.00
Tod Sloan 10.00 25.00
Lou Fontinato 10.00 25.00
Pavel Bure 25.00 50.00
Terry O'Reilly
Eddie Shack
Peter Forsberg 15.00 40.00

2010-11 ITG Ultimate Memorabilia Les Capitaines
6 ANNOUNCED PRINT RUN 9
12 ANNOUNCED PRINT RUN 24
Newsy Lalonde/9*
George Hainsworth/9*
Toe Blake/9*
Bill Durnan/9*
Maurice Richard/9*
Doug Harvey/9*
Jean Beliveau 12.00 30.00
Henri Richard 10.00 25.00
Yvan Cournoyer 10.00 25.00
Serge Savard 10.00 25.00
Bob Gainey 10.00 25.00
Guy Carbonneau 10.00 25.00
Chris Chelios 10.00 25.00
Kirk Muller 6.00 15.00
Pierre Turgeon 10.00 25.00
Vincent Damphousse 8.00 20.00
Saku Koivu 10.00 25.00
Brian Gionta 8.00 20.00

2010-11 ITG Ultimate Memorabilia Memorabilia Autographs Duals
MMON CARD 20.00 40.00
NNOUNCED PRINT RUN 19
Richard/Beliveau 30.00 60.00
Keon/Clark 25.00 50.00
Brodeur/Luongo 30.00 60.00
Thornton/Nash 25.00 50.00
Gilbert/Lafleur 30.00 60.00
Yzerman/Hull 40.00 80.00
Fuhr/Messier 30.00 60.00
Lidstrom/Bourque 30.00 60.00
Tretiak/Nabokov 30.00 60.00
P.Esposito/Bucyk 30.00 60.00
Lecavalier/St. Louis
Giguere/Bower 20.00 40.00
Bure/Neely 25.00 50.00
Hull/Mikita 25.00 50.00
M.Brodeur/Kovalchuk 30.00 60.00
Clarke/Sittler 25.00 50.00
Gaborik/Jagr 25.00 50.00

18 Price/Roy 75.00 125.00
19 Niedermayer/Selanne 30.00 60.00
20 Mahovlich/Kelly

2010-11 ITG Ultimate Memorabilia Pads and Gloves
ANNOUNCED PRINT RUN 24
1 Carey Price 40.00 100.00
2 Olaf Kolzig 10.00 25.00
3 Michael Leighton 8.00 20.00
4 Marc-Andre Fleury 15.00 40.00
5 Ilya Bryzgalov 8.00 20.00
6 Cam Ward 10.00 25.00
7 Dominik Hasek 15.00 40.00
8 Niklas Backstrom 10.00 25.00
9 Gerry Cheevers 10.00 25.00
10 Marty Turco 10.00 25.00
11 Vladislav Tretiak 12.00 30.00
12 Patrick Roy 25.00 60.00
13 Chris Osgood 10.00 25.00
14 Nikolai Khabibulin 8.00 20.00
15 Ed Belfour 10.00 25.00
16 Curtis Joseph 12.00 30.00
17 Martin Brodeur 20.00 50.00
18 Ron Hextall 12.00 30.00
19 Grant Fuhr 10.00 25.00
20 Rick DiPietro 8.00 20.00
21 Tim Thomas 8.00 20.00

2010-11 ITG Ultimate Memorabilia Past Present Future
ANNOUNCED PRINT RUN 24
1 Sittler/Giguere/Kadri 25.00 60.00
2 Perreault/Stamkos/RNH 40.00 80.00
3 Sakic/Thornton/Schenn 15.00 40.00
4 Cheevers/Thomas/Rask 10.00 25.00
5 Yzerman/Lidstrom/Helm 25.00 60.00
6 Messier/Sedin/Hodgson 30.00 80.00
7 Neely/Lucic/Seguin 30.00 80.00
8 Niedermyr/Selanne/Fowler 20.00 50.00
9 Hasek/Osgood/Howard 15.00 40.00
10 Kharlmv/Kvlchk/Tarsnko 25.00 60.00
11 Nieuwendyk/Mrrw/Glenn 10.00 25.00
12 Roy/Miller/Markstrom 25.00 60.00

2010-11 ITG Ultimate Memorabilia Stick and Jersey Autographs
ANNOUNCED PRINT RUN 19
1 Steve Yzerman 50.00 100.00
2 Ryan Getzlaf 30.00 60.00
3 Mike Modano
4 Joe Sakic
5 Mark Messier 30.00 60.00
6 Guy Lafleur 25.00 50.00
7 Vincent Lecavalier 12.00 30.00
8 Mats Sundin 15.00 40.00
9 Jean Beliveau 50.00 100.00
10 Rob Blake 12.00 30.00
11 Raymond Bourque 30.00 60.00
12 Wendel Clark 15.00 40.00
13 Marcel Dionne
14 Marian Gaborik 15.00 40.00
15 Ilya Kovalchuk 25.00 50.00
16 Steven Stamkos
17 Roberto Luongo
18 Scott Niedermayer 10.00 25.00
19 Carey Price
20 Martin Brodeur 30.00 60.00

2010-11 ITG Ultimate Memorabilia Stick Work
ANNOUNCED PRINT RUN 24
1 Peter Forsberg 25.00 60.00
2 Brad Richards 20.00 50.00
3 Eric Staal 25.00 60.00
4 Zdeno Chara 15.00 40.00
5 Miikka Kiprusoff 15.00 40.00
6 Ryan Miller 20.00 50.00
7 Johan Franzen 20.00 50.00
8 Tyler Bozak 20.00 50.00
9 Jaromir Jagr 50.00 120.00
10 Jarome Iginla 20.00 50.00
11 Chris Pronger 15.00 40.00
12 Evgeni Malkin 60.00 150.00
13 Trevor Linden 20.00 50.00
14 Simon Gagne 20.00 50.00
15 Pavel Bure 25.00 60.00
16 Ed Jovanovski 12.00 30.00
17 Jack Johnson 12.00 30.00
18 Joe Sakic 20.00 50.00
19 Steven Stamkos 40.00 100.00
20 Benoit Pouliot 12.00 30.00
21 Ryan Suter 12.00 30.00
22 Joe Thornton 20.00 50.00
23 Tyler Seguin 50.00 100.00
24 Kyle Okposo 20.00 50.00
25 Mike Richter 20.00 50.00
26 Alexander Ovechkin 80.00 200.00
27 Jonathan Toews 40.00 100.00
28 Patrick Kane 40.00 100.00
29 Phil Kessel 25.00 60.00
30 Ilya Kovalchuk 20.00 50.00

2010-11 ITG Ultimate Memorabilia Ultimate All-Stars
ANNOUNCED PRINT RUN 24
1 Teemu Selanne 10.00 25.00
2 Jaromir Jagr 20.00 50.00
3 Joe Thornton 8.00 20.00
4 Mario Lemieux 25.00 60.00
5 Rob Blake 8.00 20.00
6 Nicklas Lidstrom 8.00 20.00
7 Patrick Roy 20.00 50.00
8 Dominik Hasek 12.00 30.00
9 Sergei Fedorov 10.00 25.00
10 Joe Sakic 12.00 30.00
11 Peter Forsberg 10.00 25.00
12 Pavel Bure 10.00 25.00
13 Chris Chelios 8.00 20.00
14 Paul Coffey 8.00 20.00
15 Evgeni Nabokov 6.00 15.00
16 Martin Brodeur 15.00 40.00
17 Steve Yzerman 20.00 50.00
18 Mats Sundin 8.00 20.00
19 Mike Modano 12.00 30.00
20 Mark Messier 12.00 30.00
21 Raymond Bourque 12.00 30.00
22 Scott Niedermayer 8.00 20.00
23 Felix Potvin 12.00 30.00
24 Chris Osgood 8.00 20.00

2010-11 ITG Ultimate Memorabilia Ultimate Rivalry
ANNOUNCED PRINT RUN 19
1 Richard/Durnan/Kennedy/Broda
2 Richrd/Plnte/Howe/Sawchuk 30.00 60.00
3 Beliv/Worsly/Mahvlich/Keon 30.00 60.00
4 Richrd/Fergsn/Baun/Swchk 15.00 40.00
5 P.Espo/Drydn/Trtiak/Khrlm 30.00 60.00
6 Lemre/Cournyr/P.Espo/Orr 40.00 80.00
7 Laflr/Gainey/Mddltn/Chvrs 30.00 60.00
8 Trottr/Ptvn/T.Espo/Dvdsn
9 Grtzky/Coffy/Bossy/Smith 60.00 120.00
10 Kurri/Andrsn/McInn/Loob 12.00 30.00
11 Mess/Fuhr/McDnld/Vern 20.00 50.00
12 Nslnd/Roy/Bchrd/Ststny 25.00 60.00
13 Toews/Brodr/Millr/Prise
14 Sakic/Lemieux/Yzrmn/Drapr
15 Sndin/Domi/Alfrdsn/Hossa 25.00 50.00
16 Crsby/Mlkin/Ovech/Green 40.00 80.00

2010-11 ITG Ultimate Memorabilia When There Were Six
ANNOUNCED PRINT RUN 24
1 Boston 6 40.00 80.00
2 Chicago 6 40.00 80.00
3 Detroit 6 40.00 80.00
4 NY Rangers 6
5 Toronto 6 40.00 80.00
6 Montreal 6 75.00 150.00

2011-12 ITG Ultimate Memorabilia
ANNOUNCED PRINT RUN 62-63
1 Tony Amonte/63* 5.00 12.00
2 Hobey Baker/62* 5.00 12.00
3 Bill Barilko/62* 4.00 10.00
4 Jean Beliveau/62* 8.00 20.00
5 Mike Bossy/63* 6.00 15.00
6 Raymond Bourque/63* 10.00 25.00
7 Johnny Bower/62* 6.00 15.00
8 Turk Broda/63* 6.00 15.00
9 Pavel Bure/63* 8.00 20.00
10 Chris Chelios/62* 6.00 15.00
11 Wendel Clark/63* 6.00 15.00
12 Bobby Clarke/62* 5.00 12.00
13 Paul Coffey/63* 5.00 12.00
14 Marcel Dionne/62* 8.00 20.00
15 Phil Esposito/63* 10.00 25.00
16 Tony Esposito/63* 6.00 15.00
17 Theoren Fleury/63* 8.00 20.00
18 Peter Forsberg/63* 6.00 15.00
19 Ron Francis/63* 8.00 20.00
20 Grant Fuhr/62* 6.00 15.00
21 Bernie Geoffrion/62* 5.00 12.00
22 Ryan Getzlaf/63* 10.00 25.00
23 Ed Giacomin/62* 6.00 15.00
24 Doug Gilmour/62* 8.00 20.00
25 George Hainsworth/62* 6.00 15.00
26 Glenn Hall/62* 6.00 15.00
27 Doug Harvey/62* 6.00 15.00
28 Dominik Hasek/62* 8.00 20.00
29 Ron Hextall/63* 8.00 20.00
30 Tim Horton/63* 8.00 20.00
31 Mark Howe/62* 6.00 15.00
32 Bobby Hull/62* 6.00 15.00
33 Brett Hull/62* 8.00 20.00
34 Jaromir Jagr/62* 15.00 40.00
35 Aurel Joliat/62* 6.00 15.00
36 Curtis Joseph/62* 6.00 15.00
37 Dave Keon/62* 6.00 15.00
38 Valeri Kharlamov/63* 5.00 12.00
39 Ilya Kovalchuk/62* 6.00 15.00
40 Jari Kurri/62* 6.00 15.00
41 Elmer Lach/62* 5.00 12.00
42 Guy Lafleur/62* 8.00 20.00
43 Pat LaFontaine/63* 6.00 15.00
44 Newsy Lalonde/63* 5.00 12.00
45 Igor Larionov/62* 6.00 15.00
46 Vincent Lecavalier/63* 5.00 12.00
47 John LeClair/62* 6.00 15.00
48 Mario Lemieux/62* 20.00 50.00
49 Nicklas Lidstrom/63* 6.00 15.00
50 Pelle Lindbergh/63* 10.00 25.00
51 Trevor Linden/63* 6.00 15.00
52 Eric Lindros/62* 10.00 25.00
53 Ted Lindsay/63* 6.00 15.00
54 Henrik Lundqvist/62* 8.00 20.00
55 Roberto Luongo/63* 8.00 20.00
56 Al MacInnis/62* 6.00 15.00
57 Frank Mahovlich/62* 6.00 15.00
58 Patrick Marleau/63* 6.00 15.00
59 Mark Messier/63* 8.00 20.00
60 Mike Modano/63* 10.00 25.00
61 Howie Morenz/62* 5.00 12.00
62 Rick Nash/63* 6.00 15.00
63 Cam Neely/62* 6.00 15.00
64 Antti Niemi/62* 5.00 12.00
65 Chris Osgood/62* 6.00 15.00
66 Alexander Ovechkin/62* 15.00 40.00
67 Bernie Parent/62* 6.00 15.00
68 Gilbert Perreault/62* 6.00 15.00
69 Jacques Plante/62* 6.00 15.00
70 Denis Potvin/62* 6.00 15.00
71 Felix Potvin/62* 6.00 15.00
72 Carey Price/62* 10.00 25.00
73 Henri Richard/62* 6.00 15.00
74 Maurice Richard/63* 6.00 15.00
75 Mike Richter/63* 6.00 15.00
76 Larry Robinson/62* 6.00 15.00
77 Luc Robitaille/62* 6.00 15.00
78 Jeremy Roenick/62* 6.00 15.00
79 Patrick Roy/63* 12.00 30.00
80 Joe Sakic/62* 10.00 25.00
81 Borje Salming/62* 6.00 15.00
82 Terry Sawchuk/63* 6.00 15.00
83 Milt Schmidt/63* 6.00 15.00
84 Daniel Sedin/62* 6.00 15.00
85 Henrik Sedin/62* 6.00 15.00
86 Teemu Selanne/63* 12.00 30.00
87 Darryl Sittler/62* 6.00 15.00
88 Eric Staal/62* 8.00 20.00
89 Steven Stamkos/63* 10.00 25.00
90 Cyclone Taylor/62* 8.00 20.00
91 Tim Thomas/63* 6.00 15.00
92 Joe Thornton/62* 6.00 15.00
93 Keith Tkachuk/62* 6.00 15.00
94 Vladislav Tretiak/63* 10.00 25.00
95 Mike Vernon/63* 5.00 12.00
96 Georges Vezina/62* 6.00 15.00
97 Cam Ward/62* 6.00 15.00
98 Shea Weber/63* 5.00 12.00
99 Gump Worsley/62* 6.00 15.00
100 Steve Yzerman/63* 12.00 30.00

2011-12 ITG Ultimate Memorabilia 600 Goal Combo Memorabilia
ANNOUNCED PRINT RUN 24
1 D.Andreychuk/C.Schwab 12.00 30.00
2 D.Ciccarelli/C.Osgood 12.00 30.00
3 M.Dionne/Lemelin 12.00 30.00
4 P.Esposito/C.Maniago 15.00 40.00
5 M.Gartner/C.Terreri 12.00 30.00
6 W.Gretzky/G.Stefan 30.00 80.00
7 G.Howe/G.Worsley 20.00 50.00
8 Bo.Hull/G.Cheevers 20.00 50.00
9 Br.Hull/G.Hebert 30.00 80.00
10 J.Jagr/J.Holmqvist 15.00 40.00
11 J.Kurri/S.Fiset 15.00 40.00
12 Mario Lemieux 15.00 40.00
13 M.Messier/K.McLean 20.00 50.00
14 L.Robitaille/JS Giguere 12.00 30.00
15 Joe Sakic 15.00 40.00
16 B.Shanahan/O.Kolzig 15.00 40.00
17 T.Selanne/C.Anderson 15.00 40.00
18 S.Yzerman/T.Salo 20.00 40.00

2011-12 ITG Ultimate Memorabilia All-Stars Memorabilia
ANNOUNCED PRINT RUN 24
1 Raymond Bourque 15.00 40.00
2 Pavel Bure 10.00 25.00
3 Sergei Fedorov
4 Theoren Fleury 12.00 30.00
5 Peter Forsberg 10.00 25.00
6 Dominik Hasek 15.00 40.00
7 Brett Hull 12.00 30.00
8 Jaromir Jagr 15.00 40.00
9 Curtis Joseph 10.00 25.00
10 Brian Leetch 12.00 30.00
11 Mario Lemieux 15.00 40.00
12 Nicklas Lidstrom 12.00 30.00
13 Eric Lindros 12.00 30.00
14 Mark Messier
15 Patrick Roy 20.00 50.00
16 Steve Yzerman 15.00 40.00

2011-12 ITG Ultimate Memorabilia Autographs
ANNOUNCED PRINT RUN 19
1 Niklas Backstrom
2 Ilya Bryzgalov 15.00 40.00
3 Zdeno Chara 12.00 30.00
4 Marian Gaborik 12.00 30.00
5 Ryan Getzlaf 12.00 30.00
6 Claude Giroux 15.00 40.00
7 Mike Green
8 Jimmy Howard 15.00 30.00
9 Jaromir Jagr 40.00 80.00
10 Ryan Kesler 8.00 20.00
11 Mikko Koivu 6.00 15.00
12 Saku Koivu 8.00 20.00
13 Ilya Kovalchuk 12.00 30.00
14 Vincent Lecavalier 12.00 30.00
15 Nicklas Lidstrom
16 Henrik Lundqvist 40.00 80.00
17 Roberto Luongo 8.00 20.00
18 Patrick Marleau
19 Brenden Morrow 6.00 15.00
20 Rick Nash 8.00 20.00
21 Antti Niemi 6.00 15.00
22 Alexander Ovechkin 50.00 100.00
23 Carey Price 25.00 50.00
24 Dwayne Roloson 6.00 15.00
25 Daniel Sedin 8.00 20.00
26 Henrik Sedin 8.00 20.00
27 Teemu Selanne 12.00 30.00
28 Alexander Semin 8.00 20.00
29 Martin St. Louis 8.00 20.00
30 Eric Staal 10.00 25.00
31 Steven Stamkos 30.00 60.00
32 Joe Thornton 8.00 20.00
33 Semyon Varlamov 8.00 20.00
34 Tomas Vokoun 6.00 15.00
35 Shea Weber 6.00 15.00

2011-12 ITG Ultimate Memorabilia Blue and White Captains Memorabilia
ANNOUNCED PRINT RUN 9-24
1 Wendel Clark/24* 15.00 40.00
2 Charlie Conacher/9*
3 Doug Gilmour/24* 12.00 30.00
4 Ted Kennedy/9*
5 Dave Keon/9*
6 Darryl Sittler/24* 10.00 25.00
7 Mats Sundin/24* 10.00 25.00
8 Rick Vaive/24* 10.00 25.00

2011-12 ITG Ultimate Memorabilia Country of Origin Memorabilia
ANNOUNCED PRINT RUN 24
1 C.Chelios/B.Leetch 15.00 40.00
2 P.Forsberg/M.Sundin 12.00 30.00
3 M.Gaborik/J.Halak 15.00 40.00
4 D.Hasek/J.Jagr 20.00 50.00
5 B.Hull/M.Modano 10.00 25.00
6 V.Kharlamov/A.Yakushev 15.00 40.00
7 J.Kurri/T.Selanne 15.00 40.00
8 M.Lemieux/J.Sakic 20.00 50.00
9 P.Lindbergh/H.Lundqvist 25.00 60.00
10 M.Messier/S.Yzerman 15.00 40.00
11 A.Ovechkin/I.Kovalchuk 30.00 80.00
12 B.Salming/N.Lidstrom 15.00 40.00

2011-12 ITG Ultimate Memorabilia Cup Finals Memorabilia
ANNOUNCED PRINT RUN 4-24
1 Brlk/Brda/Kenn/Lach/Rchrd/Hrvy/4*
2 Bss/Smth/Trt/Wllm/Brd/Snps 20.00 50.00
3 Clrk/Prnt/Mclsh/Prlt/Mrt/Crzr 20.00 50.00
4 Crny/Mvl/Lpn/Esp/Stp/Mkt 20.00 50.00
5 Flry/Mac/Vrn/Roy/Nsld/Rbi 20.00 50.00
6 Fhr/Esa/Ands/Moog/Brq/Nly 20.00 50.00
7 Hain/Joli/Mrnz/Tiny/Shre/Dit/4*
8 Hort/Keon/Mvl/Rgi/Bli/Rich 25.00 60.00
9 Jari/Mss/Coff/Trot/LaFnt/Gill 25.00 60.00
10 Guy/Lmr/Rbi/Chvr/Mdlt/Park 25.00 60.00
11 Ltch/Mss/Rctr/Kirk/Lnd/Bre 30.00 80.00
12 Mrio/Jgr/Brso/Chls/Rnck/Gul 30.00 80.00
13 Sak/Roy/Brg/Mgl/Ndrm/Nwn 25.00 60.00
14 Tmu/Ndrm/Gig/Emry/Spz/Grb 20.00 50.00
15 Thm/Chr/Brgn/Lngo/Sdin/Sdin 25.00 60.00
16 Yzer/Ldst/Vrn/Lndr/LeCl/Hex 20.00 50.00

2011-12 ITG Ultimate Memorabilia Days Gone By Memorabilia
ANNOUNCED PRINT RUN 24
1 Beliveau/Clarke/Sittler/Perrlt
2 Bossy/O'Reilly/Dionne/Shutt 15.00 40.00
3 Chelios/Robit/LaFntne/Ptvin
4 Gilbert/Keon/Cournoyer/Mikita
5 Br.Hull/Sakic/Lemieux/Neely 25.00 60.00
6 Messr/Goulet/Yzerm/Gilmr 15.00 40.00
7 McDonld/Brdr/Ststny/Brque 12.00 30.00
8 Park/T.Esp/Potvn/H.Richrd 15.00 40.00
9 M.Richd/Delvc/Bucyk/Bo.Hll 15.00 40.00
10 Roenick/Leetch/Bure/Nieder 15.00 40.00
11 Roy/Hawrchk/Ciccarli/Hextll 20.00 50.00
12 Sawchuk/Hall/Giaco/Vachn 20.00 50.00

2011-12 ITG Ultimate Memorabilia Draft Day Memorabilia
ANNOUNCED PRINT RUN 24
1 MA Fleury/J.Halak 15.00 40.00
2 M.Gaborik/H.Lundqvist 15.00 40.00
3 D.Hawerchuk/J.Vanbiesbrouck 20.00 50.00
4 J.Jagr/F.Potvin
5 V.Lecavalier/A.Niittymaki
6 M.Lemieux/L.Robitaille 20.00 50.00
7 A.Ovechkin/P.Rinne 15.00 40.00
8 C.Price/D.helm
9 D.Savard/J.Kurri 8.00 20.00
10 H.Sedin/R.Miller 12.00 30.00
11 M.Sundin/P.Bure 12.00 30.00
12 S.Yzerman/D.Hasek 15.00 40.00

2011-12 ITG Ultimate Memorabilia Dynamic Duos Memorabilia
ANNOUNCED PRINT RUN 24
1 B.Barber/B.Clarke 12.00 30.00
2 P.Bure/T.Linden 15.00 40.00
3 D.Gilmour/W.Clark 20.00 50.00
4 Bo.Hull/S.Mikita 12.00 30.00
5 G.Lafleur/Y.Cournoyer 12.00 30.00
6 J.LeClair/E.Lindros 12.00 30.00
7 M.Lemieux/J.Jagr 20.00 50.00
8 M.Messier/B.Leetch 12.00 30.00
9 A.Ovechkin/A.Semin 20.00 50.00
10 D.Sittler/L.McDonald 10.00 25.00

2011-12 ITG Ultimate Memorabilia Entire Career Memorabilia
ANNOUNCED PRINT RUN 24
1 Jean Beliveau 15.00 40.00
2 Mike Bossy 8.00 20.00
3 Bobby Clarke 8.00 20.00
4 Alex Delvecchio 8.00 20.00
5 Rod Gilbert 8.00 20.00
6 Mario Lemieux 15.00 40.00
7 Stan Mikita 8.00 20.00
8 Gilbert Perreault
9 Denis Potvin 8.00 20.00
10 Henri Richard 12.00 30.00
11 Mike Richter 8.00 20.00
12 Steve Yzerman 15.00 40.00

2011-12 ITG Ultimate Memorabilia Franchise Favorites Memorabilia
ANNOUNCED PRINT RUN 24
1 Delv/Yzer/Lids/Osgd 20.00 50.00
2 Giac/Ltch/Msr/Lund 15.00 40.00
3 Glet/Stast/Bchrd/Skic 15.00 40.00
4 Hall/Br.Hll/Jsph/Mcln 15.00 40.00
5 Bo.Hll/Hwrch/Crly/Slne 15.00 40.00
6 Keon/Sitt/Slm/Sndin 15.00 40.00
7 Mrnz/M.Rich/Roy/Prce 50.00 100.00
8 Mosi/Bo.Hll/T.Esp/Svrd 15.00 40.00
9 Prnt/Clrke/Hxtll/Lndros 25.00 60.00
10 Swchk/Vchn/Dnne/Rbit 20.00 50.00
11 Shre/P.Esp/Nly/Thms
12 Wrsly/Cici/Bllws/Mdno

2011-12 ITG Ultimate Memorabilia Future Star Autograph Jerseys
ANNOUNCED PRINT RUN 30
*PATCH/19: .5X TO 1.2X BASIC JSY AU/30
1 Jake Allen 15.00 40.00
2 Sven Bartschi 10.00 25.00
3 Jonathan Bernier 10.00 25.00
4 Sergei Bobrovsky 10.00 25.00
5 Zach Boychuk 6.00 15.00
6 Jordan Caron 10.00 25.00
7 Logan Couture 10.00 25.00
8 Sean Couturier 15.00 40.00
9 Michael Del Zotto 10.00 25.00
10 Taylor Doherty 8.00 20.00
11 Oliver Ekman-Larsson 10.00 25.00
12 Lars Eller 8.00 20.00
13 Blake Geoffrion 8.00 20.00
14 Colton Gillies 6.00 15.00
15 Dougie Hamilton 12.00 30.00
16 Thomas Hickey 8.00 20.00
17 Cody Hodgson 20.00 50.00
18 Nazem Kadri 15.00 40.00
19 Adam Larsson 10.00 25.00
20 Ryan Murray 15.00 40.00
21 Greg Nemisz 12.00 30.00
22 Stuart Percy 10.00 25.00
23 Matt Puempel 10.00 25.00
24 Griffin Reinhart 12.00 30.00
25 Duncan Siemens 10.00 25.00
26 Kyle Turris 8.00 20.00
27 Dana Tyrell 6.00 15.00
28 Tyler Wotherspoon 10.00 25.00

2011-12 ITG Ultimate Memorabilia Future Star Autographs
ANNOUNCED PRINT RUN 30
1 Jake Allen 12.00 30.00
2 Sven Bartschi 8.00 20.00
3 Jonathan Bernier 8.00 20.00
4 Sergei Bobrovsky 8.00 20.00
5 Zach Boychuk 5.00 12.00
6 Jordan Caron 8.00 20.00
7 Logan Couture 8.00 20.00
8 Sean Couturier 12.00 30.00
9 Taylor Doherty 6.00 15.00
10 Oliver Ekman-Larsson 8.00 20.00
11 Lars Eller 6.00 15.00
12 Blake Geoffrion 6.00 15.00
13 Colton Gillies 5.00 12.00
14 Dougie Hamilton 10.00 25.00
15 Thomas Hickey 6.00 15.00
16 Cody Hodgson 25.00 50.00
17 Nazem Kadri 12.00 30.00
18 Adam Larsson 8.00 20.00
19 Ryan Murray 12.00 30.00
20 Greg Nemisz 6.00 15.00
21 Stuart Percy 8.00 20.00
22 Matt Puempel 8.00 20.00
23 Griffin Reinhart 8.00 20.00
24 Duncan Siemens 8.00 20.00
25 Kyle Turris 6.00 15.00
26 Dana Tyrell 5.00 12.00
27 Tyler Wotherspoon 8.00 20.00
28 Mika Zibanejad 15.00 40.00

2011-12 ITG Ultimate Memorabilia Gloves Are Off Memorabilia
ANNOUNCED PRINT RUN 24
1 Bobby Clarke 15.00 40.00
2 Marian Gaborik 8.00 20.00
3 Ryan Getzlaf 8.00 20.00
4 Brett Hull 12.00 30.00
5 Denis Potvin 8.00 20.00
6 Luc Robitaille 8.00 20.00
7 Joe Thornton 8.00 20.00
8 Bryan Trottier 8.00 20.00

2011-12 ITG Ultimate Memorabilia Goalie Autograph Jerseys
ANNOUNCED PRINT RUN 19
1 Niklas Backstrom 12.00 30.00
2 Marc-Andre Fleury 20.00 50.00
3 Jaroslav Halak 12.00 30.00
4 Henrik Lundqvist 15.00 40.00
5 Roberto Luongo 12.00 30.00
6 Antti Niemi 10.00 25.00
7 Chris Osgood 12.00 30.00
8 Carey Price 40.00 100.00
9 Jonathan Quick 25.00 50.00
10 Tim Thomas 25.00 60.00

2011-12 ITG Ultimate Memorabilia Goalie Autograph Memorabilia
ANNOUNCED PRINT RUN 19
1 Craig Anderson 12.00 30.00
2 Niklas Backstrom 12.00 30.00
3 Marc-Andre Fleury 20.00 50.00
4 Nikolai Khabibulin 15.00 40.00
5 Henrik Lundqvist 15.00 40.00
6 Roberto Luongo 12.00 30.00
7 Chris Osgood 12.00 30.00
8 Carey Price 40.00 100.00
9 Tim Thomas 30.00 60.00
10 Tomas Vokoun 10.00 25.00

2011-12 ITG Ultimate Memorabilia Goalie Generations Memorabilia
ANNOUNCED PRINT RUN 24
1 T.Esp/Vachn/Tretiak 15.00 40.00
2 Giac/Sawchk/Chvers 10.00 25.00
3 Hall/Crozier/Sawchuk 12.00 30.00
4 Hall/Worsley/Sawchuk 25.00 50.00
5 Hasek/Kolzig/Potvin 25.00 60.00
6 Moog/Brodeur/Lind 25.00 60.00
7 Osgood/Vanbies/Irbe 25.00 60.00
8 Parent/Meloche/Smith 15.00 40.00
9 Plante/Lumly/Sawchk 15.00 40.00
10 Richter/Roy/Joseph 25.00 60.00
11 Roy/Vernon/Barasso 25.00 60.00
12 Vanbies/Fuhr/Hextall

2011-12 ITG Ultimate Memorabilia Goalie Legend Autograph Jerseys
ANNOUNCED PRINT RUN 24
1 Tony Esposito 15.00 40.00
2 Ed Giacomin 12.00 30.00
3 Glenn Hall 15.00 40.00
4 Dominik Hasek 15.00 40.00
5 Arturs Irbe 12.00 30.00
6 Curtis Joseph 12.00 30.00
7 Bernie Parent 15.00 40.00
8 Patrick Roy 40.00 80.00
9 Billy Smith 12.00 30.00
10 Mike Vernon 10.00 25.00

2011-12 ITG Ultimate Memorabilia Goalie Legend Autograph Memorabilia
ANNOUNCED PRINT RUN 24
1 Sean Burke 10.00 25.00
2 Tony Esposito 15.00 40.00
3 Dominik Hasek 15.00 40.00
4 Ron Hextall 15.00 40.00
5 Arturs Irbe 12.00 30.00
6 Curtis Joseph 12.00 30.00
7 Bernie Parent 15.00 40.00
8 Patrick Roy 40.00 80.00
9 Vladislav Tretiak 25.00 50.00
10 Mike Vernon 10.00 25.00

2011-12 ITG Ultimate Memorabilia Goalie Legend Autographs
ANNOUNCED PRINT RUN 24
1 Gerry Cheevers 10.00 25.00
2 Tony Esposito 12.00 30.00
3 Grant Fuhr 10.00 25.00
4 Ed Giacomin 12.00 30.00
5 Glenn Hall 10.00 25.00
6 Dominik Hasek 12.00 30.00
7 Curtis Joseph 12.00 30.00
8 Bernie Parent 12.00 30.00
9 Patrick Roy 30.00 60.00
10 Billy Smith 10.00 25.00

2011-12 ITG Ultimate Memorabilia Hall of Famer Autographs
ANNOUNCED PRINT RUN 5-15
1 Glenn Anderson/15* 10.00 25.00
3 Andy Bathgate/15* 12.00 30.00
4 Jean Beliveau/15*
5 Mike Bossy/15*
6 Raymond Bourque/15* 25.00 50.00
7 Johnny Bower/15* 20.00 40.00
8 Scotty Bowman/15* 10.00 25.00
9 Gerry Cheevers/15* 10.00 25.00
10 Dino Ciccarelli/15* 10.00 25.00
11 Paul Coffey/15* 15.00 40.00
12 Yvan Cournoyer/15* 12.00 30.00
13 Marcel Dionne/15* 15.00 40.00
15 Phil Esposito/15* 25.00 50.00
16 Tony Esposito/15* 12.00 30.00
17 Grant Fuhr/15* 15.00 40.00
19 Mike Gartner/15* 12.00 30.00
20 Ed Giacomin/15* 10.00 25.00
21 Glenn Hall/15* 10.00 25.00
22 Dale Hawerchuk/15* 15.00 40.00
23 Harry Howell/15* 10.00 25.00
24 Bobby Hull/15* 40.00 80.00
25 Brett Hull/15* 30.00 60.00
26 Red Kelly/15* 8.00 20.00
27 Dave Keon/15*
28 Jari Kurri/15* 15.00 40.00
29 Elmer Lach/15* 15.00 40.00
30 Guy Lafleur/15* 20.00 40.00
31 Pat Lafontaine/15* 10.00 25.00
32 Rod Langway/15* 10.00 25.00
33 Jacques Laperriere/15*
35 Brian Leetch/15* 10.00 25.00
38 Lanny McDonald/15*
40 Stan Mikita/15* 15.00 40.00
41 Dickie Moore/15* 12.00 30.00
42 Cam Neely/15* 10.00 25.00
44 Bernie Parent/15* 20.00 40.00
45 Brad Park/15* 8.00 20.00
46 Gilbert Perreault/15* 20.00 40.00
47 Pierre Pilote/15* 12.00 30.00
48 Denis Potvin/15* 10.00 25.00
49 Henri Richard/15*
50 Luc Robitaille/15* 25.00 50.00
51 Patrick Roy/15* 40.00 80.00
52 Borje Salming/15* 10.00 25.00
53 Serge Savard/15* 10.00 25.00
54 Milt Schmidt/15* 12.00 30.00
55 Darryl Sittler/15* 10.00 25.00
56 Billy Smith/15* 12.00 30.00
57 Vladislav Tretiak/15* 30.00 60.00
58 Norm Ullman/15* 10.00 25.00

2011-12 ITG Ultimate Memorabilia Idols Memorabilia
ANNOUNCED PRINT RUN 24
1 J.Beliveau/G.Lafleur 12.00 30.00
2 D.Bouchard/P.Roy 20.00 50.00
3 M.Dionne/L.Robitaille
4 G.Fuhr/R.Luongo 12.00 30.00
5 Kharlamov/Ovechkin 25.00 60.00
6 J.Kurri/T.Selanne 12.00 30.00
7 G.Lafleur/M.Lemieux 20.00 50.00
8 LaFontaine/Thornton 12.00 30.00
9 L.McDonald/T.Linden 12.00 30.00
10 M.Messier/T.Amonte 10.00 25.00
11 M.Messier/E.Lindros 15.00 40.00
12 M.Naslund/M.Sundin 12.00 30.00
13 B.Parent/K.McLean
14 J.Plante/B.Parent 12.00 30.00
15 L.Robinson/R.Blake
16 P.Roy/D.Cloutier 20.00 50.00
17 B.Salming/N.Lidstrom 12.00 30.00
18 M.Sundin/R.Nash 12.00 30.00
19 B.Trottier/S.Yzerman 15.00 40.00
20 S.Yzerman/S.Stamkos 15.00 40.00

2011-12 ITG Ultimate Memorabilia Journey Jersey Memorabilia
ANNOUNCED PRINT RUN 24
1 Chris Chelios 8.00 20.00
2 Theoren Fleury 10.00 25.00
3 Peter Forsberg 8.00 20.00
4 Michel Goulet 6.00 15.00
5 Bobby Hull 12.00 30.00
6 Dave Keon 8.00 20.00
7 Ilya Kovalchuk 8.00 20.00
8 Roberto Luongo 10.00 25.00
9 Al MacInnis 6.00 15.00
10 Scott Niedermayer 6.00 15.00
11 Teemu Selanne 12.50 30.00
12 Darryl Sittler 8.00 20.00
13 Joe Thornton 8.00 20.00
14 Keith Tkachuk 8.00 20.00
15 Rogie Vachon 10.00 25.00
16 John Vanbiesbrouck 10.00 25.00

2011-12 ITG Ultimate Memorabilia Lord Stanley's Mug Memorabilia
ANNOUNCED PRINT RUN 9-24
1 Anderson/Fuhr/Messier/24* 15.00 40.00
2 Chara/Thomas/Bergeron/24* 15.00 40.00
3 Cheevers/Bucyk/Esposito/24* 15.00 40.00
4 Clarke/Barber/Parent/24* 15.00 40.00
5 Fleury/McDnld/MacInnis/24* 15.00 40.00
6 Glenn Hall/Bobby Hull/Stan Mikita/9*
7 Hasek/Larionov/Hull/24* 20.00 50.00
8 Jagr/Lemieux/Francis/24* 25.00 60.00
9 Kurri/Coffey/Messier/24* 15.00 40.00
10 Lecav/St.Louis/Khabib/24* 20.00 50.00
11 Messier/Richter/Leetch/24* 12.00 30.00
12 Osgood/Lidstrom/Chelios/24* 15.00 40.00
13 Jacques Plante/Maurice Richard/Doug Harvey/9*
14 Potvin/Bossy/Trottier/24* 12.00 30.00
15 Robinson/Roy/Naslund/24* 20.00 50.00
16 Roy/Bourque/Sakic/24* 20.00 50.00
17 Roy/Carbonneau/Savard/24* 20.00 50.00
18 Terry Sawchuk/Frank Mahovlich/Dave Keon/9*
19 Selanne/Nieder/Getzlaf/24* 20.00 50.00
20 Yzerman/Vernon/Fedor/24* 20.00 50.00

2011-12 ITG Ultimate Memorabilia Number 11 Memorabilia
ANNOUNCED PRINT RUN 24
1 Daniel Alfredsson 8.00 20.00
2 Tony Amonte 6.00 15.00
3 Mike Gartner 8.00 20.00
4 Saku Koivu 12.00 30.00
5 Anze Kopitar 10.00 25.00
6 Gary Leeman 6.00 15.00
7 Mark Messier 10.00 25.00
8 Kirk Muller 6.00 15.00
9 Ulf Nilsson 6.00 15.00
10 Mark Recchi 8.00 20.00
11 Jordan Staal 8.00 20.00

2011-12 ITG Ultimate Memorabilia Past Present Future Memorabilia
ANNOUNCED PRINT RUN 24
1 Bourq/Chara/Hamltn 15.00 40.00
2 Bure/Ovech/Trsnk 30.00 80.00
3 Franc/Staal/Bychk 12.00 30.00
4 Joseph/Halak/Allen 12.00 30.00
5 Irbe/Ward/Murphy 20.00 50.00
6 Lind/Lund/Markstrm 15.00 40.00
7 Linden/Sedin/Hdgsn 15.00 40.00
8 McDnld/Grabv/Kdri 12.00 30.00
9 Robin/Sbbn/Blieu
10 Slmng/Lids/E-Larssn 12.00 30.00
11 Selne/Thrntn/Cture 15.00 40.00
12 Vachn/Quick/Bernr 12.00 30.00

2011-12 ITG Ultimate Memorabilia Plus Minus Memorabilia
ANNOUNCED PRINT RUN 24
1 Bobby Clarke 8.00 20.00
2 Theoren Fleury 10.00 25.00
3 Ron Francis 8.00 20.00
4 Mark Howe 6.00 15.00
5 Guy Lafleur 10.00 25.00
6 Mario Lemieux 15.00 40.00
7 Larry Robinson 8.00 20.00
8 Martin St. Louis 6.00 15.00
9 Joe Sakic 8.00 20.00
10 Bryan Trottier 8.00 20.00

2011-12 ITG Ultimate Memorabilia The Boys Are Back Memorabilia
ANNOUNCED PRINT RUN 24
1 Hawerchuk/Little 10.00 25.00
2 Bo.Hull/B.Maxwell 8.00 20.00
3 Khabibulin/Mason 10.00 25.00
4 T.Selanne/A.Ladd 12.00 30.00
5 Carlyle/Selanne/Steen 15.00 40.00
6 Bo.Hll/Hawer/Tkchk 12.00 30.00
7 Khabi/Tkchk/Bo.Hull 15.00 40.00
8 Veisor/Rdick/Khab 12.00 30.00
9 Crly/Bo.Hll/Selne/Kyte 15.00 40.00
10 Hawr/Tkchk/Stn/Khbi 12.00 30.00
11 Khbi/Crlyle/Hnsy/Masn 12.00 30.00
12 Selne/Tkchk/Ldd/Lttle 15.00 40.00

2011-12 ITG Ultimate Memorabilia Ultimate Rivalry Memorabilia

ANNOUNCED PRINT RUN 4-19
2 Bli/Crn/Lma/Kn/Hrt/Mho/19* 20.00 50.00
3 Glt/Sts/Hntr/Ns/Crb/Ry/19* 30.00 80.00
4 Hal/Hul/Mkt/Crz/Ulm/Dlv/19* 15.00 40.00
5 Hed/Esp/Nls/Bss/Trt/Pot/19* 25.00 60.00
6 Mss/Fhr/Jri/Mcl/McD/Vrn/19*
7 O'Ry/Prk/Chv/Lfr/Rbi/Sht/19*
8 Rct/Mss/Ltc/Hx/LCl/Lind/19* 25.00 60.00
9 Ry/Frs/Skc/Yzr/Osg/Lids/19* 50.00 120.00
11 Stt/McD/Slm/Clrk/Prnt/Brb/19*
12 Stm/Lcv/StL/Hrt/Ws/Bw/19* 15.00 40.00

2012-13 ITG Ultimate Memorabilia

ANNOUNCED PRINT RUN 60
1 Dave Andreychuk 5.00 12.00
2 Ed Belfour 5.00 12.00
3 Jean Beliveau 5.00 12.00
4 Peter Bondra 5.00 12.00
5 Mike Bossy 5.00 12.00
6 Raymond Bourque 8.00 20.00
7 Johnny Bower 5.00 12.00
8 Turk Broda 5.00 12.00
9 Pavel Bure 6.00 15.00
10 Gerry Cheevers 5.00 12.00
11 Chris Chelios 5.00 12.00
12 Wendel Clark 5.00 12.00
13 Bobby Clarke 5.00 12.00
14 Paul Coffey 5.00 12.00
15 Marcel Dionne 6.00 15.00
16 Jonathan Drouin 10.00 25.00
17 Phil Esposito 8.00 20.00
18 Tony Esposito 5.00 12.00
19 Sergei Fedorov 6.00 15.00
20 Marc-Andre Fleury 8.00 20.00
21 Theoren Fleury 6.00 15.00
22 Peter Forsberg 5.00 12.00
23 Grant Fuhr 6.00 15.00
24 Marian Gaborik 5.00 12.00
25 Doug Gilmour 6.00 15.00
26 Claude Giroux 5.00 12.00
27 Glenn Hall 5.00 12.00
28 Doug Harvey 5.00 12.00
29 Dominik Hasek 6.00 15.00
30 Dale Hawerchuk 6.00 15.00
31 Jimmy Howard 5.00 12.00
32 Gordie Howe 10.00 25.00
33 Bobby Hull 5.00 12.00
34 Brett HullÂ• 5.00 12.00
35 Jaromir Jagr 10.00 25.00
36 Seth Jones 8.00 20.00
37 Curtis Joseph 5.00 12.00
38 Red Kelly 4.00 10.00
39 Dave Keon 5.00 12.00
40 Valeri Kharlamov 4.00 10.00
41 Jari Kurri 5.00 12.00
42 Elmer Lach 4.00 10.00
43 Guy Lafleur 6.00 15.00
44 Pat LaFontaine 5.00 12.00
45 Mario Lemieux 15.00 40.00
46 Nicklas Lidstrom 5.00 12.00
47 Pelle Lindbergh 6.00 15.00
48 Trevor Linden 5.00 12.00
49 Eric Lindros 6.00 15.00
50 Ted Lindsay 5.00 12.00
51 Henrik Lundqvist 6.00 15.00
52 Roberto Luongo 5.00 12.00
53 Al MacInnis 5.00 12.00
54 Nathan MacKinnon 8.00 20.00
55 Frank Mahovlich 5.00 12.00
56 Evgeni Malkin 15.00 40.00
57 Lanny McDonald 5.00 12.00
58 Mark Messier 6.00 15.00
59 Stan Mikita 6.00 15.00
60 Mike Modano 8.00 20.00
61 Sean Monahan 8.00 20.00
62 Howie Morenz 4.00 10.00
63 Cam Neely 5.00 12.00
64 Scott Niedermayer 5.00 12.00
65 Owen Nolan 4.00 10.00
66 Adam Oates 5.00 12.00
67 Chris Osgood 5.00 12.00
68 Alexander Ovechkin 10.00 25.00
69 Bernie Parent 5.00 12.00
70 Gilbert Perreault 5.00 12.00
71 Jacques Plante 6.00 15.00
72 Felix Potvin 8.00 20.00
73 Carey Price 15.00 40.00
74 Jonathan Quick 8.00 20.00
75 Mark Recchi 6.00 15.00
76 Henri Richard 5.00 12.00
77 Maurice Richard 5.00 12.00
78 Larry Robinson 5.00 12.00
79 Luc Robitaille 5.00 12.00
80 Jeremy Roenick 5.00 12.00
81 Patrick Roy 8.00 20.00
82 Patrick Roy 8.00 20.00
83 Joe Sakic 8.00 20.00
84 Borje Salming 5.00 12.00
85 Denis Savard 6.00 15.00
86 Terry Sawchuk 5.00 12.00
87 Daniel Sedin 5.00 12.00
88 Henrik Sedin 5.00 12.00
89 Teemu Selanne 6.00 15.00
90 Eddie Shore 4.00 10.00
91 Darryl Sittler 5.00 12.00
92 Martin St. Louis 5.00 12.00
93 Peter Stastny 4.00 10.00
94 Mats Sundin 5.00 12.00
95 Joe Thornton 5.00 12.00
96 Keith TkachukÂ• 5.00 12.00
97 Vladislav Tretiak 6.00 15.00
98 Steve Yzerman 10.00 25.00

2012-13 ITG Ultimate Memorabilia Silver

SILVER/30: .5X TO 1.2X BASIC CARD

2012-13 ITG Ultimate Memorabilia 500 Goal Scorer Stick Rack

2 Bondra/Recchi/Modano/24* 25.00 60.00
4 Ciccarelli/Lemieux/Messier/24* 50.00 100.00
5 Gartner/Goulet/Kurri/24* 30.00 60.00
6 Gretzky/McDonald/Trottier/24* 50.00 100.00
7 Lafleur/Bossy/Perreault/24* 30.00 60.00
8 Mullen/Andreychu/Robitaille/24* 30.00 60.00
10 Roenick/Tkachuk/Iginla/24* 30.00 80.00
11 Sakic/Nieuwendyk/Jagr/24* 30.00 80.00
12 Turgeon/Sundin/Selanne/24* 25.00 60.00
13 Verbeek/Francis/Shanahan/24* 40.00 80.00
14 Yzerman/Hawerchuk/Hull/24* 50.00 100.00

2012-13 ITG Ultimate Memorabilia All-Star Player Memorabilia

1 Tony Amonte 8.00 20.00
2 Raymond Bourque 15.00 40.00
3 Pavel Bure 15.00 40.00
4 Chris Chelios 10.00 25.00
5 Sergei Fedorov 15.00 40.00
6 Theoren Fleury 12.00 30.00
7 Peter Forsberg 10.00 25.00
8 Dominik Hasek 12.00 30.00
9 Jaromir Jagr 25.00 60.00
10 John LeClair 10.00 25.00
11 Mario Lemieux 30.00 60.00
12 Nicklas Lidstrom 10.00 25.00
13 Eric Lindros 15.00 40.00
14 Al MacInnis 10.00 25.00
15 Mark Messier 12.00 30.00
16 Mike Modano 15.00 40.00
17 Jeremy Roenick 20.00 40.00
18 Patrick Roy 25.00 60.00
19 Teemu Selanne 12.00 30.00
20 Mats Sundin 12.00 30.00

2012-13 ITG Ultimate Memorabilia All-Star Year Memorabilia

ANNOUNCED PRINT RUN 24
1 Amonte/Bourque/Bure 15.00 40.00
2 Belfour/Forsberg/Lindros 20.00 50.00
3 Bondra/Hasek/Fleury 12.00 30.00
4 Bure/Fleury/LeClair 15.00 40.00
5 Chelios/Hull/Messier 15.00 40.00
6 Coffey/Sundin/Yzerman 25.00 60.00
7 Fedorov/Fleury/Forsberg 15.00 40.00
8 Fedorov/Hasek/Jagr 30.00 80.00
9 Fedorov/Irbe/MacInnis 25.00 60.00
10 Fedorov/LeClair/Osgood 15.00 40.00
11 Forsberg/Hasek/Lindros 20.00 50.00
12 Gaborik/Jagr/Khabibulin 15.00 40.00
13 Hasek/Khabibulin/Roy 30.00 80.00
14 Hasek/Lemieux/Lidstrom 40.00 100.00
15 Hasek/Selanne/Bondra 12.00 30.00
16 Hasek/Roy/Belfour 20.00 50.00
17 Hebert/Nolan/Bourque 12.00 30.00
18 Hull/Joseph/Roenick 12.00 30.00
19 Irbe/Lidstrom/Modano 15.00 40.00
20 Jagr/Joseph/Kolzig 15.00 40.00
21 Khabibulin/Jagr/Chelios 30.00 80.00
22 Khabibulin/Lemieux/Nolan 15.00 40.00
23 Khabibulin/Robitaille/Selanne 15.00 40.00
24 LeClair/Lindros/MacInnis 15.00 40.00
25 LeClair/Niedermayer/Belfour 12.00 30.00
26 Lemieux/Jagr/Potvin 20.00 50.00
27 Lidstrom/Roy/Selanne 30.00 80.00
28 Lindros/Forsberg/MacInnis 25.00 50.00
29 Messier/Housley/Amonte 15.00 40.00
30 Messier/Modano/Nolan 20.00 50.00
31 Messier/Modano/Sakic 20.00 50.00
32 Messier/Recchi/Bourque 20.00 50.00
33 Nabokov/Roy/Sakic 20.00 50.00
34 Recchi/Richter/Roenick 15.00 40.00
35 Roy/Bourque/Bure 30.00 60.00
36 Roy/Selanne/Bure 25.00 60.00
37 Sundin/Tkachuk/Amonte 12.00 30.00
38 Sundin/Yzerman/Bure 25.00 60.00
39 Roy/Selanne/Lidstrom 30.00 60.00
40 Thornton/Burke/Chelios 12.00 30.00

2012-13 ITG Ultimate Memorabilia Autograph Jerseys

ANNOUNCED PRINT RUN 19
1 Marian Gaborik 12.00 30.00
2 Claude Giroux 12.00 30.00
3 Jaromir Jagr 30.00 60.00
4 Ryan Kesler 12.00 30.00
5 Henrik Lundqvist 15.00 40.00
6 Evgeni Malkin 25.00 50.00
7 Patrick Marleau 12.00 30.00
8 Alexander Ovechkin 30.00 80.00
9 Jonathan Quick 25.00 50.00
10 Daniel Sedin 12.00 30.00
11 Henrik Sedin 12.00 30.00
12 Teemu Selanne 25.00 60.00
13 Martin St. Louis 12.00 30.00
14 Joe Thornton 12.00 30.00
15 Jakub Voracek 12.00 30.00
16 Shea Weber 10.00 25.00

2012-13 ITG Ultimate Memorabilia Autographs

ANNOUNCED PRINT RUN 29
1 Marian Gaborik 10.00 25.00
2 Claude Giroux 10.00 25.00
3 Jaromir Jagr 25.00 50.00
4 Ryan Kesler 10.00 25.00
5 Henrik Lundqvist 12.00 30.00
6 Evgeni Malkin 30.00 80.00
7 Patrick Marleau 10.00 25.00
8 Alexander Ovechkin 30.00 60.00
9 Jonathan Quick 15.00 40.00
10 Daniel Sedin 10.00 25.00
11 Henrik Sedin 10.00 25.00
12 Teemu Selanne 15.00 40.00
13 Martin St. Louis 10.00 25.00
14 Joe Thornton 10.00 25.00
15 Jakub Voracek 10.00 25.00
16 Shea Weber 8.00 20.00

2012-13 ITG Ultimate Memorabilia Country of Origin Memorabilia

ANNOUNCED PRINT RUN 24
1 Bondra/Gaborik/Stastny 25.00 50.00
2 Bure/Fedorov/Khabibulin 25.00 60.00
3 Esposito/Sittler/Bossy 20.00 50.00
4 Hasek/Jagr/Holik 30.00 80.00
5 Kharlmv/Mikhailv/Tretiak 30.00 80.00
6 Kurri/Selanne/Tikkanen 30.00 80.00
7 Lemieux/Sakic/Yzerman 20.00 50.00
8 Lundqvist/Sedin/Sedin 15.00 40.00
9 Modano/Hull/Richter 20.00 50.00
10 Naslund/Salming/Loob 15.00 40.00
11 Ovechkin/Malkn/Larionv 30.00 60.00
12 Price/Luongo/Fuhr 40.00 100.00
13 Roenick/Chelios/Amonte
14 Sundin/Forsberg/Lidstrom
15 Vanbies/Howard/Tkachk 12.00 30.00

2012-13 ITG Ultimate Memorabilia Cup Finals Memorabilia

ANNOUNCED PRINT RUN 4-24
1 Blveau/Plnte/Hwe/Dlvc/24 50.00 100.00
2 Clrke/Prnt/P.Espo/Bcyk/24 20.00 50.00
3 Crnyr/Mhvlch/T.Espo/Mikt/24 20.00 50.00
4 Fleury/Mlkn/Osgd/Ldstrm/24 20.00 50.00
5 Fuhr/Coffey/Lind/Propp/24 20.00 50.00
6 Hull/Belfour/Hasek/Ray/24 20.00 50.00
7 Hull/Hasek/Irbe/Francis/24 30.00 60.00
8 Knndy/Wtsn/Rchrd/Blke/24
9 Lemx/Jgr/Belfr/Roenick/24 15.00 40.00
10 Mess/Rchtr/McLn/Bure/24 25.00 60.00
11 Potvn/Smth/Andrsn/Krri/24 15.00 40.00
12 Ranfrd/Mess/Nly/Moog/24 20.00 50.00
13 Rbnsn/Laflr/Chvers/Park/24 20.00 50.00
14 Roy/Carbon/McDon/Vrnn/24 25.00 60.00

2012-13 ITG Ultimate Memorabilia Days Gone By Memorabilia

ANNOUNCED PRINT RUN 24
1 Chelios/Nchlls/Vernon/Lemx 40.00 100.00
2 Esposito/Howe/Horton/Plante 40.00 80.00
3 Fedorov/Hasek/Messier/Bure 20.00 50.00
4 Hawerchuk/Smith/Vaive/Ciccarelli 15.00 40.00
5 Hull/MacLsh/Courn/Espo 20.00 50.00
6 Mikita/Hdge/Blveau/Baun 12.00 30.00
7 Richrd/Mahvlch/Harvey/Hall 15.00 40.00
8 Sittler/Leach/Potvin/Park 12.00 30.00
9 Trottier/Lafleur/Dnne/P.Espo 20.00 50.00
10 Vanbies/Coffey/Roy/Clark 15.00 40.00

2012-13 ITG Ultimate Memorabilia Decades Memorabilia

ANNOUNCED PRINT RUN 4-24
1 Bsy/Lem/Msr/Brq/Cfy/Fhr/24* 60.00 150.00
2 Chv/Hal/Crz/Vch/Gia/Bwr/24* 25.00 60.00
3 Clrk/Sit/Hul/Slm/Prk/Esp/24* 20.00 50.00
4 Esp/Lfl/Dio/Rbn/Ptv/Prt/24* 30.00 80.00
5 Jgr/Yzr/Rnk/Mcl/Chl/Ry/24* 50.00 125.00
6 Lml/Hwe/Pln/Hrt/Hul/Rch/24* 60.00 120.00
7 McK/Drn/Shk/Mn/Jns/Fcl/24* 30.00 80.00
8 McD/Trt/Kri/Ptv/Lng/Ilxt/24* 25.00 60.00
9 Msk/Sw/Kn/Ryn/Hrv/Mv/24*
10 Rbt/Bre/Lmx/Lds/Brq/Hk/24* 40.00 80.00

2012-13 ITG Ultimate Memorabilia Draft Day Memorabilia

ANNOUNCED PRINT RUN 24
1 Clarke/Saleski/Gilbert 15.00 40.00
2 Francis/Hawerchuk/MacInnis 15.00 40.00
3 Hextall/Bellows/Gilmour 20.00 50.00
4 Kurri/Coffey/Savard 15.00 40.00
5 Lafleur/Dionne/Robinson 12.00 30.00
6 MacKinnon/Drouin/Jones 30.00 80.00
7 McDonald/Potvin/Middleton 10.00 30.00
8 Messier/Bourque/Gartner 15.00 40.00
9 Modano/Linden/Selanne 15.00 40.00
10 Niedermayer/Lindros/Forsberg 15.00 40.00
11 Nieuwendyk/Clark/Burke 12.00 30.00
12 Nolan/Jagr/Tkachuk 30.00 80.00
13 Perreault/Sittler/MacLeish 12.00 30.00
14 Roy/Lemieux/Hull 40.00 100.00
15 Sakic/Fleury/LeClair 15.00 40.00
16 Shutt/Barber/Nystrom 10.00 25.00
17 Sundin/Lidstrom/Bure 20.00 50.00
18 Thornton/Marleau/Luongo 12.00 30.00
19 Trottier/Williams/Gillies 15.00 40.00
20 Yzerman/LaFontaine/Barrasso 25.00 60.00

2012-13 ITG Ultimate Memorabilia Dynamic Duos Memorabilia

ANNOUNCED PRINT RUN 24
1 M.Bossy/B.Trottier 12.00 30.00
2 B.Hull/S.Mikita 12.00 30.00
3 G.Lafleur/S.Shutt 10.00 25.00
4 C.Neely/A.Oates 10.00 25.00
5 B.Probert/J.Kocur 15.00 40.00
6 H.Sedin/D.Sedin 10.00 25.00
7 D.Sittler/L.McDonald 10.00 25.00
8 P.Stastny/M.Goulet 10.00 25.00
9 J.Thornton/P.Marleau 10.00 25.00
10 K.Tkachuk/T.Selanne 12.00 30.00

2012-13 ITG Ultimate Memorabilia Enforcers Memorabilia

ANNOUNCED PRINT RUN 24
1 D.Brown/C.Nilan 10.00 25.00
2 K.Chase/C.Berube 8.00 20.00
3 W.Clark/M.McSorley 15.00 40.00
4 T.Domi/R.Ray 10.00 25.00
5 S.Grimson/B.Probert 20.00 50.00
6 R.Hextall/F.Potvin 15.00 40.00
7 D.Hunter/C.Nilan 8.00 20.00
8 D.McCarty/C.Lemieux 10.00 25.00
9 M.McSorley/M.Messier 15.00 40.00
10 G.Odjick/J.Odgers 10.00 25.00
11 T.O'Reilly/D.Schultz 15.00 40.00
12 B.Probert/T.Domi 12.00 30.00
13 R.Ray/P.Laus 8.00 20.00
14 P.Roy/M.Vernon 12.00 30.00
15 T.Williams/T.O'Reilly 12.00 30.00

2012-13 ITG Ultimate Memorabilia Enshrined Autograph Jerseys

ANNOUNCED PRINT RUN 19
1 Jean Beliveau 30.00 60.00
2 Mike Bossy 15.00 40.00
3 Raymond Bourque 25.00 50.00
4 Pavel Bure 30.00 60.00
5 Bobby Clarke 25.00 50.00
6 Phil Esposito 15.00 40.00
7 Ron Francis 15.00 40.00
8 Mike Gartner 25.00 50.00
9 Ed Giacomin 15.00 40.00
10 Doug Gilmour 30.00 60.00
11 Dale Hawerchuk 15.00 40.00
12 Gordie Howe 60.00 100.00
13 Bobby Hull 25.00 50.00
14 Dave Keon 12.00 30.00
15 Jari Kurri 12.00 30.00
16 Guy Lafleur 20.00 50.00
17 Jacques Laperriere 12.00 30.00
18 Igor Larionov 30.00 60.00
19 Mario Lemieux 60.00 120.00
20 Lanny McDonald 12.00 30.00
21 Mark Messier 30.00 60.00
22 Stan Mikita 20.00 40.00
23 Joe Mullen 10.00 25.00
24 Cam Neely 15.00 40.00
25 Gilbert Perreault 20.00 50.00
26 Henri Richard 12.00 30.00
27 Luc Robitaille 15.00 40.00
28 Joe Sakic 30.00 60.00
29 Borje Salming 15.00 40.00
30 Serge Savard 12.00 30.00
31 Milt Schmidt 15.00 40.00
32 Darryl Sittler 12.00 30.00
33 Mats Sundin 30.00 60.00
34 Vladislav Tretiak 30.00 60.00
35 Steve Yzerman 40.00 80.00

2012-13 ITG Ultimate Memorabilia Enshrined Autographs

ANNOUNCED PRINT RUN 19
1 Jean Beliveau 25.00 50.00
2 Mike Bossy 12.00 30.00
3 Raymond Bourque 15.00 40.00
4 Pavel Bure 20.00 40.00
5 Bobby Clarke 12.00 30.00
6 Phil Esposito 12.00 30.00
7 Ron Francis 12.00 30.00
8 Mike Gartner 15.00 40.00
9 Ed Giacomin 12.00 30.00
10 Doug Gilmour 15.00 40.00
11 Dale Hawerchuk 12.00 30.00
12 Gordie Howe 50.00 100.00
13 Bobby Hull 15.00 40.00
14 Dave Keon 10.00 25.00
15 Jari Kurri 15.00 30.00
16 Guy Lafleur 15.00 30.00
17 Jacques Laperriere 10.00 25.00
18 Igor Larionov 20.00 40.00
19 Mario Lemieux 50.00 100.00
20 Lanny McDonald 10.00 25.00
21 Mark Messier 25.00 50.00
22 Stan Mikita 12.00 30.00
23 Joe Mullen 8.00 20.00
24 Cam Neely 12.00 30.00
25 Gilbert Perreault 20.00 40.00
26 Henri Richard 10.00 25.00
27 Luc Robitaille 12.00 30.00
28 Joe Sakic 25.00 50.00
29 Borje Salming 10.00 25.00
30 Serge Savard 10.00 25.00
31 Milt Schmidt 12.00 30.00
32 Darryl Sittler 10.00 25.00
33 Mats Sundin 25.00 50.00
34 Vladislav Tretlak 25.00 50.00
35 Steve Yzerman 30.00 60.00

2012-13 ITG Ultimate Memorabilia Entire Career Memorabilia

ANNOUNCED PRINT RUN 24
1 Jean Beliveau 10.00 25.00
2 Mike Bossy 10.00 25.00
3 Bobby Clarke 10.00 25.00
4 Ted Kennedy 10.00 25.00
5 Mario Lemieux 15.00 40.00
6 Nicklas Lidstrom 10.00 25.00
7 Stan Mikita 12.00 30.00
8 Denis Potvin 10.00 25.00
9 Henri Richard 10.00 25.00
10 Maurice Richard 10.00 25.00
11 Milt Schmidt 8.00 20.00
12 Steve Yzerman 15.00 40.00

2012-13 ITG Ultimate Memorabilia Franchise Captains Memorabilia

ANNOUNCED PRINT RUN 24
1 Arbour/Unger/Hull/MacInnis 12.00 30.00
2 Clrke/Lndrs/Prmu/Frsberg 15.00 40.00
3 Howe/Delv/Yzrmn/Lidstrm 30.00 80.00
4 Keon/Sittler/Clark/Sundin 25.00 60.00
5 Park/Mssier/P.Espo/Jagr
5 Lalnde/Rchrd/Bliv/Svrd 30.00 60.00
6 Lngwy/Hntr/Oates/Ovech 15.00 40.00
7 Lemieux/Coffey/FrancisÂ•Jagr 25.00 60.00
8 Linden/Messier/Luongo/Sedin 15.00 40.00
9 Rchrd/Courn/CarbonMuller 30.00 60.00
10 Schmdt/Brque/Bcyk/O'Reil 20.00 50.00

2012-13 ITG Ultimate Memorabilia Franchise Favorites Memorabilia

ANNOUNCED PRINT RUN 24
1 Clarke/Lindros/Parent/Lindb 40.00 80.00
2 Dionne/Taylor/Robit/Quick 20.00 50.00
3 Howe/Yzrmn/Prbert/Lidstrom 25.00 60.00
4 Kurri/Messier/Coffey/Ranford 20.00 50.00
5 Lemieux/Jagr/Malkin/Fleury 40.00 100.00
6 McDonald/MacInnis/Fleury/Vernon 15.00 40.00
7 Mikita/Esposito/Savard/Roenick 15.00 40.00
8 Richard/Lafleur/Roy/Price 40.00 80.00
9 Schmidt/Bucyk/P.Espo/Neely 15.00 40.00
10 Sittler/Clark/Gilmour/Sundin 15.00 40.00

2012-13 ITG Ultimate Memorabilia From Russia With Love Ovechkin Autographs

COMMON OVECHKIN AU/19* 40.00 80.00

2012-13 ITG Ultimate Memorabilia Future Star Autograph Jerseys

ANNOUNCED PRINT RUN 24
PATCH/24: .5X TO 1.2X BASIC JSY AU
1 Justin Bailey 10.00 25.00
2 Aleksander Barkov 40.00 80.00
3 Ben Bishop 12.00 30.00
4 William Carrier 12.00 30.00
5 Cody Ceci 10.00 25.00
6 Eric Comrie 8.00 20.00
7 Jason Dickinson 10.00 25.00
8 Max Domi 15.00 40.00
9 Jonathan Drouin 50.00 100.00
10 Anthony Duclair 20.00 50.00
11 Adam Erne 12.00 30.00
12 Zachary Fucale 25.00 60.00
13 Alex Galchenyuk 25.00 60.00
14 Frederik Gauthier 20.00 50.00
15 Stephen Harper 15.00 40.00
16 Bo Horvat 25.00 60.00
17 Seth Jones 20.00 50.00
18 Morgan Klimchuk 12.00 30.00
19 Ryan Kujawinski 10.00 25.00
20 Curtis Lazar 12.00 30.00
21 Nathan MacKinnon 50.00 100.00
22 Anthony Mantha 20.00 50.00
23 Spencer Martin 10.00 25.00
24 Connor McDavid 175.00 300.00
25 Sean Monahan 20.00 50.00
26 Josh Morrissey 12.00 30.00
27 Ryan Murphy 12.00 30.00
28 Matt Murray 12.00 30.00
29 Darnell Nurse 15.00 40.00
30 Nicolas Petan 12.00 30.00
31 Ryan Pulock 15.00 40.00
32 Eric Roy 12.00 30.00
33 Kerby Rychel 12.00 30.00
34 Hunter Shinkaruk 25.00 60.00
35 Nick Sorensen 12.00 30.00
36 Jordan Subban 15.00 40.00
37 Shea Theodore 12.00 30.00
38 Jake Virtanen 15.00 40.00
39 Nail Yakupov 40.00 80.00
40 Nikita Zadorov 12.00 30.00

2012-13 ITG Ultimate Memorabilia Future Star Autographs

ANNOUNCED PRINT RUN 24
1 Justin Bailey 8.00 20.00
2 Aleksander Barkov 25.00 60.00
3 Ben Bishop 10.00 25.00
4 William Carrier 10.00 25.00
5 Cody Ceci 8.00 20.00
6 Eric Comrie 10.00 25.00
7 Jason Dickinson 8.00 20.00
8 Max Domi 20.00 50.00
9 Jonathan Drouin 40.00 100.00
10 Anthony Duclair 15.00 40.00
11 Adam Erne 10.00 25.00
12 Zachary Fucale 20.00 50.00
13 Alex Galchenyuk 30.00 80.00
14 Frederik Gauthier 15.00 40.00
15 Stephen Harper 12.00 30.00
16 Bo Horvat 15.00 40.00
17 Seth Jones 25.00 60.00
18 Morgan Klimchuk 10.00 25.00
19 Ryan Kujawinski 8.00 20.00
20 Curtis Lazar 12.00 30.00
21 Nathan MacKinnon 40.00 80.00
22 Anthony Mantha 15.00 40.00
23 Spencer Martin 8.00 20.00
24 Connor McDavid 175.00 300.00
25 Sean Monahan 25.00 50.00
26 Josh Morrissey 10.00 25.00
27 Ryan Murphy 10.00 25.00
28 Matt Murray 10.00 25.00
29 Darnell Nurse 12.00 30.00
30 Nicolas Petan 10.00 25.00
31 Ryan Pulock 12.00 30.00
32 Eric Roy 10.00 25.00
33 Kerby Rychel 10.00 25.00
34 Hunter Shinkaruk 15.00 40.00
35 Nick Sorenson 10.00 25.00
36 Jordan Subban 12.00 30.00
37 Shea Theodore 10.00 25.00
38 Jake Virtanen 12.00 30.00
39 Nail Yakupov 40.00 80.00
40 Nikita Zadorov 10.00 25.00

2012-13 ITG Ultimate Memorabilia Gloves Are Off Memorabilia

ANNOUNCED PRINT RUN 24
1 Raymond Bourque 15.00 40.00
2 Brett Hull 10.00 25.00
3 John LeClair 10.00 25.00
4 Mario Lemieux 30.00 80.00
5 Eric Lindros 15.00 40.00
6 Cam Neely 12.00 30.00
7 Joe Sakic 15.00 40.00
8 Eddie Shore 12.00 30.00
9 Doug Weight 10.00 25.00
10 Steve Yzerman 15.00 40.00

2012-13 ITG Ultimate Memorabilia Goalie Autograph Jerseys

ANNOUNCED PRINT RUN 19
1 Ilya Bryzgalov 12.00 30.00
2 Corey Crawford 20.00 40.00
3 Rick DiPietro 10.00 25.00
4 Brian Elliott 10.00 25.00
5 Ray Emery 10.00 25.00
6 Marc-Andre Fleury 20.00 50.00
7 Jonas Hiller 10.00 25.00
8 Jimmy Howard 15.00 40.00
9 Nikolai Khabibulin 15.00 40.00
10 Kari Lehtonen 10.00 25.00
11 Henrik Lundqvist 25.00 50.00
12 Roberto Luongo 12.00 30.00
13 Evgeni Nabakov 40.00 100.00
14 Antti Niemi 10.00 25.00
15 Ondrej Pavelec 20.00 50.00
16 Carey Price 25.00 50.00
17 Jonathan Quick 25.00 60.00
18 Semyon Varlamov 12.00 30.00

2012-13 ITG Ultimate Memorabilia Goalie Autographs

ANNOUNCED PRINT RUN 19
1 Ilya Bryzgalov 10.00 25.00
2 Corey Crawford 12.00 30.00
3 Rick DiPietro 8.00 20.00
4 Brian Elliott 8.00 20.00
5 Ray Emery 8.00 20.00
6 Marc-Andre Fleury 12.00 30.00
7 Jonas Hiller 8.00 20.00
8 Jimmy Howard 12.00 30.00
9 Nikolai Khabibulin 12.00 30.00
10 Kari Lehtonen 8.00 20.00
11 Henrik Lundqvist 15.00 40.00
12 Roberto Luongo 12.00 30.00
13 Evgeni Nabakov 30.00 80.00
14 Antti Niemi 8.00 20.00
15 Ondrej Pavelec 15.00 40.00
16 Carey Price 20.00 40.00
17 Jonathan Quick 25.00 50.00
18 Semyon Varlamov 10.00 25.00

2012-13 ITG Ultimate Memorabilia Goalie Generations Memorabilia

ANNOUNCED PRINT RUN 24
1 Brodeur/Cloutier/Luongo 12.00 30.00
2 Esposito/Belfour/Crawford 15.00 40.00
3 Giacomin/Richter/Lundqvist 15.00 40.00
4 Hall/Joseph/Elliott 12.00 30.00
5 Hebert/Bryzgalov/Hiller 12.00 30.00
6 Parent/Hextall/Bryzgalov 12.00 30.00
7 Plante/Roy/Price 30.00 80.00
8 Sawchuk/Osgood/Howard 20.00 50.00
9 Smith/Snow/DiPietro 12.00 30.00
10 Vachon/Hrudey/Quick 20.00 50.00
11 Vernon/Nabokov/Niemi 10.00 25.00

2012-13 ITG Ultimate Memorabilia Goalie Legend Autograph Jerseys

ANNOUNCED PRINT RUN 19
1 Johnny Bower 12.00 30.00
2 Sean Burke 8.00 20.00
3 Gerry Cheevers 12.00 30.00
4 Tony Esposito 15.00 40.00
5 Grant Fuhr 20.00 40.00
6 Ed Giacomin 12.00 30.00
7 Glenn Hall 15.00 40.00
8 Dominik Hasek 15.00 40.00
9 Ron Hextall 40.00 80.00
10 Arturs Irbe 40.00 80.00
11 Curtis Joseph 12.00 30.00
12 Olaf Kolzig 20.00 50.00
13 Chris Osgood 12.00 30.00
14 Bernie Parent 25.00 50.00
15 Felix Potvin 20.00 50.00
16 Bill Ranford 20.00 40.00
17 Mike Richter 20.00 40.00
18 Patrick Roy 40.00 80.00
19 Vladislav Tretiak 30.00 60.00
20 John Vanbiesbrouck 30.00 60.00

2012-13 ITG Ultimate Memorabilia Goalie Legend Autographs

ANNOUNCED PRINT RUN 29
1 Johnny Bower 10.00 25.00
2 Sean Burke 6.00 15.00
3 Gerry Cheevers 10.00 25.00
4 Tony Esposito 12.00 30.00
5 Grant Fuhr 12.00 30.00
6 Ed Giacomin 10.00 25.00
7 Glenn Hall 12.00 30.00
8 Dominik Hasek 12.00 30.00
9 Ron Hextall 12.00 30.00
10 Arturs Irbe 25.00 60.00
11 Curtis Joseph 10.00 25.00
12 Olaf Kolzig 15.00 40.00
13 Chris Osgood 10.00 25.00
14 Bernie Parent 20.00 40.00
15 Felix Potvin 25.00 50.00
16 Bill Ranford 15.00 30.00
17 Mike Richter 12.00 30.00
18 Patrick Roy 30.00 60.00
19 Vladislav Tretiak 25.00 50.00
20 John Vanbiesbrouck 20.00 40.00

2012-13 ITG Ultimate Memorabilia History of the Franchise In the Net Memorabilia

ANNOUNCED PRINT RUN 24
1 Bower/Potvin/Joseph/Belfour 25.00 60.00
2 Brimsek/Chvers/Moog/Dafoe 20.00 50.00
3 Hall/T.Espo/Bclfr/Crawford 20.00 50.00
4 Plante/Vachon/Roy/Price 50.00 120.00
5 Sawchk/Osgd/Vernn/Howrd 15.00 40.00
6 Sawchk/Vachn/Hrudey/Quick 20.00 50.00

2012-13 ITG Ultimate Memorabilia Journey Jersey Memorabilia

ANNOUNCED PRINT RUN 24
1 Raymond Bourque 15.00 40.00
2 Pavel Bure 15.00 40.00
3 Marcel Dionne 12.00 30.00
4 Michel Goulet 8.00 20.00
5 Gordie Howe 25.00 60.00
6 Brett Hull 10.00 25.00
7 Jaromir Jagr 25.00 60.00
8 Guy Lafleur 12.00 30.00
9 Lanny McDonald 10.00 25.00
10 Mark Messier 12.00 30.00
11 Jeremy Roenick 10.00 25.00
12 Patrick Roy 25.00 60.00
13 Joe Sakic 15.00 40.00
14 Darryl Sittler 10.00 25.00
15 Mats Sundin 10.00 25.00

2012-13 ITG Ultimate Memorabilia Nicknames Jerseys

ANNOUNCED PRINT RUN 24
1 Ed Belfour 10.00 25.00
2 Gerry Cheevers 10.00 25.00
3 Tony Esposito 10.00 25.00
4 Peter Forsberg 10.00 25.00
5 Doug Gilmour 12.00 30.00
6 Glenn Hall 10.00 25.00
7 Gordie Howe 20.00 50.00
8 Bobby Hull 10.00 25.00
9 Brett Hull 10.00 25.00
10 Curtis Joseph 10.00 25.00
11 Guy Lafleur 12.00 30.00
12 Mario Lemieux 15.00 40.00
13 Trevor Linden 10.00 25.00
14 Mark Messier 12.00 30.00
15 Alexander Ovechkin 40.00 100.00
16 Felix Potvin 15.00 40.00
17 Jeremy Roenick 10.00 25.00
18 Teemu Selanne 20.00 50.00
19 Keith Tkachuk 10.00 25.00
20 Steve Yzerman 20.00 50.00

2012-13 ITG Ultimate Memorabilia Number 12 Memorabilia

ANNOUNCED PRINT RUN 24
1 Peter Bondra 12.00 30.00
2 Yvan Cournoyer 10.00 25.00
3 Gary Dornhoefer 6.00 15.00
4 Simon Gagne 10.00 25.00
5 Bill Guerin 10.00 25.00
6 Jarome Iginla 10.00 25.00
7 Hakan Loob 8.00 20.00
8 Patrick Marleau 10.00 25.00
9 Adam Oates 10.00 25.00
10 Eric Staal 12.00 30.00
11 Pat Stapleton 6.00 15.00
12 Pat Verbeek 8.00 20.00

2012-13 ITG Ultimate Memorabilia Overtime Heroes Jerseys

ANNOUNCED PRINT RUN 24
1 Pavel Bure 12.00 30.00
2 Theoren Fleury 12.00 30.00
3 Brett Hull 10.00 25.00
4 Pat LaFontaine 10.00 25.00
5 Brad May 6.00 15.00
6 Lanny McDonald 10.00 25.00
7 Bob Nystrom 6.00 15.00
8 Keith Primeau 8.00 20.00
9 Henri Richard 10.00 25.00
10 Henrik Sedin 10.00 25.00
11 Steve Yzerman 15.00 40.00

2012-13 ITG Ultimate Memorabilia To the Hall Autograph Jerseys

ANNOUNCED PRINT RUN 19
1 Tony Amonte 10.00 25.00
2 Dave Andreychuk 12.00 30.00
3 Peter Bondra 25.00 50.00
4 Chris Chelios 12.00 30.00
5 Wendel Clark 15.00 40.00
6 Vincent Damphousse 20.00 40.00
7 Sergei Fedorov 25.00 60.00
8 Theoren Fleury 20.00 40.00
9 Peter Forsberg 25.00 50.00
10 Danny Gare 8.00 20.00
11 Anders Hedberg 10.00 25.00
12 Phil Housley 10.00 25.00
13 Vladimir Krutov 40.00 80.00
14 Steve Larmer 20.00 50.00
15 John LeClair 25.00 50.00
16 Claude Lemieux 10.00 25.00
17 Nicklas Lidstrom 25.00 50.00
18 Trevor Linden 15.00 40.00
19 Eric Lindros 30.00 60.00
20 Mike Modano 15.00 40.00
21 Markus Naslund 15.00 40.00
22 Bernie Nicholls 15.00 40.00
23 Scott Niedermayer 12.00 30.00
24 Ulf Nilsson 8.00 20.00
25 Owen Nolan 10.00 25.00
26 Mark Recchi 15.00 40.00
27 Gary Roberts 20.00 40.00
28 Jeremy Roenick 30.00 60.00
29 Keith Tkachuk 15.00 40.00

2012-13 ITG Ultimate Memorabilia To the Hall Autographs

ANNOUNCED PRINT RUN 29
1 Tony Amonte 8.00 20.00
2 Dave Andreychuk 8.00 20.00
3 Peter Bondra 15.00 40.00
4 Chris Chelios 10.00 25.00
5 Wendel Clark 12.00 30.00
6 Vincent Damphousse 10.00 25.00
7 Sergei Fedorov 20.00 50.00
8 Theoren Fleury 20.00 40.00
9 Peter Forsberg 15.00 40.00
10 Danny Gare
11 Anders Hedberg 8.00 20.00
12 Phil Housley 8.00 20.00
13 Vladimir Krutov 30.00 60.00
14 Steve Larmer 15.00 40.00
15 John LeClair 15.00 40.00
16 Claude Lemieux 8.00 20.00
17 Nicklas Lidstrom 15.00 40.00
18 Trevor Linden 12.00 30.00
19 Eric Lindros 25.00 50.00
20 Mike Modano 12.00 30.00
21 Markus Naslund 12.00 30.00
22 Bernie Nicholls 12.00 30.00
23 Scott Niedermayer 10.00 25.00
24 Ulf Nilsson 6.00 15.00
25 Owen Nolan 8.00 20.00
26 Mark Recchi 12.00 30.00
27 Gary Roberts 10.00 25.00
28 Jeremy Roenick 15.00 30.00
29 Keith Tkachuk 12.00 30.00

2012-13 ITG Ultimate Memorabilia To the Hall Memorabilia

ANNOUNCED PRINT RUN 24
1 Chris Chelios 10.00 25.00
2 Sergei Fedorov 15.00 40.00
3 Theoren Fleury 12.00 30.00
4 Dominik Hasek 10.00 25.00
5 Phil Housley 8.00 20.00
6 Jaromir Jagr 25.00 60.00
7 Curtis Joseph 10.00 25.00
8 Nicklas Lidstrom 10.00 25.00
9 Eric Lindros 12.00 30.00
10 Mike Modano 15.00 40.00
11 Scott Niedermayer 10.00 25.00
12 Chris Osgood 10.00 25.00
13 Jeremy Roenick 10.00 25.00
14 Teemu Selanne 20.00 50.00
15 Keith Tkachuk 10.00 25.00
16 Rogie Vachon 8.00 20.00

2012-13 ITG Ultimate Memorabilia Triple Gold Club Jerseys

ANNOUNCED PRINT RUN 24
1 Peter Forsberg 10.00 25.00
2 Jaromir Jagr 25.00 60.00
3 Niklas Kronwall 8.00 20.00
4 Igor Larionov 10.00 25.00
5 Nicklas Lidstrom 12.00 30.00
6 Hakan Loob 8.00 20.00
7 Mats Naslund 10.00 25.00
8 Scott Niedermayer 6.00 15.00
9 Joe Sakic 15.00 40.00

2012-13 ITG Ultimate Memorabilia Ultimate Legacy Memorabilia Toronto Spring Expo

ARB Amnte/Rnck/Blfr
BLM Bre/Lndn/McLn
BLR Blvu/Lflr/Rchrd
BMH Blfr/Mdno/Hll
BMO Brqe/Mg/Ots
BOJ Bndra/Ovchkn/Jgr
BOK Bre/Ovchkn/Khbbln
BPL Bssy/Ptvn/LFntne
BRH Bpre/Rhds/Hsk
BRS Brqe/Ry/Skc
BSW Brdr/Snpts/Wllms
BTR Brke/Tkchk/Rnck
BVL Bre/Vnbsbrck/Lngo
CFM Cffy/Flry/Mlkn
CGP Clrk/Glmr/Ptvn
CJH Crzr/Jsph/Hwrd
CKR Chvlde/Khbbln/Rddck 12.00 30.00
CLR Clrke/Lndrs/Rnck
CSK Cltr/St.Ls/Khbbln
EPS Espsto/Prbrt/Svrd 15.00 40.00
FHT Fdrko/Hll/Tkchk
FLJ Frncs/Lmx/Jgr
FSH Fdrv/Slnne/Hllr 15.00 40.00
FSS Frsbrg/Sndn/Slmng
GDL Gbrk/Dnne/Lndqvst 12.00 30.00
GGS Grrtt/Gult/Stsny
HHM Hll/Hll/Mkta
HKF Hwe/Kn/Frncs
HRL Hsk/Ry/LaFntne
HTM Hll/Tkchk/Mdno
IFC Irbe/Frncs/Cffy
JCV Jns/Chls/Vnbsbck
KGH Klzg/Grtnr/Hntr
KPM Kcr/Prbrt/McCrty
KYK Krtv/Ykshv/Khrlmv
LBC Lch/Brbr/Clrke 20.00 40.00
LJB Lndrs/Jgr/Bre
LJP Lngo/Jsph/Prce
LSM Lflr/Shtt/Mhvlch
MCB Mdno/Cccrlli/Bllws
MCF Mssr/Cffy/Fhr 20.00 50.00
MFN McDnld/Flry/Nwndyk
MSS McDnld/Slmng/Sttlr
NCM Nslnd/Cltr/Mssr
NKM Nchlls/Krri/McSrly
NLJ Nwndyk/Lhtnn/Jgr
NNH Nwndyk/Ndrmyr/Hlk
NSS Nln/Skc/Sndn
NTM Nmi/Thrntn/Mrlu
OBM Ovchkn/Bre/Mlkn
PGF Prrlt/Gre/Fhr
PHB Prnt/Hxtll/Bryzglv
PJB Ptvn/Jsph/Blfr
PRP Prce/Ry/Plnte 50.00 100.00
RAM Rchtr/Amnte/Mdno
RDC Rbtlle/Dnne/Cffy
RSF Ry/Skc/Frsbrg
RSL Rbnsn/Svrd/Lpnte
RVL Rchtr/Vnbsbrck/Lndqvst
SFR Slnne/Frsbrg/Ry
SLB Sttlr/Lflr/Bssy
SLL Skc/Lmx/Lndrs
SLS Sdn/Lngo/Sdn
SNT Slnne/Nbkv/Thrntn
SSC Sndn/Sttlr/Clrk
STK Slnne/Tkknn/Krri
SYT St.Ls/Yzrmn/Thrntn

'KM Trtk/Khrlmv/Mkhlv
'SH Tkchk/Slnne/Hwrchk
'MD Vrck/McKnnn/Drn
'HO Yzrmn/Hsk/Osgd
'LF Yzrmn/Ldstrm/Fdrv

2012-13 ITG Ultimate Memorabilia Ultimate Rivalry Memorabilia

NNOUNCED PRINT RUN 24
Crb/Rbn/Ry/Glt/Hnt/Sty 25.00 60.00
Hdf/Prk/Gia/Smt/Nys/Ptv 20.00 50.00
Lfl/Sht/Lmr/Slm/McD/Stlr 15.00 40.00
Lnd/LeC/Hxt/Lmx/Jgr/Frn 30.00 60.00
Mcl/McD/Mln/Fhr/Msr/Kur 25.00 60.00
Nly/Brq/Mg/Ry/Lmx/Nsl 25.00 60.00
O'R/Esp/Byk/McL/Clr/Prt 20.00 50.00
Rnk/Chl/Bll/Chv/Lds/Fdv 25.00 60.00
Skc/Ry/Lmx/Yzr/Vrn/McC 30.00 80.00
0 Yzr/Prb/Fdv/Glm/Clrk/Ptv 40.00 100.00

2012-13 ITG Ultimate Memorabilia Vintage Dual Jerseys

NNOUNCED PRINT RUN 24
B.Baun/T.Sawchuk 12.00 30.00
J.Beliveau/S.Mikita 15.00 40.00
J.Bower/T.Sawchuk 12.00 30.00
B.Clarke/D.Sittler 12.00 30.00
M.Dionne/G.Lafleur 15.00 40.00
T.Horton/D.Harvey 12.00 30.00
G.Howe/G.Howe 20.00 50.00
B.Parent/R.Vachon 15.00 40.00
D.Potvin/L.Robinson 12.00 30.00
0 M.Richard/G.Howe 40.00 80.00
1 V.Tretiak/V.Kharlamov 30.00 60.00
2 R.Worters/G.Hainsworth 20.00 50.00

2014-15 ITG Ultimate Memorabilia

TATED PRINT RUN 50 SER.#'d SETS
SILVER/20: .5X TO 1.2X BASIC CARDS/50
Aaron Ekblad 10.00 25.00
Art Ross 3.00 8.00
Bobby Hull 5.00 12.00
Bryan Trottier 6.00 15.00
Cam Neely 5.00 12.00
Carey Price 15.00 40.00
Chris Chelios 5.00 12.00
Dominik Hasek 6.00 15.00
Ed Belfour 5.00 12.00
) Georges Vezina 5.00 12.00
1 Gordie Howe 10.00 25.00
2 Guy Lafleur 6.00 15.00
3 Hap Day 4.00 10.00
4 Henri Richard 5.00 12.00
5 Hobey Baker 4.00 10.00
6 Howie Morenz 4.00 10.00
7 Jacques Plante 6.00 15.00
8 Jean Beliveau 8.00 20.00
9 Joe Sakic 8.00 20.00
0 King Clancy 5.00 12.00
1 Lady Byng 3.00 8.00
2 Larry Robinson 5.00 12.00
3 Leon Draisaitl 25.00 60.00
4 Lester Patrick 5.00 12.00
5 Lord Stanley 5.00 12.00
6 Marc-Andre Fleury 8.00 20.00
7 Mario Lemieux 15.00 40.00
8 Mark Messier 5.00 12.00
9 Martin St. Louis 5.00 12.00
0 Mats Sundin 5.00 12.00
1 Maurice Richard 8.00 20.00
2 Michael Dal Colle 6.00 15.00
3 Mike Eruzione 4.00 10.00
4 Mike Modano 8.00 20.00
5 Mike Richter 5.00 12.00
6 Patrick Roy 12.00 30.00
7 Paul Coffey 5.00 12.00
8 Pelle Lindbergh 5.00 12.00
9 Peter Forsberg 5.00 12.00
0 Raymond Bourque 8.00 20.00
1 Sam Bennett 8.00 20.00
2 Sam Reinhart 15.00 40.00
3 Scott Niedermayer 5.00 12.00
4 Sid Abel 4.00 10.00
5 Steve Yzerman 10.00 25.00
6 Ted Lindsay 5.00 12.00
7 Terry Sawchuk 5.00 12.00
8 Tim Horton 5.00 12.00
9 Tony Esposito 5.00 12.00
0 Vladislav Tretiak 6.00 15.00

2014-15 ITG Ultimate Memorabilia Artistic Moments Autographs

MAD1 Alex Delvecchio/25 8.00 20.00
MBH1 Bobby Hull/25 15.00 40.00
MCC1 Chris Chelios/25 10.00 25.00
MEB1 Ed Belfour/25 10.00 25.00
MHR1 Henri Richard/25 10.00 25.00
MJB1 Jean Beliveau/25 25.00 50.00
MMM2 Mike Modano/25 15.00 40.00
MPE1 Phil Esposito/25 15.00 40.00
MRB1 Raymond Bourque/25 15.00 40.00
MVT1 Vladislav Tretiak/25 12.00 30.00

2014-15 ITG Ultimate Memorabilia Blades of Steel

S1 Bobby Hull/15 25.00 50.00
S5 Jaromir Jagr/15 25.00 60.00
S6 Jean Beliveau/15 20.00 40.00
S7 Johnny Bucyk/15 12.00 30.00
S8 King Clancy/15 10.00 25.00
S9 Mario Lemieux/15 30.00 80.00
S10 Maurice Richard/15 30.00 60.00
S11 Paul Coffey/15 10.00 25.00
S12 Paddy Moran/15 25.00 50.00
S13 Raymond Bourque/15 15.00 40.00
S14 Scott Niedermayer/15 10.00 25.00
S15 Tim Horton/15 25.00 50.00

2014-15 ITG Ultimate Memorabilia Cup Heroes Jerseys

H1 Bryan Trottier 8.00 20.00
H2 Chris Chelios 6.00 15.00
H3 Dave Keon 8.00 20.00
H4 Dominik Hasek 8.00 20.00
H5 Gordie Howe 12.00 30.00
H6 Guy Lafleur 10.00 25.00
H7 Guy Lapointe 5.00 12.00
H8 Jacques Lemaire 6.00 15.00
H9 Jari Kurri 10.00 25.00
H10 Joe Sakic 10.00 25.00
H11 Mario Lemieux 20.00 50.00
H12 Mark Messier 10.00 25.00
H13 Maurice Richard 10.00 25.00
H14 Mike Bossy 6.00 15.00
H15 Mike Modano 10.00 25.00
H16 Mike Richter 6.00 15.00
H17 Patrick Roy 15.00 40.00
H18 Paul Coffey 6.00 15.00
CH19 Phil Esposito 10.00 25.00
CH20 Steve Yzerman 12.00 30.00

2014-15 ITG Ultimate Memorabilia Decades vs. Jerseys

DV1 Hwe/Blvu/Ldsy/Mkta/Esto/Hll 50.00 100.00
DV3 Hll/Hwe/Dlvco/Esto/Lflr/Dne 50.00 100.00
DV4 Lflr/Stlr/Clrke/Msr/Lmx/Cfy 25.00 60.00
DV5 Bsy/Kri/Lmx/Yzmn/Jgr/Skc 50.00 120.00
DV6 Hwe/Ldsy/Rchd/Esto/Hll/Lflr 30.00 80.00
DV7 Yzmn/Jgr/Sdn/Thtn/St.Ls/Flry 40.00 100.00
DV8 Schk/Bwr/Plnte/Hll/Vchn/Gcmn 20.00 50.00
DV9 Hll/Wsly/Gcmn/Esto/Prnt/Vchn 20.00 50.00
DV10 Esto/Prnt/Vchn/Fhr/Smth/Brso 20.00 50.00
DV11 Hll/Wsly/Gcmn/Ry/Rchtr/Hsk 40.00 100.00
DV12 Swchk/Bwr/Plnte/Ry/Rchtr/Hsk 40.00 100.00
DV13 Hrvy/Hwe/Schk/Ry/Lmx/Brqe 50.00 120.00

2014-15 ITG Ultimate Memorabilia Dynamic Duos Autographs

DD13 R.Bourque/C.Chelios/25 15.00 40.00
DD14 R.Kelly/J.Bower/25 15.00 40.00
DD17 T.Esposito/P.Esposito/25 40.00 80.00

2014-15 ITG Ultimate Memorabilia Enshrined Autographs

EAAD1 Alex Delvecchio/25 8.00 20.00
EABH1 Bobby Hull/25 15.00 40.00
EABH2 Brett Hull/15 25.00 50.00
EABS1 Billy Smith/19 10.00 25.00
EABT1 Bryan Trottier/25 12.00 30.00
EACC1 Chris Chelios/25 10.00 25.00
EAGL1 Guy Lapointe/25 8.00 20.00
EAJB1 Johnny Bower/25 12.00 30.00
EAJB2 Johnny Bucyk/25 8.00 20.00
EAMB1 Mike Bossy/17 12.00 30.00
EAMS1 Milt Schmidt/16 8.00 20.00
EAPE1 Phil Esposito/25 15.00 40.00
EARK1 Red Kelly/25 8.00 20.00
EATE1 Tony Esposito/25 10.00 25.00
EATL1 Ted Lindsay/25 10.00 25.00
EAVT1 Vladislav Tretiak/25 12.00 30.00

2014-15 ITG Ultimate Memorabilia Franchise Legacy Jerseys

FL2 Rchrd/Lflr/Plnte 40.00 80.00
FL3 Hrtn/Slmng/Bwr 15.00 40.00
FL4 Hll/Mkta/Espsto 15.00 40.00
FL5 Mssr/Krri/Fhr 20.00 50.00
FL6 Bssy/Trttr/Smth 15.00 40.00
FL7 Lmx/Jgr/Brrsso 40.00 100.00
FL8 Hll/Mdno/Blfr 20.00 50.00

2014-15 ITG Ultimate Memorabilia Future Star Autograph Jerseys

FSAE1 Aaron Ekblad/15 15.00 40.00
FSJV1 Jake Virtanen/15 8.00 20.00
FSMM1 Matt Mistele/15 5.00 12.00
FSOLB Olivier LeBlanc/15 5.00 12.00
FSRMI Ryan MacInnis/25 5.00 12.00
FSRMK Roland McKeown/15 6.00 15.00
FSSB1 Sam Bennett/15 10.00 25.00
FSSR1 Sam Reinhart/15 12.00 30.00
FSSW1 Spencer Watson/15 6.00 15.00
FSWN1 William Nylander/15 20.00 50.00

2014-15 ITG Ultimate Memorabilia Future Star Autographs

FSAP1 Alexis Pepin/25 4.00 10.00
FSCB1 Clark Bishop/25 5.00 12.00
FSHF1 Haydn Fleury/25 5.00 12.00
FSJL1 Jaden Lindo/25 3.00 8.00
FSJV1 Jake Virtanen/25 6.00 15.00
FSMM1 Matt Mistele/25 4.00 10.00
FSNR1 Nick Ritchie/25 5.00 12.00
FSOLB Olivier LeBlanc/25 4.00 10.00
FSSB1 Sam Bennett/25 12.00 30.00
FSSR1 Sam Reinhart/17 15.00 40.00
FSWN1 William Nylander/15 12.00 30.00

2014-15 ITG Ultimate Memorabilia Gloves Are Off Memorabilia

GO1 Al MacInnis 10.00 25.00
GO2 Bobby Clarke 10.00 25.00
GO3 Cam Neely 10.00 25.00
GO4 Eddie Shore 12.00 30.00
GO5 Johnny Bower 15.00 40.00
GO6 Mario Lemieux 30.00 80.00
GO7 Paul Coffey 10.00 25.00
GO8 Raymond Bourque 15.00 40.00
GO9 Stan Mikita 12.00 30.00
GO10 Wendel Clark 10.00 25.00

2014-15 ITG Ultimate Memorabilia Goalie Legacy Jerseys

GL1 Ry/Plnte/Prce 40.00 100.00
GL2 Rchtr/Hsk/Blfr 15.00 40.00
GL3 Plnte/Gcmn/Wrsly 15.00 40.00
GL4 Swchk/Osgd/Hwrd 12.00 30.00
GL5 Espsto/Smth/Fhr 12.00 30.00
GL6 Ry/Hsk/Rchrd 30.00 80.00
GL7 Bwr/Gcmn/Ry 30.00 80.00
GL8 Hwrd/Prce/Flry 40.00 100.00

2014-15 ITG Ultimate Memorabilia Hall Bound Jerseys

HB1 Chris Osgood 10.00 25.00
HB2 Dominik Hasek 12.00 30.00
HB3 Teemu Selanne 20.00 50.00
HB4 Jaromir Jagr 25.00 60.00
HB5 Jeremy Roenick 10.00 25.00
HB6 Mike Modano 15.00 40.00
HB7 Mike Richter 10.00 25.00
HB8 Nicklas Lidstrom 10.00 25.00
HB9 Peter Forsberg 10.00 25.00
HB10 Sergei Fedorov 15.00 40.00

2014-15 ITG Ultimate Memorabilia Honoured Members Jerseys

HM2 Swchk/Blvu/Hwe/Hrvy 25.00 60.00
HM3 Bwr/Hrtn/Dlvcho/Plnte 15.00 40.00
HM4 Bcyk/Mhvlch/Wrsly/Shtt 12.00 30.00
HM5 Glbrt/Hll/Mkta/Espsto 40.00 80.00
HM6 Lmre/Prnt/Chvrs/Keon 12.00 30.00
HM7 Clrke/Gcmn/Lflr/Espsto 15.00 40.00
HM8 Lmx/Brque/Nly/Mssr 40.00 100.00
HM9 Bssy/Rbnsn/Trttr/Lpnte 15.00 40.00
HM10 Ry/Yzrmn/Hll/McInns 30.00 80.00

2014-15 ITG Ultimate Memorabilia Legendary Sweaters Jerseys

LSBH1 Bobby Hull 10.00 25.00
LSGH1 Gordie Howe 20.00 50.00
LSGL1 Guy Lafleur 12.00 30.00
LSML1 Mario Lemieux 30.00 80.00
LSMM1 Mark Messier 10.00 25.00
LSPR1 Patrick Roy 15.00 40.00
LSRB1 Raymond Bourque 15.00 40.00
LSSY1 Steve Yzerman 15.00 40.00
LSTL1 Ted Lindsay 10.00 25.00
LSVT1 Vladislav Tretiak 12.00 30.00

2014-15 ITG Ultimate Memorabilia Legendary Sweaters Six Jerseys

LS61 Hwe/Lnsy/Rch/Swk/Htn/Bwr 30.00 80.00
LS62 Lflr/Hll/Mkta/Dne/Espto/Hwe 30.00 80.00
LS64 Bwr/Swck/Plte/Wsl/Hll/Gcm 20.00 50.00
LS65 Yzmn/Lmx/Ry/Msr/Skc/Rch 50.00 120.00
LS66 Lflr/Rch/Lpn/Lmre/Mhv/Plte 20.00 50.00
LS67 Bwr/Mvch/Hrtn/Kn/Slm/Snd 20.00 50.00
LS69 Flln/Hllr/Rchrd/Lflr/Plnte/Ry 40.00 100.00

2014-15 ITG Ultimate Memorabilia Super Swatch Jerseys

SS1 Bobby Hull 8.00 20.00
SS2 Gordie Howe 25.00 50.00
SS3 Joe Sakic 12.00 30.00
SS4 Joe Thornton 8.00 20.00
SS5 Mario Lemieux 25.00 60.00
SS6 Mark Messier 8.00 20.00
SS7 Mats Sundin 8.00 20.00
SS8 Patrick Roy 20.00 50.00
SS9 Raymond Bourque 12.00 30.00
SS10 Stan Mikita 10.00 25.00
SS11 Steve Shutt 6.00 15.00
SS12 Steve Yzerman 15.00 40.00
SS13 Steve Yzerman 15.00 40.00
SS14 Teemu Selanne 15.00 40.00

2014-15 ITG Ultimate Memorabilia Ultimate Autograph Jerseys

UAMSL Martin St. Louis/15 10.00 25.00

2014-15 ITG Ultimate Memorabilia Ultimate Autographs

UAAD1 Alex Delvecchio/25 8.00 20.00
UAAE1 Aaron Ekblad/25 15.00 40.00
UACP1 Carey Price/18 30.00 80.00
UAEL1 Eddie Lack/20 8.00 20.00
UAJJ1 Jaromir Jagr/25 25.00 60.00
UAMAF Marc-Andre Fleury/25 15.00 40.00
UAMSL Martin St. Louis/25
UASR1 Sam Reinhart/15 25.00 60.00

2014-15 ITG Ultimate Memorabilia Ultimate Journey Jerseys

UJBH1 Brett Hull 10.00 25.00
UJCC1 Chris Chelios 10.00 25.00
UJEB1 Ed Belfour 8.00 20.00
UJGF1 Guy Lafleur 12.00 30.00
UJJJ1 Jaromir Jagr 25.00 60.00
UJJT1 Joe Thornton 8.00 20.00
UJMM1 Mark Messier 10.00 25.00
UJPC1 Paul Coffey 10.00 25.00
UJPF1 Peter Forsberg 10.00 25.00
UJPR1 Patrick Roy 15.00 40.00
UJRB1 Raymond Bourque 15.00 40.00
UJTS1 Teemu Selanne 20.00 50.00

2002-03 ITG Used

This 200-card set was printed on two types of card stock. Card 1-100 were printed on a shimmerboard stock and pictured players in their away jerseys. Cards 101-200 were printed on dufex card stock and pictured players in the road jerseys. Cards 81-100 and 181-200 were shortprinted rookies and were serial-numbered to just 100 copies each.

1 Adam Oates 2.00 5.00
2 Paul Kariya 2.50 6.00
3 Petr Sykora 1.50 4.00
4 Dany Heatley 2.00 5.00
5 Ilya Kovalchuk 2.50 6.00
6 Jeff O'Neill 1.25 3.00
7 Joe Thornton 2.50 6.00
8 Sergei Samsonov 1.50 4.00
9 Jarome Iginla 2.00 5.00
10 Ron Francis 2.50 6.00
11 Jocelyn Thibault 1.50 4.00
12 Alex Tanguay 1.50 4.00
13 Joe Sakic 3.00 8.00
14 Milan Hejduk 1.50 4.00
15 Patrick Roy 5.00 12.00
16 Peter Forsberg 2.50 6.00
17 Rob Blake 2.00 5.00
18 Rostislav Klesla 1.25 3.00
19 Brett Hull 2.50 6.00
20 Marty Turco 2.00 5.00
21 Mike Modano 3.00 8.00
22 Bill Guerin 2.00 5.00
23 Brendan Shanahan 2.50 6.00
24 Chris Chelios 2.00 5.00
25 Curtis Joseph 2.00 5.00
26 Luc Robitaille 2.00 5.00
27 Nicklas Lidstrom 2.00 5.00
28 Pavel Datsyuk 2.50 6.00
29 Sergei Fedorov 3.00 8.00
30 Steve Yzerman 4.00 10.00
31 Mike Comrie 2.00 5.00
32 Erik Cole 1.50 4.00
33 Kristian Huselius 1.25 3.00
34 Roberto Luongo 3.00 8.00
35 Felix Potvin 3.00 8.00
36 Jason Allison 1.50 4.00
37 Zigmund Palffy 2.00 5.00
38 Marian Gaborik 3.00 8.00
39 Jose Theodore 2.00 5.00
40 Saku Koivu 2.00 5.00
41 Martin Brodeur 4.00 10.00
42 Patrik Elias 2.00 5.00
43 Scott Gomez 1.50 4.00
44 Alexei Yashin 1.50 4.00
45 Chris Osgood 2.00 5.00
46 Rick DiPietro 1.50 4.00
47 Brian Leetch 2.00 5.00
48 Eric Lindros 3.00 8.00
49 Mark Messier 3.00 8.00
50 Mike Richter 2.00 5.00
51 Pavel Bure 2.50 6.00
52 Daniel Alfredsson 2.00 5.00
53 Marian Hossa 1.50 4.00
54 Martin Havlat 1.50 4.00
55 Jeremy Roenick 2.00 5.00
56 John LeClair 2.00 5.00
57 Mark Recchi 2.50 6.00
58 Simon Gagne 2.00 5.00
59 Nikolai Khabibulin 2.00 5.00
60 Sean Burke 1.25 3.00
61 Johan Hedberg 2.00 5.00
62 Mario Lemieux 6.00 15.00
63 Evgeni Nabokov 1.50 4.00
64 Owen Nolan 2.00 5.00
65 Teemu Selanne 4.00 10.00
66 Al MacInnis 2.00 5.00
67 Chris Pronger 1.50 4.00
68 Doug Weight 2.00 5.00
69 Keith Tkachuk 2.00 5.00
70 Vincent Lecavalier 1.50 4.00
71 Ed Belfour 2.00 5.00
72 Mats Sundin 2.00 5.00
73 Daniel Sedin 2.00 5.00
74 Henrik Sedin 2.00 5.00
75 Markus Naslund 1.50 4.00
76 Todd Bertuzzi 2.00 5.00
77 Jaromir Jagr 5.00 12.00
78 Olaf Kolzig 2.00 5.00
79 Peter Bondra 2.00 5.00
80 Tony Amonte 1.50 4.00
81 P-M Bouchard RC 6.00 15.00
82 Rick Nash RC 25.00 50.00
83 Dennis Seidenberg RC 6.00 15.00
84 Jay Bouwmeester RC 10.00 25.00
85 Stanislav Chistov RC 4.00 10.00
86 Tom Koivisto RC 4.00 10.00
87 Ivan Majesky RC 4.00 10.00
88 Chuck Kobasew RC 5.00 12.00
89 Ales Hemsky RC 15.00 40.00
90 Radovan Somik RC 4.00 10.00
91 Dmitri Bykov RC 4.00 10.00
92 Ryan Miller RC 25.00 50.00
93 Ron Hainsey RC 4.00 10.00
94 Anton Volchenkov RC 4.00 10.00
95 Dick Tarnstrom RC 4.00 10.00
96 Scottie Upshall RC 5.00 12.00
97 Jordan Leopold RC 6.00 15.00
98 Carlo Colaiacovo RC 6.00 15.00
99 Levente Szuper RC 6.00 15.00
100 Lynn Loyns RC 4.00 10.00
101 Adam Oates 2.00 5.00
102 Paul Kariya 2.50 6.00
103 Petr Sykora 1.50 4.00
104 Dany Heatley 2.00 5.00
105 Ilya Kovalchuk 2.50 6.00
106 Jeff O'Neill 1.25 3.00
107 Joe Thornton 2.50 6.00
108 Sergei Samsonov 1.50 4.00
109 Jarome Iginla 2.00 5.00
110 Ron Francis 2.50 6.00
111 Jocelyn Thibault 1.50 4.00
112 Alex Tanguay 1.50 4.00
113 Joe Sakic 3.00 8.00
114 Milan Hejduk 1.50 4.00
115 Patrick Roy 5.00 12.00
116 Peter Forsberg 2.50 6.00
117 Rob Blake 2.00 5.00
118 Rostislav Klesla 1.25 3.00
119 Brett Hull 2.50 6.00
120 Marty Turco 2.00 5.00
121 Mike Modano 3.00 8.00
122 Bill Guerin 2.00 5.00
123 Brendan Shanahan 2.50 6.00
124 Chris Chelios 2.00 5.00
125 Curtis Joseph 2.00 5.00
126 Luc Robitaille 2.00 5.00
127 Nicklas Lidstrom 2.00 5.00
128 Pavel Datsyuk 2.50 6.00
129 Sergei Fedorov 3.00 8.00
130 Steve Yzerman 4.00 10.00
131 Mike Comrie 2.00 5.00
132 Erik Cole 1.50 4.00
133 Kristian Huselius 1.25 3.00
134 Roberto Luongo 3.00 8.00
135 Felix Potvin 3.00 8.00
136 Jason Allison 1.50 4.00
137 Zigmund Palffy 2.00 5.00
138 Marian Gaborik 3.00 8.00
139 Jose Theodore 2.00 5.00
140 Saku Koivu 2.00 5.00
141 Martin Brodeur 4.00 10.00
142 Patrik Elias 2.00 5.00
143 Scott Gomez 1.50 4.00
144 Alexei Yashin 1.50 4.00
145 Chris Osgood 2.00 5.00
146 Rick DiPietro 1.50 4.00
147 Brian Leetch 2.00 5.00
148 Eric Lindros 3.00 8.00
149 Mark Messier 3.00 8.00
150 Mike Richter 2.00 5.00
151 Pavel Bure 2.50 6.00
152 Daniel Alfredsson 2.00 5.00
153 Marian Hossa 1.50 4.00
154 Martin Havlat 1.50 4.00
155 Jeremy Roenick 2.00 5.00
156 John LeClair 2.00 5.00
157 Mark Recchi 2.50 6.00
158 Simon Gagne 2.00 5.00
159 Nikolai Khabibulin 2.00 5.00
160 Sean Burke 1.25 3.00
161 Johan Hedberg 2.00 5.00
162 Mario Lemieux 6.00 15.00
163 Evgeni Nabokov 1.50 4.00
164 Owen Nolan 2.00 5.00
165 Teemu Selanne 4.00 10.00
166 Al MacInnis 2.00 5.00
167 Chris Pronger 1.50 4.00
168 Doug Weight 2.00 5.00
169 Keith Tkachuk 2.00 5.00
170 Vincent Lecavalier 1.50 4.00
171 Ed Belfour 2.00 5.00
172 Mats Sundin 2.00 5.00
173 Daniel Sedin 2.00 5.00
174 Henrik Sedin 2.00 5.00
175 Markus Naslund 1.50 4.00
176 Todd Bertuzzi 2.00 5.00
177 Jaromir Jagr 5.00 12.00
178 Olaf Kolzig 2.00 5.00
179 Peter Bondra 2.00 5.00
180 Tony Amonte 1.50 4.00
181 Shaone Morrisonn RC 4.00 10.00
182 Kari Haakana RC 4.00 10.00
183 Ray Emery RC 10.00 25.00
184 Mike Cammalleri RC 12.00 30.00
185 Ari Ahonen RC 4.00 10.00
186 Martin Gerber RC 6.00 15.00
187 Adam Hall RC 4.00 10.00
188 Lasse Pirjeta RC 4.00 10.00
189 Stephane Veilleux RC 4.00 10.00
190 Jeff Taffe RC 4.00 10.00
191 Mikael Tellqvist RC 4.00 10.00
192 Alexander Frolov RC 8.00 20.00
193 Steve Eminger RC 4.00 10.00
194 Shawn Thornton RC 5.00 12.00
195 Alexander Svitov RC 4.00 10.00
196 Alexei Smirnov RC 5.00 12.00
197 Curtis Sanford RC 6.00 15.00
198 Henrik Zetterberg RC 50.00 100.00
199 Eric Godard RC 4.00 10.00
200 Jason Spezza RC 40.00 80.00

2002-03 ITG Used Calder Jerseys

STATED PRINT RUN 50 SETS
C1 Jason Spezza 20.00 50.00
C2 Rick Nash 20.00 50.00
C3 Jay Bouwmeester 10.00 20.00
C4 Stephen Weiss 8.00 20.00
C5 Chuck Kobasew 6.00 15.00
C6 Ales Hemsky 8.00 20.00
C7 Alexander Svitov 6.00 15.00
C8 Ron Hainsey 6.00 15.00
C9 Jordan Leopold 6.00 15.00
C10 Stanislav Chistov 6.00 15.00
C11 Alexei Smirnov 6.00 15.00
C12 Ryan Miller 12.00 30.00
C13 Dennis Seidenberg 6.00 15.00
C14 Adam Hall 6.00 15.00
C15 Niko Kapanen 6.00 15.00
C16 Alexander Frolov 8.00 20.00
C17 Anton Volchenkov 6.00 15.00
C18 Radovan Somik 6.00 15.00
C19 Ivan Huml 6.00 15.00
C20 Mike Cammalleri 8.00 20.00

2002-03 ITG Used Franchise Players Jerseys

Limited to 65 copies each, this 30-card set carried swatches of game-worn jerseys.

FR1 Paul Kariya 8.00 20.00
FR2 Ilya Kovalchuk 10.00 25.00
FR3 Joe Thornton 12.50 30.00
FR4 Miroslav Satan 8.00 20.00
FR5 Jarome Iginla 10.00 25.00
FR6 Jeff O'Neill 8.00 20.00
FR7 Eric Daze 8.00 20.00
F8 Patrick Roy 18.00 40.00
FR9 Rostislav Klesla 8.00 20.00
FR10 Mike Modano 8.00 20.00
FR11 Steve Yzerman 18.00 40.00
FR12 Mike Comrie 5.00 15.00
FR13 Roberto Luongo 10.00 25.00
FR14 Zigmund Palffy 5.00 15.00
FR15 Marian Gaborik 10.00 25.00
FR16 Jose Theodore 10.00 25.00
FR17 Scott Hartnell 5.00 15.00
FR18 Martin Brodeur 18.00 40.00
FR19 Alexei Yashin 5.00 15.00
FR20 Pavel Bure 8.00 20.00
FR21 Marian Hossa 8.00 20.00
FR22 Simon Gagne 10.00 25.00
FR23 Daniel Briere 5.00 15.00
FR24 Mario Lemieux 20.00 50.00
FR25 Chris Pronger 5.00 15.00
FR26 Owen Nolan 5.00 15.00
FR27 Nikolai Khabibulin 5.00 15.00
FR28 Mats Sundin 8.00 20.00
FR29 Markus Naslund 5.00 15.00
FR30 Jaromir Jagr 10.00 25.00

2002-03 ITG Used Goalie Pad and Jersey

This 20-card set featured jersey and goalie pad swatches. Cards were limited to 50 copies each.

GP1 Jose Theodore 15.00 40.00
GP2 Patrick Roy 40.00 100.00
GP3 Martin Brodeur 30.00 80.00
GP4 Jocelyn Thibault 10.00 25.00
GP5 Mike Dunham 10.00 25.00
GP6 Ed Belfour 15.00 40.00
GP7 J-S Aubin 10.00 25.00
GP8 Dan Cloutier 10.00 25.00
GP9 Roman Turek 10.00 25.00
GP10 Chris Osgood 12.00 30.00
GP11 Marty Turco 10.00 25.00
GP12 Roman Cechmanek 10.00 25.00
GP13 Sean Burke 10.00 25.00
GP14 Tomas Vokoun 10.00 25.00
GP15 Gerry Cheevers 12.00 30.00
GP16 Bernie Parent 10.00 25.00
GP17 Brian Boucher 10.00 25.00
GP18 Jeff Hackett 10.00 25.00
GP19 Ron Hextall 12.00 30.00
GP20 Terry Sawchuk 50.00 125.00

2002-03 ITG Used International Experience Jerseys

This 28-card set featured swatches of jersey used in world championship competition. Cards were limited to 60 copies each.

IE1 Mario Lemieux 20.00 50.00
IE2 Jaromir Jagr 15.00 40.00
IE3 Mats Sundin 12.50 30.00
IE4 Steve Yzerman 25.00 60.00
IE5 Nicklas Lidstrom 12.50 30.00
IE6 Mike Modano 15.00 40.00
IE7 Peter Forsberg 15.00 40.00
IE8 Zigmund Palffy 10.00 25.00
IE9 Olaf Kolzig 12.50 30.00
IE10 Teemu Selanne 12.50 30.00
IE11 Bill Guerin 10.00 25.00
IE12 Alexander Mogilny 10.00 25.00
IE13 Alexei Yashin 10.00 25.00
IE14 Saku Koivu 10.00 25.00
IE15 Bobby Holik 10.00 25.00
IE16 Tony Amonte 10.00 25.00
IE17 Joe Sakic 15.00 40.00
IE18 Chris Chelios 10.00 25.00
IE19 Curtis Joseph 10.00 25.00
IE20 Martin Brodeur 20.00 50.00
IE21 Radek Bonk 10.00 25.00
IE22 Brian Leetch 12.50 30.00
IE23 Darius Kasparaitis 10.00 25.00
IE24 Tommy Salo 10.00 25.00
IE25 Roman Turek 10.00 25.00
IE26 Johan Hedberg 10.00 25.00
IE27 Roman Cechmanek 10.00 25.00
IE28 Nikolai Khabibulin 10.00 25.00

2002-03 ITG Used Jerseys

ATED PRINT RUN 75 SETS
GUJ1 Mario Lemieux 15.00 40.00
GUJ2 Steve Yzerman 15.00 40.00
GUJ3 Peter Forsberg 12.50 30.00
GUJ4 Patrick Roy 15.00 40.00
GUJ5 Jarome Iginla 10.00 25.00
GUJ6 Pavel Bure 8.00 20.00
GUJ7 Jaromir Jagr 8.00 20.00
GUJ8 Eric Lindros 8.00 20.00
GUJ9 Paul Kariya 8.00 20.00
GUJ10 Ilya Kovalchuk 10.00 25.00
GUJ11 Mike Modano 10.00 25.00
GUJ12 Joe Thornton 10.00 25.00
GUJ13 Jose Theodore 8.00 20.00
GUJ14 Jeremy Roenick 10.00 25.00
GUJ15 Martin Brodeur 15.00 40.00
GUJ16 Mats Sundin 8.00 20.00
GUJ17 Mark Messier 8.00 20.00
GUJ18 Alexei Yashin 8.00 20.00
GUJ19 Marian Gaborik 12.50 30.00
GUJ20 Brendan Shanahan 8.00 20.00
GUJ21 Owen Nolan 8.00 20.00
GUJ22 Joe Sakic 12.50 30.00
GUJ23 Daniel Alfredsson 8.00 20.00
GUJ24 Teemu Selanne 8.00 20.00
GUJ25 Nicklas Lidstrom 8.00 20.00
GUJ26 John LeClair 8.00 20.00
GUJ27 Keith Tkachuk 8.00 20.00
GUJ28 Brian Leetch 8.00 20.00
GUJ29 Milan Hejduk 8.00 20.00
GUJ30 Dany Heatley 8.00 20.00
GUJ31 Sergei Samsonov 8.00 20.00
GUJ32 Todd Bertuzzi 8.00 20.00
GUJ33 Markus Naslund 8.00 20.00
GUJ34 Chris Chelios 8.00 20.00
GUJ35 Rob Blake 8.00 20.00
GUJ36 Sergei Fedorov 10.00 25.00
GUJ37 Al MacInnis 8.00 20.00
GUJ38 Luc Robitaille 8.00 20.00
GUJ39 Eric Daze 8.00 20.00
GUJ40 Ron Francis 8.00 20.00
GUJ41 Alexander Mogilny 8.00 20.00
GUJ42 Chris Pronger 8.00 20.00
GUJ43 Doug Weight 8.00 20.00
GUJ44 Zigmund Palffy 8.00 20.00
GUJ45 Peter Bondra 8.00 20.00
GUJ46 Mike Comrie 8.00 20.00
GUJ47 Mark Recchi 8.00 20.00
GUJ48 Marian Hossa 8.00 20.00
GUJ49 Saku Koivu 8.00 20.00
GUJ50 Pierre Turgeon 8.00 20.00

2002-03 ITG Used Emblems

This 40-card set partially paralleled the basic jersey set but with emblem pieces. Cards were limited to 9 copies each and are not priced due to scarcity. Gold one of one's were also created.

2002-03 ITG Used Jersey and Stick

This 50-card set combined swatches of game jerseys with game-used sticks. Cards were limited to 75 copies each.

*STK/JSY: .5X TO 1.25X BASIC JERSEY

2002-03 ITG Used Magnificent Inserts

This 10-card set featured game-used equipment from the career of Mario Lemieux. Cards MI1-MI5 had a print run of 40 copies each and cards MI6-MI10 were limited to just 10 copies each. Cards MI6-MI10 are not priced due to scarcity.

MI1 2000-01 Jersey 30.00 80.00
MI2 1985-86 Jersey 30.00 80.00
MI3 2002 All-Star Jersey 30.00 80.00
MI4 1987 Canada Cup Jersey 30.00 80.00
MI5 Dual Jersey 50.00 125.00
MI6 Number
MI7 Emblem
MI8 Triple Jersey
MI9 Quad Jersey
MI10 Complete Package

2002-03 ITG Used Teammates Jerseys

Limited to 70 copies each, this 20-card set featured swatches of game jerseys from players on the same club.

T1 M.Lemieux/A.Kovalev 25.00 60.00
T2 P.Forsberg/P.Roy 15.00 40.00
T3 J.Thornton/S.Samsonov 12.50 30.00
T4 P.Bure/E.Lindros 10.00 25.00
T5 S.Yzerman/C.Chelios 25.00 60.00
T6 S.Koivu/J.Theodore 12.50 30.00
T7 I.Kovalchuk/D.Heatley 15.00 40.00
T8 C.Pronger/K.Tkachuk 10.00 25.00
T9 N.Lidstrom/B.Shanahan 12.50 30.00
T10 R.Blake/J.Sakic 12.50 30.00
T11 B.Leetch/M.Messier 12.50 30.00
T12 M.Sundin/A.Mogilny 12.50 30.00
T13 M.Modano/M.Turco 12.50 30.00
T14 M.Brodeur/S.Niedermayer 20.00 50.00
T15 S.Gagne/J.LeClair 12.50 30.00
T16 O.Nolan/T.Selanne 12.50 30.00
T17 Z.Palffy/F.Potvin 12.50 30.00
T18 J.Jagr/O.Kolzig 12.50 30.00
T19 M.Naslund/T.Bertuzzi 10.00 25.00
T20 S.Fedorov/B.Hull 15.00 40.00

2002-03 ITG Used Triple Memorabilia

This 20-card set featured three different pieces of game-used equipment. Each card was limited to just 35 copies.

TM1 Joe Thornton 25.00 60.00
TM2 Mario Lemieux 60.00 150.00
TM3 Mats Sundin 15.00 40.00
TM4 Jarome Iginla 20.00 50.00
TM5 Nicklas Lidstrom 15.00 40.00
TM6 John LeClair 15.00 40.00
TM7 Chris Chelios 15.00 40.00
TM8 Joe Sakic 30.00 80.00
TM9 Eric Lindros 15.00 40.00
TM10 Al MacInnis 15.00 40.00
TM11 Sergei Fedorov 25.00 60.00
TM12 Sergei Samsonov 10.00 30.00
TM13 Simon Gagne 15.00 40.00
TM14 Doug Weight 10.00 30.00
TM15 Alexei Yashin 10.00 30.00
TM16 Scott Niedermayer 10.00 30.00
TM17 Steve Yzerman 50.00 125.00
TM18 Rob Blake 10.00 30.00
TM19 Brett Hull 20.00 60.00
TM20 Adam Deadmarsh 10.00 30.00

2002-03 ITG Used Vintage Memorabilia

Limited to just 38 sets, this 20-card set featured swatches of game-used equipment or jersey from great players of the past.

VM1 Newsy Lalonde 30.00 80.00
VM2 Jacques Plante 30.00 80.00
VM3 Roy Worters 30.00 80.00
VM4 Tiny Thompson 12.50 30.00
VM5 Ace Bailey 40.00 100.00
VM6 Jean Beliveau 25.00 60.00
VM7 Maurice Richard 40.00 100.00
VM8 Red Kelly 20.00 50.00
VM9 Harry Lumley 20.00 50.00
VM10 Eddie Shore 20.00 50.00
VM11 Alex Delvecchio 12.50 30.00
VM12 Bill Mosienko 12.50 30.00
VM13 Tim Horton 30.00 80.00
VM14 Doug Harvey 12.50 30.00
VM15 Johnny Bower 12.50 30.00
VM16 George Hainsworth 20.00 50.00
VM17 Bill Durnan 12.50 30.00
VM18 Terry Sawchuk 30.00 80.00
VM19 Frank Brimsek 12.50 30.00
VM20 King Clancy 50.00 125.00

2003-04 ITG Used Signature Series

This 200-card set consisted of 110 veteran cards with an announced print run limited to 300 copies each, 10 legends cards (111-120) announced to be limited to 100 sets each; 30 rookie autograph cards (121-150) serial-numbered out of 135 and 50 rookie cards (151-200) serial-numbered to 390 copies each. Please note that cards 151 and 152 both had autographed parallels serial-numbered to just 25 copies each, those cards can be found in the autograph set checklist. Also note that cards 112B (Hull) and 114B (Bower) were supposedly pulled and destroyed prior to distribution. However, copies have been confirmed to be in circulation.

COMMON ROOKIE/390 3.00 8.00
ROOKIE SEMISTARS/390 4.00 10.00
ROOKIE UNL.STARS/390 5.00 12.00
1 Rick Nash 1.50 4.00
2 Tomas Vokoun 1.25 3.00
3 Alexander Frolov 1.25 3.00
4 Eric Brewer 1.00 2.50
5 Pavel Datsyuk 2.00 5.00
6 Bill Guerin 1.50 4.00
7 Rob Blake 1.50 4.00
8 Rostislav Klesla 1.00 2.50
9 Ron Francis 2.00 5.00
10 Glen Murray 1.25 3.00
11 Chris Drury 1.25 3.00
12 Alexei Yashin 1.25 3.00
13 Teemu Selanne 3.00 8.00
14 Henrik Zetterberg 2.00 5.00
15 Olli Jokinen 1.50 4.00
16 Marian Gaborik 2.50 6.00
17 Patrik Elias 1.50 4.00
18 Alex Kovalev 1.25 3.00
19 Simon Gagne 1.50 4.00
20 Martin St. Louis 1.50 4.00
21 Chris Pronger 1.25 3.00
22 Jeremy Roenick 1.50 4.00
23 Manny Fernandez 1.25 3.00
24 Zigmund Palffy 1.50 4.00
25 Erik Cole 1.25 3.00
26 Sergei Samsonov 1.25 3.00
27 Niko Kapanen 1.00 2.50
28 Ales Hemsky 1.50 4.00
29 Eric Daze 1.25 3.00
30 Vincent Lecavalier 1.25 3.00
31 Shane Doan 1.25 3.00
32 Marian Hossa 1.25 3.00
33 Scott Stevens 1.50 4.00
34 Roberto Luongo 2.50 6.00
35 Joe Thornton 2.00 5.00
36 Marc Denis 1.25 3.00
37 Marty Turco 1.50 4.00
38 Daniel Alfredsson 1.50 4.00
39 Ryan Smyth 1.25 3.00
40 Miroslav Satan 1.25 3.00
41 Nicklas Lidstrom 1.50 4.00
42 Chuck Kobasew 1.00 2.50
43 Mark Recchi 2.00 5.00
44 Rick DiPietro 1.25 3.00
45 Nikolai Khabibulin 1.50 4.00
46 Keith Tkachuk 1.50 4.00
47 Jason Spezza 1.50 4.00
48 Felix Potvin 2.50 6.00
49 Patrick Lalime 1.25 3.00
50 Milan Hejduk 1.25 3.00
51 Sergei Fedorov 2.50 6.00
52 Ed Jovanovski 1.25 3.00
53 Jarome Iginla 1.50 4.00
54 Jocelyn Thibault 1.25 3.00
55 Brian Leetch 1.50 4.00
56 Michael Ryder 1.25 3.00
57 Jay Bouwmeester 1.50 4.00
58 Saku Koivu 1.50 4.00
59 Jose Theodore 1.50 4.00
60 Anson Carter 1.25 3.00
61 John LeClair 1.50 4.00
62 Sean Burke 1.00 2.50
63 Markus Naslund 1.50 4.00
64 Olaf Kolzig 1.50 4.00
65 Peter Bondra 1.25 3.00
66 Doug Weight 1.50 4.00
67 Sergei Gonchar 1.00 2.50
68 Dwayne Roloson 1.25 3.00
69 Roman Cechmanek 1.25 3.00
70 David Legwand 1.25 3.00
71 Mike Peca 1.25 3.00
72 Mike Dunham 1.25 3.00
73 Dany Heatley 1.50 4.00
74 Chris Osgood 1.50 4.00
75 Tommy Salo 1.25 3.00
76 David Aebischer 1.25 3.00
77 Jeff O'Neill 1.00 2.50
78 Tyler Arnason 1.00 2.50
79 Roman Turek 1.25 3.00
80 Ryan Miller 1.50 4.00
81 Pasi Nurminen 1.25 3.00
82 Kevin Weekes 1.25 3.00
83 Byron Dafoe 1.25 3.00
84 Ray Whitney 1.25 3.00
85 Al MacInnis 1.50 4.00
86 Adam Oates 1.50 4.00
87 Vincent Damphousse 1.25 3.00
88 Evgeni Nabokov 1.25 3.00
89 Daymond Langkow 1.00 2.50
90 Todd Bertuzzi 1.50 4.00
91 Dan Cloutier 1.25 3.00
92 Aleksey Morozov 1.00 2.50
93 Tony Amonte 1.25 3.00
94 Brett Hull 2.00 5.00
95 Martin Biron 1.25 3.00
96 Ilya Kovalchuk 1.50 4.00
97 Andrew Raycroft 1.25 3.00
98 Curtis Joseph 1.50 4.00
99 Peter Forsberg 2.00 5.00
100 Joe Sakic 2.50 6.00
101 Steve Yzerman 8.00 20.00
102 Brendan Shanahan 4.00 10.00
103 Owen Nolan 2.50 6.00

104 Mike Modano 5.00 12.00
105 Dominik Hasek 5.00 12.00
106 Martin Brodeur 6.00 15.00
107 Eric Lindros 5.00 12.00
108 Jaromir Jagr 8.00 20.00
109 Mats Sundin 3.00 8.00
110 Mario Lemieux 10.00 25.00
111 Jean Beliveau 6.00 15.00
112 Frank Mahovlich 5.00 12.00
112B Bobby Hull SP
113 Ted Lindsay 3.00 8.00
114 Red Kelly 2.50 6.00
114B Johnny Bower SP
115 Bobby Orr 10.00 25.00
116 Ray Bourque 5.00 12.00
117 Patrick Roy 10.00 20.00
118 Guy Lafleur 4.00 10.00
119 Ted Kennedy 3.00 8.00
120 Phil Esposito 5.00 12.00
121 Tuomo Ruutu AU RC 10.00 25.00
122 Chris Higgins AU RC 12.00 30.00
123 Antoine Vermette AU RC 12.00 30.00
124 David Hale AU RC 6.00 15.00
125 Pavel Vorobiev AU RC 8.00 20.00
126 Antti Miettinen AU RC 10.00 25.00
127 Patrice Bergeron AU RC 30.00 60.00
128 Nathan Horton AU RC 15.00 40.00
129 Tim Gleason AU RC 8.00 20.00
130 Matthew Lombardi AU RC 8.00 20.00
131 Paul Martin AU RC 8.00 20.00
132 Marek Zidlicky AU RC 6.00 15.00
133 Joni Pitkanen AU RC 10.00 25.00
134 Marc-Andre Fleury AU RC 25.00 60.00
135 Jordin Tootoo AU RC 15.00 40.00
136 Eric Staal AU RC 20.00 40.00
137 Fredrik Sjostrom AU RC 10.00 25.00
138 Dustin Brown AU RC 20.00 50.00
139 Jiri Hudler AU RC 15.00 40.00
140 Derek Roy AU RC 10.00 25.00
141 Ryan Malone AU RC 12.00 30.00
142 Chris Kunitz AU RC 12.00 30.00
143 Jozef Balej AU RC 6.00 15.00
144 Boyd Gordon AU RC 8.00 20.00
145 Alexander Semin AU RC 15.00 40.00
146 Dan Fritsche AU RC 6.00 15.00
147 Brent Burns AU RC 15.00 40.00
148 Milan Michalek AU RC 12.00 30.00
149 Matt Stajan AU RC 10.00 25.00
150 Nikolai Zherdev AU RC 12.00 30.00
151 Darryl Bootland RC 4.00 10.00
152 Kari Lehtonen RC 15.00 40.00
153 Noah Clarke RC 3.00 8.00
154 Sean Bergenheim RC 4.00 10.00
155 Niklas Kronwall RC 6.00 15.00
156 Matt Murley RC 4.00 10.00
157 Mark Popovic RC 4.00 10.00
158 John-Michael Liles RC 4.00 10.00
159 Brent Krahn RC 3.00 8.00
160 Sergei Zinovjev RC 3.00 8.00
161 Trevor Daley RC 5.00 12.00
162 Matt Ellison RC 3.00 8.00
163 Timofei Shishkanov RC 3.00 8.00
164 John Pohl RC 3.00 8.00
165 Adam Munro RC 3.00 8.00
166 Rastislav Stana RC 5.00 12.00
167 Peter Sejna RC 4.00 10.00
168 Jed Ortmeyer RC 3.00 8.00
169 Aleksander Suglobov RC 3.00 8.00
170 Seamus Kotyk RC 3.00 8.00
171 Andy Chiodo RC 3.00 8.00
172 Ryan Kesler RC 10.00 25.00
173 Mikhail Yakubov RC 3.00 8.00
174 Nathan Robinson RC 3.00 8.00
175 Tom Preissing RC 4.00 10.00
176 Jeff Hamilton RC 3.00 8.00
177 Dan Hamhuis RC 4.00 10.00
178 Antero Niittymaki RC 8.00 20.00
179 Joffrey Lupul RC 8.00 20.00
180 Garth Murray RC 4.00 10.00
181 Denis Grebeshkov RC 3.00 8.00
182 Dan Ellis RC 4.00 10.00
183 Tomas Plekanec RC 10.00 25.00
184 Tuomas Pihlman RC 4.00 10.00
185 Nolan Schaefer RC 3.00 8.00
186 Joey MacDonald RC 4.00 10.00
187 Carl Corazzini RC 3.00 8.00
188 Mike Smith RC 10.00 25.00
189 Anton Babchuk RC 3.00 8.00
190 Kyle Wellwood RC 5.00 12.00
191 Marek Svatos RC 6.00 15.00
192 Ryan Barnes RC 3.00 8.00
193 Fedor Tyutin RC 3.00 8.00
194 Dominic Moore RC 3.00 8.00
195 Colton Orr RC 4.00 10.00
196 Andrew Peters RC 4.00 10.00
197 Wade Brookbank RC 4.00 10.00
198 Cody McCormick RC 4.00 10.00
199 Michal Barinka RC 3.00 8.00
200 Mikhail Kuleshov RC 3.00 8.00

2003-04 ITG Used Signature Series Gold

1-100 VETS/50: 1.5X TO 4X BASIC CARDS
101-120 RETIRED/50: .8X TO 2X BASIC CARDS
1-120 ANNOUNCED PRINT RUN 50
*151-200 ROOKIE/50: .5X TO 1.2X BASIC RC
151-200 PRINT RUN 50 SER.#'d CARDS

2003-04 ITG Used Signature Series Autographs

This 123-card set paralleled the veteran and legend subsets of the base set with certified player autographs. Announced print runs for basic veteran cards were 170 copies each unless otherwise noted. Cards listed as SP's were limited to 70 copies each. Please note that several players had two different versions of their cards, one with their former team and one with their most recent team. Those different versions are noted below with "1" and "2" designations after the card number. Also note that cards 151A and 152A are the only cards in this set featuring rookie players and carrying the same numbering as the base set; the "A" designation was added for checklisting purposes.

151A Darryl Bootland/25* 40.00 80.00
152A Kari Lehtonen/25* 100.00 250.00
AC1 Anson Carter NYR 6.00 15.00
AC2 Anson Carter LA/20*
AF Alexander Frolov 6.00 15.00
AH Ales Hemsky 6.00 15.00
AK1 Alex Kovalev NYR 6.00 15.00
AK2 Alexei Kovalev MON/20*
AM Alexei Morozov 6.00 15.00
AO Adam Oates 6.00 15.00
AR Andrew Raycroft 8.00 20.00
AY Alexei Yashin 6.00 15.00
BD Byron Dafoe 6.00 15.00
BG Bill Guerin 6.00 15.00
BJ Barret Jackman 6.00 15.00
BL Brian Leetch/100* 12.50 30.00
CD Chris Drury 6.00 15.00
CJ Curtis Joseph 8.00 20.00
CK Chuck Kobasew 6.00 15.00
CO Chris Osgood 6.00 15.00
CP Chris Pronger 6.00 15.00
DA Daniel Alfredsson 6.00 15.00
DC Dan Cloutier 6.00 15.00
DL David Legwand 6.00 15.00
DR Dwayne Roloson 6.00 15.00
DW Doug Weight 6.00 15.00
EB Eric Brewer 6.00 15.00
EC Erik Cole 6.00 15.00
ED Eric Daze 6.00 15.00
EJ Ed Jovanovski 6.00 15.00
EN Evgeni Nabokov 6.00 15.00
FP Felix Potvin 8.00 20.00
GM Glen Murray 6.00 15.00
HZ Henrik Zetterberg 10.00 25.00
IK Ilya Kovalchuk 10.00 25.00
JH Jeff Hackett 6.00 15.00
JI Jarome Iginla 10.00 25.00
JL John LeClair 8.00 20.00
JO Jeff O'Neill 6.00 15.00
JR Jeremy Roenick 8.00 20.00
JS Jason Spezza 10.00 25.00
JT Joe Thornton 12.50 30.00
KT Keith Tkachuk 8.00 20.00
KW Kevin Weekes 6.00 15.00
MD Marc Denis 6.00 15.00
MF Manny Fernandez 6.00 15.00
MG Marian Gaborik 15.00 40.00
MH Marian Hossa 8.00 20.00
MN Markus Naslund 8.00 20.00
MP Mike Peca 6.00 15.00
MR Mark Recchi 6.00 15.00
MS Martin St. Louis 6.00 15.00
MT Marty Turco 6.00 15.00
NK Niko Kapanen 6.00 15.00
NL Nicklas Lidstrom 10.00 25.00
OJ Olli Jokinen 6.00 15.00
OK Olaf Kolzig 6.00 15.00
PB1 Peter Bondra WAS 6.00 15.00
PB2 Peter Bondra OTT/20*
PD Pavel Datsyuk 12.50 30.00
PE Patrik Elias 6.00 15.00
PF Peter Forsberg 20.00 50.00
PL Patrick Lalime 6.00 15.00
PN Pasi Nurminen 6.00 15.00
PS Petr Sykora 6.00 15.00
RB Rob Blake 6.00 15.00
RC Roman Cechmanek 6.00 15.00
RD Rick DiPietro 6.00 15.00
RF1 Ron Francis CAR 6.00 15.00
RF2 Ron Francis TOR/20*
RK1 Rostislav Klesla 6.00 15.00
RL Roberto Luongo 10.00 25.00
RM Ryan Miller 8.00 20.00
RN Rick Nash/195* 10.00 25.00
RS Ryan Smyth 8.00 20.00
RT Roman Turek 6.00 15.00
RW Ray Whitney 6.00 15.00
SB1 Sean Burke PHX 6.00 15.00
SB2 Sean Burke PHI/20*
SD Shane Doan 6.00 15.00
SF Sergei Fedorov 10.00 25.00
SG Simon Gagne 8.00 20.00
SK Saku Koivu 8.00 20.00
SS Sergei Samsonov 6.00 15.00
TA Tyler Arnason 6.00 15.00
TB Todd Bertuzzi 8.00 20.00
TS Teemu Selanne 8.00 20.00
TV Tomas Vokoun 6.00 15.00
VD Vincent Damphousse 6.00 15.00
VL Vincent Lecavalier 8.00 20.00
ZP Zigmund Palffy 6.00 15.00
AMA Al MacInnis 8.00 20.00
BHU Brett Hull 8.00 20.00
DAE David Aebischer 6.00 15.00
DHE Dany Heatley 10.00 25.00
DLA Daymond Langkow 6.00 15.00
JBO Jay Bouwmeester 6.00 15.00
JHE Johan Hedberg 6.00 15.00
JSA Joe Sakic 20.00 50.00
JTH Jocelyn Thibault 6.00 15.00
MBI Martin Biron 6.00 15.00
MDU Mike Dunham 6.00 15.00
MHE Milan Hejduk 8.00 20.00
MRY Michael Ryder 10.00 25.00
MSA Miroslav Satan 6.00 15.00
NKH Nikolai Khabibulin 8.00 20.00
SGO1 Sergei Gonchar WAS 6.00 15.00
SGO2 Sergei Gonchar BOS/20*
SST Scott Stevens 6.00 15.00
TAM Tony Amonte 6.00 15.00
TSA1 Tommy Salo EDM 6.00 15.00
TSA2 Tommy Salo COL/20* 25.00 50.00
JTHE Jose Theodore 10.00 25.00
BS Brendan Shanahan/70* 60.00 150.00
DH Dominik Hasek/70* 25.00 60.00
EL Eric Lindros/70* 20.00 40.00
JJ Jaromir Jagr/70* 40.00 80.00
MB Martin Brodeur/70* 60.00 150.00
ML Mario Lemieux/70* 60.00 150.00
MM Mike Modano/70* 20.00 40.00
ON Owen Nolan/70* 10.00 25.00
SY Steve Yzerman/70* 60.00 125.00
MSU Mats Sundin/70* 25.00 60.00
BO Bobby Orr/50* 150.00 250.00
FM Frank Mahovlich/50* 20.00 50.00
GL Guy Lafleur/50* 20.00 50.00
JB Jean Beliveau/50* 20.00 50.00
PE Phil Esposito/50* 20.00 50.00
PR Patrick Roy/50* 30.00 80.00
RK Red Kelly/50* 15.00 40.00
TK Ted Kennedy/50* 20.00 50.00
TL Ted Lindsay/50* 15.00 40.00
RBO Ray Bourque/50* 20.00 50.00

2003-04 ITG Used Signature Series Autographs Gold

OLD VETS: .6X TO 1.5X BASIC AU
GOLD VET PRINT RUN 70
*GOLD ROOKIES: .8X TO 2X
GOLD ROOKIE PRINT RUN 25
134 Marc-Andre Fleury 80.00 150.00
136 Eric Staal 40.00 100.00

2003-04 ITG Used Signature Series Franchise Jerseys

INT RUN 70 SETS
1 Sergei Fedorov 10.00 25.00
2 Ilya Kovalchuk 10.00 25.00
3 Joe Thornton 10.00 25.00
4 Miroslav Satan 6.00 15.00
5 Jarome Iginla 10.00 25.00
6 Jeff O'Neill 6.00 15.00
7 Tyler Arnason 6.00 15.00
8 Peter Forsberg 10.00 25.00
9 Rick Nash 8.00 20.00
10 Mike Modano 10.00 25.00
11 Steve Yzerman 20.00 50.00
12 Ryan Smyth 6.00 15.00
13 Roberto Luongo 10.00 25.00
14 Zigmund Palffy 8.00 20.00
15 Marian Gaborik 12.50 30.00
16 Jose Theodore 10.00 25.00
17 Tomas Vokoun 8.00 20.00
18 Martin Brodeur 20.00 50.00
19 Eric Lindros 8.00 20.00
20 Rick DiPietro 8.00 20.00
21 Marian Hossa 8.00 20.00
22 Jeremy Roenick 10.00 25.00
23 Shane Doan 6.00 15.00
24 Mario Lemieux 20.00 50.00
25 Evgeni Nabokov 8.00 20.00
26 Chris Pronger 8.00 20.00
27 Vincent Lecavalier 8.00 20.00
28 Mats Sundin 8.00 20.00
29 Markus Naslund 8.00 20.00
30 Olaf Kolzig 8.00 20.00

2003-04 ITG Used Signature Series Game-Day Jerseys

INT RUN 50 SETS
1 Mats Sundin 10.00 25.00
2 Mike Modano 10.00 25.00
3 Steve Yzerman 25.00 60.00
4 Mario Lemieux 15.00 40.00
5 Ray Bourque 15.00 40.00
6 Patrick Roy 20.00 50.00
7 Martin Brodeur 15.00 40.00
8 Peter Forsberg 12.00 30.00
9 John LeClair 10.00 25.00
10 Brendan Shanahan 10.00 25.00
11 Joe Sakic 15.00 40.00

2003-04 ITG Used Signature Series Goalie Gear

1 Martin Brodeur/60* 25.00 60.00
2 Roberto Luongo/50* 12.50 30.00
3 Sean Burke/50* 8.00 20.00
4 Rick DiPietro/50* 8.00 20.00
5 Nikolai Khabibulin/60* 10.00 25.00
6 Marty Turco/60* 10.00 25.00
7 Jose Theodore/50* 10.00 25.00
8 Patrick Roy/15*
9 Jocelyn Thibault/60* 10.00 25.00
10 Tomas Vokoun/60* 8.00 20.00
11 Olaf Kolzig/60* 8.00 20.00
12 Felix Potvin/60* 15.00 40.00
13 Roman Cechmanek/60* 8.00 20.00
14 Roman Turek/60* 8.00 20.00
15 Evgeni Nabokov/60* 8.00 20.00
16 Tommy Salo/60* 8.00 20.00
17 Mike Dunham/60* 8.00 20.00
18 Jeff Hackett/60* 8.00 20.00
19 Chris Osgood/60* 8.00 20.00
20 Byron Dafoe/60* 8.00 20.00
21 David Aebischer/50* 10.00 25.00
22 Dominik Hasek/15*
23 Gerry Cheevers/15*
24 Tony Esposito/15*
25 Bernie Parent/60* 20.00 50.00
26 Patrick Lalime/60* 8.00 20.00
27 Dan Cloutier/60* 8.00 20.00
28 Jean-Sebastien Giguere/60* 8.00 20.00
29 Gump Worsley/15*
30 Glenn Hall/15*
31 Vladislav Tretiak/60* 30.00 80.00
32 Frank Brimsek/20* 20.00 40.00
33 Andrew Raycroft/60* 10.00 25.00
34 Ed Belfour/60* 10.00 25.00
35 Harry Lumley/30* 20.00 40.00
36 Roger Crozier/40* 12.50 30.00

2003-04 ITG Used Signature Series International Experience Jerseys

PRINT RUN 70 SETS
1 Martin Brodeur 15.00 40.00
2 Mario Lemieux 20.00 50.00
3 Steve Yzerman 15.00 40.00
4 Joe Sakic 12.50 30.00
5 Curtis Joseph 10.00 25.00
6 Jarome Iginla 10.00 25.00
7 Jason Spezza 10.00 25.00
8 Barret Jackman 6.00 15.00
9 Joe Nieuwendyk 6.00 15.00
10 Rob Blake 6.00 15.00
11 Paul Kariya 8.00 20.00
12 Ed Jovanovski 6.00 15.00
13 Chris Pronger 6.00 15.00
14 Dany Heatley 10.00 25.00
15 Jaromir Jagr 8.00 20.00
16 Teemu Selanne 8.00 20.00
17 Saku Koivu 8.00 20.00
18 Vladislav Tretiak 20.00 50.00
19 Alexander Mogilny 6.00 15.00
20 Alexei Yashin 6.00 15.00
21 Nikolai Khabibulin 8.00 20.00
22 Zigmund Palffy 6.00 15.00
23 Nicklas Lidstrom 8.00 20.00
24 Peter Forsberg 15.00 40.00
25 Mats Sundin 8.00 20.00
26 Mike Modano 8.00 20.00
27 Bill Guerin 6.00 15.00
28 Brian Leetch 8.00 20.00
29 Chris Chelios 8.00 20.00
30 Tony Amonte 6.00 15.00

2003-04 ITG Used Signature Series Jerseys

PRINT RUN 80 SETS
*JSY/STK/80: .5X TO 1.2X JSY
1 Alex Kovalev 4.00 10.00
2 Alexei Yashin 4.00 10.00
3 Bill Guerin 4.00 10.00
4 Bobby Orr 40.00 100.00
5 Brett Hull 10.00 25.00
6 Chris Pronger 4.00 10.00
7 Dominik Hasek 10.00 25.00
8 Eric Lindros 8.00 20.00
9 Felix Potvin 10.00 25.00
10 Henrik Zetterberg 8.00 20.00
11 Ilya Kovalchuk 10.00 25.00
12 Jarome Iginla 10.00 25.00
13 Jaromir Jagr 10.00 25.00
14 Jason Spezza 6.00 15.00
15 Jeremy Roenick 10.00 25.00
16 Joe Sakic 12.00 30.00
17 Joe Thornton 10.00 25.00
18 John LeClair 4.00 10.00
19 Jose Theodore 10.00 25.00
20 Keith Tkachuk 8.00 20.00
21 Marc-Andre Fleury 12.00 30.00
22 Marian Gaborik 10.00 25.00
23 Marian Hossa 8.00 20.00
24 Mario Lemieux 25.00 60.00
25 Martin Brodeur 15.00 40.00
26 Marty Turco 6.00 15.00
27 Mats Sundin 8.00 20.00
28 Mike Modano 10.00 25.00
29 Milan Hejduk 10.00 25.00
30 Nicklas Lidstrom 8.00 20.00
31 Nikolai Khabibulin 8.00 20.00
32 Olaf Kolzig 6.00 15.00
33 Patrick Roy 20.00 50.00
34 Pavel Datsyuk 10.00 25.00
35 Peter Forsberg 10.00 25.00
36 Ray Bourque 10.00 25.00
37 Rick Dipietro 6.00 15.00
38 Rick Nash 10.00 25.00
39 Rob Blake 4.00 10.00
40 Roberto Luongo 10.00 25.00
41 Roman Cechmanek 4.00 10.00
42 Ron Francis 4.00 10.00
43 Steve Yzerman 15.00 40.00
44 Teemu Selanne 8.00 20.00
45 Vincent Lecavalier 8.00 20.00
46 Zigmund Palffy 6.00 15.00
47 Markus Naslund 8.00 20.00
48 Todd Bertuzzi 8.00 20.00
49 Jean-Sebastien Giguere 6.00 15.00
50 Sergei Fedorov 10.00 25.00
51 Kari Lehtonen 12.00 30.00

2003-04 ITG Used Signature Series Norris Trophy

PRINT RUN 50 SETS
1 Nicklas Lidstrom 12.50 30.00
2 Chris Pronger 8.00 20.00
3 Al MacInnis 8.00 20.00
4 Rob Blake 8.00 20.00
5 Chris Chelios 8.00 20.00
6 Chris Chelios 8.00 20.00
7 Bobby Orr 40.00 80.00
8 Doug Harvey 12.50 30.00
9 Ray Bourque 15.00 40.00
10 Brian Leetch 8.00 20.00
11 Larry Robinson 8.00 20.00
12 Denis Potvin 8.00 20.00
13 Jacques Laperriere 8.00 20.00

2003-04 ITG Used Signature Series Oh Canada

PRINT RUN 50 SETS
1 Curtis Joseph 10.00 25.00
2 Martin Brodeur 20.00 50.00
3 Ed Jovanovski 8.00 20.00
4 Scott Niedermayer 8.00 20.00
5 Al MacInnis 8.00 20.00
6 Rob Blake 8.00 20.00
7 Eric Brewer 8.00 20.00
8 Owen Nolan 8.00 20.00
9 Eric Lindros 10.00 25.00
10 Paul Kariya 10.00 25.00
11 Steve Yzerman 20.00 50.00
12 Mike Peca 8.00 20.00
13 Brendan Shanahan 15.00 40.00
14 Ryan Smyth 8.00 20.00
15 Joe Nieuwendyk 8.00 20.00
16 Jarome Iginla 12.50 30.00

2003-04 ITG Used Signature Series Retrospectives

STATED PRINT RUN 50 SER.#'d SETS
1A Patrick Roy 15.00 40.00
1B Patrick Roy 15.00 40.00
1C Patrick Roy 15.00 40.00
1D Patrick Roy 15.00 40.00
1E Patrick Roy 15.00 40.00
1F Patrick Roy 15.00 40.00
2A Jaromir Jagr 10.00 25.00
2B Jaromir Jagr 10.00 25.00
2C Jaromir Jagr 10.00 25.00
2D Jaromir Jagr 10.00 25.00
2E Jaromir Jagr 10.00 25.00
2F Jaromir Jagr 10.00 25.00
3A Brett Hull 10.00 25.00
3B Brett Hull 10.00 25.00
3C Brett Hull 10.00 25.00
3D Brett Hull 10.00 25.00
3E Brett Hull 10.00 25.00
3F Brett Hull 10.00 25.00
4A Mario Lemieux 15.00 40.00
4B Mario Lemieux 15.00 40.00
4C Mario Lemieux 15.00 40.00
4D Mario Lemieux 15.00 40.00
4E Mario Lemieux 15.00 40.00
4F Mario Lemieux 15.00 40.00
5A Mats Sundin 8.00 20.00
5B Mats Sundin 8.00 20.00
5C Mats Sundin 8.00 20.00
5D Mats Sundin 8.00 20.00
5E Mats Sundin 8.00 20.00
5F Mats Sundin 8.00 20.00
6A Curtis Joseph 8.00 20.00
6B Curtis Joseph PAD 12.00 30.00
6C Curtis Joseph 8.00 20.00
6D Curtis Joseph 8.00 20.00
6E Curtis Joseph 8.00 20.00
6F Curtis Joseph 8.00 20.00
7A Paul Kariya 8.00 20.00
7B Paul Kariya 8.00 20.00
7C Paul Kariya 8.00 20.00
7D Paul Kariya 8.00 20.00
7E Paul Kariya 8.00 20.00
7F Paul Kariya 8.00 20.00
8A Pavel Bure 8.00 20.00
8B Pavel Bure 8.00 20.00
8C Pavel Bure 8.00 20.00
8D Pavel Bure 8.00 20.00
8E Pavel Bure 8.00 20.00
8F Pavel Bure 8.00 20.00
9A Ed Belfour 8.00 20.00
9B Ed Belfour 8.00 20.00
9C Ed Belfour 8.00 20.00
9D Ed Belfour 8.00 20.00
9E Ed Belfour 8.00 20.00
9F Ed Belfour 8.00 20.00
10A Mark Messier 10.00 25.00
10B Mark Messier 10.00 25.00
10C Mark Messier 10.00 25.00
10D Mark Messier 10.00 25.00
10E Mark Messier 10.00 25.00
10F Mark Messier 10.00 25.00
11A Martin Brodeur 15.00 40.00
11B Martin Brodeur 15.00 40.00
11C Martin Brodeur 15.00 40.00
11D Martin Brodeur 15.00 40.00
11E Martin Brodeur 15.00 40.00
11F Martin Brodeur 15.00 40.00
12A Dominik Hasek 10.00 25.00
12B Dominik Hasek 10.00 25.00
12C Dominik Hasek STK 10.00 25.00
12D Dominik Hasek 10.00 25.00
12E Dominik Hasek 10.00 25.00
12F Dominik Hasek 10.00 25.00
13A Steve Yzerman 15.00 40.00
13B Steve Yzerman 15.00 40.00
13C Steve Yzerman 15.00 40.00
13D Steve Yzerman 15.00 40.00
13E Steve Yzerman 15.00 40.00
13F Steve Yzerman 15.00 40.00
14A Brian Leetch 8.00 20.00
14B Brian Leetch 8.00 20.00
14C Brian Leetch 8.00 20.00
14D Brian Leetch 8.00 20.00
14E Brian Leetch 8.00 20.00
14F Brian Leetch 8.00 20.00

2003-04 ITG Used Signature Series Teammates

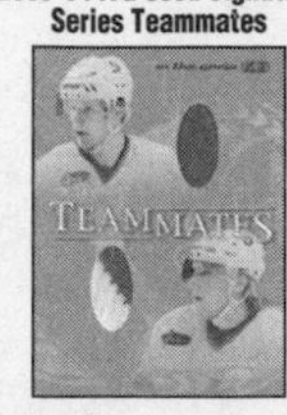

PRINT RUN 50 SETS
1 P.Kariya/T.Selanne 10.00 25.00
2 M.Recchi/J.LeClair 10.00 25.00
3 J.Spezza/M.Hossa 10.00 25.00
4 B.Hull/H. Zetterberg 15.00 40.00
5 T.Bertuzzi/M.Naslund 10.00 25.00
6 T.Amonte/J.Roenick 10.00 25.00
7 J.Sakic/P.Forsberg 12.00 30.00
8 D. Weight/K.Tkachuk 10.00 25.00
9 M.Lemieux/M.Fleury 25.00 60.00
10 E.Lindros/A.Kovalev 10.00 25.00
11 R.Luongo/J.Bouwmeester 10.00 25.00
12 M.Messier/B.Leetch 10.00 25.00
13 S.Yzerman/D.Hasek 15.00 40.00
14 J.Giguere/S.Fedorov 10.00 25.00
15 M.Sundin/E.Belfour 10.00 25.00
16 M.Brodeur/S.Stevens 15.00 40.00
17 J.Thornton/G.Murray 10.00 25.00
18 R.Bourque/C. Neely 15.00 40.00
19 M.Modano/M.Turco 10.00 25.00
20 P.Roy/R.Blake 12.00 30.00

2003-04 ITG Used Signature Series Triple Memorabilia

1 Henrik Zetterberg/30 30.00 80.00
2 Mats Sundin/15 40.00 100.00
3 Ray Bourque/20 30.00 60.00
4 Bobby Orr/20 125.00 200.00
5 Eddie Shore/15 50.00 100.00
6 Stan Mikita/25 15.00 40.00
7 Pavel Datsyuk/35 30.00 80.00
8 Aurel Joliat/20 30.00 60.00
9 Marty Turco/50 12.50 30.00
10 Martin Brodeur/40 50.00 125.00
11 Jocelyn Thibault/50 12.50 30.00
12 Sean Burke/50 12.50 30.00
13 Gerry Cheevers/45 25.00 60.00
14 Jean-Sebastien Giguere/30 12.50 30.00
15 Milan Hejduk/40 12.50 30.00
16 Jarome Iginla/40 20.00 50.00
17 Olaf Kolzig/45 12.50 30.00
18 Eric Lindros/35 20.00 50.00
19 Evgeni Nabokov/35 12.50 30.00
20 Mario Lemieux/45 40.00 100.00
21 Cam Neely/40 20.00 50.00
22 Bernie Parent/45 30.00 80.00
23 Jacques Plante/35 50.00 125.00
24 Patrick Roy/20 25.00 60.00
25 Joe Sakic/35 25.00 60.00
26 Joe Thornton/35 15.00 40.00
27 Keith Tkachuk/35 20.00 50.00
28 Alexei Yashin/40 12.50 30.00
29 Andrew Raycroft/45 15.00 40.00
30 David Aebischer/50 12.50 30.00

2003-04 ITG Used Signature Series Vintage Memorabilia

1 Bobby Orr/25 75.00 150.00
2 Ray Bourque/25 30.00 80.00
3 Phil Esposito/25 15.00 40.00
4 Tony Esposito/25 15.00 40.00
5 Ted Lindsay/25 15.00 40.00
6 Bobby Hull/25 40.00 80.00
7 Jean Beliveau/25 25.00 60.00
8 Ted Kennedy/25 15.00 40.00
9 Ed Giacomin/25 25.00 60.00
10 Red Kelly/40 20.00 50.00
11 Borje Salming/45 20.00 50.00
12 Bernie Parent/45 15.00 40.00
13 Gerry Cheevers/45 15.00 40.00
14 Guy Lafleur/25 20.00 50.00
15 Henri Richard/25 15.00 40.00
16 Bill Gadsby/45 15.00 40.00
17 Gump Worsley/25 25.00 60.00
18 Stan Mikita/45 15.00 40.00
19 Mike Bossy/45 15.00 40.00
20 Marcel Dionne/45 15.00 40.00
21 Aurel Joliat/50 20.00 50.00
22 Tiny Thompson/50 15.00 40.00
23 George Hainsworth/45 25.00 60.00
24 Eddie Shore/45 20.00 50.00
25 Tim Horton/45 25.00 60.00
26 Bill Mosienko/45 15.00 40.00
27 Chuck Gardiner/45 20.00 50.00
28 Doug Harvey/45 15.00 40.00
29 Rocket Richard/25 40.00 80.00
30 Jacques Plante/45 25.00 60.00

2003-04 ITG Used Signature Series Vintage Memorabilia Autographs

*AUTO: .75X TO 2X BASIC INSERTS
PRINT RUN 25 SETS

2013-14 ITG Used Jerseys Silver

GUJ01 Pavel Bure 6.00 15.00
GUJ02 Corey Crawford 6.00 15.00
GUJ03 Marc-Andre Fleury 8.00 20.00
GUJ04 Mario Lemieux 15.00 40.00
GUJ05 Claude Giroux 5.00 12.00
GUJ06 Jimmy Howard 5.00 12.00
GUJ07 Jaromir Jagr 12.00 30.00
GUJ08 Nicklas Lidstrom 5.00 12.00
GUJ09 Trevor Linden 5.00 12.00
GUJ10 Eric Lindros 8.00 20.00
GUJ11 Henrik Lundqvist 6.00 15.00
GUJ12 Roberto Luongo 6.00 15.00
GUJ13 Patrick Marleau 5.00 12.00
GUJ14 Cam Neely 5.00 12.00
GUJ15 Dion Phaneuf 5.00 12.00
GUJ16 Carey Price 15.00 40.00
GUJ17 Tuukka Rask 5.00 12.00
GUJ18 Joe Sakic 8.00 20.00
GUJ19 Daniel Sedin 5.00 12.00
GUJ20 Henrik Sedin 5.00 12.00
GUJ21 Teemu Selanne 8.00 20.00
GUJ22 Patrick Roy 12.00 30.00
GUJ23 Mats Sundin 5.00 12.00
GUJ24 Joe Thornton 5.00 12.00

2013-14 ITG Used Captain C Silver

CC01 Steve Yzerman 12.00 30.00
CC02 Brian Leetch 6.00 15.00
CC03 Mario Lemieux 20.00 50.00
CC04 Pavel Bure 8.00 20.00
CC05 Raymond Bourque 10.00 25.00
CC06 Mark Messier 8.00 20.00
CC07 Wendel Clark 6.00 15.00
CC08 Mike Modano 5.00 12.00
CC09 Theoren Fleury 8.00 20.00
CC10 Trevor Linden 6.00 15.00
CC11 Joe Thornton 6.00 15.00
CC12 Nicklas Lidstrom 6.00 15.00
CC13 Jaromir Jagr 15.00 40.00
CC14 Martin St. Louis 6.00 15.00
CC15 Dale Hawerchuk 8.00 20.00
CC16 Eric Lindros 10.00 25.00
CC17 Mats Sundin 6.00 15.00
CC18 Chris Chelios 6.00 15.00
CC19 Joe Sakic 10.00 25.00
CC20 Dion Phaneuf 6.00 15.00

2013-14 ITG Used Captain C Quad Jerseys Silver

QCC01 Bcyk/O'Rlly/Thrntn/Brqe 12.00 30.00
QCC02 Mkta/Chls/Amnte/Svrd 10.00 25.00
QCC03 Ldstm/Dlvch/Hwe/Yzrm 25.00 50.00
QCC04 Sndin/Clrk/Glmr/Phnf 12.00 30.00
QCC05 Svrd/Chls/Blvu/Crbnu 15.00 40.00
QCC06 Clrke/Lndrs/Frsbrg/Grx 12.00 30.00
QCC07 Jagr/Espsto/Mssr/Ltch 20.00 50.00
QCC08 Lndn/Mssr/Lngo/Nslnd 10.00 25.00
QCC09 Nln/Dmphe/Mrlu/Thrntn 10.00 25.00

2013-14 ITG Used Classic Scraps Dual Memorabilia Silver

CS01 T.Domi/B.Probert 6.00 15.00
CS02 P.Roy/C.Osgood 8.00 20.00
CS03 D.McCarty/C.Lemieux 6.00 15.00
CS04 T.Williams/T.O'Reilly 5.00 12.00
CS05 C.Chelios/R.Hextall 6.00 15.00
CS06 K.Daneyko/M.Vukota 4.00 10.00
CS07 D.Langdon/G.Odjick 4.00 10.00
CS08 D.Hunter/T.O'Reilly 5.00 12.00
CS09 C.Simon/T.Domi 5.00 12.00
CS10 P.Roy/M.Vernon 8.00 20.00
CS11 M.McSorley/M.Messier 8.00 20.00
CS12 B.Probert/W.Clark 6.00 15.00
CS13 P.Laus/R.Ray 5.00 12.00
CS14 D.Maloney/T.Williams 5.00 12.00
CS15 C.Neely/W.Clark 6.00 15.00
CS16 F.Potvin/R.Hextall 8.00 20.00
CS17 D.McCarty/C.Simon 4.00 10.00
CS18 R.Ray/T.Domi 5.00 12.00
CS19 B.Probert/C.Coxe 5.00 12.00
CS20 W.Clark/M.McSorley 5.00 12.00

2013-14 ITG Used Cup Battles Quad Jerseys Silver

CB01 Hsk/Lrnv/Frncs/Irbe 10.00 25.00
CB02 Brqe/Skic/Hlk/Ndrmyr 10.00 25.00
CB03 Hll/Blfr/Hsk/Peca 10.00 25.00
CB04 Yzrmn/Ldstrm/Bndra/Ots 10.00 25.00
CB05 Fdrv/McCrty/Lndrs/LClr 15.00 40.00
CB06 Roy/Frsbrg/Vnbsbrk/Laus 10.00 25.00
CB07 Mssr/Rchtr/Lndn/Bre 8.00 20.00
CB08 Mllr/Roy/Rbtlle/McSrly 10.00 25.00
CB09 Lmux/Brrsso/Rnck/Chls 20.00 50.00
CB10 Rnfrd/Krri/Brqe/Nly 12.00 30.00
CB11 McDn/Mclns/Crbn/Rbns 8.00 20.00
CB12 Cffy/Andrsn/Hxtll/Prpp 8.00 20.00
CB13 Roy/Nslnd/Mlln/Vrnn 10.00 25.00
CB14 Mssr/Fhr/Ptvn/LFntne 8.00 20.00
CB15 Bssy/Smth/Bodr/Wllms 8.00 20.00
CB16 Trttr/Nystrm/Brbr/McLsh 8.00 20.00
CB17 Rbnsn/Lmre/Mdltn/Chv 6.00 15.00
CB18 Lflr/Shtt/Lch/Drnhfr 8.00 20.00
CB19 Clrke/Brbr/Espsto/Bcyk 8.00 20.00
CB20 Crnyr/Lmre/Hll/Espsto 6.00 15.00

2013-14 ITG Used Decades Triple Jerseys Silver

D01 Rnhrt/Ekbld/McDvd 15.00 40.00
D02 Thrntn/Grx/St.Louis 8.00 20.00
D03 Prce/Lndqvst/Flry 12.00 30.00
D04 Jgr/Frsbrg/Ndrmyr 15.00 40.00
D05 Lmux/Nuwndk/Skic 20.00 50.00
D06 Roy/Sndn/Blfr 10.00 25.00
D07 Mssr/Flry/Ldstrm 8.00 20.00
D08 Fdrv/Lndrs/Oates 15.00 40.00
D09 Lmux/Cffy/Hsk 10.00 25.00
D10 Rnck/Hull/Bure 8.00 20.00
D11 Yzrmn/Jgr/Skic 15.00 40.00
D12 Krri/Slnne/Brque 10.00 25.00
D13 Fhr/Brrsso/Roy 15.00 40.00
D14 Dnne/Trttr/Hwrchk 8.00 20.00
D15 Lmux/Yzrmn/Roy 20.00 50.00
D16 Mssr/Svrd/McDnld 8.00 20.00
D17 Brque/Ststny/Bssy 12.00 30.00
D18 Espsto/Prrlt/Ptvin 12.00 30.00
D19 Lflr/Howe/Slmng 12.00 30.00
D20 Clrke/Dnne/Park 10.00 25.00
D21 Rbnsn/Sttler/Hull 6.00 15.00
D22 Espsto/Chvrs/Prnt 10.00 25.00

2013-14 ITG Used Enshrined Classmates Jerseys Silver

EC01 J.Sakic/A.Oates 8.00 20.00
EC02 P.Bure/M.Sundin 10.00 25.00
EC03 E.Belfour/M.Howe 6.00 15.00
EC04 D.Gilmour/J.Nieuwndyk 6.00 15.00
EC05 B.Hull/S.Yzerman 10.00 25.00
EC06 L.Robitaille/B.Leetch 5.00 12.00
EC07 R.Francis/M.Messier 6.00 15.00
EC08 C.Neely/V.Kharlamov 6.00 15.00
EC09 R.Bourque/P.Coffey 8.00 20.00
EC10 G.Fuhr/P.LaFontaine 5.00 12.00
EC11 D.Hawerchuk/J.Kurri 6.00 15.00
EC12 M.Lemieux/B.Trottier 15.00 40.00
EC13 S.Shutt/B.Smith 5.00 12.00
EC14 M.Dionne/L.McDonald 6.00 15.00
EC15 M.Bossy/D.Potvin 6.00 15.00
EC16 T.Esposito/G.Lafleur 8.00 20.00
EC17 D.Sittler/V.Tretiak 10.00 25.00
EC18 B.Clarke/E.Giacomin 8.00 20.00
EC19 S.Savard/D.Keon 8.00 20.00
EC20 Espsto/Prnt/Mkta 10.00 25.00
EC22 G.Howe/J.Beliveau 15.00 40.00

2013-14 ITG Used Forever Rivals Quad Jerseys Silver

FR01 Mhvlch/Hrtn/Blvu/Rchrd 15.00 40.00
FR02 Fhr/Mssr/Smth/Bssy 10.00 25.00
FR03 Sttlr/Slmng/Trttr/Ptvn 10.00 25.00
FR04 McDnld/Mclnns/Mssr/Cffy 10.00 25.00
FR05 Roy/Chls/Moog/Brque 12.00 30.00
FR06 Ststny/Glet/Crbnnu/Nslnd 12.00 30.00
FR07 Shtt/Lflr/Mddltn/O'Rlly 10.00 25.00
FR08 Roy/Frsbrg/Osgd/McCrty 12.00 30.00
FR09 Bssy/Nystrm/Hdbrg/Espsto 12.00 30.00

2013-14 ITG Used Game Used A Star Quad Jerseys Silver

ASQJ01 Brqe/Roy/Mssr/Rcchi 12.00 30.0
ASQJ02 Hull/Fdrv/Bure/Slnne 20.00 50.0
ASQJ03 Lndrs/Ptvn/Osgd/Lmux 15.00 40.0
ASQJ04 Nln/Cffy/Hsk/Sndn 10.00 25.0
ASQJ05 Frsbrg/Mssr/LClr/Ndrmyr 12.00 30.0
ASQJ06 Rbtlle/Irbe/Bndra/Tkchk 12.00 30.0
ASQJ07 Bre/Sndn/McInns/Rcchi 12.00 30.0
ASQJ08 Jsph/Yzrmn/Lndrs/Mdno 15.00 40.0
ASQJ09 Brqe/Flry/Skc/Roy 15.00 40.0
ASQJ10 Roy/Dmphsse/Brke/Hsk 12.00 30.0
ASQJ11 Lmux/Fdrv/Chls/Thrntn 15.00 40.0
ASQJ12 Roy/Slnne/Jgr/Ldstrm 15.00 40.0

2013-14 ITG Used Game Used Quad Jerseys Silver

QJ01 Hull/Yzrmn/Skc/Jagr 15.00 40.0
QJ02 Lndqvst/Sndn/Ldstrm/Slmng 10.00 25.0
QJ03 Thrntn/St.Ls/Grx/Slnne 8.00 20.0
QJ04 Flry/Lngo/Prce/Crwfrd 20.00 50.0
QJ05 Lndrs/Ots/Hull/Lmux 20.00 50.0
QJ06 Fdrv/Nly/Glmr/Rnck 10.00 25.0
QJ07 Mssr/Brque/Skc/Yzrmn 12.00 30.0
QJ08 Hsk/Blfr/Jsph/Roy 15.00 40.0
QJ09 Prbrt/Ray/McSrly/Clrk 10.00 25.0
QJ10 Bre/Jagr/Frsbrg/Slnne 15.00 40.0
QJ11 Ndrmyr/Brqe/Ltch/Ldstrm 10.00 25.0
QJ12 McDvd/Rnhrt/Ekbld/Nylndr 20.00 50.0

2013-14 ITG Used Game Used Stick and Memorabilia Silver

GUSM01 Mario Lemieux 25.00 60.0
GUSM02 Raymond Bourque 12.00 30.0
GUSM03 Mark Messier 10.00 25.0
GUSM04 Steve Yzerman 12.00 30.0
GUSM05 Patrick Roy 20.00 50.0
GUSM06 Joe Sakic 12.00 30.0
GUSM07 Brett Hull 10.00 25.0
GUSM08 Mats Sundin 10.00 25.0
GUSM09 Sergei Fedorov
GUSM10 Joe Thornton 8.00 20.0
GUSM11 Jeremy Roenick 8.00 20.0
GUSM12 Ron Francis 10.00 25.0

2013-14 ITG Used Goalie Gear Silver

GG01 Ed Belfour 10.00 25.0
GG02 Sean Burke 10.00 25.0
GG03 Dan Cloutier 8.00 20.0
GG04 Grant Fuhr 10.00 25.0
GG05 Dominik Hasek 15.00 40.0
GG06 Ron Hextall 20.00 50.0
GG07 Curtis Joseph 10.00 25.0
GG08 Chris Osgood 8.00 20.0
GG09 Carey Price 30.00 80.0
GG10 Patrick Roy 25.00 60.0
GG11 Patrick Roy 25.00 60.0
GG12 Patrick Lalime 10.00 25.0
GG13 Marty Turco 10.00 25.0
GG14 Henrik Lundqvist 15.00 40.0
GG15 Kelly Hrudey 10.00 25.0
GG16 Semyon Varlamov 15.00 40.0

2013-14 ITG Used Guarding the Net Triple Jerseys Silver

GTN01 Dfoe/Moog/Rsk 10.00 25.0
GTN02 Brrsso/Fhr/Hsek 12.00 30.0
GTN03 Espsto/Blfr/Crwfrd 12.00 30.0
GTN04 Osgd/Jsph/Hwrd 10.00 25.0
GTN05 Osgd/Slo/Nbkv 10.00 25.0
GTN06 Vnbsbrk/Rchtr/Lndqvst 10.00 25.0
GTN07 Bpre/Emry/Hsk 10.00 25.0
GTN08 Hxtll/Vnbsbrk/Emry 12.00 30.0
GTN09 Brrsso/Hdbrg/Flry 15.00 40.0
GTN10 Brdr/Cltr/Lngo 10.00 25.0
GTN11 Ptvn/Jsph/Blfr 15.00 40.0
GTN12 Vchn/Roy/Price 30.00 80.0
GTN13 Brrsso/Vnbsbrk/Rchtr 10.00 25.0
GTN14 Lngo/Price/Flry 30.00 80.0

2013-14 ITG Used International Influence Quad Jerseys Silver

II01 Sndn/Ldstrm/Lndqvst/Slmng 12.00 30.0
II02 Bre/Lrnv/Fdrv/Nbkv 15.00 40.0
II03 Krri/Nmi/Slnne/Rask 15.00 40.0
II04 Hll/Chls/Rnck/Vnbsbrk 10.00 25.0
II05 Lmux/Hwrchk/Yzrmn/Lndrs 25.00 60.0
II06 Skc/Thrntn/Flry/St.Ls 12.00 30.0
II07 Roy/Flry/Prce/Lngo 25.00 60.0
II08 Jgr/Hsk/Hlik/Trek 20.00 50.0

2013-14 ITG Used Kick Save Silver

KS01 Patrick Roy 15.00 40.0
KS02 Dominik Hasek 12.00 30.0
KS03 Carey Price 30.00 80.0
KS04 Ed Belfour 10.00 25.0
KS05 Marty Turco 10.00 25.0
KS06 Curtis Joseph 10.00 25.0

2013-14 ITG Used On the Move Jerseys Silver

OTM01 Roberto Luongo 5.00 12.0
OTM02 Eric Lindros 8.00 20.0
OTM03 Dion Phaneuf 5.00 12.0
OTM04 Pavel Bure 6.00 15.0
OTM05 Lanny McDonald 5.00 12.0
OTM06 Felix Potvin 8.00 20.0
OTM07 Marcel Dionne 6.00 15.0
OTM08 Darryl Sittler 5.00 12.0
OTM09 Al MacInnis 5.00 12.0
OTM10 Patrick Roy 12.00 30.0
OTM11 Jaromir Jagr 12.00 30.0
OTM12 Raymond Bourque 8.00 20.0
OTM13 Curtis Joseph 5.00 12.0
OTM14 Teemu Selanne 6.00 15.0
OTM15 Jeremy Roenick 5.00 12.0
OTM16 Dominik Hasek 6.00 15.0
OTM17 Tony Amonte 4.00 10.0
OTM18 Brett Hull 5.00 12.0
OTM19 Mark Messier 6.00 15.0
OTM20 Keith Tkachuk 5.00 12.0
OTM21 Brian Leetch 5.00 12.0
OTM22 Paul Coffey 5.00 12.0
OTM23 Mats Sundin 5.00 12.0
OTM24 Peter Forsberg 5.00 12.0

2013-14 ITG Used Past Present and Future Jerseys Silver

PPF01 Glmr/Grx/Bnntt 6.00 15.0
PPF02 Rbtlle/Mrleau/Dl Clle 6.00 15.0
PPF03 Ststny/Slnne/Drstl 12.00 30.0
PPF04 Ptvn/Phnf/Ekbld 8.00 20.0
PPF05 Flry/Flry/Flry 8.00 20.0
PPF06 Lflr/Grx/Gthr 8.00 20.0
PPF07 Rnck/Crwfrd/Hrtmn 8.00 20.0
PPF08 Lndn/Sdin/Hrvt 12.00 30.0
PPF09 Lmx/Thrntn/McDvd 20.00 50.0
PPF10 Ndrmyr/Phnf/McKwn 6.00 15.0
PPF11 Sndn/Sdn/Nylndr 6.00 15.0
PPF12 Hwrchk/Pvlc/Ptn 8.00 20.0

F13 Skc/St.Louis/Rnhrt 8.00 20.00
F14 Yzrmn/Slnne/Rtche 12.00 30.00
F15 Nly/Thrntn/Rychl 6.00 15.00
F16 Bssy/Vrck/Vrtnn 8.00 20.00

2013-14 ITG Used Prospect Game Used Jerseys Silver

01 Sam Bennett 5.00 12.00
02 Eric Cornel 3.00 8.00
03 Michael Dal Colle 4.00 10.00
04 Sean Day 5.00 12.00
05 Anthony DeAngelo 3.00 8.00
06 Leon Draisaitl 6.00 15.00
07 Nikolaj Ehlers 6.00 15.00
08 Aaron Ekblad 6.00 15.00
09 Robby Fabbri 3.00 8.00
10 Haydn Fleury 3.00 8.00
11 Frederik Gauthier 3.00 8.00
12 Nikolay Goldobin 3.00 8.00
13 Ryan Hartman 3.00 8.00
14 Bo Horvat 6.00 15.00
15 Connor McDavid 12.00 30.00
16 Roland McKeown 3.00 8.00
17 Matt Mistele 3.00 8.00
18 William Nylander 8.00 20.00
19 Brendan Perlini 5.00 12.00
20 Nicolas Petan 3.00 8.00
21 Sam Reinhart 5.00 12.00
22 Nick Ritchie 3.00 8.00
23 Kerby Rychel 3.00 8.00
24 Jake Virtanen 4.00 10.00

2013-14 ITG Used Quad Franchise Jerseys Silver

01 Hntr/Grtnr/Bndra/Klzg 12.00 30.00
02 Ltch/Mssr/Rchtr/Lndqvst 10.00 25.00
03 Yzrmn/Ldstrm/Fdrv/Hwrd 12.00 30.00
04 Mssr/Fhr/Krri/Wght 12.00 30.00
05 Nslnd/Bre/Lndn/Lngo 10.00 25.00
06 Clrke/Lndros/Hxtll/Grx 15.00 40.00
07 Prce/Lflr/Blvu/Roy 30.00 80.00
08 Flry/McInns/Nwndk/McDnld 12.00 30.00
09 Clrk/Glmr/Sndn/Phnf 12.00 30.00
10 Bssy/Ptvn/Pca/Nbkv 10.00 25.00
11 Fdrko/Hull/McInns/Tkchk 10.00 25.00
12 Mdno/Blfr/Nwndyk/Hll 15.00 40.00
13 Lmux/Jgr/Frncs/Flry 12.00 30.00
14 Roy/Skc/Frsbrg/Vrlmv 12.00 30.00
15 Slnne/Fdrv/Ndrmyr/Hllr 15.00 40.00
16 Nly/Thrntn/Rsk/Brque 15.00 40.00
17 Blfr/Amnte/Rnck/Crwfrd 12.00 30.00
18 Nbkv/Nln/Thrntn/Nmi 10.00 25.00

2013-14 ITG Used Stat Leaders Triple Jerseys Silver

01 Grtzky/Howe/Hull 30.00 80.00
02 Grtzky/Frncs/Mssr 30.00 80.00
03 Grtzky/Mssr/Howe 30.00 80.00
04 Grtzky/Jagr/Dionne 30.00 80.00
05 Andrchk/Hull/Slnne 10.00 25.00
06 Grtzky/Mssr/Yzrmn 30.00 80.00
07 Brque/Dnne/McInns 10.00 25.00
08 Brdr/Roy/Blfr 15.00 40.00
09 Brdr/Roy/Jsph 15.00 40.00
10 Grtzky/Mssr/Krri 30.00 80.00
11 Grtzky/Mssr/Brqe 30.00 80.00
12 Grtzky/Mssr/Kurri 30.00 80.00
13 Chls/Ldstrm/Roy 10.00 25.00
14 Roy/Brdr/Fuhr 15.00 40.00
15 Brdr/Roy/Jsph 15.00 40.00

2013-14 ITG Used Teammates Jerseys Silver

01 H.Sedin/D.Sedin 6.00 15.00
02 W.Clark/D.Gilmour 8.00 20.00
03 J.Thornton/P.Marleau 6.00 15.00
04 J.Sakic/P.Forsberg 8.00 20.00
05 B.Hull/A.MacInnis 10.00 25.00
06 T.Selanne/J.Hiller 10.00 25.00
07 C.Giroux/J.Voracek 6.00 15.00
08 P.Coffey/M.Messier 8.00 20.00
09 B.Nicholls/L.Robitaille 6.00 15.00
10 J.Jagr/M.Lemieux 20.00 50.00
11 M.Recchi/E.Lindros 10.00 25.00
12 M.Messier/M.Richter 8.00 20.00
13 P.Bure/T.Linden 8.00 20.00
14 E.Belfour/J.Roenick 6.00 15.00
15 C.Chelios/L.Robinson 6.00 15.00
16 O.Nolan/M.Sundin 6.00 15.00
17 M.Richard/J.Beliveau 15.00 40.00
18 D.Sittler/L.McDonald 10.00 25.00
19 G.Howe/N.Ullman 15.00 40.00
20 P.Roy/G.Carbonneau 12.00 30.00
21 R.Bourque/C.Neely 12.00 30.00
22 B.Hull/S.Mikita 12.00 30.00
23 P.Esposito/W.Cashman 15.00 40.00
24 G.Lafleur/J.Lemaire 12.00 30.00
25 H.Watson/T.Horton 10.00 25.00
26 T.Selanne/K.Tkachuk 20.00 50.00
27 S.Yzerman/S.Fedorov 20.00 50.00
28 P.Lindbergh/M.Naslund 12.00 30.00

015-16 ITG Used Jerseys Silver

OLD/15: .5X TO 1.2X SILVER/35-45
JAD1 Alex Delvecchio/25 5.00 12.00
JBH1 Brett Hull/40 5.00 12.00
JBH2 Brett Hull/45 5.00 12.00
JCJ1 Curtis Joseph/45 5.00 12.00
JCMD Connor McDavid/45 15.00 40.00
JDS1 Darryl Sittler/25 6.00 15.00
JEL1 Eric Lindros/35 8.00 20.00
JFP1 Felix Potvin/45 8.00 20.00
JGL1 Guy Lafleur/25 8.00 20.00
JJLC John LeClair/40 5.00 12.00
JJR1 Jeremy Roenick/45 5.00 12.00
JJV1 John Vanbiesbrouck/45 5.00 12.00
JLR1 Larry Robinson/25 6.00 15.00
JMD1 Marcel Dionne/25 8.00 20.00
JML1 Mario Lemieux/35 8.00 20.00
JMM1 Mark Messier/45 8.00 20.00
JMM2 Mike Modano/45 8.00 20.00
JNM1 Nathan MacKinnon/45 10.00 25.00
JNY1 Nail Yakupov/45 4.00 10.00
JPE1 Phil Esposito/25 10.00 25.00
JPR1 Patrick Roy/40 12.00 30.00
JPR2 Patrick Roy/45 12.00 30.00
JRB1 Raymond Bourque/45 8.00 20.00
JRNH Ryan Nugent-Hopkins/45 5.00 12.00
JSY1 Steve Yzerman/45 8.00 20.00
JTH1 Taylor Hall/40 10.00 25.00
JTS1 Teemu Selanne/45 10.00 25.00
JVT1 Vladimir Tarasenko/45 8.00 20.00
JWG1 Wayne Gretzky/25 30.00 80.00

015-16 ITG Used 4 Your Country Jerseys Silver

OLD/25: .5X TO 1.2X SILVER/40
C01 Clrke/Bssy/Sht/Epsto 12.00 30.00
C02 Lmx/Skc/Yzrmn/Frncs 25.00 60.00
C03 Jsph/Lndrs/Thrtn/Lngo 12.00 30.00
C04 Dnne/Sttlr/Sht/Clrke 10.00 25.00
C05 Slne/Krnsff/Kvu/Krri 12.00 30.00
C06 Mdno/Rchtr/LaFntne/Hll 12.00 30.00

4YC07 Brso/Tkchk/Chls/Ltch 8.00 20.00
4YC08 Trtk/Krtv/Mkhlv/Ykshv 12.00 30.00
4YC09 Lndbrgh/Sndn/Frsbrg/Ldstrm 10.00 25.00
4YC10 Slmng/Ldstrm/Frsbrg/Sndn 8.00 20.00

2015-16 ITG Used 50 in 50 Cut Autographs Silver

MR1 Maurice Richard 125.00 200.00

2015-16 ITG Used Dynasty Collection Jerseys Silver

*GOLD/15: .5X TO 1.2X SILVER/30-45
DCGA1 Glenn Anderson/45 6.00 15.00
DCGF1 Grant Fuhr/40 8.00 20.00
DCGL1 Guy Lafleur/35 8.00 20.00
DCGL2 Guy Lapointe/30 5.00 12.00
DCJK1 Jari Kurri/45 6.00 15.00
DCLR1 Larry Robinson/45 6.00 15.00
DCMM1 Mark Messier/45 10.00 25.00
DCSS1 Steve Shutt/45 5.00 12.00
DCWG1 Wayne Gretzky/15 40.00 100.00
DCYC1 Yvan Cournoyer/30 6.00 15.00

2015-16 ITG Used Dynasty Duo Jerseys Silver

DCD01 W.Gretzky/M.Messier/15 25.00 60.00
DCD02 M.Bossy/B.Trottier/35 8.00 20.00
DCD03 J.Kurri/G.Anderson/35 6.00 15.00
DCD04 J.Plante/J.Beliveau/15 15.00 40.00
DCD05 G.Howe/T.Lindsay/15 15.00 40.00
DCD06 T.Broda/T.Kennedy/10
DCD07 S.Shutt/L.Robinson/25 8.00 20.00
DCD08 M.Richard/J.Plante/15 15.00 40.00
DCD09 B.Geoffrion/D.Harvey/15 8.00 20.00
DCD10 P.Coffey/G.Fuhr/35 6.00 15.00

2015-16 ITG Used Fantasy Team 8's Jerseys Silver

*GOLD/15: .6X TO 1.5X SILVER/40-45
FT801 Gtz/Lx/Ry/Brq/Lds/Hk/Hl/Fd/30 75.00 135.00
FT802 Hw/Gtz/Hv/Sk/Dn/Rd/Hl/Or/15 125.00 200.00
FT803 MD/Dn/MK/Tr/Hl/RNH/Lz/Yk/45 30.00 60.00
FT804 Th/Sc/Fg/Sln/Lds/Flr/Crd/Pr/45 40.00 100.00
FT805 Lf/Cs/Brd/Pe/Rb/Ch/Yz/Kn/35 30.00 60.00
FT806 Ms/Blv/Pt/Pc/Cf/Hr/Lc/Trt/25 40.00 80.00
FT807 Wr/Ln/Lnd/Ly/Pt/Nd/Slm/Jr/35 40.00 80.00
FT808 Ry/Blf/By/Md/Brq/Cl/Clr/Dn/40 30.00 60.00

2015-16 ITG Used Hat Trick Jerseys Silver

*GOLD/15: .5X TO 1.2X SILVER/40-45
HT01 Grtzky/Lmx/Espsto/15 30.00 60.00
HT02 Hll/Dnne/Espsto/45 8.00 20.00
HT03 Hll/Slnne/Lndrs/45 8.00 20.00
HT04 Mdno/Clrk/LClr/45 10.00 25.00
HT05 Yzrmn/Lmx/Hll/45 20.00 50.00
HT06 Krri/Andrsn/Bssy/25 8.00 20.00
HT07 Crsby/Ovchkn/Mlkn/45 25.00 60.00
HT08 Jgr/Skc/Rnck/40 15.00 40.00

2015-16 ITG Used Jersey Autographs Silver

*GOLD/15: .5X TO 1.2X SILVER AU/40
GUABB1 Brian Bellows/40 8.00 20.00
GUABG1 Bill Gadsby/45 10.00 25.00
GUABH1 Bobby Hull/20 15.00 40.00
GUABH2 Brett Hull/40 15.00 40.00
GUABP1 Bernie Parent/40 15.00 40.00
GUACJ1 Curtis Joseph/30 10.00 25.00
GUAEG1 Ed Giacomin/40 15.00 40.00
GUAEL1 Eric Lindros/40 12.00 30.00
GUAJJ1 Jaromir Jagr/30 40.00 80.00
GUAJT1 Jose Theodore/40 10.00 25.00
GUAMD1 Marcel Dionne/30 12.00 30.00
GUAMM2 Mike Modano/30 15.00 40.00
GUANL1 Nicklas Lidstrom/40 10.00 25.00
GUAPR1 Patrick Roy/20 30.00 60.00
GUARB1 Raymond Bourque/30 15.00 40.00
GUASF1 Sergei Fedorov/20
GUATB1 Tom Barrasso/45 10.00 25.00
GUATL1 Ted Lindsay/45 10.00 25.00
GUATL2 Trevor Linden/40 10.00 25.00

2015-16 ITG Used Jerseys Dual Silver

*GOLD/30: .5X TO 1.2X SILVER/60
*GOLD/15-25: .5X TO 1.2X SILVER/35-55
GU2J01 C.McDavid/RNH/60 20.00 50.00
GU2J02 C.McDavid/T.Hall/60 20.00 50.00
GU2J03 McDavid/Yakupov/60 20.00 50.00
GU2J04 McDavid/S.Crosby/60 25.00 60.00
GU2J05 Gretzky/McDavid/25 40.00 80.00
GU2J06 Lemieux/Yzerman/50 15.00 40.00
GU2J07 J.Roenick/B.Hull/60 5.00 12.00
GU2J08 B.Hull/M.Modano/60 8.00 20.00
GU2J09 G.Howe/Gretzky/20 40.00 80.00
GU2J10 Lafleur/J.Beliveau/20 10.00 25.00
GU2J11 S.Fedorov/J.Jagr/50 12.00 30.00
GU2J12 D.Harvey/G.Howe/20 12.00 30.00
GU2J13 B.Salming/D.Sittler/35 8.00 20.00
GU2J14 Barrasso/M.Fleury/50 8.00 20.00
GU2J15 P.Esposito/Lafleur/40 8.00 20.00
GU2J16 Messier/G.Lafleur/45 8.00 20.00
GU2J17 Gretzky/G.Lafleur/25 30.00 80.00
GU2J18 Bourque/C.Neely/50 8.00 20.00
GU2J19 Fedorov/Selanne/50 10.00 25.00
GU2J20 B.Hull/T.Selanne/20 12.00 30.00
GU2J21 B.Trottier/M.Bossy/45 6.00 15.00
GU2J22 G.Hall/T.Esposito/25 6.00 15.00
GU2J23 Giacomin/Cheevers/20 6.00 15.00
GU2J24 Lemieux/E.Lindros/45 15.00 40.00
GU2J25 Lidstrom/S.Fedorov/55 8.00 20.00

2015-16 ITG Used Dual Patches Silver

*SLVR PATCH/15: .8X TO 2X SILVER/35-60
*SLVR PATCH/15: .6X TO 1.5X SILVER/20-25
GU2P04 McDavid/Crosby 100.00 175.00
GU2P05 Gretzky/McDavid 125.00 200.00
GU2P09 Howe/Gretzky 75.00 150.00

2015-16 ITG Used Jerseys Quad Silver

*GOLD/15-25: .5X TO 1.2X SILVER/40-55
*SLVR PATCH/15: .6X TO 1.5X SILVER/40-55
*SLVR PATCH/15: .5X TO 1.2X SILVER/20
GU4J01 McDvd/RNH/Ykpv/Hall/55 25.00 60.00
GU4J02 Hll/Lndn/Nslnd/Rnck/55 8.00 20.00
GU4J03 Roy/Jsph/Hsk/Rchtr/40 15.00 40.00
GU4J04 Mssr/Yzrmn/Lmx/Fdrv/40 20.00 50.00
GU4J05 Ldstrm/Yzrmn/Fdrv/Hll/40 10.00 25.00
GU4J06 Clrk/Kn/Sttlr/Slmng/20 12.00 30.00
GU4J07 Rbnsn/Ry/Lflr/Sht/20 20.00 50.00
GU4J08 LClr/Lndrs/Rnck/Vnbs/45 10.00 25.00
GU4J09 McDv/Crsby/Ovch/Stmk/45 25.00 60.00

2015-16 ITG Used Jerseys Trios Silver

*GOLD/15-20: .5X TO 1.2X SILVER/30-55
*SLVR PATCH/15: .6X TO 1.5X SILVER/40-55
GU3J01 Grtzky/Lflr/Mssr/25 25.00 50.00
GU3J02 McDvid/RNH/Ykpv/55 20.00 50.00
GU3J03 McDvd/Crsby/Ovch/55 25.00 60.00
GU3J04 Fdrv/Yzrmn/Ldstrm/40 12.00 30.00
GU3J05 Hwe/Hrvy/Hll/15 25.00 50.00
GU3J06 Blvu/Lflr/Rchrd/15 20.00 50.00
GU3J07 Ovchkn/Mlkn/Gtzlf/40 8.00 20.00
GU3J08 Kn/Sttlr/Slmng/35 10.00 25.00
GU3J09 Thrntn/Frsbrg/Skc/45 10.00 25.00
GU3J10 Hll/Mdno/LClr/50 8.00 20.00
GU3J11 Swchk/Vchn/Dnne/25 12.00 30.00
GU3J12 Grtzky/Rbtlle/Krri/20 30.00 60.00
GU3J13 Trsnko/Mlkn/Ovch/45 25.00 60.00
GU3J14 Brrsso/Ptvn/Jsph/45 10.00 25.00
GU3J15 Lndn/Hll/Mdno/45 8.00 20.00
GU3J16 Lndrs/Lndn/Skc/45 10.00 25.00
GU3J17 Bssy/Slnne/Lmx/30 20.00 50.00
GU3J18 Ldstrm/Brqe/Rbnsn/30 10.00 25.00

2015-16 ITG Used Locker Room Collection Jerseys Silver

LRDH1 Dominik Hasek/20 15.00 40.00
LRGC1 Gerry Cheevers/15 12.00 30.00
LRGH1 Gordie Howe/15 50.00 100.00
LRJP1 Jacques Plante/15 25.00 60.00
LRJT2 Joe Thornton/15 12.00 30.00
LRML1 Mario Lemieux/15 40.00 100.00
LRMR1 Maurice Richard/15 30.00 80.00
LRPR1 Patrick Roy/15 30.00 80.00
LRRB1 Raymond Bourque/20 20.00 50.00
LRWG1 Wayne Gretzky/8

2015-16 ITG Used Maximum Memorabilia Silver

*GOLD/20-25: .5X TO 1.2X SILVER/40-50
MMAMI Al MacInnis/50 5.00 12.00
MMBH2 Brett Hull/45 5.00 12.00
MMBS1 Brendan Shanahan/45 5.00 12.00
MMCL1 Curtis Lazar/50 3.00 8.00
MMCMD1 Connor McDavid/50 20.00 50.00
MMCMD2 Connor McDavid/50 20.00 50.00
MMDH2 Dale Hawerchuk/50 5.00 12.00
MMHL1 Henrik Lundqvist/50 5.00 12.00
MMJD1 Jonathan Drouin/50 5.00 12.00
MMJH1 Jeff Hackett/50 3.00 8.00
MMJI1 Jarome Iginla/50 4.00 10.00
MMJJ1 Jaromir Jagr/40 10.00 25.00
MMJR1 Jeremy Roenick/50 4.00 10.00
MMJT1 Jose Theodore/40 4.00 10.00
MMLR2 Luc Robitaille/50 5.00 12.00
MMMAF Marc-Andre Fleury/45 6.00 15.00
MMMG1 Marian Gaborik/50 4.00 10.00
MMMH1 Milan Hejduk/50 3.00 8.00
MMMK1 Miikka Kiprusoff/50 5.00 12.00
MMML1 Mario Lemieux/45 12.00 30.00
MMMM1 Mark Messier/40 6.00 15.00
MMMN1 Markus Naslund/50 3.00 8.00
MMMT1 Marty Turco/50 4.00 10.00
MMNK1 Nikolai Khabibulin/50 4.00 10.00
MMNM1 Nathan MacKinnon/50 8.00 20.00
MMPB1 Pavel Bure/50 6.00 15.00
MMPK1 Patrick Kane/50 8.00 20.00
MMPR1 Patrick Roy/45 10.00 25.00
MMRB2 Rob Blake/50 4.00 10.00
MMRL1 Roberto Luongo/50 4.00 10.00
MMRNH1 Ryan Nugent-Hopkins/50 4.00 10.00
MMRNH2 Ryan Nugent-Hopkins/50 4.00 10.00
MMSC1 Sidney Crosby/45 10.00 25.00
MMTH1 Taylor Hall/45 8.00 20.00
MMTV1 Tomas Vokoun/50 3.00 8.00

2015-16 ITG Used Stack The Pads Silver

SPBP1 Bernie Parent/20 12.00 30.00
SPCJ1 Curtis Joseph/20 10.00 25.00
SPCP1 Carey Price/25 30.00 80.00
SPDH1 Dominik Hasek/20 12.00 30.00
SPGC1 Gerry Cheevers/15 12.00 30.00
SPGF1 Grant Fuhr/20 12.00 30.00
SPJP1 Jacques Plante/15 30.00 60.00
SPJT1 Jose Theodore/20 10.00 25.00
SPJV1 John Vanbiesbrouck/20
SPPL1 Pelle Lindbergh/15 50.00 100.00
SPPR1 Patrick Roy/20 25.00 60.00
SPVT2 Vladislav Tretiak/15 15.00 40.00

2015-16 ITG Used Team 8's Jerseys Silver

T801 Yz/Ld/Hw/Sw/Ly/Hl/Fd/Ch/25 60.00 120.00
T802 Ry/Bv/Pn/Hy/Lr/Rc/St/Rc/25 60.00 120.00
T803 Gz/Ms/Fr/Kr/An/Cy/Lw/Rn/20 50.00 100.00
T804 Hl/Mk/Es/Hl/Ch/Ms/Rn/Br/20 30.00 60.00
T805 Hn/Br/Sr/Kn/Sm/Cl/Mh/Cn/20 40.00 80.00
T806 Bq/Tn/Cs/Sr/Es/Nl/Bk/Pk/20 30.00 60.00
T807 Ln/Pt/Ck/Vb/LC/Rk/Hx/Lh/30 40.00 80.00
T808 Lx/Br/Mk/Cy/Rb/Fr/Fy/Jr/35 40.00 80.00

2015-16 ITG Used Vintage Memorabilia Silver

VMBJ1 Busher Jackson/15 25.00 50.00
VMGH1 Gordie Howe/15 30.00 60.00
VMHM1 Howie Morenz/15
VMJP1 Jacques Plante/20 20.00 50.00
VMKC1 King Clancy/15 15.00 40.00
VMTS2 Terry Sawchuk/20 15.00 40.00

2015-16 ITG Used Vintage Memorabilia Dual Silver

VM201 G.Howe/M.Richard/25 25.00 60.00
VM202 J.Bower/T.Broda/15 15.00 40.00
VM203 W.Gretzky/M.Richard/15 60.00 150.00
VM204 T.Sawchuk/J.Plante/25 15.00 40.00
VM205 T.Kennedy/T.Horton/15 15.00 40.00
VM206 P.Lindbergh/B.Parent/30 15.00 40.00
VM207 C.Hodge/J.Plante/15 25.00 60.00
VM208 P.Esposito/B.Hull/25 20.00 50.00
VM209 H.Lumley/J.Bower/15 15.00 40.00
VM210 G.Worsley/E.Giacomin/20 15.00 40.00
VM216 B.Geoffrion/J.Beliveau/25 12.00 30.00

2016-17 ITG Used Jerseys

GU01 Al Arbour/35
GU02 Bobby Baun/20 5.00 12.00
GU03 Brett Hull/45 5.00 12.00
GU04 Curtis Joseph/45 5.00 12.00
GU05 Dave Keon/25 5.00 12.00
GU06 Gerry Cheevers/25 5.00 12.00
GU07 Grant Fuhr/45 5.00 12.00
GU08 Jacques Laperriere/25 5.00 12.00
GU09 Jeremy Roenick/45 5.00 12.00
GU10 Joe Sakic/45 8.00 20.00
GU11 Joe Thornton/45 5.00 12.00
GU12 John Vanbiesbrouck/45 5.00 12.00
GU13 Lanny McDonald/45 5.00 12.00
GU14 Larry Murphy/45 5.00 12.00
GU15 Marian Gaborik/45 5.00 12.00
GU16 Mario Lemieux/45 15.00 40.00
GU17 Matt Murray/45 8.00 20.00
GU18 P.K. Subban/45 8.00 20.00
GU19 Patrick Roy/45 12.00 30.00
GU20 Paul Coffey/45 5.00 12.00
GU21 Paul Kariya/45 6.00 15.00
GU22 Peter Forsberg/45 5.00 12.00
GU23 Peter Stastny/20 5.00 12.00
GU24 Pierre Turgeon/45 5.00 12.00
GU25 Rick Martin/20 5.00 12.00
GU26 Rick Nash/45 5.00 12.00
GU27 Ryan Nugent-Hopkins/45 5.00 12.00
GU28 Sergei Fedorov/45 8.00 20.00
GU29 Steve Shutt/25 5.00 12.00
GU30 Steven Stamkos/45 10.00 25.00
GU31 Teemu Selanne/45 10.00 25.00
GU32 Wayne Gretzky/25 25.00 60.00

2016-17 ITG Used Autographs

GUABB1 Bill Barber/30 10.00 25.00
GUABH1 Bobby Hull/30 15.00 40.00
GUABH2 Brett Hull/30 10.00 25.00
GUAGF1 Grant Fuhr/30 10.00 25.00
GUAGH1 Gordie Howe/12
GUAGL1 Guy Lafleur/30 12.00 30.00
GUAJS1 Joe Sakic/30 15.00 40.00
GUAJT1 Jose Theodore/30 10.00 25.00
GUAPB1 Pavel Bure/30 10.00 25.00
GUAPC1 Paul Coffey/30 10.00 25.00
GUAPF1 Peter Forsberg/30 10.00 25.00
GUATL1 Trevor Linden/30 12.00 30.00
GUATS1 Teemu Selanne/30 20.00 50.00
GUAVT1 Vladislav Tretiak/30 10.00 25.00
GUAWC1 Wendel Clark/30 10.00 25.00

2016-17 ITG Used Countrymen Memorabilia

C01 Yzerman/Sakic/Brodeur 15.00 40.00
Thornton/Lemieux/Joseph/Francis/Lindros
C02 Bossy/Shutt/Esposito/Sittler 8.00 20.00
Perreault/Clarke/Dionne/Goulet
C03 Crosby/Price/Fleury/Luongo 20.00 50.00
Toews/Doughty/Stamkos/Tavares
C04 Koivu/Selanne/Koivu/Nittymaki 10.00 25.00
Kurri/Tikkanen/Kiprusoff/Backstrom
C05 Samuelsson/Sundin/Lindbergh 6.00 15.00
Lidstrom/Forsberg/Zetterberg/Salming/Naslund
C06 Hull/Tkachuk/Leetch/Richter 8.00 20.00
Modano/LaFontaine/Barrasso/Chelios
C07 Yakushev/Mikhailov/Kharlamov 5.00 12.00
Maltsev/Myshkin/Krutov/Mylnikov/Tretiak

2016-17 ITG Used Fantasy Team 8's Memorabilia

FT801 Gretzky/Howe/Plante/Harvey 30.00 80.00
Lemieux/Richard/Orr/Roy/30
FT802 Hull/Cheevers/Clarke 10.00 25.00
Lidstrom/Lafleur/Esposito/Parent/Dionne/35
FT803 Delvecchio/Robinson 6.00 15.00
Esposito/Keon/Laperriere/Sittler/Giacomin/Shutt/35
FT804 Sakic/Ovechkin/Kane/Sundin 25.00 60.00
Hasek/Price/Chelios/Pronger/35
FT805 Gretzky/Lindsay/Potvin 30.00 80.00
Lemieux/Tretiak/Brodeur/Salming/Howe/35
FT806 Selanne/Bure/Lidstrom 15.00 40.00
Leetch/Roy/Brodeur/Messier/Fedorov/35
FT807 Sawchuk/Parent/McDonald 10.00 25.00
Sittler/Esposito/Robinson/Bourque/Bossy/25
FT808 Tkachuk/Turgeon/Modano 10.00 25.00
Roenick/Richter/Pronger/Belfour/Niedermayer/35
FT809 Dionne/Lemieux/MacInnis 20.00 50.00
Bourque/Fuhr/Price/Selanne/Tkachuk/35
FT810 Yzerman/Esposito/Cheevers 15.00 40.00
Roy/Robinson/Neely/Pronger/Hull/35

2016-17 ITG Used International Showdown Memorabilia

IS01 Chelios/Hull/Modano 8.00 20.00
LaFontaine/Mikhailov/Krutov/Yakushev/Kharlamov
IS02 Lemieux/Esposito/Shutt 15.00 40.00
Bossy/Hull/Richter/LaFontaine/Modano
IS03 Selanne/Koivu/Tikkanen 10.00 25.00
Kurri/Sundin/Lindbergh/Forsberg/Lidstrom
IS04 Bure/Ovechkin/Mogilny 20.00 50.00
Malkin/Sittler/Yzerman/Clarke/Sakic
IS05 Tretiak/Kharlamov 20.00 50.00
Mikhailov/Krutov/Jagr/Holik/Dzurilla/Stastnyx

2016-17 ITG Used Legends of Chicago Stadium Relics

LCS01 Bobby Hull 10.00 25.00
LCS02 Bobby Orr 20.00 50.00
LCS03 Glenn Hall 6.00 15.00
LCS04 Phil Esposito 10.00 25.00
LCS05 Pierre Pilote 6.00 15.00
LCS06 Stan Mikita 8.00 20.00
LCS07 Tony Esposito 6.00 15.00

2016-17 ITG Used Legends of Olympia Stadium Relics

LOS01 Alex Delvecchio 6.00 15.00
LOS02 Bill Gadsby 6.00 15.00
LOS03 Gordie Howe 15.00 40.00
LOS04 Harry Lumley 6.00 15.00
LOS05 Marcel Pronovost 6.00 15.00
LOS06 Norm Ullman 6.00 15.00
LOS07 Red Kelly 6.00 15.00
LOS08 Sid Abel 6.00 15.00
LOS09 Ted Lindsay 6.00 15.00
LOS10 Terry Sawchuk 6.00 15.00

2016-17 ITG Used Legendary Starting Six Memorabilia

LS601 Gretzky/Lemieux 20.00 50.00
Chelios/Roy/Pronger/Hull/30
LS602 Howe/Orr/Gretzky 20.00 50.00
Ovechkin/Hasek/Stevens/25
LS603 Lemieux/Sakic/Lidstrom 12.00 30.00
Roy/Lafleur/Housley/30
LS604 Mikita/Bure/Lidstrom 6.00 15.00
Hasek/Chelios/Fedorov/30
LS605 Savard/Lafleur/Hall 12.00 30.00
Niedermayer/Lidstrom/Lemieux/30

2016-17 ITG Used Quad Jerseys

GQ01 Baun/Plante/Salming/Keon/30 8.00 20.00
GQ02 Esposito/Hall/Belfour/Crawford/35 6.00 15.00
GQ03 Fedorov/Bure/Mogilny/Ovechkin/35 20.0050.00
GQ04 Gretzky/Lemieux/Lafleur 25.00 60.00
Esposito/35
GQ05 Howe/Delvecchio 12.00 30.00
Lindsay/Fedorov/35
GQ06 Kariya/Sakic/Forsberg/Hull/35 8.00 20.00
GQ07 Kariya/Selanne/Getzlaf/Perry/35 10.00 25.00
GQ08 MacInnis/Coffey/Murphy 5.00 12.00
Chelios/35
GQ09 Nugent-Hopkins/Hall 5.00 12.00
MacKinnon/Drouin/35x
GQ10 Vokoun/Vernon 5.00 12.00
Nabokov/Khabibulin/35

2016-17 ITG Used Quad Patches

GQP01 Baun/Plante/Salming/Keon/30 8.00 20.00
GQP02 Esposito/Hall/Belfour/Crawford/35 6.00 15.00
GQP03 Fedorov/Bure/Mogilny 20.00 50.00
Ovechkin/35
GQP04 Gretzky/Lemieux/Lafleur 25.00 60.00
Esposito/35
GQP05 Howe/Delvecchio 12.00 30.00
Lindsay/Fedorov/35
GQP06 Kariya/Sakic/Forsberg/Hull/35 8.00 20.00
GQP07 Kariya/Selanne/Getzlaf/Perry/35 10.00 25.00
GQP08 MacInnis/Coffey/Murphy 5.00 12.00
Chelios/35
GQP09 Nugent-Hopkins/Hall 10.00 25.00
MacKinnon/Drouin/35
GQP10 Vokoun/Vernon/Nabokov 5.00 12.00
Khabibulin/35

2016-17 ITG Used Super Swatch

SS01 Alexander Ovechkin 20.00 50.00
SS02 Alexei Kovalev 5.00 12.00
SS03 Arturs Irbe 4.00 10.00
SS04 Bill Guerin 5.00 12.00
SS05 Brendan Shanahan 6.00 15.00
SS06 Brett Hull 5.00 12.00
SS07 Brian Leetch 5.00 12.00
SS08 Carey Price 15.00 40.00
SS09 Chris Chelios 5.00 12.00
SS10 Chris Pronger 4.00 10.00
SS11 Corey Crawford 6.00 15.00
SS12 Daniel Alfredsson 5.00 12.00
SS13 Drew Doughty 5.00 12.00
SS14 Ed Belfour 5.00 12.00
SS15 Ed Jovanovski 5.00 12.00
SS16 Gabriel Landeskog 4.00 10.00
SS17 Ilya Kovalchuk 5.00 12.00
SS18 Jarome Iginla 5.00 12.00
SS19 Jaromir Jagr 12.00 30.00
SS20 Jeff Friesen 5.00 12.00
SS21 Jeremy Roenick 5.00 12.00
SS22 Joe Sakic 8.00 20.00
SS23 John LeClair 5.00 12.00
SS24 John Tavares 10.00 25.00
SS25 Marian Hossa 4.00 10.00
SS26 Martin Brodeur 10.00 25.00
SS27 Mats Sundin 5.00 12.00
SS28 Nathan MacKinnon 10.00 25.00
SS29 P.K. Subban 8.00 20.00
SS30 Pavol Demitra 6.00 15.00
SS31 Peter Forsberg 5.00 12.00
SS32 Rob Blake 5.00 12.00
SS33 Ryan Getzlaf 8.00 20.00
SS34 Sandis Ozolinsh 5.00 12.00
SS35 Simon Gagne 5.00 12.00
SS36 Steven Stamkos 10.00 25.00
SS37 Taylor Hall 10.00 25.00
SS38 Teemu Selanne 10.00 25.00
SS39 Tie Domi 5.00 12.00
SS40 Tommy Salo 5.00 12.00
SS41 Tony Amonte 5.00 12.00
SS42 Vincent Lecavalier 4.00 10.00

2016-17 ITG Used Triple Jerseys

GT01 Arbour/Bossy/Potvin/30 5.00 12.00
GT02 Esposito/Hall/Crawford/45 6.00 15.00
GT03 Giacomin/Richter/Lundqvist/45 5.00 12.00
GT04 Gilmour/Modano/Hull/45 8.00 20.00
GT05 Gretzky/Lemieux/Howe/30 25.00 60.00
GT06 Hall/MacKinnon/Tavares/45 10.00 25.00
GT07 Kane/Nash/Tavares/45 10.00 25.00
GT08 Khabibulin/Kolzig/Nabokov/45 5.00 12.00
GT09 Landeskog/Nugent-Hopkins/Hall/45 10.0025.00
GT10 Laperriere/Shutt/Lafleur/25 6.00 15.00
GT11 Lecavalier/Stamkos/Drouin/45 10.00 25.00
GT12 Lemieux/Hull/Sakic/45 15.00 40.00
GT13 Plante/Potvin/Joseph/25 8.00 20.00
GT14 Quick/Crawford/Price/45 15.00 40.00
GT15 Turco/Vokoun/Luongo/45 5.00 12.00

2017 ITG Used Autographs

GUAAK1 Alexei Kovalev/25 10.00 25.00
GUAAM1 Andy Moog/25 10.00 25.00
GUAAO1 Adam Oates/25 10.00 25.00
GUABL1 Brian Leetch/25 10.00 25.00
GUACO1 Chris Osgood/25 10.00 25.00
GUAEB1 Ed Belfour/25 12.00 30.00
GUAGF1 Grant Fuhr/25 12.00 30.00
GUAGP1 Gilbert Perreault/25
GUAJE1 Jack Eichel/25
GUAJK1 Joe Kocur/25 10.00 25.00
GUAJR1 Jeremy Roenick/25 10.00 25.00
GUAMR1 Manon Rheaume/25 80.00 150.00
GUANH1 Nico Hischier/40 30.00 80.00
GUANP1 Nolan Patrick/40
GUANU1 Norm Ullman/25 10.00 25.00
GUAPT1 Pierre Turgeon/25

2017 ITG Used Draft History Materials

DH01 Turgeon/Shanahan/Sakic 10.00 25.00
Richardson/LeClair/Desjardins
DH02 Clark/Burke/Richter 10.00 25.00
Nieuwendyk/Ranford/Larionov
DH03 Lemieux/Roberts 25.00 60.00
Roy/Robitaille/Hull/Muller
DH04 LaFontaine/Yzerman/Neely 15.00 40.00
Barrasso/Hasek/Fetisov
DH05 Bellows/Stevens/Housley 8.00 20.00
Andreychuk/Leeman/Gilmour
DH06 Hawerchuk/Francis/Fuhr 8.00 20.00
MacInnis/Chelios/Vanbiesbrouck
DH07 Savard/Babych/Murphy 8.00 20.00
Coffey/Kurri/Sutter
DH08 Gartner/Bourque/Goulet 8.00 20.00
Messier/Foligno/Anderson
DH09 Gillies/Valiquette/Maloney 8.00 20.00
Trottier/Howe/Williams
DH10 Potvin/McDonald/Gainey 8.00 20.00
Middleton/Davidson/Savard
DH11 Lafleur/Dionne/Martin 10.00 25.00
O'Reilly/Robinson/Garrett
DH12 Perreault/Leach/Sittler 8.00 20.00
Maloney/Smith/Meloche
DH13 Modano/Linden/Roenick 12.00 30.00
Brind'Amour/Selanne/Blake
DH14 Sundin/Guerin 12.00 30.00
Holik/Kolzig/Lidstrom/Fedorov

2017 ITG Used Jerseys

GU01 Al Secord 3.00 8.00
GU02 Alexander Ovechkin 12.00 30.00
GU03 Alexei Zhitnik 3.00 8.00
GU04 Bill Guerin 3.00 8.00
GU05 Bobby Holik 3.00 8.00
GU06 Boris Mironov 3.00 8.00
GU07 Brett Hull 3.00 8.00
GU08 Brian Leetch 3.00 8.00
GU09 Bryan Berard 3.00 8.00
GU10 Chris Drury 3.00 8.00
GU11 Chris Osgood 3.00 8.00
GU12 Chris Pronger 3.00 8.00
GU13 Dan Maloney 3.00 8.00
GU14 Darryl Sittler 3.00 8.00
GU15 Dave Maloney 3.00 8.00
GU16 Dick Redmond 3.00 8.00
GU17 Doug Jarrett 3.00 0.00
GU18 Evgeni Nabokov 3.00 8.00
GU19 Gary Dornhoefer 3.00 8.00
GU20 Gary Suter 3.00 8.00
GU21 Gilles Meloche 3.00 8.00
GU22 Jaromir Jagr 8.00 20.00
GU23 Jason Arnott 3.00 8.00
GU24 Jim Rutherford 3.00 8.00
GU25 Kevin Hatcher 3.00 8.00
GU26 Larry Murphy 3.00 8.00
GU27 Manon Rheaume 3.00 8.00
GU28 Mark Messier 3.00 8.00
GU29 Mike Gartner 3.00 8.00
GU30 Mike Peca 3.00 8.00
GU31 Nazem Kadri 3.00 8.00
GU32 Patrick Marleau 3.00 8.00
GU33 Patrick Roy 8.00 20.00
GU34 Pavel Bure 3.00 8.00
GU35 Pavel Datsyuk 5.00 12.00
GU36 Peter Forsberg 5.00 12.00
GU37 Rick Nash 3.00 8.00
GU38 Roman Cechmanek 3.00 8.00
GU39 Sandis Ozolinsh 3.00 8.00
GU40 Sergei Fedorov 5.00 12.00
GU41 Steve Larmer 3.00 8.00
GU42 Steve Mason 3.00 8.00
GU43 Teemu Selanne 5.00 12.00
GU44 Trevor Kidd 3.00 8.00
GU45 Vincent Damphousse 2.50 6.00
GU46 Zdeno Chara 3.00 8.00
GU47 Zigmund Palffy 3.00 8.00

2017 ITG Used Le Forum de Montreal Seats

LFM01 Aurele Joliat 6.00 15.00
LFM02 Bernie Geoffrion 6.00 15.00
LFM03 Bert Olmstead 6.00 15.00
LFM04 Bill Durnan 6.00 15.00
LFM05 Claude Provost 6.00 15.00
LFM06 Dickie Moore 6.00 15.00
LFM07 Doug Harvey 6.00 15.00
LFM08 Elmer Lach 6.00 15.00
LFM09 George Hainsworth 6.00 15.00
LFM10 Guy Lafleur 8.00 20.00
LFM11 Howie Morenz 6.00 15.00
LFM12 Jacques Plante 6.00 15.00
LFM13 Jean Beliveau 6.00 15.00
LFM14 Maurice Richard 6.00 15.00
LFM15 Toe Blake 6.00 15.00
LFM16 Tom Johnson 6.00 15.00

2017 ITG Used Putting on the Foll Materials

PF01 Barry Beck/15 6.00 15.00
PF02 Bob Probert/30 8.00 20.00
PF03 Craig Berube/30 6.00 15.00
PF04 Dave Manson/30 6.00 15.00
PF05 Donald Brashear/30 6.00 15.00
PF06 Dave Brown/30 6.00 15.00
PF07 Georges Laraque/30 6.00 15.00
PF08 Terry O'Reilly/30 6.00 15.00
PF09 Tie Domi/30 8.00 20.00
PF10 Tiger Williams/30 8.00 20.00

2017 ITG Used Quad Jerseys

GU401 Jarrett/White/Mikita/Redmond 5.00 12.00
GU402 Unger/Clarke/Tkaczuk/Sittler 5.00 12.00
GU403 Riggin/Beaupre/Lemelin/Meloche 5.00 12.00
GU404 Ranford/Resch/Bouchard/Vernon 5.00 12.00
GU405 Rutherford/Myre 5.00 12.00
Davidson/Meloche
GU406 Brind'Amour 5.00 12.00
Andreychuk/Recchi/Damphousse
GU407 Hatcher/Chelios 5.00 12.00
Richardson/Desjardins
GU408 Lowe/Babych/Murphy/Carlyle 5.00 12.00
GU409 Cashman/Lafleur 6.00 15.00
Tkaczuk/Mahovlich

2017 ITG Used Team Eights Materials

T801 Esposito/Orr/Bourque 25.00 60.00
Cheevers/O'Ree/Neely/Middleton/Sanderson/20
T802 Delvecchio/Crozier/Howe 15.00 40.00
Lindsay/Ullman/Giacomin/Sawchuk/Rutherford/30
T803 Yzerman/Shanahan 15.00 40.00
Lidstrom/Osgood/Hull/Hasek/Fedorov/Chelios/30
T804 Maloney/Gretzky/Robitaille 8.00 20.00
Blake/Dionne/Palffy/Sargent/Vachon/30
T805 Maloney/Rousseau/Ratelle 10.00 25.00
Gilbert/Dionne/Lafleur/Tkaczuk/Giacomin/30
T806 Lacroix/Clarke/MacLeish 8.00 20.00
Barber/Watson/Watson/Parent/Leach/30
T807 Unger/Picard/Huck/McDonald 8.00 20.00
Hall/Johnston/Federko/Arbour/30
T808 Broten/Modano/Bellows 12.00 30.00
Ciccarelli/Hartsburg/Musil/Beaupre/Payne/30
T809 Baun/Keon/Vaive 8.00 20.00
McDonald/Sittler/Salming/Williams/Valiquette/30
T810 Martin/Perreault/LaFontaine 10.00 25.00
Robert/Hasek/Zhitnik/Fuhr/Mogilny/30
T811 Bure/Brodeur/Snepsts/Tanti 8.00 20.00
Linden/Sedin/Sedin/Naslund/30
T812 Ovechkin/Bure/Malkin 8.00 20.00
Khabibulin/Mogilny/Bryzgalov/Kasparaitis/Yashin/30
T813 Bossy/Gillies/Smith/Potvin 15.00 40.00
Trottier/LaFontaine/Tavares/Nystrom/30
T814 Hull/Tkachuk/Chelios 12.00 30.00
Barrasso/Amonte/Guerin/Leetch/Modano/30
T815 Goulet/Shutt/Ciccarelli 8.00 20.00
Hawerchuk/Perreault/Unger/Sittler/Clarke/30
T816 Lemieux/Yzerman/Lindros 25.00 60.00
Joseph/Sakic/Brodeur/Thornton/Francis/30
T817 Fleury/Burns/Toews/Price 12.00 30.00
Doughty/Carter/Spezza/Bouwmeester/30
T818 Gretzky/Lemieux/Howe/Jagr 25.00 60.00
Roy/Brodeur/Yzerman/Bourque/30
T819 Orr/Clarke/Cheevers/Dionne 25.00 60.00
Lafleur/Esposito/Perreault/Sittler/30
T820 Plante/Howe/Ullman/Hall 15.00 40.00
Mikita/Giacomin/Keon/Hull/20
T821 White/Redmond/Jarrett 8.00 20.00
Mikita/Hull/Goulet/Savard/Larmer/30

2017 ITG Used Triple Jerseys

GU301 Howe/Gretzky/Orr 20.00 50.00
GU302 Bure/Ovechkin/Fedorov 10.00 25.00
GU303 Fleury/Mason/Crawford 10.00 25.00
GU304 Hasek/Roy/Brodeur 15.00 40.00
GU305 Joseph/Potvin/Khabibulin 6.00 15.00
GU306 Kariya/Lindros/Hull 6.00 15.00
GU307 Messier/Gartner/Vaive 6.00 15.00
GU308 Housley/Murphy/MacInnis 6.00 15.00
GU309 Turgeon/Oates/Sakic 6.00 15.00
GU310 Mikita/Howe/Keon 12.00 30.00
GU311 Iginla/St./Vincent 5.00 12.00
GU312 Payne/Musil/Hartsburg 6.00 15.00
GU313 Salo/Khabibulin/Turek 6.00 15.00
GU314 Suter/Roberts/MacInnis 6.00 15.00
GU315 Redmond/Sargent/Jarrett 6.00 15.00
GU316 Inness/Johnston/Davidson 5.00 12.00
GU317 Snow/Shields/Osgood 6.00 15.00
GU318 Sargent/Blake/Doughty 6.00 15.00
GU319 Vokoun/Nabokov/Khabibulin 6.00 15.00
GU320 Carlyle/Babych/Reinhart 5.00 12.00
GU321 Mikita/McDonald/Keon 6.00 15.00

2017-18 ITG Used All Time Gr8s Memorabilia

AT801 Bourque/Housley/MacInnis 6.00 15.00
Coffey/Chelios/Stevens/Blake/Lidstrom
AT802 Gretzky/Lemieux/Sakic/Hull 30.00 80.00
Turgeon/Modano/Fedorov/Bure
AT803 Howe/Lemieux/Harvey 30.00 80.00
Plante/Gretzky/Horton/Gadsby/Roy
AT804 Hull/Roenick/Turgeon 15.00 40.00
Lidstrom/Kariya/Selanne/Jagr/Lindros
AT805 Kharlamov/Krutov/Maltsev 6.00 15.00
Tretiak/Mikhailov/Mylnikov/Myshkin/Yakushev
AT806 McDavid/Ovechkin/Stamkos 25.00 60.00
Crosby/Malkin/Tavares/Kane/MacKinnon
AT807 Mikita/Howe/Hull/Ullman 15.00 40.00
Beliveau/Delvecchio/Mahovlich/Keon
AT808 Orr/Potvin/Park/Salming 20.00 50.00
Robinson/Savard/Redmond/White
AT809 Roy/Brodeur/Potvin 15.00 40.00
Joseph/Hasek/Belfour/Richter/Fuhr
AT810 Thornton/Alfredsson/Lecavalier/St.
Louis/Hossa/Iginla/Hejduk/Marleau 6.00 15.00
AT811 Unger/Esposito/Dionne 10.00 25.00
Clarke/Perreault/Sittler/Mahovlich/Martin
AT812 Vachon/Dryden/Parent 8.00 20.00
Cheevers/Smith/Giacomin/Esposito/Johnston

2003-04 ITG VIP Brightest Stars

All cards carried a "BS" prefix on the card back.
STATED PRINT RUN 30 SETS
1 Mario Lemieux 25.00 60.00
2 Marian Gaborik 20.00 50.00
3 Dany Heatley 15.00 40.00
4 Ilya Kovalchuk 15.00 40.00
5 Jason Spezza 20.00 50.00
6 Dominik Hasek 20.00 50.00
7 Peter Forsberg 25.00 60.00
8 Steve Yzerman 20.00 50.00
9 Martin Brodeur 25.00 60.00
10 Patrick Roy 25.00 60.00

2003-04 ITG VIP Collages

This set consisted of 35 sepia-toned, oversized (approx. 4"x 5") collage cards serial-numbered consecutively to a total of 6000 total cards. Cards were placed in tin "packs" and a memorabilia card was attached to the larger collage card with removable glue. Approximately 50 each of several of the collages were also autographed.

1 Mario Lemieux 10.00 25.00
2 Martin Brodeur 8.00 20.00
3 Steve Yzerman 8.00 20.00
4 Patrick Roy 8.00 20.00
5 Paul Kariya 3.00 8.00
6 Peter Forsberg 6.00 15.00
7 Joe Sakic 6.00 15.00
8 Marian Gaborik 6.00 15.00
9 Mark Messier 5.00 12.00
10 Ilya Kovalchuk 5.00 12.00
11 Mike Modano 5.00 12.00
12 Brett Hull 5.00 12.00
13 Jean-Sebastien Giguere 2.00 5.00
14 Joe Thornton 5.00 12.00
15 Pavel Bure 2.00 5.00
16 Dany Heatley 5.00 12.00
17 Rick Nash 4.00 10.00
18 Henrik Zetterberg 4.00 10.00
19 Dominik Hasek 6.00 15.00
20 Jose Theodore 4.00 10.00
21 Jason Spezza 5.00 12.00
22 Ed Belfour 3.00 8.00
23 Nicklas Lidstrom 3.00 8.00
24 Roberto Luongo 4.00 10.00
25 Tony Esposito 4.00 10.00
26 Ted Lindsay 3.00 8.00
27 Bobby Hull 6.00 15.00
28 Jacques Plante 4.00 10.00
29 Phil Esposito 2.00 5.00
30 Turk Broda 2.00 5.00
31 Georges Vezina 4.00 12.00
32 Terry Sawchuk 4.00 10.00
33 Rocket Richard 5.00 12.00
34 Jean Beliveau 3.00 8.00
35 Doug Harvey 2.00 5.00

2003-04 ITG VIP Collage Autographs

STATED PRINT RUN 20-50
1 Mario Lemieux 50.00 125.00
2 Martin Brodeur/20 50.00 125.00
3 Steve Yzerman/20 50.00 125.00
6 Peter Forsberg 30.00 80.00
7 Joe Sakic 25.00 60.00
10 Ilya Kovalchuk 20.00 50.00
12 Brett Hull 20.00 50.00
14 Joe Thornton 20.00 50.00
17 Rick Nash 20.00 50.00
18 Henrik Zetterberg 25.00 60.00
19 Dominik Hasek/20 25.00 60.00
23 Nicklas Lidstrom 15.00 40.00
24 Roberto Luongo 15.00 40.00
25 Tony Esposito 20.00 50.00
26 Ted Lindsay 12.50 30.00
27 Bobby Hull 15.00 40.00
29 Phil Esposito 12.50 30.00
34 Jean Beliveau 20.00 50.00

2003-04 ITG VIP International Experience

All cards carried an "IE" prefix on the card back.
STATED PRINT RUN 50 SETS
1 Mario Lemieux 30.00 80.00
2 Jay Bouwmeester 12.50 30.00
3 Jason Spezza 20.00 50.00
4 Mike Modano 12.50 30.00
5 Joe Sakic 25.00 60.00
6 Nicklas Lidstrom 12.50 30.00
7 Peter Forsberg 15.00 40.00
8 Mats Sundin 12.50 30.00
9 Jaromir Jagr 20.00 50.00
10 Steve Yzerman 15.00 40.00
11 Dany Healley 12.50 30.00
12 Martin Brodeur 20.00 50.00

2003-04 ITG VIP Jerseys

All cards carried a "GUJ" prefix on the card back.
STATED PRINT RUN 50 SETS
1 Joe Thornton 12.50 30.00
2 Mario Lemieux 25.00 60.00
3 Mats Sundin 8.00 20.00
4 Pavel Bure 8.00 20.00
5 Dany Heatley 15.00 40.00
6 Joe Sakic 25.00 60.00
7 Rick Nash 15.00 40.00
8 Nicklas Lidstrom 8.00 20.00

9 Markus Naslund 8.00 20.00
10 Patrick Roy 25.00 60.00
11 Peter Forsberg 20.00 50.00
12 Dominik Hasek 15.00 40.00
13 Henrik Zetterberg 15.00 40.00
14 Mike Modano 12.50 30.00
15 Jay Bouwmeester 12.50 30.00
16 Ilya Kovalchuk 12.50 30.00
17 Marian Gaborik 15.00 40.00
18 Brett Hull 12.50 30.00
19 Martin Brodeur 25.00 60.00
20 Milan Hejduk 8.00 20.00
21 Steve Yzerman 25.00 60.00
22 Jeremy Roenick 12.50 30.00
23 Jean-Sebastien Giguere 6.00 15.00
24 Brendan Shanahan 8.00 20.00
25 Todd Bertuzzi 8.00 20.00
26 Jarome Iginla 12.50 30.00
27 Al MacInnis 6.00 15.00
28 Saku Koivu 8.00 20.00
29 Jason Spezza 20.00 50.00
30 Ed Belfour 8.00 20.00

2003-04 ITG VIP Making the Bigs

All cards carried a "MTB" prefix on the card back.
STATED PRINT RUN 50 SETS
1 Jay Bouwmeester 15.00 40.00
2 Rick Nash 25.00 60.00
3 Scottie Upshall 12.50 30.00
4 Jason Spezza 20.00 50.00
5 Ron Hainsey 12.50 30.00
6 Barret Jackman 12.50 30.00
7 Dany Heatley 15.00 40.00
8 Dan Blackburn 12.50 30.00

2003-04 ITG VIP MVP

All cards carried a "MVP" prefix on the card back.
1 Howie Morenz/10
2 Roy Worters/10
3 Eddie Shore/10
4 Aurel Joliat/10
5 Maurice Richard/10
6 Ted Kennedy/10
7 Jacques Plante/10
8 Bobby Hull/50 20.00 50.00
9 Stan Mikita/50 15.00 40.00
10 Phil Esposito/50 12.00 30.00
11 Bobby Clarke/50 12.50 30.00
12 Dominik Hasek/50 15.00 40.00
13 Roger Crozier/50 15.00 40.00
14 Glenn Hall/40 20.00 50.00
15 Bernie Parent/50 20.00 50.00
16 Mike Bossy/50 12.50 30.00
17 Patrick Roy/50 30.00 80.00
18 Patrick Roy/50 30.00 80.00
19 Steve Yzerman/50 25.00 60.00
20 Jean-Sebastien Giguere/50 12.50 30.00
21 Bryan Trottier/50 12.50 30.00
22 Jean Beliveau/50 25.00 60.00
23 Guy Lafleur/50 15.00 40.00
24 Mark Messier/50 15.00 40.00
25 Mario Lemieux/50 20.00 50.00
26 Joe Sakic/50 20.00 50.00

2003-04 ITG VIP Netminders

All cards carried a "N" prefix on the card back.
STATED PRINT RUN 50 SETS
1 Martin Brodeur 15.00 40.00
2 Roberto Luongo 12.50 30.00
3 Ed Belfour 10.00 25.00
4 Patrick Roy 20.00 50.00
5 Marty Turco 10.00 25.00
6 Jean-Sebastien Giguere 10.00 25.00
7 Olaf Kolzig 10.00 25.00
8 Patrick Lalime 10.00 25.00
9 Dan Blackburn 15.00 40.00
10 Rick DiPietro 10.00 25.00
11 Ryan Miller 12.50 30.00
12 Jose Theodore 12.50 30.00

2003-04 ITG VIP Sophomores

All cards carried a "S" prefix on the card back.
STATED PRINT RUN 50 SETS
1 Rick Nash 15.00 40.00
2 Jay Bouwmeester 6.00 15.00
3 Barret Jackman 15.00 40.00
4 Henrik Zetterberg 15.00 40.00
5 Ryan Miller 12.50 30.00
6 Stanistov Chistov 6.00 15.00
7 Jason Spezza 15.00 40.00
8 Alexander Frolov 6.00 15.00

2003-04 ITG VIP Vintage Memorabilia

All cards carried a "VM" prefix on the card back.
1 Cyclone Taylor/10
2 Georges Vezina/10
3 George Hainsworth/20
4 Aurel Joliat/20
5 Charlie Conacher/10
6 Howie Morenz/10
7 Sid Abel/20
8 Frank Brimsek/20
9 Ted Lindsay/30 20.00 50.00
10 Bill Barilko/10
11 Tim Horton/30 20.00 50.00
12 Jacques Plante/30 30.00 80.00
13 Terry Sawchuk/10
14 Doug Harvey/30 12.50 30.00
15 Maurice Richard/10
16 Harry Lumley/30 15.00 40.00
17 Tony Esposito/30 12.50 30.00
18 Jean Beliveau/30 30.00 80.00
19 Frank Mahovlich/30 20.00 50.00
20 Glenn Hall/30 20.00 50.00
21 Bobby Hull/30 30.00 80.00
22 Stan Mikita/30 15.00 40.00

2009-10 ITG 1972 The Year In Hockey Blank Backs

BLANK BACK/72: 1.5X TO 4X BASIC CARDS

2009-10 ITG 1972 The Year In Hockey Autographs

B Andre Boudrias 6.00 15.00
AAD Alex Delvecchio SP 25.00 60.00
AAG Alexander Gusev 12.00 30.00
AAH Al Hamilton 5.00 12.00
AAL Andre Lacroix 6.00 15.00
AAM Al McDonough 5.00 12.00
AAW Alton White 5.00 12.00
AAY Alexander Yakushev 20.00 50.00
ABB Bill Barber SP 25.00 50.00
ABC Bobby Clarke SP 40.00 80.00
ABG Butch Goring 8.00 20.00
ABH Bryan Hextall 6.00 15.00
ABL Bob Leiter 5.00 12.00
ABM Bob MacMillan 5.00 12.00
ABN Bob Nystrom 5.00 12.00
ABP Brad Park SP 30.00 60.00
ABS Bobby Schmautz 5.00 12.00
ABW Bill White 5.00 12.00
ACB Curt Bennett 5.00 12.00
ACM Cesare Maniago 6.00 15.00
ADA Don Awrey 8.00 20.00
ADB Dan Bouchard 6.00 15.00
ADF Doug Favell 8.00 20.00
ADG Danny Grant 10.00 25.00
ADH Denis Herron 6.00 15.00
ADJ Doug Jarrett 5.00 12.00
ADK Dave Keon SP 50.00 100.00
ADL Don Lever 12.00 30.00
ADS Dallas Smith 10.00 25.00
ADT Dale Tallon Summit 15.00 40.00
ADW Dunc Wilson 8.00 20.00
AEG Ed Giacomin SP 30.00 60.00
AEJ Eddie Johnston 8.00 20.00
AES Eddie Shack 8.00 20.00
AEW Ernie Wakely 6.00 15.00
AFM Frank Mahovlich SP 50.00 100.00
AGC Gerry Cheevers 8.00 20.00
AGD Gerry Desjardins 6.00 15.00
AGE Gary Edwards 5.00 12.00
AGG Gilles Gratton 8.00 20.00
AGJ Gary Jarrett 6.00 15.00
AGL Guy Lafleur SP 40.00 80.00
AGM Gilles Meloche 8.00 20.00
AGO Gerry Odrowski 5.00 12.00
AGP Gilbert Perreault SP 8.00 20.00
AGS Gary Sabourin 6.00 15.00
AGU Garry Unger 5.00 12.00
AGV Gilles Villemure 10.00 25.00
AHH Harry Howell 6.00 15.00
AHS Harry Sinden Summit 15.00 40.00
AJB Johnny Bucyk 12.00 30.00
AJD Joe Daley 5.00 12.00
AJE Jack Egers 5.00 12.00
AJJ Joey Johnston 5.00 12.00
AJL Jacques Lemaire 10.00 25.00
AJN Jack Norris 5.00 12.00
AJS Jim Schoenfeld 5.00 12.00
AJW Joe Watson 6.00 15.00
AKB Ken Brown 6.00 15.00
AKH Ken Hodge 6.00 15.00
ALB Les Binkley 8.00 20.00
ALL Larry Lund 5.00 12.00
ALM Lowell MacDonald 5.00 12.00
ALP Larry Pleau 5.00 12.00
ALR Larry Robinson 8.00 20.00
AMA Mike Antonovich 6.00 15.00
AMC Mike Curran 6.00 15.00
AMD Marcel Dionne SP 30.00 60.00
ANF Norm Ferguson 5.00 12.00
ANL Nick Libett 6.00 15.00
ANP Noel Picard 5.00 12.00
ANU Norm Ullman 8.00 20.00
APE Phil Esposito 12.00 30.00
APH Paul Henderson 20.00 40.00
APM Phil Myre 5.00 12.00
APP Poul Popiel 6.00 15.00
APQ Pat Quinn 8.00 20.00
APS Pat Stapleton 6.00 15.00
ARB Richard Brodeur 8.00 20.00
ARE Ron Ellis SP 25.00 50.00
ARG Rod Gilbert SP 20.00 50.00
ARH Rejean Houle SP 30.00 60.00
ARK Rick Kehoe 6.00 15.00
ARL Rick Ley 5.00 12.00
ARM Rick Martin 8.00 20.00
ARP Rosaire Paiement 5.00 12.00
ARR Rene Robert 8.00 20.00
ARS Rod Seiling 6.00 15.00
ARV Rogie Vachon 20.00 40.00
ARW Ron Ward 5.00 12.00
ASA Syl Apps Jr. 8.00 20.00
ASB Serge Bernier 5.00 12.00
ASM Stan Mikita SP 25.00 50.00
ASS Serge Savard SP 15.00 40.00
ASW Stan Weir 5.00 12.00
ATE Tony Esposito SP
ATH Ted Hampson 6.00 15.00
ATO Terry O'Reilly 20.00 50.00
ATT Ted Taylor 5.00 12.00
ATW Tom Webster 5.00 12.00
AVF Val Fonteyne 6.00 15.00
AVH Vic Hadfield 6.00 15.00
AVP Vladimir Petrov 15.00 40.00
AVS Vladimir Shadrin 12.00 30.00
AVT Vladislav Tretiak 50.00 100.00
AVV Valeri Vasiliev 15.00 40.00
AWC Wayne Cashman 10.00 25.00
AWM Walt McKechnie 6.00 15.00
AWT Walt Tkaczuk 6.00 15.00
AYC Yvan Cournoyer SP
AAMC Ab McDonald 6.00 15.00
ABC2 Bobby Clarke Summit SP 40.00 80.00
ABCR Bart Crashley 5.00 12.00
ABGL Brian Glennie 10.00 25.00
ABHU Bobby Hull SP 15.00 40.00
ABMI Boris Mikhailov 25.00 50.00
ABP2 Brad Park Summit SP 25.00 50.00
ABPA Bernie Parent SP 75.00 150.00
ABSC Bob Sicinski 5.00 12.00
ABSM Billy Smith 8.00 20.00
ABW2 Bill White Summit 10.00 25.00
ACBO Christian Bordeleau 8.00 20.00
ADA2 Don Awrey Summit 8.00 20.00
ADHE Dennis Hextall 5.00 12.00
ADHU Dennis Hull 10.00 25.00
ADSA Derek Sanderson Phil.SP 15.00 40.00
ADSC Dave Schultz 8.00 20.00
ADSI Darryl Sittler SP 40.00 80.00
AEWE Ed Westfall 6.00 15.00
AFM2 Frank Mahovlich Summit SP 40.00 80.00
AGDO Gary Dornhoefer 8.00 20.00
AGLA Guy Lapointe SP 25.00 60.00
AGP2 Gilbert Perreault Summit SP 25.00 60.00
AGPI Gerry Pinder
AGVE Gary Veneruzzo 6.00 15.00
AJDO Jim Dorey 5.00 12.00
AJGG Jean-Guy Gendron 6.00 15.00
AJLO Jim Lorentz 6.00 15.00
AJMC Jim McKenny 5.00 12.00
AJPP J.P. Parise 10.00 25.00
ALMA Larry Mavety 5.00 12.00
AMD2 Marcel Dionne Summit SP 30.00 60.00
APE2 Phil Esposito Summit 20.00 50.00
APH2 Paul Henderson Summit 30.00 60.00
APMA Pete Mahovlich 25.00 50.00
APS2 Pat Stapleton Summit 12.00 30.00
ARBE Red Berenson 15.00 40.00
ARE2 Ron Ellis Summit SP 25.00 50.00
ARG2 Rod Gilbert Summit SP 15.00 40.00
ARMA Rick MacLeish 6.00 15.00
ARSM Rick Smith 6.00 15.00
ASM2 Stan Mikita Summit SP 25.00 50.00
ASS2 Serge Savard Summit SP 20.00 40.00
ASSH Steve Shutt 10.00 25.00
ATE2 Tony Esposito Summit SP 15.00 40.00
AVH2 Vic Hadfield Summit 12.00 30.00
AWC2 Wayne Cashman Summit
AWCA Wayne Carleton 5.00 12.00
AWCO Wayne Connelly 5.00 12.00
AYC2 Yvan Cournoyer Summit SP 15.00 40.00
ABGL2 Brian Glennie Summit 10.00 25.00
ADHU2 Dennis Hull Summit 10.00 25.00
ADSAN Derek Sanderson Bos.SP
AGLA2 Guy Lapointe Summit SP 25.00 60.00
AGLAB Gord Labossiere 5.00 12.00
AJMCK John McKenzie 12.00 30.00
AJMCL Jimmy McLeod 5.00 12.00
AJPP2 J.P. Parise Summit 8.00 20.00
APMA2 Pete Mahovlich Summit
ARBE2 Red Berenson Summit 15.00 40.00

2003-04 ITG VIP Rookie Debut

Cards in this 149-card set were made available for online orders after the players made their NHL debut. Collectors could order as many cards as they wanted for a period of 90 days after the debut at which time ordering was ceased. Print runs listed below were provided by BAP, the cards are not serial numbered.
1 Tuomo Ruutu/114* 4.00 10.00
2 Joffrey Lupul/101* 5.00 12.00
3 Brent Burns/71* 5.00 12.00
4 David Hale/65* 4.00 10.00
5 Paul Martin/52* 4.00 10.00
6 Patrice Bergeron/166* 8.00 20.00
7 Travis Moen/64* 5.00 12.00
8 Lasse Kukkonen/58* 4.00 10.00
9 Christoph Brandner/62* 5.00 12.00
10 Carrett Burnett/40* 4.00 10.00
11 Antti Miettinen/59* 5.00 12.00
12 Antoine Vermette/50* 4.00 10.00
13 Andrew Peters/63* 4.00 10.00
14 Joni Pitkanen/81* 5.00 12.00
15 Sean Bergenheim/54* 5.00 12.00
16 Boyd Gordon/53* 4.00 10.00
17 Dan Fritsche/54* 6.00 15.00
18 Eric Staal/165* 12.50 30.00
19 Nathan Horton/102* 6.00 15.00
20 Dustin Brown/65 6.00 15.00
21 Tim Gleason/58* 4.00 10.00
22 Esa Pirnes/54* 4.00 10.00
23 Wade Brookbank/51* 4.00 10.00
24 Dan Hamhuis/56* 5.00 12.00
25 Jordin Tootoo/156* 8.00 20.00
26 Marek Zidlicky/61* 5.00 12.00
27 Christian Ehrhoff/54* 4.00 10.00
28 Milan Michalek/58* 12.00 30.00
29 Matthew Lombardi/70* 4.00 10.00
30 John-Michael Liles/56* 4.00 10.00
31 Marek Svatos/53* 4.00 10.00
32 Marc-Andre Fleury/580* 6.00 15.00
33 Martin Strbak/66* 4.00 10.00
34 Ryan Malone/84* 8.00 20.00
35 Matt Murley/74* 4.00 10.00
36 Matthew Spiller/62* 4.00 10.00
37 Chris Higgins/67* 10.00 25.00
38 Maxim Kondratiev/62* 4.00 10.00
39 Tom Preissing/58* 4.00 10.00
40 Cody McCormick/37* 4.00 10.00
41 Pavel Vorobiev/30* 4.00 10.00
42 Alexander Semin/47* 10.00 25.00
43 Brent Krahn/32* 4.00 10.00
44 Jiri Hudler/122* 5.00 12.00
45 Boyd Kane/38* 4.00 10.00
46 Gregory Campbell/36* 4.00 10.00
47 Andrew Hutchinson/36* 4.00 10.00
48 Mike Stuart/24* 4.00 10.00
49 Sergei Zinovjev/45* 4.00 10.00
50 Trevor Daley/34* 4.00 10.00
51 Julien Vauclair/32* 4.00 10.00
52 Alan Rourke/33* 4.00 10.00
53 Tony Salmelainen/34* 4.00 10.00
54 John Pohl/36* 4.00 10.00
55 Dominic Moore/42* 4.00 10.00
56 Peter Sarno/34* 4.00 10.00
57 Rastislav Stana/66* 4.00 10.00
58 Karl Stewart/58* 4.00 10.00
59 Darryl Bootland/43* 4.00 10.00
60 Pat Rissmiller/35* 4.00 10.00
61 Jed Ortmeyer/42* 4.00 10.00
62 Nathan Smith/31* 4.00 10.00
63 Grant McNeill/31* 4.00 10.00
64 Seamus Kotyk/39* 4.00 10.00
65 Phil Osaer/35* 4.00 10.00
66 Ryan Kesler/62* 4.00 10.00
67 Libor Pivko/39* 4.00 10.00
68 Mikhail Yakubov/33* 4.00 10.00
69 Nathan Robinson/35* 4.00 10.00
70 Fredrik Sjostrom/37* 4.00 10.00
71 Tony Martensson/43* 4.00 10.00
72 Aaron Johnson/48* 4.00 10.00
73 Jeff Hamilton/47* 4.00 10.00
74 Nikolai Zherdev/255* 15.00 40.00
75 Gavin Morgan/53* 4.00 10.00
76 Patrick Leahy/50* 4.00 10.00
77 Jeff MacMillan/47* 4.00 10.00
78 Antero Niittymaki/90* 8.00 20.00
79 Niklas Kronwall/77* 12.50 30.00
80 Joey MacDonald/56* 4.00 10.00
81 Doug Doull/59* 12.50 30.00
82 Dwayne Zinger/50* 4.00 10.00
83 Jason MacDonald/47* 4.00 10.00
84 Rob Skrlac/39* 4.00 10.00
85 Derek Roy/88* 12.50 30.00
86 Ryan Barnes/39* 4.00 10.00
87 Noah Clarke/48* 12.50 30.00
88 Steve McLaren/54* 4.00 10.00
89 Tim Jackman/32* 6.00 15.00
90 Timofei Shishkanov/39* 8.00 20.00
91 Jason Pominville/40* 4.00 10.00
92 Mikko Luoma/36* 4.00 10.00
93 Jeremy Yablonski/39* 4.00 10.00
94 Tomas Plekanec/37* 10.00 25.00
95 Tuomas Pihlman/36* 4.00 10.00
96 Darcy Verot/55* 4.00 10.00
97 Mark Popovic/38* 4.00 10.00
98 Doug Lynch/36* 4.00 10.00
99 Aleksander Suglobov/31* 4.00 10.00
100 Nolan Schaefer/35* 4.00 10.00
101 Colton Orr/54* 4.00 10.00
102 Mike Smith/64* 5.00 12.00
103 Anton Babchuk/37* 4.00 10.00
104 Kyle Wellwood/41* 4.00 10.00
105 Jame Pollock/36* 4.00 10.00
106 Carl Corazzini/49* 4.00 10.00
107 Zbynek Michalek/31* 4.00 10.00
108 Chris Kunitz/27* 4.00 10.00
109 Lawrence Nycholat/37* 6.00 15.00
110 Jozef Balej/56* 8.00 20.00
111 Mike Bishai/33* 4.00 10.00
112 Garth Murray/39* 4.00 10.00
113 Matt Ellison/29* 4.00 10.00
114 Joe Motzko/36* 4.00 10.00
115 Graham Mink/54* 4.00 10.00
116 Brooks Laich/46* 4.00 10.00
117 Mike Green/27* 4.00 10.00
118 Dan Ellis/37* 4.00 10.00
119 Robert Scuderi/37* 4.00 10.00
120 Fedor Tyutin/50* 4.00 10.00
121 Michael Morrison/37* 4.00 10.00
122 Cory Larose/38* 4.00 10.00
123 Andy Chiodo/62* 4.00 10.00
124 Adam Munro/43* 4.00 10.00
125 Mikhail Kuleshov/76* 4.00 10.00
126 Matt Keith/31* 4.00 10.00
127 Denis Grebeshkov/32* 4.00 10.00
128 Quintin Laing/16* 4.00 10.00
129 Benoit Dusablon/23* 4.00 10.00
130 Matt Underhill/27* 4.00 10.00
131 Fred Meyer/20* 4.00 10.00
132 Randy Jones/23* 4.00 10.00
133 Brad Boyes/67* 12.50 30.00
134 Erik Westrum/16* 4.00 10.00
135 Bryce Lampman/23* 4.00 10.00
136 Goran Bezina/32* 4.00 10.00
137 Owen Fussey/48* 4.00 10.00
138 Josh Olson/14* 4.00 10.00
139 Michal Barinka/21* 4.00 10.00
140 Kari Lehtonen/526* 15.00 40.00
141 Matt Hussey/28* 4.00 10.00
142 Mike Stutzel/18* 4.00 10.00
143 Roman Tvrdon/34* 4.00 10.00
144 Matthew Yeats/50* 4.00 10.00
145 Thomas Pock/40* 4.00 10.00
146 Wade Dubielewicz/59* 4.00 10.00
147 Greg Mauldin/34* 4.00 10.00
148 Mike Pandolfo/32* 4.00 10.00
149 Eric Perrin/48* 4.00 10.00

2009-10 ITG 1972 The Year In Hockey

COMPLETE SET (200) 20.00 50.00
1 Phil Esposito .60 1.50
2 Johnny Bucyk .60 1.50
3 Ken Hodge .30 .75
4 Wayne Cashman .25 .60
5 Terry O'Reilly .30 .75
6 Don Awrey .40 1.00
7 Dallas Smith .50 1.25
8 Jacques Plante .60 1.50
9 Eddie Johnston .60 1.50
10 Jacques Lemaire .40 1.00
11 Frank Mahovlich .50 1.25
12 Yvan Cournoyer .40 1.00
13 Guy Lafleur .50 1.25
14 Guy Lapointe .30 .75
15 Rejean Houle .25 .60
16 Serge Savard .50 1.25
17 Larry Robinson .40 1.00
18 Michel Plasse .25 .60
19 Steve Shutt .40 1.00
20 Darryl Sittler .50 1.25
21 Rick Kehoe .30 .75
22 Dave Keon .40 1.00
23 Norm Ullman .40 1.00
24 Ron Ellis .25 .60
25 Paul Henderson .50 1.25
26 Brian Glennie .40 1.00
27 Gerry Desjardins .30 .75
28 Ed Westfall .30 .75
29 Bob Nystrom .25 .60
30 Billy Smith .40 1.00
31 Gilles Villemure .50 1.25
32 Rod Gilbert .50 1.25
33 Walt Tkaczuk .30 .75
34 Vic Hadfield .30 .75
35 Brad Park .30 .75
36 Rod Seiling .30 .75
37 Ed Giacomin .50 1.25
38 Red Berenson .75 2.00
39 Marcel Dionne .50 1.25
40 Alex Delvecchio .50 1.25
41 Nick Libett .30 .75
42 Roy Edwards .25 .60
43 Rene Robert .40 1.00
44 Gilbert Perreault .40 1.00
45 Rick Martin .40 1.00
46 Jim Lorentz .30 .75
47 Tim Horton .40 1.00
48 Roger Crozier .25 .60
49 Jim Schoenfeld .25 .60
50 Bobby Schmautz .25 .60
51 Andre Boudrias .30 .75
52 Don Lever .60 1.50
53 Dunc Wilson .40 1.00
54 Doug Jarrett .25 .60
55 Bill White .25 .60
56 Dennis Hull .50 1.25
57 Pit Martin .25 .60
58 Stan Mikita .50 1.25
59 Pat Stapleton .30 .75
60 Tony Esposito .40 1.00
61 Keith Magnuson .25 .60
62 Garry Unger .25 .60
63 Jack Egers .25 .60
64 Noel Picard .25 .60
65 Gary Sabourin .30 .75
66 Phil Myre .25 .60
67 Dan Bouchard .30 .75
68 Pat Quinn .40 1.00
69 Bob Leiter .25 .60
70 Curt Bennett .25 .60
71 Bobby Clarke .40 1.00
72 Rick MacLeish .30 .75
73 Gary Dornhoefer .40 1.00
74 Bill Flett .25 .60
75 Bill Barber .30 .75
76 Joe Watson .30 .75
77 Dave Schultz .40 1.00
78 Doug Favell .40 1.00
79 Serge Bernier .25 .60
80 Rogie Vachon .50 1.25
81 Gary Edwards .25 .60
82 Butch Goring .40 1.00
83 Harry Howell .30 .75
84 Bill Goldsworthy .25 .60
85 Dennis Hextall .25 .60
86 J.P. Parise .40 1.00
87 Gump Worsley .60 1.50
88 Danny Grant .50 1.25
89 Cesare Maniago .30 .75
90 Eddie Shack .40 1.00
91 Brian Hextall .30 .75
92 Syl Apps Jr. .40 1.00
93 Lowell MacDonald .25 .60
94 Al McDonough .25 .60
95 Denis Herron .30 .75
96 Walt McKechnie .30 .75
97 Stan Weir .25 .60
98 Joey Johnston .25 .60
99 Gilles Meloche .40 1.00
100 Checklist .25 .60
101 Rick Smith .30 .75
102 Wayne Rutledge .30 .75
103 Poul Popiel .30 .75
104 Larry Lund .25 .60
105 Ted Taylor .25 .60
106 Gord Labossiere .25 .60
107 Andre Lacroix .30 .75
108 Bernie Parent .40 1.00
109 Derek Sanderson .30 .75
110 John McKenzie .60 1.50
111 Rosaire Paiement .25 .60
112 Bob Sicinski .25 .60
113 Jim McLeod .25 .60
114 Larry Mavety .25 .60
115 Gary Jarrett .30 .75
116 Gerry Pinder .25 .60
117 Gerry Cheevers .40 1.00
118 Paul Shmyr .25 .60
119 Wayne Connelly .25 .60
120 Ted Hampson .30 .75
121 Mike Antonovich .30 .75
122 Mike Curran .30 .75
123 Bob MacMillan .25 .60
124 Bobby Hull .50 1.25
125 Joe Daley .25 .60
126 Ernie Wakely .30 .75
127 Chris Bordeleau .40 1.00
128 Ab McDonald .30 .75
129 Wayne Carleton .25 .60
130 Gilles Gratton .40 1.00
131 Les Binkley .40 1.00
132 J.C .Tremblay .25 .60
133 Richard Brodeur .40 1.00
134 Jean-Guy Gendron .30 .75
135 Ken Brown .25 .60
136 Val Fonteyne .30 .75
137 Al Hamilton .25 .60
138 Jack Norris .25 .60
139 Bill Hicke .25 .60
140 Ron Ward .25 .60
141 Norm Ferguson .25 .60
142 Kent Douglas .25 .60
143 Alton White .25 .60
144 Gary Veneruzzo .30 .75
145 Bart Crashley .25 .60
146 Gerry Odrowski .25 .60
147 Tom Webster .25 .60
148 Larry Pleau .25 .60
149 Jim Dorey .25 .60
150 Al Smith .25 .60
151 Rick Ley .25 .60
152 Don Awrey .40 1.00
153 Red Berenson .75 2.00
154 Gary Bergman .25 .60
155 Wayne Cashman .25 .60
156 Bobby Clarke .40 1.00
157 Yvan Cournoyer .40 1.00
158 Ron Ellis .25 .60
159 Phil Esposito .60 1.50
160 Tony Esposito .40 1.00
161 Rod Gilbert .50 1.25
162 Vic Hadfield .30 .75
163 Paul Henderson .50 1.25
164 Dennis Hull .50 1.25
165 Valeri Kharlamov .25 .60
166 Guy Lapointe .30 .75
167 Frank Mahovlich .50 1.25
168 Pete Mahovlich .50 1.25
169 Alexander Maltsev .25 .60
170 Bill Goldsworthy .25 .60
171 Boris Mikhailov .75 2.00
172 Stan Mikita .50 1.25
173 J.P. Parise .40 1.00
174 Brad Park .30 .75
175 Gilbert Perreault .40 1.00
176 Vladimir Petrov .75 2.00
177 Alexander Ragulin .25 .60
178 Eddie Johnston .60 1.50
179 Serge Savard .50 1.25
180 Rod Seiling .30 .75
181 Pat Stapleton .30 .75
182 Dale Tallon .40 1.00
183 Vladislav Tretiak .40 1.00
184 Valeri Vasiliev .60 1.50
185 Vladimir Shadrin .60 1.50
186 Bill White .25 .60
187 Alexander Yakushev .75 2.00
188 Harry Sinden .25 .60
189 Vsevolod Bobrov .25 .60
190 V.Kharlamov/B.Clarke .40 1.00
191 T.Esposito/V.Tretiak .40 1.00
192 P.Henderson/V.Tretiak .50 1.25
193 B.Mikhailov/P.Esposito .75 2.00
194 V.Petrov/T.Esposito .75 2.00
195 G.Bergman/A.Yakushev .75 2.00
196 B.White/B.Mikhailov .75 2.00
197 P.Henderson/Yakushev .75 2.00
198 Paul Henderson .50 1.25
199 Vladislav Tretiak .40 1.00
200 Checklist .25 .60

2009-10 ITG 1972 The Year In Hockey Coaches

COMPLETE SET (10) 10.00 25.00
C01 Scotty Bowman 1.50 4.00
C02 Tom Johnson 1.25 3.00
C03 Emile Francis 1.00 2.50
C04 Phil Goyette 1.00 2.50
C05 Billy Reay 1.00 2.50
C06 Fred Shero 1.00 2.50
C07 Al Arbour 1.25 3.00
C08 Bob Pulford 1.25 3.00
C09 Red Kelly 1.50 4.00
C10 Bernie Geoffrion 1.00 2.50

2009-10 ITG 1972 The Year In Hockey Forever Linked

FL01 Paul Henderson/Vladislav Tretiak 3.00 8.00
FL02 Bobby Hull/Gerry Cheevers 3.00 8.00
FL03 Bobby Clarke/Valeri Kharlamov 2.50 6.00
FL04 Jean Beliveau/Guy Lafleur 3.00 8.00

2009-10 ITG 1972 The Year In Hockey Game Used Jersey Black

ANNOUNCED PRINT RUN 70-90
SILVER/30: .5X TO 1.2X BASIC JSY
M01 Bill Barber 4.00 10.00
M02 Johnny Bucyk 8.00 20.00
M03 Alexander Yakushev 10.00 25.00
M04 Bobby Clarke 5.00 12.00
M05 Yvan Cournoyer 5.00 12.00
M06 Alex Delvecchio 6.00 15.00
M07 Marcel Dionne 6.00 15.00
M08 Gary Dornhoefer 5.00 12.00
M09 Phil Esposito 8.00 20.00
M10 Tony Esposito 5.00 12.00
M11 Ed Giacomin 6.00 15.00
M12 Rod Gilbert 6.00 15.00
M13 Vladislav Tretiak 5.00 12.00
M14 Pete Mahovlich 6.00 15.00
M15 Rejean Houle 3.00 8.00
M16 Bobby Hull 6.00 15.00
M17 Dennis Hull 6.00 15.00
M18 Boris Mikhailov 10.00 25.00
M19 Dave Keon 5.00 12.00
M20 Guy Lafleur 6.00 15.00
M21 Guy Lapointe 4.00 10.00
M22 Jacques Lemaire 5.00 12.00
M23 Rick MacLeish 4.00 10.00
M24 Henri Richard 12.00 30.00
M25 Rick Martin 5.00 12.00
M26 Stan Mikita 6.00 15.00
M27 Bob Nystrom 3.00 8.00
M28 Terry O'Reilly 4.00 10.00
M29 Brad Park 4.00 10.00
M30 Gilbert Perreault 6.00 15.00
M31 Vic Hadfield 4.00 10.00
M32 Valeri Kharlamov 3.00 8.00
M33 Larry Robinson 5.00 12.00
M34 Phil Myre 3.00 8.00
M35 Serge Savard 6.00 15.00
M36 Dave Schultz 5.00 12.00
M37 Steve Shutt 5.00 12.00
M38 Darryl Sittler 6.00 15.00
M39 Billy Smith 5.00 12.00
M40 Pat Stapleton 4.00 10.00
M41 Walt Tkaczuk 4.00 10.00
M42 Garry Unger 3.00 8.00
M43 Rogie Vachon 6.00 15.00
M44 Joe Watson 4.00 10.00
M45 Bill White 3.00 8.00

2009-10 ITG 1972 The Year In Hockey Great Moments

COMPLETE SET (8) 10.00 25.00
COMMON CARD .75 2.00
SEMISTARS 1.00 2.50
UNLISTED STARS 1.25 3.00
GM01 Gerry Cheevers 1.25 3.00
GM02 Johnny Bucyk 2.00 5.00
GM03 Bobby Hull 1.50 4.00
GM04 Vladislav Tretiak 1.25 3.00
GM05 Phil Esposito 2.00 5.00
GM06 Paul Henderson 1.50 4.00
GM07 Billy Smith 1.25 3.00
GM08 Les Binkley 1.25 3.00

2009-10 ITG 1972 The Year In Hockey Masked Men

COMPLETE SET (10) 15.00 40.00
MM01 Doug Favell 2.50 6.00
MM02 Gerry Cheevers 2.50 6.00
MM03 Rogie Vachon 3.00 8.00
MM04 Ed Giacomin 3.00 8.00
MM05 Gilles Villemure 3.00 8.00
MM06 Tony Esposito 2.50 6.00
MM07 Jacques Plante 4.00 10.00
MM08 Cesare Maniago 2.00 5.00
MM09 Bernie Parent 2.50 6.00
MM10 Ken Brown 1.50 4.00

2009-10 ITG 1972 The Year In Hockey Past and Present

PP01 Guy Lafleur/Carey Price 20.00 50.00
PP02 T.Esposito/Martin Brodeur 10.00 25.00
PP03 M.Dionne/Pavel Datsyuk 6.00 15.00
PP04 Bobby Clarke/Daniel Briere 5.00 12.00
PP05 Delvecchio/N.Lidstrom 6.00 15.00
PP06 Goldsworthy/Mike Modano 8.00 20.00
PP07 D.Wilson/Roberto Luongo 6.00 15.00
PP08 J.Plante/Vesa Toskala 8.00 20.00
PP09 G.Cheevers/Tim Thomas 5.00 12.00
PP10 Ed Westfall/John Tavares 15.00 40.00

2009-10 ITG 1972 The Year In Hockey Rookies

COMPLETE SET (8) 8.00 20.00
R01 Dan Bouchard/Jim Schoenfeld 1.00 2.50
R02 Denis Herron/Billy Smith 1.25 3.00
R03 Bill Barber/Dave Schultz 1.25 3.00
R04 Steve Shutt/Terry O'Reilly 1.25 3.00
R05 Bob Nystrom/Richard Brodeur 1.25 3.00
R06 Larry Robinson/Gilles Gratton 1.25 3.00
R07 Bob MacMillan/Bob Sicinski .75 2.00
R08 Don Lever/Mike Antonovich 2.00 5.00

1979-80 Islanders Transparencies

These standard postcard size cards featured black and white posed photos on a thin, transparent paper stock. Cards were unnumbered and checklisted below alphabetically.
COMPLETE SET (22) 20.00 40.00
1 Mike Bossy 7.50 15.00
2 Bob Bourne .38 .75
3 Clark Gillies .38 .75
4 Billy Harris .38 .75
5 Lerne Henning .38 .75
6 Anders Kallur .38 .75
7 Mike Kaszycki .38 .75
8 Dave Langevin .38 .75
9 Dave Lewis .38 .75
10 Bob Lorimer .38 .75
11 Wayne Merrick .38 .75
12 Bob Nystrom 1.00 2.00
13 Stefan Persson .38 .75
14 Denis Potvin 1.00 2.00
15 Jean Potvin .38 .75
16 Garry Howatt .38 .75
17 Glenn Resch 2.50 5.00
18 Bill Smith 2.50 5.00
19 Steven Tambellini .38 .75
20 John Tonelli .75 1.50
21 Bryan Trottier 2.00 4.00
22 Header Card .30 .60

1983-84 Islanders Team Issue

This 19-card set measured approximately 4" by 5 1/2" and featured the 1983-84 New York Islanders. The cards were printed on thin paper stock. The fronts had black-and-white action player photos with white borders. The player's name and the team logo appeared below the photo. The cards were unnumbered and checklisted below in alphabetical order. The set featured an early card of Kelly Hrudey pre-dating his O-Pee-Chee and Topps Rookie Cards by two years.
COMPLETE SET (19) 12.00 30.00
1 Mike Bossy 2.00 5.00
2 Bob Bourne .40 1.00
3 Billy Carroll .40 1.00
4 Clark Gillies .75 2.00
5 Mats Hallin .40 1.00
6 Kelly Hrudey 1.50 4.00
7 Tomas Jonsson .40 1.00
8 Dave Langevin .40 1.00
9 Roland Melanson .60 1.50
10 Wayne Merrick .40 1.00
11 Ken Morrow .60 1.50
12 Bob Nystrom .60 1.50
13 Denis Potvin 1.50 4.00
14 Billy Smith 1.50 4.00
15 Brent Sutter .75 2.00
16 Duane Sutter .60 1.50
17 John Tonelli .75 2.00
18 Bryan Trottier 1.50 4.00
19 Team Photo .75 2.00

1984 Islanders News

This 38-card standard-size set of New York Islanders was sponsored by Islander News and issued during the summer of 1984 to commemorate the Islanders' fourth consecutive Stanley Cup victory. The color photo on the front was framed by a thin black border. Another thin black border (with rounded corners) outlined the card front, and the space in between was pale blue. The player's name was given below the picture and sandwiched between a trophy cup icon and the New York Islanders' logo. The back had biographical information and a career summary on the player.
COMPLETE SET (38) 10.00 25.0
1 Checklist Card .20 .5
2 Mike Bossy 1.50 4.0
3 Bob Bourne .20 .5
4 Billy Carroll .20 .5
5 Greg Gilbert .20 .5
6 Clark Gillies .50 1.2
7 Butch Goring .40 1.0
8 Mats Hallin .20 .5
9 Anders Kallur .20 .5
10 Wayne Merrick .20 .5
11 Bob Nystrom .30 .7
12 Brent Sutter .50 1.2
13 Duane Sutter .40 1.0
14 John Tonelli .50 1.2
15 Bryan Trottier 1.25 3.0
16 Tomas Jonsson .20 .5
17 Gordie Lane .20 .5
18 Dave Langevin .20 .5
19 Ken Morrow .40 1.0
20 Stefan Persson .20 .5
21 Denis Potvin 1.00 2.5
22 Roland Melanson .30 .7
23 Dilly Smith .75 2.0
24 Cup Number 1 .20 .5
25 Cup Number 2 .20 .5
26 Cup Number 4 .20 .5
27 Lorne Henning CO .20 .5
28 Bill Torrey GM .20 .5
29 Al Arbour CO .40 1.0
30 Waske-Pickard .08 .2
Two Trainers
31 1979-80 Team Photo .40 1.0
32 1980-81 Team Photo .40 1.0
33 1981-82 Team Photo .40 1.0
34 1982-83 Team Photo .40 1.0
35 Mike Bossy .75 2.0
'82 Conn Smythe Winner
36 Billy Smith .50 1.2
'83 Conn Smythe Winner
37 Bryan Trottier .60 1.5
'80 Conn Smythe Winner
38 Butch Goring .30 .7
'81 Conn Smythe Winner

1985 Islanders News

This 37-card standard-size set of New York Islanders was sponsored by Islander News and issued during t summer of 1985. The color photo on the front was enframed by a thin black border. A red and blue hock stick formed the border on the left side of the picture, with the end of the stick below the picture. The words "Islander News" appeared on the end of the stick, and the player's name was given to the right. The back ha biographical information including a career summary on the player as well as the notation "Second Series". The key card in the set was the Pat LaFontaine card as it was issued concurrently with his O-Pee-Chee and Topps Rookie Cards.
COMPLETE SET (37) 12.00 30.0
1 Checklist Card .20 .5
2 Mike Bossy 1.50 4.0
3 Bob Bourne .20 .5
4 Pat Flatley .30 .7
5 Greg Gilbert .20 .5
6 Clark Gillies .40 1.0
7 Mats Hallin .20 .5
8 Anders Kallur .20 .5
9 Alan Kerr .20 .5
10 Roger Kortko .20 .5
11 Pat LaFontaine 3.00 8.0
12 Bob Nystrom .30 .7
13 Brent Sutter .40 1.0
14 Duane Sutter .30 .7
15 John Tonelli .40 1.0
16 Bryan Trottier 1.25 3.0
17 Paul Boutilier .20 .5
18 Gerald Diduck .20 .5
19 Gord Dineen .20 .5
20 Tomas Jonsson .30 .7
21 Gordie Lane .20 .5
22 Dave Langevin .20 .5
23 Ken Morrow .30 .7
24 Stefan Persson .20 .5
25 Denis Potvin 1.00 2.5
26 Kelly Hrudey 1.25 3.0
27 Billy Smith .75 2.0
28 Bill Torrey GM/P .30 .7
29 Al Arbour CO .40 1.0
30 Brian Kilrea CO .08 .2
31 Pickard .08 .2
Smith
Two Trainers
32 Mike Bossy .75 2.0
Milestone-400 Goals
33 Denis Potvin .60 1.5
Milestone-600 Assists
34 Billy Smith .40 1.0
Milestone-500 Games
35 Bryan Trottier .60 1.5
Milestone-1000 Points
36 1984-85 Team .40 1.0
37 Wales Champs .30 .7

1985 Islanders News Trottier

This 33-card standard-size set was sponsored by the New York Islander News and issued during the summer of 1985 supposedly by the Port Washington Police Department. It highlighted the early career of then-Islander, Bryan Trottier, who is credited with writing the drug and alcohol prevention tips on the back of the cards. The cards featured color or black an white photos of Trottier on the front. They were frame by a red border on two sides, and white border; the white border is in the shape of a hockey stick, with Trottier's signature across the bottom of the stick. The cards were numbered on both sides. In addition to th anti-drug or alcohol message, the back also had Trottier's own comments about each photo.
COMPLETE SET (33) 10.00 25.0
1 Penalty box .40 1.0
2 Swift Current Broncos .40 1.0
3 Three goals in first .20 .5
game at Nassau Coliseum
4 All-Star game .30 .7
5 Four goals vs. Atlanta .20 .5
6 Ross and Hart Trophies .30 .7
7 Street hockey equipment .20 .5
8 Bearing down on the .30 .7
draw against Maruk
9 Pleading with referee .20 .5
10 Trottier .20 .5
Rangers action
11 Trottier .30 .7
Holmgren action
12 Trottier .30 .7
Canadiens action
13 1980 Boston playoff .30 .7
14 1980 Final Game .30 .7

vs. Flyers
NHL Awards Luncheon .20 .50
Trottier .30 .75
Rangers action
Watching action in .20 .50
resting area
Warm-up time .20 .50
Debating with referee .20 .50
1981 Playoff with Oilers .30 .75
Trottier 4.00 10.00
Gretzky action
Trottier .30 .75
North Stars
action
Congratulating Don .30 .75
Beaupre
Second Stanley Cup .20 .50
Championship
Trottier .30 .75
Sutter celebrate
Trottier psyching himself .20 .50
Trottier .30 .75
Devils action
1983 All-Star .30 .75
Bryan Trottier 3.00 8.00
Wayne Gretzky
Fourth Stanley Cup .20 .50
Championship
Bryan Trottier .60 1.50
Denis Potvin
Bryan Trottier .75 2.00
Mike Bossy
1984 Canada Cup Series .40 1.00

1986-87 Islanders Team Issue

is 30-card set was issued by the team and used at omotional events.

OMPLETE SET (30) 10.00 25.00
Alan Kerr .20 .50
Ari Haanpaa .20 .50
Bill Smith 1.25 3.00
Bob Nystrom .30 .75
Bob Bassen .20 .50
Brad Lauer .20 .50
Brent Sutter .60 1.50
Brian Curran .20 .50
Bryan Trottier .60 1.50
Trainers .08 .25
Dale Henry .20 .50
Denis Potvin 1.25 3.00
Duane Sutter .30 .75
Gerald Diduck .20 .50
Gord Dineen .20 .50
Greg Gilbert .20 .50
Islander Emblem .02 .10
Kelly Hrudey .75 2.00
Ken Leiter .20 .50
Ken Morrow .30 .75
Mike Bossy 1.25 3.00
Mikko Makela .20 .50
Pat Lafontaine .75 2.00
Patrick Flatley .20 .50
Randy Boyd .20 .50
Richard Kromm .20 .50
Roger Kortko .20 .50
Steve Konroyd .20 .50
Terry Simpson CO .08 .25
Tomas Jonsson .20 .50

1989-90 Islanders Team Issue

is 22-card set measured approximately 3 7/8" by 7 ". The fronts featured autographed color action otos. The player's name, jersey number, position, m logo and team name were printed in the wider ttom border. The cards were unnumbered and ecklisted below in alphabetical order.

MPLETE SET (22) 4.80 12.00
Al Arbour CO .30 .75
Dean Chynoweth .20 .50
Dave Chyzowski .20 .50
Doug Crossman .20 .50
Gerald Diduck .20 .50
Tom Fitzgerald .20 .50
Mark Fitzpatrick .60 1.50
Patrick Flatley .30 .75
Glenn Healy .40 1.00
Alan Kerr .20 .50
Pat LaFontaine 1.00 2.50
Mikko Makela .20 .50
Don Maloney .20 .50
Jeff Norton .20 .50
Gary Nylund .20 .50
Rich Pilon .20 .50
Brent Sutter .30 .75
Gilles Thibaudeau .20 .50
Bryan Trottier .75 2.00
David Volek .20 .50
Mick Vukota .20 .50
Randy Wood .20 .50

1993-94 Islanders Chemical Bank Alumni

is ten-card set was issued as a promotional eaway to honor prestigious members of the anders alumni on January 28, 1994. The cards were ndard size and featured color action photos rounded by an orange border. The logos of emical Bank and the Isles adorned the corners, and player name appeared along the bottom. The two-or backs included career highlights. As the cards e unnumbered, they are listed in alphabetical order.

MPLETE SET (10) 3.00 8.00
Title Card .08 .25
Mike Bossy .75 2.00
Clark Gillies .30 .75
Gerry Hart .20 .50
Wayne Merrick .20 .50
Bob Nystrom .30 .75
Denis Potvin .60 1.50
Bill Smith .60 1.50
John Tonelli .30 .75
Eddie Westfall .20 .50

1996-97 Islander Postcards

is 23-postcard set was produced by the Islanders for omotional giveaways and autograph signings. They tured black and white action photos on the front, h a white border along the bottom containing the yer's name and the club's special 25th anniversary o. The backs were blank and unnumbered, hence alphabetical listing below.

MPLETE SET (23) 6.00 15.00
Niclas Andersson .20 .50
Derek Armstrong .20 .50
Todd Bertuzzi .30 .75
Eric Fichaud .75 2.00
Travis Green .30 .75
Doug Houda .20 .50
Brent Hughes .20 .50
Kenny Jonsson .30 .75
Derek King .30 .75

10 Paul Kruse .20 .50
11 Claude Lapointe .20 .50
12 Scott Lachance .20 .50
13 Bryan McCabe .20 .50
14 Marty McInnis .20 .50
15 Mike Milbury .20 .50
16 Zigmund Palffy 1.25 3.00
17 Dan Plante .20 .50
18 Rich Pilon .20 .50
19 Tommy Salo .60 1.50
20 Bryan Smolinski .30 .75
21 Dennis Vaske .20 .50
22 Mick Vukota .20 .50
23 Randy Wood .20 .50

1998-99 Islanders Power Play

Cards were distributed in a sealed pack and were made available through give-aways at various arenas, in conjunction with Power Play magazine. Each packet contained 4-cards, similar in design to the base set from each manufacturer, but featured a different card number on the back.

COMPLETE SET (4) 2.50 6.00
NYI1 Trevor Linden .75 2.00
NYI2 Bryan Smolinski .40 1.00
NYI3 Mike Watt .20 .50
NYI4 Zigmund Palffy 2.00 5.00

1935 J.A. Pattreiouex Sporting Events and Stars

31 Ice Hockey
Ice Skating
89 G.A. Johnson
Ice Hockey

1993-94 Jell-O Punch Outs

COMPLETE SET (8) 3.00 8.00
1 Pavel Bure .50 1.25
Kirk McLean
2 Doug Gilmour .50 1.25
Felix Potvin
3 Wayne Gretzky .75 2.00
Kelly Hrudey
4 Mario Lemieux .60 1.50
Tom Barrasso
5 Eric Lindros .50 1.25
Dominic Roussel
6 Kirk Muller .60 1.50
Patrick Roy
7 Joe Nieuwendyk .40 1.00
Mike Vernon
8 Joe Sakic .40 1.00
Stephane Fiset
AD Mario Lemieux Ad Display 4.00 10.00

1997-98 Jell-O Pinnacle Juniors To Pros

This 12-card set featured two photos of each superstar player: one from his participation in the World Junior Championships, and the other with his NHL team. The cards were found on the back of specially marked boxes of Jell-O Pudding in Canada.

COMPLETE SET (12)
1 Wayne Gretzky 2.00 5.00
2 Paul Kariya 1.00 2.50
3 Eric Lindros .40 1.00
4 Mark Messier .40 1.00
5 Patrick Roy 1.50 4.00
6 Joe Sakic .75 2.00
7 Chris Chelios .40 1.00
8 Sergei Fedorov .75 2.00
9 Jaromir Jagr .75 2.00
10 Saku Koivu .40 1.00
11 Zigmund Palffy .40 1.00
12 Mats Sundin .40 1.00

1998 Jell-O Spoons

Available one per pack in select boxes of Jell-O Pudding mix. These small stickers featured a head shot of the selected player.

COMPLETE SET (8) 6.00 15.00
1 Rod Brind'Amour .25 .60
2 Theo Fleury .30 .75
3 Wayne Gretzky 1.50 4.00
4 Curtis Joseph .30 .75
5 Paul Kariya 1.00 2.50
6 Eric Lindros .75 2.00
7 Patrick Roy 1.25 3.00
8 Joe Sakic .60 1.50

1999-00 Jell-O Goalie Collection

1 Ron Tugnutt
2 Martin Brodeur
3 Curtis Joseph
4 Dominik Hasek
5 Patrick Roy
6 Byron Dafoe

1999-00 Jell-O Partners of Power

This 12-card set was issued by Kraft to promote their Jell-O Stanley Cup 2000 sweepstakes. Cards 1-6 were available in Jell-O pudding snacks, cards 7-12 were available in Jell-O powder. Each card featured color photos of the goalie and captain of that team and opened up to reveal individual stats and contest rules.

COMPLETE SET (6) 6.00 15.00
1 S.Stevens .75 2.00
M.Brodeur
2 J.Jagr .40 1.00
T.Barrasso
3 E.Lindros .60 1.50
J.Vanbiesbrouck
4 M.Peca .40 1.00
D.Hasek
5 R.Bourque .75 2.00
B.Dafoe
6 M.Sundin .40 1.00
C.Joseph
7 D.Hatcher .30 .75
E.Belfour
8 D.Weight .20 .50
T.Salo
9 J.Sakic 2.00 5.00
P.Roy
10 S.Yzerman 1.25 3.00
C.Osgood
11 P.Kariya .75 2.00
G.Hebert
12 O.Nolan .20 .50
M.Vernon

1999-00 Jell-O Pudding Super Skills

These oversized issues came in packs of Jell-O Pudding Snacks. The cards featured an action photo on the front, along with a set checklist. The card back offered instructions on how to use the pudding paddles, which were found "inside" this card.

COMPLETE SET (6) 1.50 4.00
1 Peter Bondra .30 .75
2 Ray Bourque .60 1.50
3 John LeClair .40 1.00
4 Al MacInnis .30 .75
5 Mike Modano .40 1.00
6 Jeremy Roenick .30 .75

2000-01 Jell-O NHL Tattoos

Issued in sets of two per pack of Jell-O Pudding 4 Pack Snacks, this set included one sticker of each team in the NHL and two stickers of the NHL logo. This issue was exclusive to Canada.

COMPLETE SET (32) 8.00 20.00
COMMON DUAL TEAM (1-30) .80 2.00
COMMON NHL LOGO (31-32) .20 .50

1978-79 Jets Postcards

This 23-postcard set measured approximately 3 1/2" by 5 1/2". The fronts featured posed-on-ice borderless color player photos with a facsimile player autograph near the bottom. The backs had a postcard format and carried the player's name and a brief biography. The postcards were unnumbered and checklisted below in alphabetical order.

COMPLETE SET (23) 12.50 25.00
1 Mike Amodeo .38 .75
2 Scott Campbell .38 .75
3 Kim Clackson .50 1.00
4 Joe Daley 1.00 2.00
5 John Gray .38 .75
6 Ted Green 1.00 2.00
7 Robert Guindon .38 .75
8 Glenn Hicks .38 .75
9 Larry Hillman .38 .75
10 Bill Lesuk .50 1.00
11 Willy Lindstrom .75 1.50
12 Barry Long .38 .75
13 Morris Lukowich .75 1.50
14 Paul MacKinnon .38 .75
15 Markus Mattsson .75 1.50
16 Lyle Moffat .38 .75
17 Kent Nilsson 2.50 5.00
18 Rich Preston .50 1.00
19 Terry Ruskowski 1.25 2.50
20 Lars-Erik Sjoberg 1.25 2.50
21 Peter Sullivan .38 .75
22 Paul Terbenche .38 .75
23 Steve West .38 .75

1979-80 Jets Postcards

These 28 postcards measured approximately 3 1/2" by 5 1/2" and featured posed-on-ice color player photos on their borderless fronts. A facsimile player autograph rested near the bottom. The backs had a postcard format and carried the player's name and brief biography. The postcards were unnumbered and checklisted below in alphabetical order.

COMPLETE SET (28) 12.50 25.00
1 Mike Amodeo .38 .75
2 Al Cameron .38 .75
3 Scott Campbell .38 .75
4 Wayne Dillon .38 .75
5 Jude Drouin .38 .75
6 John Ferguson GM .50 1.00
7 Hilliard Graves .38 .75
8 Pierre Hamel .38 .75
9 Dave Hoyda .38 .75
10 Bobby Hull 4.00 8.00
11 Bill Lesuk .38 .75
12 Willy Lindstrom .75 1.50
13 Morris Lukowich .75 1.50
14 Jimmy Mann .75 1.50
15 Peter Marsh .50 1.00
16 Gord McTavish .38 .75
17 Tom McVie CO .38 .75
18 Barry Melrose 1.50 3.00
19 Lyle Moffat .38 .75
20 Craig Norwich .38 .75
21 Lars-Erik Sjoberg 1.25 2.50
22 Gary Smith .50 1.00
23 Gordon Smith .38 .75
24 Lorne Stamler .38 .75
25 Peter Sullivan .38 .75
26 Bill Sutherland ACO .25 .50
27 Ron Wilson .50 1.00
28 Title Card .25 .50

1980-81 Jets Postcards

This 23-card set of the Winnipeg Jets measured approximately 3 1/2" by 5 1/2". The fronts featured borderless black-and-white action player photos. A facsimile autograph rounded out the front. The backs were blank. The cards were unnumbered and checklisted below in alphabetical order.

COMPLETE SET (24) 10.00 20.00
1 David Babych 1.00 2.50
2 Al Cameron .40 1.00
3 Scott Campbell .40 1.00
4 Dave Chartier .40 1.00
5 Dave Christian .40 1.00
6 Jude Drouin .40 1.00
7 Norm Dupont .40 1.00
8 Dan Geoffrion .40 1.00
9 Pierre Hamel .40 1.00
10 Barry Legge .40 1.00
11 Willy Lindstrom .60 1.50
12 Barry Long .60 1.50
13 Morris Lukowich .40 1.00
14 Kris Manery .40 1.00
15 Jimmy Mann .60 1.50
16 Moe Mantha .60 1.50
17 Markus Mattsson .60 1.50
18 Richard Mulhern .40 1.00
19 Doug Smail .60 1.50
20 Don Spring .40 1.00
21 Anders Steen .40 1.00
22 Pete Sullivan .40 1.00
23 Tim Trimper .40 1.00
24 Ron Wilson .60 1.50

1981-82 Jets Postcards

This 24-card set of the Winnipeg Jets measured approximately 3 1/2" by 5 1/2". The fronts featured black-and-white action player photos with a white border and a facsimile autograph near the bottom. The backs were blank. The cards were unnumbered and checklisted below in alphabetical order. This set featured a postcard of Dale Hawerchuk that predated his RC by one year.

COMPLETE SET (24) 12.00 30.00
1 Scott Arniel .40 1.00
2 Dave Babych .60 1.50
3 Dave Christian .60 1.50
4 Lucien Deblois .40 1.00
5 Normand Dupont .30 .75
6 Dale Hawerchuk 4.00 10.00
7 Larry Hopkins .30 .75
8 Craig Levie .30 .75
9 Willy Lindstrom .40 1.00
10 Morris Lukowich .40 1.00
11 Bengt Lundholm .30 .75
12 Paul MacLean .60 1.50
13 Jimmy Mann .40 1.00
14 Bryan Maxwell .30 .75
15 Serge Savard .50 1.25
16 Doug Smail .60 1.50
17 Doug Soetaert .60 1.50
18 Don Spring .30 .75
19 Ed Staniowski .30 .75
20 Thomas Steen .75 2.00
21 Bill Sutherland CO .30 .75
22 Tim Trimper .30 .75
23 Tom Watt CO .30 .75
24 Tim Watters .30 .75

1982-83 Jets Postcards

This 28-card set measured approximately 3 1/2" by 5 1/2". The fronts featured white-bordered posed color player photos with the player's name and jersey number printed in blue inside a white bar at the bottom. The backs were blank. The cards were unnumbered and checklisted below in alphabetical order.

COMPLETE SET (28) 10.00 25.00
1 Scott Arniel .30 .75
2 Dave Babych .40 1.00
3 Jerry Butler .20 .50
4 Wade Campbell .20 .50
5 Dave Christian .40 1.00
6 Lucien DeBlois .30 .75
7 Norm Dupont .20 .50
8 Dale Hawerchuk 3.00 8.00
(Sitting holding trophy)
9 Dale Hawerchuk 3.00 8.00
10 Jim Kyte .20 .50
11 Craig Levie .20 .50
12 Willy Lindstrom .30 .75
13 Morris Lukowich .20 .50
14 Bengt Lundholm .30 .75
15 Paul MacLean .30 .75
16 Jimmy Mann .20 .50
17 Bryan Maxwell .20 .50
18 Brian Mullen .20 .50
19 Serge Savard .40 1.00
20 Doug Smail .40 1.00
21 Doug Soetaert .30 .75
22 Don Spring .20 .50
23 Ed Staniowski .20 .50
24 Thomas Steen .60 1.50
25 Bill Sutherland ACO .20 .50
26 Tom Watt CO .20 .50
27 Tim Watters .20 .50
28 Team Photo .20 .50

1983-84 Jets Postcards

This 25-card set measured 3 1/4" by 5 1/4". The fronts featured full-bleed color action photos with the player's name and jersey number at the lower right corner. The backs were blank. The cards were unnumbered and checklisted below in alphabetical order.

COMPLETE SET (25) 6.00 15.00
1 Scott Arniel .20 .50
2 Dave Babych .30 .75
3 Laurie Boschman .20 .50
4 Wade Campbell .20 .50
5 Lucien DeBlois .30 .75
6 John Ferguson VP/GM .30 .75
7 John Gibson .20 .50
8 Dale Hawerchuk 1.50 4.00
9 Brian Hayward .40 1.00
10 Jim Kyte .30 .75
11 Barry Long CO .20 .50
12 Morris Lukowich .20 .50
13 Bengt Lundholm .20 .50
14 Paul MacLean .30 .75
15 Jimmy Mann .20 .50
16 Moe Mantha .20 .50
17 Andrew McBain .20 .50
18 Brian Mullen .20 .50
19 Robert Picard .20 .50
20 Doug Smail .30 .75
21 Doug Soetaert .30 .75
22 Thomas Steen .40 1.00
23 Tim Watters .20 .50
24 Ron Wilson .20 .50
25 Tim Young .20 .50

1993-94 Jets Readers Club

This set features the Winnipeg Jets of the NHL. These are actually collectible bookmarks that were handed out to Winnipeg-area school children as a reward for reading books. The cards are unnumbered and so are listed below in alphabetical order.

COMPLETE SET (23) 6.00 15.00
1 Stu Barnes .20 .50
2 Sergei Bautin .08 .25
3 Stephane Beauregard .20 .50
4 Arto Blomsten .20 .50
5 Luciano Borsato .08 .25
6 Tie Domi .60 1.50
7 Mike Eagles .08 .25
8 Nelson Emerson .20 .50
9 Bryan Erickson .08 .25
10 Bob Essensa .20 .50
11 Yan Kaminsky .08 .25
12 Dean Kennedy .08 .25
13 Boris Mironov .08 .25
14 Teppo Numminen .40 1.00
15 Fredrik Olausson .40 1.00
16 Stephane Quintal .08 .25
17 Teemu Selanne 2.00 5.00
18 Darrin Shannon .08 .25
19 Thomas Steen .08 .25
20 Keith Tkachuk .20 .50
21 Igor Ulanov .08 .25
22 Paul Ysebaert .08 .25
23 Alexei Zhamnov .20 .50

1984-85 Jets Police

This 24-card set of Winnipeg Jets was sponsored by The Kinsmen Club of Winnipeg and all police forces in Manitoba. The cards measured approximately 2 5/8" by 3 11/16" and were issued in panels of two cards each. The front featured a color posed photo of the player shot against a blue background. The borders were white, and the player information beneath the picture was sandwiched between the Jets' and the Kinsmen logos. The back had "Jets Tips" in the form of a hockey tip paralleled by an anti-crime or safety tip. We have checklisted the cards below in alphabetical order, with the uniform number to the right of the player's name.

COMPLETE SET (24) 3.00 8.00
1 Scott Arniel 11 .08 .25
2 Dave Babych 44 .30 .75
3 Marc Behrend 29 .20 .50
4 Laurie Boschman 16 .20 .50
5 Randy Carlyle 8 .30 .75
6 Dave Ellett 2 .40 1.00
7 John Ferguson VP/GM .30 .75
8 Dale Hawerchuk 10 .75 2.00
9 Brian Hayward 1 .40 1.00
10 Jim Kyte 6 .08 .25
11 Morris Lukowich 12 .20 .50
12 Bengt Lundholm 22 .08 .25
13 Paul MacLean 15 .30 .75
14 Andrew McBain 20 .08 .25
15 Brian Mullen 19 .20 .50
16 Robert Picard 3 .08 .25
17 Paul Pooley 23 .08 .25
18 Doug Smail 9 .30 .75
19 Thomas Steen 25 .50 1.25
20 Perry Turnbull 27 .08 .25
21 Tim Watters 7 .08 .25
22 Ron Wilson 24 .08 .25
23 Assistant Coaches .08 .25
Bill Sutherland
Barry Long
Rick Bowness
24 Team Photo .30 .75

1985-86 Jets Police

This 24-card set of Winnipeg Jets was sponsored by The Kinsmen Club of Winnipeg and all police forces in Manitoba. The cards measured approximately 2 5/8" by 3 3/4" and were issued in panels of two cards each. The front featured a color action shot of the player. The borders were white, and the player information beneath the picture was sandwiched between the Jets' and the Kinsmen logos. The back had "Jets Tips" in the form of a hockey tip paralleled by an anti-crime or safety tip. We have checklisted the cards below in alphabetical order, with the uniform number to the right of the player's name.

COMPLETE SET (24) 3.00 8.00
1 Scott Arniel 11 .08 .25
2 Laurie Boschman 16 .20 .50
3 Dan Bouchard 35 .20 .50
4 Randy Carlyle 8 .30 .75
5 Dave Ellett 2 .40 1.00
6 John Ferguson VP/GM .20 .50
7 Dale Hawerchuk 10 .75 2.00
8 Brian Hayward 1 .40 1.00
9 Jim Kyte 6 .08 .25
10 Paul MacLean 15 .30 .75
11 Mario Marois 22 .08 .25
12 Andrew McBain 20 .08 .25
13 Anssi Melametsa 14 .08 .25
14 Brian Mullen 19 .20 .50
15 Ray Neufeld 28 .08 .25
16 Jim Nill 17 .08 .25
17 Dave Silk 34 .08 .25
18 Doug Smail 9 .30 .75
19 Thomas Steen 25 .50 1.25
20 Perry Turnbull 27 .08 .25
21 Tim Watters 7 .20 .50
22 Ron Wilson 24 .20 .50
23 Assistant Coaches .08 .25
Bill Sutherland
Barry Long
Rick Bowness
24 Team Photo .20 .50

1985-86 Jets Silverwood Dairy

This six-panel set of Winnipeg Jets was issued by Silverwood Dairy on the side of half-gallon milk cartons. The picture and text were printed in blue. The top of the panel featured an oval-shaped head and shoulders shot of the player, with his name immediately below the picture. The bottom of the panel presented the instructions for the Silverwood Game of the Month contest, in which ten lucky winners would win a pair of tickets to see the featured game of the month. The panels were unnumbered and checklisted below in alphabetical order.

COMPLETE SET (6) 24.00 60.00
1 Laurie Boschman 4.00 10.00
2 Randy Carlyle 5.00 12.00
3 Dave Ellett 5.00 12.00
4 Dale Hawerchuk 10.00 25.00
5 Paul MacLean 4.00 10.00
6 Brian Mullen 5.00 12.00

1986-87 Jets Postcards

This blank-backed 26-card set measured approximately 3 1/4" by 5 1/4". The fronts had borderless color action player photos. The player's name and uniform number appeared on the bottom. The cards were unnumbered and checklisted below in alphabetical order.

COMPLETE SET (26) 8.00 20.00
1 Brad Berry .30 .75
2 Laurie Boschman .40 1.00
3 Rick Bowness ACO .20 .50
Dan Maloney CO
Bill Sutherland ACO
4 Randy Carlyle .75 2.00
5 Bill Derlago .40 1.00
6 Dave Ellett .60 1.50
7 John Ferguson GM .40 1.00
8 Gilles Hamel .30 .75
9 Dale Hawerchuk 1.50 4.00
10 Hannu Jarvenpaa .30 .75
11 Jim Kyte .30 .75
12 Paul MacLean .40 1.00
13 Mario Marois .30 .75
14 Andrew McBain .30 .75
15 Brian Mullen .40 1.00
16 Ray Neufeld .30 .75
17 Jim Nill .30 .75
18 Fredrik Olausson .60 1.50
19 Steve Penney .40 1.00
20 Eldon Reddick .40 1.00
21 Doug Smail .40 1.00
22 Thomas Steen .60 1.50
23 Perry Turnbull .30 .75
24 Tim Watters .30 .75
25 Ron Wilson .30 .75
26 Team Photo .75 2.00

1987-88 Jets Postcards

This 24-card set measured approximately 3 1/4" by 5 1/4". The fronts featured autographed color action player photos with the player's jersey number and name in the lower right. The backs were blank. The cards were unnumbered and checklisted below in alphabetical order

COMPLETE SET (24) 4.80 12.00
1 Brad Berry .20 .50
2 Daniel Berthiaume .40 1.00
3 Laurie Boschman .20 .50
4 Randy Carlyle .30 .75
5 Iain Duncan .20 .50
6 Dave Ellett .30 .75
7 Pat Elynuik .20 .50
8 Gilles Hamel .20 .50
9 Dale Hawerchuk .60 1.50
10 Hannu Jarvenpaa .20 .50
11 Jim Kyte .20 .50
12 Paul MacLean .30 .75
13 Mario Marois .20 .50
14 Andrew McBain .20 .50
15 Ray Neufeld .20 .50
16 Fredrik Olausson .40 1.00
17 Eldon Reddick .40 1.00
18 Steve Rooney .30 .75
19 Doug Smail .30 .75
20 Thomas Steen .40 1.00
21 Peter Taglianetti .20 .50
22 Tim Watters .20 .50
23 Ron Wilson .20 .50
24 Team Photo .40 1.00

1988-89 Jets Police

This 24-card set of Winnipeg Jets was sponsored by The Kinsmen Club of Winnipeg and all police forces in Manitoba. The cards measured approximately 2 5/8" by 3 3/4" and were issued as 12 panels of two cards each. By uniform numbers, the panel pairs were CO/TEAM, 39/ACO, 23/4, 6/10, 16/20, 25/32, 19/22, 8/7, 27/28, 2/34, 9/12, and 31/33. The front featured a color action shot of the player. The borders were white, and the player information beneath the picture was sandwiched between the Jets' and the Kinsmen logos. The back had "Jets Tips" in the form of a hockey tip paralleled by an anti-crime or safety tip. We have checklisted the cards below in alphabetical order, with the uniform number to the right of the player's name.

COMPLETE SET (24) 3.00 8.00
1 Brent Ashton 7 .08 .25
2 Laurie Boschman 16 .20 .50
3 Randy Carlyle 8 .30 .75
4 Alain Chevrier 31 .20 .50
5 Iain Duncan 19 .08 .25
6 Dave Ellett 2 .30 .75
7 Pat Elynuik 34 .08 .25
8 Randy Gilhen 39 .08 .25
9 Dale Hawerchuk 10 .60 1.50
10 Dave Hunter 12 .08 .25
11 Hannu Jarvenpaa 23 .08 .25
12 Jim Kyte 6 .08 .25
13 Dan Maloney CO .08 .25
14 Mario Marois 22 .08 .25
15 Andrew McBain 20 .08 .25
16 Ray Neufeld 28 .08 .25
17 Teppo Numminen 27 .30 .75
18 Fredrik Olausson 4 .20 .50
19 Eldon Reddick 33 .20 .50
20 Doug Smail 9 .20 .50
21 Thomas Steen 25 .30 .75
22 Peter Taglianetti 32 .08 .25
23 Assistant Coaches .08 .25
Bill Sutherland
Bruce Southern
Rick St.Croix
24 Team Photo .30 .75

1988-89 Jets Postcards

These postcards were issued by the team at promotional events. They are unnumbered and are listed below in alphabetical order.

COMPLETE SET (24) 8.00 15.00
1 Brent Ashton .20 .50
2 Mascot .02 .10
3 Daniel Berthiaume .40 1.00
4 Laurie Boschman .20 .50
5 Randy Carlyle .30 .75
6 Iain Duncan .20 .50
7 Dave Ellett .30 .75
8 Pat Elynuik .20 .50
9 Paul Fenton .20 .50
10 Randy Gilhen .20 .50
11 Dale Hawerchuk .75 2.00
12 Hannu Jarvenpaa .20 .50
13 Brad Jones .20 .50
14 Jim Kyte .20 .50
15 Dan Maloney CO .08 .25
16 Andrew McBain .20 .50
17 Teppo Numminen .75 2.00
18 Fredrik Olausson .30 .75
19 Eldon Reddick .40 1.00
20 Doug Smail .30 .75
21 Thomas Steen .40 1.00
22 Coaches .08 .25
23 Peter Taglianetti .20 .50
24 Team Photo .40 1.00

1989-90 Jets Safeway

This 30-card set was sponsored by Safeway Limited of Canada and featured players from the Winnipeg Jets. The cards measured approximately 3 3/4" by 6 7/8". The front had a color action photo of the player, with his number and name above the picture between the Jets' and Safeway logos. The back was outlined in black boxes and included player information as well as a oversized Safeway logo and advertisement. Since the cards were unnumbered, they are listed below in alphabetical order with the player's sweater number after the name.

COMPLETE SET (30) 4.80 12.00
1 Brent Ashton 7 .20 .50
2 Stu Barnes 14 .30 .75
3 Brad Berry 29 .20 .50
4 Daniel Berthiaume 30 .30 .75
5 Laurie Boschman 16 .20 .50
6 Randy Carlyle 8 .30 .75
7 Shawn Cronin 44 .20 .50
8 Randy Cunneyworth 18 .20 .50
9 Gord Donnelly 34 .20 .50
10 Tom Draper 37 .30 .75
11 Iain Duncan 19 .20 .50
12 Dave Ellett 2 .30 .75
13 Pat Elynuik 15 .20 .50
14 Bob Essensa 35 .30 .75
15 Paul Fenton 11 .20 .50
16 Dale Hawerchuk 10 .60 1.50
17 Brent Hughes 46 .20 .50
18 Mark Kumpel 21 .20 .50
19 Moe Mantha 22 .20 .50
20 Dave McLlwain 20 .20 .50
21 Brian McReynolds 26 .20 .50
22 Teppo Numminen 27 .30 .75
23 Fredrik Olausson 4 .30 .75
24 Greg Paslawski 28 .20 .50
25 Doug Smail 12 .30 .75
26 Thomas Steen 25 .30 .75
27 Peter Taglianetti 32 .20 .50
28 Benny 00 (Mascot) .08 .25
29 Coaches Card .08 .25
Alpo Suhonen
Bob Murdoch
Clare Drake
30 Team Photo .40 1.00

1990-91 Jets IGA

This 35-card set measured approximately 3 1/2" by 6 1/2" and featured color action player photos with white borders. The team logo, sweater number, player's name, and sponsor logo appeared at the card top between two thin purple stripes. The back was divided into two sections; in the upper appeared player information, while in the lower appeared a GreenCare advertisement (environmentally safe and carried in IGA stores). The cards were unnumbered and checklisted below in alphabetical order.

COMPLETE SET (35) 4.00 10.00
1 Scott Arniel .15 .40
2 Brent Ashton .15 .40
3 Don Barber .15 .40
4 Stephane Beauregard .20 .50
5 Randy Carlyle .30 .75
6 Danton Cole .15 .40
7 Shawn Cronin .15 .40
8 Gord Donnelly .15 .40
9 Clare Drake CO .08 .25
10 Kris Draper .40 1.00
11 Iain Duncan .15 .40
12 Pat Elynuik .15 .40
13 Bob Essensa .20 .50
14 Doug Evans .15 .40
15 Phil Housley .40 1.00
16 Sergei Kharin .15 .40
17 Mark Kumpel .15 .40
18 Guy Larose .15 .40
19 Paul MacDermid .15 .40
20 Moe Mantha .15 .40
21 Brian Marchment .20 .50
22 Dave McLlwain .15 .40
23 Bob Murdoch CO .08 .25
24 Teppo Numminen .30 .75
25 Fredrik Olausson .20 .50
26 Ed Olczyk .20 .50
27 Mark Osborne .15 .40
28 Greg Paslawski .15 .40
29 Terry Simpson CO .08 .25
30 Thomas Steen .30 .75
31 Phil Sykes .15 .40
32 Rick Tabaracci .25 .60
33 Simon Wheeldon .15 .40
34 Benny (Mascot) .08 .25
35 Team Photo .40 1.00

1991 Jets Panini Team Stickers

This 32-sticker set was issued in a plastic bag that contained two 16-sticker sheets (approximately 9" by 12") and a foldout poster, "Super Poster - Hockey 91", on which the stickers could be affixed. The players' names appeared only on the poster, not on the stickers. Each sticker measured about 2 1/8" by 2 7/8" and featured a color player action shot on its white-bordered front. The back of the white sticker sheet was lined off into 16 panels, each carrying the logos for Panini, the NHL, and the NHLPA, as well as the same number that appeared on the front of the sticker. Every Canadian NHL team was featured in this promotion. Each team set was available by mail-order from Panini Canada Ltd. for 2.99 plus 50 cents for shipping and handling.

COMPLETE SET (32) 1.00 2.50
1 Scott Arniel .02 .10
2 Brent Ashton .02 .10
3 Stephane Beauregard .02 .10
4 Randy Carlyle .02 .10
5 Danton Cole .01 .05
6 Shawn Cronin .02 .10
7 Gord Donnelly .01 .05
8 Kris Draper .05 .15
9 Dave Ellett .02 .10
10 Pat Elynuik .01 .05
11 Doug Evans .01 .05
12 Paul Fenton .01 .05
13 Phil Housley .08 .25
14 Mark Kumpel .01 .05
15 Paul MacDermid .01 .05
16 Moe Mantha .01 .05
17 Dave McLlwain .01 .05
18 Teppo Numminen .05 .15
19 Fredrik Olausson .02 .10
20 Greg Paslawski .01 .05
21 Doug Smail .01 .05
22 Thomas Steen .02 .10
23 Phil Sykes .01 .05
24 Rick Tabaracci .05 .15
A Team Logo .01 .05
Left Side
B Team Logo .01 .05
Right Side
C Jets in Action .01 .05
Upper Left Corner
D Jets in Action .01 .05
Lower Left Corner
E Jets in Action .01 .05
Upper Right Corner
F Jets in Action .01 .05
Lower Right Corner
G Paul Fenton .01 .05
H Phil Housley .08 .25

1991-92 Jets IGA

This 35-card set measured approximately 3 1/2" by 6 1/2" and featured color action player photos with white borders. The IGA logo, sweater number, player's name, and a picture of Cadbury's Caramilk candy appeared at the card bottom between two thin purple stripes. The back was divided into three sections; in the top appeared player information; in the middle and bottom appeared ads for Caramilk and GreenCare, respectively. The front of the Thomas Steen card showed (in lower right corner) another Cadbury candy bar/product, "Crunchie". The cards were unnumbered and checklisted below in alphabetical order.

COMPLETE SET (35) 4.00 10.00
1 Stu Barnes .20 .50
2 Stephane Beauregard .20 .50
3 Luciano Borsato .15 .40
4 Randy Carlyle .20 .50
5 Danton Cole .15 .40
6 Shawn Cronin .15 .40
7 Burton Cummings .20 .50
8 Mike Eagles .15 .40
9 Pat Elynuik .15 .40
10 Bryan Erickson .15 .40
11 Bob Essensa .20 .50
12 Doug Evans .15 .40
13 Mike Hartman .15 .40
14 Phil Housley .30 .75
15 Dean Kennedy .15 .40
16 Paul MacDermid .15 .40
17 Moe Mantha .15 .40
18 Rob Murray .15 .40
19 Troy Murray .15 .40
20 Teppo Numminen .20 .50
21 Fredrik Olausson .20 .50
22 Ed Olczyk .15 .40
23 Mark Osborne .15 .40
24 John Paddock CO .08 .25
25 Kent Paynter .15 .40
26 Dave Prior .15 .40
27 Russ Romaniuk .15 .40
28 Darrin Shannon .20 .50
29 Terry Simpson CO .08 .25
30 Thomas Steen .20 .50
31 Phil Sykes .15 .40

32 Rick Tabaracci .20 .50
33 Glen Williamson CO .08 .25
34 Benny (Mascot) .08 .25
35 Team Photo UER .30 .75
(Incorrectly
marked 1990-91)

1993-94 Jets Ruffles

This 29-postcard set measured approximately 3 1/2" by 6 1/2" and featured color action player photos with a thin black border on a white background. The player's name was printed in white in a black bar across the bottom in the wide white border with the team logo, jersey number and sponsor logo printed in red and blue above the bar. The backs carried the player's name, jersey number, position, and biographical information in black print on a white background above a Ruffles Challenge logo and checklist for an all-star potato chip. The cards were unnumbered and checklisted below in alphabetical order.

COMPLETE SET (29) 6.00 15.00
1 Stu Barnes .30 .75
2 Sergei Bautin .15 .40
3 Stephane Beauregard .20 .50
4 Benny (Mascot) .08 .25
5 Zinetula Bilyaletdinov ACO .08 .25
6 Arto Blomsten .15 .40
7 Luciano Borsato .15 .40
8 Tie Domi .40 1.00
9 Mike Eagles .15 .40
10 Nelson Emerson .30 .75
11 Bryan Erickson .15 .40
12 Bob Essensa .20 .50
13 Yan Kaminsky .15 .40
14 Dean Kennedy .15 .40
15 Kris King .15 .40
16 Boris Mironov .25 .60
17 Andy Murray ACO .08 .25
18 Teppo Numminen .25 .60
19 Fredrik Olausson .15 .40
20 John Paddock CO .08 .25
21 Stephane Quintal .15 .40
22 Teemu Selanne 2.00 5.00
23 Darrin Shannon .15 .40
24 Thomas Steen .30 .75
25 Keith Tkachuk 1.00 2.50
26 Igor Ulanov .15 .40
27 Paul Ysebaert .15 .40
28 Alexei Zhamnov .40 1.00
29 Team Picture .20 .50

1995-96 Jets Readers Club

This set of 12 bookmarks featured the Winnipeg Jets. The top of the front featured a player photo, his name and jersey number along with a quote on the importance of reading and a pre-printed autograph. The backs displayed the logos of the various corporate sponsors of this program. The bookmarks were distributed to children who successfully read a number of books.

COMPLETE SET (12) 3.00 8.00
1 Tim Cheveldae .20 .50
2 Dallas Drake .08 .25
3 Mike Eastwood .08 .25
4 Nikolai Khabibulin .40 1.00
5 Kris King .20 .50
6 Igor Korolev .08 .25
7 Dave Manson .08 .25
8 Teppo Numminen .20 .50
9 Teemu Selanne 1.25 3.00
10 Darrin Shannon .08 .25
11 Keith Tkachuk .60 1.50
12 Alexei Zhamnov .40 1.00

1995-96 Jets Team Issue

This 26-card set measured approximately 3 1/2" by 6 1/2" and featured color action player photos in a white border. The player's name, position, and jersey number were printed in the wide bottom margin. The backs carried player information. The cards were unnumbered and checklisted below in alphabetical order.

COMPLETE SET (26) 6.00 15.00
1 Title Card .08 .25
2 Benny (Mascot) .02 .10
3 Tim Cheveldae .30 .75
4 Coaches .08 .25
5 Shane Doan .30 .75
6 Jason Doig .20 .50
7 Dallas Drake .20 .50
8 Mike Eastwood .20 .50
9 Randy Gilhen .20 .50
10 Nikolai Khabibulin .40 1.00
11 Kris King .20 .50
12 Igor Korolev .20 .50
13 Stewart Malgunas .20 .50
14 Dave Manson .20 .50
15 Jim McKenzie .20 .50
16 Teppo Numminen .30 .75
17 Eddie Olczyk .20 .50
18 Deron Quint .20 .50
19 Ed Ronan .20 .50
20 Teemu Selanne 1.50 4.00
21 Darrin Shannon .20 .50
22 Darryl Shannon .20 .50
23 Mike Stapleton .20 .50
24 Keith Tkachuk .75 2.00
25 Darren Turcotte .20 .50
26 Alexei Zhamnov .30 .75

2011-12 Jets Upper Deck Return to Winnipeg

COMPLETE SET (15) 25.00 50.00
1 Alexander Burmistrov 4.00 10.00
2 Andrew Ladd 3.00 8.00
3 Blake Wheeler 6.00 15.00
4 Bryan Little 3.00 8.00
5 Carl Klingberg 2.50 6.00
6 Chris Mason 2.50 6.00
7 Dustin Byfuglien 3.00 8.00
8 Mark Scheifele 4.00 10.00
9 Evander Kane 6.00 15.00
10 Jim Slater 2.00 5.00
11 Nik Antropov 2.50 6.00
12 Ondrej Pavelec 3.00 8.00
13 Patrice Cormier 2.00 5.00
14 Tobias Enstrom 2.00 5.00
15 Zach Bogosian 2.50 6.00
NNO Checklist 1.50 3.00

1992 Jofa/Koho

This six-card standard-size set was apparently sponsored by four major brands of hockey equipment: Jofa, Koho, Titan, and Canadien. The set was also known as "The Endorsers" and features six famous current players who endorsed their respective products. The cards were printed on thin card stock. The fronts featured color close-up player photos. The borders shade from one color to another and were studded with miniature stars. On various pastel-colored backs, biographical information was presented inside black border stripes. The cards were unnumbered and checklisted below in alphabetical order. The manufacturer's name that appears at the bottom of the card front was listed below beneath the player's name.

COMPLETE SET (6) 4.80 12.00
1 Theo Fleury .75 2.00
Jofa
2 Jari Kurri .40 1.00
Koho
3 Mario Lemieux 2.00 5.00
Koho
4 Eric Lindros 1.50 4.00
Titan
5 Denis Savard .40 1.00
Canadien
6 Mats Sundin .60 1.50
Jofa

1997-98 Katch

The 1997-98 Katch set was issued in one series totaling 168 cards. Gold and silver parallels were also created. Gold were randomly inserted at 1:48 and silver at 1:16.

COMPLETE SET (168) 100.00 100.00
COMP.GOLD SET (168) 2500.00 4000.00
*GOLD: 7.5X TO 15X HI COLUMN
COMP.SILVER SET (168) 1000.00 600.00
*SILVER: 3X TO 6X HI COLUMN
1 Guy Hebert .40 1.00
2 Paul Kariya 2.50 5.00
3 Espen Knutsen .10 .30
4 Tomas Sandstrom .10 .30
5 Teemu Selanne 1.00 2.50
6 Scott Young .10 .30
7 Per Johan Axelsson .10 .30
8 Ray Bourque .60 1.50
9 Jim Carey .40 1.00
10 Ted Donato .10 .30
11 Dimitri Khristich .40 1.00
12 Sergei Samsonov .50 1.25
13 Matthew Barnaby .40 1.00
14 Jason Dawe .10 .30
15 Dominik Hasek 1.00 2.50
16 Mike Peca .40 1.00
17 Rob Ray .40 1.00
18 Alexei Zhitnik .10 .30
19 Andrew Cassels .10 .30
20 Theo Fleury .50 1.25
21 Jarome Iginla .40 1.00
22 Sandy McCarthy .10 .30
23 Tyler Moss .10 .30
24 Cory Stillman .10 .30
25 Sean Burke .40 1.00
26 Kevin Dineen .10 .30
27 Stu Grimson .40 1.00
28 Steven Rice .10 .30
29 Keith Primeau .40 1.00
30 Geoff Sanderson .40 1.00
31 Tony Amonte .40 1.00
32 Chris Chelios .50 1.25
33 Daniel Cleary .10 .30
34 Jeff Hackett .40 1.00
35 Ethan Moreau .10 .30
36 Bob Probert .10 .30
37 Adam Deadmarsh .40 1.00
38 Peter Forsberg 1.25 3.00
39 Claude Lemieux .40 1.00
40 Sandis Ozolinsh .40 1.00
41 Patrick Roy 3.00 6.00
42 Joe Sakic 1.00 2.50
43 Ed Belfour .50 1.25
44 Derian Hatcher .10 .30
45 Jere Lehtinen .40 1.00
46 Mike Modano .60 1.50
47 Joe Nieuwendyk .40 1.00
48 Darryl Sydor .40 1.00
49 Sergei Fedorov 1.00 2.50
50 Vyacheslav Kozlov .40 1.00
51 Darren McCarty .40 1.00
52 Chris Osgood .50 1.25
53 Brendan Shanahan .75 2.00
54 Steve Yzerman 1.50 4.00
55 Jason Arnott .40 1.00
56 Boyd Devereaux .10 .30
57 Curtis Joseph .60 1.50
58 Andrei Kovalenko .10 .30
59 Ryan Smyth .40 1.00
60 Doug Weight .40 1.00
61 Ed Jovanovski .10 .30
62 Scott Mellanby .10 .30
63 David Nemirovsky .10 .30
64 Rob Niedermayer .10 .30
65 Ray Sheppard .40 1.00
66 John Vanbiesbrouck .50 1.25
67 Aki Berg .10 .30
68 Rob Blake .10 .30
69 Stephane Fiset .40 1.00
70 Donald MacLean .10 .30
71 Yanic Perreault .10 .30
72 Luc Robitaille .40 1.00
73 Valeri Bure .40 1.00
74 Vincent Damphousse .40 1.00
75 Saku Koivu .50 1.25
76 Vladimir Malakhov .10 .30
77 Mark Recchi .40 1.00
78 Jocelyn Thibault .40 1.00
79 Martin Brodeur .75 2.00
80 Patrik Elias .40 1.00
81 Doug Gilmour .50 1.25
82 Bill Guerin .40 1.00
83 Scott Niedermayer .10 .30
84 Scott Stevens .40 1.00
85 Bryan Berard .10 .30
86 Eric Fichaud .40 1.00
87 Travis Green .10 .30
88 Kenny Jonsson .10 .30
89 Bryan McCabe .10 .30
90 Zigmund Palffy .50 1.25
91 Adam Graves .40 1.00
92 Wayne Gretzky 4.00 8.00
93 Pat LaFontaine .40 1.00
94 Brian Leetch .50 1.25
95 Mike Richter .50 1.25
96 Kevin Stevens .10 .30
97 Daniel Alfredsson .40 1.00
98 Alexandre Daigle .10 .30
99 Chris Phillips .10 .30
100 Wade Redden .10 .30
101 Damian Rhodes .10 .30
102 Alexei Yashin .40 1.00
103 Paul Coffey .50 1.25
104 Chris Gratton .10 .30
105 Ron Hextall .40 1.00
106 John LeClair .75 2.00
107 Eric Lindros 1.25 3.00
108 Dainius Zubrus .10 .30
109 Mike Gartner .40 1.00
110 Brad Isbister .10 .30
111 Nikolai Khabibulin .40 1.00
112 Jeremy Roenick .50 1.25
113 Keith Tkachuk .50 1.25
114 Oleg Tverdovsky .10 .30
115 Tom Barrasso .40 1.00
116 Ron Francis .40 1.00
117 Kevin Hatcher .40 1.00
118 Jaromir Jagr 1.50 4.00
119 Alexei Morozov .10 .30
120 Petr Nedved .40 1.00
121 Patrick Marleau .40 1.00
122 Marty McSorley .10 .30
123 Bernie Nicholls .10 .30
124 Owen Nolan .40 1.00
125 Marco Sturm .40 1.00
126 Mike Vernon .40 1.00
127 Jim Campbell .40 1.00
128 Grant Fuhr .40 1.00
129 Brett Hull .60 1.50
130 Al MacInnis .40 1.00
131 Pierre Turgeon .40 1.00
132 Tony Twist .40 1.00
133 Brian Bradley .10 .30
134 Dino Ciccarelli .10 .30
135 Roman Hamrlik .10 .30
136 Daymond Langkow .10 .30
137 Daren Puppa .10 .30
138 Mikael Renberg .10 .30
139 Wendel Clark .10 .30
140 Tie Domi .40 1.00
141 Alyn McCauley .10 .30
142 Felix Potvin .40 1.00
143 Mathieu Schneider .10 .30
144 Mats Sundin .50 1.25
145 Pavel Bure 1.25 3.00
146 Trevor Linden .40 1.00
147 Kirk McLean .40 1.00
148 Mark Messier .60 1.50
149 Alexander Mogilny .40 1.00
150 Mattias Ohlund .40 1.00
151 Peter Bondra .50 1.25
152 Joe Juneau .10 .30
153 Adam Oates .40 1.00
154 Bill Ranford .40 1.00
155 Jaroslav Svejkovsky .10 .30
156 Richard Zednik .10 .30
157 Wayne Gretzky TL 1.50 4.00
158 Eric Lindros TL .60 1.50
159 Paul Kariya TL 1.00 2.50
160 Patrick Roy TL 1.25 3.00
161 Steve Yzerman TL .75 2.00
162 Jaromir Jagr TL .75 2.00
163 Brett Hull TL .30 .75
164 Joe Thornton .50 1.25
165 Vaclav Prospal .40 1.00
166 Mike Johnson .40 1.00
167 Eric Messier .40 1.00
168 Jan Bulis .40 1.00

1972 Kellogg's Iron-On Transfers

These six iron-on transfers each measured approximately 6 1/2" by 10". Each transfer consisted of a cartoon drawing of the player's body with an oversized head. The puck was comically portrayed with human characteristics (face, arms, and legs). A facsimile player autograph appeared below the drawing. At the bottom were instructions in English and French for applying the iron-on to clothing; these were to be cut off before application. These iron-on transfers were unnumbered and checklisted below in alphabetical order.

COMPLETE SET (6) 150.00 300.00
1 Ron Ellis 12.50 25.00
2 Phil Esposito 37.50 75.00
3 Rod Gilbert 20.00 40.00
4 Bobby Hull 62.50 125.00
5 Frank Mahovlich 20.00 40.00
6 Stan Mikita 25.00 50.00

1984-85 Kellogg's Accordion Discs

The entire set consisted of eight picture pucks: six different pro hockey pucks each containing action shots and personal records for six NHL players, and two different sports pucks each featuring achievements of six famous female athletes. Each puck came with a stick-on NHL Team Emblem or Sports Crest. The pucks were inserted in specially marked packages of Kellogg's Cereals in Canada. By finding instant prize messages inside the picture pucks, one could win sports equipment, such as hockey jerseys, skates, sport bags, or hockey sticks. The promotion also included a mail-in offer for a plastic collector's shield that would hold all the picture pucks and be mounted on a wall. This set of thin cardboard discs measured approximately 2" in diameter. Six discs were joined together at their sides (like the bellows of an accordion) and were issued in a thin black plastic case. The front featured a round-shaped color action photo with white border. The back provided biographical and statistical information in French and English, with the team logo at the top and a facsimile autograph at the bottom. The complete set price below includes only one of the variation pairs.

COMPLETE SET (8) 12.00 30.00
1 Dino Ciccarelli 2.50 6.00
Mike Bossy
Richard Brodeur
Michel Goulet
Jari Kurri
Paul Reinhart
2 Reed Larson 1.50 4.00
Marcel Dionne
Peter Statsny
Paul MacLean
Doug Risebrough
Larry Robinson
3A Stanley Cup 2.00 5.00
Gilbert Perreault
Rick Middleton
Bob Gainey
Kevin Lowe
Borje Salming
3B Stanley Cup 2.00 5.00
Gilbert Perreault
Rick Middleton
Guy Lafleur
Kevin Lowe
Borje Salming
4 Bernie Federko 2.00 5.00
Ron Francis
Stan Smyl
Mike Gartner
Dave Babych
Lanny McDonald
5A Barry Beck 1.50 4.00
Rick Kehoe
Dale Hawerchuk
John Anderson
Mario Tremblay
Paul Coffey
5B Barry Beck 1.50 4.00
Denis Herron
Dale Hawerchuk
Dan Daoust
Mario Tremblay
Paul Coffey
6 Thomas Gradin 1.50 4.00
Dale Hunter
Doug Wilson
Darryl Sittler
Glenn Resch
Rick Vaive
7 Tracy Austin 1.25 3.00
Tennis
Olga Korbut
Gymnastics
Kathy Kreiner
Alpine Skiing
Angela Taylor
Track and Field
Anne Ottenbrite
Swimming
Paul Martini
Skating
Barbara Underhill
Skating
8 Tatiana Kolpakova 1.25 3.00
Long Jump
Kay Thompson
Skating
Kornelia Ender
Swimming
Melanie Smith
Equestrian
Nadia Comaneci
Gymnastics
Carling Bassett
Tennis

1992 Kellogg's All-Star Posters

Posters measured approximately 14" x 10" and were full color. One posted could be found in each specially marked box of Kellogg's cereal in Canada, for a limited time.

COMPLETE SET (3) 2.00 5.00
1 Campbell Conf. All-Stars .75 2.00
2 Wales Conf. All-Stars .75 2.00
3 Snap, Crackle, Pop .40 1.00

1992 Kellogg's Trophies

Protected by a clear plastic cello pack, these 11 cards were inserted into Kellogg's Rice Krispies cereal boxes in Canada. The cards measured approximately 2 3/8" by 3 1/4" and were printed on thin card stock. The fronts featured a color photo of the trophy inside a gold border on a turquoise card face. The name of the trophy appeared in a red circle at the center of the top. The backs were red and carried text in white print about the trophy. All text on both sides is in English and French. The cards were numbered on the front at the bottom center. This set is condition sensitive.

COMPLETE SET (11) 8.00 20.00
1 Stanley Cup 1.25 3.00
2 Presidents' Trophy .75 2.00
3 Hart Memorial Trophy .75 2.00
4 Conn Smythe Trophy .75 2.00
5 Vezina Trophy .75 2.00
6 James Norris Memorial .75 2.00
T
7 Calder Memorial Trophy .75 2.00
8 Frank J. Selke Trophy .75 2.00
9 Lady Byng Memorial .75 2.00
Trop
10 Art Ross Trophy .75 2.00
11 Jack Adams Trophy .75 2.00

1992-93 Kellogg's Posters

These 9 1/4" by 14" posters were inserted inside specially marked Kellogg's products. The two-sided posters each bore the same photo, with the descriptive legend at the top written in French on one side and English on the other. The bottom of the poster featured the player's name, along with the logos of the NHL and Kellogg's. The posters were folded into card-sized squares and then placed into a protective cellophane seal. All posters, therefore, were subject to extreme creasing, and are considered in top condition in this form. The checklist below may be incomplete. Collectors with additional information are encouraged to forward it to the publisher.

COMPLETE SET 16.00 40.00
1 Mario Lemieux 8.00 20.00
2 Mark Messier 2.00 5.00
3 Luc Robitaille 1.25 3.00
4 Patrick Roy 6.00 15.00
5 Cornelius Rooster 1.25 3.00
Mascot

1995-96 Kellogg's Donruss

This six-card set was distributed in specially-marked boxes of Kellogg's Cereal in Canada and featured color photos of hockey stars Mario Lemieux and Brett Hull. The backs carried another color player photo with the card title and explanation of the title. The cards are unnumbered and listed below as Mario Lemieux (1-4) and Brett Hull (5-6).

COMPLETE SET (6) 12.00 30.00
1 Mario Lemieux 3.00 8.00
The Fiver
2 Mario Lemieux 3.00 8.00
The Cup
3 Mario Lemieux 3.00 8.00
The 500th
4 Mario Lemieux 3.00 8.00
The Comeback
5 Brett Hull/ 1.25 3.00
6 Brett Hull 1.25 3.00
The MVP

1993 Kenner Starting Lineup Cards

These cards were packaged with their corresponding individual Starting Lineup figures produced by Kenner.

COMPLETE SET (12) 40.00 100.00
1 Ed Belfour 8.00 20.00
2 Ray Bourque 1.00 2.50
3 Grant Fuhr 10.00 25.00
4 Brett Hull .75 2.00
5 Jaromir Jagr 1.25 3.00
6 Pat LaFontaine 1.00 2.50
7 Mario Lemieux 1.50 4.00
8 Eric Lindros 1.00 2.50
9 Mark Messier 1.00 2.50
10 Jeremy Roenick .75 2.00
11 Patrick Roy 2.00 5.00
12 Steve Yzerman 2.00 5.00

1994 Kenner Starting Lineup Cards

These cards were included in the packaging for Kenner Starting Lineups. Because few SLUs are broken from their packaging, these cards made for unique collectibles. This year's cards were made by Pinnacle, and featured an SLU logo on the front.

COMPLETE SET (21) 32.00 80.00
1 Tom Barrasso .75 2.00
2 Ray Bourque .75 2.00
3 Pavel Bure 1.00 2.50
4 Sergei Fedorov 1.00 2.50
5 Grant Fuhr 1.25 3.00
6 Doug Gilmour .60 1.50
7 Brett Hull .60 1.50
8 Arturs Irbe .60 1.50
9 Jaromir Jagr .60 1.50
10 Pat Lafontaine .60 1.50
11 Brian Leetch .60 1.50
12 Mario Lemieux 1.00 2.50
13 Eric Lindros .75 2.00
14 Mark Messier .60 1.50
15 Alexander Mogilny .60 1.50
16 Adam Oates .60 1.50
17 Mike Richter .75 2.00
18 Luc Robitaille .75 2.00
19 Jeremy Roenick .50 1.25
20 Teemu Selanne 1.00 2.50
21 Steve Yzerman 1.50 4.00

1995 Kenner Starting Lineup Cards

These cards were included in the packaging for Kenner Starting Lineups. Because few SLUs were broken from their packaging, these cards made for unique collectibles. This year's cards were made by Fleer, and featured an SLU logo on the front.

COMPLETE SET (21) 24.00 60.00
1 Tom Barrasso .60 1.50
2 Rob Blake .60 1.50
3 Martin Brodeur 1.50 4.00
4 Pavel Bure .60 1.50
5 Chris Chelios .75 2.00
6 Bob Corkum .30 .75
7 Sergei Fedorov .60 1.50
8 Theo Fleury .60 1.50
9 Adam Graves .30 .75
10 Dominik Hasek 1.25 3.00
11 Brett Hull .60 1.50
12 Arturs Irbe .40 1.00
13 Mike Modano .75 2.00
14 Kirk Muller .40 1.00
15 Cam Neely .60 1.50
16 Sandis Ozolinsh .60 1.50
17 Felix Potvin .75 2.00
18 Luc Robitaille .60 1.50
19 Brendan Shanahan 1.00 2.50
20 Scott Stevens .30 .75
21 Pierre Turgeon .75 2.00

1996 Kenner Starting Lineup Cards

These cards were included in the packaging for Kenner Starting Lineups. Because few SLUs are broken from their packaging, these cards make for unique collectibles. This year's cards were made by Skybox, and featured an SLU logo on the front.

COMPLETE SET (24) 24.00 60.00
1 Tom Barrasso .60 1.50
2 Brian Bradley .30 .75
3 Jim Carey .75 2.00
4 Paul Coffey .75 2.00
5 Sergei Fedorov .60 1.50
6 Ron Francis .75 2.00
7 Dominik Hasek .60 1.50
8 Paul Kariya 1.00 2.50
9 Pat Lafontaine .60 1.50
10 John LeClair .75 2.00
11 Brian Leetch .40 1.00
12 Eric Lindros .60 1.50
13 Al MacInnis .60 1.50
14 Scott Mellanby .30 .75
15 Mark Messier .60 1.50
16 Mike Modano .40 1.00
17 Adam Oates .40 1.00
18 Mikael Renberg .30 .75
19 Stephane Richer .30 .75
20 Jeremy Roenick .50 1.25
21 Patrick Roy 1.25 3.00
22 Joe Sakic 1.50 4.00
23 Brendan Shanahan .75 2.00
24 Mats Sundin .75 2.00

1997 Kenner Starting Lineup Cards

These cards were included in the packaging for Kenner Starting Lineups. Because few SLUs are broken from their packaging, these cards made for unique collectibles. This year's cards were made by Fleer, and featured an SLU logo on the front.

COMPLETE SET (20) 16.00 40.00
1 Daniel Alfredsson .30 .75
2 Jason Arnott .40 1.00
3 Peter Bondra .60 1.50
4 Martin Brodeur 1.00 2.50
5 Paul Coffey .50 1.25
6 Chris Chelios .60 1.50
7 Peter Forsberg 1.00 2.50
8 Wayne Gretzky 2.50 6.00
9 Ron Hextall .75 2.00
10 Jaromir Jagr .60 1.50
11 Patrick Lalime .60 1.50
12 Eric Lindros .60 1.50
13 Mark Messier .60 1.50
14 Chris Osgood .75 2.00
15 Sandis Ozolinsh .40 1.00
16 Zigmund Palffy .50 1.25
17 Daren Puppa .50 1.25
18 Mark Recchi .60 1.50
19 Teemu Selanne .60 1.50
20 Keith Tkachuk .60 1.50
21 John Vanbiesbrouck .60 1.50

1998 Kenner Starting Lineup Cards

These cards were included in the packaging for Kenner Starting Lineups. Because few SLUs are broken from their packaging, these cards made for unique collectibles. This year's cards were made by Upper Deck, and featured a SLU logo on the front.

COMPLETE SET (34) 20.00 50.00
1 Tony Amonte .40 1.00
2 Bryan Berard .30 .75
3 Ed Belfour .75 2.00
4 Peter Bondra .30 .75
5 Martin Brodeur 1.00 2.50
6 Jim Campbell .30 .75
7 Vincent Damphousse .30 .75
8 Theo Fleury .40 1.00
9 Grant Fuhr .60 1.50
10 Doug Gilmour .40 1.00
11 Wayne Gretzky 2.00 5.00
12 Wayne Gretzky Cup 2.00 5.00
13 Dominik Hasek .75 2.00
14 Jaromir Jagr .60 1.50
15 Paul Kariya .60 1.50
16 Trevor Kidd .40 1.00
17 Nikolai Khabibulin .40 1.00
18 Olaf Kolzig .40 1.00
19 Brian Leetch .40 1.00
20 Eric Lindros .60 1.50
21 Kirk McLean .40 1.00
22 Mark Messier .60 1.50
23 Rob Neidermayer .30 .75
24 Chris Osgood .60 1.50
25 Felix Potvin .60 1.50
26 Daren Puppa .30 .75
27 Jeremy Roenick .60 1.50
28 Patrick Roy 1.25 3.00
29 Joe Sakic Cup .75 2.00
30 Brendan Shanahan .60 1.50
31 Joe Thornton .75 2.00
32 John Vanbiesbrouck .40 1.00
33 Alexei Yashin .40 1.00
34 Steve Yzerman Cup 1.25 3.00

1980-81 Kings Card Night

The cards in this 14-card set were in color and are standard size. The set was produced during the 1980-81 season by All-Star Cards Ltd. for the Los Angeles Kings at the request of owner Jerry Buss. Reportedly 5000 sets were produced, virtually all of which were given away at the Kings' "Card Night." The fronts featured color "mug shots" of the players; the backs provided career highlights and brief biographical information.

COMPLETE SET (14) 10.00 20.00
1 Marcel Dionne 4.00 8.00
2 Glenn Goldup .30 .75
3 Doug Halward .30 .75
4 Billy Harris .40 1.00
5 Steve Jensen .40 1.00
6 Jerry Korab .30 .75
7 Mario Lessard .60 1.50
8 Dave Lewis .40 1.00
9 Mike Murphy .30 .75
10 Rob Palmer .30 .75
11 Charlie Simmer .75 2.00
12 Dave Taylor 1.25 3.00
13 Garry Unger .60 1.50
14 Jay Wells .40 1.00

1984-85 Kings Smokey

This fire safety set contained 23 cards which were numbered on the back. Players in the set were members of the Los Angeles Kings hockey team. The cards measured approximately 2 15/16" by 4 3/8" and were numbered on the back in the upper right corner. Card backs contained a fire safety cartoon and minimal information about the player. The set was sponsored by the California Department of Forestry.

COMPLETE SET (23) 8.00 20.00
1 Russ Anderson .20 .50
2 Marcel Dionne 2.00 5.00
3 Brian Engblom .30 .75
4 Daryl Evans .20 .50
5 Jim Fox .30 .75
6 Garry Galley .60 1.50
7 Anders Hakansson .20 .50
8 Mark Hardy .20 .50
9 Bob Janecyk .30 .75
10 John Paul Kelly .20 .50
11 Brian MacLellan .20 .50
12 Bernie Nicholls 1.00 2.50
13 Craig Redmond .20 .50
14 Terry Ruskowski .30 .75
15 Doug Smith .20 .50
16 Dave Taylor .75 2.00
17 Jay Wells .20 .50
18 Darren Eliot .30 .75
19 Rick Lapointe .20 .50
20 Bob Miller .20 .50
21 Steve Seguin .20 .50
22 Phil Sykes .20 .50
23 Pat Quinn CO .20 .50

1986-87 Kings 20th Anniversary Team Issue

Cards measured 4" x 6 1/4" and featured black and white photos on the front along with player name and 20th anniversary logo. Backs were blank.

COMPLETE SET (23) 10.00 25.00
1 Bob Bourne .08 .25
2 Jimmy Carson .75 2.00
3 Steve Duchesne .75 2.00
4 Darren Eliot .08 .25
5 Bryan Erickson .08 .25
6 Jim Fox .08 .25
7 Garry Galley .40 1.00
8 Paul Guay .08 .25
9 Mark Hardy .08 .25
10 Bob Janecyk .30 .75
11 Dean Kennedy .08 .25
12 Grant Ledyard .20 .50
13 Morris Lukowich .08 .25
14 Sean McKenna .08 .25
15 Roland Melanson .30 .75
16 Bernie Nicholls .75 2.00
17 Joe Paterson .08 .25
18 Larry Playfair .08 .25
19 Luc Robitaille 5.00 12.00
20 Phil Sykes .08 .25
21 Dave Taylor .30 .75
22 Jay Wells .08 .25
23 Tiger Williams .30 .75

1988-89 Kings Smokey

This fire safety set contained 25 cards and featured members of the Los Angeles Kings hockey team in their then-new silver and black colors. The cards were unnumbered; not even the player's uniform number was given on the card. The players are listed below alphabetically by name. The cards measured approximately 2 1/2" by 3 1/2". Card backs contained a fire safety cartoon and minimal information about the player. The set was sponsored by the California Department of Forestry and Fire Protection.

COMPLETE SET (25) 12.00 30.0
1 Mike Allison .20 .5
2 Ken Baumgartner .30 .7
3 Bob Carpenter .20 .5
4 Doug Crossman .20 .5
5 Dale DeGray .20 .5
6 Steve Duchesne .60 1.5
7 Ron Duguay .30 .7
8 Mark Fitzpatrick .40 1.0
9 Jim Fox .20 .5
10 Robbie Ftorek CO .20 .5
11 Wayne Gretzky 6.00 15.0
12 Gilles Hamel .20 .5
13 Glenn Healy .40 1.0
14 Mike Krushelnyski .20 .5
15 Tom Laidlaw .20 .5
16 Bryan Maxwell CO .08 .2
17 Wayne McBean .20 .5
18 Marty McSorley 1.25 3.0
19 Bernie Nicholls .60 1.5
20 Cap Raeder CO .08 .2
21 Luc Robitaille 1.50 4.0
22 Dave Taylor .60 1.5
23 John Tonelli .30 .7
24 Tim Watters .20 .5
25 Title Card .20 .5
(Checklist on back)

1989-90 Kings Smokey

This 24-card standard-size set of Los Angeles Kings was sponsored by the USDA Forest Service in cooperation with other agencies. The front featured a color action photo, banded above and below with gra[y] stripes. The Smokey the Bear logo appeared in the upper left-hand corner, and the Los Angeles Kings logo in the lower right-hand corner. A black border below and on the right of the picture created the impression of a shadow. The back provided player information, card number, and a fire prevention cartoon. The cards were numbered in the upper right corner of the reverse.

COMPLETE SET (24) 10.00 25.0
1 Wayne Gretzky 5.00 12.0
2 Tim Watters .20 .5
3 Mikael Lindholm .20 .5
4 Mike Allison .20 .5
5 Steve Kasper .20 .5
6 Dave Taylor .40 1.0
7 Larry Robinson .75 2.0
8 Luc Robitaille 1.25 3.0
9 Barry Beck .30 .7
10 Keith Crowder .20 .5
11 Petr Prajsler .20 .5
12 Mike Krushelnyski .20 .5
13 John Tonelli .30 .7
14 Steve Duchesne .40 1.0
15 Jay Miller .20 .5
16 Kelly Hrudey .60 1.5
17 Marty McSorley .75 2.0
18 Mario Gosselin .30 .7
19 Craig Duncanson .20 .5
20 Bob Kudelski .20 .5
21 Brian Benning .20 .5
22 Mikko Makela .20 .5
23 Tom Laidlaw .20 .5
24 Checklist Card .20 .5

1989-90 Kings Smokey Gretzky 8x10

This 8" by 10" blowup of Wayne Gretzky's regular Smokey issue featured a white-bordered color action shot of him on the front. The team name appeared at the top, and his name and position, along with the Kings and Smokey logos, were shown at the bottom. The black-and-white back had his name and biograp[hy] in the upper left corner and featured a cartoon of bea[r] on skates scoring a goal against a wildfire goalie whi[le] Smokey looked on. The card was unnumbered.

NNO Wayne Gretzky 6.00 15.0

1990-91 Kings Smokey

This 25-card set of Los Angeles Kings was sponsore[d] by Royal Crown Cola in cooperation with the USDA Forest Service and other agencies and features members of the Los Angeles Kings. The cards measured the standard size (2 1/2" by 3 1/2"). The fronts featured color action player photos with white borders. The player's name appeared in a silver-gray stripe above the picture, while his position and sever[al] logos appearedin a white rectangle below the picture. The backs had biographical information and a fire prevention cartoon starring Smokey, enframed by thi[n] black borders. The cards were numbered on the back [in] the upper left corner. The mascot card had a checklis[t] on its reverse.

COMPLETE SET (25) 6.00 15.0
1 Wayne Gretzky 3.00 8.0
2 Brian Benning .08 .2
3 Rob Blake .40 1.0
4 Tim Watters .08 .2
5 Todd Elik .08 .2
6 Tomas Sandstrom .20 .5
7 Steve Kasper .08 .2
8 Dave Taylor .40 1.0
9 Larry Robinson .40 1.0
10 Luc Robitaille .60 1.5
11 Tony Granato .20 .5
12 Tom Laidlaw .08 .2
13 Francois Breault .08 .2
14 John Tonelli .20 .5
15 Steve Duchesne .20 .5
16 Jay Miller .08 .2
17 Kelly Hrudey .60 1.5
18 Marty McSorley .40 1.0
19 Daniel Berthiaume .20 .5
20 Bob Kudelski .08 .2
21 Brad Jones .08 .2
22 John McIntyre .08 .2
23 Rod Buskas .08 .2
24 Kingston (Mascot) .02 .1
(Checklist on back)
NNO RC Cola Challenge .02 .1

1991-92 Kings Upper Deck Season Ticket

This approximately 5" by 3 1/2" horizontally oriented card was sent out to 7,000 Los Angeles Kings season ticket holders along with a Christmas card from Upper Deck in December 1991 celebrating the Kings' 25th anniversary. The front featured a borderless color action shot of several Kings players and opponent(s) [in] a pileup in front of the Kings' net with Kings' goalie Kelly Hrudey. The limited edition seal with production number was placed in the upper left. The Upper Deck Hockey logo was in the upper right. The horizontal back carrieda drawing of Wayne Gretzky, Rogie Vachon, Bruce McNall, Marcel Dionne, and Luc Robitaille.

NNO Los Angeles Kings 40.00 100.0
Season Ticket Holders/25th Ann

1992-93 Kings Upper Deck Season Ticket

is approximately 5" by 3 1/2" horizontally oriented d was sent out to Los Angeles Kings season ticket lders along with a Christmas card from Upper Deck December 1992. The card was numbered out of 000.

0 Los Angeles Kings 30.00 75.00
eason Ticket Holders

1993 Kings Forum

is set commemorated various athletes who appeared he Great Western Forum. Cards were standard size d full color. Only three hockey playerrs appeared in set, and they are the ones listed below.

ogie Vachon .40 1.00
larcel Dionne .40 1.00
Wayne Gretzky 4.00 10.00

1993-94 Kings Upper Deck Season Ticket

s approximately 5" by 3 1/2" horizontally oriented d was sent out to 10,000 Los Angeles Kings season ket holders along with a Christmas card from Upper k in December 1993.

0 Los Angeles Kings 20.00 50.00
eason Ticket Holders

1994-95 Kings Upper Deck Season Ticket

s approximately 5" by 3 1/2" horizontally oriented d was sent out to Los Angeles Kings season ticket ders as a seasonal greeting from the Kings and per Deck in December 1994. The front of the card ried a yuletide message over a ghosted image of yne Gretzky. The back had another message, a color ito of Gretzky, and the individual serial number out 15,000.

0 Los Angeles Kings 10.00 25.00
Vayne Gretzky

1998-99 Kings LA Times Coins

ins were given out at one coin per game for six nes.

MPLETE SET (6) 12.00 30.00
ob Blake .75 2.00
larcel Dionne 4.00 10.00
arry Robinson 2.50 6.00
uc Robitaille 4.00 10.00
ave Taylor .75 2.00
ogie Vachon 1.50 4.00

1999 Kings AAA Magnets

se magnets were issued as promotional giveaways I were sponsored by AAA.

MPLETE SET (2) 1.50 4.00
uc Robitaille 1.25 3.00
iggy Palffy .75 2.00

2002-03 Kings Game Sheets

se 8 X 10 player sheets were apparently given away ome games during the 02-03 season. The fronts ried a player image, name and jersey number. The k of the sheets carried lineups for the Kings and r opponents for that particluar game along with the nsor's logo. Please note that several players have e than one card with differing backs.

MPLETE SET (40) 30.00 75.00
ryan Smolinski 1.00 2.50
etzel's Pretzels
ryan Smolinski 1.00 2.50
ilshire Grand
mitry Yushkevich 1.00 2.50
etzel's Pretzels
mitry Yushkevich 1.00 2.50
ilshire Grand
raig Johnson 1.00 2.50
etzel's Pretzels
raig Johnson 1.00 2.50
ilshire Grand
aroslav Modry 1.00 2.50
etzel's Pretzels
aroslav Modry 1.00 2.50
ilshire Grand
ic Belanger 1.00 2.50
etzel's Pretzels
Eric Belanger 1.00 2.50
ilshire Grand
Erik Rasmussen 1.00 2.50
etzel's Pretzels
Erik Rasmussen 1.00 2.50
ilshire Grand
an Laperriere 1.00 2.50
etzel's Pretzels
an Laperriere 1.00 2.50
ilshire Grand
Felix Potvin 2.00 5.00
etzel's Pretzels
Felix Potvin 2.00 5.00
ilshire Grand
Brad Chartrand 1.00 2.50
etzel's Pretzels
Brad Chartrand 1.00 2.50
ilshire Grand
Mathieu Schneider 1.00 2.50
etzel's Pretzels
Mathieu Schneider 1.00 2.50
ilshire Grand
Mikko Eloranta 1.00 2.50
etzel's Pretzels
Mikko Eloranta 1.00 2.50
ilshire Grand
ason Allison 1.25 3.00
etzel's Pretzels
ason Allison 1.25 3.00
ilshire Grand
Mattias Norstrom 1.00 2.50
etzel's Pretzels
Mattias Norstrom 1.00 2.50
ilshire Grand
amie Storr 1.00 2.50
etzel's Pretzels
amie Storr 1.00 2.50
ilshire Grand
ubomir Visnovsky 1.00 2.50
etzel's Pretzels
ubomir Visnovsky 1.00 2.50
lshire Grand
aron Miller 1.00 2.50
etzel's Pretzels
aron Miller 1.00 2.50
lshire Grand
lexander Frolov 1.50 4.00
etzel's Pretzels
lexander Frolov 1.50 4.00
lshire Grand
igmund Palffy 1.50 4.00
etzel's Pretzels
igmund Palffy 1.50 4.00
lshire Grand
dam Deadmarsh 1.00 2.50
etzel's Pretzels
dam Deadmarsh 1.00 2.50
Wilshire Grand
39 Derek Armstrong 1.00 2.50
Wetzel's Pretzels
40 Derek Armstrong 1.00 2.50
Wilshire Grand

2002-03 Kings Team Issue

These 8X10 sheets were distributed by the Kings at public appearances. They are blank backed and do not include mention of a sponsor as do the other Kings sheets issued this season in game programs. The checklist is incomplete. If you have additional information on distribution or checklist, please write hockeymag@beckett.com.

COMPLETE SET
1 Adam Deadmarsh 1.00 2.50
2 Ziggy Palffy 1.00 2.50
3 Mattias Norstrom .75 2.00
4 Felix Potvin .75 2.00
5 Bryan Smolinski .75 2.00
6 Jason Allison .75 2.00
7 Aaron Miller .75 2.00

2005-06 Kings Team Issue

COMPLETE SET (15) 5.00 10.00
1 Header Card .02 .10
2 Luc Robitaille .75 2.00
3 Jeremy Roenick .75 2.00
4 Derek Armstrong .20 .50
5 Craig Conroy .20 .50
6 Alexander Frolov .40 1.00
7 Mathieu Garon .40 1.00
8 Joe Corvo .20 .50
9 Lubomir Visnovsky .20 .50
10 Aaron Miller .20 .50
11 Mattias Norstrom .20 .50
12 Eric Belanger .20 .50
13 Dustin Brown .40 1.00
14 Michael Cammalleri .40 1.00
15 Pavol Demitra .20 .50

1994 Kollectorfest

This five-card standard-size set was issued in conjunction with a collectibles show on October 9, 1994 in Kitchener, Ontario. The three players in this set were all Kitchener natives and donated their time for this show. Reportedly only 3,000 sets were produced, and each set had its own serial number on a title card. The fronts featured black-and-white posed player photos with team color-coded borders and the player's name on the bottom. The players' uniforms had been colorized. The backs carried player profiles. The cards were unnumbered and checklisted below in alphabetical order.

COMPLETE SET (5) 4.00 10.00
1 Woody Dumart 1.25 3.00
2 Dutch Hiller .75 2.00
3 Milt Schmidt 2.00 5.00
4 Title Card .20 .50
Kollectorfest '94
5 Title Card .20 .50
Oktoberfest 1994

1986-87 Kraft Drawings

The 1986-87 Kraft Hockey Drawings set contained 81 standard-size unnumbered cards featuring players from Canadian-based NHL teams. The fronts featured black and white drawings of the players in action, along with each player's team logo. Each back showed the entire checklist for the set. Noted sports artists Jerry Hersh and Carlton McDiarmid drew 42 and 30, respectively, of the 81 cards in the set. The cards were unnumbered and so they are presented below in alphabetical order. Prints of these cards were available through an offer detailed on the card backs. These tended to sell in the two to five times the values listed below. Dealers have reported the existence of a John Kordic print, which apparently was not released to the public. This print sells for $5-$10. An album for the cards was also offered. The set featured early cards of Wendel Clark, Stephane Richer, Patrick Roy, and Mike Vernon.

COMPLETE SET (81) 40.00 100.00
COMPLETE FACT.SET (81) 50.00 125.00
1 Glenn Anderson .40 1.00
2 Brent Ashton .20 .50
3 Laurie Boschman .20 .50
4 Richard Brodeur .30 .75
5 Guy Carbonneau .30 .75
6 Randy Carlyle .30 .75
7 Chris Chelios 1.25 3.00
8 Wendel Clark 4.00 10.00
9 Glen Cochrane .20 .50
10 Paul Coffey 1.25 3.00
11 Alain Cote .20 .50
12 Russ Courtnall .40 1.00
13 Kjell Dahlin .20 .50
14 Dan Daoust .20 .50
15 Bill Derlago .20 .50
16 Tom Fergus .20 .50
17 Grant Fuhr 1.50 4.00
18 Bob Gainey .40 1.00
19 Gaston Gingras .20 .50
20 Mario Gosselin .30 .75
21 Michel Goulet .40 1.00
22 Rick Green .20 .50
23 Wayne Gretzky 15.00 40.00
24 Doug Halward .20 .50
25 Dale Hawerchuk .60 1.50
26 Brian Hayward .30 .75
27 Dale Hunter .40 1.00
28 Mike Krushelnyski .20 .50
29 Jari Kurri 1.25 3.00
30 Mike Lalor .20 .50
31 Gary Leeman .20 .50
32 Rejean Lemelin .40 1.00
33 Claude Lemieux 2.00 5.00
34 Doug Lidster .20 .50
35 Hakan Loob .40 1.00
36 Kevin Lowe .40 1.00
37 Craig Ludwig .20 .50
38 Paul MacLean .20 .50
39 Clint Malarchuk .40 1.00
40 Mario Marois .20 .50
41 Lanny McDonald .40 1.00
42 Mike McPhee .30 .75
43 Mark Messier 4.00 10.00
44 Randy Moller .20 .50
45 Sergio Momesso .20 .50
46 Andy Moog 1.00 2.50
47 Brian Mullen .20 .50
48 Joe Mullen .40 1.00
49 Mark Napier .20 .50
50 Mats Naslund .40 1.00
51 Chris Nilan .40 1.00
52 Barry Pederson .30 .75
53 Steve Penney .30 .75
54 Jim Peplinski .20 .50
55 Brent Peterson .20 .50
56 Pat Price .20 .50
57 Paul Reinhart .20 .50
58 Stephane Richer .60 1.50
59 Doug Risebrough .20 .50
60 Larry Robinson .40 1.00
61 Patrick Roy 15.00 40.00
62 Borje Salming .40 1.00
63 Petri Skriko .20 .50
64 Brian Skrudland .30 .75
65 Bobby Smith .30 .75
66 Stan Smyl UER .30 .75
(Misspelled Syml on card front)
67 Anton Stastny .20 .50
68 Peter Stastny .40 1.00
69 Thomas Steen .30 .75
70 Patrik Sundstrom .20 .50
71 Gary Suter .60 1.50
72 Petr Svoboda .30 .75
73 Tony Tanti .20 .50
74 Greg Terrion .20 .50
75 Steve Thomas .75 2.00
76 Perry Turnbull .20 .50
77 Rick Vaive .40 1.00
78 Mike Vernon 1.50 4.00
79 Ryan Walter .20 .50
80 Carey Wilson .20 .50
81 Ken Wregget .60 1.50
ALB Album 10.00 25.00

1989-90 Kraft

This set of 64 standard-size cards featuring players from Canadian-based NHL teams was available on the package backs of specially marked boxes of Kraft Dinner, Spirals, and Egg Noodles. Also specially marked boxes of Jell-O Puddings and Pie Fillings and Kraft Singles featured additional NHL hockey cards. Each card featured a color action photo of the player, with his name, number, and team logo in different color strips running across the bottom of the picture. Kraft also issued a special album to house the cards. The cards were distributed in a variety of ways. There were 26 different Kraft boxes each with two cards on the package back. A sheet of six All-Star cards was packed in each unopened case of Kraft Dinners. Sticker sheets were found in specially marked 500g packages of Kraft Singles. Cards could also be obtained in exchange for UPCs and a small handling fee. The set numbering is listed below according to the company's checklist.

COMPLETE SET (64) 40.00 100.00
COMPLETE FACT.SET (64) 50.00 125.00
1 Doug Gilmour .75 2.00
2 Theo Fleury 1.50 4.00
3 Al MacInnis .40 1.00
4 Sergei Makarov .30 .75
5 Joe Nieuwendyk .40 1.00
6 Joel Otto .20 .50
7 Colin Patterson .20 .50
8 Sergei Priakin .20 .50
9 Paul Ranheim .20 .50
10 Glenn Anderson .40 1.00
11 Grant Fuhr .60 1.50
12 Charlie Huddy .20 .50
13 Jari Kurri .75 2.00
14 Kevin Lowe .20 .50
15 Mark Messier 1.25 3.00
16 Craig Simpson .20 .50
17 Steve Smith .20 .50
18 Esa Tikkanen .40 1.00
19 Guy Carbonneau .30 .75
20 Chris Chelios .75 2.00
21 Shayne Corson .40 1.00
22 Russ Courtnall .30 .75
23 Mats Naslund .30 .75
24 Stephane Richer .30 .75
25 Patrick Roy 2.50 6.00
26 Bobby Smith .30 .75
27 Petr Svoboda .20 .50
28 Jeff Brown .20 .50
29 Paul Gillis .20 .50
30 Michel Goulet .30 .75
31 Guy Lafleur .75 2.00
32 Joe Sakic 2.00 5.00
33 Peter Stastny .30 .75
34 Wendel Clark .60 1.50
35 Vincent Damphousse .40 1.00
36 Gary Leeman .20 .50
37 Daniel Marois .20 .50
38 Ed Olczyk .20 .50
39 Rob Ramage .20 .50
40 Vladimir Krutov .20 .50
41 Igor Larionov .40 1.00
42 Trevor Linden .40 1.00
43 Kirk McLean .40 1.00
44 Paul Reinhart .20 .50
45 Tony Tanti .20 .50
46 Brent Ashton .20 .50
47 Randy Carlyle .20 .50
48 Randy Cunneyworth .20 .50
49 Dave Ellett .20 .50
50 Dale Hawerchuk .40 1.00
51 Fredrik Olausson .20 .50
52 Ray Bourque AS .75 2.00
53 Sean Burke AS .40 1.00
54 Paul Coffey AS .75 2.00
55 Mario Lemieux AS 2.50 6.00
56 Cam Neely AS .75 2.00
57 Rick Tocchet AS .40 1.00
58 Steve Duchesne AS .20 .50
59 Wayne Gretzky AS 4.00 10.00
60 Joe Mullen AS .40 1.00
61 Gary Suter AS .20 .50
62 Mike Vernon AS .40 1.00
63 Steve Yzerman AS 2.00 5.00
64 Checklist Card .20 .50
xx Album 10.00 25.00

1989-90 Kraft All-Stars Stickers

Distributed by Kraft General Foods Canada in packages of Kraft Singles, these six bilingual sticker-sheets measured approximately 4 1/2" by 2 3/4" and each featured stickers of two players in their NHL All-Star uniforms and four NHL team logo stickers. The sheets were white, with color player action shots and color team logos on the peel-away stickers. The white back of each sticker-sheet carried a bilingual order form for the Kraft NHL Hockey sticker/card album. The stickers were numbered on the front.

COMPLETE SET (6) 8.00 20.00
1 Mike McPhee .40 1.00
Paul Reinhart
2 Wayne Gretzky 5.00 12.00
Rick Tocchet
3 Paul Coffey 2.50 6.00
Steve Yzerman
4 Mike Vernon 1.25 3.00
Ray Bourque
5 Jari Kurri 3.00 8.00
Mario Lemieux
6 Kevin Lowe .40 1.00
Sean Burke

1990-91 Kraft

This 115-card standard-size set was issued by Kraft to honor some of the stars of the NHL. There was also a special album, which included advertisements for various Kraft products, issued to store all the cards. The set was divided into three parts: Cards 1-64 were NHL star players listed alphabetically while 65-91 were the Conference All-Stars (Campbell 65-78 and Wales 79-91). Card numbers 92-115 were team photos along with three unnumbered team checklist cards. To complete the set, the consumer had to purchase items from eight different Kraft product groups. Only card number 66 (Wayne Gretzky) was available in two different product groups: Jell-O Instant Pudding (four servings) and Jell-O Lemon Pie Filling (tri-portion).

COMPLETE SET (115) 30.00 80.00
COMPLETE FACT.SET (115) 30.00 80.00
1 Dave Babych .20 .50
2 Brian Bellows .30 .75
3 Ray Bourque .60 1.50
4 Sean Burke .40 1.00
5 Jimmy Carson .20 .50
6 Chris Chelios .60 1.50
7 Dino Ciccarelli .30 .75
8 Paul Coffey .60 1.50
9 Geoff Courtnall .30 .75
10 Doug Crossman .20 .50
11 Kevin Dineen .20 .50
12 Pat Elynuik .20 .50
13 Ron Francis .40 1.00
14 Gerard Gallant .20 .50
15 Wayne Gretzky 4.00 10.00
16 Dale Hawerchuk .40 1.00
17 Ron Hextall .40 1.00
18 Phil Housley .30 .75
19 Mark Howe .30 .75
20 Brett Hull .75 2.00
21 Al Iafrate .25 .60
22 Guy Lafleur .60 1.50
23 Pat LaFontaine .40 1.00
24 Rod Langway .20 .50
25 Igor Larionov .40 1.00
26 Steve Larmer .30 .75
27 Gary Leeman .20 .50
28 Brian Leetch .60 1.50
29 Mario Lemieux 3.00 8.00
30 Trevor Linden .40 1.00
31 Mike Liut .25 .60
32 Mark Messier .75 2.00
33 Al MacInnis .30 .75
34 Mike Modano .75 2.00
35 Andy Moog .40 1.00
36 Joe Mullen .30 .75
37 Kirk Muller .30 .75
38 Petr Nedved .50 1.25
39 Cam Neely .60 1.50
40 Bernie Nicholls .30 .75
41 Joe Nieuwendyk .30 .75
42 Mats Sundin .60 1.50
43 Daren Puppa .30 .75
44 Rob Ramage .20 .50
45 Bill Ranford .40 1.00
46 Stephane Richer .30 .75
47 Larry Robinson .40 1.00
48 Luc Robitaille .40 1.00
49 Patrick Roy 3.00 8.00
50 Joe Sakic 1.25 3.00
51 Denis Savard .40 1.00
52 Craig Simpson .20 .50
53 Bobby Smith .25 .60
54 Peter Stastny .40 1.00
55 Thomas Steen .20 .50
56 Scott Stevens .30 .75
57 Brent Sutter .20 .50
58 Rick Tocchet .40 1.00
59 Pierre Turgeon .40 1.00
60 John Vanbiesbrouck .60 1.50
61 Mike Vernon .40 1.00
62 Doug Wilson .30 .75
63 Steve Yzerman 2.00 5.00
64 Checklist Card .20 .50
65 Steve Duchesne AS .20 .50
66 Wayne Gretzky AS 2.50 6.00
67 Brett Hull AS .50 1.25
68 Jari Kurri AS .40 1.00
69 Mike Gartner AS .30 .75
70 Kirk McLean AS .30 .75
71 Mark Messier AS .50 1.25
72 Joe Mullen AS .25 .60
73 Bernie Nicholls AS .25 .60
74 Joe Nieuwendyk AS .30 .75
75 Luc Robitaille AS .30 .75
76 Mike Vernon AS .30 .75
77 Doug Wilson AS .20 .50
78 Steve Yzerman AS 1.25 3.00
79 Joe Sakic AS .75 2.00
80 Ray Bourque AS .50 1.25
81 Chris Chelios AS .50 1.25
82 Paul Coffey AS .50 1.25
83 Ron Francis AS .40 1.00
84 Cam Neely AS .40 1.00
85 Phil Housley AS .25 .60
86 Pat LaFontaine AS .40 1.00
87 Mario Lemieux AS 2.00 5.00
88 Kirk Muller AS .25 .60
89 Stephane Richer AS .25 .60
90 Patrick Roy AS 2.00 5.00
91 Pierre Turgeon AS .40 1.00
92 Boston Bruins .25 .60
93 Buffalo Sabres .20 .50
94 Calgary Flames .20 .50
95 Chicago Blackhawks .25 .60
96 Detroit Red Wings .25 .60
97 Edmonton Oilers .20 .50
98 Hartford Whalers .20 .50
99 Los Angeles Kings .25 .60
100 Minnesota North Stars .20 .50
101 Montreal Canadiens .25 .60
102 New Jersey Devils .20 .50
103 New York Islanders .20 .50
104 New York Rangers .25 .60
105 Philadelphia Flyers .20 .50
106 Pittsburgh Penguins .20 .50
107 Quebec Nordiques .20 .50
108 St. Louis Blues .20 .50
109 Toronto Maple Leafs .25 .60
110 Vancouver Canucks .20 .50
111 Washington Capitals .20 .50
112 Winnipeg Jets .20 .50
113 Unnumbered Checklist .08 .25
114 Unnumbered Checklist .08 .25
115 Unnumbered Checklist .08 .25
xx Album 10.00 25.00

1991-92 Kraft

This set of 92 collectibles was sponsored by Kraft-General Foods Canada to commemorate the 75th anniversary of the NHL. It consisted of 68 standard-size cards and 24 discs. To store the set, a 75th Anniversary NHL hockey card album could be purchased. Kraft also provided the opportunity for the collector to purchase any combination of ten cards or discs through the mail to complete the set. Cards 1-40 were issued in Kraft Dinners, cards 41-56 in Kraft Spirals, and cards 57-64 in Kraft Noodles. An eight-card subset highlights "Great Moments" in NHL history. The fronts featured action player photos framed inside a team color border. The player's name was printed in black lettering across the top while the team name, team logo, and 75th NHL Anniversary logo appeared below the picture. The horizontally oriented backs were light gray with red print and carry biography, career statistics, and logos. Measuring 2 3/4" in diameter, the discs (65-88) were available under the caps of Kraft Peanut Butter. They featured action cut-out photos of two players (superimposed on a blue background), pairing today's All-Stars with legends of the past. Players' names and their teams appeared in a white semi-circular margin. The bilingual disc backs were bright yellow with black print and carried biographical and statistical information. Both discs and cards were numbered on the back.

COMPLETE SET (92) 30.00 80.00
COMPLETE FACT.SET (92) 40.00 100.00
1 Mario Lemieux 3.00 8.00
2 Mark Recchi .40 1.00
3 Jaromir Jagr 3.00 8.00
4 Mats Sundin .75 2.00
5 Adam Oates .60 1.50
6 Great Moments .60 1.50
Canadien Dynasty
Maurice Richard
Jacques Plante
7 Brendan Shanahan 1.50 4.00
8 Pat Falloon .20 .50
9 Grant Fuhr .40 1.00
10 Gary Leeman .20 .50
11 Petr Nedved .50 1.25
12 Kirk Muller .30 .75
13 Theo Fleury .75 2.00
14 Dino Ciccarelli .25 .60
15 Geoff Courtnall .20 .50
16 Mark Messier 1.00 2.50
17 Ken Hodge Jr. .20 .50
18 Chris Chelios .75 2.00
19 Mike Vernon .30 .75
20 Kevin Hatcher .25 .60
21 Stephane Richer .20 .50
22 Mark Tinordi .20 .50
23 Pat Verbeek .25 .60
24 John Cullen .20 .50
25 Pat LaFontaine .40 1.00
26 Stephan Lebeau .20 .50
27 Mike Gartner .30 .75
28 Great Moments .30 .75
Last Leaf Dynasty
Bobby Baun
29 Shayne Corson .25 .60
30 Trevor Linden .40 1.00
31 Craig Janney .25 .60
32 Al MacInnis .30 .75
33 Phil Housley .25 .60
34 Doug Wilson .20 .50
35 Tony Granato .20 .50
36 Dale Hawerchuk .30 .75
37 Bill Durnan .75 2.00
Turk Broda
38 Brian Bellows .20 .50
39 Great Moments .30 .75
Number 23 with number 23
Bob Gainey
40 Great Moments .30 .75
A Night to Remember
Darryl Sittler
41 Joe Sakic 1.50 4.00
42 Wendel Clark .40 1.00
43 Brent Sutter .20 .50
44 Bill Ranford .30 .75
45 Rick Tocchet .25 .60
46 Paul Ysebaert .20 .50
47 Adam Creighton .20 .50
48 Mike Modano .75 2.00
49 Russ Courtnall .20 .50
50 Great Moments .20 .50
Evolution of Stanley Cup
Syl Apps
51 Sergei Fedorov 1.25 3.00
52 Mike Ricci .25 .60
53 Scott Stevens .25 .60
54 Great Moments .40 1.00
The Ultimate Expansion
Bobby Clarke
55 Owen Nolan .30 .75
56 Jeremy Roenick .60 1.50
57 Ray Bourque .75 2.00
58 Gerard Gallant .20 .50
59 Andy Moog .40 1.00
60 Alexander Mogilny .50 1.25
61 Great Moments .20 .50
Islander Tradition
Denis Potvin
62 Ed Olczyk .20 .50
63 Tomas Sandstrom .20 .50
64 Checklist .20 .50
65 Wayne Gretzky 4.00 10.00
Maurice Richard
66 Brett Hull .75 2.00
Guy Lafleur
67 Jari Kurri .40 1.00
Bobby Clarke
68 Steve Yzerman 2.00 5.00
Jean Beliveau
69 Steve Larmer .30 .75
Pat Stapleton
70 Luc Robitaille .60 1.50
Ted Lindsay
71 Larry Murphy .40 1.00
Doug Harvey
72 Denis Potvin .30 .75
Gary Suter
73 Brian Leetch .75 2.00
Harry Howell
74 Paul Coffey .75 2.00
Bill Gadsby
75 Jon Casey .60 1.50
Terry Sawchuk
76 Patrick Roy 3.00 8.00
Jacques Plante
77 Denis Savard .40 1.00
Serge Savard
78 Doug Gilmour .60 1.50
Bob Baun
79 Guy Carbonneau .30 .75
Yvan Cournoyer
80 Gilbert Perreault .40 1.00
Larry Robinson
81 Red Kelly .30 .75
Craig Simpson
82 Bobby Smith .30 .75
Rod Gilbert
83 Syl Apps .30 .75
Peter Stastny
84 BoomBoom Geoffrion .60 1.50
Vincent Damphousse
85 Marcel Dionne .30 .75
Steve Smith
86 Tim Horton .75 2.00
Kevin Dineen
87 Michel Goulet .40 1.00
Frank Mahovlich
88 Mike Richter .60 1.50
Henri Richard
89 Boston Bruins logo .20 .50
New York Rangers logo
Original Six/(Unnumbered)
90 Montreal Canadiens logo .20 .50
Toronto Maple Leafs logo
Original Six/(Unnumbered)
91 Chicago Blackhawks logo .20 .50
Detroit Red Wings logo
Original Six/(Unnumbered)
92 Stanley Cup .40 1.00
(Unnumbered)
ALB Album 10.00 25.00

1992-93 Kraft

This set of 48 collectibles was sponsored by Kraft General Foods Canada to commemorate the 100th anniversary of the Stanley Cup. It consisted of 24 team cards, 12 discs, and 12 All-Star cards. To store the set, a Stanley Cup 100th anniversary album could be purchased by sending in three UPC symbols from Kraft Dinner, one UPC symbol from both Kraft Peanut Butter and Kraft Singles, and 12.99 along with sales tax and shipping and handling charges. The album included special storage sheets for the cards, the history of the Stanley Cup, and team autographs. The team cards, which measured approximately 5 3/16" by 3 7/16" and were distributed on the back of Kraft Dinner boxes, showed players in their centennial uniforms. The team name and logo appeared in a team color-coded stripe at the bottom. The backs were plain cardboard with the team history in red print. The discs, which measure approximately 2 3/4" in diameter and were distributed under the lids of Kraft Peanut Butter jars, are double-sided and feature 24 NHL goaltenders. The goalies are shown in action in a three-quarter-moon shaped picture against a team color-coded background. Statistics are included on the disc. The 12 All-Star cards, which measured approximately 1 3/4" by 2 1/2" and were distributed in groups of four in packages of Kraft Singles, carry color action player photos with white borders. A facsimile autograph was near the bottom of the picture. The player's name was printed in the wider bottom border between sponsor logos. The backs were white and included biographical information, statistics, and career highlights. Collectors who did not complete the series by purchasing the products could obtain any combination of eight cards or discs by sending the same UPC symbols, 3.00, plus shipping and handling charges. The cards were unnumbered and checklisted below in alphabetical order within each subset. The factory set price includes the album.

COMPLETE SET (48) 28.00 70.00
COMPLETE FACT.SET (48) 34.00 85.00
1 Boston Bruins .60 1.50
2 Buffalo Sabres .40 1.00
3 Calgary Flames .40 1.00
4 Chicago Blackhawks .60 1.50
5 Detroit Red Wings .60 1.50
6 Edmonton Oilers .40 1.00
7 Hartford Whalers .40 1.00
8 Los Angeles Kings .60 1.50
9 Minnesota North Stars .40 1.00
10 Montreal Canadiens .60 1.50
11 New Jersey Devils .40 1.00
12 New York Islanders .40 1.00
13 New York Rangers .60 1.50
14 Ottawa Senators .40 1.00
15 Philadelphia Flyers .40 1.00
16 Pittsburgh Penguins .60 1.50
17 Quebec Nordiques .40 1.00
18 San Jose Sharks .40 1.00
19 St. Louis Blues .40 1.00
20 Tampa Bay Lightning .40 1.00
21 Toronto Maple Leafs .60 1.50
22 Vancouver Canucks .40 1.00
23 Washington Capitals .40 1.00
24 Winnipeg Jets .40 1.00
25 Tom Barrasso .40 1.00
Wendell Young
26 Don Beaupre .40 1.00
Bob Essensa
27 Jon Casey .40 1.00
Dominic Roussel
28 Tim Cheveldae .40 1.00
Sean Burke
29 Jeff Hackett .60 1.50
Kirk McLean
30 Dominik Hasek 1.25 3.00
Chris Terreri
31 Ron Hextall .75 2.00
Curtis Joseph
32 Andy Moog .60 1.50
Mark Fitzpatrick
33 Bill Ranford .60 1.50
Kelly Hrudey
34 Patrick Roy 4.00 10.00
John Vanbiesbrouck
35 Peter Sidorkiewicz .60 1.50
Grant Fuhr
36 Mike Vernon .75 2.00
Ed Belfour
37 Ray Bourque AS .60 1.50
38 Chris Chelios AS .60 1.50
39 Paul Coffey AS .60 1.50
40 Wayne Gretzky AS 3.00 8.00
41 Brett Hull AS .75 2.00
42 Jaromir Jagr AS 1.50 4.00
43 Mario Lemieux AS 2.00 5.00
44 Trevor Linden AS .30 .75
45 Mark Messier AS .75 2.00
46 Jeremy Roenick AS .60 1.50
47 Patrick Roy AS 2.00 5.00
48 Steve Yzerman AS 1.25 3.00
ALB Album 6.00 15.00

1993-94 Kraft

This set of 72 collectibles was sponsored by Kraft General Foods Canada. It consisted of 26 team cards (1-26), 23 discs (27-49), 17 cut-outs (50-66), three Rookie cards (67-69), and three Trophy Winner cards (70-72). The album was available for purchase and contained special storage sheets for all the collectibles. It was organized by team and also included information (both in French and English) and a picture of the teams' stadiums. The team cards measured approximately 3 1/2" by 5 1/8" and were distributed on the back of Kraft Dinner boxes. The fronts showed a color action player photo with the player's name and number, and the team logo printed in a team color-coded stripe at the bottom. The backs had a ghosted light red team logo with biography (both in French and English) and statistics printed over the team logo. The discs, which measured approximately 3 3/4" in diameter and were distributed under the lids of Kraft Peanut Butter Jars, featured NHL captains and coaches. The captains' cards are double-sided and featured a blue border, while the double-sided coaches' cards had a gray border around the photo. The cut-outs, which were distributed in Jell-O boxes, featured color action poses. Also distributed in Kraft dinner boxes, the Rookie and Trophy Winner cards measured the same size as the team cards. The Trophy Winner cards showed the players with their respective trophies. The cards were unnumbered and checklisted below in alphabetical order within each subset. The factory set price includes the album.

COMPLETE SET (72) 30.00 80.00
COMPLETE FACT.SET (72) 40.00 100.00
1 Ed Belfour .60 1.50
2 Brian Bradley .20 .50
3 Pavel Bure .75 2.00
4 Paul Coffey .40 1.00
5 Russ Courtnall .20 .50
6 Alexandre Daigle .30 .75
7 Pat Falloon .20 .50
8 Theo Fleury .40 1.00
9 Doug Gilmour .40 1.00
10 Adam Graves .30 .75
11 Stu Grimson .20 .50
12 Al Iafrate .20 .50
13 Jaromir Jagr 1.25 3.00
14 Joe Juneau .30 .75
15 Eric Lindros 1.25 3.00
16 Alexander Mogilny .60 1.50
17 Kirk Muller .20 .50
18 Bill Ranford .30 .75
19 Mike Ricci .20 .50
20 Luc Robitaille .40 1.00
21 Geoff Sanderson .25 .60
22 Teemu Selanne 1.00 2.50
23 Brendan Shanahan 1.00 2.50
24 Pierre Turgeon .40 1.00
25 John Vanbiesbrouck .75 2.00
26 Valeri Zelepukin .20 .50
27 Al Arbour CO .75 2.00
28 Bob Berry CO .75 2.00
29 R.Bourque/P.Flatley 1.25 3.00
30 Scott Bowman CO 1.25 3.00
31 Pat Burns CO .75 2.00
32 Jacques Demers CO .75 2.00
33 K.Dineen/K.Hatcher .75 2.00
34 W.Gretzky/W.Clark 3.00 8.00
35 B.Hull/B.Shaw 1.25 3.00
36 Eddie Johnston CO .75 2.00
37 D.Kennedy/D.Savard .75 2.00
38 Dave King CO .75 2.00
39 P.LaFontaine/P.Verbeek 1.00 2.50
40 M.Lalor/M.Tinordi .75 2.00
41 T.Linden/T.Loney .50 1.25
42 Barry Melrose CO .75 2.00
43 M.Messier/M.Lemieux 3.00 8.00
44 John Muckler CO .75 2.00
45 J.Nieuwendyk/J.Sakic 1.00 2.50
46 Pierre Page CO .75 2.00
47 J.Roenick/G.Carbonneau 1.25 3.00
48 B.Skrudland/C.MacTavish .75 2.00
49 S.Stevens/S.Yzerman 1.50 4.00
50 Tom Barrasso .20 .50
51 Pavel Bure .75 2.00
52 Stephane Fiset .30 .75
53 Doug Gilmour .40 1.00
54 Wayne Gretzky 2.50 6.00
55 Kelly Hrudey .20 .50
56 Mario Lemieux 1.50 4.00
57 Eric Lindros 1.25 3.00
58 Kirk McLean .20 .50
59 Kirk Muller .20 .50
60 Joe Nieuwendyk .20 .50
61 Felix Potvin .40 1.00
63 Dominic Roussel .20 .50
64 Patrick Roy 1.50 4.00
65 Joe Sakic 1.00 2.50
66 Mike Vernon .20 .50
67 Jason Arnott .40 1.00
68 Rob Niedermayer .60 1.50
69 Chris Pronger .30 .75
70 Chris Chelios .30 .75
71 Mario Lemieux 1.50 4.00
72 Patrick Roy 1.50 4.00
ALB Album 10.00 25.00

1993-94 Kraft Recipes

Packaged in a folding cardboard cover, this set of recipe cards featured one card for each of the Canadian NHL teams. Each card featured a favorite recipe of a Canadian hockey star. The cards measured approximately 4 3/4" by 4 3/4" and consised of two pages bound by a perforated hinge. The front page displayed a color picture of the prepared food item, while its inside presented the recipe. On the page opposite the recipe appeared a color action player photo with a white-and-red inner border and a ice-blue outer border. The back page carried in its center a color panel displaying biography, statistics, and career summary; the wide surrounding border was a bright color (blue, green, orange, or red) and carried a player cutout as well as team and league logos. The recipe cards were unnumbered and checklisted below in alphabetical order. A Manufacturer's Rebate Coupon was also included in the package but is not considered part of the card set.

COMPLETE SET (8) 2.00 5.00
1 Vincent Damphousse .30 .75
2 Bob Essensa .20 .50
3 Doug Gilmour .50 1.25
4 Trevor Linden .30 .75
5 Al MacInnis .30 .75
6 Bill Ranford .30 .75
7 Mike Ricci .20 .50
8 Brad Shaw .20 .50

1994-95 Kraft

This set of 72 collectibles was sponsored by Kraft General Foods of Canada. Available from January to March 1995, it consisted of five distinct series: 14 Hockey Heroes cards (1-14), 16 Sharp Shooter cards (15-30), 26 Masked Defender cards (31-56), ten Award Winner discs (57-66), and six All-Star discs (67-72). Back panels of the seven different Jell-O Instant Pudding flavors showcased 14 Hockey Hero Action cards measuring 4 5/8" by 1 1/8". The horizontal fronts featured borderless color action player photos with the player's name, uniform number and team logo in a team color-coded bar alongside the left or right. The horizontal backs carried player biography, stats and sponsor logos, both in English and French. Measuring approximately 2 1/2" by 3 3/4", a pair of Sharp Shooter action cards together with an NHL team logo were inserted in Jell-O Pudding Snacks. The fronts featured borderless color action player photos on computerized backgrounds. The player's name and uniform number appeared in a team color-coded bar alongside the left or right. The backs carried player biography, stats and sponsor logos, both in English and French. Kraft Dinner boxes featured 26 oversized Masked Defenders goalie cards, measuring 3 1/2" by 5", on back panels of boxes. The fronts showed color action player photos on team color-coded backgrounds, with the player's name and uniform number in a team color-coded bar alongside the left or right, along with his nickname in stylized script. The backs carried player biography and stats, both in English and French, along with sponsor logos. Finally, two discs of 1994 Award Winners and the All-Star team were placed under each lid of Kraft Peanut Butter jars. The discs measured 2 3/4" in diameter. The Award Winner fronts had color action player photos with the player's name and uniform number, while the backs showed the trophy on a blue background. The All-Star fronts had color action player photos with the player's name and uniform number. On a ghosted player background, the backs carried player biography, season and NHL career totals. A collectible album to house all the cards was offered for 21.99. The cards were unnumbered and checklisted below in alphabetical order within each subset.

COMPLETE SET (72)	40.00	100.00
1 Dave Andreychuk	.20	.50
2 Chris Chelios	.60	1.50
3 Wendel Clark	.25	.60
4 Theo Fleury	.60	1.50
5 Wayne Gretzky	2.00	5.00
6 Breyt Hull	.75	2.00
7 Al Iafrate	.20	.50
8 Jaromir Jagr	2.00	5.00
9 Kirk Muller	.20	.50
10 Pat LaFontaine	.30	.75
11 Mark Recchi	.30	.75
12 Gary Roberts	.20	.50
13 Mats Sundin	.60	1.50
14 Steve Yzerman	2.00	5.00
15 Jason Arnott	.30	.75
16 Vincent Damphousse	.20	.50
17 Doug Gilmour	.60	1.50
18 Craig Janney	.20	.50
19 Joe Juneau	.20	.50
20 Trevor Linden	.20	.50
21 Eric Lindros	2.00	5.00
22 Mark Messier	.75	2.00
23 Mike Modano	.75	2.00
24 Alexander Mogilny	.40	1.00
25 Adam Oates	.25	.60
26 Robert Reichel	.20	.50
27 Jeremy Roenick	.40	1.00
28 Joe Sakic	1.25	3.00
29 Keith Tkachuk	.60	1.50
30 Alexei Yashin	.50	1.25
31 Tom Barrasso	.20	.50
32 Don Beaupre	.20	.50
33 Ed Belfour	.60	1.50
34 Craig Billington	.20	.50
35 Martin Brodeur	1.50	4.00
36 Sean Burke	.20	.50
37 Tim Cheveldae	.20	.50
38 Stephane Fiset	.30	.75
39 Dominik Hasek	1.25	3.00
40 Guy Hebert	.20	.50
41 Ron Hextall	.30	.75
42 Kelly Hrudey	.20	.50
43 Arthurs Irbe .00	.20	.50
44 Curtis Joseph	.75	2.00
45 Trevor Kidd	.30	.75
46 Kirk McLean	.30	.75
47 Jamie McLennan	.20	.50
48 Andy Moog	.40	1.00
49 Felix Potvin	.60	1.50
50 Daren Puppa	.30	.75
51 Bill Ranford	.30	.75
52 Mike Richter	.60	1.50
53 Vincent Riendeau	.20	.50
54 Patrick Roy	3.00	8.00
55 John Vanbiesbrouck	.60	1.50
56 Mike Vernon	.30	.75
57 Ray Bourque	.75	2.00
58 Martin Brodeur	1.50	4.00
59 Sergei Fedorov	1.25	3.00
60 Dominik Hasek	1.25	3.00
61 Jacques Lemaire	.40	1.00
62 Adam Graves	.40	1.00
63 Wayne Gretzky	4.00	10.00
64 Brian Leetch	.60	1.50
65 Cam Neely	.60	1.50
66 New York Rangers Champs	1.25	3.00
67 Ray Bourque	.75	2.00
68 Pavel Bure	1.50	4.00
69 Sergei Fedorov	1.25	3.00
70 Dominik Hasek	1.25	3.00
71 Brendan Shanahan	1.25	3.00
72 Scott Stevens	.40	1.00
NNO Collector's Album	10.00	25.00

1994-95 Kraft Goalie Masks

Inserted as a chiptopper at a rate of one per Kraft Dinner case, this set featured perforated cardboard masks of eight NHL goalies. Unassembled, the masks measured approximately 14" by 13 1/4". The fronts carried the goalie's mask with a photo of his face, along with his name, team name, and instructions on how to assemble the mask. All text was in French and English. The backs were blank. Additional masks could be ordered by mailing in three UPC's from Kraft dinner cartons plus 3.00 for shipping and handling. The masks were unnumbered and checklisted below in alphabetical order.

COMPLETE SET (8)	8.00	20.00
1 Ed Belfour	1.25	3.00
2 Guy Hebert	.60	1.50
3 Curtis Joseph	1.25	3.00
4 Andy Moog	.75	2.00
5 Felix Potvin	.75	2.00
6 Vincent Riendeau	.60	1.50
7 Patrick Roy	3.00	8.00
8 John Vanbiesbrouck	.75	2.00

1995-96 Kraft

This 79-card set continued the fine tradition of Kraft hockey series. The cards were issued in several sizes and over several Kraft products. The Hottest Ticket were issued with Jell-O Pudding, while Crease Keepers were issued with Jell-O gelatin. The first group were standard card size, while the second group of eight were about half-standard size. 12 All-Stars discs were issued with Kraft Peanut Butter, while 26 Star cards were found on the back of Kraft Dinner boxes. The 79th card was a disc picturing Conn Smythe winner Claude Lemieux and honoring the Cup champ NJ Devils. The cards were unnumbered, and so are listed below in the order in which they appeared in the factory version of the set.

COMPLETE SET (79)	30.00	80.00
1 Sergei Fedorov	.75	2.00
2 Jason Arnott	.20	.50
3 Teemu Selanne	.75	2.00
4 Pierre Turgeon	.25	.60
5 Joe Juneau	.15	.40
6 Scott Stevens	.25	.60
7 Cam Neely	.20	.50
8 Mario Lemieux	1.50	4.00
9 Wendel Clark	.20	.50
10 Alexandre Daigle	.15	.40
11 Peter Forsberg	1.00	2.50
12 Trevor Linden	.20	.50
13 Phil Housley	.15	.40
14 Doug Gilmour	.30	.75
15 Sean Burke	.25	.60
16 Dominik Hasek	.75	2.00
17 Patrick Roy	1.50	4.00
18 Kirk McLean	.20	.50
19 Blaine Lacher	.15	.40
20 Jim Carey	.20	.50
21 Martin Brodeur	1.00	2.50
22 Mike Richter	.30	.75
23 Felix Potvin	.30	.75
24 Trevor Kidd	.20	.50
25 Ed Belfour	.30	.75
26 Stephane Fiset	.20	.50
27 Ron Hextall	.20	.50
28 Grant Fuhr	.20	.50
29 Daren Puppa	.20	.50
30 Andy Moog	.20	.50
31 Mike Vernon	.20	.50
32 John Vanbiesbrouck	.40	1.00
33 Bill Ranford	.25	.60
34 Tommy Soderstrom	.20	.50
35 Tom Barrasso	.20	.50
36 Kelly Hrudey	.20	.50
37 Guy Hebert	.25	.60
38 Arturs Irbe	.20	.50
39 Tim Cheveldae	.20	.50
40 Don Beaupre	.20	.50
41 Eric Lindros	1.25	3.00
42 Jaromir Jagr	1.25	3.00
43 Paul Coffey	.30	.75
44 Chris Chelios	.30	.75
45 Dominik Hasek	.75	2.00
46 John LeClair	.60	1.50
47 Alexei Zhamnov	.15	.40
48 Keith Tkachuk	.40	1.00
49 Theo Fleury	.30	.75
50 Larry Murphy	.15	.40
51 Ray Bourque	.75	2.00
52 Ed Belfour	.40	1.00
53 Wayne Gretzky	2.00	5.00
54 Adam Oates	.25	.60
55 Paul Kariya	1.25	3.00
56 Alexander Mogilny	.25	.60
57 Dave Gagner	.15	.40
58 Theo Fleury	.30	.75
59 Jesse Belanger	.15	.40
60 Joe Sakic	.75	2.00
61 Peter Bondra	.30	.75
62 Andrew Cassels	.15	.40
63 Alexandre Daigle	.15	.40
64 Paul Coffey	.30	.75
65 Ulf Dahlen	.15	.40
66 Brett Hull	.40	1.00
67 Bernie Nicholls	.15	.40
68 Doug Weight	.25	.60
69 Brian Bradley	.15	.40
70 Mark Messier	.50	1.25
71 Stephane Richer	.15	.40
72 Eric Lindros	1.25	3.00
73 Mark Recchi	.25	.60
74 Ray Ferraro	.15	.40
75 Mats Sundin	.30	.75
76 Alexei Zhamnov	.20	.50
77 Pavel Bure	1.00	2.50
78 Jaromir Jagr	1.25	3.00
79 Claude Lemieux	10.00	25.00
NNO Binder	4.00	10.00

1996-97 Kraft Upper Deck

MVP (1-26) were found on the backs of specially marked boxes of Kraft Dinner regular or specialty flavours. All-Stars (27-32) were found on the backs of Jell-O instant pudding. Team Rivals (33-39) were available through a redemption offer found on specially marked jars of Kraft Peanut Butter. Award Winners (40-59) were found on specially marked 4 cup packs of Jell-O pudding snacks. Mascots (60-64) were found in 85g boxes of Jell-O jelly powder packs. Magnets (65-72) were found one per unopened case of Kraft Dinner. The existence of a Wayne Gretzky magnet has been reported, but not confirmed.

COMPLETE SET (72)	40.00	100.00
1 Brian Leetch	.40	1.00
2 Keith Tkachuk	.60	1.50
3 Geoff Sanderson	.30	.75
4 Owen Nolan	.30	.75
5 Saku Koivu	.60	1.50
6 Adam Oates	.30	.75
7 Mats Sundin	.40	1.00
8 Theo Fleury	.30	.75
9 Zigmund Palffy	.40	1.00
10 Alexei Yashin	.30	.75
11 Brett Hull	.40	1.00
12 Michal Pivonka	.20	.50
13 Joe Nieuwendyk	.30	.75
14 Martin Brodeur	.75	2.00
15 Ed Belfour	.40	1.00
16 Guy Hebert	.30	.75
17 Patrick Roy	1.50	4.00
18 Dominik Hasek	.75	2.00
19 John Vanbiesbrouck	.60	1.50
20 Yanic Perreault	.20	.50
21 Doug Weight	.30	.75
22 Mario Lemieux	1.50	4.00
23 Eric Lindros	1.00	2.50
24 Alexander Mogilny	.40	1.00
25 Sergei Fedorov	.75	2.00
26 Daren Puppa	.30	.75
27 Chris Chelios	.40	1.00
28 Mario Lemieux	1.50	4.00
29 Paul Kariya	1.25	3.00
30 Ray Bourque	.40	1.00
31 Chris Osgood	.40	1.00
32 Jaromir Jagr	1.25	3.00
33 Rob Blake	1.50	4.00
Paul Kariya		
Kevin Dineen		
Peter Bondra		
34 Ray Bourque	1.00	2.50
Adam Graves		
Randy Cunneyworth		
Pat L		
35 Al MacInnis	1.00	2.50
Trevor Linden		
Kris King		
Mike Modano		
36 Paul Ysebaert	1.00	2.50
Owen Nolan		
Theo Fleury		
Kelly Buch		
37 Vince Damphousse	2.00	5.00
Doug Gilmour		
Mario Lemieux		
Eri		
38 Ziggy Palffy	1.50	4.00
Scott Stevens		
Steve Yzerman		
Chris		
39 Brian Skrudland	1.50	4.00
Joe Sakic		
40 Scott Bowman CO	.40	1.00
41 Marc Crawford	.30	.75
42 Chris Chelios	.40	1.00
43 Paul Kariya	1.25	3.00
44 Ron Francis	.30	.75
45 Daniel Alfredsson	.30	.75
46 Adam Oates	.30	.75
47 Joe Sakic	.75	2.00
48 Peter Forsberg	1.00	2.50
49 Jarome Iginla	.30	.75
50 Jim Carey	.30	.75
51 C.Osgood	.40	1.00
M.Vernon		
52 Mike Richter	.40	1.00
53 Jocelyn Thibault	.30	.75
54 Mario Lemieux	1.50	4.00
55 Ed Jovanovski	.30	.75
56 Mario Lemieux	1.50	4.00
57 J.LeClair	1.25	3.00
B.Shanahan		
J.Jagr		
58 Eric Lindros	1.00	2.50
59 Sergei Fedorov	.75	2.00
60 T.Selanne	1.25	3.00
Wild Wing		
61 F.Potvin	.40	1.00
Carlton the Bear		
62 M.McSorley	.30	.75
S.J. Sharkie		
63 R.Niedermayer	.30	.75
Stanley C. Panther		
64 D.Gagner	.20	.50
Harvey the Hound		
65 Theo Fleury	.75	2.00
66 Saku Koivu	1.25	3.00
67 Mario Lemieux	4.00	10.00
68 Eric Lindros	2.00	5.00
69 Alexander Mogilny	.60	1.50
70 Mats Sundin	1.00	2.50
71 Doug Weight	.60	1.50
72 Alexei Yashin	.60	1.50

1997-98 Kraft Pinnacle

This annual set featured an international theme tied in with the 1998 Winter Olympics, the first to feature NHL players. One oversized card was found on the back of specially marked boxes of Kraft Dinner. Pinnacle logo on front and back.

COMPLETE SET (26)		
1 Vincent Damphousse	.30	.75
2 Theo Fleury	.40	1.00
3 Ron Francis	.40	1.00
4 Wayne Gretzky	2.50	6.00
5 Paul Kariya	.60	1.50
6 Eric Lindros	1.00	2.50
7 Mark Messier	1.00	2.50
8 Adam Oates	.30	.75
9 Steve Yzerman	2.00	5.00
10 Jaromir Jagr	1.00	2.50
11 Saku Koivu	.40	1.00
12 Teemu Selanne	.75	2.00
13 Uwe Krupp	.30	.75
14 Sergei Fedorov	1.00	2.50
15 Alexei Yashin	.30	.75
16 Peter Bondra	.30	.75
17 Zigmund Palffy	.30	.75
18 Jozef Stumpel	.30	.75
19 Peter Forsberg	1.00	2.50
20 Mikael Renberg	.30	.75
21 Mats Sundin	.40	1.00
22 Brett Hull	.75	2.00
23 John LeClair	.30	.75
24 Mike Modano	1.00	2.50
25 Keith Tkachuk	.40	1.00
26 Doug Weight	.30	.75

1997-98 Kraft Pinnacle 3-D World's Best

This eight card set was put out by Pinnacle in conjunction with Kraft. Each card measured 3. 1/4" X4 1/2" and is enhanced with a 3-D background.

COMPLETE SET (8)	2.50	6.00
1 Doug Weight	.25	.60
2 Mats Sundin	.30	.75
3 Alexei Yashin	.25	.60
4 Saku Koivu	.30	.75
5 Theo Fleury	.30	.75
6 Mark Messier	.40	1.00
7 Vincent Damphousse	.20	.50
8 Paul Kariya	1.25	3.00

1997-98 Kraft Team Canada

COMPLETE SET (12)	8.00	20.00
1 Ray Bourque	.75	2.00
Shayne Corson		
2 Martin Brodeur	1.25	3.00
Joe Sakic		
3 Marc Crawford	.40	1.00
Eric Lindros		
4 Eric Desjardins	.40	1.00
Adam Foote		
5 Theoren Fleury	.40	1.00
Al MacInnis		
6 Curtis Joseph	2.00	5.00
Patrick Roy		
7 Paul Kariya	.75	2.00
Rod Brind'Amour		
8 Trevor Linden	.75	2.00
Keith Primeau		
9 Joe Nieuwendyk	.40	1.00
Rob Blake		
10 Scott Stevens	.40	1.00
Rob Zamuner		
11 Brendan Shanahan	2.50	6.00
Wayne Gretzky		
12 Steve Yzerman	1.25	3.00
Chris Pronger		

1998-99 Kraft Dinners Zoomer Stickers

Available only in Kraft Dinner 12-packs, this 5-card set made by Pinnacle featured holographic 'magic motion' technology on smaller 3" X 3" cards.

COMPLETE SET	8.00	20.00
1 Atlanta Thrashers	1.50	4.00
2 Columbus Blue Jackets	1.50	4.00
3 Los Angeles Kings	1.50	4.00
4 Minnesota Wild	1.50	4.00
5 Nashville Predators	1.50	4.00

1998-99 Kraft Fearless Forwards

COMPLETE SET (13)	6.00	15.00
1 Peter Bondra	.40	1.00
2 Pavel Bure	.75	2.00
3 Vincent Damphousse	.40	1.00
4 Jaromir Jagr	1.25	3.00
5 Paul Kariya	.75	2.00
6 John Leclair	.40	1.00
7 Claude Lemieux	.40	1.00
8 Mike Modano	.75	2.00
9 Brendan Shanahan	.75	2.00
10 Cory Stillman	.40	1.00
11 Mats Sundin	.75	2.00
12 Doug Weight	.40	1.00
13 Alexei Yashin	.40	1.00

1998-99 Kraft Peanut Butter

COMPLETE SET (8)	4.00	10.00
1 Rob Blake	.75	2.00
Larry Murphy		
2 Brian Leetch	.75	2.00
Robert Svehla		
3 Patrice Brisebois	.75	2.00
Scott Niedermayer		
4 Vladimir Malakhov	.40	1.00
Darryl Sydor		
5 Al MacInnis	.40	1.00
Alexei Zhitnik		
6 Ray Bourque	1.25	3.00
Boris Mironov		
7 Mathieu Schneider	1.25	3.00
Nicklas Lidstrom		
8 Teppo Numminen	.75	2.00
Chris Chelios		

1999-00 Kraft Dinner

These oversized cards were issued on the backs of boxes of Kraft Dinner in Canada. Factory versions can also be found which were not cut from boxes. Because they tended to be in better condition, these cards earned a premium of up to 2X.

COMPLETE SET (15)	4.80	12.00
1 Shayne Corson	.20	.50
2 Jaromir Jagr	.60	1.50
3 Curtis Joseph	.40	1.00
4 Paul Kariya	.75	2.00
5 Saku Koivu	.30	.75
6 Mike Modano	.40	1.00
7 Eric Lindros	.60	1.50
8 Mattias Ohlund	.20	.50
9 Chris Pronger	.20	.50
10 Joe Sakic	.60	1.50
11 Brendan Shanahan	.40	1.00
12 Scott Stevens	.20	.50
13 Mats Sundin	.30	.75
14 Alexei Yashin	.20	.50
15 Steve Yzerman	1.25	3.00

1999-00 Upper Deck Kraft Dinner The Great One

These cards were produced by Upper Deck for Kraft Foods. Each measures roughly 3-1/4" by 5" and features Wayne Gretzky at a key moment in his career.

COMPLETE SET (4)	6.00	15.00
COMMON GRETZKY	1.50	4.00

1999-00 Kraft Face Off Rivals

COMPLETE SET (6)	4.00	10.00
1 Mats Sundin	.75	2.00
Stu Barnes		
2 Theoren Fleury	.75	2.00
Joe Nieuwendyk		
3 Pierre Turgeon	.75	2.00
Guy Carbonneau		
4 Yanic Perreault	.40	1.00
Curtis Brown		
5 Steve Yzerman	1.25	3.00
Claude Lemieux		
6 Mike Modano	.75	2.00
Mike Eastwood		

1999-00 Kraft Peanut Butter

These discs were found under the lids of specially marked jars of Kraft Peanut Butter in Canada. Discs are not numbered.

COMPLETE SET (11)	6.00	15.00
1 Ray Bourque	.75	2.00
2 Martin Brodeur	.75	2.00
3 Peter Forsberg	.75	2.00
4 Dominik Hasek	.60	1.50
5 Jaromir Jagr	.75	2.00
6 Paul Kariya	1.25	3.00
7 Nicklas Lidstrom	.40	1.00
8 Al MacInnis	.20	.50
9 Teppo Numminen	.20	.50
10 Teemu Selanne	.60	1.50
11 Brendan Shanahan	.60	1.50
12 Eric Lindros		

1999-00 Kraft Overtime Winners

COMPLETE SET (6)	2.50	6.00
1 Brett Hull	.75	2.00
2 Garry Valk	.08	.25
3 Mike Modano	.75	2.00
4 Pierre Turgeon	.40	1.00
5 Jaromir Jagr	1.25	3.00
6 Milan Hejduk	.40	1.00

1999-00 Kraft Stanley Cup Moments

COMPLETE SET (15)	2.00	5.00
1 Mark Messier	1.25	3.00
2 Eric Desjardins	.20	.50
3 Brett Hull	1.25	3.00
4 Claude Lemieux	.20	.50
5 Michael Peca	.20	.50
6 Bill Ranford	.40	1.00

1999-00 Kraft Whiz Kid

COMPLETE SET (8)	1.50	4.00
1 Milan Hejduk	.40	1.00
2 Marian Hossa	.40	1.00
3 Jan Hrdina	.08	.25
4 Tomas Kaberle	.08	.25
5 Chris Drury	.40	1.00
6 Daniil Markov	.08	.25
7 Erik Rasmussen	.08	.25
8 Brendan Morrison	.40	1.00

2000-01 Kraft

This set of 30 standard-size cards had an unusual story: they were not supposed to be issued. Despite Kraft's long history of hockey premiums, the company decided to skip a year to work on another promotion. However, it did contract In The Game to produce this set as a sales incentive for grocery store managers. While these cards were not widely distributed, a small quantity did make its way into the secondary market. The cards featured gray borders surrounding an action photo on the front, with another photo, with team and position on the back. Kraft logos appeared on both sides. Each of the cards mimicked the base cards that appeared in 2000-01 Be A Player Memorabilia, except for the cards of Scott Pellerin, which pictured him in his new Minnesota Wild sweater, and Ron Tugnutt, who was pictured with the Columbus Blue Jackets.

COMPLETE SET (30)	40.00	100.00
1 Jaromir Jagr	5.00	12.00
2 Markus Naslund	1.20	3.00
3 Luc Robitaille	1.20	3.00
4 Scott Stevens	.40	1.00
5 Mike Modano	2.50	6.00
6 Doug Weight	1.20	3.00
7 Peter Bondra	1.25	3.00
8 Paul Kariya	5.00	12.00
9 Radek Bonk	.40	1.00
10 John LeClair	2.00	5.00
11 Sandis Ozolinsh	.40	1.00
12 Steve Yzerman	10.00	25.00
13 Joe Thornton	2.00	5.00
14 Valeri Bure	.40	1.00
15 Pavel Bure	2.50	6.00
16 Cliff Ronning	.40	1.00
17 Dominik Hasek	2.50	6.00
18 Vincent Lecavalier	1.20	3.00
19 Andrew Brunette	.40	1.00
20 Chris Pronger	1.20	3.00
21 Owen Nolan	1.20	3.00
22 Joe Sakic	4.00	10.00
23 Jeremy Roenick	2.50	6.00
24 Tony Amonte	1.50	4.00
25 Mariusz Czerkawski	.40	1.00
26 Trevor Linden	1.50	4.00
27 Mats Sundin	2.00	5.00
28 Mark Messier	3.00	8.00
29 Ron Tugnutt	2.00	5.00
30 Scott Pellerin	2.00	5.00

2003-04 Kraft

These cards were issued on the backs of Kraft Dinner boxes in Canada in mid-winter, 2003/04. They are condition-sensitive as they had to be cut from the box backs.

COMPLETE SET (10)	8.00	15.00
1 Ed Belfour	1.25	3.00
2 Anson Carter	.40	1.00
3 Paul Kariya	.75	2.00
4 Trevor Linden	.40	1.00
5 Vincent Lecavalier	.75	2.00
6 Al MacInnis	.40	1.00
7 Mike Ribeiro	.40	1.00
8 Ryan Smyth	.40	1.00
9 Joe Thornton	1.25	3.00
10 Jordin Tootoo	.75	2.00

1948 Kellogg's All Wheat Sport Tips Series 1

17 Hockey: Shooting	3.00	8.00

1948 Kellogg's All Wheat Sport Tips Series 2

1 Hockey: Body Shift	3.00	8.00
2 Hockey: Poke Check	3.00	8.00
3 Hockey: Hook Check	3.00	8.00
4 Hockey:	3.00	8.00
5 Hockey: Board Trick	3.00	8.00
6 Hockey: Shoulder Feint	3.00	8.00
16 Hockey: Defensive Position	3.00	8.00
17 Hockey: Fake Pass	3.00	8.00

1979-80 Lakers/Kings Alta-Dena

This eight-card set was sponsored by Alta-Dena Dairy, and its logo adorns the bottom of both sides of the card. The cards measure approximately 2 3/4" by 4" and feature color action player photos on the fronts. While the sides of the picture have no borders, green and red-orange stripes border the picture on its top and bottom. The player's name appears in black lettering in the top red-orange stripe. The team logo appears in the bottom red-orange stripe. The back has an offer for youngsters 14-and-under, who could present the complete eight-card set in the souvenir folder to the Forum Box Office and receive a half-price discount on certain tickets to any one of the Lakers and Kings games listed on the reverse of the card. The cards are unnumbered and are checklisted below in alphabetical order. This small set features Los Angeles Kings and Los Angeles Lakers as they were both owned by Jerry Buss. Cards 1-4 are Los Angeles Lakers (NBA) and Cards 5-8 are Los Angeles Kings (NHL). The set must have been planned and produced in the late summer of 1979 since Adrian Dantley was traded to Utah for Spencer Haywood on September 13

COMPLETE SET (8)	10.00	20.00
5 Marcel Dionne	3.00	6.00
6 Butch Goring	.50	1.00
7 Mike Murphy	.50	1.00
8 Dave Taylor	1.50	3.00

1993 Lakers Forum

This set features great sports and entertainment personalities who have appeared at the Great Western Forum in Los Angeles during the past 25 years. The set was sponsored by the Los Angeles Times and "Rebuild LA" and celebrates the 25th Anniversary of the Forum with 25,000 sets produced. The set includes one randomly inserted bonus card in each pack of an outstanding Laker basketball player. The bonus cards were numbered on the back with the prefix "BC". The bonus cards were randomly inserted; one could buy five regular sets and still not guarantee a complete insert set. Noted sports artist Terry Smith designed the set. Proceeds from the 12-card sets, originally priced at 25.00 each, were intended to benefit Los Angeles-area Boys and Girls Clubs. The sets were sold at the Forum's box office and concession stands during all Forum events. Sets could also be ordered through Ticketmaster outlets. The cards measure approximately 2 1/2" by 5". The black card fronts have an inner blue border on the left, right, and upper edges. Across the top is a 25th Anniversary design printed on the border with black points along the upper border edge. The name of the highlighted athlete is printed in white with the first name along the left edge and the last name appearing on the bottom edge. The horizontal backs carry a close-up posed shot on the left with a colored panel on the right giving career highlights and significant information pertaining to their appearances at the Great Western Forum.

COMPLETE SET (11)	6.00	15.00
8 Rogie Vachon	.20	.50
9 Marcel Dionne	.40	1.00
10 Wayne Gretzky	2.00	5.00

1927-28 La Patrie

The 1927-28 La Patrie set contained 21 notebook paper-sized (approximately 8 1/2" by 11") photos. The front had a sepia-toned posed photo of the player, enframed by a thin black border. The words "La Patrie" appeared above the picture, with the player's name below it. The photo number and year appeared at the lower right corner of the picture. A patterned border completed the front. The back was blank. Reports indicate a folder may have been issued to hold the photos.

COMPLETE SET (21)	1250.00	2500.00
1 Sylvio Mantha	50.00	100.00
2 Art Gagne	30.00	60.00
3 Leo Lafrance	30.00	60.00
4 Aurel Joliat	150.00	300.00
5 Pit Lepine	40.00	80.00
6 Gizzy Hart	30.00	60.00
7 Wildor Larochelle	40.00	80.00
8 Georges Hainsworth	100.00	200.00
9 Herb Gardiner	40.00	80.00
10 Albert Leduc	40.00	80.00
11 Marty Burke	40.00	80.00
12 Charlie Langlois	30.00	60.00
13 Leonard Gaudreault	30.00	60.00
14 Howie Morenz	350.00	700.00
15 Cecil M. Hart	40.00	80.00
16 Leo Dandurand	30.00	60.00
17 Newsy Lalonde	150.00	300.00
18 Didier Pitre	30.00	60.00
19 Jack Laviolette	50.00	100.00
20 Georges Patterson	30.00	60.00
21 Georges Vezina	250.00	500.00

1927-28 La Presse Photos

1 Howie Morenz	200.00	300.00
2 Aurel Joliat	125.00	200.00
3 Sylvio Mantha	50.00	100.00
4 Pit Lepine	50.00	100.00
5 George Hainsworth	125.00	200.00
6 Art Gagne	50.00	100.00
7 Herb Gardiner	50.00	100.00
8 Art Gagne	50.00	100.00
9 Herb Gardiner	50.00	100.00
10 Albert Leduc	50.00	100.00
11 Wildor Larochelle	50.00	100.00
12 Leonard Gaudreault	50.00	100.00
13 Gizzy Hart	50.00	100.00
14 Charlie Langlois	50.00	100.00
15 Georges Vezina	200.00	300.00
16 Cattarinich	60.00	150.00
Hart		
Dandurand		
Letourneau		
17 Eddie Shore	150.00	250.00
18 Lionel Conacher	125.00	200.00
19 Red Porter	50.00	100.00
20 George Patterson	50.00	100.00

1928-29 La Presse Photos

These oversized (10 X16) photos were issued over the course of the 1928-29 season as a premium with the Montreal newspaper, La Presse. They featured color posed images on the front. Because they had standard newspaper coverage on the back, some hobbyists do not consider them true collectibles. However, recent sales information suggests there is significant interest in these pieces. Because of their age and the natural deterioration of newsprint, it is rare to find these in high grade. As they are unnumbered, they are listed below in alphabetical order.

COMPLETE SET (14)	400.00	800.00
1 Clint Benedict	50.00	100.00
2 Frank Boucher	37.50	75.00
3 George Boucher	37.50	75.00
4 Lucien Brunet	10.00	20.00
5 Marty Burke	37.50	75.00
6 Bun Cook	50.00	100.00
7 Hap Day	37.50	75.00
8 Red Dutton	37.50	75.00
9 Georges Mantha	50.00	100.00
10 Armand Mondou	37.50	75.00
11 Bill Phillips	37.50	75.00
12 Babe Siebert	50.00	100.00
13 Nels Stewart	62.50	125.00
14 Jimmy Ward	37.50	75.00

1964 Lamberts Sports and Games

Card measures approximately 1 1/2" x 3 1/2" and featured full color fronts. Came from a series of 25 cards given as a premium for Lambert tea of Norwich, England.

20 Ice Hockey	10.00	20.00

1993 Leaf Chicago National

This huge card (approximately 8 X 11) was given to dealers at the Donruss dinner during the 1993 Chicago National. It heralded the union between Donruss and their new spokesman, Mario Lemieux.

1 Mario Lemieux	5.00	12.00

1993-94 Leaf

The 1993-94 Leaf hockey set consisted of 440 standard-size cards that were issued in two series of 220. The fronts displayed color action player photos that were full-bleed except at the bottom, where a red diagonal edges the picture. Below the diagonal was a black stripe carrying the player's name in gold foil lettering, and a team color-coded triangle displaying the team logo. Against the background of the home team's skyline or another prominent architectural landmark, the backs carried a color action player cut-out overprinted at the bottom with biographical and statistical information. A holographic team logo appeared in the lower right corner. Rookie Cards included Jason Arnott, Damian Rhodes and Jocelyn Thibault. An oversized (8" by 11 3/4") blowup of Mario Lemieux's card #1 was distributed as a promotional item in advance of the release of the set. The card was primarily handed out at the National Convention in Chicago.

1 Mario Lemieux	.40	1.00
2 Curtis Joseph	.10	.25
3 Steve Leach	.05	.15
4 Vincent Damphousse	.07	.20
5 Murray Craven	.05	
6 Pat Elynuik	.05	
7 Bill Guerin	.05	
8 Zarley Zalapski	.05	
9 Rob Gaudreau RC	.10	
10 Pavel Bure	.10	
11 Brad Shaw	.05	
12 Pat LaFontaine	.10	
13 Teemu Selanne	.20	
14 Trent Klatt	.05	
15 Kevin Todd	.05	
16 Larry Murphy	.07	
17 Tony Amonte	.07	
18 Dino Ciccarelli	.07	
19 Doug Bodger	.05	
20 Luc Robitaille	.07	
21 John Tucker	.05	
22 Todd Gill	.05	
23 Mike Ricci	.05	
24 Evgeny Davydov	.05	
25 Pierre Turgeon	.07	
26 Rod Brind'Amour	.07	
27 Jeremy Roenick	.15	
28 Joel Otto	.05	
29 Jeff Brown	.05	
30 Brendan Shanahan	.12	
31 Jiri Slegr	.05	
32 Vladimir Malakhov	.05	
33 Patrick Roy	.25	
34 Kevin Hatcher	.05	
35 Alexander Semak	.05	
36 Gary Roberts	.05	
37 Tommy Soderstrom	.07	
38 Bob Essensa	.07	
39 Kelly Hrudey	.07	
40 Shawn Chambers	.05	
41 Glenn Anderson	.10	
42 Owen Nolan	.07	
43 Patrick Flatley	.05	
44 Ray Sheppard	.07	
45 Darren Turcotte	.05	
46 Shayne Corson	.05	
47 Brad May	.07	
48 Bob Kudelski	.05	
49 Pat Falloon	.05	
50 Andrew Cassels	.05	
51 Chris Chelios	.10	
52 Sylvain Cote	.05	
53 Mathieu Schneider	.05	
54 Ted Donato	.05	
55 Kirk McLean	.07	
56 Bruce Driver	.05	
57 Uwe Krupp	.05	
58 Brent Fedyk	.05	
59 Robert Reichel	.05	
60 Scott Stevens	.10	
61 Phil Housley	.07	
62 Ed Belfour	.10	
63 Dave Andreychuk	.10	
64 Claude Lapointe	.05	
65 Russ Courtnall	.05	
66 Grant Fuhr	.10	
67 Paul Coffey	.10	
68 Bill Ranford	.07	
69 Kevin Stevens	.05	
70 Brian Leetch	.10	
71 Dale Hawerchuk	.12	
72 Geoff Courtnall	.05	
73 Sandis Ozolinsh	.05	
74 Sylvain Turgeon	.05	
75 Nelson Emerson	.05	
76 Brian Bellows	.07	
77 Geoff Sanderson	.07	
78 Petr Nedved	.05	
79 Peter Bondra	.07	
80 Scott Niedermayer	.10	
81 Steve Thomas	.05	
82 Dimitri Yushkevich	.05	
83 Mike Vernon	.07	
84 Alexei Zhamnov	.07	
85 Adam Creighton	.05	
86 Dave Ellett	.05	
87 Joe Sakic	.25	
88 Mike Craig	.05	
89 Nicklas Lidstrom	.10	
90 Ed Olczyk	.05	
91 Alexander Mogilny	.07	
92 Ulf Samuelsson	.05	
93 Doug Gilmour	.12	
94 Michael Nylander	.05	
95 Steve Smith	.05	
96 Igor Korolev	.05	
97 Dixon Ward	.05	
98 John LeClair	.10	
99 Cam Neely	.10	
100 Patrick Roy Cup Champs	.25	
101 Darius Kasparaitis	.05	
102 Mike Ridley	.05	
103 Josef Beranek	.05	
104 Valeri Zelepukin	.05	
105 Keith Tkachuk	.10	
106 Tomas Sandstrom	.05	
107 Peter Zezel	.05	
108 Scott Young	.05	
109 Rick Tocchet	.07	
110 Teemu Selanne CL	.20	
111 Steve Chiasson	.05	
112 Doug Zmolek	.05	
113 Patrick Poulin	.05	
114 Stephane Matteau	.05	
115 Yves Racine	.05	
116 Steve Heinze	.05	
117 Gilbert Dionne	.05	
118 Dale Hunter	.05	
119 Derek King	.05	
120 Garry Galley	.05	
121 Ray Ferraro	.05	
122 Andrei Kovalenko	.05	
123 Alexei Zhitnik	.05	
124 Fredrik Olausson	.05	
125 Claude Lemieux	.05	
126 Joe Nieuwendyk	.07	
127 Travis Green	.07	
128 Dave Gagner	.07	
129 Sergei Fedorov	.15	
130 Adam Graves	.05	
131 Petr Svoboda	.05	
132 Sean Burke	.05	
133 Johan Garpenlov	.05	

134 Jamie Baker .05 .15
135 Teppo Numminen .05 .15
136 Mats Sundin .07 .20
137 Nikolai Borschevsky .05 .15
138 Stephane Richer .07 .20
139 Scott Lachance .05 .15
140 Gary Suter .05 .15
141 Al Iafrate .05 .15
142 Brent Sutter .05 .15
143 Dmitri Kvartalnov .05 .15
144 Pat Verbeek .05 .15
145 Ed Courtenay .05 .15
146 Mark Tinordi .05 .15
147 Alexei Kovalev .07 .20
148 Dallas Drake RC .10 .25
149 Jimmy Carson .05 .15
150 Florida Panthers .05 .15
151 Roman Hamrlik .05 .15
152 Martin Rucinsky .05 .15
153 Calle Johansson .05 .15
154 Theo Fleury .05 .15
155 Benoit Hogue .05 .15
156 Kevin Dineen .05 .15
157 Jody Hull .05 .15
158 Mark Messier .10 .25
159 Dave Manson .05 .15
160 Chris Kontos .05 .15
161 Ron Francis .12 .30
162 Steve Yzerman .25 .60
163 Igor Kravchuk .05 .15
164 Sergei Zubov .05 .15
165 Thomas Steen .05 .15
166 Wendel Clark .07 .20
167 Scott Pellerin RC .10 .25
168 Dimitri Khristich .05 .15
169 Bernie Nicholls .05 .15
170 Paul Ranheim .05 .15
171 Robert Kron .05 .15
172 Rob Blake .07 .20
173 Rob Zamuner .05 .15
174 Rob Pearson .05 .15
175 Ed Belfour CL .10 .25
176 Steve Duchesne .05 .15
177 Pelle Eklund .05 .15
178 Michal Pivonka .05 .15
179 Joe Murphy .05 .15
180 Al MacInnis .07 .20
181 Craig Janney .07 .20
182 Kirk Muller .05 .15
183 Cliff Ronning .05 .15
184 Doug Weight .07 .20
185 Mike Richter .10 .25
186 Bob Probert .07 .20
187 Robert Petrovicky .05 .15
188 Richard Smehlik .05 .15
189 Norm Maciver .05 .15
190 Stephan Lebeau .05 .15
191 Patrice Brisebois .05 .15
192 Kevin Miller .05 .15
193 Trevor Linden .07 .20
194 Darrin Shannon .05 .15
195 Tim Cheveldae .07 .20
196 Tom Barrasso .07 .20
197 Zdeno Ciger .05 .15
198 Ulf Dahlen .05 .15
199 Arturs Irbe .07 .20
200 Anaheim Mighty Ducks .05 .15
201 Tony Granato .05 .15
202 Mike Modano .15 .40
203 Eric Desjardins .07 .20
204 Bryan Smolinski .05 .15
205 Mark Recchi .12 .30
206 Darryl Sydor .05 .15
207 Valeri Kamensky .07 .20
208 Kelly Kisio .05 .15
209 Brian Bradley .05 .15
210 Mario Lemieux CL .40 1.00
211 Yuri Khmylev .05 .15
212 Derian Hatcher .05 .15
213 Mike Gartner .07 .20
214 Mike Needham UER .05 .15
215 Ray Bourque .15 .40
216 Tie Domi .05 .15
217 Shawn McEachern .05 .15
218 Joe Juneau .07 .20
219 Greg Adams .05 .15
220 Martin Straka .05 .15
221 Tom Fitzgerald .05 .15
222 Gary Shuchuk .05 .15
223 Kevin Haller .05 .15
224 Bryan Marchment .05 .15
225 Louie DeBrusk .05 .15
226 Randy Wood .05 .15
227 Bobby Holik .05 .15
228 Troy Mallette .05 .15
229 Adam Foote .05 .15
230 Bob Rouse .05 .15
231 Jyrki Lumme .05 .15
232 James Patrick .05 .15
233 Eric Lindros .30 .75
234 Joe Reekie .05 .15
235 Adam Oates .10 .25
236 Frank Musil .05 .15
237 Vladimir Konstantinov .07 .20
238 Dave Lowry .05 .15
239 Garth Butcher .05 .15
240 Jari Kurri .10 .25
241 Rick Tabaracci .05 .15
242 Sergei Bautin .05 .15
243 Scott Scissons .05 .15
244 Dominic Roussel .07 .20
245 John Cullen .05 .15
246 Sheldon Kennedy .05 .15
247 Mike Hough .05 .15
248 Paul DiPietro .05 .15
249 David Shaw .05 .15
250 Sergio Momesso .05 .15
251 Jeff Daniels .05 .15
252 Sergei Nemchinov .05 .15
253 Kris King .05 .15
254 Kelly Miller .05 .15
255 Brett Hull .15 .40
256 Dominik Hasek .20 .50
257 Chris Pronger .10 .25
258 Derek Plante RC .10 .25
259 Mark Howe .10 .25
260 Oleg Petrov .05 .15
261 Ronnie Stern .05 .15
262 Scott Mellanby .07 .20
263 Warren Rychel .05 .15
264 John MacLean .07 .20
265 Radek Hamr RC .10 .25
266 Greg Hawgood .05 .15
267 Sylvain Lefebvre .05 .15
268 Glen Wesley .05 .15
269 Joe Cirella .05 .15
270 Dirk Graham .05 .15
271 Eric Weinrich .05 .15
272 Donald Audette .05 .15
273 Jason Woolley .05 .15
274 Kjell Samuelsson .05 .15
275 Ron Sutter .05 .15
276 Keith Primeau .05 .15
277 Ron Tugnutt .07 .20
278 Jesse Belanger .05 .15
279 Mike Keane .05 .15
280 Adam Burt .05 .15
281 Don Sweeney .05 .15
282 Mike Donnelly .05 .15
283 Lyle Odelein .05 .15
284 Gord Murphy .05 .15
285 Mikael Andersson .05 .15
286 Bret Hedican .05 .15
287 Bill Berg .05 .15
288 Esa Tikkanen .05 .15
289 Markus Naslund .10 .25
290 Checklist .05 .15
291 Kerry Huffman .05 .15
292 Dana Murzyn .05 .15
293 Rob Niedermayer .07 .20
294 Andre Racicot .05 .15
295 Ken Sutton .05 .15
296 Shawn Burr .05 .15
297 Scott Pearson .05 .15
298 Joby Messier RC .10 .25
299 Darrin Madeley RC .10 .25
300 Joe Mullen .07 .20
301 Stephane Fiset .07 .20
302 Geoff Smith .05 .15
303 Slava Kozlov .07 .20
304 Wayne Gretzky .50 1.25
305 Curtis Leschyshyn .05 .15
306 Mike Sillinger .05 .15
307 Vyacheslav Butsayev .05 .15
308 Mark Lamb .05 .15
309 German Titov RC .10 .25
310 Gerard Gallant .05 .15
311 Alexandre Daigle .05 .15
312 Jim Hrivnak .05 .15
313 Corey Hirsch .07 .20
314 Craig Berube .05 .15
315 Bill Houlder .05 .15
316 Ron Wilson .05 .15
317 Glen Murray .05 .15
318 Bryan Trottier .12 .30
319 Jeff Hackett .05 .15
320 Brad Dalgarno .05 .15
321 Petr Klima .05 .15
322 Jon Casey .07 .20
323 Mikael Renberg .10 .25
324 Jimmy Waite .07 .20
325 Brian Skrudland .05 .15
326 Vitali Prokhorov .05 .15
327 Glenn Healy .07 .20
328 Brian Benning .05 .15
329 Tony Hrkac .05 .15
330 Stu Grimson .05 .15
331 Chris Gratton .07 .20
332 Dave Poulin .05 .15
333 Jarrod Skalde .05 .15
334 Christian Ruuttu .05 .15
335 Mark Fitzpatrick .05 .15
336 Martin Lapointe .05 .15
337 Cam Stewart RC .10 .25
338 Anatoli Semenov .05 .15
339 Gaetan Duchesne .05 .15
340 Checklist .05 .15
341 Ron Hextall .07 .20
342 Mikhail Tatarinov .05 .15
343 Danny Lorenz .05 .15
344 Craig Simpson .05 .15
345 Martin Brodeur .25 .60
346 Jaromir Jagr .25 .60
347 Tyler Wright .05 .15
348 Greg Gilbert .05 .15
349 Dave Tippett .05 .15
350 Stu Barnes .05 .15
351 Daniel Lacroix RC .05 .15
352 Marty McSorley .05 .15
353 Sean Hill .05 .15
354 Craig Billington .07 .20
355 Donald Dufresne .05 .15
356 Guy Hebert .07 .20
357 Neil Wilkinson .05 .15
358 Sandy McCarthy .05 .15
359 Aaron Ward RC .10 .25
360 Scott Thomas RC .10 .25
361 Corey Millen .05 .15
362 Matthew Barnaby .07 .20
363 Benoit Brunet .05 .15
364 Boris Mironov .05 .15
365 Doug Lidster .05 .15
366 Pavol Demitra .12 .30
367 Damian Rhodes RC .10 .25
368 Shawn Antoski .05 .15
369 Andy Moog .10 .25
370 Greg Johnson .05 .15
371 John Vanbiesbrouck .07 .20
372 Denis Savard .12 .30
373 Michel Goulet .05 .15
374 Dave Taylor .05 .15
375 Enrico Ciccone .05 .15
376 Sergei Zholtok .05 .15
377 Bob Errey .05 .15
378 Doug Brown .05 .15
379 Bill McDougall RC .10 .25
380 Pat Conacher .05 .15
381 Alexei Kasatonov .05 .15
382 Jason Arnott RC .20 .50
383 Jarkko Varvio .05 .15
384 Sergei Makarov .05 .15
385 Trevor Kidd .07 .20
386 Alexei Yashin .07 .20
387 Gerald Diduck .05 .15
388 Paul Ysebaert .05 .15
389 Jason Smith RC .05 .15
390 Jeff Norton .05 .15
391 Igor Larionov .05 .15
392 Pierre Sevigny .05 .15
393 Wes Walz .05 .15
394 Grant Ledyard .05 .15
395 Brad McCrimmon .05 .15
396 Martin Gelinas .05 .15
397 Paul Cavallini .05 .15
398 Brian Noonan .05 .15
399 Mike Lalor .05 .15
400 Dimitri Filimonov .05 .15
401 Andrei Lomakin .05 .15
402 Steve Junker RC .10 .25
403 Daren Puppa .05 .15
404 Jozef Stumpel .05 .15
405 Jeff Shantz RC .05 .15
406 Terry Yake .05 .15
407 Mike Peluso .05 .15
408 Vitali Karamnov .05 .15
409 Felix Potvin .20 .50
410 Steven King .05 .15
411 Roman Oksiuta RC .10 .25
412 Mark Greig .05 .15
413 Wayne McBean .05 .15
414 Nick Kypreos .05 .15
415 Dominic Lavoie .05 .15
416 Chris Simon RC .10 .25
417 Peter Popovic RC .10 .25
418 Gino Odjick .05 .15
419 Mike Rathje .05 .15
420 Keith Acton .05 .15
421 Bob Carpenter .05 .15
422 Steven Finn .05 .15
423 Ian Herbers RC .05 .15
424 Ted Drury .05 .15
425 Sergei Petrenko .05 .15
426 Mattias Norstrom RC .10 .25
427 Todd Ewen .05 .15
428 Jocelyn Thibault RC .10 .25
429 Robert Burakovsky RC .10 .25
430 Chris Terreri .07 .20
431 Michal Sykora RC .10 .25
432 Craig Ludwig .05 .15
433 Vesa Viitakoski RC .10 .25
434 Sergei Krivokrasov .05 .15
435 Darren McCarty RC .15 .40
436 Dean McAmmond .05 .15
437 J.J. Daigneault .05 .15
438 Vladimir Ruzicka .05 .15
439 Vlastimil Kroupa RC .10 .25
440 Checklist .05 .15

1993-94 Leaf Freshman Phenoms

Randomly inserted in Series II packs, these ten standard-size cards featured borderless color player action shots on their fronts. The player's name appeared in white lettering beneath the set's title in the darkened area at the bottom of the player photo. The horizontal back carried a color player action shot on one side, and player information within a black rectangle on the other.

COMPLETE SET (10) 4.00 10.00
1 Alexandre Daigle .20 .50
2 Chris Pronger 1.00 2.50
3 Chris Gratton .20 .50
4 Markus Naslund 1.00 2.50
5 Mikael Renberg .20 .50
6 Rob Niedermayer .20 .50
7 Jason Arnott .60 1.50
8 Jarkko Varvio .20 .50
9 Alexei Yashin .20 .50
10 Jocelyn Thibault .60 1.50

1993-94 Leaf Gold All-Stars

This 10-card set was randomly inserted in first (1-5) and second (6-10) series foil packs. These standard-size cards featured the NHL's top players at each position, with one player portrayed on each card side.

COMPLETE SET (10) 20.00 50.00
COMP.SERIES 1 (5) 10.00 25.00
COMP.SERIES 2 (5) 10.00 25.00
1 M.Lemieux/P.LaFontaine 4.00 10.00
2 C.Chelios/L.Murphy 1.25 3.00
3 B.Hull/T.Selanne 2.00 5.00
4 K.Stevens/Andreychuk 1.25 3.00
5 P.Roy/T.Barrasso 4.00 10.00
6 W.Gretzky/D.Gilmour 6.00 15.00
7 R.Bourque/P.Coffey 2.50 6.00
8 A.Mogilny/P.Bure 1.25 3.00
9 L.Robitaille/Shanahan 1.25 3.00
10 E.Belfour/F.Potvin 1.25 3.00

1993-94 Leaf Gold Rookies

Randomly inserted in first series foil packs, this 15-card standard-size set showcased top rookies from the 1992-93 season. Borderless horizontal fronts had a photo of the player along with "Gold Leaf Rookie 1992-93" prominent on the front. Red backs carried a player photo and rookie year highlights. The cards were numbered on back as "X of 15".

COMPLETE SET (15) 5.00 12.00
1 Teemu Selanne .60 1.50
2 Joe Juneau .20 .50
3 Eric Lindros .75 2.00
4 Felix Potvin .75 2.00
5 Alexei Zhamnov .20 .50
6 Andrei Kovalenko .20 .50
7 Shawn McEachern .20 .50
8 Alexei Zhitnik .20 .50
9 Vladimir Malakhov .20 .50
10 Patrick Poulin .20 .50
11 Keith Tkachuk .40 1.00
12 Tommy Soderstrom .20 .50
13 Darius Kasparaitis .20 .50
14 Scott Niedermayer .20 .50
15 Darryl Sydor .20 .50

1993-94 Leaf Hat Trick Artists

is 10-card set was randomly inserted in first (1-5) and second (6-10) series U.S. foil and magazine distribution packs. These standard-size cards honored players who scored three or more hat tricks in the 1992-93 season.

COMPLETE SET (10) 8.00 20.00
COMP.SERIES 1 (5) 5.00 12.00
COMP.SERIES 2 (5) 3.00 8.00
1 M.Lemieux Title Card 2.00 5.00
2 Alexander Mogilny .40 1.00
3 Teemu Selanne .75 2.00
4 Mario Lemieux 2.00 5.00
5 Pierre Turgeon .40 1.00
6 Kevin Dineen .20 .50
7 Eric Lindros .75 2.00
8 Adam Oates .40 1.00
9 Kevin Stevens .20 .50
10 Steve Yzerman 2.00 5.00

1993-94 Leaf Mario Lemieux

As part of a 10-card subset randomly inserted in first (1-5) and second (6-10) series foil packs, these standard-size cards traced Lemieux's illustrious career. Mario Lemieux personally autographed 2,000 of his cards.

COMPLETE SET (10) 8.00 20.00
COMP.SERIES 1 (5) 4.00 10.00
COMP.SERIES 2 (5) 4.00 10.00
COMMON LEMIEUX (1-10) 1.00 2.50
NNO Mario Lemieux AU/2000 60.00 120.00

1993-94 Leaf Painted Warriors

As part of a 10-card subset randomly inserted in first (1-5) and second (6-10) series foil packs, these standard-size cards featured up-close shots of NHL goalies with emphasis on mask design. The back had a small color photo, biography and career highlights.

COMPLETE SET (10) 6.00 15.00
COMP.SERIES 1 (5) 4.00 10.00
COMP.SERIES 2 (5) 2.00 5.00
1 Felix Potvin .75 2.00
2 Curtis Joseph .60 1.50
3 Kirk McLean .30 .75
4 Patrick Roy 3.00 8.00
5 Grant Fuhr .40 1.00
6 Ed Belfour .60 1.50
7 Mike Vernon .30 .75
8 John Vanbiesbrouck .30 .75
9 Tom Barrasso UER .30 .75
10 Bill Ranford .30 .75

1993-94 Leaf Studio Signature

As part of a 10-card subset randomly inserted in first (1-5) and second (6-10) series Canadian and magazine distribution foil packs, these standard-size cards spotlighted the NHL's top players. Against a colorful background of the team's uniform, the fronts displayed a cut out player photo with his gold foil signature stamped across the bottom. The backs carried a full-bleed color close-up photo and text that defines the player's personal style.

COMPLETE SET (10) 12.00 30.00
COMP.SERIES 1 (5) 10.00 20.00
COMP.SERIES 2 (5) 6.00 15.00
1 Doug Gilmour .40 1.00
2 Pat Falloon .25 .60
3 Pat LaFontaine .75 2.00
4 Wayne Gretzky 6.00 12.00
5 Steve Yzerman 5.00 10.00
6 Patrick Roy 5.00 10.00
7 Jeremy Roenick 1.00 2.50
8 Brett Hull 1.00 2.50
9 Alexandre Daigle .25 .60
10 Eric Lindros .75 2.00

1994-95 Leaf

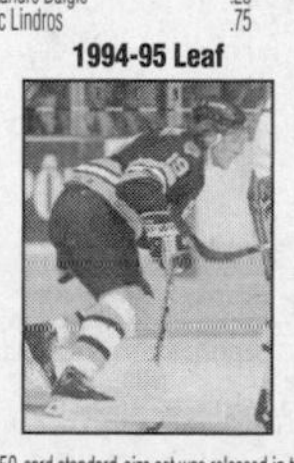

This 550-card standard-size set was released in two series. Series 1 was 330 cards while series 2 contained 220 cards. Each came in 12-card hobby and 18-card retail packs. These full-bleed cards carried a small Leaf logo above the player's name in gold foil along the bottom. The team name was stamped across the top, also in gold foil. Card backs featured four photos with brief personal and statistical information. The set contained no subsets. Rookie Cards included Mariusz Czerkawski, Byron Dafoe, Eric Fichaud, Ian Laperriere and Jason Wiemer.

1 Mario Lemieux .40 1.00
2 Tony Amonte .07 .20
3 Steve Duchesne .05 .15
4 Glen Murray .05 .15
5 John LeClair .10 .25
6 Glen Wesley .05 .15
7 Chris Chelios .10 .25
8 Alexei Zhitnik .07 .20
9 Mike Modano .15 .40
10 Pavel Bure .10 .25
11 Mark Messier .10 .25
12 Rob Blake .10 .25
13 Tony Twist .07 .20
14 Glenn Anderson .10 .25
15 Keith Redmond .07 .20
16 Brett Hull .20 .50
17 Valeri Zelepukin .05 .15
18 Mike Richter .10 .25
19 Alexei Yashin .10 .25
20 Luc Robitaille .10 .25
21 Tim Sweeney .05 .15
22 Ted Drury .05 .15
23 Guy Carbonneau .05 .15
24 Stephane Richer .07 .20
25 Ulf Dahlen .05 .15
26 Fred Brathwaite .05 .15
27 Darius Kasparaitis .05 .15
28 Kris Draper .05 .15
29 Alexander Godynyuk .05 .15
30 Brent Sutter .07 .20
31 Josef Beranek .05 .15
32 Stephane Matteau .05 .15
33 Derek Plante .05 .15
34 Vesa Viitakoski .07 .20
35 Dave Ellett .05 .15
36 Martin Straka .05 .15
37 Dimitri Yushkevich .05 .15
38 John Tucker .05 .15
39 Rob Gaudreau .05 .15
40 Doug Weight .07 .20
41 Patrick Roy .25 .60
42 Brian Bradley .05 .15
43 Bob Beers .07 .20
44 Dino Ciccarelli .07 .20
45 Dean Evason .05 .15
46 Ron Tugnutt .07 .20
47 Andy Moog .10 .25
48 Jason Dawe .05 .15
49 Ted Donato .05 .15
50 Ron Hextall .07 .20
51 Derek Armstrong RC .07 .20
52 Craig Janney .07 .20
53 Geoff Courtnall .05 .15
54 Mikael Renberg .07 .20
55 Theo Fleury .10 .25
56 Martin Brodeur .25 .60
57 Mattias Norstrom .05 .15
58 David Sacco .05 .15
59 Jeff Reese .05 .15
60 Bill Ranford .07 .20
61 Dan Quinn .07 .20
62 Joe Juneau .07 .20
63 Jeremy Roenick .20 .50
64 Donald Audette .05 .15
65 Zdeno Ciger .05 .15
66 Cliff Ronning .05 .15
67 Steve Thomas .05 .15
68 Norm Maciver .05 .15
69 Vincent Damphousse .07 .20
70 John Vanbiesbrouck .07 .20
71 Andrei Kovalenko .05 .15
72 Dave Andreychuk .10 .25
73 Stu Barnes .05 .15
74 Jamie McLennan .07 .20
75 Rudy Poeschek .07 .20
76 Ken Wregget .07 .20
77 Ray Bourque .15 .40
78 Grant Fuhr .10 .25
79 Paul Cavallini .05 .15
80 Nelson Emerson .05 .15
81 Tim Cheveldae .07 .20
82 Mariusz Czerkawski RC .10 .25
83 Pat Peake .05 .15
84 Craig Billington .07 .20
85 Sean Burke .07 .20
86 Chris Gratton .05 .15
87 Andrei Trefilov .05 .15
88 Terry Yake .05 .15
89 Mark Recchi .12 .30
90 Igor Korolev .05 .15
91 Mark Tinordi .05 .15
92 Alexei Kovalev .05 .15
93 Bob Essensa .05 .15
94 Keith Tkachuk .10 .25
95 Pat Falloon .05 .15
96 John Slaney .05 .15
97 Alexei Zhamnov .07 .20
98 Jeff Norton .05 .15
99 Doug Gilmour .12 .30
100 Rick Tocchet .07 .20
101 Robert Kron .05 .15
102 Patrik Carnback .05 .15
103 Tom Barrasso .07 .20
104 Jari Kurri .07 .20
105 Iain Fraser .05 .15
106 Mike Donnelly .05 .15
107 Ray Sheppard .07 .20
108 Scott Young .05 .15
109 Kirk McLean .07 .20
110 Checklist .05 .15
111 Sergei Zubov .05 .15
112 Ivan Droppa .05 .15
113 Brendan Shanahan .12 .30
114 Michal Pivonka .07 .20
115 Pavol Demitra .12 .30
116 Doug Brown .05 .15
117 Valeri Kamensky .07 .20
118 Alexander Karpovtsev .05 .15
119 Alexandre Daigle .05 .15
120 Dominik Hasek .20 .50
121 Murray Craven .05 .15
122 Michal Sykora .05 .15
123 Aris Brimanis RC .05 .15
124 Benoit Hogue .05 .15
125 Arto Blomsten .07 .20
126 Russ Courtnall .05 .15
127 Bryan Marchment .07 .20
128 Jeff Hackett .05 .15
129 Kevin Miller .05 .15
130 Bryan Smolinski .05 .15
131 John Druce .07 .20
132 Roman Hamrlik .07 .20
133 Jason Arnott .07 .20
134 Chris Terreri .07 .20
135 Mike Gartner .10 .25
136 Darryl Sydor .05 .15
137 Lyle Odelein .07 .20
138 Martin Gelinas .05 .15
139 Mike Rathje .05 .15
140 Sylvain Cote .05 .15
141 Nicklas Lidstrom .10 .25
142 Guy Hebert .07 .20
143 Jozef Stumpel .05 .15
144 Owen Nolan .10 .25
145 Jesse Belanger .05 .15
146 Bill Guerin .07 .20
147 Mike Stapleton .07 .20
148 Steve Yzerman .25 .60
149 Michael Nylander .07 .20
150 Rod Brind'Amour .07 .20
151 Jaromir Jagr .25 .60
152 Darcy Wakaluk .07 .20
153 Sergei Nemchinov .05 .15
154 Wes Walz .05 .15
155 Sergei Fedorov .15 .40
156 Dan Laperriere .05 .15
157 Marty McInnis .05 .15
158 Chris Joseph .05 .15
159 Matt Martin .05 .15
160 Checklist .05 .15
161 Denis Tsygurov RC .10 .25
162 Stephan Lebeau .05 .15
163 Kirk Muller .05 .15
164 Shayne Corson .05 .15
165 Joe Sakic .20 .50
166 Denis Savard .12 .30
167 Kevin Dineen .05 .15
168 Paul Coffey .10 .25
169 Sandis Ozolinsh .05 .15
170 Stewart Malgunas .05 .15
171 Petr Klima .05 .15
172 Pat Verbeek .07 .20
173 Yan Kaminsky .05 .15
174 Marty McSorley .05 .15
175 Arturs Irbe .07 .20
176 Peter Popovic .05 .15
177 Brian Skrudland .05 .15
178 John Lilley .05 .15
179 Boris Mironov .05 .15
180 Garth Snow .05 .15
181 Alexei Kudashov .05 .15
182 Scott Mellanby .07 .20
183 Dale Hunter .05 .15
184 Tommy Soderstrom .07 .20
185 Claude Lemieux .10 .25
186 Felix Potvin .10 .25
187 Corey Millen .05 .15
188 Derek King .05 .15
189 Kelly Hrudey .07 .20
190 Dimitri Khristich .05 .15
191 Sylvain Turgeon .05 .15
192 John Gruden RC .10 .25
193 Mike Peca .07 .20
194 Vladimir Malakhov .05 .15
195 Mathieu Schneider .05 .15
196 Jeff Shantz .05 .15
197 Darren McCarty .07 .20
198 Craig Simpson .05 .15
199 Jarkko Varvio .20 .50
200 Gino Odjick .05 .15
201 Martin Lapointe .05 .15
202 Paul Ysebaert .05 .15
203 Mike McPhee .05 .15
204 John MacLean .07 .20
205 Ulf Samuelsson .05 .15
206 Garry Valk .05 .15
207 Tomas Sandstrom .05 .15
208 Curtis Joseph .15 .40
209 Mikhail Shtalenkov RC .05 .15
210 Darren Turcotte .05 .15
211 Markus Naslund .10 .25
212 Al Iafrate .05 .15
213 Jim Storm .07 .20
214 Dan Plante RC .05 .15
215 Brad May .05 .15
216 Nathan Lafayette .05 .15
217 Brian Noonan .05 .15
218 Brent Hughes .05 .15
219 Geoff Sanderson .07 .20
220 Checklist .05 .15
221 Eric Weinrich .05 .15
222 Greg Adams .05 .15
223 Dominic Roussel .07 .20
224 Daren Puppa .07 .20
225 Rob Niedermayer .07 .20
226 Todd Elik .05 .15
227 Donald Brashear RC .05 .15
228 Joe Nieuwendyk .10 .25
229 Tony Granato .05 .15
230 Kirk Maltby .05 .15
231 Jocelyn Thibault .10 .25
232 Shawn McEachern .05 .15
233 Teppo Numminen .05 .15
234 Johan Garpenlov .05 .15
235 Ron Francis .12 .30
236 Slava Kozlov .07 .20
237 Scott Niedermayer .10 .25
238 Sergei Krivokrasov .05 .15
239 Dave Manson .05 .15
240 Mike Ricci .05 .15
241 Chad Penney .05 .15
242 Calle Johansson .05 .15
243 Robert Reichel .05 .15
244 Igor Kravchuk .05 .15
245 Jason Smith .07 .20
246 Neal Broten .07 .20
247 Jeff Brown .05 .15
248 Jason Bowen .05 .15
249 Larry Murphy .07 .20
250 Gord Murphy .05 .15
251 Darrin Shannon .05 .15
252 Bobby Holik .05 .15
253 Zigmund Palffy .07 .20
254 Dmitri Mironov .05 .15
255 Adam Graves .05 .15
256 Alexander Mogilny .07 .20
257 Steve Smith .05 .15
258 Jim Montgomery .05 .15
259 Danton Cole .05 .15
260 Dave McLlwain .05 .15
261 German Titov .05 .15
262 Tom Chorske .05 .15
263 Grant Ledyard .05 .15
264 Garry Galley .05 .15
265 Vlastimil Kroupa .05 .15
266 Keith Primeau .10 .25
267 Cam Neely .10 .25
268 Chris Pronger .10 .25
269 Richard Matvichuk .05 .15
270 Steve Larmer .07 .20
271 James Patrick .05 .15
272 Joel Otto .05 .15
273 Todd Nelson .05 .15
274 Joe Sacco .05 .15
275 Jason York RC .05 .15
276 Andrew Cassels .05 .15
277 Peter Bondra .07 .20
278 Pat LaFontaine .10 .25
279 Nikolai Borschevsky .05 .15
280 Dave Mackey .05 .15
281 Cam Stewart .05 .15
282 Sergei Makarov .05 .15
283 Byron Dafoe RC .30 .75
284 Joe Murphy .05 .15
285 Matthew Barnaby .07 .20
286 Derian Hatcher .05 .15
287 Jyrki Lumme .05 .15
288 Travis Green .07 .20
289 Milos Holan .05 .15
290 Ed Patterson .05 .15
291 Randy Burridge .05 .15
292 Brian Savage .05 .15
293 Stephane Quintal .05 .15
294 Zarley Zalapski .05 .15
295 Vitali Prokhorov .05 .15
296 Ed Belfour .10 .25
297 Yuri Khmylev .05 .15
298 Dean McAmmond .05 .15
299 Bob Corkum .05 .15
300 Darrin Madeley .05 .15
301 Brian Bellows .07 .20
302 Andrei Lomakin .05 .15
303 Anatoli Semenov .05 .15
304 Claude Lapointe .05 .15
305 Adam Oates .10 .25
306 Richard Smehlik .05 .15
307 Jim Dowd .05 .15
308 Mark Fitzpatrick .07 .20
309 Pierre Sevigny .05 .15
310 Glenn Healy .07 .20
311 Igor Larionov .05 .15
312 Aaron Ward .05 .15
313 Dale Hawerchuk .12 .30
314 Bob Kudelski .05 .15
315 Chris Osgood .15 .40
316 Trent Klatt .05 .15
317 Gary Suter .05 .15
318 Tie Domi .07 .20
319 Dave Gagner .07 .20
320 Kevin Smyth .05 .15
321 Philippe Bozon .07 .20
322 Trevor Kidd .07 .20
323 Warren Rychel .05 .15
324 Steven Rice .05 .15
325 Patrice Brisebois .05 .15
326 Gary Roberts .05 .15
327 Fredrik Olausson .05 .15
328 Andrei Nazarov .05 .15
329 Stephane Fiset .07 .20
330 Checklist .05 .15
331 Fred Knipscheer .05 .15
332 Shawn Chambers .05 .15
333 Kelly Buchberger .05 .15
334 Ray Ferraro .05 .15
335 Dirk Graham .05 .15
336 Ken Daneyko .05 .15
337 Mark Lamb .05 .15
338 Shaun Van Allen .05 .15
339 Chris Simon .05 .15
340 Brent Gilchrist .05 .15
341 Greg Gilbert .05 .15
342 Brent Severyn .05 .15
343 Craig Berube .05 .15
344 Randy Moller .05 .15
345 Wayne Gretzky .50 1.25
346 Shawn Anderson .05 .15
347 Mikael Andersson .05 .15
348 Jim Montgomery .05 .15
349 Scott Pearson .05 .15
350 Kevin Todd .05 .15
351 Ron Sutter .05 .15
352 Paul Kruse RC .05 .15
353 Doug Lidster .05 .15
354 Oleg Petrov .05 .15
355 Greg Johnson .05 .15
356 Kevin Stevens .05 .15
357 Doug Bodger .05 .15
358 Troy Mallette .05 .15
359 Keith Carney .05 .15
360 Petr Nedved .07 .20
361 Mark Janssens .05 .15
362 Teemu Selanne .20 .50
363 Scott Stevens .10 .25
364 Shane Churla .05 .15
365 John McIntyre .05 .15
366 Geoff Smith .05 .15
367 Pierre Turgeon .07 .20
368 Shawn Burr .05 .15
369 Kevin Hatcher .05 .15
370 Paul Ranheim .05 .15
371 Kevin Haller .05 .15
372 Scott Lachance .05 .15
373 Craig Muni .05 .15
374 Mike Ridley .05 .15
375 Joby Messier .05 .15
376 Thomas Steen .05 .15
377 Bruce Driver .05 .15
378 Mike Eastwood .05 .15
379 Brian Benning .05 .15
380 Dallas Drake .05 .15
381 Patrick Flatley .05 .15
382 Cam Russell .05 .15
383 Bobby Dollas .05 .15
384 Marc Bergevin .05 .15
385 Joe Mullen .07 .20
386 Chris Dahlquist .05 .15
387 Robert Petrovicky .05 .15
388 Yves Racine .05 .15
389 Adam Bennett .05 .15
390 Patrick Poulin .05 .15
391 Vladimir Konstantinov .07 .20
392 Frank Kucera .05 .15
393 Petr Svoboda .05 .15
394 Mike Sillinger .05 .15
395 Kris King .05 .15
396 Kelly Chase .05 .15
397 Peter Douris .05 .15
398 Bob Errey .05 .15
399 Ronnie Stern .05 .15
400 Randy McKay .05 .15
401 Benoit Brunet .05 .15
402 Gerald Diduck .05 .15
403 Brian Leetch .10 .25
404 Steve Heinze .05 .15
405 Jimmy Waite .05 .15
406 Nick Kypreos .05 .15
407 J.J. Daigneault .05 .15
408 Alexei Gusarov .07 .20
409 Paul Broten .05 .15
410 Drake Berehowsky .05 .15
411 Sandy McCarthy .05 .15
412 John Cullen .05 .15
413 Dan Quinn .07 .20
414 Dave Lowry .05 .15
415 Eric Lindros .10 .25
416 Igor Ulanov .05 .15
417 Bob Sweeney .05 .15
418 Jamie Macoun .05 .15
419 Brian Mullen .05 .15
420 Steve Leach .05 .15
421 Jamie Baker .05 .15
422 Uwe Krupp .05 .15
423 Steve Konowalchuk .05 .15
424 Craig Ludwig .05 .15
425 Bret Hedican .05 .15
426 Steve Dubinsky .05 .15
427 Rob Zamuner .05 .15
428 Dave Brown .05 .15
429 Robert Lang .05 .15
430 Dave Babych .05 .15
431 Scott Thornton .05 .15
432 Dave Archibald .05 .15
433 Eric Desjardins .07 .20
434 Jim Cummins .05 .15
435 Troy Loney .05 .15
436 Bob Carpenter .05 .15
437 Joe Reekie .05 .15
438 Mike Krushelnyski .05 .15
439 Jeff Odgers .05 .15
440 Checklist .05 .15
441 Brian Rolston .05 .15
442 Adam Deadmarsh .05 .15
443 Eric Fichaud RC .10 .25
444 Michel Petit .05 .15
445 Brett Lindros .05 .15
446 Pat Jablonski .05 .15
447 Janne Laukkanen .07 .20
448 Ray Whitney .05 .15
449 Tom Kurvers .05 .15
450 Phil Housley .07 .20
451 Viktor Kozlov .05 .15
452 Aaron Gavey .05 .15
453 Doug Zmolek .05 .15
454 Tony Twist .07 .20
455 Paul Kariya .12 .30
456 Vladislav Boulin RC .10 .25
457 Kevin Brown RC .10 .25
458 David Wilkie .07 .20
459 Jamie Pushor .07 .20
460 Glen Wesley .05 .15
461 Al MacInnis .07 .20
462 Bernie Nicholls .07 .20
463 Luc Robitaille .10 .25
464 Mike Vernon .07 .20
465 Alex Cherbayev .05 .15
466 Garth Butcher .07 .20
467 Todd Harvey .05 .15
468 Viktor Gordiouk .07 .20
469 Pat Neaton .07 .20
470 Jason Muzzatti .07 .20
471 Valeri Bure .05 .15
472 Kenny Jonsson .05 .15
473 Alexei Kasatonov .05 .15
474 Rick Tocchet .07 .20
475 Peter Forsberg .25 .60
476 Sean Hill .05 .15
477 Steven Rice .05 .15
478 David Roberts .07 .20
479 Justin Hocking RC .05 .15
480 Chris Therien .05 .15
481 Cale Hulse RC .07 .20
482 Jeff Friesen .05 .15
483 Brandon Convery .05 .15
484 Ian Laperriere RC .10 .25
485 Brent Grieve RC .05 .15
486 Valeri Karpov RC .05 .15
487 Steve Chiasson .05 .15
488 Jassen Cullimore .05 .15
489 Jason Wiemer RC .05 .15
490 Checklist .05 .15
491 Len Barrie .05 .15
492 Turner Stevenson .05 .15
493 Kelly Kisio .05 .15
494 Dwayne Norris .05 .15
495 Ron Hextall .07 .20
496 Jaroslav Modry .05 .15
497 Todd Gill .05 .15
498 Ken Sutton .05 .15

499 Sergio Momesso .10 .25
500 Dean Kennedy .05 .15
501 David Reid .05 .15
502 Jocelyn Lemieux .05 .15
503 Mark Osborne .05 .15
504 Mike Hough .05 .15
505 Todd Marchant .05 .15
506 Keith Jones .05 .15
507 Sylvain Lefebvre .05 .15
508 Sergei Zholtok .05 .15
509 Jay More .05 .15
510 Mike Craig .05 .15
511 Jason Allison .07 .20
512 Jim Paek .05 .15
513 Chris Tamer RC .05 .15
514 Craig MacTavish .05 .15
515 Mikko Makela .05 .15
516 Tom Fitzgerald .05 .15
517 Brent Fedyk .05 .15
518 Don Sweeney .05 .15
519 Kelly Miller .05 .15
520 Jiri Slegr .05 .15
521 Wayne Presley .05 .15
522 Mark Greig .05 .15
523 Doug Houda .05 .15
524 Kay Whitmore .05 .15
525 Craig Ferguson RC .05 .15
526 Kent Manderville .05 .15
527 Trevor Linden .07 .20
528 Jeff Beukeboom .05 .15
529 Adam Foote .05 .15
530 Mats Sundin .07 .20
531 Shjon Podein .05 .15
532 Louie DeBrusk .05 .15
533 Peter Zezel .05 .15
534 Greg Hawgood .05 .15
535 Pat Elynuik .05 .15
536 Mike Ramsey .05 .15
537 Bob Beers .07 .20
538 David Williams .05 .15
539 Philippe Boucher .05 .15
540 Rob Brown .05 .15
541 Marc Potvin .05 .15
542 Wendel Clark .07 .20
543 Alexander Semak .05 .15
544 Randy Wood .05 .15
545 Frank Musil .05 .15
546 Mike Peluso .05 .15
547 Gaetan Duchesne .05 .15
548 Curtis Leschyshyn .05 .15
549 Rob DiMaio .05 .15
550 Checklist .05 .15

1994-95 Leaf Crease Patrol

The ten cards in this set were randomly inserted in Leaf series 2 product at the rate of 1:9 packs. Complete sets also were available in randomly inserted Super-Packs. Cards featured a full bleed, horizontally-oriented front, with the set name, player name and logo along the bottom. Backs had a standard card look, with full stats, text, and small player photo. Cards were numbered "X of ten".

COMPLETE SET (10) 3.00 8.00
1 Patrick Roy 1.25 3.00
2 Ed Belfour .25 .60
3 Curtis Joseph .30 .75
4 Felix Potvin .30 .75
5 John Vanbiesbrouck .20 .50
6 Dominik Hasek .60 1.50
7 Kirk McLean .10 .30
8 Mike Richter .25 .60
9 Martin Brodeur .75 2.00
10 Bill Ranford .10 .30

1994-95 Leaf Fire on Ice

This 12-card set was inserted in Leaf series one packs at the rate of 1:18. Cards featured a cutout player image over the words "Fire On Ice", which embellished the silver foil background. The player name was at the bottom of the card next to the Leaf logo. Card backs featured another photo, another Fire On Ice logo and stats. Cards were numbered "X" of 12.

COMPLETE SET (12) 10.00 25.00
1 Sergei Fedorov 1.00 2.50
2 Jeremy Roenick .75 2.00
3 Pavel Bure .60 1.50
4 Wayne Gretzky 4.00 10.00
5 Doug Gilmour .30 .75
6 Eric Lindros .60 1.50
7 Joe Juneau .30 .75
8 Paul Coffey .60 1.50
9 Mario Lemieux 3.00 8.00
10 Alexander Mogilny .30 .75
11 Mike Gartner .30 .75
12 Teemu Selanne .60 1.50

1994-95 Leaf Gold Rookies

The 15 cards in this set were randomly inserted in Leaf series 1 product at the rate of 1:18 packs. Card fronts were very crowded, featuring one large color photo and three black-and-white photos. The set title was written in speckled gold foil over the large color shot. The team logo, team name and player name appeared on the right-hand side with the black and white shots. Card backs featured another photo, along with personal info and stats as well as a short blurb. The cards were numbered "X of 15".

COMPLETE SET (15) 10.00 25.00
1 Martin Brodeur 3.00 8.00
2 Jason Arnott .75 2.00
3 Alexei Yashin .75 2.00
4 Chris Gratton .75 2.00
5 Alexandre Daigle .75 2.00
6 Mikael Renberg .75 2.00
7 Rob Niedermayer .75 2.00
8 Boris Mironov .75 2.00
9 Chris Pronger 1.25 3.00
10 Chris Osgood 1.25 3.00
11 Derek Plante .75 2.00
12 Pat Peake .75 2.00
13 Jason Allison .75 2.00
14 Bryan Smolinski .75 2.00
15 Jocelyn Thibault .75 2.00

1994-95 Leaf Gold Stars

The 15 double-front cards in this set were randomly inserted in Leaf series 1 and 2 product at the rate of 1:72 packs. Cards 1-10 appeared in series 1, 11-15 in series 2. Cards featured a gold prismatic border. The player photo was in a diamond shaped gold prismatic border, surrounded by the set title. A gold foil facsimile autograph appeared under the gold diamond, just over the player name and team affiliation. One side of each card bore a serial number out of 10,000. Cards were numbered "X of 15".

COMPLETE SET (15) 60.00 150.00
1 S.Fedorov/W.Gretzky 15.00 30.00
2 D.Gilmour/J.Roenick 5.00 12.00
3 P.Roy/M.Richter 8.00 20.00
4 B.Hull/P.Bure 5.00 12.00
5 M.Messier/A.Yashin 5.00 12.00
6 R.Bourque/B.Leetch 5.00 12.00
7 C.Joseph/E.Belfour 5.00 12.00
8 M.Brodeur/D.Hasek 8.00 20.00
9 C.Neely/M.Renberg 4.00 10.00
10 M.Modano/J.Arnott 4.00 10.00
11 E.Lindros/M.Lemieux 8.00 20.00
12 S.Stevens/R.Blake 4.00 10.00
13 F.Potvin/J.Vanbiesbrouck 6.00 15.00
14 A.Oates/P.Lafontaine 4.00 10.00
15 J.Jagr/M.Recchi 4.00 10.00

1994-95 Leaf Leaf Limited Inserts

This 28-card insert set was issued in two series of 18 and 10 cards, in first and second series Leaf packs, respectively. Cards were randomly inserted at the rate of 1:18 packs, while series two could also be found randomly inserted into Super Packs. The cards were notable for the reflective silver border with rainbow lines coming out of the centered player photo. Player name was written in black at the base of the card below the team name printed in silver foil. The card backs had a ghosted photo covered by text and a small color portrait. These cards were identical in design to the Leaf Limited set issued in packs later in the season. Although the photos were different, the easiest way to determine which set your card belonged to is the numbering system. The inserts were numbered out of 28, while the regular issue cards simply bore a number. This set was condition sensitive.

COMPLETE SET (28) 20.00 50.00
1 Guy Hebert .20 .50
2 Adam Oates .40 1.00
3 Dominik Hasek 1.00 2.50
4 Robert Reichel .20 .50
5 Jeremy Roenick .75 2.00
6 Mike Modano 1.00 2.50
7 Sergei Fedorov .75 2.00
8 Jason Arnott .20 .50
9 John Vanbiesbrouck .40 1.00
10 Chris Pronger .40 1.00
11 Wayne Gretzky 5.00 12.00
12 Patrick Roy 3.00 8.00
13 Martin Brodeur 2.00 5.00
14 Pierre Turgeon .20 .50
15 Mark Messier 1.00 2.50
16 Alexei Yashin .20 .50
17 Eric Lindros .75 2.00
18 Mario Lemieux 4.00 10.00
19 Joe Sakic 1.25 3.00
20 Brendan Shanahan .75 2.00
21 Arturs Irbe .20 .50
22 Chris Gratton .20 .50
23 Doug Gilmour .40 1.00
24 Pavel Bure .75 2.00
25 Joe Juneau .20 .50
26 Teemu Selanne .75 2.00
27 Paul Kariya .75 2.00
28 Peter Forsberg 2.00 5.00

1994-95 Leaf Phenoms

The ten cards in this set were randomly inserted in Leaf series 2 product at the rate of 1:18 packs. Complete sets were also available in random Super Packs. The card fronts came out of packs with a translucent protective film as well as a white sticker which read "Remove Protective Film". The cards were made of a thick Mylar-type stock, and featured a player action photo superimposed over a black background. Set logo and player name appeared at the bottom. The back carried a brief paragraph of information over a cut-out action photo. Cards were numbered "X of 10".

COMPLETE SET (10) 10.00 25.00
1 Jamie Storr .60 1.50
2 Brett Lindros 1.25 3.00
3 Peter Forsberg 5.00 12.00
4 Jason Wiemer .40 1.00
5 Paul Kariya 1.25 3.00
6 Oleg Tverdovsky .60 1.50
7 Eric Fichaud .60 1.50
8 Viktor Kozlov .40 1.00
9 Jeff Friesen .40 1.00
10 Valeri Karpov .40 1.00

1994-95 Leaf Limited

This 120-card super-premium set was issued in five-card packs, in 20 pack boxes, which were individually numbered out of 60,000. The card designs were identical to the Limited Inserts which were randomly inserted in Leaf product earlier in the season. The cards had a large reflective silver border with rainbow lines coming out of the centered player photo. The player name was in black at the base of the card below the team name, which was printed in silver foil. The card backs had a ghosted photo covered by text and a small color portrait. Cards were numbered in silver foil. Rookie cards in the set included Mariusz Czerkawski, Eric Fichaud and Jason Wiemer. Although different photos were used, it is often difficult to distinguish a Leaf Limited card from a Leaf Limited Insert. The best way to differentiate between these cards and the Leaf Limited Inserts was the numbering system. These cards were numbered 1-120, while the inserts are numbered out of 28.

1 Mario Lemieux .75 2.00
2 Brett Hull .40 1.00
3 Ed Belfour .20 .50
4 Brian Rolston .12 .30
5 Garry Galley .12 .30
6 Steve Thomas .12 .30
7 Kevin Brown RC .20 .50
8 Doug Gilmour .25 .60
9 Bill Ranford .15 .40
10 Wayne Gretzky 1.00 2.50
11 Rob Niedermayer .15 .40
12 Larry Murphy .15 .40
13 Glen Wesley .12 .30
14 Pat Falloon .12 .30
15 Jocelyn Thibault .20 .50
16 Felix Potvin .20 .50
17 Mike Richter .20 .50
18 Jeff Brown .12 .30
19 Jesse Belanger .12 .30
20 Benoit Hogue .12 .30
21 Viktor Kozlov .12 .30
22 Chris Pronger .20 .50
23 Kirk McLean .15 .40
24 Oleg Tverdovsky .15 .40
25 Derian Hatcher .12 .30
26 Ray Sheppard .15 .40
27 Pat Verbeek .15 .40
28 Patrick Roy .50 1.25
29 Mariusz Czerkawski RC .20 .50
30 Ron Francis .25 .60
31 Wendel Clark .15 .40
32 Rob Blake .20 .50
33 Brian Leetch .20 .50
34 Dave Andreychuk .20 .50
35 Russ Courtnall .12 .30
36 Alexander Mogilny .15 .40
37 Kirk Muller .12 .30
38 Joe Juneau .15 .40
39 Robert Reichel .12 .30
40 Scott Niedermayer .20 .50
41 Owen Nolan .20 .50
42 Mats Sundin .15 .40
43 Sandis Ozolinsh .12 .30
44 Derek Plante .12 .30
45 Eric Fichaud RC .20 .50
46 Kevin Stevens .12 .30
47 Igor Larionov .12 .30
48 Mikael Renberg .15 .40
49 Cam Neely .20 .50
50 Brett Lindros .12 .30
51 Valeri Karpov RC .12 .30
52 Pierre Turgeon .15 .40
53 Doug Weight .15 .40
54 Geoff Sanderson .15 .40
55 Slava Kozlov .15 .40
56 Chris Gratton .12 .30
57 Bryan Smolinski .12 .30
58 Eric Lindros .20 .50
59 Alexei Kovalev .12 .30
60 Mike Modano .30 .75
61 Jeremy Roenick .60 1.50
62 Martin Straka .12 .30
63 Pat LaFontaine .20 .50
64 Vlastimil Kroupa .12 .30
65 Sergei Zubov .12 .30
66 Jason Arnott .15 .40
67 Petr Nedved .15 .40
68 Teemu Selanne .40 1.00
69 Geoff Courtnall .12 .30
70 Martin Brodeur .50 1.25
71 Mark Recchi .25 .60
72 John Vanbiesbrouck .15 .40
73 Adam Graves .12 .30
74 Arturs Irbe .15 .40
75 Paul Coffey .20 .50
76 Ulf Dahlen .12 .30
77 Phil Housley .15 .40
78 Rod Brind'Amour .15 .40
79 Al MacInnis .15 .40
80 Alexei Yashin .20 .50
81 Sergei Fedorov .30 .75
82 Joe Nieuwendyk .20 .50
83 Chris Chelios .20 .50
84 Ray Bourque .30 .75
85 Scott Stevens .20 .50
86 Jaromir Jagr .50 1.25
87 Alexandre Daigle .12 .30
88 Luc Robitaille .20 .50
89 Mark Messier .20 .50
90 Vincent Damphousse .15 .40
91 Craig Janney .15 .40
92 John MacLean .15 .40
93 Steve Duchesne .12 .30
94 Dale Hawerchuk .25 .60
95 Curtis Joseph .30 .75
96 Chris Osgood .30 .75
97 Brendan Shanahan .25 .60
98 Jason Allison .15 .40
99 Theo Fleury .20 .50
100 Pavel Bure .20 .50
101 Mathieu Schneider .12 .30
102 Dominik Hasek .40 1.00
103 Scott Mellanby .15 .40
104 Adam Oates .20 .50
105 Jari Kurri .15 .40
106 Joe Sakic .40 1.00
107 Paul Kariya .25 .60
108 Keith Tkachuk .20 .50
109 Daren Puppa .15 .40
110 Keith Primeau .20 .50
111 Alexei Zhitnik .15 .40
112 Trevor Linden .15 .40
113 Alexei Zhamnov .15 .40
114 Gary Roberts .12 .30
115 Kenny Jonsson .12 .30
116 Peter Forsberg .50 1.25
117 Rick Tocchet .15 .40
118 Aaron Gavey .12 .30
119 Jason Wiemer RC .12 .30
120 Steve Yzerman .50 1.25

1994-95 Leaf Limited Gold

The ten cards in this set were randomly inserted into Limited packs at the rate of 1:48 packs. The cards were designed identically to Limited except for being gold in color rather than silver and featured some of the league's most exciting players. The card backs had a ghosted photo background and featured a player profile and a small color portrait. The cards were individually numbered on the back out of 2,500.

COMPLETE SET (10) 40.00 100.00
1 Mario Lemieux 10.00 25.00
2 Brett Hull 5.00 12.00
3 Doug Gilmour 2.50 6.00
4 Eric Lindros 6.00 15.00
5 Paul Kariya 5.00 12.00
6 Jaromir Jagr 5.00 12.00
7 Wayne Gretzky 15.00 40.00
8 Jeremy Roenick 5.00 12.00
9 Sergei Fedorov 5.00 12.00
10 Pavel Bure 4.00 10.00

1994-95 Leaf Limited World Juniors Canada

The ten cards in this set were randomly inserted into Limited packs; cards from either the Canadian or U.S. World Juniors could be found at the rate of 1:12 packs. The card fronts were designed identically to Limited except for being bronze in color rather than silver. The cards featured top Canadian players who competed in the 1995 World Junior Championships. The cards were individually numbered on the back out of 5,000. Card backs also contained a small up-close photo and a brief scouting report.

COMPLETE SET (10) 30.00 60.00
1 Nolan Baumgartner 2.00 5.00
2 Eric Daze 2.00 5.00
3 Jeff Friesen 3.00 8.00
4 Todd Harvey 2.00 5.00
5 Ed Jovanovski 3.00 8.00
6 Jeff O'Neill 2.00 5.00
7 Wade Redden 4.00 10.00
8 Jamie Rivers 2.00 5.00
9 Ryan Smyth 6.00 15.00
10 Jamie Storr 2.00 5.00

1994-95 Leaf Limited World Juniors USA

The 10 cards in this set were randomly inserted into Limited packs; cards from either the U.S. or Canadian World Juniors could be found at the rate of 1:12 packs. The card fronts were designed identically to Limited save for being bronze in color rather than silver. The cards featured top American players who competed in the 1995 World Junior Championships. The cards were individually numbered on the back out of 5,000. Card backs also contained a small headshot and a brief scouting report.

COMPLETE SET (10) 20.00 40.00
1 Bryan Berard 2.00 5.00
2 Doug Bonner 2.00 5.00
3 Jason Bonsignore 2.00 5.00
4 Adam Deadmarsh 2.00 5.00
5 Rory Fitzpatrick 2.00 5.00
6 Sean Haggerty 2.00 5.00
7 Jamie Langenbrunner 4.00 8.00
8 Jeff Mitchell 2.00 5.00
9 Richard Park 2.00 5.00
10 Deron Quint 2.00 5.00

1995-96 Leaf

The 1995-96 Leaf set was released in one series of 330-cards. The 12-card packs had an SRP of $1.99. The cards boasted a simple design featuring an action photo with the team name in reflective foil along the right border. A wrapper offer on the packs gave collectors the chance to redeem two wrappers and $9.95 for a special Mario Lemieux Tribute card limited to 15,000 sequentially numbered copies.

1 Mario Lemieux .30 .75
2 Todd Harvey .05 .15
3 Blaine Lacher .07 .20
4 Alexei Zhitnik .05 .15
5 Cory Stillman .05 .15
6 Murray Craven .05 .15
7 Mike Kennedy .07 .20
8 Mike Vernon .07 .20
9 David Oliver .05 .15
10 Magnus Svensson RC .07 .20
11 Andrei Nikolishin .05 .15
12 Jamie Storr .07 .20
13 David Roberts .05 .15
14 Chris McAlpine RC .07 .20
15 Brett Lindros .05 .15
16 Pat Verbeek .07 .20
17 Tony Amonte .07 .20
18 Chris Therien .05 .15
19 Ken Wregget .07 .20
20 Peter Forsberg .25 .60
21 Jeff Friesen .05 .15
22 Patrice Tardif .07 .20
23 Jason Wiemer .05 .15
24 Kenny Jonsson .10 .25
25 Jassen Cullimore .07 .20
26 Sergei Gonchar .05 .15
27 Nikolai Khabibulin .07 .20
28 Oleg Tverdovsky .10 .25
29 Rick Tocchet .07 .20
30 Garry Galley .05 .15
31 German Titov .07 .20
32 Sergei Krivokrasov .05 .15
33 Sylvain Turgeon .05 .15
34 Sergei Fedorov .15 .40
35 Ralph Intranuovo .05 .15
36 Stu Barnes .05 .15
37 Mike Gartner .10 .25
38 Kevin Brown .07 .20
39 Valeri Bure .05 .15
40 Sergei Brylin .05 .15
41 Kirk Muller .07 .20
42 Mike Richter .10 .25
43 Stanislav Neckar .05 .15
44 Patrik Juhlin .05 .15
45 Ron Francis .12 .30
46 Janne Laukkanen .05 .15
47 Shean Donovan .05 .15
48 Igor Korolev .05 .15
49 Alexander Selivanov .07 .20
50 Frantisek Kucera .05 .15
51 Russ Courtnall .05 .15
52 Don Beaupre .07 .20
53 Michal Grosek .05 .15
54 Steve Rucchin .07 .20
55 Mariusz Czerkawski .05 .15
56 Dominik Hasek .12 .30
57 Trent Klatt .05 .15
58 Sergio Momesso .05 .15
59 Mark Lawrence .05 .15
60 Steve Yzerman .12 .30
61 Todd Marchant .05 .15
62 Jesse Belanger .05 .15
63 Sean Burke .05 .15
64 Matt Johnson .07 .20
65 Mark Recchi .12 .30
66 Martin Brodeur .25 .60
67 Mathieu Schneider .05 .15
68 Mark Messier .15 .40
69 Radim Bicanek .07 .20
70 Eric Desjardins .07 .20
71 Jaromir Jagr .25 .60
72 Adam Deadmarsh .05 .15
73 Viktor Kozlov .07 .20
74 Jeff Norton .05 .15
75 Brantt Myhres RC .05 .15
76 Darby Hendrickson .05 .15
77 Roman Oksiuta .05 .15
78 Jim Carey .07 .20
79 Keith Tkachuk .10 .25
80 Valeri Karpov .05 .15
81 Adam Oates .10 .25
82 Eric Lindros .15 .40
83 Trevor Kidd .07 .20
84 Bernie Nicholls .05 .15
85 Craig Conroy RC .07 .20
86 Bill Ranford .07 .20
87 Scott Mellanby .07 .20
88 Geoff Sanderson .05 .15
89 Wayne Gretzky .50 1.25
90 Pierre Turgeon .10 .25
91 Stephane Richer .07 .20
92 Chris Marinucci RC .07 .20
93 Brian Leetch .10 .25
94 Steve Larouche .05 .15
95 John LeClair .10 .25
96 Dmitri Mironov .05 .15
97 Jocelyn Thibault .07 .20
98 Craig Janney .05 .15
99 Ian Laperriere .05 .15
100 Dino Ciccarelli .07 .20
101 Todd Warriner .07 .20
102 Kirk McLean .07 .20
103 Jason Allison .07 .20
104 Alexei Zhamnov .10 .25
105 Keith Jones .07 .20
106 Ray Bourque .15 .40
107 John Druce .07 .20
108 Scott Walker RC .05 .15
109 Joe Murphy .05 .15
110 Checklist (1-110) .05 .15
111 Philippe DeRouville .07 .20
112 Greg Adams .05 .15
113 Cam Neely .10 .25
114 Mike Peca .07 .20
115 Theo Fleury .12 .30
116 Jeremy Roenick .12 .30
117 Kevin Hatcher .07 .20
118 Ray Sheppard .07 .20
119 Jason Arnott .07 .20
120 Mark Fitzpatrick .07 .20
121 Brendan Shanahan .12 .30
122 Jari Kurri .10 .25
123 Shayne Corson .05 .15
124 Scott Stevens .10 .25
125 Steve Thomas .07 .20
126 Sergei Zubov .07 .20
127 Denis Savard .12 .30
128 Mikael Renberg .07 .20
129 Luc Robitaille .10 .25
130 Andrei Kovalenko .05 .15
131 Andrei Nazarov .07 .20
132 Denis Chasse .05 .15
133 Chris Gratton .05 .15
134 Benoit Hogue .05 .15
135 Pavel Bure .12 .30
136 Peter Bondra .10 .25
137 Teemu Selanne .20 .50
138 Darren Van Impe RC .05 .15
139 Dimitri Khristich .05 .15
140 Pat LaFontaine .10 .25
141 Phil Housley .07 .20
142 Chris Chelios .10 .25
143 Steve Duchesne .05 .15
144 Paul Coffey .10 .25
145 Doug Weight .10 .25
146 Gord Murphy .05 .15
147 Andrew Cassels .05 .15
148 Rob Blake .07 .20
149 Vladimir Malakhov .05 .15
150 Scott Niedermayer .10 .25
151 Patrick Flatley .05 .15
152 Adam Graves .07 .20
153 Alexei Yashin .07 .20
154 Rod Brind'Amour .10 .25
155 Joe Mullen .07 .20
156 Mike Ricci .07 .20
157 Ulf Dahlen .05 .15
158 Dave Manson .05 .15
159 Brian Bradley .07 .20
160 Felix Potvin .10 .25
161 Trevor Linden .10 .25
162 Michal Pivonka .05 .15
163 Nelson Emerson .05 .15
164 Joe Sacco .05 .15
165 Todd Elik .05 .15
166 Derek Plante .05 .15
167 Mike Sullivan .07 .20
168 Randy Wood .05 .15
169 Manny Fernandez .07 .20
170 Keith Primeau .05 .15
171 Marko Tuomainen .05 .15
172 John Vanbiesbrouck .07 .20
173 Darren Turcotte .05 .15
174 Tony Granato .05 .15
175 Brian Savage .05 .15
176 John MacLean .07 .20
177 Tommy Salo RC .15 .40
178 Steve Larmer .07 .20
179 Alexandre Daigle .05 .15
180 Petr Svoboda .05 .15
181 John Cullen .05 .15
182 Joe Sakic .15 .40
183 Sandis Ozolinsh .07 .20
184 Dale Hawerchuk .12 .30
185 Paul Ysebaert .05 .15
186 Larry Murphy .10 .25
187 Alexander Mogilny .07 .20
188 Joe Juneau .07 .20
189 Craig Martin RC .05 .15
190 Jason Marshall .05 .15
191 Don Sweeney .05 .15
192 Ron Hextall .10 .25
193 Steve Chiasson .05 .15
194 Steve Smith .05 .15
195 Lyle Odelein .05 .15
196 Ryan Smyth .07 .20
197 Rob Niedermayer .07 .20
198 Steven Rice .05 .15
199 Darryl Sydor .07 .20
200 Patrick Roy .25 .60
201 Bill Guerin .07 .20
202 Scott Lachance .05 .15
203 Alexei Kovalev .05 .15
204 Ronnie Stern .05 .15
205 Kevin Dineen .07 .20
206 Ulf Samuelsson .05 .15
207 Wendel Clark .10 .25
208 Ray Whitney .07 .20
209 Brett Hull .12 .30
210 Slava Kozlov .07 .20
211 Doug Gilmour .12 .30
212 Mike Ridley .05 .15
213 Mike Torchia .07 .20
214 Tavis Hansen RC .05 .15
215 Dale Hunter .07 .20
216 Kevin Stevens .07 .20
217 Mike Donnelly .05 .15
218 Sylvain Cote .05 .15
219 Gary Suter .07 .20
220 Checklist (111-120) .05 .15
221 Richard Park .10 .25
222 Dave Gagner .05 .15
223 Jozef Stumpel .05 .15
224 Brad May .05 .15
225 Zarley Zalapski .05 .15
226 Eric Daze .20 .50
227 Mike Modano .15 .40
228 Nicklas Lidstrom .10 .25
229 Jason Bonsignore .05 .15
230 Robert Svehla RC .05 .15
231 Glen Wesley .05 .15
232 Josef Beranek .05 .15
233 Geoff Courtnall .05 .15
234 Shawn Chambers .05 .15
235 Darius Kasparaitis .05 .15
236 Sergei Nemchinov .05 .15
237 Patrick Poulin .05 .15
238 Anatoli Semenov .07 .20
239 Bryan Smolinski .05 .15
240 Owen Nolan .10 .25
241 Pat Falloon .05 .15
242 Chris Pronger .10 .25
243 Daren Puppa .07 .20
244 Mats Sundin .10 .25
245 Jeff Brown .07 .20
246 Jeff Nelson .07 .20
247 Teppo Numminen .05 .15
248 Shaun Van Allen .05 .15
249 Yanic Perreault .05 .15
250 Brian Holzinger RC .20 .50
251 Paul Kruse .05 .15
252 Jeff Shantz .05 .15
253 Martin Straka .05 .15
254 Chris Osgood .07 .20
255 Joaquin Gage RC .07 .20
256 Dave Lowry .05 .15
257 Robert Kron .05 .15
258 Dan Quinn .07 .20
259 David Wilkie .05 .15
260 Valeri Zelepukin .05 .15
261 Derek King .07 .20
262 Darren Langdon RC .20 .50
263 Radek Bonk .05 .15
264 Karl Dykhuis .05 .15
265 Tomas Sandstrom .07 .20
266 Uwe Krupp .07 .20
267 Arturs Irbe .07 .20
268 Dallas Drake .05 .15
269 John Tucker .05 .15
270 Dave Andreychuk .10 .25
271 Guy Hebert .07 .20
272 Sandy Moger RC .05 .15
273 Craig Johnson .05 .15
274 Donald Audette .07 .20
275 Cory Cross .05 .15
276 Richard Smehlik .07 .20
277 Gary Roberts .05 .15
278 Todd Gill .05 .15
279 Derian Hatcher .07 .20
280 Slava Fetisov .07 .20
281 Curtis Joseph .10 .25
282 Johan Garpenlov .05 .15
283 Vladimir Konstantinov .07 .20
284 Ray Ferraro .05 .15
285 Turner Stevenson .05 .15
286 Neal Broten .07 .20
287 Jason Wiemer RC .05 .15
288 Mattias Norstrom .07 .20
289 Michel Picard .07 .20
290 Brent Fedyk .05 .15
291 Dimitri Yushkevich .05 .15
292 Sylvain Lefebvre .05 .15
293 Sergei Makarov .05 .15
294 Brian Rolston .05 .15
295 Roman Hamrlik .05 .15
296 Mark Wotton RC .05 .15
297 Alek Stojanov RC .05 .15
298 Calle Johansson .05 .15
299 Mike Eastwood .05 .15
300 Bob Corkum .05 .15
301 Petr Nedved .07 .20
302 Vincent Damphousse .07 .20
303 Brett Harkins RC .05 .15
304 Paul Kariya .12 .30
305 Joe Nieuwendyk .10 .25
306 Dennis Bonvie RC .05 .15
307 Jason Woolley .05 .15
308 Jimmy Carson .07 .20
309 Marty McSorley .05 .15
310 Craig Rivet RC .05 .15
311 Claude Lemieux .10 .25
312 Al MacInnis .10 .25
313 Gerald Diduck .05 .15
314 Randy McKay .05 .15
315 Bob Errey .05 .15
316 Rusty Fitzgerald RC .05 .15
317 Scott Young .05 .15
318 Igor Larionov .05 .15
319 Esa Tikkanen .05 .15
320 Darren McCarty .05 .15
321 Petr Klima .05 .15
322 Jon Rohloff .05 .15
323 Steve Konowalchuk .07 .20
324 Milos Holan .05 .15
325 Checklist (221-330) .05 .15
326 Ted Donato .05 .15
327 Grant Marshall .05 .15
328 Jyrki Lumme .05 .15
329 Ed Belfour .07 .20
330 Checklist (inserts) .05 .15
NNO M.Lemieux Redemption 6.00 15.00

1995-96 Leaf Fire On Ice

This 12-card set featured some of the NHL's most dangerous snipers. The cards were sequentially numbered out of 10,000 and were randomly inserted at a rate of about 1:48 packs.

COMPLETE SET (12) 10.00 20.00
1 Pavel Bure .60 1.50
2 Eric Lindros .60 1.50
3 Alexei Zhamnov .30 .75
4 Paul Coffey .60 1.50
5 Theo Fleury .20 .50
6 Peter Forsberg 1.50 4.00
7 Sergei Fedorov .75 2.00
8 Mats Sundin .60 1.50
9 Brett Hull .75 2.00
10 Wayne Gretzky 5.00 12.00
11 Paul Kariya .60 1.50
12 Mikael Renberg .30 .75

1995-96 Leaf Freeze Frame

These eight cards, which focused on special moments for a team or player form the 1994-95 season, were randomly inserted at indeterminate odds (estimated at around 1:72). The cards were serially numbered out of 10,000.

COMPLETE SET (8) 10.00 25.00
1 Jim Carey 1.00 2.50
2 Pierre Turgeon 1.00 2.50
3 Mikael Renberg 1.00 2.50
4 Jaromir Jagr 1.50 4.00
5 Alexei Zhamnov 1.00 2.50
6 New Jersey Devils 1.00 2.50
7 Mario Lemieux 4.00 10.00
8 A.Mogilny 2.00 5.00
P.Bure

1995-96 Leaf Gold Stars

The twelve players featured in this six-card set were the tops at their position in 1994-95. The cards were individually numbered out of 5,000 and were randomly inserted in retail packs at indeterminate odds (estimated at around 1:90).

COMPLETE SET (6) 10.00 20.00
1 D.Hasek 2.50 6.00
J.Carey
2 P.Coffey 1.50 4.00
C.Chelios
3 R.Bourque 1.50 4.00
B.Leetch
4 E.Lindros 2.00 5.00
A.Zhamnov
5 J.Jagr 2.50 6.00
T.Fleury
6 B.Hull 1.50 4.00
M.Renberg

1995-96 Leaf Lemieux's Best

This set captured ten of the greatest moments in the career of one of the greatest players ever, Mario Lemieux. The cards were randomly inserted at indeterminate odds (estimated at around 1:18).

COMPLETE SET (10) 20.00 40.00
COMMON CARD (1-10) 3.00 6.00

1995-96 Leaf Road To The Cup

This ten-card set recognized several key moments from the 1994-95 Stanley Cup playoffs. The cards were serially numbered out of 5,000, and were randomly inserted into hobby packs only at indeterminate odds (estimated at around 1:90).

COMPLETE SET (10) 5.00 10.00
1 Ray Whitney .30 .75
2 Martin Brodeur 1.50 4.00
3 Jaromir Jagr 1.00 2.50
4 Eric Lindros .60 1.50
5 Paul Coffey .60 1.50
6 Chris Chelios .60 1.50
7 Neal Broten .30 .75
8 Slava Kozlov .30 .75
9 Scott Niedermayer .30 .75
10 Claude Lemieux .30 .75

1995-96 Leaf Studio Rookies

is 20-card set resembled credit cards, down to the shape, the embossed membership data on the front and the signature and metallic data strips on the back. The cards were randomly inserted into packs at indeterminate odds, estimated to be around 1:12.

COMPLETE SET (20) 15.00 30.00
1 Jim Carey 1.00 2.50
2 Peter Forsberg 2.50 6.00
3 Paul Kariya 1.50 4.00
4 David Oliver .75 2.00
5 Blaine Lacher 1.00 2.50
6 Oleg Tverdovsky .75 2.00
7 Jeff Friesen .75 2.00
8 Todd Marchant 1.00 2.50
9 Todd Harvey 1.00 2.50
10 Ian Laperriere .75 2.00
11 Eric Daze 1.00 2.50
12 Jason Bonsignore .75 2.00
13 Jamie Storr 1.00 2.50
14 Brian Holzinger 1.50 4.00
15 Brian Savage .75 2.00
16 Roman Oksiuta .75 2.00
17 Mariusz Czerkawski .75 2.00
18 Sergei Krivokrasov .75 2.00
19 Jason Wiemer .75 2.00
20 Radek Bonk .75 2.00

1996-97 Leaf

The 1996-97 Leaf set, consisting of 240 cards, was distributed in 10-card packs with a suggested retail price of $2.99. The fronts featured a color action player photo printed on common card stock with silver foil. The backs carried another player photo with season and career statistics. Marin Biron was the only rookie of note.

1 Sergei Fedorov .25 .60
2 Bill Ranford .12 .30
3 Oleg Tverdovsky .12 .30
4 Brad May .10 .25
5 Chris Pronger .12 .30
6 Martin Brodeur .30 .75
7 Yanic Perreault .10 .25
8 Garry Galley .10 .25
9 Shawn McEachern .10 .25
10 Brian Bellows .12 .30
11 Ron Francis .20 .50
12 Mike Modano .25 .60
13 Steve Yzerman .40 1.00
14 Joe Mullen .12 .30
15 Pavel Bure .20 .50
16 Dino Ciccarelli .15 .40
17 Claude Lemieux .10 .25
18 Stephane Richer .12 .30
19 Dominik Hasek .25 .60
20 Adam Graves .10 .25
21 Joe Juneau .10 .25
22 Rob Niedermayer .12 .30
23 Zigmund Palffy .15 .40
24 Dave Andreychuk .15 .40
25 Steve Thomas .10 .25
26 Tom Barrasso .12 .30
27 Eric Desjardins .12 .30
28 Curtis Joseph .15 .40
29 Russ Courtnall .10 .25
30 Stu Barnes .10 .25
31 Mark Tinordi .10 .25
32 Gary Suter .10 .25
33 Greg Johnson .10 .25
34 Joe Nieuwendyk .15 .40
35 Norm MacIver .10 .25
36 Craig Janney .12 .30
37 Mark Recchi .20 .50
38 Patrick Roy .40 1.00
39 Petr Klima .10 .25
40 Ken Wregget .12 .30
41 Rod Brind'Amour .15 .40
42 Slava Fetisov .10 .25
43 Kirk McLean .12 .30
44 Pat LaFontaine .15 .40
45 Brett Hull .75 2.00
46 Chris Chelios .15 .40
47 Damian Rhodes .12 .30
48 Kevin Hatcher .10 .25
49 Uwe Krupp .10 .25
50 Bernie Nicholls .10 .25
51 Tommy Soderstrom .12 .30
52 Teemu Selanne .30 .75
53 Mats Sundin .15 .40
54 Jeff Hackett .12 .30
55 Ulf Dahlen .10 .25
56 Dale Hunter .12 .30
57 Robert Kron .10 .25
58 Brian Bradley .10 .25
59 Pat Verbeek .10 .25
60 Kenny Jonsson .10 .25
61 Theo Fleury .30 .75
62 Alexander Selivanov .10 .25
63 Nikolai Khabibulin .12 .30
64 Grant Fuhr .15 .40
65 Phil Housley .12 .30
66 Bill Lindsay .10 .25
67 Trevor Kidd .10 .25
68 Jim Carey .15 .40
69 Brian Skrudland .10 .25
70 Todd Krygier .10 .25
71 Petr Nedved .12 .30
72 Kirk Muller .10 .25
73 Daren Puppa .12 .30
74 Doug Gilmour .20 .50
75 Nicklas Lidstrom .20 .50
76 Zdeno Ciger .10 .25

7 Robert Svehla .10 .25
8 Andrew Cassels .10 .25
9 Vincent Damphousse .12 .30
0 Alexandre Daigle .10 .25
1 Tomas Sandstrom .10 .25
2 Brent Fedyk .10 .25
3 John LeClair .15 .40
4 Mario Lemieux .50 1.25
5 Sean Burke .10 .25
6 Cam Neely .15 .40
7 Jeff Friesen .10 .25
8 Guy Hebert .12 .30
9 Jon Casey .12 .30
0 Rick Tocchet .12 .30
1 Mike Gartner .15 .40
2 Tony Amonte .12 .30
3 Jason Dawe .10 .25
4 Chris Terreri .12 .30
5 Zarley Zalapski .10 .25
6 Martin Rucinsky .10 .25
7 Garth Snow .12 .30
8 Sylvain Lefebvre .10 .25
9 Andy Moog .15 .40
00 Larry Murphy .12 .30
01 Alexei Yashin .12 .30
02 Pat Falloon .10 .25
03 Greg Adams .10 .25
04 Igor Larionov .15 .40
05 Geoff Sanderson .12 .30
06 Jaromir Jagr .40 1.00
07 Alexei Zhamnov .12 .30
08 Mikael Renberg .12 .30
09 Kelly Hrudey .12 .30
10 Vladimir Konstantinov .12 .30
11 Brian Savage .10 .25
12 Adam Oates .15 .40
13 Teppo Numminen .10 .25
14 Ray Sheppard .12 .30
15 Michael Nylander .10 .25
16 Jozef Stumpel .10 .25
17 Ed Olczyk .10 .25
8 Roman Hamrlik .12 .30
9 Kris Draper .10 .25
20 Chris Gratton .12 .30
21 Randy Burridge .10 .25
22 Ray Bourque .25 .60
23 Jyrki Lumme .10 .25
24 Dale Hawerchuk .20 .50
25 Dave Lowry .10 .25
26 Curtis Leschyshyn .10 .25
27 Martin Gelinas .10 .25
28 Owen Nolan .15 .40
29 Radek Bonk .10 .25
30 Sergei Zubov .10 .25
31 Travis Green .12 .30
32 Scott Mellanby .12 .30
33 Keith Tkachuk .15 .40
34 Luc Robitaille .15 .40
35 Alexei Kovalev .10 .25
36 Doug Weight .15 .40
37 Benoit Hogue .10 .25
38 Cory Stillman .10 .25
39 Joe Sakic .25 .60
0 Wayne Gretzky .75 2.00
1 Mike Ricci .10 .25
2 Kyle McLaren .10 .25
3 Deron Quint .10 .25
4 Ville Peltonen .10 .25
5 Todd Harvey .10 .25
6 Brendan Shanahan .20 .50
7 Mike Vernon .12 .30
8 Eric Lindros .25 .60
9 Rick Tabaracci .12 .30
0 Stephane Yelle .10 .25
1 Chris Osgood .15 .40
2 Corey Hirsch .12 .30
3 Todd Marchant .10 .25
4 Keith Primeau .10 .25
5 Alexei Zhitnik .10 .25
6 Felix Potvin .15 .40
7 Vitali Yachmenev .10 .25
8 Geoff Courtnall .10 .25
9 Peter Forsberg .25 .60
0 Radek Dvorak .12 .30
1 Bryan McCabe .10 .25
2 Alexander Mogilny .12 .30
3 Shayne Corson .10 .25
4 Paul Coffey .15 .40
5 Brian Leetch .15 .40
6 Wendel Clark .12 .30
7 Aaron Gavey .10 .25
8 Dimitri Khristich .10 .25
9 Grant Marshall .10 .25
0 Valeri Kamensky .12 .30
1 Ryan Smyth .12 .30
2 Niklas Sundstrom .10 .25
3 Cliff Ronning .10 .25
4 Al MacInnis .15 .40
5 Scott Stevens .15 .40
6 Paul Kariya .20 .50
7 Rob Blake .15 .40
8 Mike Richter .15 .40
9 Jason Arnott .12 .30
0 Mark Messier .25 .60
1 Scott Young .10 .25
2 Jocelyn Thibault .15 .40
3 Marcus Ragnarsson .10 .25
4 Darren Turcotte .10 .25
5 Joe Murphy .10 .25
6 Pierre Turgeon .15 .40
7 Trevor Linden .12 .30
8 Stephane Fiset .12 .30
9 Miroslav Satan .10 .25
0 Mathieu Schneider .10 .25
1 Jeremy Roenick .25 .60
2 Craig MacTavish .10 .25
3 John Vanbiesbrouck .15 .40
4 Ron Hextall .12 .30
5 John MacLean .12 .30
6 Vyacheslav Kozlov .10 .25
7 Sandis Ozolinsh .10 .25
8 Scott Niedermayer .15 .40
9 Ed Belfour .15 .40
0 Peter Bondra .12 .30
1 Jere Lehtinen .10 .25
2 Eric Daze .12 .30
3 Chad Kilger .10 .25
4 Saku Koivu .15 .40
5 Todd Bertuzzi .15 .40
6 Petr Sykora .10 .25
7 Valeri Bure .10 .25
8 Ed Jovanovski .12 .30
9 Jeff O'Neill .10 .25
0 Daniel Alfredsson .15 .40
1 Byron Dafoe .10 .25
2 Brian Holzinger .12 .30

213 Martin Biron RC .20 .50
214 Anders Eriksson .10 .25
215 Landon Wilson .10 .25
216 Alexei Yegorov RC .15 .40
217 Jan Caloun RC .15 .40
218 David Sacco .10 .25
219 David Nemirovsky .10 .25
220 Anders Myrvold .10 .25
221 Tommy Salo .12 .30
222 Jan Vopat .10 .25
223 Steve Staios RC .15 .40
224 Patrick Labrecque .10 .25
225 Jamie Langenbrunner .10 .25
226 Denis Pederson .10 .25
227 Marek Malik .10 .25
228 Geoff Sarjeant .10 .25
229 Chris Ferraro .10 .25
230 Zdenek Nedved .10 .25
231 Wayne Primeau .10 .25
232 Daymond Langkow .12 .30
233 Marko Kiprusoff .10 .25
234 Niklas Sundblad .10 .25
235 Jamie Ram RC .10 .25
236 Jamie Rivers .10 .25
237 Steve Washburn RC .15 .40
238 Teemu Selanne CL .30 .75
239 Steve Yzerman CL .40 1.00
240 Eric Lindros CL .25 .60

1996-97 Leaf Press Proofs

This 240-card set was a die-cut parallel rendition of the regular Leaf set. Only 1,500 sets were produced, with each card sequentially numbered. The words "Press Proof" appeared on the card front in gold foil.
*VETS: 8X TO 20X BASIC CARDS
*ROOKIES: 4X TO 10X

1996-97 Leaf Fire On Ice

This 15-card insert set, found only in retail packs, featured megastar players who heated up the ice with their play. Color player photos were printed on foil-laminated, micro-etched card stock. Only 2,500 sets were produced, with each card sequentially numbered.
COMPLETE SET (15) 25.00 50.00
1 Mario Lemieux 6.00 15.00
2 Alexander Mogilny 1.25 3.00
3 Joe Sakic 5.00 12.00
4 Paul Kariya 2.00 5.00
5 Wayne Gretzky 12.50 30.00
6 Doug Weight 1.00 2.50
7 Zigmund Palffy 1.00 2.50
8 Eric Lindros 6.00 15.00
9 Teemu Selanne 1.50 4.00
10 Doug Gilmour 1.50 4.00
11 Jeremy Roenick 3.00 8.00
12 Steve Yzerman 6.00 15.00
13 Ed Jovanovski 1.00 2.50
14 Mike Modano 2.50 6.00
15 Mark Messier 3.00 8.00

1996-97 Leaf Gold Rookies

MPLETE SET (10) 10.00 25.00
1 Ethan Moreau .75 2.00
2 Kevin Hodson .75 2.00
3 Jose Theodore 2.50 6.00
4 Peter Ferraro .75 2.00
5 Ralph Intranuovo .75 2.00
6 Nolan Baumgartner .75 2.00
7 Brandon Convery .75 2.00
8 Darcy Tucker 1.50 4.00
9 Eric Fichaud .75 2.00
10 Steve Sullivan 1.50 4.00

1996-97 Leaf Leather And Laces Promos

This 20 card set was intended to promote the upcoming Leather and Lace insert set. Unlike the regular set in which 5,000 serial numbered sets were issued, these cards were issued as Promo/5000 in the serial numbered box. Forsberg and Modano were the two most commonly found cards in this set
COMPLETE SET (20) 40.00 100.00
*PROMOS: .5X TO 1.2X BASIC INSERTS

1996-97 Leaf Leather And Laces

is 20-card set featured color action player photos of the NHL's top skaters printed on embossed leather style cards with skate laces in the background and gold foil stamping. The backs carried another player photo and player statistics on a black background. Only 5,000 of these sets were produced and were sequentially numbered.
COMPLETE SET (20) 50.00 100.00
1 Joe Sakic 5.00 12.00
2 Keith Tkachuk 1.50 4.00
3 Brett Hull 3.00 8.00
4 Paul Coffey 2.00 5.00
5 Jaromir Jagr 4.00 10.00
6 Peter Forsberg 2.50 6.00
7 Zigmund Palffy 1.25 3.00
8 Wayne Gretzky 10.00 25.00
9 Pavel Bure 2.50 6.00
10 Eric Lindros 2.50 6.00
11 Alexander Mogilny 1.25 3.00
12 Trevor Linden 2.00 5.00
13 Jeremy Roenick 3.00 8.00
14 Doug Gilmour 2.00 5.00
15 Mike Modano 2.50 6.00
16 Sergei Fedorov 3.00 8.00
17 Brendan Shanahan 2.50 6.00
18 Pierre Turgeon 1.50 4.00
19 Ed Jovanovski 1.25 3.00
20 Saku Koivu 2.00 5.00

1996-97 Leaf Shut Down

The dominant goaltenders of the NHL (as a group averaging 27 wins in 95-96), were the focus of this 15-card hobby-only chase set. The fronts featured color player photos printed on sailcloth canvas card stock while the backs carried player information. Only 2,500 of this set were produced, with each card sequentially numbered.
COMPLETE SET (15) 50.00 100.00
1 Patrick Roy 10.00 25.00
2 John Vanbiesbrouck 4.00 10.00
3 Jocelyn Thibault 2.00 5.00
4 Ed Belfour 4.00 10.00
5 Curtis Joseph 4.00 10.00
6 Martin Brodeur 8.00 20.00
7 Damian Rhodes 1.50 4.00
8 Felix Potvin 6.00 15.00
9 Nikolai Khabibulin 3.00 8.00
10 Jim Carey 2.00 5.00
11 Mike Richter 3.00 8.00
12 Corey Hirsch 1.50 4.00
13 Chris Osgood 3.00 8.00
14 Ron Hextall 4.00 10.00
15 Daren Puppa 2.00 5.00

1996-97 Leaf Sweaters Away

This 15-card insert set was printed on embossed, nylon jersey-style card stock in colors simulating the road uniforms of the league's superstars. The fronts displayed color player photos while the backs carried player information. Just 5,000 of these sets were produced and each card was sequentially numbered.
COMPLETE SET (15) 40.00 100.00
*HOME/1000: .8X TO 2X AWAY/5000
1 Mario Lemieux 10.00 25.00
2 Patrick Roy 10.00 25.00
3 Eric Lindros 5.00 12.00
4 John Vanbiesbrouck 3.00 8.00
5 Paul Kariya 4.00 10.00
6 Martin Brodeur 6.00 15.00
7 Eric Daze 2.50 6.00
8 Mark Messier 4.00 10.00
9 Jim Carey 2.50 6.00
10 Brendan Shanahan 4.00 10.00
11 Sergei Fedorov 4.00 10.00
12 Brett Hull 4.00 10.00
13 Pavel Bure 4.00 10.00
14 Daniel Alfredsson 3.00 8.00
15 Saku Koivu 3.00 8.00

1996-97 Leaf The Best Of

This nine-card insert set featured NHL record breakers and was found exclusively in pre-priced retail packs. Printed on clear plastic with holographic foil, just 1,500 of this die-cut insert set were produced, with each card sequentially numbered.
COMPLETE SET (9) 20.00 50.00
1 Jaromir Jagr 6.00 15.00
2 Eric Daze 2.00 5.00
3 Eric Lindros 3.00 8.00
4 Chris Osgood 3.00 8.00
5 Keith Tkachuk 3.00 8.00
6 Nikolai Khabibulin 3.00 8.00
7 Doug Weight 2.00 5.00
8 Peter Forsberg 6.00 15.00
9 Jocelyn Thibault 2.00 5.00

1997-98 Leaf

The 1997-98 Leaf set was issued in one series totaling 200 cards and was distributed in 10-card packs with a suggested retail price of $2.99. The fronts featured borderless color action player photos. The backs carried player information. The set contained the topical subsets: Gold Leaf Rookies (148-167), Gamers (168-187), and Day in the Life (188-197).
1 Eric Lindros .30 .75
2 Dominik Hasek .30 .75
3 Peter Forsberg .25 .60
4 Steve Yzerman .40 1.00
5 John Vanbiesbrouck .20 .50
6 Paul Kariya .25 .60
7 Martin Brodeur .40 1.00
8 Wayne Gretzky 1.00 2.50
9 Mark Messier .30 .75
10 Jaromir Jagr .50 1.25
11 Brett Hull .25 .60
12 Brendan Shanahan .25 .60
13 Ray Bourque .30 .75
14 Jarome Iginla .20 .50
15 Mike Modano .30 .75
16 Curtis Joseph .20 .50
17 Ed Jovanovski .12 .30
18 Teemu Selanne .40 1.00
19 Saku Koivu .20 .50
20 Eric Fichaud .15 .40
21 Paul Coffey .20 .50
22 Jeremy Roenick .25 .60
23 Owen Nolan .20 .50
24 Felix Potvin .20 .50
25 Alexander Mogilny .15 .40
26 Alexandre Daigle .12 .30
27 Chris Gratton .12 .30
28 Geoff Sanderson .15 .40
29 Dimitri Khristich .15 .40
30 Bryan Berard .12 .30
31 Vyacheslav Kozlov .15 .40
32 Jeff Hackett .12 .30
33 Bill Ranford .15 .40
34 Pat LaFontaine .20 .50
35 Joe Sakic .30 .75
36 Niklas Sundstrom .15 .40
37 Martin Gelinas .12 .30
38 Mikael Renberg .15 .40
39 Trevor Linden .15 .40
40 Jozef Stumpel .15 .40
41 Joe Thornton CL (1-46) .20 .50
42 Jocelyn Thibault .12 .30
43 Pierre Turgeon .20 .50
44 Ron Francis .25 .60
45 Damian Rhodes .15 .40
46 Jamie Langenbrunner .15 .40
47 Chris Osgood .20 .50
48 Vaclav Varada .12 .30
49 Ryan Smyth .15 .40
50 Daren Puppa .15 .40
51 Petr Nedved .20 .50
52 Ron Hextall .20 .50
53 Joe Juneau .15 .40
54 Jim Campbell .12 .30
55 Zigmund Palffy .20 .50
56 Roman Turek .15 .40
57 Adam Deadmarsh .12 .30
58 Rob Niedermayer .12 .30
59 Alexei Yashin .15 .40
60 Pavel Bure .25 .60
61 Jason Arnott .15 .40
62 Nikolai Khabibulin .20 .50
63 Sean Burke .12 .30
64 Chris Chelios .20 .50
65 Mike Ricci .15 .40
66 Sergei Berezin .15 .40
67 Jaroslav Svejkovsky CL .15 .40
68 Brian Savage .12 .30
69 Roman Vopat .15 .40
70 Mike Richter .20 .50
71 Jim Carey .12 .30
72 Guy Hebert .15 .40
73 Keith Tkachuk .20 .50
74 Kirk McLean .15 .40
75 Janne Niinimaa .15 .40
76 Roman Hamrlik .15 .40
77 Darcy Tucker .20 .50
78 Pat Verbeek .15 .40
79 Hnat Domenichelli .15 .40
80 Doug Gilmour .25 .60
81 Mike Grier .15 .40
82 Ken Wregget .12 .30
83 Dino Ciccarelli .20 .50
84 Steve Sullivan .15 .40
85 Anson Carter .12 .30
86 Steve Shields RC .20 .50
87 Ed Belfour .20 .50
88 Darren McCarty .15 .40
89 Adam Graves .12 .30
90 Chris Pronger .15 .40
91 Peter Bondra .15 .40
92 Oleg Tverdovsky .15 .40
93 Stephane Fiset .15 .40
94 Mike Vernon .15 .40
95 Scott Lachance .15 .40
96 Corey Schwab .15 .40
97 Eric Daze .12 .30
98 Jere Lehtinen .15 .40
99 Donald Audette .15 .40
100 John LeClair .20 .50
101 Steve Rucchin .15 .40
102 Jeff Friesen .15 .40
103 Daymond Langkow .12 .30
104 Mike Dunham .15 .40
105 Marc Denis CL .20 .50
106 Andrew Cassels .12 .30
107 Mike Peca .15 .40
108 Joe Nieuwendyk .20 .50
109 Vincent Damphousse .15 .40
110 Scott Mellanby .15 .40
111 Patrick Lalime .15 .40
112 Derek Plante .15 .40
113 Wade Redden .12 .30
114 Marcel Cousineau .15 .40
115 Ray Sheppard .15 .40
116 Dave Andreychuk .20 .50
117 Brian Leetch .20 .50
118 Sandis Ozolinsh .15 .40
119 Keith Primeau .15 .40
120 Brian Holzinger .15 .40
121 Luc Robitaille .20 .50
122 Jose Theodore .20 .50
123 Grant Fuhr .20 .50
124 Dainius Zubrus .15 .40
125 Rod Brind'Amour .20 .50
126 Trevor Kidd .12 .30
127 Mark Recchi .25 .60
128 Patrick Roy .50 1.25
129 Kevin Hatcher .12 .30
130 Adam Oates .20 .50
131 Doug Weight .20 .50
132 Vaclav Prospal RC .15 .40
133 Harry York .15 .40
134 Todd Bertuzzi .20 .50
135 Sergei Fedorov .30 .75
136 Theo Fleury .25 .60
137 Chad Kilger .15 .40
138 Jamie Storr .15 .40
139 Tony Amonte .15 .40
140 Rem Murray .12 .30
141 Chris O'Sullivan .15 .40
142 Mats Sundin .20 .50
143 Ethan Moreau .12 .30
144 Derian Hatcher .15 .40
145 Daniel Alfredsson .20 .50
146 Corey Hirsch .15 .40
147 Landon Wilson .12 .30
148 Marc Denis GLR .20 .50
149 Boyd Devereaux GLR .15 .40
150 Joe Thornton GLR .20 .50
151 Sergei Samsonov GLR .12 .30
152 Alyn McCauley GLR .15 .40
153 Erik Rasmussen GLR .15 .40
154 Patrick Marleau GLR .25 .60
155 Olli Jokinen GLR RC .25 .60
156 Chris Phillips GLR .15 .40
157 Tomas Vokoun GLR RC .20 .50
158 Chris Dingman RC GLR .20 .50
159 Daniel Cleary GLR .15 .40
160 Juha Lind GLR RC .20 .50
161 Jean-Yves Leroux RC GLR .20 .50
162 Brad Isbister GLR .15 .40
163 Vadim Sharifijanov GLR .15 .40
164 Alexei Morozov GLR .15 .40
165 Vaclav Prospal GLR .15 .40
166 Vaclav Varada GLR .12 .30
167 Jaroslav Svejkovsky GLR .15 .40
168 Eric Lindros GM .30 .75
169 Dominik Hasek GM .30 .75
170 Peter Forsberg GM .25 .60
171 Steve Yzerman GM .40 1.00
172 John Vanbiesbrouck GM .20 .50
173 Paul Kariya GM .25 .60
174 Martin Brodeur GM .40 1.00
175 Wayne Gretzky GM 1.00 2.50
176 Mark Messier GM .30 .75
177 Jaromir Jagr GM .50 1.25
178 Brett Hull GM .25 .60
179 Brendan Shanahan GM .25 .60
180 Jarome Iginla GM .20 .50
181 Mike Modano GM .30 .75
182 Teemu Selanne GM .40 1.00
183 Bryan Berard GM .12 .30
184 Ryan Smyth GM .15 .40
185 Keith Tkachuk GM .20 .50
186 Dainius Zubrus GM .15 .40
187 Patrick Roy GM .50 1.25
188 Trevor Linden DIL .15 .40
189 Trevor Linden DIL .15 .40
190 Trevor Linden DIL .15 .40
191 Trevor Linden DIL .15 .40
192 Trevor Linden DIL .15 .40
193 Trevor Linden DIL .15 .40
194 Trevor Linden DIL .15 .40
195 Trevor Linden DIL .15 .40
196 Trevor Linden DIL .15 .40
197 Trevor Linden DIL .15 .40
198 Chris Phillips CL .15 .40
199 Sergei Samsonov CL .12 .30
200 Daniel Cleary CL .15 .40
P5 Felix Potvin PROMO .60 1.50
P6 Martin Brodeur PROMO 3.00 8.00
P10 Jim Carey PROMO .50 1.25
NNO Trevor Linden AU/500 15.00 30.00

1997-98 Leaf Fractal Matrix

This 200-card set is parallel to the base set and featured color player photos with either a bronze, silver or gold finish. Only 100 cards were bronze, 60 cards were silver, and 40 cards were gold. No card was available in more than one of the color. Bronze-X cards had a stated print run 1400 sets. Bronze-Y cards had a stated print run 1600 sets. Bronze-Z cards had a stated print run 1700 sets. Silver-X cards had a stated print run of 500 sets. Silver-Y cards had a stated print run of 700 sets. Silver-Z cards had a stated print run of 800 cards. Gold-X cards had a stated print run of 50 sets. Gold-Y cards had a stated print run of 250 sets. Gold-Z cards had a stated print run of 350 sets. These cards were randomly inserted in leaf and Leaf International packs.
1 Eric Lindros GX/50* 15.00 40.00
2 Dominik Hasek GZ/350* 12.00 30.00
3 Peter Forsberg GZ/350* 8.00 20.00
4 Steve Yzerman GZ/350* 10.00 25.00
5 John Vanbiesbrouck GZ/350* 6.00 15.00
6 Paul Kariya GX/50* 20.00 50.00
7 Martin Brodeur GZ/350* 10.00 25.00
8 Wayne Gretzky GX/50* 60.00 150.00
9 Mark Messier GY/250* 5.00 12.00
10 Jaromir Jagr GZ/350* 8.00 20.00
11 Brett Hull GY/250* 6.00 15.00
12 Brendan Shanahan GZ/350* 6.00 15.00
13 Ray Bourque GY/250* 10.00 25.00
14 Jarome Iginla GY/250* 6.00 15.00
15 Mike Modano GY/250* 6.00 15.00
16 Curtis Joseph GY/250* 5.00 12.00
17 Ed Jovanovski SX/500* 2.50 6.00
18 Teemu Selanne GZ/350* 6.00 15.00
19 Saku Koivu GY/250* 5.00 12.00
20 Eric Fichaud SZ/800* 2.00 5.00
21 Paul Coffey SX/500* 3.00 8.00
22 Jeremy Roenick SX/500* 3.00 8.00
23 Owen Nolan BX/1400* 1.00 2.50
24 Felix Potvin GY/250* 8.00 20.00
25 Alexander Mogilny SZ/800* 2.50 6.00
26 Alexandre Daigle SX/500* 2.50 6.00
27 Chris Gratton SX/500* 2.00 5.00
28 Geoff Sanderson SX/500* 2.50 6.00
29 Dimitri Khristich SX/500* 2.00 5.00
30 Bryan Berard GY/250* 3.00 8.00
31 Vyacheslav Kozlov BX/1400* .75 2.00
32 Jeff Hackett BY/1600* .75 2.00
33 Bill Ranford BY/1600* .75 2.00
34 Pat LaFontaine SY/700* 2.50 6.00
35 Joe Sakic GY/250* 12.00 30.00
36 Niklas Sundstrom BX/1400* .75 2.00
37 Martin Gelinas BX/1400* .75 2.00
38 Mikael Renberg BX/1400* .75 2.00
39 Trevor Linden BX/1400* 1.25 3.00
40 Jozef Stumpel BY/1600* .75 2.00
41 Joe Thornton CL SZ/800* 4.00 10.00
42 Jocelyn Thibault GY/250* 4.00 10.00
43 Pierre Turgeon BX/1400* 1.00 2.50
44 Ron Francis BX/1400* 1.25 3.00
45 Damian Rhodes SY/700* 2.00 5.00
46 Jamie Langenbrunner SY/700* 2.50 6.00
47 Chris Osgood SZ/800* 3.00 8.00
48 Vaclav Varada SX/500* 2.00 5.00
49 Ryan Smyth GZ/350* 3.00 8.00
50 Darren Puppa BX/1400* .75 2.00
51 Petr Nedved BX/1400* .75 2.00
52 Ron Hextall BX/1400* 1.25 3.00
53 Joe Juneau BX/1400* .75 2.00
54 Jim Campbell SY/700* 2.00 5.00
55 Zigmund Palffy SZ/800* 2.50 6.00
56 Roman Turek BX/1400* .75 2.00
57 Adam Deadmarsh GY/250* 3.00 8.00
58 Rob Niedermayer BX/1400* 1.00 2.50
59 Alexei Yashin GY/250* 4.00 10.00
60 Pavel Bure GY/250* 5.00 12.00
61 Jason Arnott GY/250* 4.00 10.00
62 Nikolai Khabibulin SY/700* 2.50 6.00
63 Sean Burke SY/700* 2.50 6.00
64 Chris Chelios SX/500* 2.50 6.00
65 Mike Ricci BX/1400* 1.00 2.50
66 Sergei Berezin SY/700* 2.00 5.00
67 Jaroslav Svejkovsky GY CL/250* 3.00 8.00
68 Brian Savage BX/1400* .75 2.00
69 Roman Vopat BX/1400* .75 2.00
70 Mike Richter SX/500* 3.00 8.00
71 Jim Carey SY/700* 2.50 6.00
72 Guy Hebert BY/1600* 1.00 2.50
73 Keith Tkachuk GY/250* 5.00 12.00
74 Kirk McLean BX/1400* 1.00 2.50
75 Janne Niinimaa SY/700* 2.00 5.00
76 Roman Hamrlik SY/700* 2.50 6.00
77 Darcy Tucker SY/700* 2.00 5.00
78 Pat Verbeek BX/1400* .75 2.00
79 Hnat Domenichelli BX/1400* .75 2.00
80 Doug Gilmour SY/700* 3.00 8.00
81 Mike Grier GY/250* 3.00 8.00
82 Ken Wregget BX/1400* .75 2.00
83 Dino Ciccarelli BX/1400* 1.00 2.50
84 Steve Sullivan BX/1400* .75 2.00
85 Anson Carter SX/500* 2.00 5.00
86 Steve Shields BY/1600* .75 2.00
87 Ed Belfour SY/700* 3.00 8.00
88 Darren McCarty BX/1400* .75 2.00
89 Adam Graves BX/1400* .75 2.00
90 Chris Pronger BX/1400* 1.00 2.50
91 Peter Bondra SY/700* 2.50 6.00
92 Oleg Tverdovsky SY/700* 2.00 5.00
93 Stephane Fiset BX/1400* .75 2.00
94 Mike Vernon BY/1600* 1.25 3.00
95 Scott Lachance BX/1400* .75 2.00
96 Corey Schwab BX/1400* .75 2.00
97 Eric Daze BY/1600* .75 2.00
98 Jere Lehtinen BX/1400* 1.00 2.50
99 Donald Audette BX/1400* .75 2.00
100 John LeClair GY/250* 5.00 12.00
101 Steve Rucchin BX/1400* .75 2.00
102 Jeff Friesen SX/500* 2.00 5.00
103 Daymond Langkow SX/500* 2.00 5.00
104 Mike Dunham SY/700* 2.00 5.00
105 Marc Denis BZ CL (93-138)/1700* .75 2.00
106 Andrew Cassels BX/1400* .75 2.00
107 Mike Peca BX/1400* 1.00 2.50
108 Joe Nieuwendyk BX/1400* 1.25 3.00
109 Vincent Damphousse BX/1400* 1.00 2.50
110 Scott Mellanby BX/1400* .75 2.00
111 Patrick Lalime BX/1400* .75 2.00
112 Derek Plante SY/700* 2.00 5.00
113 Wade Redden SY/700* 2.00 5.00
114 Marcel Cousineau BY/1600* .75 2.00
115 Ray Sheppard BX/1400* .75 2.00
116 Dave Andreychuk BX/1400* 1.00 2.50
117 Brian Leetch GY/250* 5.00 12.00
118 Sandis Ozolinsh BY/1600* .75 2.00
119 Keith Primeau BX/1400* 1.00 2.50
120 Brian Holzinger BX/1400* .75 2.00
121 Luc Robitaille BX/1400* 1.00 2.50
122 Jose Theodore SX/500* 2.50 6.00
123 Grant Fuhr SY/700* 3.00 8.00
124 Dainius Zubrus GY/250* 3.00 8.00
125 Rod Brind'Amour BX/1400* 1.00 2.50
126 Trevor Kidd SY/700* 2.00 5.00
127 Mark Recchi BX/1400* 1.00 2.50
128 Patrick Roy GY/250* 20.00 50.00
129 Kevin Hatcher BX/1400* .75 2.00
130 Adam Oates SY/700* 3.00 8.00
131 Doug Weight SX/500* 2.50 6.00
132 Vaclav Prospal SX/500* 2.00 5.00
133 Harry York SY/700* 2.00 5.00
134 Todd Bertuzzi BX/1400* .75 2.00
135 Sergei Fedorov GY/250* 12.00 30.00
136 Theo Fleury SX/500* 3.00 8.00
137 Chad Kilger BY/1600* .75 2.00
138 Jamie Storr SX/500* 2.00 5.00
139 Tony Amonte BY/1600* .75 2.00
140 Rem Murray BY/1600* .75 2.00
141 Chris O'Sullivan BX/1400* .75 2.00
142 Mats Sundin SZ/800* 3.00 8.00
143 Ethan Moreau SZ/800* 2.00 5.00
144 Derian Hatcher SY/700* 2.50 6.00
145 Daniel Alfredsson SY/700* 2.50 6.00
146 Corey Hirsch BX/1400* .75 2.00
147 Landon Wilson BX/1400* .75 2.00
148 Marc Denis GLR GY/250* 3.00 8.00
149 Boyd Devereaux GLR BZ/1700* .75 2.00
150 Joe Thornton GLR GX/50* 25.00 50.00
151 Sergei Samsonov GLR GZ/350* 6.00 15.00
152 Alyn McCauley GLR SZ/800* 2.00 5.00
153 Erik Rasmussen GLR SZ/800* 2.00 5.00
154 Patrick Marleau GLR SX/500* 2.50 6.00
155 Olli Jokinen GLR BX/1400* 2.50 6.00
156 Chris Phillips GLR GY/250* 3.00 8.00
157 Tomas Vokoun GLR BX/1400* 1.00 2.50
158 Chris Dingman GLR SZ/800* 2.00 5.00
159 Daniel Cleary GLR GY/250* 3.00 8.00
160 Juha Lind GLR BX/1400* .75 2.00
161 Jean-Yves Leroux GLR BY/1600* .75 2.00
162 Brad Isbister GLR SY/700* 2.00 5.00
163 Vadim Sharifijanov GLR BX/1400* .75 2.00
164 Alexei Morozov GLR SX/500* 2.00 5.00
165 Vaclav Prospal GLR BX/1400* .75 2.00
166 Vaclav Varada GLR BY/1600* .75 2.00
167 Jaro. Svejkovsky GLR BZ/1700* .75 2.00
168 Eric Lindros GM SY/700* 4.00 10.00
169 Dominik Hasek GM BY/1600* 2.50 6.00
170 Peter Forsberg GM BY/1600* 3.00 8.00
171 Steve Yzerman GM SY/700* 10.00 25.00
172 J.Vanbiesbrouck GM BX/1400* 1.50 4.00
173 Paul Kariya GM SY/700* 5.00 12.00
174 Martin Brodeur GM BZ/1700* 3.00 8.00
175 Wayne Gretzky GM SY/700* 15.00 40.00
176 Mark Messier GM BX/1400* 1.25 3.00
177 Jaromir Jagr GM BZ/1700* 2.00 5.00
178 Brett Hull GM BX/1400* 2.00 5.00
179 Brendan Shanahan GM BY/1600* 1.25 3.00
180 Jarome Iginla GM BX/1400* 1.50 4.00
181 Mike Modano GM BY/1600* 2.00 5.00
182 Teemu Selanne GM BY/1600* 1.25 3.00
183 Bryan Berard GM BY/1600* .75 2.00
184 Ryan Smyth GM SY/700* 2.50 6.00
185 Keith Tkachuk GM BX/1400* 1.25 3.00
186 Dainius Zubrus GM BX/1400* .75 2.00
187 Patrick Roy GM BX/1400* 6.00 15.00
188 Trevor Linden BX/1400* 1.00 2.50
189 Trevor Linden BX/1400* 1.00 2.50
190 Trevor Linden BX/1400* 1.00 2.50
191 Trevor Linden BX/1400* 1.00 2.50
192 Trevor Linden BX/1400* 1.00 2.50
193 Trevor Linden BX/1400* 1.00 2.50
194 Trevor Linden BX/1400* 1.00 2.50
195 Trevor Linden BX/1400* 1.00 2.50
196 Trevor Linden BX/1400* 1.00 2.50
197 Trevor Linden BX/1400* 1.00 2.50
198 Chris Phillips BX CL/1400* .75 2.00
199 Sergei Samsonov BX CL/1400* 1.00 2.50
200 Daniel Cleary BX CL/1400* .75 2.00

1997-98 Leaf Fractal Matrix Die Cuts

Randomly inserted in packs, this 200-card set was a parallel to the base set and featured three different die-cut versions in three different finishes. Only 100 cards of the set were produced in the X-Axis cut with 75 of those bronze, 20 silver, and five gold. Only 60 were produced in the Y-Axis cut with 20 of those bronze, 30 silver and 10 gold. Only 40 were produced in the Z-Axis cut with five bronze, 10 silver, and 25 gold. X-Axis cards had a stated print run of 400 sets. Y-Axis cards had a stated print run of 200 sets. Z-Axis cards had a stated print run of 100 sets. No card was available in more than one color nor in more than one die-cut version.
BX/400: 1X TO 2.5X BX/1400*
BY/200: 2X TO 5X BY/1600*
BZ/100: 3X TO 8X BZ/1700*
SX/400: .4X TO 1X SX/500*
SY/200: 1X TO 2.5X SY/700*
SZ/100: 1.2X TO 3X SZ/800*
GX/400: .15X TO .4X GX/50*
GY/200: .4X TO 1X GY/250*
GZ/100: .6X TO 1.5X GZ/350*

1997-98 Leaf Banner Season

ndomly inserted in packs, this 24-card set featured color player photos of top players printed on die-cut banner-shaped canvas card stock. Each card was individually numbered to 3,500.
COMPLETE SET (24) 30.00 80.00
1 Paul Kariya 1.50 4.00
2 Eric Lindros 1.50 4.00
3 Wayne Gretzky 10.00 25.00
4 Jaromir Jagr 2.50 6.00
5 Steve Yzerman 8.00 20.00
6 Brendan Shanahan 1.50 4.00
7 John LeClair 1.50 4.00
8 Teemu Selanne 1.50 4.00
9 Mike Modano 2.50 6.00
10 Ryan Smyth 1.25 3.00
11 Brett Hull 2.00 5.00
12 Zigmund Palffy 1.25 3.00
13 Peter Forsberg 4.00 10.00
14 Keith Tkachuk 1.50 4.00
15 Saku Koivu 1.50 4.00
16 Sergei Fedorov 2.50 6.00
17 Brian Leetch 1.50 4.00
18 Bryan Berard .50 1.25
19 Mats Sundin 1.50 4.00
20 Jarome Iginla 2.00 5.00
21 Sergei Berezin .50 1.25
22 Dainius Zubrus 1.50 4.00
23 Mike Grier .50 1.25
24 Joe Sakic 3.00 8.00

1997-98 Leaf Fire On Ice

ndomly inserted in packs, this 16-card set featured color photos of top players on a background of fire and ice printed using dot matrix hologram technology. Each card was individually numbered to 1,000.
COMPLETE SET (16) 75.00 150.00
1 Wayne Gretzky 12.00 30.00
2 Eric Lindros 4.00 10.00
3 Jaromir Jagr 4.00 10.00
4 Steve Yzerman 8.00 25.00
5 Brendan Shanahan 2.50 20.00
6 Mike Modano 5.00 12.00
7 Joe Sakic 6.00 15.00
8 Pavel Bure 3.00 8.00
9 Ryan Smyth 2.00 5.00
10 Teemu Selanne 2.50 6.00
11 Mark Messier 2.50 6.00
12 Peter Forsberg 6.00 15.00
13 Dainius Zubrus 2.50 6.00
14 Joe Thornton 12.00 30.00
15 Sergei Samsonov 12.00 30.00
16 Paul Kariya 2.50 6.00

1997-98 Leaf Lindros Collection

Randomly inserted in packs, this five-card set featured color photos of Eric Lindros with actual pieces of game used equipment inserted into the cards. Pieces of his game-used jerseys, sticks, stirrups, and gloves were used. Each card was individually numbered to 100.
1 E.Lindros Home Jersey 30.00 60.00
2 E.Lindros Away Jersey 30.00 60.00
3 E.Lindros Stick 25.00 60.00
4 E.Lindros Glove 25.00 60.00
5 E.Lindros Stirrups 25.00 60.00

1997-98 Leaf Pipe Dreams

ndomly inserted in packs, this 16-card set featured color photos of top goalies printed on silver foil board and micro-etched. Each card was individually numbered to 2,500.
COMPLETE SET (16) 50.00 100.00
*PROMOS: .3X TO .8X BASIC INSERTS
1 Dominik Hasek 8.00 20.00
2 John Vanbiesbrouck 3.00 8.00
3 Patrick Roy 12.00 30.00
4 Curtis Joseph 3.00 8.00
5 Felix Potvin 4.00 10.00
6 Martin Brodeur 10.00 25.00
7 Guy Hebert 1.50 4.00
8 Mike Richter 3.00 8.00
9 Jose Theodore 5.00 12.00
10 Jim Carey 1.50 4.00
11 Damian Rhodes 1.50 4.00
12 Jocelyn Thibault 1.50 4.00
13 Nikolai Khabibulin 3.00 8.00
14 Chris Osgood 3.00 8.00
15 Eric Fichaud 1.50 4.00
16 Mike Dunham 1.50 4.00

2014-15 Leaf Acetate Toronto Spring Expo

COMPLETE SET (4) 4.00 10.00
CMD Connor McDavid 2.50 6.00
DS1 Dylan Strome 1.00 2.50
MB1 Mathew Barzal .75 2.00
MM1 Mitchell Marner .60 1.50

2015-16 Leaf L'Anti Expo

COMPLETE SET (1) 3.00 8.00
LAEJE1 Jack Eichel 3.00 8.00

2011 Leaf Legends of Sport

STATED PRINT RUN 6-50
NO PRICING ON CARDS #'d TO 12 OR LESS
BA8 Bernie Parent/18 12.00 30.00
BA65 Phil Esposito/40 10.00 25.00
BA83 Tony Esposito/40 10.00 25.00

2011 Leaf Legends of Sport Award Winners Autographs Bronze

STATED PRINT RUN 10-50
AW2 Bernie Parent/18 12.00 30.00

2011 Leaf Legends of Sport Moments of Greatness Autographs Bronze

STATED PRINT RUN 10-50
MG35 Tony Esposito/40 10.00 25.00
MG36 Phil Esposito/40 10.00 25.00

2011 Leaf Legends of Sport Perennial All-Stars Autographs

STATED PRINT RUN 5-24
NO PRICING ON CARDS #'d TO 13 OR LESS
PE3 Bernie Parent/5

2012 Leaf Legends of Sport

BABH1 Bobby Hull 12.00 30.00
BAGH1 Gordie Howe 50.00 100.00
UM 1980 US Hockey EXCH 300.00 600.00

2012 Leaf Legends of Sport Unsigned Bronze

ANNOUNCED PRINT RUN 70
ONLINE EXCLUSIVE

2012 Leaf Legends of Sport AKA Autographs

AKAGH1 Gordie Howe 50.00 100.00

2012 Leaf Legends of Sport Numerations Autographs

PRINT RUN 5-45
NAGH1 Gordie Howe/9

1995-96 Leaf Limited

This 120-card super-premium set was released in five-card packs with a suggested retail price of $4.99 per pack. The product was produced to order; hence 25,722 individually numbered boxes were produced, much less than the initially announced figure of 60,000. This reduction wreaked havoc with insertion ratios on the chase cards, which initially hampered interest in the product. It has since recovered nicely. Rookie Cards in this set included Daniel Alfredsson, Todd Bertuzzi, Radek Dvorak, Daymond Langkow and Marcus Ragnarsson.
1 Mario Lemieux .60 1.50
2 Peter Forsberg .50 1.25
3 Geoff Courtnall .12 .30
4 Vincent Damphousse .15 .40
5 Jason Allison .15 .40
6 Theo Fleury .25 .60
7 Shane Doan RC .60 1.50
8 Chris Gratton .12 .30
9 Paul Kariya .25 .60
10 Radek Dvorak RC .25 .60
11 Adam Graves .15 .40
12 Donald Audette .15 .40
13 Craig Janney .12 .30
14 Sean Burke .12 .30
15 Ed Belfour .15 .40
16 Ray Bourque .30 .75
17 Pavel Bure .25 .60
18 Martin Brodeur .50 1.25
19 Todd Bertuzzi RC .25 .60
20 Aki Berg RC .20 .50
21 Dave Andreychuk .20 .50
22 Jason Arnott .15 .40
23 Ron Francis .25 .60
24 Paul Coffey .20 .50
25 Daniel Alfredsson RC 1.00 2.50
26 Todd Harvey .12 .30
27 Claude Lemieux .20 .50
28 Brett Hull .25 .60
29 Felix Potvin .20 .50
30 Peter Bondra .20 .50
31 Trevor Kidd .15 .40
32 Igor Korolev .12 .30
33 Roman Hamrlik .12 .30
34 Chad Kilger RC .20 .50
35 Rob Niedermayer .15 .40
36 Richard Park .20 .50
37 Mathieu Dandenault .40 1.00
38 Alexandre Daigle .12 .30
39 Jere Lehtinen .15 .40

40 Chris Chelios .20 .50
41 Blaine Lacher .15 .40
42 Trevor Linden .20 .50
43 Scott Niedermayer .20 .50
44 Teemu Selanne .40 1.00
45 Daymond Langkow RC .20 .50
46 Oleg Tverdovsky .20 .50
47 John Vanbiesbrouck .15 .40
48 Alexei Kovalev .12 .30
49 Sergei Fedorov .30 .75
50 Alexei Yashin .15 .40
51 Mike Modano .30 .75
52 Sandis Ozolinsh .15 .40
53 Ian Laperriere .12 .30
54 Mark Recchi .25 .60
55 Jim Carey .15 .40
56 Joe Nieuwendyk .20 .50
57 Keith Tkachuk .20 .50
58 Daren Puppa .15 .40
59 Jason Bonsignore .12 .30
60 Tomas Sandstrom .15 .40
61 Chris Osgood .15 .40
62 Jeff Friesen .12 .30
63 Jeff O'Neill .20 .50
64 Joe Sakic .30 .75
65 Eric Daze .40 1.00
66 Patrick Roy .50 1.25
67 Kirk McLean .15 .40
68 Stephane Richer .15 .40
69 Rod Brind'Amour .20 .50
70 Wendel Clark .20 .50
71 Rob Blake .15 .40
72 Doug Gilmour .25 .60
73 Jaromir Jagr .50 1.25
74 Sergei Zubov .15 .40
75 Mark Messier .30 .75
76 Dominik Hasek .25 .60
77 Viktor Kozlov .15 .40
78 Marcus Ragnarsson RC .25 .60
79 Jocelyn Thibault .15 .40
80 Jeremy Roenick .25 .60
81 Cam Neely .20 .50
82 Brian Savage .12 .30
83 Alexander Mogilny .15 .40
84 Steve Thomas .15 .40
85 John LeClair .20 .50
86 Brett Lindros .12 .30
87 Wayne Gretzky 1.00 2.50
88 Kenny Jonsson .20 .50
89 David Oliver .12 .30
90 Brian Leetch .20 .50
91 Luc Robitaille .20 .50
92 Keith Primeau .12 .30
93 Owen Nolan .20 .50
94 Brendan Shanahan .25 .60
95 Al MacInnis .20 .50
96 Kevin Stevens .15 .40
97 Larry Murphy .20 .50
98 Joe Juneau .15 .40
99 Eric Lindros .30 .75
100 Travis Green .15 .40
101 Jamie Storr .15 .40
102 Pierre Turgeon .20 .50
103 Bill Ranford .15 .40
104 Niklas Sundstrom .20 .50
105 Steve Yzerman .25 .60
106 Ray Sheppard .15 .40
107 Chris Pronger .20 .50
108 Adam Oates .20 .50
109 Mike Gartner .20 .50
110 Doug Weight .20 .50
111 Jason Dawe .12 .30
112 Rick Tocchet .15 .40
113 Pat LaFontaine .20 .50
114 Scott Mellanby .15 .40
115 Vitali Yachmenev .20 .50
116 Alexei Zhamnov .20 .50
117 Brendan Witt .20 .50
118 Saku Koivu .20 .50
119 Mikael Renberg .15 .40
120 Mats Sundin .20 .50

1995-96 Leaf Limited Rookie Phenoms

This ten-card set saluted some of the league's top first year players. Each card was printed on gold patterned holographic foil and was individually numbered out of 5,000. The odds were announced at 1:24, but the reduction in production altered those somewhat; the actual odds were closer to 1:12.

COMPLETE SET (10) 5.00 12.00
1 Marcus Ragnarsson .20 .50
2 Daniel Alfredsson 2.00 5.00
3 Chad Kilger .20 .50
4 Niklas Sundstrom .20 .50
5 Vitali Yachmenev .20 .50
6 Eric Daze .40 1.00
7 Radek Dvorak .20 .50
8 Jeff O'Neill .20 .50
9 Saku Koivu 2.00 5.00
10 Todd Bertuzzi 1.00 2.50

1995-96 Leaf Limited Stars of the Game

This twelve-card set celebrated some of the biggest stars playing the game. Every card featured a photo on micro-etched silver holographic foil. Each card was sequentially numbered of 5,000. The announced odds were 1:20 packs, but the reduced production totals made the real odds closer to 1:10.

COMPLETE SET (12) 20.00 40.00
1 Mario Lemieux 5.00 12.00
2 Eric Lindros .60 1.50
3 Wayne Gretzky 6.00 15.00
4 Peter Forsberg 2.50 6.00
5 Paul Kariya .60 1.50
6 Alexander Mogilny .30 .75
7 Teemu Selanne .60 1.50
8 Jaromir Jagr 1.50 4.00
9 Mats Sundin .60 1.50
10 Brett Hull 1.25 3.00
11 Sergei Fedorov 1.25 3.00
12 Jeremy Roenick .75 2.00

1995-96 Leaf Limited Stick Side

is eight-card set was printed on an unusual wood veneer stock and featured some of the NHL's top goalies. Each card was sequentially numbered out of 2,500. The announced odds were 1:60, but the reduced production run meant the actual odds were closer to 1:30.

COMPLETE SET (8) 30.00 60.00
1 Jim Carey 5.00 12.00
2 Martin Brodeur 6.00 15.00
3 Felix Potvin 4.00 10.00
4 Patrick Roy 8.00 20.00
5 Dominik Hasek 3.00 8.00
6 John Vanbiesbrouck 6.00 15.00
7 Ron Hextall 5.00 12.00
8 Ed Belfour 2.00 5.00

1996-97 Leaf Limited

Leaf Limited was a 90-card set featuring the best players in the NHL. The product was hobby-only, with production limited to 27,000 boxes. The cards featured a silver foil effect. Each sealed box also contained an Eric Lindros card measuring 3 3/4" by 3 3/4". This card featured Lindros on the front, along with a serial number out of 27,000, while the reverse held a series checklist.

COMPLETE SET (90) 15.00 40.00
1 Chris Chelios .30 .75
2 Brendan Shanahan .40 1.00
3 Keith Tkachuk .30 .75
4 Roman Hamrlik .25 .60
5 Adam Oates .30 .75
6 Chris Osgood .30 .75
7 Wayne Gretzky 2.50 6.00
8 Alexander Mogilny .25 .60
9 Patrick Roy 2.00 5.00
10 Saku Koivu .30 .75
11 Jaromir Jagr .75 2.00
12 Wendel Clark .25 .60
13 Mike Modano .50 1.25
14 Ed Jovanovski .25 .60
15 John LeClair .30 .75
16 Jim Carey .30 .75
17 Paul Kariya .40 1.00
18 Paul Coffey .30 .75
19 Todd Bertuzzi .30 .75
20 Owen Nolan .30 .75
21 Dominik Hasek .50 1.25
22 Bill Ranford .25 .60
23 Scott Stevens .30 .75
24 Brett Hull 1.50 4.00
25 Trevor Kidd .20 .50
26 Slava Fetisov .20 .50
27 Luc Robitaille .30 .75
28 Mats Sundin .30 .75
29 Peter Forsberg .50 1.25
30 John Vanbiesbrouck .30 .75
31 Alexei Yashin .25 .60
32 Pavel Bure .40 1.00
33 Pat Verbeek .20 .50
34 Vitali Yachmenev .20 .50
35 Ron Hextall .25 .60
36 Michal Pivonka .20 .50
37 Eric Daze .25 .60
38 Pierre Turgeon .30 .75
39 Petr Nedved .25 .60
40 Steve Yzerman .75 2.00
41 Mike Richter .30 .75
42 Marcus Ragnarsson .20 .50
43 Jason Arnott .25 .60
44 Jocelyn Thibault .30 .75
45 Alexander Selivanov .20 .50
46 Claude Lemieux .20 .50
47 Eric Lindros .50 1.25
48 Grant Fuhr .30 .75
49 Ray Bourque .50 1.25
50 Scott Mellanby .25 .60
51 Craig Janney .25 .60
52 Ron Francis .40 1.00
53 Ed Belfour .30 .75
54 Petr Sykora .20 .50
55 Damian Rhodes .25 .60
56 Joe Sakic .50 1.25
57 Zigmund Palffy .30 .75
58 Daren Puppa .25 .60
59 Pat LaFontaine .30 .75
60 Nikolai Khabibulin .25 .60
61 Sergei Fedorov .50 1.25
62 Valeri Bure .20 .50
63 Peter Bondra .25 .60
64 Teemu Selanne .60 1.50
65 Mark Messier .50 1.25
66 Shayne Corson .20 .50
67 Theo Fleury .60 1.50
68 Jeff O'Neill .20 .50
69 Eric Fichaud .25 .60
70 Doug Gilmour .40 1.00
71 Doug Weight .30 .75
72 Stephane Fiset .25 .60
73 Daniel Alfredsson .30 .75
74 Trevor Linden .25 .60
75 Joe Nieuwendyk .30 .75
76 Brian Bradley .20 .50
77 Jere Lehtinen .20 .50
78 Rob Niedermayer .25 .60
79 Mikael Renberg .25 .60
80 Felix Potvin .30 .75
81 Valeri Kamensky .25 .60
82 Brian Leetch .30 .75
83 Jeff Friesen .20 .50
84 Vincent Damphousse .25 .60
85 Mario Lemieux 1.00 2.50
86 Jeremy Roenick .50 1.25
87 Martin Brodeur .60 1.50
88 Vyacheslav Kozlov .20 .50
89 Corey Hirsch .25 .60
90 Curtis Joseph .30 .75
NNO Eric Lindros CL Jumbo .50 1.25

1996-97 Leaf Limited Gold

A 90-card parallel of the regular Leaf Limited set, this gold version was randomly inserted in packs at an indeterminate rate. Only the values for the most heavily traded cards are listed below. Values for the remaining cards may be determined by using the multipliers below on the values of the regular counterparts.

*SINGLES: 2.5X TO 6X BASIC CARDS

1996-97 Leaf Limited Bash The Boards Promos

This 10-card set was intended to promote the Leaf Limited Bash the Boards insert set. Unlike the regular set which is serial numbered to 3500, these cards were numbered as Promo/2500. Doug Gilmour was the most readily found of these cards.

COMPLETE SET (10) 40.00 100.00
*PROMOS: .6X TO 1.5X BASIC INSERTS 4.00 10.00

1996-97 Leaf Limited Bash The Boards

quentially numbered to 3500, this insert featured ten players on a rigid plastic stock simulating Plexiglas. Cards were randomly inserted in packs. A limited parallel was also created. These cards were alike the base cards in everyway except that they were serial numbered out of 350.

COMPLETE SET (10) 25.00 60.00
STATED PRINT RUN 3500 SER.#'d SETS
*LIMITED EDIT: 1.5X TO 4X BASIC INSERTS
1 Eric Lindros 4.00 10.00
2 Mark Messier 4.00 10.00
3 Owen Nolan 2.00 5.00
4 Doug Gilmour 4.00 10.00
5 Keith Tkachuk 4.00 10.00
6 Claude Lemieux 2.00 5.00
7 Ed Jovanovski 2.00 5.00
8 Peter Forsberg 6.00 15.00
9 Brendan Shanahan 4.00 10.00
10 Eric Daze 2.00 5.00

1996-97 Leaf Limited Rookies

ten-card random insert, this set consisted of top rookie prospects. Fronts featured a team logo with rays of holographic foil shooting from behind a player photo, while the backs added another photo and a brief player biography. A gold parallel version of this set was known to exist, though quantity produced and distribution source was not entirely clear. Gold parallels are not priced due to scarcity.

COMPLETE SET (10) 25.00 50.00
1 Ethan Moreau .75 2.00
2 Jarome Iginla 4.00 10.00
3 Bryan Berard .75 2.00
4 Hnat Domenichelli .75 2.00
5 Wade Redden 1.25 3.00
6 Dainius Zubrus 1.25 3.00
7 Sergei Berezin .75 2.00
8 Jamie Langenbrunner 1.25 3.00
9 Tomas Holmstrom 2.00 5.00
10 Jonas Hoglund .75 2.00

1996-97 Leaf Limited Stubble

Based upon the old NHL superstition of not shaving while winning during the playoffs, Stubble was a randomly-inserted set highlighted by a felt-like treatment in the beard area. The 20 cards in the set were sequentially numbered to 1500. A promo version of the set was also produced. Those cards resembled the base set in everyway except that they were numbered Promo/1500.

COMPLETE SET (20) 75.00 150.00
1 Patrick Roy 10.00 25.00
2 Eric Lindros 6.00 15.00
3 Wayne Gretzky 12.50 30.00
4 Paul Coffey 1.50 4.00
5 Jim Carey 1.50 4.00
6 Ed Belfour 3.00 8.00
7 Mario Lemieux 10.00 25.00
8 Mike Modano 3.00 8.00
9 Todd Bertuzzi 1.50 4.00
10 Pavel Bure 3.00 8.00
11 Martin Brodeur 6.00 15.00
12 Petr Nedved 1.50 4.00
13 Alexander Mogilny 1.50 4.00
14 Steve Yzerman 10.00 25.00
15 Brett Hull 3.00 8.00
16 Joe Sakic 4.00 10.00
17 Scott Mellanby 1.50 4.00
18 Trevor Linden 2.00 5.00
19 Rob Niedermayer 1.50 4.00
20 Wendel Clark 3.00 8.00

2012 Leaf National Convention

BH1 Bobby Hull .50 1.25
BP1 Bernie Parent .40 1.00
PE1 Phil Esposito .50 1.25
TE1 Tony Esposito .30 .75

2014 Leaf National Convention

COMPLETE SET (10) 4.00 10.00
1 Mario Lemieux HK .40 1.00

2015 Leaf National Convention '90 Leaf Acetate

CMD Connor McDavid 2.50 6.00
ML1 Mario Lemieux 1.00 2.50
NP1 Nolan Patrick 1.25 3.00

2015 Leaf National Convention VIP

COMPLETE SET (11)
1 Connor McDavid
2 Mitchell Marner
3 Dylan Strome

2014 Leaf Peck and Snyder Promos

COMPLETE SET (45) 15.00 30.00
1 Aaron Ekblad HK 1.50 4.00
6 Bobby Hull HK .75 2.00
16Â•Gordie Howe HK 1.25 3.00
27 Leon Draisaitl HK 1.25 3.00
29 Mario Lemieux HK 1.25 3.00
31Â•Mike Modano HK .60 1.50
33Â•Patrick Roy HK 1.25 3.00
36Â•Sam Bennett HK .75 2.00
37Â•Sam Reinhart HK .60 1.50
40Â•Steve Yzerman HK 1.00 2.50

1996-97 Leaf Preferred

The 1996-97 Leaf Preferred set was issued in one series totaling 150 cards. Suggested retail on packs was $3.49, which included five standard cards and one metal card. Card fronts featured color action photos, a small team logo, and the player's name in team colors. One edge was also enhanced with etched silver foil with the Leaf Preferred logo. Key RCs included Dainiuis Zubrus and Sergei Berezin.

COMPLETE SET (150) 12.00 30.00
1 Patrick Roy .75 2.00
2 Alexander Mogilny .25 .60
3 Bill Ranford .25 .60
4 Jeremy Roenick .50 1.25
5 Travis Green .25 .60
6 Owen Nolan .30 .75
7 Paul Kariya .40 1.00
8 Pat Verbeek .20 .50
9 Jeff O'Neill .20 .50
10 Nikolai Khabibulin .25 .60
11 Pat LaFontaine .30 .75
12 Rob Niedermayer .25 .60
13 Luc Robitaille .30 .75
14 Mats Sundin .30 .75
15 Cory Stillman .20 .50
16 Ray Ferraro .20 .50
17 Alexei Yashin .25 .60
18 Brian Bradley .20 .50
19 Chris Chelios .30 .75
20 Jason Arnott .25 .60
21 Petr Sykora .20 .50
22 Jaromir Jagr .75 2.00
23 Jim Carey .30 .75
24 Claude Lemieux .20 .50
25 Vincent Damphousse .25 .60
26 Shayne Corson .20 .50
27 Joe Nieuwendyk .30 .75
28 Kenny Jonsson .20 .50
29 Peter Bondra .25 .60
30 Ed Belfour .30 .75
31 Brendan Shanahan .40 1.00
32 Eric Desjardins .25 .60
33 Corey Hirsch .25 .60
34 Slava Fetisov .20 .50
35 Craig Janney .25 .60
36 Felix Potvin .30 .75
37 Joe Sakic .50 1.25
38 Scott Stevens .30 .75
39 Kelly Hrudey .25 .60
40 Adam Oates .30 .75
41 John Vanbiesbrouck .30 .75
42 Brian Leetch .30 .75
43 Alexander Selivanov .20 .50
44 Mike Modano .50 1.25
45 Saku Koivu .30 .75
46 Tom Barrasso .25 .60
47 Jere Lehtinen .20 .50
48 Daniel Alfredsson .30 .75
49 Joe Juneau .20 .50
50 Chris Osgood .30 .75
51 Dave Andreychuk .30 .75
52 Marcus Ragnarsson .20 .50
53 Valeri Kamensky .25 .60
54 Doug Weight .30 .75
55 Mike Richter .30 .75
56 Teemu Selanne .60 1.50
57 Stephane Fiset .25 .60
58 Mikael Renberg .25 .60
59 Trevor Linden .25 .60
60 Bernie Nicholls .20 .50
61 Eric Daze .25 .60
62 Ron Francis .40 1.00
63 Sergei Zubov .20 .50
64 Rod Brind'Amour .30 .75
65 Sergei Fedorov .50 1.25
66 Mark Messier .50 1.25
67 Theo Fleury .60 1.50
68 Ed Jovanovski .25 .60
69 Daren Puppa .25 .60
70 Pierre Turgeon .30 .75
71 Oleg Tverdovsky .25 .60
72 Ryan Smyth .25 .60
73 Jocelyn Thibault .30 .75
74 Brendan Witt .20 .50
75 Igor Larionov .30 .75
76 Stephane Richer .25 .60
77 Ron Hextall .25 .60
78 Mike Ricci .20 .50
79 Dimitri Khristich .20 .50
80 Derian Hatcher .20 .50
81 Martin Brodeur .60 1.50
82 Petr Nedved .25 .60
83 Ray Bourque .50 1.25
84 Keith Primeau .20 .50
85 Sean Burke .20 .50
86 Geoff Sanderson .25 .60
87 Wendel Clark .25 .60
88 Valeri Bure .20 .50
89 Keith Tkachuk .30 .75
90 Roman Hamrlik .25 .60
91 Dominik Hasek .50 1.25
92 Ray Sheppard .25 .60
93 Todd Bertuzzi .30 .75
94 Pavel Bure .40 1.00
95 Alexei Zhamnov .25 .60
96 Alexei Kovalev .20 .50
97 Jeff Friesen .20 .50
98 Scott Young .20 .50
99 Vitali Yachmenev .20 .50
100 Michal Pivonka .20 .50
101 Paul Coffey .30 .75
102 Steve Yzerman .75 2.00
103 Zigmund Palffy .30 .75
104 Doug Gilmour .40 1.00
105 John LeClair .30 .75
106 Brett Hull 1.50 4.00
107 Yanic Perreault .20 .50
108 Bill Guerin .30 .75
109 Damian Rhodes .25 .60
110 Peter Forsberg .50 1.25
111 Scott Mellanby .25 .60
112 Wayne Gretzky 1.50 4.00
113 Mario Lemieux 1.00 2.50
114 Todd Harvey .20 .50
115 Mark Recchi .40 1.00
116 Trevor Kidd .20 .50
117 Eric Lindros .50 1.25
118 Jarome Iginla .40 1.00
119 Eric Fichaud .25 .60
120 Mattias Timander RC .30 .75
121 Hnat Domenichelli .20 .50
122 Chris O'Sullivan .20 .50
123 Sergei Berezin RC .50 1.25
124 Jonas Hoglund .20 .50
125 Anders Eriksson .20 .50
126 Corey Schwab .25 .60
127 Janne Niinimaa .30 .75
128 Dainius Zubrus RC .40 1.00
129 Bryan Berard .30 .75
130 Wade Redden .20 .50
131 Wayne Primeau .20 .50
132 Brandon Convery .20 .50
133 Richard Zednik RC .40 1.00
134 Darcy Tucker .20 .50
135 Christian Dube .20 .50
136 Rem Murray RC .30 .75
137 Kevin Hodson RC .30 .75
138 Steve Washburn RC .30 .75
139 Ethan Moreau RC .30 .75
140 Daymond Langkow .25 .60
141 Terry Ryan RC .30 .75
142 Curtis Brown .20 .50
143 Steve Sullivan RC .25 .60
144 Jamie Langenbrunner .20 .50
145 Daniel Goneau RC .30 .75
146 Anson Carter .25 .60
147 Jim Campbell .20 .50
148 Keith Tkachuk CL (1-76) .30 .75
149 Eric Daze CL (77-150) .25 .60
150 Mike Modano CL (inserts) .50 1.25

1996-97 Leaf Preferred Press Proofs

Paralleling the standard 150-card Leaf Preferred set, the randomly inserted Press Proofs were limited to a production run of 250. A gold strip on the left-hand side of the card distinguished this version from its regular counterpart.

*VETS: 15X TO 40X BASIC CARDS
*ROOKIES: 6X TO 15X

1996-97 Leaf Preferred Steel

Inserted one per pack, this 63-card set was the first standard-sized, all-metal hockey set. Cards are silver-colored and come with a protective covering. A gold parallel version also existed; values for these.cards can be determined by using the multipliers below. Furthermore, an Eric Lindros promo card was created. It was easy to differentiate from the regular version as it is numbered 77 of 77, and included the word SAMPLE on the back.

*GOLDS: 2X TO 5X SILVER
1 Sergei Fedorov 1.50 4.00
2 Martin Brodeur 2.50 6.00
3 Corey Hirsch .60 1.50
4 Ray Bourque 1.50 4.00
5 Saku Koivu 1.00 2.50
6 Ron Francis .60 1.50
7 Chris Chelios 1.00 2.50
8 Scott Mellanby .60 1.50
9 Ron Hextall .60 1.50
10 Doug Gilmour .60 1.50
11 Joe Sakic 2.00 5.00
12 Petr Sykora .40 1.00
13 Marcus Ragnarsson .40 1.00
14 Pat Verbeek .40 1.00
15 Stephane Fiset .60 1.50
16 Alexel Yashln .40 1.00
17 Daren Puppa .60 1.50
18 Eric Lindros 1.00 2.50
19 Jason Arnott .40 1.00
20 Todd Bertuzzi 1.00 2.50
21 Jim Carey 1.00 2.50
22 Pat LaFontaine 1.00 2.50
23 Brian Leetch 1.00 2.50
24 Trevor Linden .60 1.50
25 Eric Daze .60 1.50
26 Pierre Turgeon .60 1.50
27 Tom Barrasso .60 1.50
28 Mike Modano 1.50 4.00
29 Brendan Shanahan 1.00 2.50
30 Nikolai Khabibulin .60 1.50
31 Claude Lemieux .40 1.00
32 Zigmund Palffy .60 1.50
33 Mats Sundin 1.00 2.50
34 Paul Kariya 1.00 2.50
35 Daniel Alfredsson .60 1.50
36 Patrick Roy 5.00 12.00
37 Jaromir Jagr 1.50 4.00
38 Vyacheslav Kozlov .40 1.00
39 John LeClair 1.00 2.50
40 Bill Ranford .60 1.50
41 Vitali Yachmenev .40 1.00
42 Mark Messier 1.00 2.50
43 Valeri Bure .40 1.00
44 Roman Hamrlik .60 1.50
45 Joe Nieuwendyk .40 1.00
46 Mike Richter 1.00 2.50
47 Theo Fleury .40 1.00
48 Wendel Clark .60 1.50
49 Doug Weight .60 1.50
50 Damian Rhodes .60 1.50
51 Alexander Mogilny .60 1.50
52 Dominik Hasek 2.00 5.00
53 Eric Fichaud .60 1.50
54 Adam Oates .60 1.50
55 Jocelyn Thibault 1.00 2.50
56 Petr Nedved .40 1.00
57 Mike Vernon .60 1.50
58 Mikael Renberg .60 1.50
59 Valeri Kamensky .40 1.00
60 Peter Forsberg 2.50 6.00
61 Rob Niedermayer .40 1.00
62 Owen Nolan .60 1.50
63 Jere Lehtinen .40 1.00
77 Eric Lindros promo .40 1.00

1996-97 Leaf Preferred Masked Marauders

aturing twelve of the game's top goaltenders, the Masked Marauders were randomly inserted in Leaf Preferred packs and were sequentially numbered to 2500.

COMPLETE SET (12) 30.00 80.00
1 Jim Carey 2.00 5.00
2 Martin Brodeur 6.00 15.00
3 John Vanbiesbrouck 3.00 8.00
4 Patrick Roy 10.00 25.00
5 Felix Potvin 4.00 10.00
6 Chris Osgood 3.00 8.00
7 Dominik Hasek 5.00 12.00
8 Jocelyn Thibault 2.00 5.00
9 Nikolai Khabibulin 3.00 8.00
10 Curtis Joseph 3.00 8.00
11 Mike Richter 3.00 8.00
12 Ed Belfour 4.00 10.00

1996-97 Leaf Preferred Steel Power

With a stated print run of 2500 serial-numbered sets, the Steel Power set consisted of a dozen of the top offensive players. Card fronts featured a color action photo with silver foil at the bottom, and two lightning bolt die-cuts.

COMPLETE SET (12) 15.00 40.00
1 Joe Sakic 3.00 8.00
2 Mario Lemieux 5.00 12.00
3 Pavel Bure 2.00 5.00
4 Mark Messier 1.50 3.00
5 Wayne Gretzky 6.00 15.00
6 Peter Forsberg 2.50 6.00
7 Sergei Fedorov 2.50 6.00
8 Jaromir Jagr 3.00 8.00
9 Brett Hull 2.00 5.00
10 Teemu Selanne 1.50 3.00
11 Paul Kariya 1.50 3.00
12 Eric Lindros 2.50 6.00

1996-97 Leaf Preferred Vanity Plates

Patterned after the theme of vanity license plates, these 14 cards sported the player's nickname, team, and facsimile signature along with a photo on the front. Card backs included a brief player biography and photo. A protective coating covered the silver-colored metal cards, which were inserted randomly into packs. A tougher gold parallel version also was available.

COMPLETE SET (14) 25.00 60.00
*GOLD: .8X TO 2X SILVER
1 Wayne Gretzky 6.00 15.00
2 John Vanbiesbrouck 2.50 6.00
3 Chris Osgood 3.00 8.00
4 Steve Yzerman 3.00 8.00
5 Brett Hull 6.00 15.00
6 Mario Lemieux 4.00 10.00
7 Eric Lindros 2.00 5.00
8 Ed Jovanovski 1.00 2.50
9 Pavel Bure 2.50 6.00
10 Felix Potvin 1.25 3.00
11 Teemu Selanne 2.50 6.00
12 Keith Tkachuk 1.25 3.00
13 Curtis Joseph 1.25 3.00
14 Ed Belfour 1.25 3.00

2014 Leaf Q Autographs Silver

*GOLD/25: .5X TO 1.2X BASIC
ASY1 Steve Yzerman SP 20.00 50.00

2014 Leaf Q Memorabilia Autographs Gold

*GOLD: .6X TO 1.5X BASIC
*GOLD BAT: .4X TO 1X BASIC
*GOLD JKT: .4X TO 1X BASIC
*GOLD SHOE: .4X TO 1X BASIC
RANDOM INSERTS IN PACKS
STATED PRINT RUN 25 SER.#'d SETS
SOME NOT PRICED DUE TO LACK OF INFO

2014 Leaf Q Memorabilia Autographs Silver

AMSY1 Steve Yzerman SP 20.00 50.00

2014 Leaf Q Pure Autographs Charcoal

*BLUE/22-25: .5X TO 1.2X BASIC
PBH1 Bobby Hull 15.00 40.00
PML2 Mario Lemieux 30.00 80.00
PMM1 Mike Modano 10.00 25.00
PMM2 Mike Modano 10.00 25.00
PPE1 Phil Esposito 10.00 25.00
PPR3 Patrick Roy 20.00 50.00
PSY1 Steve Yzerman 20.00 50.00

2015-16 Leaf Signature Series Prospects Autographs

BLUE/15: .8X TO 2X BASIC AU/80-180
GRAY/45-55: .5X TO 1.2X BASIC AU/80-180
GRAY/25-40: .5X TO 1.2X BASIC AU/41-76
GRAY/20-35: .6X TO 1.5X BASIC AU/80-180
RED/15-25: .8X TO 2X BASIC AU/80-180
RED/15-25: .6X TO 1.5X BASIC AU/41-76
SPAB1 Anthony Beauvillier/44* 5.00 12.00
SPAC1 Alexandre Carrier/109* 2.50 6.00
SPAF1 Alex Forsberg/99* 2.50 6.00
SPAM1 Adam Mascherin/120* 2.50 6.00
SPAM2 Adam Musil/42* 4.00 10.00
SPAP1 Andrew Picco/109* 2.50 6.00
SPBG1 Brendan Guhle/99* 2.50 6.00
SPBH1 Brett Howden/87* 3.00 8.00
SPBM1 Beck Malenstyn/149* 4.00 10.00
SPBM2 Brett McKenzie/99* 2.50 6.00
SPBS1 Blake Speers/49* 3.00 8.00
SPBS2 Brandon Saigeon/149* 3.00 8.00
SPCA1 Cameron Askew/74* 3.00 8.00
SPCH1 Connor Hobbs/36*
SPCI1 Connor Ingram/99* 2.50 6.00
SPCJ1 Cole Johnson/87* 5.00 12.00
SPCMD Connor McDavid/7*
SPCP1 Cliff Pu/69* 3.00 8.00
SPCR1 Chaz Reddekopp/84* 3.00 8.00
SPDK1 Davis Koch/69* 3.00 8.00
SPDS1 Daniel Sprong/59* 10.00 25.00
SPDS2 Dante Salituro/109* 2.50 6.00
SPDS3 Dylan Strome/41* 10.00 25.00
SPEF1 Evan Fitzpatrick/106* 5.00 12.00
SPES1 Evan Sarthou/89* 2.50 6.00
SPES2 Evgeny Svechnikov/86* 5.00 12.00
SPFA1 Frederic Allard/111* 2.50 6.00
SPGE1 Giorgio Estephan/86* 2.50 6.00
SPGG1 Gabriel Gagne/81* 3.00 8.00
SPGG2 Glenn Gawdin/86* 2.50 6.00
SPGK1 Graham Knott/49* 3.00 8.00
SPIP1 Ivan Provorov/135* 6.00 15.00
SPJA1 Jeremiah Addison/81* 2.50 6.00
SPJA2 Jonathan Ang/99* 2.50 6.00
SPJA3 Josh Anderson/88* 4.00 10.00
SPJA4 Justin Almeida/180* 3.00 8.00
SPJB1 Jason Bell/89* 2.50 6.00
SPJC1 Jakob Chychrun/100* 5.00 12.00
SPJG1 Julien Gauthier/85* 5.00 12.00
SPJH1 Jansen Harkins/86* 4.00 10.00
SPJH2 Jordan Hollett/80* 5.00 12.00
SPJR1 Jeremy Roy/53* 5.00 12.00
SPJW1 Jaeger White/49* 3.00 8.00
SPJZ1 Jakub Zboril/159* 4.00 10.00
SPKC1 Kale Clague/114* 4.00 10.00
SPKC2 Kyle Capobianco/104* 2.50 6.00
SPKE1 Kaden Elder/104* 2.50 6.00
SPKM1 Kody McDonald/83* 3.00 8.00
SPKT1 Keoni Texeira/104* 2.50 6.00
SPLB1 Logan Brown/103* 6.00 15.00
SPLC1 Lawson Crouse/29* 10.00 25.00
SPLG1 Luke Green/84* 3.00 8.00
SPLL1 Loik Leveille/84* 3.00 8.00
SPMB1 Mackenzie Blackwood/66* 4.00 10.00
SPMB2 Mathew Barzal/41* 15.00 40.00
SPMF1 Maxime Fortier/44* 3.00 8.00
SPMG1 Matteo Gennaro/85* 2.50 6.00
SPMK1 Matthew Kreis/87* 2.50 6.00
SPMM1 Medric Mercier/84* 3.00 8.00
SPMM2 Michael McLeod/147* 4.00 10.00
SPMM3 Mitchell Marner/26* 8.00 20.00
SPMS1 Matt Spencer/67*
SPMS2 Mitchell Stephens/44* 4.00 10.00
SPNK1 Nikita Korostelev/114* 2.50 6.00
SPNK2 Nolan Kneen/86* 2.50 6.00
SPNM1 Nick Merkley/76* 6.00 15.00
SPNM2 Nicolas Meloche/100* 3.00 8.00
SPNN1 Nathan Noel/112* 3.00 8.00
SPNP1 Nolan Patrick/109* 12.00 30.00
SPNR1 Nicolas Roy/52* 4.00 10.00
SPPB1 Paul Bittner/100* 2.50 6.00
SPPD1 Pierre-Luc Dubois/84* 6.00 15.00
SPPK1 Pavel Karnaukhov/104* 2.50 6.00
SPPL1 Pascal Laberge/84* 3.00 8.00
SPPW1 Parker Wotherspoon/44* 4.00 10.00
SPPZ1 Pavel Zacha/115* 4.00 10.00
SPQB1 Quinn Benjafield/8*
SPRG1 Ryan Gropp/36*
SPRK1 Ryan Kubic/103* 2.50 6.00
SPRP1 Ryan Pilon/84* 2.50 6.00
SPSG1 Samuel Girard/89* 2.50 6.00
SPSS1 Sam Steel/80* 5.00 12.00
SPSS2 Simon Stransky/104* 4.00 10.00
SPTB1 Travis Barron/84* 3.00 8.00
SPTB2 Tyler Benson/135* 5.00 12.00
SPTK1 Tanner Kaspick/104* 2.50 6.00
SPTK2 Travis Konecny/63*
SPTM1 Timo Meier/82* 4.00 10.00
SPTR1 Ty Ronning/154* 2.50 6.00
SPTS1 Thomas Schemitsch/51* 5.00 12.00
SPTS2 Tyler Soy/85* 4.00 10.00
SPVD1 Vince Dunn/87* 2.50 6.00
SPWB1 Will Bitten/86* 2.50 6.00

2015-16 Leaf Signature Series '90 Leaf Tribute Autographs

LTBH1 Brett Hull/25 10.00 25.00
LTJLC John LeClair/25 5.00 12.00
LTMM1 Mike Modano/25 8.00 20.00
LTPF1 Peter Forsberg/25 15.00 30.00
LTPR1 Patrick Roy/25 25.00 60.00
LTSF1 Sergei Fedorov/25 20.00 50.00
LTWC1 Wendel Clark/25 5.00 12.00

2015-16 Leaf Signature Series Captains Autographs

GRAY/20-25: .6X TO 1.5X BASIC AU/60-61
*GRAY/20: .5X TO 1.2X BASIC AU/30
GRAY/20: .8X TO 2X BASIC AU/125
SCAD1 Alex Delvecchio/30 5.00 12.0
SCRB1 Raymond Bourque/61 8.00 20.0
SCRK1 Red Kelly/60 5.00 12.0
SCSS1 Serge Savard/125 5.00 12.0
SCTL1 Ted Lindsay/90 5.00 12.0
SCWC1 Wendel Clark/15
SCYC1 Yvan Cournoyer/25

2015-16 Leaf Signature Series Champions Autographs

*GRAY/25-40: .5X TO 1.2X BASIC AU/45-56
*GRAY/25-40: .6X TO 1.5X BASIC AU/72-140
*GRAY/15: .5X TO 1.2X BASIC AU/30-35
*GRAY/15: .6X TO 1.5X BASIC AU/45-56
SCHBH2 Bobby Hull/30 6.00 15.0
SCHBP1 Bernie Parent/140 8.00 20.0
SCHBT1 Bryan Trottier/45 6.00 15.0
SCHCC1 Corey Crawford/72 10.00 25.0
SCHGA1 Glenn Anderson/85 5.00 12.0
SCHGF1 Grant Fuhr/60 8.00 20.0
SCHGL1 Guy Lapointe/56 4.00 10.0
SCHHR1 Henri Richard/104 6.00 15.0
SCHJL1 Jacques Lemaire/50 5.00 12.0
SCHPR1 Patrick Roy/20 20.00 40.0
SCHSF1 Sergei Fedorov/50 10.00 25.0
SCHTL1 Ted Lindsay/90 4.00 10.0
SCHYC1 Yvan Cournoyer35 6.00 15.0

2015-16 Leaf Signature Series Decades Autographs

SDBG1 Bill Gadsby/170* 4.00 10.0
SDBP2 Brad Park/92* 3.00 8.0
SDCC1 Corey Crawford/60* 10.00 25.0
SDEG1 Ed Giacomin/169* 4.00 10.0
SDGA1 Glenn Anderson/65* 5.00 12.0
SDGL1 Guy Lapointe/56* 4.00 10.0
SDHH1 Harry Howell/170* 3.00 8.0
SDJB1 Johnny Bower/60* 6.00 15.0
SDJH2 Jimmy Howard/151* 4.00 10.0
SDJL1 Jacques Lemaire/50* 5.00 12.0
SDJLC John LeClair/122* 4.00 10.0
SDMAF Marc-Andre Fleury/32* 10.00 25.0
SDMD1 Marcel Dionne/175* 5.00 12.0
SDNU1 Norm Ullman/170* 4.00 10.0
SDPF1 Peter Forsberg/30* 8.00 20.0
SDRB1 Raymond Bourque/69* 8.00 20.0
SDRK1 Red Kelly/51* 4.00 10.0
SDTL1 Ted Lindsay/90* 4.00 10.0
SDWC1 Wendel Clark/15*
SDYC1 Yvan Cournoyer/25* 8.00 20.0

2015-16 Leaf Signature Series Decades Autographs Gray

GRAY/50: .5X TO 1.2X BASIC AU/90-175
GRAY/25-40: .5X TO 1.2X BASIC AU/50-69
GRAY/25-40: .6X TO 1.5X BASIC AU/90-175
GRAY/15: .8X TO 2X BASIC AU/90-175
GRAY/15: .6X TO 1.5X BASIC AU/50-69
SDPF1 Peter Forsberg/15 25.00 50.0

2015-16 Leaf Signature Series Dual MVP Autographs

MVP21 B.Hull/B.Hull 30.00 60.0
MVP24 P.Forsberg/J.Thornton 30.00 60.0

2015-16 Leaf Signature Series Dynasty Autographs

GRAY/20: .8X TO 2X BASIC AU/76-100
GRAY/20: .6X TO 1.5X BASIC AU/50-59
GRAY/20: .5X TO 1.2X BASIC AU/30-40
SDYAD1 Alex Delvecchio/30* 5.00 12.0
SDYBT1 Bryan Trottier/50* 6.00 15.0
SDYGA1 Glenn Anderson/76* 4.00 10.0
SDYGF1 Grant Fuhr/59* 10.00 25.0
SDYGL1 Guy Lapointe/40* 5.00 12.0
SDYHR1 Henri Richard/100* 8.00 20.0
SDYJB1 Johnny Bower/36* 8.00 20.0
SDYJL1 Jacques Lemaire/40* 6.00 15.0
SDYRK1 Red Kelly/40* 5.00 12.0
SDYSS1 Serge Savard/99* 4.00 10.0
SDYTL1 Ted Lindsay/80* 4.00 10.0
SDYYC1 Yvan Cournoyer/34* 6.00 15.0

2015-16 Leaf Signature Series Miracle Team Autographs

M80BS1 Bob Suter 15.00 40.0
M80BS2 Buzz Schneider 10.00 25.0
M80DC1 Dave Christian 10.00 25.0
M80DS1 Dave Silk 15.00 40.0
M80ES1 Eric Strobel 12.00 30.0
M80JC1 Jim Craig 15.00 40.0
M80JH1 John Harrington 12.00 30.0
M80JO1 Jack O'Callahan 12.00 30.0
M80KM1 Ken Morrow 12.00 30.0
M80ME1 Mike Eruzione 10.00 25.0
M80MP1 Mark Pavelich 10.00 25.0
M80MR1 Mike Ramsey
M80MW1 Mark Wells
M80PV1 Phil Verchota 12.00 30.0
M80RM1 Rob McClanahan 10.00 25.0
M80SJ1 Steve Janaszak

2015-16 Leaf Signature Series MVP Autographs

MVPBH2 Bobby Hull 8.00 20.0
MVPBT1 Bryan Trottier 5.00 12.0
MVPPF1 Peter Forsberg 15.00 30.0
MVPSF1 Sergei Fedorov 6.00 15.0

2015-16 Leaf Signature Series Signature Prospect Jersey Autographs

BLUE/15: .5X TO 1.2X BASIC JSY AU/30
PAJAB1 Anthony Beauvillier/30* 4.00 10.
PAJAM1 Adam Musil/30* 4.00 10.
PAJBH1 Brett Howden/30* 4.00 10.
PAJBS1 Blake Speers/30* 4.00 10.
PAJCA1 Cameron Askew/30*
PAJCH1 Connor Hobbs/30* 4.00 10.
PAJCP1 Cliff Pu/30* 4.00 10.
PAJDK1 Davis Koch/30* 8.00 20.
PAJDS1 Dylan Strome/15*
PAJGK1 Graham Knott/30*
PAJJG1 Julien Gauthier/30*
PAJJW1 Jaeger White/30*
PAJLC1 Lawson Crouse/15*
PAJMF1 Maxime Fortier/30* 4.00 10.
PAJMG1 Matteo Gennaro/30*
PAJMS1 Mitchell Stephens/30* 4.00 10.
PAJPW1 Parker Wotherspoon/30* 4.00 10.
PAJRG1 Ryan Gropp/30*
PAJTS1 Thomas Schemitsch/30* 4.00 10.
PAJVD1 Vince Dunn/30* 4.00 10.
PAJWB1 Will Bitten/30* 8.00 20.

2013 Leaf Sports Heroes

GH1 Gordie Howe 30.00 60.00
MM1 Mike Modano 10.00 25.00

1997-98 Leaf International

is 150-card set featured color player images with a ap of their home country in the background and inted on full foil board with heliogram technology d puff ink treatment. The cards were divided into inadian or U.S./Euro packs, with only Canadian ayers being found in Canadian packs and the rest of e set in the U.S./Euro version.

OMPLETE SET (150) 30.00 60.00
Eric Lindros .25 .60
Dominik Hasek .50 1.25
Peter Forsberg .60 1.50
Steve Yzerman 1.25 3.00
John Vanbiesbrouck .20 .50
Paul Kariya .25 .60
Martin Brodeur .60 1.50
Wayne Gretzky 1.50 4.00
Mark Messier .25 .60
Jaromir Jagr .40 1.00
Brett Hull .30 .75
Brendan Shanahan .25 .60
Ray Bourque .40 1.00
Jarome Iginla .30 .75
Mike Modano .40 1.00
Curtis Joseph .25 .60
Ed Jovanovski .20 .50
Teemu Selanne .25 .60
Saku Koivu .25 .60
Eric Fichaud .20 .50
Paul Coffey .25 .60
Jeremy Roenick .30 .75
Owen Nolan .20 .50
Felix Potvin .25 .60
Alexander Mogilny .20 .50
Alexandre Daigle .10 .30
Chris Gratton .20 .50
Geoff Sanderson .20 .50
Dimitri Khristich .10 .30
Bryan Berard .10 .30
Vyacheslav Kozlov .10 .30
Jeff Hackett .20 .50
Bill Ranford .20 .50
Pat LaFontaine .25 .60
Joe Sakic .50 1.25
Niklas Sundstrom .10 .30
Martin Gelinas .10 .30
Mikael Renberg .10 .30
Trevor Linden .20 .50
Jozef Stumpel .20 .50
Joe Thornton CL .10 .30
Jocelyn Thibault .20 .50
Pierre Turgeon .20 .50
Ron Francis .20 .50
Damian Rhodes .20 .50
Jamie Langenbrunner .10 .30
Chris Osgood .20 .50
Vaclav Varada .20 .50
Ryan Smyth .20 .50
Daren Puppa .20 .50
Petr Nedved .20 .50
Ron Hextall .20 .50
Joe Juneau .20 .50
Jim Campbell .10 .30
Zigmund Palffy .20 .50
Roman Turek .20 .50
Adam Deadmarsh .10 .30
Rob Niedermayer .20 .50
Alexei Yashin .10 .30
Pavel Bure .25 .60
Jason Arnott .10 .30
Nikolai Khabibulin .20 .50
Sean Burke .20 .50
Chris Chelios .25 .60
Mike Ricci .20 .50
Sergei Berezin .10 .30
Jaroslav Svejkovsky CL .10 .30
Brian Savage .10 .30
Roman Vopat .10 .30
Mike Richter .25 .60
Jim Carey .20 .50
Guy Hebert .20 .50
Keith Tkachuk .25 .60
Kirk McLean .20 .50
Janne Niinimaa .20 .50
Roman Hamrlik .10 .30
Darcy Tucker .10 .30
Pat Verbeek .10 .30
Hnat Domenichelli .10 .30
Doug Gilmour .20 .50
Mike Grier .10 .30
Ken Wregget .10 .30
Dino Ciccarelli .10 .30
Steve Sullivan .10 .30
Anson Carter .20 .50
Steve Shields RC .40 1.00
Ed Belfour .25 .60
Darren McCarty .10 .30
Adam Graves .10 .30
Chris Pronger .20 .50
Peter Bondra .20 .50
Oleg Tverdovsky .10 .30
Stephane Fiset .20 .50
Mike Vernon .20 .50
Scott Lachance .10 .30
Corey Schwab .10 .30
Eric Daze .20 .50
Jere Lehtinen .10 .30
Donald Audette .10 .30
John LeClair .25 .60
Steve Rucchin .10 .30
Jeff Friesen .10 .30
Daymond Langkow .20 .50
Mike Dunham .20 .50
Marc Denis CL .10 .30
Andrew Cassels .10 .30
Mike Peca .10 .30
Joe Nieuwendyk .20 .50
Vincent Damphousse .10 .30
Scott Mellanby .10 .30
Patrick Lalime .20 .50
Derek Plante .10 .30
Wade Redden .10 .30
Marcel Cousineau .20 .50
Ray Sheppard .10 .30
Dave Andreychuk .10 .30
Brian Leetch .25 .60
Sandis Ozolinsh .10 .30
Keith Primeau .10 .30
Brian Holzinger .10 .30
Luc Robitaille .20 .50
Jose Theodore .30 .75
Grant Fuhr .20 .50
Dainius Zubrus .25 .60
125 Rod Brind'Amour .20 .50
126 Trevor Kidd .20 .50
127 Mark Recchi .20 .50
128 Patrick Roy 1.00 2.50
129 Kevin Hatcher .10 .30
130 Adam Oates .20 .50
131 Doug Weight .20 .50
132 Vaclav Prospal RC .25 .60
133 Harry York .10 .30
134 Todd Bertuzzi .25 .60
135 Sergei Fedorov .40 1.00
136 Theo Fleury .10 .30
137 Chad Kilger .10 .30
138 Jamie Storr .20 .50
139 Tony Amonte .20 .50
140 Rem Murray .10 .30
141 Chris O'Sullivan .10 .30
142 Mats Sundin .25 .60
143 Ethan Moreau .10 .30
144 Derian Hatcher .10 .30
145 Daniel Alfredsson .20 .50
146 Corey Hirsch .20 .50
147 Landon Wilson .10 .30
148 Chris Phillips CL .10 .30
149 Sergei Samsonov CL .10 .30
(149,150 inserts)
150 Daniel Cleary CL .10 .30

1997-98 Leaf International Universal Ice

This 150-card set was parallel to the base set and was printed on holofoil board. Only 250 of each card was produced and numbered. All cards of this parallel set appeared in both Canadian packs and U.S./Euro packs.

*VETS: 4X TO 10X BASIC CARDS
*ROOKIES: 2X TO 5X BASIC CARDS

2015-16 Leaf Toronto Fall Expo Jack Eichel Patches

PJE1 Jack Eichel Patch Slvr/99 30.00 60.00
PJE2 Jack Eichel Patch Blue/35 40.00 80.00
PJE3 Jack Eichel Patch Gold/10 50.00 120.00
APJE1 Jack Eichel JSY AU Slvr/25 150.00 250.00
APJE2 Jack Eichel JSY AU Blue/15 175.00 300.00
APJE3 Jack Eichel JSY AU Gold/10 200.00 350.00

2015-16 Leaf Ultimate Signatures

USBB1 Brian Bellows/30 8.00 20.00
USBG1 Bill Gadsby/35 10.00 25.00
USBH1 Bobby Hull/30 10.00 25.00
USBH2 Brett Hull/30 10.00 25.00
USCJ1 Curtis Joseph/30 10.00 25.00
USDM1 Dickie Moore/45 8.00 20.00
USEF1 Emile Francis/30 8.00 20.00
USEG1 Ed Giacomin/45 10.00 25.00
USEL2 Eric Lindros/25 15.00 40.00
USFP1 Felix Potvin/35 15.00 40.00
USGH1 Glenn Hall/25 8.00 20.00
USJB2 Johnny Bower/45 12.00 30.00
USJB3 Johnny Bucyk/35 8.00 20.00
USJE1 Jack Eichel/45 60.00 120.00
USJP1 Jesse Puljujarvi/45 40.00 80.00
USJT1 Jose Theodore/45 10.00 25.00
USJV1 John Vanbiesbrouck/40 10.00 25.00
USKH1 Ken Hodge/45 8.00 20.00
USMB1 Martin Brodeur/30 20.00 50.00
USMD1 Marcel Dionne/40 12.00 30.00
USML1 Mario Lemieux/25 30.00 80.00
USMN1 Mats Naslund/45 10.00 25.00
USNL1 Nicklas Lidstrom/25 10.00 25.00
USPC1 Paul Coffey/15 10.00 25.00
USPH1 Phil Housley/30 10.00 25.00
USPL1 Pat LaFontaine/30 10.00 25.00
USPP1 Pierre Pilote/35 6.00 15.00
USPR1 Patrick Roy/25 25.00 60.00
USRD1 Ron Duguay/20 8.00 20.00
USRK1 Red Kelly/45 8.00 20.00
USRL1 Reggie Leach/45 8.00 20.00
USSB1 Scotty Bowman/25 8.00 20.00
USSL1 Steve Larmer/45 8.00 20.00
USSY1 Steve Yzerman/15 15.00 40.00
USTE1 Tony Esposito/35 10.00 25.00
USTL2 Trevor Linden/30 10.00 25.00
USTS1 Teemu Selanne/25 20.00 50.00
USVT1 Vladislav Tretiak/35 12.00 30.00
USWC1 Wendel Clark/40 10.00 25.00

2015-16 Leaf Ultimate Autograph Memorabilia

AMBH1 Bobby Hull/30 20.00 50.00
AMJE1 Jack Eichel/45 60.00 120.00
AMML1 Mario Lemieux/30 25.00 60.00
AMPR1 Patrick Roy/30 20.00 50.00

2015-16 Leaf Ultimate Dual Signatures

DS01 C.Joseph/F.Potvin/20 15.00 40.00
DS03 J.Eichel/P.LaFontaine/20 60.00 120.00
DS04 J.Puljujarvi/J.Eichel/25 60.00 120.00
DS06 J.Bower/C.Joseph/20 12.00 30.00
DS08 M.Lemieux/B.Hull/12 20.00 50.00
DS11 P.LaFontaine/B.Hull/20 15.00 40.00

2015-16 Leaf Ultimate Dual Ultimate Memorabilia

UD02 C.Joseph/F.Potvin/35 6.00 15.00
UD03 G.Lafleur/W.Gretzky/15 20.00 50.00
UD04 J.Eichel/M.Lemieux/25 15.00 40.00
UD05 M.Lemieux/W.Gretzky/20 20.00 50.00
UD07 M.Bossy/W.Gretzky/20 20.00 50.00
UD09 P.LaFontaine/J.Eichel/35 15.00 40.00
UD10 P.Roy/D.Hasek/35 10.00 25.00
UD11 P.Roy/M.Brodeur/30 10.00 25.00

2015-16 Leaf Ultimate Honoured Members Autographs

HMBH2 Brett Hull/15 12.50 30.00
HMCC1 Chris Chelios/10
HMDK1 Dave Keon/4 8.00 20.00
HMDM1 Dickie Moore/25 6.00 15.00
HMEF1 Emile Francis/25 6.00 15.00
HMEG1 Ed Giacomin/25 8.00 20.00
HMEL1 Elmer Lach/5
HMGC1 Gerry Cheevers/25 8.00 20.00
HMGH1 Glenn Hall/20 6.00 15.00
HMGH2 Gordie Howe/12 15.00 40.00
HMHH1 Harry Howell/10 6.00 15.00
HMHR1 Henri Richard/8 8.00 20.00
HMJB1 Jean Beliveau/5 8.00 20.00
HMJB2 Johnny Bower/25 10.00 25.00
HMJB3 Johnny Bucyk/25 6.00 15.00
HMJS1 Joe Sakic/10 12.00 30.00
HMMD1 Marcel Dionne/25 10.00 25.00
HMML1 Mario Lemieux/25 25.00 60.00
HMMM1 Mike Modano/25 12.00 30.00
HMMS1 Milt Schmidt/20 8.00 20.00
HMNL1 Nicklas Lidstrom/20 8.00 20.00
HMPC1 Paul Coffey/10 8.00 20.00
HMPH1 Phil Housley/25 8.00 20.00
HMPL1 Pat LaFontaine/25 8.00 20.00
HMPP1 Pierre Pilote/25
HMPR1 Patrick Roy/25 20.00 50.00
HMRG1 Rod Gilbert/10 6.00 15.00
HMRK1 Red Kelly/25 6.00 15.00
HMSB1 Scotty Bowman/25
HMSY1 Steve Yzerman/10 12.00 30.00
HMTL1 Ted Lindsay/10 8.00 20.00
HMYC1 Yvan Cournoyer/5 8.00 20.00

2015-16 Leaf Ultimate Journey Jerseys

UJ01 Brett Hull/15 10.00 25.00
UJ02 Brian Leetch/15 10.00 25.00
UJ03 Chris Chelios/15 10.00 25.00
UJ04 Curtis Joseph/20 10.00 25.00
UJ05 Eric Lindros/15 15.00 40.00
UJ06 Felix Potvin/20 15.00 40.00
UJ08 Jeremy Roenick/20 10.00 25.00
UJ09 Mario Lemieux/15 30.00 80.00
UJ10 Mark Messier/15 15.00 40.00
UJ11 Nicklas Lidstrom/15 10.00 25.00
UJ12 Patrick Roy/20 25.00 60.00
UJ13 Paul Kariya/20 20.00 50.00
UJ14 Pavel Bure/20 15.00 40.00
UJ15 Peter Forsberg/20 10.00 25.00
UJ16 Phil Esposito/15 15.00 40.00
UJ17 Ron Francis/15 12.00 30.00
UJ18 Sergei Fedorov/20 15.00 40.00
UJ19 Teemu Selanne/20 20.00 50.00
UJ20 Wayne Gretzky/15 50.00 120.00

2015-16 Leaf Ultimate The First Six Franchise Relics

F6F01 Fillion/Lafleur/Beliveau/Hiller/Harvey/Richard/5
F6F02 Howe/Lindsay/Yzerman/Fedorov
Sawchuk/Lidstrom/8
F6F03 Hull/Mikita/Hall/Esposito/Brimsek/Mosienko/8
F6F04 Keon/Sundin/Salming/Kennedy/Clark/Horton/8
F6F05 Lafleur/Esposito/Gilbert/Ratelle
Giacomin/Park/6
F6F06 Orr/Esposito/Cheevers
Cashman/Shore/Clapper/5

2015-16 Leaf Ultimate Time Capsule Signatures

TCEL2 Eric Lindros/30 20.00 50.00
TCGH2 Gordie Howe/9
TCJB2 Johnny Bower/40 12.00 30.00
TCJE1 Jack Eichel/40 60.00 120.00
TCJE2 Jack Eichel/25 100.00 200.00
TCJP1 Jesse Puljujarvi/40 30.00 60.00
TCML1 Mario Lemieux/20 30.00 80.00
TCPR1 Patrick Roy/25 25.00 60.00

2015-16 Leaf Ultimate Triple Signatures

TS02 Delvecchio/Kelly/Lindsay/20 20.00 50.00
TS03 Eichel/LaFontaine/Modano/20 75.00 150.00

2015-16 Leaf Ultimate Triple Ultimate Memorabilia

UT01 Barber/Clarke/Leach/30 6.00 15.00
UT02 Bourque/Lidstrom/Coffey/30 6.00 15.00
UT03 Eichel/Modano/LaFontaine/30 25.00 60.00
UT04 Fedorov/Bure/Mogilny/30 10.00 25.00
UT05 Fuhr/Potvin/Joseph/35 10.00 25.00
UT06 Gilbert/Lafleur/Esposito/30 10.00 25.00
UT07 Lemieux/Lindros/Eichel/30 25.00 60.00
UT08 Lidstrom/Shanahan/Fedorov/30 10.00 25.00
UT09 Naslund/Bellows/Koivu/35 6.00 15.00
UT10 Orr/Gretzky/Howe/12 30.00 80.00
UT11 Roy/Joseph/Belfour/30 15.00 40.00

2015-16 Leaf Ultimate Ultimate Memorabilia

UM01 Adam Oates/35
UM02 Alex Delvecchio/15
UM03 Billy Smith/35
UM04 Bobby Clarke/30
UM05 Curtis Joseph/40
UM06 Dominik Hasek/35
UM07 Felix Potvin/35
UM08 Gilbert Perreault/40
UM09 Guy Lafleur/25
UM10 Jack Eichel/40
UM11 Jari Kurri/35
UM12 Lanny McDonald/40
UM13 Mario Lemieux/40
UM14 Martin Brodeur/40
UM15 Mike Bossy/20
UM16 Mike Modano/40
UM17 Patrick Roy/40
UM18 Pavel Bure/40
UM19 Pierre Turgeon/30
UM20 Rob Blake/40
UM21 Sergei Fedorov/35
UM22 Wayne Gretzky/20

2016-17 Leaf Ultimate Quad Memorabilia

UQ01 Gretzky/Lemieux 50.00 120.00
Esposito/Howe/25
UQ02 Hull/Roenick/Lemieux/Sakic/25 30.00 80.00
UQ03 Hawerchuk/Sakic 15.00 40.00
Robitaille/Oates/25
UQ04 Chelios/Blake/Lidstrom/Pronger/25 10.0025.00
UQ05 Kariya/Selanne/Jagr/Fedorov/25 25.00 60.00
UQ06 Modano/Shanahan/Sundin/Bure/25 15.0040.00
UQ07 Howe/Delvecchio 25.00 60.00
Sawchuk/Lindsay/25
UQ08 Ovechkin/Bure/Fedorov 40.00 100.00
Mogilny/25
UQ09 Tavares/Hall/Nugent-Hopkins 20.00 50.00
Stamkos/25
UQ10 Goulet/Stastny/Gretzky/Savard/25 50.00 120.00
UQ11 Housley/Murphy/Potvin 10.00 25.00
Bourque/25
UQ12 Arbour/Potvin/Smith/Bossy/25 10.00 25.00
UQ13 Lafleur/Esposito/Clarke/Dionne/25 15.00 40.00
UQ14 Taylor/Ciccarelli/Francis/Mullen/25 12.0030.00
UQ15 Roy/Moog/Barrasso/Smith/25 25.00 60.00
UQ16 Plante/Sawchuk/Hall/Worsley/15 15.00 40.00
UQ17 Howe/Mahovlich/Mikita 25.00 60.00
Beliveau/15

2016-17 Leaf Ultimate Signature Memorabilia

SMBS1 Borje Salming/20 10.00 25.00
SMDH1 Dale Hawerchuk/20 12.00 30.00
SMDS1 Denis Savard/20 12.00 30.00
SMJE1 Jack Eichel/20 20.00 50.00
SMJM1 Joe Mullen/20 8.00 20.00
SMLM1 Larry Murphy/20 10.00 25.00
SMLR1 Larry Robinson/20 10.00 25.00
SMLR2 Luc Robitaille/20 10.00 25.00
SMMB1 Martin Brodeur/20 20.00 50.00
SMMG1 Michel Goulet/20 10.00 25.00
SMMR1 Mike Richter/20 10.00 25.00
SMRB1 Raymond Bourque/20 15.00 40.00
SMRL1 Rod Langway/20 8.00 20.00
SMSS1 Serge Savard/20 10.00 25.00
SMSS2 Steve Shutt/20 10.00 25.00
SMTB1 Tom Barrasso/20 10.00 25.00
SMTE1 Tony Esposito/20 10.00 25.00

2016-17 Leaf Ultimate Triple Memorabilia

UT01 Howe/Ullman/Lindsay 25.00 60.00
UT02 Roy/Plante/Sawchuk 25.00 60.00
UT03 McDavid/Crosby/Stamkos 50.00 125.00
UT04 Jagr/Lemieux/Malkin 30.00 80.00
UT05 McDavid/Eichel/Larkin 50.00 125.00
UT06 Gretzky/Bossy/Esposito 50.00 120.00
UT07 Ovechkin/Fedorov/Malkin 40.00 100.00
UT08 Beliveau/Joliat/Harvey 10.00 25.00
UT09 Dionne/Esposito/Clarke 15.00 40.00
UT10 Orr/Salming/Robinson 30.00 80.00
UT11 Mikita/Hull/Esposito 15.00 40.00

2017-18 Leaf Ultimate Compatriots Relics

UC02 Brodeur/Francis/Lindros 20.00 50.00
Lemieux/Yzerman/Sakic
UC03 Bure/Mogilny/Yashin 6.00 15.00
Khabibulin/Kasparaitis/Bryzgalov
UC04 Chelios/Hull/Leetch 6.00 15.00
Amonte/Barrasso/Guerin
UC05 Dzurilla/Cechmanek 6.00 15.00
Bonk/Holik/Turek/Stastny
UC06 Lindbergh/Lidstrom 10.00 25.00
Salming/Salo/Forsberg/Naslund
UC07 Perreault/Clarke 10.00 25.00
Esposito/Shutt/Sittler/Dionne
UC08 Tretiak/Mikhailov/Kharlamov 6.00 15.00
Mylnikov/Yakushev/Krutov

2017-18 Leaf Ultimate Dual Signatures

US201 B.Hull/A.Oates/15 25.00 40.00
US204 G.Lafleur/G.Lapointe/12
US206 N.Patrick/N.Hischier/25 25.00 60.00
US207 P.Esposito/M.Schmidt/12 15.00 40.00
US208 P.Pilote/B.Gadsby/12 15.00 40.00
US209 V.Tretiak/T.Esposito/12 15.00 40.00

1971-72 Letraset Action Replays

This set of 24 Hockey Action Replays was issued in Canada by Letraset. Printed on thin paper stock, each replay measured approximately 5 1/4" by 6 1/4" and was folded in the center. All replays had a common front consisting of a color photo of a face-off between Danny O'Shea of the Hawks and Jean Ratelle of the Rangers. On the reverse side, a "Know Your Signals" series illustrated arm signals used by hockey referees. The inside unfolded to display a 5" by 4 1/2" color drawings of NHL action shots. Immediately above was a description of the play plus slots for photos of the players involved in the action. The center photos and some of the players needed to complete the play were missing and supplied on a separate run-on transfer sheet. The action scene could be completed by rubbing the players on the transfer sheet onto the action scene. The replays were numbered in the white panel that presents the referee arm signals, and checklisted below accordingly.

COMPLETE SET (24) 100.00 200.00
1 Rogatien Vachon 5.00 10.00
Dave Keon
Gilles Marotte
2 Ken Dryden 10.00 20.00
Chico Maki
Jacques Laperriere
3 Gary Dornhoefer 4.00 8.00
Roger Crozier
Tracy Pratt
4 Walt Tkaczuk 4.00 8.00
Gump Worsley
Vic Hadfield
5 Dallas Smith 17.50 35.00
Bobby Orr
Walt McKechnie
6 Ab McDonald 4.00 8.00
Gary Sabourin
Garry Unger
7 Jim Rutherford 4.00 8.00
Orland Kurtenbach
Bob Woytovich
8 Gerry Cheevers 6.00 12.00
Frank Mahovlich
Don Awrey
9 Tim Ecclestone 5.00 10.00
Bob Baun
Jacques Plante
10 Stan Mikita 6.00 12.00
Ed Giacomin
Jim Pappin
11 Doug Favell 4.00 8.00
Danny Grant
Ed Van Impe
12 Ernie Wakely 4.00 8.00
Barclay Plager
Gary Croteau
13 Bryan Hextall 5.00 10.00
Tony Esposito
Pat Stapleton
14 Jean Ratelle 5.00 10.00
Rod Gilbert
Jim Roberts
15 Jacques Lemaire 6.00 12.00
Henri Richard
Yvan Cournoyer
16 George Gardiner 4.00 8.00
Dennis Hull
Lou Angotti
17 Ed Johnston 17.50 35.00
Norm Ullman
Bobby Orr
18 Gilles Meloche 4.00 8.00
Wayne Carleton
Dick Redmond
19 Al Smith 4.00 8.00
Gary Bergman
Stan Gilbertson
20 Dunc Wilson 4.00 8.00
Brad Park
Dale Tallon
21 Jude Drouin 4.00 8.00
Doug Favell
Barry Ashbee
22 Ron Ellis 10.00 20.00
Ken Dryden
Paul Henderson
23 Gary Edwards 4.00 8.00
Jean Pronovost
Ron Shock
24 Cesare Maniago 4.00 8.00
Chris Bordeleau
Ted Harris

1980 Liberty Matchbooks

This yellow matchbook was part of a multi-sport set, featuring athletes from all the major leagues and Olympics.

NNO Ray Bourque 10.00 20.00

1992-93 Lightning Sheraton

Sponsored by the Sheraton Inn Tampa Conference Center, this album and its 28 perforated cards commemorated the Tampa Bay Lightning's inaugural season. Folded closed, the album measured 10" by 13". The 28 standard-size cards folded out and feature color player action shots on their fronts. These photos were borderless on their top and right sides, and white-bordered on the left and bottom edges. The player's name appeared vertically in blue lettering in the margin on the left side, his position appeared in blue in the bottom margin, and his uniform number was shown in silver, just above the Lightning logo in the lower left. The white backs displayed the player's name, uniform number, and biography in the upper left. Below were stats from the player's previous seasons. In the upper right, the Sheraton logo rounded out the card. The cards were unnumbered and checklisted below in alphabetical order.

COMPLETE SET (28) 8.00 20.00
1 Mikael Andersson .20 .50
2 Bob Beers .20 .50
3 J.C. Bergeron .30 .75
4 Marc Bergevin .20 .50
5 Tim Bergland .20 .50
6 Brian Bradley .60 1.50
7 Marc Bureau .20 .50
8 Wayne Cashman CO .20 .50
9 Shawn Chambers .20 .50
10 Danton Cole .20 .50
11 Adam Creighton .30 .75
12 Terry Crisp CO .20 .50
13 Rob DiMaio .30 .75
14 Phil Esposito GM .75 2.00
15 Tony Esposito DIR .60 1.50
16 Roman Hamrlik .75 2.00
17 Pat Jablonski .30 .75
18 Steve Kasper .20 .50
19 Chris Kontos .20 .50
20 Steve Maltais .20 .50
21 Joe Reekie .20 .50
22 Thunderbug (Mascot) .08 .25
23 John Tucker .30 .75
24 Wendell Young .30 .75
25 Rob Zamuner .30 .75
26 Title card .20 .50
27 Inaugural season card .08 .25
28 Sheraton logo card .08 .25

1993-94 Lightning Kash n'Karry

Sponsored by Kash n'Karry, this six-card set measured approximately 5" by 7". Inside gray borders, the fronts featured color action player photos. A blue bar on the left side carried the player's name and number. The sponsor's logo appeared in the bottom gray border. The horizontal backs had a postcard design, with the player's name, position, a short biography, and career highlights on the left side. The cards were unnumbered and checklisted below in alphabetical order. The checklist below is incomplete.

COMPLETE SET (6) 3.00 8.00
1 Brian Bradley .75 2.00
2 Shawn Chambers .40 1.00
3 Chris Gratton .75 2.00
4 Adam Creighton .40 1.00
5 Rob DiMaio .40 1.00
6 Wendell Young .60 1.50

1993-94 Lightning Season in Review

Subtitled "1993-94 Season in Review," the 28 cards comprising this set of the Tampa Bay Lightning were issued in a perforated sheet, which also included a 10" by 13" title page. Each card measured approximately 2 1/2" by 3 1/4" and featured on its front a color player action shot, which was borderless at the top and right. The player's name appeared vertically within the white margin to the left of the photo; his position appeared within the white margin below. His uniform number and the team logo appeared at the lower left. The white back carried the player's name and uniform number at the top, followed below by biography and statistics. Logos for the NHL and The Sky Box Sports Cafe at the upper right roundedout the card. The cards were unnumbered and checklisted below in alphabetical order.

COMPLETE SET (28) 6.00 15.00
1 Mikael Andersson .20 .50
2 Marc Bergevin .20 .50
3 Brian Bradley .30 .75
4 Marc Bureau .20 .50
5 Wayne Cashman ACO .20 .50
6 Shawn Chambers .20 .50
7 Enrico Ciccone .20 .50
8 Danton Cole .20 .50
9 Adam Creighton .20 .50
10 Terry Crisp CO .20 .50
11 Jim Cummins .20 .50
12 Pat Elynuik .20 .50
13 Phil Esposito GM .60 1.50
14 Tony Esposito DIR .40 1.00
15 Gerard Gallant .20 .50
16 Danny Gare ACO .08 .25
17 Chris Gratton .60 1.50
18 Roman Hamrlik .60 1.50
19 Chris Joseph .20 .50
20 Petr Klima .20 .50
21 Chris LiPuma .20 .50
22 Rudy Poeschek .30 .75
23 Daren Puppa .60 1.50
24 Denis Savard .40 1.00
25 Thunderbug MASCOT .08 .25
26 John Tucker .20 .50
27 Wendell Young .25 .60
28 Rob Zamuner .20 .50

1994-95 Lightning Health Plan

This two-card set was sponsored by Health Plan of Florida and the Tampa Tribune. Twenty thousand sets were produced. The front and back panels were connected at their tops and each measure 4" by 5". The front displaysed blue-tinted action photo edged by black stripes, while the back carried a color head shot, biography, and sponsor logos. When unfolded, the inside panel measured 4" by 10" and featured a pop-up color player photo and statistics. The cards were numbered on the back at the bottom.

COMPLETE SET (2) 2.50 6.00
1 Daren Puppa 1.50 4.00
2 Chris Gratton 1.25 3.00

1994-95 Lightning Photo Album

The 1994-95 Tampa Bay Lightning Commemorative Photo Album was sponsored by the Sky Box Sports Cafe at the Sheraton Inn in Tampa. It consists of three perforated sheets, each measuring 12 1/2" by 9 3/4" and joined together to form one continuous sheet. The first panel had an array different size color shots, capturing the Lightning off and on the ice. The second and third panels each displayed three rows of player cards; if perforated, the cards would measure the standard size. The fronts featured color action photos with team color-coded borders. The team logo, player's name, position, and number were printed in the borders. On a team color-coded background, the backs carried a color head shot, biography, statistics, and career highlights. The cards were unnumbered and checklisted below in alphabetical order.

COMPLETE SET (29) 4.80 12.00
1 Mikael Andersson .15 .40
2 J.C. Bergeron .20 .50
3 Marc Bergevin .15 .40
4 Brian Bradley .30 .75
5 Marc Bureau .15 .40
6 Wayne Cashman ACO .15 .40
7 Eric Charron .15 .40
8 Enrico Ciccone .20 .50
9 Terry Crisp CO .15 .40
10 Cory Cross .15 .40
11 Phil Esposito PRES/GM .40 1.00
12 Tony Esposito DIR .20 .50
13 Danny Gare ACO .15 .40
14 Chris Gratton .30 .75
15 Bob Halkidis .15 .40
16 Roman Hamrlik .40 1.00
17 Ben Hankinson .15 .40
18 Petr Klima .15 .40
19 Brantt Myhres .15 .40
20 Adrien Plavsic .15 .40
21 Rudy Poeschek .20 .50
22 Daren Puppa .50 1.25
23 Alexander Selivanov .40 1.00
24 Alexander Semak .15 .40
25 John Tucker .20 .50
26 Jason Wiemer .30 .75
27 Paul Ysebaert .15 .40
28 Rob Zamuner .15 .40
29 Team Photo .40 1.00

1994-95 Lightning Postcards

These oversized postcards were issued by the Lightning as promotional giveaways at team events. The postcards were unnumbered, and thus are listed below in alphabetical order.

COMPLETE SET (20) 8.00 20.00
1 Mikael Andersson .30 .75
2 Brian Bradley .40 1.00
3 Shawn Burr .30 .75
4 Terry Crisp .20 .50
5 Cory Cross .30 .75
6 John Cullen .30 .75
7 Phil Esposito .75 2.00
8 Tony Esposito .75 2.00
9 Chris Gratton .40 1.00
10 Roman Hamrlik .40 1.00
11 Bill Houlder .30 .75
12 Daymond Langkow .75 2.00
13 Brantt Myhres .30 .75
14 Daren Puppa .40 1.00
15 Chris Reichart .30 .75
16 Alexander Selivanov .30 .75
17 David Shaw .30 .75
18 Jason Wiemer .30 .75
19 Paul Ysebaert .30 .75
20 Rob Zamuner .30 .75

1995-96 Lightning Team Issue

This 21-card set of the Tampa Bay Lightning measured approximately 3 3/4" by 9" and featured color action player photos with player information printed below. The cards were unnumbered and checklisted below in alphabetical order.

COMPLETE SET (21) 8.00 20.00
1 Mikael Andersson .40 1.00
2 Brian Bellows .40 1.00
3 J.C. Bergeron .50 1.25
4 Brian Bradley .50 1.25
5 Shawn Burr .40 1.00
6 Enrico Ciccone .40 1.00
7 Cory Cross .40 1.00
8 John Cullen .40 1.00
9 Aaron Gavey .40 1.00
10 Chris Gratton .60 1.50
11 Roman Hamrlik .50 1.25
12 Bill Houlder .40 1.00
13 Petr Klima .40 1.00
14 Rudy Poeschek .40 1.00
15 Daren Puppa .50 1.25
16 Alexander Selivanov .40 1.00
17 David Shaw .40 1.00
18 John Tucker .40 1.00
19 Jason Wiemer .40 1.00
20 Paul Ysebaert .40 1.00
21 Rob Zamuner .40 1.00

2002-03 Lightning Team Issue

These oversized (4X8) blank-backed cards were issued by the Lightning. The checklist below is incomplete. If you have information on distribution or additional cards, please contact hockeymag@beckett.com.

COMPLETE SET
1 Nikita Alexeev .40 1.00
2 Dave Andreychuk .75 2.00
3 Dan Boyle .75 2.00
4 Chris Dingman .40 1.00
5 Nikolai Khabibulin .75 2.00
6 Pavel Kubina .40 1.00
7 Vincent Lecavalier 2.00 5.00
8 Brad Lukowich .40 1.00
9 Fredrik Modin .40 1.00
10 Brad Richards 1.25 3.00
11 Andre Roy .40 1.00
12 Martin St-Louis .75 2.00

2003-04 Lightning Team Issue

COMPLETE SET (36) 15.00 30.00
1 Cover Card .02 .10
2 Team Card .02 .10
3 John TortorellaÂ€O .20 .50
4 Craig Ramsay ACO .20 .50
5 Jeff Reese ACO .20 .50
6 Nigel KirwanÂÂÂCO .20 .50
7 Paul KennedyÂÂÂNN .20 .50
8 Rick PeckhamÂÂÂNN .20 .50
9 Phil EspositoÂÂÂNN .75 2.00
10 Vincent Lecavalier 2.00 5.00
11 Jassen Cullimore .40 1.00
12 Ben Clymer .40 1.00
13 Martin Cibak .40 1.00
14 Eric Perrin .75 2.00
15 Brian Bradley Alumni .40 1.00
16 Chris Dingman .40 1.00
17 Pavel Kubina .40 1.00
18 John Tucker Alumni .40 1.00
19 Alexander Svitov .40 1.00
20 Ruslan Fedotenko .40 1.00
21 Brad Richards 1.50 4.00
22 Cory Sarich .40 1.00
23 Dan Boyle .40 1.00
24 Shane Willis .40 1.00
25 Dave Andreychuk .40 1.00
26 Martin St. Louis 1.25 3.00
27 Tim Taylor .40 1.00
28 Sheldon Keefe .40 1.00
29 Dmitry Afanasenkov .40 1.00
30 Fredrik Modin .40 1.00
31 Nikolai Khabibulin .75 2.00
32 Andre Roy .75 2.00
33 Brad Lukowich .40 1.00
34 Nolan Pratt .40 1.00
35 Cory Stillman .40 1.00
36 Daren Puppa Alumni .40 1.00

2005-06 Lightning Team Issue

These cards were issued by the Lightning at team events and by mail. The checklist is known to be incomplete. If you have additional information, please forward it to hockeymag@beckett.com. Thanks to Andy Hatzos for this partial list.

1 John Tortorella CO .40 1.00
2 Craig RamsayÂACO .40 1.00
3 Jeff Reese ACO .40 1.00
4 Vincent Lecavalier 2.00 5.00
5 Darryl Sydor .75 2.00
6 Chris Dingman .75 2.00
7 Vaclav Prospal .75 2.00
8 Dan Boyle .75 2.00
9 Martin St. Louis 1.25 3.00
10 Tim Taylor .75 2.00
11 Nolan Pratt .75 2.00

2006-07 Lightning Postcards

COMPLETE SET (23) 15.00 30.00
1 Logo Card .10 .25
2 Dmitry Afanasenkov .40 1.00
3 Nikita Alexeev .40 1.00
4 Dan Boyle .40 1.00
5 Ryan Craig .40 1.00
6 Marc Denis .60 1.50
7 Ruslan Fedotenko .40 1.00
8 Doug Janik .40 1.00
9 Johan Holmqvist .75 2.00
10 Andreas Karlsson .40 1.00
11 Filip Kuba .40 1.00
12 Vincent Lecavalier 2.00 5.00
13 Eric Perrin .40 1.00
14 Nolan Pratt .40 1.00
15 Vaclav Prospal .40 1.00
16 Paul Ranger .40 1.00
17 Brad Richards 1.25 3.00
18 Luke Richardson .40 1.00
19 Andre Roy .40 1.00
20 Cory Sarich .40 1.00
21 Martin St. Louis 1.25 3.00
22 Nick Tarnasky .40 1.00
23 Tim Taylor .40 1.00

2010-11 Limited

176-224 ROOKIE AU PRINT RUN 299
1 Ryan Miller 2.00 5.00
2 Henrik Sedin 2.00 5.00
3 Alex Ovechkin 8.00 20.00
4 Shane Doan 1.50 4.00
5 Phil Kessel 2.50 6.00
6 Marty Turco 2.00 5.00
7 Sidney Crosby 8.00 20.00
8 Daniel Sedin 2.00 5.00
9 Teemu Selanne 4.00 10.00
10 Kyle Okposo 2.00 5.00
11 Martin Brodeur 4.00 10.00
12 Nicklas Backstrom 3.00 8.00
13 Patrick Marleau 2.00 5.00
14 Sam Gagner 1.50 4.00
15 Tomas Vokoun 1.50 4.00
16 Jonathan Bernier 2.00 5.00
17 Steven Stamkos 4.00 10.00
18 Zach Parise 2.00 5.00
19 Claude Giroux 2.00 5.00
20 Erik Johnson 1.25 3.00
21 Roberto Luongo 2.00 5.00
22 Joe Thornton 2.00 5.00
23 Henrik Zetterberg 2.50 6.00
24 Dion Phaneuf 2.00 5.00
25 Marc Savard 1.25 3.00
26 Carey Price 8.00 20.00
27 Brad Richards 2.00 5.00
28 Marian Hossa 1.50 4.00
29 Dany Heatley 1.50 4.00
30 Chris Mason 1.50 4.00
31 Tuukka Rask 2.00 5.00
32 Evgeni Malkin 6.00 15.00
33 James Neal 2.00 5.00
34 Simon Gagne 2.00 5.00
35 Mike Modano 3.00 8.00
36 Ilya Bryzgalov 1.50 4.00
37 Pavel Datsyuk 2.50 6.00
38 Thomas Vanek 2.00 5.00
39 Marian Gaborik 2.50 6.00
40 Brent Burns 2.50 6.00
41 Jaroslav Halak 2.00 5.00
42 Paul Stastny 2.00 5.00
43 Michael Cammalleri 2.00 5.00
44 Ilya Kovalchuk 2.00 5.00
45 Nikolai Khabibulin 1.50 4.00
46 Anze Kopitar 3.00 8.00
47 Dustin Byfuglien 2.00 5.00
48 Daniel Alfredsson 2.00 5.00
49 Sergei Gonchar 1.25 3.00
50 Wojtek Wolski 1.25 3.00
51 Henrik Lundqvist 3.00 8.00
52 Eric Staal 2.50 6.00
53 Drew Doughty 2.00 5.00
54 Andrei Markov 2.00 5.00
55 Duncan Keith 2.00 5.00
56 Jonas Gustavsson 2.50 6.00
57 Vincent Lecavalier 1.50 4.00
50 Nicklas Lidstrom 2.00 5.00
59 Brandon Sutter 1.50 4.00
60 Zdeno Chara 1.50 4.00
61 Marc-Andre Fleury 3.00 8.00
62 Ryan Getzlaf 3.00 8.00
63 Alexander Frolov 1.25 3.00
64 Steve Mason 1.50 4.00
65 Ales Hemsky 1.50 4.00
66 Niklas Backstrom 2.00 5.00
67 Jonathan Toews 4.00 10.00
68 Rick Nash 2.00 5.00
69 Tomas Plekanec 2.00 5.00
70 Loui Eriksson 1.50 4.00

71 Jimmy Howard 2.50 6.00
72 Mike Richards 2.00 5.00
73 Jarome Iginla 2.00 5.00
74 Pekka Rinne 2.50 6.00
75 Mikko Koivu 2.00 5.00
76 Craig Anderson 2.00 5.00
77 Jeff Carter 2.00 5.00
78 Tyler Myers 2.00 5.00
79 Ryan Kesler 2.00 5.00
80 Mike Green 2.00 5.00
81 Miikka Kiprusoff 1.50 4.00
82 Jason Spezza 1.25 3.00
83 Shea Weber 1.50 4.00
84 Chris Pronger 1.50 4.00
85 Antti Niemi 1.50 4.00
86 Semyon Varlamov 2.00 5.00
87 Matt Duchene 2.00 5.00
88 Nathan Horton 1.50 4.00
89 Guillaume Latendresse 1.50 4.00
90 Stephen Weiss 1.50 4.00
91 Cam Ward 2.00 5.00
92 John Tavares 4.00 10.00
93 Patrick Kane 4.00 10.00
94 Wayne Simmonds 2.50 6.00
95 Jordan Staal 2.00 5.00
96 Michael Leighton 1.50 4.00
97 T.J. Oshie 3.00 8.00
98 Corey Perry 2.00 5.00
99 Tyler Bozak 2.00 5.00
100 Erik Karlsson 4.00 10.00
101 Kari Lehtonen 1.50 4.00
102 Joe Pavelski 2.00 5.00
103 Andrei Loktionov 1.50 4.00
104 Scott Gomez 1.50 4.00
105 Nikolay Zherdev 1.25 3.00
106 Nikita Filatov 1.25 3.00
107 Patrik Elias 2.00 5.00
108 Peter Mueller 1.50 4.00
109 Saku Koivu 2.00 5.00
110 Milan Lucic 2.00 5.00
111 Troy Brouwer 2.00 5.00
112 Ville Leino 1.50 4.00
113 Zach Bogosian 1.50 4.00
114 Bobby Ryan 2.00 5.00
115 Colton Orr 1.25 3.00
116 Dan Hamhuis 1.50 4.00
117 Dan Ellis 1.50 4.00
118 Tim Connolly 1.25 3.00
119 Travis Zajac 1.50 4.00
120 Dwayne Roloson 1.50 4.00
121 Milan Hejduk 1.50 4.00
122 Brian Elliott 1.50 4.00
123 Mike Comrie 1.25 3.00
124 Niclas Bergfors 1.50 4.00
125 Matthew Lombardi 1.25 3.00
126 Mario Lemieux L 5.00 12.00
127 Trevor Linden L 1.50 4.00
129 Terry O'Reilly L 1.25 3.00
130 Luc Robitaille L 1.50 4.00
131 Denis Savard L 2.00 5.00
132 Doug Gilmour L 2.00 5.00
133 Brad Park L 1.25 3.00
134 Felix Potvin L 2.50 6.00
135 Eric Lindros L 2.50 6.00
136 Jim Craig L 1.25 3.00
137 Darryl Sittler L 1.25 3.00
138 Bobby Rousseau L 1.25 3.00
139 Tony Esposito L 1.50 4.00
140 Normand Leveille L 2.00 5.00
141 Tom Barrasso L 1.50 4.00
142 Curtis Joseph L 2.00 5.00
143 Gilbert Perreault L 1.50 4.00
144 Dan Bouchard L 1.25 3.00
145 Guy Lafleur L 2.00 5.00
146 Ken Linseman L 1.50 4.00
147 Ed Belfour L 1.50 4.00
148 Jean Beliveau L 1.50 4.00
149 Simon Nolet L 1.25 3.00
150 Dale Hawerchuk L 2.00 5.00
151 Brian Leetch L 1.50 4.00
152 Cam Neely L 1.50 4.00
153 Glenn Hall L 1.50 4.00
154 Ron Hextall L 2.00 5.00
155 Joe Sakic L 2.50 6.00
156 Phil Esposito L 2.50 6.00
157 Yvan Cournoyer L 1.50 4.00
158 Patrick Roy L 4.00 10.00
159 Gerry Cheevers L 1.50 4.00
160 Al Arbour L 1.25 3.00
161 Joe Nieuwendyk L 1.50 4.00
162 Mike Bossy L 1.50 4.00
163 Johnny Bucyk L 1.50 4.00
164 Brett Hull L 2.50 6.00
165 Bobby Hull L 1.50 4.00
166 Ray Bourque L 2.50 6.00
167 Rogie Vachon L 2.00 5.00
168 Reggie Lemelin L 2.00 5.00
169 Richard Brodeur L 1.50 4.00
170 Rick Middleton L 2.00 5.00
171 Peter Stastny L 1.25 3.00
172 Stan Mikita L 2.00 5.00
173 Henri Richard L 1.50 4.00
174 Brendan Shanahan L 2.00 5.00
175 Steve Yzerman L 4.00 10.00
176 P.K. Subban AU RC 25.00 50.00
177 Eric Tangradi AU RC 6.00 15.00
178 Kevin Shattenkirk AU RC 12.00 30.00
179 Brandon Yip AU RC 6.00 15.00
180 Jamie McBain AU RC 6.00 15.00
181 Jared Cowen AU RC 6.00 15.00
182 Brandon Pirri AU RC 6.00 15.00
183 Jonas Holos AU RC 6.00 15.00
184 Zac Dalpe AU RC 6.00 15.00
185 Justin Mercier AU RC 6.00 15.00
186 Brayden Irwin AU RC 6.00 15.00
187 Nick Bonino AU RC 8.00 20.00
188 John McCarthy AU RC 6.00 15.00
189 Philip Larsen AU RC 6.00 15.00
190 Bobby Butler AU RC 6.00 15.00
191 Henrik Karlsson AU RC 6.00 15.00
192 Casey Wellman AU RC 6.00 15.00
193 Tommy Wingels AU RC 6.00 15.00
194 Robin Lehner AU RC 12.00 30.00
195 Marcus Johansson AU RC 10.00 25.00
196 Maxim Noreau AU RC 5.00 12.00
197 Nick Palmieri AU RC 6.00 15.00
198 Dustin Tokarski AU RC 6.00 15.00
199 Cam Fowler AU RC 8.00 20.00
200 Jake Muzzin AU RC 6.00 15.00
201 Justin Falk AU RC 5.00 12.00
202 Matt Taormina AU RC 6.00 15.00
203 Dana Tyrell AU RC 6.00 15.00
204 Sergei Bobrovsky AU RC 15.00 40.00
205 Mark Olver AU RC 6.00 15.00
206 T.J. Brodie AU RC 6.00 15.00
207 Tyler Seguin AU RC 35.00 60.00
208 Nazem Kadri AU RC 15.00 40.00
209 Jordan Eberle AU RC 15.00 40.00
210 Magnus Paajarvi AU RC 8.00 20.00
211 Nino Niederreiter AU RC 8.00 20.00
212 Jordan Caron AU RC 10.00 25.00
213 Derek Stepan AU RC 12.00 30.00
214 Luke Adam AU RC 6.00 15.00
215 Nick Leddy AU RC 6.00 15.00
216 Alexander Burmistrov AU RC 6.00 15.00
217 Zach Hamill AU RC 6.00 15.00
218 Nick Johnson AU RC 5.00 12.00
219 Oliver Ekman-Larsson AU RC 10.00 25.00
220 Kyle Clifford AU RC 6.00 15.00
221 Brayden Schenn AU RC 10.00 25.00
222 Anders Lindback AU RC 6.00 15.00
223 Taylor Hall AU RC 30.00 80.00
224 Steve Carlson AU 12.00 30.00
225 Dave Hanson AU 12.00 30.00

2010-11 Limited Silver Spotlight

*1-125 SILVER/49: .8X TO 2X BASIC CARDS
*126-175 SILVER LEG/49: .8X TO 2X BASE
1-175 STATED PRINT RUN 49
*176-224 ROOKIE AU: .5X TO 1.2X AU RC
176-224 ROOKIE AU PRINT RUN 30-97
12 Nicklas Backstrom 6.00 15.00
74 Pekka Rinne 5.00 12.00
183 Jonas Holos AU/50 15.00 40.00
223 Taylor Hall AU/50 60.00 120.00

2010-11 Limited Back To The Future

STATED PRINT RUN 199 SER.#'d SETS
1 D.Savard/J.Toews 4.00 10.00
2 C.Joseph/J.Gustavsson 2.50 6.00
3 C.Neely/T.Seguin 6.00 15.00
4 B.Leetch/D.Doughty 4.00 10.00
5 B.Clarke/M.Richards 4.00 10.00
6 T.Esposito/M.Turco 2.00 5.00
7 J.Iginla/T.Hall 6.00 15.00
8 P.Stastny/P.Stastny 2.00 5.00
9 R.Bourque/Z.Chara 3.00 8.00
10 P.Roy/C.Price 8.00 20.00
11 D.Maruk/A.Ovechkin 8.00 20.00
12 J.Beliveau/V.Lecavalier 2.00 5.00
13 J.Craig/R.Miller 2.00 5.00
14 M.Lemieux/E.Malkin 6.00 15.00
15 T.Barrasso/M.Fleury 3.00 8.00
16 B.Park/M.Staal 2.00 5.00
17 G.Cheevers/T.Thomas 2.00 5.00
18 D.Ciccarelli/A.Semin 2.00 5.00
19 B.Trottier/J.Tavares 4.00 10.00
20 C.Hodge/C.Schneider 1.50 4.00
21 D.Bouchard/C.Anderson 2.00 5.00
22 R.Vachon/J.Bernier 2.50 6.00
23 Y.Cournoyer/M.Paajarvi 2.00 5.00
24 P.LaFontaine/D.Roy 2.00 5.00
25 G.Hall/J.Halak 8.00 20.00

2010-11 Limited Back To The Future Signatures

STATED PRINT RUN 25 SER.#'d SETS
1 D.Savard/J.Toews 40.00 100.00
2 Joseph/Gustavsson 15.00 30.00
3 C.Neely/T.Seguin 40.00 100.00
4 B.Leetch/D.Doughty 12.00 30.00
5 B.Clarke/M.Richards 15.00 40.00
6 T.Esposito/M.Turco 15.00 40.00
7 J.Iginla/T.Hall EX 40.00 100.00
8 Stastny/Stastny 12.00 30.00
9 R.Bourque/Z.Chara 20.00 50.00
10 P.Roy/C.Price 60.00 120.00
11 D.Maruk/A.Ovechkin EX 40.00 100.00
12 J.Beliveau/V.Lecavalier 25.00 60.00
13 J.Craig/R.Miller 15.00 40.00
14 M.Lemieux/E.Malkin 75.00 150.00
15 T.Barrasso/M.Fleury 40.00 80.00
16 Park/Staal 12.00 30.00
17 Cheevers/T.Thomas 12.00 30.00
18 Ciccarelli/Semin 12.00 30.00
19 B.Trottier/J.Tavares 25.00 60.00
20 Hodge/Schneider 12.00 30.00
21 Bouchard/Anderson EX 20.00 50.00
22 R.Vachon/J.Bernier 15.00 40.00
23 Y.Cournoyer/M.Paajarvi 30.00 80.00
24 P.LaFontaine/D.Roy EX 25.00 60.00
25 G.Hall/J.Halak 12.00 30.00

2010-11 Limited Banner Season

STATED PRINT RUN 199 SER.#'d SETS
*GOLD/24: 1X TO 2.5X BASIC
*SILVER/49: .6X TO 1.5X BASIC
1 Alex Ovechkin 8.00 20.00
2 Anze Kopitar 3.00 8.00
3 Cam Ward 2.00 5.00
4 Corey Perry 2.00 5.00
5 Craig Anderson 2.00 5.00
6 Daniel Alfredsson 2.00 5.00
7 Drew Doughty 2.00 5.00
8 Evgeni Malkin 6.00 15.00
9 Henrik Sedin 2.00 5.00
10 Ilya Kovalchuk 2.00 5.00
11 Jarome Iginla 2.00 5.00
12 Jason Spezza 1.25 3.00
13 Jonathan Quick 3.00 8.00
14 Marc-Andre Fleury 3.00 8.00
15 Martin Brodeur 4.00 10.00
16 Martin St. Louis 2.00 5.00
17 Nicklas Lidstrom 2.00 5.00
18 Rick Nash 2.00 5.00
19 Teemu Selanne 4.00 10.00
20 Tim Thomas 1.50 4.00

2010-11 Limited Banner Season Materials

STATED PRINT RUN 10-99
1 Alex Ovechkin/10
2 Anze Kopitar 8.00 20.00
4 Corey Perry 5.00 12.00
5 Craig Anderson 5.00 12.00
6 Daniel Alfredsson 5.00 12.00
7 Drew Doughty/49 5.00 12.00
8 Evgeni Malkin 6.00 15.00
9 Henrik Sedin 6.00 15.00
10 Ilya Kovalchuk 5.00 12.00
11 Jarome Iginla 5.00 12.00
12 Jason Spezza 3.00 8.00
13 Jonathan Quick/50 8.00 20.00
14 Marc-Andre Fleury 8.00 20.00
15 Martin Brodeur 6.00 15.00
16 Martin St. Louis/50 5.00 12.00
17 Nicklas Lidstrom/50 5.00 12.00
18 Rick Nash/25 6.00 15.00
19 Teemu Selanne 10.00 25.00
20 Tim Thomas/10

2010-11 Limited Banner Season Materials Prime

*PRIME/25: .8X TO 2X BASIC JSY
STATED PRINT RUN 25 SER.#'d SETS
1 Alex Ovechkin 15.00 40.00
20 Tim Thomas 12.00 30.00

2010-11 Limited Banner Season Materials Signatures

STATED PRINT RUN 2-49
2 Anze Kopitar 20.00 50.00
4 Corey Perry 12.00 30.00
6 Daniel Alfredsson 12.00 30.00
7 Drew Doughty 12.00 30.00
8 Evgeni Malkin 40.00 100.00
9 Henrik Sedin 12.00 30.00
10 Ilya Kovalchuk 12.00 30.00
11 Jarome Iginla 12.00 30.00
12 Jason Spezza 10.00 25.00
13 Jonathan Quick/25 30.00 60.00
14 Marc-Andre Fleury 20.00 50.00
15 Martin Brodeur 25.00 60.00
16 Martin St. Louis 12.00 30.00
17 Nicklas Lidstrom 12.00 30.00
18 Rick Nash 12.00 30.00
19 Teemu Selanne 25.00 60.00
20 Tim Thomas 25.00 50.00

2010-11 Limited Banner Season Materials Signatures Prime

*PRIME/25: .5X TO 1.2X MAT.SIG
STATED PRINT RUN 10-25
1 Alex Ovechkin 50.00 125.00
14 Marc-Andre Fleury 25.00 60.00
18 Rick Nash 25.00 60.00

2010-11 Limited Banner Season Signatures

STATED PRINT RUN 10-25
1 Alex Ovechkin 30.00 80.00
2 Anze Kopitar 12.00 30.00
3 Cam Ward 8.00 20.00
4 Corey Perry 8.00 20.00
5 Craig Anderson 8.00 20.00
6 Daniel Alfredsson
7 Drew Doughty 8.00 20.00
8 Evgeni Malkin 20.00 50.00
9 Henrik Sedin 8.00 20.00
10 Ilya Kovalchuk
11 Jarome Iginla 8.00 20.00
12 Jason Spezza EXCH 5.00 12.00
13 Jonathan Quick 12.00 30.00
14 Marc-Andre Fleury 12.00 30.00
15 Martin Brodeur 25.00 60.00
16 Martin St. Louis/10
17 Nicklas Lidstrom 12.00 30.00
18 Rick Nash 12.00 30.00
19 Teemu Selanne 12.00 30.00
20 Tim Thomas 12.00 30.00

2010-11 Limited Brothers In Arms

STATED PRINT RUN 199 SER.#'d SETS
1 J.Hiller/C.McElhinney 4.00 10.00
3 T.Rask/T.Thomas 6.00 15.00
8 C.Anderson/P.Budaj 5.00 12.00
11 C.Mason/O.Pavelec 5.00 12.00
12 J.Deslauriers/N.Khabibulin 4.00 10.00
15 R.Luongo/C.Schneider 8.00 20.00
24 J.Gustavsson/J.Giguere 6.00 15.00

2010-11 Limited Jumbo Materials

STATED PRINT RUN 40-99
1 Teemu Selanne/40 6.00 15.00
2 Tyler Seguin 15.00 40.00
4 Jarome Iginla 4.00 10.00
5 Eric Staal 5.00 12.00
8 Matt Duchene 4.00 10.00
9 James Neal 4.00 10.00
10 Pavel Datsyuk 5.00 12.00
11 Taylor Hall 12.00 30.00
12 Jordan Eberle 8.00 20.00
14 Niklas Backstrom/49 4.00 10.00
15 Carey Price 15.00 40.00
16 Marian Gaborik 5.00 12.00
17 Daniel Alfredsson 4.00 10.00
18 Jeff Carter 5.00 12.00
19 Sidney Crosby 8.00 20.00
20 Patrick Roy 10.00 25.00
21 Steven Stamkos 12.00 30.00
22 Mario Lemieux 12.00 30.00
23 Henrik Sedin 4.00 10.00
24 Phil Kessel 5.00 12.00

2010-11 Limited Jumbo Materials Jersey Numbers

STATED PRINT RUN 8-99
1 Teemu Selanne/35 10.00 25.00
2 Tyler Seguin 20.00 50.00
4 Jarome Iginla 5.00 12.00
8 Matt Duchene/49 8.00 20.00
9 James Neal 4.00 10.00
10 Pavel Datsyuk 6.00 15.00
11 Taylor Hall 15.00 40.00
12 Jordan Eberle 12.00 30.00
14 Niklas Backstrom 5.00 12.00
15 Carey Price 20.00 50.00
16 Marian Gaborik 6.00 15.00
17 Daniel Alfredsson 5.00 12.00
18 Jeff Carter 5.00 12.00
19 Sidney Crosby 10.00 25.00
20 Patrick Roy 12.00 30.00
21 Steven Stamkos/25 15.00 40.00
22 Mario Lemieux 15.00 40.00
23 Henrik Sedin 5.00 12.00
24 Phil Kessel 6.00 15.00
25 Alex Ovechkin/8

2010-11 Limited Jumbo Materials Jersey Numbers Signatures

STATED PRINT RUN 5-50
2 Tyler Seguin 30.00 80.00
3 Ryan Miller 10.00 25.00
4 Jarome Iginla 10.00 25.00
8 Matt Duchene/30 12.00 30.00
9 James Neal 12.00 30.00
10 Pavel Datsyuk 15.00 40.00
11 Taylor Hall 40.00 100.00
12 Jordan Eberle 30.00 80.00
14 Niklas Backstrom 8.00 20.00
15 Carey Price/10
16 Marian Gaborik 12.00 30.00
17 Daniel Alfredsson 12.00 30.00
18 Jeff Carter/50 12.00 30.00
19 Sidney Crosby 75.00 150.00
20 Patrick Roy 30.00 80.00
21 Steven Stamkos 25.00 60.00
22 Mario Lemieux/5
23 Henrik Sedin 8.00 20.00
24 Phil Kessel 15.00 40.00
25 Alex Ovechkin/8

2010-11 Limited Jumbo Materials Signatures

STATED PRINT RUN 8-49
1 Teemu Selanne 15.00 40.00
2 Tyler Seguin 15.00 40.00
4 Jarome Iginla 10.00 25.00
7 Patrick Kane/30 25.00 60.00
8 Matt Duchene 10.00 25.00
9 James Neal 10.00 25.00
10 Pavel Datsyuk 12.00 30.00
11 Taylor Hall 40.00 100.00
12 Jordan Eberle 20.00 50.00
13 Drew Doughty/22 12.00 30.00
14 Niklas Backstrom 10.00 25.00
15 Carey Price 40.00 100.00
16 Marian Gaborik 12.00 30.00
18 Jeff Carter 10.00 25.00
19 Sidney Crosby 75.00 150.00
20 Patrick Roy 50.00 100.00
21 Steven Stamkos 20.00 50.00
22 Mario Lemieux 30.00 80.00
23 Henrik Sedin 12.00 30.00
24 Phil Kessel 12.00 30.00
25 Alex Ovechkin/8

2010-11 Limited Material Monikers

STATED PRINT RUN 5-25
1 Ales Hemsky/10
4 Brad Richards 12.00 30.00
5 Chris Pronger 10.00 25.00
6 Claude Giroux 12.00 30.00
7 Corey Perry 12.00 30.00
8 Daniel Alfredsson 12.00 30.00
9 Daniel Sedin 12.00 30.00
10 Dany Heatley 10.00 25.00
12 Derek Roy 12.00 30.00
13 Dion Phaneuf 12.00 30.00
15 Dustin Penner 10.00 25.00
17 Eric Staal/10
18 Erik Karlsson 15.00 40.00
19 Evgeni Malkin 40.00 100.00
20 Henrik Lundqvist 20.00 50.00
21 Henrik Sedin 12.00 30.00
22 Ilya Bryzgalov 10.00 25.00
23 Ilya Kovalchuk 20.00 40.00
24 Jarome Iginla/5
25 Jeff Carter 15.00 40.00
26 Joe Thornton 15.00 40.00
27 John Tavares 25.00 60.00
28 Jonas Hiller
29 Marc-Andre Fleury/10
30 Marian Gaborik 15.00 40.00
31 Martin Brodeur 25.00 60.00
32 Martin St. Louis 12.00 30.00
33 Matt Duchene/10
34 Michael Frolik 8.00 20.00
36 Nicklas Lidstrom
38 Pavel Datsyuk 15.00 40.00
39 Paul Stastny 12.00 30.00
40 Pekka Rinne
41 Phil Kessel 15.00 40.00
42 Rick Nash 12.00 30.00
43 Ryan Miller 12.00 30.00
44 Semyon Varlamov 12.00 30.00
45 Sidney Crosby 100.00 200.00
46 Steven Stamkos 25.00 60.00
47 Tomas Vokoun 10.00 25.00
48 Tyler Bozak 12.00 30.00
50 Zach Parise 12.00 30.00

2010-11 Limited Monikers Gold

STATED PRINT RUN 5-50
1 Ryan Miller 8.00 20.00
4 Shane Doan 6.00 15.00
5 Phil Kessel/25 10.00 25.00
8 Daniel Sedin 8.00 20.00
13 Patrick Marleau 8.00 20.00
14 Sam Gagner/25 6.00 15.00
15 Tomas Vokoun 6.00 15.00
16 Jonathan Bernier 8.00 20.00
17 Steven Stamkos 20.00 50.00
18 Zach Parise 10.00 25.00
19 Claude Giroux 8.00 20.00
22 Joe Thornton 8.00 20.00
26 Carey Price 30.00 80.00
27 Brad Richards 8.00 20.00
28 Marian Hossa 6.00 15.00
33 James Neal 8.00 20.00
34 Simon Gagne 8.00 20.00
35 Mike Modano 12.00 30.00
36 Ilya Bryzgalov 6.00 15.00
37 Pavel Datsyuk 12.00 30.00
38 Thomas Vanek 8.00 20.00
39 Marian Gaborik/25 10.00 25.00
41 Jaroslav Halak 15.00 40.00
42 Paul Stastny 12.00 30.00
43 Michael Cammalleri 8.00 20.00
46 Anze Kopitar 12.00 30.00
47 Dustin Byfuglien 10.00 25.00
50 Wojtek Wolski 5.00 12.00
51 Henrik Lundqvist 12.00 30.00
52 Eric Staal/25 10.00 25.00
53 Drew Doughty 8.00 20.00
56 Jonas Gustavsson 10.00 25.00
57 Vincent Lecavalier 6.00 15.00
59 Brandon Sutter 6.00 15.00
61 Marc-Andre Fleury 12.00 30.00
62 Ryan Getzlaf 12.00 30.00
64 Steve Mason 6.00 15.00
65 Ales Hemsky/25 12.00 30.00
66 Niklas Backstrom 8.00 20.00
68 Rick Nash 8.00 20.00
71 Jimmy Howard 10.00 25.00
72 Mike Richards 8.00 20.00
74 Pekka Rinne 10.00 25.00
76 Craig Anderson/25 8.00 20.00
77 Jeff Carter 8.00 20.00
78 Tyler Myers 8.00 20.00
79 Ryan Kesler 10.00 25.00
83 Shea Weber 6.00 15.00
84 Chris Pronger 6.00 15.00
86 Semyon Varlamov 15.00 40.00
89 Guillaume Latendresse/25 6.00 15.00
90 Stephen Weiss 6.00 15.00
91 Cam Ward 8.00 20.00
92 John Tavares 15.00 40.00
93 Patrick Kane/25 15.00 40.00
94 Wayne Simmonds 10.00 25.00
95 Jordan Staal 8.00 20.00
96 Michael Leighton 6.00 15.00
97 T.J. Oshie 12.00 30.00
98 Corey Perry/25 8.00 20.00
99 Tyler Bozak 8.00 20.00
100 Erik Karlsson 12.00 30.00
101 Kari Lehtonen 6.00 15.00
102 Joe Pavelski 8.00 20.00
104 Scott Gomez 6.00 15.00
113 Zach Bogosian 6.00 15.00
114 Bobby Ryan 8.00 20.00
115 Colton Orr 15.00 40.00
116 Joe Thornton 6.00 15.00
122 Brian Elliott 6.00 15.00
132 Doug Gilmour/25 10.00 25.00
133 Brad Park/25 6.00 15.00
134 Felix Potvin/25 12.00 30.00
135 Eric Lindros/25 30.00 60.00
136 Jim Craig/25 8.00 20.00
137 Darryl Sittler/25 8.00 20.00
138 Bobby Rousseau/25 6.00 15.00
140 Normand Leveille/25 10.00 25.00
142 Curtis Joseph/25 25.00 60.00
144 Dan Bouchard/25 6.00 15.00
145 Guy Lafleur/25 20.00 50.00
147 Ed Belfour/25 20.00 40.00
148 Jean Beliveau/25 50.00 100.00
149 Simon Nolet/25 15.00 30.00
150 Dale Hawerchuk/25 10.00 25.00
151 Brian Leetch/25 8.00 20.00
152 Cam Neely/25 8.00 20.00
154 Ron Hextall/25 15.00 40.00
155 Joe Sakic/25 15.00 40.00
156 Phil Esposito/25 12.00 30.00
157 Yvan Cournoyer/25 12.00 30.00
158 Patrick Roy/25 60.00 120.00
159 Gerry Cheevers/25 25.00 60.00
160 Al Arbour/25 6.00 15.00
161 Joe Nieuwendyk/25 8.00 20.00
162 Mike Bossy/25 8.00 20.00
163 Johnny Bucyk/25 EXCH 8.00 20.00
166 Ray Bourque/25 12.00 30.00
167 Rogie Vachon/25 10.00 25.00
168 Reggie Lemelin/25 12.00 30.00
169 Richard Brodeur/25 8.00 20.00
170 Rick Middleton/25 10.00 25.00
171 Peter Stastny/25 25.00 60.00
173 Henri Richard/25 12.00 30.00

2010-11 Limited Retired Numbers

STATED PRINT RUN 199 SER.#'d SETS
*GOLD/24: 1X TO 2.5X BASIC INSERTS
*SILVER/49: .6X TO 1.5X BASIC INSERTS
1 Ray Bourque 3.00 8.00
2 Joe Sakic 3.00 8.00
3 Marcel Dionne 2.50 6.00
4 Johnny Bucyk 2.00 5.00
5 Brett Hull 3.00 8.00
6 Patrick Roy 5.00 12.00
7 Mario Lemieux 6.00 15.00
8 Bobby Clarke 2.00 5.00
9 Elmer Lach 1.50 4.00
10 Ed Giacomin 3.00 8.00
11 Glenn Hall 2.00 5.00
12 Dale Hawerchuk 2.50 6.00
13 Guy Lafleur 2.50 6.00
15 Trevor Linden 2.00 5.00
16 Henri Richard 2.00 5.00
17 Luc Robitaille 2.00 5.00
18 Denis Savard 2.50 6.00
19 Steve Yzerman 5.00 12.00
20 Lanny McDonald 2.00 5.00

2010-11 Limited Retired Numbers Materials

STATED PRINT RUN 99 SER.#'d SETS
1 Ray Bourque 8.00 20.00
2 Joe Sakic 8.00 20.00
3 Marcel Dionne 5.00 12.00
4 Johnny Bucyk 5.00 12.00
6 Patrick Roy 12.00 30.00
7 Mario Lemieux 15.00 40.00
17 Luc Robitaille 5.00 12.00
18 Denis Savard 6.00 15.00

2010-11 Limited Retired Numbers Materials Signatures

STATED PRINT RUN 49 SER.#'d SETS
1 Ray Bourque 20.00 50.00
2 Joe Sakic 20.00 50.00
3 Marcel Dionne 15.00 40.00
4 Johnny Bucyk 12.00 30.00
6 Patrick Roy 40.00 100.00
7 Mario Lemieux 50.00 100.00
17 Luc Robitaille 12.00 30.00
18 Denis Savard 15.00 40.00

2010-11 Limited Retired Numbers Signatures

STATED PRINT RUN 10-49
1 Ray Bourque/25 25.00 50.00
2 Joe Sakic/25 20.00 50.00
3 Marcel Dionne 10.00 25.00
4 Johnny Bucyk 10.00 25.00
5 Brett Hull 15.00 40.00
6 Patrick Roy/25 30.00 80.00
7 Mario Lemieux/25 50.00 100.00
8 Bobby Clarke 10.00 25.00
9 Elmer Lach 12.00 30.00
10 Ed Giacomin 12.00 30.00
11 Glenn Hall 10.00 25.00
12 Dale Hawerchuk 10.00 25.00
13 Guy Lafleur 12.00 30.00
15 Trevor Linden 20.00 50.00
16 Henri Richard 12.00 30.00
17 Luc Robitaille/24 12.00 30.00
18 Denis Savard/24 12.00 30.00
19 Steve Yzerman/10
20 Lanny McDonald 8.00 20.00

2010-11 Limited Select Signatures

STATED PRINT RUN 49-99
1 Normand Leveille 10.00 25.00
2 Brendan Shanahan/49 40.00 80.00
3 Joe Sakic/49 20.00 50.00
4 Mario Lemieux/49 40.00 100.00
5 Steve Yzerman/49 40.00 100.00
6 Glenn Hall 8.00 20.00
7 Manon Rheaume 15.00 40.00
8 Brad Park 6.00 15.00
9 Brett Hull/49 15.00 40.00
10 Al Arbour/94 6.00 15.00
11 Bobby Rousseau 6.00 15.00

2010-11 Limited Threads

STATED PRINT RUN 5-199
*PRIME/25: .8X TO 2X BASIC THREADS
1 Ryan Miller/99 4.00 10.00
2 Henrik Sedin 4.00 10.00
4 Shane Doan 3.00 8.00
5 Phil Kessel 5.00 12.00
7 Sidney Crosby 15.00 40.00
8 Daniel Sedin/99 4.00 10.00
9 Teemu Selanne/99 8.00 20.00
10 Kyle Okposo 4.00 10.00
11 Martin Brodeur 8.00 20.00
12 Nicklas Backstrom/15 8.00 20.00
13 Patrick Marleau 4.00 10.00
14 Sam Gagner/99 3.00 8.00
15 Tomas Vokoun 3.00 8.00
17 Steven Stamkos 6.00 15.00
18 Zach Parise/99 4.00 10.00
19 Claude Giroux/25 4.00 10.00
21 Roberto Luongo 4.00 10.00
22 Joe Thornton 4.00 10.00
23 Henrik Zetterberg 5.00 12.00
24 Dion Phaneuf 4.00 10.00
26 Carey Price 15.00 40.00
27 Brad Richards 4.00 10.00
28 Marian Hossa 3.00 8.00
29 Dany Heatley 3.00 8.00
31 Tuukka Rask 4.00 10.00
32 Evgeni Malkin 12.00 30.00
33 James Neal 4.00 10.00
36 Ilya Bryzgalov 3.00 8.00
37 Pavel Datsyuk 5.00 12.00
39 Marian Gaborik 5.00 12.00
42 Paul Stastny 4.00 10.00
43 Michael Cammalleri/5
44 Ilya Kovalchuk 4.00 10.00
45 Nikolai Khabibulin/99 3.00 8.00
46 Anze Kopitar 6.00 15.00
48 Daniel Alfredsson 4.00 10.00
51 Henrik Lundqvist 6.00 15.00
52 Eric Staal/99 5.00 12.00
53 Drew Doughty/99 4.00 10.00
55 Duncan Keith 4.00 10.00
56 Jonas Gustavsson 5.00 12.00
57 Vincent Lecavalier 3.00 8.00
58 Nicklas Lidstrom/99 4.00 10.00
60 Zdeno Chara 3.00 8.00
61 Marc-Andre Fleury 6.00 15.00
62 Ryan Getzlaf 6.00 15.00
64 Steve Mason 3.00 8.00
65 Ales Hemsky 3.00 8.00
66 Niklas Backstrom 4.00 10.00
67 Jonathan Toews/85 8.00 20.00
68 Rick Nash/99 4.00 10.00
69 Tomas Plekanec 4.00 10.00
70 Loui Eriksson 3.00 8.00
73 Jarome Iginla 4.00 10.00
74 Pekka Rinne 5.00 12.00
76 Craig Anderson 4.00 10.00
77 Jeff Carter 4.00 10.00
79 Ryan Kesler 4.00 10.00
80 Mike Green 4.00 10.00
81 Miikka Kiprusoff 3.00 8.00
82 Jason Spezza 2.50 6.00
83 Shea Weber 3.00 8.00
84 Chris Pronger 3.00 8.00
86 Semyon Varlamov 4.00 10.00
87 Matt Duchene/99 4.00 10.00
90 Stephen Weiss 3.00 8.00
92 John Tavares 8.00 20.00
94 Wayne Simmonds 5.00 12.00
95 Jordan Staal 4.00 10.00
98 Corey Perry 4.00 10.00
99 Tyler Bozak/99 4.00 10.00
100 Erik Karlsson 8.00 20.00
101 Kari Lehtonen 3.00 8.00
102 Joe Pavelski 4.00 10.00
104 Scott Gomez/25 3.00 8.00
108 Peter Mueller 3.00 8.00
110 Milan Lucic 4.00 10.00
113 Zach Bogosian 3.00 8.00
115 Colton Orr 2.50 6.00
119 Travis Zajac 3.00 8.00
121 Milan Hejduk 3.00 8.00
122 Brian Elliott 3.00 8.00
124 Niclas Bergfors 3.00 8.00

2010-11 Limited Trios

STATED PRINT RUN 199 SER.#'d SETS
*SILVER/25: .6X TO 1.5X BASIC TRIOS
BTS Richards/Thornton/Sedin 2.00 5.00
DSB Doughty/Subban/Bogosian 5.00 12.00
HTS Hall/Tavares/Stamkos 6.00 15.00
IPM Iginla/Perry/Miller 2.00 5.00
KNP Kane/Nash/Perry 4.00 10.00
KPZ Kovalchuk/Parise/Zajac 2.00 5.00
KSO Kovalchuk/Stamkos/Ovechkin 8.00 20.00
ODM Ovechkin/Datsyuk/Malkin 8.00 20.00
RBG Roy/Bernier/Gustavsson 5.00 12.00
SSS Staal/Staal/Staal 2.50 6.00

2010-11 Limited Trios Materials Prime

STATED PRINT RUN 49 SER.#'d SETS
HTS Hall/Tavares/Stamkos 30.00 80.00
IPM Iginla/Perry/Miller 15.00 40.00
KNP Kane/Nash/Perry 20.00 50.00
KPZ Koval/Parise/Zajac 12.00 30.00
KSO Koval/Stamks/Ovech 15.00 40.00
ODM Ovech/Datsyk/Malkn 20.00 50.00
RTS Richrds/Thrntn/Sedin 10.00 25.00
SSS Staal/Staal/Staal 15.00 40.00

2010-11 Limited Trios Signatures

STATED PRINT RUN 9-25
BTS Richrds/Thorntn/Sedin
DSB Dougty/Subbn/Bogos 30.00 80.00
HTS Hall/Tavars/Stamks 100.00 200.00
IPM Iginla/Perry/Miller
KNP Kane/Nash/Perry 25.00 60.00
KPZ Koval/Parise/Zajac 15.00 40.00
KSO Koval/Stamks/Ovech 60.00 120.00
ODM Ovech/Datsyk/Malkin
RBG Roy/Bernier/Gustavssn 30.00 80.00
SSS Staal/Staal/Staal 20.00 50.00

2010-11 Limited Vintage Pucks

STATED PRINT RUN 20 SER.#'d SETS
1 Curtis Joseph 40.00 80.00
2 Saku Koivu 15.00 40.00
3 Shane Doan
4 Luc Robitaille 12.00 30.00
5 Brett Hull 20.00 50.00
7 Jarome Iginla
8 Martin Brodeur 25.00 60.00
9 Brian Leetch
10 Trevor Linden 25.00 60.00
11 Dino Ciccarelli
12 Eric Lindros 20.00 50.00

2011-12 Limited

1-175 STATED PRINT RUN 299
176-200 STATED PRINT RUN 99
201-264 ROOKIE AU PRINT RUN 291-598
241-264 ISSUED IN ANTHOLOGY
1 Brett Hull 2.50 6.0
2 Patrick Roy 5.00 12.0
3 Mark Messier 2.50 6.0
4 Dale Hunter 1.50 4.0
5 Trevor Linden 2.50 6.0
6 Wendel Clark 2.00 5.0
7 Cam Neely 2.00 5.0
8 Tony Esposito 2.00 5.0
9 Brendan Shanahan 2.50 6.0
10 Adam Graves 1.50 4.0
11 Brad Park 1.50 4.0
12 Eric Lindros 2.50 6.0
13 Dennis Maruk 1.50 4.0
14 Joe Mullen 1.50 4.0
15 Joe Nieuwendyk 2.00 5.0
16 Darryl Sittler 2.00 5.0
17 Dale Tallon 1.25 3.0
18 Milt Schmidt 1.50 4.0
19 Jean Beliveau 2.00 5.0
20 Charlie Simmer 1.25 3.0
21 Yvan Cournoyer 2.00 5.0
22 Steve Yzerman 3.00 8.0
23 Ron Francis 2.50 6.0
24 Brett Hull 2.50 6.0
25 Patrick Roy 5.00 12.0
26 Mark Messier 2.50 6.0
27 Dale Hunter 1.50 4.0
28 Trevor Linden 2.50 6.0
29 Wendel Clark 2.00 5.0
30 Cam Neely 2.00 5.0
31 Tony Esposito 2.00 5.0
32 Brendan Shanahan 2.50 6.0
33 Adam Graves 1.50 4.0
34 Brad Park 1.50 4.0
35 John Davidson 1.50 4.0
36 Eric Lindros 2.50 6.0
37 Pat Verbeek 1.25 3.0
38 Jeremy Roenick 2.00 5.0
39 Johnny Bower 2.00 5.0
40 Luc Robitaille 2.00 5.0
41 Mario Lemieux 6.00 15.0
42 Bobby Clarke 2.00 5.0
43 Bernie Parent 2.50 6.0
44 Bernie Nicholls 2.00 5.0
45 Ray Bourque 3.00 8.0
46 Charlie Simmer 1.25 3.0
47 Gary Simmons 2.00 5.0
48 John Davidson 1.50 4.0
49 Ed Belfour 2.00 5.0
50 Denis Savard 2.50 6.0
51 Daniel Sedin 2.00 5.0
52 Martin St. Louis 2.00 5.0
53 Corey Perry 2.00 5.0
54 Henrik Sedin 2.00 5.0
55 Steven Stamkos 4.00 10.0
56 Jarome Iginla 2.00 5.0
57 Alex Ovechkin 8.00 20.0
58 Teemu Selanne 4.00 10.0
59 Henrik Zetterberg 2.50 6.0
60 Brad Richards 2.00 5.0
61 Eric Staal 2.50 6.0
62 Jonathan Toews 4.00 10.0
63 Claude Giroux 2.00 5.0
64 Ryan Getzlaf 3.00 8.0
65 Ryan Kesler 2.00 5.0
66 Patrick Marleau 2.00 5.0
67 Thomas Vanek 2.00 5.0
68 Patrick Kane 4.00 10.0
69 Loui Eriksson 1.50 4.0
70 Anze Kopitar 3.00 8.0
71 Bobby Ryan 2.00 5.0
72 Patrick Sharp 2.00 5.0
73 Mike Ribeiro 1.50 4.0
74 Joe Thornton 2.00 5.0
75 Jay Bouwmeester 2.00 5.0
76 Danny Briere 2.00 5.0
77 Lubomir Visnovsky 1.25 3.0
78 John Tavares 4.00 10.0
79 Matt Duchene 2.00 5.0
80 Jeff Carter 2.00 5.0
81 Rick Nash 2.00 5.0
82 Sidney Crosby 8.00 20.0
83 Mike Richards 2.00 5.0
84 Joe Pavelski 2.00 5.0
85 Nicklas Backstrom 3.00 8.0
86 Phil Kessel 2.50 6.0
87 Dany Heatley 1.50 4.0
88 Jeff Skinner 2.00 5.0
89 David Backes 2.00 5.0
90 Milan Lucic 2.00 5.0
91 Ryane Clowe 1.25 3.0
92 Brent Burns 2.50 6.0
93 Clarke MacArthur 1.25 3.0
94 Mattias Tedenby 1.25 3.0
95 Mikko Koivu 1.50 4.0
96 Nicklas Lidstrom 2.50 6.0
97 David Krejci 2.00 5.0
98 Ilya Kovalchuk 2.00 5.0
99 Shane Doan 1.50 4.
100 Andrew Ladd 2.00 5.
101 Pavel Datsyuk 2.50 6.
102 Keith Yandle 2.00 5.
103 Mikhail Grabovski 1.50 4.
104 Nikolai Kulemin 2.00 5.
105 Dustin Brown 2.00 5.
106 Marian Hossa 1.50 4.
107 R.J. Umberger 1.25 3.
108 Tomas Plekanec 2.00 5.
109 Patrice Bergeron 2.50 6.
110 Paul Stastny 2.00 5.
111 Ryan Callahan 2.00 5.
112 Jason Spezza 2.00 5.
113 Tuomo Ruutu 1.50 4.
114 Ray Whitney 1.50 4.
115 Brenden Morrow 1.50 4.
116 Logan Couture 2.00 5.
117 Ryan O'Reilly 2.00 5.
118 Jamie Benn 2.50 6.
119 Johan Franzen 2.00 5.
120 Brad Boyes 1.25 3.
121 Alexander Semin 2.00 5.
122 Vincent Lecavalier 1.50 4.
123 Brandon Dubinsky 1.50 4.
124 Olli Jokinen 1.50 4.
125 Matt Moulson 1.50 4.
126 Tyler Seguin 4.00 10.
127 Tyler Myers 2.00 5.
128 Drew Stafford 2.00 5.
129 Jean-Sebastien Giguere 1.50 4.
130 Erik Johnson 1.25 3.
131 Valtteri Filppula 2.00 5.
132 Jack Johnson 1.25 3.
133 Pierre-Marc Bouchard 2.00 5.
134 Michael Cammalleri 1.50 4.

5 Michael Grabner 1.50 4.00
6 Zach Parise 2.00 5.00
7 Marian Gaborik 2.50 6.00
8 Daniel Alfredsson 2.00 5.00
9 Nikita Filatov 1.25 3.00
0 Jaromir Jagr 3.00 8.00
1 Brayden Schenn 2.00 5.00
2 Evgeni Malkin 6.00 15.00
3 Jordan Staal 2.00 5.00
4 Jordan Eberle 2.00 5.00
5 Victor Hedman 2.50 6.00
6 Luke Schenn 1.50 4.00
7 Mason Raymond 1.50 4.00
8 Mike Green 2.00 5.00
9 Alexander Burmistrov 1.50 4.00
0 Evander Kane 2.00 5.00
Nik Antropov 1.50 4.00
2 Dustin Byfuglien 2.00 5.00
3 Brooks Laich 1.25 3.00
4 Alexandre Burrows 2.00 5.00
5 Nazem Kadri 3.00 8.00
6 Dion Phaneuf 2.00 5.00
7 Chris Stewart 1.50 4.00
8 T.J. Oshie 3.00 8.00
9 Kris Letang 2.00 5.00
0 Martin Hanzal 1.25 3.00
Chris Pronger 1.50 4.00
2 James van Riemsdyk 2.00 5.00
3 Erik Karlsson 4.00 10.00
4 Derek Stepan 2.00 5.00
5 Kyle Okposo 2.00 5.00
6 Mattias Tedenby 1.25 3.00
7 Brian Gionta 1.50 4.00
8 P.K. Subban 4.00 10.00
9 Devin Setoguchi 1.50 4.00
0 Simon Gagne 2.00 5.00
Derick Brassard 2.00 5.00
2 Duncan Keith 2.00 5.00
3 Curtis Glencross 1.25 3.00
4 Tyler Ennis 1.50 4.00
5 Zdeno Chara 2.00 5.00
6 Roberto Luongo 4.00 10.00
7 Carey Price 12.00 30.00
8 Cam Ward 4.00 10.00
9 Miikka Kiprusoff 4.00 10.00
0 Jimmy Howard 4.00 10.00
Henrik Lundqvist 5.00 12.00
2 Marc-Andre Fleury 6.00 15.00
3 Ilya Bryzgalov 4.00 10.00
4 Tim Thomas 4.00 10.00
5 Jonathan Quick 6.00 15.00
6 Antti Niemi 3.00 8.00
7 Kari Lehtonen 3.00 8.00
8 Ryan Miller 4.00 10.00
9 Pekka Rinne 5.00 12.00
0 Corey Crawford 5.00 12.00
Jaroslav Halak 4.00 10.00
2 Jonas Hiller 3.00 8.00
3 Dwayne Roloson 3.00 8.00
4 Steve Mason 3.00 8.00
5 Martin Brodeur 8.00 20.00
6 Tomas Vokoun 3.00 8.00
7 Niklas Backstrom 4.00 10.00
8 Ondrej Pavelec 4.00 10.00
9 James Reimer 4.00 10.00
0 Jose Theodore 4.00 10.00
Joe Colborne AU/299 RC 5.00 12.00
Cody Hodgson AU/299 RC 10.00 25.00
Adam Henrique AU/299 RC 12.00 30.00
Marcus Kruger AU/299 RC 8.00 20.00
Blake Geoffrion AU/299 RC 5.00 12.00
Aaron Palushaj AU/299 RC 5.00 12.00
Greg Nemisz AU/299 RC 5.00 12.00
Carl Klingberg AU/299 RC 5.00 12.00
John Moore AU/299 RC 5.00 12.00
Jake Gardiner AU/299 RC 8.00 20.00
Tim Erixon AU/299 RC 5.00 12.00
D.Smith-Pelly AU/299 RC 8.00 20.00
G.Landeskog AU/299 RC 10.00 25.00
Ryan Johansen AU/299 RC 10.00 25.00
Nugent-Hopkins AU/299 RC 20.00 50.00
Adam Larsson AU/299 RC 6.00 15.00
Sean Couturier AU/299 RC 10.00 25.00
Matt Frattin AU/299 RC 5.00 12.00
Mark Scheifele AU/299 RC 12.00 30.00
Brett Connolly AU/299 RC 5.00 12.00
Mika Zibanejad AU/299 RC 12.00 30.00
Brandon Saad AU/299 RC 10.00 25.00
Roman Horak AU/299 RC 5.00 12.00
Ben Scrivens AU/299 RC 8.00 20.00
Jonathon Blum AU/299 RC 5.00 12.00
Tomas Vincour AU/299 RC 5.00 12.00
Matt Read AU/299 RC 10.00 25.00
Justin Faulk AU/299 RC 8.00 20.00
Joe Vitale AU/291 RC 5.00 12.00
S.Da Costa AU/299 RC 5.00 12.00
Craig Smith AU/299 RC 6.00 15.00
Anton Lander AU/299 RC 5.00 12.00
Gudbranson AU/299 RC 6.00 15.00
Zac Rinaldo AU/299 RC 5.00 12.00
Patrick Wiercioch AU/299 RC 5.00 12.00
Lance Bouma AU/299 RC 5.00 12.00
Brett Bulmer AU/299 RC 5.00 12.00
T.Hartikainen AU/299 RC 5.00 12.00
Alexei Emelin AU/299 RC 5.00 12.00
Erik Condra AU/299 RC 5.00 12.00
Marcus Foligno AU/299 RC 8.00 20.00
Ryan Ellis AU/299 RC 5.00 12.00
Zack Kassian AU/299 RC 6.00 15.00
Cody Eakin AU/299 RC 6.00 15.00
David Rundblad AU/299 RC 5.00 12.00
Brendan Smith AU/299 RC 5.00 12.00
Brad Malone AU/299 RC 5.00 12.00
Brayden McNabb AU/299 RC 5.00 12.00
Carl Hagelin AU/598 RC 8.00 20.00
Colin Greening AU/299 RC 5.00 12.00
David Savard AU/299 RC 5.00 12.00
Stefan Elliott AU/299 RC 5.00 12.00
Dmitry Orlov AU/299 RC 6.00 15.00
Dylan Olsen AU/299 RC 6.00 15.00
Gustav Nyquist AU/299 RC 12.00 30.00
Harry Zolnierczyk AU/299 RC 5.00 12.00
Jimmy Hayes AU/299 RC 6.00 15.00
Leland Irving AU/299 RC 5.00 12.00
Louis Leblanc AU/299 RC 5.00 12.00
Simon Despres AU/299 RC 5.00 12.00
Anders Nilsson AU/299 RC 5.00 12.00
Calvin de Haan AU/299 RC 5.00 12.00
Peter Holland AU/299 RC 5.00 12.00
Eddie Lack AU/299 RC 5.00 12.00

011-12 Limited Gold Spotlight

ENDS 1-50: 1X TO 2.5X BASIC CARDS
S 51-175: 1X TO 2.5X BASIC CARDS
LIES 176-200: .5X TO 1.2X BASIC CARDS
0 STATED PRINT RUN 25
264 ISSUED IN ANTHOLOGY
264 UNPRICED ROOKIE AU PRINT RUN 10
icklas Backstrom 8.00 20.00
Corey Crawford 6.00 15.00

2011-12 Limited Ruby Spotlight

*LEGENDS 1-50: .8X TO 2X BASIC CARDS
*VETS 51-175: .8X TO 2X BASIC CARDS
*GOALIES 176-200: .4X TO 1X BASIC CARDS
STATED PRINT RUN 49 SER.#'d SETS
85 Nicklas Backstrom 6.00 15.00
190 Corey Crawford 5.00 12.00

2011-12 Limited Silver Spotlight

*ROOKIE AU/49-50: .5X TO 1.2X BASIC AU/299
STATED PRINT RUN 49-50
241-264 ISSUED IN ANTHOLOGY
202 Cody Hodgson AU 20.00 50.00
215 Ryan Nugent-Hopkins AU 80.00 200.00

2011-12 Limited Back To The Future Signatures

STATED PRINT RUN 25 SER.#'d SETS
20 INSERTED IN ANTHOLOGY
1 H.Lundqvist/J.Davidson 25.00 50.00
2 C.Giroux/T.Kerr 25.00 50.00
3 Marchand/K.Linseman 15.00 40.00
4 S.Stamkos/S.Yzerman 40.00 100.00
6 J.Tavares/P.LaFontaine 30.00 60.00
7 R.Kesler/T.Linden
8 J.Colborne/D.Gilmour 25.00 50.00
9 J.Toews/J.Roenick 50.00 100.00
10 Z.Chara/J.Bucyk
11 J.Reimer/F.Potvin
12 J.Quick/K.Hrudey 40.00 80.00
14 T.Vanek/LaFontaine 20.00 50.00
15 Luongo/R.Brodeur 20.00 50.00
16 T.Seguin/M.Schmidt 50.00 100.00
17 Z.Parise/Niedermayer 25.00 60.00
18 A.Ovechkin/M.Messier 60.00 120.00
19 E.Kane/B.Hull 30.00 60.00
20 B.Schenn/E.Lindros
21 L.Schenn/W.Clark 25.00 50.00
22 C.Perry/B.Shanahan 25.00 60.00
23 M.Fleury/P.Roy 50.00 100.00
24 M.Duchene/J.Sakic 20.00 40.00
25 Ovechkin/M.Lemieux 100.00 200.00

2011-12 Limited Banner Season

STATED PRINT RUN 299 SER.#'d SETS
*GOLD/25: 1X TO 2.5X BASIC INSERT/199
*SILVER/49: .6X TO 1.5X BASIC INSERT/199
1 Corey Perry 2.00 5.00
2 Daniel Sedin 2.00 5.00
3 Martin St. Louis 2.00 5.00
4 Ryan Kesler 2.00 5.00
5 Steven Stamkos 4.00 10.00
6 Tim Thomas 2.00 5.00
7 Corey Crawford 2.50 6.00
8 Loui Eriksson 1.50 4.00
9 Pavel Datsyuk 2.50 6.00
10 Roberto Luongo 2.00 5.00
11 Jonathan Toews 4.00 10.00
12 Pekka Rinne 2.50 6.00
13 Taylor Hall 4.00 10.00
14 Carey Price 6.00 15.00
15 Nicklas Lidstrom 2.00 5.00
16 Keith Yandle 2.00 5.00
17 Dustin Byfuglien 2.00 5.00
18 Zdeno Chara 2.00 5.00
19 Jordan Eberle 2.00 5.00
20 Jeff Skinner 2.00 5.00
21 Jarome Iginla 2.00 5.00
22 Henrik Lundqvist 2.50 6.00
23 Cam Ward 2.00 5.00
24 Claude Giroux 2.00 5.00
25 Brad Marchand 2.50 6.00

2011-12 Limited Banner Season Materials

STATED PRINT RUN 99 SER.#'d SETS
*PRIME/50: .6X TO 1.5X BASIC JSY/99
*PRIME/25: .8X TO 2X BASIC JSY/99
1 Corey Perry 5.00 12.00
2 Daniel Sedin 5.00 12.00
3 Martin St. Louis 5.00 12.00
4 Ryan Kesler 5.00 12.00
5 Steven Stamkos 6.00 15.00
6 Tim Thomas 5.00 12.00
7 Corey Crawford 6.00 15.00
8 Loui Eriksson 4.00 10.00
9 Pavel Datsyuk 6.00 15.00
10 Roberto Luongo 5.00 12.00
11 Jonathan Toews 10.00 25.00
12 Pekka Rinne 6.00 15.00
13 Taylor Hall 10.00 25.00
14 Carey Price 15.00 40.00
15 Nicklas Lidstrom 6.00 15.00
16 Keith Yandle 5.00 12.00
17 Dustin Byfuglien 5.00 12.00
18 Zdeno Chara 5.00 12.00
19 Jordan Eberle 5.00 12.00
20 Jeff Skinner 5.00 12.00
21 Jarome Iginla 4.00 10.00
22 Henrik Lundqvist 6.00 15.00
23 Cam Ward 5.00 12.00
24 Claude Giroux 5.00 12.00
25 Brad Marchand 6.00 15.00

2011-12 Limited Banner Season Materials Signatures

STATED PRINT RUN 24-25
*PRIME/15: .6X TO 1.5X JSY AU/24-25
5/13/14/16/17/21-25 INSERTS IN ANTHOLOGY
2 Daniel Sedin 12.00 30.00
3 Martin St. Louis 12.00 30.00
4 Ryan Kesler 12.00 30.00
5 Steven Stamkos 30.00 60.00
6 Tim Thomas 12.00 30.00
8 Loui Eriksson 10.00 25.00
9 Pavel Datsyuk 15.00 40.00
10 Roberto Luongo 20.00 50.00
12 Pekka Rinne 15.00 40.00
13 Taylor Hall 25.00 50.00
14 Carey Price/24 30.00 60.00
15 Nicklas Lidstrom 20.00 40.00
16 Keith Yandle 12.00 30.00
17 Dustin Byfuglien 12.00 30.00
18 Zdeno Chara 15.00 40.00
21 Jarome Iginla 12.00 30.00
22 Henrik Lundqvist 15.00 40.00
23 Cam Ward
24 Claude Giroux 20.00 40.00
25 Brad Marchand 10.00 25.00

2011-12 Limited Banner Season Signatures

STATED PRINT RUN 24-25
5/13/14/16/17/21-25 INSERTS IN ANTHOLOGY
1 Corey Perry 10.00 25.00
2 Daniel Sedin 10.00 25.00
3 Martin St. Louis 10.00 25.00
4 Ryan Kesler 10.00 25.00
5 Steven Stamkos 20.00 40.00
6 Tim Thomas 30.00 60.00
8 Loui Eriksson 8.00 20.00
9 Pavel Datsyuk 12.00 30.00
10 Roberto Luongo 15.00 40.00
12 Pekka Rinne 12.00 30.00
13 Taylor Hall 20.00 50.00
14 Carey Price/24 30.00 80.00
15 Nicklas Lidstrom 10.00 25.00
16 Keith Yandle
17 Dustin Byfuglien 10.00 25.00
18 Zdeno Chara 12.00 30.00
21 Jarome Iginla 10.00 25.00
22 Henrik Lundqvist 20.00 40.00
23 Cam Ward 10.00 25.00
24 Claude Giroux 20.00 40.00
25 Brad Marchand 12.00 30.00

2011-12 Limited Brothers In Arms Materials

STATED PRINT RUN 99-199
*PRIME/25: .8X TO 2X BASIC DUAL/199
*PRIME/25: .6X TO 1.5X BASIC DUAL/99
1 T.Thomas/T.Rask/199 6.00 15.00
2 M.Kiprusoff/H.Karlsson/199 6.00 15.00
3 K.Lehtonen/A.Raycroft/199 5.00 12.00
4 N.Khabibulin/D.Dubnyk/199 6.00 15.00
5 J.Quick/J.Bernier/199 10.00 25.00
6 M.Brodeur/J.Hedberg/199 10.00 25.00
7 J.Halak/B.Elliott/199 6.00 15.00
8 J.Reimer/J.Gustavsson/199 6.00 15.00
9 C.Anderson/R.Lehner/199 6.00 15.00
10 M.Fleury/B.Johnson/199 5.00 12.00
11 O.Pavelec/C.Mason/199 8.00 20.00
12 H.Lundqvist/M.Biron/199 8.00 20.00
13 T.Vokoun/M.Neuvirth/199 5.00 12.00
14 J.Theodore/J.Markstrom/199 6.00 15.00
15 R.Luongo/C.Schneider/199 6.00 15.00
16 P.Rinne/A.Lindback/199 6.00 15.00
17 R.Miller/J.Enroth/99 8.00 20.00
18 E.Belfour/M.Turco/99 6.00 15.00
19 R.Luongo/M.Brodeur/99 10.00 25.00
20 R.Miller/T.Thomas/99 8.00 20.00

2011-12 Limited Crease Cleaners

STATED PRINT RUN 199 SER.#'d SETS
*GOLD/25: 1X TO 2.5X BASIC INSERT/199
*SILVER/49: .6X TO 1.5X BASIC INSERT/199
1 Tim Thomas 2.50 6.00
2 Cam Ward 2.50 6.00
3 Carey Price 8.00 20.00
4 Jaroslav Halak 2.50 6.00
5 Jonathan Quick 3.00 8.00
6 Martin Brodeur 5.00 12.00
7 Jimmy Howard 2.50 6.00
8 Kari Lehtonen 2.00 5.00
9 Pekka Rinne 3.00 8.00
10 Jonas Hiller 2.00 5.00
11 Craig Anderson 2.50 6.00
12 Niklas Backstrom 2.50 6.00
13 Jonathan Bernier 2.50 6.00
14 Nikolai Khabibulin 2.00 5.00
15 Robin Lehner 2.00 5.00
16 Corey Crawford 3.00 8.00
17 Ryan Miller 2.50 6.00
18 Ondrej Pavelec 2.50 6.00
19 Ilya Bryzgalov 2.50 6.00
20 Steve Mason 2.00 5.00

2011-12 Limited Crease Cleaners Materials

STATED PRINT RUN 99 SER.#'d SETS
*PRIME/25: .8X TO 2X BASIC JSY/99
1 Tim Thomas 5.00 12.00
2 Cam Ward 5.00 12.00
3 Carey Price 15.00 40.00
4 Jaroslav Halak 5.00 12.00
5 Jonathan Quick 8.00 20.00
6 Martin Brodeur 8.00 20.00
7 Jimmy Howard 5.00 12.00
8 Kari Lehtonen 4.00 10.00
9 Pekka Rinne 6.00 15.00
10 Jonas Hiller 4.00 10.00
11 Craig Anderson 5.00 12.00
12 Niklas Backstrom 5.00 12.00
13 Jonathan Bernier 5.00 12.00
14 Nikolai Khabibulin 4.00 10.00
15 Robin Lehner 6.00 15.00
16 Corey Crawford 6.00 15.00
17 Ryan Miller 5.00 12.00
18 Ondrej Pavelec 6.00 15.00
19 Ilya Bryzgalov 5.00 12.00
20 Steve Mason 4.00 10.00

2011-12 Limited Crease Cleaners Materials Patches Signatures

STATED PRINT RUN 5-15
2/3/5-8/10/12/14/15/17/18 INSERTS IN ANTHOLOGY
1 Tim Thomas/15
2 Cam Ward/15 12.00 30.00
3 Carey Price/15 40.00 80.00
4 Jaroslav Halak/15 15.00 40.00
5 Jonathan Quick/15
6 Martin Brodeur/15
8 Kari Lehtonen/15
9 Pekka Rinne/15 15.00 40.00
10 Jonas Hiller/15
11 Craig Anderson/15 12.00 30.00
12 Niklas Backstrom/15 15.00 40.00
13 Jonathan Bernier/15 20.00 50.00
14 Nikolai Khabibulin/15
15 Robin Lehner/15
17 Ryan Miller/15 30.00 60.00
18 Ondrej Pavelec/15
20 Steve Mason/5

2011-12 Limited Crease Cleaners Signatures

STATED PRINT RUN 25-99
2/3/5/6/8/10/12/14/15/17/18 INSERTS IN ANTHOLOGY
1 Tim Thomas/49 25.00 50.00
2 Cam Ward/99 12.00 30.00
3 Carey Price/48 20.00 40.00
4 Jaroslav Halak/99 8.00 20.00
5 Jonathan Quick/99 15.00 40.00
6 Martin Brodeur/25
7 Jimmy Howard/99 12.00 30.00
8 Kari Lehtonen/99 8.00 20.00
9 Pekka Rinne/99 10.00 25.00
10 Jonas Hiller/91 6.00 15.00
11 Craig Anderson/99 8.00 20.00
12 Niklas Backstrom/99 8.00 20.00
13 Jonathan Bernier/99 10.00 25.00
14 Nikolai Khabibulin/99 6.00 15.00
15 Robin Lehner/99 8.00 20.00
17 Ryan Miller/99 8.00 20.00
18 Ondrej Pavelec/99 10.00 25.00
20 Steve Mason/99 6.00 15.00

2011-12 Limited Freshmen Jumbo Materials Draft Position

DRAFT POSITION PRINT RUN 25-99
*DRAFT PRIME/25: .8X TO 2X DRAFT JSY/99
*BASIC JUMBO/199: 2.5X TO .6X DRFT JSY/99
*BASIC PRIME/50: .5X TO 1.2X DRFT JSY/99
*BASIC PRIME/50: .25X TO .6X DRFT JSY/25
*BASIC PRIME/25: .8X TO 2X DRFT JSY/99
1 Cody Hodgson/25 20.00 50.00
2 Joe Colborne/99 4.00 10.00
3 Gabriel Landeskog/99 10.00 25.00
4 Ryan Nugent-Hopkins/99 30.00 80.00
5 Mika Zibanejad/99 10.00 25.00
6 Brett Connolly/99 4.00 10.00
7 Ryan Johansen/99 8.00 20.00
8 Sean Couturier/99 8.00 20.00
9 Erik Gudbranson/99 5.00 12.00
10 Adam Henrique/99 10.00 25.00

2011-12 Limited Freshmen Jumbo Materials Draft Position Signatures

STATED PRINT RUN 25-99
*BASIC JSY AU/99: .4X TO 1X AU/99
1 Cody Hodgson/25 30.00 80.00
2 Joe Colborne/99 15.00 40.00
3 G.Landeskog/99 20.00 50.00
4 Ryan Nugent-Hopkins/99 50.00 120.00
5 Mika Zibanejad/99 20.00 50.00
6 Brett Connolly/99 8.00 20.00
7 Ryan Johansen/99 15.00 40.00
8 Sean Couturier/99 15.00 40.00
9 Erik Gudbranson/99 10.00 25.00
10 Adam Henrique/99 12.00 30.00

2011-12 Limited Game Pucks Signatures

STATED PRINT RUN 10-25
3/7/8/10/12-14/16 INSERTED IN ANTHOLOGY
1 Mario Lemieux/20 50.00 100.00
2 Ron Francis/20
3 Jaromir Jagr/20 40.00 100.00
4 Steve Yzerman/20 40.00 80.00
5 Curtis Joseph/20 40.00 80.00
6 Bill Ranford/20 20.00 50.00
7 Mark Messier/20 25.00 60.00
8 Eric Lindros/25 30.00 60.00
9 Trevor Linden/20 40.00 80.00
10 Carey Price/20
11 Nicklas Lidstrom/20 25.00 60.00
12 Patrick Kane/20 30.00 80.00
13 Taylor Hall/20 20.00 50.00
14 Matt Duchene/20 15.00 40.00
15 P.K. Subban/20
16 Ryan Miller/20 15.00 40.00
18 Jamie Benn/20 20.00 50.00
19 Sidney Crosby/10
20 Roberto Luongo/20 30.00 60.00

2011-12 Limited Jumbo Materials

JUMBO PRINT RUN 99 SER.#'d SETS
*JUMBO PRIME/50: .6X TO 1.5X JUMBO/99
*JUMBO PRIME/25: .8X TO 2X JUMBO/99
*JSY NUMBER/49: .5X TO 1.2X JUMBO/99
*JSY NUMBER/25: .6X TO 1.5X JUMBO/99
*JSY # PRIME/10: 1.2X TO 3X JUMBO/99
1 Alex Ovechkin 10.00 25.00
2 Rick Nash 5.00 12.00
3 Corey Perry 5.00 12.00
4 Claude Giroux 5.00 12.00
5 Sidney Crosby 12.00 30.00
6 Joe Thornton 5.00 12.00
7 Patrick Marleau 5.00 12.00
8 Ryan Kesler 6.00 15.00
9 Saku Koivu 5.00 12.00
10 Anze Kopitar 8.00 20.00
11 Tyler Myers 5.00 12.00
12 Matt Duchene 5.00 12.00
13 Jeff Skinner 5.00 12.00
14 James van Riemsdyk 3.00 8.00
15 Bobby Ryan 5.00 12.00
16 Jimmy Howard 5.00 12.00
17 Brad Marchand 6.00 15.00
18 Loui Eriksson 4.00 10.00
19 Taylor Hall 8.00 20.00
20 Marian Gaborik 6.00 15.00
21 Henrik Lundqvist 6.00 15.00
22 Antti Niemi 4.00 10.00
23 Alexander Semin 4.00 10.00
24 Ryane Clowe 3.00 8.00
25 Paul Stastny 5.00 12.00
26 Brenden Morrow 4.00 10.00
27 Ryan Getzlaf 8.00 20.00
28 Pavel Datsyuk 6.00 15.00
29 Jonathan Bernier 5.00 12.00
30 Chris Pronger 4.00 10.00
31 David Backes 5.00 12.00
32 Evgeni Malkin 8.00 20.00
33 Vincent Lecavalier 4.00 10.00
34 Martin Brodeur 10.00 25.00
35 Evander Kane 5.00 12.00
36 Daniel Alfredsson 5.00 12.00
37 Mark Letestu 4.00 10.00
38 Rene Bourque 3.00 8.00
39 P.K. Subban 10.00 25.00
40 Tim Thomas 5.00 12.00

2011-12 Limited Jumbo Materials Jersey Numbers Signatures

STATED PRINT RUN 10-25
1 Alex Ovechkin/25 40.00 100.00
3 Corey Perry/25 12.00 30.00
4 Claude Giroux/25 20.00 50.00
5 Sidney Crosby/10
6 Joe Thornton/25 15.00 40.00
7 Patrick Marleau/25 12.50 30.00
8 Ryan Kesler/25 25.00 50.00
9 Saku Koivu/25 20.00 40.00
11 Tyler Myers/25 12.00 30.00
12 Matt Duchene/25
13 Jeff Skinner/25 25.00 50.00
14 James van Riemsdyk/25 12.00 30.00
18 Loui Eriksson/25 10.00 25.00
21 Henrik Lundqvist/25 15.00 30.00
22 Antti Niemi/25 10.00 25.00
23 Alexander Semin/25 12.00 30.00
26 Brenden Morrow/25 10.00 25.00
27 Ryan Getzlaf/10
28 Pavel Datsyuk/25 20.00 40.00
29 Jonathan Bernier/25 12.00 30.00
30 Chris Pronger/25 10.00 25.00
31 David Backes/25 12.00 30.00
32 Evgeni Malkin/25 30.00 60.00
33 Vincent Lecavalier/25 10.00 25.00
35 Evander Kane/25 25.00 50.00
37 Mark Letestu/25
38 Rene Bourque/25 8.00 20.00

2011-12 Limited Jumbo Materials Prime Signatures

*PRME AU/25: .5X TO 1.2X JSY # AU/25
STATED PRINT RUN 10-25
10 Anze Kopitar/25 25.00 60.00
21 Henrik Lundqvist/25 20.00 50.00
27 Ryan Getzlaf/25
34 Martin Brodeur/25 50.00 100.00

2011-12 Limited Materials

STATED PRINT RUN 10-99
1 Brett Hull/99 6.00 15.00
2 Patrick Roy/99 12.00 30.00
6 Wendel Clark/99 6.00 15.00
7 Cam Neely/99 5.00 12.00
9 Brendan Shanahan/99 6.00 15.00
10 Adam Graves/99 4.00 10.00
12 Eric Lindros/99 6.00 15.00
14 Joe Mullen/99 4.00 10.00
15 Joe Nieuwendyk/99 5.00 12.00
16 Darryl Sittler/99 5.00 12.00
21 Yvan Cournoyer/99 5.00 12.00
22 Steve Yzerman/99 8.00 20.00
24 Brett Hull/99 6.00 15.00
25 Patrick Roy/99 12.00 30.00
26 Mark Messier/99 6.00 15.00
30 Cam Neely/99 5.00 12.00
32 Brendan Shanahan/99 6.00 15.00
36 Eric Lindros/99 6.00 15.00
37 Pat Verbeek/99 3.00 8.00
40 Luc Robitaille/99 5.00 12.00
42 Bobby Clarke/99 6.00 15.00
44 Bernie Nicholls/99 5.00 12.00
46 Charlie Simmer/99 3.00 8.00
51 Daniel Sedin/99 5.00 12.00
52 Martin St. Louis/25 6.00 15.00
53 Corey Perry/99 5.00 12.00
54 Henrik Sedin/99 5.00 12.00
55 Steven Stamkos/99 6.00 15.00
56 Jarome Iginla/99 5.00 12.00
57 Alex Ovechkin/99 5.00 12.00
58 Teemu Selanne/99 10.00 25.00
59 Henrik Zetterberg/99 6.00 15.00
60 Brad Richards/99 5.00 12.00
61 Eric Staal/99 6.00 15.00
62 Jonathan Toews/25 12.00 30.00
63 Claude Giroux/99 5.00 12.00
64 Ryan Getzlaf/99 8.00 20.00
65 Ryan Kesler/99 5.00 12.00
66 Patrick Marleau/99 5.00 12.00
67 Thomas Vanek/99 5.00 12.00
68 Patrick Kane/25 8.00 20.00
69 Loui Eriksson/99 4.00 10.00
70 Anze Kopitar/99 8.00 20.00
71 Bobby Ryan/99 5.00 12.00
72 Patrick Sharp/99 5.00 12.00
74 Joe Thornton/99 5.00 12.00
75 Jay Bouwmeester/10
76 Danny Briere/99 5.00 12.00
78 John Tavares/25 6.00 15.00
79 Matt Duchene/99 5.00 12.00
80 Jeff Carter/99 5.00 12.00
81 Rick Nash/99 5.00 12.00
82 Sidney Crosby/99 10.00 25.00
83 Mike Richards/99 5.00 12.00
84 Joe Pavelski/99 5.00 12.00
85 Nicklas Backstrom/99 8.00 20.00
86 Phil Kessel/25 8.00 20.00
87 Dany Heatley/99 4.00 10.00
88 Jeff Skinner/99 5.00 12.00
89 David Backes/10
90 Milan Lucic/99 5.00 12.00
91 Ryane Clowe/99 3.00 8.00
92 Brent Burns/99 6.00 15.00
94 Mattias Tedenby/99 3.00 8.00
95 Mikko Koivu/99 4.00 10.00
96 Nicklas Lidstrom/25 6.00 15.00
97 David Krejci/99 5.00 12.00
98 Ilya Kovalchuk/99 5.00 12.00
99 Shane Doan/99 4.00 10.00
100 Andrew Ladd/99 5.00 12.00
101 Pavel Datsyuk/99 6.00 15.00
102 Keith Yandle/99 5.00 12.00
103 Mikhail Grabovski/99 4.00 10.00
104 Nikolai Kulemin/99 5.00 12.00
105 Dustin Brown/99 5.00 12.00
106 Marian Hossa/99 4.00 10.00
108 Tomas Plekanec/99 5.00 12.00
109 Patrice Bergeron/99 6.00 15.00
110 Paul Stastny/99 5.00 12.00
111 Ryan Callahan/10
112 Jason Spezza/99 5.00 12.00
115 Brenden Morrow/99 4.00 10.00
116 Logan Couture/99 5.00 12.00
117 Ryan O'Reilly/10
118 Jamie Benn/99 6.00 15.00
119 Johan Franzen/99 5.00 12.00
121 Alexander Semin/99 5.00 12.00
122 Vincent Lecavalier/99 4.00 10.00
123 Brandon Dubinsky /99 4.00 10.00
125 Matt Moulson/99 4.00 10.00
126 Tyler Seguin/99 6.00 15.00
127 Tyler Myers/99 5.00 12.00
128 Drew Stafford/10
129 Jean-Sebastien Giguere/99 5.00 12.00
130 Erik Johnson/99 3.00 8.00
131 Valtteri Filppula/99 5.00 12.00
134 Michael Cammalleri/99 4.00 10.00
136 Zach Parise/25 6.00 15.00
137 Marian Gaborik/99 6.00 15.00
138 Daniel Alfredsson/99 5.00 12.00
140 Jaromir Jagr/10
142 Evgeni Malkin/99 8.00 20.00
143 Jordan Staal/99 5.00 12.00
144 Jordan Eberle/25 6.00 15.00
145 Victor Hedman/99 5.00 12.00
146 Luke Schenn/99 5.00 12.00
147 Mason Raymond/10
148 Mike Green/99 5.00 12.00
149 Alexander Burmistrov/99 4.00 10.00
150 Evander Kane/99 5.00 12.00
152 Dustin Byfuglien/99 5.00 12.00
153 Eric Fehr/99 3.00 8.00
154 Alexandre Burrows/99 5.00 12.00
155 Nazem Kadri/99 8.00 20.00
156 Dion Phaneuf/99 5.00 12.00
158 T.J. Oshie/10
159 Kris Letang/99 6.00 15.00
161 Chris Pronger/99 4.00 10.00
162 James van Riemsdyk/99 5.00 12.00
163 Erik Karlsson/99 5.00 12.00
164 Derek Stepan/99 5.00 12.00
165 Kyle Okposo/99 5.00 12.00
166 Mattias Tedenby/99 3.00 8.00
167 Brian Gionta/10
168 P.K. Subban/99 10.00 25.00
169 Devin Setoguchi/99 4.00 10.00
171 Derick Brassard/99 5.00 12.00
172 Duncan Keith/10
173 Curtis Glencross/99 3.00 8.00
174 Tyler Ennis/99 4.00 10.00
175 Zdeno Chara/99 5.00 12.00
176 Roberto Luongo/99 5.00 12.00
177 Carey Price/99 15.00 40.00
179 Miikka Kiprusoff/99 5.00 12.00
180 Jimmy Howard/99 5.00 12.00
181 Henrik Lundqvist/99 6.00 15.00
182 Marc-Andre Fleury/99 8.00 20.00
183 Ilya Bryzgalov/99 5.00 12.00
184 Tim Thomas/99 5.00 12.00
185 Jonathan Quick/99 8.00 20.00
186 Antti Niemi/99 4.00 10.00
187 Kari Lehtonen/99 4.00 10.00
188 Ryan Miller/99 5.00 12.00
189 Pekka Rinne/99 6.00 15.00
190 Corey Crawford/10
191 Jaroslav Halak/10
192 Jonas Hiller/99 4.00 10.00
195 Martin Brodeur/99 6.00 15.00
196 Tomas Vokoun/99 4.00 10.00
197 Niklas Backstrom/99 5.00 12.00
198 Ondrej Pavelec/99 8.00 20.00
199 James Reimer/99 5.00 12.00
200 Jose Theodore/99 5.00 12.00

2011-12 Limited Materials Prime

COMMON CARD/15-25 6.00 15.00
SEMISTARS/15-25 8.00 20.00
UNL.STARS/15-25 10.00 25.00
PRIME STATED PRINT RUN 1-25
1 Brett Hull/25 12.00 30.00
2 Patrick Roy/25 25.00 60.00
6 Wendel Clark/25 12.00 30.00
7 Cam Neely/25 10.00 25.00
9 Brendan Shanahan/25 12.00 30.00
22 Steve Yzerman/25 15.00 40.00
25 Patrick Roy/25 25.00 60.00
26 Mark Messier/25 12.00 30.00
30 Cam Neely/25 10.00 25.00
32 Brendan Shanahan/25 12.00 30.00
36 Eric Lindros/25 12.00 30.00
42 Bobby Clarke/25 12.00 30.00
54 Henrik Sedin/25 10.00 25.00
55 Steven Stamkos/25 12.00 30.00
57 Alex Ovechkin/25 12.00 30.00
59 Henrik Zetterberg/25 12.00 30.00
62 Jonathan Toews/25 20.00 50.00
63 Claude Giroux/25 10.00 25.00
65 Ryan Kesler/25 10.00 25.00
68 Patrick Kane/25 20.00 50.00
78 John Tavares/25 12.00 30.00
82 Sidney Crosby/25 20.00 50.00
85 Nicklas Backstrom/25 15.00 40.00
88 Jeff Skinner/25 10.00 25.00
117 Ryan O'Reilly/25 10.00 25.00
126 Tyler Seguin/25 12.00 30.00
127 Tyler Myers/25 10.00 25.00
129 Jean-Sebastien Giguere/25 12.00 30.00
140 Jaromir Jagr/25 25.00 60.00
142 Evgeni Malkin/25 15.00 40.00
145 Victor Hedman/25 12.00 30.00
146 Luke Schenn/25 8.00 20.00
158 T.J. Oshie/20 15.00 40.00
168 P.K. Subban/15 20.00 50.00
176 Roberto Luongo/25 10.00 25.00
177 Carey Price/25 30.00 80.00
181 Henrik Lundqvist/25 12.00 30.00
190 Corey Crawford/25 12.00 30.00

2011-12 Limited Men of Mayhem Signatures

STATED PRINT RUN 49-199
7/8 ISSUED IN ANTHOLOGY
1 Wendel Clark/199 10.00 25.00
3 Al Secord/199 8.00 20.00
7 Dale Hunter/99 8.00 20.00
8 Jody Shelley/199 8.00 20.00
9 Brendan Shanahan/49 15.00 40.00
10 Pat Verbeek/199 8.00 20.00

2011-12 Limited Monikers Gold

GOLD STATED PRINT RUN 7-25
2 Patrick Roy/25 40.00 80.00
3 Mark Messier/25 20.00 50.00
5 Trevor Linden/19 25.00 60.00
6 Wendel Clark/25 15.00 40.00
7 Cam Neely/25 15.00 40.00
8 Tony Esposito/25 15.00 40.00
10 Adam Graves/25 10.00 25.00
11 Brad Park/25 8.00 20.00
12 Eric Lindros/25 30.00 60.00
14 Joe Mullen/25 8.00 20.00
16 Darryl Sittler/25 10.00 25.00
17 Dale Tallon/25 6.00 15.00
18 Milt Schmidt/25 8.00 20.00
19 Jean Beliveau/25 30.00 60.00
20 Charlie Simmer/25 6.00 15.00
21 Yvan Cournoyer/25
22 Steve Yzerman/25 40.00 80.00
25 Patrick Roy/25 40.00 80.00
28 Trevor Linden/7
29 Wendel Clark/25 15.00 40.00
30 Cam Neely/25 25.00 50.00
31 Tony Esposito/25 15.00 40.00
33 Adam Graves/25 10.00 25.00
34 Brad Park/25 8.00 20.00
36 Eric Lindros/25 40.00 80.00
37 Pat Verbeek/25 15.00 40.00
38 Jeremy Roenick/25 30.00 60.00
39 Johnny Bower/25 15.00 40.00
40 Luc Robitaille/25 12.00 30.00
42 Bobby Clarke/25 12.00 30.00
43 Bernie Parent/25 20.00 40.00
44 Bernie Nicholls/25 10.00 25.00
46 Charlie Simmer/25 6.00 15.00
47 Gary Simmons/25 15.00 40.00
51 Daniel Sedin/25 10.00 25.00
52 Martin St. Louis/25 8.00 20.00
53 Corey Perry/25 8.00 20.00
54 Henrik Sedin/25 10.00 25.00
55 Steven Stamkos/25 15.00 40.00
56 Jarome Iginla/25 8.00 20.00
57 Alex Ovechkin/25 40.00 100.00
60 Brad Richards/25 20.00 40.00
61 Eric Staal/25 10.00 25.00
63 Claude Giroux/25 20.00 40.00
64 Ryan Getzlaf/25
65 Ryan Kesler/25 10.00 25.00
66 Patrick Marleau/25 10.00 25.00
68 Patrick Kane/25 25.00 50.00
70 Anze Kopitar/25 12.00 30.00
71 Bobby Ryan/25 10.00 25.00
74 Joe Thornton/25 12.00 30.00
75 Jay Bouwmeester/25 8.00 20.00
76 Danny Briere/25 8.00 20.00
78 John Tavares/25 20.00 40.00
79 Matt Duchene/25 12.00 30.00
80 Jeff Carter/25 8.00 20.00
82 Sidney Crosby/10
84 Joe Pavelski/25 8.00 20.00
86 Phil Kessel/25 10.00 25.00
87 Dany Heatley/25 10.00 25.00
88 Jeff Skinner/25 20.00 40.00
89 David Backes/25 8.00 20.00
92 Brent Burns/25 8.00 20.00
94 Mattias Tedenby/25 5.00 12.00
96 Nicklas Lidstrom/25 25.00 50.00
98 Ilya Kovalchuk/25
99 Shane Doan/25 6.00 15.00
100 Andrew Ladd/25 8.00 20.00
101 Pavel Datsyuk/25 15.00 40.00
102 Keith Yandle/25 8.00 20.00
104 Nikolai Kulemin/25 8.00 20.00
105 Dustin Brown/25 8.00 20.00
106 Marian Hossa/25 12.00 30.00
110 Paul Stastny/25 20.00 40.00
113 Tuomo Ruutu/25 8.00 20.00
115 Brenden Morrow/25 10.00 25.00
116 Logan Couture/25 10.00 25.00
117 Ryan O'Reilly/25 15.00 40.00
118 Jamie Benn/25
119 Johan Franzen/25 8.00 20.00
120 Brad Boyes/25 5.00 12.00
121 Alexander Semin/25 8.00 20.00
122 Vincent Lecavalier/25 6.00 15.00
125 Matt Moulson/25 6.00 15.00
126 Tyler Seguin/25
127 Tyler Myers/25 8.00 20.00
128 Drew Stafford/10
129 Jean-Sebastien Giguere/25 10.00 25.00
130 Erik Johnson/25 5.00 12.00
131 Valtteri Filppula/25 12.00 30.00
134 Michael Cammalleri/25 8.00 20.00
136 Zach Parise/25 8.00 20.00
137 Marian Gaborik/25 10.00 25.00
140 Jaromir Jagr/25 40.00 80.00
141 Brayden Schenn/25 10.00 25.00
142 Evgeni Malkin/25 25.00 50.00
143 Jordan Staal/25
144 Jordan Eberle/10
146 Luke Schenn/25 6.00 15.00
149 Alexander Burmistrov/25 6.00 15.00
150 Evander Kane/25 12.00 30.00
151 Nik Antropov/25 12.00 30.00
153 Eric Fehr/25
154 Alexandre Burrows/25 12.00 30.00
155 Nazem Kadri/22 12.00 30.00
156 Dion Phaneuf/25 12.00 30.00
157 Chris Stewart/25 6.00 15.00
158 T.J. Oshie/25 12.00 30.00
161 Chris Pronger/25 10.00 25.00
162 James van Riemsdyk/25 8.00 20.00
163 Erik Karlsson/25 15.00 40.00
164 Derek Stepan/25 12.00 30.00
165 Kyle Okposo/25 8.00 20.00
166 Mattias Tedenby/25 5.00 12.00
167 Brian Gionta/25 6.00 15.00
170 Simon Gagne/25 8.00 20.00
173 Curtis Glencross/25 8.00 20.00
174 Tyler Ennis/25 6.00 15.00
175 Zdeno Chara/25
176 Roberto Luongo/25 15.00 40.00
178 Cam Ward/25 8.00 20.00
180 Jimmy Howard/25 12.00 30.00
181 Henrik Lundqvist/25 25.00 50.00
182 Marc-Andre Fleury/25 12.00 30.00
183 Ilya Bryzgalov/25 10.00 25.00
185 Jonathan Quick/25 30.00 60.00
186 Antti Niemi/25 10.00 25.00
187 Kari Lehtonen/25 6.00 15.00
188 Ryan Miller/25 8.00 20.00
189 Pekka Rinne/25
191 Jaroslav Halak/25 8.00 20.00
192 Jonas Hiller/25 10.00 25.00
193 Dwayne Roloson/25 8.00 20.00
194 Steve Mason/25 8.00 20.00
196 Tomas Vokoun/25 6.00 15.00
197 Niklas Backstrom/25 10.00 25.00
199 James Reimer/25 15.00 40.00
200 Jose Theodore/25 8.00 20.00

2011-12 Limited Net Presence Memorabilia

STATED PRINT RUN 10-99
1 C.Price/P.Kane/99 15.00 40.00
2 C.Price/S.Stamkos/99 15.00 40.00
3 C.Price/P.Kessel/99 15.00 40.00
4 C.Price/N.Lidstrom/99 20.00 50.00
5 C.Price/A.Kopitar/25 60.00 150.00
6 T.Thomas/A.Ovechkin/99 60.00 150.00
7 T.Thomas/E.Staal/25 25.00 60.00
8 T.Thomas/R.Nash/99 15.00 40.00
9 T.Thomas/C.Perry/99 15.00 40.00
10 C.Ward/T.Hall/99 15.00 40.00
11 C.Ward/M.Duchene/25 20.00 50.00
12 C.Ward/J.Toews/98 20.00 50.00
13 C.Ward/H.Sedin/25 15.00 40.00
14 J.Hiller/A.Ovechkin/99 12.00 30.00
15 J.Hiller/J.Skinner/25 20.00 50.00
16 J.Hiller/P.Subban/25 25.00 60.00
17 J.Hiller/D.Backes/10
18 H.Lundqvist/B.Richards/99 15.00 40.00
19 H.Lundqvist/M.St. Louis/25 25.00 60.00
20 H.Lundqvist/P.Kane/99 20.00 50.00
21 H.Lundqvist/D.Stepan/25 20.00 50.00
22 M.Fleury/D.Sedin/49 20.00 50.00
23 M.Fleury/C.Giroux/99 12.00 30.00
24 M.Fleury/R.Kesler/10
25 M.Fleury/K.Letang/49 25.00 60.00

2011-12 Limited Retired Numbers

STATED PRINT RUN 199 SER.#'d SETS
*GOLD/25: .8X TO 2X BASIC INSERT/199
*SILVER/49: .5X TO 1.2X BASIC INSERT/199
1 Johnny Bucyk 3.00 8.00
2 Mark Messier 4.00 10.00
3 Steve Yzerman 5.00 12.00
4 Cam Neely 3.00 8.00
5 Bobby Clarke 3.00 8.00
6 Luc Robitaille 3.00 8.00
7 Stan Mikita 4.00 10.00
8 Patrick Roy 8.00 20.00
9 Ron Francis 4.00 10.00
10 Bryan Trottier 4.00 10.00

2011-12 Limited Retired Numbers Materials

STATED PRINT RUN 99 SER.#'d SETS
*PRIME/25: .8X TO 2X BASIC JSY/99
1 Johnny Bucyk 5.00 12.00
2 Mark Messier 6.00 15.00
3 Steve Yzerman 15.00 40.00
4 Cam Neely 5.00 12.00
5 Bobby Clarke 8.00 20.00
6 Luc Robitaille 5.00 12.00
7 Stan Mikita 6.00 15.00
8 Patrick Roy 10.00 25.00

9 Ron Francis 6.00 15.00
10 Bryan Trottier 6.00 15.00

2011-12 Limited Retired Numbers Materials Signatures

STATED PRINT RUN 25 SER.#'d SETS
1 Johnny Bucyk 15.00 40.00
2 Mark Messier 25.00 50.00
3 Steve Yzerman 50.00 100.00
4 Cam Neely 25.00 50.00
5 Bobby Clarke 30.00 60.00
6 Luc Robitaille
7 Stan Mikita 15.00 40.00
8 Patrick Roy 50.00 100.00
9 Ron Francis 15.00 40.00
10 Bryan Trottier 12.00 30.00

2011-12 Limited Retired Numbers Signatures

STATED PRINT RUN 25 SER. #'d SETS
2/7 ISSUED IN ANTHOLOGY
1 Johnny Bucyk/25 20.00 40.00
2 Mark Messier/25 30.00 60.00
3 Steve Yzerman/25 40.00 80.00
4 Cam Neely/25 15.00 40.00
5 Bobby Clarke/25 30.00 60.00
6 Luc Robitaille/25 15.00 40.00
7 Stan Mikita/25 15.00 30.00
8 Patrick Roy/25 30.00 60.00
9 Ron Francis/25 12.00 30.00
10 Bryan Trottier/25 30.00 60.00

2011-12 Limited Select Signatures

STATED PRINT RUN 25-99
3/6/8/10/11/13/14/21 INSERTED IN ANTHOLOGY
1 Ron Francis/49 12.00 30.00
2 Trevor Linden/99
3 Stan Mikita/97 12.00 30.00
4 Scott Niedermayer/25 15.00 40.00
5 Patrick Roy/25 40.00 80.00
6 Pat LaFontaine/99 10.00 25.00
7 Milt Schmidt/99 8.00 20.00
8 Mike Bossy/97 8.00 20.00
9 Johnny Bower/99 12.00 30.00
10 Jean Beliveau/99 25.00 50.00
11 Eric Lindros/49 25.00 50.00
12 Ray Bourque/99 12.00 30.00
13 Doug Gilmour/99 12.00 30.00
14 Mark Messier/25 30.00 60.00
15 Cam Neely/99 12.00 30.00
16 Dale Hawerchuk/99 8.00 20.00
17 Curtis Joseph/99 10.00 25.00
19 Jim Craig/99 10.00 25.00
20 Doug Wilson/99 6.00 15.00
21 Felix Potvin/99 15.00 40.00
22 Gilbert Perreault/99 8.00 20.00
24 Luc Robitaille/49 10.00 25.00
25 Wendel Clark/25 15.00 40.00

2011-12 Limited Stanley Cup Signatures

STATED PRINT RUN 23-100
SOME CARDS ISSUED IN ANTHOLOGY
AL Andrew Ladd/99 12.00 30.00
AN Antti Niemi/99 10.00 25.00
BG Brian Gionta/99 8.00 20.00
BH Brett Hull/23 30.00 80.00
BM Brad Marchand/99 12.00 30.00
BR Brad Richards/25 15.00 30.00
BS Brendan Shanahan/25 20.00 40.00
CP Chris Pronger/99 12.00 30.00
CW Cam Ward/99 10.00 25.00
DB Dustin Byfuglien/25 15.00 30.00
DG Doug Gilmour/99 12.00 30.00
EM Evgeni Malkin/99 40.00 80.00
ES Eric Staal/99 8.00 20.00
GF Grant Fuhr/99 10.00 25.00
JB Jean Beliveau/99 30.00 80.00
JBO Johnny Bower/79 20.00 40.00
JF Johan Franzen/99 8.00 20.00
JN Joe Nieuwendyk/98 8.00 20.00
JS Joe Sakic/25 40.00 100.00
JSG Jean-Sebastien Giguere/100 10.00 25.00
JST Jordan Staal/99 12.00 30.00
JT J.Toews/25 EXCH 30.00 80.00
KL Kris Letang/99 15.00 40.00
MB Martin Brodeur/25 50.00 100.00
MF Marc-Andre Fleury/99 15.00 40.00
MM Mark Messier/25 25.00 60.00
MS Martin St. Louis/99 10.00 25.00
NK Nikolai Khabibulin/99 8.00 20.00
NL Nicklas Lidstrom/99 25.00 50.00
PB Patrice Bergeron/25 30.00 60.00
PD Pavel Datsyuk/99
PK Patrick Kane/99 30.00 80.00
RB Ray Bourque/49 25.00 50.00
RG Ryan Getzlaf/99 10.00 25.00
SC Sidney Crosby/25 100.00 175.00
SG Scott Gomez/99 8.00 20.00
SN Scott Niedermayer/99 10.00 25.00
SY Steve Yzerman/25
TS Tyler Seguin/25
TT Tim Thomas/25 50.00 100.00
VL Vincent Lecavalier/25 15.00 30.00

2011-12 Limited Stanley Cup Winners

STATED PRINT RUN 99-199
AL Andrew Ladd 4.00 10.00
AN Antti Niemi 3.00 8.00
BG Brian Gionta 3.00 8.00
BH Brett Hull 5.00 12.00
BM Brad Marchand 5.00 12.00
BR Brad Richards 4.00 10.00
BS Brendan Shanahan 5.00 12.00
CP Corey Perry 4.00 10.00
CPR Chris Pronger 3.00 8.00
CW Cam Ward 4.00 10.00
DB Dustin Byfuglien 4.00 10.00
DG Doug Gilmour 5.00 12.00
EM Evgeni Malkin 12.00 30.00
ES Eric Staal 5.00 12.00
GF Grant Fuhr 4.00 10.00
HR Henri Richard 4.00 10.00
JB Jean Beliveau 4.00 10.00
JBO Johnny Bower 4.00 10.00
JF Johan Franzen 4.00 10.00
JN Joe Nieuwendyk 4.00 10.00
JS Joe Sakic 6.00 15.00
JSG Jean-Sebastien Giguere 3.00 8.00
JST Jordan Staal 4.00 10.00
JT Jonathan Toews 8.00 20.00
KL Kris Letang 4.00 10.00
MB Martin Brodeur 6.00 15.00
MF Marc-Andre Fleury 6.00 15.00
MM Mark Messier 5.00 12.00
MS Milt Schmidt 3.00 8.00
MSL Martin St. Louis 4.00 10.00
MT Max Talbot 3.00 8.00
NK Nikolai Khabibulin 3.00 8.00
NL Nicklas Lidstrom 5.00 12.00
PB Patrice Bergeron 6.00 15.00
PD Pavel Datsyuk 5.00 12.00
PK Patrick Kane 8.00 20.00
PR Patrick Roy 10.00 25.00
PS Patrick Sharp 4.00 10.00
RB Ray Bourque 6.00 15.00
RG Ryan Getzlaf 6.00 15.00
SC Sidney Crosby 10.00 25.00
SG Scott Gomez 3.00 8.00
SN Scott Niedermayer 4.00 10.00
ST Shawn Thornton 6.00 15.00
SY Steve Yzerman 6.00 15.00
TH Tomas Holmstrom 2.50 6.00
TS Tyler Seguin 8.00 20.00
TT Tim Thomas 8.00 20.00
VL Vincent Lecavalier 3.00 8.00
YC Yvan Cournoyer 6.00 15.00

2011-12 Limited Team Trademarks

STATED PRINT RUN 199 SER.#'d SETS
*GOLD/25: 1X TO 2.5X BASIC INSERT/199
*SILVER/49: .6X TO 1.5X BASIC INSERT/199
1 Taylor Hall 4.00 10.00
2 Nicklas Lidstrom 2.00 5.00
3 Dustin Byfuglien 2.00 5.00
4 Tyler Seguin 4.00 10.00
5 Daniel Sedin 2.00 5.00
6 Joe Thornton 2.00 5.00
7 Anze Kopitar 3.00 8.00
8 Jarome Iginla 2.00 5.00
9 Luke Schenn 1.50 4.00
10 Ryan Miller 2.00 5.00
11 Rick Nash 2.00 5.00
12 Matt Duchene 2.00 5.00
13 Jamie Benn 2.50 6.00
14 Jaroslav Halak 2.00 5.00
15 Jeff Skinner 2.00 5.00
16 Sidney Crosby 8.00 20.00
17 Henrik Lundqvist 2.50 6.00
18 John Tavares 4.00 10.00
19 Claude Giroux 2.00 5.00
20 Zach Parise 2.00 5.00

2011-12 Limited Team Trademarks Materials

STATED PRINT RUN 99 SER.#'d SETS
*PRIME/25: .8X TO 2X BASIC JSY/99
1 Taylor Hall 5.00 12.00
2 Nicklas Lidstrom 6.00 15.00
3 Dustin Byfuglien 5.00 12.00
4 Tyler Seguin 10.00 25.00
5 Daniel Sedin 5.00 12.00
6 Joe Thornton 5.00 12.00
7 Anze Kopitar 8.00 20.00
8 Jarome Iginla 5.00 12.00
9 Luke Schenn 4.00 10.00
10 Ryan Miller 5.00 12.00
11 Rick Nash 5.00 12.00
12 Matt Duchene 5.00 12.00
13 Jamie Benn 6.00 15.00
14 Jaroslav Halak 5.00 12.00
15 Jeff Skinner 5.00 12.00
16 Sidney Crosby 12.00 30.00
17 Henrik Lundqvist 5.00 12.00
18 John Tavares 6.00 15.00
19 Claude Giroux 5.00 12.00
20 Zach Parise 6.00 15.00

2011-12 Limited Team Trademarks Materials Prime Signatures

PRIME AU STATED PRINT RUN 5-25
1/3/8/10-12/18/19 INSERTED IN ANTHOLOGY
1 Taylor Hall/25 20.00 50.00
3 Dustin Byfuglien/15 15.00 40.00
5 Daniel Sedin/25 12.00 30.00
6 Joe Thornton/25 12.00 30.00
8 Jarome Iginla/25 10.00 25.00
9 Luke Schenn/25 8.00 20.00
10 Ryan Miller/25 10.00 25.00
11 Rick Nash/25 20.00 50.00
12 Matt Duchene/25 10.00 25.00
13 Jamie Benn/25 12.00 30.00
14 Jaroslav Halak/25 10.00 25.00
16 Sidney Crosby/25 75.00 150.00
17 Henrik Lundqvist/25 15.00 40.00
18 John Tavares/25 20.00 50.00
19 Claude Giroux/25 25.00 50.00
20 Zach Parise/25

2011-12 Limited Team Trademarks Materials Signatures

STATED PRINT RUN 10-49
1/3/8/10-12/18-20 INSERTED IN ANTHOLOGY
1 Taylor Hall/49 12.00 30.00
2 Nicklas Lidstrom/49 20.00 50.00
3 Dustin Byfuglien/49 10.00 25.00
5 Daniel Sedin/49 10.00 25.00
6 Joe Thornton/49 10.00 25.00
8 Jarome Iginla/49
9 Luke Schenn/49 6.00 15.00
10 Ryan Miller/19 10.00 25.00
11 Rick Nash/49 8.00 20.00
12 Matt Duchene/49 8.00 20.00
13 Jamie Benn/49 10.00 25.00
14 Jaroslav Halak/49 10.00 25.00
16 Sidney Crosby/10
17 Henrik Lundqvist/49 12.00 30.00
18 John Tavares/49 15.00 30.00
19 Claude Giroux/49 20.00 40.00
20 Zach Parise/49 8.00 20.00

2011-12 Limited Team Trademarks Signatures

STATED PRINT RUN 10-99
1/3/8/10-12/18-20 INSERTS IN ANTHOLOGY
1 Taylor Hall/99 20.00 50.00
2 Nicklas Lidstrom/99 12.00 30.00
3 Dustin Byfuglien/99 8.00 20.00
5 Daniel Sedin/99 8.00 20.00
6 Joe Thornton/49 10.00 25.00
8 Jarome Iginla/99 10.00 25.00
9 Luke Schenn/99 6.00 15.00
10 Ryan Miller/99 10.00 25.00
11 Rick Nash/99 8.00 20.00
12 Matt Duchene/99 8.00 20.00
13 Jamie Benn/99 6.00 15.00
14 Jaroslav Halak/99 12.00 30.00
16 Sidney Crosby/10
17 Henrik Lundqvist/99 12.00 30.00
18 John Tavares/99 15.00 40.00
19 Claude Giroux/49 15.00 40.00
20 Zach Parise/99 8.00 20.00

2011-12 Limited Trios Materials

STATED PRINT RUN 99 SER.#'d SETS
*PRIME/25: .8X TO 2X BASIC TRIO/99
1 Giroux/Lindros/Clarke 12.00 30.00
2 Reimer/Joseph/Fuhr 8.00 20.00
3 Hall/Eberle/Omark 10.00 25.00
4 Bergeron/Lucic/Seguin 10.00 25.00
5 Perry/Getzlaf/Ryan 12.00 30.00
6 DiPietro/Hamonic/Tavares 8.00 20.00
7 Ovechkin/Backstrom/Neuvirth 30.00 80.00
8 Kessel/Grabovski/Kulemin 10.00 25.00
9 Thornton/Pavelski/Marleau 8.00 20.00
10 Backstrom/Clutterbuck/Koivu 8.00 20.00
11 Zetterberg/Datsyuk/Franzen 10.00 25.00
12 Toews/Sharp/Hossa 8.00 20.00
13 Myers/Ennis/Roy 8.00 20.00
14 Lecavalier/St. Louis/Purcell 8.00 20.00
15 Alfredsson/Spezza/Butler 8.00 20.00
16 Staal/Malkin/Fleury 8.00 20.00
17 Brodeur/Luongo/Fleury 12.00 30.00
18 Clark/Neely/Tocchet 8.00 20.00
19 Shanahan/Verbeek/Francis 10.00 25.00
20 Lemieux/Yzerman/Sakic 12.00 30.00

2012-13 Limited

1-150 STATED PRINT RUN 299
COMMON CAPTAIN (151-180) 1.50 4.00
151-180 STATED PRINT RUN 199
181-200 STATED PRINT RUN 99
201-242 ROOK.AU PRINT RUN 299-499
1 Steven Stamkos 4.00 10.00
2 Marcus Johansson 1.50 4.00
3 Ryan Johansen 2.50 6.00
4 Jason Spezza 2.00 5.00
5 Jake Gardiner 2.00 5.00
6 James Neal 2.00 5.00
7 Claude Giroux 2.00 5.00
8 Craig Anderson 2.00 5.00
9 Ed Jovanovski 1.25 3.00
10 Nicklas Backstrom 3.00 8.00
11 Duncan Keith 2.00 5.00
12 Cam Ward 2.00 5.00
13 Zach Parise 2.00 5.00
14 Logan Couture 2.00 5.00
15 Zack Kassian 1.50 4.00
16 Patrik Elias 2.00 5.00
17 John Tavares 4.00 10.00
18 Dennis Wideman 1.25 3.00
19 Andy McDonald 1.50 4.00
20 Ryan Whitney 1.25 3.00
21 Jussi Jokinen 1.25 3.00
22 Adam Henrique 2.00 5.00
23 Scott Clemmensen 1.50 4.00
24 Jaromir Jagr 5.00 12.00
25 Brendan Smith 1.50 4.00
26 Jordan Eberle 2.00 5.00
27 Jonathan Quick 3.00 8.00
28 Daniel Sedin 2.00 5.00
29 Taylor Hall 4.00 10.00
30 Jimmy Howard 2.00 5.00
31 Devante Smith-Pelly 1.50 4.00
32 Tim Gleason 1.25 3.00
33 Brett Connolly 1.50 4.00
34 Loui Eriksson 1.50 4.00
35 Henrik Lundqvist 2.50 6.00
36 Carey Price 6.00 15.00
37 Anze Kopitar 3.00 8.00
38 Patrick Kane 4.00 10.00
39 Tuukka Rask 2.00 5.00
40 Dan Boyle 1.50 4.00
41 David Perron 1.25 3.00
42 Ryan Miller 2.00 5.00
43 Brian Campbell 1.25 3.00
44 Jack Johnson 1.25 3.00
45 Bobby Ryan 2.00 5.00
46 Adam Larsson 2.00 5.00
47 Carl Hagelin 2.00 5.00
48 Kyle Okposo 2.00 5.00
49 Brian Elliott 1.50 4.00
50 Evander Kane 2.00 5.00
51 Kris Versteeg 1.50 4.00
52 Derek Dorsett 1.25 3.00
53 Colin Greening 1.25 3.00
54 Stephen Weiss 1.50 4.00
55 Steve Downie 1.25 3.00
56 Sean Couturier 2.00 5.00
57 Mike Smith 2.00 5.00
58 Ryan Suter 1.25 3.00
59 Steve Mason 1.50 4.00
60 Semyon Varlamov 2.00 5.00
61 Corey Crawford 2.50 6.00
62 Drew Doughty 2.00 5.00
63 Joffrey Lupul 1.50 4.00
64 Cal Clutterbuck 2.00 5.00
65 Alexander Burmistrov 1.50 4.00
66 Nazem Kadri 2.00 5.00
67 Ryan Kesler 2.00 5.00
68 Ray Whitney 1.50 4.00
69 T.J. Oshie 3.00 8.00
70 David Krejci 2.00 5.00
71 Miikka Kiprusoff 1.50 4.00
72 Cam Fowler 1.50 4.00
73 Michael Grabner 1.50 4.00
74 Matt Duchene 2.00 5.00
75 Mikael Backlund 1.50 4.00
76 Mike Fisher 1.50 4.00
77 Patrice Bergeron 2.50 6.00
78 Chris Neil 1.25 3.00
79 Kari Lehtonen 1.50 4.00
80 Jay Bouwmeester 2.00 5.00
81 Braden Holtby 3.00 8.00
82 Ryan Nugent-Hopkins 2.00 5.00
83 Mike Richards 2.00 5.00
84 Jeff Skinner 2.00 5.00
85 Alex Tanguay 1.25 3.00
86 Jonas Gustavsson 2.00 5.00
87 Marian Gaborik 2.00 5.00
88 Pekka Rinne 2.50 6.00
89 Devin Setoguchi 1.50 4.00
90 Marcus Kruger 2.50 6.00
91 Martin Erat 1.25 3.00
92 Steve Ott 1.50 4.00
93 Martin Havlat 1.50 4.00
94 Martin Hanzal 1.25 3.00
95 Niklas Backstrom 1.50 4.00
96 Martin St. Louis 2.00 5.00
97 Alex Goligoski 1.25 3.00
98 Jeff Carter 2.00 5.00
99 Louis Leblanc 2.00 5.00
100 Devan Dubnyk 2.00 5.00
101 Jiri Hudler 1.50 4.00
102 Danny Briere 2.00 5.00
103 Erik Karlsson 4.00 10.00
104 Tyler Seguin 3.00 8.00
105 Cody Hodgson 2.00 5.00
106 Ilya Bryzgalov 2.00 5.00
107 Marc-Andre Fleury 3.00 8.00
108 Brad Richards 2.00 5.00
109 Cody Eakin 1.50 4.00
110 Erik Johnson 1.25 3.00
111 Ondrej Pavelec 2.00 5.00
112 Marcus Foligno 1.50 4.00
113 Pavel Datsyuk 2.50 6.00
114 Phil Kessel 2.50 6.00
115 Keith Yandle 2.00 5.00
116 Lars Eller 1.50 4.00
117 Corey Perry 2.00 5.00
118 Oliver Ekman-Larsson 2.00 5.00
119 Marc Staal 1.50 4.00
120 Rick Nash 2.00 5.00
121 Jamie Benn 2.50 6.00
122 Craig Smith 1.25 3.00
123 Jonas Hiller 1.50 4.00
124 Tuomo Ruutu 1.50 4.00
125 Jordan Staal 2.00 5.00
126 Dustin Byfuglien 2.00 5.00
127 Cory Schneider 1.50 4.00
128 Antti Niemi 1.50 4.00
129 Michael Cammalleri 1.50 4.00
130 Gabriel Landeskog 2.00 5.00
131 Milan Lucic 2.00 5.00
132 Alex Pietrangelo 1.50 4.00
133 Al Montoya 1.25 3.00
134 Matt Cullen 1.25 3.00
135 Victor Hedman 2.50 6.00
136 Max Pacioretty 2.00 5.00
137 Henrik Zetterberg 2.50 6.00
138 Patrick Marleau 2.00 5.00
139 Nathan Gerbe 1.25 3.00
140 Blake Wheeler 2.00 5.00
141 Mathieu Garon 1.50 4.00
142 Martin Brodeur 4.00 10.00
143 Dany Heatley 1.50 4.00
144 Kris Letang 2.00 5.00
145 Patrick Sharp 2.00 5.00
146 P.K. Subban 3.00 8.00
147 Kevin Bieksa 1.50 4.00
148 Tyler Myers 1.50 4.00
149 Matt Moulson 1.50 4.00
150 Evgeni Malkin 6.00 15.00
151 Ryan Getzlaf/199 C 4.00 10.00
152 Zdeno Chara/199 C 2.50 6.00
153 Jason Pominville/199 C 2.00 5.00
154 Jarome Iginla/199 C 2.50 6.00
155 Eric Staal/199 C 3.00 8.00
156 Jonathan Toews/199 C 5.00 12.00
157 Milan Hejduk/199 C 2.00 5.00
158 R.J. Umberger/199 C 1.50 4.00
159 Brenden Morrow/199 C 2.00 5.00
160 Nicklas Lidstrom/199 C 2.50 6.00
161 Shawn Horcoff/199 C 1.50 4.00
162 Ed Jovanovski/199 C 1.50 4.00
163 Dustin Brown/199 C 2.50 6.00
164 Mikko Koivu/199 C 2.00 5.00
165 Brian Gionta/199 C 2.00 5.00
166 Shea Weber/199 C 2.00 5.00
167 Ilya Kovalchuk/199 C 2.50 6.00
168 Mark Streit/199 C 1.50 4.00
169 Ryan Callahan/199 C 2.50 6.00
170 Daniel Alfredsson/199 C 2.50 6.00
171 Chris Pronger/199 C 2.00 5.00
172 Shane Doan/199 C 2.00 5.00
173 Sidney Crosby/199 C 5.00 12.00
174 David Backes/199 C 2.50 6.00
175 Joe Thornton/199 C 2.50 6.00
176 Vincent Lecavalier/199 C 2.00 5.00
177 Dion Phaneuf/199 C 2.50 6.00
178 Henrik Sedin/199 C 2.50 6.00
179 Alex Ovechkin/199 C 10.00 25.00
180 Andrew Ladd/199 C 2.50 6.00
181 Mark Messier/99 C 5.00 12.00
182 Eric Lindros/99 C 6.00 15.00
183 Steve Yzerman/99 C 8.00 20.00
184 Joe Sakic/99 C 6.00 15.00
185 Jean Beliveau/99 C 4.00 10.00
186 Bobby Clarke/99 C 4.00 10.00
187 Trevor Linden/99 C 5.00 12.00
188 Ray Bourque/99 C 6.00 15.00
189 Pat LaFontaine/99 C 4.00 10.00
190 Doug Gilmour/99 C 5.00 12.00
191 Lanny McDonald/99 C 4.00 10.00
192 Brett Hull/99 C 4.00 10.00
193 Mike Modano/99 C 6.00 15.00
194 Yvan Cournoyer/99 C 4.00 10.00
195 Mario Lemieux/99 C 12.00 30.00
196 Ron Francis/99 C 5.00 12.00
197 Luc Robitaille/99 C 4.00 10.00
198 Johnny Bucyk/99 C 3.00 8.00
199 Dale Hawerchuk/99 C 5.00 12.00
200 Gordie Howe/99 C 8.00 20.00
201 Aaron Ness AU/499 RC 4.00 10.00
202 J.T. Brown AU/499 RC 4.00 10.00
203 Brandon Bollig AU/499 RC 6.00 15.00
204 Brandon Manning AU/499 RC 4.00 10.00
205 Brenden Dillon AU/499 RC 4.00 10.00
206A C.Ashton AU/499 RC TOR 3.00 8.00
206B C.Ashton AU/499 RC TB 3.00 8.00
207 Carter Camper AU/299 RC 3.00 8.00
208 Casey Cizikas AU/499 RC 4.00 10.00
209 Chay Genoway AU/499 RC 4.00 10.00
210 Chet Pickard AU/499 RC 4.00 10.00
211 Cody Goloubef AU/499 RC 4.00 10.00
212 Colby Robak AU/499 RC 4.00 10.00
213 Dalton Prout AU/499 RC 4.00 10.00
214 Jake Allen AU/499 RC 12.00 30.00
215 Jakob Silfverberg AU/499 RC 5.00 12.00
216 Jordan Nolan AU/499 RC 4.00 10.00
217 Jussi Rynnas AU/499 RC 4.00 10.00
218 Kris Foucault AU/499 RC 4.00 10.00
219 Mat Clark AU/499 RC 4.00 10.00
220 Matt Donovan AU/499 RC 4.00 10.00
221 Max Sauve AU/299 RC 4.00 10.00
222 Tyson Sexsmith AU/499 RC 4.00 10.00
223 Michael Stone AU/499 RC 4.00 10.00
224 Mike Connolly AU/499 RC 4.00 10.00
225 Philippe Cornet AU/499 RC 4.00 10.00
226 Robert Mayer AU/499 RC 5.00 12.00
227 Scott Glennie AU/499 RC 4.00 10.00
228 Reilly Smith AU/499 RC 8.00 20.00
229 Tyler Cuma AU/299 RC 4.00 10.00
230 Tyson Barrie AU/499 RC 8.00 20.00
231 Chris Kreider AU/499 RC 12.00 30.00
232 Sven Baertschi AU/499 RC 6.00 15.00
233 Jaden Schwartz AU/499 RC 8.00 20.00
234 Riley Sheahan AU/499 RC 4.00 10.00
235 Andrew Joudrey AU/299 RC 4.00 10.00
236 Ryan Garbutt AU/299 RC 4.00 10.00
237 Travis Turnbull AU/499 RC 4.00 10.00
238 Ryan Hamilton AU/499 RC 6.00 15.00
239 Shawn Hunwick AU/299 RC 4.00 10.00
240 Gabriel Dumont AU/499 RC 4.00 10.00
241 Akim Aliu AU/499 RC 4.00 10.00
242 Jeremy Welsh AU/499 RC 4.00 10.00

2012-13 Limited Back To The Future

STATED PRINT RUN 199
BTFAG C.Ashton/D.Gilmour 4.00 10.00
BTFBN D.Brown/B.Nicholls 3.00 8.00
BTFDD A.Delvecchio/P.Datsyuk 4.00 10.00
BTFEJ L.Eriksson/J.Jagr 5.00 12.00
BTFFL M.Foligno/P.LaFontaine 3.00 8.00
BTFGE E.Lindros/G.Landeskog 5.00 12.00
BTFHN A.Henrique/J.Nieuwendyk 3.00 8.00
BTFIB J.Iginla/S.Baertschi 8.00 20.00
BTFJA C.Joseph/J.Allen 8.00 20.00
BTFLC R.Leach/S.Couturier 3.00 8.00
BTFLK T.Linden/Z.Kassian 3.00 8.00
BTFLL L.Leblanc/G.Lafleur 4.00 10.00
BTFLS N.Lidstrom/B.Smith 3.00 8.00
BTFMG M.Modano/S.Glennie 5.00 12.00
BTFMK M.Messier/C.Kreider 5.00 12.00
BTFMP A.MacInnis/A.Pietrangelo 3.00 8.00
BTFPD D.Potvin/C.de Haan 3.00 8.00
BTFPR F.Potvin/J.Rynnas 5.00 12.00
BTFPR C.Pickard/P.Rinne 6.00 15.00
BTFQB J.Quick/M.Brodeur 6.00 15.00
BTFRH B.Richards/C.Hagelin 3.00 8.00
BTFRK M.Read/T.Kerr 4.00 10.00
BTFSB M.St. Louis/J.Brown 3.00 8.00
BTFSR A.Shaw/J.Roenick 5.00 12.00
BTFSS B.Shanahan/J.Schwartz 5.00 12.00

2012-13 Limited Back To The Future Signatures

STATED PRINT RUN 25
BTFAG C.Ashton/D.Gilmour 20.00 50.00
BTFBN D.Brown/B.Nicholls 25.00 50.00
BTFDD A.Delvecchio/P.Datsyuk 25.00 50.00
BTFEJ L.Eriksson/J.Jagr 40.00 80.00
BTFFL M.Foligno/P.LaFontaine 10.00 25.00
BTFGE E.Lindros/G.Landeskog 50.00 100.00
BTFHN A.Henrique/J.Nieuwendyk 15.00 40.00
BTFIB J.Iginla/S.Baertschi 30.00 60.00
BTFJA C.Joseph/J.Allen 40.00 100.00
BTFLC R.Leach/S.Couturier 12.00 30.00
BTFLK Linden/Kassian 2.00 50.00
BTFLL L.Leblanc/G.Lafleur 15.00 40.00
BTFLS N.Lidstrom/B.Smith 15.00 40.00
BTFMG M.Modano/S.Glennie 15.00 40.00
BTFMK M.Messier/C.Kreider 25.00 50.00
BTFMP A.MacInnis/A.Pietrangelo 15.00 40.00
BTFPD D.Potvin/C.de Haan 15.00 40.00
BTFPR F.Potvin/J.Rynnas
BTFPR C.Pickard/P.Rinne 20.00 50.00
BTFQB J.Quick/M.Brodeur 20.00 50.00
BTFRH B.Richards/C.Hagelin 15.00 40.00
BTFRK M.Read/T.Kerr 12.00 30.00
BTFSB M.St. Louis/J.Brown 12.00 30.00
BTFSR A.Shaw/J.Roenick 40.00 80.00
BTFSS B.Shanahan/J.Schwartz 25.00 60.00

2012-13 Limited Board Members

STATED PRINT RUN 199
*DIECUT/25: 2X TO 5X BASIC INS
1 Alex Ovechkin 10.00 25.00
2 Eric Lindros 4.00 10.00
3 Dustin Brown 2.50 6.00
4 David Backes 2.50 6.00
5 Cam Neely 2.50 6.00
6 Dion Phaneuf 2.50 6.00
7 Shea Weber 2.00 5.00
8 Zdeno Chara 2.50 6.00
9 Duncan Keith 2.50 6.00
10 Ryan Kesler 2.50 6.00
11 Mike Richards 2.50 6.00
12 Scott Hartnell 3.00 8.00
13 Dustin Byfuglien 2.50 6.00
14 Drew Doughty 2.50 6.00
15 Milan Lucic 2.50 6.00
16 P.K. Subban 4.00 10.00
17 Ryan Getzlaf 4.00 10.00
18 Paul Bissonnette 1.50 4.00
19 Ryan Callahan 2.50 6.00
20 Steve Ott 2.00 5.00
21 Shane Doan 2.00 5.00
22 Gabriel Landeskog 2.50 6.00
23 Steven Stamkos 5.00 12.00
24 Sidney Crosby 4.00 10.00
25 Jarome Iginla 2.50 6.00
26 Henrik Zetterberg 3.00 8.00
27 Zach Parise 2.50 6.00
28 Alex Pietrangelo 2.00 5.00
29 Erik Gudbranson 2.50 6.00
30 Claude Giroux 5.00 12.00
31 Jordan Eberle 2.50 6.00
32 Chris Kreider 5.00 12.00
33 Jaden Schwartz 4.00 10.00
34 Sven Baertschi 6.00 15.00
35 Jeff Skinner 2.50 6.00
36 Ryan Nugent-Hopkins 2.50 6.00
37 John Tavares 5.00 12.00
38 Mario Lemieux 6.00 15.00
39 Mark Messier 3.00 8.00
40 Brendan Shanahan 3.00 8.00
41 Brett Hull 2.50 6.00
42 Doug Gilmour 3.00 8.00
43 Cody Hodgson 2.50 6.00
44 Andrew Ladd 2.50 6.00
45 Zack Kassian 2.00 5.00
46 Erik Karlsson 5.00 12.00
47 Keith Primeau 2.50 6.00
48 Jeremy Roenick 2.50 6.00
49 Steve Downie 1.50 4.00
50 Victor Hedman 3.00 8.00

2012-13 Limited Crease Cleaners Materials

STATED PRINT RUN 25-99
*PRIME/25: .8X TO 2X BASIC JSY/99
1 Chet Pickard/99 4.00 10.00
2 Jake Allen/99 12.00 30.00
3 Patrick Roy/99 12.00 30.00
4 Tuukka Rask/99 5.00 12.00
5 Pekka Rinne/99 6.00 15.00
6 Jimmy Howard/99 5.00 12.00
7 Cory Schneider/99 4.00 10.00
8 Jonathan Quick/99 8.00 20.00
9 Martin Brodeur/99 10.00 25.00
10 Jonas Hiller/99 4.00 10.00
11 Henrik Lundqvist/99 6.00 15.00
12 Jhonas Enroth/99 5.00 12.00
13 Kari Lehtonen/99 4.00 10.00
14 Carey Price/99 15.00 40.00
15 Ron Hextall/99 8.00 20.00
16 Felix Potvin/99 6.00 15.00
17 Johan Hedberg/99 8.00 20.00
18 Grant Fuhr/99 5.00 12.00
19 Niklas Backstrom/99 4.00 10.00
20 Ryan Miller/99 5.00 12.00
21 Mike Smith/25 8.00 20.00
22 Roberto Luongo/99 5.00 12.00
23 Craig Anderson/99 5.00 12.00
24 Tomas Vokoun/99 4.00 10.00
25 Jaroslav Halak/99 5.00 12.00
26 Braden Holtby/99 8.00 20.00
27 Marc-Andre Fleury/99 8.00 20.00
28 Brian Elliott/99 4.00 10.00
29 Ondrej Pavelec/99 5.00 12.00
30 Miikka Kiprusoff/99 4.00 10.00
32 Jonathan Bernier/99 5.00 12.00
33 Ilya Bryzgalov/99 5.00 12.00
34 Nikolai Khabibulin/99 5.00 12.00
35 Evgeni Nabokov/99 4.00 10.00
36 Antti Niemi/99 4.00 10.00
37 James Reimer/99 5.00 12.00
38 Scott Clemmensen/99 4.00 10.00
39 Curtis Joseph/99 5.00 12.00
40 Bernie Parent/99 8.00 20.00

2012-13 Limited Duels Silver

STATED PRINT RUN 99
LD1A Claude Giroux 4.00 10.00
LD1B Sidney Crosby 15.00 40.00
LD2A Dustin Brown 4.00 10.00
LD2B Shane Doan 3.00 8.00
LD3A Henrik Lundqvist 5.00 12.00
LD3B Martin Brodeur 8.00 20.00
LD4A Mike Smith 4.00 10.00
LD4B Jonathan Quick 6.00 15.00
LD5A Evgeni Malkin 12.00 30.00
LD5B Sean Couturier 4.00 10.00
LD6A Alex Ovechkin 6.00 15.00
LD6B Marian Gaborik 4.00 10.00
LD7A Ryan Kesler 4.00 10.00
LD7B Mike Richards 4.00 10.00
LD8A Loui Eriksson 3.00 8.00
LD8B Pavel Datsyuk 10.00 25.00
LD9A Ryan Nugent-Hopkins 4.00 10.00
LD9B Gabriel Landeskog 4.00 10.00
LD10A Carey Price 12.00 30.00
LD10B Tim Thomas 4.00 10.00
LD11A Dion Phaneuf 4.00 10.00
LD11B Tyler Myers 3.00 8.00
LD12A Brad Marchand 6.00 15.00
LD12B P.K. Subban 6.00 15.00
LD13A Adam Henrique 4.00 10.00
LD13B Chris Kreider 6.00 15.00
LD14A David Backes 4.00 10.00
LD14B Jonathan Toews 8.00 20.00
LD15A Steven Stamkos 8.00 20.00
LD15B James Neal 4.00 10.00
LD16A Corey Perry 4.00 10.00
LD16B Patrick Kane 8.00 20.00
LD17A John Tavares 8.00 20.00
LD17B Matt Duchene 4.00 10.00
LD18A Tyler Seguin 6.00 15.00
LD18B Taylor Hall 8.00 20.00
LD19A Scott Glennie 3.00 8.00
LD19B Jaden Schwartz 6.00 15.00
LD20A Jake Allen 10.00 25.00
LD20B Chet Pickard 3.00 8.00
LD21A Brendan Shanahan 5.00 12.00
LD21B Patrick Roy 10.00 25.00
LD22A Eric Lindros 6.00 15.00
LD22B Mark Messier 5.00 12.00
LD23A Joe Sakic 6.00 15.00
LD23B Steve Yzerman 15.00 40.00
LD24A Guy Lafleur 5.00 12.00
LD24B Bobby Clarke 4.00 10.00
LD25A Gordie Howe 8.00 20.00
LD25B Johnny Bower 4.00 10.00

2012-13 Limited Freshman Dual Jumbo Materials

STATED PRINT RUN 49
FDAR C.Ashton/J.Rynnas 10.00 25.00
FDBB S.Baertschi/T.Barrie 8.00 20.00
FDKS C.Kreider/J.Silfverberg 8.00 20.00
FDPG C.Pickard/S.Glennie 6.00 15.00
FDSA J.Schwartz/J.Allen 8.00 20.00

2012-13 Limited Freshman Jumbo Materials

*PRIME/49: .6X TO 1.5X JSY/149-199
FJCA Carter Ashton/199 2.00 5.00
FJCK Chris Kreider/199 5.00 12.00
FJCP Chet Pickard/199 2.50 6.00
FJJA Jake Allen/199 8.00 20.00
FJJB J.T. Brown/199 2.50 6.00
FJJR Jussi Rynnas/199 2.50 6.00
FJJS Jaden Schwartz/199 5.00 12.00
FJJS Jakob Silfverberg/199 5.00 12.00
FJRS Reilly Smith/199 5.00 12.00
FJSB Sven Baertschi/149 3.00 8.00
FJSG Scott Glennie/199 2.50 6.00
FJTB Tyson Barrie/199 5.00 12.00

2012-13 Limited Freshman Jumbo Materials Signatures

STATED PRINT RUN 99
FJCA Carter Ashton 5.00 12.00
FJCK Chris Kreider 10.00 25.00
FJCP Chet Pickard
FJJA Jake Allen 15.00 40.00
FJJB J.T. Brown 5.00 12.00
FJJR Jussi Rynnas 8.00 20.00
FJJS Jakob Silfverberg 12.00 30.00
FJJS Jaden Schwartz 8.00 20.00
FJRS Reilly Smith 10.00 25.00
FJSB Sven Baertschi 6.00 15.00
FJSG Scott Glennie 5.00 12.00
FJTB Tyson Barrie 10.00 25.00

2012-13 Limited Game Pucks

STATED PRINT RUN 25
GPAO Alex Ovechkin 20.00 50.00
GPBR Bobby Ryan 8.00 20.00
GPCG Claude Giroux 8.00 20.00
GPDB Dustin Brown 8.00 20.00
GPEM Evgeni Malkin 25.00 60.00
GPJA John Tavares 15.00 40.00
GPJO Joe Thornton 8.00 20.00
GPLE Loui Eriksson 6.00 15.00
GPMA Marc Staal 6.00 15.00
GPMB Martin Brodeur 15.00 40.00
GPMG Marian Gaborik 8.00 20.00
GPMS Mike Smith 8.00 20.00
GPOP Ondrej Pavelec 8.00 20.00
GPPD Pavel Datsyuk 10.00 25.00
GPRK Ryan Kesler 10.00 25.00
GPRM Ryan Miller 10.00 25.00
GPSS Steven Stamkos 15.00 40.00
GPSW Shea Weber 6.00 15.00
GPTS Tyler Seguin 12.00 30.00

2012-13 Limited Gold

*1-150 GOLD/25: 1X TO 2.5X BASIC CARDS
*151-180 GOLD/25: 1X TO 2.5X BASIC C/199
*181-200 GOLD/25: .6X TO 1.5X BASIC C/99
*201-233 GOLD AU/25: .8X TO 2X AU RC
STATED PRINT RUN 25
10 Nicklas Backstrom 8.00 20.00
61 Corey Crawford 6.00 15.00

2012-13 Limited Jumbo Materials

STATED PRINT RUN 10-99
*PRIME/49: .6X TO 1.5X JUM.JSY/50-99
*PRIME/25: .8X TO 2X JUM.JSY/50-99
JJAB Alexander Burmistrov/99 4.00 10.00
JJAL Adam Larsson/99 5.00 12.00
JJAN Antti Niemi/99 4.00 10.00
JJAO Alex Ovechkin/99 20.00 50.00
JJAX Alexandre Burrows/99 5.00 12.00
JJBL Bryan Little/99 5.00 12.00
JJCG Claude Giroux/99 5.00 12.00
JJCH Carl Hagelin/99 5.00 12.00
JJCN Chris Neil/99 3.00 8.00
JJCO Corey Perry/99 5.00 12.00
JJCP Carey Price/99 15.00 40.00
JJDG Dan Girardi/99 3.00 8.00
JJDP David Perron/99 3.00 8.00
JJDS Devin Setoguchi/75 4.00 10.00
JJEL Eric Lindros/99 8.00 20.00
JJGL Gabriel Landeskog/50 5.00 12.00
JJHL Henrik Lundqvist/99 6.00 15.00
JJJA John Tavares/99 10.00 25.00
JJJC Jeff Carter/99 5.00 12.00
JJJE Jordan Eberle/99 5.00 12.00
JJJG Josh Gorges/99 4.00 10.00
JJJH Joe Thornton/99 5.00 12.00
JJJN James Neal/99 5.00 12.00
JJJO Joe Nieuwendyk/99 5.00 12.00
JJJP Jason Pominville/99 4.00 10.00
JJJQ Jonathan Quick/99 8.00 20.00
JJJS Jordan Staal/99 5.00 12.00
JJJT Jonathan Toews/99 10.00 25.00
JJJV James van Riemsdyk/99 5.00 12.00
JJKL Kari Lehtonen/99 4.00 10.00
JJKP Keith Primeau/99 4.00 10.00
JJLE Loui Eriksson/99 4.00 10.00
JJMF Marc-Andre Fleury/99 8.00 20.00
JJMG Marian Gaborik/99 5.00 12.00
JJMH Martin Hanzal/99 3.00 8.00
JJMI Mikhail Grabovski/99 4.00 10.00
JJMK Miikka Kiprusoff/99 4.00 10.00
JJMR Matt Read/99 4.00 10.00
JJMS Mike Smith/25 15.00 30.00
JJNG Nathan Gerbe/99 3.00 8.00
JJNL Nicklas Lidstrom/99 5.00 12.00
JJPD Pavel Datsyuk/99 6.00 15.00
JJPS P.K. Subban/99 8.00 20.00
JJRF Ron Francis/99 6.00 15.00
JJRL Robin Lehner/99 4.00 10.00
JJRN Ryan Nugent-Hopkins/99 5.00 12.00
JJRS Ryan Suter/99 3.00 8.00
JJSC Sidney Crosby/99 10.00 25.00
JJSG Sam Gagner/99 4.00 10.00
JJSK Saku Koivu/99 5.00 12.00
JJSM Scott Clemmensen/99 4.00 10.00
JJSW Shea Weber/99 4.00 10.00
JJSY Steve Yzerman/99 10.00 25.00
JJTS Tyler Seguin/99 8.00 20.00

2012-13 Limited Jumbo Materials Signatures

STATED PRINT RUN 10-49
JJAB Alexander Burmistrov/49 6.00 15.00
JJAL Adam Larsson/49 EXCH 8.00 20.00
JJAN Antti Niemi/49 6.00 15.00
JJAO Alex Ovechkin/25
JJCG Claude Giroux/49 8.00 20.00
JJCH Carl Hagelin/49 8.00 20.00
JJCN Chris Neil/49 5.00 12.00
JJCO Corey Perry/49 10.00 25.00
JJCP Carey Price/49 25.00 60.00
JJDP David Perron/49
JJGL Gabriel Landeskog/49 8.00 20.00
JJJA John Tavares/49 15.00 40.00
JJJE Jordan Eberle/49 8.00 20.00
JJJH Joe Thornton/49 8.00 20.00
JJJN James Neal/49 12.00 30.00
JJJO Joe Nieuwendyk/49 8.00 20.00
JJJQ Jonathan Quick/49 25.00 60.00
JJJS Jordan Staal/49 EXCH 10.00 25.00
JJJT Jonathan Toews/49 25.00 50.00
JJJV James van Riemsdyk/49 8.00 20.00
JJKL Kari Lehtonen/49 6.00 15.00
JJKP Keith Primeau/49 6.00 15.00
JJLE Loui Eriksson/49 6.00 15.00
JJMF Marc-Andre Fleury/49 12.00 30.00
JJMG Marian Gaborik/49 8.00 20.00
JJMI Mikhail Grabovski/49 6.00 15.00
JJMR Matt Read/49
JJNG Nathan Gerbe/49 5.00 12.00
JJNL Nicklas Lidstrom/49 12.00 30.00
JJPD Pavel Datsyuk/49 15.00 40.00
JJPS P.K. Subban/49 12.00 30.00
JJRF Ron Francis/49 10.00 25.00
JJRL Robin Lehner/49 6.00 15.00
JJRN Ryan Nugent-Hopkins/49 15.00 40.00
JJSC Sidney Crosby/25
JJSG Sam Gagner/49 6.00 15.00
JJSK Saku Koivu/49 8.00 20.00
JJSW Shea Weber/49 8.00 20.00
JJTS Tyler Seguin/49 15.00 40.00

2012-13 Limited Materials

STATED PRINT RUN 49-99
*PRIME/25: .6X TO 1.5X JSY/75-99
*PRIME/25: .8X TO 1.2X JSY/49-50
LJAA Artem Anisimov/99 3.00 8.00
LJAB Alexander Burmistrov/99 3.00 8.00
LJAG Adam Graves/99 3.00 8.00
LJAK Andrei Kostitsyn/99 3.00 8.00
LJAN Antti Niemi/99 3.00 8.00
LJAT Alex Tanguay/99 2.50 6.00
LJAV Antoine Vermette/99 2.50 6.00
LJAZ Anze Kopitar/99 6.00 15.00
LJBD Brandon Dubinsky/99 3.00 8.00
LJBE Brian Boyle/99 2.50 6.00
LJBG Brian Gionta/99 3.00 8.00
LJBH Brett Hull/99 4.00 10.00
LJBL Bryan Little/99 4.00 10.00
LJBO Dan Boyle/99 3.00 8.00
LJBP Brandon Prust/99 2.50 6.00
LJBR Danny Briere/99 4.00 10.00
LJBS Brad Boyes/99 2.50 6.00
LJCC Chris Chelios/99 4.00 10.00
LJCG Curtis Glencross/99 2.50 6.00
LJCL Scott Clemmensen/99 3.00 8.00
LJCO Sean Couturier/99 4.00 10.00
LJCS Chris Stewart/99 3.00 8.00
LJCW Cam Ward/49 5.00 12.00
LJDA Daniel Alfredsson/99 4.00 10.00
LJDD Devan Dubnyk/99 4.00 10.00
LJDE Simon Despres/99 3.00 8.00
LJDG Dan Girardi/99 2.50 6.00
LJDK Dmitry Kulikov/99 2.50 6.00
LJDP David Perron/99 2.50 6.00
LJDT Dana Tyrell/99 2.50 6.00
LJEB Jordan Eberle/99 4.00 10.00
LJEK Erik Karlsson/99 8.00 20.00
LJEL Eric Lindros/99 6.00 15.00
LJEN Jhonas Enroth/99 4.00 10.00
LJES Eric Staal/50 6.00 15.00
LJGF Grant Fuhr/99 4.00 10.00
LJGI Mikhail Grabovski/99 3.00 8.00
LJGL Gabriel Landeskog/99 4.00 10.00
LJGN Mike Green/99 4.00 10.00

JGP George Parros/99 3.00 8.00
JHA Martin Hanzal/99 2.50 6.00
JHO Marian Hossa/99 3.00 8.00
JHZ Henrik Zetterberg/99 5.00 12.00
JJC Jeff Carter/99 4.00 10.00
JJH Johan Hedberg/99 3.00 8.00
JJL Jamie Langenbrunner/99 2.50 6.00
JJM Joe Mullen/99 3.00 8.00
JJN James Neal/99 4.00 10.00
JJS Jarret Stoll/99 3.00 8.00
JJV James van Riemsdyk/99 4.00 10.00
JKL Kari Lehtonen/99 3.00 8.00
JKO Niklas Kronwall/99 3.00 8.00
JKP Keith Primeau/99 3.00 8.00
JKR David Krejci/99 4.00 10.00
JKS Kevin Shattenkirk/99 4.00 10.00
JKU Nikolai Kulemin/99 3.00 8.00
JLA Adam Larsson/99 4.00 10.00
JLC Logan Couture/99 4.00 10.00
JLE Loui Eriksson/99 3.00 8.00
JLI Anders Lindback/49 3.00 8.00
JLS Luca Sbisa/99 3.00 8.00
JMA Martin Brodeur/99 8.00 20.00
JMC Michael Cammalleri/99 3.00 8.00
JMD Michael Del Zotto/99 2.50 6.00
JMF Marc-Andre Fleury/99 6.00 15.00
JMI Mikkel Boedker/99 2.50 6.00
JMR Matt Read/99 3.00 8.00
JMS Al MacInnis/99 4.00 10.00
JMZ Alec Martinez/99 2.50 6.00
JNC Nicklas Backstrom/99 6.00 15.00
JNG Nathan Gerbe/99 2.50 6.00
JNH Ryan Nugent-Hopkins/99 4.00 10.00
JNK Niklas Backstrom/75 3.00 8.00
JNO Nick Bonino/99 2.50 6.00
JPB Paul Bissonnette/99 2.50 6.00
JPC Paul Coffey/99 4.00 10.00
JPM Peter Mueller/99 2.50 6.00
JPR Pekka Rinne/99 5.00 12.00
JPS Patrick Sharp/99 4.00 10.00
JRN Rick Nash/99 4.00 10.00
JRS Ryan Smyth/99 3.00 8.00
JSA Joe Sakic/99 6.00 15.00
JSC Sidney Crosby/99 10.00 25.00
JSD Shane Doan/99 3.00 8.00
JSG Sam Gagner/99 3.00 8.00
JSH Scott Hartnell/99 4.00 10.00
JSM Derek Smith/99 2.50 6.00
JSP Jason Spezza/99 4.00 10.00
JST Paul Stastny/99 4.00 10.00
JSU Ryan Suter/99 2.50 6.00
JSV Denis Savard/99 5.00 12.00
JTA John Tavares/99 8.00 20.00
JTB Tyler Bozak/99 3.00 8.00
JTE Tyler Ennis/99 3.00 8.00
JTH Joe Thornton/99 4.00 10.00
JTO Jonathan Toews/99 10.00 25.00
JTR Tuukka Rask/99 4.00 10.00
JTS Teemu Selanne/99 8.00 20.00
JTZ Travis Zajac/99 3.00 8.00
JZC Zdeno Chara/99 4.00 10.00

2012-13 Limited Materials Signatures

ATED PRINT RUN 10-25
AB Alexander Burmistrov/25
AO Alex Ovechkin/25 30.00 60.00
AV Antoine Vermette/25
BA Bernie Parent/25 20.00 50.00
BB Brent Burns/25 15.00 40.00
BH Brett Hull/25 20.00 50.00
BI Brad Richards/25
BM Brenden Morrow/25
BR Brayden Schenn/25 12.00 30.00
BS Brad Boyes/25
BY Bobby Ryan/25
CA Craig Anderson/25 12.00 30.00
CC Chris Chelios/25 12.00 30.00
CH Carl Hagelin/25 12.00 30.00
CI Colin Wilson/25
CP Chris Pronger/25 10.00 25.00
CT Cal Clutterbuck/25
DB David Backes/25 12.00 30.00
DD Devan Dubnyk/25 12.00 30.00
DU Dustin Brown/25 12.00 30.00
EM Evgeni Malkin/25 30.00 60.00
ES Eric Staal/25 15.00 40.00
HS Henrik Sedin/25 12.00 30.00
JA Jack Johnson/25
JB Jamie Benn/25 15.00 40.00
JJ Jaromir Jagr/25 30.00 60.00
JN James Neal/25 12.00 30.00
JT Jordin Tootoo/25 10.00 25.00
KG Kris Letang/25 15.00 40.00
LA Adam Larsson/25
LE Loui Eriksson/25 10.00 25.00
MK Mike Smith/25
MS Al MacInnis/25 12.00 30.00
MT Martin St. Louis/25 12.00 30.00
MU Matt Duchene/25 12.00 30.00
MX Maxime Macenauer/25
MY Mason Raymond/25 10.00 25.00
NI Nikolai Khabibulin/25 12.00 30.00
PC Paul Coffey/25 20.00 40.00
PD Pavel Datsyuk/25 20.00 40.00
RK Ryan Kesler/25 12.00 30.00
RL Robin Lehner/25
SA Joe Sakic/25 20.00 40.00
SG Sam Gagner/25
SW Stephen Weiss/25
VL Vincent Lecavalier/25

2012-13 Limited Monikers

ATED PRINT RUN 25-99
OLD/25: .5X TO 1.2X MONIKER/99
B Alexander Burmistrov/99 8.00 20.00
O Alex Ovechkin/99 40.00 80.00
P Alex Pietrangelo/99 8.00 20.00
H Bobby Hull/25 40.00 80.00
R Bobby Ryan/99 10.00 25.00
S Brendan Shanahan/25 30.00 60.00
A Craig Anderson/99 10.00 25.00
G Claude Giroux/99 20.00 50.00
P Carey Price/99 20.00 50.00
P Chris Pronger/99 8.00 20.00
S Cory Schneider/99 8.00 20.00
D Drew Doughty/99 15.00 30.00
Eric Lindros/25 30.00 60.00
M Evgeni Malkin/99 20.00 50.00
S Eric Staal/99 12.00 30.00
H Gordie Howe/25 100.00 200.00
H Joe Thornton/99 10.00 25.00
Jarome Iginla/99 12.00 30.00
Q Jonathan Quick/99 20.00 40.00
S Joe Sakic/25 20.00 50.00
T Jonathan Toews/99 25.00 50.00
Y Keith Yandle/99 10.00 25.00
C Logan Couture/99 10.00 25.00
E Loui Eriksson/99 8.00 20.00
B Martin Brodeur/49 25.00 60.00
F Marc-Andre Fleury/99 15.00 40.00

MMG Patrick Kane/99 20.00 50.00
MMG Marian Gaborik/49 10.00 25.00
MMM Matt Moulson/99 8.00 20.00
MMM Mark Messier/25 25.00 60.00
MMS Martin St. Louis/99 10.00 25.00
MPB Patrice Bergeron/99 12.00 30.00
MPD Pavel Datsyuk/99 12.00 30.00
MPE Corey Perry/99 10.00 25.00
MPK Phil Kessel/99 12.00 30.00
MPR Patrick Roy/25 60.00 120.00
MPRI Pekka Rinne/99 12.00 30.00
MRB Ray Bourque/25 30.00 80.00
MRF Ron Francis/25 15.00 40.00
MRK Ryan Kesler/99 10.00 25.00
MRM Ryan Miller/99 10.00 25.00
MSG Sam Gagner/99 8.00 20.00
MSY Steve Yzerman/25 50.00 120.00
MVL Vincent Lecavalier/99 8.00 20.00
MZP Zach Parise/99 12.00 30.00

2012-13 Limited Monikers Silver

*SILVER/49: .5X TO 1.2X MNKR/99
*SILVER/25: .6X TO 1.5X MNKR/49-99
*SILVER/15: .4X TO 1X MNKR/25
SILVER PRINT RUN 15-49
MAO Alex Ovechkin/25 50.00 100.00
MEL Eric Lindros/15 40.00 80.00

2012-13 Limited Net Assets

STATED PRINT RUN 99
NABCKY B.Campbell/K.Yandle 10.00 25.00
NACGPK C.Giroux/P.Kane 20.00 50.00
NACPSH C.Perry/S.Hartnell 10.00 25.00
NADSHS D.Sedin/H.Sedin 15.00 40.00
NADWCP C.Price/D.Wideman 10.00 25.00
NAEMJT E.Malkin/J.Tavares 30.00 80.00
NAHLJH H.Lundqvist/J.Howard 12.00 30.00
NAJBAE A.Edler/J.Benn 12.00 30.00
NAJILO J.Iginla/L.Couture 15.00 40.00
NAJLDA D.Alfredsson/J.Lupul 8.00 20.00
NAJOTT J.Quick/T.Thomas 25.00 50.00
NAJSJE J.Spezza/J.Eberle 10.00 25.00
NAKTKL K.Timonen/K.Letang 10.00 25.00
NAMGDG D.Girardi/M.Gaborik 10.00 25.00
NAMMBE B.Elliott/M.Michalek 8.00 20.00
NAPDSS P.Datsyuk/S.Stamkos 20.00 50.00
NAPKJN J.Neal/P.Kessel 15.00 40.00
NARSEK E.Karlsson/R.Suter 10.00 25.00
NATSJP J.Pominville/T.Seguin 10.00 25.00
NAZCSH S.Weber/Z.Chara 10.00 25.00

2012-13 Limited Net Crashers

STATED PRINT RUN 25-50
NCCG Claude Giroux/50 10.00 25.00
NCCH Cody Hodgson/50 10.00 25.00
NCDP Dion Phaneuf/50 10.00 25.00
NCEM Evgeni Malkin/40 30.00 80.00
NCHS Henrik Sedin/50 10.00 25.00
NCJI Jarome Iginla/50 10.00 25.00
NCJN James Neal/50 10.00 25.00
NCJT John Tavares/50 20.00 50.00
NCKT Kimmo Timonen/50 6.00 15.00
NCMR Matt Read/50 10.00 25.00
NCPD Pavel Datsyuk/50 12.00 30.00
NCPK Phil Kessel/50 12.00 30.00
NCRD Raphael Diaz/50 6.00 15.00
NCRJ Ryan Johansen/50 12.00 30.00
NCSS Steven Stamkos/25 20.00 50.00
NCZC Zdeno Chara/50 10.00 25.00
NCCGR Colin Greening/50 6.00 15.00
NCCSM Craig Smith/50 6.00 15.00
NCDAL Daniel Alfredsson/50 10.00 25.00
NCGAB Marian Gaborik/50 8.00 20.00
NCHAG Carl Hagelin/50 10.00 25.00
NCJFA Justin Faulk/50 6.00 15.00
NCJPO Jason Pominville/50 8.00 20.00
NCKAN Patrick Kane/50 20.00 50.00
NCLAN Gabriel Landeskog/50 10.00 25.00
NCRSU Ryan Suter/50 6.00 15.00
NCSCO Sean Couturier/50 10.00 25.00
NCSED Daniel Sedin/50 10.00 25.00
NCSHA Scott Hartnell/50 10.00 25.00
NCSPE Jason Spezza/50 10.00 25.00

2012-13 Limited Rookie Redemption

STATED PRINT RUN 499
1 Etem/Rakell/Lind/Fasth 5.00 12.00
2 Hamill/Spner/Soderbrg 8.00 20.00
3 Grigor/Girgns/Pysyk/Risto 8.00 20.00
4 Monahan/Street 5.00 12.00
5 Lindholm/Staal/Murphy 5.00 12.00
6 Nordstrom/LeBlanc 5.00 12.00
7 MacKinnon/Pickard 8.00 20.00
8 Jenner/Murray 5.00 12.00
9 Nich/Chson/Rssl/Cmpbll 4.00 10.00
10 Lashoff/DeKey/Mrazek 8.00 20.00
11 Yakupov/Schultz 8.00 20.00
12 Barkv/Hber/Howden 8.00 20.00
13 Toffoli/Pearson 6.00 15.00
14 Grnlnd/Cyle/Dmba/Brdin 5.00 12.00
15 Galch/Gilghr/Bileu/Tinrdi 8.00 20.00
16 Forsberg/Jones 5.00 12.00
17 Brunner/Matteau 4.00 10.00
18 Nelson/Hickey 4.00 10.00
19 Miller/Fast 4.00 10.00
20 Conacher/Pageau 4.00 10.00
21 Laughton/McGinn 4.00 10.00
22 Brown/Lessio 3.00 8.00
23 Bennett/Maatta 6.00 15.00
24 Vladimir Tarasenko 6.00 15.00
25 Hertl/Nieto/Irwin 6.00 15.00
26 Killrn/Pank/Palat/Gudas 5.00 12.00
27 Morgan Rielly 5.00 12.00
28 Jensen/Schroeder 4.00 10.00
29 Carrick/Wilson 6.00 15.00
30 Peluso/Trouba 5.00 12.00

2012-13 Limited Silver

*1-150 SILVER/49: .5X TO 1.2X BASIC CARD
*151-180 SILVER/49: .6X TO 1.5X BASIC C/199
*181-200 SILVER/49: .4X TO 1X BASIC C/99
*201-233 SLVR AU/49: .5X TO 1.2X AU RC
STATED PRINT RUN 49
10 Nicklas Backstrom 4.00 10.00
61 Corey Crawford 3.00 8.00

2012-13 Limited Stanley Cup Winners

STATED PRINT RUN 199
SC1 Gordie Howe 10.00 25.00
SC2 Bernie Parent 5.00 12.00
SC3 Phil Esposito 8.00 20.00
SC4 Bryan Trottier 6.00 15.00
SC5 Paul Coffey 5.00 12.00
SC6 Ed Belfour 5.00 12.00
SC7 John LeClair 5.00 12.00
SC8 Mike Bossy 5.00 12.00
SC9 Red Kelly 5.00 12.00
SC10 Dave Schultz 5.00 12.00
SC11 Jaromir Jagr 12.00 30.00
SC12 Larry Robinson 5.00 12.00
SC13 Dan Boyle 4.00 10.00
SC14 Denis Potvin 5.00 12.00
SC15 Bill Barber 4.00 10.00
SC16 Dave Andreychuk 5.00 12.00
SC17 Guy Lafleur 6.00 15.00
SC18 Patrick Roy 10.00 20.00
SC19 Johnny Bucyk 4.00 10.00
SC20 Mike Modano 8.00 20.00
SC21 Jamie Langenbrunner 3.00 8.00
SC23 Lanny McDonald 5.00 12.00
SC24 Gerry Cheevers 5.00 12.00
SC25 Al MacInnis 5.00 12.00
SC26 Stan Mikita 6.00 15.00
SC27 Alex Tanguay 3.00 8.00
SC28 Bobby Clarke 6.00 15.00
SC29 Joe Nieuwendyk 5.00 12.00
SC30 Bobby Hull 5.00 12.00
SC31 Ron Francis 6.00 15.00
SC32 Brett Hull 5.00 12.00
SC33 Adam Graves 4.00 10.00
SC34 Teemu Selanne 10.00 25.00
SC35 Jonathan Quick 8.00 20.00
SC36 Dustin Brown 5.00 12.00
SC37 Anze Kopitar 8.00 20.00
SC38 Jeff Carter 5.00 12.00
SC39 Drew Doughty 5.00 12.00
SC40 Simon Gagne 5.00 12.00
SC41 Derian Hatcher 3.00 8.00
SC42 Mark Messier 6.00 15.00
SC43 Clark Gillies 5.00 12.00
SC46 Mike Richter 5.00 12.00
SC47 Grant Fuhr 6.00 15.00
SC48 Igor Larionov 5.00 12.00
SC49 Luc Robitaille 5.00 12.00
SC50 Alex Delvecchio 6.00 15.00

2012-13 Limited Stanley Cup Winners Signatures

STATED PRINT RUN 25-99
SC1 Gordie Howe/25 60.00 150.00
SC2 Bernie Parent/99 20.00 50.00
SC3 Phil Esposito/99 15.00 40.00
SC4 Bryan Trottier/99 10.00 25.00
SC5 Paul Coffey/99 10.00 25.00
SC6 Ed Belfour/99 10.00 25.00
SC7 John LeClair/99 15.00 30.00
SC8 Mike Bossy/99 10.00 25.00
SC9 Red Kelly/99 10.00 25.00
SC10 Dave Schultz/99 10.00 25.00
SC11 Jaromir Jagr/50 30.00 60.00
SC12 Larry Robinson/99 10.00 25.00
SC13 Dan Boyle/99 8.00 20.00
SC14 Denis Potvin/99 10.00 25.00
SC15 Bill Barber/99 8.00 20.00
SC16 Dave Andreychuk/99 10.00 25.00
SC17 Guy Lafleur/99 15.00 40.00
SC18 Patrick Roy/50 100.00 200.00
SC19 Johnny Bucyk/99 15.00 40.00
SC20 Mike Modano/99 15.00 40.00
SC23 Lanny McDonald/99 8.00 20.00
SC24 Gerry Cheevers/99 10.00 25.00
SC25 Al MacInnis/99 10.00 25.00
SC26 Stan Mikita/99 15.00 30.00
SC28 Bobby Clarke/99 15.00 40.00
SC29 Joe Nieuwendyk/99 10.00 25.00
SC30 Bobby Hull/50 20.00 50.00
SC31 Ron Francis/50 15.00 30.00
SC32 Brett Hull/50 20.00 50.00
SC33 Adam Graves/99 8.00 20.00
SC34 Teemu Selanne/99 20.00 50.00
SC35 Jonathan Quick/99 20.00 40.00
SC36 Dustin Brown/99 12.00 30.00
SC37 Anze Kopitar/99 20.00 50.00
SC39 Drew Doughty/99 15.00 40.00
SC41 Derian Hatcher/99 8.00 20.00
SC42 Mark Messier/25 25.00 60.00
SC43 Clark Gillies/99 10.00 25.00
SC46 Mike Richter/99 15.00 30.00
SC47 Grant Fuhr/99 15.00 30.00
SC48 Igor Larionov/99 12.00 30.00
SC49 Luc Robitaille/99 10.00 25.00
SC50 Alex Delvecchio/25 25.00 50.00

2012-13 Limited Travels Dual Jerseys

STATED PRINT RUN 199
*PRIME/49: .6X TO 1.5X DUAL JSY/199
TDAB Alexander Burmistrov 4.00 10.00
TDAC Andrew Cogliano 3.00 8.00
TDAN Antti Niemi 4.00 10.00
TDBR Brad Richards 5.00 12.00
TDCA Craig Anderson 5.00 12.00
TDEJ Erik Johnson 3.00 8.00
TDGL Guy Lafleur 6.00 15.00
TDIB Ilya Bryzgalov 5.00 12.00
TDJH Jaroslav Halak 5.00 12.00
TDJL Jamie Langenbrunner 3.00 8.00
TDJM Joe Mullen 4.00 10.00
TDJN James Neal 5.00 12.00
TDJR Jeremy Roenick 5.00 12.00
TDJS Joe Sakic 5.00 12.00
TDJV Jakub Voracek 5.00 12.00
TDKP Keith Primeau 4.00 10.00
TDLR Luc Robitaille 5.00 12.00
TDMF Mike Fisher 4.00 10.00
TDMH Marian Hossa 4.00 10.00
TDMR Mike Richards 5.00 12.00
TDNH Nathan Horton 5.00 12.00
TDNK Nikolai Khabibulin 5.00 12.00
TDOP Ondrej Pavelec 5.00 12.00
TDPR Patrick Roy 10.00 25.00
TDRB Ray Bourque 8.00 20.00
TDSV Semyon Varlamov 5.00 12.00
TDTS Teemu Selanne 8.00 20.00

2012-13 Limited Travels Triple Jerseys

STATED PRINT RUN 99
*PRIME/25: .6X TO 1.5X TRIPLE/99
TTBET Brian Elliott 5.00 12.00
TTBSH Brendan Shanahan 8.00 20.00
TTGF Grant Fuhr 6.00 15.00
TTHUL Brett Hull 6.00 15.00
TTJAG Jaromir Jagr 12.00 30.00
TTJN Joe Nieuwendyk 6.00 15.00
TTPC Paul Coffey 6.00 15.00
TTRF Ron Francis 8.00 20.00

2012-13 Limited Trophy Winners

STATED PRINT RUN 199
TW1 Corey Perry 3.00 8.00
TW2 Henrik Sedin 3.00 8.00
TW3 Alex Ovechkin 12.00 30.00
TW4 Sidney Crosby 12.00 30.00
TW5 Eric Lindros 4.00 10.00
TW6 Joe Sakic 5.00 12.00
TW7 Gabriel Landeskog 3.00 8.00
TW8 Patrick Kane 6.00 15.00
TW9 Ed Belfour 3.00 8.00
TW10 Brian Leetch 3.00 8.00
TW11 Luc Robitaille 3.00 8.00
TW12 Tim Thomas 3.00 8.00
TW13 Ryan Miller 3.00 8.00
TW14 Martin Brodeur 6.00 15.00
TW15 Patrick Roy 8.00 20.00
TW16 Ron Hextall 3.00 8.00
TW17 Evgeni Malkin 10.00 25.00
TW18 Daniel Sedin 3.00 8.00
TW19 Joe Thornton 3.00 8.00
TW20 Martin St. Louis 3.00 8.00
TW21 Jarome Iginla 3.00 8.00
TW22 Nicklas Lidstrom 3.00 8.00
TW23 Scott Niedermayer 3.00 8.00
TW24 Chris Pronger 2.50 6.00
TW25 Ray Bourque 5.00 12.00
TW26 Denis Potvin 3.00 8.00
TW27 Ryan Kesler 3.00 8.00
TW28 Pavel Datsyuk 4.00 10.00
TW29 Steve Yzerman 6.00 15.00
TW30 Ron Francis 4.00 10.00
TW31 Bobby Clarke 3.00 8.00
TW32 Steven Stamkos 6.00 15.00
TW33 Vincent Lecavalier 2.50 6.00
TW34 Milan Hejduk 2.50 6.00
TW35 Brad Richards 3.00 8.00
TW36 Joe Sakic 5.00 12.00
TW37 Brett Hull 3.00 8.00
TW38 Mike Bossy 3.00 8.00
TW39 Rick Middleton 3.00 8.00
TW40 Jonathan Toews 6.00 15.00
TW41 Jean-Sebastien Giguere 2.50 6.00
TW42 Mario Lemieux 10.00 25.00
TW43 Bernie Parent 3.00 8.00
TW44 Guy Lafleur 4.00 10.00
TW45 Mark Messier 4.00 10.00
TW46 Jonathan Quick 5.00 12.00
TW47 Phil Kessel 4.00 10.00
TW48 Cam Neely 3.00 8.00
TW49 Charlie Simmer 2.00 5.00
TW50 Jeff Skinner 3.00 8.00

2012-13 Limited Trophy Winners Signatures

STATED PRINT RUN 25-99
TW1 Corey Perry/99 10.00 25.00
TW2 Henrik Sedin/99 12.50 30.00
TW3 Alex Ovechkin/50 25.00 60.00
TW4 Sidney Crosby/25 60.00 120.00
TW5 Eric Lindros/99 20.00 50.00
TW6 Joe Sakic/50 20.00 50.00
TW7 Gabriel Landeskog/99 10.00 25.00
TW8 Patrick Kane/99 20.00 50.00
TW9 Ed Belfour/50 20.00 40.00
TW10 Brian Leetch/99 10.00 25.00
TW11 Luc Robitaille/99 10.00 25.00
TW12 Tim Thomas/99 20.00 40.00
TW13 Ryan Miller/99 10.00 25.00
TW14 Martin Brodeur/50 40.00 80.00
TW15 Patrick Roy/50 50.00 120.00
TW16 Ron Hextall/99 15.00 40.00
TW17 Evgeni Malkin/99 20.00 40.00
TW18 Daniel Sedin/99 12.50 30.00
TW19 Joe Thornton/99 10.00 25.00
TW20 Martin St. Louis/99 10.00 25.00
TW21 Jarome Iginla/50 12.00 30.00
TW22 Nicklas Lidstrom/99 15.00 40.00
TW23 Scott Niedermayer/99 10.00 25.00
TW24 Chris Pronger/99 8.00 20.00
TW25 Ray Bourque/99 20.00 50.00
TW26 Denis Potvin/99 15.00 30.00
TW27 Ryan Kesler/99 10.00 25.00
TW28 Pavel Datsyuk/99 12.00 30.00
TW29 Steve Yzerman/25 60.00 120.00
TW30 Ron Francis/50 15.00 40.00
TW31 Bobby Clarke/99 20.00 40.00
TW33 Vincent Lecavalier/99 8.00 20.00
TW34 Milan Hejduk/99 8.00 20.00
TW35 Brad Richards/99 8.00 20.00
TW36 Joe Sakic/50 20.00 50.00
TW37 Brett Hull/50 20.00 50.00
TW38 Mike Bossy/99 10.00 25.00
TW39 Rick Middleton/99 8.00 20.00
TW40 Jonathan Toews/99 25.00 50.00
TW41 Jean-Sebastien Giguere/99 12.00 30.00
TW42 Mario Lemieux/25 60.00 120.00
TW43 Bernie Parent/99 15.00 40.00
TW44 Guy Lafleur/99 15.00 40.00
TW45 Mark Messier/25 20.00 50.00
TW46 Jonathan Quick/99 20.00 50.00
TW47 Phil Kessel/99 15.00 40.00
TW48 Cam Neely/99 15.00 40.00
TW49 Charlie Simmer/99 6.00 15.00
TW50 Jeff Skinner/99 10.00 25.00

1974-75 Lipton Soup

The 1974-75 Lipton Soup NHL set contained 50 color cards measuring approximately 2 1/4" by 3 1/4". The set was issued in two-card panels on the back of Lipton Soup packages. The backs featured statistics in French and English. Both varieties of Salming were included in the complete set below.

COMPLETE SET (51) 175.00 350.00
1 Norm Ullman 4.00 8.00
2 Gilbert Perreault 4.00 8.00
3 Darryl Sittler 6.00 12.00
4 Jean-Paul Parise 2.00 4.00
5 Garry Unger 2.00 4.00
6 Ron Ellis 2.50 5.00
7 Rogatien Vachon 5.00 10.00
8 Bobby Orr 50.00 100.00
9 Wayne Cashman 2.50 5.00
10 Brad Park 3.00 6.00
11 Serge Savard 2.50 5.00
12 Walt Tkaczuk 2.00 4.00
13 Yvan Cournoyer 4.00 8.00
14 Andre Boudrias 1.50 3.00
15 Gary Smith 2.50 5.00
16 Guy Lapointe 2.00 4.00
17 Dennis Hull 2.50 5.00
18 Bernie Parent 5.00 10.00
19 Ken Dryden 25.00 50.00
20 Rick MacLeish 2.50 5.00
21 Bobby Clarke 7.50 15.00
22 Dale Tallon 2.00 4.00
23 Jim McKenny 1.50 3.00
24 Rene Robert 2.50 5.00
25 Red Berenson 2.00 4.00
26 Ed Giacomin 5.00 10.00
27 Cesare Maniago 3.00 6.00
28 Ken Hodge 2.50 5.00
29 Gregg Sheppard 1.50 3.00
30 Dave Schultz 5.00 10.00
31 Bill Barber 4.00 8.00
32 Henry Boucha 2.00 4.00
33 Richard Martin 2.50 5.00
34 Steve Vickers 2.00 4.00
35 Billy Harris 1.50 3.00
36 Jim Pappin 1.50 3.00
37 Pit Martin 1.50 3.00
38 Jacques Lemaire 4.00 8.00
39 Peter Mahovlich 2.50 5.00
40 Rod Gilbert 4.00 8.00
41A Borje Salming 6.00 12.00
(Horizontal pose)
41B Borje Salming 6.00 12.00
(Vertical pose)
42 Pete Stemkowski 1.50 3.00
43 Ron Schock 1.50 3.00
44 Dan Bouchard 3.00 6.00
45 Tony Esposito 6.00 12.00
46 Craig Patrick 2.00 4.00
47 Ed Westfall 1.50 3.00
48 Jocelyn Guevremont 1.50 3.00
49 Syl Apps 2.00 4.00
50 Dave Keon 4.00 8.00

1972-73 Los Angeles Sharks WHA

This 19-card standard-size set featured on the front black and white posed player photos, surrounded by a white border. The player's name was given in black lettering below the picture. The backs read "The Original Los Angeles Sharks, 1972-73" and had the Sharks' logo in the center.

COMPLETE SET (19) 20.00 40.00
1 Mike Byers 1.25 2.50
2 Bart Crashley 2.00 4.00
3 George Gardner 1.25 2.50
4 Russ Gillow 1.25 2.50
5 Tom Gilmore 1.25 2.50
6 Earl Heiskala 1.25 2.50
7 J.P. LeBlanc 1.50 3.00
8 Ralph McSweyn 1.25 2.50
9 Ted McCaskill 1.25 2.50
10 Jim Niekamp 1.25 2.50
11 Gerry Odrowski 1.50 3.00
12 Tom Serviss 1.25 2.50
13 Peter Slater 1.25 2.50
14 Steve Sutherland 1.25 2.50
15 Joe Szura 1.50 3.00
16 Gary Veneruzzo 1.25 2.50
17 Jim Watson 1.25 2.50
18 Alton White 1.25 2.50
19 Bill Young 1.25 2.50

1998 Lunchables Goalie Greats Rounds

Available only as a premium found in select packs of Lunchables lunch products, these cards featured color action photos on the front while backs were blank. As the title suggests, these were round, and about the size of a peanut butter lid.

COMPLETE SET (8) 4.00 10.00
1 Ed Belfour .30 .75
2 Martin Brodeur .75 2.00
3 Dominik Hasek .60 1.50
4 Olaf Kolzig .25 .60
5 Chris Osgood .30 .75
6 Damian Rhodes .25 .60
7 Mike Richter .30 .75
8 Patrick Roy 1.50 4.00

1998 Lunchables Goalie Greats Squares

Available only as a premium found in select packs of Lunchables lunch products. Color action photos were featured on the front while backs were blank. As the name suggests, these were square, while the other set was round.

COMPLETE SET (8) 4.00 10.00
1 Ed Belfour .30 .75
2 Martin Brodeur .75 2.00
3 Dominik Hasek .60 1.50
4 Olaf Kolzig .25 .60
5 Chris Osgood .30 .75
6 Damian Rhodes .25 .75
7 Mike Richter .30 .75
8 Patrick Roy 1.50 4.00

2010-11 Luxury Suite

1-75 JSY PRINT RUN 100-599
76-100 DUAL JSY PRINT RUN 599
101-125 AUTO PRINT RUN 199
126-145 JSY AU PRINT RUN 199-299
146-175 AUTO PRINT RUN 499
176-250 ROOKIE PRINT RUN 899
1 Ryan Getzlaf JSY 6.00 15.00
2 Corey Perry JSY 4.00 10.00
3 Dustin Byfuglien JSY 4.00 10.00
4 Evander Kane JSY 4.00 10.00
5 Tim Thomas JSY 4.00 10.00
6 Patrice Bergeron JSY 4.00 10.00
7 Milan Lucic JSY 4.00 10.00
8 Ryan Miller JSY 4.00 10.00
9 Thomas Vanek JSY 4.00 10.00
10 Tyler Myers JSY 4.00 10.00
11 Miikka Kiprusoff JSY 3.00 8.00
12 Jarome Iginla JSY 4.00 10.00
13 Eric Staal JSY 5.00 12.00
14 Cam Ward JSY 4.00 10.00
15 Patrick Kane JSY 8.00 20.00
16 Jonathan Toews JSY 8.00 20.00
17 Marian Hossa JSY 4.00 10.00
18 Paul Stastny JSY 4.00 10.00
19 Matt Duchene JSY 4.00 10.00
20 Steve Mason JSY/100 4.00 10.00
21 Rick Nash JSY 4.00 10.00
22 Brad Richards JSY 4.00 10.00
23 Steve Ott JSY/525 3.00 8.00
24 Henrik Zetterberg JSY 5.00 12.00
25 Nicklas Lidstrom JSY 4.00 10.00
26 Pavel Datsyuk JSY 6.00 15.00
27 Ales Hemsky JSY 3.00 8.00
28 Sam Gagner JSY 3.00 8.00
29 Tomas Vokoun JSY 3.00 8.00
30 Michael Frolik JSY 2.50 6.00
31 Anze Kopitar JSY 6.00 15.00
32 Drew Doughty JSY 4.00 10.00
33 Jonathan Bernier JSY 4.00 10.00
34 Niklas Backstrom JSY 4.00 10.00
35 Cal Clutterbuck JSY 4.00 10.00
36 Mikko Koivu JSY 4.00 10.00
37 Carey Price JSY 15.00 40.00
38 Scott Gomez JSY/525 3.00 8.00
39 Tomas Plekanec JSY 4.00 10.00
40 Ilya Kovalchuk JSY 4.00 10.00
41 Martin Brodeur JSY 8.00 20.00
42 Zach Parise JSY 4.00 10.00
43 John Tavares JSY 6.00 15.00
44 Kyle Okposo JSY 4.00 10.00
45 Sean Avery JSY 3.00 8.00
46 Marian Gaborik JSY 5.00 12.00
47 Henrik Lundqvist JSY 5.00 12.00
48 Daniel Alfredsson JSY 4.00 10.00
49 Jason Spezza JSY 2.50 6.00
50 Chris Pronger JSY 3.00 8.00
51 Jeff Carter JSY 4.00 10.00
52 Claude Giroux JSY 4.00 10.00
53 Ilya Bryzgalov JSY 3.00 8.00
54 Shane Doan JSY 3.00 8.00
55 Jordan Staal JSY 4.00 10.00
56 Sidney Crosby JSY 10.00 25.00
57 Marc-Andre Fleury JSY 6.00 15.00
58 Evgeni Malkin JSY 6.00 15.00
59 Dany Heatley JSY/525 3.00 8.00
60 Joe Thornton JSY 5.00 12.00
62 Jaroslav Halak JSY 4.00 10.00
63 T.J. Oshie JSY 6.00 15.00
64 Vincent Lecavalier JSY 3.00 8.00
65 Mike Smith JSY 4.00 10.00
66 Steven Stamkos JSY 6.00 15.00
67 Phil Kessel JSY 5.00 12.00
68 Jonas Gustavsson JSY 4.00 10.00
69 Luke Schenn JSY 5.00 12.00
70 Roberto Luongo JSY 6.00 15.00
71 Henrik Sedin JSY 5.00 12.00
72 Daniel Sedin JSY 4.00 10.00
73 Alex Ovechkin JSY 8.00 20.00
74 Nicklas Backstrom JSY 6.00 15.00
75 Alexander Semin JSY 4.00 10.00
76 S.Koivu JSY/B.Ryan JSY 5.00 12.00
77 N.Bergfors JSY/B.Little JSY 5.00 12.00
78 M.Recchi JSY/N.Horton JSY 6.00 15.00
79 R.Bourque JSY/A.Tanguay JSY 3.00 8.00
80 P.Budaj JSY/C.Anderson JSY 5.00 12.00
81 M.Hejduk JSY/M.Duchene JSY 5.00 12.00
82 S.Ott JSY/K.Barch JSY 4.00 10.00
83 T.Holmstrom JSY/J.Franzen JSY 5.00 12.00
84 N.Khabibulin JSY/D.Dubnyk JSY 5.00 12.00
85 R.Smyth JSY/D.Brown JSY 5.00 12.00
86 M.Cammalleri JSY/A.Kostitsyn JSY 5.00 12.00
87 S.Weber JSY/P.Rinne JSY 6.00 15.00
88 P.Hornqvist JSY/M.Erat JSY 4.00 10.00
89 M.Staal JSY/A.Anisimov JSY 5.00 12.00
90 N.Foligno JSY/C.Neil JSY 4.00 10.00
91 S.Hartnell JSY/V.Leino JSY 5.00 12.00
92 K.Letang JSY/M.Talbot JSY 5.00 12.00
93 R.Malone JSY/M.St. Louis JSY 5.00 12.00
95 D.Phaneuf JSY/L.Schenn JSY 6.00 15.00
96 M.Grabovski JSY/N.Kulemin JSY 4.00 10.00
97 M.Raymond JSY/R.Kesler JSY 5.00 12.00
98 A.Burrows JSY/M.Samuelsson JSY 5.00 12.00
99 M.Green JSY/S.Varlamov JSY 5.00 12.00
100 B.Laich JSY/E.Fehr JSY 3.00 8.00
101 Brad Park AU 5.00 12.00
102 Dale Hawerchuk AU 8.00 20.00
103 Darren Pang AU 6.00 15.00
104 Denis Savard AU 8.00 20.00
105 Derek Sanderson AU 6.00 15.00
106 Doug Gilmour AU 8.00 20.00
107 Jeremy Roenick AU 12.00 30.00
108 Johnny Bower AU 15.00 40.00
109 Johnny Bucyk AU 6.00 15.00
110 Keith Primeau AU 5.00 12.00
111 Ken Hodge AU 5.00 12.00
112 Marcel Dionne AU 8.00 20.00
113 Richard Brodeur AU 8.00 20.00
114 Rick Middleton AU 5.00 12.00
115 Rogie Vachon AU 8.00 20.00
116 Simon Nolet AU 5.00 12.00
117 Terry O'Reilly AU 10.00 25.00
118 Doug Wilson AU 5.00 12.00
119 Jean Ratelle AU EXCH 5.00 12.00
120 Guy Chouinard AU 5.00 12.00
121 Dirk Graham AU 5.00 12.00
122 Tim Kerr AU 8.00 20.00
123 Dale Hunter AU EXCH 5.00 12.00
124 Rick Kehoe AU 5.00 12.00
125 Al Secord AU 6.00 15.00
126 Cam Fowler JSY AU/199 RC 12.00 30.00
127 Tomas Tatar JSY AU/199 RC 15.00 40.00
128 Tyler Seguin JSY AU/199 RC 50.00 100.00
129 Jeff Skinner JSY AU/199 RC 10.00 25.00
130 Shattenkirk JSY AU/199 RC 8.00 20.00
131 Jordan Eberle JSY AU/199 RC 30.00 80.00
132 Taylor Hall JSY AU/199 RC 75.00 150.00
133 M.Paajarvi JSY AU/199 RC 10.00 25.00
134 M.Tedenby JSY AU/199 RC 6.00 15.00
135 Derek Stepan JSY AU/199 RC 15.00 40.00
136 Jordan Caron JSY AU/299 RC 6.00 15.00
137 R.McDonagh JSY AU/299 RC 20.00 40.00
138 Linus Omark JSY AU/199 RC 15.00 40.00
139 B.Schenn JSY AU/299 RC 12.00 30.00
140 A.Burmistrov JSY AU/190 RC 8.00 20.00
141 J.Markstrom JSY AU/299 RC 8.00 20.00
142 N.Niederreiter JSY AU/299 RC 8.00 20.00
143 M.Zuccarello JSY AU/299 RC 10.00 25.00
144 Ekman-Larsson JSY AU/299 RC 12.00 30.00
145 Nazem Kadri JSY AU/299 RC 15.00 40.00
146 Brandon McMillan AU RC 4.00 10.00
147 Nick Bonino AU RC 5.00 12.00
148 Jeremy Morin AU RC 4.00 10.00
149 Zach Hamill AU RC 4.00 10.00
150 Steven Kampfer AU RC 6.00 15.00
151 Zac Dalpe AU RC 4.00 10.00
152 Brandon Pirri AU RC 4.00 10.00
153 Nick Leddy AU RC 4.00 10.00
154 Brandon Yip AU RC 4.00 10.00
155 Justin Mercier AU RC 4.00 10.00
156 Kyle Clifford AU RC 4.00 10.00
157 Casey Wellman AU RC 4.00 10.00
158 Robin Lehner AU RC 8.00 20.00
159 A.Vasyunov AU RC 4.00 10.00
160 Brad Mills AU RC 4.00 10.00
161 Nick Palmieri AU RC 4.00 10.00
162 Anders Lindback AU RC 5.00 12.00
163 Travis Hamonic AU RC 5.00 12.00
164 P.K. Subban AU RC 15.00 40.00
165 Nick Spaling AU RC 4.00 10.00
166 Jared Cowen AU RC 5.00 12.00
167 Sergei Bobrovsky AU RC 6.00 15.00
168 Eric Tangradi AU RC 4.00 10.00
169 Nick Johnson AU RC 3.00 8.00
170 Ian Cole AU RC 4.00 10.00
171 Stefan Della Rovere AU RC 4.00 10.00
172 Dana Tyrell AU RC 4.00 10.00
173 Dustin Tokarski AU RC 4.00 10.00
174 Brayden Irwin AU RC 4.00 10.00
175 M.Johansson AU RC 6.00 15.00
176 Kyle Palmieri RC 5.00 12.00
177 Patrice Cormier RC 3.00 8.00
178 Jamie Arniel RC 2.50 6.00
179 Luke Adam RC 2.50 6.00
180 T.J. Brodie RC 2.50 6.00
181 Henrik Karlsson RC 2.50 6.00
182 Jon Matsumoto RC 2.50 6.00
183 Jamie McBain RC 2.50 6.00
184 Evan Brophey RC 2.50 6.00
185 Rob Klinkhammer RC 2.50 6.00
186 Ben Smith RC 2.50 6.00
187 Mark Olver RC 2.50 6.00
188 Jonas Holos RC 2.50 6.00
189 Nick Holden RC 2.50 6.00
190 Richard Bachman RC 3.00 8.00
191 Nathan Lawson RC 2.50 6.00
192 Joe Callahan RC 3.00 8.00
193 Evgeny Dadonov RC 3.00 8.00
194 Jake Muzzin RC 2.50 6.00
195 Dwight King RC 2.50 6.00
196 Matt Kassian RC 2.50 6.00
197 Jared Spurgeon RC 2.50 6.00
198 Justin Falk RC 2.00 5.00
199 Linus Klasen RC 2.50 6.00
200 Mark Dekanich RC 2.50 6.00
201 Trevor Gillies RC 2.50 6.00
202 Alex Urbom RC 2.50 6.00
203 Jacob Josefson RC 2.50 6.00
204 Olivier Magnan RC 2.50 6.00
205 Stephen Gionta RC 2.50 6.00
206 Mark Fayne RC 2.50 6.00
207 Matt Taormina RC 2.50 6.00
208 Mark Flood RC 2.00 5.00
209 Evgeny Grachev RC 2.50 6.00
210 Dale Weise RC 3.00 8.00
211 Derek Smith RC 3.00 8.00
212 Eric Wellwood RC 3.00 8.00
213 Alexander Pechurskiy RC 3.00 8.00
214 Aaron Volpatti RC 2.50 6.00
215 Mike Moore RC 2.50 6.00
216 Justin Braun RC 2.50 6.00
217 John McCarthy RC 2.50 6.00
218 Ryan Reaves RC 3.00 8.00
219 Nikita Nikitin RC 2.50 6.00
220 Nicholas Drazenovic RC 3.00 8.00
221 Adam Cracknell RC 2.50 6.00
222 Johan Harju RC 2.50 6.00
223 Keith Aulie RC 2.50 6.00
224 Korbinian Holzer RC 2.50 6.00
225 Brian Fahey RC 2.50 6.00
226 Matt Bartkowski RC 3.00 8.00
227 Grant Clitsome RC 2.50 6.00
228 Matt Calvert RC 4.00 10.00
229 Jan Mursak RC 5.00 12.00
230 Brett Rakhshani RC 2.50 6.00
231 Jeff Petry RC 3.00 8.00
232 Chris Tanev RC 6.00 15.00
233 Kevin Poulin RC 3.00 8.00
234 Jim O'Brien RC 3.00 8.00
235 Brandon Mashinter RC 3.00 8.00
236 Brett MacLean RC 3.00 8.00
237 Tommy Wingels RC 3.00 8.00
238 Cedrick Desjardins RC 3.00 8.00
239 Marcel Mueller RC 3.00 8.00
240 Jeff Frazee RC 4.00 10.00
241 Paul Byron RC 3.00 8.00
242 Colby Cohen RC 2.50 6.00
243 Andrew Desjardins RC 2.50 6.00
244 Andreas Engqvist RC 4.00 10.00
245 Chris Mueller RC 2.50 6.00
246 Chad Kolarik RC 2.50 6.00
247 Marco Scandella RC 2.50 6.00
248 Alex Stalock RC 3.00 8.00
249 Cory Emmerton RC 3.00 8.00
250 Brodie Dupont RC 3.00 8.00

2010-11 Luxury Suite Jerseys Prime

1-75 STATED PRINT RUN 5-150
76-100 STATED PRINT RUN 50
1 Ryan Getzlaf 10.00 25.00
2 Corey Perry 6.00 15.00
3 Dustin Byfuglien/125 6.00 15.00
4 Evander Kane 6.00 15.00
5 Tim Thomas 10.00 25.00
6 Patrice Bergeron 8.00 20.00
7 Milan Lucic 6.00 15.00
8 Ryan Miller 6.00 15.00
9 Thomas Vanek 6.00 15.00
10 Tyler Myers 6.00 15.00
11 Miikka Kiprusoff 5.00 12.00
12 Jarome Iginla 6.00 15.00
13 Eric Staal 8.00 20.00
14 Cam Ward 6.00 15.00
15 Patrick Kane 12.00 30.00
16 Jonathan Toews 12.00 30.00
17 Marian Hossa 5.00 12.00
18 Paul Stastny 6.00 15.00
19 Matt Duchene 6.00 15.00
20 Steve Mason/50 5.00 12.00
21 Rick Nash 6.00 15.00
22 Brad Richards 6.00 15.00
23 Steve Ott 5.00 12.00
24 Henrik Zetterberg 8.00 20.00
25 Nicklas Lidstrom 6.00 15.00
26 Pavel Datsyuk 8.00 20.00
27 Ales Hemsky 5.00 12.00
28 Sam Gagner 5.00 12.00
29 Tomas Vokoun 5.00 12.00
30 Michael Frolik 4.00 10.00
31 Anze Kopitar 10.00 25.00
32 Drew Doughty 6.00 15.00
33 Jonathan Bernier 6.00 15.00
34 Niklas Backstrom 6.00 15.00
35 Cal Clutterbuck 6.00 15.00
36 Mikko Koivu 6.00 15.00
37 Carey Price 15.00 40.00
38 Scott Gomez 5.00 12.00
39 Tomas Plekanec 8.00 20.00
40 Ilya Kovalchuk 6.00 15.00
41 Martin Brodeur 10.00 25.00
42 Zach Parise 6.00 15.00
43 John Tavares 8.00 20.00
44 Kyle Okposo 6.00 15.00
45 Sean Avery 6.00 15.00
46 Marian Gaborik 8.00 20.00
47 Henrik Lundqvist 8.00 20.00
48 Daniel Alfredsson 6.00 15.00
49 Jason Spezza 4.00 10.00
50 Chris Pronger 5.00 12.00

51 Jeff Carter 6.00 15.00
52 Claude Giroux 6.00 15.00
53 Ilya Bryzgalov 5.00 12.00
54 Shane Doan 5.00 12.00
55 Jordan Staal 8.00 20.00
56 Sidney Crosby 25.00 60.00
57 Marc-Andre Fleury 8.00 20.00
58 Evgeni Malkin 8.00 20.00
59 Dany Heatley/5
60 Joe Thornton 8.00 20.00
62 Jaroslav Halak 6.00 15.00
63 T.J. Oshie 10.00 25.00
64 Vincent Lecavalier 5.00 12.00
65 Mike Smith 6.00 15.00
66 Steven Stamkos 10.00 25.00
67 Phil Kessel 8.00 20.00
68 Jonas Gustavsson 8.00 20.00
69 Luke Schenn 8.00 20.00
70 Roberto Luongo/100 8.00 20.00
71 Henrik Sedin 6.00 15.00
72 Daniel Sedin 6.00 15.00
73 Alex Ovechkin 10.00 25.00
74 Nicklas Backstrom 10.00 25.00
75 Alexander Semin 6.00 15.00
76 B.Ryan/S.Koivu 12.00 30.00
77 N.Bergfors/B.Little 8.00 20.00
78 M.Recchi/N.Horton 10.00 25.00
79 R.Bourque/A.Tanguay 5.00 12.00
80 C.Anderson/P.Budaj 8.00 20.00
81 M.Duchene/M.Hejduk 8.00 20.00
82 S.Ott/K.Barch
83 T.Holmstrom/J.Franzen 8.00 20.00
84 N.Khabibulin/D.Dubnyk
85 D.Brown/R.Smyth 8.00 20.00
86 A.Kostitsyn/M.Cammalleri 8.00 20.00
87 S.Weber/P.Rinne 8.00 20.00
88 M.Erat/P.Hornqvist 6.00 15.00
89 M.Staal/A.Anisimov
90 N.Foligno/C.Neil 6.00 15.00
91 S.Hartnell/V.Leino 8.00 20.00
92 K.Letang/M.Talbot 12.00 30.00
94 R.Malone/M.St. Louis 8.00 20.00
95 D.Phaneuf/L.Schenn 8.00 20.00
96 M.Grabovski/N.Kulemin 8.00 20.00
97 M.Raymond/R.Kesler 10.00 25.00
98 A.Burrows/M.Samuelsson 8.00 20.00
99 M.Green/S.Varlamov 12.00 30.00
100 B.Laich/E.Fehr 5.00 12.00

2010-11 Luxury Suite Jerseys Sticks

STATED PRINT RUN 25-100
*JSY #/STCK/50: .6X TO 1.5X JSY/STCK/100
*JSY #/STCK/15-25: .8X TO 2X JSY/STCK/100
*JSY #/STCK/50: .5X TO 1.2X JSY/STCK/25
1 Ryan Getzlaf 10.00 25.00
5 Tim Thomas 10.00 25.00
6 Patrice Bergeron 8.00 20.00
7 Milan Lucic 6.00 15.00
9 Thomas Vanek 6.00 15.00
11 Miikka Kiprusoff 5.00 12.00
12 Jarome Iginla 6.00 15.00
14 Cam Ward 6.00 15.00
16 Jonathan Toews/25 15.00 40.00
17 Marian Hossa 5.00 12.00
18 Paul Stastny 6.00 15.00
21 Rick Nash 12.00 30.00
22 Brad Richards 6.00 15.00
23 Steve Ott 5.00 12.00
24 Henrik Zetterberg 8.00 20.00
25 Nicklas Lidstrom 6.00 15.00
26 Pavel Datsyuk 8.00 20.00
27 Ales Hemsky 5.00 12.00
28 Sam Gagner 5.00 12.00
29 Tomas Vokoun 5.00 12.00
30 Michael Frolik 4.00 10.00
33 Jonathan Bernier/50 6.00 15.00
35 Cal Clutterbuck 6.00 15.00
36 Mikko Koivu 6.00 15.00
37 Carey Price 25.00 60.00
38 Scott Gomez 5.00 12.00
39 Tomas Plekanec 6.00 15.00
40 Ilya Kovalchuk 6.00 15.00
41 Martin Brodeur 12.00 30.00
43 John Tavares 12.00 30.00
44 Kyle Okposo 6.00 15.00
45 Sean Avery 5.00 12.00
46 Marian Gaborik 8.00 20.00
47 Henrik Lundqvist 10.00 25.00
48 Daniel Alfredsson 6.00 15.00
49 Jason Spezza 4.00 10.00
50 Chris Pronger 5.00 12.00
51 Jeff Carter 6.00 15.00
53 Ilya Bryzgalov 5.00 12.00
54 Shane Doan 5.00 12.00
55 Jordan Staal 6.00 15.00
56 Sidney Crosby 25.00 60.00
57 Marc-Andre Fleury 12.00 30.00
58 Evgeni Malkin 20.00 50.00
59 Dany Heatley 5.00 12.00
60 Joe Thornton 6.00 15.00
62 Jaroslav Halak 6.00 15.00
64 Vincent Lecavalier 5.00 12.00
65 Mike Smith 6.00 15.00
67 Phil Kessel 8.00 20.00
70 Roberto Luongo 6.00 15.00
71 Henrik Sedin 6.00 15.00
72 Daniel Sedin 6.00 15.00
73 Alex Ovechkin/25 30.00 80.00
74 Nicklas Backstrom 10.00 25.00

2010-11 Luxury Suite Prime Patches

*PATCH/20: .6X TO 1.5X PRIME/50-150
PATCH STATED PRINT RUN 5-20
59 Dany Heatley 8.00 20.00
74 Nicklas Backstrom 15.00 40.00

2011-12 Luxury Suite

41-70 JSY AU PRINT RUN 99
1-70 INSERTED IN ROOKIE ANTHOLOGY
1 Ryan Getzlaf JSY STK 8.00 20.00
2 Blake Wheeler JSY STK 6.00 15.00
3 David Krejci JSY STK 6.00 15.00
4 Nathan Gerbe JSY STK 3.00 8.00
5 Henrik Lundqvist JSY STK 8.00 20.00
6 Saku Koivu JSY STK 5.00 12.00
7 Dion Phaneuf JSY STK 5.00 12.00
8 David Legwand JSY STK 4.00 10.00
9 Andrei Markov JSY STK 5.00 12.00
10 Derek Stepan JSY STK 5.00 12.00
11 Ilya Kovalchuk JSY STK 6.00 15.00
12 Jonas Hiller JSY STK 8.00 20.00
13 Jason Spezza JSY STK 5.00 12.00
14 Mats Zuccarello JSY STK 5.00 12.00
15 Brandon Dubinsky JSY STK 4.00 10.00
16 Alex Ovechkin JSY STK 20.00 50.00
17 Patrick Sharp JSY STK 10.00 25.00
18 Chris Pronger JSY STK 4.00 10.00
19 Shawn Thornton JSY STK 6.00 15.00
20 Ryan Callahan JSY STK 6.00 15.00
21 Pavel Datsyuk JSY STK 8.00 20.00
22 Jaromir Jagr JSY STK 10.00 25.00
23 Joe Thornton JSY STK 8.00 20.00
24 Zdeno Chara JSY STK 5.00 12.00
25 Tomas Plekanec JSY STK 5.00 12.00
26 Marc Staal JSY STK 5.00 12.00
27 Jarome Iginla JSY STK 8.00 20.00
28 Scott Gomez JSY STK 4.00 10.00
29 Carey Price JSY STK 12.00 30.00
30 Simon Gagne JSY STK 6.00 15.00
31 Semyon Varlamov JSY STK 6.00 15.00
32 Tuukka Rask JSY STK 8.00 20.00
33 Marian Gaborik JSY STK 6.00 15.00
34 Milan Hejduk JSY STK 4.00 10.00
35 Michael Del Zotto JSY STK 3.00 8.00
36 Curtis Joseph JSY STK 6.00 15.00
37 Ron Francis JSY STK 8.00 20.00
38 Ray Bourque JSY STK 8.00 20.00
39 Brian Leetch JSY STK 5.00 12.00
40 Tom Barrasso JSY STK 6.00 15.00
41 Adam Henrique JSY AU RC 25.00 60.00
42 Adam Larsson JSY AU RC 20.00 50.00
43 Blake Geoffrion JSY AU RC 12.00 30.00
44 Brandon Saad JSY AU RC 25.00 60.00
45 Brendan Smith JSY AU RC 15.00 40.00
46 Brett Connolly JSY AU RC 12.00 30.00
47 Carl Hagelin JSY AU RC 12.00 30.00
48 Cody Eakin JSY AU RC 15.00 40.00
49 Cody Hodgson JSY AU RC 12.00 30.00
50 Craig Smith JSY AU RC 10.00 25.00
51 David Rundblad JSY AU RC 10.00 25.00
52 D.Smith-Pelly JSY AU RC 10.00 25.00
53 G.Landeskog JSY AU RC 25.00 60.00
54 G.Nyquist JSY AU RC 25.00 50.00
55 J.Gardiner JSY AU RC 20.00 50.00
56 Joe Colborne JSY AU RC 20.00 50.00
57 Brett Bulmer JSY AU RC 12.00 30.00
58 L.Leblanc JSY AU RC 15.00 40.00
59 M.Scheifele JSY AU RC 15.00 40.00
60 C.de Haan JSY AU RC 12.00 30.00
61 H.Zolnierczyk JSY AU RC 12.00 30.00
62 Nugent-Hopkins JSY AU RC 60.00 120.00
63 Ryan Johansen JSY AU RC 25.00 60.00
64 Sean Couturier JSY AU RC 12.00 30.00
65 Simon Despres JSY AU RC 20.00 50.00
66 Tim Erixon JSY AU RC 10.00 25.00
67 Zack Kassian JSY AU RC 20.00 50.00
68 Aaron Palushaj JSY AU RC 8.00 20.00
69 Gudbranson JSY AU RC 12.00 30.00
70 Justin Faulk JSY AU RC 10.00 25.00

2012-13 Luxury Suite

53-100 ROOKIE JSY AU PRINT RUN 99
1 Adam Henrique STK 5.00 12.00
2 Adam Graves STK 6.00 15.00
3 Alex Ovechkin STK 10.00 25.00
4 Bernie Parent STK SP 8.00 20.00
5 Bobby Hull STK 8.00 20.00
6 Bobby Ryan STK 5.00 12.00
7 Brad Richards STK 5.00 12.00
8 Brayden Schenn STK 5.00 12.00
9 Brett Hull STK 5.00 12.00
10 Carey Price STK 15.00 40.00
11 Curtis Joseph STK 5.00 12.00
12 Daniel Sedin STK 5.00 12.00
13 Doug Gilmour STK 10.00 25.00
14 Ed Belfour STK 8.00 20.00
15 Rick Nash STK 5.00 12.00
16 Felix Potvin STK 8.00 20.00
17 Gordie Howe STK SP 20.00 50.00
18 James van Riemsdyk STK 6.00 15.00
19 Jarome Iginla STK 5.00 12.00
20 Jaroslav Halak STK 5.00 12.00
21 John Tavares STK 10.00 25.00
22 Dale Hawerchuk STK 6.00 15.00
23 Luc Robitaille STK 5.00 12.00
24 Patrik Elias STK 8.00 20.00
25 Joe Mullen STK 4.00 10.00
26 Mario Lemieux STK 6.00 15.00
27 Mark Messier STK 10.00 25.00
28 Martin Brodeur STK 12.00 30.00
29 Martin St. Louis STK 5.00 12.00
30 Michael Del Zotto STK 3.00 8.00
31 Shane Doan STK 4.00 10.00
32 Nicklas Lidstrom STK 6.00 15.00
33 Patrick Marleau STK 5.00 12.00
34 Patrick Roy STK 10.00 25.00
35 Pavel Datsyuk STK 6.00 15.00
36 Roberto Luongo STK 5.00 12.00
37 Rogie Vachon STK 10.00 25.00
38 Saku Koivu STK 8.00 20.00
39 Sean Couturier STK 8.00 20.00
40 Jaromir Jagr STK 12.00 30.00
41 Stan Mikita STK 10.00 25.00
42 Steve Yzerman STK 10.00 25.00
43 Tim Thomas STK 5.00 12.00
44 Vincent Lecavalier STK 4.00 10.00
45 Bobby Clarke STK 8.00 20.00
46 Denis Potvin STK 8.00 20.00
47 Lanny McDonald STK 6.00 15.00
48 Ray Bourque STK 8.00 20.00
49 Guy Lafleur STK 10.00 25.00
50 Adam Oates STK 6.00 15.00
51 Rick Middleton STK 6.00 15.00
52 Cam Ward STK 5.00 12.00
53 Mat Clark JSY AU RC 6.00 15.00
54 Carter Camper JSY AU RC 5.00 12.00
55 Lane MacDermid JSY AU RC 6.00 15.00
56 Max Sauve JSY AU RC 6.00 15.00
57 Torey Krug JSY AU RC 20.00 50.00
58 Michael Hutchinson JSY AU RC 10.00 25.00
59 Travis Turnbull JSY AU RC 6.00 15.00
60 Akim Aliu JSY AU RC 6.00 15.00
61 Jeremy Welsh JSY AU RC 6.00 15.00
62 Brandon Bollig JSY AU RC 6.00 15.00
63 Tyson Barrie JSY AU RC 12.00 30.00
64 Mike Connolly JSY AU RC 6.00 15.00
65 Andrew Joudrey JSY AU RC 6.00 15.00
66 Shawn Hunwick JSY AU RC 6.00 15.00
67 Cody Goloubef JSY AU RC 6.00 15.00
68 Dalton Prout JSY AU RC 6.00 15.00
69 Ryan Garbutt JSY AU RC 6.00 15.00
70 Reilly Smith JSY AU RC 12.00 30.00
71 Scott Glennie JSY AU RC 6.00 15.00
72 Brenden Dillon JSY AU RC 6.00 15.00
73 Riley Sheahan JSY AU RC 6.00 15.00
74 Philippe Cornet JSY AU RC 6.00 15.00
75 Colby Robak JSY AU RC 6.00 15.00
76 Jordan Nolan JSY AU RC 6.00 15.00
77 Kris Foucault JSY AU RC 6.00 15.00
78 Tyler Cuma JSY AU RC 6.00 15.00
79 Chay Genoway JSY AU RC 6.00 15.00
80 Jason Zucker JSY AU RC 8.00 20.00
81 Robert Mayer JSY AU RC 8.00 20.00
82 Gabriel Dumont JSY AU RC 10.00 25.00
83 Chet Pickard JSY AU RC 6.00 15.00
84 Aaron Ness JSY AU RC 6.00 15.00
85 Casey Cizikas JSY AU RC 6.00 15.00
86 Matt Donovan JSY AU RC 6.00 15.00
87 Matt Watkins JSY AU RC 6.00 15.00
88 Jakob Silfverberg JSY AU RC 15.00 30.00
89 Mark Stone JSY AU RC 12.00 30.00
90 Brandon Manning JSY AU RC 6.00 15.00
91 Michael Stone JSY AU RC 8.00 20.00
92 Tyson Sexsmith JSY AU RC 6.00 15.00
93 Jake Allen JSY AU RC 20.00 50.00
94 J.T. Brown JSY AU RC 6.00 15.00
95 Carter Ashton JSY AU RC 5.00 12.00
96 Ryan Hamilton JSY AU RC 6.00 15.00
97 Jussi Rynnas JSY AU RC 20.00 50.00
98 Chris Kreider JSY AU RC 15.00 40.00
99 Sven Baertschi JSY AU RC 8.00 20.00
100 Jaden Schwartz JSY AU RC 12.00 30.00

2012-13 Luxury Suite Autographs Gold

1-52 UNPRICED VET JSY AU PRINT RUN 5-10
*53-97 RK.JSY AU/25: .6X TO 1.5X JSY AU/99
53-97 ROOKIE PATCH AU PRINT RUN 25
98-100 UNPRICED RK.PTCH AU PRINT RUN 10

2013-14 Luxury Suite

1 Gordie Howe STK/100 12.00 30.00
2 Patrick Roy STK/199 12.00 30.00
3 Dave Andreychuk STK/199 5.00 12.00
4 Mike Richter STK/199 5.00 12.00
5 Marty Turco STK/199 5.00 12.00
6 Paul Coffey STK/199 5.00 12.00
7 Michel Goulet STK/199 4.00 10.00
8 Pierre Turgeon STK/199 5.00 12.00
9 Jonathan Toews STK/199 10.00 25.00
10 Evgeni Malkin STK/199 15.00 40.00
11 Dale Hawerchuk STK/199 6.00 15.00
12 Mark Streit STK/199 3.00 8.00
13 Paul Stastny STK/199 5.00 12.00
14 Adam Graves STK/199 4.00 10.00
15 Alex Delvecchio STK/199 4.00 10.00
16 Bobby Hull STK/199 8.00 20.00
17 Brenden Morrow STK/199 4.00 10.00
18 Curtis Joseph STK/199 5.00 12.00
19 Dale Hawerchuk STK/199 6.00 15.00
20 Dany Heatley STK/199 4.00 10.00
21 Denis Potvin STK/199 6.00 15.00
22 Doug Gilmour STK/199 6.00 15.00
23 Gerry Cheevers STK/199 5.00 12.00
24 Grant Fuhr STK/199 8.00 20.00
25 Henrik Zetterberg STK/199 6.00 15.00
26 Jimmy Howard STK/199 5.00 12.00
27 Joe Nieuwendyk STK/199 5.00 12.00
28 J.Vanbiesbrouck STK/199 6.00 15.00
29 Johnny Bower STK/199 8.00 20.00
30 Jordan Staal STK/199 5.00 12.00
31 Marc Staal STK/199 4.00 10.00
32 Marian Gaborik STK/199 6.00 15.00
33 Mario Lemieux STK/199 15.00 40.00
34 Mark Messier STK/199 6.00 15.00
35 Mikhail Grabovski STK/199 6.00 15.00
36 Nicklas Lidstrom STK/199 5.00 12.00
37 Paul Coffey STK/199 6.00 15.00
38 Phil Esposito STK/199 8.00 20.00
39 Ray Bourque STK/199 8.00 20.00
40 Roberto Luongo STK/199 8.00 20.00
41 Ron Francis STK/199 6.00 15.00
42 Ryan Callahan STK/199 5.00 12.00
43 Sheldon Souray STK/199 3.00 8.00
44 Steve Yzerman STK/199 10.00 25.00
45 Tony Esposito STK/199 5.00 12.00
46 Valtteri Filppula STK/199 5.00 12.00
47 Vincent Lecavalier STK/199 4.00 10.00
48 Zach Parise STK/199 5.00 12.00
49 Andrei Markov STK/199 5.00 12.00
50 Andrew Shaw STK/199 5.00 12.00
51 T.Selanne JSY STK/99 8.00 20.00
52 Jason Spezza JSY STK/99 8.00 20.00
53 Corey Perry JSY STK/99 6.00 15.00
54 Adam Larsson JSY STK/99 6.00 15.00
55 P.Bergeron JSY STK/99 8.00 20.00
56 Ryan Getzlaf JSY STK/99 10.00 25.00
57 Steve Ott JSY STK/99 5.00 12.00
58 Joe Pavelski JSY STK/99 6.00 15.00
59 Sam Gagner JSY STK/75 5.00 12.00
60 Marian Gaborik JSY STK/99 6.00 15.00
61 Max Pacioretty JSY STK/99 6.00 15.00
62 Stan Mikita JSY STK/99 8.00 20.00
63 B.Dubinsky JSY STK/99 5.00 12.00
64 Alex Ovechkin JSY STK/99 12.00 30.00
65 S.Stamkos JSY STK/99 12.00 30.00
66 Alex Goligoski JSY STK/99 4.00 10.00
67 Alex Tanguay JSY STK/99 4.00 10.00
68 Brad Richards JSY STK/99 6.00 15.00
69 Brendan Shanahan JSY STK/99 8.00 20.00
70 Brian Leetch JSY STK/99 6.00 15.00
71 Bryan Little JSY STK/99 6.00 15.00
72 Carey Price JSY STK/99 20.00 50.00
73 Cam Neely JSY STK/99 6.00 15.00
74 Derek Stepan JSY STK/99 6.00 15.00
75 Devan Dubnyk JSY STK/99 6.00 15.00
76 Kari Lehtonen JSY STK/99 5.00 12.00
77 Evgeni Malkin JSY STK/99 20.00 50.00
78 Gordie Howe STK/25 25.00 60.00
79 H.Lundqvist JSY STK/99 8.00 20.00
80 Henrik Sedin JSY STK/99 6.00 15.00
81 Jacob Josefson JSY STK/99 4.00 10.00
82 Jaromir Jagr JSY STK/99 15.00 40.00
83 Jaroslav Halak JSY STK/99 8.00 20.00
84 Jeff Carter JSY STK/99 6.00 15.00
85 Joe Sakic JSY STK/99 10.00 25.00
86 Joe Thornton JSY STK/99 6.00 15.00
87 Jonas Hiller JSY STK/99 4.00 10.00
88 Kris Versteeg JSY STK/99 5.00 12.00
89 Loui Eriksson JSY STK/99 5.00 12.00
90 Marc-Andre Fleury JSY/99 10.00 25.00
91 Martin St. Louis JSY STK/99 6.00 15.00
92 Martin Brodeur JSY STK/99 6.00 15.00
93 Pavel Datsyuk JSY STK/99 8.00 20.00
94 Rob Blake JSY STK/99 6.00 15.00
95 Ryan McDonagh JSY STK/99 6.00 15.00
96 Saku Koivu JSY STK/99 6.00 15.00
97 Sidney Crosby JSY STK/25 30.00 60.00
98 Tomas Plekanec JSY STK/99 6.00 15.00
99 Tyler Seguin JSY STK/99 10.00 25.00
100 Wayne Simmonds JSY STK/99 8.00 20.00
101 Nail Yakupov JSY AU RC 15.00 40.00
102 N.MacKinnon JSY AU RC 25.00 60.00
103 Ryan Murray JSY AU RC 12.00 30.00
104 A.Barkov JSY AU RC 20.00 50.00
105 A.Galchenyuk JSY AU RC 15.00 40.00
106 Seth Jones JSY AU RC 8.00 20.00
107 Morgan Rielly JSY AU RC 12.00 30.00
108 Elias Lindholm JSY AU RC 12.00 30.00
109 H.Lindholm JSY AU RC 12.00 30.00
110 Sean Monahan JSY AU RC 15.00 40.00
111 Matt Dumba JSY AU RC 8.00 20.00
113 Jacob Trouba JSY AU RC 12.00 30.00
114 V.Nichushkin JSY AU RC 8.00 20.00
115 Filip Forsberg JSY AU RC 20.00 50.00
116 M.Grigorenko JSY AU RC 10.00 25.00
117 Z.Girgensons JSY AU RC 15.00 40.00
118 Nikita Zadorov JSY AU RC 8.00 20.00
119 Tom Wilson JSY AU RC 12.00 30.00
120 Tomas Hertl JSY AU RC 15.00 40.00
121 Scott Laughton JSY AU RC 8.00 20.00
122 Olli Maatta JSY AU RC 15.00 40.00
123 Stefan Matteau JSY AU RC 6.00 15.00
124 Tanner Pearson JSY AU RC 8.00 20.00
125 Marek Mazanec JSY AU RC 8.00 20.00
126 Dougie Hamilton JSY AU RC 12.00 30.00
129 Jamie Oleksiak JSY AU RC 6.00 15.00
131 Nathan Beaulieu JSY AU RC 6.00 15.00
132 Nicklas Jensen JSY AU RC 6.00 15.00
133 Rickard Rakell JSY AU RC 8.00 20.00
134 Boone Jenner JSY AU RC 8.00 20.00
135 Magnus Hellberg JSY AU RC 8.00 20.00
136 Dmitrij Jaskin JSY AU RC 8.00 20.00
137 Matt Nieto JSY AU RC 6.00 15.00
138 Xavier Ouellet JSY AU RC 8.00 20.00
139 Lucas Lessio JSY AU RC 5.00 12.00
141 Michael Raffl JSY AU RC 6.00 15.00
142 Frank Corrado JSY AU RC 5.00 12.00
143 Jamie Devane JSY AU RC 6.00 15.00
144 Mikael Granlund JSY AU RC 12.00 30.00
145 V.Tarasenko JSY AU RC 30.00 80.00
146 Austin Watson JSY AU RC 6.00 15.00
147 Nick Bjugstad JSY AU RC 8.00 20.00
148 Beau Bennett JSY AU RC 8.00 20.00
150 Mark Pysyk JSY AU RC 6.00 15.00
151 Quinton Howden JSY AU RC 5.00 12.00
153 Emerson Etem JSY AU RC 6.00 15.00
154 Brock Nelson JSY AU RC 6.00 15.00
155 Martin Jones JSY AU RC 15.00 40.00
156 Reto Berra JSY AU RC 6.00 15.00
157 Jon Merrill JSY AU RC 6.00 15.00
158 Christian Thomas JSY AU RC 5.00 12.00
159 Ryan Spooner JSY AU RC 6.00 15.00
160 Tyler Toffoli JSY AU RC 12.00 30.00
161 Calvin Pickard JSY AU RC 6.00 15.00
162 Johan Larsson JSY AU RC 5.00 12.00
163 Max Reinhart JSY AU RC 6.00 15.00
164 Michael Bournival JSY AU RC 6.00 15.00
165 Joakim Nordstrom JSY AU RC 5.00 12.00
166 B.Gallagher JSY AU RC 15.00 40.00
167 Jesper Fast JSY AU RC 5.00 12.00
168 F.Andersen JSY AU RC 10.00 25.00
169 Viktor Fasth JSY AU RC 6.00 15.00
170 Carl Soderberg JSY AU RC 6.00 15.00
171 Jared Staal JSY AU RC 6.00 15.00
172 Connor Murphy JSY AU RC 5.00 12.00
173 Antoine Roussel JSY AU RC 6.00 15.00
174 Jack Campbell JSY AU RC 5.00 12.00
175 Alex Chiasson JSY AU RC 6.00 15.00
176 Petr Mrazek JSY AU RC 12.00 30.00
177 Kevin Connauton JSY AU RC 5.00 12.00
178 Mark Arcobello JSY AU RC 6.00 15.00
179 J.Huberdeau JSY AU RC 15.00 40.00
180 Drew Shore JSY AU RC 5.00 12.00
181 Thomas Hickey JSY AU RC 5.00 12.00
182 Cory Conacher JSY AU RC 4.00 10.00
183 Matt Irwin JSY AU RC 5.00 12.00
184 Alex Killorn JSY AU RC 6.00 15.00
186 Philipp Grubauer JSY AU RC 6.00 15.00
187 Zach Redmond JSY AU RC 5.00 12.00
188 Dylan McIlrath JSY AU RC 4.00 10.00
189 Tomas Jurco JSY AU RC 10.00 25.00
190 Sami Vatanen JSY AU RC 6.00 15.00
191 John Gibson JSY AU RC 15.00 40.00
192 D.DeKeyser JSY AU RC 8.00 20.00
193 Michael Caruso JSY AU RC 4.00 10.00
194 Tye McGinn JSY AU RC 6.00 15.00
195 Michael Kostka JSY AU RC 5.00 12.00
196 Edward Pasquale JSY AU RC 4.00 10.00
197 Darcy Kuemper JSY AU RC 6.00 15.00
198 Justin Schultz JSY AU RC 6.00 15.00
199 Chris Brown JSY AU RC 4.00 10.00
200 Ryan Strome JSY AU RC 8.00 20.00

2013-14 Luxury Suite Rookie Autographs Prime

*PRIME/25: .5X TO 1.2X BASIC INSERTS
102 Nathan MacKinnon 30.00 80.00
105 Alex Galchenyuk 30.00 60.00

1973-74 Mac's Milk

The 1973-74 Mac's Milk set contained 30 unnumbered discs measuring approximately 3" in diameter. These round discs were actually cloth stickers with a peel-off back. They were unnumbered and featured popular players in the National Hockey League. There was no identifying mark anywhere on the discs identifying the sponsor as Mac's Milk. They are checklisted below in alphabetical order by player's name.

COMPLETE SET (30) 75.00 150.00
1 Gary Bergman 1.50 3.00
2 Johnny Bucyk 2.50 5.00
3 Wayne Cashman 2.00 4.00
4 Bobby Clarke 7.50 15.00
5 Yvan Cournoyer 3.00 6.00
6 Ron Ellis 1.50 3.00
7 Rod Gilbert 2.50 5.00
8 Brian Glennie 1.50 3.00
9 Paul Henderson 2.50 5.00
10 Ed Johnston 2.50 5.00
11 Rick Kehoe 1.50 3.00
12 Orland Kurtenbach 1.50 3.00
13 Guy Lapointe 2.50 5.00
14 Jacques Lemaire 2.50 5.00
15 Frank Mahovlich 5.00 10.00
16 Pete Mahovlich 2.50 5.00
17 Richard Martin 2.00 4.00
18 Jim McKenny 1.50 3.00
19 Bobby Orr 20.00 40.00
20 Jean-Paul Parise 1.50 3.00
21 Brad Park 4.00 8.00
22 Jacques Plante 7.50 15.00
23 Jean Ratelle 2.50 5.00
24 Mickey Redmond 2.50 5.00
25 Serge Savard 2.50 5.00
26 Darryl Sittler 5.00 10.00
27 Pat Stapleton 1.50 3.00
28 Dale Tallon 1.50 3.00
29 Norm Ullman 2.50 5.00
30 Bill White 2.00 4.00

1996 Maggers

This 108 laser die-cut magnet premier edition set measured approximately 6" by 7 1/2" and was distributed one to a package with a suggested retail price of $1.99. Produced by Corporate Magnates of Ontario, the player's image could be separated from the magnet background and used alone. The magnets were checklisted below in alphabetical order.

COMPLETE SET (108) 90.00 180.00
1 Jason Arnott .50 1.25
2 Tom Barrasso .50 1.25
3 Ed Belfour .60 1.50
4 Peter Bondra .60 1.50
5 Ray Bourque 1.25 3.00
6 Martin Brodeur 1.50 4.00
7 Benoit Brunet .40 1.00
8 Pavel Bure 1.50 4.00
9 Sean Burke .50 1.25
10 Jim Carey .50 1.25
11 Chris Chelios .60 1.50
12 Steve Chiasson .40 1.00
13 Dino Ciccarelli .40 1.00
14 Zdeno Ciger .40 1.00
15 Wendel Clark .40 1.00
16 Paul Coffey .50 1.25
17 Shayne Corson .40 1.00
18 Alexandre Daigle .40 1.00
19 Vincent Damphousse .50 1.25
20 Eric Daze .40 1.00
21 Tie Domi .50 1.25
22 Sergei Fedorov 1.25 3.00
23 Eric Fichaud .40 1.00
24 Theo Fleury .60 1.50
25 Peter Forsberg 1.50 4.00
26 Ron Francis .50 1.25
27 Grant Fuhr .50 1.25
28 Doug Gilmour .60 1.50
29 Sergei Gonchar .40 1.00
30 Tony Granato .40 1.00
31 Adam Graves .50 1.25
32 Wayne Gretzky 4.00 10.00
33 Alexei Gusarov .40 1.00
34 Derian Hatcher .40 1.00
35 Dale Hawerchuk .40 1.00
36 Guy Hebert .50 1.25
37 Ron Hextall .40 1.00
38 Corey Hirsch .40 1.00
39 Phil Housley .40 1.00
40 Kelly Hrudey .40 1.00
41 Brett Hull .75 2.00
42 Jaromir Jagr 1.50 4.00
43 Ed Jovanovski .50 1.25
44 Joe Juneau .40 1.00
45 Valeri Kamensky .50 1.25
46 Paul Kariya 2.00 5.00
47 Trevor Kidd .50 1.25
48 Petr Klima .40 1.00
49 Saku Koivu .50 1.25
50 Andrei Kovalenko .40 1.00
51 Vyacheslav Kozlov .40 1.00
52 Igor Larionov .40 1.00
53 John LeClair .75 2.00
54 Brian Leetch .50 1.25
55 Claude Lemieux .50 1.25
56 Mario Lemieux 4.00 10.00
57 Trevor Linden .50 1.25
58 Eric Lindros 1.00 2.50
59 Al MacInnis .50 1.25
60 Mark Messier .75 2.00
61 Mike Modano 1.00 2.50
62 Alexander Mogilny .50 1.25
63 Andy Moog .50 1.25
64 Joe Murphy .40 1.00
65 Petr Nedved .40 1.00
66 Cam Neely .50 1.25
67 Bernie Nicholls .40 1.00
68 Joe Nieuwendyk .50 1.25
69 Owen Nolan .50 1.25
70 Adam Oates .50 1.25
71 Jeff Odgers .40 1.00
72 Chris Osgood .75 2.00
73 Sandis Ozolinsh .50 1.25
74 Zigmund Palffy .60 1.50
75 Yanic Perreault .40 1.00
76 Michal Pivonka .40 1.00
77 Felix Potvin .60 1.50
78 Keith Primeau .50 1.25
79 Chris Pronger .40 1.00
80 Daren Puppa .40 1.00
81 Bill Ranford .40 1.00
82 Mikael Renberg .40 1.00
83 Mike Ricci .40 1.00
84 Mike Richter .60 1.50
85 Gary Roberts .40 1.00
86 Luc Robitaille .60 1.50
87 Jeremy Roenick .60 1.50
88 Patrick Roy 3.00 8.00
89 Joe Sakic 1.25 3.00
90 Tomas Sandstrom .40 1.00
91 Denis Savard .40 1.00
92 Teemu Selanne 1.25 3.00
93 Brendan Shanahan 1.00 2.50
94 Kevin Stevens .40 1.00
95 Scott Stevens .40 1.00
96 Mats Sundin .60 1.50
97 Gary Suter .40 1.00
98 Chris Terreri .50 1.25
99 Jocelyn Thibault .50 1.25
100 Esa Tikkanen .40 1.00
101 German Titov .40 1.00
102 Rick Tocchet .40 1.00
103 Pierre Turgeon .50 1.25
104 John Vanbiesbrouck .60 1.50
105 Pat Verbeek .50 1.25
106 Mike Vernon .50 1.25
107 Alexei Yashin .50 1.25
108 Steve Yzerman 2.50 6.00

1963-64 Maple Leafs Team Issue

This 22-card set of postcards measured approximately 3 1/2" by 5 1/2" and featured black and white action and posed player photos with white borders. The old Toronto Maple Leafs logo was in the bottom right corner. The player's name and position appeared at the bottom. The backs were blank. The cards were unnumbered and checklisted below in alphabetical order.

COMPLETE SET (22) 62.50 125.00
1 Bob Baun (Posed) 2.50 5.00
2 Bob Baun (Posed in white uniform& position not listed) 2.50 5.00
3 Carl Brewer (White uniform) 2.50 5.00
4 Carl Brewer (Dark uniform) 2.50 5.00
5 Kent Douglas 1.50 3.00
6 Dick Duff 2.00 4.00
7 Ron Ellis 2.00 4.00
8 Billy Harris (Portrait) 1.50 3.00
9 Billy Harris (Action) 1.50 3.00
10 Larry Hillman 1.50 3.00
11 Red Kelly 4.00 8.00
12 Dave Keon (No number) 7.50 15.00
13 Dave Keon (Number 14) 7.50 15.00
14 Frank Mahovlich (Dark uniform) 7.50 15.00
15 Frank Mahovlich (Dark uniform with added line NHL All-Star) 7.50 15.00
16 Don McKenney 1.50 3.00
17 Dickie Moore 4.00 8.00
18 Bob Nevin 2.00 4.00
19 Bert Olmstead 2.50 5.00
20 Eddie Shack 5.00 10.00
21 Don Simmons 2.00 4.00
22 Allan Stanley 3.00 6.00

1965-66 Maple Leafs White Border

This 17-card set of postcards measured approximately 3 1/2" by 5 1/2" and featured black and white portrait and full length photos with white borders. The Toronto Maple Leafs logo was printed in both bottom corners. A facsimile autograph appeared at the bottom between the logos. The backs were blank. The cards were unnumbered and checklisted below in alphabetical order.

COMPLETE SET (17) 30.00 60.00
1 George Armstrong 4.00 8.00
2 Bob Baun 2.00 4.00
3 Johnny Bower 4.00 8.00
4 John Brenneman 1.50 3.00
5 Brian Conacher 1.50 3.00
6 Ron Ellis (Portrait) 2.00 4.00
7 Ron Ellis (Full length; name in print) 2.00 4.00
8 Larry Hillman 1.50 3.00
9 Larry Jeffrey 1.50 3.00
10 Bruce Gamble 2.00 4.00
11 Red Kelly 4.00 8.00
12 Dave Keon 5.00 10.00
13 Orland Kurtenbach 2.00 4.00
14 Jim Pappin 1.50 3.00
15 Marcel Pronovost 3.00 6.00
16 Eddie Shack 4.00 8.00
17 Allan Stanley 3.00 6.00

1966-67 Maple Leafs Hockey Talks

Distributed by Esso, this set of 10 albums was a popular premium among Maple Leafs fans. Set consisted of ten records inside colorful paper sleeves. Each set was also housed in a large blue Esso Hockey Talks envelope.

COMPLETE SET (10) 300.00 600.00
1 George Armstrong 30.00 60.00
2 Johnny Bower 40.00 80.00
3 Dave Keon 30.00 60.00
4 Frank Mahovlich 30.00 60.00
5 Tim Horton 30.00 60.00
6 Bob Pulford 40.00 80.00
7 Brit Selby 25.00 50.00
8 Eddie Shack 30.00 60.00
9 Ron Ellis 30.00 60.00
10 Punch Imlach 30.00 60.00
NNO Hockey Caravan Envelope 15.00 30.00

1968-69 Maple Leafs White Border

This 11-card set of postcards measured approximately 3 1/2" by 5 1/2" and featured black and white player photos with white borders. The Pelyk and Smith cards were portraits while the other cards have posed action shots. The Maple Leafs logo was at the bottom left corner. A facsimile autograph appeared at the bottom. The backs were blank. The cards were unnumbered and checklisted below in alphabetical order.

COMPLETE SET (11) 20.00 40.00
1 Johnny Bower 4.00 8.00
2 Jim Dorey 1.50 3.00
3 Paul Henderson 2.00 4.00
4 Tim Horton 5.00 10.00
5 Rick Ley 1.50 3.00
6 Murray Oliver 1.50 3.00
7 Mike Pelyk 1.50 3.00
8 Pierre Pilote 3.00 6.00
9 Darryl Sly 1.50 3.00
10 Floyd Smith 1.50 3.00
11 Bill Sutherland 1.50 3.00

1969-70 Maple Leafs White Border Glossy

This 40-card set of postcards measured approximately 3 1/2" by 5 1/2" and features glossy black and white player photos (posed action or portraits) with white borders. The Maple Leafs logo is printed in black in the bottom left corner. The player's name appears at the bottom in block letters. The backs are blank. The cards are unnumbered and checklisted below in alphabetical order.

COMPLETE SET (40) 75.00 150.00
1 George Armstrong 3.00 6.00
2 Johnny Bower 4.00 8.00
3 Wayne Carleton 1.00 2.00
4 King Clancy 3.00 6.00
5 Terry Clancy 1.00 2.00
6 Brian Conacher 1.00 2.00
7 Marv Edwards 1.50 3.00
8 Ron Ellis (Number 6) 1.50 3.00
9 Ron Ellis (Number 8) 1.50 3.00
10 Ron Ellis (No number) 1.50 3.00
11 Bruce Gamble (Front view) 1.50 3.00
12 Bruce Gamble (Side view) 1.50 3.00
13 Brian Glennie (Portrait) 1.50 3.00
14 Brian Glennie (Full length) 1.50 3.00
15 Jim Harrison 1.00 2.00
16 Larry Hillman 1.00 2.00
17 Tim Horton 5.00 10.00
18 Dave Keon (A on sweater) 3.00 6.00
19 Dave Keon (C on sweater) 3.00 6.00
20 Rick Ley 1.50 3.00
21 Frank Mahovlich 5.00 10.00
22 Jim McKenny 1.00 2.00
23 Larry Mickey 1.00 2.00
24 Murray Oliver 1.00 2.00
25 Jim Pappin 1.00 2.00
26 Mike Pelyk 1.00 2.00
27 Marcel Pronovost 2.00 4.00
28 Bob Pulford (Number on gloves) 2.50 5.00
29 Bob Pulford (No number on gloves) 2.50 5.00
30 Pat Quinn 2.00 4.00
31 Brit Selby 1.00 2.00
32 Al Smith 1.00 2.00
33 Floyd Smith 1.00 2.00
34 Allan Stanley 2.50 5.00
35 Norm Ullman 2.50 5.00
36 Mike Walton (Stick touching border) 1.50 3.00
37 Mike Walton (Stick away from border) 1.50 3.00
38 Ron Ward 1.00 2.00
39 Team Photo 1966-67 3.00 6.00
40 Punch Imlach and King Clancy 3.00 6.00

1969-70 Maple Leafs White Border Matte

This six-card set of postcards measures approximately 3 1/2" by 5 1/2" and featured matte black and white player photos with white borders. The Toronto Maple Leafs logo was printed in black in the bottom left corner. The player's name appeared at the bottom in block letters. The backs were blank. The cards were unnumbered and checklisted below in alphabetical order.

COMPLETE SET (6) 10.00 20.00
1 Brian Glennie 1.50 3.00
2 Dave Keon 4.00 8.00
3 Bill MacMillan 1.25 2.50
4 Larry McIntyre 1.25 2.50
5 Brian Spencer 2.50 5.00
6 Norm Ullman 3.00 6.00

1970-71 Maple Leafs Postcards

This 15-card set measured approximately 3 1/2" by 5 1/2" and featured matte black and white player photos with white borders. The Maple Leafs logo was printed in the bottom left corner. The player's name appeared in block letters, and a facsimile autograph was printed in black. The backs were blank. The cards were unnumbered and checklisted below in alphabetical order. Key card in the set was Darryl Sittler appearing in his Rookie Card year.

COMPLETE SET (15) 25.00 50.00
1 Jim Dorey 1.00 2.00
2 Ron Ellis 1.50 3.00
3 Bruce Gamble 1.50 3.00
4 Jim Harrison 1.00 2.00
5 Paul Henderson 1.50 3.00
6 Rick Ley 1.25 2.50
7 Bob Liddington 1.00 2.00
8 Jim McKenny 1.00 2.00
9 Garry Monahan 1.00 2.00
10 Mike Pelyk 1.00 2.00
11 Jacques Plante 6.00 12.00
12 Brad Selwood 1.00 2.00
13 Darryl Sittler 12.50 25.00
14 Guy Trottier 1.00 2.00
15 Mike Walton 1.50 3.00

1971-72 Maple Leafs Postcards

This 21-card set measured approximately 3 1/2" by 5 1/2" and featured posed color player photos with black backgrounds. (The sweaters had lace-style neck.) The cards featured a facsimile autograph. The backs are blank. The cards were unnumbered and checklisted below in alphabetical order.

COMPLETE SET (21) 25.00 50.00
1 Bob Baun 1.50 3.00
2 Jim Dorey 1.00 2.00
3 Denis Dupere 1.00 2.00
4 Ron Ellis 1.50 3.00
5 Brian Glennie 1.00 2.00
6 Jim Harrison 1.00 2.00
7 Paul Henderson 1.50 3.00
8 Dave Keon 2.50 5.00
9 Rick Ley 1.00 2.00
10 Billy MacMillan 1.00 2.00
11 Don Marshall 1.00 2.00
12 Jim McKenny 1.00 2.00
13 Garry Monahan 1.00 2.00
14 Bernie Parent 4.00 8.00
15 Mike Pelyk 1.00 2.00
16 Jacques Plante 4.00 8.00
17 Brad Selwood 1.00 2.00
18 Darryl Sittler 5.00 10.00
19 Brian Spencer 1.50 3.00
20 Guy Trottier 1.00 2.00
21 Norm Ullman 2.00 4.00

1972-73 Maple Leafs Postcards

This 30-card set measured approximately 3 1/2" by 5 1/2" and featured posed color player photos with a black background. The players were pictured wearing "V-neck" sweaters. The cards featured a facsimile autograph. The backs were blank. The cards were unnumbered and checklisted below in alphabetical order.

COMPLETE SET (30) 40.00 80.00
1 Bob Baun 1.25 2.50
2 Terry Clancy .75 1.50
3 Denis Dupere .75 1.50
4 Ron Ellis (Dark print) 1.25 2.50
5 Ron Ellis (Light print) 1.25 2.50
6 George Ferguson .75 1.50
7 Brian Glennie (Autograph touches stick) .75 1.50
8 Brian Glennie (Autograph away from stick) .75 1.50
9 John Grisdale .75 1.50
10 Paul Henderson (Light print) 1.25 2.50
11 Paul Henderson (Dark print) 1.25 2.50
12 Pierre Jarry .75 1.50
13 Rick Kehoe 1.25 2.50
14 Dave Keon (Autograph touches skate) 2.50 5.00
15 Dave Keon (Autograph away from skate) 2.50 5.00
16 Ron Low 1.25 2.50
17 Joe Lundrigan .75 1.50
18 Larry McIntyre .75 1.50
19 Jim McKenny (Blue tinge) .75 1.50
20 Jim McKenny (Red tinge) .75 1.50
21 Garry Monahan .75 1.50
22 Randy Osburn .75 1.50

3 Mike Pelyk .75 1.50
4 Jacques Plante 5.00 10.00
(Autograph through tape)
5 Jacques Plante 5.00 10.00
(Autograph under tape)
6 Darryl Sittler 5.00 10.00
(Autograph over stick)
7 Darryl Sittler 5.00 10.00
(Autograph away
from stick)
8 Errol Thompson .75 1.50
9 Norm Ullman 2.00 4.00
(Best Wishes
above blueline)
0 Norm Ullman 2.00 4.00
(Best Wishes
across blueline)

1973-74 Maple Leafs Postcards

his 29-card set measured approximately 3 1/2" by 5 /2" and featured posed color player photos with a lue-green background. The cards featured a facsimile utograph. The backs were blank. The cards were nnumbered and checklisted below in alphabetical rder. The key card in the set was Lanny McDonald, hose card predated his Rookie Card.

OMPLETE SET (29) 45.00 90.00
Johnny Bower 2.50 5.00
Willie Brossart .75 1.50
Denis Dupere .75 1.50
Ron Ellis 1.25 2.50
Doug Favell 1.50 3.00
(Standing)
Doug Favell 1.50 3.00
(Bending)
Brian Glennie .75 1.50
Jim Gregory .75 1.50
Inge Hammarstrom .75 1.50
0 Paul Henderson 1.25 2.50
1 Eddie Johnston 1.50 3.00
2 Rick Kehoe 1.50 3.00
(Same as 1972-73 set)
3 Rick Kehoe 1.50 3.00
(Bending)
4 Rick Kehoe 1.50 3.00
(Standing)
5 Red Kelly 3.00 6.00
5 Dave Keon 3.00 6.00
7 Lanny McDonald 6.00 12.00
3 Jim McKenny .75 1.50
9 Garry Monahan .75 1.50
) Bob Neely .75 1.50
1 Mike Pelyk .75 1.50
2 Borje Salming 4.00 8.00
3 Eddie Shack 3.00 6.00
4 Darryl Sittler 3.00 6.00
(Bending)
5 Darryl Sittler 3.00 6.00
(Standing)
5 Errol Thompson .75 1.50
7 Ian Turnbull .75 1.50
3 Norm Ullman 1.75 3.50
9 Dunc Wilson 1.25 2.50

1974-75 Maple Leafs Postcards

his 27-card set measured approximately 3 1/2" by 5 '2" and featured posed color player photos with a ale-blue background and a "Venetian blind" effect. he cards featured facsimile autographs. The backs ere blank. The cards were unnumbered and are hecklisted below in alphabetical order.

OMPLETE SET (27) 25.00 50.00
Claire Alexander .75 1.50
Dave Dunn .75 1.50
Ron Ellis 1.00 2.00
George Ferguson .75 1.50
(Bending)
George Ferguson .75 1.50
(Standing)
Bill Flett .75 1.50
(Front view)
Bill Flett .75 1.50
(Side view)
Brian Glennie .75 1.50
Inge Hammarstrom .75 1.50
Dave Keon 2.00 4.00
(Bending)
Dave Keon 2.00 4.00
(Standing)
Lanny McDonald 3.00 6.00
Jim McKenny .75 1.50
Gord McRae .75 1.50
Lyle Moffat .75 1.50
Bob Neely .75 1.50
Gary Sabourin .75 1.50
Borje Salming 2.00 4.00
Rod Seiling .75 1.50
Eddie Shack 2.00 4.00
Darryl Sittler 2.00 4.00
Blaine Stoughton 1.00 2.00
Errol Thompson .75 1.50
Ian Turnbull 1.00 2.00
Norm Ullman 1.50 3.00
Tiger Williams 2.00 4.00
Dunc Wilson 1.00 2.00

1975-76 Maple Leafs Postcards

is 30-card set of postcards measured approximately 1/2" by 5 1/2" and featured posed color photos of ayers in blue uniforms. The Maple Leafs logo, the ayer's name, and number appeared in a white panel the bottom. A facsimile autograph was inscribed ross the picture. The backs had player information. e cards were unnumbered and are checklisted below alphabetical order.

OMPLETE SET (30) 25.00 50.00
Claire Alexander .75 1.50
Don Ashby .75 1.50
Bending)
Don Ashby .75 1.50
Standing)
Pat Boutette .75 1.50
Dave Dunn .75 1.50
Doug Favell 1.00 2.00
George Ferguson .75 1.50
Brian Glennie .75 1.50
Inge Hammarstrom .75 1.50
Bending)
Inge Hammarstrom .75 1.50
Standing)
Greg Hubick .75 1.50
Lanny McDonald 2.50 5.00
Jim McKenny .75 1.50
Gord McRae .75 1.50
Bob Neely .75 1.50
Borje Salming 2.00 4.00
Side view)
Borje Salming 2.00 4.00
(Front view)
18 Rod Seiling .75 1.50
19 Darryl Sittler 2.00 4.00
(Bending)
20 Darryl Sittler 2.50 5.00
(Standing)
21 Blaine Stoughton 1.00 2.00
22 Wayne Thomas 1.25 2.50
(Crouching)
23 Wayne Thomas 1.25 2.50
(Standing)
24 Errol Thompson .75 1.50
25 Ian Turnbull 1.00 2.00
(Bending)
26 Ian Turnbull 1.00 2.00
(Standing)
27 Stan Weir .75 1.50
28 Tiger Williams 1.25 2.50
Bending
29 Tiger Williams 1.25 2.50
Standing
30 Maple Leaf Gardens 1.00 2.00
(Painting)

1976-77 Maple Leafs Postcards

This 24-card set in the postcard format measured approximately 3 1/2" by 5 1/2" and featured posed color photos of players in blue uniforms. A white panel at the bottom contained the Maple Leafs logo in each corner, the player's name, and uniform number. A facsimile autograph was inscribed across the picture. The cards were unnumbered and checklisted below in alphabetical order. Key card in the set was Randy Carlyle appearing prior to his Rookie Card year.

COMPLETE SET (24) 20.00 40.00
1 Claire Alexander .63 1.25
2 Don Ashby .63 1.25
3 Pat Boutette .63 1.25
4 Randy Carlyle 1.50 3.00
5 George Ferguson .63 1.25
6 Scott Garland .63 1.25
7 Brian Glennie .63 1.25
8 Inge Hammarstrom .63 1.25
9 Lanny McDonald 2.00 4.00
10 Jim McKenny .63 1.25
11 Gord McRae .63 1.25
12 Bob Neely .63 1.25
13 Mike Palmateer 2.00 4.00
14 Mike Pelyk .63 1.25
15 Borje Salming 1.50 3.00
16 Darryl Sittler 2.00 4.00
17 Wayne Thomas 1.00 2.00
18 Errol Thompson .63 1.25
19 Ian Turnbull .75 1.50
20 Ian Turnbull .75 1.50
21 Jack Valiquette .63 1.25
22 Kurt Walker .63 1.25
23 Stan Weir .63 1.25
24 Tiger Williams 2.00 4.00

1977-78 Maple Leafs Postcards

This 19-card set measures approximately 3 1/2" by 5 1/2" and featured posed color photos of players in white uniforms. At the bottom were the Toronto Maple Leafs logo in each corner, the player's uniform number, and the player's name in blue print. The backs were blank. The cards were unnumbered and checklisted below in alphabetical order.

COMPLETE SET (19) 12.50 25.00
1 Pat Boutette .50 1.00
2 Randy Carlyle 1.00 2.00
3 Ron Ellis .75 1.50
4 George Ferguson .50 1.00
5 Brian Glennie .50 1.00
6 Inge Hammarstrom .50 1.00
7 Trevor Johansen .50 1.00
8 Jimmy Jones .50 1.00
9 Lanny McDonald 2.00 4.00
10 Jim McKenny .50 1.00
11 Gord McRae .50 1.00
12 Mike Palmateer 1.50 3.00
13 Borje Salming 1.50 3.00
14 Darryl Sittler 2.00 4.00
15 Errol Thompson .50 1.00
16 Ian Turnbull .50 1.00
17 Jack Valiquette .50 1.00
18 Kurt Walker .50 1.00
19 Tiger Williams 1.50 3.00

1978-79 Maple Leafs Postcards

This 25-card set in the postcard format measured approximately 3 1/2" by 5 1/2" and featured posed color player photos. At the bottom were the Toronto Maple Leafs logo in each corner, the player's uniform number in the logo at the bottom right, and the player's name in blue print. The cards were unnumbered and checklisted below in alphabetical order.

COMPLETE SET (25) 15.00 30.00
1 John Anderson .75 1.50
2 Bruce Boudreau 1.50 4.00
3 Pat Boutette .50 1.00
4 Pat Boutette .50 1.00
5 Dave Burrows .50 1.00
6 Jerry Butler .50 1.00
7 Ron Ellis .75 1.50
8 Paul Harrison .50 1.00
9 Dave Hutchison .50 1.00
10 Trevor Johansen .50 1.00
11 Jimmy Jones .50 1.00
12 Dan Maloney .75 1.50
13 Lanny McDonald 2.00 4.00
14 Walt McKechnie .50 1.00
15 Garry Monahan .50 1.00
16 Roger Neilson 1.00 2.00
17 Mike Palmateer 1.25 2.50
18 Borje Salming 1.25 2.50
19 Darryl Sittler 2.00 4.00
20 Lorne Stamler .50 1.00
21 Ian Turnbull .50 1.00
22 Tiger Williams 1.25 2.50
23 Ron Wilson .50 1.00
24 H.Ballard/K.Clancy 1.00 2.00
25 Team Photo 1.25 2.50

1979-80 Maple Leafs Postcards

This 34-card set in the postcard format measured approximately 3 1/2" by 5 1/2" and featured posed color photos of players in blue uniforms. The Toronto Maple Leafs logo was in each bottom corner. A blue panel across the bottom contained the player's name in white print. The player's uniform number was printed in the logo at the bottom right. Most of the pictures had a light blue tint and are taken against a studio background. These cards also featured facsimile autographs on the lower portion of the picture. The backs were printed with a light blue postcard design and carry the player's name and position. The cards were unnumbered and checklisted below in alphabetical order.

COMPLETE SET (34) 20.00 40.00
1 John Anderson .50 1.00
2 Harold Ballard .75 1.50
3 Laurie Boschman .50 1.00
4 Pat Boutette .38 .75
5 Carl Brewer .75 1.50
6 Dave Burrows .38 .75
7 Jerry Butler .38 .75
8 Jiri Crha .75 1.50
9 Ron Ellis .50 1.00
10 Paul Gardner .38 .75
11 Paul Harrison .38 .75
12 Greg Hotham .38 .75
13 Dave Hutchison .38 .75
14 Punch Imlach CO 1.00 2.00
15 Jimmy Jones .38 .75
16 Mark Kirton .38 .75
17 Dan Maloney .38 .75
18 Terry Martin .50 1.00
19 Lanny McDonald 2.00 4.00
20 Walt McKechnie .38 .75
21 Mike Palmateer 1.00 2.00
22 Mike Palmateer 1.00 2.00
(Autograph at
different angle)
23 Joel Quenneville .50 1.00
24 Rocky Saganiuk .38 .75
25 Borje Salming 1.25 2.50
(Autograph touches
blue panel)
26 Borje Salming 1.25 2.50
(Autograph away
from blue panel)
27 Darryl Sittler 2.00 4.00
(Autograph closer
to blue panel)
28 Darryl Sittler 2.00 4.00
29 Floyd Smith .38 .75
30 Bob Stephenson .50 1.00
(Action shot taken at
rink; borderless; no
facsimile autograph;
black print on back)
31 Ian Turnbull .38 .75
32 Tiger Williams 1.00 2.00
33 Ron Wilson .38 .75
34 Faceoff with Cardinal .63 1.25

1980-81 Maple Leafs Postcards

This 28-card set measured approximately 3 1/2" by 5 1/2" and featured horizontally oriented color player photos on the left half of the card. The right half displayed player information, blue logos, and a facsimile autograph printed in sky blue along with the team logo and a maple leaf carrying the player's jersey number. The backs were blank. The cards were unnumbered and checklisted below in alphabetical order.

COMPLETE SET (28) 12.50 25.00
1 John Anderson .40 1.00
2 Harold Ballard .60 1.50
3 Laurie Boschman .40 1.00
(Portrait)
4 Laurie Boschman .40 1.00
(Action)
5 Johnny Bower 1.25 3.00
6 King Clancy .75 2.00
7 Jiri Crha .60 1.50
8 Joe Crozier CO .30 .75
9 Bill Derlago .40 1.00
10 Dick Duff .40 1.00
11 Vitezslav Duris .30 .75
12 Dave Farrish .30 .75
13 Stewart Gavin .40 1.00
14 Paul Harrison .30 .75
15 Pat Hickey .30 .75
16 Mark Kirton .30 .75
17 Terry Martin .30 .75
18 Gerry McNamara .30 .75
19 Wilf Paiement .40 1.00
20 Robert Picard .30 .75
21 Curt Ridley .30 .75
22 Rocky Saganiuk .30 .75
23 Borje Salming .75 2.00
24 Dave Shand .30 .75
25 Darryl Sittler 1.50 4.00
(Portrait)
26 Darryl Sittler 1.50 4.00
(Action)
27 Ian Turnbull .30 .75
28 Rick Vaive .60 1.50

1981-82 Maple Leafs Postcards

This 26-card set in the postcard format measured approximately 3 1/2" by 5 1/2" and featured full-bleed color photos of players posed on the ice against a dark background. A white Maple Leafs logo appeared in each top corner and the player's name in white between the logos. The player's number was printed in the right top logo. These cards also featured facsimile autographs. The backs were white and have a basic postcard design printed in light blue. The cards were unnumbered and checklisted below in alphabetical order.

COMPLETE SET (26) 10.00 25.00
1 John Anderson .40 1.00
2 Harold Ballard .75 2.00
(Painting)
3 Jim Benning .30 .75
4 Fred Boimistruck .30 .75
5 Laurie Boschman .30 .75
6 Bill Derlago .40 1.00
7 Stewart Gavin .40 1.00
8 Bunny Larocque .60 1.50
9 Don Luce .30 .75
10 Dan Maloney .30 .75
11 Bob Manno .30 .75
12 Paul Marshall .30 .75
13 Terry Martin .30 .75
14 Bob McGill .30 .75
15 Barry Melrose .60 1.50
16 Mike Nykoluk CO .30 .75
17 Wilf Paiement .40 1.00
18 Rene Robert .40 1.00
19 Rocky Saganiuk .30 .75
20 Borje Salming .75 2.00
21 Darryl Sittler 1.50 4.00
22 Vincent Tremblay .30 .75
23 Rick Vaive .60 1.50
24 Gary Yaremchuk .30 .75
25 Ron Zanussi .30 .75
26 Frank J. Selke and .60 1.50
Harold Ballard

1982-83 Maple Leafs Postcards

This 37-card set in the postcard format measured approximately 3 1/2" by 5 1/2" and featured color photos of players on the ice against a dark background. A white Maple Leafs logo, the sweater number, and the player's name appeared in a blue panel at the bottom. A facsimile autograph appeared near the bottom of the picture. A blue Maple Leafs logo was printed in one of the top corners. The postcard backs were printed in light blue, in contrast to the 1984-85 issue, which featured black print on the back. The cards were unnumbered and checklisted below in alphabetical order.

COMPLETE SET (37) 10.00 25.00
1 Russ Adam .30 .75
2 John Anderson .40 1.00
3 Normand Aubin .30 .75
4 Jim Benning .30 .75
5 Fred Boimistruck .30 .75
6 Serge Boisvert .30 .75
7 Dan Daoust .30 .75
8 Bill Derlago .40 1.00
(Autograph 1
8
from border)
9 Bill Derlago .40 1.00
(Autograph 1
4
from border)
10 Vitezslav Duris .30 .75
11 Miroslav Frycer .30 .75
(Autograph touching
skate blade)
12 Miroslav Frycer .30 .75
(Autograph away
from skate blade
13 Stewart Gavin .40 1.00
14 Gaston Gingras .30 .75
(Dark background)
15 Gaston Gingras .30 .75
(Light background)
16 Billy Harris .30 .75
17 Paul Higgins .30 .75
18 Peter Inhacak .30 .75
19 Jim Korn .30 .75
20 Bunny Larocque .40 1.00
(Bunny touching stick)
21 Bunny Larocque .40 1.00
(Bunny touching
goalie pad)
22 Dan Maloney .40 1.00
23 Terry Martin .30 .75
24 Bob McGill .30 .75
25 Frank Nigro .30 .75
26 Mike Nykoluk CO .30 .75
27 Gary Nylund .30 .75
28 Mike Palmateer .75 2.00
29 Walt Poddubny .40 1.00
30 Borje Salming .75 2.00
(Autograph 1
8
from skate)
31 Borje Salming .75 2.00
(Autograph 1
4
from skate)
32 Rick St. Croix .40 1.00
33 Greg Terrion .30 .75
(Dark background)
34 Greg Terrion .30 .75
(Light background)
35 Vincent Tremblay .30 .75
36 Rick Vaive .50 1.25
(Autograph touching
blade)
37 Rick Vaive .50 1.25
(Autograph touching
toe of skate)

1983-84 Maple Leafs Postcards

This 26-card set in the postcard format measured approximately 3 1/2" by 5 1/2" and featured posed color photos of players on the ice. A pale blue border contained a blue Maple Leafs logo in the bottom right corner. The player's name and number was printed running up the left side and across the top in the left corner. A facsimile autograph was printed in black on the front near the bottom of the photo. The backs were white and carry a basic postcard design in light blue. The cards were unnumbered and checklisted below in alphabetical order.

COMPLETE SET (26) 8.00 20.00
1 John Anderson .40 1.00
2 Jim Benning .30 .75
3 Dan Daoust .30 .75
4 Bill Derlago .40 1.00
5 Dave Farrish .30 .75
6 Miroslav Frycer .30 .75
7 Stewart Gavin .40 1.00
8 Gaston Gingras .30 .75
9 Pat Graham .30 .75
10 Billy Harris .30 .75
11 Peter Inhacak .30 .75
12 Jim Korn .30 .75
13 Gary Leeman .40 1.00
14 Dan Maloney .30 .75
15 Terry Martin .30 .75
16 Basil McRae .40 1.00
17 Frank Nigro .30 .75
18 Mike Nykoluk CO .30 .75
19 Gary Nylund .30 .75
20 Mike Palmateer .60 1.50
21 Walt Poddubny .40 1.00
22 Borje Salming .75 2.00
23 Bill Stewart .30 .75
24 Rick St. Croix .40 1.00
25 Greg Terrion .30 .75
26 Rick Vaive .50 1.25

1984-85 Maple Leafs Postcards

This 25-card set in the postcard format measured approximately 3 1/2" by 5 1/2" and featured posed color photos of players on the ice with facsimile autographs. A blue panel at the bottom contained the player's name, sweater number, and a white Maple Leafs logo. A blue Toronto Maple Leafs logo appeared in one of the top corners. The backs had a basic postcard design printed in black. The cards were unnumbered and checklisted below in alphabetical order. Both Russ Courtnall and Al Iafrate appeared in this set prior to their Rookie Card year. This set could be distinguished from the similarly designed 1982-83 postcard set by the black jersey number and black outline around the team logo in the bottom border stripe.

COMPLETE SET (25) 10.00 25.00
1 John Anderson .40 1.00
2 Jim Benning .30 .75
3 Allan Bester .50 1.25
4 John Brophy CO .40 1.00
5 Jeff Brubaker .30 .75
6 Russ Courtnall 1.25 3.00
7 Dan Daoust .30 .75
8 Bill Derlago .30 .75
9 Miroslav Frycer .30 .75
10 Stewart Gavin .40 1.00
11 Al Iafrate 1.50 4.00
12 Peter Inhacak .30 .75
13 Jeff Jackson .30 .75
14 Jim Korn .30 .75
15 Gary Leeman .40 1.00
16 Dan Maloney CO .30 .75
17 Bob McGill .30 .75
18 Gary Nylund .30 .75
19 Walt Poddubny .40 1.00
20 Bill Root .30 .75
21 Borje Salming .75 2.00
22 Bill Stewart .30 .75
23 Greg Terrion .30 .75
24 Rick Vaive .50 1.25
25 Ken Wregget 1.00 2.50

1985-86 Maple Leafs Postcards

This 34-card set in the postcard format measured approximately 3 1/2" by 5 1/2" and featured color action photos of players on the ice. A blue panel at the bottom contained the player's name, number, and a white Maple Leafs logo. The cards were unnumbered and checklisted below in alphabetical order. Wendel Clark appeared in this set the year before his Rookie Card. In addition to the regular set, a special John Bower card was also available.

COMPLETE SET (35) 12.00 30.00
1 Harold Ballard PRES .40 1.00
2 Jim Benning .30 .75
3 Tim Bernhardt .40 1.00
4 Johnny Bower ACO .60 1.50
5 Jeff Brubaker .30 .75
6 Wendel Clark 4.00 10.00
7 Russ Courtnall .75 2.00
(Dark uniform)
8 Russ Courtnall .75 2.00
(Light uniform)
9 Dan Daoust .30 .75
10 Don Edwards .60 1.50
11 Tom Fergus .30 .75
12 Miroslav Frycer .30 .75
13 Dan Hodgson .30 .75
14 Al Iafrate 1.25 3.00
15 Miroslav Inhacak .30 .75
16 Peter Inhacak .30 .75
17 Jim Korn .30 .75
18 Chris Kotsopoulos .30 .75
19 Gary Leeman .30 .75
20 Brad Maxwell .40 1.00
(Dark uniform)
21 Brad Maxwell .40 1.00
(Light uniform)
22 Bob McGill .30 .75
23 Gary Nylund .30 .75
24 Walt Poddubny .40 1.00
25 Bill Root .30 .75
26 Borje Salming .75 2.00
27 Marian Stastny .30 .75
28 Greg Terrion .30 .75
29 Steve Thomas 1.00 2.50
30 Rick Vaive .40 1.00
(Taking slapshot
31 Rick Vaive .40 1.00
(Light uniform)
32 Blake Wesley .30 .75
33 Ken Wregget .60 1.50
34 Team Photo 1.25 3.00
(5 1/2 by 8 1/2)
35 John Bower SPECIAL .30 .75

1986-87 Maple Leafs Postcards

This 22-card set measured approximately 3 1/2" by 5 1/2". The fronts featured full-bleed color action player photos; the player's name, number and team logo were printed in a blue-and-white bar at the top or bottom. The backs were white and show a postcard design. The cards were unnumbered and checklisted below in alphabetical order.

COMPLETE SET (22) 10.00 25.00
1 Mike Allison .30 .75
2 Harold Ballard PR .60 1.50
3 Tim Bernhardt .40 1.00
4 Wendel Clark 2.00 5.00
5 Russ Courtnall .75 2.00
6 Vincent Damphousse 2.00 5.00
7 Jerome Dupont .30 .75
8 Tom Fergus .30 .75
9 Miroslav Frycer .30 .75
10 Todd Gill .30 .75
11 Al Iafrate 1.25 3.00
12 Peter Ihnacak .30 .75
13 Jeff Jackson .30 .75
14 Terry Johnson .30 .75
15 Chris Kotsopoulos .30 .75
16 Gary Leeman .30 .75
17 Borje Salming .75 2.00
18 Brad Smith .40 1.00
19 Greg Terrion .30 .75
20 Steve Thomas .60 1.50
21 Rick Vaive .40 1.00
22 Ken Wregget 1.00 2.50

1987-88 Maple Leafs PLAY

This set contained 30 P.L.A.Y. (Police, Law and Youth) cards, and it was sponsored by Kellogg Salada Canada Inc. in conjunction with the Toronto Maple Leafs and various police agencies. The cards could be collected from members of the London City Police and the Ontario Provincial Police, at a rate of three new cards per week. Three special "make-up weeks" were held to acquire any cards that were missed. The cards measured approximately 2 3/4" by 3 1/4".

COMPLETE SET (30) 8.00 20.00
1 N.Laverne Shipley .02 .10
(Police Chief)
2 Tom Gosnell (Mayor) .02 .10
3 Sponsor's Card .02 .10
Kellogg Salada
4 Harold E. Ballard PR .20 .50
5 D. Almond .02 .10
(Police Superintendent)
6 Wendel Clark 17 2.00 5.00
7 Tom Fergus 19 .30 .75
8 Borje Salming 21 .60 1.50
9 Ed Olczyk 16 .30 .75
10 Gary Leeman 11 .30 .75
11 Rick Lanz 4 .20 .50
12 Allan Bester 30 .30 .75
13 Todd Gill 23 .30 .75
14 Al Secord 20 .30 .75
15 Miroslav Frycer 14 .20 .50
16 Chris Kotsopoulos 26 .20 .50
17 Vincent Damphousse 10 1.50 4.00
18 Mike Allison 8 .20 .50
19 Al Iafrate 33 .75 2.00
20 Dan Daoust 24 .20 .50
21 Greg Terrion 7 .20 .50
22 Brad Smith 29 .30 .75
23 Mark Osborne 12 .20 .50
24 Peter Ihnacak 18 .20 .50
25 Dale Degray 3 .20 .50
26 Dave Semenko 27 .30 .75
27 Luke Richardson 2 .30 .75
28 John Brophy CO .20 .50
29 Ken Wregget 31 .60 1.50
30 Russ Courtnall 9 .40 1.00

1987-88 Maple Leafs Postcards

Measuring approximately 5" by 8", this set of oversized postcards featured the Toronto Maple Leafs. The fronts had full-bleed color action player photos; the player's name, number, and team logo were printed in a blue-and-white bar at the bottom. The backs were white and show a postcard design. The cards were unnumbered and checklisted below in alphabetical order.

COMPLETE SET (21) 8.00 20.00
1 Allan Bester .30 .75
2 Wendel Clark 2.00 5.00
3 Russ Courtnall .40 1.00
4 Vincent Damphousse 1.50 4.00
5 Dan Daoust .20 .50
6 Tom Fergus .30 .75
7 Miroslav Frycer .20 .50
8 Todd Gill .30 .75
9 Al Iafrate .75 2.00
10 Peter Ihnacak .20 .50
11 Chris Kotsopoulos .20 .50
12 Rick Lanz .20 .50
13 Gary Leeman .30 .75
14 Ed Olczyk .30 .75
15 Mark Osborne .20 .50
16 Luke Richardson .30 .75
17 Borje Salming .60 1.50
18 Al Secord .30 .75
19 Dave Semenko .30 .75
20 Ken Wregget .60 1.50
21 Team Photo .75 2.00

1987-88 Maple Leafs Postcards Oversized

This set was similar in design and checklist to the regular size set, yet measures 6" x 10".

COMPLETE SET (21) 8.00 20.00
1 Allan Bester .30 .75
2 Wendel Clark 2.00 5.00
3 Russ Courtnall .40 1.00
4 Vincent Damphousse 1.50 4.00
5 Dan Daoust .20 .50
6 Tom Fergus .30 .75
7 Miroslav Frycer .20 .50
8 Todd Gill .30 .75
9 Al Iafrate .75 2.00
10 Peter Ihnacak .20 .50
11 Chris Kotsopoulos .20 .50
12 Rick Lanz .20 .50
13 Gary Leeman .30 .75
14 Ed Olczyk .30 .75
15 Mark Osborne .20 .50
16 Luke Richardson .30 .75
17 Borje Salming .60 1.50
18 Al Secord .30 .75
19 Dave Semenko .30 .75
20 Ken Wregget .60 1.50
21 Team Photo .75 2.00

1988-89 Maple Leafs PLAY

This set contained 30 P.L.A.Y. (Police, Law and Youth) cards, and it was sponsored by Kellogg's in conjunction with Toronto Maple Leafs and various police agencies. The cards could be collected from members of the London City Police and the Ontario Provincial Police, at a rate of three new cards per week. Three special "make-up weeks" were held to acquire any cards that were missed. After collecting the first 12 cards, they were to be brought to police stations in order to obtain the collector album, which measured approximately 7" by 10". The P.L.A.Y. cards measured 2 3/4" by 3 1/2" and the album had three slots per page in a horizontal format. Below each picture the album had the player's name, number, and a hockey tip paralleled by an anti-crime message.

COMPLETE SET (30) 4.80 12.00
1 Rules and Tips .08 .25
2 Wendel Clark 17 .75 2.00
3 Tom Fergus 19 .20 .50
4 D. Almond .08 .25
(Superintendent)
5 Borje Salming 21 .60 1.50
6 Ed Olczyk 16 .20 .50
7 Sponsor's Card .08 .25
Kellogg Canada
8 Gary Leeman 11 .20 .50
9 Rick Lanz 4 .20 .50
10 N.LaVerne Shipley .08 .25
(Chief of Police)
11 Allan Bester 30 .30 .75
12 Todd Gill 23 .20 .50
13 Harold E. Ballard PR .40 1.00
14 Al Secord 20 .30 .75
15 Daniel Marois 32 .20 .50
16 Chris Kotsopoulos 26 .20 .50
17 Vincent Damphousse 10 .75 2.00
18 Craig Laughlin 14 .20 .50
19 Al Iafrate 33 .40 1.00
20 Dan Daoust 24 .20 .50
21 Derek Laxdal 35 .20 .50
22 Darren Veitch 25 .20 .50
23 Mark Osborne 12 .20 .50
24 David Reid 34 .30 .75
25 Brad Marsh 3 .30 .75
26 Brian Curran 28 .20 .50
27 Sean McKenna 8 .20 .50
28 John Brophy CO .20 .50
29 Ken Wregget 31 .40 1.00
30 Russ Courtnall 9 .40 1.00

1990-91 Maple Leafs Postcards

This postcard-like issue featured color action photos on the front, with an unusual design element of Leafs logos surrounding the action. It was believed that the cards were distributed by local police officers to children. The cards were unnumbered, so are listed in alphabetical order.

COMPLETE SET (21) 4.80 12.00
1 Aaron Broten .20 .50
2 Vincent Damphousse .60 1.50
3 Dave Ellett .20 .50
4 Paul Fenton .20 .50
5 Tom Fergus .20 .50
6 Lou Franceschetti .30 .75
7 Al Iafrate .30 .75
8 Peter Ing .30 .75
9 Mike Krushelnyski .30 .75
10 Tom Kurvers .20 .50
11 Gary Leeman .30 .75
12 Kevin Maguire .30 .75
13 Brad Marsh .30 .75
14 Scott Pearson .20 .50
15 Michel Petit .20 .50
16 Rob Ramage .20 .50
17 Dave Reid .20 .50
18 Luke Richardson .20 .50
19 Joe Sacco .20 .50
20 Doug Shedden .20 .50
21 Scott Thornton .20 .50

1991 Maple Leafs Panini Team Stickers

This 32-sticker set was issued in a plastic bag that contained two 16-sticker sheets (approximately 9" by 12") and a foldout poster, "Super Poster - Hockey 91", on which the stickers could be affixed. The players' names appeared only on the poster, not on the stickers. Each sticker measured about 2 1/8" by 2 7/8" and featured a color player action shot on its white-bordered front. The back of the white sticker sheet was lined off into 16 panels, each carrying the logos for Panini, the NHL, and the NHLPA, as well as the same number that appeared on the front of the sticker. Every Canadian NHL team was featured in this promotion. Each team set was available by mail-order from Panini Canada Ltd. for 2.99 plus 50 cents for shipping and handling.

COMPLETE SET (32) 1.25 3.00
1 Drake Berehowsky .01 .05
2 Allan Bester .02 .10
3 Wendel Clark .20 .50
4 Brian Curran .01 .05
5 Vincent Damphousse .20 .50
6 Lou Franceschetti .01 .05
7 Todd Gill .01 .05
8 Dave Hannan .01 .05
9 Al Iafrate .02 .10
10 Peter Ing .02 .10
11 Tom Kurvers .01 .05
12 Gary Leeman .01 .05
13 Kevin Maguire .01 .05
14 Daniel Marois .01 .05
15 Brad Marsh .02 .10
16 John McIntyre .01 .05
17 Ed Olczyk .01 .05
18 Mark Osborne .01 .05
19 Scott Pearson .01 .05
20 Rob Ramage .02 .10
21 Jeff Reese .02 .10
22 Dave Reid .02 .10
23 Luke Richardson .01 .05
24 Maple Leafs in Action .01 .05
A Team Logo .01 .05
Left Side
B Team Logo .01 .05
Right Side
C Maple Leafs in Action .01 .05
Upper Left Corner
Al Iafrate
Dave Reid
D Maple Leafs in Action .01 .05
Lower Left Corner
Al Iafrate
Dave Reid
E Maple Leafs in Action .01 .05
Upper Right Corner
Al Iafrate
Dave Reid
F Maple Leafs in Action .01 .05
Lower Right Corner
Al Iafrate
Dave Reid
G Al Iafrate .05 .15
Ken Wregget
H Gary Leeman .08 .25
John Kordic

1991-92 Maple Leafs PLAY

This postcard-like set featured action photos on the front, along with player information. The cards were handed out by local police officers to children.

COMPLETE SET (30) 6.00 15.00
1 Glenn Anderson .40 1.00
2 Craig Berube .20 .50
3 Brian Bradley .20 .50
4 Mike Bullard .20 .50
5 Rob Cimetta .20 .50
6 Wendel Clark .75 2.00
7 Bryan Cousineau .20 .50
8 Lucien Deblois .20 .50
9 Dave Ellett .20 .50
10 Tom Fergus .20 .50
11 Cliff Fletcher .08 .25
12 Mike Foligno .20 .50
13 Grant Fuhr .75 2.00
14 Todd Gill .20 .50
15 Alexander Godynyuk .20 .50
16 Bob Halkidis .20 .50
17 Dave Hannan .20 .50
19 Mike Krushelnyski .20 .50
20 Lanny the Police Dog .02 .10
21 Gary Leeman .30 .75
22 Claude Loiselle .20 .50
23 Daniel Marois .20 .50
24 Rob Pearson .20 .50
25 Michel Petit .20 .50
26 Jeff Reese .25 .60
27 Bob Rouse .20 .50
28 Darryl Shannon .20 .50
29 Tom Watt .08 .25
30 Peter Zezel .20 .50

1992-93 Maple Leafs Kodak

This oversized set (4" X 6 1/8") featured full color photos on Kodak paper. The backs were blank. The cards were believed to have been issued as a game-night promotion, although that has not been confirmed.

COMPLETE SET (22) 8.00 20.00
1 Glenn Anderson .30 .75
2 Dave Andreychuk .30 .75
3 Dave Andreychuk .30 .75
(In front of the net
4 Ken Baumgartner .20 .50
5 Drake Berehowsky .20 .50
6 Bill Berg .20 .50
7 Nikolai Borschevsky .20 .50
8 Wendel Clark .75 2.00
9 John Cullen .20 .50
10 Mike Eastwood .20 .50
11 Dave Ellett .20 .50
12 Doug Gilmour .75 2.00
13 Sylvain Lefebvre .20 .50
14 Jamie Macoun .20 .50
15 Kent Manderville .20 .50
16 Dave McIlwain .20 .50
17 Dmitri Mironov .20 .50
18 Mark Osborne .20 .50
19 Rob Pearson .20 .50
20 Felix Potvin 1.25 3.00
21 Bob Rouse .20 .50

22 Peter Zezel .20 .50
23 Mike Foligno .20 .50
24 Grant Fuhr .60 1.50
25 Todd Gill .20 .50
26 Mike Krushelnyski .20 .50
27 Guy Larose .20 .50
28 Bob McGill .20 .50
29 Dave McLLwain .20 .50
30 Daren Puppa .30 .75
31 Joe Sacco .20 .50
32 Darryl Shannon .20 .50
33 Rick Wamsley .30 .75

1993-94 Maple Leafs Score Black's

This 24-card, standard-size Toronto Maple Leafs team set was produced by Score and sponsored by Black's Photography. The cards were distributed free in four-card packs, when a customer brought in film for developing, or with a second order of prints, or when purchasing two rolls of Black's P.I. film. The fronts featured a pop-up photo cut-out. The pop-up was accomplished by gently bending the card to pop up the player's head and then pulling a tab at the top to stand the player up. The fronts had an white outer border with a wider purple inner border overlaid with a thin red and purple line. The words "Collector's Edition" were printed in white at the top of the picture. The logo for Black's Photography was printed on the upper left vertical side. Player identification appearsed under the action photo. The purple backs had a white border with a second player portrait and biography. The Black's Photography logo was printed in the upper left corner. The cards were numbered on the front. There was also an album available for this set; it is not included in the complete set price below.

COMPLETE SET (24) 12.00 30.00
1 Wendel Clark 1.50 4.00
2 Doug Gilmour 2.00 5.00
3 Glenn Anderson .60 1.50
4 Peter Zezel .30 .75
5 Bob Rouse .20 .50
6 Rob Pearson .20 .50
7 Mark Osborne .20 .50
8 Dmitri Mironov .40 1.00
9 Dave McLlwain .20 .50
10 Kent Manderville .20 .50
11 Jamie Macoun .20 .50
12 Sylvain Lefebvre .30 .75
13 Dave Andreychuk .75 2.00
14 Drake Berehowsky .20 .50
15 Bill Berg .20 .50
16 John Cullen .30 .75
17 Ken Baumgartner .30 .75
18 Nikolai Borschevsky .20 .50
19 Mike Eastwood .20 .50
20 Dave Ellett .30 .75
21 Mike Foligno .30 .75
22 Todd Gill .20 .50
23 Mike Krushelnyski .20 .50
24 Felix Potvin 3.00 8.00
NNO Album 2.00 5.00

1994-95 Maple Leafs Gangsters

This 17-card set measured approximately 4 3/4" by 7". The fronts had borderless color action player photos. The backs carried black-and-white player portraits with a 1920's style gangster motif.

COMPLETE SET (17) 4.80 12.00
1 Dave Andreychuk .40 1.00
2 Ken Baumgartner .20 .50
3 Bill Berg .20 .50
4 Nikolai Borschevsky .20 .50
5 Mike Eastwood .20 .50
6 Dave Ellett .30 .75
7 Mike Gartner .40 1.00
8 Todd Gill .30 .75
9 Doug Gilmour .75 2.00
10 Alexei Kudashov .20 .50
11 Jamie Macoun .20 .50
12 Kent Manderville .20 .50
13 Dmitri Mironov .20 .50
14 Mark Osborne .20 .50
15 Felix Potvin .75 2.00
16 Damian Rhodes .40 1.00
17 Title Card .08 .25

1994-95 Maple Leafs Kodak

This set measured approximately 4" x 6" and featured full color action photos on the front. Cards featured blank backs and are checklisted below in alphabetical order.

COMPLETE SET (30) 6.00 15.00
1 Dave Andreychuk .40 1.00
2 Ken Baumgartner .20 .50
3 Drake Berehowsky .20 .50
4 Bill Berg .20 .50
5 Nikolai Borschevsky .20 .50
6 Pat Burns .08 .25
7 Garth Butcher .20 .50
8 Mike Craig .20 .50
9 Paul Dipietro .08 .25
10 Tie Domi .30 .75
11 Mike Gartner .40 1.00
12 Todd Gill .30 .75
13 Doug Gilmour .75 2.00
14 David Harlock .30 .75
15 Benoit Hogue .20 .50
16 Grant Jennings .08 .25
17 Kenny Jonsson .30 .75
18 Jamie Macoun .20 .50
19 Terry Martin .08 .25
20 Dmitri Mironov .20 .50
21 Felix Potvin 1.25 3.00
22 Damian Rhodes .40 1.00
23 Mike Ridley .20 .50
24 Warren Rychel .08 .25
25 Mats Sundin .75 2.00
26 Rich Sutter .08 .25
27 Dixon Ward .20 .50
28 Todd Warriner .20 .50
29 Randy Wood .08 .25
30 Terry Yake .08 .25

1994-95 Maple Leafs Pin-up Posters

Cards measure 11 1/2" x 15" and were issued in Saturday and Sunday Toronto Sun newspapers. 1995 MAPLE LEAFS appeared in red at the bottom of the pin-up.

COMPLETE SET (30) 6.00 15.00
1 Mats Sundin .75 2.00
2 Doug Gilmour .75 2.00
3 Dave Ellett .20 .50
4 Mike Eastland .20 .50
5 Garth Butcher .20 .50
6 Nikolai Borschevsky .20 .50
7 Kenny Jonsson .30 .75
8 Todd Gill .20 .50
9 Bill Berg .20 .50
10 Jamie Macoun .20 .50
11 Damian Rhodes .30 .75
12 Mike Ridley .20 .50
13 Terry Yake .08 .25
14 Felix Potvin 1.25 3.00
15 Warren Rychel .08 .25
16 Randy Wood .08 .25
17 Kent Manderville .20 .50
18 Dave Andreychuk .30 .75
19 Ken Baumgartner .20 .50
20 Dmitri Mironov .20 .50
21 Mike Craig .20 .50
21A Mike Gartner .30 .75
23 Matt Martin .20 .50
24 Tie Domi .40 1.00
25 Paul DiPietro .08 .25
26 Rich Sutter .08 .25
27 Grant Jennings .08 .25
28 Benoit Hogue .20 .50
29 Darby Hendrickson .20 .50
30 Pat Burns CL .08 .25

1994-95 Maple Leafs Postcards

Sponsored by Coca-Cola, this four-card set measured approximately 5 3/4" by 4". The horizontal and vertical fronts featured borderless color action player photos. The words "1995 Collector Postcard" and Coca-Cola's logo appeared on the bottom. The backs had a postcard format and carried a short description of the scene depicted on the front. The cards were distributed to fans at Maple Leaf Gardens before a game in March, 1995, and came attached to a series of coupons for Beckers convenience stores. The cards were unnumbered and checklisted below in alphabetical order.

COMPLETE SET (4) 3.00 8.00
1 Dave Andreychuk 1.00 2.50
Todd Gill
Doug Gilmour
Jamie Ma
2 Garth Butcher 1.25 3.00
Doug Gilmour
Felix Potvin
Mats Su
3 Dmitri Mironov .60 1.50
Mike Ridley
Mats Sundin
4 Felix Potvin 1.00 2.50

1995-96 Maple Leafs Postcards

COMPLETE SET (6) 3.00 8.00
1 Dave Andreychuk 1.00 2.50
Doug Gilmour
2 Tie Domi .50 1.25
Gary Suter
3 Felix Potvin 1.25 3.00
Kenny Jonsson
Mike Ricci
Claude Lapointe
4 Mats Sundin .60 1.50
Tommy Salo
5 Cover Card .40 1.00
6 Becker's Coupon .40 1.00

1996-97 Maple Leafs Postcards

These four postcard-sized singles were available for sale at Maple Leaf Gardens souvenir stands throughout this season. They featured the Leafs' most popular players in action.

COMPLETE SET (4) 2.50 6.00
1 Sundin/Clark/Gilmour .75 2.00
2 Potvin/Lemieux 1.25 3.00
3 Wendel Clark .75 2.00
4 Domi/Berezin .40 1.00

1997-98 Maple Leafs Postcards

limited edition of postcards, with just 10,000 sets made, these collectibles were distributed by Beckers to commemorate the 65th Anniversary of Maple Leaf Gardens.

COMPLETE SET 4.00 10.00
1 Mats Sundin 1.00 2.50
2 Felix Potvin 1.00 2.50
3 Wendel Clark 1.00 2.50
4 Tie Domi 1.00 2.50
Sergei Berezin

1999-00 Maple Leafs Pizza Pizza

Released by Pizza Pizza, this 20-card set featured the 1999-2000 Toronto Maple Leafs. The set was divided up into four sheets of five cards each. One sheet was available each week from March 27 to April 23 with the purchase of a Big Bacon 16-inch pizza.

COMPLETE SET (20) 4.80 12.00
1 Dimitri Khristich .20 .50
2 Jonas Hoglund .20 .50
3 Tomas Kaberle .20 .50
4 Garry Valk .20 .50
5 Curtis Joseph AS 1.25 3.00
6 Danny Markov .20 .50
7 Bryan Berard .20 .50
8 Kevyn Adams .20 .50
9 Alexander Karpovtsev .20 .50
10 Steve Thomas .20 .50
11 Alyn McCauley .20 .50
12 Tie Domi .60 1.50
13 Nikolai Antropov .40 1.00
14 Sergei Berezin .20 .50
15 Alexander Karpovtsev AS .20 .50
16 Igor Korolev .20 .50
17 Darcy Tucker .30 .75
18 Glenn Healy .30 .75
19 Yanic Perreault .20 .50
20 Mats Sundin AS .60 1.50

2000-01 Maple Leafs Pizza Pizza

COMPLETE SET (20) 4.00 10.00
1 Dmitri Khristich .20 .50
2 Jonas Hoglund .20 .50
3 Tomas Kaberle .20 .50
4 Garry Valk .20 .50
5 Curtis Joseph 1.00 2.50
6 Danil Markov .20 .50
7 Bryan Berard .20 .50
8 Kevyn Adams .20 .50
9 Alexander Karpovtsev .20 .50
10 Steve Thomas .20 .50
11 Alyn McCauley .20 .50
12 Tie Domi .60 1.50
13 Nikolai Antropov .40 1.00
14 Sergei Berezin .20 .50
15 Dmitri Yushkevich .20 .50
16 Igor Korolev .20 .50
17 Darcy Tucker .20 .50
18 Glenn Healy .20 .50
19 Yanic Perreault .20 .50
20 Mats Sundin .60 1.50

2002-03 Maple Leafs Platinum Collection

Produced by Topps and available through MLG, this 120-card set featured current players and former Maple Leaf greats. Each box set also contained a Maple Leafs pin and one autographed card. Cards were also available at the ACC in five different 22-card packs.

COMPLETE SET (120) 30.00 80.00
1 Wade Belak .20 .50
2 Ed Belfour 1.25 3.00
3 Aki Berg .20 .50
4 Shayne Corson .30 .75
5 Tie Domi .75 2.00
6 Tom Fitzgerald .20 .50
7 Travis Green .20 .50
8 Jonas Hoglund .20 .50
9 Tomas Kaberle .20 .50
10 Trevor Kidd .30 .75
11 Jyrki Lumme .20 .50
12 Bryan McCabe .20 .50
13 Alyn McCauley .20 .50
14 Alexander Mogilny .30 .75
15 Robert Reichel .20 .50
16 Mikael Renberg .30 .75
17 Gary Roberts .30 .75
18 Mats Sundin .75 2.00
19 Robert Svehla .20 .50
20 Darcy Tucker .30 .75
21 Nik Antropov .30 .75
22 Karel Pilar .20 .50
23 Richard Jackman .20 .50
24 Carlo Colaiacovo .30 .75
25 Dave Andreychuk .30 .75
26 Andy Bathgate .30 .75
27 Wendel Clark .75 2.00
28 Bill Derlago .20 .50
29 Todd Gill .20 .50
30 Doug Gilmour .75 2.00
31 Billy Harris .20 .50
32 Curtis Joseph 1.25 3.00
33 Bob Nevin .20 .50
34 Felix Potvin 1.25 3.00
35 Eddie Shack .40 1.00
36 Sid Smith .20 .50
37 Ron Stewart .20 .50
38 Ian Turnbull .30 .75
39 Tiger Williams .75 2.00
40 Syl Apps .40 1.00
41 George Armstrong .40 1.00
42 Ace Bailey .75 2.00
43 Max Bentley .30 .75
44 Johnny Bower .75 2.00
45 Turk Broda .75 2.00
46 King Clancy .75 2.00
47 Charlie Conacher .40 1.00
48 Hap Day .30 .75
49 Gordie Drillon .30 .75
50 Babe Dye .30 .75
51 Mike Gartner .30 .75
52 Red Horner .30 .75
53 Tim Horton 1.25 3.00
54 Busher Jackson .30 .75
55 Red Kelly .30 .75
56 Ted Kennedy .40 1.00
57 Harry Lumley .40 1.00
58 Frank Mahovlich .40 1.00
59 Lanny McDonald .30 .75
60 Babe Pratt .30 .75
61 Joe Primeau .30 .75
62 Marcel Pronovost .30 .75
63 Bob Pulford .40 1.00
64 Borje Salming .40 1.00
65 Terry Sawchuk 1.25 3.00
66 Sweeney Schriner .30 .75
67 Darryl Sittler .40 1.00
68 Allan Stanley .30 .75
69 Norm Ullman .30 .75
70 Harry Watson .30 .75
71 Bobby Baun .30 .75
72 Ron Ellis .30 .75
73 Pat Quinn .30 .75
74 Rick Vaive .30 .75
75 Paul Henderson .30 .75
76 Red Kelly .30 .75
77 Frank Mahovlich .40 1.00
78 Lanny McDonald .30 .75
79 Jim McKenny .20 .50
80 Mike Palmateer .40 1.00
81 John Anderson .20 .50
82 Laurie Boschman .20 .50
83 Randy Carlyle .20 .50
84 Wendel Clark .75 2.00
85 Ron Ellis .30 .75
86 Jim McKenny .20 .50
87 Gary Nylund .20 .50
88 Mike Palmateer .40 1.00
89 Joel Quenneville .30 .75
90 Borje Salming .40 1.00
91 Brit Selby .20 .50
92 Darryl Sittler .40 1.00
93 MLG Opening Night .20 .50
94 MLG Closing Night .20 .50
95 AAC Opening Night .20 .50
96 Bill Barilko .40 1.00
The Goal
97 1991-92 St. Pats .20 .50
98 1st NHL All-Star Game .20 .50
99 50th NHL All-Star Game .20 .50
100 Tim Horton 1.25 3.00
101 Darryl Sittler/10 Point Night .40 1.00
102 Gordie Drillon .30 .75
Art Ross Trophy
103 Ted Kennedy .40 1.00
Hart Memorial Trophy
104 Sid Smith .20 .50
Lady Byng Trophy
105 Terry Sawchuk 1.25 3.00
Johnny Bower
Vezina Trophy
106 Harry Lumley .40 1.00
Bickell Memorial Trophy
107 Curtis Joseph 1.25 3.00
King Clancy Memorial Trophy
108 Borje Salming .40 1.00
Molson Cup
109 Doug Gilmour .75 2.00
Selke Trophy
110 Pat Burns .30 .75
Jack Adams Trophy
111 Gus Bodnar .30 .75
Calder Trophy
112 1931-92 Stanley Cup Winners .30 .75
113 1941-42 Stanley Cup Winners .30 .75
114 1946-47 Stanley Cup Winners .30 .75
115 1948-49 Stanley Cup Winners .30 .75
116 1961-62 Stanley Cup Winners .30 .75
117 1962-63 Stanley Cup Winners .30 .75
118 1963-64 Stanley Cup Winners .30 .75
119 1966-67 Stanley Cup Winners .30 .75
120 Checklist .04 .10

2002-03 Maple Leafs Team Issue

This postcard-size team issue features glossy prints on actual Kodak photo paper. The fronts include player and sponsor names and the backs are blank. If you have information about additional singles in this set, please forward to hockeymag@beckett.com.

COMPLETE SET 8.00 20.00
1 Nik Antropov .40 1.00
2 Ed Belfour 1.25 3.00
3 Tie Domi .75 2.00
4 Tom Fitzgerald .40 1.00
5 Travis Green .40 1.00
6 Tomas Kaberle .40 1.00
7 Trevor Kidd .60 1.50
8 Alexander Mogilny .60 1.50
9 Robert Reichel .40 1.00
10 Mikael Renberg .40 1.00
11 Mats Sundin 1.25 3.00
12 Robert Svehla .40 1.00
13 Mikael Tellqvist .75 2.00
14 Darcy Tucker .60 1.50

2007 Maple Leafs 1967 Commemorative

COMPLETE SET (30) 10.00 25.00
1 Bob Baun .20 .50
2 Johnny Bower .40 1.00
3 John Brennemman .10 .25
4 Wayne Carleton .20 .50
5 Brian Conacher .20 .50
6 Kent Douglas .20 .50
7 Ron Ellis .20 .50
8 Aut Erickson .20 .50
9 Bob Haggert .20 .50
10 Larry Hillman .20 .50
11 Tim Horton .75 2.00
12 Larry Jeffrey .20 .50
13 Red Kelly .20 .50
14 Dave Keon .75 2.00
15 Frank Mahovlich .40 1.00
16 Frank Mahovlich .40 1.00
Red Kelly
17 Milan Marcetta .20 .50
18 Jim McKenny .20 .50
19 Jim Pappin .20 .50
20 Marcel Pronovost .20 .50
21 Bob Pulford .20 .50
22 Terry Sawchuk .75 2.00
23 Brit Selby .20 .50
24 Eddie Shack .40 1.00
25 Allan Stanley .20 .50
26 Pete Stemkowski .20 .50
27 Mike Walton .20 .50
28 Group Photo .10 .25
29 Victory Parade .10 .25
30 Johnny Bower CL .20 .50

2007 Maple Leafs 1967 Commemorative Autographs

RANDOM INSERTS IN SEALED SETS
ABB1 Bob Baun 12.00 30.00
ABB2 Bob Baun 12.00 30.00
ABC1 Brian Conacher 6.00 15.00
ABC2 Brian Conacher 6.00 15.00
ABP1 Bob Pulford 12.00 30.00
ABP2 Bob Pulford 12.00 30.00
AES1 Eddie Shack 15.00 40.00
AES2 Eddie Shack 15.00 40.00
AJB1 Johnny Bower 15.00 40.00
AJB2 Johnny Bower 15.00 40.00
ALJ1 Larry Jeffrey 6.00 15.00
ALJ2 Larry Jeffrey 6.00 15.00
ARE1 Ron Ellis 12.00 30.00
ARE2 Ron Ellis 12.00 30.00
ARK1 Red Kelly 12.00 30.00
ARK2 Red Kelly 12.00 30.00

2007 Maple Leafs 1967 Commemorative Box Topper

ML67 Group Photo .40 1.00

2007 Maple Leafs 1967 Commemorative Jerseys

RANDOM INSERTS IN SEALED SETS
JES Eddie Shack 6.00 15.00
JJB Johnny Bower 8.00 20.00

2007 Maple Leafs 1967 Commemorative Sticks

RANDOM INSERTS IN SEALED SETS
SDK Dave Keon 30.00 80.00
SFM Frank Mahovlich 30.00 80.00

2003 Marc-Andre Fleury Stadium Giveaways

This 4-card set of Penguins' goalie Marc-Andre Fleury was given away during a game in October 2003.

COMPLETE SET (4) 15.00 35.00
COMMON CARD (1-4) 4.00 10.00

2004 MasterCard Priceless Moments

is 10-card set was produced by MasterCard and highlighted Stanley Cup winners of the past 5 decades. The cards were available at participating restaurants in Canada during the 2004 playoffs.

COMPLETE SET (10) 20.00
1 Scotty Bowman 1.25 3.00
2002 Stanley Cup
2 Mark Messier 1.50 4.00
1994 Stanley Cup
3 Bobby Baun 1.25 3.00
1964 Stanley Cup
4 Bobby Orr 4.00 10.00
1970 Stanley Cup
5 Bob Nystrom 1.25 3.00
1980 Stanley Cup
6 Jari Kurri 1.50 4.00
1984 Stanley Cup
7 Martin Brodeur 3.00 8.00
2003 Stanley Cup
8 Lanny McDonald 1.25 3.00
1989 Stanley Cup
9 Mario Lemieux 5.00 12.00
Larry Murphy
1991 Stanley Cup
10 Ray Bourque 2.00 5.00
2001 Stanley Cup

1971 Mattel Mini-Records

This set was designed to be played on a special Mattel mini-record player, which is not included in the complete set price. Each black plastic disc, approximately 2 1/2" in diameter, features a recording on one side and a color drawing of the player on the other. The picture appears on a paper disk that is glued onto the smooth unrecorded side of the mini-record. On the recorded side, the player's name and the set's subtitle appear in arcs stamped in the central portion of the mini-record. The hand-engraved player's name appears again along with a production number, copyright symbol, and the Mattel name and year of production in the ring between the central portion of the record and the grooves. The ivory discs are the ones which are double sided and are considered to be tougher than the black discs. They were also known as "Mattel Show 'N Tell". The discs are unnumbered and checklisted below in alphabetical order according to sport

COMPLETE SET (18) 200.00 400.00
HK1 Yvan Cournoyer 5.00 10.00
HK2 Tony Esposito 6.00 12.00
HK3 Phil Esposito 7.50 15.00
HK4 Ed Giacomin 5.00 10.00
HK5 Gordie Howe 20.00 40.00
HK6 Frank Mahovlich 6.00 12.00
HK7 Bobby Orr 25.00 50.00
HK8 Jacques Plante 12.50 25.00

1982-83 McDonald's Stickers

This set consisted of 36 full-color stickers measuring 2" by 2 1/2". A 12-page album was also available. The stickers were only issued in the province of Quebec. The stickers were numbered on the front and on the back. The sticker numbering was by position, i.e., goalies (1-5), right wings (6-10), left wings (11-15), all-stars (16-21), centers (22-26), and defensemen (27-36). The all-star stickers were gold foils; the other stickers all had a distinctive red border and showed the McDonald's logo in the lower right corner.

COMPLETE SET (36) 15.00 40.00
1 Dan Bouchard .20 .50
2 Richard Brodeur .25 .60
3 Gilles Meloche .20 .50
4 Billy Smith .40 1.00
5 Rick Wamsley .20 .50
6 Mike Bossy .75 2.00
7 Dino Ciccarelli .30 .75
8 Guy Lafleur .75 2.00
9 Rick Middleton .30 .75
10 Marian Stastny .15 .40
11 Bill Barber .25 .60
12 Bob Gainey .40 1.00
13 Clark Gillies .20 .50
14 Michel Goulet .30 .75
15 Mark Messier 3.00 8.00
16 Billy Smith AS .75 2.00
17 Larry Robinson AS 1.00 2.50
18 Denis Potvin AS .75 2.00
19 Michel Goulet AS .75 2.00
20 Wayne Gretzky AS 8.00 20.00
21 Mike Bossy AS 2.50 6.00
22 Wayne Gretzky 6.00 15.00
23 Denis Savard .30 .75
24 Peter Stastny .30 .75
25 Bryan Trottier .40 1.00
26 Doug Wickenheiser .15 .40
27 Barry Beck .15 .40
28 Ray Bourque 1.25 3.00
29 Brian Engblom .15 .40
30 Craig Hartsburg .20 .50
31 Mark Howe .40 1.00
32 Rod Langway .20 .50
33 Denis Potvin .30 .75
34 Larry Robinson .40 1.00
35 Normand Rochefort .15 .40
36 Doug Wilson .25 .60
NNO Album 2.00 5.00

1991-92 McDonald's Upper Deck

is 31-card standard-size set, which featured 25 regular cards and six hologram cards and was produced by Upper Deck for McDonald's Restaurants across Canada to honor NHL All-Stars. For 29 cents plus tax, with the purchase of any soft drink, customers could receive a pack with three regular cards and one hologram sticker card. The fronts featured a mix of posed and action pictures enclosed in red and white borders. The Upper Deck logo appeared in the upper right corner while the McDonald's All-Stars logo appeared in a red circle in the lower right corner. The player's name and position appeared in the bottom white border. The backs carried a second color photo and career summary was presented in English and French. Upper Deck's unique anti-counterfeiting device appeared in the upper right corner in the shape of McDonald's golden arches. Six players wearing their 1991 All-Star uniforms on the regular cards appeared on the hologram cards in their regular team uniforms. The holograms had blank backs and were numbered on the front. The card numbers showed a "Mc" prefix.

COMPLETE SET (31) 6.00 15.00
1 Cam Neely .20 .50
2 Rick Tocchet .15 .40
3 Kevin Stevens .15 .40
4 Mark Recchi .25 .60
5 Joe Sakic .60 1.50
6 Pat LaFontaine .20 .50
7 Darren Turcotte .15 .40
8 Patrick Roy .50 1.25
9 Andy Moog .15 .40
10 Ray Bourque .30 .75
11 Paul Coffey .15 .40
12 Brian Leetch .15 .40
13 Brett Hull .30 .75
14 Luc Robitaille .15 .40
15 Steve Larmer .15 .40
16 Vincent Damphousse .15 .40
17 Wayne Gretzky 1.00 2.50
18 Theo Fleury .15 .40
19 Steve Yzerman .60 1.50
20 Mike Vernon .15 .40
21 Bill Ranford .15 .40
22 Chris Chelios .20 .50
23 Al MacInnis .15 .40
24 Scott Stevens .20 .50
25 Checklist .12 .30
H1 Wayne Gretzky 1.00 2.50
H2 Chris Chelios .20 .50
H3 Ray Bourque .30 .75
H4 Brett Hull .30 .75
H5 Cam Neely .20 .50
H6 Patrick Roy .50 1.25

1992-93 McDonald's Upper Deck Iron-Ons

inted in Canada, these 26 iron-on transfers measured approximately 3" by 3". They featured the NHL team logos and commemorated the 44th All-Star Game in Montreal. The backs carried ironing instructions. These iron-ons were a test issue to be distributed along with the McDonald's All-Star cards, and surfaced just in parts of Quebec. The iron-ons were unnumbered and checklisted below in alphabetical order.

COMPLETE SET (26) 16.00 40.00
1 Boston Bruins .75 2.00
2 Buffalo Sabres .75 2.00
3 Calgary Flames .75 2.00
4 Chicago Blackhawks .75 2.00
5 Minnesota North Stars .75 2.00
6 Detroit Red Wings .75 2.00
7 Edmonton Oilers .75 2.00
8 Hartford Whalers .75 2.00
9 Los Angeles Kings .75 2.00
10 Montreal Canadiens .75 2.00
11 New Jersey Devils .75 2.00
12 New York Islanders .75 2.00
13 New York Rangers .75 2.00
14 Ottawa Senators .75 2.00
15 Philadelphia Flyers .75 2.00
16 Pittsburgh Penguins .75 2.00
17 Quebec Nordiques .75 2.00
18 St. Louis Blues .75 2.00
19 San Jose Sharks .75 2.00
20 Tampa Bay Lightning .75 2.00
21 Toronto Maple Leafs .75 2.00
22 Vancouver Canucks .75 2.00
23 Washington Capitals .75 2.00
24 Winnipeg Jets .75 2.00
25 All-Stars Logo .75 2.00
26 44th NHL All-Star Game 2.00 5.00

1992-93 McDonald's Upper Deck

oduced by Upper Deck for McDonald's of Canada, this set consisted of 27 regular cards and six hologram cards in honor of 33 of hockey's most exciting players. Four-card packs were available for 39 cents plus tax with a purchase at participating McDonald's restaurants. All cards measured the standard size. The regular cards featured color action photos of the players in their 1992 All-Star uniforms. A black border, which edged the photo on three sides, contained the player's name and position. Featuring six NHL post-season First Team All-Stars, the six hologram cards were randomly inserted in a limited number of card packs. The full-bleed cards featured a small, cut-out action player photos against a facial shot. The player's name appeared in a stripe across the bottom. The backs of the regular cards and holograms were identical, each showing a narrow, vertical player photo against a white background with a bilingual (English and French) player profile to the right. The regular cards were arranged according to conference: Campbell (1-14) and Wales (15-27). The cards were numbered on the back with an "McD" prefix.

1 Ed Belfour .20 .50
2 Brian Bellows .15 .40
3 Chris Chelios .20 .50
4 Vincent Damphousse .15 .40
5 Dave Ellett .12 .30
6 Sergei Fedorov .30 .75
7 Theo Fleury .30 .75
8 Phil Housley .12 .30
9 Trevor Linden .15 .40
10 Al MacInnis .15 .40
11 Adam Oates .20 .50
12 Luc Robitaille .15 .40
13 Jeremy Roenick .30 .75
14 Steve Yzerman .50 1.25
15 Don Beaupre .15 .40
16 Rod Brind'Amour .12 .30
17 Paul Coffey .20 .50
18 John Cullen .12 .30
19 Kevin Hatcher .12 .30
20 Jaromir Jagr .50 1.25
21 Mario Lemieux .75 2.00
22 Alexander Mogilny .15 .40
23 Kirk Muller .12 .30
24 Owen Nolan .12 .30
25 Mike Richter .20 .50
26 Joe Sakic .50 1.25
27 Scott Stevens .20 .50
H1 Mark Messier HOLO .60 1.50
H2 Brett Hull HOLO 1.00 2.50
H3 Kevin Stevens HOLO .50 1.25
H4 Brian Leetch HOLO .60 1.50
H5 Ray Bourque HOLO 1.50 4.00
H6 Patrick Roy HOLO 1.50 4.00
NNO Checklist UER SP .75 2.00

1993-94 McDonald's Upper Deck

oduced by Upper Deck for McDonald's of Canada, this set was similar in concept to the previous year's Upper Deck McDonald's set. The 27 regular cards and six hologram-type cards honored 33 of the NHL's most exciting players. The holograms were random inserts in the four-card packs. An oversized (4" by 5 1/2") Patrick Roy card (23) was also available via a redemption card randomly inserted in packs. The redemption card could be redeemed at McDonald's or through the mail. A number of redemption cards for other prizes, such as trips to games, autographed pucks and sticks, etc, also were included. These cards obviously were extremely difficult to locate, but also experience limited demand from collectors at this point. Most would be valued in the $10-$20 range. Also, Upper Deck had confirmed that the unnumbered checklist card was short-printed. All cards measured the standard size. The regular cards featured on their fronts white-bordered color action shots of players in their 1993 All-Star uniforms. The hologram cards were horizontal on their fronts and backs. The front of each card featured a hologram-type action photo of a first team All-Star on the right and a posed close-up on the left. The player's name and position appeared within blue, black, and gray stripes near the bottom. The back carried the player's All-Star highlights in both English and French. Variations of the cards with incorrect backs were known to exist. The regular cards were arranged according to conference: Campbell (1-13) and Wales (14-27). The regular cards were numbered on the back with an "McD" prefix; the hologram-types are numbered with an "McH" prefix.

COMPLETE SET (34) 6.00 15.00
1 Brian Bradley .08 .25
2 Pavel Bure .50 1.25
3 Jon Casey .08 .25
4 Paul Coffey .25 .60
5 Doug Gilmour .25 .60
6 Phil Housley .08 .25
7 Brett Hull .40 1.00
8 Jari Kurri .08 .25
9 Dave Manson .08 .25
10 Mike Modano .40 1.00
11 Gary Roberts .08 .25
12 Jeremy Roenick .25 .60
13 Steve Yzerman .60 1.50
14 Steve Duchesne .08 .25
15 Mike Gartner .08 .25
16 Al Iafrate .08 .25
17 Jaromir Jagr .60 1.50
18 Pat LaFontaine .15 .40
19 Alexander Mogilny .15 .40
20A Kirk Muller ERR .08 .25
20B Kirk Muller COR .08 .25
21 Adam Oates .15 .40
22 Mark Recchi .15 .40
23 Patrick Roy 1.25 3.00
23L Patrick Roy jumbo 5.00 12.00
24 Joe Sakic .60 1.50
25 Kevin Stevens .08 .25
26 Scott Stevens .08 .25
27 Pierre Turgeon .15 .40
H1 Mario Lemieux 2.00 5.00
H2 Teemu Selanne .75 2.00
H3 Luc Robitaille .25 .60
H4 Ray Bourque .25 .60
H5 Chris Chelios .25 .60
H6 Ed Belfour .40 1.00
NNO Checklist SP 1.00 2.50

1994-95 McDonald's Upper Deck

oduced by Upper Deck for McDonald's of Canada, this set consisted of 40 standard-size cards and honored some of hockey's most exciting players. Three-card packs were available for 39 cents plus tax with a purchase of a soft drink at participating McDonald's restaurants across Canada. The offer began March 24 and ran as long as supplies lasted. The horizontal fronts featured color action player cutouts on holographic backgrounds. The player's name appeared in a team color-coded bar alongside the left, while a small color player portrait in his 1994 All-Star uniform was on the right. The bilingual backs carried another small color player portrait, with profile and statistics. The cards were arranged as follows: 1994 NHL All-Stars Eastern Conference (1-10), 1994 NHL All-Stars Western Conference (11-20), Hat Tricks Eastern Conference (21-25), Hat Tricks Western Conference (26-30), Future NHL All-Stars Eastern Conference (31-35), and Future NHL All-Stars Western Conference (36-39). An unnumbered checklist card featuring All-Star Game MVP Mike Richter completed the set. This card was thought by some to be short printed. Since we cannot confirm this, we have not applied this designation.

COMPLETE SET (40) 10.00 25.00
McD1 Joe Sakic .60 1.50
McD2 Adam Graves .08 .25
McD3 Alexei Yashin .08 .25
McD4 Patrick Roy 1.50 4.00
McD5 Ray Bourque .40 1.00
McD6 Brian Leetch .25 .60
McD7 Scott Stevens .08 .25
McD8 Alexander Mogilny .15 .40
McD9 Eric Lindros .75 2.00
McD10 Jaromir Jagr 1.00 2.50
McD11 Sandis Ozonlish .08 .25
McD12 Sergei Fedorov .60 1.50
McD13 Brett Hull .40 1.00
McD14 Felix Potvin .15 .40
McD15 Al MacInnis .08 .25
McD16 Chris Chelios .25 .60
McD17 Rob Blake .08 .25
McD18 Dave Andreychuk .08 .25
McD19 Paul Coffey .25 .60
McD20 Jeremy Roenick .25 .60
McD21 Joe Nieuwendyk .15 .40
McD22 Cam Neely .15 .40
McD23 Pavel Bure .75 2.00
McD24 Wendel Clark .15 .40
McD25 Teemu Selanne .60 1.50
McD26 Pierre Turgeon .15 .40
McD27 Alexei Zhamnov .08 .25
McD28 Doug Gilmour .25 .60
McD29 Vincent Damphousse .08 .25
McD30 Brendan Shanahan .50 1.25
McD31 Peter Forsberg 1.00 2.50
McD32 Paul Kariya 1.25 3.00
McD33 Viktor Kozlov .08 .25
McD34 Brett Lindros .08 .25
McD35 Martin Brodeur .75 2.00
McD36 Alexandre Daigle .08 .25
McD37 Jason Arnott .15 .40
McD38 Alexei Kovalev .08 .25
McD39 Mikael Renberg .25 .60
NNO Mike Richter CL .25 .60

1995-96 McDonald's Pinnacle

is 41-card set featured borderless color player cut-out photos on a 3-D, lenticular background. The backs carried information about the player in both English and French. The cards were divided into three categories as follows: Game Winners (McD-1-McD-24), Game Savers (McD-25-McD-30), and Future Game Winners (McD-31-McD-40). They were available in 3-card packs for 79 cents (with purchase) at participating McDonald's restaurants in Canada.

COMPLETE SET (41) 10.00 25.00
MCD1 Jaromir Jagr .75 2.00
MCD2 Eric Lindros .60 1.50
MCD3 Alexei Zhamnov .08 .25
MCD4 Paul Coffey .25 .60
MCD5 Mark Messier .30 .75
MCD6 Brett Hull .30 .75
MCD7 Peter Forsberg .60 1.50
MCD8 Pavel Bure .60 1.50
MCD9 Doug Gilmour .25 .60
MCD10 Owen Nolan .25 .60
MCD11 Paul Kariya 1.00 2.50
MCD12 Joe Nieuwendyk .15 .40
MCD13 Pierre Turgeon .15 .40
MCD14 Jason Arnott .15 .40
MCD15 Mario Lemieux 1.25 3.00
MCD16 Jeremy Roenick .25 .60
MCD17 Sergei Fedorov .40 1.00
MCD18 Mats Sundin .25 .60
MCD19 Teemu Selanne .40 1.00
MCD20 John LeClair .40 1.00
MCD21 Alexander Mogilny .25 .60
MCD22 Mikael Renberg .08 .25
MCD23 Chris Chelios .25 .60
MCD24 Mark Recchi .15 .40
MCD25 Patrick Roy 1.25 3.00
MCD26 Felix Potvin .08 .25
MCD27 Martin Brodeur .60 1.50
MCD28 Dominik Hasek .40 1.00
MCD29 Ed Belfour .25 .60
MCD30 Kirk McLean .15 .40
MCD31 Jeff Friesen .15 .40
MCD32 Todd Harvey .08 .25
MCD33 Brett Lindros .08 .25
MCD34 Valeri Bure .15 .40
MCD35 Oleg Tverdovsky .08 .25
MCD36 Kenny Jonsson .08 .25
MCD37 Mariusz Czerkawski .08 .25
MCD38 Alexandre Daigle .08 .25
MCD39 Saku Koivu .25 .60
MCD40 Jim Carey .15 .40
NNO Joe Sakic CL .25 .60

1996-97 McDonald's Pinnacle

is 40-card set was available through McDonald's Restaurants of Canada and featured advanced 3D and ull-Motion Video technology. The set contained three bsets: IceBreakers (3D Cards #1-20 which consisted 20 of the top NHL players), Premier IceBreakers ull-Motion Video Cards #21-31 which showcased proximately three seconds of live footage of 11 tstanding NHL players), and Caged IceBreakers (3D rds #32-40 which featured nine of the league's best altenders).

OMPLETE SET (40) 15.00 30.00
Paul Coffey .10 .30
Teemu Selanne .40 1.00
Eric Daze .08 .25
John LeClair .40 1.00
Saku Koivu .30 .75
Ed Jovanovski .25 .60
Chris Osgood .30 .75
Chris Chelios .10 .30
Daniel Alfredsson .08 .25
Joe Sakic .50 1.25
Alexander Mogilny .08 .25
Jeremy Roenick .10 .30
Keith Tkachuk .30 .75
Doug Gilmour .10 .30
Theo Fleury .25 .60
Doug Weight .08 .25
Steve Yzerman .60 1.50
Zigmund Palffy .25 .60
Pierre Turgeon .08 .25
Brian Leetch .10 .30
Mario Lemieux SP 2.00 5.00
Mark Messier SP .60 1.50
Jaromir Jagr SP 1.25 3.00
Brett Hull SP .60 1.50
Eric Lindros SP 1.25 3.00
Sergei Fedorov SP .75 2.00
Pavel Bure SP 1.00 2.50
Peter Forsberg SP 1.00 2.50
Paul Kariya SP 1.50 4.00
Patrick Roy SP 2.00 5.00
Ray Bourque SP .50 1.25
Jim Carey .20 .50
Martin Brodeur .60 1.50
Trevor Kidd .15 .40
John Vanbiesbrouck .50 1.25
Jocelyn Thibault .20 .50
Ed Belfour .25 .60
Felix Potvin .25 .60
Damian Rhodes .15 .40
Curtis Joseph .30 .75
O Checklist .01 .05

1997 McDonald's Team Canada Coins

OMPLETE SET (10) 10.00 25.00
Rod Brind'Amour .75 2.00
Trevor Linden
Rob Blake .75 2.00
Al MacInnis
Martin Brodeur 1.25 3.00
Curtis Joseph
Ray Bourque 1.25 3.00
Chris Pronger
Shayne Corson .75 2.00
Brendan Shanahan
Eric DesJardins .75 2.00
Adam Foote
Theoren Fleury .75 2.00
Paul Kariya
Wayne Gretzky 1.50 4.00
Joe Sakic
Eric Lindros .75 2.00
Joe Nieuwendyk
Keith Primeau 1.25 3.00
Steve Yzerman
Patrick Roy 1.25 3.00
Olympic Games Logo
Scott Stevens .75 2.00
Rob Zamuner

1997-98 McDonald's Upper Deck

40-card set was available through McDonald's staurants of Canada and featured a design similar to at of the 1996-97 Upper Deck Ice set. Redemption rds for various Wayne Gretzky prizes were also serted randomly into packs. These prizes included tographed sticks, photos and jerseys, these items are t priced due to scarcity.

OMPLETE SET (40) 12.50 25.00
Wayne Gretzky 2.50 6.00
Theo Fleury .25 .60
Pavel Bure .60 1.50
Saku Koivu .25 .60
Joe Sakic .50 1.25
Wade Redden .08 .25
Keith Tkachuk .30 .75
Eric Lindros .75 2.00
Paul Kariya 1.00 2.50
Bryan Berard .15 .40
Teemu Selanne .50 1.25
Jarome Iginla .15 .40
Mats Sundin .25 .60
Brendan Shanahan .50 1.25
Peter Forsberg .60 1.50
Brett Hull .30 .75
Ray Bourque .25 .60
Doug Weight .15 .40
Steve Yzerman .75 2.00
Jaromir Jagr .75 2.00
Vincent Damphousse .15 .40
Trevor Linden .15 .40
Patrick Roy 1.25 3.00
John Vanbiesbrouck .25 .60
Martin Brodeur .60 1.50
Dominik Hasek .50 1.25
Curtis Joseph .30 .75
Andy Moog .15 .40
Mike Richter .25 .60
Damian Rhodes .15 .40
Felix Potvin .25 .60
Chris Osgood .25 .60
Joe Thornton .40 1.00
Patrick Marleau .40 1.00
Jaroslav Svejkovsky .15 .40
Daniel Cleary .15 .40
Chris Phillips .08 .25
Alexei Morozov .15 .40
Vaclav Prospal .25 .60
Sergei Samsonov .40 1.00

1997-98 McDonald's Upper Deck Game Film

s 10-card set was randomly inserted into packs of Donalds hockey cards. Each set featured a design ilar to a strip of film.

MPLETE SET (10) 25.00 60.00
Wayne Gretzky 10.00 25.00
Alexander Mogilny 1.50 4.00
Steve Yzerman 6.00 15.00
Eric Lindros 2.00 5.00
Patrick Roy 8.00 20.00
Paul Kariya 6.00 15.00
Ray Bourque 2.50 6.00

8 Saku Koivu 2.00 5.00
9 Theo Fleury 1.50 4.00
10 Mats Sundin 2.50 6.00

1998-99 McDonald's Upper Deck

sued by McDonald's of Canada, these cards were available with any french fry purchase for 79 cents. Cards featured color action photos and statistical information. The Gretzky jersey card was issued at a later date by Upper Deck.

COMPLETE SET (28) 7.50 15.00
1 Wayne Gretzky 2.00 5.00
2 Theo Fleury .20 .50
3 Joe Sakic .60 1.50
4 Saku Koivu .20 .50
5 Brendan Shanahan .40 1.00
6 Steve Yzerman 1.25 3.00
7 Peter Forsberg .60 1.50
8 Paul Kariya .75 2.00
9 Alexei Yashin .15 .40
10 Eric Lindros .60 1.50
11 Jaromir Jagr .60 1.50
12 Mats Sundin .20 .50
13 Sergei Samsonov .20 .50
14 Pavel Bure .60 1.50
15 Patrick Roy 1.25 3.00
16 Dominik Hasek .40 1.00
17 Martin Brodeur .60 1.50
18 Curtis Joseph .40 1.00
19 Jocelyn Thibault .20 .50
20 Chris Osgood .20 .50
21 Ed Belfour .20 .50
22 Mattias Ohlund .15 .40
23 Marian Hossa .20 .50
24 Brendan Morrison .15 .40
25 Jason Botterill .15 .40
26 Cameron Mann .15 .40
27 Daniel Briere .20 .50
28 Terry Ryan .15 .40
NNO Wayne Gretzky JSY/198 250.00 450.00

1998-99 McDonald's Upper Deck Gretzky's Moments

ndom inserts in packs of McDonalds cards. Entire set featured some of Gretzky's greatest accomplishments.

COMPLETE SET (10) 25.00 30.00
COMMON CARD (1-10) 1.50 4.00

1998-99 McDonald's Upper Deck Gretzky's Teammates

ndom inserts in packs of McDonalds cards. Each card featured Gretzky along with a past or present teammate.

COMPLETE SET (13) 2.00 5.00
T1 Walter Gretzky .50 1.25
T2 Gordie Howe .75 2.00
T3 Marty McSorley .10 .30
T4 Brian Leetch .20 .50
T5 Brett Hull .30 .75
T6 Esa Tikkanen .10 .30
T7 Grant Fuhr .20 .50
T8 Mike Richter .20 .50
T9 Jari Kurri .20 .50
T10 Paul Coffey .20 .50
T11 Rob Blake .20 .50
T12 Mario Lemieux .75 2.00
T13 Luc Robitaille .20 .50

1999-00 McDonald's Upper Deck Gretzky Performance for the Record

COMPLETE SET (24) 12.00 30.00
COMMON RECORD (1-15) .75 2.00
COMMON CHECKLIST (C1-C9) .60 1.50

1999-00 McDonald's Upper Deck

Produced by Upper Deck in conjunction with McDonalds of Canada at the cost of an order of french fries and 89 cents, this 35-card set utilized set designs from Upper Deck and Upper Deck Retro.

COMPLETE SET (35) 8.00 20.00
MCD1 Paul Kariya .50 1.25
MCD1R Paul Kariya .50 1.25
MCD2 Eric Lindros .20 .50
MCD2R Eric Lindros .20 .50
MCD3 Dominik Hasek .40 1.00
MCD3R Dominik Hasek .40 1.00
MCD4 Steve Yzerman 1.00 2.50
MCD4R Steve Yzerman 1.00 2.50
MCD5 Jarome Iginla .20 .50
MCD5R Jarome Iginla .20 .50
MCD6 Jaromir Jagr .30 .75
MCD6R Jaromir Jagr .30 .75
MCD7 Brett Hull .25 .60
MCD7R Brett Hull .25 .60
MCD8 Ed Belfour .20 .50
MCD8R Ed Belfour .20 .50
MCD9 Mats Sundin .20 .50
MCD9R Mats Sundin .20 .50
MCD10 Peter Forsberg .50 1.25
MCD10R Peter Forsberg .50 1.25
MCD11 Doug Weight .20 .50
MCD11R Doug Weight .20 .50
MCD12 Curtis Joseph .20 .50
MCD12R Curtis Joseph .20 .50
MCD13 Michael Peca .20 .50
MCD13R Michael Peca .20 .50
MCD14 Saku Koivu .20 .50
MCD14R Saku Koivu .20 .50
MCD15 Patrick Roy .75 2.00
MCD15R Patrick Roy .75 2.00
MCD16 Jose Theodore .20 .50
MCD17 David Legwand .20 .50
MCD18 Chris Drury .20 .50
MCD19 Milan Hejduk .20 .50
MCD20 Marian Hossa .20 .50
NNO Wayne Gretzky 5 x 7 4.00 10.00

1999-00 McDonald's Upper Deck Game Jerseys

ndomly inserted in McDonald's Upper Deck Packs, this 11-card set featured players coupled with a swatch of game jersey. Stated print run for the set was 300, with Wayne Gretzky limited to 99, and a special autographed version of the Gretzky card.

GJCP Chris Pronger 15.00 40.00
GJDS Darryl Sydor 12.00 30.00
GJEL Eric Lindros 50.00 100.00
GJGF Grant Fuhr 30.00 80.00
GJJJ Jaromir Jagr 30.00 80.00
GJMM Mike Modano 15.00 40.00
GJPB Peter Bondra 15.00 40.00
GJPF Peter Forsberg 30.00 80.00
GJSS Scott Stevens 15.00 4.00
GJTA Tony Amonte 15.00 40.00
GJWG Wayne Gretzky/99 600.00 1000.00
GJWG Wayne Gretzky AU 750.00 1500.00

1999-00 McDonald's Upper Deck Signatures

Randomly inserted in McDonald's packs, this 16-card set featured player action photography coupled with an authentic player autograph. Each card was sequentially numbered to 500. The Gretzky card was known to exist, but it is not priced due to scarcity.

AY Alexei Yashin 15.00 40.00
BH Brett Hull 30.00 80.00
CJ Curtis Joseph 30.00 80.00
CO Chris Osgood 15.00 40.00
EB Ed Belfour 25.00 50.00
GF Grant Fuhr 15.00 40.00
JL John LeClair 15.00 40.00
JT Jose Theodore 15.00 40.00
LR Luc Robitaille 15.00 40.00
RB Ray Bourque 40.00 100.00
SK Saku Koivu 15.00 40.00
ST Steve Thomas 15.00 40.00
SY Steve Yzerman 80.00 150.00
TA Tony Amonte 15.00 40.00
TD Tie Domi 30.00 80.00
WG Wayne Gretzky/25

1999-00 McDonald's Upper Deck The Great Career

Randomly inserted in McDonald's Upper Deck packs at the rate of one in six, this five card set payed tribute to the great career of Wayne Gretzky.

COMPLETE SET (5) 4.00 10.00
COMMON CARD .75 2.00

2000-01 McDonald's Pacific

Released by Pacific in conjunction with McDonald's, this 36-card set was available through McDonald's of Canada with the purchase of a large french fry or hash brown and 89 cents from December 18, 2000 through January 11, 2001. Cards utilized the 00-01 Pacific Prism card stock and carried both English and French on the card backs.

COMPLETE SET (36) 6.00 15.00
1 Paul Kariya .25 .60
2 Teemu Selanne .40 1.00
3 Patrik Stefan .15 .40
4 Joe Thornton .30 .75
5 Dominik Hasek .30 .75
6 Valeri Bure .15 .40
7 Ray Bourque .30 .75
8 Peter Forsberg .25 .60
9 Patrick Roy .50 1.25
10 Joe Sakic .30 .75
11 Brett Hull .30 .75
12 Mike Modano .30 .75
13 Chris Osgood .20 .50
14 Brendan Shanahan .25 .60
15 Steve Yzerman .60 1.50
16 Doug Weight .20 .50
17 Pavel Bure .25 .60
18 Jeff Hackett .12 .30
19 Saku Koivu .20 .50
20 Martin Brodeur .40 1.00
21 Scott Gomez .15 .40
22 Scott Stevens .20 .50
23 Marian Hossa .15 .40
24 Brian Boucher .15 .40
25 John LeClair .20 .50
26 Eric Lindros .30 .75
27 Jaromir Jagr .50 1.25
28 Chris Pronger .15 .40
29 Roman Turek .15 .40
30 Vincent Lecavalier .15 .40
31 Nikolai Antropov .15 .40
32 Curtis Joseph .25 .60
33 Mats Sundin .20 .50
34 Mattias Ohlund .12 .30
35 Felix Potvin .30 .75
36 Olaf Kolzig .20 .50

2000-01 McDonald's Pacific Blue

ndomly inserted in packs at the rate of one in four, this 36-card set paralleled the base McDonald's Pacific set enhanced with a blue foil background.

COMPLETE SET (36) 15.00 40.00
*BLUE: 2X TO 5X BASIC CARDS

2000-01 McDonald's Pacific Checklists

ndomly inserted in packs at the rate of one in one, this nine card set featured full color player action photography set on a card with white borders, and contained a checklist of the McDonald's Pacific set on the back.

COMPLETE SET (9) 1.50 3.00
1 Valeri Bure .10 .25
2 Doug Weight .15 .40
3 Jeff Hackett .15 .40
4 Saku Koivu .20 .50
5 Marian Hossa .20 .50
6 Curtis Joseph .20 .50
7 Mats Sundin .20 .50
8 Mattias Ohlund .10 .25
9 Felix Potvin .20 .50

2000-01 McDonald's Pacific Dial-A-Stats

ndomly inserted in McDonald's Pacific packs at the rate of one in 16, this six card set featured a framed player action shot on the top half of the card and a rotating wheel and display window that when turned displays the featured player's career statistics versus selected NHL teams. Cards contained gold foil highlights.

COMPLETE SET (6) 7.50 15.00
1 Paul Kariya 2.50 6.00
2 Steve Yzerman 5.00 12.00
3 Pavel Bure 1.00 2.50
4 Eric Lindros 1.00 2.50
5 Jaromir Jagr 1.50 4.00
6 Mats Sundin 1.00 2.50

2000-01 McDonald's Pacific Glove Side Net Fusions

Randomly inserted in packs at the rate of one in 16, this six card set featured a die cut card around a white goalie glove with actual "netting" in the die cut holes for the glove netting. Goalie action photography was set in front of the backdrop and names were highlighted in gold foil.

COMPLETE SET (6) 8.00 20.00
1 Dominik Hasek 2.00 5.00
2 Patrick Roy 5.00 12.00
3 Chris Osgood 1.00 2.50
4 Martin Brodeur 2.50 6.00
5 Brian Boucher 1.00 2.50
6 Curtis Joseph 1.00 2.50

2000-01 McDonald's Pacific Gold Crown Die Cuts

ndomly inserted in McDonald's Pacific packs at the rate of one in eight, this six card set featuresd player action shots set against a green background and a maroon die-cut crown along the top of the card. Both the crown and the name box along the bottom of the card were highlighted in gold foil.

COMPLETE SET (6) 4.00 8.00
1 Patrik Stefan .60 1.50
2 Alex Tanguay .60 1.50
3 David Legwand .60 1.50
4 Scott Gomez .60 1.50
5 Tim Connolly .60 1.50
6 Vincent Lecavalier .60 1.50

2000-01 McDonald's Pacific Game Jerseys

ndomly inserted in McDonald's Pacific packs at the rate of one in 11,915, this 10-card set featured player action photography coupled with a circular game jersey swatch. Cards were accented with gold foil highlights.

1 Teemu Selanne 15.00 40.00
2 Peter Forsberg 15.00 40.00
3 Patrick Roy 40.00 100.00
4 Mike Modano 15.00 40.00
5 Steve Yzerman 15.00 40.00
6 Pavel Bure 15.00 40.00
7 Martin Brodeur 25.00 60.00
8 Eric Lindros 20.00 50.00
9 Jaromir Jagr 30.00 80.00
10 Mats Sundin 15.00 40.00

2001-02 McDonald's Pacific

oduced by Pacific in conjunction with McDonalds of Canada at the cost of an order of french fries or hash browns and 89 cents, this 42-card set utilized set designs from Pacific Prism Gold. Card backs carried stats and player bios in both English and French.

COMPLETE SET (42) 12.50 25.00
1 Paul Kariya .30 .75
2 Joe Thornton .30 .75
3 Jarome Iginla .25 .60
4 Ray Bourque .40 1.00
5 Peter Forsberg .30 .75
6 Patrick Roy SP 1.25 3.00
7 Joe Sakic .40 1.00
8 Ed Belfour SP .50 1.25
9 Brett Hull .30 .75
10 Mike Modano .40 1.00
11 Sergei Fedorov .40 1.00
12 Dominik Hasek SP .75 2.00
13 Chris Osgood SP .50 1.25
14 Brendan Shanahan .30 .75
15 Steve Yzerman .75 2.00
16 Tommy Salo SP .40 1.00
17 Ryan Smyth .20 .50
18 Pavel Bure .30 .75
19 Felix Potvin SP .75 2.00
20 Marian Gaborik .40 1.00
21 Saku Koivu .25 .60
22 Jose Theodore SP .50 1.25
23 Jason Arnott .20 .50
24 Martin Brodeur SP 1.00 2.50
25 Rick DiPietro SP .40 1.00
26 Marian Hossa .20 .50
27 Patrick Lalime SP .40 1.00
28 Roman Cechmanek SP .40 1.00
29 John LeClair .25 .60
30 Johan Hedberg SP .40 1.00
31 Mario Lemieux SP 1.50 4.00
32 Fred Brathwaite SP .40 1.00
33 Chris Pronger .20 .50
34 Doug Weight .25 .60
35 Evgeni Nabokov SP .40 1.00
36 Teemu Selanne .50 1.25
37 Vincent Lecavalier .20 .50
38 Curtis Joseph SP .50 1.25
39 Mats Sundin .25 .60
40 Dan Cloutier SP .40 1.00
41 Markus Naslund .25 .60
42 Jaromir Jagr SP 1.25 3.00

2001-02 McDonald's Pacific Cosmic Force

Inserted at odds of 1:16, this 6-card set featured a "starlight" sparkle effect which revealed a player silhouette when tilted in the light.

COMPLETE SET (6) 15.00 30.00
1 Pavel Bure 2.00 5.00
2 Mario Lemieux 5.00 12.00
3 Doug Weight 1.50 4.00
4 Teemu Selanne 2.00 5.00
5 Mats Sundin 2.00 5.00
6 Jaromir Jagr 2.00 5.00

2001-02 McDonald's Pacific Future Legends

serted at 1:16, this 6-card die-cut set featured both large profile photos in black-and-white and smaller color action photos.

COMPLETE SET (6) 15.00 30.00
1 Mike Comrie 2.00 5.00
2 Rick DiPietro 2.00 5.00
3 Martin Havlat 2.00 5.00
4 Evgeni Nabokov 2.00 5.00
5 Daniel Sedin 2.50 6.00
6 Henrik Sedin 2.50 6.00

2001-02 McDonald's Pacific Glove-Side Net-Fusion

serted at 1:16, this 6-card die-cut set featured color goalie photos over a goalie trapper background. Realistic "netting" was used in the die-cut pocket of the glove.

COMPLETE SET (6) 12.00 30.00
1 Patrick Roy 4.00 10.00
2 Tommy Salo 2.00 5.00
3 Jose Theodore 2.50 6.00
4 Martin Brodeur 3.00 8.00
5 Johan Hedberg 2.50 6.00
6 Curtis Joseph 2.00 5.00

2001-02 McDonald's Pacific Hockey Greats

serted at 1:16, this 6-card set featured bronzed player profiles on sepia toned card fronts.

COMPLETE SET (6) 15.00 30.00
1 Ray Bourque 3.00 8.00
2 Joe Sakic 3.00 8.00
3 Brett Hull 2.50 6.00
4 Dominik Hasek 3.00 8.00
5 Steve Yzerman 5.00 12.00
6 Mark Messier 2.00 5.00

2001-02 McDonald's Pacific Hometown Pride

is 10-card set was inserted one per pack and featured dual player photos on the card fronts and set checklists on the card backs.

COMPLETE SET (10) 5.00 10.00
1 J.Friesen/W.Redden .40 1.00
2 P.Kariya/B.Morrison .40 1.00
3 S.Pellerin/D.Sweeney .40 1.00
4 M.Comrie/J.Iginla .40 1.00
5 B.Richards/G.Sanderson .40 1.00
6 E.Belfour/T.Fleury .60 1.50
7 L.Robitaille/V.Lecavalier .40 1.00
8 D.Cleary/H.Druken .40 1.00
9 A.MacInnis/C.White .40 1.00
10 G.Roberts/S.Thomas .40 1.00

2001-02 McDonald's Pacific Jersey Patches Silver

is 20-card set featured game-worn swatches of jersey patches. Each card was serial-numbered to a number equal to 250 minus their jersey numbers. Actual redeemed numbers are listed below.

1 Jarome Iginla/238 30.00 80.00
2 Peter Forsberg/229 30.00 80.00
3 Patrick Roy/217 30.00 80.00
4 Joe Sakic/231 20.00 50.00
5 Ed Belfour/230 20.00 50.00
6 Brett Hull/234 25.00 60.00
7 Mike Modano/241 25.00 60.00
8 Joe Nieuwendyk/225 15.00 40.00
9 Dominik Hasek/211 30.00 80.00
10 Brendan Shanahan/236 25.00 60.00
11 Steve Yzerman/231 40.00 80.00
12 Saku Koivu/239 25.00 60.00
13 Theo Fleury/236 25.00 60.00
14 Daniel Alfredsson/239 15.00 40.00
15 Mario Lemieux/184 50.00 120.00
16 Teemu Selanne/242 30.00 80.00
17 Vincent Lecavalier/246 15.00 40.00
18 Curtis Joseph/219 25.00 60.00
19 Mats Sundin/237 30.00 80.00
20 Jaromir Jagr/182 40.00 100.00

2001-02 McDonald's Pacific Jersey Patches Gold

is 20-card set paralleled the base jersey set but was on gold card stock. Each card was serial-numbered to the player's jersey number. Actual redeemed numbers are listed below.

3 Patrick Roy/33 200.00 400.00
8 Joe Nieuwendyk/25 150.00 300.00
9 Dominik Hasek/39 150.00 300.00
15 Mario Lemieux/66 200.00 400.00
18 Curtis Joseph/31
20 Jaromir Jagr/68 150.00 300.00

2002-03 McDonald's Pacific

Produced by Pacific in conjunction with McDonalds of Canada at the cost of an order of french fries or hash browns and 89 cents, this 42-card set utilized set designs from Pacific Prism Platinum. Card backs carried stats and player bios in both English and French.

COMPLETE SET (42) 12.50 30.00
COMP.SET w/CL's (52) 15.00 40.00
COMP.MASTER SET (76) 40.00 100.00
1 Paul Kariya .40 1.00
2 Dany Heatley .30 .75
3 Ilya Kovalchuk .40 1.00
4 Joe Thornton .40 1.00
5 Jarome Iginla .30 .75
6 Derek Morris .20 .50
7 Roman Turek .30 .75
8 Peter Forsberg .40 1.00
9 Patrick Roy .75 2.00
10 Joe Sakic .50 1.25
11 Dominik Hasek .50 1.25
12 Brendan Shanahan .40 1.00
13 Steve Yzerman .60 1.50
14 Anson Carter .25 .60
15 Mike Comrie .30 .75
16 Ryan Smyth .25 .60
17 Roberto Luongo .50 1.25
18 Jason Allison .25 .60
19 Marian Gaborik .50 1.25
20 Doug Gilmour .40 1.00
21 Saku Koivu .30 .75
22 Jose Theodore .30 .75
23 Martin Brodeur .60 1.50
24 Michael Peca .25 .60
25 Alexei Yashin .25 .60
26 Pavel Bure .40 1.00
27 Eric Lindros .50 1.25
28 Daniel Alfredsson .30 .75
29 Marian Hossa .25 .60
30 Patrick Lalime .25 .60
31 Simon Gagne .30 .75
32 Mario Lemieux 1.00 2.50
33 Chris Pronger .25 .60
34 Evgeni Nabokov .25 .60
35 Teemu Selanne .60 1.50
36 Curtis Joseph .30 .75
37 Gary Roberts .20 .50
38 Mats Sundin .30 .75
39 Todd Bertuzzi .30 .75
40 Brendan Morrison .25 .60
41 Markus Naslund .25 .60
42 Jaromir Jagr .75 2.00

2002-03 McDonald's Pacific Atomic

ndomly inserted into packs at 1:16, this 6-card set borrowed from the Pacific Atomic diecut design.

COMPLETE SET (6)
1 Paul Kariya 1.50 4.00
2 Ron Francis 1.50 4.00
3 Brett Hull 2.00 5.00
4 Steve Yzerman 5.00 12.00
5 Mats Sundin 1.50 4.00
6 Jaromir Jagr 1.50 4.00

2002-03 McDonald's Pacific Clear Advantage

serted at 1:16, this 6-card set featured color photos of up and coming stars on sparkle effect backgrounds.

COMPLETE SET (6) 12.50 30.00
1 Dany Heatley 2.50 6.00
2 Ilya Kovalchuk 4.00 10.00
3 Jarome Iginla 3.00 8.00
4 Mike Comrie 3.00 8.00
5 Martin Havlat 2.00 5.00
6 Todd Bertuzzi 2.00 5.00

2002-03 McDonald's Pacific Cup Contenders Die-Cuts

Inserted at 1:16, this 6-card set featured full color action player photos skating over an image of the Stanley Cup. All cards were die-cut.

COMPLETE SET (6) 15.00 30.00
1 Joe Thornton 2.50 6.00
2 Patrick Roy 5.00 12.00
3 Sergei Fedorov 2.50 6.00
4 Saku Koivu 2.00 5.00
5 Daniel Alfredsson 1.50 4.00
6 Mats Sundin 1.50 4.00

2002-03 McDonald's Pacific Glove Side Net-Fusions

serted at 1:16, this 6-card die-cut set featured color goalie photos over a goalie trapper background. Realistic "netting" was used in the die-cut pocket of the glove.

COMPLETE SET (6) 12.00 30.00
1 Patrick Roy 4.00 10.00
2 Dominik Hasek 2.50 6.00
3 Tommy Salo 2.00 5.00
4 Jose Theodore 2.50 6.00
5 Patrick Lalime 2.50 6.00
6 Evgeni Nabokov 2.00 5.00

2002-03 McDonald's Pacific Jersey Patches Silver

ndomly inserted into packs as redemption cards, this 20-card set featured authentic game-worn jersey patches of the featured players. Both silver and gold variations were produced for a total of 250 cards of each player. Gold versions were serial-numbered to the player's jersey and silver versions were numbered to the remainder.

1 Dany Heatley/235 50.00 100.00
2 Ilya Kovalchuk/233 50.00 100.00
3 Ron Francis/240 50.00 100.00
4 Joe Sakic/231 60.00 120.00
5 Dominik Hasek/211 60.00 120.00
6 Mike Comrie/161 50.00 100.00
7 Yanic Perreault/156 40.00 80.00
8 Jose Theodore/190 40.00 80.00
9 Martin Brodeur/220 60.00 120.00
10 Pavel Bure/241 60.00 120.00
11 Eric Lindros/162 50.00 100.00
12 Daniel Alfredsson/239 25.00 60.00
13 Adam Oates/173 40.00 80.00
14 Mario Lemieux/184 75.00 150.00
15 Chris Pronger/206 50.00 120.00
16 Curtis Joseph/219 50.00 100.00
17 Alexander Mogilny/161 40.00 80.00
18 Gary Roberts/243 40.00 80.00
19 Markus Naslund/231 40.00 80.00
20 Jaromir Jagr/182 60.00 120.00

2002-03 McDonald's Pacific Jersey Patches Gold

This 20-card set paralleled the base jersey set but was on gold card stock. Each card was serial-numbered to the player's jersey number. Print runs less than 25 were not priced due to scarcity.

1 Dany Heatley/15
2 Ilya Kovalchuk/17
3 Ron Francis/10
4 Joe Sakic/19
5 Dominik Hasek/39 125.00 250.00
6 Mike Comrie/89 150.00 300.00
7 Yanic Perreault/94
8 Jose Theodore/60
9 Martin Brodeur/30 150.00 300.00
10 Pavel Bure/9
11 Eric Lindros/88 125.00 250.00
12 Daniel Alfredsson/11
13 Adam Oates/77 75.00 150.00
14 Mario Lemieux/66 200.00 400.00
15 Chris Pronger/44 75.00 150.00
16 Curtis Joseph/31 125.00 250.00
17 Alexander Mogilny/89 60.00 120.00
18 Gary Roberts/7
19 Markus Naslund/19
20 Jaromir Jagr/68 150.00 300.00

2002-03 McDonald's Pacific Salt Lake Gold

ndomly inserted in packs, this 10-card set features players who were members of the 2002 gold medal Canadian Olympic team. Card backs carry checklists for the rest of the product.

COMPLETE SET (10) 5.00 10.00
1 M.Brodeur .40 1.00
C.Joseph
E.Belfour
2 A.Foote .25 .60
R.Blake
S.Niedermayer
3 E.Jovanovski .25 .60
C.Pronger
A.MacInnis
4 R.Smyth .25 .60
E.Brewer
5 B.Shanahan 1.25 3.00
S.Yzerman
6 E.Lindros .30 .75
T.Fleury
7 P.Kariya .25 .60
J.Nieuwendyk
8 J.Iginla .25 .60
O.Nolan
9 J.Sakic .25 .60
M.Peca
10 M.Lemieux 1.25 3.00
S.Gagne

2003-04 McDonald's Pacific

2003-04, Pacific Trading Cards utilized their Atomic brand for the McDonald's promotion. This set consisted of 55 veteran cards and 6 rookie autograph cards originally found in packs as redemption cards. The redeemed cards were serial-numbered out of 100.

COMP.SET w/o SP's (55) 12.00 25.00
COMP.SET w/CL's (65) 15.00 30.00
COMP.MASTER SET (89) 50.00 100.00
1 Jean-Sebastien Giguere .25 .60
2 Dany Heatley .40 1.00
3 Ilya Kovalchuk .40 1.00
4 Joe Thornton .50 1.25
5 Martin Biron .25 .60
6 Chris Drury .25 .60
7 Jarome Iginla .40 1.00
8 Chuck Kobasew .12 .30
9 Jocelyn Thibault .25 .60
10 Peter Forsberg .60 1.50
11 Milan Hejduk .30 .75
12 Paul Kariya .30 .75
13 Joe Sakic .60 1.50
14 Rick Nash .40 1.00
15 Mike Modano .50 1.25
16 Marty Turco .25 .60
17 Sergei Fedorov .40 1.00
18 Curtis Joseph .30 .75
19 Steve Yzerman 1.25 3.00
20 Henrik Zetterberg .40 .75
21 Mike Comrie .25 .60
22 Georges Laraque .12 .30
23 Ryan Smyth .12 .30
24 Jay Bouwmeester .12 .30
25 Roberto Luongo .40 1.00
26 Marian Gaborik .50 1.25
27 Marcel Hossa .30 .75
28 Saku Koivu .30 .75
29 Jose Theodore .40 1.00
30 Martin Brodeur 1.00 2.50
31 Scott Stevens .25 .60
32 Michael Peca .12 .30
33 Eric Lindros .30 .75
34 Mark Messier .30 .75
35 Daniel Alfredsson .25 .60
36 Marian Hossa .30 .75
37 Patrick Lalime .25 .60
38 Simon Gagne .30 .75
39 Jeremy Roenick .40 1.00
40 Sean Burke .25 .60
41 Mario Lemieux 2.00 4.00
42 Barret Jackman .25 .60
43 Peter Sejna .30 .75
44 Vincent Lecavalier .30 .75
45 Martin St. Louis .25 .60
46 Ed Belfour .30 .75
47 Tie Domi .25 .60
48 Owen Nolan .25 .60
49 Matt Stajan .30 .75
50 Mats Sundin .30 .75
51 Todd Bertuzzi .30 .75
52 Ed Jovanovski .25 .60
53 Brendan Morrison .25 .60
54 Markus Naslund .30 .75
55 Jaromir Jagr .50 1.25
56 Eric Staal AU 175.00 300.00
57 Tuomo Ruutu AU 100.00 200.00
58 Nathan Horton AU 100.00 200.00
59 Chris Higgins AU 75.00 150.00
60 Jordin Tootoo AU 100.00 200.00
61 Marc-Andre Fleury AU 80.00 200.00

2003-04 McDonald's Pacific Canadian Pride

MPLETE SET (6) 12.00 25.00
STATED ODDS 1:16
1 Dany Heatley 1.50 4.00
2 Joe Thornton 2.00 5.00
3 Rick Nash 2.00 5.00
4 Jay Bouwmeester 1.25 3.00
5 Jason Spezza 2.00 5.00
6 Vincent Lecavalier 1.25 3.00

2003-04 McDonald's Pacific Etched in Time

MPLETE SET (6) 12.00 25.00
STATED ODDS 1:16
1 Joe Sakic 2.50 6.00
2 Brett Hull 1.50 4.00
3 Steve Yzerman 4.00 10.00
4 Mark Messier 1.50 4.00
5 Mario Lemieux 5.00 12.00
6 Jaromir Jagr 2.50 6.00

2003-04 McDonald's Pacific Hockey Roots Checklists

MPLETE SET (10) 3.00 6.00
STATED ODDS 1:1
1 Dany Heatley .25 .60
2 Joe Thornton .25 .60
3 Jarome Iginla .30 .75
4 Rob Blake .30 .75
5 Paul Kariya .25 .60
6 Rick Nash .25 .60
7 Jeff Friesen .25 .60
8 Vincent Lecavalier .30 .75
9 Brad Richards .30 .75
10 Gary Roberts .25 .60

2003-04 McDonald's Pacific Patches Silver

ndomly inserted into packs as redemption cards, this 25-card set featured authentic game-worn jersey patches of the featured players. Each card was serial-numbered out of 150, though there is no information currently as to how many cards were actually redeemed.

UNLISTED STARS 40.00 100.00
COMMON CARD (1-25) 40.00 100.00
STATED PRINT RUN 150 SER.#'d SETS
1 Paul Kariya 40.00 100.00
2 Dany Heatley 40.00 100.00
3 Joe Thornton 60.00 120.00
4 Jarome Iginla 40.00 100.00
5 Peter Forsberg 40.00 100.00
6 Ilya Kovalchuk 50.00 125.00
7 Joe Sakic 60.00 120.00
8 Mike Modano 40.00 100.00
9 Marty Turco 40.00 100.00
10 Brendan Shanahan 40.00 100.00
11 Steve Yzerman 60.00 120.00
12 Mike Comrie 40.00 100.00
13 Ryan Smyth 40.00 100.00
14 Saku Koivu 40.00 100.00
15 Jose Theodore 40.00 100.00
16 Martin Brodeur 60.00 150.00
17 Marian Hossa 40.00 100.00
18 Patrick Lalime 40.00 100.00
19 Jason Spezza 60.00 120.00
20 Mario Lemieux 60.00 120.00
21 Vincent Lecavalier 40.00 100.00
22 Ed Belfour 60.00 120.00
23 Mats Sundin 40.00 100.00
24 Todd Bertuzzi 40.00 100.00
25 Markus Naslund 40.00 100.00

2003-04 McDonald's Pacific Patches Gold

OLD: 1X TO 2X SILVER JSY
STATED PRINT RUN 100 SER.#'d SETS

2003-04 McDonald's Pacific Patches and Sticks

COMMON CARD (1-25) 60.00 150.00
UNLISTED STARS 100.00 200.00
*PATCH/STK: .8X TO 2X BASE JSY
STATED PRINT RUN 50 SETS
1 Paul Kariya 125.00 250.00
2 Dany Heatley 125.00 250.00
3 Joe Thornton 150.00 400.00
4 Jarome Iginla 150.00 400.00
5 Peter Forsberg 125.00 250.00
6 Ilya Kovalchuk 125.00 250.00
7 Joe Sakic 150.00 400.00
8 Mike Modano 100.00 200.00
9 Marty Turco 100.00 200.00
10 Brendan Shanahan 100.00 200.00
11 Steve Yzerman 150.00 400.00
12 Mike Comrie 60.00 150.00
13 Ryan Smyth 100.00 200.00

14 Saku Koivu 100.00 200.00
15 Jose Theodore 125.00 250.00
16 Martin Brodeur 200.00 400.00
17 Marian Hossa 125.00 250.00
18 Patrick Lalime 100.00 200.00
19 Jason Spezza 150.00 400.00
20 Mario Lemieux 250.00 500.00
21 Vincent Lecavalier 125.00 250.00
22 Ed Belfour 150.00 300.00
23 Mats Sundin 100.00 200.00
24 Todd Bertuzzi 125.00 250.00
25 Markus Naslund 125.00 250.00

2003-04 McDonald's Pacific Net Fusions

MPLETE SET (6) 10.00 20.00
STATED ODDS 1:16
1 Jean-Sebastien Giguere 1.25 3.00
2 Curtis Joseph 1.50 4.00
3 Roberto Luongo 1.50 4.00
4 Jose Theodore 1.50 4.00
5 Martin Brodeur 2.00 5.00
6 Ed Belfour 1.50 4.00

2003-04 McDonald's Pacific Saturday Night Rivals

MPLETE SET (1-6) 8.00 15.00
UNLISTED STARS 2.00 5.00
STATED ODDS 1:16
1 J.Iginla/M.Comrie 1.50 4.00
2 T.Bertuzzi/R.Smyth 1.50 4.00
3 B.Morrison/C.Conroy 1.25 3.00
4 M.Sundin/S.Koivu 2.00 5.00
5 P.Lalime/E.Belfour 2.00 5.00
6 Mar.Hossa/Marc.Hossa 2.00 5.00

2005-06 McDonald's Upper Deck

MPLETE SET (51) 15.00 40.00
1 Jay Bouwmeester .40 1.00
2 Eric Lindros .60 1.50
3 Sergei Fedorov .60 1.50
4 Vincent Lecavalier .30 .75
5 Miikka Kiprusoff .30 .75
6 Scott Niedermayer .40 1.00
7 Chris Pronger .30 .75
8 Joe Thornton .50 1.25
9 Rick Nash .40 1.00
10 Saku Koivu .40 1.00
11 Wade Redden .25 .60
12 Mats Sundin .40 1.00
13 Jason Smith .25 .60
14 Tuomo Ruutu .40 1.00
15 Olaf Kolzig .40 1.00
16 Simon Gagne .40 1.00
17 Brendan Shanahan .50 1.25
18 Jean-Sebastien Giguere .40 1.00
19 Roberto Luongo .60 1.50
20 Michael Ryder .30 .75
21 Ed Jovanovski .30 .75
22 Daniel Briere .40 1.00
23 Jarome Iginla .40 1.00
24 Joe Sakic .60 1.50
25 Dany Heatley .40 1.00
26 Steve Yzerman 1.00 2.50
27 Mike Ribeiro .30 .75
28 Mario Lemieux 1.25 3.00
29 Brendan Morrison .25 .60
30 Brad Richards .40 1.00
31 Luc Robitaille .40 1.00
32 Daniel Alfredsson .40 1.00
33 Andrew Raycroft .30 .75
34 Eric Staal .50 1.25
35 Jose Theodore .40 1.00
36 Jaromir Jagr 1.00 2.50
37 Jeremy Roenick .40 1.00
38 Martin St. Louis .40 1.00
39 Ed Belfour .40 1.00
40 Mike Modano .60 1.50
41 Marian Hossa .30 .75
42 Ilya Kovalchuk .40 1.00
43 Jonathan Cheechoo .40 1.00
44 Ryan Smyth .30 .75
45 Peter Forsberg .50 1.25
46 Shean Donovan .25 .60
47 Marian Gaborik .60 1.50
48 Martin Brodeur .75 2.00
49 Bryan McCabe .25 .60
50 Markus Naslund .40 1.00
51 Sidney Crosby 5.00 12.00

2005-06 McDonald's Upper Deck Autographs

COMMON CARD
PRINT RUN 50 SER.#'d SETS
MA1 Wayne Gretzky 400.00 750.00
MA2 Markus Naslund 50.00 125.00
MA3 Joe Thornton 100.00 200.00
MA4 Dominik Hasek 100.00 200.00
MA5 Jarome Iginla 125.00 250.00
MA6 Martin Brodeur 250.00 400.00
MA7 Rick Nash 125.00 250.00
MA8 Jose Theodore 150.00 300.00
MA9 Mats Sundin 150.00 300.00

2005-06 McDonald's Upper Deck Chasing the Cup

PRINT RUN 100 SER.#'d SETS
CC1 Simon Gagne 30.00 60.00
CC2 Jose Theodore 40.00 80.00
CC3 Jarome Iginla 40.00 80.00
CC4 Markus Naslund 40.00 80.00
CC5 Jason Spezza 50.00 100.00
CC6 Mats Sundin 50.00 100.00
CC7 Joe Thornton 60.00 120.00
CC8 Ilya Kovalchuk 50.00 100.00

2005-06 McDonald's Upper Deck CHL Graduates

MPLETE SET (6) 2.00 4.00
STATED ODDS 1:1
CG1 Joe Sakic .50 1.25
CG2 Jarome Iginla .30 .75
CG3 Wade Redden .25 .60
CG4 Vincent Lecavalier .25 .60
CG5 Joe Thornton .40 1.00
CG6 Rick Nash .30 .75

2005-06 McDonald's Upper Deck Goalie Factory

COMPLETE SET (15) 20.00 50.00
STATED ODDS 1:14
GF1 Dominik Hasek 3.00 8.00
GF2 Roberto Luongo 2.50 6.00
GF3 Martin Brodeur 4.00 10.00
GF4 Marty Turco 2.00 5.00
GF5 Miikka Kiprusoff 2.00 5.00
GF6 Jean-Sebastien Giguere 2.00 5.00
GF7 Tomas Vokoun 2.00 5.00
GF8 Dan Cloutier 2.00 5.00
GF9 Jose Theodore 2.00 5.00
GF10 Nikolai Khabibulin 2.00 5.00
GF11 Marc-Andre Fleury 2.50 6.00
GF12 Kari Lehtonen 2.00 5.00
GF13 Ed Belfour 2.00 5.00
GF14 Curtis Joseph 2.00 5.00
GF15 Andrew Raycroft 2.00 5.00

2005-06 McDonald's Upper Deck Goalie Gear

PRINT RUN 50 SER.#'d SETS
MG1 Marc-Andre Fleury 125.00 250.00
MG2 Jocelyn Thibault 60.00 150.00
MG3 Roberto Luongo 75.00 200.00
MG4 Rick DiPietro 60.00 150.00
MG5 Olaf Kolzig 100.00 200.00
MG6 Jose Theodore 75.00 150.00
MG7 Andrew Raycroft 60.00 150.00
MG8 Marty Turco 60.00 150.00
MG9 Dominik Hasek 125.00 250.00
MG10 Ed Belfour 125.00 250.00
MG11 Chris Osgood 60.00 150.00
MG12 Curtis Joseph 40.00 100.00

2005-06 McDonald's Upper Deck Jerseys

PRINT RUN 120 SER.#'d SETS
MJ1 Mario Lemieux 125.00 250.00
MJ2 Joe Thornton 75.00 200.00
MJ3 Mats Sundin 60.00 150.00
MJ4 Markus Naslund 60.00 150.00
MJ5 Dany Heatley 60.00 150.00
MJ6 Martin Brodeur 150.00 300.00
MJ7 Steve Yzerman 150.00 300.00
MJ8 Saku Koivu 75.00 150.00
MJ9 Jose Theodore 75.00 150.00
MJ10 Ed Belfour 100.00 200.00
MJ11 Jarome Iginla 125.00 250.00
MJ12 Jason Spezza 75.00 150.00
MJ13 Martin Havlat 40.00 100.00
MJ14 Sergei Fedorov 75.00 150.00
MJ15 Jeremy Roenick 50.00 120.00

2005-06 McDonald's Upper Deck Next Generation

COMPLETE SET (15) 20.00 50.00
STATED ODDS 1:18
NG1 Andrew Raycroft 2.50 6.00
NG2 Rick Nash 3.00 8.00
NG3 Marc-Andre Fleury 3.00 8.00
NG4 Nikolai Zherdev 2.00 5.00
NG5 Tuomo Ruutu 2.00 5.00
NG6 Jonathan Cheechoo 2.50 6.00
NG7 Kari Lehtonen 2.50 6.00
NG8 Jason Spezza 3.00 8.00
NG9 Alexander Frolov 2.00 5.00
NG10 Stephen Weiss 2.50 6.00
NG11 Patrice Bergeron 2.50 6.00
NG12 Derek Roy 2.00 5.00
NG13 Eric Staal 3.00 8.00
NG14 Michael Ryder 2.50 6.00
NG15 Matthew Lombardi 2.00 5.00

2005-06 McDonald's Upper Deck Superstar Spotlight

COMPLETE SET (10) 30.00 60.00
COMMON CARD (SS1-SS10) 1.50 4.00
STATED ODDS 1:16
SS1 Mario Lemieux 6.00 15.00
SS2 Joe Thornton 2.50 6.00
SS3 Mats Sundin 1.50 4.00
SS4 Jarome Iginla 2.00 5.00
SS5 Martin Brodeur 5.00 12.00
SS6 Jose Theodore 2.00 5.00
SS7 Martin St. Louis 1.50 4.00
SS8 Joe Sakic 3.00 8.00
SS9 Steve Yzerman 5.00 12.00
SS10 Vincent Lecavalier 1.50 4.00

2005-06 McDonald's Upper Deck Top Scorers

MPLETE SET (15) 100.00 175.00
STATED ODDS 1:18
TS1 Wayne Gretzky 15.00 40.00
TS2 Martin St. Louis 4.00 10.00
TS3 Joe Sakic 8.00 25.00
TS4 Mario Lemieux 10.00 25.00
TS5 Peter Forsberg 8.00 20.00
TS6 Steve Yzerman 12.00 30.00
TS7 Mike Modano 8.00 20.00
TS8 Mike Ribeiro 4.00 10.00
TS9 Mats Sundin 6.00 15.00
TS10 Markus Naslund 6.00 15.00
TS11 Jarome Iginla 8.00 20.00
TS12 Daniel Alfredsson 6.00 15.00
TS13 Ilya Kovalchuk 6.00 15.00
TS14 Rick Nash 8.00 20.00
TS15 Joe Thornton 8.00 20.00

2006-07 McDonald's Upper Deck

MPLETE SET (56) 15.00 40.00
1 Teemu Selanne 1.00 2.50
2 Ilya Kovalchuk .50 1.25
3 Patrice Bergeron .60 1.50
4 Ryan Miller .50 1.25
5 Jarome Iginla .50 1.25
6 Miikka Kiprusoff .40 1.00
7 Dion Phaneuf .50 1.25
8 Eric Staal .60 1.50
9 Nikolai Khabibulin .50 1.25
10 Joe Sakic .75 2.00
11 Milan Hejduk .40 1.00
12 Rick Nash .50 1.25
13 Mike Modano .75 2.00
14 Marty Turco .50 1.25
15 Steve Yzerman 1.25 3.00
16 Brendan Shanahan .60 1.50
17 Jarret Stoll .40 1.00
18 Ales Hemsky .40 1.00
19 Ryan Smyth .40 1.00
20 Jay Bouwmeester .50 1.25
21 Alexander Frolov .30 .75
22 Marian Gaborik .60 1.50
23 Saku Koivu .50 1.25
24 Michael Ryder .30 .75
25 Mike Ribeiro .40 1.00
26 Paul Kariya .60 1.50
27 Martin Brodeur 1.00 2.50
28 Miroslav Satan .40 1.00
29 Jaromir Jagr 1.25 3.00
30 Henrik Lundqvist 1.00 2.50
31 Jason Spezza .50 1.25
32 Dany Heatley .50 1.25
33 Daniel Alfredsson .50 1.25
34 Peter Forsberg .60 1.50
35 Simon Gagne .50 1.25
36 Shane Doan .40 1.00
37 Marc-Andre Fleury .75 2.00
38 Joe Thornton .60 1.50
39 Jonathan Cheechoo .50 1.25
40 Keith Tkachuk .50 1.25
41 Brad Richards .50 1.25
42 Martin St. Louis .50 1.25
43 Vincent Lecavalier .40 1.00
44 Darcy Tucker .40 1.00
45 Mats Sundin .50 1.25
46 Alexander Steen .50 1.25
47 Markus Naslund .40 1.00
48 Ed Jovanovski .40 1.00
49 Brendan Morrison .30 .75
50 Alexander Ovechkin 2.00 5.00
51 Saku Koivu CL .75 2.00
52 Mats Sundin CL .75 2.00
53 Jarome Iginla CL .75 2.00
54 Markus Naslund CL .60 1.50
55 Daniel Alfredsson CL .75 2.00
56 Jason Smith CL .50 1.25

2006-07 McDonald's Upper Deck Autographs

STATED ODDS 1:4,000
PRINT RUN 25 SER. #'d SETS
AAH Ales Hemsky 125.00 250.00
AAO Alexander Ovechkin
AAT Alex Tanguay 75.00 150.00
ABM Bryan McCabe 75.00 150.00
ADP Dion Phaneuf 100.00 175.00
AES Eric Staal 100.00 200.00
AHL Henrik Lundqvist 125.00 250.00
AHZ Henrik Zetterberg 125.00 250.00
AIK Ilya Kovalchuk 125.00 300.00
AJC Jonathan Cheechoo 100.00 200.00
AJI Jarome Iginla 125.00 250.00
AJT Joe Thornton
AKD Kris Draper 100.00 175.00
ALR Luc Robitaille 100.00 200.00
AMB Martin Brodeur
AMF Marc-Andre Fleury 125.00 250.00
AMK Miikka Kiprusoff 100.00 200.00
AMN Markus Naslund 100.00 200.00
AMP Michael Peca 75.00 150.00
AMR Michael Ryder 75.00 150.00
AMT Marty Turco 60.00 125.00
APB Patrice Bergeron 75.00 150.00
APM Patrick Marleau 75.00 150.00
ARL Roberto Luongo 150.00 250.00
ARM Ryan Miller 125.00 225.00
ARN Rick Nash 125.00 225.00
ARS Ryan Smyth 100.00 200.00
ASH Shawn Horcoff 75.00 150.00
ASK Saku Koivu
AVL Vincent Lecavalier

2006-07 McDonald's Upper Deck Clear Cut Winners

MPLETE SET (10) 300.00 400.00
STATED ODDS 1:100
CC1 Joe Sakic 20.00 50.00
CC2 Jarome Iginla 20.00 50.00
CC3 Rick Nash 15.00 40.00
CC4 Eric Staal 15.00 40.00
CC5 Saku Koivu 20.00 50.00
CC6 Martin Brodeur 20.00 50.00
CC7 Dany Heatley 15.00 40.00
CC8 Joe Thornton 15.00 40.00
CC9 Mats Sundin 15.00 40.00
CC10 Ryan Smyth 15.00 40.00

2006-07 McDonald's Upper Deck Hardware Heroes

MPLETE SET (10) 15.00 40.00
STATED ODDS 1:6
HH1 Joe Thornton 5.00 12.00
HH2 Alexander Ovechkin 6.00 15.00
HH3 Nicklas Lidstrom 2.50 6.00
HH4 Joe Thornton 5.00 12.00
HH5 Cam Ward 3.00 8.00
HH6 Miikka Kiprusoff 4.00 10.00
HH7 Jonathan Cheechoo 2.50 6.00
HH8 Eric Staal 3.00 8.00
HH9 Ryan Smyth 2.50 6.00
HH10 Rod Brind`Amour 2.50 6.00

2006-07 McDonald's Upper Deck Hot Gloves

MPLETE SET (10) 20.00 50.00
STATED ODDS 1:20
HG1 Martin Brodeur 5.00 12.00
HG2 Dominik Hasek 5.00 12.00
HG3 Dwayne Roloson 2.50 6.00
HG4 Miikka Kiprusoff 5.00 12.00
HG5 Cristobal Huet 2.50 6.00
HG6 Jean-Sebastien Giguere 3.00 8.00
HG7 Roberto Luongo 3.00 8.00
HG8 Marty Turco 2.50 6.00
HG9 Marc-Andre Fleury 4.00 10.00
HG10 Henrik Lundqvist 4.00 10.00

2006-07 McDonald's Upper Deck Jerseys

ATED PRINT RUN 100 SER.#'d SETS
JAH Ales Hemsky 30.00 80.00
JAO Alexander Ovechkin 75.00 150.00
JAT Alex Tanguay 30.00 80.00
JBS Brendan Shanahan 50.00 120.00
JCP Chris Pronger 30.00 80.00
JDH Dany Heatley 50.00 120.00
JDT Darcy Tucker 25.00 60.00
JES Eric Staal 30.00 80.00
JHZ Henrik Zetterberg 75.00 150.00
JIK Ilya Kovalchuk 50.00 120.00
JJG Jean-Sebastien Giguere 40.00 100.00
JJI Jarome Iginla 30.00 80.00
JJJ Jaromir Jagr 50.00 120.00
JJS Joe Sakic 50.00 120.00
JJT Joe Thornton 40.00 100.00
JMB Martin Brodeur 60.00 150.00
JMK Miikka Kiprusoff 40.00 100.00
JMN Markus Naslund 40.00 100.00
JMR Michael Ryder 25.00 60.00
JMS Mats Sundin 40.00 100.00
JMT Marty Turco 30.00 80.00
JPB Patrice Bergeron 40.00 100.00
JPF Peter Forsberg 30.00 80.00
JPK Paul Kariya 40.00 100.00
JRL Roberto Luongo 30.00 80.00
JRN Rick Nash 40.00 100.00
JSC Brad Richards 50.00 120.00
JSK Saku Koivu 40.00 100.00
JSP Jason Spezza 30.00 80.00
JVL Vincent Lecavalier 50.00 120.00

2006-07 McDonald's Upper Deck Rookie Review

MPLETE SET (15) 10.00 25.00
STATED ODDS 1:20
RR1 Kyle Wellwood 1.50 4.00
RR2 Alexander Ovechkin 5.00 12.00
RR3 Henrik Lundqvist 2.50 6.00
RR4 Dion Phaneuf 2.50 6.00
RR5 Alexander Steen 1.50 4.00
RR6 Thomas Vanek 2.00 5.00
RR7 Corey Perry 2.00 5.00
RR8 Andrej Meszaros 1.50 4.00
RR9 Jeff Carter 2.00 5.00
RR10 Patrick Eaves 1.50 4.00
RR11 Ryan Miller 2.00 5.00
RR12 Marek Svatos 1.50 4.00
RR13 Brad Boyes 1.50 4.00
RR14 Chris Higgins 2.00 5.00
RR15 Cam Ward 2.00 5.00

2007-08 McDonald's Upper Deck

MPLETE SET (50) 10.00 25.00
1 Alexander Ovechkin 2.00 5.00
2 Markus Naslund .50 1.25
3 Roberto Luongo .60 1.50
4 Daniel Sedin .50 1.25
5 Mats Sundin .50 1.25
6 Bryan McCabe .30 .75
7 Darcy Tucker .40 1.00
8 Vincent Lecavalier .40 1.00
9 Martin St. Louis .50 1.25
10 Doug Weight .50 1.25
11 Joe Thornton .60 1.50
12 Jonathan Cheechoo .50 1.25
13 Marc-Andre Fleury .75 2.00
14 Jordan Staal .50 1.25
15 Evgeni Malkin 1.50 4.00
16 Shane Doan .40 1.00
17 Simon Gagne .50 1.25
18 Dany Heatley .50 1.25
19 Ray Emery .40 1.00
20 Jason Spezza .50 1.25
21 Jaromir Jagr 1.25 3.00
22 Henrik Lundqvist .60 1.50
23 Rick DiPietro .40 1.00
24 Martin Brodeur 1.00 2.50
25 Alexander Radulov .50 1.25
26 Saku Koivu .50 1.25
27 Guillaume Latendresse .40 1.00
28 Cristobal Huet .40 1.00
29 Marian Gaborik .60 1.50
30 Anze Kopitar .75 2.00
31 Nathan Horton .50 1.25
32 Ales Hemsky .40 1.00
33 Dwayne Roloson .40 1.00
34 Rob Schremp RC .40 1.00
35 Nicklas Lidstrom .50 1.25
36 Henrik Zetterberg .60 1.50
37 Pavel Datsyuk .60 1.50
38 Marty Turco .50 1.25
39 Rick Nash .50 1.25
40 Joe Sakic .75 2.00
41 Martin Havlat .50 1.25
42 Eric Staal .60 1.50
43 Jarome Iginla .50 1.25
44 Miikka Kiprusoff .40 1.00
45 Dion Phaneuf .50 1.25
46 Thomas Vanek .60 1.50
47 Ryan Miller .50 1.25
48 Patrice Bergeron .60 1.50
49 Marian Hossa .40 1.00
50 Scott Niedermayer .50 1.25

2007-08 McDonald's Upper Deck Autographs

STATED PRINT RUN 30 #'d SETS
MAAH Ales Hemsky 80.00 200.00
MAAR Andrew Raycroft 80.00 200.00
MAAS Alexander Steen 100.00 250.00
MAAT Alex Tanguay 60.00 150.00
MABM Brendan Morrison 60.00 150.00
MACH Chris Higgins 60.00 150.00
MACW Cam Ward 100.00 250.00
MADB Daniel Briere 100.00 250.00
MADH Dany Heatley 150.00 300.00
MADR Dwayne Roloson 80.00 200.00
MAEC Erik Cole 80.00 200.00
MAEM Evgeni Malkin 150.00 300.00
MAES Eric Staal 120.00 300.00
MAGL Guillaume Latendresse 80.00 200.00
MAHU Cristobal Huet 80.00 200.00
MAJC Jonathan Cheechoo 100.00 250.00
MAJI Jarome Iginla 100.00 250.00
MAJS Jarret Stoll 80.00 200.00
MAKL Kari Lehtonen 80.00 200.00
MAMF Marc-Andre Fleury 150.00 300.00
MAMR Michael Ryder 60.00 150.00
MAMT Marty Turco 40.00 100.00
MAPM Patrick Marleau 100.00 250.00
MAPS Paul Stastny 100.00 250.00
MARL Roberto Luongo 150.00 300.00
MARN Rick Nash 100.00 250.00
MASK Saku Koivu 100.00 250.00
MAST Jordan Staal 150.00 300.00
MATV Thomas Vanek 125.00 300.00
MAWR Wade Redden 60.00 150.00

2007-08 McDonald's Upper Deck In the Crease

MPLETE SET (6) 10.00 25.00
STATED ODDS 1:15
ICDH Dominik Hasek 2.50 6.00
ICMB Martin Brodeur 4.00 10.00
ICMF Marc-Andre Fleury 3.00 8.00
ICMK Miikka Kiprusoff 1.50 4.00
ICRL Roberto Luongo 2.50 6.00
ICRM Ryan Miller 2.00 5.00

2007-08 McDonald's Upper Deck Jerseys

STATED PRINT RUN 100 SER.#'d SETS
MJAH Ales Hemsky 25.00 60.00
MJAO Alexander Ovechkin 75.00 150.00
MJAR Andrew Raycroft 25.00 60.00
MJAT Alex Tanguay 20.00 50.00
MJBS Brendan Shanahan 40.00 100.00
MJCH Cristobal Huet 25.00 60.00
MJDH Dany Heatley 30.00 80.00
MJDR Dwayne Roloson 25.00 60.00
MJEM Evgeni Malkin 100.00 200.00
MJES Eric Staal 40.00 100.00
MJIK Ilya Kovalchuk 30.00 80.00
MJJC Jonathan Cheechoo 30.00 80.00
MJJI Jarome Iginla 30.00 80.00
MJJS Joe Sakic 50.00 125.00
MJJT Joe Thornton 30.00 80.00
MJMB Martin Brodeur 40.00 100.00
MJMK Miikka Kiprusoff 25.00 60.00
MJMN Markus Naslund 30.00 80.00
MJMR Michael Ryder 20.00 50.00
MJMS Martin St. Louis 30.00 80.00
MJMT Marty Turco 30.00 80.00
MJPB Patrice Bergeron 40.00 100.00
MJPK Paul Kariya 40.00 100.00
MJRL Roberto Luongo 40.00 100.00
MJRN Rick Nash 30.00 80.00
MJSG Simon Gagne 30.00 80.00
MJSK Saku Koivu 30.00 80.00
MJSP Jason Spezza 30.00 80.00
MJSU Mats Sundin 30.00 80.00
MJVL Vincent Lecavalier 25.00 60.00

2007-08 McDonald's Upper Deck Pride of Canada

COMPLETE SET (6) 8.00 20.00
STATED ODDS 1:15
PC1 Joe Sakic 2.50 6.00
PC2 Rick Nash 1.50 4.00
PC3 Joe Thornton 2.00 5.00
PC4 Vincent Lecavalier 1.25 3.00
PC5 Eric Staal 2.00 5.00
PC6 Jarome Iginla 1.50 4.00

2007-08 McDonald's Upper Deck Season in Review

COMPLETE SET (6) 10.00 25.00
STATED ODDS 1:15
SR1 Evgeni Malkin 5.00 12.00
SR2 Mats Sundin 1.50 4.00
SR3 Mike Modano 2.50 6.00
SR4 Martin Brodeur 3.00 8.00
SR5 Roberto Luongo 2.00 5.00
SR6 Joe Sakic 2.50 6.00

2007-08 McDonald's Upper Deck Superstar Spotlight

MPLETE SET (10) 15.00 40.00
STATED ODDS 1:15
SS1 Ray Emery 1.25 3.00
SS2 Joe Sakic 2.50 6.00
SS3 Alexander Ovechkin 6.00 15.00
SS4 Dany Heatley 1.50 4.00
SS5 Martin St. Louis 1.50 4.00
SS6 Jaromir Jagr 4.00 10.00
SS7 Jarome Iginla 1.50 4.00
SS8 Joe Thornton 2.00 5.00
SS9 Vincent Lecavalier 1.25 3.00
SS10 Teemu Selanne 3.00 8.00

2007-08 McDonald's Upper Deck Three Stars Checklists

MPLETE SET (6) 1.00 2.50
ONE PER PACK
CL1 Koivu/Ryder/Huet .20 .50
CL2 Sundin/Tucker/McCabe .20 .50
CL3 Spezza/Heatley/Emery .20 .50
CL4 Horcoff/Roloson/Hemsky .15 .40
CL5 Iginla/Kiprusoff/Phaneuf .20 .50
CL6 Naslund/Luongo/Sedin .25 .60

2008-09 McDonald's Upper Deck

COMPLETE SET (50) 8.00 20.00
1 Ryan Getzlaf .75 2.00
2 Teemu Selanne 1.00 2.50
3 Ilya Kovalchuk .50 1.25
4 Patrice Bergeron .60 1.50
5 Ryan Miller .50 1.25
6 Jarome Iginla .50 1.25
7 Miikka Kiprusoff .40 1.00
8 Dion Phaneuf .50 1.25
9 Eric Staal .60 1.50
10 Patrick Kane 1.00 2.50
11 Jonathan Toews 1.25 3.00
12 Paul Stastny .50 1.25
13 Peter Forsberg .60 1.50
14 Joe Sakic .75 2.00
15 Rick Nash .50 1.25
16 Marty Turco .50 1.25
17 Mike Modano .75 2.00
18 Henrik Zetterberg .60 1.50
19 Chris Osgood .50 1.25
20 Nicklas Lidstrom .50 1.25
21 Sam Gagner .40 1.00
22 Ales Hemsky .40 1.00
23 Andrew Cogliano .40 1.00
24 Anze Kopitar .75 2.00
25 Marian Gaborik .60 1.50
26 Carey Price 2.00 5.00
27 Saku Koivu .50 1.25
28 Alex Kovalev .40 1.00
29 Martin Brodeur 1.00 2.50
30 Rick DiPietro .40 1.00
31 Marc Staal .50 1.25
32 Henrik Lundqvist .60 1.50
33 Dany Heatley .50 1.25
34 Daniel Alfredsson .50 1.25
35 Jason Spezza .50 1.25
36 Simon Gagne .50 1.25
37 Shane Doan .40 1.00
38 Jordan Staal .50 1.25
39 Evgeni Malkin 1.50 4.00
40 Marc-Andre Fleury .75 2.00
41 Joe Thornton .60 1.50
42 Paul Kariya .60 1.50
43 Vincent Lecavalier .40 1.00
44 Martin St. Louis .50 1.25
45 Mats Sundin .50 1.25
46 Vesa Toskala .40 1.00
47 Tomas Kaberle .30 .75
48 Roberto Luongo .60 1.50
49 Markus Naslund .40 1.00
50 Alexander Ovechkin 2.00 5.00

2008-09 McDonald's Upper Deck Gold

*GOLD: 10X TO 25X BASE

2008-09 McDonald's Upper Deck Autographs

STATED PRINT RUN 25 SERIAL #'d SETS
AAC Andrew Cogliano 150.00 250.00
AAH Ales Hemsky
AAK Anze Kopitar 150.00 250.00
AAO Alexander Ovechkin 175.00 300.00
ACP Carey Price
ADH Dany Heatley 125.00 200.00
AEJ Erik Johnson
AEM Evgeni Malkin
AES Eric Staal 100.00 175.00
AHZ Henrik Zetterberg 250.00 400.00
AIK Ilya Kovalchuk
AJI Jarome Iginla
AJJ Jack Johnson
AJT Jonathan Toews 200.00 350.00
AKE Phil Kessel 75.00 150.00
AMG Marian Gaborik
AMM Mike Modano
AMS Martin St. Louis 175.00 300.00
AMT Marty Turco 30.00 60.00
ANF Nick Foligno 125.00 200.00
ANL Nicklas Lidstrom
APK Patrick Kane
APM Peter Mueller
APS Paul Stastny 150.00 250.00
ARG Ryan Getzlaf
ARM Ryan Miller 75.00 150.00
ASG Sam Gagner 100.00 200.00
ASK Saku Koivu 200.00 350.00
ATH Joe Thornton 100.00 200.00
ATK Tomas Kaberle

2008-09 McDonald's Upper Deck Canadian Goalie Checklist

COMPLETE SET (6) 5.00 12.00
CLCGY Miikka Kiprusoff .75 2.00
CLEDM Mathieu Garon .75 2.00
CLMTL Carey Price 4.00 10.00
CLOTT Martin Gerber .75 2.00
CLTOR Vesa Toskala .75 2.00
CLVAN Roberto Luongo 1.25 3.00

2008-09 McDonald's Upper Deck Clear Path to Greatness

COMPLETE SET (14) 250.00 500.00
CP1 Joe Sakic 15.00 40.00
CP2 Alexander Ovechkin 15.00 40.00
CP3 Vincent Lecavalier 8.00 20.00
CP4 Dany Heatley 10.00 25.00
CP5 Ilya Kovalchuk 10.00 25.00
CP6 Joe Thornton 12.00 30.00
CP7 Jaromir Jagr 25.00 60.00
CP8 Martin Brodeur 15.00 40.00
CP9 Henrik Zetterberg 12.00 30.00
CP10 Markus Naslund 8.00 20.00
CP11 Mats Sundin 10.00 25.00
CP12 Jarome Iginla 10.00 25.00
CP13 Mike Modano 15.00 40.00
CP14 Evgeni Malkin 20.00 40.00

2008-09 McDonald's Upper Deck Jerseys

STATED PRINT RUN 100 SERIAL #'d SETS
JAO Alexander Ovechkin 150.00 250.00
JBS Brendan Shanahan 50.00 120.00
JDA Daniel Alfredsson 40.00 100.00
JDH Dany Heatley 40.00 100.00
JDS Daniel Sedin 40.00 100.00
JEM Evgeni Malkin 125.00 300.00
JES Eric Staal 50.00 120.00
JGA Simon Gagne 40.00 100.00
JHZ Henrik Zetterberg 125.00 250.00
JIK Ilya Kovalchuk 100.00 200.00
JJI Jarome Iginla 100.00 200.00
JJJ Jaromir Jagr 100.00 250.00
JJS Joe Sakic 60.00 150.00
JJT Joe Thornton 50.00 125.00
JKA Patrick Kane 40.00 100.00
JMB Martin Brodeur 150.00 250.00
JMG Marian Gaborik 75.00 150.00
JMK Miikka Kiprusoff 30.00 80.00
JMM Mike Modano 60.00 150.00
JMS Mats Sundin 40.00 100.00
JNL Nicklas Lidstrom 40.00 100.00
JPF Peter Forsberg 50.00 125.00
JPK Paul Kariya 50.00 125.00
JRG Ryan Getzlaf 60.00 150.00
JRL Roberto Luongo 100.00 200.00
JRM Ryan Miller
JRN Rick Nash 40.00 100.00
JSG Sam Gagner 125.00 250.00
JSK Saku Koivu 40.00 100.00
JVL Vincent Lecavalier

2008-09 McDonald's Upper Deck Profiles

COMPLETE SET (10) 15.00 40.00
PRO1 Roberto Luongo 4.00 10.00
PRO2 Mats Sundin 3.00 8.00
PRO3 Jarome Iginla 3.00 8.00
PRO4 Dany Heatley 3.00 8.00
PRO5 Saku Koivu 3.00 8.00
PRO6 Vincent Lecavalier 2.50 6.00
PRO7 Martin Brodeur 6.00 15.00
PRO8 Alexander Ovechkin 12.00 30.00
PRO9 Nicklas Lidstrom 3.00 8.00
PRO10 Joe Thornton 4.00 10.00

2008-09 McDonald's Upper Deck Speed Skaters

COMPLETE SET (10) 30.00 60.00
SS1 Martin St. Louis 4.00 10.00
SS2 Paul Kariya 5.00 12.00
SS3 Teemu Selanne 8.00 20.00
SS4 Marian Hossa 3.00 8.00
SS5 Jaromir Jagr 10.00 25.00
SS6 Marian Gaborik 5.00 12.00
SS7 Simon Gagne 4.00 10.00
SS8 Ilya Kovalchuk 4.00 10.00
SS9 Alexander Ovechkin 15.00 40.00
SS10 Scott Niedermayer 4.00 10.00

2008-09 McDonald's Upper Deck Superstar Spotlight

MPLETE SET (14) 20.00 50.00
IS1 Carey Price 8.00 20.00
IS2 Vincent Lecavalier 1.50 4.00
IS3 Jonathan Toews 5.00 12.00
IS4 Vesa Toskala 1.50 4.00
IS5 Miikka Kiprusoff 1.50 4.00
IS6 Joe Thornton 2.50 6.00
IS7 Pavel Datsyuk 2.50 6.00
IS8 Evgeni Malkin 6.00 15.00
IS9 Roberto Luongo 2.50 6.00
IS10 Jarome Iginla 2.00 5.00
IS11 Daniel Alfredsson 2.00 5.00
IS12 Jaromir Jagr 5.00 12.00
IS13 Alexander Ovechkin 8.00 20.00
IS14 Martin Brodeur 4.00 10.00

2009-10 McDonald's Upper Deck

MPLETE SET (50) 8.00 20.00
1 Ryan Getzlaf .60 1.50
2 Ilya Kovalchuk .40 1.00
3 Tim Thomas .40 1.00
4 Marc Savard .25 .60
5 Thomas Vanek .40 1.00
6 Ryan Miller .40 1.00
7 Jarome Iginla .40 1.00
8 Miikka Kiprusoff .30 .75
9 Dion Phaneuf .50 1.25
10 Eric Staal .50 1.25
11 Jonathan Toews .75 2.00
12 Patrick Kane .75 2.00
13 Paul Stastny .40 1.00
14 Rick Nash .30 .75
15 Steve Mason .30 .75
16 Marty Turco .40 1.00
17 Henrik Zetterberg .50 1.25
18 Pavel Datsyuk .50 1.25
19 Andrew Cogliano .30 .75
20 Sheldon Souray .25 .60
21 Ales Hemsky .30 .75
22 Drew Doughty .50 1.25
23 Niklas Backstrom .40 1.00
24 Carey Price 1.50 4.00
25 Andrei Markov .40 1.00
26 Saku Koivu .40 1.00
27 Shea Weber .30 .75
28 Martin Brodeur .75 2.00
29 Zach Parise .40 1.00
30 Rick DiPietro .30 .75
31 Henrik Lundqvist .60 1.5
32 Dany Heatley .40 1.0
33 Jason Spezza .40 1.0
34 Daniel Alfredsson .40 1.0
35 Jeff Carter .40 1.0
36 Mike Richards .40 1.0
37 Shane Doan .30 .7
38 Evgeni Malkin 1.25 3.0
39 Marc-Andre Fleury .60 1.5
40 Joe Thornton .40 1.0
41 Patrick Marleau .40 1.0
42 Paul Kariya .50 1.2
43 Steven Stamkos .75 2.0
44 Vincent Lecavalier .30 .7
45 Matt Stajan .30 .7
46 Luke Schenn .30 .7
47 Ryan Kesler .40 1.0
48 Roberto Luongo .50 1.2
49 Alexander Ovechkin 1.50 4.0
50 Mike Green .40 1.0

2009-10 McDonald's Upper Deck Checklists

MPLETE SET (6) 2.50 6.0
STATED ODDS 1:4
CL1 Patrick Roy 1.00 2.5
CL2 Jarome Iginla .40 1.0
CL3 Roberto Luongo .50 1.2
CL4 Grant Fuhr .40 1.0
CL5 Jason Spezza .40 1.0
CL6 Doug Gilmour .50 1.2

2009-10 McDonald's Upper Deck Goaltending Greats

MPLETE SET (6) 8.00 20.0
STATED ODDS 1:10
GG1 Carey Price 4.00 10.0
GG2 Roberto Luongo 1.25 3.0
GG3 Miikka Kiprusoff .75 2.0
GG4 Steve Mason .75 2.0
GG5 Marc-Andre Fleury 1.50 4.0
GG6 Martin Brodeur 2.00 5.0

2009-10 McDonald's Upper Deck Horizons

MPLETE SET (14) 20.00 50.0
STATED ODDS 1:20
H1 Tim Thomas 2.00 5.0
H2 Jarome Iginla 2.00 5.0
H3 Jonathan Toews 4.00 10.0
H4 Henrik Zetterberg 2.50 6.0
H5 Andrew Cogliano 1.50 4.0
H6 Carey Price 8.00 20.0
H7 Henrik Lundqvist 3.00 8.0
H8 Dany Heatley 2.00 5.0
H9 Luke Schenn 1.50 4.0
H10 Roberto Luongo 2.50 6.0
H11 Drew Doughty 2.50 6.0
H12 Marty Turco 2.00 5.0
H13 Evgeni Malkin 6.00 15.0
H14 Alexander Ovechkin 8.00 20.0

2009-10 McDonald's Upper Deck In the Spotlight

MPLETE SET (10) 100.00 200.0
STATED ODDS 1:60
IS1 Alexander Ovechkin 20.00 50.0
IS2 Evgeni Malkin 8.00 20.0
IS3 Joe Thornton 5.00 12.0
IS4 Jarome Iginla 5.00 12.0
IS5 Ilya Kovalchuk 6.00 15.0
IS6 Carey Price 20.00 50.0
IS7 Martin Brodeur 10.00 25.0
IS8 Steven Stamkos 10.00 25.0
IS9 Jonathan Toews 10.00 25.0
IS10 Vincent Lecavalier 4.00 10.0

2009-10 McDonald's Upper Deck Pride of Canada

MPLETE SET (14) 75.00 150.0
STATED ODDS 1:40
PC1 Dany Heatley 6.00 15.0
PC2 Vincent Lecavalier 5.00 12.0
PC3 Jarome Iginla 6.00 15.0
PC4 Rick Nash 5.00 12.0
PC5 Mike Richards 6.00 15.0
PC6 Joe Thornton 6.00 15.0
PC7 Ryan Getzlaf 10.00 25.0
PC8 Mike Green 6.00 15.0
PC9 Jeff Carter 6.00 15.0
PC10 Jonathan Toews 12.00 30.0
PC11 Dion Phaneuf 8.00 20.0
PC12 Chris Pronger 5.00 12.0
PC13 Martin Brodeur 12.00 30.0
PC14 Roberto Luongo 8.00 20.0

2011-12 McDonald's Upper Deck Canadiens

COMPLETE SET (25)
*GOLD: 20X TO 50X BASIC CARDS
1 Alexei Emelin .30 .7
2 Andrei Kostitsyn .30 .7
3 Andrei Markov .40 1.0
4 Brian Gionta .30 .7
5 Carey Price 1.25 3.0
6 Chris Campoli .30 .7
7 David Desharnais .50 1.2
8 Erik Cole .30 .7
9 Hal Gill .25 .6
10 Tomas Kaberle .25 .6
11 Josh Gorges .25 .6
12 Lars Eller .30 .7
13 Max Pacioretty .40 1.0
14 Michael Cammalleri .30 .7
15 P.K. Subban .75 2.0
16 Peter Budaj .30 .7
17 Petteri Nokelainen .25 .6
18 Raphael Diaz .30 .7
19 Ryan White .25 .6
20 Scott Gomez .30 .7
21 Tomas Plekanec .40 1.0
22 Travis Moen .25 .6
23 Yannick Weber .30 .7
24 Mathieu Darche .30 .7
25 Youppi mascot .25 .6

1906 McGill Men at Hockey Postcard

Standard sized postcard featured a photo of unknown men playing ice hockey. Back featured U.P.S. Montreal Series No 402.

NNO McGill Men at Hockey Montreal 60.00 120.0

1995-96 Metal

The 1995-96 Fleer Metal set was issued in one series totaling 200 cards. The 8-card packs had a suggested retail of $2.49 each. The hand-engraved etched cards each featured a colorful action photo with the player cutting through a unique metallic foil background. The cards were grouped alphabetically within teams. The Joe Sakic SkyMint Exchange card was randomly inserted 1:360 packs. When exchanged collectors

eceived a unique card with a dime-sized coin featuring he Avalanche star embedded in the corner. The xchange offer expired January 1, 1997. Rookie Cards n this set included Daniel Alfredsson, Radek Dvorak, had Kilger, Daymond Langkow, and Kyle McLaren.
Guy Hebert .12 .30
Paul Kariya .20 .50
Todd Krygier .10 .25
Steve Rucchin .12 .30
Oleg Tverdovsky .15 .40
Ray Bourque .25 .60
Blaine Lacher .12 .30
Shawn McEachern .10 .25
Cam Neely .15 .40
0 Adam Oates .15 .40
1 Kevin Stevens .12 .30
2 Donald Audette .12 .30
3 Randy Burridge .10 .25
4 Jason Dawe .10 .25
5 Dominik Hasek .20 .50
6 Pat LaFontaine .15 .40
7 Alexei Zhitnik .10 .25
8 Theo Fleury .20 .50
9 Phil Housley .12 .30
0 Trevor Kidd .12 .30
1 Joe Nieuwendyk .15 .40
2 Michael Nylander .10 .25
3 Ed Belfour .12 .30
4 Chris Chelios .15 .40
5 Joe Murphy .10 .25
6 Bernie Nicholls .10 .25
7 Patrick Poulin .10 .25
8 Jeremy Roenick .20 .50
9 Gary Suter .12 .30
0 Adam Deadmarsh .10 .25
1 Stephane Fiset .12 .30
2 Peter Forsberg .40 1.00
3 Valeri Kamensky .12 .30
4 Claude Lemieux .15 .40
5 Sandis Ozolinsh .12 .30
6 Joe Sakic .25 .60
7 Greg Adams .10 .25
8 Dave Gagner .10 .25
9 Todd Harvey .10 .25
0 Derian Hatcher .12 .30
1 Kevin Hatcher .12 .30
2 Mike Modano .25 .60
3 Andy Moog .15 .40
4 Paul Coffey .15 .40
5 Sergei Fedorov .25 .60
6 Vladimir Konstantinov .12 .30
7 Slava Kozlov .12 .30
8 Nicklas Lidstrom .15 .40
9 Chris Osgood .12 .30
0 Keith Primeau .10 .25
1 Steve Yzerman .20 .50
2 Jason Arnott .12 .30
3 Zdeno Ciger .12 .30
4 Todd Marchant .10 .25
5 David Oliver .10 .25
6 Bill Ranford .12 .30
7 Doug Weight .15 .40
8 Stu Barnes .10 .25
9 Jody Hull .10 .25
0 Scott Mellanby .12 .30
1 Rob Niedermayer .12 .30
2 John Vanbiesbrouck .12 .30
3 Sean Burke .10 .25
4 Andrew Cassels .10 .25
5 Nelson Emerson .10 .25
6 Geoff Sanderson .10 .25
7 Brendan Shanahan .20 .50
8 Glen Wesley .10 .25
9 Rob Blake .12 .30
0 Tony Granato .10 .25
1 Wayne Gretzky .75 2.00
2 Dimitri Khristich .10 .25
3 Yanic Perreault .10 .25
4 Rick Tocchet .12 .30
5 Benoit Brunet .10 .25
6 Vincent Damphousse .12 .30
7 Mark Recchi .20 .50
8 Patrick Roy .40 1.00
9 Brian Savage .10 .25
0 Pierre Turgeon .15 .40
1 Martin Brodeur .40 1.00
2 Neal Broten .12 .30
3 John MacLean .12 .30
4 Scott Niedermayer .15 .40
5 Scott Stevens .12 .30
6 Stephane Richer .15 .40
7 Esa Tikkanen .12 .30
8 Steve Thomas .10 .25
9 Wendel Clark .15 .40
0 Travis Green .12 .30
1 Kirk Muller .12 .30
2 Zigmund Palffy .15 .40
3 Mathieu Schneider .10 .25
4 Ray Ferraro .10 .25
5 Alexei Kovalev .10 .25
6 Brian Leetch .15 .40
7 Mark Messier .25 .60
8 Mike Richter .15 .40
9 Luc Robitaille .15 .40
00 Ulf Samuelsson .10 .25
01 Pat Verbeek .12 .30
02 Radek Bonk .10 .25
03 Don Beaupre .12 .30
04 Alexandre Daigle .10 .25
05 Steve Duchesne .10 .25
06 Dan Quinn .12 .30
07 Martin Straka .10 .25
08 Rod Brind'Amour .15 .40
09 Eric Desjardins .12 .30
10 Ron Hextall .15 .40
11 John LeClair .15 .40
12 Eric Lindros .25 .60
13 Mikael Renberg .12 .30
14 Chris Therien .10 .25
15 Tom Barrasso .12 .30
16 Ron Francis .20 .50
17 Jaromir Jagr .40 1.00
18 Mario Lemieux .50 1.25
19 Tomas Sandstrom .12 .30
20 Bryan Smolinski .10 .25
21 Sergei Zubov .12 .30
22 Shayne Corson .10 .25
23 Grant Fuhr .15 .40
24 Dale Hawerchuk .20 .50
25 Brett Hull .20 .50
26 Al MacInnis .15 .40
27 Chris Pronger .15 .40
28 Ulf Dahlen .10 .25
29 Jeff Friesen .10 .25
30 Arturs Irbe .12 .30
31 Craig Janney .10 .25
32 Andrei Nazarov .12 .30
33 Owen Nolan .15 .40
34 Ray Sheppard .12 .30
35 Brian Bradley .12 .30
36 Chris Gratton .10 .25
137 Roman Hamrlik .10 .25
138 Petr Klima .10 .25
139 Daren Puppa .12 .30
140 Alexander Selivanov .12 .30
141 Dave Andreychuk .15 .40
142 Mike Gartner .15 .40
143 Doug Gilmour .20 .50
144 Kenny Jonsson .15 .40
145 Larry Murphy .15 .40
146 Felix Potvin .15 .40
147 Mats Sundin .15 .40
148 Jeff Brown .12 .30
149 Pavel Bure .20 .50
150 Russ Courtnall .10 .25
151 Trevor Linden .15 .40
152 Kirk McLean .12 .30
153 Alexander Mogilny .12 .30
154 Roman Oksiuta .10 .25
155 Mike Ridley .10 .25
156 Peter Bondra .15 .40
157 Jim Carey .12 .30
158 Sylvain Cote .10 .25
159 Sergei Gonchar .10 .25
160 Keith Jones .12 .30
161 Joe Juneau .12 .30
162 Nikolai Khabibulin .12 .30
163 Igor Korolev .10 .25
164 Teppo Numminen .10 .25
165 Teemu Selanne .30 .75
166 Keith Tkachuk .15 .40
167 Darren Turcotte .10 .25
168 Alexei Zhamnov .15 .40
169 Daniel Alfredsson RC .75 2.00
170 Aki Berg RC .15 .40
171 Todd Bertuzzi RC .20 .50
172 Jason Bonsignore .10 .25
173 Byron Dafoe .12 .30
174 Eric Daze .30 .75
175 Shane Doan RC .50 1.25
176 Radek Dvorak RC .20 .50
177 Brian Holzinger RC .30 .75
178 Ed Jovanovski .15 .40
179 Chad Kilger RC .15 .40
180 Saku Koivu .15 .40
181 Darren Langdon RC .30 .75
182 Daymond Langkow RC .15 .40
183 Jere Lehtinen .12 .30
184 Kyle McLaren RC .10 .25
185 Marty Murray .15 .40
186 Jeff O'Neill .15 .40
187 Richard Park .15 .40
188 Deron Quint .12 .30
189 Marcus Ragnarsson RC .20 .50
190 Miroslav Satan RC .20 .50
191 Tommy Salo RC .25 .60
192 Jamie Storr .12 .30
193 Niklas Sundstrom .15 .40
194 Robert Svehla RC .10 .25
195 Denis Pederson .40 1.00
196 Antti Tormanen RC .10 .25
197 Brendan Witt .15 .40
198 Vitali Yachmenev .15 .40
199 Checklist (1-114) .05 .15
200 Checklist (115-200 inserts) UER .05 .15
NNO Joe Sakic EXCH .75 2.00
NNO Joe Sakic Coin Card 8.00 20.00

1995-96 Metal Heavy Metal

ndomly inserted in packs at a rate of 1:30 packs, this 12-card set highlighted some of the league's top players. The fronts featured an isolated player photo over a dynamic starburst metallic background. The backs included another photo, and the card number out of 12.

COMPLETE SET (12) 15.00 40.00
1 Pavel Bure 1.25 3.00
2 Sergei Fedorov 1.25 3.00
3 Theo Fleury .60 1.50
4 Wayne Gretzky 8.00 20.00
5 Brett Hull 1.25 3.00
6 Jaromir Jagr 2.00 5.00
7 Paul Kariya 1.25 3.00
8 Brian Leetch .60 1.50
9 Mario Lemieux 6.00 15.00
10 Mike Modano 2.00 5.00
11 Adam Oates .60 1.50
12 Joe Sakic 3.00 8.00

1995-96 Metal International Steel

ndomly inserted in packs at a rate of 1:3 packs, this 24-card set featured the top skaters from around the globe. The checklist card for this set found in the regular Fleer Metal series suggested that card number one is Aki-Petteri Berg. This was incorrect as this card did not exist. The remaining cards existed as checklisted, save for their number being one less than listed.

COMPLETE SET (24) 15.00 30.00
1 Pavel Bure .60 1.50
2 Chris Chelios .40 1.00
3 Sergei Fedorov .75 2.00
4 Peter Forsberg 1.25 3.00
5 Wayne Gretzky 2.50 6.00
6 Roman Hamrlik .20 .50
7 Dominik Hasek 1.25 3.00
8 Brett Hull .75 2.00
9 Jaromir Jagr 1.00 2.50
10 Saku Koivu .60 1.50
11 Pat LaFontaine .40 1.00
12 Brian Leetch .40 1.00
13 Jere Lehtinen .40 1.00
14 Mario Lemieux 2.00 5.00
15 Alexander Mogilny .40 1.00
16 Mikael Renberg .20 .50
17 Jeremy Roenick .60 1.50
18 Joe Sakic 1.25 3.00
19 Teemu Selanne .60 1.50
20 Mats Sundin .60 1.50
21 Niklas Sundstrom .20 .50
22 Vitali Yachmenev .20 .50
23 Alexei Zhamnov .20 .50
24 Sergei Zubov .20 .50

1995-96 Metal Iron Warriors

Randomly inserted in packs at a rate of 1:12 packs, this 15-card set had a razor-sharp design and featured the NHL's toughest competitors.

COMPLETE SET (15) 20.00 40.00
1 Jason Arnott .60 1.50
2 Ed Belfour 1.25 3.00
3 Theo Fleury .60 1.50
4 Ron Francis .75 2.00
5 John LeClair .75 2.00
6 Claude Lemieux .60 1.50
7 Eric Lindros 2.00 5.00
8 Mark Messier 2.00 5.00
9 Cam Neely 2.00 5.00
10 Keith Primeau .60 1.50
11 Kevin Stevens .60 1.50
12 Scott Stevens .60 1.50
13 Brendan Shanahan 2.00 5.00
14 Keith Tkachuk 1.25 3.00
15 Rick Tocchet .75 2.00

1995-96 Metal Promo Panel

Measuring 7" by 7", this promo panel was issued to preview the 1995-96 Fleer Metal series. Its left side consisted of a 2" by 7" strip with ad copy; to the right were four standard-size perforated cards. The fronts displayed color action cutouts on a silver metallic background. On a background consisting of a close-up photo and a jagged ice design, the backs carried biography and a bar graph presenting statistics. The cards were numbered "SAMPLE X" in the upper left corner.

COMPLETE SHEET .75 2.00
1 Felix Potvin .40 1.00
2 Jeremy Roenick .30 .75
3 Theo Fleury .20 .50
4 Richard Park .08 .25
PAN Uncut Panel .75 2.00
Felix Potvin
Jeremy Roenick
Theo Fleury
Richard Park

1995-96 Metal Winners

Randomly inserted in packs at a rate of 1:60 packs , this 9-card set emblazoned on a high-tech design, showed players who have won medals in international competitions such as the Olympics or World Championships.

COMPLETE SET (9) 8.00 20.00
1 Peter Forsberg 4.00 10.00
2 Saku Koivu 2.00 5.00
3 Alexei Kovalev .40 1.00
4 Eric Lindros 2.00 5.00
5 Alexander Mogilny .75 2.00
6 Tommy Salo .75 2.00
7 Brian Savage .40 1.00
8 Sergei Zubov .40 1.00
9 Alexei Zhamnov .40 1.00

1996-97 Metal Universe

Issued in eight-card packs with a SRP of $2.49, this single-series set consisted of 200 cards. The design is comprised of a cutout player photo placed atop a surrealistic, etched-metal background. Key rookies include Dainius Zubrus, Mike Grier, and Sergei Berezin.

1 Guy Hebert .12 .30
2 Paul Kariya .20 .50
3 Jari Kurri .15 .40
4 Roman Oksiuta .10 .25
5 Steve Rucchin .10 .25
6 Teemu Selanne .30 .75
7 Ray Bourque .25 .60
8 Kyle McLaren .10 .25
9 Adam Oates .15 .40
10 Bill Ranford .12 .30
11 Rick Tocchet .12 .30
12 Donald Audette .10 .25
13 Jason Dawe .10 .25
14 Dominik Hasek .25 .60
15 Pat LaFontaine .15 .40
16 Derek Plante .10 .25
17 Wayne Primeau .10 .25
18 Theo Fleury .30 .75
19 Dave Gagner .15 .40
20 Trevor Kidd .10 .25
21 James Patrick .10 .25
22 Robert Reichel .10 .25
23 German Titov .10 .25
24 Tony Amonte .12 .30
25 Ed Belfour .15 .40
26 Chris Chelios .15 .40
27 Eric Daze .12 .30
28 Gary Suter .10 .25
29 Alexei Zhamnov .12 .30
30 Adam Deadmarsh .10 .25
31 Adam Foote .10 .25
32 Peter Forsberg .25 .60
33 Valeri Kamensky .12 .30
34 Uwe Krupp .10 .25
35 Claude Lemieux .10 .25
36 Sandis Ozolinsh .10 .25
37 Patrick Roy .40 1.00
38 Joe Sakic .25 .60
39 Derian Hatcher .10 .25
40 Mike Modano .25 .60
41 Andy Moog .15 .40
42 Joe Nieuwendyk .15 .40
43 Pat Verbeek .10 .25
44 Sergei Zubov .10 .25
45 Sergei Fedorov .25 .60
46 Vladimir Konstantinov .12 .30
47 Slava Kozlov .10 .25
48 Nicklas Lidstrom .20 .50
49 Chris Osgood .15 .40
50 Brendan Shanahan .20 .50
51 Steve Yzerman .40 1.00
52 Jason Arnott .12 .30
53 Curtis Joseph .15 .40
54 Andrei Kovalenko .10 .25
55 Miroslav Satan .10 .25
56 Doug Weight .15 .40
57 Radek Dvorak .12 .30
58 Per Gustafsson RC .15 .40
59 Ed Jovanovski .12 .30
60 Scott Mellanby .12 .30
61 Rob Niedermayer .12 .30
62 Ray Sheppard .12 .30
63 Robert Svehla .10 .25
64 John Vanbiesbrouck .15 .40
65 Jeff Brown .10 .25
66 Sean Burke .10 .25
67 Paul Coffey .15 .40
68 Nelson Emerson .10 .25
69 Jeff O'Neill .10 .25
70 Keith Primeau .10 .25
71 Geoff Sanderson .12 .30
72 Aki Berg .10 .25
73 Rob Blake .15 .40
74 Stephane Fiset .12 .30
75 Dimitri Khristich .10 .25
76 Petr Klima .10 .25
77 Ed Olczyk .10 .25
78 Vitali Yachmenev .10 .25
79 Vincent Damphousse .12 .30
80 Saku Koivu .15 .40
81 Mark Recchi .20 .50
82 Stephane Richer .12 .30
83 Jocelyn Thibault .15 .40
84 Pierre Turgeon .15 .40
85 Dave Andreychuk .15 .40
86 Martin Brodeur .30 .75
87 Scott Niedermayer .15 .40
88 Scott Stevens .15 .40
89 Petr Sykora .10 .25
90 Steve Thomas .10 .25
91 Todd Bertuzzi .15 .40
92 Travis Green .12 .30
93 Kenny Jonsson .10 .25
94 Bryan McCabe .10 .25
95 Zigmund Palffy .15 .40
96 Wayne Gretzky .75 2.00
97 Alexei Kovalev .10 .25
98 Brian Leetch .15 .40
99 Mark Messier .25 .60
100 Mike Richter .15 .40
101 Luc Robitaille .15 .40
102 Niklas Sundstrom .10 .25
103 Daniel Alfredsson .15 .40
104 Radek Bonk .10 .25
105 Alexandre Daigle .10 .25
106 Steve Duchesne .10 .25
107 Damian Rhodes .12 .30
108 Alexei Yashin .12 .30
109 Rod Brind'Amour .15 .40
110 Eric Desjardins .12 .30
111 Dale Hawerchuk .20 .50
112 Ron Hextall .12 .30
113 John LeClair .15 .40
114 Eric Lindros .25 .60
115 Mikael Renberg .12 .30
116 Mike Gartner .15 .40
117 Craig Janney .12 .30
118 Nikolai Khabibulin .12 .30
119 Dave Manson .10 .25
120 Teppo Numminen .10 .25
121 Jeremy Roenick .25 .60
122 Keith Tkachuk .15 .40
123 Oleg Tverdovsky .12 .30
124 Tom Barrasso .12 .30
125 Ron Francis .20 .50
126 Kevin Hatcher .10 .25
127 Jaromir Jagr .40 1.00
128 Mario Lemieux .50 1.25
129 Petr Nedved .12 .30
130 Shayne Corson .10 .25
131 Grant Fuhr .15 .40
132 Brett Hull .75 2.00
133 Al MacInnis .15 .40
134 Joe Murphy .10 .25
135 Chris Pronger .12 .30
136 Kelly Hrudey .12 .30
137 Al Iafrate .10 .25
138 Bernie Nicholls .10 .25
139 Owen Nolan .15 .40
140 Marcus Ragnarsson .10 .25
141 Darren Turcotte .10 .25
142 Brian Bradley .10 .25
143 Dino Ciccarelli .15 .40
144 Chris Gratton .12 .30
145 Roman Hamrlik .12 .30
146 Daren Puppa .12 .30
147 Alexander Selivanov .10 .25
148 Wendel Clark .12 .30
149 Doug Gilmour .20 .50
150 Kirk Muller .10 .25
151 Larry Murphy .12 .30
152 Felix Potvin .15 .40
153 Mathieu Schneider .10 .25
154 Mats Sundin .15 .40
155 Pavel Bure .20 .50
156 Russ Courtnall .10 .25
157 Trevor Linden .12 .30
158 Kirk McLean .12 .30
159 Alexander Mogilny .12 .30
160 Esa Tikkanen .10 .25
161 Peter Bondra .12 .30
162 Jim Carey .15 .40
163 Sergei Gonchar .10 .25
164 Phil Housley .12 .30
165 Calle Johansson .12 .30
166 Joe Juneau .10 .25
167 Michal Pivonka .10 .25
168 Brendan Witt .10 .25
169 Nolan Baumgartner .10 .25
170 Bryan Berard .15 .40
171 Sergei Berezin RC .25 .60
172 Curtis Brown .10 .25
173 Jan Caloun RC .15 .40
174 Andreas Dackell RC .15 .40
175 Hnat Domenichelli .10 .25
176 Christian Dube .10 .25
177 Anders Eriksson .10 .25
178 Peter Ferraro .10 .25
179 Eric Fichaud .12 .30
180 Daniel Goneau RC .15 .40
181 Mike Grier RC .20 .50
182 Jarome Iginla .20 .50
183 Steve Kelly RC .12 .30
184 Jamie Langenbrunner .10 .25
185 Daymond Langkow .12 .30
186 Jay McKee RC .10 .25
187 Ethan Moreau RC .15 .40
188 Rem Murray RC .15 .40
189 Janne Niinimaa .15 .40
190 Wade Redden .10 .25
191 Ruslan Salei RC .15 .40
192 Jamie Storr .10 .25
193 Darren Van Impe .10 .25
194 Roman Vopat .10 .25
195 David Wilkie .10 .25
196 Landon Wilson .10 .25
197 Richard Zednik RC .20 .50
198 Dainius Zubrus RC .20 .50
199 Checklist (1-118) .05 .15
200 Checklist (119-200 inserts) .05 .15

1996-97 Metal Universe Armor Plate

Randomly inserted in packs at a rate of 1:72, this 12-card set was comprised of hockey's top netminders. Cutout player photos were placed over a bubbled metallic surface, with a short write-up and photo on the reverse. A Super Power parallel with enhanced holographic foil backgrounds was inserted one per 720 packs. There was no distinction other than the special holofoil treatment.

COMPLETE SET (12) 30.00 80.00
*SUPER POWER: 2X TO 5X BASIC INSERTS
1 Ed Belfour 3.00 8.00
2 Martin Brodeur 8.00 20.00
3 Jim Carey 2.00 5.00
4 Dominik Hasek 6.00 15.00
5 Ron Hextall 2.50 6.00
6 Chris Osgood 3.00 0.00
7 Felix Potvin 6.00 15.00
8 Daren Puppa 2.00 5.00
9 Damian Rhodes 2.00 5.00
10 Mike Richter 3.00 8.00
11 Patrick Roy 12.00 30.00
12 John Vanbiesbrouck 3.00 8.00

1996-97 Metal Universe Cool Steel

Randomly inserted in packs at a rate of 1:48, this 12-card set featured cutout player photos on a brushed metal background. Two photos graced the reverse, including an extreme face close-up, as well as a description of each player's strengths. A Super Power parallel with an enhanced holographic foil background was inserted one per 480 packs. There was no distinction between the two versions other than the special holofoil treatment.

COMPLETE SET (12) 25.00 50.00
*SUPER POWER: 1.5X TO 4X BASIC INSERTS
1 Chris Chelios 2.00 5.00
2 Peter Forsberg 3.00 8.00
3 Ron Francis 1.50 4.00
4 Dominik Hasek 4.00 10.00
5 Ed Jovanovski 1.50 4.00
6 Vladimir Konstantinov 1.50 4.00
7 Eric Lindros 3.00 10.00
8 Mark Messier 2.50 6.00
9 Patrick Roy 10.00 25.00
10 Brendan Shanahan 2.00 5.00
11 Keith Tkachuk 2.00 5.00
12 John Vanbiesbrouck 1.50 4.00

1996-97 Metal Universe Ice Carvings

This 12-card set was randomly inserted in retail packs at a rate of 1:24. An etched, blue-foil player image accompanied a cutout photo on the front, while the flip side added a close-up photo and interesting text on each player. A Super Power parallel with an enhanced holographic foil background was inserted one per 240 packs. There was no distinction between the two versions other than the special holofoil treatment.

COMPLETE SET (12) 30.00 60.00
*SUPER POWER: 1.5X TO 4X BASIC INSERTS
1 Martin Brodeur 6.00 15.00
2 Pavel Bure 4.00 10.00
3 Jim Carey 2.00 5.00
4 Paul Coffey 4.00 10.00
5 Sergei Fedorov 3.00 8.00
6 Jaromir Jagr 3.00 8.00
7 Paul Kariya 4.00 10.00
8 Pat LaFontaine 2.00 5.00
9 Brian Leetch 4.00 10.00
10 Mario Lemieux 10.00 25.00
11 Alexander Mogilny 2.00 5.00
12 Joe Sakic 4.00 10.00

1996-97 Metal Universe Lethal Weapons

e most common of the Metal inserts, this 20-card set was randomly inserted 1:12 packs and featured the top scorers in the NHL. Cutout player photos leaped off of bronze metallic backgrounds with a second photo on the card back as well as a description of each player's scoring prowess. Super Power parallels were inserted every 120 packs and differed only by an enhanced holographic foil background.

COMPLETE SET (20) 20.00 50.00
*SUPER POWER: 1.5X TO 4X BASIC INSERTS
1 Peter Bondra 1.00 2.50
2 Pavel Bure 1.50 4.00
3 Sergei Fedorov 1.50 4.00
4 Peter Forsberg 2.50 6.00
5 Ron Francis 1.50 4.00
6 Wayne Gretzky 6.00 15.00
7 Brett Hull 1.25 3.00
8 Jaromir Jagr 1.50 4.00
9 Paul Kariya 1.50 4.00
10 John LeClair 1.50 4.00
11 Mario Lemieux 5.00 12.00
12 Eric Lindros 2.00 5.00
13 Mark Messier 1.50 4.00
14 Alexander Mogilny 1.00 2.50
15 Adam Oates 1.00 2.50
16 Joe Sakic 2.50 6.00
17 Teemu Selanne 1.50 4.00
18 Brendan Shanahan 1.50 4.00
19 Keith Tkachuk 1.50 4.00
20 Doug Weight 1.50 4.00

1996 Metallic Ice Series

Produced by Cityscope Digital Imaging, this standard size card was given out at a Dallas Stars game in 1996. It was made of metal and weighed significantly more than a standard card. Card is serial numbered out of 1000.

NNO Mike Modano 4.00 10.00

1972-73 Minnesota Fighting Saints Postcards WHA

These borderless postcards featured action photos on the front, along with player name and biographical information. They were issued as promotional giveaways at autograph signings and to by-mail requesters.

COMPLETE SET (25) 35.00 70.00
1 Mike Antonovich 2.00 4.00
2 John Arbour 1.50 3.00
3 Terry Ball 1.50 3.00
4 Keith Christiansen 1.50 3.00
5 Wayne Connelly 2.50 5.00
6 Mike Curran 1.50 3.00
7 Craig Falkman 1.50 3.00
8 Ted Hampson 2.00 4.00
9 Jimmy Johnson 1.50 3.00
10 Bill Klatt 1.50 3.00
11 George Konik 1.50 3.00
12 Leonard Lilyholm 1.50 3.00
13 Bob MacMillan 1.50 3.00
14 Jack McCartan 2.50 5.00
15 Mike McMahon 1.50 3.00
16 George Morrison 1.50 3.00
17 Dick Paradise 1.50 3.00
18 Mel Pearson 1.50 3.00
19 Terry Ryan 1.50 3.00
20 Blaine Rydman 1.50 3.00
21 Frank Sanders 1.50 3.00
22 Glen Sonmor CO 1.50 3.00
23 Fred Speck 1.50 3.00
24 Bill Young 1.50 3.00
25 Carl Wetzel 1.50 3.00

1974-75 Minnesota Fighting Saints WHA

These cards set measure 3 1/2" x 5 1/2" and featured borderless color action photos on the front. Backs featured a head shot and statistics, along with the players position. The Saints logo could be found in black along the top of card back. Several cards are as yet unconfirmed.

1 Mike Antonovich 2.00 4.00
2 John Arbour 1.50 3.00
3 Terry Ball (unconfirmed)
4 Bob Boyd (unconfirmed)
5 Ron Busniuk 1.50 3.00
6 Wayne Connelly 2.00 4.00
7 Mike Curran 1.50 3.00
8 Gord Gallant 2.00 4.00
9 Gary Gambucci 1.50 3.00
10 John Garrett 5.00 10.00
11 Ted Hampson 2.00 4.00
12 Murray Heatley 1.50 3.00
13 Fran Huck 1.50 3.00
14 Jim Johnson 1.50 3.00
15 Jack McCartan (unconfirmed)
16 Mike McMahon 1.50 3.00
17 George Morrison (unconfirmed)
18 Harry Neale (unconfirmed)
19 Danny O'Shea (unconfirmed)
20 Rich Smith 1.50 3.00
21 Glen Sonmor (unconfirmed)
22 Don Tannahill (unconfirmed)
23 Mike Walton 2.50 5.00

1982 Montreal News

This 21-card set was cut out of the Montreal News and features various size color player photos of stars of different sports. The paper is printed in French. The cards are unnumbered and checklisted below in alphabetical order.

COMPLETE SET (21) 16.00 40.00
7 Rejean Houle HK .80 2.00
8 Mark Hunter HK .40 1.00
11 Wilfrid Paiement HK .40 1.00

1910 Murad College Silks S21

Each of these silks was issued by Murad Cigarettes around 1910 with a college emblem and an artist's rendering of a generic athlete on the front. The backs are blank. Each of the S21 silks measures roughly 5" by 7" and there was a smaller version created (roughly 3 1/2" by 5 1/2") of each and cataloged as S22.

*SMALLER S22: .3X TO .8X LARGER S21
1HK Army (West Point) hockey 30.00 60.00
2HK Brown hockey 30.00 60.00
3HK California hockey 30.00 60.00
4HK Chicago hockey 30.00 60.00
5HK Colorado hockey 30.00 60.00
6HK Columbia hockey 30.00 60.00
7HK Cornell hockey 30.00 60.00
8HK Dartmouth hockey 30.00 60.00
9HK Georgetown hockey 30.00 60.00
10HK Harvard hockey 30.00 60.00
11HK Illinois hockey 30.00 60.00
12HK Michigan hockey 30.00 60.00
13HK Minnesota hockey 30.00 60.00
14HK Missouri hockey 30.00 60.00
15HK Navy (Annapolis) hockey 30.00 60.00
16HK Ohio State hockey 30.00 60.00
17HK Pennsylvania hockey 30.00 60.00
18HK Purdue hockey 30.00 60.00
19HK Stanford hockey 30.00 60.00
20HK Stanford hockey 30.00 60.00
21HK Syracuse hockey 30.00 60.00
22HK Texas hockey 30.00 60.00
23HK Wisconsin hockey 30.00 60.00
24HK Yale hockey 30.00 60.00

1911 Murad College Series T51

These colorful cigarette cards featured several colleges and a variety of sports and recreations of the day and were issued in packs of Murad Cigarettes. The cards measure approximately 2" by 3". Two variations of each of the first 50 cards were produced; one variation says "College Series" on back, the other, "2nd Series". The drawings on cards of the 2nd Series are slightly different from those of the College Series. There are 6 different series of 25 in the College Series and they are listed here in the order that they appear on the checklist on the cardbacks. There is also a larger version (5" x 8") that was available for the first 25 cards as a premium (catalog designation T6) offer that could be obtained in exchange for 15 Murad cigarette coupons; the offers expired June 30, 1911.

*2ND SERIES: .4X TO 1X COLLEGE SERIES
18 Rochester Ice Hockey 25.00 50.00

1911 Murad College Series Premiums T6

18 Rochester Ice Hockey 250.00 400.00

1974 Nabisco Sugar Daddy

This set of 25 tiny (approximately 1 1/16" by 2 3/4") cards features athletes from a variety of popular pro sports. One card was included in specially marked Sugar Daddy and Sugar Mama candy bars. The cards were designed to be placed on a 18" by 24" poster, which could only be obtained through a mail-in offer direct from Nabisco. The set is referred to as "Pro Faces" as the cards show an enlarged head photo with a small caricature body. Cards 1-10 are football players, cards 11-16 and 22 are hockey players, and cards 17-21 and 23-25 are basketball players. Each card was produced in two printings. The first printing has a copyright date of 1973 printed on the backs (although the cards are thought to have been released in early 1974) and the second printing is missing a copyright date altogether.

COMPLETE SET (25) 75.00 150.00
11 Phil Esposito 4.00 8.00
12 Dennis Hull 1.50 4.00
13 Reg Fleming 1.50 4.00
14 Garry Unger 1.50 4.00
15 Derek Sanderson 2.50 5.00
16 Jerry Korab 1.50 4.00
22 Mickey Redmond 1.50 4.00

1975 Nabisco Sugar Daddy

This set of 25 tiny (approximately 1 1/16" by 2 3/4") cards features athletes from a variety of popular pro sports. One card was included in specially marked Sugar Daddy and Sugar Mama candy bars. The cards were designed to be placed on a 18" by 24" poster, which could only be obtained through a mail-in offer direct from Nabisco. The set is referred to as "Sugar Daddy All-Stars". As with the set of the previous year, the cards show an enlarged head photo with a small caricature body with a flag background of stars and stripes. This set is referred on the back as Series No. 2 and has a red, white, and blue background behind the picture on the front of the card. Cards 1-10 are pro football players and the remainder are pro basketball (17-21, 23-25) and hockey (11-16, 22) players.

COMPLETE SET (25) 75.00 150.00
11 Phil Esposito 4.00 8.00
12 Dennis Hull 1.50 4.00
13 Brad Park 2.00 5.00
14 Tom Lysiak 1.50 4.00
15 Bernie Parent 2.00 5.00
16 Mickey Redmond 1.50 4.00
22 Don Awrey 1.50 4.00

1976 Nabisco Sugar Daddy 1

This set of 25 tiny (approximately 1 1/16" by 2 3/4") cards features action scenes from a variety of popular sports from around the world. One card was included in specially marked Sugar Daddy and Sugar Mama candy bars. The set is referred to as "Sugar Daddy Sports World - Series 1" on the backs of the cards. The cards are in color with a relatively wide white border around the front of the cards.

COMPLETE SET (25) 40.00 80.00
1 Hockey 5.00 10.00

1976 Nabisco Sugar Daddy 2

This set of 25 tiny (approximately 1 1/16" by 2 3/4") cards features action scenes from a variety of popular sports from around the world. One card was included in specially marked Sugar Daddy and Sugar Mama candy bars. The set is referred to as "Sugar Daddy Sports World - Series 2" on the backs of the cards. The cards are in color with a relatively wide white border around the front of the cards.

COMPLETE SET (25) 40.00 80.00
11 Hockey 5.00 10.00

2004 National Trading Card Day

This 53-card set (49 basic cards plus four cover cards) was given out in five separate sealed packs (one from each of the following manufacturers: Donruss, Fleer, Press Pass, Topps and Upper Deck). One of the five packs was distributed at no cost to each patron that visited a participating sports card shop on April 3rd, 2004 as part of the National Trading Card Day promotion in an effort to increase awareness of collecting sports cards. The 50-card set is composed of 16 baseball, 9 basketball, 10 football, 4 golf, 5 hockey and 4 NASCAR cards. Of note, first year cards of NBA rookie stars LeBron James and Carmelo Anthony were included respectively within the UD and Fleer packs. An early Alex Rodriguez Yankees card was also highlighted within the Fleer pack.

F1-F9 ISSUED IN FLEER PACK
T1-T12 ISSUED IN TOPPS PACK
DP1-DP6 ISSUED IN DONRUSS PACK
PP1-PP7 ISSUED IN PRESS PASS PACK
UD1-UD15 ISSUED IN UPPER DECK PACK
T7 Rick Nash .20 .50
T8 Jean-Sebastien Giguere .30 .75
T12 Jaromir Jagr .40 1.00
UD10 Patrick Roy .40 1.00
UD15 Wayne Gretzky .50 1.25

1982-83 Neilson's Gretzky

This 50-card set was issued to honor Wayne Gretzky. The cards measured 2 1/2" by 3 1/2". The first nine cards featured vintage black and white photos from Gretzky's childhood up to age 17. The rest of the cards featured color action photos highlighting Gretzky's pro career. All the pictures on the cards are framed by white and orange borders in a dark blue frame. The card number appears in a star at the upper left hand corner of the card front. A facsimile autograph was inscribed across the bottom of each picture. The card backs had captions to the pictures and include a discussion of some aspect of the game. The card backs were bilingual, i.e., French and English. Many of these discussions were accompanied by illustrations. The cards were issued as inserts with Neilson's candy bars.

COMPLETE SET (50) 60.00 150.00
1 Discard Broken Stick 4.00 10.00
2 Handling the Puck 2.00 5.00
3 Offsides 2.00 5.00
4 Penalty Shot 2.00 5.00
5 Icing the Puck 2.00 5.00
6 Taping your Stick 2.00 5.00
7 Skates 2.00 5.00
8 The Helmet 2.00 5.00
9 Selecting Skates 2.00 5.00
10 Choosing a Stick (with Gordie Howe) 15.00 30.00
11 General Equipment Care 2.00 5.00
12 The Hook Check (with Marcel Dionne) 3.00 8.00
13 The Hip Check 2.00 5.00
14 Forward Skating (With Mike Gartner) 4.00 10.00
15 Stopping 2.00 5.00
16 Sharp Turning 2.00 5.00
17 Fast Starts 2.00 5.00
18 Backward Skating 2.00 5.00
19 The Grip 2.00 5.00
20 The Wrist Shot 2.00 5.00
21 The Back Hand Shot 2.00 5.00
22 The Slap Shot 2.00 5.00
23 The Flip Shot 2.00 5.00
24 Pass Receiving 2.00 5.00
25 Faking 2.00 5.00
26 Puck Handling 2.00 5.00
27 Deflecting Shots 2.00 5.00
28 One On One 2.00 5.00
29 Keep Your Head Up 2.00 5.00
30 Passing to the Slot 2.00 5.00
31 Winning Face-Offs (with Guy Lafleur and Mike Bossy) 5.00 12.00
32 Forechecking 2.00 5.00
33 Body Checking 2.00 5.00
34 Breaking Out 2.00 5.00
35 The Drop Pass 2.00 5.00
36 Backchecking (with Phil Esposito) 4.00 10.00
37 Using the Boards 2.00 5.00
38 The Power Play 3.00 8.00
39 Passing the Puck 2.00 5.00
40 Clear the Slot 2.00 5.00
41 Leg Lifts 2.00 5.00
42 Balance Exercise 2.00 5.00
43 Leg Stretches 2.00 5.00
44 Hip and Groin Stretch 2.00 5.00
45 Toe Touches (with Mark Messier) 4.00 10.00
46 Goalie Warm Up Drill 2.00 5.00
47 Leg Exercises 2.00 5.00
48 Arm Exercises 2.00 5.00
49 Wrist Exercises 2.00 5.00
50 Flip Pass 3.00 8.00

2002 Nextel NHL All-Star Game

Handed out exclusively at the Nextel booth at the All-Star Fantasy, this 4-card set featured three players per card of either the World or North American team. Collectors had to answer trivia questions to receive the cards. Each card was approximately 7 1/2" x 3 1/2". The cards were unnumbered.

COMPLETE SET (4) 4.00 10.00
1 Rob Blake 1.60 4.00

Patrick Roy
Chris Pronger
2 Brendan Shanahan .80 2.00
Vincent Damphousse
Owen Nolan
3 Jaromir Jagr 1.20 3.00
Sergei Fedorov
Teemu Selanne
4 Nicklas Lidstrom .80 2.00
Dominik Hasek
Sandis Ozolinsh

1974 New York News This Day in Sports

These cards are newspaper clippings of drawings by Hollreiser and are accompanied by textual description highlighting a player's unique sports feat. Cards are approximately 2" X 4 1/4". These are multisport cards and aranged in chronological order.

COMPLETE SET 50.00 120.00
34 Bobby Orr 2.00 4.00
Nov. 15, 1973

1974-75 NHL Action Stamps

This set of NHL Action Stamps was distributed throughout North America in large grocery chains such as Loblaw's, IGA, A and P, and Acme. Some of these small stickers (or stamps) mentioned the particular grocery store on back; others had blank backs. A strip of eight player stamps was given out with a grocery purchase. The stamps measured approximately 1 5/8" by 2 1/8". These unnumbered stamps were ordered below alphabetically by teams as follows, Atlanta Flames (1-18), Boston Bruins (19-36), Buffalo Sabres (37-54), California Golden Seals (55-72), Chicago Blackhawks (73-90), Detroit Red Wings (91-108), Los Angeles Kings (109-126), Minnesota North Stars (127-144), Montreal Canadiens (145-162), New York Islanders (163-180), New York Rangers (181-198), Philadelphia Flyers (199-216), Pittsburgh Penguins (217-234), St. Louis Blues (235-252), Toronto Maple Leafs (253-270), Vancouver Canucks (271-288), Kansas City Scouts (289-306), and Washington Capitals (307-324). An album was available for this set which included 20 stamps in the back. Some of the stamps (29, 57, 94, and 164) were only available in the album. Intact strips would be valued at 50 to 75 percent more than the sum of the respective player prices listed below.

COMPLETE SET (324) 100.00 200.00
1 Eric Vail .25 .50
2 Jerry Byers .18 .35
3 Rey Comeau .18 .35
4 Curt Bennett .18 .35
5 Bob Murray .18 .35
6 Don Bouchard .50 1.00
7 Pat Quinn .50 1.00
8 Larry Romanchych .18 .35
9 Randy Manery .18 .35
10 Phil Myre .50 1.00
11 Buster Harvey .18 .35
12 Keith McCreary .18 .35
13 Jean Lemieux .18 .35
14 Arnie Brown .18 .35
15 Bob Leiter .18 .35
16 Jacques Richard .25 .50
17 Noel Price .18 .35
18 Tom Lysiak .38 .75
19 Bobby Orr 10.00 20.00
20 Al Sims .25 .50
21 Don Marcotte .18 .35
22 Terry O'Reilly .50 1.00
23 Carol Vadnais .18 .35
24 Gilles Gilbert .75 1.50
25 Bobby Schmautz .25 .50
26 Phil Esposito 2.50 5.00
27 Walt McKechnie .25 .50
28 Ken Hodge .38 .75
29 Dave Forbes .18 .35
30 Wayne Cashman .38 .75
31 Johnny Bucyk .75 1.50
32 Ross Brooks .25 .50
33 Dallas Smith .18 .35
34 Darryl Edestrand .18 .35
35 Gregg Sheppard .18 .35
36 Andre Savard .25 .50
37 Jim Schoenfeld .38 .75
38 Brian Spencer .38 .75
39 Rick Dudley .25 .50
40 Craig Ramsay .18 .35
41 Gary Bromley .38 .75
42 Lee Fogolin .18 .35
43 Jerry Korab .18 .35
44 Larry Mickey .18 .35
45 Roger Crozier .50 1.00
46 Larry Carriere .18 .35
47 Norm Gratton .18 .35
48 Jim Lorentz .18 .35
49 Rene Robert .38 .75
50 Gilbert Perreault 2.00 4.00
(74/75 season on back)
51 Mike Robitaille .18 .35
52 Don Luce .18 .35
53 Richard Martin .38 .75
54 Gerry Meehan .25 .50
55 Bruce Affleck .18 .35
56 Wayne King .18 .35
57 Joseph Johnston .18 .35
58 Ron Huston .18 .35
59 Dave Hrechkosy .18 .35
60 Stan Gilbertson .18 .35
61 Mike Christie .18 .35
62 Larry Wright .18 .35
63 Stan Weir .18 .35
64 Larry Patey .18 .35
65 Al MacAdam .25 .50
66 Ted McAneeley .18 .35
67 Jim Neilson .18 .35
68 Rick Hampton .18 .35
69 Len Frig .18 .35
70 Gilles Meloche .38 .75
71 Robert Stewart .18 .35
72 Craig Patrick .38 .75
73 Dennis Hull .38 .75
74 Dale Tallon .25 .50
75 Bill White .25 .50
76 Jim Pappin .18 .35
77 Cliff Koroll .18 .35
78 Tony Esposito 2.50 5.00
79 Doug Jarrett .18 .35
80 John Marks .18 .35
81 Stan Mikita 2.00 4.00
82 Darcy Rota .18 .35
83 J.P. Bordeleau .18 .35
84 Ivan Boldirev .18 .35
85 Germaine Gagnon UER .18 .35
86 Dick Redmond .18 .35
87 Pit Martin .18 .35
88 Keith Magnuson .25 .50
89 Phil Russell .18 .35
90 Chico Maki .25 .50
91 Jean Hamel .18 .35
92 Nick Libett .25 .50
93 Hank Nowak .18 .35
94 Guy Charron .25 .50
95 Bryan Watson .18 .35
96 Nelson Pyatt .18 .35
97 Billy Lochead .18 .35
98 Danny Grant .25 .50
99 Bill Hogaboam .18 .35
100 Jim Rutherford .50 1.00
101 Doug Grant .18 .35
102 Pierre Jarry .18 .35
103 Doug Roberts .18 .35
104 Red Berenson .38 .75
105 Marcel Dionne 1.75 3.50
106 Mickey Redmond .75 1.50
107 Jack Lynch .18 .35
108 Thommie Bergman .18 .35
109 Mike Corrigan .18 .35
110 Frank St.Marseille .18 .35
111 Gene Carr .18 .35
112 Neil Komadoski .18 .35
113 Gary Edwards .38 .75
114 Sheldon Kannegiesser .18 .35
115 Bob Murdoch .18 .35
116 Rogatien Vachon 1.25 3.00
117 Dave Hutchinson .18 .35
118 Tom Williams .18 .35
119 Butch Goring .38 .75
120 Bob Berry .25 .50
121 Dan Maloney .25 .50
122 Mike Murphy .18 .35
123 Juha Widing .25 .50
124 Don Kozak .18 .35
125 Bob Nevin .18 .35
126 Terry Harper .25 .50
127 Bill Goldsworthy .38 .75
128 Dennis O'Brien .18 .35
129 Dennis Hextall .25 .50
130 Murray Oliver .18 .35
131 Lou Nanne .25 .50
132 Fred Stanfield .18 .35
133 Jean-Paul Parise .25 .50
134 Tom Reid .18 .35
135 Fred Barrett .18 .35
136 Gary Bergman .18 .35
137 Barry Gibbs .18 .35
138 Cesare Maniago .50 1.00
139 Jude Drouin .18 .35
140 Blake Dunlop .18 .35
141 Henry Boucha .25 .50
142 Fern Rivard .18 .35
143 Chris Ahrens .18 .35
144 Don Martineau .18 .35
145 Jacques Lemaire .75 1.50
146 Peter Mahovlich .38 .75
147 Yvon Lambert .18 .35
148 Yvan Cournoyer 1.25 2.50
149 Michel Larocque .38 .75
150 Guy Lapointe .50 1.00
151 Steve Shutt 1.50 3.00
152 Guy Lafleur 3.50 7.00
153 Larry Robinson 1.00 2.00
154 Jacques Laperriere .38 .75
155 Chuck Lefley .18 .35
156 Henri Richard 1.25 2.50
157 Claude Larose .18 .35
158 Ken Dryden 6.00 12.00
159 Pierre Bouchard .18 .35
160 Murray Wilson .18 .35
161 Jim Roberts .25 .50
162 Serge Savard .50 1.00
163 Clark Gillies 1.25 2.50
164 Garry Howatt .18 .35
165 Ernie Hicke .18 .35
166 Craig Cameron .18 .35
167 Ralph Stewart .18 .35
168 Lorne Henning .18 .35
169 Glenn Resch .50 1.00
170 Bill MacMillan .18 .35
171 Doug Rombough .18 .35
172 Jean Potvin .18 .35
173 Gerry Hart .18 .35
174 Bert Marshall .18 .35
175 Billy Harris .18 .35
176 Bob Nystrom .38 .75
177 Dave Lewis .18 .35
178 Billy Smith 1.00 2.00
179 Denis Potvin 4.00 8.00
180 Ed Westfall .25 .50
181 Jerry Butler .18 .35
182 Bobby Rousseau .25 .50
183 Ron Harris .18 .35
184 Bill Fairbairn .18 .35
185 Derek Sanderson 1.50 3.00
186 Jean Ratelle 1.00 2.00
187 Greg Polis .18 .35
188 Rod Gilbert 1.00 2.00
189 Ed Giacomin 1.00 2.00
190 Rod Seiling .18 .35
191 Dale Rolfe .18 .35
192 Walt Tkaczuk .25 .50
193 Pete Stemkowski .25 .50
194 Gilles Villemure .38 .75
195 Ted Irvine .18 .35
196 Brad Park 1.00 2.00
197 Gilles Marotte .25 .50
198 Steve Vickers .25 .50
199 Ross Lonsberry .18 .35
200 Bob Kelly .25 .50
201 Reggie Leach .38 .75
202 Bernie Parent 1.75 3.50
203 Terry Crisp .38 .75
204 Bill Clement .50 1.00
205 Bill Barber .50 1.00
206 Dave Schultz .50 1.00
207 Ed Van Impe .18 .35
208 Jimmy Watson .25 .50
209 Tom Bladon .18 .35
210 Rick MacLeish .38 .75
211 Andre Dupont .25 .50
212 Orest Kindrachuk .25 .50
213 Gary Dornhoefer .38 .75
214 Joe Watson .25 .50
215 Don Saleski .18 .35
216 Bobby Clarke 3.00 6.00
217 Jean Pronovost .38 .75
218 Ab DeMarco .18 .35
219 Wayne Bianchin .18 .35
220 Dave Burrows .18 .35
221 Ron Lalonde .18 .35
222 Syl Apps .38 .75
223 Bob Kelly .18 .35
224 Chuck Arnason .18 .35
225 Steve Durbano .18 .35
226 Ron Schock .18 .35
227 Bob Paradise .18 .35
228 Ron Stackhouse .18 .35
229 Lowell MacDonald .25 .50
230 Bob Johnson .18 .35
231 Rick Kehoe .38 .75
232 Nelson Debenedet .18 .35
233 Vic Hadfield .25 .50
234 Denis Herron .50 1.00
235 Phil Roberto .18 .35
236 Floyd Thomson .18 .35
237 Don Awrey .18 .35
238 Rick Wilson .18 .35
239 John Davidson 1.50 3.00
240 Pierre Plante .18 .35
241 Barclay Plager .38 .75
242 Larry Giroux .18 .35
243 Bob Gassoff .38 .75
244 Dave Gardner .18 .35
245 Brian Ogilvie .18 .35
246 Ed Johnston .50 1.00
247 Bob Plager .25 .50
248 Wayne Merrick .18 .35
249 Larry Sacharuk .18 .35
250 Bill Collins .18 .35
251 Garnet Bailey .18 .35
252 Garry Unger .38 .75
253 Gary Sabourin .18 .35
254 Willie Brossart .18 .35
255 Tim Ecclestone .18 .35
256 Dave Keon .75 1.50
257 Darryl Sittler 1.50 3.00
258 Inge Hammarstrom .18 .35
259 Ian Turnbull .25 .50
260 Jim McKenny .18 .35
261 Norm Ullman .75 1.50
262 Doug Favell .50 1.00
263 Bob Neely .18 .35
264 Lanny McDonald 1.50 3.00
265 Dunc Wilson .38 .75
266 Errol Thompson .18 .35
267 Brian Glennie .18 .35
268 Bill Flett .18 .35
269 Borje Salming .75 1.50
270 Ron Ellis .25 .50
271 Dave Dunn .18 .35
272 Chris Oddleifson .18 .35
273 Barry Wilkins .18 .35
274 Gary Smith .38 .75
275 Dennis Ververgaert .18 .35
276 Jocelyn Guevremont .18 .35
277 Andre Boudrias .25 .50
278 John Gould .18 .35
279 Jim Wiley .18 .35
280 Bob Dailey .18 .35
281 Tracy Pratt .18 .35
282 Ken Lockett .18 .35
283 Paulin Bordeleau .18 .35
284 Gerry O'Flaherty .18 .35
285 Bryan McSheffrey .18 .35
286 Gregg Boddy .18 .35
287 Don Lever .25 .50
288 Dennis Kearns .18 .35
289 Robin Burns .18 .35
290 Gary Coalter .18 .35
291 John Wright .18 .35
292 Peter McDuffe .38 .75
293 Simon Nolet .18 .35
294 Ted Snell .18 .35
295 Gary Croteau .18 .35
296 Lynn Powis .18 .35
297 Dave Hudson .18 .35
298 Richard Lemieux .18 .35
299 Bryan Lefley .18 .35
300 Doug Horbul .18 .35
301 Brent Hughes .18 .35
302 Ed Gilbert .18 .35
303 Michel Plasse .38 .75
304 Dennis Patterson .18 .35
305 Randy Rota .18 .35
306 Chris Evans .18 .35
307 Bill Mikkelson .18 .35
308 Ron Low .50 1.00
309 Doug Mohns .25 .50
310 Joe Lundrigan .18 .35
311 Steve Atkinson .18 .35
312 Ron Anderson .18 .35
313 Mike Marson .38 .75
314 Lew Morrison .18 .35
315 Jack Egers .18 .35
316 Gordy Brooks .18 .35
317 Pete Laframboise .18 .35
318 Mike Bloom .18 .35
319 Bob Collyard .18 .35
320 Dave Kryskow .18 .35
321 Greg Joly .18 .35
322 Jim Hrycuik .18 .35
323 Bob Gryp .18 .35
324 Larry Fullan .18 .35
NNO Album 10.00 20.00

1974-75 NHL Action Stamps Update

A group of 43 previously uncatalogued NHL Action (Loblaw's) stamps had been reported. Thirty-six of these stamps are recropped or airbrushed versions of original stamps listing the player's new team. The remaining seven were completely new stamps to replace nine originals dropped from the set. The discrepancy between the seven added and the nine dropped stamps had led some to speculate that there were at least two other stamps in the set, all the more so since two teams (Islanders and Vancouver) have one less player than all the other teams. These stamps were grouped alphabetically within teams and checklisted below alphabetically according to teams as follows: Atlanta Flames (1), Boston Bruins (2), Buffalo Sabres (3-5), California Golden Seals (6-8), Detroit Red Wings (9-13), Kansas City Scouts (14-16), Minnesota North Stars (17-21), Montreal Canadiens (22-23), New York Islanders (24-25), New York Rangers (26), Pittsburgh Penguins (27-29), St. Louis Blues (30-34), Toronto Maple Leafs (35-37), Vancouver Canucks (38-40), and Washington Capitals (41-43).

COMPLETE SET (43) 25.00 50.00
1 Barry Gibbs .50 1.00
2 Henry Nowak .50 1.00
3 Jocelyn Guevremont .50 1.00
4 Bryan McSheffrey .50 1.00
5 Fred Stanfield .50 1.00
6 Dave Gardner .50 1.00
7 Morris Mott NEW .50 1.00
8 Gary Simmons NEW 2.00 4.00
9 Gary Bergman .75 1.50
10 Dave Kryskow .50 1.00
11 Walt McKechnie .50 1.00
12 Phil Roberto .50 1.00
13 Ted Snell .50 1.00
14 Guy Charron .75 1.50
15 Jean-Guy Lagace NEW .50 1.00
16 Denis Herron 2.00 4.00
17 Craig Cameron .50 1.00
18 John Flesch NEW .50 1.00
19 Norm Gratton .50 1.00
20 Ernie Hicke .50 1.00
21 Doug Rombough .50 1.00
22 Don Awrey .50 1.00
23 Wayne Thomas NEW 2.00 4.00
24 Jude Drouin .50 1.00
25 Jean Paul Parise .50 1.00
26 Rick Middleton NEW 2.50 5.00
27 Lew Morrison .50 1.00
28 Michel Plasse 2.00 4.00
29 Barry Wilkins .50 1.00
30 Red Berenson .75 1.50
31 Chris Evans .50 1.00
32 Claude Larose .50 1.00
33 Chuck Lefley .50 1.00
34 Craig Patrick .75 1.50
35 Dave Dunn .50 1.00
36 George Ferguson NEW .50 1.00
37 Rod Seiling .50 1.00
38 Ab Demarco .50 1.00
39 Gerry Meehan .50 1.00
40 Mike Robitaille .50 1.00
41 Willie Brossart .50 1.00
42 Ron Lalonde .50 1.00
43 Jack Lynch .50 1.00

1995-96 NHL Aces Playing Cards

This 55 standard-size playing card set featured National Hockey League players. The fronts of these rounded-corner cards featured full-color action player shots. The team logo appear in the upper right of each picture. The player's name and position appeared in either a blue or aqua stripe at the bottom. The backs had the NHL Aces design and sponsor logos on a black background. Since this set was similar to a playing card set, the set was checklisted below as if it were a playing card deck. In the checklist C meant Clubs, D meant Diamonds, H meant Hearts and S meant Spades. The cards were checklisted in playing order by suits and numbers are assigned to Aces (1), Jacks (11), Queens (12) and Kings (13).

COMPLETE SET (55) 6.00 15.00
1C Paul Coffey .25 .60
1D Wayne Gretzky 1.25 3.00
1H Eric Lindros .60 1.50
1S Patrick Roy 1.00 2.50
2C Scott Stevens .01 .05
2D Al MacInnis .01 .05
2H Craig Janney .01 .05
2S Kirk Muller .01 .05
3C Bill Ranford .05 .15
3D Mike Modano .25 .60
3H Doug Gilmour .25 .60
3S Steve Yzerman .60 1.50
4C Brian Bradley .01 .05
4D Alexandre Daigle .01 .05
4H Claude Lemieux .05 .15
4S Felix Potvin .15 .40
5C Ed Belfour .25 .60
5D Jeremy Roenick .25 .60
5H Trevor Linden .02 .10
5S Pat Lafontaine .05 .15
6C Brian Leetch .25 .60
6D Jason Arnott .02 .10
6H Geoff Sanderson .01 .05
6S Jim Carey .15 .40
7C Ron Francis .05 .15
7D Peter Bondra .25 .60
7H Paul Kariya .75 2.00
7S John Vanbiesbrouck .20 .50
8C Teemu Selanne .40 1.00
8D Ray Bourque .25 .60
8H Pierre Turgeon .05 .15
8S Alexei Yashin .15 .40
9C Martin Brodeur .50 1.25
9D Pavel Bure .50 1.25
9H Peter Forsberg .50 1.25
9S Chris Chelios .25 .60
10C Joe Nieuwendyk .07 .20
10D Mats Sundin .25 .60
10H Adam Oates .05 .15
10S Cam Neely .07 .20
11C Mark Messier .25 .60
11D Brett Hull .25 .60
11H Sergei Fedorov .40 1.00
11S Keith Tkachuk .25 .60
12C Mikael Renberg .05 .15
12D Jaromir Jagr .60 1.50
12H Mario Lemieux 1.00 2.50
12S John Leclair .30 .75
13C Joe Sakic .40 1.00
13D Dominik Hasek .40 1.00
13H Alexei Zhamnov .02 .10
13S Theo Fleury .25 .60
NNO Eastern Conference Logo .01 .05
NNO Checklist of Players in Deck .01 .05
NNO Western Conference Logo .01 .05

1996-97 NHL Aces Playing Cards

This 55-card set was standard playing card size and featured NHL players in action. A color action photo took up the bulk of the front, with the team logo in the upper right corner. The suits and numbers were located in the upper left and lower right hand corners. Player name and position could be found along the bottom. If the player was a finalist for or winner of any major NHL award, that achievement was noted with a golden icon in the lower left corner. The backs carried a uniformly indistinguishable NHL Hockey Aces logo.

COMPLETE SET (55) 4.80 12.00
1 Daniel Alfredsson .10 .30
2 Jason Arnott .10 .30
3 Ray Bourque .30 .75
4 Rod Brind'Amour .10 .30
5 Martin Brodeur .30 .75
6 Pavel Bure .30 .75
7 Jim Carey .08 .25
8 Chris Chelios .10 .30
9 Vincent Damphousse .05 .15
10 Eric Daze .08 .25
11 Sergei Fedorov .30 .75
12 Ray Ferraro .02 .10
13 Theo Fleury .10 .30
14 Peter Forsberg .30 .75
15 Ron Francis .10 .30
16 Grant Fuhr .07 .20
17 Mike Gartner .05 .15
18 Doug Gilmour .10 .30
19 Travis Green .02 .10
20 Wayne Gretzky .75 2.00
21 Roman Hamrlik .05 .15
22 Brett Hull .15 .40
23 Jaromir Jagr .40 1.00
24 Ed Jovanovski .07 .20
25 Joe Juneau .07 .20
26 Paul Kariya .40 1.00
27 Pat LaFontaine .08 .25
28 Brian Leetch .10 .30
29 Mario Lemieux .60 1.50
30 Trevor Linden .10 .30
31 Eric Lindros .30 .75
32 Mark Messier .15 .40
33 Mike Modano .15 .40
34 Alexander Mogilny .08 .25
35 Owen Nolan .10 .30
36 Adam Oates .10 .30
37 Chris Osgood .10 .30
38 Daren Puppa .05 .15
39 Gary Roberts .05 .15
40 Jeremy Roenick .10 .30
41 Patrick Roy .60 1.50
42 Joe Sakic .30 .75
43 Teemu Selanne .30 .75
44 Brendan Shanahan .30 .75
45 Mats Sundin .10 .30
46 Jocelyn Thibault .08 .25
47 Keith Tkachuk .10 .30
48 Pierre Turgeon .08 .25
49 John Vanbiesbrouck .10 .30
50 Doug Weight .10 .30
51 Alexei Yashin .08 .25
52 Steve Yzerman .60 1.50
NNO Checklist .02 .10
NNO Western Conference .02 .10
NNO Eastern Conference .02 .10

1997-98 NHL Aces Playing Cards

COMPLETE SET (55) 8.00 20.00
1 Dominik Hasek .40 1.00
2 Mike Vernon .08 .25
3 Doug Gilmour .20 .50
4 Dimitri Kristich .02 .10
5 Mark Recchi .08 .25
6 Daniel Alfredsson .08 .25
7 Eric Lindros .08 .25
8 Keith Tkachuk .08 .25
9 Pavel Bure .30 .75
10 Brendan Shanahan .30 .75
11 Sandis Ozolinsh .02 .10
12 Mark Messier .30 .75
13 Patrick Roy .75 2.00
14 Paul Kariya .30 .75
15 Ray Bourque .40 1.00
16 Ryan Smyth .08 .25
17 Jarome Iginla .40 1.00
18 Chris Gratton .02 .10
19 Jeremy Roenick .40 1.00
20 Mike Modano .40 1.00
21 Doug Weight .08 .25
22 Jim Campbell .02 .10
23 Sheldon Kennedy .02 .10
24 Jason Arnott .02 .10
25 Peter Forsberg .40 1.00
26 Brian Leetch .40 1.00
27 Mike Peca .02 .10
28 Jere Lehtinen .08 .25
29 Trevor Linden .40 1.00
30 John Leclair .08 .25
31 Owen Nolan .08 .25
32 Pierre Turgeon .02 .10
33 Tony Amonte .02 .10
34 Alexei Yashin .02 .10
35 Mats Sundin .40 1.00
36 Jaromir Jagr .60 1.50
37 Wayne Gretzky 1.25 3.00
38 Martin Brodeur .60 1.50
39 Tony Granato .02 .10
40 Bryan Berard .02 .10
41 Geoff Sanderson .02 .10
42 Chris Chelios .20 .50
43 Felix Potvin .30 .75
44 Adam Oates .08 .25
45 Roman Hamrlik .02 .10
46 Theoren Fleury .08 .25
47 Vincent Damphousse .02 .10
48 Zigmund Palffy .08 .25
49 Saku Koivu .40 1.00
50 Teemu Selanne .40 1.00
51 John Vanbiesbrouck .20 .50
52 Vladimir Konstantinov .40 1.00
NNO Checklist .01 .01
NNO Eastern Conference .01 .01
NNO Western Conference .01 .01

1998-99 NHL Aces Playing Cards

COMPLETE SET (55) 6.00 15.00
1 Olaf Kolzig .20 .50
2 Marcel Cousineau .08 .25
3 Corey Schwab .08 .25
4 Dwayne Roloson .08 .25
5 Mark Fitzpatrick .08 .25
6 Guy Herbert .08 .25
7 Jamie McLennan .08 .25
8 Rick Tabaracci .08 .25
9 Jose Theodore .40 1.00
10 Grant Fuhr .40 1.00
11 Ed Belfour .40 1.00
12 Felix Potvin .40 1.00
13 Damian Rhodes .08 .25
14 Patrick Roy 1.00 2.50
15 Ken Wregget .08 .25
16 Bill Ranford .08 .25
17 Jamie Storr .08 .25
18 Chris Terreri .08 .25
19 Kelly Hrudey .08 .25
20 Ron Tugnutt .08 .25
21 Mike Vernon .08 .25
22 Mikhail Shtalenkov .08 .25
23 Darren Puppa .08 .25
24 Bryon Dafoe .08 .25
25 Arthurs Irbe .20 .50
26 Chris Osgood .20 .50
27 Dominik Hasek .60 1.50
28 Robbie Tallas .08 .25
29 Kirk McLean .08 .25
30 Peter Skudra .08 .25
31 Eric Fichaud .08 .25
32 Bob Essensa .08 .25
33 Sean Burke .08 .25
34 Jocelyn Thibault .08 .25
35 Ron Hextall .40 1.00
36 Nikolai Khabibulin .40 1.00
37 Mike Richter .40 1.00
38 Tommy Salo .08 .25
39 John Vanbiesbrouck .40 1.00
40 Curtis Joseph .40 1.00
41 Glenn Healy .08 .25
42 Mike Dunham .08 .25
43 Roman Turek .08 .25
44 Steve Shields .08 .25
45 Garth Snow .08 .25
46 Kevin Hodson .08 .25
47 Craig Billington .08 .25
48 Trevor Kidd .08 .25
49 Jeff Hackett .08 .25
50 Stephane Fiset .08 .25
51 Tom Barrasso .20 .50
52 Martin Brodeur .75 2.00
NNO Checklist .01 .01
NNO Eastern Conference .01 .01
NNO Western Conference .01 .01

1995-96 NHL Cool Trade

This 20-card standard-size set was the result of a unique collaboration between the NHL, the NHLPA and the five card manufacturers. Each of the latter created four cards for inclusion in the set, which was available to collectors who sent in 20 wrappers plus postage and handling to a mailing address. The set also was available at the NHLPA booth at the 1996 National Convention for between five and ten wrappers, depending upon when you went to the booth. The set included five different designs, one unique to each contributing manufacturer. There also was the possibility of acquiring limited-edition upgrade versions of the cards. Cool Trade exchange cards were randomly inserted in packs of Bowman, Donruss Elite, Summit, Ultra series 2, and Upper Deck series 2. These could be mailed in to the participating licensee for redemption. The Emotion exchange card inserted in '95-96 Ultra series two was by far the most difficult to acquire. The redemption cards are priced individually below, and have an RP prefix amended to them for cataloguing purposes only, the RP prefix is not on the actual cards.

COMPLETE SET (20) 3.00 10.00
1 Cam Neely .20 .50
2 Wayne Gretzky 1.50 4.00
3 Jeremy Roenick .20 .50
4 Mario Lemieux 1.00 2.50
5 Mark Messier .30 .75
6 Ray Bourque .20 .50
7 Sergei Fedorov .40 1.00
8 Paul Kariya .40 1.00
9 Eric Lindros .40 1.00
10 Pavel Bure .30 .75
11 Chris Chelios .20 .50
12 Peter Forsberg .50 1.25
13 Saku Koivu .20 .50
14 Ed Belfour .20 .50
15 Brett Hull .30 .75
16 Patrick Roy 1.00 2.50
17 Doug Gilmour .20 .50
18 Martin Brodeur .40 1.00
19 Alexander Mogilny .20 .50
20 Jaromir Jagr .30 .75
RP1 Cam Neely .75 2.00
RP2 Wayne Gretzky 6.00 15.00
RP3 Jeremy Roenick 4.00 10.00
RP4 Mario Lemieux 3.00 8.00
RP5 Mark Messier 2.00 5.00
RP6 Ray Bourque 1.00 2.50
RP7 Sergei Fedorov 1.50 4.00
RP8 Paul Kariya 10.00 25.00
RP9 Eric Lindros 1.00 2.50
RP10 Pavel Bure 3.00 8.00
RP11 Chris Chelios .75 2.00
RP12 Peter Forsberg 1.25 3.00
RP13 Saku Koivu 4.00 10.00
RP14 Ed Belfour 1.00 2.50
RP15 Brett Hull 3.00 6.00
RP16 Patrick Roy 5.00 10.00
RP17 Doug Gilmour .75 2.00
RP18 Martin Brodeur 8.00 20.00
RP19 Alexander Mogilny 1.00 2.50
RP20 Jaromir Jagr 2.50 6.00

1996-97 NHL Pro Stamps

This set of 130 postage stamp-style collectibles was released by Chris Martin Enterprises. The series was issued in 12 numbered sheets of 12 stamps each. There were several double prints-they are noted below with a DP suffix.

COMPLETE SET (130) 7.20 18.00
1 Stephane Fiset .05 .15
2 Peter Forsberg .20 .50
3 Claude Lemieux DP .05 .15
4 Mike Ricci .02 .10
5 Joe Sakic .15 .40
6 Ed Belfour .08 .25
7 Chris Chelios .08 .25
8 Joe Murphy .02 .10
9 Bernie Nicholls .02 .10
10 Jeremy Roenick DP .08 .25
11 Geoff Courtnall .02 .10
12 Brett Hull .15 .40
13 Al MacInnis .05 .15
14 Chris Pronger .05 .15
15 Esa Tikkanen .05 .15
16 Ray Bourque .08 .25
17 Blaine Lacher .05 .15
18 Cam Neely .07 .20
19 Adam Oates DP .07 .20
20 Kevin Stevens .02 .10
21 Valeri Bure .02 .10
22 Vincent Damphousse .05 .15
23 Mark Recchi .05 .15
24 Patrick Roy .30 .75
25 Pierre Turgeon .07 .20
26 Pavel Bure .15 .40
27 Trevor Linden .05 .15
28 Kirk McLean .05 .15
29 Alexander Mogilny .08 .25
30 Cliff Ronning .02 .10
31 Jason Allison .02 .10
32 Jim Carey .10 .30
33 Dale Hunter .02 .10
34 Joe Juneau DP .07 .20
35 Brendan Witt .02 .10
36 Martin Brodeur DP .15 .40
37 John MacLean .05 .15
38 Scott Niedermayer .05 .15
39 Stephane Richer .02 .10
40 Scott Stevens .05 .15
41 Patrik Carnback .02 .10
42 Guy Hebert .07 .20
43 Paul Kariya .25 .60
44 Oleg Tverdovsky .05 .15
45 Garry Valk .02 .10
46 Theo Fleury .07 .20
47 Trevor Kidd .05 .15
48 Joe Nieuwendyk .05 .15
49 Gary Roberts .02 .10
50 German Titov .02 .10
51 Rod Brind'Amour .05 .15
52 Ron Hextall .05 .15
53 John LeClair .10 .30
54 Eric Lindros .20 .50
55 Mikael Renberg .07 .20
56 Brett Lindros .02 .10
57 Wendel Clark .05 .15
58 Patrick Flatley .02 .10
59 Kirk Muller .02 .10
60 Mathieu Schneider .02 .10
61 Tim Cheveldae .05 .15
62 Dallas Drake .02 .10
63 Teemu Selanne .15 .40
64 Keith Tkachuk .10 .30
65 Alexei Zhamnov .05 .15
66 Rob Blake .05 .15
67 Wayne Gretzky DP .40 1.00
68 Jari Kurri .05 .15
69 Jamie Storr .05 .15
70 Rick Tocchet .05 .15
71 Brian Bradley .02 .10
72 Chris Gratton .05 .15
73 Roman Hamrlik .05 .15
74 Paul Ysebaert .02 .10
75 Rob Zamuner .02 .10
76 Dave Andreychuk .05 .15
77 Doug Gilmour .08 .25
78 Kenny Jonsson .05 .15
79 Felix Potvin .10 .30
80 Mats Sundin .07 .20
81 Jason Arnott .07 .20
82 Jason Bonsignore .02 .10
83 Todd Marchant .02 .10
84 Bill Ranford .07 .20
85 Doug Weight .07 .20
86 Jody Hull .02 .10
87 Bob Kudelski .02 .10
88 Scott Mellanby .05 .15
89 Rob Niedermayer .05 .15
90 John Vanbiesbrouck .08 .25
91 Ron Francis .07 .20
92 Jaromir Jagr .20 .50
93 Mario Lemieux DP .30 .75
94 Bryan Smolinski .02 .10
95 Sergei Zubov .02 .10
96 Adam Graves .05 .15
97 Brian Leetch .07 .20
98 Mark Messier DP .15 .40
99 Mike Richter .08 .25
100 Luc Robitaille .07 .20
101 Paul Coffey .07 .20
102 Sergei Fedorov DP .15 .40
103 Nicklas Lidstrom .05 .15
104 Ray Sheppard .02 .10
105 Steve Yzerman .20 .50
106 Donald Audette .02 .10
107 Dominik Hasek DP .15 .40
108 Yuri Khmylev .02 .10
109 Pat LaFontaine .05 .15
110 Alexei Zhitnik .02 .10
111 Radek Bonk .02 .10
112 Randy Cunneyworth .02 .10
113 Alexandre Daigle .05 .15
114 Steve Larouche .02 .10
115 Martin Straka .02 .10
116 Ulf Dahlen .02 .10
117 Pat Falloon .02 .10
118 Jeff Friesen .05 .15
119 Arturs Irbe DP .05 .15
120 Craig Janney .02 .10
121 Shane Churla .02 .10
122 Todd Harvey .02 .10
123 Derian Hatcher .02 .10
124 Mike Modano .07 .20
125 Andy Moog .07 .20
126 Sean Burke .05 .15
127 Andrew Cassels .02 .10
128 Geoff Sanderson .05 .15
129 Brendan Shanahan .15 .40
130 Darren Turcotte .02 .10

1994 NHLPA Phone Cards

This set was issued by the Player's Association in 1994. The photos are from the 4 on 4 tournament held in Canada during the NHL lockout. Each card carried the player's name and the denomination of the card on front.

COMPLETE SET (9) 16.00 40.00
1 Doug Gilmour 1.50 4.00
2 Brett Hull 2.00 5.00
3 Paul Kariya 3.00 8.00
4 Eric Lindros 2.50 6.00
5 Luc Robitaille 1.50 4.00
6 Jeremy Roenick 1.50 4.00
7 Patrick Roy 4.00 10.00
8 John Vanbiesbrouck 1.50 4.00
9 Team Ontario 1.25 3.00

2003 NHL Sticker Collection

This 300-card sticker set was sold in packs of 10 stickers. The stickers measured approximately 2" X 1 1/2". A collector album was also available with pages separated by team.

COMPLETE SET (300) 25.00 50.00
1 Atlanta Thrashers .10 .25
Home Logo
2 Atlanta Thrashers .10 .25
Away Logo
3 Dany Heatley .20 .50
4 Ilya Kovalchuk .20 .50
5 Patrik Stefan .10 .25
6 Frantisek Kaberle .10 .25
7 Yannick Tremblay .10 .25
8 Tony Hrkac .10 .25
9 Shawn Mceachern .10 .25
10 Byron Dafoe .10 .25
11 Boston Bruins .10 .25
Home Logo
12 Boston Bruins .10 .25
Away Logo
13 Martin Lapointe .10 .25
14 Glen Murray .20 .50
15 Brian Rolston .10 .25
16 Sergei Samsonov .20 .50
17 Joe Thornton .40 1.00
18 Jozef Stumpel .10 .25
19 Nick Boynton .10 .25
20 Steve Shields .10 .25
21 Buffalo Sabres .10 .25
Home Logo
22 Buffalo Sabres .10 .25
Away Logo
23 Stu Barnes .10 .25
24 Curtis Brown .10 .25
25 Miroslav Satan .20 .50
26 Jochen Hecht .10 .25
27 Tim Connolly .10 .25
28 Jay McKee .10 .25
29 Chris Gratton .10 .25
30 Martin Biron .20 .50

31 Carolina Hurricanes Home Logo .10 .25
32 Carolina Hurricanes Away Logo .10 .25
33 Rod Brind'Amour .20 .50
34 Erik Cole .10 .25
35 Ron Francis .20 .50
36 Sami Kapanen .10 .25
37 Jeff O'Neill .10 .25
38 Bret Hedican .10 .25
39 Sean Hill .10 .25
40 Kevin Weekes .10 .25
41 Florida Panthers Home Logo .10 .25
42 Florida Panthers Away Logo .10 .25
43 Valeri Bure .10 .25
44 Olli Jokinen .10 .25
45 Marcus Nilsson .10 .25
46 Stephen Weiss .10 .25
47 Kristian Huselius .10 .25
48 Sandis Ozolinsh .10 .25
49 Jay Bouwmeester .20 .50
50 Roberto Luongo .60 1.50
51 Montreal Canadians Home Logo .10 .25
52 Montreal Canadians Away Logo .10 .25
53 Randy McKay .10 .25
54 Richard Zednik .10 .25
55 Doug Gilmour .40 1.00
56 Saku Koivu .40 1.00
57 Yanic Perreault .10 .25
58 Craig Rivet .10 .25
59 Patrice Brisebois .10 .25
60 Jose Theodore .30 .75
61 New Jersey Devils Home Logo .10 .25
62 New Jersey Devils Away Logo .10 .25
63 Patrik Elias .10 .25
64 Jeff Friesen .10 .25
65 Joe Nieuwendyk .20 .50
66 Sergei Brylin .10 .25
67 Jamie Langenbrunner .10 .25
68 Scott Stevens .10 .25
69 Scott Niedermayer .20 .50
70 Martin Brodeur .40 1.00
71 New York Islanders Home Logo .10 .25
72 New York Islanders Away Logo .10 .25
73 Shawn Bates .10 .25
74 Brad Isbister .10 .25
75 Mark Parrish .10 .25
76 Michael Peca .10 .25
77 Alexei Yashin .10 .25
78 Kenny Jonsson .10 .25
79 Roman Hamrlik .10 .25
80 Chris Osgood .20 .50
81 New York Rangers Home Logo .10 .25
82 New York Rangers Away Logo .10 .25
83 Pavel Bure .40 1.00
84 Bobby Holik .10 .25
85 Eric Lindros .40 1.00
86 Mark Messier .40 1.00
87 Petr Nedved .10 .25
88 Brian Leetch .20 .50
89 Darius Kasparitis .10 .25
90 Mike Richter .20 .50
91 Ottawa Senators Home Logo .10 .25
92 Ottawa Senators .10 .25
93 Daniel Alfredsson .20 .50
94 Jason Spezza .20 .50
95 Marian Hossa .30 .75
96 Magnus Arvedson .10 .25
97 Martin Havlat .20 .50
98 Wade Redden .10 .25
99 Chris Phillips .10 .25
100 Patrick Lalime .10 .25
101 Philadelphia Flyers Home Logo .10 .25
102 Philadelphia Flyers Away Logo .10 .25
103 Simon Gagne .20 .50
104 John LeClair .10 .25
105 Keith Primeau .10 .25
106 Mark Recchi .20 .50
107 Jeremy Roenick .40 1.00
108 Eric Desjardins .10 .25
109 Kim Johnsson .10 .25
110 Roman Cechmanek .10 .25
111 Pittsburgh Penguins Home Logo .10 .25
112 Pittsburgh Penguins Away Logo .10 .25
113 Jan Hrdina .10 .25
114 Alexei Kovalev .10 .25
115 Mario Lemieux .75 2.00
116 Alexei Morozov .10 .25
117 Wayne Primeau .10 .25
118 Michal Rozsival .10 .25
119 Dick Tarnstrom .10 .25
120 Johan Hedberg .10 .25
121 Tampa Bay Lightning Home Logo .10 .25
122 Tampa Bay Lightning Away Logo .10 .25
123 Dave Andreychuk .10 .25
124 Vincent Lecavalier .40 1.00
125 Vaclav Prospal .10 .25
126 Brad Richards .20 .50
127 Martin St. Louis .20 .50
128 Pavel Kubina .10 .25
129 Dan Boyle .10 .25
130 Nikolai Khabibulin .40 1.00
131 Toronto Maple Leafs Home Logo .10 .25
132 Toronto Maple Leafs Away Logo .10 .25
133 Mats Sundin .40 1.00
134 Tie Domi .10 .25
135 Darcy Tucker .10 .25
136 Alexander Mogilny .10 .25
137 Gary Roberts .10 .25
138 Tomas Kaberle .10 .25
139 Bryan McCabe .10 .25
140 Ed Belfour .40 1.00
141 Washington Capitals Home Logo .10 .25
142 Washington Capitals Away Logo .10 .25
143 Peter Bondra .10 .25
144 Jaromir Jagr .30 .75
145 Robert Lang .10 .25
146 Jeff Halpern .10 .25
147 Sergei Gonchar .10 .25
148 Dainius Zubrus .10 .25
149 Steve Konowalchuk .10 .25
150 Olaf Kolzig .20 .50
151 Anaheim Mighty Ducks Home Logo .10 .25
152 Anaheim Mighty Ducks Away Logo .10 .25
153 Paul Kariya .40 1.00
154 Matt Cullen .10 .25
155 Steve Rucchin .10 .25
156 Mike Leclerc .10 .25
157 Petr Sykora .10 .25
158 Stanislav Chistov .10 .25
159 Keith Carney .10 .25
160 Jean-Sebastien Giguere .20 .50
161 Calgary Flames Home Logo .10 .25
162 Calgary Flames Away Logo .10 .25
163 Craig Conroy .10 .25
164 Jarome Iginla .40 1.00
165 Chris Drury .20 .50
166 Martin Gelinas .10 .25
167 Stephane Yelle .10 .25
168 Denis Gauthier .10 .25
169 Bob Boughner .10 .25
170 Roman Turek .10 .25
171 Chicago Blackhawks Home Logo .10 .25
172 Chicago Blackhawks Away Logo .10 .25
173 Eric Daze .10 .25
174 Steve Sullivan .10 .25
175 Alexei Zhamnov .10 .25
176 Kyle Calder .10 .25
177 Phil Housley .10 .25
178 Tyler Arnason .10 .25
179 Lyle Odelein .10 .25
180 Jocelyn Thibault .20 .50
181 Colorado Avalanche Home Logo .10 .25
182 Colorado Avalanche Away Logo .10 .25
183 Peter Forsberg .40 1.00
184 Milan Hejduk .20 .50
185 Joe Sakic .40 1.00
186 Alex Tanguay .20 .50
187 Rob Blake .10 .25
188 Adam Foote .10 .25
189 Derek Morris .10 .25
190 Patrick Roy .75 2.00
191 Columbus Blue Jackets Home Logo .10 .25
192 Columbus Blue Jackets Away Logo .10 .25
193 Rick Nash .40 1.00
194 Geoff Sanderson .10 .25
195 Andrew Cassels .10 .25
196 Ray Whitney .10 .25
197 Luke Richardson .10 .25
198 Scott Lachance .10 .25
199 Mike Sillinger .10 .25
200 Marc Denis .10 .25
201 Dallas Stars Home Logo .10 .25
202 Dallas Stars Away Logo .10 .25
203 Ulf Dahlen .10 .25
204 Bill Guerin .10 .25
205 Mike Modano .30 .75
206 Pierre Turgeon .10 .25
207 Scott Young .10 .25
208 Sergei Zubov .10 .25
209 Darryl Sydor .10 .25
210 Marty Turco .20 .50
211 Detriot Red Wings Home Logo .10 .25
212 Detriot Red Wings Away Logo .10 .25
213 Sergei Fedorov .20 .50
214 Brett Hull .30 .75
215 Brendan Shanahan .20 .50
216 Steve Yzerman .75 2.00
217 Chris Chelios .20 .50
218 Nicklas Lidstrom .20 .50
219 Kris Draper .10 .25
220 Curtis Joseph .20 .50
221 Edmonton Oilers Home Logo .10 .25
222 Edmonton Oilers Away Logo .10 .25
223 Anson Carter .10 .25
224 Mike Comrie .10 .25
225 Ryan Smyth .20 .50
226 Mike York .10 .25
227 Eric Brewer .10 .25
228 Jason Smith .10 .25
229 Janne Niinimaa .10 .25
230 Tommy Salo .10 .25
231 Los Angeles Kings Home Logo .10 .25
232 Los Angeles Kings Away Logo .10 .25
233 Jason Allison .10 .25
234 Adam Deadmarsh .10 .25
235 Bryan Smolinski .10 .25
236 Mathieu Schneider .10 .25
237 Jaroslav Modry .10 .25
238 Zigmund Palffy .20 .50
239 Lubomir Visnovsky .10 .25
240 Felix Potvin .20 .50
241 Minnesota Wild Home Logo .10 .25
242 Minnesota Wild Away Logo .10 .25
243 Andrew Brunette .10 .25
244 Marian Gaborik .40 1.00
245 Cliff Ronning .10 .25
246 Sergei Zholtok .10 .25
247 Jim Dowd .10 .25
248 Antti Laaksonen .10 .25
249 Willie Mitchell .10 .25
250 Manny Fernandez .20 .50
251 Nashville Predators Home Logo .10 .25
252 Nashville Predators Away Logo .10 .25
253 Andreas Johansson .10 .25
254 Greg Johnson .10 .25
255 Denis Arkhipov .10 .25
256 David Legwand .10 .25
257 Vladimir Orszagh .10 .25
258 Andy Delmore .10 .25
259 Kimmo Timonen .10 .25
260 Tomas Vokoun .20 .50
261 Phoenix Coyotes Home Logo .10 .25
262 Phoenix Coyotes Away Logo .10 .25
263 Tony Amonte .10 .25
264 Daniel Briere .10 .25
265 Shane Doan .10 .25
266 Daymond Langkow .10 .25
267 Ladislav Nagy .10 .25
268 Teppo Numminen .10 .25
269 Danny Markov .10 .25
270 Sean Burke .20 .50
271 St. Louis Blues Home Logo .10 .25
272 St. Louis Blues Away Logo .10 .25
273 Pavol Demitra .10 .25
274 Cory Stillman .10 .25
275 Keith Tkachuk .20 .50
276 Doug Weight .10 .25
277 Al MacInnis .20 .50
278 Chris Pronger .20 .50
279 Eric Boguniecki .10 .25
280 Brent Johnson .10 .25
281 San Jose Sharks Home Logo .10 .25
282 San Jose Sharks Away Logo .10 .25
283 Vincent Damphousse .10 .25
284 Adam Graves .10 .25
285 Patrick Marleau .20 .50
286 Owen Nolan .10 .25
287 Teemu Selanne .30 .75
288 Marco Sturm .10 .25
289 Mike Ricci .10 .25
290 Evgeni Nabokov .20 .50
291 Vancouver Canucks Home Logo .10 .25
292 Vancouver Canucks Away Logo .10 .25
293 Todd Bertuzzi .20 .50
294 Trevor Linden .40 1.00
295 Brendan Morrison .10 .25
296 Markus Naslund .20 .50
297 Henrik Sedin .10 .25
298 Ed Jovanovski .10 .25
299 Mattias Ohlund .10 .25
300 Dan Cloutier .10 .25

1996 No Fear

This eight-card jumbo-sized set was issued through No Fear. It is a multi-sport set that features a posed color player shot on the front and a white back featuring a slogan by No Fear. The mode of distribution is unclear. The cards are not numbered and checklisted below in alphabetical order.

COMPLETE SET (8) 5.00 12.00
2 Theoren Fleury HK .40 1.00
3 Grant Fuhr HK 1.20 3.00

1972-73 Nordiques Postcards

This standard size postcard featured color photos surrounded by a white border. Card fronts featured a facsimile autograph and were issued by Pro Star Promotions. Backs were blank. The postcards were unnumbered and checklisted below in alphabetical order.

COMPLETE SET (22) 20.00 40.00
1 Michel Archambeault 1.00 2.00
2 Serge Aubry 1.00 2.00
3 Yves Bergeron 1.00 2.00
4 Jacques Blain 1.00 2.00
5 Alain Caron 1.00 2.00
6 Ken Desjardine 1.00 2.00
7 Maurice Filion 1.00 2.00
8 Andre Gaudette 1.00 2.00
9 Jean-Guy Gendron 1.00 2.00
10 Rejean Giroux 1.00 2.00
11 Frank Golembrosky 1.00 2.00
12 Robert Guindon 1.00 2.00
13 Pierre Guite 1.00 2.00
14 Francois Lacombe 1.00 2.00
15 Paul Larose 1.00 2.00
16 Jacques Lemelin 1.00 2.00
17 Michel Parizeau 1.00 2.00
18 Jean Payette 1.00 2.00
19 Michel Rouleau 1.00 2.00
20 Pierre Roy 1.00 2.00
21 J.C. Tremblay 1.50 3.00
NNO Header Card .50 1.00

1973-74 Nordiques Team Issue

This 21-card team issue set featured the 1973-74 Quebec Nordiques of the World Hockey Association. The oversized cards measured approximately 3 1/2" by 5 1/2". The fronts featured glossy color posed photos with white borders. The team and WHA logos were superimposed in the upper corners of the picture. A facsimile autograph was inscribed across the bottom of the picture. The backs were blank. The cards were unnumbered and checklisted below in alphabetical order.

COMPLETE SET (21) 25.00 50.00
1 Mike Archambault 1.25 2.50
2 Serge Aubry 1.25 2.50
3 Yves Bergeron 1.25 2.50
4 Jacques Blain 1.25 2.50
5 Richard Brodeur 4.00 8.00
6 Alain Caron 1.25 2.50
7 Ken Desjardine 1.25 2.50
8 Maurice Filion 1.25 2.50
9 Andre Gaudette 1.25 2.50
10 Jean-Guy Gendron 1.50 3.00
11 Rejean Giroux 1.25 2.50
12 Frank Golembrosky 1.25 2.50
13 Bob Guindon 1.25 2.50
14 Pierre Guite 1.25 2.50
15 Frank Lacombe 1.25 2.50
16 Paul Larose 1.25 2.50
17 Michel Parizeau 1.25 2.50
18 Jean Payette 1.25 2.50
19 Michel Rouleau 1.25 2.50
20 Pierre Roy 1.25 2.50
21 J.C. Tremblay 2.50 5.00

1976 Nordiques Marie Antoinette

This 14-card set measured approximately 8" by 10 1/2" and featured on the fronts color player portraits of the Quebec Nordiques by the artist Claude Laroche. The player's name was printed in black in the lower right with the card logo on the left. The backs were blank. The cards were unnumbered and checklisted below in alphabetical order.

COMPLETE SET (14) 30.00 60.00
1 Paul Baxter 2.00 4.00
2 Serge Bernier 2.00 4.00
3 Paulin Bordeleau 2.00 4.00
4 Andre Boudrias 2.50 5.00
5 Curt Brackenbury 2.00 4.00
6 Richard Brodeur 4.00 8.00
7 Real Cloutier 3.00 6.00
8 Charles Constantin 2.00 4.00
9 Bob Fitchner 2.00 4.00
10 Richard Grenier 2.00 4.00
11 Marc Tardif 3.00 6.00
12 Jean-Claude Tremblay 3.00 6.00
13 Steve Sutherland 2.00 4.00
14 Wally Weir 2.00 4.00

1976-77 Nordiques Postcards

These 20 postcards measured approximately 3 1/2" by 5 1/2" and featured posed-on-ice color player photos on their borderless fronts. A facsimile player autograph rested near the bottom. The backs carried the player's name, uniform number, brief biography, and Nordiques team logo at the upper left. Places for stamp and address appeared on the right. All text is in French. The postcards are unnumbered and checklisted below in alphabetical order.

COMPLETE SET (20) 15.00 30.00
1 Serge Aubry .75 1.50
2 Paul Baxter 1.00 2.00
3 Jean Bernier .75 1.50
4 Serge Bernier 1.50 3.00
5 Christian Bordeleau .75 1.50
6 Paulin Bordeleau 1.00 2.00
7 Andre Boudrias 1.00 2.00
8 Curt Brackenbury .75 1.50
9 Richard Brodeur 2.00 4.00
10 Real Cloutier 1.50 3.00
11 Charles Constantin .75 1.50
12 Jim Dorey 1.00 2.00
13 Robert Fitchner .75 1.50
14 Richard Grenier .75 1.50
15 Francois Lacombe .75 1.50
16 Pierre Roy .75 1.50
17 Steve Sutherland .75 1.50
18 Marc Tardif 1.50 3.00
19 J.C. Tremblay 1.50 3.00
20 Wally Weir .75 1.50

1980-81 Nordiques Postcards

Printed in Canada, this 24-card set measured approximately 3" by 5 1/2" and featured members of the 1980-81 Quebec Nordiques. The fronts had borderless, posed color player photos. The backs were in postcard format with a short player biography both in French and in English. The text on some cards was printed in royal blue and on other cards in turquoise. The cards were unnumbered and checklisted below in alphabetical order.

COMPLETE SET (29) 20.00 40.00
1 Michel Bergeron .40 1.00
2 Serge Bernier .75 2.00
3 Daniel Bouchard .40 1.00
4 Ron Chipperfield .40 1.00
5 Kim Clackson .60 1.50
6 Real Cloutier .75 2.00
7 Alain Cote .60 1.50
8 Michel Dion .60 1.50
9 Andre Dupont .60 1.50
10 Robbie Ftorek .75 2.00
11 Michel Goulet 2.50 5.00
12 Ron Grahame .40 1.00
13 Jamie Hislop .40 1.00
14 Dale Hoganson .40 1.00
15 Dale Hunter 2.50 5.00
16 Pierre Lacroix .40 1.00
17 Garry Lariviere .40 1.00
18 Richard Leduc .40 1.00
19 Lee Norwood .60 1.50
20 John Paddock .60 1.50
21 Dave Pichette .40 1.00
22 Michel Plasse .75 2.00
23 Jacques Richard .60 1.50
24 Normand Rochefort .40 1.00
25 Anton Stastny .75 2.00
26 Peter Stastny 4.00 8.00
27 Marc Tardif .75 2.00
28 Wally Weir .40 1.00
29 John Wensink .60 1.50

1981-82 Nordiques Postcards

Printed in Canada, this 21-card set measured approximately 3" by 5 1/2" and featured members of the 1981-82 Quebec Nordiques. The fronts had borderless, posed color player portraits. The backs were in postcard format with a short player biography both in French and in English. The cards were unnumbered and checklisted below in alphabetical order.

COMPLETE SET (21) 10.00 25.00
1 Pierre Aubry .40 1.00
2 Michel Bergeron CO .60 1.50
3 Daniel Bouchard .75 2.00
4 Real Cloutier .75 2.00
5 Alain Cote .40 1.00
6 Andre Dupont .40 1.00
7 Miroslav Frycer UER (Last and first names are reversed) .40 1.00
8 Michel Goulet 1.50 4.00
9 Dale Hunter 1.25 3.00
10 Pierre Lacroix .40 1.00
11 Mario Marois .40 1.00
12 Dave Pichette .40 1.00
13 Michel Plasse .60 1.50
14 Jacques Richard .60 1.50
15 Normand Rochefort .40 1.00
16 Anton Stastny .60 1.50
17 Peter Stastny 2.00 5.00
18 Marian Stastny 1.00 2.50
19 Marc Tardif .60 1.50
20 Charles Thiffault CO .30 .75
21 Wally Weir .40 1.00

1982-83 Nordiques Postcards

This 24-card set measured approximately 3" by 5 1/2" and featured members of the 1982-83 Quebec Nordiques. The fronts had borderless color action player photos. The backs were in postcard format with a short player biography both in French and in English and a facsimile player autograph on the bottom. The cards were unnumbered and checklisted below in alphabetical order.

COMPLETE SET (25) 10.00 25.00
1 Pierre Aubry .30 .75
2 Michel Bergeron CO .60 1.50
3 Daniel Bouchard .20 .50
4 Real Cloutier .75 2.00
5 Alain Cote .30 .75
6 Andre Dupont .40 1.00
7 John Garrett .60 1.50
8 Michel Goulet 1.25 3.00
9 Jean Hamel .30 .75
10 Dale Hunter 1.00 2.50
11 Rick Lapointe .40 1.00
12 Clint Malarchuk .75 2.00
13 Mario Marois .30 .75
14 Randy Moller .30 .75
15 Wilf Paiement .40 1.00
16 Dave Pichette .30 .75
17 Jacques Richard .60 1.50
18 Normand Rochefort .30 .75
19 Louis Sleigher .30 .75
20 Anton Stastny .60 1.50
21 Marian Stastny .60 1.50
22 Peter Stastny 1.25 3.00
23 Marc Tardif .60 1.50
24 Charles Thiffault ACO .20 .50
25 Wally Weir .30 .75

1983-84 Nordiques Postcards

This 32-card set measured approximately 3 1/2" by 5 1/2" and featured members of the 1983-84 Quebec Nordiques. This set featured borderless full-color action shots on the front. The back was in postcard format with a brief identification of the player written in blue ink. This unnumbered set had been checklisted in alphabetical order.

COMPLETE SET (32) 10.00 25.00
1 Pierre Aubry .30 .75
2 Michel Bergeron CO .40 1.00
3 Dan Bouchard .50 1.25
4 Real Cloutier .60 1.50
5 Alain Cote .30 .75
6 Andre Dore .30 .75
7 Andre Dupont .40 1.00
8 John Garrett .50 1.25
9 Paul Gillis .30 .75
10 Mario Gosselin .50 1.25
11 Michel Goulet 1.00 2.50
12 Jean Hamel .30 .75
13 Dale Hunter .60 1.50
14 Rick Lapointe .30 .75
15 Clint Malarchuk .60 1.50
16 Jimmy Mann .40 1.00
17 Mario Marois .40 1.00
18 Randy Moller .40 1.00
19 Wilf Paiement .40 1.00
20 Dave Pichette .30 .75
21 Pat Price .30 .75
22 Jacques Richard .40 1.00
23 Normand Rochefort .30 .75
24 Jean-Francois Sauve .30 .75
25 Andre Savard .30 .75
26 Louis Sleigher .30 .75
27 Anton Stastny .40 1.00
28 Marian Stastny .40 1.00
29 Peter Stastny 1.00 2.50
30 Marc Tardif .50 1.25
31 Wally Weir .30 .75
32 Blake Wesley .30 .75

1984-85 Nordiques Postcards

This 27-card set measured approximately 3" by 5 1/2" and featured members of the 1984-85 Quebec Nordiques. The fronts had borderless color action player photos. The backs were in postcard format with a short player biography both in French and in English. The years "84-85" appeared in the spot where the stamp is supposed to go. The cards were unnumbered and checklisted below in alphabetical order.

COMPLETE SET (27) 8.00 20.00
1 Brent Ashton .30 .75
2 Bruce Bell .30 .75
3 Michel Bergeron CO .40 1.00
4 Daniel Bouchard .40 1.00
5 Alain Cote .30 .75
6 Gord Donnelly .30 .75
7 Luc Dufour .30 .75
8 Jean-Marc Gaulin .30 .75
9 Paul Gillis .30 .75
10 Mario Gosselin .40 1.00
11 Michel Goulet 1.00 2.50
12 Dale Hunter .60 1.50
13 Guy Lapointe ACO .40 1.00
14 Jimmy Mann .30 .75
15 Mario Marois .30 .75
16 Brad Maxwell .30 .75
17 Randy Moller .30 .75
18 Simon Nolet ACO .30 .75
19 Wilf Paiement .40 1.00
20 Pat Price .30 .75
21 Normand Rochefort .40 1.00
22 Jean-Francois Sauve .30 .75
23 Andre Savard .30 .75
24 Richard Sevigny .40 1.00
25 Anton Stastny .40 1.00
26 Marian Stastny .40 1.00
27 Peter Stastny 1.00 2.50

1985-86 Nordiques General Foods

These 27 cards measured approximately 3 1/2" by 5 1/2". The fronts featured color close-ups of the players against a light background. The pictures were full-bleed, except at the bottom where the player's number, name and the sponsor's logo appeared in a white bar. The backs were blank. The cards were unnumbered and checklisted below in alphabetical order.

COMPLETE SET (27) 12.00 30.00
1 John Anderson .40 1.00
2 Brent Ashton .40 1.00
3 Michel Bergeron CO .40 1.00
4 Alain Cote .40 1.00
5 Gilbert Delorme .40 1.00
6 Mike Eagles .40 1.00
7 Steven Finn .40 1.00
8 Jean-Marc Gaulin .40 1.00
9 Paul Gillis .40 1.00
10 Mario Gosselin .60 1.50
11 Michel Goulet 1.00 2.50
12 Ron Harris CO .20 .50
13 Dale Hunter 1.00 2.50
14 Mark Kumpel .40 1.00
15 Clint Malarchuk .60 1.50
16 Jimmy Mann .40 1.00
17 Mario Marois .40 1.00
18 Randy Moller .40 1.00
19 Simon Nolet CO .20 .50
20 Pat Price .40 1.00
21 Normand Rochefort .40 1.00
22 Jean-Francois Sauve .40 1.00
23 Richard Sevigny .60 1.50
24 David Shaw .40 1.00
25 Anton Stastny .60 1.50
26 Peter Stastny 1.50 4.00
27 Trevor Stienburg .40 1.00

1985-86 Nordiques McDonald's

This 22-card set measured approximately 3 1/2" by 5 1/2" and featured members of the 1985-86 Quebec Nordiques. The fronts featured borderless color action player photos. The sponsors' logos (McDonald's, Le Soleil and CHRC 80) appeared across the bottom; there were no player names on the fronts. The backs were blank. The cards were unnumbered and checklisted below in alphabetical order.

COMPLETE SET (22) 10.00 25.00
1 Brent Ashton .40 1.00
2 Jeff Brown 1.00 2.50
3 Alain Cote .40 1.00
4 Gilbert Delorme .40 1.00
5 Gord Donnelly .40 1.00
6 Mike Eagles .40 1.00
7 Paul Gillis .40 1.00
8 Mario Gosselin .60 1.50
9 Michel Goulet 1.00 2.50
10 Dale Hunter 1.00 2.50
11 Mark Kumpel .40 1.00
12 Jason Lafreniere .40 1.00
13 Clint Malarchuk .60 1.50
14 Randy Moller .40 1.00
15 Robert Picard .40 1.00
16 Pat Price .40 1.00
17 Normand Rochefort .40 1.00
18 Richard Sevigny .60 1.50
19 David Shaw .40 1.00
20 Risto Siltanen .40 1.00
21 Anton Stastny .60 1.50
22 Peter Stastny 1.50 4.00

1985-86 Nordiques Placemats

This 6-card placemat set of the Quebec Nordiques was sponsored by Pepsi-Cola and Seven-up and measured approximately 11" by 17". The fronts featured a painted portrait, action shot, and facsimile autograph on a yellow background with white border. The player's name, position, jersey number, date and place of birth, and career statistics in French were also found on the front. The sponsors' logos appeared in the upper right corner. The backs carried the sponsors' and team logos on a white background with thin blue, white, and purple borders. The mats were unnumbered, and one placemat showed portraits of all twelve players with their facsimile autographs.

COMPLETE SET (6) 8.00 20.00
1 Brent Ashton Randy Moller 1.25 3.00
2 Mario Gosselin Clint Malarchuk 1.50 4.00
3 Dale Hunter Michel Goulet 2.00 5.00
4 Pat Price Robert Picard 1.25 3.00
5 Peter Stastny Anton Stastny 2.00 5.00
6 Player Portraits Dale Hunter Michel Goulet Peter Stastny Anton Stastny Brent Ashton Randy Moller Pat Price Robert Picard Mario Gosselin Clint Malarchuk Alain Cote John Anderson 2.00 5.00

1985-86 Nordiques Provigo

This 25-sticker set of Quebec Nordiques was released through Provigo. The puffy stickers measured approximately 1 1/8" by 2 1/4" and featured a color head and shoulders photo of the player, with the player's number and name bordered by star-studded banners across the bottom of the picture. The player's signature was inscribed just above the banner. The Nordiques' logo was superimposed over the banner at its right end. The backs were blank. We have checklisted them below in alphabetical order, with the uniform number to the right of the player's name. The 25 Styrofoam stickers were to be attached to a cardboard poster. The poster measured approximately 20" by 11" and had 25 white spaces (designated for the stickers) on blue background. At the center was a picture of a goalie mask, with the Nordiques' logo above and slightly to the right. The back of the poster had a checklist, stripes in the team's colors, and two team logos.

COMPLETE SET (25) 8.00 20.00
1 John Anderson 14 .40 1.00
2 Brent Ashton 9 .30 .75
3 Wayne Babych 18 .40 1.00
4 Michel Bergeron CO .30 .75
5 Alain Cote 19 .30 .75
6 Gilbert Delorme 6 .30 .75
7 Mike Eagles 11 .30 .75
8 Steven Finn 25 .30 .75
9 Paul Gillis 23 .30 .75
10 Mario Gosselin 33 .40 1.00
11 Michel Goulet 16 .75 2.00
12 Dale Hunter 32 .75 2.00
13 Mark Kumpel 17 .30 .75
14 Clint Malarchuk 30 .40 1.00
15 Jimmy Mann 10 .40 1.00
16 Mario Marois 22 .40 1.00
17 Randy Moller 21 .30 .75
18 Wilf Paiement 27 .40 1.00
19 Pat Price 7 .30 .75
20 Normand Rochefort 5 .30 .75
21 J.F. Sauve 15 .30 .75
22 Richard Sevigny 1 .40 1.00
23 David Shaw 4 .30 .75
24 Anton Stastny 20 .40 1.00
25 Peter Stastny 26 1.25 3.00
NNO Poster 2.00 5.00

1985-86 Nordiques Team Issue

This 27-card set measured approximately 3 1/2" by 5 1/2" and featured members of the 1985-86 Quebec Nordiques. The fronts featured posed color close-up shots of the players against a light background. The pictures were borderless except at the bottom, where the player's name, uniform number and the team logo appeared in a white bar. The backs were blank. The cards were unnumbered and checklisted below in alphabetical order.

COMPLETE SET (27) 10.00 25.00
1 Brent Ashton .40 1.00
2 Michel Bergeron CO .40 1.00
3 Jeff Brown 1.00 2.50
4 Alain Cote .40 1.00
5 Gilbert Delorme .40 1.00
6 Gord Donnelly .40 1.00
7 Mike Eagles .40 1.00
8 Paul Gillis .40 1.00
9 Mario Gosselin .60 1.50
10 Michel Goulet 1.00 2.50
11 Dale Hunter 1.00 2.50
12 Mark Kumpel .40 1.00
13 Jason Lafreniere .40 1.00
14 Clint Malarchuk .60 1.50
15 Randy Moller .40 1.00
16 Simon Nolet CO .20 .50
17 Robert Picard .40 1.00
18 Pat Price .40 1.00
19 Ken Quinney .40 1.00
20 Normand Rochefort .40 1.00
21 Richard Sevigny .60 1.50
22 David Shaw .40 1.00
23 Risto Siltanen .40 1.00
24 Anton Stastny .60 1.50
25 Peter Stastny 1.50 4.00
26 Charles Thiffault CO .20 .50
27 Richard Zemlak .40 1.00

1986-87 Nordiques General Foods

This 28-card set measured approximately 3 1/2" by 5 1/2" and featured members of the 1986-87 Quebec Nordiques. The fronts featured posed color close-up shots of the players against a light background. The pictures were borderless except at the bottom, where the player's name, uniform number and the sponsor's logo appeared in a white bar. The backs were blank. The cards were unnumbered and checklisted below in alphabetical order.

COMPLETE SET (28) 10.00 25.00
1 Brent Ashton .30 .75
2 Michel Bergeron CO .60 1.50
3 Jeff Brown .60 1.50
4 Alain Cote .30 .75
5 Gilbert Delorme .30 .75
6 Gord Donnelly .30 .75
7 Mike Eagles .30 .75
8 Paul Gillis .30 .75
9 Mario Gosselin .60 1.50
10 Michel Goulet .75 2.00
11 Mike Hough .30 .75
12 Dale Hunter .60 1.50
13 Mark Kumpel .30 .75
14 Jason Lafreniere .30 .75
15 Clint Malarchuk .50 1.25
16 Randy Moller .30 .75
17 Simon Nolet CO .20 .50
18 Robert Picard .30 .75

1986-87 Nordiques General Foods

This 28-card set measured approximately 3 1/2" by 5 1/2" and featured members of the 1986-87 Quebec Nordiques. The fronts featured posed color close-up shots of the players against a light background. The pictures were borderless except at the bottom, where the player's name, uniform number and the sponsor's logo appeared in a white bar. The backs were blank. The cards were unnumbered and checklisted below in alphabetical order.

19 Pat Price .30 .75
20 Ken Quinney .30 .75
21 Normand Rochefort .30 .75
22 Richard Sevigny .50 1.25
23 David Shaw .30 .75
24 Risto Siltanen .30 .75
25 Anton Stastny .40 1.00
26 Peter Stastny 1.25 3.00
27 Charles Thiffault CO .20 .50
28 Richard Zemlak .40 1.00

1986-87 Nordiques McDonald's

This 25-card set measured approximately 3 1/2" by 5 1/2" and featured members of the 1986-87 Quebec Nordiques. The fronts featured borderless color action player photos. The sponsors' logos (McDonald's and Le Soleil) appeared across the bottom; there were no player names on the fronts. The backs were blank. The cards were unnumbered and checklisted below in alphabetical order.

COMPLETE SET (25) 12.00 30.00
1 John Anderson .60 1.50
2 Brent Ashton .40 1.00
3 Jeff Brown .75 2.00
4 Alain Cote .40 1.00
5 Gilbert Delorme .40 1.00
6 Mike Eagles .40 1.00
7 Steven Finn .40 1.00
8 Paul Gillis .40 1.00
9 Mario Gosselin .60 1.50
10 Michel Goulet 1.00 2.50
11 Mike Hough .40 1.00
12 Dale Hunter .75 2.00
13 Mark Kumpel .40 1.00
14 Alain Lemieux .40 1.00
15 Clint Malarchuk .60 1.50
16 Jimmy Mann .60 1.50
17 Randy Moller .40 1.00
18 Wilf Paiement .60 1.50
19 Pat Price .40 1.00
20 Normand Rochefort .40 1.00
21 Jean-Francois Sauve .40 1.00
22 Richard Sevigny .60 1.50
23 David Shaw .40 1.00
24 Anton Stastny .60 1.50
25 Peter Stastny 1.50 4.00

1986-87 Nordiques Team Issue

This 29-card set measured approximately 3 1/2" by 5 1/2" and featured members of the 1986-87 Quebec Nordiques. The fronts featured borderless color action photos. The player's name and number appeared in white or black lettering at the lower right corner. The backs were blank. The cards were unnumbered and checklisted below in alphabetical order.

COMPLETE SET (29) 8.00 20.00
1 Jeff Brown .75 2.00
2 Alain Cote .30 .75
3 Bill Derlago .30 .75
4 Gord Donnelly .30 .75
5 Mike Eagles .30 .75
6 Steven Finn .30 .75
7 Paul Gillis .30 .75
8 Mario Gosselin .40 1.00
9 Michel Goulet .75 2.00
10 Mike Hough .30 .75
11 Dale Hunter .60 1.50
12 Jason Lafreniere .30 .75
13 Clint Malarchuk .50 1.25
14 Basil McRae .40 1.00
15 Randy Moller .30 .75
16 John Ogrodnick .40 1.00
17 Robert Picard .30 .75
18 Pat Price .30 .75
19 Normand Rochefort .30 .75
20 Richard Sevigny .50 1.25
21 David Shaw .30 .75
22 Doug Shedden .30 .75
23 Risto Siltanen .30 .75
24 Anton Stastny .40 1.00
25 Peter Stastny 1.25 3.00

1986-87 Nordiques Yum-Yum

Each card in this ten-card set measured approximately 2" by 2 1/2". The fronts featured color action player photos with blue, white, and red borders. The player's name and number, along with sponsor and team logos, appearedon the front. The backs carried a team checklist. The cards were unnumbered and checklisted below in alphabetical order.

COMPLETE SET (10) 10.00 25.00
1 Alain Cote .75 2.00
2 Gilbert Delorme .75 2.00
3 Paul Gillis .75 2.00
4 Michel Goulet 2.00 5.00
5 Dale Hunter 1.50 4.00
6 Clint Malarchuk 1.25 3.00
7 Robert Picard .75 2.00
8 Normand Rochefort .75 2.00
9 Anton Stastny 1.00 2.50
10 Peter Stastny 2.50 6.00

1987-88 Nordiques General Foods

Each card in this 32-card set measured approximately 3 3/4" by 5 5/8". The fronts featured a full color action photo of the player, with the Quebec Nordiques' logo superimposed at the upper left-hand corner of the picture. At the bottom the player's number and name were given in the white triangle. The backs were blank. The set was issued in two versions, one with and one without the General Foods logo at the lower right corner. Both versions are valued equally. The set featured an early card of Ron Tugnutt pre-dating his O-Pee-Chee rookie card by two years.

COMPLETE SET (32) 8.00 20.00
1 Tommy Albelin 28 .20 .50
2 Jeff Brown 22 .50 1.25
3 Mario Brunetta 30 .30 .75
4 Terry Carkner 4 .30 .75
5 Alain Cote 19 .20 .50
6 Gord Donnelly 34 .20 .50
7 Gaetan Duchesne 14 .30 .75
8 Mike Eagles 11 .20 .50
9 Steven Finn 29 .20 .50
10 Paul Gillis 23 .20 .50
11 Mario Gosselin 33 .40 1.00
12 Michel Goulet 16 .75 2.00
13 Stephane Guerard 46 .20 .50
14 Alan Haworth 15 .20 .50
15 Mike Hough 18 .20 .50
16 Jeff Jackson 25 .20 .50
17 Stu Kulak 17 .20 .50
18 Jason Lafreniere 10 .20 .50
19 Lane Lambert 7 .20 .50
20 David Latta 27 .20 .50
21 Max Middendorf 12 .20 .50
22 Randy Moller 21 .20 .50
23 Robert Picard 24 .20 .50
24 Daniel Poudrier 2 .20 .50
25 Ken Quinney 54 .20 .50
26 Normand Rochefort 5 .20 .50
27 Richard Sevigny 1 .30 .75
28 Anton Stastny 20 .30 .75
29 Peter Stastny 26 1.25 3.00
30 Ron Tugnutt 50 1.50 4.00
31 Alain Chainey .08 .25
Andre Savard
Guy Lapointe
32 Badaboum (Mascot) .08 .25

1987-88 Nordiques Team Issue

COMPLETE SET (32) 15.00 30.00
1 Richard Sevigny .75 2.00
2 Daniel Poudrier .40 1.00
3 Terry Carkner .40 1.00
4 Normand Rochefort .40 1.00
5 Lane Lambert .40 1.00
6 Jason Lafreniere .40 1.00
7 Mike Eagles .40 1.00
8 Max Middendorf .40 1.00
9 Gaetan Duchesne .40 1.00
10 Alan Haworth .40 1.00
11 Michel Goulet .75 2.00
12 Stu Kulak .40 1.00
13 Mike Hough .40 1.00
14 Alain Cote .40 1.00
15 Anton Stastny .75 2.00
16 Randy Moller .40 1.00
17 Jeff Brown .40 1.00
18 Paul Gillis .40 1.00
19 Robert Picard .40 1.00
20 Jeff Jackson .40 1.00
21 Peter Stastny 1.50 4.00
22 David Latta .40 1.00
23 Tommy Albelin .40 1.00
24 Steven Finn .40 1.00
25 Mario Brunetta .40 1.00
26 Mario Gosselin .75 2.00
27 Gord Donnelly .40 1.00
28 Stephane Guerard .40 1.00
29 Ron Tugnutt .75 2.00
30 Ken Quinney .40 1.00
31 Badaboum on sled .08 .25
32 Alain Chainey .20 .50
Andre Savard
Guy Lapointe

1987-88 Nordiques Yum-Yum

Each card in this ten-card set measured approximately 2" by 2 1/2". The front had a color action photo of the player, enframed by red, white, and blue borders. At the bottom the player's number and name was sandwiched between the Nordiques' logo and the Yum-Yum potato chips logo. The back was printed in red, white, and blue, and presented in two columns a checklist of the ten players. We have checklisted the cards below in alphabetical order, with the uniform number to the right of the player's name.

COMPLETE SET (10) 8.00 20.00
1 Alain Cote 19 .60 1.50
2 Paul Gillis 23 .60 1.50
3A Mario Gosselin 33 ERR 1.25 3.00
(Reverse has number 83)
3B Mario Gosselin 33 COR 1.25 3.00
4 Michel Goulet 16 1.50 4.00
5 Alan Haworth 15 UER .60 1.50
(Reverse has 38
for sweater number)
6 Jason Lefreniere 10 UER .60 1.50
(Reverse has 30
for sweater number)
7 Robert Picard 24 .60 1.50
8 Normand Rochefort 5 .60 1.50
9 Anton Stastny 20 .75 2.00
10 Peter Stastny 26 2.00 5.00

1988-89 Nordiques General Foods

The 31 blank-backed cards comprising this set measured approximately 3 3/4" by 5 5/8" and feature white-bordered color player action shots. The Nordiques logo is displayed at the upper right. The player's first name appears at the lower left of the photo. His last name appears in cursive lettering in the wide white margin below. The player's uniform number and the logos for General Foods, Le Journal de Quebec, and CHRC Sport Radio appear at the bottom right. The cards are unnumbered and checklisted below in alphabetical order. Joe Sakic's card predates his Rookie Card by one year.

COMPLETE SET (31) 14.00 35.00
1 Tommy Albelin .20 .50
2 Badaboum MASCOT .20 .50
3 Joel Baillargeon .20 .50
4 Jeff Brown .30 .75
5 Mario Brunetta .30 .75
6 Coaches .20 .50
Serge Aubry
Ron Lapointe
Guy Lapointe
Alain Chainey
7 Alain Cote .20 .50
8 Gord Donnelly .30 .75
9 Daniel Dore .20 .50
10 Gaetan Duchesne .30 .75
11 Steven Finn .20 .50
12 Marc Fortier .20 .50
13 Paul Gillis .20 .50
14 Mario Gosselin .30 .75
15 Michel Goulet .60 1.50
16 Jari Gronstrand .20 .50
17 Stephane Guerard .20 .50
18 Mike Hough .20 .50
19 Jeff Jackson .20 .50
20 Iiro Jarvi .20 .50
21 Darin Kimble .40 1.00
22 Lane Lambert .20 .50
23 David Latta .20 .50
24 Curtis Leschyshyn .40 1.00
25 Bob Mason .30 .75
26 Mario Marois .20 .50
27 Ken McRae .20 .50
28 Randy Moller .20 .50
29 Robert Picard .20 .50
30 Walt Poddubny .30 .75
31 Joe Sakic 6.00 15.00
32 Greg Smyth .20 .50
33 Anton Stastny .40 1.00
34 Peter Stastny 1.00 2.50
35 Trevor Steinberg .20 .50
36 Ron Tugnutt .75 2.00
37 Mark Vermette .20 .50
38 Team Picture .40 1.00

1988-89 Nordiques Team Issue

The 41 blank-backed cards comprising this set measure approximately 3 3/4" by 5 5/8" and featured white-bordered player action shots. The team logo was displayed at the upper right. The player's first name in all capital letters appeared at the lower left of the photo. His last name was a facsimile autograph in the wide white margin right below, with his uniform number next to it. The cards were unnumbered and checklisted below in alphabetical order. The Joe Sakic issue predated his RC by one year.

COMPLETE SET (33) 15.00 30.00
1 Tommy Albelin .20 .50
2 Serge Aubry CO .30 .75
Ron Lapointe CO
Guy Lapointe CO
Alain Chainey CO
3 Badaboum (Mascot) .08 .25
4 Joel Baillargeon .20 .50
5 Jeff Brown .60 1.50
6 Mario Brunetta .30 .75
7 Alain Cote .20 .50
8 Gord Donnelly .30 .75
9 Daniel Dore .20 .50
10 Gaetan Duchesne .30 .75
11 Steven Finn .20 .50
12 Marc Fortier .20 .50
13 Paul Gillis .20 .50
14 Mario Gosselin .30 .75
15 Michel Goulet .75 2.00
16 Jari Gronstrand .20 .50
17 Stephane Guerard .20 .50
18 Jeff Jackson .20 .50
19 Iiro Jarvi .20 .50
20 Lane Lambert .20 .50
21 David Latta .20 .50
22 Curtis Leschyshyn .40 1.00
23 Bob Mason .30 .75
24 Randy Moller .20 .50
25 Robert Picard .20 .50
26 Walt Poddubny .30 .75
27 Joe Sakic 6.00 15.00
28 Greg Smyth .20 .50
29 Anton Stastny .30 .75
30 Peter Stastny 1.00 2.50
31 Trevor Steinburg .20 .50
32 Mark Vermette .20 .50
33 Team Photo .75 2.00
34 Bobby Dollas .20 .50
35 Mike Hough .20 .50
36 Darin Kimble .20 .50
37 Ken McRae .20 .50
38 Martin Madded .20 .50
39 Ron Tugnutt .40 1.00
40 Mario Marois .20 .50
41 Jean Perron .20 .50

1989-90 Nordiques Team Issue

This 39-card set of the Quebec Nordiques printed on white card stock measured approximately 5 5/8" by 3 3/4" and featured a borderless posed head shot of the player against a blue background. The team logo and the player's name and jersey number appeared to the left of each picture. The backs were blank. The cards were unnumbered and checklisted below in alphabetical order.

COMPLETE SET (39) 10.00 25.00
1 Serge Aubry .20 .50
2 Michel Bergeron CO .20 .50
3 Jeff Brown .30 .75
4 Alain Chainey .20 .50
5 Joe Cirella .20 .50
6 Lucien DeBlois .20 .50
7 Daniel Dore .20 .50
8 Steven Finn .20 .50
9 Stephane Fiset .60 1.50
10 Bryan Fogarty .20 .50
11 Marc Fortier .20 .50
12 Paul Gillis .20 .50
13 Michel Goulet .40 1.00
14 Jari Gronstrand .20 .50
15 Stephane Guerard .20 .50
16 Mike Hough .20 .50
17 Tony Hrkac .20 .50
18 Jeff Jackson .20 .50
19 Iiro Jarvi .20 .50
20 Kevin Kaminski .20 .50
21 Darin Kimble .20 .50
22 Guy Lafleur 1.00 2.50
23 Guy Lapointe .20 .50
24 David Latta .20 .50
25 Brian Lawton .20 .50
26 Curtis Leschyshyn .30 .75
27 Claude Loiselle .20 .50
28 Mario Marois .20 .50
29 Tony McKegney .20 .50
30 Ken McRae .20 .50
31 Greg Millen .30 .75
32 Randy Moller .20 .50
33 Sergei Mylnikov .30 .75
34 Michel Petit .20 .50
35 Robert Picard .20 .50
36 Joe Sakic 6.00 15.00
37 Peter Stastny .60 1.50
38 Ron Tugnutt .60 1.50
39 Team Picture .20 .50

1989-90 Nordiques General Foods

This 30-card set of Quebec Nordiques printed on white card stock measured approximately 5 5/8" by 3 3/4" and featured a borderless posed head shot of the player against a blue background. It was essentially the same as the 1989-90 Quebec Nordiques set save for the smaller set size and the appearance of a General Foods logo in the lower left corner. Card backs were blank and unnumbered; thus the cards are listed below alphabetically. Joe Sakic's card appeared during his Rookie Card year.

COMPLETE SET (30) 10.00 25.00
1 Michel Bergeron CO .20 .50
2 Jeff Brown .30 .75
3 Joe Cirella .20 .50
4 Lucien DeBlois .20 .50
5 Daniel Dore .20 .50
6 Steven Finn .20 .50
7 Stephane Fiset .60 1.50
8 Marc Fortier .20 .50
9 Paul Gillis .20 .50
10 Michel Goulet .40 1.00
11 Jari Gronstrand .20 .50
12 Stephane Guerard .20 .50
13 Mike Hough .20 .50
14 Jeff Jackson .20 .50
15 Iiro Jarvi .20 .50
16 Kevin Kaminski .20 .50
17 Darin Kimble .20 .50
18 Guy Lafleur 1.00 2.50
19 David Latta .20 .50
20 Curtis Leschyshyn .30 .75
21 Claude Loiselle .20 .50
22 Mario Marois .20 .50
23 Ken McRae .20 .50
24 Sergei Mylnikov .30 .75
25 Michel Petit .20 .50
26 Robert Picard .20 .50
27 Joe Sakic 6.00 15.00
28 Peter Stastny .60 1.50
29 Ron Tugnutt .60 1.50
30 Team Photo .60 1.50

1989-90 Nordiques Police

This 27-card police set of Quebec Nordiques was sponsored by the city of Vanier. The cards measured approximately 4" by 2 3/4" and featured a borderless posed head and shoulders photo against a blue background. The team logo appeared to the left of each player picture. The backs, which read "Un Project Stupefiant..Sss" across the top, were printed in French and present biography and an anti-drug or alcohol message on the left side. The right side had a local police number and slot for a police officer's signature. The cards were unnumbered and checklisted below in alphabetical order. Joe Sakic's card appears during his Rookie Card year.

COMPLETE SET (27) 8.00 20.00
1 Jeff Brown .30 .75
2 Joe Cirella .20 .50
3 Lucien DeBlois .20 .50
4 Daniel Dore .20 .50
5 Steven Finn .20 .50
6 Stephane Fiset .60 1.50
7 Marc Fortier .20 .50
8 Paul Gillis .20 .50
9 Michel Goulet .40 1.00
10 Stephane Guerard .20 .50
11 Mike Hough .20 .50
12 Jeff Jackson .20 .50
13 Iiro Jarvi .20 .50
14 Darin Kimble .20 .50
15 Guy Lafleur 1.00 2.50
16 David Latta .20 .50
17 Curtis Leschyshyn .30 .75
18 Claude Loiselle .20 .50
19 Mario Marois .20 .50
20 Ken McRae .20 .50
21 Sergei Mylnikov .30 .75
22 Michel Petit .20 .50
23 Robert Picard .20 .50
24 Jean-Marc Routhier .20 .50
25 Joe Sakic 6.00 15.00
26 Peter Stastny .60 1.50
27 Ron Tugnutt .60 1.50

1990-91 Nordiques Petro-Canada

These blank-backed cards measured approximately 3 3/4" by 5 5/8" and featured white-bordered color player action shots. The player's name, uniform number, Nordiques logo, and Petro-Canada logo appeared on the bottom. The words "Les Nordiques" in blue letters was printed in the upper right corner. The cards were unnumbered and checklisted below in alphabetical order.

COMPLETE SET (28) 15.00 30.00
1 Aaron Broten .20 .50
2 Dave Chambers CO .20 .50
3 Joe Cirella .30 .75
4 Lucien DeBlois .20 .50
5 Steven Finn .20 .50
6 Bryan Fogarty .20 .50
7 Marc Fortier .20 .50
8 Robbie Ftorek ACO .20 .50
9 Paul Gillis .20 .50
10 Scott Gordon .30 .75
11 Mike Hough .20 .50
12 Tony Hrkac .30 .75
13 Darin Kimble .30 .75
14 Guy Lafleur .75 2.00
15 Curtis Leschyshyn .20 .50
16 Claude Loiselle .20 .50
17 Jacques Martin ACO .20 .50
18 Tony McKegney .20 .50
19 Owen Nolan 1.00 2.50
20 Michel Petit .20 .50
21 Joe Sakic 2.00 5.00
22 Everett Sanipass .20 .50
23 Mats Sundin 1.25 3.00
24 John Tanner .30 .75
25 Ron Tugnutt .40 1.00
26 Daniel Vincelette .20 .50
27 Craig Wolanin .20 .50
28 Team Photo .30 .75
29 Shawn Anderson .20 .50
30 Jacques Cloutier .30 .75
31 Alexei Gusarov .20 .50
32 Jeff Jackson .20 .50
33 Claude Lapointe .20 .50
34 Stephane Morin .20 .50
35 Scott Pearson .20 .50
36 Ken Quinney .20 .50
37 Serge Roberge .20 .50
38 Tony Twist .40 1.00
39 Randy Velischek .20 .50
40 Wayne Van Dorp .40 1.00
41 Mark Vermette .20 .50
42 Badaboum MASCOT .08 .25

1990-91 Nordiques Team Issue

The 25 blank-backed cards comprising this set measured approximately 5 5/8" by 3 3/4" and featured white-bordered posed color player head shots against blue backgrounds. The Quebec Nordiques logo was prominently displayed to the left of the player. The player's name and uniform number appeared in white lettering below the logo. The cards were unnumbered and checklisted below in alphabetical order.

COMPLETE SET (25) 6.00 15.00
1 Joe Cirella .20 .50
2 Lucien DeBlois .20 .50
3 Daniel Dore .20 .50
4 Steven Finn .20 .50
5 Stephane Fiset .60 1.50
6 Bryan Fogarty .20 .50
7 Marc Fortier .20 .50
8 Paul Gillis .20 .50
9 Michel Goulet .50 1.25
10 Stephane Guerard .20 .50
11 Mike Hough .20 .50
12 Tony Hrkac .25 .60
13 Jeff Jackson .20 .50
14 Iiro Jarvi .20 .50
15 Kevin Kaminski .20 .50
16 Darin Kimble .25 .60
17 David Latta .20 .50
18 Curtis Leschyshyn .20 .50
19 Claude Loiselle .20 .50
20 Mario Marois .20 .50
21 Tony McKegney .20 .50
22 Ken McRae .20 .50
23 Michel Petit .20 .50
24 Peter Stastny .60 1.50
25 Ron Tugnutt .40 1.00

1991 Nordiques Panini Team Stickers

This 32-sticker set was issued in a plastic bag that contained two 16-sticker sheets (approximately 9" by 12") and a foldout poster, "Super Poster - Hockey 91", on which the stickers could be affixed. The players' names appeared only on the poster, not on the stickers. Each sticker measured about 2 1/8" by 2 7/8" and featured a color player action shot on its white-bordered front. The back of the white sticker sheet was lined off into 16 panels, each carried the logos for Panini, the NHL, and the NHLPA, as well as the same number that appears on the front of the sticker. Every Canadian NHL team was featured in this promotion. Each team set was available by mail-order from Panini Canada Ltd. for 2.99 plus 50 cents for shipping and handling.

COMPLETE SET (32) 2.00 5.00
1 Joe Cirella .01 .05
2 Daniel Dore .01 .05
3 Steven Finn .01 .05
4 Bryan Fogarty .01 .05
5 Marc Fortier .01 .05
6 Paul Gillis .01 .05
7 Scott Gordon .02 .10
8 Stephane Guerard .01 .05
9 Mike Hough .01 .05
10 Tony Hrkac .01 .05
11 Darin Kimble .01 .05
12 Guy Lafleur .20 .50
13 Curtis Leschyshyn .02 .10
14 Claude Loiselle .01 .05
15 Tony McKegney .01 .05
16 Ken McRae .01 .05
17 Owen Nolan .20 .50
18 Joe Sakic .50 1.25
19 Everett Sanipass .01 .05
20 Mats Sundin .30 .75
21 John Tanner .02 .10
22 Ron Tugnutt .05 .15
23 Randy Velischek .01 .05
24 Craig Wolanin .01 .05
A Team Logo .01 .05
Left Side
B Team Logo .01 .05
Right Side
C Guy Lafleur .08 .25
Upper Left Corner
D Guy Lafleur .08 .25
Lower Left Corner
E Benoit Hogue .02 .10
Upper Right Corner
F Benoit Hogue .02 .10
Lower Right Corner
G Guy Lafleur .20 .50
H Mats Sundin .30 .75

1991-92 Nordiques Petro-Canada

These blank-backed cards measured approximately 3 1/2" by 5 5/8" and featured white-bordered color player action shots. The player's name, uniform number, Nordiques logo, and Petro-Canada logo appeared within the purplish margin on the left and below the photo. The cards were unnumbered and checklisted below in alphabetical order.

COMPLETE SET (35) 8.00 20.00
1 Badaboum (Mascot) .08 .25
2 Don Barber .20 .50
3 Jacques Cloutier .30 .75
4 Steven Finn .20 .50
5 Stephane Fiset .50 1.25
6 Bryan Fogarty .20 .50
7 Adam Foote .40 1.00
8 Marc Fortier .20 .50
9 Alexei Gusarov .20 .50
10 Mike Hough .20 .50
11 Don Jackson ACO .08 .25
12 Valeri Kamensky .60 1.50
13 John Kordic .30 .75
14 Claude Lapointe .20 .50
15 Curtis Leschyshyn .25 .60
16 Jacques Martin ACO .20 .50
17 Mike McNeill .20 .50
18 Ken McRae .20 .50
19 Kip Miller .20 .50
20 Stephane Morin .20 .50
21 Owen Nolan .60 1.50
22 Pierre Page GM/CO .20 .50
23 Greg Paslawski .20 .50
24 Herb Raglan .20 .50
25 Joe Sakic 1.50 4.00
26 Doug Smail .20 .50
27 Greg Smyth .20 .50
28 Mats Sundin .75 2.00
29 Mikhail Tatarinov .20 .50
30 Ron Tugnutt .30 .75
31 Tony Twist .50 1.25
32 Wayne Van Dorp .20 .50
33 Randy Velischek .20 .50
34 Mark Vermette .20 .50
35 Craig Wolanin .20 .50

1992-93 Nordiques Petro-Canada

These blank-backed cards measured approximately 3 1/2" by 5 5/8" and featured white-bordered color player action shots. The player's name, uniform number, Nordiques logo, and Petro-Canada logo appeaed within the purplish margin on the left and below the photo. The cards were unnumbered and checklisted below in alphabetical order.

COMPLETE SET (39) 8.00 20.00
1 Badaboum (Mascot) .08 .25
2 Daniel Bouchard CO .20 .50
3 Gino Cavallini .20 .50
4 Jacques Cloutier .30 .75
5 Steve Duchesne .20 .50
6 Steven Finn .20 .50
7 Stephane Fiset .40 1.00
8 Adam Foote .40 1.00
9 Alexei Gusarov .20 .50
10 Ron Hextall .40 1.00
11 Mike Hough .20 .50
12 Kerry Huffman .20 .50
13 Tim Hunter .20 .50
14 Don Jackson ACO .08 .25
15 Valeri Kamensky .20 .50
16 David Karpa .20 .50
17 Andrei Kovalenko .20 .50
18 Claude Lapointe .20 .50
19 Curtis Leschyshyn .20 .50
20 Bill Lindsay .20 .50
21 Jacques Martin ACO .08 .25
22 Owen Nolan .40 1.00
23 Pierre Page GM/CO .08 .25
24 Scott Pearson .20 .50
25 Herb Raglan .20 .50
26 Mike Ricci .30 .75
27 Martin Rucinsky .20 .50
28 Joe Sakic 1.50 4.00
29 Andre Savard ACO .08 .25
30 Chris Simon .40 1.00
31 Mats Sundin .75 2.00
32 John Tanner .25 .60
33 Mikhail Tatarinov .20 .50
34 Tony Twist .30 .75
35 Wayne Van Dorp .30 .75
36 Mark Vermette .20 .50
37 Craig Wolanin .20 .50
38 Scott Young .30 .75
39 Team Photo .08 .25

1994-95 Nordiques Burger King

Sponsored by Burger King, this 24-card set measured approximately 3 1/2" by 6" and featured members of the 1994-95 Quebec Nordiques. The fronts had white-bordered color action player shots, with the player's name and uniform number was a team color-coded bar alongside the left or right. A small color player portrait with red borders appeared on the bottom. The backs carried another small blue-toned action shot, along with biography, career statistics and highlights (both in English and French) and the sponsor logo. The cards were unnumbered and checklisted below in alphabetical order.

COMPLETE SET (28) 8.00 20.00
1 Badaboum .20 .50
2 Bob Bassen .20 .50
3 Wendel Clark .40 1.00
4 Adam Deadmarsh .40 1.00
5 Steven Finn .20 .50
6 Stephane Fiset .40 1.00
7 Adam Foote .30 .75
8 Peter Forsberg 2.00 5.00
9 Alexei Gusarov .20 .50
10 Valeri Kamensky .20 .50
11 Jon Klemm .20 .50
12 Andrei Kovalenko .20 .50
13 Uwe Krupp .20 .50
14 Claude Lapointe .20 .50
15 Janne Laukkanen .20 .50
16 Sylvain Lefebvre .20 .50
17 Curtis Leschyshyn .20 .50
18 Paul MacDermid .20 .50
19 Owen Nolan .60 1.50
20 Mike Ricci .30 .75
21 Martin Rucinsky .30 .75
22 Joe Sakic 1.25 3.00
23 Reggie Savage .20 .50
24 Chris Simon .20 .50
25 Jocelyn Thibault .60 1.50
26 Craig Wolanin .20 .50
27 Scott Young .30 .75
28 Team Card .20 .50

2001 Nortel All-Star Game Sheets

Sponsored by Nortel Networks, this 10-card set featured two sheets containing six perforated cards each of the NHL's Top All-Stars. The sheets were given to participants in a shooting contest at the All-Star Fan Fest, and so are extremely difficult to acquire. Each card featured a full color player action photo set against the colored All-Star Game logo for 2001. The cards were bound together by a gray sheet that displayed the Nortel Networks logo and the North America vs. The World logo.

COMPLETE SET (12) 24.00 60.00
1 Jaromir Jagr 3.00 7.50
2 Peter Forsberg 3.00 7.50
3 Pavel Bure 1.00 2.50
4 Nicklas Lidstrom 1.00 2.50
5 Dominik Hasek 2.00 5.00
6 Sandis Ozolinsh .40 1.00
7 Paul Kariya 4.00 10.00
8 Joe Sakic 3.00 7.50
9 Theo Fleury 1.00 2.50
10 Ray Bourque 3.00 7.50
11 Patrick Roy 6.00 15.00
12 Chris Pronger 1.00 2.50

1970-71 North Stars Postcards

This 10-card set measured 3 1/2" by 5 1/2" and was stapled together in a booklet with the team name and logo above two hockey sticks on a pale green background. The fronts featured posed, color player photos. The backs carried the player's name, biographical information and career highlights printed in blue on a white background. The cards were unnumbered and checklisted below in alphabetical order.

COMPLETE SET (10) 17.50 35.00
1 Barry Gibbs 1.00 2.00
2 Bill Goldsworthy 2.50 5.00
3 Danny Grant 2.00 4.00
4 Ted Harris 1.00 2.00
5 Cesare Maniago 3.00 6.00
6 Jean Paul Parise 1.50 3.00
7 Tom Reid 1.00 2.00
8 Bobby Rousseau 1.00 2.00
9 Tom Williams 1.00 2.00
10 Lorne Worsley 5.00 10.00

1972-73 North Stars Glossy Photos

These 20 blank-backed approximately 8" by 10" glossy white-bordered black-and-white photo sheets featured a suited-up posed player photo on the right and, on the left, a posed player head shot. Below the head shot appeared the player's name and the Minnesota North Stars name and logo. The photos were unnumbered and checklisted below in alphabetical order.

COMPLETE SET (20) 10.00 20.00
1 Fred Barrett .50 1.00
2 Charlie Burns .50 1.00
3 Jude Drouin .50 1.00
4 Barry Gibbs .50 1.00
5 Bill Goldsworthy 1.25 2.50
6 Danny Grant .75 1.50
7 Ted Harris .50 1.00
8 Fred(Buster) Harvey .50 1.00
9 Dennis Hextall .75 1.50
10 Cesare Maniago 1.00 2.00
11 Doug Mohns .75 1.50
12 Lou Nanne .75 1.50
13 Bob Nevin .50 1.00
14 Dennis O'Brien .50 1.00
15 Murray Oliver .50 1.00
16 J.P. Parise .50 1.00
17 Dean Prentice .75 1.50
18 Tom Reid .50 1.00
19 Gump Worsley 2.50 5.00
20 W.Blair/J.Gordon .50 1.00

1973-74 North Stars Action Posters

These 14 x 20 color action posters were distributed by Mr. Steak restaurants in the Minneapolis area. They were distributed one every two weeks for twenty weeks.

COMPLETE SET (10) 10.00 20.00
1 Henry Boucha 1.00 2.00
2 Jude Drouin 1.00 2.00
3 Barry Gibbs 1.00 2.00
4 Bill Goldsworthy 1.50 3.00
5 Dennis Hextall 1.00 2.00
6 Cesare Maniago 1.50 3.00
7 Lou Nanne 1.50 3.00
8 Dennis O'Brien 1.00 2.00
9 J.P. Parise 1.50 3.00
10 Tom Reid 1.00 2.00

1973-74 North Stars Postcards

These postcard sized cards featured black and white posed photos on the front, and were blank backed. Cards were unnumbered and checklisted below alphabetically.

COMPLETE SET (20) 10.00 20.00
1 Fred Barrett .38 .75
2 Gary Bergman .38 .75
3 Jude Drouin .38 .75
4 Tony Featherstone .38 .75
5 Barry Gibbs .38 .75
6 Bill Goldsworthy .63 1.25
7 Danny Grant .38 .75
8 Buster Harvey .38 .75
9 Dennis Hextall .50 1.00
10 Parker MacDonald .38 .75
11 Cesare Maniago .50 1.00
12 Lou Nanne .50 1.00
13 Rod Norrish .38 .75
14 Dennis O'Brien .38 .75
15 Murray Oliver .38 .75
16 Jean-Paul Parise .38 .75
17 Dean Prentice .50 1.00
18 Tom Reid .38 .75
19 Fred Stanfield .63 1.25
20 Lorne Worsley 1.50 3.00

1978-79 North Stars Cloverleaf Dairy

This ten-panel set of Minnesota North Stars was issued on the side of half gallon milk cartons as part of a sweepstakes. The picture and text were printed in either red or purple. The panels measured approximately 3 3/4" by 7 5/8", with two players per panel. The North Stars' logo, the team name, year, and panel number appeared at the top of each panel. Each panel featured a "mug shot" and brief biographical information on two players. A North Stars question was included at the bottom of each panel. There were ten questions in all: one per panel, and a tenth question on the final entry panel, which also included a list of all ten questions and gave complete entry information. The unnumbered panel described the sweepstakes promotion and lists the prizes.

COMPLETE SET (11) 60.00 120.00
1 Gilles Meloche 7.50 15.00
Gary Sargent
2 Fred Barrett and 6.00 12.00
Per-Olov Brasar
3 Jean-Paul Parise and 6.00 12.00
Greg Smith
4 Al MacAdam and 6.00 12.00
Kent-Erik Andersson
5 Gary Edwards and 12.50 25.00
Bobby Smith
6 Mike Polich and 6.00 12.00
Brad Maxwell
7 Steve Payne and 6.00 12.00
Glen Sharpley
8 Tim Young and 6.00 12.00
Kris Manery
9 Ron Zanussi and 6.00 12.00
Tom Younghans
10 Final Entry Panel 6.00 12.00
NNO Sweepstakes Promotion 2.50 5.00

1979-80 North Stars Postcards

This 21-card set measured approximately 3 1/2" by 5 1/2" and featured the 1979-80 Minnesota North Stars. The fronts had borderless black-and-white player action photos. The backs had a postcard format and carry the player's name, position, short biography, and the team logo. The cards were unnumbered and checklisted below in alphabetical order.

COMPLETE SET (21) 10.00 20.00
1 Kent-Erik Andersson .38 .75
2 Fred Barrett .38 .75
3 Gary Edwards .75 1.50
4 Mike Fidler .38 .75
5 Craig Hartsburg 1.00 2.00
6 Al MacAdam .50 1.00
7 Kris Manery .38 .75
8 Brad Maxwell .38 .75
9 Tom McCarthy .50 1.00
10 Gilles Meloche 1.00 2.00
11 Steve Payne .50 1.00
12 Mike Polich .38 .75
13 Gary Sargent .50 1.00
14 Glen Sharpley .38 .75
15 Paul Shmyr .38 .75
16 Bobby Smith 1.50 3.00
17 Greg Smith .38 .75
18 Glen Sonmor CO .38 .75
19 Tim Young .50 1.00
20 Tom Younghans .38 .75
21 Ron Zanussi .38 .75

1980-81 North Stars Postcards

This 24-card set measured approximately 3 1/2" by 5 1/2" and featured the 1980-81 Minnesota North Stars. The fronts had borderless color posed player photos with facsimile autographs across the bottom. The backs had a postcard format and carry a short player biography and the team logo in green print. The cards were unnumbered and checklisted below in alphabetical order.

COMPLETE SET (24) 8.00 20.00
1 Kent-Erik Andersson .30 .75
2 Fred Barrett .30 .75
3 Don Beaupre 1.00 2.50
4 Jack Carlson 1.00 2.50
5 Steve Christoff .40 1.00
6 Mike Eaves .30 .75
7 Gary Edwards .60 1.50
8 Curt Giles .40 1.00
9 Craig Hartsburg .75 2.00
10 Al MacAdam .40 1.00
11 Brad Maxwell .30 .75
12 Tom McCarthy .30 .75
13 Gilles Meloche .60 1.50
14 Murray Oliver ACO .30 .75
J.P. Parise ACO
Glen Sonmor CO
15 Steve Payne .30 .75
16 Mike Polich .30 .75
17 Gary Sargent .40 1.00
18 Glen Sharpley .30 .75
19 Paul Shmyr .30 .75
20 Bobby Smith 1.00 2.50
21 Greg Smith .30 .75
22 Tim Young .30 .75
23 Tom Younghans .30 .75
24 Ron Zanussi .30 .75

1981-82 North Stars Postcards

This 24-card set measured approximately 3 1/2" by 5 1/2" and featured color player photos on the fronts. The backs had a green postcard design with the North Stars' logo printed in pale green on the left side. The player's name, position, and biographical information appeared in the upper left corner. The season and team name appeared vertically in the middle, bisecting the cards. The cards were unnumbered and checklisted below in alphabetical order.

COMPLETE SET (24) 10.00 25.00
1 Kent-Erik Andersson .30 .75
2 Fred Barrett .30 .75
3 Don Beaupre 1.00 2.50
4 Neal Broten 1.50 4.00
5 Jack Carlson .75 2.00
6 Steve Christoff .30 .75
7 Dino Ciccarelli 2.50 6.00
8 Mike Eaves .30 .75
9 Curt Giles .40 1.00
10 Anders Hakansson .30 .75
11 Craig Hartsburg .60 1.50
12 Al Macadam .30 .75
13 Brad Maxwell .30 .75
14 Kevin Maxwell .30 .75
15 Tom McCarthy .30 .75
16 Gilles Meloche .60 1.50
17 Bill Nyrop .30 .75
18 Steve Payne .30 .75
19 Brad Palmer .30 .75
20 Gordie Roberts .30 .75
21 Gary Sargent .30 .75
22 Bobby Smith .75 2.00
23 Glen Sonmor CO .30 .75
J.P. Parise ACO
Murray Oliver ACO
24 Tim Young .30 .75

1982-83 North Stars Postcards

This 25-card set measured approximately 3 1/2" by 5 1/2" and featured color player photos on the fronts. The backs had a green postcard design with the North Stars' logo printed in pale green on the left side. The player's name, position, and biographical information appeared in the upper left corner. The season and team name appeared vertically in the middle, bisecting the cards. The cards were unnumbered and checklisted below in alphabetical order.

COMPLETE SET (24) 10.00 25.00
1 Fred Barrett .30 .75
2 Don Beaupre .60 1.50
3 Brian Bellows 1.25 3.00
4 Neal Broten 1.00 2.50
5 Dino Ciccarelli 1.50 4.00
6 Dino Ciccarelli 1.00 2.50
Neal Broten
7 Jordy Douglas .30 .75
8 Mike Eaves .30 .75
9 George Ferguson .30 .75
10 Ron Friest .30 .75
11 Curt Giles .40 1.00
12 Craig Hartsburg .60 1.50
13 Al MacAdam .30 .75
14 Dan Mandich .30 .75
15 Brad Maxwell .30 .75
16 Tom McCarthy .30 .75
17 Gilles Meloche .60 1.50
18 Steve Payne .30 .75
19 Willi Plett .40 1.00
20 Gordie Roberts .30 .75
21 Gary Sargent .30 .75
22 Bobby Smith .75 2.00
23 Ken Solheim .30 .75
24 Tim Young .30 .75
25 Team Photo .60 1.50

1983-84 North Stars Postcards

This 27-card set measured approximately 3 1/2" by 5 1/2" and featured color player photos on the fronts. The backs had a green postcard design with the North Stars' logo printed in pale green on the left side. The player's name, position, and biographical information appeared in the upper left corner. The season and team name appeared vertically in the middle, bisecting the cards. The cards wereunnumbered and checklisted below in alphabetical order.

COMPLETE SET (27)	8.00	20.00
1 Keith Acton	.30	.75
2 Brent Ashton	.30	.75
3 Don Beaupre	.60	1.50
4 Brian Bellows	.75	2.00
5 Neal Broten	.75	2.00
6 Dino Ciccarelli	1.00	2.50
7 Jordy Douglas	.30	.75
8 George Ferguson	.30	.75
9 Curt Giles	.40	1.00
10 Craig Hartsburg	.40	1.00
11 Brian Lawton	.30	.75
12 Craig Levie	.30	.75
13 Lars Lindgren	.30	.75
14 Al MacAdam	.30	.75
15 Bill Mahoney CO	.20	.50
16 Dan Mandich	.30	.75
17 Dennis Maruk	.50	1.25
18 Brad Maxwell	.30	.75
19 Tom McCarthy	.30	.75
20 Gilles Meloche	.40	1.00
21 Mark Napier	.30	.75
22 Steve Payne	.30	.75
23 Willi Plett	.40	1.00
24 Dave Richter	.30	.75
25 Gordie Roberts	.30	.75
26 Randy Velischek	.30	.75
27 Team Photo	.60	1.50

1984-85 North Stars 7-Eleven

This 12-card safety set was sponsored by the Southland Corporation in cooperation with the Fire Marshalls Assn. of Minnesota and the Minnesota North Stars. The cards measured 2 5/8" by 4 1/8". The front had a color action photo enframed by a thin green border on white card stock. The green box below the picture gave the uniform number, player's name, position, the team name, and team logo. The card number on the back was sandwiched between the North Stars' and 7-Eleven logos. The back also had basic biographical information, career scoring statistics, and a fire prevention tip in a yellow box on the lower portion of the card back.

COMPLETE SET (12)	3.00	8.00
1 Neal Broten	.50	1.25
2 Willi Plett	.30	.75
3 Craig Hartsburg	.50	1.25
4 Brian Bellows	.75	2.00
5 Gordie Roberts	.20	.50
6 Keith Acton	.30	.75
7 Paul Holmgren	.30	.75
8 Gilles Meloche	.30	.75
9 Dennis Maruk	.50	1.25
10 Tom McCarthy	.20	.50
11 Steve Payne	.30	.75
12 Dino Ciccarelli	.75	2.00

1984-85 North Stars Postcards

This 25-card set measured approximately 3 1/2" by 5 1/2" and featured full-bleed, posed, color player photos. The backs had a green postcard design. The North Stars' logo was printed in pale green on the left side. The player's name and biographical information appeared in the upper left corner. The season and team name appeared vertically in the middle, bisecting the cards. The cards were unnumbered and checklisted below in alphabetical order.

COMPLETE SET (29)	6.00	15.00
1 Keith Acton	.30	.75
2 Don Beaupre	.60	1.50
3 Brian Bellows	.75	2.00
4 Scott Bjugstad	.20	.50
5 Neal Broten	.60	1.50
6 Dino Ciccarelli	.75	2.00
7 Curt Giles	.30	.75
8 Curt Giles w/captain's C	.20	.50
9 Craig Hartsburg	.60	1.50
10 Tom Hirsch	.20	.50
11 Paul Holmgren	.40	1.00
12 Brian Lawton	.20	.50
13 Dan Mandich	.20	.50
14 Dennis Maruk	.60	1.50
15 Brad Maxwell	.20	.50
16 Tom McCarthy	.20	.50
17 Tony McKegney	.20	.50
18 Roland Melanson	.30	.75
19 Gilles Meloche	.30	.75
20 Mark Napier	.30	.75
21 Steve Payne	.30	.75
22 Willi Plett	.30	.75
23 Dave Richter	.20	.50
24 Gordie Roberts	.20	.50
25 Bob Rouse	.20	.50
26 Gord Sherven	.20	.50
27 Harold Snepsts	.40	1.00
28 Ken Solheim	.20	.50
29 Randy Velischek	.20	.50

1985-86 North Stars 7-Eleven

This 12-card safety set was sponsored by the Southland Corporation in cooperation with the Fire Marshalls Assn. of Minnesota and the Minnesota North Stars. The cards measured the standard size, 2 1/2" by 3 1/2". The front had a color action photo enframed by a thin green border on white card stock. The green box below the picture gave the uniform number, player's name, position, the team name, and team logo. The card number on the back was sandwiched between the North Stars' and 7-Eleven logos. The back also had basic biographical information, career scoring statistics, and a fire prevention tip in a yellow box on the lower portion of the card back.

COMPLETE SET (12)	3.00	8.00
1 Dino Ciccarelli	.75	2.00
2 Scott Bjugstad	.20	.50
3 Curt Giles	.30	.75
4 Don Beaupre	.40	1.00
5 Tony McKegney	.20	.50
6 Neal Broten	.60	1.50
7 Willi Plett	.30	.75
8 Craig Hartsburg	.40	1.00
9 Brian Bellows	.40	1.00
10 Keith Acton	.30	.75
11 Dave Langevin	.20	.50
12 Dirk Graham	.60	1.50

1985-86 North Stars Postcards

This 27-card set measured 3 1/2" by 5 1/2" and featured full-bleed, posed, color player photos on thin card stock. The backs had a green postcard design. The North Stars' logo was printed in pale green outline lettering on the left side. The player's name and biographical information appeared in the upper left corner. The cards were unnumbered and checklisted below in alphabetical order. The year of the set is established by the Dave Langevin card; he played with the North Stars only during the 1985-86 season.

COMPLETE SET (27)	6.00	15.00
1 Keith Acton	.30	.75
2 Don Beaupre	.40	1.00
3 Brian Bellows	.40	1.00
4 Bo Berglund	.20	.50
5 Scott Bjugstad	.20	.50
6 Neal Broten	.60	1.50
7 Jon Casey	.60	1.50
8 Dino Ciccarelli	.75	2.00
9 Tim Coulis	.20	.50
10 Curt Giles	.30	.75
11 Dirk Graham	.60	1.50
12 Mats Hallin	.20	.50
13 Craig Hartsburg	.40	1.00
14 Tom Hirsch	.20	.50
15 Dave Langevin	.20	.50
16 Brian Lawton	.20	.50
17 Craig Levie	.20	.50
18 Dan Mandich	.20	.50
19 Dennis Maruk	.40	1.00
20 Tom McCarthy	.20	.50
21 Tony McKegney	.20	.50
22 Roland Melanson	.30	.75
23 Steve Payne	.20	.50
24 Willi Plett	.30	.75
25 Gordie Roberts	.20	.50
26 Bob Rouse	.30	.75
27 Gord Sherven	.20	.50

1986-87 North Stars 7-Eleven

This 12-card safety set was sponsored by the Southland Corporation in cooperation with the Fire Marshalls Assn. of Minnesota and the Minnesota North Stars. The cards measured the standard size, 2 1/2" by 3 1/2". The front had a color action photo enframed by a thin green border on white card stock. The green box below the picture gave the uniform number, player's name, position, the team name, and team logo. The card number on the back was sandwiched between the North Stars' and 7-Eleven logos. The back also had basic biographical information, career scoring statistics, and a fire prevention tip in a yellow box on the lower portion of the card back. The copyright notice on the back said 1987.

COMPLETE SET (12)	3.00	8.00
1 Neal Broten	.40	1.00
2 Brian MacLellan	.20	.50
3 Willi Plett	.30	.75
4 Scott Bjugstad	.20	.50
5 Don Beaupre	.40	1.00
6 Dino Ciccarelli	.75	2.00
7 Craig Hartsburg	.40	1.00
8 Dennis Maruk	.60	1.50
9 Bob Rouse	.20	.50
10 Gordie Roberts	.20	.50
11 Bob Brooke	.20	.50
12 Brian Bellows	.60	1.50

1987-88 North Stars Postcards

This 31-card set of Minnesota North Stars featured color action photos without borders. The cards measured approximately 3 1/2" by 5 3/8" and are of the postcard type format. The backs were printed in green, provided brief biographical information, and had the North Stars' logo on the left-hand portion. These cards were unnumbered and we have checklisted them below in alphabetical order.

COMPLETE SET (31)	8.00	20.00
1 Keith Acton	.25	.60
2 Dave Archibald	.20	.50
3 Warren Babe	.20	.50
4 Don Beaupre	.40	1.00
5 Brian Bellows	.40	1.00
6 Mike Berger	.20	.50
7 Scott Bjugstad	.20	.50
8 Bob Brooke	.20	.50
9 Herb Brooks CO	.30	.75
10 Neal Broten	.40	1.00
11 Dino Ciccarelli	.60	1.50
12 Larry DePalma	.20	.50
13 Dave Gagner	1.00	2.50
14 Curt Giles	.30	.75
15 Dirk Graham	.40	1.00
16 Craig Hartsburg	.40	1.00
17 Tom Hirsch	.20	.50
18 Brian Lawton	.20	.50
19 Brian MacLellan	.20	.50
20 Dennis Maruk	.30	.75
21 Basil McRae	.30	.75
22 Frantisek Musil	.20	.50
23 Steve Payne	.25	.60
24 Pat Price	.20	.50
25 Chris Pryor	.20	.50
26 Gordie Roberts	.20	.50
27 Bob Rouse	.25	.60
28 Terry Ruskowski	.25	.60
29 Kari Takko	.30	.75
30 Ron Wilson	.20	.50
31 Richard Zemlak	.20	.50

1988-89 North Stars ADA

This 23-card set measured 3 1/2" by 7 1/8" and was sponsored by the American Dairy Association and Pro Ex Photo Systems. The fronts featured color action player photos with the team logo, player's name, and sponsors' logos at the bottom in the wide white margin. On the horizontal backs, the left box carried the team logo and player information. The right box displayed a nutrition tip from the American Dairy Association of Minnesota. The cards were unnumbered and checklisted below in alphabetical order.

COMPLETE SET (23)	5.00	12.00
1 Brian Bellows	.40	1.00
2 Bob Brooke	.20	.50
3 Neal Broten	.40	1.00
4 Jon Casey	.60	1.50
5 Shawn Chambers	.20	.50
6 Dino Ciccarelli	.75	2.00
7 Larry DePalma	.20	.50
8 Curt Fraser	.20	.50
9 Link Gaetz	.30	.75
10 Dave Gagner	.75	2.00
11 Stewart Gavin	.20	.50
12 Curt Giles	.20	.50
13 Marc Habscheid	.20	.50
14 Mark Hardy	.20	.50
15 Craig Hartsburg	.40	1.00
16 Brian MacLellan	.20	.50
17 Moe Mantha	.20	.50
18 Basil McRae	.30	.75
19 Frantisek Musil	.20	.50
20 Dusan Pasek	.20	.50
21 Bob Rouse	.20	.50
22 Terry Ruskowski	.20	.50
23 Kari Takko	.30	.75

1989-90 North Stars ADA

This postcard-sized set featured the old Minnesota North Stars. The cards were issued as a promotional giveaway, likely at one home game. The set was noteworthy for the inclusion of a card on Mike Modano, a full year before his RC appearance.

COMPLETE SET (23)	8.00	20.00
1 Brian Bellows	.20	.50
2 Perry Berezan	.08	.25
3 Bob Brooke	.08	.25
4 Neal Broten	.40	1.00
5 Jon Casey	.30	.75
6 Shawn Chambers	.08	.25
7 Shane Churla	.40	1.00
8 Clark Donatelli	.08	.25
9 Gaetan Duchesne	.08	.25
10 Curt Fraser	.08	.25
11 Dave Gagner	.20	.50
12 Mike Gartner	.30	.75
13 Stewart Gavin	.08	.25
14 Curt Giles	.20	.50
15 Ken Leiter	.08	.25
16 Basil McRae	.30	.75
17 Mike Modano	4.00	10.00
18 Larry Murphy	.30	.75
19 Frantisek Musil	.08	.25
20 Pierre Page	.08	.25
21 Ville Siren	.08	.25
22 Kari Takko	.30	.75
23 Mark Tinordi	.08	.25

1990 Oakville Horton

Card was produced to promote a show in Oakville, Ontario.

1 Tim Horton	1.50	4.00

1979-80 Oilers Postcards

Measuring approximately 3 1/2" by 5 1/4", this 24-card set featured borderless posed-on-ice photos of the Edmonton Oilers on the fronts. The postcard format had each of the horizontal backs bisected by a vertical line, with the player's name, position, and biography on the left side, and the team logo on the right. The cards were unnumbered and checklisted below in alphabetical order. Early cards of Wayne Gretzky, Kevin Lowe, and Mark Messier were featured in this set. The complete set price includes both Mio variations.

COMPLETE SET (24)	50.00	100.00
1 Brett Callighen	.50	1.00
2 Colin Campbell	1.00	2.00
3 Ron Chipperfield	.50	1.00
4 Cam Connor	.50	1.00
5 Peter Driscoll	.50	1.00
6 Dave Dryden	1.00	2.00
7 Bill Flett	.50	1.00
8 Lee Fogolin	.50	1.00
9 Wayne Gretzky	30.00	60.00
10 Al Hamilton	.50	1.00
11 Doug Hicks	.50	1.00
12 Dave Hunter	.50	1.00
13 Kevin Lowe	2.00	4.00
14 Dave Lumley	.50	1.00
15 Blair MacDonald	.50	1.00
16 Kari Makkonen	.50	1.00
17 Mark Messier	12.50	25.00
18A Ed Mio ERR	1.00	2.00
18B Ed Mio COR	1.00	2.00
19 Pat Price	.50	1.00
20 Dave Semenko	1.00	2.00
21 Bobby Schmautz	.50	1.00
22 Risto Siltanen	.75	1.50
23 Stan Weir	.50	1.00

1980-81 Oilers Zellers

1 Wayne Gretzky	500.00	1000.00
2 Dave Lumley	5.00	10.00
3 Blair MacDonald	5.00	10.00

1981-82 Oilers Red Rooster

This 30-card set of Edmonton Oilers was sponsored by Red Rooster Food Stores in conjunction with Sun-Rype, Jell-O, Maxwell House, and Post. The player cards could be collected from any police officer or Red Rooster store. The cards measured approximately 2 3/4" by 3 9/16". The front had a color photo (with rounded corners) of the player, with the Oilers' logo and player's signature across the bottom of the picture. The player's name, uniform number, and a hockey tip were given below the photo. The back had the Red Rooster logo at the upper left-hand corner as well as biographical and statistical information on the player. The bottom included logos of the sponsors and an anti-crime message. The original printing included four "long-hair" Gretzky cards as well as coaches' cards of Billy Harris and Ted Green. Reportedly those involved didn't approve of the photos and thus most of the offending pictures were destroyed. Consequently, the new poses were much more common and the old ones more scarce. The mass-produced second printing produced six variations so that the total possible cards is 36. These (original) other six cards were very hard to find as they were apparently not released to the general collecting public. The set is checklisted below using sweater numbers for reference.

COMPLETE SET (30)	25.00	60.00
1 Grant Fuhr	1.50	4.00
2 Lee Fogolin	.20	.50
4 Kevin Lowe	.60	1.50
5 Doug Hicks	.20	.50
6 Garry Lariviere	.20	.50
7 Paul Coffey	3.00	8.00
8 Risto Siltanen	.20	.50
9 Glenn Anderson	1.25	3.00
10 Matti Hagman	.20	.50
11 Mark Messier	3.00	8.00
12 Dave Hunter	.20	.50
15 Curt Brackenbury	.20	.50
16 Pat Hughes	.20	.50
17 Jari Kurri	2.00	5.00
18 Brett Callighen	.20	.50
20 Dave Lumley	.20	.50
21 Stan Weir	.20	.50
26 Mike Forbes	.20	.50
27 Dave Semenko	.40	1.00
30 Ron Low	.40	1.00
35 Andy Moog	1.50	4.00
77 Garry Unger	.30	.75
99A Wayne Gretzky	30.00	80.00
99B Wayne Gretzky	5.00	12.00
99C Wayne Gretzky	5.00	12.00
99D Wayne Gretzky	5.00	12.00
99E Wayne Gretzky	5.00	12.00
99F Wayne Gretzky Physical size is not Long hair		
99G Wayne Gretzky Headman the puck Long hair		
99H Wayne Gretzky Penalties don't help Long hair		
99I Wayne Gretzky In order to play(Long hair		
99J Wayne Gretzky The positions on a Long hair		
NNO Team Autographs	.40	1.00
xx Glen Sather CO	.30	.75
xx Billy Harris CO	.20	.50
xx Ted Green CO	.20	.50

1981-82 Oilers West Edmonton Mall

These nine blank-backed photos measured approximately 5" by 7" and featured white-bordered black-and-white player head shots. The player's name and uniform number, along with the name and logo of the West Edmonton Mall, appeared in the wide bottom white margin. The photos were unnumbered and checklisted below in alphabetical order.

COMPLETE SET (9)	50.00	125.00
1 Lee Fogolin	1.50	4.00
2 Grant Fuhr	6.00	15.00
3 Wayne Gretzky	40.00	100.00
4 Billy Harris ACO	1.50	4.00
5 Charlie Huddy	2.00	5.00
6 Gary Lariviere	1.50	4.00
7 Dave Lumley	1.50	4.00
8 Risto Siltanen	1.50	4.00
9 Stan Weir	1.50	4.00

1982-83 Oilers Red Rooster

This 30-card set of Edmonton Oilers was sponsored by Red Rooster Food Stores, and the player cards could be collected at any of these stores. The cards measured approximately 2 3/4" by 3 9/16" and the set includes four different cards of Wayne Gretzky. The front had a color photo (with rounded corners) of the player, with the Edmonton Oilers' logo and player's signature across the bottom of the picture. The player's name, uniform number, and a hockey tip were given below the photo. The back had the Red Rooster logo at the upper left-hand corner as well as biographical and statistical information on the player. The bottom had an anti-crime message. The set is checklisted below using sweater numbers for reference.

COMPLETE SET (30)	15.00	40.00
2 Lee Fogolin	.20	.50
4 Kevin Lowe	.40	1.00
6 Garry Lariviere	.20	.50
7 Paul Coffey	1.50	4.00
9 Glenn Anderson	.50	1.25
10 Jaroslav Pouzar	.20	.50
11 Mark Messier	2.00	5.00
12 Dave Hunter	.20	.50
13 Ken Linseman	.20	.50
14 Laurie Boschman	.20	.50
16 Pat Hughes	.20	.50
17 Jari Kurri	1.25	3.00
20 Dave Lumley	.20	.50
21 Randy Gregg	.20	.50
22 Charlie Huddy	.30	.75
23 Marc Habscheid	.20	.50
24 Tom Roulston	.20	.50
27 Dave Semenko	.30	.75
29 Don Jackson	.20	.50
30 Ron Low	.30	.75
31 Grant Fuhr	1.00	2.50
35 Andy Moog	1.00	2.50
77 Garry Unger	.30	.75
99A Wayne Gretzky	4.00	10.00
99B Wayne Gretzky	4.00	10.00
99C Wayne Gretzky	4.00	10.00
99D Wayne Gretzky	4.00	10.00
NNO Glen Sather CO	.30	.75
NNO John Muckler ACO	.20	.50
NNO Ted Green ACO	.20	.50

1983-84 Oilers Dollars

These seven cards, measuring approximately 3" by 5" and perforated on each end, were issued with Hockey Dollars or what may be better described as silver-colored coins. Each coin displayed an engraving of the player's face on the obverse and the team logo on the reverse. The card fronts were gray with tan lettering. They hadthe player's name, number, year, team logo, and a picture of the coin. In a horizontal format, the backs carried biography, career highlights, and career statistics. The cards were numbered on the back in the upper right corner. The prices below refer to the coin-card combination intact.

COMPLETE SET (7)	30.00	75.00
H14 Wayne Gretzky	4.00	10.00
H15 Andy Moog	2.00	5.00
H16 Dave Hunter	1.25	3.00
H17 Ken Linseman SP	12.00	30.00
H18 Lee Fogolin SP	12.00	30.00
H19 Dave Semenko	2.00	5.00
H20 Mark Messier	3.00	8.00

1983-84 Oilers McDonald's

This 25-card set of Edmonton Oilers (entitled McDonald's Playoff Action Album) was issued in seven panels. After perforation, the standard issue cards measured 1 1/2" by 2 1/2" and number 22; three cards (3, 19, and 20) are oversized and measure 3" by 2 1/2". The card fronts featured color action photos with dark blue borders. The card backs gave the player's name and number and often included a bit of trivia about player's career or preferences. Cards could be collected from participating McDonald's restaurants and pasted in a playoff album. An adhesive strip on the back could be used to stick the card in a special album. We have checklisted the names below according to the order of the album.

COMPLETE SET (25)	10.00	25.00
1 Ken Linseman 13	.20	.50
2 Dave Semenko 27	.20	.50
3 Andy Moog 35	.75	2.00
4 Raimo Summanen 25	.15	.40
5 Jari Kurri 17	.75	2.00
6 Rick Chartraw 6	.15	.40
7 Don Jackson 29	.15	.40
8 Dave Hunter 12	.15	.40
9 Charlie Huddy 22	.20	.50
10 Emery Award	.15	.40
11 Pat Conacher 15	.15	.40
12 Lee Fogolin 2	.15	.40
13 Kevin Lowe 4	.30	.75
14 Randy Gregg 21	.20	.50
15 Pat Hughes 16	.15	.40
16 Kevin McClelland 24	.15	.40
17 Willy Lindstrom 19	.15	.40
18 Mark Messier 11	1.50	4.00
19 Grant Fuhr 31	.75	2.00
20 Coaches Ted Green Glen Sather John Muckler	.30	.75
21 Wayne Gretzky 99	4.00	10.00
22 Dave Lumley 20	.15	.40
23 Jaroslav Pouzar 10	.15	.40
24 Glenn Anderson 9	.40	1.00
25 Paul Coffey 7	1.00	2.50
xx Playoff Album	1.25	3.00

1984-85 Oilers Red Rooster

This 30-card set of Edmonton Oilers was sponsored by Red Rooster Food Stores in conjunction with Old Dutch Potato Chips and Post. The player cards could be collected at Red Rooster stores. The cards measured approximately 2 3/4" by 3 9/16" and the set included four different cards of Wayne Gretzky featuring the same pose but different text on the front. The front had a color photo of the player, with the Oilers' logo and player's signature across the bottom of the picture. The player's name, uniform number, and a hockey tip were given below the photo. The top half of the back had biographical and statistical information on the player, while the bottom half had company logos and an anti-crime message. There was a second print version of Glen Sather, which color corrected his first print card to reduce the redness in his face. The set is checklisted below using sweater numbers for reference.

COMPLETE SET (30)	12.00	30.00
2 Lee Fogolin	.15	.40
4 Kevin Lowe	.20	.50
7 Paul Coffey	1.00	2.50
8 Dave Lumley	.15	.40
9 Glenn Anderson	.40	1.00
10 Jaroslav Pouzar	.15	.40
11 Mark Messier	1.50	4.00
12 Dave Hunter	.15	.40
16 Pat Hughes	.15	.40
17 Jari Kurri	.75	2.00
18 Mark Napier	.15	.40
19 Willy Lindstrom	.15	.40
20 Billy Carroll	.15	.40
21 Randy Gregg	.15	.40
22 Charlie Huddy	.15	.40
23 Marc Habscheid	.15	.40
24 Kevin McClelland	.15	.40
26 Mike Krushelnyski	.15	.40
27 Dave Semenko	.20	.50
28 Larry Melnyk	.15	.40
29 Don Jackson	.15	.40
31 Grant Fuhr	.75	2.00
35 Andy Moog	.75	2.00
99A Wayne Gretzky You try to be aware	3.00	8.00
99B Wayne Gretzky	3.00	8.00
99C Wayne Gretzky	3.00	8.00
99D Wayne Gretzky	3.00	8.00
NNO Ted Green ACO	.15	.40
NNO John Muckler ACO	.15	.40
NNO Glen Sather CO P1 (Facsimile autograph	.20	.50
NNO Glen Sather CO P2 (No facsimile autograph	2.00	5.00

1984-85 Oilers Team Issue

Each of these collectibles measured approximately 4 1/2" by 6 1/2" and was printed on thin glossy paper. The set was packaged in a plastic bag that included three small stickers. Two of the stickers ("Go 2 It Oilers" and "do it again Oilers") determined the date of the set as 1984-85, the season following the Oilers' 1983-84 championship. On the top half, the front featured player information on the left and a color portrait with a light blue studio background on the right. On the bottom half, a white-bordered 4" by 3" color action player photo appeared. The backs were blank. The cards were unnumbered and checklisted below in alphabetical order.

COMPLETE SET (23)	12.00	30.00
1 Glenn Anderson	.50	1.25
2 Billy Carroll	.20	.50
3 Paul Coffey	1.25	3.00
4 Lee Fogolin	.20	.50
5 Grant Fuhr	.75	2.00
6 Randy Gregg	.20	.50
7 Wayne Gretzky	4.00	10.00
8 Charlie Huddy	.20	.50
9 Pat Hughes	.20	.50
10 Dave Hunter	.20	.50
11 Don Jackson	.20	.50
12 Mike Krushelnyski	.30	.75
13 Jari Kurri	.75	2.00
14 Willy Lindstrom	.20	.50
15 Kevin Lowe	.40	1.00
16 Dave Lumley	.20	.50
17 Kevin McClelland	.20	.50
18 Larry Melnyk	.20	.50
19 Mark Messier	2.00	5.00
20 Andy Moog	.75	2.00
21 Mark Napier	.20	.50
22 Jaroslav Pouzar	.20	.50
23 Dave Semenko	.30	.75

1985-86 Oilers Red Rooster

This 30-card set of Edmonton Oilers was sponsored by Red Rooster Food Stores in conjunction with Old Dutch Potato Chips and Post. The player cards could be collected from any Red Rooster stores. The cards measured approximately 2 3/4" by 3 9/16" and the set included three different cards of Wayne Gretzky. The front had a color photo (with rounded corners) of the player, with the player's signature across the bottom of the picture. The player's name, uniform number, and a hockey tip were given below the photo. In contrast to earlier issues, the team logo appeared beneath the picture. The top half of the back had biographical and statistical information on the player, while the bottom half had company logos and an anti-crime message. The cards of Marty McSorley, Steve Smith, and Esa Tikkanen predated their O-Pee-Chee Rookie Cards by at least a year. The set is checklisted below using sweater numbers for reference.

COMPLETE SET (30)	15.00	40.00
2 Lee Fogolin	.15	.40
4 Kevin Lowe	.20	.50
5 Steve Smith	.60	1.50
7 Paul Coffey	1.00	2.50
8 Gord Sherven	.15	.40
9 Glenn Anderson	.30	.75
10 Esa Tikkanen	1.25	3.00
11 Mark Messier	1.50	4.00
12 Dave Hunter	.15	.40
14 Craig MacTavish	.30	.75
17 Jari Kurri	.75	2.00
18 Mark Napier	.20	.50
19 Mike Rogers	.15	.40
20 Dave Lumley	.15	.40
21 Randy Gregg	.15	.40
22 Charlie Huddy	.15	.40
24 Kevin McClelland	.15	.40
25 Raimo Summanen	.15	.40
26 Mike Krushelnyski	.15	.40
27 Dave Semenko	.20	.50
29 Don Jackson	.15	.40
31 Grant Fuhr	.75	2.00
33 Marty McSorley	1.00	2.50
35 Andy Moog	.75	2.00
99A Wayne Gretzky	3.00	8.00
99B Wayne Gretzky	3.00	8.00
99C Wayne Gretzky	3.00	8.00
NNO Bob McCammon ACO	.15	.40
NNO John Muckler ACO	.15	.40
NNO Glen Sather CO	.20	.50

1986-87 Oilers Red Rooster

This 30-card set of Edmonton Oilers was sponsored by Red Rooster Food Stores in conjunction with Old Dutch Potato Chips. The player cards could be collected from any Red Rooster stores. The cards measured approximately 2 3/4" by 3 9/16" and the set included two different cards of Wayne Gretzky and of Andy Moog. The front had a color photo (with rounded corners) of the player, with the player's signature across the bottom of the picture. The player's name, uniform number, the team logo, and a safety tip were given below the photo. The top half of the back had biographical and statistical information on the player, while the bottom half had the sponsor's advertisements and the anti-crime slogan "Support Crime Stoppers." The set is checklisted below using sweater numbers for reference.

COMPLETE SET (30)	10.00	25.00
2 Lee Fogolin	.15	.40
4 Kevin Lowe	.20	.50
5 Steve Smith	.30	.75
6 Jeff Beukeboom	.20	.50
7 Paul Coffey	.75	2.00
8 Stu Kulak	.15	.40
9 Glenn Anderson	.30	.75
10 Esa Tikkanen	.75	2.00
11 Mark Messier	1.25	3.00
12 Dave Hunter	.15	.40
14 Craig MacTavish	.40	1.00
15 Steve Graves	.15	.40
17 Jari Kurri	.60	1.50
18 Danny Gare	.20	.50
21 Randy Gregg	.15	.40
22 Charlie Huddy	.20	.50
24 Kevin McClelland	.15	.40
25 Raimo Summanen	.15	.40
26 Mike Krushelnyski	.15	.40
28 Craig Muni	.15	.40
31 Grant Fuhr	.60	1.50
33 Marty McSorley	.75	2.00
35A Andy Moog	.60	1.50
35B Andy Moog	.60	1.50
65 Mark Napier	.20	.50
99A Wayne Gretzky	3.00	8.00
99B Wayne Gretzky	3.00	8.00
NNO Ted Green ACO	.15	.40
NNO John Muckler ACO	.08	.25
NNO Glen Sather CO	.20	.50

1986-87 Oilers Team Issue

This set of Edmonton Oilers consisted of 24 cards, each measuring approximately 3 11/16" by 6 13/16". The front featured a full color action shot of the player on white card stock, with a color "mug shot" superimposed for the most part at one of the lower corners of the picture. The player's uniform number, name, Oilers' logo, and brief biographical information were given above the photo. The back of each card was blank. The set is checklisted below using sweater numbers for reference.

COMPLETE SET (24)	15.00	40.00
2 Lee Fogolin	.20	.50
4 Kevin Lowe	.30	.75
5 Steve Smith	.30	.75
6 Jeff Beukeboom	.30	.75
7 Paul Coffey	1.25	3.00
8 Stu Kulak	.20	.50
9 Glenn Anderson	.40	1.00
10 Esa Tikkanen	1.25	3.00
11 Mark Messier	2.00	5.00
12 Dave Hunter	.20	.50
14 Craig MacTavish	.40	1.00
17 Jari Kurri	1.00	2.50
20 Jaroslav Pouzar	.20	.50
21 Randy Gregg	.20	.50
22 Charlie Huddy	.20	.50
24 Kevin McClelland	.20	.50
25 Raimo Summanen	.20	.50
26 Mike Krushelnyski	.20	.50
28 Craig Muni	.20	.50
31 Grant Fuhr	1.00	2.50
33 Marty McSorley	1.25	3.00
35 Andy Moog	1.00	2.50
65 Mark Napier	.30	.75
99 Wayne Gretzky	6.00	15.00

1987-88 Oilers Team Issue

This set of Edmonton Oilers consisted of 22 cards, each measuring approximately 3 11/16" by 6 13/16". The front featured a full color action shot of the player on white card stock, with a color "mug shot" superimposed for the most part at one of the lower corners of the picture. The player's uniform number, name, Oilers' logo, and brief biographical information were given above the photo. The back of each card was blank. The set is checklisted below using sweater numbers for reference.

COMPLETE SET (22)	12.00	30.00
4 Kevin Lowe	.30	.75
5 Steve Smith	.40	1.00
6 Jeff Beukeboom	.40	1.00
9 Glenn Anderson	.40	1.00
10 Esa Tikkanen	.60	1.50
11 Mark Messier	1.50	4.00
12 Dave Hannan	.20	.50
14 Craig MacTavish	.30	.75
17 Jari Kurri	.75	2.00
18 Craig Simpson	.40	1.00
19 Normand Lacombe	.20	.50
22 Charlie Huddy	.20	.50
23 Keith Acton	.30	.75
24 Kevin McClelland	.20	.50
26 Mike Krushelnyski	.20	.50
28 Craig Muni	.20	.50
29 Daryl Reaugh	.30	.75
30 Warren Skorodenski	.30	.75
31 Grant Fuhr	.75	2.00
33 Marty McSorley	.60	1.50
36 Selmar Odelein	.20	.50
99 Wayne Gretzky	6.00	15.00

1988-89 Oilers Tenth Anniversary

This set contained 164 cards and commemorateed the tenth anniversary of the Edmonton Oilers. The cards were issued in four card panels, and each regular season edition of Action Magazine (Edmonton Oilers game program) contained one panel. The panels measured approximately 9 1/4 by 7 7/16", and the horizontally oriented cards were in between a gray stripe at the top and card information at the bottom. The cards were not perforated, but after cutting they measure approximately 2 9/16" by 4 5/16". The front featured a color action photo of the player, with a thin black border on white card stock. The box below the picture had player identification and three logos. The back had biographical and statistical information in a horizontal format concerning the player's history with the Oilers.

COMPLETE SET (164)	50.00	125.00
1 Garry Unger	.40	1.00
2 Chris Joseph	.20	.50
3 Raimo Summanen	.20	.50
4 Mike Zanier	.30	.75
5 Kevin Lowe	.60	1.50
6 Dave Semenko	.40	1.00
7 Peter Driscoll	.20	.50
8 Ken Solheim	.20	.50
9 Glenn Anderson	1.00	2.50
10 Curt Brackenbury	.20	.50
11 Ron Shudra	.20	.50
12 Gord Sherven	.20	.50
13 Randy Gregg	.30	.75
14 Larry Melnyk	.20	.50
15 Tom Roulston	.20	.50
16 Billy Carroll	.20	.50
17 Jeff Beukeboom	.30	.75
18 Jaroslav Pouzar	.20	.50
19 Jeff Brubaker	.20	.50
20 Danny Gare	.30	.75
21 Craig MacTavish	.30	.75
22 Reijo Routsalainen	.30	.75
23 Willy Lindstrom	.20	.50
24 Pat Hughes	.20	.50
25 Jim Wiemer	.20	.50
26 Selmar Odelein	.20	.50
27 Kent Nilsson	.40	1.00
28 Mark Napier	.30	.75
29 Esa Tikkanen	1.00	2.50
30 John Miner	.20	.50
31 Tom McMurchy	.20	.50
32 Steve Graves	.20	.50
33 Craig Muni	.20	.50
34 Moe Mantha	.20	.50
35 Dave Lumley	.30	.75
36 Ron Low	.30	.75
37 Marty McSorley	1.00	2.50
38 Steve Dykstra	.20	.50
39 Risto Jalo	.20	.50
40 Dave Hunter	.20	.50
41 Jari Kurri	2.00	5.00
42 Lee Fogolin	.20	.50
43 Moe Lemay	.20	.50
44 Stu Kulak	.20	.50
45 Charlie Huddy	.30	.75
46 Wayne Gretzky	15.00	40.00
47 Ken Linseman	.30	.75
48 Risto Siltanen	.30	.75
49 Glen Sather	.40	1.00
50 Brett Callighen	.20	.50
51 Eddie Mio	.30	.75
52 Ken Hammond	.20	.50
53 Jimmy Carson	.30	.75
54 Paul Coffey	2.00	5.00
55 Wayne Gretzky 1050th	10.00	25.00
56 Reed Larson	.20	.50
57 Ted Green	.30	.75
58 Matti Hagman	.20	.50
59 Marc Habscheid	.20	.50
60 Bill Ranford	2.00	5.00
61 Mark Lamb	.20	.50
62 Daryl Reaugh	.40	1.00
63 Al Hamilton	.20	.50
64 Paul Coffey's 47th	1.25	3.00
65 Grant Fuhr	2.00	5.00
66 Stan Weir	.20	.50
67 Ken Berry	.20	.50
68 John Muckler CO	.30	.75
69 Doug Smith	.20	.50
70 Lance Nethery	.20	.50
71 Bill Flett	.20	.50
72 Mike Forbes	.20	.50
73 Martin Gelinas	.40	1.00
74 Ron Chipperfield	.20	.50
75 Reg Kerr	.20	.50
76 Don Jackson	.20	.50
77 Keith Acton	.30	.75
78 Gary Edwards	.30	.75
79 Mike Krushelnyski	.30	.75
80 Trainers Lyle Kulchisky Peter Millar Barrie Stafford	.20	.50
81 Normand Lacombe	.20	.50
82 Pat Price	.20	.50
83 Dave Hannan	.20	.50
84 Garry Lariviere	.20	.50
85 Greg Adams	.20	.50
86 Poul Popiel	.20	.50
87 Tom Gorence	.20	.50
88 Geoff Courtnall	.75	2.00
89 Mark Messier	3.00	8.00
90 Dave Dryden	.30	.75
91 Andy Moog	2.00	5.00
92 Jim Ennis	.20	.50
93 Craig Simpson	.40	1.00
94 Laurie Boschman	.20	.50
95 Doug Hicks	.20	.50
96 Rick Chartraw	.20	.50
97 1984 Stanley Cup Champs	.40	1.00
98 Ron Carter	.20	.50
99 Blair MacDonald	.20	.50
100 Dean Clark	.20	.50
101 Glen Cochrane	.20	.50

Card	Low	High
102 Lindsay Middlebrook	.20	.50
103 Ron Areshenkoff	.20	.50
104 Billy Harris CO	.20	.50
105 Conn Smythe Trophy	.30	.75
106 John Blum	.20	.50
107 Wayne Bianchin	.20	.50
108 Tom Bladon	.20	.50
109 Kevin McClelland	.20	.50
110 Roy Sommer	.20	.50
111 Mike Toal	.20	.50
112 Don Ashby	.20	.50
113 Don Nachbaur	.20	.50
114 1985 Stanley Cup Champs	.40	1.00
115 Jim Corsi	.20	.50
116 John Hughes	.20	.50
117 Coach of the Year Glen Sather	.40	1.00
118 Bob Dupuis	.20	.50
119 Jim Harrison	.20	.50
120 Don Murdoch	.20	.50
121 Steve Smith	.40	1.00
122 Pete Lopresti	.20	.50
123 Colin Campbell	.40	1.00
124 Bryan Watson	.20	.50
125 John Bednarski	.20	.50
126 1987 Stanley Cup Champs (Marty McSorley)	.40	1.00
127 Scott Metcalfe	.20	.50
128 Mike Rogers	.20	.50
129 Dan Newman	.20	.50
130 Fuhr's 75th	.75	2.00
131 Warren Skorodenski	.30	.75
132 Todd Strueby	.20	.50
133 Kelly Buchberger	.40	1.00
134 Cam Connor	.20	.50
135 Dean Hopkins	.20	.50
136 Mike Moller	.20	.50
137 1988 Stanley Cup Champs (Wayne Gretzky)	3.00	8.00
138 Bryon Baltimore	.20	.50
139 Pat Conacher	.20	.50
140 Ray Cote	.20	.50
141 Walt Poddubny	.20	.50
142 Jim Playfair	.20	.50
143 Nick Fotiu	.20	.50
144 Kari Makkonen	.20	.50
145 Dave Brown	.30	.75
146 Terry Martin	.20	.50
147 Francois Leroux	.20	.50
148 Kari Jalonen	.20	.50
149 Tomas Jonsson	.30	.75
150 Dave Donnelly	.20	.50
151 Mike Ware	.20	.50
152 Don Cutts	.20	.50
153 Miroslav Frycer	.20	.50
154 Bruce MacGregor GM	.20	.50
155 Kim Issel	.20	.50
156 Marco Baron	.30	.75
157 Doug Halward	.20	.50
158 Barry Fraser DIR	.20	.50
159 Alan May	.20	.50
160 Bobby Schmautz	.20	.50
161 Craig Redmond	.20	.50
162 Oilers Host '89 All-Star Game	.30	.75
163 Alex Tidey	.20	.50
164 Wayne Van Dorp	.20	.50

1988-89 Oilers Team Issue

This 27-card set measured approximately 3 3/4" by 6 7/8". On a white background, the fronts featured a color action player photo with a color player portrait superimposed in one of the corners. The player's name, uniform number, a short biography, and the team logo appeared above the picture. The backs were blank. The cards are unnumbered and checklisted below in alphabetical order.

Card	Low	High
COMPLETE SET (27)	8.00	20.00
1 Glenn Anderson	.40	1.00
2 Jeff Beukeboom	.40	1.00
3 Dave Brown	.30	.75
4 Kelly Buchberger	.40	1.00
5 Jimmy Carson	.30	.75
6 Miroslav Frycer	.20	.50
7 Grant Fuhr	.75	2.00
8 Randy Gregg	.30	.75
9 Doug Halward	.20	.50
10 Charlie Huddy	.30	.75
11 Dave Hunter	.20	.50
12 Tomas Jonsson	.30	.75
13 Chris Joseph	.20	.50
14 Jari Kurri	.60	1.50
15 Normand Lacombe	.20	.50
16 Mark Lamb	.20	.50
17 John LeBlanc	.20	.50
18 Kevin Lowe	.30	.75
19 Craig MacTavish	.30	.75
20 Kevin McClelland	.20	.50
21 Mark Messier	1.50	4.00
22 Craig Muni	.20	.50
23 Bill Ranford	1.25	3.00
24 Craig Redmond	.20	.50
25 Craig Simpson	.30	.75
26 Steve Smith	.40	1.00
27 Esa Tikkanen	.60	1.50

1989-90 Oilers Team Issue

This standard size set featured color action photos on a white background. Players name, number, and a short bio appeared at the top of the card. Cards featured blank backs and are checklisted below alphabetically.

Card	Low	High
COMPLETE SET (24)	10.00	25.00
1 Glenn Anderson	.30	.75
2 Jeff Beukeboom	.25	.60
3 Dave Brown	.25	.60
4 Kelly Buchberger	.25	.60
5 Peter Eriksson	.15	.40
6 Grant Fuhr	.60	1.50
7 Martin Gelinas	.75	2.00
8 Adam Graves	1.50	4.00
9 Randy Gregg	.25	.60
10 Charlie Huddy	.25	.60
11 Petr Klima	.30	.75
12 Jari Kurri	.60	1.50
13 Normand Lacombe	.15	.40
14 Mark Lamb	.15	.40
15 Kevin Lowe	.25	.60
16 Craig Mactavish	.25	.60
17 Mark Messier	1.25	3.00
18 Craig Muni	.15	.40
19 Joe Murphy	.75	2.00
20 Bill Ranford	.75	2.00
21 Craig Simpson	.25	.60
22 Geoff Smith	.25	.60
23 Steve Smith	.30	.75
24 Esa Tikkanen	.30	.75

1990-91 Oilers IGA

This 30-card standard-size set was sponsored by IGA food stores in conjunction with McGavin's, a distributor of bread and other products in Alberta. Protected by a cello pack, one card was inserted in bread loaves distributed by McGavin's to IGA stores in Calgary and Edmonton. Calgary consumers received a Flames' card, while Edmonton consumers received an Oilers' card. Checklist and coaches cards were not inserted in the loaves but were included on five hundred individually numbered and uncut sheets not offered to the general public. The cards were printed on thin card stock. The fronts had posed color player photos, with a border that shades from blue to orange and back to blue. Most of the photos were shot against the background of the equipment room or dressing room. The player's name was printed in the bottom border, and his uniform number was printed in a circle in the upper left corner of each picture. The horizontally oriented backs featured biographical information, with year-by-year statistics presented in a pink rectangle. Sponsor logos at the bottom rounded out the back. The cards were unnumbered and checklisted below in alphabetical order. Adam Graves appears during his Rookie Card year.

Card	Low	High
COMPLETE SET (30)	14.00	35.00
1 Glenn Anderson	.60	1.50
2 Jeff Beukeboom	.30	.75
3 Dave Brown	.40	1.00
4 Kelly Buchberger	.40	1.00
5 Martin Gelinas	.40	1.00
6 Adam Graves	1.50	4.00
7 Ted Green CO SP	1.25	3.00
8 Charlie Huddy	.30	.75
9 Chris Joseph	.30	.75
10 Petr Klima	.20	.50
11 Mark Lamb	.20	.50
12 Ken Linseman	.30	.75
13 Ron Low CO SP	1.25	3.00
14 Kevin Lowe	.50	1.25
15 Craig MacTavish	.30	.75
16 Mark Messier	2.50	6.00
17 Joey Moss	.20	.50
18 John Muckler CO SP	1.25	3.00
19 Craig Muni	.20	.50
20 Joe Murphy	.30	.75
21 Bill Ranford	1.25	3.00
22 Anatoli Semenov	.20	.50
23 Craig Simpson	.20	.50
24 Geoff Smith	.20	.50
25 Steve Smith	.40	1.00
26 Kari Takko	.30	.75
27 Esa Tikkanen	.60	1.50
28 Training Staff SP	.60	1.50
29 Edmonton Oilers Year-by-Year Record	.20	.50
30 Checklist Card SP	1.25	3.00

1991 Oilers Panini Team Stickers

This 32-sticker set was issued in a plastic bag that contained two 16-sticker sheets (approximately 9" by 12") and a foldout poster, "Super Poster - Hockey 91", on which the stickers could be affixed. The players' names appeared only on the poster, not on the stickers. Each sticker measured about 2 1/8" by 2 7/8" and featured a color player action shot on its white-bordered front. The back of the white sticker sheet was lined off into 16 panels, each carried the logos for Panini, the NHL, and the NHLPA, as well as the same number that appeared on the front of the sticker. Every Canadian NHL team was featured in this promotion. Each team set was available by mail-order from Panini Canada Ltd. for 2.99 plus 50 cents for shipping and handling.

Card	Low	High
COMPLETE SET (32)	1.50	4.00
1 Glenn Anderson	.07	.20
2 Jeff Beukeboom	.01	.05
3 Dave Brown	.01	.05
4 Kelly Buchberger	.02	.10
5 Martin Gelinas	.02	.10
6 Adam Graves	.15	.40
7 Charlie Huddy	.01	.05
8 Chris Joseph	.01	.05
9 Petr Klima	.02	.10
10 Mark Lamb	.01	.05
11 Ken Linesman	.01	.05
12 Kevin Lowe	.05	.15
13 Craig MacTavish	.02	.10
14 Mark Messier	.20	.50
15 Craig Muni	.01	.05
16 Joe Murphy	.02	.10
17 Bill Ranford	.15	.40
18 Eldon Reddick	.02	.10
19 Anatoli Semenov	.01	.05
20 Craig Simpson	.02	.10
21 Geoff Smith	.01	.05
22 Steve Smith	.02	.10
23 Esa Tikkanen	.07	.20
24 Oilers In Action	.05	.15
A Team Logo Left Side	.01	.05
B Team Logo Right Side	.01	.05
C Oilers in Action Upper Left Corner	.01	.05
D Oilers in Action Lower Left Corner	.01	.05
E Bill Ranford Upper Right Corner	.08	.25
F Bill Ranford Lower Right Corner	.08	.25
G Mark Messier	.20	.50
H Action in the Crease	.05	.15

1991-92 Oilers IGA

This 30-card standard-size set of Edmonton Oilers was sponsored by IGA food stores and included manufacturers' discount coupons. One pack of cards was distributed in Calgary and Edmonton IGA stores with any grocery purchase of 10.00 or more. The cards were printed on thin card stock. The fronts have posed color action photos bordered in dark blue. The player's name was printed vertically in the wider left border, and his uniform number and the team name appeared at the bottom of the picture. In black print on a white background, the backs presented biography and statistics (regular season and playoff). Packs were kept under the cash till drawer, and therefore many of the cards were creased. Each pack contained three Oilers and two Flame cards. The checklist and coaches cards for both teams were not included in the packs but were available on a very limited basis through an uncut team sheet offer. The cards were unnumbered and checklisted below in alphabetical order, with the coaches cards listed after the players.

Card	Low	High
COMPLETE SET (30)	8.00	20.00
1 Josef Beranek	.20	.50
2 Kelly Buchberger	.30	.75
3 Vincent Damphousse	.60	1.50
4 Louie DeBrusk	.20	.50
5 Martin Gelinas	.30	.75
6 Peter Ing	.25	.60
7 Petr Klima	.20	.50
8 Mark Lamb	.20	.50
9 Kevin Lowe	.30	.75
10 Norm Maciver	.20	.50
11 Craig MacTavish	.30	.75
12 Troy Mallette	.20	.50
13 Dave Manson	.40	1.00
14 Scott Mellanby	.40	1.00
15 Craig Muni	.20	.50
16 Joe Murphy	.30	.75
17 Bill Ranford	.75	2.00
18 Steven Rice	.20	.50
19 Luke Richardson	.20	.50
20 Anatoli Semenov	.20	.50
21 David Shaw	.20	.50
22 Craig Simpson	.30	.75
23 Geoff Smith	.20	.50
24 Scott Thornton	.20	.50
25 Esa Tikkanen	.40	1.00
26 Training Staff SP	.60	1.50
27 Ted Green CO SP	1.00	2.50
28 Ron Low CO SP	1.00	2.50
29 Kevin Primeau CO SP	1.00	2.50
30 Checklist Card SP	1.00	2.50

1991-92 Oilers Team Issue

Printed on thin card stock, this 28-card set measured approximately 3 3/4" by 6 7/8". On the fronts, the white-bordered color action shots had player information and team logo in the top white border. The backs were blank. The cards were unnumbered and checklisted below in alphabetical order.

Card	Low	High
COMPLETE SET (28)	6.00	15.00
1 Josef Beranek	.20	.50
2 Jeff Beukeboom	.20	.50
3 Kelly Buchberger	.30	.75
4 Vincent Damphousse	.60	1.50
5 Louie DeBrusk	.20	.50
6 Martin Gelinas	.20	.50
7 Peter Ing	.25	.60
8 Chris Joseph	.20	.50
9 Petr Klima	.20	.50
10 Mark Lamb	.20	.50
11 Kevin Lowe	.30	.75
12 Norm Maciver	.20	.50
13 Craig MacTavish	.20	.50
14 Troy Mallette	.20	.50
15 Dave Manson	.40	1.00
16 Scott Mellanby	.40	1.00
17 Craig Muni	.20	.50
18 Joe Murphy	.30	.75
19 Bill Ranford	.75	2.00
20 Pokey Reddick	.30	.75
21 Steve Rice	.20	.50
22 Luke Richardson	.20	.50
23 Martin Rucinsky	.60	1.50
24 Anatoli Semenov	.20	.50
25 Craig Simpson	.20	.50
26 Geoff Smith	.20	.50
27 Scott Thornton	.20	.50
28 Esa Tikkanen	.40	1.00

1992-93 Oilers IGA

Sponsored by IGA food stores, the 30 standard-size cards comprising this Special Edition Collector Series set featured color player action shots on their fronts. Each photo was trimmed with a black line and offset flush with the thin white border on the right, which surrounds the card. On the remaining three sides, the picture was edged with a gray and white netlike pattern. The player's name appeared in the upper right and the Oilers logo rests in the lower left. The back carried the player's name at the top, with his position, uniform number, biography, and stat table set within a bluish-gray screened background. The Oilers logo in the upper right rounded out the card.

Card	Low	High
COMPLETE SET (30)	6.00	15.00
1 Checklist	.08	.25
2 Joseph Beranek	.20	.50
3 Kelly Buchberger	.30	.75
4 Shayne Corson	.40	1.00
5 Louie DeBrusk	.20	.50
6 Martin Gelinas	.30	.75
7 Brent Gilchrist	.20	.50
8 Brian Glynn	.20	.50
9 Greg Hawgood	.20	.50
10 Petr Klima	.20	.50
11 Chris Joseph	.20	.50
12 Craig MacTavish	.20	.50
13 Dan Currie	.20	.50
14 Dave Manson	.20	.50
15 Scott Mellanby	.20	.50
16 Craig Muni	.20	.50
17 Bernie Nicholls	.30	.75
18 Bill Ranford	.40	1.00
19 Luke Richardson	.20	.50
20 Craig Simpson	.25	.60
21 Geoff Smith	.20	.50
22 Vladimir Vujtek	.20	.50
23 Esa Tikkanen	.40	1.00
24 Ron Tugnutt	.60	1.50
25 Shaun Van Allen	.20	.50
26 Glen Sather GM	.20	.50
27 Ted Green CO	.20	.50
28 Ron Low CO	.20	.50
29 Kevin Primeau CO	.08	.25
30 Oilers Yearly Record	.08	.25

1992-93 Oilers Team Issue

The 22 blank-backed cards comprising this set were printed on thin white card stock and measured approximately 3 3/4" by 6 7/8". They featured white-bordered color player action photos and displayed the Oilers logo, the player's name, jersey number, and brief biography within the broad white border at the top. The cards were unnumbered and checklisted below in alphabetical order.

Card	Low	High
COMPLETE SET (22)	4.80	12.00
1 Kelly Buchberger	.25	.60
2 Zdeno Ciger	.20	.50
3 Shayne Corson	.30	.75
4 Louie DeBrusk	.20	.50
5 Todd Elik	.20	.50
6 Brian Glynn	.20	.50
7 Mike Hudson	.20	.50
8 Chris Joseph	.20	.50
9 Igor Kravchuk	.20	.50
10 Francois Leroux	.20	.50
11 Craig MacTavish	.20	.50
12 Dave Manson	.20	.50
13 Shjon Podein	.20	.50
14 Bill Ranford	.40	1.00
15 Steve Rice	.20	.50
16 Luke Richardson	.20	.50
17 Craig Simpson	.25	.60
18 Geoff Smith	.20	.50
19 Kevin Todd	.20	.50
20 Vladimir Vujtek	.20	.50
21 Doug Weight	.75	2.00
22 Brad Werenka	.20	.50

1996-97 Oilers Postcards

This 27-card set of Oilers postcards was the first to picture the team in their new sweaters. These odd size postcards (3 3/4" by 6 7/8") featured sharp action photography on the front, along with team logo, player name and biographical data. The backs were blank. As the players' jersey numbers were displayed prominently on the upper left corner, they are listed below accordingly.

Card	Low	High
COMPLETE SET (27)	6.00	15.00
2 Boris Mironov	.20	.50
4 Kevin Lowe	.20	.50
5 Greg de Vries	.20	.50
6 Jeff Norton	.15	.40
7 Jason Arnott	.40	1.00
8 Sean Brown	.15	.40
10 Steve Kelly	.20	.50
14 Mats Lindgren	.20	.50
16 Kelly Buchberger	.20	.50
17 Rem Murray	.20	.50
18 Miroslav Satan	.60	1.50
19 Boyd Devereaux	.40	1.00
21 Mariusz Czerkawski	.20	.50
22 Luke Richardson	.20	.50
23 Dan McGillis	.20	.50
24 Bryan Marchment	.20	.50
25 Mike Grier	.60	1.50
26 Todd Marchant	.20	.50
29 Louie DeBrusk	.15	.40
30 Bob Essensa	.30	.75
31 Curtis Joseph	.75	2.00
34 Donald Dufresne	.15	.40
37 Dean McAmmond	.15	.40
39 Doug Weight	.40	1.00
51 Andrei Kovalenko	.20	.50
85 Petr Klima	.15	.40
94 Ryan Smyth	.75	2.00

2000-01 Oilers Postcards

Card	Low	High
COMPLETE SET (25)	5.00	12.00
1 Eric Brewer	.20	.50
2 Tom Poti	.20	.50
3 Frank Musil	.20	.50
4 Josh Green	.20	.50
5 Domenic Pittis	.20	.50
6 Rem Murray	.20	.50
7 Ethan Moreau	.20	.50
8 Jason Smith	.20	.50
9 Anson Carter	.75	2.00
10 Sean Brown	.20	.50
11 Mike Grier	.30	.75
12 Todd Marchant	.20	.50
13 Georges Laraque	.75	2.00
14 Dominic Roussel	.20	.50
15 Scott Ferguson	.20	.50
16 Dan LaCouture	.20	.50
17 Sergei Zholtok	.20	.50
18 Tommy Salo	.40	1.00
19 Shawn Horcoff	.20	.50
20 Doug Weight	.40	1.00
21 Janne Niinimaa	.20	.50
22 Paul Comrie	.20	.50
23 Igor Ulanov	.20	.50
24 Mike Comrie	.20	.50
25 Ryan Smyth	1.00	2.50

2001-02 Oilers Postcards

Card	Low	High
COMPLETE SET (23)	5.00	12.00
1 Shawn Horcoff	.20	.50
2 Josh Green	.20	.50
3 Domenic Pittis	.20	.50
4 Marty Reasoner	.30	.75
5 Rem Murray	.20	.50
6 Ethan Moreau	.20	.50
7 Jochen Hecht	.20	.50
8 Jason Smith	.20	.50
9 Anson Carter	.60	1.50
10 Sean Brown	.20	.50
11 Steve Staios	.20	.50
12 Mike Grier	.30	.75
13 Todd Marchant	.20	.50
14 Georges Laraque	.60	1.50
15 Jussi Markkanen	.20	.50
16 Scott Ferguson	.20	.50
17 Tommy Salo	.40	1.00
18 Janne Niinimaa	.20	.50
19 Mike Comrie	.20	.50
20 Ryan Smyth	1.00	2.50
21 Eric Brewer	.20	.50
22 Tom Poti	.20	.50
23 Daniel Cleary	.20	.50

2002-03 Oilers Postcards

This 22-card set was issued by the team. Cards measure approximately 4" x 7" and are unnumbered. The checklist below is in order by jersey number.

Card	Low	High
COMPLETE SET (22)	8.00	20.00
1 Eric Brewer	.20	.50
2 Daniel Cleary	.20	.50
3 Ales Pisa	.20	.50
4 Shawn Horcoff	.20	.50
5 Mike York	.20	.50
6 Ethan Moreau	.20	.50
7 Marty Reasoner	.20	.50
8 Jason Smith	.20	.50
9 Anson Carter	.40	1.00
10 Steve Staios	.20	.50
11 Todd Marchant	.20	.50
12 Georges Laraque	.60	1.50
14 Jussi Markkanen	.40	1.00
15 Scott Ferguson	.20	.50
16 Jiri Dopita	.20	.50
17 Tommy Salo	.40	1.00
18 Brian Swanson	.20	.50
19 Janne Niinimaa	.20	.50
20 Ales Hemsky	1.25	3.00
21 Mike Comrie	.75	2.00
22 Ryan Smyth	.75	2.00
113 Jason Chimera	.20	.50

2003-04 Oilers Postcards

These postcards were offered by the team in singles form at club events and in response to fan requests. It is believed that this list is complete.

Card	Low	High
COMPLETE SET (22)	8.00	20.00
1 Marc-Andre Bergeron	.30	.75
2 Eric Brewer	.30	.75
3 Jason Chimera	.20	.50
4 Ty Conklin	.40	1.00
5 Cory Cross	.30	.75
6 Radek Dvorak	.30	.75
7 Scott Ferguson	.20	.50
8 Ales Hemsky	.60	1.50
9 Shawn Horcoff	.20	.50
10 Brad Isbister	.30	.75
11 Georges Laraque	.40	1.00
12 Ethan Moreau	.40	1.00
13 Fernando Pisani	.40	1.00
14 Marty Reasoner	.30	.75
15 Tommy Salo	.40	1.00
16 Alexei Semenov	.30	.75
17 Jason Smith	.20	.50
18 Ryan Smyth	.75	2.00
19 Steve Staios	.30	.75
20 Jarret Stoll	.40	1.00
21 Raffi Torres	.40	1.00
22 Mike York	.40	1.00

1932-33 O'Keefe Maple Leafs

This 20-card set was issued by O'Keefe's Beverages and featured the Toronto Maple Leafs, 1931-32 Stanley Cup Champions. Each was designed for use as a coaster. The shape of each card is an eight-pointed star, which measures approximately 5" from one point across to its opposite. Inside a blue border, the front had a black and blue ink portrait or drawing of the player, which was surrounded by cartoons and captions presenting player information. The backs read "O'Keefe's Big 4" and "Each a Leader in its Class." The coasters were numbered on the front near the top and are checklisted below accordingly. Card numbers 13 and 15 are unknown, although many collectors believe it likely that the NNO Doraty and Thoms cards were slated to fill those slots.

Card	Low	High
COMPLETE SET (20)	6000.00	12000.00
1 Lorne Chabot	250.00	600.00
2 Red Horner	250.00	600.00
3 Alex Levinsky	200.00	500.00
4 Hap Day	200.00	500.00
5 Andy Blair	200.00	500.00
6 Ace Bailey	500.00	1200.00
7 King Clancy	500.00	1200.00
8 Harold Cotton	250.00	600.00
9 Charlie Conacher	400.00	1000.00
10 Joe Primeau	400.00	1000.00
11 Harvey Jackson	400.00	1000.00
12 Frank Finnigan	200.00	500.00
14 Bob Gracie	200.00	500.00
16 Harold Darragh	200.00	500.00
17 Benny Grant	200.00	500.00
18 Fred Robertson	200.00	500.00
19 Conn Smythe	400.00	1000.00
20 Dick Irvin	300.00	800.00
NNO Ken Doraty	250.00	600.00
NNO Bill Thoms	250.00	600.00

1933-34 O-Pee-Chee V304A

This first of five O-Pee-Chee 1930's hockey card issues featured a black and white photo of the player portrayed on a colored field of stars. The cards in the set were approximately 2 5/16" by 3 9/16". The player's name appeared in a rectangle at the bottom of the front of the card. Four possible color background fields existed, red, blue, orange and green. The cards were numbered on the back, and a short biography in both English and French is also contained on the back. The catalog designation for this set is V304A. The existence of an album designed to store the cards has been confirmed. It is valued at approximately $250.

Card	Low	High
COMPLETE SET (48)	9000.00	15000.00
WRAPPER (1-CENT)	175.00	350.00
1 Danny Cox RC	150.00	250.00
2 Joe Lamb RC	60.00	100.00
3 Eddie Shore RC	900.00	1500.00
4 Ken Doraty RC	60.00	100.00
5 Fred Hitchman	60.00	100.00
6 Nels Stewart RC	500.00	800.00
7 Walter Galbraith RC	60.00	100.00
8 Dit Clapper RC	400.00	600.00
9 Harry Oliver RC	200.00	400.00
10 Red Horner RC	175.00	300.00
11 Alex Levinsky RC	90.00	150.00
12 Joe Primeau RC	400.00	600.00
13 Ace Bailey RC	300.00	500.00
14 George Patterson RC	60.00	100.00
15 George Hainsworth RC	250.00	400.00
16 Ott Heller RC	60.00	100.00
17 Art Somers RC	60.00	100.00
18 Lorne Chabot RC	250.00	400.00
19 Johnny Gagnon RC	90.00	150.00
20 Pit Lepine RC	60.00	100.00
21 Wildor Larochelle RC	90.00	150.00
22 Georges Mantha RC	90.00	150.00
23 Howie Morenz	1200.00	2500.00
24 Syd Howe RC	200.00	350.00
25 Frank Finnigan	90.00	150.00
26 Bill Touhey RC	90.00	150.00
27 Cooney Weiland RC	200.00	400.00
28 Leo Bourgeault RC	60.00	100.00
29 Normie Himes RC	90.00	150.00
30 Johnny Sheppard RC	60.00	100.00
31 King Clancy	600.00	1000.00
32 Hap Day	150.00	250.00
33 Harvey Jackson RC	300.00	500.00
34 Charlie Conacher RC	600.00	1000.00
35 Harold Cotton RC	125.00	200.00
36 Butch Keeling RC	60.00	100.00
37 Murray Murdoch RC	60.00	100.00
38 Bill Cook UER RC	150.00	250.00
39 Ivan Johnson RC	300.00	600.00
40 Happy Emms RC	90.00	150.00
41 Bert McInenly RC	60.00	100.00
42 John Sorrell RC	90.00	150.00
43 Bill Phillips RC	60.00	100.00
44 Charley McVeigh RC	60.00	100.00
45 Roy Worters RC	250.00	400.00
46 Albert Leduc RC	100.00	200.00
47 Nick Wasnie RC	60.00	100.00
48 Armand Mondou RC	125.00	200.00

1933-34 O-Pee-Chee V304B

The second O-Pee-Chee hockey series of the 1930's contained 24 cards and continues the numbering sequence of the Series A cards. The format was exactly the same as the cards of Series A. The cards in the set measureed approximately 2 5/16" by 3 9/16". The catalog designation for this set is V304B.

Card	Low	High
COMPLETE SET (24)	3000.00	5000.00
WRAPPER (1-CENT)	175.00	350.00
49 Babe Siebert RC	250.00	400.00
50 Aurel Joliat	500.00	800.00
51 Larry Aurie RC	175.00	300.00
52 Ebbie Goodfellow RC	150.00	300.00
53 John Roach	125.00	200.00
54 Bill Beveridge RC	125.00	200.00
55 Earl Robinson RC	90.00	150.00
56 Jimmy Ward RC	90.00	150.00
57 Archie Wilcox RC	90.00	150.00
58 Lorne Duguid RC	90.00	150.00
59 Dave Kerr RC	125.00	200.00
60 Baldy Northcott RC	100.00	200.00
61 Marvin Wentworth RC	125.00	200.00
62 Dave Trottier RC	100.00	200.00
63 Wally Kilrea RC	90.00	150.00
64 Glen Brydson RC	125.00	200.00
65 Vernon Ayres RC	90.00	150.00
66 Bob Gracie RC	90.00	150.00
67 Vic Ripley RC	90.00	150.00
68 Tiny Thompson RC	300.00	500.00
69 Alex Smith RC	90.00	150.00
70 Andy Blair RC	90.00	150.00
71 Cecil Dillon RC	90.00	150.00
72 Bun Cook RC	250.00	400.00

1935-36 O-Pee-Chee V304C

While Series C in the O-Pee-Chee 1930's hockey card set continued the numbering sequence of the previous two years, this 24-card set differed significantly in both format and size. The cards in this set measured approximately 2 3/8" by 2 7/8". Each black and white photo portraying the player on the front could be found on four possible color fields, green, orange, maroon, or yellow. The field consisted of a star in the center and cartooned hockey players flanking the center of the card. The backs contained the player's name, the card number, and biographical data in both English and French. The catalog designation for this set is V304C.

Card	Low	High
COMPLETE SET (24)	2500.00	4000.00
WRAPPER (1-CENT)	175.00	350.00
73 Wilfred Cude RC	175.00	300.00
74 Jack McGill RC	75.00	125.00
75 Russ Blinco RC	75.00	125.00
76 Hooley Smith	150.00	250.00
77 Herb Cain RC	90.00	150.00
78 Gus Marker RC	75.00	125.00
79 Lynn Patrick RC	175.00	300.00
80 Johnny Gottselig	75.00	125.00
81 Marty Barry	125.00	200.00
82 Sylvio Mantha	150.00	250.00
83 Flash Hollett RC	90.00	150.00
84 Nick Metz RC	75.00	125.00
85 Bill Thoms	75.00	125.00
86 Hec Kilrea	75.00	125.00
87 Pep Kelly RC	75.00	125.00
88 Art Jackson RC	75.00	125.00
89 Allan Shields RC	75.00	125.00
90 Buzz Boll	75.00	125.00
91 Jean Pusie RC	75.00	125.00
92 Roger Jenkins RC	75.00	125.00
93 Arthur Coulter RC	90.00	150.00
94 Art Chapman	75.00	125.00
95 Paul Haynes	75.00	125.00
96 Leroy Goldsworthy RC	150.00	250.00

1936-37 O-Pee-Chee V304D

The most significant difference between Series D cards and cards from the previous three O-Pee-Chee sets was the fact that these cards are die-cut and could be folded to give a stand-up figure, like the 1934-36 Batter-Up baseball cards. The cards were in black and white with no colored background field. The cards in the set measured approximately 2 3/8" by 2 15/16". As these cards are difficult to find without the backs missing, this set was the most valuable of the 1930's O-Pee-Chee sets. The backs contained the card number and biographical data in English and French. The player's name was given on the front of the card only. The catalog designation for this set is V304D.

Card	Low	High
COMPLETE SET (36)	9000.00	15000.00
WRAPPER (1-CENT)	175.00	350.00
97 Turk Broda RC	700.00	1200.00
98 Sweeney Schriner RC	250.00	400.00
99 Jack Shill RC	100.00	150.00
100 Bob Davidson RC	125.00	200.00
101 Syl Apps RC	500.00	800.00
102 Lionel Conacher	400.00	600.00
103 Jimmy Fowler RC	125.00	200.00
104 Al Murray RC	100.00	150.00
105 Neil Colville RC	175.00	300.00
106 Paul Runge RC	100.00	150.00
107 Mike Karakas RC	125.00	200.00
108 John Gallagher RC	100.00	150.00
109 Alex Shibicky RC	150.00	250.00
110 Herb Cain	150.00	250.00
111 Bill McKenzie	100.00	150.00
112 Harold Jackson	100.00	150.00
113 Art Wiebe RC	100.00	150.00
114 Joffre Desilets RC	100.00	150.00
115 Earl Robinson	100.00	150.00
116 Cy Wentworth	150.00	250.00
117 Ebbie Goodfellow	125.00	200.00
118 Eddie Shore	1200.00	1800.00
119 Buzz Boll	100.00	150.00
120 Wilfred Cude	125.00	200.00
121 Howie Morenz	1400.00	2200.00
122 Red Horner	250.00	400.00
123 Charlie Conacher	500.00	800.00
124 Busher Jackson	300.00	500.00
125 King Clancy	600.00	1000.00
126 Dave Trottier	100.00	150.00
127 Russ Blinco	100.00	150.00
128 Lynn Patrick	300.00	500.00
129 Aurel Joliat	500.00	800.00
130 Baldy Northcott	100.00	150.00
131 Larry Aurie	100.00	150.00
132 Hooley Smith	250.00	400.00

1937-38 O-Pee-Chee V304E

Series E cards continued the numerical series of the 1930's O-Pee-Chee sets and featured a black and white photo of the player within a serrated, colored (blue or purple) frame. A facsimile autograph and a cartooned hockey player appeared on the front in the same color as the frame. The cards in the set measured approximately 2 3/8" by 2 7/8". The backs contained the card number, the player's name, and biographical data in both English and French. The catalog designation for this set is V304E.

Card	Low	High
COMPLETE SET (48)	4000.00	7500.00
WRAPPER (1-CENT)	150.00	300.00
133 Turk Broda	400.00	600.00
134 Red Horner	125.00	200.00
135 Jimmy Fowler	60.00	100.00
136 Bob Davidson	60.00	100.00
137 Reg. Hamilton RC	60.00	100.00
138 Charlie Conacher	300.00	500.00
139 Busher Jackson	175.00	300.00
140 Buzz Boll	60.00	100.00
141 Syl Apps	250.00	400.00
142 Gordie Drillon RC	175.00	300.00
143 Bill Thoms	60.00	100.00
144 Nick Metz	60.00	100.00
145 Pep Kelly	60.00	100.00
146 Murray Armstrong RC	60.00	100.00
147 Murph Chamberlain RC	60.00	100.00
148 Des Smith RC	60.00	100.00
149 Wilfred Cude	90.00	150.00
150 Babe Siebert	125.00	200.00
151 Bill MacKenzie	60.00	100.00
152 Aurel Joliat	300.00	500.00
153 Georges Mantha	60.00	100.00
154 Johnny Gagnon	60.00	100.00
155 Paul Haynes	60.00	100.00
156 Joffre Desilets	60.00	100.00
157 George Allen Brown RC	60.00	100.00
158 Paul Drouin RC	60.00	100.00
159 Pit Lepine	60.00	100.00
160 Toe Blake RC	500.00	800.00
161 Bill Beveridge	90.00	150.00
162 Allan Shields	60.00	100.00
163 Cy Wentworth	125.00	200.00
164 Stew Evans RC	60.00	100.00
165 Earl Robinson	60.00	100.00
166 Baldy Northcott	90.00	150.00
167 Paul Runge	60.00	100.00
168 Dave Trottier	60.00	100.00
169 Russ Blinco	60.00	100.00
170 Jimmy Ward	60.00	100.00
171 Bob Gracie	60.00	100.00
172 Herb Cain	125.00	200.00
173 Gus Marker	60.00	100.00
174 Walter Buswell RC	60.00	100.00
175 Carl Voss RC	125.00	200.00
176 Rod Lorraine RC	60.00	100.00
177 Armand Mondou	60.00	100.00
178 Cliff Goupille RC	60.00	100.00
179 Jerry Shannon RC	60.00	100.00
180 Tom Cook RC	125.00	200.00

1939-40 O-Pee-Chee V301-1

This O-Pee-Chee set of 100 large cards was apparently issued during the 1939-40 season. The catalog designation for this set is V301-1. The cards are black and white and measured approximately 5" by 7". The card backs were blank. The cards were numbered on the front in the lower right corner. Cards in the set were identified on the front by name, team, and position. These cards were premiums and were issued one per cello pack.

Card	Low	High
COMPLETE SET (100)	4000.00	7000.00
1 Reg Hamilton	35.00	60.00
2 Turk Broda	175.00	300.00
3 Bingo Kampman RC	25.00	50.00
4 Gordie Drillon	50.00	80.00
5 Bob Davidson	25.00	50.00
6 Syl Apps	125.00	200.00
7 Pete Langelle RC	25.00	50.00
8 Don Metz RC	25.00	50.00
9 Pep Kelly	25.00	50.00
10 Red Horner	60.00	100.00
11 Wally Stanowsky RC	25.00	50.00
12 Murph Chamberlain	25.00	50.00
13 Bucko MacDonald	25.00	50.00
14 Sweeney Schriner	60.00	100.00
15 Billy Taylor RC	25.00	50.00
16 Gus Marker	25.00	50.00
17 Hooley Smith	60.00	100.00
18 Art Chapman	25.00	50.00
19 Murray Armstrong	25.00	50.00
20 Busher Jackson	90.00	150.00
21 Buzz Boll	25.00	50.00
22 Cliff(Red) Goupille	25.00	50.00
23 Rod Lorraine	25.00	50.00
24 Paul Drouin	25.00	50.00
25 Johnny Gagnon	25.00	50.00
26 Georges Mantha	25.00	50.00
27 Armand Mondou	25.00	50.00
28 Claude Bourque RC	25.00	50.00
29 Ray Getliffe RC	25.00	50.00
30 Cy Wentworth	50.00	80.00
31 Paul Haynes	25.00	50.00
32 Walter Buswell	25.00	50.00
33 Ott Heller	25.00	50.00
34 Arthur Coulter	35.00	60.00
35 Clint Smith RC	60.00	100.00
36 Lynn Patrick	60.00	100.00
37 Dave Kerr	50.00	80.00
38 Murray Patrick RC	25.00	50.00
39 Neil Colville	60.00	100.00
40 Jack Portland RC	25.00	50.00
41 Flash Hollett	25.00	50.00
42 Herb Cain	50.00	80.00
43 Mud Bruneteau	25.00	50.00
44 Joffre DeSilets	25.00	50.00
45 Mush March	25.00	50.00
46 Cully Dahlstrom RC	25.00	50.00
47 Mike Karakas	35.00	60.00
48 Bill Thoms	25.00	50.00
49 Art Wiebe	25.00	50.00
50 Johnny Gottselig	25.00	50.00
51 Nick Metz	25.00	50.00
52 Jack Church RC	25.00	50.00
53 Bob Heron RC	25.00	50.00
54 Hank Goldup RC	25.00	50.00
55 Jimmy Fowler	25.00	50.00
56 Charlie Sands	25.00	50.00
57 Marty Barry	35.00	60.00
58 Doug Young	25.00	50.00
59 Charlie Conacher	150.00	250.00
60 John Sorrell	25.00	50.00
61 Tommy Anderson RC	25.00	50.00
62 Lorne Carr	25.00	50.00
63 Earl Robertson RC	35.00	60.00
64 Wilfy Field RC	25.00	50.00
65 Jimmy Orlando RC	25.00	50.00
66 Ebbie Goodfellow	35.00	60.00
67 Jack Keating RC	25.00	50.00
68 Sid Abel RC	250.00	400.00
69 Gus Giesebrecht RC	25.00	50.00
70 Don Deacon RC	25.00	50.00
71 Hec Kilrea	25.00	50.00
72 Syd Howe	60.00	100.00
73 Eddie Wares RC	25.00	50.00
74 Carl Liscombe RC	25.00	50.00
75 Tiny Thompson	90.00	150.00
76 Earl Seibert RC	25.00	50.00
77 Des Smith RC	25.00	50.00
78 Les Cunningham RC	25.00	50.00
79 George Allen RC	25.00	50.00
80 Bill Carse RC	25.00	50.00
81 Bill McKenzie	25.00	50.00
82 Ab DeMarco RC	25.00	50.00
83 Phil Watson	30.00	50.00
84 Alf Pike RC	25.00	50.00
85 Babe Pratt RC	50.00	80.00
86 Bryan Hextall Sr. RC	50.00	80.00
87 Kilby MacDonald RC	25.00	50.00

88 Alex Shibicky 25.00 50.00
89 Dutch Hiller RC 25.00 50.00
90 Mac Colville 25.00 50.00
91 Roy Conacher RC 60.00 100.00
92 Cooney Weiland 60.00 100.00
93 Art Jackson 25.00 50.00
94 Woody Dumart RC 75.00 150.00
95 Dit Clapper 125.00 200.00
96 Mel Hill RC 25.00 50.00
97 Frank Brimsek RC 150.00 300.00
98 Bill Cowley RC 75.00 150.00
99 Bobby Bauer RC 50.00 100.00
100 Eddie Shore 400.00 600.00

1940-41 O-Pee-Chee V301-2

This O-Pee-Chee set was continuously numbered from the 1939-40 O-Pee-Chee set. These large cards were apparently issued during the 1940-41 season. The catalog designation for this set is V301-2. The cards were sepia and measure approximately 5" by 7". The second series numbers were somewhat larger than the numbers used for the first series. The card backs were blank. The cards were numbered on the front in the lower right corner. Cards in the set were identified on the front by name, team, and position. These cards were premiums and were issued one per cello pack.

COMPLETE SET (50) 3000.00 5000.00
101 Toe Blake 175.00 300.00
102 Charlie Sands 30.00 50.00
103 Wally Stanowski 30.00 50.00
104 Jack Adams 30.00 50.00
105 Johnny Mowers RC 50.00 80.00
106 Johnny Quilty RC 30.00 50.00
107 Billy Taylor 30.00 50.00
108 Turk Broda 175.00 300.00
109 Bingo Kampman 30.00 50.00
110 Gordie Drillon 75.00 125.00
111 Don Metz 30.00 50.00
112 Paul Haynes 30.00 50.00
113 Gus Marker 30.00 50.00
114 Alex Singbush RC 30.00 50.00
115 Alex Motter RC 30.00 50.00
116 Ken Reardon RC 90.00 150.00
117 Pete Langelle 30.00 50.00
118 Syl Apps 125.00 200.00
119 Reg. Hamilton 30.00 50.00
120 Cliff(Red) Goupille 30.00 50.00
121 Joe Benoit RC 30.00 50.00
122 Sweeney Schriner 75.00 125.00
123 Joe Carveth RC 30.00 50.00
124 Jack Stewart RC 75.00 125.00
125 Elmer Lach RC 125.00 200.00
126 Jack Schewchuk RC 50.00 80.00
127 Norman Larson RC 50.00 80.00
128 Don Grosso RC 50.00 80.00
129 Lester Douglas RC 50.00 80.00
130 Turk Broda 250.00 400.00
131 Max Bentley RC 175.00 300.00
132 Milt Schmidt RC 250.00 400.00
133 Nick Metz 50.00 80.00
134 Jack Crawford RC 50.00 80.00
135 Bill Benson RC 50.00 80.00
136 Lynn Patrick 90.00 150.00
137 Cully Dahlstrom 50.00 80.00
138 Mud Bruneteau 50.00 80.00
139 Dave Kerr 90.00 150.00
140 Bob(Red) Heron 50.00 80.00
141 Nick Metz 50.00 80.00
142 Ott Heller 50.00 80.00
143 Phil Hergesheimer RC 50.00 80.00
144 Tony Demers RC 50.00 80.00
145 Archie Wilder RC 50.00 80.00
146 Syl Apps 150.00 250.00
147 Ray Getliffe 50.00 80.00
148 Lex Chisholm RC 50.00 80.00
149 Eddie Wiseman RC 50.00 80.00
150 Paul Goodman RC 60.00 120.00

1968-69 O-Pee-Chee

The 1968-69 O-Pee-Chee set contained 216 standard-size color cards. Included are players from the six expansion teams: Philadelphia, Pittsburgh, St. Louis, Minnesota, Los Angeles and Oakland. The cards were originally sold in five-cent wax packs. The horizontally oriented fronts featured the player in the foreground with an artistically rendered hockey scene in the background. The bilingual backs were printed in red and black ink. The player's 1967-68 and career statistics, a short biography, and a cartoon-illustrated fact about the player were included on the back. The cards were printed in Canada and were issued by O-Pee-Chee, even though the Topps Gum copyright is found on the reverse. For the most part, the cards were grouped by teams. However, numerous cards are updated to reflect off-season transactions. The O-Pee-Chee set featured many different poses from the corresponding Topps cards. Card No. 193 can be found either numbered or unnumbered. Rookie Cards in this set included Bernie Parent, Mickey Redmond, Gary Smith and Garry Unger.

COMPLETE SET (216) 1500.00 2500.00
1 Doug Harvey 25.00 60.00
2 Bobby Orr 200.00 400.00
3 Don Awrey UER 5.00 8.00
4 Ted Green 6.00 10.00
5 Johnny Bucyk 9.00 15.00
6 Derek Sanderson 25.00 50.00
7 Phil Esposito 25.00 40.00
8 Ken Hodge 6.00 10.00
9 John McKenzie 6.00 10.00
10 Fred Stanfield 5.00 8.00
11 Tom Williams 5.00 8.00
12 Denis DeJordy 6.00 10.00
13 Doug Jarrett 5.00 8.00
14 Gilles Marotte 5.00 8.00
15 Pat Stapleton 6.00 10.00
16 Bobby Hull 50.00 75.00
17 Chico Maki 5.00 8.00
18 Pit Martin 6.00 10.00
19 Doug Mohns 5.00 8.00
20 John Ferguson 6.00 10.00
21 Jim Pappin 5.00 8.00
22 Ken Wharram 5.00 8.00
23 Roger Crozier 6.00 10.00
24 Bob Baun 6.00 10.00
25 Gary Bergman 5.00 8.00
26 Kent Douglas 5.00 8.00
27 Ron Harris RC 5.00 8.00
28 Alex Delvecchio 9.00 15.00
29 Gordie Howe 60.00 100.00
30 Bruce MacGregor 5.00 8.00
31 Frank Mahovlich 12.00 20.00
32 Dean Prentice 5.00 8.00
33 Pete Stemkowski 5.00 8.00
34 Terry Sawchuk 30.00 50.00
35 Larry Cahan 5.00 8.00
36 Real Lemieux RC 5.00 8.00
37 Bill White RC 7.00 12.00
38 Gord Labossiere RC 5.00 8.00
39 Ted Irvine RC 5.00 8.00
40 Eddie Joyal 5.00 8.00
41 Dale Rolfe RC 5.00 8.00
42 Lowell MacDonald RC 7.00 12.00
43 Skip Krake UER 5.00 8.00
44 Terry Gray 5.00 8.00
45 Cesare Maniago 6.00 10.00
46 Mike McMahon 5.00 8.00
47 Wayne Hillman 5.00 8.00
48 Larry Hillman 5.00 8.00
49 Bob Woytowich 5.00 8.00
50 Wayne Connelly 5.00 8.00
51 Claude Larose 5.00 8.00
52 Danny Grant UER 10.00 20.00
John Vanderburg pictured
53 Andre Boudrias RC 5.00 8.00
54 Ray Cullen RC 6.00 10.00
55 Parker MacDonald 5.00 8.00
56 Gump Worsley 9.00 15.00
57 Terry Harper 5.00 8.00
58 Jacques Laperriere 6.00 10.00
59 J.C. Tremblay 6.00 10.00
60 Ralph Backstrom 6.00 10.00
61 Checklist 1 125.00 200.00
62 Yvan Cournoyer 12.00 20.00
63 Jacques Lemaire 15.00 25.00
64 Mickey Redmond RC 40.00 70.00
65 Bobby Rousseau 5.00 8.00
66 Gilles Tremblay 5.00 8.00
67 Ed Giacomin 12.00 20.00
68 Arnie Brown 5.00 8.00
69 Harry Howell 6.00 10.00
70 Al Hamilton RC 5.00 8.00
71 Rod Seiling 5.00 8.00
72 Rod Gilbert 7.00 12.00
73 Phil Goyette 5.00 8.00
74 Larry Jeffrey 5.00 8.00
75 Don Marshall 5.00 8.00
76 Bob Nevin 6.00 10.00
77 Jean Ratelle 7.00 12.00
78 Charlie Hodge 6.00 10.00
79 Bert Marshall 5.00 8.00
80 Billy Harris 5.00 8.00
81 Carol Vadnais 6.00 10.00
82 Howie Young 5.00 8.00
83 John Brenneman RC 5.00 8.00
84 Gerry Ehman 5.00 8.00
85 Ted Hampson 5.00 8.00
86 Bill Hicke 5.00 8.00
87 Gary Jarrett 5.00 8.00
88 Doug Roberts 5.00 8.00
89 Bernie Parent RC 100.00 250.00
90 Joe Watson 5.00 8.00
91 Ed Van Impe 5.00 8.00
92 Larry Zeidel 5.00 8.00
93 John Miszuk RC 5.00 8.00
94 Gary Dornhoefer 6.00 10.00
95 Leon Rochefort RC 5.00 8.00
96 Brit Selby 5.00 8.00
97 Forbes Kennedy 5.00 8.00
98 Ed Hoekstra RC 5.00 8.00
99 Garry Peters 5.00 8.00
100 Les Binkley RC 10.00 20.00
101 Leo Boivin 6.00 10.00
102 Earl Ingarfield 5.00 8.00
103 Lou Angotti 5.00 8.00
104 Andy Bathgate 7.00 12.00
105 Wally Boyer 5.00 8.00
106 Ken Schinkel 5.00 8.00
107 Ab McDonald 5.00 8.00
108 Charlie Burns 5.00 8.00
109 Val Fonteyne 5.00 8.00
110 Noel Price 5.00 8.00
111 Glenn Hall 12.00 20.00
112 Bob Plager RC 12.50 25.00
113 Jim Roberts 5.00 8.00
114 Red Berenson 6.00 10.00
115 Larry Keenan 5.00 8.00
116 Camille Henry 5.00 8.00
117 Gary Sabourin RC 5.00 8.00
118 Ron Schock 5.00 8.00
119 Gary Veneruzzo RC 5.00 8.00
120 Gerry Melnyk 5.00 8.00
121 Checklist 2 150.00 250.00
122 Johnny Bower 9.00 15.00
123 Tim Horton 15.00 25.00
124 Pierre Pilote 7.00 12.00
125 Marcel Pronovost 6.00 10.00
126 Ron Ellis 6.00 10.00
127 Paul Henderson 6.00 10.00
128 Al Arbour 6.00 10.00
129 Bob Pulford 6.00 10.00
130 Floyd Smith 5.00 8.00
131 Norm Ullman 7.00 12.00
132 Mike Walton 6.00 10.00
133 Ed Johnston DP 6.00 10.00
134 Glen Sather 9.00 15.00
135 Ed Westfall DP 6.00 10.00
136 Dallas Smith DP 5.00 8.00
137 Eddie Shack DP 7.00 12.00
138 Gary Doak DP 5.00 8.00
139 Ron Murphy DP 5.00 8.00
140 Gerry Cheevers DP 12.00 20.00
141 Bob Falkenberg RC 5.00 8.00
142 Garry Unger DP RC 18.00 30.00
143 Peter Mahovlich DP 6.00 10.00
144 Roy Edwards 6.00 10.00
145 Gary Bauman DP RC 5.00 8.00
146 Bob McCord DP 5.00 8.00
147 Elmer Vasko DP 5.00 8.00
148 Bill Goldsworthy RC 7.00 12.00
149 Jean-Paul Parise RC 7.00 12.00
150 Dave Dryden 6.00 10.00
151 Howie Young DP 5.00 8.00
152 Matt Ravlich DP 5.00 8.00
153 Dennis Hull DP 6.00 10.00
154 Eric Nesterenko DP 6.00 10.00
155 Stan Mikita DP 18.00 30.00
156 Bob Wall DP 5.00 8.00
157 Dave Amadio RC 5.00 8.00
158 Howie Hughes DP RC 5.00 8.00
159 Bill Flett RC 7.00 12.00
160 Doug Robinson 5.00 8.00
161 Dick Duff DP 6.00 10.00
162 Ted Harris DP 5.00 8.00
163 Claude Provost DP 5.00 8.00
164 Rogatien Vachon DP 25.00 40.00
165 Henri Richard DP 12.00 20.00
166 Jean Beliveau DP 20.00 40.00
167 Reg Fleming DP 5.00 8.00
168 Ron Stewart DP 5.00 8.00
169 Dave Balon 5.00 8.00
170 Orland Kurtenbach DP 5.00 8.00
171 Vic Hadfield DP 6.00 10.00
172 Jim Neilson DP 5.00 8.00
173 Bryan Watson DP 5.00 8.00
174 George Swarbrick DP RC 5.00 8.00
175 Joe Szura RC 5.00 8.00
176 Gary Smith RC 10.00 20.00
177 Barclay Plager UER DP RC 9.00 15.00
178 Tim Ecclestone DP RC 5.00 8.00
179 Jean-Guy Talbot DP 6.00 10.00
180 Ab McDonald DP 5.00 8.00
181 Jacques Plante DP 25.00 60.00
182 Bill McCreary RC 5.00 8.00
183 Allan Stanley DP 7.00 12.00
184 Andre Lacroix RC 7.00 12.00
185 Jean-Guy Gendron DP 5.00 8.00
186 Jim Johnson RC 5.00 8.00
187 Simon Nolet RC 7.00 12.00
188 Joe Daley DP RC 7.00 12.00
189 John Arbour DP RC 5.00 8.00
190 Billy Dea DP 5.00 8.00
191 Bob Dillabough DP 5.00 8.00
192 Bob Woytowich DP 5.00 8.00
193 Keith McCreary RC 5.00 8.00
194 Murray Oliver DP 5.00 8.00
195 Larry Mickey RC 5.00 8.00
196 Bill Sutherland DP RC 5.00 8.00
197 Bruce Gamble DP 6.00 10.00
198 Dave Keon DP 9.00 15.00
199 Gump Worsley AS1 7.00 12.00
200 Bobby Orr AS1 90.00 150.00
201 Tim Horton AS1 8.00 15.00
202 Stan Mikita AS1 9.00 15.00
203 Gordie Howe AS1 40.00 60.00
204 Bobby Hull AS1 30.00 50.00
205 Ed Giacomin AS2 9.00 15.00
206 J.C. Tremblay AS2 6.00 10.00
207 Jim Neilson AS2 5.00 8.00
208 Phil Esposito AS2 15.00 25.00
209 Rod Gilbert AS2 6.00 10.00
210 Johnny Bucyk AS2 6.00 10.00
211 Stan Mikita Triple 9.00 15.00
212 Worsley/Vachon Vezina 25.00 40.00
213 D.Sanderson Calder 25.00 50.00
214 B.Orr Norris 90.00 150.00
215 G.Hall Smythe 7.00 12.00
216 C.Provost Masterson 7.50 15.00

1968-69 O-Pee-Chee Puck Stickers

This set consisted of 22 numbered (on the front), full-color stickers measuring 2 1/2" by 3 1/2". The card backs were blank and contained an adhesive. These stickers were printed in Canada and were inserted one per pack in 1968-69 O-Pee-Chee regular issue hockey packs. The pucks were perforated so that they could be punched out. This was obviously not recommended. Sticker card 22 is a special card honoring Gordie Howe's 700th goal.

COMPLETE SET (22) 250.00 500.00
1 Stan Mikita 10.00 25.00
2 Frank Mahovlich 10.00 25.00
3 Bobby Hull 25.00 50.00
4 Bobby Orr 125.00 250.00
5 Phil Esposito 15.00 30.00
6 Gump Worsley 10.00 20.00
7 Jean Beliveau 15.00 30.00
8 Elmer Vasko 7.50 15.00
9 Rod Gilbert 10.00 20.00
10 Roger Crozier 10.00 20.00
11 Lou Angotti 7.50 15.00
12 Charlie Hodge 7.50 15.00
13 Glenn Hall 10.00 25.00
14 Doug Harvey 10.00 25.00
15 Jacques Plante 25.00 50.00
16 Allan Stanley 7.50 15.00
17 Johnny Bower 15.00 30.00
18 Tim Horton 15.00 30.00
19 Dave Keon 15.00 40.00
20 Terry Sawchuk 25.00 50.00
21 Henri Richard 10.00 25.00
22 Gordie Howe Special 30.00 60.00

1969-70 O-Pee-Chee

The 1969-70 O-Pee-Chee set contained 231 standard-size cards issued in two series of 132 and 99. The cards were issued in ten-cent wax packs. Bilingual backs contain 1968-69 and career statistics, a short biography and a cartoon-illustrated fact about the player. The cards were printed in Canada with the Topps Gum Company copyright appearing on the reverse. Many player poses in this set were different from the corresponding player poses of the Topps set of this year. Card 193, Gordie Howe "Mr. Hockey" existed with or without the card number. Stamps inserted in wax packs could be placed on the back of the corresponding player's regular-issue cards in a space provided. A card with a stamp on the back was considered to be of less value than one without the stamp. Rookie Cards include Tony Esposito and Serge Savard.

COMPLETE SET (231) 1200.00 2000.00
1 Gump Worsley 20.00 35.00
2 Ted Harris 4.00 6.00
3 Jacques Laperriere 5.00 8.00
4 Serge Savard RC 90.00 150.00
5 J.C. Tremblay 5.00 8.00
6 Yvan Cournoyer 6.00 10.00
7 John Ferguson 5.00 8.00
8 Jacques Lemaire 6.00 10.00
9 Bobby Rousseau 4.00 6.00
10 Jean Beliveau 15.00 25.00
11 Dick Duff 5.00 8.00
12 Glenn Hall 7.00 12.00
13 Bob Plager 4.00 6.00
14 Ron Anderson RC 4.00 6.00
15 Jean-Guy Talbot 5.00 8.00
16 Andre Boudrias 4.00 6.00
17 Camille Henry 4.00 6.00
18 Ab McDonald 4.00 6.00
19 Gary Sabourin 4.00 6.00
20 Red Berenson 4.00 6.00
21 Phil Goyette 4.00 6.00
22 Gerry Cheevers 9.00 15.00
23 Ted Green 4.00 6.00
24 Bobby Orr 125.00 250.00
25 Dallas Smith 4.00 6.00
26 Johnny Bucyk 8.00 12.00
27 Ken Hodge 5.00 8.00
28 John McKenzie 5.00 8.00
29 Ed Westfall 5.00 8.00
30 Phil Esposito 18.00 30.00
31 Checklist 2 100.00 150.00
32 Fred Stanfield 4.00 6.00
33 Ed Giacomin 9.00 15.00
34 Arnie Brown 4.00 8.00
35 Jim Neilson 4.00 6.00
36 Rod Seiling 4.00 6.00
37 Rod Gilbert 6.00 10.00
38 Vic Hadfield 5.00 8.00
39 Don Marshall 4.00 6.00
40 Bob Nevin 4.00 6.00
41 Ron Stewart 4.00 6.00
42 Jean Ratelle 6.00 10.00
43 Walt Tkaczuk RC 6.00 10.00
44 Bruce Gamble 5.00 8.00
45 Jim Dorey RC 4.00 6.00
46 Ron Ellis 5.00 8.00
47 Paul Henderson 5.00 8.00
48 Brit Selby 4.00 6.00
49 Floyd Smith 4.00 6.00
50 Mike Walton 5.00 8.00
51 Dave Keon 6.00 10.00
52 Murray Oliver 4.00 6.00
53 Bob Pulford 5.00 8.00
54 Norm Ullman 6.00 10.00
55 Roger Crozier 5.00 8.00
56 Roy Edwards 5.00 8.00
57 Bob Baun 5.00 8.00
58 Gary Bergman 4.00 6.00
59 Carl Brewer 5.00 8.00
60 Wayne Connelly 4.00 6.00
61 Gordie Howe 60.00 120.00
62 Frank Mahovlich 7.50 15.00
63 Bruce MacGregor 4.00 6.00
64 Ron Harris 4.00 6.00
65 Pete Stemkowski 4.00 6.00
66 Denis DeJordy 5.00 8.00
67 Doug Jarrett 4.00 6.00
68 Gilles Marotte 4.00 6.00
69 Pat Stapleton 5.00 8.00
70 Bobby Hull 40.00 80.00
71 Dennis Hull 5.00 8.00
72 Doug Mohns 4.00 6.00
73 Howie Menard RC 4.00 6.00
74 Ken Wharram 4.00 6.00
75 Pit Martin 5.00 8.00
76 Stan Mikita 12.00 20.00
77 Charlie Hodge 5.00 8.00
78 Gary Smith 5.00 8.00
79 Harry Howell 5.00 8.00
80 Bert Marshall 4.00 6.00
81 Doug Roberts 4.00 6.00
82 Carol Vadnais 5.00 8.00
83 Gerry Ehman 4.00 6.00
84 Brian Perry RC 4.00 6.00
85 Gary Jarrett 4.00 6.00
86 Ted Hampson 4.00 6.00
87 Earl Ingarfield 4.00 6.00
88 Doug Favell RC 9.00 15.00
89 Bernie Parent 25.00 40.00
90 Larry Hillman 4.00 6.00
91 Wayne Hillman 4.00 6.00
92 Ed Van Impe 4.00 6.00
93 Joe Watson 4.00 6.00
94 Gary Dornhoefer 5.00 8.00
95 Reg Fleming 4.00 6.00
96 Ralph McSweyn RC 4.00 6.00
97 Jim Johnson 4.00 6.00
98 Andre Lacroix 5.00 8.00
99 Gerry Desjardins RC 7.00 12.00
100 Dale Rolfe 4.00 6.00
101 Bill White 4.00 6.00
102 Bill Flett 4.00 6.00
103 Ted Irvine 4.00 6.00
104 Ross Lonsberry 4.00 6.00
105 Leon Rochefort 4.00 6.00
106 Bryan Campbell RC 4.00 6.00
107 Dennis Hextall RC 6.00 10.00
108 Eddie Joyal 4.00 6.00
109 Gord Labossiere 4.00 6.00
110 Les Binkley 5.00 8.00
111 Tracy Pratt RC 4.00 6.00
112 Bryan Watson 4.00 6.00
113 Bob Blackburn RC 4.00 6.00
114 Keith McCreary 4.00 6.00
115 Dean Prentice 4.00 6.00
116 Glen Sather 5.00 8.00
117 Ken Schinkel 4.00 6.00
118 Wally Boyer 4.00 6.00
119 Val Fonteyne 4.00 6.00
120 Ron Schock 4.00 6.00
121 Cesare Maniago 5.00 8.00
122 Leo Boivin 5.00 8.00
123 Bob McCord 4.00 6.00
124 John Miszuk 4.00 6.00
125 Danny Grant 5.00 8.00
126 Bill Collins RC 4.00 6.00
127 Jean-Paul Parise 5.00 8.00
128 Tom Williams 4.00 6.00
129 Charlie Burns 4.00 6.00
130 Ray Cullen 4.00 6.00
131 Danny O'Shea RC 5.00 8.00
132 Checklist 1 150.00 250.00
133 Jim Pappin 4.00 6.00
134 Lou Angotti 4.00 6.00
135 Terry Cafery RC 5.00 8.00
136 Eric Nesterenko 5.00 8.00
137 Chico Maki 5.00 8.00
138 Tony Esposito RC 75.00 150.00
139 Eddie Shack 6.00 10.00
140 Bob Wall 4.00 6.00
141 Skip Krake 5.00 8.00
142 Howie Hughes 4.00 6.00
143 Jimmy Peters RC 5.00 8.00
144 Brent Hughes RC 5.00 8.00
145 Bill Hicke 4.00 6.00
146 Norm Ferguson RC 5.00 8.00
147 Dick Mattiussi RC 5.00 8.00
148 Mike Laughton RC 5.00 8.00
149 Gene Ubriaco RC 5.00 8.00
150 Bob Dillabough 4.00 6.00
151 Bob Woytowich 4.00 6.00
152 Joe Daley 5.00 8.00
153 Duane Rupp 4.00 6.00
154 Bryan Hextall RC 6.00 10.00
155 Jean Pronovost RC 6.00 10.00
156 Jim Morrison 4.00 6.00
157 Alex Delvecchio 8.00 12.00
158 Paul Popiel 4.00 6.00
159 Garry Unger 6.00 10.00
160 Garry Monahan 4.00 6.00
161 Matt Ravlich 4.00 6.00
162 Nick Libett RC 6.00 10.00
163 Henri Richard 7.00 12.00
164 Terry Harper 5.00 8.00
165 Rogatien Vachon 10.00 20.00
166 Ralph Backstrom 5.00 8.00
167 Claude Provost 5.00 8.00
168 Gilles Tremblay 5.00 8.00
169 Jean Guy Gendron 5.00 8.00
170 Earl Heiskala RC 5.00 8.00
171 Garry Peters 4.00 6.00
172 Bill Sutherland 4.00 6.00
173 Dick Cherry RC 5.00 8.00
174 Jim Roberts 5.00 8.00
175 Noel Picard RC 5.00 8.00
176 Barclay Plager 5.00 8.00
177 Frank St. Marseille RC 5.00 8.00
178 Al Arbour 5.00 8.00
179 Tim Ecclestone 4.00 6.00
180 Jacques Plante 25.00 40.00
181 Bill McCreary 4.00 6.00
182 Tim Horton 12.00 20.00
183 Rick Ley RC 6.00 10.00
184 Wayne Carleton 4.00 6.00
185 Marv Edwards RC 6.00 10.00
186 Pat Quinn RC 9.00 15.00
187 Johnny Bower 7.00 12.00
188 Orland Kurtenbach 5.00 8.00
189 Terry Sawchuk UER 25.00 40.00
190 Real Lemieux 4.00 6.00
191 Dave Balon 4.00 6.00
192 Al Hamilton 4.00 6.00
193A G.Howe Mr. HK ERR 90.00 150.00
193B G.Howe Mr. HK COR 100.00 175.00
194 Claude Larose 4.00 6.00
195 Bill Goldsworthy 5.00 8.00
196 Bob Barlow RC 4.00 6.00
197 Ken Broderick RC 5.00 8.00
198 Lou Nanne RC 6.00 10.00
199 Tom Polonic RC 5.00 8.00
200 Ed Johnston 5.00 8.00
201 Derek Sanderson 15.00 25.00
202 Gary Doak 4.00 6.00
203 Don Awrey 4.00 6.00
204 Ron Murphy 4.00 6.00
205A P.Esposito Double ERR 15.00 25.00
205B P.Esposito Double COR 12.00 20.00
206 Alex Delvecchio Byng 4.00 6.00
207 J.Plante/G.Hall Vezina 30.00 50.00
208 Danny Grant Calder 4.00 6.00
209 Bobby Orr Norris 50.00 100.00
210 Serge Savard Smythe 4.00 6.00
211 Glenn Hall AS 9.00 15.00
212 Bobby Orr AS 50.00 100.00
213 Tim Horton AS 12.00 20.00
214 Phil Esposito AS 12.00 20.00
215 Gordie Howe AS 30.00 50.00
216 Bobby Hull AS 20.00 35.00
217 Ed Giacomin AS 7.00 12.00
218 Ted Green AS 4.00 6.00
219 Ted Harris AS 4.00 6.00
220 Jean Beliveau AS 20.00 35.00
221 Yvan Cournoyer AS 4.00 6.00
222 Frank Mahovlich AS 7.50 15.00
223 Art Ross Trophy 5.00 8.00
224 Hart Trophy 5.00 8.00
225 Lady Byng Trophy 5.00 8.00
226 Vezina Trophy 6.00 10.00
227 Calder Trophy 5.00 8.00
228 James Norris Trophy 5.00 8.00
229 Conn Smythe Trophy 5.00 8.00
230 Prince of Wales 5.00 8.00
231 The Stanley Cup 25.00 60.00

1969-70 O-Pee-Chee Four-in-One

The 1969-70 O-Pee-Chee Four-in-One set contained 18 four-player adhesive-backed color cards. The cards were standard size, 2 1/2" by 3 1/2", whereas the individual mini-cards were approximately 1" by 1 1/2". These small cards could be separated and then stuck in a small team album/booklet that was also available that year from O-Pee-Chee. This set was distributed as an insert with the second series of regular 1969-70 O-Pee-Chee cards. Cards that had been separated into the mini-cards have very little value. The cards were unnumbered and so they are checklisted below alphabetically by the (upper left corner) player's name.

COMPLETE SET (18) 600.00 1000.00
1 Baun/Schink/Hort/Parent 30.00 60.00
2 Bink/Hodge/Flem/Laper 30.00 60.00
3 Courn/Neil/Sabo/Misz 30.00 60.00
4 Gamb/Vadn/Mahov/Hillman 30.00 60.00
5 Giac/Beliv/Joyal/Boivin 30.00 60.00
6 Goye/Jarret/Green/Hicke 30.00 60.00
7 Hamp/Brewer/DeJordy/Roche 30.00 60.00
8 Hodge/Quinn/Sand/Rupp 30.00 60.00
9 Ingfld/Robrts/Wors/Hull 50.00 100.00
10 Lacro/Wall/Savard/Croz 30.00 60.00
11 Mani/Orr/Keon/Gendron 150.00 300.00
12 McCr/Larose/Gilb/Cheev 30.00 60.00
13 Mikita/Arbo/Seili/Schock 30.00 60.00
14 Mohn/Woyt/Howe/Desj 75.00 150.00
15 Nev/Plante/Walt/Cullen 30.00 60.00
16 Pulf/Rich/Beren/Shack 40.00 80.00
17 Stapl/Grant/Marsh/Ratel 30.00 60.00
18 VanImp/Rolf/Delv/Espo 30.00 60.00

1969-70 O-Pee-Chee Stamps

The 1969-70 O-Pee-Chee Stamps set contained 26 black and white stamps measuring approximately 1 1/2" by 1 1/4". The stamps were distributed with the first series of regular 1969-70 O-Pee-Chee hockey cards and may also have been available in some of the Topps wax packs of that year as well. The stamps were unnumbered and hence are checklisted below alphabetically for convenience. OPC intended for the stamps to be stuck on the blank space provided on the backs of the corresponding regular card; collectors are strongly encouraged NOT to follow that procedure. The stamps were produced as pairs; intact pairs are now valued at 1.5 to 2 times the sum of the individual player prices listed below.

COMPLETE SET (26) 125.00 250.00
1 Jean Beliveau 7.50 15.00
2 Red Berenson 4.00 8.00
3 Les Binkley 5.00 10.00
4 Yvan Cournoyer 6.00 12.00
5 Ray Cullen 4.00 8.00
6 Gerry Desjardins 5.00 10.00
7 Phil Esposito 7.50 15.00
8 Ed Giacomin 6.00 12.00
9 Rod Gilbert 6.00 12.00
10 Danny Grant 4.00 8.00
11 Glenn Hall 7.50 15.00
12 Ted Hampson 4.00 8.00
13 Ken Hodge 4.00 8.00
14 Gordie Howe 20.00 40.00
15 Bobby Hull 15.00 30.00
16 Eddie Joyal 4.00 8.00
17 Dave Keon 7.50 15.00
18 Andre Lacroix 4.00 8.00
19 Frank Mahovlich 6.00 12.00
20 Keith McCreary 4.00 8.00
21 Stan Mikita 7.50 15.00
22 Bobby Orr 25.00 60.00
23 Bernie Parent 7.50 15.00
24 Jean Ratelle 5.00 10.00
25 Norm Ullman 5.00 10.00
26 Carol Vadnais 4.00 8.00

1970-71 O-Pee-Chee

The 1970-71 O-Pee-Chee set contained 264 standard-size cards. Players from expansion Buffalo and Vancouver are included. Bilingual backs featured a short biography as well as the player's 1969-70 and career statistics. The cards were printed in Canada, and the O-Pee-Chee copyright, and not the Topps, appeared on the back for the first time. Many player poses were different from the Topps set of this year. Cards were grouped by teams. However, there are a number of cards that had updated team names reflecting off-season trades. Card no. 231 is a special memorial to Terry Sawchuk, who passed away in 1970. Card nos. 111, Brit Selby, and 175 Mickey Redmond, could be found with or without a line of text acknowledging trades. Rookie Cards included Wayne Cashman, Bobby Clarke, Brad Park, Guy Lapointe, Gilbert Perreault, and Darryl Sittler.

COMPLETE SET (264) 1200.00 2000.00
1 Gerry Cheevers 10.00 25.00
2 Johnny Bucyk 2.50 6.00
3 Bobby Orr 150.00 250.00
4 Don Awrey 1.50 4.00
5 Fred Stanfield 1.50 4.00
6 John McKenzie 2.50 6.00
7 Wayne Cashman RC 8.00 20.00
8 Ken Hodge 2.50 6.00
9 Wayne Carleton 1.50 4.00
10 Garnet Bailey RC 2.50 6.00
11 Phil Esposito 10.00 25.00
12 Lou Angotti 1.50 4.00
13 Jim Pappin 1.50 4.00
14 Dennis Hull 2.50 6.00
15 Bobby Hull 25.00 50.00
16 Doug Mohns 1.50 4.00
17 Pat Stapleton 2.50 6.00
18 Pit Martin 2.50 6.00
19 Eric Nesterenko 2.50 6.00
20 Stan Mikita 8.00 20.00
21 Roy Edwards 2.50 6.00
22 Frank Mahovlich 5.00 12.00
23 Ron Harris 1.50 4.00
24 Checklist 1 100.00 200.00
25 Pete Stemkowski 1.50 4.00
26 Garry Unger 1.50 4.00
27 Bruce MacGregor 1.50 4.00
28 Larry Jeffrey 1.50 4.00
29 Gordie Howe 40.00 80.00
30 Billy Dea 1.50 4.00
31 Denis DeJordy 2.50 6.00
32 Matt Ravlich 1.50 4.00
33 Dave Amadio 1.50 4.00
34 Gilles Marotte 1.50 4.00
35 Eddie Shack 5.00 12.00
36 Bob Pulford 2.50 6.00
37 Ross Lonsberry 2.50 6.00
38 Gord Labossiere 1.50 4.00
39 Eddie Joyal 1.50 4.00
40 Gump Worsley 5.00 12.00
41 Bob McCord 1.50 4.00
42 Leo Boivin 2.50 6.00
43 Tom Reid RC 1.50 4.00
44 Charlie Burns 1.50 4.00
45 Bob Barlow 1.50 4.00
46 Bill Goldsworthy 2.50 6.00
47 Danny Grant 2.50 6.00
48 Norm Beaudin RC 1.50 4.00
49 Rogatien Vachon 5.00 12.00
50 Yvan Cournoyer 5.00 12.00
51 Serge Savard 5.00 12.00
52 Jacques Laperriere 2.50 6.00
53 Terry Harper 1.50 4.00
54 Ralph Backstrom 2.50 6.00
55 Jean Beliveau 5.00 12.00
56 Claude Larose 1.50 4.00
57 Jacques Lemaire 5.00 12.00
58 Peter Mahovlich 4.00 10.00
59 Tim Horton 6.00 15.00
60 Bob Nevin 1.50 4.00
61 Dave Balon 1.50 4.00
62 Vic Hadfield 2.50 6.00
63 Rod Gilbert 5.00 12.00
64 Ron Stewart 1.50 4.00
65 Ted Irvine 1.50 4.00
66 Arnie Brown 1.50 4.00
67 Brad Park RC 20.00 40.00
68 Ed Giacomin 5.00 12.00
69 Gary Smith 2.50 6.00
70 Carol Vadnais 2.50 6.00
71 Doug Roberts 1.50 4.00
72 Harry Howell 2.50 6.00
73 Joe Szura 1.50 4.00
74 Mike Laughton 1.50 4.00
75 Gary Jarrett 1.50 4.00
76 Bill Hicke 1.50 4.00
77 Paul Andrea RC 1.50 4.00
78 Bernie Parent 10.00 25.00
79 Joe Watson 1.50 4.00
80 Ed Van Impe 1.50 4.00
81 Larry Hillman 1.50 4.00
82 George Swarbrick 1.50 4.00
83 Bill Sutherland 1.50 4.00
84 Andre Lacroix 2.50 6.00
85 Gary Dornhoefer 2.50 6.00
86 Jean-Guy Gendron 1.50 4.00
87 Al Smith RC 2.50 6.00
88 Bob Woytowich 1.50 4.00
89 Duane Rupp 1.50 4.00
90 Jim Morrison 1.50 4.00
91 Ron Schock 1.50 4.00
92 Ken Schinkel 1.50 4.00
93 Keith McCreary 1.50 4.00
94 Bryan Hextall 2.50 6.00
95 Wayne Hicks RC 1.50 4.00
96 Gary Sabourin 1.50 4.00
97 Ernie Wakely RC 2.50 6.00
98 Bob Wall 1.50 4.00
99 Barclay Plager 2.50 6.00
100 Jean-Guy Talbot 1.50 4.00
101 Gary Veneruzzo 1.50 4.00
102 Tim Ecclestone 1.50 4.00
103 Red Berenson 2.50 6.00
104 Larry Keenan 1.50 4.00
105 Bruce Gamble 2.50 6.00
106 Jim Dorey 1.50 4.00
107 Mike Pelyk RC 1.50 4.00
108 Rick Ley 1.50 4.00
109 Mike Walton 1.50 4.00
110 Norm Ullman 5.00 12.00
111A Brit Selby no trade 1.50 4.00
111B Brit Selby trade 8.00 20.00
112 Garry Monahan 1.50 4.00
113 George Armstrong 5.00 12.00
114 Gary Doak 1.50 4.00
115 Darryl Sly RC 1.50 4.00
116 Wayne Maki 1.50 4.00
117 Orland Kurtenbach 1.50 4.00
118 Murray Hall 1.50 4.00
119 Marc Reaume 1.50 4.00
120 Pat Quinn 5.00 12.00
121 Andre Boudrias 1.50 4.00
122 Paul Popiel 1.50 4.00
123 Paul Terbenche 1.50 4.00
124 Howie Menard 1.50 4.00
125 Gerry Meehan RC 2.50 6.00
126 Skip Krake 1.50 4.00
127 Phil Goyette 1.50 4.00
128 Reg Fleming 1.50 4.00
129 Don Marshall 2.50 6.00
130 Bill Inglis RC 1.50 4.00
131 Gilbert Perreault RC 100.00 200.00
132 Checklist 2 100.00 200.00
133 Ed Johnston 2.50 6.00
134 Ted Green 2.50 6.00
135 Rick Smith RC 1.50 4.00
136 Derek Sanderson 8.00 20.00
137 Dallas Smith 1.50 4.00
138 Don Marcotte RC 2.50 6.00
139 Ed Westfall 2.50 6.00
140 Floyd Smith 1.50 4.00
141 Randy Wyrozub RC 1.50 4.00
142 Cliff Schmautz RC 1.50 4.00
143 Mike McMahon 1.50 4.00
144 Jim Watson 1.50 4.00
145 Roger Crozier 2.50 6.00
146 Tracy Pratt 1.50 4.00
147 Cliff Koroll RC 2.50 6.00
148 Gerry Pinder RC 2.50 6.00
149 Chico Maki 1.50 4.00
150 Doug Jarrett 1.50 4.00
151 Keith Magnuson RC 5.00 12.00
152 Gerry Desjardins 2.50 6.00
153 Tony Esposito 25.00 50.00
154 Gary Bergman 1.50 4.00
155 Tom Webster RC 2.50 6.00
156 Dale Rolfe 1.50 4.00
157 Alex Delvecchio 5.00 12.00
158 Nick Libett 1.50 4.00
159 Wayne Connelly 1.50 4.00
160 Mike Byers RC 1.50 4.00
161 Bill Flett 1.50 4.00
162 Larry Mickey 1.50 4.00
163 Noel Price 1.50 4.00
164 Larry Cahan 1.50 4.00
165 Jack Norris RC 2.50 6.00
166 Ted Harris 1.50 4.00
167 Murray Oliver 1.50 4.00
168 Jean-Paul Parise 2.50 6.00
169 Tom Williams 1.50 4.00
170 Bobby Rousseau 1.50 4.00
171 Jude Drouin RC 2.50 6.00
172 Walt McKechnie RC 2.50 6.00
173 Cesare Maniago 2.50 6.00
174 Rejean Houle RC 5.00 12.00
175A Mickey Redmond trade 2.50 6.00
175B Mickey Redmond no trade 6.00 15.00
176 Henri Richard 6.00 15.00
177 Guy Lapointe RC 8.00 20.00
178 J.C. Tremblay 2.50 6.00
179 Marc Tardif RC 5.00 12.00
180 Walt Tkaczuk 2.50 6.00
181 Jean Ratelle 5.00 12.00
182 Pete Stemkowski 1.50 4.00
183 Gilles Villemure 2.50 6.00
184 Rod Seiling 1.50 4.00
185 Jim Neilson 1.50 4.00
186 Dennis Hextall 2.50 6.00
187 Gerry Ehman 1.50 4.00
188 Bert Marshall 1.50 4.00
189 Gary Croteau RC 1.50 4.00
190 Ted Hampson 1.50 4.00
191 Earl Ingarfield 1.50 4.00
192 Dick Mattiussi 1.50 4.00
193 Earl Heiskala 1.50 4.00
194 Simon Nolet 1.50 4.00
195 Bobby Clarke RC 60.00 120.00
196 Garry Peters 1.50 4.00
197 Lew Morrison RC 1.50 4.00
198 Wayne Hillman 1.50 4.00
199 Doug Favell 5.00 12.00
200 Les Binkley 2.50 6.00
201 Dean Prentice 1.50 4.00
202 Jean Pronovost 2.50 6.00
203 Wally Boyer 1.50 4.00
204 Bryan Watson 1.50 4.00
205 Glen Sather 2.50 6.00
206 Lowell MacDonald 1.50 4.00
207 Andy Bathgate 2.50 6.00
208 Val Fonteyne 1.50 4.00
209 Jim Lorentz RC 1.50 4.00
210 Glenn Hall 5.00 12.00
211 Bob Plager 2.50 6.00
212 Noel Picard 1.50 4.00
213 Jim Roberts 2.50 6.00
214 Frank St.Marseille 1.50 4.00
215 Ab McDonald 1.50 4.00
216 Brian Glennie RC 1.50 4.00
217 Paul Henderson 3.00 8.00
218 Darryl Sittler RC 75.00 125.00
219 Dave Keon 5.00 12.00
220 Jim Harrison RC 1.50 4.00
221 Ron Ellis 2.50 6.00
222 Jacques Plante 10.00 25.00
223 Bob Baun 2.50 6.00
224 George Gardner RC 1.50 4.00
225 Dale Tallon RC 2.50 6.00
226 Rosaire Paiement RC 1.50 4.00
227 Mike Corrigan RC 1.50 4.00
228 Ray Cullen 1.50 4.00
229 Charlie Hodge 2.50 6.00
230 Len Lunde 1.50 4.00
231 Terry Sawchuk Mem 30.00 60.00
232 Bruins Team Champs 5.00 12.00
233 Espo/Cashman/Hodge 10.00 25.00
234 Tony Esposito AS1 10.00 25.00
235 Bobby Hull AS1 10.00 25.00
236 Bobby Orr AS1 30.00 60.00
237 Phil Esposito AS1 6.00 15.00

238 Gordie Howe AS1	20.00	40.00
239 Brad Park AS1	6.00	15.00
240 Stan Mikita AS2	5.00	12.00
241 John McKenzie AS2	1.50	4.00
242 Frank Mahovlich AS2	2.50	6.00
243 Carl Brewer AS2	1.50	4.00
244 Ed Giacomin AS2	2.50	6.00
245 Jacques Laperriere AS2	1.50	4.00
246 Bobby Orr Hart	30.00	60.00
247 Tony Esposito Calder	10.00	25.00
248A B.Orr Norris Howe	30.00	60.00
248B B.Orr Norris no Howe	30.00	60.00
249 Bobby Orr Ross	30.00	60.00
250 Tony Esposito Vezina	10.00	25.00
251 Phil Goyette Lady Byng	1.50	4.00
252 Bobby Orr Smythe	30.00	60.00
253 Pit Martin Bill Masterton Trophy	1.50	4.00
254 Stanley Cup Trophy	6.00	15.00
255 Wales Trophy	2.50	6.00
256 Conn Smythe Trophy	2.50	6.00
257 James Norris Trophy	2.50	6.00
258 Calder Trophy	2.50	6.00
259 Vezina Trophy	2.50	6.00
260 Lady Byng Trophy	2.50	6.00
261 Hart Trophy	2.50	6.00
262 Art Ross Trophy	2.50	6.00
263 Clarence Campbell Bowl	2.50	6.00
264 John Ferguson	5.00	12.00

1970-71 O-Pee-Chee Deckle

This set consisted of 48 numbered black and white deckle edge cards measuring approximately 2 1/8" by 3 1/8". The set was issued as an insert with the second series regular issue of the same year. The set was printed in Canada.

COMPLETE SET (48)	200.00	400.00
1 Pat Quinn	2.00	5.00
2 Eddie Shack	3.00	6.00
3 Eddie Joyal	2.00	5.00
4 Bobby Orr	40.00	80.00
5 Derek Sanderson	6.00	12.00
6 Phil Esposito	7.50	15.00
7 Fred Stanfield	2.00	5.00
8 Bob Woytowich	2.00	5.00
9 Ron Schock	2.00	5.00
10 Les Binkley	3.00	6.00
11 Roger Crozier	3.00	6.00
12 Reg Fleming	2.00	5.00
13 Charlie Burns	2.00	5.00
14 Bobby Rousseau	2.00	5.00
15 Leo Boivin	2.00	5.00
16 Garry Unger	2.00	5.00
17 Frank Mahovlich	5.00	10.00
18 Gordie Howe	25.00	50.00
19 Jacques Lemaire	3.00	8.00
20 Jacques Laperriere	2.00	5.00
21 Jean Beliveau	10.00	20.00
22 Rogatien Vachon	4.00	10.00
23 Yvan Cournoyer	3.00	8.00
24 Henri Richard	6.00	12.00
25 Red Berenson	2.00	5.00
26 Frank St.Marseille	2.00	5.00
27 Glenn Hall	5.00	10.00
28 Gary Sabourin	2.00	5.00
29 Doug Mohns	2.00	5.00
30 Bobby Hull	20.00	40.00
31 Ray Cullen	2.00	5.00
32 Tony Esposito	10.00	20.00
33 Gary Dornhoefer	2.00	5.00
34 Ed Van Impe	2.00	5.00
35 Doug Favell	3.00	6.00
36 Carol Vadnais	2.00	5.00
37 Harry Howell	2.00	5.00
38 Bill Hicke	2.00	5.00
39 Rod Gilbert	3.00	6.00
40 Jean Ratelle	3.00	6.00
41 Walt Tkaczuk	3.00	6.00
42 Ed Giacomin	4.00	8.00
43 Brad Park	6.00	15.00
44 Bruce Gamble	3.00	6.00
45 Orland Kurtenbach	2.00	5.00
46 Ron Ellis	2.00	6.00
47 Dave Keon	5.00	10.00
48 Norm Ullman	3.00	6.00

1971-72 O-Pee-Chee

The 1971-72 O-Pee-Chee set contained 264 standard-size cards. The unopened wax packs consisted of eight cards plus a piece of bubble gum. Player photos were framed in an oval. Bilingual backs featured a short biography, year-by-year statistics and a cartoon-illustrated fact about the player. Rookie Cards in this set included Marcel Dionne, Ken Dryden, Butch Goring, Guy Lafleur, Reggie Leach, Richard Martin, and Rick MacLeish.

COMPLETE SET (264)	900.00	1500.00
1 Paul Popiel	3.00	8.00
2 Pierre Bouchard RC	2.00	5.00
3 Don Awrey	1.50	4.00
4 Paul Curtis RC	1.50	4.00
5 Guy Trottier RC	1.50	4.00
6 Paul Shmyr RC	1.50	4.00
7 Fred Stanfield	1.50	4.00
8 Mike Robitaille RC	1.50	4.00
9 Vic Hadfield	2.00	5.00
10 Jim Harrison	1.50	4.00
11 Bill White	1.50	4.00
12 Andre Boudrias	1.50	4.00
13 Gary Sabourin	1.50	4.00
14 Arnie Brown	1.50	4.00
15 Yvan Cournoyer	3.00	8.00
16 Bryan Hextall	2.00	5.00
17 Gary Croteau	1.50	4.00
18 Gilles Villemure	2.00	5.00
19 Serge Bernier RC	2.00	5.00
20 Phil Esposito	8.00	20.00
21 Tom Reid	1.50	4.00
22 Doug Barrie RC	1.50	4.00
23 Eddie Joyal	1.50	4.00
24 Dunc Wilson RC	3.00	8.00
25 Pat Stapleton	2.00	5.00
26 Garry Unger	2.00	5.00
27 Al Smith	2.00	5.00
28 Bob Woytowich	1.50	4.00
29 Marc Tardif	2.00	5.00
30 Norm Ullman	3.00	8.00
31 Tom Williams	1.50	4.00
32 Ted Harris	1.50	4.00
33 Andre Lacroix	2.00	5.00
34 Mike Byers	1.50	4.00
35 Johnny Bucyk	3.00	8.00
36 Roger Crozier	2.00	5.00
37 Alex Delvecchio	4.00	10.00
38 Frank St.Marseille	1.50	4.00
39 Pit Martin	2.00	5.00
40 Brad Park	6.00	15.00
41 Greg Polis RC	1.50	4.00
42 Orland Kurtenbach	1.50	4.00
43 Jim McKenny RC	1.50	4.00
44 Bob Nevin	1.50	4.00
45 Ken Dryden RC	200.00	300.00
46 Carol Vadnais	2.00	5.00
47 Bill Flett	1.50	4.00
48 Jim Johnson	1.50	4.00
49 Al Hamilton	1.50	4.00
50 Bobby Hull	15.00	40.00
51 Chris Bordeleau RC	1.50	4.00
52 Tim Ecclestone	1.50	4.00
53 Rod Seiling	1.50	4.00
54 Gerry Cheevers	4.00	10.00
55 Bill Goldsworthy	2.00	5.00
56 Ron Schock	1.50	4.00
57 Jim Dorey	1.50	4.00
58 Wayne Maki	1.50	4.00
59 Terry Harper	1.50	4.00
60 Gilbert Perreault	10.00	25.00
61 Ernie Hicke RC	1.50	4.00
62 Wayne Hillman	1.50	4.00
63 Denis DeJordy	2.00	5.00
64 Ken Schinkel	1.50	4.00
65 Derek Sanderson	5.00	12.00
66 Barclay Plager	2.00	5.00
67 Paul Henderson	2.00	5.00
68 Jude Drouin	1.50	4.00
69 Keith Magnuson	2.00	5.00
70 Ron Harris	1.50	4.00
71 Jacques Lemaire	3.00	8.00
72 Doug Favell	2.00	5.00
73 Bert Marshall	1.50	4.00
74 Ted Irvine	1.50	4.00
75 Walt Tkaczuk	2.00	5.00
76 Bob Berry RC	3.00	8.00
77 Syl Apps RC	3.00	8.00
78 Tom Webster	2.00	5.00
79 Danny Grant	2.00	5.00
80 Dave Keon	3.00	8.00
81 Ernie Wakely	2.00	5.00
82 John McKenzie	2.00	5.00
83 Ron Stackhouse RC	1.50	4.00
84 Peter Mahovlich	2.00	5.00
85 Dennis Hull	2.00	5.00
86 Juha Widing RC	1.50	4.00
87 Gary Doak	1.50	4.00
88 Phil Goyette	1.50	4.00
89 Lew Morrison	1.50	4.00
90 Ab DeMarco RC	1.50	4.00
91 Red Berenson	2.00	5.00
92 Mike Pelyk	1.50	4.00
93 Gary Jarrett	1.50	4.00
94 Bob Pulford	2.00	5.00
95 Dan Johnson RC	1.50	4.00
96 Eddie Shack	3.00	8.00
97 Jean Ratelle	3.00	8.00
98 Jim Pappin	1.50	4.00
99 Roy Edwards	2.00	5.00
100 Bobby Orr	50.00	100.00
101 Ted Hampson	1.50	4.00
102 Mickey Redmond	3.00	8.00
103 Bob Plager	3.00	8.00
104 Barry Ashbee RC	2.00	5.00
105 Frank Mahovlich	4.00	10.00
106 Dick Redmond RC	1.50	4.00
107 Tracy Pratt	1.50	4.00
108 Ralph Backstrom	2.00	5.00
109 Murray Hall	1.50	4.00
110 Tony Esposito	15.00	40.00
111 Checklist Card	300.00	500.00
112 Jim Neilson	1.50	4.00
113 Ron Ellis	2.00	5.00
114 Bobby Clarke	30.00	60.00
115 Ken Hodge	2.00	5.00
116 Jim Roberts	2.00	5.00
117 Cesare Maniago	2.00	5.00
118 Jean Pronovost	2.00	5.00
119 Gary Bergman	1.50	4.00
120 Henri Richard	4.00	10.00
121 Ross Lonsberry	1.50	4.00
122 Pat Quinn	2.00	5.00
123 Rod Gilbert	3.00	8.00
124 Walt McKechnie	2.00	5.00
125 Stan Mikita	6.00	15.00
126 Ed Van Impe	1.50	4.00
127 Terry Crisp RC	4.00	10.00
128 Fred Barrett RC	1.50	4.00
129 Wayne Cashman	3.00	8.00
130 J.C. Tremblay	2.00	5.00
131 Bernie Parent	8.00	20.00
132 Bryan Watson	2.00	5.00
133 Marcel Dionne RC	75.00	150.00
134 Ab McDonald	2.00	5.00
135 Leon Rochefort	2.00	5.00
136 Serge Lajeunesse RC	2.00	5.00
137 Joe Daley	2.50	6.00
138 Brian Conacher	2.00	5.00
139 Bill Collins	2.00	5.00
140 Nick Libett	2.00	5.00
141 Bill Sutherland	2.00	5.00
142 Bill Hicke	2.00	5.00
143 Serge Savard	4.00	10.00
144 Jacques Laperriere	2.50	6.00
145 Guy Lapointe	2.50	6.00
146 Claude Larose UER	2.00	5.00
147 Rejean Houle	2.50	6.00
148 Guy Lafleur UER RC	100.00	200.00
149 Dale Hoganson RC	2.00	5.00
150 Al McDonough RC	2.00	5.00
151 Gilles Marotte	2.00	5.00
152 Butch Goring RC	4.00	10.00
153 Harry Howell	2.50	6.00
154 Real Lemieux	2.00	5.00
155 Gary Edwards RC	2.50	6.00
156 Rogatien Vachon	4.00	10.00
157 Mike Corrigan	2.00	5.00
158 Floyd Smith	2.00	5.00
159 Dave Dryden	2.50	6.00
160 Gerry Meehan	2.50	6.00
161 Richard Martin RC	8.00	20.00
162 Steve Atkinson RC	2.00	5.00
163 Ron Anderson	2.00	5.00
164 Dick Duff	2.50	6.00
165 Jim Watson	2.00	5.00
166 Don Luce RC	2.00	5.00
167 Larry Mickey	2.00	5.00
168 Larry Hillman	2.00	5.00
169 Ed Westfall	2.50	6.00
170 Dallas Smith	2.00	5.00
171 Mike Walton	2.00	5.00
172 Ed Johnston	2.50	6.00
173 Ted Green	2.50	6.00
174 Rick Smith	2.00	5.00
175 Reggie Leach RC	8.00	20.00
176 Don Marcotte	2.00	5.00
177 Bobby Sheehan RC	2.00	5.00
178 Wayne Carleton	2.00	5.00
179 Norm Ferguson	2.00	5.00
180 Don O'Donoghue RC	2.00	5.00
181 Gary Kurt RC	2.50	6.00
182 Joey Johnston RC	2.00	5.00
183 Stan Gilbertson RC	2.00	5.00
184 Craig Patrick RC	4.00	10.00
185 Gerry Pinder	2.00	5.00
186 Tim Horton	5.00	12.00
187 Darryl Edestrand RC	2.00	5.00
188 Keith McCreary	2.00	5.00
189 Val Fonteyne	2.00	5.00
190 S.Kannegiesser RC	2.00	5.00
191 Nick Harbaruk RC	2.00	5.00
192 Les Binkley	2.50	6.00
193 Darryl Sittler	15.00	40.00
194 Rick Ley	2.00	5.00
195 Jacques Plante	12.00	30.00
196 Bob Baun	2.50	6.00
197 Brian Glennie	2.00	5.00
198 Brian Spencer RC	4.00	10.00
199 Don Marshall	2.50	6.00
200 Denis Dupere RC	2.00	5.00
201 Bruce Gamble	2.50	6.00
202 Gary Dornhoefer	2.00	5.00
203 Bob Kelly RC	2.50	6.00
204 Jean-Guy Gendron	2.00	5.00
205 Brent Hughes	2.00	5.00
206 Simon Nolet	2.00	5.00
207 Rick MacLeish RC	8.00	20.00
208 Doug Jarrett	2.00	5.00
209 Cliff Koroll	2.00	5.00
210 Chico Maki	2.00	5.00
211 Danny O'Shea	2.00	5.00
212 Lou Angotti	2.00	5.00
213 Eric Nesterenko	2.50	6.00
214 Bryan Campbell	2.00	5.00
215 Bill Fairbairn RC	2.00	5.00
216 Bruce MacGregor	2.00	5.00
217 Pete Stemkowski	2.00	5.00
218 Bobby Rousseau	2.00	5.00
219 Dale Rolfe	2.00	5.00
220 Ed Giacomin	4.00	10.00
221 Glen Sather	2.50	6.00
222 Carl Brewer	2.50	6.00
223 George Morrison RC	2.00	5.00
224 Noel Picard	2.00	5.00
225 Peter McDuffe RC	2.50	6.00
226 Brit Selby	2.00	5.00
227 Jim Lorentz	2.00	5.00
228 Phil Roberto RC	2.00	5.00
229 Dave Balon	2.00	5.00
230 Barry Wilkins RC	2.00	5.00
231 Dennis Kearns RC	2.00	5.00
232 Jocelyn Guevremont RC	2.50	6.00
233 Rosaire Paiement	2.00	5.00
234 Dale Tallon	2.00	5.00
235 George Gardner	2.00	5.00
236 Ron Stewart	2.00	5.00
237 Wayne Connelly	2.00	5.00
238 Charlie Burns	2.00	5.00
239 Murray Oliver	2.00	5.00
240 Lou Nanne	2.50	6.00
241 Gump Worsley	4.00	10.00
242 Doug Mohns	2.00	5.00
243 Jean-Paul Parise	2.00	5.00
244 Dennis Hextall	2.50	6.00
245 Bobby Orr Double	20.00	50.00
246 Gilbert Perreault Calder	6.00	15.00
247 Phil Esposito Ross	4.00	10.00
248 Giacmn/Ville Vezina	2.50	6.00
249 Johnny Bucyk Byng	2.50	6.00
250 Ed Giacomin AS1	2.50	6.00
251 Bobby Orr AS1	20.00	50.00
252 J.C. Tremblay AS1	2.50	6.00
253 Phil Esposito AS1 UER	5.00	12.00
254 Ken Hodge AS1	2.50	6.00
255 Johnny Bucyk AS1	2.50	6.00
256 Jacques Plante AS2 UER	6.00	15.00
257 Brad Park AS2	2.50	6.00
258 Pat Stapleton AS2	2.50	6.00
259 Dave Keon AS2	3.00	8.00
260 Yvan Cournoyer AS2	2.50	6.00
261 Bobby Hull AS2	10.00	25.00
262 Gordie Howe Retires	50.00	100.00
263 Jean Beliveau Retires	30.00	60.00
264 Checklist Card	100.00	175.00

1971-72 O-Pee-Chee/Topps Booklets

This set consisted of 24 colorful comic booklets (eight pages in format) each measuring 2 1/2" by 3 1/2". The booklets were included as an insert with the regular issue of the same year and gave a mini-biography of the player. These booklets were also put out by Topps and were printed in the United States. They could be found in either French or English language versions. The booklets were numbered on the fronts with a complete set checklist on the backs. The prices below are valid as well for the 1971-72 Topps version of these booklets although the English version is probably a little easier to find.

COMPLETE SET (24)	50.00	125.00
1 Bobby Hull	6.00	15.00
2 Phil Esposito	3.00	6.00
3 Dale Tallon	1.25	3.00
4 Jacques Plante	4.00	8.00
5 Roger Crozier	1.25	3.00
6 Henri Richard	1.25	3.00
7 Ed Giacomin	2.50	5.00
8 Gilbert Perreault	3.00	6.00
9 Greg Polis	1.25	3.00
10 Bobby Clarke	5.00	10.00
11 Danny Grant	1.25	3.00
12 Alex Delvecchio	1.25	3.00
13 Tony Esposito	3.00	6.00
14 Garry Unger	1.25	3.00
15 Frank St.Marseille	1.25	3.00
16 Dave Keon	2.50	5.00
17 Ken Dryden	8.00	20.00
18 Rod Gilbert	1.25	3.00
19 Juha Widing	1.25	3.00
20 Orland Kurtenbach	1.25	3.00
21 Jude Drouin	1.25	3.00
22 Gary Smith	1.25	3.00
23 Gordie Howe	8.00	20.00
24 Bobby Orr	10.00	25.00

1971-72 O-Pee-Chee Posters

The 1971-72 O-Pee-Chee Posters set contained 24 color pictures measuring approximately 10" by 18". They were originally issued (as a separate issue) in folded form, two to a wax pack. Attached pairs are still sometimes found; these pairs are valued at 25 percent greater than the sum of the individual players included in the pair. The current scarcity of these posters suggests that they may have been a test issue. These posters are numbered and blank backed.

COMPLETE SET (24)	600.00	1000.00
1 Bobby Orr	125.00	250.00
2 Bob Pulford	10.00	20.00
3 Dave Keon	15.00	30.00
4 Yvan Cournoyer	15.00	30.00
5 Dale Tallon	10.00	20.00
6 Richard Martin	7.50	15.00
7 Rod Gilbert	15.00	30.00
8 Tony Esposito	20.00	40.00
9 Bobby Hull	25.00	50.00
10 Red Berenson	7.50	15.00
11 Norm Ullman	8.00	20.00
12 Orland Kurtenbach	7.50	15.00
13 Guy Lafleur	50.00	100.00
14 Gilbert Perreault	20.00	40.00
15 Jacques Plante	25.00	50.00
16 Bruce Gamble	10.00	25.00
17 Walt McKechnie	7.50	15.00
18 Tim Horton	25.00	50.00
19 Jean Ratelle	15.00	30.00
20 Garry Unger	7.50	15.00
21 Phil Esposito	25.00	50.00
22 Ken Dryden	75.00	150.00
23 Gump Worsley	15.00	30.00
24 Montreal Canadiens	20.00	40.00

1972-73 O-Pee-Chee

The 1972-73 O-Pee-Chee set featured 340 standard-size cards that were printed in Canada. The set featured players from the expansion New York Islanders and Atlanta Flames. Unopened packs consisted of eight cards plus a bubble-gum piece. Tan borders on the front included the team name on the left-hand side. Bilingual backs featured a year-by-year record of the player's career, a short biography and a cartoon-illustrated fact about the player. There were a number of In-Action (IA) cards of popular players distributed throughout the set. Card number 208 was never issued. The last series (290-341), which was printed in lesser quantities, featured players from the newly formed World Hockey Association. Based upon uncut sheets that are known and observed, there were apparently 22 double-printed cards in the first series (1-110) and 22 known double-printed cards in the second series (111-209). These cards were identified by DP in the checklist below.

103190702

1972-73 O-Pee-Chee

COMPLETE SET (340)	900.00	1500.00
1 Johnny Bucyk DP	3.00	8.00
2 Rene Robert RC	2.00	5.00
3 Gary Croteau	1.00	2.50
4 Pat Stapleton	1.00	2.50
5 Ron Harris	1.00	2.50
6 Checklist 1	20.00	50.00
7 Playoff Game 1	1.00	2.50
8 Marcel Dionne	10.00	25.00
9 Bob Berry	1.00	2.50
10 Lou Nanne	1.00	2.50
11 Marc Tardif	1.00	2.50
12 Jean Ratelle	1.50	4.00
13 Craig Cameron RC	1.00	2.50
14 Bobby Clarke	12.00	30.00
15 Jim Rutherford RC	4.00	10.00
16 Andre Dupont RC	1.50	4.00
17 Mike Pelyk	1.00	2.50
18 Dunc Wilson	1.00	2.50
19 Checklist 2	20.00	50.00
20 Playoff Game 2	1.00	2.50
21 Dallas Smith	1.00	2.50
22 Gerry Meehan	1.00	2.50
23 Rick Smith UER	1.00	2.50
24 Pit Martin	1.00	2.50
25 Keith McCreary	1.00	2.50
26 Alex Delvecchio	1.50	4.00
27 Gilles Marotte	1.00	2.50
28 Gump Worsley	1.50	4.00
29 Yvan Cournoyer	1.50	4.00
30 Playoff Game 3	1.00	2.50
31 Vic Hadfield	1.00	2.50
32 Tom Miller RC	1.00	2.50
33 Ed Van Impe	1.00	2.50
34 Greg Polis	1.00	2.50
35 Barclay Plager	1.00	2.50
36 Ron Ellis	1.00	2.50
37 Jocelyn Guevremont	1.00	2.50
38 Playoff Game 4	1.00	2.50
39 Carol Vadnais	1.00	2.50
40 Steve Atkinson	1.00	2.50
41 Ivan Boldirev RC	2.50	6.00
42 Jim Pappin	1.00	2.50
43 Phil Myre RC	3.00	8.00
44 Yvan Cournoyer IA	1.25	3.00
45 Nick Libett	1.00	2.50
46 Juha Widing	1.00	2.50
47 Jude Drouin	1.00	2.50
48A Jean Ratelle IA Def	1.50	4.00
48B Jean Ratelle IA Cent	1.25	3.00
49 Ken Hodge	1.00	2.50
50 Roger Crozier	1.00	2.50
51 Reggie Leach	1.50	4.00
52 Dennis Hull	1.00	2.50
53 Larry Hale RC	1.00	2.50
54 Playoff Game 5	1.00	2.50
55 Tim Ecclestone	1.00	2.50
56 Butch Goring	1.25	3.00
57 Danny Grant	1.00	2.50
58 Bobby Orr IA	15.00	40.00
59 Guy Lafleur	25.00	60.00
60 Jim Neilson	1.00	2.50
61 Brian Spencer	1.00	2.50
62 Joe Watson	1.00	2.50
63 Playoff Game 6	1.00	2.50
64 Jean Pronovost	1.00	2.50
65 Frank St.Marseille	1.00	2.50
66 Bob Baun	1.00	2.50
67 Paul Popiel	1.00	2.50
68 Wayne Cashman	1.00	2.50
69 Tracy Pratt	1.00	2.50
70 Stan Gilbertson	1.00	2.50
71 Keith Magnuson	1.00	2.50
72 Ernie Hicke	1.00	2.50
73 Gary Doak	1.00	2.50
74 Mike Corrigan	1.00	2.50
75 Doug Mohns	1.00	2.50
76 Phil Esposito IA	3.00	8.00
77 Jacques Lemaire	1.50	4.00
78 Pete Stemkowski	1.00	2.50
79 Bill Mikkelson RC	1.00	2.50
80 Rick Foley RC	1.00	2.50
81 Ron Schock	1.00	2.50
82 Phil Roberto	1.00	2.50
83 Jim McKenny	1.00	2.50
84 Wayne Maki	1.00	2.50
85A Brad Park IA Cent	3.00	8.00
85B Brad Park IA Def	2.00	5.00
86 Guy Lapointe	1.25	3.00
87 Bill Fairbairn	1.00	2.50
88 Terry Crisp	1.00	2.50
89 Doug Favell	1.00	2.50
90 Bryan Watson	1.00	2.50
91 Gary Sabourin	1.00	2.50
92 Jacques Plante	8.00	20.00
93 Andre Boudrias	1.00	2.50
94 Mike Walton	1.00	2.50
95 Don Luce	1.00	2.50
96 Joey Johnston	1.00	2.50
97 Doug Jarrett	1.00	2.50
98 Bill MacMillan RC	1.00	2.50
99 Mickey Redmond	1.25	3.00
100 Rogatien Vachon UER	1.50	4.00
101 Barry Gibbs RC	1.00	2.50
102 Frank Mahovlich DP	1.50	4.00
103 Bruce MacGregor	1.00	2.50
104 Ed Westfall	1.00	2.50
105 Rick MacLeish	2.00	5.00
106 Nick Harbaruk	1.00	2.50
107 Jack Egers RC	1.00	2.50
108 Dave Keon	1.50	4.00
109 Barry Wilkins	1.00	2.50
110 Walt Tkaczuk	1.00	2.50
111 Phil Esposito	6.00	15.00
112 Gilles Meloche RC	3.00	8.00
113 Gary Edwards	1.25	3.00
114 Brad Park	4.00	10.00
115 Syl Apps DP	1.25	3.00
116 Jim Lorentz	1.25	3.00
117 Gary Smith	1.25	3.00
118 Ted Harris	1.25	3.00
119 Gerry Desjardins DP	.60	1.50
120 Garry Unger	1.25	3.00
121 Dale Tallon	1.25	3.00
122 Bill Plager RC	1.50	4.00
123 Red Berenson DP	.60	1.50
124 Peter Mahovlich DP	1.25	3.00
125 Simon Nolet	1.25	3.00
126 Paul Henderson	1.25	3.00
127 Hart Trophy Winners	1.25	3.00
128 Frank Mahovlich IA	1.25	3.00
129 Bobby Orr	40.00	80.00
130 Bert Marshall	1.25	3.00
131 Ralph Backstrom	1.25	3.00
132 Gilles Villemure	1.25	3.00
133 Dave Burrows RC	1.25	3.00
134 Calder Trophy Winners	1.25	3.00
135 Dallas Smith IA	1.25	3.00
136 Gilbert Perreault DP	5.00	12.00
137 Tony Esposito DP	8.00	20.00
138 Cesare Maniago DP	.60	1.50
139 Gerry Hart RC	1.25	3.00
140 Jacques Caron RC	1.50	4.00
141 Orland Kurtenbach	1.25	3.00
142 Norris Trophy Winners	1.25	3.00
143 Lew Morrison	1.25	3.00
144 Arnie Brown	1.25	3.00
145 Ken Dryden DP	20.00	40.00
146 Gary Dornhoefer	1.25	3.00
147 Norm Ullman	2.00	5.00
148 Art Ross Trophy	1.25	3.00
149 Orland Kurtenbach IA	1.25	3.00
150 Fred Stanfield	1.25	3.00
151 Dick Redmond DP	.60	1.50
152 Serge Bernier	1.25	3.00
153 Rod Gilbert	2.00	5.00
154 Duane Rupp	1.25	3.00
155 Vezina Trophy Winners	1.25	3.00
156 Stan Mikita IA	2.00	5.00
157 Richard Martin DP	2.00	5.00
158 Bill White DP	.60	1.50
159 Bill Goldsworthy DP	.60	1.50
160 Jack Lynch RC	1.25	3.00
161 Bob Plager DP	.60	1.50
162 Dave Balon UER	1.25	3.00
163 Noel Price	1.25	3.00
164 Gary Bergman DP	.60	1.50
165 Pierre Bouchard	1.25	3.00
166 Ross Lonsberry	1.25	3.00
167 Denis Dupere	1.25	3.00
168 Byng Trophy Winners DP	.60	1.50
169 Ken Hodge	1.25	3.00
170 Don Awrey DP	.60	1.50
171 Marshall Johnston DP RC	.60	1.50
172 Terry Harper	1.25	3.00
173 Ed Giacomin	2.00	5.00
174 Bryan Hextall DP	.60	1.50
175 Conn Smythe Trophy Winners	1.25	3.00
176 Larry Hillman	1.25	3.00
177 Stan Mikita DP	3.00	8.00
178 Charlie Burns	1.25	3.00
179 Brian Marchinko	1.25	3.00
180 Noel Picard DP	.60	1.50
181 Bobby Schmautz RC	1.50	4.00
182 Richard Martin IA UER	1.50	4.00
183 Pat Quinn	1.25	3.00
184 Denis DeJordy UER	1.25	3.00
185 Serge Savard	2.00	5.00
186 Eddie Shack	1.50	4.00
187 Bill Flett	1.25	3.00
188 Darryl Sittler	8.00	20.00
189 Gump Worsley IA	1.50	4.00
190 Checklist 2	25.00	60.00
191 Garnet Bailey DP	.60	1.50
192 Walt McKechnie	1.25	3.00
193 Harry Howell	1.25	3.00
194 Rod Seiling	1.25	3.00
195 Darryl Edestrand	1.25	3.00
196 Tony Esposito IA	3.00	8.00
197 Tim Horton	3.00	8.00
198 Chico Maki DP	.60	1.50
199 Jean-Paul Parise	1.25	3.00
200 Germaine Gagnon UER RC	1.25	3.00
201 Danny O'Shea	1.25	3.00
202 Richard Lemieux RC	1.25	3.00
203 Dan Bouchard RC	4.00	10.00
204 Leon Rochefort	1.25	3.00
205 Jacques Laperriere	1.50	4.00
206 Barry Ashbee	1.25	3.00
207 Garry Monahan	1.25	3.00
209 Dave Keon IA	2.00	5.00
210 Rejean Houle	2.00	5.00
211 Dave Hudson RC	1.50	4.00
212 Ted Irvine	1.50	4.00
213 Don Saleski RC	2.00	5.00
214 Lowell MacDonald	1.50	4.00
215 Mike Murphy RC	2.50	6.00
216 Brian Glennie	1.50	4.00
217 Bobby Lalonde RC	1.50	4.00
218 Bob Leiter	1.50	4.00
219 Don Marcotte	1.50	4.00
220 Jim Schoenfeld RC	5.00	12.00
221 Craig Patrick	1.50	4.00
222 Cliff Koroll	1.50	4.00
223 Guy Charron RC	2.00	5.00
224 Jim Peters	1.50	4.00
225 Dennis Hextall	1.50	4.00
226 Tony Esposito AS1	6.00	15.00
227 Orr/Park AS1	15.00	40.00
228 Bobby Hull AS1	12.00	30.00
229 Rod Gilbert AS1	1.50	4.00
230 Phil Esposito AS1	4.00	10.00
231 Claude Larose UER	1.50	4.00
232 Jim Mair RC	1.50	4.00
233 Bobby Rousseau	1.50	4.00
234 Brent Hughes	1.50	4.00
235 Al McDonough	1.50	4.00
236 Chris Evans RC	1.50	4.00
237 Pierre Jarry RC	1.50	4.00
238 Don Tannahill RC	1.50	4.00
239 Rey Comeau RC	1.50	4.00
240 Gregg Sheppard UER RC	1.50	4.00
241 Dave Dryden	1.50	4.00
242 Ted McAneeley RC	1.50	4.00
243 Lou Angotti	1.50	4.00
244 Len Fontaine RC	1.50	4.00
245 Bill Lesuk RC	1.50	4.00
246 Fred Harvey RC	1.50	4.00
247 Ken Dryden AS2	12.00	30.00
248 Bill White AS2	1.50	4.00
249 Pat Stapleton AS2	1.50	4.00
250 Ratel/Cour/Hadfld LL	2.50	6.00
251 Henri Richard	2.50	6.00
252 Bryan Lefley RC	1.50	4.00
253 Stanley Cup Trophy	6.00	15.00
254 Steve Vickers RC	3.00	8.00
255 Wayne Hillman	1.50	4.00
256 Ken Schinkel UER	1.50	4.00
257 Kevin O'Shea RC	1.50	4.00
258 Ron Low RC	6.00	15.00
259 Don Lever RC	10.00	25.00
260 Randy Manery RC	1.50	4.00
261 Ed Johnston	2.00	5.00
262 Craig Ramsay RC	3.00	8.00
263 Pete Laframboise RC	1.50	4.00
264 Dan Maloney RC	2.50	6.00
265 Bill Collins	1.50	4.00
266 Paul Curtis	1.50	4.00
267 Bob Nevin	1.50	4.00
268 Watson/Magnuson LL	2.00	5.00
269 Jim Roberts	1.50	4.00
270 Brian Lavender RC	1.50	4.00
271 Dale Rolfe	1.50	4.00
272 Espo/Hadf/B.Hull LL	8.00	20.00
273 Michel Belhumeur RC	3.00	8.00
274 Eddie Shack	2.50	6.00
275 Wayne Stephenson RC UER	4.00	10.00
276 Bruins SC Winner	6.00	15.00
277 Rick Kehoe RC	3.00	8.00
278 Gerry O'Flaherty RC	1.50	4.00
279 Jacques Richard RC	2.00	5.00
280 Espo/Orr/Ratelle LL	10.00	25.00
281 Nick Beverley RC	3.00	8.00
282 Larry Carriere RC	1.50	4.00
283 Orr/Espo/Ratelle LL	10.00	25.00
284 Rick Smith IA	2.00	5.00
285 Jerry Korab RC	2.50	6.00
286 Espo/Villem/Worsley LL	5.00	12.00
287 Ron Stackhouse	1.50	4.00
288 Barry Long RC	2.00	5.00
289 Dean Prentice	2.00	5.00
290 Norm Beaudin	3.00	6.00
291 Mike Amodeo RC	3.00	8.00
292 Jim Harrison	3.00	8.00
293 J.C. Tremblay	3.00	8.00
294 Murray Hall	3.00	8.00
295 Bart Crashley	3.00	8.00
296 Wayne Connelly	3.00	8.00
297 Bobby Sheehan	3.00	8.00
298 Ron Anderson	3.00	8.00
299 Chris Bordeleau	3.00	8.00
300 Les Binkley	3.00	8.00
301 Ron Walters	3.00	8.00
302 Jean-Guy Gendron	3.00	8.00
303 Gord Labossiere	3.00	8.00
304 Gerry Odrowski	3.00	8.00
305 Mike McMahon	3.00	8.00
306 Gary Kurt	3.00	8.00
307 Larry Cahan	3.00	8.00
308 Wally Boyer	3.00	8.00
309 Bob Charlebois RC	3.00	8.00
310 Bob Falkenberg	3.00	8.00
311 Jean Payette RC	3.00	8.00
312 Ted Taylor	3.00	8.00
313 Joe Szura	3.00	8.00
314 George Morrison	3.00	8.00
315 Wayne Rivers	3.00	8.00
316 Reg Fleming	4.00	10.00
317 Larry Hornung RC	3.00	8.00
318 Ron Climie RC	3.00	8.00
319 Val Fonteyne	3.00	8.00
320 Michel Archambault RC	3.00	8.00
321 Ab McDonald	3.00	8.00
322 Bob Leduc RC	3.00	8.00
323 Bob Wall	3.00	8.00
324 Alain Caron RC	3.00	8.00
325 Bob Woytowich	3.00	8.00
326 Guy Trottier	3.00	8.00
327 Bill Hicke	3.00	8.00
328 Guy Dufour RC	3.00	8.00
329 Wayne Rutledge RC	4.00	10.00
330 Gary Veneruzzo	3.00	8.00
331 Fred Speck RC	3.00	8.00
332 Ron Ward RC	3.00	8.00
333 Rosaire Paiement	3.00	8.00
334A Checklist 3 ERR	40.00	80.00
334B Checklist 3 COR	25.00	60.00
335 Michel Parizeau RC	3.00	8.00
336 Bobby Hull	25.00	60.00
337 Wayne Carleton	3.00	8.00
338 John McKenzie	4.00	10.00
339 Jim Dorey	3.00	8.00
340 Gerry Cheevers	12.00	30.00
341 Gerry Pinder	8.00	20.00

1972-73 O-Pee-Chee Player Crests

This set consisted of 22 full-color cardboard stickers measuring 2 1/2" by 3 1/2". The set was issued as an insert with the regular issue of the same year in with the first series wax packs. Cards were numbered on the front and have a blank adhesive back. Although the cards were designed so that the crest could be popped out, this is strongly discouraged. These stickers were printed in Canada.

COMPLETE SET (22)	100.00	200.00
1 Pat Quinn	3.00	10.00
2 Phil Esposito	8.00	20.00
3 Bobby Orr	30.00	80.00
4 Richard Martin	2.50	6.00
5 Stan Mikita	4.00	10.00
6 Bill White	2.50	6.00
7 Red Berenson	2.50	6.00
8 Gary Bergman	2.50	6.00
9 Gary Edwards	2.50	6.00
10 Bill Goldsworthy	2.50	6.00
11 Jacques Laperriere	2.50	6.00
12 Ken Dryden	20.00	40.00
13 Ed Westfall	2.50	6.00
14 Walt Tkaczuk	2.50	6.00
15 Brad Park	5.00	12.00
16 Doug Favell	5.00	12.00
17 Eddie Shack	5.00	10.00
18 Jacques Caron	2.50	6.00
19 Paul Henderson	4.00	10.00
20 Jim Harrison	2.50	6.00
21 Dale Tallon	2.50	6.00
22 Orland Kurtenbach	2.50	6.00

1972-73 O-Pee-Chee Team Canada

This attractive set consisted of 28 unnumbered color cards measuring 2 1/2" by 3 1/2". The 28 players are those who represented Team Canada against Russia in the 1972 Summit Series. Only the players' heads were shown surrounded by a border of maple leaves with a Canadian and Russian flag in each corner. The card back provided a summary of that player's performance in the eight-game series. The set was issued as an insert with the second series of the 1972-73 O-Pee-Chee regular issue. Backs were written in both French and English. The cards were printed in Canada.

COMPLETE SET (28)	150.00	300.00
1 Don Awrey	3.00	8.00
2 Red Berenson	3.00	8.00
3 Gary Bergman	3.00	8.00
4 Wayne Cashman	4.00	10.00
5 Bobby Clarke	12.50	25.00
6 Yvan Cournoyer	7.50	15.00
7 Ken Dryden	25.00	50.00
8 Ron Ellis	5.00	12.00
9 Phil Esposito	12.50	25.00
10 Tony Esposito	15.00	30.00
11 Rod Gilbert	5.00	12.00
12 Bill Goldsworthy	3.00	8.00
13 Vic Hadfield	3.00	8.00
14 Paul Henderson	15.00	30.00
15 Dennis Hull	3.00	8.00
16 Guy Lapointe	3.00	8.00
17 Frank Mahovlich	7.50	15.00
18 Pete Mahovlich	3.00	8.00
19 Stan Mikita	10.00	20.00
20 Jean-Paul Parise	3.00	8.00
21 Brad Park	5.00	12.00
22 Gilbert Perreault	3.00	8.00
23 Jean Ratelle	5.00	12.00
24 Mickey Redmond	5.00	12.00
25 Serge Savard	4.00	10.00
26 Rod Seiling	3.00	8.00
27 Pat Stapleton	3.00	8.00
28 Bill White	3.00	8.00

1972-73 O-Pee-Chee Team Logos

This set of 30 team logo pushouts included logos for the 15 NHL established teams as well as the two new NHL teams, the 12 WHA teams, and the WHA League emblem. The cards were die-cut and adhesive backed. They were inserted in with the third series of the 1972-73 O-Pee-Chee wax packs. The expansion and WHA emblems were more difficult to find and are listed as SP in the checklist below. These inserts were standard size, 2 1/2" by 3 1/2". These team logos cards were distinguished by their lack of instructions on the front.

ONE PER SER. 3 OPC PACK

1 NHL Logo	10.00	25.00
2 Atlanta Flames SP	100.00	200.00
3 Boston Bruins	5.00	12.00
4 Buffalo Sabres	5.00	12.00
5 California Seals	10.00	25.00
6 Chicago Blackhawks	5.00	12.00
7 Detroit Red Wings	5.00	12.00
8 Los Angeles Kings	5.00	12.00
9 Minnesota North Stars	6.00	15.00
10 Montreal Canadiens	5.00	12.00
11 New York Islanders SP	60.00	120.00
12 New York Rangers	6.00	15.00
13 Philadelphia Flyers	5.00	12.00
14 Pittsburgh Penguins	6.00	15.00
15 St. Louis Blues	5.00	12.00
16 Toronto Maple Leafs	5.00	12.00
17 Vancouver Canucks	8.00	20.00
18 WHA Logo SP	30.00	60.00
19 Chicago Cougars SP	30.00	60.00
20 Cleveland Crusaders SP	40.00	80.00
21 Edmonton Oilers SP	40.00	80.00
22 Houston Aeros SP	40.00	80.00
23 Los Angeles Sharks SP	30.00	60.00
24 Minnesota Fighting Saints SP	50.00	100.00
25 New England Whalers SP	40.00	80.00
26 New York Raiders SP	30.00	60.00
27 Ottawa Nationals SP	40.00	80.00
28 Phila. Blazers SP	40.00	80.00
29 Quebec Nordiques SP	30.00	60.00
30 Winnipeg Jets SP	50.00	100.00

1973-74 O-Pee-Chee

The 1973-74 O-Pee-Chee NHL set featured 264 standard-size cards. The cards measured 2 1/2" by 3 1/2". The border color on the fronts differed from the Topps set. Cards 1-198 had a red border and cards 199-264 had a green border. Topps cards were a mix of blue and green. Bilingual backs contained 1972-73 and career statistics, a short biography and a cartoon-illustrated fact about the player. Team cards (92-107) contained team and player records on the back. The cards were printed in Canada on both cream or gray card stock. Rookie Cards in this set included Bill Barber, Terry O'Reilly, Larry Robinson, Dave Schultz, and Billy Smith.

COMPLETE SET (264) 300.00 500.00
1 Alex Delvecchio 2.50 5.00
2 Gilles Meloche 1.25 3.00
3 Phil Roberto 1.25 3.00
4 Orland Kurtenbach 1.00 2.50
5 Gilles Marotte 1.00 2.50
6 Stan Mikita 4.00 8.00
7 Paul Henderson 1.25 3.00
8 Gregg Sheppard 1.00 2.50
9 Rod Seiling 1.00 2.50
10 Red Berenson 1.25 3.00
11 Jean Pronovost 1.25 3.00
12 Dick Redmond 1.00 2.50
13 Keith McCreary 1.00 2.50
14 Bryan Watson 1.00 2.50
15 Garry Unger 1.25 3.00
16 Neil Komadoski RC 1.00 2.50
17 Marcel Dionne 6.00 15.00
18 Ernie Hicke 1.00 2.50
19 Andre Boudrias 1.00 2.50
20 Bill Flett 1.00 2.50
21 Marshall Johnston 1.00 2.50
22 Gerry Meehan 1.00 2.50
23 Ed Johnston 1.25 3.00
24 Serge Savard 2.50 5.00
25 Walt Tkaczuk 1.25 3.00
26 Ken Hodge 1.25 3.00
27 Norm Ullman 2.50 5.00
28 Cliff Koroll 1.00 2.50
29 Rey Comeau 1.00 2.50
30 Bobby Orr 25.00 50.00
31 Wayne Stephenson 1.25 3.00
32 Dan Maloney 1.25 3.00
33 Henry Boucha RC 2.50 5.00
34 Gerry Hart 1.00 2.50
35 Bobby Schmautz 1.00 2.50
36 Ross Lonsberry 1.00 2.50
37 Ted McAneeley 1.00 2.50
38 Don Luce 1.00 2.50
39 Jim McKenny 1.00 2.50
40 Jacques Laperriere 1.25 3.00
41 Bill Fairbairn 1.00 2.50
42 Craig Cameron 1.00 2.50
43 Bryan Hextall 1.00 2.50
44 Chuck Lefley RC 1.00 2.50
45 Dan Bouchard 1.25 3.00
46 Jean-Paul Parise 1.00 2.50
47 Barclay Plager 1.25 3.00
48 Mike Corrigan 1.00 2.50
49 Nick Libett 1.00 2.50
50 Bobby Clarke 10.00 20.00
51 Bert Marshall 1.00 2.50
52 Craig Patrick 1.25 3.00
53 Richard Lemieux 1.00 2.50
54 Tracy Pratt 1.00 2.50
55 Ron Ellis 1.25 3.00
56 Jacques Lemaire 2.50 5.00
57 Steve Vickers 1.25 3.00
58 Carol Vadnais 1.00 2.50
59 Jim Rutherford 1.25 3.00
60 Rick Kehoe 1.25 3.00
61 Pat Quinn 1.25 3.00
62 Bill Goldsworthy 1.25 3.00
63 Dave Dryden 1.25 3.00
64 Rogatien Vachon 2.50 6.00
65 Gary Bergman 1.00 2.50
66 Bernie Parent 6.00 10.00
67 Ed Westfall 1.25 3.00
68 Ivan Boldirev 1.25 3.00
69 Don Tannahill 1.00 2.50
70 Gilbert Perreault 7.00 12.00
71 Mike Pelyk 1.00 2.50
72 Guy Lafleur 15.00 25.00
73 Pit Martin 1.25 3.00
74 Gilles Gilbert RC 5.00 8.00
75 Jim Lorentz 1.00 2.50
76 Syl Apps 1.25 3.00
77 Phil Myre 1.25 3.00
78 Bill White 1.00 2.50
79 Jack Egers 1.00 2.50
80 Terry Harper 1.00 2.50
81 Bill Barber RC 12.00 20.00
82 Roy Edwards 1.25 3.00
83 Brian Spencer 1.25 3.00
84 Reggie Leach 1.25 3.00
85 Wayne Cashman 1.25 3.00
86 Jim Schoenfeld 2.50 5.00
87 Henri Richard 2.50 5.00
88 Dennis O'Brien RC 1.00 2.50
89 Al McDonough 1.00 2.50
90 Tony Esposito 6.00 12.00
91 Joe Watson 1.00 2.50
92 Flames Team 2.50 5.00
93 Bruins Team 2.50 5.00
94 Sabres Team 2.50 5.00
95 Golden Seals Team 2.50 5.00
96 Blackhawks Team 2.50 5.00
97 Red Wings Team 2.50 5.00
98 Kings Team 2.50 5.00
99 North Stars Team 2.50 5.00
100 Canadiens Team 4.00 8.00
101 Islanders Team 2.50 5.00
102 Rangers Team 2.50 5.00
103 Flyers Team 2.50 5.00
104 Penguins Team 2.50 5.00
105 Blues Team 2.50 5.00
106 Maple Leafs Team 4.00 8.00
107 Canucks Team 2.50 5.00
108 Vic Hadfield 1.25 3.00
109 Tom Reid 1.00 2.50
110 Hilliard Graves RC 1.00 2.50
111 Don Lever 1.25 3.00
112 Jim Pappin 1.00 2.50
113 Andre Dupont 1.00 2.50
114 Guy Lapointe 1.25 3.00
115 Dennis Hextall 1.00 2.50
116 Checklist 1 20.00 40.00
117 Bob Leiter 1.00 2.50
118 Ab DeMarco 1.00 2.50
119 Gilles Villemure 1.25 3.00
120 Phil Esposito 5.00 10.00
121 Mike Robitaille 1.00 2.50
122 Real Lemieux 1.00 2.50
123 Jim Neilson 1.00 2.50
124 Steve Durbano RC 1.25 3.00
125 Jude Drouin 1.00 2.50
126 Gary Smith 1.25 3.00
127 Cesare Maniago 1.25 3.00
128 Lowell MacDonald 1.00 2.50
129 Checklist 2 20.00 40.00
130 Billy Harris RC 1.25 3.00
131 Randy Manery 1.00 2.50
132 Darryl Sittler 7.50 15.00
133 P.Espo/MacLeish LL 2.50 5.00
134 P.Espo/B.Clarke LL 2.50 5.00
135 P.Espo/B.Clarke LL 2.50 5.00
136 K.Dryden/T.Espo LL 6.00 10.00
137 Schultz/Schnfeld LL 2.50 5.00
138 P.Espo/MacLeish LL 2.50 5.00
139 Rene Robert 1.25 3.00
140 Dave Burrows 1.00 2.50
141 Jean Ratelle 2.50 5.00
142 Billy Smith RC 25.00 50.00
143 Jocelyn Guevremont 1.00 2.50
144 Tim Ecclestone 1.00 2.50
145 Frank Mahovlich 2.50 5.00
146 Rick MacLeish 2.50 5.00
147 Johnny Bucyk 2.50 5.00
148 Bob Plager 1.25 3.00
149 Curt Bennett RC 1.00 2.50
150 Dave Keon 2.50 5.00
151 Keith Magnuson 1.25 3.00
152 Walt McKechnie 1.00 2.50
153 Roger Crozier 1.25 3.00
154 Ted Harris 1.00 2.50
155 Butch Goring 1.25 3.00
156 Rod Gilbert 2.50 5.00
157 Yvan Cournoyer 2.50 5.00
158 Doug Favell 1.25 3.00
159 Juha Widing 1.00 2.50
160 Ed Giacomin 2.50 5.00
161 Germaine Gagnon UER 1.00 2.50
162 Dennis Kearns 1.00 2.50
163 Bill Collins 1.00 2.50
164 Peter Mahovlich 1.25 3.00
165 Brad Park 3.00 6.00
166 Dave Schultz RC 7.50 15.00
167 Dallas Smith 1.00 2.50
168 Gary Sabourin 1.00 2.50
169 Jacques Richard 1.00 2.50
170 Brian Glennie 1.00 2.50
171 Dennis Hull 1.25 3.00
172 Joey Johnston 1.00 2.50
173 Richard Martin 2.50 5.00
174 Barry Gibbs 1.00 2.50
175 Bob Berry 1.00 2.50
176 Greg Polis 1.00 2.50
177 Dale Rolfe 1.00 2.50
178 Gerry Desjardins 1.25 3.00
179 Bobby Lalonde 1.00 2.50
180 Mickey Redmond 1.25 3.00
181 Jim Roberts 1.00 2.50
182 Gary Dornhoefer 1.25 3.00
183 Derek Sanderson 2.50 5.00
184 Brent Hughes 1.00 2.50
185 Larry Romanchych RC 1.00 2.50
186 Pierre Jarry 1.00 2.50
187 Doug Jarrett 1.00 2.50
188 Bob Stewart RC 1.25 3.00
189 Tim Horton 4.00 8.00
190 Fred Harvey 1.00 2.50
191 Series A/Cand/Sabr .75 2.00
192 Series B/Flyrs/Stars .75 2.00
193 Series C/Hwks/Blues .75 2.00
194 Series D/Rngr/Bruins .75 2.00
195 Series E/Cndn/Flyr .75 2.00
196 Series F/Blckh/Rngr .75 2.00
197 Series G/Cndn/Hawk .75 2.00
198 Canadiens Champs 2.50 5.00
199 Gary Edwards 1.25 3.00
200 Ron Schock 1.00 2.50
201 Bruce MacGregor 1.00 2.50
202 Bob Nystrom RC 3.00 6.00
203 Jerry Korab 1.00 2.50
204 Thommie Bergman RC 1.00 2.50
205 Bill Lesuk 1.00 2.50
206 Ed Van Impe 1.00 2.50
207 Doug Roberts 1.00 2.50
208 Chris Evans 1.00 2.50
209 Lynn Powis RC 1.00 2.50
210 Denis Dupere 1.00 2.50
211 Dale Tallon 1.00 2.50
212 Stan Gilbertson 1.00 2.50
213 Craig Ramsay 1.25 3.00
214 Danny Grant 1.25 3.00
215 Doug Volmar RC 1.00 2.50
216 Darryl Edestrand 1.00 2.50
217 Pete Stemkowski 1.00 2.50
218 Lorne Henning RC 1.25 3.00
219 Bryan McSheffrey RC 1.00 2.50
220 Guy Charron 1.25 3.00
221 Wayne Thomas RC 2.50 5.00
222 Simon Nolet 1.00 2.50
223 Fred O'Donnell RC 1.00 2.50
224 Lou Angotti 1.00 2.50
225 Arnie Brown 1.00 2.50
226 Garry Monahan 1.00 2.50
227 Chico Maki 1.00 2.50
228 Gary Croteau 1.00 2.50
229 Paul Terbenche 1.00 2.50
230 Gump Worsley 3.00 8.00
231 Jim Peters 1.00 2.50
232 Jack Lynch 1.00 2.50
233 Bobby Rousseau 1.00 2.50
234 Dave Hudson 1.00 2.50
235 Gregg Boddy RC 1.00 2.50
236 Ron Stackhouse 1.00 2.50
237 Larry Robinson RC 40.00 80.00
238 Bobby Taylor RC 2.50 5.00
239 Nick Beverley 1.00 2.50
240 Don Awrey 1.00 2.50
241 Doug Mohns 1.00 2.50
242 Eddie Shack 2.50 5.00
243 Phil Russell RC 2.50 5.00
244 Pete Laframboise 1.00 2.50
245 Steve Atkinson 1.00 2.50
246 Lou Nanne 1.25 3.00
247 Yvon Labre RC 1.25 3.00
248 Ted Irvine 1.00 2.50
249 Tom Miller 1.00 2.50
250 Gerry O'Flaherty 1.00 2.50
251 Larry Johnston RC 1.00 2.50
252 Michel Plasse RC 2.50 5.00
253 Bob Kelly 1.00 2.50
254 Terry O'Reilly RC 10.00 20.00
255 Pierre Plante RC 1.00 2.50
256 Noel Price 1.00 2.50
257 Dunc Wilson 1.25 3.00
258 J.P. Bordeleau RC 1.25 3.00
259 Terry Murray RC 1.25 3.00
260 Larry Carriere 1.00 2.50
261 Pierre Bouchard 1.25 3.00
262 Frank St.Marseille 1.00 2.50
263 Checklist 3 20.00 40.00
264 Fred Barrett 1.25 3.00

1973-74 O-Pee-Chee Rings

The 1973-74 O-Pee-Chee Rings set contained 17 standard-size cards, featuring the NHL league and team logos. The fronts have a push-out cardboard ring and instructions in English and French. The rings are yellow-colored and feature a NHL team logo in the team's colors. The cards are numbered on the front and the backs are blank.

COMPLETE SET (17) 75.00 175.00
1 Vancouver Canucks 3.00 8.00
2 Montreal Canadiens 5.00 12.00
3 Toronto Maple Leafs 3.00 8.00
4 NHL Logo 3.00 8.00
5 Minnesota North Stars 3.00 8.00
6 New York Rangers 3.00 8.00
7 California Seals 8.00 20.00
8 Pittsburgh Penguins 5.00 12.00
9 Philadelphia Flyers 3.00 8.00
10 Chicago Blackhawks 3.00 8.00
11 Boston Bruins 3.00 8.00
12 Los Angeles Kings 3.00 8.00
13 Detroit Red Wings 3.00 8.00
14 St. Louis Blues 3.00 8.00
15 Buffalo Sabres 3.00 8.00
16 Atlanta Flames 8.00 20.00
17 New York Islanders 3.00 8.00

1973-74 O-Pee-Chee Team Logos

The 1973-74 O-Pee-Chee Team Logos set contains 17 unnumbered, standard-size color stickers, featuring the NHL league and team logos. The cards were die-cut and adhesive backed. After the NHL logo, they were ordered below alphabetically by team city/location. This set was distinguished from the similar set of the previous year by the presence of written instructions on the fronts.

COMPLETE SET (17) 25.00 60.00
1 NHL Logo 2.00 5.00
2 Atlanta Flames 6.00 15.00
3 Boston Bruins 3.00 6.00
4 Buffalo Sabres 2.00 5.00
5 California Seals 5.00 10.00
6 Chicago Blackhawks 2.00 5.00
7 Detroit Red Wings 3.00 6.00
8 Los Angeles Kings 2.00 5.00
9 Minnesota North Stars 3.00 6.00
10 Montreal Canadiens 3.00 6.00
11 New York Islanders 5.00 10.00
12 New York Rangers 2.00 5.00
13 Philadelphia Flyers 2.00 5.00
14 Pittsburgh Penguins 3.00 6.00
15 St. Louis Blues 2.00 5.00
16 Toronto Maple Leafs 3.00 6.00
17 Vancouver Canucks 2.00 5.00

1973-74 O-Pee-Chee WHA Posters

Players featured in this set are from the World Hockey Association (WHA). The set consisted of 20 large posters each measuring approximately 7 1/2" by 13 3/4" and was a separate issue in wax packs. The packs contained two posters and gum; gum stains are frequently seen. Posters were numbered on the front and were issued folded. As a result, folded copies are accepted as being in near mint condition. The posters are blank backed.

COMPLETE SET (20) 50.00 100.00
1 Al Smith 2.50 5.00
2 J.C. Tremblay 2.50 5.00
3 Guy Dufour 1.50 3.00
4 Pat Stapleton 2.50 5.00
5 Rosaire Paiement 1.50 3.00
6 Gerry Cheevers 5.00 10.00
7 Gerry Pinder 2.00 4.00
8 Wayne Carleton 1.50 3.00
9 Bob Leduc 1.50 3.00
10 Andre Lacroix 2.50 5.00
11 Jim Harrison 1.50 3.00
12 Ron Climie 1.50 3.00
13 Gordie Howe 12.50 25.00
14 The Howe Family 12.50 25.00
15 Mike Walton 2.00 4.00
16 Bobby Hull 10.00 20.00
17 Chris Bordeleau 1.50 3.00
18 Claude St.Sauveur 1.50 3.00
19 Bryan Campbell 1.50 3.00
20 Marc Tardif 2.50 5.00

1974-75 O-Pee-Chee

The 1974-75 O-Pee-Chee NHL set contained 396 standard-size cards. The first 264 cards are identical to those of Topps in terms of numbering and photos. Wax packs consisted of eight cards plus a piece of bubble gum. Bilingual backs featured the player's 1973-74 and career statistics, a short biography and a cartoon-illustrated fact about the player. The first six cards in the set (1-6) featured league leaders of the previous season. The set included players from the expansion Washington Capitals and Kansas City Scouts (presently New Jersey Devils). The set marked the return of coach cards, including Rookie Cards of Don Cherry and Scotty Bowman.

COMPLETE SET (396) 300.00 500.00
1 P.Espo/Gldswrthy LL 2.50 5.00
2 B.Orr/D.Hextall LL 9.00 15.00
3 P.Espo/B.Clarke LL 3.00 6.00
4 Favell/B.Parent LL .75 2.00
5 Watson/D.Schulz LL .75 2.00
6 Redmond/MacLsh LL .75 2.00
7 Gary Bromley RC 1.00 2.50
8 Bill Barber 3.00 6.00
9 Emile Francis CO .75 2.00
10 Gilles Gilbert 1.00 2.50
11 John Davidson RC 10.00 15.00
12 Ron Ellis 1.00 2.50
13 Syl Apps .75 2.00
14 Richard/Lysiak TL .75 2.00
15 Dan Bouchard 1.00 2.50
16 Ivan Boldirev 1.00 2.50
17 Gary Coalter RC .75 2.00
18 Bob Berry .75 2.00
19 Red Berenson 1.00 2.50
20 Stan Mikita 3.00 6.00
21 Fred Shero CO RC 4.00 8.00
22 Gary Smith 1.00 2.50
23 Bill Mikkelson .75 2.00
24 Jacques Lemaire UER 1.50 3.00
25 Gilbert Perreault 4.00 8.00
26 Cesare Maniago 1.00 2.50
27 Bobby Schmautz .75 2.00
28 Espo/Orr/Bucyk TL 9.00 15.00
29 Steve Vickers 1.00 2.50
30 Lowell MacDonald UER .75 2.00
31 Fred Stanfield .75 2.00
32 Ed Westfall 1.00 2.50
33 Curt Bennett .75 2.00
34 Bep Guidolin CO .75 2.00
35 Cliff Koroll .75 2.00
36 Gary Croteau .75 2.00
37 Mike Corrigan .75 2.00
38 Henry Boucha .75 2.00
39 Ron Low 1.00 2.50
40 Darryl Sittler 6.00 10.00
41 Tracy Pratt .75 2.00
42 Martin/Robert TL .75 2.00
43 Larry Carriere .75 2.00
44 Gary Dornhoefer .75 2.00
45 Denis Herron RC 2.50 5.00
46 Doug Favell 1.00 2.50
47 Dave Gardner RC .75 2.00
48 Morris Mott RC .75 2.00
49 Marc Boileau CO .75 2.00
50 Brad Park 2.50 5.00
51 Bob Leiter .75 2.00
52 Tom Reid .75 2.00
53 Serge Savard 1.50 3.00
54 Checklist 1-132 UER 18.00 30.00
55 Terry Harper .75 2.00
56 Seals Leaders .75 2.00
57 Guy Charron 1.00 2.50
58 Pit Martin .75 2.00
59 Chris Evans .75 2.00
60 Bernie Parent 3.00 6.00
61 Jim Lorentz .75 2.00
62 Dave Kryskow RC .75 2.00
63 Lou Angotti CO .75 2.00
64 Bill Flett .75 2.00
65 Vic Hadfield 1.00 2.50
66 Wayne Merrick RC .75 2.00
67 Andre Dupont .75 2.00
68 Tom Lysiak RC 1.50 3.00
69 Pappin/Mikita/Bord TL 1.00 2.50
70 Guy Lapointe 1.00 2.50
71 Gerry O'Flaherty .75 2.00
72 Marcel Dionne 6.00 10.00
73 Butch Deadmarsh RC .75 2.00
74 Butch Goring 1.00 2.50
75 Keith Magnuson .75 2.00
76 Red Kelly CO .75 2.00
77 Pete Stemkowski .75 2.00
78 Jim Roberts .75 2.00
79 Don Luce .75 2.00
80 Don Awrey .75 2.00
81 Rick Kehoe 1.00 2.50
82 Billy Smith 6.00 10.00
83 Jean-Paul Parise .75 2.00
84 Rdmnd/Dnne/Hoga TL 1.00 2.50
85 Ed Van Impe .75 2.00
86 Randy Manery .75 2.00
87 Barclay Plager 1.00 2.50
88 Inge Hammarstrom RC .75 2.00
89 Ab DeMarco .75 2.00
90 Bill White .75 2.00
91 Al Arbour CO 1.50 3.00
92 Bob Stewart .75 2.00
93 Jack Egers .75 2.00
94 Don Lever 1.00 2.50
95 Reggie Leach 1.00 2.50
96 Dennis O'Brien .75 2.00
97 Peter Mahovlich 1.00 2.50
98 Grng/St.Mrsle/Kzk TL .75 2.00
99 Gerry Meehan .75 2.00
100 Bobby Orr 25.00 50.00
101 Jean Potvin RC .75 2.00
102 Rod Seiling .75 2.00
103 Keith McCreary .75 2.00
104 Phil Maloney CO RC .75 2.00
105 Denis Dupere .75 2.00
106 Steve Durbano .75 2.00
107 Bob Plager UER 1.00 2.50
108 Chris Oddleifson RC .75 2.00
109 Jim Neilson .75 2.00
110 Jean Pronovost 1.00 2.50
111 Don Kozak RC .75 2.00
112 Gldswrthy/Hxtall TL .75 2.00
113 Jim Pappin .75 2.00
114 Richard Lemieux .75 2.00
115 Dennis Hextall .75 2.00
116 Bill Hogaboam RC .75 2.00
117 Vrgrt/Schmt/Boud TL .75 2.00
118 Jimmy Anderson CO .75 2.00
119 Walt Tkaczuk 1.00 2.50
120 Mickey Redmond 1.00 2.50
121 Jim Schoenfeld 1.00 2.50
122 Jocelyn Guevremont .75 2.00
123 Bob Nystrom 1.00 2.50
124 Cour/F.Mahov/Lrse TL 1.50 3.00
125 Lew Morrison .75 2.00
126 Terry Murray 1.00 2.50
127 Richard Martin AS .75 2.00
128 Ken Hodge AS .75 2.00
129 Phil Esposito AS 2.00 4.00
130 Bobby Orr AS 12.00 20.00
131 Brad Park AS 1.00 2.50
132 Gilles Gilbert AS .75 2.00
133 Lowell MacDonald AS .75 2.00
134 Bill Goldsworthy AS .75 2.00
135 Bobby Clarke AS 3.00 6.00
136 Bill White AS .75 2.00
137 Dave Burrows AS .75 2.00
138 Bernie Parent AS 1.50 3.00
139 Jacques Richard .75 2.00
140 Yvan Cournoyer 1.50 3.00
141 R.Gilbert/B.Park TL 1.50 3.00
142 Rene Robert 1.00 2.50
143 J. Bob Kelly RC .75 2.00
144 Ross Lonsberry .75 2.00
145 Jean Ratelle 1.50 3.00
146 Dallas Smith .75 2.00
147 Bernie Geoffrion CO 2.00 4.00
148 Ted McAneeley .75 2.00
149 Pierre Plante .75 2.00
150 Dennis Hull 1.00 2.50
151 Dave Keon 1.50 3.00
152 Dave Dunn RC .75 2.00
153 Michel Belhumeur 1.00 2.50
154 Clarke/D.Schultz TL 2.00 4.00
155 Ken Dryden 15.00 25.00
156 John Wright RC .75 2.00
157 Larry Romanchych .75 2.00
158 Ralph Stewart RC .75 2.00
159 Mike Robitaille .75 2.00
160 Ed Giacomin 2.00 4.00
161 Don Cherry CO RC 30.00 60.00
162 Checklist 133-264 18.00 30.00
163 Rick MacLeish 1.00 2.50
164 Greg Polis .75 2.00
165 Carol Vadnais .75 2.00
166 Pete Laframboise .75 2.00
167 Ron Schock .75 2.00
168 Lanny McDonald RC 15.00 25.00
169 Scouts Emblem 1.00 2.50
170 Tony Esposito 4.00 8.00
171 Pierre Jarry .75 2.00
172 Dan Maloney 1.00 2.50
173 Peter McDuffe 1.00 2.50
174 Danny Grant 1.00 2.50
175 John Stewart RC .75 2.00
176 Floyd Smith CO .75 2.00
177 Bert Marshall .75 2.00
178 Chuck Lefley UER .75 2.00
179 Gilles Villemure 1.00 2.50
180 Borje Salming RC 15.00 30.00
181 Doug Mohns .75 2.00
182 Barry Wilkins .75 2.00
183 MacDonald/Apps TL .75 2.00
184 Gregg Sheppard .75 2.00
185 Joey Johnston .75 2.00
186 Dick Redmond .75 2.00
187 Simon Nolet .75 2.00
188 Ron Stackhouse .75 2.00
189 Marshall Johnston .75 2.00
190 Richard Martin 1.00 2.50
191 Andre Boudrias .75 2.00
192 Steve Atkinson .75 2.00
193 Nick Libett .75 2.00
194 Bob Murdoch Kings RC .75 2.00
195 Denis Potvin RC 30.00 50.00
196 Dave Schultz 2.00 4.00
197 Unger/Plante TL .75 2.00
198 Jim McKenny .75 2.00
199 Gerry Hart .75 2.00
200 Phil Esposito 3.00 6.00
201 Rod Gilbert 1.50 3.00
202 Jacques Laperriere 1.00 2.50
203 Barry Gibbs .75 2.00
204 Billy Reay CO 1.00 2.50
205 Gilles Meloche 1.00 2.50
206 Wayne Cashman 1.00 2.50
207 Dennis Ververgaert RC .75 2.00
208 Phil Roberto .75 2.00
209 Quarter Finals .75 2.00
210 Quarter Finals .75 2.00
211 Quarter Finals .75 2.00
212 Quarter Finals .75 2.00
213 Semi-Finals .75 2.00
214 Semi-Finals .75 2.00
215 Stanley Cup Finals .75 2.00
216 Flyers Champions 1.00 2.50
217 Joe Watson .75 2.00
218 Wayne Stephenson 1.00 2.50
219 Sittlr/Ullmn/Hend TL 1.00 2.50
220 Bill Goldsworthy 1.00 2.50
221 Don Marcotte .75 2.00
222 Alex Delvecchio CO .75 2.00
223 Stan Gilbertson .75 2.00
224 Mike Murphy .75 2.00
225 Jim Rutherford 1.00 2.50
226 Phil Russell .75 2.00
227 Lynn Powis .75 2.00
228 Billy Harris .75 2.00
229 Bob Pulford CO 1.00 2.50
230 Ken Hodge 1.00 2.50
231 Bill Fairbairn .75 2.00
232 Guy Lafleur 7.50 15.00
233 Harr/Stw/Ptvn TL UER 2.00 4.00
234 Fred Barrett .75 2.00
235 Rogatien Vachon 2.00 5.00
236 Norm Ullman 1.50 3.00
237 Garry Unger 1.00 2.50
238 Jack Gordon CO RC .75 2.00
239 Johnny Bucyk 1.50 3.00
240 Bob Dailey RC .75 2.00
241 Dave Burrows .75 2.00
242 Len Frig RC .75 2.00
243 Henri Richard Mstrsn 1.00 2.50
244 Phil Esposito Hart 2.00 4.00
245 Johnny Bucyk Byng 1.00 2.50
246 Phil Esposito Ross 2.00 4.00
247 Wales Trophy .75 2.00
248 Bobby Orr Norris 12.00 20.00
249 Bernie Parent Vezina 1.00 2.50
250 Philadelphia Flyers SC 2.00 5.00
251 Bernie Parent Smythe 1.00 2.50
252 Denis Potvin Calder 6.00 10.00
253 Campbell Trophy .75 2.00
254 Pierre Bouchard .75 2.00
255 Jude Drouin .75 2.00
256 Capitals Emblem 1.00 2.50
257 Michel Plasse 1.00 2.50
258 Juha Widing .75 2.00
259 Bryan Watson .75 2.00
260 Bobby Clarke UER 7.00 12.00
261 Scotty Bowman CO RC 30.00 60.00
262 Craig Patrick 1.00 2.50
263 Craig Cameron .75 2.00
264 Ted Irvine .75 2.00
265 Ed Johnston 1.00 2.50
266 Dave Forbes RC .75 2.00
267 Red Wings Team CL 2.00 4.00
268 Rick Dudley RC 1.00 2.50
269 Darcy Rota RC 1.00 2.50
270 Phil Myre 1.00 2.50
271 Larry Brown RC .75 2.00
272 Bob Neely RC .75 2.00
273 Jerry Byers RC .75 2.00
274 Penguins Team CL 2.00 4.00
275 Glenn Goldup RC .75 2.00
276 Ron Harris .75 2.00
277 Joe Lundrigan RC .75 2.00
278 Mike Christie RC .75 2.00
279 Doug Rombough RC .75 2.00
280 Larry Robinson 12.00 20.00
281 Blues Team CL 2.00 4.00
282 John Marks RC .75 2.00
283 Don Saleski 1.00 2.50
284 Rick Wilson RC .75 2.00
285 Andre Savard RC .75 2.00
286 Pat Quinn 1.00 2.50
287 Kings Team CL 2.00 4.00
288 Norm Gratton .75 2.00
289 Ian Turnbull RC 1.00 2.50
290 Derek Sanderson 2.00 4.00
291 Murray Oliver .75 2.00
292 Wilf Paiement RC 1.50 3.00
293 Nelson Debenedet RC .75 2.00
294 Greg Joly RC .75 2.00
295 Terry O'Reilly 2.00 4.00
296 Rey Comeau .75 2.00
297 Michel Larocque RC 2.50 5.00
298 Floyd Thomson RC .75 2.00
299 Jean-Guy Lagace RC .75 2.00
300 Flyers Team CL 2.00 4.00
301 Al MacAdam RC 1.50 3.00
302 George Ferguson RC .75 2.00
303 Jimmy Watson RC 1.50 3.00
304 Rick Middleton RC 12.00 20.00
305 Craig Ramsay UER .75 2.00
306 Hilliard Graves .75 2.00
307 Islanders Team CL 2.00 4.00
308 Blake Dunlop RC .75 2.00
309 J.P. Bordeleau .75 2.00
310 Brian Glennie .75 2.00
311 Checklist 265-396 UER 18.00 30.00
312 Doug Roberts .75 2.00
313 Darryl Edestrand .75 2.00
314 Ron Anderson .75 2.00
315 Blackhawks Team CL 2.00 4.00
316 Steve Shutt RC 15.00 30.00
317 Doug Horbul RC .75 2.00
318 Billy Lochead RC .75 2.00
319 Fred Harvey .75 2.00
320 Gene Carr RC .75 2.00
321 Henri Richard 1.50 3.00
322 Canucks Team CL 2.00 4.00
323 Tim Ecclestone .75 2.00
324 Dave Lewis RC .75 2.00
325 Lou Nanne 1.00 2.50
326 Bobby Rousseau .75 2.00
327 Dunc Wilson 1.00 2.50
328 Brian Spencer .75 2.00
329 Rick Hampton RC .75 2.00
330 Canadiens Team CL UER 2.00 4.00
331 Jack Lynch .75 2.00
332 Garnet Bailey .75 2.00
333 Al Sims RC .75 2.00
334 Orest Kindrachuk RC 1.00 2.50
335 Dave Hudson .75 2.00
336 Bob Murray RC 1.00 2.50
337 Sabres Team CL 2.00 4.00
338 Sheldon Kannegiesser .75 2.00
339 Bill MacMillan .75 2.00
340 Paulin Bordeleau RC .75 2.00
341 Dale Rolfe .75 2.00
342 Yvon Lambert RC 1.00 2.50
343 Bob Paradise RC .75 2.00
344 Germaine Gagnon UER .75 2.00
345 Yvon Labre .75 2.00
346 Chris Ahrens RC .75 2.00
347 Doug Grant RC .75 2.00
348 Blaine Stoughton RC 2.00 4.00
349 Gregg Boddy .75 2.00
350 Bruins Team CL 2.00 4.00
351 Doug Jarrett .75 2.00
352 Terry Crisp 1.00 2.50
353 Glenn Resch UER RC 12.00 20.00
354 Jerry Korab .75 2.00
355 Stan Weir RC .75 2.00
356 Noel Price .75 2.00
357 Bill Clement RC 9.00 15.00
358 Neil Komadoski .75 2.00
359 Murray Wilson RC .75 2.00
360 Dale Tallon UER .75 2.00
361 Gary Doak .75 2.00
362 Randy Rota RC .75 2.00
363 North Stars Team CL 2.00 4.00
364 Bill Collins .75 2.00
365 Thommie Bergman UER .75 2.00
366 Dennis Kearns .75 2.00
367 Lorne Henning .75 2.00
368 Gary Sabourin .75 2.00
369 Mike Bloom RC .75 2.00
370 Rangers Team CL 2.00 4.00
371 Gary Simmons RC 2.50 5.00
372 Dwight Bialowas RC .75 2.00
373 Gilles Marotte .75 2.00
374 Frank St.Marseille .75 2.00
375 Garry Howatt RC .75 2.00
376 Ross Brooks RC 1.00 2.50
377 Flames Team CL 2.00 4.00
378 Bob Nevin .75 2.00
379 Lyle Moffat RC .75 2.00
380 Bob Kelly .75 2.00
381 John Gould RC .75 2.00
382 Dave Fortier RC .75 2.00
383 Jean Hamel RC .75 2.00
384 Bert Wilson RC .75 2.00
385 Chuck Arnason RC .75 2.00
386 Bruce Cowick RC .75 2.00
387 Ernie Hicke .75 2.00
388 Bob Gainey RC 18.00 30.00
389 Vic Venasky RC .75 2.00
390 Maple Leafs Team CL 2.00 4.00
391 Eric Vail RC 1.00 2.50
392 Bobby Lalonde .75 2.00
393 Jerry Butler RC .75 2.00
394 Tom Williams .75 2.00
395 Chico Maki .75 2.00
396 Tom Bladon RC 2.00 4.00

1974-75 O-Pee-Chee WHA

The 1974-75 O-Pee-Chee WHA set consisted of 66 color standard-size cards. The cards were originally sold in eight-card ten-cent wax packs. Bilingual backs featured a short biography, the player's 1973-74 and career WHA statistics as well as a cartoon-illustrated hockey fact or interpretation of a referee's signal. Rookie Cards in this set included Anders Hedberg and Ulf Nilsson, although some collectors and dealers considered the Howe Family card to be the Rookie Card for Mark and Marty Howe.

COMPLETE SET (66) 75.00 200.00
1 Gord/Mark/Marty Howe 40.00 75.00
2 Bruce MacGregor 1.50 3.00
3 Wayne Dillon RC 1.50 3.00
4 Ulf Nilsson RC 7.00 12.00
5 Serge Bernier 2.00 4.00
6 Dryan Campbell 1.50 3.00
7 Rosaire Paiement 1.50 3.00
8 Tom Webster 2.00 4.00
9 Gerry Pinder 1.50 3.00
10 Mike Walton 1.50 3.00
11 Norm Beaudin 1.50 3.00
12 Bob Whitlock RC 1.50 3.00
13 Wayne Rivers 1.50 3.00
14 Gerry Odrowski 1.50 3.00
15 Ron Climie 1.50 3.00
16 Tom Simpson RC 1.50 3.00
17 Anders Hedberg RC 7.00 12.00
18 J.C. Tremblay 1.50 3.00
19 Mike Pelyk 1.50 3.00
20 Dave Dryden 2.00 4.00
21 Ron Ward 1.50 3.00
22 Larry Lund RC 1.50 3.00
23 Ron Buchanan RC 1.50 3.00
24 Pat Hickey RC 2.00 4.00
25 Danny Lawson RC 2.00 4.00
26 Bob Guindon RC 1.50 3.00
27 Gene Peacosh RC 1.50 3.00
28 Fran Huck 1.50 3.00
29 Al Hamilton 1.50 3.00
30 Gerry Cheevers 7.50 15.00
31 Heikki Riihiranta RC 2.00 4.00
32 Don Burgess RC 1.50 3.00
33 John French RC 1.50 3.00
34 Jim Wiste RC 1.50 3.00
35 Pat Stapleton 4.00 8.00
36 J.P. LeBlanc RC 1.50 3.00
37 Mike Antonovich RC 1.50 3.00
38 Joe Daley 2.00 4.00
39 Ross Perkins RC 1.50 3.00
40 Frank Mahovlich 7.00 12.00
41 Rejean Houle 1.50 3.00
42 Ron Chipperfield RC 3.00 6.00
43 Marc Tardif 1.50 3.00
44 Murray Keogan RC 1.50 3.00
45 Wayne Carleton 1.50 3.00
46 Andre Gaudette RC 1.50 3.00
47 Ralph Backstrom 2.00 4.00
48 Don McLeod RC 2.00 4.00
49 Vaclav Nedomansky RC 3.00 6.00
50 Bobby Hull 20.00 35.00
51 Rusty Patenaude RC 1.50 3.00
52 Michel Parizeau 1.50 3.00
53 Checklist 20.00 40.00
54 Wayne Connelly 2.00 4.00
55 Gary Veneruzzo 1.50 3.00
56 Dennis Sobchuk RC 2.00 4.00
57 Paul Henderson 2.00 4.00
58 Andy Brown RC 3.00 6.00
59 Paul Popiel 1.50 3.00
60 Andre Lacroix 2.00 4.00
61 Gary Jarrett 1.50 3.00
62 Claude St.Sauveur RC 1.50 3.00
63 Real Cloutier RC 3.00 6.00
64 Jacques Plante 20.00 35.00
65 Gilles Gratton RC 4.00 8.00
66 Lars-Erik Sjoberg RC 4.00 8.00

1975-76 O-Pee-Chee

The 1975-76 O-Pee-Chee NHL set consisted of 396 color standard-size cards. The cards were originally sold in ten-cent wax packs. The first 330 cards had identical fronts (except perhaps for a short traded line) to the Topps set of this year. Number 395 was not issued; however, the set contained two of number 267, which are checklist cards. Team cards (81-98) had a team checklist on the back. Bilingual backs contained year-by-year and career statistics, a short biography and a cartoon-illustrated NHL fact or interpretation of a referee's signal.

COMPLETE SET (396) 200.00 400.00
1 Stanley Cup Finals 1.50 3.00
2 Semi-Finals .40 1.25
3 Semi-Finals .40 1.25
4 Quarter Finals .40 1.25
5 Quarter Finals .40 1.25
6 Quarter Finals .40 1.25
7 Quarter Finals .40 1.25
8 Curt Bennett .40 1.25
9 Johnny Bucyk 1.00 2.50
10 Gilbert Perreault 3.00 6.00
11 Darryl Edestrand .40 1.25
12 Ivan Boldirev .40 1.25
13 Nick Libett .40 1.25
14 Jim McElmury RC .40 1.25
15 Frank St.Marseille .40 1.25
16 Blake Dunlop .40 1.25
17 Yvon Lambert .60 1.50
18 Gerry Hart .40 1.25
19 Steve Vickers .40 1.25
20 Rick MacLeish .60 1.50
21A Bob Paradise NoTR .40 1.25
21B Bob Paradise TR .60 1.50
22 Red Berenson .60 1.50
23 Lanny McDonald 4.00 7.00
24 Mike Robitaille .40 1.25
25 Ron Low .60 1.50
26A Bryan Hextall NoTR .40 1.25
26B Bryan Hextall TR .40 1.25
27A Carol Vadnais NoTR .40 1.25
27B Carol Vadnais TR .40 1.25
28 Jim Lorentz .40 1.25
29 Gary Simmons .60 1.50
30 Stan Mikita 2.50 5.00
31 Bryan Watson .40 1.25
32 Guy Charron .40 1.25
33 Bob Murdoch .40 1.25
34 Norm Gratton .40 1.25
35 Ken Dryden 12.00 20.00
36 Jean Potvin .40 1.25
37 Rick Middleton 2.50 5.00
38 Ed Van Impe .40 1.25
39 Rick Kehoe .60 1.50
40 Garry Unger .60 1.50
41 Ian Turnbull .60 1.50
42 Dennis Ververgaert .40 1.25
43 Mike Marson RC .60 1.50
44 Randy Manery .40 1.25
45 Gilles Gilbert .60 1.50
46 Rene Robert .60 1.50
47 Bob Stewart .40 1.25
48 Pit Martin .40 1.25
49 Danny Grant .60 1.50
50 Peter Mahovlich .60 1.50
51 Dennis Patterson RC .40 1.25
52 Mike Murphy .40 1.25
53 Dennis O'Brien .40 1.25
54 Garry Howatt .40 1.25
55 Ed Giacomin 1.00 2.50
56 Andre Dupont .40 1.25
57 Chuck Arnason .40 1.25
58 Bob Gassoff RC .40 1.25
59 Ron Ellis .60 1.50
60 Andre Boudrias .40 1.25
61 Yvon Labre .40 1.25
62 Hilliard Graves .40 1.25
63 Wayne Cashman .60 1.50
64 Danny Gare RC 1.50 3.00
65 Rick Hampton .40 1.25
66 Darcy Rota .40 1.25
67 Bill Hogaboam .40 1.25
68 Denis Herron .60 1.50
69 Sheldon Kannegiesser .40 1.25
70 Yvan Cournoyer 1.00 2.50
71 Ernie Hicke .40 1.25
72 Bert Marshall .40 1.25
73 Derek Sanderson 2.00 4.00
74 Tom Bladon .40 1.25
75 Ron Schock .40 1.25
76 Larry Sacharuk RC .40 1.25
77 George Ferguson .40 1.25
78 Ab DeMarco .40 1.25
79 Tom Williams .40 1.25
80 Phil Roberto .40 1.25
81 Bruins Team 2.00 4.00
82 Seals Team 2.00 4.00
83 Sabres Team 2.00 4.00
84 Blackhawks Team 2.00 4.00
85 Flames Team 2.00 4.00
86 Kings Team 2.00 4.00
87 Red Wings Team 2.00 4.00
88 Scouts Team 2.00 4.00
89 North Stars Team 2.00 4.00
90 Canadiens Team 2.00 4.00
91 Maple Leafs Team 2.00 4.00
92 Islanders Team 2.00 4.00
93 Penguins Team 2.00 4.00
94 Rangers Team 2.00 4.00
95 Flyers Team 2.00 4.00
96 Blues Team 2.00 4.00
97 Canucks Team 2.00 4.00
98 Capitals Team 2.00 4.00
99 Checklist 1-110 8.00 15.00
100 Bobby Orr 20.00 30.00
101 Germain Gagnon UER .40 1.25
102 Phil Russell .40 1.25

103 Billy Lochead .40 1.25
104 Robin Burns RC .40 1.25
105 Gary Edwards .60 1.50
106 Dwight Bialowas .40 1.25
107 Doug Risebrough UER RC 2.00 4.00
108 Dave Lewis .40 1.25
109 Bill Fairbairn .40 1.25
110 Ross Lonsberry .40 1.25
111 Ron Stackhouse .40 1.25
112 Claude Larose .40 1.25
113 Don Luce .40 1.25
114 Errol Thompson RC .60 1.50
115 Gary Smith .60 1.50
116 Jack Lynch .40 1.25
117 Jacques Richard .40 1.25
118 Dallas Smith .40 1.25
119 Dave Gardner .40 1.25
120 Mickey Redmond .60 1.50
121 John Marks .40 1.25
122 Dave Hudson .40 1.25
123 Bob Nevin .40 1.25
124 Fred Barrett .40 1.25
125 Gerry Desjardins .60 1.50
126 Guy Lafleur UER 9.00 15.00
127 Jean-Paul Parise .40 1.25
128 Walt Tkaczuk .60 1.50
129 Gary Dornhoefer .60 1.50
130 Syl Apps .40 1.25
131 Bob Plager .60 1.50
132 Stan Weir .40 1.25
133 Tracy Pratt .40 1.25
134 Jack Egers .40 1.25
135 Eric Vail .40 1.25
136 Al Sims .40 1.25
137 Larry Patey RC .40 1.25
138 Jim Schoenfeld .60 1.50
139 Cliff Koroll .40 1.25
140 Marcel Dionne 3.00 8.00
141 Jean-Guy Lagace .40 1.25
142 Juha Widing .40 1.25
143 Lou Nanne .60 1.50
144 Serge Savard 1.00 2.50
145 Glenn Resch 2.50 5.00
146 Ron Greschner RC 1.50 3.00
147 Dave Schultz 1.00 2.50
148 Barry Wilkins .40 1.25
149 Floyd Thomson .40 1.25
150 Darryl Sittler 4.00 8.00
151 Paulin Bordeleau .40 1.25
152 Ron Lalonde RC .40 1.25
153 Larry Romanchych .40 1.25
154 Larry Carriere .40 1.25
155 Andre Savard .40 1.25
156 Dave Hrechkosy RC .40 1.25
157 Bill White .40 1.25
158 Dave Kryskow .40 1.25
159 Denis Dupere .40 1.25
160 Rogatien Vachon 1.50 4.00
161 Doug Rombough .40 1.25
162 Murray Wilson .40 1.25
163 Bob Bourne RC 1.50 3.00
164 Gilles Marotte .40 1.25
165 Vic Hadfield .60 1.50
166 Reggie Leach .60 1.50
167 Jerry Butler .40 1.25
168 Inge Hammarstrom .40 1.25
169 Chris Oddleifson .40 1.25
170 Greg Joly .40 1.25
171 Checklist 111-220 8.00 15.00
172 Pat Quinn .60 1.50
173 Dave Forbes .40 1.25
174 Len Frig .40 1.25
175 Richard Martin .60 1.50
176 Keith Magnuson .40 1.25
177 Dan Maloney .40 1.25
178 Craig Patrick .60 1.50
179 Tom Williams .40 1.25
180 Bill Goldsworthy .60 1.50
181 Steve Shutt 2.50 5.00
182 Ralph Stewart .40 1.25
183 John Davidson 2.50 5.00
184 Bob Kelly .40 1.25
185 Ed Johnston .60 1.50
186 Dave Burrows .40 1.25
187 Dave Dunn .40 1.25
188 Dennis Kearns .40 1.25
189 Bill Clement 2.50 5.00
190 Gilles Meloche .60 1.50
191 Bob Leiter .40 1.25
192 Jerry Korab .40 1.25
193 Joey Johnston .40 1.25
194 Walt McKechnie .40 1.25
195 Wilf Paiement .60 1.50
196 Bob Berry .40 1.25
197 Dean Talafous RC .40 1.25
198 Guy Lapointe .60 1.50
199 Clark Gillies RC 6.00 12.00
200A Phil Esposito NoTR 4.00 8.00
200B Phil Esposito TR 2.50 5.00
201 Greg Polis .40 1.25
202 Jimmy Watson .60 1.50
203 Gord McRae RC .60 1.50
204 Lowell MacDonald .40 1.25
205 Barclay Plager .60 1.50
206 Don Lever .40 1.25
207 Bill Mikkelson .40 1.25
208 Espo/Lafleur/Martin LL 2.50 5.00
209 Clarke/Orr/P.Mahv LL 4.00 8.00
210 Orr/Espo/Dionne LL 4.00 8.00
211 Schltz/Dupnt/Rssll LL 2.00 4.00
212 Espo/Martin/Grant LL 1.50 3.00
213 Parnt/Vach/Drydn LL 4.00 8.00
214 Barry Gibbs .40 1.25
215 Ken Hodge .60 1.50
216 Jocelyn Guevremont .40 1.25
217 Warren Williams RC .40 1.25
218 Dick Redmond .40 1.25
219 Jim Rutherford .60 1.50
220 Simon Nolet .40 1.25
221 Butch Goring .60 1.50
222 Glen Sather .60 1.50
223 Mario Tremblay UER RC 2.50 5.00
224 Jude Drouin .40 1.25
225 Rod Gilbert 1.00 2.50
226 Bill Barber 2.00 4.00
227 Gary Inness RC .60 1.50
228 Wayne Merrick .40 1.25
229 Rod Seiling .40 1.25
230 Tom Lysiak .60 1.50
231 Bob Dailey .40 1.25
232 Michel Belhumeur .60 1.50
233 Bill Hajt RC .40 1.25
234 Jim Pappin .40 1.25
235 Gregg Sheppard .40 1.25
236A Gary Bergman NoTR .40 1.25
236B Gary Bergman TR .40 1.25
237 Randy Rota .40 1.25
238 Neil Komadoski .40 1.25
239 Craig Cameron .40 1.25
240 Tony Esposito 3.00 6.00
241 Larry Robinson 7.00 12.00
242 Billy Harris .40 1.25
243A Jean Ratelle NoTR 1.50 3.00
243B Jean Ratelle TR 1.00 2.50
244 Ted Irvine UER .40 1.25
245 Bob Neely .40 1.25
246 Bobby Lalonde .40 1.25
247 Ron Jones RC .40 1.25
248 Rey Comeau .40 1.25
249 Michel Plasse .60 1.50
250 Bobby Clarke 5.00 10.00
251 Bobby Schmautz .40 1.25
252 Peter McNab RC 2.00 4.00
253 Al MacAdam .40 1.25
254 Dennis Hull .60 1.50
255 Terry Harper .40 1.25
256 Peter McDuffe .60 1.50
257 Jean Hamel .40 1.25
258 Jacques Lemaire 1.00 2.50
259 Bob Nystrom .60 1.50
260A Brad Park NoTR 2.00 4.00
260B Brad Park TR 1.50 3.00
261 Cesare Maniago .60 1.50
262 Don Saleski .40 1.25
263 J. Bob Kelly .40 1.25
264 Bob Hess RC .40 1.25
265 Blaine Stoughton .60 1.50
266 John Gould .40 1.25
267A Checklist 221-330 8.00 15.00
267B Checklist 331-396 8.00 15.00
268 Dan Bouchard .60 1.50
269 Don Marcotte .40 1.25
270 Jim Neilson .40 1.25
271 Craig Ramsay .40 1.25
272 Grant Mulvey RC .60 1.50
273 Larry Giroux RC .40 1.25
274 Real Lemieux .40 1.25
275 Denis Potvin 7.00 12.00
276 Don Kozak .40 1.25
277 Tom Reid .40 1.25
278 Bob Gainey 4.00 7.00
279 Nick Beverley .40 1.25
280 Jean Pronovost .60 1.50
281 Joe Watson .40 1.25
282 Chuck Lefley .40 1.25
283 Borje Salming 4.00 8.00
284 Garnet Bailey .40 1.25
285 Gregg Boddy .40 1.25
286 Bobby Clarke AS1 2.50 5.00
287 Denis Potvin AS1 2.50 5.00
288 Bobby Orr AS1 9.00 15.00
289 Richard Martin AS1 .60 1.50
290 Guy Lafleur AS1 3.00 6.00
291 Bernie Parent AS1 1.00 2.50
292 Phil Esposito AS2 2.00 4.00
293 Guy Lapointe AS2 1.00 2.50
294 Borje Salming AS2 2.00 4.00
295 Steve Vickers AS2 .60 1.50
296 Rene Robert AS2 .60 1.50
297 Rogatien Vachon AS2 1.00 2.50
298 Buster Harvey RC .40 1.25
299 Gary Sabourin .40 1.25
300 Bernie Parent 2.00 4.00
301 Terry O'Reilly 1.00 2.50
302 Ed Westfall .60 1.50
303 Pete Stemkowski .40 1.25
304 Pierre Bouchard .40 1.25
305 Pierre Larouche RC 4.00 8.00
306 Lee Fogolin RC .60 1.50
307 Gerry O'Flaherty .40 1.25
308 Phil Myre .60 1.50
309 Pierre Plante .40 1.25
310 Dennis Hextall .40 1.25
311 Jim McKenny .40 1.25
312 Vic Venasky .40 1.25
313 Vail/Lysiak TL .40 1.25
314 P.Espo/Orr/Bucyk TL 9.00 15.00
315 R.Martin/R.Robert TL .60 1.50
316 Hrchsy/Ptey/Weir TL .40 1.25
317 S.Mikita/J.Pappin TL 1.00 2.50
318 D.Grant/M.Dionne TL 1.00 2.50
319 Nolet/Pmnt/Charn TL .40 1.25
320 Nevin/Wdng/Brry TL .40 1.25
321 Gldswrthy/Hextall TL .40 1.25
322 Lafleur/P.Mahov TL 1.50 3.00
323 Nystrm/Potvin/Gill TL 1.00 2.50
324 Vick/Gilbert/Ratle TL 1.00 2.50
325 R.Leach/B.Clarke TL 1.00 2.50
326 Pronovost/Schock TL .40 1.25
327 G.Unger/Sacharuk TL .60 1.50
328 Darryl Sittler TL 1.00 2.50
329 Lever/Boudrias TL .40 1.25
330 Williams/Bailey TL .40 1.25
331 Noel Price .40 1.25
332 Fred Stanfield .40 1.25
333 Doug Jarrett .40 1.25
334 Gary Coalter .40 1.25
335 Murray Oliver .40 1.25
336 Dave Fortier .40 1.25
337 Terry Crisp UER .40 1.25
338 Bert Wilson .40 1.25
339 John Grisdale RC .40 1.25
340 Ken Broderick .60 1.50
341 Frank Spring RC .40 1.25
342 Mike Korney RC .40 1.25
343 Gene Carr .40 1.25
344 Don Awrey .40 1.25
345 Pat Hickey .40 1.25
346 Colin Campbell RC 1.00 2.50
347 Wayne Thomas .60 1.50
348 Bob Gryp RC .40 1.25
349 Bill Flett .40 1.25
350 Roger Crozier .60 1.50
351 Dale Tallon .40 1.25
352 Larry Johnston .40 1.25
353 John Flesch RC .40 1.25
354 Lorne Henning .40 1.25
355 Wayne Stephenson .60 1.50
356 Rick Wilson .40 1.25
357 Garry Monahan .40 1.25
358 Gary Doak .40 1.25
359A Pierre Jarry NoTR .40 1.25
359B Pierre Jarry TR .40 1.25
360 George Pesut RC .40 1.25
361 Mike Corrigan .40 1.25
362 Michel Larocque 1.00 2.50
363 Wayne Dillon .40 1.25
364 Pete Laframboise .40 1.25
365 Brian Glennie .40 1.25
366 Mike Christie .40 1.25
367 Jean Lemieux RC .40 1.25
368 Gary Bromley .60 1.50
369 J.P. Bordeleau .40 1.25
370 Ed Gilbert RC .40 1.25
371 Chris Ahrens .40 1.25
372 Billy Smith 3.00 6.00
373 Larry Goodenough RC .40 1.25
374 Leon Rochefort .40 1.25
375 Doug Gibson RC .40 1.25
376 Mike Bloom .40 1.25
377 Larry Brown .40 1.25
378 Jim Roberts .40 1.25
379 Gilles Villemure .60 1.50
380 Dennis Owchar RC .40 1.25
381 Doug Favell .60 1.50
382 Stan Gilbertson UER .40 1.25
383 Ed Kea RC .40 1.25
384 Brian Spencer .40 1.25
385 Mike Veisor RC .60 1.50
386 Bob Murray .40 1.25
387 Andre St.Laurent RC .40 1.25
388 Rick Chartraw RC .60 1.50
389 Orest Kindrachuk .40 1.25
390 Dave Hutchinson RC .60 1.50
391 Glenn Goldup .40 1.25
392 Jerry Holland RC .40 1.25
393 Peter Sturgeon RC .40 1.25
394 Alain Daigle RC .40 1.25
396 Harold Snepsts RC 12.00 20.00

1975-76 O-Pee-Chee WHA

The 1975-76 O-Pee-Chee WHA set consisted of 132 color cards. Printed in Canada, the cards measured 2 1/2" by 3 1/2". Bilingual backs featured 1974-75 and career WHA statistics as well as a short biography.

COMPLETE SET (132) 250.00 400.00
1 Bobby Hull 25.00 50.00
2 Dale Hoganson 2.50 5.00
3 Serge Aubry 3.00 6.00
4 Ron Chipperfield 2.00 4.00
5 Paul Shmyr 2.00 4.00
6 Perry Miller RC 2.00 4.00
7 Mark Howe RC 20.00 50.00
8 Mike Rogers RC 3.00 6.00
9 Bryon Baltimore 2.00 4.00
10 Andre Lacroix 2.50 5.00
11 Nick Harbaruk 2.00 4.00
12 John Garrett RC 6.00 12.00
13 Lou Nistico RC 2.00 4.00
14 Rick Ley 2.00 4.00
15 Veli-Pekka Ketola RC 4.00 8.00
16 Real Cloutier 2.50 5.00
17 Pierre Guite RC 2.00 4.00
18 Duane Rupp 2.00 4.00
19 Robbie Ftorek RC 7.50 15.00
20 Gerry Cheevers 7.50 15.00
21 John Schella RC 2.00 4.00
22 Bruce MacGregor 2.00 4.00
23 Ralph Backstrom 2.50 5.00
24 Gene Peacosh 2.00 4.00
25 Pierre Roy 2.00 4.00
26 Mike Walton 3.00 6.00
27 Vaclav Nedomansky 2.50 5.00
28 Christer Abrahamsson RC 6.00 10.00
29 Thommie Bergman 2.00 4.00
30 Marc Tardif 2.00 4.00
31 Bryan Campbell 2.00 4.00
32 Don McLeod 2.50 5.00
33 Al McDonough 2.00 4.00
34 Jacques Plante 20.00 35.00
35 Andre Hinse RC 2.00 4.00
36 Eddie Joyal 2.00 4.00
37 Ken Baird RC 2.00 4.00
38 Wayne Rivers 2.00 4.00
39 Ron Buchanan 2.00 4.00
40 Anders Hedberg 3.00 6.00
41 Rick Smith 2.00 4.00
42 Paul Henderson 2.50 5.00
43 Wayne Carleton 2.50 5.00
44 Richard Brodeur RC 7.00 12.00
45 John Hughes RC 2.00 4.00
46 Larry Israelson RC 2.00 4.00
47 Jim Harrison 2.00 4.00
48 Cam Connor RC 2.00 4.00
49 Al Hamilton 2.00 4.00
50 Ron Grahame RC 3.00 6.00
51 Frank Rochon RC 2.00 4.00
52 Ron Climie 2.00 4.00
53 Murray Heatley RC 2.00 4.00
54 John Arbour 2.00 4.00
55 Jim Shaw RC 2.50 5.00
56 Larry Pleau RC 3.00 6.00
57 Ted Green 3.00 6.00
58 Rick Dudley 2.00 4.00
59 Butch Deadmarsh 2.00 4.00
60 Serge Bernier 3.00 6.00
61 Ron Grahame AS 2.00 4.00
62 J.C. Tremblay AS 2.00 4.00
63 Kevin Morrison AS 2.00 4.00
64 Andre Lacroix AS 2.00 4.00
65 Bobby Hull AS 12.00 20.00
66 Gordie Howe AS 18.00 30.00
67 Gerry Cheevers AS 4.00 8.00
68 Poul Popiel AS 2.00 4.00
69 Barry Long AS 2.00 4.00
70 Serge Bernier AS 2.00 4.00
71 Marc Tardif AS 2.00 4.00
72 Anders Hedberg AS 2.00 4.00
73 Ron Ward 2.00 4.00
74 Michel Cormier RC 2.00 4.00
75 Marty Howe RC 3.00 6.00
76 Rusty Patenaude 2.00 4.00
77 John McKenzie 2.50 5.00
78 Mark Napier RC 3.00 6.00
79 Henry Boucha 2.00 4.00
80 Kevin Morrison RC 2.00 4.00
81 Tom Simpson 2.00 4.00
82 Brad Selwood RC 3.00 6.00
83 Ulf Nilsson 3.00 6.00
84 Rejean Houle 2.50 5.00
85 Normand Lapointe RC UER 2.00 4.00
86 Danny Lawson 2.50 5.00
87 Gary Jarrett 2.00 4.00
88 Al McLeod RC 2.00 4.00
89 Gord Labossiere 2.00 4.00
90 Barry Long 2.50 5.00
91 Rick Morris RC 2.00 4.00
92 Norm Ferguson 2.00 4.00
93 Bob Whitlock 2.00 4.00
94 Jim Dorey 2.00 4.00
95 Tom Webster 2.50 5.00
96 Gordie Gallant 2.00 4.00
97 Dave Keon 3.00 6.00
98 Ron Plumb RC 2.50 5.00
99 Rick Jodzio RC 2.00 4.00
100 Gordie Howe 30.00 50.00
101 Joe Daley 3.00 6.00
102 Wayne Muloin RC 2.00 4.00
103 Gavin Kirk RC 2.00 4.00
104 Dave Dryden 2.50 5.00
105 Bob Liddington RC 2.00 4.00
106 Rosaire Paiement 2.00 4.00
107 John Sheridan 4.00 8.00
108 Nick Fotiu RC 6.00 12.00
109 Lars-Erik Sjoberg 2.00 4.00
110 Frank Mahovlich 3.00 6.00
111 Mike Antonovich 2.00 4.00
112 Paul Terbenche 2.00 4.00
113 Rich Leduc RC 2.00 4.00
114 Jack Norris 2.50 5.00
115 Dennis Sobchuk 2.00 4.00
116 Chris Bordeleau 2.00 4.00
117 Doug Barrie 2.00 4.00
118 Hugh Harris RC 2.00 4.00
119 Cam Newton RC 2.50 5.00
120 Poul Popiel 2.00 4.00
121 Fran Huck 2.00 4.00
122 Tony Featherstone 2.00 4.00
123 Bob Woytowich 2.00 4.00
124 Claude St.Sauveur 2.00 4.00
125 Heikki Riihiranta 2.50 5.00
126 Gary Kurt 2.50 5.00
127 Thommy Abrahamsson RC 3.00 5.00
128 Danny Gruen RC 2.00 4.00
129 Jacques Locas RC 2.00 4.00
130 J.C. Tremblay 2.50 5.00
131 Checklist Card 25.00 50.00
132 Ernie Wakely 4.00 8.00

1976-77 O-Pee-Chee

The 1976-77 O-Pee-Chee NHL set consisted of 396 color standard-size cards. Printed in Canada, the cards contained both the O-Pee-Chee and the NHL Players Association copyright. The wax packs issued contained eight cards in ten-cent packs along with a bubble-gum slab. Several Record Breaker (RB) cards featured achievements from the previous season. Team cards (132-149) had a team checklist on the back. Bilingual backs contained the player's statistics from the 1975-76 season, career numbers, a short biography and a cartoon-illustrated fact about the player. Cards that featured California players in the 1976-77 Topps set had been updated in this set to show them with the Cleveland Barons. One of those was card 176 Gary Simmons. There are reportedly three variations of the Simmons card. In addition to the basic card, one version had "Team transferred to Colorado" on front. This is an error in itself because the Barons disbanded with players going to Minnesota. The other version had the text shaded or airbrushed out. Information on values and scarcities is not known at this time. Rookie Cards included Bryan Trottier and Dave "Tiger" Williams.

COMPLETE SET (396) 150.00 300.00
1 Leach/Lafleur/Larou LL 1.50 3.00
2 Clarke/Lafleur/Perr LL 1.50 3.00
3 Lafleur/Clarke/Perr LL 1.50 3.00
4 Durbno/Watsn/Schltz LL .40 1.00
5 Espo/Lafleur/Potvin LL 1.50 3.00
6 Dryden/Resch/Laroc LL 2.50 5.00
7 Gary Doak .40 1.00
8 Jacques Richard .40 1.00
9 Wayne Dillon .40 1.00
10 Bernie Parent .75 2.00
11 Ed Westfall .40 1.00
12 Dick Redmond .40 1.00
13 Bryan Hextall .40 1.00
14 Jean Pronovost .40 1.00
15 Peter Mahovlich .60 1.50
16 Danny Grant .40 1.00
17 Phil Myre .40 1.00
18 Wayne Merrick .40 1.00
19 Steve Durbano .40 1.00
20 Derek Sanderson .75 2.00
21 Mike Murphy .40 1.00
22 Borje Salming 2.50 5.00
23 Mike Walton .40 1.00
24 Randy Manery .40 1.00
25 Ken Hodge .40 1.00
26 Mel Bridgman RC 1.00 2.50
27 Jerry Korab .40 1.00
28 Gilles Gratton .40 1.00
29 Andre St.Laurent .40 1.00
30 Yvan Cournoyer .75 2.00
31 Phil Russell .40 1.00
32 Dennis Hextall .40 1.00
33 Lowell MacDonald .40 1.00
34 Dennis O'Brien .40 1.00
35 Gerry Meehan .40 1.00
36 Gilles Meloche .60 1.50
37 Wilf Paiement .40 1.00
38 Bob MacMillan RC .75 2.00
39 Ian Turnbull .40 1.00
40 Rogatien Vachon 1.00 2.50
41 Nick Beverley .40 1.00
42 Rene Robert .60 1.50
43 Andre Savard .40 1.00
44 Bob Gainey 2.00 4.00
45 Joe Watson .40 1.00
46 Billy Smith 2.50 5.00
47 Darcy Rota .40 1.00
48 Rick Lapointe RC .40 1.00
49 Pierre Jarry .40 1.00
50 Syl Apps .40 1.00
51 Eric Vail .40 1.00
52 Greg Joly .40 1.00
53 Don Lever .40 1.00
54 Bob Murdoch Seals .40 1.00
55 Denis Herron .40 1.00
56 Mike Bloom .40 1.00
57 Bill Fairbairn .40 1.00
58 Fred Stanfield .40 1.00
59 Steve Shutt .75 2.00
60 Brad Park .75 2.00
61 Gilles Villemure .40 1.00
62 Bert Marshall .40 1.00
63 Chuck Lefley .40 1.00
64 Simon Nolet .40 1.00
65 Reggie Leach RB .40 1.00
66 Darryl Sittler RB .75 2.00
67 Bryan Trottier RB 5.00 10.00
68 Garry Unger RB .40 1.00
69 Ron Low .40 1.00
70 Bobby Clarke 3.00 6.00
71 Michel Bergeron RC .40 1.00
72 Ron Stackhouse .40 1.00
73 Bill Hogaboam .40 1.00
74 Bob Murdoch Kings .40 1.00
75 Steve Vickers .40 1.00
76 Pit Martin .40 1.00
77 Gerry Hart .40 1.00
78 Craig Ramsay .40 1.00
79 Michel Larocque .40 1.00
80 Jean Ratelle .75 2.00
81 Don Saleski .40 1.00
82 Bill Clement .75 2.00
83 Dave Burrows .40 1.00
84 Wayne Thomas .40 1.00
85 John Gould .40 1.00
86 Dennis Maruk RC 1.50 3.00
87 Ernie Hicke .40 1.00
88 Jim Rutherford .40 1.00
89 Dale Tallon .40 1.00
90 Rod Gilbert .75 2.00
91 Marcel Dionne 3.00 6.00
92 Chuck Arnason .40 1.00
93 Jean Potvin .40 1.00
94 Don Luce .40 1.00
95 Johnny Bucyk .75 2.00
96 Larry Goodenough .40 1.00
97 Mario Tremblay .60 1.50
98 Nelson Pyatt RC .40 1.00
99 Brian Glennie .40 1.00
100 Tony Esposito 2.00 4.00
101 Dan Maloney .40 1.00
102 Dunc Wilson .40 1.00
103 Dean Talafous .40 1.00
104 Ed Staniowski RC .60 1.50
105 Dallas Smith .40 1.00
106 Jude Drouin .40 1.00
107 Pat Hickey .40 1.00
108 Jocelyn Guevremont .40 1.00
109 Doug Risebrough .75 2.00
110 Reggie Leach .60 1.50
111 Dan Bouchard .60 1.50
112 Chris Oddleifson .40 1.00
113 Rick Hampton .40 1.00
114 John Marks .40 1.00
115 Bryan Trottier RC 25.00 60.00
116 Checklist 1-132 6.00 10.00
117 Greg Polis .40 1.00
118 Peter McNab .75 2.00
119 Jim Roberts Mont .40 1.00
120 Gerry Cheevers 1.50 3.00
121 Rick MacLeish .60 1.50
122 Billy Lochead .40 1.00
123 Tom Reid .40 1.00
124 Rick Kehoe .40 1.00
125 Keith Magnuson .40 1.00
126 Clark Gillies .75 2.00
127 Rick Middleton .75 2.00
128 Bill Hajt .40 1.00
129 Jacques Lemaire .75 2.00
130 Terry O'Reilly .75 2.00
131 Andre Dupont .40 1.00
132 Flames Team 1.50 3.00
133 Bruins Team 1.50 3.00
134 Sabres Team 1.50 3.00
135 Seals Team 1.50 3.00
136 Blackhawks Team 1.50 3.00
137 Red Wings Team 1.50 3.00
138 Scouts Team 1.50 3.00
139 Kings Team 1.50 3.00
140 North Stars Team 1.50 3.00
141 Canadiens Team 1.50 3.00
142 Islanders Team 1.50 3.00
143 Rangers Team 1.50 3.00
144 Flyers Team 1.50 3.00
145 Penguins Team 1.50 3.00
146 Blues Team 1.50 3.00
147 Maple Leafs Team 1.50 3.00
148 Canucks Team 1.50 3.00
149 Capitals Team 1.50 3.00
150 Dave Schultz .75 2.00
151 Larry Robinson 3.00 6.00
152 Al Smith .60 1.50
153 Bob Nystrom .60 1.50
154 Ron Greschner .40 1.00
155 Gregg Sheppard .40 1.00
156 Alain Daigle .40 1.00
157 Ed Van Impe .40 1.00
158 Tim Young RC .60 1.50
159 Bryan Lefley .40 1.00
160 Ed Giacomin .75 2.00
161 Yvon Labre .40 1.00
162 Jim Lorentz .40 1.00
163 Guy Lafleur 7.00 12.00
164 Tom Bladon .40 1.00
165 Wayne Cashman .60 1.50
166 Pete Stemkowski .40 1.00
167 Grant Mulvey .40 1.00
168 Yves Belanger RC .60 1.50
169 Bill Goldsworthy .60 1.50
170 Denis Potvin 3.00 6.00
171 Nick Libett .40 1.00
172 Michel Plasse .40 1.00
173 Lou Nanne .40 1.00
174 Tom Lysiak .40 1.00
175 Dennis Ververgaert .40 1.00
176 Gary Simmons .60 1.50
177 Pierre Bouchard .40 1.00
178 Bill Barber .75 2.00
179 Darryl Edestrand .40 1.00
180 Gilbert Perreault 1.50 3.00
181 Dave Maloney RC .75 2.00
182 Jean-Paul Parise .40 1.00
183 Jim Harrison .40 1.00
184 Pete Lopresti RC .60 1.50
185 Don Kozak .40 1.00
186 Guy Charron .40 1.00
187 Stan Gilbertson .40 1.00
188 Bill Nyrop RC .60 1.50
189 Bobby Schmautz .40 1.00
190 Wayne Stephenson .40 1.00
191 Brian Spencer .40 1.00
192 Gilles Marotte .40 1.00
193 Lorne Henning .40 1.00
194 Bob Neely .40 1.00
195 Dennis Hull .40 1.00
196 Walt McKechnie .40 1.00
197 Curt Ridley RC .60 1.50
198 Dwight Bialowas .40 1.00
199 Pierre Larouche .75 2.00
200 Ken Dryden 10.00 20.00
201 Ross Lonsberry .40 1.00
202 Curt Bennett .40 1.00
203 Hartland Monahan RC .40 1.00
204 John Davidson 1.50 3.00
205 Serge Savard .75 2.00
206 Garry Howatt .40 1.00
207 Darryl Sittler 2.50 5.00
208 J.P. Bordeleau .40 1.00
209 Henry Boucha .40 1.00
210 Richard Martin .60 1.50
211 Vic Venasky .40 1.00
212 Buster Harvey .40 1.00
213 Bobby Orr 20.00 50.00
214 Martin/Perreault/Robert 2.00 4.00
215 Barber/Clarke/Leach 2.00 4.00
216 Gillies/Trottier/Harris 2.50 5.00
217 Gainey/Jarvis/Roberts 1.00 2.50
218 Bicentennial Line .40 1.00
219 Bob Kelly .40 1.00
220 Walt Tkaczuk .40 1.00
221 Dave Lewis .40 1.00
222 Danny Gare .75 2.00
223 Guy Lapointe .60 1.50
224 Hank Nowak RC .40 1.00
225 Stan Mikita 2.00 4.00
226 Vic Hadfield .40 1.00
227 Bernie Wolfe RC .60 1.50
228 Bryan Watson .40 1.00
229 Ralph Stewart .40 1.00
230 Gerry Desjardins .60 1.50
231 John Bednarski RC .40 1.00
232 Yvon Lambert .40 1.00
233 Orest Kindrachuk .40 1.00
234 Don Marcotte .40 1.00
235 Bill White .40 1.00
236 Red Berenson .40 1.00
237 Al MacAdam .40 1.00
238 Rick Blight RC .40 1.00
239 Butch Goring .60 1.50
240 Cesare Maniago .60 1.50
241 Jim Schoenfeld .60 1.50
242 Cliff Koroll .40 1.00
243 Scott Garland RC .40 1.00
244 Rick Chartraw .40 1.00
245 Phil Esposito 2.00 4.00
246 Dave Forbes .40 1.00
247 Jimmy Watson .40 1.00
248 Ron Schock .40 1.00
249 Fred Barrett .40 1.00
250 Glenn Resch 1.50 3.00
251 Ivan Boldirev .40 1.00
252 Billy Harris .40 1.00
253 Lee Fogolin .40 1.00
254 Murray Wilson .40 1.00
255 Gilles Gilbert .60 1.50
256 Gary Dornhoefer .60 1.50
257 Carol Vadnais .40 1.00
258 Checklist 133-264 6.00 10.00
259 Errol Thompson .40 1.00
260 Garry Unger .60 1.50
261 J. Bob Kelly .40 1.00
262 Terry Harper .40 1.00
263 Blake Dunlop .40 1.00
264 Canadiens Champs 1.25 2.50
265 Richard Mulhern RC .40 1.00
266 Gary Sabourin .40 1.00
267 Bill McKenzie UER RC .40 1.00
268 Mike Corrigan .40 1.00
269 Rick Smith .40 1.00
270 Stan Weir .40 1.00
271 Ron Sedlbauer RC .40 1.00
272 Jean Lemieux .40 1.00
273 Hilliard Graves .40 1.00
274 Dave Gardner .40 1.00
275 Tracy Pratt .40 1.00
276 Frank St.Marseille .40 1.00
277 Bob Hess .40 1.00
278 Bobby Lalonde .40 1.00
279 Tony White RC .40 1.00
280 Rod Seiling .40 1.00
281 Larry Romanchych .40 1.00
282 Ralph Klassen RC .40 1.00
283 Gary Croteau .40 1.00
284 Neil Komadoski .40 1.00
285 Ed Johnston .40 1.00
286 George Ferguson .40 1.00
287 Gerry O'Flaherty .40 1.00
288 Jack Lynch .40 1.00
289 Pat Quinn .60 1.50
290 Gene Carr .40 1.00
291 Bob Stewart .40 1.00
292 Doug Favell .60 1.50
293 Rick Wilson .40 1.00
294 Jack Valiquette RC .40 1.00
295 Garry Monahan .40 1.00
296 Michel Belhumeur .40 1.00
297 Larry Carriere .40 1.00
298 Fred Ahern RC .40 1.00
299 Dave Hudson .40 1.00
300 Bob Berry .40 1.00
301 Bob Gassoff .40 1.00
302 Jim McKenny .40 1.00
303 Gord Smith RC .40 1.00
304 Garnet Bailey .40 1.00
305 Bruce Affleck RC .40 1.00
306 Doug Halward RC .40 1.00
307 Lew Morrison .40 1.00
308 Bob Sauve RC 1.50 3.00
309 Bob Murray RC 1.25 3.00
310 Claude Larose .40 1.00
311 Don Awrey .40 1.00
312 Bill MacMillan .40 1.00
313 Doug Jarvis RC 1.50 4.00
314 Dennis Owchar .40 1.00
315 Jerry Holland .40 1.00
316 Guy Chouinard RC .75 2.00
317 Gary Smith .60 1.50
318 Pat Price RC .40 1.00
319 Tom Williams .40 1.00
320 Larry Patey .40 1.00
321 Claire Alexander .40 1.00
322 Larry Bolonchuk RC .40 1.00
323 Bob Sirois RC .40 1.00
324 Joe Zanussi RC .40 1.00
325 Joey Johnston .40 1.00
326 J.P. LeBlanc .40 1.00
327 Craig Cameron .40 1.00
328 Dave Fortier .40 1.00
329 Ed Gilbert .40 1.00
330 John Van Boxmeer RC .60 1.50
331 Gary Inness .60 1.50
332 Bill Flett .40 1.00
333 Mike Christie .40 1.00
334 Denis Dupere .40 1.00
335 Sheldon Kannegiesser .40 1.00
336 Jerry Butler .40 1.00
337 Gord McRae .40 1.00
338 Dennis Kearns .40 1.00
339 Ron Lalonde .40 1.00
340 Jean Hamel .40 1.00
341 Barry Gibbs .40 1.00
342 Mike Pelyk .40 1.00
343 Rey Comeau .40 1.00
344 Jim Neilson .40 1.00
345 Phil Roberto .40 1.00
346 Dave Hutchinson .40 1.00
347 Ted Irvine .40 1.00
348 Lanny McDonald 2.00 5.00
349 Jim Moxey RC .40 1.00
350 Bob Dailey .40 1.00
351 Tim Ecclestone .40 1.00
352 Len Frig .40 1.00
353 Randy Rota .40 1.00
354 Juha Widing .40 1.00
355 Larry Brown .40 1.00
356 Floyd Thomson .40 1.00
357 Richard Nantais RC .40 1.00
358 Inge Hammarstrom .40 1.00
359 Mike Robitaille .40 1.00
360 Rejean Houle .40 1.00
361 Ed Kea .40 1.00
362 Bob Girard RC .40 1.00
363 Bob Murray Vancv .40 1.00
364 Dave Hrechkosy .40 1.00
365 Gary Edwards .40 1.00
366 Harold Snepsts 2.00 4.00
367 Pat Boutette RC .75 2.00
368 Bob Paradise .40 1.00
369 Bob Plager .60 1.50
370 Tim Jacobs RC .40 1.00
371 Pierre Plante .40 1.00
372 Colin Campbell .60 1.50
373 Tiger Williams RC 12.50 25.00
374 Ab DeMarco .40 1.00
375 Mike Lampman RC .40 1.00
376 Mark Heaslip RC .40 1.00
377 Checklist Card 6.00 10.00
378 Bert Wilson .40 1.00
379 Bntt/Lysk/Qnn/St.S TL .40 1.00
380 Gre/Perrlt/Mrtin TL .40 1.00
381 Bucyk/Ratle/O'Rei TL 1.25 2.50
382 Mrtn/Tln/Rsll/Kroll TL .40 1.00
383 Seals/McAd/Mrdch TL .40 1.00
384 Charron/Durbano TL .40 1.00
385 Brgrn/McKch/Wtsn TL .40 1.00
386 Dione/Htch/Corrig TL .40 1.00
387 Hoga/Yng/O'Brien TL .40 1.00
388 Laflr/P.Mahv/Rise TL 1.50 3.00
389 Gillies/Potvin/How TL 1.25 2.50
390 Gilbert/Vick/Espo TL 1.25 2.50
391 Leach/Clrke/Brbr TL 1.25 2.50
392 Lrch/Apps/Schck TL .40 1.00
393 Lefly/Ungr/Gssf TL .40 1.00
394 Thmpsn/Sittlr/Will TL .40 1.00
395 Vgrt/Odl/Krns/Snpst TL .40 1.00
396 Pyatt/Mhn/Lbr/Whte TL .40 1.00

1976-77 O-Pee-Chee WHA

The 1976-77 O-Pee-Chee WHA set consisted of 132 color cards featuring WHA players. Cards were 2 1/2" by 3 1/2". The cards were originally sold in ten-cent wax packs. The backs, in both French and English, told a short biography of the player and career statistics. The cards were printed in Canada. Cards 1-6 featured the league leaders from the previous season in various statistical categories. The backs of cards 62-65, 67, and 71 formed a puzzle of Gordie Howe. A puzzle of Bobby Hull was derived from the backs of cards 61, 66, 68-70 and 72. These cards (61-72) comprised the All-Star subset.

COMPLETE SET (132) 100.00 200.00
1 Tardif/Clout/Nedom LL 2.00 4.00
2 Tardif/Trembl/Nils LL 1.50 3.00
3 Tardif/B.Hull/Nils LL 4.00 8.00
4 Penalties Leaders 1.00 2.00
5 Tardif/B.Hull/Nils LL 4.00 8.00
6 Goals Against Avg. Leaders 1.00 2.00
7 Barry Long .60 1.50
8 Danny Lawson .60 1.50
9 Ulf Nilsson 1.25 3.00
10 Kevin Morrison .60 1.50
11 Gerry Pinder .60 1.50
12 Richard Brodeur 3.00 5.00
13 Robbie Ftorek 4.00 8.00
14 Tom Webster .75 2.00
15 Marty Howe 1.25 3.00
16 Bryan Campbell .60 1.50
17 Rick Dudley .60 1.50
18 Jim Turkiewicz RC .60 1.50
19 Rusty Patenaude .60 1.50
20 Joe Daley .75 2.00
21 Gary Veneruzzo .60 1.50
22 Chris Evans .60 1.50
23 Mike Antonovich .60 1.50
24 Jim Dorey .60 1.50
25 John Gray RC .60 1.50
26 Larry Pleau .60 1.50
27 Poul Popiel .60 1.50
28 Renald Leclerc RC .60 1.50
29 Dennis Sobchuk .60 1.50
30 Lars-Erik Sjoberg .60 1.50
31 Wayne Wood RC .75 2.00
32 Ron Chipperfield .60 1.50
33 Tim Sheehy RC .60 1.50
34 Brent Hughes .60 1.50
35 Ron Ward .60 1.50
36 Ron Huston RC .60 1.50
37 Rosaire Paiement .60 1.50
38 Terry Ruskowski RC 3.00 5.00
39 Hugh Harris .60 1.50
40 J.C. Tremblay .60 1.50
41 Rich Leduc .60 1.50
42 Peter Sullivan RC .60 1.50
43 Jerry Rollins RC .60 1.50
44 Ken Broderick .75 2.00
45 Peter Driscoll RC .60 1.50
46 Joe Noris RC .60 1.50
47 Al McLeod .60 1.50
48 Bruce Landon RC .75 2.00
49 Chris Bordeleau .60 1.50
50 Gordie Howe 20.00 40.00
51 Thommie Bergman .60 1.50
52 Dave Keon 1.25 3.00
53 Butch Deadmarsh .60 1.50
54 Bryan Maxwell .60 1.50
55 John Garrett .75 2.00
56 Glen Sather .75 2.00
57 John Miszuk .60 1.50
58 Heikki Riihiranta .75 2.00
59 Richard Grenier RC .60 1.50
60 Gene Peacosh .60 1.50
61 Joe Daley AS 1.00 2.00
62 J.C. Tremblay AS 1.00 2.00
63 Lars-Erik Sjoberg AS 1.00 2.00
64 Vaclav Nedomansky AS 1.00 2.00
65 Bobby Hull AS 10.00 20.00
66 Anders Hedberg AS 1.00 2.00
67 Chris Abrahamsson AS 1.00 2.00
68 Kevin Morrison AS 1.00 2.00
69 Paul Shmyr AS 1.00 2.00
70 Andre Lacroix AS 1.00 2.00
71 Gene Peacosh AS 1.00 2.00
72 Gordie Howe AS 15.00 25.00
73 Bob Nevin .60 1.50

4 Richard Lemieux .60 1.50
5 Mike Ford RC .60 1.50
6 Real Cloutier .75 2.00
7 Al McDonough .60 1.50
8 Del Hall RC .60 1.50
9 Thommy Abrahamsson .60 1.50
0 Andre Lacroix .75 2.00
1 Frank Hughes RC .60 1.50
2 Reg Thomas RC .60 1.50
3 Dave Inkpen RC .60 1.50
4 Paul Henderson 1.25 3.00
5 Dave Dryden .75 2.00
6 Lynn Powis .60 1.50
7 Andre Boudrias .60 1.50
8 Veli-Pekka Ketola .75 2.00
9 Cam Connor .60 1.50
0 Claude St.Sauveur .60 1.50
1 Garry Swain RC .60 1.50
2 Ernie Wakely .75 2.00
3 Blair MacDonald RC .75 2.00
4 Ron Plumb .60 1.50
5 Mark Howe 7.00 12.00
6 Peter Marrin RC 1.25 3.00
7 Al Hamilton .75 2.00
8 Paulin Bordeleau .60 1.50
9 Gavin Kirk .60 1.50
100 Bobby Hull 15.00 30.00
101 Rick Ley .60 1.50
102 Gary Kurt .75 2.00
103 John McKenzie .75 2.00
104 Al Karlander RC .60 1.50
105 John French .60 1.50
106 John Hughes .60 1.50
107 Ron Grahame .75 2.00
108 Mark Napier .75 2.00
109 Serge Bernier .75 2.00
110 Christer Abrahamsson .75 2.00
111 Frank Mahovlich 3.50 6.00
112 Ted Green .75 2.00
113 Rick Jodzio .60 1.50
114 Michel Dion RC 3.00 6.00
115 Rich Preston RC .75 2.00
116 Pekka Rautakallio RC 3.00 6.00
117 Checklist Card 12.00 30.00
118 Marc Tardif .75 2.00
119 Doug Barrie .60 1.50
120 Vaclav Nedomansky .75 2.00
121 Bill Lesuk .60 1.50
122 Wayne Connelly .60 1.50
123 Pierre Guite .60 1.50
124 Ralph Backstrom .75 2.00
125 Anders Hedberg 1.25 3.00
126 Norm Ullman 1.25 3.00
127 Steve Sutherland RC .60 1.50
128 John Schella .60 1.50
129 Don McLeod .75 2.00
130 Canadian Finals 1.50 4.00
131 U.S. Finals 1.50 4.00
132 World Trophy Final 6.00 15.00

1977-78 O-Pee-Chee

The 1977-78 O-Pee-Chee NHL set consisted of 396 color standard-size cards. Unopened packs consisted of 12 cards plus a bubble-gum stick. Cards 203 and 255 featured different players than corresponding Topps cards. Bilingual backs contained yearly statistics and a cartoon-illustrated fact about the player. Cards 322-339 had a team logo on the front with team records on the back. Rookie Cards included Mike Milbury, Mike Palmateer and Paul Holmgren. The Rick Bourbonnais card (312) actually depicted Bernie Federko, predating his Rookie Card by one year.

COMPLETE SET (396) 75.00 150.00
1 Shutt/Lafleur/Dionne LL 1.50 3.00
2 Lafleur/Dionne/Sal/ LL 1.00 2.00
3 Lafleur/Dionne/Shutt LL 1.25 2.50
4 Wills/Polnch/Gassoff LL .30 .75
5 McDonald/Espo/Will LL .40 1.00
6 Laroc/Dryden/Resch LL 2.00 4.00
7 Perr/Shutt/Lafleur LL 1.25 2.50
8 Dryden/Vach/Parent LL 2.50 5.00
9 Brian Spencer .25 .60
10 Denis Potvin AS2 2.00 4.00
11 Nick Fotiu .40 1.00
12 Bob Murray .25 .60
13 Pete Lopresti .30 .75
14 J. Bob Kelly .25 .60
15 Rick MacLeish .30 .75
16 Terry Harper .25 .60
17 Willi Plett RC 1.50 3.00
18 Peter McNab .30 .75
19 Wayne Thomas .30 .75
20 Pierre Bouchard .25 .60
21 Dennis Maruk .40 1.00
22 Mike Murphy .25 .60
23 Cesare Maniago .30 .75
24 Paul Gardner RC .40 1.00
25 Rod Gilbert .40 1.00
26 Orest Kindrachuk .25 .60
27 Bill Hajt .25 .60
28 John Davidson .75 1.50
29 Jean-Paul Parise .25 .60
30 Larry Robinson AS1 2.50 5.00
31 Yvon Labre .25 .60
32 Walt McKechnie .25 .60
33 Rick Kehoe .30 .75
34 Randy Holt RC .25 .60
35 Garry Unger .30 .75
36 Lou Nanne .25 .60
37 Dan Bouchard .30 .75
38 Darryl Sittler 1.50 3.00
39 Bob Murdoch .25 .60
40 Jean Ratelle .40 1.00
41 Dave Maloney .25 .60
42 Danny Gare .30 .75
43 Jimmy Watson .25 .60
44 Tom Williams .25 .60
45 Serge Savard .40 1.00
46 Derek Sanderson 1.00 2.00
47 John Marks .25 .60
48 Al Cameron RC .25 .60
49 Dean Talafous .25 .60
50 Glenn Resch 1.00 2.00
51 Ron Schock .25 .60
52 Gary Croteau .25 .60
53 Gerry Meehan .25 .60
54 Ed Staniowski .25 .60
55 Phil Esposito UER 1.50 3.00
56 Dennis Ververgaert .25 .60
57 Rick Wilson .25 .60
58 Jim Lorentz .25 .60
59 Bobby Schmautz .25 .60
60 Guy Lapointe AS2 .30 .75
61 Ivan Boldirev .25 .60
62 Bob Nystrom .25 .60
63 Rick Hampton .25 .60
64 Jack Valiquette .25 .60
65 Bernie Parent 1.25 2.50
66 Dave Burrows .25 .60
67 Butch Goring .30 .75
68A Checklist 1-132 ERR 4.00 8.00
68B Checklist 1-132 COR 4.00 8.00
69 Murray Wilson .25 .60
70 Ed Giacomin .75 1.50
71 Flames Team .75 2.00
72 Bruins Team .75 2.00
73 Sabres Team .75 2.00
74 Blackhawks Team .75 2.00
75 Barons Team .75 2.00
76 Rockies Team .75 2.00
77 Red Wings Team .75 2.00
78 Kings Team .75 2.00
79 North Stars Team .75 2.00
80 Canadiens Team .75 2.00
81 Islanders Team .75 2.00
82 Rangers Team .75 2.00
83 Flyers Team .75 2.00
84 Penguins Team .75 2.00
85 Blues Team .75 2.00
86 Maple Leafs Team .75 2.00
87 Canucks Team .75 2.00
88 Capitals Team .75 2.00
89 Keith Magnuson .25 .60
90 Walt Tkaczuk .30 .75
91 Bill Nyrop .25 .60
92 Michel Plasse .30 .75
93 Bob Bourne .30 .75
94 Lee Fogolin .25 .60
95 Gregg Sheppard .25 .60
96 Hartland Monahan .25 .60
97 Curt Bennett .25 .60
98 Bob Dailey .25 .60
99 Bill Goldsworthy .30 .75
100 Ken Dryden AS1 7.50 15.00
101 Grant Mulvey .25 .60
102 Pierre Larouche .40 1.00
103 Nick Libett .25 .60
104 Rick Smith .25 .60
105 Bryan Trottier 8.00 20.00
106 Pierre Jarry .25 .60
107 Red Berenson .30 .75
108 Jim Schoenfeld .30 .75
109 Gilles Meloche .30 .75
110 Lanny McDonald AS2 1.25 2.50
111 Don Lever .25 .60
112 Greg Polis .25 .60
113 Gary Sargent RC .25 .60
114 Earl Anderson RC .25 .60
115 Bobby Clarke 2.50 5.00
116 Dave Lewis .25 .60
117 Darcy Rota .25 .60
118 Andre Savard .25 .60
119 Denis Herron .30 .75
120 Steve Shutt AS1 1.00 2.00
121 Mel Bridgman .25 .60
122 Buster Harvey .25 .60
123 Roland Eriksson RC .25 .60
124 Dale Tallon .25 .60
125 Gilles Gilbert .30 .75
126 Billy Harris .25 .60
127 Tom Lysiak .30 .75
128 Jerry Korab .25 .60
129 Bob Gainey 1.25 2.50
130 Wilf Paiement .30 .75
131 Tom Bladon .25 .60
132 Ernie Hicke .25 .60
133 J.P. LeBlanc .25 .60
134 Mike Milbury RC 4.00 8.00
135 Pit Martin .25 .60
136 Steve Vickers .25 .60
137 Don Awrey .25 .60
138 Bernie Wolfe .30 .75
139 Doug Jarvis .30 .75
140 Borje Salming AS1 1.50 3.00
141 Bob MacMillan .25 .60
142 Wayne Stephenson .30 .75
143 Dave Forbes .25 .60
144 Jean Potvin .25 .60
145 Guy Charron .25 .60
146 Cliff Koroll .25 .60
147 Danny Grant .30 .75
148 Bill Hogaboam .25 .60
149 Al MacAdam .25 .60
150 Gerry Desjardins .30 .75
151 Yvon Lambert .25 .60
152 Rick Lapointe .25 .60
153 Ed Westfall .30 .75
154 Carol Vadnais .25 .60
155 Johnny Bucyk .40 1.00
156 J.P. Bordeleau .25 .60
157 Ron Stackhouse .25 .60
158 Glen Sharpley RC .25 .60
159 Michel Bergeron .25 .60
160 Rogatien Vachon AS2 .75 2.00
161 Fred Stanfield .25 .60
162 Gerry Hart .25 .60
163 Mario Tremblay .30 .75
164 Andre Dupont .25 .60
165 Don Marcotte .25 .60
166 Wayne Dillon .25 .60
167 Claude Larose .25 .60
168 Eric Vail .25 .60
169 Tom Edur RC .25 .60
170 Tony Esposito 1.50 3.00
171 Andre St.Laurent .25 .60
172 Dan Maloney .25 .60
173 Dennis O'Brien .25 .60
174 Blair Chapman RC .25 .60
175 Dennis Kearns .25 .60
176 Wayne Merrick .25 .60
177 Michel Larocque .30 .75
178 Bob Kelly .25 .60
179 Dave Farrish RC .25 .60
180 Richard Martin AS2 .30 .75
181 Gary Doak .25 .60
182 Jude Drouin .25 .60
183 Barry Dean RC .25 .60
184 Gary Smith .30 .75
185 Reggie Leach .30 .75
186 Ian Turnbull .30 .75
187 Vic Venasky .25 .60
188 Wayne Bianchin RC .25 .60
189 Doug Risebrough .30 .75
190 Brad Park 1.00 2.50
191 Craig Ramsay .25 .60
192 Ken Hodge .30 .75
193 Phil Myre .30 .75
194 Garry Howatt .25 .60
195 Stan Mikita 1.50 3.00
196 Garnet Bailey .25 .60
197 Dennis Hextall .25 .60
198 Nick Beverley .25 .60
199 Larry Patey .25 .60
200 Guy Lafleur AS1 6.00 10.00
201 Don Edwards RC 2.00 4.00
202 Gary Dornhoefer .30 .75
203 Bob Paradise .25 .60
204 Alex Pirus RC .25 .60
205 Peter Mahovlich .30 .75
206 Bert Marshall .25 .60
207 Gilles Gratton .30 .75
208 Alain Daigle .25 .60
209 Chris Oddleifson .25 .60
210 Gilbert Perreault AS2 1.25 2.50
211 Mike Palmateer RC 4.00 8.00
212 Billy Lochead .25 .60
213 Dick Redmond .25 .60
214 Guy Lafleur RB 1.25 2.50
215 Ian Turnbull RB .25 .60
216 Guy Lafleur RB 1.25 2.50
217 Steve Shutt RB .30 .75
218 Guy Lafleur RB 1.25 2.50
219 Lorne Henning .25 .60
220 Terry O'Reilly .30 .75
221 Pat Hickey .25 .60
222 Rene Robert .30 .75
223 Tim Young .25 .60
224 Dunc Wilson .30 .75
225 Dennis Hull .30 .75
226 Rod Seiling .25 .60
227 Bill Barber .40 1.00
228 Dennis Polonich RC .25 .60
229 Billy Smith 1.25 2.50
230 Yvan Cournoyer .40 1.00
231 Don Luce .25 .60
232 Mike McEwen RC .25 .60
233 Don Saleski .25 .60
234 Wayne Cashman .30 .75
235 Phil Russell .25 .60
236 Mike Corrigan .25 .60
237 Guy Chouinard .30 .75
238 Steve Jensen RC .25 .60
239 Jim Rutherford .30 .75
240 Marcel Dionne AS1 2.00 4.00
241 Rejean Houle .25 .60
242 Jocelyn Guevremont .25 .60
243 Jim Harrison .25 .60
244 Don Murdoch RC .40 1.00
245 Rick Green RC .40 1.00
246 Rick Middleton 1.00 2.00
247 Joe Watson .25 .60
248 Syl Apps .25 .60
249 Checklist 133-264 4.00 8.00
250 Clark Gillies .30 .75
251 Bobby Orr 15.00 25.00
252 Nelson Pyatt .25 .60
253 Gary McAdam RC .25 .60
254 Jacques Lemaire .40 1.00
255 Bob Girard .25 .60
256 Ron Greschner .30 .75
257 Ross Lonsberry .25 .60
258 Dave Gardner .25 .60
259 Rick Blight .25 .60
260 Gerry Cheevers 1.00 2.00
261 Jean Pronovost .30 .75
262 Cup Semi-Finals .25 .60
263 Cup Semi-Finals .25 .60
264 Canadiens Champs .40 1.00
265 Rick Bowness RC .75 2.00
266 George Ferguson .25 .60
267 Mike Kitchen RC .25 .60
268 Bob Berry .25 .60
269 Greg Smith RC .25 .60
270 Stan Jonathan RC 1.00 3.00
271 Dwight Bialowas .25 .60
272 Pete Stemkowski .25 .60
273 Greg Joly .25 .60
274 Ken Houston RC .25 .60
275 Brian Glennie .25 .60
276 Ed Johnston .30 .75
277 John Grisdale .25 .60
278 Craig Patrick .30 .75
279 Ken Breitenbach RC .25 .60
280 Fred Ahern .25 .60
281 Jim Roberts .25 .60
282 Harvey Bennett RC .25 .60
283 Ab DeMarco .25 .60
284 Pat Boutette .25 .60
285 Bob Plager .30 .75
286 Hilliard Graves .25 .60
287 Gordie Lane RC .25 .60
288 Ron Andruff RC .25 .60
289 Larry Brown .25 .60
290 Mike Fidler RC .25 .60
291 Fred Barrett .25 .60
292 Bill Clement .30 .75
293 Errol Thompson .25 .60
294 Doug Grant .30 .75
295 Harold Snepsts 1.00 2.00
296 Rick Bragnalo RC .25 .60
297 Bryan Lefley .25 .60
298 Gene Carr .25 .60
299 Bob Stewart .25 .60
300 Lew Morrison .25 .60
301 Ed Kea .25 .60
302 Scott Garland .25 .60
303 Bill Fairbairn .25 .60
304 Larry Carriere .25 .60
305 Ron Low .30 .75
306 Tom Reid .25 .60
307 Paul Holmgren RC 2.50 5.00
308 Pat Price .25 .60
309 Kirk Bowman RC .25 .60
310 Bobby Simpson RC .25 .60
311 Ron Ellis .30 .75
312 Rick Bourbonnais RC UER .60 1.50
313 Bobby Lalonde .25 .60
314 Tony White .25 .60
315 John Van Boxmeer .30 .75
316 Don Kozak .25 .60
317 Jim Neilson .25 .60
318 Terry Martin RC .25 .60
319 Barry Gibbs .25 .60
320 Inge Hammarstrom .25 .60
321 Darryl Edestrand .25 .60
322 Flames Logo .75 2.00
323 Bruins Logo .75 2.00
324 Sabres Logo .75 2.00
325 Blackhawks Logo .75 2.00
326 Barons Logo .75 2.00
327 Rockies Logo .75 2.00
328 Red Wings Logo .75 2.00
329 Kings Logo .75 2.00
330 North Stars Logo .75 2.00
331 Canadiens Logo .75 2.00
332 Islanders Logo .75 2.00
333 Rangers Logo .75 2.00
334 Flyers Logo .75 2.00
335 Penguins Logo .75 2.00
336 Blues Logo .75 2.00
337 Maple Leafs Logo .75 2.00
338 Canucks Logo .75 2.00
339 Capitals Logo .75 2.00
340 Chuck Lefley .25 .60
341 Garry Monahan .25 .60
342 Bryan Watson .25 .60
343 Dave Hudson .25 .60
344 Neil Komadoski .25 .60
345 Gary Edwards .30 .75
346 Rey Comeau .25 .60
347 Bob Neely .25 .60
348 Jean Hamel .25 .60
349 Jerry Butler .25 .60
350 Mike Walton .25 .60
351 Bob Sirois .25 .60
352 Jim McElmury .25 .60
353 Dave Schultz .30 .75
354 Doug Palazzari RC .25 .60
355 David Shand RC .25 .60
356 Stan Weir .25 .60
357 Mike Christie .25 .60
358 Floyd Thomson .25 .60
359 Larry Goodenough .25 .60
360 Bill Riley RC .25 .60
361 Doug Hicks RC .25 .60
362 Dan Newman RC .25 .60
363 Rick Chartraw .25 .60
364 Tim Ecclestone .25 .60
365 Don Ashby RC .25 .60
366 Jacques Richard .25 .60
367 Yves Belanger .25 .60
368 Ron Sedlbauer .25 .60
369 Jack Lynch UER .25 .60
370 Doug Favell .30 .75
371 Bob Murdoch .25 .60
372 Ralph Klassen .25 .60
373 Richard Mulhern .25 .60
374 Jim McKenny .25 .60
375 Mike Bloom .25 .60
376 Bruce Affleck .25 .60
377 Gerry O'Flaherty .25 .60
378 Ron Lalonde .25 .60
379 Chuck Arnason .25 .60
380 Dave Hutchinson .25 .60
381A Checklist ERR 4.00 8.00
381B Checklist COR 4.00 8.00
382 John Gould .25 .60
383 Tiger Williams 2.00 4.00
384 Len Frig .25 .60
385 Pierre Plante .25 .60
386 Ralph Stewart .25 .60
387 Gord Smith .25 .60
388 Denis Dupere .25 .60
389 Randy Manery .25 .60
390 Lowell MacDonald .25 .60
391 Dennis Owchar .25 .60
392 Jim Roberts RC .25 .60
393 Mike Veisor .30 .75
394 Bob Hess .25 .60
395 Curt Ridley .25 .60
396 Mike Lampman .40 1.00

1977-78 O-Pee-Chee WHA

The 1977-78 O-Pee-Chee WHA set consistedof 66 color standard-size cards. Printed in Canada, the cards were originally sold in 15-cent wax packs containing 12 cards and gum. Bilingual backs featured player statistics and a short biography. Card number 1 featured Gordie Howe's 1000th career goal. There were no key Rookie Cards in this set. This was the final WHA set. The league disbanded following the 1978-79 season with the four surviving teams (Edmonton, New England/Hartford, Quebec and Winnipeg) merging with the NHL.

COMPLETE SET (66) 35.00 70.00
1 Gordie Howe 15.00 30.00
2 Jean Bernier RC .30 .75
3 Anders Hedberg .75 2.00
4 Ken Broderick .60 1.50
5 Joe Noris .30 .75
6 Blaine Stoughton .60 1.50
7 Claude St.Sauveur .30 .75
8 Real Cloutier .60 1.50
9 Joe Daley .60 1.50
10 Ron Chipperfield .30 .75
11 Wayne Rutledge .60 1.50
12 Mark Napier .60 1.50
13 Rich Leduc .30 .75
14 Don McLeod .60 1.50
15 Ulf Nilsson .75 2.00
16 Blair MacDonald .30 .75
17 Mike Rogers .60 1.50
18 Gary Inness .60 1.50
19 Larry Lund .30 .75
20 Marc Tardif .60 1.50
21 Lars-Erik Sjoberg .60 1.50
22 Bryan Campbell .30 .75
23 John Garrett .60 1.50
24 Ron Plumb .30 .75
25 Mark Howe 3.00 6.00
26 Garry Lariviere RC .30 .75
27 Peter Sullivan .30 .75
28 Dave Dryden .60 1.50
29 Reg Thomas .30 .75
30 Andre Lacroix .60 1.50
31 Paul Henderson 1.25 3.00
32 Paulin Bordeleau .30 .75
33 Juha Widing .60 1.50
34 Mike Antonovich .30 .75
35 Robbie Ftorek .60 1.50
36 Rosaire Paiement .30 .75
37 Terry Ruskowski .60 1.50
38 Richard Brodeur 1.75 3.00
39 Willy Lindstrom RC 1.00 2.50
40 Al Hamilton .30 .75
41 John McKenzie .60 1.50
42 Wayne Wood .60 1.50
43 Claude Larose .30 .75
44 J.C. Tremblay .30 .75
45 Gary Bromley .60 1.50
46 Ken Baird .30 .75
47 Bobby Sheehan .30 .75
48 Don Larway RC .30 .75
49 Al Smith .60 1.50
50 Bobby Hull 10.00 20.00
51 Peter Marrin .30 .75
52 Norm Ferguson .30 .75
53 Dennis Sobchuk .30 .75
54 Norm Dube RC .30 .75
55 Tom Webster .30 .75
56 Jim Park RC .60 1.50
57 Dan Labraaten RC .75 2.00
58 Checklist Card 6.00 10.00
59 Paul Shmyr .30 .75
60 Serge Bernier .60 1.50
61 Frank Mahovlich 2.00 4.00
62 Michel Dion .60 1.50
63 Poul Popiel .30 .75
64 Lyle Moffat .30 .75
65 Marty Howe .60 1.50
66 Don Burgess .75 2.00

1978-79 O-Pee-Chee

The 1978-79 O-Pee-Chee set consisted of 396 standard-size cards. Bilingual backs featured the card number (pictured in a hockey skate), year-by-year player statistics, a short biography and a facsimile autograph. Unlike Topps, All-Star designations did not appear on the front of cards of those players named to the All-Star team. An All-Star subset (325-336) served to recognize these players. Card number 300 honored Bobby Orr's retirement early in the season.

COMPLETE SET (396) 100.00 200.00
1 Mike Bossy HL 6.00 12.00
2 Phil Esposito HL .75 1.50
3 Guy Lafleur HL .75 1.50
4 Darryl Sittler HL .30 .75
5 Garry Unger HL .20 .50
6 Gary Edwards .20 .50
7 Rick Blight .15 .40
8 Larry Patey .15 .40
9 Craig Ramsay .15 .40
10 Bryan Trottier 5.00 10.00
11 Don Murdoch .15 .40
12 Phil Russell .15 .40
13 Doug Jarvis .20 .50
14 Gene Carr .15 .40
15 Bernie Parent 1.00 2.00
16 Perry Miller .15 .40
17 Kent-Erik Andersson RC .20 .50
18 Gregg Sheppard .15 .40
19 Dennis Owchar .15 .40
20 Rogatien Vachon .40 1.00
21 Dan Maloney .15 .40
22 Guy Charron .15 .40
23 Dick Redmond .15 .40
24 Checklist 1-132 2.50 5.00
25 Anders Hedberg .20 .50
26 Mel Bridgman .15 .40
27 Lee Fogolin .15 .40
28 Gilles Meloche .20 .50
29 Garry Howatt .15 .40
30 Darryl Sittler 1.25 2.50
31 Curt Bennett .15 .40
32 Andre St.Laurent .15 .40
33 Blair Chapman .15 .40
34 Keith Magnuson .15 .40
35 Pierre Larouche .20 .50
36 Michel Plasse .20 .50
37 Gary Sargent .15 .40
38 Mike Walton .15 .40
39 Robert Picard RC .20 .50
40 Terry O'Reilly .20 .50
41 Dave Farrish .15 .40
42 Gary McAdam .15 .40
43 Joe Watson .15 .40
44 Yves Belanger .20 .50
45 Steve Jensen .15 .40
46 Bob Stewart .15 .40
47 Darcy Rota .15 .40
48 Dennis Hextall .15 .40
49 Bert Marshall .15 .40
50 Ken Dryden 6.00 12.00
51 Peter Mahovlich .20 .50
52 Dennis Ververgaert .15 .40
53 Inge Hammarstrom .15 .40
54 Doug Favell .20 .50
55 Steve Vickers .15 .40
56 Syl Apps .15 .40
57 Errol Thompson .15 .40
58 Don Luce .15 .40
59 Mike Milbury .30 .75
60 Yvan Cournoyer .30 .75
61 Kirk Bowman .15 .40
62 Billy Smith .75 1.50
63 Lafleur/Bossy/Shutt LL 2.50 5.00
64 Trott/Lafleur/Sitt LL 1.25 2.50
65 Lafleur/Trott/Sitt LL 1.25 2.50
66 Schltz/Will/Polnich LL .30 .75
67 Bossy/Espo/Shutt LL 2.00 4.00
68 Dryden/Parent/Gilb LL 2.00 4.00
69 Lafleur/Barber/Sitt LL 1.00 2.00
70 Parent/Dryden/Espo LL 2.50 5.00
71 Bob Kelly .15 .40
72 Ron Stackhouse .15 .40
73 Wayne Dillon .15 .40
74 Jim Rutherford .20 .50
75 Stan Mikita 1.25 2.50
76 Bob Gainey .75 1.50
77 Gerry Hart .15 .40
78 Lanny McDonald .75 1.50
79 Brad Park .75 1.50
80 Richard Martin .20 .50
81 Bernie Wolfe .20 .50
82 Bob MacMillan .15 .40
83 Brad Maxwell RC .15 .40
84 Mike Fidler .15 .40
85 Carol Vadnais .15 .40
86 Don Lever .15 .40
87 Phil Myre .20 .50
88 Paul Gardner .15 .40
89 Bob Murray .15 .40
90 Guy Lafleur 4.00 7.00
91 Bob Murdoch .15 .40
92 Ron Ellis .20 .50
93 Jude Drouin .15 .40
94 Jocelyn Guevremont .15 .40
95 Gilles Gilbert .20 .50
96 Bob Sirois .15 .40
97 Tom Lysiak .20 .50
98 Andre Dupont .15 .40
99 Per-Olov Brasar RC .15 .40
100 Phil Esposito 1.50 3.00
101 J.P. Bordeleau .15 .40
102 Pierre Mondou RC .40 1.00
103 Wayne Bianchin .15 .40
104 Dennis O'Brien .15 .40
105 Glenn Resch .30 .75
106 Dennis Polonich .15 .40
107 Kris Manery RC .15 .40
108 Bill Hajt .15 .40
109 Jere Gillis RC .15 .40
110 Garry Unger .20 .50
111 Nick Beverley .15 .40
112 Pat Hickey .15 .40
113 Rick Middleton .30 .75
114 Orest Kindrachuk .15 .40
115 Mike Bossy RC 50.00 100.00
116 Pierre Bouchard .15 .40
117 Alain Daigle .15 .40
118 Terry Martin .15 .40
119 Tom Edur .15 .40
120 Marcel Dionne 1.50 3.00
121 Barry Beck RC 1.25 2.50
122 Billy Lochead .15 .40
123 Paul Harrison RC .20 .50
124 Wayne Cashman .20 .50
125 Rick MacLeish .20 .50
126 Bob Bourne .20 .50
127 Ian Turnbull .15 .40
128 Gerry Meehan .15 .40
129 Eric Vail .15 .40
130 Gilbert Perreault .30 .75
131 Bob Dailey .15 .40
132 Dale McCourt RC .30 .75
133 John Wensink RC .50 1.25
134 Bill Nyrop .15 .40
135 Ivan Boldirev .15 .40
136 Lucien DeBlois RC .15 .40
137 Brian Spencer .15 .40
138 Tim Young .15 .40
139 Ron Sedlbauer .15 .40
140 Gerry Cheevers .75 1.50
141 Dennis Maruk .20 .50
142 Barry Dean .15 .40
143 Bernie Federko RC 5.00 10.00
144 Stefan Persson RC .20 .50
145 Wilf Paiement .20 .50
146 Dale Tallon .15 .40
147 Yvon Lambert .15 .40
148 Greg Joly .15 .40
149 Dean Talafous .15 .40
150 Don Edwards .20 .50
151 Butch Goring .20 .50
152 Tom Bladon .15 .40
153 Bob Nystrom .15 .40
154 Ron Greschner .20 .50
155 Jean Ratelle .30 .75
156 Russ Anderson RC .15 .40
157 John Marks .15 .40
158 Michel Larocque .20 .50
159 Paul Woods RC .30 .75
160 Mike Palmateer .20 .50
161 Jim Lorentz .15 .40
162 Dave Lewis .15 .40
163 Harvey Bennett .15 .40
164 Rick Smith .15 .40
165 Reggie Leach .20 .50
166 Wayne Thomas .20 .50
167 Dave Forbes .15 .40
168 Doug Wilson RC 6.00 12.00
169 Dan Bouchard .20 .50
170 Steve Shutt .30 .75
171 Mike Kaszycki RC .15 .40
172 Denis Herron .20 .50
173 Rick Bowness .20 .50
174 Rick Hampton .15 .40
175 Glen Sharpley .15 .40
176 Bill Barber .30 .75
177 Ron Duguay RC 4.00 8.00
178 Jim Schoenfeld .20 .50
179 Pierre Plante .15 .40
180 Jacques Lemaire .30 .75
181 Stan Jonathan .15 .40
182 Billy Harris .15 .40
183 Chris Oddleifson .15 .40
184 Jean Pronovost .20 .50
185 Fred Barrett .15 .40
186 Ross Lonsberry .15 .40
187 Mike McEwen .15 .40
188 Rene Robert .20 .50
189 J. Bob Kelly .15 .40
190 Serge Savard .30 .75
191 Dennis Kearns .15 .40
192 Flames Team .40 1.00
193 Bruins Team .40 1.00
194 Sabres Team .40 1.00
195 Blackhawks Team .40 1.00
196 Rockies Team .40 1.00
197 Red Wings Team .40 1.00
198 Kings Team .40 1.00
199 North Stars Team .40 1.00
200 Canadiens Team .40 1.00
201 Islanders Team .40 1.00
202 Rangers Team .40 1.00
203 Flyers Team .40 1.00
204 Penguins Team .40 1.00
205 Blues Team .40 1.00
206 Maple Leafs Team .40 1.00
207 Canucks Team .40 1.00
208 Capitals Team .40 1.00
209 Danny Gare .20 .50
210 Larry Robinson 1.25 2.50
211 John Davidson .30 .75
212 Peter McNab .20 .50
213 Rick Kehoe .20 .50
214 Terry Harper .15 .40
215 Bobby Clarke 1.50 3.00
216 Bryan Maxwell UER .15 .40
217 Ted Bulley RC .15 .40
218 Red Berenson .20 .50
219 Ron Grahame .20 .50
220 Clark Gillies .20 .50
221 Dave Maloney .15 .40
222 Derek Smith RC .15 .40
223 Wayne Stephenson .20 .50
224 John Van Boxmeer .15 .40
225 Dave Schultz .20 .50
226 Reed Larson RC .50 1.25
227 Rejean Houle .15 .40
228 Doug Hicks .15 .40
229 Mike Murphy .15 .40
230 Pete Lopresti .20 .50
231 Jerry Korab .15 .40
232 Ed Westfall .20 .50
233 Greg Malone RC .30 .75
234 Paul Holmgren .20 .50
235 Walt Tkaczuk .20 .50
236 Don Marcotte .15 .40
237 Ron Low .20 .50
238 Rick Chartraw .15 .40
239 Cliff Koroll .15 .40
240 Borje Salming 1.00 2.00
241 Roland Eriksson .15 .40
242 Ric Seiling RC .15 .40
243 Jim Bedard RC .30 .75
244 Peter Lee RC .20 .50
245 Denis Potvin 1.25 2.50
246 Greg Polis .15 .40
247 Jimmy Watson .15 .40
248 Bobby Schmautz .15 .40
249 Doug Risebrough .20 .50
250 Tony Esposito 1.25 2.50
251 Nick Libett .15 .40
252 Ron Zanussi RC .15 .40
253 Andre Savard .15 .40
254 Dave Burrows .15 .40
255 Ulf Nilsson .30 .75
256 Richard Mulhern .15 .40
257 Don Saleski .15 .40
258 Wayne Merrick .15 .40
259 Checklist 133-264 2.50 5.00
260 Guy Lapointe .20 .50
261 Grant Mulvey .15 .40
262 Stanley Cup Semifinals .30 .75
263 Stanley Cup Semifinals .30 .75
264 Stanley Cup Finals .30 .75
265 Bob Sauve .20 .50
266 Randy Manery .15 .40
267 Bill Fairbairn .15 .40
268 Garry Monahan .15 .40
269 Colin Campbell .20 .50
270 Dan Newman .15 .40
271 Dwight Foster RC .15 .40
272 Larry Carriere .15 .40
273 Michel Bergeron .15 .40
274 Scott Garland .15 .40
275 Bill McKenzie .20 .50
276 Garnet Bailey .15 .40
277 Ed Kea .15 .40
278 Dave Gardner .15 .40
279 Bruce Affleck .15 .40
280 Bruce Boudreau RC .75 2.00
281 Jean Hamel .15 .40
282 Kurt Walker RC .15 .40
283 Denis Dupere .15 .40
284 Gordie Lane .15 .40
285 Bobby Lalonde .15 .40
286 Pit Martin .15 .40
287 Jean Potvin .15 .40
288 Jimmy Jones RC .15 .40
289 Dave Hutchinson .15 .40
290 Pete Stemkowski .15 .40
291 Mike Christie .15 .40
292 Bill Riley .15 .40
293 Rey Comeau .15 .40
294 Jack McIlhargey RC .20 .50
295 Tom Younghans RC .15 .40
296 Mario Faubert RC .15 .40
297 Checklist 265-396 2.50 5.00
298 Rob Palmer RC .15 .40
299 Dave Hudson .15 .40
300 Bobby Orr 25.00 40.00
301 Lorne Stamler RC .15 .40
302 Curt Ridley .15 .40
303 Greg Smith .15 .40
304 Jerry Butler .15 .40
305 Gary Doak .15 .40
306 Danny Grant .20 .50
307 Mark Suzor RC .15 .40
308 Rick Bragnalo .15 .40
309 John Gould .15 .40
310 Sheldon Kannegiesser .15 .40
311 Bobby Sheehan .15 .40
312 Randy Carlyle RC 3.00 6.00
313 Lorne Henning .15 .40
314 Tom Williams .15 .40
315 Ron Andruff .15 .40
316 Bryan Watson .15 .40
317 Willi Plett .15 .40
318 John Grisdale .15 .40
319 Brian Sutter RC 4.00 8.00
320 Trevor Johansen RC .15 .40
321 Vic Venasky .15 .40
322 Rick Lapointe .15 .40
323 Ron Delorme RC .20 .50
324 Yvon Labre .15 .40
325 Bryan Trottier AS UER 2.00 4.00
326 Guy Lafleur AS 1.25 2.50
327 Clark Gillies AS .20 .50
328 Borje Salming AS .20 .50
329 Larry Robinson AS .30 .75
330 Ken Dryden AS 2.50 5.00
331 Darryl Sittler AS .30 .75
332 Terry O'Reilly AS .30 .75
333 Steve Shutt AS .20 .50
334 Denis Potvin AS .30 .75
335 Serge Savard AS .20 .50
336 Don Edwards AS .30 .75
337 Glenn Goldup .15 .40
338 Mike Kitchen .15 .40
339 Bob Girard .15 .40
340 Guy Chouinard .20 .50
341 Randy Holt .15 .40
342 Jim Roberts .15 .40
343 Dave Logan RC .15 .40
344 Walt McKechnie .15 .40
345 Brian Glennie .15 .40
346 Ralph Klassen .15 .40
347 Gord Smith .15 .40
348 Ken Houston .15 .40
349 Bob Manno RC .15 .40
350 Jean-Paul Parise .15 .40
351 Don Ashby .15 .40
352 Fred Stanfield .15 .40
353 Dave Taylor RC 18.00 30.00
354 Nelson Pyatt .15 .40
355 Blair Stewart RC .15 .40
356 David Shand .15 .40
357 Hilliard Graves .15 .40
358 Bob Hess .15 .40
359 Tiger Williams .75 1.50
360 Larry Wright RC .15 .40
361 Larry Brown .15 .40
362 Gary Croteau .15 .40
363 Rick Green .20 .50
364 Bill Clement .20 .50
365 Gerry O'Flaherty .15 .40
366 John Baby RC .15 .40
367 Nick Fotiu .20 .50
368 Pat Price .15 .40
369 Bert Wilson .15 .40
370 Bryan Lefley .15 .40
371 Ron Lalonde .15 .40
372 Bobby Simpson .15 .40
373 Doug Grant .20 .50
374 Pat Boutette .15 .40
375 Bob Paradise .15 .40
376 Mario Tremblay .20 .50
377 Darryl Edestrand .15 .40
378 Andy Spruce RC .15 .40
379 Jack Brownschidle RC .15 .40
380 Harold Snepsts .30 .75
381 Al MacAdam .15 .40
382 Neil Komadoski .15 .40
383 Don Awrey .15 .40
384 Ron Schock .15 .40
385 Gary Simmons .20 .50
386 Fred Ahern .15 .40

387 Larry Bolonchuk .15 .40
388 Brad Gassoff RC .15 .40
389 Chuck Arnason .15 .40
390 Barry Gibbs .15 .40
391 Jack Valiquette .15 .40
392 Doug Halward .15 .40
393 Hartland Monahan .15 .40
394 Rod Seiling .15 .40
395 George Ferguson .15 .40
396 Al Cameron .30 .75

1979-80 O-Pee-Chee

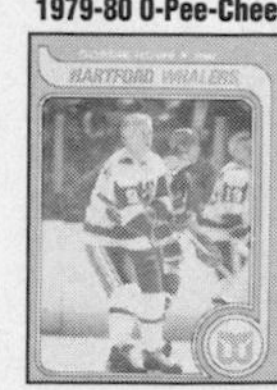

The 1979-80 O-Pee-Chee set consisted of 396 standard-size cards. Cards 81, 82, 141, 163, and 263 differed from that of the corresponding Topps issue. Wax packs had 14 cards plus a bubble-gum piece. The fronts featured distinctive blue borders (that are prone to chipping), while bilingual backs featured 1978-79 and career stats, a short biography and a cartoon-illustrated fact about the player. Team cards (#244-261) had checklist backs. The Rookie Card of Wayne Gretzky (No. 18) had been illegally reprinted. Most of the reprints were discovered and then destroyed or clearly marked as reprints. However some still exist in the market. The reprint is difficult to distinguish from the real card, hence, collectors and dealers should be careful.

COMPLETE SET (396) 700.00 1400.00
1 Bossy/Dionne/Lafleur LL 2.50 5.00
2 Trott/Lafleur/Dionne LL 1.50 3.00
3 Trott/Dionne/Lafleur LL 1.50 4.00
4 Williams/Holt/Schultz LL .60 1.50
5 Bossy/Dionne/Gardner LL 1.50 4.00
6 Dryden/Resch/Parent LL 2.50 6.00
7 Lafleur/Bossy/Trott/ LL 2.00 4.00
8 Dryden/Espo/Parent LL 2.50 6.00
9 Greg Malone .30 .75
10 Rick Middleton .60 1.50
11 Greg Smith .30 .75
12 Rene Robert .40 1.00
13 Doug Risebrough .40 1.00
14 Bob Kelly .30 .75
15 Walt Tkaczuk .40 1.00
16 John Marks .30 .75
17 Willie Huber RC .30 .75
18 Wayne Gretzky RC 500.00 800.00
19 Ron Sedlbauer .30 .75
20 Glenn Resch AS2 .60 1.50
21 Blair Chapman .30 .75
22 Ron Zanussi .30 .75
23 Brad Park .60 1.50
24 Yvon Lambert .30 .75
25 Andre Savard .30 .75
26 Jimmy Watson .30 .75
27 Hal Philipoff RC .30 .75
28 Dan Bouchard .40 1.00
29 Bob Sirois .30 .75
30 Ulf Nilsson .40 1.00
31 Mike Murphy .30 .75
32 Stefan Persson .30 .75
33 Garry Unger .40 1.00
34 Rejean Houle .30 .75
35 Barry Beck .40 1.00
36 Tim Young .30 .75
37 Rick Dudley .30 .75
38 Wayne Stephenson .40 1.00
39 Peter McNab .40 1.00
40 Borje Salming AS2 .60 1.50
41 Tom Lysiak .30 .75
42 Don Maloney RC .75 2.00
43 Mike Rogers .40 1.00
44 Dave Lewis .30 .75
45 Peter Lee .30 .75
46 Marty Howe .60 1.50
47 Serge Bernier .30 .75
48 Paul Woods .30 .75
49 Bob Sauve .40 1.00
50 Larry Robinson AS1 1.00 2.50
51 Tom Gorence RC .30 .75
52 Gary Sargent .30 .75
53 Thomas Gradin RC .75 2.00
54 Dean Talafous .30 .75
55 Bob Murray .30 .75
56 Bob Bourne .40 1.00
57 Larry Patey .30 .75
58 Ross Lonsberry .30 .75
59 Rick Smith UER .30 .75
60 Guy Chouinard .40 1.00
61 Danny Gare .40 1.00
62 Jim Bedard .40 1.00
63 Dale McCourt UER .40 1.00
64 Steve Payne RC .30 .75
65 Pat Hughes RC .30 .75
66 Mike McEwen .30 .75
67 Reg Kerr RC .30 .75
68 Walt McKechnie .30 .75
69 Michel Plasse .40 1.00
70 Denis Potvin AS1 .75 2.00
71 Dave Dryden .60 1.50
72 Gary McAdam .30 .75
73 Andre St.Laurent .30 .75
74 Jerry Korab .30 .75
75 Rick MacLeish .60 1.50
76 Dennis Kearns .30 .75
77 Jean Pronovost .40 1.00
78 Ron Greschner .40 1.00
79 Wayne Cashman .60 1.50
80 Tony Esposito 1.00 2.50
81 Jets Logo CL 6.00 15.00
82 Oilers Logo CL 20.00 50.00
83 Stanley Cup Finals 2.50 6.00
84 Brian Sutter 1.00 2.50
85 Gerry Cheevers .60 1.50
86 Pat Hickey .30 .75
87 Mike Kaszycki .30 .75
88 Grant Mulvey .30 .75
89 Derek Smith .30 .75
90 Steve Shutt .60 1.50
91 Robert Picard .30 .75
92 Dan Labraaten .30 .75
93 Glen Sharpley .30 .75
94 Denis Herron .40 1.00
95 Reggie Leach .60 1.50
96 John Van Boxmeer .30 .75
97 Tiger Williams .60 1.50
98 Butch Goring .40 1.00
99 Don Marcotte .30 .75
100 Bryan Trottier AS1 2.00 4.00
101 Serge Savard AS2 .60 1.50
102 Cliff Koroll .30 .75
103 Gary Smith .40 1.00
104 Al MacAdam .30 .75
105 Don Edwards .40 1.00
106 Errol Thompson .30 .75
107 Andre Lacroix .40 1.00
108 Marc Tardif .40 1.00
109 Rick Kehoe .40 1.00
110 John Davidson .60 1.50
111 Behn Wilson RC .40 1.00
112 Doug Jarvis .40 1.00
113 Tom Rowe RC .30 .75
114 Mike Milbury .60 1.50
115 Billy Harris .30 .75
116 Greg Fox RC .30 .75
117 Curt Fraser RC .40 1.00
118 Jean-Paul Parise .30 .75
119 Ric Seiling .30 .75
120 Darryl Sittler .60 1.50
121 Rick Lapointe .30 .75
122 Jim Rutherford .40 1.00
123 Mario Tremblay .60 1.50
124 Randy Carlyle .60 1.50
125 Bobby Clarke 1.25 3.00
126 Wayne Thomas .40 1.00
127 Ivan Boldirev .30 .75
128 Ted Bulley .30 .75
129 Dick Redmond .30 .75
130 Clark Gillies AS1 .60 1.50
131 Checklist 1-132 20.00 40.00
132 Vaclav Nedomansky .30 .75
133 Richard Mulhern .30 .75
134 Dave Schultz .60 1.50
135 Guy Lapointe .40 1.00
136 Gilles Meloche .60 1.50
137 Randy Pierce RC .30 .75
138 Cam Connor .30 .75
139 George Ferguson .30 .75
140 Bill Barber .60 1.50
141 Terry Ruskowski UER .40 1.00
142 Wayne Babych RC .60 1.50
143 Phil Russell .30 .75
144 Bobby Schmautz .30 .75
145 Carol Vadnais .30 .75
146 John Tonelli RC 3.00 8.00
147 Peter Marsh RC .30 .75
148 Thommie Bergman .30 .75
149 Richard Martin .60 1.50
150 Ken Dryden AS1 8.00 20.00
151 Kris Manery .30 .75
152 Guy Charron .30 .75
153 Lanny McDonald .75 2.00
154 Ron Stackhouse .30 .75
155 Stan Mikita 1.25 3.00
156 Paul Holmgren .30 .75
157 Perry Miller .30 .75
158 Gary Croteau .30 .75
159 Dave Maloney .30 .75
160 Marcel Dionne AS2 1.50 3.00
161 Mike Bossy RB 2.00 4.00
162 Don Maloney RB .30 .75
163 Whalers Logo CL 6.00 15.00
164 Brad Park RB .30 .75
165 Bryan Trottier RB .60 1.50
166 Al Hill RC .30 .75
167 Gary Bromley UER .40 1.00
168 Don Murdoch .30 .75
169 Wayne Merrick .30 .75
170 Bob Gainey .60 1.50
171 Jim Schoenfeld .60 1.50
172 Gregg Sheppard .30 .75
173 Dan Bolduc RC .30 .75
174 Blake Dunlop .30 .75
175 Gordie Howe 15.00 25.00
176 Richard Brodeur .60 1.50
177 Tom Younghans .30 .75
178 Andre Dupont .30 .75
179 Ed Johnstone RC .40 1.00
180 Gilbert Perreault .60 1.50
181 Bob Lorimer RC .30 .75
182 John Wensink .30 .75
183 Lee Fogolin .30 .75
184 Greg Carroll RC .30 .75
185 Bobby Hull 15.00 25.00
186 Harold Snepsts .30 .75
187 Peter Mahovlich .40 1.00
188 Eric Vail .30 .75
189 Phil Myre .40 1.00
190 Wilf Paiement .40 1.00
191 Charlie Simmer RC 3.00 8.00
192 Per-Olov Brasar .30 .75
193 Lorne Henning .30 .75
194 Don Luce .30 .75
195 Steve Vickers .30 .75
196 Bob Miller RC .30 .75
197 Mike Palmateer .40 1.00
198 Nick Libett .30 .75
199 Pat Ribble RC .30 .75
200 Guy Lafleur AS1 4.00 10.00
201 Mel Bridgman .40 1.00
202 Morris Lukowich RC .40 1.00
203 Don Lever .30 .75
204 Tom Bladon .30 .75
205 Garry Howatt .30 .75
206 Bobby Smith RC 4.00 10.00
207 Craig Ramsay .40 1.00
208 Ron Duguay .60 1.50
209 Gilles Gilbert .40 1.00
210 Bob MacMillan .30 .75
211 Pierre Mondou .30 .75
212 J.P. Bordeleau .30 .75
213 Reed Larson .40 1.00
214 Dennis Ververgaert .30 .75
215 Bernie Federko 2.50 5.00
216 Mark Howe 1.50 4.00
217 Bob Nystrom .30 .75
218 Orest Kindrachuk .30 .75
219 Mike Fidler .30 .75
220 Phil Esposito .75 2.00
221 Bill Hajt .30 .75
222 Mark Napier .40 1.00
223 Dennis Maruk .40 1.00
224 Dennis Polonich .30 .75
225 Jean Ratelle .60 1.50
226 Bob Dailey .30 .75
227 Alain Daigle .30 .75
228 Ian Turnbull .30 .75
229 Jack Valiquette .30 .75
230 Mike Bossy AS2 10.00 20.00
231 Brad Maxwell .30 .75
232 Dave Taylor 2.00 5.00
233 Pierre Larouche .60 1.50
234 Rod Schutt RC .30 .75
235 Rogatien Vachon .60 1.50
236 Ryan Walter RC .75 2.00
237 Checklist 133-264 UER 20.00 50.00
238 Terry O'Reilly .60 1.50
239 Real Cloutier .40 1.00
240 Anders Hedberg .40 1.00
241 Ken Linseman RC 2.00 5.00
242 Billy Smith .60 1.50
243 Rick Chartraw .30 .75
244 Flames Team 1.50 4.00
245 Bruins Team 1.50 4.00
246 Sabres Team 1.50 4.00
247 Blackhawks Team 1.50 4.00
248 Rockies Team 1.50 4.00
249 Red Wings Team 1.50 4.00
250 Kings Team 1.50 4.00
251 North Stars Team 1.50 4.00
252 Canadiens Team 5.00 12.00
253 Islanders Team 2.00 5.00
254 Rangers Team 1.50 4.00
255 Flyers Team 1.50 4.00
256 Penguins Team 1.50 4.00
257 Blues Team 1.50 4.00
258 Maple Leafs Team 2.00 5.00
259 Canucks Team 2.00 5.00
260 Capitals Team 1.50 4.00
261 Nordiques Team 6.00 15.00
262 Jean Hamel .30 .75
263 Stan Jonathan .30 .75
264 Russ Anderson .30 .75
265 Gordie Roberts RC .40 1.00
266 Bill Flett .30 .75
267 Robbie Ftorek .40 1.00
268 Mike Amodeo .30 .75
269 Vic Venasky .30 .75
270 Bob Manno .30 .75
271 Dan Maloney .30 .75
272 Al Sims .30 .75
273 Greg Polis .30 .75
274 Doug Favell .60 1.50
275 Pierre Plante .30 .75
276 Bob Murdoch .30 .75
277 Lyle Moffat .30 .75
278 Jack Brownschidle .30 .75
279 Dave Keon .60 1.50
280 Darryl Edestrand .30 .75
281 Greg Millen RC 2.00 4.00
282 John Gould .30 .75
283 Rich Leduc .30 .75
284 Ron Delorme .30 .75
285 Gord Smith .30 .75
286 Nick Fotiu .40 1.00
287 Kevin McCarthy RC .40 1.00
288 Jimmy Jones .30 .75
289 Pierre Bouchard .30 .75
290 Wayne Bianchin .30 .75
291 Garry Lariviere .30 .75
292 Steve Jensen .30 .75
293 John Garrett .40 1.00
294 Hilliard Graves .30 .75
295 Bill Clement .40 1.00
296 Michel Larocque .60 1.50
297 Bob Stewart .30 .75
298 Doug Patey RC .30 .75
299 Dave Farrish .30 .75
300 Al Smith .40 1.00
301 Billy Lochead .30 .75
302 Dave Hutchinson .30 .75
303 Bill Riley .30 .75
304 Barry Gibbs .30 .75
305 Chris Oddleifson .30 .75
306 J. Bob Kelly UER .30 .75
307 Al Hangsleben RC .30 .75
308 Curt Brackenbury RC .30 .75
309 Rick Green .40 1.00
310 Ken Houston .30 .75
311 Greg Joly .30 .75
312 Bill Lesuk .30 .75
313 Bill Stewart RC .30 .75
314 Rick Ley .30 .75
315 Brett Callighen RC .30 .75
316 Michel Dion .40 1.00
317 Randy Manery .30 .75
318 Barry Dean .30 .75
319 Pat Boutette .30 .75
320 Mark Heaslip .30 .75
321 Dave Inkpen .30 .75
322 Jere Gillis .30 .75
323 Larry Brown .30 .75
324 Alain Cote RC .30 .75
325 Gordie Lane .30 .75
326 Bobby Lalonde .30 .75
327 Ed Staniowski .30 .75
328 Ron Plumb .30 .75
329 Jude Drouin .30 .75
330 Rick Hampton .30 .75
331 Stan Weir .30 .75
332 Blair Stewart .30 .75
333 Mike Polich RC .30 .75
334 Jean Potvin .30 .75
335 Jordy Douglas RC .30 .75
336 Joel Quenneville RC .40 1.00
337 Glen Hanlon RC 1.25 3.00
338 Dave Hoyda RC .30 .75
339 Colin Campbell .40 1.00
340 John Smrke .30 .75
341 Brian Glennie .30 .75
342 Don Kozak .30 .75
343 Yvon Labre .30 .75
344 Curt Bennett .30 .75
345 Mike Christie .30 .75
346 Checklist 265-396 20.00 40.00
347 Pat Price .30 .75
348 Ron Low .40 1.00
349 Mike Antonovich .30 .75
350 Roland Eriksson .30 .75
351 Bob Murdoch .30 .75
352 Rob Palmer .30 .75
353 Brad Gassoff .30 .75
354 Bruce Boudreau .30 .75
355 Al Hamilton .30 .75
356 Blaine Stoughton .40 1.00
357 John Baby .30 .75
358 Gary Inness .40 1.00
359 Wayne Dillon .30 .75
360 Darcy Rota .30 .75
361 Brian Engblom RC .60 1.50
362 Bill Hogaboam .30 .75
363 Dave Debol RC .30 .75
364 Pete Lopresti .40 1.00
365 Gerry Hart .30 .75
366 Syl Apps .30 .75
367 Jack McIlhargey .30 .75
368 Willy Lindstrom .30 .75
369 Don Laurence RC .30 .75
370 Chuck Luksa RC .30 .75
371 Dave Semenko RC 4.00 10.00
372 Paul Baxter RC .40 1.00
373 Ron Ellis .40 1.00
374 Leif Svensson RC .30 .75
375 Dennis O'Brien .30 .75
376 Glenn Goldup .30 .75
377 Terry Richardson .30 .75
378 Peter Sullivan .30 .75
379 Doug Hicks .30 .75
380 Jamie Hislop RC .30 .75
381 Jocelyn Guevremont .30 .75
382 Willi Plett .40 1.00
383 Larry Goodenough .30 .75
384 Jim Warner RC .30 .75
385 Rey Comeau .30 .75
386 Barry Melrose RC 5.00 10.00
387 Dave Hunter RC .60 1.50
388 Wally Weir RC .30 .75
389 Mario Lessard RC .60 1.50
390 Ed Kea .30 .75
391 Bob Stephenson RC .30 .75
392 Dennis Hextall .30 .75
393 Jerry Butler .30 .75
394 David Shand .30 .75
395 Rick Blight .30 .75
396 Lars-Erik Sjoberg 1.00 3.00

1980-81 O-Pee-Chee

Card fronts of this 396-card standard-size set contained the player's name and position (bilingual text) in a hockey puck on the lower right of the front. Unlike the Topps set of this year, the puck was not issued with a black scratch-off covering. The team name was listed to the left of the puck. The cards were originally sold in 10-card 20-cent wax packs. Bilingual backs featured a short list of career milestones, 1979-80 season and career statistics along with short trivia comments. Members of the U.S. Olympic hockey team (USA in checklist below) were honored with the USA hockey emblem on the card front. Beware when purchasing the cards of Ray Bourque and Mark Messier as they have been counterfeited.

COMPLETE SET (396) 150.00 300.00
1 Philadelphia Flyers RB .60 1.50
2 Ray Bourque RB 8.00 20.00
3 Wayne Gretzky RB 8.00 20.00
4 Charlie Simmer RB .60 1.50
5 Billy Smith RB .40 1.00
6 Jean Ratelle .40 1.00
7 Dave Maloney .30 .75
8 Phil Myre .40 1.00
9 Ken Morrow OLY RC 1.25 3.00
10 Guy Lafleur 1.25 3.00
11 Bill Derlago RC .30 .75
12 Doug Wilson .60 1.50
13 Craig Ramsay .25 .60
14 Pat Boutette .25 .60
15 Eric Vail .25 .60
16 Mike Foligno TL .75 2.00
17 Bobby Smith .75 2.00
18 Rick Kehoe .30 .75
19 Joel Quenneville .25 .60
20 Marcel Dionne .75 2.00
21 Kevin McCarthy .25 .60
22 Jim Craig OLY RC 4.00 10.00
23 Steve Vickers .25 .60
24 Ken Linseman .40 1.00
25 Mike Bossy 3.00 8.00
26 Serge Savard .50 1.25
27 Grant Mulvey TL .30 .75
28 Pat Hickey .25 .60
29 Peter Sullivan .25 .60
30 Blaine Stoughton .30 .75
31 Mike Liut RC 6.00 15.00
32 Blair MacDonald .25 .60
33 Rick Green .25 .60
34 Al MacAdam .30 .75
35 Robbie Ftorek .25 .60
36 Dick Redmond .25 .60
37 Ron Duguay .30 .75
38 Danny Gare TL .30 .75
39 Brian Propp RC 2.50 6.00
40 Bryan Trottier 1.00 2.50
41 Rich Preston .25 .60
42 Pierre Mondou .25 .60
43 Reed Larson .25 .60
44 George Ferguson .25 .60
45 Guy Chouinard .40 1.00
46 Billy Harris .25 .60
47 Gilles Meloche .40 1.00
48 Blair Chapman .25 .60
49 Mike Gartner TL 2.50 6.00
50 Darryl Sittler .50 1.25
51 Richard Martin .40 1.00
52 Ivan Boldirev .25 .60
53 Craig Norwich RC .25 .60
54 Dennis Polonich .25 .60
55 Bobby Clarke .60 1.50
56 Terry O'Reilly .40 1.00
57 Carol Vadnais .25 .60
58 Bob Gainey .50 1.25
59 Blaine Stoughton TL .30 .75
60 Billy Smith .40 1.00
61 Mike O'Connell RC .60 1.50
62 Lanny McDonald .50 1.25
63 Lee Fogolin .25 .60
64 Rocky Saganiuk RC .25 .60
65 Rolf Edberg RC .25 .60
66 Paul Shmyr .25 .60
67 Michel Goulet RC 5.00 12.00
68 Dan Bouchard .40 1.00
69 Mark Johnson OLY RC .50 1.25
70 Reggie Leach .30 .75
71 Bernie Federko TL .75 2.00
72 Peter Mahovlich .40 1.00
73 Anders Hedberg .40 1.00
74 Brad Park .30 .75
75 Clark Gillies .40 1.00
76 Doug Jarvis .25 .60
77 John Garrett .40 1.00
78 Dave Hutchinson .25 .60
79 John Anderson RC .50 1.25
80 Gilbert Perreault .40 1.00
81 Marcel Dionne AS1 .75 2.00
82 Guy Lafleur AS1 1.25 3.00
83 Charlie Simmer AS1 .60 1.50
84 Larry Robinson AS1 .50 1.25
85 Borje Salming AS1 .30 .75
86 Tony Esposito AS1 .60 1.50
87 Wayne Gretzky AS2 10.00 25.00
88 Danny Gare AS2 .30 .75
89 Steve Shutt AS2 .30 .75
90 Barry Beck AS2 .30 .75
91 Mark Howe AS2 .60 1.50
92 Don Edwards AS2 .30 .75
93 Tom McCarthy RC .25 .60
94 P.McNab/R.Middleton TL .40 1.00
95 Mike Palmateer .40 1.00
96 Jim Schoenfeld .40 1.00
97 Jordy Douglas .25 .60
98 Keith Brown RC .30 .75
99 Dennis Ververgaert .25 .60
100 Phil Esposito .60 1.50
101 Jack Brownschidle .25 .60
102 Bob Nystrom .25 .60
103 Steve Christoff OLY RC .40 1.00
104 Rob Palmer .25 .60
105 Tiger Williams .30 .75
106 Kent Nilsson TL .30 .75
107 Morris Lukowich .40 1.00
108 Jack Valiquette .25 .60
109 Richie Dunn RC .25 .60
110 Rogatien Vachon .50 1.25
111 Mark Napier .25 .60
112 Gordie Roberts .25 .60
113 Stan Jonathan .25 .60
114 Brett Callighen .25 .60
115 Rick MacLeish .40 1.00
116 Ulf Nilsson .40 1.00
117 Rick Kehoe TL .30 .75
118 Dan Maloney .25 .60
119 Terry Ruskowski .25 .60
120 Denis Potvin .50 1.25
121 Wayne Stephenson .40 1.00
122 Rich Leduc .25 .60
123 Checklist 1-132 3.00 8.00
124 Don Lever .25 .60
125 Jim Rutherford .40 1.00
126 Ray Allison RC .25 .60
127 Mike Ramsey OLY RC 1.25 3.00
128 Stan Smyl TL .60 1.50
129 Al Secord RC 3.00 8.00
130 Denis Herron .40 1.00
131 Bob Dailey .25 .60
132 Dean Talafous .25 .60
133 Ian Turnbull .25 .60
134 Ron Sedlbauer .25 .60
135 Tom Bladon .25 .60
136 Bernie Federko 1.50 4.00
137 Dave Taylor 1.50 4.00
138 Bob Lorimer .25 .60
139 A.MacAdam/S.Payne TL .30 .75
140 Ray Bourque RC 30.00 80.00
141 Glen Hanlon .40 1.00
142 Willy Lindstrom .25 .60
143 Mike Rogers .25 .60
144 Tony McKegney RC .30 .75
145 Behn Wilson .25 .60
146 Lucien DeBlois .25 .60
147 Dave Burrows .25 .60
148 Paul Woods .25 .60
149 Phil Esposito TL .60 1.50
150 Tony Esposito .60 1.50
151 Pierre Larouche .40 1.00
152 Brad Maxwell .25 .60
153 Stan Weir .25 .60
154 Ryan Walter .25 .60
155 Dale Hoganson .25 .60
156 Anders Kallur RC .25 .60
157 Paul Reinhart RC .75 2.00
158 Greg Millen .40 1.00
159 Ric Seiling .25 .60
160 Mark Howe .60 1.50
161 Goals Leaders .60 1.50
162 Gretzky/Dionne/Lafleur LL 8.00 20.00
163 Dionne/Gretzky/Lafleur LL 12.00 30.00
164 Penalty Minutes LL .40 1.00
165 Sim/Dnne/Gre/Shtt/Stlr LL .75 2.00
166 Goals Against Avg. LL .40 1.00
167 Game-Winning Goals LL .30 .75
168 Espo/Chvrs/Sve/Vach LL .60 1.50
169 Perry Turnbull RC .25 .60
170 Barry Beck .30 .75
171 Charlie Simmer TL .60 1.50
172 Paul Holmgren .40 1.00
173 Willie Huber .25 .60
174 Tim Young .25 .60
175 Gilles Gilbert .40 1.00
176 Dave Christian OLY RC 1.25 3.00
177 Lars Lindgren RC .25 .60
178 Real Cloutier .30 .75
179 Laurie Boschman RC .30 .75
180 Steve Shutt .30 .75
181 Bob Murray .25 .60
182 Wayne Gretzky TL 8.00 20.00
183 John Van Boxmeer .25 .60
184 Nick Fotiu .40 1.00
185 Mike McEwen .25 .60
186 Greg Malone .25 .60
187 Mike Foligno RC 2.00 5.00
188 Dave Langevin RC .25 .60
189 Mel Bridgman .25 .60
190 John Davidson .40 1.00
191 Mike Milbury .40 1.00
192 Ron Zanussi .25 .60
193 Darryl Sittler TL .50 1.25
194 John Marks .25 .60
195 Mike Gartner RC 12.00 30.00
196 Dave Lewis .25 .60
197 Kent Nilsson RC 2.50 6.00
198 Rick Ley .25 .60
199 Derek Smith .25 .60
200 Bill Barber .40 1.00
201 Guy Lapointe .40 1.00
202 Vaclav Nedomansky .25 .60
203 Don Murdoch .25 .60
204 Mike Bossy TL 1.25 3.00
205 Pierre Hamel RC .40 1.00
206 Mike Eaves RC .25 .60
207 Doug Halward .25 .60
208 Stan Smyl RC .60 1.50
209 Mike Zuke RC .25 .60
210 Borje Salming .30 .75
211 Walt Tkaczuk .40 1.00
212 Grant Mulvey .30 .75
213 Rob Ramage RC 3.00 8.00
214 Tom Rowe .25 .60
215 Don Edwards .30 .75
216 G.Lafleur/P.Larouche TL 1.00 3.00
217 Dan Labraaten .25 .60
218 Glen Sharpley .25 .60
219 Stefan Persson .25 .60
220 Peter McNab .30 .75
221 Doug Hicks .25 .60
222 Bengt Gustafsson RC .25 .60
223 Michel Dion .40 1.00
224 Jimmy Watson .25 .60
225 Wilf Paiement .25 .60
226 Phil Russell .25 .60
227 Morris Lukowich TL .40 1.00
228 Ron Stackhouse .25 .60
229 Ted Bulley .25 .60
230 Larry Robinson .50 1.25
231 Don Maloney .25 .60
232 Rob McClanahan OLY RC .30 .75
233 Al Sims .25 .60
234 Errol Thompson .25 .60
235 Glenn Resch .40 1.00
236 Bob Miller .25 .60
237 Gary Sargent .25 .60
238 Real Cloutier TL .30 .75
239 Rene Robert .50 1.25
240 Charlie Simmer .60 1.50
241 Thomas Gradin .25 .60
242 Rick Vaive RC 6.00 15.00
243 Ron Wilson RC .25 .60
244 Brian Sutter .75 2.00
245 Dale McCourt .25 .60
246 Yvon Lambert .25 .60
247 Tom Lysiak .25 .60
248 Ron Greschner .25 .60
249 Reggie Leach TL .30 .75
250 Wayne Gretzky 30.00 80.00
251 Rick Middleton .40 1.00
252 Al Smith .40 1.00
253 Fred Barrett .25 .60
254 Butch Goring .40 1.00
255 Robert Picard .25 .60
256 Marc Tardif .25 .60
257 Checklist 133-264 3.00 6.00
258 Barry Long .25 .60
259 Rene Robert TL .50 1.25
260 Danny Gare .30 .75
261 Rejean Houle .25 .60
262 Islanders/Sabres .30 .75
263 Flyers/North Stars .30 .75
264 Stanley Cup Finals .50 1.25
265 Bobby Lalonde .25 .60
266 Bob Sauve .40 1.00
267 Bob MacMillan .25 .60
268 Greg Fox .25 .60
269 Hardy Astrom RC .50 1.25
270 Greg Joly .25 .60
271 Dave Lumley RC .25 .60
272 Dave Keon .40 1.00
273 Garry Unger .40 1.00
274 Steve Payne .25 .60
275 Doug Risebrough .25 .60
276 Bob Bourne .25 .60
277 Ed Johnstone .25 .60
278 Peter Lee .25 .60
279 Pete Peeters RC 2.50 6.00
280 Ron Chipperfield .25 .60
281 Wayne Babych .40 1.00
282 David Shand .25 .60
283 Jere Gillis .25 .60
284 Dennis Maruk .40 1.00
285 Jude Drouin .25 .60
286 Mike Murphy .25 .60
287 Curt Fraser .25 .60
288 Gary McAdam .25 .60
289 Mark Messier UER RC 40.00 100.00
290 Vic Venasky .25 .60
291 Per-Olov Brasar .25 .60
292 Orest Kindrachuk .25 .60
293 Dave Hunter .25 .60
294 Steve Jensen .25 .60
295 Chris Oddleifson .25 .60
296 Larry Playfair RC .25 .60
297 Mario Tremblay .25 .60
298 Gilles Lupien RC .25 .60
299 Pat Price .25 .60
300 Jerry Korab .25 .60
301 Darcy Rota .25 .60
302 Don Luce .25 .60
303 Ken Houston .25 .60
304 Brian Engblom .25 .60
305 John Tonelli .75 2.00
306 Doug Sulliman RC .25 .60
307 Rod Schutt .25 .60
308 Norm Barnes RC .25 .60
309 Serge Bernier .25 .60
310 Larry Patey .25 .60
311 Dave Farrish .25 .60
312 Harold Snepsts .40 1.00
313 Bob Sirois .25 .60
314 Peter Marsh .25 .60
315 Risto Siltanen RC .25 .60
316 Andre St.Laurent .25 .60
317 Craig Hartsburg RC 2.50 6.00
318 Wayne Cashman .40 1.00
319 Lindy Ruff RC 2.50 6.00
320 Willi Plett .40 1.00
321 Ron Delorme .25 .60
322 Gaston Gingras RC .25 .60
323 Gordie Lane .25 .60
324 Doug Soetaert RC .40 1.00
325 Gregg Sheppard .25 .60
326 Mike Busniuk RC .25 .60
327 Jamie Hislop .25 .60
328 Ed Staniowski .25 .60
329 Ron Ellis .40 1.00
330 Gary Bromley UER .40 1.00
331 Mark Lofthouse RC .25 .60
332 Dave Hoyda .25 .60
333 Ron Low .25 .60
334 Barry Gibbs .25 .60
335 Gary Edwards 1.25 3.00
336 Don Marcotte .25 .60
337 Bill Hajt .25 .60
338 Brad Marsh RC 2.00 5.00
339 J.P. Bordeleau .25 .60
340 Randy Pierce .25 .60
341 Eddie Mio RC .50 1.25
342 Randy Manery .25 .60
343 Tom Younghans .25 .60
344 Rod Langway RC 3.00 8.00
345 Wayne Merrick .25 .60
346 Steve Baker RC .40 1.00
347 Pat Hughes .25 .60
348 Al Hill .25 .60
349 Gerry Hart .25 .60
350 Richard Mulhern .25 .60
351 Jerry Butler .25 .60
352 Guy Charron .25 .60
353 Jimmy Mann RC .40 1.00
354 Brad McCrimmon RC 2.00 5.00
355 Rick Dudley .25 .60
356 Pekka Rautakallio .25 .60
357 Tim Trimper RC .25 .60
358 Mike Christie .25 .60
359 John Ogrodnick RC 2.00 5.00
360 Dave Semenko 1.50 4.00
361 Mike Veisor .40 1.00
362 Syl Apps .25 .60
363 Mike Polich .25 .60
364 Rick Chartraw .25 .60
365 Steve Tambellini RC .40 1.00
366 Ed Hospodar RC .25 .60
367 Randy Carlyle .40 1.00
368 Tom Gorence .25 .60
369 Pierre Plante .25 .60
370 Blake Dunlop .25 .60
371 Mike Kaszycki .25 .60
372 Rick Blight .25 .60
373 Pierre Bouchard .25 .60
374 Gary Doak .25 .60
375 Andre Savard .25 .60
376 Bill Clement .40 1.00
377 Reg Kerr .25 .60
378 Walt McKechnie .25 .60
379 George Lyle RC .25 .60
380 Colin Campbell .25 .60
381 Dave Debol .25 .60
382 Glenn Goldup .25 .60
383 Kent-Erik Andersson .25 .60
384 Tony Currie RC .25 .60
385 Richard Sevigny RC 3.00 8.00
386 Garry Howatt .25 .60
387 Cam Connor .25 .60
388 Ross Lonsberry .25 .60
389 Frank Bathe RC .25 .60
390 John Wensink .25 .60
391 Paul Harrison .40 1.00
392 Dennis Kearns .25 .60
393 Pat Ribble .25 .60
394 Markus Mattsson RC .40 1.00
395 Chuck Lefley .25 .60
396 Checklist 265-396 4.00 10.00

1980-81 O-Pee-Chee Super

These large (approximately 5" by 7") full-color photos were numbered on the back. They were made of thicker cardboard stock and issued as a separate release rather than as an insert. A mail-in offer card was issued in late print run packs of 1981-82 O-Pee-Chee that could be exchanged for one of the cards.

COMPLETE SET (24) 20.00 40.00
1 Brad Park 1.00 2.50
2 Gilbert Perreault .60 1.50
3 Kent Nilsson .40 1.00
4 Tony Esposito .75 2.00
5 Lanny McDonald .60 1.50
6 Pete Mahovlich .30 .75
7 Wayne Gretzky 10.00 20.00
8 Marcel Dionne 1.00 2.50
9 Bob Gainey 1.25 3.00
10 Guy Lafleur 2.50 6.00
11 Larry Robinson .75 2.00
12 Mike Bossy 3.00 6.00
13 Denis Potvin .60 1.50
14 Phil Esposito 1.25 3.00
15 Anders Hedberg .30 .75
16 Bobby Clarke 1.25 3.00
17 Marc Tardif .20 .50
18 Bernie Federko .60 1.50
19 Borje Salming .40 1.00
20 Darryl Sittler .75 2.00
21 Ian Turnbull .20 .50
22 Glen Hanlon .25 .60
23 Mike Palmateer .60 1.50
24 Morris Lukowich .20 .50

1981-82 O-Pee-Chee

The 396 standard-size cards in this set featured the player's name, position and team logo along the front bottom border. The team name appeared in bold letters across the lower portion of the photo. Bilingual backs featured yearly and career statistics and biographical data. Super Action (SA) cards were designated in the list below. The set was essentially numbered in team order with the team leader (TL) card typically portrayed the team's leading scorer. However, team names were updated to reflect off-season trades. Beware when purchasing the Rookie Card of Paul Coffey as it has been counterfeited. Finally, a mail-in offer card was issued in late print run packs that could be exchanged, for a fee, for a single card from the 1980-81 O-Pee-Chee super set.

COMPLETE SET (396) 125.00 250.00
1 Ray Bourque 12.00 30.00
2 Rick Middleton .25 .60
3 Dwight Foster .25 .60
4 Steve Kasper RC .75 2.00
5 Peter McNab .25 .60
6 Mike O'Connell .30 .75
7 Terry O'Reilly .30 .75
8 Brad Park .30 .75
9 Dick Redmond .25 .60
10 Rogatien Vachon .40 1.00
11 Wayne Cashman .30 .75
12 Mike Gillis RC .30 .75
13 Stan Jonathan .25 .60
14 Don Marcotte .25 .60
15 Brad McCrimmon .30 .75
16 Mike Milbury .30 .75
17 Ray Bourque SA 3.00 8.00
18 Rick Middleton SA .25 .60
19 Rick Middleton TL .25 .60
20 Danny Gare .25 .60
21 Don Edwards .25 .60
22 Tony McKegney .25 .60
23 Bob Sauve .30 .75
24 Andre Savard .25 .60
25 Derek Smith .25 .60
26 John Van Boxmeer .25 .60
27 Danny Gare SA .25 .60
28 Danny Gare TL .25 .60
29 Richie Dunn .25 .60
30 Gilbert Perreault .40 1.00
31 Craig Ramsay .25 .60
32 Ric Seiling .25 .60
33 Guy Chouinard .30 .75
34 Kent Nilsson .25 .60
35 Willi Plett .25 .60
36 Paul Reinhart .25 .60
37 Pat Riggin RC .50 1.25
38 Eric Vail .25 .60
39 Bill Clement .30 .75
40 Jamie Hislop .25 .60
41 Randy Holt .25 .60
42 Dan Labraaten .25 .60
43 Kevin Lavallee RC .25 .60
44 Rejean Lemelin RC 2.50 6.00
45 Don Lever .25 .60
46 Bob MacMillan .25 .60
47 Brad Marsh .30 .75
48 Bob Murdoch .25 .60
49 Jim Peplinski RC 1.25 3.00
50 Pekka Rautakallio .25 .60
51 Phil Russell .25 .60
52 Kent Nilsson SA .25 .60
53 Kent Nilsson TL .25 .60
54 Tony Esposito .30 .75
55 Keith Brown .25 .60
56 Ted Bulley .25 .60
57 Tim Higgins RC .25 .60
58 Reg Kerr .25 .60
59 Tom Lysiak .25 .60
60 Grant Mulvey .25 .60
61 Bob Murray .25 .60
62 Terry Ruskowski .25 .60
63 Denis Savard RC 10.00 25.00
64 Glen Sharpley .25 .60
65 Darryl Sutter RC 1.00 2.50
66 Doug Wilson .30 .75

67 Tony Esposito SA .30 .75
68 Murray Bannerman RC .50 1.25
69 Greg Fox .25 .60
70 John Marks .25 .60
71 Peter Marsh .25 .60
72 Al Secord .30 .75
73 Tom Lysia TL .25 .60
74 Lucien DeBlois .25 .60
75 Paul Gagne RC .25 .60
76 Merlin Malinowski RC .25 .60
77 Lanny McDonald .25 .60
78 Joel Quenneville .25 .60
79 Rob Ramage .30 .75
80 Glenn Resch .30 .75
81 Steve Tambellini .25 .60
82 Ron Delorme .25 .60
83 Mike Kitchen .25 .60
84 Yvon Vautour RC .25 .60
85 Lanny McDonald TL .25 .60
86 Dale McCourt .25 .60
87 Mike Foligno .30 .75
88 Gilles Gilbert .30 .75
89 Willie Huber .25 .60
90 Mark Kirton RC .25 .60
91 Jim Korn RC .25 .60
92 Reed Larson .25 .60
93 Gary McAdam .25 .60
94 Vaclav Nedomansky .25 .60
95 John Ogrodnick .25 .60
96 Dale McCourt SA .25 .60
97 Jean Hamel .25 .60
98 Glen Hicks RC .25 .60
99 Larry Lozinski RC .30 .75
100 George Lyle .25 .60
101 Perry Miller .25 .60
102 Brad Maxwell .25 .60
103 Brad Smith RC .30 .75
104 Paul Woods .25 .60
105 Dale McCourt TL .25 .60
106 Wayne Gretzky 15.00 40.00
107 Jari Kurri RC 15.00 40.00
108 Glenn Anderson RC 8.00 20.00
109 Curt Brackenbury .25 .60
110 Brett Callighen .25 .60
111 Paul Coffey RC 20.00 50.00
112 Lee Fogolin .25 .60
113 Matti Hagman RC .25 .60
114 Doug Hicks .25 .60
115 Dave Hunter .25 .60
116 Garry Lariviere .25 .60
117 Kevin Lowe RC 5.00 12.00
118 Mark Messier 10.00 25.00
119 Eddie Mio .30 .75
120 Andy Moog RC 10.00 25.00
121 Dave Semenko .30 .75
122 Risto Siltanen .25 .60
123 Garry Unger .30 .75
124 Stan Weir .25 .60
125 Wayne Gretzky SA 10.00 25.00
126 Wayne Gretzky TL 5.00 12.00
127 Mike Rogers .25 .60
128 Mark Howe .40 1.00
129 Dave Keon .40 1.00
130 Warren Miller RC .25 .60
131 Al Sims .25 .60
132 Blaine Stoughton .30 .75
133 Rick MacLeish .30 .75
134 Greg Millen .30 .75
135 Mike Rogers SA .25 .60
136 Mike Fidler .25 .60
137 John Garrett .25 .60
138 Don Nachbaur RC .25 .60
139 Tom Rowe .25 .60
140 Mike Rogers TL .25 .60
141 Marcel Dionne .50 1.25
142 Charlie Simmer .30 .75
143 Dave Taylor .60 1.50
144 Billy Harris .25 .60
145 Jerry Korab .25 .60
146 Mario Lessard .30 .75
147 Don Luce .25 .60
148 Larry Murphy RC 8.00 20.00
149 Mike Murphy .25 .60
150 Marcel Dionne SA .50 1.25
151 Charlie Simmer SA .30 .75
152 Dave Taylor SA .30 .75
153 Jim Fox RC .30 .75
154 Steve Jensen .25 .60
155 Greg Terrion RC .25 .60
156 Marcel Dionne TL .50 1.25
157 Bobby Smith .25 .60
158 Kent-Erik Andersson .25 .60
159 Don Beaupre RC 2.00 5.00
160 Steve Christoff .25 .60
161 Dino Ciccarelli RC 8.00 20.00
162 Craig Hartsburg .25 .60
163 Al MacAdam .25 .60
164 Tom McCarthy .25 .60
165 Gilles Meloche .30 .75
166 Steve Payne .25 .60
167 Gordie Roberts .25 .60
168 Greg Smith .25 .60
169 Tim Young .25 .60
170 Bobby Smith SA .25 .60
171 Mike Eaves .25 .60
172 Mike Polich .25 .60
173 Tom Younghans .25 .60
174 Bobby Smith TL .25 .60
175 Brian Engblom .25 .60
176 Bob Gainey .30 .75
177 Guy Lafleur 1.00 2.50
178 Mark Napier .25 .60
179 Larry Robinson .40 1.00
180 Steve Shutt .25 .60
181 Keith Acton RC .50 1.25
182 Gaston Gingras .25 .60
183 Rejean Houle .25 .60
184 Doug Jarvis .25 .60
185 Yvon Lambert .25 .60
186 Rod Langway .60 1.50
187 Pierre Larouche .30 .75
188 Pierre Mondou .25 .60
189 Robert Picard .25 .60
190 Doug Risebrough .25 .60
191 Richard Sevigny .25 .60
192 Mario Tremblay .25 .60
193 Doug Wickenheiser RC .60 1.50
194 Bob Gainey SA .30 .75
195 Guy Lafleur SA 1.25 3.00
196 Larry Robinson SA .40 1.00
197 Steve Shutt TL .25 .60
198 Mike Bossy 1.50 4.00
199 Denis Potvin .50 1.25
200 Bryan Trottier .60 1.50
201 Bob Bourne .25 .60
202 Clark Gillies .40 1.00
203 Butch Goring .30 .75
204 Anders Kallur .25 .60
205 Ken Morrow .30 .75
206 Stefan Persson .25 .60
207 Billy Smith .40 1.00
208 Mike Bossy SA .60 1.50
209 Denis Potvin SA .50 1.25
210 Bryan Trottier SA .50 1.25
211 Duane Sutter RC .60 1.50
212 Gordie Lane .25 .60
213 Dave Langevin .25 .60
214 Bob Lorimer .25 .60
215 Mike McEwen .25 .60
216 Wayne Merrick .25 .60
217 Bob Nystrom .25 .60
218 John Tonelli .40 1.00
219 Mike Bossy TL 1.25 3.00
220 Barry Beck .40 1.00
221 Mike Allison RC .25 .60
222 John Davidson .40 1.00
223 Ron Duguay .30 .75
224 Ron Greschner .25 .60
225 Anders Hedberg .25 .60
226 Ed Johnstone .25 .60
227 Dave Maloney .25 .60
228 Don Maloney .25 .60
229 Ulf Nilsson .40 1.00
230 Barry Beck SA .40 1.00
231 Steve Baker .40 1.00
232 Jere Gillis .25 .60
233 Ed Hospodar .25 .60
234 Tom Laidlaw RC .40 1.00
235 Dean Talafous .25 .60
236 Carol Vadnais .25 .60
237 Anders Hedberg TL .25 .60
238 Bill Barber .25 .60
239 Behn Wilson .25 .60
240 Bobby Clarke .40 1.00
241 Bob Dailey .25 .60
242 Paul Holmgren .40 1.00
243 Reggie Leach .40 1.00
244 Ken Linseman .40 1.00
245 Pete Peeters .60 1.50
246 Brian Propp .75 2.00
247 Bill Barber SA .25 .60
248 Mel Bridgman .25 .60
249 Mike Busniuk .25 .60
250 Tom Gorence .25 .60
251 Tim Kerr RC 2.50 6.00
252 Rick St.Croix RC .40 1.00
253 Bill Barber TL .25 .60
254 Rick Kehoe .25 .60
255 Pat Boutette .25 .60
256 Randy Carlyle .40 1.00
257 Paul Gardner .25 .60
258 Peter Lee .25 .60
259 Rod Schutt .25 .60
260 Rick Kehoe SA .25 .60
261 Mario Faubert .25 .60
262 George Ferguson .25 .60
263 Ross Lonsberry .25 .60
264 Greg Malone .25 .60
265 Pat Price .25 .60
266 Ron Stackhouse .25 .60
267 Rick Kehoe TL .25 .60
268 Jacques Richard .25 .60
269 Peter Stastny RC 8.00 20.00
270 Dan Bouchard .40 1.00
271 Kim Clackson RC .40 1.00
272 Alain Cote .25 .60
273 Andre Dupont .25 .60
274 Robbie Ftorek .25 .60
275 Michel Goulet 1.25 3.00
276 Dale Hoganson .25 .60
277 Dale Hunter RC 4.00 10.00
278 Pierre Lacroix .25 .60
279 Mario Marois RC .25 .60
280 Dave Pichette RC .25 .60
281 Michel Plasse .40 1.00
282 Anton Stastny RC .50 1.25
283 Marc Tardif .25 .60
284 Wally Weir .25 .60
285 Jacques Richard SA .25 .60
286 Peter Stastny SA 2.00 5.00
287 Peter Stastny TL 1.25 3.00
288 Bernie Federko .60 1.50
289 Mike Liut .60 1.50
290 Wayne Babych .25 .60
291 Blair Chapman .25 .60
292 Tony Currie .25 .60
293 Blake Dunlop .25 .60
294 Ed Kea .25 .60
295 Rick Lapointe .25 .60
296 Jorgen Pettersson RC .25 .60
297 Brian Sutter .40 1.00
298 Perry Turnbull .25 .60
299 Mike Zuke .25 .60
300 Bernie Federko SA .25 .60
301 Mike Liut SA .40 1.00
302 Jack Brownschidle .25 .60
303 Larry Patey .25 .60
304 Bernie Federko TL .25 .60
305 Bill Derlago .25 .60
306 Wilf Paiement .25 .60
307 Borje Salming .40 1.00
308 Darryl Sittler .40 1.00
309 Ian Turnbull .25 .60
310 Rick Vaive .40 1.00
311 Wilf Paiement SA .25 .60
312 Darryl Sittler SA .40 1.00
313 John Anderson .25 .60
314 Laurie Boschman .40 1.00
315 Jiri Crha RC .50 1.25
316 Vitezslav Duris RC .25 .60
317 Dave Farrish .25 .60
318 Pat Hickey .25 .60
319 Michel Larocque .40 1.00
320 Dan Maloney .25 .60
321 Terry Martin .25 .60
322 Rene Robert .40 1.00
323 Rocky Saganiuk .25 .60
324 Ron Sedlbauer .25 .60
325 Ron Zanussi .25 .60
326 Wilf Paiement TL .25 .60
327 Thomas Gradin .25 .60
328 Stan Smyl .40 1.00
329 Ivan Boldirev .25 .60
330 Per-Olov Brasar UER .25 .60
(Brent Ashton pictured)
331 Richard Brodeur .40 1.00
332 Jerry Butler .25 .60
333 Colin Campbell .25 .60
334 Curt Fraser .25 .60
335 Doug Halward .25 .60
336 Glen Hanlon .40 1.00
337 Dennis Kearns .25 .60
338 Rick Lanz RC UER .25 .60
339 Pat Ribble .25 .60
340 Blair MacDonald .25 .60
341 Kevin McCarthy .25 .60
342 Gerry Minor RC .25 .60
343 Darcy Rota .25 .60
344 Harold Snepsts .25 .60
345 Tiger Williams .25 .60
346 Thomas Gradin TL .25 .60
347 Mike Gartner 5.00 12.00
348 Rick Green .25 .60
349 Bob Kelly .25 .60
350 Dennis Maruk .25 .60
351 Mike Palmateer .25 .60
352 Ryan Walter .25 .60
353 Bengt Gustafsson .25 .60
354 Al Hangsleben .25 .60
355 Jean Pronovost .40 1.00
356 Dennis Ververgaert .25 .60
357 Dennis Maruk TL .25 .60
358 Dave Babych RC .60 1.50
359 Dave Christian .25 .60
360 Dave Christian SA .25 .60
361 Rick Bowness .40 1.00
362 Rick Dudley .25 .60
363 Norm Dupont RC .25 .60
364 Dan Geoffrion RC .25 .60
365 Pierre Hamel .30 .75
366 Dave Hoyda UER .25 .60
(Photo actually
Doug Lecuyer)
367 Doug Lecuyer RC .25 .60
368 Willy Lindstrom .25 .60
369 Barry Long .25 .60
370 Morris Lukowich .25 .60
371 Kris Manery .25 .60
372 Jimmy Mann .30 .75
373 Moe Mantha RC .30 .75
374 Markus Mattsson .30 .75
375 Don Spring RC .25 .60
376 Tim Trimper .25 .60
377 Ron Wilson .25 .60
378 Dave Christian TL .25 .60
379 Checklist 1-132 3.00 8.00
380 Checklist 133-264 3.00 8.00
381 Checklist 265-396 3.00 8.00
382 Mike Bossy LL 1.25 3.00
383 Wayne Gretzky LL 4.00 10.00
384 Wayne Gretzky LL 4.00 10.00
385 Tiger Williams LL .25 .60
386 Mike Bossy LL 1.25 3.00
387 Richard Sevigny LL .25 .60
388 Mike Bossy LL 1.25 3.00
389 Don Edward .30 .75
Glenn Resch LL
390 Mike Bossy RB 1.25 3.00
391 Dionne/Sims/Taylor RB 1.00 2.50
392 Wayne Gretzky RB 4.00 10.00
393 Larry Murphy RB 1.25 3.00
394 Mike Palmateer RB .25 .60
395 Peter Stastny RB 1.25 3.00
396 Bob Manno .30 .75

1982-83 O-Pee-Chee

Because Topps did not issue a set for a two-year period, this 396-card set marks the first time since the pre-war era that O-Pee-Chee manufactured hockey cards without competition. Card fronts displayed the player's name, team and position at the top. The backs had yearly statistics, highlights and a section devoted to team records. A team logo appeared at the bottom. Highlight cards, team scoring leaders cards, league leaders cards and In-Action cards were contained within the set. The cards were essentially in team order. However, text on front was updated to reflect off-season trades.

COMPLETE SET (396) 60.00 120.00
1 Wayne Gretzky HL 4.00 10.00
2 Mike Bossy HL .75 2.00
3 Dale Hawerchuk HL 2.00 5.00
4 Mikko Leinonen HL .20 .50
5 Bryan Trottier HL .40 1.00
6 Rick Middleton .30 .75
7 Ray Bourque 5.00 12.00
8 Wayne Cashman .30 .75
9 Bruce Crowder RC .20 .50
10 Keith Crowder RC .20 .50
11 Tom Fergus RC .30 .75
12 Steve Kasper .20 .50
13 Normand Leveille RC .60 1.50
14 Don Marcotte .20 .50
15 Rick Middleton .30 .75
16 Peter McNab .20 .50
17 Mike O'Connell .20 .50
18 Terry O'Reilly .30 .75
19 Brad Park .30 .75
20 Barry Pederson RC .60 1.50
21 Brad Palmer RC .20 .50
22 Pete Peeters .40 1.00
23 Rogatien Vachon .40 1.00
24 Ray Bourque IA 2.00 5.00
25 Gilbert Perreault TL .40 1.00
26 Mike Foligno .30 .75
27 Yvon Lambert .20 .50
28 Dale McCourt .20 .50
29 Tony McKegney .20 .50
30 Gilbert Perreault .40 1.00
31 Lindy Ruff .20 .50
32 Mike Ramsey .20 .50
33 J.F. Sauve RC .20 .50
34 Bob Sauve .30 .75
35 Ric Seiling .20 .50
36 John Van Boxmeer .20 .50
37 John Van Boxmeer IA .20 .50
38 Lanny McDonald .30 .75
39 Mel Bridgman .20 .50
40 Mel Bridgman IA .20 .50
41 Guy Chouinard .20 .50
42 Steve Christoff .20 .50
43 Denis Cyr RC .20 .50
44 Bill Clement .30 .75
45 Richie Dunn .20 .50
46 Don Edwards .20 .50
47 Jamie Hislop .20 .50
48 Steve Konroyd RC .30 .75
49 Kevin Lavallee .20 .50
50 Rejean Lemelin .40 1.00
51 Lanny McDonald .30 .75
52 Lanny McDonald IA .30 .75
53 Bob Murdoch .20 .50
54 Kent Nilsson .30 .75
55 Jim Peplinski .20 .50
56 Paul Reinhart .20 .50
57 Doug Risebrough .20 .50
58 Phil Russell .20 .50
59 Howard Walker RC .20 .50
60 Al Secord .30 .75
61 Murray Bannerman .30 .75
62 Keith Brown .20 .50
63 Doug Crossman RC .40 1.00
64 Tony Esposito .40 1.00
65 Greg Fox .20 .50
66 Tim Higgins .20 .50
67 Reg Kerr .20 .50
68 Tom Lysiak .20 .50
69 Grant Mulvey .20 .50
70 Bob Murray .20 .50
71 Rich Preston .20 .50
72 Terry Ruskowski .20 .50
73 Denis Savard 1.50 4.00
74 Al Secord .30 .75
75 Glen Sharpley .20 .50
76 Darryl Sutter .30 .75
77 Doug Wilson .30 .75
78 Doug Wilson IA .30 .75
79 John Ogrodnick .20 .50
80 John Barrett RC .20 .50
81 Mike Blaisdell RC .20 .50
82 Colin Campbell .20 .50
83 Danny Gare .30 .75
84 Gilles Gilbert .30 .75
85 Willie Huber .20 .50
86 Greg Joly .20 .50
87 Mark Kirton .20 .50
88 Reed Larson .20 .50
89 Reed Larson IA .20 .50
90 Reggie Leach .30 .75
91 Walt McKechnie .20 .50
92 John Ogrodnick .20 .50
93 Mark Osborne RC .30 .75
94 Jim Schoenfeld .30 .75
95 Derek Smith .20 .50
96 Greg Smith .20 .50
97 Eric Vail .20 .50
98 Paul Woods .20 .50
99 Wayne Gretzky TL 3.00 8.00
100 Glenn Anderson 1.00 2.50
101 Paul Coffey 3.00 8.00
102 Paul Coffey IA 2.50 6.00
103 Brett Callighen .20 .50
104 Lee Fogolin .20 .50
105 Grant Fuhr RC 15.00 40.00
106 Wayne Gretzky 12.00 30.00
107 Wayne Gretzky IA 5.00 12.00
108 Matti Hagman .20 .50
109 Pat Hughes .20 .50
110 Dave Hunter .20 .50
111 Jari Kurri 3.00 8.00
112 Ron Low .20 .50
113 Kevin Lowe UER .60 1.50
114 Dave Lumley .20 .50
115 Ken Linseman .30 .75
116 Garry Lariviere .20 .50
117 Mark Messier 3.00 8.00
118 Tom Roulston RC .20 .50
119 Dave Semenko .30 .75
120 Garry Unger .30 .75
121 Checklist 1-132 1.00 2.50
122 Blaine Stoughton .30 .75
123 Ron Francis RC 10.00 25.00
124 Chris Kotsopoulos RC .20 .50
125 Pierre Larouche .30 .75
126 Greg Millen .30 .75
127 Warren Miller .20 .50
128 Merlin Malinowski .20 .50
129 Risto Siltanen .20 .50
130 Blaine Stoughton .30 .75
131 Blaine Stoughton IA .30 .75
132 Doug Sulliman .20 .50
133 Blake Wesley RC .20 .50
134 Steve Tambellini .20 .50
135 Brent Ashton RC .30 .75
136 Aaron Broten RC .20 .50
137 Joe Cirella RC .30 .75
138 Dwight Foster .20 .50
139 Paul Gagne .20 .50
140 Garry Howatt .20 .50
141 Don Lever .20 .50
142 Bob Lorimer .20 .50
143 Bob MacMillan .20 .50
144 Rick Meagher RC .30 .75
145 Glenn Resch .30 .75
146 Glenn Resch IA .30 .75
147 Steve Tambellini .20 .50
148 Carol Vadnais .20 .50
149 Marcel Dionne TL .40 1.00
150 Dan Bonar RC .20 .50
151 Steve Bozek RC .30 .75
152 Marcel Dionne .40 1.00
153 Marcel Dionne IA .40 1.00
154 Jim Fox .20 .50
155 Mark Hardy RC .30 .75
156 Mario Lessard .20 .50
157 Dave Lewis .20 .50
158 Larry Murphy 1.25 3.00
159 Charlie Simmer .40 1.00
160 Doug Smith RC .20 .50
161 Dave Taylor .30 .75
162 Dino Ciccarelli TL .40 1.00
163 Don Beaupre .40 1.00
164 Neal Broten RC 4.00 10.00
165 Dino Ciccarelli 1.25 3.00
166 Curt Giles RC .60 1.50
167 Craig Hartsburg .20 .50
168 Brad Maxwell .20 .50
169 Tom McCarthy .20 .50
170 Gilles Meloche .30 .75
171 Al MacAdam .20 .50
172 Steve Payne .20 .50
173 Willi Plett .20 .50
174 Gordie Roberts .20 .50
175 Bobby Smith .30 .75
176 Bobby Smith IA .30 .75
177 Tim Young .20 .50
178 Mark Napier .20 .50
179 Keith Acton .20 .50
180 Keith Acton IA .20 .50
181 Bob Gainey .40 1.00
182 Gaston Gingras .20 .50
183 Rick Green .20 .50
184 Rejean Houle .20 .50
185 Mark Hunter RC .30 .75
186 Guy Lafleur .40 1.00
187 Guy Lafleur IA .40 1.00
188 Pierre Mondou .20 .50
189 Mark Napier .20 .50
190 Robert Picard .20 .50
191 Larry Robinson .40 1.00
192 Steve Shutt .20 .50
193 Mario Tremblay .20 .50
194 Ryan Walter .20 .50
195 Rick Wamsley RC .60 1.50
196 Doug Wickenheiser .20 .50
197 Mike Bossy TL .75 2.00
198 Bob Bourne .20 .50
199 Mike Bossy .75 2.00
200 Butch Goring .30 .75
201 Clark Gillies .40 1.00
202 Tomas Jonsson RC .20 .50
203 Anders Kallur .20 .50
204 Dave Langevin .20 .50
205 Wayne Merrick .20 .50
206 Ken Morrow .30 .75
207 Mike McEwen .20 .50
208 Bob Nystrom .20 .50
209 Stefan Persson .20 .50
210 Denis Potvin .40 1.00
211 Billy Smith .40 1.00
212 Duane Sutter .20 .50
213 John Tonelli .40 1.00
214 Bryan Trottier .40 1.00
215 Bryan Trottier IA .40 1.00
216 Brent Sutter RC .60 1.50
217 Ron Duguay .30 .75
218 Kent-Erik Andersson .20 .50
219 Barry Beck .20 .50
220 Barry Beck IA .20 .50
221 Ron Duguay .30 .75
222 Nick Fotiu .30 .75
223 Robbie Ftorek .20 .50
224 Ron Greschner .20 .50
225 Anders Hedberg .30 .75
226 Ed Johnstone .20 .50
227 Tom Laidlaw .20 .50
228 Dave Maloney .20 .50
229 Don Maloney .20 .50
230 Eddie Mio .30 .75
231 Mark Pavelich RC .40 1.00
232 Mike Rogers .30 .75
233 Reijo Ruotsalainen RC .40 1.00
234 Steve Weeks RC .40 1.00
235 Wayne Gretzky LL 3.00 8.00
236 Paul Gardner LL .20 .50
237 W.Gretzky/M.Goulet LL 2.50 6.00
238 Paul Baxter LL .20 .50
239 Denis Herron LL .30 .75
240 Wayne Gretzky LL 3.00 8.00
241 Denis Herron LL .30 .75
242 Wayne Gretzky LL 3.00 8.00
243 Wayne Gretzky LL 3.00 8.00
244 Bill Barber TL .30 .75
245 Fred Arthur RC .20 .50
246 Bill Barber .30 .75
247 Bill Barber IA .30 .75
248 Bobby Clarke .40 1.00
249 Ron Flockhart RC .30 .75
250 Tom Gorence .20 .50
251 Paul Holmgren .30 .75
252 Mark Howe .40 1.00
253 Tim Kerr .60 1.50
254 Brad Marsh .20 .50
255 Brad McCrimmon .30 .75
256 Brian Propp .60 1.50
257 Darryl Sittler .40 1.00
258 Rick St.Croix .20 .50
259 Jimmy Watson .20 .50
260 Behn Wilson .20 .50
261 Checklist 133-264 1.00 2.50
262 Mike Bullard .40 1.00
263 Pat Boutette .20 .50
264 Mike Bullard RC .40 1.00
265 Randy Carlyle .20 .50
266 Randy Carlyle IA .20 .50
267 Michel Dion .30 .75
268 George Ferguson .20 .50
269 Paul Gardner .20 .50
270 Denis Herron .30 .75
271 Rick Kehoe .30 .75
272 Greg Malone .20 .50
273 Rick MacLeish .30 .75
274 Pat Price .20 .50
275 Ron Stackhouse .20 .50
276 Peter Stastny TL 1.00 3.00
277 Pierre Aubry RC .20 .50
278 Dan Bouchard .30 .75
279 Real Cloutier .20 .50
280 Real Cloutier IA .20 .50
281 Alain Cote .20 .50
282 Andre Dupont .20 .50
283 John Garrett .20 .50
284 Michel Goulet .75 2.00
285 Dale Hunter .75 2.00
286 Pierre Lacroix .20 .50
287 Mario Marois .20 .50
288 Wilf Paiement .20 .50
289 Dave Pichette .20 .50
290 Jacques Richard .20 .50
291 Normand Rochefort RC .20 .50
292 Peter Stastny 1.00 3.00
293 Peter Stastny IA 1.00 3.00
294 Anton Stastny .30 .75
295 Marian Stastny RC .30 .75
296 Marc Tardif .20 .50
297 Wally Weir .20 .50
298 Brian Sutter .30 .75
299 Wayne Babych .20 .50
300 Jack Brownschidle .20 .50
301 Blake Dunlop .20 .50
302 Bernie Federko .30 .75
303 Bernie Federko IA .30 .75
304 Pat Hickey .20 .50
305 Guy Lapointe .30 .75
306 Mike Liut .40 1.00
307 Joe Mullen RC 4.00 10.00
308 Larry Patey .20 .50
309 Jorgen Pettersson .20 .50
310 Rob Ramage .20 .50
311 Brian Sutter .30 .75
312 Perry Turnbull .20 .50
313 Mike Zuke .20 .50
314 Rick Vaive .20 .50
315 John Anderson .20 .50
316 Normand Aubin RC .20 .50
317 Jim Benning RC .20 .50
318 Fred Boimistruck RC .20 .50
319 Bill Derlago .20 .50
320 Bill Derlago IA .20 .50
321 Miroslav Frycer RC .20 .50
322 Billy Harris .20 .50
323 Jim Korn .20 .50
324 Michel Larocque .30 .75
325 Bob Manno .20 .50
326 Dan Maloney .20 .50
327 Bob McGill RC .30 .75
328 Barry Melrose .30 .75
329 Terry Martin .20 .50
330 Rene Robert .30 .75
331 Rocky Saganiuk .20 .50
332 Borje Salming .30 .75
333 Greg Terrion .20 .50
334 Vincent Tremblay RC .20 .50
335 Rick Vaive .20 .50
336 Rick Vaive IA .20 .50
337 Thomas Gradin .20 .50
338 Ivan Boldirev .20 .50
339 Richard Brodeur .30 .75
340 Richard Brodeur IA .30 .75
341 Tony Currie .20 .50
342 Marc Crawford RC .75 2.00
343 Curt Fraser .20 .50
344 Thomas Gradin .20 .50
345 Thomas Gradin IA .20 .50
346 Ivan Hlinka UER RC .30 .75
347 Ron Delorme .20 .50
348 Rick Lanz .20 .50
349 Lars Lindgren .20 .50
350 Blair MacDonald .20 .50
351 Kevin McCarthy .20 .50
352 Gerry Minor .20 .50
353 Lars Molin RC .20 .50
354 Gary Lupul RC .20 .50
355 Darcy Rota .20 .50
356 Stan Smyl .20 .50
357 Harold Snepsts .20 .50
358 Tiger Williams .30 .75
359 Dennis Maruk .30 .75
360 Ted Bulley .20 .50
361 Bobby Carpenter RC .60 1.50
362 Brian Engblom .20 .50
363 Mike Gartner 2.00 5.00
364 Bengt Gustafsson .20 .50
365 Doug Hicks .20 .50
366 Ken Houston .20 .50
367 Doug Jarvis .20 .50
368 Rod Langway .40 1.00
369 Dennis Maruk .30 .75
370 Dennis Maruk IA .30 .75
371 Dave Parro RC .30 .75
372 Pat Riggin .30 .75
373 Chris Valentine RC .20 .50
374 Dale Hawerchuk TL 1.00 3.00
375 Dave Babych .20 .50
376 Dave Babych IA .20 .50
377 Dave Christian .30 .75
378 Norm Dupont .20 .50
379 Lucien DeBlois .20 .50
380 Dale Hawerchuk RC 6.00 15.00
381 Dale Hawerchuk IA 1.00 3.00
382 Craig Levie RC .20 .50
383 Morris Lukowich .20 .50
384 Willy Lindstrom .20 .50
385 Bengt Lundholm RC .20 .50
386 Paul MacLean UER RC .40 1.00
387 Bryan Maxwell .20 .50
388 Doug Smail RC .30 .75
389 Doug Soetaert .30 .75
390 Serge Savard .40 1.00
391 Thomas Steen RC 1.25 3.00
392 Don Spring .20 .50
393 Ed Staniowski .20 .50
394 Tim Trimper .20 .50
395 Tim Watters RC .30 .75
396 Checklist 265-396 1.00 2.50

1983-84 O-Pee-Chee

This 396-card standard-size set featured card fronts that contain player name, position, team name and team logo at the top. The player's position appeared within an area that resembles a hockey stick blade with the team logo fronting the blade as if to be a puck. Bilingual backs contained yearly, career statistics and a section devoted to team records. Each team had a Highlight (HL) and scoring leaders (SL) card. However, updated text on front reflected off-season trades. For the second straight year, Topps did not produce a set.

COMPLETE SET (396) 40.00 100.00
1 Mike Bossy TL .40 1.00
2 Denis Potvin HL .20 .50
3 Mike Bossy .40 1.00
4 Bob Bourne .10 .30
5 Billy Carroll RC .10 .30
6 Clark Gillies .20 .50
7 Butch Goring .20 .50
8 Mats Hallin RC .10 .30
9 Tomas Jonsson .10 .30
10 Gordie Lane .10 .30
11 Dave Langevin .10 .30
12 Rollie Melanson RC .40 1.00
13 Ken Morrow .10 .30
14 Bob Nystrom .10 .30
15 Stefan Persson .10 .30
16 Denis Potvin .30 .75
17 Billy Smith .20 .50
18 Brent Sutter .30 .75
19 Duane Sutter .10 .30
20 John Tonelli .20 .50
21 Bryan Trottier .30 .75
22 Wayne Gretzky TL 2.50 6.00
23 M.Messier/W.Gretzky HL 10.00 25.00
24 Glenn Anderson .60 1.50
25 Paul Coffey 4.00 10.00
26 Lee Fogolin .10 .30
27 Grant Fuhr 3.00 8.00
28 Randy Gregg RC .30 .75
29 Wayne Gretzky 12.00 30.00
30 Charlie Huddy RC .40 1.00
31 Pat Hughes .10 .30
32 Dave Hunter .10 .30
33 Don Jackson RC .10 .30
34 Jari Kurri 3.00 8.00
35 Willy Lindstrom .10 .30
36 Ken Linseman .20 .50
37 Kevin Lowe .30 .75
38 Dave Lumley .10 .30
39 Mark Messier 2.50 6.00
40 Andy Moog 3.00 6.00
41 Jaroslav Pouzar RC .10 .30
42 Tom Roulston .10 .30
43 Rick Middleton SL .20 .50
44 Pete Peeters HL .20 .50
45 Ray Bourque UER 5.00 10.00
46 Bruce Crowder .10 .30
47 Keith Crowder .10 .30
48 Luc Dufour RC .20 .50
49 Tom Fergus .10 .30
50 Steve Kasper .10 .30
51 Gord Kluzak RC .30 .75
52 Mike Krushelnyski RC .20 .50
53 Peter McNab .10 .30
54 Rick Middleton .20 .50
55 Mike Milbury .20 .50
56 Mike O'Connell .10 .30
57 Barry Pederson .10 .30
58 Pete Peeters .20 .50
59 Jim Schoenfeld .20 .50
60 Tony McKegney SL .10 .30
61 Bob Sauve HL .20 .50
62 Real Cloutier .10 .30
63 Mike Foligno .20 .50
64 Bill Hajt .10 .30
65 Phil Housley RC 2.50 6.00
66 Dale McCourt .10 .30
67 Gilbert Perreault .30 .75
68 Brent Peterson RC .10 .30
69 Craig Ramsay .10 .30
70 Mike Ramsey .10 .30
71 Bob Sauve .20 .50
72 Ric Seiling .10 .30
73 John Van Boxmeer .10 .30
74 Lanny McDonald SL .20 .50
75 Lanny McDonald HL .20 .50
76 Ed Beers RC .10 .30
77 Steve Bozek .10 .30
78 Guy Chouinard .10 .30
79 Mike Eaves .10 .30
80 Don Edwards .10 .30
81 Kari Eloranta RC .10 .30
82 Dave Hindmarch RC .10 .30
83 Jamie Hislop .10 .30
84 Jim Jackson RC .10 .30
85 Steve Konroyd .10 .30
86 Rejean Lemelin .30 .75
87 Lanny McDonald .20 .50
88 Greg Meredith RC .10 .30
89 Kent Nilsson .20 .50
90 Jim Peplinski .10 .30
91 Paul Reinhart .10 .30
92 Doug Risebrough .10 .30
93 Steve Tambellini .10 .30
94 Mickey Volcan RC .10 .30
95 Al Secord SL .20 .50
96 Denis Savard HL .20 .50
97 Murray Bannerman .20 .50
98 Keith Brown .10 .30
99 Tony Esposito .30 .75
100 Dave Feamster RC .10 .30
101 Greg Fox .10 .30
102 Curt Fraser .10 .30
103 Bill Gardner RC .10 .30
104 Tim Higgins .10 .30
105 Steve Larmer UER RC 3.00 8.00
106 Steve Ludzik UER RC .75 2.00
107 Tom Lysiak .10 .30
108 Bob Murray .10 .30
109 Rick Paterson RC .10 .30
110 Rich Preston .10 .30
111 Denis Savard 1.00 2.50
112 Al Secord .20 .50
113 Darryl Sutter .10 .30
114 Doug Wilson .30 .75
115 John Ogrodnick SL .10 .30
116 Corrado Micalef HL .10 .30
117 John Barrett .10 .30
118 Ivan Boldirev .10 .30
119 Colin Campbell .10 .30
120 Murray Craven RC .30 .75
121 Ron Duguay .10 .30
122 Dwight Foster .10 .30
123 Danny Gare .20 .50
124 Ed Johnstone .10 .30
125 Reed Larson .10 .30
126 Corrado Micalef RC .10 .30
127 Eddie Mio .20 .50
128 John Ogrodnick .10 .30
129 Brad Park .20 .50
130 Greg Smith .10 .30
131 Ken Solheim RC .10 .30
132 Bob Manno .10 .30
133 Paul Woods .10 .30
134 Checklist 1-132 1.00 2.50
135 Blaine Stoughton SL .20 .50
136 Blaine Stoughton HL .20 .50
137 Richie Dunn .10 .30
138 Ron Francis 3.00 6.00
139 Marty Howe .20 .50
140 Mark Johnson .10 .30
141 Paul Lawless RC .10 .30
142 Merlin Malinowski .10 .30
143 Greg Millen .20 .50
144 Ray Neufeld RC .10 .30
145 Joel Quenneville .10 .30
146 Risto Siltanen .10 .30
147 Blaine Stoughton .20 .50
148 Doug Sulliman .10 .30
149 Bob Sullivan RC .10 .30
150 Marcel Dionne TL .20 .50
151 Marcel Dionne HL .20 .50
152 Marcel Dionne .30 .75
153 Daryl Evans RC .10 .30
154 Jim Fox .10 .30
155 Mark Hardy .10 .30
156 Gary Laskoski RC .10 .30
157 Kevin Lavallee .10 .30
158 Dave Lewis .10 .30
159 Larry Murphy .60 1.50
160 Bernie Nicholls RC 2.50 6.00
161 Terry Ruskowski .10 .30
162 Charlie Simmer .20 .50
163 Dave Taylor .30 .75
164 Dino Ciccarelli TL .20 .50
165 Brian Bellows HL .30 .75
166 Don Beaupre .30 .75
167 Brian Bellows RC 2.00 5.00
168 Neal Broten .30 .75
169 Steve Christoff .10 .30
170 Dino Ciccarelli 1.00 2.50
171 George Ferguson .10 .30
172 Craig Hartsburg .10 .30
173 Al MacAdam .10 .30
174 Dennis Maruk .20 .50
175 Brad Maxwell .10 .30
176 Tom McCarthy .10 .30
177 Gilles Meloche .20 .50
178 Steve Payne .10 .30
179 Willi Plett .10 .30
180 Gordie Roberts .10 .30
181 Bobby Smith .20 .50
182 Mark Napier SL .10 .30
183 Guy Lafleur HL .30 .75
184 Keith Acton .10 .30
185 Guy Carbonneau RC 5.00 12.00
186 Gilbert Delorme RC .10 .30
187 Bob Gainey .30 .75
188 Rick Green .10 .30
189 Guy Lafleur .30 .75
190 Craig Ludwig RC .40 1.00
191 Pierre Mondou .10 .30
192 Mark Napier .10 .30
193 Mats Naslund UER RC 3.00 8.00
194 Chris Nilan RC .60 1.50
195 Larry Robinson .20 .50

196 Bill Root RC .10 .30
197 Richard Sevigny .20 .50
198 Steve Shutt .10 .30
199 Mario Tremblay .10 .30
200 Ryan Walter .10 .30
201 Rick Wamsley .20 .50
202 Doug Wickenheiser .10 .30
203 Wayne Gretzky Hart 3.00 8.00
204 Wayne Gretzky Ross 3.00 8.00
205 Mike Bossy Byng .30 .75
206 Steve Larmer Calder 1.25 3.00
207 Rod Langway Norris .10 .30
208 Lanny McDonald Masterton .10 .30
209 Pete Peeters Vezina .10 .30
210 Mike Bossy RB .30 .75
211 Marcel Dionne RB .20 .50
212 Wayne Gretzky RB 2.50 6.00
213 Pat Hughes RB .10 .30
214 Rick Middleton RB .20 .50
215 Wayne Gretzky LL 2.50 6.00
216 Wayne Gretzky LL 2.50 6.00
217 Wayne Gretzky LL 3.00 8.00
218 Brian Propp LL .10 .30
219 Paul Gardner Al Secord LL .10 .30
220 Randy Holt LL .10 .30
221 Pete Peeters LL .20 .50
222 Pete Peeters LL .20 .50
223 Steve Tambellini TL .10 .30
224 Don Lever HL .10 .30
225 Brent Ashton .10 .30
226 Mel Bridgman .10 .30
227 Aaron Broten .10 .30
228 Murray Brumwell RC .10 .30
229 Garry Howatt .10 .30
230 Jeff Larmer RC .10 .30
231 Don Lever .10 .30
232 Bob Lorimer .10 .30
233 Ron Low .10 .30
234 Bob MacMillan .10 .30
235 Hector Marini RC .10 .30
236 Glenn Resch .20 .50
237 Phil Russell .10 .30
238 Mark Pavelich SL .20 .50
239 Mark Pavelich HL .20 .50
240 Bill Baker RC .30 .75
241 Barry Beck .10 .30
242 Mike Blaisdell .10 .30
243 Nick Fotiu .20 .50
244 Robbie Ftorek .10 .30
245 Anders Hedberg .20 .50
246 Willie Huber .10 .30
247 Tom Laidlaw .10 .30
248 Mikko Leinonen RC .10 .30
249 Dave Maloney .10 .30
250 Don Maloney .10 .30
251 Rob McClanahan .10 .30
252 Mark Osborne .10 .30
253 Mark Pavelich .20 .50
254 Mike Rogers .10 .30
255 Reijo Ruotsalainen .10 .30
256 Checklist 133-264 1.00 2.50
257 Darryl SittlerSL .20 .50
258 Darryl Sittler HL .20 .50
259 Ray Allison .10 .30
260 Bill Barber .20 .50
261 Lindsay Carson RC .10 .30
262 Bobby Clarke .30 .75
263 Doug Crossman .10 .30
264 Ron Flockhart .10 .30
265 Bob Froese RC .30 .75
266 Paul Holmgren .20 .50
267 Mark Howe .30 .75
268 Pelle Lindbergh RC 10.00 25.00
269 Brad Marsh .10 .30
270 Brad McCrimmon .20 .50
271 Brian Propp .30 .75
272 Darryl Sittler .30 .75
273 Mark Taylor RC .10 .30
274 Rick Kehoe SL .20 .50
275 Paul Gardner HL .10 .30
276 Pat Boutette .10 .30
277 Mike Bullard .10 .30
278 Randy Carlyle .10 .30
279 Michel Dion .10 .30
280 Paul Gardner .10 .30
281 Dave Hannan RC .20 .50
282 Rick Kehoe .20 .50
283 Randy Boyd RC .10 .30
284 Greg Malone .10 .30
285 Doug Shedden RC .20 .50
286 Andre St.Laurent .10 .30
287 Michel Goulet TL .30 .75
288 Michel Goulet HL .30 .75
289 Pierre Aubry .10 .30
290 Dan Bouchard .20 .50
291 Alain Cote .10 .30
292 Michel Goulet .30 .75
293 Dale Hunter .30 .75
294 Rick Lapointe .10 .30
295 Mario Marois .10 .30
296 Tony McKegney .10 .30
297 Randy Moller RC .10 .30
298 Wilf Paiement .10 .30
299 Dave Pichette .10 .30
300 Normand Rochefort .10 .30
301 Louis Sleigher RC .10 .30
302 Anton Stastny .20 .50
303 Marian Stastny .20 .50
304 Peter Stastny .60 1.50
305 Marc Tardif .10 .30
306 Wally Weir .10 .30
307 Blake Wesley .10 .30
308 Brian Sutter SL .20 .50
309 Mike Liut HL .20 .50
310 Wayne Babych .10 .30
311 Jack Brownschidle .10 .30
312 Mike Crombeen RC .10 .30
313 Andre Dore RC .10 .30
314 Blake Dunlop .10 .30
315 Bernie Federko .30 .75
316 Mike Liut .30 .75
317 Joe Mullen 1.00 2.50
318 Jorgen Pettersson .10 .30
319 Rob Ramage .10 .30
320 Brian Sutter .20 .50
321 Perry Turnbull .10 .30
322 Mike Zuke .10 .30
323 Rick Vaive SL .10 .30
324 Rick Vaive HL .10 .30
325 John Anderson .10 .30
326 Jim Benning .10 .30
327 Bill Derlago .10 .30
328 Dan Daoust RC .10 .30
329 Dave Farrish .10 .30
330 Miroslav Frycer .10 .30
331 Stewart Gavin RC .10 .30
332 Gaston Gingras .10 .30
333 Billy Harris .10 .30
334 Peter Inhacak RC .10 .30
335 Jim Korn .10 .30
336 Terry Martin .10 .30
337 Frank Nigro RC .10 .30
338 Mike Palmateer .20 .50
339 Walt Poddubny RC .20 .50
340 Rick St.Croix .10 .30
341 Borje Salming .20 .50
342 Greg Terrion .10 .30
343 Rick Vaive .10 .30
344 Darcy Rota SL .10 .30
345 Darcy Rota HL .10 .30
346 Richard Brodeur .20 .50
347 Jiri Bubla RC .10 .30
348 Ron Delorme .10 .30
349 John Garrett .10 .30
350 Thomas Gradin .10 .30
351 Doug Halward .10 .30
352 Mark Kirton .10 .30
353 Rick Lanz .10 .30
354 Lars Lindgren .10 .30
355 Gary Lupul .10 .30
356 Kevin McCarthy .10 .30
357 Jim Nill RC .10 .30
358 Darcy Rota .10 .30
359 Stan Smyl .10 .30
360 Harold Snepsts .10 .30
361 Patrik Sundstrom RC .20 .50
362 Tony Tanti RC .30 .75
363 Tiger Williams .20 .50
364 Mike Gartner TL .30 .75
365 Rod Langway HL .20 .50
366 Bobby Carpenter .10 .30
367 Dave Christian .10 .30
368 Brian Engblom .10 .30
369 Mike Gartner 1.50 4.00
370 Bengt Gustafsson .10 .30
371 Ken Houston .10 .30
372 Doug Jarvis .10 .30
373 Al Jensen RC .30 .75
374 Rod Langway .20 .50
375 Craig Laughlin RC .20 .50
376 Scott Stevens RC 6.00 15.00
377 Dale Hawerchuk TL .30 .75
378 Lucien DeBlois HL .10 .30
379 Scott Arniel RC .10 .30
380 Dave Babych .10 .30
381 Laurie Boschman .10 .30
382 Wade Campbell RC .10 .30
383 Lucien DeBlois .10 .30
384 Murray Eaves RC .10 .30
385 Dale Hawerchuk 1.50 4.00
386 Morris Lukowich .10 .30
387 Bengt Lundholm .10 .30
388 Paul MacLean .10 .30
389 Brian Mullen RC .20 .50
390 Doug Smail .10 .30
391 Doug Soetaert .20 .50
392 Don Spring .10 .30
393 Thomas Steen .30 .75
394 Tim Watters .10 .30
395 Tim Young .10 .30
396 Checklist 265-396 1.00 2.50

1984-85 O-Pee-Chee

This 396-card standard-size set featured two player photos on the front. A small head shot appeared in a circle toward the bottom of the card. Bilingual backs contained yearly and career statistics and career highlights. All-Stars were featured on cards 207-218. Cards 352-372 featured each team's leading goal scorer on the front and team individual scoring statistics on the back. The cards were essentially in team order. However, updated text on some card fronts reflected off-season trades. The Instant Winner card (one in 662 packs) could be redeemed for prizes including Stanley Cup Finals tickets, hockey equipment and sets of uncut card sheets from this year.

COMPLETE SET (396) 100.00 200.00
1 Ray Bourque 3.00 8.00
2 Keith Crowder .20 .50
3 Luc Dufour .30 .75
4 Tom Fergus .20 .50
5 Doug Keans RC .30 .75
6 Gord Kluzak .20 .50
7 Ken Linseman .30 .75
8 Nevin Markwart RC .20 .50
9 Rick Middleton .30 .75
10 Mike Milbury .20 .50
11 Jim Nill .20 .50
12 Mike O'Connell .20 .50
13 Terry O'Reilly .30 .75
14 Barry Pederson .20 .50
15 Pete Peeters .30 .75
16 Dave Silk RC .20 .50
17 Dave Andreychuk RC 4.00 10.00
18 Tom Barrasso RC 3.00 8.00
19 Real Cloutier .20 .50
20 Mike Foligno .30 .75
21 Bill Hajt .20 .50
22 Gilles Hamel RC .20 .50
23 Phil Housley .40 1.00
24 Gilbert Perreault .40 1.00
25 Brent Peterson .20 .50
26 Larry Playfair .20 .50
27 Craig Ramsay .20 .50
28 Mike Ramsey .20 .50
29 Lindy Ruff .20 .50
30 Bob Sauve .30 .75
31 Ric Seiling .20 .50
32 Murray Bannerman .30 .75
33 Keith Brown .20 .50
34 Curt Fraser .20 .50
35 Bill Gardner .20 .50
36 Jeff Larmer .20 .50
37 Steve Larmer 1.00 2.50
38 Steve Ludzik .20 .50
39 Tom Lysiak .20 .50
40 Bob MacMillan .20 .50
41 Bob Murray .20 .50
42 Troy Murray RC .40 1.00
43 Jack O'Callahan RC .30 .75
44 Rick Paterson .20 .50
45 Denis Savard .40 1.00
46 Al Secord .30 .75
47 Darryl Sutter .20 .50
48 Doug Wilson .30 .75
49 John Barrett .30 .75
50 Ivan Boldirev .20 .50
51 Colin Campbell .20 .50
52 Ron Duguay .30 .75
53 Dwight Foster .20 .50
54 Danny Gare .20 .50
55 Ed Johnstone .20 .50
56 Kelly Kisio RC .30 .75
57 Lane Lambert .20 .50
58 Reed Larson .20 .50
59 Bob Manno .20 .50
60 Randy Ladouceur RC .20 .50
61 Eddie Mio .30 .75
62 John Ogrodnick .20 .50
63 Brad Park .30 .75
64 Greg Smith .20 .50
65 Greg Stefan RC .30 .75
66 Paul Woods .30 .75
67 Steve Yzerman RC 30.00 80.00
68 Bob Crawford RC .20 .50
69 Richie Dunn .20 .50
70 Ron Francis 1.50 4.00
71 Marty Howe .20 .50
72 Mark Johnson .20 .50
73 Chris Kotsopoulos .20 .50
74 Greg Malone .20 .50
75 Greg Millen .30 .75
76 Ray Neufeld .20 .50
77 Joel Quenneville .20 .50
78 Risto Siltanen .20 .50
79 Sylvain Turgeon RC .30 .75
80 Mike Zuke .20 .50
81 Steve Christoff .20 .50
82 Marcel Dionne .40 1.00
83 Brian Engblom .20 .50
84 Jim Fox .20 .50
85 Anders Hakansson RC .20 .50
86 Mark Hardy .20 .50
87 Brian MacLellan RC .20 .50
88 Bernie Nicholls .75 2.00
89 Terry Ruskowski .20 .50
90 Charlie Simmer .30 .75
91 Doug Smith .20 .50
92 Dave Taylor .30 .75
93 Keith Acton .20 .50
94 Don Beaupre .30 .75
95 Brian Bellows .30 .75
96 Neal Broten .40 1.00
97 Dino Ciccarelli .40 1.00
98 Craig Hartsburg .20 .50
99 Tom Hirsch RC .20 .50
100 Paul Holmgren .30 .75
101 Dennis Maruk .30 .75
102 Brad Maxwell .20 .50
103 Tom McCarthy .20 .50
104 Gilles Meloche .30 .75
105 Mark Napier .20 .50
106 Steve Payne .20 .50
107 Gordie Roberts .20 .50
108 Harold Snepsts .20 .50
109 Mel Bridgman .20 .50
110 Joe Cirella .20 .50
111 Tim Higgins .20 .50
112 Don Lever .20 .50
113 Dave Lewis .20 .50
114 Bob Lorimer .20 .50
115 Ron Low .20 .50
116 Jan Ludvig RC .20 .50
117 Gary McAdam .20 .50
118 Rich Preston .20 .50
119 Glenn Resch .30 .75
120 Phil Russell .20 .50
121 Pat Verbeek RC 4.00 10.00
122 Mike Bossy .75 2.00
123 Bob Bourne .20 .50
124 Pat Flatley RC .40 1.00
125 Greg Gilbert RC .30 .75
126 Clark Gillies .40 1.00
127 Butch Goring .30 .75
128 Tomas Jonsson .20 .50
129 Pat LaFontaine RC 6.00 15.00
130 Rollie Melanson .30 .75
131 Ken Morrow .20 .50
132 Bob Nystrom .20 .50
133 Stefan Persson .20 .50
134 Denis Potvin .40 1.00
135 Billy Smith .40 1.00
136 Brent Sutter .20 .50
137 Duane Sutter .20 .50
138 John Tonelli .30 .75
139 Bryan Trottier .40 1.00
140 Barry Beck .20 .50
141 Ron Greschner .20 .50
142 Glen Hanlon .30 .75
143 Anders Hedberg .30 .75
144 Tom Laidlaw .20 .50
145 Pierre Larouche .30 .75
146 Dave Maloney .20 .50
147 Don Maloney .20 .50
148 Mark Osborne .20 .50
149 Larry Patey .20 .50
150 James Patrick RC .40 1.00
151 Mark Pavelich .20 .50
152 Mike Rogers .20 .50
153 Reijo Ruotsalainen .20 .50
154 Blaine Stoughton .30 .75
155 Peter Sundstrom RC .30 .75
156 Bill Barber .30 .75
157 Doug Crossman .20 .50
158 Thomas Eriksson RC .20 .50
159 Bob Froese .30 .75
160 Paul Guay RC .20 .50
161 Mark Howe .40 1.00
162 Tim Kerr .30 .75
163 Brad Marsh .20 .50
164 Brad McCrimmon .30 .75
165 Dave Poulin RC .60 1.50
166 Brian Propp .30 .75
167 Ilkka Sinisalo RC .30 .75
168 Darryl Sittler .40 1.00
169 Rich Sutter RC .30 .75
170 Ron Sutter RC .40 1.00
171 Pat Boutette .20 .50
172 Mike Bullard .20 .50
173 Michel Dion .30 .75
174 Ron Flockhart .20 .50
175 Greg Fox .20 .50
176 Denis Herron .30 .75
177 Rick Kehoe .30 .75
178 Kevin McCarthy .20 .50
179 Tom Roulston .20 .50
180 Mark Taylor .20 .50
181 Wayne Babych .20 .50
182 Tim Bothwell RC .20 .50
183 Kevin Lavallee .20 .50
184 Bernie Federko .30 .75
185 Doug Gilmour RC 15.00 40.00
186 Terry Johnson RC .20 .50
187 Mike Liut .30 .75
188 Joe Mullen .60 1.50
189 Jorgen Pettersson .20 .50
190 Rob Ramage .20 .50
191 Dwight Schofield RC .20 .50
192 Brian Sutter .30 .75
193 Doug Wickenheiser .20 .50
194 Bobby Carpenter .20 .50
195 Dave Christian .20 .50
196 Bob Gould RC .20 .50
197 Mike Gartner 1.00 3.00
198 Bengt Gustafsson .20 .50
199 Alan Haworth RC .20 .50
200 Doug Jarvis .20 .50
201 Al Jensen .30 .75
202 Rod Langway .30 .75
203 Craig Laughlin .20 .50
204 Larry Murphy .40 1.00
205 Pat Riggin .30 .75
206 Scott Stevens 1.00 3.00
207 Michel Goulet AS .30 .75
208 Wayne Gretzky AS 1.50 4.00
209 Mike Bossy AS .75 2.00
210 Rod Langway AS .30 .75
211 Ray Bourque AS 1.00 3.00
212 Tom Barrasso AS 1.50 4.00
213 Mark Messier AS 2.00 5.00
214 Bryan Trottier AS .40 1.00
215 Jari Kurri AS .75 2.00
216 Denis Potvin AS .40 1.00
217 Paul Coffey AS .60 1.50
218 Pat Riggin AS .30 .75
219 Ed Beers .20 .50
220 Steve Bozek .20 .50
221 Mike Eaves .20 .50
222 Don Edwards .30 .75
223 Kari Eloranta .20 .50
224 Dave Hindmarch .20 .50
225 Jim Jackson .20 .50
226 Steve Konroyd .20 .50
227 Richard Kromm RC .20 .50
228 Rejean Lemelin .30 .75
229 Hakan Loob RC 1.00 3.00
230 Jamie Macoun RC .30 .75
231 Lanny McDonald .30 .75
232 Kent Nilsson .30 .75
233 Jim Peplinski .20 .50
234 Dan Quinn RC .40 1.00
235 Paul Reinhart .20 .50
236 Doug Risebrough .20 .50
237 Steve Tambellini .20 .50
238 Glenn Anderson .40 1.00
239 Paul Coffey 2.50 6.00
240 Lee Fogolin .20 .50
241 Grant Fuhr 2.50 6.00
242 Randy Gregg .20 .50
243 Wayne Gretzky 10.00 25.00
244 Charlie Huddy .30 .75
245 Pat Hughes .20 .50
246 Dave Hunter .20 .50
247 Don Jackson .20 .50
248 Mike Krushelnyski .20 .50
249 Jari Kurri 2.00 5.00
250 Willy Lindstrom .20 .50
251 Kevin Lowe .40 1.00
252 Dave Lumley .20 .50
253 Kevin McClelland RC .20 .50
254 Mark Messier 2.50 6.00
255 Andy Moog 1.50 4.00
256 Jaroslav Pouzar .20 .50
257 Guy Carbonneau .40 1.00
258 John Chabot RC .20 .50
259 Chris Chelios RC 10.00 25.00
260 Lucien DeBlois .20 .50
261 Bob Gainey .40 1.00
262 Rick Green .20 .50
263 Jean Hamel .20 .50
264 Guy Lafleur .40 1.00
265 Craig Ludwig .20 .50
266 Pierre Mondou .20 .50
267 Mats Naslund .40 1.00
268 Chris Nilan .20 .50
269 Steve Penney RC .30 .75
270 Larry Robinson .40 1.00
271 Bill Root .20 .50
272 Steve Shutt .20 .50
273 Bobby Smith .30 .75
274 Mario Tremblay .20 .50
275 Ryan Walter .20 .50
276 Bo Berglund RC .20 .50
277 Dan Bouchard .30 .75
278 Alain Cote .20 .50
279 Andre Dore .20 .50
280 Michel Goulet .30 .75
281 Dale Hunter .30 .75
282 Mario Marois .20 .50
283 Tony McKegney .20 .50
284 Randy Moller .20 .50
285 Wilf Paiement .20 .50
286 Pat Price .20 .50
287 Normand Rochefort .20 .50
288 Andre Savard .20 .50
289 Richard Sevigny .20 .50
290 Louis Sleigher .20 .50
291 Anton Stastny .30 .75
292 Marian Stastny .30 .75
293 Peter Stastny .40 1.00
294 Blake Wesley .20 .50
295 John Anderson .20 .50
296 Jim Benning .20 .50
297 Allan Bester UER RC .30 .75
298 Rich Costello RC .20 .50
299 Dan Daoust .20 .50
300 Bill Derlago .20 .50
301 Dave Farrish .20 .50
302 Stewart Gavin .20 .50
303 Gaston Gingras .20 .50
304 Jim Korn .20 .50
305 Gary Leeman RC .40 1.00
306 Terry Martin .20 .50
307 Gary Nylund RC .20 .50
308 Mike Palmateer .30 .75
309 Walt Poddubny .20 .50
310 Rick St.Croix .20 .50
311 Borje Salming .30 .75
312 Greg Terrion .20 .50
313 Rick Vaive .20 .50
314 Richard Brodeur .30 .75
315 Jiri Bubla .20 .50
316 Ron Delorme .20 .50
317 John Garrett .30 .75
318 Jere Gillis .20 .50
319 Thomas Gradin .20 .50
320 Doug Halward .20 .50
321 Rick Lanz .20 .50
322 Moe Lemay RC .20 .50
323 Gary Lupul .20 .50
324 Al MacAdam .20 .50
325 Rob McClanahan .20 .50
326 Peter McNab .20 .50
327 Cam Neely RC 12.00 30.00
328 Darcy Rota .20 .50
329 Andy Schliebener RC .20 .50
330 Stan Smyl .20 .50
331 Patrik Sundstrom .20 .50
332 Tony Tanti .20 .50
333 Scott Arniel .20 .50
334 Dave Babych .20 .50
335 Laurie Boschman .20 .50
336 Wade Campbell .20 .50
337 Randy Carlyle .20 .50
338 Jordy Douglas .20 .50
339 Dale Hawerchuk 1.00 3.00
340 Morris Lukowich .20 .50
341 Bengt Lundholm .20 .50
342 Paul MacLean .20 .50
343 Andrew McBain RC .20 .50
344 Brian Mullen .20 .50
345 Robert Picard .20 .50
346 Doug Smail .20 .50
347 Doug Soetaert .30 .75
348 Thomas Steen .20 .50
349 Perry Turnbull .20 .50
350 Tim Watters .20 .50
351 Tim Young .20 .50
352 Rick Middleton SL .30 .75
353 Dave Andreychuk TL 1.00 3.00
354 Ed Beers SL .20 .50
355 Denis Savard TL .40 1.00
356 John Ogrodnick SL .20 .50
357 Wayne Gretzky TL 1.50 4.00
358 Charlie Simmer SL .30 .75
359 Brian Bellows TL .30 .75
360 Guy Lafleur TL .40 1.00
361 Mel Bridgman SL .20 .50
362 Mike Bossy TL .75 2.00
363 Pierre Larouche SL .30 .75
364 Tim Kerr SL .30 .75
365 Mike Bullard SL .20 .50
366 Michel Goulet TL .30 .75
367 Federko/Mullen UER SL .60 1.50
368 Rick Vaive .20 .50
369 Tony Tanti .20 .50
370 Mike Gartner TL 1.00 3.00
371 Paul MacLean SL .20 .50
372 Sylvain Turgeon SL .30 .75
373 Wayne Gretzky Ross 1.50 4.00
374 Wayne Gretzky Hart 1.50 4.00
375 Tom Barrasso Calder 1.50 4.00
376 Mike Bossy Byng .75 2.00
377 Rod Langway Norris .30 .75
378 Brad Park TW .30 .75
379 Tom Barrasso Vezina 1.50 4.00
380 Wayne Gretzky LL 1.50 4.00
381 Wayne Gretzky LL 1.50 4.00
382 Wayne Gretzky LL 1.50 4.00
383 Wayne Gretzky LL 1.50 4.00
384 Michel Goulet LL .30 .75
385 Steve Yzerman LL 5.00 12.00
386 Pat Riggin LL .30 .75
387 Rollie Melanson LL .30 .75
388 Wayne Gretzky RB 1.50 4.00
389 Denis Potvin RB .40 1.00
390 Brad Park RB .30 .75
391 Michel Goulet RB .30 .75
392 Pat LaFontaine RB 1.00 3.00
393 Dale Hawerchuk RB 1.00 3.00
394 Checklist 1-132 1.00 2.50
395 Checklist 133-264 UER (185 Gilmore) 1.00 2.50
396 Checklist 265-396 1.00 2.50

1984-85 O-Pee-Chee Stanley Cup Sweepstakes Entry

1 Centreman .75 2.00
2 Left Wing .75 2.00
3 Right Defense .75 2.00
4 Right Wing .75 2.00
5 Instant Winner 50.00 100.00

1985-86 O-Pee-Chee

The 1985-86 O-Pee-Chee set contained 264 standard-size cards. The fronts had player name and position at the bottom with team logo at the top right or left. Bilingual backs contained yearly and career stats and highlights. The key Rookie Card in this set was Mario Lemieux. Printed later than Topps, O-Pee-Chee was able to issue a Memorial card of the late Pelle Lindbergh. Beware when purchasing the Rookie Card of Mario Lemieux as it has been counterfeited.

COMPLETE SET (264) 175.00 350.00
1 Lanny McDonald .75 2.00
2 Mike O'Connell .30 .75
3 Curt Fraser .30 .75
4 Steve Penney .30 .75
5 Brian Engblom .30 .75
6 Ron Sutter .30 .75
7 Joe Mullen .30 .75
8 Rod Langway .30 .75
9 Mario Lemieux RC 60.00 150.00
10 Dave Babych .30 .75
11 Bob Nystrom .30 .75
12 Andy Moog 2.50 6.00
13 Dino Ciccarelli .30 .75
14 Dwight Foster .30 .75
15 James Patrick .30 .75
16 Thomas Gradin .30 .75
17 Mike Foligno .30 .75
18 Mario Gosselin RC .30 .75
19 Mike Zuke .30 .75
20 John Anderson .30 .75
21 Dave Pichette .30 .75
22 Nick Fotiu .30 .75
23 Tom Lysiak .25 .60
24 Peter Zezel RC 1.00 2.50
25 Denis Potvin .25 .60
26 Bob Carpenter .25 .60
27 Murray Bannerman .25 .60
28 Gordie Roberts .25 .60
29 Steve Yzerman 12.00 30.00
30 Phil Russell .25 .60
31 Peter Stastny .25 .60
32 Craig Ramsay .25 .60
33 Terry Ruskowski .25 .60
34 Kevin Dineen RC 2.50 6.00
35 Mark Howe .30 .75
36 Glenn Resch .25 .60
37 Danny Gare .25 .60
38 Doug Bodger RC .25 .60
39 Mike Rogers .30 .75
40 Ray Bourque 3.00 8.00
41 John Tonelli .25 .60
42 Mel Bridgman .30 .75
43 Sylvain Turgeon .25 .60
44 Mark Johnson .30 .75
45 Doug Wilson .25 .60
46 Mike Gartner 1.50 4.00
47 Brent Peterson .30 .75
48 Paul Reinhart .25 .60
49 Mike Krushelnyski .30 .75
50 Brian Bellows .25 .60
51 Chris Chelios 3.00 8.00
52 Barry Pederson .30 .75
53 Murray Craven .25 .60
54 Pierre Larouche .25 .60
55 Reed Larson .25 .60
56 Pat Verbeek .25 .60
57 Randy Carlyle .25 .60
58 Ray Neufeld .25 .60
59 Keith Brown .30 .75
60 Bryan Trottier .40 1.00
61 Jim Fox .30 .75
62 Scott Stevens 1.50 4.00
63 Phil Housley .25 .60
64 Rick Middleton .25 .60
65 Steve Payne .25 .60
66 Dave Lewis .25 .60
67 Mike Bullard .25 .60
68 Stan Smyl .25 .60
69 Mark Pavelich .25 .60
70 John Ogrodnick .25 .60
71 Bill Derlago .25 .60
72 Brad Marsh .25 .60
73 Denis Savard .40 1.00
74 Mark Fusco RC .25 .60
75 Pete Peeters .25 .60
76 Doug Gilmour 4.00 10.00
77 Mike Ramsey .25 .60
78 Anton Stastny .25 .60
79 Steve Kasper .25 .60
80 Bryan Erickson RC .25 .60
81 Clark Gillies .30 .75
82 Keith Acton .25 .60
83 Pat Flatley .25 .60
84 Kirk Muller RC 1.50 4.00
85 Paul Coffey 2.00 5.00
86 Ed Olczyk RC .30 .75
87 Charlie Simmer .30 .75
88 Mike Liut .30 .75
89 Dave Maloney .30 .75
90 Marcel Dionne .40 1.00
91 Tim Kerr .30 .75
92 Ivan Boldirev .30 .75
93 Ken Morrow .30 .75
94 Don Maloney .30 .75
95 Rejean Lemelin .30 .75
96 Curt Giles .30 .75
97 Bob Bourne .30 .75
98 Joe Cirella .30 .75
99 Dave Christian .30 .75
100 Darryl Sutter .30 .75
101 Kelly Kisio .30 .75
102 Mats Naslund .30 .75
103 Joel Quenneville .30 .75
104 Bernie Federko .30 .75
105 Tom Barrasso .30 .75
106 Rick Vaive .30 .75
107 Brent Sutter .30 .75
108 Wayne Babych .25 .60
109 Dale Hawerchuk 1.50 4.00
110 Pelle Lindbergh Mem. 6.00 15.00
111 Dennis Maruk .20 .50
112 Reijo Ruotsalainen .20 .50
113 Tom Fergus .20 .50
114 Bob Murray .20 .50
115 Patrik Sundstrom .25 .60
116 Ron Duguay .25 .60
117 Alan Haworth .20 .50
118 Greg Malone .20 .50
119 Bill Hajt .20 .50
120 Wayne Gretzky 15.00 40.00
121 Craig Redmond RC .20 .50
122 Kelly Hrudey RC 3.00 8.00
123 Tomas Sandstrom RC 2.50 6.00
124 Neal Broten .25 .60
125 Moe Mantha .25 .60
126 Greg Gilbert .25 .60
127 Bruce Driver RC .30 .75
128 Dave Poulin .25 .60
129 Morris Lukowich .25 .60
130 Mike Bossy .75 2.00
131 Larry Playfair .25 .60
132 Steve Larmer .25 .60
133 Doug Keans .25 .60
134 Bob Manno .30 .75
135 Brian Sutter .30 .75
136 Pat Riggin .30 .75
137 Pat LaFontaine 2.50 6.00
138 Barry Beck .30 .75
139 Rich Preston .30 .75
140 Ron Francis 2.00 5.00
141 Brian Propp .30 .75
142 Don Beaupre .30 .75
143 Dave Andreychuk .30 .75
144 Ed Beers .25 .60
145 Paul MacLean .25 .60
146 Troy Murray .30 .75
147 Larry Robinson .30 .75
148 Bernie Nicholls .30 .75
149 Glen Hanlon .30 .75
150 Michel Goulet .30 .75
151 Doug Jarvis .30 .75
152 Warren Young RC .25 .60
153 Tony Tanti .25 .60
154 Tomas Jonsson .25 .60
155 Jari Kurri 2.00 5.00
156 Tony McKegney .25 .60
157 Greg Stefan .25 .60
158 Brad McCrimmon .25 .60
159 Keith Crowder .25 .60
160 Gilbert Perreault .30 .75
161 Tim Bothwell .25 .60
162 Bob Crawford .25 .60
163 Paul Gagne .25 .60
164 Dan Daoust .25 .60
165 Checklist 1-132 3.00 8.00
166 Tim Bernhardt RC .25 .60
167 Gord Kluzak .25 .60
168 Glenn Anderson .30 .75
169 Bob Gainey .25 .60
170 Brent Ashton .25 .60
171 Ron Flockhart .25 .60
172 Gary Nylund .25 .60
173 Moe Lemay .25 .60
174 Bob Sauve .25 .60
175 Doug Smail .25 .60
176 Dan Quinn .25 .60
177 Mark Messier 2.50 6.00
178 Jay Wells RC .20 .50
179 Dale Hunter .20 .50
180 Richard Brodeur .20 .50
181 Bobby Smith .20 .50
182 Ron Greschner .20 .50
183 Don Edwards .20 .50
184 Hakan Loob .20 .50
185 Dave Ellett RC .30 .75
186 Denis Herron .30 .75
187 Charlie Huddy .30 .75
188 Ilkka Sinisalo .30 .75
189 Doug Halward .25 .60
190 Craig Laughlin .25 .60
191 Carey Wilson RC .25 .60
192 Craig Ludwig .25 .60
193 Bob MacMillan .25 .60
194 Mario Marois .25 .60
195 Brian Mullen .25 .60
196 Rob Ramage .25 .60
197 Rick Lanz .25 .60
198 Miroslav Frycer .25 .60
199 Randy Gregg .25 .60
200 Corrado Micalef .25 .60
201 Jamie Macoun .25 .60
202 Bob Brooke RC .25 .60
203 Billy Carroll .25 .60
204 Brian MacLellan .25 .60
205 Alain Cote .25 .60
206 Thomas Steen .25 .60
207 Grant Fuhr 2.50 6.00
208 Rich Sutter .25 .60
209 Al MacAdam .25 .60
210 Al Iafrate RC 3.00 8.00
211 Pierre Mondou .30 .75
212 Randy Hillier RC .30 .75
213 Mike Eaves .20 .50
214 Dave Taylor .20 .50
215 Robert Picard .20 .50
216 Randy Ladouceur .20 .50
217 Willy Lindstrom .20 .50
218 Torrie Robertson RC .20 .50
219 Tom Kurvers RC .25 .60
220 John Garrett .25 .60
221 Greg Millen .20 .50
222 Richard Kromm .20 .50
223 Bob Janecyk RC .20 .50
224 Brad Maxwell .20 .50
225 Mike McPhee RC .20 .50
226 Brian Hayward RC .25 .60
227 Duane Sutter .25 .60
228 Cam Neely 4.00 10.00
229 Doug Wickenheiser .25 .60
230 Rollie Melanson .25 .60
231 Bruce Bell RC .25 .60
232 Harold Snepsts .25 .60
233 Guy Carbonneau .25 .60
234 Doug Sulliman .25 .60
235 Lee Fogolin .30 .75
236 Larry Murphy .30 .75
237 Al MacInnis RC 20.00 50.00
238 Don Lever .30 .75
239 Kevin Lowe .30 .75
240 Randy Moller .30 .75
241 Doug Lidster RC .30 .75
242 Craig Hartsburg .25 .60
243 Doug Risebrough .25 .60
244 John Chabot .25 .60
245 Mario Tremblay .25 .60
246 Dan Bouchard .25 .60
247 Doug Shedden .25 .60
248 Borje Salming .25 .60
249 Aaron Broten .30 .75
250 Jim Benning .20 .50
251 Laurie Boschman .20 .50
252 George McPhee RC .25 .60
253 Mark Napier .30 .75
254 Perry Turnbull .30 .75
255 Warren Skorodenski RC .25 .60
256 Checklist 133-264 3.00 8.00
257 Wayne Gretzky LL 3.00 8.00
258 Wayne Gretzky LL 3.00 8.00
259 Wayne Gretzky LL 3.00 8.00
260 Tim Kerr LL .30 .75
261 Jari Kurri LL .50 1.25
262 Mario Lemieux LL 12.00 30.00
263 Tom Barrasso LL .30 .75
264 Warren Skorodenski LL .25 .60

1985-86 O-Pee-Chee Box Bottoms

This sixteen-card standard-size set was issued in sets of four on the bottom of the 1985-86 O-Pee-Chee wax pack boxes. Complete box bottom panels are valued at a 25 percent premium above the prices listed below. The card back included statistical information,and was written in English and French. The cards were lettered rather than numbered. The key card in the set was obviously Mario Lemieux, pictured in his rookie year for cards.

COMPLETE SET (16) 40.00 100.00
A Brian Bellows .30 .75
B Ray Bourque 2.00 5.00
C Bob Carpenter .20 .50
D Chris Chelios 2.00 5.00
E Marcel Dionne .75 2.00
F Ron Francis 1.25 3.00
G Wayne Gretzky 12.00 30.00
H Tim Kerr .20 .50
I Mario Lemieux 40.00 100.00
J John Ogrodnick .20 .50
K Gilbert Perreault .40 1.00
L Glenn Resch .40 1.00
M Reijo Ruotsalainen .20 .50
N Brian Sutter .30 .75
O John Tonelli .20 .50
P Doug Wilson .30 .75

1986-87 O-Pee-Chee

This 1986-87 O-Pee-Chee set consisted of 264 standard-size cards. Card fronts featured player name, team, team logo and position at the bottom. Bilingual backs featured yearly and career statistics as well as the number of game-winning goals scored in 1985-86. The key Rookie Card in this set was Patrick Roy. Beware when purchasing the Patrick Roy card from this set as it has been counterfeited.

COMPLETE SET (264) 125.00 250.00
1 Ray Bourque 2.50 5.00
2 Pat LaFontaine 1.25 3.00
3 Wayne Gretzky 10.00 25.00
4 Lindy Ruff .08 .25
5 Brad McCrimmon .08 .25
6 Tiger Williams .20 .50
7 Denis Savard .50 1.25
8 Lanny McDonald .20 .50
9 John Vanbiesbrouck RC 8.00 20.00
10 Greg Adams RC .60 1.50
11 Steve Yzerman 10.00 25.00
12 Craig Hartsburg .08 .25

3 John Anderson .08 .25
4 Bob Bourne .08 .25
5 Kjell Dahlin RC .08 .25
6 Dave Andreychuk .50 1.25
7 Rob Ramage .08 .25
8 Ron Greschner .08 .25
9 Bruce Driver .20 .50
10 Peter Stastny .20 .50
11 Dave Christian .08 .25
12 Doug Keans .08 .25
13 Scott Bjugstad RC .08 .25
14 Doug Bodger .08 .25
15 Troy Murray .08 .25
16 Al Iafrate .40 1.00
17 Kelly Hrudey .40 1.00
18 Doug Jarvis .08 .25
19 Rich Sutter .08 .25
20 Marcel Dionne .20 .50
21 Curt Fraser .08 .25
22 Doug Lidster .08 .25
23 Brian MacLellan .08 .25
24 Barry Pederson .08 .25
25 Craig Laughlin .08 .25
26 Ilkka Sinisalo .08 .25
27 John MacLean RC 1.50 4.00
28 Brian Mullen .08 .25
29 Duane Sutter .08 .25
30 Brian Engblom .08 .25
31 Chris Cichocki RC .08 .25
32 Gordie Roberts .08 .25
33 Ron Francis 1.00 2.50
34 Joe Mullen .40 1.00
35 Moe Mantha .08 .25
36 Pat Verbeek .08 .25
37 Clint Malarchuk RC .60 1.50
38 Bob Brooke .08 .25
39 Darryl Sutter .08 .25
40 Stan Smyl .08 .25
41 Greg Stefan .20 .50
42 Bill Hajt .08 .25
43 Patrick Roy RC 60.00 150.00
44 Gord Kluzak .08 .25
45 Bob Froese .20 .50
46 Grant Fuhr 1.00 2.50
47 Mark Hunter .08 .25
48 Dana Murzyn RC .40 1.00
49 Mike Gartner .40 1.00
50 Dennis Maruk .08 .25
51 Rich Preston .08 .25
52 Larry Robinson .20 .50
53 Dave Taylor .20 .50
54 Bob Murray .08 .25
55 Ken Morrow .08 .25
56 Mike Ridley RC .40 1.00
57 John Tucker RC .20 .50
58 Miroslav Frycer .08 .25
59 Danny Gare .20 .50
60 Randy Burridge RC .40 1.00
61 Dave Poulin .08 .25
62 Brian Sutter .20 .50
63 Dave Babych .08 .25
64 Dale Hawerchuk .50 1.25
65 Brian Bellows .40 1.00
66 Dave Pasin RC .08 .25
67 Pete Peeters .20 .50
68 Tomas Jonsson .08 .25
69 Gilbert Perreault .20 .50
70 Glenn Anderson .50 1.25
71 Don Maloney .08 .25
72 Ed Olczyk .08 .25
73 Mike Bullard .08 .25
74 Tom Fergus .08 .25
75 Dave Lewis .08 .25
76 Brian Propp .20 .50
77 John Ogrodnick .08 .25
78 Kevin Dineen .40 1.00
79 Don Beaupre .20 .50
80 Mike Bossy .60 1.50
81 Tom Barrasso .40 1.00
82 Michel Goulet .20 .50
83 Doug Gilmour 2.50 5.00
84 Kirk Muller .40 1.00
85 Larry Melnyk RC .08 .25
86 Bob Gainey .40 1.00
87 Steve Kasper .08 .25
88 Petr Klima RC .40 1.00
89 Neal Broten .20 .50
100 Al Secord .08 .25
101 Bryan Erickson .08 .25
102 Rejean Lemelin .20 .50
103 Sylvain Turgeon .08 .25
104 Bob Nystrom .08 .25
105 Bernie Federko .20 .50
106 Doug Wilson .20 .50
107 Alan Haworth .08 .25
108 Jari Kurri 1.00 2.50
109 Ron Sutter .08 .25
110 Reed Larson .08 .25
111 Terry Ruskowski .08 .25
112 Mark Johnson .08 .25
113 James Patrick .08 .25
114 Paul MacLean .08 .25
115 Mike Ramsey .08 .25
116 Kelly Kisio .08 .25
117 Brent Sutter .08 .25
118 Joel Quenneville .08 .25
119 Curt Giles .08 .25
120 Tony Tanti .08 .25
121 Doug Sulliman .08 .25
122 Mario Lemieux 15.00 40.00
123 Mark Howe .20 .50
124 Bob Sauve .20 .50
125 Anton Stastny .08 .25
126 Scott Stevens .40 1.00
127 Mike Foligno .08 .25
128 Reijo Ruotsalainen .08 .25
129 Denis Potvin .20 .50
130 Keith Crowder .08 .25
131 Bob Janecyk .20 .50
132 John Tonelli .08 .25
133 Mike Liut .20 .50
134 Tim Kerr .20 .50
135 Al Jensen .08 .25
136 Mel Bridgman .08 .25
137 Paul Coffey 1.50 4.00
138 Dino Ciccarelli .40 1.00
139 Steve Larmer .40 1.00
140 Mike O'Connell .08 .25
141 Clark Gillies .20 .50
142 Phil Russell .08 .25
143 Dirk Graham RC .60 1.50
144 Randy Carlyle .08 .25
145 Charlie Simmer .20 .50
146 Ron Flockhart .08 .25
147 Tom Laidlaw .08 .25
148 Dave Tippett RC .20 .50
149 Wendel Clark RC 15.00 30.00
150 Bob Carpenter .08 .25
151 Bill Watson RC .08 .25
152 Roberto Romano RC .20 .50
153 Doug Shedden .08 .25
154 Phil Housley .40 1.00
155 Bryan Trottier .40 1.00
156 Patrik Sundstrom .08 .25
157 Rick Middleton .20 .50
158 Glenn Resch .20 .50
159 Bernie Nicholls .20 .50
160 Ray Ferraro RC 2.50 6.00
161 Mats Naslund .20 .50
162 Pat Flatley .08 .25
163 Joe Cirella .08 .25
164 Rod Langway .20 .50
165 Checklist 1-132 1.25 3.00
166 Carey Wilson .08 .25
167 Murray Craven .20 .50
168 Paul Gillis RC .08 .25
169 Borje Salming .08 .25
170 Perry Turnbull .08 .25
171 Chris Chelios 2.00 5.00
172 Keith Acton .08 .25
173 Al MacInnis 3.00 6.00
174 Russ Courtnall RC 1.50 4.00
175 Brad Marsh .20 .50
176 Guy Carbonneau .20 .50
177 Ray Neufeld .08 .25
178 Craig MacTavish RC .75 2.00
179 Rick Lanz .08 .25
180 Murray Bannerman .08 .25
181 Brent Ashton .08 .25
182 Jim Peplinski .08 .25
183 Mark Napier .08 .25
184 Laurie Boschman .08 .25
185 Larry Murphy .40 1.00
186 Mark Messier .75 2.00
187 Risto Siltanen .08 .25
188 Bobby Smith .20 .50
189 Gary Suter RC 1.25 3.00
190 Peter Zezel .08 .25
191 Rick Vaive .08 .25
192 Dale Hunter .20 .50
193 Mike Krushelnyski .08 .25
194 Scott Arniel .08 .25
195 Larry Playfair .08 .25
196 Doug Risebrough .08 .25
197 Kevin Lowe .20 .50
198 Checklist 133-264 1.25 3.00
199 Chris Nilan .08 .25
200 Paul Cyr RC .08 .25
201 Ric Seiling .08 .25
202 Doug Smith .08 .25
203 Jamie Macoun .08 .25
204 Dan Quinn .08 .25
205 Paul Reinhart .08 .25
206 Keith Brown .08 .25
207 Jack O'Callahan .08 .25
208 Steve Richmond RC .08 .25
209 Warren Young .08 .25
210 Lee Fogolin .08 .25
211 Charlie Huddy .08 .25
212 Andy Moog 1.00 2.50
213 Wayne Babych .08 .25
214 Torrie Robertson .08 .25
215 Jim Fox .08 .25
216 Phil Sykes RC .08 .25
217 Jay Wells .08 .25
218 Dave Langevin .08 .25
219 Steve Payne .08 .25
220 Craig Ludwig .08 .25
221 Mike McPhee .08 .25
222 Steve Penney .08 .25
223 Mario Tremblay .08 .25
224 Ryan Walter .08 .25
225 Alain Chevrier RC .20 .50
226 Uli Hiemer RC .08 .25
227 Tim Higgins .08 .25
228 Billy Smith .20 .50
229 Richard Kromm .08 .25
230 Tomas Sandstrom .40 1.00
231 Jim Johnson RC .20 .50
232 Willy Lindstrom .08 .25
233 Alain Cote .08 .25
234 Gilbert Delorme .08 .25
235 Mario Gosselin .20 .50
236 David Shaw RC .40 1.00
237 Dave Barr RC .40 1.00
238 Ed Beers .08 .25
239 Charlie Bourgeois RC .08 .25
240 Rick Wamsley .08 .25
241 Dan Daoust .08 .25
242 Brad Maxwell .08 .25
243 Gary Nylund .08 .25
244 Greg Terrion .08 .25
245 Steve Thomas RC 2.00 5.00
246 Richard Brodeur .20 .50
247 Joel Otto UER RC .40 1.00
248 Doug Halward .08 .25
249 Moe Lemay UER .08 .25
Photo is Joel Otto
250 Cam Neely 2.00 5.00
251 Brent Peterson .08 .25
252 Petri Skriko RC .40 1.00
253 Greg C.Adams RC .20 .50
254 Bill Derlago .08 .25
255 Brian Hayward .20 .50
256 Doug Smail .08 .25
257 Thomas Steen .08 .25
258 Jari Kurri LL .40 1.00
259 Wayne Gretzky LL 2.50 6.00
260 Wayne Gretzky LL 2.50 6.00
261 Tim Kerr LL .08 .25
262 Kjell Dahlin LL .08 .25
263 Bob Froese LL .20 .50
264 Bob Froese LL .20 .50

1986-87 O-Pee-Chee Box Bottoms

This sixteen-card standard-size set was issued in sets of four on the bottom of the 1986-87 O-Pee-Chee wax pack boxes. Complete box bottom panels are valued at a 25 percent premium above the prices listed below. This set featured some of the leading NHL players including Mike Bossy, Wayne Gretzky, Mario Lemieux, and Bryan Trottier. The front presented a color action photo with various color borders, with the team's logo in the lower right hand corner. The back included statistical information, was written in English and French, and was printed in blue with black ink. The cards were lettered rather than numbered.

COMPLETE SET (16) 16.00 40.00
A Greg Adams .20 .50
B Mike Bossy .60 1.50
C Dave Christian .08 .25
D Mike Foligno .20 .50
E Michel Goulet .30 .75
F Wayne Gretzky 8.00 20.00
G Tim Kerr .08 .25
H Jari Kurri 1.00 2.50
I Mario Lemieux 10.00 25.00
J Lanny McDonald .30 .75
K Bernie Nicholls .30 .75
L Mike Ridley .30 .75
M Larry Robinson .30 .75
N Denis Savard .30 .75
O Brian Sutter .08 .25
P Bryan Trottier .40 1.00

1987-88 O-Pee-Chee

Card fronts in this 264-card standard-size set featured a bottom border that contains the design of a hockey stick with which the player's name appears. Also, the team name appeared within a puck. Bilingual backs contain yearly and career statistics along with highlights. Beware when purchasing the cards of Wayne Gretzky, Adam Oates and Luc Robitaille from this set as they have been counterfeited.

COMPLETE SET (264) 60.00 120.00
COMP.FACT.SET (264) 75.00 150.00
1 Denis Potvin .25 .60
2 Rick Tocchet RC 4.00 10.00
3 Dave Andreychuk .30 .75
4 Stan Smyl .25 .60
5 Dave Babych .25 .60
6 Pat Verbeek .25 .60
7 Esa Tikkanen RC 3.00 8.00
8 Mike Ridley .25 .60
9 Randy Carlyle UER .25 .60
(Misspelled Calryle
10 Greg Paslawski RC .25 .60
11 Neal Broten .25 .60
12 Wendel Clark 2.50 6.00
13 Bill Ranford RC 4.00 10.00
14 Doug Wilson .25 .60
15 Mario Lemieux 10.00 25.00
16 Mats Naslund .25 .60
17 Mel Bridgman .25 .60
18 James Patrick .25 .60
19 Rollie Melanson .25 .60
20 Lanny McDonald .25 .60
21 Peter Stastny .25 .60
22 Murray Craven .25 .60
23 Ulf Samuelsson RC 2.50 6.00
24 Michael Thelven RC .25 .60
25 Scott Stevens .30 .75
26 Petr Klima .25 .60
27 Brent Sutter .25 .60
28 Tomas Sandstrom .25 .60
29 Tim Bothwell .25 .60
30 Bob Carpenter .25 .60
31 Brian MacLellan .25 .60
32 John Chabot .25 .60
33 Phil Housley .25 .60
34 Patrik Sundstrom .25 .60
35 Dave Ellett .25 .60
36 John Vanbiesbrouck 3.00 8.00
37 Dave Lewis .25 .60
38 Tom McCarthy .25 .60
39 Dave Poulin .25 .60
40 Mike Foligno .25 .60
41 Gordie Roberts .25 .60
42 Luc Robitaille RC 12.00 30.00
43 Duane Sutter .25 .60
44 Pete Peeters .25 .60
45 John Anderson .25 .60
46 Aaron Broten .25 .60
47 Keith Brown .25 .60
48 Bobby Smith .25 .60
49 Don Maloney .25 .60
50 Mark Hunter .25 .60
51 Moe Mantha .25 .60
52 Charlie Simmer .25 .60
53 Wayne Gretzky 10.00 25.00
54 Mark Howe .30 .75
55 Bob Gould .25 .60
56 Steve Yzerman 5.00 12.00
57 Larry Playfair .25 .60
58 Alain Chevrier .25 .60
59 Steve Larmer .25 .60
60 Bryan Trottier .40 1.00
61 Stewart Gavin .30 .75
62 Russ Courtnall .30 .75
63 Mike Ramsey .30 .75
64 Bob Brooke .30 .75
65 Rick Wamsley .30 .75
66 Ken Morrow .30 .75
67 Gerard Gallant UER RC .30 .75
68 Kevin Hatcher RC .75 2.00
69 Cam Neely 1.00 2.50
70 Sylvain Turgeon .30 .75
71 Peter Zezel .30 .75
72 Al MacInnis 2.00 5.00
73 Terry Ruskowski .30 .75
74 Troy Murray .30 .75
75 Jim Fox .30 .75
76 Kelly Kisio .30 .75
77 Michel Goulet .30 .75
78 Tom Barrasso .30 .75
79 Bruce Driver .30 .75
80 Craig Simpson RC .50 1.25
81 Dino Ciccarelli .30 .75
82 Gary Nylund .30 .75
83 Bernie Federko .30 .75
84 John Tonelli .30 .75
85 Brad McCrimmon .30 .75
86 Dave Tippett .30 .75
87 Ray Bourque 2.00 5.00
88 Dave Christian .30 .75
89 Glen Hanlon .30 .75
90 Brian Curran RC .30 .75
91 Paul MacLean .30 .75
92 Jimmy Carson RC .30 .75
93 Willie Huber .30 .75
94 Brian Bellows .25 .60
95 Doug Jarvis .30 .75
96 Clark Gillies .30 .75
97 Tony Tanti .30 .75
98 Pelle Eklund RC .30 .75
99 Paul Coffey 1.50 4.00
100 Brent Ashton .30 .75
101 Mark Johnson .30 .75
102 Greg Johnston RC .30 .75
103 Ron Flockhart .30 .75
104 Ed Olczyk .30 .75
105 Mike Bossy 1.00 2.50
106 Chris Chelios 1.50 4.00
107 Gilles Meloche .30 .75
108 Rod Langway .30 .75
109 Ray Ferraro .30 .75
110 Ron Duguay .25 .60
111 Al Secord .30 .75
112 Mark Messier .30 .75
113 Ron Sutter .30 .75
114 Darren Veitch RC .30 .75
115 Rick Middleton .30 .75
116 Doug Sulliman .30 .75
117 Dennis Maruk .30 .75
118 Dave Taylor .30 .75
119 Kelly Hrudey .30 .75
120 Tom Fergus .30 .75
121 Christian Ruuttu RC .30 .75
122 Brian Benning RC .30 .75
123 Adam Oates RC 6.00 15.00
124 Kevin Dineen .30 .75
125 Doug Bodger .30 .75
126 Joe Mullen .30 .75
127 Denis Savard .40 1.00
128 Brad Marsh .30 .75
129 Marcel Dionne .40 1.00
130 Bryan Erickson .30 .75
131 Reed Larson .30 .75
132 Don Beaupre .30 .75
133 Larry Murphy .30 .75
134 John Ogrodnick .30 .75
135 Greg Adams .30 .75
136 Pat Flatley .30 .75
137 Scott Arniel .30 .75
138 Dana Murzyn .30 .75
139 Greg C. Adams .20 .50
140 Bob Sauve .20 .50
141 Mike O'Connell .20 .50
142 Walt Poddubny .20 .50
143 Paul Reinhart .20 .50
144 Tim Kerr .20 .50
145 Brian Lawton RC .20 .50
146 Gino Cavallini RC .20 .50
147 Doug Keans .20 .50
148 Jari Kurri .20 .50
149 Dale Hawerchuk .40 1.00
150 Randy Cunneyworth RC .25 .60
151 Jay Wells .20 .50
152 Mike Liut .20 .50
153 Steve Konroyd .20 .50
154 John Tucker .20 .50
155 Rick Vaive .20 .50
156 Bob Murray .20 .50
157 Kirk Muller .20 .50
158 Brian Propp .20 .50
159 Ron Greschner .20 .50
160 Rob Ramage .20 .50
161 Craig Laughlin .20 .50
162 Steve Kasper .25 .60
163 Patrick Roy 8.00 20.00
164 Shawn Burr RC .25 .60
165 Craig Hartsburg .25 .60
166 Dean Evason RC .25 .60
167 Bob Bourne .25 .60
168 Mike Gartner .25 .60
169 Ron Hextall RC 6.00 15.00
170 Joe Cirella .25 .60
171 Dan Quinn .25 .60
172 Tony McKegney .25 .60
173 Pat LaFontaine .30 .75
174 Allen Pedersen RC .25 .60
175 Doug Gilmour .40 1.00
176 Gary Suter .25 .60
177 Barry Pederson .25 .60
178 Grant Fuhr .60 1.50
179 Wayne Presley RC .25 .60
180 Wilf Paiement .25 .60
181 Doug Smail .30 .75
182 Doug Crossman .30 .75
183 Bernie Nicholls UER .30 .75
(Misspelled Nichols
on both sides)
184 Dirk Graham UER .30 .75
(Misspelled Dick)
185 Anton Stastny .30 .75
186 Greg Stefan .30 .75
187 Ron Francis .40 1.00
188 Steve Thomas .30 .75
189 Kelly Miller RC .30 .75
190 Tomas Jonsson .30 .75
191 John MacLean .30 .75
192 Larry Robinson .25 .60
193 Doug Wickenheiser .25 .60
194 Keith Crowder .25 .60
195 Bob Froese .25 .60
196 Jim Johnson .25 .60
197 Checklist 1-132 .60 1.50
198 Checklist 133-264 .60 1.50
199 Glenn Anderson .30 .75
200 Kevin Lowe .25 .60
201 Kevin McClelland .20 .50
202 Mike Krushelnyski .20 .50
203 Craig MacTavish .20 .50
204 Andy Moog .75 2.00
205 Marty McSorley RC 3.00 8.00
206 Craig Muni RC .20 .50
207 Charlie Huddy .20 .50
208 Hakan Loob .20 .50
209 Jim Peplinski .20 .50
210 Mike Bullard .20 .50
211 Carey Wilson .20 .50
212 Joel Otto .20 .50
213 Neil Sheehy RC .20 .50
214 Jamie Macoun .20 .50
215 Mike Vernon RC 4.00 10.00
216 Steve Bozek .20 .50
217 Daniel Berthiaume RC .20 .50
218 Gilles Hamel .20 .50
219 Tim Watters .20 .50
220 Mario Marois .25 .60
221 Thomas Steen .25 .60
222 Laurie Boschman .25 .60
223 Steve Rooney RC .25 .60
224 Ron Wilson .25 .60
225 Fredrik Olausson RC .25 .60
226 Jim Kyte RC .25 .60
227 Claude Lemieux RC 4.00 10.00
228 Bob Gainey .25 .60
229 Gaston Gingras .25 .60
230 Brian Hayward .25 .60
231 Ryan Walter .25 .60
232 Guy Carbonneau .25 .60
233 Stephane Richer RC 3.00 8.00
234 Rick Green .25 .60
235 Brian Skrudland RC .75 2.00
236 Allan Bester .25 .60
237 Borje Salming .25 .60
238 Al Iafrate .25 .60
239 Rick Lanz .25 .60
240 Gary Leeman .25 .60
241 Greg Terrion .25 .60
242 Ken Wregget RC 1.25 3.00
243 Vincent Damphousse RC 4.00 10.00
244 Chris Kotsopoulos .25 .60
245 Dale Hunter .25 .60
246 Clint Malarchuk .25 .60
247 Paul Gillis .25 .60
248 Robert Picard .25 .60
249 Doug Shedden .25 .60
250 Mario Gosselin .25 .60
251 Randy Moller .25 .60
252 David Shaw .25 .60
253 Mike Eagles RC .25 .60
254 Alain Cote .25 .60
255 Petri Skriko .25 .60
256 Doug Lidster .20 .50
257 Richard Brodeur UER .20 .50
(Photo actually
Frank Caprice)
258 Rich Sutter .25 .60
259 Steve Tambellini .25 .60
260 Jim Benning .25 .60
261 Dave Richter RC .25 .60
262 Michel Petit RC .25 .60
263 Brent Peterson .25 .60
264 Jim Sandlak RC .25 .60

1987-88 O-Pee-Chee Box Bottoms

This sixteen-card set was issued in sets of four on the bottom of the 1987-88 O-Pee-Chee wax pack boxes. Complete box bottom panels are valued at a 25 percent premium above the prices listed below. The cards were in the same design as the 1987-88 O-Pee-Chee regular issues except they were bordered in yellow. The backs were printed in red and black ink and give statistical information. The cards were lettered rather than numbered.

COMPLETE SET (16) 14.00 35.00
A Wayne Gretzky 6.00 15.00
B Tim Kerr .15 .40
C Steve Yzerman 3.00 8.00
D Luc Robitaille 3.00 8.00
E Doug Gilmour .75 2.00
F Ray Bourque .75 2.00
G Joe Mullen .30 .75
H Larry Murphy .30 .75
I Dale Hawerchuk .40 1.00
J Ron Francis .75 2.00
K Walt Poddubny .08 .25
L Mats Naslund .20 .50
M Michel Goulet .30 .75
N Denis Savard .30 .75
O Bryan Trottier .40 1.00
P Russ Courtnall .30 .75

1987-88 O-Pee-Chee Minis

The 1987-88 O-Pee-Chee Minis set contained 42 cards measuring approximately 2 1/8" by 3". The fronts were white with vignette-style color photos and player names in navy blue. The backs were pale pink and blue, and show 1986-87 stats. The cards were distributed five per cello pack at a suggested retail price of 25 cents.

COMPLETE SET (42) 8.00 20.00
1 Glenn Anderson .08 .25
2 Brian Benning .02 .10
3 Daniel Berthiaume .05 .15
4 Ray Bourque .40 1.00
5 Shawn Burr .02 .10
6 Jimmy Carson .05 .15
7 Dino Ciccarelli .08 .25
8 Paul Coffey .40 1.00
9 Pelle Eklund .02 .10
10 Ron Francis .40 1.00
11 Doug Gilmour .40 1.00
12 Michel Goulet .08 .25
13 Wayne Gretzky 2.50 6.00
14 Glen Hanlon .05 .15
15 Brian Hayward .05 .15
16 Ron Hextall .75 2.00
17 Phil Housley .08 .25
18 Mark Howe .05 .15
19 Doug Jarvis .02 .10
20 Tim Kerr .05 .15
21 Jari Kurri .20 .50
22 Pat LaFontaine .20 .50
23 Mario Lemieux 2.50 6.00
24 Mike Liut .07 .20
25 Kevin Lowe .05 .15
26 Al MacInnis .15 .40
27 Brad McCrimmon .02 .10
28 Mark Messier .60 1.50
29 Joe Mullen .08 .25
30 Craig Muni .02 .10
31 Larry Murphy .08 .25
32 Dave Poulin .05 .15
33 Brian Propp .05 .15
34 Paul Reinhart .05 .15
35 Luc Robitaille 1.50 4.00
36 Patrick Roy 4.00 10.00
37 Christian Ruuttu .02 .10
38 Tomas Sandstrom .08 .25
39 Denis Savard .08 .25
40 Petri Skriko .02 .10
41 Bryan Trottier .20 .50
42 Checklist 1-42 .02 .10

1988-89 O-Pee-Chee

The 1988-89 O-Pee-Chee set consisted of 264 cards. The card fronts contain the player's name within a team-colored banner, position and team logo at the top. Bilingual backs had yearly and career statistics, number of game winning goals from previous season, playoff scoring records and highlights. Printed later than Topps, O-Pee-Chee was able to get Wayne Gretzky (120) in a Kings uniform in an arena setting. In the Topps set, Gretzky was holding a Kings jersey during a press conference. Beware when purchasing the cards of Gretzky, Hull, Lemieux, Nieuwendyk, and Turgeon as they have been counterfeited.

COMPLETE SET (264) 40.00 100.00
COMP.FACT.SET (264) 75.00 200.00
1 Mario Lemieux 5.00 12.00
2 Bob Joyce RC .30 .75
3 Joel Quenneville .25 .60
4 Tony McKegney .25 .60
5 Stephane Richer .25 .60
6 Mark Howe .30 .75
7 Brent Sutter .25 .60
8 Gilles Meloche .25 .60
9 Jimmy Carson .25 .60
10 John MacLean .25 .60
11 Gary Leeman .25 .60
12 Gerard Gallant .25 .60
13 Marcel Dionne .40 1.00
14 Dave Christian .25 .60
15 Gary Nylund .25 .60
16 Joe Nieuwendyk RC 5.00 12.00
17 Billy Smith .30 .75
18 Christian Ruuttu .25 .60
19 Randy Cunneyworth .25 .60
20 Brian Lawton .25 .60
21 Scott Mellanby RC 1.00 2.50
22 Peter Stastny .25 .60
23 Gord Kluzak .25 .60
24 Sylvain Turgeon .25 .60
25 Clint Malarchuk .25 .60
26 Denis Savard .40 1.00
27 Craig Simpson .25 .60
28 Petr Klima .25 .60
29 Pat Verbeek .25 .60
30 Moe Mantha .25 .60
31 Chris Nilan .25 .60
32 Barry Pederson .25 .60
33 Randy Burridge .25 .60
34 Ron Hextall 1.00 2.50
35 Gaston Gingras .25 .60
36 Kevin Dineen .25 .60
37 Tom Laidlaw .25 .60
38 Paul MacLean .25 .60
39 John Chabot .25 .60
40 Lindy Ruff .25 .60
41 Dan Quinn .25 .60
42 Don Beaupre .25 .60
43 Gary Suter .25 .60
44 Mikko Makela RC .25 .60
45 Mark Johnson .25 .60
46 Dave Taylor .25 .60
47 Ulf Dahlen RC .25 .60
48 Jeff Sharples RC .25 .60
49 Chris Chelios .75 2.00
50 Mike Gartner .25 .60
51 Darren Pang RC 1.00 2.50
52 Ron Francis .40 1.00
53 Ken Morrow .25 .60
54 Michel Goulet .25 .60
55 Ray Sheppard RC 1.00 2.50
56 Doug Gilmour .40 1.00
57 David Shaw .25 .60
58 Cam Neely .75 2.00
59 Grant Fuhr .60 1.50
60 Scott Stevens .30 .75
61 Bob Brooke .30 .75
62 Dave Hunter .30 .75
63 Alan Kerr RC .30 .75
64 Brad Marsh .30 .75
65 Dale Hawerchuk .40 1.00
66 Brett Hull RC 15.00 40.00
67 Patrik Sundstrom .30 .75
68 Greg Stefan .30 .75
69 James Patrick .30 .75
70 Dale Hunter .30 .75
71 Al Iafrate .30 .75
72 Bob Carpenter .30 .75
73 Ray Bourque 1.00 2.50
74 John Tucker .30 .75
75 Carey Wilson .30 .75
76 Joe Mullen .30 .75
77 Rick Vaive .30 .75
78 Shawn Burr .30 .75
79 Murray Craven .30 .75
80 Clark Gillies .30 .75
81 Bernie Federko .30 .75
82 Tony Tanti .30 .75
83 Greg Gilbert .30 .75
84 Kirk Muller .30 .75
85 Dave Tippett .30 .75
86 Kevin Hatcher .30 .75
87 Rick Middleton .30 .75
88 Bobby Smith .30 .75
89 Doug Wilson .30 .75
90 Scott Arniel .30 .75
91 Brian Mullen .30 .75
92 Mike O'Connell .20 .50
93 Mark Messier .60 1.50
94 Sean Burke RC 2.00 5.00
95 Brian Bellows .25 .60
96 Doug Bodger .20 .50
97 Bryan Trottier .40 1.00
98 Anton Stastny .20 .50
99A Checklist 1-99 .30 .75
(found in vending cases)
99B Checklist 1-132 .30 .75
(found in wax cases)
100 Dave Poulin .20 .50
101 Bob Bourne .20 .50
102 John Vanbiesbrouck .20 .50
103 Allen Pedersen .20 .50
104 Mike Ridley .20 .50
105 Andrew McBain .20 .50
106 Troy Murray .20 .50
107 Tom Barrasso .20 .50
108 Tomas Jonsson .20 .50
109 Rob Brown RC .20 .50
110 Hakan Loob .20 .50
111 Ilkka Sinisalo .20 .50
112 Dave Archibald RC .20 .50
113 Doug Halward .20 .50
114 Ray Ferraro .20 .50
115 Doug Brown RC .20 .50
116 Patrick Roy 6.00 15.00
117 Greg Millen .20 .50
118 Ken Linseman .20 .50
119 Phil Housley .20 .50
120 Wayne Gretzky UER 6.00 15.00
121 Tomas Sandstrom .20 .50
122 Brendan Shanahan RC 10.00 25.00
123 Pat LaFontaine .30 .75
124 Luc Robitaille 2.50 6.00
125 Ed Olczyk .20 .50
126 Ron Sutter .20 .50
127 Mike Liut .20 .50
128 Brent Ashton .20 .50
129 Tony Hrkac RC .20 .50
130 Kelly Miller .20 .50
131 Alan Haworth .20 .50
132 Dave McLlwain RC .20 .50
133 Mike Ramsey .20 .50
134 Bob Sweeney RC .25 .60
135 Dirk Graham .25 .60
136 Ulf Samuelsson .25 .60
137 Petri Skriko .25 .60
138 Aaron Broten .25 .60
139 Jim Fox .25 .60
140 Randy Wood RC .25 .60
141 Larry Murphy .25 .60
142 Daniel Berthiaume .25 .60
143 Kelly Kisio .25 .60
144 Neal Broten .25 .60
145 Reed Larson .25 .60
146 Peter Zezel .25 .60
147 Jari Kurri .25 .60
148 Jim Johnson .25 .60
149 Gino Cavallini .25 .60
150 Glen Hanlon .25 .60
151 Bengt Gustafsson .25 .60
152 Mike Bullard .25 .60
153 John Ogrodnick .25 .60
154 Steve Larmer .25 .60
155 Kelly Hrudey .25 .60
156 Mats Naslund .25 .60
157 Bruce Driver .25 .60
158 Randy Hillier .25 .60
159 Craig Hartsburg .25 .60
160 Rollie Melanson .25 .60
161 Adam Oates 2.00 5.00
162 Greg Adams .20 .50
163 Dave Andreychuk .30 .75
164 Dave Babych .25 .60
165 Brian Noonan RC .25 .60
166 Glen Wesley RC .25 .60
167 Dave Ellett .25 .60
168 Brian Propp .25 .60
169 Bernie Nicholls .25 .60
170 Walt Poddubny .25 .60
171 Steve Konroyd .25 .60
172 Doug Sulliman .25 .60
173 Mario Gosselin .25 .60
174 Brian Benning .25 .60
175 Dino Ciccarelli .25 .60
176 Steve Kasper .25 .60
177 Rick Tocchet .75 2.00
178 Brad McCrimmon .25 .60
179 Paul Coffey .60 1.50
180 Pete Peeters .25 .60
181 Bob Probert RC 4.00 10.00
182 Steve Duchesne RC .75 2.00
183 Russ Courtnall .25 .60
184 Mike Foligno .25 .60
185 Wayne Presley .25 .60
186 Rejean Lemelin .25 .60
187 Mark Hunter .25 .60
188 Joe Cirella .25 .60
189 Glenn Anderson .30 .75
190 John Anderson .20 .50
191 Pat Flatley .20 .50
192 Rod Langway .20 .50
193 Brian MacLellan .25 .60
194 Pierre Turgeon RC 5.00 12.00
195 Brian Hayward .25 .60
196 Steve Yzerman 3.00 8.00
197 Doug Crossman .25 .60
198A Checklist 100-198 .30 .75
(Found in vending cases)
198B Checklist 133-264 UER .30 .75
(Found in wax cases)
199 Greg C. Adams .25 .60
200 Laurie Boschman .25 .60
201 Jeff Brown RC .25 .60
202 Garth Butcher RC .25 .60
203 Guy Carbonneau .25 .60
204 Randy Carlyle .25 .60
205 Alain Cote .25 .60
206 Keith Crowder .25 .60
207 Vincent Damphousse .75 2.00
208 Gaetan Duchesne RC .25 .60
209 Iain Duncan RC .25 .60
210 Tommy Albelin RC .25 .60
211 Pelle Eklund .25 .60
212 Jan Erixon RC .25 .60
213 Paul Fenton RC .25 .60
214 Tom Fergus .25 .60
215 Dave Gagner RC .50 1.25
216 Bob Gainey .25 .60
217 Stewart Gavin .25 .60
218 Charlie Huddy .25 .60
219 Jeff Jackson RC .25 .60
220 Uwe Krupp RC .50 1.25
221 Mike Krushelnyski .25 .60
222 Tom Kurvers .25 .60
223 Jason Lafreniere RC .25 .60
224 Lane Lambert .25 .60
225 Rick Lanz .25 .60
226 Brad Lauer RC .25 .60
227 Claude Lemieux 1.25 3.00
228 Doug Lidster .25 .60
229 Kevin Lowe UER .25 .60
230 Craig Ludwig .25 .60
231 Al MacInnis .60 1.50
232 Craig MacTavish .25 .60
233 Mario Marois .25 .60
misspelled Marios
234 Lanny McDonald .25 .60
235 Rick Meagher .25 .60
236 Craig Muni .25 .60
237 Mike McPhee .20 .50
238 Ric Nattress RC .20 .50
239 Ray Neufeld .20 .50
240 Lee Norwood RC .20 .50
241 Mark Osborne UER .20 .50
(Misspelled Osbourne
242 Joel Otto .20 .50
243 Jim Peplinski .20 .50
244 Rob Ramage .20 .50
245 Luke Richardson RC .20 .50
246 Larry Robinson .20 .50
247 Borje Salming .20 .50
248 David Saunders RC .20 .50
249 Al Secord .20 .50
250 Charlie Simmer .20 .50
251 Doug Smail .20 .50
252 Steve Smith UER RC .20 .50
253 Stan Smyl .20 .50
254 Thomas Steen .20 .50
255 Rich Sutter .20 .50
256 Petr Svoboda RC .20 .50
257 Peter Taglianetti RC .20 .50
258 Steve Tambellini .20 .50
259 Steve Thomas .20 .50
260 Esa Tikkanen .60 1.50
261 Mike Vernon .60 1.50
262 Ryan Walter .20 .50
263 Doug Wickenheiser .20 .50
264 Ken Wregget .25 .60

1988-89 O-Pee-Chee Box Bottoms

This sixteen-card set was issued in sets of four on the bottom of the 1988-89 O-Pee-Chee wax pack boxes. Complete box bottom panels are valued at a 25 percent premium above the prices listed below. The cards were in the same design as the 1988-89 O-Pee-Chee regular issues. The backs were printed in purple on orange background and give statistical information. The cards were lettered rather than numbered.

COMPLETE SET (16) 6.00 15.00
A Ron Francis .40 1.00
B Wayne Gretzky 3.00 8.00
C Pat LaFontaine .40 1.00
D Bobby Smith .15 .40
E Bernie Federko .15 .40
F Kirk Muller .30 .75

G Ed Olczyk .08 .25
H Denis Savard .30 .75
I Ray Bourque .75 2.00
J Murray Craven .08 .25
Brian Propp
K Dale Hawerchuk .30 .75
L Steve Yzerman 2.00 5.00
M Dave Andreychuk .20 .50
N Mike Gartner .30 .75
O Hakan Loob .15 .40
P Luc Robitaille .60 1.50

1988-89 O-Pee-Chee Minis

The 1988-89 O-Pee-Chee Minis set contained 46 numbered cards measuring approximately 2 1/8" by 3". The fronts were white with vignette-style color photos and player names in navy blue. The backs were pale pink and blue, and show 1987-88 stats. The key card in the set was Brett Hull, appearing in his Rookie Card year. The set numbering was alphabetical by player's name.

COMPLETE SET (46) 8.00 20.00
1 Tom Barrasso .08 .25
2 Bob Bourne .01 .05
3 Ray Bourque .30 .75
4 Guy Carbonneau .05 .15
5 Jimmy Carson .02 .10
6 Paul Coffey .30 .75
7 Ulf Dahlen .05 .15
8 Marcel Dionne .15 .40
9 Grant Fuhr .20 .50
10 Michel Goulet .08 .25
11 Wayne Gretzky 2.50 6.00
12 Dale Hawerchuk .15 .40
13 Brian Hayward .05 .15
14 Ron Hextall .20 .50
15 Tony Hrkac .01 .05
16 Brett Hull 2.00 5.00
17 Steve Larmer .08 .25
18 Rejean Lemelin .05 .15
19 Mario Lemieux 2.00 5.00
20 Mike Liut .05 .15
21 Hakan Loob .08 .25
22 Al MacInnis .08 .25
23 Paul MacLean .02 .10
24 Brad McCrimmon .01 .05
25 Mark Messier .60 1.50
26 Mats Naslund .08 .25
27 Cam Neely .30 .75
28 Bernie Nicholls .08 .25
29 Joe Nieuwendyk .75 2.00
30 Pete Peeters .05 .15
31 Stephane Richer .15 .40
32 Luc Robitaille .30 .75
33 Patrick Roy 2.00 5.00
34 Denis Savard .15 .40
35 Ray Sheppard .08 .25
36 Craig Simpson .02 .10
37 Peter Stastny .15 .40
38 Greg Stefan .02 .10
39 Scott Stevens .08 .25
40 Gary Suter .05 .15
41 Petr Svoboda .02 .10
42 John Vanbiesbrouck 1.25 3.00
43 Pat Verbeek .15 .40
44 Mike Vernon .20 .50
45 Carey Wilson .01 .05
46 Checklist Card .01 .05

1989-90 O-Pee-Chee

This 330-card standard-size set was O-Pee-Chee's largest issue since 1984-85. The fronts featured color action photos with "blue ice" borders and player name and team logo at the lower right-hand corner. Solid blue borders appeared at the top and bottom on the card face. Bilingual backs were tinted red with black lettering and provided career and playoff statistics as well as highlights. The team cards in the set (298-318) were actually action scenes with no players explicitly identified. This set was produced in mass quantity as O-Pee-Chee gave dealers the option to order vending cases following the initial printing. A second printing allowed for these orders to be filled, saturating the market. Most dealers believe that this O-Pee-Chee set was produced in an amount much greater than the Topps production of this year. One complete sheet of 1989-90 O-Pee-Chee cards was printed on white back "test" card stock produced by paper supplier Tembec. Tembec became the new supplier for O-Pee-Chee cards the following year. A much scarcer version of 132-cards in the set were created and can be identified by the bright, almost white, card stock on the backs compared to the more gray color used in the standard printing. It is commonly thought that roughly 100 copies of each of the cards were issued on this white stock.

COMPLETE SET (330) 12.00 30.00
COMP.FACT.SET (330) 15.00 35.00
*WHITE BACKS: 6X TO 15X BASIC CARDS
1 Mario Lemieux 1.25 3.00
2 Ulf Dahlen .30 .75
3 Terry Carkner RC .30 .75
4 Tony McKegney .30 .75
5 Denis Savard .40 1.00
6 Derek King RC .30 .75
7 Lanny McDonald .30 .75
8 John Tonelli .30 .75
9 Tom Kurvers .30 .75
10 Dave Archibald .30 .75
11 Peter Sidorkiewicz RC .30 .75
12 Esa Tikkanen .30 .75
13 Dave Barr .30 .75
14 Brent Sutter .30 .75
15 Cam Neely .30 .75
16 Calle Johansson RC .25 .60
17 Patrick Roy 1.00 2.50
18 Dale DeGray RC .25 .60
19 Phil Bourque RC .25 .60
20 Kevin Dineen .25 .60
21 Mike Bullard .25 .60
22 Gary Leeman .25 .60
23 Greg Stefan .25 .60
24 Brian Mullen .25 .60
25 Pierre Turgeon .60 1.50
26 Bob Rouse RC .25 .60
27 Peter Zezel .25 .60
28 Jeff Brown .25 .60
29 Andy Brickley RC .25 .60
30 Mike Gartner .25 .60
31 Darren Pang .25 .60
32 Pat Verbeek .25 .60
33 Petri Skriko .25 .60
34 Tom Laidlaw .25 .60
35 Randy Wood .25 .60
36 Tom Barrasso .25 .60
37 John Tucker .25 .60
38 Andrew McBain .25 .60
39 David Shaw .25 .60
40 Rejean Lemelin .25 .60
41 Dino Ciccarelli .25 .60
42 Jeff Sharples .25 .60
43 Jari Kurri .25 .60
44 Murray Craven .25 .60
45 Cliff Ronning RC 1.00 2.50
46 Dave Babych .25 .60
47 Bernie Nicholls .25 .60
48 Jon Casey RC .25 .60
49 Al MacInnis .25 .60
50 Bob Errey RC .25 .60
51 Glen Wesley .25 .60
52 Dirk Graham .25 .60
53 Guy Carbonneau .25 .60
54 Tomas Sandstrom .25 .60
55 Rod Langway .25 .60
56 Patrik Sundstrom .25 .60
57 Michel Goulet .25 .60
58 Dave Taylor .25 .60
59 Phil Housley .25 .60
60 Pat LaFontaine .30 .75
61 Kirk McLean RC .40 1.00
62 Ken Linseman .25 .60
63 Randy Cunneyworth .25 .60
64 Tony Hrkac .25 .60
65 Mark Messier .25 .60
66 Carey Wilson .25 .60
67 Stephen Leach RC .25 .60
68 Christian Ruuttu .25 .60
69 Dave Ellett .25 .60
70 Ray Ferraro .25 .60
71 Colin Patterson RC .25 .60
72 Tim Kerr .25 .60
73 Bob Joyce .25 .60
74 Doug Gilmour .40 1.00
75 Lee Norwood .25 .60
76 Dale Hunter .25 .60
77 Jim Johnson .25 .60
78 Mike Foligno .30 .75
79 Al Iafrate .30 .75
80 Rick Tocchet .30 .75
81 Greg Hawgood RC .30 .75
82 Steve Thomas .30 .75
83 Steve Yzerman .75 2.00
84 Mike McPhee .30 .75
85 David Volek RC .30 .75
86 Brian Benning .30 .75
87 Neal Broten .30 .75
88 Luc Robitaille .30 .75
89 Trevor Linden RC 1.00 2.50
90 James Patrick .30 .75
91 Brian Lawton .30 .75
92 Sean Burke .30 .75
93 Scott Stevens .30 .75
94 Pat Elynuik RC .30 .75
95 Paul Coffey .30 .75
96 Jan Erixon .30 .75
97 Mike Liut .30 .75
98 Wayne Presley .30 .75
99 Craig Simpson .30 .75
100 Kjell Samuelsson RC .30 .75
101 Shawn Burr .30 .75
102 John MacLean .30 .75
103 Tom Fergus .30 .75
104 Mike Krushelnyski .30 .75
105 Gary Nylund .30 .75
106 Dave Andreychuk .30 .75
107 Bernie Federko .30 .75
108 Gary Suter .30 .75
109 Dave Gagner .30 .75
110 Ray Bourque .50 1.25
111 Geoff Courtnall RC .60 1.50
112 Doug Wilson .30 .75
113 Joe Sakic RC 8.00 20.00
114 John Vanbiesbrouck .30 .75
115 Dave Poulin .30 .75
116 Rick Meagher .20 .50
117 Kirk Muller .20 .50
118 Mats Naslund .20 .50
119 Ray Sheppard .20 .50
120 Jeff Norton RC .25 .60
121 Randy Burridge .20 .50
122 Dale Hawerchuk .40 1.00
123 Steve Duchesne .20 .50
124 John Anderson .20 .50
125 Rick Vaive .20 .50
126 Randy Hillier .20 .50
127 Jimmy Carson .20 .50
128 Larry Murphy .20 .50
129 Paul MacLean .20 .50
130 Joe Cirella .20 .50
131 Kelly Miller .20 .50
132 Alain Chevrier .20 .50
133 Ed Olczyk .20 .50
134 Dave Tippett .20 .50
135 Bob Sweeney .20 .50
136 Brian Leetch RC 2.50 6.00
137 Greg Millen .20 .50
138 Joe Nieuwendyk .20 .50
139 Brian Propp .20 .50
140 Mike Ramsey .20 .50
141 Mike Allison .20 .50
142 Shawn Chambers RC .20 .50
143 Peter Stastny .20 .50
144 Glen Hanlon .20 .50
145 John Cullen RC .25 .60
146 Kevin Hatcher .25 .60
147 Brendan Shanahan .40 1.00
148 Paul Reinhart .25 .60
149 Bryan Trottier .40 1.00
150 Dave Manson RC .25 .60
151 Marc Habscheid RC .25 .60
152 Dan Quinn .25 .60
153 Stephane Richer .25 .60
154 Doug Bodger .25 .60
155 Ron Hextall .25 .60
156 Wayne Gretzky 1.50 4.00
157 Steve Tuttle RC .30 .75
158 Charlie Huddy .30 .75
159 Dave Christian .30 .75
160 Andy Moog .30 .75
161 Tony Granato RC .30 .75
162 Sylvain Cote RC .30 .75
163 Mike Vernon .40 1.00
164 Steve Chiasson RC .25 .60
165 Mike Ridley .25 .60
166 Kelly Hrudey .25 .60
167 Bob Carpenter .25 .60
168 Zarley Zalapski RC .25 .60
169 Derek Laxdal RC .30 .75
170 Clint Malarchuk .30 .75
171 Kelly Kisio .30 .75
172 Gerard Gallant .30 .75
173 Ron Sutter .30 .75
174 Chris Chelios .30 .75
175 Ron Francis .40 1.00
176 Gino Cavallini .25 .60
177 Brian Bellows .25 .60
178 Greg C. Adams .25 .60
179 Steve Larmer .25 .60
180 Aaron Broten .25 .60
181 Brent Ashton .25 .60
182 Gerald Diduck RC .25 .60
183 Paul MacDermid RC .25 .60
184 Walt Poddubny .25 .60
185 Adam Oates .30 .75
186 Brett Hull .40 1.00
187 Scott Arniel .25 .60
188 Bobby Smith .25 .60
189 Guy Lafleur .40 1.00
190 Craig Janney RC .40 1.00
191 Mark Howe .30 .75
192 Grant Fuhr .60 1.50
193 Rob Brown .20 .50
194 Steve Kasper .20 .50
195 Pete Peeters .20 .50
196 Joe Mullen .20 .50
197 Checklist 1-110 .20 .50
198 Checklist 111-220 .20 .50
199 Keith Crowder .20 .50
200 Daren Puppa RC .40 1.00
201 Benoit Hogue RC .20 .50
202 Gary Roberts RC .40 1.00
203 Brad McCrimmon .20 .50
204 Rick Wamsley .20 .50
205 Joel Otto .20 .50
206 Jim Peplinski .20 .50
207 Jamie Macoun .20 .50
208 Brian MacLellan .20 .50
209 Scott Young RC .50 1.25
210 Ulf Samuelsson .20 .50
211 Joel Quenneville UER .20 .50
Misspelled Quennville
212 Tim Watters .20 .50
213 Curt Giles .20 .50
214 Stewart Gavin .20 .50
215 Bob Brooke .25 .60
216 Basil McRae RC .25 .60
217 Frantisek Musil RC .25 .60
218 Adam Creighton RC .25 .60
219 Troy Murray .25 .60
220 Steve Konroyd .25 .60
221 Duane Sutter .25 .60
222 Trent Yawney RC .25 .60
223 Mike O'Connell .30 .75
224 Jim Nill .30 .75
225 John Chabot .30 .75
226 Glenn Anderson .30 .75
227 Kevin Lowe .30 .75
228 Steve Smith .25 .60
229 Randy Gregg .25 .60
230 Craig MacTavish .25 .60
231 Craig Muni .25 .60
232 Theo Fleury RC 3.00 8.00
233 Bill Ranford .25 .60
234 Claude Lemieux .25 .60
235 Larry Robinson .25 .60
236 Craig Ludwig .25 .60
237 Brian Hayward .25 .60
238 Petr Svoboda .25 .60
239 Russ Courtnall .25 .60
240 Ryan Walter .25 .60
241 Tommy Albelin .25 .60
242 Doug Brown .25 .60
243 Ken Daneyko RC .25 .60
244 Mark Johnson .25 .60
245 Randy Velischek RC .25 .60
246 Brad Dalgarno RC .25 .60
247 Mikko Makela .25 .60
248 Shayne Corson RC .50 1.25
249 Marc Bergevin RC .25 .60
250 Pat Flatley .20 .50
251 Michel Petit .20 .50
252 Mark Hardy .20 .50
253 Scott Mellanby .20 .50
254 Keith Acton .20 .50
255 Ken Wregget .20 .50
256 Gord Dineen RC .20 .50
257 Dave Hannan .20 .50
258 Mario Gosselin .20 .50
259 Randy Moller .20 .50
260 Mario Marois .20 .50
261 Robert Picard .20 .50
262 Marc Fortier RC .20 .50
263 Ron Tugnutt RC .75 2.00
264 Iiro Jarvi RC .20 .50
265 Paul Gillis .25 .60
266 Mike Hough RC .25 .60
267 Jim Sandlak .25 .60
268 Greg Paslawski .25 .60
269 Paul Cavallini RC .25 .60
270 Gaston Gingras .25 .60
271 Allan Bester .25 .60
272 Vincent Damphousse .25 .60
273 Daniel Marois RC .25 .60
274 Mark Osborne UER .30 .75
Misspelled Osbourne
275 Craig Laughlin .25 .60
276 Brad Marsh .25 .60
277 Dan Daoust .25 .60
278 Borje Salming .25 .60
279 Chris Kotsopoulos .25 .60
280 Tony Tanti .25 .60
281 Barry Pederson .25 .60
282 Rich Sutter .25 .60
283 Stan Smyl .25 .60
284 Doug Lidster .25 .60
285 Steve Weeks .20 .50
286 Harold Snepsts .20 .50
287 Brian Bradley RC .25 .60
288 Larry Melnyk .25 .60
289 Bob Gould .25 .60
290 Thomas Steen .25 .60
291 Randy Carlyle .25 .60
292 Hannu Jarvenpaa RC .20 .50
293 Iain Duncan .20 .50
294 Doug Smail .20 .50
295 Jim Kyte .25 .60
296 Daniel Berthiaume .25 .60
297 Peter Taglianetti .25 .60
298 Bruins/Janney .25 .60
299 Buffalo Sabres .25 .60
300 Calgary Flames .25 .60
301 Chicago Blackhawks .25 .60
302 Detroit Red Wings .25 .60
303 Edmonton Oilers .25 .60
304 Hartford Whalers .25 .60
305 Los Angeles Kings .25 .60
306 Minnesota North Stars .25 .60
307 Montreal Canadiens .25 .60
308 New Jersey Devils .25 .60
309 New York Islanders .25 .60
310 New York Rangers .25 .60
311 Flyers/Hextall .25 .60
312 Penguins/Lemieux .30 .75
313 Nordiques/Sakic .30 .75
314 St. Louis Blues .25 .60
315 Toronto Maple Leafs .25 .60
316 Vancouver Canucks .25 .60
Action Scene/(Jim Sandlak, Ray Bourque defending)
317 Washington Capitals .25 .60
318 Winnipeg Jets .25 .60
319 Mario Lemieux Ross 1.25 3.00
320 Wayne Gretzky Hart 1.50 4.00
321 Brian Leetch Calder 1.00 2.50
322 Patrick Roy Vezina 1.00 2.50
323 Norris Trophy .25 .60
324 Lady Byng Trophy .25 .60
325 Wayne Gretzky HL 1.50 4.00
326 Brian Leetch HL UER 1.00 2.50
327 Mario Lemieux HL 1.25 3.00
328 1988-89 Highlight .25 .60
329 Coupe Stanley Cup .25 .60
330 Checklist 221-330 .25 .60

1989-90 O-Pee-Chee Box Bottoms

This sixteen-card set was issued in sets of four on the bottom of the 1989-90 O-Pee-Chee wax pack boxes. Complete box bottom panels are valued at a 25 percent premium above the prices listed below. The cards featured sixteen NHL star players who were scoring leaders on their teams. A color action photo appeared on the front and the player's name, team, and team logo at the bottom of the picture. The back was printed in red and black ink and gave the player's position and statistical information. The cards were lettered rather than numbered.

COMPLETE SET (16) 4.00 10.00
A Mario Lemieux 1.50 4.00
B Mike Ridley .08 .25
C Tomas Sandstrom .08 .25
D Petri Skriko .08 .25
E Wayne Gretzky 1.50 4.00
F Brett Hull .75 2.00
G Tim Kerr .08 .25
H Mats Naslund .08 .25
I Jari Kurri .20 .50
J Steve Larmer .20 .50
K Cam Neely .30 .75
L Steve Yzerman .75 2.00
M Kevin Dineen .08 .25
N Dave Gagner .15 .40
O Joe Mullen .15 .40
P Pierre Turgeon .30 .75

1989-90 O-Pee-Chee Sticker Back Cards

This set was essentially part of the 1989-90 O-Pee-Chee sticker set. The cards measured approximately 2 1/8" by 3" and were actually the backs of the stickers base set. Each of the first 34-cards feature a color action player photo cut out and superimposed on a solid color background (red, orange, or green). The player's name, position, and team appeared next to the cut-out picture along with a card number. The remainder of the cards in the set feature triva questions.

COMPLETE SET (76) 3.00 8.00
1 Greg Hawgood .02 .10
2 Craig Janney .08 .25
3 Bob Joyce .02 .10
4 Benoit Hogue .07 .20
5 Jiri Hrdina .02 .10
6 Peter Sidorkiewicz .07 .20
7 Scott Young .08 .25
8 Sean Burke .10 .30
9 Dave Volek .02 .10
10 Tony Granato .07 .20
11 Brian Leetch .40 1.00
12 Gord Murphy .02 .10
13 John Cullen .07 .20
14 Zarley Zalapski .07 .20
15 Iiro Jarvi .02 .10
16 Joe Sakic .60 1.50
17 Vincent Riendeau .07 .20
18 Dan Marois .02 .10
19 Trevor Linden .30 .75
20 Pat Elynuik .02 .10
21 Bob Essensa .07 .20
22 Checklist .02 .10
23 Joe Mullen .07 .20
24 Mario Lemieux .60 1.50
25 Gerard Gallant .02 .10
26 Chris Chelios .20 .50
27 Al MacInnis .08 .25
28 Patrick Roy .60 1.50
29 Geoff Courtnall .08 .25
30 Wayne Gretzky .75 2.00
31 Rob Brown .02 .10
32 Steve Duchesne .08 .25
33 Ray Bourque .20 .50
34 Mike Vernon .08 .25
Q35 Trivia Question 35 .01 .05
Q36 Trivia Question 36 .01 .05
Q37 Trivia Question 37 .01 .05
Q38 Trivia Question 38 .01 .05
Q39 Trivia Question 39 .01 .05
Q40 Trivia Question 40 .01 .05
Q41 Trivia Question 41 .01 .05
Q42 Trivia Question 42 .01 .05
Q43 Trivia Question 43 .01 .05
Q44 Trivia Question 44 .01 .05
Q45 Trivia Question 45 .01 .05
Q46 Trivia Question 46 .01 .05
Q47 Trivia Question 47 .01 .05
Q48 Trivia Question 48 .01 .05
Q49 Trivia Question 49 .01 .05
Q50 Trivia Question 50 .01 .05
Q51 Trivia Question 51 .01 .05
Q52 Trivia Question 52 .01 .05
Q53 Trivia Question 53 .01 .05
Q54 Trivia Question 54 .01 .05
Q55 Trivia Question 55 .01 .05
A56 Trivia Answer 56 .01 .05
A57 Trivia Answer 57 .01 .05
A58 Trivia Answer 58 .01 .05
A59 Trivia Answer 59 .01 .05
A60 Trivia Answer 60 .01 .05
A61 Trivia Answer 61 .01 .05
A62 Trivia Answer 62 .01 .05
A63 Trivia Answer 63 .01 .05
A64 Trivia Answer 64 .01 .05
A65 Trivia Answer 65 .01 .05
A66 Trivia Answer 66 .01 .05
A67 Trivia Answer 67 .01 .05
A68 Trivia Answer 68 .01 .05
A69 Trivia Answer 69 .01 .05
A70 Trivia Answer 70 .01 .05
A71 Trivia Answer 71 .01 .05
A72 Trivia Answer 72 .01 .05
A73 Trivia Answer 73 .01 .05
A74 Trivia Answer 74 .01 .05
A75 Trivia Answer 75 .01 .05
A76 Trivia Answer 76 .01 .05

1990-91 O-Pee-Chee

At 528 cards, this was the largest set ever issued by O-Pee-Chee. Cards measured the standard 2 1/2" by 3 1/2". The fronts featured color photos bordered by team colors. A hockey stick is superimposed over the picture at the top border. Bilingual backs had blue lettering on a pale green background and had biographical information and career statistics.

COMPLETE SET (528) 12.00 25.00
COMP.FACT.SET (528) 20.00 50.00
1 Wayne Gretzky Indy 1.00 2.50
2 Wayne Gretzky Oilers 1.00 2.50
3 Wayne Gretzky LA 1.00 2.50
4 Brett Hull HL .40 1.00
5 Jari Kurri HL .25 .60
6 Bryan Trottier HL .25 .60
7 Jeremy Roenick RC .60 1.50
8 Brian Propp .20 .50
9 Jim Hrivnak RC .20 .50
10 Mick Vukota RC .20 .50
11 Tom Kurvers .20 .50
12 Ulf Dahlen .20 .50
13 Bernie Nicholls .20 .50
14 Peter Sidorkiewicz .20 .50
15 Peter Zezel .20 .50
16 Mike Hartman RC .20 .50
17 Kings Team .20 .50
18 Jim Sandlak .20 .50
19 Rob Brown .40 1.00
20 Paul Ranheim RC .20 .50
21 Rick Zombo RC .20 .50
22 Paul Gillis .15 .40
23 Brian Hayward .20 .50
24 Brent Ashton .20 .50
25 Mark Lamb .20 .50
26 Rick Tocchet .20 .50
27 Slava Fetisov RC .40 1.00
28 Denis Savard .25 .60
29 Chris Chelios .20 .50
30 Janne Ojanen RC .20 .50
31 Don Maloney .20 .50
32 Allan Bester .20 .50
33 Geoff Smith RC .20 .50
34 Daniel Shank RC .20 .50
35 Mikael Andersson RC .20 .50
36 Gino Cavallini .20 .50
37 Rob Murphy RC .20 .50
38 Flames Team .25 .60
39 Laurie Boschman .15 .40
40 Craig Wolanin RC .15 .40
41 Phil Bourque .15 .40
42 Alexander Mogilny RC .60 1.50
43 Ray Bourque .30 .75
44 Mike Liut .15 .40
45 Ron Sutter .15 .40
46 Bob Kudelski RC .15 .40
47 Larry Murphy .15 .40
48 Darren Turcotte RC .15 .40
49 Paul Ysebaert RC .15 .40
50 Alan Kerr .15 .40
51 Randy Carlyle .15 .40
52 Iiro Jarvi .15 .40
53 Don Barber RC .15 .40
54 Carey Wilson .15 .40
55 Joey Kocur RC .40 1.00
56 Steve Larmer .15 .40
57 Paul Cavallini .15 .40
58 Shayne Corson .15 .40
59 Canucks Team .15 .40
60 Sergei Makarov RC .40 1.00
61 Kjell Samuelsson .15 .40
62 Tony Granato .15 .40
63 Tom Fergus .15 .40
64 Martin Gelinas RC .40 1.00
65 Tom Barrasso .15 .40
66 Pierre Turgeon .15 .40
67 Randy Cunneyworth .15 .40
68 Michal Pivonka RC .15 .40
69 Cam Neely .20 .50
70 Brian Bellows .15 .40
71 Pat Elynuik .15 .40
72 Doug Crossman .15 .40
73 Sylvain Turgeon .15 .40
74 Shawn Burr .15 .40
75 John Vanbiesbrouck .15 .40
76 Steve Bozek .15 .40
77 Brett Hull .40 1.00
78 Zarley Zalapski .15 .40
79 Wendel Clark .20 .50
80 Flyers Team .20 .50
81 Kelly Miller .12 .30
82 Mark Pederson RC .20 .50
83 Adam Creighton .12 .30
84 Scott Young .12 .30
85 Petr Klima .12 .30
86 Steve Duchesne .12 .30
87 Joe Nieuwendyk .12 .30
88 Andy Brickley .12 .30
89 Phil Housley .15 .40
90 Neal Broten .12 .30
91 Al Iafrate .12 .30
92 Steve Thomas .12 .30
93 Guy Carbonneau .12 .30
94 Steve Chiasson .12 .30
95 Mike Tomlak RC .20 .50
96 Roger Johansson RC .20 .50
97 Randy Wood .12 .30
98 Jim Johnson .12 .30
99 Bob Sweeney .12 .30
100 Dino Ciccarelli .20 .50
101 Rangers Team .20 .50
102 Mike Ramsey .12 .30
103 Kelly Hrudey .12 .30
104 Dave Ellett .12 .30
105 Bob Brooke .12 .30
106 Greg Adams .12 .30
107 Joe Cirella .12 .30
108 Jari Kurri .25 .60
109 Pete Peeters .12 .30
110 Paul MacLean .15 .40
111 Doug Wilson .20 .50
112 Pat Verbeek .15 .40
113 Bob Beers RC .15 .40
114 Mike O'Connell .15 .40
115 Brian Bradley .15 .40
116 Paul Coffey .20 .50
117 Doug Brown .15 .40
118 Aaron Broten .15 .40
119 Bob Essensa RC .30 .75
120 Wayne Gretzky 1.00 2.50
121 Vincent Damphousse .15 .40
122 Nordiques Team .15 .40
123 Mike Foligno .15 .40
124 Russ Courtnall .20 .50
125 Rick Meagher .15 .40
126 Craig Fisher RC .20 .50
127 Al MacInnis .15 .40
128 Derek King .20 .50
129 Dale Hunter .20 .50
130 Mark Messier UER .40 1.00
131 James Patrick UER .20 .50
should be orange border
132 Checklist 1-132 .20 .50
133 Red Wings Team .60 1.50
134 Barry Pederson .15 .40
135 Gary Leeman .15 .40
136 Doug Gilmour .25 .60
137 Mike McPhee .15 .40
138 Bob Murray .15 .40
139 Bob Carpenter .15 .40
140 Sean Burke .15 .40
141 Dale Hawerchuk .25 .60
142 Guy Lafleur .25 .60
143 Lindy Ruff .15 .40
144 Whalers Team .20 .50
145 Glenn Anderson .20 .50
146 Dave Chyzowski RC .15 .40
147 Kevin Hatcher .15 .40
148 Rick Vaive .15 .40
149 Adam Oates .20 .50
150 Garth Butcher .15 .40
151 Basil McRae .15 .40
152 Ilkka Sinisalo .15 .40
153 Steve Kasper .15 .40
154 Greg Paslawski .15 .40
155 Brad Marsh .15 .40
156 Esa Tikkanen .15 .40
157 Tony Tanti .15 .40
158 Mario Marois UER .15 .40
159 Sylvain Lefebvre RC .15 .40
160 Troy Murray .15 .40
161 Gary Roberts .20 .50
162 Randy Ladouceur .20 .50
163 John Chabot .20 .50
164 Calle Johansson .20 .50
165 Bruins Team .30 .75
166 Jeff Norton .20 .50
167 Mike Krushelnyski .20 .50
168 Dave Gagner .20 .50
169 Dave Andreychuk .20 .50
170 Dave Capuano RC .20 .50
171 Curtis Joseph RC .60 1.50
172 Bruce Driver .20 .50
173 Scott Mellanby .20 .50
174 John Ogrodnick .20 .50
175 Mario Lemieux .75 2.00
176 Marc Fortier .15 .40
177 Vincent Riendeau RC .20 .50
178 Mark Johnson .15 .40
179 Dirk Graham .15 .40
180 Jets Team .20 .50
181 Robb Stauber RC .20 .50
182 Christian Ruuttu .15 .40
183 Dave Tippett .15 .40
184 Pat LaFontaine .20 .50
185 Mark Howe .20 .50
186 Stephane Richer .20 .50
187 Jan Erixon .20 .50
188 Neil Sheehy .20 .50
189 Craig MacTavish .15 .40
190 Randy Burridge .15 .40
191 Bernie Federko .15 .40
192 Shawn Chambers .15 .40
193 Mark Messier AS1 .40 1.00
194 Luc Robitaille AS1 .20 .50
195 Brett Hull AS1 .40 1.00
196 Ray Bourque AS1 .30 .75
197 Al MacInnis AS1 .15 .40
198 Patrick Roy AS1 .50 1.25
199 Wayne Gretzky AS2 1.00 2.50
200 Brian Bellows AS2 .15 .40
201 Cam Neely AS2 .20 .50
202 Paul Coffey AS2 .20 .50
203 Doug Wilson AS2 .20 .50
204 Daren Puppa AS2 .15 .40
205 Gary Suter .20 .50
206 Ed Olczyk .20 .50
207 Doug Lidster .20 .50
208 John Cullen .20 .50
209 Luc Robitaille .20 .50
210 Tim Kerr .20 .50
211 Scott Stevens .20 .50
212 Craig Janney .20 .50
213 Kevin Dineen .20 .50
214 Jimmy Waite RC .20 .50
215 Benoit Hogue .20 .50
216 Curtis Leschyshyn RC .15 .40
217 Brad Lauer .15 .40
218 Joe Mullen .15 .40
219 Patrick Roy .50 1.25
220 Blues Team .20 .50
221 Brian Leetch .25 .60
222 Steve Yzerman .60 1.50
223 Stephane Beauregard RC .15 .40
224 John MacLean .15 .40
225 Trevor Linden .15 .40
226 Bill Ranford .15 .40
227 Mark Osborne .15 .40
228 Curt Giles .15 .40
229 Mikko Makela .15 .40
230 Bob Errey .15 .40
231 Jimmy Carson .15 .40
232 Kay Whitmore RC .15 .40
233 Gary Nylund .15 .40
234 Jiri Hrdina RC .15 .40
235 Stephen Leach .15 .40
236 Greg Hawgood .15 .40
237 Jocelyn Lemieux RC .15 .40
238 Daren Puppa .15 .40
239 Kelly Kisio .15 .40
240 Craig Simpson .15 .40
241 Maple Leafs Team .15 .40
242 Fredrik Olausson .15 .40
243 Ron Hextall .15 .40
244 Sergio Momesso RC .15 .40
245 Kirk Muller .15 .40
246 Petr Svoboda .15 .40
247 Daniel Berthiaume .15 .40
248 Andrew McBain .15 .40
249 Jeff Jackson UER .15 .40
250 Randy Gilhen RC .12 .30
251 Oilers .40 1.00
Adam Graves
252 Rick Bennett RC .12 .30
253 Don Beaupre .12 .30
254 Pelle Eklund .12 .30
255 Greg Gilbert .12 .30
256 Gordie Roberts .12 .30
257 Kirk McLean .12 .30
258 Brent Sutter .15 .40
259 Brendan Shanahan .25 .60
260 Todd Krygier RC .15 .40
261 Larry Robinson UER .15 .40
262 Sabres Team .15 .40
263 Dave Christian .15 .40
264 Checklist 133-264 .20 .50
265 Jamie Macoun .15 .40
266 Glen Hanlon .15 .40
267 Daniel Marois .15 .40
268 Doug Smail .15 .40
269 Jon Casey .20 .50
270 Brian Skrudland .15 .40
271 Michel Petit .15 .40
272 Dan Quinn .15 .40
273 Geoff Courtnall .15 .40
274 Mike Bullard .15 .40
275 Randy Gregg .15 .40
276 Keith Brown .15 .40
277 Troy Mallette RC .15 .40
278 Steve Tuttle .15 .40
279 Brad Shaw RC .15 .40
280 Mark Recchi RC .60 1.50
281 John Tonelli .15 .40
282 Doug Bodger .15 .40
283 Thomas Steen .15 .40
284 Devils Team .40 1.00
285 Lee Norwood .15 .40
286 Brian MacLellan .15 .40
287 Bobby Smith .15 .40
288 Rob Cimetta RC .15 .40
289 Rob Zettler RC .15 .40
290 David Reid RC .20 .50
291 Bryan Trottier .25 .60
292 Brian Mullen .20 .50
293 Paul Reinhart .20 .50
294 Andy Moog .20 .50
295 Jeff Brown .20 .50
296 Ryan Walter .20 .50
297 Trent Yawney .20 .50
298 John Druce RC .20 .50
299 Dave McLlwain .20 .50
300 David Volek .20 .50
301 Tomas Sandstrom .20 .50
302 Gord Murphy RC .20 .50
303 Lou Franceschetti RC .20 .50
304 Dana Murzyn .20 .50
305 North Stars Team .20 .50
306 Patrik Sundstrom .20 .50
307 Kevin Lowe .20 .50
308 Dave Barr .20 .50
309 Wendell Young RC .20 .50
310 Darrin Shannon RC .20 .50
311 Ron Francis .25 .60
312 Stephane Fiset RC .40 1.00
313 Paul Fenton .20 .50
314 Dave Taylor .20 .50
315 Islanders Team .20 .50
316 Petri Skriko .20 .50
317 Rob Ramage .20 .50
318 Murray Craven .20 .50
319 Gaetan Duchesne .20 .50
320 Brad McCrimmon .20 .50
321 Grant Fuhr .20 .50
322 Gerard Gallant .12 .30
323 Tommy Albelin .12 .30
324 Scott Arniel .12 .30
325 Mike Keane RC .12 .30
326 Penguins Team .20 .50
327 Mike Ridley .12 .30
328 Dave Babych .12 .30
329 Michel Goulet .12 .30
330 Mike Richter RC .60 1.50
331 Garry Galley RC .12 .30
332 Rod Brind'Amour RC .40 1.00
333 Tony McKegney .12 .30
334 Peter Stastny .15 .40
335 Greg Millen .15 .40
336 Ray Ferraro .15 .40
337 Miloslav Horava RC .15 .40
338 Paul MacDermid .15 .40
339 Craig Coxe RC .15 .40
340 Dave Snuggerud RC .15 .40
341 Mike Lalor RC .15 .40
342 Marc Habscheid .15 .40
343 Rejean Lemelin .15 .40
344 Charlie Huddy .15 .40
345 Ken Linseman .15 .40
346 Canadiens Team .20 .50
347 Troy Loney RC .20 .50
348 Mike Modano RC .60 1.50
349 Jeff Reese RC .20 .50
350 Pat Flatley .20 .50
351 Mike Vernon .20 .50
352 Todd Elik RC .20 .50
353 Rod Langway .20 .50
354 Moe Mantha .20 .50
355 Keith Acton .20 .50
356 Scott Pearson RC .20 .50
357 Perry Berezan RC .20 .50
358 Alexei Kasatonov RC .20 .50
359 Igor Larionov RC .40 1.00
360 Kevin Stevens RC .40 1.00
361 Yves Racine RC .20 .50
362 Dave Poulin .20 .50
363 Blackhawks Team .20 .50
364 Yvon Corriveau RC .15 .40
365 Brian Benning .15 .40
366 Hubie McDonough RC .15 .40
367 Ron Tugnutt .15 .40
368 Steve Smith .15 .40
369 Joel Otto .15 .40
370 Dave Lowry RC .15 .40
371 Clint Malarchuk .15 .40
372 Mathieu Schneider RC .15 .40
373 Mike Gartner .20 .50
374 John Tucker .15 .40
375 Chris Terreri RC .40 1.00
376 Dean Evason .15 .40
377 Jamie Leach RC .15 .40
378 Jacques Cloutier RC .15 .40
379 Glen Wesley .15 .40
380 Vladimir Krutov RC .40 1.00
381 Terry Carkner .15 .40
382 John McIntyre RC .15 .40
383 Ville Siren RC .15 .40

384 Joe Sakic .60 1.50
385 Teppo Numminen RC .40 1.00
386 Theo Fleury .25 .60
387 Glen Featherstone RC .15 .40
388 Stephan Lebeau RC .15 .40
389 Kevin McClelland .15 .40
390 Uwe Krupp .20 .50
391 Mark Janssens RC .20 .50
392 Marty McSorley .20 .50
393 Vladimir Ruzicka RC .20 .50
394 Capitals Team .20 .50
395 Mark Fitzpatrick RC .15 .40
396 Checklist 265-396 .20 .50
397 Dave Manson .20 .50
398 Bob Gould .20 .50
399 Bill Houlder RC .20 .50
400 Glenn Healy RC .40 1.00
401 John Kordic RC .40 1.00
402 Stewart Gavin .20 .50
403 David Shaw .20 .50
404 Ed Kastelic RC .20 .50
405 Rich Sutter .20 .50
406 Grant Ledyard RC .20 .50
407 Steve Weeks .20 .50
408 Randy Hillier .20 .50
409 Rick Wamsley .20 .50
410 Doug Houda RC .20 .50
411 Ken McRae RC .20 .50
412 Craig Ludwig .20 .50
413 Doug Evans RC .20 .50
414 Ken Baumgartner RC .20 .50
415 Ken Wregget .20 .50
416 Eric Weinrich RC .20 .50
417 Mike Allison .15 .40
418 Joel Quenneville .15 .40
419 Larry Melnyk .15 .40
420 Colin Patterson .15 .40
421 Gerald Diduck .15 .40
422 Brent Gilchrist RC .15 .40
423 Craig Muni .15 .40
424 Mike Hudson RC .15 .40
425 Eric Desjardins RC .40 1.00
426 Walt Poddubny .15 .40
427 Mike Hough .15 .40
428 Luke Richardson .15 .40
429 Joe Murphy RC .15 .40
430 Tim Cheveldae RC .15 .40
431 Adam Burt RC .15 .40
432 Kelly Chase RC .40 1.00
433 Robert Nordmark RC .15 .40
434 Tim Hunter RC .15 .40
435 Peter Taglianetti .15 .40
436 Alain Chevrier .15 .40
437 Darin Kimble RC .40 1.00
438 David Maley RC .20 .50
439 Jim Wiemer RC .20 .50
440 Nick Kypreos RC .20 .50
441 Lucien DeBlois .15 .40
442 Mario Gosselin .15 .40
443 Neil Wilkinson RC .15 .40
444 Mark Kumpel RC .12 .30
445 Sergei Mylnikov RC .12 .30
446 Ray Sheppard .12 .30
447 Ron Greschner .12 .30
448 Craig Berube RC .12 .30
449 Dave Hannan .12 .30
450 Jim Korn .12 .30
451 Claude Lemieux .12 .30
452 Eldon Reddick RC .40 1.00
453 Randy Velischek .12 .30
454 Chris Nilan .12 .30
455 Jim Benning .12 .30
456 Wayne Presley .12 .30
457 Jon Morris RC .12 .30
458 Clark Donatelli RC .12 .30
459 Ric Nattress .12 .30
460 Rob Murray RC .12 .30
461 Tim Watters .12 .30
462 Checklist 397-528 .20 .50
463 Derrick Smith RC .15 .40
464 Lyndon Byers RC .15 .40
465 Jeff Chychrun RC .15 .40
466 Duane Sutter .15 .40
467 Conn Smythe Trophy .15 .40
468 Anatoli Semenov RC .15 .40
469 Konstantin Kurashov RC .15 .40
470 Gord Dineen .15 .40
471 Jeff Beukeboom RC .15 .40
472 Andrei Lomakin RC .15 .40
473 Doug Sulliman .15 .40
474 Alexander Kerch RC .15 .40
475 Norris Trophy .30 .75
476 Keith Crowder .15 .40
477 Oleg Znarok RC .15 .40
478 Dimitri Zinovyev RC .15 .40
479 Igor Esmantovich RC .15 .40
480 Adam Graves RC .40 1.00
481 Petr Prajsler RC .15 .40
482 Sergei Yashin RC .15 .40
483 Jeff Bloemberg RC .15 .40
484 Yuri Strakhov RC .15 .40
485 Sergei B. Makarov RC .15 .40
486 Jennings Trophy .20 .50
487 Sergei Zaltsev RC .15 .40
488 Selke Trophy .15 .40
489 Yuri Kusnetsov RC .15 .40
490 Tom Chorske RC .15 .40
491 Igor Akulinin RC .15 .40
492 Mikhail Panin RC .15 .40
493 Sergei Nemchinov RC .15 .40
494 Vladimir Yurzinov RC .15 .40
495 Gord Kluzak .15 .40
496 Sergei Skosyrev RC .15 .40
497 Jeff Parker RC .15 .40
498 Tom Tilley RC .15 .40
499 Alexander Smirnov RC .15 .40
500 Alexander Lysenko RC .15 .40
501 Arturs Irbe UER RC .75 2.00
502 Alexei Frolikov RC .15 .40
503 Sergei Makarov Calder .40 1.00
504 Nikolai Varjanov RC .15 .40
505 Allen Pedersen .15 .40
506 Vladimir Shashov RC .15 .40
507 Tim Bergland RC .15 .40
508 Gennady Lebedev RC .20 .50
509 Rod Buskas RC .20 .50
510 Grant Jennings RC .20 .50
511 Ulf Samuelsson .20 .50
512 Patrick Roy Vezina .50 1.25
513 Brett Hull Byng .40 1.00
514 Dimitri Mironov RC .20 .50
515 Randy Moller .20 .50
516 Kerry Huffman RC .20 .50
517 Gilbert Delorme .20 .50
518 Greg C. Adams .20 .50
519 Hart Trophy .40 1.00
520 Sheldon Kennedy RC .20 .50
521 Harijs Vitolins RC .20 .50
522 Wayne Gretzky Ross 1.00 2.50
523 Dmitri Frolov RC .20 .50
524 Tom Laidlaw .20 .50
525 Oleg Bratash RC .20 .50
526 Kris King RC .20 .50
527 Wayne Van Dorp RC .20 .50
528 Chris Dahlquist RC .20 .50

1990-91 O-Pee-Chee Box Bottoms

This sixteen-card set was issued in sets of four on the bottom of the 1990-91 O-Pee-Chee wax pack boxes. Complete box bottom panels are valued at a 25 percent premium above the prices listed below. The cards are lettered rather than numbered.

COMPLETE SET (16) 5.00 12.00
A Alexander Mogilny .30 .75
B Jon Casey .15 .40
C Paul Coffey .30 .75
D Wayne Gretzky 1.50 4.00
E Patrick Roy 1.00 2.50
F Mike Modano .40 1.00
G Mario Lemieux 1.00 2.50
H Al MacInnis .20 .50
I Ray Bourque .30 .75
J Steve Yzerman 1.00 2.50
K Darren Turcotte .08 .25
L Mike Vernon .20 .50
M Pierre Turgeon .20 .50
N Doug Wilson .08 .25
O Don Beaupre .15 .40
P Sergei Makarov .20 .50

1990-91 O-Pee-Chee Red Army

This 22-card standard-size set was distributed one card per 1990-91 O-Pee-Chee wax pack. The fronts featured color action photos surrounded by red borders. The words "Central Red Army" appeared above the photos in the red border. The horizontally designed backs contained the player's statistics compiled from the Super Series tour against the NHL. The statistical information on the back was superimposed over a white Soviet star and a "hammer and sickle" insignia. The card number was followed by an R suffix. Parts of the first print run suffered from pin punctures and other quality control flaws. First cards of Sergei Fedorov, Arturs Irbe, and Valeri Kamensky were a part of this set. Because this was an insert set, these cards are not considered Rookie Cards.

COMPLETE SET (22) 5.00 12.00
1R Ilya Byalsin .15 .40
2R Vladimir Malakhov .15 .40
3R Andrei Khomutov .15 .40
4R Valeri Kamensky .20 .50
5R Dimitri Motkov .15 .40
6R Evgeny Shastin .15 .40
7R Arturs Irbe UER .60 1.50
8R Igor Chibirev .15 .40
9R Maxim Mikhailovsky .20 .50
10R Viacheslav Bykov .15 .40
11R Central Red Army Team .15 .40
12R Central Red Army Team .15 .40
13R Valeri Shirjaev .15 .40
14R Igor Maslennikov .15 .40
15R Igor Malykhin .15 .40
16R Dimitri Khristich .15 .40
17R Viktor Tikhonov CO .30 .75
18R Eugeny Davydov .15 .40
19R Sergei Fedorov 1.25 3.00
20R Pavel Kostichkin .15 .40
21R Vladimir Konstantinov .60 1.50
22R Checklist Card .15 .40

1991-92 O-Pee-Chee

This 528-card set parallels the Topps set of the same season. See the Topps listing for complete prices and checklist.

COMPLETE SET (528) 10.00 25.00
COMP.FACT.SET (528) 12.00 30.00
*O-PEE-CHEE: .5X TO 1.25X TOPPS

1991-92 O-Pee-Chee Inserts

Inserted one per 1991-92 O-Pee-Chee nine-card wax pack, this 66-card standard-size set features ten cards of San Jose Sharks (1S-10S) and 56 Russian hockey players (11R-66R). Among the 56 Russian player cards are those from Central Red Army (11R-30R), Dynamo Moscow (31R-48R), and Khimik (49R-66R). The Sharks' cards have either posed or action player photos with gray and teal border stripes. Card backs present biography and statistics. The Russian player cards have color action player photos enclosed by yellow and red borders. On a red and white background, the backs carry a blue hammer and sickle emblem, a blue Russian star, biography, and statistics versus NHL clubs while touring.

1S Link Gaetz .12 .30
2S Bengt Gustafsson .12 .30
3S Dan Keczmer .12 .30
4S Dean Kolstad .12 .30
5S Peter Lappin .12 .30
6S Jeff Madill .12 .30
7S Mike McHugh .12 .30
8S Jarmo Myllys UER .12 .30
9S Doug Zmolek .12 .30
10S Sharks Checklist .08 .25
11R Vadim Brezgunov .12 .30
12R Vyacheslav Butsayev .12 .30
13R Ilya Byakin .12 .30
14R Igor Chibirev .12 .30
15R Victor Gordiouk .12 .30
16R Yuri Khmylev .12 .30
17R Pavel Kostichkin .12 .30
18R Andrei Kovalenko .12 .30
19R Igor Kravchuk .15 .40
20R Igor Malykhin .12 .30
21R Igor Maslennikov .12 .30
22R Maxim Mikhailovsky .12 .30
23R Dimitri Mironov .12 .30
24R Sergei Nemchinov .12 .30
25R Alexander Prokopjev .12 .30
26R Igor Stelnov .12 .30
27R Sergei Vostrikov .12 .30
28R Sergei Zubov .12 .30
29R Central Red Army Team .05 .15
30R Central Red Army Team .12 .30
31R Alexander Andreivsky .12 .30
32R Igor Dorofeyev .12 .30
33R Alexander Galchenyuk .12 .30
34R Roman Ilyin .12 .30
35R Alexander Karpovtsev .12 .30
36R Ravil Khaidarov .12 .30
37R Igor Korolytov .12 .30
38R Andrei Kovalyov .12 .30
39R Yuri Leonov .12 .30
40R Andrei Lomakin UER .12 .30
name misspelled
41R Evgeny Popikhin .12 .30
42R Alexander Semak .15 .40
43R Mikhail Shtalenkov .12 .30
44R Sergei Sorokin .12 .30
45R Andrei Trefilov .12 .30
46R Ravil Yakubov .12 .30
47R Alexander Yudin .12 .30
48R Alexei Zhamnov .12 .30
49R Andrei Basalgin .12 .30
50R Lev Berdichevsky .12 .30
51R Konstantin Kapkaikin .12 .30
52R Konstantin Kurashov .12 .30
53R Andrei Kvartalnov UER .12 .30
54R Albert Malgin .12 .30
55R Nikolai Maslov .12 .30
56R Anatoli Naida .12 .30
57R Roman Oksiuta .12 .30
58R Sergei Selyanin .12 .30
59R Valeri Shiryev .12 .30
60R Alexander Smirnov .12 .30
61R Leonid Trukhno .12 .30
62R Igor Ulanov UER .15 .40
63R Andrei Yakovenko .12 .30
64R Oleg Yashin .12 .30
65R Valeri Zelepukin .15 .40
66R Russian Checklist .05 .15

1992-93 O-Pee-Chee

The 1992-93 set marks O-Pee-Chee's 25th consecutive year of manufacturing hockey cards. The set contains 396 standard-size cards. The set includes 25 special 25th Anniversary Tribute cards. The same 25 players are featured in a 25th Anniversary wax pack insert set. O-Pee-Chee produced 12,000 Special Anniversary Collector sets which included the complete 396-card set and the 26-card (including checklist) anniversary insert set. Also, 750 additional factory sets were allocated across Canada for confectionary customers and O-Pee-Chee employees to purchase. Card fronts feature color player photos bordered by a metallic blue stripe on the left and full-bleed on the other three sides. The player's name, team name, and position appear in a gray stripe toward the bottom of the card. The bilingual backs carry the team logo, biography, complete statistics, and player profile. Guy Hebert is the only Rookie Card of note.

COMPLETE SET (396) 15.00 35.00
COMP.FACT.SET (396) 15.00 35.00
COMP.ANN.FACT.SET (422) 50.00 100.00
1 Kevin Todd .01 .05
2 Robert Kron .01 .05
3 David Volek .01 .05
4 Teppo Numminen .01 .05
5 Paul Coffey .02 .10
6 Luc Robitaille .02 .10
7 Steven Finn .01 .05
8 Gord Hynes .01 .05
9 Dave Ellett .01 .05
10 Alexander Godynyuk .01 .05
11 Darryl Sydor .01 .05
12 Randy Carlyle .01 .05
13 Chris Chelios .08 .25
14 Kent Manderville .01 .05
15 Wayne Gretzky .60 1.50
16 Jon Casey .02 .10
17 Mark Tinordi .01 .05
18 Dale Hunter .02 .10
19 Martin Gelinas UER .01 .05
20 Todd Elik .01 .05
21 Bob Sweeney .01 .05
22 Chris Dahlquist .01 .05
23 Joe Mullen .02 .10
24 Shawn Burr .01 .05
25 Pavel Bure .08 .25
26 Randy Gilhen .01 .05
27 Brian Bradley .01 .05
28 Don Beaupre .02 .10
29 Kevin Stevens .01 .05
30 Michal Pivonka .01 .05
31 Grant Fuhr .02 .10
32 Steve Larmer .02 .10
33 Gary Leeman .01 .05
34 Tony Tanti .01 .05
35 Denis Savard .02 .10
36 Paul Ranheim .01 .05
37 Andrei Lomakin .01 .05
38 Perry Anderson .01 .05
39 Stu Barnes .01 .05
40 Don Sweeney .01 .05
41 Jamie Baker .01 .05
42 Ray Ferraro .01 .05
43 Bobby Clarke 70 .08 .25
44 Kelly Hrudey .02 .10
45 Brian Skrudland .01 .05
46 Paul Ysebaert .01 .05
47 Pierre Turgeon .02 .10
48 Keith Brown .01 .05
49 Rod Brind'Amour .02 .10
50 Wayne McBean .01 .05
51 Doug Lidster .01 .05
52 Bernie Nicholls .02 .10
53 Daren Puppa .02 .10
54 Joe Sakic .15 .40
55 Joe Sakic 89 .30 .75
56 Dave Manson .01 .05
57 Denis Potvin 74 .02 .10
58 Daniel Marois .01 .05
59 Martin Brodeur .30 .75
60 Brent Sutter .01 .05
61 Steve Yzerman .40 1.00
62 Neal Broten .02 .10
63 Darcy Wakaluk .02 .10
64 Troy Murray .01 .05
65 Tony Granato .01 .05
66 Frank Musil .01 .05
67 Claude Lemieux .01 .05
68 Brian Benning .01 .05
69 Stephane Matteau .01 .05
70 Tomas Forslund .01 .05
71 Dmitri Mironov .01 .05
72 Gary Roberts .01 .05
73 Felix Potvin .15 .40
74 Glen Murray UER .01 .05
75 Stephane Fiset .02 .10
76 Stephane Richer .02 .10
77 Jeff Reese .01 .05
78 Marc Bureau .01 .05
79 Derek King .01 .05
80 Dave Gagner .01 .05
81 Ed Belfour .08 .25
82 Joel Otto .01 .05
83 Anatoli Semenov .01 .05
84 Ron Hextall .02 .10
85 Adam Creighton .01 .05
86 Kris King .01 .05
87 Brett Hull .10 .30
88 Zdeno Ciger .01 .05
89 Petr Nedved .02 .10
90 Sergei Makarov .01 .05
91 Tomas Sandstrom .02 .10
92 Steve Heinze .01 .05
93 Robert Reichel .01 .05
94 Cliff Ronning .01 .05
95 Eric Weinrich .01 .05
96 Wendel Clark .02 .10
97 Rick Zombo .01 .05
98 Ric Nattress .01 .05
99 Theo Fleury .01 .05
100 Joe Murphy .01 .05
101 Gord Murphy .01 .05
102 Jaromir Jagr .10 .30
103 Mike Craig .01 .05
104 John Cullen .01 .05
105 John Druce .01 .05
106 Peter Bondra .02 .10
107 Bryan Trottier 76 .08 .25
108 Steve Smith .01 .05
109 Petr Svoboda .01 .05
110 Mats Sundin .08 .25
111 Patrick Roy 86 .75 2.00
112 Steve Leach .01 .05
113 Jacques Cloutier .02 .10
114 Doug Weight .08 .25
115 Frank Pietrangelo .02 .10
116 Guy Hebert RC .25 .60
117 Donald Audette .01 .05
118 Craig MacTavish .01 .05
119 Grant Fuhr 82 .15 .40
120 Trevor Linden .02 .10
121 Fredrik Olausson .01 .05
122 Geoff Sanderson .02 .10
123 Derian Hatcher .01 .05
124 Brett Hull 88 .25 .60
125 Kelly Buchberger .01 .05
126 Ray Bourque .15 .40
127 Murray Craven .01 .05
128 Tim Cheveldae .02 .10
129 Ulf Dahlen .01 .05
130 Bryan Trottier .02 .10
131 Bob Carpenter .01 .05
132 Benoit Hogue .01 .05
133 Claude Vilgrain .01 .05
134 Glenn Anderson .02 .10
135 Marty McInnis .01 .05
136 Rob Pearson .01 .05
137 Bill Ranford .02 .10
138 Mario Lemieux .40 1.00
139 Bob Bassen .01 .05
140 Scott Mellanby .01 .05
141 Dave Andreychuk .02 .10
142 Kelly Miller .01 .05
143 Gaetan Duchesne .01 .05
144 Mike Sullivan .01 .05
145 Kevin Hatcher .01 .05
146 Doug Bodger .01 .05
147 Craig Berube .01 .05
148 Rick Tocchet .02 .10
149 Luciano Borsato .01 .05
150 Glen Wesley .01 .05
151 Mike Donnelly .01 .05
152 Jimmy Carson .01 .05
153 Jocelyn Lemieux .01 .05
154 Ray Sheppard .01 .05
155 Tony Amonte .02 .10
156 Adrien Plavsic .01 .05
157 Mark Pederson .01 .05
158 Adam Graves .01 .05
159 Igor Larionov .01 .05
160 Steve Chiasson .01 .05
161 Igor Kravchuk .01 .05
162 Slava Fetisov .01 .05
163 Gerard Gallant .01 .05
164 Patrick Roy .40 1.00
165 Ken Sutton .01 .05
166 Mathieu Schneider .01 .05
167 Larry Robinson 73 .08 .25
168 Jim Sandlak .01 .05
169 Joey Kocur .02 .10
170 Rob Brown .01 .05
171 Luke Richardson .01 .05
172 Adam Oates 87 .10 .30
173 Uwe Krupp .01 .05
174 Cam Neely .08 .25
175 Peter Sidorkiewicz .02 .10
176 Geoff Courtnall .01 .05
177 Doug Gilmour .02 .10
178 Josef Beranek .01 .05
179 Michel Picard .01 .05
180 Terry Carkner .01 .05
181 Nelson Emerson .01 .05
182 Perry Berezan .01 .05
183 Checklist C .01 .05
184 Andy Moog .08 .25
185 Michel Petit .01 .05
186 Mark Greig .01 .05
187 Paul Coffey 81 .08 .25
188 Ron Francis .02 .10
189 Joe Juneau .02 .10
190 Jeff Odgers .01 .05
191 Darryl Sittler 75 .02 .10
192 Vincent Damphousse .01 .05
193 Greg Paslawski .01 .05
194 Tony Esposito 69 .08 .25
195 Sergei Fedorov .10 .30
196 Doug Smail .01 .05
197 Pat Verbeek .01 .05
198 Dominic Roussel .02 .10
199 Mike McPhee .01 .05
200 Kevin Dineen .01 .05
201 Pat Elynuik .01 .05
202 Tom Kurvers .01 .05
203 Chris Joseph .01 .05
204 Mark Fitzpatrick .02 .10
205 Jari Kurri .08 .25
206 Guy Carbonneau .02 .10
207 Jan Erixon .01 .05
208 Mark Messier .08 .25
209 Larry Murphy .02 .10
210 Dirk Graham .01 .05
211 Ron Tugnutt .02 .10
212 Dale Hawerchuk .02 .10
213 Dave Babych .01 .05
214 Mikael Andersson .01 .05
215 James Patrick .01 .05
216 Peter Stastny .02 .10
217 Bernie Parent 68 .08 .25
218 Jeff Hackett .02 .10
219 Dave Lowry .01 .05
220 Wayne Gretzky 79 5.00 12.00
221 Brent Gilchrist .01 .05
222 Andrew Cassels .01 .05
223 Calle Johansson .01 .05
224 Joe Reekie .01 .05
225 Craig Simpson .01 .05
226 Bob Essensa .02 .10
227 Pat Falloon .01 .05
228 Vladimir Ruzicka .01 .05
229 Igor Ulanov .01 .05
230 Kjell Samuelsson .01 .05
231 Shayne Corson .01 .05
232 Kelly Kisio .01 .05
233 Gordie Roberts .01 .05
234 Brian Noonan .01 .05
235 Slava Kozlov .02 .10
236 Checklist B .01 .05
237 Jeff Beukeboom .01 .05
238 Steve Konroyd .01 .05
239 Patrice Brisebois .01 .05
240 Mario Lemieux Smythe .20 .50
241 Dana Murzyn .01 .05
242 Pelle Eklund .01 .05
243 Rob Blake .02 .10
244 Brendan Shanahan .08 .25
245 Mike Gartner HL .01 .05
246 David Bruce .01 .05
247 Mike Vernon .02 .10
248 Zarley Zalapski .01 .05
249 Dino Ciccarelli .02 .10
250 David Williams RC .01 .05
251 Scott Stevens 83 .10 .30
252 Bob Probert .02 .10
253 Mikhail Tatarinov .01 .05
254 Bobby Holik .02 .10
255 Tony Amonte 91 .02 .10
256 Brad May .01 .05
257 Philippe Bozon .01 .05
258 Mark Messier 80 .15 .40
259 Mike Richter .08 .25
260 Brian Mullen .01 .05
261 Marty McSorley .01 .05
262 Glenn Healy .02 .10
263 Russ Romaniuk .01 .05
264 Dan Quinn .01 .05
265 Jyrki Lumme .01 .05
266 Valeri Kamensky .01 .05
267 Vladimir Konstantinov .08 .25
268 Peter Ahola .01 .05
269 Guy Larose .01 .05
270 Ulf Samuelsson .01 .05
271 Dale Craigwell .01 .05
272 Adam Oates .02 .10
273 Pat MacLeod .01 .05
274 Mike Keane .01 .05
275 John Vanbiesbrouck .02 .10
276 Brian Lawton .01 .05
277 Sylvain Cote .01 .05
278 Gary Suter .01 .05
279 Alexander Mogilny .02 .10
280 Garth Butcher .01 .05
281 Doug Wilson .02 .10
282 Chris Terreri .02 .10
283 Phil Esposito 77 UER .08 .25
284 Russ Courtnall .01 .05
285 Pat LaFontaine .08 .25
286 Dimitri Khristich .01 .05
287 John LeBlanc RC .01 .05
288 Randy Velischek .01 .05
289 Dave Christian .01 .05
290 Kevin Haller .01 .05
291 Kevin Miller .01 .05
292 Mario Lemieux 85 .75 2.00
293 Stephan Lebeau .01 .05
294 Marcel Dionne 71 .08 .25
295 Barry Pederson .01 .05
296 Steve Duchesne .01 .05
297 Yves Racine .01 .05
298 Phil Housley .02 .10
299 Randy Ladouceur .01 .05
300 Mike Gartner .02 .10
301 Dominik Hasek .30 .75
302 Kevin Lowe .02 .10
303 Sylvain Lefebvre .01 .05
304 J.J. Daigneault .01 .05
305 Mike Ridley .01 .05
306 Curtis Leschyshyn .01 .05
307 Gilbert Dionne .01 .05
308 Bill Guerin RC .30 .75
309 Gerald Diduck .01 .05
310 Rick Wamsley .02 .10
311 Pat Jablonski UER .02 .10
312 Jay More .01 .05
313 Mike Modano .20 .50
314 Checklist A .01 .05
315 Slyvain Turgeon .01 .05
316 Sergei Nemchinov .01 .05
317 Garry Galley .01 .05
318 Paul Coffey HL .05 .15
319 Esa Tikkanen .01 .05
320 Claude LaPointe .01 .05
321 Steve Yzerman 84 .75 2.00
322 Mark Lamb .01 .05
323 Bob Errey .01 .05
324 Pavel Bure 92 .08 .25
325 Craig Janney .02 .10
326 Bob Kudelski .01 .05
327 Kirk Muller .01 .05
328 Jim Paek .01 .05
329 Mike Ricci .02 .10
330 Al MacInnis .02 .10
331 Mike Hudson .01 .05
332 Darrin Shannon .01 .05
333 Doug Brown .01 .05
334 Corey Millen .01 .05
335 Mike Krushelnyski .01 .05
336 Scott Stevens .02 .10
337 Peter Zezel .01 .05
338 Geoff Smith .01 .05
339 Curtis Joseph .08 .25
340 Tom Barrasso .02 .10
341 Al Iafrate .02 .10
342 Kirk McLean .02 .10
343 Gerry Cheevers 72 .05 .15
344 Norm Maciver .01 .05
345 Jeremy Roenick .10 .30
346 Keith Tkachuk UER .08 .25
347 Rod Langway .01 .05
348 Ray Bourque HL .07 .20
349 Kirk McLean .02 .10
350 Brian Propp .01 .05
351 John Ogrodnick .01 .05
352 Benoit Brunet .01 .05
353 Alexei Kasatonov .01 .05
354 Joe Nieuwendyk .02 .10
355 Joe Sacco .01 .05
356 Tom Fergus .01 .05
357 Dan Lambert .01 .05
358 Michel Goulet .02 .10
359 Shawn McEachern .01 .05
360 Eric Desjardins .02 .10
361 Paul Stanton .01 .05
362 Ron Sutter .01 .05
363 Derrick Smith .01 .05
364 Paul Broten .01 .05
365 Greg Adams .01 .05
366 Rob Zettler .01 .05
367 Dave Poulin .01 .05
368 Keith Acton .01 .05
369 Nicklas Lidstrom .08 .25
370 Randy Burridge .01 .05
371 Jamie Macoun .01 .05
372 Craig Billington .02 .10
373 Mark Recchi .02 .10
374 Kris Draper .02 .10
375 Ed Olczyk .01 .05
376 Tom Draper .01 .05
377 Sergio Momesso .01 .05
378 Brian Leetch .08 .25
379 Paul Cavallini .01 .05
380 Paul Fenton .01 .05
381 Dean Evason .01 .05
382 Owen Nolan .02 .10
383 Jeremy Roenick 90 .10 .30
384 Brian Bellows .01 .05
385 Thomas Steen .01 .05
386 John LeClair .15 .40
387 Darren Turcotte .01 .05
388 James Black .01 .05
389 Alexei Gusarov .01 .05
390 Scott Lachance .01 .05
391 Mike Bossy 78 .10 .30
392 Mike Hough .01 .05
393 Grant Ledyard .01 .05
394 Tom Fitzgerald .01 .05
395 Steve Thomas .02 .10
396 Bobby Smith .02 .10

1992-93 O-Pee-Chee 25th Anniversary

This insert was included in 1992-93 O-Pee-Chee wax packs. The first 25 cards commemorate each of the past 25 years, beginning with the 1968-69 series. The cards measure the standard size and each one is a reproduction of the actual card design from each of the past 25 years; the front is bordered in silver metallic ink with a "watermark" mat varnish logo to commemorate the 25th Anniversary. The cards are numbered on the back as originally issued; however, the set has been renumbered on the front at the lower left and are checklisted below accordingly. Cards can be found with and without the 25th Anniversary emblem embossed on the front.

COMPLETE SET (26) 8.00 20.00
1 Bernie Parent .20 .50
2 Tony Esposito .20 .50
3 Bobby Clarke .07 .20
4 Marcel Dionne .07 .20
5 Gerry Cheevers .20 .50
6 Larry Robinson .07 .20
7 Denis Potvin .07 .20
8 Darryl Sittler .07 .20
9 Bryan Trottier .07 .20
10 Phil Esposito .20 .50
11 Mike Bossy .20 .50
12 Wayne Gretzky 5.00 12.00
13 Mark Messier .40 1.00
14 Paul Coffey .30 .75
15 Grant Fuhr .20 .50
16 Scott Stevens .07 .20
17 Steve Yzerman 1.25 3.00
18 Mario Lemieux 2.00 5.00
19 Patrick Roy 1.50 3.00
20 Adam Oates .20 .50
21 Brett Hull .30 .75
22 Joe Sakic .50 1.25
23 Jeremy Roenick .30 .75
24 Tony Amonte .07 .20
25 Pavel Bure .60 1.50
NNO Checklist .07 .20

1992-93 O-Pee-Chee Trophy Winners

These four oversized cards measure approximately 4 7/8" by 6 3/4" and were bottoms from 1992-93 O-Pee-Chee pack boxes. Each features on its front a white-bordered color shot of the player in a tuxedo, holding his trophy and standing in front of an NHL backdrop. The player's name, team, and the trophy name appear in a dark gray stripe near the bottom. O-Pee-Chee appears vertically in a blue stripe along the left edge of the photo. In both French and English, the back has the trophy name, player name and team, and stats in blue lettering. The cards are unnumbered and checklisted below in alphabetical order.

COMPLETE SET (4) 2.00 5.00
1 Pavel Bure .60 1.50
2 Brian Leetch .20 .50
3 Mark Messier .25 .60
4 Patrick Roy 1.00 2.50

1993 O-Pee-Chee Canadiens Hockey Fest

Sold initially only at Hockey Fest '93 (February 4-7, 1993) and the Montreal Forum, this 66-card standard-size set features tribute cards to the Stanley Cup, the Montreal Forum, and past and present stars of the Montreal Canadiens. The production run was 5,000 sets, and each set came in a puck-shaped display box that bore the set serial number. A portion of the proceeds went to the Montreal Canadiens Old Timers Association. Current players are shown in color action photos with white borders and a red stripe at the top. Cards showing former players and people associated with the team have either color or sepia-tone photos framed by red borders on a white card face. The backs of all cards display a variegated pale blue panel containing text or statistics. The current player cards also carry a close-up player photo on the back. Former player cards have a red border around the panel. All the cards have a royal blue outer border.

COMPLETE SET (66) 28.00 70.00
1 Montreal Forum 1924 .40 1.00
2 Emile Bouchard .08 .25
3 Henri Richard .75 2.00
4 Serge Savard .20 .50
5 Toe Blake CO HL .75 2.00
6 Maurice Richard HL 2.00 5.00
7 Stephan Lebeau .08 .25
8 Kevin Haller .08 .25
9 Guy Carbonneau .20 .50
10 Jacques Demers CO .15 .40
11 Serge Savard .20 .50
12 Montreal Forum 1968 .40 1.00
13 Howie Morenz 2.00 5.00
14 Jean Beliveau 1.25 3.00
15 Jacques Laperriere .20 .50
16 Bob Gainey .30 .75
17 Guy Lafleur HL .75 2.00
18 Jacques Raymond .08 .25
19 Sean Hill .08 .25
20 Eric Desjardins .15 .40
21 Aurel Joliat .75 2.00
22 Doug Harvey .75 2.00
23 Yvan Cournoyer .30 .75
24 Frank Mahovlich HL .40 1.00
25 J.J. Daigneault .08 .25
26 Kirk Muller .15 .40
27 Jean Beliveau 1.50 4.00
28 Georges Vezina 2.00 5.00
29 Maurice Richard 3.00 8.00
30 Patrick Roy 5.00 12.00
31 Benoit Brunet .08 .25
32 Jacques Plante HL 1.25 3.00
33 Ralph Backstrom .08 .25
34 Elmer Lach .40 1.00
35 Stanley Cup Champions .20 .50
36 Jacques Laperriere .20 .50
37 Montreal Individual Records--Playoffs .08 .25
38 Vincent Damphousse .30 .75
39 Frank Mahovlich .75 2.00
40 Jacques Plante 2.00 5.00
41 Stanley Cup Champions Montreal .20 .50
42 Kenny Reardon .30 .75
43 Claude Provost .08 .25
44 Jean Beliveau HL 1.00 2.50
45 Edward Ronan .08 .25
46 Canadiens NHL Individual Records .08 .25
47 Bill Durnan .75 2.00
48 Stanley Cup .20 .50
49 Patrice Brisebois .08 .25
50 Denis Savard .30 .75
51 Ken Dryden 2.00 5.00
52 Lou Fontinato .15 .40
53 Jean-Guy Talbot .20 .50
54 BoomBoom Geoffrion .75 2.00
55 Joe Malone .40 1.00
56 Oleg Petrov .08 .25
57 Guy Lafleur 1.00 2.50
58 Bert Olmstead .20 .50
59 The Dream Team Jacques 2.00 5.00
60 Brian Bellows .15 .40
61 Henri Richard HL .40 1.00
62 Jacques Lemaire .30 .75
63 Dickie Moore .60 1.50
64 Lorne Worsley .60 1.50
65 Toe Blake .75 2.00
66 Checklist Card .02 .10
NNO Advertisement Card .01

1993 O-Pee-Chee Canadiens Panel

This approximately 5" by 7" panel displays samples of the O-Pee-Chee Canadiens Hockey Fest cards. If the cards were cut, they would measure the standard size. The front features three cards with posed color player photos with red borders, and one sepia-tone action player photo with red borders. The cards are printed on a white card face. The back show variegated pale blue panels containing statistics. The panels are bordered in dark blue and set on a red background.

1 Canadiens Panel 6.00 15.00

1999-00 O-Pee-Chee

This 286-card set parallels the Topps set of the same season. See the Topps listings for complete prices and checklists.

COMPLETE SET (286) 20.00 50.00
*O-PEE-CHEE: .5X TO 1.2X TOPPS

1999-00 O-Pee-Chee All-Topps

COMPLETE SET (15) 20.00 40.00
*O-PEE-CHEE: .4X TO 1X TOPPS
STATED ODDS 1:16 OPC
AT1 Dominik Hasek 1.50 4.00
AT2 Martin Brodeur 2.00 5.00
AT3 Ray Bourque 1.25 3.00
AT4 Al MacInnis .60 1.50
AT5 Nicklas Lidstrom .75 2.00
AT6 Brian Leetch .75 2.00
AT7 John LeClair 1.00 2.50
AT8 Paul Kariya 2.00 5.00
AT9 Keith Tkachuk .75 2.00
AT10 Eric Lindros 1.25 3.00
AT11 Peter Forsberg 2.00 5.00
AT12 Steve Yzerman 4.00 10.00
AT13 Jaromir Jagr 1.25 3.00
AT14 Teemu Selanne 1.50 4.00
AT15 Pavel Bure 1.00 2.50

1999-00 O-Pee-Chee Autographs

Randomly inserted in Topps packs at the rate of 1:517, this 10-card set features authentic player autographs

STATED ODDS 1:517 OPC
TA1 John LeClair 20.00 50.00
TA2 Dominik Hasek 30.00 80.00
TA3 Curtis Joseph 15.00 40.00
TA4 Alexei Yashin 12.00 30.00
TA5 Mats Sundin 15.00 40.00
TA6 Chris Drury 12.00 30.00
TA7 Milan Hejduk 15.00 40.00
TA8 Marian Hossa 15.00 40.00
TA9 Vincent Lecavalier 12.00 30.00
TA10 Joe Thornton 20.00 50.00

1999-00 O-Pee-Chee Ice Masters

COMPLETE SET (20) 40.00 80.00
*O-PEE-CHEE: .4X TO 1X TOPPS
STATED ODDS 1:25 OPC
IM1 Joe Sakic 5.00 12.00
IM2 Dominik Hasek 5.00 12.00
IM3 Eric Lindros 3.00 8.00
IM4 Jaromir Jagr 3.00 8.00
IM5 John LeClair 2.00 5.00
IM6 Mats Sundin 2.00 5.00
IM7 Ray Bourque 3.00 8.00
IM8 Mike Modano 3.00 8.00
IM9 Peter Forsberg 4.00 10.00
IM10 Brian Leetch 2.00 5.00
IM11 Martin Brodeur 6.00 15.00
IM12 Al MacInnis 1.50 4.00

IM13 Paul Kariya 4.00 10.00
IM14 Alexei Yashin 1.50 4.00
IM15 Steve Yzerman 10.00 25.00
IM16 Ed Belfour 4.00 10.00
IM17 Keith Tkachuk 2.00 5.00
IM18 Patrick Roy 10.00 25.00
IM19 Nicklas Lidstrom 4.00 10.00
IM20 Teemu Selanne 3.00 8.00

1999-00 O-Pee-Chee Now Starring

COMPLETE SET (15) 10.00 20.00
*O-PEE-CHEE: .4X TO 1X TOPPS
STATED ODDS 1:16 OPC

1999-00 O-Pee-Chee A-Men

COMPLETE SET (6) 5.00 12.00
*O-PEE-CHEE: .4X TO 1X TOPPS
STATED ODDS 1::8 OPC

1999-00 O-Pee-Chee Fantastic Finishers

COMPLETE SET (6) 3.00 8.00
*O-PEE-CHEE: .4X TO 1X TOPPS
STATED ODDS 1:10 TOPPS/1:8 OPC

1999-00 O-Pee-Chee Ice Futures

COMPLETE SET (6) 1.25 3.00
*O-PEE-CHEE: .4X TO 1X TOPPS
STATED ODDS 1:8 OPC

1999-00 O-Pee-Chee Positive Performers

COMPLETE SET (6) 2.50 6.00
*O-PEE-CHEE: .4X TO 1X TOPPS
STATED ODDS 1:8 OPC

1999-00 O-Pee-Chee Postmasters

COMPLETE SET (6) 5.00 12.00
*O-PEE-CHEE: .4X TO 1X TOPPS
STATED ODDS 1:8 OPC

1999-00 O-Pee-Chee Top of the World

COMPLETE SET (20) 30.00 80.00
*O-PEE-CHEE: .4X TO 1X TOPPS

2000-01 O-Pee-Chee

Released as a 330-card set, O-Pee-Chee features action player photography on each card with silver borders and gold foil highlights. OPC was packaged in 36-pack boxes with packs containing 10 cards and carried a suggested retail price of $1.29. The Topps release was essentially a parallel to O-Pee-Chee except for the company logo on the fronts and that card numbers 251-270 were exclusive to either Topps or O-Pee-Chee.

251 Yannick Tremblay .10 .25
252 Grant Fuhr .15 .40
253 Cory Stillman .10 .25
254 Jason Wiemer .10 .25
255 Martin Gelinas .10 .25
256 Mike Keane .12 .30
257 Ethan Moreau .10 .25
258 Jason Smith .10 .25
259 Kelly Buchberger .12 .30
260 Benoit Brunet .10 .25
261 Brian Savage .10 .25
262 Sheldon Souray .10 .25
263 Greg Johnson .10 .25
264 Magnus Arvedson .10 .25
265 Patrick Lalime .12 .30
266 Wayne Primeau .10 .25
267 Igor Korolev .10 .25
268 Yanic Perreault .10 .25
269 Adrian Aucoin .10 .25
270 Andrew Cassels .10 .25

2000-01 O-Pee-Chee Foil Parallel

Randomly inserted in Topps packs at the rate of 1:39 and OPC packs at the rate of 1:31, this 330-card set parallels the base Topps/OPC set on cards enhanced with an all foil card stock. Each card is sequentially numbered to 100. Topps Parallels are found in O-Pee-Chee packs and O-Pee-Chee Parallels are found in Topps packs. Card numbers 251-270 were exclusive to either Topps or OPC.
*OPC FOIL/100: .15X TO 40X BASIC OPC

2000-01 O-Pee-Chee 1000 Point Club

*O-PEE-CHEE: .4X TO 1X TOPPS
STATED ODDS 1:27

2000-01 O-Pee-Chee Combos

COMPLETE SET (10) 15.00 40.00
*O-PEE-CHEE: .4X TO 1X TOPPS
STATED ODDS 1:24
*OPC JUMBO: .4X TO 1X TOPPS JUMBO
TC1 P.Bure/V.Bure 1.50 4.00
TC2 T.Selanne/P.Kariya 1.25 3.00
TC3 J.LeClair/T.Amonte 1.00 2.50
TC4 C.Joseph/D.Hasek 2.00 5.00
TC5 M.Modano/P.Forsberg 2.00 5.00
TC6 R.Bourque/C.Pronger 2.00 5.00
TC7 V.Lecavalier/J.Thornton 2.00 5.00
TC8 P.Roy/M.Brodeur 4.00 10.00
TC9 S.Yzerman/B.Hull 3.00 8.00
TC10 J.Jagr/M.Lemieux 3.00 8.00

2000-01 O-Pee-Chee Hobby Masters

COMPLETE SET (10) 12.00 30.00
*O-PEE-CHEE: .4X TO 1X TOPPS
STATED ODDS 1:20 OPC

2000-01 O-Pee-Chee NHL Draft

COMPLETE SET (14) 20.00 40.00
*O-PEE-CHEE: .4X TO 1X TOPPS
STATED ODDS 1:31

2000-01 O-Pee-Chee Own the Game

COMPLETE SET (30) 20.00 50.00
*O-PEE-CHEE: .4X TO 1X TOPPS
STATED ODDS 1:7

2001-02 O-Pee-Chee

This 360-card set parallels the Topps set of the same season. See the Topps listing for complete prices and checklist. Pack SRP was $1.49 for a 10-card pack and there were 36 packs per box. Ten Update Topps and O-Pee-Chee base cards were randomly seeded in 2001-02 Topps Chrome packs at the rate of 1:4.
COMPLETE SET (360) 150.00 300.00
*VETS: .4X TO 1X TOPPS
*ROOKIES: .5X TO 1.2X TOPPS
*UPDATES: .5X TO 1.2X BASIC CARDS
UPDATE ODDS 1:4 TOPPS CHROME
55 Mark Messier .30 .75

2001-02 O-Pee-Chee Heritage Parallel

Inserted at a rate of 1:1, this 110-card set parallels the first 110 cards of the O-Pee-Chee base set. The card fronts carry the same photo as the base cards, but use the 1971-72 O-Pee-Chee design. Card backs are the same as the base set. A limited parallel to these inserts were also created, these parallels look the same but carry different colored foil and serial numbering out of 50.
*OPC HERITAGE: 1X TO 2.5X OPC
55 Mark Messier .75 2.00

2001-02 O-Pee-Chee Heritage Parallel Limited

This 110-card set parallels the first 110 cards of the O-Pee-Chee base set. The card fronts carry the same photo as the base cards, but use the 1971-72 O-Pee-Chee design. Card backs are the same as the base set. A limited parallel to these inserts were also created, these parallels look the same but carry different colored foil and serial numbering out of 50.
*LIMITED/50: 15X TO 40X BASIC OPC
55 Mark Messier 12.00 30.00

2001-02 O-Pee-Chee Premier Parallel

This parallel to the base set was inserted at 1:4 packs. Cards from this set were stamped with a OPC Premier silver foil stamp on the card fronts.
*OPC PREMIER: 1.5X TO 4X BASIC OPC
55 Mark Messier 1.25 3.00

2001-02 O-Pee-Chee Jumbos

Inserted in retail value boxes only as box toppers, very little is known about these eight oversized cards other than that they were numbered "X of 8".
1 Mario Lemieux 2.00 5.00
2 Steve Yzerman 2.00 5.00
3 Martin Brodeur .75 2.00
4 Paul Kariya 1.00 2.50
5 Patrick Roy 2.00 5.00
6 Curtis Joseph .75 2.00
7 Martin Havlat .75 2.00
8 Mike Comrie .40 1.00

2002-03 O-Pee-Chee

Available in Canada only, this 341-card set is a parallel to the basic Topps issue except for the O-Pee-Chee logo. Cards 331-340 were available via mail-in redemption.
COMPLETE SET (340) 30.00 60.00
COMP.SET w/o SP's (330) 20.00 50.00
*1-330 VETERANS: .4X TO 1X TOPPS
*331-340 ROOKIES: .5X TO 1.2X TOPPS RC
242 Mark Messier .30 .75

2002-03 O-Pee-Chee Jumbos

Inserted as boxtoppers in OPC boxes, this 25-card set consists of jumbo-sized reprints of 25 base cards.
COMPLETE SET (25) 30.00 60.00
1 Joe Thornton 2.00 5.00
2 Jarome Iginla 1.25 3.00
3 Roman Turek .75 2.00
4 Ron Francis .75 2.00
5 Patrick Roy 4.00 10.00
6 Joe Sakic 3.00 8.00
7 Steve Yzerman 4.00 10.00
8 Brendan Shanahan 2.00 5.00
9 Mike Comrie 1.25 3.00
10 Ryan Smyth .75 2.00
11 Paul Kariya 2.00 5.00
12 Jose Theodore 1.25 3.00
13 Saku Koivu 1.25 3.00
14 Martin Brodeur 2.00 5.00
15 Mike Peca .40 1.00
16 Daniel Alfredsson .40 1.00
17 Martin Havlat 1.25 3.00
18 Sean Burke .75 2.00
19 Mario Lemieux 4.00 10.00
20 Owen Nolan .75 2.00
21 Chris Pronger .75 2.00
22 Mats Sundin 1.25 3.00
23 Curtis Joseph 1.25 3.00
24 Markus Naslund .75 2.00
25 Todd Bertuzzi .75 2.00

2002-03 O-Pee-Chee Premier Blue

This set paralleled the base set but carried blue borders and blue foil accents. The OPC Premier logo was stamped on the card fronts in blue foil and each card was serial-numbered out of 500.
*1-330 VETS/500: 4X TO 10X OPC
*331-340 ROOKIE/500: 2X TO 5X OPC

2002-03 O-Pee-Chee Premier Red

Issued as a redemption, this parallel set carried red borders and red foil accents. The OPC Premier logo was stamped on the card fronts in red foil and each card was serial-numbered out of 100.
*1-330 VETS/100: 6X TO 15X OPC
*331-340 ROOKIE/100: 4X TO 10X OPC
242 Mark Messier 5.00 12.00

2002-03 O-Pee-Chee Factory Set

COMPLETE FACTORY SET 30.00 60.00
*VETS: .6X TO 1.5X BASIC OPC
*ROOKIES: .8X TO 2X BASIC OPC
ISSUED WITH GOLD FOIL HIGHLIGHTS
242 Mark Messier .50 1.25

2002-03 O-Pee-Chee Hometown Heroes

COMPLETE SET (20) 6.00 15.00
STATED ODDS 1:12 OPC
*FACT.SET: .4X TO 1X BASIC INSERTS
HHC1 Jarome Iginla .40 1.00
HHC2 Ed Jovanovski .40 1.00
HHC3 Ryan Smyth .40 1.00
HHC4 Mike York .40 1.00
HHC5 Mats Sundin .50 1.25
HHC6 Todd Bertuzzi .40 1.00
HHC7 Markus Naslund .40 1.00
HHC8 Saku Koivu .40 1.00
HHC9 Jose Theodore .50 1.25
HHC10 Daniel Alfredsson .40 1.00
HHC11 Patrick Lalime .40 1.00
HHC12 Roman Turek .40 1.00
HHC13 Mike Comrie .40 1.00
HHC14 Tommy Salo .40 1.00
HHC15 Anson Carter .40 1.00
HHC16 Doug Gilmour .40 1.00
HHC17 Yanic Perreault .40 1.00
HHC18 Radek Bonk .40 1.00
HHC19 Darcy Tucker .40 1.00
HHC20 Curtis Joseph .60 1.50

2003-04 O-Pee-Chee

Released in late-August, this 340-card set consisted of 330-base cards and a special 10-card rookie redemption subset. Rookie redemption cards were seeded at 1:36.
COMPLETE SET (340) 30.00 80.00
*O-PEE-CHEE: .5X TO 1.2X TOPPS
101 Mark Messier .40 1.00

2003-04 O-Pee-Chee Blue

This 330-card set paralleled the base set but carried blue borders. These parallels were inserted at 1:5 and each card was serial numbered out of 500. The Rookie Redemption parallel card was inserted at 1:1562.
*VETS/500: 3X TO 8X BASIC TOPPS
*309-317 ROOKIES/500: 1.5X TO 4X TOPPS RC
*331-340 ROOKIES/500: .8X TO 2X TOPPS RC

2003-04 O-Pee-Chee Gold

This 330-card set paralleled the base set but carried gold glitter borders and the Topps logo. These parallels were inserted at 1:23 and each card was serial numbered out of 50. The Rookie Redemption parallel card was inserted at 1:7485.
*VETS/50: 10X TO 25X BASIC CARDS
*309-317 ROOKIES/50: 6X TO 12X BASIC RC
*331-340 ROOKIES/50: 2.5X TO 6X BASIC RC

2003-04 O-Pee-Chee Red

This 330-card set paralleled the base set but carried red borders. These parallels were inserted at 2:36 and each card was serial numbered out of 100. The Rookie Redemption parallel card was inserted at 1:5852.
*VETS/100: 6X TO 15X BASIC CARDS
*309-317 ROOKIES/100: 3X TO 8X BASIC RC
*331-340 ROOKIES/100: 1.5X TO 4X BASIC RC

2006-07 O-Pee-Chee

This 700-card set was released in March, 2007. The set was issued into the hobby in six-card packs, with a $1.59 SRP, which came 36 packs to a box and 12 boxes to a case. Cards numbered 1-500 feature veterans and the rest of the set is broken down into subsets. Cards numbered 501-600 are Rookie Cards, while cards 601-615 are Stat Leaders, Cards numbered 616-645 are Rookie/Sophmore Showdowns, Cards numbered 646-670 is an Hall Worthy subset and the set concludes with Team Checklists from cards 671-700.
COMPLETE SET (700) 100.00 200.00
COMP. SET w/o SPs (500) 30.00 80.00
1 Chris Pronger .20 .50
2 Samuel Pahlsson .15 .40
3 Andy McDonald .20 .50
4 Todd Fedoruk .15 .40
5 Teemu Selanne .50 1.25
6 Chris Kunitz .25 .60
7 Scott Niedermayer .25 .60
8 Corey Perry .25 .60
9 Sean O'Donnell .15 .40
10 Ryan Getzlaf .40 1.00
11 Francois Beauchemin .15 .40
12 Dustin Penner .20 .50
13 Rob Niedermayer .20 .50
14 Todd Marchant .15 .40
15 Ilya Bryzgalov .25 .60
16 Stanislav Chistov .15 .40
17 Jean-Sebastien Giguere .25 .60
18 Andy Sutton .15 .40
19 Steve Rucchin .15 .40
20 Greg de Vries .15 .40
21 Vitaly Vishnevski .15 .40
22 Ilya Kovalchuk .25 .60
23 Scott Mellanby .15 .40
24 Jim Slater .15 .40
25 Kari Lehtonen .20 .50
26 Johan Hedberg .20 .50
27 Niclas Havelid .15 .40
28 Marian Hossa .20 .50
29 Bobby Holik .15 .40
30 Garnet Exelby .15 .40
31 Steve McCarthy .15 .40
32 Niko Kapanen .15 .40
33 Slava Kozlov .15 .40
34 P.J. Axelsson .15 .40
35 Hannu Toivonen .20 .50
36 Patrice Bergeron .30 .75
37 Tim Thomas .30 .75
38 Marc Savard .15 .40
39 Nathan Dempsey .15 .40
40 Glen Murray .20 .50
41 Brad Stuart .15 .40
42 Shean Donovan .15 .40
43 Marco Sturm .15 .40
44 Mark Mowers .15 .40
45 Paul Mara .15 .40
46 Andrew Alberts .15 .40
47 Brad Boyes .15 .40
48 Wayne Primeau .15 .40
49 Milan Jurcina .15 .40
50 Jason York .15 .40
51 Zdeno Chara .25 .60
52 Jiri Novotny .15 .40
53 Derek Roy .15 .40
54 Teppo Numminen .20 .50
55 Jason Pominville .25 .60
56 Henrik Tallinder .15 .40
57 Adam Mair .15 .40
58 Daniel Briere .25 .60
59 Chris Drury .20 .50
60 Ryan Miller .25 .60
61 Ales Kotalik .15 .40
62 Thomas Vanek .30 .75
63 Brian Campbell .20 .50
64 Paul Gaustad .15 .40
65 Jaroslav Spacek .15 .40
66 Jochen Hecht .15 .40
67 Maxim Afinogenov .15 .40
68 Martin Biron .20 .50
69 Robyn Regehr .15 .40
70 Dion Phaneuf .25 .60
71 Miikka Kiprusoff .20 .50
72 Jamie Lundmark .15 .40
73 Roman Hamrlik .20 .50
74 Kristian Huselius .15 .40
75 Darren McCarty .15 .40
76 Stephane Yelle .15 .40
77 Marcus Nilson .15 .40
78 Daymond Langkow .15 .40
79 Jamie McLennan .20 .50
80 Tony Amonte .20 .50
81 Chuck Kobasew .15 .40
82 Jarome Iginla .25 .60
83 Alex Tanguay .15 .40
84 Andrew Ference .15 .40
85 Matthew Lombardi .15 .40
86 Jeff Friesen .15 .40
87 Glen Wesley .15 .40
88 Cory Stillman .15 .40
89 John Grahame .15 .40
90 Erik Cole .20 .50
91 Chad Larose .15 .40
92 Andrew Ladd .25 .60
93 Craig Adams .15 .40
94 Eric Staal .30 .75
95 Rod Brind'Amour .25 .60
96 Mike Commodore .15 .40
97 Ray Whitney .20 .50
98 Justin Williams .20 .50
99 Kevyn Adams .15 .40
100 Cam Ward .25 .60
101 Eric Belanger .15 .40
102 Scott Walker .15 .40
103 Bret Hedican .15 .40
104 Tim Gleason .15 .40
105 Adrian Aucoin .15 .40
106 Nikolai Khabibulin .25 .60
107 Michal Handzus .20 .50
108 Tuomo Ruutu .25 .60
109 Martin Lapointe .15 .40
110 Jim Vandermeer .15 .40
111 Martin Havlat .15 .40
112 Bryan Smolinski .15 .40
113 Michael Holmqvist .15 .40
114 Rene Bourque .15 .40
115 Brandon Bochenski .15 .40
116 Patrick Sharp .25 .60
117 Brent Seabrook .25 .60
118 Duncan Keith .30 .75
119 Jeffrey Hamilton .15 .40
120 Radim Vrbata .20 .50
121 Joe Sakic .40 1.00
122 Peter Budaj .20 .50
123 Tyler Arnason .15 .40
124 Mark Rycroft .15 .40
125 John-Michael Liles .15 .40
126 Milan Hejduk .20 .50
127 Andrew Brunette .15 .40
128 Ian Laperriere .15 .40
129 Antti Laaksonen .15 .40
130 Marek Svatos .15 .40
131 Wojtek Wolski .20 .50
132 Patrice Brisebois .15 .40
133 Pierre Turgeon .25 .60
134 Brett McLean .15 .40
135 Karlis Skrastins .15 .40
136 Brad Richardson .20 .50
137 Brett Clark .15 .40
138 Jose Theodore .25 .60
139 Rick Nash .25 .60
140 Nikolai Zherdev .15 .40
141 Rostislav Klesla .15 .40
142 David Vyborny .15 .40
143 Anders Eriksson .15 .40
144 Adam Foote .15 .40
145 Jody Shelley .15 .40
146 Duvie Westcott .15 .40
147 Gilbert Brule .20 .50
148 Jason Chimera .15 .40
149 Pascal Leclaire .20 .50
150 Manny Malhotra .15 .40
151 Ron Hainsey .15 .40
152 Anson Carter .20 .50
153 Fredrik Modin .15 .40
154 Dan Fritsche .15 .40
155 Sergei Fedorov .40 1.00
156 Marty Turco .25 .60
157 Jussi Jokinen .20 .50
158 Steve Ott .20 .50
159 Jaroslav Modry .15 .40
160 Patrik Stefan .15 .40
161 Matthew Barnaby .15 .40
162 Jeff Halpern .15 .40
163 Eric Lindros .40 1.00
164 Sergei Zubov .20 .50
165 Darryl Sydor .15 .40
166 Brenden Morrow .20 .50
167 Antti Miettinen .15 .40
168 Jere Lehtinen .15 .40
169 Philippe Boucher .15 .40
170 Mike Ribeiro .20 .50
171 Stu Barnes .15 .40
172 Mike Modano .40 1.00
173 Dominik Hasek .30 .75
174 Tomas Holmstrom .20 .50
175 Johan Franzen .25 .60
176 Robert Lang .15 .40
177 Mathieu Schneider .15 .40
178 Nicklas Lidstrom .25 .60
179 Chris Osgood .25 .60
180 Jason Williams .15 .40
181 Mikael Samuelsson .15 .40
182 Chris Chelios .25 .60
183 Pavel Datsyuk .30 .75
184 Dan Cleary .20 .50
185 Kirk Maltby .15 .40
186 Kris Draper .15 .40
187 Andreas Lilja .15 .40
188 Brett Lebda .15 .40
189 Jiri Hudler .25 .60
190 Henrik Zetterberg .30 .75
191 Ales Hemsky .20 .50
192 Fernando Pisani .15 .40
193 Joffrey Lupul .20 .50
194 Dwayne Roloson .20 .50
195 Matt Greene .15 .40
196 Jason Smith .15 .40
197 Ethan Moreau .15 .40
198 Jarret Stoll .20 .50
199 Jussi Markkanen .15 .40
200 Brad Winchester .15 .40
201 Marc-Andre Bergeron .15 .40
202 Raffi Torres .15 .40
203 Petr Sykora .20 .50
204 Shawn Horcoff .15 .40
205 Steve Staios .15 .40
206 Ryan Smyth .20 .50
207 Jay Bouwmeester .25 .60
208 Ed Belfour .25 .60
209 Ruslan Salei .15 .40
210 Stephen Weiss .15 .40
211 Rostislav Olesz .15 .40
212 Mike Van Ryn .15 .40
213 Jozef Stumpel .15 .40
214 Nathan Horton .25 .60
215 Alexander Auld .15 .40
216 Juraj Kolnik .15 .40
217 Martin Gelinas .15 .40
218 Joe Nieuwendyk .25 .60
219 Gary Roberts .15 .40
220 Todd Bertuzzi .25 .60
221 Chris Gratton .15 .40
222 Bryan Allen .15 .40
223 Olli Jokinen .25 .60
224 Alexander Frolov .15 .40
225 Mathieu Garon .20 .50
226 Dustin Brown .25 .60
227 Lubomir Visnovsky .15 .40
228 Sean Avery .15 .40
229 Brent Sopel .15 .40
230 Craig Conroy .15 .40
231 Aaron Miller .15 .40
232 Scott Thornton .15 .40
233 Mattias Norstrom .15 .40
234 Dan Cloutier .20 .50
235 Mike Cammalleri .15 .40
236 Oleg Tverdovsky .15 .40
237 Derek Armstrong .15 .40
238 Tom Kostopoulos .15 .40
239 Rob Blake .25 .60
240 Marian Gaborik .30 .75
241 Derek Boogaard .15 .40
242 Brian Rolston .20 .50
243 Keith Carney .15 .40
244 Mark Parrish .15 .40
245 Wes Walz .15 .40
246 Todd White .15 .40
247 Pierre-Marc Bouchard .25 .60
248 Nick Schultz .15 .40
249 Kurtis Foster .15 .40
250 Pascal Dupuis .15 .40
251 Mikko Koivu .20 .50
252 Manny Fernandez .20 .50
253 Wyatt Smith .15 .40
254 Brent Burns .30 .75
255 Kim Johnsson .15 .40
256 Pavol Demitra .30 .75
257 Michael Ryder .15 .40
258 David Aebischer .20 .50
259 Andrei Markov .25 .60
260 Alexander Perezhogin .15 .40
261 Sheldon Souray .15 .40
262 Cristobal Huet .20 .50
263 Chris Higgins .15 .40
264 Steve Begin .15 .40
265 Radek Bonk .15 .40
266 Janne Niinimaa .15 .40
267 Mike Komisarek .15 .40
268 Tomas Plekanec .25 .60
269 Sergei Samsonov .20 .50
270 Alexei Kovalev .20 .50
271 Craig Rivet .15 .40
272 Mathieu Dandenault .15 .40
273 Mike Johnson .15 .40
274 Saku Koivu .25 .60
275 Tomas Vokoun .20 .50
276 Scott Hartnell .25 .60
277 Marek Zidlicky .15 .40
278 Josef Vasicek .15 .40
279 Jordin Tootoo .25 .60
280 Ryan Suter .20 .50
281 Martin Erat .15 .40
282 David Legwand .20 .50
283 Kimmo Timonen .15 .40
284 Chris Mason .20 .50
285 Steve Sullivan .15 .40
286 Jason Arnott .20 .50
287 Dan Hamhuis .20 .50
288 J.P. Dumont .15 .40
289 Darcy Hordichuk .15 .40
290 Paul Kariya .30 .75
291 Martin Brodeur .50 1.25
292 Brian Gionta .20 .50
293 Paul Martin .15 .40
294 John Madden .15 .40
295 Brian Rafalski .20 .50
296 Colin White .15 .40
297 Zach Parise .30 .75
298 Jay Pandolfo .15 .40
299 Jamie Langenbrunner .15 .40
300 Scott Gomez .20 .50
301 Sergei Brylin .15 .40
302 Scott Clemmensen .15 .40
303 Jim Fahey .15 .40
304 Erik Rasmussen .15 .40
305 Brad Lukowich .15 .40
306 Patrik Elias .25 .60
307 Rick DiPietro .20 .50
308 Jason Blake .15 .40
309 Tom Poti .15 .40
310 Trent Hunter .15 .40
311 Brendan Witt .15 .40
312 Chris Simon .15 .40
313 Arron Asham .15 .40
314 Alexei Yashin .20 .50
315 Mike Sillinger .15 .40
316 Alexei Zhitnik .15 .40
317 Jeff Tambellini .15 .40
318 Mike Dunham .15 .40
319 Mike York .15 .40
320 Shawn Bates .15 .40
321 Viktor Kozlov .15 .40
322 Miroslav Satan .20 .50
323 Henrik Lundqvist .50 1.25
324 Fedor Tyutin .15 .40
325 Michal Rozsival .15 .40
326 Michael Nylander .15 .40
327 Sandis Ozolinsh .15 .40
328 Matt Cullen .15 .40
329 Brendan Shanahan .30 .75
330 Darius Kasparaitis .15 .40
331 Kevin Weekes .20 .50
332 Petr Prucha .20 .50
333 Martin Straka .15 .40
334 Aaron Ward .15 .40
335 Marek Malik .15 .40
336 Blair Betts .15 .40
337 Jason Ward .15 .40
338 Jaromir Jagr .60 1.50
339 Dany Heatley .25 .60
340 Wade Redden .15 .40
341 Peter Schaefer .15 .40
342 Mike Fisher .15 .40
343 Ray Emery .20 .50
344 Tom Preissing .15 .40
345 Patrick Eaves .15 .40
346 Daniel Alfredsson .25 .60
347 Chris Phillips .15 .40
348 Andrej Meszaros .15 .40
349 Martin Gerber .20 .50
350 Joe Corvo .15 .40
351 Antoine Vermette .20 .50
352 Chris Neil .15 .40
353 Anton Volchenkov .15 .40
354 Chris Kelly .20 .50
355 Jason Spezza .25 .60
356 Simon Gagne .25 .60
357 Antero Niittymaki .20 .50
358 Joni Pitkanen .15 .40
359 Jeff Carter .25 .60
360 Randy Jones .15 .40
361 R.J. Umberger .15 .40
362 Mike Knuble .15 .40
363 Derian Hatcher .15 .40
364 Sami Kapanen .15 .40
365 Frederick Meyer .15 .40
366 Mike Richards .25 .60
367 Robert Esche .20 .50
368 Randy Robitaille .15 .40
369 Stefan Ruzicka .15 .40
370 Geoff Sanderson .15 .40
371 Kyle Calder .15 .40
372 Peter Forsberg .30 .75
373 Curtis Joseph .25 .60
374 Ladislav Nagy .15 .40
375 Nick Boynton .15 .40
376 Dave Scatchard .15 .40
377 Derek Morris .15 .40
378 Mike Comrie .20 .50
379 Ed Jovanovski .20 .50
380 Georges Laraque .20 .50
381 Oleg Saprykin .15 .40
382 Keith Ballard .15 .40
383 Steven Reinprecht .15 .40
384 Jeremy Roenick .25 .60
385 Zbynek Michalek .15 .40
386 Owen Nolan .20 .50
387 Fredrik Sjostrom .15 .40
388 David Leneveu .20 .50
389 Shane Doan .20 .50
390 Marc-Andre Fleury .40 1.00
391 Sergei Gonchar .15 .40
392 Dominic Moore .15 .40
393 Ryan Whitney .20 .50
394 Nils Ekman .15 .40
395 Brooks Orpik .20 .50
396 Mark Eaton .15 .40
397 Jocelyn Thibault .20 .50
398 Andre Roy .15 .40
399 Colby Armstrong .20 .50
400 Ryan Malone .15 .40
401 Jarkko Ruutu .15 .40
402 Mark Recchi .30 .75
403 John LeClair .25 .60
404 Josef Melichar .15 .40
405 Sidney Crosby 1.00 2.50
406 Jonathan Cheechoo .25 .60
407 Steve Bernier .15 .40
408 Evgeni Nabokov .20 .50
409 Marcel Goc .20 .50
410 Christian Ehrhoff .15 .40
411 Mark Bell .15 .40
412 Mike Grier .15 .40
413 Patrick Marleau .25 .60
414 Scott Hannan .15 .40
415 Mark Smith .15 .40
416 Milan Michalek .15 .40
417 Ville Nieminen .15 .40
418 Kyle McLaren .15 .40
419 Vesa Toskala .20 .50
420 Josh Gorges .15 .40
421 Joe Thornton .30 .75
422 Keith Tkachuk .25 .60
423 Barret Jackman .15 .40
424 Lee Stempniak .15 .40
425 Jay McClement .15 .40
426 Dallas Drake .15 .40
427 Curtis Sanford .20 .50
428 Petr Cajanek .15 .40
429 Eric Brewer .15 .40
430 Bill Guerin .25 .60
431 Jamal Mayers .15 .40
432 Manny Legace .20 .50
433 Christian Backman .15 .40
434 Martin Rucinsky .15 .40
435 Dennis Wideman .15 .40
436 Jay McKee .15 .40
437 Doug Weight .25 .60
438 Brad Richards .25 .60
439 Ruslan Fedotenko .15 .40
440 Johan Holmqvist .25 .60
441 Filip Kuba .15 .40
442 Dimitry Afanasenkov .15 .40
443 Ryan Craig .15 .40
444 Dan Boyle .20 .50
445 Paul Ranger .15 .40
446 Marc Denis .20 .50
447 Vaclav Prospal .15 .40
448 Tim Taylor .15 .40
449 Martin St. Louis .25 .60
450 Cory Sarich .15 .40
451 Nikita Alexeev .15 .40
452 Nolan Pratt .15 .40
453 Vincent Lecavalier .20 .50
454 Mats Sundin .25 .60
455 Darcy Tucker .20 .50
456 Kyle Wellwood .20 .50
457 Nik Antropov .20 .50
458 Tomas Kaberle .15 .40
459 Hal Gill .15 .40
460 Jean-Sebastien Aubin .20 .50
461 Matt Stajan .20 .50
462 Alexander Steen .25 .60
463 Bryan McCabe .15 .40
464 Jeff O'Neill .15 .40
465 Wade Belak .15 .40
466 Michael Peca .20 .50
467 Carlo Colaiacovo .15 .40
468 Chad Kilger .15 .40
469 Alexei Ponikarovsky .15 .40
470 Andrew Raycroft .20 .50
471 Roberto Luongo .40 1.00
472 Ryan Kesler .30 .75
473 Jan Bulis .15 .40
474 Matt Cooke .15 .40
475 Sami Salo .15 .40
476 Brendan Morrison .15 .40
477 Henrik Sedin .25 .60
478 Daniel Sedin .25 .60
479 Mattias Ohlund .15 .40
480 Willie Mitchell .15 .40
481 Dany Sabourin .15 .40
482 Lukas Krajicek .15 .40
483 Marc Chouinard .15 .40
484 Trevor Linden .25 .60
485 Taylor Pyatt .15 .40
486 Markus Naslund .20 .50
487 Olaf Kolzig .25 .60
488 Donald Brashear .15 .40
489 Chris Clark .15 .40
490 Dainius Zubrus .15 .40
491 Matt Pettinger .20 .50
492 Jamie Heward .15 .40
493 Bryan Muir .15 .40
494 Steve Eminger .15 .40
495 Brian Pothier .15 .40
496 Brian Sutherby .15 .40
497 Richard Zednik .15 .40
498 Brent Johnson .20 .50
499 Matt Bradley .15 .40
500 Alexander Ovechkin 1.00 2.50
501 Dustin Byfuglien RC 2.50 6.00
502 Yan Stastny RC 1.00 2.50
503 Mark Stuart RC 1.00 2.50
504 Eric Fehr RC 1.50 4.00
505 Bill Thomas RC 1.00 2.50
506 Joel Perrault RC 1.00 2.50
507 Frank Doyle RC 1.25 3.00
508 Carsen Germyn RC 1.00 2.50
509 Ryan Potulny RC 1.00 2.50
510 David Printz RC 1.00 2.50
511 Rob Collins RC 1.00 2.50
512 Steve Regier RC 1.25 3.00
513 Matt Koalska RC 1.00 2.50
514 Ryan Caldwell RC 1.00 2.50
515 Masi Marjamaki RC 1.00 2.50
516 Cole Jarrett RC 1.00 2.50
517 Konstantin Pushkarev RC 1.25 3.00
518 Ben Ondrus RC 1.00 2.50
519 Brendan Bell RC 1.00 2.50
520 Ian White RC 1.25 3.00
521 Jeremy Williams RC 1.00 2.50
522 Marc-Antoine Pouliot RC 1.00 2.50
523 Noah Welch RC 1.00 2.50
524 Michel Ouellet RC 1.25 3.00
525 Shea Weber RC 2.50 6.00
526 Jarkko Immonen RC 1.00 2.50
527 David Liffiton RC 1.00 2.50
528 Tomas Kopecky RC 1.25 3.00
529 Billy Thompson RC 1.00 2.50
530 Filip Novak RC 1.00 2.50
531 Matt Carle RC 1.00 2.50
532 Dan Jancevski RC 1.00 2.50
533 Erik Reitz RC 1.00 2.50
534 Miroslav Kopriva RC 1.00 2.50
535 Jonas Johansson RC 1.00 2.50
536 Shane O'Brien RC 1.00 2.50
537 Ryan Shannon RC 1.00 2.50
538 Patrick O'Sullivan RC 1.50 4.00
539 Anze Kopitar RC 4.00 10.00
540 John Oduya RC 1.50 4.00
541 Travis Zajac RC 2.00 5.00
542 Fredrik Norrena RC 1.00 2.50
543 Phil Kessel RC 2.50 6.00
544 Guillaume Latendresse RC 1.50 4.00
545 Nigel Dawes RC 1.00 2.50
546 Jordan Staal RC 3.00 8.00
547 Kristopher Letang RC 3.00 8.00
548 Paul Stastny RC 3.00 8.00
549 Niklas Backstrom RC 2.00 5.00
550 D.J. King RC 1.00 2.50
551 Marc-Edouard Vlasic RC 1.00 2.50
552 Patrick Thoresen RC 1.00 2.50
553 Ladislav Smid RC 1.00 2.50
554 Loui Eriksson RC 1.50 4.00
555 Patrick Fischer RC 1.00 2.50
556 Mikko Lehtonen RC 1.25 3.00
557 Roman Polak RC 1.25 3.00
558 Luc Bourdon RC 1.50 4.00
559 Keith Yandle RC 2.00 5.00
560 Enver Lisin RC 1.00 2.50
561 Adam Burish RC 1.50 4.00
562 Alexei Kaigorodov RC 1.00 2.50
563 Alex Brooks RC 1.00 2.50
564 Evgeni Malkin RC 6.00 15.00
565 Nate Thompson RC 1.00 2.50
566 Janis Sprukts RC 1.00 2.50
567 Alexander Radulov RC 2.00 5.00
568 Alexei Mikhnov RC 1.00 2.50
569 Dave Bolland RC 1.50 4.00
570 Michael Blunden RC 1.00 2.50
571 Lars Jonsson RC 1.00 2.50
572 Triston Grant RC 1.00 2.50
573 Matt Lashoff RC 1.00 2.50
574 Dustin Boyd RC 1.00 2.50
575 Brandon Prust RC 1.00 2.50
576 Alexander Edler RC 1.50 4.00
577 Jan Hejda RC 1.00 2.50
578 Drew Stafford RC 1.50 4.00
579 Kelly Guard RC 1.25 3.00
580 Patrick Coulombe RC 1.00 2.50
581 Nathan McIver RC 1.00 2.50
582 Mike Brown RC 1.00 2.50
583 Jean-Francois Racine RC 1.25 3.00
584 Adam Dennis RC 1.00 2.50
585 Drew Larman RC 1.00 2.50
586 Mike Card RC 1.00 2.50
587 Michael Funk RC 1.00 2.50
588 Stefan Liv RC 1.00 2.50
589 David Booth RC 1.25 3.00
590 Blair Jones RC 1.00 2.50
591 Jussi Timonen RC 1.25 3.00
592 David McKee RC 1.00 2.50
593 Michael Ryan RC 1.00 2.50
594 Peter Harrold RC 1.00 2.50
595 Joe Pavelski RC 5.00 12.00
596 Karl Goehring RC 1.25 3.00
597 Benoit Pouliot RC 1.25 3.00
598 Jesse Schultz RC 1.00 2.50
599 Jeff Drouin-Deslauriers RC 1.00 2.50
600 Martin Houle RC 1.25 3.00
601 Joe Thornton .30 .75
602 Jonathan Cheechoo .25 .60
603 Wade Redden .15 .40
604 Michal Rozsival .15 .40
605 Ilya Kovalchuk .25 .60
606 Marian Hossa .20 .50
607 Sean Avery .15 .40
608 Martin Brodeur .50 1.25
609 Miikka Kiprusoff .20 .50
610 Cristobal Huet .20 .50
611 Eric Staal .30 .75
612 Fernando Pisani .15 .40
613 Dwayne Roloson .20 .50
614 Ilya Bryzgalov .25 .60
615 Alexander Ovechkin 1.00 2.50
616 P.Eaves/A.Kaigorodov .75 2.00
617 K.Ballard/K.Yandle .75 2.00
618 D.Phaneuf/L.Bourdon .75 2.00
619 J.Jokinen/L.Eriksson .75 2.00
620 M.Svatos/P.Stastny .75 2.00

21 S.Crosby/E.Malkin 2.00 5.00
22 C.Higgins/G.Latendresse .75 2.00
23 B.Boyes/P.Kessel .75 2.00
24 A.Ovechkin/E.Malkin 1.25 3.00
25 P.Prucha/N.Dawes .75 2.00
26 A.Meszaros/L.Smid .75 2.00
27 J.Carter/P.O'Sullivan .75 2.00
28 Z.Parise/T.Zajac .75 2.00
29 R.Whitney/N.Welch .75 2.00
30 R.Suter/S.Weber .75 2.00
31 J.Gorges/M.Carle .75 2.00
32 R.Getzlaf/R.Shannon 1.00 2.50
33 M.Richards/R.Potulny .75 2.00
34 P.LeClaire/F.Norrena .75 2.00
35 B.Winchester/M.Pouliot .75 2.00
36 M.Koivu/A.Kopitar 1.00 2.50
37 A.Alberts/M.Stuart .75 2.00
38 T.Vanek/D.Stafford 1.00 2.50
39 J.Franzen/T.Kopecky .75 2.00
40 C.Colaiacovo/I.White .75 2.00
41 F.Beauchemin/S.O'Brien .75 2.00
42 S.Bernier/E.Fehr .75 2.00
43 C.Perry/J.Staal 1.25 3.00
44 A.Steen/P.Thoresen .75 2.00
45 B.Seabrook/K.Letang .75 2.00
646 Teemu Selanne .50 1.25
647 Joe Sakic .40 1.00
648 Mike Modano .40 1.00
649 Eric Lindros .40 1.00
650 Dominik Hasek .30 .75
651 Nicklas Lidstrom .25 .60
652 Chris Chelios .25 .60
653 Joe Nieuwendyk .25 .60
654 Ed Belfour .25 .60
655 Rob Blake .25 .60
656 Saku Koivu .25 .60
657 Paul Kariya .30 .75
658 Martin Brodeur .50 1.25
659 Jaromir Jagr .60 1.50
660 Brendan Shanahan .30 .75
661 Daniel Alfredsson .25 .60
662 Peter Forsberg .30 .75
663 Jeremy Roenick .25 .60
664 Curtis Joseph .25 .60
665 Sidney Crosby 1.00 2.50
666 Mark Recchi .30 .75
667 Doug Weight .25 .60
668 Keith Tkachuk .25 .60
669 Mats Sundin .25 .60
670 Markus Naslund .20 .50
671 Teemu Selanne .50 1.25
672 Ilya Kovalchuk .25 .60
673 Patrice Bergeron .30 .75
674 Ryan Miller .25 .60
675 Miikka Kiprusoff .20 .50
676 Eric Staal .30 .75
677 Nikolai Khabibulin .25 .60
678 Rick Nash .25 .60
679 Joe Sakic .40 1.00
680 Mike Modano .40 1.00
681 Nicklas Lidstrom .25 .60
682 Ryan Smyth .20 .50
683 Olli Jokinen .25 .60
684 Rob Blake .25 .60
685 Marian Gaborik .30 .75
686 Saku Koivu .25 .60
687 Martin Brodeur .50 1.25
688 Paul Kariya .30 .75
689 Miroslav Satan .20 .50
690 Jaromir Jagr .60 1.50
691 Daniel Alfredsson .25 .60
692 Peter Forsberg .30 .75
693 Shane Doan .20 .50
694 Sidney Crosby 1.00 2.50
695 Patrick Marleau .25 .60
696 Keith Tkachuk .25 .60
697 Vincent Lecavalier .20 .50
698 Mats Sundin .25 .60
699 Markus Naslund .20 .50
700 Alexander Ovechkin 1.00 2.50

2006-07 O-Pee-Chee Rainbow

*RAINBOW: 10X to 25X BASE HI
PRINT RUN 100 #'d SETS
5 Teemu Selanne 12.00 30.00
121 Joe Sakic 20.00 50.00
173 Dominik Hasek 12.00 30.00
291 Martin Brodeur 20.00 50.00
405 Sidney Crosby 25.00 60.00
500 Alexander Ovechkin 30.00 80.00
539 Anze Kopitar 30.00 80.00
544 Guillaume Latendresse 10.00 25.00
546 Jordan Staal 12.00 30.00
548 Paul Stastny 15.00 40.00
564 Evgeni Malkin 40.00 100.00
567 Alexander Radulov 12.00 30.00
608 Martin Brodeur 20.00 50.00
615 Alexander Ovechkin 40.00 100.00
621 S.Crosby/E.Malkin 50.00 100.00
624 A.Ovechkin/E.Malkin 15.00 40.00
643 C.Perry/J.Staal 10.00 25.00
647 Joe Sakic 12.00 30.00
650 Dominik Hasek 8.00 20.00
658 Martin Brodeur 10.00 25.00
665 Sidney Crosby 25.00 60.00
679 Joe Sakic 12.00 30.00
687 Martin Brodeur 10.00 25.00
694 Sidney Crosby 25.00 60.00
700 Alexander Ovechkin 20.00 50.00

2006-07 O-Pee-Chee Autographs

AAH Ales Hemsky 6.00 15.00
AAM Andy McDonald 10.00 25.00
AAN Antero Niittymaki SP 40.00 80.00
AAR Andrew Raycroft SP 20.00 50.00
ABB Brad Boyes SP 30.00 60.00
ABG Brian Gionta 6.00 15.00
ABM Brendan Morrison 6.00 15.00
ABO Bobby Orr SP 400.00 700.00
ACC Chris Campoli 6.00 15.00
ACH Cristobal Huet 12.00 30.00
ACK Chris Kunitz 8.00 20.00
ACS Cory Stillman 8.00 20.00
ACW Cam Ward SP 40.00 100.00
ADB Daniel Briere 15.00 30.00
ADH Dany Heatley SP 30.00 60.00
ADR Dwayne Roloson 12.00 30.00
AEM Evgeni Malkin 125.00 200.00
AGB Gilbert Brule SP 20.00 50.00
AHA Dominik Hasek SP 40.00 80.00
AHT Hannu Toivonen 12.00 30.00
AIK Ilya Kovalchuk SP 30.00 80.00
AJA Jason Arnott 6.00 15.00
AJC Jeff Carter 10.00 25.00
AJI Jarome Iginla SP 40.00 80.00
AJL John-Michael Liles 6.00 15.00
AJS Jordan Staal 12.00 30.00
AJT Joe Thornton SP
AKB Keith Dallard 6.00 15.00
AKC Kyle Calder 10.00 25.00
AKD Kris Draper SP
AKO Mikko Koivu 6.00 15.00
AMC Mike Cammalleri 10.00 25.00
AMG Marian Gaborik SP 50.00 100.00
AMP Marc-Antoine Pouliot 8.00 20.00
AMR Mike Richards 10.00 25.00
AMS Marek Svatos 6.00 15.00
ANA Rick Nash 20.00 50.00
ANH Nathan Horton 10.00 25.00
ANL Nicklas Lidstrom SP 40.00 100.00
AOJ Olli Jokinen SP
APB Pierre-Marc Bouchard 6.00 15.00
APK Phil Kessel SP 60.00 125.00
APP Petr Prucha 8.00 20.00
APS Paul Stastny 30.00 60.00
ARB Rob Blake 10.00 25.00
ARL Roberto Luongo SP 75.00 150.00
ARM Ryan Malone 8.00 20.00
ARN Robert Nilsson 6.00 15.00
ARS Ryan Smyth 8.00 20.00
ASB Steve Bernier 10.00 25.00
ASW Stephen Weiss 6.00 15.00
AWR Wade Redden 6.00 15.00
AWW Wojtek Wolski 12.00 30.00

2006-07 O-Pee-Chee Swatches

STATED ODDS 1:24
SAA Arron Asham 5.00 12.00
SAE David Aebischer 6.00 15.00
SAF Alexander Frolov 5.00 12.00
SAH Ales Hemsky 6.00 15.00
SAM Andrej Meszaros 5.00 12.00
SAO Alexander Ovechkin 15.00 40.00
SAS Alexander Steen 8.00 20.00
SAT Alex Tanguay 5.00 12.00
SAY Alexei Yashin 6.00 15.00
SBB Brandon Bochenski 5.00 12.00
SBM Brendan Morrison 5.00 12.00
SBS Brad Stuart 5.00 12.00
SCC Chris Chelios 8.00 20.00
SCD Chris Drury 6.00 15.00
SCH Jonathan Cheechoo 8.00 20.00
SCK Chuck Kobasew 5.00 12.00
SCP Chris Pronger 6.00 15.00
SDA Daniel Alfredsson 8.00 20.00
SDE Pavol Demitra 10.00 25.00
SDH Dominik Hasek 10.00 25.00
SDK Duncan Keith 10.00 25.00
SDT Darcy Tucker 6.00 15.00
SDW Doug Weight 8.00 20.00
SEN Evgeni Nabokov 6.00 15.00
SES Eric Staal 10.00 25.00
SFP Fernando Pisani 5.00 12.00
SGA Mathieu Garon 6.00 15.00
SGL Guy Lafleur SP 50.00 125.00
SGM Glen Murray 6.00 15.00
SGR Gary Roberts 5.00 12.00
SHA Martin Havlat 5.00 12.00
SHE Milan Hejduk 6.00 15.00
SHO Shawn Horcoff 5.00 12.00
SHS Henrik Sedin 8.00 20.00
SHT Hannu Toivonen 6.00 15.00
SJA Jason Arnott 6.00 15.00
SJB Jay Bouwmeester 8.00 20.00
SJC Jeff Carter 8.00 20.00
SJG Jean-Sebastien Giguere 8.00 20.00
SJI Jarome Iginla 8.00 20.00
SJJ Jaromir Jagr 20.00 50.00
SJL Jere Lehtinen 5.00 12.00
SJP Joni Pitkanen 5.00 12.00
SJR Jeremy Roenick 8.00 20.00
SJS Jason Spezza 8.00 20.00
SKL Kari Lehtonen 6.00 15.00
SLE Jordan Leopold 5.00 12.00
SLX Mario Lemieux SP 25.00 60.00
SMA Maxim Afinogenov 5.00 12.00
SMB Martin Brodeur 15.00 40.00
SMC Mike Cammalleri 5.00 12.00
SMD Marc Denis 6.00 15.00
SMF Manny Fernandez 6.00 15.00
SMG Marian Gaborik 10.00 25.00
SMH Marian Hossa 6.00 15.00
SMI Miroslav Satan 6.00 15.00
SML Manny Legace 6.00 15.00
SMM Mike Modano 12.00 30.00
SMN Markus Naslund 6.00 15.00
SMR Mark Recchi 10.00 25.00
SMS Martin St. Louis SP 25.00 60.00
SMT Marty Turco 8.00 20.00
SNL Nicklas Lidstrom 8.00 20.00
SOJ Olli Jokinen 8.00 20.00
SOT Steve Ott 6.00 15.00
SPB Patrice Bergeron 10.00 25.00
SPD Pavel Datsyuk 10.00 25.00
SPF Peter Forsberg 10.00 25.00
SPK Paul Kariya 10.00 25.00
SPL Pascal LeClaire 6.00 15.00
SPM Patrick Marleau 8.00 20.00
SPR Patrick Roy 20.00 50.00
SPS Peter Stastny 8.00 20.00
SRB Rod Brind`Amour 8.00 20.00
SRD Rick DiPietro 6.00 15.00
SRE Robert Esche 6.00 15.00
SRF Ruslan Fedotenko 5.00 12.00
SRI Mike Ribeiro 6.00 15.00
SRK Rostislav Klesla 5.00 12.00
SRL Robert Lang 5.00 12.00
SRM Ryan Miller 8.00 20.00
SRN Rick Nash 8.00 20.00
SRS Ryan Smyth 6.00 15.00
SRY Michael Ryder 5.00 12.00
SSA Joe Sakic 10.00 25.00
SSB Steve Bernier 5.00 12.00
SSC Sidney Crosby SP 90.00 150.00
SSD Shane Doan 6.00 15.00
SSF Sergei Fedorov 12.00 30.00
SSG Scott Gomez 6.00 15.00
SSH Brendan Shanahan 10.00 25.00
SSO Sandis Ozolinsh 5.00 12.00
SSS Sergei Samsonov 6.00 15.00
SST Martin Straka 5.00 12.00
SSU Mats Sundin 8.00 20.00
STR Tuomo Ruutu 8.00 20.00
STS Teemu Selanne 15.00 40.00
STV Tomas Vokoun 6.00 15.00
SVL Vincent Lecavalier 6.00 15.00
SZC Zdeno Chara 8.00 20.00

2007-08 O-Pee-Chee

This 600-card set was released in December, 2007. The set was issued into the hobby in six-card packs, with a $1.59 SRP, which came 36 packs to a box and 12 boxes to a case. Cards numbered 1-500 feature veterans while cards numbered 501-600 are Rookie Cards. Those Rookie Cards were inserted into packs at a stated rate of one in two.

COMPLETE SET (600) 100.00 200.00
COMP.SET w/o SP's (500) 40.00 80.00
MARQUEE ROOKIE STATED ODDS 1:2
1 Jean-Sebastien Giguere .25 .60
2 Andy McDonald .20 .50
3 Teemu Selanne .50 1.25
4 Travis Moen .15 .40
5 George Parros .15 .40
6 Samuel Pahlsson .15 .40
7 Rob Niedermayer .20 .50
8 Scott Niedermayer .25 .60
9 Francois Beauchemin .15 .40
10 Dustin Penner .20 .50
11 Ryan Getzlaf .40 1.00
12 Corey Perry .25 .60
13 Chris Kunitz .25 .60
14 Chris Pronger .20 .50
15 Ilya Bryzgalov .25 .60
16 Mathieu Schneider .15 .40
17 Todd Bertuzzi .25 .60
18 Marian Hossa .20 .50
19 Bobby Holik .15 .40
20 Eric Belanger .15 .40
21 Ken Klee .15 .40
22 Alexei Zhitnik .15 .40
23 Johan Hedberg .20 .50
24 Steve Rucchin .15 .40
25 Ilya Kovalchuk .25 .60
26 Niclas Havelid .15 .40
27 Jim Slater .15 .40
28 Kari Lehtonen .20 .50
29 Garnet Exelby .15 .40
30 Slava Kozlov .15 .40
31 Chris Thorburn .15 .40
32 Pascal Dupuis .15 .40
33 Andy Sutton .15 .40
34 Patrice Bergeron .30 .75
35 Phil Kessel .30 .75
36 Manny Fernandez .20 .50
37 Aaron Ward .15 .40
38 Zdeno Chara .25 .60
39 Glen Murray .20 .50
40 Marco Sturm .15 .40
41 Chuck Kobasew .15 .40
42 P.J. Axelsson .15 .40
43 Dennis Wideman .15 .40
44 Tim Thomas .30 .75
45 Andrew Ference .15 .40
46 Mark Mowers .15 .40
47 Marc Savard .15 .40
48 Brandon Bochenski .15 .40
49 Andrew Alberts .15 .40
50 Shean Donovan .15 .40
51 Ryan Miller .25 .60
52 Thomas Vanek .30 .75
53 Derek Roy .15 .40
54 Jochen Hecht .15 .40
55 Dmitri Kalinin .15 .40
56 Jason Pominville .25 .60
57 Daniel Paille .15 .40
58 Drew Stafford .20 .50
59 Brian Campbell .20 .50
60 Nathan Paetsch .15 .40
61 Jocelyn Thibault .20 .50
62 Andrew Peters .15 .40
63 Teppo Numminen .20 .50
64 Tim Connolly .15 .40
65 Ales Kotalik .15 .40
66 Maxim Afinogenov .15 .40
67 Jarome Iginla .25 .60
68 Matthew Lombardi .15 .40
69 Rhett Warrener .15 .40
70 Robyn Regehr .15 .40
71 Daymond Langkow .15 .40
72 David Hale .15 .40
73 Miikka Kiprusoff .20 .50
74 Stephane Yelle .15 .40
75 Adrian Aucoin .15 .40
76 Mark Giordano .20 .50
77 Alex Tanguay .15 .40
78 Kristian Huselius .15 .40
79 Owen Nolan .20 .50
80 Dion Phaneuf .25 .60
81 Craig Conroy .15 .40
82 Cory Sarich .15 .40
83 Cam Ward .25 .60
84 Ray Whitney .20 .50
85 Erik Cole .20 .50
86 Mike Commodore .15 .40
87 Eric Staal .30 .75
88 Chad Larose .15 .40
89 Justin Williams .20 .50
90 Tim Gleason .15 .40
91 Andrew Ladd .25 .60
92 David Tanabe .15 .40
93 John Grahame .15 .40
94 Cory Stillman .15 .40
95 Craig Adams .15 .40
96 Rod Brind`Amour .25 .60
97 Scott Walker .15 .40
98 Jeffrey Hamilton .15 .40
99 Glen Wesley .15 .40
100 Martin Havlat .25 .60
101 Rene Bourque .15 .40
102 Andrei Zyuzin .15 .40
103 Duncan Keith .25 .60
104 Jim Vandermeer .15 .40
105 Patrick Sharp .25 .60
106 Martin Lapointe .15 .40
107 Tuomo Ruutu .25 .60
108 Patrick Lalime .20 .50
109 Jason Williams .15 .40
110 Radim Vrbata .20 .50
111 Brent Seabrook .25 .60
112 Robert Lang .15 .40
113 Cam Barker .15 .40
114 Sergei Samsonov .20 .50
115 Nikolai Khabibulin .25 .60
116 Nikita Alexeev .15 .40
117 Joe Sakic .40 1.00
118 Peter Budaj .20 .50
119 Andrew Brunette .15 .40
120 John-Michael Liles .15 .40
121 Ian Laperriere .15 .40
122 Scott Hannan .15 .40
123 Marek Svatos .15 .40
124 Brett Clark .15 .40
125 Jose Theodore .25 .60
126 Jordan Leopold .15 .40
127 Tyler Arnason .15 .40
128 Wojtek Wolski .20 .50
129 Kurt Sauer .15 .40
130 Paul Stastny .25 .60
131 Brad Richardson .20 .50
132 Ryan Smyth .20 .50
133 Milan Hejduk .20 .50
134 Rick Nash .25 .60
135 Nikolai Zherdev .15 .40
136 Jody Shelley .15 .40
137 Adam Foote .15 .40
138 Ole-Kristian Tollefsen .15 .40
139 Jason Chimera .15 .40
140 Fredrik Norrena .15 .40
141 Sergei Fedorov .40 1.00
142 Rostislav Klesla .15 .40
143 Dan Fritsche .15 .40
144 Fredrik Modin .15 .40
145 Manny Malhotra .15 .40
146 Jiri Novotny .15 .40
147 David Vyborny .15 .40
148 Alexander Svitov .15 .40
149 Gilbert Brule .20 .50
150 Pascal Leclaire .20 .50
151 Mike Modano .40 1.00
152 Sergei Zubov .20 .50
153 Mike Smith .25 .60
154 Jussi Jokinen .15 .40
155 Philippe Boucher .15 .40
156 Trevor Daley .15 .40
157 Antti Miettinen .15 .40
158 Steve Ott .15 .40
159 Brenden Morrow .20 .50
160 Loui Eriksson .25 .60
161 Todd Fedoruk .15 .40
162 Mike Ribeiro .20 .50
163 Jere Lehtinen .15 .40
164 Stu Barnes .15 .40
165 Jeff Halpern .15 .40
166 Mattias Norstrom .15 .40
167 Marty Turco .25 .60
168 Nicklas Lidstrom .25 .60
169 Dan Cleary .20 .50
170 Kris Draper .15 .40
171 Chris Osgood .25 .60
172 Andreas Lilja .15 .40
173 Henrik Zetterberg .30 .75
174 Brett Lebda .15 .40
175 Chris Chelios .25 .60
176 Tomas Holmstrom .20 .50
177 Pavel Datsyuk .30 .75
178 Jiri Hudler .20 .50
179 Kyle Quincey .15 .40
180 Valtteri Filppula .25 .60
181 Brian Rafalski .20 .50
182 Johan Franzen .25 .60
183 Mikael Samuelsson .15 .40
184 Dominik Hasek .30 .75
185 Ales Hemsky .20 .50
186 Mathieu Garon .20 .50
187 Jarret Stoll .20 .50
188 Ladislav Smid .15 .40
189 Marc-Antoine Pouliot .15 .40
190 Matt Greene .15 .40
191 Joni Pitkanen .15 .40
192 Marty Reasoner .15 .40
193 Shawn Horcoff .15 .40
194 Steve Staios .15 .40
195 Ethan Moreau .15 .40
196 Patrick Thoresen .15 .40
197 Dwayne Roloson .20 .50
198 Fernando Pisani .15 .40
199 Geoff Sanderson .15 .40
200 Jean-Francois Jacques .15 .40
201 Raffi Torres .15 .40
202 Olli Jokinen .20 .50
203 Mike Van Ryn .15 .40
204 Stephen Weiss .15 .40
205 Bryan Allen .15 .40
206 Richard Zednik .15 .40
207 Steve Montador .15 .40
208 Alexander Auld .15 .40
209 Nathan Horton .25 .60
210 Ruslan Salei .15 .40
211 Rostislav Olesz .15 .40
212 David Booth .15 .40
213 Gregory Campbell .15 .40
214 Noah Welch .15 .40
215 Brett McLean .15 .40
216 Tomas Vokoun .20 .50
217 Jay Bouwmeester .25 .60
218 Radek Dvorak .15 .40
219 Rob Blake .25 .60
220 Patrick O'Sullivan .20 .50
221 Derek Armstrong .15 .40
222 Dan Cloutier .20 .50
223 Scott Thornton .15 .40
224 Michal Handzus .20 .50
225 Anze Kopitar .40 1.00
226 Dustin Brown .25 .60
227 Raitis Ivanans .15 .40
228 Kyle Calder .15 .40
229 Brad Stuart .15 .40
230 Mike Cammalleri .20 .50
231 Ladislav Nagy .15 .40
232 Jason LaBarbera .20 .50
233 Lubomir Visnovsky .15 .40
234 Alexander Frolov .15 .40
235 Marian Gaborik .30 .75
236 Kim Johnsson .15 .40
237 Niklas Backstrom .25 .60
238 Branko Radivojevic .15 .40
239 Dominic Moore .15 .40
240 Pavol Demitra .30 .75
241 Nick Schultz .15 .40
242 Brian Rolston .20 .50
243 Josh Harding .25 .60
244 Derek Boogaard .15 .40
245 Kurtis Foster .15 .40
246 Stephane Veilleux .15 .40
247 Keith Carney .15 .40
248 Mikko Koivu .20 .50
249 Mark Parrish .15 .40
250 Brent Burns .30 .75
251 Pierre-Marc Bouchard .25 .60
252 Saku Koivu .25 .60
253 Chris Higgins .15 .40
254 Mike Komisarek .15 .40
255 Maxim Lapierre .15 .40
256 Guillaume Latendresse .20 .50
257 Bryan Smolinski .15 .40
258 Sheldon Souray .15 .40
259 Andrei Kostitsyn .20 .50
260 Cristobal Huet .20 .50
261 Michael Ryder .15 .40
262 Andrei Markov .25 .60
263 Josh Gorges .15 .40
264 Alexander Perezhogin .15 .40
265 Tomas Plekanec .25 .60
266 Roman Hamrlik .20 .50
267 Mark Streit .15 .40
268 Alexei Kovalev .20 .50
269 Jerred Smithson .15 .40
270 Jason Arnott .20 .50
271 Dan Hamhuis .20 .50
272 Jordin Tootoo .25 .60
273 Darcy Hordichuk .15 .40
274 Vernon Fiddler .15 .40
275 Steve Sullivan .15 .40
276 Shea Weber .20 .50
277 Alexander Radulov .25 .60
278 Marek Zidlicky .15 .40
279 David Legwand .20 .50
280 Radek Bonk .15 .40
281 Ryan Suter .20 .50
282 Chris Mason .20 .50
283 Greg de Vries .15 .40
284 J.P. Dumont .15 .40
285 Martin Erat .15 .40
286 Brian Gionta .20 .50
287 Travis Zajac .20 .50
288 Johnny Oduya .20 .50
289 Jamie Langenbrunner .15 .40
290 Colin White .15 .40
291 Sergei Brylin .15 .40
292 Dainius Zubrus .15 .40
293 Jay Pandolfo .15 .40
294 Cam Janssen .15 .40
295 Martin Brodeur .50 1.25
296 Zach Parise .30 .75
297 Paul Martin .15 .40
298 John Madden .15 .40
299 Mike Rupp .15 .40
300 Kevin Weekes .20 .50
301 Patrik Elias .25 .60
302 Rick DiPietro .20 .50
303 Mike Sillinger .15 .40
304 Marc-Andre Bergeron .15 .40
305 Mike Comrie .20 .50
306 Jon Sim .15 .40
307 Chris Campoli .15 .40
308 Ruslan Fedotenko .15 .40
309 Bill Guerin .25 .60
310 Trent Hunter .15 .40
311 Radek Martinek .15 .40
312 Frederick Meyer .15 .40
313 Richard Park .15 .40
314 Jeff Tambellini .15 .40
315 Wade Dubielewicz .20 .50
316 Brendan Witt .15 .40
317 Andy Hilbert .15 .40
318 Miroslav Satan .20 .50
319 Jaromir Jagr .60 1.50
320 Sean Avery .15 .40
321 Michal Rozsival .15 .40
322 Petr Prucha .15 .40
323 Matt Cullen .15 .40
324 Marcel Hossa .15 .40
325 Paul Mara .15 .40
326 Scott Gomez .20 .50
327 Blair Betts .15 .40
328 Colton Orr .15 .40
329 Marek Malik .15 .40
330 Chris Drury .20 .50
331 Martin Straka .15 .40
332 Nigel Dawes .15 .40
333 Ryan Hollweg .15 .40
334 Fedor Tyutin .15 .40
335 Henrik Lundqvist .30 .75
336 Dany Heatley .25 .60
337 Wade Redden .15 .40
338 Joe Corvo .15 .40
339 Jason Spezza .25 .60
340 Patrick Eaves .15 .40
341 Chris Kelly .20 .50
342 Mike Fisher .15 .40
343 Ray Emery .20 .50
344 Andrej Meszaros .15 .40
345 Peter Schaefer .15 .40
346 Anton Volchenkov .15 .40
347 Chris Neil .15 .40
348 Chris Phillips .15 .40
349 Christoph Schubert .15 .40
350 Antoine Vermette .15 .40
351 Martin Gerber .20 .50
352 Daniel Alfredsson .25 .60
353 Jason Smith .15 .40
354 Simon Gagne .25 .60
355 Antero Niittymaki .20 .50
356 Joffrey Lupul .20 .50
357 Jeff Carter .25 .60
358 Ben Eager .15 .40
359 Scott Hartnell .25 .60
360 Martin Biron .20 .50
361 Mike Richards .25 .60
362 Kimmo Timonen .15 .40
363 R.J. Umberger .15 .40
364 Daniel Briere .25 .60
365 Scottie Upshall .15 .40
366 Mike Knuble .15 .40
367 Shane Doan .20 .50
368 Niko Kapanen .15 .40
369 Mathias Tjarnqvist .15 .40
370 Zbynek Michalek .15 .40
371 Fredrik Sjostrom .15 .40
372 Bill Thomas .15 .40
373 Josh Gratton .15 .40
374 Mikael Tellqvist .20 .50
375 Derek Morris .15 .40
376 Kevyn Adams .15 .40
377 Michael Zigomanis .15 .40
378 Ed Jovanovski .20 .50
379 David Leneveu .20 .50
380 Steven Reinprecht .15 .40
381 Nick Boynton .15 .40
382 Keith Ballard .15 .40
383 Marc-Andre Fleury .40 1.00
384 Jordan Staal .25 .60
385 Gary Roberts .15 .40
386 Georges Laraque .20 .50
387 Ryan Whitney .20 .50
388 Petr Sykora .20 .50
389 Jarkko Ruutu .15 .40
390 Evgeni Malkin .75 2.00
391 Brooks Orpik .20 .50
392 Maxime Talbot .25 .60
393 Mark Recchi .30 .75
394 Ryan Malone .15 .40
395 Colby Armstrong .15 .40
396 Sergei Gonchar .15 .40
397 Erik Christensen .15 .40
398 Darryl Sydor .15 .40
399 Sidney Crosby 1.00 2.50
400 Evgeni Nabokov .20 .50
401 Milan Michalek .15 .40
402 Marc-Edouard Vlasic .15 .40
403 Patrick Marleau .25 .60
404 Christian Ehrhoff .15 .40
405 Pat Rissmiller .15 .40
406 Craig Rivet .15 .40
407 Jonathan Cheechoo .25 .60
408 Joe Pavelski .25 .60
409 Curtis Brown .15 .40
410 Mike Grier .15 .40
411 Kyle McLaren .15 .40
412 Steve Bernier .15 .40
413 Matt Carle .15 .40
414 Marcel Goc .20 .50
415 Ryane Clowe .20 .50
416 Joe Thornton .30 .75
417 Manny Legace .20 .50
418 Brad Boyes .15 .40
419 Eric Brewer .15 .40
420 Jay McClement .15 .40
421 Martin Rucinsky .15 .40
422 Jay McKee .15 .40
423 Petr Cajanek .15 .40
424 Doug Weight .25 .60
425 Christian Backman .15 .40
426 Jamal Mayers .15 .40
427 Jeff Woywitka .15 .40
428 Lee Stempniak .15 .40
429 David Backes .25 .60
430 Barret Jackman .15 .40
431 Paul Kariya .30 .75
432 Keith Tkachuk .25 .60
433 Bryce Salvador .15 .40
434 Vincent Lecavalier .20 .50
435 Paul Ranger .15 .40
436 Vaclav Prospal .15 .40
437 Shane O'Brien .15 .40
438 Michel Ouellet .15 .40
439 Marc Denis .20 .50
440 Jason Ward .15 .40
441 Martin St. Louis .25 .60
442 Blair Jones .15 .40
443 Filip Kuba .15 .40
444 Ryan Craig .15 .40
445 Tim Taylor .15 .40
446 Dan Boyle .20 .50
447 Nick Tarnasky .15 .40
448 Johan Holmqvist .20 .50
449 Brad Richards .25 .60
450 Andre Roy .15 .40
451 Mats Sundin .25 .60
452 Kyle Wellwood .20 .50
453 Bryan McCabe .15 .40
454 Jason Blake .15 .40
455 Ian White .15 .40
456 Alexei Ponikarovsky .15 .40
457 Hal Gill .15 .40
458 Pavel Kubina .15 .40
459 Andrew Raycroft .20 .50
460 Alexander Steen .25 .60
461 Nik Antropov .20 .50
462 Mark Bell .15 .40
463 Carlo Colaiacovo .15 .40
464 Matt Stajan .20 .50
465 Tomas Kaberle .15 .40
466 Vesa Toskala .20 .50
467 Darcy Tucker .20 .50
468 Roberto Luongo .30 .75
469 Sami Salo .15 .40
470 Ryan Kesler .30 .75
471 Trevor Linden .25 .60
472 Kevin Bieksa .20 .50
473 Matt Cooke .15 .40
474 Aaron Miller .15 .40
475 Henrik Sedin .25 .60
476 Mattias Ohlund .15 .40
477 Brendan Morrison .15 .40
478 Willie Mitchell .15 .40
479 Curtis Sanford .20 .50
480 Markus Naslund .25 .60
481 Taylor Pyatt .15 .40
482 Alexandre Burrows .25 .60
483 Lukas Krajicek .15 .40
484 Daniel Sedin .25 .60
485 Alexander Ovechkin 1.00 2.50
486 Chris Clark .15 .40
487 Milan Jurcina .15 .40
488 Boyd Gordon .15 .40
489 Michael Nylander .15 .40
490 Donald Brashear .15 .40
491 Shaone Morrisonn .15 .40
492 Steve Eminger .15 .40
493 Olaf Kolzig .25 .60
494 Matt Pettinger .15 .40
495 Viktor Kozlov .15 .40
496 Brooks Laich .15 .40
497 Mike Green .25 .60
498 Jakub Klepis .15 .40
499 Brent Johnson .20 .50
500 Alexander Semin .25 .60
501 Bobby Ryan RC 2.00 5.00
502 Drew Miller RC 1.00 2.50
503 Aaron Rome RC 1.00 2.50
504 Ryan Carter RC .75 2.00
505 Jonas Hiller RC 1.50 4.00
506 Kent Huskins RC .75 2.00
507 Bjorn Melin RC .75 2.00
508 Bryan Little RC 1.25 3.00
509 Brett Sterling RC .75 2.00
510 Tobias Enstrom RC 1.25 3.00
511 David Krejci RC 2.50 6.00
512 Jonathan Sigalet RC .75 2.00
513 Milan Lucic RC 4.00 10.00
514 Curtis McElhinney RC 1.25 3.00
515 David Moss RC 1.25 3.00
516 Tomi Maki RC .75 2.00
517 Jonathan Toews RC 5.00 12.00
518 Patrick Kane RC 6.00 15.00
519 Colin Fraser RC .75 2.00
520 Bryan Bickell RC 1.50 4.00
521 Magnus Johansson RC .75 2.00
522 Pierre Parenteau RC 1.00 2.50
523 Jonas Nordqvist RC .75 2.00
524 David Koci RC .75 2.00
525 Tyler Weiman RC 1.00 2.50
526 Jaroslav Hlinka RC 1.00 2.50
527 Jeff Finger RC .75 2.00
528 Kris Russell RC 1.00 2.50
529 Danny Bois RC .75 2.00
530 Tomas Popperle RC 1.00 2.50
531 Marc Methot RC .75 2.00
532 Jared Boll RC 1.00 2.50
533 Curtis Glencross RC 1.25 3.00
534 Matt Niskanen RC 1.25 3.00
535 Tobias Stephan RC 1.00 2.50
536 Joel Lundqvist RC .75 2.00
537 Krys Barch RC 1.00 2.50
538 Chris Conner RC .75 2.00
539 Matt Ellis RC 1.00 2.50
540 Sam Gagner RC 1.50 4.00
541 Andrew Cogliano RC 1.25 3.00
542 Rob Schremp RC 1.00 2.50
543 Tom Gilbert RC 1.00 2.50
544 Bryan Young RC .75 2.00
545 Zack Stortini RC .75 2.00
546 Sebastien Bisaillon RC .75 2.00
547 Martin Lojek RC .75 2.00
548 Cory Murphy RC .75 2.00
549 Jack Johnson RC 1.00 2.50
550 Jonathan Bernier RC 2.00 5.00
551 Lauri Tukonen RC .75 2.00
552 Brady Murray RC .75 2.00
553 John Zeiler RC .75 2.00
554 Gabe Gauthier RC .75 2.00
555 Shay Stephenson RC .75 2.00
556 Joe Piskula RC .75 2.00
557 Petr Kalus RC .75 2.00
558 James Sheppard RC .75 2.00
559 Joel Ward RC 1.25 3.00
560 Carey Price RC 10.00 25.00
561 Kyle Chipchura RC 1.25 3.00
562 Jaroslav Halak RC 2.00 5.00
563 Duncan Milroy RC .75 2.00
564 Ville Koistinen RC .75 2.00
565 Rich Peverley RC 1.25 3.00
566 Nicklas Bergfors RC .75 2.00
567 Andy Greene RC 1.00 2.50
568 Mark Fraser RC .75 2.00
569 David Clarkson RC 1.25 3.00
570 Rod Pelley RC .75 2.00
571 Frans Nielsen RC 1.25 3.00
572 Marc Staal RC 1.25 3.00
573 Brandon Dubinsky RC 1.50 4.00
574 Ryan Callahan RC 1.50 4.00
575 Daniel Girardi RC 1.00 2.50
576 Nick Foligno RC 1.50 4.00
577 Brian Elliott RC 1.50 4.00
578 Ryan Parent RC .75 2.00
579 Scott Munroe RC .75 2.00
580 Denis Tolpeko RC .75 2.00
581 Riley Cote RC 1.00 2.50
582 Nathan Guenin RC 1.00 2.50
583 Peter Mueller RC 1.00 2.50
584 Martin Hanzal RC 1.00 2.50
585 Craig Weller RC .75 2.00
586 Daniel Winnik RC 1.00 2.50
587 Daniel Carcillo RC 1.00 2.50
588 Mark Mancari RC 1.00 2.50
589 Torrey Mitchell RC 1.00 2.50
590 Thomas Plihal RC 1.00 2.50
591 Erik Johnson RC 1.25 3.00
592 Darcy Campbell RC .75 2.00
593 Steve Wagner RC .75 2.00
594 Matt Smaby RC .75 2.00
595 Mike Lundin RC .75 2.00
596 Mason Raymond RC 1.25 3.00
597 Jannik Hansen RC 1.00 2.50
598 Nicklas Backstrom RC 2.50 6.00
599 Jeff Schultz RC 1.00 2.50
600 Jamie Hunt RC .75 2.00

2007-08 O-Pee-Chee Micromotion

*MICRO: 2.5X TO 6X
STATED ODDS 1:6

2007-08 O-Pee-Chee Micromotion Black

*MICRO BLACK: 6X TO 15X
*MICRO BLACK ROOKIES: 1.2X TO 3X
STATED PRINT RUN 100 SER.#'d SETS

2007-08 O-Pee-Chee Silver

*SILVER: 1X TO 2.5X

2007-08 O-Pee-Chee 3x5 Toys R' Us

INSERTS IN TOYS R US PACKS
TRU1 Saku Koivu 4.00 10.00
TRU2 Michael Ryder 2.50 6.00
TRU3 Guillaume Latendresse 3.00 8.00
TRU4 Cristobal Huet 3.00 8.00
TRU5 Alexei Kovalev 3.00 8.00
TRU6 Chris Higgins 2.50 6.00
TRU7 Miikka Kiprusoff 3.00 8.00
TRU8 Jarome Iginla 4.00 10.00
TRU9 Dion Phaneuf 4.00 10.00
TRU10 Alex Tanguay 2.50 6.00
TRU11 Daymond Langkow 2.50 6.00
TRU12 Kristian Huselius 2.50 6.00
TRU13 Ray Emery 3.00 8.00
TRU14 Dany Heatley 4.00 10.00
TRU15 Daniel Alfredsson 4.00 10.00
TRU16 Jason Spezza 4.00 10.00
TRU17 Wade Redden 2.50 6.00
TRU18 Mike Fisher 2.50 6.00
TRU19 Roberto Luongo 5.00 12.00
TRU20 Markus Naslund 4.00 10.00
TRU21 Daniel Sedin 4.00 10.00
TRU22 Henrik Sedin 4.00 10.00
TRU23 Brendan Morrison 2.50 6.00
TRU24 Ryan Kesler 5.00 12.00
TRU25 Mats Sundin 4.00 10.00
TRU26 Jason Blake 2.50 6.00
TRU27 Darcy Tucker 3.00 8.00
TRU28 Alexander Steen 4.00 10.00
TRU29 Tomas Kaberle 2.50 6.00
TRU30 Vesa Toskala 3.00 8.00
TRU31 Ales Hemsky 3.00 8.00
TRU32 Dwayne Roloson 3.00 8.00
TRU33 Joni Pitkanen 2.50 6.00
TRU34 Geoff Sanderson 2.50 6.00
TRU35 Jarret Stoll 3.00 8.00
TRU36 Shawn Horcoff 2.50 6.00
TRU37 Sidney Crosby 15.00 40.00
TRU38 Martin Brodeur 8.00 20.00

Card	Low	High
TRU39 Nicklas Lidstrom	4.00	10.00
TRU40 Evgeni Malkin	12.00	30.00
TRU41 Scott Niedermayer	4.00	10.00
TRU42 Sidney Crosby	15.00	40.00

2007-08 O-Pee-Chee Bobby Orr Panoramic Cards

Card	Low	High
COMPLETE SET (6)	30.00	60.00
COMMON ORR	6.00	15.00

2007-08 O-Pee-Chee In Action

Card	Low	High
COMPLETE SET (20)	12.00	30.00
IA1 Sidney Crosby	2.00	5.00
IA2 Alexander Ovechkin	2.00	5.00
IA3 Evgeni Malkin	1.50	4.00
IA4 Dany Heatley	.50	1.25
IA5 Rick Nash	.50	1.25
IA6 Ilya Kovalchuk	.50	1.25
IA7 Vincent Lecavalier	.40	1.00
IA8 Jaromir Jagr	1.25	3.00
IA9 Thomas Vanek	.60	1.50
IA10 Jarome Iginla	.50	1.25
IA11 Henrik Zetterberg	.60	1.50
IA12 Michael Ryder	.30	.75
IA13 Mats Sundin	.50	1.25
IA14 Joe Sakic	.75	2.00
IA15 Martin Brodeur	1.00	2.50
IA16 Roberto Luongo	.60	1.50
IA17 Ray Emery	.40	1.00
IA18 Ryan Miller	.50	1.25
IA19 Joe Thornton	.60	1.50
IA20 Ryan Getzlaf	.75	2.00

2007-08 O-Pee-Chee Materials Quad

Card	Low	High
STATED ODDS 1:144		
QMANGE Alf/Nied/Gig/Emery	8.00	20.00
QMASHE Alf/Spez/Heat/Emery	8.00	20.00
QMASOW Antro/Staj/Ond/White	6.00	15.00
QMBEGP Brod/Eli/Gion/Parise	15.00	40.00
QMBFCK Blake/Frol/Cam/Kopit	12.00	30.00
QMBJBH Belf/Jos/Brod/Hasek	15.00	40.00
QMCBMA Con/Afino/Miller/Vanek	10.00	25.00
QMCBTK Char/Berg/Thom/Kess	10.00	25.00
QMCHOD Chel/Hasek/Osg/Drap	10.00	25.00
QMDGHB Dem/Gab/Hall/Bouch	10.00	25.00
QMDLAF Leg/Arn/Fors/Dumont	10.00	25.00
QMDNLW Doan/Nash/Lom/Ward	8.00	20.00
QMGBRC Gag/Briere/Rich/Cart	8.00	20.00
QMGFCM Gonc/Fleu/Cros/Malk	15.00	40.00
QMITKP Iginla/Tang/Kipr/Phan	8.00	20.00
QMJBWH Jok/Bouw/Weiss/Hort	8.00	20.00
QMJDSB Jovo/Doan/Sjo/Bell	6.00	15.00
QMJHEH Jagr/Hejd/Elias/Havlat	20.00	50.00
QMJHSH Jagr/Hoss/St. Lo/Heat	20.00	50.00
QMJROM Jack/Ray/Ov/Malkin	25.00	60.00
QMJSLP Jagr/Strak/Lund/Pruc	20.00	50.00
QMKHHK Koivu/Huet/Higg/Kov	8.00	20.00
QMKMOJ Kolz/Morr/Ov/Jurcina	15.00	40.00
QMKOMR Kov/Ov/Malk/Radu	12.00	30.00
QMLHDZ Lids/Holm/Dats/Zett	10.00	25.00
QMLLMK Luo/Lind/Morr/Kesler	10.00	25.00
QMLNFB LeClr/Nash/Fed/Brule	12.00	30.00
QMLNMG Lids/Nied/McC/Gonc	8.00	20.00
QMLREK Luon/Ray/Emery/Kipr	10.00	25.00
QMLRSC Lecav/Rich/St. L/Craig	8.00	20.00
QMMLRT Mo/Leht/Rib/Turco	12.00	30.00
QMMTNC Marl/Thor/Nab/Chee	10.00	25.00
QMNSOS Nasl/Sedin/Ohl/Sedin	8.00	20.00
QMRNGW Rich/Nied/Gig/Ward	8.00	20.00
QMSBTI Sakic/Brod/Thorn/Ig	15.00	40.00
QMSCCL Still/Commo/Cole/Ladd	8.00	20.00
QMSDRD Sakic/Dem/Rich/Dats	12.00	30.00
QMSGDH Guer/Sat/DiPie/Hunt	8.00	20.00
QMSHRH Stoll/Horc/Rolo/Hem	6.00	15.00
QMSHRK Sam/Havl/Ruut/Khabi	8.00	20.00
QMSHSB Sakic/Hejd/Svat/Bud	12.00	30.00
QMSJSS Sakic/Shan/Jagr/Sun	20.00	50.00
QMSKAI Sundin/Koivu/Alf/Ig	8.00	20.00
QMSLHO Sel/Lecav/Heat/Ov	15.00	40.00
QMSLKJ Sel/Leht/Koivu/Jokin	15.00	40.00
QMSLTC Sak/Lecav/Thorn/Cros	15.00	40.00
QMSMKB Sav/Murr/Kob/Boch	6.00	15.00
QMSMSR Sel/Mo/Sund/Recchi	15.00	40.00
QMSNGG Sel/Nied/Gig/Getzlaf	15.00	40.00
QMSNLF Sund/Nas/Lids/Fors	10.00	25.00
QMSOVM Sedin/Ov/Van/Malk	12.00	30.00
QMSSKW Sharp/Seab/Keith/Will	8.00	20.00
QMSTMS Sun/Tuck/McC/Steen	8.00	20.00
QMTFSC Thorn/Fors/St. L/Cros	20.00	50.00
QMTLLW Theo/Leo/Lile/Wolski	8.00	20.00
QMTPPP Torr/Pisan/Pit/Pouliot	5.00	12.00
QMVSZP Vyb/Shel/Zher/Picard	5.00	12.00
QMWBSW Will/Brind/Staal/Ward	10.00	25.00
QMWJLB Weight/Jack/Leg/Boy	8.00	20.00
QMZMOJ Zubov/Morr/Ott/Jok	6.00	15.00

2007-08 O-Pee-Chee Record Breakers

Card	Low	High
COMPLETE SET (10)	8.00	20.00
RB1 Mike Modano	.75	2.00
RB2 Martin Brodeur	1.00	2.50
RB3 Paul Stastny	.50	1.25
RB4 Vincent Lecavalier	.40	1.00
RB5 Sidney Crosby	2.00	5.00
RB6 Sheldon Souray	.30	.75
RB7 Evgeni Malkin	1.50	4.00
RB8 Jaromir Jagr	1.25	3.00
RB9 Alexander Ovechkin	2.00	5.00
RB10 Roberto Luongo	.60	1.50

2007-08 O-Pee-Chee Season Highlights

Card	Low	High
COMPLETE SET (19)	10.00	25.00
SH1 Scott Niedermayer	.50	1.25
SH2 Daniel Alfredsson	.50	1.25
SH3 Ryan Miller	.50	1.25
SH4 Evgeni Malkin	1.50	4.00
SH5 Joe Sakic	.75	2.00
SH6 Daniel Briere	.50	1.25
SH7 Sidney Crosby	2.00	5.00
SH8 Brendan Shanahan	.60	1.50
SH9 Jaromir Jagr	1.25	3.00
SH10 Mats Sundin	.50	1.25
SH11 Teemu Selanne	1.00	2.50
SH12 Dean McAmmond	.30	.75
SH13 Jean-Sebastien Giguere	.50	1.25
SH14 Wade Dubielewicz	.40	1.00
SH15 Sidney Crosby	2.00	5.00
SH16 Roberto Luongo	.60	1.50
SH17 Dominik Hasek	.60	1.50
SH18 Joe Thornton	.60	1.50
SH19 Nicklas Lidstrom	.50	1.25
SH20 Jordan Staal	.50	1.25

2007-08 O-Pee-Chee Signatures

Card	Low	High
STATED ODDS 1:432		
SAB Adam Burish	8.00	20.00
SAD Adam Dennis	8.00	20.00
SAE Alexander Edler	6.00	15.00
SAF Alexander Frolov	6.00	15.00
SAO Alexander Ovechkin SP	250.00	350.00
SAT Alex Tanguay SP		
SBA Christian Backman	6.00	15.00
SBJ Blair Jones	6.00	15.00
SBM Brenden Morrow		
SBO Ben Ondrus	6.00	15.00
SBP Benoit Pouliot	6.00	15.00
SBR Alex Brooks	6.00	15.00
SBW Ben Walter	6.00	15.00
SCK Chuck Kobasew	6.00	15.00
SCP Chris Phillips	6.00	15.00
SCT Chris Thorburn	6.00	15.00
SCW Cam Ward	10.00	25.00
SDB Dave Bolland	8.00	20.00
SDH Dany Heatley SP		
SDL Drew Larman	6.00	15.00
SDS Drew Stafford	8.00	20.00
SDW Doug Weight	10.00	25.00
SEC Erik Christensen		
SEL Patrik Elias	25.00	60.00
SEM Evgeni Malkin	50.00	120.00
SES Eric Staal SP		
SFN Filip Novak	6.00	15.00
SFP Fernando Pisani	6.00	15.00
SGA Simon Gagne SP		
SGH Gordie Howe SP	75.00	150.00
SHL Henrik Lundqvist SP		
SIW Ian White	6.00	15.00
SJC Jeff Carter	10.00	25.00
SJG Jean-Sebastien Giguere SP	25.00	60.00
SJI Jarome Iginla SP		
SJM Jay McClement	6.00	15.00
SJP Joe Pavelski	10.00	25.00
SJS Jordan Staal	10.00	25.00
SJT Joe Thornton SP	150.00	250.00
SMC Mike Cammalleri		
SMG Marian Gaborik SP		
SMH Marian Hossa SP		
SMJ Milan Jurcina	6.00	15.00
SML Mario Lemieux SP		
SMM Mark Messier SP		
SMO Michel Ouellet	6.00	15.00
SMP Marc-Antoine Pouliot	6.00	15.00
SMR Michael Ryder		
SMV Marc-Edouard Vlasic	6.00	15.00
SNG Niklas Grossman	6.00	15.00
SNZ Nikolai Zherdev	6.00	15.00
SOR Bobby Orr SP		
SPE Corey Perry	10.00	25.00
SPM Paul Mara	6.00	15.00
SPR Brandon Prust	6.00	15.00
SPS Paul Stastny	10.00	25.00
SRA Paul Ranger	6.00	15.00
SRC Ryan Clowe SP		
SRG Ryan Getzlaf	15.00	40.00
SRI Mike Richards	10.00	25.00
SRM Ryan Malone	6.00	15.00
SRN Rick Nash SP	40.00	80.00
SRY Ryan Miller	10.00	25.00
SSB Steve Bernier	6.00	15.00
SSC Sidney Crosby SP	400.00	600.00
SSG Scott Gomez	8.00	20.00
SSO Shane O'Brien	6.00	15.00
SST Martin St. Louis SP	50.00	100.00
SSW Shea Weber	8.00	20.00
STV Tomas Vokoun		
SVL Vincent Lecavalier SP	75.00	150.00
SWW Wojtek Wolski	8.00	20.00

2007-08 O-Pee-Chee Stat Leaders

Card	Low	High
COMPLETE SET (20)	12.00	30.00
SL1 Selanne/Lecavalier/Heatley	1.00	2.50
SL2 Thornton/Savard/Crosby	2.00	5.00
SL3 Lecavalier/Thornton/Crosby	2.00	5.00
SL4 Lidstrom/Alfredsson/Vanek	.60	1.50
SL5 Selanne/Kovalchuk/Souray	1.00	2.50
SL6 Lecavalier/Draper/Staal	.50	1.25
SL7 Selanne/Zetterberg/Heatley	1.00	2.50
SL8 Neil/Gratton/Eager	.30	.75
SL9 Brodeur/Hasek/Backstrom	1.00	2.50
SL10 Brodeur/Luongo/Kiprusoff	1.00	2.50
SL11 Brodeur/Mason/Backstrom	1.00	2.50
SL12 Brodeur/Hasek/Kiprusoff	1.00	2.50
SL13 Alfredsson/McDonald/Datsyuk	.60	1.50
SL14 Lidstrom/Spezza/Heatley	.50	1.25
SL15 Alfredsson/Spezza/Heatley	.50	1.25
SL16 Pronger/Numminen/Pahlsson	.40	1.00
SL17 Drury/Alfredsson/Getzlaf	.75	2.00
SL18 Hasek/Giguere/Emery	.60	1.50
SL19 Hasek/Luongo/Turco	.60	1.50
SL20 Niedermayer/Gonchar/Souray	.50	1.25

2007-08 O-Pee-Chee Team Checklists

Card	Low	High
COMPLETE SET (30)	20.00	50.00
STATED ODDS 1:14		
CL1 Anaheim Ducks	1.00	2.50
CL2 Atlanta Thrashers	1.00	2.50
CL3 Boston Bruins	1.00	2.50
CL4 Buffalo Sabres	1.00	2.50
CL5 Calgary Flames	1.00	2.50
CL6 Carolina Hurricanes	1.00	2.50
CL7 Chicago Blackhawks	1.00	2.50
CL8 Colorado Avalanche	1.00	2.50
CL9 Columbus Blue Jackets	1.00	2.50
CL10 Dallas Stars	1.00	2.50
CL11 Detroit Red Wings	1.00	2.50
CL12 Edmonton Oilers	1.00	2.50
CL13 Florida Panthers	1.00	2.50
CL14 Los Angeles Kings	1.00	2.50
CL15 Minnesota Wild	1.00	2.50
CL16 Montreal Canadiens	1.00	2.50
CL17 Nashville Predators	1.00	2.50
CL18 New Jersey Devils	1.00	2.50
CL19 New York Islanders	1.00	2.50
CL20 New York Rangers	1.00	2.50
CL21 Ottawa Senators	1.00	2.50
CL22 Philadelphia Flyers	1.00	2.50
CL23 Phoenix Coyotes	1.00	2.50
CL24 Pittsburgh Penguins	1.00	2.50
CL25 San Jose Sharks	1.00	2.50
CL26 St. Louis Blues	1.00	2.50
CL27 Tampa Bay Lightning	1.00	2.50
CL28 Toronto Maple Leafs	1.00	2.50
CL29 Vancouver Canucks	1.00	2.50
CL30 Washington Capitals	1.00	2.50

2008-09 O-Pee-Chee

This set was released on October 7, 2008. The base set consists of 600 cards, including rookies as cards 501-560.

Card	Low	High
COMPLETE SET (800)	100.00	250.00
COMP.SER.1 SET (600)	40.00	100.00
COMP.SET w/o RCs (500)	40.00	100.00
COMP.UPDATE SET (200)	60.00	120.00
1 Markus Naslund	.20	.50
2 Dan Hinote	.15	.40
3 Pascal Dupuis	.15	.40
4 Frantisek Kaberle	.15	.40
5 Derek Morris	.15	.40
6 Scottie Upshall	.15	.40
7 Richard Park	.15	.40
8 Josh Gorges	.15	.40
9 Rob Blake	.25	.60
10 Cory Murphy	.15	.40
11 Sheldon Souray	.15	.40
12 Mike Modano	.40	1.00
13 Wojtek Wolski	.20	.50
14 Hal Gill	.15	.40
15 Dustin Boyd	.15	.40
16 Jason Pominville	.25	.60
17 Slava Kozlov	.15	.40
18 Sidney Crosby	1.00	2.50
19 Kamil Kreps	.15	.40
20 Bryan McCabe	.15	.40
21 Karri Ramo	.20	.50
22 Joe Pavelski	.25	.60
23 Mikael Tellqvist	.20	.50
24 Braydon Coburn	.15	.40
25 Nigel Dawes	.15	.40
26 Jay Pandolfo	.15	.40
27 Niklas Backstrom	.25	.60
28 Shaone Morrisonn	.15	.40
29 Bryan Allen	.15	.40
30 Jiri Hudler	.20	.50
31 Marc-Andre Bergeron	.15	.40
32 Pascal Leclaire	.20	.50
33 Tim Gleason	.15	.40
34 Patrice Bergeron	.30	.75
35 Eric Perrin	.15	.40
36 Francois Beauchemin	.15	.40
37 Fredrik Norrena	.15	.40
38 Mats Sundin	.25	.60
39 Jay McClement	.15	.40
40 Jarkko Ruutu	.15	.40
41 Ladislav Smid	.15	.40
42 Daniel Carcillo	.15	.40
43 Ryan Parent	.15	.40
44 Antoine Vermette	.15	.40
45 Brendan Shanahan	.30	.75
46 Josef Vasicek	.15	.40
47 Roman Hamrlik	.20	.50
48 Michal Handzus	.20	.50
49 Ales Hemsky	.20	.50
50 Brooks Orpik	.20	.50
51 Scott Parker	.15	.40
52 Chad Larose	.15	.40
53 Ryan Miller	.25	.60
54 Tobias Enstrom	.15	.40
55 George Parros	.15	.40
56 Viktor Kozlov	.15	.40
57 Kyle Wellwood	.20	.50
58 Evgeni Nabokov	.20	.50
59 Corey Perry	.25	.60
60 Boyd Gordon	.15	.40
61 Dan Cleary	.20	.50
62 Mike Fisher	.15	.40
63 John Madden	.15	.40
64 Tomas Plekanec	.25	.60
65 Nathan Horton	.20	.50
66 Dwayne Roloson	.20	.50
67 Niklas Kronwall	.20	.50
68 Radim Vrbata	.20	.50
69 Manny Malhotra	.15	.40
70 Martin Havlat	.25	.60
71 Curtis Joseph	.25	.60
72 Saku Koivu	.25	.60
73 Bryan Little	.20	.50
74 Marc-Edouard Vlasic	.15	.40
75 Jonas Hiller	.20	.50
76 Brendan Morrison	.15	.40
77 Nikolai Antropov	.20	.50
78 Ryan Johnson	.15	.40
79 Craig Rivet	.15	.40
80 Marian Hossa	.20	.50
81 Simon Gagne	.25	.60
82 Cory Stillman	.15	.40
83 Chris Campoli	.15	.40
84 Zach Parise	.25	.60
85 David Legwand	.20	.50
86 Andrei Kostitsyn	.20	.50
87 Maxim Afinogenov	.15	.40
88 Kyle Calder	.15	.40
89 Henrik Zetterberg	.30	.75
90 Rostislav Klesla	.15	.40
91 Travis Zajac	.20	.50
92 Brent Seabrook	.25	.60
93 Toni Lydman	.15	.40
94 Todd White	.15	.40
95 Tomas Fleischmann	.15	.40
96 Devin Setoguchi	.20	.50
97 Henrik Sedin	.25	.60
98 Boyd Devereaux	.15	.40
99 Michel Ouellet	.15	.40
100 Matt Carle	.15	.40
101 Zbynek Michalek	.15	.40
102 Scott Gomez	.20	.50
103 Dainius Zubrus	.15	.40
104 Nikolai Khabibulin	.25	.60
105 James Sheppard	.15	.40
106 Richard Zednik	.25	.60
107 Chris Osgood	.25	.60
108 Alexander Semin	.25	.60
109 Paul Stastny	.25	.60
110 Justin Williams	.20	.50
111 Eric Nystrom	.15	.40
112 Tuukka Rask	.25	.60
113 Mathieu Schneider	.15	.40
114 Mikael Samuelsson	.15	.40
115 Vincent Lecavalier	.20	.50
116 Eric Brewer	.15	.40
117 Pat Rissmiller	.15	.40
118 Niko Kapanen	.15	.40
119 Jaromir Jagr	.60	1.50
120 Paul Martin	.15	.40
121 Guillaume Latendresse	.15	.40
122 Pierre-Marc Bouchard	.25	.60
123 Olli Jokinen	.20	.50
124 Brian Rafalski	.20	.50
125 Rob Niedermayer	.20	.50
126 Jiri Novotny	.15	.40
127 Matt Cullen	.15	.40
128 Tim Thomas	.25	.60
129 Dennis Wideman	.15	.40
130 Garnet Exelby	.15	.40
131 Nicklas Lidstrom	.25	.60
132 Sami Salo	.15	.40
133 Alexei Ponikarovsky	.15	.40
134 Paul Ranger	.15	.40
135 Andy McDonald	.20	.50
136 Chris Kunitz	.25	.60
137 Mike Richards	.25	.60
138 Andrej Meszaros	.15	.40
139 Michal Rozsival	.15	.40
140 Brendan Witt	.15	.40
141 Marek Zidlicky	.15	.40
142 Mark Parrish	.15	.40
143 Craig Anderson	.25	.60
144 Mathieu Garon	.20	.50
145 Brett Lebda	.15	.40
146 Loui Eriksson	.25	.60
147 Marek Svatos	.15	.40
148 Scott Walker	.15	.40
149 Anders Eriksson	.15	.40
150 Aaron Ward	.15	.40
151 Nicklas Backstrom	.40	1.00
152 Anton Stralman	.15	.40
153 Dmitri Kalinin	.15	.40
154 Mike Grier	.15	.40
155 Keith Yandle	.25	.60
156 Ray Emery	.20	.50
157 Chris Drury	.20	.50
158 Blake Comeau	.15	.40
159 Kevin Weekes	.20	.50
160 Marian Gaborik	.30	.75
161 Rostislav Olesz	.15	.40
162 Tomas Kopecky	.15	.40
163 Jason Chimera	.15	.40
164 Tuomo Ruutu	.25	.60
165 Henrik Tallinder	.15	.40
166 Matt Stajan	.20	.50
167 Marc Savard	.15	.40
168 Alexei Zhitnik	.15	.40
169 Scott Niedermayer	.25	.60
170 Mike Green	.25	.60
171 Pavel Kubina	.15	.40
172 David Perron	.20	.50
173 Jaroslav Halak	.25	.60
174 Torrey Mitchell	.15	.40
175 Shane Doan	.20	.50
176 Johnny Oduya	.20	.50
177 Carey Price	1.00	2.50
178 David Backes	.25	.60
179 Martin Skoula	.15	.40
180 David Booth	.15	.40
181 Kris Draper	.15	.40
182 Paul Gaustad	.15	.40
183 Donald Brashear	.15	.40
184 Roberto Luongo	.30	.75
185 Brooks Laich	.15	.40
186 Craig MacDonald	.15	.40
187 Patrick Marleau	.25	.60
188 Steven Reinprecht	.15	.40
189 Chris Kelly	.20	.50
190 Ryan Hollweg	.15	.40
191 Andy Hilbert	.15	.40
192 Andy Greene	.15	.40
193 Jason Arnott	.20	.50
194 Nick Schultz	.15	.40
195 Jozef Stumpel	.15	.40
196 Matt Niskanen	.20	.50
197 John-Michael Liles	.15	.40
198 Dave Bolland	.20	.50
199 Patrick Eaves	.15	.40
200 Cory Sarich	.15	.40
201 Marco Sturm	.15	.40
202 Martin St. Louis	.25	.60
203 Jeff Schultz	.15	.40
204 Alexander Steen	.25	.60
205 Shane O'Brien	.15	.40
206 Thomas Greiss	.25	.60
207 Nick Boynton	.15	.40
208 Daniel Girardi	.15	.40
209 Alex Kovalev	.20	.50
210 Henrik Lundqvist	.30	.75
211 Shea Weber	.20	.50
212 Mikko Koivu	.20	.50
213 Karlis Skrastins	.15	.40
214 Jere Lehtinen	.15	.40
215 Fredrik Modin	.15	.40
216 Peter Budaj	.20	.50
217 Andrew Ladd	.25	.60
218 Joe Corvo	.15	.40
219 Zdeno Chara	.25	.60
220 Sean O'Donnell	.15	.40
221 Ian White	.15	.40
222 Andre Roy	.15	.40
223 Steve Wagner	.15	.40
224 Ty Conklin	.20	.50
225 Daniel Winnik	.15	.40
226 Jason Spezza	.25	.60
227 Martin Brodeur	.50	1.25
228 Ryan Callahan	.25	.60
229 Ryan O'Byrne	.15	.40
230 Brian Rolston	.20	.50
231 Ladislav Nagy	.15	.40
232 Tomas Holmstrom	.20	.50
233 Kris Russell	.15	.40
234 Jason LaBarbera	.20	.50
235 Ben Guite	.15	.40
236 Rene Bourque	.15	.40
237 David Moss	.15	.40
238 Jaroslav Spacek	.15	.40
239 Jean-Sebastien Giguere	.25	.60
240 Jason Blake	.15	.40
241 Dan Boyle	.20	.50
242 Joe Thornton	.30	.75
243 Ilya Bryzgalov	.20	.50
244 Martin Gerber	.20	.50
245 Andy Sutton	.15	.40
246 Patrik Elias	.25	.60
247 Mike Komisarek	.15	.40
248 Eric Belanger	.15	.40
249 Andrew Raycroft	.20	.50
250 David Vyborny	.15	.40
251 Pavel Datsyuk	.30	.75
252 Ron Hainsey	.15	.40
253 Patrick Sharp	.25	.60
254 Mike Sillinger	.15	.40
255 Adrian Aucoin	.15	.40
256 Thomas Vanek	.25	.60
257 Derek Armstrong	.15	.40
258 Teemu Selanne	.50	1.25
259 Ryan Kesler	.30	.75
260 Darcy Tucker	.20	.50
261 Alexander Frolov	.15	.40
262 Erik Johnson	.20	.50
263 Willie Mitchell	.15	.40
264 Ryan Whitney	.25	.60
265 Jeff Carter	.25	.60
266 Bruno Gervais	.15	.40
267 Brent Sopel	.15	.40
268 Martin Erat	.15	.40
269 Raitis Ivanans	.15	.40
270 Drew Stafford	.20	.50
271 Robert Nilsson	.15	.40
272 Lee Stempniak	.15	.40
273 Dan Fritsche	.15	.40
274 Ryan Smyth	.20	.50
275 Owen Nolan	.20	.50
276 David Krejci	.25	.60
277 Jim Slater	.15	.40
278 Alexander Ovechkin	1.00	2.50
279 Drew MacIntyre	.25	.60
280 Stephane Robidas	.15	.40
281 Manny Legace	.25	.60
282 Jordan Staal	.25	.60
283 Scott Hartnell	.25	.60
284 Brandon Dubinsky	.20	.50
285 Bill Guerin	.25	.60
286 R.J. Umberger	.15	.40
287 Ryan Suter	.20	.50
288 Lubomir Visnovsky	.15	.40
289 Joni Pitkanen	.15	.40
290 Dominik Hasek	.30	.75
291 Niklas Hagman	.15	.40
292 Jordan Leopold	.15	.40
293 Miroslav Satan	.25	.60
294 Erik Cole	.20	.50
295 Kristian Huselius	.15	.40
296 Kari Lehtonen	.20	.50
297 Mason Raymond	.25	.60
298 Marc Denis	.20	.50
299 Dan Ellis	.15	.40
300 Randy Jones	.15	.40
301 Cam Ward	.25	.60
302 Tom Gilbert	.15	.40
303 Daniel Alfredsson	.25	.60
304 Radek Martinek	.15	.40
305 Vernon Fiddler	.15	.40
306 Tyler Kennedy	.20	.50
307 Patrick O'Sullivan	.20	.50
308 Chris Thorburn	.15	.40
309 Dany Heatley	.25	.60
310 Denis Grebeshkov	.15	.40
311 Steve Ott	.15	.40
312 Ian Laperriere	.15	.40
313 Adam Burish	.20	.50
314 Stephane Yelle	.15	.40
315 Ilya Kovalchuk	.25	.60
316 Brian Willsie	.15	.40
317 Olaf Kolzig	.25	.60
318 Daniel Sedin	.25	.60
319 Filip Kuba	.15	.40
320 Chris Neil	.15	.40
321 Hannu Toivonen	.20	.50
322 Milan Michalek	.15	.40
323 Martin Hanzal	.20	.50
324 Dean McAmmond	.15	.40
325 Marc Staal	.25	.60
326 Mike Rupp	.15	.40
327 Kim Johnsson	.15	.40
328 Stephen Weiss	.15	.40
329 Chris Chelios	.25	.60
330 Mike Ribeiro	.20	.50
331 Tyler Arnason	.15	.40
332 Duncan Keith	.25	.60
333 Rod Brind'Amour	.25	.60
334 Peter Schaefer	.15	.40
335 Colby Armstrong	.15	.40
336 Ryan Carter	.15	.40
337 Lukas Krajicek	.15	.40
338 Mike Smith	.25	.60
339 Maxime Talbot	.25	.60
340 Steve Downie	.25	.60
341 Christoph Schubert	.15	.40
342 Jeff Halpern	.15	.40
343 Jeff Tambellini	.15	.40
344 Jordin Tootoo	.25	.60
345 Anze Kopitar	.40	1.00
346 Evgeni Malkin	.75	2.00
347 Zach Stortini	.15	.40
348 Dustin Penner	.20	.50
349 Trevor Daley	.15	.40
350 Milan Hejduk	.20	.50
351 Corey Crawford	.30	.75
352 Robyn Regehr	.15	.40
353 Daniel Paille	.15	.40
354 Milan Lucic	.40	1.00
355 Chris Pronger	.20	.50
356 Taylor Pyatt	.15	.40
357 Jussi Jokinen	.15	.40
358 Petr Sykora	.20	.50
359 Jack Johnson	.15	.40
360 Daymond Langkow	.15	.40
361 Antero Niittymaki	.20	.50
362 Trent Hunter	.15	.40
363 Aaron Voros	.15	.40
364 Craig Conroy	.15	.40
365 Brett McLean	.15	.40
366 Jarret Stoll	.20	.50
367 Marty Turco	.25	.60
368 Gilbert Brule	.15	.40
369 Joe Sakic	.40	1.00
370 Mike Knuble	.15	.40
371 Jarome Iginla	.25	.60
372 Stephane Veilleux	.15	.40
373 Mark Stuart	.15	.40
374 Mattias Ohlund	.15	.40
375 Mike Lundin	.15	.40
376 Sergei Gonchar	.15	.40
377 Ed Jovanovski	.20	.50
378 Kimmo Timonen	.15	.40
379 Rick DiPietro	.20	.50
380 J.P. Dumont	.15	.40
381 Mattias Norstrom	.15	.40
382 Andrei Markov	.25	.60
383 Josh Harding	.25	.60
384 Steve Staios	.15	.40
385 Francis Bouillon	.20	.50
386 Brenden Morrow	.20	.50
387 Scott Hannan	.15	.40
388 Dustin Byfuglien	.25	.60
389 Bret Hedican	.15	.40
390 Matthew Lombardi	.15	.40
391 Derek Roy	.15	.40
392 Phil Kessel	.30	.75
393 Milan Jurcina	.15	.40
394 Nick Foligno	.25	.60
395 Jiri Tlusty	.20	.50
396 Jonathan Cheechoo	.25	.60
397 Peter Mueller	.20	.50
398 Daniel Briere	.25	.60
399 Anton Volchenkov	.15	.40
400 Brian Pothier	.15	.40
401 Sergei Brylin	.15	.40
402 Sergei Kostitsyn	.15	.40
403 Tomas Vokoun	.20	.50
404 Valtteri Filppula	.25	.60
405 Bobby Ryan	.25	.60
406 Antti Miettinen	.15	.40
407 Nikolai Zherdev	.15	.40
408 Jack Skille	.20	.50
409 Jochen Hecht	.15	.40
410 Chuck Kobasew	.15	.40
411 Brad Richards	.25	.60
412 Todd Bertuzzi	.25	.60
413 Trevor Linden	.25	.60
414 Nick Tarnasky	.15	.40
415 Brian Campbell	.20	.50
416 Marc-Andre Fleury	.40	1.00
417 Martin Biron	.20	.50
418 Dan Hamhuis	.20	.50
419 Petr Prucha	.15	.40
420 David Clarkson	.20	.50
421 Scott Nichol	.15	.40
422 Christian Backman	.15	.40
423 Brent Burns	.30	.75
424 Pavol Demitra	.30	.75
425 Sam Gagner	.20	.50
426 Fernando Pisani	.15	.40
427 Philippe Boucher	.15	.40
428 Peter Forsberg	.30	.75
429 Cam Barker	.15	.40
430 Miikka Kiprusoff	.20	.50
431 Clarke MacArthur	.15	.40
432 Glen Murray	.20	.50
433 Ruslan Fedotenko	.15	.40
434 Ales Kotalik	.15	.40
435 Vesa Toskala	.20	.50
436 Keith Tkachuk	.25	.60
437 Ryan Malone	.15	.40
438 Joffrey Lupul	.20	.50
439 Chris Phillips	.15	.40
440 Frederick Meyer	.15	.40
441 P.J. Axelsson	.15	.40
442 Colin White	.15	.40
443 Chris Mason	.20	.50
444 Mark Streit	.15	.40
445 Andrew Cogliano	.20	.50
446 Michael Ryder	.15	.40
447 Rick Nash	.25	.60
448 Patrick Kane	.50	1.25
449 Steve Bernier	.15	.40
450 Alexandre Burrows	.25	.60
451 Ondrej Pavelec	.30	.75
452 Alexander Edler	.15	.40
453 Tomas Kaberle	.15	.40
454 Jay McKee	.15	.40
455 Christian Ehrhoff	.15	.40
456 Kristopher Letang	.25	.60
457 Vaclav Prospal	.15	.40
458 Fedor Tyutin	.15	.40
459 Jamie Langenbrunner	.15	.40
460 Barret Jackman	.15	.40
461 Chris Higgins	.15	.40
462 Kyle Brodziak	.15	.40
463 Mike Cammalleri	.20	.50
464 Johan Franzen	.25	.60
465 Jared Boll	.15	.40
466 Andrew Brunette	.15	.40
467 Robert Lang	.15	.40
468 Glen Wesley	.15	.40
469 Tim Connolly	.15	.40
470 Niclas Havelid	.15	.40
471 Cristobal Huet	.20	.50
472 Kevin Bieksa	.20	.50
473 Jason Ward	.15	.40
474 Brad Boyes	.15	.40
475 Brian Gionta	.20	.50
476 Kyle McLaren	.15	.40
477 Keith Ballard	.15	.40
478 Wade Redden	.15	.40
479 Martin Straka	.15	.40
480 Radek Bonk	.15	.40
481 Ray Whitney	.20	.50
482 Kurtis Foster	.15	.40
483 Dustin Brown	.25	.60
484 Mike Van Ryn	.15	.40
485 Sergei Zubov	.20	.50
486 T.J. Hensick	.20	.50
487 Eric Staal	.30	.75
488 Alexander Radulov	.25	.60
489 Alex Tanguay	.15	.40
490 Manny Fernandez	.20	.50
491 Jamal Mayers	.15	.40
492 Colton Orr	.15	.40
493 Jay Bouwmeester	.25	.60
494 Jonathan Toews	.60	1.50
495 Ryan Getzlaf	.40	1.00
496 Checklist	.15	.40
497 Checklist	.15	.40
498 Checklist	.15	.40
499 Checklist	.15	.40
500 Checklist	.15	.40
501 Sami Lepisto RC	1.00	2.50
502 Mike Brown RC	1.50	4.00
503 Zach Fitzgerald RC	1.25	3.00
504 Robbie Earl RC	.75	2.00
505 Darryl Boyce RC	1.00	2.50
506 Alex Foster RC	1.00	2.50
507 Mike Iggulden RC	1.00	2.50
508 Tom Cavanagh RC	1.00	2.50
509 Alex Goligoski RC	1.50	4.00
510 Jon Filewich RC	1.00	2.50
511 Ryan Stone RC	.75	2.00
512 Chris Minard RC	1.25	3.00
513 Kyle Turris RC	2.00	5.00
514 Claude Giroux RC	2.50	6.00
515 Kyle Greentree RC	1.25	3.00
516 Brian Lee RC	1.00	2.50
517 Ilya Zubov RC	1.00	2.50
518 Jesse Winchester RC	.75	2.00
519 Kyle Okposo RC	1.25	3.00
520 Mike Mole RC	1.00	2.50
521 Jack Hillen RC	1.00	2.50
522 Jordan LaVallee RC	1.25	3.00
523 Matt D'Agostini RC	1.00	2.50
524 Corey Locke RC	1.00	2.50
525 Brian Boyle RC	1.00	2.50
526 Teddy Purcell RC	1.50	4.00
527 Danny Taylor RC	1.00	2.50
528 Erik Ersberg RC	1.00	2.50
529 Shawn Matthias RC	1.25	3.00
530 David Brine RC	.75	2.00
531 Tyler Plante RC	1.00	2.50
532 Theo Peckham RC	1.25	3.00
533 Tom Sestito RC	1.25	3.00
534 Justin Abdelkader RC	2.00	5.00
535 Jonathan Ericsson RC	1.25	3.00
536 Darren Helm RC	1.25	3.00
537 Mattias Ritola RC	1.00	2.50
538 Garrett Stafford RC	1.25	3.00
539 Mark Fistric RC	1.00	2.50
540 B.J. Crombeen RC	.75	2.00
541 Derick Brassard RC	1.00	2.50
542 Steve Mason RC	2.00	5.00
543 Adam Pineault RC	1.00	2.50
544 Dan LaCosta RC	1.25	3.00
545 Andrew Murray RC	1.00	2.50
546 Clay Wilson RC	.75	2.00
547 Cody McLeod RC	1.00	2.50
548 Jordan Hendry RC	1.00	2.50
549 Niklas Hjalmarsson RC	2.00	5.00
550 Brandon Nolan RC	1.00	2.50
551 Tim Conboy RC	1.00	2.50
552 Joey Mormina RC	1.00	2.50
553 Joe Jensen RC	1.25	3.00
554 Tim Ramholt RC	1.00	2.50
555 Marc-Andre Gragnani RC	1.00	2.50
556 Pascal Pelletier RC	.75	2.00
557 Boris Valabik RC	1.25	3.00
558 Colin Stuart RC	1.00	2.50
559 Kevin Doell RC	.75	2.00
560 Andrew Ebbett RC	.75	2.00
561 Checklist	.15	.40
562 Dale Hawerchuk	1.00	2.50
563 Bobby Hull	1.25	3.00
564 Richard Brodeur	.60	1.50
565 Borje Salming	.75	2.00
566 Johnny Bower	1.00	2.50
567 Eddie Shack	.75	2.00
568 Doug Wilson	.60	1.50
569 Peter Stastny	.75	2.00
570 Mario Lemieux	2.50	6.00
571 Joe Mullen	.60	1.50
572 Ron Hextall	1.25	3.00
573 Rick MacLeish	.60	1.50
574 Bernie Parent	.75	2.00
575 Mark Messier	1.00	2.50
576 Brian Leetch	.75	2.00
577 Mike Bossy	.75	2.00
578 Pat LaFontaine	.75	2.00
579 Guy Lafleur	1.00	2.50
580 Jean Beliveau	.75	2.00
581 Frank Mahovlich	.75	2.00
582 Dino Ciccarelli	.75	2.00
583 Rogie Vachon	1.00	2.50
584 Wayne Gretzky	4.00	10.00
585 Glenn Anderson	.75	2.00
586 Grant Fuhr	.75	2.00
587 Luc Robitaille	.75	2.00
588 Scotty Bowman	.75	2.00
589 Alex Delvecchio	1.00	2.50
590 Patrick Roy	2.00	5.00
591 Jari Kurri	.75	2.00
592 Denis Savard	1.00	2.50
593 Tony Esposito	.75	2.00
594 Stan Mikita	1.00	2.50
595 Lanny McDonald	.75	2.00
596 Gilbert Perreault	.75	2.00
597 Ray Bourque	1.25	3.00
598 Cam Neely	.75	2.00
599 Phil Esposito	1.25	3.00
600 Bobby Orr	2.50	6.00
601 Steve Montador	.15	.40
602 Brendan Morrison	.15	.40
603 Mathieu Schneider	.15	.40
604 Ron Hainsey	.15	.40
605 Michael Ryder	.15	.40
606 Patrick Lalime	.20	.50
607 Craig Rivet	.15	.40
608 Teppo Numminen	.20	.50
609 Todd Bertuzzi	.25	.60
610 Mike Cammalleri	.20	.50
611 Curtis Glencross	.15	.40
612 Rene Bourque	.15	.40
613 Jarome Iginla	.25	.60
614 Joni Pitkanen	.15	.40
615 Brian Campbell	.20	.50
616 Cristobal Huet	.20	.50
617 Adam Foote	.15	.40
618 Darcy Tucker	.20	.50
619 Andrew Raycroft	.20	.50
620 Joe Sakic	.40	1.00
621 Kristian Huselius	.15	.40
622 R.J. Umberger	.15	.40
623 Mike Commodore	.15	.40
624 Sean Avery	.15	.40
625 Mark Parrish	.15	.40
626 Marian Hossa	.20	.50
627 Ty Conklin	.20	.50
628 Lubomir Visnovsky	.15	.40
629 Erik Cole	.20	.50
630 Jeff Drouin-Deslauriers	.15	.40
631 Keith Ballard	.15	.40
632 Cory Stillman	.15	.40
633 Bryan McCabe	.15	.40
634 Jarret Stoll	.20	.50
635 Andrew Brunette	.15	.40
636 Owen Nolan	.20	.50
637 Marek Zidlicky	.15	.40
638 Marc-Andre Bergeron	.15	.40
639 Craig Weller	.15	.40
640 Antti Miettinen	.15	.40
641 Alex Tanguay	.15	.40
642 Marc Denis	.20	.50
643 Georges Laraque	.20	.50
644 Robert Lang	.15	.40
645 Joel Ward	.15	.40
646 Brian Rolston	.20	.50
647 Doug Weight	.25	.60
648 Mark Streit	.15	.40
649 Nikolai Zherdev	.15	.40
650 Wade Redden	.15	.40
651 Markus Naslund	.20	.50
652 Filip Kuba	.15	.40
653 Alex Auld	.15	.40
654 Alexandre Picard	.15	.40
655 Ryan Shannon	.15	.40
656 Jason Smith	.15	.40

7 Brendan Bell .15 .40
8 Samuel Pahlsson .15 .40
9 Matt Carle .15 .40
0 Arron Asham .15 .40
1 Ossi Vaananen .15 .40
2 Olli Jokinen .20 .50
3 Joakim Lindstrom .15 .40
4 Todd Fedoruk .15 .40
5 Ken Klee .15 .40
6 Eric Godard .15 .40
7 Miroslav Satan .25 .60
8 Ruslan Fedotenko .15 .40
9 Matt Cooke .15 .40
0 Sidney Crosby 1.00 2.50
1 Evgeni Malkin .75 2.00
2 Rob Blake .25 .60
3 Dan Boyle .20 .50
4 Jody Shelley .15 .40
5 Chris Mason .20 .50
6 Andy McDonald .20 .50
7 David Koci .15 .40
8 Andy Wozniewski .15 .40
9 Matt Foy .15 .40
0 Brad Winchester .15 .40
1 Mark Recchi .30 .75
2 Radim Vrbata .20 .50
3 Ryan Malone .15 .40
4 Vaclav Prospal .15 .40
5 Andrej Meszaros .15 .40
6 Gary Roberts .15 .40
7 Olaf Kolzig .25 .60
8 Steve Eminger .15 .40
9 Vincent Lecavalier .20 .50
0 Curtis Joseph .25 .60
1 Jeff Finger .15 .40
2 Ryan Hollweg .15 .40
3 Niklas Hagman .15 .40
4 Pavol Demitra .30 .75
5 Steve Bernier .15 .40
6 Shane O'Brien .15 .40
7 Darcy Hordichuk .15 .40
8 Rob Davison .15 .40
9 Jose Theodore .25 .60
0 Checklist .15 .40
1 Checklist .15 .40
2 Bret Hedican .15 .40
3 Cory Schneider RC 3.00 8.00
4 Jason Williams .15 .40
5 Karl Alzner RC .75 2.00
6 Johan Hedberg .20 .50
7 Erik Christensen .15 .40
8 Stephane Yelle .15 .40
9 Andrew Ference .15 .40
0 Andrej Sekera .15 .40
1 Andrew Peters .15 .40
2 Wayne Primeau .15 .40
3 Brandon Prust .15 .40
4 Sergei Samsonov .20 .50
5 Michael Leighton .20 .50
6 Nathan Gerbe RC 1.25 3.00
7 Kris Versteeg .30 .75
8 Aaron Johnson .15 .40
9 Ben Eager .15 .40
20 David Jones .15 .40
21 Brett Clark .15 .40
22 Raffi Torres .15 .40
23 Michael Peca .20 .50
24 Kenndal McArdle RC 1.00 2.50
25 Kirk Maltby .15 .40
26 Ethan Moreau .15 .40
27 Marc-Antoine Pouliot .15 .40
28 Wade Belak .15 .40
29 Kyle Quincey .15 .40
30 Matt Greene .15 .40
31 Derek Boogaard .15 .40
32 Cal Clutterbuck .20 .50
33 Maxim Lapierre .15 .40
34 Pekka Rinne .30 .75
35 Scott Clemmensen .15 .40
36 Mike Comrie .20 .50
37 Joey MacDonald .25 .60
38 Michal Repik RC 1.25 3.00
39 Jesse Winchester .15 .40
40 Riley Cote .15 .40
41 Dany Sabourin .15 .40
42 Brad Lukowich .15 .40
43 Brian Boucher .20 .50
44 Doug Murray .15 .40
45 Adam Hall .15 .40
46 Mikhail Grabovski .25 .60
47 Mike Van Ryn .15 .40
48 Chris Stewart RC 1.25 3.00
49 Zach Bogosian RC 1.25 3.00
50 Nathan Oystrick RC 1.25 3.00
51 Blake Wheeler RC 3.00 8.00
52 Adam Pardy RC 1.00 2.50
53 Zach Boychuk RC 1.25 3.00
54 Brandon Sutter RC 1.25 3.00
55 Dwight Helminen RC 1.25 3.00
56 Patrick Dwyer RC 1.25 3.00
57 Nikita Filatov RC 1.25 3.00
58 Jakub Voracek RC 2.50 6.00
59 Derek Dorsett RC 1.50 4.00
60 James Neal RC 2.50 6.00
61 Fabian Brunnstrom RC 1.00 2.50
62 Steve MacIntyre RC 1.25 3.00
63 Michael Frolik RC 1.25 3.00
64 Wayne Simmonds RC 2.00 5.00
65 Oscar Moller RC 1.00 2.50
66 Drew Doughty RC 3.00 8.00
67 Colton Gillies RC 1.00 2.50
68 Patric Hornqvist RC 1.25 3.00
69 Ryan Jones RC 1.25 3.00
70 Pierre-Luc Letourneau-Leblond RC .75 2.00
71 Patrick Davis RC 1.00 2.50
72 Anssi Salmela RC 1.25 3.00
73 Matthew Halischuk RC .75 2.00
74 Petr Vrana RC .75 2.00
75 Josh Bailey RC 1.50 4.00
76 Brett Skinner RC 1.00 2.50
77 Mitch Fritz RC 1.00 2.50
78 Jared Ross RC 1.25 3.00
79 Andreas Nodl RC .75 2.00
80 Luca Sbisa RC .75 2.00
81 Darroll Powe RC 1.25 3.00
82 Ben Maxwell RC 1.25 3.00
83 Kevin Porter RC 1.00 2.50
84 Viktor Tikhonov RC 1.00 2.50
85 Mikkel Boedker RC 1.50 4.00
86 Janne Pesonen RC 1.00 2.50
87 Brad Staubitz RC 1.00 2.50
88 Jamie McGinn RC 1.25 3.00
89 Ben Bishop RC 2.00 5.00
90 T.J. Oshie RC 2.50 6.00
91 Patrik Berglund RC 1.00 2.50
92 Chris Porter RC 1.25 3.00
93 Alex Pietrangelo RC 1.50 4.00
94 Vladimir Mihalik RC .75 2.00
795 Steven Stamkos RC 8.00 20.00
796 John Mitchell RC 1.00 2.50
797 Jonas Frogren RC .75 2.00
798 Luke Schenn RC 1.50 4.00
799 Nikolai Kulemin RC 1.25 3.00
800 Simeon Varlamov RC 2.50 6.00

2008-09 O-Pee-Chee 1979-80 Retro

COMPLETE SET (800) 300.00 600.00
COMP.SER.1 SET (600) 200.00 400.00
COMP.UPDATE SET (200) 100.00 200.00
*1-500/601-747 RETRO: 2X TO 5X
*510-560/748-800 ROOKIE: .6X TO 1.5X
*561-600 RETRO SP: .8X TO 2X
151 Nicklas Backstrom 2.00 5.00

2008-09 O-Pee-Chee 1979-80 Retro Blank Backs

*1-500/601-747 BLANK: 25X TO 60X BASE
*501-560/748-800 ROOKIE: 4X TO 10X
*561-600 BLANK SP: 5X TO 12X BASE
151 Nicklas Backstrom 25.00 60.00

2008-09 O-Pee-Chee 1979-80 Retro Rainbow

*RAINBOW VETS: 8X TO 20X BASE
*RAINBOW ROOKIES: 2X TO 5X BASE
*RAINBOW RETIRED: 2.5X TO 6X BASE
STATED PRINT RUN 100 SER.#'d SETS
151 Nicklas Backstrom 8.00 20.00

2008-09 O-Pee-Chee Gold

*1-500/601-747 GOLD: 2.5X TO 6X BASE
*501-560/748-800 ROOKIE: .6X TO 1.5X
*561-600 GOLD SP: 1X TO 2.5X BASE
151 Nicklas Backstrom 2.50 6.00
795 Steven Stamkos 20.00 50.00

2008-09 O-Pee-Chee Metal

*METAL: 1.5X TO 4X BASE
*METAL ROOKIE: .5X TO 1.2X BASE RC
*METAL 561-600: .8X TO 2X BASE
TWO PER UPDATE PACK
151 Nicklas Backstrom 1.50 4.00

2008-09 O-Pee-Chee Metal X

*METAL X: 3X TO 8 X BASE
*METAL X ROOKIE: 1X TO 2.5X BASE RC
*METAL X 561-600: 1.2X TO 3X BASE
STATED ODDS 1:4 UPDATE PACKS
151 Nicklas Backstrom 3.00 8.00

2008-09 O-Pee-Chee All-Rookie Team

COMPLETE SET (6) 8.00 20.00
STATED ODDS 1:4
ARTCP Carey Price 3.00 8.00
ARTJT Jonathan Toews 2.00 5.00
ARTNB Nicklas Backstrom 1.25 3.00
ARTPK Patrick Kane 1.50 4.00
ARTTE Tobias Enstrom .50 1.25
ARTTG Tom Gilbert .50 1.25

2008-09 O-Pee-Chee Autographed Buybacks

STATED ODDS 1:432
BBAG Andy Greene 10.00 25.00
BBBE Brian Elliott 12.00 30.00
BBBR Bobby Ryan 12.00 30.00
BBCG Clark Gillies 15.00 40.00
BBCM Cory Murphy 8.00 20.00
BBDC Daniel Carcillo 10.00 25.00
BBDG Daniel Girardi 12.00 30.00
BBDH Dale Hawerchuk 15.00 40.00
BBDS Denis Savard 89-90 OPC 12.00 30.00
BBDW Doug Wilson 8.00 20.00
BBDY Ron Duguay 10.00 25.00
BBGF Grant Fuhr 25.00 60.00
BBGP Gilbert Perreault 15.00 40.00
BBHA Jaroslav Halak 12.00 30.00
BBJJ Jack Johnson 20.00 40.00
BBJS James Sheppard 10.00 25.00
BBLI Bryan Little 12.00 30.00
BBLT Lauri Tukonen 12.00 30.00
BDMD Mike Bossy 25.00 60.00
BBMC Curtis McElhinney 10.00 25.00
BBMD Lanny McDonald 89-90 OPC 15.00 40.00
BBMF Mark Fraser 8.00 20.00
BBMK Mark Mancari 8.00 20.00
BBMR Mason Raymond 20.00 50.00
BBMS Marc Staal 15.00 40.00
BBNB Neal Broten 89-90 OPC 25.00 50.00
BBPE Phil Esposito 20.00 50.00
BBPP Pete Peeters 12.00 30.00
BBPS Peter Stastny 15.00 40.00
BBPV Rich Peverley 10.00 25.00
BBRC Ryan Carter 8.00 20.00
BBRL Rod Langway 80-81 OPC 15.00 40.00
BBRO Luc Robitaille 89-90 OPC 12.00 30.00
BBRP Rod Pelley 8.00 20.00
BBRS Rob Schremp 15.00 40.00
BBRY Ryan Callahan 12.00 30.00
BBSG Sam Gagner 25.00 60.00
BBSM Matt Smaby 8.00 20.00
BBST Brett Sterling 8.00 20.00
BBSW Steve Wagner 10.00 25.00
BBTE Tobias Enstrom 20.00 50.00
BBTO Terry O'Reilly 25.00 60.00
BBTW Tyler Weiman 12.00 30.00
BBVK Ville Koistinen 8.00 20.00

2008-09 O-Pee-Chee Box Bottoms

IGIN/LUON/KOVAL/GABK 2.50 6.00
LECAV/NASH/STAAL/LUNDQ 1.50 4.00
BROD/THORN/ZETTER/TOEWS 1.50 4.00
OVECH/ALFRED/PRICE/SUND 2.50 6.00
STAM/SUTT/FILA/OKPOSO 2.50 6.00
VORCK/BOEDK/GILLIES/SCHEN 1.50 4.00
BRUNN/BRASS/OSHI/BOGO 2.00 5.00
TURRIS/WHEEL/BOYC/DOUGH 2.00 5.00
NNO Fabian Brunnstrom U .12 .30
NNO Derick Brassard U .12 .30
NNO T.J. Oshie U .30 .75
NNO Zach Bogosian U .15 .40
NNO Kyle Turris U .25 .60
NNO Blake Wheeler U .40 1.00
NNO Zach Boychuk U .15 .40
NNO Drew Doughty U .40 1.00
NNO Jakub Voracek U .30 .75
NNO Mikkel Boedker U .20 .50
NNO Colton Gillies U .12 .30
NNO Luke Schenn U .20 .50
NNO Steven Stamkos U 1.00 2.50
NNO Brandon Sutter U .15 .40
NNO Nikita Filatov U .15 .40
NNO Kyle Okposo U .15 .40
NNO Daniel Alfredsson .15 .40
NNO Martin Brodeur .30 .75
NNO Marian Gaborik .20 .50
NNO Jarome Iginla .15 .40
NNO Ilya Kovalchuk .15 .40
NNO Vincent LeCavalier .12 .30
NNO Henrik Lundqvist .20 .50
NNO Roberto Luongo .20 .50
NNO Rick Nash .15 .40
NNO Alexander Ovechkin .60 1.50
NNO Carey Price .60 1.50
NNO Eric Staal .20 .50
NNO Mats Sundin .15 .40
NNO Joe Thornton .20 .50
NNO Jonathan Toews .40 1.00
NNO Henrik Zetterberg .20 .50

2008-09 O-Pee-Chee First Team All-Stars

COMPLETE SET (6) 8.00 20.00
STATED ODDS 1:4
1STAO Alexander Ovechkin 5.00 12.00
1STDP Dion Phaneuf 1.25 3.00
1STEM Evgeni Malkin 4.00 10.00
1STEN Evgeni Nabokov 1.00 2.50
1STJI Jarome Iginla 1.25 3.00
1STNL Nicklas Lidstrom 1.25 3.00

2008-09 O-Pee-Chee Materials Triple

STATED ODDS 1:108
3MADR Radulov/Arnott/Dumont 6.00 15.00
3MASH Heatley/Alfreds/Spezz 6.00 15.00
3MASZ Alfredssn/Zetter/Sedin 8.00 20.00
3MBBJ Brown/Blake/Johnson 6.00 15.00
3MBBK Kopitar/Brown/Blake 10.00 25.00
3MBBP Price/Bouilln/Brisebs 25.00 60.00
3MBCP Phan/Cammalleri/Bertuz 6.00 15.00
3MBDL Brodr/Lundq/DiPiet 12.00 30.00
3MBEP Brodeur/Parise/Elias 12.00 30.00
3MBHH Higgins/Bouillon/Hamrlik 5.00 12.00
3MBLG Brodeur/Luong/Gigur 12.00 30.00
3MBLR Briere/Richards/Lupul 6.00 15.00
3MBMR Brque/Robin/MacInn SP
3MBOT Turris/Okposo/Brassard 10.00 25.00
3MBPM Salming/Forsbrg/Sundn 8.00 20.00
3MBRE Brind'Amour/Ruutu/Eavs 6.00 15.00
3MBSP Boyes/Perron/Stempniak 5.00 12.00
3MBSW Staal/Ward/Brind'Amour 8.00 20.00
3MCBP Connolly/Paille/Bernier 4.00 10.00
3MCFH Hunter/Comrie/Fedotenko 5.00 12.00
3MCHO Hasek/Osgood/Chelios 8.00 20.00
3MCOK Crosby/Ovechkin/Kane 25.00 60.00
3MCPC Parise/Cole/Carle 6.00 15.00
3MCRL Lidstrm/Chelio/Rafalsk 6.00 15.00
3MCSK Kopitar/Stoll/Calder 10.00 25.00
3MDGK Gaborik/Koivu/Demitra 8.00 20.00
3MDMJ Doan/Mueller/Jokinen 5.00 12.00
3MDSG DiPietro/Satan/Guerin 6.00 15.00
3MFCM Crosby/Malkin/Fleury 25.00 60.00
3MFCT Thoms/Ferndz/Chara 6.00 15.00
3MFIN Selanne/Koivu/Koivu 12.00 30.00
3MFTW Forsberg/Wolski/Tucker 8.00 20.00
3MGAC Gionta/Clarkson/Asham 5.00 12.00
3MGCM Crosby/Malkin/Gnchr 25.00 60.00
3MGKM Getzlaf/Mueller/Kopitar 10.00 25.00
3MGLN Gagne/Lupul/Niittymaki 6.00 15.00
3MGNL Lundqv/Naslund/Gomez 8.00 20.00
3MGRC Gagne/Richards/Carter 6.00 15.00
3MGRP Gomez/Redden/Prucha 5.00 12.00
3MGSD Drury/Gomez/Straka 5.00 12.00
3MGWL Gonchar/Whitney/Letang 6.00 15.00
3MHGS Gaborik/Hossa/Svatos 8.00 20.00
3MHHG Gagner/Hemsky/Horcoff 5.00 12.00
3MHLH Lidstrm/Hossa/Holmstrm 6.00 15.00
3MHMS Hossa/Staal/Malone 6.00 15.00
3MHSD Holmstrom/Draper/Stuart 5.00 12.00
3MHSG Gaborik/Hossa/Satan 8.00 20.00
3MHSV Heatley/Vanek/Steen 6.00 15.00
3MHTK Kane/Toews/Havlat 12.00 30.00
3MHTS Stastny/Hejduk/Tucker 6.00 15.00
3MICP Iginla/Cammalleri/Phan
3MIGS Iginla/Gagne/Staal 8.00 20.00
3MISH Iginla/St. Louis/Heatley 6.00 15.00
3MITP Iginla/Tanguay/Phaneuf 6.00 15.00
3MJBH Brodeur/Hasek/Joseph 12.00 30.00
3MJDM Mueller/Doan/Jokinen 5.00 12.00
3MJEM Jagr/Elias/Michalek 15.00 40.00
3MJLJ Legace/Johnson/Jackmn 6.00 15.00
3MJNJ Johnson/Johnson/Niskanen 5.00 12.00
3MJTS Toskala/Joseph/Stajan 6.00 15.00
3MKGH Kolzig/Huet/Green 6.00 15.00
3MKKP Koivu/Price/Kovalev 25.00 60.00
3MKLE Koval/Leht/Enstrom 6.00 15.00
3MKLH Howe/Lafleur/Kurri SP
3MKMC Malone/Kolzig/Carle 6.00 15.00
3MKOR Koval/Ovech/Radulov 25.00 60.00
3MKPK Koivu/Komisarek/Plekanec 6.00 15.00
3MKSF Fedorov/Semin/Kozlov 10.00 25.00
3MKSS Kane/Keith/Seabrook
3MKTB Kariya/Tkachuk/Boyes 8.00 20.00
3MKWP Kariya/Perron/Woznw 8.00 20.00
3MKZO Ovech/Koval/Zherdev 25.00 60.00
3MLCT Lecav/Cheechoo/Toews 15.00 40.00
3MLDZ Zetter/Lidstrm/Dtsyuk 8.00 20.00
3MLEZ Legwand/Erat/Zidlicky 5.00 12.00
3MLGM Gretzky/Lemix/Messr SP
3MLMK Kesler/Linden/Morrison 8.00 20.00
3MLMO Morrow/Lehtinen/Ott 5.00 12.00
3MLNP Lidstrom/Phan/Nieder 6.00 15.00
3MLNZ Nash/Zherdev/Leclaire 6.00 15.00
3MLOB Luongo/Ohlund/Bernier 8.00 20.00
3MLOE Luongo/Ohlund/Edler 8.00 20.00
3MLRV Luongo/Toskala/Roloson 8.00 20.00
3MLSJ Lecav/St.Louis/Jokin 6.00 15.00
3MLSW Lang/Sharp/Williams 6.00 15.00
3MLTT Lecav/Thornton/Toews 12.00 30.00
3MMCM Cheechoo/Marleau/Michalek 6.00 15.00
3MMCW McCabe/White/Colaiacovo 4.00 10.00
3MMFG Mason/Fistric/Goligoski 10.00 25.00
3MMHK Kovalev/Higgins/Markov 6.00 15.00
3MMKL Murray/Kobasew/Lucic 10.00 25.00
3MMKP Modano/Kariya/Parise 10.00 25.00
3MMRR Modano/Ribeiro/Richards 10.00 25.00
3MMRT Modano/Roenick/Tkachuk 10.00 25.00
3MMSS Spezza/Stajan/Matthias 6.00 15.00
3MMVS Miller/Vanek/Stafford 6.00 15.00
3MNJL Iginla/Lombardi/Nolan 6.00 15.00
3MNLR Lehtonen/Niittymaki/Rask 6.00 15.00
3MNSS Naslund/Sedin/Sedin 6.00 15.00
3MPRB Rolston/Bouchard/Parrish 6.00 15.00
3MPRM Redden/Phillips/Meszaros 4.00 10.00
3MRCL Craig/Lundin/Recchi 8.00 20.00
3MRDS Spezza/Doan/Richards 6.00 15.00
3MRFH Roy/Fuhr/Hextall SP
3MRGH Heatley/Gerber/Redden 6.00 15.00
3MRHA Recchi/Holik/Armstrong 8.00 20.00
3MRHL Ryder/Latendresse/Higgins 4.00 10.00
3MRHS Robitaille/Hull/Shutt SP
3MRK1 Stamks/Dghty/Bogsian 20.00 50.00
3MRK2 Brassard/Turris/Okposo 10.00 25.00
3MRTL Ryder/Thomas/Lucic 10.00 25.00
3MSAS Steen/Antropov/Stajan 6.00 15.00
3MSBK Bergeron/Savard/Kessel 8.00 20.00
3MSBR Brind'Am/Samsonov/Ruutu 6.00 15.00
3MSBS Staal/Briere/Sakic 6.00 15.00
3MSBT Sundin/Tucker/Blake 6.00 15.00
3MSCW Cole/Williams/Samsonov 5.00 12.00
3MSDL Doan/Smyth/Lupul 5.00 12.00
3MSFB Forsb/Sund/Backstrm 10.00 25.00
3MSFS Sakic/Forsberg/Smyth 10.00 25.00
3MSGN Selanne/Getzlaf/Nieder 12.00 30.00
3MSJL Jagr/Shanahan/Lundq 15.00 40.00
3MSKA Sundin/Koivu/Alfredsson 6.00 15.00
3MSKK Khabibulin/Sharp/Keith 6.00 15.00
3MSKT Kariya/Shanahan/Selanne 12.00 30.00
3MSLB Sakic/Budaj/Liles 10.00 25.00
3MSLJ Selanne/Lehtinen/Jokinen 12.00 30.00
3MSNG Giguere/Selanne/Nieder 12.00 30.00
3MSOB Ovech/Bckstrm/Semin 12.00 30.00
3MSSS Staal/Staal/Staal 8.00 20.00
3MSWS Stastny/Svatos/Wolski 6.00 15.00
3MTLU Leclaire/Umberger/Torres 5.00 12.00
3MTRM Thorntn/Roenik/Mrl 8.00 20.00
3MTTL Toivonen/Lehtonen/Toskala 5.00 12.00
3MVKB Vyborny/Brule/Klesla 4.00 10.00
3MVWH Vokoun/Weiss/Horton 5.00 12.00
3MWPG Getzlaf/Perry/Weight 10.00 25.00
3MWPG Weight/Parise/Gomez 6.00 15.00
3MZBW Weiss/Bouwmeester/Zednik 6.00 15.00
3MZEG Giroux/Zubov/Earl 12.00 30.00
3MZKA Khabibulin/Zherdev/Antropov 6.00 15.00
3MZRT Turco/Ribeiro/Zubov 6.00 15.00
3MZTN Turco/Zubov/Niskanen 6.00 15.00

2008-09 O-Pee-Chee Oversized Cards

COMPLETE SET (42) 15.00 40.00
TRU1 Alexander Ovechkin 2.00 5.00
TRU2 Markus Naslund .40 1.00
TRU3 Roberto Luongo .60 1.50
TRU4 Mats Sundin .50 1.25
TRU5 Vincent Lecavalier .40 1.00
TRU6 Martin St. Louis .50 1.25
TRU7 Joe Thornton .60 1.50
TRU8 Sidney Crosby 2.00 5.00
TRU9 Evgeni Malkin 1.50 4.00
TRU10 Marc-Andre Fleury .75 2.00
TRU11 Shane Doan .40 1.00
TRU12 Mike Richards .50 1.25
TRU13 Brendan Shanahan .60 1.50
TRU14 Jaromir Jagr 1.25 3.00
TRU15 Henrik Lundqvist .60 1.50
TRU16 Martin Brodeur 1.00 2.50
TRU17 Alexander Radulov .50 1.25
TRU18 Saku Koivu .50 1.25
TRU19 Carey Price 2.00 5.00
TRU20 Marian Gaborik .60 1.50
TRU21 Anze Kopitar .75 2.00
TRU22 Sam Gagner .40 1.00
TRU23 Andrew Cogliano .40 1.00
TRU24 Henrik Zetterberg .60 1.50
TRU25 Nicklas Lidstrom .50 1.25
TRU26 Pavel Datsyuk .60 1.50
TRU27 Dominik Hasek .60 1.50
TRU28 Mike Modano .75 2.00
TRU29 Marty Turco .50 1.25
TRU30 Brad Richards .50 1.25
TRU31 Rick Nash .50 1.25
TRU32 Paul Stastny .50 1.25
TRU33 Joe Sakic .75 2.00
TRU34 Patrick Kane 1.00 2.50
TRU35 Jonathan Toews 1.25 3.00
TRU36 Eric Staal .60 1.50
TRU37 Jarome Iginla .50 1.25
TRU38 Miikka Kiprusoff .40 1.00
TRU39 Ryan Miller .50 1.25
TRU40 Patrice Bergeron .60 1.50
TRU41 Ilya Kovalchuk .50 1.25
TRU42 Ryan Getzlaf .75 2.00

2008-09 O-Pee-Chee Season Highlights

COMPLETE SET (19) 20.00 50.00
STATED ODDS 1:4
SH1 Alexander Ovechkin 4.00 10.00
SH2 Alexander Ovechkin 4.00 10.00
SH3 Andrew Cogliano .75 2.00
SH4 Chris Chelios 1.00 2.50
SH5 Evgeni Nabokov .75 2.00
SH6 Jarome Iginla 1.00 2.50
SH7 Jarome Iginla 1.00 2.50
SH8 Jeremy Roenick 1.00 2.50
SH9 Joe Sakic 1.50 4.00
SH10 Marian Gaborik 1.25 3.00
SH11 Martin Brodeur 2.00 5.00
SH12 Mats Sundin 1.00 2.50
SH13 Mike Modano 1.50 4.00
SH14 Paul Kariya 1.25 3.00
SH15 Robert Nilsson .60 1.50
SH16 Sidney Crosby 4.00 10.00
SH17 Carey Price 4.00 10.00
SH18 Johan Franzen 1.00 2.50
SH19 Jonathan Toews 2.50 6.00

2008-09 O-Pee-Chee Second Team All-Stars

COMPLETE SET (6) 5.00 12.00
STATED ODDS 1:4
2NDAK Alex Kovalev 1.25 3.00
2NDBC Brian Campbell 1.25 3.00
2NDHZ Henrik Zetterberg 2.00 5.00
2NDJT Joe Thornton 2.00 5.00
2NDMB Martin Brodeur 3.00 8.00
2NDZC Zdeno Chara 1.50 4.00

2008-09 O-Pee-Chee Signatures

STATED ODDS 1:432
SAK Anze Kopitar 25.00 50.00
SAO Alexander Ovechkin
SBC Blake Comeau
SBD Brandon Dubinsky 15.00 40.00
SBE Jonathan Bernier
SBL Michael Blunden 6.00 15.00
SBO Bobby Orr 100.00 200.00
SBR Bobby Ryan 10.00 25.00
SBY Dustin Byfuglien 20.00 50.00
SCA Casey Borer 10.00 25.00
SCB Cam Barker
SCD Chris Drury 8.00 20.00
SCH Chris Higgins 15.00 40.00
SCK Chris Kunitz 12.00 30.00
SCM Cory Murphy 6.00 15.00
SDA Daniel Carcillo 6.00 15.00
SDB Dan Boyle 8.00 20.00
SDC Dan Cleary 15.00 40.00
SDG Daniel Girardi 15.00 40.00
SDJ David Jones 6.00 15.00
SDP Daniel Paille 6.00 15.00
SDS Daniel Sedin 15.00 40.00
SDU Dustin Penner
SEJ Erik Johnson
SEN Eric Nystrom
SFN Frans Nielsen 6.00 15.00
SGL Guillaume Latendresse 30.00 60.00
SGM Greg Moore
SHA Josh Harding 10.00 25.00
SHE T.J. Hensick 8.00 20.00
SHI Jonas Hiller 8.00 20.00
SHL Jaroslav Hlinka 6.00 15.00
SHS Henrik Sedin 12.00 30.00
SHZ Henrik Zetterberg
SJB Jared Boll 6.00 15.00
SJC Jeff Carter 20.00 50.00
SJH Jaroslav Halak
SJJ Jack Johnson 15.00 40.00
SJO Johnny Boychuk 6.00 15.00
SJP Jason Pominville 12.00 30.00
SJS Jack Skille 15.00 40.00
SJT Jiri Tlusty 12.00 30.00
SKA Petr Kalus 8.00 20.00
SKC Kyle Chipchura 12.00 30.00
SKE Phil Kessel 15.00 40.00
SKY Keith Yandle
SLK Lukas Kaspar 6.00 15.00
SMA Mark Fraser 8.00 20.00
SMAN Mark Mancari
SMB Martin Brodeur 60.00 120.00
SME Matt Ellis 6.00 15.00
SMI Milan Michalek 6.00 15.00
SML Matt Lashoff 6.00 15.00
SMM Marc Methot 6.00 15.00
SMN Matt Niskanen 12.00 30.00
SMR Mike Ribeiro 8.00 20.00
SMS Matt Smaby 8.00 20.00
SMT Marty Turco
SNA Evgeni Nabokov 12.00 30.00
SNB Nicklas Backstrom 25.00 60.00
SNG Niklas Grossman
SNH Nathan Horton
SNI Nicklas Bergfors 10.00 25.00
SNK Niklas Kronwall
SOP Ondrej Pavelec 12.00 30.00
SPA Ryan Parent 15.00 40.00
SPB Peter Budaj 8.00 20.00
SPE David Perron 12.00 30.00
SPI Pierre-Marc Bouchard 10.00 25.00
SPK Patrick Kane 50.00 100.00
SPM Peter Mueller 12.00 30.00
SPS Paul Stastny
SRC Ryan Callahan 12.00 30.00
SRG Ryan Getzlaf
SRI Mike Richards 20.00 50.00
SRO Rostislav Olesz
SRP Rod Pelley 6.00 15.00
SRS Ryan Smyth
SRY Ryan Carter 6.00 15.00
SSC Sidney Crosby 125.00 200.00
SSD Steve Downie 12.50 30.00
SSE Devin Setoguchi 12.00 30.00
SSG Sam Gagner 20.00 50.00
SSH James Sheppard 6.00 15.00
SSJ Jordan Staal 25.00 60.00
SSK Sergei Kostitsyn
SSM Matt Stajan 12.00 30.00
SST Drew Stafford 8.00 20.00
STA Maxime Talbot 10.00 25.00
STE Tobias Enstrom 15.00 40.00
STG Tom Gilbert 15.00 40.00
STH Joe Thornton 25.00 60.00
STK Tomas Kaberle
STO Jonathan Toews 50.00 100.00
STP Tomas Plihal 8.00 20.00
STR Tuukka Rask 20.00 50.00
STS Tobias Stephan 8.00 20.00
STV Tomas Vokoun
STW Tyler Weiman 12.00 30.00
STY Tyler Kennedy 12.00 30.00
OPSAB Adam Burish 8.00 20.00
OPSAE Andrew Ebbett
OPSBB Brian Boyle
OPSBE Brendan Bell 6.00 15.00
OPSBG Brian Gionta 8.00 20.00
OPSBJ Jonathan Bernier 12.00 30.00
OPSBL Brian Lee 8.00 20.00
OPSBM Brenden Morrow
OPSBO Brad Boyes
OPSBW Blake Wheeler
OPSCG Colton Gillies
OPSCP Chris Phillips 6.00 15.00
OPSCR Sidney Crosby 125.00 200.00
OPSDC David Clarkson 8.00 20.00
OPSDG Daniel Girardi 6.00 15.00
OPSDL Dan LaCosta 10.00 25.00
OPSDP Daniel Paille 6.00 15.00
OPSDU Dustin Boyd
OPSEF Eric Fehr 6.00 15.00
OPSEL Patrik Elias 10.00 25.00
OPSFB Fabian Brunnstrom 20.00 50.00
OPSFR Michael Frolik 10.00 25.00
OPSHA Michal Handzus
OPSHE Josh Hennessy 6.00 15.00
OPSJA Jarret Stoll
OPSJD Jeff Drouin-Deslauriers
OPSJH Jannik Hansen 10.00 25.00
OPSJI Jarome Iginla
OPSJJ Jack Johnson 6.00 15.00
OPSJL John-Michael Liles
OPSJM Jamie McGinn 10.00 25.00
OPSJO Joel Perrault
OPSJP Jason Pominville 10.00 25.00
OPSJS James Sheppard 6.00 15.00
OPSJT Jiri Tlusty 8.00 20.00
OPSKD Kris Draper
OPSKN Kevin Nastiuk 6.00 15.00
OPSKQ Kyle Quincey 6.00 15.00
OPSKT Kyle Turris 15.00 40.00
OPSKV Kris Versteeg 40.00 80.00
OPSLA Drew Larman 6.00 15.00
OPSLI Bryan Little 8.00 20.00
OPSLS Luke Schenn
OPSMA Mark Fraser 8.00 20.00
OPSMB Mikkel Boedker
OPSMC Bryan McCabe 6.00 15.00
OPSME Matt Ellis 6.00 15.00
OPSMF Mark Fistric 8.00 20.00
OPSMG Martin Gerber 8.00 20.00
OPSMH Martin Havlat 10.00 25.00
OPSMI Mike Iggulden
OPSMK Mike Knuble 6.00 15.00
OPSMM Mark Mancari 8.00 20.00
OPSMP Marc-Antoine Pouliot 6.00 15.00
OPSMR Mattias Ritola 8.00 20.00
OPSMS Marco Sturm 6.00 15.00
OPSNB Nicklas Backstrom 25.00 60.00
OPSND Nigel Dawes 6.00 15.00
OPSNF Nikita Filatov 25.00 60.00
OPSNK Nikolai Kulemin 10.00 25.00
OPSNW Noah Welch 6.00 15.00
OPSOP Ondrej Pavelec 12.00 30.00
OPSPA Dimitri Patzold
OPSPD Dustin Penner 8.00 20.00
OPSPO Ryan Potulny 6.00 15.00
OPSRA Mason Raymond 10.00 25.00
OPSRC Ryane Clowe 8.00 20.00
OPSRP Rich Peverley 8.00 20.00
OPSSA Miroslav Satan 15.00 40.00
OPSSC Marek Schwarz
OPSSM Stefan Meyer
OPSSS Steven Stamkos 75.00 150.00
OPSSW Steve Wagner
OPSTG Tom Gilbert 8.00 20.00
OPSTO T.J. Oshie 20.00 50.00
OPSTS Tom Sestito 10.00 25.00
OPSTW Tyler Weiman 6.00 15.00
OPSVF Valtteri Filppula 10.00 25.00
OPSVT Viktor Tikhonov
OPSZB Zach Bogosian 10.00 25.00

2008-09 O-Pee-Chee Stat Leaders

COMPLETE SET (14) 12.00 30.00
STATED ODDS 1:4
SL1 Ovechkin/Malkin/Iginla 3.00 8.00
SL2 Ovechkin/Kovalchuk/Iginla 3.00 8.00
SL3 Thornton/Datsyuk/Savard 1.00 2.50
SL4 Datsyuk/Lidstrom/Heatley 1.00 2.50
SL5 Carcillo/Boll/Burish .60 1.50
SL6 Lidstrom/Gonchar/Streit .75 2.00
SL7 Nabokov/Brodeur/Kiprusoff 1.50 4.00
SL8 Osgood/Giguere/Hasek 1.00 2.50
SL9 Lundqvist/Leclaire/Nabokov 1.00 2.50
SL10 Ellis/Conklin/Giguere .75 2.00
SL11 Kane/Backstrom/Toews 2.00 5.00
SL12 Crosby/Zetterberg/Hossa 3.00 8.00
SL13 Franzen/Zetterberg/Hossa 1.00 2.50
SL14 Osgood/Fleury/Turco 1.25 3.00

2008-09 O-Pee-Chee Team Checklists

COMPLETE SET (30) 20.00 50.00
STATED ODDS 1:4
CL1 Anaheim Ducks 1.25 3.00
CL2 Atlanta Thrashers 1.25 3.00
CL3 Boston Bruins 1.25 3.00
CL4 Buffalo Sabres 1.25 3.00
CL5 Calgary Flames 1.25 3.00
CL6 Carolina Hurricanes 1.25 3.00
CL7 Chicago Blackhawks 1.25 3.00
CL8 Colorado Avalanche 1.25 3.00
CL9 Columbus Blue Jackets 1.25 3.00
CL10 Dallas Stars 1.25 3.00
CL11 Detroit Red Wings 1.25 3.00
CL12 Edmonton Oilers 1.25 3.00
CL13 Florida Panthers 1.25 3.00
CL14 Los Angeles Kings 1.25 3.00
CL15 Minnesota Wild 1.25 3.00
CL16 Montreal Canadiens 1.25 3.00
CL17 Nashville Predators 1.25 3.00
CL18 New Jersey Devils 1.25 3.00
CL19 New York Islanders 1.25 3.00
CL20 New York Rangers 1.25 3.00
CL21 Ottawa Senators 1.25 3.00
CL22 Philadelphia Flyers 1.25 3.00
CL23 Phoenix Coyotes 1.25 3.00
CL24 Pittsburgh Penguins 1.25 3.00
CL25 San Jose Sharks 1.25 3.00
CL26 St. Louis Blues 1.25 3.00
CL27 Tampa Bay Lightning 1.25 3.00
CL28 Toronto Maple Leafs 1.25 3.00
CL29 Vancouver Canucks 1.25 3.00
CL30 Washington Capitals 1.25 3.00

2008-09 O-Pee-Chee Trophy Cards

COMPLETE SET (19) 15.00 40.00
STATED ODDS 1:4
AWDAL Art Ross 1.00 2.50
AWDAO Hart Memorial 1.00 2.50
AWDDA Lady Byng 1.00 2.50
AWDDE Roger Crozier 1.00 2.50
AWDDR Clarence Campbell 1.00 2.50
AWDDW Stanley Cup 1.00 2.50
AWDHO William Jennings 1.00 2.50
AWDHZ Conn Smythe 1.00 2.50
AWDJB Bill Masterton 1.00 2.50
AWDMB Vezina 1.00 2.50
AWDNL James Norris 1.00 2.50
AWDOA Maurice Richard 1.00 2.50
AWDOV Lester B Pearson 1.00 2.50
AWDPD Frank J Selke 1.00 2.50
AWDPK Calder 1.00 2.50
AWDPP Prince of Whales 1.00 2.50
AWDPV Plus Minus Award 1.00 2.50
AWDRE Presidents' Trophy 1.00 2.50
AWDVL King Clancy Memorial Trophy 1.00 2.50

2008-09 O-Pee-Chee Wayne Gretzky Panoramic Cards

COMMON GRETAZKY 8.00 20.00

2008-09 O-Pee-Chee Wayne Gretzky Retro Cards

COMPLETE SET (4) 150.00 300.00
COMMON GRETZKY 40.00 80.00

2008-09 O-Pee-Chee Winter Classic Highlights

OVERALL STATED ODDS 1:36
WC1 Buffalo Sabres 4.00 10.00
WC2 Brian Campbell 4.00 10.00
WC3 Brian Campbell 4.00 10.00
WC4 Erik Christensen 3.00 8.00
WC5 Ty Conklin 4.00 10.00
WC6 Ty Conklin 4.00 10.00
WC7 Ty Conklin 4.00 10.00
WC8 Daniel Paille 3.00 8.00
WC9 Sidney Crosby 8.00 20.00
WC10 Sidney Crosby 8.00 20.00
WC11 Pittsburgh Penguins 4.00 10.00
WC12 Paul Gaustad 3.00 8.00
WC13 Sergei Gonchar 3.00 8.00
WC14 Sergei Gonchar 3.00 8.00
WC15 Tyler Kennedy 4.00 10.00
WC16 Ales Kotalik 3.00 8.00
WC17 Buffalo Sabres 4.00 10.00
WC18 Georges Laraque 4.00 10.00
WC19 Evgeni Malkin 15.00 40.00
WC20 Ryan Malone 3.00 8.00
WC21 Ryan Miller 5.00 12.00
WC22 Derek Roy 3.00 8.00
WC23 Michael Ryan 3.00 8.00
WC24 Colby Armstrong 3.00 8.00
WC25 Jaroslav Spacek 3.00 8.00
WC26 Jordan Staal 5.00 12.00
WC27 Ralph Wilson Stadium 3.00 8.00
WC28 Thomas Vanek 5.00 12.00
WC29 Jason Pominville 5.00 12.00
WC30 Maxim Afinogenov 3.00 8.00
WC31 Jordan Staal SP 12.00 30.00
WC32 Ryan Miller SP 12.00 30.00
WC33 Evgeni Malkin SP 20.00 50.00
WC34 Thomas Vanek SP 10.00 25.00
WC35 Thomas Vanek SP 10.00 25.00
WC36 Evgeni Malkin SP 25.00 60.00
WC37 Sidney Crosby SP 15.00 40.00
WC38 Sidney Crosby SP 15.00 40.00
WC39 Sidney Crosby SP 15.00 40.00
WC40 Sidney Crosby SP 15.00 40.00

2009-10 O-Pee-Chee

COMPLETE SET (800) 100.00 200.00
COMP.SET w/SPs (600) 60.00 120.00
COMP.SET w/o SPs (500) 25.00 60.00
COMP.FACT.UPDATE (205) 20.00 50.00
STATED ROOKIE ODDS 1:2
STATED LEGEND ODDS 1:2
1 Roberto Luongo .30 .75
2 Zdeno Chara .25 .60
3 Patrick Lalime .20 .50
4 Sergei Samsonov .15 .40
5 Troy Brouwer .15 .40
6 Mike Commodore .15 .40
7 Marian Hossa .20 .50
8 Alexander Ovechkin 1.00 2.50
9 Alexander Frolov .20 .50
10 Colton Gillies .25 .60
11 Jamie Langenbrunner .15 .40
12 Paul Mara .15 .40
13 Scottie Upshall .15 .40
14 Jordan Staal .25 .60
15 Anton Stralman .15 .40
16 Andrej Meszaros .15 .40
17 Henrik Sedin .25 .60
18 Karl Alzner .15 .40
19 Jonathan Toews .50 1.25
20 Jim Slater .15 .40
21 Andrew Ference .15 .40
22 David Moss .20 .50
23 Bruno Gervais .15 .40
24 David Jones .15 .40
25 James Neal .25 .60
26 Ty Conklin .20 .50
27 Gregory Campbell .15 .40
28 Jonathan Quick .50 1.25
29 Roman Hamrlik .15 .40
30 Martin Brodeur .50 1.25
31 Carey Price 1.00 2.50
32 Alex Auld .20 .50
33 Martin Hanzal .20 .50
34 Eric Godard .15 .40
35 Chris Mason .20 .50
36 Tomas Kaberle .15 .40
37 Erik Cole .20 .50
38 Joel Ward .15 .40
39 Colby Armstrong .15 .40
40 Stephane Yelle .15 .40
41 Craig Conroy .15 .40
42 Mike Comrie .20 .50
43 Cody McLeod .15 .40
44 Loui Eriksson .20 .50
45 Jiri Tlusty .20 .50
46 Cory Stillman .15 .40
47 Erik Ersberg .20 .50
48 Sergei Kostitsyn .15 .40
49 Brendan Shanahan .30 .75
50 Scott Gomez .20 .50
51 Chris Phillips .15 .40
52 Steven Reinprecht .15 .40
53 Ryan Whitney .15 .40
54 T.J. Oshie .40 1.00
55 Alexei Ponikarovsky .15 .40
56 Willie Mitchell .15 .40
57 David Legwand .20 .50
58 Brendan Mikkelson .15 .40
59 Milan Lucic .20 .50
60 Adam Mair .15 .40
61 Joni Pitkanen .20 .50
62 Ryan Smyth .20 .50
63 Michael Peca .20 .50
64 Jiri Hudler .20 .50
65 Sam Gagner .20 .50
66 Patrick O'Sullivan .20 .50
67 Josh Harding .25 .60
68 Dainius Zubrus .15 .40
69 Daniel Alfredsson .25 .60
70 Daniel Briere .25 .60
71 Alex Goligoski .20 .50
72 Brian Boucher .20 .50
73 Paul Ranger .15 .40
74 Mats Sundin .25 .60
75 Rick Rypien .25 .60
76 Zbynek Michalek .15 .40
77 Corey Perry .25 .60
78 Zach Bogosian .20 .50
79 Ales Kotalik .15 .40
80 Cory Sarich .15 .40
81 Andrew Ladd .25 .60
82 Andrew Raycroft .20 .50
83 Fabian Brunnstrom .20 .50
84 Ales Hemsky .20 .50
85 Keith Ballard .15 .40
86 Marek Zidlicky .15 .40
87 Sidney Crosby 1.00 2.50
88 Patrick Kane .50 1.25
89 Daniel Girardi .15 .40
90 Jeff Carter .25 .60
91 Viktor Tikhonov .20 .50
92 Dan Boyle .20 .50
93 Barret Jackman .15 .40
94 Nikolai Kulemin .20 .50
95 Alexander Semin .25 .60
96 Wade Belak .15 .40
97 Jonas Hiller .20 .50
98 Chuck Kobasew .15 .40

Card	Low	High
99 Craig Rivet	.15	.40
100 Adam Pardy	.15	.40
101 Milan Hejduk	.20	.50
102 Kris Russell	.25	.60
103 Brian Rafalski	.15	.40
104 Dwayne Roloson	.20	.50
105 Kyle Quincey	.15	.40
106 Niklas Backstrom	.25	.60
107 Johnny Oduya	.20	.50
108 Jason Spezza	.25	.60
109 Luca Sbisa	.25	.60
110 Kristopher Letang	.25	.60
111 Evgeni Nabokov	.20	.50
112 Evgeni Artyukhin	.15	.40
113 Kevin Bieksa	.20	.50
114 Donald Brashear	.15	.40
115 Jonas Frogren	.20	.50
116 Rob Niedermayer	.15	.40
117 Patrice Bergeron	.30	.75
118 Jochen Hecht	.15	.40
119 Chad LaRose	.15	.40
120 Paul Stastny	.25	.60
121 Jared Boll	.15	.40
122 Nicklas Lidstrom	.25	.60
123 Jeff Drouin-Deslauriers	.15	.40
124 Michal Handzus	.20	.50
125 Andrei Markov	.25	.60
126 David Clarkson	.20	.50
127 Filip Kuba	.15	.40
128 Martin Biron	.20	.50
129 Pascal Dupuis	.15	.40
130 Brad Boyes	.15	.40
131 Ty Wishart	.20	.50
132 Pavol Demitra	.30	.75
133 Matt Bradley	.15	.40
134 Steve Montador	.15	.40
135 Matt Hunwick	.15	.40
136 Jarome Iginla	.25	.60
137 Justin Williams	.20	.50
138 Wojtek Wolski	.15	.40
139 Rostislav Klesla	.25	.60
140 Johan Franzen	.25	.60
141 Robert Nilsson	.15	.40
142 Drew Doughty	.30	.75
143 Robert Lang	.15	.40
144 John Madden	.15	.40
145 Antoine Vermette	.15	.40
146 Antero Niittymaki	.25	.60
147 Marc-Andre Fleury	.40	1.00
148 Keith Tkachuk	.25	.60
149 Mike Smith	.25	.60
150 Alexandre Burrows	.25	.60
151 Boyd Gordon	.15	.40
152 Teemu Selanne	.50	1.25
153 Phil Kessel	.30	.75
154 Teppo Numminen	.20	.50
155 Eric Staal	.30	.75
156 Ben Eager	.20	.50
157 Jakub Voracek	.25	.60
158 Marty Turco	.25	.60
159 Tom Gilbert	.15	.40
160 Craig Anderson	.25	.60
161 James Sheppard	.15	.40
162 Zach Parise	.25	.60
163 Trevor Smith	.15	.40
164 Colton Orr	.15	.40
165 Joffrey Lupul	.20	.50
166 Chris Drury	.20	.50
167 Christian Ehrhoff	.15	.40
168 Ryan Malone	.15	.40
169 Justin Pogge	.25	.60
170 Tomas Fleischmann	.15	.40
171 Kyle Brodziak	.15	.40
172 Ilya Kovalchuk	.25	.60
173 Tim Thomas	.25	.60
174 Mike Cammalleri	.20	.50
175 Brandon Sutter	.20	.50
176 John-Michael Liles	.15	.40
177 Nikita Filatov	.20	.50
178 Mikael Samuelsson	.15	.40
179 Steve Staios	.15	.40
180 Oscar Moller	.15	.40
181 Alex Kovalev	.25	.60
182 Paul Martin	.15	.40
183 Mike Fisher	.15	.40
184 Arron Asham	.20	.50
185 Mathieu Garon	.25	.60
186 David Perron	.15	.40
187 Ryan Bayda	.15	.40
188 Steve Bernier	.15	.40
189 Jean-Pierre Dumont	.15	.40
190 Todd White	.15	.40
191 Manny Fernandez	.20	.50
192 Daymond Langkow	.15	.40
193 Zach Boychuk	.20	.50
194 Marek Svatos	.15	.40
195 Steve Mason	.20	.50
196 Tomas Holmstrom	.20	.50
197 Marc-Antoine Pouliot	.20	.50
198 Wayne Simmonds	.30	.75
199 Andrei Kostitsyn	.20	.50
200 Brian Rolston	.20	.50
201 Chris Kelly	.20	.50
202 Riley Cote	.15	.40
203 Tyler Kennedy	.20	.50
204 Patrik Berglund	.15	.40
205 Vladimir Mihalik	.25	.60
206 Alexander Edler	.15	.40
207 Martin Erat	.15	.40
208 Slava Kozlov	.15	.40
209 P.J. Axelsson	.25	.60
210 Todd Bertuzzi	.25	.60
211 Dennis Seidenberg	.20	.50
212 Jordan Leopold	.15	.40
213 Pascal Leclaire	.25	.60
214 Niklas Kronwall	.20	.50
215 Stephen Weiss	.15	.40
216 Trevor Lewis	.20	.50
217 Saku Koivu	.25	.60
218 Colin White	.15	.40
219 Alexandre Picard	.20	.50
220 Shane Doan	.20	.50
221 Matt Cooke	.15	.40
222 David Backes	.25	.60
223 Nik Antropov	.20	.50
224 Jannik Hansen	.15	.40
225 Shea Weber	.20	.50
226 Brad Winchester	.15	.40
227 Boris Valabik	.25	.60
228 Derek Roy	.20	.50
229 Mark Giordano	.20	.50
230 Patrick Sharp	.25	.60
231 Adam Foote	.15	.40
232 Steve Ott	.15	.40
233 Brad Stuart	.15	.40
234 Radek Dvorak	.15	.40
235 Antti Miettinen	.15	.40
236 Patrice Brisebois	.15	.40
237 Bill Guerin	.25	.60
238 Michal Rozsival	.15	.40
239 Brian Lee	.25	.60
240 Mikkel Boedker	.15	.40
241 Patrick Marleau	.25	.60
242 Carlo Colaiacovo	.15	.40
243 Lee Stempniak	.15	.40
244 Shane O'Brien	.15	.40
245 Vernon Fiddler	.15	.40
246 Tobias Enstrom	.25	.60
247 Thomas Vanek	.25	.60
248 Matthew Lombardi	.15	.40
249 Kris Versteeg	.25	.60
250 Darcy Tucker	.20	.50
251 Trevor Daley	.15	.40
252 Chris Osgood	.25	.60
253 Michael Frolik	.20	.50
254 Mikko Koivu	.25	.60
255 Maxim Lapierre	.15	.40
256 Doug Weight	.25	.60
257 Brandon Dubinsky	.20	.50
258 Brian Elliott	.20	.50
259 Keith Yandle	.25	.60
260 Joe Thornton	.25	.60
261 Manny Legace	.20	.50
262 Niklas Hagman	.15	.40
263 Cory Schneider	.30	.75
264 Dan Hamhuis	.20	.50
265 Sami Salo	.25	.60
266 Dennis Wideman	.15	.40
267 Maxim Afinogenov	.15	.40
268 Rod Brind`Amour	.25	.60
269 Nikolai Khabibulin	.25	.60
270 Fredrik Modin	.15	.40
271 Tobias Stephan	.15	.40
272 Denis Grebeshkov	.15	.40
273 Dustin Brown	.20	.50
274 Benoit Pouliot	.15	.40
275 Patrik Elias	.25	.60
276 Rick DiPietro	.20	.50
277 Henrik Lundqvist	.40	1.00
278 Kimmo Timonen	.20	.50
279 Petr Sykora	.20	.50
280 Jonathan Cheechoo	.25	.60
281 Steve Eminger	.15	.40
282 John Mitchell	.15	.40
283 Sergei Fedorov	.40	1.00
284 Fernando Pisani	.15	.40
285 Travis Moen	.15	.40
286 Michael Ryder	.15	.40
287 Ryan Miller	.25	.60
288 Tuomo Ruutu	.15	.40
289 Cristobal Huet	.25	.60
290 Jason Arnott	.20	.50
291 Pavel Datsyuk	.30	.75
292 Dustin Penner	.15	.40
293 Anze Kopitar	.40	1.00
294 Marian Gaborik	.30	.75
295 Travis Zajac	.20	.50
296 Joey MacDonald	.20	.50
297 Stephen Valiquette	.15	.40
298 Braydon Coburn	.15	.40
299 Miroslav Satan	.15	.40
300 Mike Grier	.15	.40
301 Steven Stamkos	.50	1.25
302 Daniel Sedin	.25	.60
303 Milan Jurcina	.15	.40
304 Cal Clutterbuck	.15	.40
305 Ryan Getzlaf	.40	1.00
306 Kari Lehtonen	.20	.50
307 Jason Pominville	.25	.60
308 Dustin Boyd	.15	.40
309 Brian Campbell	.20	.50
310 Brett Clark	.15	.40
311 Stephane Robidas	.15	.40
312 Brett Lebda	.15	.40
313 Bryan McCabe	.20	.50
314 Pierre-Marc Bouchard	.25	.60
315 Max Pacioretty	.30	.75
316 Trent Hunter	.15	.40
317 Ryan Callahan	.25	.60
318 Ilya Zubov	.20	.50
319 Kyle Turris	.25	.60
320 Devin Setoguchi	.20	.50
321 Jay McClement	.15	.40
322 Mikhail Grabovski	.25	.60
323 George Parros	.15	.40
324 Jordin Tootoo	.25	.60
325 Scott Niedermayer	.25	.60
326 Mathieu Schneider	.15	.40
327 Clarke MacArthur	.15	.40
328 Curtis Glencross	.15	.40
329 Duncan Keith	.25	.60
330 Rick Nash	.20	.50
331 Jere Lehtinen	.20	.50
332 Shawn Horcoff	.15	.40
333 Anthony Stewart	.15	.40
334 Eric Belanger	.15	.40
335 Jaroslav Halak	.25	.60
336 Kyle Okposo	.25	.60
337 Nigel Dawes	.15	.40
338 Mike Richards	.25	.60
339 Daniel Carcillo	.15	.40
340 Joe Pavelski	.25	.60
341 Martin St. Louis	.25	.60
342 Ian White	.20	.50
343 Mike Green	.25	.60
344 Dan Ellis	.15	.40
345 Francois Beauchemin	.15	.40
346 Blake Wheeler	.25	.60
347 Daniel Paille	.20	.50
348 Joe Corvo	.15	.40
349 Jack Skille	.15	.40
350 Manny Malhotra	.15	.40
351 Henrik Zetterberg	.30	.75
352 Ethan Moreau	.15	.40
353 Jarret Stoll	.20	.50
354 Derek Boogaard	.15	.40
355 Brian Gionta	.20	.50
356 Dany Heatley	.25	.60
357 Matt Carle	.20	.50
358 Ruslan Fedotenko	.15	.40
359 Jeremy Roenick	.25	.60
360 Jussi Jokinen	.15	.40
361 Ryan Kesler	.25	.60
362 Jose Theodore	.25	.60
363 Derek Morris	.15	.40
364 Bobby Ryan	.25	.60
365 Eric Perrin	.15	.40
366 Jaroslav Spacek	.15	.40
367 Miikka Kiprusoff	.20	.50
368 Cam Barker	.15	.40
369 Kristian Huselius	.15	.40
370 Matt Niskanen	.20	.50
371 Sheldon Souray	.15	.40
372 Shawn Matthias	.25	.60
373 Owen Nolan	.25	.60
374 Chris Higgins	.15	.40
375 Andy Hilbert	.15	.40
376 Aaron Voros	.15	.40
377 Simon Gagne	.25	.60
378 Mike Weaver	.15	.40
379 Milan Michalek	.15	.40
380 Vincent Lecavalier	.20	.50
381 Jeff Finger	.15	.40
382 Viktor Kozlov	.15	.40
383 Pekka Rinne	.30	.75
384 Chris Kunitz	.25	.60
385 David Krejci	.25	.60
386 Paul Gaustad	.20	.50
387 Ray Whitney	.20	.50
388 Brent Seabrook	.20	.50
389 Derick Brassard	.25	.60
390 Darryl Sydor	.15	.40
391 Andrew Cogliano	.20	.50
392 Tomas Vokoun	.20	.50
393 Brent Burns	.30	.75
394 Matt D'Agostini	.20	.50
395 Josh Bailey	.20	.50
396 Lauri Korpikoski	.15	.40
397 Mike Knuble	.15	.40
398 Evgeni Malkin	.75	2.00
399 Marc-Edouard Vlasic	.15	.40
400 Vaclav Prospal	.15	.40
401 Vesa Toskala	.25	.60
402 Michael Nylander	.15	.40
403 Anton Babchuk	.20	.50
404 Rich Peverley	.20	.50
405 Marco Sturm	.15	.40
406 Adrian Aucoin	.15	.40
407 Martin Havlat	.20	.50
408 Chris Stewart	.20	.50
409 Mike Modano	.40	1.00
410 Chris Chelios	.25	.60
411 Jay Bouwmeester	.25	.60
412 Jack Johnson	.15	.40
413 Guillaume Latendresse	.20	.50
414 Mark Streit	.15	.40
415 Jamal Mayers	.15	.40
416 Chris Neil	.15	.40
417 Ed Jovanovski	.15	.40
418 Philippe Boucher	.15	.40
419 Paul Kariya	.30	.75
420 Dominic Moore	.25	.60
421 Mattias Ohlund	.15	.40
422 Radek Bonk	.15	.40
423 Jean-Sebastien Giguere	.25	.60
424 Johan Hedberg	.20	.50
425 Drew Stafford	.25	.60
426 Robyn Regehr	.20	.50
427 Dave Bolland	.20	.50
428 Peter Budaj	.20	.50
429 Brenden Morrow	.20	.50
430 Kirk Maltby	.15	.40
431 Michal Repik	.20	.50
432 Andrew Brunette	.15	.40
433 Mike Komisarek	.20	.50
434 Richard Park	.15	.40
435 Wade Redden	.15	.40
436 Jesse Winchester	.20	.50
437 Enver Lisin	.15	.40
438 Ryane Clowe	.20	.50
439 Mason Raymond	.25	.60
440 Pavel Kubina	.15	.40
441 Nicklas Backstrom	.40	1.00
442 Patric Hornqvist	.20	.50
443 Ron Hainsey	.15	.40
444 Mark Stuart	.15	.40
445 Dion Phaneuf	.30	.75
446 Brooks Orpik	.20	.50
447 Tyler Arnason	.15	.40
448 Brad Richards	.25	.60
449 Valtteri Filppula	.25	.60
450 Nathan Horton	.25	.60
451 Raitis Ivanans	.15	.40
452 Tomas Plekanec	.25	.60
453 Bobby Holik	.15	.40
454 Nikolai Zherdev	.15	.40
455 Jarkko Ruutu	.15	.40
456 Peter Mueller	.20	.50
457 Maxime Talbot	.25	.60
458 Andy McDonald	.20	.50
459 Matt Stajan	.20	.50
460 Kyle Wellwood	.20	.50
461 Ryan Suter	.25	.60
462 Chris Pronger	.20	.50
463 Marc Savard	.15	.40
464 Tim Connolly	.15	.40
465 Curtis McElhinney	.20	.50
466 Dustin Byfuglien	.25	.60
467 R.J. Umberger	.20	.50
468 Sergei Zubov	.15	.40
469 Lubomir Visnovsky	.15	.40
470 Kenndal McArdle	.20	.50
471 Marc-Andre Bergeron	.15	.40
472 Alexander Steen	.25	.60
473 Chris Campoli	.15	.40
474 Marc Staal	.25	.60
475 Scott Hartnell	.25	.60
476 Ilya Bryzgalov	.20	.50
477 Rob Blake	.25	.60
478 Mark Recchi	.30	.75
479 Luke Schenn	.20	.50
480 Brooks Laich	.25	.60
481 Steve Sullivan	.15	.40
482 Bryan Little	.25	.60
483 Jason Blake	.15	.40
484 Rene Bourque	.15	.40
485 Cam Ward	.25	.60
486 T.J. Hensick	.15	.40
487 Mike Ribeiro	.20	.50
488 Dan Cleary	.25	.60
489 David Booth	.15	.40
490 Brian Boyle	.15	.40
491 Alex Tanguay	.15	.40
492 Scott Clemmensen	.20	.50
493 Brendan Witt	.15	.40
494 Nick Foligno	.20	.50
495 Olli Jokinen	.20	.50
496 Checklist	.15	.40
497 Checklist	.15	.40
498 Checklist	.15	.40
499 Checklist	.15	.40
500 Checklist	.15	.40
501 Yannick Weber RC	1.25	3.00
502 Ville Leino RC	1.00	2.50
503 Troy Bodie RC	1.00	2.50
504 Tom Wandell RC	1.25	3.00
505 Tim Wallace RC	.75	2.00
506 Tim Stapleton RC	1.25	3.00
507 T.J. Galiardi RC	1.25	3.00
508 Spencer Machacek RC	1.25	3.00
509 Sean Collins RC	1.00	2.50
510 Scott Lehman RC	.75	2.00
511 Christian Hanson RC	1.25	3.00
512 Riley Armstrong RC	1.00	2.50
513 Riku Helenius RC	1.25	3.00
514 Phil Oreskovic RC	1.25	3.00
515 Peter Regin RC	1.00	2.50
516 Mike Santorelli RC	1.25	3.00
517 Mike McKenna RC	1.00	2.50
518 Mikael Backlund RC	1.25	3.00
519 Michal Neuvirth RC	2.00	5.00
520 Michael Vernace RC	1.00	2.50
521 Matt Hendricks RC	1.00	2.50
522 Matt Beleskey RC	1.00	2.50
523 Luca Caputi RC	1.25	3.00
524 Kurtis McLean RC	1.00	2.50
525 Kris Chucko RC	1.00	2.50
526 Kevin Westgarth RC	1.00	2.50
527 Kevin Quick RC	.75	2.00
528 John Scott RC	1.25	3.00
529 Joel Rechlicz RC	.75	2.00
530 Jhonas Enroth RC	1.50	4.00
531 Jesse Joensuu RC	1.00	2.50
532 Jay Beagle RC	1.50	4.00
533 Jaime Sifers RC	1.00	2.50
534 Taylor Chorney RC	1.25	3.00
535 Grant Lewis RC	1.00	2.50
536 Derek Peltier RC	.75	2.00
537 Davis Drewiske RC	1.25	3.00
538 David Van Der Gulik RC	1.00	2.50
539 David Schlemko RC	1.00	2.50
540 John Negrin RC	1.25	3.00
541 Cal O'Reilly RC	1.00	2.50
542 Byron Bitz RC	1.00	2.50
543 Ivan Vishnevskiy RC	1.00	2.50
544 Brian Salcido RC	1.00	2.50
545 Brandon Segal RC	1.00	2.50
546 Ben Lovejoy RC	1.25	3.00
547 Artem Anisimov RC	1.25	3.00
548 Antti Niemi RC	2.00	5.00
549 Andrew MacDonald RC	.75	2.00
550 Alexander Sulzer RC	.75	2.00
551 Wayne Gretzky L	4.00	10.00
552 Denis Potvin L	.75	2.00
553 Steve Shutt L	.75	2.00
554 Dale Hawerchuk L	1.00	2.50
555 Don Cherry L	.75	2.00
556 Stan Mikita L	1.00	2.50
557 Al MacInnis L	.75	2.00
558 Denis Savard L	1.00	2.50
559 Bernie Federko L	.60	1.50
560 Darryl Sutter L	.60	1.50
561 Alex Delvecchio L	1.00	2.50
562 Rod Langway L	.60	1.50
563 Johnny Bucyk L	1.25	3.00
564 Mark Messier L	1.00	2.50
565 Ted Lindsay L	.60	1.50
566 Bobby Hull L	1.00	2.50
567 Scotty Bowman L	.75	2.00
568 Clark Gillies L	.75	2.00
569 Red Kelly L	.75	2.00
570 Gilbert Perreault L	.75	2.00
571 Terry O'Reilly L	.60	1.50
572 Jean Beliveau L	.75	2.00
573 Ron Ellis L	.50	1.25
574 Harry Howell L	.60	1.50
575 Guy Carbonneau L	1.25	3.00
576 Butch Bouchard L	.60	1.50
577 Frank Mahovlich L	1.00	2.50
578 Lanny McDonald L	.75	2.00
579 Peter Stastny L	.75	2.00
580 Dick Duff L	.60	1.50
581 Grant Fuhr L	.75	2.00
582 Cam Neely L	.75	2.00
583 Rogie Vachon L	1.00	2.50
584 Phil Esposito L	1.25	3.00
585 Theoren Fleury L	1.25	3.00
586 Bobby Orr L	2.50	6.00
587 Johnny Bower L	1.00	2.50
588 Luc Robitaille L	.75	2.00
589 Jari Kurri L	.75	2.00
590 Doug Wilson L	.60	1.50
591 Borje Salming L	.75	2.00
592 Marty McSorley L	.60	1.50
593 Bob Bourne L	.60	1.50
594 Doug Gilmour L	1.00	2.50
595 Mike Bossy L	.75	2.00
596 Bobby Clarke L	.75	2.00
597 Mario Lemieux L	2.50	6.00
598 Patrick Roy L	2.00	5.00
599 Tony Esposito L	.75	2.00
600 Gordie Howe L	2.00	5.00
601 Justin Williams	.20	.50
602 Jason Williams	.15	.40
603 Rob Scuderi	.15	.40
604 Aaron Ward	.15	.40
605 Rickard Wallin	.15	.40
606 Niclas Wallin	.15	.40
607 Stephane Veilleux	.15	.40
608 Ole-Kristian Tollefsen	.15	.40
609 Alex Tanguay	.15	.40
610 Petr Sykora	.20	.50
611 Darryl Sydor	.15	.40
612 Jaroslav Spacek	.15	.40
613 Ryan Smyth	.20	.50
614 Dennis Seidenberg	.20	.50
615 Jeff Schultz	.15	.40
616 Rob Schremp	.15	.40
617 Luca Sbisa	.25	.60
618 Mikael Samuelsson	.15	.40
619 Dwayne Roloson	.20	.50
620 Andrew Raycroft	.20	.50
621 Kyle Quincey	.15	.40
622 Vaclav Prospal	.15	.40
623 Chris Pronger	.20	.50
624 Wayne Primeau	.15	.40
625 Roman Polak	.15	.40
626 Patrick O'Sullivan	.20	.50
627 Colton Orr	.15	.40
628 Mattias Ohlund	.15	.40
629 Antero Niittymaki	.25	.60
630 Rob Niedermayer	.15	.40
631 Scott Nichol	.15	.40
632 Cory Murphy	.15	.40
633 Matt Moulson	.20	.50
634 Brendan Morrison	.20	.50
635 Steve Montador	.15	.40
636 Travis Moen	.15	.40
637 Drew Miller	.15	.40
638 Milan Michalek	.15	.40
639 Steve McCarthy	.15	.40
640 Paul Mara	.15	.40
641 Manny Malhotra	.15	.40
642 John Madden	.15	.40
643 Joey MacDonald	.20	.50
644 Joffrey Lupul	.20	.50
645 Pascal Leclaire	.25	.60
646 Ian Laperriere	.15	.40
647 Robert Lang	.15	.40
648 Quintin Lang	.20	.50
649 Jason LaBarbera	.20	.50
650 Pavel Kubina	.15	.40
651 Alex Kovalev	.25	.60
652 Ales Kotalik	.15	.40
653 Lauri Korpikoski	.15	.40
654 Mike Komisarek	.20	.50
655 Saku Koivu	.25	.60
656 Chuck Kobasew	.15	.40
657 Mike Knuble	.15	.40
658 Nikolai Khabibulin	.25	.60
659 Phil Kessel	.30	.75
660 Boyd Kane	.15	.40
661 Ryan Johnson	.15	.40
662 Brent Johnson	.15	.40
663 Cam Janssen	.15	.40
664 Marian Hossa	.20	.50
665 Darcy Hordichuk	.15	.40
666 Chris Higgins	.15	.40
667 Dany Heatley	.25	.60
668 Martin Havlat	.20	.50
669 Jeff Halpern	.15	.40
670 Scott Gomez	.20	.50
671 Brian Gionta	.20	.50
672 Hal Gill	.15	.40
673 Mathieu Garon	.25	.60
674 Marian Gaborik	.30	.75
675 Maxim Afinogenov	.15	.40
676 Todd Fedoruk	.15	.40
677 Garnet Exelby	.15	.40
678 Ray Emery	.20	.50
679 Christian Ehrhoff	.15	.40
680 Andrew Ebbett	.15	.40
681 Steve Downie	.15	.40
682 Nigel Dawes	.15	.40
683 Ty Conklin	.20	.50
684 Mike Comrie	.20	.50
685 Scott Clemmensen	.20	.50
686 Jonathan Cheechoo	.25	.60
687 Mike Cammalleri	.20	.50
688 Jay Bouwmeester	.25	.60
689 Chris Bourque	.25	.60
690 Paul Bissonnette	.15	.40
691 Martin Biron	.20	.50
692 Todd Bertuzzi	.25	.60
693 Marc-Andre Bergeron	.15	.40
694 Francois Beauchemin	.15	.40
695 Alex Auld	.20	.50
696 Keith Aucoin	.30	.75
697 Evgeni Artyukhin	.15	.40
698 Nik Antropov	.20	.50
699 Craig Anderson	.25	.60
700 Checklist	.15	.40
701 Checklist	.15	.40
702 Toni Lydman	.15	.40
703 Brian McGrattan	.15	.40
704 Matt Ellis	.15	.40
705 Fredrik Sjostrom	.15	.40
706 Tomas Kopecky	.20	.50
707 Brent Sopel	.15	.40
708 Bryan Bickell	.25	.60
709 Niklas Hjalmarsson	.20	.50
710 Henrik Tallinder	.15	.40
711 Nathan Paetsch	.15	.40
712 Mike Grier	.15	.40
713 Jordan Hendry	.20	.50
714 Aaron Johnson	.15	.40
715 Johnny Boychuk	.20	.50
716 Derek Morris	.15	.40
717 Daniel Paille	.20	.50
718 Steve Begin	.15	.40
719 Ondrej Pavelec	.30	.75
720 Christoph Schubert	.15	.40
721 Eric Boulton	.15	.40
722 Chris Thorburn	.15	.40
723 Ryan Carter	.15	.40
724 Erik Christensen	.15	.40
725 Sheldon Brookbank	.15	.40
726 Petteri Nokelainen	.15	.40
727 Nick Boynton	.15	.40
728 Ruslan Salei	.15	.40
729 Scott Hannan	.15	.40
730 David Koci	.15	.40
731 Stephane Yelle	.15	.40
732 Tom Kostopoulos	.15	.40
733 Georges Laraque	.20	.50
734 Ryan Shannon	.20	.50
735 Anton Volchenkov	.15	.40
736 Steve MacIntyre	.15	.40
737 Gilbert Brule	.30	.75
738 Jean-Francois Jacques	.15	.40
739 Derek Meech	.15	.40
740 Jimmy Howard	.30	.75
741 Kyle Chipchura	.20	.50
742 Matt Carkner	.15	.40
743 Ryan Stone	.15	.40
744 Anton Stralman	.15	.40
745 Derek Dorsett	.20	.50
746 Patrick Eaves	.15	.40
747 Brad May	.15	.40
748 Mathieu Roy	.15	.40
749 Tanner Glass	.15	.40
750 Shean Donovan	.15	.40
751 Craig Adams	.15	.40
752 Martin Skoula	.15	.40
753 Steven Zalewski RC	.40	1.00
754 Matthew Corrente RC	.40	1.00
755 Bryan Rodney RC	.40	1.00
756 Ryan Vesce RC	.40	1.00
757 David Sloane RC	.50	1.25
758 Lars Eller RC	.50	1.25
759 Tyson Strachan RC	.30	.75
760 Wes O'Neill RC	.50	1.25
761 Matt Climie RC	.40	1.00
762 Daniel Larsson RC	.40	1.00
763 James Wright RC	.50	1.25
764 Teemu Laakso RC	.30	.75
765 Devan Dubnyk RC	1.00	2.50
766 Jason Demers RC	.75	2.00
767 Benn Ferriero RC	.50	1.25
768 Frazer McLaren RC	.40	1.00
769 Johan Backlund RC	.50	1.25
770 Mika Pyorala RC	.40	1.00
771 Tyler Myers RC	.75	2.00
772 Ryan O'Reilly RC	.75	2.00
773 Jamie Benn RC	1.50	4.00
774 Dmitry Kulikov RC	.50	1.25
775 Alec Martinez RC	.60	1.50
776 Matt Gilroy RC	.50	1.25
777 Michael Del Zotto RC	.50	1.25
778 Jay Rosehill RC	.50	1.25
779 Sergei Shirokov RC	.30	.75
780 Tyler Ennis RC	.60	1.50
781 Chris Butler RC	.50	1.25
782 James Reimer RC	1.25	3.00
783 Perttu Lindgren RC	.40	1.00
784 Bobby Sanguinetti RC	.30	.75
785 Braden Holtby RC	1.25	3.00
786 Ryan Wilson RC	.50	1.25
787 Aaron Gagnon RC	.30	.75
788 Viktor Stalberg RC	.50	1.25
789 Erik Karlsson RC	1.50	4.00
790 Brad Marchand RC	1.25	3.00
791 Colin Wilson RC	.50	1.25
792 Michael Grabner RC	.50	1.25
793 Tyler Bozak RC	.75	2.00
794 Logan Couture RC	1.00	2.50
795 Evander Kane RC	1.00	2.50
796 Jonas Gustavsson RC	.60	1.50
797 Victor Hedman RC	1.00	2.50
798 James van Riemsdyk RC	1.00	2.50
799 Matt Duchene RC	1.00	2.50
800 John Tavares RC	3.00	8.00

2009-10 O-Pee-Chee Rainbow

*SINGLES: 2.5X TO 6X BASIC CARDS
*ROOKIES: .6X TO 1.5X BASIC
*LEGENDS: 1X TO 2.5X BASIC
STATED ODDS 1:4
*UPD (601-752): 3X TO 8X BASIC CARDS
*UPD ROOKIES (753-800): 2X TO 5X
UPDATE STATED ODDS 2-5 PER FACT.SET

Card	Low	High
162 Zach Parise	1.50	4.00
441 Nicklas Backstrom	2.50	6.00
501 Yannick Weber	2.00	5.00
523 Luca Caputi	2.00	5.00
800 John Tavares	10.00	25.00

2009-10 O-Pee-Chee Retro

*SINGLES: 2X TO 5X BASIC CARDS
*ROOKIES:.5 X TO 1.2X BASIC CARDS
*LEGENDS: .8X TO 2X BASIC CARDS
STATED ODDS 1 PER PACK

Card	Low	High
441 Nicklas Backstrom	2.00	5.00

2009-10 O-Pee-Chee Retro Blank Backs

*BLANK: 25X TO 60X BASIC CARDS
*BLANK RCs: 4X TO 10X BASIC CARDS
*BLANK SPs: 5X TO 12X BASIC CARDS

Card	Low	High
COMMON CLs	4.00	10.00
441 Nicklas Backstrom	25.00	60.00

2009-10 O-Pee-Chee Retro Rainbow

*SINGLES: 6X TO 15X BASIC CARDS
*ROOKIES: 1.2X TO 3X BASIC
*LEGENDS: 2.5X TO 6X BASIC
STATED PRINT RUN 100 SER. #'d SETS

Card	Low	High
441 Nicklas Backstrom	6.00	15.00

2009-10 O-Pee-Chee All Rookie Team

Card	Low	High
COMPLETE SET (6)	6.00	15.00
STATED ODDS 1:4		
ART1 Steve Mason	.60	1.50
ART2 Drew Doughty	1.00	2.50
ART3 Luke Schenn	.60	1.50
ART4 Patrik Berglund	.50	1.25
ART5 Bobby Ryan	.75	2.00
ART6 Kris Versteeg	.75	2.00

2009-10 O-Pee-Chee All Star Team

Card	Low	High
COMPLETE SET (12)	10.00	25.00
STATED ODDS 1:4		
AST1 Tim Thomas	.75	2.00
AST2 Mike Green	.75	2.00
AST3 Zdeno Chara	.75	2.00
AST4 Evgeni Malkin	2.50	6.00
AST5 Jarome Iginla	.75	2.00
AST6 Alexander Ovechkin	3.00	8.00
AST7 Steve Mason	.60	1.50
AST8 Nicklas Lidstrom	.75	2.00
AST9 Dan Boyle	.60	1.50
AST10 Pavel Datsyuk	1.00	2.50
AST11 Marian Hossa	.60	1.50
AST12 Zach Parise	.75	2.00

2009-10 O-Pee-Chee Box Bottoms

Card	Low	High
COMPLETE SET (16)	6.00	15.00
IGINLA/LECV/KOVAL/NASH	1.25	3.00
BRIND'A/MALKIN/ZETTER/STAMKOS	1.25	3.00
OVECH/LNGO/TOEWS/SCHENN	1.50	4.00
CRSBY/THRNTN/PRICE/LDSTRM	1.50	4.00
NNO Jarome Iginla	.25	.60
NNO Vincent Lecavalier	.20	.50
NNO Ilya Kovalchuk	.25	.60
NNO Rick Nash	.20	.50
NNO Rod Brind`Amour	.25	.60
NNO Evgeni Malkin	.75	2.00
NNO Henrik Zetterberg	.30	.75
NNO Steven Stamkos	.50	1.25
NNO Alexander Ovechkin	1.00	2.50
NNO Roberto Luongo	.30	.75
NNO Jonathan Toews	.50	1.25
NNO Luke Schenn	.20	.50
NNO Sidney Crosby	1.00	2.50
NNO Joe Thornton	.25	.60
NNO Carey Price	1.00	2.50
NNO Nicklas Lidstrom	.25	.60

2009-10 O-Pee-Chee Buyback Autographs

Card	Low	High
BBCG Claude Giroux '08-09	30.00	60.00
BBHW Dale Hawerchuk '08-09 LL	10.00	25.00

2009-10 O-Pee-Chee Canadian Heroes

Card	Low	High
COMPLETE SET (42)	15.00	40.00
STATED ODDS 1:4		
CBBC Braydon Coburn	.50	1.25
CBBK Becky Kellar	.50	1.25
CBCH Chris Mason	.60	1.50
CBCL Charline Labonte	.50	1.25
CBCM Carla MacLeod	.50	1.25
CBCO Caroline Ouellette	.50	1.25
CBCP Chris Phillips	.50	1.25
CBCS Colleen Sostorics	.50	1.25
CBCW Catherine Ward	.50	1.25
CBDD Drew Doughty	1.00	2.50
CBDH Dan Hamhuis	.60	1.50
CBDR Dwayne Roloson	.60	1.50
CBGA Gillian Apps	.50	1.25
CBGF Gillian Ferrari	.50	1.25
CBGK Gina Kingsbury	.50	1.25
CBHA Josh Harding	.75	2.00
CBHE Dany Heatley	.75	2.00
CBHI Haley Irwin	.50	1.25
CBHW Hayley Wickenheiser	.50	1.25
CBIW Ian White	.60	1.50
CBJB Jennifer Botterill	.50	1.25
CBJH Jayna Hefford	.50	1.25
CBJS Jason Spezza	.75	2.00
CBKS Kim St. Pierre	.50	1.25
CBLS Luke Schenn	.60	1.5
CBMA Meghan Agosta	.50	1.2
CBML Matthew Lombardi	.50	1.2
CBMM Meaghan Mikkelson	.50	1.2
CBMP Marie-Philip Poulin	.50	1.2
CBMS Martin St. Louis	.75	2.0
CBMV Marc-Edouard Vlasic	.50	1.2
CBRJ Rebecca Johnston	.50	1.2
CBRO Derek Roy	.60	1.5
CBSD Shane Doan	.60	1.5
CBSH Shawn Horcoff	.50	1.2
CBSS Shannon Szabados	.50	1.2
CBST Steven Stamkos	1.50	4.0
CBSU Scottie Upshall	.50	1.2
CBSV Sarah Vaillancourt	.50	1.2
CBSW Shea Weber	.60	1.5
CBTB Tessa Bonhomme	.50	1.2
CBTZ Travis Zajac	.60	1.5

2009-10 O-Pee-Chee Canadian Heroes Autographs

Card	Low	High
CBABO Bobby Orr		
CBACP Carey Price	150.00	300.0
CBADD Drew Doughty	30.00	80.0
CBADH Dany Heatley	30.00	80.0
CBADP Dion Phaneuf	25.00	60.0
CBADR Dwayne Roloson		
CBAGH Gordie Howe	125.00	250.0
CBAHA Josh Harding	25.00	60.0
CBAJI Jarome Iginla	125.00	250.0
CBAJT Jonathan Toews	75.00	150.0
CBALS Luke Schenn	50.00	100.0
CBAML Mario Lemieux	125.00	250.0
CBAMM Mark Messier	100.00	200.0
CBAMR Mike Richards	60.00	150.0
CBAMS Martin St. Louis		
CBAPR Patrick Roy	250.00	400.0
CBARB Ray Bourque	125.00	250.0
CBARN Rick Nash	125.00	250.0
CBASC Sidney Crosby	125.00	250.0
CBAST Steven Stamkos	100.00	200.0
CBAWG Wayne Gretzky	400.00	600.0

2009-10 O-Pee-Chee Canadian Heroes Foil

Card	Low	High
STATED ODDS 1:36		
CBH1 Wayne Gretzky	12.00	30.0
CBH2 Gordie Howe	8.00	20.0
CBH3 Bobby Orr	10.00	25.0
CBH4 Steven Stamkos	6.00	15.0
CBH5 Mark Messier	4.00	10.0
CBH6 Sidney Crosby	12.00	30.0
CBH7 Phil Esposito	5.00	12.0
CBH8 Tony Esposito	3.00	8.0
CBH9 Gilbert Perreault	3.00	8.0
CBH10 Lanny McDonald	3.00	8.0
CBH11 Ray Bourque	5.00	12.0
CBH12 Theoren Fleury	5.00	12.0
CBH13 Luc Robitaille	3.00	8.0
CBH14 Manon Rheaume	6.00	15.0
CBH15 Mike Bossy	3.00	8.0
CBH16 Bobby Clarke	3.00	8.0
CBH17 Patrick Roy	8.00	20.0
CBH18 Mario Lemieux	10.00	25.0
CBH19 Joe Thornton	3.00	8.0
CBH20 Jarome Iginla	3.00	8.0
CBH21 Vincent Lecavalier	2.50	6.0
CBH22 Ryan Getzlaf	5.00	12.0
CBH23 Patrick Marleau	3.00	8.00
CBH24 Martin St. Louis	3.00	8.00
CBH25 Mike Richards	3.00	8.00
CBH26 Shane Doan	2.50	6.00
CBH27 Jonathan Toews	6.00	15.00
CBH28 Steve Mason	2.50	6.00
CBH29 Martin Brodeur	6.00	15.00
CBH30 Marc-Andre Fleury	5.00	12.00
CBH31 Roberto Luongo	4.00	10.00
CBH32 Mike Green	3.00	8.00
CBH33 Brian Campbell	2.50	6.00
CBH34 Scott Niedermayer	3.00	8.00
CBH35 Dion Phaneuf	4.00	10.00
CBH36 Joe Sakic	5.00	12.00
CBH37 Marty Turco	3.00	8.00
CBH38 Carey Price	8.00	20.00
CBH39 Jason Spezza	3.00	8.00
CBH40 Rick Nash	2.50	6.00

2009-10 O-Pee-Chee In Action

Card	Low	High
COMPLETE SET (12)	12.00	30.00
STATED ODDS 1:4		
ACT1 Sidney Crosby	3.00	8.00
ACT2 Evgeni Malkin	2.50	6.00
ACT3 Alexander Ovechkin	3.00	8.00
ACT4 Jarome Iginla	.75	2.00
ACT5 Bobby Ryan	.75	2.00
ACT6 Jonathan Toews	1.50	4.00
ACT7 Ilya Kovalchuk	.75	2.00
ACT8 Henrik Zetterberg	1.00	2.50
ACT9 Ales Hemsky	.60	1.50
ACT10 Zach Parise	.75	2.00
ACT11 Dany Heatley	.75	2.00
ACT12 Mikko Koivu	.75	2.00

2009-10 O-Pee-Chee Materials

Card	Low	High
STATED ODDS 1:144		
JBEES Wheel/Savard/Berg/Kessl	8.00	20.00
JBLUE Perrn/Tkac/Berglnd/Kariya	8.00	20.00
JBOLT St.L/Stamk/Prospl/Lecav	12.00	30.00
JBOST Ferndz/Ryder/Lucic/Rask	6.00	15.00
JCANE Ward/Staal/Cole/Brind	8.00	20.00
JCAPS Ovech/Grn/Back/Flsch	25.00	60.00
JCATS Booth/Hortn/Wiss/Vokn	6.00	15.00
JCNDS Kovalv/Kost/Mrkv/Kmsk	6.00	15.00
JCNKS Edler/Sedin/Bksa/Luong	8.00	20.00
JCOLO Sakic/Svts/Ststny/Wlski	10.00	25.00
JCYTE Lmbrdi/Bdkr/Muelr/Doan	5.00	12.00
JDEVL Clrksn/Brodr/Elias/Parise	12.00	30.00
JDRFT Dougty/Schn/Bdkr/Stmk	12.00	30.00
JDUCK Prnger/Perry/Gigre/Gtzlf	10.00	25.00
JEURO Sundn/Kolzig/Fdrv/Slne	12.00	30.00
JFLAM Phanf/Iginla/Kprsff/Jokin	8.00	20.00
JFLYR Ntymki/Crtr/Rchr/Ggne	6.00	15.00
JGCML Mario/Messi/Crsby/Gretz	60.00	125.00
JHABS Tang/Prce/Koivu/Plknc	25.00	60.00
JHAWK Sbrk/Toews/Kne/Sharp	12.00	30.00
JISLE Wght/Tmbl/DiPt/Hntr SP		
JJACK Vorck/Umbrgr/Nsh/Klsla	6.00	15.00
JKING Frolv/Kpitr/Dghty/Brwn	10.00	25.00
JKMLP Tucker/Ignla/Niedr/Doan	6.00	15.00
JLEAF Blake/Schn/Stjn/Tskla	6.00	15.00
JLGND Howe/Messier/Roy/Gretz	60.00	125.00
JOILR Coglio/Poul/Ggnr/Horcff	8.00	20.00
JPENS Malkn/Staal/Flry/Crosby	25.00	60.00
JRBLF Fleury/Brdr/Roy/Luongo	15.00	40.00
JRNGR Dubin/Lund/Staal/Nslnd	10.00	25.00
JSABR Roy/Pomin/Miller/Vanek	6.00	15.00
JSBBS Shanahn/Skic/Brdr/Blke	12.00	30.00
JSENS Campli/Phillips/Htly/Spez	6.00	15.00
JSHRK Setog/Nabk/Trntn/Marlu	6.00	15.00
JSTAR Turco/Niskn/Mdno/Zubv	10.00	25.00

Card	Low	High
THRS Little/Koval/Leht/Enstrom	6.00	15.00
VANC Sndin/Ohlnd/Luong/Bern	8.00	20.00
WILD Gabrik/Koiv/Noln/Bouch	8.00	20.00
WING Zetter/Hossa/Lids/Datsyk	8.00	20.00
WNGS Raflski/Cheli/Osgd/Draper	6.00	15.00
PREDS Legwnd/Rine/Web/Sullivn	8.00	20.00

2009-10 O-Pee-Chee Record Breakers

Card	Low	High
COMPLETE SET (10)	10.00	25.00
STATED ODDS 1:4		
B1 Zdeno Chara	.75	2.00
B2 Alexander Ovechkin	3.00	8.00
B3 Steve Mason	.60	1.50
B4 Patrik Elias	.75	2.00
B5 Jarome Iginla	.75	2.00
B6 Miikka Kiprusoff	.60	1.50
B7 Mike Green	.75	2.00
B8 Martin Brodeur	1.50	4.00
B9 Brendan Shanahan	1.00	2.50
B10 Mike Richards	.75	2.00

2009-10 O-Pee-Chee Signatures

Card	Low	High
STATED ODDS 1:216		
SAP Adam Pineault	8.00	20.00
SBB Ben Bishop	10.00	25.00
SBL Brian Lee	10.00	25.00
SBM Brendan Mikkelson	6.00	15.00
SBO Bobby Orr	150.00	250.00
SBR Brian Boyle	6.00	15.00
SBS Brandon Sutter	8.00	20.00
SBU Peter Budaj	8.00	20.00
SBW Blake Wheeler	10.00	25.00
SCB Cam Barker	6.00	15.00
SCG Colton Gillies	10.00	25.00
SCK Chris Kunitz	10.00	25.00
SCL David Clarkson	8.00	20.00
SCO Cory Schneider	12.00	30.00
SCP Carey Price	30.00	60.00
SCS Chris Stewart	8.00	20.00
SDC Daniel Carcillo	6.00	15.00
SDD Drew Doughty	12.00	30.00
SDJ David Jones	6.00	15.00
SDP Dion Phaneuf	12.00	30.00
SDR Dwayne Roloson		
SDS Daniel Sedin	10.00	25.00
SEN Evgeni Nabokov	8.00	20.00
SFB Fabian Brunnstrom	8.00	20.00
SGA Marian Gaborik	12.00	30.00
SGH Gordie Howe		
SGI Claude Giroux	20.00	40.00
SGL Guillaume Latendresse	8.00	20.00
SHL Henrik Lundqvist	40.00	80.00
SHS Henrik Sedin	20.00	40.00
SHU Matt Hunwick	6.00	15.00
SJB Josh Bailey	8.00	20.00
SJD Jean-Pierre Dumont	6.00	15.00
SJH Jonas Hiller	8.00	20.00
SJI Jarome Iginla	25.00	50.00
SJM Jamie McGinn	8.00	20.00
SJN James Neal	10.00	25.00
SJP Justin Pogge	10.00	25.00
SJS Jack Skille	6.00	15.00
SJT Joe Thornton	10.00	25.00
SJV Jakub Voracek		
SKA Karl Alzner	6.00	15.00
SKE Tyler Kennedy	8.00	20.00
SKM Kenndal McArdle	8.00	20.00
SKO Kyle Okposo	10.00	25.00
SKV Kris Versteeg	15.00	40.00
SLS Luke Schenn	8.00	20.00
SMA Steve Mason	8.00	20.00
SMB Mikkel Boedker	6.00	15.00
SMD Matt D'Agostini	8.00	20.00
SMG Mike Green	10.00	25.00
SMH Matthew Halischuk		
SMI Michael Peca	8.00	20.00
SMK Mike Knuble	6.00	15.00
SMM Milan Michalek	6.00	15.00
SMN Markus Naslund	8.00	20.00
SMO Brendan Morrison	8.00	20.00
SMP Max Pacioretty	12.00	30.00
SMR Michal Repik	8.00	20.00
SMS Marc Staal	10.00	25.00
SMX Ben Maxwell	8.00	20.00
SNB Nicklas Backstrom	15.00	40.00
SNF Nikita Filatov	8.00	20.00
SNG Nathan Gerbe	8.00	20.00
SNI Matt Niskanen	8.00	20.00
SNK Nikolai Kulemin	8.00	20.00
SPB Patrik Berglund	6.00	15.00
SPD Pavel Datsyuk	20.00	40.00
SPE Patrik Elias	10.00	25.00
SPH Chris Phillips	6.00	15.00
SPI Alex Pietrangelo	8.00	20.00
SPO Jason Pominville	10.00	25.00
SRI Mike Ribeiro	8.00	20.00
SRS Ryan Smyth	8.00	20.00
SRY Bobby Ryan	10.00	25.00
SSC Sidney Crosby	125.00	200.00
SSD Steve Downie	6.00	15.00
SSG Simon Gagne	10.00	25.00
SSM Matt Smaby	8.00	20.00
SSS Steven Stamkos		
SST Marco Sturm		
SSV Simeon Varlamov	40.00	80.00
SSW Stephen Weiss	6.00	15.00
STE Tobias Enstrom		
STG Tom Gilbert	6.00	15.00
STH Tomas Holmstrom	8.00	20.00
STK Tim Kennedy	8.00	20.00
STL Trevor Lewis	8.00	20.00
STO T.J. Oshie	15.00	40.00
STV Tomas Vokoun	8.00	20.00
STW Ty Wishart	8.00	20.00
SVT Viktor Tikhonov	8.00	20.00
SWG Wayne Gretzky	250.00	450.00
SZA Zach Boychuk	8.00	20.00
SZB Zach Bogosian	8.00	20.00

2009-10 O-Pee-Chee Stat Leaders

Card	Low	High
COMPLETE SET (17)	15.00	40.00
STATED ODDS 1:4		
SL1 Evgeni Malkin	2.50	6.00
SL2 Alexander Ovechkin	3.00	8.00
SL3 Evgeni Malkin	2.50	6.00
SL4 Mike Richards	.75	2.00
SL5 David Krejci	.75	2.00
SL6 Daniel Carcillo	.50	1.25
SL7 Thomas Vanek	.75	2.00
SL8 Alexander Ovechkin	3.00	8.00
SL9 Jeff Carter	.75	2.00
SL10 Alexander Ovechkin	3.00	8.00
SL11 Cal Clutterbuck	.50	1.25
SL12 Evgeni Malkin	2.50	6.00
SL13 Steve Mason	.60	1.50
SL14 Miikka Kiprusoff	.60	1.50
SL15 Tim Thomas	.75	2.00
SL16 Tim Thomas	.75	2.00
SL17 Henrik Lundqvist	1.25	3.00

2009-10 O-Pee-Chee Top Draws Triple Jerseys

Card	Low	High
RANDOM INSERTS IN UPDATE SETS		
TJATL E.Kane/Antropov/Koval	15.00	40.00
TJBOS Ryder/Lucic/Rask	15.00	40.00
TJCGY Pelech/Backlund/Chucko	12.00	30.00
TJGR8 Lemieux/Yzermn/Gretzky	50.00	120.00
TJHOF Shutt/Stastny/McDonald	12.00	30.00
TJBEES Neely/Oates/Bourque	20.00	50.00
TJBUFF Vanek/Pominville/Roy	15.00	40.00
TJCALG MacInnis/Fleury/McDon	12.00	30.00
TJCAPS Green/Ovechkin/Back	20.00	50.00
TJCOUV Bernier/Grabnr/Shirokv	15.00	40.00
TJDALL Benn/Modano/Turco	12.00	30.00
TJNEXT van Riems/Tavr/Duchn	20.00	50.00
TJPHIL van Riems/Bartulis/Girx	15.00	40.00
TJRANG Gilroy/Anisimov/Del Zot	20.00	50.00
TJSANJ Ferriero/Coutre/Demrs	12.00	30.00
TJCANES Staal/Brind/Ward	15.00	40.00
TJFLAME Iginla/Kiprusoff/Phanf	12.00	30.00
TJFLYER Richards/Carter/Emery	15.00	40.00
TJHTOWN Holmstrm/Osgd/Franzn	15.00	40.00
TJKINGS Martinez/Frolov/Smyth	15.00	40.00
TJROOKD Hedman/Myers/Karlssn	15.00	40.00
TJROOKF Duchen/van Rms/Kane	12.00	30.00
TJROOKG Niemi/Gustav/Enroth	15.00	40.00
TJTHRSH Kane/Machck/Koval	15.00	40.00
TJPHILLY van Rms/Cartr/Rchrds	15.00	40.00

2009-10 O-Pee-Chee Trophy Winners

Card	Low	High
COMPLETE SET (13)	6.00	15.00
STATED ODDS 1:4		
TW1 Alexander Ovechkin	3.00	8.00
TW2 Alexander Ovechkin	3.00	8.00
TW3 Alexander Ovechkin	3.00	8.00
TW4 Steve Sullivan	.50	1.25
TW5 Tim Thomas	.75	2.00
TW6 Pavel Datsyuk	1.00	2.50
TW7 Pavel Datsyuk	1.00	2.50
TW8 Zdeno Chara	.75	2.00
TW9 Steve Mason	.60	1.50
TW10 Evgeni Malkin	2.50	6.00
TW11 Ethan Moreau	.50	1.25
TW12 Evgeni Malkin	2.50	6.00
TW13 Pittsburgh Penguins	2.00	5.00

2010-11 O-Pee-Chee

Card	Low	High
COMPLETE SET (620)	100.00	200.00
COMP.SET w/o SPs (500)	30.00	80.00
COMP.UPD.SET (20)	8.00	20.00
MARQUEE ROOKIE STATED ODDS 1:2		
LEGENDS STATED ODDS 1:2		
UPDATE ODDS 1:9H, 1:18R: 11-12 OPC		
1 Corey Perry	.25	.60
2 T.J. Oshie	.40	1.00
3 Sami Salo	.15	.40
4 Mikhail Grabovski	.20	.50
5 Carey Price	1.00	2.50
6 Saku Koivu	.25	.60
7 Dainius Zubrus	.15	.40
8 Sidney Crosby	1.00	2.50
9 Brandon Sutter	.20	.50
10 Cal Clutterbuck	.25	.60
11 Tyler Ennis	.20	.50
12 Marco Sturm	.15	.40
13 Steve Sullivan	.15	.40
14 Lubomir Visnovsky	.15	.40
15 Scott Parse	.15	.40
16 Ben Eager	.15	.40
17 Fernando Pisani	.15	.40
18 Jonas Hiller	.20	.50
19 Brian Rolston	.20	.50
20 Ryan Suter	.15	.40
21 Niklas Hjalmarsson	.15	.40
22 Johnny Oduya	.20	.50
23 Chris Higgins	.15	.40
24 Matt Niskanen	.20	.50
25 Niklas Backstrom	.25	.60
26 Luca Caputi	.20	.50
27 John Madden	.15	.40
28 Mike Commodore	.15	.40
29 Luca Sbisa	.20	.50
30 Eric Belanger	.15	.40
31 Joffrey Lupul	.20	.50
32 Brian Elliott	.20	.50
33 Fedor Tyutin	.15	.40
34 Rostislav Klesla	.15	.40
35 Zenon Konopka	.20	.50
36 Milan Lucic	.25	.60
37 Craig Rivet	.15	.40
38 Francois Beauchemin	.15	.40
39 Bobby Sanguinetti	.15	.40
40 Zach Bogosian	.20	.50
41 Logan Couture	.25	.60
42 Pekka Rinne	.30	.75
43 Mike Grier	.15	.40
44 Mike Smith	.25	.60
45 Craig Anderson	.25	.60
46 Tomas Plekanec	.25	.60
47 Pavel Datsyuk	.30	.75
48 Brent Sopel	.15	.40
49 Chad LaRose	.15	.40
50 Alexander Frolov	.15	.40
51 Thomas Vanek	.25	.60
52 Scott Hannan	.15	.40
53 Jay McKee	.15	.40
54 Mason Raymond	.20	.50
55 Michael Leighton	.20	.50
56 Michael Del Zotto	.20	.50
57 Colin White	.15	.40
58 Doug Murray	.15	.40
59 Ville Leino	.20	.50
60 Henrik Lundqvist	.40	1.00
61 Sam Gagner	.20	.50
62 Ondrej Pavelec	.25	.60
63 Kyle Cumiskey	.15	.40
64 Steve Bernier	.15	.40
65 Andy Greene	.15	.40
66 Patrick Marleau	.25	.60
67 Christian Ehrhoff	.15	.40
68 Marty Turco	.25	.60
69 Ryan Whitney	.15	.40
70 Tomas Holmstrom	.15	.40
71 Drew Doughty	.25	.60
72 Tom Kostopoulos	.15	.40
73 Patric Hornqvist	.20	.50
74 Ron Hainsey	.15	.40
75 Paul Stastny	.25	.60
76 Miikka Kiprusoff	.20	.50
77 Erik Christensen	.15	.40
78 Phil Kessel	.30	.75
79 T.J. Galiardi	.20	.50
80 Niklas Hagman	.15	.40
81 Michal Handzus	.20	.50
82 Jason Arnott	.20	.50
83 Ryan Malone	.15	.40
84 Joe Corvo	.15	.40
85 Anton Stralman	.15	.40
86 John-Michael Liles	.15	.40
87 Nikolai Kulemin	.20	.50
88 Mike Green	.25	.60
89 Jeff Deslauriers	.15	.40
90 Martin Brodeur	.50	1.25
91 David Legwand	.20	.50
92 Henrik Zetterberg	.30	.75
93 Ivan Vishnevskiy	.15	.40
94 Robyn Regehr	.15	.40
95 Brian Gionta	.20	.50
96 Artem Anisimov	.20	.50
97 Drew Stafford	.25	.60
98 Matt Carle	.20	.50
99 Ales Hemsky	.20	.50
100 Cam Barker	.15	.40
101 Tom Poti	.15	.40
102 J.P. Dumont	.15	.40
103 Steve Montador	.15	.40
104 Kimmo Timonen	.15	.40
105 Jonas Gustavsson	.30	.75
106 Tom Wandell	.15	.40
107 Bruno Gervais	.15	.40
108 Blake Wheeler	.25	.60
109 Tyler Bozak	.25	.60
110 Scottie Upshall	.15	.40
111 Jonathan Bernier	.25	.60
112 Alex Tanguay	.15	.40
113 Scott Nichol	.15	.40
114 Joni Pitkanen	.20	.50
115 Matthew Lombardi	.15	.40
116 Jonathan Ericsson	.15	.40
117 David Steckel	.15	.40
118 Tuomo Ruutu	.20	.50
119 Josh Gorges	.15	.40
120 Bobby Ryan	.25	.60
121 Jonathan Toews	.50	1.25
122 Jaroslav Spacek	.15	.40
123 Jack Johnson	.15	.40
124 Andrej Meszaros	.15	.40
125 Jay McClement	.15	.40
126 Anze Kopitar	.40	1.00
127 David Krejci	.25	.60
128 Roman Hamrlik	.20	.50
129 Brooks Orpik	.20	.50
130 Patrick O'Sullivan	.15	.40
131 Dustin Byfuglien	.25	.60
132 Patrik Berglund	.15	.40
133 Rob Schremp	.15	.40
134 Bryan Allen	.15	.40
135 Mike Ribeiro	.20	.50
136 Valtteri Filppula	.25	.60
137 Eric Nystrom	.15	.40
138 Scott Hartnell	.25	.60
139 Ian White	.20	.50
140 Jarret Stoll	.20	.50
141 Zbynek Michalek	.15	.40
142 Michael Frolik	.15	.40
143 Radim Vrbata	.20	.50
144 Samuel Pahlsson	.15	.40
145 Ryan Smyth	.20	.50
146 Ryan Jones	.15	.40
147 Radek Dvorak	.15	.40
148 Matt Gilroy	.15	.40
149 Dan Boyle	.20	.50
150 Milan Michalek	.15	.40
151 Dany Heatley	.20	.50
152 Josh Bailey	.20	.50
153 Johan Hedberg	.20	.50
154 Curtis McElhinney	.20	.50
155 Alex Kovalev	.25	.60
156 Adam Foote	.15	.40
157 Dave Bolland	.20	.50
158 Toby Petersen	.15	.40
159 Jamie Langenbrunner	.15	.40
160 Dominic Moore	.15	.40
161 Tuukka Rask	.25	.60
162 Matt Stajan	.20	.50
163 David Backes	.25	.60
164 Maxime Talbot	.25	.60
165 Claude Giroux	.25	.60
166 Gilbert Brule	.25	.60
167 Ray Whitney	.20	.50
168 Tom Pyatt	.15	.40
169 Marek Zidlicky	.15	.40
170 Daniel Sedin	.25	.60
171 Shawn Horcoff	.15	.40
172 Dennis Seidenberg	.20	.50
173 Simon Gagne	.25	.60
174 Anton Volchenkov	.15	.40
175 Guillaume Latendresse	.20	.50
176 B.J. Crombeen	.15	.40
177 Jason Spezza	.15	.40
178 Alexander Semin	.25	.60
179 Peter Mueller	.20	.50
180 Colby Armstrong	.15	.40
181 Troy Brouwer	.25	.60
182 Zdeno Chara	.20	.50
183 Alexandre Burrows	.25	.60
184 Frans Nielsen	.15	.40
185 Andrew Ebbett	.15	.40
186 Tobias Enstrom	.15	.40
187 Tyler Kennedy	.15	.40
188 Fabian Brunnstrom	.15	.40
189 Vernon Fiddler	.15	.40
190 Ryan Kesler	.25	.60
191 Teemu Selanne	.50	1.25
192 Dmitry Kulikov	.20	.50
193 Mark Stuart	.15	.40
194 Corey Crawford	.30	.75
195 Carl Gunnarsson	.15	.40
196 Alexander Edler	.15	.40
197 Adam Burish	.15	.40
198 Ian Laperriere	.15	.40
199 Semyon Varlamov	.25	.60
200 Colin Wilson	.20	.50
201 Erik Johnson	.15	.40
202 Pierre-Marc Bouchard	.25	.60
203 Brooks Laich	.15	.40
204 Wojtek Wolski	.15	.40
205 Shane O'Brien	.15	.40
206 Dan Ellis	.20	.50
207 Martin Erat	.15	.40
208 Antti Miettinen	.15	.40
209 Ilya Bryzgalov	.20	.50
210 Cory Schneider	.20	.50
211 Tomas Fleischmann	.15	.40
212 Cody McLeod	.15	.40
213 Daniel Paille	.15	.40
214 Kris Draper	.15	.40
215 Chris Phillips	.15	.40
216 Kyle Brodziak	.15	.40
217 Patrick Dwyer	.15	.40
218 Tom Gilbert	.15	.40
219 Jarome Iginla	.25	.60
220 John Carlson	.30	.75
221 Sean O'Donnell	.15	.40
222 Daniel Winnik	.15	.40
223 Maxim Lapierre	.15	.40
224 Roberto Luongo	.25	.60
225 Niclas Bergfors	.20	.50
226 Vaclav Prospal	.15	.40
227 Matt Cooke	.15	.40
228 Jay Bouwmeester	.30	.75
229 Niclas Wallin	.15	.40
230 Steven Reinprecht	.15	.40
231 David Jones	.15	.40
232 Jaroslav Halak	.25	.60
233 Mikael Backlund	.15	.40
234 Bryan McCabe	.15	.40
235 Andy McDonald	.20	.50
236 Jordan Staal	.25	.60
237 Brad Richards	.25	.60
238 Milan Hejduk	.20	.50
239 Scott Clemmensen	.20	.50
240 Marian Gaborik	.30	.75
241 Nathan Horton	.20	.50
242 Zach Boychuk	.20	.50
243 Mattias Ohlund	.15	.40
244 Derek Morris	.15	.40
245 Erik Karlsson	.50	1.25
246 Daymond Langkow	.15	.40
247 Lee Stempniak	.15	.40
248 Cody Franson	.15	.40
249 Jordan Leopold	.15	.40
250 Nicklas Lidstrom	.25	.60
251 R.J. Umberger	.15	.40
252 Tomas Kopecky	.20	.50
253 Kris Russell	.15	.40
254 Keith Ballard	.15	.40
255 Wayne Simmonds	.30	.75
256 Tyler Myers	.25	.60
257 Patrick Sharp	.25	.60
258 Alex Auld	.20	.50
259 Arron Asham	.15	.40
260 Justin Williams	.20	.50
261 Chris Butler	.15	.40
262 Brian Campbell	.15	.40
263 Derek Dorsett	.15	.40
264 Ilya Kovalchuk	.25	.60
265 Andrei Markov	.25	.60
266 Brent Seabrook	.25	.60
267 Marc Savard	.15	.40
268 Rene Bourque	.15	.40
269 Tim Gleason	.15	.40
270 Shea Weber	.20	.50
271 Dan Hamhuis	.20	.50
272 Kristopher Letang	.25	.60
273 Vincent Lecavalier	.20	.50
274 Marian Hossa	.20	.50
275 Brad Richardson	.20	.50
276 Jarkko Ruutu	.15	.40
277 Chris Osgood	.25	.60
278 Benoit Pouliot	.15	.40
279 Alexander Steen	.25	.60
280 Shane Doan	.20	.50
281 Nicklas Backstrom	.40	1.00
282 Mike Komisarek	.15	.40
283 Kristian Huselius	.15	.40
284 Sheldon Souray	.15	.40
285 Craig Conroy	.15	.40
286 Alexander Ovechkin	1.00	2.50
287 Brandon Dubinsky	.20	.50
288 Greg Zanon	.15	.40
289 Jiri Hudler	.20	.50
290 James Neal	.25	.60
291 Joe Thornton	.25	.60
292 Todd White	.15	.40
293 Alex Pietrangelo	.20	.50
294 Matt Walker	.15	.40
295 Matt Hunwick	.15	.40
296 David Booth	.15	.40
297 Jason Blake	.15	.40
298 Pascal Dupuis	.15	.40
299 Curtis Glencross	.15	.40
300 Matt Carkner	.20	.50
301 Mike Knuble	.15	.40
302 Blake Comeau	.15	.40
303 Daniel Carcillo	.15	.40
304 Adrian Aucoin	.15	.40
305 Luke Schenn	.20	.50
306 Daniel Girardi	.15	.40
307 Paul Ranger	.15	.40
308 George Parros	.20	.50
309 Sean Avery	.20	.50
310 Matt Bradley	.15	.40
311 Trevor Daley	.15	.40
312 Sergei Kostitsyn	.15	.40
313 Jeff Carter	.25	.60
314 Craig Adams	.15	.40
315 Chris Drury	.20	.50
316 Duncan Keith	.25	.60
317 Martin St. Louis	.25	.60
318 Sergei Gonchar	.15	.40
319 Bryce Salvador	.15	.40
320 Dustin Penner	.15	.40
321 Chris Kunitz	.25	.60
322 Mikael Samuelsson	.15	.40
323 Kyle Quincey	.15	.40
324 Matt Cullen	.15	.40
325 Ryan Shannon	.15	.40
326 David Moss	.15	.40
327 Marc-Edouard Vlasic	.15	.40
328 Evander Kane	.25	.60
329 Brian Rafalski	.15	.40
330 Stephane Robidas	.15	.40
331 Cory Stillman	.15	.40
332 Zach Parise	.25	.60
333 Andrew Ladd	.25	.60
334 Jean-Sebastien Giguere	.20	.50
335 Joe Pavelski	.25	.60
336 Braydon Coburn	.15	.40
337 Dion Phaneuf	.25	.60
338 Milan Jurcina	.15	.40
339 Clarke MacArthur	.15	.40
340 Ethan Moreau	.15	.40
341 Chris Stewart	.20	.50
342 James Wisniewski	.15	.40
343 Alexei Ponikarovsky	.15	.40
344 Martin Biron	.20	.50
345 Dan Sexton	.20	.50
346 David Perron	.15	.40
347 Devin Setoguchi	.20	.50
348 Mike Richards	.25	.60
349 Colin Fraser	.15	.40
350 Brenden Morrow	.20	.50
351 Mike Modano	.40	1.00
352 Daniel Alfredsson	.25	.60
353 Mark Recchi	.30	.75
354 Karlis Skrastins	.15	.40
355 Andrew Brunette	.15	.40
356 Francis Bouillon	.15	.40
357 Barret Jackman	.15	.40
358 Manny Malhotra	.20	.50
359 Keith Yandle	.25	.60
360 Marc-Andre Fleury	.40	1.00
361 Jared Boll	.15	.40
362 Ryane Clowe	.15	.40
363 Antti Niemi	.20	.50
364 Colton Orr	.15	.40
365 Jason Pominville	.25	.60
366 Todd Bertuzzi	.20	.50
367 Nick Boynton	.15	.40
368 Tomas Vokoun	.20	.50
369 Mikko Koivu	.25	.60
370 Erik Cole	.20	.50
371 Johan Franzen	.25	.60
372 Steven Stamkos	.50	1.25
373 Kari Lehtonen	.20	.50
374 James van Riemsdyk	.40	1.00
375 Kurtis Foster	.15	.40
376 Paul Gaustad	.15	.40
377 Kent Huskins	.15	.40
378 Teddy Purcell	.25	.60
379 Brad Boyes	.15	.40
380 Chris Mason	.20	.50
381 Derick Brassard	.25	.60
382 Karl Alzner	.15	.40
383 Michal Rozsival	.15	.40
384 Petr Prucha	.15	.40
385 Patrick Kane	.50	1.25
386 David Clarkson	.15	.40
387 Jim Howard	.30	.75
388 Travis Moen	.15	.40
389 Jakub Voracek	.25	.60
390 John Mitchell	.15	.40
391 Evgeni Malkin	.75	2.00
392 Michael Ryder	.15	.40
393 Nick Foligno	.20	.50
394 Ryan Miller	.25	.60
395 Brett Clark	.15	.40
396 Mark Streit	.15	.40
397 Dustin Brown	.25	.60
398 Eric Staal	.30	.75
399 Toni Lydman	.15	.40
400 Roman Polak	.15	.40
401 Daniel Briere	.25	.60
402 Todd Marchant	.15	.40
403 Jason Chimera	.15	.40
404 Pascal Leclaire	.20	.50
405 Steve Ott	.20	.50
406 Ryan O'Reilly	.25	.60
407 John Scott	.15	.40
408 Mark Giordano	.20	.50
409 Mike Lundin	.15	.40
410 Tim Connolly	.15	.40
411 Olli Jokinen	.20	.50
412 Ryan Getzlaf	.40	1.00
413 Derek Roy	.25	.60
414 Kevin Bieksa	.20	.50
415 Dwayne Roloson	.20	.50
416 Pavel Kubina	.15	.40
417 Scott Gomez	.20	.50
418 Eric Fehr	.15	.40
419 Jonathan Quick	.40	1.00
420 Raffi Torres	.15	.40
421 Andrei Kostitsyn	.20	.50
422 Sergei Samsonov	.20	.50
423 Ryan Callahan	.25	.60
424 Steve Downie	.15	.40
425 Brent Burns	.30	.75
426 Jochen Hecht	.15	.40
427 Rob Scuderi	.15	.40
428 Matt Duchene	.25	.60
429 Chris Kelly	.20	.50
430 Matt Moulson	.20	.50
431 Doug Weight	.25	.60
432 Rostislav Olesz	.15	.40
433 Nick Schultz	.15	.40
434 Chris Neil	.15	.40
435 Steve Mason	.20	.50
436 Filip Kuba	.15	.40
437 Trent Hunter	.15	.40
438 Jussi Jokinen	.15	.40
439 Tim Thomas	.20	.50
440 Kris Versteeg	.20	.50
441 Patrik Elias	.25	.60
442 Zach Stortini	.15	.40
443 Kevin Klein	.15	.40
444 Kyle Okposo	.25	.60
445 Fredrik Sjostrom	.15	.40
446 Cam Ward	.25	.60
447 Dustin Boyd	.15	.40
448 Jason Demers	.15	.40
449 Joel Ward	.15	.40
450 Ed Jovanovski	.15	.40
451 Matt Beleskey	.20	.50
452 Nikita Filatov	.15	.40
453 Ryan Parent	.15	.40
454 Matt Greene	.15	.40
455 Alex Goligoski	.20	.50
456 Loui Eriksson	.20	.50
457 John Tavares	.50	1.25
458 Jeff Schultz	.15	.40
459 Antoine Vermette	.15	.40
460 Andrew Cogliano	.15	.40
461 Nikolai Khabibulin	.20	.50
462 Paul Martin	.15	.40
463 Nik Antropov	.20	.50
464 Niklas Kronwall	.15	.40
465 Jamie Benn	.30	.75
466 Hal Gill	.15	.40
467 Victor Hedman	.30	.75
468 Henrik Tallinder	.15	.40
469 Martin Hanzal	.15	.40
470 Anton Babchuk	.15	.40
471 Dan Cleary	.25	.60
472 Travis Zajac	.20	.50
473 Antero Niittymaki	.20	.50
474 Mike Cammalleri	.25	.60
475 Taylor Pyatt	.15	.40
476 Martin Havlat	.20	.50
477 Sean Bergenheim	.15	.40
478 Marc Staal	.25	.60
479 Willie Mitchell	.15	.40
480 Chris Pronger	.20	.50
481 Mike Fisher	.25	.60
482 Dennis Wideman	.15	.40
483 Henrik Sedin	.25	.60
484 Eric Brewer	.15	.40
485 Rick Nash	.25	.60
486 Rich Peverley	.25	.60
487 Rob Niedermayer	.15	.40
488 Carlo Colaiacovo	.15	.40
489 Peter Regin	.20	.50
490 Stephen Weiss	.20	.50
491 Brad Stuart	.15	.40
492 Mark Eaton	.15	.40
493 Patrice Bergeron	.30	.75
494 Bryan Little	.25	.60
495 Jason Strudwick	.15	.40
496 Checklist	.15	.40
497 Checklist	.15	.40
498 Checklist	.15	.40
499 Checklist	.15	.40
500 Checklist	.15	.40
501 Dana Tyrell RC	1.00	2.50
502 Jordan Caron RC	1.50	4.00
503 Nino Niederreiter RC	1.25	3.00
504 P.K. Subban RC	3.00	8.00
505 Justin Falk RC	.75	2.00
506 Brandon Pirri RC	1.00	2.50
507 Robin Lehner RC	2.00	5.00
508 Taylor Hall RC	4.00	10.00
509 Oliver Ekman-Larsson RC	1.50	4.00
510 Nazem Kadri RC	3.00	8.00
511 Marcus Johansson RC	1.50	4.00
512 Cam Fowler RC	1.25	3.00
513 Sergei Bobrovsky RC	2.50	6.00
514 Kyle Clifford RC	1.00	2.50
515 Jared Cowen RC	1.00	2.50
516 Brandon Yip RC	1.00	2.50
517 Matt Taormina RC	1.00	2.50
518 Jamie McBain RC	1.00	2.50
519 Jordan Eberle RC	2.50	6.00
520 Alexander Burmistrov RC	1.00	2.50
521 Dustin Tokarski RC	1.00	2.50
522 Philip Larsen RC	1.00	2.50
523 Nick Spaling RC	1.00	2.50
524 Jake Muzzin RC	1.00	2.50
525 Ryan Reaves RC	1.25	3.00
526 Maxim Noreau RC	.75	2.00
527 Zach Hamill RC	1.00	2.50
528 Henrik Karlsson RC	1.00	2.50
529 Jacob Josefson RC	1.00	2.50
530 Luke Adam RC	1.00	2.50
531 Eric Tangradi RC	1.00	2.50
532 Alexander Urbom RC	1.00	2.50
533 Alexander Vasyunov RC	1.00	2.50
534 Matt Martin RC	1.50	4.00
535 Tommy Wingels RC	1.00	2.50
536 Tyler Seguin RC	4.00	10.00
537 Alex Plante RC	1.00	2.50
538 Derek Stepan RC	2.00	5.00
539 Zac Dalpe RC	1.00	2.50
540 T.J. Brodie RC	1.00	2.50
541 Nick Leddy RC	1.00	2.50
542 Mark Olver RC	1.00	2.50
543 Anders Lindback RC	1.00	2.50
544 Nick Johnson RC	.75	2.00
545 Cody Almond RC	1.00	2.50
546 Nick Palmieri RC	1.00	2.50
547 Brayden Schenn RC	1.50	4.00
548 Jeff Skinner RC	2.00	5.00
549 Evan Brophey RC	1.00	2.50
550 Magnus Paajarvi RC	1.25	3.00
551 Dominik Hasek L	1.25	3.00
552 Mark Messier L	1.25	3.00
553 Luc Robitaille L	.75	2.00
554 Gilbert Perreault L	.75	2.00
555 Doug Gilmour L	1.00	2.50
556 Denis Savard L	1.00	2.50
557 Markus Naslund L	.60	1.50
558 Guy Lafleur L	1.00	2.50
559 Jari Kurri L	.75	2.00
560 Bobby Hull L	.75	2.00
561 Phil Esposito L	1.25	3.00
562 Mike Bossy L	.75	2.00
563 Stan Mikita L	1.00	2.50
564 Ray Bourque L	1.25	3.00
565 Johnny Bucyk L	.75	2.00
566 Marcel Dionne L	1.00	2.50
567 Larry Robinson L	.75	2.00
568 Red Kelly L	.75	2.00
569 Tony Esposito L	.75	2.00
570 Grant Fuhr L	.75	2.00
571 Peter Stastny L	.60	1.50
572 Brian Leetch L	.75	2.00
573 Borje Salming L	.75	2.00
574 Frank Mahovlich L	.75	2.00
575 Andy Bathgate L	.75	2.00
576 Al MacInnis L	.75	2.00
577 Ted Lindsay L	.75	2.00
578 Darryl Sittler L	.60	1.50
579 Alex Delvecchio L	.60	1.50
580 Brent Sutter L	.50	1.25
581 Adam Oates L	.75	2.00
582 Dale Hawerchuk L	1.00	2.50
583 Joe Mullen L	.60	1.50
584 Bob Bourne L	.50	1.25
585 Ron Hextall L	1.00	2.50
586 Guy Carbonneau L	.75	2.00
587 Doug Wilson L	.60	1.50
588 Butch Bouchard L	.60	1.50
589 Dave Schultz L	.75	2.00
590 Clark Gillies L	.75	2.00
591 Cam Neely L	.75	2.00
592 Rogie Vachon L	1.00	2.50
593 Johnny Bower L	1.00	2.50
594 Patrick Roy L	2.00	5.00
595 Steve Yzerman L	2.00	5.00
596 Mario Lemieux L	2.50	6.00
597 Bobby Orr L	2.50	6.00
598 Gordie Howe L	2.00	5.00
599 Wayne Gretzky L	4.00	10.00
600 Rookies Checklist	.15	.40
601 Cory Emmerton RC	1.25	3.00
602 Eric Wellwood RC	1.25	3.00
603 Evgeny Grachev RC	1.00	2.50
604 Ian Cole RC	1.00	2.50
605 Jacob Markstrom RC	1.50	4.00
606 Jan Mursak RC	2.00	5.00
607 Keith Aulie RC	1.00	2.50
608 Kevin Shattenkirk RC	2.00	5.00
609 Linus Omark RC	2.50	6.00
610 Marcel Mueller RC	1.25	3.00
611 Mats Zuccarello RC	1.50	4.00
612 Matt Calvert RC	1.50	4.00
613 Matt Hackett RC	1.25	3.00
614 Mattias Tedenby RC	.75	2.00
615 Patrice Cormier RC	1.25	3.00
616 Ryan McDonagh RC	2.50	6.00
617 Stefan Della Rovere RC	1.00	2.50
618 Thomas McCollum RC	1.25	3.00
619 Tomas Tatar RC	2.00	5.00
620 Travis Hamonic RC	1.25	3.00

2010-11 O-Pee-Chee Retro

Card	Low	High
COMPLETE SET (620)	200.00	300.00
COMP.UPD.SET (20)	20.00	50.00
*RETRO 1-500: 2X TO 5X BASE		
*RETRO ROOKIES 501-550: .5X TO 1.2X		
*RETRO LEGENDS 551-600: .8X TO 2X		
1-600 RETRO ODDS 1 PER PACK		
*RETRO UPD.ROOKIES 601-620: .5X TO 1.2X		
601-620 UPDATE ODDS 1:36H 1:72R		
194 Corey Crawford	1.50	4.00
281 Nicklas Backstrom	2.00	5.00

2010-11 O-Pee-Chee Retro Black Rainbow

Card	Low	High
*BLACK RAINBOW 1-500: 6X TO 15X BASE		
*BLACK RAIN.501-550: 1.2X TO 3X BASE RC		
*BLACK RAIN.551-600: 2.5X TO 6X BASE		
*BLACK RAIN.601-620: 1.2X TO 3X BASE RC		
STATED PRINT RUN 100 SER.#'d SETS		
194 Corey Crawford	5.00	12.00
281 Nicklas Backstrom	6.00	15.00
504 P.K. Subban	30.00	80.00
508 Taylor Hall	30.00	80.00
519 Jordan Eberle	40.00	80.00
536 Tyler Seguin	40.00	80.00

2010-11 O-Pee-Chee Retro Rainbow

Card	Low	High
*RAINBOW 1-500: 2.5X TO 6X BASE		
*RAINBOW 501-550: .6X TO 1.5X BASE RC		
*RAINBOW 551-600: 1X TO 2.5X BASE		
(1-600) STATED ODDS 1:4		
*RAINBOW 601-620: .6X TO 1.5X BASE RC		
(601-620) STATED ODDS 1:144H 1:288R		
194 Corey Crawford	2.00	5.00
281 Nicklas Backstrom	2.50	6.00

2010-11 O-Pee-Chee All Rookie Team

Card	Low	High
COMPLETE SET (6)	6.00	15.00
STATED ODDS 1:4		
AR1 Jim Howard	1.00	2.50
AR2 Tyler Myers	.75	2.00
AR3 Michael Del Zotto	.60	1.50
AR4 John Tavares	1.50	4.00
AR5 Matt Duchene	.75	2.00
AR6 Niclas Bergfors	.60	1.50

2010-11 O-Pee-Chee Box Bottoms

Card	Low	High
COMPLETE SET (16)	5.00	12.00
PANEL: TWS/MLK/TVRS/MARL	1.25	3.00
PANEL: CRSBY/STMK/DCH/KAD	1.50	4.00
PANEL: OVCH/KNE/BRDR/DGH	1.50	4.00
PANEL: LNGO/IGN/DATS/GRN	1.25	3.00
NNO Jonathan Toews	.50	1.25
NNO Evgeni Malkin	.75	2.00
NNO John Tavares	.50	1.25
NNO Patrick Marleau	.25	.60
NNO Sidney Crosby	1.00	2.50
NNO Steven Stamkos	.50	1.25
NNO Matt Duchene	.25	.60
NNO Nazim Kadri	.60	1.50
NNO Alexander Ovechkin	1.00	2.50
NNO Patrick Kane	.50	1.25
NNO Martin Brodeur	.50	1.25
NNO Drew Doughty	.25	.60
NNO Roberto Luongo	.25	.60
NNO Jarome Iginla	.25	.60
NNO Pavel Datsyuk	.30	.75
NNO Mike Green	.25	.60

2010-11 O-Pee-Chee In Action

Card	Low	High
COMP.SET w/o SPs (30)	75.00	150.00
STATED ODDS 1:36		
SP STATED ODDS 1:360		
IA1 Pavel Datsyuk	4.00	10.00
IA2 Alexandre Burrows	3.00	8.00
IA3 Alexander Semin	3.00	8.00
IA4 Tomas Plekanec	3.00	8.00
IA5 Jarome Iginla	3.00	8.00
IA6 Chris Pronger	2.50	6.00
IA7 Marc-Andre Fleury	5.00	12.00
IA8 Ilya Bryzgalov	2.50	6.00
IA9 Carey Price	12.00	30.00
IA10 Henrik Lundqvist	5.00	12.00
IA11 Jim Howard	4.00	10.00
IA12 Matt Duchene	3.00	8.00
IA13 Anze Kopitar	5.00	12.00
IA14 Drew Doughty	3.00	8.00
IA15 Nicklas Backstrom	5.00	12.00
IA16 Mike Green	3.00	8.00
IA17 Martin St. Louis	3.00	8.00
IA18 Brad Richards	3.00	8.00
IA19 Patrick Marleau	3.00	8.00
IA20 Ryan Getzlaf	5.00	12.00
IA21 Phil Kessel	4.00	10.00
IA22 Joe Thornton	3.00	8.00
IA23 Mike Richards	3.00	8.00
IA24 Dustin Penner	2.00	5.00
IA25 Paul Stastny	3.00	8.00
IA26 Daniel Alfredsson	3.00	8.00
IA27 Daniel Sedin	3.00	8.00
IA28 Mikko Koivu	3.00	8.00
IA29 Eric Staal	4.00	10.00
IA30 Jeff Carter	3.00	8.00
IA31 Rick Nash SP	6.00	15.00
IA32 Ryan Miller SP	6.00	15.00
IA33 Jonathan Toews SP	12.00	30.00
IA34 Henrik Sedin SP	6.00	15.00
IA35 Steven Stamkos SP	12.00	30.00
IA36 Patrick Kane SP	12.00	30.00
IA37 Marian Gaborik SP	8.00	20.00
IA38 Martin Brodeur SP	12.00	30.00
IA39 Alexander Ovechkin SP	25.00	60.00
IA40 Sidney Crosby SP	25.00	60.00

2010-11 O-Pee-Chee Season Highlights

Card	Low	High
COMPLETE SET (15)	12.00	30.00
STATED ODDS 1:4		
SH1 Nicklas Lidstrom	.75	2.00
SH2 Alexander Ovechkin	3.00	8.00
SH3 Keith Tkachuk	.75	2.00
SH4 Mike Cammalleri	.75	2.00
SH5 Paul Kariya	1.00	2.50
SH6 Martin Brodeur	1.50	4.00
SH7 Scott Niedermayer	.75	2.00
SH8 Teemu Selanne	1.50	4.00
SH9 Martin Brodeur	1.50	4.00
SH10 Sidney Crosby	3.00	8.00
SH11 Henrik Sedin	.75	2.00
SH12 Alexander Ovechkin	3.00	8.00
SH13 Mike Richards	.75	2.00
SH14 Steven Stamkos	1.50	4.00
SH15 Patrick Kane	1.50	4.00

2010-11 O-Pee-Chee Signatures

STATED ODDS 1:144
OSAC Andrew Cogliano 5.00 12.00
OSAM Al MacInnis SP 50.00 100.00
OSAO Alexander Ovechkin SP 40.00 100.00
OSBA Barry Melrose 6.00 15.00
OSBH Bobby Hull SP 15.00 40.00
OSBL Brian Leetch SP 25.00 60.00
OSBM Brad Marchand 12.00 30.00
OSBO Bobby Orr SP 125.00 200.00
OSBR Bobby Ryan 8.00 20.00
OSBS Bobby Sanguinetti 5.00 12.00
OSCH Christian Hanson 5.00 12.00
OSCS Cory Schneider 6.00 15.00
OSCW Colin Wilson 6.00 15.00
OSDC Daniel Carcillo 5.00 12.00
OSDL Dan LaCosta 5.00 12.00
OSDO Don Cherry SP 25.00 60.00
OSDP Daniel Paille SP 15.00 40.00
OSDS Devin Setoguchi 6.00 15.00
OSEK Erik Karlsson 15.00 40.00
OSET Eric Tangradi 4.00 10.00
OSEV Evander Kane 8.00 20.00
OSGI Jean-Sebastien Giguere SP 25.00 60.00
OSJB Johnny Bucyk 8.00 20.00
OSJE Jhonas Enroth 8.00 20.00
OSJG Jonas Gustavsson
OSJI Jarome Iginla 12.00 30.00
OSJV James van Riemsdyk 12.00 30.00
OSKC Kris Chucko 5.00 12.00
OSMA Andrei Markov 8.00 20.00
OSMD Matt Duchene 8.00 20.00
OSMF Mark Fraser 5.00 12.00
OSMG Matt Gilroy 5.00 12.00
OSMH Matt Hendricks 5.00 12.00
OSMN Michal Neuvirth 6.00 15.00
OSMR Mike Ribeiro 6.00 15.00
OSMS Michael Sauer 5.00 12.00
OSNB Nicklas Backstrom 12.00 30.00
OSNH Nathan Horton 6.00 15.00
OSNK Nazem Kadri 25.00 60.00
OSPE Phil Esposito SP 15.00 40.00
OSPK Patrick Kane 25.00 60.00
OSPS P.K. Subban 12.00 30.00
OSRH Riku Helenius 5.00 12.00
OSRO Ryan O'Reilly 8.00 20.00
OSSC Sidney Crosby SP 100.00 200.00
OSSG Simon Gagne 10.00 25.00
OSSH Sergei Shirokov 6.00 15.00
OSSL Marc Staal 8.00 20.00
OSSS Steven Stamkos SP 20.00 50.00
OSST Peter Stastny 12.00 30.00
OSSV Marek Svatos 5.00 12.00
OSSW Chris Stewart 6.00 15.00
OSSY Steve Yzerman SP 60.00 120.00
OSTM Tyler Myers 8.00 20.00
OSVH Victor Hedman 10.00 25.00
OSWG Wayne Gretzky SP
OSYW Yannick Weber 6.00 15.00

2010-11 O-Pee-Chee Souvenirs

STATED ODDS 1:144
SV1ST Kne/Stam/Crsby/Tvres 25.00 60.00
SVATL Kane/Antr/Enstm/Byfg 6.00 15.00
SVCAR Jokin/Staal/Wrd/Cole 10.00 25.00
SVCBJ Mason/Nash/Brsrd/Vrck 6.00 15.00
SVCGY Bou/Stajan/Iginla/Kiprsff 8.00 20.00
SVCHI Hosa/Tws/Seabrk/Kne 15.00 40.00
SVDRW Lids/Holms/Osgd/Zetter 8.00 20.00
SVEDM Cogli/Horcf/Khbib/Ggnr 5.00 12.00
SVFLA Booth/Vokn/Stillmn/Weiss 8.00 20.00
SVGR8 Yzer/Gretzky/Mesr/Lem 30.00 80.00
SVLAK Anze/Johnsn/Brwn/Dghty 10.00 25.00
SVMTL Hamr/Price/Plekan/Kostits 25.00 60.00
SVNYR Lundq/Staal/Drury/Gabrik 6.00 15.00
SVRUS Ovch/Semin/Kvlck/Kvalv 25.00 60.00
SVSJS Setog/Thrn/Heat/Pavlsk 6.00 15.00
SVSTL Jckmn/Kriya/Jhnsn/Back 8.00 20.00
SVSWE Lids/Zettr/Bckstrm/Lndq 10.00 25.00
SVTML McDon/Salm/Sittler/Mahv 10.00 25.00
SVUSA Parise/Backs/Keslr/Kane 12.00 30.00
SVVAN Tambl/Sedin/Luong/Sdin 6.00 15.00
SV2002 Bowman/Holms/Yzer/Lids 15.00 40.00
SVBEES Hortn/Thmas/Rask/Chra 15.00 40.00
SVBUFF Miller/Roy/Stafford/Vanek 8.00 20.00
SVCAPS Backs/Semin/Ovch/Green 15.00 40.00
SVHABS Price/Kostits/Hamr/Gionta 10.00 25.00
SVLEAF Kessl/Kaberl/Gigre/Kulem 12.00 30.00
SVPENS Fleury/Malkn/Crsby/Staal 20.00 50.00
SVPITT Mullen/Lemx/Crsby/Malkn 20.00 50.00
SVPRED Webr/Dumnt/Rin/Lgwnd 8.00 20.00
SVSCUP Carter/Rchrds/Kane/Tws 10.00 25.00
SVSENS Kovlv/Folig/Leclre/Spez 8.00 20.00
SVWILD Backs/Koivu/Bouch/Havlt 10.00 25.00

2010-11 O-Pee-Chee Stat Kings

COMPLETE SET (20) 12.00 30.00
STATED ODDS 1:4
SK1 Sidney Crosby 3.00 8.00
SK2 Steven Stamkos 1.50 4.00
SK3 Henrik Sedin .75 2.00
SK4 Henrik Sedin .75 2.00
SK5 Zenon Konopka .60 1.50
SK6 Steven Stamkos 1.50 4.00
SK7 Alexander Ovechkin 3.00 8.00
SK8 Dany Heatley .60 1.50
SK9 Mike Green .75 2.00
SK10 Mike Green .75 2.00
SK11 Matt Duchene .75 2.00
SK12 Jeff Schultz .50 1.25
SK13 Cal Clutterbuck .75 2.00
SK14 Daniel Briere .75 2.00
SK15 Mike Cammalleri .75 2.00
SK16 Martin Brodeur 1.50 4.00
SK17 Tuukka Rask .75 2.00
SK18 Tuukka Rask .75 2.00
SK19 Martin Brodeur 1.50 4.00
SK20 Craig Anderson .75 2.00

2010-11 O-Pee-Chee Team Leaders

COMPLETE SET (30) 15.00 40.00
STATED ODDS 1:4
TL1 Hiller/Ryan/Getzlaf 1.25 3.00
TL2 Hedberg/Kovalchuk/Enstrom .75 2.00
TL3 Rask/Chara/Sturm .75 2.00
TL4 Connolly/Miller/Vanek .75 2.00
TL5 Iginla/Iginla/Kiprusoff .75 2.00
TL6 Staal/Ward/Jokinen 1.00 2.50
TL7 Niemi/Kane/Kane 1.50 4.00
TL8 Anderson/Stastny/Stewart .75 2.00
TL9 Huselius/Mason/Nash .75 2.00
TL10 Turco/Eriksson/Richards .75 2.00
TL11 Datsyuk/Howard/Zetterberg 1.00 2.50
TL12 Penner/Penner/Deslauriers .50 1.25
TL13 Horton/Vokoun/Weiss .60 1.50
TL14 Kopitar/Kopitar/Quick 1.25 3.00
TL15 Latendresse/Backstrom/Koivu .75 2.00
TL16 Gomez/Gionta/Halak .75 2.00
TL17 Sullivan/Rinne/Hornqvist 1.00 2.50
TL18 Parise/Parise/Brodeur 1.50 4.00
TL19 Roloson/Moulson/Streit .60 1.50
TL20 Gaborik/Gaborik/Lundqvist 1.25 3.00
TL21 Elliott/Fisher/Alfredsson .75 2.00
TL22 Carter/Pronger/Leighton .75 2.00
TL23 Vrbata/Doan/Bryzgalov .60 1.50
TL24 Fleury/Crosby/Crosby 3.00 8.00
TL25 Marleau/Thornton/Nabokov .75 2.00
TL26 Mason/Steen/McDonald .75 2.00
TL27 Stamkos/Niittymaki/St. Louis 1.50 4.00
TL28 Kessel/Kaberle/Gustavsson 1.00 2.50
TL29 Sedin/Luongo/Burrows .75 2.00
TL30 Backstrom/Ovechkin/Theodore 3.00 8.00

2010-11 O-Pee-Chee Trophy Winners

COMPLETE SET (13) 10.00 25.00
STATED ODDS 1:4
TW1 Henrik Sedin .75 2.00
TW2 Alexander Ovechkin 3.00 8.00
TW3 S.Stamkos/S.Crosby 3.00 8.00
TW4 Duncan Keith .75 2.00
TW5 Ryan Miller .75 2.00
TW6 Tyler Myers .75 2.00
TW7 Pavel Datsyuk 1.00 2.50
TW8 Martin St. Louis .75 2.00
TW9 Jose Theodore .75 2.00
TW10 Martin Brodeur 1.50 4.00
TW11 Shane Doan .60 1.50
TW12 Jonathan Toews 1.50 4.00
TW13 Henrik Sedin .75 2.00

2010-11 O-Pee-Chee Winter Classic

COMPLETE SET (16) 10.00 25.00
STATED ODDS 1:4
WC1 Daniel Briere .75 2.00
WC2 Scott Hartnell .75 2.00
WC3 Jeff Carter .75 2.00
WC4 Mike Richards .75 2.00
WC5 Chris Pronger .60 1.50
WC6 Daniel Carcillo .50 1.25
WC7 Michael Leighton .60 1.50
WC8 B.Clarke/B.Orr 2.50 6.00
WC9 Mark Recchi 1.00 2.50
WC10 Marco Sturm .50 1.25
WC11 Zdeno Chara .60 1.50
WC12 Patrice Bergeron 1.00 2.50
WC13 Marc Savard .50 1.25
WC14 David Krejci .75 2.00
WC15 Shawn Thornton .50 1.25
WC16 Tim Thomas .60 1.50

2011-12 O-Pee-Chee

COMPLETE SET (600) 60.00 120.00
COMP.SET w/o SPs (500) 25.00 60.00
501-600 STATED ODDS 1:2
601-610 UPDATE ODDS 1:20 SER.2 UD H
611-625 UPDATE ODDS 1:14 SER.2 UD H
1 Scott Hartnell .25 .60
2 Paul Mara .15 .40
3 Marian Hossa .20 .50
4 Duncan Keith .25 .60
5 Henrik Zetterberg .30 .75
6 Maxime Talbot .20 .50
7 Brian Campbell .15 .40
8 Todd Bertuzzi .20 .50
9 J.P. Dumont .15 .40
10 Claude Giroux .25 .60
11 Chris Phillips .15 .40
12 Dan Cleary .25 .60
13 Jordan Staal .25 .60
14 Ryan Kesler .25 .60
15 George Parros .20 .50
16 Joe Thornton .25 .60
17 Johan Franzen .25 .60
18 Patrick Kane .50 1.25
19 Mike Richards .25 .60
20 Patrick Sharp .25 .60
21 Jeff Carter .25 .60
22 Dan Boyle .20 .50
23 Daniel Sedin .25 .60
24 Henrik Sedin .25 .60
25 Eric Staal .30 .75
26 Pascal Dupuis .15 .40
27 Olli Jokinen .20 .50
28 Guillaume Latendresse .20 .50
29 Jonathan Toews .50 1.25
30 Kris Versteeg .20 .50
31 Roberto Luongo .25 .60
32 Patrick Marleau .25 .60
33 Martin St. Louis .25 .60
34 Saku Koivu .25 .60
35 Cam Ward .25 .60
36 Tomas Holmstrom .15 .40
37 Antti Niemi .20 .50
38 Matt Cullen .15 .40
39 Raffi Torres .15 .40
40 Tim Thomas .25 .60
41 Jarome Iginla .25 .60
42 Joe Pavelski .25 .60
43 Fernando Pisani .15 .40
44 Chris Drury .20 .50
45 Brian Gionta .20 .50
46 Ryan Smyth .20 .50
47 Alexander Ovechkin 1.00 2.50
48 Daniel Briere .25 .60
49 Marc-Andre Fleury .40 1.00
50 Sidney Crosby 1.00 2.50
51 Jonas Hiller .20 .50
52 Adam McQuaid .15 .40
53 Steve Ott .20 .50
54 Andrei Loktionov .20 .50
55 Erik Cole .20 .50
56 Alec Martinez .15 .40
57 Lauri Korpikoski .15 .40
58 Keith Yandle .25 .60
59 Jay Bouwmeester .25 .60
60 Jay McClement .15 .40
61 Toni Lydman .15 .40
62 Brian Elliott .20 .50
63 Shawn Horcoff .15 .40
64 Devan Dubnyk .25 .60
65 Nate Thompson .15 .40
66 Douglas Murray .15 .40
67 Matt Hendricks .15 .40
68 Nick Schultz .15 .40
69 Jamie McBain .15 .40
70 Jannik Hansen .20 .50
71 Matt Calvert .20 .50
72 Victor Hedman .30 .75
73 Shea Weber .20 .50
74 David Perron .15 .40
75 David Clarkson .15 .40
76 Travis Zajac .20 .50
77 Michael Grabner .20 .50
78 Kevin Bieksa .20 .50
79 Viktor Stalberg .15 .40
80 Jim Howard .25 .60
81 Ryan McDonagh .25 .60
82 Valtteri Filppula .25 .60
83 Chris Pronger .20 .50
84 Ian White .20 .50
85 Tomas Kaberle .15 .40
86 Jason Pominville .20 .50
87 Filip Kuba .15 .40
88 Clarke MacArthur .15 .40
89 Niclas Bergfors .20 .50
90 Ron Hainsey .15 .40
91 Bobby Butler .20 .50
92 Jeff Halpern .15 .40
93 James Reimer .25 .60
94 Jamie Benn .30 .75
95 Dustin Brown .25 .60
96 Jonathan Quick .40 1.00
97 Mikkel Boedker .15 .40
98 Michal Rozsival .15 .40
99 T.J. Galiardi .20 .50
100 John-Michael Liles .15 .40
101 Jordan Eberle .25 .60
102 Ryan Whitney .15 .40
103 Torrey Mitchell .15 .40
104 David Booth .15 .40
105 Mathieu Garon .20 .50
106 Alexander Edler .15 .40
107 John Carlson .30 .75
108 Mike Santorelli .15 .40
109 Nick Spaling .15 .40
110 B.J. Crombeen .15 .40
111 Nikita Nikitin .15 .40
112 Adam Mair .15 .40
113 Dennis Wideman .15 .40
114 Trent Hunter .15 .40
115 Radek Martinek .15 .40
116 Niklas Kronwall .20 .50
117 Ryan Callahan .25 .60
118 Jack Skille .20 .50
119 James van Riemsdyk .25 .60
120 Daniel Paille .15 .40
121 Drew Stafford .25 .60
122 Mike Weber .15 .40
123 Mikhail Grabovski .20 .50
124 Brett Lebda .15 .40
125 Jim Slater .15 .40
126 P.K. Subban .50 1.25
127 Ryan Shannon .15 .40
128 Adam Burish .15 .40
129 Tuomo Ruutu .20 .50
130 Kyle Clifford .15 .40
131 Tom Poti .15 .40
132 Michal Handzus .15 .40
133 Sean Bergenheim .15 .40
134 Ryan Getzlaf .40 1.00
135 Eric Belanger .15 .40
136 Vincent Lecavalier .20 .50
137 Mark Giordano .20 .50
138 Ryan O'Reilly .25 .60
139 Scott Clemmensen .20 .50
140 Joni Pitkanen .20 .50
141 Brandon McMillan .15 .40
142 Devin Setoguchi .20 .50
143 Rene Bourque .15 .40
144 Martin Havlat .20 .50
145 Alexander Semin .25 .60
146 Jared Boll .15 .40
147 Fedor Tyutin .15 .40
148 Cody Franson .15 .40
149 Marty Reasoner .15 .40
150 Ian Cole .15 .40
151 Dmitry Kulikov .15 .40
152 Martin Brodeur .50 1.25
153 Travis Hamonic .20 .50
154 Niklas Hjalmarsson .15 .40
155 Brandon Prust .15 .40
156 Pavel Datsyuk .30 .75
157 Evgeni Malkin .75 2.00
158 David Krejci .25 .60
159 Derek Roy .20 .50
160 Sergei Gonchar .15 .40
161 Braden Holtby .50 1.25
162 Nazem Kadri .40 1.00
163 Andrew Ladd .25 .60
164 Dustin Byfuglien .25 .60
165 Ondrej Pavelec .25 .60
166 Michal Neuvirth .20 .50
167 Travis Moen .15 .40
168 Tyler Kennedy .15 .40
169 Kari Lehtonen .20 .50
170 Steve Downie .15 .40
171 Anze Kopitar .40 1.00
172 Shane Doan .20 .50
173 Lubomir Visnovsky .15 .40
174 Jeff Skinner .25 .60
175 Cory Sarich .15 .40
176 Cam Fowler .20 .50
177 Matt Duchene .25 .60
178 David Jones .15 .40
179 Corey Perry .25 .60
180 Ryan Malone .15 .40
181 Ales Hemsky .20 .50
182 James Neal .25 .60
183 Dustin Penner .20 .50
184 Andrew Brunette .15 .40
185 Luca Sbisa .20 .50
186 Mikko Koivu .20 .50
187 Sami Salo .15 .40
188 Troy Brouwer .20 .50
189 R.J. Umberger .15 .40
190 Martin Erat .15 .40
191 Colin Wilson .20 .50
192 Patrik Berglund .20 .50
193 Patric Hornqvist .20 .50
194 Ty Conklin .20 .50
195 Zach Parise .25 .60
196 Colin White .15 .40
197 Josh Bailey .20 .50
198 Taylor Pyatt .15 .40
199 Artem Anisimov .20 .50
200 Brian Rafalski .15 .40
201 Wojtek Wolski .15 .40
202 Michael Sauer .15 .40
203 Jiri Hudler .20 .50
204 Kimmo Timonen .15 .40
205 Chris Kunitz .25 .60
206 Brent Johnson .20 .50
207 Zdeno Chara .25 .60
208 Tim Connolly .15 .40
209 Jhonas Enroth .25 .60
210 Tyler Bozak .25 .60
211 Jason Arnott .20 .50
212 Nik Antropov .20 .50
213 Zach Bogosian .20 .50
214 Jaroslav Spacek .15 .40
215 Chris Neil .15 .40
216 Antti Miettinen .15 .40
217 Loui Eriksson .20 .50
218 Wayne Simmonds .30 .75
219 Martin Hanzal .15 .40
220 Matt Stajan .20 .50
221 Milan Hejduk .20 .50
222 Jiri Tlusty .20 .50
223 Andrew Cogliano .15 .40
224 Kyle Quincey .15 .40
225 Joe Corvo .15 .40
226 Gilbert Brule .25 .60
227 Bobby Ryan .25 .60
228 Trevor Daley .15 .40
229 Jarret Stoll .20 .50
230 Ray Whitney .20 .50
231 Robyn Regehr .15 .40
232 Kevin Porter .15 .40
233 Brandon Sutter .20 .50
234 Brandon Yip .15 .40
235 Steven Stamkos .50 1.25
236 Sam Gagner .20 .50
237 Francois Beauchemin .15 .40
238 Cory Stillman .15 .40
239 Paul Stastny .25 .60
240 Dominic Moore .15 .40
241 Alexandre Burrows .25 .60
242 Alex Tanguay .15 .40
243 Marc-Andre Bergeron .15 .40
244 Cody Hodgson .60 1.50
245 Kurtis Foster .15 .40
246 Jussi Jokinen .15 .40
247 Michael Frolik .15 .40
248 Derick Brassard .25 .60
249 Evgeny Dadonov .20 .50
250 Rick Nash .25 .60
251 Luke Schenn .20 .50
252 Alexander Burmistrov .20 .50
253 Jason Chimera .15 .40
254 Anthony Stewart .15 .40
255 Marcus Johansson .20 .50
256 Brooks Laich .15 .40
257 Mathieu Perreault .20 .50
258 Roman Hamrlik .20 .50
259 Daniel Alfredsson .25 .60
260 Tomas Plekanec .25 .60
261 Jose Theodore .25 .60
262 Manny Malhotra .20 .50
263 Dave Bolland .20 .50
264 Jakub Voracek .25 .60
265 Shawn Matthias .15 .40
266 Kris Russell .15 .40
267 Francis Bouillon .15 .40
268 Alex Pietrangelo .20 .50
269 Mattias Tedenby .15 .40
270 Zenon Konopka .20 .50
271 Al Montoya .15 .40
272 Brad Stuart .15 .40
273 Mike Knuble .15 .40
274 Braydon Coburn .15 .40
275 Karl Alzner .15 .40
276 Jochen Hecht .15 .40
277 Dwayne Roloson .20 .50
278 Bryan Little .25 .60
279 Carey Price .75 2.00
280 Benoit Pouliot .15 .40
281 Teemu Selanne .50 1.25
282 Evander Kane .25 .60
283 Niklas Hagman .15 .40
284 Tim Gleason .15 .40
285 Nick Leddy .15 .40
286 Erik Johnson .15 .40
287 Derek Dorsett .15 .40
288 Mike Ribeiro .20 .50
289 Nicklas Lidstrom .25 .60
290 Drew Doughty .25 .60
291 Dennis Seidenberg .20 .50
292 Derek Stepan .25 .60
293 Dion Phaneuf .25 .60
294 Eric Nystrom .15 .40
295 Erik Karlsson .50 1.25
296 Blake Comeau .15 .40
297 Blake Wheeler .50 1.25
298 Brad Boyes .15 .40
299 Brandon Dubinsky .20 .50
300 Miikka Kiprusoff .25 .60
301 Daniel Winnik .15 .40
302 Adrian Aucoin .15 .40
303 Alex Goligoski .20 .50
304 Alexander Steen .25 .60
305 Mason Raymond .20 .50
306 Mats Zuccarello .25 .60
307 Matt Carkner .20 .50
308 Mike Fisher .25 .60
309 Nicklas Backstrom .40 1.00
310 Brenden Morrow .20 .50
311 Niklas Backstrom .25 .60
312 Nikolai Kulemin .25 .60
313 Radim Vrbata .20 .50
314 Oliver Ekman-Larsson .25 .60
315 Andrej Meszaros .15 .40
316 Anders Lindback .20 .50
317 Andreas Nodl .15 .40
318 Antero Niittymaki .20 .50
319 Brent Burns .30 .75
320 Brent Seabrook .25 .60
321 Brian Boyle .15 .40
322 Brian Lee .20 .50
323 Brooks Orpik .20 .50
324 Michal Repik .15 .40
325 Stephane Robidas .15 .40
326 Jonathan Bernier .25 .60
327 Tomas Fleischmann .15 .40
328 Teddy Purcell .25 .60
329 Ladislav Smid .15 .40
330 Cal Clutterbuck .25 .60
331 Logan Couture .25 .60
332 Mikael Backlund .25 .60
333 Christian Ehrhoff .15 .40
334 Antoine Vermette .15 .40
335 Cal O'Reilly .15 .40
336 Carlo Colaiacovo .15 .40
337 Rod Pelley .15 .40
338 Kyle Okposo .25 .60
339 Patrick Eaves .15 .40
340 Henrik Lundqvist .30 .75
341 Matt Carle .20 .50
342 Eric Tangradi .15 .40
343 Nathan Horton .25 .60
344 Jamal Mayers .15 .40
345 Mike Komisarek .20 .50
346 Milan Michalek .15 .40
347 Jamie Langenbrunner .15 .40
348 Justin Williams .20 .50
349 Lee Stempniak .15 .40
350 Chad LaRose .15 .40
351 Dana Tyrell .15 .40
352 Taylor Hall .50 1.25
353 John Madden .15 .40
354 Ryane Clowe .15 .40
355 Marek Zidlicky .15 .40
356 Keith Ballard .15 .40
357 Steve Mason .20 .50
358 Ryan Suter .15 .40
359 Jason Garrison .15 .40
360 Johan Hedberg .20 .50
361 P.A. Parenteau .15 .40
362 Marian Gaborik .30 .75
363 Darroll Powe .15 .40
364 Tyler Seguin .50 1.25
365 Chris Butler .15 .40
366 Carl Gunnarsson .15 .40
367 Jason Spezza .25 .60
368 Josh Gorges .15 .40
369 Pekka Rinne .30 .75
370 Patrice Bergeron .30 .75
371 Willie Mitchell .15 .40
372 Tyler Myers .25 .60
373 Tyler Ennis .20 .50
374 Ty Wishart .15 .40
375 Tuukka Rask .25 .60
376 Matt Moulson .20 .50
377 Tom Wandell .15 .40
378 Tom Gilbert .15 .40
379 Tobias Enstrom .15 .40
380 Thomas Vanek .25 .60
381 Theo Peckham .15 .40
382 T.J. Oshie .40 1.00
383 Chris Kelly .20 .50
384 Stephen Weiss .20 .50
385 David Backes .25 .60
386 Mark Stuart .15 .40
387 Sergei Bobrovsky .25 .60
388 Andy McDonald .20 .50
389 David Steckel .15 .40
390 Anton Stralman .15 .40
391 Anton Volchenkov .15 .40
392 Arron Asham .15 .40
393 Barret Jackman .15 .40
394 Brad Marchand .30 .75
395 Brett Clark .15 .40
396 Brian Rolston .20 .50
397 Cam Barker .15 .40
398 Chris Mason .20 .50
399 Chris Stewart .20 .50
400 Cody McCormick .15 .40
401 Colby Armstrong .15 .40
402 Colton Orr .15 .40
403 Corey Crawford .30 .75
404 Cory Schneider .20 .50
405 Simon Gagne .25 .60
406 Dan Hamhuis .20 .50
407 Ryan Miller .25 .60
408 Robin Lehner .20 .50
409 Rich Peverley .25 .60
410 Sergei Kostitsyn .15 .40
411 Linus Omark .25 .60
412 Jason Demers .15 .40
413 Mikael Samuelsson .15 .40
414 Kristian Huselius .15 .40
415 Justin Abdelkader .20 .50
416 Peter Regin .15 .40
417 Mark Dekanich .15 .40
418 Kevin Shattenkirk .20 .50
419 Ilya Kovalchuk .25 .60
420 Jacob Markstrom .25 .60
421 Andrew MacDonald .15 .40
422 Erik Christensen .15 .40
423 Daniel Carcillo .15 .40
424 Matt Cooke .15 .40
425 Paul Gaustad .15 .40
426 Jonas Gustavsson .25 .60
427 Scott Gomez .20 .50
428 Andrei Kostitsyn .20 .50
429 Michael Ryder .15 .40
430 Andrew Raycroft .20 .50
431 Andy Greene .15 .40
432 Brad Richards .25 .60
433 Jack Johnson .15 .40
434 Curtis Glencross .15 .40
435 Dany Heatley .20 .50
436 Steve Sullivan .15 .40
437 Dainius Zubrus .15 .40
438 John Tavares .50 1.25
439 Jonathan Ericsson .20 .50
440 Michael Del Zotto .15 .40
441 Brian Boucher .20 .50
442 Matt Niskanen .20 .50
443 Phil Kessel .30 .75
444 Patrice Cormier .15 .40
445 Michael Cammalleri .20 .50
446 Max Pacioretty .25 .60
447 Keith Aulie .20 .50
448 Mark Letestu .20 .50
449 Ville Leino .20 .50
450 Johnny Boychuk .15 .40
451 Mark Fistric .15 .40
452 Rob Scuderi .15 .40
453 Kyle Turris .15 .40
454 Magnus Paajarvi .20 .50
455 Pierre-Marc Bouchard .25 .60
456 Marc-Edouard Vlasic .15 .40
457 Greg Zanon .15 .40
458 Samuel Pahlsson .15 .40
459 Ray Emery .20 .50
460 David Legwand .20 .50
461 Matt D'Agostini .15 .40
462 Patrik Elias .25 .60
463 Jeff Schultz .15 .40
464 Mike Weaver .15 .40
465 Henrik Tallinder .15 .40
466 Jesse Joensuu .15 .40
467 Pavel Kubina .15 .40
468 Bryan Bickell .15 .40
469 Jason Blake .15 .40
470 Marc Staal .25 .60
471 Darren Helm .20 .50
472 Mike Comrie .15 .40
473 Milan Lucic .25 .60
474 Mike Green .25 .60
475 Johnny Oduya .20 .50
476 James Wisniewski .15 .40
477 Semyon Varlamov .25 .60
478 Alex Kovalev .25 .60
479 Lars Eller .20 .50
480 Matt Greene .15 .40
481 Sergei Samsonov .20 .50
482 Anton Babchuk .15 .40
483 Rick DiPietro .20 .50
484 Kristopher Letang .25 .60
485 Joffrey Lupul .20 .50
486 Nick Foligno .20 .50
487 Derek Morris .15 .40
488 Liam Reddox .15 .40
489 Jordin Tootoo .20 .50
490 Jaroslav Halak .25 .60
491 David Moss .15 .40
492 Matt Martin .15 .40
493 Frans Nielsen .15 .40
494 Sean Avery .20 .50
495 Daniel Girardi .15 .40
496 Checklist .15 .40
497 Checklist .15 .40
498 Checklist .15 .40
499 Checklist .15 .40
500 Checklist .15 .40
501 Dale Hawerchuk L 1.00 2.50
502 Mike Gartner L .75 2.00
503 Richard Brodeur L .75 2.00
504 Tony Tanti L .50 1.25
505 Al Iafrate L .60 1.50
506 Brett Hull L 1.00 2.50
507 Mario Lemieux L 2.50 6.00
508 Bobby Clarke L .75 2.00
509 Eric Lindros L 1.25 3.00
510 Reggie Leach L .60 1.50
511 Bill Barber L .75 2.00
512 Rick MacLeish L .60 1.50
513 Dave Schultz L .75 2.00
514 Tim Kerr L .60 1.50
515 Mark Messier L 1.00 2.50
516 Andy Bathgate L .75 2.00
517 Mike Bossy L .75 2.00
518 Denis Potvin L .75 2.00
519 Patrick Roy L 2.00 5.00
520 Jean Beliveau L .75 2.00
521 Guy Lafleur L 1.00 2.50
522 Larry Robinson L .75 2.00
523 Claude Lemieux L .60 1.50
524 Russ Courtnall L .50 1.25
525 Neal Broten L .60 1.50
526 Marcel Dionne L 1.00 2.50
527 Rogie Vachon L 1.00 2.50
528 Bernie Nicholls L .75 2.00
529 Dave Taylor L .60 1.50
530 Ron Francis L 1.00 2.50
531 Wayne Gretzky L 4.00 10.00
532 Jari Kurri L .75 2.00
533 Bill Ranford L .75 2.00
534 Paul Coffey L .75 2.00
535 Ted Lindsay L .75 2.00
536 Red Kelly L .60 1.50
537 Igor Larionov L .75 2.00
538 Alex Delvecchio L .60 1.50
539 Joe Sakic L 1.25 3.00
540 Bobby Hull L .75 2.00
541 Stan Mikita L 1.00 2.50
542 Doug Wilson L .60 1.50
543 Steve Larmer L .60 1.50
544 Bobby Orr L 2.50 6.00
545 Ray Bourque L 1.25 3.00
546 Phil Esposito L 1.25 3.00
547 Johnny Bucyk L .75 2.00
548 Cam Neely L .75 2.00
549 Milt Schmidt L .60 1.50
550 Brad Park L .60 1.50
551 Todd Ford RC 1.25 3.00
552 Cody Hodgson RC 2.00 5.00
553 Yann Suave RC 1.00 2.50
554 Joe Colborne RC 1.00 2.50
555 Ben Scrivens RC 1.50 4.00
556 Matt Frattin RC 1.00 2.50
557 Alex Stalock 1.00 2.50
558 Brian Strait RC 1.25 3.00
559 Joe Vitale RC 1.00 2.50
560 Ben Holmstrom RC 1.00 2.50
561 Erik Gustafsson RC 1.25 3.00
562 Zac Rinaldo RC 1.00 2.50
563 Patrick Wiercioch RC 1.00 2.50
564 Erik Condra RC 1.00 2.50
565 Roman Wick RC 1.25 3.00
566 Colin Greening RC 1.00 2.50
567 Andre Benoit RC 1.25 3.00
568 Stephane Da Costa RC 1.00 2.50
569 Cam Talbot RC 2.50 6.00
570 Matt Campanale RC 1.00 2.50
571 Shane Sims RC 1.00 2.50
572 Mikko Koskinen RC 1.25 3.00
573 Jamie Doornbosch RC 1.00 2.50
574 Mark Katic RC 1.00 2.50
575 Justin DiBenedetto RC .75 2.00
576 Adam Henrique RC 2.50 6.00
577 Jonathon Blum RC 1.00 2.50
578 Blake Geoffrion RC 1.00 2.50
579 Aaron Palushaj RC 1.00 2.50
580 Brendon Nash RC 1.00 2.50
581 Drew Bagnall RC 1.00 2.50
582 Carson McMillan RC 1.25 3.00
583 Hugh Jessiman RC 1.00 2.50
584 Scott Timmins RC 1.00 2.50
585 Teemu Hartikainen RC 1.00 2.50
586 Chris Vande Velde RC 1.50 4.00
587 Tomas Vincour RC 1.00 2.50
588 Colton Sceviour RC 1.00 2.50
589 John Moore RC 1.00 2.50
590 Tomas Kubalik RC 1.00 2.50
591 Cameron Gaunce RC .75 2.00
592 Marcus Kruger RC 1.50 4.00
593 Greg Nemisz RC 1.00 2.50
594 Lance Bouma RC 1.00 2.50
595 Paul Postma RC 1.00 2.50
596 Andrei Zubarev RC 1.25 3.00
597 Carl Klingberg RC 1.00 2.50
598 Timo Pielmeier 1.25 3.00
599 Jean-Philippe Levasseur 1.00 2.50
600 Checklist .50 1.25
601 Semyon Varlamov .40 1.00
602 Jeff Carter .40 1.00
603 Mike Richards .40 1.00
604 Jaromir Jagr 1.00 2.50
605 Ilya Bryzgalov .40 1.00
606 Tomas Vokoun .30 .75
607 Ondrej Pavelec .40 1.00
608 Dustin Byfuglien .40 1.00
609 Alexander Burmistrov .30 .75
610 Evander Kane .40 1.00
611 Gabriel Landeskog RC 3.00 8.00
612 Ryan Johansen RC 2.00 5.00
613 Zack Kassian RC 1.25 3.00
614 Ryan Nugent-Hopkins RC 4.00 10.00
615 Erik Gudbranson RC 1.25 3.00
616 Craig Smith RC 1.25 3.00
617 Adam Larsson RC 1.25 3.00
618 David Rundblad RC 1.00 2.50
619 Mika Zibanejad RC 2.50 6.00
620 Sean Couturier RC 2.00 5.00
621 Matt Read RC 2.00 5.00
622 Brett Connolly RC 1.00 2.50
623 Louis Leblanc RC 1.00 2.50
624 Cody Eakin RC 1.25 3.00
625 Mark Scheifele RC 2.50 6.00

2011-12 O-Pee-Chee Black Rainbow

*1-500 VETS: 6X TO 15X BASIC CARDS
*501-600 LEGENDS : 2.5X TO 6X BASE
*551-599 ROOKIES: 1.5X TO 4X BASE RC
STATED PRINT RUN 100 SER.#'d SETS
244 Cody Hodgson 15.00 40.00
309 Nicklas Backstrom 6.00 15.00
403 Corey Crawford 5.00 12.00
552 Cody Hodgson 15.00 40.00

2011-12 O-Pee-Chee Rainbow

*1-500 VETS: 2.5X TO 6X BASIC CARDS
*501-600 LEGENDS: 1X TO 2.5X BASE
*551-599 ROOKIES: .6X TO 1.5X BASE
1-600 STATED ODDS 1:4
244 Cody Hodgson 6.00 15.00
309 Nicklas Backstrom 2.50 6.00
403 Corey Crawford 2.00 5.00
552 Cody Hodgson 6.00 15.00

2011-12 O-Pee-Chee Retro

*1-500 VETS: 2X TO 5X BASIC CARDS
*501-550 LEGENDS: .8X TO 2X BASE
*551-600 ROOKIES: .5X TO 1.2X BASE
1-600 ONE PER O-PEE-CHEE PACK
*601-610 VETS: 2X TO 5X BASIC CARDS
601-610 UPDATE ODDS 1:60 SER.2 UD HOB
*611-625 ROOKIES: .6X TO 1.5X BASE
601-610 UPDATE ODDS 1:60 SER.2 UD HOB
309 Nicklas Backstrom 2.00 5.00
403 Corey Crawford 1.50 4.00

2011-12 O-Pee-Chee Box Bottoms

COMPLETE SET (16) 6.00 15.00
1 Patrice Bergeron .30 .75
2 Martin Brodeur .50 1.25
3 Sidney Crosby 1.00 2.50
4 Claude Giroux .25 .60
5 Taylor Hall .50 1.25
6 Jarome Iginla .25 .60
7 Patrick Kane .50 1.25
8 Ryan Kesler .25 .60
9 Henrik Lundqvist .30 .75
10 Roberto Luongo .25 .60
11 Alexander Ovechkin 1.00 2.50
12 Carey Price .75 2.00
13 Martin St. Louis .25 .60
14 Steven Stamkos .50 1.25
15 Jonathan Toews .50 1.25
16 Henrik Zetterberg .30 .75
P1 Stamkos/Iginla/Zett/Lundq 1.50 4.00
P2 Ovech/Keslr/Brod/Girox 1.50 4.00
P3 Toews/Luong/Berg/Hall 1.50 4.00
P4 Sid/Kane/St.Louis/Price 1.50 4.00

2011-12 O-Pee-Chee In Action

STATED ODDS 1:36
SP STATED ODDS 1:360
A1 Corey Perry 3.00 8.00
A2 Nathan Horton 3.00 8.00
A3 Derek Roy 2.50 6.00
A4 Jeff Skinner 3.00 8.00
A5 Patrick Sharp 3.00 8.00
A6 Matt Duchene 3.00 8.00
A7 Rick Nash 3.00 8.00
A8 Brad Richards 3.00 8.00
A9 Pavel Datsyuk 4.00 10.00
A10 Henrik Zetterberg 4.00 10.00
A11 Jordan Eberle 3.00 8.00
A12 Taylor Hall 6.00 15.00
A13 Drew Doughty 3.00 8.00
A14 Mikko Koivu 2.50 6.00
A15 P.K. Subban 6.00 15.00
A16 Ilya Kovalchuk 3.00 8.00
A17 John Tavares 6.00 15.00
A18 Marian Gaborik 4.00 10.00
A19 Jason Spezza 3.00 8.00
A20 Erik Karlsson 6.00 15.00
A21 Mike Richards 3.00 8.00
A22 Jeff Carter 3.00 8.00
A23 Evgeni Malkin 10.00 25.00
A24 Logan Couture 3.00 8.00
A25 Antti Niemi 2.50 6.00
A26 Phil Kessel 4.00 10.00
A27 Daniel Sedin 3.00 8.00
A28 Alexandre Burrows 3.00 8.00
A29 Alexander Semin 3.00 8.00
A30 Nicklas Backstrom 5.00 12.00
A31 Alexander Ovechkin SP 25.00 60.00
A32 Roberto Luongo SP 12.00 30.00
A33 Ryan Kesler SP 6.00 15.00
A34 Steven Stamkos SP 12.00 30.00
A35 Sidney Crosby SP 25.00 60.00
A36 Henrik Lundqvist SP 10.00 25.00
A37 Martin Brodeur SP 12.00 30.00
A38 Carey Price SP 20.00 50.00
A39 Patrick Kane SP 12.00 30.00
A40 Jonathan Toews SP 15.00 40.00

2011-12 O-Pee-Chee League Leaders

COMPLETE SET (10) 8.00 20.00
STATED ODDS 1:4
LL1 Perry/Stamkos/Iginla 1.50 4.00
LL2 Sedin/St. Louis/Sedin .75 2.00
LL3 Sedin/St. Louis/Perry .75 2.00
LL4 Konopka/Neil/Peckham .60 1.50
LL5 Sedin/Stamkos/Selanne 1.50 4.00
LL6 Clutterbuck/Ruutu/Brown .75 2.00
LL7 Luongo/Price/Ward 2.50 6.00
LL8 Thomas/Luongo/Rinne 1.00 2.50
LL9 Thomas/Rinne/Luongo 1.00 2.50
LL10 Lundqvist/Thomas/Price 2.50 6.00

2011-12 O-Pee-Chee Marquee Legends

COMPLETE SET (10) 15.00 40.00
RANDOM INSERT IN WALMART PACKS
L1 Paul Coffey 1.50 4.00
L2 Eric Lindros 2.50 6.00
L3 Bobby Orr 5.00 12.00
L4 Bobby Hull 1.50 4.00
L5 Wayne Gretzky 10.00 25.00
L6 Mario Lemieux 5.00 12.00

Patrick Roy 4.00 10.00
Ron Francis 2.00 5.00
Mike Bossy 1.50 4.00
0 Bobby Clarke 1.50 4.00

2011-12 O-Pee-Chee Playoff Beard

hese cards parallel the first 50 cards of the base set, owever each has a unique photo and carries silver text r the player's name instead of the gold that is used r the base set.
BEARD: 2.5X TO 6X BASE
Scott Hartnell 1.50 4.00
Paul Mara 1.00 2.50
Marian Hossa 1.25 3.00
Duncan Keith 1.50 4.00
Henrik Zetterberg 2.00 5.00
Maxime Talbot 1.25 3.00
Brian Campbell 1.00 2.50
Todd Bertuzzi 1.25 3.00
J.P. Dumont 1.00 2.50
Claude Giroux 1.50 4.00
Chris Phillips 1.00 2.50
Dan Cleary 1.50 4.00
Jordan Staal 1.50 4.00
Ryan Kesler 1.50 4.00
George Parros 1.25 3.00
Joe Thornton 1.50 4.00
Johan Franzen 1.50 4.00
Patrick Kane 3.00 8.00
Mike Richards 1.50 4.00
Patrick Sharp 1.50 4.00
Jeff Carter 1.50 4.00
Dan Boyle 1.25 3.00
Daniel Sedin 1.50 4.00
Henrik Sedin 1.50 4.00
Eric Staal 2.00 5.00
Pascal Dupuis 1.00 2.50
Olli Jokinen 1.25 3.00
Guillaume Latendresse 1.25 3.00
Jonathan Toews 3.00 8.00
Kris Versteeg 1.25 3.00
Roberto Luongo 1.50 4.00
Patrick Marleau 1.50 4.00
Martin St. Louis 1.50 4.00
Saku Koivu 1.50 4.00
Cam Ward 1.50 4.00
Tomas Holmstrom 1.00 2.50
Antti Niemi 1.25 3.00
Matt Cullen 1.00 2.50
Raffi Torres 1.00 2.50
Tim Thomas 1.50 4.00
Jarome Iginla 1.50 4.00
Joe Pavelski 1.50 4.00
Fernando Pisani 1.00 2.50
Chris Drury 1.25 3.00
Brian Gionta 1.25 3.00
Ryan Smyth 1.25 3.00
Alexander Ovechkin 6.00 15.00
Daniel Briere 1.50 4.00
Marc-Andre Fleury 2.50 6.00
Sidney Crosby 6.00 15.00

2011-12 O-Pee-Chee Signatures

VERALL STATED ODDS 1:144 UD1
ROUP A ANNC'D ODDS 1:103,626
ROUP B ANNC'D ODDS 1:8726
ROUP C ANNC'D ODDS 1:5527
ROUP D ANNC'D ODDS 1:937
ROUP E ANNC'D ODDS 1:307
PDATE STATED ODDS 1:1800 UD2
PD GRP A ANNC'D ODDS 1:6136 UD2
PD GRP B ANNC'D ODDS 1:2547 UD2
SAH Ales Hemsky B 10.00 25.00
SAK Arturs Kulda E 5.00 12.00
SAL Andrew Ladd D 8.00 20.00
SAO Alexander Ovechkin B 60.00 120.00
SAS Alex Stalock D 6.00 15.00
SBB Brian Boyle A
SBM Brett MacLean E 5.00 12.00
SDB David Backes C 8.00 20.00
SDS Drayson Bowman D 5.00 12.00
SJA Jamie Arniel E 6.00 15.00
SJM Justin Mercier E 5.00 12.00
SJO Jim O'Brien D 8.00 20.00
SJV Jakub Voracek D 8.00 20.00
SKD Kaspars Daugavins D 5.00 12.00
SKS Kevin Shattenkirk D 6.00 15.00
SKV Kris Versteeg C 6.00 15.00
SMA Jacob Markstrom E 8.00 20.00
SMO John Moore B
SMT Mattias Tedenby E 5.00 12.00
SMZ Mats Zuccarello E 15.00 40.00
SNB Niclas Bergfors B
SPB Patrik Berglund E 6.00 15.00
SPM Peter Mueller C 6.00 15.00
SRB Richard Bachman E 6.00 15.00
SRM Ryan McDonagh E 8.00 20.00
STM Thomas McCollum E 6.00 15.00
STT Tomas Tatar E 10.00 25.00
PCAL Andrew Ladd Upd. B 12.00 30.00
PCAO A.Ovechkin Upd. A 100.00 175.00
PCBM Brett MacLean Upd. B 8.00 20.00
PCBO Bobby Orr Upd. A 250.00 400.00
PCDB D.Bowman Upd. B 8.00 20.00
PCGL G.Latendresse Upd. A 40.00 80.00
PCJE Jordan Eberle Upd. A
PCJM J.Markstrom Upd. B 10.00 25.00
PCMU Peter Mueller Upd. B 10.00 25.00
PCNH Nathan Horton Upd. A 15.00 40.00
PCRY Nugent-Hopkins Upd. A 150.00 250.00
PCSC Sidney Crosby Upd. A 150.00 250.00
PCSW Stephen Weiss Upd. A 12.00 30.00
PCTM T.McCollum Upd. A 15.00 40.00
PCWG Wayne Gretzky Upd. A

2011-12 O-Pee-Chee Souvenirs

VERALL STATED ODDS 1:144
ROUP A STATED ODDS 1:37,404
ROUP B STATED ODDS 1:29,923
ROUP C STATED ODDS 1:14,962
ROUP D STATED ODDS 1:2494
ROUP E STATED ODDS 1:156
1#2 Grtz/Lem/Crsby/Ovch A 300.00 400.00
LUES Halk/Brgl/Bcks/Pern E 6.00 15.00
OLTS Stmks/Lecv/St.L/Hdm E 10.00 25.00
OS Chra/Berg/Rask/Thms E 12.00 30.00
UF Vanek/Myrs/Grbe/Enn E 6.00 15.00
APS Ovch/Bckstr/Smin/Grn C 25.00 60.00
BJ Brass/Nash/Vrck/Filat E 8.00 20.00
GY Ignl/Kipr/Bwmtr/Brque E 6.00 15.00
HI Tws/Kne/Hossa/Sbrk E 12.00 30.00
AL Benn/Rich/Erik/Gligki E 8.00 20.00
ET Zettr/Frnzn/Lidstr/Dtsy D 8.00 20.00
LYER Brre/Crtr/Hrtnll/Crcillo E 12.00 30.00
R8 Lem/Mess/Sakc/Yzrm A 125.00 250.00
AK Qck/Dghty/Kptr/Smyth E 10.00 25.00
BBR Sbn/Prce/Plkn/Cmmlri D 20.00 50.00
ASH Rne/Wber/Ster/Hrnq E 8.00 20.00

NJD Zajc/Elias/Prse/Clrksn E 10.00 25.00
NUCKS Lngo/Brrws/Kslr/Edlr E 6.00 15.00
NYI Bley/Mlson/Okps/DiPtr E 8.00 20.00
NYR Lndq/Staal/Gbrik/Stpn E 8.00 20.00
OTT Spez/Flino/Alfrd/Gnchr E 6.00 15.00
PENS Mlkn/Staal/Crsby/Flry D 25.00 60.00
PIM Orr/Carc/Crknr/Parros B
POE1 Tvres/Hdgsn/Ebrl/Kne E 15.00 40.00
POE2 Sbn/Myrs/Ptrnglo/Aie E 12.00 30.00
POE3 Crmr/Benn/Dlla/Bychk E 8.00 20.00
SABRE Roy/Mill/Stff/Pmnvlle E 6.00 15.00
SJS Thrnt/Htley/Mrl/Stchi E 6.00 15.00
VAN Keslr/Sedins/Hodgson E 15.00 40.00
WILD Thdre/Bchr/Kvu/Bcks E 6.00 15.00
WPG Byfgln/Pvlc/Kne/Enstr E 10.00 25.00

2011-12 O-Pee-Chee Team Canada Signatures

OVERALL STATED ODDS 1:432 UD1
GROUP A ANNC'D ODDS 1:1836 UD1
GROUP B ANNC'D ODDS 1:1407 UD1
GROUP C ANNC'D ODDS 1:944 UD1
UPDATE STATED ODDS 1:1800 UD2
UPD GRP A ANNC'D ODDS 1:6101 UD2
UPD GRP B ANNC'D ODDS 1:2553 UD2
TCAC Andrew Cogliano A 40.00 80.00
TCAH Adam Henrique Upd. B 30.00 60.00
TCAP Alex Pietrangelo A 40.00 80.00
TCBC Brett Connolly Upd. B 30.00 60.00
TCBO Bobby Orr A 300.00 500.00
TCBS Brandon Sutter C 8.00 20.00
TCBY Brayden Schenn A 25.00 60.00
TCCA Jordan Caron C 12.00 30.00
TCCE Cody Eakin Upd. B 25.00 50.00
TCCH Cody Hodgson B 15.00 40.00
TCCM Clarke MacArthur Upd. B 25.00 50.00
TCDD Drew Doughty A 40.00 80.00
TCDR Sean Couturier Upd. A 20.00 50.00
TCEG Derek Roy Upd. B 15.00 40.00
TCEK Evander Kane A 15.00 40.00
TCGL Guillaume Latendresse B 15.00 40.00
TCGN Erik Gudbranson Upd. A 25.00 50.00
TCHA Taylor Hall A
TCJC Jared Cowen B 10.00 25.00
TCJE Jordan Eberle A 60.00 120.00
TCJS Greg Nemisz Upd. B
TCJT John Tavares A 50.00 120.00
TCKA Karl Alzner B 6.00 15.00
TCKA Jeff Skinner Upd. A 40.00 80.00
TCLC Logan Couture A 30.00 60.00
TCMD Matt Duchene A 40.00 80.00
TCMS Marco Scandella C 6.00 15.00
TCMT Maxime Talbot A 15.00 40.00
TCPC Patrice Cormier C 12.00 30.00
TCPM Patrick Marleau A 50.00 100.00
TCPS P.K. Subban A 75.00 150.00
TCRJ Keith Aulie Upd. B 10.00 25.00
TCRJ Ryan Johansen Upd. A 30.00 80.00
TCRY R.Nugent-Hopkins Upd. A 100.00 200.00
TCSC Sidney Crosby A 125.00 250.00
TCSD Stefan Della Rovere B 20.00 50.00
TCSG Simon Gagne A 50.00 120.00
TCSS Steven Stamkos A 75.00 150.00
TCTE Tyler Ennis C 8.00 20.00
TCTH Travis Hamonic B 8.00 20.00
TCWG Wayne Gretzky A 175.00 350.00

2011-12 O-Pee-Chee Team Leaders

COMPLETE SET (30) 20.00 50.00
STATED ODDS 1:4
TL1 Perry/Getzlaf/Selanne/Hiller 1.50 4.00
TL2 Ladd/Enstrom/Ladd/Pavelec .75 2.00
TL3 Lucic/Krejci/Chara/Thomas .75 2.00
TL4 Vanek/Vanek/Stafford/Miller .75 2.00
TL5 Iginla/Tanguay/Iginla/Kiprsff .75 2.00
TL6 Staal/Staal/Staal/Ward 1.00 2.50
TL7 Sharp/Kane/Sharp/Crawford 1.50 4.00
TL8 Jones/Dchne/Hejdk/Budaj .75 2.00
TL9 Nash/Nash/Umbrgr/Mason .75 2.00
TL10 Mornw/Ribro/Erkssn/Lehton .60 1.50
TL11 Franzn/Zettr/Hlmstrm/Hwrd 1.00 2.50
TL12 Hall/Hmsky/Hall/Dubnyk 1.50 4.00
TL13 Booth/Weiss/Booth/Vokoun .60 1.50
TL14 Brown/Kopitar/Smyth/Quick 1.25 3.00
TL15 Havlt/Koivu/Brns/Bckstrm 1.00 2.50
TL16 Gionta/Plek/Subban/Price 2.50 6.00
TL17 Kostitsyn/Suter/Erat/Rinne 1.00 2.50
TL18 Kovalchuk/Elias/Brodeur 1.50 4.00
TL19 Grabnr/Tavrs/Mlson/Mntya 1.50 4.00
TL20 Dubinsky/Callahan/Lundqv 1.00 2.50
TL21 Spezza/Alfredsson/Elliott .75 2.00
TL22 Carter/Giroux/Bobrovsky .75 2.00
TL23 Yandle/Doan/Bryzgalov .75 2.00
TL24 Letang/Crosby/Fleury 3.00 8.00
TL25 Mrleau/Thrntn/Htly/Niemi .75 2.00
TL26 Backs/Pietr/Brglnd/Halak .75 2.00
TL27 St. Louis/Stamkos/Roloson 1.50 4.00
TL28 MacArthur/Kessel/Reimer 1.00 2.50
TL29 Kesler/Sedins/Luongo .75 2.00
TL30 Ovechkin/Knuble/Neuvirth 3.00 8.00

2011-12 O-Pee-Chee Trophy Winners

COMPLETE SET (10) 6.00 15.00
STATED ODDS 1:4
TW1 Corey Perry .75 2.00
TW2 Daniel Sedin .75 2.00
TW3 Daniel Sedin .75 2.00
TW4 Corey Perry .75 2.00
TW5 Nicklas Lidstrom .75 2.00
TW6 Tim Thomas .75 2.00
TW7 Tim Thomase .75 2.00
TW8 Jeff Skinner .75 2.00
TW9 Ryan Kesler .75 2.00
TW10 Martin St. Louis .75 2.00

2012-13 O-Pee-Chee

COMP.SET w/o SP's (500) 25.00 60.00
501-600 STATED ODDS 1:2 HOB
1 Marian Gaborik .25 .60
2 Matt Moulson .20 .50
3 Ryan Nugent-Hopkins .25 .60
4 Justin Williams .20 .50
5 Luca Sbisa .20 .50
6 Duncan Keith .25 .60
7 Martin Brodeur .50 1.25
8 Johnny Boychuk .15 .40
9 Kris Versteeg .20 .50
10 Marco Scandella .15 .40
11 Bryan Bickell .15 .40
12 Anton Stralman .15 .40
13 Mikael Backlund .20 .50
14 Alex Goligoski .15 .40
15 Todd Bertuzzi .20 .50
16 Carl Hagelin .25 .60
17 Oliver Ekman-Larsson .25 .60
18 Miikka Kiprusoff .20 .50
19 Blake Geoffrion .25 .60
20 Thomas Vanek .25 .60
21 Jaroslav Halak .25 .60
22 Mark Stuart .15 .40
23 Jared Cowen .25 .60
24 Michael Grabner .20 .50
25 Alexandre Burrows .25 .60
26 Dan Ellis .20 .50
27 Tim Gleason .15 .40
28 Vaclav Prospal .15 .40
29 Tom Pyatt .15 .40
30 Ryan Whitney .15 .40
31 Rostislav Klesla .15 .40
32 Eric Staal .30 .75
33 Kari Lehtonen .20 .50
34 Marcel Goc .20 .50
35 Devin Setoguchi .20 .50
36 Torrey Mitchell .15 .40
37 Dmitry Orlov .25 .60
38 Zdeno Chara .25 .60
39 Nathan Gerbe .15 .40
40 Max Pacioretty .25 .60
41 Carl Gunnarsson .15 .40
42 Kyle Brodziak .15 .40
43 Daniel Winnik .15 .40
44 Teddy Purcell .25 .60
45 Erik Condra .15 .40
46 Patric Hornqvist .20 .50
47 Dave Bolland .20 .50
48 Ed Jovanovski .15 .40
49 Andrew Ladd .25 .60
50 Brett Connolly .20 .50
51 Jean-Sebastien Giguere .20 .50
52 Brayden Schenn .25 .60
53 Raphael Diaz .15 .40
54 Marc-Andre Gragnani .15 .40
55 Kristopher Letang .25 .60
56 Steve Mason .20 .50
57 Jhonas Enroth .25 .60
58 Loui Eriksson .20 .50
59 Alex Tanguay .15 .40
60 Willie Mitchell .15 .40
61 Arron Asham .15 .40
62 Karl Alzner .15 .40
63 Jamie McBain .15 .40
64 Patrick Marleau .25 .60
65 Jonas Gustavsson .25 .60
66 Milan Michalek .15 .40
67 Patrik Berglund .15 .40
68 Marc Methot .15 .40
69 Mason Raymond .20 .50
70 Stephane Robidas .15 .40
71 P.K. Subban .40 1.00
72 Henrik Sedin .25 .60
73 Sean Couturier .25 .60
74 David Clarkson .15 .40
75 Chad LaRose .15 .40
76 Ryan O'Reilly .25 .60
77 Saku Koivu .25 .60
78 Dion Phaneuf .25 .60
79 Nathan Horton .25 .60
80 Jonathan Ericsson .20 .50
81 Shawn Horcoff .15 .40
82 Mark Fayne .15 .40
83 Scott Hartnell .25 .60
84 Dennis Wideman .15 .40
85 Matt D'Agostini .15 .40
86 Ryane Clowe .15 .40
87 Mike Smith .25 .60
88 Jason Garrison .15 .40
89 Al Montoya .15 .40
90 Alexander Radulov .25 .60
91 Tobias Enstrom .15 .40
92 Chris Kunitz .25 .60
93 Shane O'Brien .15 .40
94 Teemu Selanne .50 1.25
95 Sergei Bobrovsky .25 .60
96 Ryan Callahan .25 .60
97 Rob Scuderi .15 .40
98 Johan Franzen .25 .60
99 David Legwand .20 .50
100 Steve Ott .20 .50
101 Nikolai Khabibulin .25 .60
102 Matt Read .20 .50
103 Pascal Dupuis .15 .40
104 Mike Richards .25 .60
105 Derek Roy .20 .50
106 Johnny Oduya .20 .50
107 Tomas Kaberle .15 .40
108 Andrew MacDonald .15 .40
109 Ryan Jones .20 .50
110 David Backes .25 .60
111 Chris Phillips .15 .40
112 Tomas Fleischmann .15 .40
113 George Parros .20 .50
114 Alexander Steen .25 .60
115 Shea Weber .20 .50
116 Niklas Backstrom .20 .50
117 Jaromir Jagr .60 1.50
118 Erik Cole .20 .50
119 David Krejci .25 .60
120 Brad Richards .25 .60
121 Milan Hejduk .20 .50
122 Andrei Kostitsyn .20 .50
123 Jonathan Toews .50 1.25
124 Corey Perry .25 .60
125 Josh Bailey .20 .50
126 Antoine Vermette .15 .40
127 Matt Greene .15 .40
128 Kyle Okposo .25 .60
129 Douglas Murray .15 .40
130 Shawn Thornton .20 .50
131 Brent Seabrook .25 .60
132 Trevor Daley .15 .40
133 James Reimer .25 .60
134 Craig Smith .15 .40
135 Dan Boyle .20 .50
136 Benoit Pouliot .15 .40
137 Zach Bogosian .20 .50
138 Jannik Hansen .20 .50
139 R.J. Umberger .15 .40
140 Taylor Hall .50 1.25
141 Jeff Skinner .25 .60
142 Ryan Malone .15 .40
143 David Perron .15 .40
144 Kyle Clifford .15 .40
145 Jordin Tootoo .20 .50
146 Brent Burns .30 .75
147 Brandon Dubinsky .20 .50
148 Robyn Regehr .15 .40
149 Boyd Gordon .15 .40
150 Kyle Turris .15 .40
151 Drew Miller .15 .40
152 Tyler Bozak .20 .50
153 Lauri Korpikoski .15 .40
154 John Carlson .30 .75
155 Josh Harding .25 .60
156 Christian Ehrhoff .15 .40
157 Scott Clemmensen .20 .50
158 Dustin Byfuglien .25 .60
159 Shane Doan .20 .50
160 Derek Mackenzie .15 .40
161 Nick Leddy .15 .40
162 Jiri Tlusty .20 .50
163 Olli Jokinen .20 .50
164 B.J. Crombeen .15 .40
165 Ian White .20 .50
166 Marc-Andre Fleury .40 1.00
167 David Jones .15 .40
168 Alexander Ovechkin 1.00 2.50
169 Jake Gardiner .25 .60
170 Tanner Glass .15 .40
171 Braydon Coburn .15 .40
172 Kevin Bieksa .20 .50
173 Andy Greene .15 .40
174 Darren Helm .20 .50
175 Brandon Prust .15 .40
176 Brooks Laich .15 .40
177 Guillaume Latendresse .20 .50
178 Jan Hejda .15 .40
179 Brandon Sutter .20 .50
180 Jay Bouwmeester .25 .60
181 Mike Commodore .15 .40
182 Johan Hedberg .20 .50
183 Marc Staal .20 .50
184 Pavel Datsyuk .30 .75
185 Travis Moen .15 .40
186 Tim Thomas .25 .60
187 Curtis Sanford .20 .50
188 Anze Kopitar .40 1.00
189 Eric Brewer .15 .40
190 Ryan Kesler .25 .60
191 Cam Fowler .20 .50
192 Brenden Morrow .20 .50
193 Craig Anderson .25 .60
194 Mike Green .25 .60
195 Stephen Weiss .20 .50
196 Matt Stajan .20 .50
197 Matt Niskanen .20 .50
198 Fedor Tyutin .15 .40
199 Nicklas Lidstrom .25 .60
200 Ilya Kovalchuk .25 .60
201 Matt Martin .15 .40
202 Raffi Torres .15 .40
203 Mikhail Grabovski .20 .50
204 Jason Chimera .15 .40
205 Corey Crawford .30 .75
206 Logan Couture .25 .60
207 Valtteri Filppula .25 .60
208 Ryan Suter .15 .40
209 Blake Comeau .15 .40
210 Nikolai Kulemin .20 .50
211 Ville Leino .20 .50
212 Brian Rolston .20 .50
213 Ruslan Fedotenko .15 .40
214 Ray Whitney .20 .50
215 Kyle Wellwood .20 .50
216 Manny Malhotra .20 .50
217 Joel Ward .15 .40
218 Jamie Langenbrunner .15 .40
219 Francois Beauchemin .15 .40
220 Chris Kelly .20 .50
221 Cam Ward .25 .60
222 Jonathan Quick .40 1.00
223 P.A. Parenteau .15 .40
224 Kimmo Timonen .15 .40
225 Michal Handzus .15 .40
226 Bobby Butler .20 .50
227 Ryan Getzlaf .40 1.00
228 Stefan Elliott .20 .50
229 Evgeni Malkin .75 2.00
230 Patrick Kane .50 1.25
231 Derick Brassard .25 .60
232 Jamie Benn .30 .75
233 Lars Eller .20 .50
234 Michael Cammalleri .20 .50
235 Toni Lydman .15 .40
236 T.J. Oshie .40 1.00
237 Paul Martin .15 .40
238 Matt Ellis .15 .40
239 Steven Stamkos .50 1.25
240 Jakub Voracek .25 .60
241 Jack Johnson .15 .40
242 Gabriel Landeskog .25 .60
243 Mark Giordano .20 .50
244 Jim Slater .15 .40
245 Drew Stafford .25 .60
246 Cody Franson .15 .40
247 Mathieu Darche .15 .40
248 Tom Gilbert .15 .40
249 Marc-Andre Bergeron .15 .40
250 Mike Fisher .20 .50
251 Jeff Carter .25 .60
252 Brent Johnson .20 .50
253 Milan Jurcina .20 .50
254 Ryan Smyth .20 .50
255 Brian Gionta .20 .50
256 Adam Larsson .25 .60
257 Andrej Meszaros .15 .40
258 Chris Higgins .15 .40
259 Steve Sullivan .15 .40
260 Colin Greening .15 .40
261 Brian Lee .20 .50
262 Daymond Langkow .15 .40
263 Devan Dubnyk .25 .60
264 Erik Gudbranson .25 .60
265 Roberto Luongo .25 .60
266 Hal Gill .15 .40
267 Tuukka Rask .25 .60
268 Nicklas Backstrom .40 1.00
269 Adam Henrique .25 .60
270 Nick Johnson .20 .50
271 Corey Potter .20 .50
272 Vernon Fiddler .15 .40
273 Nik Antropov .20 .50
274 Filip Kuba .15 .40
275 Joey MacDonald .20 .50
276 Jamie McGinn .15 .40
277 Thomas Greiss .20 .50
278 Viatcheslav Voynov .25 .60
279 Artem Anisimov .20 .50
280 Braden Holtby .40 1.00
281 Brad Marchand .30 .75
282 Jay Harrison .15 .40
283 Victor Hedman .30 .75
204 Jiri Hudler .20 .50
285 Daniel Carcillo .15 .40
286 Radek Dvorak .15 .40
287 Matt Cullen .15 .40
288 Henrik Lundqvist .30 .75
289 Jason Arnott .20 .50
290 Mattias Tedenby .15 .40
291 Daniel Alfredsson .25 .60
292 Jose Theodore .25 .60
293 Niklas Hjalmarsson .15 .40
294 Matthew Halischuk .15 .40
295 Mike Santorelli .15 .40
296 Anthony Stewart .15 .40
297 Simon Gagne .25 .60
298 Nick Foligno .20 .50
299 Matt Cooke .15 .40
300 Lubomir Visnovsky .15 .40
301 Bryan Little .25 .60
302 Chris Butler .15 .40
303 Ryan Miller .25 .60
304 Brett Clark .15 .40
305 Erik Christensen .15 .40
306 Mike Komisarek .20 .50
307 Joe Corvo .15 .40
308 Evgeni Nabokov .20 .50
309 Derek Dorsett .15 .40
310 Rene Bourque .15 .40
311 Antti Niemi .20 .50
312 Evander Kane .25 .60
313 Brian Boyle .15 .40
314 Henrik Zetterberg .30 .75
315 Dustin Penner .20 .50
316 Cory Schneider .20 .50
317 Wayne Simmonds .30 .75
318 Eric Belanger .15 .40
319 Sean Bergenheim .15 .40
320 Peter Mueller .15 .40
321 Petr Sykora .20 .50
322 Mike Ribeiro .20 .50
323 Mikko Koivu .20 .50
324 Matt Hendricks .15 .40
325 Mark Letestu .20 .50
326 Kyle Quincey .15 .40
327 Jason Spezza .25 .60
328 Paul Stastny .25 .60
329 Ryan McDonagh .25 .60
330 T.J. Galiardi .20 .50
331 Sheldon Souray .15 .40
332 Tyler Seguin .40 1.00
333 Steve Staios .15 .40
334 Peter Budaj .20 .50
335 Alexander Semin .25 .60
336 Clarke MacArthur .15 .40
337 Chris Stewart .20 .50
338 Maxime Talbot .20 .50
339 Andrei Loktionov .20 .50
340 Patrice Bergeron .30 .75
341 Niklas Hagman .15 .40
342 Roman Horak .20 .50
343 Pierre-Marc Bouchard .25 .60
344 Ryan Johansen .30 .75
345 Marcus Johansson .20 .50
346 Pekka Rinne .30 .75
347 Niklas Kronwall .20 .50
348 Dwayne Roloson .20 .50
349 Andrew Cogliano .15 .40
350 Alex Pietrangelo .20 .50
351 Keith Yandle .25 .60
352 Marian Hossa .20 .50
353 Tomas Kopecky .20 .50
354 Derek Stepan .25 .60
355 Erik Johnson .15 .40
356 Dan Hamhuis .20 .50
357 Zenon Konopka .20 .50
358 Jussi Jokinen .15 .40
359 Zbynek Michalek .15 .40
360 Tomas Holmstrom .15 .40
361 Drew Doughty .25 .60
362 Luke Adam .20 .50
363 Sam Gagner .20 .50
364 Martin St. Louis .25 .60
365 Luke Schenn .15 .40
366 Tom Wandell .15 .40
367 Henrik Tallinder .15 .40
368 Sidney Crosby 1.00 2.50
369 Marc-Edouard Vlasic .15 .40
370 Bobby Ryan .25 .60
371 Zack Smith .15 .40
372 Brad Boyes .15 .40
373 Daniel Briere .25 .60
374 Josh Gorges .20 .50
375 Nick Spaling .15 .40
376 Theo Peckham .15 .40
377 Chris Mason .20 .50
378 Martin Hanzal .15 .40
379 Darroll Powe .15 .40
380 Curtis Glencross .15 .40
381 Rich Peverley .25 .60
382 Alexander Burmistrov .20 .50
383 Barret Jackman .15 .40
384 Brian Campbell .15 .40
385 Michael Del Zotto .15 .40
386 David Booth .15 .40
387 Marek Zidlicky .15 .40
388 Tyler Kennedy .15 .40
389 Steve Downie .15 .40
390 Nikita Nikitin .15 .40
391 Ray Emery .20 .50
392 Jordan Leopold .15 .40
393 Derek Morris .15 .40
394 Zach Parise .25 .60
395 Mark Streit .15 .40
396 Phil Kessel .30 .75
397 Michael Ryder .15 .40
398 Daniel Girardi .15 .40
399 Sami Salo .15 .40
400 Joni Pitkanen .20 .50
401 Tyler Myers .20 .50
402 Cody McLeod .15 .40
403 Tuomo Ruutu .20 .50
404 Matt Carle .20 .50
405 Brooks Orpik .20 .50
406 Radim Vrbata .20 .50
407 Daniel Sedin .25 .60
408 Eric Nystrom .15 .40
409 Nino Niederreiter .15 .40
410 Patrik Elias .25 .60
411 James Wisniewski .15 .40
412 T.J. Brodie .15 .40
413 Erik Karlsson .50 1.25
414 Claude Giroux .25 .60
415 Dan Cleary .25 .60
416 Shawn Matthias .15 .40
417 Dainius Zubrus .15 .40
418 Zack Kassian .20 .50
419 Jonas Hiller .20 .50
420 Ron Hainsey .15 .40
421 Dominic Moore .15 .40
422 Steve Montador .15 .40
423 Milan Lucic .25 .60
424 Mathieu Garon .20 .50
425 Colin Wilson .20 .50
426 Matt Beleskey .15 .40
427 Chris Neil .15 .40
428 Joffrey Lupul .20 .50
429 Anton Volchenkov .15 .40
430 Dustin Brown .25 .60
431 Alexander Edler .15 .40
432 Cody Hodgson .25 .60
433 Dennis Seidenberg .20 .50
434 Martin Biron .20 .50
435 Martin Havlat .20 .50
436 John Moore .15 .40
437 James van Riemsdyk .25 .60
438 Jarome Iginla .25 .60
439 Martin Erat .15 .40
440 Tomas Plekanec .25 .60
441 Frans Nielsen .15 .40
442 Troy Brouwer .20 .50
443 James Neal .25 .60
444 Jared Spurgeon .15 .40
445 Matt Duchene .25 .60
446 Dmitry Kulikov .15 .40
447 Ilya Bryzgalov .25 .60
448 John Tavares .50 1.25
449 Ondrej Pavelec .25 .60
450 Jarret Stoll .20 .50
451 Kevin Shattenkirk .25 .60
452 Chris Campoli .15 .40
453 Adrian Aucoin .15 .40
454 Patrick Sharp .25 .60
455 Brad Stuart .15 .40
456 John-Michael Liles .15 .40
457 Tim Jackman .15 .40
458 Jaroslav Spacek .15 .40
459 Carey Price .75 2.00
460 Tomas Vokoun .20 .50
461 Kevin Klein .15 .40
462 Marcus Kruger .30 .75
463 Sergei Gonchar .15 .40
464 Travis Hamonic .20 .50
465 Tim Connolly .15 .40
466 Joe Thornton .25 .60
467 Jordan Staal .25 .60
468 Kris Russell .15 .40
469 Michal Neuvirth .20 .50
470 Dany Heatley .20 .50
471 Blake Wheeler .25 .60
472 Viktor Stalberg .15 .40
473 Ladislav Smid .15 .40
474 Justin Faulk .15 .40
475 David Desharnais .25 .60
476 Grant Clitsome .15 .40
477 Jordan Eberle .25 .60
478 Semyon Varlamov .25 .60
479 Vincent Lecavalier .20 .50
480 Mikkel Boedker .15 .40
481 Jim Howard .25 .60
482 Cal Clutterbuck .25 .60
483 Lee Stempniak .15 .40
484 Ales Hemsky .20 .50
485 Sergei Kostitsyn .15 .40
486 Brian Elliott .20 .50
487 Joe Pavelski .25 .60
488 Brad Richardson .20 .50
489 Tim Brent .15 .40
490 Nick Schultz .15 .40
491 Richard Bachman .20 .50
492 Rick Nash .25 .60
493 Nate Thompson .15 .40
494 Jason Pominville .20 .50
495 Mikael Samuelsson .15 .40
496 Checklist .15 .40
497 Checklist .15 .40
498 Checklist .15 .40
499 Checklist .15 .40
500 Checklist .15 .40
501 Bobby Orr L 2.50 6.00
502 Cam Neely L .75 2.00
503 Johnny Bucyk L .60 1.50
504 Milt Schmidt L .60 1.50
505 Phil Esposito L 1.25 3.00
506 Ray Bourque L 1.25 3.00
507 Bobby Hull L .75 2.00
508 Denis Savard L 1.00 2.50
509 Doug Wilson L .60 1.50
510 Stan Mikita L 1.00 2.50
511 Alex Delvecchio L .60 1.50
512 Red Kelly L .60 1.50
513 Ted Lindsay L .75 2.00
514 Bill Ranford L .75 2.00
515 Mark Messier L 1.00 2.50
516 Paul Coffey L .75 2.00
517 Ron Francis L 1.00 2.50
518 Jari Kurri L .75 2.00
519 Marcel Dionne L 1.00 2.50
520 Rogie Vachon L 1.00 2.50
521 Dino Ciccarelli L .75 2.00
522 Mike Modano L 1.25 3.00
523 Neal Broten L .60 1.50
524 Guy Lafleur L 1.00 2.50
525 Jean Beliveau L .75 2.00
526 Larry Robinson L .75 2.00
527 Claude Lemieux L .60 1.50
528 Scott Niedermayer L .75 2.00
529 Brent Sutter L .50 1.25
530 Bryan Trottier L 1.00 2.50
531 Denis Potvin L .75 2.00
532 Duane Sutter L .50 1.25
533 Mike Bossy L .75 2.00
534 Andy Bathgate L .75 2.00
535 Brad Park L .60 1.50
536 Bill Barber L .60 1.50
537 Bobby Clarke L .75 2.00
538 Dave Schultz L .75 2.00
539 Eric Lindros L 1.25 3.00
540 Tim Kerr L .60 1.50
541 Peter Stastny L .60 1.50
542 Brendan Shanahan L 1.00 2.50
543 Brett Hull L .75 2.00
544 Tony Twist L .50 1.25
545 Curtis Joseph L .75 2.00
546 Wendel Clark L .75 2.00
547 Markus Naslund L .60 1.50
548 Richard Brodeur L .75 2.00
549 Mike Gartner L .75 2.00
550 Dale Hawerchuk L 1.00 2.50
551 Checklist .75 2.00
552 Carter Camper RC .75 2.00
553 Maxime Sauve RC 1.00 2.50
554 Lane MacDermid RC 1.00 2.50
555 Torey Krug RC 4.00 10.00
556 Michael Hutchinson RC 2.00 5.00
557 Travis Turnbull RC 1.00 2.50
558 Sven Baertschi RC 1.25 3.00
559 Akim Aliu RC 1.00 2.50
560 Jeremy Welsh RC 1.00 2.50
561 Brandon Bollig RC 1.00 2.50
562 Tyson Barrie RC 2.00 5.00
563 Mike Connolly RC 1.00 2.50
564 Dalton Prout RC 1.00 2.50
565 Cody Goloubef RC 1.00 2.50
566 Shawn Hunwick RC 1.00 2.50
567 Ryan Garbutt RC 1.00 2.50
568 Reilly Smith RC 2.00 5.00
569 Brenden Dillon RC 1.00 2.50
570 Scott Glennie RC 1.00 2.50
571 Riley Sheahan RC 1.00 2.50
572 Philippe Cornet RC 1.00 2.50
573 Colby Robak RC 1.00 2.50
574 Jordan Nolan RC 1.00 2.50
575 Kristopher Foucault RC 1.00 2.50
576 Jason Zucker RC 1.25 3.00
577 Tyler Cuma RC 1.00 2.50
578 Chay Genoway RC 1.00 2.50
579 Gabriel Dumont RC 1.00 2.50
580 Robert Mayer RC 1.25 3.00
581 Chet Pickard RC 1.00 2.50
582 Aaron Ness RC 1.00 2.50
583 Casey Cizikas RC 1.00 2.50
584 Matt Donovan RC 1.00 2.50
585 Chris Kreider RC 2.00 5.00
586 Brandon Manning RC 1.00 2.50
587 Michael Stone RC 1.00 2.50
588 Matt Watkins RC 1.00 2.50
589 Tyson Sexsmith RC 1.00 2.50
590 Jake Allen RC 3.00 8.00
591 Jaden Schwartz RC 2.00 5.00
592 J.T. Brown RC 1.00 2.50
593 Carter Ashton RC .75 2.00
594 Ryan Hamilton RC 1.00 2.50
595 Jussi Rynnas RC 1.00 2.50
596 Joe Sakic MR 1.25 3.00
597 Mario Lemieux MR 2.50 6.00
598 Patrick Roy MR 2.00 5.00
599 Pelle Lindbergh MR 1.00 2.50
600 Wayne Gretzky MR 4.00 10.00

2012-13 O-Pee-Chee Black Rainbow

*1-500 VETS: 6X TO 15X BASIC CARDS
*501-600 LEGENDS: 2.5X TO 6X BASIC CARDS
*552-595 ROOKIES: 1.5X TO 4X BASIC CARDS
STATED PRINT RUN 100 SER.#'d SETS
205 Corey Crawford 5.00 12.00
268 Nicklas Backstrom 6.00 15.00
558 Sven Baertschi 5.00 12.00
585 Chris Kreider 15.00 40.00

2012-13 O-Pee-Chee Rainbow

*1-500 VETS: 2.5X TO 6X BASIC CARDS
*501-600 LEGENDS: 1X TO 2.5X BASIC CARDS
*552-595 ROOKIES: .6X TO 1.5X BASIC CARDS
STATED ODDS 1:4 HOBBY
205 Corey Crawford 2.00 5.00
268 Nicklas Backstrom 2.50 6.00

2012-13 O-Pee-Chee Red

*1-500 VETS: 6X TO 15X BASIC CARDS
*501-600 LEGENDS: 2.5X TO 6X BASIC CARDS
*552-595 ROOKIES: 2.5X TO 6X BASIC CARDS
4-CARD PACK PER WRAPPER REDEMPTION
205 Corey Crawford 5.00 12.00
268 Nicklas Backstrom 6.00 15.00

2012-13 O-Pee-Chee Retro

*1-500 VETS: 2X TO 5X BASIC CARDS
*501-600 LEGENDS: .8X TO 2X BASIC CARDS
*552-595 ROOKIES: .5X TO 1.2X BASIC CARDS
ONE RETRO PER HOBBY PACK
205 Corey Crawford 1.50 4.00
268 Nicklas Backstrom 2.00 5.00
346 Pekka Rinne 1.50 4.00

2012-13 O-Pee-Chee All Stars

ONE PER 50 WRAPPER REDEMPTION
AS1 Alexander Ovechkin 20.00 50.00
AS2 Bobby Hull 5.00 12.00
AS3 Bobby Orr 15.00 40.00
AS4 Brad Marchand 6.00 15.00
AS5 Brett Hull 5.00 12.00
AS6 Bryan Trottier 6.00 15.00
AS7 Carey Price 12.00 30.00
AS8 Claude Giroux 5.00 12.00
AS9 Curtis Joseph 5.00 12.00
AS10 Daniel Sedin 5.00 12.00
AS11 Dominik Hasek 6.00 15.00
AS12 Ed Belfour 5.00 12.00
AS13 Eric Lindros 8.00 20.00
AS14 Evgeni Malkin 15.00 40.00
AS15 Henrik Lundqvist 6.00 15.00
AS16 Henrik Sedin 5.00 12.00
AS17 Henrik Zetterberg 6.00 15.00
AS18 Ilya Kovalchuk 5.00 12.00
AS19 Jarome Iginla 5.00 12.00
AS20 Jean Beliveau 5.00 12.00
AS21 Jeff Skinner 5.00 12.00
AS22 Joe Sakic 8.00 20.00
AS23 John Tavares 10.00 25.00
AS24 Jonathan Toews 12.00 30.00
AS25 Jordan Eberle 5.00 12.00
AS26 Mario Lemieux 15.00 40.00
AS27 Mark Messier 6.00 15.00
AS28 Martin Brodeur 10.00 25.00
AS29 Matt Duchene 5.00 12.00
AS30 Mike Gartner 5.00 12.00
AS31 Nicklas Backstrom 8.00 20.00
AS32 Nicklas Lidstrom 5.00 12.00
AS33 Ondrej Pavelec 5.00 12.00
AS34 P.K. Subban 8.00 20.00
AS35 Patrice Bergeron 6.00 15.00
AS36 Patrick Kane 10.00 25.00
AS37 Paul Coffey 5.00 12.00
AS38 Rick Nash 5.00 12.00
AS39 Roberto Luongo 5.00 12.00
AS40 Ron Francis 6.00 15.00
AS41 Ryan Miller 5.00 12.00
AS42 Ryan Nugent-Hopkins 5.00 12.00
AS43 Sidney Crosby 25.00 50.00
AS44 Steven Stamkos 10.00 25.00
AS45 Taylor Hall 10.00 25.00
AS46 Tim Thomas 5.00 12.00
AS47 Tyler Seguin 8.00 20.00
AS48 Wayne Gretzky 40.00 80.00
AS49 Zach Parise 5.00 12.00
AS50 Zdeno Chara 5.00 12.00

2012-13 O-Pee-Chee Black and White

1 Alex Ovechkin 100.00 250.00
2 Alexandre Burrows 25.00 60.00
3 Antti Niemi 20.00 50.00
4 Bobby Orr 90.00 150.00
5 Brett Hull 25.00 60.00
6 Carey Price 80.00 200.00
7 Claude Giroux 25.00 60.00
8 Curtis Joseph 25.00 60.00
9 Daniel Alfredsson 25.00 60.00
10 Drew Doughty 25.00 60.00

11 Eric Lindros 40.00 100.00
12 Erik Karlsson 50.00 125.00
13 Henrik Lundqvist 30.00 80.00
14 Ilya Kovalchuk 25.00 60.00
15 Jaromir Jagr 60.00 150.00
16 Jason Spezza 25.00 60.00
17 Joe Sakic 40.00 100.00
18 John Tavares 50.00 125.00
19 Jonathan Toews 40.00 100.00
20 Jordan Eberle 25.00 60.00
21 Mario Lemieux 60.00 120.00
22 Martin Brodeur 50.00 125.00
23 Milan Lucic 25.00 60.00
24 Nicklas Lidstrom 25.00 60.00
25 Ondrej Pavelec 25.00 60.00
26 P.K. Subban 40.00 100.00
27 Patrick Roy 100.00 175.00
28 Patrick Sharp 25.00 60.00
29 Pavel Datsyuk 30.00 80.00
30 Pelle Lindbergh 30.00 80.00
31 Roberto Luongo 25.00 60.00
32 Ryan Nugent-Hopkins 100.00 200.00
33 Sidney Crosby 125.00 200.00
35 Wayne Gretzky 100.00 200.00
36 Wendel Clark 25.00 60.00

2012-13 O-Pee-Chee Blaster Box Bottoms

1 Sidney Crosby A 1.00 2.50
2 Jonathan Toews A .50 1.25
3 Ryan Nugent-Hopkins B .25 .60
4 Alex Ovechkin B 1.00 2.50
5 Martin Brodeur C .50 1.25
6 Steven Stamkos C .50 1.25
P1 S.Crosby/J.Toews 1.00 2.50
P2 A.Ovechkin/Nugent-Hopkins .75 2.00
P3 M.Brodeur/S.Stamkos .75 2.00

2012-13 O-Pee-Chee Buyback Autographs

8 A.Ovechkin 09-10 OPCR/22 40.00 80.00
87 S.Crosby 09-10 OPCR/20 75.00 135.00

2012-13 O-Pee-Chee League Leaders

ODDS 1:10 SPECIAL CANADIAN BLASTER
LL Bergeron/Seguin/Chara 10.00 25.00
LLGL Stamkos/Malkin/Gaborik 20.00 50.00
LLSO Quick/Elliott/Smith 10.00 25.00
LLSV Elliott/Schndr/Lndqvst 8.00 20.00
LLAST Sedin/Giroux/Karlsson 12.00 30.00
LLPIM Dorsett/Rinaldo/Konopka 5.00 12.00
LLPNT Malkin/Stamkos/Giroux 20.00 50.00
LLPPG Neal/Hartnell/Perry 8.00 20.00
LLWIN Rinne/Fleury/Lundqvist 10.00 25.00

2012-13 O-Pee-Chee Marquee Legends Gold

INSERTS IN RETAIL HANGER PACKS
G1 Bobby Orr 20.00 50.00
G2 Bobby Hull 6.00 15.00
G3 Patrick Roy 15.00 40.00
G4 Joe Sakic 10.00 25.00
G5 Mark Messier 8.00 20.00
G6 Wayne Gretzky 15.00 40.00
G7 Jean Beliveau 6.00 15.00
G8 Eric Lindros 10.00 25.00
G9 Mario Lemieux 20.00 50.00
G10 Brett Hull 6.00 15.00

2012-13 O-Pee-Chee Pop Ups

COMMON CARD (PU1-PU50) 1.25 3.00
UNLISTED STARS 1.50 4.00
STATED ODDS 1:16 HOB, 1:32 RET
PU1 Corey Perry 1.50 4.00
PU2 Bobby Orr 5.00 12.00
PU3 Tyler Seguin 2.50 6.00
PU4 Tim Thomas 1.50 4.00
PU5 Ryan Miller 1.50 4.00
PU6 Jarome Iginla 1.50 4.00
PU7 Jeff Skinner 1.50 4.00
PU8 Jonathan Toews 3.00 8.00
PU9 Marian Hossa 1.25 3.00
PU10 Patrick Kane 3.00 8.00
PU11 Matt Duchene 1.50 4.00
PU12 Rick Nash 1.50 4.00
PU13 Jamie Benn 2.00 5.00
PU14 Henrik Zetterberg 2.00 5.00
PU15 Jim Howard 1.50 4.00
PU16 Nicklas Lidstrom 1.50 4.00
PU17 Pavel Datsyuk 2.00 5.00
PU18 Ryan Nugent-Hopkins 1.50 4.00
PU19 Paul Coffey 1.50 4.00
PU20 Taylor Hall 3.00 8.00
PU21 Wayne Gretzky 8.00 20.00
PU22 Brendan Shanahan 2.00 5.00
PU23 Ron Francis 2.00 5.00
PU24 Anze Kopitar 2.50 6.00
PU25 Drew Doughty 1.50 4.00
PU26 Jean Beliveau 1.50 4.00
PU27 Carey Price 3.00 8.00
PU28 Patrick Roy 4.00 10.00
PU29 P.K. Subban 2.50 6.00
PU30 Ilya Kovalchuk 1.50 4.00
PU31 Martin Brodeur 3.00 8.00
PU32 Zach Parise 1.50 4.00
PU33 John Tavares 3.00 8.00
PU34 Henrik Lundqvist 2.00 5.00
PU35 Mark Messier 2.00 5.00
PU36 Daniel Alfredsson 1.50 4.00
PU37 Claude Giroux 1.50 4.00
PU38 Eric Lindros 2.50 6.00
PU39 Pelle Lindbergh 3.00 8.00
PU40 Evgeni Malkin 5.00 12.00
PU41 Mario Lemieux 5.00 12.00
PU42 Sidney Crosby 6.00 15.00
PU43 Jaroslav Halak 1.50 4.00
PU44 Steven Stamkos 3.00 8.00
PU45 Phil Kessel 2.00 5.00
PU46 Daniel Sedin 1.50 4.00
PU47 Henrik Sedin 1.50 4.00
PU48 Roberto Luongo 1.50 4.00
PU49 Alexander Ovechkin 3.00 8.00
PU50 Ondrej Pavelec 1.50 4.00

2012-13 O-Pee-Chee Retro Hobby Box Bottoms

1 Sidney Crosby A 1.00 2.50
2 Pavel Datsyuk A .30 .75
3 John Tavares A .50 1.25
4 Tim Thomas A .25 .60
5 Phil Kessel B .30 .75
6 Gabriel Landeskog B .25 .60
7 Henrik Lundqvist B .30 .75
8 Alex Ovechkin B 1.00 2.50
9 Claude Giroux C .25 .60
10 Ryan Nugent-Hopkins C .25 .60
11 Carey Price C .75 2.00
12 Steven Stamkos C .50 1.25
13 Martin Brodeur D .50 1.25
14 Evgeni Malkin D .75 2.00
15 Eric Staal D .30 .75
16 Jonathan Toews D .50 1.25
P1 Crsby/Dtsyk/Tvres/Thmas 1.50 4.00
P2 Ovch/Kssl/Lndqst/Lndskg 1.25 3.00
P3 Stmkos/RNH/Girx/Price 1.50 4.00
P4 Tws/Brdr/Mlkin/E.Staal 1.25 3.00

2012-13 O-Pee-Chee Signatures

GROUP A ODDS 1:6212 HOB
GROUP B ODDS 1:2323 HOB
GROUP C ODDS 1:1429 HOB
GROUP D ODDS 1:240 HOB
OVERALL ODDS 1:192 HOB, 1:768 RET
OPCAO Alexander Ovechkin A 50.00 100.00
OPCBO Bobby Orr A
OPCCS Cory Schneider B 15.00 40.00
OPCDH Dale Hawerchuk A 20.00 50.00
OPCEK Evander Kane B 10.00 25.00
OPCEN Evgeni Nabokov C 8.00 20.00
OPCGL Gabriel Landeskog A 15.00 40.00
OPCJE Jonathan Ericsson D 6.00 15.00
OPCJH Jonas Hiller C 6.00 15.00
OPCJP Joe Pavelski B 12.00 30.00
OPCKA Karl Alzner D 5.00 12.00
OPCKC Kyle Clifford D 5.00 12.00
OPCMA Matt Hackett B 8.00 20.00
OPCMB Matt Beleskey D 5.00 12.00
OPCMF Michael Frolik D 5.00 12.00
OPCMH Marian Hossa A 40.00 100.00
OPCML Maxim Lapierre D 6.00 15.00
OPCMN Markus Naslund A 20.00 50.00
OPCMS Matt Stajan C 6.00 15.00
OPCNF Nick Foligno D 6.00 15.00
OPCNG Nicklas Grossman D 5.00 12.00
OPCPM Peter Mueller C 6.00 15.00
OPCPR Pekka Rinne A 25.00 50.00
OPCRO Ryan O'Reilly D 8.00 20.00
OPCSC Sidney Crosby A
OPCSG Sam Gagner D 6.00 15.00
OPCSS Steven Stamkos B 30.00 60.00
OPCSW Stephen Weiss D 6.00 15.00
OPCWG Wayne Gretzky A

2012-13 O-Pee-Chee Sport Royalty Autographs

GROUP B ODDS 1:26,988 HOB
PR Patrick Roy A
WG Wayne Gretzky B 250.00 400.00

2012-13 O-Pee-Chee Stickers

COMPLETE SET (100) 40.00 80.00
STATED ODDS 1:3 HOB, 1:6 RET
S1 Teemu Selanne 1.25 3.00
S2 Ryan Getzlaf 1.00 2.50
S3 Bobby Ryan .60 1.50
S4 Jonas Hiller .50 1.25
S5 Corey Perry .60 1.50
S6 Tyler Seguin 1.00 2.50
S7 Zdeno Chara .60 1.50
S8 Tim Thomas .60 1.50
S9 David Krejci .60 1.50
S10 Nathan Horton .60 1.50
S11 Brad Marchand .75 2.00
S12 Bobby Orr 2.00 5.00
S13 Tyler Myers .50 1.25
S14 Thomas Vanek .60 1.50
S15 Ryan Miller .60 1.50
S16 Michael Cammalleri .50 1.25
S17 Jarome Iginla .60 1.50
S18 Miikka Kiprusoff .50 1.25
S19 Eric Staal .75 2.00
S20 Cam Ward .60 1.50
S21 Jeff Skinner .60 1.50
S22 Duncan Keith .60 1.50
S23 Corey Crawford .75 2.00
S24 Jonathan Toews 1.25 3.00
S25 Patrick Kane 1.25 3.00
S26 Marian Hossa .50 1.25
S27 Gabriel Landeskog .60 1.50
S28 Jean-Sebastien Giguere .50 1.25
S29 Matt Duchene .60 1.50
S30 Paul Stastny .60 1.50
S31 Joe Sakic 1.00 2.50
S32 Rick Nash .60 1.50
S33 Jamie Benn .75 2.00
S34 Brenden Morrow .50 1.25
S35 Jim Howard .60 1.50
S36 Henrik Zetterberg .75 2.00
S37 Pavel Datsyuk .75 2.00
S38 Nicklas Lidstrom .60 1.50
S39 Johan Franzen .60 1.50
S40 Ryan Nugent-Hopkins .60 1.50
S41 Sam Gagner .50 1.25
S42 Paul Coffey .60 1.50
S43 Jordan Eberle .60 1.50
S44 Taylor Hall 1.25 3.00
S45 Ryan Smyth .50 1.25
S46 Wayne Gretzky 3.00 8.00
S47 Stephen Weiss .50 1.25
S48 Tomas Fleischmann .40 1.00
S49 Drew Doughty .60 1.50
S50 Anze Kopitar 1.00 2.50
S51 Mike Richards .60 1.50
S52 Dany Heatley .50 1.25
S53 Mikko Koivu .50 1.25
S54 Niklas Backstrom .50 1.25
S55 Patrick Roy 1.50 4.00
S56 Carey Price 2.00 5.00
S57 P.K. Subban 1.00 2.50
S58 Jean Beliveau .60 1.50
S59 Pekka Rinne .75 2.00
S60 Shea Weber .50 1.25
S61 Martin Brodeur 1.25 3.00
S62 Zach Parise .60 1.50
S63 Ilya Kovalchuk .60 1.50
S64 P.A. Parenteau .40 1.00
S65 Evgeni Nabokov .50 1.25
S66 John Tavares 1.25 3.00
S67 Mark Messier .75 2.00
S68 Henrik Lundqvist .75 2.00
S69 Marian Gaborik .60 1.50
S70 Jason Spezza .60 1.50
S71 Daniel Alfredsson .60 1.50
S72 Jaromir Jagr 1.50 4.00
S73 Claude Giroux .60 1.50
S74 Eric Lindros 1.00 2.50
S75 Pelle Lindbergh .75 2.00
S76 Mario Lemieux 2.00 5.00
S77 Sidney Crosby 2.50 6.00
S78 Evgeni Malkin 2.00 5.00
S79 Marc-Andre Fleury 1.00 2.50
S80 Joe Thornton .60 1.50
S81 Patrick Marleau .60 1.50
S82 Logan Couture .60 1.50
S83 Jaroslav Halak .60 1.50
S84 Steven Stamkos 1.25 3.00
S85 James Reimer .60 1.50
S86 Dion Phaneuf .60 1.50
S87 Phil Kessel .75 2.00
S88 Ryan Kesler .60 1.50
S89 Roberto Luongo .60 1.50
S90 Daniel Sedin .60 1.50
S91 Henrik Sedin .60 1.50
S92 Alexandre Burrows .60 1.50
S93 Alexander Semin .60 1.50
S94 Alexander Ovechkin 2.50 6.00
S95 Nicklas Backstrom 1.00 2.50
S96 Mike Green .60 1.50
S97 Andrew Ladd .60 1.50
S98 Alexander Burmistrov .50 1.25
S99 Ondrej Pavelec .60 1.50
S100 Evander Kane .60 1.50

2012-13 O-Pee-Chee Team Canada Signatures

GROUP A ODDS 1:7144 HOB
GROUP B ODDS 1:1633 HOB
GROUP C ODDS 1:520 HOB
OVERAL ODDS 1:384 HOB, 1:1536 RET
TCAH Adam Henrique C 10.00 25.00
TCBC Brett Connolly C 10.00 25.00
TCBO Bobby Orr A 350.00 500.00
TCCD Calvin de Haan C 10.00 25.00
TCCE Cody Eakin C 10.00 25.00
TCCJ Curtis Joseph A 50.00 100.00
TCCO Sean Couturier B 15.00 40.00
TCDH Dale Hawerchuk A
TCDO Shane Doan C 10.00 25.00
TCDP Dion Phaneuf B 12.00 30.00
TCEB Ed Belfour A 40.00 80.00
TCGF Grant Fuhr A 40.00 80.00
TCJC Jared Cowen B 30.00 60.00
TCJH Josh Harding C 12.00 30.00
TCKT Kyle Turris B 12.00 30.00
TCLC Logan Couture B 30.00 60.00
TCLL Louis Leblanc B 50.00 100.00
TCMF Marcus Foligno C 12.00 30.00
TCMS Martin St. Louis B 20.00 40.00
TCNA Rick Nash B 40.00 80.00
TCRE Ryan Ellis C 8.00 20.00
TCRN Ryan Nugent-Hopkins A
TCRS Ryan Smyth B 15.00 40.00
TCSC Sidney Crosby A 250.00 400.00
TCSD Simon Despres C 10.00 25.00
TCSG Simon Gagne B 20.00 40.00
TCSS Steven Stamkos B 30.00 80.00
TCSW Stephen Weiss C 10.00 25.00
TCWG Wayne Gretzky A 350.00 500.00
TCZK Zack Kassian C 10.00 25.00

2012-13 O-Pee-Chee Team Logo Patches

TL1-TL50 STATED ODDS 1:125 HOB
TL51-TL62 STATED ODDS 1:852 HOB
TL63-TL73 STATED ODDS 1:1704 HOB
TL74-TL86 STATED ODDS 1:1922 HOB
TL87-TL96 STATED ODDS 1:3748 HOB
OVERALL STATED ODDS 1:96
TL1 NHL primary 10.00 25.00
TL2 Eastern Conf primary 8.00 20.00
TL3 Western Conf primary 8.00 20.00
TL4 Anaheim Ducks primary 10.00 25.00
TL5 Boston Bruins primary 15.00 40.00
TL6 Buffalo Sabres primary 10.00 25.00
TL7 Calgary Flames primary 15.00 40.00
TL8 Hurricanes primary 10.00 25.00
TL9 Blackhawks primary 12.00 30.00
TL10 Avalanche primary 12.00 30.00
TL11 Blue Jackets primary 10.00 25.00
TL12 Dallas Stars primary 10.00 25.00
TL13 Red Wings primary 15.00 40.00
TL14 Edmonton Oilers primary 12.00 30.00
TL15 Florida Panthers primary 8.00 20.00
TL16 L.A. Kings primary 15.00 30.00
TL17 Minnesota Wild primary 10.00 25.00
TL18 Canadiens primary 15.00 40.00
TL19 Nash. Predators primary 8.00 20.00
TL20 NJ Devils primary 12.00 30.00
TL21 NY Islanders primary 12.50 30.00
TL22 NY Rangers primary 10.00 25.00
TL23 Ottawa Senators primary 10.00 25.00
TL24 Flyers primary 10.00 25.00
TL25 Phoenix Coyotes primary 8.00 20.00
TL26 Penguins primary 15.00 40.00
TL27 SJ Sharks primary 10.00 25.00
TL28 St. Louis Blues primary 10.00 25.00
TL29 T.B. Lightning primary 15.00 40.00
TL30 Maple Leafs primary 12.00 30.00
TL31 Canucks primary 8.00 20.00
TL32 Capitals primary 10.00 25.00
TL33 Winnipeg Jets primary 20.00 40.00
TL34 NHL primary 10.00 25.00
TL35 Eastern Conference alt 8.00 20.00
TL36 Western Conference alt 8.00 20.00
TL37 Playoffs primary 10.00 25.00
TL38 Stanley Cup Final alt 10.00 25.00
TL39 All-Star Game primary 10.00 25.00
TL40 All-Star Game alt 10.00 25.00
TL41 Winter Classic alt 15.00 30.00
TL42 Heritage Classic alt 15.00 50.00
TL43 Boston Bruins alt 15.00 30.00
TL44 Boston Bruins script 15.00 30.00
TL45 Chicago Blackhawks alt 20.00 40.00
TL46 Minnesota Wild script 15.00 30.00
TL47 Canadiens script 20.00 40.00
TL48 Que Nordiques alt 30.00 60.00
TL49 Maple Leafs second 25.00 60.00
TL50 Winnipeg Jets script 20.00 40.00
TL51 Atl Thrashers 10ANN 20.00 40.00
TL52 Buffalo Sabres 10ANN 25.00 50.00
TL53 Calgary Flames 10ANN 20.00 40.00
TL54 Avalanche 10ANN 20.00 40.00
TL55 Edmonton Oilers 10ANN 30.00 60.00
TL56 Hart Whalers 10ANN 25.00 50.00
TL57 Nash Predators 10ANN 20.00 40.00
TL58 NJ Devils 10ANN 30.00 80.00
TL59 Ottawa Senators 10ANN 20.00 40.00
TL60 Que Nordiques 10ANN 25.00 50.00
TL61 SJ Sharks 10ANN 20.00 40.00
TL62 Winnipeg Jets 10ANN 30.00 60.00
TL63 Atlanta Flames primary 30.00 60.00
TL64 Cal. Golden Seals primary 30.00 80.00
TL65 Colorado Rockies primary 40.00 80.00
TL66 K.C. Scouts primary 50.00 120.00
TL67 LA Kings primary 30.00 60.00
TL68 North Stars primary 40.00 80.00
TL69 N.Y. Islanders primary 40.00 80.00
TL70 Penguins primary 40.00 80.00
TL71 St. Louis Blues primary 60.00 120.00
TL72 Canucks primary 50.00 100.00
TL73 Capitals primary 30.00 80.00
TL74 Boston Bruins primary 100.00 200.00
TL75 Blackhawks primary 50.00 100.00
TL76 Detroit Cougars primary 60.00 125.00
TL77 Red Wings primary 50.00 100.00
TL78 Hamilton Tigers primary 25.00 50.00
TL79 Canadiens primary 50.00 100.00
TL80 Maroons primary 50.00 100.00
TL81 N.Y. Americans primary 100.00 175.00
TL82 N.Y. Rangers primary 30.00 80.00
TL83 Ottawa Senators primary 50.00 100.00
TL84 St. Louis Eagles primary 40.00 80.00
TL85 Toronto Arenas primary 40.00 80.00
TL86 Maple Leafs primary 60.00 120.00
TL87 Avalanche Joe Sakic 40.00 80.00
TL88 Oilers Gretzky HOF 100.00 200.00
TL89 Oilers Messier 11 40.00 80.00
TL90 L.A. Kings Gretzky 802 150.00 300.00
TL91 N.J. Devils Brodeur 552 75.00 125.00
TL92 N.Y. Rangers Gretzky 75.00 150.00
TL93 N.Y. Rangers Shanahan 40.00 80.00
TL94 St. Louis Blues Hull 75.00 150.00
TL95 Caps 9-11 Memorial 175.00 300.00
TL96 Winn.Jets Memories 75.00 150.00
TL97 Predators cartoon
TL98 Red Wings cartoon
TL99 Whalers cartoon
TL100 Canucks cartoon

2013-14 O-Pee-Chee

COMP.SERIES 1 (600) 90.00 150.00
COMP.SER. 1 w/o RC's (500) 30.00 60.00
COMP.SERIES 2 (42) 25.00 60.00
501-600 ROOKIE ODDS 1:2 HOB/RET
601-612 ODDS 1:17H/R, 1:34 BL UD SER.2
613-642 ODDS 1:7H/R, 1:14 BL UD SER.2
1 Phil Kessel .30 .75
2 Benoit Pouliot .15 .40
3 Semyon Varlamov .25 .60
4 Andrew Ference .15 .40
5 Jonathan Bernier .25 .60
6 Daniel Girardi .15 .40
7 Douglas Murray .15 .40
8 Ray Whitney .20 .50
9 Daniel Briere .25 .60
10 Johan Franzen .25 .60
11 Pavel Bure .30 .75
12 Nick Spaling .15 .40
13 Dwight King .15 .40
14 Devin Setoguchi .20 .50
15 Andrej Sekera .15 .40
16 Patrick Dwyer .15 .40
17 John-Michael Liles .15 .40
18 Michael Grabner .20 .50
19 Guillaume Latendresse .20 .50
20 Derick Brassard .25 .60
21 Matt Read .15 .40
22 Duncan Keith .25 .60
23 Colin Wilson .20 .50
24 Jordan Eberle .25 .60
25 Drayson Bowman .15 .40
26 Jordin Tootoo .20 .50
27 Justin Williams .20 .50
28 Kyle Wellwood .20 .50
29 Larry Robinson .25 .60
30 Tyler Kennedy .15 .40
31 Kevin Klein .15 .40
32 Loui Eriksson .20 .50
33 Alexander Semin .25 .60
34 Cody Franson .15 .40
35 Erik Condra .15 .40
36 Nik Antropov .20 .50
37 Peter Holland .15 .40
38 Drew Miller .15 .40
39 Henrik Sedin .25 .60
40 Curtis Glencross .15 .40
41 Mike Richards .25 .60
42 Ryane Clowe .15 .40
43 Carl Gunnarsson .15 .40
44 Evgeni Nabokov .20 .50
45 James Wisniewski .15 .40
46 Brian Gionta .20 .50
47 Scott Hartnell .25 .60
48 Shawn Matthias .15 .40
49 Jonathan Toews .50 1.25
50 Luc Robitaille .25 .60
51 Joey MacDonald .15 .40
52 Alex Pietrangelo .20 .50
53 Brayden Schenn .25 .60
54 Paul Gaustad .15 .40
55 Radim Vrbata .20 .50
56 Mark Fistric .15 .40
57 Cory Emmerton .15 .40
58 Matt Carle .20 .50
59 John Carlson .30 .75
60 Zenon Konopka .20 .50
61 Jiri Tlusty .20 .50
62 Alex Tanguay .15 .40
63 Viktor Stalberg .15 .40
64 Daniel Alfredsson .25 .60
65 Colin McDonald .20 .50
66 Dennis Seidenberg .20 .50
67 Steven Stamkos .50 1.25
68 R.J. Umberger .15 .40
69 Rob Scuderi .15 .40
70 Nikolai Khabibulin .25 .60
71 Jaroslav Halak .25 .60
72 Steve Ott .20 .50
73 Joni Pitkanen .20 .50
74 Henrik Zetterberg .30 .75
75 Jason Chimera .15 .40
76 Victor Hedman .30 .75
77 Sergei Bobrovsky .25 .60
78 Oliver Ekman-Larsson .20 .50
79 Mark Messier .30 .75
80 Martin Erat .15 .40
81 Wayne Simmonds .30 .75
82 Jordan Leopold .15 .40
83 Craig Smith .15 .40
84 Matt Cooke .15 .40
85 Jay McClement .15 .40
86 Fedor Tyutin .15 .40
87 Rick Nash .25 .60
88 Kyle Turris .15 .40
89 Andrew MacDonald .15 .40
90 Bobby Orr .75 2.00
91 Vernon Fiddler .15 .40
92 Joffrey Lupul .20 .50
93 Patrik Berglund .15 .40
94 Braden Holtby .40 1.00
95 Patrick Kane .50 1.25
96 Steve Sullivan .15 .40
97 Martin Hanzal .15 .40
98 Cam Atkinson .25 .60
99 James Sheppard .15 .40
100 T.J. Oshie .40 1.00
101 Brooks Orpik .20 .50
102 Derek Roy .20 .50
103 Mike Weber .15 .40
104 Blake Comeau .15 .40
105 Colton Orr .15 .40
106 Jussi Jokinen .15 .40
107 Patrice Bergeron .30 .75
108 Justin Abdelkader .20 .50
109 Robin Lehner .20 .50
110 Teemu Selanne .50 1.25
111 Peter Mueller .15 .40
112 Cal Clutterbuck .25 .60
113 Troy Brouwer .20 .50
114 Mike Bossy .25 .60
115 Paul Martin .15 .40
116 Joe Pavelski .25 .60
117 Tom Pyatt .15 .40
118 Jan Hejda .15 .40
119 Brandon Sutter .20 .50
120 Marcus Foligno .15 .40
121 Pierre-Marc Bouchard .25 .60
122 Chris Neil .15 .40
123 Filip Kuba .15 .40
124 David Perron .15 .40
125 Jonathan Ericsson .20 .50
126 Doug Gilmour .30 .75
127 P.K. Subban .40 1.00
128 Sheldon Souray .15 .40
129 Marc Staal .20 .50
130 Stephen Gionta .15 .40
131 Tom Gilbert .15 .40
132 Jacob Markstrom .20 .50
133 Jim Howard .25 .60
134 Jay Harrison .15 .40
135 Chris Kelly .20 .50
136 Mark Letestu .20 .50
137 Nick Schultz .15 .40
138 Taylor Pyatt .15 .40
139 Mikhail Grabovski .20 .50
140 Tomas Kopecky .20 .50
141 Mikkel Boedker .15 .40
142 Cody Eakin .15 .40
143 Dustin Byfuglien .25 .60
144 Richard Clune .15 .40
145 Kevin Bieksa .20 .50
146 Anton Volchenkov .15 .40
147 Francois Beauchemin .15 .40
148 Gregory Campbell .15 .40
149 Carey Price .75 2.00
150 Casey Cizikas .15 .40
151 Reilly Smith .25 .60
152 Marc-Andre Fleury .40 1.00
153 Brian Campbell .15 .40
154 Brandon Saad .25 .60
155 Clayton Stoner .15 .40
156 Jakub Kindl .15 .40
157 Zack Smith .15 .40
158 Alexander Edler .15 .40
159 Andrew Ladd .25 .60
160 Raffi Torres .15 .40
161 John Tavares .50 1.25
162 Dmitry Kulikov .15 .40
163 Ryan Ellis .15 .40
164 Teddy Purcell .25 .60
165 Tyson Barrie .25 .60
166 Mathieu Perreault .15 .40
167 Dale Hawerchuk .30 .75
168 Marian Hossa .20 .50
169 Luca Sbisa .20 .50
170 Shawn Horcoff .15 .40
171 James Neal .25 .60
172 Mike Fisher .20 .50
173 Henrik Lundqvist .30 .75
174 Brett Hull .25 .60
175 Stephen Weiss .20 .50
176 Saku Koivu .25 .60
177 Sam Gagner .20 .50
178 Mike Ribeiro .20 .50
179 Tuukka Rask .25 .60
180 Marc Methot .15 .40
181 David Backes .25 .60
182 Jiri Hudler .20 .50
183 Steve Yzerman .50 1.25
184 Shea Weber .20 .50
185 Philip Larsen .15 .40
186 Brad Marchand .30 .75
187 Jamie McBain .15 .40
188 Ryan Nugent-Hopkins .25 .60
189 Chris Phillips .15 .40
190 Mike Green .25 .60
191 Frans Nielsen .15 .40
192 Ruslan Fedotenko .15 .40
193 Kyle Brodziak .15 .40
194 Ryan Carter .15 .40
195 Niklas Hjalmarsson .15 .40
196 Marcel Goc .20 .50
197 Ryan McDonagh .25 .60
198 Joe Corvo .15 .40
199 Dion Phaneuf .25 .60
200 Tomas Vokoun .20 .50
201 Craig Anderson .25 .60
202 Dan Hamhuis .20 .50
203 Logan Couture .25 .60
204 Kari Lehtonen .20 .50
205 Vincent Lecavalier .20 .50
206 Devan Dubnyk .25 .60
207 Roman Josi .25 .60
208 Barret Jackman .15 .40
209 Evgeni Malkin .75 2.00
210 Dany Heatley .20 .50
211 Jochen Hecht .15 .40
212 Marcus Johansson .20 .50
213 Matt Calvert .15 .40
214 Boyd Gordon .15 .40
215 Alexandre Burrows .25 .60
216 Erik Johnson .15 .40
217 Erik Karlsson .50 1.25
218 Eric Brewer .15 .40
219 Tomas Fleischmann .15 .40
220 Brandon Prust .15 .40
221 Daniel Winnik .15 .40
222 Brent Burns .30 .75
223 Andrew Shaw .25 .60
224 Torrey Mitchell .15 .40
225 Gustav Nyquist .20 .50
226 Patrick Wiercioch .15 .40
227 Trevor Daley .15 .40
228 Nazem Kadri .25 .60
229 Keith Yandle .25 .60
230 Mark Stuart .15 .40
231 Michael Del Zotto .15 .40
232 Nick Foligno .20 .50
233 David Desharnais .25 .60
234 Bryan Bickell .15 .40
235 Jakub Voracek .25 .60
236 Brian McGrattan .15 .40
237 Rob Klinkhammer .15 .40
238 Joel Ward .15 .40
239 Marian Gaborik .25 .60
240 Ryan Miller .25 .60
241 Josh Gorges .20 .50
242 Travis Hamonic .15 .40
243 Carl Hagelin .25 .60
244 Tobias Enstrom .15 .40
245 Scott Gomez .20 .50
246 Corey Crawford .30 .75
247 Francis Bouillon .15 .40
248 Miikka Kiprusoff .20 .50
249 Nate Thompson .15 .40
250 Lauri Korpikoski .15 .40
251 Alexander Ovechkin 1.00 2.50
252 Jake Muzzin .15 .40
253 Ryan Kesler .25 .60
254 Pascal Dupuis .15 .40
255 Ray Bourque .40 1.00
256 Kimmo Timonen .15 .40
257 Andy McDonald .20 .50
258 Corey Perry .25 .60
259 Matt Hendricks .15 .40
260 Marcus Kruger .25 .60
261 Milan Hejduk .20 .50
262 Tyler Ennis .20 .50
263 John Moore .15 .40
264 Kris Versteeg .20 .50
265 Chad LaRose .15 .40
266 David Legwand .20 .50
267 Daniel Sedin .25 .60
268 Martin St. Louis .25 .60
269 Patrick Eaves .15 .40
270 James van Riemsdyk .25 .60
271 Jay Bouwmeester .25 .60
272 Nicklas Backstrom .40 1.00
273 Andre Benoit .15 .40
274 Nikita Nikitin .15 .40
275 Brad Boyes .15 .40
276 Andrei Markov .25 .60
277 Matt Beleskey .15 .40
278 Brian Elliott .20 .50
279 Chris Butler .15 .40
280 Ilya Kovalchuk .25 .60
281 Lubomir Visnovsky .15 .40
282 Ray Emery .20 .50
283 Mikko Koivu .20 .50
284 Dominik Hasek .30 .75
285 Alex Goligoski .15 .40
286 Marc-Edouard Vlasic .15 .40
287 Vaclav Prospal .15 .40
288 Antoine Vermette .15 .40
289 David Jones .15 .40
290 Brian Boyle .15 .40
291 Kris Letang .25 .60
292 Justin Peters .15 .40
293 Simon Gagne .25 .60
294 Rich Peverley .25 .60
295 Gabriel Landeskog .20 .50
296 Adam Larsson .25 .60
297 Kyle Okposo .25 .60
298 Martin Havlat .20 .50
299 Maxime Talbot .20 .50
300 B.J. Crombeen .15 .40
301 Karl Alzner .15 .40
302 Eric Staal .30 .75
303 Ryan Whitney .15 .40
304 Kyle Clifford .15 .40
305 Sean Couturier .25 .60
306 Matthew Lombardi .15 .40
307 Michael Ryder .15 .40
308 Brenden Morrow .20 .50
309 Dan Cleary .25 .60
310 Theoren Fleury .30 .75
311 Cory Schneider .20 .50
312 Johan Hedberg .20 .50
313 Matt Martin .15 .40
314 Cody Hodgson .25 .60
315 Tyler Seguin .40 1.00
316 Brent Seabrook .25 .60
317 Ryan O'Reilly .25 .60
318 Patrick Roy .60 1.50
319 Ryan Garbutt .15 .40
320 Jack Johnson .15 .40
321 Lee Stempniak .15 .40
322 Patrick Sharp .25 .60
323 Milan Lucic .25 .60
324 Anders Lindback .15 .40
325 Eric Tangradi .15 .40
326 Jamie Benn .30 .75
327 Tyler Bozak .20 .50
328 Martin Brodeur .50 1.25
329 Roberto Luongo .25 .60
330 Pekka Rinne .30 .75
331 Clarke MacArthur .15 .40
332 Michal Neuvirth .20 .50
333 Colin Greening .15 .40
334 Robyn Regehr .15 .40
335 Bryce Salvador .15 .40
336 Jared Spurgeon .15 .40
337 Grant Clitsome .15 .40
338 Nikolai Kulemin .20 .50
339 Jonas Hiller .20 .50
340 Derek Stepan .25 .60
341 David Krejci .25 .60
342 Jack Skille .20 .50
343 Andy Greene .15 .40
344 Dan Ellis .20 .50
345 Nick Bonino .15 .40
346 Eric Lindros .40 1.00
347 Ladislav Smid .15 .40
348 Chris Higgins .15 .40
349 Matt Frattin .20 .50
350 Steve Begin .15 .40
351 John Mitchell .15 .40
352 Anton Khudobin .20 .50
353 Tim Jackman .15 .40
354 Patrik Elias .25 .60
355 Drew Doughty .25 .60
356 Ryan Smyth .20 .50
357 Aaron Palushaj .20 .50
358 Thomas Vanek .25 .60
359 Derek Morris .15 .40
360 Marek Zidlicky .15 .40
361 Niklas Kronwall .20 .50
362 Matt Moulson .20 .50
363 Matt Cullen .15 .40
364 Matt Stajan .20 .50
365 Zac Rinaldo .20 .50
366 Antti Niemi .20 .50
367 Shane Doan .20 .50
368 Eric Nystrom .15 .40
369 Josh Bailey .20 .50
370 Vladimir Sobotka .15 .40
371 Brandon Dubinsky .20 .50
372 Bobby Clarke .25 .60
373 Cam Fowler .20 .50
374 Matt Duchene .25 .60
375 Brandon Yip .15 .40
376 Ryan Callahan .25 .60
377 Justin Faulk .15 .40
378 Jason LaBarbera .20 .50
379 Cody McLeod .15 .40
380 Kyle Palmieri .20 .50
381 Sami Salo .15 .40
382 Valtteri Filppula .25 .60
383 Zdeno Chara .25 .60
384 Ilya Bryzgalov .25 .60
385 Jeff Skinner .20 .50
386 Ben Scrivens .20 .50
387 Joe Thornton .25 .60
388 Jarret Stoll .20 .50
389 Anton Stralman .15 .40
390 Jannik Hansen .20 .50
391 Jeff Petry .20 .50
392 P.A. Parenteau .15 .40
393 Ales Hemsky .15 .40
394 Ian White .20 .50
395 Michal Handzus .15 .40
396 Ryan Getzlaf .40 1.00
397 Wayne Gretzky 1.25 3.00
398 Tyler Myers .20 .50
399 Brad Stuart .15 .40
400 George Parros .20 .50
401 Mason Raymond .20 .50
402 Adrian Aucoin .15 .40
403 Daniel Paille .15 .40
404 Travis Zajac .20 .50
405 Taylor Hall .50 1.25
406 Jamie McGinn .15 .40
407 Evander Kane .25 .60
408 Alexei Emelin .20 .50
409 Magnus Paajarvi .25 .60
410 Erik Cole .20 .50
411 Christian Ehrhoff .15 .40
412 Jeff Carter .25 .60
413 Ryan Johansen .30 .75
414 Eric Fehr .15 .40
415 David Moss .15 .40
416 David Clarkson .15 .40
417 Ville Leino .20 .50
418 Nick Leddy .15 .40
419 Andrew Cogliano .15 .40
420 Gabriel Bourque .20 .50
421 Jonathan Quick .40 1.00
422 Nathan Horton .25 .60
423 Paul Coffey .25 .60
424 Nathan Gerbe .15 .40
425 Ryan Suter .15 .40
426 Ryan Malone .15 .40
427 Rene Bourque .15 .40
428 Alexander Burmistrov .20 .50
429 Sergei Kostitsyn .15 .40
430 Nicklas Lidstrom .25 .60
431 Mike Smith .25 .60
432 Bryan Trottier .30 .75
433 Paul Stastny .25 .60
434 Jaden Schwartz .30 .75
435 Artem Anisimov .20 .50
436 Michael Cammalleri .20 .50
437 Bobby Ryan .25 .60
438 Rostislav Klesla .15 .40
439 Jason Garrison .15 .40
440 Max Pacioretty .25 .60
441 Olli Jokinen .20 .50
442 Zach Parise .25 .60
443 Chris Kunitz .25 .60
444 Anze Kopitar .40 1.00
445 Kevin Shattenkirk .25 .60
446 Jakob Silfverberg .20 .50
447 Andrei Loktionov .15 .40
448 Tommy Wingels .15 .40
449 Lars Eller .20 .50
450 Ondrej Pavelec .25 .60
451 Drew Stafford .25 .60
452 Pavel Datsyuk .30 .75
453 Dustin Brown .25 .60
454 Alexander Steen .25 .60
455 Ben Bishop .25 .60
456 Erik Gudbranson .25 .60
457 Maxim Lapierre .15 .40
458 Adam Henrique .25 .60
459 Jordan Staal .25 .60
460 Milan Michalek .15 .40
461 Dave Bolland .15 .40
462 Adam Burish .15 .40
463 Mark Streit .15 .40
464 Jaromir Jagr .60 1.50
465 James Reimer .25 .60
466 Jason Pominville .20 .50
467 Trevor Lewis .15 .40
468 Stephane Robidas .15 .40
469 Dennis Wideman .15 .40
470 Bryan Little .25 .60
471 Kyle Chipchura .15 .40
472 Roman Polak .15 .40
473 Tomas Plekanec .25 .60
474 Mark Giordano .20 .50
475 Sidney Crosby 1.00 2.50
476 Blake Wheeler .25 .60
477 Luke Schenn .15 .40
478 Niklas Backstrom .20 .50
479 Brad Richards .25 .60
480 Sergei Gonchar .15 .40
481 Cam Ward .25 .60
482 Jarome Iginla .25 .60
483 Keaton Ellerby .15 .40
484 Dan Boyle .20 .50
485 Raphael Diaz .15 .40
486 Patric Hornqvist .20 .50
487 T.J. Brodie .15 .40
488 Claude Giroux .25 .60
489 Scott Clemmensen .20 .50
490 Joe Sakic .40 1.00
491 Slava Voynov .20 .50
492 Justin Falk .15 .40
493 Chris Stewart .20 .50
494 Ron Hainsey .15 .40
495 Patrick Marleau .25 .60
496 Checklist .15 .40
497 Checklist .15 .40
498 Checklist .15 .40
499 Checklist .15 .40
500 Checklist .15 .40
501 Nail Yakupov RC 6.00 15.00
502 Ryan Murphy RC 1.25 3.00
503 Jon Rheault RC .75 2.00
504 Sean Collins RC 1.00 2.50
505 Roman Cervenka RC 1.00 2.50
506 Quinton Howden RC 1.00 2.50
507 Matt Anderson RC .75 2.00
508 Matt Tennyson RC .75 2.00
509 Christian Thomas RC 1.00 2.50
510 Chris Brown RC .75 2.00
511 Mark Barberio RC .75 2.00
512 Zach Redmond RC 1.00 2.50
513 Steve Pinizzotto RC 1.25 3.00
514 Calvin Pickard RC 1.25 3.00
515 Jean-Gabriel Pageau RC 1.00 2.50
516 Darcy Kuemper RC 1.25 3.00

17 Viktor Fasth RC 1.25 3.00
18 Brett Bellemore RC 1.00 2.50
19 Dan DeKeyser RC 1.50 4.00
20 Brendan Gallagher RC 4.00 10.00
21 Oliver Lauridsen RC 1.00 2.50
22 Leo Komarov RC 1.25 3.00
23 Michal Jordan RC .75 2.00
24 Nick Petrecki RC .75 2.00
25 Filip Forsberg RC 3.00 8.00
26 Michael Sgarbossa RC 1.00 2.50
27 Mikhail Grigorenko RC 1.50 4.00
28 Emerson Etem RC 1.25 3.00
29 Alex Chiasson RC 1.25 3.00
30 Ben Street RC .75 2.00
31 Dougie Hamilton RC 2.50 6.00
32 Mark Arcobello RC 1.25 3.00
33 Victor Bartley RC 1.00 2.50
34 Beau Bennett RC 1.50 4.00
35 Steve Oleksy RC 1.25 3.00
36 Radko Gudas RC 1.25 3.00
37 Vladimir Tarasenko RC 5.00 12.00
38 Eric Gryba RC 1.00 2.50
39 Jarred Tinordi RC 1.25 3.00
40 Eric Selleck RC 1.00 2.50
41 Patrick Bordeleau RC 1.25 3.00
42 Sami Vatanen RC 1.25 3.00
43 Brian Lashoff RC 1.00 2.50
44 Drew Shore RC 1.00 2.50
45 Cameron Schilling RC .75 2.00
46 David Dziurzynski RC 1.00 2.50
47 Mike Kostka RC 1.00 2.50
48 Anthony Peluso RC .75 2.00
49 Thomas Hickey RC 1.00 2.50
50 Daniel Bang RC 1.00 2.50
51 Greg Pateryn RC 1.25 3.00
52 Tye McGinn RC 1.25 3.00
53 Stefan Matteau RC 1.00 2.50
54 Charlie Coyle RC 1.25 3.00
55 Jonathan Huberdeau RC 3.00 8.00
56 Petr Mrazek RC 2.50 6.00
57 Max Reinhart RC 1.25 3.00
58 Rickard Rakell RC 1.25 3.00
59 Anders Lee RC 2.00 5.00
60 Tyler Toffoli RC 2.50 6.00
61 Tyler Johnson RC 3.00 8.00
62 Philipp Grubauer RC 1.25 3.00
63 Brian Flynn RC 1.00 2.50
64 Mark Pysyk RC 1.25 3.00
65 Ryan Spooner RC 1.25 3.00
66 Cory Conacher RC .75 2.00
67 Andrej Sustr RC .75 2.00
68 Justin Schultz RC 1.25 3.00
69 Jamie Oleksiak RC 1.00 2.50
70 Jamie Tardif RC .75 2.00
71 Michael Caruso RC .75 2.00
72 Derek Grant RC 1.00 2.50
73 Nicklas Jensen RC 1.00 2.50
74 Dmitrij Jaskin RC 1.25 3.00
75 Alex Galchenyuk RC 6.00 15.00
76 Jonas Brodin RC 1.00 2.50
77 Richard Panik RC 1.25 3.00
78 J.T. Miller RC 1.25 3.00
79 Nathan Beaulieu RC 1.00 2.50
80 Ondrej Palat RC 1.50 4.00
81 Scott Laughton RC 1.25 3.00
82 Austin Watson RC 1.00 2.50
83 Jordan Schroeder RC 1.25 3.00
84 Chris Terry RC .75 2.00
85 Jonathan Audy-Marchessault RC 2.50 6.00
86 Christopher Nilstorp RC 1.00 2.50
87 Harri Pesonen RC 1.00 2.50
88 Matthew Irwin RC 1.00 2.50
89 Johan Larsson RC 1.00 2.50
90 Damien Brunner RC 1.00 2.50
91 Mikael Granlund RC 2.00 5.00
92 Chad Ruhwedel RC .75 2.00
93 Alex Killorn RC 1.25 3.00
94 Nicolas Blanchard RC 1.00 2.50
95 Nick Bjugstad RC 1.50 4.00
96 Ben Hanowski RC 1.00 2.50
97 Antoine Roussel RC 1.25 3.00
98 Sami Aittokallio RC 1.25 3.00
99 Jack Campbell RC 1.00 2.50
00 Checklist .75 2.00
01 Jarome Iginla 1.25 3.00
02 Jaromir Jagr 3.00 8.00
03 Daniel Briere 1.25 3.00
04 Bobby Ryan 1.25 3.00
05 David Perron .75 2.00
06 Loui Eriksson 1.00 2.50
07 Daniel Alfredsson 1.25 3.00
08 Tyler Seguin 2.00 5.00
09 David Clarkson .75 2.00
10 Jonathan Bernier 1.25 3.00
11 Cory Schneider 1.00 2.50
12 Vincent Lecavalier 1.00 2.50
13 Sean Monahan RC 1.50 4.00
14 Antti Raanta RC 1.25 3.00
15 Aleksander Barkov RC 2.50 6.00
16 Martin Jones RC 2.50 6.00
17 Mathew Dumba RC 1.00 2.50
18 Freddie Hamilton RC 1.00 2.50
19 Lucas Lessio RC .60 1.50
20 Nathan MacKinnon RC 4.00 10.00
21 Carl Soderberg RC 1.00 2.50
22 Jacob Trouba RC 1.50 4.00
23 Ryan Strome RC 1.25 3.00
24 Tomas Jurco RC 1.50 4.00
25 Tomas Hertl RC 3.00 8.00
26 Ryan Murray RC 1.50 4.00
27 Reto Berra RC 1.00 2.50
28 Michael Bournival RC 1.00 2.50
29 Rasmus Ristolainen RC 1.50 4.00
30 Olli Maatta RC 1.50 4.00
31 Marek Mazanec RC 1.00 2.50
32 Jon Merrill RC 1.00 2.50
33 Matt Nieto RC .75 2.00
34 Valeri Nichushkin RC 1.00 2.50
35 Nikita Zadorov RC 1.00 2.50
36 Seth Jones RC 1.00 2.50
37 Elias Lindholm RC 1.50 4.00
38 Jesper Fast RC .75 2.00
39 Morgan Rielly RC 2.50 6.00
40 Justin Fontaine RC 1.00 2.50
41 Boone Jenner RC 1.00 2.50
42 Zemgus Girgensons RC 2.00 5.00

2013-14 O-Pee-Chee Black Rainbow

-500 VETS: 8X TO 20X BASIC CARDS
501-600 ROOK: 1.5X TO 4X BASIC RC
TATED PRINT RUN 100 SER.#'d SETS
46 Corey Crawford 6.00 15.00
01 Nail Yakupov 15.00 40.00
75 Alex Galchenyuk 40.00 80.00

2013-14 O-Pee-Chee Rainbow

*1-500 VETS: 2.5X TO 6X BASIC CARDS
*501-600 ROOKIES: .5X TO 1.2X BASIC RC
STATED ODDS 1:4 HOB, 1:8 RET, 1:7 BLST
246 Corey Crawford 2.00 5.00

2013-14 O-Pee-Chee Red

*1-500 VETS: 6X TO 15X BASIC CARDS
*501-600 ROOKIES: 1.2X TO 3X BASIC RC
FOUR PER 50 WRAPPER REDEMPTION
*601-612 VETS: 1.5X TO 4X BASIC CARDS
601-612 ODDS 1:840 HOB UD SER.2
*613-642 ROOK: 2X TO 5X BASIC RC
613-642 ODDS 1:336 HOB UD SER.2
246 Corey Crawford 5.00 12.00

2013-14 O-Pee-Chee Retro

*1-500 VETS: 2X TO 5X BASIC CARDS
*501-600 ROOK: .5X TO 1.2X BASIC RC
1-600 ODDS 1:1 HOB, 1:2 RET, 1:2 BLST
*601-612 VETS: .6X TO 1.5X BASIC CARDS
601-612 ODDS 1:42 H/R, 1:85 BL UD SER.2
*613-642 ROOK: .6X TO 1.5X BASIC RC
601-612 ODDS 1:17 H/R, 1:34 BL UD SER.2
246 Corey Crawford 1.50 4.00

2013-14 O-Pee-Chee Blaster Box Bottoms

TWO PER BLASTER BOX BOTTOM
AG Alex Galchenyuk 1.25 3.00
AO Alexander Ovechkin 1.25 3.00
NY Nail Yakupov .75 2.00
SC Sidney Crosby 1.25 3.00
SS Steven Stamkos .60 1.50
VT Vladimir Tarasenko 1.00 2.50

2013-14 O-Pee-Chee Buyback Autographs

8 Ovechkin '09-10 OPC/23 75.00 125.00
87 Crosby '09-10 OPC/20 100.00 200.00
161 Rask/10 /'10-11 OPC Rtr ser.2
372R Stamkos/25 /'10-11 OPC Rtr ser.2
372 Stamkos/25 /'10-11 OPC ser.2

2013-14 O-Pee-Chee Glossy

1 Teemu Selanne 50.00 125.00
2 Corey Perry 25.00 60.00
3 Bobby Orr 75.00 135.00
4 Milan Lucic 25.00 60.00
5 Zdeno Chara 25.00 60.00
6 Tyler Seguin 40.00 100.00
7 Brad Marchand 30.00 80.00
8 Theo Fleury 30.00 80.00
9 Miikka Kiprusoff 20.00 50.00
10 Jarome Iginla 25.00 60.00
11 Jonathan Toews 50.00 100.00
12 Patrick Sharp 25.00 60.00
13 Patrick Kane 50.00 125.00
14 Matt Duchene 25.00 60.00
15 Brett Hull 40.00 80.00
16 Nicklas Lidstrom 25.00 60.00
17 Pavel Datsyuk 30.00 80.00
18 Jimmy Howard 25.00 60.00
19 Nail Yakupov 75.00 135.00
20 Jordan Eberle 25.00 60.00
21 Ryan Nugent-Hopkins 50.00 100.00
22 Wayne Gretzky 125.00 225.00
23 Taylor Hall 50.00 125.00
24 Pavel Bure 40.00 100.00
25 Jonathan Huberdeau 50.00 100.00
26 Drew Doughty 25.00 60.00
27 Mike Richards 25.00 60.00
28 Jonathan Quick 40.00 100.00
29 Mikko Koivu 20.00 50.00
30 Alex Galchenyuk 90.00 150.00
31 Carey Price 50.00 100.00
32 Patrick Roy 75.00 135.00
33 Pekka Rinne 30.00 80.00
34 Ilya Kovalchuk 25.00 60.00
35 Martin Brodeur 40.00 100.00
36 John Tavares 50.00 125.00
37 Henrik Lundqvist 30.00 80.00
38 Chris Kreider 25.00 60.00
39 Jason Spezza 25.00 60.00
40 Erik Karlsson 50.00 125.00
41 Pelle Lindbergh 25.00 60.00
42 Brayden Schenn 25.00 60.00
43 Eric Lindros 40.00 80.00
44 Mario Lemieux 50.00 100.00
45 Evgeni Malkin 40.00 80.00
46 Sidney Crosby 75.00 150.00
47 Joe Sakic 40.00 80.00
48 Mats Sundin 25.00 60.00
49 TBD
50 Steven Stamkos 40.00 80.00
51 Nazem Kadri 25.00 60.00
52 Wendel Clark 25.00 60.00
53 Alexandre Burrows 25.00 60.00
54 Roberto Luongo 25.00 60.00
55 Daniel Sedin 25.00 60.00
56 Henrik Sedin 25.00 60.00
57 Alex Ovechkin 50.00 100.00
58 Braden Holtby 40.00 100.00
59 Ondrej Pavelec 25.00 60.00
60 Evander Kane 25.00 60.00

2013-14 O-Pee-Chee League Leaders

STATED ODDS 1:10 CAN.TIRE BLASTER
LL Dpuis/Kntz/Toews 6.00 15.00
LLA St.Louis/Crsby/Bckstrm 12.00 30.00
LLSO Hwrd/Rask/Rinne 5.00 12.00
LLGAA Andrsn/Brner/Crwfrd 4.00 10.00
LLGLS Ovchkn/Stmks/Tvres 12.00 30.00
LLPIM Orr/Neil/Brown 3.00 8.00
LLPPG Ovchkn/Stmks/Vnek 12.00 30.00
LLPTS St. Louis/Stmks/Crsby 12.00 30.00
LLRPTS Ykpv/Hbrdeau/Cncher 5.00 12.00
LLWINS Lndqvst/Nmi/Bckstrm 4.00 10.00

2013-14 O-Pee-Chee Marquee Legends

STATED ODDS 1:4 FAT PACK
ML1 Wayne Gretzky 12.00 30.00
ML2 Bobby Orr 10.00 25.00
ML3 Steve Yzerman 8.00 20.00
ML4 Patrick Roy 10.00 25.00
ML5 Mark Messier 5.00 12.00
ML6 Joe Sakic 6.00 15.00
ML7 Eric Lindros 6.00 15.00
ML8 Theoren Fleury 5.00 12.00
ML9 Dominik Hasek 5.00 12.00
ML10 Pavel Bure 5.00 12.00

2013-14 O-Pee-Chee Retro Hobby Box Bottoms

FOUR PER HOBBY BOX BOTTOM
1 Sidney Crosby A 1.00 2.50
2 Ryan Getzlaf A .40 1.00
3 Jonathan Huberdeau A .40 1.00
4 Henrik Lundqvist A .30 .75
5 Martin Brodeur B .50 1.25
6 Alex Galchenyuk B .75 2.00
7 Steven Stamkos B .50 1.25
8 Henrik Zetterberg B .30 .75
9 Patrick Kane C .50 1.25
10 Alexander Ovechkin C 1.00 2.50
11 Carey Price C .75 2.00
12 Vladimir Tarasenko C .60 1.50
13 Tuukka Rask D .25 .60
14 John Tavares D .50 1.25
15 Jonathan Toews D .50 1.25
16 Nail Yakupov D .50 1.25
P1 Crosby/Getlaf/Huber/Lund 1.25 3.00
P2 Brodr/Galch/Stamk/Zettr 1.25 3.00
P3 Kane/Ovch/Price/Taras 1.25 3.00
P4 Rask/Tavr/Toews/Yakpv 1.25 3.00

2013-14 O-Pee-Chee Rings

STATED ODDS 1:16 HOB, 1:32 RET/BLST
R1 Anaheim Ducks 1.50 4.00
R2 Boston Bruins 2.00 5.00
R3 Buffalo Sabres 1.50 4.00
R4 Calgary Flames 1.50 4.00
R5 Carolina Hurricanes 1.50 4.00
R6 Chicago Blackhawks 1.50 4.00
R7 Colorado Avalanche 1.50 4.00
R8 Columbus Blue Jackets 1.50 4.00
R9 Dallas Stars 1.50 4.00
R10 Detroit Red Wings 1.50 4.00
R11 Edmonton Oilers 2.00 5.00
R12 Florida Panthers 1.50 4.00
R13 Los Angeles Kings 1.50 4.00
R14 Minnesota Wild 1.50 4.00
R15 Montreal Canadiens 2.00 5.00
R16 Nashville Predators 1.50 4.00
R17 New Jersey Devils 1.50 4.00
R18 New York Islanders 1.50 4.00
R19 New York Rangers 1.50 4.00
R20 Ottawa Senators 1.50 4.00
R21 Philadelphia Flyers 1.50 4.00
R22 Phoenix Coyotes 1.50 4.00
R23 Pittsburgh Penguins 2.00 5.00
R24 San Jose Sharks 1.50 4.00
R25 St. Louis Blues 1.50 4.00
R26 Tampa Bay Lightning 1.50 4.00
R27 Toronto Maple Leafs 2.00 5.00
R28 Vancouver Canucks 1.50 4.00
R29 Washington Capitals 1.50 4.00
R30 Winnipeg Jets 1.50 4.00
R31 Wayne Gretzky 10.00 25.00
R32 Bobby Orr 6.00 15.00
R33 Mario Lemieux 6.00 15.00
R34 Patrick Roy 5.00 12.00
R35 Dave Schultz 2.00 5.00
R36 Terry O'Reilly 1.50 4.00
R37 Tie Domi 2.00 5.00
R38 Bob Probert 2.00 5.00
R39 Marty McSorley 1.50 4.00
R40 Daniel Carcillo 1.25 3.00
R41 Zenon Konopka 1.50 4.00
R42 George Parros 1.50 4.00
R43 Sidney Crosby 8.00 20.00
R44 Alexander Ovechkin 8.00 20.00
R45 Jonathan Toews 4.00 10.00
R46 Steven Stamkos 4.00 10.00
R47 Martin Brodeur 4.00 10.00
R48 Henrik Lundqvist 2.50 6.00
R49 Carey Price 6.00 15.00
R50 Jonathan Quick 3.00 8.00

2013-14 O-Pee-Chee Signatures

GROUP C ODDS 1:218
GROUP B ODDS 1:1747
GROUP A ODDS 1:17,472
OVERALL ODDS 1:192H, 1:400R, 1:800 BST
GROUP B2 ODDS 1:10,080 UD SER.2
USAG Alex Galchenyuk B 2 40.00 80.00
USJH Jonathan Huberdeau B 2 75.00 125.00
USNY Nail Yakupov B 2
USTH Tomas Hertl B 2 15.00 40.00
USVN Valeri Nichushkin B 2 20.00 40.00
OPCAB Adam Burish C 3.00 8.00
OPCAG Alex Goligoski B 8.00 20.00
OPCBL Brian Lee C 3.00 8.00
OPCBM Brayden McNabb C 3.00 8.00
OPCBO Bobby Orr A 175.00 300.00
OPCBS Brendan Smith B 6.00 15.00
OPCCK Chris Kunitz B 8.00 20.00
OPCCO Cal O'Reilly C 3.00 8.00
OPCDC Daniel Carcillo C 3.00 8.00
OPCEN Evgeni Nabokov B 6.00 15.00
OPCET Eric Tangradi C 4.00 10.00
OPCHS Harri Sateri C 3.00 8.00
OPCJB Josh Bailey C 4.00 10.00
OPCJE Jonathan Ericsson B 6.00 15.00
OPCJF Justin Falk C 3.00 8.00
OPCLB Lance Bouma C 3.00 8.00
OPCLI Leland Irving B 6.00 15.00
OPCMI Brendan Mikkelson C 3.00 8.00
OPCML Mario Lemieux A 100.00 175.00
OPCMS Mark Streit B 6.00 15.00
OPCNG Nicklas Grossman C 3.00 8.00
OPCPB Pavel Bure A
OPCPR Patrick Roy A 100.00 175.00
OPCRW Roman Wick C 3.00 8.00
OPCSU Mats Sundin A 50.00 100.00
OPCTL Trevor Lewis C 3.00 8.00
OPCVF Valtteri Filppula C 5.00 12.00
OPCVS Viktor Stalberg B 5.00 12.00
OPCWG Wayne Gretzky A 250.00 400.00
OPCYS Yann Sauve C 3.00 8.00

2013-14 O-Pee-Chee Sport Royalty Autographs

BO Bobby Orr 150.00 300.00

2013-14 O-Pee-Chee Stamps

ONE PER 50 WRAPPER REDEMPTION
STAO Alexander Ovechkin 15.00 40.00
STAP Alex Pietrangelo 3.00 8.00
STBO Bobby Orr 10.00 25.00
STCG Claude Giroux 4.00 10.00
STCP Corey Perry 4.00 10.00
STCS Cory Schneider 3.00 8.00
STDD Drew Doughty 4.00 10.00
STDS Daniel Sedin 4.00 10.00
STEK Erik Karlsson 8.00 20.00
STEL Eric Lindros 6.00 15.00
STEM Evgeni Malkin 12.00 30.00
STHL Henrik Lundqvist 5.00 12.00
STHS Henrik Sedin 4.00 10.00
STHZ Henrik Zetterberg 5.00 12.00
STIK Ilya Kovalchuk 4.00 10.00
STJB Jamie Benn 5.00 12.00
STJH Jim Howard 4.00 10.00
STJI Jarome Iginla 4.00 10.00
STJJ Jack Johnson 2.50 6.00
STJO Joe Sakic 6.00 15.00
STJQ Jonathan Quick 6.00 15.00
STJS Jeff Skinner 3.00 8.00
STJT Jonathan Toews 8.00 20.00
STKA Evander Kane 4.00 10.00
STKE Phil Kessel 5.00 12.00
STMB Martin Brodeur 8.00 20.00
STMD Matt Duchene 4.00 10.00
STML Mario Lemieux 12.00 30.00
STMM Mark Messier 5.00 12.00
STMS Mats Sundin 4.00 10.00
STOP Ondrej Pavelec 4.00 10.00
STPB Pavel Bure 5.00 12.00
STPC Paul Coffey 4.00 10.00
STPD Pavel Datsyuk 5.00 12.00
STPK Patrick Kane 8.00 20.00
STPR Carey Price 12.00 30.00
STPS P.K. Subban 6.00 15.00
STRF Ron Francis 5.00 12.00
STRM Ryan Miller 4.00 10.00
STRN Ryan Nugent-Hopkins 4.00 10.00
STRO Patrick Roy 10.00 25.00
STSC Sidney Crosby 15.00 40.00
STSS Steven Stamkos 8.00 20.00
STTA John Tavares 8.00 20.00
STTD Tie Domi 4.00 10.00
STTH Taylor Hall 8.00 20.00
STTS Tyler Seguin 6.00 15.00
STWG Wayne Gretzky 20.00 50.00
STZC Zdeno Chara 4.00 10.00
STZP Zach Parise 4.00 10.00

2013-14 O-Pee-Chee Stickers

STATED ODDS 1:4 HOB, 1:6 RET/BLST
SAB Alexandre Burrows .75 2.00
SAN Antti Niemi .60 1.50
SAO Alexander Ovechkin 3.00 8.00
SBC Bobby Clarke .75 2.00
SBE Jean Beliveau .75 2.00
SBH Braden Holtby 1.25 3.00
SBM Brad Marchand 1.00 2.50
SBO Bobby Orr 2.50 6.00
SBR Bobby Ryan .75 2.00
SBU Alexander Burmistrov .60 1.50
SCA Carey Price 2.50 6.00
SCC Corey Crawford 1.00 2.50
SCG Claude Giroux .75 2.00
SCK Chris Kreider .75 2.00
SCP Corey Perry .75 2.00
SCW Cam Ward .75 2.00
SDA Daniel Alfredsson .75 2.00
SDD Drew Doughty .75 2.00
SDH Dany Heatley .60 1.50
SDK David Krejci .75 2.00
SDP Dion Phaneuf .75 2.00
SDS Daniel Sedin .75 2.00
SEK Evander Kane .75 2.00
SEL Eric Lindros 1.25 3.00
SEM Evgeni Malkin 2.50 6.00
SES Eric Staal 1.00 2.50
SGL Gabriel Landeskog .60 1.50
SGR Mike Green .75 2.00
SHA Jaroslav Halak .75 2.00
SHL Henrik Lundqvist 1.00 2.50
SHO Jim Howard .75 2.00
SHS Henrik Sedin .75 2.00
SHZ Henrik Zetterberg 1.00 2.50
SIK Ilya Kovalchuk .75 2.00
SJA Jaromir Jagr 2.00 5.00
SJB Jamie Benn 1.00 2.50
SJE Jordan Eberle .75 2.00
SJF Johan Franzen .75 2.00
SJH Jonas Hiller .60 1.50
SJI Jarome Iginla .75 2.00
SJJ Jack Johnson .50 1.25
SJN James Neal .75 2.00
SJO Joe Thornton .75 2.00
SJQ Jonathan Quick 1.25 3.00
SJS Jeff Skinner .60 1.50
SJT Jonathan Toews 1.50 4.00
SKE Duncan Keith .75 2.00
SKO Mikko Koivu .60 1.50
SKV Kris Versteeg .60 1.50
SLC Logan Couture .75 2.00
SMB Martin Brodeur 1.50 4.00
SMC Michael Cammalleri .60 1.50
SMD Matt Duchene .75 2.00
SMF Marc-Andre Fleury 1.25 3.00
SMG Marian Gaborik .75 2.00
SMH Marian Hossa .60 1.50
SMI Mike Bossy .75 2.00
SMK Miikka Kiprusoff .60 1.50
SML Mario Lemieux 2.50 6.00
SMM Mark Messier 1.00 2.50
SMO Brenden Morrow .60 1.50
SMR Mike Richards .75 2.00
SMS Mark Scheifele 1.00 2.50
SNB Niklas Backstrom .60 1.50
SNH Nathan Horton .75 2.00
SNL Nicklas Lidstrom .75 2.00
SOP Ondrej Pavelec .75 2.00
SPB Pavel Bure 1.00 2.50
SPC Paul Coffey .75 2.00
SPD Pavel Datsyuk 1.00 2.50
SPH Phil Kessel 1.00 2.50
SPK Patrick Kane 1.50 4.00
SPM Patrick Marleau .75 2.00
SPR Patrick Roy 2.00 5.00
SPS Paul Stastny .75 2.00
SRG Ryan Getzlaf 1.25 3.00
SRI Pekka Rinne 1.00 2.50
SRK Ryan Kesler .75 2.00
SRM Ryan Miller .75 2.00
SRN Ryan Nugent-Hopkins .75 2.00
SRS Ryan Smyth .60 1.50
SSA Joe Sakic 1.25 3.00
SSC Sidney Crosby 3.00 8.00
SSE Tyler Seguin 1.25 3.00
SSG Sam Gagner .60 1.50
SSP Jason Spezza .75 2.00
SSS Steven Stamkos 1.50 4.00
SSU P.K. Subban 1.25 3.00
SSW Stephen Weiss .60 1.50
STA John Tavares 1.50 4.00
STD Tie Domi .75 2.00
STH Taylor Hall 1.50 4.00
STM Tyler Myers .60 1.50
STR Tuukka Rask .75 2.00
STS Teemu Selanne 1.50 4.00
STV Thomas Vanek .75 2.00
SWE Shea Weber .60 1.50
SWG Wayne Gretzky 4.00 10.00
SZC Zdeno Chara .75 2.00
SZP Zach Parise .75 2.00

2013-14 O-Pee-Chee Team Canada Signatures

UNPRICED GROUP A ODDS 1: 32,371
GROUP B ODDS 1:4856
GROUP C ODDS 1:3237
GROUP D ODDS 1:1646
GROUP E ODDS 1:689
OVERALL ODDS 1:382 HOB
TCAH Adam Henrique B 30.00 60.00
TCAP Alex Pietrangelo B 20.00 50.00
TCAT Alex Tanguay C 12.00 30.00
TCBO Bobby Orr A
TCCA Carter Ashton D 4.00 10.00
TCCD Calvin de Haan E 4.00 10.00
TCCE Cody Eakin E 4.00 10.00
TCCS Chris Stewart D 5.00 12.00
TCDH Dale Hawerchuk B 30.00 60.00
TCDO Dylan Olsen B 15.00 40.00
TCDP Dion Phaneuf B 15.00 40.00
TCJB Jamie Benn B 25.00 50.00
TCJH Josh Harding E 6.00 15.00
TCJT John Tavares C 30.00 60.00
TCKA Keith Aulie E 4.00 10.00
TCLL Louis Leblanc D 6.00 15.00
TCMF Marcus Foligno C 15.00 40.00
TCMH Matthew Halischuk E 4.00 10.00
TCMR Mike Ribeiro E 5.00 12.00
TCMS Martin St. Louis C 20.00 50.00
TCRE Ryan Ellis E 4.00 10.00
TCRN Ryan Nugent-Hopkins A 100.00 175.00
TCSC Sean Couturier B 25.00 50.00
TCSM Shawn Matthias E 5.00 12.00
TCSS Steven Stamkos B 30.00 80.00
TCTM Tyler Myers D 5.00 12.00
TCWC Wendel Clark C 40.00 80.00
TCWG Wayne Gretzky A 250.00 400.00
TCZK Zack Kassian D 8.00 20.00

2013-14 O-Pee-Chee Team Logo Patches

TL101-TL150 ODDS 1:125
TL151-TL162 ODDS 1:979
TL163-TL176 ODDS 1:1146
TL177-TL188 ODDS 1:1973
TL189-TL196 ODDS 1:5074
UNPRICED TL197-TL200 ODDS 1:17,760
TL101 NHL alternate 10.00 25.00
TL102 All-Star Game 80-81 primary 12.00 30.00
TL103 All-Star Game 90-91 primary 12.00 30.00
TL104 NHL Draft 06 primary 12.00 30.00
TL105 NHL Draft 12 primary 10.00 25.00
TL106 Winter Classic primary 10.00 25.00
TL107 Atl. Thrashers primary 10.00 25.00
TL108 Boston Bruins primary 15.00 40.00
TL109 Boston Bruins alt 12.00 30.00
TL110 Buffalo Sabres primary 10.00 25.00
TL111 Calgary Flames primary 10.00 25.00
TL112 Calgary Flames alt 10.00 25.00
TL113 Blue Jackets primary 10.00 25.00
TL114 Blue Jackets alt 10.00 25.00
TL115 Red Wings Hockeytown 40.00 40.00
TL116 Edmonton Oilers primary 12.00 30.00
TL117 Edmonton Oilers alt 15.00 40.00
TL118 Harford Whalers primary 12.00 30.00
TL119 Harford Whalers script 12.00 30.00
TL120 L.A. Kings primary 12.00 30.00
TL121 L.A. Kings primary 15.00 40.00
TL122 North Stars alt 15.00 40.00
TL123 Montreal Canadiens alt 20.00 50.00
TL124 Nash Predators primary 10.00 25.00
TL125 Nash Predators alt 10.00 25.00
TL126 NJ Devils primary 10.00 25.00
TL127 N.Y. Islanders alt 10.00 25.00
TL128 N.Y. Islanders primary 10.00 25.00
TL129 N.Y. Rangers alt 12.00 30.00
TL130 Ottaway Senators alt 10.00 25.00
TL131 Ottaway Senators primary 10.00 25.00
TL132 Flyers script 10.00 25.00
TL133 Flyers alt 15.00 40.00
TL134 Phoenix Coyotes alt 10.00 25.00
TL135 Phoenix Coyotes alt 10.00 25.00
TL136 Penguins primary 10.00 25.00
TL137 Penguins script 10.00 25.00
TL138 Que Nordiques alt 15.00 40.00
TL139 Que Nordiques alt 12.00 30.00
TL140 S.J. Sharks primary 10.00 25.00
TL141 St. Louis Blues primary 12.00 30.00
TL142 St. Louis Blues alt 12.00 30.00
TL143 T.B. Lighting primary 10.00 25.00
TL144 Maple Leafs primary 12.00 30.00
TL145 Maple Leafs secondary 12.00 30.00
TL146 Canucks primary 12.00 30.00
TL147 Canucks alt 15.00 40.00
TL148 Capitals primary 15.00 40.00
TL149 Winnipeg Jets alt 12.00 30.00
TL150 Winnipeg Jets primary 12.00 30.00
TL151 Buffalo Sabres 25ANN 30.00 60.00
TL152 Calgary Flames 25ANN 20.00 40.00
TL153 Edmonton Oilers 25ANN 25.00 50.00
TL154 L.A. Kings 30ANN 15.00 40.00
TL155 N.J. Devils 25ANN 20.00 40.00
TL156 N.Y. Islanders 25ANN 20.00 40.00
TL157 Flyers 40ANN 60.00 100.00
TL158 Penguins 25ANN 25.00 50.00
TL159 St. Louis Blues 25ANN 30.00 60.00
TL160 Canucks 25ANN 20.00 40.00
TL161 Canucks 40ANN 20.00 40.00
TL162 Capitals 25ANN 25.00 50.00
TL163 Golden Seals alt 40.00 100.00
TL164 Golden Seals primary 40.00 80.00
TL165 Cleveland Barons primary 30.00 60.00
TL166 CO Rockies alt 15.00 40.00
TL167 CO Rockies script 30.00 60.00
TL168 L.A. Kings alt 40.00 80.00
TL169 Penguins primary 25.00 50.00
TL170 Canucks alt 25.00 50.00
TL171 Boston Bruins primary 50.00 100.00
TL172 Blackhawks primary 30.00 60.00
TL173 N.Y. Rangers primary 35.00 60.00
TL174 Maple Leafs primary 35.00 60.00
TL175 Maple Leafs secondary 25.00 50.00
TL176 Maple Leafs primary 30.00 60.00
TL177 Boston Bruins primary 40.00 80.00
TL178 Boston Bruins primary 75.00 125.00
TL179 Blackhawks primary 75.00 125.00
TL180 Red Wings primary 100.00 200.00
TL181 Hamilton Tigers primary
TL182 Canadiens primary 60.00 120.00
TL183 Canadiens alt 60.00 120.00
TL184 Canadiens primary 60.00 120.00
TL185 N.Y. Americans primary 60.00 100.00
TL186 N.Y. Americans primary 60.00 100.00
TL187 Maple Leafs secondary 75.00 150.00
TL188 Toronto St. Pats primary 60.00 100.00
TL189 Brooklyn Americans primary 125.00 250.00
TL190 Detroit Cougars alt 150.00 250.00
TL191 Detroit Falcons primary
TL192 Wanderers primary 150.00 250.00
TL193 Quakers primary
TL194 Pirates primary 150.00 250.00
TL195 Pirates alt
TL196 Toronto St. Pats primary 150.00 250.00
TL197 Blue Jackets cartoon
TL198 Hamilton Tigers cartoon
TL199 L.A. Kings cartoon
TL200 Phoenix Coyotes cartoon

2014-15 O-Pee-Chee

COMP.SET w/o RC's (500) 30.00 60.00
COMP.SET w/o SP's (600) 75.00 150.00
501-600 STATED ODDS 1:4 HOB/RET/BL
1 Martin Brodeur .50 1.25
2 Teemu Selanne .50 1.25
3 Jean-Sebastien Giguere .20 .50
4 Daniel Alfredsson .25 .60
5 Jaromir Jagr .60 1.50
6 Jarret Stoll .20 .50
7 Andrew Ference .15 .40
8 Chris Kreider .25 .60
9 P.K. Subban .40 1.00
10 Brent Seabrook .25 .60
11 Milan Lucic .25 .60
12 Ryan Garbutt .15 .40
13 Bobby Ryan .25 .60
14 Dany Heatley .20 .50
15 Mark Letestu .20 .50
16 Oliver Ekman-Larsson .20 .50
17 Tyler Ennis .20 .50
18 Sean Monahan .25 .60
19 Cam Ward .25 .60
20 Sean Bergenheim .15 .40
21 Kyle Palmieri .20 .50
22 Craig Smith .15 .40
23 Tom Sestito .15 .40
24 Jarome Iginla .25 .60
25 Olli Jokinen .20 .50
26 Teddy Purcell .25 .60
27 Mason Raymond .20 .50
28 Mikkel Boedker .15 .40
29 Jamie McGinn .15 .40
30 Ryan McDonagh .25 .60
31 Rich Peverley .25 .60
32 Marian Hossa .20 .50
33 Calvin de Haan .15 .40
34 Viktor Fasth .20 .50
35 Max Pacioretty .25 .60
36 Marcel Goc .15 .40
37 Jonas Brodin .15 .40
38 Pavel Datsyuk .30 .75
39 Luke Schenn .15 .40
40 Tyler Toffoli .25 .60
41 Carl Hagelin .25 .60
42 Joe Thornton .25 .60
43 Andy Greene .15 .40
44 Brock Nelson .20 .50
45 Alexander Ovechkin 1.00 2.50
46 Elias Lindholm .25 .60
47 Sven Baertschi .15 .40
48 Jimmy Hayes .20 .50
49 Alex Pietrangelo .20 .50
50 Marc-Andre Fleury .40 1.00
51 Brian Flynn .15 .40
52 Nathan Horton .25 .60
53 Nino Niederreiter .15 .40
54 Alex Killorn .20 .50
55 Zdeno Chara .25 .60
56 Ben Smith .20 .50
57 Frederik Andersen .20 .50
58 Jordan Eberle .25 .60
59 Shawn Matthias .15 .40
60 Radim Vrbata .20 .50
61 Ryan O'Reilly .25 .60
62 Dustin Brown .20 .50
63 Alex Chiasson .20 .50
64 Roman Josi .25 .60
65 Jonas Gustavsson .20 .50
66 Jiri Hudler .20 .50
67 Wayne Simmonds .30 .75
68 Chris Stewart .20 .50
69 Brandon Pirri .15 .40
70 Lubomir Visnovsky .15 .40
71 Vladimir Tarasenko .40 1.00
72 Andrei Markov .25 .60
73 Jordan Staal .25 .60
74 Tommy Wingels .15 .40
75 Darcy Kuemper .20 .50
76 Jake Gardiner .25 .60
77 Michael Ryder .15 .40
78 Brandon Dubinsky .20 .50
79 Mats Zuccarello-Aasen .25 .60
80 Jared Cowen .15 .40
81 Mike Green .25 .60
82 Tobias Enstrom .15 .40
83 Ondrej Palat .20 .50
84 Corey Perry .25 .60
85 Alexandre Burrows .25 .60
86 Alexei Emelin .20 .50
87 David Krejci .25 .60
88 Viktor Stalberg .15 .40
89 Antoine Vermette .15 .40
90 Ladislav Smid .15 .40
91 Ben Scrivens .20 .50
92 P.A. Parenteau .15 .40
93 Dwight King .15 .40
94 Zemgus Girgensons .25 .60
95 Jamie Benn .30 .75
96 David Legwand .20 .50
97 Matt Niskanen .20 .50
98 Matt Read .15 .40
99 Joffrey Lupul .20 .50
100 Justin Faulk .15 .40
101 Nick Bjugstad .20 .50
102 Evgeni Nabokov .20 .50
103 Bryan Bickell .15 .40
104 Artem Anisimov .20 .50
105 Matt Irwin .15 .40
106 Alex Galchenyuk .40 1.00
107 Derick Brassard .25 .60
108 Cam Fowler .20 .50
109 Patrik Elias .25 .60
110 Ryan Smyth .20 .50
111 Mikko Koivu .20 .50
112 Zack Smith .15 .40
113 Andrew Ladd .25 .60
114 Jaroslav Halak .20 .50
115 Nate Thompson .15 .40
116 Michael Del Zotto .15 .40
117 Shane Doan .20 .50
118 Jaden Schwartz .30 .75
119 Sergei Gonchar .15 .40
120 Maxime Talbot .20 .50
121 Mike Santorelli .15 .40
122 Eric Staal .30 .75
123 Chad Johnson .20 .50
124 Dennis Wideman .15 .40
125 Cory Conacher .15 .40
126 Brayden Schenn .25 .60
127 Niklas Kronwall .20 .50
128 Sidney Crosby 1.00 2.50
129 Trevor Lewis .15 .40
130 James Reimer .25 .60
131 James Wisniewski .15 .40
132 Tomas Fleischmann .15 .40
133 Daniel Briere .20 .50
134 Andrew Shaw .25 .60
135 Ryan Ellis .15 .40
136 Frans Nielsen .15 .40
137 Ben Lovejoy .15 .40
138 Tomas Hertl .25 .60
139 Erik Karlsson .50 1.25
140 Brian Boyle .15 .40
141 Michael Frolik .15 .40
142 Nick Holden .15 .40
143 Brooks Laich .15 .40
144 Andrej Sekera .15 .40
145 Brian Elliott .20 .50
146 Erik Cole .20 .50
147 Gabriel Bourque .20 .50
148 Danny DeKeyser .20 .50
149 Jussi Jokinen .15 .40
150 Scott Hartnell .25 .60
151 Tuukka Rask .25 .60
152 Jannik Hansen .20 .50
153 Tyler Bozak .20 .50
154 Al Montoya .15 .40
155 Josh Gorges .15 .40
156 Marian Gaborik .25 .60
157 Drew Stafford .25 .60
158 Jack Johnson .15 .40
159 Zach Parise .25 .60
160 Pat Maroon .15 .40
161 Derek Stepan .25 .60
162 Ryan Malone .15 .40
163 Kyle Okposo .25 .60
164 Nathan MacKinnon .50 1.25
165 Roberto Luongo .25 .60
166 Kyle Turris .25 .60
167 Patrik Berglund .15 .40
168 Adam Henrique .25 .60
169 Ryan Jones .15 .40
170 Patrick Kane .50 1.25
171 Martin Havlat .20 .50
172 Alex Goligoski .15 .40
173 Joe Colborne .15 .40
174 Eric Fehr .15 .40
175 Andrej Meszaros .15 .40
176 Pascal Dupuis .15 .40
177 Willie Mitchell .15 .40
178 Eddie Lack .20 .50
179 Vincent Lecavalier .20 .50
180 Mark Stuart .15 .40
181 Rene Bourque .15 .40
182 Riley Nash .15 .40
183 Ryan Suter .25 .60
184 Nick Spaling .15 .40
185 Ryan Murray .15 .40
186 Ryan Callahan .25 .60
187 Milan Michalek .15 .40
188 Matt Beleskey .15 .40
189 Tanner Pearson .15 .40
190 Lee Stempniak .15 .40
191 Alexander Steen .25 .60
192 Mike Ribeiro .20 .50
193 Tyson Barrie .25 .60
194 Torey Krug .25 .60
195 Cory Schneider .20 .50
196 Nick Leddy .15 .40
197 Tyler Kennedy .15 .40
198 Jonathan Huberdeau .25 .60
199 Jonathan Ericsson .20 .50
200 Matt Stajan .20 .50
201 Cody Hodgson .25 .60
202 Nicklas Backstrom .40 1.00
203 Martin Jones .25 .60
204 Brian Gionta .20 .50
205 Drayson Bowman .15 .40
206 Alexander Edler .15 .40
207 Ryan Nugent-Hopkins .25 .60
208 Chris Neil .15 .40
209 Henrik Lundqvist .30 .75
210 Brenden Dillon .15 .40
211 Mikael Granlund .20 .50
212 Cam Atkinson .25 .60
213 Carter Hutton .25 .60
214 Sami Vatanen .15 .40
215 Sean Couturier .25 .60
216 Thomas Greiss .20 .50
217 James Neal .25 .60
218 Steve Ott .20 .50
219 J.T. Brown .15 .40
220 Erik Johnson .15 .40
221 Tuomo Ruutu .20 .50
222 Daniel Paille .15 .40
223 Justin Braun .15 .40
224 Michael Cammalleri .20 .50
225 James van Riemsdyk .25 .60
226 Slava Voynov .25 .60
227 Aleksander Barkov .25 .60
228 Marcus Foligno .15 .40
229 Zach Bogosian .20 .50
230 Casey Cizikas .15 .40
231 Peter Budaj .20 .50
232 Martin St. Louis .25 .60
233 Jiri Tlusty .20 .50
234 Niklas Hjalmarsson .15 .40
235 Jeff Petry .15 .40
236 Dustin Penner .20 .50
237 Eric Nystrom .15 .40
238 Kari Lehtonen .20 .50
239 Brenden Morrow .20 .50
240 Mathieu Perreault .15 .40
241 Boone Jenner .15 .40
242 Steve Mason .20 .50
243 Gustav Nyquist .20 .50
244 Marco Scandella .15 .40
245 Martin Erat .15 .40
246 Paul Martin .15 .40
247 Ryane Clowe .15 .40
248 Curtis Glencross .15 .40
249 Loui Eriksson .20 .50
250 Ales Hemsky .15 .40
251 Cody McLeod .15 .40
252 Anze Kopitar .40 1.00
253 Chris Higgins .15 .40
254 Erik Gudbranson .25 .60
255 Jhonas Enroth .25 .60
256 Jonathan Toews .50 1.25
257 Evander Kane .25 .60
258 David Desharnais .25 .60
259 Patrick Dwyer .15 .40
260 John Moore .15 .40
261 Valeri Nichushkin .20 .50
262 Jakob Silfverberg .20 .50
263 Boyd Gordon .15 .40
264 Fedor Tyutin .15 .40
265 Valtteri Filppula .25 .60

266 Antti Niemi .20 .50
267 Anders Lee .25 .60
268 John Carlson .30 .75
269 Paul Bissonnette .15 .40
270 Johan Franzen .25 .60
271 Matt Bartkowski .15 .40
272 Phil Kessel .30 .75
273 John Mitchell .15 .40
274 Travis Zajac .20 .50
275 Matt Moulson .20 .50
276 Colin Wilson .15 .40
277 Mark Giordano .20 .50
278 Mark Streit .15 .40
279 Mike Richards .25 .60
280 Tom Gilbert .15 .40
281 Robin Lehner .20 .50
282 Kevin Shattenkirk .25 .60
283 Devin Setoguchi .20 .50
284 Andre Benoit .15 .40
285 Daniel Sedin .25 .60
286 Ryan Murphy .15 .40
287 Kris Versteeg .20 .50
288 Brooks Orpik .20 .50
289 Ville Leino .20 .50
290 Nick Foligno .20 .50
291 Anton Stralman .15 .40
292 Ray Whitney .20 .50
293 Victor Hedman .30 .75
294 Mark Arcobello .15 .40
295 Tomas Plekanec .25 .60
296 Hampus Lindholm .20 .50
297 Jim Howard .25 .60
298 Patrick Marleau .25 .60
299 Matt Martin .15 .40
300 Adam McQuaid .15 .40
301 Mikael Backlund .20 .50
302 Josh Harding .20 .50
303 Lauri Korpikoski .15 .40
304 David Clarkson .15 .40
305 Troy Brouwer .20 .50
306 Kimmo Timonen .15 .40
307 Jason Spezza .25 .60
308 Dainius Zubrus .15 .40
309 Christopher Tanev .20 .50
310 Matt Cullen .15 .40
311 Dylan Olsen .15 .40
312 Michal Neuvirth .20 .50
313 Brandon Saad .25 .60
314 Vladimir Sobotka .15 .40
315 Jake Muzzin .15 .40
316 Bryan Little .25 .60
317 Steven Stamkos .50 1.25
318 Brad Richards .25 .60
319 Tim Thomas .25 .60
320 Craig Adams .15 .40
321 Anton Belov .25 .60
322 Thomas Vanek .25 .60
323 Carl Soderberg .25 .60
324 Marc-Edouard Vlasic .15 .40
325 Matt Calvert .15 .40
326 Brendan Smith .20 .50
327 Braden Holtby .40 1.00
328 Charlie Coyle .20 .50
329 Colin Greening .15 .40
330 Jeff Skinner .25 .60
331 Saku Koivu .25 .60
332 Carl Gunnarsson .15 .40
333 Paul Stastny .25 .60
334 Michael Raffl .15 .40
335 Antti Raanta .25 .60
336 Thomas Hickey .15 .40
337 Henrik Sedin .25 .60
338 Justin Schultz .20 .50
339 Brad Boyes .15 .40
340 T.J. Oshie .40 1.00
341 Martin Hanzal .15 .40
342 Seth Jones .20 .50
343 Kris Russell .15 .40
344 Benoit Pouliot .15 .40
345 Blake Wheeler .25 .60
346 Radko Gudas .15 .40
347 Alex Stalock .20 .50
348 Mark Pysyk .15 .40
349 Kris Letang .25 .60
350 Reilly Smith .25 .60
351 Justin Williams .20 .50
352 Eric Gelinas .20 .50
353 Carey Price .75 2.00
354 Ryan Johansen .30 .75
355 Karl Alzner .15 .40
356 Jordie Benn .15 .40
357 Matt Duchene .25 .60
358 Clarke MacArthur .15 .40
359 Derek Roy .20 .50
360 Kyle Quincey .15 .40
361 Morgan Rielly .25 .60
362 Anton Khudobin .20 .50
363 Rob Klinkhammer .15 .40
364 David Perron .15 .40
365 Erik Haula .20 .50
366 Ryan Kesler .25 .60
367 Johnny Oduya .20 .50
368 Cal Clutterbuck .25 .60
369 T.J. Brodie .15 .40
370 Braydon Coburn .15 .40
371 Ondrej Pavelec .25 .60
372 Chris Kunitz .25 .60
373 Nick Bonino .15 .40
374 Patric Hornqvist .20 .50
375 Rick Nash .25 .60
376 Dan Boyle .20 .50
377 Robyn Regehr .15 .40
378 Richard Panik .15 .40
379 Brendan Gallagher .25 .60
380 Mika Zibanejad .25 .60
381 Marek Zidlicky .15 .40
382 Derek Morris .15 .40
383 Drew Miller .15 .40
384 Joel Ward .15 .40
385 Antoine Roussel .15 .40
386 Sergei Bobrovsky .25 .60
387 Dougie Hamilton .25 .60
388 Nikolai Kulemin .20 .50
389 Patrick Sharp .25 .60
390 Joe Pavelski .25 .60
391 Jared Spurgeon .15 .40
392 Henrik Tallinder .15 .40
393 David Backes .25 .60
394 Ben Bishop .25 .60
395 Jason Garrison .15 .40
396 Alexander Semin .25 .60
397 Dmitry Kulikov .15 .40
398 Claude Giroux .25 .60
399 Dustin Byfuglien .25 .60
400 Nail Yakupov .20 .50
401 Marc Staal .20 .50
402 Karri Ramo .20 .50
403 Damien Brunner .15 .40
404 Jan Hejda .15 .40
405 Dave Bolland .15 .40
406 Cody Ceci .15 .40
407 Michael Grabner .20 .50
408 Corey Crawford .30 .75
409 Logan Couture .25 .60
410 David Moss .15 .40
411 Mikhail Grabovski .20 .50
412 Cody Eakin .15 .40
413 Patrice Bergeron .30 .75
414 Tomas Tatar .20 .50
415 Lars Eller .20 .50
416 Evgeni Malkin .75 2.00
417 Ryan Miller .25 .60
418 Matt Cooke .15 .40
419 Andrew Cogliano .15 .40
420 Mike Fisher .20 .50
421 Nikita Kucherov .40 1.00
422 Steve Downie .15 .40
423 Drew Doughty .25 .60
424 Jamie McBain .15 .40
425 David Jones .15 .40
426 Semyon Varlamov .25 .60
427 Chris Phillips .15 .40
428 Zack Kassian .20 .50
429 Dion Phaneuf .25 .60
430 Marcus Kruger .25 .60
431 Brian Campbell .15 .40
432 Mark Scheifele .30 .75
433 Jason Demers .15 .40
434 Tom Wilson .25 .60
435 Brandon Sutter .20 .50
436 Taylor Hall .50 1.25
437 Cam Talbot .30 .75
438 Shea Weber .20 .50
439 Ryan Strome .20 .50
440 Steve Bernier .15 .40
441 Henrik Zetterberg .30 .75
442 Jason Pominville .20 .50
443 R.J. Umberger .15 .40
444 Matt Carle .15 .40
445 Jonas Hiller .20 .50
446 Nazem Kadri .25 .60
447 Brandon Prust .15 .40
448 Ron Hainsey .15 .40
449 Johnny Boychuk .15 .40
450 Jeff Carter .25 .60
451 Jakub Voracek .25 .60
452 Brandon Bollig .20 .50
453 Olli Maatta .25 .60
454 Craig Anderson .25 .60
455 Jesse Winchester .15 .40
456 Barret Jackman .15 .40
457 Brent Burns .30 .75
458 Trevor Daley .15 .40
459 Dan Hamhuis .15 .40
460 Tyler Johnson .25 .60
461 Christian Ehrhoff .15 .40
462 Jason Chimera .15 .40
463 Jacob Trouba .20 .50
464 Bryce Salvador .15 .40
465 Gabriel Landeskog .20 .50
466 Pekka Rinne .30 .75
467 Sam Gagner .20 .50
468 Keith Yandle .25 .60
469 Rob Scuderi .15 .40
470 Justin Fontaine .20 .50
471 T.J. Galiardi .20 .50
472 David Savard .15 .40
473 Daniel Girardi .15 .40
474 Andrew MacDonald .15 .40
475 Josh Bailey .20 .50
476 Ryan Getzlaf .40 1.00
477 Justin Abdelkader .20 .50
478 Jonathan Bernier .25 .60
479 Nathan Gerbe .15 .40
480 Jay Bouwmeester .25 .60
481 Duncan Keith .25 .60
482 Kevin Bieksa .20 .50
483 Scottie Upshall .15 .40
484 Mike Smith .25 .60
485 Grant Clitsome .15 .40
486 Brad Marchand .30 .75
487 Sami Salo .15 .40
488 Marc Methot .15 .40
489 Tyler Seguin .40 1.00
490 Andrew Desjardins .15 .40
491 John Tavares .50 1.25
492 Cody Franson .15 .40
493 Marcus Johansson .20 .50
494 Jonathan Quick .40 1.00
495 Tyler Myers .20 .50
496 Checklist 1 .15 .40
497 Checklist 2 .15 .40
498 Checklist 3 .15 .40
499 Checklist 4 .15 .40
500 Checklist 5 .15 .40
501 Andrey Makarov RC 1.25 3.00
502 Adam Payerl RC 1.00 2.50
503 Ty Rattie RC 1.50 4.00
504 Jake McCabe RC 1.25 3.00
505 Vincent Trocheck RC 1.50 4.00
506 Paul Carey RC .75 2.00
507 Teuvo Teravainen RC 2.00 5.00
508 Oscar Klefbom RC 2.50 6.00
509 Laurent Brossoit RC 1.25 3.00
510 Connor Knapp RC .75 2.00
511 Calle Jarnkrok RC 1.25 3.00
512 Brandon Gormley RC 1.25 3.00
513 Andrew Campbell RC 1.00 2.50
514 Markus Granlund RC 2.00 5.00
515 Joonas Nattinen RC 1.25 3.00
516 Landon Ferraro RC .75 2.00
517 Phil Varone RC 1.00 2.50
518 Nicolas Deschamps RC 1.25 3.00
519 Cedric Paquette RC 1.25 3.00
520 Bill Arnold RC 1.00 2.50
521 Alexander Khokhlachev RC 1.25 3.00
522 Patrik Nemeth RC 1.25 3.00
523 Kristers Gudlevskis RC 1.25 3.00
524 Jonathan Racine RC 1.25 3.00
525 Corban Knight RC 1.25 3.00
526 Simon Moser RC .75 2.00
527 Matt Carey RC 1.00 2.50
528 Petter Granberg RC 1.00 2.50
529 Andrew Hammond RC 2.00 5.00
530 Nathan Lieuwen RC 1.00 2.50
531 Joey Hishon RC 1.50 4.00
532 Joni Ortio RC 1.50 4.00
533 Evgeny Kuznetsov RC 5.00 12.00
534 Mitch Callahan RC .75 2.00
535 Kellan Lain RC .75 2.00
536 Greg McKegg RC 1.00 2.50
537 Christian Folin RC 1.25 3.00
538 Matt Lindblad RC 1.00 2.50
539 Colton Sissons RC 1.25 3.00
540 Peter LeBlanc RC .75 2.00
541 Johan Sundstrom RC 1.25 3.00
542 Scott Mayfield RC 1.00 2.50
543 Tyler Wotherspoon RC 1.25 3.00
544 Johnny Gaudreau RC 4.00 10.00
545 Teemu Pulkkinen RC 1.50 4.00
546 Vladislav Namestnikov RC 2.00 5.00
547 Ryan Sproul RC 1.25 3.00
548 Mike Halmo RC .75 2.00
549 Joe Whitney RC .75 2.00
550 Mark Visentin RC 1.25 3.00
551 Rogie Vachon 1.25 3.00
552 Brian Bellows .75 2.00
553 Scotty Bowman 1.00 2.50
554 John LeClair 1.00 2.50
555 Steve Yzerman 2.00 5.00
556 Olaf Kolzig 1.00 2.50
557 Mike Bossy 1.00 2.50
558 Phil Esposito 1.50 4.00
559 Mike Modano 1.50 4.00
560 Guy Carbonneau 1.00 2.50
561 Adam Oates 1.00 2.50
562 Brian Leetch 1.00 2.50
563 Trevor Linden 1.00 2.50
564 Guy Lafleur 1.25 3.00
565 Bill Guerin 1.00 2.50
566 Jeremy Roenick 1.00 2.50
567 Bobby Hull 1.00 2.50
568 Bill Ranford 1.00 2.50
569 Tony Esposito 1.00 2.50
570 Stan Mikita 1.25 3.00
571 Bobby Orr 2.50 6.00
572 Rob Brown .75 2.00
573 Doug Harvey 1.00 2.50
574 Al MacInnis 1.00 2.50
575 Felix Potvin 1.50 4.00
576 Doug Gilmour 1.25 3.00
577 Mike Richter 1.00 2.50
578 Arturs Irbe .75 2.00
579 Jean Beliveau 1.00 2.50
580 Nicklas Lidstrom 1.00 2.50
581 Grant Fuhr 1.00 2.50
582 Pierre Turgeon 1.00 2.50
583 Dominik Hasek 1.25 3.00
584 Joe Sakic 1.50 4.00
585 Ray Bourque 1.50 4.00
586 Mike Gartner 1.00 2.50
587 Wayne Gretzky 5.00 12.00
588 Vincent Damphousse .75 2.00
589 Ron Francis 1.25 3.00
590 Patrick Roy 2.50 6.00
591 Jari Kurri 1.00 2.50
592 Larry Robinson 1.00 2.50
593 Dwayne Roloson .60 1.50
594 Doug Wilson .75 2.00
595 Richard Brodeur 1.00 2.50
596 Darryl Sittler 1.00 2.50
597 Terry O'Reilly .75 2.00
598 Eric Lindros 1.50 4.00
599 Peter Forsberg 1.00 2.50
600 Checklist .40 1.00
601 Sidney Crosby AW 20.00 50.00
602 Sidney Crosby AW 20.00 50.00
603 Tuukka Rask AW 5.00 12.00
604 Duncan Keith AW 5.00 12.00
605 Alex Ovechkin AW 20.00 50.00
606 Nathan MacKinnon AW 10.00 25.00
607 Patrice Bergeron AW 6.00 15.00
608 Justin Williams AW 4.00 10.00
609 Sidney Crosby AW 20.00 50.00
610 Wayne Gretzky AT 50.00 120.00
611 Nicklas Lidstrom AT 10.00 25.00
612 Jean Beliveau AT 10.00 25.00
613 Mario Lemieux AT 30.00 80.00
614 Dominik Hasek AT 12.00 30.00
615 Mike Bossy AT 10.00 25.00
616 Bobby Orr AT 30.00 80.00
617 Patrick Roy AT 25.00 60.00
618 Wayne Gretzky GO 40.00 100.00

2014-15 O-Pee-Chee Rainbow

*1-500 VETS: 2.5X TO 6X BASIC CARDS
*501-550 ROOKIES: .5X TO 1.2X BASIC RC
*551-600 LEGEND.6 TO 1.5X BASIC LGD
STATED ODDS 1:4 HOB, 1:8 RET, 1:7 BLST
202 Nicklas Backstrom 2.50 6.00

2014-15 O-Pee-Chee Red

*1-500 VETS: 5X TO 12X BASIC CARDS
*501-550 ROOKIES: 1X TO 2.5X BASIC CARDS
*551-600 LEGEND: 2X TO 5X BASIC LEG
FIVE PER WRAPPER REDEMPTION
202 Nicklas Backstrom 5.00 12.00
408 Corey Crawford 4.00 10.00
571 Bobby Orr 30.00 60.00
587 Wayne Gretzky 30.00 60.00

2014-15 O-Pee-Chee Retro

*1-500 VETS: 2X TO 5X BASIC CARDS
*501-550 ROOK: .5X TO 1.2X BASIC RC
*551-600 LEGEND: .6X TO 1.5X BASIC LGD
1-600 ODDS 1:1 HOB, 1:2 RET, 1:2 BLST
202 Nicklas Backstrom 2.00 5.00
408 Corey Crawford 1.50 4.00

2014-15 O-Pee-Chee Black Rainbow

*1-500 VETS/100: 6X TO 15X BASIC CARDS
*501-550 ROOK/100: 1.2X TO 3X BASIC RC
*551-600 LGD/100: 2X TO 5X BASIC LGD
STATED ODDS 1:16 HOBBY
STATED PRINT RUN 100 SER.#'d SETS
202 Nicklas Backstrom 6.00 15.00
587 Wayne Gretzky 20.00 50.00
590 Patrick Roy 12.00 30.00

2014-15 O-Pee-Chee 3-D

1 Jaromir Jagr 50.00 100.00
2 Pavel Datsyuk 40.00 100.00
3 Carey Price 75.00 150.00
4 Evgeni Malkin 75.00 150.00
5 Steve Yzerman 75.00 150.00
6 Alex Ovechkin 125.00 200.00
7 Jonathan Toews 90.00 150.00
8 Jordan Eberle 40.00 80.00
9 Arturs Irbe 75.00 125.00
10 P.K. Subban 40.00 100.00
11 Rick Nash 60.00 120.00
12 Bobby Orr 100.00 175.00
13 Anze Kopitar 50.00 125.00
14 Henrik Zetterberg 60.00 120.00
15 Ryan Nugent-Hopkins 40.00 100.00
16 Bobby Hull 75.00 135.00
17 Brett Hull 60.00 120.00
18 Martin Brodeur 75.00 150.00
19 Curtis Joseph 30.00 80.00
20 Wayne Gretzky 250.00 400.00
21 Mario Lemieux 75.00 150.00
22 Ryan Miller 30.00 80.00
23 Sidney Crosby 150.00 250.00
24 Nathan MacKinnon 100.00 200.00
25 Pavel Bure 150.00 250.00
26 Felix Potvin 60.00 120.00
27 Phil Kessel 40.00 100.00
28 Teemu Selanne 60.00 120.00
29 Shea Weber 25.00 60.00
30 Erik Karlsson 60.00 150.00
31 Steven Stamkos 90.00 150.00
32 Taylor Hall 40.00 80.00
33 Jonathan Quick 60.00 120.00
34 Henrik Lundqvist 75.00 150.00
35 Mats Sundin 30.00 80.00
36 John Tavares 60.00 120.00
37 Ryan Getzlaf 50.00 120.00
38 Ray Bourque 75.00 125.00
39 Patrick Roy 125.00 200.00
40 Joe Sakic 75.00 150.00
41 Patrick Kane 75.00 125.00
42 Zdeno Chara 30.00 80.00

2014-15 O-Pee-Chee Blaster Box Bottoms

TWO PER BLASTER BOX BOTTOM
AO Alexander Ovechkin B 2.00 5.00
CP Carey Price A 1.50 4.00
EM Evgeni Malkin A 1.50 4.00
HL Henrik Lundqvist B .60 1.50
JQ Jonathan Quick C .75 2.00
JT Jonathan Toews C 1.00 2.50

2014-15 O-Pee-Chee Mini Tall Boys

ONE PER WRAPPER REDEMPTION PACK
1 Erik Karlsson 8.00 20.00
2 Nazem Kadri 4.00 10.00
3 Martin Brodeur 8.00 20.00
4 Vladislav Namestnikov 4.00 10.00
5 Ryan Getzlaf 6.00 15.00
6 Carey Price 12.00 30.00
7 Alexander Ovechkin 15.00 40.00
8 P.K. Subban 6.00 15.00
9 Zdeno Chara 4.00 10.00
10 Jonathan Bernier 4.00 10.00
11 Phil Kessel 5.00 12.00
12 John Tavares 8.00 20.00
13 Pavel Datsyuk 5.00 12.00
14 Sidney Crosby 15.00 40.00
15 Steven Stamkos 8.00 20.00
16 Claude Giroux 4.00 10.00
17 Tuukka Rask 5.00 12.00
18 Ryan Miller 4.00 10.00
19 Patrick Kane 8.00 20.00
20 Nathan MacKinnon 8.00 20.00
21 Teemu Selanne 8.00 20.00
22 Taylor Hall 8.00 20.00
23 Valeri Nichushkin 3.00 8.00
24 Henrik Lundqvist 5.00 12.00
25 Jonathan Toews 8.00 20.00
26 Evgeny Kuznetsov 15.00 40.00
27 Evgeni Malkin 12.00 30.00
28 Jonathan Quick 6.00 15.00
29 Jaromir Jagr 10.00 25.00
30 Brandon Gormley 4.00 10.00
31 Brett Hull 12.50 25.00
32 Pavel Bure 5.00 12.00
33 Joe Sakic 6.00 15.00
34 Mario Lemieux 8.00 20.00
35 Mark Messier 10.00 20.00
36 Dominik Hasek 5.00 12.00
37 Arturs Irbe 6.00 15.00
38 Nicklas Lidstrom 4.00 10.00
39 Wayne Gretzky 30.00 60.00
40 Bobby Orr 25.00 50.00
41 Steve Yzerman 8.00 20.00
42 Patrick Roy 20.00 40.00

2014-15 O-Pee-Chee Retro Hobby Box Bottoms

FOUR PER HOBBY BOX BOTTOM
AG Alex Galchenyuk B .40 1.00
AO Alexander Ovechkin C 1.00 2.50
CG Claude Giroux B .25 .60
CP Carey Price A .75 2.00
EM Evgeni Malkin A .75 2.00
HL Henrik Lundqvist C .30 .75
HZ Henrik Zetterberg D .30 .75
JQ Jonathan Quick D .40 1.00
JT Jonathan Toews B .50 1.25
NM Nathan MacKinnon C .50 1.25
NY Nail Yakupov D .20 .50
PK Phil Kessel A .30 .75
RG Ryan Getzlaf C .40 1.00
SS Steven Stamkos D .50 1.25
VT Vladimir Tarasenko A .40 1.00
MAF Marc-Andre Fleury B .40 1.00

2014-15 O-Pee-Chee Signatures

GROUP A ODDS 1:7,565
GROUP B ODDS 1: 4,530
GROUP C ODDS 1:2,771
GROUP D ODDS 1:1,250
GROUP E ODDS 1:272
OVERALL ODDS 1:192H,1:400R,1:800B
SAL Alex Pietrangelo A
SAP Aaron Palushaj E 5.00 12.00
SCK Chris Kreider B 40.00 80.00
SDG Daniel Girardi E 2.50 6.00
SHE Milan Hejduk A
SHO Peter Holland E 3.00 8.00
SJA Justin Abdelkader C 4.00 10.00
SJB Jordie Benn E 3.00 8.00
SJF Justin Faulk C 3.00 8.00
SJG John Gibson E 5.00 12.00
SJO Johnny Oduya D 4.00 10.00
SJS Jack Skille E 3.00 8.00
SJT Jiri Tlusty B
SKS Kevin Shattenkirk D 5.00 12.00
SLS Luke Schenn A 12.00 30.00
SMH Martin Hanzal D 3.00 8.00
SMK Mike Kostka E 4.00 10.00
SML Maxim Lapierre E 3.00 8.00
SMP Magnus Paajarvi A
SNG Nathan Gerbe D 3.00 8.00
SPH Patric Hornqvist C 4.00 10.00
SRD Raphael Diaz E 2.50 6.00
SRE Ray Emery E 4.00 10.00
SSB Sergei Bobrovsky A
SSH Shawn Horcoff E 3.00 8.00
SSS Sheldon Souray E 3.00 8.00
STR Tuukka Rask B 15.00 40.00
STV Tomas Vokoun B 12.00 30.00

2014-15 O-Pee-Chee Sport Royalty Autographs

SRAIS Sidney Crosby 125.00 200.00

2014-15 O-Pee-Chee Stickers

STATED ODDS 1:3 H, 1:3 R, 1:6 B
ST1 Seth Jones .60 1.50
ST2 Pavel Bure 1.00 2.50
ST3 Henrik Zetterberg 1.00 2.50
ST4 Martin Brodeur 1.50 4.00
ST5 Patrick Kane 1.50 4.00
ST6 Corey Crawford 1.00 2.50
ST7 Martin St. Louis .75 2.00
ST8 Steven Stamkos 1.50 4.00
ST9 P.K. Subban 1.25 3.00
ST10 Jordan Eberle .75 2.00
ST11 Alex Galchenyuk 1.25 3.00
ST12 Duncan Keith .75 2.00
ST13 Joe Sakic 1.25 3.00
ST14 Bobby Hull .75 2.00
ST15 Marian Hossa .60 1.50
ST16 Luc Robitaille .75 2.00
ST17 Nail Yakupov .60 1.50
ST18 Erik Karlsson 1.50 4.00
ST19 Mario Lemieux 2.50 6.00
ST20 Marian Gaborik .75 2.00
ST21 Shea Weber .60 1.50
ST22 Sergei Bobrovsky .75 2.00
ST23 Peter Forsberg .75 2.00
ST24 Teuvo Teravainen 1.25 3.00
ST25 Darryl Sittler .75 2.00
ST26 Danny DeKeyser .60 1.50
ST27 Mark Messier .75 2.00
ST28 David Backes .75 2.00
ST29 Jonathan Bernier .75 2.00
ST30 Nathan MacKinnon 1.50 4.00
ST31 Brett Hull .75 2.00
ST32 Pekka Rinne 1.00 2.50
ST33 Curtis Joseph .75 2.00
ST34 Jacob Trouba .60 1.50
ST35 Tuukka Rask .75 2.00
ST36 Ron Francis 1.00 2.50
ST37 Mike Modano 1.25 3.00
ST38 Dominik Hasek 1.00 2.50
ST39 Jonas Hiller .60 1.50
ST40 Patrick Sharp .75 2.00
ST41 Bobby Clarke .75 2.00
ST42 Dustin Byfuglien .75 2.00
ST43 Jonathan Quick 1.25 3.00
ST44 Tyler Seguin 1.25 3.00
ST45 Tomas Hertl .75 2.00
ST46 Ray Bourque 1.25 3.00
ST47 John Tavares 1.50 4.00
ST48 Evgeny Kuznetsov 3.00 8.00
ST49 Zach Parise .75 2.00
ST50 Nazem Kadri .75 2.00
ST51 Ryan Miller .75 2.00
ST52 Ryan Nugent-Hopkins .75 2.00
ST53 Vladimir Tarasenko 1.25 3.00
ST54 Joe Pavelski .75 2.00
ST55 Mats Sundin .75 2.00
ST56 Roberto Luongo .75 2.00
ST57 James van Riemsdyk .75 2.00
ST58 Nicklas Lidstrom .75 2.00
ST59 Ryan Getzlaf 1.25 3.00
ST60 Joe Thornton .75 2.00
ST61 Steve Yzerman 1.50 4.00
ST62 Shane Doan .60 1.50
ST63 Jason Spezza .75 2.00
ST64 Ryan Suter .75 2.00
ST65 Patrick Roy 2.00 5.00
ST66 Mike Bossy .75 2.00
ST67 Matt Duchene .75 2.00
ST68 Antti Niemi .60 1.50
ST69 Carey Price 2.50 6.00
ST70 Phil Kessel 1.00 2.50
ST71 Marcel Dionne 1.00 2.50
ST72 Brandon Gormley .75 2.00
ST73 Teemu Selanne 1.50 4.00
ST74 Mike Gartner .75 2.00
ST75 Calle Jarnkrok .75 2.00
ST76 Claude Giroux .75 2.00
ST77 Henrik Lundqvist 1.00 2.50
ST78 Sidney Crosby 3.00 8.00
ST79 Cam Neely .75 2.00
ST80 Alexander Ovechkin 3.00 8.00
ST81 Taylor Hall 1.50 4.00
ST82 Jamie Benn 1.00 2.50
ST83 Patrice Bergeron 1.00 2.50
ST84 Evgeni Malkin 2.50 6.00
ST85 Evander Kane .75 2.00
ST86 Grant Fuhr .75 2.00
ST87 Brendan Gallagher .75 2.00
ST88 Ryan Kesler .75 2.00
ST89 Jonathan Toews 1.50 4.00
ST90 Vladislav Namestnikov 1.25 3.00
ST91 Arturs Irbe .60 1.50
ST92 Oscar Klefbom 1.50 4.00
ST93 Brian Leetch .75 2.00
ST94 Jaromir Jagr 2.00 5.00
ST95 Corey Perry .75 2.00
ST96 John LeClair .75 2.00
ST97 Sean Monahan .75 2.00
ST98 Pavel Datsyuk 1.00 2.50
ST99 Wayne Gretzky 4.00 10.00
ST100 Drew Doughty .75 2.00

2014-15 O-Pee-Chee Team Canada Signatures

GROUP A ODDS 1:6297 HOBBY
GROUP B ODDS 1:6649 HOBBY
GROUP C ODDS 1:5937 HOBBY
GROUP D ODDS 1:1062 HOBBY
GROUP E ODDS 1:831 HOBBY
(OVERALL ODDS 1:384H,1:1200R, 1:2400B
TCSAB Alexandre Burrows D 10.00 25.00
TCSAH Adam Henrique A
TCSAL Andrew Ladd D 10.00 25.00
TCSBH Braden Holtby E 15.00 40.00
TCSBO Bobby Orr B 150.00 300.00
TCSBS Brayden Schenn E 6.00 15.00
TCSCK Chris Kunitz D 10.00 25.00
TCSDP Dion Phaneuf A 10.00 25.00
TCSGL Guy Lafleur A
TCSJB Jonathan Bernier D 10.00 25.00
TCSJG Jean-Sebastien Giguere A 100.00 200.00
TCSJT John Tavares B 30.00 80.00
TCSLA Guillaume Latendresse C 10.00 25.00
TCSLC Logan Couture A
TCSLR Larry Robinson B 90.00 150.00
TCSMH Matthew Halischuk E 6.00 15.00
TCSMR Mike Ribeiro C 10.00 25.00
TCSMS Martin St. Louis A
TCSMU Ryan Murray C 8.00 20.00
TCSRM Ryan Murphy D 6.00 15.00
TCSRT Raffi Torres E 6.00 15.00
TCSRV Rogie Vachon B 12.00 30.00
TCSSG Simon Gagne A
TCSSM Steve Mason A 30.00 60.00
TCSSS Steve Shutt B 60.00 120.00
TCSTP Teddy Purcell D 10.00 25.00
TCSWG Wayne Gretzky B 250.00 500.00

2014-15 O-Pee-Chee Team Logo Patches

201-250 STATED ODDS 1:123
251-262 STATED ODDS 1:852
263-278 STATED ODDS 1:1171
279-289 STATED ODDS 1:2272
UNPRICED 290-297 ODDS 1:4685
UNPRICED 298-300 ODDS 1:18,741
OVERALL STATED ODDS 1:96
201 NHL 2005-06 Alt 10.00 25.00
202 Eastern Conf primary 10.00 25.00
203 Western Conf. primary 10.00 25.00
204 Winter Classic primary 12.00 30.00
205 Ducks alt 12.00 30.00
206 Ducks alt 10.00 25.00
207 Thrashers Inaugural 10.00 25.00
208 Bruins alt 15.00 40.00
209 Sabres alt 10.00 25.00
210 Sabres script 10.00 25.00
211 Flames alt 10.00 25.00
212 Flames script 12.00 30.00
213 Hurricanes script 10.00 25.00
214 Blackhawks alt 10.00 25.00
215 Avalanche secondary 12.00 30.00
216 Avalanche script 10.00 25.00
217 Blue Jackets alt 10.00 25.00
218 Stars primary 10.00 25.00
219 Stars secondary 10.00 25.00
220 Red Wings primary 12.00 30.00
221 Oilers alt 12.00 30.00
222 Oilers alt 12.00 30.00
223 Panthers alt 10.00 25.00
224 Panthers secondary 10.00 25.00
225 Panthers secondary 10.00 25.00
226 Whalers alt 10.00 25.00
227 Kings primary 10.00 25.00
228 Wild Inaugural 10.00 25.00
229 Wild primary 10.00 25.00
230 Predators Inaugural 10.00 25.00
231 Predators alt 10.00 25.00
232 Predators alt 10.00 25.00
233 Predators secondary 10.00 25.00
234 Devils script 10.00 25.00
235 Islanders primary 10.00 25.00
236 Rangers alt 15.00 40.00
237 Senators alt 10.00 25.00
238 Senators alt 10.00 25.00
239 Coyotes Inaugural 10.00 25.00
240 Sharks green 12.00 30.00
241 Sharks white 12.00 30.00
242 Blues primary 12.00 30.00
243 Blues primary 12.00 30.00
244 Lightning primary 10.00 25.00
245 Maple Leafs alt 12.00 30.00
246 Canucks primary 12.00 30.00
247 Capitals primary 12.00 30.00
248 Capitals alt 12.00 30.00
249 Jets primary 12.00 30.00
250 Jets alt 12.00 30.00
251 Bruins 80th Anniv. 25.00 50.00
252 Bruins 90th Anniv. 30.00 60.00
253 Blackhawks 75th Anniv. 20.00 40.00
254 Red Wings 50th Anniv. 25.00 50.00
255 Red Wings 75th Anniv. 25.00 50.00
256 Canadiens 75th Anniv. 30.00 60.00
257 Canadiens 100th Anniv. 30.00 60.00
258 Rangers 85th Anniv. 25.00 50.00
259 Maple Leafs 50th Anniv. 25.00 50.00
260 Maple Leafs 75th Anniv. 25.00 50.00
261 NHL 75th Anniv. 20.00 40.00
262 Stanley Cup 100th Anniv. 25.00 50.00
263 NHL alt 20.00 50.00
264 Campbell Conf. primary 20.00 50.00
265 Wales Conf. primary 20.00 50.00
266 Bruins primary 30.00 60.00
267 Sabres primary 20.00 50.00
268 Golden Seals primary 50.00 100.00
269 Blackhawks alt 60.00 120.00
270 Blackhawks alt 60.00 100.00
271 Kings primary 30.00 60.00
272 Seals secondary 30.00 60.00
273 North Stars primary 50.00 100.00
274 Canadiens script 30.00 60.00
275 Rangers primary 50.00 100.00
276 Penguins primary 60.00 120.00
277 Maple Leafs alt 60.00 120.00
278 Maple Leafs primary 30.00 60.00
279 Bruins primary
280 Bruins primary 75.00 150.00
281 Cougars alt 100.00 200.00
282 Red Wings V for Victory
283 Canadiens primary 90.00 150.00
284 Canadiens primary 100.00 200.00
285 Maroons alt 75.00 150.00
286 Americans primary 40.00 80.00
287 Senators World Champs
288 Eagles alt 150.00 250.00
289 St. Pats primary 90.00 150.00
290 Bruins Boston Gardens
291 Hurricanes Francis 10
292 Red Wings Believe
293 Oilers Glenn Anderson 9
294 Whalers Thanks
295 Kings Gretzky 99
296 Kings Luc Robitaille 20
297 Maple Leafs Gardens
298 Thrashers Cartoon
299 Sabres Cartoon
300 Red Wings Cartoon

2014-15 O-Pee-Chee V Series A

STATED ODDS 1:16 H, 1:32 R, 1:32 B
S1 Jaromir Jagr 5.00 12.00
S2 Phil Kessel 2.50 6.00
S3 Jonathan Quick 3.00 8.00
S4 Martin Brodeur 4.00 10.00
S5 Nathan MacKinnon 4.00 10.00
S6 Mike Gartner 2.00 5.00
S7 Brian Bellows 1.50 4.00
S8 Patrick Kane 4.00 10.00
S9 Dominik Hasek 2.50 6.00
S10 Pavel Bure 2.50 6.00
S11 Pekka Rinne 2.50 6.00
S12 Evgeny Kuznetsov 8.00 20.00
S13 Alexander Ovechkin 8.00 20.00
S14 Steven Stamkos 4.00 10.00
S15 Ryan Miller 2.00 5.00
S16 Zdeno Chara 2.00 5.00
S17 Ed Belfour 2.00 5.00
S18 Jonathan Toews 4.00 10.00
S19 Sergei Bobrovsky 2.00 5.00
S20 Mats Sundin 2.00 5.00
S21 Alexander Steen 2.00 5.00
S22 Tyler Seguin 3.00 8.00
S23 Patrice Bergeron 2.50 6.0
S24 Henrik Lundqvist 2.50 6.0
S25 Wayne Gretzky 10.00 25.0
S26 Sidney Crosby 8.00 20.0
S27 Carey Price 6.00 15.0
S28 Pavel Datsyuk 2.50 6.0
S29 Steve Yzerman 4.00 10.0
S30 Bobby Hull 2.00 5.0
S31 John LeClair 2.00 5.0
S32 Mike Bossy 2.00 5.0
S33 Mario Lemieux 6.00 15.0
S34 Rick Nash 2.00 5.0
S35 Evgeni Malkin 6.00 15.0
S36 Mark Messier 2.00 5.0
S37 Ryan Getzlaf 3.00 8.0
S38 Teuvo Teravainen 3.00 8.0
S39 Brad Marchand 2.50 6.0
S40 John Tavares 4.00 10.0
S41 Claude Giroux 2.00 5.0
S42 Ryan Nugent-Hopkins 2.00 5.0
S43 P.K. Subban 3.00 8.0
S44 Drew Doughty 2.00 5.0
S45 Grant Fuhr 2.00 5.0

2015-16 O-Pee-Chee

COMPLETE SET (600) 75.00 135.0
COMP.SET w/o SP's (500) 25.00 50.0
501-600 ODDS 1:4 HOB/RET/BL
601-609 AW ODDS 1:312 H, 1:6240 R/BL
610-617 AT ODDS 1:352 H, 1:7040 R/BL
618 SC ODDS 1:2810 HOB, 1:56,200 R/BL
601-618 PRINTED ON RETRO STOCK
1 Scott Darling .25 .6
2 Francois Beauchemin .15 .4
3 Jaroslav Halak AS .20 .5
4 Niklas Hjalmarsson .15 .4
5 David Perron .15 .4
6 David Booth .15 .4
7 Darren Helm .15 .4
8 Michael Stone .15 .4
9 Jeff Petry .15 .4
10 Erik Haula .15 .4
11 Ben Smith .15 .4
12 Jaromir Jagr .60 1.5
13 Michael Del Zotto .15 .4
14 Eric Nystrom .15 .4
15 Maxime Talbot .20 .5
16 Curtis McElhinney .15 .4
17 Kyle Clifford .15 .4
18 Andy Greene .15 .4
19 Kari Lehtonen .20 .5
20 T.J. Brodie .15 .4
21 Jake Allen .30 .7
22 Andrew Ference .15 .4
23 John Mitchell .15 .4
24 Mikhail Grabovski .20 .5
25 Jonathan Drouin AS .30 .7
26 Tyler Ennis .20 .5
27 Chris Kreider .25 .6
28 Ryan Kesler .25 .6
29 Mathieu Perreault .15 .4
30 Chris Kunitz .25 .6
31 Aleksander Barkov .25 .6
32 P.K. Subban .40 1.0
33 Mike Santorelli .15 .4
34 Andrew Shaw .25 .6
35 Braden Holtby .40 1.0
36 Jonathan Ericsson .20 .5
37 Scott Hartnell .25 .6
38 Eric Staal .30 .7
39 Steve Mason .20 .5
40 Jay Bouwmeester .25 .6
41 Nick Bonino .15 .4
42 Andrej Nestrasil .15 .4
43 Morgan Rielly .20 .5
44 Michael Cammalleri .20 .5
45 Bryan Little .20 .5
46 Patrik Berglund .15 .4
47 Matt Carle .15 .4
48 Dennis Wideman .15 .4
49 Curtis Glencross .15 .4
50 Evgeni Malkin .75 2.0
51 Checklist .15 .4
52 Bobby Ryan AS .20 .5
53 Rick Nash AS .25 .6
54 Loui Eriksson .20 .5
55 Alec Martinez .15 .4
56 Nathan Beaulieu .20 .5
57 Jason Zucker .20 .5
58 Brayden Schenn .25 .6
59 Ales Hemsky .15 .4
60 Peter Holland .15 .4
61 Antti Niemi .20 .5
62 Alexander Wennberg .20 .5
63 Niklas Kronwall .20 .5
64 Cody McLeod .15 .4
65 Mika Zibanejad .25 .6
66 Ben Scrivens .20 .5
67 Nate Thompson .15 .4
68 Nicklas Backstrom .40 1.0
69 Ryan McDonagh .20 .5
70 Shea Weber AS .20 .5
71 Johnny Oduya .20 .5
72 Mikael Backlund .20 .5
73 Trevor Lewis .15 .4
74 Chris Higgins .15 .4
75 Oliver Ekman-Larsson AS .20 .5
76 Patrice Bergeron AS .30 .7
77 Cam Ward .25 .6
78 James Reimer .25 .6
79 Nail Yakupov .20 .5
80 Tomas Jurco .25 .6
81 Kevin Shattenkirk AS .20 .5
82 Sean Bergenheim .15 .4
83 James Wisniewski .15 .4
84 Jhonas Enroth .25 .6
85 Joel Ward .15 .4
86 Joe Thornton .25 .6
87 Josh Bailey .20 .5
88 Jimmy Hayes .20 .5
89 Evander Kane .25 .6
90 Scott Gomez .20 .5
91 Brayden McNabb .15 .4
92 Craig Smith .15 .4
93 Steve Downie .15 .4
94 Tobias Enstrom .15 .4
95 Sergei Bobrovsky .25 .6
96 Karl Alzner .15 .4
97 Brad Richardson .15 .4
98 Sean Monahan .25 .6
99 Victor Rask .15 .4
100 Steven Stamkos AS .50 1.2
101 Jason Pominville .20 .5
102 Jarome Iginla .25 .6
103 Sergei Gonchar .15 .4
104 Kevin Hayes .25 .6
105 Patrick Sharp .25 .6
106 Andrew MacDonald .15 .4

07 Michael Hutchinson .25 .60
08 Frans Nielsen .15 .40
09 Jakob Silfverberg .20 .50
10 Jaden Schwartz .30 .75
11 Tuukka Rask .25 .60
12 Teddy Purcell .25 .60
13 Andrew Hammond .75 2.00
14 Paul Martin .15 .40
15 Jared Spurgeon .15 .40
16 Tom Wilson .25 .60
17 Mason Raymond .20 .50
18 Tomas Hertl .25 .60
19 John Klingberg .20 .50
20 Leo Komarov .20 .50
21 Rasmus Ristolainen .20 .50
22 Mikkel Boedker .15 .40
23 Brian Boyle .15 .40
24 Radim Vrbata AS .20 .50
25 Aaron Ekblad AS .25 .60
26 Justin Abdelkader .20 .50
27 Michael Ryder .15 .40
28 Michael Frolik .15 .40
29 Anders Lee .25 .60
30 Roman Josi .25 .60
31 Matt Duchene .25 .60
32 Marian Hossa .20 .50
33 Andre Burakovsky .20 .50
34 David Pastrnak .40 1.00
35 Dominic Moore .15 .40
36 Nathan Gerbe .15 .40
37 Matt Hendricks .15 .40
38 Ben Bishop .25 .60
39 Joe Pavelski .25 .60
40 Steve Bernier .15 .40
41 Roman Polak .15 .40
42 Max Pacioretty .25 .60
43 Brian Elliott AS .20 .50
44 Matt Moulson .20 .50
45 Claude Giroux AS .25 .60
46 Devan Dubnyk .25 .60
47 Blake Comeau .15 .40
48 Erik Cole .20 .50
49 Colin Wilson .15 .40
50 Jonathan Quick .40 1.00
51 Checklist .15 .40
52 Kevan Miller .15 .40
53 Kyle Palmieri .15 .40
54 Mark Giordano AS .25 .60
55 Leon Draisaitl .25 .60
56 Johan Franzen .25 .60
57 Kevin Connauton .15 .40
58 Jussi Jokinen .15 .40
59 Mark Streit .15 .40
60 Anders Lindback .15 .40
61 Mark Stuart .15 .40
62 Duncan Keith AS .25 .60
63 Valtteri Filppula .20 .50
64 Lars Eller .20 .50
65 Colton Sceviour .15 .40
66 Marco Scandella .15 .40
67 Carl Hagelin .20 .50
68 Jannik Hansen .15 .40
69 Robin Lehner .20 .50
70 Bryce Salvador .15 .40
71 Logan Couture .25 .60
72 Nick Spaling .15 .40
73 Dave Bolland .15 .40
74 Adam Lowry .15 .40
75 Pavel Datsyuk .30 .75
76 Gabriel Landeskog .25 .60
77 Brock Nelson .20 .50
78 Derek Roy .20 .50
79 Sam Reinhart .25 .60
80 Cody Ceci .15 .40
81 Marcus Johansson .20 .50
82 Vladislav Namestnikov .25 .60
83 Marian Gaborik .25 .60
84 Daniel Sedin .25 .60
85 Tomas Fleischmann .15 .40
86 Shane Doan .20 .50
87 Elias Lindholm .15 .40
88 Drew Stafford .25 .60
89 Kris Versteeg .20 .50
90 Taylor Beck .15 .40
91 Nikolai Kulemin .20 .50
92 Markus Granlund .20 .50
93 Jack Johnson .15 .40
94 Evgeny Kuznetsov .40 1.00
95 Tomas Tatar .20 .50
96 Cody Eakin .15 .40
97 Alex Pietrangelo .20 .50
98 Ryan Carter .15 .40
99 Dennis Seidenberg .20 .50
00 Carey Price AS .75 2.00
01 Curtis Lazar .20 .50
02 Marc-Andre Fleury AS .40 1.00
03 Pat Maroon .15 .40
04 Patrick Kane AS .50 1.25
05 Ryan Miller .25 .60
06 Zach Redmond .15 .40
07 Gustav Nyquist .25 .60
08 Derek Stepan .25 .60
09 Anton Stralman .15 .40
10 Jason Spezza .20 .50
11 Andrej Sekera .15 .40
12 Justin Braun .15 .40
13 Brandon Pirri .15 .40
14 Josh Gorges .15 .40
15 Andrew Cogliano .15 .40
16 Lance Bouma .15 .40
17 Nino Niederreiter .15 .40
18 Kyle Okposo .25 .60
19 Lee Stempniak .15 .40
20 Carter Hutton .25 .60
21 Boone Jenner .15 .40
22 Mark Arcobello .15 .40
23 Nathan MacKinnon .50 1.25
24 Brooks Orpik .20 .50
25 Vladimir Tarasenko AS .40 1.00
26 Phil Kessel AS .40 1.00
27 Zdeno Chara .25 .60
28 Patric Hornqvist .20 .50
29 Tomas Plekanec .25 .60
30 Drew Doughty AS .25 .60
31 Teuvo Teravainen .25 .60
32 Vernon Fiddler .15 .40
33 Adam Henrique .25 .60
34 Connor Murphy .15 .40
35 Derick Brassard .25 .60
36 Mike Hoffman AS .20 .50
37 Frederik Andersen .20 .50
38 Dmitry Kulikov .15 .40
39 Jim Howard .25 .60
40 David Jones .15 .40
41 Matt Cullen .15 .40
42 Jordan Eberle .25 .60
43 Mike Weber .15 .40
44 Nick Foligno AS .20 .50
245 Jordan Staal .25 .60
246 Nikita Kucherov .40 1.00
247 Shawn Matthias .15 .40
248 Martin Havlat .20 .50
249 Seth Griffith .20 .50
250 John Tavares AS .50 1.25
251 Checklist .15 .40
252 Andrew Ladd .25 .60
253 Joe Colborne .15 .40
254 David Backes .25 .60
255 Bo Horvat .40 1.00
256 Michael Raffl .15 .40
257 Ryan O'Reilly .25 .60
258 Eric Fehr .15 .40
259 Keith Yandle .25 .60
260 Dion Phaneuf .25 .60
261 Danny DeKeyser .20 .50
262 Dustin Brown .20 .50
263 Michal Neuvirth .20 .50
264 Lauri Korpikoski .15 .40
265 Marcus Kruger .25 .60
266 Jason Demers .15 .40
267 Alex Chiasson .20 .50
268 Richard Panik .15 .40
269 Marko Dano .20 .50
270 Jason Garrison .15 .40
271 Brad Richards .25 .60
272 Niklas Svedberg .20 .50
273 Vincent Lecavalier .20 .50
274 Troy Brouwer .20 .50
275 Zach Parise .25 .60
276 Seth Jones .20 .50
277 Riley Sheahan .20 .50
278 John Gibson .25 .60
279 Damon Severson .20 .50
280 Calvin Pickard .20 .50
281 Anze Kopitar AS .40 1.00
282 Jiri Hudler .20 .50
283 Riley Nash .15 .40
284 Christopher Tanev .20 .50
285 Daniel Girardi .15 .40
286 Nick Leddy .15 .40
287 Brian Flynn .15 .40
288 Tobias Rieder .15 .40
289 Viktor Fasth .20 .50
290 Steve Ott .20 .50
291 Ray Emery .20 .50
292 Chris Stewart .15 .40
293 Matt Calvert .15 .40
294 Daniel Winnik .15 .40
295 Marcus Foligno .15 .40
296 Torey Krug .25 .60
297 Vincent Trocheck .20 .50
298 Mark Stone .20 .50
299 Jay McClement .15 .40
300 Jonathan Toews AS .50 1.25
301 Brendan Gallagher .30 .75
302 Brooks Laich .15 .40
303 Tanner Pearson .15 .40
304 Milan Lucic .20 .50
305 Joakim Lindstrom .15 .40
306 Taylor Hall .50 1.25
307 Alex Killorn .20 .50
308 Alex Stalock .15 .40
309 Artem Anisimov .20 .50
310 Daniel Briere .20 .50
311 Erik Condra .15 .40
312 Andrei Markov .25 .60
313 Alexander Steen .25 .60
314 Derrick Pouliot .20 .50
315 Derek Dorsett .15 .40
316 Jiri Tlusty .20 .50
317 Hampus Lindholm .20 .50
318 Mike Ribeiro .20 .50
319 Jake Muzzin .15 .40
320 Erik Gudbranson .25 .60
321 Ondrej Palat .20 .50
322 Tommy Wingels .15 .40
323 Tyson Barrie .25 .60
324 Kyle Turris .20 .50
325 Johnny Gaudreau AS .40 1.00
326 Anton Khudobin .20 .50
327 Darcy Kuemper .20 .50
328 Brian Gionta .20 .50
329 Cam Talbot .30 .75
330 Brad Marchand .30 .75
331 Alex Goligoski .15 .40
332 Jake Gardiner .25 .60
333 Cory Schneider .20 .50
334 Tyler Toffoli .25 .60
335 Ondrej Pavelec .25 .60
336 Barret Jackman .15 .40
337 Matt Beleskey .15 .40
338 Luke Schenn .15 .40
339 Marek Zidlicky .15 .40
340 Mike Smith .25 .60
341 Justin Fontaine .15 .40
342 Kimmo Timonen .15 .40
343 Tyler Kennedy .15 .40
344 Victor Hedman .30 .75
345 Barclay Goodrow .15 .40
346 Tyler Bozak .20 .50
347 Trevor Daley .15 .40
348 Devante Smith-Pelly .20 .50
349 Willie Mitchell .15 .40
350 Henrik Lundqvist .30 .75
351 Checklist .15 .40
352 Jared Cowen .15 .40
353 Ryan Ellis .15 .40
354 Thomas Vanek .25 .60
355 Dustin Byfuglien AS .25 .60
356 Alexander Edler .15 .40
357 Mike Green .25 .60
358 Matt Stajan .20 .50
359 Matt Martin .15 .40
360 Oscar Klefbom .40 1.00
361 Travis Zajac .20 .50
362 David Desharnais .20 .50
363 Cody Hodgson .25 .60
364 Marc-Edouard Vlasic .15 .40
365 Sam Gagner .20 .50
366 David Savard .15 .40
367 Beau Bennett .15 .40
368 Martin Jones .25 .60
369 Semyon Varlamov .25 .60
370 Brian Campbell .15 .40
371 Jonathan Bernier .25 .60
372 Corey Perry .25 .60
373 Calle Jarnkrok .20 .50
374 Brendan Smith .20 .50
375 Carl Soderberg .20 .50
376 Cedric Paquette .15 .40
377 Alexandre Burrows .20 .50
378 Wayne Simmonds .30 .75
379 Charlie Coyle .20 .50
380 Matt Nieto .15 .40
381 Dmitrij Jaskin .15 .40
382 Alexei Emelin .20 .50
383 Ryan Nugent-Hopkins AS .25 .60
384 Nicolas Deslauriers .15 .40
385 Shawn Horcoff .15 .40
386 Martin Erat .15 .40
387 David Krejci .20 .50
388 Chris Neil .15 .40
389 Jeff Skinner .20 .50
390 Christian Ehrhoff .15 .40
391 Eddie Lack .20 .50
392 Antoine Vermette .15 .40
393 Cody Franson .15 .40
394 Boyd Gordon .15 .40
395 Ryan Strome .20 .50
396 Matt Read .15 .40
397 Dan Boyle .20 .50
398 Melker Karlsson .15 .40
399 Jori Lehtera .20 .50
400 Alexander Ovechkin AS 1.00 2.50
401 Patrik Elias AS .25 .60
402 P.A. Parenteau .15 .40
403 Mikael Granlund .20 .50
404 Dougie Hamilton .25 .60
405 Nazem Kadri .20 .50
406 Ryan Callahan .25 .60
407 Dwight King .15 .40
408 Cam Atkinson .25 .60
409 Mark Scheifele .30 .75
410 R.J. Umberger .15 .40
411 Corey Crawford AS .30 .75
412 Zemgus Girgensons AS .20 .50
413 Brenden Dillon .15 .40
414 Henrik Sedin .25 .60
415 Marc Staal .20 .50
416 Nick Holden .15 .40
417 Jamie Benn .30 .75
418 Ron Hainsey .15 .40
419 Justin Schultz .20 .50
420 Jonas Hiller .20 .50
421 Mike Fisher .20 .50
422 David Legwand .20 .50
423 Sean Couturier .25 .60
424 Brad Boyes .15 .40
425 Henrik Zetterberg .30 .75
426 Brandon Sutter .20 .50
427 Matt Niskanen .20 .50
428 Simon Despres .15 .40
429 Martin Hanzal .15 .40
430 Brandon Prust .15 .40
431 Johnny Boychuk .15 .40
432 Brandon Saad .25 .60
433 James Neal .25 .60
434 Kris Russell .15 .40
435 Ryan Suter AS .15 .40
436 Erik Karlsson .50 1.25
437 Joffrey Lupul .20 .50
438 Brett Connolly .15 .40
439 Benoit Pouliot .15 .40
440 Jeff Carter .25 .60
441 Paul Stastny .25 .60
442 Justin Faulk AS .25 .60
443 Adam Larsson .25 .60
444 Blake Wheeler .25 .60
445 Dan Hamhuis .15 .40
446 Fedor Tyutin .15 .40
447 Nick Bjugstad .20 .50
448 Nikita Zadorov .20 .50
449 Kyle Chipchura .15 .40
450 Ryan Getzlaf AS .40 1.00
451 Checklist .15 .40
452 Andrei Vasilevskiy .30 .75
453 Kevin Klein .15 .40
454 Kris Letang .25 .60
455 Craig Anderson .25 .60
456 Jakub Voracek AS .25 .60
457 Bryan Bickell .15 .40
458 Erik Johnson .15 .40
459 Reilly Smith .25 .60
460 Filip Forsberg AS .30 .75
461 John Carlson .30 .75
462 Antoine Roussel .15 .40
463 James van Riemsdyk .25 .60
464 Justin Williams .20 .50
465 Brent Burns AS .30 .75
466 Jiri Sekac AS .20 .50
467 Travis Hamonic .15 .40
468 Calvin de Haan .15 .40
469 Eric Gelinas .15 .40
470 Linden Vey .15 .40
471 Roberto Luongo AS .25 .60
472 Alex Galchenyuk .30 .75
473 Jonathan Huberdeau .25 .60
474 Ryan Johansen AS .30 .75
475 Martin St. Louis .25 .60
476 Tyler Myers .20 .50
477 Karri Ramo .20 .50
478 Zach Bogosian .20 .50
479 Jay Beagle .20 .50
480 Alexander Semin .25 .60
481 Alex Tanguay .15 .40
482 Cam Fowler .20 .50
483 John Moore .15 .40
484 Petr Mrazek .30 .75
485 Jacob Trouba .20 .50
486 Chris Vande Velde .15 .40
487 Nikita Nikitin .15 .40
488 Dale Weise .15 .40
489 Clarke MacArthur .15 .40
490 Jon Merrill .15 .40
491 Patrick Marleau .25 .60
492 Mikko Koivu .20 .50
493 Tyler Johnson .20 .50
494 Tyler Seguin AS .40 1.00
495 Pekka Rinne .30 .75
496 T.J. Oshie .40 1.00
497 Thomas Hickey .15 .40
498 Brent Seabrook AS .25 .60
499 Mats Zuccarello .20 .50
500 Sidney Crosby 1.00 2.50
501 Louis Domingue RC 1.25 3.00
502 Malcolm Subban RC 3.00 8.00
503 Alex Biega RC .75 2.00
504 Mike Lee RC .75 2.00
505 David Wolf RC 1.25 3.00
506 Ryan Hartman RC 1.50 4.00
507 Josh Anderson RC 1.25 3.00
508 Nick Shore RC 1.25 3.00
509 Jacob de la Rose RC 1.25 3.00
510 Anthony Bitetto RC .75 2.00
511 Mackenzie Skapski RC 1.25 3.00
512 Shane Prince RC 1.00 2.50
513 Anthony Stolarz RC 1.25 3.00
514 Petr Straka RC 1.00 2.50
515 Daniil Tarasov RC 1.00 2.50
516 Luke Witkowski RC 1.00 2.50
517 Antoine Bibeau RC 1.25 3.00
518 Ronalds Kenins RC 1.25 3.00
519 Jean-Francois Berube RC 1.00 2.50
520 Brian Ferlin RC .75 2.00
521 Jordan Oesterle RC .75 2.00
522 Kael Mouillierat RC 1.00 2.50
523 Matt Puempel RC 1.00 2.50
524 Brendan Ranford RC 1.00 2.50
525 Henrik Samuelsson RC 1.00 2.50
526 Emile Poirier RC 1.25 3.00
527 Oscar Dansk RC 1.50 4.00
528 Oscar Lindberg RC 1.25 3.00
529 Mark Alt RC .75 2.00
530 Chris Driedger RC 1.00 2.50
531 Sam Brittain RC 1.25 3.00
532 Rasmus Rissanen RC 1.00 2.50
533 Andrew MacWilliam RC .75 2.00
534 Kevin Fiala RC 1.25 3.00
535 Danny Biega RC .75 2.00
536 Andrew Miller RC 1.00 2.50
537 Viktor Arvidsson RC 1.50 4.00
538 Nick Cousins RC 1.25 3.00
539 Casey Bailey RC 1.25 3.00
540 Sam Bennett RC 1.50 4.00
541 Stefan Noesen RC 1.00 2.50
542 Kyle Baun RC 1.25 3.00
543 Slater Koekkoek RC 1.00 2.50
544 Andrew Copp RC 1.25 3.00
545 Brett Kulak RC 1.00 2.50
546 Duncan Siemens RC 1.50 4.00
547 Stanislav Galiev RC 1.25 3.00
548 David Musil RC 1.00 2.50
549 Bryan Lerg RC .75 2.00
550 Michael Paliotta RC 1.00 2.50
551 Brett Hull 1.00 2.50
552 Patrick Roy 2.50 6.00
553 Mike Modano 1.50 4.00
554 Bobby Hull 1.00 2.50
555 Andy Moog 1.00 2.50
556 John Vanbiesbrouck 1.00 2.50
557 Bobby Orr 3.00 8.00
558 Marty McSorley 1.00 2.50
559 Mario Lemieux 3.00 8.00
560 Teemu Selanne 2.00 5.00
561 Martin Brodeur 2.00 5.00
562 Mike Bossy 1.00 2.50
563 Steve Yzerman 1.50 4.00
564 Trevor Linden 1.00 2.50
565 Jean Beliveau 1.00 2.50
566 Mark Messier 1.50 4.00
567 Mike Gartner 1.00 2.50
568 Nicklas Lidstrom 1.00 2.50
569 Pierre Turgeon 1.00 2.50
570 Mats Sundin 1.00 2.50
571 Curtis Joseph 1.00 2.50
572 Brad Park .75 2.00
573 Adam Oates 1.00 2.50
574 Terry Sawchuk 1.00 2.50
575 Pelle Lindbergh 1.00 2.50
576 Olaf Kolzig 1.00 2.50
577 Darryl Sittler 1.00 2.50
578 Vincent Damphousse .75 2.00
579 Grant Fuhr 1.00 2.50
580 Arturs Irbe .75 2.00
581 Felix Potvin 1.50 4.00
582 Rob Brown .60 1.50
583 Wayne Gretzky 5.00 12.00
584 Chris Chelios 1.00 2.50
585 Tom Barrasso 1.00 2.50
586 Ray Bourque 1.50 4.00
587 Cam Neely 1.00 2.50
588 Pete Peeters .75 2.00
589 Marcel Dionne 1.25 3.00
590 Mike Liut .60 1.50
591 Steve Larmer .75 2.00
592 Dave Schultz 1.00 2.50
593 Denis Savard 1.25 3.00
594 Phil Esposito 1.50 4.00
595 Doug Harvey 1.00 2.50
596 Doug Weight 1.00 2.50
597 Brian Bellows .75 2.00
598 Wendel Clark 1.00 2.50
599 Denis Potvin 1.00 2.50
600 Checklist .60 1.50
601 Carey Price AW 25.00 60.00
602 Jamie Benn AW 10.00 25.00
603 Carey Price AW 25.00 60.00
604 Erik Karlsson AW 8.00 20.00
605 Alexander Ovechkin AW 30.00 80.00
606 Aaron Ekblad AW 8.00 20.00
607 Patrice Bergeron AW 10.00 25.00
608 Duncan Keith AW 10.00 25.00
609 Carey Price AW 20.00 35.00
610 Wayne Gretzky AT 40.00 100.00
611 Bobby Orr AT 25.00 60.00
612 Brad Park AT 6.00 15.00
613 Mark Messier AT 12.00 30.00
614 Mario Lemieux AT 25.00 60.00
615 Cam Neely AT 8.00 20.00
616 Curtis Joseph AT 8.00 20.00
617 Vincent Damphousse AT 6.00 15.00
618 Stanley Cup 25.00 50.00

2015-16 O-Pee-Chee Rainbow

*1-500 VETS: 2.5X TO 6X BASIC CARDS
*501-550 ROOKIES: .5X TO 1.2X BASIC RC
*551-600 LEGENDS: .6X TO 1.5X BASIC SP
STATED ODDS 1:4 HOB, 1:7 RET, 1:8 BL
25 Jonathan Drouin AS 2.00 5.00
68 Nicklas Backstrom 2.50 6.00
194 Evgeny Kuznetsov 2.50 6.00
411 Corey Crawford AS 2.00 5.00
506 Ryan Hartman 2.00 5.00

2015-16 O-Pee-Chee Rainbow Black

*1-500 VETS/100: 6X TO 15X BASIC CARDS
*501-550 ROOKIE/100: 1.2X TO 3X BASIC RC
*551-600 LEGEND/100: 1.5X TO 4X BASIC SP
25 Jonathan Drouin AS 5.00 12.00
68 Nicklas Backstrom 6.00 15.00
194 Evgeny Kuznetsov 6.00 15.00
411 Corey Crawford AS 5.00 12.00
506 Ryan Hartman 5.00 12.00
583 Wayne Gretzky 15.00 40.00

2015-16 O-Pee-Chee Red

*1-500 VETS: 5X TO 12X BASIC CARDS
*501-550 ROOKIES: 1X TO 2.5X BASIC RC
*551-600 LEGENDS: 1.5X TO 4X BASIC RC
FIVE PER WRAPPER REDEMPTION
25 Jonathan Drouin AS 4.00 10.00
68 Nicklas Backstrom 5.00 12.00
194 Evgeny Kuznetsov 5.00 12.00
411 Corey Crawford AS 4.00 10.00
506 Ryan Hartman 4.00 10.00
540 Sam Bennett 12.00 30.00
552 Patrick Roy 12.00 30.00
557 Bobby Orr 12.00 30.00
583 Wayne Gretzky 15.00 40.00

2015-16 O-Pee-Chee Retro

*1-500 VETS: 1.5X TO 4X BASIC CARDS
*501-550 ROOKIES: .4X TO 1X BASIC RC
*551-600 LEGENDS: .5X TO 1.2X BASIC SP
STATED ODDS 1:1 HOB, 1:2 RET/BL
25 Jonathan Drouin AS 1.25 3.00
68 Nicklas Backstrom 1.50 4.00
194 Evgeny Kuznetsov 1.50 4.00
411 Corey Crawford AS 1.25 3.00
506 Ryan Hartman 1.50 4.00

2015-16 O-Pee-Chee All-Star Glossy

1-45 ODDS 1:9 HOB/RET, 1:18 BL
46-49 ODDS 1:100 HOB/RET, 1:200 BL
50 ODDS 1:400 HOB/RET, 1:800 BL
AS1 N.Foligno/J.Toews .75 2.00
AS2 Nick Foligno .75 2.00
AS3 Patrick Kane 2.00 5.00
AS4 Drew Doughty 1.00 2.50
AS5 Ryan Johansen 1.25 3.00
AS6 Duncan Keith 1.00 2.50
AS7 Anze Kopitar 1.50 4.00
AS8 Steven Stamkos 2.00 5.00
AS9 Phil Kessel 1.50 4.00
AS10 Carey Price 3.00 8.00
AS11 Claude Giroux 1.00 2.50
AS12 Dustin Byfuglien 1.00 2.50
AS13 Marc-Andre Fleury 1.50 4.00
AS14 Brian Elliott .75 2.00
AS15 Brent Burns 1.25 3.00
AS16 Jonathan Drouin 1.25 3.00
AS17 Jiri Sekac .75 2.00
AS18 Kevin Shattenkirk .75 2.00
AS19 Bobby Ryan .75 2.00
AS20 Radim Vrbata .75 2.00
AS21 Oliver Ekman-Larsson .75 2.00
AS22 Zemgus Girgensons .75 2.00
AS23 Alexander Ovechkin 4.00 10.00
AS24 Ryan Nugent-Hopkins 1.00 2.50
AS25 Jonathan Toews 2.00 5.00
AS26 Ryan Getzlaf 1.50 4.00
AS27 Rick Nash 1.00 2.50
AS28 Tyler Seguin 1.50 4.00
AS29 Shea Weber .75 2.00
AS30 Jakub Voracek 1.00 2.50
AS31 Corey Crawford 1.25 3.00
AS32 John Tavares 2.00 5.00
AS33 Roberto Luongo 1.00 2.50
AS34 Brent Seabrook 1.00 2.50
AS35 Vladimir Tarasenko 1.50 4.00
AS36 Patrice Bergeron 1.25 3.00
AS37 Jaroslav Halak .75 2.00
AS38 Johnny Gaudreau 1.50 4.00
AS39 Mike Hoffman .75 2.00
AS40 Aaron Ekblad 1.00 2.50
AS41 Patrik Elias 1.00 2.50
AS42 Ryan Suter .60 1.50
AS43 Mark Giordano 1.00 2.50
AS44 Justin Faulk 1.00 2.50
AS45 Filip Forsberg 1.25 3.00
AS46 Jonathan Drouin FS 1.50 4.00
AS47 Ryan Johansen Brk 1.50 4.00
AS48 Patrick Kane Acc 2.50 6.00
AS49 Shea Weber HS 1.00 2.50
AS50 Ryan Johansen MVP 1.50 4.00

2015-16 O-Pee-Chee Buyback Autographs

199 N.Lidstrom 12-13 Rtr/20 75.00 125.00

2015-16 O-Pee-Chee Draft Pick Puzzle

COMMON PUZZLE 2.00 5.00
PUZZLE PIECE ODDS 1:104 HOB/RET/BL
EXCH EXPIRATION: 12/1/2015
OPCCM Connor McDavid/97 500.00 800.00

2015-16 O-Pee-Chee Mini Glossy

ONE PER WRAPPER REDEMPTION PACK
1 Ryan Getzlaf 5.00 12.00
2 Oliver Ekman-Larsson 2.50 6.00
3 Patrice Bergeron 4.00 10.00
4 Zemgus Girgensons 2.50 6.00
5 Johnny Gaudreau 5.00 12.00
6 Jiri Hudler 2.50 6.00
7 Patrick Kane 6.00 15.00
8 Jonathan Toews 6.00 15.00
9 Jarome Iginla 4.00 10.00
10 Tyler Seguin 5.00 12.00
11 Henrik Zetterberg 4.00 10.00
12 Jordan Eberle 3.00 8.00
13 Taylor Hall 6.00 15.00
14 Aaron Ekblad 3.00 8.00
15 Tyler Toffoli 3.00 8.00
16 Max Pacioretty 4.00 10.00
17 P.K. Subban 5.00 12.00
18 Filip Forsberg 4.00 10.00
19 Pekka Rinne 4.00 10.00
20 John Tavares 6.00 15.00
21 Kyle Okposo 3.00 8.00
22 Keith Yandle 3.00 8.00
23 Rick Nash 3.00 8.00
24 Pavel Datsyuk 4.00 10.00
25 Erik Karlsson 6.00 15.00
26 Jakub Voracek 3.00 8.00
27 Claude Giroux 4.00 10.00
28 Sidney Crosby 12.00 30.00
29 Evgeni Malkin 10.00 25.00
30 Vladimir Tarasenko 5.00 12.00
31 Tyler Johnson 2.50 6.00
32 Steven Stamkos 6.00 15.00
33 James van Riemsdyk 3.00 8.00
34 Nazem Kadri 2.50 6.00
35 Ryan Miller 3.00 8.00
36 Alexander Ovechkin 12.00 30.00
37 Wayne Gretzky 15.00 40.00
38 Bobby Orr 6.00 15.00
39 Martin Brodeur 8.00 20.00
40 Mario Lemieux 10.00 25.00
41 Steve Yzerman 6.00 15.00
42 Patrick Roy 10.00 25.00

2015-16 O-Pee-Chee Box Bottoms

BL ODDS TWO PER BLASTER BOX
HOD ODDS FOUR PER HOBBY BOX
32 P.K. Subban HOB .40 1.00
50 Evgeni Malkin HOB .75 2.00
53 Rick Nash AS HOB .25 .60
70 Shea Weber AS HOB .20 .50
76 Patrice Bergeron AS HOB .30 .75
100 Steven Stamkos AS HOB .50 1.25
145 Claude Giroux AS HOB .25 .60
150 Jonathan Quick BL/HOB .40 1.00
200 Carey Price AS BL HOB .75 2.00
204 Patrick Kane AS HOB .50 1.25
226 Phil Kessel AS HOB .40 1.00
239 Jim Howard HOB .25 .60
250 John Tavares AS BL .75 2.00
383 Ryan Nugent-Hopkins AS HOB .25 .60
400 Alexander Ovechkin AS HOB 1.00 2.50
436 Erik Karlsson HOB .50 1.25
450 Ryan Getzlaf AS HOB .40 1.00
463 James van Riemsdyk BL .40 1.00
494 Tyler Seguin AS HOB .40 1.00
495 Pekka Rinne BL .50 1.25
500 Sidney Crosby BL 1.50 4.00

2015-16 O-Pee-Chee Glossy Rookies

R1 Connor McDavid 15.00 40.00
R2 Robby Fabbri 2.50 6.00
R3 Dylan Larkin 6.00 15.00
R4 Artemi Panarin 6.00 15.00
R5 Jake Virtanen 2.50 6.00
R6 Sam Bennett 2.50 6.00
R7 Zachary Fucale 2.00 5.00
R8 Max Domi 4.00 10.00
R9 Nikolaj Ehlers 4.00 10.00
R10 Jack Eichel 8.00 20.00

2015-16 O-Pee-Chee Glossy Rookies Black

COMPLETE SET (10)
*BLACK: 1X TO 2.5X BASIC INSERTS
STATED ODDS 1:18 MEGA BOX BONUS
R1 Connor McDavid 100.00 200.00

2015-16 O-Pee-Chee Glossy Rookies Red

COMPLETE SET (10)
*RED: .6X TO 1.5X BASIC INSERTS
STATED ODDS 1:4 MEGA BOX BONUS
R1 Connor McDavid 40.00 80.00

2015-16 O-Pee-Chee Signatures

UNPRICED GRP A ODDS 1:10,283
GROUP B ODDS 1:2666
GROUP C ODDS 1:2637
GROUP D ODDS 1:1314
GROUP E ODDS 1:278
OVERALL ODDS 1:192 H,1:400 R,1:800 BL
SAV Andrei Vasilevskiy E 6.00 15.00
SBR Brett Ritchie E 3.00 8.00
SCC Charlie Coyle E 4.00 10.00
SCF Cody Franson D 3.00 8.00
SCG Cody Goloubef E 3.00 8.00
SCH Carl Hagelin B 8.00 20.00
SDS Derek Stepan B 10.00 25.00
SJB Jonathan Bernier A
SJE Jordie Benn E 3.00 8.00
SJH Jonathan Huberdeau B 10.00 25.00
SJM John Moore E 3.00 8.00
SJS Justin Schultz D 4.00 10.00
SKQ Kyle Quincey E 3.00 8.00
SKT Kyle Turris E 4.00 10.00
SLE Lars Eller E 4.00 10.00
SLK Lauri Korpikoski E 3.00 8.00
SMB Matt Beleskey E 3.00 8.00
SMG Mikael Granlund C 6.00 15.00
SMN Matt Nieto E 3.00 8.00
SMP Max Pacioretty A
SMR Mikhail Grigorenko D 4.00 10.00
SNY Nail Yakupov A
SPB Derrick Pouliot D 4.00 10.00
SRH Ryan Nugent-Hopkins A
SRK Ryan Kesler B 10.00 25.00
SRM Ryan McDonagh C 8.00 20.00
SSL Scott Laughton C 8.00 20.00
STH Tomas Hertl B 10.00 25.00
STK Torey Krug B
SZR Zach Redmond E 3.00 8.00

2015-16 O-Pee-Chee Sport Royalty Autographs

GAO Alexander Ovechkin 100.00 200.00

2015-16 O-Pee-Chee Team Canada Signatures

UNPRICED GRP A ODDS 1:18,643
GROUP B ODDS 1:7170
GROUP C ODDS 1:1819
GROUP D ODDS 1:1325
GROUP E ODDS 1:904
OVERALL ODDS 1:384H, 1:1200R, 1:2400BL
TCSAC Andrew Cogliano E 4.00 10.00
TCSBD Brenden Dillon E 4.00 10.00
TCSBJ Boone Jenner E 4.00 10.00
TCSBS Ben Scrivens B 8.00 20.00
TCSCP Corey Perry A
TCSCS Sean Couturier D 8.00 20.00
TCSDH Dougie Hamilton D 8.00 20.00
TCSDN Darnell Nurse D 8.00 20.00
TCSDP Derrick Pouliot D 6.00 15.00
TCSJB Jonathan Bernier B 10.00 25.00
TCSJC Jared Cowen D 5.00 12.00
TCSJH Jonathan Huberdeau C 10.00 25.00
TCSJN James Neal C 8.00 20.00
TCSJS Jeff Skinner B
TCSJU Justin Schultz B 8.00 20.00
TCSJZ Jason Spezza B 20.00 40.00
TCSKT Kyle Turris D 6.00 15.00
TCSLL Louis Leblanc D 6.00 15.00
TCSLS Luke Schenn C 6.00 15.00
TCSMD Matt Duchene C 10.00 25.00
TCSMJ Martin Jones E 6.00 15.00
TCSMR Morgan Rielly D 15.00 30.00
TCSRJ Ryan Johansen C 12.00 30.00
TCSRS Ryan Spooner E 5.00 12.00
TCSSH Scott Hartnell C 10.00 25.00
TCSSM Steve Mason A
TCSSW Shea Weber C 8.00 20.00
TCSTH Thomas Hickey E 4.00 10.00
TCSWG Wayne Gretzky A

2015-16 O-Pee-Chee Patches

1-40 PLAYER PATCH ODDS 1:147
41-50 PLAYER PATCH ODDS 1:900
51-75 GOLD OPC PATCH ODDS 1:540
76-85 GREEN OPC PATCH ODDS 1:1874
86-90 NEON OPC PATCH ODDS 1:4998
91-100 STATED ODDS 1:4685
OVERALL STATED ODDS 1:96
P1 Corey Perry 5.00 12.00
P2 Ryan Getzlaf 8.00 20.00
P3 Oliver Ekman-Larsson 4.00 10.00
P4 Patrice Bergeron 6.00 15.00
P5 Zemgus Girgensons 4.00 10.00
P6 Jonas Hiller 4.00 10.00
P7 Eric Staal 6.00 15.00
P8 Patrick Kane 10.00 25.00
P9 Marian Hossa 4.00 10.00
P10 Nathan MacKinnon 10.00 25.00
P11 Sergei Bobrovsky 5.00 12.00
P12 Jamie Benn 6.00 15.00
P13 Jim Howard 5.00 12.00
P14 Pavel Datsyuk 6.00 15.00
P15 Jordan Eberle 5.00 12.00
P16 Jaromir Jagr 12.00 30.00
P17 Anze Kopitar 8.00 20.00
P18 Jonathan Quick 8.00 20.00
P19 Zach Parise 5.00 12.00
P20 Max Pacioretty 5.00 12.00
P21 P.K. Subban 8.00 20.00
P22 Filip Forsberg 6.00 15.00
P23 Adam Henrique 5.00 12.00
P24 John Tavares 10.00 25.00
P25 Rick Nash 5.00 12.00
P26 Henrik Lundqvist 6.00 15.00
P27 Bobby Ryan 4.00 10.00
P28 Claude Giroux 5.00 12.00
P29 Marc-Andre Fleury 8.00 20.00
P30 Sidney Crosby 20.00 50.00
P31 Joe Pavelski 5.00 12.00
P32 Vladimir Tarasenko 8.00 20.00
P33 Tyler Johnson 4.00 10.00
P34 Steven Stamkos 10.00 25.00
P35 Phil Kessel 8.00 20.00
P36 James van Riemsdyk 5.00 12.00
P37 Daniel Sedin 5.00 12.00
P38 Nicklas Backstrom 8.00 20.00
P39 Alexander Ovechkin 20.00 50.00
P40 Bryan Little 4.00 10.00
P41 Wayne Gretzky 25.00 50.00
P42 Mark Messier 10.00 25.00
P43 Mario Lemieux 20.00 50.00
P44 Patrick Roy 30.00 60.00
P45 Brett Hull 6.00 15.00
P46 Malcolm Subban 15.00 40.00
P47 Jacob de la Rose 6.00 15.00
P48 Kevin Fiala 6.00 15.00
P49 Matt Puempel 5.00 12.00
P50 Ryan Hartman 8.00 20.00
P51 Ryan Getzlaf 12.00 30.00
P52 Evgeni Malkin 25.00 60.00
P53 Alexander Ovechkin 30.00 80.00
P54 Steven Stamkos 15.00 40.00
P55 Jonathan Toews 15.00 40.00
P56 Carey Price 15.00 40.00
P57 Tuukka Rask 8.00 20.00
P58 Johnny Gaudreau 12.00 30.00
P59 Henrik Zetterberg 10.00 25.00
P60 Aaron Ekblad 8.00 20.00
P61 Jonathan Quick 12.00 30.00
P62 Pekka Rinne 10.00 25.00
P63 Jaromir Jagr 20.00 50.00
P64 John Tavares 15.00 40.00
P65 Martin St. Louis 8.00 20.00
P66 Erik Karlsson 15.00 40.00
P67 Jakub Voracek 8.00 20.00
P68 Sidney Crosby 30.00 80.00
P69 Logan Couture 8.00 20.00
P70 Vladimir Tarasenko 12.00 30.00
P71 Jonathan Bernier 8.00 20.00
P72 Ryan Miller 8.00 20.00
P73 Blake Wheeler 8.00 20.00
P74 Shea Weber 6.00 15.00
P75 Tyler Seguin 12.00 30.00
P76 Wayne Gretzky 75.00 135.00
P77 Bobby Orr 50.00 100.00
P78 Steve Yzerman 50.00 100.00
P79 Pavel Bure 30.00 60.00
P80 Grant Fuhr 25.00 50.00
P81 Mark Messier 25.00 50.00
P82 Mario Lemieux 50.00 100.00
P83 Patrick Roy 50.00 100.00
P84 Teemu Selanne 25.00 50.00
P85 Felix Potvin 40.00 80.00
P86 Sidney Crosby 60.00 120.00
P87 Alexander Ovechkin 50.00 100.00
P88 Steven Stamkos 50.00 100.00
P89 Jonathan Toews 50.00 100.00
P90 Carey Price 50.00 120.00
P91 Youppi!
P92 Bernie the St. Bernard
P93 SJ Sharkie
P94 Wild Wing
P95 Al The Octopus
P96 Bailey
P97 Gnash
P98 Spartacat
P99 Stinger
P100 Stanley Panther

2015-16 O-Pee-Chee V Series B

STATED ODDS 1:16 HOB, 1:32 RET/BL
S1 Jonathan Quick 2.50 6.00
S2 Pekka Rinne 2.00 5.00
S3 Mark Messier 2.50 6.00
S4 Curtis Joseph 1.50 4.00
S5 Steven Stamkos 3.00 8.00
S6 Carey Price 5.00 12.00
S7 Aaron Ekblad 1.50 4.00
S8 Zdeno Chara 1.50 4.00
S9 Sidney Crosby 6.00 15.00
S10 Pierre Turgeon 1.50 4.00
S11 Tyler Seguin 2.50 6.00
S12 Jakub Voracek 1.50 4.00
S13 Ryan Getzlaf 2.50 6.00
S14 Tyler Johnson 1.25 3.00
S15 Vladimir Tarasenko 2.50 6.00
S16 John Tavares 3.00 8.00
S17 Rick Nash 1.50 4.00
S18 Wayne Gretzky 8.00 20.00
S19 Evgeni Malkin 5.00 12.00
S20 Claude Giroux 1.50 4.00
S21 Patrick Kane 3.00 8.00
S22 Joe Pavelski 1.50 4.00
S23 Ryan Miller 1.50 4.00
S24 Brett Hull 1.50 4.00
S25 Jiri Hudler 1.25 3.00
S26 Johnny Gaudreau 2.50 6.00
S27 Jonathan Bernier 1.50 4.00
S28 Jonathan Drouin 2.00 5.00
S29 John Carlson 2.00 5.00
S30 Filip Forsberg 2.00 5.00
S31 Michael Hutchinson 1.50 4.00
S32 Corey Crawford 2.00 5.00
S33 James van Riemsdyk 1.50 4.00
S34 Jamie Benn 2.00 5.00
S35 Corey Perry 1.50 4.00
S36 Nikita Kucherov 2.50 6.00
S37 Jaromir Jagr 4.00 10.00
S38 Malcolm Subban 4.00 10.00
S39 Ryan Hartman 2.00 5.00
S40 Jacob de la Rose 1.50 4.00

2015-16 O-Pee-Chee Woodies

WW1 Alex Ovechkin
WW2 P.K. Subban
WW3 Tyler Seguin
WW4 Ryan Miller
WW5 Wayne Gretzky
WW6 Jonathan Toews
WW7 Johnny Gaudreau
WW8 Patrick Roy
WW9 Eric Staal
WW10 Nicklas Backstrom
WW11 Patrice Bergeron

WW12 Marty McSorley
WW13 Aaron Ekblad
WW14 Sergei Bobrovski
WW15 T.J. Oshie
WW16 Erik Karlsson
WW17 Sidney Crosby
WW18 Mario Lemieux
WW19 Patrick Kane
WW20 Ben Bishop
WW21 Mike Gartner
WW22 Frederik Andersen
WW23 Evgeni Malkin 40.00 80.00
WW24 Jaromir Jagr
WW25 Henrik Zetterberg
WW26 Tuukka Rask
WW27 Martin St. Louis
WW28 Carey Price
WW29 Claude Giroux
WW30 Bobby Orr

2016-17 O-Pee-Chee

1 Jonathan Quick .40 1.00
2 Colton Sceviour .20 .50
3 Ben Hutton .25 .60
4 Sergei Kalinin .20 .50
5 Ryan Callahan .25 .60
6 Andrew Shaw .25 .60
7 Cody Ceci .20 .50
8 Deryk Engelland .15 .40
9 Matt Moulson .20 .50
10 Nicolas Petan .20 .50
11 J.T. Miller .20 .50
12 Henrik Sedin .25 .60
13 Wayne Simmonds .30 .75
14 Johnny Boychuk .25 .60
15 Andreas Athanasiou .25 .60
16 Sami Vatanen .20 .50
17 Kris Russell .20 .50
18 Jordan Staal .25 .60
19 Brett Connolly .20 .50
20 Beau Bennett .20 .50
21 Brent Burns .30 .75
22 Trevor Lewis .20 .50
23 Brandon Sutter .20 .50
24 Louis Domingue .20 .50
25 Leon Draisaitl .30 .75
26 Josh Bailey .20 .50
27 Jonathan Huberdeau .25 .60
28 Mark Scheifele .30 .75
29 Roman Josi .25 .60
30 Kris Versteeg .20 .50
31 Max Domi .30 .75
32 Ryan O'Reilly .25 .60
33 Craig Anderson .25 .60
34 Kevin Hayes .20 .50
35 Damon Severson .20 .50
36 Rickard Rakell .25 .60
37 Boone Jenner .25 .60
38 Joni Ortio .20 .50
39 Ian Cole .20 .50
40 Dan Hamhuis .20 .50
41 John Tavares .50 1.25
42 Henrik Zetterberg .30 .75
43 Calle Jarnkrok .20 .50
44 Jason Pominville .20 .50
45 Garret Sparks .20 .50
46 Johnny Oduya .20 .50
47 Jake Allen .30 .75
48 Nikita Zadorov .20 .50
49 Brian Campbell .20 .50
50 Valtteri Filppula .20 .50
51 Trevor Daley .20 .50
52 Brendan Smith .20 .50
53 Andrei Markov .25 .60
54 Dustin Brown .20 .50
55 Jamie Benn .30 .75
56 Ryan Suter .20 .50
57 Nicklas Backstrom .40 1.00
58 Willie Mitchell .20 .50
59 Michal Rozsival .20 .50
60 Chris Kreider .25 .60
61 Frederik Andersen .20 .50
62 Nick Leddy .15 .40
63 Brendan Gallagher .30 .75
64 Carter Hutton .25 .60
65 Zemgus Girgensons .20 .50
66 Cam Talbot .30 .75
67 Brian Dumoulin .20 .50
68 Joe Thornton .25 .60
69 Colin Miller .15 .40
70 Andrei Vasilevskiy .30 .75
71 Milan Michalek .15 .40
72 Tom Wilson .25 .60
73 Mike Brown .15 .40
74 John Klingberg .25 .60
75 Derick Brassard .25 .60
76 Ryan Ellis .20 .50
77 Erik Johnson .15 .40
78 Jaromir Jagr .60 1.50
79 Zach Bogosian .20 .50
80 Joel Ward .20 .50
81 Alex Tanguay .15 .40
82 Jake Muzzin .20 .50
83 Olli Maatta .25 .60
84 Brad Marchand .30 .75
85 Danny DeKeyser .15 .40
86 Patrik Berglund .15 .40
87 Andre Burakovsky .20 .50
88 Joonas Korpisalo .15 .40
89 James Neal .20 .50
90 Mattias Janmark .15 .40
91 Marc-Andre Fleury .40 1.00
92 Martin Marincin .20 .50
93 Marc Staal .15 .40
94 Andrew Cogliano .15 .40
95 J.T. Brown .15 .40
96 Luke Glendening .20 .50
97 David Krejci .25 .60
98 Justin Braun .15 .40
99 Erik Gudbranson .25 .60
100 Anze Kopitar .40 1.00
101 Steven Stamkos .50 1.25
102 Joakim Nordstrom .15 .40
103 Matt Read .20 .50
104 Brad Richardson .20 .50
105 Michael Grabner .20 .50
106 Carey Price .75 2.00
107 Evgeny Medvedev .15 .40
108 Matt Niskanen .20 .50
109 Jordan Eberle .25 .60
110 Checklist 1-110 .15 .40
111 Mikael Granlund .20 .50
112 Niklas Hjalmarsson .20 .50
113 Marek Zidlicky .15 .40
114 Tyler Johnson .20 .50
115 Devante Smith-Pelly .20 .50
116 Matt Stajan .15 .40
117 Tyler Myers .20 .50
118 Ryan McDonagh .20 .50
119 Francois Beauchemin .20 .50
120 Adam McQuaid .15 .40
121 Jean-Gabriel Pageau .20 .50
122 Jhonas Enroth .25 .60
123 Jamie McGinn .20 .50
124 Dion Phaneuf .25 .60
125 Josh Gorges .15 .40
126 Teddy Purcell .25 .60
127 Brian Boyle .15 .40
128 Justin Fontaine .20 .50
129 Benoit Pouliot .20 .50
130 Jori Lehtera .20 .50
131 Michael Stone .15 .40
132 Ryan Kesler .25 .60
133 Elias Lindholm .25 .60
134 Jeff Carter .25 .60
135 Keith Kinkaid .20 .50
136 Braydon Coburn .15 .40
137 Barret Jackman .20 .50
138 Tobias Enstrom .15 .40
139 Troy Brouwer .20 .50
140 Derek Mackenzie .15 .40
141 Jason Spezza .25 .60
142 Rick Nash .25 .60
143 Paul Martin .20 .50
144 Cam Fowler .20 .50
145 Dalton Prout .15 .40
146 Marian Hossa .20 .50
147 Nathan Gerbe .20 .50
148 Mark Pysyk .15 .40
149 Dwight King .20 .50
150 John Mitchell .15 .40
151 Jaroslav Halak .25 .60
152 Karl Alzner .15 .40
153 Roman Polak .15 .40
154 John-Michael Liles .20 .50
155 Jay McClement .15 .40
156 Trevor van Riemsdyk .20 .50
157 Sam Reinhart .20 .50
158 Patrik Elias .25 .60
159 Jay Bouwmeester .25 .60
160 Stefan Matteau .15 .40
161 Mathieu Perreault .20 .50
162 Connor Murphy .15 .40
163 Dennis Wideman .15 .40
164 Oscar Lindberg .15 .40
165 Evgeni Malkin .75 2.00
166 Connor McDavid 1.25 3.00
167 Shawn Matthias .15 .40
168 Kevan Miller .15 .40
169 Jarret Stoll .20 .50
170 Dale Weise .15 .40
171 Matt Bartkowski .15 .40
172 Mark Stuart .15 .40
173 Joonas Donskoi .20 .50
174 Pavel Datsyuk .30 .75
175 Braden Holtby .40 1.00
176 Patric Hornqvist .20 .50
177 Brian Elliott .20 .50
178 Mikael Backlund .20 .50
179 Valeri Nichushkin .20 .50
180 Blake Wheeler .25 .60
181 Jannik Hansen .15 .40
182 Rasmus Ristolainen .20 .50
183 Ryan Spooner .20 .50
184 P.K. Subban .40 1.00
185 Matt Duchene .25 .60
186 Brenden Dillon .15 .40
187 Kevin Bieksa .15 .40
188 Calvin de Haan .15 .40
189 Nick Bonino .15 .40
190 Oliver Ekman-Larsson .20 .50
191 Adam Lowry .15 .40
192 Mark Letestu .20 .50
193 Sven Baertschi .15 .40
194 Victor Rask .20 .50
195 William Karlsson .50 1.25
196 Chris Neil .15 .40
197 Antti Raanta .25 .60
198 Nino Niederreiter .25 .60
199 Frans Nielsen .20 .50
200 Taylor Hall .50 1.25
201 Nick Spaling .15 .40
202 Riley Sheahan .20 .50
203 Jacob Markstrom .20 .50
204 Loui Eriksson .25 .60
205 Nathan MacKinnon .50 1.25
206 Lars Eller .20 .50
207 Adam Henrique .25 .60
208 Dmitry Kulikov .20 .50
209 Nick Foligno .20 .50
210 Steve Mason .20 .50
211 Jonathan Toews .50 1.25
212 Drew Stafford .20 .50
213 Henrik Lundqvist .25 .60
214 Viktor Arvidsson .30 .75
215 Antoine Vermette .20 .50
216 Vincent Lecavalier .20 .50
217 Jaccob Slavin .15 .40
218 Jason Garrison .20 .50
219 Adam Larsson .25 .60
220 Checklist 111-220 .15 .40
221 Joffrey Lupul .20 .50
222 Kris Letang .25 .60
223 Patrice Bergeron .30 .75
224 Andrej Sekera .15 .40
225 Jonas Hiller .20 .50
226 Daniel Winnik .20 .50
227 Alexandre Burrows .20 .50
228 Cody Franson .15 .40
229 Roberto Luongo .25 .60
230 Shea Weber .20 .50
231 Niklas Kronwall .15 .40
232 Eric Staal .30 .75
233 Alexander Wennberg .20 .50
234 Joe Colborne .15 .40
235 Kyle Okposo .25 .60
236 Vladimir Tarasenko .40 1.00
237 Ryan Nugent-Hopkins .25 .60
238 Alec Martinez .15 .40
239 Chris Kunitz .25 .60
240 Ron Hainsey .20 .50
241 Jordan Martinook .15 .40
242 Al Montoya .20 .50
243 Mathew Dumba .20 .50
244 Brent Seabrook .20 .50
245 Zdeno Chara .25 .60
246 Jarome Iginla .25 .60
247 Ben Bishop .25 .60
248 Antti Niemi .20 .50
249 John Gibson .25 .60
250 Joseph Blandisi .20 .50
251 Eddie Lack .20 .50
252 Jake McCabe .20 .50
253 Pekka Rinne .30 .75
254 Sergei Bobrovsky .25 .60
255 Thomas Vanek .20 .50
256 Torey Krug .25 .60
257 Calvin Pickard .15 .40
258 Alexander Steen .25 .60
259 Vincent Trocheck .25 .60
260 Evander Kane .25 .60
261 Mark Streit .20 .50
262 Karri Ramo .20 .50
263 Jonathan Ericsson .15 .40
264 Mark Stone .25 .60
265 Christopher Tanev .20 .50
266 Filip Forsberg .30 .75
267 Casey Cizikas .15 .40
268 Martin Hanzal .20 .50
269 Brooks Laich .15 .40
270 Michael Frolik .20 .50
271 Ales Hemsky .20 .50
272 Robin Lehner .20 .50
273 Philipp Grubauer .25 .60
274 Jiri Hudler .20 .50
275 Andrew Ladd .25 .60
276 Shea Theodore .20 .50
277 Chris Thorburn .15 .40
278 Derek Stepan .20 .50
279 Paul Gaustad .15 .40
280 Jake Virtanen .30 .75
281 Tyler Seguin .40 1.00
282 Patrick Marleau .25 .60
283 Sidney Crosby 1.00 2.50
284 Brett Pesce .15 .40
285 Erik Karlsson .50 1.25
286 Luke Schenn .15 .40
287 Michael Cammalleri .20 .50
288 Phil Kessel .30 .75
289 Corey Crawford .30 .75
290 Jyrki Jokipakka .20 .50
291 Dylan Larkin .40 1.00
292 Alex Goligoski .15 .40
293 James van Riemsdyk .25 .60
294 Carl Gunnarsson .15 .40
295 Justin Faulk .20 .50
296 Milan Lucic .20 .50
297 Ondrej Pavelec .25 .60
298 Mike Richards .15 .40
299 Mike Smith .25 .60
300 Marco Scandella .20 .50
301 Mike Hoffman .20 .50
302 Jordie Benn .15 .40
303 Seth Jones .20 .50
304 Joe Pavelski .25 .60
305 Nick Bjugstad .20 .50
306 Mattias Ekholm .15 .40
307 Noah Hanifin .25 .60
308 Brayden McNabb .15 .40
309 Michal Neuvirth .20 .50
310 T.J. Oshie .40 1.00
311 Teuvo Teravainen .25 .60
312 Mika Zibanejad .25 .60
313 Josh Manson .20 .50
314 Charlie Coyle .20 .50
315 Nick Holden .15 .40
316 Chris Tierney .15 .40
317 Pat Maroon .15 .40
318 Colin Wilson .25 .60
319 Jim Howard .20 .50
320 Thomas Hickey .15 .40
321 Scottie Upshall .15 .40
322 Tyler Toffoli .25 .60
323 Sean Couturier .25 .60
324 Mike Condon .25 .60
325 Curtis Lazar .15 .40
326 Teemu Pulkkinen .15 .40
327 Tomas Fleischmann .20 .50
328 Erik Haula .20 .50
329 Dmitry Orlov .20 .50
330 Checklist 221-330 .15 .40
331 Brandon Dubinsky .25 .60
332 Marian Gaborik .25 .60
333 Travis Zajac .20 .50
334 Kevin Connauton .20 .50
335 Mikhail Grabovski .15 .40
336 Peter Holland .15 .40
337 Matt Beleskey .20 .50
338 Reilly Smith .25 .60
339 Shawn Horcoff .20 .50
340 Blake Comeau .15 .40
341 Victor Hedman .30 .75
342 Sam Gagner .20 .50
343 Sam Bennett .30 .75
344 Michael Hutchinson .15 .40
345 Nail Yakupov .20 .50
346 Tyler Bozak .20 .50
347 Carl Hagelin .25 .60
348 Cody Eakin .20 .50
349 Dan Boyle .20 .50
350 David Backes .25 .60
351 Cory Schneider .20 .50
352 Miikka Salomaki .15 .40
353 Jared Spurgeon .15 .40
354 Alexei Emelin .15 .40
355 Patrick Kane .50 1.25
356 Aleksander Barkov .25 .60
357 Scott Laughton .15 .40
358 Matt Hunwick .20 .50
359 Justin Abdelkader .20 .50
360 Lee Stempniak .20 .50
361 Cam Atkinson .25 .60
362 Tobias Rieder .15 .40
363 Vernon Fiddler .15 .40
364 Michael Ferland .15 .40
365 Tanner Pearson .20 .50
366 Brandon Saad .25 .60
367 Nikita Kucherov .40 1.00
368 Gabriel Landeskog .20 .50
369 Andy Greene .15 .40
370 Andrew Hammond .20 .50
371 Jimmy Hayes .15 .40
372 Matt Nieto .15 .40
373 Dmitrij Jaskin .15 .40
374 Tyler Ennis .20 .50
375 Brad Richards .25 .60
376 Matt Calvert .15 .40
377 Justin Williams .20 .50
378 Jeff Skinner .25 .60
379 Anders Lee .25 .60
380 Derek Dorsett .15 .40
381 Aaron Ekblad .25 .60
382 Tyson Barrie .25 .60
383 David Jones .15 .40
384 Daniel Girardi .15 .40
385 Jake Gardiner .25 .60
386 Jaden Schwartz .30 .75
387 Jeff Petry .15 .40
388 Alexander Burmistrov .15 .40
389 Marcus Johansson .25 .60
390 Riley Nash .15 .40
391 Matt Hendricks .15 .40
392 Marc Methot .20 .50
393 Bo Horvat .40 1.00
394 Ryan Strome .20 .50
395 Kevin Klein .15 .40
396 Nathan Beaulieu .15 .40
397 David Schlemko .15 .40
398 Robby Fabbri .25 .60
399 Brandon Pirri .15 .40
400 David Savard .15 .40
401 Torrey Mitchell .15 .40
402 Rob Scuderi .15 .40
403 Radim Vrbata .20 .50
404 Mats Zuccarello .25 .60
405 Tommy Wingels .15 .40
406 Ondrej Palat .20 .50
407 Kevin Shattenkirk .20 .50
408 Shayne Gostisbehere .30 .75
409 Griffin Reinhart .20 .50
410 T.J. Brodie .20 .50
411 Jay Beagle .20 .50
412 Mikkel Boedker .20 .50
413 Jakub Voracek .25 .60
414 Ty Rattie .15 .40
415 Brad Boyes .15 .40
416 Devan Dubnyk .25 .60
417 Jakob Silfverberg .25 .60
418 Ryan Miller .25 .60
419 Erik Gustafsson .15 .40
420 Nikolai Kulemin .15 .40
421 Johnny Gaudreau .40 1.00
422 Jesper Fast .15 .40
423 Claude Giroux .25 .60
424 Nate Schmidt .15 .40
425 Petr Mrazek .25 .60
426 Logan Couture .25 .60
427 Alex Pietrangelo .20 .50
428 Jason Demers .15 .40
429 Zach Parise .25 .60
430 Jonathan Drouin .30 .75
431 Alexander Ovechkin 1.00 2.50
432 Michael Raffl .15 .40
433 Andrew Desjardins .15 .40
434 Andrej Sustr .15 .40
435 Dominic Moore .15 .40
436 Tuukka Rask .25 .60
437 Alex Galchenyuk .30 .75
438 Leo Komarov .25 .60
439 Radko Gudas .15 .40
440 Checklist 331-440 .15 .40
441 Mike Ribeiro .20 .50
442 Jonas Brodin .15 .40
443 Dustin Byfuglien .25 .60
444 Vladislav Namestnikov .15 .40
445 John Moore .15 .40
446 Martin Jones .25 .60
447 John Carlson .30 .75
448 Artem Anisimov .20 .50
449 Ryan Murray .15 .40
450 Gustav Nyquist .25 .60
451 Cody McLeod .15 .40
452 Sean Monahan .25 .60
453 Alexander Edler .15 .40
454 Patrick Sharp .20 .50
455 Ryan Johansen .30 .75
456 Cal Clutterbuck .15 .40
457 Keith Yandle .25 .60
458 Marcus Kruger .25 .60
459 Tomas Plekanec .25 .60
460 Brian Gionta .20 .50
461 Lauri Korpikoski .15 .40
462 Radek Faksa .15 .40
463 Jussi Jokinen .25 .60
464 Mike Fisher .20 .50
465 Andrew Copp .15 .40
466 Brooks Orpik .20 .50
467 Zack Smith .15 .40
468 Reto Berra .15 .40
469 P.A. Parenteau .15 .40
470 Shane Doan .20 .50
471 Dougie Hamilton .25 .60
472 Kyle Palmieri .20 .50
473 Matt Cullen .25 .60
474 Scott Darling .15 .40
475 Brayden Schenn .25 .60
476 Mikhail Grigorenko .15 .40
477 Ryan Reaves .15 .40
478 Darren Helm .15 .40
479 James Reimer .25 .60
480 Sven Andrighetto .20 .50
481 Anton Stralman .20 .50
482 Craig Smith .15 .40
483 David Pastrnak .40 1.00
484 David Perron .20 .50
485 Scott Hartnell .25 .60
486 Brandon Davidson .15 .40
487 Darcy Kuemper .15 .40
488 Travis Hamonic .15 .40
489 Marcus Foligno .15 .40
490 Bryan Rust .25 .60
491 Daniel Sedin .25 .60
492 Nazem Kadri .20 .50
493 Reid Boucher .15 .40
494 Jason Chimera .15 .40
495 Mark Giordano .20 .50
496 Darnell Nurse .20 .50
497 Marc-Edouard Vlasic .15 .40
498 Jack Johnson .15 .40
499 Anthony Duclair .25 .60
500 Alex Killorn .15 .40
501 Kyle Turris .20 .50
502 Andrej Nestrasil .20 .50
503 Drew Doughty .25 .60
504 Ben Lovejoy .15 .40
505 Nick Schultz .15 .40
506 Sergei Plotnikov .15 .40
507 Ryan Getzlaf .40 1.00
508 Oscar Klefbom .40 1.00
509 Carl Soderberg .15 .40
510 Mike Green .25 .60
511 Jack Eichel .50 1.25
512 Paul Stastny .25 .60
513 Patrick Wiercioch .20 .50
514 Yannick Weber .15 .40
515 Antoine Roussel .15 .40
516 Connor Hellebuyck .40 1.00
517 Viktor Stalberg .20 .50
518 Matt Carle .15 .40
519 Jakub Kindl .15 .40
520 Semyon Varlamov .25 .60
521 Matt Murray .40 1.00
522 Hampus Lindholm .15 .40
523 Duncan Keith .25 .60
524 Brock Nelson .20 .50
525 David Desharnais .20 .50
526 Jonathan Bernier .25 .60
527 Nikolaj Ehlers .25 .60
528 Jared McCann .15 .40
529 Jason Zucker .20 .50
530 Jacob Trouba .20 .50
531 Michael Del Zotto .20 .50
532 Corey Perry .25 .60
533 Tomas Tatar .20 .50
534 Nick Shore .20 .50
535 Bryan Little .20 .50
536 Morgan Rielly .20 .50
537 Max Pacioretty .25 .60
538 Justin Schultz .20 .50
539 Colton Parayko .25 .60
540 Artemi Panarin .30 .75
541 Kari Lehtonen .20 .50
542 Cam Ward .25 .60
543 Alex Petrovic .15 .40
544 Evgeny Kuznetsov .40 1.00
545 Bobby Ryan .20 .50
546 Mikko Koivu .20 .50
547 Dennis Seidenberg .15 .40
548 Tomas Hertl .25 .60
549 Thomas Greiss .20 .50
550 Checklist 441-550 .15 .40
551 Mike Reilly RC 1.00 2.50
552 Mark McNeill RC 1.25 3.00
553 J.C. Lipon RC 1.25 3.00
554 Daniel Altshuller RC 1.00 2.50
555 Chris Bigras RC 1.00 2.50
556 Oliver Bjorkstrand RC 1.00 2.50
557 Esa Lindell RC 1.25 3.00
558 Brendan Leipsic RC 1.25 3.00
559 Hudson Fasching RC 1.25 3.00
560 Oliver Kylington RC 1.00 2.50
561 Zach Hyman RC 1.50 4.00
562 Justin Bailey RC 1.25 3.00
563 Connor Brown RC 2.00 5.00
564 Oskar Sundqvist RC 1.25 3.00
565 Alan Quine RC 1.25 3.00
566 Kevin Gravel RC 1.50 4.00
567 Alex Friesen RC 1.50 4.00
568 Sonny Milano RC 1.50 4.00
569 Marek Hrivik RC 1.50 4.00
570 Kasperi Kapanen RC 2.50 6.00
571 Michael Matheson RC 1.25 3.00
572 Pontus Aberg RC 1.50 4.00
573 Nick Paul RC 1.50 4.00
574 Ryan Pulock RC 1.25 3.00
575 Garnet Hathaway RC 1.50 4.00
576 William Nylander RC 5.00 12.00
577 Jared Coreau RC 1.50 4.00
578 Darren Dietz RC 1.50 4.00
579 Nikita Soshnikov RC .75 2.00
580 Aaron Dell RC 1.50 4.00
581 Kyle Rau RC 1.50 4.00
582 Steven Santini RC 1.00 2.50
583 Noel Acciari RC 1.50 4.00
584 Josh Morrissey RC 1.50 4.00
585 Charlie Lindgren RC 2.50 6.00
586 Tobias Lindberg RC 2.00 5.00
587 Anthony Mantha RC 3.00 8.00
588 Trevor Carrick RC 1.25 3.00
589 Scott Kosmachuk RC 1.25 3.00
590 Nikita Tryamkin RC 1.00 2.50
591 Dominik Simon RC 1.25 3.00
592 Steve Michalek RC 1.50 4.00
593 Rinat Valiev RC 1.50 4.00
594 Jason Dickinson RC 1.00 2.50
595 Frederik Gauthier RC 1.00 2.50
596 Miles Wood RC 1.00 2.50
597 Nic Dowd RC 1.25 3.00
598 Sergey Tolchinsky RC 1.00 2.50
599 Evan Rodrigues RC 1.50 4.00
600 Pavel Zacha RC 1.50 4.00
601 Connor McDavid SH 5.00 12.00
602 Corey Perry SH 1.00 2.50
603 Alexander Ovechkin SH 4.00 10.00
604 Steven Stamkos SH 2.00 5.00
605 Patrick Kane SH 2.00 5.00
606 Henrik Zetterberg SH 1.25 3.00
607 Patrick Marleau SH 1.00 2.50
608 Drew Doughty SH 1.00 2.50
609 Jarome Iginla SH 1.00 2.50
610 Joe Thornton SH 1.00 2.50
611 Jonathan Quick SH 1.50 4.00
612 Braden Holtby SH 1.50 4.00
613 Jaromir Jagr SH 2.50 6.00
614 Jonathan Toews SH 2.00 5.00
615 Daniel Sedin SH 1.00 2.50
616 Anaheim Ducks CL .25 .60
617 Arizona Coyotoes CL .25 .60
618 Boston Bruins CL .25 .60
619 Buffalo Sabres CL .25 .60
620 Calgary Flames CL .25 .60
621 Carolina Hurricanes CL .25 .60
622 Chicago Blackhawks CL .25 .60
623 Colorado Avalanche CL .25 .60
624 Columbus Blue Jackets CL .25 .60
625 Dallas Stars CL .25 .60
626 Detroit Red Wings CL .25 .60
627 Edmonton Oilers CL .25 .60
628 Florida Panthers CL .25 .60
629 Los Angeles Kings CL .25 .60
630 Minnesota Wild CL .25 .60
631 Montreal Canadiens CL .25 .60
632 Nashville Predators CL .25 .60
633 New Jersey Devils CL .25 .60
634 New York Islanders CL .25 .60
635 New York Rangers CL .25 .60
636 Ottawa Senators CL .25 .60
637 Philadelphia Flyers CL .25 .60
638 Pittsburgh Penguins CL .25 .60
639 San Jose Sharks CL .25 .60
640 St. Louis Blues CL .25 .60
641 Tampa Bay Lightning CL .25 .60
642 Toronto Maple Leafs CL .25 .60
643 Vancouver Canucks CL .25 .60
644 Washington Capitals CL .25 .60
645 Winnipeg Jets CL .25 .60
646 Artemi Panarin LL 1.25 3.00
647 Derek Dorsett LL .60 1.50
648 Tyler Toffoli LL 1.00 2.50
649 Jean-Gabriel Pageau LL .75 2.00
650 Alexander Ovechkin LL 4.00 10.00
651 Jonathan Toews LL 2.00 5.00
652 Joe Pavelski LL 1.00 2.50
653 Brian Elliott LL .75 2.00
654 Ben Bishop LL 1.00 2.50
655 Corey Crawford LL 1.25 3.00
656 Braden Holtby LL 1.50 4.00
657 Erik Karlsson LL 2.00 5.00
658 Alexander Ovechkin LL 4.00 10.00
659 Patrick Kane LL 2.00 5.00
660 Checklist 551-660 .60 1.50
661A Patrick Kane - Hart Trophy 15.00 40.00
661B Taylor Hall 1.00 2.50
662A Braden Holtby - Vezina Trophy 12.00 30.00
662B David Backes .50 1.25
663A Drew Doughty - Norris Trophy 8.00 20.00
663B Kyle Okposo .50 1.25
664A Patrick Kane - Art Ross Trophy 15.00 40.00
664B Mikkel Boedker .40 1.00
665A Alex Ovechkin - Rocket Richard Trophy 30.00 80.00
665B Milan Lucic .40 1.00
666A Anze Kopitar - Frank J. Selke Trophy 12.0030.00
666B Shea Weber .40 1.00
667A Patrick Kane - Ted Lindsay Award 15.00 40.00
667B P.K. Subban .75 2.00
668A Sidney Crosby - Conn Smythe Trophy 30.00 80.00
668B Frederik Andersen .40 1.00
669A Artemi Panarin - Calder Trophy 10.00 25.00
669B Thomas Vanek .40 1.00
670A Bobby Hull 12.00 30.00
670B David Perron .75 2.00
671A Dominik Hasek 8.00 20.00
671B Tyler Motte RC 1.00 2.50
672A Nicklas Lidstrom 8.00 20.00
672B Mitch Marner RC 5.00 12.00
673A Patrick Roy 20.00 50.00
673B Zach Sanford RC 1.00 2.50
674A Mike Modano 12.00 30.00
674B A.J. Greer RC 1.00 2.50
675A Steve Yzerman 10.00 25.00
675B Jake Guentzel RC 4.00 10.00
676A Chris Chelios 8.00 20.00
676B Kyle Connor RC 2.50 6.00
677A Milt Schmidt 8.00 20.00
677B Artturi Lehkonen RC 1.00 2.50
678A Sidney Crosby 30.00 80.00
678B Zach Werenski RC 2.00 5.00
679 Patrik Laine RC 4.00 10.00
680 Nikita Zaitsev RC 1.00 2.50
681 Matthew Tkachuk RC 3.00 8.00
682 Brayden Point RC 2.50 6.00
683 Thomas Chabot RC 2.00 5.00
684 Jimmy Vesey RC 2.00 5.00
685 Danton Heinen RC 1.50 4.00
686 Ivan Provorov RC 2.00 5.00
687 Sebastian Aho RC 2.00 5.00
688 Dylan Strome RC 2.00 5.00
689 Mathew Barzal RC 3.00 8.00
690 Julius Honka RC 1.00 2.50
691 Jakob Chychrun RC 1.00 2.50
692 Travis Konecny RC 2.00 5.00
693 Kevin Labanc RC 1.00 2.50
694 Auston Matthews RC 6.00 15.00
695 Tom Kuhnhackl RC .75 2.00
696 Christian Dvorak RC 1.00 2.50
697 Joel Eriksson Ek RC 1.00 2.50
698 Jacob Larsson RC 1.50 4.00
699 Anthony DeAngelo RC 1.00 2.50
700 Pavel Buchnevich RC 1.50 4.00
701 Nick Schmaltz RC 1.00 2.50
702 Troy Stecher RC 1.00 2.50
703 Brandon Carlo RC 1.00 2.50
704 Jesse Puljujarvi RC 2.50 6.00
705 Anthony Beauvillier RC 1.00 2.50
706 Drake Caggiula RC 1.00 2.50
707 Mikhail Sergachev RC 2.00 5.00
708 Nick Baptiste RC 1.00 2.50
709 Denis Malgin RC 1.00 2.50
710 Nick Lappin RC 1.00 2.50

2016-17 O-Pee-Chee Rainbow Black

*1-550 VETS: 6X TO 15X BASIC CARDS
*551-710 ROOKIES: 1.2X TO 3X BASIC CARDS
601-660 SH/LL 1.5X TO 4X BASIC SP
57 Nicklas Backstrom 5.00 12.00
289 Corey Crawford 4.00 10.00
430 Jonathan Drouin 4.00 10.00
544 Evgeny Kuznetsov 5.00 12.00
655 Corey Crawford LL 4.00 10.00
672 Mitch Marner 50.00 125.00
679 Patrik Laine 50.00 120.00
694 Auston Matthews 100.00 225.00

2016-17 O-Pee-Chee Retro

*1-550 VETS: 2.5X TO 1.2X BASIC CARDS
*551-600 ROOKIES: .6X TO 1.5X BASIC CARDS
601-660 SH/LL .6X TO 1.50X BASIC SP
694 Auston Matthews 15.00 40.00

2016-17 O-Pee-Chee Patches

P1 John Gibson 5.00 12.00
P2 Max Domi 6.00 15.00
P3 David Krejci 5.00 12.00
P4 Jack Eichel 10.00 25.00
P5 Sam Bennett 6.00 15.00
P6 Noah Hanifin 5.00 12.00
P7 Jonathan Toews 10.00 25.00
P8 Duncan Keith 5.00 12.00
P9 Artemi Panarin 6.00 15.00
P10 Gabriel Landeskog 4.00 10.00
P11 Brandon Saad 5.00 12.00
P12 Tyler Seguin 8.00 20.00
P13 John Klingberg 5.00 12.00
P14 Dylan Larkin 8.00 20.00
P15 Connor McDavid 25.00 60.00
P16 Taylor Hall 10.00 25.00
P17 Aleksander Barkov 5.00 12.00
P18 Drew Doughty 5.00 12.00
P19 Jeff Carter 5.00 12.00
P20 Ryan Suter 4.00 10.00
P21 Carey Price 15.00 40.00
P22 Brendan Gallagher 6.00 15.00
P23 Pekka Rinne 6.00 15.00
P24 Shea Weber 4.00 10.00
P25 Cory Schneider 4.00 10.00
P26 Jaroslav Halak 5.00 12.00
P27 Mats Zuccarello 5.00 12.00
P28 Derek Stepan 4.00 10.00
P29 Erik Karlsson 10.00 25.00
P30 Wayne Simmonds 6.00 15.00
P31 Kris Letang 5.00 12.00
P32 Evgeni Malkin 15.00 40.00
P33 Logan Couture 5.00 12.00
P34 Alex Pietrangelo 4.00 10.00
P35 Victor Hedman 6.00 15.00
P36 Morgan Rielly 4.00 10.00
P37 Henrik Sedin 5.00 12.00
P38 Evgeny Kuznetsov 8.00 20.00
P39 Braden Holtby 8.00 20.00
P40 Dustin Byfuglien 5.00 12.00
P41 Wayne Gretzky LEG 30.00 80.00
P42 Jari Kurri LEG 6.00 15.00
P43 Joe Sakic LEG 10.00 25.00
P44 Dominik Hasek LEG 6.00 15.00
P45 Steve Yzerman LEG 8.00 20.00
P46 Mike Reilly 5.00 12.00
P47 William Nylander 25.00 60.00
P48 Michael Matheson 6.00 15.00
P49 Chris Bigras 5.00 12.00
P50 Nick Paul 8.00 20.00
P51 Shea Weber '16 AS 6.00 15.00
P52 Braden Holtby '16 AS 12.00 30.00
P53 Patrick Kane '16 AS 15.00 40.00
P54 Taylor Hall '16 AS 15.00 40.00
P55 Jaromir Jagr '16 AS 20.00 50.00
P56 Drew Doughty '16 AS 8.00 20.00
P57 Johnny Gaudreau '16 AS 12.00 30.00
P58 Justin Faulk '16 AS 6.00 15.00
P59 Dylan Larkin '16 AS 12.00 30.00
P60 Tyler Seguin '16 AS 12.00 30.00
P61 Carey Price '15 AS 20.00 50.00
P62 Anze Kopitar '15 AS 10.00 25.00
P63 Jonathan Toews '15 AS 12.00 30.00
P64 Steven Stamkos '15 AS 12.00 30.00
P65 John Tavares '15 AS 12.00 30.00
P66 Claude Giroux '12 AS 6.00 15.00
P67 Phil Kessel '12 AS 8.00 20.00
P68 Jason Spezza '12 AS 6.00 15.00
P69 Henrik Lundqvist '12 AS 6.00 15.00
P70 James Neal '12 AS 5.00 12.00
P71 Brent Burns '11 AS 8.00 20.00
P72 Rick Nash '11 AS 6.00 15.00
P73 Patrick Sharp '11 AS 5.00 12.00
P74 Mike Green '11 AS 6.00 15.00
P75 Duncan Keith '11 AS 6.00 15.00
P76 Joe Thornton '09 AS 6.00 15.00
P77 Evgeni Malkin '09 AS 20.00 50.00
P78 Zach Parise '09 AS 6.00 15.00
P79 Ryan Getzlaf '09 AS 10.00 25.00
P80 Jeff Carter '09 AS 6.00 15.00
P81 Pavel Datsyuk '08 AS 8.00 20.00
P82 Jarome Iginla '08 AS 6.00 15.00
P83 Eric Staal '08 AS 8.00 20.00
P84 Marian Hossa '08 AS 5.00 12.00
P85 Corey Perry '08 AS 6.00 15.00
P86 Wayne Gretzky '88 AS 250.00 600.00
P87 Larry Robinson '88 AS 50.00 125.00
P88 Patrick Roy '88 AS 125.00 300.00
P89 Steve Yzerman '88 AS 60.00 150.00
P90 Mario Lemieux '88 AS 150.00 400.00
P91 Mick E. Moose
P92 N.J. Devil
P93 Iceburgh
P94 Slapshot
P95 Blades The Bruin
P96 Fin The Whale
P97 Louie
P98 Tommy Hawk
P99 Harvey The Hound RARE
P100 Carlton RARE

2016-17 O-Pee-Chee Playing Cards

2C Daniel Sedin 1.25 3.00
2D Shayne Gostisbehere 1.50 4.00
2H Morgan Rielly 1.00 2.50
2S Brad Marchand 1.50 4.00
3C Henrik Sedin 1.25 3.00
3D Dylan Larkin 2.00 5.00
3H Mats Zuccarello 1.25 3.00
3S Adam Henrique 1.25 3.00
4C Mark Scheifele 1.50 4.00
4D Aleksander Barkov 1.25 3.00
4H Ryan Suter 1.00 2.50
4S Brian Elliott 1.00 2.50
5C Brandon Saad 1.25 3.00
5D Ben Bishop 1.25 3.00
5H Henrik Zetterberg 1.50 4.00
5S Brent Burns 1.50 4.00
6C Dustin Byfuglien 1.25 3.00
6D Sean Monahan 1.25 3.00
6H Shea Weber 1.00 2.50
6S Zach Parise 1.25 3.00
7C Pekka Rinne 1.50 4.00
7D Anze Kopitar 2.00 5.00
7H Cory Schneider 1.00 2.50
7S Claude Giroux 1.25 3.00
8C Matt Duchene 1.25 3.00
8D Patrice Bergeron 1.50 4.00
8H Johnny Gaudreau 2.00 5.00
8S Oliver Ekman-Larsson 1.00 2.50
9C Artemi Panarin 1.50 4.00
9D Taylor Hall 2.50 6.00
9H Nathan MacKinnon 2.50 6.00
9S Tyler Seguin 2.00 5.00
AC Connor McDavid 8.00 20.00
AD Sidney Crosby 6.00 15.00
AH Henrik Lundqvist 1.50 4.00
AS Erik Karlsson 3.00 8.00
JC Jamie Benn 1.50 4.00
JD Ryan Getzlaf 2.00 5.00
JH Joe Thornton 1.25 3.00
JS Vladimir Tarasenko 2.00 5.00
KC Jack Eichel 2.50 6.00
KD Alexander Ovechkin 5.00 12.00
KH Steven Stamkos 2.50 6.00
KS Jonathan Toews 2.50 6.00
QC Drew Doughty 1.25 3.00
QD Jaromir Jagr 3.00 8.00
QH Patrick Kane 2.50 6.00
QS John Tavares 2.50 6.00
10C Corey Perry 1.25 3.00
10D Braden Holtby 2.00 5.00
10H Evgeni Malkin 4.00 10.00
10S Carey Price 4.00 10.00

2016-17 O-Pee-Chee Puck Stickers

1 Teemu Selanne 3.00 8.00
2 Oliver Ekman-Larsson 1.25 3.00
3 Patrice Bergeron 2.00 5.00
4 Jack Eichel 3.00 8.00
5 Sam Bennett 2.00 5.00
6 Rod Brind'Amour 1.50 4.00
7 Patrick Kane 3.00 8.00
8 Matt Duchene 1.50 4.00
9 Brandon Saad 1.50 4.00
10 Jamie Benn 2.00 5.00
11 Henrik Zetterberg 2.00 5.00
12 Connor McDavid 8.00 20.00
13 Aaron Ekblad 1.50 4.00
14 Drew Doughty 1.50 4.00
15 Ryan Suter 1.25 3.00
16 P.K. Subban 2.50 6.00
17 Filip Forsberg 2.00 5.00
18 Adam Henrique 1.50 4.00
19 Jaroslav Halak 1.50 4.00
20 Mark Messier 2.00 5.00
21 Bobby Ryan 1.25 3.00
22 Jakub Voracek 1.50 4.00
23 Mario Lemieux 5.00 12.00
24 Brent Burns 2.00 5.00
25 Jake Allen 2.00 5.00
26 Victor Hedman 2.00 5.00
27 Morgan Rielly 1.25 3.00
28 Bo Horvat 2.50 6.00
29 Evgeny Kuznetsov 2.50 6.00
30 Blake Wheeler 1.50 4.00

2016-17 O-Pee-Chee Glossy Rookies

Auston Matthews 8.00 20.00
Mitch Marner 5.00 12.00
Zach Werenski 2.00 5.00
William Nylander 4.00 10.00
Matthew Tkachuk 3.00 8.00
Jesse Puljujarvi 2.50 6.00
Jimmy Vesey 2.00 5.00
Travis Konecny 2.00 5.00
Pavel Zacha 1.25 3.00
) Patrik Laine 4.00 10.00

016-17 O-Pee-Chee Signatures

A Andy Andreoff E 4.00 10.00
B Aleksander Barkov D 5.00 12.00
H Andrew Hammond D 4.00 10.00
S Andrew Shaw C 8.00 20.00
B Brent Burns B 12.00 30.00
C Barclay Goodrow E 4.00 10.00
G Claude Giroux B 10.00 25.00
D David Desharnais D 4.00 10.00
K David Krejci D 5.00 12.00
C Frank Corrado E 4.00 10.00
J Joe Colborne B 6.00 15.00
F Justin Fontaine E 4.00 10.00
H Jiri Hudler D 4.00 10.00
P Jean-Gabriel Pageau E 4.00 10.00
V James van Riemsdyk B 10.00 25.00
T Kyle Turris E 4.00 10.00
B Matt Beleskey D 4.00 10.00
D Matt Duchene B 10.00 25.00
M Matt Moulson D 4.00 10.00
R Morgan Rielly D 4.00 10.00
S Mark Scheifele E 6.00 15.00
D Nicolas Deslauriers E 4.00 10.00
F Nick Foligno D 4.00 10.00
E Oliver Ekman-Larsson A
K Oscar Klefbom D 8.00 20.00
J Tyler Johnson D 4.00 10.00
P Teemu Pulkkinen C 5.00 12.00
T Tyler Toffoli C 8.00 20.00
AB Anthony Beauvillier E 5.00 12.00
AM Auston Matthews A
BP Brayden Point E 12.00 30.00
DH Danton Heinen E 8.00 20.00
HF Hudson Fasching E 5.00 12.00
JP Jesse Puljujarvi B 25.00 60.00
KC Kyle Connor C 20.00 50.00
MA Anthony Mantha C 20.00 50.00
MM Mitch Marner C 40.00 100.00
MT Matthew Tkachuk C 25.00 60.00
MW Miles Wood E 4.00 10.00
NS Nick Schmaltz D 5.00 12.00
PB Pavel Buchnevich D 8.00 20.00
PL Patrik Laine B 125.00 250.00
PZ Pavel Zacha C 10.00 25.00
SM Sonny Milano E 6.00 15.00
TM Tyler Motte E 5.00 12.00
WN William Nylander C 30.00 80.00
ZW Zach Werenski D 10.00 25.00

2016-17 O-Pee-Chee Team Canada Signatures

SAD Anthony Duclair E 6.00 15.00
SAE Aaron Ekblad B 15.00 40.00
SAH Adam Henrique C 10.00 25.00
SAP Alex Pietrangelo C 8.00 20.00
SBG Brendan Gallagher B 20.00 50.00
SBO Bobby Orr A
SCM Connor McDavid A
SCW Cam Ward C 10.00 25.00
SDN Darnell Nurse B 12.00 30.00
SES Eric Staal C 12.00 30.00
SJB Jamie Benn A
SJH Jonathan Huberdeau D 6.00 15.00
SJS Jordan Staal C 10.00 25.00
SJV Jake Virtanen C 12.00 30.00
SKT Kyle Turris D 5.00 12.00
SMR Morgan Rielly E 5.00 12.00
SMS Mark Scheifele D 8.00 20.00
SRF Robby Fabbri E 6.00 15.00
SRN Rick Nash B 15.00 40.00
SRO Ryan O'Reilly A
SSB Sam Bennett C 12.00 30.00
SSK Jeff Skinner C 10.00 25.00
SSL Martin St. Louis A
SSM Sean Monahan C 10.00 25.00
STH Taylor Hall B 30.00 80.00
STT Tyler Toffoli E 6.00 15.00
SWG Wayne Gretzky A

016-17 O-Pee-Chee V Series C

Cory Schneider 1.25 3.00
Justin Faulk 1.25 3.00
Claude Giroux 1.50 4.00
Ryan Johansen 2.00 5.00
Mike Modano 2.50 6.00
Brandon Saad 1.50 4.00
Sidney Crosby 6.00 15.00
Victor Hedman 2.00 5.00
Corey Perry 1.50 4.00
Tyler Seguin 2.50 6.00
Connor McDavid 8.00 20.00
Patrick Kane 3.00 8.00
Nathan MacKinnon 3.00 8.00
John Tavares 3.00 8.00
Alex Pietrangelo 1.25 3.00
Oliver Ekman-Larsson 1.25 3.00
Pavel Bure 1.50 4.00
Carey Price 5.00 12.00
Wayne Gretzky 8.00 20.00
Bobby Orr 5.00 12.00
Artemi Panarin 2.00 5.00
Patrice Bergeron 2.00 5.00
Taylor Hall 3.00 8.00
Morgan Rielly 1.25 3.00
P.K. Subban 2.50 6.00
Joe Pavelski 1.50 4.00
Dylan Larkin 2.50 6.00
Dustin Byfuglien 1.50 4.00
Jack Eichel 3.00 8.00
Henrik Lundqvist 1.50 4.00
Ryan Suter 1.25 3.00
Aleksander Barkov 1.50 4.00
Sean Monahan 1.50 4.00
Vladimir Tarasenko 2.50 6.00
Alexander Ovechkin 6.00 15.00
Ryan Getzlaf 2.50 6.00
Erik Karlsson 3.00 8.00
Daniel Sedin 1.50 4.00
Drew Doughty 1.50 4.00
Mario Lemieux 5.00 12.00

2017-18 O-Pee-Chee

uston Matthews 1.00 2.50
ler Seguin .40 1.00
evin Shattenkirk .25 .60
arian Hossa .20 .50
5 Evgeni Malkin .75 2.00
6 Cam Talbot .25 .60
7 Jeff Carter .25 .60
8 Max Pacioretty .25 .60
9 Tom Pyatt .15 .40
10 Nicklas Backstrom .40 1.00
11 Slater Koekkoek .20 .50
12 Alan Quine .15 .40
13 Marc-Andre Fleury .40 1.00
14 Sven Andrighetto .15 .40
15 Patrik Laine .40 1.00
16 Jakub Voracek .25 .60
17 Mike Fisher .20 .50
18 Eric Staal .30 .75
19 Patrik Berglund .15 .40
20 Lawson Crouse .20 .50
21 William Carrier .20 .50
22 Matthew Tkachuk .25 .60
23 Elias Lindholm .20 .50
24 Marian Gaborik .25 .60
25 Brent Burns .30 .75
26 David Perron .25 .60
27 Connor Carrick .20 .50
28 Jack Skille .15 .40
29 Micheal Ferland .15 .40
30 Henrik Zetterberg .25 .60
31 Jakob Silfverberg .20 .50
32 Sam Gagner .20 .50
33 Adam Larsson .25 .60
34 Ben Bishop .25 .60
35 Adam Henrique .20 .50
36 Craig Anderson .25 .60
37 Nikita Kucherov .40 1.00
38 Cody Eakin .20 .50
39 Martin Jones .25 .60
40 Leo Komarov .15 .40
41 Josh Bailey .20 .50
42 Mikko Rantanen .25 .60
43 Andrew Copp .20 .50
44 David Pastrnak .40 1.00
45 Paul Stastny .25 .60
46 Ryan Getzlaf .25 .60
47 Joonas Donskoi .20 .50
48 Patric Hornqvist .20 .50
49 Anthony Beauvillier .25 .60
50 Carey Price .75 2.00
51 Colton Sissons .20 .50
52 Devante Smith-Pelly .20 .50
53 Matt Dumba .20 .50
54 Reilly Smith .25 .60
55 Dustin Brown .20 .50
56 Mike Green .20 .50
57 Devin Shore .20 .50
58 Noah Hanifin .25 .60
59 Trevor van Riemsdyk .25 .60
60 Brandon Carlo .20 .50
61 Christian Dvorak .20 .50
62 John Gibson .25 .60
63 Pekka Rinne .30 .75
64 Mats Zuccarello .25 .60
65 Vladimir Tarasenko .40 1.00
66 Vincent Trocheck .20 .50
67 Teuvo Teravainen .20 .50
68 Sam Reinhart .20 .50
69 Loui Eriksson .20 .50
70 J.T. Brown .20 .50
71 Nick Cousins .20 .50
72 Matt Cullen .20 .50
73 Jannik Hansen .20 .50
74 Bo Horvat .25 .60
75 Erik Karlsson .30 .75
76 Ryan Strome .20 .50
77 Calle Jarnkrok .20 .50
78 Jason Zucker .20 .50
79 Darren Helm .15 .40
80 Ryan Nugent-Hopkins .25 .60
81 Dougie Hamilton .20 .50
82 Evander Kane .25 .60
83 Ryan Spooner .20 .50
84 Antoine Vermette .20 .50
85 Cam Atkinson .25 .60
86 Anthony DeAngelo .20 .50
87 Jay Beagle .20 .50
88 Ivan Provorov .25 .60
89 Ryan McDonagh .20 .50
90 Andrei Markov .25 .60
91 Curtis McKenzie .20 .50
92 Mathieu Perreault .20 .50
93 Justin Williams .20 .50
94 Radim Vrbata .15 .40
95 Artemi Panarin .25 .60
96 Oscar Lindberg .20 .50
97 Connor McDavid 1.00 2.50
98 Michael Cammalleri .20 .50
99 Colton Sceviour .15 .40
100 Checklist .25 .60
101 Alexander Ovechkin 1.00 2.50
102 Henrik Sedin .25 .60
103 Blake Wheeler .25 .60
104 Austin Watson .20 .50
105 Matt Murray .40 1.00
106 Mike Hoffman .20 .50
107 Jimmy Vesey .25 .60
108 Calvin de Haan .20 .50
109 Pavel Zacha .25 .60
110 Ryan Johansen .25 .60
111 Phillip Danault .15 .40
112 Jason Pominville .20 .50
113 David Krejci .20 .50
114 Aleksander Barkov .25 .60
115 Jordan Eberle .25 .60
116 Gustav Nyquist .25 .60
117 Antoine Roussel .20 .50
118 Brandon Dubinsky .20 .50
119 Mikhail Grigorenko .15 .40
120 Richard Panik .20 .50
121 Sebastian Aho .25 .60
122 Sean Monahan .25 .60
123 Drew Stafford .15 .40
124 Anze Kopitar .40 1.00
125 Oliver Ekman-Larsson .25 .60
126 Nikolaj Ehlers .25 .60
127 Joel Eriksson Ek .25 .60
128 Oliver Bjorkstrand .20 .50
129 William Nylander .40 1.00
130 Jonathan Drouin .25 .60
131 Roberto Luongo .25 .60
132 Jake Virtanen .25 .60
133 Danny DeKeyser .25 .60
134 Jakub Vrana .25 .60
135 Mikko Koivu .20 .50
136 Nikita Soshnikov .15 .40
137 Joe Pavelski .25 .60
138 Phil Kessel .30 .75
139 Claude Giroux .25 .60
140 Henrik Lundqvist .40 1.00
141 Jason Chimera .15 .40
142 Craig Smith .15 .40
143 Brendan Gallagher .25 .60
144 Mikael Granlund .25 .60
145 Mark Pysyk .15 .40
146 Drake Caggiula .20 .50
147 Riley Sheahan .15 .40
148 Esa Lindell .20 .50
149 Rene Bourque .15 .40
150 Marcus Kruger .25 .60
151 Brock McGinn .20 .50
152 Troy Brouwer .20 .50
153 Brian Gionta .20 .50
154 Zdeno Chara .25 .60
155 Jordan Martinook .20 .50
156 Alexander Wennberg .20 .50
157 Matt Nieto .15 .40
158 Brayden Point .25 .60
159 Kevin Labanc .15 .40
160 Chad Johnson .15 .40
161 Jaden Schwartz .30 .75
162 Jacob Trouba .20 .50
163 Michael Chaput .20 .50
164 Paul Martin .15 .40
165 Patrick Eaves .20 .50
166 Ian Cole .20 .50
167 Travis Konecny .25 .60
168 Chris Wideman .15 .40
169 Michael Grabner .15 .40
170 John Tavares .50 1.25
171 Kyle Palmieri .20 .50
172 John Carlson .30 .75
173 Alexander Radulov .25 .60
174 Erik Haula .15 .40
175 Derek Forbort .20 .50
176 Jason Demers .15 .40
177 Andrej Sekera .15 .40
178 Andreas Athanasiou .25 .60
179 John Klingberg .20 .50
180 William Karlsson .50 1.25
181 Tuukka Rask .25 .60
182 Gabriel Landeskog .20 .50
183 Duncan Keith .25 .60
184 Lee Stempniak .15 .40
185 Michael Frolik .15 .40
186 Kyle Okposo .20 .50
187 Louis Domingue .15 .40
188 Zach Hyman .20 .50
189 Hampus Lindholm .20 .50
190 Stefan Noesen .15 .40
191 Tomas Hertl .25 .60
192 Matthew Benning .15 .40
193 Colton Parayko .25 .60
194 Nicolas Petan .20 .50
195 Lars Eller .20 .50
196 James Neal .20 .50
197 Kris Letang .25 .60
198 Mark Stone .25 .60
199 J.T. Miller .20 .50
200 Checklist .25 .60
201 Jonathan Toews .50 1.25
202 Victor Rask .25 .60
203 Johnny Gaudreau .40 1.00
204 Jake McCabe .15 .40
205 Brad Marchand .30 .75
206 Tobias Rieder .15 .40
207 Alexander Steen .25 .60
208 Tyler Toffoli .20 .50
209 Brett Pesce .15 .40
210 Niklas Hjalmarsson .15 .40
211 Andreas Martinsen .15 .40
212 Shane Doan .20 .50
213 Nikita Zaitsev .20 .50
214 Steve Mason .20 .50
215 Cedric Paquette .20 .50
216 Joel Edmundson .20 .50
217 Darnell Nurse .20 .50
218 David Schlemko .15 .40
219 Ondrej Kase .15 .40
220 Adam Lowry .20 .50
221 Daniel Winnik .15 .40
222 Jacob Markstrom .15 .40
223 Morgan Rielly .25 .60
224 Nick Bonino .20 .50
225 Brayden Schenn .25 .60
226 Brady Skjei .20 .50
227 Anders Lee .25 .60
228 Travis Zajac .15 .40
229 Viktor Arvidsson .20 .50
230 Andrew Shaw .20 .50
231 Tanner Pearson .20 .50
232 Jonathan Marchessault .25 .60
233 Leon Draisaitl .40 1.00
234 Brett Ritchie .15 .40
235 Seth Jones .20 .50
236 Tyson Barrie .25 .60
237 Vincent Hinostroza .15 .40
238 Justin Faulk .20 .50
239 Matt Moulson .15 .40
240 David Backes .20 .50
241 Jonathan Bernier .20 .50
242 Shea Weber .20 .50
243 Nazem Kadri .20 .50
244 Vladislav Namestnikov .20 .50
245 Josh Anderson .15 .40
246 Mark Scheifele .30 .75
247 Sven Baertschi .15 .40
248 Melker Karlsson .15 .40
249 Jay Bouwmeester .25 .60
250 Matt Niskanen .20 .50
251 Blake Comeau .15 .40
252 Troy Stecher .20 .50
253 Conor Sheary .25 .60
254 Dion Phaneuf .20 .50
255 Derek Stepan .20 .50
256 Cory Schneider .20 .50
257 Mattias Ekholm .15 .40
258 Zach Parise .25 .60
259 Corey Crawford .30 .75
260 Corey Perry .25 .60
261 Nick Shore .20 .50
262 Michael Matheson .20 .50
263 Benoit Pouliot .15 .40
264 Dylan Larkin .25 .60
265 Jason Spezza .25 .60
266 Brandon Saad .25 .60
267 Brent Seabrook .20 .50
268 Sam Bennett .20 .50
269 Jack Eichel .40 1.00
270 Derick Brassard .25 .60
271 Brendan Perlini .20 .50
272 Andrew Ladd .25 .60
273 Victor Hedman .30 .75
274 Jonathan Quick .40 1.00
275 Connor Hellebuyck .40 1.00
276 Braden Holtby .40 1.00
277 Daniel Sedin .25 .60
278 Mikkel Boedker .20 .50
279 Anthony Mantha .25 .60
280 Scott Wilson .15 .40
281 Sean Couturier .20 .50
282 Mike Condon .20 .50
283 Austin Czarnik .25 .60
284 Pavel Buchnevich .20 .50
285 Thomas Greiss .20 .50
286 Logan Couture .25 .60
287 Andrew Cogliano .15 .40
288 John Moore .20 .50
289 Ryan Ellis .20 .50
290 Artturi Lehkonen .20 .50
291 Jonas Brodin .20 .50
292 Jake Muzzin .20 .50
293 Jussi Jokinen .20 .50
294 Mark Letestu .20 .50
295 Xavier Ouellet .20 .50
296 Stephen Johns .20 .50
297 David Savard .20 .50
298 Joe Colborne .20 .50
299 Chris Stewart .20 .50
300 Checklist .25 .60
301 Sidney Crosby 1.00 2.50
302 Radko Gudas .20 .50
303 Zack Smith .15 .40
304 Nick Holden .20 .50
305 P.K. Subban .25 .60
306 Nathan Beaulieu .20 .50
307 Trevor Lewis .20 .50
308 Oscar Klefbom .20 .50
309 Jaromir Jagr .60 1.50
310 Tomas Tatar .25 .60
311 Patrick Sharp .20 .50
312 Nick Foligno .20 .50
313 Matt Duchene .25 .60
314 Artem Anisimov .20 .50
315 Kris Versteeg .15 .40
316 Rasmus Ristolainen .25 .60
317 Patrice Bergeron .30 .75
318 Max Domi .25 .60
319 Rickard Rakell .20 .50
320 Ryan Miller .20 .50
321 Cody Ceci .15 .40
322 Cody Franson .15 .40
323 Johnny Boychuk .20 .50
324 Keith Kinkaid .15 .40
325 Matt Calvert .15 .40
326 Martin Hanzal .20 .50
327 Cam Ward .20 .50
328 Peter Budaj .15 .40
329 Mitch Marner .40 1.00
330 Chris Kreider .25 .60
331 Robby Fabbri .25 .60
332 Brandon Sutter .20 .50
333 Matt Beleskey .15 .40
334 Josh Morrissey .15 .40
335 Andre Burakovsky .20 .50
336 Johan Larsson .15 .40
337 Joe Thornton .25 .60
338 Jake Guentzel .30 .75
339 Jean-Gabriel Pageau .15 .40
340 Brandon Pirri .15 .40
341 Carter Hutton .25 .60
342 Nick Leddy .15 .40
343 Taylor Hall .50 1.25
344 Filip Forsberg .30 .75
345 Alex Galchenyuk .30 .75
346 Nino Niederreiter .20 .50
347 Drew Doughty .25 .60
348 Anton Slepyshev .15 .40
349 Alex Killorn .20 .50
350 Justin Abdelkader .20 .50
351 Radek Faksa .20 .50
352 Calvin Pickard .15 .40
353 Tanner Kero .15 .40
354 Jaccob Slavin .15 .40
355 Ryan Reaves .15 .40
356 Riley Nash .15 .40
357 Jakob Chychrun .20 .50
358 Josh Manson .15 .40
359 Mark Giordano .20 .50
360 Valtteri Filppula .15 .40
361 Evgeny Kuznetsov .40 1.00
362 Tyler Bozak .20 .50
363 Milan Lucic .25 .60
364 Scott Hartnell .15 .40
365 Alex Pietrangelo .20 .50
366 Dustin Byfuglien .25 .60
367 Alexander Edler .15 .40
368 Carl Hagelin .25 .60
369 Wayne Simmonds .30 .75
370 Rick Nash .25 .60
371 Casey Cizikas .15 .40
372 Juuse Saros .25 .60
373 Alexei Emelin .15 .40
374 Marcus Johansson .20 .50
375 Ryan Suter .15 .40
376 Kyle Clifford .15 .40
377 Thomas Vanek .20 .50
378 Petr Mrazek .25 .60
379 Ondrej Palat .25 .60
380 Jack Johnson .15 .40
381 Francois Beauchemin .15 .40
382 Ryan Hartman .25 .60
383 Jordan Staal .25 .60
384 Marcus Foligno .15 .40
385 Dominic Moore .15 .40
386 Nick Ritchie .15 .40
387 Michael Del Zotto .15 .40
388 Jamie McGinn .15 .40
389 Steven Stamkos .50 1.25
390 Kari Lehtonen .20 .50
391 Steven Santini .15 .40
392 Chris Tierney .15 .40
393 Brett Connolly .15 .40
394 Jeff Petry .15 .40
395 Frederik Andersen .20 .50
396 Chris Kunitz .25 .60
397 Beau Bennett .15 .40
398 Jonathan Huberdeau .20 .50
399 Alex Chiasson .20 .50
400 Checklist .25 .60
401 Patrick Kane .50 1.25
402 Ryan Kesler .25 .60
403 Torey Krug .25 .60
404 Zemgus Girgensons .15 .40
405 Jamie Benn .30 .75
406 Zack Kassian .15 .40
407 Alec Martinez .15 .40
408 Jared Spurgeon .15 .40
409 Tomas Plekanec .20 .50
410 Roman Josi .25 .60
411 Miles Wood .15 .40
412 Mika Zibanejad .25 .60
413 Bryan Rust .25 .60
414 Ben Hutton .15 .40
415 Tom Wilson .25 .60
416 Timo Meier .20 .50
417 Zach Sanford .15 .40
418 Robin Lehner .15 .40
419 Anthony Duclair .15 .40
420 P.A. Parenteau .15 .40
421 Dale Weise .15 .40
422 Andrei Vasilevskiy .30 .75
423 Alexandre Burrows .15 .40
424 Kevin Bieksa .15 .40
425 Colin Miller .15 .40
426 Brian Elliott .20 .50
427 Carl Soderberg .15 .40
428 Luke Glendening .15 .40
429 Keith Yandle .15 .40
430 Jarome Iginla .25 .60
431 Daniel Carr .15 .40
432 Damon Severson .20 .50
433 Nikolay Kulemin .20 .50
434 Ryan Dzingel .15 .40
435 Justin Schultz .25 .60
436 Patrick Marleau .25 .60
437 Dmitry Orlov .20 .50
438 Joel Armia .15 .40
439 Connor Brown .25 .60
440 Tyler Johnson .20 .50
441 Jori Lehtera .15 .40
442 Curtis Lazar .15 .40
443 Dennis Seidenberg .15 .40
444 Jim Howard .15 .40
445 Joseph Cramarossa .15 .40
446 Sami Vatanen .15 .40
447 Tim Schaller .15 .40
448 Mikael Backlund .15 .40
449 Derek Ryan .20 .50
450 Dennis Rasmussen .20 .50
451 Boone Jenner .20 .50
452 Antti Niemi .20 .50
453 Patrick Maroon .20 .50
454 Aaron Ekblad .25 .60
455 Charlie Coyle .20 .50
456 Paul Byron .20 .50
457 Colin Wilson .20 .50
458 Jake Gardiner .20 .50
459 Kevin Hayes .20 .50
460 Shayne Gostisbehere .25 .60
461 Trevor Daley .20 .50
462 Marc-Edouard Vlasic .15 .40
463 Cam Fowler .20 .50
464 Bryan Little .20 .50
465 Devan Dubnyk .25 .60
466 Markus Granlund .20 .50
467 Bobby Ryan .20 .50
468 Nail Yakupov .20 .50
469 James van Riemsdyk .25 .60
470 Kevin Fiala .20 .50
471 Brock Nelson .20 .50
472 Jesper Fast .20 .50
473 T.J. Oshie .40 1.00
474 Matt Read .20 .50
475 Sergei Bobrovsky .25 .60
476 Joel Ward .20 .50
477 Nic Dowd .20 .50
478 Alex Goligoski .20 .50
479 Kyle Connor .25 .60
480 Patrick Wiercioch .20 .50
481 Jake Allen .30 .75
482 Joseph Blandisi .20 .50
483 Torrey Mitchell .20 .50
484 Anton Stralman .20 .50
485 Joakim Nordstrom .20 .50
486 Niklas Kronwall .20 .50
487 Kyle Turris .25 .60
488 Mike Smith .25 .60
489 Frank Vatrano .25 .60
490 Ryan O'Reilly .25 .60
491 T.J. Brodie .20 .50
492 Jeff Skinner .20 .50
493 Nick Schmaltz .20 .50
494 James Reimer .25 .60
495 Zach Werenski .25 .60
496 Brian Boyle .15 .40
497 Frans Nielsen .20 .50
498 Jesse Puljujarvi .30 .75
499 Nathan MacKinnon .50 1.25
500 Checklist .25 .60
501 Alexander Nylander RC 1.50 4.00
502 Valentin Zykov RC 1.00 2.50
503 Robert Hagg RC 1.00 2.50
504 Brock Boeser RC 5.00 12.00
505 Colin White RC 1.00 2.50
506 Marcus Sorensen RC .75 2.00
507 Ivan Barbashev RC 1.00 2.50
508 Carter Rowney RC .75 2.00
509 J.T. Compher RC 1.25 3.00
510 Evgeny Svechnikov RC 2.00 5.00
511 Jack Roslovic RC 1.25 3.00
512 Jake Dotchin RC .75 2.00
513 Josh Ho-Sang RC 1.25 3.00
514 Alexandre Carrier RC .75 2.00
515 Gabriel Carlsson RC .75 2.00
516 Christian Fischer RC 1.25 3.00
517 Kalle Kossila RC .75 2.00
518 Jakob Forsbacka-Karlsson RC 1.00 2.50
519 Ian McCoshen RC 1.00 2.50
520 Alex Tuch RC 2.50 6.00
521 Samuel Morin RC 1.00 2.50
522 Eric Comrie RC .75 2.00
523 Peter Cehlarik RC 1.00 2.50
524 Robbie Russo RC 1.00 2.50
525 Adrian Kempe RC 1.25 3.00
526 Remi Elie RC .75 2.00
527 Griffen Molino RC .75 2.00
528 Jordan Schmaltz RC 1.25 3.00
529 Rasmus Andersson RC 1.00 2.50
530 Nicolas Kerdiles RC 1.00 2.50
531 Chris DiDomenico RC .75 2.00
532 Paul LaDue RC .75 2.00
533 Tyson Jost RC 2.00 5.00
534 T.J. Tynan RC .75 2.00
535 Nikita Scherbak RC 2.00 5.00
536 Charlie McAvoy RC 3.00 8.00
537 Lucas Wallmark RC 1.00 2.50
538 Denis Gurianov RC 1.00 2.50
539 Jonny Brodzinski RC 1.00 2.50
540 Clayton Keller RC 2.50 6.00
541 Mike Vecchione RC .75 2.00
542 Jon Gillies RC 1.00 2.50
543 Blake Coleman RC .75 2.00
544 John Hayden RC .75 2.00
545 Riley Barber RC .75 2.00
546 C.J. Smith RC .75 2.00
547 Connor Jones RC .75 2.00
548 Alex Nedeljkovic RC .75 2.00
549 Dan Renouf RC .75 2.00
550 Vladislav Kamenev RC 1.50 4.00
551 Sidney Crosby SH 4.00 10.00
552 Marian Hossa SH .75 2.00
553 Jaromir Jagr SH 2.50 6.00
554 Auston Matthews SH 4.00 10.00
555 Connor McDavid SH 4.00 10.00
556 Joe Thornton SH 1.00 2.50
557 Patrick Marleau SH 1.00 2.50
558 Mitch Marner SH 1.50 4.00
559 Henrik Lundqvist SH 1.50 4.00
560 Alexander Ovechkin SH 4.00 10.00
561 Anaheim Ducks CL .25 .60
562 Arizona Coyotes CL .25 .60
563 Boston Bruins CL .25 .60
564 Buffalo Sabres CL .25 .60
565 Calgary Flames CL .25 .60
566 Carolina Hurricanes CL .25 .60
567 Chicago Blackhawks CL .25 .60
568 Colorado Avalanche CL .25 .60
569 Columbus Blue Jackets CL .25 .60
570 Dallas Stars CL .25 .60
571 Detroit Red Wings CL .25 .60
572 Edmonton Oilers CL .25 .60
573 Florida Panthers CL .25 .60
574 Los Angeles Kings CL .25 .60
575 Minnesota Wild CL .25 .60
576 Montreal Canadiens CL .25 .60
577 Nashville Predators CL .25 .60
578 New Jersey Devils CL .25 .60
579 New York Islanders CL .25 .60
580 New York Rangers CL .25 .60
581 Ottawa Senators CL .25 .60
582 Philadelphia Flyers CL .25 .60
583 Pittsburgh Penguins CL .25 .60
584 San Jose Sharks CL .25 .60
585 St. Louis Blues CL .25 .60
586 Tampa Bay Lightning CL .25 .60
587 Toronto Maple Leafs CL .25 .60
588 Vancouver Canucks CL .25 .60
509 Washington Capitals CL .25 .60
590 Winnipeg Jets CL .25 .60
591 Connor McDavid LL 4.00 10.00
592 Braden Holtby LL 1.50 4.00
593 Sidney Crosby LL 4.00 10.00
594 Mark Borowiecki LL 1.25 3.00
595 Brent Burns LL 1.25 3.00
596 Ryan Suter LL .60 1.50
597 Sergei Bobrovsky LL 1.00 2.50
598 Auston Matthews LL 4.00 10.00
599 Connor McDavid LL 4.00 10.00
600 Checklist LL .25 .60
601 Marc-Andre Fleury .40 1.00
602 Brayden Schenn .25 .60
603 Jaromir Jagr .60 1.50
604 Chris Kunitz .25 .60
605 Jonathan Drouin .25 .60
606 Alexander Radulov .25 .60
607 Patrick Marleau .25 .60
608 Kevin Shattenkirk .25 .60
609 Brandon Saad .25 .60
610 Artemi Panarin .25 .60
611 Kailer Yamamoto RC 3.00 8.00
612 Alex Iafallo RC 1.25 3.00
613 Travis Sanheim RC 1.25 3.00
614 Oscar Fantenberg RC 1.25 3.00
615 Andreas Borgman RC 1.25 3.00
616 Jake DeBrusk RC 2.00 5.00
617 Kurtis MacDermid RC 1.25 3.00
618 Tage Thompson RC 2.00 5.00
619 Andrei Mironov RC 1.25 3.00
620 Haydn Fleury RC 1.25 3.00
621 Tucker Poolman RC 1.25 3.00
622 Victor Mete RC 1.25 3.00
623 Dylan Ferguson RC 1.25 3.00
624 Luke Kunin RC 1.25 3.00
625 Logan Brown RC 1.25 3.00
626 Madison Bowey RC 1.00 2.50
627 Jesper Bratt RC 2.00 5.00
628 Giovanni Fiore RC 1.25 3.00
629 Samuel Girard RC 1.25 3.00
630 Nathan Walker RC 1.25 3.00
631 Janne Kuokkanen RC 1.25 3.00
632 Pierre-Luc Dubois RC 2.50 6.00
633 Martin Necas RC 1.25 3.00
634 Anders Bjork RC 1.50 4.00
635 Vince Dunn RC 1.25 3.00
636 Will Butcher RC 1.50 4.00
637 Calle Rosen RC 1.25 3.00
638 Christian Jaros RC 1.25 3.00
639 Filip Chytil RC 1.25 3.00
640 Nolan Patrick RC 2.50 6.00
641 Jan Rutta RC 1.25 3.00
642 Owen Tippett RC 2.50 6.00
643 Christian Djoos RC 1.25 3.00
644 Brendan Lemieux RC 1.25 3.00
645 Alex DeBrincat RC 3.00 8.00
646 Viktor Antipin RC 1.25 3.00
647 Alex Formenton RC 1.25 3.00
648 Alex Kerfoot RC 1.25 3.00
649 Nico Hischier RC 4.00 10.00
650 Alex Tuch RC 3.00 8.00

2017-18 O-Pee-Chee Rainbow Black

*VETS/100: 2.5X TO 6X BASIC CARDS
*SP/RC/100: 1X TO 2.5X BASIC CARDS
1 Auston Matthews 20.00 50.00
504 Brock Boeser 50.00 125.00
554 Auston Matthews SH 20.00 50.00
598 Auston Matthews LL 25.00 60.00

2017-18 O-Pee-Chee Red

1 Auston Matthews 15.00 40.00
504 Brock Boeser 25.00 60.00

2017-18 O-Pee-Chee Hobby Box Bottoms

AO Alex Ovechkin G4 2.00 5.00
BB Brent Burns G2 .60 1.50
CG Claude Giroux G3 .50 1.25
CM Connor McDavid G2 2.00 5.00
CP Carey Price G3 1.50 4.00
EK Erik Karlsson G1 .60 1.50
EM Evgeni Malkin G3 1.50 4.00
HS Henrik Sedin G1 .50 1.25
JB Jamie Benn G4 .60 1.50
JQ Jonathan Quick G2 .75 2.00
JT Jonathan Toews G3 1.00 2.50
MM Mitch Marner G4 .75 2.00
PK Patrick Kane G1 1.00 2.50
PL Patrick Laine G1 .75 2.00
SS Steven Stamkos G2 1.00 2.50
SW Shea Weber G4 .40 1.00

2017-18 O-Pee-Chee Glossy Rookies

R1 Josh Ho-Sang 1.00 2.50
R2 Brock Boeser 4.00 10.00
R3 Pierre-Luc Dubois 1.50 4.00
R4 Charlie McAvoy 2.50 6.00
R5 Alex DeBrincat 2.00 5.00
R6 Will Butcher 1.00 2.50
R7 Nolan Patrick 1.50 4.00
R8 Tyson Jost 1.50 4.00
R9 Nico Hischier 2.50 6.00
R10 Clayton Keller 2.00 5.00

2017-18 O-Pee-Chee Mini

M1 Nicklas Backstrom 1.25 3.00
M2 Mitch Marner 1.25 3.00
M3 Brayden Schenn .75 2.00
M4 Phil Kessel 1.00 2.50
M5 Alex Galchenyuk 1.00 2.50
M6 Jack Eichel 1.25 3.00
M7 Sean Monahan .75 2.00
M8 Aleksander Barkov .75 2.00
M9 Tyler Seguin 1.25 3.00
M10 Cam Talbot .75 2.00
M11 Anthony Mantha .75 2.00
M12 Ryan Getzlaf .75 2.00
M13 David Pastrnak 1.25 3.00
M14 Jeff Carter .75 2.00
M15 Artemi Panarin .75 2.00
M16 Eric Staal 1.00 2.50
M17 Kyle Turris .75 2.00
M18 Filip Forsberg 1.00 2.50
M19 Shea Weber .60 1.50
M20 Joe Pavelski .75 2.00
M21 Daniel Sedin .75 2.00
M22 Nikita Kucherov 1.25 3.00
M23 Loui Eriksson .60 1.50
M24 Mark Scheifele 1.00 2.50
M25 Oliver Ekman-Larsson .75 2.00
M26 Kyle Palmieri .60 1.50
M27 Jeff Skinner .60 1.50
M28 Mikko Rantanen .75 2.00
M29 Jake Allen 1.00 2.50
M30 Andrew Ladd .75 2.00
M31 Tuukka Rask .75 2.00
M32 Derek Stepan .60 1.50
M33 William Nylander 1.25 3.00
M34 Logan Couture .75 2.00
M35 Anze Kopitar 1.25 3.00
M36 Ryan O'Reilly .75 2.00
M37 Cam Atkinson .75 2.00
M38 Devan Dubnyk .75 2.00
M39 Patrik Laine 1.25 3.00
M40 Matt Murray 1.25 3.00
M41 Tomas Tatar .75 2.00
M42 Leon Draisaitl 1.25 3.00
M43 Corey Perry .75 2.00
M44 Jonathan Drouin .75 2.00
M45 Evgeny Kuznetsov 1.25 3.00
M46 Tyson Jost 1.50 4.00
M47 Nikita Scherbak 1.50 4.00
M48 Evgeny Svechnikov 1.50 4.00
M49 Brock Boeser 4.00 10.00
M50 Ivan Barbashev .75 2.00
M51 Clayton Keller SP 4.00 10.00
M52 Alexander Nylander SP 2.50 6.00
M53 Auston Matthews SP 6.00 15.00
M54 Jonathan Toews SP 3.00 8.00
M55 Brent Burns SP 2.00 5.00
M56 Sergei Bobrovsky SP 1.50 4.00
M57 Taylor Hall SP 3.00 8.00
M58 Jamie Benn SP 2.00 5.00
M59 Evgeni Malkin SP 5.00 12.00
M60 Henrik Zetterberg SP 1.50 4.00
M61 Nathan MacKinnon SP 3.00 8.00
M62 Max Pacioretty SP 1.50 4.00
M63 Erik Karlsson SP 2.00 5.00
M64 Vladimir Tarasenko SP 2.50 6.00
M65 Alexander Ovechkin SP 6.00 15.00
M66 Carey Price RARE 12.00 30.00
M67 Patrick Kane RARE 8.00 20.00
M68 Henrik Sedin RARE 4.00 10.00
M69 Brad Marchand RARE 5.00 12.00
M70 Sidney Crosby RARE 15.00 40.00
M71 Johnny Gaudreau RARE 6.00 15.00
M72 Henrik Lundqvist RARE 6.00 15.00
M73 Jaromir Jagr RARE 10.00 25.00
M74 John Tavares RARE 8.00 20.00
M75 P.K. Subban RARE 4.00 10.00
M76 Steven Stamkos RARE 8.00 20.00
M77 Connor McDavid RARE 15.00 40.00

2017-18 O-Pee-Chee Mini Back Variation

M77 Connor McDavid 50.00 125.00

2017-18 O-Pee-Chee Patches

P1 Corey Perry 8.00 20.00
P2 Mike Smith 8.00 20.00
P3 Patrice Bergeron 10.00 25.00
P4 Ryan O'Reilly 8.00 20.00
P5 Sean Monahan 8.00 20.00
P6 Sebastian Aho 8.00 20.00
P7 Artemi Panarin 8.00 20.00
P8 Matt Duchene 8.00 20.00
P9 Nick Foligno 6.00 15.00
P10 Tyler Seguin 12.00 30.00
P11 Dylan Larkin 8.00 20.00
P12 Connor McDavid 30.00 80.00
P13 Aaron Ekblad 8.00 20.00
P14 Jeff Carter 8.00 20.00
P15 Devan Dubnyk 8.00 20.00
P16 Shea Weber 6.00 15.00
P17 Filip Forsberg 10.00 25.00
P18 Kyle Palmieri 6.00 15.00
P19 Andrew Ladd 8.00 20.00
P20 Derek Stepan 6.00 15.00
P21 Mike Hoffman 6.00 15.00
P22 Jakub Voracek 8.00 20.00
P23 Sidney Crosby 30.00 80.00
P24 Joe Pavelski 8.00 20.00
P25 Jaden Schwartz 10.00 25.00
P26 Nikita Kucherov 12.00 30.00
P27 Mitch Marner 12.00 30.00
P28 Daniel Sedin 8.00 20.00
P29 Alexander Ovechkin 30.00 80.00
P30 Patrik Laine 12.00 30.00
P31 Ivan Barbashev 12.00 30.00
P32 Vladislav Kamenev 20.00 50.00
P33 Nikita Scherbak 25.00 60.00
P34 Alex Tuch 30.00 80.00
P35 Nicolas Kerdiles 12.00 30.00
P36 Riley Barber 10.00 25.00
P37 Clayton Keller 30.00 80.00
P38 Christian Fischer 15.00 40.00
P39 Adrian Kempe 15.00 40.00
P40 Peter Cehlarik 12.00 30.00
P41 Sidney Crosby 100 40.00 100.00
P42 Carey Price 100 30.00 80.00
P43 Jonathan Toews 100 20.00 50.00
P44 Jaromir Jagr 100 25.00 60.00
P45 Connor McDavid 100 150.00 250.00
P46 Vladimir Tarasenko 100 15.00 40.00
P47 Claude Giroux 100 10.00 25.00
P48 Roberto Luongo 100 10.00 25.00
P49 John Tavares 100 20.00 50.00
P50 P.K. Subban 100 10.00 25.00
P51 Steven Stamkos 100 20.00 50.00
P52 Henrik Zetterberg 100 10.00 25.00
P53 Henrik Sedin 100 10.00 25.00
P54 Brent Burns 100 12.00 30.00
P55 Auston Matthews 100 80.00 150.00

P56 Henrik Lundqvist 100 15.00 40.00
P57 Ryan Kesler 100 10.00 25.00
P58 Anze Kopitar 100 15.00 40.00
P59 Brad Marchand 100 12.00 30.00
P60 Patrick Kane 100 20.00 50.00
P61 Erik Karlsson 100 12.00 30.00
P62 Nathan MacKinnon 100 20.00 50.00
P63 Johnny Gaudreau 100 15.00 40.00
P64 Oliver Ekman-Larsson 100 10.00 25.00
P65 Max Pacioretty 100 10.00 25.00
P66 Taylor Hall 100 20.00 50.00
P67 Jamie Benn 100 12.00 30.00
P68 Evgeni Malkin 100 30.00 80.00
P69 Tuukka Rask 100 10.00 25.00
P70 Alexander Ovechkin 100 40.00 100.00
P71 Wayne Gretzky 100 120.00 300.00
P72 Mark Messier 100 40.00 100.00
P73 Steve Yzerman 100 30.00 80.00
P74 Mike Bossy 100 40.00 100.00
P75 Darryl Sittler 100 25.00 60.00
P76 Mario Lemieux 100 80.00 200.00
P77 Bobby Orr 100 80.00 200.00
P78 Milt Schmidt 100 25.00 60.00
P79 Patrick Roy 100 60.00 150.00
P80 Stan Mikita 100 30.00 80.00
P81 Johnny Bower 100 25.00 60.00
P82 Eddie Shore 100 25.00 60.00
P83 Stormy 50.00 125.00
P84 Hunter 50.00 125.00
P85 Howler 50.00 125.00
P86 Sabretooth 50.00 125.00
P87 Victor E. Green 40.00 100.00
P88 Sparky The Dragon 50.00 125.00
P89 Thunderbug RARE
P90 Nordy RARE

2017-18 O-Pee-Chee Playing Cards

2C Vincent Trocheck 1.00 2.50
2D Loui Eriksson 1.00 2.50
2H Jakub Voracek 1.25 3.00
2S Mike Hoffman 1.00 2.50
3C Jaden Schwartz 1.50 4.00
3D Cam Atkinson 1.25 3.00
3H Gustav Nyquist 1.25 3.00
3S Ryan O'Reilly 1.25 3.00
4C Jeff Skinner 1.00 2.50
4D Logan Couture 1.25 3.00
4H Max Domi 1.25 3.00
4S Derek Stepan 1.00 2.50
5C Henrik Sedin 1.25 3.00
5D Sergei Bobrovsky 1.25 3.00
5H Shea Weber 1.00 2.50
5S Victor Hedman 1.50 4.00
6C Mark Scheifele 1.50 4.00
6D Ryan Johansen 1.25 3.00
6H Ryan Kesler 1.25 3.00
6S Nicklas Backstrom 2.00 5.00
7C Alex Galchenyuk 1.50 4.00
7D Jeff Carter 1.25 3.00
7H Devan Dubnyk 1.25 3.00
7S Brad Marchand 1.50 4.00
8C William Nylander 2.00 5.00
8D Wayne Simmonds 1.50 4.00
8H Johnny Gaudreau 2.00 5.00
8S Taylor Hall 2.50 6.00
9C Joe Pavelski 1.25 3.00
9D David Pastrnak 2.00 5.00
9H Nathan MacKinnon 2.50 6.00
9S Tyler Seguin 2.00 5.00
AC Connor McDavid 20.00 50.00
AD Sidney Crosby 15.00 40.00
AH Alexander Ovechkin 8.00 20.00
AS Auston Matthews 15.00 40.00
JC Nikita Kucherov 2.00 5.00
JD Corey Crawford 1.50 4.00
JH Leon Draisaitl 2.00 5.00
JS Vladimir Tarasenko 2.00 5.00
KC Patrik Laine 2.00 5.00
KD Jaromir Jagr 3.00 8.00
KH Patrick Kane 2.50 6.00
KS Henrik Lundqvist 2.00 5.00
QC Mitch Marner 2.00 5.00
QD Henrik Zetterberg 1.25 3.00
QH Jonathan Quick 2.00 5.00
QS John Tavares 2.50 6.00
10C P.K. Subban 1.25 3.00
10D Ryan Getzlaf 1.25 3.00
10H Phil Kessel 1.50 4.00
10S Max Pacioretty 1.25 3.00

2017-18 O-Pee-Chee Playing Cards Foil

*SINGLES: .6X TO 1.5X BASIC INSERTS
AC Connor McDavid 25.00 60.00
AD Sidney Crosby 25.00 60.00
AH Alexander Ovechkin 12.00 30.00
AS Auston Matthews 25.00 60.00

2017-18 O-Pee-Chee Retro Award Winners

AWAM Auston Matthews Calder 30.00 80.00
AWBB Brent Burns Norris 25.00 60.00
AWCM Connor McDavid Hart 30.00 80.00
AWCO Connor McDavid Art Ross 30.00 80.00
AWMC Connor McDavid Ted Lindsay 30.00 80.00
AWSB Sergei Bobrovsky Vezina 15.00 40.00
AWSC Sidney Crosby Richard 30.00 80.00

2017-18 O-Pee-Chee Retro Cup Captain

CCSC Sidney Crosby 40.00 100.00

2017-18 O-Pee-Chee Retro Top 10 Point Seasons

T1 Wayne Gretzky '85-86 20.00 50.00
T2 Wayne Gretzky '81-82 20.00 50.00
T3 Wayne Gretzky '84-85 20.00 50.00
T4 Wayne Gretzky '83-84 20.00 50.00
T5 Mario Lemieux '88-89 12.00 30.00
T6 Wayne Gretzky '82-83 20.00 50.00
T7 Wayne Gretzky '86-87 20.00 50.00
T8 Mario Lemieux '87-88 12.00 30.00
T9 Wayne Gretzky '88-89 20.00 50.00
T10 Wayne Gretzky '80-81 20.00 50.00

2017-18 O-Pee-Chee Team Logo Patches

301 NHL Centennial Classic '16-17 30.00 80.00
302 Pittsburgh Penguins '16-17 50th Season 150.00 250.00
303 New York Rangers '16-17 90th Anniversary 80.00 150.00
304 St. Louis Blues '16-17 50th Anniversary 60.00 150.00
305 Toronto Maple Leafs '16-17 100th Anniversary 60.00 150.00
306 Vegas Golden Knights Logo 80.00 150.00
307 LA Kings '16-17 50th Anniversary 80.00 150.00
308 Philadelphia Flyers '16-17 50th Season 80.00 150.00
309 Detroit Red Wings Joe Louis Arena Farewell 60.00 150.00
310 Florida Panthers '16-17 Primary 60.00 150.00

1998-99 O-Pee-Chee Chrome

The 1998-99 OPC Chrome set was issue in one series by Topps totaling 242 cards and was distributed in four card packs with a suggested retail price of $3. The fronts feature color action photos of veteran players, 1998 NHL Draft Picks, and CHL All-Stars. The backs carry player information and career statistics.

COMPLETE SET (242) 40.00 100.00
1 Peter Forsberg 1.00 2.50
2 Petr Sykora .20 .50
3 Byron Dafoe .30 .75
4 Ron Francis .30 .75
5 Alexei Yashin .20 .50
6 Dave Ellett .20 .50
7 Jamie Langenbrunner .20 .50
8 Doug Weight .30 .75
9 Jason Woolley .20 .50
10 Paul Coffey .40 1.00
11 Uwe Krupp .20 .50
12 Tomas Sandstrom .20 .50
13 Scott Mellanby .20 .50
14 Vladimir Tsyplakov .20 .50
15 Martin Rucinsky .20 .50
16 Mikael Renberg .30 .75
17 Marco Sturm .20 .50
18 Eric Lindros .40 1.00
19 Sean Burke .30 .75
20 Martin Brodeur 1.25 3.00
21 Boyd Devereaux .20 .50
22 Kelly Buchberger .20 .50
23 Scott Stevens .30 .75
24 Jamie Storr .30 .75
25 Anders Eriksson .20 .50
26 Gary Suter .20 .50
27 Theo Fleury .20 .50
28 Steve Leach .20 .50
29 Felix Potvin .40 1.00
30 Brett Hull .60 1.50
31 Mike Grier .20 .50
32 Cale Hulse .20 .50
33 Larry Murphy .30 .75
34 Rick Tocchet .30 .75
35 Eric Desjardins .30 .75
36 Igor Kravchuk .20 .50
37 Rob Niedermayer .20 .50
38 Bryan Smolinski .20 .50
39 Valeri Kamensky .20 .50
40 Ryan Smyth .30 .75
41 Bruce Driver .20 .50
42 Mike Johnson .20 .50
43 Rob Zamuner .20 .50
44 Steve Duchesne .20 .50
45 Martin Straka .20 .50
46 Bill Houlder .20 .50
47 Craig Conroy .20 .50
48 Guy Hebert .30 .75
49 Colin Forbes .20 .50
50 Mike Modano .60 1.50
51 Jamie Pushor .20 .50
52 Jarome Iginla .75 2.00
53 Paul Kariya .40 1.00
54 Mattias Ohlund .30 .75
55 Sergei Berezin .30 .75
56 Peter Zezel .20 .50
57 Teppo Numminen .20 .50
58 Dale Hunter .20 .50
59 Sandy Moger .20 .50
60 John LeClair .40 1.00
61 Wade Redden .20 .50
62 Patrik Elias .30 .75
63 Rob Blake .30 .75
64 Todd Marchant .20 .50
65 Claude Lemieux .20 .50
66 Trevor Kidd .30 .75
67 Sergei Fedorov .60 1.50
68 Joe Sakic 1.00 2.50
69 Derek Morris .20 .50
70 Alexei Morozov .20 .50
71 Mats Sundin .40 1.00
72 Daymond Langkow .30 .75
73 Kevin Hatcher .20 .50
74 Damian Rhodes .30 .75
75 Brian Leetch .40 1.00
76 Saku Koivu .40 1.00
77 Rick Tabaracci .30 .75
78 Bernie Nicholls .30 .75
79 Alyn McCauley .30 .75
80 Patrice Brisebois .20 .50
81 Bret Hedican .20 .50
82 Sandy McCarthy .20 .50
83 Viktor Kozlov .20 .50
84 Derek King .20 .50
85 Alexander Selivanov .20 .50
86 Mike Vernon .30 .75
87 Jeff Beukeboom .20 .50
88 Tommy Salo .30 .75
89 Adam Graves .20 .50
90 Randy McKay .20 .50
91 Rich Pilon .20 .50
92 Richard Zednik .20 .50
93 Jeff Hackett .30 .75
94 Michael Peca .20 .50
95 Brent Gilchrist .20 .50
96 Stu Grimson .20 .50
97 Bob Probert .20 .50
98 Stu Barnes .20 .50
99 Ruslan Salei .20 .50
100 Al MacInnis .30 .75
101 Ken Daneyko .20 .50
102 Paul Ranheim .20 .50
103 Marty McInnis .20 .50
104 Marian Hossa .40 1.00
105 Darren McCarty .20 .50
106 Guy Carbonneau .20 .50
107 Dallas Drake .20 .50
108 Sergei Samsonov .30 .75
109 Teemu Selanne .40 1.00
110 Checklist .20 .50
111 Jaromir Jagr 1.00 2.50
112 Joe Thornton 1.00 2.50
113 Jon Klemm .20 .50
114 Grant Fuhr .30 .75
115 Nikolai Khabibulin .30 .75
116 Rod Brind'Amour .30 .75
117 Trevor Linden .30 .75
118 Vincent Damphousse .20 .50
119 Dino Ciccarelli .30 .75
120 Pat Verbeek .20 .50
121 Sandis Ozolinsh .20 .50
122 Garth Snow .30 .75
123 Ed Belfour .40 1.00
124 Keith Primeau .20 .50
125 Jason Allison .20 .50
126 Peter Bondra .30 .75
127 Ulf Samuelsson .20 .50
128 Jeff Friesen .20 .50
129 Jason Bonsignore .20 .50
130 Daniel Alfredsson .30 .75
131 Bobby Holik .20 .50
132 Jozef Stumpel .30 .75
133 Brian Bellows .20 .50
134 Chris Osgood .30 .75
135 Alexei Zhamnov .20 .50
136 Mattias Norstrom .20 .50
137 Drake Berehowsky .20 .50
138 Mark Messier .40 1.00
139 Geoff Courtnall .20 .50
140 Marc Bureau .20 .50
141 Don Sweeney .20 .50
142 Wendel Clark .30 .75
143 Scott Niedermayer .20 .50
144 Chris Therien .20 .50
145 Kirk Muller .20 .50
146 Wayne Primeau .20 .50
147 Tony Granato .20 .50
148 Derian Hatcher .20 .50
149 Daniel Briere .20 .50
150 Fredrik Olausson .20 .50
151 Joe Juneau .30 .75
152 Michal Grosek .20 .50
153 Janne Laukkanen .20 .50
154 Keith Tkachuk .40 1.00
155 Marty McSorley .20 .50
156 Owen Nolan .30 .75
157 Mark Tinordi .20 .50
158 Steve Washburn .20 .50
159 Luke Richardson .20 .50
160 Kris King .20 .50
161 Joe Nieuwendyk .30 .75
162 Travis Green .20 .50
163 Dominik Hasek 1.00 2.50
164 Dimitri Khristich .20 .50
165 Dave Manson .20 .50
166 Chris Chelios .40 1.00
167 Claude LaPointe .20 .50
168 Kris Draper .20 .50
169 Brad Isbister .20 .50
170 Patrick Marleau .20 .50
171 Jeremy Roenick .60 1.50
172 Darren Langdon .20 .50
173 Kevin Dineen .20 .50
174 Luc Robitaille .30 .75
175 Steve Yzerman 1.50 4.00
176 Sergei Zubov .20 .50
177 Ed Jovanovski .20 .50
178 Sami Kapanen .20 .50
179 Adam Oates .30 .75
180 Pavel Bure .40 1.00
181 Chris Pronger .30 .75
182 Pat Falloon .20 .50
183 Darcy Tucker .20 .50
184 Zigmund Palffy .30 .75
185 Curtis Brown .20 .50
186 Curtis Joseph .40 1.00
187 Valeri Zelepukin .20 .50
188 Russ Courtnall .20 .50
189 Adam Foote .20 .50
190 Patrick Roy 1.50 4.00
191 Cory Stillman .20 .50
192 Alexei Zhitnik .20 .50
193 Olaf Kolzig .30 .75
194 Mark Fitzpatrick .20 .50
195 Eric Daze .30 .75
196 Zarley Zalapski .20 .50
197 Niklas Sundstrom .20 .50
198 Bryan Berard .30 .75
199 Jason Arnott .20 .50
200 Mike Richter .40 1.00
201 Ken Baumgartner .20 .50
202 Jason Dawe .20 .50
203 Nicklas Lidstrom .40 1.00
204 Tony Amonte .30 .75
205 Kjell Samuelsson .20 .50
206 Ray Bourque .60 1.50
207 Alexander Mogilny .30 .75
208 Pierre Turgeon .30 .75
209 Tom Barrasso .30 .75
210 Richard Matvichuk .20 .50
211 Sergei Krivokrasov .20 .50
212 Ted Drury .20 .50
213 Matthew Barnaby .20 .50
214 Denis Pederson .20 .50
215 John Vanbiesbrouck .30 .75
216 Brendan Shanahan .40 1.00
217 Jocelyn Thibault .30 .75
218 Nelson Emerson .20 .50
219 Wayne Gretzky 2.00 5.00
220 Checklist .20 .50
221 Ramzi Abid RC .40 1.00
222 Mark Bell RC .75 2.00
223 Michael Henrich RC .40 1.00
224 Vincent Lecavalier .75 2.00
225 Rico Fata .40 1.00
226 Bryan Allen .40 1.00
227 Daniel Tkaczuk .40 1.00
228 Brad Stuart RC .75 2.00
229 Derrick Walser RC .40 1.00
230 Jonathan Cheechoo RC 1.50 4.00
231 Sergei Varlamov .40 1.00
232 Scott Gomez RC 1.00 2.50
233 Jeff Heerema RC .40 1.00
234 David Legwand .40 1.00
235 Manny Malhotra .40 1.00
236 Michael Rupp RC .40 1.00
237 Alex Tanguay .40 1.00
238 Mathieu Biron RC .40 1.00
239 Bujar Amidovski RC .40 1.00
240 Brian Finley RC .40 1.00
241 Philippe Sauve RC .40 1.00
242 Jiri Fischer RC .40 1.00

1998-99 O-Pee-Chee Chrome Refractors

Randomly inserted in packs at the rate of 1:12, this 242-card set is a refractive parallel version of the base set.

*VETERANS: 4X TO 10X BASIC CARDS
*ROOKIES: .8X TO 2X BASIC CARDS

1998-99 O-Pee-Chee Chrome Blast From the Past

Randomly inserted into packs at the rate of 1:28, this 10-card set features reprints of the rookie cards of selected great retired as well as current stars. A refractor parallel version of this set was also produced with an insertion rate of 1:112.

COMPLETE SET (10) 60.00 120.00
*REFRACTORS: 1.2X TO 3X BASIC INSERTS
1 Wayne Gretzky 40.00 80.00
2 Mark Messier 3.00 8.00
3 Ray Bourque 5.00 12.00
4 Patrick Roy 6.00 15.00
5 Grant Fuhr 3.00 8.00
6 Brett Hull 3.00 8.00
7 Gordie Howe 8.00 20.00
8 Stan Mikita 4.00 10.00
9 Bobby Hull 5.00 12.00
10 Phil Esposito 4.00 10.00

1998-99 O-Pee-Chee Chrome Board Members

Randomly inserted into packs at the rate of 1:12, this 15-card set features color action photos of some of the great defensive superstars of the NHL. A refractor parallel version of this set was also produced with an insertion rate of 1:36.

COMPLETE SET (15) 30.00 60.00
*REFRACTORS: .8X TO 2X BASIC INSERTS
B1 Chris Pronger 2.00 5.00
B2 Chris Chelios 3.00 8.00
B3 Brian Leetch 2.00 5.00
B4 Ray Bourque 5.00 12.00
B5 Mattias Ohlund 2.00 5.00
B6 Nicklas Lidstrom 3.00 8.00
B7 Sergei Zubov 2.00 5.00
B8 Scott Niedermayer 1.25 3.00
B9 Larry Murphy 2.00 5.00
B10 Sandis Ozolinsh 1.25 3.00
B11 Rob Blake 2.00 5.00
B12 Scott Stevens 2.00 5.00
B13 Derian Hatcher 1.25 3.00
B14 Kevin Hatcher 1.25 3.00
B15 Wade Redden 1.25 3.00

1998-99 O-Pee-Chee Chrome Season's Best

Randomly inserted into packs at the rate of 1:8, this 30-card set features color action photos of top players in five distinct categories: Net Minders, the league's top goalies; Sharpshooters, the top scoring leaders; Puck Providers, assist leaders; Performers Plus, leaders in ice time by plus/minus ratio; and Ice Hot, powerful rookies. A refractor parallel version of this set was also produced with an insertion rate of 1:24.

COMPLETE SET (30) 30.00 60.00
*REFRACTORS: 1X TO 2.5X BASIC INSERTS
SB1 Dominik Hasek 2.00 5.00
SB2 Martin Brodeur 2.50 6.00
SB3 Ed Belfour 1.00 2.50
SB4 Curtis Joseph 1.00 2.50
SB5 Jeff Hackett .75 2.00
SB6 Tom Barrasso .75 2.00
SB7 Mike Johnson .40 1.00
SB8 Sergei Samsonov .75 2.00
SB9 Patrik Elias .75 2.00
SB10 Patrick Marleau .75 2.00
SB11 Mattias Ohlund .75 2.00
SB12 Marco Sturm .75 2.00
SB13 Teemu Selanne 1.00 2.50
SB14 Peter Bondra .75 2.00
SB15 Pavel Bure 1.00 2.50
SB16 John LeClair 1.00 2.50
SB17 Zigmund Palffy .75 2.00
SB18 Keith Tkachuk 1.00 2.50
SB19 Jaromir Jagr 1.50 4.00
SB20 Wayne Gretzky 6.00 15.00
SB21 Peter Forsberg 2.50 6.00
SB22 Ron Francis .40 1.00
SB23 Adam Oates .40 1.00
SB24 Jozef Stumpel .40 1.00
SB25 Chris Pronger .75 2.00
SB26 Larry Murphy .40 1.00
SB27 Jason Allison .40 1.00
SB28 John LeClair 1.00 2.50
SB29 Randy McKay .40 1.00
SB30 Dainius Zubrus .40 1.00

1999-00 O-Pee-Chee Chrome

COMPLETE SET (297) 200.00 400.00
*OPC CHROME: .6X TO 1.5X TOPPS CHROME

1999-00 O-Pee-Chee Chrome All Topps

COMPLETE SET (15) 15.00 40.00
*O-PEE-CHEE: .4X TO 1X TOPPS CHROME
STATED ODDS 1:24 OPC
*REFRACTORS: 1.2X TO 3X OPC INSERTS
REFRACTOR ODDS 1:120 OPC

1999-00 O-Pee-Chee Chrome Ice Masters

COMPLETE SET (20) 25.00 50.00
*O-PEE-CHEE: .4X TO 1X TOPPS CHROME
STATED ODDS 1:18 OPC
*REFRACTORS: 1.2X TO 3X OPC INSERTS
REFRACTOR ODDS 1:90 OPC

1999-00 O-Pee-Chee Chrome A-Men

COMPLETE SET (6) 10.00 20.00
*O-PEE-CHEE: .4X TO 1X TOPPS CHROME
STATED ODDS 1:24 OPC
*REFRACTORS: 1.2X TO 3X OPC INSERTS
REFRACTOR ODDS 1:120 OPC

1999-00 O-Pee-Chee Chrome Fantastic Finishers

COMPLETE SET (6) 6.00 15.00
*O-PEE-CHEE: .4X TO 1X TOPPS CHROME
STATED ODDS 1:24 OPC
*REFRACTORS: 1.2X TO 3X OPC INSERTS
REFRACTOR ODDS 1:120 OPC

1999-00 O-Pee-Chee Chrome Ice Futures

COMPLETE SET (6) 5.00 12.00
*O-PEE-CHEE: .4X TO 1X TOPPS CHROME
STATED ODDS 1:24 OPC
*REFRACTORS: 1.2X TO 3X OPC INSERTS
REFRACTOR ODDS 1:120 OPC

1999-00 O-Pee-Chee Chrome Positive Performers

COMPLETE SET (6) 3.00 8.00
*O-PEE-CHEE: .4X TO 1X TOPPS CHROME
STATED ODDS 1:24 OPC
*REFRACTORS: 1.2X TO 3X OPC INSERTS
REFRACTOR ODDS 1:120 OPC

1999-00 O-Pee-Chee Chrome Postmasters

COMPLETE SET (6) 10.00 20.00
*O-PEE-CHEE: .4X TO 1X TOPPS CHROME
STATED ODDS 1:24
*REFRACTORS: 1.2X TO 3X OPC INSERTS

2014-15 O-Pee-Chee Platinum

SP STATED ODDS 1:160 H, 1:320 B
1 Martin Brodeur .75 2.00
2 Alex Galchenyuk .60 1.50
3 Milan Lucic .40 1.00
4 Mikko Koivu .30 .75
5 Shane Doan .30 .75
6 Eric Staal .50 1.25
7 Brayden Schenn .40 1.00
8A Sidney Crosby 1.50 4.00
8B Sidney Crosby SP 8.00 20.00
9 Bobby Ryan .40 1.00
10 Tomas Hertl .40 1.00
11 Erik Karlsson .75 2.00
12 Scott Hartnell .40 1.00
13 Tuukka Rask .40 1.00
14 Tyler Bozak .30 .75
15 Marian Gaborik .40 1.00
16 Zach Parise .40 1.00
17 Emerson Etem .30 .75
18 Derek Stepan .40 1.00
19 Kyle Okposo .40 1.00
20A Nathan MacKinnon .75 2.00
20B Nathan MacKinnon SP 8.00 20.00
21 Roberto Luongo .40 1.00
22 Kyle Turris .40 1.00
23 Adam Henrique .40 1.00
24 Tyler Ennis .30 .75
25A Patrick Kane .75 2.00
25B Patrick Kane SP
26 Nino Niederreiter .25 .60
27A Sean Monahan .40 1.00
27B Sean Monahan SP 3.00 8.00
28 Ryan Callahan .40 1.00
29 Cam Ward .40 1.00
30 Alexander Steen .40 1.00
31 Cory Schneider .30 .75
32 Jonathan Huberdeau .40 1.00
33 Matt Beleskey .25 .60
34 Cody Hodgson .40 1.00
35 Nicklas Backstrom .60 1.50
36A Ryan Nugent-Hopkins .40 1.00
36B Ryan Nugent-Hopkins SP
37 Henrik Lundqvist .50 1.25
38 Sean Couturier .40 1.00
39 James Neal .40 1.00
40 Michael Cammalleri .30 .75
41A James van Riemsdyk .40 1.00
41B James van Riemsdyk SP 3.00 8.00
42 Aleksander Barkov .40 1.00
43A Martin St. Louis .40 1.00
43B Martin St. Louis SP 3.00 8.00
44 Kari Lehtonen .30 .75
45 Jarome Iginla .40 1.00
46 Steve Mason .30 .75
47 Gustav Nyquist .30 .75
48A Anze Kopitar .60 1.50
48B Anze Kopitar SP 6.00 15.00
49A Jonathan Toews .75 2.00
49B Jonathan Toews 6.00 15.00
50 Evander Kane .40 1.00
51 Valeri Nichushkin .30 .75
52 Valtteri Filppula .40 1.00
53 Antti Niemi .30 .75
54A Phil Kessel .50 1.25
54B Phil Kessel SP 4.00 10.00
55 Daniel Sedin .40 1.00
56 Tomas Plekanec .40 1.00
57 Jim Howard .40 1.00
58 Patrick Marleau .40 1.00
59 P.A. Parenteau .25 .60
60 Jason Spezza .40 1.00
61 Bryan Little .40 1.00
62 Steven Stamkos .75 2.00
63 Brad Richards .40 1.00
64 Marian Hossa .30 .75
65 Thomas Vanek .40 1.00
66 Marc-Edouard Vlasic .25 .60
67 Braden Holtby .60 1.50
68 Jeff Skinner .40 1.00
69 Paul Stastny .40 1.00
70 Henrik Sedin .40 1.00
71 T.J. Oshie .60 1.50
72A Seth Jones .30 .75
72B Seth Jones SP 2.50 6.00
73 Blake Wheeler .40 1.00
74 Kris Letang .40 1.00
75 Max Pacioretty .40 1.00
76A Carey Price 1.25 3.00
76B Carey Price SP 12.00 30.00
77 Ryan Johansen .50 1.25
78A Matt Duchene .40 1.00
78B Matt Duchene SP 3.00 8.00
79 David Perron .25 .60
80 Ryan Kesler .40 1.00
81 Ondrej Pavelec .40 1.00
82 Chris Kunitz .40 1.00
83 Patric Hornqvist .30 .75
84 Rick Nash .40 1.00
85 Brendan Gallagher .40 1.00
86A Pavel Datsyuk .50 1.25
86B Pavel Datsyuk SP 4.00 10.00
87 Joel Ward .25 .60
88 Sergei Bobrovsky .40 1.00
89 Patrick Sharp .40 1.00
90 Luke Schenn .25 .60
91A Joe Pavelski .40 1.00
91B Joe Pavelski SP 3.00 8.00
92 David Backes .40 1.00
93 Ben Bishop .40 1.00
94A Claude Giroux .40 1.00
94B Claude Giroux SP 3.00 8.00
95 Dustin Byfuglien .40 1.00
96 Tomas Tatar .30 .75
97 Tyler Toffoli .40 1.00
98 Nail Yakupov .30 .75
99 Corey Crawford .50 1.25
100A Logan Couture .40 1.00
100B Logan Couture SP 3.00 8.00
101 Patrice Bergeron .50 1.25
102A Evgeni Malkin 1.25 3.00
102B Evgeni Malkin SP 10.00 25.00
103 Ryan Miller .40 1.00
104 Joe Thornton .40 1.00
105 Drew Doughty .40 1.00
106 Semyon Varlamov .40 1.00
107A Dion Phaneuf .40 1.00
107B Dion Phaneuf SP 3.00 8.00
108 Mark Scheifele .50 1.25
109A Taylor Hall .75 2.00
109B Taylor Hall SP 6.00 15.00
110A Shea Weber .30 .75
110B Shea Weber SP 2.50 6.00
111 Ryan Strome .30 .75
112 Henrik Zetterberg .50 1.25
113 Jason Pominville .30 .75
114 Nazem Kadri .40 1.00
115A Alexander Ovechkin 1.50 4.00
115B Alexander Ovechkin SP
116 Jeff Carter .40 1.00
117 Jakub Voracek .40 1.00
118 Craig Anderson .40 1.00
119 Tyler Johnson .40 1.00
120 Gabriel Landeskog .30 .75
121A Pekka Rinne .50 1.25
121B Pekka Rinne SP 4.00 10.00
122 Keith Yandle .40 1.00
123 Ryan Getzlaf .60 1.50
124A Jonathan Bernier .40 1.00
124B Jonathan Bernier SP 3.00 8.00
125 Duncan Keith .40 1.00
126 Mike Smith .40 1.00
127A Tyler Seguin .60 1.50
127B Tyler Seguin SP 5.00 12.00
128 Alex Pietrangelo .30 .75
129 John Tavares .75 2.00
130 Jonathan Quick .60 1.50
131 Tyler Myers .30 .75
132 Jaromir Jagr 1.00 2.50
133 Marc-Andre Fleury .60 1.50
134 Zdeno Chara .40 1.00
135 Frederik Andersen .30 .75
136 Jordan Eberle .40 1.00
137 Ryan O'Reilly .40 1.00
138 Jiri Hudler .30 .75
139 Wayne Simmonds .50 1.25
140 Vladimir Tarasenko .60 1.50
141 Brandon Dubinsky .30 .75
142 Mats Zuccarello .40 1.00
143 Mike Green .40 1.00
144 Ondrej Palat .30 .75
145 Corey Perry .40 1.00
146 Alexandre Burrows .40 1.00
147 David Krejci .40 1.00
148 Antoine Vermette .25 .60
149 P.K. Subban .60 1.50
150 Jamie Benn .50 1.25
151 Scott Darling RC 2.00 5.00
152 Mirco Mueller RC .75 2.00
153A Ty Rattie RC 1.00 2.50
153B Ty Rattie SP 4.00 10.00
154A Sven Andrighetto RC 1.00 2.50
154B Josh McCabe SP 3.00 8.00
155A Vincent Trocheck RC 1.00 2.50
155B Vincent Trocheck SP 4.00 10.00
156 Stuart Percy RC .75 2.00
157A Teuvo Teravainen RC 1.25 3.00
157B Teuvo Teravainen SP 5.00 12.00
158A Aaron Ekblad RC 3.00 8.00
158B Aaron Ekblad SP 12.00 30.00
159A Leon Draisaitl RC 4.00 10.00
159B Leon Draisaitl SP
160 Josh Jooris RC .75 2.00
161A Calle Jarnkrok RC .75 2.00
161B Calle Jarnkrok SP 3.00 8.00
162A Brandon Gormley RC .75 2.00
162B Brandon Gormley SP 3.00 8.00
163 Andre Burakovsky RC 1.25 3.00
164 Adam Lowry RC .75 2.00
165 Jori Lehtera RC 1.00 2.50
166 Andrei Vasilevskiy RC 2.50 6.00
167A Adam Clendening RC .75 2.00
167B Oscar Klefbom SP 6.00 15.00
168 Shayne Gostisbehere RC 3.00 8.00
169A Anthony Duclair RC 1.25 3.00
169B Anthony Duclair SP
170 Ryan Sproul RC .75 2.00
171A Alexander Khokhlachev RC .75 2.00
171B Alexander Khokhlachev SP 3.00 8.00
172 Barclay Goodrow RC .75 2.00
173A Bo Horvat RC 2.50 6.00
173B Bo Horvat SP 10.00 25.00
174 Derrick Pouliot RC 1.00 2.50
175A Corban Knight RC .75 2.00
175B Corban Knight SP 3.00 8.00
176 Curtis McKenzie RC .60 1.50
177 David Pastrnak RC 3.00 8.00
178 Kevin Hayes RC 2.50 6.00
179 Kerby Rychel RC .60 1.50
180 Brett Ritchie RC .75 2.00
181A Rocco Grimaldi RC .75 2.00
181B Joey Hishon SP 4.00 10.00
182 Tobias Rieder RC .75 2.00
183A Evgeny Kuznetsov RC 3.00 8.00
183B Evgeny Kuznetsov SP 10.00 25.00
184 Jiri Sekac RC .75 2.00
185A Jonathan Drouin RC 2.00 5.00
185B Jonathan Drouin SP
186A Curtis Lazar RC 1.00 2.50
186B Curtis Lazar SP 4.00 10.00
187 Marko Dano RC .75 2.00
188A Alexander Wennberg RC 1.50 4.00
188B Alexander Wennberg SP 6.00 15.00
189 John Klingberg RC 2.50 6.00
190 Victor Rask RC .75 2.00
191A Damon Severson RC .75 2.00
191B Damon Severson SP
192A Griffin Reinhart RC 1.00 2.50
192B Griffin Reinhart SP 4.00 10.00
193 Markus Granlund RC 1.25 3.00
194A Johnny Gaudreau RC 2.50 6.00
194B Johnny Gaudreau SP 10.00 25.00
195A Teemu Pulkkinen RC 1.00 2.50
195B Teemu Pulkkinen SP 4.00 10.00
196 Vladislav Namestnikov RC 1.25 3.00
197A Darnell Nurse RC 2.50 6.00
197B Darnell Nurse SP 10.00 25.
198A Sam Reinhart RC 2.50 6.
198B Sam Reinhart SP 10.00 25.
199A Seth Griffith RC 1.00 2.
199B Seth Griffith SP 4.00 10.
200 William Karlsson RC 3.00 8.

2014-15 O-Pee-Chee Platinum Black Ice

*VETS/65: 5X TO 12X BASIC CARDS
*ROOKIES/65:2.5X TO 6X BASIC CARDS
1 Martin Brodeur 15.00 40.
8 Sidney Crosby 30:00 60.
35 Nicklas Backstrom 8.00 20.
115 Alexander Ovechkin 15.00 40.
157 Teuvo Teravainen 30.00 60.
168 Shayne Gostisbehere 20.00 40.

2014-15 O-Pee-Chee Platinum Blue Cubes

*VETS/65: 4X TO 10X BASIC CARDS
*ROOKIES/65: 2X TO 5X BASIC CARDS
1 Martin Brodeur 8.00 20.
8 Sidney Crosby 10.00 25.
35 Nicklas Backstrom 6.00 15.

2014-15 O-Pee-Chee Platinum Rainbow

*RAINBOW: .5X TO X 1.2BASIC CARDS
35 Nicklas Backstrom .75 2.

2014-15 O-Pee-Chee Platinum Red Prism

*VETS/135: 2X TO 5X BASIC CARDS
*ROOKIES/135: 1X TO 2.5X BASIC CARDS
1 Martin Brodeur 8.00 20.
35 Nicklas Backstrom 3.00 8.

2014-15 O-Pee-Chee Platinum Seismic Gold

*VETS/50: 4X TO 10X BASIC CARDS
*ROOKIES/50: 2X TO 5X BASIC CARDS
1 Martin Brodeur 10.00 25.
8 Sidney Crosby 10.00 25.
35 Nicklas Backstrom 6.00 15.
76 Carey Price 12.00 30.
132 Jaromir Jagr 10.00 25.
177 David Pastrnak 15.00 40.
194 Johnny Gaudreau 12.00 30.

2014-15 O-Pee-Chee Platinum Legends

LS1 Wayne Gretzky 8.00 20.
LS2 Steve Yzerman 6.00 15.
LS3 Bobby Orr 6.00 15.
LS4 Pierre Turgeon 2.00 5.
LS5 Brett Hull 2.00 5.
LS6 Doug Gilmour 2.50 6.
LS7 Nicklas Lidstrom 2.00 5.
LS8 Dominik Hasek 2.50 6.
LS9 Guy Carbonneau 2.00 5.
LS10 Stan Mikita 2.50 6.
LS11 Marcel Dionne 2.50 6.
LS12 Phil Esposito 3.00 8.
LS13 Larry Robinson 2.00 5.
LS14 Ray Bourque 3.00 8.
LS15 Mike Gartner 2.00 5.
LS16 Mario Lemieux 6.00 15.
LS17 Mark Messier 2.00 5.
LS18 Theoren Fleury 2.50 6.
LS19 Patrick Roy 8.00 20.
LS20 Jean Beliveau 2.00 5.

2014-15 O-Pee-Chee Platinum Retro

STATED ODDS 1:3 H, 1:6 B
*RAIN. VETS: 1.2X TO 3X BASIC INSERT
*RAIN. ROOKIES: .6X TO 1.5X BASIC INSERT
*RED VETS: 1.5X TO 4X BASIC INSERTS
*RED ROOK.: .75X TO 8X BASIC INSERTS
*BLACK VETS/100: 2X TO 5X BASIC INSERTS
*BLACK ROOK./100: 1X TO 2.5X BASIC INSERTS
1 Sidney Crosby 2.00 5.0
2 Ryan Getzlaf .75 2.0
3 Claude Giroux .50 1.2
4 T.J. Oshie .75 2.0
5 Mikko Koivu .40 1.0
6 David Backes .50 1.2
7 Sean Monahan .50 1.2
8 Anze Kopitar .75 2.0
9 Ondrej Palat .40 1.0
10 Martin St. Louis .50 1.2
11 James van Riemsdyk .50 1.2
12 Tyler Seguin .75 2.0
13 Johan Franzen .50 1.2
14 Shea Weber .40 1.0
15 Jonathan Toews 1.00 2.5
16 John Tavares 1.00 2.5
17 Evgeni Malkin 1.50 4.0
18 Jonathan Bernier .50 1.2
19 Joe Pavelski .50 1.2
20 Ryan Nugent-Hopkins .50 1.2
21 Seth Jones .40 1.0
22 Matt Duchene .50 1.2
23 Patrick Sharp .50 1.2
24 Logan Couture .50 1.2
25 Phil Kessel .60 1.5
26 Pavel Datsyuk .60 1.5
27 Nathan MacKinnon 1.00 2.5
28 Carey Price 1.50 4.0
29 Pekka Rinne .60 1.5
30 Dion Phaneuf .50 1.2
31 Tomas Hertl .50 1.2
32 Nicklas Backstrom .75 2.0
33 Tuukka Rask .50 1.2
34 Tomas Plekanec .50 1.2
35 Patrick Kane 1.00 2.5
36 Paul Stastny .50 1.2
37 Duncan Keith .50 1.2
38 Taylor Hall 1.00 2.5
39 Kari Lehtonen .40 1.0
40 Adam Henrique .50 1.2
41 Cody Hodgson .50 1.2
42 Henrik Zetterberg .60 1.5
43 Ryan Miller .50 1.2
44 Jason Spezza .50 1.2
45 Chris Kunitz .50 1.2
46 Gustav Nyquist .40 1.0
47 Sergei Bobrovsky .50 1.2
48 Eric Staal .60 1.5
49 Zdeno Chara .50 1.2
50 Antti Niemi .40 1.0
51 Evander Kane .50 1.2
52 Bobby Ryan .50 1.2
53 Zach Parise .50 1.2
54 Keith Yandle .50 1.2
55 Corey Perry .50 1.2
56 Patrice Bergeron .60 1.5
57 Marian Gaborik .50 1.2
58 Shane Doan .40 1.0

Jonathan Quick .75 2.00
Dustin Byfuglien .50 1.25
Jarome Iginla .50 1.25
Alexander Ovechkin 2.00 5.00
Drew Doughty .50 1.25
Jordan Eberle .50 1.25
Jamie Benn .60 1.50
Alex Galchenyuk .75 2.00
Mats Zuccarello .50 1.25
Henrik Lundqvist .60 1.50
P.K. Subban .75 2.00
Steven Stamkos 1.00 2.50
Kevin Hayes 3.00 8.00
Darnell Nurse 3.00 8.00
Corban Knight 1.00 2.50
Bo Horvat 3.00 8.00
Sam Reinhart 3.00 8.00
Seth Griffith 1.25 3.00
Alexander Wennberg 2.00 5.00
Jiri Sekac 1.00 2.50
Leon Draisaitl 5.00 12.00
Teuvo Teravainen 1.50 4.00
Griffin Reinhart 1.25 3.00
Brandon Gormley 1.00 2.50
Stuart Percy 1.00 2.50
William Karlsson 4.00 10.00
Aaron Ekblad 4.00 10.00
Evgeny Kuznetsov 4.00 10.00
Jori Lehtera 1.25 3.00
Oscar Klefbom 2.00 5.00
Curtis Lazar 1.25 3.00
Johnny Gaudreau 3.00 8.00
Vincent Trocheck 1.25 3.00
Mirco Mueller 1.00 2.50
Chris Tierney 1.00 2.50
Calle Jarnkrok 1.00 2.50
Andre Burakovsky 1.50 4.00
Alexander Khokhlachev 1.00 2.50
Teemu Pulkkinen 1.25 3.00
Joey Hishon 1.25 3.00
Ty Rattie 1.25 3.00
Anthony Duclair 1.50 4.00

2014-15 O-Pee-Chee Platinum Retro Rainbow Autographs

TATED ODDS 1:160
avid Backes 6.00 15.00
nze Kopitar 10.00 25.00
Tyler Seguin 15.00 40.00
Shea Weber 5.00 12.00
Jonathan Toews 60.00 120.00
John Tavares 15.00 40.00
Patrick Sharp 20.00 50.00
Pavel Datsyuk 15.00 40.00
Carey Price 75.00 150.00
Tomas Hertl 6.00 15.00
Taylor Hall 12.00 30.00
Kari Lehtonen 5.00 12.00
Adam Henrique 6.00 15.00
Gustav Nyquist 5.00 12.00
Eric Staal 8.00 20.00
Bobby Ryan 6.00 15.00
Zach Parise 8.00 20.00
Corey Perry 75.00 150.00
Jarome Iginla 12.00 30.00
Alexander Ovechkin 30.00 80.00
Darnell Nurse 15.00 30.00
Bo Horvat 20.00 50.00
Sam Reinhart 20.00 50.00
Seth Griffith 8.00 20.00
Alexander Wennberg 12.00 30.00
Leon Draisaitl 30.00 80.00
Teuvo Teravainen 10.00 25.00
Brandon Gormley 6.00 15.00
Stuart Percy 6.00 15.00
William Karlsson 25.00 60.00
Aaron Ekblad 25.00 60.00
Evgeny Kuznetsov 25.00 60.00
Jori Lehtera 8.00 20.00
Curtis Lazar 8.00 20.00
Johnny Gaudreau 40.00 100.00
Mirco Mueller 6.00 15.00
Calle Jarnkrok 6.00 15.00
Alexander Khokhlachev 6.00 15.00
Joey Hishon 8.00 20.00
Ty Rattie 8.00 20.00
Anthony Duclair 10.00 25.00

2014-15 O-Pee-Chee Platinum Rookie Autographs

1 Jonathan Drouin 20.00 50.00
2 Bo Horvat 15.00 40.00
3 Aaron Ekblad 12.00 30.00
4 Alexander Wennberg 6.00 15.00
5 Leon Draisaitl 25.00 60.00
6 Griffin Reinhart EXCH 4.00 10.00
7 Johnny Gaudreau 20.00 50.00
8 Teuvo Teravainen 5.00 12.00
9 Curtis Lazar 4.00 10.00
10 Evgeny Kuznetsov 15.00 40.00
11 Darnell Nurse 10.00 25.00
12 Stuart Percy 3.00 8.00
13 Ty Rattie 4.00 10.00
14 Brandon Gormley 3.00 8.00
15 Alexander Khokhlachev 3.00 8.00
16 Jiri Sekac EXCH 3.00 8.00
17 Seth Griffith 4.00 10.00
18 Anthony Duclair 5.00 12.00
19 Marko Dano 3.00 8.00
20 Adam Lowry 3.00 8.00
21 Andre Burakovsky EXCH 5.00 12.00
22 Victor Rask 3.00 8.00
23 Jori Lehtera 4.00 10.00
24 Mirco Mueller 3.00 8.00
25 Damon Severson 3.00 8.00
26 Calle Jarnkrok 3.00 8.00
27 Kevin Hayes 15.00 40.00
28 Corban Knight EXCH 3.00 8.00
29 Chris Tierney 3.00 8.00
30 William Karlsson 15.00 40.00

2014-15 O-Pee-Chee Platinum Rookie Autographs Black Ice

Jonathan Drouin 40.00 100.00
Bo Horvat 30.00 80.00
Leon Draisaitl 80.00 150.00
Johnny Gaudreau 40.00 100.00
Jiri Sekac EXCH 8.00 20.00
Andre Burakovsky EXCH 20.00 50.00
Kevin Hayes 25.00 60.00

2014-15 O-Pee-Chee Platinum Rookie Autographs Blue Rainbow

UE/25: 1X TO 2.5X BASIC AU
Jonathan Drouin 100.00 200.00
Bo Horvat 60.00 150.00
Aaron Ekblad 100.00 200.00
Leon Draisaitl 150.00 250.00

RA7 Johnny Gaudreau 80.00 150.00
RA21 Andre Burakovsky EXCH 50.00 120.00
RA27 Kevin Hayes 40.00 100.00

2014-15 O-Pee-Chee Platinum Rookie Autographs Red Rainbow

*RED/50: 1X TO 2.5X BASIC AU
RA1 Jonathan Drouin 50.00 120.00
RA2 Bo Horvat 40.00 100.00
RA3 Aaron Ekblad 30.00 80.00
RA5 Leon Draisaitl 90.00 150.00
RA7 Johnny Gaudreau 25.00 60.00
RA21 Andre Burakovsky EXCH 25.00 60.00
RA27 Kevin Hayes 30.00 80.00

2014-15 O-Pee-Chee Platinum Superstars

PS1 John Tavares 4.00 10.00
PS2 Nathan MacKinnon 4.00 10.00
PS3 Claude Giroux 2.00 5.00
PS4 Zach Parise 2.00 5.00
PS5 Jonathan Toews 4.00 10.00
PS6 Patrick Kane 4.00 10.00
PS7 Phil Kessel 2.50 6.00
PS8 Shea Weber 1.50 4.00
PS9 Martin Brodeur 4.00 10.00
PS10 Martin St. Louis 2.00 5.00
PS11 Patrick Marleau 2.00 5.00
PS12 Carey Price 6.00 15.00
PS13 Tyler Seguin 3.00 8.00
PS14 Taylor Hall 4.00 10.00
PS15 Evgeni Malkin 6.00 15.00
PS16 Anze Kopitar 3.00 8.00
PS17 Corey Perry 2.00 5.00
PS18 Matt Duchene 2.00 5.00
PS19 Joe Pavelski 2.00 5.00
PS20 Jarome Iginla 2.00 5.00

2015-16 O-Pee-Chee Platinum

SP STATED ODDS 1:160 H, 1:320 B
GRP A STATED ODDS 1:2,932
GRP B STATED ODDS 1:2,697
GRP C STATED ODDS 1:704
GRP D STATED ODDS 1:420
GRP E STATED ODDS 1:170
GRP F STATED ODDS 1:91
*PURPLE VETS: 8X TO 20X BASIC CARDS
1 Sidney Crosby 1.50 4.00
2 Oliver Ekman-Larsson .30 .75
3 Corey Crawford .50 1.25
4 Ryan Nugent-Hopkins .40 1.00
5 Rick Nash .40 1.00
6 Loui Eriksson .30 .75
7 Filip Forsberg .50 1.25
8 Drew Doughty .40 1.00
9 Patric Hornqvist .30 .75
10 John Tavares .75 2.00
11 Jason Spezza .30 .75
12 Mike Hoffman .30 .75
13 Mike Smith .40 1.00
14 Anders Lee .40 1.00
15 Erik Karlsson .75 2.00
16 Derek Stepan .40 1.00
17 Teuvo Teravainen .40 1.00
18 Radim Vrbata .30 .75
19 Joe Thornton .40 1.00
20 Corey Perry .40 1.00
21 Nazem Kadri .30 .75
22 Daniel Sedin .40 1.00
23 James Neal .40 1.00
24 Brian Elliott .30 .75
25 Evgeni Malkin 1.25 3.00
26 Michael Cammalleri .30 .75
27 Mark Scheifele .50 1.25
28 Keith Yandle .40 1.00
29 Taylor Hall .75 2.00
30 Claude Giroux .40 1.00
31 Jonas Hiller .30 .75
32 Frederik Andersen .30 .75
33 Henrik Sedin .40 1.00
34 Max Pacioretty .40 1.00
35 Zach Parise .40 1.00
36 Mark Stone .40 1.00
37 Jiri Hudler .30 .75
38 Jaroslav Halak .30 .75
39 Cam Ward .40 1.00
40 Henrik Zetterberg .50 1.25
41 Shane Doan .30 .75
42 Tyler Bozak .30 .75
43 Semyon Varlamov .40 1.00
44 Vladimir Tarasenko .60 1.50
45 Jamie Benn .60 1.50
46 Ryan Strome .30 .75
47 Nino Niederreiter .25 .60
48 Andrew Hammond 1.25 3.00
49 Kyle Okposo .30 .75
50 Steven Stamkos .75 2.00
51 Aaron Ekblad .40 1.00
52 Jonathan Quick .60 1.50
53 Ryan Kesler .40 1.00
54 Kris Letang .40 1.00
55 Tuukka Rask .40 1.00
56 Brayden Schenn .40 1.00
57 Blake Wheeler .40 1.00
58 Nail Yakupov .30 .75
59 James van Riemsdyk .40 1.00
60 Ryan Miller .40 1.00
61 Bo Horvat .60 1.50
62 Steve Mason .30 .75
63 Ryan O'Reilly .40 1.00
64 Sam Reinhart .40 1.00
65 Johnny Gaudreau .60 1.50
66 Victor Hedman .50 1.25
67 Tyler Johnson .30 .75
68 Jaromir Jagr 1.00 2.50
69 Matt Duchene .40 1.00
70 Pavel Datsyuk .50 1.25
71 Jaden Schwartz .50 1.25
72 Pekka Rinne .50 1.25
73 Eric Staal .50 1.25
74 Patrice Bergeron .50 1.25
75 Carey Price 1.25 3.00
76 Joe Pavelski .40 1.00
77 Jeff Carter .30 .75
78 Kari Lehtonen .30 .75
79 Milan Lucic .30 .75
80 P.K. Subban .60 1.50
81 Jonathan Bernier .40 1.00
82 Andrew Ladd .40 1.00
83 Patrik Elias .40 1.00
84 Patrick Sharp .40 1.00
85 Jarome Iginla .40 1.00
86 Nicklas Backstrom .60 1.50
87 Shea Weber .40 1.00
88 Sergei Bobrovsky .40 1.00
89 David Backes .40 1.00
90 Tyler Seguin .60 1.50
91 Brendan Gallagher .50 1.25
92 Nick Foligno .30 .75
93 Evgeny Kuznetsov .60 1.50
94 Nikita Kucherov .60 1.50
95 Nathan MacKinnon .75 2.00
96 Justin Abdelkader .30 .75
97 Braden Holtby .60 1.50
98 Adam Henrique .40 1.00
99 Ryan Johansen .50 1.25
100 Henrik Lundqvist .50 1.25
101 Thomas Vanek .40 1.00
102 Brad Marchand .50 1.25
103 Jim Howard .40 1.00
104 Matt Moulson .30 .75
105 Anze Kopitar .60 1.50
106 Martin Jones .40 1.00
107 Mark Giordano .40 1.00
108 Kyle Turris .30 .75
109 Gabriel Landeskog .40 1.00
110 Roberto Luongo .40 1.00
111 Mike Ribeiro .30 .75
112 Zemgus Girgensons .30 .75
113 Cam Talbot .50 1.25
114 Marc-Andre Fleury .60 1.50
115 Chris Kreider .40 1.00
116 Derick Brassard .40 1.00
117 Sean Monahan .40 1.00
118 Logan Couture .40 1.00
119 Marcus Johansson .30 .75
120 Patrick Kane .75 2.00
121 Justin Faulk .40 1.00
122 Ben Bishop .40 1.00
123 Tomas Plekanec .40 1.00
124 Duncan Keith .40 1.00
125 Jonathan Toews .75 2.00
126 Bryan Little .30 .75
127 Jason Pominville .30 .75
128 Alex Galchenyuk .50 1.25
129 Cory Schneider .40 1.00
130 Phil Kessel .60 1.50
131 Marian Gaborik .40 1.00
132 Alexandre Burrows .30 .75
133 Wayne Simmonds .50 1.25
134 Mike Green .40 1.00
135 Bobby Ryan .30 .75
136 Matt Beleskey .25 .60
137 John Carlson .50 1.25
138 Jakub Voracek .40 1.00
139 Jordan Eberle .40 1.00
140 Ryan Getzlaf .60 1.50
141 Alexander Steen .40 1.00
142 Brandon Saad .40 1.00
143 Gustav Nyquist .40 1.00
144 Dion Phaneuf .40 1.00
145 Marian Hossa .30 .75
146 Dustin Byfuglien .40 1.00
147 Devan Dubnyk .40 1.00
148 Tyler Ennis .30 .75
149 Ondrej Pavelec .40 1.00
150 Alexander Ovechkin 1.50 4.00
151 Mike Gartner 1.50 4.00
152 Doug Weight 1.50 4.00
153 Ron Francis 2.00 5.00
154 Felix Potvin 2.50 6.00
155 Mike Bossy 1.50 4.00
156 Grant Fuhr 1.50 4.00
157 Denis Potvin 1.50 4.00
158 John Vanbiesbrouck 1.50 4.00
159 Marcel Dionne 2.00 5.00
160 Cam Neely 1.50 4.00
161 Malcolm Subban C AU RC 15.00 40.00
162 Kevin Fiala E AU RC 6.00 15.00
163 Jacob de la Rose E AU RC 6.00 15.00
164 Henrik Samuelsson F AU RC 5.00 12.00
165 Dylan Larkin D AU RC 30.00 80.00
166 Sergei Plotnikov F AU RC 5.00 12.00
167 Nick Shore A AU RC 6.00 15.00
168 Matt Puempel E AU RC 5.00 12.00
169 Shane Prince E AU RC 5.00 12.00
170 Sam Bennett D AU RC 8.00 20.00
171 Nick Cousins E AU RC 6.00 15.00
172 Antoine Bibeau F AU RC 6.00 15.00
173 Nikolaj Ehlers D AU RC 12.00 30.00
174 Ryan Hartman F AU RC 8.00 20.00
175 Jordan Weal F AU RC 6.00 15.00
176 Jake Virtanen D AU RC 8.00 20.00
177 Ronalds Kenins F AU RC 6.00 15.00
178 Nicolas Petan D AU RC 6.00 15.00
179 Jared McCann E AU RC 8.00 20.00
180 Robby Fabbri C AU RC 8.00 20.00
181 Mikko Rantanen C AU RC 12.00 30.00
182 Nikolay Goldobin E AU RC 6.00 15.00
183 Daniel Sprong E AU RC 12.00 30.00
184 Emile Poirier F AU RC 6.00 15.00
185 Viktor Arvidsson F AU RC 8.00 20.00
186 Artemi Panarin B AU RC 20.00 50.00
187 Noah Hanifin A AU RC 8.00 20.00
188 Connor Hellebuyck A AU RC 15.00 40.00
189 Max Domi B AU RC 25.00 60.00
190 Connor McDavid C AU RC 175.00 250.00

2015-16 O-Pee-Chee Platinum Black Ice

*VETS/99: 5X TO 12X BASIC CARDS
SP/50: 1.5X TO 4X BASIC CARDS
*ROOKIES/50: .75X TO 2X BASIC CARDS
165 Dylan Larkin AU 100.00 200.00
174 Ryan Hartman AU 15.00 40.00
190 Connor McDavid AU 400.00 500.00

2015-16 O-Pee-Chee Platinum Rainbow

*VETS: .5X TO 1.25X BASIC CARDS
*SP: .5X TO 1.25X BASIC CARDS
*ROOKIES: .5X TO 1.25X BASIC CARDS
*VETS STATED ODDS 1:5 H 1:10 B
*SP STATED ODDS 1:160 H 1:1,600 B
RC GRP A STATED ODDS 1:38,354
RC GRP B STATED ODDS 1:10,201
RC GRP C STATED ODDS 1:1,073
RC GRP D STATED ODDS 1:693
RC GRP E STATED ODDS 1:215
NO GRP A PRICING DUE TO SCARCITY
3 Corey Crawford .60 1.50
86 Nicklas Backstrom .75 2.00
93 Evgeny Kuznetsov .75 2.00
165 Dylan Larkin C AU 25.00 60.00
174 Ryan Hartman E AU 6.00 15.00
190 Connor McDavid B AU 350.00 500.00

2015-16 O-Pee-Chee Platinum Red Prism

*VETS/149: 2X TO 5X BASIC CARDS
SP/75: 1X TO 2.5X BASIC CARDS
*ROOKIES/75: .6X TO 1.6X BASIC CARDS
3 Corey Crawford 2.50 6.00
86 Nicklas Backstrom 3.00 8.00
93 Evgeny Kuznetsov 3.00 8.00
165 Dylan Larkin AU 60.00 150.00
174 Ryan Hartman AU 12.00 30.00
190 Connor McDavid AU 325.00 425.00

2015-16 O-Pee-Chee Platinum Traxx

*SINGLES: 1.5X TO 4X BASIC INSERTS
*SP: .6X TO 1.5X BASIC INSERTS
*RC: .6X TO 1.5X BASIC INSERTS
STATED ODD 1:10 H 1:10 B
RC PRINT RUN 125 SER. #'D SETS
3 Corey Crawford 2.00 5.00
86 Nicklas Backstrom 2.50 6.00
93 Evgeny Kuznetsov 2.50 6.00
165 Dylan Larkin AU 30.00 80.00
174 Ryan Hartman AU 10.00 25.00
190 Connor McDavid AU 200.00 400.00

2015-16 O-Pee-Chee Platinum White Ice

*VETS: 2X TO 5X BASIC CARDS
*SP: 1X TO 2.5X BASIC CARDS
*ROOKIES: .6X TO 1.5X BASIC CARDS
VETS STATED PRINT RUN 199 SER.#'d SETS
SP AND RC STATED PRINT RUN 99 SER.#'D SETS
3 Corey Crawford 2.50 6.00
86 Nicklas Backstrom 3.00 8.00
93 Evgeny Kuznetsov 3.00 8.00
165 Dylan Larkin AU 75.00 150.00
174 Ryan Hartman AU 12.00 30.00
190 Connor McDavid AU 550.00 650.00

2015-16 O-Pee-Chee Platinum Marquee Rookies

RANDOM INSERTS IN PACKS
*RAINBOW: .5X TO 1.2X BASIC INSERTS
M1 Connor McDavid 10.00 25.00
M2 Emile Poirier 1.25 3.00
M3 Ryan Hartman 1.50 4.00
M4 Jacob de la Rose 1.25 3.00
M5 Malcolm Subban 3.00 8.00
M6 Kevin Fiala 1.25 3.00
M7 Garret Sparks 1.50 4.00
M8 Taylor Leier 1.25 3.00
M9 Shane Prince 1.00 2.50
M10 Sam Bennett 1.50 4.00
M11 Matt Puempel 1.00 2.50
M12 Brock McGinn 1.25 3.00
M13 Linus Ullmark 1.50 4.00
M14 Devin Shore 1.25 3.00
M15 Daniel Sprong 2.50 6.00
M16 Joonas Donskoi 1.25 3.00
M17 Mattias Janmark 1.25 3.00
M18 Nick Shore 1.25 3.00
M19 Nikolay Goldobin 1.25 3.00
M20 Jared McCann 1.25 3.00
M21 Hunter Shinkaruk 1.25 3.00
M22 Sergei Plotnikov 1.00 2.50
M23 Ben Hutton 1.25 3.00
M24 Colton Parayko 1.50 4.00
M25 Artemi Panarin 4.00 10.00
M26 Robby Fabbri 1.50 4.00
M27 Juuse Saros 1.50 4.00
M28 Stanislav Galiev 1.25 3.00
M29 Matt Murray 6.00 15.00
M30 Max Domi 2.50 6.00
M31 Chandler Stephenson 1.25 3.00
M32 Mike Condon 1.25 3.00
M33 Andreas Athanasiou 3.00 8.00
M34 Oscar Lindberg 1.25 3.00
M35 Brendan Gaunce 1.50 4.00
M36 Connor Hellebuyck 3.00 8.00
M37 Zachary Fucale 1.25 3.00
M38 Nikolaj Ehlers 2.50 6.00
M39 Mike McCarron 1.50 4.00
M40 Jake Virtanen 1.50 4.00
M41 Noah Hanifin 1.50 4.00
M42 Mikko Rantanen 2.50 6.00
M43 Nicolas Petan 1.25 3.00
M44 Gustav Olofsson 1.25 3.00
M45 Dylan Larkin 4.00 10.00
M46 Charles Hudon 1.25 3.00
M47 Adam Pelech 1.00 2.50
M48 Andrew Copp 1.25 3.00
M49 Nick Ritchie 1.25 3.00
M50 Jack Eichel 5.00 12.00

2015-16 O-Pee-Chee Platinum Marquee Rookies Black Ice

*BLACK ICE: 1X TO 2.5X BASIC INSERTS
RANDOM INSERTS IN PACKS
STATED PRINT RUN 99 SER.#'d SETS
M1 Connor McDavid 60.00 120.00
M3 Ryan Hartman 5.00 12.00
M29 Matt Murray 40.00 80.00
M45 Dylan Larkin 25.00 60.00

2015-16 O-Pee-Chee Platinum Marquee Rookies Blue Cubes

*SINGLES: 1.25X TO 3X BASIC INSERTS
RANDOM INSERTS IN HOBBY PACKS
STATED PRINT RUN 75 SER.#'D SETS
M1 Connor McDavid 125.00 200.00
M3 Ryan Hartman 6.00 15.00
M29 Matt Murray 40.00 80.00

2015-16 O-Pee-Chee Platinum Marquee Rookies Red Prism

*RED PRISM: 1X TO 2.5X BASIC INSERTS
RANDOM INSERTS IN PACKS
STATED PRINT RUN 149 SER.#'d SETS
M1 Connor McDavid 60.00 120.00
M3 Ryan Hartman 5.00 12.00
M29 Matt Murray 30.00 60.00

2015-16 O-Pee-Chee Platinum Marquee Rookies Seismic Gold

*SINGLES: 1.5X TO 4X BASIC INSERTS
RANDOM INSERTS IN HOBBY PACKS
STATED PRINT RUN 50 SER.#'d SETS
M1 Connor McDavid 175.00 250.00
M3 Ryan Hartman 8.00 20.00
M25 Artemi Panarin 30.00 80.00
M29 Matt Murray 80.00 150.00
M45 Dylan Larkin 30.00 80.00
M50 Jack Eichel 30.00 80.00

2015-16 O-Pee-Chee Platinum Marquee Rookies Traxx

*TRAXX: .6X TO 1.5X BASIC INSERTS
STATED ODDS 1:10 H, 1:10 B
M1 Connor McDavid 30.00 80.00

2015-16 O-Pee-Chee Platinum Marquee Rookies White Ice

*WHITE ICE: .75 X TO 2X BASIC INSERTS
RANDOM INSERTS IN PACKS
STATED PRINT RUN 199 SER.#'d SETS
M1 Connor McDavid 30.00 80.00
M3 Ryan Hartman 4.00 10.00
M29 Matt Murray 25.00 60.00

2015-16 O-Pee-Chee Platinum Retro

STATED ODDS 1:3.3 H 1:3.3 B
*RAINBOW: .5X TO 1.25X BASIC INSERTS
RAINBOW STATED ODDS 1:20 H 1:20 B
*GOLD: 1.25X TO 3X BASIC INSERTS
GOLD RAND INSERTS IN HOBBY PACKS
R1 Wayne Gretzky 8.00 20.00
R2 Phil Esposito 2.50 6.00
R3 Martin Brodeur 3.00 8.00
R4 Bobby Orr 5.00 12.00
R5 Mike Bossy 1.50 4.00
R6 Doug Weight 1.50 4.00
R7 John Vanbiesbrouck 1.50 4.00
R8 Ray Bourque 2.50 6.00
R9 Glenn Anderson 1.50 4.00
R10 Steve Yzerman 2.50 6.00
R11 Marty Turco 1.50 4.00
R12 Mario Lemieux 5.00 12.00
R13 Bobby Hull 1.50 4.00
R14 Markus Naslund 1.25 3.00
R15 Marty McSorley 1.50 4.00
R16 Patrick Roy 4.00 10.00
R17 Cam Neely 1.50 4.00
R18 Denis Potvin 1.50 4.00
R19 Rob Blake 1.50 4.00
R20 Grant Fuhr 1.50 4.00
R21 John Tavares 3.00 8.00
R22 Sidney Crosby 6.00 15.00
R23 Alexander Ovechkin 6.00 15.00
R24 Jakub Voracek 1.50 4.00
R25 Jamie Benn 2.00 5.00
R26 Carey Price 5.00 12.00
R27 Steve Mason 1.25 3.00
R28 Taylor Hall 3.00 8.00
R29 Eric Staal 2.00 5.00
R30 Sean Monahan 1.50 4.00
R31 Anze Kopitar 2.50 6.00
R32 Joe Pavelski 1.50 4.00
R33 Jonathan Toews 3.00 8.00
R34 Zach Parise 1.50 4.00
R35 Jarome Iginla 1.50 4.00
R36 Bobby Ryan 1.25 3.00
R37 David Backes 1.50 4.00
R38 Ben Bishop 1.50 4.00
R39 Rick Nash 1.50 4.00
R40 Tyler Seguin 2.50 6.00
R41 Jiri Hudler 1.25 3.00
R42 Claude Giroux 1.50 4.00
R43 Steven Stamkos 3.00 8.00
R44 Evgeni Malkin 5.00 12.00
R45 Ryan Getzlaf 2.50 6.00
R46 Corey Perry 1.50 4.00
R47 Max Pacioretty 1.50 4.00
R48 Erik Karlsson 3.00 8.00
R49 Johnny Gaudreau 2.50 6.00
R50 Patrick Kane 3.00 8.00
R51 Filip Forsberg 2.00 5.00
R52 Devan Dubnyk 1.50 4.00
R53 Pekka Rinne 2.00 5.00
R54 Henrik Lundqvist 2.00 5.00
R55 Pavel Datsyuk 2.00 5.00
R56 Radim Vrbata 1.25 3.00
R57 Vladimir Tarasenko 2.50 6.00
R58 Phil Kessel 2.50 6.00
R59 Oliver Ekman-Larsson 1.25 3.00
R60 Patrice Bergeron 2.00 5.00
R61 Tyler Ennis 1.25 3.00
R62 Nick Foligno 1.25 3.00
R63 Jaromir Jagr 4.00 10.00
R64 Adam Henrique 1.50 4.00
R65 Andrew Ladd 1.50 4.00
R66 Henrik Zetterberg 2.00 5.00
R67 P.K. Subban 2.50 6.00
R68 Jonathan Bernier 1.50 4.00
R69 Andrew Hammond 5.00 12.00
R70 Jonathan Quick 2.50 6.00
R71 Malcolm Subban 4.00 10.00
R72 Emile Poirier 1.50 4.00
R73 Ryan Hartman 2.00 5.00
R74 Jacob de la Rose 1.50 4.00
R75 Sam Bennett 2.00 5.00
R76 Kevin Fiala 1.50 4.00
R77 Matt Puempel 1.25 3.00
R78 Noah Hanifin 2.00 5.00
R79 Artemi Panarin 5.00 12.00
R80 Nikolaj Ehlers 3.00 8.00
R81 Slater Koekkoek 1.25 3.00
R82 Oscar Lindberg 1.25 3.00
R83 Shane Prince 1.25 3.00
R84 Kyle Baun 1.50 4.00
R85 Max Domi 3.00 8.00
R86 Anthony Stolarz 1.50 4.00
R87 Josh Anderson 1.50 4.00
R88 Mikko Rantanen 1.50 4.00
R89 Connor Hellebuyck 4.00 10.00
R90 Dylan Larkin 5.00 12.00
R91 Daniel Sprong 3.00 8.00
R92 Antoine Bibeau 1.50 4.00
R93 Nikolay Goldobin 1.50 4.00
R94 Nick Cousins 1.50 4.00
R95 Robby Fabbri 2.00 5.00
R96 Ronalds Kenins 1.50 4.00
R97 Connor McDavid 12.00 30.00
R98 Nicolas Petan 1.50 4.00
R99 Jake Virtanen 2.00 5.00
R100 Jack Eichel 6.00 15.00

2015-16 O-Pee-Chee Platinum Retro Rainbow Gold

R73 Ryan Hartman 6.00 15.00

2015-16 O-Pee-Chee Platinum Retro Rainbow Orange

*ORANGE: 1.5X TO 4X BASIC INSERTS
RANDOM INSERTS IN PACKS
STATED PRINT RUN 49 SER.#'d SETS
R73 Ryan Hartman 10.00 25.00
R97 Connor McDavid 100.00 200.00

2015-16 O-Pee-Chee Platinum Retro Rainbow Blue Autographs

GRP A VETS STATED ODDS 1:5,734
GRP B VETS STATED ODDS 1:3,209
GRP C VETS STATED ODDS 1:2,168
GRP D VETS STATED ODDS 1:1,390
GRP A RC STATED ODDS 1:17,981
GRP B RC STATED ODDS 1:5,800
GRP C RC STATED ODDS 1:607
GRP D RC STATED ODDS 1:229
R1 Wayne Gretzky A 300.00 500.00
R3 Martin Brodeur A 75.00 150.00
R4 Bobby Orr A 100.00 200.00
R5 Mike Bossy A 40.00 80.00
R6 Doug Weight C 8.00 20.00
R7 John Vanbiesbrouck C 8.00 20.00
R8 Ray Bourque 12.00 30.00
R9 Glenn Anderson 8.00 20.00
R10 Steve Yzerman A 30.00 80.00
R11 Marty Turco C 8.00 20.00
R12 Mario Lemieux C 100.00 200.00
R13 Bobby Hull 25.00 60.00
R14 Markus Naslund 6.00 15.00
R15 Marty McSorley C 8.00 20.00
R16 Patrick Roy A 50.00 120.00
R17 Cam Neely B 8.00 20.00
R18 Denis Potvin
Inserted in '17-18 O-Pee-Chee Platinum
R20 Grant Fuhr B 25.00 60.00
R21 John Tavares 15.00 40.00
R22 Sidney Crosby A 100.00 250.00
R23 Alexander Ovechkin A 60.00 150.00
R24 Jakub Voracek 8.00 20.00
R26 Carey Price B 50.00 100.00
R27 Steve Mason 6.00 15.00
R28 Taylor Hall B 50.00 100.00
R29 Eric Staal C 10.00 25.00
R31 Anze Kopitar 12.00 30.00
R32 Joe Pavelski C 8.00 20.00
R33 Jonathan Toews 15.00 40.00
R34 Zach Parise B 15.00 40.00
R35 Jarome Iginla B 8.00 20.00
R36 Bobby Ryan B 12.00 30.00
R37 David Backes A 15.00 40.00
R39 Rick Nash B 25.00 60.00
R41 Jiri Hudler D 6.00 15.00
R46 Corey Perry B 8.00 20.00
R47 Max Pacioretty C 15.00 40.00
R52 Devan Dubnyk D 8.00 20.00
R53 Pekka Rinne 10.00 25.00
R55 Pavel Datsyuk B 25.00 60.00
R62 Nick Foligno D 6.00 15.00
R63 Jaromir Jagr B 50.00 100.00
R64 Adam Henrique D 8.00 20.00
R65 Andrew Ladd D 8.00 20.00
R68 Jonathan Bernier C 8.00 20.00
R69 Andrew Hammond D 25.00 60.00
R71 Malcolm Subban 20.00 50.00
R72 Emile Poirier D 8.00 20.00
R73 Ryan Hartman D 10.00 25.00
R74 Jacob de la Rose C 8.00 20.00
R75 Sam Bennett C 10.00 25.00
R76 Kevin Fiala D 8.00 20.00
R77 Matt Puempel C 6.00 15.00
R78 Noah Hanifin C 10.00 25.00
R80 Nikolaj Ehlers D 15.00 40.00
R81 Slater Koekkoek 6.00 15.00
R82 Oscar Lindberg C 6.00 15.00
R83 Shane Prince C 6.00 15.00
R84 Kyle Baun D 8.00 20.00
R86 Anthony Stolarz D 8.00 20.00
R88 Mikko Rantanen C 15.00 40.00
R89 Connor Hellebuyck B 20.00 50.00
R90 Dylan Larkin A 50.00 120.00
R91 Daniel Sprong C 15.00 40.00
R92 Antoine Bibeau D 8.00 20.00
R93 Nikolay Goldobin C 8.00 20.00
R94 Nick Cousins D 8.00 20.00
R95 Robby Fabbri 10.00 25.00
R96 Ronalds Kenins D 8.00 20.00
R97 Connor McDavid B 150.00 300.00
R98 Nicolas Petan D 8.00 20.00
R99 Jake Virtanen C 10.00 25.00

2015-16 O-Pee-Chee Platinum Superstars Die Cuts

STATED ODDS 1:37 H 1:37 B
SS1 Alexander Ovechkin 10.00 25.00
SS2 Sidney Crosby 10.00 25.00
SS3 Jakub Voracek 2.50 6.00
SS4 Max Pacioretty 2.50 6.00
SS5 Steven Stamkos 5.00 12.00
SS6 Bobby Ryan 2.00 5.00
SS7 Jamie Benn 3.00 8.00
SS8 Jonathan Toews 5.00 12.00
SS9 Vladimir Tarasenko 4.00 10.00
SS10 Taylor Hall 5.00 12.00
SS11 Joe Pavelski 2.50 6.00
SS12 Corey Perry 2.50 6.00
SS13 Johnny Gaudreau 4.00 10.00
SS14 Filip Forsberg 3.00 8.00
SS15 Mark Stone 2.00 5.00
SS16 Bobby Hull 2.50 6.00
SS17 Wayne Gretzky 12.00 30.00
SS18 Mike Bossy 2.50 6.00

2015-16 O-Pee-Chee Platinum Superstars Die Cuts Rainbow Autographs

SS1 Alexander Ovechkin B 50.00 120.00
SS2 Sidney Crosby A 150.00 250.00
SS3 Jakub Voracek 12.00 30.00
SS4 Max Pacioretty C 15.00 40.00
SS5 Steven Stamkos 25.00 60.00
SS8 Jonathan Toews 25.00 60.00
SS10 Taylor Hall C 25.00 60.00
SS11 Joe Pavelski C 12.00 30.00
SS12 Corey Perry B 30.00 80.00
SS15 Mark Stone C 8.00 20.00
SS16 Bobby Hull 20.00 50.00
SS17 Wayne Gretzky A 300.00 500.00
SS18 Mike Bossy B 20.00 50.00

2015-16 O-Pee-Chee Platinum Team Logo Die Cuts

T1 Ryan Getzlaf 4.00 10.00
T2 Shane Doan 2.00 5.00
T3 Patrice Bergeron 3.00 8.00
T4 Tyler Ennis 2.00 5.00
T5 Sean Monahan 2.50 6.00
T6 Eric Staal 3.00 8.00
T7 Jonathan Toews 5.00 12.00
T8 Jarome Iginla 2.50 6.00
T9 Nick Foligno 2.00 5.00
T10 Jamie Benn 3.00 8.00
T11 Pavel Datsyuk 3.00 8.00
T12 Taylor Hall 5.00 12.00
T13 Jaromir Jagr 6.00 15.00
T14 Anze Kopitar 4.00 10.00
T15 Devan Dubnyk 2.50 6.00
T16 Carey Price 8.00 20.00
T17 Pekka Rinne 3.00 8.00
T18 Cory Schneider 2.00 5.00
T19 John Tavares 5.00 12.00
T20 Rick Nash 2.50 6.00
T21 Erik Karlsson 5.00 12.00
T22 Jakub Voracek 2.50 6.00
T23 Sidney Crosby 10.00 25.00
T24 Joe Pavelski 2.50 6.00
T25 Vladimir Tarasenko 4.00 10.00
T26 Steven Stamkos 5.00 12.00
T27 James van Riemsdyk 2.50 6.00
T28 Ryan Miller 2.50 6.00
T29 Alexander Ovechkin 10.00 25.00
T30 Andrew Ladd 2.50 6.00
T31 Mike Modano 4.00 10.00
T32 Ron Francis 3.00 8.00
T33 Joe Sakic 4.00 10.00
T34 Teemu Selanne 5.00 12.00
T35 Mario Lemieux 8.00 20.00
T36 Wayne Gretzky 12.00 30.00

2015-16 O-Pee-Chee Platinum Trophied Talent Die Cuts

STATED ODDS 1:66 H 1:66 B
TT1 Wayne Gretzky 8.00 20.00
TT2 Bobby Orr 5.00 12.00
TT3 Teemu Selanne 3.00 8.00
TT4 Martin Brodeur 3.00 8.00
TT5 Patrick Roy 4.00 10.00
TT6 Carey Price 5.00 12.00
TT7 Jiri Hudler 1.25 3.00
TT8 Aaron Ekblad 1.50 4.00
TT9 Jamie Benn 2.00 5.00
TT10 Devan Dubnyk 1.50 4.00

2015-16 O-Pee-Chee Platinum Trophied Talent Die Cuts Rainbow Autographs

GRP A STATED ODDS 1:18,307
GRP B STATED ODDS 1:22,375
GRP A STATED ODDS 1:8,136
NO PRICING FOR GRP A DUE TO SCARCITY
TT1 Wayne Gretzky A 250.00 500.00
TT2 Bobby Orr A 80.00 150.00
TT3 Teemu Selanne B 30.00 80.00
TT4 Martin Brodeur A
TT5 Patrick Roy A 150.00 250.00
TT6 Carey Price B 80.00 150.00
TT7 Jiri Hudler C 20.00 50.00
TT8 Aaron Ekblad C 20.00 50.00
TT10 Devan Dubnyk 15.00 40.00

2016-17 O-Pee-Chee Platinum

1 Connor McDavid 2.00 5.00
2 Tyler Seguin .60 1.50
3 Nathan MacKinnon .75 2.00
4 Mika Zibanejad .40 1.00
5 Jonathan Toews .75 2.00
6 Brandon Saad .40 1.00
7 Tuukka Rask .40 1.00
8 Anze Kopitar .60 1.50
9 Jonathan Huberdeau .40 1.00
10 Henrik Zetterberg .50 1.25
11 Filip Forsberg .50 1.25
12 Nino Niederreiter .40 1.00
13 Jordan Staal .40 1.00
14 Ryan Getzlaf .60 1.50
15 Oliver Ekman-Larsson .30 .75
16 Adam Henrique .40 1.00
17 Brock Nelson .30 .75
18 Alex Galchenyuk .50 1.25
19 Mark Stone .40 1.00
20 Johnny Gaudreau .60 1.50
21 Alexander Steen .40 1.00
22 Brent Burns .50 1.25
23 Nikita Kucherov .60 1.50
24 Ryan O'Reilly .40 1.00
25 Sidney Crosby 1.50 4.00
26 Blake Wheeler .40 1.00
27 Leo Komarov .40 1.00
28 Daniel Sedin .40 1.00
29 Shayne Gostisbehere .50 1.25
30 Braden Holtby .60 1.50
31 Jarome Iginla .40 1.00
32 David Backes .40 1.00
33 Artemi Panarin .50 1.25
34 Justin Abdelkader .30 .75
35 Brendan Gallagher .50 1.25
36 Andre Burakovsky .30 .75
37 Taylor Hall .75 2.00
38 Ryan Nugent-Hopkins .40 1.00
39 Kris Letang .40 1.00
40 Jaromir Jagr 1.00 2.50
41 Drew Doughty .40 1.00
42 Logan Couture .40 1.00
43 Shane Doan .30 .75
44 Cam Atkinson .40 1.00
45 Jake Allen .50 1.25
46 Tyler Johnson .30 .75
47 Rickard Rakell .40 1.00
48 James Neal .30 .75
49 Gabriel Landeskog .30 .75
50 Patrick Kane .75 2.00
51 Anders Lee .40 1.00
52 Tomas Tatar .30 .75
53 Henrik Lundqvist .40 1.00
54 Jimmy Hayes .25 .60
55 Mikko Koivu .30 .75
56 Nazem Kadri .30 .75
57 Jeff Skinner .40 1.00
58 Phil Kessel .50 1.25
59 Bo Horvat .60 1.50
60 P.K. Subban .60 1.50
61 Joe Thornton .40 1.00
62 Claude Giroux .40 1.00
63 Mark Scheifele .50 1.25
64 Jack Eichel .75 2.00
65 Jonathan Quick .60 1.50
66 Nicklas Backstrom .60 1.50
67 Aaron Ekblad .40 1.00
68 Vladimir Tarasenko .60 1.50
69 Kyle Okposo .40 1.00
70 Max Pacioretty .40 1.00
71 Steven Stamkos .75 2.00
72 Pekka Rinne .50 1.25
73 Leon Draisaitl .50 1.25
74 John Gibson .40 1.00
75 Jamie Benn .50 1.25
76 Marcus Johansson .40 1.00
77 Bobby Ryan .30 .75
78 Milan Lucic .30 .75
79 Erik Karlsson .75 2.00
80 Vincent Trocheck .40 1.00
81 Tomas Plekanec .40 1.00
82 Rick Nash .40 1.00
83 Sean Monahan .40 1.00
84 Patric Hornqvist .30 .75
85 Patrick Marleau .40 1.00
86 Artem Anisimov .30 .75
87 Jake Virtanen .50 1.25
88 Zach Parise .40 1.00
89 Kyle Palmieri .30 .75
90 Shea Weber .40 1.00
91 Jeff Carter .40 1.00
92 Patrice Bergeron .50 1.25
93 Morgan Rielly .30 .75
94 Jakob Silfverberg .30 .75
95 Derek Stepan .30 .75
96 Dylan Larkin .60 1.50
97 Elias Lindholm .40 1.00
98 Ben Bishop .40 1.00
99 Boone Jenner .40 1.00
100 Alexander Ovechkin 1.50 4.00
101 Robby Fabbri .40 1.00
102 Andrew Ladd .40 1.00
103 Sam Reinhart .40 1.00
104 Jordan Eberle .40 1.00

105 Wayne Simmonds .50 1.25
106 John Klingberg .40 1.00
107 Matt Duchene .40 1.00
108 Reilly Smith .40 1.00
109 Bryan Little .30 .75
110 Max Domi .50 1.25
111 Rasmus Ristolainen .30 .75
112 Tyler Toffoli .40 1.00
113 Gustav Nyquist .40 1.00
114 Matt Murray .60 1.50
115 Ryan Kesler .40 1.00
116 Jean-Gabriel Pageau .30 .75
117 Joe Pavelski .40 1.00
118 Brian Elliott .30 .75
119 Duncan Keith .40 1.00
120 Nikolaj Ehlers .40 1.00
121 Mats Zuccarello .40 1.00
122 David Pastrnak .60 1.50
123 Cory Schneider .30 .75
124 Scott Hartnell .40 1.00
125 Carey Price 1.25 3.00
126 Ondrej Palat .30 .75
127 Carl Soderberg .25 .60
128 Evgeny Kuznetsov .60 1.50
129 Jason Spezza .40 1.00
130 Sam Bennett .50 1.25
131 Devan Dubnyk .40 1.00
132 Chris Kreider .40 1.00
133 Victor Rask .30 .75
134 Michael Raffl .25 .60
135 Corey Perry .40 1.00
136 Evgeni Malkin 1.25 3.00
137 Tyler Bozak .30 .75
138 Corey Crawford .50 1.25
139 Henrik Sedin .40 1.00
140 Anthony Duclair .40 1.00
141 Tanner Pearson .30 .75
142 Mike Hoffman .30 .75
143 Ryan Johansen .50 1.25
144 Jussi Jokinen .40 1.00
145 Petr Mrazek .40 1.00
146 Brad Marchand .50 1.25
147 Kevin Shattenkirk .30 .75
148 Patrick Sharp .30 .75
149 Martin Jones .40 1.00
150 John Tavares .75 2.00
151 Auston Matthews RC 10.00 25.00
152 Matthew Tkachuk RC 3.00 8.00
153 Michael Matheson RC 1.00 2.50
154 Nick Schmaltz RC 1.00 2.50
155 William Nylander RC 4.00 10.00
156 Ivan Provorov RC 2.00 5.00
157 Chris Bigras RC .75 2.00
158 Danton Heinen RC 1.50 4.00
159 Oliver Bjorkstrand RC .75 2.00
160 Jesse Puljujarvi RC 2.50 6.00
161 Mikhail Sergachev RC 2.00 5.00
162 Frederik Gauthier RC .75 2.00
163 Brandon Carlo RC 1.00 2.50
164 Nikita Tryamkin RC .75 2.00
165 Hudson Fasching RC 1.00 2.50
166 Dylan Strome RC 2.00 5.00
167 Pavel Buchnevich RC 1.50 4.00
168 Tobias Lindberg RC 1.50 4.00
169 Jacob Larsson RC 1.50 4.00
170 Pavel Zacha RC 1.25 3.00
171 Anthony Beauvillier RC 1.00 2.50
172 Josh Morrissey RC 1.25 3.00
173 Sebastian Aho RC 2.00 5.00
174 Thomas Chabot RC 2.00 5.00
175 Connor Brown RC 1.50 4.00
176 Patrik Laine RC 4.00 10.00
177 Tom Kuhnhackl RC .75 2.00
178 Lawson Crouse RC .75 2.00
179 Trevor Carrick RC 1.00 2.50
180 Mitch Marner RC 5.00 12.00
181 Nick Sorensen RC 1.00 2.50
182 Sonny Milano RC 1.25 3.00
183 Gustav Forsling RC 1.00 2.50
184 Brayden Point RC 2.50 6.00
185 Anthony Mantha RC 2.50 6.00
186 Artturi Lehkonen RC 1.00 2.50
187 Kasperi Kapanen RC 2.00 5.00
188 Mathew Barzal RC 3.00 8.00
189 Nikita Soshnikov RC .60 1.50
190 Jimmy Vesey RC 2.00 5.00
191 Jakob Chychrun RC 1.00 2.50
192 Joel Eriksson Ek RC 1.00 2.50
193 Tyler Motte RC 1.00 2.50
194 Steven Santini RC .75 2.00
195 Brendan Leipsic RC 1.00 2.50
196 Zach Werenski RC 2.00 5.00
197 Kyle Connor RC 2.50 6.00
198 Zach Sanford RC 1.00 2.50
199 Travis Konecny RC 2.00 5.00
200 Christian Dvorak RC 1.00 2.50

2016-17 O-Pee-Chee Platinum Ice Blue Traxx

*TRAXX VET: 1.25X TO 3X BASIC CARDS
*TRAXX RC: .6X TO 1.5X BASIC CARDS
66 Nicklas Backstrom 2.00 5.00
128 Evgeny Kuznetsov 2.00 5.00
138 Corey Crawford 1.50 4.00
151 Auston Matthews 20.00 50.00

2016-17 O-Pee-Chee Platinum Rainbow Color Wheel

151 Auston Matthews 25.00 60.00

2016-17 O-Pee-Chee Platinum Rainbow Orange

*ORANGE/25: 5X TO 12X BASIC CARDS
*ORANGE RC/25: 3X TO 8X BASIC CARDS
1 Connor McDavid 40.00 100.00
66 Nicklas Backstrom 8.00 20.00
125 Carey Price 20.00 50.00
128 Evgeny Kuznetsov 8.00 20.00
138 Corey Crawford 6.00 15.00
151 Auston Matthews 100.00 200.00
176 Patrik Laine 50.00 120.00

2016-17 O-Pee-Chee Platinum Red Prism

*RED PRISM/199: 1.5X TO 4X BASIC CARDS
*RED PRISM RC/199: 1X TO 2.5X BASIC CARDS
1 Connor McDavid 15.00 40.00
66 Nicklas Backstrom 2.50 6.00
128 Evgeny Kuznetsov 2.50 6.00
138 Corey Crawford 2.00 5.00
151 Auston Matthews 30.00 80.00
155 William Nylander 15.00 40.00
176 Patrik Laine 25.00 60.00
180 Mitch Marner 20.00 50.00

2016-17 O-Pee-Chee Platinum Royal Blue Cubes

*BLUE CUBES/99: 2X TO 5X BASIC CARDS
*BLUE CUBES RC/99: 1.25X TO 3X BASIC CARDS
1 Connor McDavid 25.00 60.00
25 Sidney Crosby 6.00 15.00
66 Nicklas Backstrom 3.00 8.00
125 Carey Price 12.00 30.00
128 Evgeny Kuznetsov 3.00 8.00
138 Corey Crawford 2.50 6.00
151 Auston Matthews 40.00 100.00
155 William Nylander 20.00 50.00
176 Patrik Laine 30.00 80.00
180 Mitch Marner 25.00 60.00

2016-17 O-Pee-Chee Platinum Seismic Gold

*GOLD/50: 3X TO 10X BASIC CARDS
*GOLD RC/50: 2X TO 5X BASIC CARDS
1 Connor McDavid 30.00 80.00
50 Patrick Kane 8.00 20.00
66 Nicklas Backstrom 6.00 15.00
125 Carey Price 15.00 40.00
128 Evgeny Kuznetsov 6.00 15.00
138 Corey Crawford 5.00 12.00
151 Auston Matthews 90.00 150.00
155 William Nylander 25.00 60.00
173 Sebastian Aho 15.00 40.00
176 Patrik Laine 40.00 100.00
180 Mitch Marner 30.00 80.00

2016-17 O-Pee-Chee Platinum NHL Logo Crest Die Cuts

NHLLD1 Wayne Gretzky 5.00 12.00
NHLLD2 Bobby Orr 3.00 8.00
NHLLD3 Mario Lemieux 3.00 8.00
NHLLD4 Henrik Lundqvist 1.00 2.50
NHLLD5 Alexander Ovechkin 4.00 10.00
NHLLD6 Connor McDavid 5.00 12.00
NHLLD7 Jaromir Jagr 2.50 6.00
NHLLD8 Evgeni Malkin 3.00 8.00
NHLLD9 Patrick Kane 2.00 5.00
NHLLD10 Sidney Crosby 4.00 10.00
NHLLD11 Jamie Benn 1.25 3.00
NHLLD12 Henrik Zetterberg 1.25 3.00
NHLLD13 Jonathan Toews 2.00 5.00
NHLLD14 John Tavares 2.00 5.00
NHLLD15 Carey Price 3.00 8.00

2016-17 O-Pee-Chee Platinum Platinum Phenoms Die Cuts

OPPAK Anze Kopitar 3.00 8.00
OPPAL Andrew Ladd 2.00 5.00
OPPAM Auston Matthews 12.00 30.00
OPPBO Bobby Orr 6.00 15.00
OPPCH Carl Hagelin 2.00 5.00
OPPCM Connor McDavid 10.00 25.00
OPPCP Corey Perry 2.00 5.00
OPPDK David Krejci 2.00 5.00
OPPDS Dylan Strome 4.00 10.00
OPPHL Henrik Lundqvist 2.00 5.00
OPPHZ Henrik Zetterberg 2.50 6.00
OPPJP Joe Pavelski 2.00 5.00
OPPJT Jonathan Toews 4.00 10.00
OPPMM Mark Messier 2.50 6.00
OPPMU Matt Murray 3.00 8.00
OPPNM Nathan MacKinnon 4.00 10.00
OPPPL Patrik Laine 8.00 20.00
OPPPR Patrick Roy 5.00 12.00
OPPPZ Pavel Zacha 2.50 6.00
OPPSC Sidney Crosby 8.00 20.00
OPPSY Steve Yzerman 2.50 6.00
OPPTS Tyler Seguin 3.00 8.00
OPPWG Wayne Gretzky 10.00 25.00
OPPWN William Nylander 8.00 20.00
OPPZP Zach Parise 2.00 5.00

2016-17 O-Pee-Chee Platinum Puck Personas Die Cuts

PP1 Mario Lemieux 5.00 12.00
PP2 Martin Brodeur 3.00 8.00
PP3 Steve Yzerman 2.00 5.00
PP4 John Tavares 3.00 8.00
PP5 Roberto Luongo 1.50 4.00
PP6 Evgeni Malkin 5.00 12.00
PP7 Patrick Kane 3.00 8.00
PP8 Brent Burns 2.00 5.00
PP9 Alex Galchenyuk 2.00 5.00
PP10 Alexander Ovechkin 6.00 15.00
PP11 Mats Zuccarello 1.50 4.00
PP12 Matt Duchene 1.50 4.00
PP13 Max Pacioretty 1.50 4.00
PP14 Tyler Toffoli 1.50 4.00
PP15 Taylor Hall 3.00 8.00

2016-17 O-Pee-Chee Platinum Retro

R1 Henrik Zetterberg 2.00 5.00
R2 Andrew Ladd 1.50 4.00
R3 Alex Galchenyuk 2.00 5.00
R4 Ryan Spooner 1.25 3.00
R5 Sidney Crosby 6.00 15.00
R6 Ryan O'Reilly 1.50 4.00
R7 Nikita Kucherov 2.50 6.00
R8 David Krejci 1.50 4.00
R9 Wayne Simmonds 2.00 5.00
R10 Taylor Hall 3.00 8.00
R11 Jonathan Huberdeau 1.50 4.00
R12 Brent Burns 2.00 5.00
R13 Jake Muzzin 1.25 3.00
R14 Oliver Ekman-Larsson 1.25 3.00
R15 Jonathan Toews 3.00 8.00
R16 Jaroslav Halak 1.50 4.00
R17 Nathan MacKinnon 3.00 8.00
R18 Mark Scheifele 2.00 5.00
R19 Jamie Benn 2.00 5.00
R20 Henrik Lundqvist 1.50 4.00
R21 Aaron Ekblad 1.50 4.00
R22 Jake Allen 2.00 5.00
R23 Jaden Schwartz 2.00 5.00
R24 Victor Rask 1.25 3.00
R25 Connor McDavid 8.00 20.00
R26 Matt Murray 2.50 6.00
R27 Johnny Gaudreau 2.50 6.00
R28 Jason Pominville 1.25 3.00
R29 Roman Josi 1.50 4.00
R30 Alexander Ovechkin 6.00 15.00
R31 Roberto Luongo 1.50 4.00
R32 Tyler Toffoli 1.50 4.00
R33 Dylan Larkin 2.50 6.00
R34 Bo Horvat 2.50 6.00
R35 Sam Bennett 2.00 5.00
R36 Rasmus Ristolainen 1.25 3.00
R37 Noah Hanifin 1.50 4.00
R38 Mats Zuccarello 1.50 4.00
R39 Carl Hagelin 1.50 4.00
R40 Carey Price 5.00 12.00
R41 Morgan Rielly 1.25 3.00
R42 Kyle Palmieri 1.25 3.00
R43 Jason Spezza 1.50 4.00
R44 Brendan Gallagher 2.00 5.00
R45 Derek Stepan 1.25 3.00
R46 Jaromir Jagr 4.00 10.00
R47 John Tavares 3.00 8.00
R48 Leon Draisaitl 2.00 5.00
R49 Robby Fabbri 1.50 4.00
R50 Zach Parise 1.50 4.00
R51 Bobby Ryan 1.25 3.00
R52 Brandon Saad 1.50 4.00
R53 John Gibson 1.50 4.00
R54 Evgeny Kuznetsov 2.50 6.00
R55 Joe Pavelski 1.50 4.00
R56 Tyson Barrie 1.50 4.00
R57 Ryan Johansen 2.00 5.00
R58 Andrew Shaw 1.50 4.00
R59 Andreas Athanasiou 1.50 4.00
R60 Anze Kopitar 2.50 6.00
R61 Nino Niederreiter 1.50 4.00
R62 Boone Jenner 1.50 4.00
R63 Artemi Panarin 2.00 5.00
R64 Evgeni Malkin 5.00 12.00
R65 Pekka Rinne 2.00 5.00
R66 Auston Matthews 10.00 25.00
R67 Charlie Lindgren 3.00 8.00
R68 Dylan Strome 3.00 8.00
R69 Oliver Bjorkstrand 1.25 3.00
R70 Travis Konecny 3.00 8.00
R71 Michael Matheson 1.50 4.00
R72 Kyle Connor 4.00 10.00
R73 William Nylander 6.00 15.00
R74 Mikhail Sergachev 3.00 8.00
R75 Oliver Kylington 1.25 3.00
R76 Jesse Puljujarvi 4.00 10.00
R77 Sonny Milano 2.00 5.00
R78 Brayden Point 4.00 10.00
R79 Pavel Zacha 2.00 5.00
R80 Mathew Barzal 5.00 12.00
R81 Kasperi Kapanen 3.00 8.00
R82 Sebastian Aho 3.00 8.00
R83 Anthony Mantha 4.00 10.00
R84 Pavel Buchnevich 2.50 6.00
R85 Ryan Pulock 1.50 4.00
R86 Matthew Tkachuk 5.00 12.00
R87 Hudson Fasching 1.50 4.00
R88 Mitch Marner 8.00 20.00
R89 Josh Morrissey 2.00 5.00
R90 Zach Werenski 3.00 8.00
R91 Brendan Leipsic 1.50 4.00
R92 Ivan Provorov 3.00 8.00
R93 Justin Bailey 1.50 4.00
R94 Jimmy Vesey 3.00 8.00
R95 Connor Brown 2.50 6.00
R96 Jakob Chychrun 1.50 4.00
R97 Lawson Crouse 1.25 3.00
R98 Christian Dvorak 1.50 4.00
R99 Patrik Laine 6.00 15.00
R100 Joel Eriksson Ek 1.50 4.00

2016-17 O-Pee-Chee Platinum Retro Rainbow Black

R1 Henrik Zetterberg AU A 20.00 50.00
R3 Alex Galchenyuk AU A 25.00 60.00
R7 Nikita Kucherov AU C 15.00 40.00
R9 Wayne Simmonds AU B 25.00 60.00
R12 Brent Burns AU B 15.00 40.00
R16 Jaroslav Halak AU B 25.00 60.00
R18 Mark Scheifele AU C 15.00 40.00
R20 Henrik Lundqvist AU A 30.00 80.00
R26 Matt Murray AU C 20.00 50.00
R31 Roberto Luongo AU A 30.00 80.00
R34 Bo Horvat AU C 25.00 60.00
R45 Derek Stepan AU B 15.00 40.00
R46 Jaromir Jagr AU A 150.00 250.00
R47 John Tavares AU A 30.00 80.00
R48 Leon Draisaitl AU B 20.00 50.00
R50 Zach Parise AU A 40.00 100.00
R58 Andrew Shaw AU C 15.00 40.00
R67 Charlie Lindgren AU E 20.00 50.00
R68 Dylan Strome AU D 25.00 60.00
R70 Travis Konecny AU F 20.00 40.00
R74 Mikhail Sergachev AU D 20.00 50.00
R86 Matthew Tkachuk AU E 30.00 80.00
R94 Jimmy Vesey AU E 15.00 40.00
R100 Joel Eriksson Ek AU F 10.00 25.00

2016-17 O-Pee-Chee Platinum Retro Rainbow Gold

*GOLD/149: 1X TO 2.5X BASIC INSERTS
R54 Evgeny Kuznetsov 6.00 15.00
R66 Auston Matthews 50.00 120.00

2016-17 O-Pee-Chee Platinum Retro Rainbow Orange

*ORANGE/49: 2X TO 5X BASIC INSERTS
R25 Connor McDavid 30.00 80.00
R66 Auston Matthews 100.00 200.00

2016-17 O-Pee-Chee Platinum Rookie Autographs

RAB Anthony Beauvillier E 5.00 12.00
RAM Auston Matthews A 300.00 400.00
RAN Anthony Mantha A 20.00 50.00
RBA Mathew Barzal C 40.00 100.00
RBL Brendan Leipsic A 5.00 12.00
RBP Brayden Point A 20.00 50.00
RBR Connor Brown A 8.00 20.00
RCB Chris Bigras D 4.00 10.00
RCD Christian Dvorak E 5.00 12.00
RCL Charlie Lindgren C 12.00 30.00
RDS Dominik Simon E 5.00 12.00
REL Esa Lindell E 5.00 12.00
RHF Hudson Fasching C 5.00 12.00
RIP Ivan Provorov B 10.00 25.00
RJD Jason Dickinson A 4.00 10.00
RJM Josh Morrissey A 6.00 15.00
RJP Jesse Puljujarvi B 12.00 30.00
RJV Jimmy Vesey B 10.00 25.00
RKC Kyle Connor C 12.00 30.00
RLC Lawson Crouse E 4.00 10.00
RMA Michael Matheson A 8.00 20.00
RMM Mitch Marner A 30.00 80.00
RMR Mike Reilly E 4.00 10.00
RMS Mikhail Sergachev B 12.00 30.00
RMT Matthew Tkachuk B 15.00 40.00
RMW Miles Wood E 4.00 10.00
RNS Nikita Soshnikov C 3.00 8.00
ROB Oliver Bjorkstrand C 4.00 10.00
ROK Oliver Kylington E 4.00 10.00
ROS Oskar Sundqvist E 5.00 12.00
RPB Pavel Buchnevich A 8.00 20.00
RPL Patrik Laine B 80.00 150.00
RPZ Pavel Zacha A 6.00 15.00
RRP Ryan Pulock E 5.00 12.00
RSA Sebastian Aho D 10.00 25.00
RSC Nick Schmaltz C 12.00 30.00
RSM Sonny Milano E 6.00 15.00
RSS Steven Santini E 4.00 10.00
RST Dylan Strome A 10.00 25.00
RTC Trevor Carrick D 5.00 12.00
RTM Timo Meier E 5.00 12.00
RVR Jakub Vrana E 5.00 12.00
RWN William Nylander A 40.00 100.00
RZW Zach Werenski B 10.00 25.00

2016-17 O-Pee-Chee Platinum Rookie Autographs Rainbow

*RAINBOW: .5X TO 1.25X BASIC INSERTS
RAM Auston Matthews A 250.00 400.00
RJP Jesse Puljujarvi B 25.00 60.00
RMM Mitch Marner A 80.00 150.00
RMS Mikhail Sergachev B 25.00 60.00
RPL Patrik Laine B 80.00 150.00
RWN William Nylander A 60.00 150.00

2017-18 O-Pee-Chee Platinum

1 Sidney Crosby 1.50 4.00
2 Max Pacioretty .40 1.00
3 Brad Marchand .50 1.25
4 Nikita Kucherov .60 1.50
5 Henrik Lundqvist .60 1.50
6 Corey Perry .40 1.00
7 Tyler Seguin .60 1.50
8 Patrik Laine .60 1.50
9 Leon Draisaitl .60 1.50
10 Patrick Kane .75 2.00
11 Ryan O'Reilly .40 1.00
12 Evgeny Kuznetsov .60 1.50
13 Henrik Sedin .40 1.00
14 Jaden Schwartz .50 1.25
15 Sergei Bobrovsky .40 1.00
16 Adam Henrique .30 .75
17 Anthony Mantha .40 1.00
18 Gabriel Landeskog .30 .75
19 Aaron Ekblad .40 1.00
20 P.K. Subban .40 1.00
21 Sean Monahan .40 1.00
22 Mikael Granlund .40 1.00
23 Max Domi .40 1.00
24 Jeff Carter .40 1.00
25 Auston Matthews 1.50 4.00
26 Matt Duchene .40 1.00
27 Wayne Simmonds .50 1.25
28 Sebastian Aho .40 1.00
29 Logan Couture .40 1.00
30 John Tavares .75 2.00
31 Marc-Andre Fleury .60 1.50
32 Ryan Kesler .40 1.00
33 Jake Guentzel .50 1.25
34 Jonathan Drouin .40 1.00
35 Victor Hedman .50 1.25
36 David Krejci .30 .75
37 Jamie Benn .50 1.25
38 Cam Talbot .40 1.00
39 Brandon Saad .40 1.00
40 Taylor Hall .75 2.00
41 Chris Kreider .40 1.00
42 Jack Eichel .60 1.50
43 Jakub Voracek .40 1.00
44 Nick Foligno .30 .75
45 Martin Jones .40 1.00
46 Charlie Coyle .30 .75
47 Nick Bonino .30 .75
48 Henrik Zetterberg .40 1.00
49 Johnny Gaudreau .60 1.50
50 Connor McDavid 1.50 4.00
51 Aleksander Barkov .40 1.00
52 Vladimir Tarasenko .60 1.50
53 James Neal .30 .75
54 Mark Scheifele .50 1.25
55 Anze Kopitar .60 1.50
56 Alex Galchenyuk .50 1.25
57 Erik Karlsson .50 1.25
58 John Klingberg .30 .75
59 Derek Stepan .30 .75
60 Mitch Marner .60 1.50
61 Loui Eriksson .30 .75
62 Scott Darling .30 .75
63 Nick Leddy .25 .60
64 Cam Fowler .30 .75
65 Brent Burns .50 1.25
66 Evgeni Malkin 1.25 3.00
67 Nathan MacKinnon .75 2.00
68 Ryan Hartman .40 1.00
69 T.J. Oshie .60 1.50
70 Steven Stamkos .75 2.00
71 Artemi Panarin .40 1.00
72 Dustin Byfuglien .40 1.00
73 Frans Nielsen .30 .75
74 Ryan Strome .30 .75
75 Alexander Ovechkin 1.50 4.00
76 Matt Beleskey .25 .60
77 Alexander Radulov .40 1.00
78 Claude Giroux .40 1.00
79 Pekka Rinne .50 1.25
80 Nazem Kadri .30 .75
81 Brayden Point .40 1.00
82 Mats Zuccarello .40 1.00
83 Oliver Ekman-Larsson .40 1.00
84 Brayden Schenn .40 1.00
85 Matthew Tkachuk .40 1.00
86 Cory Schneider .30 .75
87 Christian Dvorak .30 .75
88 Duncan Keith .40 1.00
89 Braden Holtby .60 1.50
90 Matt Murray .60 1.50
91 Reilly Smith .40 1.00
92 Jonathan Quick .60 1.50
93 Brandon Sutter .30 .75
94 Jonathan Huberdeau .30 .75
95 Joe Thornton .40 1.00
96 Rickard Rakell .30 .75
97 Zach Parise .40 1.00
98 Brandon Dubinsky .30 .75
99 Tyson Barrie .40 1.00
100 Carey Price 1.25 3.00
101 Sam Gagner .30 .75
102 Bobby Ryan .30 .75
103 Jason Pominville .30 .75
104 Jordan Eberle .40 1.00
105 Tuukka Rask .40 1.00
106 Nicklas Backstrom .60 1.50
107 Ryan Johansen .40 1.00
108 William Nylander .60 1.50
109 Kevin Hayes .30 .75
110 Nick Bjugstad .30 .75
111 Andrei Vasilevskiy .50 1.25
112 Dylan Larkin .40 1.00
113 Nikolaj Ehlers .40 1.00
114 Jonathan Marchessault .40 1.00
115 Jeff Skinner .30 .75
116 Sean Couturier .30 .75
117 Mikko Rantanen .40 1.00
118 David Pastrnak .60 1.50
119 Viktor Arvidsson .30 .75
120 Jaromir Jagr 1.00 2.50
121 Joe Pavelski .40 1.00
122 Alec Martinez .25 .60
123 Oscar Klefbom .30 .75
124 Ben Bishop .40 1.00
125 Jonathan Toews .75 2.00
126 Andrew Ladd .40 1.00
127 Kevin Shattenkirk .40 1.00
128 William Karlsson .75 2.00
129 Cam Atkinson .40 1.00
130 Ryan Getzlaf .40 1.00
131 Kyle Palmieri .30 .75
132 Patrick Marleau .40 1.00
133 Mike Smith .40 1.00
134 Kyle Okposo .30 .75
135 Mike Hoffman .30 .75
136 Andreas Athanasiou .40 1.00
137 Andrew Shaw .30 .75
138 Justin Faulk .30 .75
139 Devan Dubnyk .40 1.00
140 Phil Kessel .50 1.25
141 Mario Lemieux 1.25 3.00
142 Pavel Bure .40 1.00
143 Joe Sakic .50 1.25
144 Mark Recchi .50 1.25
145 Ed Belfour .50 1.25
146 Steve Yzerman .50 1.25
147 Teemu Selanne .50 1.25
148 Patrick Roy 1.00 2.50
149 Pat LaFontaine .40 1.00
150 Wayne Gretzky 2.00 5.00
151 Nico Hischier RC 3.00 8.00
152 Alex DeBrincat RC 2.50 6.00
153 Victor Mete RC 1.00 2.50
154 Adrian Kempe RC 1.25 3.00
155 Charlie McAvoy RC 3.00 8.00
156 Carter Rowney RC .75 2.00
157 Robert Hagg RC 1.00 2.50
158 Evgeny Svechnikov RC 2.00 5.00
159 Filip Chlapik RC 1.00 2.50
160 Clayton Keller RC 2.50 6.00
161 Jack Roslovic RC 1.25 3.00
162 Vince Dunn RC 1.00 2.50
163 Kailer Yamamoto RC 2.50 6.00
164 Samuel Girard RC 1.00 2.50
165 Brock Boeser RC 5.00 12.00
166 Rasmus Andersson RC 1.00 2.50
167 Logan Brown RC 1.00 2.50
168 Calle Rosen RC 1.00 2.50
169 Christian Jaros RC 1.00 2.50
170 Pierre-Luc Dubois RC 2.00 5.00
171 Samuel Blais RC 1.00 2.50
172 Anders Bjork RC 1.25 3.00
173 Travis Sanheim RC 1.00 2.50
174 Henrik Haapala RC 1.00 2.50
175 Will Butcher RC 1.25 3.00
176 Alex Kerfoot RC 1.00 2.50
177 Colin White RC 1.00 2.50
178 Luke Kunin RC 1.00 2.50
179 J.T. Compher RC 1.25 3.00
180 Alexander Nylander RC 1.50 4.00
181 Filip Chytil RC 1.00 2.50
182 Martin Necas RC 1.00 2.50
183 Andreas Borgman RC 1.00 2.50
184 Nikita Scherbak RC 2.00 5.00
185 Josh Ho-Sang RC 1.25 3.00
186 Ville Husso RC 1.00 2.50
187 Jake DeBrusk RC 1.50 4.00
188 Christian Djoos RC 1.00 2.50
189 John Hayden RC .75 2.00
190 Owen Tippett RC 2.00 5.00
191 Haydn Fleury RC 1.00 2.50
192 Tage Thompson RC 1.50 4.00
193 Alex Formenton RC 1.00 2.50
194 Alex Tuch RC 2.50 6.00
195 Tyson Jost RC 2.00 5.00
196 Eric Comrie RC .75 2.00
197 Jesper Bratt RC 1.50 4.00
198 Christian Fischer RC 1.25 3.00
199 Michael Amadio RC 1.00 2.50
200 Nolan Patrick RC 2.00 5.00

2017-18 O-Pee-Chee Platinum Orange Checkers

*ORANGE/25: 5X TO 12X BASIC CARDS
*ORANGE.RC/25: 2.5X TO 6X BASIC CARDS
165 Brock Boeser 60.00 150.00

2017-18 O-Pee-Chee Platinum Seismic Gold

*GOLD/50: 4X TO 10X BASIC CARDS
*GOLD.RC/50: 2X TO 5X BASIC CARDS
165 Brock Boeser 50.00 125.00

2017-18 O-Pee-Chee Platinum Destined For Glory

DG1 Connor McDavid 3.00 8.00
DG2 Matt Murray 1.25 3.00
DG3 Dylan Larkin .75 2.00
DG4 Jake Guentzel 1.00 2.50
DG5 Mitch Marner 1.25 3.00
DG6 Artemi Panarin .75 2.00
DG7 Jack Eichel 1.25 3.00
DG8 William Nylander 1.25 3.00
DG9 Anthony Mantha .75 2.00
DG10 Auston Matthews 3.00 8.00
DG11 Patrik Laine 1.25 3.00
DG12 Clayton Keller 2.00 5.00
DG13 Charlie McAvoy 2.50 6.00
DG14 Nico Hischier 2.50 6.00
DG15 Nolan Patrick 1.50 4.00

2017-18 O-Pee-Chee Platinum In Action

IA1 Alexander Ovechkin 4.00 10.00
IA2 Carey Price 2.50 6.00
IA3 Vladimir Tarasenko 1.25 3.00
IA4 Henrik Zetterberg .75 2.00
IA5 Auston Matthews 3.00 8.00
IA6 P.K. Subban .75 2.00
IA7 Jamie Benn 1.00 2.50
IA8 Johnny Gaudreau 1.25 3.00
IA9 Connor McDavid 3.00 8.00
IA10 Steven Stamkos 1.50 4.00
IA11 Brent Burns 1.00 2.50
IA12 Henrik Lundqvist 1.25 3.00
IA13 Sidney Crosby 3.00 8.00
IA14 Jonathan Drouin .75 2.00
IA15 Wayne Simmonds 1.00 2.50
IA16 Anze Kopitar 1.25 3.00
IA17 Patrick Kane 1.50 4.00
IA18 Mitch Marner 1.25 3.00
IA19 Matt Murray 1.25 3.00
IA20 John Tavares 1.50 4.00
IA21 Charlie McAvoy 2.50 6.00
IA22 Brock Boeser 4.00 10.00
IA23 Nico Hischier 2.50 6.00
IA24 Nolan Patrick 1.50 4.00
IA25 Pierre-Luc Dubois 1.50 4.00

2017-18 O-Pee-Chee Platinum Platinum Records

PR1 Wayne Gretzky 3.00 8.00
PR2 Wayne Gretzky 3.00 8.00
PR3 Wayne Gretzky 3.00 8.00
PR4 Wayne Gretzky 3.00 8.00
PR5 Wayne Gretzky 3.00 8.00
PR6 Teemu Selanne .75 2.00
PR7 Dave Andreychuk .60 1.50
PR8 Ian Turnbull .50 1.25
PR9 Darryl Sittler .60 1.50
PR10 Martin Brodeur 1.25 3.00
PR11 Auston Matthews 2.50 6.00
PR12 Jake Guentzel .75 2.00
PR13 Grant Fuhr .75 2.00
PR14 Mark Messier 1.00 2.50
PR15 Chris Chelios .60 1.50

2017-18 O-Pee-Chee Platinum Retro

R1 Auston Matthews 4.00 10.00
R2 Brad Marchand 1.25 3.00
R3 Johnny Gaudreau 1.50 4.00
R4 Oliver Ekman-Larsson 1.00 2.50
R5 Patrick Kane 2.00 5.00
R6 Vladimir Tarasenko 1.50 4.00
R7 Nathan MacKinnon 2.00 5.00
R8 Aleksander Barkov 1.00 2.50
R9 Brent Burns 1.25 3.00
R10 Jake Guentzel 1.25 3.00
R11 Max Pacioretty 1.00 2.50
R12 Henrik Lundqvist 1.50 4.00
R13 Jeff Skinner .75 2.00
R14 Steven Stamkos 2.00 5.00
R15 Tyler Seguin 1.50 4.00
R16 Cam Atkinson 1.00 2.50
R17 Daniel Sedin 1.00 2.50
R18 Jonathan Quick 1.50 4.00
R19 Nicklas Backstrom 1.50 4.00
R20 Connor McDavid 4.00 10.00
R21 Mikael Granlund 1.00 2.50
R22 P.K. Subban 1.00 2.50
R23 Anders Lee 1.00 2.50
R24 Corey Perry 1.00 2.50
R25 Shayne Gostisbehere 1.00 2.50
R26 Henrik Zetterberg 1.00 2.50
R27 Marc-Andre Fleury 1.50 4.00
R28 Adam Henrique .75 2.00
R29 Jack Eichel 1.50 4.00
R30 Erik Karlsson 1.25 3.00
R31 Nikolaj Ehlers 1.00 2.50
R32 Marcus Johansson .75 2.00
R33 Artemi Panarin 1.00 2.50
R34 Sidney Crosby 4.00 10.00
R35 Martin Jones 1.00 2.50
R36 Zdeno Chara 1.00 2.50
R37 Tyler Johnson .75 2.00
R38 Carey Price 3.00 8.00
R39 Jordan Eberle 1.00 2.50
R40 Mitch Marner 1.50 4.00
R41 Sean Monahan 1.00 2.50
R42 Ryan Kesler 1.00 2.50
R43 Mark Scheifele 1.25 3.00
R44 Jordan Staal 1.00 2.50
R45 Jakub Voracek 1.00 2.50
R46 Braden Holtby 1.50 4.00
R47 Drew Doughty 1.00 2.50
R48 Colton Parayko 1.00 2.50
R49 Conor Sheary 1.00 2.50
R50 Jonathan Toews 2.00 5.00
R51 Vincent Trocheck .75 2.00
R52 Loui Eriksson .75 2.00
R53 Tomas Tatar 1.00 2.50
R54 Devan Dubnyk 1.00 2.50
R55 Chris Kreider 1.00 2.50
R56 Jonathan Drouin 1.00 2.50
R57 James Neal .75 2.00
R58 John Tavares 2.00 5.00
R59 Viktor Arvidsson .75 2.00
R60 Kyle Okposo .75 2.00
R61 Ben Bishop 1.00 2.50
R62 Mikko Rantanen 1.00 2.50
R63 Kyle Turris 1.00 2.50
R64 Phil Kessel 1.25 3.00
R65 Frederik Andersen .75 2.00
R66 Nico Hischier 3.00 8.00
R67 Brock Boeser 5.00 12.00
R68 Alex DeBrincat 2.50 6.00
R69 Clayton Keller 2.50 6.00
R70 Nolan Patrick 2.00 5.00
R71 Tyson Jost 2.00 5.00
R72 Anders Bjork 1.25 3.00
R73 Colin White 1.00 2.50
R74 Filip Chytil 1.00 2.50
R75 Josh Ho-Sang 1.25 3.00
R76 Kailer Yamamoto 2.50 6.00
R77 Evgeny Svechnikov 2.00 5.00
R78 Logan Brown 1.00 2.50
R79 Ivan Barbashev 1.00 2.50
R80 Pierre-Luc Dubois 2.00 5.00
R81 Jack Roslovic 1.25 3.00
R82 Tage Thompson 1.50 4.00
R83 Alexander Nylander 1.50 4.00
R84 Jake DeBrusk 1.50 4.00
R85 Alex Tuch 2.50 6.00
R86 Jon Gillies 1.00 2.50
R87 J.T. Compher 1.25 3.00
R88 Riley Barber .75 2.00
R89 Remi Elie .75 2.00
R90 Christian Fischer 1.25 3.00
R91 Lucas Wallmark 1.00 2.50
R92 Jordan Schmaltz 1.25 3.00
R93 Mike Vecchione .75 2.00
R94 Gabriel Carlsson .75 2.00
R95 Nikita Scherbak 2.00 5.00
R96 Adrian Kempe 1.25 3.00
R97 Vladislav Kamenev 1.50 4.00
R98 Jakob Forsbacka-Karlsson 1.00 2.50
R99 Janne Kuokkanen 1.00 2.50
R100 Charlie McAvoy 3.00 8.00

2017-18 O-Pee-Chee Platinum Retro Rainbow Green

*GREEN/49: 2X TO 5X BASIC INSERTS
R67 Brock Boeser 40.00 100.00

2017-18 O-Pee-Chee Platinum Rookie Autographs

RAB Anders Bjork A 10.00 25.00
RAD Alex DeBrincat A 20.00 50.00
RAK Adrian Kempe A 10.00 25.00
RAN Alexander Nylander A 12.00 30.00
RAT Alex Tuch A 20.00 50.00
RBB Brock Boeser A 60.00 150.00
RBR Jesper Bratt B 12.00 30.00
RCF Christian Fischer B 10.00 25.00
RCK Clayton Keller A 20.00 50.00
RCM Charlie McAvoy A 25.00 60.00
RDG Denis Gurianov C 8.00 20.00
RES Evgeny Svechnikov C 15.00 40.00
RFC Filip Chytil B 8.00 20.00
RHF Haydn Fleury C 8.00 20.00
RIB Ivan Barbashev C 8.00 20.00
RJD Jake DeBrusk A 12.00 30.00
RJH Josh Ho-Sang A 10.00 25.00
RJK Jakob Forsbacka-Karlsson C 8.00 20.00
RJR Jack Roslovic C 10.00 25.00
RKE Alex Kerfoot B 8.00 20.00
RKY Kailer Yamamoto A 20.00 50.00
RLK Luke Kunin B 8.00 20.00
RMN Martin Necas B 8.00 20.00
RNS Nikita Scherbak C 15.00 40.00
ROT Owen Tippett A 15.00 40.00
RPD Pierre-Luc Dubois A 15.00 40.00
RSM Samuel Morin A 8.00 20.00
RTJ Tyson Jost A 15.00 40.00
RTS Travis Sanheim A 8.00 20.00
RTT Tage Thompson C 12.00 30.00
RVK Vladislav Kamenev B 12.00 30.00
RVM Victor Mete B 8.00 20.00
RVZ Valentin Zykov C 8.00 20.00
RWB Will Butcher B 10.00 25.00

2017-18 O-Pee-Chee Platinum Rookie Autographs Rainbow

*RAINBOW: .6X TO 1.5X BASIC INSERTS
RBB Brock Boeser A 80.00 150.00

2017-18 O-Pee-Chee Platinum Rookie Autographs Rainbow Seismic Gold

GOLD/25: 1.25X TO 3X BASIC INSERTS
RBB Brock Boeser 200.00 300.00

2017-18 O-Pee-Chee Platinum Rookie Autographs Red Prism

*RED/50: 1X TO 2.5X BASIC INSERTS

1990-91 OPC Premier

The 1990-91 O-Pee-Chee Premier hockey set contained 132 standard-size cards. The fronts featured color action photos of the players and have the words "O-Pee-Chee Premier" in a gold border above the picture. Border colors according to team framed the photo. Horizontal backs contained 1989-90 and career statistics. A player photo appeared in the upper left hand corner. The checklist was numbered alphabetically.

COMPLETE SET (132) 12.00 30.00
COMP.FACT.SET (132) 30.00 60.00
1 Scott Arniel .25 .60
2 Jergus Baca RC .30 .75
3 Brian Bellows .30 .75
4 Jean-Claude Bergeron RC .40 1.00
5 Daniel Berthiaume .30 .75
6 Rob Blake RC 2.50 6.00
7 Peter Bondra RC 1.50 4.00
8 Laurie Boschman .30 .75
9 Ray Bourque .60 1.50
10 Aaron Broten .30 .75
11 Greg Brown RC .40 1.00
12 Jimmy Carson .30 .75
13 Chris Chelios .40 1.00
14 Dino Ciccarelli .40 1.00
15 Zdeno Ciger RC .40 1.00
16 Paul Coffey .40 1.00
17 Danton Cole RC .40 1.00
18 Geoff Courtnall .30 .75
19 Mike Craig UER RC .40 1.00
20 John Cullen .40 1.00
21 Vincent Damphousse .30 .75
22 Gerald Diduck .30 .75
23 Kevin Dineen .40 1.00
24 Per Djoos RC .40 1.00
25 Tie Domi RC 1.50 4.00
26 Peter Douris RC .40 1.00
27 Rob DiMaio RC .40 1.00
28 Pat Elynuik .30 .75
29 Bob Essensa RC .60 1.50
30 Sergei Fedorov RC 4.00 10.00
31 Brent Fedyk RC .40 1.00
32 Ron Francis .50 1.25
33 Link Gaetz RC .40 1.00
34 Troy Gamble RC .40 1.00
35 Johan Garpenlov RC .40 1.00
36 Mike Gartner .40 1.00
37 Rick Green .40 1.00
38 Wayne Gretzky 2.00 5.00
39 Jeff Hackett RC .60 1.50
40 Dale Hawerchuk .50 1.25
41 Ron Hextall .30 .75
42 Bruce Hoffort RC .40 1.00
43 Bobby Holik RC .40 1.00
44 Martin Hostak RC .40 1.00
45 Phil Housley .30 .75
46 Jody Hull RC .40 1.00
47 Brett Hull .75 2.00
48 Al Iafrate .25 .60
49 Peter Ing RC .40 1.00
50 Jaromir Jagr RC 12.00 30.00
51 Curtis Joseph RC 2.50 6.00
52 Robert Kron RC .40 1.00
53 Frantisek Kucera RC .40 1.00
54 Dale Kushner RC .40 1.00
55 Guy Lafleur .50 1.25
56 Pat LaFontaine .40 1.00
57 Mike Lalor RC .30 .75
58 Steve Larmer .30 .75
59 Jiri Latal RC .40 1.00
60 Jamie Leach RC .30 .75
61 Brian Leetch .50 1.25
62 Claude Lemieux .25 .60
63 Mario Lemieux 2.00 5.00
64 Craig Ludwig .40 1.00
65 Al MacInnis .30 .75
66 Mikko Makela .30 .75
67 David Marcinyshyn RC .40 1.00
68 Stephane Matteau RC .40 1.00
69 Brad McCrimmon .40 1.00
70 Kirk McLean .25 .60
71 Mark Messier .75 2.00
72 Kelly Miller .25 .60
73 Kevin Miller RC .40 1.00
74 Mike Modano RC 3.00 8.00
75 Alexander Mogilny RC 1.25 3.00
76 Andy Moog .40 1.00
77 Joe Mullen .30 .75
78 Kirk Muller .30 .75
79 Pat Murray RC .40 1.00
80 Jarmo Myllys RC .40 1.00
81 Petr Nedved RC .40 1.00
82 Cam Neely .40 1.00
83 Bernie Nicholls .40 1.00
84 Joe Nieuwendyk .25 .60
85 Chris Nilan .25 .60
86 Owen Nolan RC 1.25 3.00
87 Brian Noonan .40 1.00
88 Adam Oates .40 1.00

9 Greg Parks RC .40 1.00
0 Adrien Plavsic RC .40 1.00
Keith Primeau RC .60 1.50
2 Brian Propp .40 1.00
3 Dan Quinn .30 .75
4 Bill Ranford .30 .75
5 Robert Reichel RC .40 1.00
5 Mike Ricci RC .40 1.00
7 Steven Rice RC .40 1.00
3 Stephane Richer .40 1.00
9 Luc Robitaille .40 1.00
00 Jeremy Roenick RC 3.00 8.00
01 Patrick Roy 2.00 5.00
02 Joe Sakic 1.25 3.00
03 Denis Savard .50 1.25
04 Anatoli Semenov RC .30 .75
05 Brendan Shanahan .50 1.25
06 Ray Sheppard .25 .60
07 Mike Sillinger RC .40 1.00
08 Ilkka Sinisalo .30 .75
09 Bobby Smith .30 .75
10 Paul Stanton RC .40 1.00
11 Kevin Stevens RC .75 2.00
12 Scott Stevens .40 1.00
13 Alan Stewart RC .40 1.00
14 Mats Sundin RC 2.50 6.00
15 Brent Sutter .30 .75
16 Tim Sweeney RC .40 1.00
17 Peter Taglianetti .30 .75
18 John Tanner RC .40 1.00
19 Dave Tippett .30 .75
20 Rick Tocchet .40 1.00
21 Bryan Trottier .50 1.25
22 John Tucker .30 .75
23 Darren Turcotte RC .30 .75
24 Pierre Turgeon .30 .75
25 Randy Velischek .25 .60
26 Mike Vernon .40 1.00
27 Wes Walz RC .40 1.00
28 Carey Wilson .30 .75
29 Doug Wilson .40 1.00
30 Steve Yzerman 1.25 3.00
31 Peter Zezel .40 1.00
32 Checklist 1-132 .20 .50

1991-92 OPC Premier

he 1991-92 O-Pee-Chee Premier hockey set contains 98 standard-size cards. Color player photos are ordered above and below in gold. Player name, team nd position appear at the bottom. The backs have a mall color player photo, biography, team logo and atistics. A Konstantinov variation can be found with dstrom's photo on the back. Very few of these riations have been located. To commemorate the 5th Anniversary of the NHL, throwback sweaters were orn several times during the 1991-92 campaign by e original six teams. Cards portraying players in ose sweaters are indicated by ORIG6.

OMPLETE SET (198) 6.00 15.00
OMP.FACT.SET (198) 8.00 20.00
Dale Hawerchuk .05 .15
Ray Sheppard .01 .05
Wayne Gretzky UER .60 1.50
John MacLean .05 .15
Pat Verbeek .01 .05
Doug Wilson .05 .15
Adam Oates .05 .15
Bob McGill .01 .05
Mike Vernon .05 .15
0 Glenn Anderson .05 .15
Tony Amonte RC .60 1.50
2 Stephen Leach .01 .05
Steve Duchesne .01 .05
Patrick Roy .50 1.25
Jarmo Myllys .01 .05
Yanic Dupre RC .01 .05
Chris Chelios .08 .25
Bill Ranford .05 .15
Ed Belfour .08 .25
Michel Picard RC .01 .05
Rob Zettler .01 .05
Kevin Todd RC .01 .05
Mike Ricci .08 .25
Jaromir Jagr .15 .40
Sergei Nemchinov .01 .05
Kevin Stevens .01 .05
Dan Quinn .01 .05
Adam Graves .05 .15
Pat Jablonski RC .05 .15
Scott Mellanby .01 .05
Tomas Forslund RC .01 .05
Doug Weight RC .50 1.25
Peter Ing .05 .15
Luc Robitaille .05 .15
Scott Niedermayer .01 .05
Dean Evason .01 .05
John Tonelli .01 .05
Ron Hextall .05 .15
Troy Mallette .01 .05
Tony Hrkac .01 .05
Ken Hodge Jr. .01 .05
Kip Miller .01 .05
Randy Burridge .01 .05
Rob Blake .05 .15
Sergei Makarov .01 .05
Luke Richardson .01 .05
Craig Berube .01 .05
Joe Nieuwendyk .05 .15
Brett Hull .10 .30
Phil Housley .05 .15
Mark Messier .08 .25
Jeremy Roenick .08 .25
Dave Christian .01 .05
Dave Barr .01 .05
Sergio Momesso .01 .05
Pat Falloon .01 .05
Brian Leetch .08 .25
Russ Courtnall .01 .05
Pierre Turgeon .05 .15
Steve Larmer .05 .15
Petr Klima .01 .05
Mikhail Tatarinov .01 .05
Rick Tocchet .05 .15
Pat LaFontaine .08 .25
Rob Pearson RC .01 .05
Glen Featherstone .01 .05
Pavel Bure .08 .25
Sergei Fedorov .15 .40
Kelly Kisio .01 .05
Joe Sakic .20 .50
Denis Savard .05 .15
Andrew Cassels .01 .05
Steve Yzerman .50 1.25
Todd Elik .01 .05
Troy Murray .01 .05
Rob Ramage .01 .05
Trevor Linden .05 .15
Mike Richter .08 .25

79 Paul Coffey .08 .25
80 Craig Ludwig .01 .05
81 Al MacInnis .05 .15
82 Tomas Sandstrom .01 .05
83 Tim Kerr .01 .05
84 Scott Stevens .05 .15
85 Steve Kasper .01 .05
86 Kirk Muller .01 .05
87 Pat MacLeod RC .01 .05
88 Kevin Hatcher .05 .15
89 Wayne Presley .01 .05
90 Darryl Sydor .05 .15
91 Tom Chorske .01 .05
92 Theo Fleury .01 .05
93 Craig Janney .05 .15
94 Rod Brind'Amour .08 .25
95 Ron Sutter .01 .05
96 Matt DelGuidice RC .01 .05
97 Rollie Melanson .05 .15
98 Tom Kurvers .01 .05
99 Bryan Marchment RC .05 .15
100 Grant Fuhr .08 .25
101 Geoff Courtnall .05 .15
102 Joel Otto .01 .05
103 Tom Barrasso .05 .15
104 Vincent Damphousse .01 .05
105 John LeClair RC .60 1.50
106 Gary Leeman .01 .05
107 Cam Neely .08 .25
108 Jeff Hackett .05 .15
109 Stu Barnes .01 .05
110 Neil Wilkinson .01 .05
111 Jari Kurri .08 .25
112 Jon Casey .05 .15
113 Stephane Richer .05 .15
114 Mario Lemieux .60 1.50
115 Brad Jones .01 .05
116 Wendel Clark .05 .15
117 Nicklas Lidstrom RC .60 1.50
118A Vladimir Konstantinov ERR RC 12.50 25.00
118B Vladimir Konstantinov COR RC .40 1.00
119 Ray Bourque .15 .40
120 Ron Francis .05 .15
121 Esa Tikkanen .01 .05
122 Randy Hillier .01 .05
123 Randy Gilhen .01 .05
124 Barry Pederson .01 .05
125 Charlie Huddy .01 .05
126 Gary Roberts .05 .15
127 John Cullen .01 .05
128 Dave Gagner .01 .05
129 Bob Kudelski .01 .05
130 Brendan Shanahan .08 .25
131 Dirk Graham .01 .05
132 Checklist 1-99 .01 .05
133 Andy Moog .08 .25
134 Gary Leeman ORIG6 .01 .05
135 Steve Larmer ORIG6 .05 .15
136 Steve Smith .01 .05
137 Dave Manson .01 .05
138 Nelson Emerson .01 .05
139 Doug Weight ORIG6 .08 .25
140 Uwe Krupp .01 .05
141 Peter Douris ORIG6 .01 .05
142 Steve Yzerman ORIG6 .30 .75
143 Derian Hatcher .05 .15
144 Vladimir Ruzicka ORIG6 .01 .05
145 Kirk Muller ORIG6 .01 .05
146 Darrin Shannon .01 .05
147 Mike Gartner ORIG6 .05 .15
148 Bob Carpenter ORIG6 .01 .05
149 Josef Beranek RC .01 .05
150 Chris Chelios ORIG6 .08 .25
151 Bob Rouse ORIG6 .01 .05
152 Guy Carbonneau ORIG6 .05 .15
153 Joe Mullen .05 .15
154 Ken Hodge Jr. ORIG6 .01 .05
155 Vladimir Konstantinov ORIG6 .08 .25
156 Brent Sutter .01 .05
157 Eric Desjardins ORIG6 .05 .15
158 Kirk McLean .05 .15
159 John Tonelli ORIG6 .01 .05
160 Rob Cimetta ORIG6 .01 .05
161 Shayne Corson .01 .05
162 Russ Romaniuk RC .01 .05
163 Nicklas Lidstrom ORIG6 .08 .25
164 Mike Gartner .05 .15
165 Curtis Joseph .08 .25
166 Brian Mullen .01 .05
167 Jimmy Carson .01 .05
168 Petr Svoboda ORIG6 .01 .05
169 Troy Crowder .01 .05
170 Patrick Roy ORIG6 .30 .75
171 Adam Creighton .01 .05
172 James Patrick ORIG6 .01 .05
173 Sergei Fedorov ORIG6 .15 .40
174 Jeremy Roenick ORIG6 .08 .25
175 Tim Cheveldae ORIG6 .05 .15
176 Dimitri Khristich .01 .05
177 Wendel Clark ORIG6 .08 .20
178 Andrei Lomakin .01 .05
179 Benoit Hogue .01 .05
180 Dave Ellett ORIG6 .01 .05
181 Mathieu Schneider ORIG6 .01 .05
182 Kay Whitmore .05 .15
183 Brian Leetch ORIG6 .08 .25
184 Sylvain Turgeon ORIG6 .01 .05
185 Brian Bradley ORIG6 .01 .05
186 John LeClair ORIG6 .20 .50
187 Paul Fenton .01 .05
188 Alain Cote ORIG6 .01 .05
189 Mike Krushelnyski ORIG6 .01 .05
190 Brian Bradley .01 .05
191 Grant Fuhr ORIG6 .08 .25
192 Ray Bourque ORIG6 .08 .25
193 Owen Nolan .08 .25
194 Russ Courtnall ORIG6 .01 .05
195 Steve Thomas .01 .05
196 Ed Olczyk .01 .05
197 Chris Terreri .05 .15
198 Checklist 100-198 .01 .05

1992-93 OPC Premier

The 1992-93 O-Pee-Chee Premier hockey set consists of 132 standard-sized cards. The fronts feature action color player photos with white borders. A team color-coded stripe accents the top edge of each picture. The O-Pee-Chee logo overlaps the picture at the lower right corner. The player's name and position appear in the bottom border. The backs show a slightly offset, pale, team color-coded panel which carries a close-up photo and biographical data. A darker team color-coded bar with a speckled effect presents statistics and appears at the bottom. The team logo overlaps the picture panel at the lower left corner of the photo. Each pack contained an insert from either the Top Rookie set or the 22-card Star Performers set. According to O-Pee-Chee, every ninth pack contained a Top Rookie card as its insert with the other packs containing a Star Performers card. The production quantity reportedly was 7,500 20-box wax cases.

1 Dave Christian .05 .15
2 Christian Ruuttu .05 .15
3 Vincent Damphousse .07 .20
4 Chris Lindberg .05 .15
5 Bill Lindsay RC .05 .15
6 Dmitri Kvartalnov RC .05 .15
7 Darcy Loewen .05 .15
8 Ed Courtenay .05 .15
9 Sergei Krivokrasov .05 .15
10 Shawn Antoski .05 .15
11 Andre Racicot .07 .20
12 Marty McInnis .05 .15
13 Alexei Zhamnov .07 .20
14 Keith Jones RC .10 .25
15 Steve Konowalchuk RC .07 .20
16 Darryl Sydor .05 .15
17 Janne Ojanen .05 .15
18 Doug Zmolek RC .05 .15
19 Michael Nylander RC .05 .15
20 Russ Courtnall .05 .15
21 Martin Straka RC .20 .50
22 Kevin Dahl RC .05 .15
23 Kent Manderville .05 .15
24 Steve Heinze .05 .15
25 Philippe Bozon .05 .15
26 Brent Fedyk .05 .15
27 Kris Draper .05 .15
28 Brad Schlegel .05 .15
29 Patric Kjellberg RC .10 .25
30 Ted Donato .05 .15
31 Vyatcheslav Butsayev RC .05 .15
32 Tyler Wright .05 .15
33 Tom Pederson RC .07 .20
34 Jim Hiller RC .05 .15
35 Chris Luongo RC .05 .15
36 Robert Petrovicky RC .05 .15
37 Jean-Francois Quintin RC .05 .15
38 Chris Dahlquist .07 .20
39 Daniel Laperriere RC .05 .15
40 Guy Hebert RC .15 .40
41 Ed Ronan RC .05 .15
42 Shawn Cronin .05 .15
43 Keith Tkachuk .10 .25
44 Dino Ciccarelli .07 .20
45 Doug Evans .05 .15
46 Roman Hamrlik RC .20 .50
47 Robert Lang RC .05 .15
48 Kerry Huffman .05 .15
49 Pat Conacher .05 .15
50 Dominik Hasek .20 .50
51 Dominic Roussel .07 .20
52 Glen Murray .05 .15
53 Igor Korolev RC .05 .15
54 Jiri Slegr .05 .15
55 Mikael Andersson .05 .15
56 Bob Babcock RC .05 .15
57 Ron Hextall .07 .20
58 Jeff Daniels .05 .15
59 Doug Crossman .07 .20
60 Viktor Gordijuk RC .05 .15
61 Adam Creighton .05 .15
62 Rob DiMaio .05 .15
63 Eric Weinrich .05 .15
64 Vitali Prokhorov RC .05 .15
65 Dimitri Yushkevich RC .05 .15
66 Evgeny Davydov .05 .15
67 Dixon Ward RC .07 .20
68 Teemu Selanne .20 .50
69 Rob Zamuner RC .07 .20
70 Joe Reekie .05 .15
71 Slava Kozlov .07 .20
72 Philippe Boucher .05 .15
73 Phil Bourque .05 .15
74 Yvon Corriveau .05 .15
75 Brian Bellows .07 .20
76 Wendell Young .07 .20
77 Bobby Holik .07 .20
78 Bob Carpenter .05 .15
79 Scott Lachance .05 .15
80 John Druce .05 .15
81 Keith Carney RC .20 .50
82 Neil Brady .05 .15
83 Richard Matvichuk RC .07 .20
84 Sergei Bautin RC .05 .15
85 Patrick Poulin .05 .15
86 Gordie Roberts .07 .20
87 Kay Whitmore .07 .20
88 Steph Beauregard .07 .20
89 Vladimir Malakhov .05 .15
90 Richard Smehlik RC .05 .15
91 Mike Ricci .07 .20
92 Sean Burke .07 .20
93 Andrei Kovalenko RC .15 .40
94 Shawn McEachern .05 .15
95 Pat Jablonski .07 .20
96 Oleg Petrov RC .05 .15
97 Glenn Mulvenna RC .05 .15
98 Jason Woolley RC .05 .15
99 Mark Greig .07 .20
100 Nikolai Borschevsky RC .05 .15
101 Joe Juneau .05 .15
102 Eric Lindros .30 .75
103 Darius Kasparaitis .05 .15
104 Sandis Ozolinsh .05 .15
105 Stan Drulia RC .05 .15
106 Mike Needham RC .05 .15
107 Norm Maciver .05 .15
108 Sylvain Lefebvre .05 .15
109 Tommy Sjodin RC .05 .15
110 Bob Sweeney .05 .15
111 Brian Mullen .05 .15
112 Peter Sidorkiewicz .05 .15
113 Scott Niedermayer .10 .25
114 Felix Potvin .20 .50
115 Robb Stauber .07 .20
116 Sylvain Turgeon .05 .15
117 Mark Janssens .05 .15
118 Darren Banks RC .05 .15
119 Pat Elynuik .05 .15
120 Bill Guerin RC .60 1.50
121 Reggie Savage .05 .15
122 Enrico Ciccone .05 .15
123 Chris Kontos RC .05 .15
124 Martin Rucinsky .05 .15
125 Alexei Zhitnik .05 .15
126 Alexei Kovalev .07 .20
127 Tim Kerr .05 .15
128 Guy Larose .05 .15
129 Brent Gilchrist .05 .15
130 Steve Duchesne .05 .15
131 Drake Berehowsky .05 .15
132 Checklist 1-132 .05 .15

1992-93 OPC Premier Star Performers

This 22-card standard-size set was randomly inserted in 1992-93 O-Pee-Chee Premier foil packs. According to O-Pee-Chee, the insertion rate was eight out of every nine packs. The other packs contained Top Rookie inserts.

COMPLETE SET (22) 4.00 10.00
1 Ray Ferraro .05 .15
2 Dale Hunter .15 .40
3 Murray Craven .05 .15
4 Paul Coffey .20 .50
5 Jeremy Roenick .25 .60
6 Denis Savard .15 .40
7 Jon Casey .15 .40
8 Doug Gilmour .15 .40
9 Rod Brind'Amour .15 .40
10 Pavel Bure .20 .50
11 Joe Sakic .40 1.00
12 Pat Falloon .05 .15
13 Adam Oates .15 .40
14 Gary Roberts .05 .15
15 Mark Messier .20 .50
16 Phil Housley .05 .15
17 Pat LaFontaine .20 .50
18 Stephane Richer .15 .40
19 Bill Ranford .15 .40
20 Sergei Fedorov .30 .75
21 Brett Hull .30 .75
22 Mario Lemieux 1.00 2.50

1992-93 OPC Premier Top Rookies

This four-card standard-size set was randomly inserted in 1992-93 O-Pee-Chee Premier foil packs. According to O-Pee-Chee, eight out of nine packs contained a Star Performer insert card, while the ninth pack contained a Top Rookie card as its insert.

COMPLETE SET (4) .60 1.50
1 Eric Lindros .20 .50
2 Roman Hamrlik .30 .75
3 Dominic Roussel .08 .25
4 Felix Potvin .60 1.50

1993-94 OPC Premier

1 Patrick Roy .25 .60
2 Alexei Zhitnik .05 .15
3 Uwe Krupp .05 :15
4 Todd Gill .05 .15
5 Paul Stanton .05 .15
6 Petr Nedved .05 .15
7 Dale Hawerchuk .12 .30
8 Kevin Miller .05 .15
9 Nicklas Lidstrom .10 .25
10 Joe Sakic .25 .60
11 Thomas Steen .05 .15
12 Peter Bondra .07 .20
13 Brian Noonan .05 .15
14 Glen Featherstone .05 .15
15 Mike Vernon .07 .20
16 Janne Ojanen .05 .15
17 Neil Brady .05 .15
18 Dimitri Yushkevich .05 .15
19 Rob Zamuner .05 .15
20 Zarley Zalapski .05 .15
21 Mike Sullivan .05 .15
22 Jamie Baker .05 .15
23 Craig MacTavish .05 .15
24 Mark Tinordi .05 .15
25 Brian Leetch .10 .25
26 Brian Skrudland .05 .15
27 Keith Tkachuk .10 .25
28 Patrick Flatley .05 .15
29 Doug Bodger .05 .15
30 Felix Potvin .20 .50
31 Shawn Antoski .05 .15
32 Eric Desjardins .07 .20
33 Mike Donnelly .05 .15
34 Kjell Samuelsson .05 .15
35 Nelson Emerson .05 .15
36 Phil Housley .07 .20
37 Mario Lemieux LL .40 1.00
38 Shayne Corson .05 .15
39 Steve Smith .05 .15
40 Bob Kudelski .05 .15
41 Joe Cirella .05 .15
42 Sergei Nemchinov .05 .15
43 Kerry Huffman .05 .15
44 Bob Beers .05 .15
45 Al Iafrate .05 .15
46 Mike Modano .15 .40
47 Pat Verbeek .05 .15
48 Joel Otto .05 .15
49 Dino Ciccarelli .07 .20
50 Adam Oates .10 .25
51 Pat Elynuik .05 .15
52 Bobby Holik .05 .15
53 Johan Garpenlov .05 .15
54 Jeff Beukeboom .05 .15
55 Tommy Soderstrom .07 .20
56 Rob Blake .07 .20
57 Marty McInnis .05 .15
58 Dixon Ward .05 .15
59 Patrice Brisebois .05 .15
60 Ed Belfour .10 .25
61 Donald Audette .05 .15
62 Mike Ricci .05 .15
63 Fredrik Olausson .05 .15
64 Norm Maciver .05 .15
65 Andrew Cassels .05 .15
66 Tim Cheveldae .07 .20
67 David Reid .05 .15
68 Philippe Bozon .05 .15
69 Drake Berehowsky .05 .15
70 Tony Amonte .07 .20
71 Dave Manson .05 .15
72 Rick Tocchet .07 .20
73 Steve Kasper .05 .15
74 Assist Leader .10 .25
75 Ulf Dahlen .05 .15
76 Chris Lindberg .05 .15
77 Doug Wilson .05 .15
78 Mike Ridley .05 .15
79 Viacheslav Butsayev .05 .15
80 Scott Stevens .10 .25
81 Cliff Ronning .05 .15
82 Andrei Lomakin .05 .15
83 Shawn Burr .05 .15
84 Benoit Brunet .05 .15
85 Valeri Kamensky .07 .20
86 Randy Carlyle .05 .15
87 Chris Joseph .05 .15
88 Dirk Graham .05 .15
89 Ken Sutton .05 .15
90 Luc Robitaille AS .07 .20
91 Mario Lemieux AS .40 1.00
92 Teemu Selanne AS .20 .50
93 Ray Bourque AS .15 .40
94 Chris Chelios AS .10 .25
95 Ed Belfour AS .10 .25
96 Keith Jones .05 .15
97 Sylvain Turgeon .05 .15
98 Jim Johnson .05 .15
99 Michael Nylander .05 .15
100 Theo Fleury .05 .15
101 Shawn Chambers .05 .15
102 Alexander Semak .05 .15
103 Ron Sutter .05 .15
104 Glenn Anderson .10 .25
105 Jaromir Jagr .25 .60
106 Adam Graves .05 .15
107 Nikolai Borschevsky .05 .15
108 Vladimir Konstantinov .07 .20
109 Robb Stauber .05 .15
110 Arturs Irbe .07 .20
111 Felix Potvin LL .20 .50
112 Darius Kasparaitis .05 .15
113 Kirk McLean .07 .20
114 Glen Wesley .05 .15
115 Rod Brind'Amour .07 .20
116 Mike Eagles .05 .15
117 Brian Bradley .05 .15
118 Dave Christian .05 .15
119 Randy Wood .05 .15
120 Craig Janney .07 .20
121 Eric Lindros SR .30 .75
122 Tommy Soderstrom SR .07 .20
123 Shawn McEachern SR .05 .15
124 Andrei Kovalenko SR .05 .15
125 Joe Juneau SR .07 .20
126 Felix Potvin SR .20 .50
127 Dixon Ward SR .05 .15
128 Alexei Zhamnov SR .07 .20
129 Vladimir Malakhov SR .05 .15
130 Teemu Selanne SR .20 .50
131 Neal Broten .07 .20
132 Ulf Samuelsson .05 .15
133 Mark Janssens .05 .15
134 Claude Lemieux .05 .15
135 Mike Richter .10 .25
136 Doug Weight .07 .20
137 Rob Pearson .05 .15
138 Sylvain Cote .05 .15
139 Mike Keane .05 .15
140 Benoit Hogue .05 .15
141 Michel Petit .05 .15
142 Mark Freer .05 .15
143 Doug Zmolek .05 .15
144 Tony Granato .05 .15
145 Paul Coffey .10 .25
146 Ted Donato .05 .15
147 Brent Sutter .05 .15
148 A.Mogilny T.Selanne LL .20 .50
149 James Patrick .05 .15
150 Mikael Andersson .05 .15
151 Steve Duchesne .05 .15
152 Terry Carkner .05 .15
153 Russ Courtnall .05 .15
154 Brian Mullen .05 .15
155 Martin Straka .05 .15
156 Geoff Sanderson .07 .20
157 Mark Howe .10 .25
158 Stephane Richer .07 .20
159 Doug Crossman .05 .15
160 John Vanbiesbrouck .07 .20
161 Bob Essensa .07 .20
162 Wayne Presley .05 .15
163 Mathieu Schneider .05 .15
164 Jiri Slegr .05 .15
165 Stephane Fiset .07 .20
166 Wendell Young .05 .15
167 Kevin Dineen .05 .15
168 Sandis Ozolinsh .05 .15
169 Mike Krushelnyski .05 .15
170 Kevin Stevens AS .05 .15
171 Pat LaFontaine AS .10 .25
172 Alexander Mogilny AS .07 .20
173 Larry Murphy AS .07 .20
174 Al Iafrate AS .05 .15
175 Tom Barrasso AS .07 .20
176 Derek King .05 .15
177 Bob Probert .07 .20
178 Gary Suter .05 .15
179 David Shaw .05 .15
180 Luc Robitaille .07 .20
181 John LeClair .10 .25
182 Troy Murray .05 .15
183 Dave Gagner .07 .20
184 Darcy Loewen .05 .15
185 Mario Lemieux LL .40 1.00
186 Pat Jablonski .05 .15
187 Alexei Kovalev .07 .20
188 Todd Krygier .05 .15
189 Larry Murphy .07 .20
190 Pierre Turgeon .07 .20
191 Craig Ludwig .05 .15
192 Brad May .07 .20
193 John MacLean .07 .20
194 Ron Wilson .05 .15
195 Eric Weinrich .05 .15
196 Steve Chiasson .05 .15
197 Dmitri Kvartalnov .05 .15
198 Andrei Kovalenko .05 .15
199 Rob Gaudreau RC .10 .25
200 Evgeny Davydov .05 .15
201 Adrien Plavsic .05 .15
202 Brian Bellows .07 .20
203 Doug Evans .05 .15
204 Win Leader Tom Barrasso .07 .20
205 Joe Nieuwendyk .07 .20
206 Jari Kurri .10 .25
207 Bob Rouse .05 .15
208 Yvon Corriveau .05 .15
209 John Blue .07 .20
210 Dimitri Khristich .05 .15
211 Brent Fedyk .05 .15
212 Jody Hull .05 .15
213 Chris Terreri .07 .20
214 Mike McPhee .05 .15
215 Chris Kontos .05 .15
216 Greg Gilbert .05 .15
217 Sergei Zubov .05 .15
218 Grant Fuhr .10 .25
219 Charlie Huddy .05 .15
220 Mario Lemieux .40 1.00
221 Sheldon Kennedy .05 .15
222 Curtis Joseph St. Louis Blues Save Pct. Leader .10 .25
223 Brad Dalgarno .05 .15
224 Bret Hedican .05 .15
225 Trevor Linden .07 .20
226 Darryl Sydor .05 .15
227 Jay More .05 .15
228 Dave Poulin .05 .15
229 Frank Musil .05 .15
230 Mark Recchi .12 .30
231 Craig Simpson .05 .15
232 Gino Cavallini .05 .15
233 Vincent Damphousse .07 .20
234 Luciano Borsato .05 .15
235 Dave Andreychuk .10 .25
236 Ken Daneyko .05 .15
237 Chris Chelios .10 .25
238 Andrew McBain .05 .15
239 Rick Tabaracci .05 .15
240 Steve Larmer .07 .20
241 Sean Burke .05 .15
242 Rob DiMaio .05 .15
243 Jim Paek .05 .15
244 Dave Lowry .05 .15
245 Alexander Mogilny .07 .20
246 Darren Turcotte .05 .15
247 Brendan Shanahan .12 .30
248 Peter Taglianetti .05 .15
249 Scott Mellanby .07 .20
250 Guy Carbonneau .05 .15
251 Claude LaPointe .05 .15
252 Pat Conacher .05 .15
253 Roger Johansson .05 .15
254 Cam Neely .10 .25
255 Garry Galley .05 .15
256 Keith Primeau .05 .15
257 Scott Lachance .05 .15
258 Bill Ranford .07 .20
259 Pat Fallon .05 .15
260 Pavel Bure .10 .25
261 Darrin Shannon .05 .15
262 Mike Foligno .05 .15
263 Checklist 1-132 .05 .15
264 Checklist 133-264 .05 .15
265 Peter Douris .05 .15
266 Warren Rychel .05 .15
267 Owen Nolan .07 .20
268 Mark Osborne .05 .15
269 Teppo Numminen .05 .15
270 Rob Niedermayer .07 .20
271 Mark Lamb .05 .15
272 Curtis Joseph .10 .25
273 Joe Murphy .05 .15
274 Bernie Nicholls .05 .15
275 Gord Roberts .05 .15
276 Al MacInnis .07 .20
277 Ken Wregget .05 .15
278 Calle Johansson .05 .15
279 Tom Kurvers .05 .15
280 Steve Yzerman .25 .60
281 Roman Hamrlik .05 .15
282 Esa Tikkanen .05 .15
283 Darrin Madeley RC .10 .25
284 Robert Dirk .05 .15
285 Derek Plante RC .10 .25
286 Ron Tugnutt .07 .20
287 Frank Pietrangelo .07 .20
288 Paul DiPietro .05 .15
289 Alexander Godynyuk .05 .15
290 Kirk Maltby RC .10 .25
291 Olaf Kolzig .07 .20
292 Vitali Karamnov .05 .15
293 Alexei Gusarov .05 .15
294 Bryan Erickson .05 .15
295 Jocelyn Lemieux .05 .15
296 Bryan Trottier .12 .30
297 Dave Ellett .05 .15
298 Tim Watters .05 .15
299 Joe Juneau .07 .20
300 Steve Thomas .05 .15
301 Mark Greig .05 .15
302 Jeff Reese .05 .15
303 Steven King .05 .15
304 Don Beaupre .07 .20
305 Denis Savard .12 .30
306 Greg Smyth .05 .15
307 Jaroslav Modry RC .10 .25
308 Petr Svoboda .05 .15
309 Mike Craig .05 .15
310 Eric Lindros .30 .75
311 Dana Murzyn .05 .15
312 Sean Hill .05 .15
313 Andre Racicot .05 .15
314 John Vanbiesbrouck .07 .20
315 Doug Lidster .05 .15
316 Garth Butcher .05 .15
317 Alexei Yashin .07 .20
318 Sergei Fedorov .15 .40
319 Louie DeBrusk .05 .15
320 Dominik Hasek CZE .20 .50
321 Michal Pivonka .05 .15
322 Bobby Holik .05 .15
323 Roman Hamrlik CZE .05 .15
324 Petr Svoboda .05 .15
325 Jaromir Jagr CZE .25 .60
326 Steven Finn .05 .15
327 Stephane Richer .07 .20
328 Claude Loiselle .05 .15
329 Joe Sacco .05 .15
330 Wayne Gretzky .50 1.25
331 Sylvain Lefebvre .05 .15
332 Sergei Bautin .05 .15
333 Craig Simpson .05 .15
334 Don Sweeney .05 .15
335 Dominic Roussel .07 .20
336 Scott Thomas RC .10 .25
337 Geoff Courtnall .05 .15
338 Tom Fitzgerald .05 .15
339 Kevin Haller .05 .15
340 Troy Loney .05 .15
341 Ronnie Stern .05 .15
342 Mark Astley RC .10 .25
343 Jeff Daniels .05 .15
344 Marc Bureau .05 .15
345 Micah Aivazoff RC .10 .25
346 Matthew Barnaby .07 .20
347 C.J. Young .05 .15
348 Dale Craigwell .05 .15
349 Ray Ferraro .05 .15
350 Ray Bourque .15 .40
351 Stu Barnes .05 .15
352 Alan Conroy RC .05 .15
353 Shawn McEachern .05 .15
354 Garry Valk .05 .15
355 Christian Ruuttu .05 .15
356 Darren Rumble .05 .15
357 Stu Grimson .05 .15
358 Alexander Karpovtsev .05 .15
359 Wendel Clark .07 .20
360 Michal Pivonka .05 .15
361 Peter Popovic RC .10 .25
362 Kevin Dahl .05 .15
363 Jeff Brown .05 .15
364 Daren Puppa .05 .15
365 Dallas Drake RC .10 .25
366 Dean McAmmond .05 .15
367 Martin Rucinsky .05 .15
368 Shane Churla .05 .15
369 Todd Ewen .05 .15
370 Kevin Stevens .05 .15
371 David Volek .05 .15
372 J.J. Daigneault .05 .15
373 Marc Bergevin .05 .15
374 Craig Billington .07 .20
375 Mike Gartner .07 .20
376 Jimmy Carson .05 .15
377 Bruce Driver .05 .15
378 Steve Heinze .05 .15
379 Patrick Carnback RC .10 .25
380 Wayne Gretzky CAN .50 1.25
381 Jeff Brown CAN .05 .15
382 Gary Roberts CAN .05 .15
383 Ray Bourque CAN .15 .40
384 Mike Gartner CAN .07 .20
385 Felix Potvin CAN .20 .50
386 Michel Goulet .05 .15
387 Dave Tippett .05 .15
388 Jim Waite .07 .20
389 Yuri Khmylev .05 .15
390 Doug Gilmour .12 .30
391 Brad McCrimmon .05 .15
392 Brent Severyn RC .10 .25
393 Jocelyn Thibault RC .10 .25
394 Boris Mironov .05 .15
395 Marty McSorley .05 .15
396 Shaun Van Allen .05 .15
397 Gary Leeman .05 .15
398 Ed Olczyk .05 .15
399 Darcy Wakaluk .05 .15
400 Murray Craven .05 .15
401 Martin Brodeur .25 .60
402 Paul Laus RC .05 .15
403 Bill Houlder .05 .15
404 Robert Reichel .05 .15
405 Alexandre Daigle .05 .15
406 Brent Thompson .05 .15
407 Keith Acton .05 .15
408 Dave Karpa .05 .15
409 Igor Korolev .05 .15
410 Chris Gratton .07 .20
411 Vincent Riendeau .05 .15
412 Darren McCarty RC .15 .40
413 Bob Carpenter .05 .15
414 Joe Cirella .05 .15
415 Stephane Matteau .05 .15
416 Jozef Stumpel .05 .15
417 Rich Pilon .05 .15
418 Mattias Norstrom RC .10 .25
419 Dmitri Moronov .05 .15
420 Alexei Zhamnov .07 .20
421 Bill Guerin .05 .15
422 Greg Hawgood .05 .15
423 Randy Cunneyworth .05 .15
424 Ron Francis .12 .30
425 Brett Hull .15 .40
426 Tim Sweeney .05 .15
427 Mike Rathje .05 .15
428 Dave Babych .05 .15
429 Chris Tancill .05 .15
430 Mark Messier .10 .25
431 Bob Sweeney .05 .15
432 Terry Yake .05 .15
433 Joe Reekie .05 .15
434 Tomas Sandstrom .05 .15
435 Kevin Hatcher .05 .15
436 Bill Lindsay .05 .15
437 Jon Casey .07 .20
438 Dennis Vaske .05 .15
439 Allen Pedersen .05 .15
440 Pavel Bure RUS .10 .25
441 Sergei Fedorov RUS .15 .40
442 Arturs Irbe LAT .07 .20
443 Darius Kasparaitis .05 .15
444 Evgeny Davydov .05 .15
445 Vladimir Malakhov .05 .15
446 Tom Barrasso .07 .20
447 Jeff Norton .05 .15
448 David Emma .05 .15
449 Pelle Eklund .05 .15
450 Jeremy Roenick .15 .40
451 Jesse Belanger .05 .15
452 Vitali Prokhorov .05 .15
453 Arto Blomsten .05 .15
454 Peter Zezel .05 .15
455 Kelly Kisio .05 .15
456 Zdeno Ciger .05 .15
457 Greg Johnson .05 .15
458 Dave Archibald .05 .15
459 Vladimir Vujtek .05 .15
460 Mats Sundin .07 .20
461 Dan Keczmer .05 .15
462 Stephan Lebeau .05 .15
463 Dominik Hasek .20 .50
464 Kevin Lowe .05 .15
465 Gord Murphy .05 .15
466 Bryan Smolinski .05 .15
467 Josef Beranek .05 .15
468 Ron Hextall .07 .20
469 Randy Ladouceur .05 .15
470 Scott Niedermayer .10 .25
471 Kelly Hrudey .07 .20
472 Mike Needham .05 .15
473 John Tucker .05 .15
474 Kelly Miller .05 .15
475 Jyrki Lumme .05 .15
476 Andy Moog .10 .25
477 Glen Murray .05 .15
478 Mark Ferner RC .05 .15
479 John Cullen .05 .15
480 Gilbert Dionne .05 .15

481 Paul Ranheim	.05	.15
482 Mike Hough	.05	.15
483 Teemu Selanne	.20	.50
484 Aaron Ward RC	.10	.25
485 Chris Pronger	.10	.25
486 Glenn Healy	.07	.20
487 Curtis Leschyshyn	.05	.15
488 Jim Montgomery RC	.10	.25
489 Travis Green	.07	.20
490 Pat LaFontaine	.10	.25
491 Bobby Dollas RC	.05	.15
492 Alexei Kasatonov	.05	.15
493 Corey Millen	.05	.15
494 Slava Kozlov	.07	.20
495 Igor Kravchuk	.05	.15
496 Dimitri Filimonov	.05	.15
497 Jeff Odgers	.05	.15
498 Joe Mullen	.07	.20
499 Gary Shuchuk	.05	.15
500 Jeremy Roenick USA	.15	.40
501 Tom Barrasso USA	.07	.20
502 Keith Tkachuk USA	.10	.25
503 Phil Housley USA	.07	.20
504 Tony Granato USA	.05	.15
505 Brian Leetch USA	.10	.25
506 Anatoli Semenov	.05	.15
507 Steve Leach	.05	.15
508 Brian Skrudland	.05	.15
509 Kirk Muller	.05	.15
510 Gary Roberts	.05	.15
511 Gerard Gallant	.05	.15
512 Joey Kocur	.05	.15
513 Tie Domi	.05	.15
514 Kay Whitmore	.05	.15
515 Vladimir Malakhov	.05	.15
516 Stewart Malgunas RC	.10	.25
517 Jamie Macoun	.05	.15
518 Alan May	.05	.15
519 Guy Hebert	.07	.20
520 Derian Hatcher	.05	.15
521 Richard Smehlik	.05	.15
522 Joby Messier RC	.10	.25
523 Trent Klatt	.05	.15
524 Tom Chorske	.05	.15
525 Iain Fraser RC	.10	.25
526 Dan Laperriere	.05	.15
527 Checklist	.05	.15
528 Checklist	.05	.15

1993-94 OPC Premier Gold

COMPLETE SET (528)	60.00	120.00
COMP.SERIES 1 (264)	25.00	60.00
COMP.SERIES 2 (264)	25.00	60.00

*GOLD: 2.5X TO 6X BASIC CARDS
ONE PER OPC PACK/FOUR PER OPC JUMBO
CARD BACKS WRITTEN IN FRENCH

1993-94 OPC Premier Black Gold

These 24 standard-size Black Gold cards were randomly inserted in O-Pee-Chee packs. The white-bordered fronts feature color player action shots with darkened backgrounds. Gold-foil stripes above and below the photo carry multiple-set logos. The player's name appears in white lettering within a black stripe through the lower gold-foil stripe. The white-bordered and horizontal back carries a color player cutout on one side, and career highlights in French and English within a purple rectangle on the other.

1 Wayne Gretzky	8.00	20.00
2 Vincent Damphousse	1.25	3.00
3 Adam Oates	1.50	4.00
4 Phil Housley	1.00	2.50
5 Mike Vernon	1.25	3.00
6 Mats Sundin	1.50	4.00
7 Pavel Bure	3.00	8.00
8 Patrick Roy	4.00	10.00
9 Tom Barrasso	1.00	2.50
10 Alexander Mogilny	1.25	3.00
11 Doug Gilmour	1.50	4.00
12 Eric Lindros	6.00	15.00
13 Theo Fleury	1.50	4.00
14 Pat LaFontaine	1.25	3.00
15 Joe Sakic	2.00	5.00
16 Ed Belfour	1.50	4.00
17 Felix Potvin	3.00	8.00
18 Mario Lemieux	5.00	12.00
19 Jaromir Jagr	2.50	6.00
20 Teemu Selanne	2.50	6.00
21 Ray Bourque	1.50	4.00
22 Brett Hull	2.00	5.00
23 Steve Yzerman	2.50	6.00
24 Kirk Muller	1.00	2.50

1993-94 OPC Premier Team Canada

Randomly inserted in second-series OPC Premier packs, these 19 standard-size cards feature borderless color player action shots on their fronts. The player's name and the Hockey Canada logo appear at the bottom. The red back carries the player's name and position at the top, followed below by biography, player photo, career highlights in English and French, and statistics. The cards are numbered on the back as "X of 19."

COMPLETE SET (19)	10.00	25.00
1 Brett Lindros	.75	2.00
2 Manny Legace	.75	2.00
3 Adrian Aucoin	.60	1.50
4 Ken Lovsin	.60	1.50
5 Craig Woodcroft	.60	1.50
6 Derek Mayer	.60	1.50
7 Fabian Joseph	.60	1.50
8 Todd Brost	.60	1.50
9 Chris Therien	.75	2.00
10 Brad Turner	.60	1.50
11 Trevor Sim	.60	1.50
12 Todd Hlushko	.60	1.50
13 Dwayne Norris	.60	1.50
14 Chris Kontos	.60	1.50
15 Petr Nedved	.75	2.00
16 Brian Savage	.75	2.00
17 Paul Kariya	1.50	4.00
18 Corey Hirsch	.75	2.00
19 Todd Warriner	.75	2.00

1994-95 OPC Premier

1 Mark Messier	.10	.25
2 Darren Turcotte	.05	.15
3 Mikhail Shtalenkov RC	.05	.15
4 Rob Gaudreau	.05	.15
5 Tony Amonte	.07	.20
6 Stephane Quintal	.05	.15
7 Iain Fraser	.05	.15
8 Doug Weight	.07	.20
9 German Titov	.05	.15
10 Larry Murphy	.07	.20
11 Danton Cole	.05	.15
12 Pat Peake	.05	.15
13 Chris Terreri	.07	.20
14 Yuri Khmylev	.05	.15
15 Paul Coffey	.10	.25
16 Brian Savage	.05	.15
17 Rod Brind'Amour	.07	.20
18 Nathan Lafayette	.05	.15
19 Gord Murphy	.05	.15
20 Al Iafrate	.05	.15
21 Kevin Miller	.05	.15
22 Peter Zezel	.05	.15
23 Sylvain Turgeon	.05	.15
24 Mark Tinordi	.05	.15
25 Jari Kurri	.07	.20
26 Benoit Hogue	.05	.15
27 Jeff Reese	.05	.15
28 Brian Noonan	.05	.15
29 Denis Tsygurov RC	.10	.25
30 James Patrick	.05	.15
31 Bob Corkum	.05	.15
32 Valeri Kamensky	.07	.20
33 Ray Whitney	.05	.15
34 Joe Murphy	.05	.15
35 Dominik Hasek AS	.20	.50
36 Ray Bourque AS	.15	.40
37 Brian Leetch AS	.10	.25
38 Dave Andreychuk AS	.10	.25
39 Pavel Bure AS	.10	.25
40 Sergei Fedorov AS	.15	.40
41 Bob Beers	.07	.20
42 Byron Dafoe RC	.30	.75
43 Lyle Odelein	.07	.20
44 Markus Naslund	.10	.25
45 Dean Chynoweth RC	.05	.15
46 Trent Klatt	.05	.15
47 Murray Craven	.05	.15
48 Dave Mackey	.05	.15
49 Norm Maciver	.05	.15
50 Alexander Mogilny	.07	.20
51 David Reid	.05	.15
52 Nicklas Lidstrom	.10	.25
53 Tom Fitzgerald	.05	.15
54 Roman Hamrlik	.07	.20
55 Wendel Clark	.07	.20
56 Dominic Roussel	.07	.20
57 Alexei Zhitnik	.07	.20
58 Valeri Zelepukin	.05	.15
59 Calle Johansson	.05	.15
60 Craig Janney	.07	.20
61 Randy Wood	.05	.15
62 Curtis Leschyshyn	.05	.15
63 Stephan Lebeau	.05	.15
64 Dallas Drake	.05	.15
65 Vincent Damphousse	.07	.20
66 Scott Lachance	.05	.15
67 Dirk Graham	.05	.15
68 Kevin Smyth	.05	.15
69 Denis Savard	.12	.30
70 Mike Richter	.10	.25
71 Ronnie Stern	.05	.15
72 Kirk Maltby	.05	.15
73 Kjell Samuelsson	.05	.15
74 Neal Broten	.07	.20
75 Trevor Linden	.07	.20
76 Todd Elik	.05	.15
77 Andrew McBain	.05	.15
78 Alexei Kudashov	.05	.15
79 Ken Daneyko	.05	.15
80 D.Hasek	.20	.50
G.Fuhr GD		
81 Andy Moog	.10	.25
Dallas Stars		
Darcy Wakaluk DUO		
Dallas		
82 Vanbiesbrouck	.07	.20
Fitz. GD		
83 M.Brodeur	.25	.60
Terreri GD		
84 Tom Barrasso	.07	.20
Pittsburgh Penguins		
Ken Wregget DUO		
85 Kirk McLean	.07	.20
Vancouver Canucks		
Kay Whitmore DUO/		
86 Darryl Sydor	.05	.15
87 Chris Osgood	.15	.40
88 Ted Donato	.05	.15
89 Dave Lowry	.05	.15
90 Mark Recchi	.12	.30
91 Jim Montgomery	.05	.15
92 Bill Houlder	.05	.15
93 Richard Smehlik	.05	.15
94 Benoit Brunet	.05	.15
95 Teemu Selanne	.20	.50
96 Paul Ranheim	.05	.15
97 Andrei Kovalenko	.05	.15
98 Grant Ledyard	.05	.15
99 Brent Grieve RC	.05	.15
100 Joe Juneau	.07	.20
101 Martin Gelinas	.05	.15
102 Jamie Macoun	.05	.15
103 Craig MacTavish	.05	.15
104 Micah Aivazoff	.05	.15
105 Stephane Richer	.07	.20
106 Eric Weinrich	.05	.15
107 Pat Elynuik	.05	.15
108 Tomas Sandstrom	.05	.15
109 Darrin Madeley	.05	.15
110 Al MacInnis	.07	.20
111 Cam Stewart	.05	.15
112 Dixon Ward	.05	.15
113 Vlastimil Kroupa	.05	.15
114 Rob DiMaio	.05	.15
115 Pierre Turgeon	.07	.20
116 Mike Hough	.05	.15
117 John LeClair	.10	.25
118 Dave Hannan	.05	.15
119 Todd Ewen	.05	.15
121 Dave Manson	.05	.15
122 Jocelyn Lemieux	.05	.15
123 Jocelyn Thibault	.10	.25
124 Scott Pearson	.05	.15
125 Patrick Roy AS	.25	.60
126 Scott Stevens AS	.10	.25
127 Al MacInnis AS	.07	.20
128 Adam Graves AS	.05	.15
129 Cam Neely AS	.10	.25
130 Wayne Gretzky AS	.50	1.25
131 Tom Chorske	.05	.15
132 John Tucker	.05	.15
133 Steve Smith	.05	.15
134 Kay Whitmore	.05	.15
135 Adam Oates	.10	.25
136 Bill Berg	.05	.15
137 Wes Walz	.05	.15
138 Jeff Beukeboom	.05	.15
139 Ron Francis	.12	.30
140 Alexandre Daigle	.05	.15
141 Josef Beranek	.05	.15
142 Tom Pederson	.05	.15
143 Jamie McLennan	.07	.20
144 Scott Mellanby	.07	.20
145 Slava Kozlov	.07	.20
146 Marty McSorley	.05	.15
147 Tim Sweeney	.05	.15
148 Luciano Borsato	.05	.15
149 Jason Dawe	.05	.15
150 Wayne Gretzky LL	.50	1.25
151 Pavel Bure LL	.10	.25
152 Dominik Hasek LL	.20	.50
153 Scott Stevens LL	.10	.25
154 Wayne Gretzky LL	.50	1.25
155 Mike Richter LL	.10	.25
156 Dominik Hasek LL	.20	.50
157 Ted Drury	.05	.15
158 Peter Popovic	.05	.15
159 Alexei Kasatonov	.05	.15
160 Mats Sundin	.07	.20
161 Brad Shaw	.05	.15
162 Bret Hedican	.05	.15
163 Mike McPhee	.05	.15
164 Martin Straka	.05	.15
165 Dmitri Mironov	.05	.15
166 Andrei Trefilov	.05	.15
167 Joe Reekie	.05	.15
168 Gary Suter	.05	.15
169 Greg Gilbert	.05	.15
170 Igor Larinov	.05	.15
171 Mike Sillinger	.05	.15
172 Igor Kravchuk	.05	.15
173 Glen Murray	.05	.15
174 Shawn Chambers	.05	.15
175 John MacLean	.07	.20
176 Yves Racine	.05	.15
177 Andrei Lomakin	.05	.15
178 Patrick Flatley	.05	.15
179 Igor Ulanov	.05	.15
180 Pat LaFontaine	.10	.25
181 Mathieu Schneider	.05	.15
182 Peter Stastny	.07	.20
183 Tony Granato	.05	.15
184 Peter Douris	.05	.15
185 Alexei Kovalev	.05	.15
186 Geoff Courtnall	.05	.15
187 Richard Matvichuk	.05	.15
188 Troy Murray	.05	.15
189 Todd Gill	.05	.15
190 Martin Brodeur RS	.25	.60
191 Mikael Renberg RS	.07	.20
192 Alexei Yashin RS	.10	.25
193 Jason Arnott RS	.07	.20
194 Derek Plante RS	.05	.15
195 Alexandre Daigle RS	.05	.15
196 Bryan Smolinski RS	.05	.15
197 Jesse Belanger RS	.05	.15
198 Chris Pronger RS	.10	.25
199 Chris Osgood RS	.15	.40
200 Jeremy Roenick	.20	.50
201 Johan Garpenlov	.05	.15
202 Dave Karpa	.05	.15
203 Darren McCarty	.05	.15
204 Claude Lemieux	.10	.25
205 Geoff Sanderson	.07	.20
206 Tom Barrasso	.07	.20
207 Kevin Dineen	.05	.15
208 Sylvain Cote	.05	.15
209 Brent Gretzky	.05	.15
210 Shayne Corson	.05	.15
211 Darius Kasparaitis	.05	.15
212 Peter Andersson	.05	.15
213 Robert Reichel	.05	.15
214 Jozef Stumpel	.05	.15
215 Brendan Shanahan	.12	.30
216 Craig Muni	.05	.15
217 Alexei Zhamnov	.07	.20
218 Robert Lang	.05	.15
219 Brian Bellows	.07	.20
220 Steven King	.05	.15
221 Sergei Zubov	.05	.15
222 Kelly Miller	.05	.15
223 Ilya Byakin	.05	.15
224 Chris Tamer RC	.05	.15
225 Doug Gilmour	.12	.30
226 Shawn Antoski	.05	.15
227 Andrew Cassels	.05	.15
228 Craig Wolanin	.05	.15
229 Jon Casey	.07	.20
230 Mike Modano	.15	.40
231 Bill Guerin	.07	.20
232 Gaetan Duchesne	.05	.15
233 Steve Dubinsky	.05	.15
234 Jason Bowen	.05	.15
235 Steve Yzerman	.25	.60
236 Dave Poulin	.05	.15
237 Michael Nylander	.07	.20
238 Felix Potvin TF	.10	.25
239 Sandis Ozolinsh FUT	.05	.15
240 Scott Niedermayer FUT	.10	.25
241 Eric Lindros TF	.10	.25
242 Keith Tkachuk TF	.10	.25
243 Teemu Selanne TF	.20	.50
244 Marty McInnis	.05	.15
245 Bob Kudelski	.05	.15
246 Paul Cavallini	.05	.15
247 Brian Bradley	.05	.15
248 Robb Stauber	.05	.15
249 Jay Wells	.05	.15
250 Mario Lemieux	.40	1.00
251 Tommy Albelin	.05	.15
252 Paul DePietro	.05	.15
253 Mike Gartner	.10	.25
254 Darrin Shannon	.05	.15
255 Alexander Karpovtsev	.05	.15
256 Dave Babych	.05	.15
257 Greg Johnson	.05	.15
258 Frank Musil	.05	.15
259 Michal Pivonka	.07	.20
260 Arturs Irbe	.07	.20
261 Paul Broten	.05	.15
262 Don Sweeney	.05	.15
263 Doug Brown	.05	.15
264 Bobby Dollas	.05	.15
265 Brian Skrudland	.05	.15
266 Dan Plante RC	.05	.15
267 Chad Penney	.05	.15
268 Steve Leach	.05	.15
269 Damian Rhodes	.07	.20
270 Glenn Anderson	.10	.25
271 Randy McKay	.05	.15
272 Jeff Brown	.05	.15
273 Steve Konowalchuk	.05	.15
276 Sergei Fedorov TOTG	.15	.40
277 Adam Oates TOTG	.10	.25
278 Mark Messier TOTG	.10	.25
279 Doug Gilmour TOTG	.12	.30
280 Wayne Gretzky TOTG	.50	1.25
281 Rick Tocchet	.07	.20
282 Guy Carbonneau	.05	.15
283 Peter Bondra	.07	.20
284 Valeri Karpov RC	.05	.15
285 Ed Belfour	.10	.25
286 Petr Nedved	.07	.20
287 Mikael Andersson	.05	.15
288 Boris Mironov	.05	.15
289 Donald Audette	.05	.15
290 Kevin Stevens	.05	.15
291 Cliff Ronning	.05	.15
292 Bruce Driver	.05	.15
293 Mariusz Czerkawski RC	.10	.25
294 Mikael Renberg	.07	.20
295 Theo Fleury	.10	.25
296 Robert Kron	.05	.15
297 Wendel Clark	.07	.20
298 Dave Gagner	.07	.20
299 Ulf Dahlen	.05	.15
300 Keith Tkachuk	.10	.25
301 Mike Ridley	.05	.15
302 Mike Vernon	.07	.20
303 Troy Mallette	.05	.15
304 Derek King	.05	.15
305 Kirk Muller	.05	.15
306 Rob Niedermayer	.07	.20
307 Ian Laperriere RC	.10	.25
308 Mike Donnelly	.05	.15
309 Joe Sacco	.05	.15
310 Patrick Roy TOTG	.25	.60
311 Tom Barrasso	.07	.20
312 Dominik Hasek TOTG	.20	.50
313 Felix Potvin TOTG	.10	.25
314 Mike Richter	.10	.25
315 Bobby Holik	.05	.15
316 Patrick Poulin	.05	.15
317 Stephane Matteau	.05	.15
318 Petr Klima	.05	.15
319 Fredrik Olausson	.05	.15
320 Dale Hawerchuk	.12	.30
321 Jim Dowd	.05	.15
322 Chris Therien	.05	.15
323 Ravil Gusmanov RC	.05	.15
324 Vincent Riendeau	.05	.15
325 Pavel Bure	.10	.25
326 Jimmy Carson	.05	.15
327 Steve Chiasson	.05	.15
328 Ken Wregget	.07	.20
329 Kenny Jonsson	.05	.15
330 Keith Primeau	.10	.25
331 Bob Errey	.05	.15
332 Derian Hatcher	.05	.15
333 Stephane Fiset	.07	.20
334 Brent Severyn	.05	.15
335 Ray Ferraro	.05	.15
336 Pavol Demitra	.12	.30
337 Valeri Bure	.05	.15
338 Guy Hebert	.07	.20
339 Matt Johnson RC	.05	.15
340 Curtis Joseph	.15	.40
341 Rob Pearson	.05	.15
342 Jeff Shantz	.05	.15
343 Eric Charron RC	.10	.25
344 Jason Smith	.07	.20
345 M.Sundin	.07	.20
W.Clark TRA		
346 Rick Tocchet	.07	.20
Los Angeles Kings		
Luc Robitaille		
P		
347 Al MacInnis	.07	.20
St. Louis Blues		
Phil Housley		
Calgar		
348 Mike Vernon	.07	.20
Detroit Red Wings		
Steve Chiasson		
Ca		
349 Craig Simpson	.05	.15
350 Adam Graves	.05	.15
351 Kevin Haller	.05	.15
352 Nelson Emerson	.05	.15
353 Phil Housley	.07	.20
354 Shawn McEachern	.05	.15
355 Felix Potvin	.10	.25
356 Sergio Momesso	.10	.25
357 Glen Wesley	.05	.15
358 David Shaw	.05	.15
359 Terry Carkner	.05	.15
360 John Vanbiesbrouck	.07	.20
361 Dean Evason	.05	.15
362 Michal Sykora	.05	.15
363 Troy Loney	.05	.15
364 Sylvain Lefebvre	.05	.15
365 Alexei Yashin	.10	.25
366 Gilbert Dionne	.05	.15
367 Rick Tabaracci	.07	.20
368 Paul Ysebaert	.05	.15
369 Craig Johnson	.05	.15
370 Scott Stevens	.10	.25
371 Phillippe Boucher	.05	.15
372 Garry Valk	.05	.15
373 Jason Muzzatti	.07	.20
374 Chris Joseph	.05	.15
375 Wayne Gretzky	.50	1.25
376 Teppo Numminen	.05	.15
377 Oleg Petrov	.05	.15
378 Patrik Juhlin RC	.05	.15
379 Zarley Zalapski	.05	.15
380 Martin Brodeur TOTF	.25	.60
381 Chris Pronger TOTF	.10	.25
382 Sergei Zubov TOTF	.05	.15
383 Mikael Renberg TOTF	.07	.20
384 Brett Lindros TOTF	.05	.15
385 Peter Forsberg TOTF	.25	.60
386 Brandon Convery	.05	.15
387 Steve Heinze	.05	.15
388 Glenn Healy	.07	.20
389 Brian Benning	.05	.15
390 Pat Verbeek	.07	.20
391 Ulf Samuelsson	.05	.15
392 Turner Stevenson	.05	.15
393 Bob Rouse	.05	.15
394 Steve Konroyd	.05	.15
395 Russ Courtnall	.05	.15
396 Sergei Makarov	.05	.15
397 Kirk McLean	.07	.20
398 Steven Finn	.05	.15
399 Yan Kaminsky	.05	.15
400 Eric Lindros	.10	.25
401 Steve Duchesne	.05	.15
402 John Slaney	.05	.15
403 Bernie Nicholls	.07	.20
Chicago Black Hawks		
404 Kelly Buchberger	.05	.15
405 Paul Kariya	.12	.30
406 Michel Petit	.05	.15
407 Cale Hulse RC	.07	.20
408 Sheldon Kennedy	.05	.15
409 Brad May	.05	.15
410 Daren Puppa	.07	.20
411 Janne Laukkanen	.07	.20
412 Mats Sundin	.07	.20
413 Trevor Kidd	.07	.20
414 Greg Adams	.05	.15
415 Pavel Bure TOTG	.10	.25
416 Teemu Selanne TOTG	.20	.50
417 Brett Hull TOTG	.20	.50
418 Steve Larmer	.07	.20
419 Cam Neely TOTG	.10	.25
420 Ray Bourque	.15	.40
421 Andrei Nikolishin	.05	.15
422 Jim Paek	.05	.15
423 John Cullen	.05	.15
424 Darcy Wakaluk	.07	.20
425 Peter Forsberg	.25	.60
426 Yves Racine	.05	.15
427 Jody Hull	.05	.15
428 Ron Sutter	.05	.15
429 Ray Sheppard	.07	.20
430 Sandis Ozolinsh	.05	.15
431 Brent Grieve	.05	.15
432 Shaun Van Allen	.05	.15
433 Craig Berube	.05	.15
434 Vladislav Boulin RC	.10	.25
435 Bill Ranford	.07	.20
436 Denny Felsner	.05	.15
437 Jamie Storr	.07	.20
438 Brian Rolston	.05	.15
439 Chris Gratton	.05	.15
440 Dominik Hasek	.20	.50
441 Garth Butcher	.07	.20
442 Jyrki Lumme	.05	.15
443 Sergei Nemchinov	.05	.15
444 Tie Domi	.07	.20
445 Gary Roberts	.05	.15
446 Dave McLlwain	.05	.15
447 John Gruden RC	.05	.15
448 Vladimir Konstantinov	.07	.20
449 Adam Deadmarsh	.05	.15
450 Brian Leetch TOTG	.10	.25
451 Scott Stevens	.10	.25
452 Mark Tinordi	.05	.15
453 Al Iafrate	.05	.15
454 Ray Bourque TOTG	.15	.40
455 Patrick Roy	.25	.60
456 Viktor Gordiouk	.07	.20
457 Owen Nolan	.10	.25
458 Stu Barnes	.05	.15
459 Zigmund Palffy	.07	.20
460 Jaromir Jagr	.25	.60
461 Andrei Nazarov	.05	.15
462 Kelly Hrudey	.07	.20
463 Jason Wiemer RC	.05	.15
464 Oleg Tverdovsky	.07	.20
465 Brett Hull	.20	.50
466 Luke Richardson	.05	.15
467 Jason Allison	.07	.20
468 Dimitri Yushkevich	.05	.15
469 Todd Simon RC	.05	.15
470 Martin Brodeur	.25	.60
471 Thomas Steen	.05	.15
472 Vesa Viitakoski	.07	.20
473 Todd Harvey	.05	.15
474 Kent Manderville	.05	.15
475 Chris Chelios	.10	.25
476 Joby Messier	.05	.15
477 Jassen Cullimore	.05	.15
478 Jamie Pushor	.07	.20
479 Bryan Smolinski	.05	.15
480 Joe Sakic	.20	.50
481 David Wilkie	.07	.20
482 Craig Billington	.07	.20
483 Pat Neaton	.07	.20
484 Chris Pronger	.10	.25
485 Brian Leetch POW	.10	.25
486 Chris Chelios	.10	.25
487 Jeff Brown	.05	.15
488 Al MacInnis	.07	.20
489 Paul Coffey	.10	.25
490 Ray Bourque POW	.15	.40
491 Phil Housley	.07	.20
492 Larry Murphy	.07	.20
493 Sergei Zubov POW	.05	.15
494 Scott Stevens	.10	.25
495 Steve Thomas	.05	.15
496 Jim Waite	.05	.15
497 Mike Keane	.05	.15
498 Rob Blake	.10	.25
499 John Lilley	.05	.15
500 Brian Leetch	.10	.25
501 Derek Plante	.05	.15
502 Tim Cheveldae	.07	.20
503 Vladimir Vujtek	.05	.15
504 Esa Tikkanen	.05	.15
505 Cam Neely	.10	.25
506 Dale Hunter	.05	.15
507 Marc Bergevin	.05	.15
508 Joel Otto	.05	.15
509 Brent Fedyk	.05	.15
510 Dave Andreychuk	.10	.25
511 Andy Moog	.10	.25
512 Jaroslav Modry	.05	.15
513 Sergei Krivokrasov	.05	.15
514 Brett Lindros	.05	.15
515 Cory Stillman RC	.05	.15
516 Jon Rohloff RC	.10	.25
517 Joe Mullen	.07	.20
518 Evgeny Davydov	.05	.15
519 Scott Young	.05	.15
520 Sergei Fedorov	.15	.40
521 Pat Falloon	.05	.15
522 Bill Lindsay	.05	.15
523 Ron Tugnutt	.07	.20
524 Anatoli Semenov	.05	.15
525 Geoff Courtnall	.05	.15
526 Luc Robitaille	.10	.25
527 Geoff Sanderson	.07	.20
528 Esa Tikkanen	.05	.15
529 Brendan Shanahan TOTG	.12	.30
530 Jason Arnott	.07	.20
531 Michal Grosek RC	.05	.15
532 Steve Larmer	.07	.20
533 Eric Fichaud RC	.10	.25
534 Dimitri Khristich	.05	.15
535 Garry Galley	.05	.15
536 Aaron Gavey	.05	.15
537 Joe Nieuwendyk	.10	.25
538 Mike Craig	.05	.15
539 Scott Niedermayer	.10	.25
540 Luc Robitaille	.10	.25
541 Dino Ciccarelli	.07	.20
542 Sean Burke	.07	.20
543 Jiri Slegr	.05	.15
544 Jesse Belanger	.05	.15
545 Sean Hill	.05	.15
546 Vladimir Malakhov	.05	.15
547 Jeff Friesen	.05	.15
548 Mike Ricci	.05	.15

1994-95 OPC Premier Finest Inserts

The 23 cards in this set were randomly inserted at a rate of 1:36 OPC Premier series 1 packs. The set includes top rookies of 1993-94. Cards feature an isolated player photo over a textured rainbow background. A reflective rainbow border is broken up by the player name. Premier Finest is written across the top of the card. Backs have a small player photo with brief personal information, and statistical breakdown. Cards are numbered "X of 23".

COMPLETE SET (23)	20.00	50.00
1 Patrik Carnback	.60	1.50
2 Bryan Smolinski	.60	1.50
3 Derek Plante	.60	1.50
4 Alexander Karpovtsev	.60	1.50
5 Trevor Kidd	1.25	3.00
6 Iain Fraser	.60	1.50
7 Alexandre Daigle	.60	1.50
8 Chris Osgood	2.00	5.00
9 Rob Niedermayer	.60	1.50
10 Jason Arnott	.60	1.50
11 Chris Pronger	2.00	5.00
12 Jesse Belanger	.60	1.50
13 Oleg Petrov	.60	1.50
14 Martin Brodeur	8.00	20.00
15 Alexei Yashin	.60	1.50
16 Mikael Renberg	1.25	3.00
17 Boris Mironov	.60	1.50
18 Damian Rhodes	1.25	3.00
19 Darren McCarty	.60	1.50
20 Chris Gratton	1.25	3.00
21 Jamie McLennan	.60	1.50
22 Nathan Lafayette	.60	1.50
23 Jeff Shantz	.60	1.50

1994-95 OPC Premier Special Effects

*OPC SE: .6X TO 1.5X TOPPS SPEC.EFFECT

2007-08 OPC Premier

STATED PRINT RUN 299 SERIAL #'d SETS

1 Bernie Parent	2.50	6.00
2 Al MacInnis	2.50	6.00
3 Rob Blake	2.50	6.00
4 Bobby Orr	8.00	20.00
5 Denis Potvin	2.50	6.00
6 Nicklas Lidstrom	2.50	6.00
7 Phil Esposito	4.00	10.00
8 Cam Neely	2.50	6.00
9 Gordie Howe	6.00	15.00
10 Guy Lafleur	3.00	8.00
11 Mark Messier	4.00	10.00
12 Jarome Iginla	2.50	6.00
13 Mats Sundin	2.50	6.00
14 Brendan Shanahan	3.00	8.00
15 Dany Heatley	2.50	6.00
16 Bobby Clarke	2.50	6.00
17 Jari Kurri	2.50	6.00
18 Larry Robinson	2.50	6.00
19 Joe Sakic	4.00	10.00
20 Dino Ciccarelli	2.50	6.00
21 Borje Salming	2.50	6.00
22 Mike Bossy	2.50	6.00
23 Milan Hejduk	2.00	5.00
24 Bernie Federko	1.50	4.00
25 Stan Mikita	3.00	8.00
26 Peter Stastny	2.00	5.00
27 Frank Mahovlich	3.00	8.00
28 Alexander Semin	2.50	6.00
29 Marc-Andre Fleury	4.00	10.00
30 Martin Brodeur	5.00	12.00
31 Grant Fuhr	2.50	6.00
32 Billy Smith	2.50	6.00
33 Patrick Roy	6.00	15.00
34 Miikka Kiprusoff	2.00	5.00
35 Tony Esposito	2.50	6.00
36 Jean-Sebastien Giguere	2.50	6.00
37 Patrice Bergeron	3.00	8.00
38 Dominik Hasek	3.00	8.00
39 Henrik Zetterberg	3.00	8.00
40 Lee Stempniak	1.50	4.00
41 Keith Tkachuk	2.50	6.00
42 Alexander Ovechkin	10.00	25.00
43 Zach Parise	3.00	8.00
44 Andy Bathgate	2.00	5.00
45 Rick DiPietro	2.00	5.00
46 Alexander Radulov	2.50	6.00
47 Daniel Briere	2.50	6.00
48 Jason Spezza	2.50	6.00
49 Ray Emery	2.00	5.00
50 Marian Gaborik	3.00	8.00
51 Simon Gagne	2.50	6.00
52 Roberto Luongo	3.00	8.00
53 Saku Koivu	2.50	6.00
54 Paul Kariya	3.00	8.00
55 Lanny McDonald	2.50	6.00
56 Darryl Sittler	2.00	5.00
57 Scott Stevens	2.50	6.00
58 Joe Thornton	3.00	8.00
59 Mike Modano	4.00	10.00
60 Clark Gillies	2.50	6.00
61 Rick Nash	2.50	6.00
62 Dale Hawerchuk	3.00	8.00
63 Anze Kopitar	4.00	10.00
64 Gilbert Perreault	2.50	6.00
65 Daniel Alfredsson	2.50	6.00
66 Mario Lemieux	8.00	20.00
67 Brad Richards	2.50	6.00
68 Jaromir Jagr	6.00	15.00
69 Bobby Hull	4.00	10.00
70 Mark Recchi	3.00	8.00
71 Evgeni Malkin	8.00	20.00
72 Jordan Staal	2.50	6.00
73 Michael Ryder	1.50	4.00
74 Eric Staal	3.00	8.00
75 Olli Jokinen	2.00	5.00
76 Pavel Datsyuk	3.00	8.00
77 Ray Bourque	4.00	10.00
78 Vincent Lecavalier	2.00	5.00
79 Dwayne Roloson	2.00	5.00
80 Henrik Lundqvist	3.00	8.00
81 Phil Kessel	3.00	8.00
82 Tomas Vokoun	2.00	5.00
83 Steve Shutt	2.50	6.00
84 Thomas Vanek	3.00	8.00
85 Patrik Elias	2.50	6.00
86 Martin St. Louis	2.50	6.00
87 Sidney Crosby	10.00	25.00
88 Paul Stastny	2.50	6.00
89 Cam Ward	2.50	6.00
90 Marty Turco	2.50	6.00
91 Sergei Fedorov	4.00	10.00
92 Patrick Marleau	2.50	6.00
93 Jason Arnott	2.00	5.00
94 Jonathan Cheechoo	2.50	6.00
95 Ryan Getzlaf	4.00	10.00
96 Shane Doan	2.00	5.00
97 Ryan Miller	2.50	6.00
98 Markus Naslund	2.50	6.00
99 Wayne Gretzky	12.00	30.00
100 Alexander Frolov	1.50	4.00
101 Andrew Cogliano JSY AU RC	8.00	20.00
102 Andy Greene JSY AU RC	6.00	15.00
103 Anton Stralman JSY AU RC	5.00	12.00
104 Bobby Ryan JSY AU RC	12.00	30.00
105 Brandon Dubinsky JSY AU RC	10.00	25.00
106 Brian Elliott JSY AU RC	10.00	25.00
107 Bryan Little JSY AU RC	8.00	20.00
108 Carey Price JSY AU RC	75.00	125.00
109 Cory Murphy JSY AU RC	5.00	12.00
110 Curtis McElhinney JSY AU RC	8.00	20.00
111 Casey Borer JSY AU RC	5.00	12.00
112 David Krejci JSY AU RC	20.00	40.00
113 David Perron JSY AU RC	8.00	20.00
114 Drew Miller JSY AU RC	6.00	15.00
115 Erik Johnson JSY AU RC	8.00	20.00
116 Frans Nielsen JSY AU RC	8.00	20.00
117 Devin Setoguchi JSY AU RC	8.00	20.00
118 Jack Johnson JSY AU RC	6.00	15.00
119 James Sheppard JSY AU RC	5.00	12.00
120 Jannik Hansen JSY AU RC	6.00	15.00
121 Jared Boll JSY AU RC	6.00	15.00
122 Jaroslav Halak JSY AU RC	12.00	30.00
123 Jaroslav Hlinka JSY AU RC	6.00	15.00
124 Jiri Tlusty JSY AU RC	8.00	20.00
125 Jack Skille JSY AU RC	6.00	15.00
126 Jonathan Bernier JSY AU RC	12.00	30.00
127 Jonathan Sigalet JSY AU RC	5.00	12.00
128 Jonathan Toews JSY AU RC	75.00	135.00
129 Tuukka Rask JSY AU RC	25.00	50.00
130 Kyle Chipchura JSY AU RC	8.00	20.00
131 Lauri Tukonen JSY AU RC	5.00	12.00
132 Sergei Kostitsyn JSY AU RC	6.00	15.00
133 Marc Staal JSY AU RC	8.00	20.00
134 Martin Hanzal JSY AU RC	6.00	15.00
135 Mason Raymond JSY AU RC	8.00	20.00
136 T.J. Hensick JSY AU RC	6.00	15.00
137 Matt Niskanen JSY AU RC	8.00	20.00
138 Matt Smaby JSY AU RC	5.00	12.00
139 Milan Lucic JSY AU RC	12.00	30.00
140 Nick Foligno JSY AU RC	10.00	25.00
141 Nicklas Backstrom JSY AU RC	15.00	40.00
142 Nicklas Bergfors JSY AU RC	5.00	12.00
143 Ondrej Pavelec JSY AU RC	10.00	25.00
144 Patrick Kane JSY AU RC	100.00	200.00
145 Peter Mueller JSY AU RC	6.00	15.00
146 Petr Kalus JSY AU RC	5.00	12.00
147 Rob Schremp JSY AU RC	6.00	15.00
148 Rod Pelley JSY AU RC	5.00	12.00
149 Ryan Callahan JSY AU RC	10.00	25.00
150 Ryan Carter JSY AU RC	5.00	12.00
151 Steve Downie JSY AU RC	6.00	15.00
152 Sam Gagner JSY AU RC	10.00	25.00
153 Stefan Meyer JSY AU RC	6.00	15.00
154 Steve Wagner JSY AU RC	5.00	12.00
155 Tobias Enstrom JSY AU RC	8.00	20.00
156 Tobias Stephan JSY AU RC	6.00	15.00
157 David Jones JSY AU RC	5.00	12.00
158 Torrey Mitchell JSY AU RC	6.00	15.00
159 Tyler Weiman JSY AU RC	6.00	15.00
160 Ville Koistinen JSY AU RC	5.00	12.00

2007-08 OPC Premier Gold

*VETS/75: .4X TO 1X BASIC CARDS
STATED PRINT RUN 75 SER.#'d SETS
*ROOK.JSY AU/50: .6X TO 1.5X BASIC RC
GOLD JSY AU PRINT RUN 50 SER.#'d SETS

108 Carey Price JSY AU	100.00	175.00
128 Jonathan Toews JSY AU	125.00	200.00
144 Patrick Kane JSY AU	150.00	250.00

2007-08 OPC Premier Silver Spectrum

*SILVER SPECTRUM: .8X TO 2X
STATED PRINT RUN 25 SER.#'d SETS
*SILVER SPECTRUM JSY AU: .6X TO 1.5X
JSY AU PRINT RUN 35 SER.#'d SETS

108 Carey Price JSY AU	100.00	175.00
128 Jonathan Toews JSY AU	100.00	200.00

2007-08 OPC Premier Autographed Premier Stitchings

STATED PRINT RUN 50 SERIAL #'d SETS

APSAB Andy Bathgate	12.00	30.00
APSAK Anze Kopitar	25.00	60.00
APSBC Bobby Clarke	15.00	40.00
APSBY Mike Bossy	25.00	60.00
APSCN Cam Neely	15.00	40.00
APSCW Cam Ward	15.00	40.00
APSDS Darryl Sittler	12.00	30.00
APSES Eric Staal	30.00	60.00
APSIK Ilya Kovalchuk	40.00	80.00
APSJB Johnny Bucyk	15.00	40.00
APSJC Jonathan Cheechoo	15.00	40.00
APSJG Jean-Sebastien Giguere	15.00	40.00
APSJI Jarome Iginla	20.00	50.00
APSLR Larry Robinson	12.00	30.00
APSMF Marc-Andre Fleury	25.00	60.00
APSMM Mike Modano	25.00	60.00
APSMN Markus Naslund	15.00	40.00
APSMR Michael Ryder	10.00	25.00
APSMS Martin St. Louis	15.00	40.00
APSMT Marty Turco	15.00	40.00
APSNL Nicklas Lidstrom	25.00	50.00
APSPS Peter Stastny	12.00	30.00
APSRN Rick Nash	20.00	50.00
APSSA Borje Salming	15.00	40.00
APSSD Shane Doan	12.00	30.00
APSSG Simon Gagne	15.00	40.00
APSSK Saku Koivu	25.00	50.00
APSSM Stan Mikita	20.00	50.00
APSST Paul Stastny	20.00	50.00
APSTV Thomas Vanek	15.00	40.00
APSVL Vincent Lecavalier	12.00	30.00
APSVO Tomas Vokoun	12.00	30.00

2007-08 OPC Premier Autographs Duos

STATED PRINT RUN 75 SERIAL #'d SETS

PP2BC J.Bucyk/B.Clarke	12.00	30.00
PP2BF M.Brodeur/M.Fleury	40.00	100.00
PP2BK P.Bergeron/P.Kessel	15.00	40.00
PP2BT A.Bathgate/W.Tkaczuk		

'2CH B.Clarke/R.Hextall 20.00 50.00
'2DF Lidstrom/Salming 15.00 40.00
'2DH S.Doan/D.Heatley
'2EJ E.Staal/J.Staal
'2EM T.Esposito/S.Mikita 25.00 50.00
'2FM B.Federko/J.Mullen 10.00 25.00
'2FR G.Fuhr/B.Ranford 30.00 60.00
'2FS M.Fleury/J.Staal 20.00 50.00
'2GK M.Gaborik/P.Kalus 15.00 40.00
'2GO B.Orr/G.Howe 150.00 300.00
'2GS S.Gagne/M.St. Louis 12.00 30.00
'2GT J.Giguere/M.Turco 12.00 30.00
'2HK M.Hossa/I.Kovalchuk 12.00 30.00
'2IC J.Iginla/J.Cheechoo 15.00 40.00
'2IN J.Iginla/R.Nash 15.00 40.00
'2IT J.Iginla/A.Tanguay 15.00 40.00
'2KR Kovalchuk/Radulov 12.00 30.00
'2LB Lecavalier/D.Boyle 10.00 25.00
'2LK T.Lindsay/R.Kelly 12.00 30.00
'2LR J.Lupul/M.Richards
'2LS G.Lafleur/S.Shutt 20.00 50.00
'2MB M.Modano/B.Morrow 20.00 50.00
'2NB C.Neely/R.Bourque 20.00 50.00
'2NK M.Naslund/R.Kesler 20.00 50.00
'2OM A.Ovechkin/E.Malkin 50.00 100.00
'2PG C.Perry/R.Getzlaf 15.00 40.00
'2RG R.Nash/G.Brule 12.00 30.00
'2RL Ryder/Latendresse
'2SJ R.Schremp/J.Johnson 10.00 25.00
'2SS M.Svatos/P.Stastny 12.00 30.00
'2TB Tanguay/Bergeron
'2VH T.Vokoun/D.Hasek 15.00 40.00
'2VM Lecavalier/M.St. Louis 12.00 30.00

2007-08 OPC Premier Autographs Trios

iginally five cards were released in packs as
change cards: Gagne/Lupul/Carter,
ll/Steen/Hawerchuk, Iginla/Gagne/Cheechoo,
ndsay/Howe/Kelly and St. Louis/Heatley/Nash.
ATED PRINT RUN 35 SERIAL #'d SETS
3AMS Armstrong/Malkin/Staal
3CHP Clarke/Hextall/Parent
3CKJ Cammalleri/Kopitar/Johnson 25.00 60.00
3EHM Esposito/Hull/Mikita 75.00 150.00
3FKM Fuhr/Kurri/Messier 100.00 200.00
3GGP Giguere/Perry/Getzlaf 30.00 60.00
3GLC Gagne/Lupul/Carter 15.00 40.00
3HSH Hull/Steen/Hawer 50.00 100.00
3HWS Hejduk/Wolski/Stastny
3IGC Iginla/Gagne/Chech 25.00 60.00
3KRL Koivu/Ryder/Latendresse 20.00 50.00
3LHK Lindsay/Howe/Kelly 75.00 150.00
3LSB Lecavalier/St. Louis/Boyle 30.00 60.00
3LSR Lafleur/Shutt/Robinson 50.00 100.00
3MRM Modano/Ribeiro/Morrow 25.00 60.00
3NMK Naslund/Morrison/Kesler 20.00 50.00
3OGH Orr/Gretzky/Howe 600.00 900.00
3RLO Lemieux/Roy/Orr 200.00 300.00
3SBK Savard/Bergeron/Kessel 50.00 100.00
3SHN St. Louis/Heatley/Nash 50.00 100.00
3WSW Williams/Staal/Ward 15.00 40.00

2007-08 OPC Premier Autographs Foursomes

ATED PRINT RUN 15 SERIAL #'d SETS
4BHMH Belv/Hll/Mhv/Hwe 250.00 400.00
4DGHM Dne/Grt/Hwe/Msr 300.00 450.00
4DSFH Dne/Stst/Fdr/Hwr 75.00 150.00
4GSCN Ggn/St.L/Chc/Nsh 75.00 150.00
4HSGS Hsa/Stn/Gbk/Svt 100.00 200.00
4LTIH Lcv/Thrn/Ign/Htly
4RBFE Roy/Brd/Fhr/Espo 200.00 350.00
4RUSS Ovch/Mlkn/Rdl/Kvl 125.00 200.00
4SPKS Svt/Prch/Kptr/Stny 125.00 200.00
4SSSS Staal/Stastny Bros. 125.00 200.00

2007-08 OPC Premier Original Six Signatures

ATED PRINT RUN 100 SERIAL #'d SETS
AB Andy Bathgate 6.00 15.00
BB Butch Bouchard
BD Bill Dineen 8.00 20.00
BH Bobby Hull 20.00 50.00
BO Bobby Orr 75.00 150.00
BS Borje Salming 8.00 20.00
DM Dickie Moore
DS Darryl Sittler 6.00 15.00
DW Doug Wilson 6.00 15.00
EG Ed Giacomin 8.00 20.00
EL Elmer Lach 8.00 20.00
FM Frank Mahovlich 10.00 25.00
GC Gerry Cheevers 8.00 20.00
GH Gordie Howe 30.00 80.00
GL Guy Lafleur 15.00 40.00
JB Jean Beliveau 50.00 100.00
LR Larry Robinson 6.00 15.00
MS Milt Schmidt 10.00 25.00
PE Phil Esposito
PH Paul Henderson 6.00 15.00
PP Pierre Pilote 10.00 25.00
RD Ron Duguay 6.00 15.00
RE Ron Ellis 6.00 15.00
RG Ron Greschner 5.00 12.00
RK Red Kelly 6.00 15.00
SS Steve Shutt 6.00 15.00
TE Tony Esposito 12.00 30.00
TL Ted Lindsay 10.00 25.00
TO Terry O'Reilly 6.00 15.00
WT Walt Tkaczuk 8.00 20.00

2007-08 OPC Premier Original Six Signatures Gold

OLD: .8X TO 2X BASE
ATED PRINT RUN 25 SERIAL #'d SETS
BD Bill Dineen 12.00 30.00
BO Bobby Orr 100.00 200.00
GH Gordie Howe 60.00 120.00
RK Red Kelly 12.00 30.00
TL Ted Lindsay 12.00 30.00
TO Terry O'Reilly 8.00 20.00

2007-08 OPC Premier Original Six Signatures Silver

LVER: .6X TO 1.5X BASE
ATED PRINT RUN 50 SERIAL #'d SETS
BH Bobby Hull 25.00 60.00
BO Bobby Orr 100.00 200.00
BS Borje Salming 12.00 30.00
DS Darryl Sittler 12.00 30.00
DW Doug Wilson 10.00 25.00
GH Gordie Howe 75.00 150.00

2007-08 OPC Premier Pairings Autographed Jerseys

ATED PRINT RUN 50 SERIAL #'d SETS
AS C.Armstrong/J.Staal 15.00 40.00
BB J.Bucyk/R.Bourque 25.00 60.00
BP J.Bucyk/G.Perreault 12.00 30.00
BS M.Bossy/S.Shutt 12.00 30.00
PCCB Cammalleri/Brown 12.00 30.00
PCCK Cammalleri/Kopitar 12.00 30.00
PCCP C.Neely/P.Kessel 15.00 40.00
PCDF Lidstrom/Salming 25.00 50.00
PCDH M.Dionne/D.Hawerchuk 30.00 60.00
PCDN M.Dionne/B.Nicholls 15.00 40.00
PCEC E.Staal/C.Ward
PCEJ E.Malkin/J.Staal 25.00 60.00
PCFR G.Fuhr/B.Ranford 30.00 60.00
PCGD S.Gagne/S.Doan 10.00 25.00
PCHG M.Hossa/M.Gaborik 15.00 40.00
PCHK M.Hossa/I.Kovalchuk 20.00 50.00
PCIM J.Iginla/L.McDonald 30.00 60.00
PCIT J.Iginla/A.Tanguay 12.00 30.00
PCLB P.Leclaire/G.Brule 10.00 25.00
PCLG M.Lemieux/W.Gretzky 200.00 400.00
PCLM Leetch/Messier 60.00 120.00
PCLN P.Leclaire/R.Nash 12.00 30.00
PCLS Lecavalier/M.St. Louis 15.00 40.00
PCLT Lecavalier/Thornton 12.00 30.00
PCMB M.Turco/B.Morrow 15.00 40.00
PCMC M.Ryder/S.Shutt 15.00 40.00
PCMH MacInnis/Hawerchuk 12.00 30.00
PCMK B.Morrison/R.Kesler 15.00 40.00
PCMM M.Modano/J.Mullen 12.00 30.00
PCMO G.Lafleur/L.Robinson 25.00 60.00
PCMR M.Modano/M.Ribeiro 12.00 30.00
PCMS S.Mikita/D.Savard 15.00 40.00
PCNB R.Nash/G.Brule 12.00 30.00
PCNM M.Naslund/B.Morrison 15.00 40.00
PCNO C.Neely/A.Oates 25.00 50.00
PCNS Tanguay/Zetterberg 20.00 50.00
PCOM A.Ovechkin/E.Malkin 75.00 150.00
PCPD P.Stastny/D.Hawerchuk 30.00 60.00
PCPE P.Bergeron/E.Staal 15.00 40.00
PCPG C.Perry/R.Getzlaf 20.00 50.00
PCRB P.Roy/R.Bourque 60.00 120.00
PCRT M.Ribeiro/M.Turco 12.00 30.00
PCSH M.St. Louis/N.Horton 10.00 25.00
PCSM S.Gagne/A.Tanguay 12.00 30.00
PCSW M.Svatos/W.Wolski 12.00 30.00
PCTR D.Tucker/A.Raycroft
PCWH T.Vokoun/N.Horton 12.00 30.00
PCWS J.Williams/E.Staal 12.00 30.00

2007-08 OPC Premier Pairings Autographed Jerseys Patch

STATED PRINT RUN 25 SERIAL #'d SETS
PCAS C.Armstrong/J.Staal 15.00 40.00
PCBB J.Bucyk/R.Bourque 50.00 100.00
PCBP J.Bucyk/G.Perreault 15.00 40.00
PCBS M.Bossy/S.Shutt 20.00 50.00
PCCB Cammalleri/Brown 15.00 40.00
PCCK Cammalleri/Kopitar
PCCP C.Neely/P.Kessel 30.00 60.00
PCDF Lidstrom/Salming 40.00 80.00
PCDH M.Dionne/D.Hawerchuk 25.00 50.00
PCDN M.Dionne/B.Nicholls
PCEC E.Staal/C.Ward 40.00 80.00
PCEJ E.Malkin/J.Staal 25.00 60.00
PCFR G.Fuhr/B.Ranford
PCGD S.Gagne/S.Doan 10.00 25.00
PCHG M.Hossa/M.Gaborik 40.00 80.00
PCHK M.Hossa/I.Kovalchuk 25.00 50.00
PCIM J.Iginla/L.McDonald 60.00 120.00
PCIT J.Iginla/A.Tanguay 25.00 60.00
PCKB R.Kesler/K.Bieksa 25.00 60.00
PCLB P.Leclaire/G.Brule 20.00 50.00
PCLM B.Leetch/M.Messier 60.00 120.00
PCLN P.Leclaire/R.Nash 20.00 50.00
PCLS Lecavalier/M.St. Louis
PCLT Lecavalier/Thornton 25.00 60.00
PCMB M.Turco/B.Morrow 20.00 50.00
PCMH MacInnis/Hawerchuk 15.00 40.00
PCMK B.Morrison/R.Kesler 20.00 50.00
PCMM M.Modano/J.Mullen 12.00 30.00
PCMO G.Lafleur/L.Robinson 40.00 80.00
PCMR M.Modano/M.Ribeiro 15.00 40.00
PCMS S.Mikita/D.Savard 25.00 60.00
PCNB R.Nash/G.Brule 20.00 50.00
PCNM M.Naslund/B.Morrison 15.00 40.00
PCNO C.Neely/A.Oates 30.00 60.00
PCNS Tanguay/Zetterberg 40.00 80.00
PCOM A.Ovechkin/E.Malkin 100.00 200.00
PCPD P.Stastny/D.Hawerchuk
PCPE P.Bergeron/E.Staal 15.00 40.00
PCRB P.Roy/R.Bourque 100.00 175.00
PCRT M.Ribeiro/M.Turco 15.00 40.00
PCSH M.St. Louis/N.Horton 15.00 40.00
PCSM S.Gagne/A.Tanguay 15.00 40.00
PCSW M.Svatos/W.Wolski
PCTR D.Tucker/A.Raycroft 20.00 50.00
PCWH T.Vokoun/N.Horton 20.00 50.00
PCWS J.Williams/E.Staal 12.00 30.00

2007-08 OPC Premier Penmanship

STATED PRINT RUN 100 SER.#'d SETS
PPAK Anze Kopitar 12.00 30.00
PPBF Bernie Federko 5.00 12.00
PPCG Clark Gillies 8.00 20.00
PPDH Dany Heatley 8.00 20.00
PPDR Dwayne Roloson 6.00 15.00
PPEM Evgeni Malkin 15.00 40.00
PPHJ Milan Hejduk 8.00 20.00
PPHX Ron Hextall 12.00 30.00
PPIK Ilya Kovalchuk 10.00 25.00
PPJG Jean-Sebastien Giguere 8.00 20.00
PPJK Jari Kurri 8.00 20.00
PPJS Jordan Staal 10.00 25.00
PPMG Marian Gaborik 10.00 25.00
PPMN Markus Naslund 8.00 20.00
PPMR Michael Ryder
PPMT Marty Turco 8.00 20.00
PPNL Nicklas Lidstrom 12.00 30.00
PPPB Patrice Bergeron 8.00 20.00
PPPS Paul Stastny 8.00 20.00
PPRG Ryan Getzlaf 12.00 30.00
PPSC Sidney Crosby 75.00 150.00
PPSD Shane Doan 6.00 15.00
PPSG Simon Gagne 8.00 20.00
PPSK Saku Koivu 8.00 20.00
PPVL Vincent Lecavalier 6.00 15.00
PPVO Tomas Vokoun 6.00 15.00

2007-08 OPC Premier Penmanship Gold

*GOLD: .8X TO 2X BASE
STATED PRINT RUN 25 SERIAL #'d SETS
PPEM Evgeni Malkin 40.00 80.00

2007-08 OPC Premier Penmanship Silver

*SILVER: .6X TO 1.5X BASE
STATED PRINT RUN 50 SERIAL #'d SETS
PPEM Evgeni Malkin 30.00 80.00
PPSC Sidney Crosby 125.00 200.00

2007-08 OPC Premier Rare Remnants Triples

STATED PRINT RUN 50 SERIAL #'d SETS
PTAJD Aebiscr/Jovanvski/Doan 15.00 40.00
PTAMV Afinogenov/Miller/Vanek 15.00 40.00
PTAVS Afinogenv/Vanek/Staffd 12.00 30.00
PTBES Brodeur/Elias/Stevens 20.00 50.00
PTBGP Brodeur/Gionta/Parise 15.00 40.00
PTBLB Blake/Lecav/Bourdon 15.00 40.00
PTBLK Brodeur/Luongo/Kiprusoff 20.00 50.00
PTBLM Beliveau/Lafleur/Mahov 15.00 40.00
PTBPS Bossy/Potvin/Smith 15.00 40.00
PTBRS Bourque/Robinsn/Stevns 15.00 40.00
PTBSW Brind'Amour/Staal/Ward 12.00 30.00
PTCFM Fleury/Crosby/Malkin 25.00 60.00
PTCGH Clarke/Gagne/Hextall 20.00 50.00
PTCMS Crosby/Malkin/Hextall 50.00 100.00
PTDFM Datsyuk/Fedorov/Malkin 15.00 40.00
PTDGK Demitra/Gaborik/Koivu 15.00 40.00
PTFBK Fernandz/Bergern/Kessel 12.00 30.00
PTFCK Frolov/Cammalleri/Kopitar 12.00 30.00
PTFCT Fernandz/Chara/Thomas 10.00 25.00
PTGBL Gagne/Briere/Lupul 15.00 40.00
PTGDP Gomez/Drury/Prucha 12.00 30.00
PTGRC Gagne/Richards/Carter 15.00 40.00
PTGSD Guerin/Satan/DiPietro 15.00 40.00
PTHDG Hossa/Demitra/Gaborik 12.00 30.00
PTHHK Huet/Higgins/Kovalev 12.00 30.00
PTHKL Hossa/Koval/Lehton 15.00 40.00
PTHLD Hasek/Lidstrom/Datsyuk 15.00 40.00
PTHRK Havlat/Ruutu/Khabibulin 12.00 30.00
PTHSW Hejduk/Svatos/Wolski 12.00 30.00
PTIKP Iginla/Kiprusoff/Phaneuf 10.00 25.00
PTJHE Jagr/Hasek/Elias 20.00 50.00
PTKOF Kolzig/Ovechkin/Fehr 15.00 40.00
PTKOR Koval/Ovech/Radulov 12.00 30.00
PTKRK Koivu/Ryder/Kovalev 12.00 30.00
PTKSK Koivu/Staal/Kopitar 15.00 40.00
PTKST Kariya/Tkachuk/Stemp 12.00 30.00
PTLEK Luongo/Emery/Kiprusoff 12.00 30.00
PTLHZ Lidstrm/Holmstrm/Zetter 15.00 40.00
PTLRS Lecavalier/Richards/St. Louis 12.00 30.00
PTMGM McDonald/Gilmour/Macln 12.00 30.00
PTMSR Modano/Sundin/Recchi 12.00 30.00
PTMTK Modano/Tkachuk/Kessel 15.00 40.00
PTNBO Neely/Bourque/Oates 15.00 40.00
PTNLM Naslund/Luongo/Morrison 10.00 25.00
PTNSS Naslund/Sedin/Sedin 10.00 25.00
PTNZF Nash/Zherdev/Fedorov 10.00 25.00
PTPGB Parrish/Gaborik/Bouchard 10.00 25.00
PTRLG Roy/Lemieux/Gretzky 75.00 150.00
PTROV Richards/Ott/Vaive 10.00 25.00
PTRRM Roberts/Recchi/Malone 15.00 40.00
PTSBS Spezza/Bergeron/Staal 10.00 25.00
PTSFA Sundin/Forsberg/Alfredsson 15.00 40.00
PTSHP Stoll/Hemsky/Pouliot 12.00 30.00
PTSJL Shanahan/Jagr/Lundqvist 10.00 25.00
PTSLJ Selanne/Lehtinen/Jokinen 15.00 40.00
PTSNG Selanne/Nieder/Giguere 15.00 40.00
PTSOH Stastny/Oates/Hawerchuk 10.00 25.00
PTSRT Sakic/Richards/Thornton 12.00 30.00
PTSSN Nolan/Sakic/Sundin 15.00 40.00
PTSTS Sakic/Theodore/Smyth 12.00 30.00
PTTSC Thornton/St.L/Crosby 20.00 50.00
PTVNB Vyborny/Nash/Brule 10.00 25.00

2007-08 OPC Premier Rare Remnants Quads

STATED PRINT RUN 25 SERIAL #'d SETS
PQASHE Alf/Spez/Heat/Emry 25.00 60.00
PQBBLP Bucy/Bosy/Laflr/Perrlt
PQBLMF Brodr/Luon/Miller/Flery 30.00 80.00
PQBSHS Brodr/Hask/Smith/Hxtl 30.00 80.00
PQCFMS Fleu/Crsby/Malkn/Stal 60.00 120.00
PQCWPS Cheli/Will/Prb/Stvns 25.00 60.00
PQGBBC Gag/Brier/Birn/Cartr 10.00 25.00
PQHLDZ Hask/Lids/Dats/Zetter
PQITKP Igin/Tang/Kipr/Phanf 20.00 50.00
PQJFIC Jagr/Fors/Igin/Crsby 60.00 120.00
PQKSTL Kari/Tkac/Legc/Stmp
PQLCGM Mrio/Crsby/Grtz/Mess 60.00 120.00
PQLHRK Lng/Hvlt/Rutu/Khab
PQLNFB Lclre/Nsh/Fdrv/Brul 20.00 50.00
PQMTCC Mrlu/Thrn/Chec/Crle 25.00 60.00
PQPGBK Prsh/Gbk/Bchrd/Kvu
PQRNWS BRch/Nder/Wrd/Stvns 25.00 60.00
PQSICM Sak/Igin/Crsby/Mess 40.00 100.00
PQSJDL Shan/Jgr/Druy/Lndq 50.00 100.00
PQSKBI Sakic/Krya/Brodr/Igin 20.00 50.00
PQSKRD Sakic/Krya/BRich/Dts 15.00 40.00
PQSLLA Sundn/Leht/Lids/Alf
PQSOMA Selne/Alf/Ovch/Mlkn 60.00 120.00
PQSPNG Selne/Prng/Nder/Ggy 20.00 50.00
PQTNCO Thrn/Nsh/Crsby/Ovch 30.00 80.00

2007-08 OPC Premier Remnants Triples

STATED PRINT RUN 50-100
*PATCH/15-35: 1X TO 2.5X JSY/50-100
PRAF Alexander Frolov/100 4.00 10.00
PRAK Alex Kovalev/100 5.00 12.00
PRAO Alexander Ovechkin/100 10.00 25.00
PRAS Alexander Steen/100 6.00 15.00
PRBL Rob Blake/100 6.00 15.00
PRBM Brendan Morrison/100 4.00 10.00
PRBO Mike Bossy/100 6.00 15.00
PRBR Rod Brind'Amour/100 6.00 15.00
PRBS Billy Smith/100 6.00 15.00
PRCH Jonathan Cheechoo/100 6.00 15.00
PRCW Cam Ward/100 6.00 15.00
PRDA Daniel Alfredsson/100 6.00 15.00
PRDE Pavol Demitra/100 8.00 20.00
PRDH Dale Hawerchuk/100 8.00 20.00
PRDL David Legwand/100 5.00 12.00
PRDR Dwayne Roloson/100 5.00 12.00
PRDS Darryl Sittler/100 5.00 12.00
PREB Ed Belfour/100 6.00 15.00
PREJ Ed Jovanovski/100 5.00 12.00
PREL Eric Lindros/100 8.00 20.00
PREM Evgeni Malkin/100 20.00 50.00
PRES Eric Staal/100 8.00 20.00
PRGA Simon Gagne/100 6.00 15.00
PRGP Gilbert Perreault/100 6.00 15.00
PRHA Dominik Hasek/100 8.00 20.00
PRHE Dany Heatley/75 8.00 20.00
PRHL Henrik Lundqvist/100 8.00 20.00
PRHM Milan Hejduk/100 5.00 12.00
PRHZ Henrik Zetterberg/100 8.00 20.00
PRIK Ilya Kovalchuk/100 6.00 15.00
PRJA Jason Arnott/100 5.00 12.00
PRJB Jay Bouwmeester/100 6.00 15.00
PRJC Jeff Carter/75 6.00 15.00
PRJG Jean-Sebastien Giguere/100 6.00 15.00
PRJI Jarome Iginla/100 6.00 15.00
PRJJ Jaromir Jagr/100
PRJO Joe Sakic/100 8.00 20.00
PRJP Joni Pitkanen/100 4.00 10.00
PRJS Jason Spezza/100 6.00 15.00
PRJT Joe Thornton/100 8.00 20.00
PRJW Justin Williams/100 5.00 12.00
PRKL Kari Lehtonen/100 5.00 12.00
PRKO Mikko Koivu/100 5.00 12.00
PRLM Lanny McDonald/100 6.00 15.00
PRLR Larry Robinson/100 6.00 15.00
PRMA Martin Havlat/100 6.00 15.00
PRMB Martin Brodeur/100 12.00 30.00
PRMC Mike Cammalleri/100 5.00 12.00
PRMG Marian Gaborik/100 8.00 20.00
PRMH Marian Hossa/100 12.50 30.00
PRMI Mike Richards/100 6.00 15.00
PRMK Miikka Kiprusoff/100 5.00 12.00
PRML Mario Lemieux/100 20.00 50.00
PRMM Mike Modano/100 10.00 25.00
PRMN Markus Naslund/100 6.00 15.00
PRMR Mark Recchi/100 8.00 20.00
PRMS Marc Savard/100 4.00 10.00
PRMT Marty Turco/100 6.00 15.00
PRNH Nathan Horton/100 6.00 15.00
PRNL Nicklas Lidstrom/100 6.00 15.00
PROJ Olli Jokinen/100 5.00 12.00
PROK Olaf Kolzig/100 6.00 15.00
PRPB Patrice Bergeron/100 8.00 20.00
PRPD Pavel Datsyuk/100 8.00 20.00
PRPE Patrik Elias/100 6.00 15.00
PRPF Peter Forsberg/100 8.00 20.00
PRPI Pierre-Marc Bouchard/100 6.00 15.00
PRPK Paul Kariya/100 8.00 20.00
PRPM Patrick Marleau/100 6.00 15.00
PRPR Patrick Roy/100 15.00 40.00
PRPS Peter Stastny/100 5.00 12.00
PRRB Ray Bourque/100 10.00 25.00
PRRD Rick DiPietro/100 5.00 12.00
PRRI Mike Ribeiro/100 5.00 12.00
PRRL Roberto Luongo/100 8.00 20.00
PRRM Ryan Miller/100 6.00 15.00
PRRN Rick Nash/100 6.00 15.00
PRRS Ryan Smyth/100 5.00 12.00
PRRY Michael Ryder/100 4.00 10.00
PRSA Borje Salming/100 6.00 15.00
PRSC Sidney Crosby/100 30.00 80.00
PRSD Shane Doan/100 5.00 12.00
PRSE Sergei Samsonov/50 5.00 12.00
PRSF Sergei Fedorov/100 10.00 25.00
PRSG Scott Gomez/100 5.00 12.00
PRSH Brendan Shanahan/100 8.00 20.00
PRSK Saku Koivu/100 6.00 15.00
PRSM Miroslav Satan/100 5.00 12.00
PRSS Steve Shutt/100 6.00 15.00
PRST Martin St. Louis/100 6.00 15.00
PRSU Mats Sundin/100 6.00 15.00
PRSV Marek Svatos/100 4.00 10.00
PRTB Todd Bertuzzi/100 6.00 15.00
PRTH Tomas Holmstrom/100 5.00 12.00
PRTR Tuomo Ruutu/100 6.00 15.00
PRTS Teemu Selanne/100 12.00 30.00
PRTV Tomas Vokoun/100 5.00 12.00
PRVL Vincent Lecavalier/100 5.00 12.00
PRZC Zdeno Chara/100

2007-08 OPC Premier Remnants Quads

STATED PRINT RUN 25 SERIAL #'d SETS
*PATCH/20: .6X TO 1.5X QUAD/25
PRAF Alexander Frolov 12.00 30.00
PRAK Alex Kovalev 15.00 40.00
PRAO Alexander Ovechkin 25.00 60.00
PRAS Alexander Steen 20.00 50.00
PRBM Brendan Morrison 12.00 30.00
PRBO Mike Bossy 20.00 50.00
PRBR Rod Brind'Amour 20.00 50.00
PRBS Billy Smith 12.00 30.00
PRCH Jonathan Cheechoo 20.00 50.00
PRCW Cam Ward 20.00 50.00
PRDE Pavol Demitra 25.00 60.00
PRDH Dale Hawerchuk 25.00 60.00
PRDS Darryl Sittler 15.00 40.00
PREB Ed Belfour 20.00 50.00
PREJ Ed Jovanovski 15.00 40.00
PREL Eric Lindros 30.00 80.00
PREM Evgeni Malkin 20.00 50.00
PRES Eric Staal 25.00 60.00
PRGA Simon Gagne 20.00 50.00
PRHE Dany Heatley 20.00 50.00
PRHL Henrik Lundqvist 25.00 60.00
PRHM Milan Hejduk 15.00 40.00
PRHZ Henrik Zetterberg 20.00 50.00
PRIK Ilya Kovalchuk 12.00 30.00
PRJA Jason Arnott 15.00 40.00
PRJB Jay Bouwmeester 20.00 50.00
PRJC Jeff Carter 20.00 50.00
PRJG Jean-Sebastien Giguere 20.00 50.00
PRJI Jarome Iginla 20.00 50.00
PRJJ Jaromir Jagr 25.00 60.00
PRJO Joe Sakic 20.00 50.00
PRJP Joni Pitkanen 12.00 30.00
PRJS Jason Spezza 20.00 50.00
PRJT Joe Thornton 15.00 40.00
PRKL Kari Lehtonen 15.00 40.00
PRLM Lanny McDonald 12.00 30.00
PRLR Larry Robinson 20.00 50.00
PRMA Martin Havlat 12.00 30.00
PRMB Martin Brodeur 30.00 60.00
PRMC Mike Cammalleri 12.00 30.00
PRMG Marian Gaborik 25.00 60.00
PRMH Marian Hossa 15.00 40.00
PRMI Mike Richards 20.00 50.00
PRML Mario Lemieux 40.00 80.00
PRMM Mike Modano 12.00 30.00
PRMN Markus Naslund 20.00 50.00
PRMR Mark Recchi 25.00 60.00
PRMS Marc Savard 12.00 30.00
PRMT Marty Turco 20.00 50.00
PRNH Nathan Horton 12.00 30.00
PRNL Nicklas Lidstrom 20.00 50.00
PROJ Olli Jokinen 15.00 40.00
PROK Olaf Kolzig 12.00 30.00
PRPB Patrice Bergeron 25.00 60.00
PRPF Peter Forsberg 12.00 30.00
PRPI Pierre-Marc Bouchard 20.00 50.00
PRPK Paul Kariya 15.00 40.00
PRPM Patrick Marleau 20.00 50.00
PRPR Patrick Roy 30.00 80.00
PRPS Peter Stastny 15.00 40.00
PRRB Ray Bourque 30.00 80.00
PRRD Rick DiPietro 15.00 40.00
PRRI Mike Ribeiro 15.00 40.00
PRRM Ryan Miller 20.00 50.00
PRRN Rick Nash 20.00 50.00
PRRS Ryan Smyth 15.00 40.00
PRSA Borje Salming 20.00 50.00
PRSC Sidney Crosby 30.00 80.00
PRSD Shane Doan 15.00 40.00
PRSE Sergei Samsonov 15.00 40.00
PRSF Sergei Fedorov 30.00 80.00
PRSG Scott Gomez 15.00 40.00
PRSH Brendan Shanahan 12.00 30.00
PRSK Saku Koivu 20.00 50.00
PRSM Miroslav Satan/15 15.00 40.00
PRSS Steve Shutt 20.00 50.00
PRST Martin St. Louis 20.00 50.00
PRSU Mats Sundin 12.00 30.00
PRTH Tomas Holmstrom 12.00 30.00
PRTS Teemu Selanne 40.00 100.00
PRTV Tomas Vokoun 15.00 40.00
PRVL Vincent Lecavalier 15.00 40.00

2007-08 OPC Premier Stitchings

STATED PRINT RUN 199 SERIAL #'d SETS
PSAB Andy Bathgate 5.00 12.00
PSAO Alexander Ovechkin 12.00 30.00
PSBC Bobby Clarke 6.00 15.00
PSBH Bobby Hull 10.00 25.00
PSBL Rob Blake 6.00 15.00
PSBO Bobby Orr 25.00 50.00
PSBP Bernie Parent 6.00 15.00
PSBR Brad Richards/25 12.50 30.00
PSBS Brendan Shanahan 8.00 20.00
PSCD Chris Drury 5.00 12.00
PSCN Cam Neely 6.00 15.00
PSCT Cyclone Taylor 6.00 15.00
PSDA Daniel Alfredsson 6.00 15.00
PSDH Dany Heatley 6.00 15.00
PSDS Darryl Sittler 6.00 15.00
PSEG Ed Giacomin 6.00 15.00
PSEJ Ed Jovanovski 5.00 12.00
PSEM Evgeni Malkin 20.00 50.00
PSES Eddie Shack 6.00 15.00
PSFN Frank Nighbor 6.00 15.00
PSGC Gerry Cheevers 6.00 15.00
PSGH Gordie Howe 12.00 30.00
PSGR Wayne Gretzky 20.00 50.00
PSIK Ilya Kovalchuk 6.00 15.00
PSJB Jean Beliveau 8.00 20.00
PSJI Jarome Iginla 8.00 20.00
PSJJ Jaromir Jagr 15.00 40.00
PSJL Jacques Lemaire 5.00 12.00
PSJS Jason Spezza 6.00 15.00
PSJT Joe Thornton 8.00 20.00
PSKL Kari Lehtonen 5.00 12.00
PSLR Larry Robinson 6.00 15.00
PSMA Martin Brodeur 10.00 25.00
PSMH Martin Havlat 6.00 15.00
PSMK Miikka Kiprusoff 5.00 12.00
PSML Mario Lemieux 12.00 30.00
PSMM Mark Messier 10.00 25.00
PSMS Mats Sundin 6.00 15.00
PSOK Olaf Kolzig 6.00 15.00
PSPD Pavel Datsyuk 8.00 20.00
PSPE Phil Esposito 10.00 25.00
PSPK Paul Kariya 8.00 20.00
PSPL Pat LaFontaine 6.00 15.00
PSPR Patrick Roy 20.00 40.00
PSRA Ray Bourque 10.00 25.00
PSRB Richard Brodeur 5.00 12.00
PSRK Red Kelly 5.00 12.00
PSRL Roberto Luongo 8.00 20.00
PSRO Patrick Roy 12.00 30.00
PSSA Joe Sakic 10.00 25.00
PSSF Sergei Fedorov 10.00 25.00
PSSM Billy Smith 6.00 15.00
PSST Jordan Staal 6.00 15.00
PSTE Tony Esposito 6.00 15.00
PSTS Teemu Selanne 12.00 30.00
PSVL Vincent Lecavalier 5.00 12.00
PSWA Wayne Gretzky 15.00 40.00
PSWG Wayne Gretzky/100 20.00 50.00

2007-08 OPC Premier Stitchings 25

*STITCHINGS/25: .6X TO 1.5X BASE JSY
STATED PRINT RUN 25 SERIAL #'d SETS

2007-08 OPC Premier Stitchings 50

*STITCHINGS/50: .5X TO 1.2X BASE JSY
STATED PRINT RUN 50 SERIAL #'d SETS
PSBR Brad Richards 8.00 20.00

2007-08 OPC Premier Stitchings Variation

STATED PRINT RUN 99 SERIAL #'d SETS
*STITCHINGS/25: .6X TO 1.5X BASE JSY
PSAB Andy Bathgate 5.00 12.00
PSAO Alexander Ovechkin 12.00 30.00
PSBC Bobby Clarke 6.00 15.00
PSBH Bobby Hull 10.00 25.00
PSBL Rob Blake 6.00 15.00
PSBO Bobby Orr 20.00 50.00
PSBP Bernie Parent 6.00 15.00
PSBR Brad Richards 6.00 15.00
PSBS Brendan Shanahan 8.00 20.00
PSCD Chris Drury 5.00 12.00
PSCN Cam Neely 10.00 25.00
PSCT Cyclone Taylor 6.00 15.00
PSDA Daniel Alfredsson 6.00 15.00
PSDH Dany Heatley 6.00 15.00
PSDS Darryl Sittler 6.00 15.00
PSEG Ed Giacomin/50 6.00 15.00
PSEJ Ed Jovanovski 5.00 12.00
PSEM Evgeni Malkin 12.00 30.00
PSES Eddie Shack 6.00 15.00
PSFN Frank Nighbor 6.00 15.00
PSGC Gerry Cheevers 6.00 15.00
PSGR Wayne Gretzky 30.00 80.00
PSIK Ilya Kovalchuk 6.00 15.00
PSJB Jean Beliveau 8.00 20.00
PSJI Jarome Iginla 15.00 40.00
PSJJ Jaromir Jagr 15.00 40.00
PSJL Jacques Lemaire 5.00 12.00
PSJS Jason Spezza 6.00 15.00
PSJT Joe Thornton 8.00 20.00
PSKL Kari Lehtonen 5.00 12.00
PSLR Larry Robinson 6.00 15.00
PSMA Martin Brodeur 15.00 40.00
PSMH Martin Havlat 6.00 15.00
PSMK Miikka Kiprusoff 5.00 12.00
PSML Mario Lemieux 20.00 50.00
PSMM Mark Messier 10.00 25.00
PSMS Mats Sundin 6.00 15.00
PSOK Olaf Kolzig 6.00 15.00
PSPD Pavel Datsyuk 8.00 20.00
PSPE Phil Esposito 10.00 25.00
PSPK Paul Kariya 8.00 20.00
PSPR Patrick Roy 15.00 40.00
PSRA Ray Bourque 10.00 25.00
PSRB Richard Brodeur 5.00 12.00
PSRK Red Kelly 5.00 12.00
PSRL Roberto Luongo 8.00 20.00
PSRO Patrick Roy 15.00 40.00
PSSF Sergei Fedorov 10.00 25.00
PSSM Billy Smith 6.00 15.00
PSST Jordan Staal 6.00 15.00
PSTE Tony Esposito 6.00 15.00
PSTS Teemu Selanne 12.00 30.00
PSVL Vincent Lecavalier 5.00 12.00
PSWA Wayne Gretzky 30.00 80.00
PSWG Wayne Gretzky 25.00 60.00

2008-09 OPC Premier

COMP.SET w/o SPs (42) 175.00 300.00
STATED PRINT RUN 299 SER.#'d SETS
1 Wayne Gretzky 10.00 25.00
2 Vincent Lecavalier 1.50 4.00
3 Tony Esposito 2.00 5.00
4 Sidney Crosby 8.00 20.00
5 Saku Koivu 2.00 5.00
6 Rick Nash 2.00 5.00
7 Ray Bourque 3.00 8.00
8 Phil Esposito 3.00 8.00
9 Peter Mueller 1.50 4.00
10 Pavel Datsyuk 2.50 6.00
11 Paul Stastny 2.00 5.00
12 Patrick Roy 5.00 12.00
13 Patrick Kane 4.00 10.00
14 Nicklas Lidstrom 2.00 5.00
15 Mike Bossy 2.00 5.00
16 Martin St. Louis 2.00 5.00
17 Martin Brodeur 4.00 10.00
18 Mark Messier 2.50 6.00
19 Mario Lemieux 6.00 15.00
20 Marian Gaborik 2.50 6.00
21 Jonathan Toews 5.00 12.00
22 Jonathan Cheechoo 2.00 5.00
23 Joe Thornton 2.50 6.00
24 Joe Sakic 3.00 8.00
25 Jarome Iginla 2.00 5.00
26 Jari Kurri 2.00 5.00
27 Ilya Kovalchuk 2.00 5.00
28 Henrik Zetterberg 2.50 6.00
29 Guy Lafleur 2.50 6.00
30 Grant Fuhr 2.00 5.00
31 Gordie Howe 5.00 12.00
32 Gilbert Perreault 2.00 5.00
33 Evgeni Malkin 6.00 15.00
34 Eric Staal 2.50 6.00
35 Dany Heatley 2.00 5.00
36 Dale Hawerchuk 2.50 6.00
37 Carey Price 8.00 20.00
38 Cam Neely 2.00 5.00
39 Bobby Orr 6.00 15.00
40 Bobby Hull 3.00 8.00
41 Bobby Clarke 2.00 5.00
42 Alexander Ovechkin 8.00 20.00
43 Zach Bogosian JSY AU RC 5.00 12.00
44 Blake Wheeler JSY AU RC 12.00 30.00
45 Zach Boychuk JSY AU RC 5.00 12.00
46 Brandon Sutter JSY AU RC 5.00 12.00
47 Nikita Filatov JSY AU RC 5.00 12.00
48 Jakub Voracek JSY AU RC 20.00 40.00
49 Derick Brassard JSY AU RC 4.00 10.00
50 Steve Mason JSY AU RC 12.00 30.00
51 Justin Pogge JSY AU RC 5.00 12.00
52 Fabian Brunnstrom JSY AU RC 4.00 10.00
53 James Neal JSY AU RC 15.00 30.00
54 Justin Abdelkader JSY AU RC 8.00 20.00
55 Darren Helm JSY AU RC 5.00 12.00
56 Mattias Ritola JSY AU RC 4.00 10.00
57 Michael Frolik JSY AU RC 5.00 12.00
58 Shawn Matthias JSY AU RC 5.00 12.00
59 Drew Doughty JSY AU RC 20.00 40.00
60 Oscar Moller JSY AU RC 4.00 10.00
61 Erik Ersberg JSY AU RC 4.00 10.00
62 Brian Boyle JSY AU RC 4.00 10.00
63 Colton Gillies JSY AU RC 4.00 10.00
64 Patric Hornqvist JSY AU RC 5.00 12.00
65 Ben Maxwell JSY AU RC 5.00 12.00
66 Josh Bailey JSY AU RC 6.00 15.00
67 Kyle Okposo JSY AU RC 5.00 12.00
68 Lauri Korpikoski JSY AU RC 3.00 8.00
69 Ilya Zubov JSY AU RC 4.00 10.00
70 Claude Giroux JSY AU RC 30.00 60.00
71 Luca Sbisa JSY AU RC 3.00 8.00
72 Viktor Tikhonov JSY AU RC 4.00 10.00
73 Mikkel Boedker JSY AU RC 6.00 15.00
74 Kyle Turris JSY AU RC 8.00 20.00
75 Alex Goligoski JSY AU RC 6.00 15.00
76 Jamie McGinn JSY AU RC 5.00 12.00
77 Alex Pietrangelo JSY AU RC 6.00 15.00
78 Patrik Berglund JSY AU RC 4.00 10.00
79 T.J. Oshie JSY AU RC 15.00 40.00
80 Ben Bishop JSY AU RC 12.50 25.00
81 Steven Stamkos JSY AU RC 75.00 150.00
82 Luke Schenn JSY AU RC 6.00 15.00
83 Nikolai Kulemin JSY AU RC 5.00 12.00
84 Cory Schneider JSY AU RC 12.00 30.00

2008-09 OPC Premier Gold Spectrum

1-42 UNPRICED VET PRINT RUN 5
*ROOKIE JSY AU/15: 1.2X TO 3X BASIC RC
ROOKIE PRINT RUN 15 SERIAL #'d SETS

2008-09 OPC Premier Silver

*SINGLES: .6X TO 1.5X BASIC CARDS
STATED PRINT RUN 75 SER.#'d SETS

2008-09 OPC Premier Duos Autographs

STATED PRINT RUN 75 SER.#'d SETS
PP2BF D.Brassard/N.Filatov 8.00 20.00
PP2BN F.Brunnstrom/J.Neal 12.00 30.00
PP2DH P.Datsyuk/M.Hossa EXCH 15.00 40.00
PP2DK A.Delvecchio/R.Kelly 15.00 40.00
PP2DZ N.Zherdev/C.Drury
PP2EN P.Esposito/C.Neely 30.00 80.00
PP2FA G.Fuhr/G.Anderson 12.00 30.00
PP2FH T.Holmstrom/J.Franzen
PP2GG C.Gillies/C.Gillies 12.00 30.00
PP2GM W.Gretzky/M.Messier 150.00 250.00
PP2HE B.Hull/T.Esposito 50.00 100.00
PP2HO B.Orr/G.Howe 150.00 250.00
PP2KR J.Kurri/L.Robitaille 15.00 40.00
PP2KT J.Toews/P.Kane 125.00 200.00
PP2LN M.Naslund/H.Lundqvist 30.00 80.00
PP2LS V.Lecavalier/M.St. Louis 10.00 25.00
PP2MF E.Malkin/M.Fleury 30.00 80.00
PP2MK E.Malkin/I.Kovalchuk 20.00 50.00
PP2ML B.Leetch/M.Messier 50.00 100.00
PP2OB B.Orr/R.Bourque 100.00 200.00
PP2PV T.Vanek/G.Perreault 12.00 30.00
PP2RP C.Price/P.Roy 50.00 100.00
PP2SB Z.Boychuk/B.Sutter 12.00 30.00
PP2TC J.Cheechoo/J.Thornton 12.00 30.00
PP2TM K.Turris/P.Mueller 12.00 30.00
PP2ZL N.Lidstrom/H.Zetterberg 25.00 60.00

2008-09 OPC Premier Dynasty Duos Autographs

STATED PRINT RUN 100 SER.#'d SETS
DDAF G.Fuhr/G.Anderson 12.00 30.00
DDBP M.Bossy/D.Potvin 12.00 30.00
DDDH T.Holmstrom/P.Datsyuk 15.00 40.00
DDGM M.Messier/W.Gretzky 125.00 250.00
DDLK T.Lindsay/R.Kelly 15.00 40.00
DDLS S.Shutt/G.Lafleur 15.00 40.00
DDMB F.Mahovlich/J.Bower 12.00 30.00
DDOE B.Orr/P.Esposito 100.00 200.00

2008-09 OPC Premier Dynasty Duos Autographs Gold Spectrum

*SINGLES: .6X TO 1.5X BASIC INSERTS
STATED PRINT RUN 25 SER.#'d SETS

2008-09 OPC Premier Inductions Ink

STATED PRINT RUN 100 SER.#'d SETS
PIAM Al MacInnis 8.00 20.00
PIBS Borje Salming 8.00 20.00
PIDS Denis Savard 10.00 25.00
PIJM Joe Mullen 6.00 15.00
PILM Lanny McDonald 8.00 20.00
PIMD Marcel Dionne 10.00 25.00
PIPS Peter Stastny 8.00 20.00
PIRB Ray Bourque 12.00 30.00
PISS Steve Shutt 8.00 20.00

2008-09 OPC Premier Inductions Ink Dual

STATED PRINT RUN 50 SER.#'d SETS
2PIBP D.Potvin/M.Bossy 15.00 40.00
2PIDM M.Dionne/L.McDonald 20.00 50.00
2PIEL G.Lafleur/T.Esposito 20.00 50.00
2PIGL R.Langway/C.Gillies 15.00 40.00
2PIHB Beliveau/Howe EXCH 75.00 150.00
2PIKH J.Kurri/D.Hawerchuk 20.00 50.00
2PIMM Messier/MacInnis 30.00 80.00
2PIMS J.Mullen/D.Savard 20.00 50.00
2PIOH H.Howell/B.Orr 75.00 150.00

2008-09 OPC Premier Inductions Ink Gold Spectrum

*SINGLES: .5X TO 1.2X BASIC INSERTS
STATED PRINT RUN 25 SER.#'d SETS

2008-09 OPC Premier Penmanship

STATED PRINT RUN 100 SER.#'d SETS
PPAK Anze Kopitar 12.00 30.00
PPAO Alexander Ovechkin 40.00 80.00
PPCP Carey Price 25.00 50.00
PPDH Dany Heatley 8.00 20.00
PPEM Evgeni Malkin 25.00 60.00
PPHZ Henrik Zetterberg 12.00 30.00
PPJG Jean-Sebastien Giguere 8.00 20.00
PPJS Jordan Staal 8.00 20.00
PPMH Milan Hejduk 6.00 15.00
PPMR Mike Richards 8.00 20.00
PPMT Marty Turco 8.00 20.00
PPPK Patrick Kane 30.00 60.00
PPPS Paul Stastny 8.00 20.00
PPRG Ryan Getzlaf 12.00 30.00
PPRH Ron Hextall 10.00 25.00
PPSC Sidney Crosby 75.00 125.00
PPSG Simon Gagne 8.00 20.00
PPTH Joe Thornton 10.00 25.00
PPTV Thomas Vanek 8.00 20.00
PPVL Vincent Lecavalier 6.00 15.00

2008-09 OPC Premier Penmanship Gold Spectrum

*SINGLES: .6X TO 1.5X BASIC INSERTS
STATED PRINT RUN 25 SER.#'d SETS

2008-09 OPC Premier Rare Remnants Triples

STATED PRINT RUN 20 SERIAL #'d SETS
RR3BON Adam Oates 20.00 50.00
Ray Bourque
Cam Neely
RR3GML Mark Messier 75.00 150.00
Wayne Gretzky
Mario Lemieux
RR3HSW Milan Hejduk
Marek Svatos
Wojtek Wolski
RR3LNG Ryan Getzlaf 12.00 30.00
Rick Nash
Vincent Lecavalier
RR3PMK Phil Kessel 12.00 30.00
Peter Mueller
Zach Parise
RR3RBH Martin Brodeur 30.00 75.00
Dominik Hasek
Patrick Roy
RR3RLB Patrick Roy 30.00 75.00
Martin Brodeur
Roberto Luongo
RR3SBV Fabian Brunnstrom 15.00 40.00
Jakub Voracek
Steven Stamkos
RR3SDB Zach Bogosian 20.00 50.00
Drew Doughty
Luke Schenn
RR3SRL Steve Shutt 12.00 30.00
Rod Langway
Larry Robinson
RR3SSB Patrice Bergeron 15.00 40.00
Eric Staal
Jason Spezza
RR3ZLH Henrik Zetterberg 20.00 50.00
Nicklas Lidstrom
Tomas Holmstrom

2008-09 OPC Premier Remnants Quads

STATED PRINT RUN 25 SER.#'d SETS
PRAO Adam Oates 8.00 20.00
PRBS Borje Salming 8.00 20.00
PRCP Carey Price 30.00 80.00
PRDH Dale Hawerchuk 10.00 25.00
PRDS Darryl Sittler 8.00 20.00
PREM Evgeni Malkin 25.00 60.00
PRES Eric Staal 10.00 25.00
PRHA Dominik Hasek 10.00 25.00
PRHL Henrik Lundqvist 10.00 25.00
PRHZ Henrik Zetterberg 10.00 25.00

PRIK Ilya Kovalchuk 8.00 20.00
PRJC Jonathan Cheechoo 8.00 20.00
PRJI Jarome Iginla 8.00 20.00
PRKB Nicklas Backstrom 12.00 30.00
PRLM Lanny McDonald 8.00 20.00
PRLR Larry Robinson 8.00 20.00
PRMB Martin Brodeur 15.00 40.00
PRMG Marian Gaborik 10.00 25.00
PRMK Mikko Koivu 6.00 15.00
PRML Mario Lemieux 25.00 60.00
PRMM Mike Modano 12.00 30.00
PRMR Mike Richards 8.00 20.00
PRNL Nicklas Lidstrom 8.00 20.00
PROV Alexander Ovechkin 30.00 80.00
PRPB Patrice Bergeron 10.00 25.00
PRPM Peter Mueller 6.00 15.00
PRPR Patrick Roy 20.00 50.00
PRRB Ray Bourque 12.00 30.00
PRRL Roberto Luongo 10.00 25.00
PRRN Rick Nash 8.00 20.00
PRSC Sidney Crosby 30.00 80.00
PRSD Shane Doan 6.00 15.00
PRSG Simon Gagne 8.00 20.00
PRSK Saku Koivu 8.00 20.00
PRSS Steve Shutt 8.00 20.00
PRTR Tuomo Ruutu 8.00 20.00
PRVL Vincent Lecavalier 6.00 15.00
PRZP Marian Hossa 6.00 15.00

2008-09 OPC Premier Remnants Quads Gold

*GOLD: .5X TO 1.2X BASIC
STATED PRINT RUN 20 SERIAL #'d SETS
PRKB Nicklas Backstrom 20.00 50.00

2008-09 OPC Premier Remnants Triples

STATED PRINT RUN 100 SER.#'d SETS
*GOLD/35: .8X TO 2X BASIC TRIPLE
PRAO Adam Oates 5.00 12.00
PRBS Borje Salming 5.00 12.00
PRCP Carey Price 20.00 50.00
PRDH Dale Hawerchuk 6.00 15.00
PRDS Darryl Sittler 5.00 12.00
PREM Evgeni Malkin 15.00 40.00
PRES Eric Staal 6.00 15.00
PRHA Dominik Hasek 6.00 15.00
PRHL Henrik Lundqvist 6.00 15.00
PRHZ Henrik Zetterberg 6.00 15.00
PRIK Ilya Kovalchuk 5.00 12.00
PRJC Jonathan Cheechoo 5.00 12.00
PRJI Jarome Iginla 5.00 12.00
PRKB Nicklas Backstrom 8.00 20.00
PRLM Lanny McDonald 5.00 12.00
PRLR Larry Robinson 5.00 12.00
PRMB Martin Brodeur 10.00 25.00
PRMG Marian Gaborik 8.00 20.00
PRMK Mikko Koivu 4.00 10.00
PRML Mario Lemieux 15.00 40.00
PRMM Mike Modano 8.00 20.00
PRMR Mike Richards 5.00 12.00
PRNL Nicklas Lidstrom 5.00 12.00
PROV Alexander Ovechkin 20.00 50.00
PRPB Patrice Bergeron 6.00 15.00
PRPM Peter Mueller 4.00 10.00
PRPR Patrick Roy 12.00 30.00
PRRB Ray Bourque 8.00 20.00
PRRN Rick Nash 5.00 12.00
PRSC Sidney Crosby 20.00 50.00
PRSD Shane Doan 4.00 10.00
PRSG Simon Gagne 5.00 12.00
PRSK Saku Koivu 5.00 12.00
PRSS Steve Shutt 5.00 12.00
PRTR Tuomo Ruutu 5.00 12.00
PRVL Vincent Lecavalier 4.00 10.00
PRZP Marian Hossa 4.00 10.00

2008-09 OPC Premier Stitchings

STATED PRINT RUN 99 SER.#'d SETS
*BLUE/25: .6X TO 1.5X STITCHINGS
PSBH Bobby Hull 5.00 12.00
PSBO Bobby Orr 10.00 25.00
PSCN Cam Neely 3.00 8.00
PSCP Carey Price 12.00 30.00
PSDH Dany Heatley 3.00 8.00
PSEM Evgeni Malkin 10.00 25.00
PSGH Gordie Howe 8.00 20.00
PSHL Henrik Lundqvist 4.00 10.00
PSHZ Henrik Zetterberg 4.00 10.00
PSIK Ilya Kovalchuk 3.00 8.00
PSJI Jarome Iginla 3.00 8.00
PSJS Joe Sakic 5.00 12.00
PSJT Joe Thornton 4.00 10.00
PSMB Martin Brodeur 6.00 15.00
PSME Mark Messier 4.00 10.00
PSMG Marian Gaborik 4.00 10.00
PSML Mario Lemieux 10.00 25.00
PSMM Mike Modano 4.00 10.00
PSOV Alexander Ovechkin 12.00 30.00
PSPD Pavel Datsyuk 4.00 10.00
PSPE Phil Esposito 5.00 12.00
PSPK Patrick Kane 6.00 15.00
PSPR Patrick Roy 8.00 20.00
PSRB Ray Bourque 5.00 12.00
PSRL Roberto Luongo 6.00 15.00
PSRN Rick Nash 3.00 8.00
PSSS Steven Stamkos 8.00 20.00
PSTO Jonathan Toews 8.00 20.00
PSVL Vincent Lecavalier 2.50 6.00
PSWG Wayne Gretzky 15.00 40.00

2008-09 OPC Premier Stitchings Autographs

STATED PRINT RUN 15-50
APSBH Bobby Hull 30.00 60.00
APSBO Bobby Orr/15 125.00 200.00
APSCN Cam Neely 20.00 50.00
APSCP Carey Price 40.00 100.00
APSEM Evgeni Malkin/15
APSGH Gordie Howe/15 75.00 150.00
APSGP Gilbert Perreault 10.00 25.00
APSHE Dany Heatley
APSHZ Henrik Zetterberg 25.00 60.00
APSJI Jarome Iginla 8.00 20.00
APSJT Joe Thornton 10.00 25.00
APSMB Martin Brodeur 50.00 100.00
APSML Mario Lemieux/15 100.00 200.00
APSMM Mark Messier/15 50.00 100.00
APSPE Phil Esposito 20.00 50.00
APSPK Patrick Kane 15.00 40.00
APSPR Patrick Roy/15 75.00 150.00
APSTO Jonathan Toews 20.00 50.00
APSWG Wayne Gretzky/15 175.00 300.00

2008-09 OPC Premier Stitchings Variation

*VARIATION: .5X TO 1.2X STITCHINGS
STATED PRINT RUN 75 SER.#'d SETS

2008-09 OPC Premier Trios

STATED PRINT RUN 35 SER.#'d SETS
PP3BPF Price/Fleury/Brodeur 40.00 100.00
PP3BPG Gillies/Potvin/Bossy 50.00 100.00
PP3BVF Filatov/Voracek/Brassrd 30.00 60.00
PP3GOH Howe/Gretzky/Orr 250.00 400.00
PP3HTK Kane/Hull/Toews 100.00 175.00
PP3MLS Messier/Stamks/Mario
PP3RFH Hextall/Roy/Fuhr 125.00 200.00
PP3TBW Wheeler/Brunnstrom/Turris

2009-10 OPC Premier

61-102 JSY AU PRINT RUN 299
1 Al MacInnis 2.00 5.00
2 Alexander Ovechkin 8.00 20.00
3 Anze Kopitar 3.00 8.00
4 Bobby Hull 2.50 6.00
5 Bobby Orr 6.00 15.00
6 Brian Leetch 2.00 5.00
7 Cam Neely 2.00 5.00
8 Carey Price 8.00 20.00
9 Dale Hawerchuk 2.50 6.00
10 Daniel Sedin 2.00 5.00
11 Dany Heatley 2.00 5.00
12 Dion Phaneuf 2.50 6.00
13 Eric Staal 2.50 6.00
14 Evgeni Malkin 6.00 15.00
15 Gordie Howe 5.00 12.00
16 Grant Fuhr 2.00 5.00
17 Guy Lafleur 2.50 6.00
18 Henrik Sedin 2.00 5.00
19 Henrik Zetterberg 2.50 6.00
20 Ilya Kovalchuk 2.00 5.00
21 Jari Kurri 2.00 5.00
22 Jarome Iginla 2.00 5.00
23 Jason Spezza 2.00 5.00
24 Jean Beliveau 2.00 5.00
25 Joe Thornton 2.00 5.00
26 Jonathan Toews 4.00 10.00
27 Luc Robitaille 2.00 5.00
28 Marc-Andre Fleury 3.00 8.00
29 Marian Gaborik 2.50 6.00
30 Mario Lemieux 6.00 15.00
31 Mark Messier 2.50 6.00
32 Martin Brodeur 4.00 10.00
33 Martin St. Louis 2.00 5.00
34 Marty Turco 2.00 5.00
35 Mike Richards 2.00 5.00
36 Nicklas Backstrom 3.00 8.00
37 Nicklas Lidstrom 2.00 5.00
38 Patrick Kane 4.00 10.00
39 Patrick Roy 5.00 12.00
40 Paul Stastny 2.00 5.00
41 Pavel Datsyuk 2.50 6.00
42 Phil Esposito 3.00 8.00
43 Ray Bourque 3.00 8.00
44 Rick Nash 1.50 4.00
45 Roberto Luongo 2.50 6.00
46 Ron Hextall 3.00 8.00
47 Ryan Getzlaf 3.00 8.00
48 Ryan Miller 2.00 5.00
49 Saku Koivu 2.00 5.00
50 Sam Gagner 1.50 4.00
51 Sidney Crosby 10.00 25.00
52 Steve Mason 1.50 4.00
53 Steve Yzerman 5.00 12.00
54 Steven Stamkos 4.00 10.00
55 Teemu Selanne 4.00 10.00
56 Thomas Vanek 2.00 5.00
57 Tony Esposito 2.00 5.00
58 Vincent Lecavalier 1.50 4.00
59 Walt Tkaczuk 1.50 4.00
60 Wayne Gretzky 10.00 25.00
61 John Tavares JSY AU RC 40.00 100.00
62 J.van Riemsdyk JSY AU RC 12.00 30.00
63 Evander Kane JSY AU RC 12.00 30.00
64 Victor Hedman JSY AU RC 12.00 30.00
65 Jonas Gustavsson JSY AU RC 8.00 20.00
66 Matt Duchene JSY AU RC 12.00 30.00
67 Colin Wilson JSY AU RC 6.00 15.00
68 T.J. Galiardi JSY AU RC 6.00 15.00
69 Yannick Weber JSY AU RC 6.00 15.00
70 Spencer Machacek JSY AU RC 6.00 15.00
71 Antti Niemi JSY AU RC 10.00 25.00
72 Viktor Stalberg JSY AU RC 6.00 15.00
73 Michael Del Zotto JSY AU RC 6.00 15.00
74 Dmitry Kulikov JSY AU RC 6.00 15.00
75 Jamie Benn JSY AU RC 15.00 30.00
76 Ryan O'Reilly JSY AU RC 10.00 25.00
77 Tyler Myers JSY AU RC 12.50 25.00
78 Erik Karlsson JSY AU RC 25.00 50.00
79 Matt Gilroy JSY AU RC 6.00 15.00
80 Sergei Shirokov JSY AU RC 4.00 10.00
81 Ville Leino JSY AU RC 5.00 12.00
82 Riku Helenius JSY AU RC 6.00 15.00
83 Mikael Backlund JSY AU RC 6.00 15.00
84 Michal Neuvirth JSY AU RC 10.00 25.00
85 Cody Franson JSY AU RC 6.00 15.00
86 Luca Caputi JSY AU RC 5.00 12.00
87 Kris Chucko JSY AU RC 5.00 12.00
88 Jhonas Enroth JSY AU RC 8.00 20.00
89 Ivan Vishnevskiy JSY AU RC 5.00 12.00
90 Jakub Kindl JSY AU RC 6.00 15.00
91 Artem Anisimov JSY AU RC 6.00 15.00
92 Taylor Chorney JSY AU RC 6.00 15.00
93 Benn Ferriero JSY AU RC 6.00 15.00
94 Cal O'Reilly JSY AU RC 5.00 12.00
95 Matthew Corrente JSY AU RC 5.00 12.00
96 Jason Demers JSY AU RC 10.00 25.00
97 Ryan Stoa JSY AU RC 5.00 12.00
98 Lars Eller JSY AU RC 6.00 15.00
99 Ryan O'Marra JSY AU RC 4.00 10.00
100 Logan Couture JSY AU RC 12.00 30.00
101 Brad Marchand JSY AU RC 12.50 30.00
102 Michael Grabner JSY AU RC 6.00 15.00

2009-10 OPC Premier Gold

*GOLD/25: .8X TO 2X BASIC CARDS
STATED PRINT RUN 25 SER.#'d SETS
36 Nicklas Backstrom 6.00 15.00

2009-10 OPC Premier Gold Spectrum

61-102 PATCH AU PRINT RUN 35
61 John Tavares PATCH AU 100.00 200.00
62 J.van Riemsdyk PATCH AU 40.00 100.00
63 Evander Kane PATCH AU 30.00 80.00
64 Victor Hedman PATCH AU 15.00 40.00
65 Jonas Gustavsson PATCH AU 20.00 50.00
66 Matt Duchene PATCH AU 40.00 100.00
67 Colin Wilson PATCH AU 15.00 40.00
68 T.J. Galiardi PATCH AU 15.00 40.00
69 Yannick Weber PATCH AU 15.00 40.00
70 Spencer Machacek PATCH AU 15.00 40.00
71 Antti Niemi PATCH AU 40.00 80.00
72 Viktor Stalberg PATCH AU 15.00 40.00
73 Michael Del Zotto PATCH AU 15.00 40.00
74 Dmitry Kulikov PATCH AU 15.00 40.00
75 Jamie Benn PATCH AU 50.00 125.00
76 Ryan O'Reilly PATCH AU 25.00 60.00
77 Tyler Myers PATCH AU 25.00 60.00
78 Erik Karlsson PATCH AU 60.00 120.00
79 Matt Gilroy PATCH AU 15.00 40.00
80 Sergei Shirokov PATCH AU 10.00 25.00
81 Ville Leino PATCH AU 12.00 30.00
82 Riku Helenius PATCH AU 15.00 40.00
83 Mikael Backlund PATCH AU 15.00 40.00
84 Michal Neuvirth PATCH AU 25.00 60.00
85 Cody Franson PATCH AU 15.00 40.00
86 Luca Caputi PATCH AU 12.00 30.00
87 Kris Chucko PATCH AU 12.00 30.00
88 Jhonas Enroth PATCH AU 20.00 50.00
89 Ivan Vishnevskiy PATCH AU 12.00 30.00
90 Jakub Kindl PATCH AU 15.00 40.00
91 Artem Anisimov PATCH AU 15.00 40.00
92 Taylor Chorney PATCH AU 15.00 40.00
93 Benn Ferriero PATCH AU 15.00 40.00
94 Cal O'Reilly PATCH AU 12.00 30.00
95 Matthew Corrente PATCH AU 12.00 30.00
96 Jason Demers PATCH AU 25.00 60.00
97 Ryan Stoa PATCH AU 12.00 30.00
98 Lars Eller PATCH AU 15.00 40.00
99 Ryan O'Marra PATCH AU 10.00 25.00
100 Logan Couture PATCH AU 30.00 80.00
101 Brad Marchand PATCH AU 40.00 100.00
102 Michael Grabner PATCH AU 15.00 40.00

2009-10 OPC Premier Foursomes

All cards have a 4J prefix.
STATED PRINT RUN 25 SER.#'d SETS
AVKS Anism/Shirk/Kulk/Vshnv 15.00 40.00
CKWM Cout/Kan/Wlsn/Mrchd 12.00 30.00
CTDM Corrnt/Tavrs/Zott/Myrs 25.00 60.00
DENG Gustv/Niem/Enrth/Dbnk 15.00 40.00
DKOM Ovch/Mlkn/Kovl/Datsk 20.00 50.00
DMKH Hdmn/Ztto/Karlssn/Myrs 25.00 60.00
EBHH Espo/Beliv/Hull/Howe
EMEB Enroth/Myers/Ennis/Butlr 20.00 50.00
FCMS Fleury/Sid/Malkn/Staal 30.00 80.00
GMCP Pric/Gmz/Cammllr/Mark 30.00 60.00
HGBS Gustv/Bzk/Stlbrg/Hnsn 30.00 80.00
ISHN Iginla/Htley/Nash/St.Lou 8.00 20.00
JIKP Iginl/Kprsff/Phanf/Jokn
KCOT Koval/Crsby/Ovch/Tvrs 25.00 60.00
LDZF Ldstrm/Dtsyk/Zttr/Frnzn
LSSK Sedn/Sedn/Ksler/Lngo 30.00 60.00
LTSS Spez/Stl/Lcav/Thorntn 10.00 25.00
LYCO Mario/Yzer/Crsby/Ovch 75.00 150.00
LYGM Messi/Grtz/Mrio/Yzrmn 75.00 150.00
MPOV Rms/Mdno/Prse/Okps 12.00 30.00
MTNS Thorn/Mrleau/Set/Nbkv 12.00 30.00
NCTS Crsby/Nsh/Stamk/Tvrs 40.00 100.00
RBLF Roy/Brdr/Lngo/Fleury 20.00 50.00
RBTL Thms/Lcic/Berg/Rder 15.00 40.00
RCGV Riems/Rich/Cartr/Girx 25.00 60.00
SDSG Zott/Gilry/Sngti/Sauer 10.00 25.00
SGDO Ststny/Glrdi/Dchn/O'Re 25.00 60.00
SSGS Sedin/Sdin/Shrkv/Grb 20.00 50.00
TKDH Tavrs/Kne/Dchn/Hdmn 15.00 40.00
TWPM Masn/Prce/Wrd/Turco 30.00 80.00

2009-10 OPC Premier Rare Remnants Triples

STATED PRINT RUN 35 SER.#'d SETS
*PATCH/25: .8X TO 2X BASIC JSY
PRTAN Antti Niemi 8.00 20.00
PRTAO Alexander Ovechkin 15.00 40.00
PRTBA Mikael Backlund 12.00 30.00
PRTBH Bobby Hull 6.00 15.00
PRTBL Brian Leetch 5.00 12.00
PRTBM Brad Marchand 12.00 30.00
PRTCN Cam Neely 5.00 12.00
PRTCP Carey Price 15.00 40.00
PRTCW Colin Wilson 5.00 12.00
PRTDB Derick Brassard 5.00 12.00
PRTDE Michael Del Zotto 5.00 12.00
PRTDH Dany Heatley 5.00 12.00
PRTDP Dion Phaneuf 6.00 15.00
PRTEK Evander Kane 8.00 20.00
PRTEM Evgeni Malkin 15.00 40.00
PRTES Eric Staal 8.00 20.00
PRTGH Gordie Howe 12.00 30.00
PRTGR Michael Grabner 5.00 12.00
PRTHL Henrik Lundqvist 8.00 20.00
PRTHZ Henrik Zetterberg 6.00 15.00
PRTIK Ilya Kovalchuk 5.00 12.00
PRTJB Jamie Benn 15.00 40.00
PRTJC Jeff Carter 8.00 20.00
PRTJG Jonas Gustavsson 6.00 15.00
PRTJI Jarome Iginla 5.00 12.00
PRTJS Jordan Staal 5.00 12.00
PRTJT Joe Thornton 5.00 12.00
PRTJV James van Riemsdyk 10.00 25.00
PRTKE Phil Kessel 6.00 15.00
PRTLC Logan Couture 10.00 25.00
PRTLE Lars Eller 10.00 25.00
PRTMB Martin Brodeur 15.00 40.00
PRTMD Matt Duchene 12.00 30.00
PRTMF Marc-Andre Fleury 10.00 25.00
PRTMG Marian Gaborik 6.00 15.00
PRTMK Miikka Kiprusoff 8.00 20.00
PRTML Mario Lemieux 15.00 40.00
PRTMM Mark Messier 12.00 30.00
PRTMO Mike Modano 8.00 20.00
PRTMR Mike Richards 5.00 12.00
PRTMS Martin St. Louis 5.00 12.00
PRTMT Marty Turco 5.00 12.00
PRTNB Nicklas Backstrom 8.00 20.00
PRTNL Nicklas Lidstrom 5.00 12.00
PRTPD Pavel Datsyuk 10.00 25.00
PRTPK Patrick Kane 12.00 30.00
PRTPM Patrick Marleau 5.00 12.00
PRTPR Patrick Roy 12.00 30.00
PRTPS Paul Stastny 5.00 12.00
PRTRB Ray Bourque 8.00 20.00
PRTRL Roberto Luongo 6.00 15.00
PRTRN Rick Nash 8.00 20.00
PRTRO Ryan O'Reilly 8.00 20.00
PRTSC Sidney Crosby 20.00 50.00
PRTSM Steve Mason 4.00 10.00
PRTSP Jason Spezza 5.00 12.00
PRTSS Steven Stamkos 10.00 25.00
PRTSY Steve Yzerman 20.00 50.00
PRTTA John Tavares 20.00 50.00
PRTTB Tyler Bozak 8.00 20.00
PRTTM Tyler Myers 8.00 20.00
PRTTO Jonathan Toews 12.50 30.00
PRTTT Tim Thomas 10.00 25.00
PRTTV Tomas Vokoun 4.00 10.00
PRTVH Victor Hedman 10.00 25.00
PRTVI Ville Leino 6.00 15.00
PRTVL Vincent Lecavalier 4.00 10.00
PRTWA Cam Ward 8.00 20.00
PRTWG Wayne Gretzky 25.00 60.00
PRTZP Zach Parise 8.00 20.00

2009-10 OPC Premier Remnants Quad Jerseys

STATED PRINT RUN 25 SER.#'d SETS
PRQAO Alexander Ovechkin 25.00 60.00
PRQDP Dion Phaneuf 8.00 20.00
PRQEK Evander Kane 12.00 30.00
PRQEM Evgeni Malkin 20.00 50.00
PRQGH Gordie Howe 15.00 40.00
PRQHL Henrik Lundqvist 25.00 60.00
PRQHZ Henrik Zetterberg 8.00 20.00
PRQIK Ilya Kovalchuk 6.00 15.00
PRQJB Jamie Benn 10.00 25.00
PRQJC Jeff Carter 10.00 25.00
PRQJG Jonas Gustavsson 8.00 20.00
PRQJI Jarome Iginla 6.00 15.00
PRQJT John Tavares 25.00 60.00
PRQJV James van Riemsdyk 15.00 40.00
PRQMB Martin Brodeur 12.00 30.00
PRQMD Matt Duchene 15.00 40.00
PRQMF Marc-Andre Fleury 10.00 25.00
PRQMG Michael Grabner 6.00 15.00
PRQMK Miikka Kiprusoff 10.00 25.00
PRQML Mario Lemieux 20.00 50.00
PRQMM Mark Messier 8.00 20.00
PRQMR Mike Richards 25.00 60.00
PRQNB Nicklas Backstrom 10.00 25.00
PRQNL Nicklas Lidstrom 10.00 25.00
PRQPR Patrick Roy 15.00 40.00
PRQRL Roberto Luongo 10.00 25.00
PRQSC Sidney Crosby 25.00 60.00
PRQSS Steven Stamkos 12.00 30.00
PRQSY Steve Yzerman 15.00 40.00
PRQWG Wayne Gretzky 50.00 100.00

2009-10 OPC Premier Remnants Triple Autographs

STATED PRINT RUN 25 SER.#'d SETS
AR3AO Alexander Ovechkin 40.00 100.00
AR3BH Bobby Hull 20.00 50.00
AR3BL Brian Leetch 12.00 30.00
AR3BW Blake Wheeler 10.00 25.00
AR3CN Cam Neely 10.00 25.00
AR3CP Carey Price 30.00 60.00
AR3CW Cam Ward 12.00 30.00
AR3DP Dion Phaneuf 12.00 30.00
AR3EM Evgeni Malkin 30.00 60.00
AR3ES Eric Staal 12.00 30.00
AR3GA Glenn Anderson 15.00 40.00
AR3GH Gordie Howe 60.00 120.00
AR3HL Henrik Lundqvist 15.00 40.00
AR3HZ Henrik Zetterberg 25.00 50.00
AR3IK Ilya Kovalchuk
AR3JC Jeff Carter 10.00 25.00
AR3JI Jarome Iginla 10.00 25.00
AR3JK Jari Kurri 20.00 50.00
AR3JT Joe Thornton 10.00 25.00
AR3LR Luc Robitaille 20.00 50.00
AR3MB Martin Brodeur 50.00 100.00
AR3MF Marc-Andre Fleury 15.00 40.00
AR3MG Marian Gaborik 12.00 30.00
AR3ML Mario Lemieux 50.00 100.00
AR3MM Mark Messier 20.00 50.00
AR3MR Mike Richards
AR3NB Nicklas Backstrom 15.00 40.00
AR3NL Nicklas Lidstrom 15.00 40.00
AR3PD Pavel Datsyuk 15.00 40.00
AR3PR Patrick Roy 50.00 100.00
AR3RB Ray Bourque 25.00 60.00
AR3RM Ryan Miller 20.00 50.00
AR3RN Rick Nash 15.00 40.00
AR3SC Sidney Crosby 75.00 150.00
AR3SM Steve Mason 8.00 20.00
AR3SS Steven Stamkos 40.00 80.00
AR3SY Steve Yzerman 50.00 100.00
AR3TO Jonathan Toews 30.00 60.00
AR3VL Vincent Lecavalier 12.00 30.00
AR3WG Wayne Gretzky 125.00 200.00

2009-10 OPC Premier Signings

STATED PRINT RUN 50 SER.#'d SETS
PSAA Artem Anisimov 10.00 25.00
PSAK Anze Kopitar 15.00 40.00
PSAN Antti Niemi 15.00 40.00
PSAT Alex Tanguay 6.00 15.00
PSBA David Backes 10.00 25.00
PSBH Bobby Hull 15.00 40.00
PSBL Brian Leetch 10.00 25.00
PSBO Bobby Orr 60.00 120.00
PSBR Martin Brodeur 25.00 60.00
PSBW Blake Wheeler 10.00 25.00
PSCP Carey Price 40.00 100.00
PSCR Sidney Crosby 75.00 150.00
PSCS Sidney Crosby 75.00 150.00
PSCW Cam Ward 10.00 25.00
PSDB Derick Brassard 10.00 25.00
PSDD Drew Doughty 15.00 40.00
PSDE Michael Del Zotto 6.00 15.00
PSDG Doug Gilmour 15.00 40.00
PSDH Dany Heatley
PSDP Dion Phaneuf 8.00 20.00
PSDS Daniel Sedin 10.00 25.00
PSEK Evander Kane 12.00 30.00
PSEM Evgeni Malkin 20.00 50.00
PSEP Phil Esposito 12.00 30.00
PSES Eric Staal 12.00 30.00
PSGA Glenn Anderson
PSGH Gordie Howe 40.00 100.00
PSGI Matt Gilroy
PSGO Scott Gomez
PSGP Gilbert Perreault 10.00 25.00
PSGR Mike Green 10.00 25.00
PSHL Henrik Lundqvist 12.00 30.00
PSHS Henrik Sedin
PSHZ Henrik Zetterberg 12.00 30.00
PSIK Ilya Kovalchuk
PSJA Jason Arnott 8.00 20.00
PSJB Jean Beliveau 25.00 50.00
PSJC Jeff Carter 10.00 25.00
PSJE Jhonas Enroth 8.00 20.00
PSJG Jonas Gustavsson 15.00 40.00
PSJI Jarome Iginla 15.00 40.00
PSJS Jordan Staal 10.00 25.00
PSJT Jonathan Toews 20.00 50.00
PSJV Jakub Voracek 10.00 25.00
PSKA Erik Karlsson 20.00 50.00
PSKE Phil Kessel 12.00 30.00
PSLE Vincent Lecavalier 8.00 20.00
PSLR Luc Robitaille 12.00 30.00
PSLS Luke Schenn 10.00 25.00
PSMB Mikael Backlund 10.00 25.00
PSMD Matt Duchene 12.00 30.00
PSME Mark Messier 25.00 60.00
PSMF Marc-Andre Fleury 10.00 25.00
PSMG Marian Gaborik 12.00 30.00
PSMH Milan Hejduk 8.00 20.00
PSML Mario Lemieux 30.00 60.00
PSMM Mike Modano 15.00 40.00
PSMN Markus Naslund 8.00 20.00
PSMR Mike Ribeiro 8.00 20.00
PSMS Martin St. Louis 10.00 25.00
PSMT Marty Turco 10.00 25.00
PSNB Nicklas Backstrom 15.00 40.00
PSNF Tony Esposito 15.00 40.00
PSNL Nicklas Lidstrom 10.00 25.00
PSOV Alexander Ovechkin 50.00 100.00
PSPB Patrice Bergeron
PSPD Pavel Datsyuk 15.00 40.00
PSPE Patrik Elias 10.00 25.00
PSPK Patrick Kane 20.00 50.00
PSPR Patrick Roy 40.00 80.00
PSPS Paul Stastny 10.00 25.00
PSRB Ray Bourque 15.00 40.00
PSRG Ryan Getzlaf
PSRI Mike Richards
PSRM Ryan Miller 10.00 25.00
PSRN Rick Nash 8.00 20.00
PSRO Ryan O'Reilly 10.00 25.00
PSRS Ryan Stoa 8.00 20.00
PSSC Sidney Crosby 75.00 150.00
PSSD Shane Doan 8.00 20.00
PSSG Sam Gagner 8.00 20.00
PSSH Sergei Shirokov
PSSI Simon Gagne 10.00 25.00
PSSK Saku Koivu
PSSM Steve Mason 10.00 25.00
PSSS Steven Stamkos 20.00 50.00
PSST Peter Stastny
PSSV Steve Shutt 10.00 25.00
PSSW Shea Weber 8.00 20.00
PSSY Steve Yzerman 25.00 60.00
PSTA John Tavares 25.00 60.00
PSTH Joe Thornton 15.00 40.00
PSTM Tyler Myers 15.00 40.00
PSTV Thomas Vanek 10.00 25.00
PSVA James van Riemsdyk 15.00 40.00
PSVH Victor Hedman 12.00 30.00
PSVL Ville Leino 8.00 20.00
PSVO Tomas Vokoun 8.00 20.00
PSWG Wayne Gretzky 125.00 200.00
PSZB Zach Bogosian 8.00 20.00

2009-10 OPC Premier Signings Duals

STATED PRINT RUN 25 SER.#'d SETS
PS2AO J.Arnott/C.O'Reilly
PS2BO D.Backes/T.Oshie
PS2BT J.Tavares/M.Bossy 50.00 100.00
PS2BV Vishnevskiy/Benn 10.00 25.00
PS2BW Bergeron/B.Wheeler
PS2CV B.Clarke/J.Riemsdyk 20.00 50.00
PS2DM S.Doan/P.Mueller
PS2DW Dumont/Weber 10.00 25.00
PS2EO P.Esposito/B.Orr 75.00 150.00
PS2FA G.Fuhr/G.Anderson
PS2FF Foligno/Foligno 10.00 25.00
PS2FK G.Fuhr/J.Kurri 12.00 30.00
PS2FL V.Filppula/V.Leino 12.00 30.00
PS2GB N.Backstrom/M.Green 15.00 40.00
PS2GC Carter/Gagne 10.00 25.00
PS2GG Gillies/Gillies 10.00 25.00
PS2GL Gaborik/H.Lundqvist 20.00 50.00
PS2GM W.Gretzky/M.Messier 150.00 250.00
PS2GZ M.Gaborik/M.Zotto 15.00 40.00
PS2HD G.Howe/A.Delvecchio 60.00 100.00
PS2HG Gustavsson/C.Hanson 15.00 40.00
PS2HM B.Hull/S.Mikita 25.00 60.00
PS2HS Heatley/D.Setoguchi
PS2HT B.Hull/J.Toews 40.00 80.00
PS2IB J.Iginla/M.Backlund 15.00 40.00
PS2IO Kovalchuk/Ovechkin
PS2JD J.Johnson/D.Doughty
PS2JV J.Tavares/V.Hedman 50.00 100.00
PS2KB J.Bailey/K.Okposo
PS2KM E.Malkin/I.Kovalchuk
PS2KS P.Kane/S.Stamkos 25.00 60.00
PS2KV P.Kane/J.Riemsdyk 25.00 60.00
PS2LB Leetch/Bathgate 12.00 30.00
PS2LE N.Lidstrom/J.Ericsson 12.00 30.00
PS2LG Gustavsson/Lundqvist 20.00 50.00
PS2LI V.Lecavalier/J.Iginla 20.00 50.00
PS2LK T.Lindsay/R.Kelly 20.00 40.00
PS2LS G.Lafleur/S.Shutt 15.00 40.00
PS2ME R.Miller/J.Enroth 15.00 40.00
PS2MH Hawerchuk/Mullen 15.00 40.00
PS2NV Varlamov/M.Neuvirth
PS2NW C.Neely/B.Wheeler 20.00 50.00
PS2OB B.Orr/R.Bourque 75.00 150.00
PS2OC T.O'Reilly/D.Carcillo
PS2OM A.Ovechkin/E.Malkin 100.00 200.00
PS2PM Phaneuf/A.MacInnis
PS2PP Stastny/Stastny 12.00 30.00
PS2RB P.Roy/M.Brodeur 30.00 80.00
PS2RC M.Richards/J.Carter 25.00 50.00
PS2RO Ovechkin/L.Robitaille 40.00 100.00
PS2SD H.Sedin/D.Sedin
PS2SG S.Shirokov/M.Grabner 20.00 50.00
PS2SH V.Hedman/S.Stamkos 25.00 60.00
PS2SS M.St. Louis/S.Stamkos 30.00 60.00
PS2SW D.Savard/D.Wilson
PS2TD J.Tavares/M.Duchene 25.00 60.00
PS2TH J.Thornton/D.Heatley
PS2TV J.Toews/K.Versteeg
PS2VG T.Vanek/M.Grabner 15.00 40.00
PS2YL S.Yzerman/N.Lidstrom 60.00 120.00

2009-10 OPC Premier Stitchings

STATED PRINT RUN 199 SER.#'d SETS
PSAC Andrew Cogliano 2.50 6.00
PSAO Alexander Ovechkin 8.00 20.00
PSBA Mikael Backlund 3.00 8.00
PSBF Benn Ferriero 10.00 25.00
PSBH Bobby Hull 4.00 10.00
PSBL Brian Leetch 3.00 8.00
PSBO Bobby Orr 10.00 25.00
PSBR Bobby Ryan 3.00 8.00
PSBW Blake Wheeler 3.00 8.00
PSCG Clark Gillies 3.00 8.00
PSCN Cam Neely 3.00 8.00
PSCP Carey Price 12.00 30.00
PSCW Cam Ward 3.00 8.00
PSDC Don Cherry 8.00 20.00
PSDH Dany Heatley 3.00 8.00
PSDP Dion Phaneuf 4.00 10.00
PSDP Denis Potvin 4.00 10.00
PSEM Evgeni Malkin 10.00 25.00
PSES Eric Staal 4.00 10.00
PSGH Gordie Howe 8.00 20.00
PSGP Gilbert Perreault 4.00 10.00
PSHL Henrik Lundqvist 5.00 12.00
PSHZ Henrik Zetterberg 4.00 10.00
PSIK Ilya Kovalchuk 3.00 8.00
PSJF Johan Franzen 3.00 8.00
PSJI Jarome Iginla 3.00 8.00
PSJK Jari Kurri 6.00 15.00
PSJN John Tavares 8.00 20.00
PSJS Jason Spezza 3.00 8.00
PSJT Joe Thornton 3.00 8.00
PSKA Paul Kariya 4.00 10.00
PSLR Luc Robitaille 4.00 10.00
PSLK Luke Schenn 2.50 6.00
PSMB Martin Brodeur 8.00 20.00
PSMD Matt Duchene 8.00 20.00
PSMF Marc-Andre Fleury 5.00 12.00
PSMG Marian Gaborik 4.00 10.00
PSMI Mike Bossy 2.50 6.00
PSMK Miikka Kiprusoff 2.50 6.00
PSML Mario Lemieux 8.00 20.00
PSMM Mark Messier 4.00 10.00
PSMN Markus Naslund 2.50 6.00
PSMO Mike Modano 5.00 12.00
PSMR Mike Richards 3.00 8.00
PSMS Martin St. Louis 3.00 8.00
PSNB Nicklas Backstrom 5.00 12.00
PSNL Nicklas Lidstrom 3.00 8.00
PSPD Pavel Datsyuk 6.00 15.00
PSPE Phil Esposito 5.00 12.00
PSPK Patrick Kane 6.00 15.00
PSPR Patrick Roy 8.00 20.00
PSRB Ray Bourque 5.00 12.00
PSRL Roberto Luongo 4.00 10.00
PSRM Ryan Miller 5.00 12.00
PSRN Rick Nash 2.50 6.00
PSSC Sidney Crosby 15.00 40.00
PSSG Sam Gagner 2.50 6.00
PSSM Steve Mason 2.50 6.00
PSSS Steven Stamkos 6.00 15.00
PSSY Steve Yzerman 8.00 20.00
PSTO Jonathan Toews 6.00 15.00
PSTS Teemu Selanne 6.00 15.00
PSTV Thomas Vanek 3.00 8.00
PSVL Vincent Lecavalier 2.50 6.00
PSWG Wayne Gretzky 15.00 40.00

2009-10 OPC Premier Stitchings Autographs

STATED PRINT RUN 25 SER.#'d SETS
APSAC Andrew Cogliano 8.00 20.00
APSAO Alexander Ovechkin 60.00 120.00
APSBH Bobby Hull 20.00 50.00
APSBL Brian Leetch 12.00 30.00
APSBO Bobby Orr 100.00 150.00
APSBR Martin Brodeur 50.00 100.00
APSCG Clark Gillies 10.00 25.00
APSCN Cam Neely 15.00 40.00
APSCP Carey Price 20.00 50.00
APSCW Cam Ward 10.00 25.00
APSDC Don Cherry 60.00 120.00
APSDH Dany Heatley 15.00 40.00
APSDP Denis Potvin 8.00 20.00
APSEM Evgeni Malkin 50.00 100.00
APSES Eric Staal 15.00 40.00
APSGH Gordie Howe 60.00 120.00
APSGP Gilbert Perreault 12.00 30.00
APSGR Wayne Gretzky 200.00 300.00
APSHL Henrik Lundqvist
APSHZ Henrik Zetterberg 30.00 60.00
APSJI Jarome Iginla 20.00 50.00
APSJK Jari Kurri 15.00 40.00
APSJN John Tavares 30.00 80.00
APSKA Patrick Kane 30.00 80.00
APSLR Luc Robitaille
APSLK Luke Schenn 5.00 12.00
APSMA Mark Messier 30.00 60.00
APSMD Matt Duchene 40.00 80.00
APSMG Marian Gaborik 12.00 30.00
APSML Mario Lemieux 50.00 100.00
APSMM Mike Modano 15.00 40.00
APSMS Martin St. Louis 8.00 20.00
APSNB Nicklas Backstrom 10.00 25.00
APSNL Nicklas Lidstrom 15.00 40.00
APSPD Pavel Datsyuk 15.00 40.00
APSPE Phil Esposito 10.00 25.00
APSPH Dion Phaneuf 8.00 20.00
APSPK Phil Kessel
APSPS Paul Stastny
APSRB Ray Bourque/24 25.00 60.00
APSRM Ryan Miller 15.00 40.00
APSRN Rick Nash 15.00 40.00
APSRO Patrick Roy 40.00 80.00
APSRY Bobby Ryan 12.00 30.00
APSSC Sidney Crosby 100.00 200.00
APSSG Sam Gagner 8.00 20.00
APSSM Steve Mason 5.00 12.00
APSSS Steven Stamkos 25.00 50.00
APSSY Steve Yzerman 50.00 100.00
APSTE Tony Esposito
APSTH Joe Thornton 15.00 40.00
APSTV Thomas Vanek 12.00 30.00
APSTW Jonathan Toews 30.00 60.00
APSVL Vincent Lecavalier 12.00 30.00

2009-10 OPC Premier Trios Jerseys

STATED PRINT RUN 50 SER.#'d SETS
*PATCH/15: 1X TO 2.5X TRIO JSY
3JAKA Afinogenv/Koval/Antropv 5.00 12.00
3JASK Alfredssn/Spez/Kovalv 8.00 20.00
3JBGB Bossy/Gillies/Bourne
3JBMR Robinsn/MacIns/Bourque 8.00 20.00
3JBSW Ward/Staal/Brind'Amour 8.00 20.00
3JCBP Pelech/Backlund/Chucko 5.00 12.00
3JCDF Couture/Demers/Ferriero 10.00 25.00
3JCTS Crosby/Stamkos/Tavares 40.00 80.00
3JCWM Marchnd/Wilsn/Couture 12.00 30.00
3JDGL Lundqvist/Gaborik/Drury 8.00 20.00
3JDMO Dubnyk/McDon/O'Mrra 10.00 25.00
3JDSG Zotto/Gilroy/Sauer 5.00 12.00
3JEHH Howe/Hull/Esposito
3JEME Enroth/Myers/Ennis 8.00 20.00
3JENW Esposito/Neely/Wheeler
3JFCS Fleury/Crosby/Staal 12.00 30.00
3JFOW Wilson/O'Reilly/Franson 5.00 12.00
3JGBS Gustavs/Stalbrg/Bozak 8.00 20.00
3JGDO Duchne/O'Reilly/Galrdi 12.00 30.00
3JGKH Gustav/Hedmn/Karlssn 15.00 40.00
3JHGV Voracek/Gaborik/Hossa
3JHTK Toews/Kane/Hossa 15.00 40.00
3JIKP Phaneuf/Kiprusoff/Iginla
3JKAM Messier/Kurri/Anderson 12.00 30.00
3JKBS Kessel/Bozak/Stalberg 8.00 20.00
3JKLN Kiprusoff/Lehton/Niemi 8.00 20.0
3JKOM Ovech/Malkin/Koval 20.00 50.0
3JKSS Kurri/Selanne/Koivu 15.00 40.0
3JLAM Leetch/Andrsn/Messier 15.00 40.0
3JLCM Lemieux/Crosby/Malkin 20.00 50.0
3JLEG Lundq/Enroth/Gustav 8.00 20.0
3JLIN Lecavalier/Iginla/Nash 5.00 12.0
3JLMP Leetch/Modano/Parise 10.00 25.0
3JLPM Luongo/Price/Mason 12.50 30.0
3JLSH Hedmn/Salming/Lidstrm 12.00 30.0
3JLSS Lecav/St.Louis/Stamks 10.00 25.0
3JLVB Benn/Vishnev/Lindgren 15.00 40.0
3JLYM Lemieux/Yzermn/Messr 25.00 60.0
3JLYT Yzermn/Lemieux/Tavres 25.00 60.0
3JLZF Lidstrom/Zetter/Franzen
3JMGK McDnld/Gilmour/Kessel 12.00 30.0
3JMMG McDnld/Mullen/Gilmour 6.00 15.0
3JMTS Thrntn/Marleu/Setoguc 5.00 12.0
3JMVM Miller/Vanek/Myers 8.00 20.0
3JNBM Mason/Nash/Brassard 5.00 12.0
3JOCM Ovechkin/Crosby/Malkin 25.00 60.0
3JPGW Phaneuf/Green/Weber
3JPKW Parise/Kane/Wilson 10.00 25.0
3JRBF Roy/Brodeur/Fleury 25.00 60.0
3JRBL Roy/Brodeur/Luongo 25.00 60.0
3JRCG Richards/Carter/Giroux 15.00 40.0
3JRCR Roy/Carbon/Robinson
3JRCV Richrds/Carter/Riemsdyk 15.00 40.0
3JRDG Gretzky/Robitlle/Dionne 25.00 60.0
3JRNG Gretzky/Robitlle/Nicholls 25.00 60.0
3JSDG Zotto/Gilroy/Sanguinetti 5.00 12.0
3JSDO Stastny/Duchne/O'Reilly 10.00 25.0
3JSGH Satan/Gaborik/Hossa 12.00 30.0
3JSGR Getzlaf/Ryan/Selanne 10.00 25.0
3JSHN St. Louis/Heatley/Nash 5.00 12.0
3JSKK Spezza/Kovalev/Karlsson 15.00 40.0
3JSOG Semin/Ovechkin/Green 15.00 40.0
3JSRL Shutt/Robinson/Lemaire
3JSSL Luongo/Sedin/Sedin 6.00 15.0
3JTDH Tavares/Hedmn/Duchne 15.00 40.0
3JTKD Tavares/Kane/Duchene 20.00 50.0
3JTVD Duchene/Tavares/Riems 20.00 50.0
3JVWG Riemsdyk/Wilson/Gilroy 10.00 25.0
3JYGM Yzerman/Gretzky/Messier 25.00 60.0
3JYLH Lidstrom/Howe/Yzerman 12.00 30.0
3JYZH Howe/Yzerman/Zetterberg 40.00 80.0

1981-82 O-Pee-Chee Stickers

Similar in size and format to the baseball and footbal stickers of recent years, this 269-sticker set featured foil cards of significant events and star players. Stickers measured approximately 1 15/16" by 2 9/16 The backs printed in both English and French contained the card number, the player's name and team, an advertisement for an O-Pee-Chee hockey sticker album, and a 1981 O-Pee-Chee copyright dat The sticker number also appeared within the border a the lower left corner on the front. On the inside back cover of the sticker album the company offered (via direct mail-order) any ten different stickers (but no more than two foil) of your choice for one dollar; this one reason why the values of the most popular playe in these sticker sets are somewhat depressed compared to traditional card set prices.

COMPLETE SET (269) 20.00 50.0
1 The Stanley Cup FOIL .75 2.0
2 The Stanley Cup FOIL .75 2.0
3 The Stanley Cup FOIL .75 2.0
4 The Stanley Cup FOIL .75 2.0
5 The Stanley Cup FOIL .75 2.0
6 The Stanley Cup FOIL .75 2.0
7 Oilers vs. Islanders .20 .5
8 Oilers vs. Islanders .20 .5
9 Oilers vs. Islanders .20 .5
10 Oilers vs. Islanders .20 .5
11 Jari Kurri 1.50 4.0
12 Pat Riggin .10 .2
13 Flames vs. Flyers .08 .2
14 Flames vs. Flyers .08 .2
15 Flames vs. Flyers .08 .2
16 Flames vs. Flyers .08 .2
17 Stanley Cup Winner/1980-81 .08 .2
18 Stanley Cup Winner/1980-81 .08 .2
19 Conn Smythe Trophy FOIL .60 1.5
20 Butch Goring .08 .2
21 North Stars vs. Islanders .08 .2
22 Steve Payne .08 .2
23 North Stars vs. Islanders .08 .2
24 North Stars vs. Islanders .08 .2
25 North Stars vs. Islanders .08 .2
26 North Stars vs. Islanders .08 .2
27 Prince of Wales Trophy FOIL .60 1.5
28 Prince of Wales Trophy FOIL .60 1.5
29 Guy Lafleur .40 1.0
30 Bob Gainey .10 .2
31 Larry Robinson .20 .5
32 Steve Shutt .10 .2
33 Brian Engblom .08 .2
34 Doug Jarvis .08 .2
35 Yvon Lambert .08 .2
36 Mark Napier .08 .2
37 Rejean Houle .08 .2
38 Pierre Larouche .15 .4
39 Rod Langway .15 .4
40 Richard Sevigny .15 .4
41 Guy Lafleur .40 1.0
42 Larry Robinson .20 .5
43 Bob Gainey .15 .4
44 Steve Shutt .10 .2
45 Rick Middleton .10 .2
46 Peter McNab .08 .2
47 Rogatien Vachon .15 .4
48 Brad Park .15 .4
49 Ray Bourque 1.25 3.0
50 Terry O'Reilly .10 .2
51 Steve Kasper .08 .2
52 Dwight Foster .08 .2
53 Danny Gare .10 .2
54 Andre Savard .08 .2
55 Don Edwards .08 .2
56 Bob Sauve .10 .2
57 Tony McKegney .08 .2
58 John Van Boxmeer .08 .2
59 Derek Smith .08 .2
60 Gilbert Perreault .15 .4
61 Mike Rogers .08 .2
62 Mark Howe .15 .4
63 Blaine Stoughton .15 .4
64 Rick Ley .08 .2
65 Jordy Douglas .08 .2

Al Sims .08 .20
Norm Barnes .08 .20
John Garrett .10 .25
Peter Stastny .60 1.50
Anton Stastny .10 .25
Jacques Richard .08 .20
Robbie Ftorek .08 .20
Dan Bouchard .10 .25
Real Cloutier .08 .20
Michel Goulet .30 .75
Marc Tardif .08 .20
Capitals vs. Maple Leafs .08 .20
Capitals vs. Maple Leafs .08 .20
Capitals vs. Maple Leafs .08 .20
Capitals vs. Maple Leafs .08 .20
Whalers vs. Capitals .08 .20
Whalers vs. Capitals .08 .20
Canadiens vs. Capitals .08 .20
Dan Bouchard .10 .25
North Stars vs. .08 .20
apitals
North Stars vs. .08 .20
apitals
Bruins vs. Capitals .08 .20
Bobby Smith .10 .25
Don Beaupre .10 .25
Al MacAdam .08 .20
Craig Hartsburg .10 .25
Steve Payne .08 .20
Gilles Meloche .10 .25
Tim Young .08 .20
Tom McCarthy .08 .20
Wilf Paiement .08 .20
Darryl Sittler .15 .40
Borje Salming .15 .40
Bill Derlago .08 .20
Ian Turnbull .08 .20
Rick Vaive .10 .25
Dan Maloney .08 .20
Laurie Boschman .08 .20
Pat Hickey .08 .20
Michel Larocque .10 .25
Jiri Crha .08 .20
John Anderson .08 .20
Bill Derlago .08 .20
Darryl Sittler .10 .25
Wilf Paiement .08 .20
Borje Salming .10 .25
Denis Savard 1.00 2.50
Tony Esposito .30 .75
Tom Lysiak .10 .25
Keith Brown .08 .20
Glen Sharpley .08 .20
Terry Ruskowski .08 .20
Reg Kerr .08 .20
Bob Murray .08 .20
Dale McCourt .08 .20
John Ogrodnick .10 .25
Mike Foligno .10 .25
Gilles Gilbert .10 .25
Reed Larson .08 .20
Vaclav Nedomansky .08 .20
Willie Huber .08 .20
Jim Korn .08 .20
Bernie Federko .20 .50
Mike Liut .15 .40
Wayne Babych .08 .20
Blake Dunlop .08 .20
Mike Zuke .08 .20
Brian Sutter .10 .25
Rick Lapointe .08 .20
Jorgen Pettersson .08 .20
Dave Christian .10 .25
Dave Babych .08 .20
Morris Lukowich .08 .20
Norm Dupont .08 .20
Ron Wilson .08 .20
Dan Geoffrion .08 .20
Barry Long .08 .20
Pierre Hamel .08 .20
Charlie Simmer AS .60 1.50
IL
Mark Howe AS FOIL .75 2.00
Don Beaupre AS FOIL .60 1.50
Marcel Dionne AS .75 2.00
IL
Larry Robinson AS .75 2.00
IL
Dave Taylor AS FOIL .60 1.50
Mike Bossy AS FOIL 1.00 2.50
Denis Potvin AS FOIL .75 2.00
Bryan Trottier AS .75 2.00
IL
Mike Liut AS FOIL .60 1.50
Rob Ramage AS FOIL .60 1.50
Bill Barber AS FOIL .60 1.50
Campbell Bowl FOIL .60 1.50
Campbell Bowl FOIL .60 1.50
Mike Bossy .40 1.00
Denis Potvin .15 .40
Bryan Trottier .20 .50
Billy Smith .15 .40
Anders Kallur .08 .20
Bob Bourne .08 .20
Clark Gillies .08 .20
Ken Morrow .15 .40
Anders Hedberg .10 .25
Ron Greschner .10 .25
Barry Beck .08 .20
Ed Johnstone .08 .20
Don Maloney .10 .25
Ron Duguay .10 .25
Ulf Nilsson .08 .20
Dave Maloney .08 .20
Bill Barber .20 .50
Behn Wilson .08 .20
Ken Linseman .10 .25
Pete Peeters .20 .50
Bobby Clarke .40 1.00
Paul Holmgren .10 .25
Brian Propp .08 .20
Reggie Leach .10 .25
Rick Kehoe .08 .20
Randy Carlyle .08 .20
George Ferguson .08 .20
Peter Lee .08 .20
Rod Schutt .08 .20
Paul Gardner .08 .20
Ron Stackhouse .08 .20
Mario Faubert .08 .20
Mike Gartner .50 1.25
Dennis Maruk .08 .20
Ryan Walter .10 .25
Rick Green .08 .20
Mike Palmateer .15 .40
Bob Kelly .08 .20
Jean Pronovost .08 .20
Al Hangsleben .08 .20

198 Flames vs. Capitals .08 .20
199 Oilers vs. Islanders .40 1.00
200 Oilers vs. Islanders .40 1.00
201 Oilers vs. Islanders .40 1.00
202 Oilers vs. Islanders .40 1.00
203 Rangers vs. Islanders .08 .20
204 Rangers vs. Islanders .08 .20
205 Flyers vs. Capitals .08 .20
206 Flyers vs. Capitals .08 .20
207 Rangers vs. Capitals .08 .20
208 Canadiens vs. Capitals .08 .20
209 Wayne Gretzky 4.00 10.00
210 Mark Messier 2.00 5.00
211 Jari Kurri 1.50 4.00
212 Brett Callighen .08 .20
213 Matti Hagman .08 .20
214 Risto Siltanen .10 .25
215 Lee Fogolin .08 .20
216 Eddie Mio .08 .20
217 Glenn Anderson .60 1.50
218 Kent Nilsson .10 .25
219 Guy Chouinard .08 .20
220 Eric Vail .08 .20
221 Pat Riggin .10 .25
222 Willi Plett .08 .20
223 Pekka Rautakallio .08 .20
224 Paul Reinhart .10 .25
225 Brad Marsh .10 .25
226 Phil Russell .08 .20
227 Lanny McDonald .15 .40
228 Merlin Malinowski .08 .20
229 Rob Ramage .10 .25
230 Glenn Resch .15 .40
231 Ron Delorme .08 .20
232 Lucien DeBlois .08 .20
233 Paul Gagne .08 .20
234 Joel Quenneville .08 .20
235 Marcel Dionne .20 .50
236 Charlie Simmer .15 .40
237 Dave Taylor .15 .40
238 Mario Lessard .08 .20
239 Larry Murphy .50 1.25
240 Jerry Korab .08 .20
241 Mike Murphy .08 .20
242 Billy Harris .08 .20
243 Thomas Gradin .10 .25
244 Per-Olov Brasar .08 .20
245 Glen Hanlon .10 .25
246 Chris Oddleifson .08 .20
247 Tiger Williams .20 .50
248 Kevin McCarthy .08 .20
249 Dennis Kearns .08 .20
250 Harold Snepsts .15 .40
251 Art Ross Trophy FOIL .60 1.50
252 Wayne Gretzky 4.00 10.00
253 Mike Bossy .40 1.00
254 Norris Trophy FOIL .60 1.50
255 Randy Carlyle .08 .20
256 Richard Sevigny .15 .40
257 Vezina Trophy FOIL .60 1.50
258 Denis Herron .08 .20
259 Michel Larocque .10 .25
260 Lady Byng Trophy FOIL .60 1.50
261 Rick Kehoe .08 .20
262 Calder Trophy FOIL .60 1.50
263 Peter Stastny .60 1.50
264 Wayne Gretzky 4.00 10.00
265 Hart Trophy FOIL .60 1.50
266 Charlie Simmer .15 .40
267 Marcel Dionne .20 .50
268 Dave Taylor .15 .40
269 Bob Gainey .15 .40
xx Sticker Album 2.00 5.00

1982-83 O-Pee-Chee Stickers

This set of 263 stickers was exactly the same as the Topps stickers issued this year except for minor back differences. Foil cards of players and trophies were contained within this set. The stickers in the set were 1 15/16" by 2 9/16". The card numbers appeared at the lower right within the border on the fronts of the cards as well as appearing on the back. The backs of the stickers contained an ad for an O-Pee-Chee hockey sticker album (in both English and French), the player's name and team, a 1982 Topps copyright date, and a statement to the fact that these cards were made in Italy. The checklist and prices below apply to both O-Pee-Chee and Topps stickers for this year. On the inside back cover of the sticker album the company offered (via direct mail-order) any ten different stickers (but no more than two foil) of your choice for one dollar; this is one reason why the values of the most popular players in these sticker sets are somewhat depressed compared to traditional card set prices.

COMPLETE SET (263) 18.00 45.00
*TOPPS: .4X TO 1X O-PEE-CHEE
1 Mike Bossy .20 .50
2 Conn Smythe Trophy .08 .25
FOIL
3 1981-82 Stanley Cup .01 .05
Winners
4 1981-82 Stanley Cup .01 .05
Winners
5 Stanley Cup Finals .08 .25
6 Stanley Cup Finals .08 .25
7 Richard Brodeur .08 .25
8 Victory .01 .05
Victoire
9 Stanley Cup Finals .08 .25
10 Stanley Cup Finals .08 .25
11 Canucks vs. Chicago .01 .05
12 Canucks vs. Chicago .01 .05
13 Canucks vs. Chicago .01 .05
14 Tom Lysiak .08 .25
15 Peter Stastny .30 .75
16 Islanders vs. Quebec .01 .05
17 Islanders vs. Quebec .01 .05
18 Islanders vs. Quebec .01 .05
19 Peter Stastny .30 .75
20 Marian Stastny .01 .05
21 Marc Tardif .08 .25
22 Wilf Paiement .01 .05
23 Real Cloutier .01 .05
24 Anton Stastny .08 .25
25 Michel Goulet .20 .50
26 Dale Hunter .08 .25
27 Dan Bouchard .08 .25
28 Guy Lafleur .20 .50
29 Guy Lafleur .20 .50
30 Mario Tremblay .08 .25
31 Larry Robinson .08 .25
32 Steve Shutt .08 .25
33 Steve Shutt .08 .25
34 Rod Langway .08 .25
35 Pierre Mondou .01 .05
36 Bob Gainey .08 .25
37 Rick Wamsley .08 .25
38 Mark Napier .08 .25
39 Mark Napier .08 .25
40 Doug Jarvis .08 .25
41 Denis Herron .08 .25
42 Keith Acton .01 .05
43 Keith Acton .01 .05
44 Prince of Wales .08 .25
Trophy FOIL
45 Prince of Wales .08 .25
Trophy FOIL
46 Denis Potvin .08 .25
47 Bryan Trottier .08 .25
48 Bryan Trottier .08 .25
49 John Tonelli .08 .25
50 Mike Bossy .20 .50
51 Mike Bossy .20 .50
52 Duane Sutter .08 .25
53 Bob Bourne .01 .05
54 Clark Gillies .08 .25
55 Clark Gillies .08 .25
56 Brent Sutter .08 .25
57 Anders Kallur .01 .05
58 Ken Morrow .08 .25
59 Bob Nystrom .08 .25
60 Billy Smith .08 .25
61 Billy Smith .08 .25
62 Rick Vaive .08 .25
63 Rick Vaive .08 .25
64 Jim Benning .01 .05
65 Miroslav Frycer .01 .05
66 Terry Martin .01 .05
67 Bill Derlago .01 .05
68 Bill Derlago .01 .05
69 Rocky Saganiuk .01 .05
70 Vincent Tremblay .01 .05
71 Bob Manno .01 .05
72 Dan Maloney .08 .25
73 John Anderson .01 .05
74 John Anderson .01 .05
75 Borje Salming .08 .25
76 Borje Salming .08 .25
77 Michel Larocque .08 .25
78 Rick Middleton .08 .25
79 Rick Middleton .08 .25
80 Keith Crowder .01 .05
81 Steve Kasper .08 .25
82 Brad Park .10 .30
83 Peter McNab .08 .25
84 Peter McNab .08 .25
85 Terry O'Reilly .08 .25
86 Ray Bourque .60 1.50
87 Ray Bourque .60 1.50
88 Tom Fergus .01 .05
89 Mike O'Connell .01 .05
90 Brad McCrimmon .08 .25
91 Don Marcotte .01 .05
92 Barry Pederson .08 .25
93 Barry Pederson .08 .25
94 Mark Messier 1.50 4.00
95 Grant Fuhr .75 2.00
96 Kevin Lowe .20 .50
97 Wayne Gretzky 2.50 6.00
98 Wayne Gretzky 2.50 6.00
99 Glenn Anderson .20 .50
100 Glenn Anderson .20 .50
101 Dave Lumley .01 .05
102 Dave Hunter .01 .05
103 Matti Hagman .01 .05
104 Paul Coffey .75 2.00
105 Paul Coffey .75 2.00
106 Lee Fogolin .01 .05
107 Ron Low .08 .25
108 Jari Kurri .40 1.00
109 Jari Kurri .40 1.00
110 Bill Barber .08 .25
111 Brian Propp .08 .25
112 Ken Linseman .08 .25
113 Ron Flockhart .08 .25
114 Darryl Sittler .08 .25
115 Bobby Clarke .20 .50
116 Paul Holmgren .08 .25
117 Pete Peeters .08 .25
118 Gilbert Perreault .08 .25
119 Dale McCourt .01 .05
120 Mike Foligno .08 .25
121 John Van Boxmeer .01 .05
122 Tony McKegney .08 .25
123 Ric Seiling .01 .05
124 Don Edwards .08 .25
125 Yvon Lambert .01 .05
126 Blaine Stoughton .08 .25
127 Pierre Larouche .08 .25
128 Doug Sulliman .01 .05
129 Ron Francis 1.25 3.00
130 Greg Millen .08 .25
131 Mark Howe .08 .25
132 Chris Kotsopoulos .01 .05
133 Garry Howatt .01 .05
134 Ron Duguay .08 .25
135 Barry Beck .08 .25
136 Mike Rogers .01 .05
137 Don Maloney .08 .25
138 Mark Pavelich .08 .25
139 Ed Johnstone .01 .05
140 Dave Maloney .01 .05
141 Steve Weeks .08 .25
142 Eddie Mio .08 .25
143 Rick Kehoe .08 .25
144 Randy Carlyle .08 .25
145 Paul Gardner .01 .05
146 Michel Dion .08 .25
147 Rick MacLeish .08 .25
148 Pat Boutette .08 .25
149 Mike Bullard .08 .25
150 George Ferguson .01 .05
151 Dennis Maruk .08 .25
152 Ryan Walter .08 .25
153 Mike Gartner .20 .50
154 Bob Carpenter .20 .50
155 Chris Valentine .01 .05
156 Rick Green .08 .25
157 Bengt Gustafsson .01 .05
158 Dave Parro .01 .05
159 Mark Messier AS FOIL 1.50 4.00
160 Paul Coffey AS FOIL 1.25 3.00
161 Grant Fuhr AS FOIL 1.25 3.00
162 Wayne Gretzky AS 4.00 10.00
FOIL
163 Doug Wilson AS FOIL .20 .50
164 Dave Taylor AS FOIL .20 .50
165 Mike Bossy AS FOIL .40 1.00
166 Ray Bourque AS FOIL 1.00 2.50
167 Peter Stastny AS .40 1.00
FOIL
168 Michel Dion AS FOIL .08 .25
169 Larry Robinson AS .20 .50
FOIL
170 Bill Barber AS FOIL .20 .50
171 Denis Savard .20 .50
172 Doug Wilson .08 .25
173 Grant Mulvey .08 .25
174 Tom Lysiak .08 .25
175 Al Secord .08 .25
176 Reg Kerr .01 .05
177 Tim Higgins .01 .05
178 Terry Ruskowski .08 .25
179 John Ogrodnick .08 .25
180 Reed Larson .01 .05
181 Bob Sauve .08 .25
182 Mark Osborne .01 .05
183 Jim Schoenfeld .08 .25
184 Danny Gare .08 .25
185 Willie Huber .01 .05
186 Walt McKechnie .01 .05
187 Paul Woods .08 .25
188 Bobby Smith .08 .25
189 Dino Ciccarelli .30 .75
190 Neal Broten .20 .50
191 Steve Payne .08 .25
192 Craig Hartsburg .08 .25
193 Don Beaupre .08 .25
194 Steve Christoff .08 .25
195 Gilles Meloche .08 .25
196 Mike Liut .08 .25
197 Bernie Federko .08 .25
198 Brian Sutter .08 .25
199 Blake Dunlop .01 .05
200 Joe Mullen .40 1.00
201 Wayne Babych .01 .05
202 Jorgen Pettersson .01 .05
203 Perry Turnbull .01 .05
204 Dale Hawerchuk 1.00 2.50
205 Morris Lukowich .01 .05
206 Dave Christian .08 .25
207 Dave Babych .08 .25
208 Paul MacLean .08 .25
209 Willy Lindstrom .01 .05
210 Ed Staniowski .01 .05
211 Doug Soetaert .08 .25
212 Lucien DeBlois .01 .05
213 Mel Bridgman .08 .25
214 Lanny McDonald .08 .25
215 Guy Chouinard .08 .25
216 Jim Peplinski .08 .25
217 Kent Nilsson .08 .25
218 Pekka Rautakallio .08 .25
219 Paul Reinhart .08 .25
220 Kevin Lavallee .01 .05
221 Ken Houston .01 .05
222 Glenn Resch .08 .25
223 Rob Ramage .08 .25
224 Don Lever .01 .05
225 Bob MacMillan .01 .05
226 Steve Tambellini .01 .05
227 Brent Ashton .01 .05
228 Bob Lorimer .01 .05
229 Merlin Malinowski .01 .05
230 Marcel Dionne .08 .25
231 Dave Taylor .08 .25
232 Larry Murphy .20 .50
233 Steve Bozek .01 .05
234 Greg Terrion .01 .05
235 Jim Fox .01 .05
236 Mario Lessard .08 .25
237 Charlie Simmer .08 .25
238 Campbell Bowl FOIL .08 .25
239 Campbell Bowl FOIL .08 .25
240 Thomas Gradin .08 .25
241 Ivan Boldirev .01 .05
242 Stan Smyl .08 .25
243 Harold Snepsts .08 .25
244 Curt Fraser .01 .05
245 Lars Molin .01 .05
246 Kevin McCarthy .01 .05
247 Richard Brodeur .08 .25
248 Calder Trophy FOIL .08 .25
249 Dale Hawerchuk 1.00 2.50
250 Vezina Trophy FOIL .08 .25
251 Billy Smith .08 .25
252 Denis Herron .10 .25
Rick Wamsley
253 Steve Kasper .08 .25
254 Doug Wilson .08 .25
255 Norris Trophy FOIL .08 .25
256 Wayne Gretzky 2.50 6.00
257 Wayne Gretzky 2.50 6.00
258 Wayne Gretzky 2.50 6.00
259 Wayne Gretzky 2.50 6.00
260 Hart Trophy FOIL .08 .25
261 Art Ross Trophy FOIL .08 .25
262 Rick Middleton .08 .25
263 Lady Byng Trophy FOIL .08 .25
NNO Sticker Album 2.00 5.00

1983-84 O-Pee-Chee Stickers

This sticker set consisted of 330 stickers in full color and was put out by both O-Pee-Chee and Topps. The foil stickers were numbers 1-4, 15, 22-24, 299-300, 304-305, 308-311, 314-315, 319-330. Stickers measured 1 15/16" by 2 9/16". An album was available for these stickers. The Topps set was distinguishable only by minor back differences. The checklist and prices below apply to both O-Pee-Chee and Topps stickers for this year. On the inside back cover of the sticker album the company offered (via direct mail-order) any ten different stickers of your choice for one dollar; this is one reason why the values of the most popular players in these sticker sets are somewhat depressed compared to traditional card set prices.

COMPLETE SET (330) 16.00 40.00
1 Marcel Dionne FOIL .20 .50
2 Guy Lafleur FOIL .40 1.00
3 Darryl Sittler FOIL .20 .50
4 Gilbert Perreault FOIL .20 .50
5 Bill Barber .08 .25
6 Steve Shutt .08 .25
7 Wayne Gretzky 2.50 6.00
8 Lanny McDonald .08 .25
9 Reggie Leach .08 .25
10 Mike Bossy .20 .50
11 Rick Kehoe .08 .25
12 Bobby Clarke .08 .25
13 Butch Goring .08 .25
14 Rick Middleton .08 .25
15 Conn Smythe .05 .15
Trophy FOIL
16 Billy Smith .08 .25
17 Lee Fogolin .01 .05
18 Stanley Cup Finals .08 .25
19 Stanley Cup Finals .08 .25
20 Stanley Cup Finals .08 .25
21 Stanley Cup Finals .08 .25
22 Stanley Cup FOIL .08 .25
23 Stanley Cup FOIL .08 .25
24 Stanley Cup FOIL .08 .25
25 Rick Vaive .08 .25
26 Rick Vaive .08 .25
27 Billy Harris .01 .05
28 Dan Daoust .01 .05
29 Dan Daoust .01 .05
30 John Anderson .01 .05
31 John Anderson .01 .05
32 Peter Ihnacak .01 .05
33 Borje Salming .08 .25
34 Borje Salming .08 .25
35 Bill Derlago .01 .05
36 Rick St.Croix .08 .25
37 Greg Terrion .01 .05
38 Miroslav Frycer .01 .05
39 Mike Palmateer .08 .25
40 Gaston Gingras .01 .05
41 Pete Peeters .08 .25
42 Pete Peeters .08 .25
43 Mike Krushelnyski .08 .25
44 Rick Middleton .08 .25
45 Rick Middleton .08 .25
46 Ray Bourque .40 1.00
47 Ray Bourque .40 1.00
48 Brad Park .08 .25
49 Barry Pederson .08 .25
50 Barry Pederson .08 .25
51 Peter McNab .08 .25
52 Mike O'Connell .01 .05
53 Steve Kasper .08 .25
54 Marty Howe .08 .25
55 Tom Fergus .01 .05
56 Keith Crowder .01 .05
57 Steve Shutt .08 .25
58 Guy Lafleur .20 .50
59 Guy Lafleur .20 .50
60 Larry Robinson .08 .25
61 Larry Robinson .08 .25
62 Ryan Walter .08 .25
63 Ryan Walter .08 .25
64 Mark Napier .01 .05
65 Mark Napier .08 .25
66 Bob Gainey .08 .25
67 Doug Wickenheiser .01 .05
68 Pierre Mondou .01 .05
69 Mario Tremblay .08 .25
70 Gilbert Delorme .01 .05
71 Mats Naslund .08 .25
72 Rick Wamsley .08 .25
73 Ken Morrow .08 .25
74 John Tonelli .08 .25
75 John Tonelli .08 .25
76 Bryan Trottier .08 .25
77 Bryan Trottier .08 .25
78 Mike Bossy .20 .50
79 Mike Bossy .20 .50
80 Bob Bourne .01 .05
81 Denis Potvin .08 .25
82 Denis Potvin .08 .25
83 Dave Langevin .01 .05
84 Clark Gillies .08 .25
85 Bob Nystrom .08 .25
86 Billy Smith .08 .25
87 Tomas Jonsson .01 .05
88 Rollie Melanson .08 .25
89 Wayne Gretzky 2.50 6.00
90 Wayne Gretzky 2.50 6.00
91 Willy Lindstrom .01 .05
92 Glenn Anderson .20 .50
93 Glenn Anderson .20 .50
94 Paul Coffey .40 1.00
95 Paul Coffey ..40 1.00
96 Charlie Huddy .08 .25
97 Mark Messier .75 2.00
98 Mark Messier .75 2.00
99 Andy Moog .40 1.00
100 Lee Fogolin .01 .05
101 Kevin Lowe .08 .25
102 Ken Linseman .08 .25
103 Tom Roulston .01 .05
104 Jari Kurri .40 1.00
105 Darryl Sutter .08 .25
106 Denis Savard .08 .25
107 Denis Savard .08 .25
108 Steve Larmer .75 2.00
109 Bob Murray .01 .05
110 Tom Lysiak .08 .25
111 Al Secord .08 .25
112 Doug Wilson .08 .25
113 Murray Bannerman .08 .25
114 Gordie Roberts .01 .05
115 Tom McCarthy .01 .05
116 Bobby Smith .08 .25
117 Craig Hartsburg .08 .25
118 Dino Ciccarelli .20 .50
119 Dino Ciccarelli .20 .50
120 Neal Broten .08 .25
121 Steve Payne .01 .05
122 Don Beaupre .08 .25
123 Jorgen Pettersson .01 .05
124 Perry Turnbull .01 .05
125 Bernie Federko .08 .25
126 Mike Crombeen .01 .05
127 Brian Sutter .08 .25
128 Brian Sutter .08 .25
129 Mike Liut .08 .25
130 Rob Ramage .08 .25
131 Blake Dunlop .01 .05
132 Ivan Boldirev .01 .05
133 Dwight Foster .01 .05
134 Reed Larson .01 .05
135 Danny Gare .08 .25
136 Jim Schoenfeld .08 .25
137 John Ogrodnick .08 .25
138 John Ogrodnick .08 .25
139 Willie Huber .01 .05
140 Greg Smith .01 .05
141 Ed Beers .01 .05
142 Brian Bellows .20 .50
143 Jiri Bubla .01 .05
144 Daryl Evans .01 .05
145 Randy Gregg .01 .05
146 Jim Jackson .01 .05
147 Corrado Micalef .01 .05
148 Brian Mullen .08 .25
149 Frank Nigro .01 .05
150 Walt Poddubny .01 .05
151 Jaroslav Pouzar .01 .05
152 Patrik Sundstrom .08 .25
153 Denis Savard .20 .50
154 Dave Hunter .01 .05
155 Andy Moog .40 1.00
156 Al Secord .08 .25
157 Mark Messier .75 2.00
158 Glenn Anderson .20 .50
159 Jaroslav Pouzar .01 .05
160 Al Secord AS .01 .05
161 Wayne Gretzky AS 2.50 6.00
162 Lanny McDonald AS .08 .25
163 Dave Babych AS .01 .05
164 Murray Bannerman AS .08 .25
165 Doug Wilson AS .01 .05
166 Michel Goulet AS .08 .25
167 Peter Stastny AS .20 .50
168 Marian Stastny AS .08 .25
169 Denis Potvin AS .08 .25
170 Pete Peeters AS .08 .25
171 Mark Howe AS .08 .25
172 Luc Dufour .01 .05
173 Ray Bourque .40 1.00
174 Bob Bourne .01 .05
175 Denis Potvin .08 .25
176 Mike Bossy .20 .50
177 Butch Goring .08 .25
178 Brad Park .08 .25
179 Murray Brumwell .01 .05
180 Guy Carbonneau .40 1.00
181 Lindsay Carson .01 .05
182 Luc Dufour .01 .05
183 Bob Froese .08 .25
184 Mats Hallin .01 .05
185 Gord Kluzak .08 .25
186 Jeff Larmer .01 .05
187 Milan Novy .01 .05
188 Scott Stevens .75 2.00
189 Bob Sullivan .01 .05
190 Mark Taylor .01 .05
191 Darryl Sittler .08 .25
192 Ron Flockhart .01 .05
193 Brad McCrimmon .08 .25
194 Bill Barber .08 .25
195 Mark Howe .08 .25
196 Mark Howe .08 .25
197 Pelle Lindbergh 1.50 4.00
198 Bobby Clarke .08 .25
199 Brian Propp .08 .25
200 Ken Houston .01 .05
201 Rod Langway .08 .25
202 Al Jensen .08 .25
203 Brian Engblom .01 .05
204 Dennis Maruk .08 .25
205 Dennis Maruk .08 .25
206 Bob Carpenter .08 .25
207 Mike Gartner .20 .50
208 Doug Jarvis .08 .25
209 Eddie Mio .08 .25
210 Barry Beck .08 .25
211 Dave Maloney .08 .25
212 Don Maloney .08 .25
213 Mark Pavelich .08 .25
214 Mark Pavelich .01 .05
215 Anders Hedberg .08 .25
216 Reijo Ruotsalainen .01 .05
217 Mike Rogers .01 .05
218 Don Lever .01 .05
219 Steve Tambellini .01 .05
220 Bob MacMillan .01 .05
221 Hector Marini .01 .05
222 Glenn Resch .08 .25
223 Glenn Resch .08 .25
224 Carol Vadnais .01 .05
225 Joel Quenneville .01 .05
226 Aaron Broten .01 .05
227 Randy Carlyle .08 .25
228 Doug Shedden .01 .05
229 Greg Malone .01 .05
230 Paul Gardner .01 .05
231 Rick Kehoe .08 .25
232 Rick Kehoe .08 .25
233 Pat Boutette .01 .05
234 Michel Dion .08 .25
235 Mike Bullard .08 .25
236 Dale McCourt .01 .05
237 Mike Foligno .08 .25
238 Phil Housley .40 1.00
239 Tony McKegney .08 .25
240 Gilbert Perreault .08 .25
241 Gilbert Perreault .08 .25
242 Bob Sauve .08 .25
243 Mike Ramsey .08 .25
244 John Van Boxmeer .01 .05
245 Dan Bouchard .08 .25
246 Real Cloutier .01 .05
247 Marc Tardif .08 .25
248 Randy Moller .01 .05
249 Michel Goulet .08 .25
250 Michel Goulet .08 .25
251 Marian Stastny .08 .25
252 Anton Stastny .08 .25
253 Peter Stastny .20 .50
254 Mark Johnson .08 .25
255 Ron Francis .60 1.50
256 Doug Sulliman .01 .05
257 Risto Siltanen .01 .05
258 Blaine Stoughton .08 .25
259 Blaine Stoughton .08 .25
260 Ray Neufeld .01 .05
261 Pierre Lacroix .01 .05
262 Greg Millen .08 .25
263 Lanny McDonald .08 .25
264 Paul Reinhart .08 .25
265 Mel Bridgman .08 .25
266 Rejean Lemelin .08 .25
267 Kent Nilsson .08 .25
268 Kent Nilsson .08 .25
269 Doug Risebrough .08 .25
270 Kari Eloranta .01 .05
271 Phil Russell .01 .05
272 Darcy Rota .01 .05
273 Thomas Gradin .08 .25
274 Stan Smyl .08 .25
275 John Garrett .08 .25
276 Richard Brodeur .08 .25
277 Richard Brodeur .08 .25
278 Doug Halward .01 .05
279 Kevin McCarthy .01 .05
280 Rick Lanz .01 .05
281 Morris Lukowich .01 .05
282 Dale Hawerchuk .40 1.00
283 Paul MacLean .08 .25
284 Lucien DeBlois .01 .05
285 Dave Babych .08 .25
286 Dave Babych .01 .05
287 Doug Smail .01 .05
288 Doug Soetaert .01 .05
289 Thomas Steen .08 .25
290 Charlie Simmer .08 .25
291 Terry Ruskowski .08 .25
292 Bernie Nicholls .75 2.00
293 Jim Fox .01 .05
294 Marcel Dionne .08 .25
295 Marcel Dionne .08 .25
296 Gary Laskoski .01 .05
297 Jerry Korab .01 .05
298 Larry Murphy .20 .50
299 Hart Trophy FOIL .05 .15
300 Hart Trophy FOIL .05 .15
301 Wayne Gretzky 2.50 6.00
302 Bobby Clarke .08 .25
303 Lanny McDonald .08 .25
304 Lady Byng .05 .15
Trophy FOIL
305 Lady Byng .05 .15
Trophy FOIL
306 Mike Bossy .20 .50
307 Wayne Gretzky 2.50 6.00
308 Art Ross .05 .15
Trophy FOIL
309 Art Ross .05 .15
Trophy FOIL
310 Calder Trophy FOIL .05 .15
311 Calder Trophy FOIL .05 .15
312 Steve Larmer .60 1.50
313 Rod Langway .08 .25
314 Norris Trophy FOIL .05 .15
315 Norris Trophy FOIL .05 .15
316 Billy Smith .08 .25
317 Roland Melanson .08 .25
318 Pete Peeters .08 .25
319 Vezina Trophy FOIL .05 .15
320 Vezina Trophy FOIL .05 .15
321 Mike Bossy FOIL .20 .50
322 Mike Bossy FOIL .20 .50
323 Marcel Dionne FOIL .20 .50
324 Marcel Dionne FOIL .20 .50
325 Wayne Gretzky FOIL 3.00 8.00
326 Wayne Gretzky FOIL 3.00 8.00
327 Pat Hughes FOIL .05 .15
328 Pat Hughes FOIL .05 .15
329 Rick Middleton FOIL .05 .15
330 Rick Middleton FOIL .05 .15
xx Sticker Album 1.50 4.00

1984-85 O-Pee-Chee Stickers

This sticker set consisted of 270 stickers in full color and was put out by O-Pee-Chee. The foil stickers are listed in the checklist below explicitly. The stickers measured approximately 1 15/16" by 2 9/16". An album was available for these stickers. Those stickers which are pairs are indicated in the checklist below by noting parenthetically the other member of the pair. On the inside back cover of the sticker album the company offered (via direct mail-order) any ten different stickers of your choice for one dollar; this is one reason why the values of the most popular players in these sticker sets are somewhat depressed compared to traditional card set prices.

COMPLETE SET (270) 16.00 40.00
1 Stanley Cup .20 .50
2 Stanley Cup .20 .50
3 Stanley Cup .20 .50
4 Stanley Cup .20 .50
5 Mark Messier .50 1.25
6 Maple Leafs Logo FOIL .30 .75
23. Blackhawks Logo FOIL
7 Borje Salming .05 .15
8 Borje Salming .05 .15
9 Dan Daoust .05 .15
10 Dan Daoust .05 .15
11 Rick Vaive .05 .15
12 Rick Vaive .05 .15
13 Dale McCourt .05 .15
14 Bill Derlago .05 .15
15 Gary Nylund .05 .15
16 Gary Nylund .05 .15
17 Jim Korn .05 .15
18 John Anderson .05 .15
19 Greg Terrion .05 .15
20 Allan Bester .08 .25
21 Jim Benning .05 .15
22 Mike Palmateer .08 .25
24 Denis Savard .20 .50
25 Denis Savard .20 .50
26 Bob Murray .05 .15
27 Doug Wilson .05 .15
28 Keith Brown .05 .15
29 Steve Larmer .20 .50
30 Darryl Sutter .05 .15
31 Tom Lysiak .05 .15
32 Murray Bannerman .08 .25
33 Red Wings Logo FOIL .20 .50
43. North Stars Logo FOIL
34 John Ogrodnick .05 .15
35 John Ogrodnick .05 .15
36 Reed Larson .05 .15
37 Steve Yzerman 5.00 12.00
38 Brad Park .08 .25
39 Ivan Boldirev .05 .15
40 Kelly Kisio .05 .15
41 Greg Stefan .08 .25
42 Ron Duguay .05 .15
44 Brian Bellows .08 .25
45 Brian Bellows .08 .25
46 Neal Broten .15 .40
47 Dino Ciccarelli .20 .50
48 Dennis Maruk .05 .15
49 Steve Payne .05 .15
50 Brad Maxwell .05 .15
51 Gilles Meloche .08 .25
52 Tom McCarthy .05 .15
53 Blues Logo FOIL .15 .40
67. Devils Logo FOIL
54 Bernie Federko .08 .25
55 Bernie Federko .08 .25
56 Brian Sutter .05 .15
57 Mike Liut .15 .40
58 Doug Wickenheiser .05 .15
59 Jorgen Pettersson .05 .15
60 Doug Gilmour 1.50 4.00
61 Joe Mullen .15 .40
62 Rob Ramage .05 .15
63 Wayne Gretzky FOIL 2.50 6.00
64. Michel Goulet FOIL
65 Pat Riggin FOIL .15 .40
66. Denis Potvin FOIL
68 Glenn Resch .08 .25
69 Glenn Resch .08 .25
70 Don Lever .05 .15
71 Mel Bridgman .05 .15
72 Bob MacMillan .05 .15
73 Pat Verbeek .20 .50
74 Joe Cirella .05 .15
75 Phil Russell .05 .15
76 Jan Ludvig .05 .15
77 Islanders Logo FOIL .15 .40
94. Rangers Logo FOIL
78 Denis Potvin .15 .40
79 Denis Potvin .15 .40
80 John Tonelli .05 .15
81 John Tonelli .05 .15
82 Mike Bossy .20 .50
83 Mike Bossy .20 .50
84 Butch Goring .05 .15
85 Bob Nystrom .05 .15
86 Bryan Trottier .15 .40
87 Bryan Trottier .15 .40
88 Brent Sutter .05 .15

89 Bob Bourne .05 .15
90 Greg Gilbert .05 .15
91 Billy Smith .15 .40
92 Rollie Melanson .08 .25
93 Ken Morrow .08 .25
95 Don Maloney .05 .15
96 Don Maloney .05 .15
97 Mark Pavelich .05 .15
98 Glen Hanlon .08 .25
99 Mike Rogers .05 .15
100 Barry Beck .05 .15
101 Reijo Ruotsalainen .05 .15
102 Anders Hedberg .05 .15
103 Pierre Larouche .08 .25
104 Flyers Logo FOIL .15 .40
114. Penguins Logo FOIL
105 Tim Kerr .05 .15
106 Tim Kerr .05 .15
107 Ron Sutter .08 .25
108 Darryl Sittler .08 .25
109 Mark Howe .15 .40
110 Dave Poulin .05 .15
111 Rich Sutter .08 .25
112 Brian Propp .05 .15
113 Bob Froese .08 .25
115 Ron Flockhart .05 .15
116 Ron Flockhart .05 .15
117 Rick Kehoe .05 .15
118 Mike Bullard .05 .15
119 Kevin McCarthy .05 .15
120 Doug Shedden .05 .15
121 Mark Taylor .05 .15
122 Denis Herron .05 .15
123 Tom Roulston .05 .15
124 Capitals Logo FOIL .30 .75
146. Canadiens Logo FOIL
125 Rod Langway .05 .15
126 Rod Langway .05 .15
127 Larry Murphy .08 .25
128 Al Jensen .05 .15
129 Doug Jarvis .05 .15
130 Bengt Gustafsson .05 .15
131 Mike Gartner .20 .50
132 Bob Carpenter .05 .15
133 Dave Christian .05 .15
134 Paul Coffey FOIL .50 1.25
135 Murray Bannerman FOIL .08 .25
136 Rob Ramage FOIL .08 .25
137 John Ogrodnick FOIL .08 .25
138 Wayne Gretzky FOIL 2.50 6.00
139 Rick Vaive FOIL .08 .25
140 Michel Goulet FOIL .20 .50
141 Peter Stastny FOIL .20 .50
142 Rick Middleton FOIL .08 .25
143 Ray Bourque FOIL .50 1.25
144 Pete Peeters FOIL .08 .25
145 Denis Potvin FOIL .20 .50
147 Larry Robinson .08 .25
148 Larry Robinson .08 .25
149 Guy Lafleur .20 .50
150 Guy Lafleur .20 .50
151 Bobby Smith .05 .15
152 Bobby Smith .05 .15
153 Bob Gainey .08 .25
154 Craig Ludwig .05 .15
155 Mats Naslund .08 .25
156 Mats Naslund .08 .25
157 Rick Wamsley .08 .25
158 Jean Hamel .05 .15
159 Ryan Walter .05 .15
160 Guy Carbonneau .15 .40
161 Mario Tremblay .05 .15
162 Pierre Mondou .05 .15
163 Nordiques Logo FOIL .15 .40
180. Bruins Logo FOIL
164 Peter Stastny .20 .50
165 Peter Stastny .20 .50
166 Mario Marois .05 .15
167 Mario Marois .05 .15
168 Michel Goulet .15 .40
169 Michel Goulet .15 .40
170 Andre Savard .05 .15
171 Tony McKegney .05 .15
172 Dan Bouchard .08 .25
173 Dan Bouchard .08 .25
174 Randy Moller .05 .15
175 Wilf Paiement .05 .15
176 Normand Rochefort .05 .15
177 Marian Stastny .05 .15
178 Anton Stastny .05 .15
179 Dale Hunter .08 .25
181 Rick Middleton .08 .25
182 Rick Middleton .08 .25
183 Ray Bourque .30 .75
184 Pete Peeters .08 .25
185 Mike O'Connell .05 .15
186 Gord Kluzak .05 .15
187 Barry Pederson .05 .15
188 Mike Krushelnyski .05 .15
189 Tom Fergus .05 .15
190 Whalers Logo FOIL .20 .50
200. Sabres Logo FOIL
191 Sylvain Turgeon .05 .15
192 Sylvain Turgeon .05 .15
193 Mark Johnson .05 .15
194 Greg Malone .05 .15
195 Mike Zuke .05 .15
196 Ron Francis .40 1.00
197 Bob Crawford .05 .15
198 Greg Millen .08 .25
199 Ray Neufeld .05 .15
201 Gilbert Perreault .15 .40
202 Gilbert Perreault .15 .40
203 Phil Housley .20 .50
204 Phil Housley .20 .50
205 Tom Barrasso .30 .75
206 Tom Barrasso .30 .75
207 Larry Playfair .05 .15
208 Bob Sauve .08 .25
209 Dave Andreychuk .40 1.00
210 Dave Andreychuk .40 1.00
211 Mike Ramsey .05 .15
212 Mike Foligno .05 .15
213 Lindy Ruff .05 .15
214 Bill Hajt .05 .15
215 Craig Ramsay .05 .15
216 Ric Seiling .05 .15
217 Hart Trophy FOIL .15 .40
224. Selke Trophy FOIL
218 Vezina Trophy FOIL .15 .40
223. Masterton Trophy FOIL
219 Jennings Trophy FOIL .15 .40
221. Art Ross Trophy FOIL
220 Calder Trophy FOIL .15 .40
225. Lady Byng Trophy FOIL
222 Norris Trophy FOIL .15 .40
283. Jets Logo FOIL
226 Wayne Gretzky 1.50 4.00
227. Tom Barrasso
228 Tom Barrasso 1.50 4.00
229. Wayne Gretzky
230 Rod Langway .08 .25
{ 231. Brad Park
232 Al Jensen .08 .25
{ 233. Pat Riggin
234 Doug Jarvis .15 .40
{ 235. Mike Bossy
236 Flames Logo FOIL .15 .40
246. Oilers Logo FOIL
237 Lanny McDonald .08 .25
238 Lanny McDonald .08 .25
239 Steve Tambellini .05 .15
240 Rejean Lemelin .08 .25
241 Doug Risebrough .05 .15
242 Hakan Loob .08 .25
243 Ed Beers .05 .15
244 Mike Eaves .05 .15
245 Kent Nilsson .05 .15
247 Glenn Anderson .08 .25
248 Glenn Anderson .08 .25
249 Jari Kurri .20 .50
250 Jari Kurri .20 .50
251 Paul Coffey .30 .75
252 Paul Coffey .30 .75
253 Kevin Lowe .15 .40
254 Lee Fogolin .05 .15
255 Wayne Gretzky 1.50 4.00
256 Wayne Gretzky 1.50 4.00
257 Randy Gregg .05 .15
258 Charlie Huddy .05 .15
259 Grant Fuhr .20 .50
260 Willy Lindstrom .05 .15
261 Mark Messier .50 1.25
262 Andy Moog .20 .50
263 Kings Logo FOIL .15 .40
273. Canucks Logo FOIL
264 Marcel Dionne .08 .25
265 Marcel Dionne .08 .25
266 Charlie Simmer .05 .15
267 Dave Taylor .05 .15
268 Jim Fox .05 .15
269 Bernie Nicholls .20 .50
270 Terry Ruskowski .05 .15
271 Brian Engblom .05 .15
272 Mark Hardy .05 .15
274 Tony Tanti .05 .15
275 Tony Tanti .05 .15
276 Rick Lanz .05 .15
277 Richard Brodeur .08 .25
278 Doug Halward .05 .15
279 Patrik Sundstrom .08 .25
280 Darcy Rota .05 .15
281 Stan Smyl .05 .15
282 Thomas Gradin .05 .15
284 Dale Hawerchuk .20 .50
285 Dale Hawerchuk .20 .50
286 Scott Arniel .05 .15
287 Dave Babych .05 .15
288 Laurie Boschman .05 .15
289 Paul MacLean .05 .15
290 Lucien DeBlois .05 .15
291 Randy Carlyle .05 .15
292 Thomas Steen .05 .15
NNO Sticker Album 2.00 5.00

1985-86 O-Pee-Chee Stickers

This sticker set consisted of 163 stickers in full color and was put out by O-Pee-Chee. The foil stickers are listed in the checklist below explicitly. The stickers measured approximately 2 1/8" by 3". An album was available for these stickers. Those stickers which are pairs are indicated in the checklist below by noting parenthetically the other member of the pair. On the inside back cover of the sticker album the company offered (via direct mail-order) any ten different stickers of your choice for one dollar; this is one reason why the values of the most popular players in these sticker sets are somewhat depressed compared to traditional card set prices. For example, anyone wanting Mario Lemieux, Wayne Gretzky, and eight others could get them for one dollar directly through this offer.

COMPLETE SET (163) 16.00 40.00
1 Stanley Cup Finals .08 .25
2 Stanley Cup Finals .02 .10
3 Stanley Cup Finals .02 .10
4 Stanley Cup Finals .02 .10
5 Wayne Gretzky 2.00 5.00
6 Rick Vaive .02 .10
7 Bill Derlago .02 .10
8 Rick St. Croix .02 .10
136. Doug Soetaert
9 Tim Bernhardt .02 .10
137. Mark Hunter
10 John Anderson .02 .10
{ 138. Bob Gainey
11 Dan Daoust .02 .10
139. Petr Svoboda
12 Borje Salming .02 .10
13 Al Iafrate .20 .50
143. Dan Bouchard
14 Gary Nylund .02 .10
144. Mario Marois
15 Bob McGill .02 .10
145. Randy Moller
16 Jim Benning .08 .25
146. Mario Gosselin
17 Stewart Gavin .02 .10
148. Normand Rochefort
18 Greg Terrion .02 .10
149. Alain Cote
19 Peter Ihnacak .02 .10
150. Paul Gillis
20 Russ Courtnall .20 .50
151. Dale Hunter
21 Miroslav Frycer .02 .10
22 Denis Savard .08 .25
23 Steve Yzerman .75 2.00
152. Wilf Paiement
24 Curt Fraser .02 .10
153. Brent Ashton
25 Doug Wilson .02 .10
26 Ed Olczyk .08 .25
154. Brad Maxwell
27 Murray Bannerman .02 .10
155. J.F. Sauve
28 Steve Larmer .08 .25
158. Charlie Simmer
29 Troy Murray .02 .10
159. Rick Middleton
30 Steve Yzerman 1.25 3.00
31 Greg Stefan .02 .10
161. Mike O'Connell
32 Ron Duguay .02 .10
162. Terry O'Reilly
33 Reed Larson .02 .10
{ 163. Keith Crowder
34 Ivan Boldirev .02 .10
164. Tom Fergus
35 Danny Gare .02 .10
166. Greg Malone
36 Darryl Sittler .02 .10
167. Bob Crawford
37 John Ogrodnick .02 .10
38 Keith Acton .02 .10
39 Dino Ciccarelli .08 .25
168. Kevin Dineen
40 Neal Broten .08 .25
169. Mike Liut
41 Brian Bellows .08 .25
42 Steve Payne .02 .10
170. Joel Quenneville
43 Gordie Roberts .02 .10
171. Ray Neufeld
44 Harold Snepsts .02 .10
175. Craig Ramsay
45 Tony McKegney .02 .10
176. Bill Hajt
46 Brian Sutter .02 .10
47 Joe Mullen .08 .25
177. Dave Maloney
48 Doug Gilmour .40 1.00
178. Brent Peterson
49 Tim Bothwell .02 .10
180. Mike Ramsey
50 Mark Johnson .02 .10
181. Bob Sauve
51 Greg Millen .02 .10
182. Ric Seiling
52 Doug Wickenheiser .02 .10
183. Paul Cyr
53 Bernie Federko .02 .10
54 Wayne Gretzky FOIL 1.50 4.00
197. Vezina Trophy FOIL
55 Tom Barrasso FOIL .08 .25
203. Hart Trophy FOIL
56 Paul Coffey FOIL .20 .50
204. Calder Trophy FOIL
57 Mel Bridgman .02 .10
58 Phil Russell .02 .10
184. John Tucker
59 Dave Lewis .02 .10
185. Gilles Hamel
60 Paul Gagne .02 .10
186. Malcolm Davis
61 Glenn Resch .08 .25
187. Dave Andreychuk
62 Aaron Broten .08 .25
189. Tom Barrasso
63 Dave Pichette .02 .10
190. Bob Sauve
64 Kirk Muller .40 1.00
65 Bryan Trottier .08 .25
66 Mike Bossy .08 .25
67 Bob Bourne .08 .25
191. Paul Coffey
68 Clark Gillies .02 .10
192. Craig Ramsay
69 Bob Nystrom .75 2.00
193. Pelle Lindbergh
70 Denis Potvin 1.50 4.00
198. Wayne Gretzky
71 Brent Sutter .02 .10
72 Duane Sutter 3.00 8.00
199. Mario Lemieux
73 Pat Flatley .02 .10
200. Anders Hedberg
74 Pat LaFontaine .40 1.00
201. Jari Kurri
75 Greg Gilbert 1.50 4.00
202. Wayne Gretzky
76 Billy Smith .08 .25
209. Paul Reinhart
77 Gordie Lane .02 .10
210. Rejean Lemelin
78 Tomas Jonsson .75 2.00
211. Al MacInnis
79 Kelly Hrudey .30 .75
212. Jamie Macoun
80 John Tonelli .02 .10
81 Reijo Ruotsalainen .02 .10
82 Barry Beck .08 .25
213. Carey Wilson
83 James Patrick .08 .25
214. Ed Beers
84 Mark Pavelich .02 .10
85 Pierre Larouche .02 .10
86 Mike Rogers .08 .25
219. Kevin Lowe
87 Glen Hanlon .08 .25
220. Andy Moog
88 John Vanbiesbrouck 1.25 3.00
221. Grant Fuhr
89 Dave Poulin .02 .10
90 Brian Propp .02 .10
223. Mike Krushelnyski
91 Pelle Lindbergh .75 2.00
224. Billy Carroll
92 Brad McCrimmon .02 .10
225. Randy Gregg
93 Mark Howe .08 .25
226. Willy Lindstrom
94 Peter Zezel .08 .25
227. Glenn Anderson
95 Murray Craven .20 .50
228. Mark Messier
96 Tim Kerr .02 .10
97 Mario Lemieux 6.00 15.00
98 Moe Mantha .02 .10
229. Pat Hughes
99 Doug Bodger .02 .10
230. Kevin McClelland
100 Warren Young .02 .10
101 John Chabot .02 .10
233. Brian Engblom
102 Doug Shedden .02 .10
234. Mark Hardy
103 Wayne Babych .02 .10
236. Jim Fox
104 Mike Bullard .02 .10
237. Terry Ruskowski
105 Rod Langway .02 .10
106 Pat Riggin .02 .10
238. Dave Taylor
107 Scott Stevens .08 .25
239. Bob Janecyk
108 Alan Haworth .02 .10
241. Patrik Sundstrom
109 Doug Jarvis .02 .10
242. Al MacAdam
110 Dave Christian .02 .10
243. Doug Halward
111 Mike Gartner .08 .25
244. Peter McNab
112 Bob Carpenter .02 .10
113 Rod Langway FOIL .05 .15
114 Tom Barrasso FOIL .08 .25
115 Ray Bourque FOIL .40 1.00
116 John Tonelli FOIL .05 .15
117 Brent Sutter FOIL .05 .15
118 Mike Bossy FOIL .20 .50
119 John Ogrodnick FOIL .05 .15
120 Wayne Gretzky FOIL 2.00 5.00
121 Jari Kurri FOIL .30 .75
122 Doug Wilson FOIL .05 .15
123 Andy Moog FOIL .20 .50
124 Paul Coffey FOIL .40 1.00
125 Chris Chelios .40 1.00
126 Steve Penney .02 .10
127 Chris Nilan .02 .10
245. Tony Tanti
128 Ron Flockhart .02 .10
246. Moe Lemay
129 Tom Kurvers .02 .10
249. Dave Babych
130 Craig Ludwig .02 .10
250. Paul MacLean
131 Mats Naslund .02 .10
132 Bobby Smith .02 .10
252. Robert Picard
133 Pierre Mondou .02 .10
253. Thomas Steen
134 Mario Tremblay .02 .10
254. Laurie Boschman
135 Guy Carbonneau .08 .25
255. Doug Smail
140 Larry Robinson .08 .25
141 Michel Goulet .08 .25
142 Bruce Bell .02 .10
147 Anton Stastny .02 .10
156 Peter Stastny .08 .25
157 Ray Bourque .20 .50
160 Pete Peeters .02 .10
165 Sylvain Turgeon .02 .10
172 Ron Francis .20 .50
173 Phil Housley .08 .25
174 Mike Foligno .02 .10
179 Tom Barrasso .08 .25
188 Gilbert Perreault .08 .25
194 Jennings Trophy FOIL .02 .10
205. Masterton Trophy FOIL
195 Norris Trophy FOIL .02 .10
206. Lady Byng Trophy FOIL
196 Selke Trophy FOIL .02 .10
207. Art Ross Trophy FOIL
208 Kent Nilsson .02 .10
215 Lanny McDonald .08 .25
216 Charlie Huddy .02 .10
217 Paul Coffey .20 .50
222 Wayne Gretzky 2.00 5.00
231 Jari Kurri .20 .50
232 Bernie Nicholls .08 .25
235 Marcel Dionne .08 .25
240 Thomas Gradin .02 .10
247 Stan Smyl .02 .10
248 Dale Hawerchuk .20 .50
251 Randy Carlyle .02 .10
NNO Sticker Album 2.00 5.00

1986-87 O-Pee-Chee Stickers

This sticker set consisted of 167 stickers in full color and was put out by O-Pee-Chee. The foil stickers are listed in the checklist below explicitly. The stickers measured approximately 2 1/8" by 3". An album was available for these stickers. Those stickers which are pairs are indicated in the checklist below by noting the other member of the pair. On the inside back cover of the sticker album the company offered (via direct mail-order) any ten different stickers of your choice for one dollar; this is one reason why the values of the most popular players in these sticker sets are somewhat depressed compared to traditional card set prices.

COMPLETE SET (167) 15.00 40.00
1 Stanley Cup Action .20 .50
2 Stanley Cup Action .08 .25
3 Stanley Cup Action .08 .25
4 Stanley Cup Action .08 .25
5 Patrick Roy FOIL 6.00 15.00
6 Chris Chelios .15 .40
{ 151. Darryl Sutter
7 Guy Carbonneau .02 .05
{ 152. Bob Sauve
8 Larry Robinson .02 .10
9 Mario Tremblay FOIL .02 .05
154. Troy Murray
10 Tom Kurvers .02 .05
{ 155. Al Secord
11 Mats Naslund .02 .10
12 Bob Gainey .30 .75
13 Bobby Smith .02 .10
14 Craig Ludwig .08 .25
{ 156. Ed Olczyk
15 Mike McPhee .08 .25
{ 157. Steve Larmer
16 Doug Soetaert .02 .05
{ 159. Danny Gare
17 Petr Svoboda .02 .05
{ 160. Petr Svoboda
18 Kjell Dahlin .02 .10
19 Patrick Roy 4.00 10.00
20 Alain Cote 1.00 2.50
{ 161. Steve Yzerman
21 Mario Gosselin .02 .05
{ 162. Petr Klima
22 Michel Goulet .08 .25
23 J.F. Sauve .02 .05
{ 163. Kelly Kisio
24 Paul Gillis .02 .05
{ 164. Doug Shedden
25 Brent Ashton .02 .10
26 Peter Stastny .08 .25
27 Anton Stastny .02 .10
28 Gilbert Delorme .02 .05
{ 167. Brian Bellows
29 Risto Siltanen .02 .05
168. Scott Bjugstad
30 Robert Picard .02 .05
{ 170. Dennis Maruk
31 David Shaw .08 .25
{ 171. Dirk Graham
32 Dale Hunter .02 .10
33 Clint Malarchuk .15 .40
34 Ray Bourque .20 .50
35 Rick Middleton .02 .05
{ 172. Curt Giles
36 Charlie Simmer .02 .05
{ 173. Craig Hartsburg
37 Keith Crowder .02 .10
38 Barry Pederson .02 .05
{ 175. Brian Sutter
39 Reed Larson .02 .05
176. Ron Flockhart
40 Steve Kasper .20 .50
{ 177. Doug Gilmour
41 Pat Riggin .02 .05
{ 178. Charlie Bourgeois
42 Mike Foligno .02 .10
43 Gilbert Perreault .02 .05
179. Rick Wamsley
44 Mike Ramsey .02 .05
180. Rob Ramage
45 Tom Barrasso .15 .40
{ 186. Bob Froese
46 Brian Engblom .02 .05
{ 187. Darren Jensen
47 Phil Housley .20 .50
{ 188. Paul Coffey
48 John Tucker .02 .05
{ 189. Troy Murray
49 Dave Andreychuk .08 .25
50 Dave Babych .02 .10
51 Ron Francis .40 1.00
{ 190. John Vanbiesbrouck
52 Mike Liut 1.50 4.00
{ 191. Wayne Gretzky
53 Sylvain Turgeon .02 .10
54 John Anderson .02 .05
{ 192. Gary Suter
55 Joel Quenneville .02 .05
{ 193. Bob Froese
56 Kevin Dineen .08 .25
{ 194. Mike Bossy
57 Ray Ferraro 1.50 4.00
{ 195. Wayne Gretzky
58 Action Sticker .02 .10
59 Action Sticker .02 .10
60 Action Sticker .02 .10
61 Action Sticker .02 .10
62 Action Sticker .02 .10
63 Action Sticker .02 .10
64 Action Sticker .02 .10
65 Action Sticker .02 .10
66 Andy Moog .15 .40
{ 197. Dave Lewis
67 Grant Fuhr .15 .40
{ 198. Joe Cirella
68 Paul Coffey .20 .50
69 Charlie Huddy .02 .05
{ 199. Rich Preston
70 Kevin Lowe .08 .25
{ 200. Mark Johnson
71 Lee Fogolin .02 .10
72 Wayne Gretzky 2.00 5.00
73 Jari Kurri .10 .30
74 Mike Krushelnyski .08 .25
201. Kirk Muller
75 Mark Napier .08 .25
{ 202. Pat Verbeek
76 Craig MacTavish .02 .05
{ 204. Bob Nystrom
77 Kevin McClelland .02 .05
205. Clark Gillies
78 Glenn Anderson .10 .30
79 Mark Messier .30 .75
80 Lanny McDonald .10 .30
81 John Tonelli .02 .05
{ 207. Pat Flatley
82 Joe Mullen .08 .25
{ 208. Bob Bourne
83 Reggie Lemelin .08 .25
84 Jim Peplinski .20 .50
{ 212. Kelly Hrudey
85 Jamie Macoun .08 .25
{ 213. Billy Smith
86 Al MacInnis .20 .50
{ 214. Tomas Jonsson
87 Dan Quinn .02 .05
{ 215. Ken Morrow
88 Marcel Dionne .08 .25
89 Jim Fox .15 .40
{ 217. Mike Bossy
90 Dave Taylor .02 .05
{ 219. Bob Brooke
91 Bob Janecyk .02 .05
222. Ron Greschner
92 Jay Wells .02 .05
{ 223. Tom Laidlaw
93 Bryan Erickson .02 .05
{ 224. Larry Melnyk
94 Tiger Williams .02 .05
225. Reijo Ruotsalainen
95 Bernie Nicholls .08 .25
96 Stan Smyl .02 .10
97 Doug Halward .02 .05
{ 227. Willy Lindstrom
98 Richard Brodeur .02 .05
{ 228. Mike Bullard
99 Tony Tanti .02 .10
100 Brent Peterson .02 .05
229. Roberto Romano
101 Patrik Sundstrom .02 .05
230. John Chabot
102 Doug Lidster .02 .05
{ 231. Moe Mantha
103 Petri Skriko .02 .05
{ 232. Doug Bodger
104 Dale Hawerchuk .08 .25
105 Bill Derlago .08 .25
{ 234. Glenn Resch
106 Ray Neufeld .02 .05
{ 235. Brad Marsh
107 Randy Carlyle .02 .05
{ 237. Doug Crossman
108 Paul MacLean .02 .05
{ 238. Ilkka Sinisalo
109 Brian Mullen .02 .05
{ 242. Rich Sutter
110 Thomas Steen .02 .05
243. Ron Sutter
111 Laurie Boschman .02 .10
112 Paul Coffey FOIL .30 .75
126. Kjell Dahlin FOIL
113 Michel Goulet .20 .50
{ 127. Pelle Eklund FOIL
114 John Vanbiesbrouck FOIL 1.25 3.00
128. Jim Johnson FOIL
115 Wayne Gretzky 2.50 6.00
{ 129. Petr Klima FOIL
116 Mark Howe FOIL .15 .40
130. Joel Otto FOIL
117 Mike Bossy FOIL .30 .75
131. Mike Ridley FOIL
118 Jari Kurri FOIL 4.00 10.00
132. Patrick Roy FOIL
119 Ray Bourque FOIL .30 .75
133. David Shaw FOIL
120 Mario Lemieux FOIL 1.25 3.00
134. Gary Suter FOIL
121 Grant Fuhr FOIL .20 .50
135. Steve Thomas FOIL
122 Mats Naslund FOIL .15 .40
182. Bob Froese FOIL
123 Larry Robinson 2.00 5.00
{ 183. Wayne Gretzky FOIL
124 Chris Cichocki FOIL .15 .40
184. Mark Howe FOIL
125 Wendel Clark FOIL 1.00 2.50
185. Jari Kurri FOIL
136 Borje Salming .02 .05
{ 244. Murray Craven
137 Gary Nylund .02 .05
{ 245. Peter Zezel
138 Rick Vaive .02 .10
139 Don Edwards .02 .05
249. Rod Langway
140 Steve Thomas .08 .25
{ 250. Bob Carpenter
141 Wendel Clark .50 1.25
142 Miroslav Frycer .02 .10
143 Tom Fergus .02 .10
144 Marian Stastny .02 .05
{ 252. Al Jensen
145 Brad Maxwell .02 .05
{ 253. Craig Laughlin
146 Dan Daoust .08 .25
254. Scott Stevens
147 Greg Terrion .02 .05
{ 255. Alan Haworth
148 Al Iafrate .15 .40
149 Russ Courtnall .08 .25
150 Denis Savard .08 .25
153 Doug Wilson .02 .10
158 John Ogrodnick .02 .10
165 Greg Stefan .02 .10
166 Neal Broten .08 .25
169 Dino Ciccarelli .08 .25
174 Bernie Federko .02 .10
181 Mark Hunter .02 .10
196 Greg Adams .02 .10
203 Mel Bridgman .02 .10
206 Pat LaFontaine .30 .75
209 Denis Potvin .08 .25
210 Duane Sutter .02 .10
211 Brent Sutter .02 .10
216 Bryan Trottier .08 .25
217 Mike Bossy .15 .40
218 John Vanbiesbrouck .75 2.00
221 Mike Ridley .08 .25
226 Terry Ruskowski .02 .10
233 Mario Lemieux 3.00 8.00
236 Bob Froese .02 .10
239 Brian Propp .02 .10
240 Tim Kerr .02 .10
241 Dave Poulin .40 1.00
246 Mark Howe .02 .10
247 Brad McCrimmon .02 .10
248 Dave Christian .02 .10
251 Mike Gartner .08 .25
NNO Sticker Album 1.50 4.00

1987-88 O-Pee-Chee Stickers

This sticker set consisted of 168 stickers in full color and was put out by O-Pee-Chee. There were no foil stickers in this set. The stickers measured approximately 2 1/8" by 3". An album was available for these stickers. Those stickers which are pairs are indicated in the checklist below by noting parenthetically the other member of the pair. On the inside back cover of the sticker album the company offered (via direct mail-order) up to 25 different stickers of your choice for ten cents each; this is one reason why the values of the most popular players in these sticker sets are somewhat depressed compared to traditional card set prices.

COMPLETE SET (168) 12.00 30.00
1 Ron Hextall MVP .08 .25
2 Stanley Cup Action .08 .25
3 Stanley Cup Action .08 .25
4 Stanley Cup Action .08 .25
5 Stanley Cup Action .08 .25
6 Mats Naslund .08 .25
7 Guy Carbonneau .08 .25
{ 146. Steve Dykstra
8 Gaston Gingras .08 .25
{ 147. Dave Andreychuk
9 Chris Chelios .20 .50
10 Bobby Smith .08 .25
11 Rick Green .02 .10
{ 149. Mike Ramsey
12 Bob Gainey .08 .25
{ 150. Mike Foligno
13 Patrick Roy 3.00 8.00
14 Kjell Dahlin .02 .10
{ 153. Greg Terrion
15 Chris Nilan .08 .25
{ 154. Steve Thomas
16 Larry Robinson .08 .25
17 Ryan Walter .02 .10
{ 157. Rick Lanz
18 Petr Svoboda .02 .10
{ 158. Miroslav Frycer
19 Claude Lemieux .60 1.50
20 Rob Ramage .08 .25
{ 160. Al Iafrate
21 Mark Hunter .02 .10
{ 161. Gary Leeman
22 Rick Wamsley .02 .10
163. Todd Gill
23 Greg Paslawski .10 .30
{ 164. Ken Wregget
24 Bernie Federko .08 .25
25 Ron Flockhart .08 .25
{ 166. Craig Simpson
26 Tim Bothwell .02 .10
{ 167. Terry Ruskowski
27 Doug Gilmour .20 .50
28 Kelly Kisio .02 .10
{ 168. Gilles Meloche
29 Don Maloney .02 .10
{ 169. John Chabot
30 James Patrick .02 .10
{ 171. Moe Mantha
31 Willie Huber .02 .10
{ 172. Jim Johnson
32 Walt Poddubny .02 .10
33 John Vanbiesbrouck .20 .50
{ 178. Ray Bourque
34 Marcel Dionne .08 .25
{ 179. Dave Poulin
35 Tomas Sandstrom .08 .25
36 Joe Mullen .08 .25
37 Mike Bullard 1.25 3.00
{ 180. Wayne Gretzky Hart Tr.
38 Neil Sheehy 1.25 3.00
{ 181. Wayne Gretzky Ross Tr.
39 Paul Reinhart .02 .10
40 Al MacInnis .08 .25
41 Mike Vernon .20 .50
{ 182. Ron Hextall
42 Joel Otto .02
{ 183. Doug Jarvis
43 Lanny McDonald .08
44 Hakan Loob .08
{ 184. Brian Hayward
45 Carey Wilson 1.25 3
{ 185. Patrick Roy
46 Jim Peplinski .02
47 John Tonelli .08
{ 186. Joe Mullen
48 Jamie Macoun .30
{ 187. Luc Robitaille
49 Gary Suter .08
50 Dennis Maruk .02
{ 189. Richard Brodeur
51 Don Beaupre .08
{ 190. Dave Richter
52 Neal Broten .08
{ 193. Rich Sutter
53 Brian Bellows .08
{ 194. Jim Sandlak
54 Craig Hartsburg .02
55 Gordie Roberts .02
{ 196. Michel Petit
56 Steve Payne .02
{ 197. Jim Benning
57 Dino Ciccarelli .08
58 Pat Verbeek .02
{ 199. Brent Peterson
59 Doug Sulliman .08
200. Garth Butcher
60 Bruce Driver .02
{ 202. Kevin Dineen
61 Joe Cirella .02
{ 203. Sylvain Turgeon
62 Aaron Broten .02
63 Alain Chevrier .02
{ 204. John Anderson
64 Mark Johnson .08
{ 205. Ulf Samuelsson
65 Kirk Muller .08
66A Face-Off Action .02
(Jim Sandlak)
66B Face-Off Action .02
(Steve Kasper)
67 Action Sticker .02
68 Action Sticker .02
69 Murray Craven IA .02
70 Bruins Action .02
71 Islanders Action .02
72 Action Sticker .02
73 Action Sticker .02
74 Al Secord .02
{ 207. Doug Jarvis
75 Bob Sauve .02
{ 208. Dave Babych
76 Ed Olczyk .08
{ 210. Jimmy Carson
77 Doug Wilson .02
{ 211. Larry Playfair
78 Denis Savard .08
79 Troy Murray .02
{ 212. Jay Wells
80 Gary Nylund .02
{ 213. Rollie Melanson
81 Steve Larmer .08
82 Jari Kurri .08
83 Esa Tikkanen .20
{ 215. Dave Taylor
84 Kevin Lowe .02
{ 216. Jim Fox
85 Grant Fuhr .08
86 Wayne Gretzky 1.50 4
87 Charlie Huddy .02
{ 219. Jason Lafreniere
88 Kent Nilsson .02
{ 220. Mike Hough
89 Paul Coffey .20
90 Mike Krushelnyski .02
223. David Shaw
91 Craig MacTavish .02
{ 224. Bill Derlago
92 Mark Messier .40 1
93 Andy Moog .08
{ 226. Doug Shedden
94 Randy Gregg .02
{ 227. Basil McRae
95 Glenn Anderson .08
96 Peter Zezel .08
{ 229. Randy Moller
97 Brian Propp .08
{ 230. Robert Picard
98 Dave Poulin .08
{ 232. Larry Murphy
99 Brad McCrimmon .08
{ 233. Scott Stevens
100 Mark Howe .08
101 Ron Hextall .20
{ 234. Mike Ridley
102 Ron Sutter .02
{ 235. Dave Christian
103 Tim Kerr .02
104 Petr Klima .08
{ 237. Bob Gould
105 Adam Oates .60 1
{ 238. Bob Mason
106 Gerard Gallant .08
{ 240. Bryan Trottier
107 Mike O'Connell .02
{ 241. Brent Sutter
108 Brent Ashton .02
109 Glen Hanlon .08
{ 242. Kelly Hrudey
110 Harold Snepsts .20
{ 243. Pat LaFontaine
111 Steve Yzerman .40 1
112 Mark Howe .08
{ 124. Brian Benning
113 Michel Goulet .08
{ 125. Shawn Burr
114 Ron Hextall .20
{ 126. Jimmy Carson
115 Wayne Gretzky 1.25 3
{ 127. Shayne Corson
116 Ray Bourque .20
{ 128. Vincent Damphousse
117 Jari Kurri .20
{ 129. Ron Hextall
118 Dino Ciccarelli .08
{ 130. Jason Lafreniere
119 Larry Murphy .08
{ 131. Ken Leiter
120 Mario Lemieux .75 2
{ 132. Allen Pedersen
121 Mike Liut .30
{ 133. Luc Robitaille
122 Luc Robitaille .40 1
{ 134. Christian Ruuttu

23 Al MacInnis .08 .25
(135. Jim Sandlak
36 Keith Crowder .02 .10
(245. Pat Flatley
37 Charlie Simmer .02 .10
(246. Ken Morrow
38 Rick Middleton .02 .10
(248. Randy Carlyle
39 Doug Keans .08 .25
(249. Daniel Berthiaume
40 Ray Bourque .08 .25
41 Tom McCarthy .02 .10
(250. Mario Marois
42 Reed Larson .02 .10
(251. Dave Ellett
43 Cam Neely .20 .50
44 Christian Ruuttu .02 .10
253. Gilles Hamel
45 John Tucker .02 .10
(254. Doug Smail
48 Tom Barrasso .08 .25
51 Phil Housley .08 .25
52 Wendel Clark .20 .50
55 Rick Vaive .02 .10
56 Russ Courtnall .08 .25
59 Tom Fergus .02 .10
62 Allan Bester .08 .25
65 Borje Salming .08 .25
70 Mario Lemieux 1.25 3.00
73 Dan Quinn .02 .10
74 Wayne Gretzky 1.25 3.00
(176. Mark Howe
75 Brian Hayward .30 .75
(177. Luc Robitaille
88 Barry Pederson .02 .10
91 Doug Lidster .02 .10
92 Petri Skriko .02 .10
95 Tony Tanti .02 .10
98 Stan Smyl .02 .10
01 Patrik Sundstrom .02 .10
06 Ron Francis .20 .50
09 Mike Liut .08 .25
14 Bernie Nicholls .08 .25
17 Luc Robitaille 1.25 3.00
18 John Ogrodnick .02 .10
21 Paul Gillis .02 .10
22 Peter Stastny .08 .25
25 Michel Goulet .08 .25
28 Anton Stastny .02 .10
31 Mario Gosselin .08 .25
36 Rod Langway .08 .25
39 Mike Gartner .08 .25
44 Mike Bossy .08 .25
47 Denis Potvin .08 .25
52 Paul MacLean .02 .10
55 Dale Hawerchuk .08 .25
NO Sticker Album 1.50 4.00

1988-89 O-Pee-Chee Stickers

his set consisted of 181 stickers in full color and was ut out by O-Pee-Chee. There were no foil stickers in is set. The stickers measured approximately 2 1/8" 3". An album was available for these stickers. Those ickers which are pairs are indicated in the checklist elow by noting the other member of the pair. The acks of the stickers were three types: trivia questions d answers (42 different red Level I and blue Level II), rious souvenir offers, and the colorful Future Stars hich are considered a separate set in their own ght). On the inside back cover of the sticker album the ompany offered (via direct mail-order) up to 20 ferent stickers of your choice for ten cents each; this one reason why the values of the most popular ayers in these sticker sets are somewhat depressed mpared to traditional card set prices.

OMPLETE SET (182) 8.00 20.00
Wayne Gretzky MVP 1.50 4.00
Oilers/Bruins Action .02 .10
Oilers/Bruins Action .08 .25
Oilers/Bruins Action .08 .25
Oilers/Bruins Action .02 .10
Doug Wilson .08 .25
135. Darren Pang
Dirk Graham .08 .25
136. Kirk McLean
Darren Pang .02 .10
137. Doug Smail
Rick Vaive .02 .10
138. Thomas Steen
Troy Murray .02 .10
139. Laurie Boschman
Brian Noonan .02 .10
140. Iain Duncan
Kirk McLean (back)
Steve Larmer .08 .25
Denis Savard .08 .25
Mark Hunter .02 .10
141. Ray Neufeld
Brian Sutter .02 .10
142. Mario Marois
Brett Hull .75 2.00
145. Jim Kyte
Tony McKegney .02 .10
146. Pokey Reddick
Brian Benning .02 .10
151. Roland Melanson
Darren Pang (back)
Tony Hrkac .08 .25
152. Steve Duchesne
Doug Gilmour .20 .50
Bernie Federko .02 .10
Cam Neely .20 .50
Ray Bourque .20 .50
Doug Brown (back)
Rejean Lemelin .02 .10
153. Bob Carpenter
Gord Kluzak .02 .10
154. Jim Fox
Rick Middleton .08 .25
155. Dave Taylor
Steve Kasper .08 .25
156. Bernie Nicholls
Bob Sweeney .02 .10
168. Mark Osborne
Randy Burridge .02 .10
169. Dan Daoust
Bruins/Whalers Action .02 .10
Canadiens/Bruins .02 .10
Action
Canadiens/Bruins .02 .10
Action
Blues/Red Wings .02 .10
Action
Canadiens/Bruins .02 .10
Action
Canadiens/Bruins .02 .10
Action
Canadiens/Bruins .02 .10
Action
Tony Hrkac (back)
37 Canadiens/Bruins .02 .10
Action
38 Canadiens/Bruins .02 .10
Action
39 Larry Robinson .08 .25
170. Tom Fergus
40 Ryan Walter .08 .25
171. Vincent Damphousse
41 Guy Carbonneau .08 .25
172. Wendel Clark
42 Bob Gainey .08 .25
173. Luke Richardson
43 Claude Lemieux .20 .50
176. Rick Lanz
44 Petr Svoboda .08 .25
177. Ken Wregget
45 Patrick Roy 1.25 3.00
46 Bobby Smith .08 .25
47 Mike McPhee .02 .10
182. Normand Rochefort
48 Craig Ludwig .02 .10
183. Lane Lambert
49 Stephane Richer .08 .25
50 Mats Naslund .02 .10
51 Chris Chelios .20 .50
52 Brian Hayward .08 .25
53 Larry Melnyk .02 .10
184. Tommy Albelin
David Archibald (back)
54 Garth Butcher .02 .10
185. Jason Lafreniere
55 Kirk McLean .08 .25
186. Alain Cote
56 Doug Wickenheiser .02 .10
187. Gaetan Duchesne
57 Rich Sutter .02 .10
190. Jeff Jackson
58 Jim Benning .02 .10
191. Mike Eagles
59 Tony Tanti .02 .10
60 Stan Smyl .02 .10
61 David Saunders .08 .25
196. Don Beaupre
62 Steve Tambellini .02 .10
197. Brian MacLellan
63 Doug Lidster .02 .10
Rob Brown (back)
64 Petri Skriko .02 .10
65 Barry Pederson .02 .10
66 Greg Adams .02 .10
67 Mike Gartner .08 .25
68 Scott Stevens .08 .25
Bob Sweeney (back)
69 Rod Langway .02 .10
198. Brian Lawton
Pierre Turgeon (back)
70 Dave Christian .02 .10
199. Craig Hartsburg
71 Larry Murphy .02 .10
200. Moe Mantha
72 Clint Malarchuk .08 .25
201. Neal Broten
73 Dale Hunter .60 1.50
204. Mario Lemieux
74 Mike Ridley .08 .25
205. Joe Nieuwendyk
Jeff Sharples (back)
75 Kirk Muller .08 .25
76 Aaron Broten .02 .10
77 Bruce Driver .02 .10
206. Brad McCrimmon
78 John MacLean .08 .25
207. Pete Peeters
79 Joe Cirella .08 .25
208. Norris Trophy Winner
Ray Bourque
80 Doug Brown .02 .10
209. Selke Trophy Winner
Guy Carbonneau
81 Pat Verbeek 1.50 4.00
210. Hart Trophy Winner
Mario Lemieux
Brett Hull (back)
82 Sean Burke .40 1.00
211. Ross Trophy Winner
Mario Lemiuex
83 Joel Otto .08 .25
212. Vezina Trophy Winner
Grant Fuhr
84 Rob Ramage .02 .10
213. Masterton Trophy Winner
Bob Bourne
85 Lanny McDonald .08 .25
215. Lady Byng Trophy Win
Mats Naslund
Glen Wesley (back)
86 Mike Vernon .20 .50
216. Calder Trophy Winner
Joe Nieuwendyk
87 John Tonelli .02 .10
217. Craig MacTavish
88 Jim Peplinski .02 .10
218. Chris Joseph
89 Gary Suter .08 .25
90 Joe Nieuwendyk .40 1.00
Craig Janney (back)
91 Ric Nattress .02 .10
219. Kevin Lowe
92 Al MacInnis .20 .50
220. Esa Tikkanen
93 Mike Bullard .02 .10
94 Hakan Loob .02 .10
95 Joe Mullen .08 .25
96 Brad McCrimmon .02 .10
97 Brian Propp .02 .10
221. Charlie Huddy
98 Murray Craven .08 .25
222. Geoff Courtnall
99 Rick Tocchet .20 .50
225. Steve Smith
100 Doug Crossman .02 .10
226. Mike Krushelnyski
101 Brad Marsh .08 .25
233. Paul Coffee
102 Peter Zezel .02 .10
234. Doug Bodger
103 Ron Hextall .08 .25
104 Mark Howe .08 .25
105 Brent Sutter .02 .10
235. Dave Hunter
106 Alan Kerr .02 .10
236. Dan Quinn
107 Randy Wood .02 .10
237. Rob Brown
108 Mikko Makela .02 .10
238. Gilles Meloche
Iain Duncan (back)
109 Kelly Hrudey .20 .50
241. John Vanbiesbrouck
110 Steve Konroyd .02 .10
242. Tomas Sandstrom
111 Pat LaFontaine .20 .50
112 Bryan Trottier .08 .25
113 Gary Suter .02 .10
243. David Shaw
114 Luc Robitaille .20 .50
244. Marcel Dionne
115 Patrick Roy .60 1.50
245. Chris Nilan
116 Mario Lemieux .60 1.50
246. James Patrick
117 Ray Bourque .20 .50
247. Bob Probert
118 Hakan Loob .02 .10
248. Mike O'Connell
119 Mike Bullard .02 .10
249. Jeff Sharples
120 Brad McCrimmon .02 .10
250. Brent Ashton
121 Wayne Gretzky .75 2.00
251. Petr Klima
122 Grant Fuhr .08 .25
252. Greg Stefan
123 Craig Simpson .08 .25
255. Phil Housley
Glenn Healy (back)
124 Mark Howe .02 .10
256. Christian Ruuttu
125 Joe Nieuwendyk .08 .25
257. Mike Foligno
126 Ray Sheppard .08 .25
258. Scott Arniel
Ulf Dahlen (back)
127 Brett Hull .75 2.00
259. Tom Barrasso
128 Ulf Dahlen .08 .25
260. Mike Ramsey
129 Tony Hrkac .02 .10
265. Ulf Samuelsson
130 Bob Sweeney .02 .10
266. Carey Wilson
131 Rob Brown .08 .25
267. Dave Babych
132 Iain Duncan .02 .10
268. Ray Ferraro
133 Pierre Turgeon .40 1.00
269. Kevin Dineen
134 Calle Johansson .02 .10
270. John Anderson
Joe Nieuwendyk (back)
143 Dale Hawerchuk .08 .25
144 Paul MacLean .02 .10
147 Andrew McBain .02 .10
Brian Noonan (back)
148 Randy Carlyle .02 .10
149 Daniel Berthiaume .08 .25
150 Dave Ellett .02 .10
157 Luc Robitaille .30 .75
158 Jimmy Carson .20 .50
Sean Burke (back)
159 Canadiens/Bruins .02 .10
Action
160 Devils/Nordiques .02 .10
Action
161 Devils/Nordiques .02 .10
Action
Ray Sheppard (back)
162 Devils/North Stars .02 .10
Action
163 Oilers/Flames Action .02 .10
164 Oilers/Flames Action .02 .10
165 Oilers/Flames Action .02 .10
166 Oilers/Flames Action .02 .10
167 Canadiens/Bruins .02 .10
Action
174 Borje Salming .08 .25
175 Russ Courtnall .08 .25
178 Gary Leeman .02 .10
179 Al Secord .02 .10
180 Al Iafrate .08 .25
181 Ed Olczyk .02 .10
188 Michel Goulet .08 .25
189 Peter Stastny .08 .25
Brian Leetch (back)
192 Jeff Brown .20 .50
193 Mario Gosselin .08 .25
194 Anton Stastny .02 .10
195 Alan Haworth .02 .10
202 Dino Ciccarelli .08 .25
Randy Wood (back)
203 Brian Bellows .02 .10
223 Grant Fuhr .08 .25
224 Wayne Gretzky 1.50 4.00
227 Jari Kurri .08 .25
228 Craig Simpson .02 .10
229 Glenn Anderson .08 .25
230 Mark Messier .20 .50
231 Randy Cunneyworth .02 .10
232 Mario Lemieux 1.25 3.00
239 Kelly Kisio .02 .10
240 Walt Poddubny .02 .10
253 Steve Yzerman .40 1.00
254 Gerard Gallant .08 .25
Calle Johansson (back)
261 Dave Andreychuk .08 .25
262 Ray Sheppard .08 .25
263 Mike Liut .08 .25
264 Ron Francis .20 .50
NNO Sticker Album 1.25 3.00

1988-89 O-Pee-Chee Sticker Back Cards

COMPLETE SET (106) 3.00 8.00
1 David Archibald .02 .10
2 Doug Brown .02 .10
3 Rob Brown .02 .10
4 Sean Burke .07 .20
5 Ulf Dahlen .07 .20
6 Iain Duncan .02 .10
7 Glenn Healy .02 .10
8 Tony Hrkac .02 .10
9 Brett Hull 1.00 2.50
10 Craig Janney .07 .20
11 Calle Johansson .07 .20
12 Brian Leetch .40 1.00
13 Kirk McLean .10 .30
14 Joe Nieuwendyk .40 1.00
15 Brian Noonan .02 .10
16 Darren Pang .02 .10
17 Jeff Sharples .02 .10
18 Ray Sheppard .02 .10
19 Bob Sweeney .02 .10
20 Pierre Turgeon .20 .50
21 Glen Wesley .02 .10
22 Randy Wood .02 .10
A1 Answer 1 .01 .05
A2 Answer 2 .01 .05
A3 Answer 3 .01 .05
A4 Answer 4 .01 .05
A5 Answer 5 .01 .05
A6 Answer 6 .01 .05
A7 Answer 7 .01 .05
A8 Answer 8 .01 .05
A9 Answer 9 .01 .05
Q1 Question 1 .01 .05
Q2 Question 2 .01 .05
Q3 Question 3 .01 .05
Q4 Question 4 .01 .05
Q5 Question 5 .01 .05
Q6 Question 6 .01 .05
Q7 Question 7 .01 .05
Q8 Question 8 .01 .05
Q9 Question 9 .01 .05
A10 Answer 10 .01 .05
A11 Answer 11 .01 .05
A12 Answer 12 .01 .05
A13 Answer 13 .01 .05
A14 Answer 14 .01 .05
A15 Answer 15 .01 .05
A16 Answer 16 .01 .05
A17 Answer 17 .01 .05
A18 Answer 18 .01 .05
A19 Answer 19 .01 .05
A20 Answer 20 .01 .05
A21 Answer 21 .01 .05
A22 Answer 22 .01 .05
A23 Answer 23 .01 .05
A24 Answer 24 .01 .05
A25 Answer 25 .01 .05
A26 Answer 26 .01 .05
A27 Answer 27 .01 .05
A28 Answer 28 .01 .05
A29 Answer 29 .01 .05
A30 Answer 30 .01 .05
A31 Answer 31 .01 .05
A32 Answer 32 .01 .05
A33 Answer 33 .01 .05
A34 Answer 34 .01 .05
A35 Answer 35 .01 .05
A36 Answer 36 .01 .05
A37 Answer 37 .01 .05
A38 Answer 38 .01 .05
A39 Answer 39 .01 .05
A40 Answer 40 .01 .05
A41 Answer 41 .01 .05
A42 Answer 42 .01 .05
Q10 Question 10 .01 .05
Q11 Question 11 .01 .05
Q12 Question 12 .01 .05
Q13 Question 13 .01 .05
Q14 Question 14 .01 .05
Q15 Question 15 .01 .05
Q16 Question 16 .01 .05
Q17 Question 17 .01 .05
Q18 Question 18 .01 .05
Q19 Question 19 .01 .05
Q20 Question 20 .01 .05
Q21 Question 21 .01 .05
Q22 Question 22 .01 .05
Q23 Question 23 .01 .05
Q24 Question 24 .01 .05
Q25 Question 25 .01 .05
Q26 Question 26 .01 .05
Q27 Question 27 .01 .05
Q28 Question 28 .01 .05
Q29 Question 29 .01 .05
Q30 Question 30 .01 .05
Q31 Question 31 .01 .05
Q32 Question 32 .01 .05
Q33 Question 33 .01 .05
Q34 Question 34 .01 .05
Q35 Question 35 .01 .05
Q36 Question 36 .01 .05
Q37 Question 37 .01 .05
Q38 Question 38 .01 .05
Q39 Question 39 .01 .05
Q40 Question 40 .01 .05
Q41 Question 41 .01 .05
Q42 Question 42 .01 .05

1989-90 O-Pee-Chee Stickers

The 1989-90 O-Pee-Chee set contained 270 stickers. The standard size stickers measured 2 1/8" by 3"; some stickers consisted of two half-size stickers. The fronts featured color action photos of players, teams, and trophies. The sticker backs were of four types: trivia questions and answers (green Level III), souvenir offers, Future Stars, and All-Stars. A full-color glossy album was issued with the set for holding the stickers. Some team action shots were a composite of two or four stickers; in the checklist below these stickers are denoted by L (left half) and R (right half), with the additional prefixes U (upper) and L (lower) for the four sticker pictures. The stickers were numbered on the front and are checklisted below accordingly. For those stickers that consist of two half-size stickers, we have noted the other number of the pair parenthetically after the player's name.

COMPLETE SET (182) 8.00 20.00
1 Flames/Canadiens .02 .10
action UL
2 Flames/Canadiens .08 .25
action UR
3 Flames/Canadiens .02 .10
action LL
4 Flames/Canadiens .02 .10
action LR
5 Al MacInnis .08 .25
Conn Smythe Trophy Win
6 Flames/Canadiens .02 .10
action UL
7 Flames/Canadiens .02 .10
action UR
8 Flames/Canadiens .02 .10
action LL
9 Flames/Canadiens .02 .10
action LR
10 Darren Pang .08 .25
150. Steve Duchesne
Tony Granato FS (back)
11 Troy Murray .02 .10
151. Dave Taylor
12 Dirk Graham .02 .10
152. Steve Kasper
13 Dave Manson .02 .10
153. Mike Krushelnyski
14 Doug Wilson .60 1.50
156. Chris Chelios
Patrick Roy AS (back)
15 Steve Thomas .02 .10
157. Gerard Gallant
16 Denis Savard .08 .25
17 Steve Larmer .08 .25
18 Paul MacLean .40 1.00
158. Mario Lemieux
19 Paul Cavallini .02 .10
159. Al MacInnis
20 Cliff Ronning .08 .25
160. Joe Mullen
21 Gaston Gingras .40 1.00
161. Patrick Roy
Al MacInnis AS (back)
22 Brett Hull .40 1.00
23 Peter Zezel .02 .10
24 Brian Benning .08 .25
162. Ray Bourque
25 Tony Hrkac .02 .10
163. Rob Brown
26 Ken Linseman .02 .10
164. Geoff Courtnall
27 Glen Wesley .02 .10
165. Steve Duchesne
28 Randy Burridge .60 1.50
166. Wayne Gretzky
29 Craig Janney .08 .25
167. Mike Vernon
30 Andy Moog .08 .25
170. David Reid
31 Bob Joyce .02 .10
171. Craig Laughlin
32 Ray Bourque .20 .50
Gerard Gallant AS (back)
33 Cam Neely .20 .50
34 Sean Burke .02 .10
174. Mark Osborne
35 Pat Elynuik .20 .50
175. Brad Marsh
Craig Janney FS (back)
36 Tony Granato .02 .10
176. Daniel Marois
37 Benoit Hogue .08 .25
177. Dan Daoust
38 Craig Janney .08 .25
180. Chris Kotsopoulos
39 Brian Leetch .20 .50
181. Derek Laxdal
40 Trevor Linden .20 .50
184. Jeff Jackson
41 Joe Sakic 1.00 2.50
185. Mario Marois
Joe Sakic FS (back)
42 Peter Sidorkiewicz .02 .10
188. Bob Mason
43 Dave Volek .02 .10
189. Marc Fortier
44 Scott Young .02 .10
190. Robert Picard
45 Zarley Zalapski .02 .10
191. Steven Finn
46 Mats Naslund .02 .10
47 Bobby Smith .75 2.00
Wayne Gretzky AS (back)
48 Guy Carbonneau .02 .10
194. Gaetan Duchesne
49 Shayne Corson .02 .10
195. Randy Moller
50 Brian Hayward .02 .10
51 Stephane Richer .02 .10
52 Claude Lemieux .08 .25
196. Mike Gartner
53 Russ Courtnall .08 .25
197. Jon Casey
54 Petr Svoboda .20 .50
198. Marc Habscheid
Chris Chelios AS (back)
55 Larry Robinson .60 1.50
199. Larry Murphy
Mario Lemieux AS (back)
56 Chris Chelios .20 .50
57 Patrick Roy .60 1.50
58 Bob Gainey .02 .10
200. Brian Bellows
59 Mike McPhee .02 .10
201. Dave Archibald
60 Barry Pederson .02 .10
Jiri Hrdina AS (back)
61 Trevor Linden .30 .75
Joe Mullen AS (back)
62 Rich Sutter .02 .10
204. Vezina Trophy
63 Brian Bradley .08 .25
205. Jennings Trophy
Bob Essensa FS (back)
64 Kirk McLean .08 .25
John Cullen FS (back)
65 Paul Reinhart .08 .25
Steve Duchesne AS (back)
66 Robert Nordmark .02 .10
206. Selke Trophy
Pat Elynuik FS (back)
67 Steve Bozek .02 .10
207. Masterton Trophy
Greg Hawgood FS (back)
68 Stan Smyl .40 1.00
208. Mario Lemieux
69 Doug Lidster .01 1.50
209. Wayne Gretzky
70 Petri Skriko .02 .10
71 Tony Tanti .02 .10
72 Garth Butcher .40 1.00
210. Patrick Roy
Ray Bourque AS (back)
73 Larry Melnyk .08 .25
212. Chris Chelios
74 Kelly Miller .02 .10
213. Guy Carbonneau
75 Dino Ciccarelli .02 .10
214. Joe Mullen
76 Scott Stevens .20 .50
215. Brian Leetch
Mike Vernon AS (back)
77 Rod Langway .08 .25
216. Tim Kerr
Benoit Hogue FS (back)
78 Dave Christian .08 .25
219. Esa Tikkanen
79 Stephen Leach .02 .10
220. Charlie Huddy
80 Geoff Courtnall .08 .25
81 Mike Ridley .02 .10
82 Patrik Sundstrom .02 .10
223. Steve Smith
83 Kirk Muller .02 .10
224. Kevin Lowe
84 Tom Kurvers .02 .10
225. Chris Joseph
85 Walt Poddubny .02 .10
226. Craig MacTavish
86 Sean Burke .08 .25
87 John MacLean .02 .10
88 Aaron Broten (229) .02 .10
Gordon Murphy FS
89 Brendan Shanahan .40 1.00
230. Bill Ranford
90 Joe Mullen .08 .25
91 Brad McCrimmon .40 1.00
Brian Leetch FS (back)
92 Lanny McDonald .08 .25
231. John Cullen
93 Rick Wamsley .02 .10
232. Zarley Zalapski
94 Mike Vernon .08 .25
95 Al MacInnis .08 .25
96 Joel Otto .02 .10
233. Bob Errey
Scott Young FS (back)
97 Jiri Hrdina .02 .10
234. Dan Quinn
98 Gary Roberts .08 .25
235. Tom Barrasso
99 Jim Peplinski .02 .10
236. Rob Brown
100 Gary Suter .02 .10
101 Joe Nieuwendyk .08 .25
102 Colin Patterson .02 .10
239. Carey Wilson
Dan Marois FS (back)
103 Doug Gilmour .20 .50
240. Brian Leetch
104 Mike Bullard .02 .10
241. Tony Granato
105 Pelle Eklund .02 .10
242. James Patrick
106 Brian Propp .08 .25
245. Guy Lafleur
107 Ron Sutter .20 .50
246. John Vanbiesbrouck
Geoff Courtnall AS (back)
108 Rick Tocchet .08 .25
247. Bernie Federko
109 Mark Howe .02 .10
248. Greg Stefan
110 Tim Kerr .02 .10
111 Ron Hextall .08 .25
112 Mikko Makela .30 .75
249. Mike O'Connell
Trevor Linden AS (back)
113 Dave Volek .08 .25
250. Dave Barr
114 Gary Nylund .02 .10
251. Lee Norwood
115 Brent Sutter .02 .10
252. Shawn Burr
116 Derek King .08 .25
255. Christian Ruuttu
117 Gerald Diduck .02 .10
256. Rick Vaive
Rob Brown AS (back)
118 Bryan Trottier .08 .25
Peter Sidorkiewicz FS (back)
119 Pat LaFontaine .20 .50
120 Blues/Bruins action L .02 .10
121 Blues/Bruins action R .02 .10
122 Bruins/Rangers action L .02 .10
123 Bruins/Rangers action R .02 .10
124 Blackhawks action .02 .10
125 Bruins/Canadiens action .08 .25
(Ray Bourque)
126 Devils/Bruins action .02 .10
127 Flames/Devils action .02 .10
128 Canadiens/Flyers action .02 .10
129 Flyers/Oilers action .02 .10
130 Canucks/Bruins action L .02 .10
131 Canucks/Bruins action R .02 .10
132 North Stars/Bruins action L .02 .10
133 North Stars/Bruins action R .02 .10
134 Dale Hawerchuk .08 .25
135 Andrew McBain .02 .10
136 Iain Duncan .02 .10
257. Doug Bodger
137 Eldon Reddick .02 .10
258. Dave Andreychuk
138 Brent Ashton .02 .10
139 Dave Ellett .02 .10
140 Jim Kyte .02 .10
259. Ray Sheppard
141 Doug Smail .02 .10
260. Mike Foligno
142 Pat Elynuik .02 .10
263. Ray Ferraro
143 Randy Carlyle .02 .10
264. Scott Young
144 Thomas Steen .02 .10
145 Hannu Jarvenpaa .02 .10
146 Peter Taglianetti .02 .10
265. Dave Babych
Vincent Riendeau FS (back)
147 Laurie Boschman .02 .10
266. Paul MacDermid
148 Luc Robitaille .20 .50
267. Mike Liut
149 Kelly Hrudey .02 .10
268. Dave Tippett
154 Wayne Gretzky .75 2.00
155 Bernie Nicholls .02 .10
168 Gary Leeman .02 .10
169 Allan Bester .02 .10
172 Ed Olczyk .02 .10
173 Tom Fergus .02 .10
178 Al Iafrate .08 .25
179 Vincent Damphousse .08 .25
182 Peter Stastny .08 .25
183 Paul Gillis .02 .10
186 Michel Goulet .08 .25
187 Joe Sakic 1.50 4.00
Dave Volek FS (back)
192 Iiro Jarvi .02 .10
193 Jeff Brown .08 .25
202 Neal Broten .02 .10
203 Dave Gagner .20 .50
Sean Burke FS (back)
211 Patrick Roy .30 .75
Brian Hayward
(Jennings Trophy Winners)
217 Craig Simpson .02 .10
218 Glenn Anderson .02 .10
221 Jari Kurri .08 .25
222 Jimmy Carson .02 .10
227 Mark Messier .20 .50
228 Grant Fuhr .08 .25
237 Paul Coffey .20 .50
238 Mario Lemieux .60 1.50
243 Brian Mullen .02 .10
244 Tomas Sandstrom .02 .10
253 Gerard Gallant .02 .10
254 Steve Yzerman .30 .75
261 Phil Housley .08 .25
262 Pierre Turgeon .20 .50
269 Ron Francis .20 .50
270 Kevin Dineen .02 .10
NNO Sticker Album .75 2.00

2014-15 O-Pee-Chee Update

U1-U12 VET ODDS 1:17H/R, 1:33B UD SER.2
U13-U42 ROOK.ODDS 1:7H/R, 1:13B UD SER.2
*RED VETS: 2.5X TO 6X BASIC INSERTS
*RED ROOK: 2.5X TO 6X BASIC INSERTS
*RETRO VETS: .6X TO 1.5X BASIC INSERTS
*RETRO ROOK: .5X TO 1.2X BASIC INSERTS
U1 Jason Spezza .75 2.00
U2 Jarome Iginla .75 2.00
U3 Ryan Kesler .75 2.00
U4 Ryan Miller .75 2.00
U5 James Neal .75 2.00
U6 Radim Vrbata .60 1.50
U7 Matt Niskanen .60 1.50
U8 Thomas Vanek .75 2.00
U9 Paul Stastny .75 2.00
U10 Brad Richards .75 2.00
U11 Matt Moulson .60 1.50
U12 Brooks Orpik .60 1.50
U13 Leon Draisaitl 5.00 12.00
U14 Derrick Pouliot 1.25 3.00
U15 Andrei Vasilevskiy 3.00 8.00
U16 Seth Griffith 1.25 3.00
U17 Adam Lowry 1.00 2.50
U18 Sam Reinhart 3.00 8.00
U19 Jiri Sekac 1.00 2.50
U20 Alexander Wennberg 2.00 5.00
U21 Curtis Lazar 1.25 3.00
U22 Shayne Gostisbehere 4.00 10.00
U23 Victor Rask 1.00 2.50
U24 Jori Lehtera 1.25 3.00
U25 Chris Tierney 1.00 2.50
U26 William Karlsson 4.00 10.00
U27 Jonathan Drouin 3.00 8.00
U28 Mirco Mueller 1.00 2.50
U29 Trevor van Riemsdyk 1.50 4.00
U30 Aaron Ekblad 4.00 10.00
U31 Darnell Nurse 3.00 8.00
U32 Curtis McKenzie .75 2.00
U33 Stuart Percy 1.00 2.50
U34 Bo Horvat 3.00 8.00
U35 Andre Burakovsky 1.50 4.00
U36 Rocco Grimaldi 1.00 2.50
U37 Kevin Hayes 3.00 8.00
U38 Tobias Rieder 1.00 2.50
U39 Damon Severson 1.00 2.50
U40 Marko Dano 1.00 2.50
U41 Anthony Duclair 1.50 4.00
U42 Griffin Reinhart 1.25 3.00

2014-15 O-Pee-Chee Update Signatures

UNPRICED GRP A ODDS 1:58,240 UD SER.2 HOB
UNPRICED GRP B ODDS 1:4660 UD SER.2 HOB
GROUP C ODDS 1:1370 UD SER.2 HOB
OVERALL ODDS 1:1040 UD SER.2 HOB
USAB Andre Burakovsky C 6.00 15.00
USAD Anthony Duclair B 8.00 20.00
USAE Aaron Ekblad B 20.00 50.00
USAW Alexander Wennberg C 8.00 20.00
USBH Bo Horvat A 20.00 40.00
USCL Curtis Lazar C 12.00 30.00
USDN Darnell Nurse C 6.00 15.00
USDS Damon Severson C 6.00 15.00
USGR Griffin Reinhart C 5.00 12.00
USJD Jonathan Drouin B 30.00 60.00
USLD Leon Draisaitl B 20.00 50.00
USSR Sam Reinhart B 60.00 120.00

2015-16 O-Pee-Chee Update

U1-U10 VET ODDS 1:24H/R, 1:48B UD SER.2
U11-U50 ROOK.ODDS 1:6H/R, 1:12B UD SER.2
U1 Ryan O'Reilly .75 2.00
U2 Dougie Hamilton .75 2.00
U3 Brandon Saad .75 2.00
U4 Patrick Sharp .75 2.00
U5 Mike Green .75 2.00
U6 Milan Lucic .60 1.50
U7 Phil Kessel 1.25 3.00
U8 Martin Jones .75 2.00
U9 Troy Brouwer .60 1.50
U10 T.J. Oshie 1.25 3.00
U11 Connor McDavid 10.00 25.00
U12 Nikolaj Ehlers 2.00 5.00
U13 Connor Brickley .75 2.00
U14 Anton Slepyshev .75 2.00
U15 Dylan DeMelo .75 2.00
U16 Jake Virtanen 1.25 3.00
U17 Matt O'Connor .75 2.00
U18 Colton Parayko 1.25 3.00
U19 Ben Hutton 1.00 2.50
U20 Dylan Larkin 3.00 8.00
U21 Colin Miller .75 2.00
U22 Joel Edmundson .75 2.00
U23 Sergei Plotnikov .75 2.00
U24 Robby Fabbri 1.25 3.00
U25 Brock McGinn 1.00 2.50
U26 Mike Condon 1.00 2.50
U27 Vincent Hinostroza .60 1.50
U28 Sergei Kalinin .75 2.00
U29 Nicolas Petan 1.00 2.50
U30 Mattias Janmark 1.00 2.50
U31 Chris Wideman 1.00 2.50
U32 Jared McCann 1.00 2.50
U33 Joonas Kemppainen .75 2.00
U34 Tyler Randell 1.00 2.50
U35 Max Domi 2.00 5.00
U36 Jordan Weal 1.00 2.50
U37 Andreas Athanasiou 2.50 6.00
U38 Chandler Stephenson 1.00 2.50
U39 Brendan Gaunce 1.25 3.00
U40 Daniel Sprong 2.00 5.00
U41 Joonas Donskoi 1.00 2.50
U42 Linus Ullmark 1.25 3.00
U43 Derek Forbort .75 2.00
U44 Radek Faksa 1.00 2.50
U45 Artemi Panarin 3.00 8.00
U46 Noah Hanifin 1.25 3.00
U47 Connor Hellebuyck 2.50 6.00
U48 Nikolay Goldobin 1.00 2.50
U49 Mikko Rantanen 2.00 5.00
U50 Jack Eichel 4.00 10.00

2015-16 O-Pee-Chee Update Rainbow Foil

*RAINBOW: .5X TO 1.2X BASIC INSERTS
U1-U10 VET ODDS 1:120H/R, 1:240B UD SER.2
U11-U50 ROOK.ODDS 1:30H/R, 1:60B UD SER.2
U11 Connor McDavid 20.00 50.00

2015-16 O-Pee-Chee Update Rainbow Foil Black

*BLACK VETS/100: 1.5X TO 4X BASIC INSERTS
*BLACK ROOK/100: 1.2X TO 3X BASIC INSERTS
RANDOM INSERTS IN PACKS
RANDOM INSERTS IN PACKS

U11 Connor McDavid	150.00	250.00
U45 Artemi Panarin	40.00	80.00
U50 Jack Eichel	60.00	120.00

2015-16 O-Pee-Chee Update Red

*RED: 2.5X TO 6X BASIC INSERTS

U11 Connor McDavid	60.00	120.00

2015-16 O-Pee-Chee Update Retro

*RETRO: .5X TO 1.2X BASIC INSERTS
U11-U50 ROOK.ODDS 1:17H/R, 1:34B UD SER.2

U11 Connor McDavid	10.00	25.00

2015-16 O-Pee-Chee Update Signatures

COMPLETE SET (17)
GROUP A ODDS 1:16,476
GROUP B ODDS 1:6,824
GROUP C ODDS 1:2,516
GROUP D ODDS 1:2,037
GROUP E ODDS 1:1,562
OVERALL STATED ODDS 1:576

USCS Carl Soderberg C	4.00	10.00
USDD Devan Dubnyk B	15.00	40.00
USDL David Legwand D	4.00	10.00
USEE Emerson Etem E	4.00	10.00
USGL Gabriel Landeskog C	5.00	12.00
USJQ Jonathan Quick B	30.00	80.00
USLA Dylan Larkin D	100.00	200.00
USMB Matt Beleskey C	6.00	15.00
USMD Matt Duchene C	10.00	25.00
USMF Matt Fraser E	4.00	10.00
USNG Nikolay Goldobin C	5.00	12.00
USOM Olli Maatta A	20.00	50.00
USRR Rickard Rakell A	8.00	20.00
USRS Ryan Spooner D	4.00	10.00
USSR Sam Reinhart D	5.00	12.00
USSU Ryan Suter B	10.00	25.00
USVT Vincent Trocheck E	4.00	10.00

1976 Old Timers

This 18-card set of indeterminate origin measures approximately 2 1/2" by 3 5/8" and features black-and-white player photos in a white border. Members of the Red Wings, Maple Leafs and Blackhawks are pictured. The backs are blank. The cards are unnumbered and checklisted below in alphabetical order.

COMPLETE SET (18)	30.00	60.00
1 Gerry Abel	1.25	2.50
2 Sid Abel	4.00	8.00
3 Doug Barkley	1.25	2.50
4 Joe Carveth	1.25	2.50
5 Billy Dea	1.25	2.50
6 Alex Delvecchio	7.50	15.00
7 Bill Gadsby	1.25	2.50
8 Hal Jackson	1.25	2.50
9 Joe Klukay	1.25	2.50
10 Ted Lindsay	7.50	15.00
11 Jim Orlando	1.25	2.50
12 Marty Pavlich	1.25	2.50
13 Jim Peters	1.25	2.50
14 Marcel Pronovost	1.25	2.50
15 Marc Reaume	1.25	2.50
16 Leo Reise Jr.	1.25	2.50
17 Glen Skov	1.25	2.50
18 Jack Stewart	1.25	2.50

1999-00 Oscar Mayer Lunchables

These cards were featured on the backs of Oscar Mayer Lunchables packages. Each package contained both a 3 x 5 player card and a postcard size artist rendition of the player as a comic book superhero. The inside of each package contained a checklist of the set, player stats, and one part of the twelve part comic series.

COMPLETE SET (12)	6.00	15.00
1 Ray Bourque	.60	1.50
2 Pavel Bure	.75	2.00
3 Dominik Hasek	.60	1.50
4 Jaromir Jagr	1.00	2.50
5 Curtis Joseph	.40	1.00
6 Paul Kariya	1.25	3.00
7 Saku Koivu	.30	.75
8 Eric Lindros	1.00	2.50
9 Al MacInnis	.20	.50
10 Mark Messier	.40	1.00
11 Mats Sundin	.40	1.00
12 Alexei Yashin	.25	.60

1997-98 Pacific

The 1997-98 inaugural issue of the Pacific Crown Collection NHL Hockey cards was issued in one series totaling 350 cards and was distributed in eight-card packs. The fronts feature color action player photos with gold foil highlights. The backs carry player information. Pacific chose not to print a card #66, as a tribute to Mario Lemieux

COMPLETE SET (350)	20.00	40.00
1 Ray Bourque	.15	.40
2 Brian Leetch	.10	.25
3 Claude Lemieux	.07	.20
4 Mike Modano	.15	.40
5 Zigmund Palffy	.10	.25
6 Nikolai Khabibulin	.10	.25
7 Chris Chelios	.10	.25
8 Teemu Selanne	.20	.50
9 Paul Kariya	.12	.30
10 John LeClair	.10	.25
11 Mark Messier	.15	.40
12 Jarome Iginla	.10	.25
13 Petr Nedved	.10	.25
14 Brendan Shanahan	.12	.30
15 Dino Ciccarelli	.10	.25
16 Brett Hull	.12	.30
17 Wendel Clark	.10	.25
18 Peter Bondra	.07	.20
19 Steve Yzerman	.20	.50
20 Ed Belfour	.10	.25
21 Peter Forsberg	.12	.30
22 Mike Gartner	.10	.25
23 Jim Carey	.05	.15
24 Mike Vernon	.07	.20
25 Vincent Damphousse	.07	.20
26 Adam Graves	.05	.15
27 Ron Hextall	.10	.25
28 Keith Tkachuk	.10	.25
29 Felix Potvin	.10	.25
30 Martin Brodeur	.20	.50
31 Rod Brind'Amour	.10	.25
32 Pierre Turgeon	.10	.25
33 Patrick Roy	.25	.60
34 John Vanbiesbrouck	.10	.25
35 Andy Moog	.10	.25
36 Sergei Berezin	.07	.20
37 Adam Oates	.10	.25
38 Joe Sakic	.15	.40
39 Dominik Hasek	.15	.40
40 Patrick Lalime	.07	.20
41 Bobby Dollas	.05	.15
42 Kyle McLaren	.05	.15
43 Wayne Primeau	.07	.20
44 Stephane Richer	.05	.15
45 Theo Fleury	.12	.30
46 Kevin Miller	.05	.15
47 Adam Deadmarsh	.05	.15
48 Darryl Sydor	.05	.15
49 Igor Larionov	.05	.15
50 Radek Dvorak	.07	.20
51 Andrei Kovalenko	.05	.15
52 Keith Primeau	.07	.20
53 Ray Ferraro	.05	.15
54 David Wilkie	.05	.15
55 Bobby Holik	.05	.15
56 Tommy Salo	.05	.15
57 Jeff Beukeboom	.07	.20
58 Daniel Alfredsson	.10	.25
59 Mikael Renberg	.07	.20
60 Norm Maciver	.05	.15
61 Darius Kasparaitis	.07	.20
62 Geoff Courtnall	.05	.15
63 Jeff Friesen	.07	.20
64 Brian Bradley	.05	.15
65 Tie Domi	.10	.25
67 Martin Gelinas	.05	.15
68 Jaromir Jagr	.25	.60
69 Steve Konowalchuk	.07	.20
70 Brian Bellows	.07	.20
71 Jozef Stumpel	.07	.20
72 Darryl Shannon	.05	.15
73 Todd Simpson	.07	.20
74 Ulf Dahlen	.05	.15
75 Sandis Ozolinsh	.07	.20
76 Sergei Zubov	.07	.20
77 Paul Coffey	.10	.25
78 Nicklas Lidstrom	.10	.25
79 Jason Arnott	.07	.20
80 Ray Sheppard	.07	.20
81 Sean Burke	.05	.15
82 Vladimir Tsyplakov	.07	.20
83 Darcy Tucker	.10	.25
84 Dave Andreychuk	.10	.25
85 Scott Lachance	.07	.20
86 Niklas Sundstrom	.07	.20
87 Ron Tugnutt	.10	.25
88 Eric Lindros	.15	.40
89 Alexander Mogilny	.07	.20
90 Kris King	.05	.15
91 Sergei Fedorov	.15	.40
92 Ed Olczyk	.05	.15
93 Doug Gilmour	.12	.30
94 Ryan Smyth	.07	.20
95 Scott Pellerin	.05	.15
96 Pavel Bure	.12	.30
97 Jeremy Roenick	.12	.30
98 Todd Gill	.07	.20
99 Wayne Gretzky	.50	1.25
100 Roman Hamrlik	.07	.20
101 Rob Zettler	.05	.15
102 Sergei Nemchinov	.05	.15
103 Sergei Gonchar	.05	.15
104 Steve Rucchin	.07	.20
105 Landon Wilson	.05	.15
106 Anatoli Semenov	.05	.15
107 Corey Millen	.05	.15
108 Eric Daze	.05	.15
109 Mike Ricci	.07	.20
110 Jamie Langenbrunner	.07	.20
111 Slava Fetisov	.05	.15
112 Rem Murray	.05	.15
113 Tom Fitzgerald	.05	.15
114 Robert Kron	.05	.15
115 Kevin Stevens	.05	.15
116 Valeri Bure	.05	.15
117 Bill Guerin	.10	.25
118 Bryan McCabe	.05	.15
119 Alexei Kovalev	.05	.15
120 Alexei Yashin	.07	.20
121 Eric Desjardins	.05	.15
122 Teppo Numminen	.07	.20
123 Ron Francis	.12	.30
124 Chris Pronger	.07	.20
125 Viktor Kozlov	.07	.20
126 Corey Schwab	.07	.20
127 Fredrik Modin	.07	.20
128 Markus Naslund	.07	.20
129 Dale Hunter	.07	.20
130 Warren Rychel	.07	.20
131 Anson Carter	.05	.15
132 Miroslav Satan	.05	.15
133 Trevor Kidd	.05	.15
134 Sergei Krivokrasov	.05	.15
135 Adam Foote	.05	.15
136 Brent Gilchrist	.10	.25
137 Chris Osgood	.10	.25
138 Doug Weight	.10	.25
139 Martin Straka	.05	.15
140 Jeff O'Neill	.07	.20
141 Byron Dafoe	.05	.15
142 Brian Savage	.05	.15
143 Lyle Odelein	.05	.15
144 Niklas Andersson	.05	.15
145 Luc Robitaille	.10	.25
146 Damian Rhodes	.07	.20
147 Garth Snow	.07	.20
148 Craig Janney	.05	.15
149 Fredrik Olausson	.07	.20
150 Joe Murphy	.07	.20
151 Owen Nolan	.10	.25
152 Shawn Burr	.05	.15
153 Dimitri Yushkevich	.05	.15
154 Trevor Linden	.07	.20
155 Joe Juneau	.07	.20
156 Sean Pronger	.05	.15
157 Jeff Odgers	.05	.15
158 Brian Holzinger	.07	.20
159 Dave Gagner	.05	.15
160 Jeff Hackett	.05	.15
161 Eric Lacroix	.05	.15
162 Pat Verbeek	.07	.20
163 Darren McCarty	.07	.20
164 Mike Grier	.07	.20
165 Per Gustafsson	.07	.20
166 Andrew Cassels	.05	.15
167 Vitali Yachmenev	.07	.20
168 Jocelyn Thibault	.05	.15
169 John MacLean	.05	.15
170 Travis Green	.07	.20
171 Ulf Samuelsson	.10	.25
172 Bruce Gardiner RC	.07	.20
173 Janne Niinimaa	.07	.20
174 Jim Johnson	.07	.20
175 Stu Barnes	.05	.15
176 Harry York	.07	.20
177 Al Iafrate	.07	.20
178 Paul Ysebaert	.07	.20
179 Mathieu Schneider	.07	.20
180 Corey Hirsch	.07	.20
181 Mark Tinordi	.07	.20
182 Kevin Todd	.05	.15
183 Tim Sweeney	.05	.15
184 Donald Audette	.07	.20
185 Jonas Hoglund	.07	.20
186 Brent Sutter	.05	.15
187 Scott Young	.07	.20
188 Arturs Irbe	.07	.20
189 Vladimir Konstantinov	.05	.15
190 Mats Lindgren	.05	.15
191 David Nemirovsky	.05	.15
192 Sami Kapanen	.07	.20
193 Rob Blake	.10	.25
194 Sebastien Bordeleau	.07	.20
195 Steve Thomas	.07	.20
196 Bryan Smolinski	.07	.20
197 Mike Richter	.10	.25
198 Randy Cunneyworth	.05	.15
199 Pat Falloon	.05	.15
200 Cliff Ronning	.05	.15
201 Ken Wregget	.05	.15
202 Al MacInnis	.10	.25
203 Tony Granato	.07	.20
204 Rob Zamuner	.05	.15
205 Mats Sundin	.10	.25
206 Mike Ridley	.05	.15
207 Sylvain Cote	.05	.15
208 Joe Sacco	.07	.20
209 Ted Donato	.05	.15
210 Matthew Barnaby	.07	.20
211 Cory Stillman	.07	.20
212 Gary Suter	.05	.15
213 Valeri Kamensky	.07	.20
214 Derian Hatcher	.07	.20
215 Jamie Pushor	.05	.15
216 Mariusz Czerkawski	.05	.15
217 Kirk Muller	.05	.15
218 Kevin Dineen	.07	.20
219 Dimitri Khristich	.07	.20
220 Martin Rucinsky	.07	.20
221 Denis Pederson	.05	.15
222 Bryan Berard	.05	.15
223 Alexander Karpovtsev	.05	.15
224 Shawn McEachern	.05	.15
225 Dale Hawerchuk	.12	.30
226 Bob Corkum	.07	.20
227 Kevin Hatcher	.05	.15
228 Grant Fuhr	.10	.25
229 Darren Turcotte	.07	.20
230 Patrick Poulin	.05	.15
231 Jamie Macoun	.05	.15
232 Jyrki Lumme	.07	.20
233 Bill Ranford	.07	.20
234 Dmitri Mironov	.07	.20
235 Mattias Timander	.07	.20
236 Alexei Zhitnik	.05	.15
237 Hnat Domenichelli	.07	.20
238 Murray Craven	.05	.15
239 Mike Keane	.05	.15
240 Benoit Hogue	.07	.20
241 Martin Lapointe	.05	.15
242 Curtis Joseph	.10	.25
243 Robert Svehla	.07	.20
244 Glen Wesley	.05	.15
245 Stephane Fiset	.07	.20
246 Shayne Corson	.05	.15
247 Scott Niedermayer	.10	.25
248 Steve Webb RC	.10	.25
249 Esa Tikkanen	.05	.15
250 Alexandre Daigle	.05	.15
251 Trent Klatt	.07	.20
252 Oleg Tverdovsky	.07	.20
253 Dave Roche	.05	.15
254 Tony Twist	.07	.20
255 Bernie Nicholls	.07	.20
256 Rick Tabaracci	.07	.20
257 Todd Warriner	.07	.20
258 Kirk McLean	.07	.20
259 Phil Housley	.07	.20
260 Guy Hebert	.07	.20
261 Steve Heinze	.05	.15
262 Derek Plante	.07	.20
263 German Titov	.05	.15
264 Tony Amonte	.07	.20
265 Uwe Krupp	.05	.15
266 Joe Nieuwendyk	.10	.25
267 Vyacheslav Kozlov	.07	.20
268 Kelly Buchberger	.07	.20
269 Rob Niedermayer	.05	.15
270 Geoff Sanderson	.07	.20
271 Jan Vopat	.05	.15
272 Saku Koivu	.10	.25
273 Scott Stevens	.10	.25
274 Eric Fichaud	.07	.20
275 Russ Courtnall	.05	.15
276 Wade Redden	.05	.15
277 Petr Svoboda	.05	.15
278 Andreas Dackell	.07	.20
279 Jason Woolley	.07	.20
280 Stephane Matteau	.05	.15
281 Stephen Guolla RC	.05	.15
282 John Cullen	.05	.15
283 Steve Sullivan	.07	.20
284 Bret Hedican	.05	.15
285 Michal Pivonka	.05	.15
286 Darren Van Impe	.07	.20
287 Rob DiMaio	.05	.15
288 Garry Galley	.05	.15
289 Kent Manderville	.05	.15
290 Bob Probert	.05	.15
291 Keith Jones	.05	.15
292 Guy Carbonneau	.10	.25
293 Tomas Sandstrom	.05	.15
294 Daniel McGillis RC	.07	.20
295 Brian Skrudland	.05	.15
296 Stu Grimson	.07	.20
297 Doug Zmolek	.05	.15
298 Mark Recchi	.12	.30
299 Valeri Zelepukin	.07	.20
300 Derek Armstrong	.05	.15
301 Eric Cairns RC	.10	.25
302 Steve Duchesne	.05	.15
303 Dainius Zubrus	.07	.20
304 Deron Quint	.05	.15
305 Joe Dziedzic	.05	.15
306 Mike Peluso	.05	.15
307 Andrei Nazarov	.05	.15
308 Chris Gratton	.05	.15
309 Mike Craig	.05	.15
310 Lonny Bohonos	.07	.20
311 Rick Tocchet	.05	.15
312 Ted Drury	.07	.20
313 Jean-Yves Roy	.05	.15
314 Jason Dawe	.07	.20
315 Jamie Allison	.07	.20
316 Alexei Zhamnov	.05	.15
317 Aaron Miller	.05	.15
318 Todd Krygier	.05	.15
319 Tomas Holmstrom	.05	.15
320 Todd Marchant	.07	.20
321 Scott Mellanby	.07	.20
322 Marek Malik	.05	.15
323 Dan Bylsma	.07	.20
324 Stephane Quintal	.07	.20
325 Ken Daneyko	.07	.20
326 Robert Reichel	.07	.20
327 Daniel Goneau	.07	.20
328 Sergei Zholtok	.07	.20
329 Kjell Samuelsson	.05	.15
330 Shane Doan	.07	.20
331 Radek Bonk	.05	.15
332 Jim Campbell	.05	.15
333 Marty McSorley	.05	.15
334 Brantt Myhres	.05	.15
335 Mike Johnson RC	.07	.20
336 Mike Sillinger	.05	.15
337 Kelly Hrudey	.07	.20
338 Joel Bouchard	.05	.15
339 Brian Noonan	.05	.15
340 Dean Chynoweth	.07	.20
341 Michael Peca	.07	.20
342 Jeff Toms RC	.05	.15
343 Denis Savard	.05	.15
344 Stephane Yelle	.05	.15
345 Grant Ledyard	.05	.15
346 Ronnie Stern	.05	.15
347 Petr Klima	.05	.15
348 Johan Garpenlov	.05	.15
349 Nelson Emerson	.07	.20
350 Matt Johnson	.05	.15
351 Ken Belanger RC	.10	.25
CM1 Mark Messier	.15	.40

1997-98 Pacific Copper

*COPPER: 2.5X TO 6X BASIC CARDS
COPPER STATED ODDS 1:1 HOBBY

1997-98 Pacific Emerald Green

*GREEN: 3X TO 8X BASIC CARDS
GREEN ODDS 1:1 CANADIAN ONLY

1997-98 Pacific Ice Blue

ICE BLUE/67: 20X TO 50X BASIC CARDS
ICE BLUE/67* STATED ODDS 1:73

1997-98 Pacific Red

*RED: 5X TO 12X BASIC CARDS
STATED ODDS 1:1 TREAT PACKS

1997-98 Pacific Silver

*SILVER: 2.5X TO 6X BASIC CARDS
SILVER ODDS 1:1 RETAIL PACKS

1997-98 Pacific Card-Supials

Randomly inserted at a rate of 1:37 packs, this 20-card set features color action player photos of some of the great players in Hockey. A smaller card is made to pair with the regular size card of the same player. The backs carry a slot for insertion of the small card.

COMPLETE SET (40)	40.00	80.00
*MINIS: .25X TO .6X LARGE		
1 Paul Kariya	1.50	4.00
2 Teemu Selanne	1.50	4.00
3 Jarome Iginla	2.00	5.00
4 Peter Forsberg	2.50	6.00
5 Mike Modano	2.00	5.00
6 Sergei Fedorov	2.00	5.00
7 Vladimir Konstantinov	1.00	2.50
8 Steve Yzerman	4.00	10.00
9 John Vanbiesbrouck	1.00	2.50
10 Martin Brodeur	3.00	8.00
11 Doug Gilmour	1.00	2.50
12 Wayne Gretzky	6.00	15.00
13 Mark Messier	1.50	4.00
14 John LeClair	1.00	2.50
15 Eric Lindros	1.50	4.00
16 Jeremy Roenick	1.50	4.00
17 Keith Tkachuk	1.00	2.50
18 Brett Hull	1.50	4.00
19 Felix Potvin	1.50	4.00
20 Pavel Bure	1.50	4.00

1997-98 Pacific Cramer's Choice

Randomly inserted in packs at the rate of 1:721, this 10-card set features top NHL Hockey players as chosen by Pacific President and CEO, Michael Cramer. The fronts display a color action player cut-out on a pyramid die-cut shaped background.

COMPLETE SET (10)	40.00	100.00
1 Paul Kariya	5.00	12.00
2 Dominik Hasek	8.00	20.00
3 Jarome Iginla	5.00	12.00
4 Peter Forsberg	10.00	25.00
5 Patrick Roy	20.00	50.00
6 Steve Yzerman	20.00	50.00
7 Wayne Gretzky	25.00	60.00
8 Mark Messier	5.00	12.00
9 Eric Lindros	6.00	15.00
10 Jaromir Jagr	8.00	20.00

1997-98 Pacific Gold Crown Die-Cuts

COMPLETE SET (20)	30.00	80.00
STATED ODDS 1:37		
1 Paul Kariya	1.50	4.00
2 Teemu Selanne	1.25	3.00
3 Dominik Hasek	3.00	8.00
4 Michael Peca	.75	2.00
5 Jarome Iginla	1.50	4.00
6 Chris Chelios	.75	2.00
7 Peter Forsberg	2.00	5.00
8 Patrick Roy	8.00	20.00
9 Joe Sakic	3.00	8.00
10 Brendan Shanahan	1.50	4.00
11 Steve Yzerman	6.00	15.00
12 Ryan Smyth	.75	2.00
13 John Vanbiesbrouck	1.25	3.00
14 Martin Brodeur	4.00	10.00
15 Wayne Gretzky	8.00	20.00
16 Mark Messier	1.50	4.00
17 Eric Lindros	1.25	3.00
18 Jaromir Jagr	2.00	5.00
19 Brett Hull	1.25	3.00
20 Pavel Bure	1.50	4.00

1997-98 Pacific In The Cage Laser Cuts

Randomly inserted in packs at the rate of 1:145, this 20-card set honors top goalies of the NHL. The laser-cut fronts feature color player photos with the net as the background. The backs carry player information.

COMPLETE SET (20)	40.00	100.00
1 Guy Hebert	2.00	5.00
2 Dominik Hasek	5.00	12.00
3 Trevor Kidd	2.00	5.00
4 Jeff Hackett	2.00	5.00
5 Patrick Roy	8.00	20.00
6 Andy Moog	2.00	5.00
7 Chris Osgood	2.00	5.00
8 Mike Vernon	2.00	5.00
9 Curtis Joseph	4.00	10.00
10 John Vanbiesbrouck	4.00	10.00
11 Jocelyn Thibault	2.00	5.00
12 Martin Brodeur	6.00	15.00
13 Mike Richter	4.00	10.00
14 Ron Hextall	4.00	10.00
15 Garth Snow	2.00	5.00
16 Nikolai Khabibulin	4.00	10.00
17 Patrick Lalime	2.00	5.00
18 Grant Fuhr	4.00	10.00
19 Ed Belfour	4.00	10.00
20 Felix Potvin	4.00	10.00

1997-98 Pacific Slap Shots Die-Cuts

Randomly inserted in packs at the rate of 1:73, this 36-card set features color player photos of top NHL players. Three cards of players from the same team were made to fit on top of each other to form a hockey stick on the cards' right sides with the words, "Pacific Trading Cards," printed on the middle section of the stick. The cards that go together have the same number with the letters, "A, B, or C" after the number to indicate where the cards should be placed to form the giant hockey stick.

COMPLETE SET (36)	50.00	125.00
1A Paul Kariya	2.00	5.00
1B Jari Kurri	1.50	4.00
1C Teemu Selanne	1.50	4.00
2A Peter Forsberg	3.00	8.00
2B Joe Sakic	4.00	10.00
2C Claude Lemieux	1.00	2.50
3A Brendan Shanahan	2.00	5.00
3B Sergei Fedorov	2.00	5.00
3C Steve Yzerman	6.00	15.00
4A Mark Recchi	1.00	2.50
4B Vincent Damphousse	1.00	2.50
4C Stephane Richer	1.00	2.50
5A Wayne Gretzky	10.00	25.00
5B Mark Messier	2.00	5.00
5C Brian Leetch	1.50	4.00
6A Rod Brind'Amour	1.00	2.50
6B Eric Lindros	2.00	5.00
6C John LeClair	1.00	2.50
7A Keith Tkachuk	1.00	2.50
7B Jeremy Roenick	2.00	5.00
7C Mike Gartner	1.00	2.50
8A Petr Nedved	1.00	2.50
8B Ron Francis	1.00	2.50
8C Jaromir Jagr	3.00	8.00
9A Geoff Courtnall	1.00	2.50
9B Pierre Turgeon	1.00	2.50
9C Brett Hull	2.00	5.00
10A Wendel Clark	3.00	8.00
10B Mats Sundin	1.50	4.00
10C Sergei Berezin	1.00	2.50
11A Pavel Bure	2.50	6.00
11B Trevor Linden	1.50	4.00
11C Alexander Mogilny	1.00	2.50
12A Joe Juneau	1.00	2.50
12B Adam Oates	1.00	2.50
12C Peter Bondra	1.00	2.50

1997-98 Pacific Team Checklists

Randomly inserted in packs at the rate of 1:73, this 26-card set features color player photos with the player's team logo in a circle next to the player's image. The backs carry the checklist of the team the player plays on.

COMPLETE SET (26)	40.00	100.00
1 Teemu Selanne	2.00	5.00
2 Ray Bourque	2.00	5.00
3 Dominik Hasek	4.00	8.00
4 Jarome Iginla	2.50	6.00
5 Keith Primeau	.75	2.00
6 Chris Chelios	1.25	3.00
7 Patrick Roy	6.00	15.00
8 Mike Modano	2.00	5.00
9 Steve Yzerman	5.00	12.00
10 Curtis Joseph	1.25	3.00
11 John Vanbiesbrouck	1.25	3.00
12 Rob Blake	.75	2.00
13 Stephane Richer	.75	2.00
14 Martin Brodeur	4.00	10.00
15 Zigmund Palffy	1.25	3.00
16 Wayne Gretzky	10.00	25.00
17 Alexandre Daigle	.75	2.00
18 Eric Lindros	1.25	3.00
19 Jeremy Roenick	2.00	5.00
20 Jaromir Jagr	3.00	8.00
21 Brett Hull	2.00	5.00
22 Owen Nolan	.75	2.00
23 Dino Ciccarelli	.75	2.00
24 Felix Potvin	1.25	3.00
25 Pavel Bure	2.00	5.00
26 Peter Bondra	.75	2.00

1998-99 Pacific

The 1998-99 Pacific set was issued in one series totaling 450 cards and was distributed in 10-card packs. The fronts features borderless action color player photos. The backs carry player information and career statistics.

COMPLETE SET (450)	25.00	40.00
1 Damian Rhodes	.05	.15
2 Mattias Ohlund	.05	.15
3 Craig Ludwig	.05	.15
4 Rob Blake	.15	.40
5 Nicklas Lidstrom	.20	.50
6 Calle Johansson	.05	.15
7 Chris Chelios	.20	.50
8 Teemu Selanne	.20	.50
9 Paul Kariya	.20	.50
10 Pavel Bure	.20	.50
11 Mark Messier	.20	.50
12 Peter Bondra	.15	.40
13 Mats Sundin	.20	.50
14 Brendan Shanahan	.20	.50
15 Jamie Langenbrunner	.05	.15
16 Brett Hull	.25	.60
17 Rod Brind'Amour	.15	.40
18 Adam Deadmarsh	.05	.15
19 Steve Yzerman	1.00	2.50
20 Ed Belfour	.20	.50
21 Peter Forsberg	.50	1.25
22 Dino Ciccarelli	.05	.15
23 Brian Bellows	.05	.15
24 Janne Niinimaa	.05	.15
25 Joe Nieuwendyk	.15	.40
26 Patrik Elias	.15	.40
27 Michael Peca	.05	.15
28 Tie Domi	.15	.40
29 Felix Potvin	.20	.50
30 Martin Brodeur	.50	1.25
31 Grant Fuhr	.15	.40
32 Trevor Linden	.05	.15
33 Patrick Roy	1.00	2.50
34 John Vanbiesbrouck	.15	.40
35 Tom Barrasso	.15	.40
36 Matthew Barnaby	.05	.15
37 Olaf Kolzig	.15	.40
38 Pavol Demitra	.15	.40
39 Dominik Hasek	.40	1.00
40 Chris Terreri	.15	.40
41 Jason Allison	.05	.15
42 Richard Smehlik	.05	.15
43 Frank Banham	.05	.15
44 Chris Pronger	.15	.40
45 Matt Cullen	.05	.15
46 Mike Rucinski RC	.05	.15
47 Mike Crowley RC	.15	.40
48 Scott Young	.05	.15
49 Brian Savage	.05	.15
50 Travis Green	.05	.15
51 John LeClair	.20	.50
52 Adam Foote	.05	.15
53 Derek Morris	.05	.15
54 Guy Hebert	.15	.40
55 Chris Gratton	.15	.40
56 Sergei Zubov	.05	.15
57 Dave Karpa	.05	.15
58 Sergei Varlamov	.05	.15
59 Josef Marha	.05	.15
60 Jason Marshall	.05	.15
61 Jeff Nielsen RC	.05	.15
62 Steve Rucchin	.05	.15
63 Tomas Sandstrom	.05	.15
64 Jason Bonsignore	.05	.15
65 Mikhail Shtalenkov	.05	.15
67 Tom Askey RC	.05	.15
68 Jaromir Jagr	.30	.75
69 Per Axelsson	.05	.15
70 Ken Baumgartner	.05	.15
71 Jiri Slegr	.05	.15
72 Mathieu Schneider	.05	.15
73 Anson Carter	.15	.40
74 Byron Dafoe	.15	.40
75 Rob DiMaio	.05	.15
76 Ted Donato	.05	.15
77 Ray Bourque	.30	.75
78 Dave Ellett	.05	.15
79 Steve Heinze	.05	.15
80 Geoff Sanderson	.15	.40
81 Miroslav Satan	.15	.40
82 Martin Straka	.05	.15
83 Dimitri Khristich	.05	.15
84 Grant Ledyard	.05	.15
85 Cameron Mann	.05	.15
86 Kyle McLaren	.05	.15
87 Sergei Samsonov	.15	.40
88 Eric Lindros	.20	.50
89 Alexander Mogilny	.15	.40
90 Joe Juneau	.05	.15
91 Sergei Fedorov	.30	.75
92 Rick Tocchet	.05	.15
93 Doug Gilmour	.15	.40
94 Ryan Smyth	.05	.15
95 Alexei Morozov	.05	.15
96 Phil Housley	.05	.15
97 Jeremy Roenick	.25	.60
98 Jay More	.05	.15
99 Wayne Gretzky	1.25	3.00
100 Robbie Tallas	.05	.15
101 Tim Taylor	.05	.15
102 Joe Thornton	.30	.75
103 Donald Audette	.05	.15
104 Curtis Brown	.05	.15
105 Michal Grosek	.05	.15
106 Brian Holzinger	.05	.15
107 Derek Plante	.05	.15
108 Rob Ray	.05	.15
109 Darryl Shannon	.05	.15
110 Steve Shields	.15	.40
111 Vaclav Varada	.05	.15
112 Dixon Ward	.05	.15
113 Jason Woolley	.05	.15
114 Alexei Zhitnik	.05	.15
115 Andrew Cassels	.05	.15
116 Hnat Domenichelli	.05	.15
117 Theo Fleury	.05	.15
118 Denis Gauthier	.05	.15
119 Cale Hulse	.05	.15
120 Jarome Iginla	.25	.60
121 Marty McInnis	.05	.15
122 Tyler Moss	.05	.15
123 Michael Nylander	.05	.15
124 Dwayne Roloson	.05	.15
125 Cory Stillman	.05	.15
126 Rick Tabaracci	.05	.15
127 German Titov	.05	.15
128 Jason Wiemer	.05	.15
129 Steve Chiasson	.05	.15
130 Kevin Dineen	.05	.15
131 Nelson Emerson	.05	.15
132 Martin Gelinas	.05	.15
133 Stu Grimson	.05	.15
134 Sami Kapanen	.05	.15
135 Trevor Kidd	.15	.40
136 Robert Kron	.05	.15
137 Jeff O'Neill	.05	.15
138 Keith Primeau	.05	.15
139 Paul Ranheim	.05	.15
140 Gary Roberts	.05	.15
141 Glen Wesley	.05	.15
142 Tony Amonte	.15	.40
143 Eric Daze	.15	.40
144 Jeff Hackett	.15	.40
145 Greg Johnson	.05	.15
146 Chad Kilger	.05	.15
147 Sergei Krivokrasov	.05	.15
148 Christian LaFlamme	.05	.15
149 Jean-Yves Leroux	.05	.15
150 Dmitri Nabokov	.05	.15
151 Jeff Shantz	.05	.15
152 Gary Suter	.05	.15
153 Eric Weinrich	.05	.15
154 Todd White RC	.05	.1
155 Alexei Zhamnov	.05	.1
156 Wade Belak	.05	.1
157 Craig Billington	.05	.1
158 Rene Corbet	.05	.1
159 Shean Donovan	.05	.1
160 Valeri Kamensky	.05	.1
161 Uwe Krupp	.05	.1
162 Jari Kurri	.15	.4
163 Eric Lacroix	.05	.1
164 Claude Lemieux	.05	.1
165 Eric Messier	.05	.1
166 Jeff Odgers	.05	.1
167 Sandis Ozolinsh	.05	.1
168 Warren Rychel	.05	.1
169 Joe Sakic	.40	1.0
170 Stephane Yelle	.05	.1
171 Greg Adams	.05	.1
172 Jason Botterill	.05	.1
173 Guy Carbonneau	.05	.1
174 Shawn Chambers	.05	.1
175 Manny Fernandez	.05	.1
176 Derian Hatcher	.05	.1
177 Benoit Hogue	.05	.1
178 Mike Keane	.05	.1
179 Jere Lehtinen	.05	.1
180 Juha Lind	.05	.1
181 Mike Modano	.30	.7
182 Brian Skrudland	.05	.1
183 Darryl Sydor	.05	.1
184 Roman Turek	.15	.4
185 Pat Verbeek	.05	.1
186 Jamie Wright	.05	.1
187 Doug Brown	.05	.1
188 Kris Draper	.05	.1
189 Anders Eriksson	.05	.1
190 Slava Fetisov	.05	.1
191 Brent Gilchrist	.05	.1
192 Kevin Hodson	.05	.1
193 Tomas Holmstrom	.05	.1
194 Michael Knuble	.15	.4
195 Joey Kocur	.05	.1
196 Vyacheslav Kozlov	.15	.4
197 Martin Lapointe	.05	.1
198 Igor Larionov	.05	.1
199 Kirk Maltby	.05	.1
200 Norm Maracle RC	.30	.7
201 Darren McCarty	.05	.1
202 Dmitri Mironov	.05	.1
203 Larry Murphy	.15	.4
204 Chris Osgood	.15	.4
205 Kelly Buchberger	.05	.1
206 Bob Essensa	.15	.4
207 Scott Fraser	.05	.1
208 Mike Grier	.05	.1
209 Bill Guerin	.15	.4
210 Tony Hrkac	.05	.1
211 Curtis Joseph	.20	.5
212 Mats Lindgren	.05	.1
213 Todd Marchant	.05	.1
214 Dean McAmmond	.05	.1
215 Craig Millar	.05	.1
216 Boris Mironov	.05	.1
217 Doug Weight	.15	.4
218 Valeri Zelepukin	.05	.1
219 Roman Hamrlik	.05	.1
220 Radek Dvorak	.05	.1
221 Dave Gagner	.05	.1
222 Ed Jovanovski	.05	.1
223 Viktor Kozlov	.05	.1
224 Paul Laus	.05	.1
225 Kirk McLean	.05	.1
226 Scott Mellanby	.05	.1
227 Kirk Muller	.05	.1
228 Robert Svehla	.05	.1
229 Steve Washburn	.05	.1
230 Kevin Weekes	.15	.4
231 Ray Whitney	.05	.1
232 Peter Worrell RC	.25	.6
233 Russ Courtnall	.05	.1
234 Stephane Fiset	.15	.4
235 Garry Galley	.05	.1
236 Craig Johnson	.05	.1
237 Ian Laperriere	.05	.1
238 Donald MacLean	.05	.1
239 Steve McKenna	.05	.1
240 Sandy Moger	.05	.1
241 Glen Murray	.05	.1
242 Sean O'Donnell	.05	.1
243 Yanic Perreault	.05	.1
244 Luc Robitaille	.15	.4
245 Jamie Storr	.15	.4
246 Jozef Stumpel	.05	.1
247 Vladimir Tsyplakov	.05	.1
248 Benoit Brunet	.05	.1
249 Shayne Corson	.05	.1
250 Vincent Damphousse	.05	.1
251 Eric Houde RC	.05	.1
252 Saku Koivu	.20	.5
253 Vladimir Malakhov	.05	.1
254 Dave Manson	.05	.1
255 Andy Moog	.15	.4
256 Mark Recchi	.15	.4
257 Martin Rucinsky	.05	.1
258 Jocelyn Thibault	.15	.4
259 Mick Vukota	.05	.1
260 Dave Andreychuk	.15	.4
261 Jason Arnott	.05	.1
262 Mike Dunham	.15	.4
263 Bobby Holik	.05	.1
264 Randy McKay	.05	.1
265 Brendan Morrison	.15	.4
266 Scott Niedermayer	.05	.1
267 Lyle Odelein	.05	.1
268 Krzysztof Oliwa	.05	.1
269 Denis Pederson	.05	.1
270 Brian Rolston	.05	.1
271 Sheldon Souray RC	.30	.7
272 Scott Stevens	.05	.1
273 Petr Sykora	.05	.1
274 Steve Thomas	.05	.1
275 Bryan Berard	.15	.4
276 Zdeno Chara	.15	.4
277 Vladimir Chebaturkin RC	.05	.1
278 Tom Chorske	.05	.1
279 Mariusz Czerkawski	.05	.1
280 Jason Dawe	.05	.1
281 Wade Flaherty	.15	.4
282 Kenny Jonsson	.05	.1
283 Sergei Nemchinov	.05	.1
284 Zigmund Palffy	.15	.4
285 Rich Pilon	.05	.1
286 Robert Reichel	.05	.1
287 Joe Sacco	.05	.1
288 Tommy Salo	.15	.4
289 Bryan Smolinski	.05	.1
290 Jeff Beukeboom	.05	.1
291 Dan Cloutier	.15	.4

2 Bruce Driver .05 .15
3 Adam Graves .05 .15
4 Alexei Kovalev .15 .40
5 Pat LaFontaine .20 .50
6 Darren Langdon .05 .15
7 Brian Leetch .20 .50
8 Mike Richter .20 .50
9 Ulf Samuelsson .05 .15
0 Marc Savard .05 .15
1 Kevin Stevens .05 .15
2 Niklas Sundstrom .05 .15
3 Tim Sweeney .05 .15
4 Vladimir Vorobiev .05 .15
5 Daniel Alfredsson .15 .40
6 Magnus Arvedson .05 .15
7 Radek Bonk .05 .15
8 Andreas Dackell .05 .15
9 Bruce Gardiner .05 .15
0 Igor Kravchuk .05 .15
1 Denny Lambert .05 .15
2 Janne Laukkanen .05 .15
3 Shawn McEachern .05 .15
4 Chris Phillips .05 .15
5 Wade Redden .05 .15
6 Ron Tugnutt .15 .40
7 Shaun Van Allen .05 .15
8 Alexei Yashin .05 .15
9 Jason York .05 .15
0 Sergei Zholtok .05 .15
1 Sean Burke .15 .40
2 Paul Coffey .20 .50
3 Alexandre Daigle .05 .15
4 Eric Desjardins .15 .40
5 Colin Forbes .05 .15
6 Ron Hextall .15 .40
7 Trent Klatt .05 .15
8 Dan McGillis .05 .15
9 Joel Otto .05 .15
0 Shjon Podein .05 .15
1 Mike Sillinger .05 .15
2 Chris Therien .05 .15
3 Dainius Zubrus .05 .15
4 Bob Corkum .05 .15
5 Jim Cummins .05 .15
6 Jason Doig .05 .15
7 Dallas Drake .05 .15
8 Mike Gartner .15 .40
9 Brad Isbister .05 .15
0 Craig Janney .05 .15
1 Nikolai Khabibulin .15 .40
2 Teppo Numminen .05 .15
3 Cliff Ronning .05 .15
4 Keith Tkachuk .20 .50
5 Oleg Tverdovsky .05 .15
6 Jim Waite .15 .40
7 Juha Ylonen .05 .15
8 Stu Barnes .05 .15
9 Rob Brown .05 .15
0 Robert Dome .05 .15
1 Ron Francis .15 .40
2 Kevin Hatcher .05 .15
3 Alex Hicks .05 .15
4 Darius Kasparaitis .05 .15
5 Robert Lang .05 .15
6 Fredrik Olausson .05 .15
7 Ed Olczyk .05 .15
8 Peter Skudra .05 .15
9 Chris Tamer .05 .15
0 Ken Wregget .05 .15
1 Blair Atcheynum .05 .15
2 Jim Campbell .05 .15
3 Kelly Chase .05 .15
4 Craig Conroy .05 .15
5 Geoff Courtnall .05 .15
6 Steve Duchesne .15 .40
7 Todd Gill .05 .15
8 Al MacInnis .15 .40
9 Jamie McLennan .05 .15
0 Scott Pellerin .05 .15
1 Pascal Rheaume .05 .15
2 Jamie Rivers .15 .40
3 Darren Turcotte .05 .15
4 Pierre Turgeon .15 .40
5 Tony Twist .05 .15
6 Terry Yake .05 .15
7 Richard Brennan .05 .15
8 Murray Craven .05 .15
9 Jeff Friesen .05 .15
0 Tony Granato .05 .15
1 Bill Houlder .05 .15
2 Kelly Hrudey .15 .40
3 Alexander Korolyuk .15 .40
4 John MacLean .05 .15
5 Bryan Marchment .05 .15
6 Patrick Marleau .12 .30
7 Stephane Matteau .05 .15
8 Marty McSorley .05 .15
9 Bernie Nicholls .05 .15
0 Owen Nolan .15 .40
1 Mike Ricci .15 .40
2 Marco Sturm .05 .15
3 Mike Vernon .15 .40
4 Andrei Zyuzin .05 .15
5 Mikael Andersson .05 .15
6 Zac Bierk RC .05 .15
7 Enrico Ciccone .05 .15
8 Louie DeBrusk .05 .15
9 Karl Dykhuis .05 .15
0 Daymond Langkow .05 .15
Mike McBain .05 .15
2 Sandy McCarthy .05 .15
3 Daren Puppa .15 .40
4 Mikael Renberg .15 .40
5 Stephane Richer .15 .40
6 Alexander Selivanov .05 .15
7 Darcy Tucker .05 .15
8 Paul Ysebaert .05 .15
9 Rob Zamuner .05 .15
0 Sergei Berezin .05 .15
Wendel Clark .05 .15
2 Sylvain Cote .05 .15
Mike Johnson .05 .15
Derek King .05 .15
Kris King .05 .15
Igor Korolev .05 .15
Daniil Markov RC .05 .15
Alyn McCauley .05 .15
Fredrik Modin .05 .15
Martin Prochazka .05 .15
Jason Smith .05 .15
Steve Sullivan .05 .15
Yannick Tremblay .05 .15
Todd Bertuzzi .20 .50
Donald Brashear .05 .15
Bret Hedican .05 .15
Arturs Irbe .15 .40
Jyrki Lumme .05 .15
Brad May .05 .15
430 Bryan McCabe .05 .15
431 Markus Naslund .20 .50
432 Brian Noonan .05 .15
433 Dave Scatchard .05 .15
434 Garth Snow .15 .40
435 Scott Walker RC .05 .15
436 Peter Zezel .05 .15
437 Craig Berube .05 .15
438 Jeff Brown .05 .15
439 Andrew Brunette .15 .40
440 Jan Bulis .05 .15
441 Sergei Gonchar .05 .15
442 Dale Hunter .15 .40
443 Steve Konowalchuk .05 .15
444 Kelly Miller .05 .15
445 Adam Oates .15 .40
446 Bill Ranford .15 .40
447 Jaroslav Svejkovsky .05 .15
448 Esa Tikkanen .05 .15
449 Mark Tinordi .05 .15
450 Brendan Witt .05 .15
451 Richard Zednik .05 .15
S181 Mike Modano SAMPLE .60 1.50

1998-99 Pacific Ice Blue

*VETERANS: 6X TO 15X BASIC CARDS
*ROOKIES: 1.2X TO 3X BASIC CARDS

1998-99 Pacific Red

*VETERANS: 3X TO 8X BASIC CARDS
*ROOKIES: 1.5X TO 4X BASIC CARDS

1998-99 Pacific Cramer's Choice

Randomly inserted in packs at the rate of 1:721, this 10-card set features action color photos of players picked by President/CEO Michael Cramer and printed on die-cut trophy cards.

COMPLETE SET (10) 100.00 200.00
1 Sergei Samsonov 4.00 10.00
2 Dominik Hasek 8.00 20.00
3 Peter Forsberg 12.50 30.00
4 Patrick Roy 20.00 50.00
5 Mike Modano 8.00 20.00
6 Martin Brodeur 12.50 30.00
7 Wayne Gretzky 25.00 60.00
8 Eric Lindros 5.00 12.00
9 Jaromir Jagr 8.00 20.00
10 Pavel Bure 5.00 12.00

1998-99 Pacific Dynagon Ice Inserts

Randomly inserted in packs at the rate of 4:37, this 20-card set features color photos of some of the NHL's most exciting players printed on mirror-patterned full-foil cards. A titanium parallel was also created and randomly inserted in packs. Titanium Ice parallels were numbered to just 99.

COMPLETE SET (20) 15.00 40.00
1 Paul Kariya .75 2.00
2 Teemu Selanne .75 2.00
3 Sergei Samsonov .60 1.50
4 Dominik Hasek 1.50 4.00
5 Peter Forsberg 2.00 5.00
6 Patrick Roy 4.00 10.00
7 Joe Sakic 1.50 4.00
8 Mike Modano 1.25 3.00
9 Sergei Fedorov 1.25 3.00
10 Steve Yzerman 4.00 10.00
11 Saku Koivu .75 2.00
12 Martin Brodeur 2.00 5.00
13 Wayne Gretzky 5.00 12.00
14 John LeClair .75 2.00
15 Eric Lindros .75 2.00
16 Jaromir Jagr 1.25 3.00
17 Pavel Bure .75 2.00
18 Mark Messier .75 2.00
19 Peter Bondra .60 1.50
20 Olaf Kolzig .60 1.50

1998-99 Pacific Titanium Ice

Randomly inserted into packs, this 20-card set is an insert to the Pacific base set. Only 99 serially numbered sets were made.

STATED PRINT RUN 99 SER.#'d SETS
1 Paul Kariya 10.00 25.00
2 Teemu Selanne 10.00 25.00
3 Sergei Samsonov 8.00 20.00
4 Dominik Hasek 20.00 50.00
5 Peter Forsberg 25.00 60.00
6 Patrick Roy 50.00 120.00
7 Joe Sakic 20.00 50.00
8 Mike Modano 15.00 40.00
9 Sergei Fedorov 15.00 40.00
10 Steve Yzerman 50.00 120.00
11 Saku Koivu 10.00 25.00
12 Martin Brodeur 25.00 60.00
13 Wayne Gretzky 60.00 150.00
14 John LeClair 10.00 25.00
15 Eric Lindros 10.00 25.00
16 Jaromir Jagr 15.00 40.00
17 Pavel Bure 10.00 25.00
18 Mark Messier 10.00 25.00
19 Peter Bondra 8.00 20.00
20 Olaf Kolzig 8.00 20.00

1998-99 Pacific Gold Crown Die-Cuts

Randomly inserted in packs at the rate of 1:37, this 36-card set features color photos of top NHL stars printed on die-cut crown design 24-point card stock with laser cutting and dual foil.

COMPLETE SET (36) 75.00 150.00
1 Paul Kariya 2.00 5.00
2 Teemu Selanne 2.00 5.00
3 Sergei Samsonov 1.50 4.00
4 Dominik Hasek 4.00 10.00
5 Michael Peca .75 2.00
6 Theo Fleury .75 2.00
7 Chris Chelios .75 2.00
8 Peter Forsberg 5.00 12.00
9 Patrick Roy 10.00 25.00
10 Joe Sakic 4.00 10.00
11 Ed Belfour 2.00 5.00
12 Mike Modano 3.00 8.00
13 Sergei Fedorov 2.50 6.00
14 Chris Osgood 1.50 4.00
15 Brendan Shanahan 2.00 5.00
16 Steve Yzerman 10.00 25.00
17 Saku Koivu 2.00 5.00
18 Martin Brodeur 6.00 15.00
19 Patrik Elias .75 2.00
20 Doug Gilmour 1.50 4.00
21 Trevor Linden .75 2.00
22 Zigmund Palffy .75 2.00
23 Wayne Gretzky 12.00 30.00
24 John LeClair .75 2.00
25 Eric Lindros 2.00 5.00
26 Dainius Zubrus .75 2.00
27 Keith Tkachuk .75 2.00
28 Tom Barrasso 1.50 4.00
29 Jaromir Jagr 3.00 8.00
30 Brett Hull 2.50 6.00
31 Felix Potvin 2.00 5.00
32 Mats Sundin 2.00 5.00
33 Pavel Bure 2.00 5.00
34 Mark Messier 2.00 5.00
35 Peter Bondra .75 2.00
36 Olaf Kolzig 1.50 4.00

1998-99 Pacific Martin Brodeur Show Promo

This card was created by Pacific to honor its relationship with new spokesman Martin Brodeur. It was given away free at three shows in early 1999 to those who opened complete boxes of Pacific product at the company's booth. It was reported that 5,000 copies were produced, but few ever make their way onto market.

COMPLETE SET (1) 10.00
1 Martin Brodeur 4.00 10.00

1998-99 Pacific Team Checklists

COMPLETE SET (30) 15.00 30.00
STATED ODDS 2:37
1 Paul Kariya .40 1.00
2 Sergei Samsonov .30 .75
3 Dominik Hasek .75 2.00
4 Theo Fleury .10 .30
5 Keith Primeau .10 .30
6 Chris Chelios .40 1.00
7 Patrick Roy 2.00 5.00
8 Mike Modano .60 1.50
9 Steve Yzerman 2.00 5.00
10 Ryan Smyth .10 .30
11 John Vanbiesbrouck .30 .75
12 Jozef Stumpel .10 .30
13 Saku Koivu .40 1.00
14 Mike Dunham .30 .75
15 Martin Brodeur 1.00 2.50
16 Zigmund Palffy .30 .75
17 Wayne Gretzky 2.50 6.00
18 Alexei Yashin .10 .30
19 Eric Lindros .40 1.00
20 Keith Tkachuk .40 1.00
21 Jaromir Jagr .60 1.50
22 Brett Hull .50 1.25
23 Patrick Marleau .15 .40
24 Rob Zamuner .10 .30
25 Mats Sundin .40 1.00
26 Pavel Bure .40 1.00
27 Olaf Kolzig .30 .75
28 Atlanta Thrashers .40 1.00
29 Minnesota Wild .40 1.00
30 Columbus Blue Jackets .40 1.00

1998-99 Pacific Timelines

COMPLETE SET (20) 60.00 150.00
STATED ODDS 1:181
1 Teemu Selanne 3.00 8.00
2 Dominik Hasek 6.00 15.00
3 Peter Forsberg 6.00 15.00
4 Patrick Roy 12.00 30.00
5 Joe Sakic 6.00 15.00
6 Ed Belfour 3.00 8.00
7 Brendan Shanahan 3.00 8.00
8 Steve Yzerman 10.00 25.00
9 Mike Modano 4.00 10.00
10 Doug Gilmour 2.50 6.00
11 Wayne Gretzky 15.00 40.00
12 Pat LaFontaine 3.00 8.00
13 John LeClair 3.00 8.00
14 Eric Lindros 3.00 8.00
15 Keith Tkachuk 3.00 8.00
16 Jaromir Jagr 4.00 10.00
17 Brett Hull 4.00 10.00
18 Mats Sundin 3.00 8.00
19 Pavel Bure 3.00 8.00
20 Mark Messier 3.00 8.00

1998-99 Pacific Trophy Winners

COMPLETE SET (10) 10.00 25.00
1 Martin Brodeur 2.50 6.00
2 Dominik Hasek 1.50 4.00
3 Jaromir Jagr 1.25 3.00
4 Sergei Samsonov .25 .60
5 Sergei Fedorov 1.00 2.50
6 Nicklas Lidstrom .75 2.00
7 Darren McCarty .25 .60
8 Chris Osgood .25 .60
9 Brendan Shanahan .75 2.00
10 Steve Yzerman 3.00 8.00

1999-00 Pacific

Among the first sets released during the 1999-00 hockey season, these cards featured near full bleed photography on the front, along with stars and biographical information on the back. Cards #451-466 were not found in packs. They were available only as part of an arena giveaway program. As such, they are not considered part of the base set. Card #461 was not issued.

COMPLETE SET (450) 25.00 60.00
1 Matt Cullen .10 .25
2 Johan Davidsson .10 .25
3 Scott Ferguson RC .10 .25
4 Travis Green .10 .25
5 Stu Grimson .12 .30
6 Kevin Haller .10 .25
7 Guy Hebert .15 .40
8 Paul Kariya .20 .50
9 Marty McInnis .10 .25
10 Jim McKenzie .10 .25
11 Fredrik Olausson .10 .25
12 Dominic Roussel .10 .25
13 Steve Rucchin .10 .25
14 Ruslan Salei .10 .25
15 Tomas Sandstrom .10 .25
16 Teemu Selanne .30 .75
17 Jason Allison .12 .30
18 P.J. Axelsson .10 .25
19 Shawn Bates .10 .25
20 Ray Bourque .25 .60
21 Anson Carter .12 .30
22 Byron Dafoe .10 .25
23 Hal Gill .10 .25
24 Steve Heinze .10 .25
25 Dimitri Khristich .10 .25
26 Cameron Mann .10 .25
27 Kyle McLaren .10 .25
28 Sergei Samsonov .12 .30
29 Robbie Tallas .10 .25
30 Joe Thornton .25 .60
31 Landon Wilson .10 .25
32 J.Girard/A.Savage RC .10 .25
33 Stu Barnes .12 .30
34 Martin Biron .12 .30
35 Curtis Brown .10 .25
36 Michal Grosek .10 .25
37 Dominik Hasek .25 .60
38 Brian Holzinger .10 .25
39 Joe Juneau .12 .30
40 Jay McKee .10 .25
41 Michael Peca .12 .30
42 Erik Rasmussen .10 .25
43 Rob Ray .10 .25
44 Geoff Sanderson .12 .30
45 Miroslav Satan .12 .30
46 Darryl Shannon .10 .25
47 Vaclav Varada .10 .25
48 Dixon Ward .10 .25
49 Jason Woolley .10 .25
50 Alexei Zhitnik .10 .25
51 Fred Brathwaite .10 .25
52 Valeri Bure .10 .25
53 Andrew Cassels .10 .25
54 Rene Corbet .10 .25
55 Jean-Sebastien Giguere .15 .40
56 Phil Housley .10 .25
57 Jarome Iginla .15 .40
58 Derek Morris .10 .25
59 Andrei Nazarov .10 .25
60 Jeff Shantz .10 .25
61 Todd Simpson .10 .25
62 Cory Stillman .10 .25
63 Jason Wiemer .10 .25
64 Clarke Wilm .10 .25
65 Ken Wregget .10 .25
66 R.Fata RC/T.Garner .10 .25
67 Bates Battaglia .10 .25
68 Paul Coffey .15 .40
69 Kevin Dineen .10 .25
70 Ron Francis .20 .50
71 Martin Gelinas .10 .25
72 Arturs Irbe .12 .30
73 Sami Kapanen .10 .25
74 Trevor Kidd .10 .25
75 Andrei Kovalenko .10 .25
76 Robert Kron .10 .25
77 Kent Manderville .10 .25
78 Jeff O'Neill .10 .25
79 Keith Primeau .10 .25
80 Gary Roberts .10 .25
81 Ray Sheppard .10 .25
82 Glen Wesley .10 .25
83 Byron Ritchie RC .15 .40
Craig MacDonald
84 Tony Amonte .12 .30
85 Eric Daze .12 .30
86 J-P Dumont .12 .30
87 Anders Eriksson .10 .25
88 Mark Fitzpatrick .10 .25
89 Doug Gilmour .20 .50
90 J.Y. Leroux .10 .25
91 Dave Manson .10 .25
92 Josef Marha .10 .25
93 Dean McAmmond .10 .25
94 Boris Mironov .10 .25
95 Ed Olczyk .10 .25
96 Bob Probert .12 .30
97 Jocelyn Thibault .12 .30
98 Alexei Zhamnov .10 .25
99 Remi Royer .10 .25
Ty Jones
100 Craig Billington .10 .25
101 Adam Deadmarsh .10 .25
102 Chris Drury .12 .30
103 Theo Fleury .20 .50
104 Adam Foote .12 .30
105 Peter Forsberg .15 .40
106 Milan Hejduk .12 .30
107 Dale Hunter .12 .30
108 Valeri Kamensky .10 .25
109 Sylvain Lefebvre .10 .25
110 Claude Lemieux .12 .30
111 Aaron Miller .10 .25
112 Jeff Odgers .10 .25
113 Sandis Ozolinsh .10 .25
114 Patrick Roy .60 1.50
115 Joe Sakic .25 .60
116 Stephane Yelle .10 .25
117 Ed Belfour .15 .40
118 Derian Hatcher .12 .30
119 Benoit Hogue .10 .25
120 Brett Hull .25 .60
121 Mike Keane .12 .30
122 Jamie Langenbrunner .10 .25
123 Jere Lehtinen .12 .30
124 Brad Lukowich RC .12 .30
125 Grant Marshall .10 .25
126 Mike Modano .25 .60
127 Joe Nieuwendyk .15 .40
128 Derek Plante .10 .25
129 Darryl Sydor .12 .30
130 Roman Turek .12 .30
131 Pat Verbeek .12 .30
132 Sergei Zubov .10 .25
133 Jonathan Sim RC .15 .40
Blake Sloan
134 Doug Brown .10 .25
135 Chris Chelios .15 .40
136 Wendel Clark .12 .30
137 Kris Draper .12 .30
138 Sergei Fedorov .25 .60
139 Tomas Holmstrom .10 .25
140 Vyacheslav Kozlov .10 .25
141 Martin Lapointe .12 .30
142 Igor Larionov .15 .40
143 Nicklas Lidstrom .15 .40
144 Darren McCarty .10 .25
145 Larry Murphy .12 .30
146 Chris Osgood .15 .40
147 Bill Ranford .12 .30
148 Ulf Samuelsson .10 .25
149 Brendan Shanahan .20 .50
150 Aaron Ward .10 .25
151 Steve Yzerman .50 1.25
152 Josef Beranek .10 .25
153 Pat Falloon .12 .30
154 Mike Grier .10 .25
155 Bill Guerin .15 .40
156 Roman Hamrlik .12 .30
157 Chad Kilger .10 .25
158 Georges Laraque RC .30 .75
159 Todd Marchant .10 .25
160 Ethan Moreau .10 .25
161 Rem Murray .10 .25
162 Janne Niinimaa .10 .25
163 Tom Poti .10 .25
164 Tommy Salo .12 .30
165 Alexander Selivanov .10 .25
166 Ryan Smyth .12 .30
167 Doug Weight .15 .40
168 Steve Passmore RC .12 .30
169 Pavel Bure .20 .50
170 Sean Burke .10 .25
171 Dino Ciccarelli .15 .40
172 Radek Dvorak .10 .25
173 Viktor Kozlov .10 .25
174 Oleg Kvasha .10 .25
175 Paul Laus .10 .25
176 Bill Lindsay .10 .25
177 Kirk McLean .12 .30
178 Scott Mellanby .10 .25
179 Rob Niedermayer .10 .25
180 Mark Parrish .10 .25
181 Jaroslav Spacek .10 .25
182 Robert Svehla .10 .25
183 Ray Whitney .12 .30
184 Peter Worrell .10 .25
185 D.Boyle RC/M.Nilson .12 .30
186 Donald Audette .10 .25
187 Rob Blake .15 .40
188 Russ Courtnall .10 .25
189 Ray Ferraro .10 .25
190 Stephane Fiset .12 .30
191 Craig Johnson .10 .25
192 Olli Jokinen .12 .30
193 Glen Murray .12 .30
194 Mattias Norstrom .10 .25
195 Sean O'Donnell .10 .25
196 Luc Robitaille .15 .40
197 Pavel Rosa .10 .25
198 Jamie Storr .10 .25
199 Jozef Stumpel .10 .25
200 Vladimir Tsyplakov .10 .25
201 Benoit Brunet .10 .25
202 Shayne Corson .10 .25
203 Jeff Hackett .10 .25
204 Matt Higgins .10 .25
205 Saku Koivu .15 .40
206 Vladimir Malakhov .10 .25
207 Patrick Poulin .10 .25
208 Stephane Quintal .10 .25
209 Martin Rucinsky .10 .25
210 Brian Savage .10 .25
211 Turner Stevenson .10 .25
212 Jose Theodore .15 .40
213 Eric Weinrich .10 .25
214 Sergei Zholtok .10 .25
215 Dainius Zubrus .12 .30
216 Terry Ryan .10 .25
Miloslav Guren
217 Drake Berehowsky .10 .25
218 Sebastien Bordeleau .10 .25
219 Bob Boughner .10 .25
220 Andrew Brunette .10 .25
221 Patrick Cote .10 .25
222 Mike Dunham .10 .25
223 Tom Fitzgerald .10 .25
224 Jamie Heward .10 .25
225 Greg Johnson .10 .25
226 Patric Kjellberg .10 .25
227 Sergei Krivokrasov .10 .25
228 Denny Lambert .10 .25
229 David Legwand .10 .25
230 Mark Mowers RC .10 .25
231 Cliff Ronning .10 .25
232 Tomas Vokoun .15 .40
233 Scott Walker .10 .25
234 Jason Arnott .12 .30
235 Martin Brodeur .30 .75
236 Ken Daneyko .10 .25
237 Patrik Elias .15 .40
238 Bobby Holik .10 .25
239 John Madden RC .15 .40
240 Randy McKay .10 .25
241 Brendan Morrison .12 .30
242 Scott Niedermayer .15 .40
243 Lyle Odelein .10 .25
244 Krzysztof Oliwa .10 .25
245 Jay Pandolfo .10 .25
246 Brian Rolston .12 .30
247 Vadim Sharifijanov .10 .25
248 Petr Sykora .12 .30
249 Chris Terreri .12 .30
250 Scott Stevens .15 .40
251 Eric Brewer .10 .25
252 Zdeno Chara .15 .40
253 Mariusz Czerkawski .10 .25
254 Wade Flaherty .10 .25
255 Kenny Jonsson .10 .25
256 Claude Lapointe .12 .30
257 Mark Lawrence .10 .25
258 Trevor Linden .15 .40
259 Mats Lindgren .10 .25
260 Warren Luhning .10 .25
261 Zigmund Palffy .15 .40
262 Rich Pilon .10 .25
263 Felix Potvin .25 .60
264 Barry Richter .10 .25
265 Bryan Smolinski .10 .25
266 Mike Watt .10 .25
267 Dan Cloutier .10 .25
268 Brent Fedyk .10 .25
269 Adam Graves .12 .30
270 Todd Harvey .10 .25
271 Mike Knuble .10 .25
272 Brian Leetch .15 .40
273 John MacLean .12 .30
274 Manny Malhotra .12 .30
275 Rumun Ndur .10 .25
276 Petr Nedved .10 .25
277 Peter Popovic .10 .25
278 Mike Richter .15 .40
279 Marc Savard .10 .25
280 Mathieu Schneider .10 .25
281 Kevin Stevens .12 .30
282 Niklas Sundstrom .10 .25
283 Daniel Alfredsson .15 .40
284 Magnus Arvedson .10 .25
285 Radek Bonk .10 .25
286 Andreas Dackell .10 .25
287 Bruce Gardiner .10 .25
288 Marian Hossa .12 .30
289 Andreas Johansson .10 .25
290 Igor Kravchuk .10 .25
291 Shawn McEachern .10 .25
292 Vaclav Prospal .10 .25
293 Wade Redden .10 .25
294 Damian Rhodes .10 .25
295 Sami Salo .12 .30
296 Ron Tugnutt .12 .30
297 Alexei Yashin .12 .30
298 Jason York .10 .25
299 Rod Brind'Amour .15 .40
300 Adam Burt .10 .25
301 Eric Desjardins .12 .30
302 Ron Hextall .15 .40
303 Jody Hull .10 .25
304 Keith Jones .10 .25
305 Daymond Langkow .12 .30
306 John LeClair .15 .40
307 Eric Lindros .25 .60
308 Sandy McCarthy .10 .25
309 Dan McGillis .10 .25
310 Mark Recchi .20 .50
311 Mikael Renberg .10 .25
312 Chris Therien .10 .25
313 John Vanbiesbrouck .12 .30
314 Valeri Zelepukin .10 .25
315 Greg Adams .10 .25
316 Keith Carney .10 .25
317 Bob Corkum .10 .25
318 Jim Cummins .10 .25
319 Shane Doan .12 .30
320 Dallas Drake .10 .25
321 Nikolai Khabibulin .12 .30
322 Jyrki Lumme .10 .25
323 Teppo Numminen .10 .25
324 Robert Reichel .10 .25
325 Jeremy Roenick .15 .40
326 Mikhail Shtalenkov .10 .25
327 Mike Stapleton .10 .25
328 Keith Tkachuk .15 .40
329 Rick Tocchet .12 .30
330 Oleg Tverdovsky .10 .25
331 Juha Ylonen .10 .25
332 R.Esche RC/S.Langkow .15 .40
333 Matthew Barnaby .12 .30
334 Tom Barrasso .15 .40
335 Rob Brown .10 .25
336 Kevin Hatcher .10 .25
337 Jan Hrdina .10 .25
338 Jaromir Jagr .40 1.00
339 Darius Kasparaitis .12 .30
340 Dan Kesa .10 .25
341 Alexei Kovalev .12 .30
342 Robert Lang .10 .25
343 Kip Miller .10 .25
344 Alexei Morozov .12 .30
345 Peter Skudra .12 .30
346 Jiri Slegr .10 .25
347 Martin Straka .10 .25
348 German Titov .10 .25
349 Brad Werenka .10 .25
350 J.S. Aubin RC .12 .30
Brian Bonin
351 Blair Atcheynum .10 .25
352 Lubos Bartecko .10 .25
353 Craig Conroy .10 .25
354 Geoff Courtnall .12 .30
355 Pavol Demitra .20 .50
356 Grant Fuhr .15 .40
357 Michal Handzus .12 .30
358 Al MacInnis .15 .40
359 Jamal Mayers .10 .25
360 Jamie McLennan .12 .30
361 Scott Pellerin .10 .25
362 Chris Pronger .12 .30
363 Pascal Rheaume .10 .25
364 Pierre Turgeon .15 .40
365 Tony Twist .12 .30
366 Scott Young .10 .25
367 J.Hecht RC/B.Johnson .25 .60
368 Tyson Nash RC .10 .25
Marty Reasoner
369 Vincent Damphousse .12 .30
370 Jeff Friesen .12 .30
371 Tony Granato .10 .25
372 Bill Houlder .10 .25
373 Alexander Korolyuk .10 .25
374 Bryan Marchment .12 .30
375 Patrick Marleau .15 .40
376 Stephane Matteau .10 .25
377 Joe Murphy .10 .25
378 Owen Nolan .15 .40
379 Mike Rathje .10 .25
380 Mike Ricci .12 .30
381 Steve Shields .12 .30
382 Ronnie Stern .10 .25
383 Marco Sturm .12 .30
384 Mike Vernon .12 .30
385 Scott Hannan RC .10 .25
Shawn Heins
386 Cory Cross .10 .25
387 Alexandre Daigle .10 .25
388 Colin Forbes .10 .25
389 Chris Gratton .10 .25
390 Kevin Hodson .10 .25
391 Pavel Kubina .10 .25
392 Vincent Lecavalier .12 .30
393 Michael Nylander .10 .25
394 Stephane Richer .12 .30
395 Corey Schwab .10 .25
396 Mike Sillinger .10 .25
397 Petr Svoboda .12 .30
398 Darcy Tucker .10 .25
399 Rob Zamuner .10 .25
400 Paul Mara RC .10 .25
Mario Larocque
401 Bryan Berard .10 .25
402 Sergei Berezin .10 .25
403 Lonny Bohonos .10 .25
404 Sylvain Cote .10 .25
405 Tie Domi .12 .30
406 Mike Johnson .12 .30
407 Curtis Joseph .15 .40
408 Tomas Kaberle .10 .25
409 Alexander Karpovtsev .10 .25
410 Derek King .10 .25
411 Igor Korolev .10 .25
412 Adam Mair RC .10 .25
413 Alyn McCauley .12 .30
414 Yanic Perreault .10 .25
415 Steve Sullivan .10 .25
416 Mats Sundin .15 .40
417 Steve Thomas .10 .25
418 Garry Valk .10 .25
419 Adrian Aucion .10 .25
420 Todd Bertuzzi .12 .30
421 Donald Brashear .10 .25
422 Dave Gagner .10 .25
423 Josh Holden .10 .25
424 Ed Jovanovski .12 .30
425 Bryan McCabe .12 .30
426 Mark Messier .25 .60
427 Alexander Mogilny .12 .30
428 Bill Muckalt .10 .25
429 Markus Naslund .15 .40
430 Mattias Ohlund .12 .30
431 Dave Scatchard .10 .25
432 Peter Schaefer .10 .25
433 Garth Snow .12 .30
434 Kevin Weekes .10 .25
435 Brian Bellows .12 .30
436 James Black .10 .25
437 Peter Bondra .12 .30
438 Jan Bulis .10 .25
439 Sergei Gonchar .10 .25
440 Benoit Gratton RC .10 .25
441 Calle Johansson .10 .25
442 Ken Klee .10 .25
443 Olaf Kolzig .15 .40
444 Steve Konowalchuk .10 .25
445 Andrei Nikolishin .10 .25
446 Adam Oates .15 .40
447 Jaroslav Svejkovsky .10 .25
448 Rick Tabaracci .10 .25
449 Richard Zednik .10 .25
450 Baumgartner/Tezikov RC .15 .40
451 Ladislav Kohn AG .40 1.00
452 Petr Buzek AG .40 1.00
453 Robyn Regehr AG .40 1.00
454 David Tanabe AG .40 1.00
455 Jiri Fischer AG .40 1.00
456 Paul Comrie AG .50 1.25
457 Brad Chartrand AG .40 1.00
458 Scott Gomez AG .50 1.25
459 Roberto Luongo AG .75 2.00
460 Mike York AG .40 1.00
462 Trevor Letowski AG .40 1.00
463 Brad Stuart AG .50 1.25
464 Ben Clymer AG .40 1.00
465 Nikolai Antropov AG .75 2.00
466 Jeff Halpern AG .40 1.00
235S Martin Brodeur Sample .75 2.00

1999-00 Pacific Copper

*COPPER/99: 8X TO 20X BASIC CARDS
STATED PRINT RUN 99 SER.#'d SETS
426 Mark Messier 5.00 12.00

1999-00 Pacific Emerald Green

*GREEN/199: 6X TO 15X BASIC CARDS
STATED PRINT RUN 199 SER.#'d SETS
426 Mark Messier 4.00 10.00

1999-00 Pacific Gold

*GOLD/199: 6X TO 15X BASIC CARDS
426 Mark Messier 4.00 10.00

1999-00 Pacific Ice Blue

*ICE BLUE/75: 10X TO 25X BASIC CARDS
426 Mark Messier 6.00 15.00

1999-00 Pacific Premiere Date

*PREM.DATE/46: 15X TO 40X BASIC CARDS
426 Mark Messier 10.00 25.00

1999-00 Pacific Red

*RED: 1X TO 2.5X BASIC CARDS

1999-00 Pacific Center Ice

Randomly inserted in the 7-eleven pack release, this set identifies some of the NHL's top stars. A parallel proof version of this set was released also where cards are sequentially numbered to 10. Proofs are not priced due to scarcity.

COMPLETE SET (20) 12.00 30.00
1 Paul Kariya .75 2.00
2 Teemu Selanne .75 2.00
3 Dominik Hasek 1.50 4.00
4 Jarome Iginla 1.00 2.50
5 Theo Fleury .60 1.50
6 Peter Forsberg 2.00 5.00
7 Patrick Roy 4.00 10.00
8 Joe Sakic 1.50 4.00
9 Mike Modano 1.25 3.00
10 Brendan Shanahan .75 2.00
11 Steve Yzerman 4.00 10.00
12 Doug Weight .60 1.50
13 Trevor Linden .30 .75
14 Martin Brodeur 2.00 5.00
15 Alexei Yashin .30 .75
16 Eric Lindros .75 2.00
17 Jaromir Jagr 1.25 3.00
18 Curtis Joseph .75 2.00
19 Mats Sundin .75 2.00
20 Mark Messier .75 2.00

1999-00 Pacific Cramer's Choice

Randomly inserted into packs, this set continues the tradition of the Cramer's Choice Awards. For the first time, these cards are serial numbered out of 299.

COMPLETE SET (10) 175.00 350.00
1 Paul Kariya 8.00 20.00
2 Dominik Hasek 15.00 40.00
3 Peter Forsberg 10.00 25.00
4 Patrick Roy 30.00 80.00
5 Joe Sakic 15.00 40.00
6 Mike Modano 12.50 30.00
7 Steve Yzerman 30.00 80.00
8 Eric Lindros 8.00 20.00
9 Jaromir Jagr 12.50 30.00
10 Curtis Joseph 8.00 20.00

1999-00 Pacific Gold Crown Die-Cuts

COMPLETE SET (36) 100.00 200.00
STATED ODDS 1:25
1 Paul Kariya 2.00 5.00
2 Teemu Selanne 2.00 5.00
3 Ray Bourque 3.00 8.00
4 Byron Dafoe 1.25 3.00
5 Dominik Hasek 4.00 10.00
6 Michael Peca 1.25 3.00
7 Chris Drury 1.25 3.00
8 Theo Fleury 1.25 3.00
9 Peter Forsberg 5.00 12.00
10 Milan Hejduk 1.25 3.00
11 Patrick Roy 10.00 25.00
12 Joe Sakic 4.00 10.00
13 Ed Belfour 2.00 5.00
14 Brett Hull 2.50 6.00
15 Mike Modano 2.50 6.00
16 Chris Chelios 1.25 3.00
17 Brendan Shanahan 2.00 5.00
18 Steve Yzerman 10.00 25.00
19 Pavel Bure 2.00 5.00
20 David Legwand 1.25 3.00
21 Martin Brodeur 6.00 15.00
22 Felix Potvin 2.00 5.00
23 Mike Richter 2.00 5.00
24 Alexei Yashin 1.25 3.00
25 John LeClair 1.25 3.00
26 Eric Lindros 2.00 5.00
27 Mark Recchi 1.25 3.00
28 John Vanbiesbrouck 1.25 3.00
29 Jeremy Roenick 2.50 6.00
30 Keith Tkachuk 1.25 3.00
31 Jaromir Jagr 3.00 8.00
32 Vincent Lecavalier 2.00 5.00

33 Sergei Berezin 1.25 3.00
34 Curtis Joseph 2.00 5.00
35 Mats Sundin 2.00 5.00
36 Mark Messier 2.00 5.00

1999-00 Pacific Home and Away

Inserted 2:25 packs, these cards feature players in both their Home and Away jerseys. Cards 1-10 can be found in retail packs, while cards 11-20 can be found in hobby packs.

COMPLETE SET (20) 50.00 100.00
1 Paul Kariya 1.25 3.00
2 Teemu Selanne 1.25 3.00
3 Dominik Hasek 2.50 6.00
4 Peter Forsberg 3.00 8.00
5 Patrick Roy 6.00 15.00
6 Mike Modano 2.00 5.00
7 Steve Yzerman 6.00 15.00
8 John LeClair 1.25 3.00
9 Eric Lindros 1.25 3.00
10 Jaromir Jagr 2.00 5.00
11 Paul Kariya 1.25 3.00
12 Teemu Selanne 1.25 3.00
13 Dominik Hasek 2.50 6.00
14 Peter Forsberg 3.00 8.00
15 Patrick Roy 6.00 15.00
16 Mike Modano 2.00 5.00
17 Steve Yzerman 6.00 15.00
18 John LeClair 1.25 3.00
19 Eric Lindros 1.25 3.00
20 Jaromir Jagr 2.00 5.00

1999-00 Pacific In the Cage Net-Fusions

Inserted 1:97 packs, these cards are die-cut and feature actual netting as the background. Cards are full color and feature goalie action shots.

COMPLETE SET (20) 50.00 100.00
1 Guy Hebert 2.50 6.00
2 Byron Dafoe 2.00 5.00
3 Dominik Hasek 5.00 12.00
4 Arturs Irbe 2.00 5.00
5 Patrick Roy 12.50 30.00
6 Ed Belfour 3.00 8.00
7 Chris Osgood 3.00 8.00
8 Tommy Salo 2.50 6.00
9 Jeff Hackett 2.00 5.00
10 Martin Brodeur 6.00 15.00
11 Felix Potvin 3.00 8.00
12 Mike Richter 3.00 8.00
13 Ron Tugnutt 2.50 6.00
14 John Vanbiesbrouck 3.00 8.00
15 Nikolai Khabibulin 2.50 6.00
16 Tom Barrasso 2.00 5.00
17 Grant Fuhr 3.00 8.00
18 Mike Vernon 2.50 6.00
19 Curtis Joseph 3.00 8.00
20 Olaf Kolzig 2.50 6.00

1999-00 Pacific Past and Present

A hobby only insert seeded 1:49 that features 20 of the NHL's top stars in both their old and current uniforms.

COMPLETE SET (20) 100.00 200.00
1 Paul Kariya 2.00 5.00
2 Teemu Selanne 2.00 5.00
3 Ray Bourque 3.00 8.00
4 Dominik Hasek 6.00 15.00
5 Theo Fleury 1.50 4.00
6 Peter Forsberg 8.00 20.00
7 Patrick Roy 12.00 30.00
8 Joe Sakic 6.00 15.00
9 Ed Belfour 2.00 5.00
10 Brett Hull 3.00 8.00
11 Mike Modano 3.00 8.00
12 Brendan Shanahan 2.00 5.00
13 Steve Yzerman 12.00 30.00
14 Pavel Bure 2.00 5.00
15 Martin Brodeur 8.00 20.00
16 John LeClair 1.50 4.00
17 Eric Lindros 2.00 5.00
18 John Vanbiesbrouck 1.50 4.00
19 Jaromir Jagr 4.00 10.00
20 Curtis Joseph 2.00 5.00

1999-00 Pacific Team Leaders

Randomly inserted in packs at the rate of 2:25, this set features 27 of the NHL's premier team leaders. Each card features holographic foil with a complete team checklist on the back.

COMPLETE SET (28) 30.00 60.00
1 Paul Kariya 1.00 2.50
2 Atlanta Thrashers .40 1.00
3 Ray Bourque 1.50 4.00
4 Dominik Hasek 2.00 5.00
5 Jarome Iginla 1.25 3.00
6 Arturs Irbe .75 2.00
7 Doug Gilmour .75 2.00
8 Patrick Roy 5.00 12.00
9 Mike Modano 1.50 4.00
10 Steve Yzerman 5.00 12.00
11 Bill Guerin .75 2.00
12 Pavel Bure 1.00 2.50
13 Luc Robitaille .75 2.00
14 Saku Koivu 1.00 2.50
15 Mike Dunham .75 2.00
16 Martin Brodeur 2.50 6.00
17 Zigmund Palffy .75 2.00
18 Mike Richter 1.00 2.50
19 Alexei Yashin .40 1.00
20 Eric Lindros 1.00 2.50
21 Keith Tkachuk 1.00 2.50
22 Jaromir Jagr 1.50 4.00
23 Grant Fuhr .75 2.00
24 Mike Vernon .75 2.00
25 Vincent Lecavalier 1.00 2.50
26 Curtis Joseph 1.00 2.50
27 Mark Messier 1.00 2.50
28 Peter Bondra .75 2.00

2000-01 Pacific

Released as a 450-card set, Pacific features full color action shots and cards enhanced with silver foil highlights. Pacific was packaged in 36-pack boxes with packs containing 12 cards each and carried a suggested retail price of $2.99.

COMPLETE SET (450) 15.00 40.00
1 Maxim Balmochnyk .10 .25
2 Matt Cullen .10 .25
3 Ted Donato .10 .25
4 Guy Hebert .12 .30
5 Paul Kariya .20 .50
6 Ladislav Kohn .10 .25
7 Marty McInnis .12 .30
8 Kip Miller .10 .25
9 Dominic Roussel .10 .25
10 Steve Rucchin .10 .25
11 Teemu Selanne .30 .75
12 Oleg Tverdovsky .10 .25
13 Vitali Vishnevski .10 .25
14 Donald Audette .12 .30
15 Andrew Brunette .10 .25
16 Petr Buzek .10 .25
17 Hnat Domenichelli .10 .25
18 Ray Ferraro .10 .25
19 Steve Guolla .10 .25
20 Denny Lambert .10 .25
21 Damian Rhodes .10 .25
22 Mike Stapleton .10 .25
23 Patrik Stefan .12 .30
24 Per Svartvadet .10 .25
25 Dean Sylvester .10 .25
26 Yannick Tremblay .10 .25
27 B.Adams RC/Fankhouser .10 .25
28 Vasilijevs RC/Vyshedkevich RC .10 .25
29 Jason Allison .12 .30
30 Per Johan Axelsson .10 .25
31 Anson Carter .12 .30
32 Byron Dafoe .12 .30
33 Hal Gill .10 .25
34 John Grahame .10 .25
35 Steve Heinze .10 .25
36 Joe Hulbig .10 .25
37 Mike Knuble .10 .25
38 Kyle McLaren .10 .25
39 Eric Nickulas RC .10 .25
40 Brian Rolston .12 .30
41 Sergei Samsonov .12 .30
42 Andre Savage .10 .25
43 Joe Thornton .25 .60
44 Darren Van Impe .10 .25
45 N.Boynton/J.Aitken RC .10 .25
46 Maxim Afinogenov .10 .25
47 Stu Barnes .12 .30
48 Martin Biron .12 .30
49 Curtis Brown .10 .25
50 Doug Gilmour .20 .50
51 Chris Gratton .10 .25
52 Dominik Hasek .25 .60
53 Michael Peca .12 .30
54 Erik Rasmussen .10 .25
55 Rob Ray .10 .25
56 Geoff Sanderson .12 .30
57 Miroslav Satan .10 .25
58 Vladimir Tsyplakov .10 .25
59 Vaclav Varada .10 .25
60 Jason Woolley .10 .25
61 Fred Brathwaite .12 .30
62 Valeri Bure .12 .30
63 Bobby Dollas .10 .25
64 Jean-Sebastien Giguere .12 .30
65 Phil Housley .12 .30
66 Jarome Iginla .15 .40
67 Andreas Johansson .10 .25
68 Sergei Krivokrasov .10 .25
69 Bill Lindsay .10 .25
70 Derek Morris .10 .25
71 Andrei Nazarov .10 .25
72 Oleg Saprykin .10 .25
73 Marc Savard .12 .30
74 Jeff Shantz .10 .25
75 Cory Stillman .10 .25
76 Jason Wiemer .10 .25
77 C.Clark/S.Varlamov .10 .25
78 Bates Battaglia .10 .25
79 Rod Brind'Amour .15 .40
80 Paul Coffey .15 .40
81 Ron Francis .20 .50
82 Sean Hill .10 .25
83 Arturs Irbe .12 .30
84 Sami Kapanen .10 .25
85 Dave Karpa .10 .25
86 Andrei Kovalenko .10 .25
87 Robert Kron .10 .25
88 Jeff O'Neill .12 .30
89 Gary Roberts .10 .25
90 Dave Tanabe .10 .25
91 Tommy Westlund .10 .25
92 Tony Amonte .12 .30
93 Eric Daze .12 .30
94 Kevin Dean .10 .25
95 Michal Grosek .10 .25
96 Dean McAmmond .10 .25
97 Bryan McCabe .10 .25
98 Steven McCarthy .10 .25
99 Boris Mironov .10 .25
100 Michael Nylander .10 .25
101 Bob Probert .12 .30
102 Steve Sullivan .10 .25
103 Jocelyn Thibault .12 .30
104 Ryan Vandenbussche .10 .25
105 Alexei Zhamnov .12 .30
106 Dave Andreychuk .15 .40
107 Ray Bourque .25 .60
108 Adam Deadmarsh .12 .30
109 Marc Denis .12 .30
110 Greg DeVries .10 .25
111 Chris Drury .12 .30
112 Adam Foote .12 .30
113 Peter Forsberg .20 .50
114 Alexei Gusarov .10 .25
115 Milan Hejduk .12 .30
116 Eric Messier .10 .25
117 Sandis Ozolinsh .12 .30
118 Shjon Podein .10 .25
119 Dave Reid .10 .25
120 Patrick Roy .40 1.00
121 Joe Sakic .25 .60
122 Martin Skoula .12 .30
123 Alex Tanguay .12 .30
124 Stephane Yelle .10 .25
125 S.Aubin RC/V.Nieminen RC .12 .30
126 Ed Belfour .15 .40
127 Guy Carbonneau .12 .30
128 Sylvain Cote .10 .25
129 Manny Fernandez .12 .30
130 Derian Hatcher .12 .30
131 Brett Hull .25 .60
132 Mike Keane .12 .30
133 Jamie Langenbrunner .12 .30
134 Jere Lehtinen .12 .30
135 Dave Manson .10 .25
136 Richard Matvichuk .10 .25
137 Mike Modano .25 .60
138 Brenden Morrow .12 .30
139 Joe Nieuwendyk .15 .40
140 Blake Sloan .10 .25
141 Darryl Sydor .12 .30
142 Scott Thornton .12 .30
143 Sergei Zubov ERR .12 .30
144 Doug Brown .10 .25
145 Chris Chelios .15 .40
146 Kris Draper .10 .25
147 Sergei Fedorov .25 .60
148 Tomas Holmstrom .12 .30
149 Vyacheslav Kozlov .12 .30
150 Darryl Laplante .10 .25
151 Martin Lapointe .12 .30
152 Igor Larionov .15 .40
153 Nicklas Lidstrom .15 .40
154 Kirk Maltby .10 .25
155 Darren McCarty .10 .25
156 Larry Murphy .12 .30
157 Chris Osgood .15 .40
158 Brendan Shanahan .20 .50
159 Pat Verbeek .12 .30
160 Jesse Wallin .10 .25
161 Ken Wregget .12 .30
162 Steve Yzerman .50 1.25
163 Boyd Devereaux .10 .25
164 Jim Dowd .10 .25
165 Mike Grier .10 .25
166 Bill Guerin .15 .40
167 Roman Hamrlik .12 .30
168 Georges Laraque .12 .30
169 Todd Marchant .10 .25
170 Ethan Moreau .10 .25
171 Tom Poti .10 .25
172 Tommy Salo .12 .30
173 Alexander Selivanov .10 .25
174 Ryan Smyth .12 .30
175 German Titov .10 .25
176 Doug Weight .15 .40
177 Pavel Bure .20 .50
178 Trevor Kidd .10 .25
179 Viktor Kozlov .12 .30
180 Oleg Kvasha .10 .25
181 Paul Laus .10 .25
182 Scott Mellanby .10 .25
183 Rob Niedermayer .12 .30
184 Ivan Novoseltsev .10 .25
185 Mark Parrish .10 .25
186 Mikhail Shtalenkov .10 .25
187 Robert Svehla .10 .25
188 Mike Vernon .12 .30
189 Ray Whitney .12 .30
190 Peter Worrell .10 .25
191 E.Boguniecki/B.Ference .10 .25
192 Aki Berg .10 .25
193 Rob Blake .15 .40
194 Kelly Buchberger .12 .30
195 Nelson Emerson .10 .25
196 Stephane Fiset .10 .25
197 Garry Galley .10 .25
198 Glen Murray .10 .25
199 Jan Nemecek .10 .25
200 Zigmund Palffy .15 .40
201 Luc Robitaille .15 .40
202 Bryan Smolinski .12 .30
203 Jamie Storr .12 .30
204 Jozef Stumpel .10 .25
205 Patrice Brisebois .10 .25
206 Benoit Brunet .10 .25
207 Shayne Corson .10 .25
208 Jeff Hackett .10 .25
209 Saku Koivu .15 .40
210 Trevor Linden .15 .40
211 Oleg Petrov .10 .25
212 Martin Rucinsky .10 .25
213 Brian Savage .10 .25
214 Sheldon Souray .10 .25
215 Jose Theodore .20 .50
216 Eric Weinrich .10 .25
217 Sergei Zholtok .10 .25
218 Dainius Zubrus .10 .25
219 Sebastien Bordeleau .10 .25
220 Mike Dunham .10 .25
221 Tom Fitzgerald .10 .25
222 Greg Johnson .10 .25
223 David Legwand .15 .40
224 Craig Millar .10 .25
225 Cliff Ronning .10 .25
226 Kimmo Timonen .10 .25
227 Tomas Vokoun .12 .30
228 Scott Walker .10 .25
229 A.Boikov RC/M.Moro RC .10 .25
230 D.Gosselin RC/C.Mason RC .20 .50
231 Jason Arnott .12 .30
232 Martin Brodeur .30 .75
233 Patrik Elias .15 .40
234 Scott Gomez .12 .30
235 Bobby Holik .10 .25
236 Claude Lemieux .12 .30
237 John Madden .12 .30
238 Vladimir Malakhov .10 .25
239 Randy McKay .10 .25
240 Alexander Mogilny .12 .30
241 Scott Niedermayer .15 .40
242 Brian Rafalski .10 .25
243 Scott Stevens .15 .40
244 Petr Sykora .12 .30
245 Chris Terreri .10 .25
246 W.Mitchell RC/C.White RC .15 .40
247 Tim Connolly .10 .25
248 Mariusz Czerkawski .10 .25
249 Josh Green .10 .25
250 Brad Isbister .10 .25
251 Jason Krog .10 .25
252 Claude Lapointe .10 .25
253 Roberto Luongo .25 .60
254 Petr Mika RC .10 .25
255 Dave Scatchard .10 .25
256 Steve Valiquette RC .12 .30
257 Kevin Weekes .10 .25
258 Alexandre Daigle .12 .30
259 Radek Dvorak .12 .30
260 Theo Fleury .20 .50
261 Adam Graves .12 .30
262 Jan Hlavac .10 .25
263 Kim Johnsson .10 .25
264 Valeri Kamensky .10 .25
265 Brian Leetch .15 .40
266 John MacLean .12 .30
267 Kirk McLean .10 .25
268 Petr Nedved .12 .30
269 Mike Richter .15 .40
270 Mathieu Schneider .10 .25
271 Johan Witehall RC .10 .25
272 Mike York .10 .25
273 Daniel Alfredsson .15 .40
274 Magnus Arvedson .10 .25
275 Tom Barrasso .12 .30
276 Radek Bonk .12 .30
277 Mike Fisher .12 .30
278 Marian Hossa .12 .30
279 Jani Hurme RC .10 .25
280 Joe Juneau .12 .30
281 Patrick Lalime .12 .30
282 Grant Ledyard .10 .25
283 Shawn McEachern .10 .25
284 Chris Phillips .10 .25
285 Vaclav Prospal .10 .25
286 Wade Redden .10 .25
287 Sami Salo .10 .25
288 Alexei Yashin .12 .30
289 Jason York .10 .25
290 Rob Zamuner .10 .25
291 E.Goldmann RC/P.Schastlivy .10 .25
292 Craig Berube .10 .25
293 Brian Boucher .12 .30
294 Andy Delmore .10 .25
295 Eric Desjardins .12 .30
296 Simon Gagne .15 .40
297 Jody Hull .10 .25
298 Keith Jones .10 .25
299 Daymond Langkow .10 .25
300 John LeClair .15 .40
301 Eric Lindros .25 .60
302 Kent Manderville .10 .25
303 Dan McGillis .10 .25
304 Gino Odjick .10 .25
305 Keith Primeau .12 .30
306 Mark Recchi .20 .50
307 Chris Therien .10 .25
308 Rick Tocchet .12 .30
309 John Vanbiesbrouck .12 .30
310 Valeri Zelepukin .10 .25
311 Sean Burke .10 .25
312 Keith Carney .10 .25
313 Louie DeBrusk .10 .25
314 Shane Doan .12 .30
315 Dallas Drake .10 .25
316 Travis Green .10 .25
317 Nikolai Khabibulin .25 .60
318 Trevor Letowski .10 .25
319 Jyrki Lumme .10 .25
320 Mikael Renberg .10 .25
321 Jeremy Roenick .15 .40
322 Keith Tkachuk .15 .40
323 R.Esche/W.Smith .10 .25
324 Jean-Sebastien Aubin .12 .30
325 Matthew Barnaby .12 .30
326 Pat Falloon .12 .30
327 Jan Hrdina .10 .25
328 Jaromir Jagr .40 1.00
329 Darius Kasparaitis .12 .30
330 Alexei Kovalev .12 .30
331 Robert Lang .10 .25
332 Janne Laukkanen .10 .25
333 Stephen Leach .10 .25
334 Alexei Morozov .10 .25
335 Michal Rozsival .10 .25
336 Jiri Slegr .10 .25
337 Martin Straka .12 .30
338 Ron Tugnutt .12 .30
339 Lubos Bartecko .10 .25
340 Marc Bergevin .10 .25
341 Pavol Demitra .20 .50
342 Mike Eastwood .10 .25
343 Dave Ellett .10 .25
344 Michal Handzus .10 .25
345 Jochen Hecht .10 .25
346 Al MacInnis .15 .40
347 Jamie McLennan .10 .25
348 Tyson Nash .10 .25
349 Chris Pronger .12 .30
350 Marty Reasoner .10 .25
351 Stephane Richer .10 .25
352 Roman Turek .12 .30
353 Pierre Turgeon .15 .40
354 Scott Young .10 .25
355 D.Bekar RC/L.Nagy .10 .25
356 Vincent Damphousse .12 .30
357 Jeff Friesen .10 .25
358 Todd Harvey .12 .30
359 Alexander Korolyuk .10 .25
360 Patrick Marleau .15 .40
361 Stephane Matteau .10 .25
362 Evgeni Nabokov .12 .30
363 Owen Nolan .15 .40
364 Mike Ricci .12 .30
365 Steve Shields .10 .25
366 Brad Stuart .12 .30
367 Marco Sturm .12 .30
368 Gary Suter .12 .30
369 Dan Cloutier .12 .30
370 Stan Drulia .10 .25
371 Matt Elich RC .12 .30
372 Brian Holzinger .10 .25
373 Mike Johnson .10 .25
374 Ryan Johnson .10 .25
375 Dieter Kochan RC .10 .25
376 Pavel Kubina .10 .25
377 Vincent Lecavalier .12 .30
378 Fredrik Modin .10 .25
379 Wayne Primeau .10 .25
380 Cory Sarich .10 .25
381 Petr Svoboda .10 .25
382 K.Astashenko RC/K.Freadrich RC .10 .25
383 G.Dwyer/M.Posmyk .10 .25
384 Nikolai Antropov .12 .30
385 Sergei Berezin .10 .25
386 Wendel Clark .12 .30
387 Tie Domi .25 .60
388 Gerald Diduck .10 .25
389 Jeff Farkas .10 .25
390 Glenn Healy .10 .25
391 Jonas Hoglund .10 .25
392 Curtis Joseph .20 .50
393 Tomas Kaberle .10 .25
394 Alexander Karpovtsev .10 .25
395 Dimitri Khristich .10 .25
396 Igor Korolev .10 .25
397 Yanic Perreault .10 .25
398 DJ Smith .10 .25
399 Mats Sundin .15 .40
400 Steve Thomas .10 .25
401 Darcy Tucker .10 .25
402 Dimitri Yushkevich .10 .25
403 Adrian Aucoin .10 .25
404 Todd Bertuzzi .12 .30
405 Donald Brashear .10 .25
406 Andrew Cassels .10 .25
407 Harold Druken .10 .25
408 Ed Jovanovski .12 .30
409 Steve Kariya .10 .25
410 Trent Klatt .10 .25
411 Mark Messier .25 .60
412 Markus Naslund .12 .30
413 Mattias Ohlund .10 .25
414 Felix Potvin .25 .60
415 Peter Schaefer .10 .25
416 Garth Snow .12 .30
417 A.Michaud/J.Ruutu .15 .40
418 Peter Bondra .12 .30
419 Martin Brochu RC .10 .25
420 Jan Bulis .10 .25
421 Sergei Gonchar .10 .25
422 Jeff Halpern .10 .25
423 Calle Johansson .10 .25
424 Ken Klee .10 .25
425 Olaf Kolzig .15 .40
426 Steve Konowalchuk .10 .25
427 Glen Metropolit .10 .25
428 Adam Oates .15 .40
429 Chris Simon .10 .25
430 Richard Zednik .10 .25
431 Jorgen Jonsson SF .10 .25
432 Teemu Selanne SF .30 .75
433 Sami Kapanen SF .10 .25
434 Peter Forsberg SF .20 .50
435 Jere Lehtinen SF .12 .30
436 Nicklas Lidstrom SF .15 .40
437 Janne Niinimaa SF .10 .25
438 Tommy Salo SF .12 .30
439 Saku Koivu SF .15 .40
440 Patric Kjellberg SF .10 .25
441 Olli Jokinen SF .12 .30
442 Kenny Jonsson SF .10 .25
443 Daniel Alfredsson SF .15 .40
444 Andreas Dackell SF .10 .25
445 Teppo Numminen SF .10 .25
446 Marcus Ragnarsson SF .10 .25
447 Niklas Sundstrom SF .10 .25
448 Mats Sundin SF .15 .40
449 Markus Naslund SF .12 .30
450 Ulf Dahlen SF .10 .25

2000-01 Pacific Copper

*COPPER/40: 20X TO 50X BASIC CARDS
STATED PRINT RUN 40 SER.#'d SETS
STATED ODDS 1:37 HOBBY

2000-01 Pacific Gold

*GOLD/50: 20X TO 50X BASIC CARDS
STATED ODDS 1:37 RETAIL
STATED PRINT RUN 50 SER.#'d SETS

2000-01 Pacific Ice Blue

*VETS: 20X TO 50X BASIC CARDS
STATED ODDS 1:73
STATED PRINT RUN 45 SER.#'d SETS

2000-01 Pacific Premiere Date

*PREM.DATE/40: 15X TO 40X BASIC CARDS
STATED PRINT RUN 40 SERIAL #'d SETS

2000-01 Pacific 2001: Ice Odyssey

COMPLETE SET (20) 25.00 60.00
STATED ODDS 1:37
1 Paul Kariya 2.00 5.00
2 Teemu Selanne 2.00 5.00
3 Martin Biron 1.25 3.00
4 Jarome Iginla 2.50 6.00
5 Chris Drury .75 2.00
6 Peter Forsberg 3.00 8.00
7 Milan Hejduk 1.25 3.00
8 Patrick Roy 6.00 15.00
9 Steve Yzerman 6.00 15.00
10 Pavel Bure 2.00 5.00
11 Jose Theodore 2.00 5.00
12 Martin Brodeur 4.00 10.00
13 Patrik Elias .75 2.00
14 Scott Gomez .75 2.00
15 Roberto Luongo 2.50 6.00
16 Marian Hossa 1.25 3.00
17 Brian Boucher 1.25 3.00
18 Jaromir Jagr 3.00 8.00
19 Vincent Lecavalier 2.00 5.00
20 Mats Sundin 2.00 5.00

2000-01 Pacific Autographs

Randomly inserted in packs, this 20-card set utilizes the base card design and number. Each card is autographed by the featured player and contains a Pacific stamp of authenticity. This set is skip numbered. Card number 262 has recently been confirmed. It appears that they arrived to late to be inserted into packs and were held back at the Pacific offices. When the company folded, the cards were sold to Fairfield, a repackager, and only recently have begun to appear. Each card is serial numbered, and the totals are listed beside the player's name below.

57 Miroslav Satan/500 5.00 12.00
123 Alex Tanguay/250 15.00 30.00
126 Ed Belfour/250 6.00 15.00
137 Mike Modano/250 15.00 30.00
138 Brenden Morrow/500 5.00 12.00
169 Todd Marchant/250 5.00 12.00
172 Tommy Salo/500 5.00 12.00
215 Jose Theodore/250 10.00 25.00
223 David Legwand/250 5.00 12.00
233 Patrik Elias/500 5.00 12.00
234 Scott Gomez/500 5.00 12.00
251 Jason Krog/500 5.00 12.00
262 Jan Hlavac/500 6.00 15.00
272 Mike York/500 5.00 12.00
296 Simon Gagne/1000 6.00 15.00
300 John LeClair/250 12.50 30.00
352 Roman Turek/500 5.00 12.00
377 Vincent Lecavalier/1000 6.00 15.00
384 Nikolai Antropov/250 5.00 12.00

2000-01 Pacific Cramer's Choice

Randomly inserted in packs at the rate of 1:721, this 10-card set features a die-cut holographic foil card stock showcasing Michael Cramer's top player choices.

COMPLETE SET (10) 100.00 200.00
1 Paul Kariya 5.00 12.00
2 Teemu Selanne 5.00 12.00
3 Peter Forsberg 10.00 25.00
4 Patrick Roy 15.00 40.00
5 Steve Yzerman 15.00 40.00
6 Pavel Bure 5.00 12.00
7 Martin Brodeur 10.00 25.00
8 Scott Gomez 3.00 8.00
9 Jaromir Jagr 8.00 20.00
10 Mats Sundin 5.00 12.00

2000-01 Pacific Euro-Stars

COMPLETE SET (10) 30.00 60.00
STATED ODDS 1:37
1 Teemu Selanne 2.50 6.00
2 Dominik Hasek 5.00 12.00
3 Peter Forsberg 6.00 15.00
4 Sergei Fedorov 5.00 12.00
5 Pavel Bure 3.00 8.00
6 Jaromir Jagr 4.00 10.00
7 Pavol Demitra 2.00 5.00
8 Roman Turek 2.00 5.00
9 Mats Sundin 2.50 6.00
10 Olaf Kolzig 2.00 5.00

2000-01 Pacific Jerseys

1 Ray Bourque 10.00 25.00
2 Eric Messier 4.00 10.00
3 Patrick Roy 12.50 30.00
4 Joe Sakic 10.00 25.00
5 Mike Modano 6.00 15.00
6 Darryl Sydor 4.00 10.00
7 Brendan Shanahan 4.00 10.00
8 Steve Yzerman 12.50 30.00
9 Pavel Bure 4.00 10.00
10 Eric Desjardins 4.00 10.00
11 Daymond Langkow 4.00 10.00
12 Shane Doan 4.00 10.00
13 Jaromir Jagr 10.00 25.00
14 Mark Messier 4.00 10.00
15 Olaf Kolzig 4.00 10.00

2000-01 Pacific Gold Crown Die Cuts

Randomly seeded in packs at the rate of 1:37, this 36-card set features top NHL players on a crown die-cut card with enhanced holofoil and gold foil stamping. Card number 12 was not released.

COMPLETE SET (36) 60.00 150.00
1 Paul Kariya 2.00 5.00
2 Teemu Selanne 2.00 5.00
3 Joe Thornton 3.00 8.00
4 Dominik Hasek 4.00 10.00
5 Valeri Bure 1.25 3.00
6 Tony Amonte 1.25 3.00
7 Ray Bourque 3.00 8.00
8A Peter Forsberg 3.00 8.00
8B Milan Hejduk 1.25 3.00
9 Joe Sakic 4.00 10.00
10 Patrick Roy 8.00 20.00
11 Brett Hull 2.50 5.00
13 Mike Modano 3.00 5.00
14 Brendan Shanahan 3.00 5.00
15 Steve Yzerman 6.00 15.00
16 Pavel Bure 2.50 6.00
17 Luc Robitaille 1.50 4.00
18 Martin Brodeur 5.00 12.00
19 Scott Gomez 1.25 3.00
20 Roberto Luongo 2.50 6.00
21 Marian Hossa 1.25 3.00
22 Brian Boucher 1.25 3.00
23 John LeClair 1.25 3.00
24 Eric Lindros 2.00 5.00
25 Mark Recchi 1.25 3.00
26 Keith Tkachuk 1.25 3.00
27 Jeremy Roenick 2.50 5.00
28 Jaromir Jagr 3.00 8.00
29 Chris Pronger 1.25 3.00
30 Roman Turek 1.25 3.00
31 Owen Nolan 1.25 3.00
32 Vincent Lecavalier 2.00 5.00
33 Mats Sundin 2.00 5.00
34 Curtis Joseph 2.00 4.00
35 Mark Messier 2.50 5.00
36 Olaf Kolzig 1.50 4.00

2000-01 Pacific In the Cage Net-Fusions

Inserted at 1:73 packs, these cards are die-cut and feature a goalie game action photograph where the goal itself has been die cut out and replaced with "netting."

COMPLETE SET (10) 30.00 60.00
1 Dominik Hasek 5.00 12.00
2 Fred Brathwaite 2.00 5.00
3 Patrick Roy 12.50 30.00
4 Mike Vernon 2.00 5.00
5 Stephane Fiset 2.00 5.00
6 Jeff Hackett 2.00 5.00
7 Martin Brodeur 6.00 15.00
8 Mike Richter 2.50 6.00
9 Brian Boucher 2.50 6.00
10 Curtis Joseph 2.50 6.00

2000-01 Pacific North American Stars

COMPLETE SET (10) 50.00 100.00
STATED ODDS 1:37
1 Paul Kariya 2.50 6.00
2 Joe Sakic 5.00 12.00
3 Patrick Roy 12.50 30.00
4 Mike Modano 4.00 10.00
5 Brendan Shanahan 4.00 10.00
6 Steve Yzerman 12.50 30.00
7 Martin Brodeur 6.00 15.00
8 Scott Gomez 2.50 6.00
9 John LeClair 3.00 8.00
10 Curtis Joseph 2.50 6.00

2000-01 Pacific Reflections

Randomly inserted in packs at the rate of 1:145, this 20-card set features a die cut base card in the shape of a helmet. Each helmet has an iridescent visor that shows the reflection of the featured player.

COMPLETE SET (20) 60.00 150.00
STATED ODDS 1:145
1 Paul Kariya 2.50 6.00
2 Teemu Selanne 2.50 6.00
3 Doug Gilmour 2.00 5.00
4 Ray Bourque 4.00 10.00
5 Peter Forsberg 8.00 20.00
6 Joe Sakic 6.00 15.00
7 Brett Hull 3.00 8.00
8 Mike Modano 4.00 10.00
9 Brendan Shanahan 3.00 8.00
10 Steve Yzerman 12.00 30.00
11 Pavel Bure 3.00 8.00
12 Zigmund Palffy 2.00 5.00
13 Scott Gomez 2.00 5.00
14 Marian Hossa 2.00 5.00
15 John LeClair 2.00 5.00
16 Eric Lindros 3.00 8.00
17 Jaromir Jagr 4.00 10.00
18 Vincent Lecavalier 2.50 6.00
19 Mats Sundin 2.50 6.00
20 Mark Messier 3.00 8.00

2001-02 Pacific

Pacific was released as a 452-card set with the last 10 cards of the set available only by mail-in redemption. Cards 444-451 were issued as autographed cards numbered to 500 and card 452 had stated odds of 1 per case. The card front design had only 1 border, with the featured player's name and team, and it was highlighted with silver-foil. The 'Pacific 2002' logo was also done with silver-foil to let it stand out. The card backs had player stats by season and there was a brief synopsis of the career highlights.

1 Matt Cullen .12 .30
2 Jim Cummins .12 .30
3 Jeff Friesen .12 .30
4 Jean-Sebastien Giguere .15 .40
5 Tony Hrkac .12 .30
6 Paul Kariya .25
7 Mike Leclerc .12
8 Marty McInnis .15
9 Steve Rucchin .12
10 Ruslan Salei .12
11 Steve Shields .15
12 Oleg Tverdovsky .12
13 Bob Wren RC .12
14 Andrew Brunette .12
15 Hnat Domenichelli .12
16 Ray Ferraro .12
17 Stephen Guolla .12
18 Milan Hnilicka .15
19 Tomi Kallio .12
20 Norm Maracle .12
21 Rumun Ndur .12
22 Jeff Odgers .12
23 Damian Rhodes .15
24 Jiri Slegr .12
25 Patrik Stefan .15
26 J.P. Vigier .12
27 Jason Allison .15
28 P.J. Axelsson .12
29 Byron Dafoe .15
30 John Grahame .15
31 Bill Guerin .20
32 Mike Knuble .12
33 Andrei Kovalenko .12
34 Eric Manlow .12
35 Andrei Nazarov .12
36 Brian Rolston .15
37 Sergei Samsonov .15
38 Peter Skudra .15
39 Don Sweeney .12
40 Joe Thornton .25
41 Eric Weinrich .12
42 Maxim Afinogenov .12
43 Dave Andreychuk .20
44 Donald Audette .12
45 Stu Barnes .15
46 Martin Biron .15
47 J-P Dumont .12
48 Doug Gilmour .25
49 Chris Gratton .12
50 Dominik Hasek .30
51 Steve Heinze .12
52 Erik Rasmussen .12
53 Rob Ray .12
54 Miroslav Satan .15
55 Alexei Zhitnik .12
56 Tommy Albelin .12
57 Fred Brathwaite .15
58 Valeri Bure .12
59 Craig Conroy .12
60 Phil Housley .15
61 Jarome Iginla .20
62 Dave Lowry .12
63 Derek Morris .12
64 Oleg Saprykin .12
65 Marc Savard .12
66 Daniel Tkaczuk .12
67 Mike Vernon .15
68 Jason Wiemer .12
69 Bates Battaglia .12
70 Rod Brind'Amour .20
71 Ron Francis .25
72 Martin Gelinas .12
73 Kevin Hatcher .12
74 Arturs Irbe .15
75 Sami Kapanen .12
76 Dave Karpa .12
77 Tyler Moss .12
78 Jeff O'Neill .12
79 Sandis Ozolinsh .12
80 Scott Pellerin .12
81 Shane Willis .12
82 Tony Amonte .15
83 Mark Bell .12
84 Eric Daze .15
85 Steve Dubinsky .12
86 Chris Herperger .12
87 Michel Larocque .12
88 Michael Nylander .12
89 Steve Passmore .12
90 Bob Probert .15
91 Stephane Quintal .12
92 Steve Sullivan .12
93 Jocelyn Thibault .15
94 Alexei Zhamnov .15
95 David Aebischer .15
96 Rick Berry .12
97 Rob Blake .20
98 Ray Bourque .30
99 Chris Drury .15
100 Adam Foote .15
101 Peter Forsberg .25
102 Milan Hejduk .15
103 Ville Nieminen .12
104 Shjon Podein .12
105 Steven Reinprecht .12
106 Patrick Roy .50
107 Joe Sakic .30
108 Alex Tanguay .15
109 Serge Aubin .12
110 Mathieu Darche RC .20
111 Matt Davidson RC .12
112 Marc Denis .15
113 Rostislav Klesla .12
114 Espen Knutsen .12
115 Chris Nielsen .12
116 Geoff Sanderson .12
117 Martin Spanhel RC .12
118 Ron Tugnutt .15
119 David Vyborny .12
120 Ray Whitney .12
121 Tyler Wright .12
122 Ed Belfour .20
123 Steve Gainey .12
124 Derian Hatcher .12
125 Sami Helenius .12
126 Brett Hull .25
127 Jamie Langenbrunner .12
128 Jere Lehtinen .15
129 Brad Lukowich .12
130 Grant Marshall .12
131 Mike Modano .30
132 Brenden Morrow .15
133 Kirk Muller .15
134 Joe Nieuwendyk .20
135 Darryl Sydor .12
136 Marty Turco .20
137 Sergei Zubov .15
138 Chris Chelios .20
139 Sergei Fedorov .30

140 Todd Gill .12 .30
141 Tomas Holmstrom .12 .30
142 Slava Kozlov .15 .40
143 Martin Lapointe .12 .30
144 Igor Larionov .20 .50
145 Manny Legace .15 .40
146 Nicklas Lidstrom .20 .50
147 Darren McCarty .12 .30
148 Chris Osgood .20 .50
149 Brendan Shanahan .25 .60
150 Pat Verbeek .15 .40
151 Aaron Ward .12 .30
152 Steve Yzerman .60 1.50
153 Anson Carter .15 .40
154 Jason Chimera RC .12 .30
155 Daniel Cleary .15 .40
156 Mike Comrie .15 .40
157 Mike Grier .12 .30
158 Shawn Horcoff .15 .40
159 Georges Laraque .15 .40
160 Todd Marchant .12 .30
161 Rem Murray .15 .40
162 Janne Niinimaa .12 .30
163 Dominic Roussel .12 .30
164 Tommy Salo .15 .40
165 Jason Smith .12 .30
166 Ryan Smyth .15 .40
167 Doug Weight .20 .50
168 Kevyn Adams .12 .30
169 Pavel Bure .25 .60
170 Anders Eriksson .12 .30
171 Trevor Kidd .12 .30
172 Viktor Kozlov .12 .30
173 Roberto Luongo .30 .75
174 Rob Niedermayer .15 .40
175 Marcus Nilsson .12 .30
176 Andrej Podkonicky RC .12 .30
177 Robert Svehla .12 .30
178 Peter Worrell .12 .30
179 Eric Belanger .12 .30
180 Adam Deadmarsh .15 .40
181 Stu Grimson .12 .30
182 Andreas Lilja .12 .30
183 Glen Murray .15 .40
184 Zigmund Palffy .20 .50
185 Felix Potvin .30 .75
186 Luc Robitaille .20 .50
187 Mathieu Schneider .12 .30
188 Bryan Smolinski .12 .30
189 Jamie Storr .15 .40
190 Jozef Stumpel .12 .30
191 Lubomir Visnovsky .12 .30
192 Jim Dowd .12 .30
193 Manny Fernandez .15 .40
194 Marian Gaborik .30 .75
195 Derek Gustafson .12 .30
196 Matt Johnson .12 .30
197 Filip Kuba .12 .30
198 Antti Laaksonen .12 .30
199 Jamie McLennan .12 .30
00 Lubomir Sekeras .12 .30
01 Wes Walz .12 .30
02 Francis Belanger RC .15 .40
03 Patrice Brisebois .12 .30
04 Jan Bulis .12 .30
05 Karl Dykhuis .12 .30
06 Mathieu Garon .15 .40
07 Jeff Hackett .15 .40
08 Chad Kilger .12 .30
09 Saku Koivu .20 .50
10 Oleg Petrov .12 .30
11 Martin Rucinsky .12 .30
12 Brian Savage .12 .30
13 Jose Theodore .20 .50
14 Richard Zednik .15 .40
15 Marian Cisar .12 .30
16 Mike Dunham .15 .40
17 Scott Hartnell .20 .50
18 Greg Johnson .12 .30
19 Patric Kjellberg .12 .30
20 David Legwand .15 .40
21 Cliff Ronning .12 .30
22 Tomas Vokoun .15 .40
23 Scott Walker .12 .30
24 Vitali Yachmenev .12 .30
25 Jason Arnott .15 .40
26 Jiri Bicek .12 .30
27 Martin Brodeur .40 1.00
28 Sergei Brylin .12 .30
29 Patrik Elias .20 .50
30 Scott Gomez .15 .40
31 Bobby Holik .12 .30
32 John Madden .15 .40
33 Randy McKay .12 .30
34 Jim McKenzie .12 .30
35 Alexander Mogilny .15 .40
36 Sergei Nemchinov .12 .30
37 Scott Niedermayer .20 .50
38 Scott Stevens .20 .50
39 Petr Sykora .12 .30
40 John Vanbiesbrouck .20 .50
41 Ed Ward .12 .30
42 Zdeno Chara .20 .50
43 Tim Connolly .12 .30
44 Mariusz Czerkawski .12 .30
45 Rick DiPietro .15 .40
46 Garry Galley .12 .30
47 Kevin Haller .12 .30
48 Roman Hamrlik .12 .30
49 Brad Isbister .12 .30
50 Kenny Jonsson .12 .30
51 Claude Lapointe .12 .30
52 Mark Parrish .12 .30
53 Dave Scatchard .12 .30
54 Chris Terreri .15 .40
55 Radek Dvorak .15 .40
56 Theo Fleury .25 .60
57 Adam Graves .15 .40
58 Guy Hebert .20 .50
59 Jan Hlavac .12 .30
60 Valeri Kamensky .12 .30
61 Brian Leetch .20 .50
62 Sylvain Lefebvre .12 .30
63 Sandy McCarthy .12 .30
64 Mark Messier .30 .75
65 Petr Nedved .15 .40
66 Rich Pilon .12 .30
67 Mike Richter .20 .50
68 Mike York .12 .30
69 Daniel Alfredsson .20 .50
70 Magnus Arvedson .12 .30
71 Radek Bonk .12 .30
72 Martin Havlat .15 .40
73 Marian Hossa .15 .40
74 Jani Hurme .15 .40
75 Patrick Lalime .15 .40
76 Shawn McEachern .12 .30
77 Chris Phillips .12 .30
278 Wade Redden .12 .30
279 Andre Roy .12 .30
280 Mike Sillinger .12 .30
281 Alexei Yashin .15 .40
282 Rob Zamuner .12 .30
283 Brian Boucher .15 .40
284 Roman Cechmanek .15 .40
285 Eric Desjardins .15 .40
286 Ruslan Fedotenko .12 .30
287 Simon Gagne .20 .50
288 Daymond Langkow .15 .40
289 John LeClair .20 .50
290 Eric Lindros .30 .75
291 Dan McGillis .12 .30
292 Keith Primeau .15 .40
293 Paul Ranheim .12 .30
294 Mark Recchi .25 .60
295 Rick Tocchet .12 .30
296 Justin Williams .12 .30
297 Joel Bouchard .12 .30
298 Daniel Briere .15 .40
299 Sean Burke .12 .30
300 Keith Carney .12 .30
301 Shane Doan .15 .40
302 Robert Esche .12 .30
303 Michal Handzus .12 .30
304 Mike Johnson .12 .30
305 Joe Juneau .15 .40
306 Claude Lemieux .15 .40
307 Teppo Numminen .12 .30
308 Jeremy Roenick .20 .50
309 Landon Wilson .12 .30
310 Jean-Sebastien Aubin .15 .40
311 Jan Hrdina .12 .30
312 Jaromir Jagr .50 1.25
313 Darius Kasparaitis .12 .30
314 Alexei Kovalev .15 .40
315 Robert Lang .12 .30
316 Mario Lemieux .60 1.50
317 Garth Snow .15 .40
318 Kevin Stevens .12 .30
319 Martin Straka .12 .30
320 Sebastien Bordeleau .12 .30
321 Pavol Demitra .25 .60
322 Dallas Drake .12 .30
323 Jochen Hecht .12 .30
324 Brent Johnson .15 .40
325 Reed Low .12 .30
326 Al MacInnis .20 .50
327 Scott Mellanby .12 .30
328 Jaroslav Obsut RC .12 .30
329 Chris Pronger .15 .40
330 Darren Rumble .12 .30
331 Cory Stillman .12 .30
332 Keith Tkachuk .20 .50
333 Roman Turek .15 .40
334 Pierre Turgeon .20 .50
335 Scott Young .12 .30
336 Vincent Damphousse .15 .40
337 Miikka Kiprusoff .20 .50
338 Bryan Marchment .12 .30
339 Patrick Marleau .20 .50
340 Evgeni Nabokov .15 .40
341 Owen Nolan .20 .50
342 Jeff Norton .12 .30
343 Mike Ricci .15 .40
344 Teemu Selanne .40 1.00
345 Brad Stuart .12 .30
346 Marco Sturm .12 .30
347 Niklas Sundstrom .15 .40
348 Scott Thornton .15 .40
349 Matthew Barnaby .12 .30
350 Brian Holzinger .12 .30
351 Nikolai Khabibulin .20 .50
352 Alexander Kharitonov .12 .30
353 Pavel Kubina .12 .30
354 Kristian Kudroc .12 .30
355 Vincent Lecavalier .15 .40
356 Fredrik Modin .12 .30
357 Brad Richards .20 .50
358 Martin St. Louis .20 .50
359 Kevin Weekes .15 .40
360 Thomas Ziegler RC .15 .40
361 Sergei Berezin .12 .30
362 Shayne Corson .12 .30
363 Cory Cross .12 .30
364 Tie Domi .15 .40
365 Glenn Healy .12 .30
366 Jonas Hoglund .12 .30
367 Curtis Joseph .20 .50
368 Don MacLean .12 .30
369 Dave Manson .12 .30
370 Yanic Perreault .12 .30
371 Alexei Ponikarovsky .12 .30
372 Gary Roberts .12 .30
373 Mats Sundin .20 .50
374 Steve Thomas .12 .30
375 Darcy Tucker .12 .30
376 Murray Baron .12 .30
377 Todd Bertuzzi .20 .50
378 Donald Brashear .12 .30
379 Andrew Cassels .12 .30
380 Dan Cloutier .15 .40
381 Bob Essensa .15 .40
382 Ed Jovanovski .15 .40
383 Brendan Morrison .15 .40
384 Markus Naslund .20 .50
385 Mattias Ohlund .12 .30
386 Peter Schaefer .12 .30
387 Daniel Sedin .20 .50
388 Henrik Sedin .20 .50
389 Craig Billington .12 .30
390 Peter Bondra .20 .50
391 Ulf Dahlen .12 .30
392 Sergei Gonchar .12 .30
393 Jeff Halpern .12 .30
394 Dmitri Khristich .12 .30
395 Olaf Kolzig .20 .50
396 Steve Konowalchuk .12 .30
397 Trevor Linden .20 .50
398 Adam Oates .20 .50
399 Chris Simon .12 .30
400 Dainius Zubrus .12 .30
401 P.Kariya/J.Cummins .25 .60
402 R.Ferraro/J.Odgers .12 .30
403 J.Allison/K.Belanger .15 .40
404 J.Dumont/R.Ray .12 .30
405 J.Iginla/J.Wiemer .20 .50
406 R.Francis/D.Langdon .25 .60
407 S.Sullivan/B.Probert .15 .40
408 J.Sakic/S.Parker .30 .75
409 M.Modano/G.Marshall .30 .75
410 S.Yzerman/D.McCarty .60 1.50
411 R.Smyth/G.Laraque .15 .40
412 P.Bure/P.Worrell .25 .60
413 Z.Palffy/S.Grimson .20 .50
414 P.Elias/C.White .20 .50
415 Czerkawski/Z.Chara .20 .50
416 T.Fleury/S.McCarthy .25 .60
417 M.Hossa/A.Roy .15 .40
418 J.Roenick/L.DeBrusk .20 .50
419 M.Lemieux/K.Oliwa .60 1.50
420 P.Turgeon/R.Low .20 .50
421 T.Selanne/Marchment .40 1.00
422 Lecavalier/M.Barnaby .15 .40
423 M.Sundin/T.Domi .20 .50
424 M.Naslund/D.Brashear .20 .50
425 P.Bondra/C.Simon .20 .50
426 J.Allison/J.Thornton .25 .60
427 J.Sakic/P.Roy .50 1.25
428 M.Modano/B.Hull .30 .75
429 S.Fedorov/N.Lidstrom .30 .75
430 D.Weight/R.Smyth .20 .50
431 P.Bure/R.Luongo .30 .75
432 L.Robitaille/Z.Palffy .20 .50
433 P.Elias/A.Mogilny .20 .50
434 Czerkawski/R.DiPietro .15 .40
435 T.Fleury/B.Leetch .25 .60
436 A.Yashin/M.Hossa .15 .40
437 K.Primeau/Cechmanek .15 .40
438 J.Roenick/S.Burke .20 .50
439 J.Jagr/M.Lemieux .60 1.50
440 P.Turgeon/B.Johnson .20 .50
441 T.Selanne/E.Nabokov .40 1.00
442 M.Sundin/C.Joseph .20 .50
443 A.Oates/P.Bondra .20 .50
444 David Aebischer AU/500 10.00 25.00
445 Steven Reinprecht AU/500 8.00 20.00
446 Marty Turco AU/500 12.00 30.00
447 Marian Gaborik AU/500 15.00 40.00
448 Martin Havlat AU/500 10.00 25.00
449 Brent Johnson AU/500 10.00 25.00
450 Evgeni Nabokov AU/500 10.00 25.00
451 Brad Richards AU/500 12.00 30.00
452 Johan Hedberg SP 2.00 5.00
453 Timo Parssinen RC 1.50 4.00
454 Ilya Kovalchuk RC 6.00 15.00
455 Vaclav Nedorost RC 1.25 3.00
456 Kristian Huselius RC 2.00 5.00
457 Jaroslav Bednar RC 1.25 3.00
458 Dan Blackburn RC 1.50 4.00
459 Jiri Dopita RC 1.25 3.00
460 Krystofer Kolanos RC 1.25 3.00
461 Jeff Jillson RC 1.25 3.00
462 Nikita Alexeev RC 1.25 3.00

2001-02 Pacific Extreme LTD

Randomly inserted at 1 per hobby box or 1:2 retail boxes, this set parallels the base set except that the words "Extreme LTD" are embossed across the front of the card diagonally. These cards were limited to 49 serial-numbered sets.

*EXTREME/49: 8X TO 20X BASIC CARDS
264 Mark Messier 8.00 20.00

2001-02 Pacific Gold

Randomly inserted in packs of 2001-02 Pacific, this 43-card set featured a gold version of the base set cards 401-443. Each card was serial numbered to 100, and featured 2 players on the cards.

*GOLD/100: 5X TO 12X BASIC CARDS

2001-02 Pacific Hobby LTD

Randomly inserted, this set parallels the base set except that the words "Hobby LTD" are embossed across the front of the card diagonally. These cards were limited to 99 serial-numbered sets.

*HOBBY LTD/99: 5X TO 12X BASIC CARDS
264 Mark Messier 3.00 8.00

2001-02 Pacific Premiere Date

Randomly inserted in packs of 2001-02 Pacific, this 400-card set was a parallel to the base set along with the 'Premiere Date' stamp on these and each card was serial numbered to 45.

*PREM.DATE/45: 8X TO 20X BASIC CARDS
264 Mark Messier 8.00 20.00

2001-02 Pacific Retail LTD

Randomly inserted, this set parallels the base set except that the words "Retail LTD" are embossed across the front of the card diagonally. These cards were limited to 149 serial-numbered sets.

*LTD/149: 5X TO 12X BASIC CARDS
264 Mark Messier 5.00 12.00

2001-02 Pacific All-Stars

Randomly inserted in packs of 2001-02 Pacific at a rate of 1:37, this 20-card set featured 10 World All Stars and 10 North America All Stars. The cards were die-cut and featured silver-foil lettering and highlights.

COMPLETE SET (20) 60.00 125.00
W1 Dominik Hasek 3.00 8.00
W2 Peter Forsberg 4.00 10.00
W3 Sergei Fedorov 3.00 8.00
W4 Pavel Bure 2.00 5.00
W5 Zigmund Palffy 1.25 3.00
W6 Marian Hossa 1.50 4.00
W7 Roman Cechmanek 3.00 8.00
W8 Alexei Kovalev 1.50 4.00
W9 Evgeni Nabokov 3.00 8.00
W10 Mats Sundin 1.50 4.00
NA1 Paul Kariya 1.50 4.00
NA2 Bill Guerin 1.25 3.00
NA3 Ray Bourque 6.00 15.00
NA4 Patrick Roy 8.00 20.00
NA5 Joe Sakic 3.00 8.00
NA6 Brett Hull 2.00 5.00
NA7 Doug Weight 1.25 3.00
NA8 Luc Robitaille 1.25 3.00
NA9 Martin Brodeur 4.00 10.00
NA10 Mario Lemieux 10.00 25.00

2001-02 Pacific Cramer's Choice

Randomly inserted in packs of 2001-02 Pacific, this 10-card set was serial numbered to 49.

1 Paul Kariya 8.00 20.00
2 Ray Bourque 20.00 50.00
3 Patrick Roy 40.00 100.00
4 Joe Sakic 20.00 50.00
5 Steve Yzerman 30.00 80.00
6 Pavel Bure 10.00 25.00
7 Martin Brodeur 25.00 60.00
8 Jaromir Jagr 12.00 30.00
9 Mario Lemieux 40.00 100.00
10 Curtis Joseph 15.00 40.00

2001-02 Pacific Jerseys

STATED ODDS 2:37 HOB, 1:145 RET
STATED PRINT RUN 110-1135
1 Andre Savage/510 2.50 6.00
2 Eric Weinrich/510 2.50 6.00
3 Jay McKee/1135 2.50 6.00
4 Fred Brathwaite/1135 3.00 8.00
5 Marc Savard/760 2.50 6.00
6 Tony Amonte/1135 3.00 8.00
7 Alexei Zhamnov/1135 2.50 6.00
8 Chris Dingman/510 2.50 6.00
9 Joe Sakic/510 6.00 15.00
10 Derian Hatcher/1135 2.50 6.00
11 Jamie Langenbrunner/1135 2.50 6.00
12 Sergei Zubov/760 4.00 10.00
13 Mathieu Dandenault/1135 2.50 6.00
14 Chris Osgood/760 4.00 10.00
15 Doug Weight/260 3.00 8.00
16 Aaron Miller/510 2.50 6.00
17 Cliff Ronning/510 2.50 6.00
18 Bobby Holik/760 2.50 6.00
19 Mariusz Czerkawski/510 2.50 6.00
20 Chris Terreri/1135 2.50 6.00
21 Guy Hebert/760 3.00 8.00
22 Mike Richter/760 3.00 8.00
23 Mika Alatalo/510 2.50 6.00
24 Shane Doan/310 2.50 6.00
25 Jyrki Lumme/1135 2.50 6.00
26 Jan Hrdina/510 2.50 6.00
27 Jaromir Jagr/210 6.00 15.00
28 Mario Lemieux/110 20.00 50.00
29 Kip Miller/1135 2.50 6.00
30 Ian Moran/1135 2.50 6.00
31 Martin Straka/110 5.00 12.00
32 Cory Stillman/1135 2.50 6.00
33 Vincent Damphousse/1010 2.50 6.00
34 Teemu Selanne/1135 4.00 10.00
35 Mats Sundin/760 3.00 8.00
36 Dainius Zubrus/760 2.50 6.00

2001-02 Pacific Gold Crown Die-Cuts

COMPLETE SET (20) 60.00 125.00
STATED ODDS 1:73
1 Paul Kariya 1.50 4.00
2 Joe Thornton 2.50 6.00
3 Dominik Hasek 4.00 10.00
4 Ray Bourque 3.00 8.00
5 Peter Forsberg 5.00 12.00
6 Patrick Roy 8.00 20.00
7 Joe Sakic 4.00 10.00
8 Mike Modano 2.50 6.00
9 Sergei Fedorov 2.50 6.00
10 Steve Yzerman 8.00 20.00
11 Pavel Bure 1.50 4.00
12 Martin Brodeur 6.00 15.00
13 Rick DiPietro 1.50 4.00
14 Mark Messier 2.50 6.00
15 Marian Hossa 1.50 4.00
16 Jaromir Jagr 3.00 8.00
17 Mario Lemieux 12.00 30.00
18 Keith Tkachuk 1.50 4.00
19 Evgeni Nabokov 2.50 6.00
20 Curtis Joseph 1.50 4.00

2001-02 Pacific Impact Zone

COMPLETE SET (20) 15.00 40.00
STATED ODDS 1:37
1 Paul Kariya 1.50 4.00
2 Byron Dafoe .75 2.00
3 Doug Gilmour .75 2.00
4 Dominik Hasek 3.00 8.00
5 Ron Francis .75 2.00
6 Ray Bourque 3.00 8.00
7 Patrick Roy 6.00 15.00
8 Ed Belfour 1.50 4.00
9 Derian Hatcher .40 1.00
10 Mike Modano 2.50 6.00
11 Chris Osgood .75 2.00
12 Martin Brodeur 4.00 10.00
13 Marian Hossa .75 2.00
14 Patrick Lalime .75 2.00
15 Roman Cechmanek .40 1.00
16 Chris Pronger .75 2.00
17 Tie Domi .40 1.00
18 Curtis Joseph 1.50 4.00
19 Mats Sundin 1.50 4.00
20 Andrew Cassels .40 1.00

2001-02 Pacific 97-98 Update

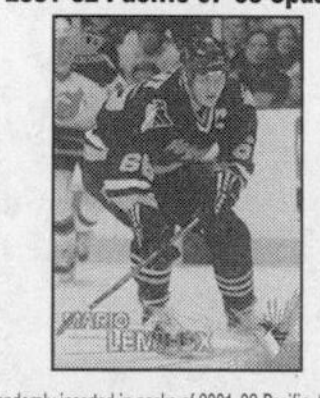

Randomly inserted in packs of 2001-02 Pacific, this 7-card set was issued as an update to the 1997-98 set. The cards featured a similar design as that of the original set and added 7 players who were not originally included in the set. There was also a gold version available in random retail packs. Gold cards were serial-numbered to 100.

COMPLETE SET (7) 10.00 20.00
*GOLD/100: 8X TO 20X BASIC INSERT
66 Mario Lemieux 2.50 6.00
352 Mike LeClerc 1.25 3.00
353 Sergei Samsonov 1.50 4.00
354 Joe Thornton 2.50 6.00
355 Steve Shields 1.25 3.00
356 Patrik Elias 1.25 3.00
357 Marian Hossa 1.50 4.00

2001-02 Pacific Steel Curtain

COMPLETE SET (20) 30.00 60.00
STATED ODDS 2:37
1 Steve Shields 1.00 2.50
2 Byron Dafoe 1.00 2.50
3 Dominik Hasek 2.50 6.00
4 Jocelyn Thibault 1.00 2.50
5 Patrick Roy 6.00 15.00
6 Ed Belfour 1.25 3.00
7 Manny Legace 1.00 2.50
8 Tommy Salo 1.00 2.50
9 Roberto Luongo 1.50 4.00
10 Jose Theodore 1.50 4.00
11 Martin Brodeur 3.00 8.00
12 Rick DiPietro 1.00 2.50
13 Mike Richter 1.25 3.00
14 Patrick Lalime 1.00 2.50
15 Roman Cechmanek 1.00 2.50
16 Sean Burke 1.00 2.50
17 Roman Turek 1.00 2.50
10 Evgeni Nabokov 1.00 2.50
19 Curtis Joseph 1.25 3.00
20 Olaf Kolzig 1.00 2.50

2001-02 Pacific Top Draft Picks

Randomly inserted in packs of 2001-02 Pacific at a rate of 1:37, this 10-card set featured some of the top draft picks from the last 20 years. These cards were identical to the Promos with the exception of gold-foil instead of silver, and these were not serial numbered.

COMPLETE SET (10) 10.00 25.00
1 Rick DiPietro .75 2.00
2 Patrik Stefan .40 1.00
3 Vincent Lecavalier 1.25 3.00
4 Joe Thornton 2.00 5.00
5 Eric Lindros 1.25 3.00
6 Owen Nolan .75 2.00
7 Mats Sundin 1.25 3.00
8 Mike Modano 2.00 5.00
9 Pierre Turgeon .75 2.00
10 Mario Lemieux 4.00 10.00

2001 Pacific Top Draft Picks Draft Day Promos

This 10-card set was given away at the 2001 NHL Draft. Collectors could obtain one card in exchange for a Titanium Draft Day wrapper, or combination of other Pacific wrappers. Although the cards mirror the inserts found in 2001-02 Pacific, these cards differ in that they are serial numbered to 499, and are highlighted by silver foil lettering. It is believed that far fewer than 499 sets were actually distributed.

COMPLETE SET (10) 40.00 100.00
1 Rick DiPietro 6.00 15.00
2 Patrik Stefan 2.00 5.00
3 Vincent LeCavalier 4.80 12.00
4 Joe Thornton 6.00 15.00
5 Eric Lindros 4.80 12.00
6 Owen Nolan 4.00 10.00
7 Mats Sundin 4.80 12.00
8 Mike Modano 6.00 15.00
9 Pierre Turgeon 4.00 10.00
10 Mario Lemieux 12.00 30.00

2002-03 Pacific

This 400-card set was released in late-July 2002 and carried an SRP of $2.99 for a 10-card pack. A red parallel of this set was also created and inserted 1:2 packs. Cards 401-410 were available as a mail-in redemption only and were serial-numbered out of 999.

COMPLETE SET (400) 50.00 100.00
1 Matt Cullen .12 .30
2 Jeff Friesen .12 .30
3 Jean-Sebastien Giguere .20 .50
4 Paul Kariya .25 .60
5 Mike Leclerc .12 .30
6 Andy McDonald .20 .50
7 Steve Rucchin .12 .30
8 Steve Shields .15 .40
9 German Titov .12 .30
10 Oleg Tverdovsky .12 .30
11 Jason York .12 .30
12 Lubos Bartecko .12 .30
13 Dany Heatley .20 .50
14 Milan Hnilicka .15 .40
15 Tony Hrkac .12 .30
16 Frantisek Kaberle .12 .30
17 Tomi Kallio .12 .30
18 Ilya Kovalchuk .25 .60
19 Jeff Odgers .12 .30
20 Damian Rhodes .12 .30
21 Patrik Stefan .15 .40
22 Daniel Tjarnqvist .12 .30
23 Nicholas Boynton .12 .30
24 Sean Brown .12 .30
25 Byron Dafoe .15 .40
26 Hal Gill .12 .30
27 John Grahame .12 .30
28 Bill Guerin .20 .50
29 Martin Lapointe .15 .40
30 Glen Murray .15 .40
31 Brian Rolston .15 .40
32 Sergei Samsonov .15 .40
33 P.J. Stock .12 .30
34 Jozef Stumpel .12 .30
35 Joe Thornton .25 .60
36 Maxim Afinogenov .12 .30
37 Stu Barnes .12 .30
38 Martin Biron .15 .40
39 Curtis Brown .12 .30
40 Tim Connolly .12 .30
41 J-P Dumont .12 .30
42 Chris Gratton .12 .30
43 Ales Kotalik .12 .30
44 Slava Kozlov .12 .30
45 Jay McKee .12 .30
46 Mika Noronen .15 .40
47 Rob Ray .12 .30
48 Miroslav Satan .20 .50
49 Alexei Zhitnik .15 .40
50 Bob Boughner .12 .30
51 Chris Clark .12 .30
52 Craig Conroy .12 .30
53 Denis Gauthier .12 .30
54 Jarome Iginla .20 .50
55 Toni Lydman .12 .30
56 Dean McAmmond .12 .30
57 Derek Morris .12 .30
58 Rob Niedermayer .15 .40
59 Marc Savard .12 .30
60 Roman Turek .20 .50
61 Mike Vernon .15 .40
62 Bates Battaglia .12 .30
63 Rod Brind'Amour .20 .50
64 Erik Cole .15 .40
65 Ron Francis .25 .60
66 Bret Hedican .12 .30
67 Arturs Irbe .15 .40
68 Sami Kapanen .12 .30
69 Jeff O'Neill .12 .30
70 Dave Tanabe .12 .30
71 Josef Vasicek .12 .30
72 Kevin Weekes .15 .40
73 Tony Amonte .15 .40
74 Mark Bell .12 .30
75 Kyle Calder .12 .30
76 Eric Daze .12 .30
77 Phil Housley .15 .40
78 Jon Klemm .12 .30
79 Boris Mironov .12 .30
80 Steve Passmore .12 .30
81 Bob Probert .20 .50
82 Steve Sullivan .12 .30
83 Jocelyn Thibault .15 .40
84 Steve Thomas .12 .30
85 Alexei Zhamnov .15 .40
86 David Aebischer .15 .40
87 Rob Blake .20 .50
88 Chris Drury .20 .50
89 Adam Foote .12 .30
90 Peter Forsberg .25 .60
91 Milan Hejduk .15 .40
92 Darius Kasparaitis .12 .30
93 Scott Parker .12 .30
94 Steven Reinprecht .12 .30
95 Patrick Roy .50 1.25
96 Joe Sakic .30 .75
97 Alex Tanguay .15 .40
98 Radim Vrbata .15 .40
99 Marc Denis .15 .40
100 Rostislav Klesla .12 .30
101 Espen Knutsen .12 .30
102 Grant Marshall .12 .30
103 Deron Quint .12 .30
104 Geoff Sanderson .15 .40
105 Jody Shelley .12 .30
106 Mike Sillinger .12 .30
107 Ron Tugnutt .15 .40
108 David Vyborny .12 .30
109 Ray Whitney .15 .40
110 Jason Arnott .15 .40
111 Ed Belfour .20 .50
112 Derian Hatcher .15 .40
113 Jere Lehtinen .20 .50
114 Mike Modano .30 .75
115 Brenden Morrow .15 .40
116 Kirk Muller .12 .30
117 Scott Pellerin .12 .30
118 Darryl Sydor .12 .30
119 Marty Turco .20 .50
120 Pierre Turgeon .20 .50
121 Pat Verbeek .12 .30
122 Sergei Zubov .15 .40
123 Chris Chelios .20 .50
124 Pavel Datsyuk .25 .60
125 Boyd Devereaux .12 .30
126 Kris Draper .12 .30
127 Sergei Fedorov .30 .75
128 Dominik Hasek .30 .75
129 Brett Hull .25 .60
130 Igor Larionov .20 .50
131 Manny Legace .20 .50
132 Nicklas Lidstrom .20 .50
133 Luc Robitaille .20 .50
134 Brendan Shanahan .25 .60
135 Jiri Slegr .12 .30
136 Jason Williams .12 .30
137 Steve Yzerman .40 1.00
138 Eric Brewer .12 .30
139 Anson Carter .15 .40
140 Daniel Cleary .15 .40
141 Mike Comrie .20 .50
142 Mike Grier .12 .30
143 Jochen Hecht .12 .30
144 Georges Laraque .15 .40
145 Todd Marchant .12 .30
146 Jussi Markkanen .12 .30
147 Janne Niinimaa .12 .30
148 Tommy Salo .15 .40
149 Ryan Smyth .15 .40
150 Mike York .12 .30
151 Eric Beaudoin .12 .30
152 Valeri Bure .15 .40
153 Niklas Hagman .12 .30
154 Kristian Huselius .12 .30
155 Trevor Kidd .12 .30
156 Roberto Luongo .30 .75
157 Marcus Nilsson .12 .30
158 Sandis Ozolinsh .15 .40
159 Nick Smith .12 .30
160 Robert Svehla .12 .30
161 Stephen Weiss .20 .50
162 Jason Wiemer .12 .30
163 Peter Worrell .12 .30
164 Jason Allison .15 .40
165 Adam Deadmarsh .15 .40
166 Steve Heinze .12 .30
167 Craig Johnson .12 .30
168 Ian Laperriere .15 .40
169 Aaron Miller .12 .30
170 Jaroslav Modry .12 .30
171 Zigmund Palffy .20 .50
172 Felix Potvin .30 .75
173 Cliff Ronning .12 .30
174 Mathieu Schneider .12 .30
175 Bryan Smolinski .15 .40
176 Jamie Storr .15 .40
177 Andrew Brunette .12 .30
178 Hnat Domenichelli .12 .30
179 Jim Dowd .12 .30
180 Pascal Dupuis .12 .30
181 Manny Fernandez .15 .40
182 Marian Gaborik .30 .75
183 Darby Hendrickson .12 .30
184 Filip Kuba .12 .30
185 Antti Laaksonen .12 .30
186 Stacy Roest .12 .30
187 Dwayne Roloson .12 .30
188 Wes Walz .12 .30
189 Sergei Zholtok .12 .30
190 Donald Audette .12 .30
191 Sergei Berezin .12 .30
192 Patrice Brisebois .12 .30
193 Andreas Dackell .12 .30
194 Stephane Fiset .12 .30
195 Mathieu Garon .15 .40
196 Doug Gilmour .25 .60
197 Joe Juneau .15 .40
198 Saku Koivu .20 .50
199 Andrei Markov .20 .50
200 Yanic Perreault .12 .30
201 Oleg Petrov .12 .30
202 Mike Ribeiro .15 .40
203 Jose Theodore .20 .50
204 Richard Zednik .12 .30
205 Denis Arkhipov .12 .30
206 Andy Delmore .12 .30
207 Mike Dunham .15 .40
208 Martin Erat .12 .30
209 Stu Grimson .12 .30
210 Scott Hartnell .20 .50
211 Greg Johnson .12 .30
212 David Legwand .15 .40
213 Vladimir Orszagh .12 .30
214 Kimmo Timonen .12 .30
215 Tomas Vokoun .15 .40
216 Scott Walker .12 .30
217 Vitali Yachmenev .12 .30
218 Martin Brodeur .40 1.00
219 Sergei Brylin .12 .30
220 Patrik Elias .20 .50
221 Brian Gionta .15 .40
222 Scott Gomez .15 .40
223 Bobby Holik .12 .30
224 Jamie Langenbrunner .15 .40
225 John Madden .12 .30
226 Scott Niedermayer .20 .50
227 Joe Nieuwendyk .20 .50
228 Brian Rafalski .12 .30
229 Scott Stevens .20 .50
230 Petr Sykora .15 .40
231 John Vanbiesbrouck .20 .50
232 Adrian Aucoin .12 .30
233 Shawn Bates .12 .30
234 Mariusz Czerkawski .12 .30
235 Rick DiPietro .15 .40
236 Roman Hamrlik .12 .30
237 Brad Isbister .12 .30
238 Kenny Jonsson .12 .30
239 Kip Miller .12 .30
240 Chris Osgood .20 .50
241 Mark Parrish .12 .30
242 Michael Peca .15 .40
243 Garth Snow .15 .40
244 Raffi Torres .12 .30
245 Alexei Yashin .15 .40
246 Matthew Barnaby .12 .30
247 Bryan Berard .12 .30
248 Dan Blackburn .15 .40
249 Pavel Bure .25 .60
250 Radek Dvorak .15 .40
251 Theo Fleury .25 .60
252 Brian Leetch .20 .50
253 Eric Lindros .30 .75
254 Vladimir Malakhov .12 .30
255 Sandy McCarthy .12 .30
256 Mark Messier .30 .75
257 Petr Nedved .12 .30
258 Mike Richter .20 .50
259 Martin Rucinsky .12 .30
260 Daniel Alfredsson .20 .50
261 Magnus Arvedson .12 .30
262 Chris Bala .12 .30
263 Radek Bonk .15 .40
264 Zdeno Chara .20 .50
265 Mike Fisher .12 .30
266 Martin Havlat .15 .40
267 Marian Hossa .15 .40
268 Jani Hurme .15 .40
269 Patrick Lalime .15 .40
270 Shawn McEachern .12 .30
271 Chris Phillips .12 .30
272 Wade Redden .12 .30
273 Sami Salo .12 .30
274 Todd White .12 .30
275 Brian Boucher .15 .40
276 Donald Brashear .12 .30
277 Roman Cechmanek .15 .40
278 Eric Desjardins .12 .30
279 Jiri Dopita .12 .30
280 Simon Gagne .20 .50
281 Kim Johnsson .12 .30
282 John LeClair .20 .50
283 Neil Little .12 .30
284 Adam Oates .20 .50
285 Keith Primeau .20 .50
286 Mark Recchi .25 .60
287 Jeremy Roenick .20 .50
288 Bill Tibbetts .12 .30
289 Eric Weinrich .12 .30
290 Justin Williams .15 .40
291 Daniel Briere .15 .40
292 Sean Burke .12 .30
293 Shane Doan .15 .40
294 Robert Esche .12 .30
295 Michal Handzus .15 .40
296 Mike Johnson .15 .40
297 Krystofer Kolanos .12 .30
298 Daymond Langkow .15 .40
299 Claude Lemieux .15 .40
300 Daniil Markov .12 .30
301 Ladislav Nagy .12 .30
302 Andrei Nazarov .15 .40
303 Teppo Numminen .15 .40
304 Brian Savage .12 .30
305 J-S Aubin .12 .30
306 Kris Beech .12 .30
307 Johan Hedberg .20 .50
308 Jan Hrdina .12 .30
309 Alexei Kovalev .20 .50
310 Milan Kraft .12 .30
311 Robert Lang .12 .30
312 Mario Lemieux .60 1.50
313 Alexei Morozov .12 .30
314 Toby Petersen .12 .30
315 Wayne Primeau .15 .40
316 Randy Robitaille .12 .30
317 Michal Rozsival .15 .40
318 Martin Straka .15 .40
319 Fred Brathwaite .15 .40
320 Pavol Demitra .25 .60
321 Dallas Drake .15 .40
322 Ray Ferraro .15 .40
323 Brent Johnson .15 .40
324 Reed Low .12 .30
325 Al MacInnis .20 .50
326 Scott Mellanby .12 .30
327 Chris Pronger .15 .40
328 Cory Stillman .12 .30
329 Keith Tkachuk .20 .50
330 Doug Weight .20 .50
331 Scott Young .12 .30
332 Vincent Damphousse .15 .40
333 Adam Graves .15 .40
334 Jeff Jillson .12 .30
335 Bryan Marchment .15 .40
336 Patrick Marleau .20 .50
337 Evgeni Nabokov .15 .40
338 Owen Nolan .20 .50
339 Mike Ricci .15 .40
340 Teemu Selanne .40 1.00
341 Brad Stuart .12 .30
342 Marco Sturm .12 .30
343 Gary Suter .15 .40
344 Scott Thornton .12 .30
345 Nikita Alexeev .12 .30
346 Dave Andreychuk .20 .50
347 Ben Clymer .12 .30
348 Nikolai Khabibulin .20 .50
349 Dieter Kochan .12 .30
350 Pavel Kubina .12 .30
351 Vincent Lecavalier .15 .40
352 Fredrik Modin .12 .30
353 Vaclav Prospal .12 .30
354 Brad Richards .20 .50
355 Martin St.Louis .20 .50
356 Shane Willis .12 .30
357 Tom Barrasso .15 .40
358 Shayne Corson .12 .30
359 Tie Domi .15 .40
360 Travis Green .12 .30
361 Curtis Joseph .20 .50
362 Tomas Kaberle .12 .30
363 Bryan McCabe .12 .30
364 Alyn McCauley .12 .30
365 Alexander Mogilny .15 .40
366 Robert Reichel .12 .30
367 Mikael Renberg .12 .30
368 Gary Roberts .12 .30
369 Corey Schwab .15 .40
370 Mats Sundin .20 .50
371 Darcy Tucker .12 .30
372 Dimitri Yushkevich .12 .30
373 Todd Bertuzzi .20 .50
374 Andrew Cassels .12 .30
375 Dan Cloutier .15 .40
376 Matt Cooke .12 .30
377 Jan Hlavac .12 .30

378 Ed Jovanovski	.15	.40
379 Trevor Linden	.20	.50
380 Brendan Morrison	.15	.40
381 Markus Naslund	.15	.40
382 Mattias Ohlund	.12	.30
383 Daniel Sedin	.20	.50
384 Henrik Sedin	.20	.50
385 Peter Skudra	.12	.30
386 Brent Sopel	.12	.30
387 Craig Billington	.12	.30
388 Peter Bondra	.20	.50
389 Ulf Dahlen	.12	.30
390 Sergei Gonchar	.15	.40
391 Jeff Halpern	.12	.30
392 Jaromir Jagr	.50	1.25
393 Calle Johansson	.12	.30
394 Dimitri Khristich	.12	.30
395 Olaf Kolzig	.20	.50
396 Steve Konowalchuk	.12	.30
397 Andrei Nikolishin	.12	.30
398 Stephen Peat	.12	.30
399 Chris Simon	.12	.30
400 Dainius Zubrus	.12	.30
401 Stanislav Chistov RC	1.00	2.50
402 Alexei Smirnov RC	1.25	3.00
403 Chuck Kobasew RC	1.25	3.00
404 Rick Nash RC	8.00	20.00
405 Henrik Zetterberg RC	10.00	25.00
406 Ales Hemsky RC	4.00	10.00
407 Jay Bouwmeester RC	3.00	8.00
408 Alexander Frolov RC	2.00	5.00
409 P-M Bouchard RC	1.50	4.00
410 Alexander Svitov RC	1.00	2.50

2002-03 Pacific Blue

This 400-card set paralleled the base set but carried blue foil highlights in place of the silver foil on the base set. Cards in this set were serial-numbered out of 45.

*BLUE/45: 8X TO 20X BASIC CARDS

256 Mark Messier	8.00	20.00

2002-03 Pacific Red

Inserted at 1:2 packs, this 400-card set paralleled the base set but carried red foil highlights in place of the silver foil on the base set.

*RED: .6X TO 1.5X BASIC CARDS

256 Mark Messier	.60	1.50

2002-03 Pacific Cramer's Choice

This 10-card set was inserted at 1:732 packs. Each card was serial-numbered to just 95 copies.

1 Dany Heatley	6.00	15.00
2 Ilya Kovalchuk	6.00	15.00
3 Joe Thornton	6.00	15.00
4 Peter Forsberg	10.00	25.00
5 Patrick Roy	25.00	60.00
6 Dominik Hasek	8.00	20.00
7 Steve Yzerman	25.00	60.00
8 Martin Brodeur	15.00	40.00
9 Mario Lemieux	30.00	75.00
10 Mats Sundin	4.00	10.00

2002-03 Pacific Impact Zone

This 10-card set was inserted at 1:9 packs.

COMPLETE SET (10)	8.00	15.00
1 Paul Kariya	.40	1.00
2 Ilya Kovalchuk	.50	1.25
3 Joe Thornton	.60	1.50
4 Jarome Iginla	.60	1.50
5 Joe Sakic	.75	2.00
6 Brendan Shanahan	.60	1.50
7 Saku Koivu	.40	1.00
8 Eric Lindros	.60	1.50
9 Mario Lemieux	2.50	6.00
10 Teemu Selanne	.40	1.00

2002-03 Pacific Jerseys

Inserted at 2:37, this 50-card set featured swatches of game-worn jerseys. The NNO card at the end of this set was inserted at a stated rate of 1:732 and was serial-numbered out of 500. A holo-silver hobby only parallel was also created and serial-numbered to 40 sets. The parallel had a silver foil border around the jersey swatch.

*HOLOSILVER/40: 1X TO 2.5X BASIC JSY

1 Dany Heatley	5.00	12.00
2 Milan Hnilicka	3.00	8.00
3 Joe Thornton	6.00	15.00
4 Miroslav Satan	3.00	8.00
5 Roman Turek	3.00	8.00
6 Arturs Irbe	3.00	8.00
7 Tony Amonte	3.00	8.00
8 Steve Sullivan	3.00	8.00
9 Rob Blake	3.00	8.00
10 Chris Drury	3.00	8.00
11 Joe Sakic	8.00	20.00
12 Marc Denis	3.00	8.00
13 Ron Tugnutt	3.00	8.00
14 Jason Arnott	3.00	8.00
15 Mike Modano	6.00	15.00
16 Sergei Fedorov	5.00	12.00
17 Dominik Hasek	12.50	30.00
18 Jason Williams	3.00	8.00
19 Tommy Salo	3.00	8.00
20 Wade Flaherty	3.00	8.00
21 Jason Allison	3.00	8.00
22 Aaron Miller	3.00	8.00
23 Cliff Ronning	3.00	8.00
24 Manny Fernandez	3.00	8.00
25 Sergei Berezin	3.00	8.00
26 Yanic Perreault	3.00	8.00
27 Jose Theodore	5.00	12.00
28 Martin Erat	3.00	8.00
29 Jukka Hentunen	3.00	8.00
30 Jamie Langenbrunner SP	3.00	8.00
31 Joe Nieuwendyk SP	3.00	8.00
32 Michael Peca	3.00	8.00
33 Alexei Yashin	3.00	8.00
34 Pavel Bure	4.00	10.00
35 Theo Fleury	3.00	8.00
36 Mark Messier	4.00	10.00
37 Martin Havlat	3.00	8.00
38 Jiri Dopita	3.00	8.00
39 Simon Gagne	4.00	10.00
40 Adam Oates	3.00	8.00
41 Daymond Langkow	3.00	8.00
42 Mario Lemieux	10.00	25.00
43 Pavol Demitra	3.00	8.00
44 Ray Ferraro	3.00	8.00
45 Evgeni Nabokov	3.00	8.00
46 Fredrik Modin	3.00	8.00
47 Alexander Mogilny	3.00	8.00
48 Darcy Tucker	3.00	8.00
49 Dan Cloutier	3.00	8.00
50 Jaromir Jagr	6.00	15.00
NNO I.Kovalchuk AU/500	15.00	40.00

2002-03 Pacific Lamplighters

This 14-card set was inserted at 1:20 packs.

COMPLETE SET (14)	25.00	50.00
1 Dany Heatley	1.00	2.50
2 Ilya Kovalchuk	1.00	2.50
3 Joe Thornton	1.25	3.00
4 Jarome Iginla	1.00	2.50
5 Peter Forsberg	2.00	5.00
6 Joe Sakic	1.50	4.00
7 Steve Yzerman	3.00	8.00
8 Alexei Yashin	.75	2.00
9 Pavel Bure	1.25	3.00
10 Eric Lindros	.75	2.00
11 Mario Lemieux	4.00	10.00
12 Mats Sundin	.75	2.00
13 Todd Bertuzzi	.75	2.00
14 Jaromir Jagr	1.25	3.00

2002-03 Pacific Main Attractions

This 20-card set was inserted at 1:12 packs.

COMPLETE SET (20)	15.00	30.00
1 Paul Kariya	.40	1.00
2 Ilya Kovalchuk	1.50	4.00
3 Joe Thornton	.60	1.50
4 Jarome Iginla	.60	1.50
5 Patrick Roy	2.00	5.00
6 Mike Modano	.60	1.50
7 Steve Yzerman	2.00	5.00
8 Mike Comrie	.30	.75
9 Jason Allison	.30	.75
10 Jose Theodore	.50	1.25
11 Martin Brodeur	1.50	4.00
12 Alexei Yashin	.30	.75
13 Pavel Bure	.60	1.50
14 Daniel Alfredsson	.30	.75
15 Jeremy Roenick	.50	1.25
16 Mario Lemieux	2.50	6.00
17 Keith Tkachuk	.40	1.00
18 Mats Sundin	.40	1.00
19 Markus Naslund	.40	1.00
20 Jaromir Jagr	.60	1.50

2002-03 Pacific Maximum Impact

This 16-card set was inserted at 1:12 packs.

COMPLETE SET (16)	12.50	25.00
1 Roman Turek	.30	.75
2 Patrick Roy	2.00	5.00
3 Dominik Hasek	.75	2.00
4 Jose Theodore	.60	1.50
5 Martin Brodeur	1.25	3.00
6 Sean Burke	.30	.75
7 Evgeni Nabokov	.30	.75
8 Curtis Joseph	.40	1.00
9 Ilya Kovalchuk	1.50	4.00
10 Joe Thornton	.60	1.50
11 Jarome Iginla	.60	1.50
12 Joe Sakic	.75	2.00
13 Steve Yzerman	2.00	5.00
14 Eric Lindros	.40	1.00
15 Mario Lemieux	2.50	6.00
16 Mats Sundin	.40	1.00

2002-03 Pacific Shining Moments

This 10-card set was inserted at 1:20 packs.

COMPLETE SET (10)	20.00	40.00
1 Dany Heatley	2.50	6.00
2 Ilya Kovalchuk	3.00	8.00
3 Erik Cole	1.50	4.00
4 Radim Vrbata	1.50	4.00
5 Pavel Datsyuk	2.50	6.00
6 Kristian Huselius	1.50	4.00
7 Stephen Weiss	1.50	4.00
8 Mike Ribeiro	1.50	4.00
9 Dan Blackburn	2.00	5.00
10 Krystofer Kolanos	1.50	4.00

2003-04 Pacific

Released in late July 2003, this 350-card set was the first of the 2003-04 season. Cards 351-360 were available only by a mail-in/internet redemption offer and cards 361-368 were available in packs of Pacific Calder.

COMPLETE SET (368)	60.00	120.00
COMP.SET w/o SP's (350)	15.00	40.00
351-360 STATED PRINT RUN 999		
361-368 STATED PRINT RUN 1225		
1 Stanislav Chistov	.15	.40
2 Martin Gerber	.15	.40
3 Jean-Sebastien Giguere	.25	.60
4 Niclas Havelid	.15	.40
5 Paul Kariya	.30	.75
6 Mike Leclerc	.15	.40
7 Adam Oates	.25	.60
8 Sandis Ozolinsh	.15	.40
9 Steve Rucchin	.15	.40
10 Petr Sykora	.20	.50
11 Steve Thomas	.15	.40
12 Byron Dafoe	.20	.50
13 Joe DiPenta RC	.40	1.00
14 Dany Heatley	.25	.60
15 Milan Hnilicka	.15	.40
16 Ilya Kovalchuk	.25	.60
17 Slava Kozlov	.20	.50
18 Shawn McEachern	.15	.40
19 Pasi Nurminen	.20	.50
20 Jeff Odgers	.15	.40
21 Marc Savard	.20	.50
22 Patrik Stefan	.15	.40
23 P.J. Axelsson	.15	.40
24 Bryan Berard	.20	.50
25 Nick Boynton	.15	.40
26 Jeff Hackett	.20	.50
27 Mike Knuble	.15	.40
28 Glen Murray	.20	.50
29 Brian Rolston	.20	.50
30 Sergei Samsonov	.20	.50
31 Steve Shields	.20	.50
32 P.J. Stock	.15	.40
33 Jozef Stumpel	.15	.40
34 Joe Thornton	.30	.75
35 Milan Bartovic RC	.40	1.00
36 Martin Biron	.20	.50
37 Daniel Briere	.25	.60
38 Curtis Brown	.15	.40
39 Tim Connolly	.15	.40
40 J-P Dumont	.15	.40
41 Ales Kotalik	.15	.40
42 Ryan Miller	.25	.60
43 Mika Noronen	.15	.40
44 Taylor Pyatt	.15	.40
45 Miroslav Satan	.20	.50
46 Alexei Zhitnik	.20	.50
47 Craig Conroy	.15	.40
48 Chris Drury	.20	.50
49 Martin Gelinas	.15	.40
50 Jarome Iginla	.25	.60
51 Chuck Kobasew	.15	.40
52 Jordan Leopold	.15	.40
53 Toni Lydman	.15	.40
54 Dean McAmmond	.15	.40
55 Jamie McLennan	.15	.40
56 Roman Turek	.20	.50
57 Stephane Yelle	.15	.40
58 Ryan Bayda	.15	.40
59 Rod Brind'Amour	.25	.60
60 Erik Cole	.20	.50
61 Ron Francis	.30	.75
62 Jeff Heerema	.15	.40
63 Sean Hill	.15	.40
64 Arturs Irbe	.20	.50
65 Jeff O'Neill	.15	.40
66 Radim Vrbata	.20	.50
67 Kevin Weekes	.20	.50
68 Craig Andersson	.25	.60
69 Tyler Arnason	.15	.40
70 Mark Bell	.15	.40
71 Kyle Calder	.15	.40
72 Eric Daze	.20	.50
73 Theoren Fleury	.30	.75
74 Steve Passmore	.15	.40
75 Chris Simon	.15	.40
76 Steve Sullivan	.15	.40
77 Jocelyn Thibault	.20	.50
78 Alexei Zhamnov	.20	.50
79 David Aebischer	.20	.50
80 Bates Battaglia	.15	.40
81 Rob Blake	.25	.60
82 Adam Foote	.15	.40
83 Peter Forsberg	.30	.75
84 Milan Hejduk	.20	.50
85 Derek Morris	.15	.40
86 Vaclav Nedorost	.15	.40
87 Steven Reinprecht	.15	.40
88 Patrick Roy	.60	1.50
89 Joe Sakic	.40	1.00
90 Alex Tanguay	.20	.50
91 Andrew Cassels	.15	.40
92 Marc Denis	.20	.50
93 Rostislav Klesla	.15	.40
94 Pascal Leclaire	.15	.40
95 Kent McDonell RC	.40	1.00
96 Rick Nash	.25	.60
97 Geoff Sanderson	.15	.40
98 Mike Sillinger	.15	.40
99 David Vyborny	.15	.40
100 Ray Whitney	.20	.50
101 Tyler Wright	.15	.40
102 Jason Arnott	.20	.50
103 Ulf Dahlen	.15	.40
104 Bill Guerin	.25	.60
105 Derian Hatcher	.15	.40
106 Jere Lehtinen	.20	.50
107 Mike Modano	.40	1.00
108 Brenden Morrow	.20	.50
109 Steve Ott	.20	.50
110 Ron Tugnutt	.20	.50
111 Marty Turco	.25	.60
112 Pierre Turgeon	.25	.60
113 Scott Young	.15	.40
114 Sergei Zubov	.20	.50
115 Chris Chelios	.25	.60
116 Pavel Datsyuk	.30	.75
117 Sergei Fedorov	.40	1.00
118 Tomas Holmstrom	.20	.50
119 Brett Hull	.30	.75
120 Curtis Joseph	.25	.60
121 Igor Larionov	.25	.60
122 Manny Legace	.15	.40
123 Nicklas Lidstrom	.25	.60
124 Luc Robitaille	.25	.60
125 Mathieu Schneider	.15	.40
126 Brendan Shanahan	.30	.75
127 Steve Yzerman	.60	1.50
128 Henrik Zetterberg	.30	.75
129 Eric Brewer	.15	.40
130 Jason Chimera	.15	.40
131 Mike Comrie	.20	.50
132 Ales Hemsky	.25	.60
133 Brad Isbister	.15	.40
134 Georges Laraque	.20	.50
135 Todd Marchant	.15	.40
136 Jussi Markkanen	.15	.40
137 Tommy Salo	.20	.50
138 Ryan Smyth	.20	.50
139 Mike York	.15	.40
140 Jaroslav Bednar	.15	.40
141 Jay Bouwmeester	.25	.60
142 Matt Cullen	.15	.40
143 Jani Hurme	.15	.40
144 Kristian Huselius	.15	.40
145 Olli Jokinen	.25	.60
146 Viktor Kozlov	.15	.40
147 Roberto Luongo	.40	1.00
148 Marcus Nilsson	.15	.40
149 Stephen Weiss	.15	.40
150 Peter Worrell	.15	.40
151 Jason Allison	.20	.50
152 Jared Aulin	.15	.40
153 Michael Cammalleri	.25	.60
154 Adam Deadmarsh	.20	.50
155 Alexander Frolov	.20	.50
156 Cristobal Huet	.20	.50
157 Jaroslav Modry	.15	.40
158 Zigmund Palffy	.25	.60
159 Felix Potvin	.40	1.00
160 Jamie Storr	.20	.50
161 Pierre-Marc Bouchard	.25	.60
162 Andrew Brunette	.15	.40
163 Pascal Dupuis	.15	.40
164 Manny Fernandez	.20	.50
165 Marian Gaborik	.40	1.00
166 Filip Kuba	.15	.40
167 Antti Laaksonen	.15	.40
168 Richard Park	.15	.40
169 Dwayne Roloson	.20	.50
170 Cliff Ronning	.15	.40
171 Wes Walz	.15	.40
172 Sergei Zholtok	.15	.40
173 Donald Audette	.15	.40
174 Patrice Brisebois	.15	.40
175 Jan Bulis	.15	.40
176 Mathieu Garon	.15	.40
177 Marcel Hossa	.15	.40
178 Saku Koivu	.25	.60
179 Andrei Markov	.25	.60
180 Yanic Perreault	.15	.40
181 Mike Ribeiro	.20	.50
182 Niklas Sundstrom	.15	.40
183 Jose Theodore	.25	.60
184 Richard Zednik	.15	.40
185 Denis Arkhipov	.15	.40
186 Andy Delmore	.15	.40
187 Adam Hall	.15	.40
188 Scott Hartnell	.25	.60
189 Andreas Johansson	.15	.40
190 David Legwand	.20	.50
191 Oleg Petrov	.15	.40
192 Kimmo Timonen	.15	.40
193 Scottie Upshall	.20	.50
194 Tomas Vokoun	.20	.50
195 Scott Walker	.15	.40
196 Martin Brodeur	.50	1.25
197 Patrik Elias	.25	.60
198 Jeff Friesen	.15	.40
199 Brian Gionta	.20	.50
200 Scott Gomez	.20	.50
201 Jamie Langenbrunner	.20	.50
202 John Madden	.15	.40
203 Scott Niedermayer	.25	.60
204 Joe Nieuwendyk	.25	.60
205 Brian Rafalski	.20	.50
206 Scott Stevens	.25	.60
207 Oleg Tverdovsky	.15	.40
208 Arron Asham	.15	.40
209 Shawn Bates	.15	.40
210 Jason Blake	.15	.40
211 Rick DiPietro	.20	.50
212 Roman Hamrlik	.20	.50
213 Mark Parrish	.15	.40
214 Michael Peca	.20	.50
215 Dave Scatchard	.15	.40
216 Garth Snow	.20	.50
217 Mattias Weinhandl	.15	.40
218 Alexei Yashin	.20	.50
219 Matthew Barnaby	.20	.50
220 Dan Blackburn	.20	.50
221 Pavel Bure	.30	.75
222 Anson Carter	.20	.50
223 Mike Dunham	.20	.50
224 Bobby Holik	.15	.40
225 Alex Kovalev	.20	.50
226 Brian Leetch	.25	.60
227 Eric Lindros	.40	1.00
228 Mark Messier	.40	1.00
229 Petr Nedved	.15	.40
230 Tom Poti	.15	.40
231 Mike Richter	.25	.60
232 Daniel Alfredsson	.25	.60
233 Magnus Arvedson	.15	.40
234 Radek Bonk	.20	.50
235 Zdeno Chara	.25	.60
236 Mike Fisher	.15	.40
237 Martin Havlat	.25	.60
238 Marian Hossa	.20	.50
239 Patrick Lalime	.20	.50
240 Martin Prusek	.15	.40
241 Wade Redden	.15	.40
242 Bryan Smolinski	.15	.40
243 Jason Spezza	.25	.60
244 Vaclav Varada	.15	.40
245 Todd White	.15	.40
246 Tony Amonte	.20	.50
247 Donald Brashear	.15	.40
248 Roman Cechmanek	.20	.50
249 Eric Desjardins	.20	.50
250 Robert Esche	.15	.40
251 Simon Gagne	.25	.60
252 Michal Handzus	.20	.50
253 Kim Johnsson	.15	.40
254 John LeClair	.25	.60
255 Keith Primeau	.25	.60
256 Mark Recchi	.30	.75
257 Jeremy Roenick	.25	.60
258 Zac Bierk	.15	.40
259 Brian Boucher	.20	.50
260 Sean Burke	.15	.40
261 Shane Doan	.20	.50
262 Chris Gratton	.15	.40
263 Jan Hrdina	.15	.40
264 Mike Johnson	.15	.40
265 Daymond Langkow	.15	.40
266 Ladislav Nagy	.15	.40
267 Teppo Numminen	.15	.40
268 Jeff Taffe	.15	.40
269 Ramzi Abid	.15	.40
270 Rico Fata	.15	.40
271 Johan Hedberg	.20	.50
272 Brian Holzinger	.15	.40
273 Mathias Johansson	.15	.40
274 Mario Lemieux	.75	2.00
275 Alexei Morozov	.15	.40
276 Martin Straka	.15	.40
277 Tomas Surovy	.15	.40
278 Dick Tarnstrom	.15	.40
279 Eric Boguniecki	.15	.40
280 Pavol Demitra	.30	.75
281 Dallas Drake	.15	.40
282 Barret Jackman	.15	.40
283 Brent Johnson	.20	.50
284 Al MacInnis	.25	.60
285 Scott Mellanby	.15	.40
286 Chris Osgood	.25	.60
287 Chris Pronger	.20	.50
288 Peter Sejna RC	.40	1.00
289 Cory Stillman	.15	.40
290 Keith Tkachuk	.25	.60
291 Doug Weight	.25	.60
292 Jonathan Cheechoo	.20	.50
293 Vincent Damphousse	.20	.50
294 Niko Dimitrakos	.15	.40
295 Miikka Kiprusoff	.20	.50
296 Patrick Marleau	.25	.60
297 Alyn McCauley	.15	.40
298 Evgeni Nabokov	.20	.50
299 Mike Ricci	.20	.50
300 Teemu Selanne	.50	1.25
301 Marco Sturm	.15	.40
302 Vesa Toskala	.15	.40
303 Dave Andreychuk	.25	.60
304 Dan Boyle	.20	.50
305 Ruslan Fedotenko	.15	.40
306 John Grahame	.15	.40
307 Nikolai Khabibulin	.25	.60
308 Vincent Lecavalier	.20	.50
309 Fredrik Modin	.15	.40
310 Vaclav Prospal	.15	.40
311 Brad Richards	.25	.60
312 Martin St. Louis	.25	.60
313 Alexander Svitov	.15	.40
314 Nik Antropov	.20	.50
315 Ed Belfour	.25	.60
316 Tie Domi	.20	.50
317 Doug Gilmour	.30	.75
318 Tomas Kaberle	.15	.40
319 Trevor Kidd	.15	.40
320 Alexander Mogilny	.20	.50
321 Owen Nolan	.20	.50
322 Gary Roberts	.15	.40
323 Matt Stajan RC	.50	1.25
324 Mats Sundin	.25	.60
325 Robert Svehla	.15	.40
326 Darcy Tucker	.20	.50
327 Todd Bertuzzi	.25	.60
328 Dan Cloutier	.20	.50
329 Matt Cooke	.15	.40
330 Ed Jovanovski	.20	.50
331 Trent Klatt	.15	.40
332 Trevor Linden	.25	.60
333 Brendan Morrison	.20	.50
334 Markus Naslund	.25	.60
335 Daniel Sedin	.25	.60
336 Henrik Sedin	.25	.60
337 Peter Skudra	.20	.50
338 Brent Sopel	.15	.40
339 Sergei Berezin	.15	.40
340 Peter Bondra	.20	.50
341 Sebastien Charpentier	.15	.40
342 Sergei Gonchar	.15	.40
343 Mike Grier	.15	.40
344 Jeff Halpern	.15	.40
345 Jaromir Jagr	.60	1.50
346 Olaf Kolzig	.25	.60
347 Robert Lang	.15	.40
348 Kip Miller	.15	.40
349 Michael Nylander	.15	.40
350 Dainius Zubrus	.15	.40
351 Joffrey Lupul RC	1.50	4.00
352 Eric Staal RC	3.00	8.00
353 Tuomo Ruutu RC	1.00	2.50
354 Pavel Vorobiev RC	.75	2.00
355 Nathan Horton RC	1.50	4.00
356 Dustin Brown RC	1.25	3.00
357 Jordin Tootoo RC	1.25	3.00
358 Marc-Andre Fleury RC	4.00	10.00
359 Milan Michalek RC	1.25	3.00
360 Boyd Gordon RC	.75	2.00
361 Derek Roy RC	1.00	2.50
362 Matthew Lombardi RC	.75	2.00
363 Nikolai Zherdev RC	1.25	3.00
364 Jiri Hudler RC	1.50	4.00
365 Niklas Kronwall RC	1.25	3.00
366 Fredrik Sjostrom RC	1.00	2.50
367 Ryan Malone RC	1.25	3.00
368 Ryan Kesler RC	3.00	8.00

2003-04 Pacific Blue

*BLUE/250: 1.2X TO 3X BASIC CARDS

2003-04 Pacific Red

*RED: .6X TO 1.5X BASIC CARDS

STATED ODDS: 1:3

228 Mark Messier	.60	1.50

2003-04 Pacific Cramer's Choice

STATED PRINT RUN 99 SER.#'d SETS

1 Peter Forsberg	12.00	30.00
2 Patrick Roy	25.00	60.00
3 Rick Nash	12.00	30.00
4 Mike Modano	8.00	20.00
5 Steve Yzerman	20.00	50.00
6 Henrik Zetterberg	10.00	25.00
7 Martin Brodeur	20.00	50.00
8 Mario Lemieux	30.00	80.00
9 Markus Naslund	4.00	10.00
10 Jaromir Jagr	10.00	25.00

2003-04 Pacific In the Crease

COMPLETE SET (12)	10.00	20.00
STATED ODDS 1:10		
1 Jean-Sebastien Giguere	.60	1.50
2 Jocelyn Thibault	.60	1.50
3 Patrick Roy	1.50	4.00
4 Marty Turco	.60	1.50
5 Curtis Joseph	.75	2.00
6 Jose Theodore	1.00	2.50
7 Martin Brodeur	1.25	3.00
8 Patrick Lalime	.60	1.50
9 Roman Cechmanek	.60	1.50
10 Sean Burke	.60	1.50
11 Ed Belfour	.75	2.00
12 Dan Cloutier	.60	1.50

2003-04 Pacific Jerseys

STATED ODDS 1:19

*GOLD/50: 1X TO 2.5X BASIC JSY

1 Paul Kariya	2.50	6.00
2 Dany Heatley	3.00	8.00
3 Milan Hnilicka	2.00	5.00
4 Ilya Kovalchuk	3.00	8.00
5 Joe Thornton	5.00	12.00
6 J-P Dumont	2.00	5.00
7 Chris Drury	2.00	5.00
8 Peter Forsberg	6.00	15.00
9 Patrick Roy	10.00	25.00
10 Joe Sakic	5.00	12.00
11 Alex Tanguay	2.00	5.00
12 Geoff Sanderson	2.00	5.00
13 Mike Modano	3.00	8.00
14 Marty Turco	2.00	5.00
15 Brendan Shanahan	2.50	6.00
16 Steve Yzerman	8.00	20.00
17 Ryan Smyth	2.00	5.00
18 Ziggy Palffy	2.00	5.00
19 Filip Kuba	2.00	5.00
20 Saku Koivu	2.50	6.00
21 Jose Theodore	3.00	8.00
22 Scott Walker	2.00	5.00
23 Martin Brodeur	8.00	20.00
24 Alexei Yashin	2.00	5.00
25 Pavel Bure	2.50	6.00
26 Eric Lindros	2.50	6.00
27 Daniel Alfredsson	2.00	5.00
28 Jason Spezza	5.00	12.00
29 Roman Cechmanek	2.00	5.00
30 Jeremy Roenick	3.00	8.00
31 Mario Lemieux	10.00	25.00
32 Brent Johnson	2.00	5.00
33 Keith Tkachuk	2.50	6.00
34 Miikka Kiprusoff	2.00	5.00
35 Vincent Lecavalier	2.00	5.00
36 Fredrik Modin	2.00	5.00
37 Ed Belfour	3.00	8.00
38 Todd Bertuzzi	2.50	6.00
39 Dan Cloutier	2.00	5.00
40 Jaromir Jagr	3.00	8.00

2003-04 Pacific Main Attractions

STATED ODDS 1:10

1 Paul Kariya	.60	1.50
2 Ilya Kovalchuk	.75	2.00
3 Joe Thornton	.75	2.00
4 Peter Forsberg	1.25	3.00
5 Mike Modano	.75	2.00
6 Steve Yzerman	1.50	4.00
7 Marian Gaborik	1.00	2.50
8 Saku Koivu	.60	1.50
9 Pavel Bure	.60	1.50
10 Marian Hossa	.60	1.50
11 John LeClair	.60	1.50
12 Mario Lemieux	2.00	5.00
13 Teemu Selanne	.60	1.50
14 Mats Sundin	.60	1.50
15 Markus Naslund	.60	1.50
16 Jaromir Jagr	.75	2.00

2003-04 Pacific Marty Turco

This 6-card set highlighted the young career of Marty Turco and was inserted at 1:37.

COMPLETE SET (6)	8.00	15.00
COMMON CARD (1-6)	1.25	3.00

2003-04 Pacific Marty Turco Autographs

This 6-card set paralleled the regular insert set but carried certified autographs. Cards #1-5 were serial-numbered to 99 and card #6 was serial-numbered to 35 copies.

COMMON AUTO/99 (1-5)	15.00	40.00
COMMON AUTO/35 (6)	40.00	100.00

2003-04 Pacific Maximum Impact

COMPLETE SET (10)	10.00	20.00
STATED ODDS 1:19		
1 Joe Thornton	1.25	3.00
2 Jarome Iginla	1.00	2.50
3 Rick Nash	1.00	2.50
4 Brendan Shanahan	.75	2.00
5 Michael Peca	.60	1.50
6 Eric Lindros	.75	2.00
7 Mark Messier	.75	2.00
8 Jeremy Roenick	1.00	2.50
9 Owen Nolan	.60	1.50
10 Todd Bertuzzi	.75	2.00

2003-04 Pacific Milestones

COMPLETE SET (8)	10.00	20.00
STATED ODDS 1:19		
1 Patrick Roy	2.50	6.00
2 Joe Sakic	1.50	4.00
3 Mike Modano	1.25	3.00
4 Marty Turco	.60	1.50
5 Brett Hull	1.00	2.50
6 Joe Nieuwendyk	.60	1.50
7 Mats Sundin	.75	2.00
8 Jaromir Jagr	1.25	3.00

2003-04 Pacific View from the Crease

COMPLETE SET (8)	15.00	30.00
STATED ODDS 1:37		
1 Paul Kariya	1.25	3.00
2 Joe Thornton	2.00	5.00
3 Joe Sakic	2.50	6.00
4 Mike Modano	2.00	5.00
5 Sergei Fedorov	1.50	4.00
6 Brett Hull	1.50	4.00
7 Marian Gaborik	2.50	6.00
8 Todd Bertuzzi	1.25	3.00

2004-05 Pacific

This 300-card set was issued in the summer of 2004 before the eventual NHL lockout. It was the last set produced by Pacific Trading Cards.

COMPLETE SET (300)	15.00	40.00
1 Stanislav Chistov	.12	.30
2 Sergei Fedorov	.30	.75
3 Martin Gerber	.15	.40
4 Jean-Sebastien Giguere	.20	.50
5 Joffrey Lupul	.15	.40
6 Vaclav Prospal	.12	.30
7 Steve Rucchin	.12	.30
8 Martin Skoula	.12	.30
9 Petr Sykora	.15	.40
10 Dany Heatley	.20	.50
11 Ilya Kovalchuk	.20	.50
12 Slava Kozlov	.15	.40
13 Shawn McEachern	.12	.30
14 Pasi Nurminen	.15	.40
15 Ronald Petrovicky	.12	.30
16 Randy Robitaille	.12	.30
17 Marc Savard	.12	.30
18 Patrik Stefan	.12	.30
19 Patrice Bergeron	.25	.60
20 Sergei Gonchar	.15	.40
21 Mike Knuble	.12	.30
22 Glen Murray	.15	.40
23 Felix Potvin	.25	.60
24 Andrew Raycroft	.15	.40
25 Brian Rolston	.15	.40
26 Sergei Samsonov	.15	.40
27 Joe Thornton	.25	.60
28 Maxim Afinogenov	.12	.30
29 Martin Biron	.15	.40
30 Daniel Briere	.20	.50
31 Chris Drury	.15	.40
32 J-P Dumont	.12	.30
33 Jochen Hecht	.12	.30
34 Mika Noronen	.15	.40
35 Derek Roy	.12	.30
36 Miroslav Satan	.15	.40
37 Craig Conroy	.12	.30
38 Shean Donovan	.12	.30
39 Martin Gelinas	.12	.30
40 Jarome Iginla	.20	.50
41 Miikka Kiprusoff	.15	.40
42 Jordan Leopold	.12	.30
43 Matthew Lombardi	.12	.30
44 Steven Reinprecht	.12	.30
45 Chris Simon	.12	.30
46 Rod Brind'Amour	.20	.50
47 Erik Cole	.15	.40
48 Sean Hill	.12	.30
49 Jeff O'Neill	.12	.30
50 Eric Staal	.25	.60
51 Josef Vasicek	.12	.30
52 Radim Vrbata	.15	.40
53 Kevin Weekes	.15	.40
54 Justin Williams	.12	.30
55 Craig Andersson	.20	.50
56 Tyler Arnason	.12	.30
57 Mark Bell	.12	.30
58 Bryan Berard	.15	.40
59 Kyle Calder	.12	.30
60 Eric Daze	.15	.40
61 Brett McLean	.12	.30
62 Tuomo Ruutu	.15	.40
63 Jocelyn Thibault	.15	.40
64 David Aebischer	.15	.40
65 Rob Blake	.20	.50
66 Peter Forsberg	.25	.60
67 Milan Hejduk	.15	.40
68 Paul Kariya	.25	.60
69 Joe Sakic	.30	.75
70 Tommy Salo	.15	.40
71 Teemu Selanne	.40	1.00
72 Alex Tanguay	.15	.40
73 Andrew Cassels	.12	.30
74 Marc Denis	.15	.40
75 Anders Eriksson	.12	.30
76 Trevor Letowski	.12	.30
77 Manny Malhotra	.12	.30
78 Todd Marchant	.12	.30
79 Rick Nash	.20	.50
80 David Vyborny	.12	.30
81 Nikolai Zherdev	.15	.40
82 Jason Arnott	.15	.40
83 Valeri Bure	.15	.40
84 Bill Guerin	.20	.50
85 Jere Lehtinen	.20	.50
86 Mike Modano	.30	.75
87 Brenden Morrow	.20	.50
88 Marty Turco	.20	.50
89 Pierre Turgeon	.20	.50
90 Sergei Zubov	.15	.40
91 Pavel Datsyuk	.25	.60
92 Kris Draper	.12	.30
93 Brett Hull	.25	.60
94 Curtis Joseph	.20	.50
95 Robert Lang	.12	.30
96 Manny Legace	.15	.40
97 Nicklas Lidstrom	.20	.50
98 Brendan Shanahan	.25	.60
99 Steve Yzerman	.60	1.50
100 Ty Conklin	.15	.40
101 Radek Dvorak	.12	.30
102 Ales Hemsky	.20	.50
103 Shawn Horcoff	.15	.40
104 Ethan Moreau	.12	.30
105 Petr Nedved	.12	.30
106 Ryan Smyth	.15	.40
107 Raffi Torres	.12	.30
108 Mike York	.12	.30
109 Jay Bouwmeester	.20	.50
110 Niklas Hagman	.15	.40
111 Nathan Horton	.20	.50
112 Kristian Huselius	.12	.30
113 Olli Jokinen	.15	.40
114 Juraj Kolnik	.12	.30
115 Roberto Luongo	.30	.75
116 Mike Van Ryn	.12	.30
117 Stephen Weiss	.12	.30
118 Derek Armstrong	.12	.30
119 Dustin Brown	.20	.50
120 Roman Cechmanek	.15	.40
121 Alexander Frolov	.15	.40
122 Cristobal Huet	.15	.40
123 Trent Klatt	.12	.30
124 Ziggy Palffy	.20	.50
125 Luc Robitaille	.20	.50
126 Jozef Stumpel	.12	.30
127 Andrew Brunette	.12	.30
128 Brent Burns	.25	.60
129 Alexandre Daigle	.12	.30
130 Pascal Dupuis	.12	.30
131 Manny Fernandez	.15	.40
132 Marian Gaborik	.30	.75
133 Filip Kuba	.12	.30
134 Antti Laaksonen	.12	.30
135 Dwayne Roloson	.15	.40
136 Patrice Brisebois	.12	.30
137 Saku Koivu	.20	.50
138 Alex Kovalev	.12	.30
139 Yanic Perreault	.12	.30
140 Mike Ribeiro	.15	.40
141 Michael Ryder	.15	.40
142 Sheldon Souray	.12	.30
143 Jose Theodore	.20	.50
144 Richard Zednik	.12	.30
145 Martin Erat	.12	.30
146 Adam Hall	.12	.30
147 Scott Hartnell	.20	.50
148 David Legwand	.15	.40
149 Steve Sullivan	.12	.30
150 Jordin Tootoo	.12	.30
151 Tomas Vokoun	.15	.40
152 Scott Walker	.12	.30
153 Marek Zidlicky	.12	.30
154 Martin Brodeur	.40	1.00
155 Patrik Elias	.20	.50
156 Jeff Friesen	.12	.30
157 Brian Gionta	.15	.40
158 Scott Gomez	.15	.40
159 Jamie Langenbrunner	.15	.40
160 John Madden	.12	.30
161 Scott Niedermayer	.20	.50
162 Scott Stevens	.20	.50
163 Adrian Aucoin	.12	.3
164 Jason Blake	.12	.3
165 Mariusz Czerkawski	.12	.3
166 Rick DiPietro	.15	.4
167 Trent Hunter	.12	.3
168 Oleg Kvasha	.12	.3
169 Mark Parrish	.12	.3
170 Michael Peca	.15	.4
171 Alexei Yashin	.15	.4
172 Mike Dunham	.15	.4
173 Jan Hlavac	.12	.3
174 Bobby Holik	.12	.3
175 Jaromir Jagr	.50	1.2
176 Eric Lindros	.30	.7
177 Mark Messier	.50	1.2
178 Boris Mironov	.12	.3
179 Tom Poti	.12	.3
180 Fedor Tyutin	.12	.3
181 Daniel Alfredsson	.20	.5
182 Peter Bondra	.15	.4
183 Zdeno Chara	.20	.5
184 Martin Havlat	.20	.5
185 Marian Hossa	.15	.4
186 Patrick Lalime	.15	.4
187 Wade Redden	.12	.3
188 Bryan Smolinski	.15	.4
189 Jason Spezza	.20	.5
190 Tony Amonte	.15	.4
191 Sean Burke	.12	.3
192 Robert Esche	.15	.4
193 Simon Gagne	.20	.5
194 Michal Handzus	.12	.3
195 John LeClair	.20	.5
196 Joni Pitkanen	.12	.3
197 Mark Recchi	.25	.6
198 Jeremy Roenick	.20	.5

Brian Boucher .15 .40
Mike Comrie .15 .40
Shane Doan .15 .40
Daymond Langkow .12 .30
Paul Mara .12 .30
Derek Morris .12 .30
Ladislav Nagy .12 .30
Fredrik Sjostrom .12 .30
Jeff Taffe .12 .30
Jean-Sebastien Aubin .12 .30
Rico Fata .12 .30
Marc-Andre Fleury .50 1.25
Ric Jackman .12 .30
Milan Kraft .12 .30
Mario Lemieux .60 1.50
Ryan Malone .12 .30
Aleksey Morozov .12 .30
Dick Tarnstrom .12 .30
Pavol Demitra .25 .60
Dallas Drake .12 .30
Barret Jackman .12 .30
Al MacInnis .20 .50
Chris Osgood .20 .50
Chris Pronger .15 .40
Mark Rycroft .12 .30
Keith Tkachuk .20 .50
Doug Weight .20 .50
Jonathan Cheechoo .15 .40
Vincent Damphousse .15 .40
Nils Ekman .12 .30
Alex Korolyuk .12 .30
Patrick Marleau .20 .50
Alyn McCauley .12 .30
Evgeni Nabokov .15 .40
Marco Sturm .12 .30
Vesa Toskala .12 .30
Dave Andreychuk .20 .50
John Grahame .15 .40
Nikolai Khabibulin .20 .50
Pavel Kubina .12 .30
Vincent Lecavalier .15 .40
Fredrik Modin .12 .30
Brad Richards .20 .50
Martin St. Louis .20 .50
Cory Stillman .12 .30
Ed Belfour .20 .50
Brian Leetch .20 .50
Bryan McCabe .12 .30
Alexander Mogilny .15 .40
Joe Nieuwendyk .20 .50
Owen Nolan .15 .40
Gary Roberts .12 .30
Mats Sundin .20 .50
Darcy Tucker .12 .30
Todd Bertuzzi .20 .50
Dan Cloutier .15 .40
Ed Jovanovski .15 .40
Trevor Linden .20 .50
Brendan Morrison .15 .40
Markus Naslund .20 .50
Mattias Ohlund .12 .30
Daniel Sedin .20 .50
Henrik Sedin .20 .50
Sebastien Charpentier .15 .40
Jeff Halpern .12 .30
Olaf Kolzig .20 .50
Kip Miller .12 .30
Maxime Ouellet .12 .30
Matt Pettinger .12 .30
Brian Willsie .12 .30
Brendan Witt .12 .30
Dainius Zubrus .12 .30
Chris Kunitz .25 .60
Kari Lehtonen .25 .60
Brett Lysak .12 .30
Matt Keith .12 .30
Adam Munro .12 .30
Mikhail Kuleshov .12 .30
John-Michael Liles .12 .30
Marek Svatos .12 .30
Dan Fritsche .12 .30
Greg Mauldin .12 .30
Mike Pandolfo .12 .30
Dan Ellis .15 .40
Mike Bishai .12 .30
Lukas Krajicek .12 .30
Denis Grebeshkov .12 .30
Tomas Plekanec .20 .50
Timofei Shishkanov .12 .30
Scottie Upshall .12 .30
Thomas Pihlman .12 .30
Aleksander Suglobov .12 .30
Jozef Balej .12 .30
Bryce Lampman .12 .30
Randy Jones .12 .30
Antero Niittymaki .12 .30
Mike Stutzel .12 .30
Niko Dimitrakos .12 .30
Marcel Goc RC .20 .50
Matt Stajan .15 .40
Alexander Semin .20 .50
Roman Tvrdon .12 .30

2004-05 Pacific Blue

UE/250: 2X TO 5X BASIC CARDS
TED PRINT RUN 250 SER.#'d SETS

2004-05 Pacific Red

D: .8X TO 2X BASIC CARDS
TED ODDS 1:3

2004-05 Pacific All-Stars

MPLETE SET (12) 8.00 15.00
TED ODDS 1:10
a Kovalchuk .75 2.00
e Thornton .75 2.00
e Sakic 1.25 3.00
ck Nash .75 2.00
ike Modano 1.00 2.50
arty Turco .50 1.25
bert Lang .50 1.25
cklas Lidstrom .60 1.50
se Theodore .75 2.00
Martin Brodeur 1.50 4.00
Patrick Marleau .50 1.25
Martin St. Louis .50 1.25

04-05 Pacific Cramer's Choice

TED ODDS 1:721
IT RUN 99 SER.#'d SETS
a Kovalchuk 12.00 30.00
e Thornton 12.00 30.00
rome Iginla 12.00 30.00
e Sakic 15.00 40.00
ck Nash 12.00 30.00
eve Yzerman 20.00 50.00
artin Brodeur 15.00 40.00
ario Lemieux 20.00 50.00
artin St. Louis 8.00 20.00
d Belfour 8.00 20.00

2004-05 Pacific Global Connection

COMPLETE SET (8) 8.00 15.00
STATED ODDS 1:19
1 D.Heatley
I.Kovalchuk 1.25 3.00
2 S.Samsonov/J.Thornton 1.00 2.50
3 P.Forsberg/J.Sakic 1.50 4.00
4 P.Kariya/T.Selanne 1.00 2.50
5 P.Datsyuk/H.Zetterberg 1.25 3.00
6 B.Hull/N.Lidstrom 1.00 2.50
7 M.Havlat/M.Hossa 1.00 2.50
8 A.Mogilny/M.Sundin 1.00 2.50

2004-05 Pacific Gold Crown Die-Cuts

COMPLETE SET (8) 10.00 25.00
STATED ODDS 1:37
1 Ilya Kovalchuk 2.00 5.00
2 Andrew Raycroft 1.50 4.00
3 Eric Staal 2.50 6.00
4 Henrik Zetterberg 2.50 6.00
5 Michael Ryder 1.50 4.00
6 Jordin Tootoo 1.25 3.00
7 Jason Spezza 2.00 5.00
8 Jonathan Cheechoo 1.50 4.00

2004-05 Pacific In The Crease

COMPLETE SET (10) 8.00 15.00
STATED ODDS 1:19
1 Andrew Raycroft .75 2.00
2 Miikka Kiprusoff .75 2.00
3 David Aebischer .75 2.00
4 Marty Turco .75 2.00
5 Dominik Hasek 1.25 3.00
6 Roberto Luongo 1.25 3.00
7 Jose Theodore 1.25 3.00
8 Martin Brodeur 1.50 4.00
9 Nikolai Khabibulin 1.00 2.50
10 Ed Belfour 1.00 2.50

2004-05 Pacific Jerseys

Card #45 in this 45-card set featured the Richard Trophy winners for 2003-04. The card carried jersey swatches of both Ilya Kovlachuk and Jarome Iginla on front and a certified Rick Nash autograph on the back.
STAT.ODDS 2:36 HBBY/1:36 RETAIL
CARD#45 PRINT RUN 100 SER.#'d SETS
*GOLD: 1X TO 2X
1 Sergei Fedorov 4.00 10.00
2 Patrice Bergeron 3.00 8.00
3 Sergei Samsonov 3.00 8.00
4 Joe Thornton 5.00 12.00
5 Ales Kotalik 2.00 5.00
6 Mark Bell 2.00 5.00
7 Jocelyn Thibault 2.00 5.00
8 Peter Forsberg 6.00 15.00
9 Paul Kariya 4.00 10.00
10 Joe Sakic 6.00 15.00
11 Mike Modano 5.00 12.00
12 Derian Hatcher 2.00 5.00
13 Jason Williams 2.00 5.00
14 Steve Yzerman 10.00 25.00
15 Ryan Smyth 2.00 5.00
16 Roberto Luongo 3.00 8.00
17 Vaclav Nedorost 2.00 5.00
18 Jason Allison 2.00 5.00
19 Alex Kovalev 2.00 5.00
20 Martin Brodeur 10.00 25.00
21 Alexei Yashin 2.00 5.00
22 Pavel Bure 3.00 8.00
23 Eric Lindros 4.00 10.00
24 Daniel Alfredsson 3.00 8.00
25 Martin Havlat 3.00 8.00
26 Jeff Hackett 2.00 5.00
27 Joni Pitkanen 2.00 5.00
28 Jeremy Roenick 3.00 8.00
29 Brent Johnson 2.00 5.00
30 Krystofer Kolanos 2.00 5.00
31 Kris Beech 2.00 5.00
32 Mike Eastwood 2.00 5.00
33 Rico Fata 2.00 5.00
34 Mario Lemieux 10.00 25.00
35 Chris Osgood 2.00 5.00
36 Peter Sejna 2.00 5.00
37 Vincent Lecavalier 3.00 8.00
38 Ed Belfour 3.00 8.00
39 Matt Stajan 1.50 4.00
40 Mats Sundin 3.00 8.00
41 Todd Bertuzzi 3.00 8.00
42 Dan Cloutier 2.00 5.00
43 Brendan Morrison 2.00 5.00
44 Olaf Kolzig 3.00 8.00
45 Kovy J/Iginla J/Nash AU 75.00 200.00

2004-05 Pacific Milestones

COMPLETE SET (6) 10.00 20.00
STATED ODDS 1:37
1 Steve Yzerman 3.00 8.00
2 Martin Brodeur 3.00 8.00
3 Jaromir Jagr 1.50 4.00
4 Mark Messier 1.00 2.50
5 Mario Lemieux 4.00 10.00
6 Ed Belfour 1.00 2.50

2004-05 Pacific Philadelphia

COMPLETE SET (16) 10.00 25.00
STATED ODDS 1:10
1 Sergei Fedorov 1.00 2.50
2 Joe Sakic 1.00 2.50
3 Chris Chelios .60 1.50
4 Dominik Hasek 1.00 2.50
5 Brett Hull .75 2.00
6 Steve Yzerman 2.00 5.00
7 Luc Robitaille .60 1.50
8 Jaromir Jagr 1.50 4.00
9 Eric Lindros 1.00 2.50
10 Mark Messier 1.50 4.00
11 John LeClair .60 1.50
12 Jeremy Roenick .60 1.50
13 Mario Lemieux 2.00 5.00
14 Keith Tkachuk .60 1.50
15 Ron Francis .75 2.00
16 Brian Leetch .60 1.50

2001-02 Pacific Adrenaline

Released in December 2001, this 225-card set carried an SRP of $3.50 for a 5-card pack. Base cards carried full color action photos on white card fronts. Short printed rookies were serial-numbered out of 984, and the Kovalchuk autographed card was inserted at a rate of 1:721 hobby packs/1:1921 retail packs and serial-numbered to 500. The 500 Kovalchuk cards were inserted in both hobby and retail packs.
1 Jeff Friesen .12 .30
2 Jean-Sebastien Giguere .15 .40
3 Paul Kariya .25 .60
4 Marty McInnis .15 .40
5 Steve Shields .15 .40
6 Oleg Tverdovsky .12 .30
7 Ray Ferraro .12 .30
8 Milan Hnilicka .15 .40
9 Tomi Kallio .12 .30
10 Damian Rhodes .15 .40
11 Patrik Stefan .15 .40
12 Byron Dafoe .15 .40
13 Bill Guerin .20 .50
14 Martin Lapointe .12 .30
15 Sergei Samsonov .15 .40
16 Jozef Stumpel .12 .30
17 Joe Thornton .25 .60
18 Stu Barnes .15 .40
19 Martin Biron .15 .40
20 Tim Connolly .12 .30
21 J-P Dumont .12 .30
22 Chris Gratton .12 .30
23 Slava Kozlov .15 .40
24 Miroslav Satan .15 .40
25 Jarome Iginla .20 .50
26 Derek Morris .12 .30
27 Rob Niedermayer .15 .40
28 Marc Savard .12 .30
29 Roman Turek .15 .40
30 Mike Vernon .15 .40
31 Rod Brind'Amour .20 .50
32 Ron Francis .25 .60
33 Martin Gelinas .12 .30
34 Arturs Irbe .15 .40
35 Sami Kapanen .12 .30
36 Jeff O'Neill .12 .30
37 Shane Willis .12 .30
38 Tony Amonte .15 .40
39 Eric Daze .15 .40
40 Michael Nylander .12 .30
41 Steve Sullivan .12 .30
42 Jocelyn Thibault .15 .40
43 Alexei Zhamnov .15 .40
44 David Aebischer .15 .40
45 Rob Blake .20 .50
46 Chris Drury .15 .40
47 Peter Forsberg .25 .60
48 Milan Hejduk .15 .40
49 Patrick Roy .50 1.25
50 Joe Sakic .30 .75
51 Alex Tanguay .15 .40
52 Marc Denis .15 .40
53 Rostislav Klesla .12 .30
54 Espen Knutsen .12 .30
55 Geoff Sanderson .12 .30
56 Ron Tugnutt .15 .40
57 Donald Audette .12 .30
58 Ed Belfour .20 .50
59 Mike Modano .30 .75
60 Joe Nieuwendyk .20 .50
61 Marty Turco .20 .50
62 Pierre Turgeon .20 .50
63 Chris Chelios .20 .50
64 Sergei Fedorov .30 .75
65 Dominik Hasek .30 .75
66 Brett Hull .25 .60
67 Nicklas Lidstrom .20 .50
68 Luc Robitaille .20 .50
69 Brendan Shanahan .25 .60
70 Steve Yzerman .60 1.50
71 Eric Brewer .12 .30
72 Anson Carter .15 .40
73 Daniel Cleary .15 .40
74 Mike Comrie .15 .40
75 Mike Grier .12 .30
76 Jochen Hecht .12 .30
77 Tommy Salo .15 .40
78 Ryan Smyth .15 .40
79 Pavel Bure .25 .60
80 Valeri Bure .12 .30
81 Trevor Kidd .12 .30
82 Viktor Kozlov .12 .30
83 Roberto Luongo .30 .75
84 Marcus Nilsson .12 .30
85 Jason Allison .15 .40
86 Adam Deadmarsh .15 .40
87 Zigmund Palffy .20 .50
88 Felix Potvin .30 .75
89 Mathieu Schneider .12 .30
90 Bryan Smolinski .12 .30
91 Manny Fernandez .15 .40
92 Marian Gaborik .30 .75
93 Darby Hendrickson .12 .30
94 Lubomir Sekeras .12 .30
95 Wes Walz .12 .30
96 Joe Juneau .15 .40
97 Yanic Perreault .12 .30
98 Oleg Petrov .12 .30
99 Martin Rucinsky .12 .30
100 Brian Savage .12 .30
101 Jose Theodore .20 .50
102 Richard Zednik .15 .40
103 Mike Dunham .15 .40
104 Scott Hartnell .20 .50
105 Patric Kjellberg .12 .30
106 David Legwand .15 .40
107 Cliff Ronning .12 .30
108 Tomas Vokoun .15 .40
109 Scott Walker .12 .30
110 Jason Arnott .15 .40
111 Martin Brodeur .40 1.00
112 Sergei Brylin .12 .30
113 Patrik Elias .20 .50
114 Scott Gomez .15 .40
115 John Madden .15 .40
116 Randy McKay .12 .30
117 Scott Stevens .20 .50
118 Mariusz Czerkawski .12 .30
119 Rick DiPietro .15 .40
120 Brad Isbister .12 .30
121 Chris Osgood .20 .50
122 Michael Peca .15 .40
123 Alexei Yashin .15 .40
124 Radek Dvorak .15 .40
125 Theo Fleury .25 .60
126 Brian Leetch .20 .50
127 Eric Lindros .30 .75
128 Mark Messier .30 .75
129 Petr Nedved .15 .40
130 Mike Richter .20 .50
131 Daniel Alfredsson .20 .50
132 Radek Bonk .12 .30
133 Martin Havlat .15 .40
134 Marian Hossa .15 .40
135 Patrick Lalime .15 .40
136 Shawn McEachern .12 .30
137 Wade Redden .12 .30
138 Roman Cechmanek .15 .40
139 Simon Gagne .20 .50
140 John LeClair .20 .50
141 Keith Primeau .15 .40
142 Mark Recchi .25 .60
143 Jeremy Roenick .20 .50
144 Justin Williams .12 .30
145 Sergei Berezin .12 .30
146 Sean Burke .12 .30
147 Shane Doan .15 .40
148 Michal Handzus .12 .30
149 Daymond Langkow .15 .40
150 Claude Lemieux .15 .40
151 Johan Hedberg .15 .40
152 Jan Hrdina .12 .30
153 Alexei Kovalev .15 .40
154 Robert Lang .12 .30
155 Mario Lemieux .60 1.50
156 Martin Straka .12 .30
157 Fred Brathwaite .15 .40
158 Pavol Demitra .25 .60
159 Brent Johnson .15 .40
160 Al MacInnis .20 .50
161 Chris Pronger .15 .40
162 Cory Stillman .12 .30
163 Keith Tkachuk .20 .50
164 Doug Weight .20 .50
165 Miikka Kiprusoff .20 .50
166 Patrick Marleau .20 .50
167 Evgeni Nabokov .15 .40
168 Owen Nolan .20 .50
169 Mike Ricci .15 .40
170 Teemu Selanne .40 1.00
171 Marco Sturm .12 .30
172 Brian Holzinger .12 .30
173 Nikolai Khabibulin .20 .50
174 Vincent Lecavalier .15 .40
175 Fredrik Modin .12 .30
176 Brad Richards .20 .50
177 Martin St. Louis .20 .50
178 Kevin Weekes .15 .40
179 Tie Domi .15 .40
180 Jonas Hoglund .12 .30
181 Curtis Joseph .20 .50
182 Tomas Kaberle .12 .30
183 Alexander Mogilny .15 .40
184 Gary Roberts .12 .30
185 Mats Sundin .20 .50
186 Darcy Tucker .12 .30
187 Todd Bertuzzi .20 .50
188 Andrew Cassels .12 .30
189 Dan Cloutier .15 .40
190 Brendan Morrison .15 .40
191 Markus Naslund .20 .50
192 Daniel Sedin .20 .50
193 Henrik Sedin .20 .50
194 Peter Bondra .20 .50
195 Sergei Gonchar .12 .30
196 Jeff Halpern .12 .30
197 Jaromir Jagr .50 1.25
198 Olaf Kolzig .20 .50
199 Steve Konowalchuk .12 .30
200 Adam Oates .20 .50
201 Ilja Bryzgalov RC 3.00 8.00
202 Timo Parssinen RC 1.50 4.00
203 I.Kovalchuk AU/500 RC 15.00 40.00
204 Kamil Piros RC 1.25 3.00
205 Erik Cole RC 2.50 6.00
206 Vaclav Nedorost RC 1.25 3.00
207 Pavel Datsyuk RC 8.00 20.00
208 Ty Conklin RC 2.00 5.00
209 Niklas Hagman RC 1.50 4.00
210 Kristian Huselius RC 2.00 5.00
211 Jaroslav Bednar RC 1.25 3.00
212 Nick Schultz RC 1.25 3.00
213 Martin Erat RC 2.00 5.00
214 Scott Clemmensen RC 1.25 3.00
215 Andreas Salomonsson RC 1.25 3.00
216 Radek Martinek RC 1.25 3.00
217 Dan Blackburn RC 1.50 4.00
218 Chris Neil RC 1.50 4.00
219 Pavel Brendl SP 1.25 3.00
220 Jiri Dopita RC 1.25 3.00
221 Krystofer Kolanos RC 1.25 3.00
222 Mark Rycroft RC 1.50 4.00
223 Jeff Jillson RC 1.25 3.00
224 Nikita Alexeev RC 1.25 3.00
225 Brian Sutherby RC 1.25 3.00

2001-02 Pacific Adrenaline Blue

This 225-card set directly parallels the base set, with the only difference being a blue foil stamp rather than gold and serial numbering out of 62 on the card front. The cards were inserted randomly in hobby packs at a rate of 1:25.
*1-200 VETS/62: 6X TO 15X BASIC CARDS
*201-225 ROOKIES/62: .8X TO 2X
128 Mark Messier 6.00 15.00
203 Ilya Kovalchuk 12.00 30.00

2001-02 Pacific Adrenaline Premiere Date

This 225-card set directly parallels the base set, with the only difference being a gold premiere date stamp and serial numbering out of 62 on the card front. The cards were inserted randomly in hobby packs at a rate of 1:25.
*1-200 VETS/62: 6X TO 15X BASIC CARDS
*201-225 ROOKIES/62: .8X TO 2X
128 Mark Messier 6.00 15.00
203 Ilya Kovalchuk 12.00 30.00

2001-02 Pacific Adrenaline Red

Randomly inserted into retail packs at a rate of one per box, this 225 card set paralleled the base set but carried red foil and was serial-numbered to 54 sets.
*1-200 VETS/54: 8X TO 20X BASIC CARDS
*201-225 ROOKIE/54: 1X TO 2.5X
128 Mark Messier 8.00 20.00
203 Ilya Kovalchuk 15.00 40.00

2001-02 Pacific Adrenaline Retail

Though similar to the hobby version, the retail set had silver foil highlights and short prints were non-serial numbered. SP's were inserted at a rate of 4:25. There were two versions of the Kovalchuk card, a non serial-numbered regular card and a serial-numbered out of 500 autographed card. Odds for the Kovalchuk auto card were 1:1921 for retail packs and the cards were inserted in both retail and hobby packs.
*RETAIL VETS: .4X TO 1X HOBBY
*RETAIL ROOKIES: .15X TO .4X HOBBY
128 Mark Messier .40 1.00
203 Ilya Kovalchuk RC 5.00 12.00

2001-02 Pacific Adrenaline Blade Runners

Inserted into hobby packs at a rate of 1:481, this 10-card set featured a color action photo of the featured player on a blue and gold micro-chip design background. Borders were white with the same micro-chip design, and each card was serial-numbered out of 63.
1 Paul Kariya 10.00 25.00
2 Patrick Roy 20.00 50.00
3 Joe Sakic 12.00 30.00
4 Dominik Hasek 12.00 30.00
5 Steve Yzerman 25.00 60.00
6 Pavel Bure 10.00 25.00
7 Martin Brodeur 15.00 40.00
8 Eric Lindros 12.00 30.00
9 Mario Lemieux 25.00 60.00
10 Jaromir Jagr 20.00 50.00

2001-02 Pacific Adrenaline Creased Lightning

COMPLETE SET (20) 15.00 40.00
STATED ODDS 1:25 HOB, 1:49 RET
1 Martin Biron .75 2.00
2 Arturs Irbe .75 2.00
3 Jocelyn Thibault .75 2.00
4 Patrick Roy 2.50 6.00
5 Ed Belfour 1.00 2.50
6 Dominik Hasek 1.50 4.00
7 Tommy Salo .75 2.00
8 Roberto Luongo 1.50 4.00
9 Felix Potvin 1.50 4.00
10 Jose Theodore 1.00 2.50
11 Martin Brodeur 2.00 5.00
12 Rick DiPietro .75 2.00
13 Mike Richter 1.00 2.50
14 Patrick Lalime .75 2.00
15 Roman Cechmanek .75 2.00
16 Sean Burke .75 2.00
17 Johan Hedberg .75 2.00
18 Brent Johnson .75 2.00
19 Evgeni Nabokov .75 2.00
20 Curtis Joseph 1.00 2.50

2001-02 Pacific Adrenaline Jerseys

STATED ODDS 2:25 HOB, 1:73 RET
1 Oleg Tverdovsky 2.00 5.00
2 Sergei Samsonov 4.00 10.00
3 J-P Dumont 2.00 5.00
4 Jay McKee 2.00 5.00
5 Jarome Iginla 6.00 15.00
6 Roman Turek 2.00 5.00
7 Tony Amonte 4.00 10.00
8 Alexei Zhamnov 2.00 5.00
9 Patrick Roy 12.50 30.00
10 Joe Sakic 8.00 20.00
11 Ed Belfour 4.00 10.00
12 Derian Hatcher 2.00 5.00
13 Joe Nieuwendyk 4.00 10.00
14 Pierre Turgeon 4.00 10.00
15 Brett Hull 6.00 15.00
16 Steve Yzerman 12.00 30.00
17 Jochen Hecht 2.00 5.00
18 Valeri Bure 2.00 5.00
19 Robert Svehla 2.00 5.00
20 Felix Potvin 5.00 12.00
21 Jamie McLennan 2.00 5.00
22 Saku Koivu 4.00 10.00
23 Patric Kjellberg 2.00 5.00
24 Kimmo Timonen 2.00 5.00
25 Martin Brodeur 8.00 20.00
26 Petr Sykora 2.00 5.00
27 Chris Osgood 4.00 10.00
28 Eric Lindros 5.00 12.00
29 Petr Nedved 2.00 5.00
30 Mike Richter 4.00 10.00
31 Zdeno Chara 2.50 6.00
32 John LeClair 2.00 5.00
33 Shane Doan 2.00 5.00
34 Daymond Langkow 2.00 5.00
35 Alexei Kovalev 2.00 5.00
36 Milan Kraft 2.00 5.00
37 Robert Lang 2.00 5.00
38 Mario Lemieux 12.00 30.00
39 Fred Brathwaite 2.00 5.00
40 Cory Stillman 2.00 5.00
41 Doug Weight 4.00 10.00
42 Scott Young 2.00 5.00
43 Teemu Selanne 4.00 10.00
44 Nikolai Khabibulin 4.00 10.00
45 Vincent Lecavalier 5.00 12.00
46 Shayne Corson 2.00 5.00
47 Mats Sundin 5.00 12.00
48 Dimitri Yushkevich 2.00 5.00
49 Andrew Cassels 2.00 5.00
50 Jaromir Jagr 8.00 20.00

2001-02 Pacific Adrenaline Playmakers

COMPLETE SET (10) 10.00 25.00
STATED ODDS 1:49 HOB, 1:97 RET
1 Joe Thornton 2.50 6.00
2 Milan Hejduk .75 2.00
3 Mike Modano 2.50 6.00
4 Brett Hull 1.50 4.00
5 Mike Comrie .75 2.00
6 Marian Gaborik 2.50 6.00
7 Martin Havlat 1.25 3.00
8 Teemu Selanne 1.50 4.00
9 Daniel Sedin 1.25 3.00
10 Henrik Sedin 1.25 3.00

2001-02 Pacific Adrenaline Power Play

This 36-card set was inserted at a rate of 1:1. The cards were sponsored by Power Play magazine and the NHLPA. This set featured the top goalies of the league.
COMPLETE SET (36) 8.00 20.00
1 Jean-Sebastien Giguere .20 .50
2 Steve Shields .20 .50
3 Milan Hnilicka .20 .50
4 Byron DaFoe .20 .50
5 Martin Biron .20 .50
6 Roman Turek .20 .50
7 Arturs Irbe .20 .50
8 Jocelyn Thibault .20 .50
9 Patrick Roy 1.50 4.00
10 Marc Denis .20 .50
11 Ron Tugnutt .20 .50
12 Ed Belfour .30 .75
13 Marty Turco .30 .75
14 Dominik Hasek .60 1.50
15 Tommy Salo .20 .50
16 Trevor Kidd .20 .50
17 Roberto Luongo .40 1.00
18 Felix Potvin .30 .75
19 Manny Fernandez .20 .50
20 Jose Theodore .40 1.00
21 Mike Dunham .20 .50
22 Martin Brodeur .75 2.00
23 Rick DiPietro .30 .75
24 Mike Richter .30 .75
25 Patrick Lalime .20 .50
26 Roman Cechmanek .20 .50
27 Sean Burke .20 .50
28 Johan Hedberg .20 .50
29 Fred Brathwaite .20 .50
30 Brent Johnson .20 .50
31 Miikka Kiprusoff .40 1.00
32 Evgeni Nabokov .20 .50
33 Nikolai Khabibulin .30 .75
34 Curtis Joseph .30 .75
35 Dan Cloutier .20 .50
36 Olaf Kolzig .40 1.00

2001-02 Pacific Adrenaline Rookie Report

COMPLETE SET (20) 15.00 40.00
STATED ODDS 2:25 HOB, 1:25 RET
1 Ilja Bryzgalov 1.25 3.00
2 Dany Heatley 3.00 8.00
3 Ilya Kovalchuk 8.00 20.00
4 Erik Cole 2.00 5.00
5 Mark Bell .40 1.00
6 Vaclav Nedorost .40 1.00
7 Rostislav Klesla .40 1.00
8 Pavel Datsyuk 5.00 12.00
9 Kristian Huselius .40 1.00
10 Jaroslav Bednar .40 1.00
11 Rick DiPietro 2.00 5.00
12 Dan Blackburn .40 1.00
13 Pavel Brendl .40 1.00
14 Krystofer Kolanos .40 1.00
15 Kris Beech .40 1.00
16 Johan Hedberg .40 1.00
17 Jeff Jillson .40 1.00
18 Miikka Kiprusoff 2.00 5.00
19 Nikita Alexeev .40 1.00
20 Brian Sutherby .40 1.00

2001-02 Pacific Adrenaline World Beaters

COMPLETE SET (20) 25.00 50.00
STATED ODDS 3:25 HOB, 2:25 RET
1 Paul Kariya .75 2.00
2 Chris Drury .60 1.50
3 Joe Sakic 1.25 3.00
4 Mike Modano 1.00 2.50
5 Brett Hull .75 2.00
6 Steve Yzerman 3.00 8.00
7 Pavel Bure .75 2.00
8 Zigmund Palffy .60 1.50
9 Marian Gaborik 1.50 4.00
10 Patrik Elias .60 1.50
11 Alexei Yashin .60 1.50
12 Eric Lindros 1.00 2.50
13 Martin Havlat .60 1.50
14 John LeClair .75 2.00
15 Alexei Kovalev .60 1.50
16 Mario Lemieux 4.00 10.00
17 Keith Tkachuk .75 2.00
18 Teemu Selanne .75 2.00
19 Mats Sundin .75 2.00
20 Jaromir Jagr 1.00 2.50

2003 Pacific All-Star Game-Used Goal Net Cards

Given away exclusivley at the 2003 NHL All-Star block party as a wrapper redemption, this 2-card set featured swatches of the actual goal netting used during the 2002 NHL All-Star game. Each card was serial-numbered out of 500.
COMPLETE SET (2) 20.00 40.00
1 North American All-Star Team 20.00 25.00
2 World All-Star Team 20.00 25.00

2001-02 Pacific Arena Exclusives

Produced by Pacific as arena giveaways, this 444-card set paralleled the base set except for a silver foiled "Arena Exclusive" stamp and serial numbering to just 50 each on the card front.
*ARENA/50: 8X TO 20X BASIC CARDS
*452 HEDBERG/50: .8X TO 2X BASIC CARDS
264 Mark Messier 8.00 20.00

2003 Pacific Atlantic City National Convention

Available via wrapper redemption at the Pacific booth during the 2003 Atlantic City National Sports Collectors Convention, this 6-card dual player set was numbered to just 500 copies.
COMPLETE SET (6) 12.50 30.00
1 Rick Nash
John LeClair 3.00 8.00
2 Henrik Zetterberg
Ilya Kovalchuk 4.00 10.00
3 Ryan Miller
Martin Brodeur 2.50 6.00
4 Jay Bouwmeester
Scott Stevens 2.00 5.00
5 Jason Spezza
Jeremy Roenick 3.00 8.00
6 Stanislav Chistov
Paul Kariya 2.00 5.00

2002 Pacific Calder Collection All-Star Fantasy

Available via wrapper redemption from the Pacific booth at the NHL All-Star Fantasy show, this 10-card set featured top rookies from the 2001-02 season. Each card was serial numbered out of 2000.
COMPLETE SET (10) 20.00 50.00
1 Dany Heatley 3.20 8.00
2 Ilya Kovalchuk 8.00 20.00
3 Erik Cole 2.40 6.00
4 Vaclav Nedorost 2.40 6.00
5 Kristian Huselius 2.40 6.00
6 Jaroslav Bednar 1.20 3.00
7 Martin Erat 1.20 3.00
8 Dan Blackburn 3.20 8.00
9 Krys Kolanos 2.40 6.00
10 Jeff Jillson 1.60 4.00

2003 Pacific Calder Collection NHL All-Star Block Party

Given away as wrapper redemptions exclusively at the Pacific booth during the 2003 NHL All-Star block party, this 10-card set featured players eligible for Calder consideration. Each card was serial-numbered out of 500.
COMPLETE SET 10.00 25.00
1 Stanislav Chistov .75 2.00
2 Chuck Kobasew .75 2.00
3 Jordan Leopold .75 2.00
4 Rick Nash 4.00 10.00
5 Henrik Zetterberg 4.00 10.00
6 Jay Bouwmeester 2.50 6.00
7 Alexander Frolov 2.00 5.00
8 P-M Bouchard 2.00 5.00
9 Jason Spezza 3.00 8.00
10 Alexander Svitov .75 2.00

2003 Pacific Calder Contenders NHL Entry Draft

Distributed exclusively at the 2003 NHL Entry Draft, this 10-card set paralleled the regular Calder Contenders set in Pacific Quest for the Cup, but carried a foil Draft stamp and gold background. Each card was serial-numbered to just 500 copies.
COMPLETE SET 15.00 40.00
1 Stanislav Chistov .75 2.00
2 Ales Kotalik .75 2.00
3 Ryan Miller 2.00 5.00
4 Tyler Arnason .75 2.00
5 Pascal Leclaire 1.25 3.00
6 Rick Nash 4.00 10.00
7 Henrik Zetterberg 3.00 8.00
8 Ales Hemsky .75 2.00
9 Jay Bouwmeester 1.50 4.00
10 Jason Spezza 3.00 8.00

2002-03 Pacific Calder

Released in June, this 150-card set featured veteran players who were nominated for the Calder trophy and rookies. Rookie cards were serial-numbered to 825.
COMP.SET w/o SP'S (100) 15.00 30.00
1 Dany Heatley .30 .75
2 Ilya Kovalchuk .40 1.00
3 Evgeni Nabokov .25 .60
4 Brad Richards .30 .75
5 Scott Gomez .25 .60
6 Brad Stuart .20 .50
7 Chris Drury .30 .75
8 Marian Hossa .25 .60
9 Sergei Samsonov .25 .60
10 Mattias Ohlund .20 .50
11 Bryan Berard .20 .50
12 Jarome Iginla .30 .75
13 Daniel Alfredsson .30 .75
14 Eric Daze .20 .50
15 Peter Forsberg .40 1.00
16 Martin Brodeur .60 1.50
17 Jason Arnott .25 .60
18 Teemu Selanne .60 1.50
19 Pavel Bure .40 1.00
20 Nicklas Lidstrom .30 .75
21 Ed Belfour .30 .75
22 Sergei Fedorov .50 1.25
23 Mike Modano .50 1.25
24 Brian Leetch .30 .75
25 Joe Nieuwendyk .30 .75
26 Luc Robitaille .30 .75
27 Mario Lemieux 1.00 2.50
28 Chris Chelios .30 .75
29 Steve Yzerman .60 1.50
30 Paul Kariya .40 1.00
31 Joe Thornton .40 1.00
32 Theoren Fleury .40 1.00
33 Milan Hejduk .25 .60
34 Patrick Roy .75 2.00
35 Joe Sakic .50 1.25
36 Marty Turco .30 .75
37 Brett Hull .40 1.00
38 Curtis Joseph .30 .75
39 Brendan Shanahan .40 1.00
40 Mike Comrie .30 .75
41 Marian Gaborik .50 1.25
42 Saku Koivu .30 .75
43 Jose Theodore .30 .75
44 Alexei Yashin .25 .60
45 Alex Kovalev .30 .75
46 Eric Lindros .50 1.25
47 Mark Messier .50 1.25
48 Tony Amonte .25 .60
49 Vincent Lecavalier .25 .60
50 Mats Sundin .30 .75
51 Markus Naslund .25 .60
52 Jaromir Jagr .75 2.00
53 Dan Snyder .20 .50
54 Lee Goren .20 .50
55 Ivan Huml .20 .50
56 Andrew Raycroft .25 .60
57 Ales Kotalik .20 .50
58 Mika Noronen .25 .60
59 Henrik Tallinder .20 .50
60 Pavel Brendl .20 .50
61 Jeff Heerema .20 .50
62 Jaroslav Svoboda .20 .50
63 Tyler Arnason .30 .75
64 Riku Hahl .20 .50
65 Vaclav Nedorost .20 .50
66 Niko Kapanen .25 .60
67 Jesse Wallin .20 .50
68 Jason Chimera .20 .50
69 Jani Rita .20 .50
70 Raffi Torres .20 .50
71 Jaroslav Bednar .20 .50
72 Stephen Weiss .30 .75
73 Joe Corvo .20 .50
74 Kyle Wanvig .20 .50
75 Mathieu Garon .25 .60
76 Marcel Hossa .20 .50
77 Jan Lasak .25 .60
78 Christian Berglund .20 .50
79 Jiri Bicek .20 .50
80 Michael Rupp .20 .50
81 Rick DiPietro .25 .60
82 Justin Mapletoft .20 .50
83 Mattias Weinhandl .20 .50
84 Jamie Lundmark .25 .60
85 Ales Pisa .20 .50
86 Toni Dahlman .20 .50
87 Eric Chouinard .20 .50
88 Ramzi Abid .20 .50
89 Sebastien Caron .25 .60
90 Dan Focht .20 .50
91 Barret Jackman .25 .60
92 Justin Papineau .20 .50
93 Jonathan Cheechoo .25 .60
94 Miikka Kiprusoff .25 .60
95 Vesa Toskala .20 .50
96 Karel Pilar .20 .50
97 Fedor Fedorov .20 .50
98 Sebastien Charpentier .20 .50
99 Joel Kwiatkowski .20 .50
100 Brian Sutherby .20 .50
101 Stanislav Chistov RC 1.00 2.50
102 Kurt Sauer RC 1.00 2.50
103 Alexei Smirnov RC 1.25 3.00
104 Shaone Morrisonn RC 1.00 2.50
105 Kris Vernarsky RC 1.00 2.50
106 Ryan Miller RC 5.00 12.00
107 Chuck Kobasew RC 1.25 3.00
108 Jordan Leopold RC 1.50 4.00

109 Ryan Bayda RC 1.00 2.50
110 Igor Radulov RC 1.00 2.50
111 Pascal Leclaire RC 1.25 3.00
112 Rick Nash RC 8.00 20.00
112AU Rick Nash AU/100 40.00 100.00
113 Jason Bacashihua RC 1.25 3.00
114 Steve Ott RC 2.00 5.00
115 Dmitri Bykov RC 1.00 2.50
116 Henrik Zetterberg RC 8.00 20.00
117 Ales Hemsky RC 4.00 10.00
118 Fernando Pisani RC 1.00 2.50
119 Jay Bouwmeester RC 3.00 8.00
120 Jared Aulin RC 1.00 2.50
121 Michael Cammalleri RC 3.00 8.00
122 Alexander Frolov RC 2.00 5.00
123 Cristobal Huet RC 2.00 5.00
124 P-M Bouchard RC 1.50 4.00
125 Stephane Veilleux RC 1.00 2.50
126 Ron Hainsey RC 1.00 2.50
127 Mike Komisarek RC 1.50 4.00
128 Vernon Fiddler RC 1.25 3.00
129 Adam Hall RC 1.00 2.50
130 Scottie Upshall RC 1.25 3.00
131 Eric Godard RC 1.00 2.50
132 Ray Emery RC 3.00 8.00
133 Jason Spezza RC 6.00 15.00
134 Anton Volchenkov RC 1.00 2.50
135 Dennis Seidenberg RC 1.50 4.00
136 Radovan Somik RC 1.00 2.50
137 Jim Vandermeer RC 1.00 2.50
138 Jeff Taffe RC 1.00 2.50
139 Brooks Orpik RC 1.50 4.00
140 Tomas Surovy RC 1.00 2.50
141 Curtis Sanford RC 1.50 4.00
142 Matt Walker RC 1.00 2.50
143 Niko Dimitrakos RC 1.00 2.50
144 Jim Fahey RC 1.00 2.50
145 Lynn Loyns RC 1.00 2.50
146 Alexander Svitov RC 1.00 2.50
147 Carlo Colaiacovo RC 1.50 4.00
148 Mikael Tellqvist RC 1.00 2.50
149 Steve Eminger RC 1.00 2.50
150 Alex Henry RC 1.25 3.00

2002-03 Pacific Calder Silver

*1-100 VETS/299: 1.5X TO 4X BASIC CARDS
*101-150 ROOKIES/299: .4X TO 1X BASIC RC
47 Mark Messier 2.00 5.00

2002-03 Pacific Calder Chasing Glory

COMPLETE SET (10) 8.00 20.00
STATED ODDS 1:13
1 Joe Thornton 1.00 2.50
2 Peter Forsberg 1.00 2.50
3 Patrick Roy 2.00 5.00
4 Mike Modano 1.25 3.00
5 Marty Turco .75 2.00
6 Martin Brodeur 1.50 4.00
7 Marian Hossa .60 1.50
8 Mario Lemieux 2.50 6.00
9 Ed Belfour .75 2.00
10 Markus Naslund .60 1.50

2002-03 Pacific Calder Hardware Heroes

COMPLETE SET (12) 8.00 20.00
STATED ODDS 1:9
1 Dany Heatley .60 1.50
2 Patrick Roy 2.00 5.00
3 Joe Sakic 1.00 2.50
4 Brett Hull .60 1.50
5 Nicklas Lidstrom .50 1.25
6 Steve Yzerman 2.00 5.00
7 Jose Theodore .60 1.50
8 Eric Lindros .50 1.25
9 Mark Messier .50 1.25
10 Mario Lemieux 2.50 6.00
11 Ed Belfour .50 1.25
12 Jaromir Jagr .75 2.00

2002-03 Pacific Calder Hart Stoppers

COMPLETE SET (8) 10.00 20.00
STATED ODDS 1:13
1 Joe Thornton 1.00 2.50
2 Peter Forsberg 1.50 4.00
3 Patrick Roy 2.00 5.00
4 Mike Modano 1.00 2.50
5 Marty Turco .60 1.50
6 Martin Brodeur 1.50 4.00
7 Marian Hossa .60 1.50
8 Markus Naslund .60 1.50

2002-03 Pacific Calder Jerseys

STATED ODDS 1:13
1 Dany Heatley 5.00 12.00
2 Patrik Stefan 3.00 8.00
3 Glen Murray 3.00 8.00
4 Joe Thornton 5.00 12.00
5 Miroslav Satan 3.00 8.00
6 Alexei Zhamnov 3.00 8.00
7 Peter Forsberg 8.00 20.00
8 Patrick Roy 8.00 20.00
9 Marty Turco 4.00 10.00
10 Luc Robitaille 3.00 8.00
11 Olli Jokinen 3.00 8.00
12 Yanic Perreault 3.00 8.00
13 Tomas Vokoun 3.00 8.00
14 Rick DiPietro 3.00 8.00
15 Daniel Alfredsson 3.00 8.00
16 Jason Spezza 6.00 15.00
17 Roman Cechmanek 3.00 8.00
18 Mario Lemieux 8.00 20.00
19 Valeri Bure 3.00 8.00
20 Doug Weight 3.00 8.00
21 Ed Belfour 4.00 10.00
22 Mats Sundin 4.00 10.00
23 Brendan Morrison 3.00 8.00
24 Markus Naslund 3.00 8.00
25 Jaromir Jagr 6.00 15.00

2002-03 Pacific Calder Reflections

COMPLETE SET (20) 12.00 30.00
STATED ODDS 1:5
1 Stanislav Chistov .50 1.25
2 Ivan Huml .50 1.25
3 Ales Kotalik .50 1.25
4 Ryan Miller 1.50 4.00
5 Jordan Leopold .75 2.00
6 Tyler Arnason .75 2.00
7 Pascal Leclaire .60 1.50
8 Rick Nash 2.00 5.00
9 Henrik Zetterberg 2.50 6.00
10 Ales Hemsky 1.00 2.50
11 Jay Bouwmeester .75 2.00
12 Stephen Weiss .75 2.00
13 Michael Cammalleri .75 2.00
14 Alexander Frolov .50 1.25
15 P-M Bouchard .75 2.00
16 Marcel Hossa .50 1.25
17 Rick DiPietro .60 1.50
18 Jason Spezza 1.50 4.00
19 Barret Jackman .60 1.50
20 Jonathan Cheechoo .60 1.50

2003-04 Pacific Calder

The last Pacific brand of the season, Calder focused on rookies and prospects. Cards 101-140 were serial-numbered to 775 copies each. Cards 141 through 175 were jersey cards.

OVERALL JERSEY ODDS 2:24
1 Sergei Fedorov .50 1.25
2 Jean-Sebastien Giguere .30 .75
3 Dany Heatley .30 .75
4 Ilya Kovalchuk .30 .75
5 Marc Savard .25 .60
6 Sergei Gonchar .20 .50
7 Glen Murray .25 .60
8 Andrew Raycroft .25 .60
9 Joe Thornton .40 1.00
10 Martin Biron .25 .60
11 Daniel Briere .30 .75
12 Mika Noronen .20 .50
13 Jarome Iginla .30 .75
14 Miikka Kiprusoff .25 .60
15 Chuck Kobasew .20 .50
16 Erik Cole .25 .60
17 Josef Vasicek .20 .50
18 Justin Williams .25 .60
19 Tyler Arnason .20 .50
20 Mark Bell .20 .50
21 Kyle Calder .20 .50
22 Peter Forsberg .40 1.00
23 Milan Hejduk .25 .60
24 Paul Kariya .40 1.00
25 Joe Sakic .50 1.25
26 Philippe Sauve .25 .60
27 Alex Tanguay .25 .60
28 Marc Denis .25 .60
29 Rick Nash .30 .75
30 Valeri Bure .20 .50
31 Bill Guerin .30 .75
32 Mike Modano .50 1.25
33 Marty Turco .30 .75
34 Pavel Datsyuk .40 1.00
35 Kris Draper .20 .50
36 Dominik Hasek .50 1.25
37 Brett Hull .40 1.00
38 Curtis Joseph .30 .75
39 Robert Lang .20 .50
40 Brendan Shanahan .40 1.00
41 Steve Yzerman .75 2.00
42 Ryan Smyth .25 .60
43 Raffi Torres .20 .50
44 Mike York .20 .50
45 Jay Bouwmeester .30 .75
46 Olli Jokinen .30 .75
47 Roberto Luongo .50 1.25
48 Roman Cechmanek .25 .60
49 Alexander Frolov .25 .60
50 Ziggy Palffy .30 .75
51 Alexandre Daigle .25 .60
52 Marian Gaborik .50 1.25
53 Dwayne Roloson .25 .60
54 Saku Koivu .30 .75
55 Alex Kovalev .25 .60
56 Mike Ribeiro .25 .60
57 Michael Ryder .25 .60
58 Jose Theodore .30 .75
59 Scott Hartnell .30 .75
60 Scottie Upshall .25 .60
61 Tomas Vokoun .25 .60
62 Martin Brodeur .60 1.50
63 Patrik Elias .30 .75
64 Jeff Friesen .20 .50
65 Rick DiPietro .25 .60
66 Trent Hunter .20 .50
67 Jaromir Jagr .75 2.00
68 Eric Lindros .50 1.25
69 Mark Messier .50 1.25
70 Daniel Alfredsson .30 .75
71 Martin Havlat .30 .75
72 Marian Hossa .25 .60
73 Jason Spezza .30 .75
74 Mark Recchi .40 1.00
75 Jeremy Roenick .30 .75
76 Brian Boucher .25 .60
77 Mike Comrie .25 .60
78 Shane Doan .25 .60
79 Ladislav Nagy .20 .50
80 Rico Fata .20 .50
81 Mario Lemieux 1.00 2.50
82 Pavol Demitra .40 1.00
83 Chris Osgood .30 .75
84 Keith Tkachuk .30 .75
85 Doug Weight .30 .75
86 Jonathan Cheechoo .25 .60
87 Patrick Marleau .30 .75
88 Evgeni Nabokov .25 .60
89 Nikolai Khabibulin .30 .75
90 Vincent Lecavalier .25 .60
91 Martin St. Louis .30 .75
92 Ed Belfour .30 .75
93 Owen Nolan .25 .60
94 Gary Roberts .20 .50
95 Mats Sundin .30 .75
96 Todd Bertuzzi .30 .75
97 Dan Cloutier .25 .60
98 Jason King .20 .50
99 Brendan Morrison .25 .60
100 Markus Naslund .30 .75
101 Chris Kunitz RC 2.00 5.00
102 Kari Lehtonen RC 5.00 12.00
103 Jason Pominville RC 2.50 6.00
104 Derek Roy RC 1.50 4.00
105 Brent Krahn RC 1.00 2.50
106 Eric Staal RC 5.00 12.00
107 Adam Munro RC 1.00 2.50
108 Tuomo Ruutu RC 1.50 4.00
109 Pavel Vorobiev RC 1.25 3.00
110 Cody McCormick RC 1.25 3.00
111 Dan Fritsche RC 1.00 2.50
112 Tim Jackman RC 1.25 3.00
113 Nikolai Zherdev RC 2.00 5.00
114 Dan Ellis RC 1.25 3.00
115 Jiri Hudler RC 2.50 6.00
116 Niklas Kronwall RC 2.00 5.00
117 Nathan Robinson RC 1.00 2.50
118 Doug Lynch RC 1.00 2.50
119 Scott Barney 1.00 2.50
120 Noah Clarke RC 1.00 2.50
121 Brent Burns RC 2.50 6.00
122 Dan Hamhuis RC 1.25 3.00
123 Timofei Shishkanov RC 1.00 2.50
124 Marek Zidlicky RC 1.00 2.50
125 Tuomas Pihlman RC 1.25 3.00
126 Jozef Balej RC 1.00 2.50
127 Dominic Moore RC 1.00 2.50
128 Chad Wiseman 1.00 2.50
129 Fredrik Sjostrom RC 1.50 4.00
130 Marc-Andre Fleury RC 8.00 20.00
131 Ryan Malone RC 2.00 5.00
132 Matt Murley RC 1.25 3.00
133 John Pohl RC 1.00 2.50
134 Milan Michalek RC 2.00 5.00
135 Kyle Wellwood RC 1.50 4.00
136 Wade Brookbank RC 1.25 3.00
137 Ryan Kesler RC 5.00 12.00
138 Peter Sarno RC 1.00 2.50
139 Alexander Semin RC 3.00 8.00
140 Rastislav Stana RC 1.50 4.00
141 Jean-Sebastien Giguere JSY 2.50 6.00
142 Ilya Kovalchuk JSY 8.00 20.00
143 Joe Thornton JSY/200 6.00 15.00
144 Jarome Iginla JSY 6.00 15.00
145 Peter Forsberg JSY 8.00 20.00
146 Milan Hejduk JSY 2.50 6.00
147 Rick Nash JSY/500 4.00 10.00
148 Marty Turco JSY 4.00 10.00
149 Roman Cechmanek JSY 2.50 6.00
150 Martin Brodeur JSY/200 12.00 30.00
151 Jaromir Jagr JSY 6.00 15.00
152 Daniel Alfredsson JSY/500 3.00 8.00
153 Marian Hossa JSY 2.50 6.00
154 Jeff Hackett JSY/500 2.50 6.00
155 Mario Lemieux JSY/66 25.00 60.00
156 Chris Osgood JSY/500 3.00 8.00
157 Vincent Lecavalier .25 .60
158 Ed Belfour JSY 3.00 8.00
159 Todd Bertuzzi JSY 3.00 8.00
160 Brendan Morrison JSY/500 2.50 6.00
161 Olaf Kolzig JSY 3.00 8.00
162 Joffrey Lupul JSY RC 5.00 12.00
163 Patrice Bergeron JSY RC 10.00 25.00
164 Matthew Lombardi JSY RC 2.50 6.00
165 Antti Miettinen JSY RC 3.00 8.00
166 Nathan Horton JSY RC 5.00 12.00
167 Dustin Brown JSY RC 4.00 10.00
168 Chris Higgins JSY RC 4.00 10.00
169 Jordin Tootoo JSY RC 4.00 10.00
170 Sean Bergenheim JSY RC 2.50 6.00
171 Antoine Vermette JSY RC 4.00 10.00
172 Joni Pitkanen JSY RC 3.00 8.00
173 Peter Sejna JSY RC 2.50 6.00
174 Matt Stajan JSY RC 3.00 8.00
175 Boyd Gordon JSY RC 2.50 6.00
176 Andrew Raycroft AU/250 10.00 25.00

2003-04 Pacific Calder Silver

*1-110 VETS/575: 1.5X TO 4X BASIC CARDS
*111-140 ROOKIE/575: .4X TO 1X BASIC RC

2003-04 Pacific Calder Reflections

COMPLETE SET 15.00 30.00
STATED ODDS 1:13
1 Joffrey Lupul 2.00 5.00
2 Patrice Bergeron 3.00 8.00
3 Andrew Raycroft 2.50 6.00
4 Eric Staal 2.50 6.00
5 Michael Ryder 2.00 5.00
6 Trent Hunter 2.00 5.00
7 Marc-Andre Fleury 4.00 10.00
8 Ryan Malone 2.00 5.00

2002 Pacific Chicago National

Available via a wrapper redemption at the Pacific booth during the 2002 Chicago National Convention, this 8-card set was serial-numbered to just 500 copies. Collectors had to open a box of 2002 Pacific football or 2001-02 Pacific hockey product to receive the set. Each card featured an NHL player and an NFL player on either side.

COMPLETE SET (8) 12.00 30.00
1 Ilya Kovalchuk 2.00 5.00
Michael Vick
2 Joe Thornton 4.00 10.00
Tom Brady
3 Eric Daze 2.00 5.00
Anthony Thomas
4 Peter Forsberg 2.00 5.00
Brian Griese
5 Mike Modano 2.50 6.00
Emmitt Smith
6 Steve Yzerman 2.00 5.00
Joey Harrington
7 Eric Lindros 1.50 4.00
Ron Dayne
8 Chris Pronger 2.00 5.00
Kurt Warner

2002-03 Pacific Complete

This 600-card super set was inserted into various Pacific products throughout the season. A red parallel set was also created and sold via an online offer.

*RED/100: 6X TO 15X BASIC CARDS
1 Nicklas Lidstrom .20 .50
2 Mika Noronen .15 .40
3 Alexei Kovalev .20 .50
4 Jason Allison .15 .40
5 Erik Cole .15 .40
6 Sami Kapanen .12 .30
7 Marty Turco .20 .50
8 Brad Isbister .12 .30
9 Saku Koivu .20 .50
10 Jarome Iginla .20 .50
11 Jean-Sebastien Giguere .20 .50
12 Roman Turek .20 .50
13 Joe Sakic .30 .75
14 Peter Bondra .20 .50
15 Dany Heatley .20 .50
16 Vincent Lecavalier .15 .40
17 Manny Fernandez .15 .40
18 Simon Gagne .20 .50
19 Rick DiPietro .15 .40
20 Mark Recchi .25 .60
21 Mike Richter .20 .50
22 Daymond Langkow .15 .40
23 Pavel Datsyuk .25 .60
24 Mark Messier .30 .75
25 Ed Belfour .20 .50
26 Michael Peca .15 .40
27 Krystofer Kolanos .12 .30
28 Alexander Mogilny .15 .40
29 Martin Straka .15 .40
30 Shane Willis .12 .30
31 Alyn McCauley .12 .30
32 Ryan Smyth .15 .40
33 Tomi Kallio .12 .30
34 Doug Weight .20 .50
35 Nicholas Boynton .12 .30
36 Pascal Dupuis .12 .30
37 Jaroslav Svoboda .12 .30
38 Al MacInnis .20 .50
39 Peter Forsberg .25 .60
40 Rostislav Klesla .12 .30
41 Kimmo Timonen .12 .30
42 Darren McCarty .15 .40
43 Brian Savage .12 .30
44 Ethan Moreau .12 .30
45 Peter Worrell .12 .30
46 Doug Gilmour .25 .60
47 David Aebischer .15 .40
48 Aaron Miller .12 .30
49 Nick Schultz .12 .30
50 Magnus Arvedson .12 .30
51 Cale Hulse .12 .30
52 Brian Gionta .15 .40
53 Trevor Linden .20 .50
54 Raffi Torres .12 .30
55 Jean-Sebastien Aubin .12 .30
56 Zdeno Chara .20 .50
57 Mattias Ohlund .12 .30
58 Travis Green .12 .30
59 Michael Nylander .12 .30
60 Andreas Dackell .12 .30
61 Craig Billington .12 .30
62 Chris Therien .12 .30
63 Eric Brewer .12 .30
64 Shayne Corson .12 .30
65 Patrice Brisebois .12 .30
66 Sean O'Donnell .12 .30
67 Sergei Varlamov .15 .40
68 Donald Brashear .12 .30
69 Vaclav Prospal .12 .30
70 Mike Ricci .15 .40
71 Fredrik Modin .12 .30
72 Stu Grimson .12 .30
73 Jeff Jillson .12 .30
74 Andre Roy .12 .30
75 Filip Kuba .12 .30
76 Martin Skoula .12 .30
77 Sandis Ozolinsh .15 .40
78 Robert Reichel .12 .30
79 Wes Walz .12 .30
80 Keith Carney .12 .30
81 Steve Kariya .12 .30
82 Dave Tanabe .12 .30
83 Robert Svehla .12 .30
84 Rob Ray .12 .30
85 Niklas Hagman .12 .30
86 Stu Barnes .12 .30
87 Scott Gomez .15 .40
88 Rob Niedermayer .15 .40
89 Dave Scatchard .12 .30
90 Petr Nedved .12 .30
91 Bob Probert .20 .50
92 Dallas Drake .15 .40
93 Mike Leclerc .12 .30
94 Janne Niinimaa .12 .30
95 Rob Zamuner .12 .30
96 Jim Dowd .12 .30
97 Richard Matvichuk .12 .30
98 Boyd Devereaux .12 .30
99 Jamie Storr .15 .40
100 Rem Murray .12 .30
101 Jaromir Jagr .50 1.25
102 Todd Bertuzzi .20 .50
103 Mike Modano .30 .75
104 Sergei Fedorov .30 .75
105 Ilya Kovalchuk .25 .60
106 Patrik Elias .20 .50
107 Marian Hossa .15 .40
108 Paul Kariya .25 .60
109 Manny Legace .20 .50
110 Milan Hejduk .15 .40
111 Adam Deadmarsh .15 .40
112 Owen Nolan .20 .50
113 Patrick Marleau .20 .50
114 Adam Oates .20 .50
115 Donald Audette .12 .30
116 Steven Reinprecht .12 .30
117 Jere Lehtinen .20 .50
118 Joe Nieuwendyk .20 .50
119 Roman Cechmanek .15 .40
120 Brian Rolston .15 .40
121 Chris Drury .20 .50
122 J-P Dumont .12 .30
123 Denis Arkhipov .12 .30
124 Sergei Zubov .15 .40
125 Scott Hartnell .20 .50
126 Espen Knutsen .12 .30
127 Slava Kozlov .12 .30
128 Roberto Luongo .30 .75
129 John LeClair .20 .50
130 Daniel Sedin .20 .50
131 Justin Williams .15 .40
132 Kyle Calder .12 .30
133 Bryan Smolinski .15 .40
134 Scott Mellanby .12 .30
135 Martin Lapointe .15 .40
136 Dwayne Roloson .12 .30
137 Niklas Sundstrom .12 .30
138 Ladislav Nagy .12 .30
139 Mathieu Schneider .12 .30
140 Scott Walker .12 .30
141 Marcus Nilsson .12 .30
142 Steve Thomas .12 .30
143 Kevin Weekes .15 .40
144 Vladimir Orszagh .12 .30
145 Brad Stuart .12 .30
146 Shawn Bates .12 .30
147 Oleg Tverdovsky .12 .30
148 Andy Delmore .12 .30
149 Stanislav Neckar .12 .30
150 Phil Housley .15 .40
151 Matt Cooke .12 .30
152 Scott Niedermayer .20 .50
153 Jeff Hackett .15 .40
154 Ruslan Fedotenko .12 .30
155 Daniel Cleary .15 .40
156 Martin Prusek .12 .30
157 Matt Cullen .12 .30
158 Jason Woolley .12 .30
159 Fred Brathwaite .15 .40
160 Adam Graves .15 .40
161 Kenny Jonsson .12 .30
162 Todd Marchant .12 .30
163 Jason Williams .12 .30
164 Joe Juneau .15 .40
165 Patrick Roy .50 1.25
166 Tie Domi .15 .40
167 Adrian Aucoin .12 .30
168 Dan Blackburn .15 .40
169 Vitali Yachmenev .12 .30
170 Derian Hatcher .15 .40
171 Mike Ribeiro .15 .40
172 Mike Van Ryn .12 .30
173 Brian Willsie .12 .30
174 Chris Phillips .12 .30
175 Jason York .12 .30
176 Kris Draper .12 .30
177 Sean Burke .12 .30
178 Kevin Dineen .12 .30
179 Toni Lydman .12 .30
180 Artem Chubarov .12 .30
181 Trevor Letowski .12 .30
182 P.J. Axelsson .12 .30
183 Lubos Bartecko .12 .30
184 Mike Knuble .12 .30
185 Ossi Vaananen .12 .30
186 David Vyborny .12 .30
187 Kevyn Adams .12 .30
188 Johan Hedberg .20 .50
189 Brent Gilchrist .15 .40
190 Eric Boguniecki .12 .30
191 Marcus Ragnarsson .12 .30
192 Eric Weinrich .12 .30
193 Yannick Tremblay .12 .30
194 Mike Keane .15 .40
195 Chad Kilger .12 .30
196 Glen Metropolit .12 .30
197 Stephane Quintal .12 .30
198 Tyler Arnason .20 .50
199 Jan Bulis .12 .30
200 Patric Kjellberg .12 .30
201 Eric Lindros .30 .75
202 Markus Naslund .15 .40
203 Ziggy Palffy .20 .50
204 Brian Rafalski .12 .30
205 Miroslav Satan .20 .50
206 Marian Gaborik .30 .75
207 Tony Amonte .15 .40
208 Tomas Kaberle .12 .30
209 Ray Whitney .15 .40
210 Ron Francis .25 .60
211 Steve Sullivan .12 .30
212 Bryan Berard .12 .30
213 Keith Primeau .20 .50
214 Vincent Damphousse .15 .40
215 Richard Zednik .12 .30
216 Ed Jovanovski .15 .40
217 Valeri Bure .15 .40
218 Jozef Stumpel .12 .30
219 Alexei Zhamnov .15 .40
220 Mariusz Czerkawski .12 .30
221 John Grahame .12 .30
222 Mark Parrish .12 .30
223 Mike York .12 .30
224 Chris Osgood .20 .50
225 Scott Young .12 .30
226 Derek Morris .12 .30
227 Brendan Morrison .15 .40
228 Mike Sillinger .12 .30
229 Todd White .12 .30
230 Tom Poti .12 .30
231 Sergei Zholtok .12 .30
232 Kip Miller .12 .30
233 Pasi Nurminen .12 .30
234 Michal Handzus .15 .40
235 Henrik Sedin .20 .50
236 Steve McCarthy .12 .30
237 Jeff Halpern .12 .30
238 Stephen Weiss .20 .50
239 Pavel Kubina .12 .30
240 Luc Robitaille .20 .50
241 Michal Rozsival .15 .40
242 Martin Gelinas .12 .30
243 Curtis Brown .12 .30
244 Steve Passmore .12 .30
245 Tony Hrkac .12 .30
246 Alexei Yashin .15 .40
247 Richard Park .12 .30
248 Viktor Kozlov .12 .30
249 Andrei Markov .20 .50
250 Dan Boyle .15 .40
251 Paul Mara .12 .30
252 Jeremy Roenick .20 .50
253 Randy McKay .12 .30
254 Tommy Salo .15 .40
255 Jaroslav Spacek .12 .30
256 Adam Foote .12 .30
257 Martin Erat .12 .30
258 Jamal Mayers .12 .30
259 Chris Neil .12 .30
260 Mark Bell .12 .30
261 Matt Bradley .12 .30
262 Boris Mironov .12 .30
263 Trevor Kidd .12 .30
264 Dave Andreychuk .20 .50
265 Jaroslav Modry .12 .30
266 Vaclav Varada .12 .30
267 Marty Murray .12 .30
268 Ben Clymer .12 .30
269 Mikael Renberg .12 .30
270 Sean Hill .12 .30
271 Eric Belanger .12 .30
272 Andy McDonald .20 .50
273 Miikka Kiprusoff .15 .40
274 Brad May .12 .30
275 Dan LaCouture .12 .30
276 Andy Sutton .12 .30
277 Kirk Maltby .12 .30
278 Kirk Muller .12 .30
279 Alex Tanguay .15 .40
280 Bryan Marchment .15 .40
281 Jason Smith .12 .30
282 Dan Bylsma .12 .30
283 Jyrki Lumme .12 .30
284 Chris Gratton .12 .30
285 Chris Clark .12 .30
286 David Legwand .15 .40
287 Alexander Khavanov .12 .30
288 Marc Chouinard .12 .30
289 Rob DiMaio .12 .30
290 Sean Avery .15 .40
291 Tommy Albelin .12 .30
292 Jean-Francois Fortin .12 .30
293 Matthew Barnaby .12 .30
294 Jan Hrdina .12 .30
295 Harold Druken .12 .30
296 Jody Hull .12 .30
297 Shjon Podein .12 .30
298 Jochen Hecht .12 .30
299 Glen Murray .15 .40
300 Sergei Brylin .12 .30
301 Pavel Bure .25 .60
302 Mike Comrie .20 .50
303 Mario Lemieux .60 1.50
304 Mats Sundin .20 .50
305 Jason Blake .12 .30
306 Robert Lang .12 .30
307 Bill Guerin .20 .50
308 Brad Richards .20 .50
309 Radek Bonk .15 .40
310 Craig Conroy .12 .30
311 Brett Hull .25 .60
312 Dainius Zubrus .12 .30
313 Petr Sykora .15 .40
314 Craig Rivet .12 .30
315 Andrew Brunette .12 .30
316 Kristian Huselius .12 .30
317 Rod Brind'Amour .20 .50
318 Tim Connolly .12 .30
319 Anson Carter .15 .40
320 Cory Stillman .12 .30
321 Teppo Numminen .15 .40
322 Jason Arnott .15 .40
323 Oleg Petrov .12 .30
324 Shawn McEachern .12 .30
325 Scott Thornton .12 .30
326 Oleg Kvasha .12 .30
327 Byron Dafoe .15 .40
328 Glen Wesley .12 .30
329 Eric Messier .12 .30
330 Brad Lukowich .12 .30
331 Jon Klemm .12 .30
332 Tomas Vokoun .15 .40
333 Scott Hannan .12 .30
334 Mike Eastwood .12 .30
335 Peter Skudra .12 .30
336 Roman Hamrlik .12 .30
337 Josef Vasicek .12 .30
338 Bryan McCabe .12 .30
339 Igor Larionov .20 .50
340 Darryl Sydor .12 .30
341 Mike Fisher .12 .30
342 Greg Johnson .12 .30
343 Danny Markov .12 .30
344 Frantisek Kaberle .12 .30
345 Michal Grosek .12 .30
346 Ivan Novoseltsev .12 .30
347 Marty McInnis .12 .30
348 Eric Desjardins .12 .30
349 Jason Wiemer .12 .30
350 Fredrik Olausson .12 .30
351 Bill Muckalt .12 .30
352 Ville Nieminen .12 .30
353 Taylor Pyatt .12 .30
354 Mike Rathje .12 .30
355 Trent Klatt .12 .30
356 Bret Hedican .12 .30
357 Tyler Wright .12 .30
358 Greg deVries .12 .30
359 Lubomir Sekeras .12 .30
360 Jonas Hoglund .12 .30
361 Mike Grier .12 .30
362 Wade Redden .12 .30
363 Nik Antropov .15 .40
364 Philippe Boucher .12 .30
365 Clarke Wilm .12 .30
366 Erik Rasmussen .12 .30
367 Per Svartvadet .12 .30
368 Felix Potvin .30 .75
369 Igor Korolev .12 .30
370 Vladimir Malakhov .12 .30
371 Mathieu Dandenault .12 .30
372 Brent Johnson .15 .40
373 Shaun Van Allen .12 .30
374 Scott Pellerin .12 .30
375 Radim Vrbata .15 .40
376 Mike Johnson .15 .40
377 Mikael Samuelsson .12 .30
378 Radek Martinek .12 .30
379 Curtis Joseph .20 .50
380 Craig Johnson .12 .30
381 Kelly Buchberger .15 .40
382 Todd Harvey .12 .30
383 Jason Chimera .12 .30
384 Claude Lapointe .12 .30
385 Marc Denis .15 .40
386 Lyle Odelein .12 .30
387 Dimitri Kalinin .12 .30
388 Scott Nichol .12 .30
389 Tom Fitzgerald .12 .30
390 Darius Kasparaitis .12 .30
391 Bryan Allen .12 .30
392 Jamie McLennan .12 .30
393 Martin St. Louis .20 .50
394 Landon Wilson .12 .30
395 Kim Johnsson .12 .30
396 Pavel Trnka .12 .30
397 P.J. Stock .12 .30
398 Alexandre Daigle .12 .30
399 Andrew Cassels .12 .30
400 Wayne Primeau .15 .40
401 Theo Fleury .25 .60
402 Cliff Ronning .12 .30
403 Sergei Samsonov .15 .40
404 Jean-Francois Labbe .12 .30
405 Darcy Tucker .12 .30
406 Daniel Briere .15 .40
407 Marc Savard .12 .30
408 Blake Sloan .15 .40
409 Sergei Berezin .12 .30
410 Ron Tugnutt .15 .40
411 Jocelyn Thibault .15 .40
412 Jose Theodore .20 .50
413 Sheldon Keefe .12 .30
414 Yanic Perreault .12 .30
415 Jason Krog .12 .30
416 John Madden .12 .30
417 Jonathan Girard .12 .30
418 Niclas Havelid .12 .30
419 Daniel Alfredsson .20 .50
420 Dean McAmmond .12 .30
421 Brenden Morrow .15 .40
422 Dimitri Yushkevich .12 .30
423 Alexei Zhitnik .15 .40
424 Jani Hurme .15 .40
425 Antti Laaksonen .12 .30
426 Corey Schwab .15 .40
427 Geoff Sanderson .15 .40
428 Brian Leetch .20 .50
429 Brad Tapper .12 .30
430 Derek Armstrong .12 .30
431 Evgeni Nabokov .15 .40
432 Jan Hlavac .12 .30
433 Bob Boughner .12 .30
434 Andreas Johansson .12 .30
435 Jeff Odgers .12 .30
436 Teemu Selanne .40 1.00
437 Pavol Demitra .25 .60
438 Tomas Holmstrom .12 .30
439 Jeff Friesen .12 .30
440 Eric Boulton .12 .30
441 Oleg Saprykin .12
442 Chris Chelios .20
443 Stephane Yelle .12
444 Martin Havlat .15
445 Jeff O'Neill .12
446 Dan Cloutier .15
447 Nikolai Khabibulin .20
448 Grant Marshall .12
449 Pierre Turgeon .20
450 Jamie Langenbrunner .15
451 Steve Staios .12
452 Alexei Morozov .12
453 Shawn Horcoff .15
454 Adam Mair .12
455 Ruslan Salei .12
456 Robert Esche .12
457 Brent Sopel .12
458 Aaron Ward .12
459 Martin Biron .15
460 Brian Boucher .15
461 Richard Jackman .12
462 Jarkko Ruutu .12
463 Bates Battaglia .12
464 Sergei Gonchar .15
465 Martin Brodeur .40
466 Patrik Stefan .15
467 Scott Stevens .20
468 Gary Roberts .12
469 Shane Doan .15
470 Keith Tkachuk .20
471 Brendan Witt .12
472 Todd Fedoruk .12
473 Patrick Lalime .15
474 Mike Dunham .15
475 Ulf Dahlen .12
476 Olli Jokinen .20
477 Garth Snow .15
478 Sean Pronger .12
479 Milan Kraft .12
480 Aki Berg .12
481 Steve Shields .15
482 Sami Salo .12
483 Brendan Shanahan .25
484 Niclas Wallin .12
485 Sandy McCarthy .12
486 Olaf Kolzig .20
487 Cory Sarich .12
488 Zac Bierk .12
489 Luke Richardson .12
490 Colin White .12
491 Reed Low .12
492 Joe Thornton .25
493 Rob Blake .20
494 Bobby Holik .12
495 Chris Simon .12
496 Wade Belak .12
497 Eric Daze .12
498 Hal Gill .12
499 Chris Pronger .15
500 Steve Yzerman .40
501 Justin Papineau .12
502 Alex Auld .12
503 Niko Kapanen .15
504 Michael Cammalleri .40
505 Sebastien Charpentier .12
506 Stanislav Chistov .12
507 Jiri Bicek .12
508 Ryan Flinn .12
509 Christian Berglund .12
510 Vernon Fiddler .15
511 Andrej Nedorost .12
512 Lynn Loyns .12
513 Niko Dimitrakos .12
514 Ryan Bayda .12
515 Curtis Sanford .20
516 Pierre-Marc Bouchard .20
517 Sebastien Caron .15
518 Steve Ott .25
519 Dan Snyder .12
520 Mattias Weinhandl .12
521 Henrik Zetterberg 1.25
522 Tomas Surovy .12
523 Ales Hemsky .50
524 Jamie Lundmark .15
525 Barret Jackman .15
526 Toni Dahlman .12
527 Jaroslav Bednar .12
528 Ales Pisa .12
529 Joel Kwiatkowski .12
530 Jan Lasak .15
531 Jim Fahey .12
532 Pavel Brendl .12
533 Stephane Veilleux .12
534 Vaclav Nedorost .12
535 Tomas Malec .12
536 Jeff Heerema .12
537 Dmitri Bykov .12
538 Dennis Seidenberg .20
539 Jonathan Cheechoo .15
540 Fernando Pisani .12
541 Riku Hahl .12
542 Jani Rita .12
543 Jim Vandermeer .12
544 Jordan Leopold .20
545 Joe Corvo .12
546 Ales Kotalik .12
547 Ryan Miller .75
548 Tomas Kurka .12
549 Arturs Irbe .15
550 Radovan Somik .12
551 Mathieu Garon .15
552 Jesse Wallin .12
553 Steve Eminger .12
554 Jason Bacashihua .15
555 Ramzi Abid .12
556 Marcel Hossa .12
557 Rick Nash 1.00
558 Kris Vernarsky .12
559 Brian Sutherby .12
560 Adam Hall .12
561 Eric Chouinard .12
562 Henrik Tallinder .12
563 Alexander Svitov .12
564 Kurt Sauer .12
565 Matt Walker .12
566 Ray Emery .40
567 Eric Godard .12
568 Jay Bouwmeester .40
569 Kip Brennan .12
570 Mike Komisarek .20
571 Alex Henry .15
572 Scottie Upshall .15
573 Chuck Kobasew .15
574 Anton Volchenkov .12
575 Carlo Colaiacovo .20
576 Pascal Leclaire .15
577 Jason Spezza .75
578 Jeff Taffe .12

79 Alexander Frolov .25 .60
80 Shaone Morrisonn .12 .30
81 Ron Hainsey .12 .30
82 Alexei Smirnov .15 .40
83 Andrew Raycroft .15 .40
84 Brooks Orpik .20 .50
85 Dan Focht .12 .30
86 Fedor Fedorov .12 .30
87 Ivan Huml .12 .30
88 Jared Aulin .12 .30
89 Justin Mapletoft .12 .30
90 Karel Pilar .12 .30
91 Kyle Wanvig .12 .30
92 Lee Goren .12 .30
93 Cristobal Huet .25 .60
94 Mikael Tellqvist .12 .30
95 Igor Radulov .12 .30
96 Kirill Safronov .12 .30
97 Jerred Smithson .12 .30
98 Vesa Toskala .12 .30
99 Dick Tarnstrom .12 .30
00 Martin Gerber .20 .50

2003-04 Pacific Complete

his 600-card super set was inserted into various acific products throughout the season. A red parallel et was also created and available randomly.
RED/100: 5X TO 12X BASIC CARDS
RED STAR ROOKIES/100: 3X TO 8X

Donald Brashear .12 .30
Chris Gratton .12 .30
Alyn McCauley .12 .30
Mats Sundin .20 .50
Brenden Morrow .15 .40
Jaroslav Modry .12 .30
Brian Rafalski .15 .40
Mike Grier .12 .30
Marco Sturm .12 .30
0 Mike Comrie .15 .40
1 Derek Morris .12 .30
2 Scott Niedermayer .20 .50
3 Dainius Zubrus .12 .30
4 Jason Krog .12 .30
5 Brian Rolston .15 .40
6 Dany Heatley .20 .50
7 Dean McAmmond .12 .30
8 Glen Murray .15 .40
9 Adam Mair .12 .30
0 Tony Amonte .15 .40
1 David Vyborny .12 .30
2 Tyler Wright .12 .30
3 Doug Gilmour .25 .60
4 Andy Sutton .12 .30
5 Ivan Huml .12 .30
6 Olli Jokinen .20 .50
7 Kimmo Timonen .12 .30
8 Donald Audette .12 .30
9 Martin St. Louis .20 .50
0 Martin Skoula .12 .30
1 Wade Redden .12 .30
2 Kyle Calder .12 .30
3 Shawn Bates .12 .30
4 Brendan Shanahan .25 .60
5 Martin Havlat .20 .50
6 Radim Vrbata .15 .40
7 Eric Daze .15 .40
8 J-P Dumont .12 .30
9 Scott Mellanby .12 .30
0 Brad Richards .20 .50
1 Jason Allison .15 .40
2 Rostislav Klesla .12 .30
3 Tyler Arnason .12 .30
4 Henrik Sedin .20 .50
5 Markus Naslund .20 .50
6 Daniel Sedin .20 .50
7 Niklas Sundstrom .12 .30
8 Rod Brind'Amour .20 .50
9 Martin Straka .12 .30
0 Craig Conroy .12 .30
1 Tomas Kaberle .12 .30
2 Robyn Regehr .12 .30
3 Scott Hartnell .20 .50
4 Sergei Zholtok .12 .30
5 Pierre Turgeon .20 .50
6 Mike Ricci .15 .40
7 Brad Tapper .12 .30
8 Martin Gelinas .12 .30
9 Philippe Boucher .12 .30
0 Alex Tanguay .15 .40
1 Niclas Havelid .12 .30
2 Kristian Huselius .12 .30
3 Dave Lowry .12 .30
4 Tim Connolly .12 .30
5 Robert Lang .12 .30
6 Taylor Pyatt .12 .30
7 Bryan Smolinski .12 .30
8 Keith Primeau .20 .50
9 Anson Carter .15 .40
0 Dallas Drake .12 .30
1 Curtis Brown .12 .30
2 Nik Antropov .15 .40
3 Aaron Ward .12 .30
4 Tie Domi .15 .40
5 Mike Leclerc .12 .30
6 Tom Poti .12 .30
7 Kris Draper .12 .30
8 Joe Juneau .15 .40
9 Milan Kraft .12 .30
0 Marty Reasoner .12 .30
1 Shaun Van Allen .12 .30
2 Kenny Jonsson .12 .30
3 Alexander Khavanov .12 .30
4 Pavel Kubina .12 .30
5 Vladimir Malakhov .12 .30
6 Willie Mitchell .12 .30
7 Jason Smith .12 .30
8 Radoslav Suchy .12 .30
9 Mattias Timander .12 .30
0 Eric Weinrich .12 .30
1 Andrei Zyuzin .12 .30
2 Christian Berglund .12 .30
3 Jamie Lundmark .12 .30
4 Kirk Maltby .12 .30
5 Brian Savage .12 .30
6 Petr Schastlivy .12 .30
7 Ian Laperriere .12 .30
8 Alexei Morozov .12 .30
9 Justin Williams .15 .40
00 Jason Chimera .12 .30
01 Patrick Marleau .20 .50
02 Ryan Smyth .15 .40
03 Michal Handzus .15 .40
04 Brett Hull .25 .60
105 Tom Fitzgerald .12 .30
106 Ben Clymer .12 .30
107 Rick Nash .20 .50
108 Scott Walker .12 .30
109 Rob Niedermayer .15 .40
110 Sergei Gonchar .12 .30
111 Chris Chelios .20 .50
112 Brian Leetch .20 .50
113 David Legwand .15 .40
114 Sean Hill .12 .30
115 Brad Isbister .12 .30
116 Pavel Datsyuk .25 .60
117 Alexei Yashin .15 .40
118 Jere Lehtinen .15 .40
119 Jason Spezza .20 .50
120 Daniel Briere .20 .50
121 Andreas Dackell .12 .30
122 Shane Doan .15 .40
123 Josef Vasicek .12 .30
124 Dan McGillis .12 .30
125 Geoff Sanderson .12 .30
126 Teemu Selanne .40 1.00
127 Andreas Johansson .12 .30
128 Al MacInnis .20 .50
129 Ruslan Fedotenko .12 .30
130 Scott Stevens .20 .50
131 Frantisek Kaberle .12 .30
132 Toni Lydman .12 .30
133 Kip Miller .12 .30
134 Dan Hinote .12 .30
135 Mike Modano .30 .75
136 Scott Thornton .15 .40
137 Eric Lindros .30 .75
138 Grant Marshall .12 .30
139 Vincent Damphousse .15 .40
140 Mario Lemieux .60 1.50
141 Patrice Brisebois .12 .30
142 Sergei Samsonov .15 .40
143 Sergei Zubov .15 .40
144 Alexei Zhamnov .15 .40
145 Oleg Kvasha .12 .30
146 Brendan Morrison .15 .40
147 Jason York .12 .30
148 Eric Boguniecki .12 .30
149 Henrik Zetterberg .25 .60
150 Nick Boynton .12 .30
151 Trevor Linden .20 .50
152 Joe Nieuwendyk .20 .50
153 Filip Kuba .12 .30
154 Matthew Barnaby .15 .40
155 Ales Hemsky .20 .50
156 Jan Bulis .12 .30
157 Yannick Tremblay .12 .30
158 Andre Roy .12 .30
159 Jaroslav Bednar .12 .30
160 Stephane Yelle .12 .30
161 Paul Mara .12 .30
162 Sandis Ozolinsh .12 .30
163 Trent Klatt .12 .30
164 Brian Gionta .15 .40
165 Jaroslav Spacek .12 .30
166 Rob Blake .20 .50
167 Ziggy Palffy .20 .50
168 Chris Clark .12 .30
169 John LeClair .20 .50
170 Landon Wilson .12 .30
171 Mark Bell .12 .30
172 Simon Gagne .20 .50
173 Michael Nylander .12 .30
174 Andy McDonald .15 .40
175 Todd Bertuzzi .20 .50
176 Dick Tarnstrom .12 .30
177 Radek Dvorak .15 .40
178 Antti Laaksonen .12 .30
179 Steve Rucchin .12 .30
180 Steve Sullivan .12 .30
181 Viktor Kozlov .12 .30
182 Miroslav Satan .15 .40
183 Lubomir Visnovsky .12 .30
184 Stephen Weiss .12 .30
185 John Madden .12 .30
186 Mike Knuble .12 .30
187 Michael Peca .15 .40
188 Adam Foote .12 .30
189 Steve McKenna .12 .30
190 Adam Deadmarsh .15 .40
191 Barret Jackman .12 .30
192 Marian Gaborik .30 .75
193 Zdeno Chara .20 .50
194 Chris Drury .15 .40
195 Sami Salo .12 .30
196 Daniel Tjarnqvist .12 .30
197 Vaclav Varada .12 .30
198 Shawn McEachern .12 .30
199 Kevyn Adams .12 .30
200 Roman Hamrlik .15 .40
201 Keith Carney .12 .30
202 Scott Gomez .15 .40
203 Marcus Nilsson .12 .30
204 Tomas Surovy .12 .30
205 Vladimir Orszagh .12 .30
206 Owen Nolan .15 .40
207 Matt Cooke .12 .30
208 Jeremy Roenick .20 .50
209 Andrew Cassels .12 .30
210 Jim Dowd .12 .30
211 Todd Marchant .12 .30
212 Joe Sakic .30 .75
213 Krystofer Kolanos .12 .30
214 Chris Phillips .12 .30
215 Stanislav Chistov .12 .30
216 Steve Yzerman .50 1.25
217 Jamie Langenbrunner .15 .40
218 Daymond Langkow .12 .30
219 Jarome Iginla .20 .50
220 Darryl Sydor .12 .30
221 Mark Messier .30 .75
222 Richard Matvichuk .12 .30
223 Jay Bouwmeester .20 .50
224 Sheldon Souray .12 .30
225 Niklas Hagman .12 .30
226 Bill Lindsay .12 .30
227 Ray Whitney .15 .40
228 Jordan Leopold .12 .30
229 Daniel Alfredsson .20 .50
230 Kyle McLaren .12 .30
231 Vincent Lecavalier .15 .40
232 Bobby Holik .12 .30
233 Adam Hall .12 .30
234 Mark Recchi .25 .60
235 Alexander Mogilny .15 .40
236 Alexei Zhitnik .15 .40
237 Jay McKee .12 .30
238 Jaromir Jagr .50 1.25
239 Ladislav Nagy .12 .30
240 Radek Bonk .15 .40
241 Mike Van Ryn .12 .30
242 Joe Thornton .25 .60
243 Peter Bondra .15 .40
244 Keith Tkachuk .20 .50
245 Luc Robitaille .20 .50
246 Alexandre Daigle .15 .40
247 Jason Blake .12 .30
248 Jonathan Cheechoo .15 .40
249 Alexander Frolov .15 .40
250 Danny Markov .12 .30
251 Oleg Saprykin .12 .30
252 Maxim Afinogenov .12 .30
253 Alexander Karpovtsev .12 .30
254 Peter Forsberg .25 .60
255 Espen Knutsen .12 .30
256 Erik Cole .15 .40
257 Dan Boyle .15 .40
258 Marc Savard .15 .40
259 Adrian Aucoin .12 .30
260 Brian Holzinger .12 .30
261 Cory Stillman .12 .30
262 Mattias Ohlund .12 .30
263 Petr Sykora .15 .40
264 Jeff Halpern .12 .30
265 Patrik Stefan .12 .30
266 Jeff Jillson .12 .30
267 Mariusz Czerkawski .12 .30
268 Jeff O'Neill .12 .30
269 Brad Stuart .12 .30
270 Ron Francis .25 .60
271 Mike Johnson .12 .30
272 Richard Park .12 .30
273 Yanic Perreault .12 .30
274 Eric Belanger .12 .30
275 Stu Barnes .12 .30
276 Nathan Dempsey .12 .30
277 Bryan McCabe .12 .30
278 Andrew Brunette .12 .30
279 Ville Nieminen .12 .30
280 Greg Johnson .12 .30
281 Alex Kovalev .15 .40
282 Raffi Torres .12 .30
283 Drake Berehowsky .12 .30
284 Steve McCarthy .12 .30
285 Martin Erat .12 .30
286 Pavol Demitra .25 .60
287 Saku Koivu .20 .50
288 Milan Hejduk .15 .40
289 Sami Kapanen .12 .30
290 Nicklas Lidstrom .20 .50
291 Eric Brewer .12 .30
292 Martin Lapointe .15 .40
293 Andrei Markov .20 .50
294 Doug Weight .20 .50
295 Jason Arnott .15 .40
296 Mike York .12 .30
297 Jay Pandolfo .12 .30
298 Ed Jovanovski .15 .40
299 Bill Guerin .20 .50
300 Petr Cajanek .12 .30
301 Shawn Horcoff .12 .30
302 Ales Kotalik .12 .30
303 Chris Dingman .12 .30
304 Arron Asham .12 .30
305 Steve Staios .12 .30
306 Artem Chubarov .12 .30
307 Karlis Skrastins .12 .30
308 Nick Schultz .12 .30
309 Rico Fata .12 .30
310 Jan Hrdina .12 .30
311 Brendan Witt .12 .30
312 Lyle Odelein .12 .30
313 Pascal Dupuis .12 .30
314 Paul Kariya .25 .60
315 Petr Nedved .12 .30
316 Tim Taylor .12 .30
317 Ethan Moreau .12 .30
318 Shean Donovan .12 .30
319 Ruslan Salei .12 .30
320 Rem Murray .12 .30
321 Eric Nickulas .12 .30
322 Rob DiMaio .12 .30
323 Steven Reinprecht .12 .30
324 Cory Cross .12 .30
325 Kim Johnsson .12 .30
326 Chris Simon .12 .30
327 Gary Roberts .12 .30
328 Ken Klee .12 .30
329 Krzysztof Oliwa .12 .30
330 Marian Hossa .15 .40
331 Valeri Bure .12 .30
332 Bret Hedican .12 .30
333 Pavel Trnka .12 .30
334 Darcy Tucker .15 .40
335 Peter Schaefer .12 .30
336 Sergei Brylin .12 .30
337 Hal Gill .12 .30
338 Jason Woolley .12 .30
339 Mike Rathje .12 .30
340 Marty Murray .12 .30
341 Todd White .12 .30
342 Brent Sopel .12 .30
343 Glen Wesley .12 .30
344 Jozef Stumpel .12 .30
345 Scott Nichol .12 .30
346 Derrick Walser .12 .30
347 Marc Bergevin .12 .30
348 Richard Zednik .12 .30
349 Mike Ribeiro .15 .40
350 Mike Eastwood .12 .30
351 Trevor Letowski .12 .30
352 Fredrik Modin .12 .30
353 Mark Parrish .12 .30
354 Sandy McCarthy .12 .30
355 Tomas Holmstrom .15 .40
356 Dmitri Kalinin .12 .30
357 Janne Niinimaa .12 .30
358 Dave Andreychuk .20 .50
359 Boyd Devereaux .12 .30
360 Sergei Fedorov .30 .75
361 Josef Melichar .12 .30
362 Stephane Quintal .12 .30
363 Lasse Pirjeta .12 .30
364 Denis Arkhipov .12 .30
365 Matt Cullen .12 .30
366 Teppo Numminen .12 .30
367 Ilya Kovalchuk .20 .50
368 Reed Low .12 .30
369 Jochen Hecht .12 .30
370 Martin Rucinsky .12 .30
371 Mark Eaton .12 .30
372 Nils Ekman .12 .30
373 Slava Kozlov .15 .40
374 Scott Young .12 .30
375 Mathieu Schneider .12 .30
376 Scott Hannan .12 .30
377 Brad May .12 .30
378 Jeff Friesen .12 .30
379 P.J. Axelsson .12 .30
380 Brian Sutherby .12 .30
381 David Tanabe .12 .30
382 Pierre-Marc Bouchard .20 .50
383 Steve Konowalchuk .12 .30
384 Chris Pronger .15 .40
385 Craig Rivet .12 .30
386 Eric Desjardins .15 .40
387 Jody Shelley .12 .30
388 Vaclav Prospal .12 .30
389 Aaron Miller .12 .30
390 Deron Quint .12 .30
391 Joel Kwiatkowski .12 .30
392 Branko Radivojevic .12 .30
393 Niko Kapanen .12 .30
394 Wayne Primeau .12 .30
395 Patrik Elias .20 .50
396 Ronald Petrovicky .12 .30
397 Mike Cammalleri .20 .50
398 Bryan Berard .15 .40
399 Jason Doig .12 .30
400 Marcus Ragnarsson .12 .30
401 Aaron Downey .12 .30
402 Byron Dafoe .15 .40
403 Jean-Sebastien Giguere .20 .50
404 Dwayne Roloson .15 .40
405 Marc-Andre Fleury 2.00 5.00
406 Ray Emery .15 .40
407 Derek Armstrong .12 .30
408 Randy Robitaille .12 .30
409 Manny Fernandez .15 .40
410 Jeff Hackett .15 .40
411 Nikolai Khabibulin .20 .50
412 Tomas Vokoun .15 .40
413 Chris Neil .12 .30
414 Andrei Nikolishin .12 .30
415 Garth Snow .15 .40
416 Marty Turco .20 .50
417 Roberto Luongo .30 .75
418 Mikael Tellqvist .15 .40
419 Chris Osgood .20 .50
420 Jocelyn Thibault .15 .40
421 Olaf Kolzig .20 .50
422 Tommy Salo .15 .40
423 Corey Schwab .15 .40
424 Johan Hedberg .15 .40
425 Travis Green .12 .30
426 Pascal Leclaire .12 .30
427 Craig Andersson .20 .50
428 John Grahame .12 .30
429 Pasi Nurminen .15 .40
430 Trevor Kidd .12 .30
431 Scott Lachance .12 .30
432 Brent Johnson .15 .40
433 Jamie Storr .15 .40
434 Miikka Kiprusoff .15 .40
435 Cristobal Huet .15 .40
436 Jose Theodore .20 .50
437 Ty Conklin .15 .40
438 Curtis Joseph .20 .50
439 Jussi Markkanen .12 .30
440 Patrick Lalime .15 .40
441 Vesa Toskala .12 .30
442 Dan Cloutier .15 .40
443 Kevin Weekes .15 .40
444 Peter Worrell .12 .30
445 Zac Bierk .12 .30
446 Evgeni Nabokov .15 .40
447 Martin Biron .15 .40
448 Rick DiPietro .15 .40
449 Ed Belfour .20 .50
450 Martin Gerber .12 .30
451 Reinhard Divis .12 .30
452 Brian Finley .12 .30
453 Jason Bacashihua .12 .30
454 Mika Noronen .12 .30
455 Scott Clemmensen .12 .30
456 Brian Boucher .15 .40
457 Jason LaBarbera .12 .30
458 Mike Dunham .15 .40
459 Sean Burke .12 .30
460 Felix Potvin .30 .75
461 Martin Brodeur .40 1.00
462 Sebastien Caron .15 .40
463 Rob Zamuner .12 .30
464 Igor Larionov .20 .50
465 Andrew Raycroft .15 .40
466 Mathieu Garon .12 .30
467 Roman Turek .15 .40
468 Steve Passmore .12 .30
469 Chris Mason .12 .30
470 Jean-Sebastien Aubin .12 .30
471 Milan Hnilicka .12 .30
472 Steve Shields .15 .40
473 Arturs Irbe .15 .40
474 Ilja Bryzgalov .15 .40
475 Roman Cechmanek .15 .40
476 Steve Ott .15 .40
477 Mattias Weinhandl .12 .30
478 Brent Krahn .12 .30
479 Jamie McLennan .12 .30
480 Michael Leighton .12 .30
481 Ryan Miller .20 .50
482 Dominik Hasek .30 .75
483 Marc Denis .15 .40
484 Rastislav Stana .20 .50
485 Alex Auld .12 .30
486 Fred Brathwaite .15 .40
487 Martin Prusek .12 .30
488 Robert Esche .12 .30
489 Sebastien Charpentier .12 .30
490 David Aebischer .15 .40
491 Manny Legace .12 .30
492 Philippe Sauve .15 .40
493 Bob Boughner .12 .30
494 Maxime Ouellet .15 .40
495 Ron Tugnutt .15 .40
496 J.P. Vigier .12 .30
497 Steve Thomas .12 .30
498 Manny Malhotra .12 .30
499 Dany Sabourin .12 .30
500 Pavel Brendl .12 .30
501 Derek Roy .20 .50
502 Lawrence Nycholat .15 .40
503 Simon Gamache .12 .30
504 Dan Fritsche .12 .30
505 Chris Higgins .25 .60
506 Pierre Hedin .15 .40
507 Marc-Andre Fleury 2.00 5.00
508 Tony Salmelainen .12 .30
509 Ryan Kesler .60 1.50
510 John-Michael Liles .15 .40
511 Zbynek Michalek .12 .30
512 Trent Hunter .12 .30
513 Matthew Lombardi .15 .40
514 Matt Stajan .20 .50
515 Gregory Campbell .12 .30
516 Chad Wiseman .12 .30
517 Konstantin Koltsov .12 .30
518 Joffrey Lupul .75 2.00
519 Jeff MacMillan .15 .40
520 Wade Brookbank .15 .40
521 Timofei Shishkanov .12 .30
522 Eric Staal 1.50 4.00
523 Nathan Horton .75 2.00
524 Julien Vauclair .12 .30
525 Tom Preissing .15 .40
526 Kent McDonell .15 .40
527 Antoine Vermette .25 .60
528 Anton Babchuk .12 .30
529 Grant McNeill .12 .30
530 Chris Hajt .15 .40
531 Burke Henry .12 .30
532 Kyle Rossiter .15 .40
533 Joni Pitkanen .20 .50
534 Maxim Kondratiev .12 .30
535 Peter Sejna .15 .40
536 Sergei Zinovjev .12 .30
537 Nathan Robinson .12 .30
538 Tuomas Pihlman .15 .40
539 Lasse Kukkonen .12 .30
540 Tomas Plekanec .40 1.00
541 Alexander Semin 1.00 2.50
542 Fredrik Sjostrom .20 .50
543 Kari Lehtonen 1.50 4.00
544 Matt Murley .15 .40
545 Dustin Brown .25 .60
546 Tuomo Ruutu .20 .50
547 Dominic Moore .12 .30
548 Garnet Exelby .12 .30
549 Dan Hamhuis .15 .40
550 Ryan Malone .25 .60
551 Milan Michalek .60 1.50
552 Aaron Johnson .12 .30
553 Matthew Spiller .15 .40
554 Christian Ehrhoff .15 .40
555 Doug Lynch .12 .30
556 Andrew Peters .15 .40
557 Aleksander Suglobov .12 .30
558 Chuck Kobasew .12 .30
559 Sean Bergenheim .15 .40
560 Jason Pominville .75 2.00
561 Andrew Hutchinson .12 .30
562 Garrett Burnett .12 .30
563 Nikolai Zherdev .60 1.50
564 Tony Martensson .12 .30
565 Antti Miettinen .20 .50
566 Scott Barney .12 .30
567 Jordin Tootoo .60 1.50
568 Brad Leeb .12 .30
569 Peter Sarno .12 .30
570 Jed Ortmeyer .12 .30
571 Kyle Wellwood .20 .50
572 Brent Krahn .12 .30
573 Dmitri Afanasenkov .15 .40
574 Jarret Stoll .12 .30
575 Marek Zidlicky .12 .30
576 Karl Stewart .12 .30
577 Darryl Bootland .15 .40
578 Niklas Kronwall .25 .60
579 Paul Martin .15 .40
580 Adam Munro .12 .30
581 Pat Leahy .15 .40
582 Cody McCormick .15 .40
583 Jozef Balej .12 .30
584 Boyd Gordon .15 .40
585 Jason King .12 .30
586 Trevor Daley .20 .50
587 Robert Schnabel .15 .40
588 Chris Kunitz .25 .60
589 Mike Danton .12 .30
590 Mikhail Yakubov .12 .30
591 John Pohl .12 .30
592 Brent Burns .30 .75
593 Patrice Bergeron 1.50 4.00
594 Jiri Hudler .75 2.00
595 David Hale .12 .30
596 Travis Moen .15 .40
597 Michael Ryder .15 .40
598 Tim Gleason .15 .40
599 Christian Backman .20 .50
600 Pavel Vorobiev .15 .40

1997-98 Pacific Dynagon

The 1997-98 Pacific Dynagon set was issued in one series totaling 156 cards and was distributed in three-card packs with a suggested retail price of $2.49. The fronts feature color action player photos printed on fully foiled and double etched cards. The backs carry a small circular player head photo and player information.

COMPLETE SET (156) 25.00 60.00
1 Brian Bellows .30 .75
2 Guy Hebert .30 .75
3 Paul Kariya .50 1.25
4 Steve Rucchin .30 .75
5 Teemu Selanne .75 2.00
6 Jason Allison .30 .75
7 Ray Bourque .60 1.50
8 Jim Carey .25 .60
9 Jozef Stumpel .30 .75
10 Dominik Hasek .60 1.50
11 Brian Holzinger .30 .75
12 Michael Peca .30 .75
13 Derek Plante .30 .75
14 Miroslav Satan .25 .60
15 Theo Fleury .50 1.25
16 Jonas Hoglund .30 .75
17 Jarome Iginla .40 1.00
18 Trevor Kidd .25 .60
19 German Titov .25 .60
20 Sean Burke .25 .60
21 Andrew Cassels .25 .60
22 Keith Primeau .30 .75
23 Geoff Sanderson .30 .75
24 Tony Amonte .30 .75
25 Chris Chelios .40 1.00
26 Eric Daze .25 .60
27 Jeff Hackett .25 .60
28 Ethan Moreau .25 .60
29 Peter Forsberg .50 1.25
30 Valeri Kamensky .30 .75
31 Claude Lemieux .30 .75
32 Sandis Ozolinsh .30 .75
33 Patrick Roy 1.00 2.50
34 Joe Sakic .60 1.50
35 Derian Hatcher .30 .75
36 Jamie Langenbrunner .30 .75
37 Mike Modano .60 1.50
38 Joe Nieuwendyk .40 1.00
39 Darryl Sydor .25 .60
40 Sergei Zubov .30 .75
41 Sergei Fedorov .60 1.50
42 Vladimir Konstantinov .25 .60
43 Chris Osgood .40 1.00
44 Brendan Shanahan .50 1.25
45 Mike Vernon .30 .75
46 Steve Yzerman .75 2.00
47 Kelly Buchberger .30 .75
48 Mike Grier .30 .75
49 Curtis Joseph .40 1.00
50 Rem Murray .25 .60
51 Ryan Smyth .30 .75
52 Doug Weight .40 1.00
53 Ed Jovanovski .25 .60
54 Scott Mellanby .30 .75
55 Ray Sheppard .30 .75
56 Robert Svehla .30 .75
57 John Vanbiesbrouck .40 1.00
58 Rob Blake .40 1.00
59 Ray Ferraro .25 .60
60 Dimitri Khristich .30 .75
61 Vladimir Tsyplakov .30 .75
62 Vincent Damphousse .30 .75
63 Saku Koivu .40 1.00
64 Mark Recchi .50 1.25
65 Stephane Richer .25 .60
66 Jocelyn Thibault .25 .60
67 Dave Andreychuk .40 1.00
68 Martin Brodeur .75 2.00
69 Doug Gilmour .50 1.25
70 Bobby Holik .25 .60
71 John MacLean .25 .60
72 Bryan Berard .25 .60
73 Travis Green .30 .75
74 Zigmund Palffy .40 1.00
75 Tommy Salo .25 .60
76 Bryan Smolinski .30 .75
77 Adam Graves .25 .60
78 Wayne Gretzky 2.00 5.00
79 Alexei Kovalev .25 .60
80 Brian Leetch .40 1.00
81 Mark Messier .60 1.50
82 Mike Richter .40 1.00
83 Daniel Alfredsson .40 1.00
84 Alexandre Daigle .25 .60
85 Wade Redden .25 .60
86 Damian Rhodes .30 .75
87 Alexei Yashin .30 .75
88 Rod Brind'Amour .40 1.00
89 Ron Hextall .40 1.00
90 John LeClair .40 1.00
91 Eric Lindros .60 1.50
92 Janne Niinimaa .30 .75
93 Garth Snow .30 .75
94 Dainius Zubrus .30 .75
95 Mike Gartner .40 1.00
96 Nikolai Khabibulin .40 1.00
97 Jeremy Roenick .50 1.25
98 Keith Tkachuk .40 1.00
99 Oleg Tverdovsky .30 .75
100 Ron Francis .50 1.25
101 Kevin Hatcher .25 .60
102 Jaromir Jagr 1.00 2.50
103 Patrick Lalime .30 .75
104 Petr Nedved .40 1.00
105 Jim Campbell .25 .60
106 Grant Fuhr .40 1.00
107 Brett Hull .50 1.25
108 Pierre Turgeon .40 1.00
109 Harry York .30 .75
110 Jeff Friesen .30 .75
111 Tony Granato .30 .75
112 Stephen Guolla RC .25 .60
113 Viktor Kozlov .30 .75
114 Owen Nolan .40 1.00
115 Dino Ciccarelli .40 1.00
116 John Cullen .25 .60
117 Chris Gratton .25 .60
118 Roman Hamrlik .30 .75
119 Daymond Langkow .25 .60
120 Sergei Berezin .30 .75
121 Wendel Clark .40 1.00
122 Felix Potvin .40 1.00
123 Steve Sullivan .30 .75
124 Mats Sundin .40 1.00
125 Pavel Bure .50 1.25
126 Martin Gelinas .25 .60
127 Trevor Linden .30 .75
128 Kirk McLean .30 .75
129 Alexander Mogilny .30 .75
130 Peter Bondra .30 .75
131 Joe Juneau .30 .75
132 Steve Konowalchuk .30 .75
133 Adam Oates .40 1.00
134 Bill Ranford .30 .75
135 Paul Kariya .75 2.00
Teemu Selanne
136 Dominik Hasek .60 1.50
Mike Peca
137 T.Fleury/J.Iginla .50 1.25
138 P.Forsberg/P.Roy 1.00 2.50
139 B.Shanahan/S.Yzerman .75 2.00
140 W.Gretzky/M.Messier 2.00 5.00
141 J.LeClair/E.Lindros .60 1.50
142 J.Jagr/P.Lalime 1.00 2.50
143 J.Campbell/B.Hull .50 1.25
144 S.Berezin/M.Sundin .40 1.00
NNO1 Shawn Bates RC .30 .75
NNO2 Daniel Cleary .30 .75
NNO3 Marian Hossa RC .50 1.25
NNO4 Olli Jokinen RC .50 1.25
NNO5 Espen Knutsen RC .40 1.00
NNO6 Patrick Marleau .50 1.25
NNO7 Alyn McCauley .30 .75
NNO8 Mattias Ohlund .30 .75
NNO9 Chris Phillips .30 .75
NNO10 Erik Rasmussen .30 .75
NNO11 Sergei Samsonov .25 .60
NNO12 Joe Thornton .40 1.00

1997-98 Pacific Dynagon Copper

Randomly inserted in hobby packs only at the rate of 2:37, this 156-card set is a parallel version of the base set and is distinguished by the copper foil enhancements.
*VETS: 5X TO 12X BASIC CARDS
*ROOKIE STAR: 2X TO 5X BASIC CARDS

1997-98 Pacific Dynagon Dark Gray

Randomly inserted in hobby packs only at the rate of 2:37, this 156-card set is a parallel version of the base set and is distinguished by the gray foil enhancements.
*VETS: 5X TO 12X BASIC CARDS
*ROOKIE STAR: 2X TO 5X BASIC CARDS

1997-98 Pacific Dynagon Emerald Green

Randomly inserted in Canadian packs only at the rate of 2:37, this 156-card set is a parallel version of the base set and is distinguished by the green foil enhancements.
*VETS: 5X TO 12X BASIC CARDS
*ROOKIE STAR: 2X TO 5X BASIC CARDS

1997-98 Pacific Dynagon Ice Blue

Randomly inserted in packs at the rate of 1:73, this 156-card set is a parallel version of the base set and is distinguished by the blue foil enhancements.
*VETS: 8X TO 15X BASIC CARDS
*ROOKIE STAR: 2.5X TO 8X BASIC CARDS

1997-98 Pacific Dynagon Red

Randomly inserted in packs at the rate of 2:37 Treat packs, this 156-card set is a parallel version of the base set and is distinguished by the red foil enhancements.
*VETS: 5X TO 12X BASIC CARDS
*ROOKIE STAR: 2X TO 5X BASIC CARDS

1997-98 Pacific Dynagon Silver

Randomly inserted in retail packs only at the rate of 2:37, this 156-card set is a parallel version of the base set and is distinguished by the silver foil enhancements.
*VETS: 5X TO 12X BASIC CARDS
*ROOKIE STAR: 2X TO 5X BASIC CARDS

1997-98 Pacific Dynagon Best Kept Secrets

Randomly inserted one per pack, this 110-card set features color action player photos of the top NHL players made to resemble a picture paper clipped to a file. A small slide-look version of the player's picture appears at the top. The backs carry player information and career statistics.

COMPLETE SET (110) 12.50 25.00
1 J.J. Daigneault .02 .10
2 Paul Kariya .15 .40
3 Dave Karpa .02 .10
4 Teemu Selanne .15 .40
5 Ray Bourque .25 .60
6 Jim Carey .08 .25
7 Davis Payne .02 .10
8 Paxton Schafer .02 .10
9 Bob Boughner .02 .10
10 Dominik Hasek .30 .75
11 Brad May .02 .10
12 Cale Hulse .02 .10
13 Jarome Iginla .20 .50
14 James Patrick .02 .10
15 Zarley Zalapski .02 .10
16 Jeff Brown .02 .10
17 Keith Primeau .08 .25
18 Steven Rice .02 .10
19 James Black .02 .10
20 Chris Chelios .15 .40
21 Steve Dubinsky .02 .10
22 Steve Smith .02 .10
23 Craig Billington .08 .25
24 Peter Forsberg .40 1.00
25 Jon Klemm .02 .10
26 Patrick Roy .75 2.00
27 Joe Sakic .30 .75
28 Neal Broten .02 .10
29 Richard Matvichuk .02 .10
30 Mike Modano .25 .60
31 Andy Moog .08 .25
32 Sergei Fedorov .30 .75
33 Kirk Maltby .02 .10
34 Brendan Shanahan .25 .60
35 Tim Taylor .02 .10
36 Steve Yzerman .75 2.00
37 Louie DeBrusk .02 .10
38 Joe Hulbig .02 .10
39 Ryan Smyth .08 .25
40 Mike Hough .02 .10
41 Jody Hull .02 .10
42 Paul Laus .08 .25
43 John Vanbiesbrouck .15 .40
44 Aki Berg .02 .10
45 Ray Ferraro .02 .10
46 Craig Johnson .02 .10
47 Ian Laperriere .02 .10
48 Vincent Damphousse .08 .25
49 Dave Manson .02 .10
50 Stephane Richer .08 .25
51 Craig Rivet .02 .10
52 Martin Brodeur .40 1.00
53 Jay Pandolfo .02 .10
54 Brian Rolston .02 .10
55 Doug Houda .02 .10
56 Brent Hughes .02 .10
57 Zigmund Palffy .15 .40
58 Adam Graves .08 .25
59 Wayne Gretzky 1.00 2.50
60 Chris Ferraro .02 .10
61 Glenn Healy .08 .25
62 Brian Leetch .15 .40
63 Mark Messier .20 .50
64 Radim Bicanek .02 .10
65 Philip Crowe .02 .10
66 Christer Olsson .02 .10
67 Jason York .02 .10
68 Rod Brind'Amour .08 .25
69 John Druce .02 .10
70 Daniel Lacroix .02 .10
71 John LeClair .20 .50
72 Eric Lindros .30 .75
73 Murray Baron .02 .10
74 Mike Gartner .08 .25
75 Brad McCrimmon .02 .10
76 Keith Tkachuk .15 .40
77 Jaromir Jagr .25 .60
78 Patrick Lalime .08 .25
79 Ian Moran .02 .10
80 Petr Nedved .08 .25
81 Brett Hull .20 .50
82 Robert Petrovicky .02 .10
83 Pierre Turgeon .08 .25
84 Trent Yawney .02 .10
85 Tim Hunter .02 .10
86 Marcus Ragnarsson .02 .10
87 Dody Wood .02 .10
88 Dino Ciccarelli .02 .10
89 Alexander Selivanov .02 .10
90 Jason Wiemer .02 .10

91 Sergei Berezin .08 .25
92 Felix Potvin .15 .40
93 Mats Sundin .15 .40
94 Craig Wolanin .02 .10
95 Pavel Bure .25 .60
96 Troy Crowder .02 .10
97 Dana Murzyn .02 .10
98 Gino Odjick .08 .25
99 Craig Berube .02 .10
100 Peter Bondra .15 .40
101 Mike Eagles .02 .10
102 Andrei Nikolishin .02 .10
103 Paul Kariya .15 .40
104 Dominik Hasek .30 .75
105 Michael Peca .02 .10
106 M.Brodeur/M.Dunham .20 .50
107 Bryan Berard .08 .25
108 Brian Leetch .15 .40
109 Tony Granato .02 .10
110 Trevor Linden .08 .25

1997-98 Pacific Dynagon Dynamic Duos

Randomly inserted in packs at the rate of 1:37, this 30-card set features color action images of the NHL's top teammates printed on a die-cut gold foil card and framed with a textured hockey puck border. When placed side by side, the matching cards are joined together by their team logo.

COMPLETE SET (30) 30.00 80.00
1A Paul Kariya 1.50 4.00
1B Teemu Selanne 1.50 4.00
2A Ray Bourque 2.00 5.00
2B Jim Carey .75 2.00
3A Dominik Hasek 3.00 8.00
3B Michael Peca .40 1.00
4A Theo Fleury .75 2.00
4B Jarome Iginla 2.00 5.00
5A Peter Forsberg 2.50 6.00
5B Claude Lemieux .40 1.00
6A Patrick Roy 8.00 20.00
6B Joe Sakic 3.00 8.00
7A Sergei Fedorov 1.50 4.00
7B Vladimir Konstantinov .75 2.00
8A Brendan Shanahan 1.50 4.00
8B Steve Yzerman 6.00 15.00
9A Bryan Berard .40 1.00
9B Zigmund Palffy .75 2.00
10A Wayne Gretzky 10.00 25.00
10B Mark Messier 1.50 4.00
11A Eric Lindros 1.50 4.00
11B Dainius Zubrus .40 1.00
12A Jeremy Roenick 2.00 5.00
12B Keith Tkachuk 1.25 3.00
13A Jaromir Jagr 2.50 6.00
13B Patrick Lalime .75 2.00
14A Jim Campbell .40 1.00
14B Brett Hull 1.50 4.00
15A Pavel Bure 1.50 4.00
15B Alexander Mogilny .75 2.00

1997-98 Pacific Dynagon Kings of the NHL

COMPLETE SET (10) 30.00 80.00
STATED ODDS 1:361
1 Paul Kariya 3.00 8.00
2 Peter Forsberg 6.00 15.00
3 Patrick Roy 12.00 30.00
4 Joe Sakic 6.00 15.00
5 John Vanbiesbrouck 2.50 6.00
6 Wayne Gretzky 20.00 50.00
7 Mark Messier 3.00 8.00
8 Eric Lindros 3.00 8.00
9 Jaromir Jagr 5.00 12.00
10 Pavel Bure 3.00 8.00

1997-98 Pacific Dynagon Stonewallers

COMPLETE SET (20) 25.00 60.00
STATED ODDS 1:73
1 Guy Hebert 1.25 3.00
2 Jim Carey 1.25 3.00
3 Dominik Hasek 4.00 10.00
4 Trevor Kidd 1.25 3.00
5 Jeff Hackett 1.25 3.00
6 Patrick Roy 10.00 25.00
7 Chris Osgood 1.25 3.00
8 Mike Vernon 1.50 4.00
9 Curtis Joseph 1.50 4.00
10 John Vanbiesbrouck 1.50 4.00
11 Jocelyn Thibault 1.25 3.00
12 Martin Brodeur 6.00 15.00
13 Tommy Salo 1.25 3.00
14 Mike Richter 1.50 4.00
15 Ron Hextall 1.50 4.00
16 Garth Snow 1.25 3.00
17 Nikolai Khabibulin 1.50 4.00
18 Patrick Lalime 1.25 3.00
19 Grant Fuhr 1.50 4.00
20 Felix Potvin 2.00 5.00

1997-98 Pacific Dynagon Tandems

Randomly inserted in packs at the rate of 1:37, this 72-card set features color player images printed on double front, holographic fully foiled, double etched cards.

COMPLETE SET (72) 60.00 150.00
1 W.Gretzky/E.Lindros 10.00 25.00
2 J.Sakic/P.Kariya 4.00 10.00
3 J.Iginla/M.Messier 4.00 10.00
4 P.Roy/D.Hasek 8.00 20.00
5 P.Forsberg/J.Jagr 4.00 10.00
6 B.Shanahan/K.Tkachuk 1.25 3.00
7 S.Yzerman/T.Selanne 4.00 10.00
8 S.Fedorov/B.Hull 4.00 10.00
9 D.Zubrus/P.Lalime .75 2.00
10 S.Berezin/M.Grier .75 2.00
11 Z.Palffy/C.Joseph 1.25 3.00
12 C.Osgood/M.Brodeur 4.00 10.00
13 J.Vanbiesbr./J.Thibault 1.25 3.00
14 S.Koivu/P.Bure 2.00 5.00
15 J.LeClair/P.Bondra 1.25 3.00
16 M.Sundin/J.Niinimaa 1.25 3.00
17 F.Potvin/J.Carey 3.00 8.00
18 Fuhr/Hull/Campbell 2.00 5.00
19 Gretzky/Messier/Leetch 8.00 20.00
20 Lindros/LeClair/B'Amour 2.00 5.00
21 Hasek/Peca/Satan 2.00 5.00
22 Jagr/Lalime/Nedved 2.00 5.00
23 Iginla/Fleury/Kidd 2.00 5.00
24 Kariya/Selanne/Hebert 2.00 5.00
25 Forsberg/Roy/Lemieux 8.00 20.00
26 Yzerman/Shanahan/Konst. 8.00 20.00
27 Sundin/Berezin/Clark 2.00 5.00
28 R.Bourque/D.Plante 2.00 5.00
29 B.Bellows/J.Allison .75 2.00
30 S.Rucchin/K.Primeau 1.00 2.50
31 J.Stumpel/E.Daze .75 2.00
32 B.Holzinger/J.Langenbrunner .75 2.00
33 M.Peca/T.Amonte .75 2.00
34 G.Titov/D.Sydor .75 2.00
35 T.Fleury/C.Chelios 1.25 3.00
36 J.Hoglund/D.Khristich .75 2.00
37 S.Burke/D.Andreychuk 1.00 2.50
38 G.Sanderson/D.Hatcher .75 2.00
39 A.Cassels/J.Hackett .75 2.00
40 E.Moreau/R.Ferraro .75 2.00
41 S.Ozolinsh/D.Gilmour 1.00 2.50
42 V.Kamensky/M.Modano 1.25 3.00
43 J.Nieuwendyk/V.Tsyplakov 1.00 2.50
44 S.Zubov/M.Vernon 1.00 2.50
45 R.Blake/B.Holik 1.00 2.50
46 V.Damphousse/D.Weight 1.00 2.50
47 M.Recchi/R.Smyth 1.00 2.50
48 S.Richer/J.MacLean .75 2.00
49 K.Buchberger/E.Jovanovski .75 2.00
50 R.Murray/O.Nolan .75 2.00
51 R.Svehla/B.Ranford .75 2.00
52 R.Sheppard/S.Sullivan .75 2.00
53 S.Mellanby/J.Cullen .75 2.00
54 G.Snow/A.Daigle .75 2.00
55 R.Hextall/A.Mogilny 1.25 3.00
56 K.McLean/A.Oates 1.00 2.50
57 J.Juneau/D.Ciccarelli 1.00 2.50
58 S.Konowalchuk/J.Campbell .75 2.00
59 T.Linden/P.Turgeon 1.25 3.00
60 M.Gelinas/J.Friesen .75 2.00
61 R.Hamrlik/H.York 1.00 2.50
62 K.Hatcher/C.Gratton .75 2.00
63 R.Francis/J.Roenick 1.50 4.00
64 N.Khabibulin/V.Kozlov 1.00 2.50
65 D.Langkow/M.Gartner .75 2.00
66 O.Tverdovsky/S.Guolla .75 2.00
67 T.Granato/T.Salo .75 2.00
68 B.Smolinski/W.Redden .75 2.00
69 A.Graves/D.Rhodes .75 2.00
70 M.Richter/A.Yashin 1.25 3.00
71 D.Alfredsson/B.Berard 1.00 2.50
72 T.Green/A.Kovalev .75 2.00

1998-99 Pacific Dynagon Ice

The 1998-99 Pacific Dynagon Ice set was issued in one series totaling 200 cards and was distributed in five-card packs with a suggested retail price of $2.49. The set features color action player photos printed on gold foil cards with player highlights and statistics displayed on the backs.

COMPLETE SET (200) 25.00 50.00
1 Travis Green .08 .25
2 Guy Hebert .25 .60
3 Paul Kariya .30 .75
4 Steve Rucchin .08 .25
5 Tomas Sandstrom .08 .25
6 Teemu Selanne .30 .75
7 Jason Allison .08 .25
8 Ray Bourque .50 1.25
9 Byron Dafoe .25 .60
10 Anson Carter .25 .60
11 Dimitri Khristich .08 .25
12 Antti Laaksonen RC .08 .25
13 Peter Nordstrom RC .08 .25
14 Sergei Samsonov .25 .60
15 Joe Thornton .50 1.25
16 Matthew Barnaby .08 .25
17 Michal Grosek .08 .25
18 Dominik Hasek .60 1.50
19 Brian Holzinger .08 .25
20 Michael Peca .08 .25
21 Miroslav Satan .25 .60
22 Vaclav Varada .08 .25
23 Andrew Cassels .08 .25
24 Rico Fata .08 .25
25 Theo Fleury .08 .25
26 Phil Housley .08 .25
27 Jarome Iginla .40 1.00
28 Martin St. Louis RC 2.00 5.00
29 Ken Wregget .25 .60
30 Kevin Dineen .08 .25
31 Ron Francis .25 .60
32 Martin Gelinas .08 .25
33 Arturs Irbe .25 .60
34 Sami Kapanen .08 .25
35 Trevor Kidd .25 .60
36 Robert Kron .08 .25
37 Keith Primeau .08 .25
38 Tony Amonte .25 .60
39 Chris Chelios .30 .75
40 Eric Daze .25 .60
41 Doug Gilmour .25 .60
42 Jeff Hackett .25 .60
43 Ty Jones .25 .60
44 Bob Probert .08 .25
45 Adam Deadmarsh .08 .25
46 Chris Drury .25 .60
47 Peter Forsberg .75 2.00
48 Milan Hejduk RC 1.25 3.00
49 Valeri Kamensky .08 .25
50 Claude Lemieux .08 .25
51 Patrick Roy 1.50 4.00
52 Joe Sakic .60 1.50
53 Ed Belfour .30 .75
54 Sergey Gusev RC .08 .25
55 Derian Hatcher .08 .25
56 Brett Hull .40 1.00
57 Jamie Langenbrunner .08 .25
58 Jere Lehtinen .08 .25
59 Mike Modano .50 1.25
60 Joe Nieuwendyk .25 .60
61 Sergei Zubov .08 .25
62 Sergei Fedorov .50 -1.25
63 Vyacheslav Kozlov .25 .60
64 Uwe Krupp .08 .25
65 Nicklas Lidstrom .30 .75
66 Darren McCarty .08 .25
67 Chris Osgood .25 .60
68 Brendan Shanahan .30 .75
69 Steve Yzerman 1.50 4.00
70 Bob Essensa .25 .60
71 Mike Grier .08 .25
72 Bill Guerin .25 .60
73 Roman Hamrlik .08 .25
74 Janne Niinimaa .08 .25
75 Tom Poti .08 .25
76 Ryan Smyth .25 .60
77 Doug Weight .25 .60
78 Sean Burke .08 .25
79 Dino Ciccarelli .25 .60
80 Dave Gagner .08 .25
81 Ed Jovanovski .08 .25
82 Viktor Kozlov .08 .25
83 Oleg Kvasha RC .30 .75
84 Paul Laus .08 .25
85 Mark Parrish RC .40 1.00
86 Rob Blake .25 .60
87 Stephane Fiset .25 .60
88 Josh Green RC .08 .25
89 Yanic Perreault .08 .25
90 Luc Robitaille .25 .60
91 Jozef Stumpel .25 .60
92 Vladimir Tsyplakov .08 .25
93 Brad Brown .08 .25
94 Shayne Corson .25 .60
95 Vincent Damphousse .08 .25
96 Saku Koivu .30 .75
97 Mark Recchi .25 .60
98 Jocelyn Thibault .25 .60
99 Sergei Zholtok .08 .25
100 Andrew Brunette .25 .60
101 Mike Dunham .25 .60
102 Tom Fitzgerald .08 .25
103 Patrik Kjellberg .08 .25
104 Sergei Krivokrasov .08 .25
105 Darren Turcotte .08 .25
106 Dave Andreychuk .25 .60
107 Jason Arnott .08 .25
108 Martin Brodeur .75 2.00
109 Patrik Elias .25 .60
110 Bobby Holik .08 .25
111 Brendan Morrison .25 .60
112 Scott Stevens .25 .60
113 Bryan Berard .25 .60
114 Eric Brewer .08 .25
115 Trevor Linden .25 .60
116 Zigmund Palffy .25 .60
117 Robert Reichel .08 .25
118 Tommy Salo .25 .60
119 Bryan Smolinski .08 .25
120 Adam Graves .08 .25
121 Wayne Gretzky 2.00 5.00
122 Alexei Kovalev .08 .25
123 Brian Leetch .30 .75
124 Manny Malhotra .25 .60
125 Mike Richter .30 .75
126 Daniel Alfredsson .25 .60
127 Igor Kravchuk .08 .25
128 Shawn McEachern .08 .25
129 Vaclav Prospal .25 .60
130 Damian Rhodes .25 .60
131 Sami Salo RC .25 .60
132 Alexei Yashin .08 .25
133 Rod Brind'Amour .25 .60
134 Alexandre Daigle .08 .25
135 Chris Gratton .25 .60
136 Ron Hextall .25 .60
137 John LeClair .30 .75
138 Eric Lindros .30 .75
139 Mike Maneluk RC .08 .25
140 John Vanbiesbrouck .25 .60
141 Dainius Zubrus .08 .25
142 Brad Isbister .08 .25
143 Nikolai Khabibulin .25 .60
144 Jeremy Roenick .40 1.00
145 Keith Tkachuk .30 .75
146 Rick Tocchet .25 .60
147 Oleg Tverdovsky .08 .25
148 Tom Barrasso .25 .60
149 Kevin Hatcher .08 .25
150 Jan Hrdina RC .50 1.25
151 Jaromir Jagr .50 1.25
152 Alexei Morozov .08 .25
153 Jiri Slegr .08 .25
154 Martin Straka .08 .25
155 Jim Campbell .08 .25
156 Geoff Courtnall .08 .25
157 Grant Fuhr .25 .60
158 Michal Handzus RC .40 1.00
159 Al MacInnis .25 .60
160 Jamie McLennan .25 .60
161 Chris Pronger .25 .60
162 Marty Reasoner .25 .60
163 Pierre Turgeon .25 .60
164 Jeff Friesen .08 .25
165 Tony Granato .08 .25
166 Scott Hannan RC .25 .60
167 Patrick Marleau .15 .40
168 Owen Nolan .25 .60
169 Marco Sturm .08 .25
170 Mike Vernon .25 .60
171 Wendel Clark .25 .60
172 John Cullen .08 .25
173 Vincent Lecavalier 1.00 2.50
174 Stephane Richer .25 .60
175 Paul Ysebaert .08 .25
176 Rob Zamuner .08 .25
177 Sergei Berezin .25 .60
178 Tie Domi .25 .60
179 Mike Johnson .08 .25
180 Curtis Joseph .30 .75
181 Tomas Kaberle RC .40 1.00
182 Igor Korolev .08 .25
183 Alyn McCauley .08 .25
184 Mats Sundin .30 .75
185 Todd Bertuzzi .30 .75
186 Donald Brashear .08 .25
187 Pavel Bure .30 .75
188 Matt Cooke RC .08 .25
189 Mark Messier .30 .75
190 Alexander Mogilny .25 .60
191 Mattias Ohlund .08 .25
192 Garth Snow .25 .60
193 Peter Bondra .25 .60
194 Matthew Herr RC .08 .25
195 Calle Johansson .08 .25
196 Joe Juneau .25 .60
197 Olaf Kolzig .25 .60
198 Adam Oates .25 .60
199 Jaroslav Svejkovsky .08 .25
200 Richard Zednik .08 .25

1998-99 Pacific Dynagon Ice Blue

Randomly inserted into packs, this 200-card set is a blue foil parallel version of the base set. Only 67 serially numbered sets were made.

*BLUE/67: 10X TO 25X BASIC CARDS
*ROOKIE STAR/67: 4X TO 10X

1998-99 Pacific Dynagon Ice Red

Randomly inserted into Treat retail packs only at the rate of 4:37, this 200-card set is a red foil parallel version of the base set made especially for Treat Entertainment.

*VETERANS: 1.5X TO 4X BASIC CARDS
*ROOKIES: 1.5X TO 4X BASIC CARDS

1998-99 Pacific Dynagon Ice Adrenaline Rush Bronze

Randomly inserted into Canadian retail packs only at the rate of 1:37, this 10-card set is a Canadian insert to the Pacific Dynagon Ice base set. Four limited edition parallel sets were also made and inserted into packs: Bronze with only 180 sets made, Ice Blue with 10 sets made, Red with 79 sets made, and Silver with 120 sets made.

COMPLETE SET (10) 60.00 120.00
*RED/79: .8X TO 2X BRONZE/180
*SILVER1/120: .5X TO 1.2X BRONZE/180
1 Paul Kariya 2.00 5.00
2 Teemu Selanne 3.00 8.00
3 Dominik Hasek 5.00 12.00
4 Peter Forsberg 6.00 15.00
5 Patrick Roy 10.00 25.00
6 Joe Sakic 5.00 12.00
7 Steve Yzerman 12.50 30.00
8 Wayne Gretzky 20.00 50.00
9 Eric Lindros 3.00 8.00
10 Jaromir Jagr 4.00 10.00

1998-99 Pacific Dynagon Ice Forward Thinking

COMPLETE SET (20) 12.00 30.00
1 Paul Kariya 1.25 3.00
2 Teemu Selanne 1.25 3.00
3 Michael Peca .40 1.00
4 Doug Gilmour .75 2.00
5 Peter Forsberg 2.00 5.00
6 Joe Sakic 2.00 5.00
7 Brett Hull 1.50 4.00
8 Mike Modano 1.50 4.00
9 Sergei Fedorov 1.50 4.00
10 Brendan Shanahan 1.25 3.00
11 Steve Yzerman 3.00 8.00
12 Saku Koivu 1.25 3.00
13 Wayne Gretzky 4.00 10.00
14 John LeClair .40 1.00
15 Eric Lindros 1.25 3.00
16 Jaromir Jagr 2.00 5.00
17 Vincent Lecavalier 1.50 4.00
18 Mats Sundin 1.25 3.00
19 Mark Messier 1.25 3.00
20 Peter Bondra .75 2.00

1998-99 Pacific Dynagon Ice Watchmen

COMPLETE SET (10) 20.00 50.00
1 Dominik Hasek 6.00 15.00
2 Patrick Roy 12.00 30.00
3 Ed Belfour 2.00 5.00
4 Chris Osgood 2.00 5.00
5 Martin Brodeur 8.00 20.00
6 Mike Richter 2.00 5.00
7 John Vanbiesbrouck 2.00 5.00
8 Grant Fuhr 2.00 5.00
9 Curtis Joseph 3.00 8.00
10 Olaf Kolzig 2.00 5.00

1998-99 Pacific Dynagon Ice Preeminent Players

COMPLETE SET (10) 60.00 150.00
STATED ODDS 1:181
1 Paul Kariya 4.00 10.00
2 Dominik Hasek 8.00 20.00
3 Peter Forsberg 6.00 15.00
4 Patrick Roy 12.00 30.00
5 Mike Modano 5.00 12.00
6 Steve Yzerman 12.00 30.00
7 Martin Brodeur 10.00 25.00
8 Wayne Gretzky 15.00 40.00
9 Eric Lindros 4.00 10.00
10 Jaromir Jagr 6.00 15.00

1998-99 Pacific Dynagon Ice Rookies

COMPLETE SET (10) 15.00 40.00
STATED ODDS 1:73 HOBBY
1 Chris Drury 2.00 5.00
2 Milan Hejduk 2.00 5.00
3 Mark Parrish .75 2.00
4 Brendan Morrison 2.00 5.00
5 Mike Maneluk .75 2.00
6 Jan Hrdina .75 2.00
7 Marty Reasoner .75 2.00
8 Vincent Lecavalier 10.00 25.00
9 Tomas Kaberle .75 2.00
10 Bill Muckalt .75 2.00

1998-99 Pacific Dynagon Ice Team Checklists

COMPLETE SET (27) 25.00 60.00
STATED ODDS 2:37
1 Paul Kariya 1.25 3.00
2 Ray Bourque 1.25 3.00
3 Dominik Hasek 2.50 6.00
4 Theo Fleury .40 1.00
5 Keith Primeau .40 1.00
6 Chris Chelios .75 2.00
7 Patrick Roy 6.00 15.00
8 Mike Modano 1.50 4.00
9 Steve Yzerman 4.00 10.00
10 Ryan Smyth .75 2.00
11 Dino Ciccarelli .40 1.00
12 Rob Blake .75 2.00
13 Saku Koivu 1.25 3.00
14 Mike Dunham .75 2.00
15 Martin Brodeur 3.00 8.00
16 Trevor Linden .75 2.00
17 Wayne Gretzky 8.00 20.00
18 Alexei Yashin .40 1.00
19 Eric Lindros 1.25 3.00
20 Keith Tkachuk .75 2.00
21 Jaromir Jagr 2.00 5.00
22 Grant Fuhr .75 2.00
23 Mike Vernon .75 2.00
24 Vincent Lecavalier 2.00 5.00
25 Mats Sundin 1.25 3.00
26 Mark Messier 1.25 3.00
27 Peter Bondra .75 2.00

1999-00 Pacific Dynagon Ice

Released as a 206-card set, Dynagon Ice features base cards with full color action photography set against each respective player's team logo and feature silver foil highlights. Dynagon Ice was packaged in 36-pack boxes with packs containing five cards and carried a suggested retail price of $2.49.

COMPLETE SET (206) 15.00 40.00
COMP.SET w/o SP's (200) 35.00 70.00
1 Steve Kariya SP RC 1.50 4.00
2 Simon Gagne SP 2.50 6.00
3 Mike Fisher SP RC 2.50 6.00
4 Mike Ribeiro SP 1.50 4.00
5 Oleg Saprykin SP RC 4.00 10.00
6 Patrik Stefan SP RC 4.00 10.00
7 Ted Donato .08 .25
8 Niclas Havelid RC .30 .75
9 Guy Hebert .25 .60
10 Paul Kariya .30 .75
11 Steve Rucchin .08 .25
12 Teemu Selanne .30 .75
13 Oleg Tverdovsky .08 .25
14 Kelly Buchberger .08 .25
15 Nelson Emerson .08 .25
16 Ray Ferraro .08 .25
17 Norm Maracle .25 .60
18 Damian Rhodes .25 .60
19 Per Svartvadet RC .08 .25
20 Jason Allison .08 .25
21 Ray Bourque .50 1.25
22 Anson Carter .25 .60
23 Byron Dafoe .25 .60
24 John Grahame RC .60 1.50
25 Sergei Samsonov .25 .60
26 Joe Thornton .50 1.25
27 Stu Barnes .08 .25
28 Martin Biron .25 .60
29 Curtis Brown .08 .25
30 Michal Grosek .08 .25
31 Dominik Hasek .60 1.50
32 Michael Peca .25 .60
33 Miroslav Satan .25 .60
34 Valeri Bure .08 .25
35 Grant Fuhr .25 .60
36 Jarome Iginla .40 1.00
37 Derek Morris .08 .25
38 Marc Savard .08 .25
39 Cory Stillman .08 .25
40 Ron Francis .25 .60
41 Arturs Irbe .25 .60
42 Sami Kapanen .08 .25
43 Keith Primeau .08 .25
44 Dave Tanabe .08 .25
45 Tommy Westlund RC .25 .60
46 Tony Amonte .25 .60
47 Wendel Clark .08 .25
48 Eric Daze .25 .60
49 J-P Dumont .25 .60
50 Doug Gilmour .25 .60
51 Steve McCarthy .08 .25
52 Jocelyn Thibault .25 .60
53 Alexei Zhamnov .08 .25
54 Adam Deadmarsh .08 .25
55 Chris Drury .25 .60
56 Peter Forsberg .75 2.00
57 Milan Hejduk .30 .75
58 Dan Hinote RC .25 .60
59 Patrick Roy 1.50 4.00
60 Joe Sakic .60 1.50
61 Martin Skoula RC .75 2.00
62 Alex Tanguay .25 .60
63 Ed Belfour .30 .75
64 Derian Hatcher .08 .25
65 Brett Hull .40 1.00
66 Jamie Langenbrunner .08 .25
67 Jere Lehtinen .25 .60
68 Mike Modano .50 1.25
69 Joe Nieuwendyk .25 .60
70 Pavel Patera RC .08 .25
71 Yuri Butsayev RC .08 .25
72 Chris Chelios .30 .75
73 Sergei Fedorov .50 1.25
74 Vyacheslav Kozlov .08 .25
75 Nicklas Lidstrom .30 .75
76 Darren McCarty .08 .25
77 Chris Osgood .25 .60
78 Brendan Shanahan .30 .75
79 Steve Yzerman 1.50 4.00
80 Paul Comrie RC .25 .60
81 Mike Grier .08 .25
82 Tom Poti .08 .25
83 Bill Ranford .25 .60
84 Tommy Salo .25 .60
85 Ryan Smyth .08 .25
86 Doug Weight .25 .60
87 Pavel Bure .30 .75
88 Sean Burke .25 .60
89 Trevor Kidd .25 .60
90 Viktor Kozlov .08 .25
91 Ivan Novoseltsev RC .60 1.50
92 Mark Parrish .08 .25
93 Ray Whitney .08 .25
94 Jason Blake RC .25 .60
95 Rob Blake .25 .60
96 Stephane Fiset .25 .60
97 Zigmund Palffy .25 .60
98 Luc Robitaille .25 .60
99 Jozef Stumpel .25 .60
100 Shayne Corson .08 .25
101 Jeff Hackett .25 .60
102 Saku Koivu .30 .75
103 Trevor Linden .08 .25
104 Martin Rucinsky .08 .25
105 Brian Savage .08 .25
106 Mike Dunham .25 .60
107 Greg Johnson .08 .25
108 Sergei Krivokrasov .08 .25
109 David Legwand .25 .60
110 Ville Peltonen .08 .25
111 Cliff Ronning .08 .25
112 Scott Walker .08 .25
113 Jason Arnott .08 .25
114 Martin Brodeur .75 2.00
115 Patrik Elias .25 .60
116 Scott Gomez .08 .25
117 Bobby Holik .08 .25
118 Scott Niedermayer .08 .25
119 Brian Rafalski RC .60 1.50
120 Petr Sykora .08 .25
121 Mathieu Biron .25 .60
122 Tim Connolly .08 .25
123 Mariusz Czerkawski .08 .25
124 Olli Jokinen .25 .60
125 Jorgen Jonsson RC .08 .25
126 Kenny Jonsson .08 .25
127 Felix Potvin .30 .75
128 Theo Fleury .08 .25
129 Adam Graves .08 .25
130 Kim Johnsson RC .25 .60
131 Valeri Kamensky .25 .60
132 Brian Leetch .30 .75
133 Petr Nedved .25 .60
134 Mike Richter .30 .75
135 Mike York .08 .25
136 Daniel Alfredsson .25 .60
137 Magnus Arvedson .08 .25
138 Radek Bonk .08 .25
139 Marian Hossa .30 .75
140 Patrick Lalime .25 .60
141 Ron Tugnutt .25 .60
142 Alexei Yashin .08 .25
143 Rob Zamuner .08 .25
144 Brian Boucher .30 .75
145 Rod Brind'Amour .25 .60
146 Mark Eaton RC .30 .75
147 John LeClair .30 .75
148 Eric Lindros .30 .75
149 Mark Recchi .25 .60
150 John Vanbiesbrouck .25 .60
151 Travis Green .08 .25
152 Nikolai Khabibulin .25 .60
153 Jeremy Roenick .40 1.00
154 Mikhail Shtalenkov .25 .60
155 Keith Tkachuk .30 .75
156 Rick Tocchet .25 .60
157 Matthew Barnaby .08 .25
158 Tom Barrasso .25 .60
159 Jaromir Jagr .50 1.25
160 Alexei Kovalev .08 .25
161 Alexei Morozov .08 .25
162 Michal Rozsival RC .08 .25
163 Martin Straka .08 .25
164 German Titov .08 .25
165 Pavol Demitra .25 .60
166 Al MacInnis .25 .60
167 Chris Pronger .25 .60
168 Roman Turek .25 .60
169 Pierre Turgeon .25 .60
170 Scott Young .08 .25
171 Vincent Damphousse .08 .25
172 Jeff Friesen .08 .25
173 Patrick Marleau .30 .75
174 Owen Nolan .25 .60
175 Steve Shields .25 .60
176 Brad Stuart .25 .60
177 Niklas Sundstrom .08 .25
178 Mike Vernon .25 .60
179 Dan Cloutier .25 .60
180 Chris Gratton .08 .25
181 Vincent Lecavalier .30 .75
182 Fredrik Modin .08 .25
183 Darcy Tucker .08 .25
184 Nikolai Antropov RC .75 2.00
185 Sergei Berezin .08 .25
186 Tie Domi .25 .60
187 Jonas Hoglund .08 .25
188 Mike Johnson .08 .25
189 Curtis Joseph .30 .75
190 Mats Sundin .30 .75
191 Steve Thomas .08 .25
192 Andrew Cassels .08 .25
193 Artem Chubarov .08 .25
194 Mark Messier .30 .75
195 Alexander Mogilny .25 .60
196 Bill Muckalt .08 .25
197 Markus Naslund .30 .75
198 Kevin Weekes .25 .60
199 Peter Bondra .25 .60
200 Jan Bulis .08 .25
201 Jeff Halpern RC .75 2.00
202 Olaf Kolzig .25 .60
203 Adam Oates .25 .60
204 Chris Simon .08 .25
205 Alexander Volchkov RC .25 .60
206 Richard Zednik .08 .25
NNO Martin Brodeur SAMPLE 1.50 4.00

1999-00 Pacific Dynagon Ice Blue

Randomly inserted in packs, this 206-card set parallels the base Dynagon Ice set and is enhanced with blue foil highlights. Each card set sequentially numbered to 67.

*ICE BLUE 1-6: 2.5X TO 6X BASIC CARDS
*ICE BLUE 7-200: 15X TO 40X BASIC CARDS

1999-00 Pacific Dynagon Ice Copper

Randomly inserted in Retail packs, this 206-card set parallels the base Dynagon Ice set and is enhanced with copper foil highlights. Each card set sequentially numbered to 99.

*COPPER 1-6: 1.5X TO 4X BASIC CARDS
*COPPER 7-200: 10X TO 25X BASIC CARDS
STATED PRINT RUN 99 SER.#'d SETS

1999-00 Pacific Dynagon Ice Gold

Randomly inserted in Retail packs, this 206-card set parallels the base Dynagon Ice set and is enhanced with gold foil highlights. Each card set sequentially numbered to 199.

*GOLD 1-6: .8X TO 2X BASIC SP
*GOLD 7-200: 4X TO 10X BASIC CARDS
GOLD PRINT RUN 199 SER.#'d SETS

1999-00 Pacific Dynagon Ice Premiere Date

Randomly inserted in packs, this 206-card set parallels the base Dynagon Ice set and is enhanced with a Premier Date stamp. Each card set sequentially numbered to 63.

*1-6 PREM.DATE: 2.5X TO 6X BASIC SP
*7-200 PREM.DATE: 15X TO 40X BASIC CARDS
STATED PRINT RUN 63 SER.#'d SETS

1999-00 Pacific Dynagon Ice 2000 All-Star Preview

Randomly inserted in Hobby packs at the rate of 2:37, this 20-card set features color player photos set against a circular panoramic shot of a live hockey game and the 1999-2000 All-Star game logo in the lower left corner.

COMPLETE SET (20) 50.00 100.00
1 Paul Kariya 1.25 3.00
2 Teemu Selanne 1.25 3.00
3 Ray Bourque 2.00 5.00
4 Dominik Hasek 2.50 6.00
5 Patrick Roy 6.00 15.00
6 Joe Sakic 2.50 6.00
7 Nicklas Lidstrom 1.25 3.00
8 Steve Yzerman 6.00 15.00
9 Ed Belfour 1.25 3.00
10 Jere Lehtinen 1.00 2.50
11 Mike Modano 2.00 5.00
12 Pavel Bure 1.50 4.00
13 Martin Brodeur 3.00 8.00
14 John LeClair 1.50 4.00
15 Eric Lindros 2.00 5.00
16 Jaromir Jagr 2.00 5.00
17 Keith Tkachuk 1.25 3.00
18 Curtis Joseph 1.25 3.00
19 Mats Sundin 1.25 3.00
20 Peter Bondra 1.00 2.50

1999-00 Pacific Dynagon Ice Checkmates American

Randomly inserted in American packs at the rate of two in 37, this 30-card set pairs a top goal scorer on the card front and an enforcer on the card back for numbers 1-15, then switches to enforcer on the front and scorer on the back for card numbers 16-30.

COMPLETE SET (30) 40.00 100.00
1 P.Kariya/S.Kariya .60 1.50
2 T.Selanne/B.Shanahan .60 1.50
3 P.Stefan/E.Lindros .60 1.50
4 T.Amonte/C.Pronger .60 1.50
5 C.Drury/P.Forsberg 3.00 8.00
6 J.Sakic/T.Fleury 2.50 6.00
7 S.Yzerman/C.Chelios 5.00 12.00
8 B.Hull/M.Peca 1.50 4.00
9 M.Modano/D.Hatcher 2.00 5.00
10 P.Bure/R.Bourque 1.50 4.00
11 Z.Palffy/K.Tkachuk 1.00 2.50
12 M.Hossa/J.LeClair 1.25 3.00
13 J.Jagr/M.Barnaby 2.00 5.00
14 P.Marleau/O.Nolan .60 1.50
15 M.Sundin/T.Domi 1.00 2.50
16 S.Kariya/P.Kariya .60 1.50
17 B.Shanahan/T.Selanne .60 1.50
18 E.Lindros/P.Stefan 1.25 3.00
19 C.Pronger/T.Amonte 1.00 2.50
20 P.Forsberg/C.Drury 3.00 8.00
21 T.Fleury/J.Sakic 2.50 6.00
22 C.Chelios/S.Yzerman 5.00 12.00
23 M.Peca/B.Hull 1.50 4.00
24 D.Hatcher/M.Modano 2.00 5.00
25 R.Bourque/P.Bure 1.50 4.00
26 K.Tkachuk/Z.Palffy 1.00 2.50
27 J.LeClair/M.Hossa 1.25 3.00
28 M.Barnaby/J.Jagr 2.00 5.00
29 O.Nolan/P.Marleau 1.25 3.00
30 T.Domi/M.Sundin 1.25 3.00

1999-00 Pacific Dynagon Ice Checkmates Canadian

Randomly inserted in Canadian packs at a rate of 2:37, this 30-cards set features top NHL players in both their home and away jerseys.

COMPLETE SET (30) 40.00 80.00
1 Steve Kariya .60 1.50
2 Brendan Shanahan 2.00 5.00
3 Eric Lindros 2.00 5.00
4 Chris Pronger 1.00 2.50
5 Peter Forsberg 3.00 8.00
6 Theo Fleury .60 1.50
7 Chris Chelios 1.25 3.00
8 Michael Peca 1.00 2.50
9 Derian Hatcher .60 1.50
10 Ray Bourque 2.00 5.00
11 Keith Tkachuk 1.25 3.00
12 John LeClair 1.25 3.00
13 Matthew Barnaby .60 1.50
14 Owen Nolan 1.00 2.50
15 Tie Domi .60 1.50
16 Paul Kariya 1.25 3.00
17 Teemu Selanne 1.25 3.00
18 Patrik Stefan 1.00 2.50
19 Tony Amonte 1.00 2.50
20 Chris Drury 1.00 2.50
21 Joe Sakic 2.50 6.00
22 Steve Yzerman 5.00 12.00
23 Brett Hull 1.50 4.00
24 Mike Modano 2.00 5.00
25 Pavel Bure 1.50 4.00
26 Zigmund Palffy 1.00 2.50
27 Marian Hossa 1.25 3.00
28 Jaromir Jagr 2.00 5.00
29 Patrick Marleau 1.25 3.00
30 Mats Sundin 1.25 3.00

1999-00 Pacific Dynagon Ice Lamplighter Net-Fusions

Randomly inserted in packs at the rate of 1:73, this 10-card set features a laser cut background that has been filled in with actual "netting."

COMPLETE SET (10) 40.00 80.00
1 Paul Kariya 2.50 6.00
2 Teemu Selanne 2.50 6.00
3 Patrik Stefan 2.00 5.00
4 Joe Sakic 5.00 12.00
5 Steve Yzerman 12.50 30.00
6 Pavel Bure 3.00 8.00
7 Theo Fleury 2.50 6.00
8 John LeClair 3.00 8.00
9 Eric Lindros 4.00 10.00
10 Jaromir Jagr 4.00 10.00

1999-00 Pacific Dynagon Ice Lords of the Rink

COMPLETE SET (10) 15.00 40.00
STATED ODDS 1:181
1 Paul Kariya 8.00 20.00
2 Teemu Selanne 10.00 25.00
3 Dominik Hasek 6.00 15.00
4 Peter Forsberg 8.00 20.00
5 Patrick Roy 15.00 40.00
6 Joe Sakic 8.00 20.00
7 Steve Yzerman 12.00 30.00
8 Martin Brodeur 10.00 25.00
9 Eric Lindros 6.00 15.00
10 Jaromir Jagr 6.00 15.00

1999-00 Pacific Dynagon Ice Masks

Randomly inserted in packs at the rate of 1:37, this 10-card set showcases some of the NHL's to goalies' masks. Each card is enhanced with holographic foil stamping. Card numbers 1-5 are found only in hobby packs, and card numbers 6-10 are only found in retail packs.

COMPLETE SET (10) 12.00 30.00
1 Patrick Roy 6.00 15.00
2 Martin Brodeur 5.00 12.00
3 Mike Richter 1.00 2.50
4 John Vanbiesbrouck 1.00 2.50
5 Curtis Joseph 1.00 2.50
6 Patrick Roy 6.00 15.00
7 Martin Brodeur 3.00 8.00
8 Mike Richter 1.00 2.50
9 John Vanbiesbrouck 1.00 2.50
10 Curtis Joseph 1.00 2.50

2002 Pacific Entry Draft

Available as a wrapper redemption at the 2002 NHL Entry Draft, held in Toronto. Each card was serial-numbered on the back out of 500.

COMPLETE SET (10) 24.00 40.00
1 Ilya Kovalchuk 10.00 20.00
2 Erik Cole 3.20 5.00
3 Mark Bell 1.20 2.00
4 Marcel Hossa 2.00 3.00
5 Mike Ribeiro 1.20 2.00
6 Rick DiPietro 4.00 5.00
7 Raffi Torres 2.00 2.00
8 Dan Blackburn 4.00 5.00
9 Krys Kolanos 3.20 5.00
10 Jeff Jillson 2.00 3.00

2002-03 Pacific Exclusive

his 200-card set consisted of 175 veteran cards, 17 rospect cards and 8 autographed rookie cards hortprinted to 1000 copies each. A glitch during roduction caused two different versions of card #179 be inserted into packs. Both Alex Henry and Jason pezza cards were created and have been verified, they e labeled below with "A" and "B" suffixes for hecklisting only.

OMP.SET w/o SP's (175) 25.00 60.00
Jean-Sebastien Giguere .30 .75
Paul Kariya .40 1.00
Adam Oates .30 .75
Petr Sykora .25 .60
Dany Heatley .30 .75
Milan Hnilicka .25 .60
Tomi Kallio .20 .50
Ilya Kovalchuk .40 1.00
Patrik Stefan .25 .60
0 Nick Boynton .20 .50
1 Glen Murray .25 .60
2 Brian Rolston .25 .60
3 Sergei Samsonov .25 .60
4 Steve Shields .25 .60
5 Joe Thornton .40 1.00
6 Martin Biron .25 .60
7 Tim Connolly .20 .50
8 J-P Dumont .20 .50
9 Mika Noronen .25 .60
0 Miroslav Satan .30 .75
1 Craig Conroy .20 .50
2 Chris Drury .30 .75
3 Jarome Iginla .30 .75
4 Roman Turek .30 .75
5 Bates Battaglia .20 .50
6 Rod Brind'Amour .30 .75
7 Erik Cole .25 .60
8 Ron Francis .40 1.00
9 Arturs Irbe .25 .60
0 Sami Kapanen .20 .50
1 Jeff O'Neill .20 .50
2 Jaroslav Svoboda .20 .50
3 Josef Vasicek .20 .50
4 Mark Bell .20 .50
5 Eric Daze .20 .50
6 Theo Fleury .40 1.00
7 Jocelyn Thibault .25 .60
8 Alexei Zhamnov .25 .60
9 Rob Blake .30 .75
0 Peter Forsberg .40 1.00
1 Milan Hejduk .25 .60
2 Dean McAmmond .20 .50
3 Derek Morris .20 .50
4 Steven Reinprecht .20 .50
5 Patrick Roy .75 2.00
6 Joe Sakic .50 1.25
7 Alex Tanguay .25 .60
8 Radim Vrbata .25 .60
9 Andrew Cassels .20 .50
0 Marc Denis .25 .60
1 Rostislav Klesla .20 .50
2 Espen Knutsen .20 .50
3 Ray Whitney .25 .60
4 Jason Arnott .25 .60
5 Bill Guerin .30 .75
6 Jere Lehtinen .30 .75
7 Mike Modano .50 1.25
8 Marty Turco .30 .75
9 Pierre Turgeon .30 .75
0 Chris Chelios .30 .75
1 Pavel Datsyuk .40 1.00
2 Sergei Fedorov .50 1.25
3 Brett Hull .40 1.00
4 Curtis Joseph .30 .75
5 Nicklas Lidstrom .30 .75
6 Luc Robitaille .30 .75
7 Brendan Shanahan .40 1.00
8 Steve Yzerman .60 1.50
9 Anson Carter .25 .60
70 Mike Comrie .30 .75
71 Tommy Salo .25 .60
72 Jason Smith .20 .50
73 Ryan Smyth .25 .60
74 Mike York .20 .50
75 Valeri Bure .25 .60
76 Kristian Huselius .20 .50
77 Roberto Luongo .50 1.25
78 Stephen Weiss .30 .75
79 Jason Allison .25 .60
80 Adam Deadmarsh .25 .60
81 Zigmund Palffy .30 .75
82 Felix Potvin .50 1.25
83 Bryan Smolinski .25 .60
84 Andrew Brunette .20 .50
85 Pascal Dupuis .20 .50
86 Manny Fernandez .25 .60
87 Marian Gaborik .50 1.25
88 Cliff Ronning .20 .50
89 Mariusz Czerkawski .20 .50
90 Marcel Hossa .20 .50
91 Saku Koivu .30 .75
92 Yanic Perreault .20 .50
93 Oleg Petrov .20 .50
94 Jose Theodore .30 .75
95 Richard Zednik .20 .50
96 Denis Arkhipov .20 .50
97 Mike Dunham .25 .60
98 Scott Hartnell .30 .75
99 Greg Johnson .20 .50
100 David Legwand .25 .60
101 Christian Berglund .20 .50
102 Martin Brodeur .60 1.50
103 Patrik Elias .30 .75
104 Jeff Friesen .20 .50
105 Joe Nieuwendyk .30 .75
106 Rick DiPietro .25 .60
107 Brad Isbister .20 .50
108 Chris Osgood .30 .75
109 Mark Parrish .20 .50
110 Michael Peca .25 .60
111 Alexei Yashin .25 .60
112 Dan Blackburn .25 .60
113 Pavel Bure .40 1.00
114 Bobby Holik .20 .50
115 Brian Leetch .30 .75
116 Eric Lindros .50 1.25
117 Mark Messier .50 1.25
118 Mike Richter .30 .75
119 Daniel Alfredsson .30 .75
120 Radek Bonk .25 .60
121 Martin Havlat .25 .60
122 Marian Hossa .25 .60
123 Patrick Lalime .25 .60
124 Pavel Brendl .20 .50
125 Roman Cechmanek .25 .60
126 Simon Gagne .30 .75
127 John LeClair .30 .75
128 Mark Recchi .40 1.00
129 Jeremy Roenick .30 .75
130 Tony Amonte .25 .60
131 Brian Boucher .25 .60
132 Daniel Briere .25 .60
133 Sean Burke .20 .50
134 Krystofer Kolanos .20 .50
135 Daymond Langkow .25 .60
136 Johan Hedberg .30 .75
137 Alexei Kovalev .30 .75
138 Mario Lemieux 1.00 2.50
139 Alexei Morozov .20 .50
140 Martin Straka .25 .60
141 Pavol Demitra .40 1.00
142 Barret Jackman .25 .60
143 Brent Johnson .25 .60
144 Al MacInnis .30 .75
145 Chris Pronger .25 .60
146 Keith Tkachuk .30 .75
147 Doug Weight .30 .75
148 Vincent Damphousse .25 .60
149 Patrick Marleau .30 .75
150 Evgeni Nabokov .25 .60
151 Owen Nolan .30 .75
152 Teemu Selanne .60 1.50
153 Scott Thornton .20 .50
154 Dave Andreychuk .30 .75
155 Nikolai Khabibulin .30 .75
156 Vincent Lecavalier .25 .60
157 Brad Richards .30 .75
158 Shane Willis .20 .50
159 Ed Belfour .30 .75
160 Alyn McCauley .20 .50
161 Alexander Mogilny .25 .60
162 Gary Roberts .20 .50
163 Mats Sundin .30 .75
164 Darcy Tucker .20 .50
165 Todd Bertuzzi .30 .75
166 Dan Cloutier .25 .60
167 Ed Jovanovski .25 .60
168 Brendan Morrison .25 .60
169 Markus Naslund .25 .60
170 Peter Bondra .30 .75
171 Sergei Gonchar .25 .60
172 Jaromir Jagr .75 2.00
173 Olaf Kolzig .30 .75
174 Robert Lang .20 .50
175 Dainius Zubrus .20 .50
176 Martin Gerber RC 1.50 4.00
177 Dmitri Bykov RC 1.00 2.50
178 Ales Hemsky RC 4.00 10.00
179A Alex Henry RC 1.25 3.00
179B Jason Spezza RC 6.00 15.00
180 P-M Bouchard RC 1.50 4.00
181 Ron Hainsey RC 1.00 2.50
182 Adam Hall RC 1.00 2.50
183 Scottie Upshall RC 1.25 3.00
184 Mike Danton .20 .50
185 Jamie Lundmark .25 .60
186 Anton Volchenkov RC 1.00 2.50
187 Dennis Seidenberg RC 1.50 4.00
188 Patrick Sharp RC 3.00 8.00
189 Petr Cajanek .20 .50
190 Jonathan Cheechoo .25 .60
191 Fedor Fedorov .20 .50
192 Steve Eminger RC 1.00 2.50
193 Stanislav Chistov AU RC 2.50 6.00
194 Alexei Smirnov AU RC 3.00 8.00
195 Chuck Kobasew AU RC 3.00 8.00
196 Rick Nash AU RC 15.00 30.00
197 Henrik Zetterberg AU RC 15.00 40.00
198 Jay Bouwmeester AU RC 8.00 20.00
199 Alexander Frolov AU RC 5.00 12.00
200 Alexander Svitov AU RC 2.50 6.00

2002-03 Pacific Exclusive Blue

Inserted into hobby packs at a stated rate of 1:11, this 25-card set paralleled the last 25 cards of the base set but carried blue foil backgrounds on the card fronts. No cards in this parallel set were autographed. Each card was serial-numbered out of 699.

*BLUE/699: 1.5X TO 4X BASIC CARDS
*BLUE/699: .3X TO .8X BASIC RC

2002-03 Pacific Exclusive Gold

This 200-card set was inserted at 1:1 hobby and 1:2 retail packs and directly paralleled the base set but card fronts carried a gold foil background. Cards 193-200 were not autographed as in the base set.

*VETS: 1X TO 2.5X BASIC CARDS
*ROOKIE SP's: .2X TO .5X BASIC RC
117 Mark Messier 1.25 3.00
193 Stanislav Chistov .50 1.25
194 Alexei Smirnov .60 1.50
195 Chuck Kobasew .60 1.50
196 Rick Nash 4.00 10.00
197 Henrik Zetterberg 5.00 12.00
198 Jay Bouwmeester 1.50 4.00
199 Alexander Frolov 1.00 2.50
200 Alexander Svitov .50 1.25

2002-03 Pacific Exclusive Retail

The only cards that were different in retail packs than hobby packs of 2002-03 Pacific Exclusive were cards 193-200. Those retail cards were unsigned and carried the same dot matrix pattern as the other players. All other players had the same card in both hobby and retail.

193 Stanislav Chistov RC .75 2.00
194 Alexei Smirnov RC 1.00 2.50
195 Chuck Kobasew RC 1.00 2.50
196 Rick Nash RC 6.00 15.00
197 Henrik Zetterberg RC 8.00 20.00
198 Jay Bouwmeester RC 2.50 6.00
199 Alexander Frolov RC 1.50 4.00
200 Alexander Svitov RC .75 2.00

2002-03 Pacific Exclusive Advantage

COMPLETE SET (15) 8.00 20.00
STATED ODDS 1:6 HOBBY/1:13 RETAIL
1 Jean-Sebastien Giguere .50 1.25
2 Roman Turek .50 1.25
3 Arturs Irbe .50 1.25
4 Patrick Roy 2.00 5.00
5 Marc Denis .50 1.25
6 Marty Turco .50 1.25
7 Curtis Joseph .60 1.50
8 Roberto Luongo 1.00 2.50
9 Felix Potvin .60 1.50
10 Jose Theodore .75 2.00
11 Martin Brodeur 1.50 4.00
12 Mike Richter .60 1.50
13 Brent Johnson .50 1.25
14 Evgeni Nabokov .50 1.25
15 Ed Belfour .60 1.50

2002-03 Pacific Exclusive Destined

COMPLETE SET (10) 6.00 15.00
STATED ODDS 1:11 HOBBY/1:25 RETAIL
1 Stanislav Chistov .60 1.50
2 Dany Heatley 1.25 3.00
3 Ilya Kovalchuk 1.50 4.00
4 Ivan Huml .60 1.50
5 Rick Nash 2.00 5.00
6 Pavel Datsyuk 1.50 3.50
7 Kristian Huselius .60 1.50
8 Stephen Weiss .75 2.00
9 Jamie Lundmark .60 1.50
10 Jonathan Cheechoo 1.25 3.00

2002-03 Pacific Exclusive Etched in Stone

COMPLETE SET (10) 12.00 30.00
STATED ODDS 1:21 HOBBY/1:25 RETAIL
1 Paul Kariya .75 2.00
2 Ron Francis .75 2.00
3 Patrick Roy 4.00 10.00
4 Joe Sakic 2.00 5.00
5 Brett Hull 1.25 3.00
6 Steve Yzerman 5.00 12.00
7 Martin Brodeur 3.00 8.00
8 Eric Lindros .75 2.00
9 Mario Lemieux 5.00 12.00
10 Jaromir Jagr 1.50 4.00

2002-03 Pacific Exclusive Great Expectations

COMPLETE SET (15) 12.50 25.00
STATED ODDS 1:6 HOBBY/1:13 RETAIL
1 Dany Heatley 1.25 3.00
2 Ilya Kovalchuk 1.25 3.00
3 Ivan Huml .75 2.00
4 Erik Cole .75 2.00
5 Radim Vrbata .75 2.00
6 Pavel Datsyuk 1.00 2.50
7 Mike Comrie .75 2.00
8 Kristian Huselius .75 2.00
9 Stephen Weiss .75 2.00
10 Marian Gaborik 1.50 4.00
11 Marcel Hossa .75 2.00
12 Rick DiPietro 1.00 2.50
13 Dan Blackburn .75 2.00
14 Krystofer Kolanos .75 2.00
15 Barret Jackman .75 2.00

2002-03 Pacific Exclusive Jerseys

COMMON CARD (1-25) 3.00 8.00
STATED ODDS 2:21 HOBBY/1:49 RETAIL
*GOLD/25: .8X TO 2X BASIC JERSEY
1 Tomi Kallio 3.00 8.00
2 Joe Thornton 8.00 20.00
3 Miroslav Satan 4.00 10.00
4 Theo Fleury 3.00 8.00
5 Milan Hejduk 5.00 12.00
6 Pierre Turgeon 4.00 10.00
7 Sergei Fedorov 8.00 20.00
8 Nicklas Lidstrom 5.00 12.00
9 Tommy Salo 4.00 10.00
10 Kristian Huselius 3.00 8.00
11 Roberto Luongo 8.00 20.00
12 Bryan Smolinski 3.00 8.00
13 Manny Fernandez 4.00 10.00
14 Mariusz Czerkawski 3.00 8.00
15 David Legwand 4.00 10.00
16 Bobby Holik 3.00 8.00
17 Eric Lindros 5.00 12.00
18 Marian Hossa 5.00 12.00
19 Michal Handzus 3.00 8.00
20 Alexei Kovalev 4.00 10.00
21 Keith Tkachuk 5.00 12.00
22 Patrick Marleau 4.00 10.00
23 Brad Richards 5.00 12.00
24 Mats Sundin 5.00 12.00
25 Olaf Kolzig 4.00 10.00

2002-03 Pacific Exclusive Maximum Overdrive

COMPLETE SET (20) 15.00 30.00
STATED ODDS 1:6 HOBBY/1:13 RETAIL
1 Paul Kariya .40 1.00
2 Dany Heatley .50 1.25
3 Ilya Kovalchuk .50 1.25
4 Joe Thornton .60 1.50
5 Jarome Iginla .60 1.50
6 Peter Forsberg 1.00 2.50
7 Joe Sakic .75 2.00
8 Mike Modano .60 1.50
9 Sergei Fedorov .75 2.00
10 Steve Yzerman 2.00 5.00
11 Saku Koivu .40 1.00
12 Patrik Elias .40 1.00
13 Alexei Yashin .40 1.00
14 Pavel Bure .40 1.00
15 Simon Gagne .40 1.00
16 Mario Lemieux 2.50 6.00
17 Teemu Selanne .40 1.00
18 Mats Sundin .40 1.00
19 Markus Naslund .40 1.00
20 Jaromir Jagr .60 1.50

2003-04 Pacific Exhibit

This 225-card set was released in early-October and consisted of four distinct subsets. Cards 1-150 were regular base cards, cards 151-200 were oversized cards measuring approximately 3.5" X 5"and cards 201-215 were oversized jersey cards serial numbered of 465. Cards 216-225 made up the "Time Warp" subset, the cards were oversized and contained a jersey swatch of a current player and an authentic autograph of a retired great, each serial-numbered out of 565. Cards 226-235 were rookies, serial numbered of 975, and available in packs of Pacific Calder.

COMP.SET w/o SP's (150) 25.00 60.00
COMP.SET w/o JSYS (200) 25.00 60.00
1 Stanislav Chistov .15 .40
2 Mike Leclerc .15 .40
3 Adam Oates .25 .60
4 Sandis Ozolinsh .15 .40
5 Vaclav Prospal .15 .40
6 Steve Rucchin .15 .40
7 Steve Thomas .15 .40
8 Byron Dafoe .20 .50
9 Joe DiPenta RC .20 .50
10 Slava Kozlov .20 .50
11 Patrik Stefan .15 .40
12 Bryan Berard .20 .50
13 Mike Knuble .15 .40
14 Glen Murray .20 .50
15 Brian Rolston .20 .50
16 Milan Bartovic RC .20 .50
17 Daniel Briere .25 .60
18 Chris Drury .20 .50
19 J-P Dumont .15 .40
20 Ales Kotalik .15 .40
21 Ryan Miller .25 .60
22 Miroslav Satan .20 .50
23 Craig Conroy .15 .40
24 Martin Gelinas .15 .40
25 Roman Turek .20 .50
26 Rod Brind'Amour .25 .60
27 Erik Cole .20 .50
28 Arturs Irbe .20 .50
29 Jeff O'Neill .15 .40
30 Tyler Arnason .15 .40
31 Kyle Calder .15 .40
32 Eric Daze .20 .50
33 Theoren Fleury .30 .75
34 Alexei Zhamnov .20 .50
35 David Aebischer .20 .50
36 Rob Blake .25 .60
37 Milan Hejduk .20 .50
38 Derek Morris .15 .40
39 Teemu Selanne .50 1.25
40 Alex Tanguay .20 .50
41 Andrew Cassels .15 .40
42 Marc Denis .20 .50
43 Kent McDonell RC .20 .50
44 Geoff Sanderson .15 .40
45 Ray Whitney .20 .50
46 Jason Arnott .20 .50
47 Bill Guerin .25 .60
48 Jere Lehtinen .20 .50
49 Brenden Morrow .20 .50
50 Teppo Numminen .15 .40
51 Chris Chelios .25 .60
52 Pavel Datsyuk .30 .75
53 Derian Hatcher .15 .40
54 Nicklas Lidstrom .25 .60
55 Brendan Shanahan .30 .75
56 Henrik Zetterberg .30 .75
57 Mike Comrie .20 .50
58 Ales Hemsky .25 .60
59 Georges Laraque .20 .50
60 Tommy Salo .20 .50
61 Mike York .15 .40
62 Jay Bouwmeester .25 .60
63 Kristian Huselius .15 .40
64 Olli Jokinen .25 .60
65 Stephen Weiss .15 .40
66 Jason Allison .20 .50
67 Roman Cechmanek .20 .50
68 Adam Deadmarsh .20 .50
69 Alexander Frolov .20 .50
70 Felix Potvin .40 1.00
71 Andrew Brunette .15 .40
72 Manny Fernandez .20 .50
73 Filip Kuba .15 .40
74 Dwayne Roloson .20 .50
75 Cliff Ronning .15 .40
76 Mathieu Garon .15 .40
77 Marcel Hossa .15 .40
78 Yanic Perreault .15 .40
79 Richard Zednik .15 .40
80 Scott Hartnell .25 .60
81 Andreas Johansson .15 .40
82 Tomas Vokoun .20 .50
83 Scott Walker .15 .40
84 Patrik Elias .25 .60
85 Jeff Friesen .15 .40
86 Scott Gomez .20 .50
87 Jamie Langenbrunner .20 .50
88 John Madden .15 .40
89 Joe Nieuwendyk .25 .60
90 Scott Stevens .25 .60
91 Jason Blake .15 .40
92 Rick DiPietro .20 .50
93 Roman Hamrlik .20 .50
94 Mark Parrish .15 .40
95 Dan Blackburn .20 .50
96 Anson Carter .20 .50
97 Mike Dunham .20 .50
98 Bobby Holik .15 .40
99 Alex Kovalev .20 .50
100 Tom Poti .15 .40
101 Daniel Alfredsson .25 .60
102 Zdeno Chara .25 .60
103 Mike Fisher .15 .40
104 Martin Havlat .25 .60
105 Bryan Smolinski .15 .40
106 Jason Spezza .25 .60
107 Todd White .15 .40
108 Tony Amonte .20 .50
109 Simon Gagne .25 .60
110 Jeff Hackett .20 .50
111 Keith Primeau .25 .60
112 Mark Recchi .30 .75
113 Shane Doan .20 .50
114 Chris Gratton .15 .40
115 Mike Johnson .15 .40
116 Daymond Langkow .15 .40
117 Johan Hedberg .20 .50
118 Aleksey Morozov .15 .40
119 Martin Straka .15 .40
120 Dick Tarnstrom .15 .40
121 Pavol Demitra .30 .75
122 Al MacInnis .25 .60
123 Chris Pronger .20 .50
124 Peter Sejna RC .20 .50
125 Keith Tkachuk .25 .60
126 Doug Weight .25 .60
127 Jonathan Cheechoo .20 .50
128 Vincent Damphousse .20 .50
129 Patrick Marleau .25 .60
130 Dave Andreychuk .25 .60
131 John Grahame .15 .40
132 Brad Richards .25 .60
133 Martin St. Louis .25 .60
134 Nik Antropov .20 .50
135 Tie Domi .20 .50
136 Doug Gilmour .30 .75
137 Alexander Mogilny .20 .50
138 Matt Stajan RC .25 .60
139 Darcy Tucker .20 .50
140 Dan Cloutier .20 .50
141 Ed Jovanovski .20 .50
142 Trevor Linden .25 .60
143 Brendan Morrison .20 .50
144 Daniel Sedin .25 .60
145 Henrik Sedin .25 .60
146 Sergei Berezin .15 .40
147 Peter Bondra .20 .50
148 Sebastien Charpentier .15 .40
149 Sergei Gonchar .15 .40
150 Michael Nylander .15 .40
151 Sergei Fedorov .75 2.00
152 Jean-Sebastien Giguere .50 1.25
153 Dany Heatley .50 1.25
154 Ilya Kovalchuk .50 1.25
155 Joe Thornton .60 1.50
156 Martin Biron .40 1.00
157 Jarome Iginla .50 1.25
158 Ron Francis .60 1.50
159 Jocelyn Thibault .40 1.00
160 Peter Forsberg .60 1.50
161 Paul Kariya .60 1.50
162 Patrick Roy 1.25 3.00
163 Joe Sakic .75 2.00
164 Rick Nash .50 1.25
165 Mike Modano .75 2.00
166 Marty Turco .50 1.25
167 Dominik Hasek .75 2.00
168 Brett Hull .60 1.50
169 Steve Yzerman 1.25 3.00
170 Ryan Smyth .40 1.00
171 Roberto Luongo .75 2.00
172 Ziggy Palffy .50 1.25
173 Marian Gaborik .75 2.00
174 Saku Koivu .50 1.25
175 Jose Theodore .50 1.25
176 David Legwand .40 1.00
177 Martin Brodeur 1.00 2.50
178 Michael Peca .40 1.00
179 Alexei Yashin .40 1.00
180 Pavel Bure .60 1.50
181 Eric Lindros .75 2.00
182 Mark Messier .75 2.00
183 Marian Hossa .40 1.00
184 Patrick Lalime .40 1.00
185 John LeClair .50 1.25
186 Jeremy Roenick .50 1.25
187 Sean Burke .30 .75
188 Mario Lemieux 1.50 4.00
189 Barret Jackman .30 .75
190 Chris Osgood .50 1.25
191 Evgeni Nabokov .40 1.00
192 Nikolai Khabibulin .50 1.25
193 Vincent Lecavalier .40 1.00
194 Ed Belfour .50 1.25
195 Owen Nolan .40 1.00
196 Mats Sundin .50 1.25
197 Todd Bertuzzi .50 1.25
198 Markus Naslund .50 1.25
199 Jaromir Jagr 1.25 3.00
200 Olaf Kolzig .50 1.25
201 Stanislav Chistov JSY 4.00 10.00
202 Martin Biron JSY 5.00 12.00
203 Eric Daze JSY 5.00 12.00
204 Milan Hejduk JSY 5.00 12.00
205 Bill Guerin JSY 6.00 15.00
206 Marty Turco JSY 6.00 15.00
207 Jason Allison JSY 5.00 12.00
208 Roman Cechmanek JSY 5.00 12.00
209 David Legwand JSY 5.00 12.00
210 Patrick Lalime JSY 5.00 12.00
211 Tony Amonte JSY 5.00 12.00
212 Jeff Hackett JSY 5.00 12.00
213 Sean Burke JSY 4.00 10.00
214 Chris Osgood JSY 6.00 15.00
215 Nikolai Khabibulin JSY 6.00 15.00
216 B.Hull JSY/B.Hull AU 12.00 30.00
217 Yzerman JSY/T.Espo AU 12.50 30.00
218 P.Roy JSY/Beliveau AU 30.00 60.00
219 Kovalchuk JSY/Lafleur AU 12.50 30.00
220 Heatley JSY/G.Hall AU 15.00 30.00
221 Lemieux JSY/J.Bower AU 15.00 40.00
222 Theodore JSY/Sittler AU 10.00 25.00
223 P.Kariya JSY/M.Dionne AU 10.00 25.00
224 Brodeur JSY/Mahovlich AU 20.00 50.00
225 J.Sakic JSY/B.Park AU 15.00 30.00
226 Joffrey Lupul RC 2.00 5.00
227 Patrice Bergeron RC 4.00 10.00
228 Matthew Lombardi RC 1.00 2.50
229 Eric Staal RC 4.00 10.00
230 Nikolai Zherdev RC 1.50 4.00
231 Nathan Horton RC 2.00 5.00
232 Brent Burns RC 2.00 5.00
233 Joni Pitkanen RC 1.25 3.00
234 Marc-Andre Fleury RC 6.00 15.00
235 Ryan Malone RC 1.50 4.00

2003-04 Pacific Exhibit Blue Backs

*1-150 BLUE/275: 2X TO 5X BASIC CARDS
1-150 STATED ODDS 1:10 HOB,1:13 RET
1-150 STATED PRINT RUN 275
*151-200 BLUE/425: 1X TO 2.5X BASIC CARDS
151-200 STATED ODDS 1:15 HOB,1:25 RET
151-200 STATED PRINT RUN 425

2003-04 Pacific Exhibit Yellow Backs

*YELLOW BACK: .6X TO 1.5X BASIC CARDS
ONE PER HOBBY PACK

2003-04 Pacific Exhibit History Makers

COMPLETE SET (8) 12.50 25.00
STATED ODDS 1:29 HOBBY/1:25 RETAIL
1 Paul Kariya .60 1.50
2 Peter Forsberg 1.50 4.00
3 Joe Sakic 1.25 3.00
4 Brett Hull .75 2.00
5 Steve Yzerman 2.50 6.00
6 Mario Lemieux 3.00 8.00
7 Todd Bertuzzi .60 1.50
8 Markus Naslund .60 1.50

2003-04 Pacific Exhibit Pursuing Prominence

COMPLETE SET (12) 8.00 15.00
STATED ODDS 1:15 HOBBY/1:13 RETAIL
1 Dany Heatley 1.00 2.50
2 Ilya Kovalchuk 1.00 2.50
3 Joe Thornton 1.00 2.50
4 Rick Nash 1.25 3.00
5 Henrik Zetterberg 1.25 3.00
6 Ales Hemsky .50 1.25
7 Jay Bouwmeester .50 1.25
8 Marian Gaborik 1.25 3.00
9 Marian Hossa .50 1.25
10 Jason Spezza 1.25 3.00
11 Barret Jackman .50 1.25
12 Vincent Lecavalier .50 1.25

2003-04 Pacific Exhibit Standing on Tradition

COMPLETE SET (10) 10.00 20.00
STATED ODDS 1:29 HOBBY/1:25 RETAIL
1 Jean-Sebastien Giguere .60 1.50
2 Jocelyn Thibault .60 1.50
3 Patrick Roy 2.50 6.00
4 Marty Turco .60 1.50
5 Dominik Hasek 1.50 4.00
6 Roberto Luongo 1.00 2.50
7 Jose Theodore .75 2.00
8 Martin Brodeur 2.00 5.00
9 Patrick Lalime .60 1.50
10 Ed Belfour .75 2.00

2001-02 Pacific Heads Up

Released in mid-November 2001, this 120-card set carried an SRP of $3.99 for a five-card hobby pack with 18 packs per box. The set consisted of 100 veteran cards and 20 shortprinted Rookie Cards available in hobby packs only. Rookies (Cards 101-120) were serial-numbered to 999 sets.

1 Paul Kariya .30 .75
2 Steve Shields .20 .50
3 Ray Ferraro .15 .40
4 Milan Hnilicka .20 .50
5 Patrik Stefan .20 .50
6 Jason Allison .20 .50
7 Byron Dafoe .20 .50
8 Bill Guerin .25 .60
9 Sergei Samsonov .20 .50
10 Joe Thornton .30 .75
11 J-P Dumont .15 .40
12 Jarome Iginla .25 .60
13 Marc Savard .15 .40
14 Roman Turek .20 .50
15 Ron Francis .30 .75
16 Arturs Irbe .20 .50
17 Jeff O'Neill .15 .40
18 Tony Amonte .20 .50
19 Steve Sullivan .15 .40
20 Jocelyn Thibault .20 .50
21 Rob Blake .25 .60
22 Chris Drury .20 .50
23 Peter Forsberg .30 .75
24 Milan Hejduk .20 .50
25 Patrick Roy .60 1.50
26 Joe Sakic .40 1.00
27 Marc Denis .20 .50
28 Geoff Sanderson .15 .40
29 Ed Belfour .25 .60
30 Brett Hull .30 .75
31 Mike Modano .40 1.00
32 Joe Nieuwendyk .25 .60
33 Pierre Turgeon .25 .60
34 Sergei Fedorov .40 1.00
35 Dominik Hasek .40 1.00
36 Chris Osgood .25 .60
37 Luc Robitaille .25 .60
38 Brendan Shanahan .30 .75
39 Steve Yzerman .75 2.00
40 Mike Comrie .20 .50
41 Tommy Salo .20 .50
42 Ryan Smyth .20 .50
43 Pavel Bure .30 .75
44 Roberto Luongo .40 1.00
45 Steve Heinze .15 .40
46 Zigmund Palffy .25 .60
47 Felix Potvin .40 1.00
48 Manny Fernandez .20 .50
49 Marian Gaborik .40 1.00
50 Saku Koivu .25 .60
51 Brian Savage .15 .40
52 Jose Theodore .25 .60
53 Mike Dunham .20 .50
54 David Legwand .20 .50
55 Jason Arnott .20 .50
56 Martin Brodeur .50 1.25
57 Patrik Elias .25 .60
58 Scott Stevens .25 .60
59 Mariusz Czerkawski .15 .40
60 Rick DiPietro .20 .50
61 Mike Peca .20 .50
62 Alexei Yashin .20 .50
63 Theo Fleury .30 .75
64 Brian Leetch .25 .60
65 Mark Messier .40 1.00
66 Mike Richter .25 .60
67 Daniel Alfredsson .25 .60
68 Martin Havlat .20 .50
69 Marian Hossa .20 .50
70 Patrick Lalime .20 .50
71 Roman Cechmanek .20 .50
72 John LeClair .25 .60
73 Mark Recchi .30 .75
74 Jeremy Roenick .25 .60
75 Sean Burke .15 .40
76 Johan Hedberg .20 .50
77 Alexei Kovalev .20 .50
78 Mario Lemieux .75 2.00
79 Fred Brathwaite .20 .50
80 Chris Pronger .20 .50
81 Keith Tkachuk .25 .60
82 Doug Weight .25 .60
83 Patrick Marleau .25 .60
84 Evgeni Nabokov .20 .50
85 Teemu Selanne .50 1.25
86 Nikolai Khabibulin .25 .60
87 Vincent Lecavalier .20 .50
88 Brad Richards .25 .60
89 Curtis Joseph .25 .60
90 Alexander Mogilny .20 .50
91 Gary Roberts .15 .40
92 Mats Sundin .25 .60
93 Dan Cloutier .20 .50
94 Markus Naslund .25 .60
95 Daniel Sedin .25 .60
96 Henrik Sedin .25 .60
97 Peter Bondra .25 .60
98 Jaromir Jagr .60 1.50
99 Olaf Kolzig .25 .60
100 Adam Oates .25 .60
101 Ilja Bryzgalov RC 3.00 8.00
102 Timo Parssinen RC 1.50 4.00
103 Ilya Kovalchuk RC 10.00 25.00
104 Erik Cole RC 2.50 6.00
105 Vaclav Nedorost RC 1.25 3.00
106 Pavel Datsyuk RC 12.00 30.00
107 Kristian Huselius RC 2.00 5.00
108 Jaroslav Bednar RC 1.25 3.00
109 Pascal Dupuis RC 2.00 5.00
110 Martin Erat RC 2.00 5.00
111 Scott Clemmensen RC 1.25 3.00
112 Dan Blackburn RC 1.50 4.00
113 Chris Neil RC 1.50 4.00
114 Pavel Brendl SP 1.25 3.00
115 Jiri Dopita RC 1.25 3.00
116 Krystofer Kolanos RC 1.25 3.00
117 Mark Rycroft RC 1.50 4.00
118 Jeff Jillson RC 1.25 3.00
119 Nikita Alexeev RC 1.25 3.00
120 Brian Sutherby RC 1.25 3.00

2001-02 Pacific Heads Up Blue

Randomly inserted in packs at a rate of 1:37 hobby packs, This 100-card set paralleled the base set but featured full color action card fronts with a blue holographic background. Each card was serial-numbered to 55 on the card fronts.

*BLUE/55: 8X TO 20X BASIC CARDS
65 Mark Messier 10.00 25.00

2001-02 Pacific Heads Up Premiere Date

Randomly inserted into hobby packs at the rate of one per box, this 100-card set paralleled the base set but was enhanced with a foil premiere date box on the card front. Each card was serial-numbered out of 105.

*PREM.DATE/105: 5X TO 12X BASIC CARDS
65 Mark Messier 6.00 15.00

2001-02 Pacific Heads Up Red

Randomly inserted in retail packs at a rate of 2:25 , this 100 card set paralleled the base set but carried a red holographic background. Each card was serial-numbered to 165.

*RED/165: 4X TO 10X BASIC CARDS
65 Mark Messier 5.00 12.00

2001-02 Pacific Heads Up Silver

Randomly inserted into packs at 1:145 hobby and 1:241 retail, this 100-card set paralleled the base set but featured a silver holographic card front. Each card was serial-numbered to 27.

*SILVER/27: 12X TO 30X BASIC CARDS
65 Mark Messier 15.00 40.00

2001-02 Pacific Heads Up All-Star Net

Randomly inserted in packs at a rate of 1:1153 hobby and 1:2401 retail. This set featured 2 player action color photos on the card front along with a swatch of game-used NHL All-Star goal net located in a gold box at the bottom center of card. Cards were serial-numbered to 65.

1 Nabokov/Cechmanek 20.00 50.00
2 M.Brodeur/R.Blake 25.00 60.00
3 B.Guerin/D.Weight 20.00 50.00
4 P.Bure/Z.Palffy 12.00 30.00
5 P.Kariya/M.Sundin 10.00 25.00
6 C.Pronger/N.Lidstrom 12.00 30.00

2001-02 Pacific Heads Up Bobble Heads

Randomly inserted in hobby boxes at a rate of 1 per box and in retail packs as redemption cards at 1:121, this 12-player ceramic bobble head doll set featured the Pacific logo on the base along with the Pacific Heads-Up logo with the last name of each player. Please note that the Comrie bobble head was not produced and was redeemable for another randomly chosen bobble head as a replacement. Collectors receiving a bobble head of Pacific president Mike Cramer also received a redemption card good for the entire set. Approximately 12 of these dolls were randomly inserted into boxes.

1 Paul Kariya 12.50 30.00
2 Patrick Roy 15.00 40.00
3 Joe Sakic 12.50 30.00
4 Dominik Hasek 12.50 30.00
5 Steve Yzerman 15.00 40.00
7 Martin Brodeur 15.00 40.00
8 Mark Messier 12.50 30.00
9 Johan Hedberg 12.50 -30.00
10 Mario Lemieux 20.00 50.00
11 Curtis Joseph 12.50 30.00
12 Jaromir Jagr 12.50 30.00

2001-02 Pacific Heads Up Breaking the Glass

COMPLETE SET (20) 30.00 60.00
STATED ODDS 1:19 HOB, 1:25 RET
1 Milan Hnilicka 1.25 3.00
2 Patrik Stefan 1.25 3.00
3 J-P Dumont 1.25 3.00
4 Shane Willis 1.25 3.00
5 David Aebischer 1.25 3.00
6 Chris Drury 1.25 3.00
7 Alex Tanguay 2.00 5.00
8 Marc Denis 1.25 3.00
9 Marty Turco 1.25 3.00
10 Mike Comrie 1.25 3.00
11 Roberto Luongo 1.50 4.00
12 Marian Gaborik 3.00 8.00
13 David Legwand 1.25 3.00
14 Rick DiPietro 1.25 3.00
15 Martin Havlat 1.25 3.00
16 Johan Hedberg 1.25 3.00
17 Evgeni Nabokov 1.25 3.00
18 Brad Richards 1.25 3.00
19 Daniel Sedin 2.00 5.00
20 Henrik Sedin 2.00 5.00

2001-02 Pacific Heads Up HD NHL

Cards 1-10 in this 20-card set were only available in hobby packs at rate of 1:19. Cards 11-20 were only available in retail packs at an insertion rate of 1:25. Cards featured color player photos on silver metallic card stock.

COMPLETE SET (20) 8.00 20.00
1 Paul Kariya .75 2.00
2 Peter Forsberg 2.00 5.00
3 Joe Sakic 1.50 4.00
4 Mike Modano 1.25 3.00
5 Steve Yzerman 4.00 10.00
6 Pavel Bure 1.00 2.50
7 Mario Lemieux 5.00 12.00
8 Teemu Selanne .75 2.00
9 Mats Sundin .75 2.00
10 Jaromir Jagr 1.25 3.00
11 Roman Turek .60 1.50
12 Ed Belfour .75 2.00
13 Chris Osgood .60 1.50
14 Tommy Salo .60 1.50
15 Felix Potvin .75 2.00
16 Jose Theodore 1.00 2.50
17 Martin Brodeur 2.00 5.00
18 Mike Richter .75 2.00
19 Roman Cechmanek .60 1.50
20 Curtis Joseph .75 2.00

2001-02 Pacific Heads Up Prime Picks

COMPLETE SET (10) 15.00 40.00
STATED ODDS 1:73 HOB, 1:121 RET
1 Mike Comrie 1.50 4.00
2 Roberto Luongo 4.00 10.00
3 Marian Gaborik 4.00 10.00
4 Rick DiPietro 1.50 4.00
5 Martin Havlat 1.50 4.00
6 Johan Hedberg 1.50 4.00
7 Evgeni Nabokov 1.50 4.00
8 Brad Richards 2.00 5.00

9 Daniel Sedin 2.50 6.00
10 Henrik Sedin 2.50 6.00

2001-02 Pacific Heads Up Quad Jerseys

Randomly inserted in packs at a rate of 2:19 hobby and 1:97 retail, this 29-card set featured color action photo's along with game-used jersey swatches on both card front and back for a total of 4 per card.

1 Gig/Leclerc/Selanne/Hebert 6.00 15.00
2 Thorn/Sams/McLaren/Dafoe 8.00 20.00
3 Niedmyr/Holik/Axels/Sween 8.00 20.00
4 Hasek/Barnes/Czer/Jonsson 6.00 15.00
5 Iginla/V.Bure/Savard/Fata 6.00 15.00
6 Amonte/Daze/Thibault/Calder 6.00 15.00
7 Gig/Leclerc/Selanne/Hebert 6.00 15.00
8 Forsbrg/Sakic/Miller/Reid 10.00 25.00
9 Roy/Dingman/deVries/Klemm 8.00 20.00
10 Modano/Nieuw/Sydor/Hatch 6.00 15.00
11 Shan/Chelios/Dandnlt/Osgd 8.00 20.00
12 Brunet/Zholtok/Zubrus/Dahlen 6.00 15.00
13 Dunham/Legwnd/Fitz/Walker 6.00 15.00
14 Fleury/Leetch/Richtr/Nedvd 6.00 15.00
15 LeClair/Desjdns/Stevns/Millr 6.00 15.00
16 Roenick/Burke/Alatalo/Doan 6.00 15.00
17 Lemieux/Jagr/Hrdina/Kaspts 15.00 40.00
18 Straka/Kov/Aubin/Parent 6.00 15.00
19 Domi/Healy/Alfron/Cloutier 6.00 15.00
20 Roy/Jos./Hasek/Richter 20.00 50.00
21 Lemieux/Sakic/Moda./Bure 30.00 80.00
22 Weight/Cheli./Hatch./Ltch. 10.00 25.00
23 Zhitnik/Rasmsn/Ray/Smehlik 6.00 15.00
24 Lehtinen/Keane/Hogue/Sloan 6.00 15.00
25 York/Graves/Lefebvre/Malhtra 6.00 15.00
26 Burke/Nummin/Suchy/Lumme 6.00 15.00
27 Lecvalr/Primeau/Barnby/Kraft 6.00 15.00
28 Straka/Morzv/Berank/Bghnr 6.00 15.00
29 Kovalev/Rozsivl/Parent/Kasp 6.00 15.00

2001-02 Pacific Heads Up Rink Immortals

Randomly inserted in packs at a rate of 1:289 packs, this 10-card set featured full color action shots with a grey silhouette background. Cards were serial numbered to 105 of each on the front of the card in lower right hand corner.

1 Paul Kariya 8.00 20.00
2 Patrick Roy 20.00 50.00
3 Joe Sakic 10.00 25.00
4 Brett Hull 8.00 20.00
5 Dominik Hasek 10.00 25.00
6 Steve Yzerman 15.00 40.00
7 Pavel Bure 6.00 15.00
8 Martin Brodeur 12.00 30.00
9 Mario Lemieux 25.00 60.00
10 Jaromir Jagr 10.00 25.00

2001-02 Pacific Heads Up Showstoppers

COMPLETE SET (20) 20.00 40.00
STATED ODDS 2:19 HOB, 2:25 RET
1 Steve Shields .60 1.50
2 Byron Dafoe .60 1.50
3 Roman Turek .60 1.50
4 Patrick Roy 4.00 10.00
5 Ed Belfour .75 2.00
6 Dominik Hasek 1.50 4.00
7 Chris Osgood .60 1.50
8 Tommy Salo .60 1.50
9 Roberto Luongo 1.00 2.50
10 Felix Potvin .75 2.00
11 Jose Theodore 1.00 2.50
12 Martin Brodeur 2.00 5.00
13 Rick DiPietro .60 1.50
14 Mike Richter .60 1.50
15 Patrick Lalime .60 1.50
16 Roman Cechmanek .60 1.50
17 Johan Hedberg .60 1.50
18 Evgeni Nabokov .60 1.50
19 Curtis Joseph .75 2.00
20 Olaf Kolzig .60 1.50

2001-02 Pacific Heads Up Stat Masters

COMPLETE SET (20) 25.00 50.00
STATED ODDS 2:19 HOB, 2:25 RET
1 Paul Kariya .60 1.50
2 Joe Thornton 1.00 2.50
3 Peter Forsberg 1.50 4.00
4 Joe Sakic 1.25 3.00
5 Brett Hull .75 2.00
6 Mike Modano 1.00 2.50
7 Steve Yzerman 3.00 8.00
8 Pavel Bure .75 2.00
9 Zigmund Palffy .50 1.25
10 Jason Arnott .50 1.25
11 Theo Fleury .50 1.25
12 Marian Hossa .60 1.50
13 Jeremy Roenick .75 2.00
14 Mario Lemieux 4.00 10.00
15 Keith Tkachuk .60 1.50
16 Teemu Selanne .60 1.50
17 Vincent Lecavalier .60 1.50
18 Brad Richards .50 1.25
19 Mats Sundin .60 1.50
20 Jaromir Jagr 1.00 2.50

2002-03 Pacific Heads Up

This 125-card set contained 125 veteran cards and 20 shortprinted rookie cards. Rookies were serial-numbered to 1000 each and were only available via a mail in redemption card found in packs.

COMPLETE SET (145) 40.00 80.00
COMP.SET w/o SP's (125) 12.00 30.00
1 Jean-Sebastien Giguere .30 .75
2 Paul Kariya .40 1.00
3 Adam Oates .30 .75
4 Dany Heatley .30 .75
5 Milan Hnilicka .25 .60
6 Ilya Kovalchuk .40 1.00
7 Byron Dafoe .25 .60
8 Glen Murray .25 .60
9 Brian Rolston .25 .60
10 Sergei Samsonov .25 .60
11 Joe Thornton .40 1.00
12 Martin Biron .25 .60
13 J-P Dumont .20 .50
14 Miroslav Satan .30 .75
15 Craig Conroy .20 .50
16 Jarome Iginla .30 .75
17 Dean McAmmond .20 .50
18 Roman Turek .30 .75
19 Erik Cole .25 .60
20 Ron Francis .40 1.00
21 Arturs Irbe .25 .60
22 Sami Kapanen .20 .50
23 Jeff O'Neill .20 .50
24 Tony Amonte .25 .60
25 Eric Daze .20 .50
26 Jocelyn Thibault .25 .60
27 Alexei Zhamnov .25 .60
28 Rob Blake .30 .75
29 Chris Drury .30 .75
30 Peter Forsberg .40 1.00
31 Milan Hejduk .25 .60
32 Patrick Roy .75 2.00
33 Joe Sakic .50 1.25
34 Marc Denis .25 .60
35 Rostislav Klesla .20 .50
36 Ray Whitney .25 .60
37 Jason Arnott .25 .60
38 Bill Guerin .30 .75
39 Mike Modano .50 1.25
40 Marty Turco .30 .75
41 Sergei Fedorov .50 1.25
42 Dominik Hasek .50 1.25
43 Brett Hull .40 1.00
44 Curtis Joseph .30 .75
45 Nicklas Lidstrom .30 .75
46 Luc Robitaille .30 .75
47 Brendan Shanahan .40 1.00
48 Steve Yzerman .60 1.50
49 Mike Comrie .30 .75
50 Tommy Salo .25 .60
51 Ryan Smyth .25 .60
52 Kristian Huselius .20 .50
53 Roberto Luongo .50 1.25
54 Stephen Weiss .30 .75
55 Jason Allison .25 .60
56 Adam Deadmarsh .25 .60
57 Zigmund Palffy .30 .75
58 Felix Potvin .50 1.25
59 Andrew Brunette .20 .50
60 Manny Fernandez .25 .60
61 Marian Gaborik .50 1.25
62 Donald Audette .20 .50
63 Doug Gilmour .40 1.00
64 Saku Koivu .30 .75
65 Yanic Perreault .20 .50
66 Jose Theodore .30 .75
67 Denis Arkhipov .20 .50
68 Scott Hartnell .30 .75
69 David Legwand .25 .60
70 Martin Brodeur .60 1.50
71 Patrik Elias .30 .75
72 Joe Nieuwendyk .30 .75
73 Chris Osgood .30 .75
74 Mark Parrish .20 .50
75 Michael Peca .25 .60
76 Alexei Yashin .25 .60
77 Daniel Blackburn .25 .60
78 Pavel Bure .40 1.00
79 Theo Fleury .40 1.00
80 Bobby Holik .20 .50
81 Brian Leetch .30 .75
82 Eric Lindros .50 1.25
83 Mike Richter .30 .75
84 Daniel Alfredsson .30 .75
85 Radek Bonk .25 .60
86 Martin Havlat .25 .60
87 Marian Hossa .25 .60
88 Patrick Lalime .25 .60
89 Roman Cechmanek .25 .60
90 Simon Gagne .30 .75
91 John LeClair .30 .75
92 Mark Recchi .40 1.00
93 Jeremy Roenick .30 .75
94 Daniel Briere .25 .60
95 Sean Burke .20 .50
96 Krystofer Kolanos .20 .50
97 Daymond Langkow .25 .60
98 Johan Hedberg .30 .75
99 Alexei Kovalev .30 .75
100 Mario Lemieux 1.00 2.50
101 Alexei Morozov .20 .50
102 Pavol Demitra .40 1.00
103 Brent Johnson .25 .60
104 Chris Pronger .25 .60
105 Keith Tkachuk .30 .75
106 Doug Weight .30 .75
107 Patrick Marleau .30 .75
108 Evgeni Nabokov .25 .60
109 Owen Nolan .30 .75
110 Teemu Selanne .60 1.50
111 Nikolai Khabibulin .30 .75
112 Vincent Lecavalier .25 .60
113 Brad Richards .30 .75
114 Ed Belfour .30 .75
115 Alyn McCauley .20 .50
116 Alexander Mogilny .25 .60
117 Gary Roberts .20 .50
118 Mats Sundin .30 .75
119 Todd Bertuzzi .30 .75
120 Dan Cloutier .25 .60
121 Brendan Morrison .25 .60
122 Markus Naslund .25 .60
123 Peter Bondra .30 .75
124 Jaromir Jagr .75 2.00
125 Olaf Kolzig .30 .75
126 Stanislav Chistov RC .60 1.50
127 Martin Gerber RC 1.00 2.50
128 Alexei Smirnov RC .75 2.00
129 Chuck Kobasew RC .75 2.00
130 Rick Nash RC 5.00 12.00
131 Dmitri Bykov RC .60 1.50
132 Henrik Zetterberg RC 6.00 15.00
133 Ales Hemsky RC 2.50 6.00
134 Jay Bouwmeester RC 2.00 5.00
135 Alexander Frolov RC 1.25 3.00
136 Sylvain Blouin RC .60 1.50
137 P-M Bouchard RC 1.00 2.50
138 Ron Hainsey RC .60 1.50
139 Scottie Upshall RC .75 2.00
140 Mike Danton SP .60 1.50
141 Ray Schultz RC .60 1.50
142 Anton Volchenkov RC .60 1.50
143 Dennis Seidenberg RC 1.00 2.50
144 Alexander Svitov RC .60 1.50
145 Steve Eminger RC .60 1.50

2002-03 Pacific Heads Up Blue

*BLUE/240: 2X TO 5X BASIC CARDS
STATED PRINT RUN 240 SER.#'d SETS

2002-03 Pacific Heads Up Purple

*PURPLE/30: 12X TO 30X BASIC CARDS
PURPLE/30 STATED ODDS 1:73

2002-03 Pacific Heads Up Red

*RED/80: 6X TO 15X BASIC CARDS
RED/80 ODDS 1:19 HOBBY

2002-03 Pacific Heads Up Bobble Heads

Randomly inserted on per hobby box, this 14-player ceramic bobble head doll set featured the Pacific logo on the base along with the Pacific Heads-Up logo with the last name of each player.

1 Jason Allison 10.00 25.00
2 Pavel Bure 10.00 25.00
3 Mike Comrie 10.00 25.00
4 Peter Forsberg 15.00 50.00
5 Jarome Iginla 15.00 40.00
6 Saku Koivu 10.00 25.00
7 Ilya Kovalchuk 15.00 40.00
8 Eric Lindros 10.00 25.00
9 Evgeni Nabokov 10.00 25.00
10 Brendan Shanahan 10.00 25.00
11 Mats Sundin 10.00 25.00
12 Jose Theodore 15.00 40.00
13 Joe Thornton 15.00 40.00
14 Alexei Yashin 10.00 25.00

2002-03 Pacific Heads Up Etched in Time

This 15-card set was inserted at a rate of 1:289 and each card was serial-numbered to just 85 copies.

1 Paul Kariya 6.00 15.00
2 Ilya Kovalchuk 12.50 30.00
3 Joe Thornton 8.00 20.00
4 Jarome Iginla 8.00 20.00
5 Ron Francis 6.00 15.00
6 Peter Forsberg 15.00 40.00
7 Patrick Roy 20.00 50.00
8 Joe Sakic 12.50 30.00
9 Dominik Hasek 12.00 30.00
10 Steve Yzerman 20.00 50.00
11 Martin Brodeur 15.00 40.00
12 Eric Lindros 6.00 15.00
13 Mario Lemieux 25.00 60.00
14 Mats Sundin 6.00 15.00
15 Jaromir Jagr 8.00 20.00

2002-03 Pacific Heads Up Head First

This 16-card set was inserted at a rate of 1:19.

COMPLETE SET (16) 12.00 30.00
1 Dany Heatley 1.25 3.00
2 Ilya Kovalchuk 1.50 4.00
3 Sergei Samsonov .75 2.00
4 Joe Thornton 1.50 4.00
5 Stephen Weiss .75 2.00
6 Marian Gaborik 1.50 4.00
7 Scott Hartnell .75 2.00
8 Rick DiPietro 1.00 2.50
9 Raffi Torres .75 2.00
10 Dan Blackburn .75 2.00
11 Martin Havlat 1.00 2.50
12 Simon Gagne 1.25 3.00
13 Krystofer Kolanos .75 2.00
14 Vincent Lecavalier 1.25 3.00
15 Daniel Sedin 1.25 3.00
16 Henrik Sedin 1.25 3.00

2002-03 Pacific Heads Up Inside the Numbers

This 24-card set was inserted at a rate of 1:10.

COMPLETE SET (24) 12.00 30.00
1 Adam Oates .60 1.50
2 Dany Heatley 1.00 2.50
3 Ilya Kovalchuk 1.00 2.50
4 Joe Thornton 1.25 3.00
5 Jarome Iginla 1.50 3.00
6 Ron Francis .60 1.50
7 Patrick Roy 3.00 8.00
8 Joe Sakic 1.50 4.00
9 Mike Modano 1.25 3.00
10 Dominik Hasek 1.50 4.00
11 Brendan Shanahan .75 2.00
12 Jose Theodore 1.00 2.50
13 Martin Brodeur 2.50 6.00
14 Alexei Yashin .60 1.50
15 Eric Lindros .75 2.00
16 Daniel Alfredsson .60 1.50
17 Mario Lemieux 4.00 10.00
18 Pavol Demitra .60 1.50
19 Evgeni Nabokov .60 1.50
20 Nikolai Khabibulin .75 2.00
21 Mats Sundin .75 2.00
22 Todd Bertuzzi .75 2.00
23 Markus Naslund .75 2.00
24 Jaromir Jagr 1.25 3.00

2002-03 Pacific Heads Up Postseason Picks

This 10-card set was inserted at a rate of 1:37.

COMPLETE SET (10) 20.00 40.00
1 Erik Cole .75 2.00
2 Ron Francis .75 2.00
3 Peter Forsberg 2.00 5.00
4 Patrick Roy 4.00 10.00
5 Joe Sakic 1.50 4.00
6 Dominik Hasek 1.50 4.00
7 Brendan Shanahan 1.00 2.50
8 Steve Yzerman 4.00 10.00
9 Jose Theodore 1.00 2.50
10 Mats Sundin .75 2.00

2002-03 Pacific Heads Up Quad Jerseys

Inserted at 2:19, this 36-card set featured four swatches of game-used jerseys. Two swatches appeared on the card front and two on the card back.

COMPLETE SET (36)
COMMON CARD (1-36) 5.00 12.00
STATED ODDS 2:19
1 Friesen/Tver/Allison/Deadmrsh 5.00 12.00
2 Kovlchk/Stefan/Hnilicka/Kallio 5.00 12.00
3 Sams/Thorntn/McLrn/Swney 5.00 12.00
4 Dumont/Biron/Mckee/Satan 5.00 12.00
5 Turek/Savrd/Comrie/Smyth 5.00 12.00
6 Franc/Irbe/Brdmour/O'Neill 12.50 30.00
7 Amonte/Daze/Bell/Sulli 5.00 12.00
8 Drury/Hejduk/Tngy/Nedrst 5.00 12.00
9 Blake/Sakic/Rbtlle/Fedorov 15.00 40.00
10 Denis/Tugntt/Klesla/Sandrsn 5.00 12.00
11 Belfour/Turco/Trgeon/Mdno 6.00 15.00
12 Hasek/Hull/Lidstrm/Williams 10.00 25.00
13 Allison/Palffy/Potvin/Smlnski 4.00 10.00
14 Gbrik/Kuba/McLnn/Ferndz 6.00 15.00
15 Theod/Prrlt/Berzn/Koivu 6.00 15.00
16 Erat/Legwnd/Walkr/Hntnen 5.00 12.00
17 Brodeur/Elias/Gomez/Stevens 12.50 30.00
18 Peca/Yash/Lndros/Fleury 5.00 12.00
19 Alfrdsson/Lalime/Havlat/Hossa 10.00 25.00
20 Oates/Roenk/Cech/Dopita 5.00 12.00
21 Klnos/Handzs/Lngkow/Doan 5.00 12.00
22 Hedbrg/Lang/Petrsn/Beech 5.00 12.00
23 Prngr/Tkck/Demtra/Vrlmov 5.00 12.00
24 Nabkv/Nolan/Kipsff/Marleau 8.00 20.00
25 Khabi/Richrd/Bure/Luongo 10.00 25.00
26 Cujo/Robrts/Moglny/Tuckr 10.00 25.00
27 Cltier/Brtzzi/D.Sedin/H.Sedin 8.00 20.00
28 Lemx/Prnger/Brodeur/Cujo 15.00 40.00
29 Guerin/Mdno/Hull/Leetch 12.50 30.00
30 Bure/Khabi./Fedrov/Yashin 12.50 30.00
31 Sundin/Alfr-son/Salo/Hdbrg 5.00 12.00
32 Jagr/Hasek/Hejduk/Elias 10.00 25.00
33 Selne/Lehtn./Lumme/Kallio 5.00 12.00
34 Bndra/Gbrik/Demitra/Plffy 8.00 20.00
35 Kovlchk/Heat./Klnos/Cole 10.00 25.00
36 Hslius/Dopita/Erat/Hntnen 5.00 12.00

2002-03 Pacific Heads Up Showstoppers

This 20-card set was inserted at a rate of 1:10 and featured goalies only.

COMPLETE SET (20) 25.00 50.00
1 Jean-Sebastien Giguere .40 1.00
2 Byron Dafoe .40 1.00
3 Roman Turek .40 1.00
4 Arturs Irbe .40 1.00
5 Jocelyn Thibault .40 1.00
6 Patrick Roy 2.50 6.00
7 Marty Turco .40 1.00
8 Dominik Hasek 1.25 3.00
9 Curtis Joseph .60 1.50
10 Roberto Luongo .75 2.00
11 Felix Potvin .60 1.50
12 Jose Theodore .60 2.00
13 Martin Brodeur 1.50 4.00
14 Chris Osgood .60 1.50
15 Patrick Lalime .40 1.00
16 Sean Burke .40 1.00
17 Brent Johnson .40 1.00
18 Evgeni Nabokov .40 1.00
19 Nikolai Khabibulin .60 1.50
20 Dan Cloutier .40 1.00

2002-03 Pacific Heads Up Stat Masters

This 15-card set was inserted at a rate of 1:73.

COMPLETE SET (15) 40.00 80.00
1 Paul Kariya 1.25 3.00
2 Dany Heatley 1.50 4.00
3 Ilya Kovalchuk 1.50 4.00
4 Joe Thornton 2.00 5.00
5 Jarome Iginla 1.50 4.00
6 Ron Francis 1.25 3.00
7 Joe Sakic 2.50 6.00
8 Brett Hull 1.50 4.00
9 Steve Yzerman 6.00 15.00
10 Pavel Bure 1.50 4.00
11 Eric Lindros 1.25 3.00
12 Mario Lemieux 8.00 20.00
13 Mats Sundin 1.25 3.00
14 Todd Bertuzzi 1.25 3.00
15 Jaromir Jagr 2.00 5.00

2003-04 Pacific Heads Up

This 136-card set consisted of 100 veteran cards and 36 short-printed rookie cards (101-136). Rookie cards were serial-numbered to just 899 copies each.

COMPLETE SET (136) 30.00 80.00
COMP.SET w/o SP's (100) 15.00 30.00
1 Sergei Fedorov .60 1.50
2 Jean-Sebastien Giguere .40 1.00
3 Steve Rucchin .25 .60
4 Ilya Kovalchuk .40 1.00
5 Shawn McEachern .25 .60
6 Pasi Nurminen .30 .75
7 Mike Knuble .25 .60
8 Andrew Raycroft .30 .75
9 Brian Rolston .30 .75
10 Joe Thornton .50 1.25
11 Martin Biron .30 .75
12 Daniel Briere .40 1.00
13 J-P Dumont .25 .60
14 Jarome Iginla .40 1.00
15 Jamie McLennan .25 .60
16 Steven Reinprecht .25 .60
17 Ron Francis .50 1.25
18 Josef Vasicek .25 .60
19 Kevin Weekes .30 .75
20 Mark Bell .25 .60
21 Michael Leighton .25 .60
22 Jocelyn Thibault UER .30 .75
23 David Aebischer .30 .75
24 Peter Forsberg .50 1.25
25 Paul Kariya .50 1.25
26 Joe Sakic .60 1.50
27 Alex Tanguay .30 .75
28 Marc Denis .30 .75
29 Rick Nash .40 1.00
30 David Vyborny .25 .60
31 Bill Guerin .40 1.00
32 Mike Modano .60 1.50
33 Marty Turco .40 1.00
34 Pavel Datsyuk .50 1.25
35 Dominik Hasek .60 1.50
36 Brett Hull .50 1.25
37 Brendan Shanahan .50 1.25
38 Steve Yzerman 1.00 2.50
39 Henrik Zetterberg .50 1.25
40 Ty Conklin .30 .75
41 Ales Hemsky .40 1.00
42 Ryan Smyth .30 .75
43 Jay Bouwmeester .40 1.00
44 Olli Jokinen .40 1.00
45 Roberto Luongo .60 1.50
46 Roman Cechmanek .30 .75
47 Cristobal Huet .30 .75
48 Ziggy Palffy .40 1.00
49 Pierre-Marc Bouchard .40 1.00
50 Marian Gaborik .60 1.50
51 Dwayne Roloson .30 .75
52 Saku Koivu .40 1.00
53 Mike Ribeiro .30 .75
54 Michael Ryder UER .30 .75
55 Jose Theodore .40 1.00
56 Scott Hartnell .40 1.00
57 David Legwand .30 .75
58 Martin Brodeur .75 2.00
59 Patrik Elias .40 1.00
60 Jamie Langenbrunner .30 .75
61 Mariusz Czerkawski .25 .60
62 Rick DiPietro .30 .75
63 Trent Hunter .25 .60
64 Alexei Yashin .30 .75
65 Alex Kovalev .30 .75
66 Eric Lindros .60 1.50
67 Mark Messier .60 1.50
68 Daniel Alfredsson .40 1.00
69 Marian Hossa .30 .75
70 Patrick Lalime .30 .75
71 Jason Spezza .40 1.00
72 Tony Amonte .30 .75
73 Robert Esche .25 .60
74 Jeremy Roenick .40 1.00
75 Justin Williams .30 .75
76 Sean Burke .25 .60
77 Ladislav Nagy .25 .60
78 Rico Fata .25 .60
79 Mario Lemieux 1.25 3.00
80 Barret Jackman .25 .60
81 Chris Osgood .40 1.00
82 Chris Pronger .30 .75
83 Patrick Marleau .40 1.00
84 Alyn McCauley .25 .60
85 Marco Sturm .25 .60
86 Nikolai Khabibulin .40 1.00
87 Vincent Lecavalier .30 .75
88 Martin St. Louis .40 1.00
89 Cory Stillman .25 .60
90 Ed Belfour .40 1.00
91 Alexander Mogilny .30 .75
92 Owen Nolan .30 .75
93 Mats Sundin .40 1.00
94 Todd Bertuzzi .40 1.00
95 Dan Cloutier .30 .75
96 Jason King .25 .60
97 Brendan Morrison .30 .75
98 Markus Naslund .40 1.00
99 Jaromir Jagr 1.00 2.50
100 Robert Lang .25 .60
101 Joffrey Lupul RC 2.00 5.00
102 Patrice Bergeron RC 4.00 10.00
103 Pat Leahy RC 1.00 2.50
104 Brent Krahn RC .75 2.00
105 Matthew Lombardi RC 1.00 2.50
106 Eric Staal RC 4.00 10.00
107 Tuomo Ruutu RC 1.25 3.00
108 Mikhail Yakubov RC .75 2.00
109 Cody McCormick RC 1.00 2.50
110 Dan Fritsche RC .75 2.00
111 Nikolai Zherdev RC 1.50 4.00
112 Antti Miettinen RC 1.25 3.00
113 Darryl Bootland RC 1.00 2.50
114 Jiri Hudler RC 2.00 5.00
115 Nathan Robinson RC .75 2.00
116 Tony Salmelainen RC .75 2.00
117 Peter Sarno RC .75 2.00
118 Nathan Horton RC 2.00 5.00
119 Dustin Brown RC 1.50 4.00
120 Brent Burns RC 2.00 5.00
121 Christopher Higgins RC 1.50 4.00
122 Dan Hamhuis RC 1.00 2.50
123 Jordin Tootoo RC 1.50 4.00
124 Marek Zidlicky RC .75 2.00
125 Paul Martin RC 1.00 2.50
126 Dominic Moore RC .75 2.00
127 Antoine Vermette RC 1.50 4.00
128 Joni Pitkanen RC 1.25 3.00
129 Fredrik Sjostrom RC 1.25 3.00
130 Marc-Andre Fleury RC 5.00 12.00
131 John Pohl RC .75 2.00
132 Peter Sejna RC 1.00 2.50
133 Milan Michalek RC 1.50 4.00
134 Matt Stajan RC 1.25 3.00
135 Boyd Gordon RC 1.00 2.50
136 Alexander Semin RC 2.50 6.00

2003-04 Pacific Heads Up Hobby LTD

*1-100 VETS/299: 2X TO 5X BASIC CARDS
1-100 STATED PRINT RUN 299
*101-136 ROOK/250: .6X TO 1.5X BASIC RC
101-136 ROOKIE PRINT RUN 250

2003-04 Pacific Heads Up Retail LTD

*STARS: .5X TO 1.2X
*ROOKIES: .25X TO .5X
STATED ODDS 1:2 RETAIL PACKS

2003-04 Pacific Heads Up Fast Forwards

STATED ODDS 1:9
*LTD: .75X TO 2X
LTD PRINT RUN 175 SER.#'d SETS
1 Sergei Fedorov 1.00 2.50
2 Ilya Kovalchuk 1.00 2.50
3 Rick Nash 1.00 2.50
4 Mike Modano 1.25 3.00
5 Marian Gaborik 1.50 4.00
6 Marian Hossa .75 2.00
7 Jeremy Roenick 1.00 2.50
8 Alexander Mogilny .75 2.00
9 Markus Naslund .75 2.00

2003-04 Pacific Heads Up In Focus

STATED ODDS 1:13
*LTD: .75X TO 2X
LTD PRINT RUN 175 SER.#'d SETS
1 Sergei Fedorov 1.00 2.50
2 Ilya Kovalchuk 1.00 2.50
3 Eric Staal 1.00 2.50
4 Joe Sakic 1.50 4.00
5 Alex Tanguay .75 2.00
6 Rick Nash 1.00 2.50
7 Henrik Zetterberg .75 2.00
8 Jay Bouwmeester .75 2.00
9 Jason Spezza .75 2.00
10 Todd Bertuzzi .75 2.00

2003-04 Pacific Heads Up Jerseys

This 25-card memorabilia set was inserted at 2 per 24-pack box. Known SP's are noted below.

1 Joffrey Lupul 3.00 8.00
2 Ilya Kovalchuk SP 8.00 20.00
3 Joe Thornton SP 10.00 25.00
4 Ales Kotalik 2.00 5.00
5 Ryan Miller 4.00 10.00
6 Matthew Lombardi 2.00 5.00
7 David Aebischer 3.00 8.00
8 Peter Forsberg SP 8.00 20.00
9 Antti Miettinen 2.00 5.00
10 Steve Yzerman SP 12.50 30.00
11 Ales Hemsky 2.00 5.00
12 Jay Bouwmeester 2.00 5.00
13 Nathan Horton 3.00 8.00
14 Dustin Brown 4.00 10.00
15 Ziggy Palffy 2.00 5.00
16 Chris Higgins 3.00 8.00
17 Jordin Tootoo 5.00 12.00
18 Martin Brodeur 10.00 25.00
19 Rick DiPietro 3.00 8.00
20 Jason Spezza 6.00 15.00
21 Antoine Vermette 2.00 5.00
22 Mario Lemieux SP 15.00 40.00
23 Barret Jackman 2.00 5.00
24 Owen Nolan 2.00 5.00
25 Boyd Gordon 2.00 5.00

2003-04 Pacific Heads Up Mini Sweaters

Inserted at one per hobby box, these small replica sweaters measured about 6" high.

1 Marc-Andre Fleury 12.00 30.00
2 Ilya Kovalchuk 12.00 30.00
3 Joe Thornton 12.00 30.00
4 Peter Forsberg 12.00 30.00
5 Steve Yzerman 15.00 40.00
6 Martin Brodeur 15.00 40.00
7 Marian Gaborik 12.00 30.00
8 Ed Belfour 8.00 20.00
9 Todd Bertuzzi 8.00 20.00

2003-04 Pacific Heads Up Prime Prospects

COMPLETE SET (10) 10.00 20.00
STATED ODDS 1:7
*LTD: .6X TO 1.5X
LTD PRINT RUN 175 SER.#'d SETS
1 Joffrey Lupul .75 2.00
2 Patrice Bergeron 1.50 4.00
3 Ryan Miller 1.25 3.00
4 Matthew Lombardi .40 1.00
5 Eric Staal 2.00 5.00
6 Philippe Sauve .40 1.00
7 Nikolai Zherdev 1.25 3.00
8 Jiri Hudler .75 2.00
9 Nathan Horton .75 2.00
10 Dustin Brown .50 1.25
11 Brent Burns .40 1.00
12 Christopher Higgins 1.25 3.00
13 Michael Ryder 1.25 3.00
14 Jordin Tootoo 1.25 3.00
15 Antoine Vermette .40 1.00
16 Joni Pitkanen .75 2.00
17 Marc-Andre Fleury 2.00 5.00
18 Milan Michalek .75 2.00
19 Matt Stajan .75 2.00
20 Jason King .40 1.00

2003-04 Pacific Heads Up Rink Immortals

STATED ODDS 1:13
*LTD: .75X TO 2X
LTD PRINT RUN 175 SER.#'d SETS
1 Joe Thornton 1.00 2.50
2 Peter Forsberg 2.00 5.00
3 Joe Sakic 1.50 4.00
4 Dominik Hasek 1.50 4.00
5 Brett Hull 1.00 2.50
6 Steve Yzerman 2.50 6.00
7 Martin Brodeur 2.50 6.00
8 Mark Messier 1.00 2.50
9 Mario Lemieux 3.00 8.00
10 Ed Belfour 1.00 2.50

2003-04 Pacific Heads Up Stonewallers

STATED ODDS 1:9
*LTD: .75X TO 2X
LTD.PRINT RUN 175 SER.#'d SETS
1 Jean-Sebastien Giguere .60 1.50
2 Pasi Nurminen .60 1.50
3 David Aebischer .60 1.50
4 Marty Turco .60 1.50
5 Dominik Hasek 1.50 4.00
6 Jose Theodore 1.00 2.50
7 Martin Brodeur 2.50 6.00
8 Rick DiPietro .60 1.50
9 Patrick Lalime .60 1.50
10 Nikolai Khabibulin .75 2.00
11 Ed Belfour .75 2.00
12 Dan Cloutier .60 1.50

2001-02 Pacific High Voltage

Available via a mail-in offer advertised in Powerplay magazine, this 10-card set featured hot rookies from the 2001-02 season. To receive a set, collectors had to send in wrappers from other Pacific products.

COMPLETE SET (10) 20.00 50.00
1 Dany Heatley 2.50 6.00
2 Ilya Kovalchuk 10.00 25.00
3 Erik Cole 3.00 8.00
4 Vaclav Nedorost 2.50 6.00
5 Kristian Huselius 3.00 8.00
6 Martin Erat .75 2.00
7 Dan Blackburn 1.00 2.50
8 Krystofer Kolanos 2.50 6.00
9 Jeff Jillson 1.50 4.00
10 Nikita Alexeev 1.50 4.00

1997-98 Pacific Invincible

The 1997-98 Pacific Invincible set was issued in one series totaling 150 cards and distributed in three-card packs. The fronts feature color action player images with gold foil background enhancements and a small player head photo in a clear, circular "window" at the bottom. The backs carry player information.

1 Brian Bellows .30 .75
2 Guy Hebert .30 .75
3 Paul Kariya .50 1.25
4 Teemu Selanne .75 2.00
5 Darren Van Impe .30 .75
6 Jason Allison .30 .75
7 Ray Bourque .60 1.50
8 Jim Carey .25 .60
9 Ted Donato .25 .60
10 Jozef Stumpel .30 .75
11 Jason Dawe .30 .75
12 Dominik Hasek .60 1.50
13 Michael Peca .30 .75
14 Derek Plante .30 .75
15 Miroslav Satan .25 .60
16 Theo Fleury .50 1.25
17 Dave Gagner .25 .60
18 Jonas Hoglund .30 .75
19 Jarome Iginla .40 1.00
20 Trevor Kidd .25 .60
21 German Titov .25 .60
22 Sean Burke .25 .60
23 Andrew Cassels .25 .60
24 Derek King .30 .75
25 Keith Primeau .30 .75
26 Geoff Sanderson .30 .75
27 Tony Amonte .30 .75
28 Chris Chelios .40 1.00
29 Eric Daze .25 .60
30 Jeff Hackett .25 .60
31 Ethan Moreau .25 .60
32 Alexei Zhamnov .25 .60
33 Adam Deadmarsh .25 .60
34 Peter Forsberg .50 1.25
35 Valeri Kamensky .30 .75
36 Claude Lemieux .30 .75
37 Sandis Ozolinsh .30 .75
38 Patrick Roy 1.00 2.50
39 Joe Sakic .60 1.50
40 Jamie Langenbrunner .30 .75
41 Mike Modano .60 1.50
42 Andy Moog .40 1.00
43 Joe Nieuwendyk .40 1.00
44 Pat Verbeek .30 .75
45 Sergei Zubov .30 .75
46 Sergei Fedorov .60 1.50
47 Vladimir Konstantinov .25 .60
48 Vyacheslav Kozlov .30 .75
49 Nicklas Lidstrom .40 1.00
50 Chris Osgood .40 1.00
51 Brendan Shanahan .50 1.25
52 Mike Vernon .30 .75
53 Steve Yzerman .75 2.00
54 Jason Arnott .30 .75
55 Mike Grier .30 .75
56 Curtis Joseph .40 1.00
57 Rem Murray .25 .60
58 Ryan Smyth .30 .75
59 Doug Weight .40 1.00
60 Ed Jovanovski .25 .60
61 Scott Mellanby .30 .75
62 Kirk Muller .25 .60
63 Ray Sheppard .30 .75
64 John Vanbiesbrouck .40 1.00
65 Rob Blake .40 1.00
66 Ray Ferraro .25 .60
67 Stephane Fiset .30 .75
68 Dimitri Khristich .30 .75
69 Vladimir Tsyplakov .30 .75
70 Vincent Damphousse .30 .75
71 Saku Koivu .40 1.00
72 Mark Recchi .50 1.25
73 Stephane Richer .25 .60
74 Jocelyn Thibault .25 .60
75 Dave Andreychuk .40 1.00
76 Martin Brodeur .75 2.00
77 Doug Gilmour .50 1.25
78 Bobby Holik .25 .60
79 Denis Pederson .25 .60
80 Bryan Berard .25 .60
81 Travis Green .30 .75
82 Zigmund Palffy .40 1.00
83 Tommy Salo .25 .60
84 Bryan Smolinski .30 .75
85 Adam Graves .25 .60
86 Wayne Gretzky 2.00 5.00
87 Alexei Kovalev .25 .60
88 Brian Leetch .40 1.00
89 Mark Messier .60 1.50
90 Mike Richter .40 1.00
91 Luc Robitaille .40 1.00
92 Daniel Alfredsson .40 1.00
93 Alexandre Daigle .25 .60
94 Steve Duchesne .25 .60
95 Wade Redden .25 .60
96 Ron Tugnutt .40 1.00
97 Alexei Yashin .30 .75
98 Rod Brind'Amour .40 1.00
99 Paul Coffey .40 1.00
100 Ron Hextall .40 1.00
101 John LeClair .40 1.00
102 Eric Lindros .60 1.50
103 Janne Niinimaa .30 .75
104 Mikael Renberg .30 .75
105 Dainius Zubrus .30 .75
106 Mike Gartner .40 1.00
107 Nikolai Khabibulin .40 1.00
108 Jeremy Roenick .50 1.25
109 Keith Tkachuk .40 1.00
110 Oleg Tverdovsky .30 .75
111 Ron Francis .50 1.25
112 Kevin Hatcher .25 .60
113 Jaromir Jagr 1.00 2.50
114 Patrick Lalime .30 .75
115 Petr Nedved .40 1.00
116 Ed Olczyk .25 .60
117 Jim Campbell .25 .60
118 Geoff Courtnall .25 .60
119 Grant Fuhr .40 1.00
120 Brett Hull .50 1.25
121 Sergio Momesso .25 .60
122 Pierre Turgeon .40 1.00
123 Ed Belfour .40 1.00
124 Jeff Friesen .30 .75
125 Tony Granato .30 .75
126 Stephen Guolla RC .25 .60
127 Bernie Nicholls .30 .75
128 Owen Nolan .40 1.00
129 Dino Ciccarelli .40 1.00
130 John Cullen .25 .60
131 Chris Gratton .25 .60
132 Roman Hamrlik .30 .75
133 Daymond Langkow .25 .60
134 Paul Ysebaert .30 .75
135 Sergei Berezin .30 .75
136 Wendel Clark .40 1.00
137 Felix Potvin .40 1.00
138 Steve Sullivan .30 .75
139 Mats Sundin .40 1.00
140 Pavel Bure .50 1.25
141 Martin Gelinas .25 .60
142 Trevor Linden .30 .75
143 Kirk McLean .30 .75
144 Alexander Mogilny .30 .75
145 Peter Bondra .30 .75
146 Dale Hunter .30 .75
147 Joe Juneau .30 .75
148 Steve Konowalchuk .30 .75
149 Adam Oates .40 1.00
150 Bill Ranford .30 .75
S41 Mike Modano Sample .60 1.50

1997-98 Pacific Invincible Copper

Randomly inserted in U.S. hobby packs only at the rate of 2:37, this 150-card set is parallel to the regular gold foil base set only with copper foil enhancements.

*COPPER: 3X TO 8X BASIC CARDS

1997-98 Pacific Invincible Emerald Green

Randomly inserted in Canadian packs only at the rate of 2:37, this 150-card set is parallel to the regular gold foil base set only with green foil enhancements.

*GREEN: 3X TO 8X BASIC CARDS

1997-98 Pacific Invincible Ice Blue

Randomly inserted in packs at the rate of 1:73, this 150-card set is parallel to the regular gold foil base set only with blue foil enhancements.

*ICE BLUE: 10X TO 25X BASIC CARDS

1997-98 Pacific Invincible Red

Randomly inserted at the rate of 2:37 into special packs found only in Wal-Mart stores, this 150-card set is parallel to the regular gold foil base set only with red foil enhancements.

*RED: 4X TO 10X BASIC CARDS

1997-98 Pacific Invincible Silver

Randomly inserted in U.S. retail packs only at the rate of 2:37, this 150-card set is parallel to the regular gold foil base set only with silver foil enhancements.

*SILVER: 4X TO 10X BASIC CARDS

1997-98 Pacific Invincible Attack Zone

Randomly inserted in packs at the rate of 1:37, this 24-card set features color action player images on a bright, colorful background. The backs carry player information.

COMPLETE SET (24) 50.00 100.00
1 Paul Kariya 2.50 6.00

emu Selanne 2.50 6.00
chael Peca 1.00 2.50
rome Iginla 3.00 8.00
ter Forsberg 6.00 15.00
aude Lemieux 1.00 2.50
e Sakic 5.00 12.00
ke Modano 4.00 10.00
rgei Fedorov 4.00 10.00
rendan Shanahan 2.50 6.00
teve Yzerman 10.00 25.00
ryan Berard 2.00 5.00
igmund Palffy 2.00 5.00
ayne Gretzky 12.50 30.00
rian Leetch 2.50 6.00
ark Messier 2.50 6.00
ohn LeClair 2.50 6.00
ric Lindros 3.00 8.00
on Francis 2.00 5.00
aromir Jagr 4.00 10.00
rett Hull 3.00 8.00
ino Ciccarelli 1.00 2.50
avel Bure 2.50 6.00
lexander Mogilny 2.00 5.00

1997-98 Pacific Invincible Feature Performers

domly inserted in packs at the rate of 2:37, this 36- set features color action player made to look as if are breaking through the ice.

MPLETE SET (36) 15.00 40.00
aul Kariya 1.25 3.00
emu Selanne 1.25 3.00
y Bourque 2.00 5.00
ominik Hasek 3.00 8.00
rome Iginla 2.00 5.00
hris Chelios 1.25 3.00
eter Forsberg 2.50 6.00
laude Lemieux .40 1.00
atrick Roy 6.00 15.00
Joe Sakic 3.00 8.00
Mike Modano 1.50 4.00
Sergei Fedorov 1.25 3.00
Vladimir Konstantinov 1.25 3.00
Brendan Shanahan 1.25 3.00
Mike Vernon .75 2.00
Steve Yzerman 4.00 10.00
John Vanbiesbrouck .75 2.00
Saku Koivu 1.25 3.00
Martin Brodeur 4.00 10.00
Zigmund Palffy .75 2.00
Wayne Gretzky 8.00 20.00
Mark Messier 1.25 3.00
Alexandre Daigle .40 1.00
John LeClair .75 2.00
Eric Lindros 1.25 3.00
Janne Niinimaa .40 1.00
Jeremy Roenick 2.00 5.00
Jaromir Jagr 2.50 6.00
Patrick Lalime .75 2.00
Jim Campbell .40 1.00
Brett Hull 1.25 3.00
Sergei Berezin .40 1.00
Felix Potvin 1.25 3.00
Mats Sundin 1.25 3.00
Alexander Mogilny .75 2.00
Peter Bondra .75 2.00

1997-98 Pacific Invincible NHL Regime

ndomly inserted one in every pack, this 220-card set tures color action player photos with a faint lavender rder. The backs carry player information.

MPLETE SET (220) 8.00 20.00
Ken Baumgartner .05 .15
Mark Janssens .05 .15
Jean-Francois Jomphe .05 .15
Paul Kariya .10 .30
Jason Marshall .05 .15
Richard Park .05 .15
Teemu Selanne .10 .30
Mikhail Shtalenkov .05 .15
Bob Beers .05 .15
Ray Bourque .20 .50
Jim Carey .05 .15
Brett Harkins .05 .15
Sheldon Kennedy .05 .15
Troy Mallette .05 .15
Sandy Moger .05 .15
Jon Rohloff .05 .15
Don Sweeney .05 .15
Randy Burridge .05 .15
Michal Grosek .05 .15
Dominik Hasek .25 .60
Rob Ray .05 .15
Steve Shields .08 .25
Richard Smehlik .05 .15
Dixon Ward .05 .15
Mike Wilson .05 .15
Tommy Albelin .05 .15
Aaron Gavey .05 .15
Todd Hlushko .05 .15
Jarome Iginla .15 .40
Yves Racine .05 .15
1 Dwayne Roloson .08 .25
2 Mike Sullivan .05 .15
3 Ed Ward .05 .15
4 Adam Burt .05 .15
5 Nelson Emerson .05 .15
6 Kevin Haller .05 .15
7 Derek King .05 .15
8 Curtis Leschyshyn .05 .15
9 Chris Murray .05 .15
0 Jason Muzzatti .05 .15
1 Keith Carney .05 .15
2 Chris Chelios .10 .30
3 Enrico Ciccone .05 .15
4 Jim Cummins .05 .15
5 Cam Russell .05 .15
6 Jeff Shantz .05 .15
7 Michal Sykora .05 .15
8 Chris Terreri .08 .25
9 Eric Weinrich .05 .15
0 Rene Corbet .05 .15
1 Peter Forsberg .30 .75
2 Alexei Gusarov .05 .15
53 Uwe Krupp .05 .15
54 Sylvain Lefebvre .05 .15
55 Eric Messier .08 .25
56 Patrick Roy .60 1.50
57 Joe Sakic .25 .60
58 Brent Severyn .05 .15
59 Greg Adams .05 .15
60 Todd Harvey .05 .15
61 Jere Lehtinen .05 .15
62 Craig Ludwig .05 .15
63 Mike Modano .20 .50
64 Andy Moog .08 .25
65 Dave Reid .05 .15
66 Roman Turek .05 .15
67 Doug Brown .05 .15
68 Kris Draper .05 .15
69 Sergei Fedorov .20 .50
70 Joey Kocur .05 .15
71 Kirk Maltby .05 .15
72 Bob Rouse .05 .15
73 Brendan Shanahan .10 .30
74 Aaron Ward .05 .15
75 Steve Yzerman .60 1.50
76 Greg DeVries .05 .15
77 Bob Essensa .08 .25
78 Kevin Lowe .05 .15
79 Bryan Marchment .05 .15
80 Dean McAmmond .05 .15
81 Boris Mironov .05 .15
82 Luke Richardson .05 .15
83 Ryan Smyth .08 .25
84 Terry Carkner .05 .15
85 Ed Jovanovski .08 .25
86 Bill Lindsay .05 .15
87 Dave Lowry .05 .15
88 Gord Murphy .05 .15
89 John Vanbiesbrouck .08 .25
90 Steve Washburn .05 .15
91 Chris Wells .05 .15
92 Philippe Boucher .05 .15
93 Steven Finn .05 .15
94 Mattias Norstrom .05 .15
95 Kai Nurminen .05 .15
96 Sean O'Donnell .05 .15
97 Yanic Perreault .05 .15
98 Jeff Shevalier .05 .15
99 Brad Smyth .05 .15
100 Brad Brown .05 .15
101 Jassen Cullimore .05 .15
102 Vincent Damphousse .05 .15
103 Vladimir Malakhov .05 .15
104 Peter Popovic .05 .15
105 Stephane Richer .08 .25
106 Turner Stevenson .05 .15
107 Jose Theodore .15 .40
108 Martin Brodeur .30 .75
109 Bob Carpenter .05 .15
110 Mike Dunham .08 .25
111 Patrik Elias .08 .25
112 Dave Ellett .05 .15
113 Doug Gilmour .08 .25
114 Randy McKay .05 .15
115 Todd Bertuzzi .10 .30
116 Kenny Jonsson .05 .15
117 Paul Kruse .05 .15
118 Claude Lapointe .05 .15
119 Zigmund Palffy .08 .25
120 Rich Pilon .05 .15
121 Dan Plante .05 .15
122 Dennis Vaske .05 .15
123 Shane Churla .05 .15
124 Bruce Driver .05 .15
125 Mike Eastwood .05 .15
126 Patrick Flatley .05 .15
127 Adam Graves .05 .15
128 Wayne Gretzky .75 2.00
129 Brian Leetch .10 .30
130 Doug Lidster .05 .15
131 Mark Messier .10 .30
132 Tom Chorske .05 .15
133 Sean Hill .05 .15
134 Denny Lambert .05 .15
135 Janne Laukkanen .05 .15
136 Frank Musil .05 .15
137 Lance Pitlick .05 .15
138 Shaun Van Allen .05 .15
139 Rod Brind'Amour .08 .25
140 Paul Coffey .10 .30
141 Karl Dykhuis .05 .15
142 Dan Kordic .05 .15
143 Daniel Lacroix .05 .15
144 John LeClair .10 .30
145 Eric Lindros .10 .30
146 Joel Otto .05 .15
147 Shjon Podein .05 .15
148 Chris Therien .05 .15
149 Shane Doan .05 .15
150 Dallas Drake .05 .15
151 Jeff Finley .05 .15
152 Mike Gartner .08 .25
153 Nikolai Khabibulin .08 .25
154 Darrin Shannon .05 .15
155 Mike Stapleton .05 .15
156 Keith Tkachuk .10 .30
157 Tom Barrasso .08 .25
158 Josef Beranek .05 .15
159 Alex Hicks .05 .15
160 Jaromir Jagr .20 .50
161 Patrick Lalime .08 .25
162 Francois Leroux .05 .15
163 Petr Nedved .08 .25
164 Roman Oksiuta .05 .15
165 Chris Tamer .05 .15
166 Marc Bergevin .05 .15
167 Jon Casey .08 .25
168 Craig Conroy .05 .15
169 Brett Hull .15 .40
170 Igor Kravchuk .05 .15
171 Stephen Leach .05 .15
172 Ricard Persson .05 .15
173 Pierre Turgeon .08 .25
174 Ed Belfour .10 .30
175 Doug Bodger .05 .15
176 Shean Donovan .05 .15
177 Bob Errey .05 .15
178 Todd Ewen .05 .15
179 Wade Flaherty .05 .15
180 Mike Rathje .05 .15
181 Ron Sutter .05 .15
182 Mikael Andersson .05 .15
183 Dino Ciccarelli .05 .15
184 Cory Cross .05 .15
185 Jamie Huscroft .05 .15
186 Rudy Poeschek .05 .15
187 Daren Puppa .08 .25
188 David Shaw .05 .15
189 Jay Wells .05 .15
190 Jamie Baker .05 .15
191 Sergei Berezin .08 .25
192 Brandon Convery .05 .15
193 Darby Hendrickson .05 .15
194 Matt Martin .05 .15
195 Felix Potvin .10 .30
196 Jason Smith .05 .15
197 Craig Wolanin .05 .15
198 Adrian Aucoin .05 .15
199 Dave Babych .05 .15
200 Donald Brashear .05 .15
201 Pavel Bure .10 .30
202 Chris Joseph .05 .15
203 Alexander Mogilny .08 .25
204 David Roberts .05 .15
205 Scott Walker .05 .15
206 Peter Bondra .08 .25
207 Andrew Brunette .08 .25
208 Calle Johansson .05 .15
209 Ken Klee .05 .15
210 Olaf Kolzig .08 .25
211 Kelly Miller .05 .15
212 Joe Reekie .05 .15
213 Chris Simon .05 .15
214 Brendan Witt .05 .15
215 Paul Kariya TL .10 .30
216 Peter Forsberg TL .10 .30
217 Patrick Roy TL .10 .30
218 Wayne Gretzky TL .10 .30
219 Eric Lindros TL .10 .30
220 Jaromir Jagr TL .10 .30

1997-98 Pacific Invincible Off The Glass

Randomly inserted in packs at the rate of 1:73, this 20-card set features borderless color action photos of top hockey players with gold foil highlights.

COMPLETE SET (20) 25.00 60.00
1 Paul Kariya 1.25 3.00
2 Teemu Selanne 1.25 3.00
3 Michael Peca .75 2.00
4 Jarome Iginla 2.00 5.00
5 Peter Forsberg 3.00 8.00
6 Joe Sakic 4.00 10.00
7 Sergei Fedorov 1.50 4.00
8 Brendan Shanahan 1.25 3.00
9 Steve Yzerman 6.00 15.00
10 Mike Grier .75 2.00
11 Saku Koivu 1.25 3.00
12 Wayne Gretzky 10.00 25.00
13 Mark Messier 1.50 4.00
14 Eric Lindros 1.25 3.00
15 Dainius Zubrus .75 2.00
16 Keith Tkachuk 1.25 3.00
17 Jaromir Jagr 3.00 8.00
18 Brett Hull 1.50 4.00
19 Sergei Berezin .75 2.00
20 Pavel Bure 1.50 4.00

2003-04 Pacific Invincible

This 125-card set consisted of 100 veteran cards (1-100) and 25 shortprinted rookie cards (101-125). Rookies were serial-numbered to 799.

COMPLETE SET (125)
COMP.SET w/o SP's (100) 12.00 30.00
1 Stanislav Chistov .25 .60
2 Sergei Fedorov .60 1.50
3 Jean-Sebastien Giguere .40 1.00
4 Dany Heatley .40 1.00
5 Ilya Kovalchuk .40 1.00
6 Glen Murray .30 .75
7 Sergei Samsonov .30 .75
8 Joe Thornton .50 1.25
9 Martin Biron .30 .75
10 Ryan Miller .40 1.00
11 Miroslav Satan .30 .75
12 Craig Conroy .25 .60
13 Jarome Iginla .40 1.00
14 Roman Turek .30 .75
15 Ron Francis .50 1.25
16 Jeff O'Neill .25 .60
17 Eric Daze .30 .75
18 Jocelyn Thibault .30 .75
19 Alexei Zhamnov .30 .75
20 David Aebischer .30 .75
21 Peter Forsberg .50 1.25
22 Milan Hejduk .30 .75
23 Paul Kariya .50 1.25
24 Patrick Roy 1.00 2.50
25 Joe Sakic .60 1.50
26 Teemu Selanne .75 2.00
27 Marc Denis .30 .75
28 Rick Nash .40 1.00
29 Bill Guerin .40 1.00
30 Mike Modano .60 1.50
31 Marty Turco .40 1.00
32 Dominik Hasek .60 1.50
33 Brett Hull .50 1.25
34 Nicklas Lidstrom .40 1.00
35 Brendan Shanahan .50 1.25
36 Steve Yzerman 1.00 2.50
37 Henrik Zetterberg .50 1.25
38 Mike Comrie .30 .75
39 Ales Hemsky .40 1.00
40 Ryan Smyth .30 .75
41 Jay Bouwmeester .40 1.00
42 Olli Jokinen .40 1.00
43 Roberto Luongo .60 1.50
44 Jason Allison .30 .75
45 Roman Cechmanek .30 .75
46 Zigmund Palffy .40 1.00
47 Manny Fernandez .30 .75
48 Marian Gaborik .60 1.50
49 Marcel Hossa .25 .60
50 Saku Koivu .40 1.00
51 Jose Theodore .40 1.00
52 David Legwand .30 .75
53 Scottie Upshall .30 .75
54 Tomas Vokoun .30 .75
55 Martin Brodeur .75 2.00
56 Patrik Elias .40 1.00
57 Jeff Friesen .25 .60
58 Jamie Langenbrunner .30 .75
59 Scott Stevens .40 1.00
60 Rick DiPietro .30 .75
61 Mark Parrish .30 .75
62 Michael Peca .30 .75
63 Alexei Yashin .30 .75
64 Pavel Bure .50 1.25
65 Alex Kovalev .30 .75
66 Eric Lindros .60 1.50
67 Mark Messier .60 1.50
68 Daniel Alfredsson .40 1.00
69 Marian Hossa .30 .75
70 Patrick Lalime .30 .75
71 Jason Spezza .40 1.00
72 Tony Amonte .30 .75
73 Jeff Hackett .30 .75
74 John LeClair .40 1.00
75 Jeremy Roenick .40 1.00
76 Sean Burke .25 .60
77 Daymond Langkow .25 .60
78 Mario Lemieux 1.25 3.00
79 Pavol Demitra .50 1.25
80 Barret Jackman .25 .60
81 Chris Osgood .40 1.00
82 Doug Weight .40 1.00
83 Patrick Marleau .40 1.00
84 Evgeni Nabokov .30 .75
85 John Grahame .25 .60
86 Nikolai Khabibulin .40 1.00
87 Vincent Lecavalier .30 .75
88 Martin St. Louis .40 1.00
89 Ed Belfour .40 1.00
90 Alexander Mogilny .30 .75
91 Owen Nolan .30 .75
92 Mats Sundin .40 1.00
93 Todd Bertuzzi .40 1.00
94 Dan Cloutier .30 .75
95 Johan Hedberg .30 .75
96 Brendan Morrison .30 .75
97 Markus Naslund .40 1.00
98 Peter Bondra .30 .75
99 Jaromir Jagr 1.00 2.50
100 Olaf Kolzig .40 1.00
101 Joffrey Lupul RC 3.00 8.00
102 Patrice Bergeron RC 6.00 15.00
103 Milan Bartovic RC 1.50 4.00
104 Matthew Lombardi RC 1.50 4.00
105 Eric Staal RC 6.00 15.00
106 Tuomo Ruutu RC 2.00 5.00
107 Pavel Vorobiev RC 1.50 4.00
108 Dan Fritsche RC 1.25 3.00
109 Kent McDonell RC 1.50 4.00
110 Antti Miettinen RC 2.00 5.00
111 Nathan Horton RC 3.00 8.00
112 Dustin Brown RC 2.50 6.00
113 Tim Gleason RC 1.50 4.00
114 Brent Burns RC 3.00 8.00
115 Christopher Higgins RC 2.50 6.00
116 Dan Hamhuis RC 1.50 4.00
117 Jordin Tootoo RC 2.50 6.00
118 Sean Bergenheim RC 1.50 4.00
119 Antoine Vermette RC 2.50 6.00
120 Joni Pitkanen RC 2.00 5.00
121 Marc-Andre Fleury RC 8.00 20.00
122 Peter Sejna RC 1.50 4.00
123 Milan Michalek RC 2.50 6.00
124 Matt Stajan RC 2.00 5.00
125 Boyd Gordon RC 1.50 4.00

2003-04 Pacific Invincible Blue

*1-100 VETS/350: 2X TO 5X BASIC CARDS
*101-125 ROOK/350: .5X TO 1.2X RC
67 Mark Messier 3.00 8.00

2003-04 Pacific Invincible Red

This retail only parallel carried a red foil logo and was serial-numbered out of 850.

*1-100 VETS/850: 1.5X TO 4X BASIC CARDS
*101-125 ROOKIES/850: .3X TO .8X RC
67 Mark Messier 2.50 6.00

2003-04 Pacific Invincible Retail

*1-100 VETS: .4X TO 1X HOBBY
*101-125 ROOKIES: .25X TO .6X
67 Mark Messier .60 1.50

2003-04 Pacific Invincible Afterburners

STAT.ODDS 1:41 HBBY/1:49 RETAIL
1 Ilya Kovalchuk 1.25 3.00
2 Paul Kariya .75 2.00
3 Teemu Selanne .75 2.00
4 Mike Modano 1.25 3.00
5 Henrik Zetterberg 1.00 2.50
6 Marian Gaborik 1.25 3.00
7 Pavel Bure .75 2.00
8 Marian Hossa .75 2.00
9 Martin St. Louis .75 2.00
10 Markus Naslund .75 2.00

2003-04 Pacific Invincible Featured Performers

COMPLETE SET (30) 10.00 25.00
STAT.ODDS 1:11 HBBY/1:25 RETAIL
1 Jean-Sebastien Giguere .40 1.00
2 Dany Heatley .75 2.00
3 Joe Thornton 1.00 2.50
4 Miroslav Satan .40 1.00
5 Jarome Iginla .50 1.25
6 Ron Francis .40 1.00
7 Jocelyn Thibault .40 1.00
8 Peter Forsberg 1.50 4.00
9 Rick Nash .75 2.00
10 Mike Modano 1.00 2.50
11 Steve Yzerman 2.00 5.00
12 Ales Hemsky .40 1.00
13 Olli Jokinen .40 1.00
14 Ziggy Palffy .40 1.00
15 Marian Gaborik 1.25 3.00
16 Jose Theodore .50 1.25
17 David Legwand .40 1.00
18 Martin Brodeur 1.50 4.00
19 Michael Peca .40 1.00
20 Eric Lindros .40 1.00
21 Jason Spezza .75 2.00
22 Jeremy Roenick .50 1.25
23 Sean Burke .40 1.00
24 Mario Lemieux 2.50 6.00
25 Pavol Demitra .40 1.00
26 Patrick Marleau .40 1.00
27 Vincent Lecavalier .40 1.00
28 Mats Sundin .40 1.00
29 Todd Bertuzzi .40 1.00
30 Jaromir Jagr 1.00 2.50

2003-04 Pacific Invincible Freeze Frame

COMPLETE SET (24) 10.00 20.00
STAT.ODDS 1:11/1:25 RETAIL
1 Jean-Sebastien Giguere .30 .75
2 Ryan Miller .60 1.50
3 Jocelyn Thibault .30 .75
4 Patrick Roy 2.00 5.00
5 Marc Denis .30 .75
6 Marty Turco .30 .75
7 Dominik Hasek 1.00 2.50
8 Roberto Luongo .60 1.50
9 Roman Cechmanek .30 .75
10 Jose Theodore .50 1.25
11 Tomas Vokoun .30 .75
12 Martin Brodeur 1.50 4.00
13 Rick DiPietro .30 .75
14 Garth Snow .30 .75
15 Mike Dunham .30 .75
16 Patrick Lalime .30 .75
17 Sean Burke .30 .75
18 Chris Osgood .30 .75
19 Evgeni Nabokov .30 .75
20 John Grahame .30 .75
21 Nikolai Khabibulin .30 .75
22 Ed Belfour .40 1.00
23 Dan Cloutier .30 .75
24 Olaf Kolzig .30 .75

2003-04 Pacific Invincible Jerseys

STATED ODDS 1:11 HOB/1:25 RET
1 Byron Dafoe 2.50 6.00
2 Milan Hnilicka 2.50 6.00
3 Martin Biron 2.50 6.00
4 Jamie McLennan 2.50 6.00
5 Roman Turek 3.00 8.00
6 Patrick Roy SP 12.00 30.00
7 Fred Brathwaite SP 4.00 10.00
8 Marc Denis 3.00 8.00
9 Ron Tugnutt 3.00 8.00
10 Marty Turco 3.00 8.00
11 Dominik Hasek SP 10.00 25.00
12 Curtis Joseph 4.00 10.00
13 Roman Cechmanek 2.50 6.00
14 Felix Potvin 5.00 12.00
15 Manny Fernandez 3.00 8.00
16 Jose Theodore 4.00 10.00
17 Tomas Vokoun 3.00 8.00
18 Martin Brodeur 8.00 20.00
19 Rick DiPietro 4.00 10.00
20 Mike Richter 3.00 8.00
21 Patrick Lalime 2.50 6.00
22 Jeff Hackett 2.50 6.00
23 Sean Burke 3.00 8.00
24 Johan Hedberg 3.00 8.00
25 Brent Johnson 2.50 6.00
26 Chris Osgood 3.00 8.00
27 Miikka Kiprusoff 4.00 10.00
28 Evgeni Nabokov 4.00 10.00
29 Nikolai Khabibulin 3.00 8.00
30 Ed Belfour SP 6.00 15.00
31 Dan Cloutier 3.00 8.00
32 Olaf Kolzig 4.00 10.00

2003-04 Pacific Invincible New Sensations

STAT.ODDS 1:21 HBBY/1:49 RETAIL
1 Stanislav Chistov .60 1.50
2 Dany Heatley 1.25 3.00
3 Ilya Kovalchuk 1.25 3.00
4 Ales Kotalik .60 1.50
5 Ryan Miller .75 2.00
6 Chuck Kobasew .60 1.50
7 Jordan Leopold .60 1.50
8 Tyler Arnason .60 1.50
9 Rick Nash 1.00 2.50
10 Pavel Datsyuk .75 2.00
11 Henrik Zetterberg 1.00 2.50
12 Ales Hemsky .60 1.50
13 Jay Bouwmeester .60 1.50
14 Alexander Frolov .60 1.50
15 Marcel Hossa .60 1.50
16 Rick DiPietro .60 1.50
17 Mattias Weinhandl .60 1.50
18 Jason Spezza 1.00 2.50
19 Barret Jackman .60 1.50
20 Jonathan Cheechoo .75 2.00

2003-04 Pacific Invincible Top Line

STATED ODDS 1:41 HOBBY
1 Sergei Fedorov 1.50 3.00
2 Peter Forsberg 2.00 5.00
3 Paul Kariya 1.00 2.50
4 Joe Sakic 2.00 5.00
5 Brett Hull 1.25 3.00
6 Steve Yzerman 3.00 8.00
7 Marian Gaborik 2.00 5.00
8 Mario Lemieux 4.00 10.00
9 Markus Naslund 1.00 2.50
10 Jaromir Jagr 1.50 4.00

2002 Pacific Les Gardiens

This 7-card set was available via a wrapper redemption at the Pacific booth during the Montreal show in October 2002. Each card was serial-numbered to just 199 copies. A gold parallel was also created and available randomly.

COMPLETE SET (7) 30.00
*GOLD/99: .6X TO 1.5X BASIC CARDS
1 Jean-Sebastien Giguere 2.00 5.00
2 Jocelyn Thibault 2.00 3.00
3 Patrick Roy 4.80 10.00
4 Roberto Luongo 2.00 5.00
5 Jose Theodore 3.20 5.00
6 Martin Brodeur 4.00 8.00
7 Patrick Lalime 2.00 3.00

2003-04 Pacific Luxury Suite

This mostly memorabilia set consisted of 23 veteran cards with up to 4 versions of each player; 25 dual-player cards with as many as 4 versions of each card; 30 short-printed rookie cards and 20 short-printed rookie cards that carried certified autographs and memorabilia swatches. Single player stick/blade cards were serial-numbered out of 20 and single player patch/blade cards were serial-numbered out of 10. Dual-player jerseys were serial-numbered out of 650 (unless otherwise noted below); dual-player patch cards were serial-numbered out of 100 (unless otherwise noted); dual-player blade cards were serial-numbered out of 10 and dual-player patch/blade cards were serial-numbered out of 10. Rookie cards #51-80 were serial-numbered out of 599 and rookie autograph/memorabilia cards #81-100 were serial numbered out of 299.

1A Sergei Fedorov J/S-150 12.50 30.00
1B Sergei Fedorov J/P-100 15.00 40.00
1C Sergei Fedorov S/B
1D Sergei Fedorov P/B
2A Ilya Kovalchuk J/S-300 12.50 30.00
2B Ilya Kovalchuk J/P-100 15.00 40.00
2C Ilya Kovalchuk S/B
2D Ilya Kovalchuk P/B
3A Jarome Iginla J/S-150 15.00 40.00
3B Jarome Iginla J/P-100 20.00 50.00
3C Jarome Iginla S/B
3D Jarome Iginla P/B
4A Ron Francis P/S-65 30.00 80.00
4B Ron Francis S/B
4C Ron Francis P/B
5A Peter Forsberg J/S-150 15.00 40.00
5B Peter Forsberg J/P-100 20.00 50.00
5C Peter Forsberg S/B
5D Peter Forsberg P/B
6A Joe Sakic J/S-300 15.00 30.00
6B Joe Sakic J/P-100 20.00 50.00
6C Joe Sakic S/B
6D Joe Sakic P/B
7A Marc Denis P/S-175 12.50 30.00
7B Marc Denis S/B
7C Marc Denis P/B
8A Mike Modano J/S-150 15.00 40.00
8B Mike Modano J/P-100 15.00 40.00
8C Mike Modano S/B
8D Mike Modano P/B
9A Dominik Hasek P/S-30 50.00 100.00
9B Dominik Hasek S/B-20 50.00 100.00
9C Dominik Hasek P/B
10A Steve Yzerman J/S-150 30.00 80.00
10B Steve Yzerman J/P-100 30.00 80.00
10C Steve Yzerman S/B
10D Steve Yzerman P/B
11A Ziggy Palffy J/S-150 8.00 20.00
11B Ziggy Palffy J/P-100 12.50 30.00
11C Ziggy Palffy S/B
11D Ziggy Palffy P/B
12A Jose Theodore J/S-300 15.00 40.00
12B Jose Theodore J/P-100 20.00 50.00
12C Jose Theodore S/B
12D Jose Theodore P/B
13A Martin Brodeur J/S-300 15.00 40.00
13B Martin Brodeur J/P-100 25.00 60.00
13C Martin Brodeur S/B
13D Martin Brodeur P/B
14A Jason Spezza J/S-300 10.00 25.00
14B Jason Spezza J/P-50 25.00 60.00
14C Jason Spezza S/B
14D Jason Spezza P/B
15A Mike Comrie J/S-300 6.00 15.00
15B Mike Comrie J/P-50 10.00 25.00
15C Mike Comrie S/B
15D Mike Comrie P/B
16A Mario Lemieux J/S-100 30.00 80.00
16B Mario Lemieux S/B
16C Mario Lemieux P/B
17A Nikolai Khabibulin J/S-150 12.50 30.00
17B Nikolai Khabibulin J/P-50 25.00 60.00
17C Nikolai Khabibulin S/B
17D Nikolai Khabibulin P/B
18A Vincent Lecavalier J/S-100 15.00 40.00
18B Vincent Lecavalier J/P-50 25.00 60.00
18C Vincent Lecavalier S/B
18D Vincent Lecavalier P/B
19A Ed Belfour J/S-300 12.50 30.00
19B Ed Belfour J/P-50 15.00 40.00
19C Ed Belfour S/B
19D Ed Belfour P/B
20A Mats Sundin J/S-300 12.00 30.00
20B Mats Sundin J/P-50 15.00 40.00
20C Mats Sundin S/B
20D Mats Sundin P/B
21A Todd Bertuzzi J/S-300 12.50 30.00
21B Todd Bertuzzi J/P-50 20.00 50.00
21C Todd Bertuzzi S/B
21D Todd Bertuzzi P/B
22A Markus Naslund J/S-300 8.00 20.00
22B Markus Naslund J/P-50 15.00 40.00
22C Markus Naslund S/B
22D Markus Naslund P/B
23A Olaf Kolzig J/S-150 6.00 15.00
23B Olaf Kolzig J/P-50 15.00 40.00
23C Olaf Kolzig S/B
23D Olaf Kolzig P/B
24A S.Fedorov/J.Giguere J/J 8.00 20.00
24B S.Fedorov/J.Giguere P/P 12.50 30.00
24C S.Fedorov/J.Giguere P/B
25A Kovalchuk/Heatley J/J-475 10.00 25.00
25B Kovalchuk/Heatley P/P-50 30.00 80.00
25C Kovalchuk/Heatley B/B
26A J.Thornton/S.Samsonov J/J 8.00 20.00
26B J.Thornton/S.Samsonov P/P 15.00 40.00
26C J.Thornton/S.Samsonov J/S 12.50 30.00
26D J.Thornton/S.Samsonov P/B
27A R.Miller/A.Kotalik J/J 8.00 20.00
27B R.Miller/A.Kotalik P/P 15.00 40.00
28A P.Forsberg/J.Sakic J/J 10.00 25.00
28B P.Forsberg/J.Sakic P/P 40.00 100.00
28C P.Forsberg/J.Sakic B/B
29A P.Kariya/T.Selanne J/J 5.00 12.00
29B P.Kariya/T.Selanne P/P 25.00 60.00
29C P.Kariya/T.Selanne P/B
30A P.Kariya/M.Hejduk J/J 10.00 25.00
30B P.Kariya/M.Hejduk P/P 25.00 60.00
30C P.Kariya/M.Hejduk P/B
31A T.Selanne/D.Aebischer J/J 8.00 20.00
31B T.Selanne/D.Aebischer P/P 15.00 40.00
32A M.Modano/M.Turco J/J 6.00 15.00
32B M.Modano/M.Turco P/P 15.00 40.00
32C M.Modano/M.Turco B/B
33A B.Hull/B. Shanahan J/J 10.00 25.00
33B B.Hull/B. Shanahan P/P 20.00 50.00
33C B.Hull/B. Shanahan P/B
34A C.Chelios/N.Lidstrom P/P 40.00 100.00
34B C.Chelios/N.Lidstrom B/B
35A R.Smyth/A.Hemsky J/J 6.00 15.00
35B R.Smyth/A.Hemsky P/P 25.00 60.00
35C R.Smyth/A.Hemsky P/B
36A Bouwmeester/Luongo J/J 6.00 15.00
36B Bouwmeester/Luongo P/P 20.00 50.00
37A Palffy/Deadmarsh J/J-400 5.00 12.00
37B Palffy/Deadmarsh P/P 12.00 30.00
37C Palffy/Deadmarsh B/B 15.00 40.00
38A S.Koivu/J.Theodore J/J 10.00 25.00
38B S.Koivu/J.Theodore P/P 25.00 60.00
38C S.Koivu/J.Theodore B/B
39A Vokoun/Walker J/J-350 5.00 12.00
39B Vokoun/Walker P/P 15.00 40.00
39C Vokoun/Walker J/S-100 8.00 20.00
39D T.Vokoun/S.Walker P/B
40A M.Brodeur/P.Elias J/J 8.00 20.00
40B M.Brodeur/P.Elias P/P 30.00 80.00
40C M.Brodeur/P.Elias P/B
41A A.Yashin/R.DiPietro J/J 8.00 20.00
41B A.Yashin/R.DiPietro P/P 20.00 50.00
42A Lindros/Leetch J/J 8.00 20.00
42B Lindros/Leetch P/P-75 20.00 50.00
42C Lindros/Leetch B/B
43A M. Hossa/P.Lalime J/J 6.00 15.00
43B M. Hossa/P.Lalime P/P 20.00 50.00
43C M. Hossa/P.Lalime B/B
44A J.Roenick/J.Hackett J/J 8.00 20.00
44B J.Roenick/J.Hackett P/P 15.00 40.00
45A Jackman/Pronger J/J-250 8.00 20.00
45B Jackman/Pronger P/P-50 20.00 50.00
46A D.Weight/C.Osgood J/J 8.00 20.00
46B D.Weight/C.Osgood P/P 20.00 50.00
46C D.Weight/C.Osgood B/B
47A N.Khabibulin/V.Lecavalier J/J 10.00 25.00
47B N.Khabibulin/V.Lecavalier P/P 15.00 40.00
47C N.Khabibulin/V.Lecavalier B/B
48A Sundin/Mogilny J/J-500 6.00 15.00
48B Sundin/Mogilny P/P-25 25.00 60.00
48C Sundin/Mogilny B/B
49A B.Morrison/D.Cloutier J/J 6.00 15.00
49B B.Morrison/D.Cloutier P/P 12.50 30.00
50A J.Jagr/P.Bondra J/J-400 8.00 20.00
50B J.Jagr/P.Bondra P/P 25.00 60.00
50C J.Jagr/P.Bondra B/B
51 Garrett Burnett RC 3.00 8.00
52 Tony Martensson RC 3.00 8.00
53 Sergei Zinovjev RC 3.00 8.00
54 Andrew Peters RC 3.00 8.00
55 Matthew Lombardi RC 3.00 8.00
56 Travis Moen RC 3.00 8.00
57 Pavel Vorobiev RC 3.00 8.00
58 Mikhail Yakubov RC 3.00 8.00
59 Cody McCormick RC 3.00 8.00
60 Dan Fritsche RC 3.00 8.00
61 Kent McDonell RC 3.00 8.00
62 Nikolai Zherdev RC 8.00 20.00
63 Darryl Bootland RC 3.00 8.00
64 Nathan Robinson RC 3.00 8.00
65 Tony Salmelainen RC 3.00 8.00
66 Peter Sarno RC 3.00 8.00
67 Gregory Campbell RC 3.00 8.00
68 Dan Hamhuis RC 3.00 8.00
69 Marek Zidlicky RC 3.00 8.00
70 David Hale RC 3.00 8.00
71 Paul Martin RC 3.00 8.00
72 Dominic Moore RC 3.00 8.00
73 Fredrik Sjostrom RC 3.00 8.00
74 Matt Murley RC 3.00 8.00
75 John Pohl RC 3.00 8.00
76 Tom Preissing RC 3.00 8.00
77 Maxim Kondratiev RC 3.00 8.00
78 Ryan Kesler RC 6.00 15.00
79 Alexander Semin RC 10.00 25.00
80 Rastislav Stana RC 4.00 10.00
81 Joffrey Lupul JSY AU RC 12.00 30.00
82 Patrice Bergeron JSY AU RC 25.00 50.00
83 Brent Krahn PCK AU RC 8.00 20.00
84 Eric Staal PCK AU RC 10.00 25.00
85 Tuomo Ruutu PCK AU RC 10.00 25.00
86 Antti Miettinen JSY AU RC 8.00 20.00
87 Jiri Hudler PCK AU RC 12.00 30.00
88 Nathan Horton PCK AU RC 15.00 40.00
89 Dustin Brown JSY AU RC 15.00 30.00
90 Brent Burns PCK AU RC 12.00 30.00
91 Chris Higgins JSY AU RC 12.50 30.00
92 Jordin Tootoo JSY AU RC 15.00 40.00
93 S.Bergenheim PCK AU RC 8.00 20.00
94 Antoine Vermette JSY AU RC 10.00 25.00
95 Joni Pitkanen JSY AU RC 8.00 20.00
96 M.Fleury PCK AU RC 40.00 80.00
97 Peter Sejna PCK AU RC 8.00 20.00
98 Milan Michalek PCK AU RC 15.00 40.00
99 Matt Stajan PCK AU RC 8.00 20.00
100 Boyd Gordon JSY AU RC 8.00 20.00

2003 Pacific Montreal International

This set was issued at the Spring 2003 Montreal show as a wrapper redemption by Pacific. The cards feature members of the Montreal Canadiens on one side and Montreal Alouettes on the other.

COMPLETE SET (6) 15.00
1 Saku Koivu 2.00 5.00
Anthony Calvillo
2 Jose Theodore 2.00 5.00
Jermaine Copeland
3 Yanic Perreault .75 2.00
Ben Cahoon
4 Richard Zednik .75 2.00
Eric Lapointe
5 Jan Bulis .75 2.00
Bruno Heppell
6 Patrice Brisebois .75 2.00
Kevin Johnson

2003 Pacific Montreal Olympic Stadium Show

Serial-numbered to 299, this 8-card set was available via wrapper redemption at the Pacific booth during the 2003 Spring " Collections Sport et Jouet" in Montreal at the Olympic Stadium. A gold version was also created and numbered to 99.

COMPLETE SET (8) 15.00 40.00
*GOLD/99: .8X TO 2X BASIC CARDS
1 Stanislav Chistov 1.25 3.00
2 Pascal Leclaire 1.25 3.00
3 Rick Nash 4.00 10.00
4 Henrik Zetterberg 4.00 10.00
5 Jay Bouwmeester 2.50 6.00
6 Alexander Frolov 1.25 3.00
7 Ron Hainsey 1.25 3.00
8 Jason Spezza 4.00 10.00

2004 Pacific Montreal International

Available via redemption only at the 2004 Montreal International show, this 8-card set featured promising prospects.

COMPLETE SET (8) 6.00 15.00
STATED PRINT RUN 499 SER.#'d SETS
*GOLD: 2X TO 4X BASIC CARDS
GOLD PRINT RUN 99 SER.#'d SETS
1 Patrice Bergeron 1.50 4.00
2 Eric Staal .75 2.00
3 Nathan Horton .75 2.00
4 Chris Higgins .40 1.00
5 Jordin Tootoo .75 2.00
6 Antoine Vermette .40 1.00
7 Joni Pitkanen .75 2.00
8 Marc-Andre Fleury 1.50 4.00

2004 Pacific NHL All-Star FANtasy

This 10-card set was available via wrapper redemption at the Pacific booth during the 2004 NHL All-Star FANtasy. Cards were serial-numbered out of 499.

COMPLETE SET (10) 8.00 20.00
1 Joffrey Lupul .60 1.50
2 Patrice Bergeron 1.50 4.00
3 Eric Staal 1.00 2.50
4 Jiri Hudler .75 2.00
5 Brent Burns .60 1.50
6 Jordin Tootoo 1.00 2.50
7 Joni Pitkanen .75 2.00
8 Marc-Andre Fleury 1.50 4.00
9 Peter Sejna .40 1.00
10 Matt Stajan .75 2.00

2004 Pacific NHL All-Star Nets

These cards were available via redemption at the Pacific booth during the 2004 NHL All-Star FANtasy. Cards were serial-numbered out of 499. A gold parallel was also created and available randomly.
*GOLD: 1X TO 2.5X BASIC CARDS
GOLD PRINT RUN 99 SER.#'d SETS
1 Eastern Team 12.50 30.00
Joe Thornton
Martin Brodeur
Marian
2 Western Team 15.00 25.00
Mike Modano
Marty Turco
Marian Gab

2004 Pacific NHL Draft All-Star Nets

Available via wrapper redemption at the Pacific booth during the 2004 NHL Draft, this 3-card set features pieces of netting from the 2004 All-Star game. Each card was serial numbered out of 250.
COMPLETE SET (3) 60.00 125.00
1 I.Kovalchuk 20.00 50.00
R.Nash
2 M.St.Louis 15.00 40.00
J.Sakic
3 M.Turco 20.00 50.00
M.Brodeur

2004 Pacific NHL Draft Show Calder Reflections

COMPLETE SET (8)
1 Joffrey Lupul .75 2.00
2 Patrice Bergeron 1.50 4.00
3 Andrew Raycroft 1.25 3.00
4 Eric Staal .75 2.00
5 Michael Ryder .75 2.00
6 Trent Hunter .40 1.00
7 Marc-Andre Fleury 1.50 4.00
8 Ryan Malone .40 1.00

1997-98 Pacific Omega

The 1997-98 Pacific Omega set was issued in one series totaling 250 cards and was distributed in six-card packs with a suggested retail price of $1.99. The fronts feature color action photos etched in foil of players who are popular with fans. The backs carry another photo and the player's accomplishments.
COMPLETE SET (250) 12.00 30.00
1 Matt Cullen RC .12 .30
2 Guy Hebert .12 .30
3 Paul Kariya .20 .50
4 Dmitri Mironov .12 .30
5 Steve Rucchin .12 .30
6 Tomas Sandstrom .10 .25
7 Teemu Selanne .30 .75
8 Mikhail Shtalenkov .12 .30
9 Pavel Trnka .10 .25
10 Jason Allison .12 .30
11 Per Axelsson .15 .40
12 Ray Bourque .25 .60
13 Anson Carter .10 .25
14 Byron Dafoe .10 .25
15 Ted Donato .10 .25
16 Hal Gill RC .10 .25
17 Dimitri Khristich .12 .30
18 Sergei Samsonov .10 .25
19 Joe Thornton .15 .40
20 Jason Dawe .12 .30
21 Michal Grosek .10 .25
22 Dominik Hasek .25 .60
23 Brian Holzinger .12 .30
24 Michael Peca .12 .30
25 Derek Plante .12 .30
26 Miroslav Satan .10 .25
27 Steve Shields RC .15 .40
28 Andrew Cassels .10 .25
29 Theo Fleury .20 .50
30 Jarome Iginla .15 .40
31 Derek Morris RC .15 .40
32 Tyler Moss RC .12 .30
33 Michael Nylander .12 .30
34 Dwayne Roloson .12 .30
35 Cory Stillman .12 .30
36 Rick Tabaracci .12 .30
37 German Titov .10 .25
38 Bates Battaglia RC .12 .30
39 Nelson Emerson .12 .30
40 Martin Gelinas .10 .25
41 Sami Kapanen .12 .30
42 Trevor Kidd .10 .25
43 Kevin Dineen .12 .30
44 Keith Primeau .12 .30
45 Gary Roberts .12 .30
46 Tony Amonte .12 .30
47 Keith Carney .10 .25
48 Chris Chelios .15 .40
49 Eric Daze .10 .25
50 Brian Felsner .10 .25
51 Jeff Hackett .10 .25
52 Christian LaFlamme RC .15 .40
53 Alexei Zhamnov .10 .25
54 Craig Billington .10 .25
55 Adam Deadmarsh .10 .25
56 Peter Forsberg .20 .50
57 Valeri Kamensky .12 .30
58 Uwe Krupp .10 .25
59 Jari Kurri .15 .40
60 Claude Lemieux .12 .30
61 Eric Messier RC .15 .40
62 Jeff Odgers .10 .25
63 Sandis Ozolinsh .12 .30
64 Patrick Roy .40 1.00
65 Joe Sakic .25 .60
66 Greg Adams .12 .30
67 Ed Belfour .15 .40
68 Manny Fernandez .10 .25
69 Derian Hatcher .12 .30
70 Jamie Langenbrunner .12 .30
71 Jere Lehtinen .12 .30
72 Juha Lind RC .15 .40
73 Mike Modano .25 .60
74 Joe Nieuwendyk .15 .40
75 Darryl Sydor .10 .25
76 Pat Verbeek .12 .30
77 Sergei Zubov .12 .30
78 Slava Fetisov .10 .25
79 Brent Gilchrist .15 .40
80 Kevin Hodson .12 .30
81 Vyacheslav Kozlov .12 .30
82 Igor Larionov .10 .25
83 Nicklas Lidstrom .15 .40
84 Darren McCarty .12 .30
85 Larry Murphy .15 .40
86 Chris Osgood .15 .40
87 Brendan Shanahan .20 .50
88 Steve Yzerman .30 .75
89 Kelly Buchberger .12 .30
90 Mike Grier .12 .30
91 Bill Guerin .15 .40
92 Roman Hamrlik .12 .30
93 Curtis Joseph .15 .40
94 Boris Mironov .10 .25
95 Ryan Smyth .12 .30
96 Doug Weight .15 .40
97 Dino Ciccarelli .15 .40
98 Dave Gagner .10 .25
99 Ed Jovanovski .10 .25
100 Scott Mellanby .12 .30
101 Robert Svehla .12 .30
102 John Vanbiesbrouck .15 .40
103 Steve Washburn .10 .25
104 Kevin Weekes RC .12 .30
105 Ray Whitney .12 .30
106 Rob Blake .15 .40
107 Stephane Fiset .12 .30
108 Garry Galley .10 .25
109 Steve McKenna RC .20 .50
110 Glen Murray .10 .25
111 Yanic Perreault .12 .30
112 Luc Robitaille .15 .40
113 Jamie Storr .12 .30
114 Jozef Stumpel .12 .30
115 Vladimir Tsyplakov .12 .30
116 Shayne Corson .10 .25
117 Vincent Damphousse .12 .30
118 Saku Koivu .15 .40
119 Vladimir Malakhov .10 .25
120 Andy Moog .15 .40
121 Mark Recchi .20 .50
122 Martin Rucinsky .12 .30
123 Brian Savage .10 .25
124 Jocelyn Thibault .10 .25
125 Jason Arnott .12 .30
126 Brad Bombardir RC .12 .30
127 Martin Brodeur .30 .75
128 Patrik Elias RC .25 .60
129 Doug Gilmour .20 .50
130 Bobby Holik .10 .25
131 Randy McKay .12 .30
132 Scott Niedermayer .15 .40
133 Krzysztof Oliwa RC .15 .40
134 Scott Stevens .15 .40
135 Petr Sykora .10 .25
136 Bryan Berard .10 .25
137 Travis Green .12 .30
138 Bryan McCabe .10 .25
139 Sergei Nemchinov .10 .25
140 Zigmund Palffy .15 .40
141 Robert Reichel .12 .30
142 Tommy Salo .10 .25
143 Bryan Smolinski .12 .30
144 Adam Graves .10 .25
145 Wayne Gretzky .75 2.00
146 Pat LaFontaine .15 .40
147 Brian Leetch .15 .40
148 Mike Richter .15 .40
149 Kevin Stevens .10 .25
150 Niklas Sundstrom .12 .30
151 Tim Sweeney .10 .25
152 Daniel Alfredsson .15 .40
153 Magnus Arvedson .15 .40
154 Andreas Dackell .12 .30
155 Igor Kravchuk .10 .25
156 Shawn McEachern .10 .25
157 Damian Rhodes .12 .30
158 Ron Tugnutt .15 .40
159 Alexei Yashin .12 .30
160 Rod Brind'Amour .15 .40
161 Paul Coffey .15 .40
162 Eric Desjardins .10 .25
163 Colin Forbes .15 .40
164 Chris Gratton .10 .25
165 Ron Hextall .15 .40
166 Trent Klatt .12 .30
167 John LeClair .15 .40
168 Eric Lindros .25 .60
169 Joel Otto .10 .25
170 Garth Snow .12 .30
171 Dainius Zubrus .12 .30
172 Dallas Drake .12 .30
173 Mike Gartner .15 .40
174 Nikolai Khabibulin .15 .40
175 Teppo Numminen .12 .30
176 Jeremy Roenick .20 .50
177 Keith Tkachuk .15 .40
178 Rick Tocchet .10 .25
179 Oleg Tverdovsky .12 .30
180 Juha Ylonen .12 .30
181 Stu Barnes .10 .25
182 Tom Barrasso .12 .30
183 Rob Brown .12 .30
184 Ron Francis .20 .50
185 Kevin Hatcher .10 .25
186 Jaromir Jagr .40 1.00
187 Alexei Morozov .12 .30
188 Ed Olczyk .10 .25
189 Jim Campbell .10 .25
190 Geoff Courtnall .10 .25
191 Pavol Demitra .20 .50
192 Steve Duchesne .10 .25
193 Grant Fuhr .15 .40
194 Brett Hull .20 .50
195 Al MacInnis .15 .40
196 Chris Pronger .12 .30
197 Pascal Rheaume RC .12 .30
198 Jamie Rivers .12 .30
199 Pierre Turgeon .15 .40
200 Jeff Friesen .12 .30
201 Tony Granato .12 .30
202 John MacLean .10 .25
203 Patrick Marleau .20 .50
204 Marty McSorley .10 .25
205 Owen Nolan .15 .40
206 Marco Sturm RC .15 .40
207 Mike Vernon .12 .30
208 Andrei Zyuzin RC .10 .25
209 Karl Dykhuis .10 .25
210 Daymond Langkow .10 .25
211 Louie DeBrusk .10 .25
212 Daren Puppa .12 .30
213 Mikael Renberg .12 .30
214 Alexander Selivanov .10 .25
215 Paul Ysebaert .12 .30
216 Rob Zamuner .10 .25
217 Sergei Berezin .12 .30
218 Wendel Clark .15 .40
219 Marcel Cousineau .12 .30
220 Tie Domi .15 .40
221 Mike Johnson RC .12 .30
222 Igor Korolev .10 .25
223 Felix Potvin .15 .40
224 Mathieu Schneider .12 .30
225 Mats Sundin .15 .40
226 Yannick Tremblay RC .12 .30
227 Donald Brashear .12 .30
228 Pavel Bure .20 .50
229 Sean Burke .10 .25
230 Trevor Linden .12 .30
231 Mark Messier .25 .60
232 Alexander Mogilny .12 .30
233 Markus Naslund .12 .30
234 Mattias Ohlund .12 .30
235 Dave Scatchard RC .12 .30
236 Peter Bondra .12 .30
237 Andrew Brunette .12 .30
238 Phil Housley .12 .30
239 Dale Hunter .12 .30
240 Calle Johansson .12 .30
241 Joe Juneau .12 .30
242 Olaf Kolzig .12 .30
243 Adam Oates .15 .40
244 Richard Zednik .12 .30
245 Chris Chelios .15 .40
Keith Tkachuk
246 Mike Modano .25 .60
Ed Belfour
247 Teemu Selanne .30 .75
Saku Koivu
248 Eric Lindros .25 .60
Shayne Corson
249 Patrick Roy .40 1.00
Martin Brodeur
250 Wayne Gretzky .75 2.00
Mark Messier
NNO Mike Modano SAMPLE .25 .60

1997-98 Pacific Omega Copper

Inserted one in every hobby pack, this 250-card set is parallel to the base set with copper foil highlights.
*COPPER: 2X TO 5X BASIC CARDS
*COPPER ROOKIE STAR: 1.2X TO 3X

1997-98 Pacific Omega Dark Gray

Inserted one in every Canadian retail pack, this 250-card set is parallel to the base set with dark gray foil highlights.
*DARK GRAY: 2X TO 5X BASIC CARDS
*DARK GRAY ROOKIE STAR: 1.2X TO 3X

1997-98 Pacific Omega Emerald Green

Inserted one in every Canadian pack only, this 250-card set is parallel to the base set with green foil highlights.
*GREEN: 2X TO 5X BASIC CARDS
*GREEN ROOKIE STAR: 1.2X TO 3X

1997-98 Pacific Omega Gold

Inserted one in every U.S. retail pack only, this 250-card set is parallel to the base set with gold foil highlights.
*GOLD: 2X TO 5X BASIC CARDS
*GOLD ROOKIE STAR: 1.2X TO 3X BASIC CARDS

1997-98 Pacific Omega Ice Blue

Randomly inserted in both Canadian and U.S. hobby and retail packs at the rate of 1:73, this 250-card set is parallel to the base set with blue foil highlights.
*ICE BLUE VETS: 10X TO 25X BASIC CARDS
*ICE BLUE ROOKIE STAR: 6X TO 15X

1997-98 Pacific Omega Game Face

Randomly inserted in hobby and retail packs at the rate of 1:37, this 20-card set features color photos of top goalies printed on die-cut helmet-shaped cards with a cel facemask. The backs carry player information and describe his talents as a goalie.
COMPLETE SET (20) 12.00 30.00
1 Paul Kariya .60 1.50
2 Teemu Selanne .60 1.50
3 Peter Forsberg 1.50 4.00
4 Joe Sakic 2.00 5.00
5 Mike Modano 1.25 3.00
6 Nicklas Lidstrom .60 1.50
7 Brendan Shanahan .60 1.50
8 Steve Yzerman 3.00 8.00
9 Ryan Smyth .50 1.25
10 Saku Koivu .60 1.50
11 Wayne Gretzky 4.00 10.00
12 John LeClair .60 1.50
13 Eric Lindros 1.25 3.00
14 Dainius Zubrus .60 1.50
15 Keith Tkachuk .60 1.50
16 Jaromir Jagr 1.25 3.00
17 Brett Hull .75 2.00
18 Pavel Bure .60 1.50
19 Mark Messier .60 1.50
20 Peter Bondra .50 1.25

1997-98 Pacific Omega No Scoring Zone

COMPLETE SET (10) 6.00 12.00
STATED ODDS 2:37
1 Dominik Hasek 1.00 2.50
2 Patrick Roy 2.50 6.00
3 Ed Belfour .50 1.25
4 Chris Osgood .40 1.00
5 John Vanbiesbrouck .40 1.00
6 Andy Moog .40 1.00
7 Martin Brodeur 1.25 3.00
8 Mike Richter .50 1.25
9 Ron Hextall .40 1.00
10 Felix Potvin .50 1.25

1997-98 Pacific Omega Silks

Randomly inserted in hobby and retail packs at the rate of 1:73, this 12-card set features color photos of top players printed on a silk-like fabric card stock.
COMPLETE SET (12) 30.00 60.00
1 Paul Kariya 1.25 3.00
2 Teemu Selanne 2.50 6.00
3 Peter Forsberg 3.00 8.00
4 Patrick Roy 6.00 15.00
5 Joe Sakic 2.50 6.00
6 Steve Yzerman 6.00 15.00
7 Martin Brodeur 3.00 8.00
8 Wayne Gretzky 8.00 20.00
9 Eric Lindros 1.25 3.00
10 Jaromir Jagr 2.00 5.00
11 Pavel Bure 1.25 3.00
12 Mark Messier 1.25 3.00

1997-98 Pacific Omega Stick Handle Laser Cuts

Randomly inserted in hobby and retail packs at the rate of 1:145, this 20-card set features color photos of popular players printed on full foil card stock with laser-cut hockey sticks crossing in the background. The backs carry a description of the player's accomplishments on ice.
COMPLETE SET (20) 60.00 120.00
1 Paul Kariya 5.00 12.00
2 Teemu Selanne 6.00 15.00
3 Theo Fleury 2.00 5.00
4 Chris Chelios 2.00 5.00
5 Peter Forsberg 6.00 15.00
6 Joe Sakic 4.00 10.00
7 Mike Modano 3.00 8.00
8 Brendan Shanahan 2.00 5.00
9 Steve Yzerman 12.50 30.00
10 Saku Koivu 2.00 5.00
11 Doug Gilmour 2.00 5.00
12 Zigmund Palffy 2.00 5.00
13 Wayne Gretzky 15.00 40.00
14 Pat LaFontaine 2.00 5.00
15 John LeClair 2.00 5.00
16 Eric Lindros 2.00 5.00
17 Jaromir Jagr 3.00 8.00
18 Mats Sundin 2.00 5.00
19 Pavel Bure 2.00 5.00
20 Mark Messier 2.00 5.00

1997-98 Pacific Omega Team Leaders

COMPLETE SET (20) 15.00 30.00
STATED ODDS 2:48 CANADIAN PACKS
1 Paul Kariya .50 1.25
2 Ray Bourque .75 2.00
3 Theo Fleury .20 .50
4 Patrick Roy 2.50 6.00
5 Joe Sakic 1.00 2.50
6 Ed Belfour .50 1.25
7 Joe Nieuwendyk .40 1.00
8 Brendan Shanahan .50 1.25
9 Steve Yzerman 2.50 6.00
10 Ryan Smyth .40 1.00
11 Shayne Corson .20 .50
12 Mark Recchi .40 1.00
13 Martin Brodeur 1.25 3.00
14 Wayne Gretzky 3.00 8.00
15 Rod Brind'Amour .40 1.00
16 Eric Lindros .50 1.25
17 Chris Pronger .40 1.00
18 Felix Potvin .50 1.25
19 Pavel Bure .50 1.25
20 Mark Messier .50 1.25

1998-99 Pacific Omega

The 1998-99 Pacific Omega set was issued in one series totaling 250 cards and was distributed in six-card packs with a suggested retail price of $1.99. The fronts feature color action photos of the NHL's greatest stars and most exciting rookies printed on etched silver foil cards. The backs carry player information and career statistics.
COMPLETE SET (252) 40.00 80.00
COMP.SET w/o SP's (1-250) 30.00 60.00
1 Travis Green .05 .15
2 Stu Grimson .05 .15
3 Guy Hebert .10 .30
4 Paul Kariya .15 .40
5 Marty McInnis .05 .15
6 Fredrik Olausson .05 .15
7 Steve Rucchin .05 .15
8 Teemu Selanne .15 .40
9 Johan Davidsson .15 .40
Antti Aalto
10 Jason Allison .05 .15
11 Ken Belanger .05 .15
12 Ray Bourque .25 .60
13 Anson Carter .10 .30
14 Byron Dafoe .10 .30
15 Steve Heinze .05 .15
16 Dimitri Khristich .05 .15
17 Sergei Samsonov .10 .30
18 Robbie Tallas .10 .30
19 Joe Thornton .25 .60
20 Matthew Barnaby .10 .30
21 Curtis Brown .05 .15
22 Michal Grosek .05 .15
23 Domink Hasek .30 .75
24 Brian Holzinger .10 .30
25 Micael Peca .10 .30
26 Rob Ray .05 .15
27 Geoff Sanderson .10 .30
28 Miroslav Satan .10 .30
29 Dixon Ward .05 .15
30 Valeri Bure .05 .15
31 Theo Fleury .05 .15
32 Jean-Sebastien Giguere .10 .30
33 Jarome Iginla .20 .50
34 Tyler Moss .05 .15
35 Cory Stillman .05 .15
36 Jason Wiemer .05 .15
37 Clarke Wilm RC .05 .15
38 M.St.Louis RC/R.Fata 2.00 5.00
39 Paul Coffey .15 .40
40 Ron Francis .10 .30
41 Martin Gelinas .05 .15
42 Arturs Irbe .10 .30
43 Sami Kapanen .05 .15
44 Trevor Kidd .10 .30
45 Keith Primeau .05 .15
46 Gary Roberts .05 .15
47 Ray Sheppard .10 .30
48 Tony Amonte .10 .30
49 Chris Chelios .15 .40
50 Eric Daze .10 .30
51 Nelson Emerson .05 .15
52 Doug Gilmour .10 .30
53 Mike Maneluk RC .05 .15
54 Bob Probert .05 .15
55 Jocelyn Thibault .10 .30
56 Alexei Zhamnov .05 .15
57 Todd White RC .05 .15
Brad Brown
58 Adam Deadmarsh .05 .15
59 Marc Denis .10 .30
60 Peter Forsberg .40 1.00
61 Claude Lemieux .05 .15
62 Jeff Odgers .05 .15
63 Sandis Ozolinsh .05 .15
64 Patrick Roy .75 2.00
65 Joe Sakic .30 .75
66 Wade Belak RC .10 .30
Scott Parker
67 C.Drury/M.Hejduk RC 2.00 5.00
68 Ed Belfour .15 .40
69 Derian Hatcher .05 .15
70 Brett Hull .20 .50
71 Jamie Langenbrunner .05 .15
72 Jere Lehtinen .10 .30
73 Mike Modano .25 .60
74 Joe Nieuwendyk .10 .30
75 Darryl Sydor .05 .15
76 Roman Turek .10 .30
77 Sergei Zubov .05 .15
78 Sergei Gusev RC .05 .15
Jamie Wright
79 Sergei Fedorov .25 .60
80 Joey Kocur .05 .15
81 Martin LaPointe .05 .15
82 Igor Larionov .05 .15
83 Nicklas Lidstrom .15 .40
84 Darren McCarty .05 .15
85 Larry Murphy .10 .30
86 Chris Osgood .10 .30
87 Brendan Shanahan .15 .40
88 Steve Yzerman .75 2.00
89 N.Maracle RC/S.Roest RC .25 .60
90 Josef Beranek .05 .15
91 Sean Brown .05 .15
92 Bill Guerin .10 .30
93 Roman Hamrlik .05 .15
94 Janne Niinimaa .05 .15
95 Mikhail Shtalenkov .05 .15
96 Ryan Smyth .10 .30
97 Doug Weight .10 .30
98 Tom Poti .10 .30
Craig Millar
99 Pavel Bure .15 .40
100 Sean Burke .10 .30
101 Dino Ciccarelli .10 .30
102 Bret Hedican .05 .15
103 Viktor Kozlov .05 .15
104 Paul Laus .05 .15
105 Rob Niedermayer .05 .15
106 Mark Parrish RC .10 .30
107 Ray Whitney .05 .15
108 O.Kvasha RC/P.Worrell RC .20 .50
109 Rob Blake .10 .30
110 Stephane Fiset .10 .30
111 Glen Murray .05 .15
112 Luc Robitaille .10 .30
113 Jamie Storr .10 .30
114 Jozef Stumpel .10 .30
115 Vladimir Tsyplakov .05 .15
116 M.Visheau RC .05 .15
J.Green RC
117 Olli Jokinen RC .10 .30
Pavel Rosa
118 Benoit Brunet .05 .15
119 Shayne Corson .10 .30
120 Vincent Damphousse .05 .15
121 Jeff Hackett .10 .30
122 Matt Higgins RC .05 .15
123 Saku Koivu .15 .40
124 Mark Recchi .10 .30
125 Martin Rucinsky .05 .15
126 Brian Savage .05 .15
127 Andrew Brunette .10 .30
128 Mike Dunham .10 .30
129 Greg Johnson .05 .15
130 Sergei Krivokrasov .05 .15
131 Denny Lambert .05 .15
132 Cliff Ronning .05 .15
133 Tomas Vokoun .05 .15
134 Patrick Cote .10 .30
Kimmo Timonen
135 Jason Arnott .05 .15
136 Martin Brodeur .40 1.00
137 Patrik Elias .10 .30
138 Bobby Holik .05 .15
139 Brendan Morrison .10 .30
140 Krzysztof Oliwa .05 .15
141 Brian Rolston .05 .15
142 Vadim Sharifijanov .05 .15
143 Scott Stevens .10 .30
144 Petr Sykora .05 .15
145 Ted Donato .05 .15
146 Kenny Jonsson .05 .15
147 Trevor Linden .10 .30
148 Gino Odjick .05 .15
149 Zigmund Palffy .10 .30
150 Felix Potvin .15 .40
151 Robert Reichel .05 .15
152 Tommy Salo .10 .30
153 Mike Watt .10 .30
Eric Brewer
154 Dan Cloutier .10 .30
155 Adam Graves .05 .15
156 Wayne Gretzky 1.00 2.50
157 Todd Harvey .05 .15
158 Brian Leetch .15 .40
159 Manny Malhotra .10 .30
160 Petr Nedved .10 .30
161 Mike Richter .15 .40
162 Esa Tikkanen .05 .15
163 Daniel Alfredsson .10 .30
164 Marian Hossa .15 .40
165 Andreas Johansson .05 .15
166 Shawn McEachern .05 .15
167 Wade Redden .05 .15
168 Damian Rhodes .10 .30
169 Ron Tugnutt .10 .30
170 Alexei Yashin .05 .15
171 Patrick Traverse RC .05 .15
Sami Salo
172 Rod Brind'Amour .10 .30
173 Eric Desjardins .10 .30
174 Ron Hextall .10 .30
175 Keith Jones .10 .30
176 John LeClair .15 .40
177 Eric Lindros .15 .40
178 Mikael Renberg .10 .30
179 Dimitri Tertyshny RC .05 .15
180 John Vanbiesbrouck .10 .30
181 Dainius Zubrus .05 .15
182 Daniel Briere .05 .15
183 Dallas Drake .05 .15
184 Nikolai Khabibulin .10 .30
185 Jyrki Lumme .05 .15
186 Teppo Numminen .05 .15
187 Jeremy Roenick .20 .50
188 Keith Tkachuk .15 .40
189 Rick Tocchet .10 .30
190 Oleg Tverdovsky .05 .15
191 Jim Waite .10 .30
192 Jean-Sebastien Aubin RC .30 .75
193 Stu Barnes .05 .15
194 Tom Barrasso .10 .30
195 Jaromir Jagr .25 .60
196 Alexei Kovalev .05 .15
197 Robert Lang .05 .15
198 Alexei Morozov .05 .15
199 Martin Straka .05 .15
200 J.Hrdina RC/M.Galanov RC .25 .60
201 Pavol Demitra .10 .30
202 Grant Fuhr .10 .30
203 Al MacInnis .10 .30
204 Jamie McLennan .10 .30
205 Chris Pronger .10 .30
206 Pierre Turgeon .10 .30
207 Tony Twist .05 .15
208 M.Reasoner RC/L.Bartecko .30 .75
209 Jeff Friesen .05 .15
210 Bryan Marchment .05 .15
211 Patrick Marleau .15 .40
212 Owen Nolan .10 .30
213 Mike Ricci .10 .30
214 Steve Shields .10 .30
215 Marco Sturm .10 .30
216 Mike Vernon .10 .30
217 Wendel Clark .10 .30
218 Chris Gratton .05 .15
219 Vincent Lecavalier .50 1.25
220 Sandy McCarthy .05 .15
221 Stephane Richer .10 .30
222 Darcy Tucker .05 .15
223 Rob Zamuner .05 .15
224 P.Kubina RC/Z.Bierk RC .50 1.25
225 Bryan Berard .05 .15
226 Tie Domi .10 .30
227 Mike Johnson .10 .30
228 Curtis Joseph .15 .40
229 Igor Korolev .05 .15
230 Alyn McCauley .05 .15
231 Mats Sundin .15 .40
232 Steve Thomas .05 .15
233 T.Kaberle RC/D.Markov RC .20 .50
234 Adrian Aucoin .05 .15
235 Corey Hirsch .10 .30
236 Mark Messier .15 .40
237 Alexander Mogilny .10 .30
238 Bill Muckalt RC .05 .15
239 Markus Naslund .15 .40
240 Mattias Ohlund .10 .30
241 Garth Snow .10 .30
242 Matt Cooke RC .05 .15
Peter Schaefer
243 Brian Bellows .05 .15
244 Craig Berube .05 .15
245 Peter Bondra .10 .30
246 Matt Herr RC .05 .15
247 Joe Juneau .10 .30
248 Olaf Kolzig .10 .30
249 Adam Oates .10 .30
250 Richard Zednik .05 .15
251 Last Game at MLG SP 2.00 5.00
252 First Game at ACC SP 2.00 5.00
S136 Martin Brodeur SAMPLE .20 .50

1998-99 Pacific Omega Red

Found at a rate of 4:25 Treat packs, this tough insert features red foil on the front as its distinguishing mark.

*VETERANS: 2X TO 5X BASIC CARDS
*ROOKIES: .8X TO 2X BASIC CARDS

1998-99 Pacific Omega Opening Day Issue

Randomly inserted into packs, this 250-card set is parallel to the base set. Only 56 serially numbered sets were made.
*VETERANS: 30X TO 80X BASIC CARDS
*ROOKIES: 8X TO 20X BASIC CARDS

1998-99 Pacific Omega Championship Spotlight

Randomly inserted in special packs at the rate of 1:49, this 10-card set features color action photos of top NHL players with player information on the backs. Three limited edition parallel sets were also produced to be inserted into Treat packs. Only 50 serially numbered Green parallel versions were made, 10 serially numbered Red parallel versions, and one Gold parallel version. Gold parallels not priced due to scarcity.
COMPLETE SET (10) 75.00 150.00
*GREEN/50: 1.5X TO 4X BASIC INSERTS
1 Paul Kariya 4.00 10.00
2 Dominik Hasek 6.00 15.00
3 Patrick Roy 12.00 30.00
4 Steve Yzerman 10.00 25.00
5 Pavel Bure 4.00 10.00
6 Martin Brodeur 8.00 20.00
7 Wayne Gretzky 20.00 50.00
8 Eric Lindros 5.00 12.00
9 Jaromir Jagr 5.00 12.00
10 Curtis Joseph 4.00 10.00

1998-99 Pacific Omega EO Portraits

Randomly inserted into packs at the rate of 1:73, this 20-card set features color player images of some of hockey's biggest superstars printed using Electro-Optical technology to laser-cut the player image into every card. A special one of a kind Hobby only parallel set was also produced with "1/1" laser-cut into each card, they are not priced due to scarcity.
COMPLETE SET (20) 15.00 40.00
1 Paul Kariya .75 2.00
2 Teemu Selanne .75 2.00
3 Dominik Hasek 1.50 4.00
4 Peter Forsberg 2.00 5.00
5 Patrick Roy 4.00 10.00
6 Joe Sakic 1.50 4.00
7 Brett Hull 1.25 3.00
8 Mike Modano 1.25 3.00
9 Sergei Fedorov 1.25 3.00
10 Brendan Shanahan .75 2.00
11 Steve Yzerman 4.00 10.00
12 Pavel Bure .75 2.00
13 Martin Brodeur 2.00 5.00
14 Wayne Gretzky 5.00 12.00
15 John LeClair .75 2.00
16 Eric Lindros .75 2.00
17 Keith Tkachuk .75 2.00
18 Jaromir Jagr 1.25 3.00
19 Mats Sundin .75 2.00
20 Mark Messier .75 2.00

1998-99 Pacific Omega Face to Face

Randomly inserted into packs at the rate of 1:145, this 10-card set features color portraits of top NHL players printed on silver-foiled and etched cards. Two players are matched on every card creating an all-star face-off effect.
COMPLETE SET (10) 75.00 150.00
1 P.Roy/M.Brodeur 12.50 30.00
2 W. Gretzky/P.Kariya 15.00 40.00
3 D.Hasek/J.Jagr 5.00 12.00
4 S.Fedorov/P.Bure 5.00 12.00
5 K.Tkachuk/B.Shanahan 4.00 10.00
6 S.Yzerman/J.Sakic 12.50 30.00
7 T.Selanne/S.Koivu 4.00 10.00
8 P.Forsberg/M.Sundin 10.00 25.00
9 M.Modano/J.LeClair 5.00 12.
10 E.Lindros/M.Messier 4.00 10.

1998-99 Pacific Omega Onlin

Randomly inserted into packs at the rate of 4:37, thi 36-card set features color photos of NHL stars with interesting player facts on the backs. Each card invi fans to learn more about each player and team by logging on to their respective internet sites at www.nhlpa.com and www.nhl.com.
COMPLETE SET (36) 10.00 20.
1 Paul Kariya .20
2 Teemu Selanne .20
3 Ray Bourque .30
4 Dominik Hasek .20
5 Theo Fleury .07
6 Chris Chelios .20
7 Doug Gilmour .15
8 Peter Forsberg .50 1.
9 Patrick Roy 1.00 2.
10 Joe Sakic .40 1.
11 Ed Belfour .20
12 Brett Hull .25
13 Mike Modano .30
14 Sergei Fedorov .30
15 Brendan Shanahan .20
16 Steve Yzerman 1.00 2.
17 Pavel Bure .20
18 Saku Koivu .20
19 Martin Brodeur .50 1.
20 Brendan Morrison .15
21 Zigmund Palffy .15
22 Felix Potvin .20
23 Wayne Gretzky 1.25 3.
24 Alexei Yashin .07
25 John LeClair .20
26 Eric Lindros .20
27 John Vanbiesbrouck .15
28 Nikolai Khabibulin .15
29 Keith Tkachuk .20
30 Jaromir Jagr .30
31 Vincent Lecavalier .60 1.
32 Curtis Joseph .20
33 Mats Sundin .20
34 Mark Messier .20
35 Bill Muckalt .07
36 Peter Bondra .15

1998-99 Pacific Omega Planet Ice

Randomly inserted into hobby packs only with an insertion rate of 4:37, this 30-card set features action color photos of top NHL players. The backs carry player information.
COMPLETE SET (30) 8.00 15.0
*1-6 PARALLEL/100: 6X TO 15X BASIC INSERTS
*7-12 PARALLEL/75: 8X TO 20X BASIC INSERTS
*13-18 PARALLEL/50: 12X TO 30X BASIC INSERTS
*19-24 PARALLEL/25: 25X TO 60X BASIC INSERTS
1 Ray Bourque .30 .7
2 Chris Chelios .15 .4
3 Vincent Lecavalier .08 .2
4 Mark Parrish .08 .2
5 Felix Potvin .15 .4
6 Alexei Yashin .08 .2
7 Ed Belfour .15 .4
8 Peter Bondra .08 .2
9 Brett Hull .25 .6
10 Mark Messier .25 .6
11 Mats Sundin .08 .2
12 John Vanbiesbrouck .08 .2
13 Sergei Fedorov .30 .7
14 Curtis Joseph .15 .4
15 John LeClair .15 .4
16 Mike Modano .30 .7
17 Brendan Shanahan .15 .4
18 Keith Tkachuk .15 .4
19 Martin Brodeur 1.00 2.5
20 Pavel Bure .15 .4
21 Dominik Hasek .40 1.0
22 Joe Sakic .40 1.0
23 Teemu Selanne .15 .4
24 Steve Yzerman 1.00 2.5
25 Peter Forsberg .50 1.2
26 Wayne Gretzky 1.25 3.0
27 Jaromir Jagr .30 .7
28 Paul Kariya .15 .4
29 Eric Lindros .15 .4
30 Patrick Roy 1.00 2.5

1998-99 Pacific Omega Prism

COMPLETE SET (20) 20.00 40.00
STATED ODDS 1:37
1 Paul Kariya .60 1.50
2 Teemu Selanne .60 1.50
3 Dominik Hasek .60 1.50
4 Peter Forsberg 1.50 4.00
5 Patrick Roy 3.00 8.00
6 Joe Sakic 1.25 3.00
7 Mike Modano 1.00 2.50
8 Sergei Fedorov 1.00 2.50
9 Brendan Shanahan .60 1.50
10 Steve Yzerman 3.00 8.00
11 Pavel Bure .60 1.50
12 Martin Brodeur 1.50 4.00
13 Wayne Gretzky 4.00 10.00
14 Alexei Yashin .25 .60
15 John LeClair .60 1.50
16 Eric Lindros .60 1.50
17 Keith Tkachuk .60 1.50
18 Jaromir Jagr 1.00 2.50
19 Mats Sundin .60 1.50
20 Mark Messier .60 1.50

1999-00 Pacific Omega

The 1999-00 Pacific Omega set was released as a 250 card set. It is available in both hobby and retail version, limiting certain inserts to hobby only or retail only. The base card features full-color photography and a silver foil player portrait in the bottom right corner, while prospect cards contain two players in split screen format. Each pack contains 6 cards, and carries a suggested retail price of $1.99.
COMPLETE SET (250) 30.00 60.00
1 Matt Cullen .12 .30
2 Guy Hebert .20 .50
3 Paul Kariya .25 .60
4 Marty McInnis .12 .30
5 Steve Rucchin .12 .30
6 Teemu Selanne .40 1.00
7 Pascal Trepanier .12 .30
8 L.Kohn .15 .40
V.Vishnevski
9 Andrew Brunette .12 .30
10 Nelson Emerson .12 .30
11 Ray Ferraro .12 .30
12 Damian Rhodes .12 .30
13 Patrik Stefan RC .20 .50

14 Dean Sylvester RC .12 .30
15 P.Buzek .12 .30
S.Fankhouser RC
16 Jason Allison .15 .40
17 Dave Andreychuk .20 .50
18 Ray Bourque .30 .75
19 Anson Carter .15 .40
20 Byron Dafoe .12 .30
21 Sergei Samsonov .15 .40
22 Joe Thornton .30 .75
23 J.GrahameRC .15 .40
J.HendersonRC
24 Maxim Afinogenov .12 .30
25 Martin Biron .15 .40
26 Curtis Brown .12 .30
27 Brian Campbell RC .20 .50
28 Dominik Hasek .30 .75
29 Dimitri Kalinin RC .20 .50
30 Michael Peca .15 .40
31 Miroslav Satan .15 .40
32 Rhett Warrener .12 .30
33 J.L.Grand-Pierre RC .12 .30
D.Moravec RC
34 Fred Brathwaite .12 .30
35 Valeri Bure .12 .30
36 Grant Fuhr .20 .50
37 Phil Housley .12 .30
38 Jarome Iginla .20 .50
39 Oleg Saprykin RC .20 .50
40 Marc Savard .12 .30
41 Cory Stillman .12 .30
42 T.Bingley RC .12 .30
R.Regehr
43 Ron Francis .25 .60
44 Sean Hill .12 .30
45 Arturs Irbe .15 .40
46 Sami Kapanen .12 .30
47 Curtis Leschyshyn .12 .30
48 Jeff O'Neill .12 .30
49 Gary Roberts .12 .30
50 D.Tanabe .12 .30
T.Westlund RC
51 Tony Amonte .15 .40
52 Eric Daze .15 .40
53 Doug Gilmour .25 .60
54 Michael Nylander .12 .30
55 Steve Sullivan .12 .30
56 Jocelyn Thibault .15 .40
57 Alexei Zhamnov .12 .30
58 J-P Dumont .15 .40
M.Lamothe RC
59 C.Herperger RC .12 .30
S.McCarthy
60 Adam Deadmarsh 2.00 5.00
61 Chris Drury .15 .40
62 Peter Forsberg .20 .50
63 Milan Hejduk .15 .40
64 Sandis Ozolinsh .12 .30
65 Patrick Roy .75 2.00
66 Joe Sakic .30 .75
67 Alex Tanguay .15 .40
68 M.Denis .15 .40
M.Skoula RC
69 S.Helenius RC .15 .40
B.Willsie
70 Ed Belfour .20 .50
71 Manny Fernandez .15 .40
72 Brett Hull .30 .75
73 Jere Lehtinen .15 .40
74 Mike Modano .30 .75
75 Brenden Morrow .20 .50
76 Joe Nieuwendyk .20 .50
77 Sergei Zubov .12 .30
78 R.Christie RC .12 .30
R.Lyashenko
79 R.Jackman .20 .50
A.Letang RC
80 Chris Chelios .20 .50
81 Sergei Fedorov .30 .75
82 Igor Larionov .20 .50
83 Nicklas Lidstrom .20 .50
84 Chris Osgood .20 .50
85 Brendan Shanahan .25 .60
86 Pat Verbeek .15 .40
87 Ken Wregget .12 .30
88 Steve Yzerman .60 1.50
89 Paul Comrie RC .30 .75
90 Bill Guerin .20 .50
91 Tom Poti .12 .30
92 Bert Robertsson RC .12 .30
93 Tommy Salo .15 .40
94 Alexander Selivanov .12 .30
95 Ryan Smyth .15 .40
96 Doug Weight .20 .50
97 Pavel Bure .25 .60
98 Viktor Kozlov .12 .30
99 Mark Parrish .12 .30
100 Mikhail Shtalenkov .12 .30
101 Robert Svehla .12 .30
102 Mike Vernon .15 .40
103 Ray Whitney .15 .40
104 D.DuerdenRC/I.Nvsltsv RC .25 .60
105 J.Jakopin RC .12 .30
F.Kuba RC
106 Rob Blake .20 .50
107 Stephane Fiset .15 .40
108 Jaroslav Modry .12 .30
109 Glen Murray .15 .40
110 Zigmund Palffy .20 .50
111 Luc Robitaille .20 .50
112 Bryan Smolinski .12 .30
113 Jamie Storr .15 .40
114 Marko Tuomainen .12 .30
115 B.Chartrand RC .12 .30
F.Kaberle
116 Shayne Corson .12 .30
117 Craig Darby .12 .30
118 Jeff Hackett .12 .30
119 Saku Koivu .20 .50
120 Trevor Linden .20 .50
121 Martin Rucinsky .12 .30
122 Brian Savage .12 .30
123 Jose Theodore .20 .50
124 F.Bouillon RC .20 .50
S.Robidas RC
125 Mike Ribeiro .15 .40
J.Ward
126 Mike Dunham .12 .30
127 Patric Kjellberg .12 .30
128 Cliff Ronning .12 .30
129 Tomas Vokoun .20 .50
130 D.Legwand .12 .30
R.Robitaille
131 R.Lintner RC .12 .30
K.Skrastins RC
132 Jason Arnott .15 .40
133 Martin Brodeur .40 1.00
134 Patrik Elias .20 .50
135 Scott Gomez .15 .40
136 Bobby Holik .12 .30
137 Claude Lemieux .15 .40
138 Petr Sykora .15 .40
139 J.Madden RC .20 .50
B.Rafalski RC
140 Mariusz Czerkawski .12 .30
141 Brad Isbister .12 .30
142 Jorgen Jonsson RC .12 .30
143 Roberto Luongo .25 .60
144 Bill Muckalt .12 .30
145 Kevin Weekes .12 .30
146 T.Connolly .12 .30
E.Korolev RC
147 Alexandre Daigle .12 .30
148 Radek Dvorak .12 .30
149 Theo Fleury .25 .60
150 Adam Graves .15 .40
151 Brian Leetch .20 .50
152 Petr Nedved .12 .30
153 Mike Richter .20 .50
154 Michael York .12 .30
155 J.Hlavac .12 .30
K.Johnsson RC
156 Daniel Alfredsson .20 .50
157 Magnus Arvedson .12 .30
158 Radek Bonk .12 .30
159 Marian Hossa .15 .40
160 Patrick Lalime .15 .40
161 Shawn McEachern .12 .30
162 Petr Schastlivy RC .12 .30
163 Ron Tugnutt .15 .40
164 Shaun Van Allen .12 .30
165 Alexei Yashin .15 .40
166 M.Fisher RC .20 .50
A.Roy RC
167 Brian Boucher .20 .50
168 Eric Desjardins .15 .40
169 Simon Gagne .20 .50
170 Daymond Langkow .15 .40
171 John LeClair .20 .50
172 Eric Lindros .30 .75
173 Keith Primeau .12 .30
174 Mark Recchi .25 .60
175 Mikael Renberg .12 .30
176 John Vanbiesbrouck .15 .40
177 A.Delmore RC .12 .30
M.Eaton RC
178 Shane Doan .15 .40
179 Dallas Drake .12 .30
180 Robert Esche RC .20 .50
181 Travis Green .12 .30
182 Nikolai Khabibulin .15 .40
183 Teppo Numminen .12 .30
184 Jeremy Roenick .20 .50
185 Keith Tkachuk .20 .50
186 T.Letowski .30 .75
R.Suchy RC
187 Jan Hrdina .12 .30
188 Jaromir Jagr .50 1.25
189 Hans Jonsson RC .12 .30
190 Alexei Kovalev .15 .40
191 Martin Straka .12 .30
192 German Titov .12 .30
193 Tyler Wright .12 .30
194 J.S.Aubin .15 .40
M.Rozsival RC
195 Pavol Demitra .25 .60
196 Al MacInnis .20 .50
197 Jamie McLennan .15 .40
198 Tyson Nash RC .12 .30
199 Chris Pronger .15 .40
200 Todd Reirden RC .12 .30
201 Roman Turek .15 .40
202 Pierre Turgeon .20 .50
203 J.Hecht RC .30 .75
L.Nagy RC
204 Vincent Damphousse .15 .40
205 Jeff Friesen .15 .40
206 Todd Harvey .12 .30
207 Alexander Korolyuk .12 .30
208 Patrick Marleau .20 .50
209 Owen Nolan .20 .50
210 Steve Shields .15 .40
211 Gary Suter .12 .30
212 Evgeni Nabokov RC 2.50 6.00
Brad Stuart
213 Dan Cloutier .12 .30
214 Stan Drulia .12 .30
215 Chris Gratton .12 .30
216 Vincent Lecavalier .15 .40
217 Steve Martins RC .12 .30
218 Fredrik Modin .12 .30
219 Mike Sillinger .12 .30
220 B.Clymer RC .12 .30
N.Ekman RC
221 Nikolai Antropov RC .50 1.25
222 Sergei Berezin .12 .30
223 Tie Domi .15 .40
224 Jonas Hoglund .12 .30
225 Curtis Joseph .20 .50
226 Tomas Kaberle .12 .30
227 Dimitri Khristich .12 .30
228 Mats Sundin .20 .50
229 Steve Thomas .12 .30
230 A.Mair RC .12 .30
D.Yakushin RC
231 Todd Bertuzzi .15 .40
232 Andrew Cassels .12 .30
233 Steve Kariya RC .20 .50
234 Mark Messier .30 .75
235 Alexander Mogilny .15 .40
236 Markus Naslund .20 .50
237 Felix Potvin .60 1.50
238 R.Bonni RC .12 .30
Z.Komarniski
239 H.Druken .12 .30
P.Schaefer
240 B.Leeb RC .20 .50
A.Michaud RC
241 Peter Bondra .15 .40
242 Jan Bulis .12 .30
243 Olaf Kolzig .20 .50
244 Steve Konowalchuk .12 .30
245 Adam Oates .20 .50
246 J.Halpern RC .20 .50
G.Mrpit RC
247 A.Tezikov RC .20 .50
A.Volchkov RC
248 North American All-Stars .15 .40
249 World All-Stars .15 .40
250 P.Bure .25 .60
V.Bure
NNO Martin Brodeur SAMPLE .40 1.00

1999-00 Pacific Omega Copper

Randomly inserted in packs, this 250-card Hobby Only set parallels the base set and enhances the base card design with copper foil on the text and on the player portrait in the bottom right front corner. Just above the player portrait is a box that contains each card's serial number. Each of the Copper parallel version cards are numbered out of 99.
*VETS: 4X TO 10 BASE
*ROOKIES: 2X TO 5X BASE
234 Mark Messier 5.00 12.00

1999-00 Pacific Omega Gold

Randomly inserted in packs, this 250-card Retail Only set parallels the base set and enhances the base card design with gold foil on the text and on the player portrait in the bottom right front corner. Just above the player portrait is a box that contains each card's serial number. Each of the Gold parallel version cards are numbered out of 299.
*VETS: 2X TO 5X BASE
*ROOKIES: 1X TO 2.5X BASE
234 Mark Messier 3.00 8.00

1999-00 Pacific Omega Ice Blue

Randomly inserted in packs, this 250-card set parallels the base set and enhances the base card design with blue foil on the text and on the player portrait in the bottom right front corner. Just above the player portrait is a box that contains each card's serial number. Each of the Ice Blue parallel version cards are numbered out of 75. This set was available in both Hobby and Retail packs.
*VETS: 5X TO 12X BASIC CARDS
*ROOKIES: 2.5X TO 6X BASIC CARDS
234 Mark Messier 5.00 12.00

1999-00 Pacific Omega Premiere Date

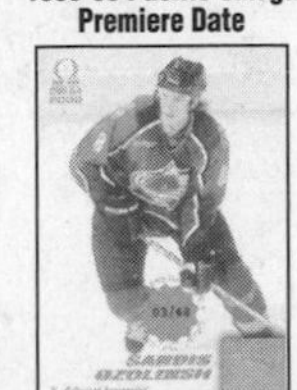

Randomly inserted in packs at a rate of 1:37, this 250 card set paralleled the base set except for a gold foil stamp just above the player's name. The stamps carried a serial number out of 68. The date of the player's 'premiere' in the NHL is under the stamp.
*VETS: 6X TO 15X BASE
*ROOKIES: 3X TO 8X BASE
234 Mark Messier 5.00 12.00

1999-00 Pacific Omega Cup Contenders

COMPLETE SET (20) 25.00 60.00
STATED ODDS 1:37
1 Paul Kariya 1.25 3.00
2 Dominik Hasek 1.50 4.00
3 Peter Forsberg 1.00 2.50
4 Patrick Roy 4.00 10.00
5 Joe Sakic 1.50 4.00
6 Brett Hull 1.50 4.00
7 Mike Modano 1.50 4.00
8 Sergei Fedorov 1.50 4.00
9 Brendan Shanahan 1.25 3.00
10 Steve Yzerman 3.00 8.00
11 Pavel Bure 1.25 3.00
12 Martin Brodeur 2.00 5.00
13 Theo Fleury 1.25 3.00
14 Mike Richter 1.00 2.50
15 John LeClair 1.00 2.50
16 Jeremy Roenick 1.00 2.50
17 Jaromir Jagr 2.50 6.00
18 Al MacInnis 1.00 2.50
19 Curtis Joseph 1.00 2.50
20 Mark Messier 1.50 4.00

1999-00 Pacific Omega EO Portraits

Randomly inserted in packs at 1:73, this 20-card set features laser-cut player images on one side and a full color photo on the other. Parallels numbered 1/1 also exist; they are not priced due to scarcity.
COMPLETE SET (20) 20.00 50.00
1 Paul Kariya 1.25 3.00
2 Teemu Selanne 2.00 5.00
3 Patrik Stefan 1.00 2.50
4 Dominik Hasek 1.50 4.00
5 Peter Forsberg 1.00 2.50
6 Patrick Roy 4.00 10.00
7 Mike Modano 1.50 4.00
8 Brendan Shanahan 1.25 3.00
9 Steve Yzerman 3.00 8.00
10 Pave Bure 1.25 3.00
11 Martin Brodeur 2.00 5.00
12 Scott Gomez .75 2.00
13 Eric Lindros 1.50 4.00
14 John Vanbiesbrouck .75 2.00
15 Keith Tkachuk 1.00 2.50
16 Jaromir Jagr 2.50 6.00
17 Vincent Lecavalier .75 2.00
18 Curtis Joseph 1.00 2.50
19 Mats Sundin 1.00 2.50
20 Mark Messier 1.50 4.00

1999-00 Pacific Omega Game-Used Jerseys

Randomly inserted in packs at 1:180, this 10-card set features a swatch of game used jersey on each card. This set was not announced in the initial release, and was a last minute addition.
1 Teemu Selanne 10.00 25.00
2 Mike Modano 8.00 20.00
3 Steve Yzerman 10.00 25.00
4 Martin Brodeur 10.00 25.00
5 Mike Richter 5.00 12.00
6 John LeClair 5.00 12.00
7 Eric Lindros 8.00 20.00
8 John Vanbiesbrouck 4.00 10.00
9 Jaromir Jagr 12.00 30.00
10 Mats Sundin 5.00 12.00

1999-00 Pacific Omega NHL Generations

Randomly seeded in packs at one in 1:145, this 10-card set features two players on each card. The left side pictures an NHL standout veteran paired with a top rated prospect on the right. The green background on each side contains a silhouette of both respective players.
COMPLETE SET (10) 60.00 120.00
1 P.Kariya/S.Kariya 4.00 10.00
2 T.Selanne/M.Hejduk 6.00 15.00
3 P.Forsberg/C.Drury 3.00 8.00
4 P.Roy/R.Luongo 12.00 30.00
5 M.Modano/D.Legwand 5.00 12.00
6 S.Yzerman/M.Hossa 10.00 25.00
7 P.Bure/M.Hossa 4.00 10.00
8 J.LeClair/S.Gagne 3.00 8.00
9 E.Lindros/V.Lecavalier 5.00 12.00
10 J.Jagr/P.Stefan 8.00 20.00

1999-00 Pacific Omega North American All-Stars

Randomly inserted in packs at 2:37, this 10-card die-cut set pictured some of North America's most dominating All-Stars set against the Toronto All-Star logo.
COMPLETE SET (10) 8.00 20.00
1 Paul Kariya 1.00 2.50
2 Ray Bourque 1.25 3.00
3 Joe Sakic 1.25 3.00
4 Mike Modano 1.25 3.00
5 Brendan Shanahan 1.00 2.50
6 Steve Yzerman 2.50 6.00
7 Martin Brodeur 1.50 4.00
8 Scott Gomez .60 1.50
9 Curtis Joseph .75 2.00
10 Mark Messier 1.25 3.00

1999-00 Pacific Omega 5 Star Talents

Randomly inserted in Hobby packs at the rate of 4:37, this 30-card set segments NHL players into five different groups of six cards each. Card #'s 1-6 are top prospects (Rookies), card #'s 7-12 are power players (Power Game), card #'s 13-18 are some of the NHL's quickest (Speed Merchants), card #'s 19-24 are some of the top set-up guys (Playmakers), and card #'s 25-30 are some of the NHL's most dominating goaltenders (Netminders). A five-tier serial #'d parallel of this set was released also.
COMPLETE SET (30) 20.00 40.00
STATED ODDS 4:37 HOBBY
1 Patrik Stefan .60 1.50
2 Alex Tanguay .50 1.25
3 David Legwand .40 1.00
4 Scott Gomez .50 1.25
5 Roberto Luongo .75 2.00
6 Steve Kariya .60 1.50
7 Brendan Shanahan .75 2.00
8 John LeClair .60 1.50
9 Eric Lindros 1.00 2.50
10 Keith Tkachuk .60 1.50
11 Owen Nolan .60 1.50
12 Mark Messier 1.00 2.50
13 Paul Kariya .60 1.50
14 Teemu Selanne 1.25 3.00
15 Pavel Bure .75 2.00
16 Theo Fleury .75 2.00
17 Marian Hossa .50 1.25
18 Jaromir Jagr 1.50 4.00
19 Peter Forsberg .60 1.50
20 Mike Modano 1.00 2.50
21 Steve Yzerman 2.00 5.00
22 Mark Recchi .75 2.00
23 Vincent Lecavalier .50 1.25
24 Mats Sundin .60 1.50
25 Dominik Hasek 1.00 2.50
26 Patrick Roy 2.50 6.00
27 Ed Belfour .60 1.50
28 Martin Brodeur 1.25 3.00
29 John Vanbiesbrouck .50 1.25
30 Curtis Joseph .60 1.50

1999-00 Pacific Omega 5 Star Talents Parallel

*1-6 PARALLEL/100: 2X TO 5X BASIC INSERT
1-6 PARALLEL PRINT RUN 100
*7-12 PARALLEL/75: 2.5X TO 6X BASIC INSERT
7-12 PARALLEL PRINT RUN 75
*13-18 PARALLEL/50: 3X TO 8X BASIC INSERT
13-18 PARALLEL PRINT RUN 50
*19-24 PARALLEL/25: 4X TO 10X BASIC INSERT
19-24 PARALLEL PRINT RUN 25
25-30 UNPRICED PARALLEL PRINT RUN 1
12 Mark Messier 6.00 15.00

1999-00 Pacific Omega World All-Stars

Randomly inserted in packs at 2:37, this 10-card die-cut set pictured some of the World's most dominating All-Stars set against the Toronto All-Star logo.
COMPLETE SET (10) 6.00 12.00
1 Teemu Selanne 1.50 4.00
2 Valeri Bure .50 1.25
3 Nicklas Lidstrom .75 2.00
4 Pavel Bure 1.00 2.50
5 Viktor Kozlov .50 1.25
6 Jaromir Jagr 2.00 5.00
7 Pavol Demitra 1.00 2.50
8 Roman Turek .60 1.50
9 Mats Sundin .75 2.00
10 Olaf Kolzig .75 2.00

1999-00 Pacific Prism

The 1999-00 Pacific Prism set was released in both hobby and retail versions as a 150-card set featuring both veterans and prospects. The base cards are printed on silver holo-foil, and the prospects are denoted by a red diamond in the lower front right corner. Prism was packaged in 20-pack boxes with three cards per pack.
COMPLETE SET (150) 30.00 60.00
1 Guy Hebert .15 .40
2 Paul Kariya .20 .50
3 Mike Leclerc .10 .30
4 Steve Rucchin .10 .30
5 Teemu Selanne .20 .50
6 Andrew Brunette .15 .40
7 Petr Buzek .15 .40
8 Damian Rhodes .10 .30
9 Patrik Stefan RC .75 2.00
10 Jason Allison .10 .30
11 Dave Andreychuk .15 .40
12 Ray Bourque .30 .75
13 Byron Dafoe .15 .40
14 Sergei Samsonov .15 .40
15 Joe Thornton .30 .75
16 Maxim Afinogenov .10 .30
17 Martin Biron .15 .40
18 Curtis Brown .10 .30
19 Dominik Hasek .40 1.00
20 Michael Peca .10 .30
21 Miroslav Satan .15 .40
22 Valeri Bure .10 .30
23 Grant Fuhr .15 .40
24 Jarome Iginla .25 .60
25 Oleg Saprykin RC .60 1.50
26 Cory Stillman .10 .30
27 Bates Battaglia .10 .30
28 Ron Francis .10 .30
29 Arturs Irbe .15 .40
30 Sami Kapanen .10 .30
31 Keith Primeau .10 .30
32 Tony Amonte .15 .40
33 J-P Dumont .15 .40
34 Doug Gilmour .15 .40
35 Jocelyn Thibault .15 .40
36 Alexei Zhamnov .10 .30
37 Chris Drury .15 .40
38 Peter Forsberg .50 1.25
39 Milan Hejduk .20 .50
40 Patrick Roy 1.00 2.50
41 Joe Sakic .40 1.00
42 Alex Tanguay .15 .40
43 Ed Belfour .20 .50
44 Brett Hull .25 .60
45 Roman Lyashenko .10 .30
46 Mike Modano .30 .75
47 Joe Nieuwendyk .15 .40
48 Brendan Shanahan .20 .50
49 Chris Chelios .20 .50
50 Sergei Fedorov .30 .75
51 Jiri Fischer .10 .30
52 Nicklas Lidstrom .20 .50
53 Chris Osgood .15 .40
54 Steve Yzerman 1.00 2.50
55 Bill Guerin .10 .30
56 Tommy Salo .15 .40
57 Alexander Selivanov .10 .30
58 Ryan Smyth .10 .30
59 Doug Weight .15 .40
60 Pavel Bure .20 .50
61 Trevor Kidd .10 .30
62 Viktor Kozlov .15 .40
63 Mark Parrish .10 .30
64 Ray Whitney .15 .40
65 Rob Blake .15 .40
66 Stephane Fiset .15 .40
67 Frantisek Kaberle .10 .30
68 Zigmund Palffy .15 .40
69 Luc Robitaille .15 .40
70 Francis Bouillon RC .20 .50
71 Jeff Hackett .15 .40
72 Saku Koivu .20 .50
73 Trevor Linden .15 .40
74 Brian Savage .10 .30
75 Mike Dunham .15 .40
76 David Legwand .20 .50
77 Cliff Ronning .15 .40
78 Rob Valicevic RC .20 .50
79 Martin Brodeur .50 1.25
80 Patrik Elias .15 .40
81 Scott Gomez .10 .30
82 Bobby Holik .10 .30
83 Claude Lemieux .10 .30
84 Petr Sykora .10 .30
85 Tim Connolly .10 .30
86 Mariusz Czerkawski .10 .30
87 Brad Isbister .10 .30
88 Roberto Luongo .25 .60
89 Theo Fleury .10 .30
90 Jan Hlavac .10 .30
91 Brian Leetch .20 .50
92 Mike Richter .20 .50
93 Mike York .10 .30
94 Daniel Alfredsson .15 .40
95 Radek Bonk .10 .30
96 Marian Hossa .20 .50
97 Shawn McEachern .10 .30
98 Ron Tugnutt .15 .40
99 Alexei Yashin .10 .30
100 Brian Boucher .20 .50
101 Simon Gagne .20 .50
102 John LeClair .20 .50
103 Eric Lindros .20 .50
104 Mark Recchi .15 .40
105 John Vanbiesbrouck .15 .40
106 Mike Alatalo RC .20 .50
107 Travis Green .10 .30
108 Nikolai Khabibulin .15 .40
109 Jeremy Roenick .25 .60
110 Keith Tkachuk .20 .50
111 Rick Tocchet .15 .40
112 Jean-Sebastien Aubin .15 .40
113 Andrew Ference .10 .30
114 Jaromir Jagr .30 .75
115 Alexei Kovalev .10 .30
116 Martin Straka .10 .30
117 Pavol Demitra .15 .40
118 Jochen Hecht RC .75 2.00
119 Al MacInnis .15 .40
120 Chris Pronger .15 .40
121 Roman Turek .15 .40
122 Pierre Turgeon .15 .40
123 Vincent Damphousse .10 .30
124 Jeff Friesen .10 .30
125 Patrick Marleau .15 .40
126 Owen Nolan .15 .40
127 Steve Shields .15 .40
128 Brad Stuart .15 .40
129 Dan Cloutier .10 .30
130 Ben Clymer RC .20 .50
131 Chris Gratton .10 .30
132 Vincent Lecavalier .20 .50
133 Darcy Tucker .10 .30
134 Nikolai Antropov RC 1.25 3.00
135 Sergei Berezin .10 .30
136 Tie Domi .15 .40
137 Curtis Joseph .20 .50
138 Dimitri Khristich .10 .30
139 Mats Sundin .20 .50
140 Steve Kariya RC .60 1.50
141 Mark Messier .20 .50
142 Alfie Michaud RC .40 1.00
143 Alexander Mogilny .15 .40
144 Jarkko Ruutu RC .20 .50
145 Peter Schaefer .15 .40
146 Peter Bondra .15 .40
147 Jan Bulis .10 .30
148 Olaf Kolzig .15 .40
149 Glen Metropolit RC .60 1.50
150 Adam Oates .15 .40
NNO Martin Brodeur SAMPLE .75 2.00

1999-00 Pacific Prism Holographic Blue

Randomly inserted in packs, this 150-card set parallels the base set in a holographic blue foil version. Each card is numbered out of 80 in the top left-hand corner.
*VETS: 6X TO 15X BASIC CARDS
*ROOKIES: 3X TO 8X BASIC CARDS

1999-00 Pacific Prism Holographic Gold

Randomly inserted in packs, this 150-card set parallels the base set in a holographic gold foil version. Each card is numbered out of 480 in the top left-hand corner.
*VETS: 1.2X TO 3X BASIC CARDS
*ROOKIES: .8X TO 2X BASIC CARDS

1999-00 Pacific Prism Holographic Mirror

Randomly inserted in packs, this 150-card set parallels the base set in a holographic silver rainbow foil version. Each card is numbered out of 160 in the top left-hand corner.
*VETS: 4X TO 10X BASIC CARDS
*ROOKIES: 2X TO 5X BASIC CARDS
STATED PRINT RUN 160 SER.#'d SETS

1999-00 Pacific Prism Holographic Purple

Randomly inserted in hobby packs, this 150-card set parallels the base set in a holographic purple foil version. Each card is numbered out of 99 in the top left-hand corner.
*VETS: 5X TO 12X BASIC CARDS
*ROOKIES: 2.5X TO 6X BASIC CARDS

1999-00 Pacific Prism Premiere Date

Randomly inserted in packs, the 150-card set parallels the base set and is serial numbered in the upper-left front corner out of 69. The center of the cards also contains a "premiere date" embossed stamp.
*VETS: 8X TO 20X BASIC CARDS
*ROOKIES: 4X TO 10X BASIC CARDS

1999-00 Pacific Prism Clear Advantage

Randomly seeded in packs at 2:25, this 20-card set features 20 of hockey's most exciting players. Action player photos are set against an icy-looking blue background.
COMPLETE SET (20) 20.00 40.00
1 Paul Kariya .60 1.50
2 Teemu Selanne .60 1.50
3 Dominik Hasek 1.25 3.00
4 Peter Forsberg 1.50 4.00
5 Patrick Roy 3.00 8.00
6 Alex Tanguay .50 1.25
7 Brett Hull .75 2.00
8 Brendan Shanahan 1.00 2.50
9 Steve Yzerman 3.00 8.00
10 Pavel Bure .75 2.00
11 Zigmund Palffy .50 1.25
12 Martin Brodeur 1.50 4.00
13 Theo Fleury .50 1.25
14 Marian Hossa .60 1.50
15 John LeClair .75 2.00
16 Eric Lindros 1.00 2.50
17 Mark Recchi .50 1.25
18 Jaromir Jagr 1.00 2.50
19 Vincent Lecavalier .60 1.50
20 Mats Sundin .60 1.50

1999-00 Pacific Prism Ice Prospects

Randomly inserted in hobby packs at 1:97, this 10-card set features some of hockey's up and coming prospects.
COMPLETE SET (10) 30.00 60.00
1 Patrik Stefan 3.00 8.00
2 Martin Biron 3.00 8.00
3 Alex Tanguay 3.00 8.00
4 David Legwand 3.00 8.00
5 Scott Gomez 3.00 8.00
6 Simon Gagne 3.00 8.00
7 Brad Stuart 3.00 8.00
8 Nikolai Antropov 3.00 8.00
9 Steve Kariya 3.00 8.00
10 Peter Schaefer 3.00 8.00

1999-00 Pacific Prism Dial-a-Stats

Randomly inserted in packs at 1:193, this 20-card set showcases NHL superstars that boast impressive statistics. The card is cut and fitted with a fastener in the middle to allow a wheel with stat numbers on it to be spun to display the player's career statistics versus the various NHL teams faced.
COMPLETE SET (10) 40.00 80.00
1 Paul Kariya 6.00 15.00
2 Teemu Selanne 6.00 15.00
3 Dominik Hasek 4.00 10.00
4 Peter Forsberg 5.00 12.00
5 Patrick Roy 10.00 25.00
6 Mike Modano 3.00 8.00
7 Steve Yzerman 10.00 25.00
8 Eric Lindros 3.00 8.00
9 Jaromir Jagr 3.00 8.00
10 Mark Messier 2.50 6.00

1999-00 Pacific Prism Sno-Globe Die-Cuts

Randomly seeded in packs at one in 1:25, this 20-card set features NHL greats on a full foil die-cut card shaped like a glass sno-globe.
COMPLETE SET (20) 20.00 40.00
1 Paul Kariya .60 1.50
2 Teemu Selanne .60 1.50
3 Ray Bourque 1.00 2.50
4 Dominik Hasek 1.25 3.00
5 Peter Forsberg 1.50 4.00
6 Patrick Roy 3.00 8.00
7 Joe Sakic 1.25 3.00
8 Ed Belfour .60 1.50
9 Mike Modano 1.00 2.50
10 Brendan Shanahan 1.00 2.50
11 Steve Yzerman 3.00 8.00
12 Pavel Bure .75 2.00
13 Martin Brodeur 1.50 4.00
14 Theo Fleury .60 1.50
15 John LeClair .75 2.00
16 Eric Lindros 1.00 2.50
17 John Vanbiesbrouck .60 1.50
18 Keith Tkachuk .60 1.50
19 Jaromir Jagr 1.00 2.50
20 Curtis Joseph .60 1.50

2003-04 Pacific Prism

Released in mid-August, this 150-card set consisted of 100 base cards and 50 jersey cards. Jersey cards were one per pack and were serial-numbered. Numbering for individual cards can be found below. Cards 151-160 were available only in packs of Pacific Calder.
COMP.SET w/o JSY's (100) 20.00 50.00
JERSEY PRINT RUN 185-1185
1 Stanislav Chistov .20 .50
2 Jean-Sebastien Giguere .30 .75
3 Adam Oates .30 .75
4 Petr Sykora .25 .60
5 Joe DiPenta RC 1.00 2.50
6 Slava Kozlov .25 .60
7 Marc Savard .25 .60
8 Patrik Stefan .20 .50
9 Jeff Hackett .25 .60
10 Miko Knuble .20 .50
11 Sergei Samsonov .25 .60
12 Steve Shields .25 .60
13 Milan Bartovic RC 1.00 2.50
14 Martin Biron .25 .60
15 Daniel Briere .30 .75
16 Ryan Miller .30 .75
17 Miroslav Satan .25 .60
18 Craig Conroy .20 .50
19 Roman Turek .25 .60
20 Ron Francis .40 1.00
21 Arturs Irbe .25 .60
22 Jeff O'Neill .20 .50
23 Tyler Arnason .20 .50
24 Theo Fleury .40 1.00
25 Jocelyn Thibault .25 .60
26 Alexei Zhamnov .25 .60
27 Rob Blake .30 .75
28 Alex Tanguay .25 .60
29 Marc Denis .25 .60
30 Kent McDonell RC 1.00 2.50
31 Rick Nash .30 .75
32 Geoff Sanderson .20 .50
33 Ray Whitney .25 .60
34 Jason Arnott .25 .60
35 Jere Lehtinen .25 .60
36 Pavel Datsyuk .40 1.00
37 Brett Hull .40 1.00
38 Curtis Joseph .30 .75
39 Henrik Zetterberg .40 1.00
40 Ales Hemsky .30 .75
41 Tommy Salo .25 .60
42 Ryan Smyth .25 .60
43 Jay Bouwmeester .30 .75
44 Olli Jokinen .30 .75
45 Roberto Luongo .50 1.25
46 Stephen Weiss .20 .50
47 Michael Cammalleri .30 .75
48 Adam Deadmarsh .25 .60
49 Alexander Frolov .25 .60
50 Felix Potvin .50 1.25
51 Andrew Brunette .20 .50
52 Manny Fernandez .25 .60
53 Marian Gaborik .50 1.25
54 Dwayne Roloson .25 .60
55 Cliff Ronning .20 .50
56 Marcel Hossa .20 .50
57 Yanic Perreault .20 .50
58 Scottie Upshall .25 .60
59 Tomas Vokoun .25 .60
60 Scott Walker .20 .50
61 Patrik Elias .30 .75
62 Jamie Langenbrunner .25 .60
63 John Madden .20 .50
64 Joe Nieuwendyk .30 .75
65 Scott Stevens .30 .75
66 Jason Blake .20 .50
67 Rick DiPietro .25 .60
68 Mark Parrish .20 .50
69 Mike Dunham .25 .60
70 Alex Kovalev .25 .60
71 Brian Leetch .30 .75
72 Mark Messier .50 1.25
73 Zdeno Chara .30 .75
74 Martin Havlat .30 .75
75 Todd White .20 .50
76 John LeClair .30 .75
77 Mark Recchi .40 1.00
78 Shane Doan .25 .60
79 Mike Johnson .20 .50
80 Johan Hedberg .25 .60
81 Martin Straka .20 .50
82 Pavol Demitra .40 1.00
83 Barret Jackman .20 .50
84 Al MacInnis .30 .75
85 Peter Sejna RC 1.00 2.50
86 Keith Tkachuk .30 .75
87 Patrick Marleau .30 .75
88 Evgeni Nabokov .25 .60
89 Teemu Selanne .60 1.50
90 Dave Andreychuk .30 .75
91 Brad Richards .30 .75
92 Alexander Mogilny .25 .60
93 Owen Nolan .25 .60
94 Matt Stajan RC 1.25 3.00
95 Ed Jovanovski .25 .60
96 Daniel Sedin .30 .75
97 Henrik Sedin .30 .75
98 Peter Bondra .25 .60
99 Sergei Gonchar .20 .50
100 Olaf Kolzig .30 .75
101 Paul Kariya JSY/935 5.00 12.00
102 Dany Heatley JSY/924 4.00 10.00
103 Ilya Kovalchuk JSY/935 4.00 10.00
104 Glen Murray JSY/1185 3.00 8.00
105 Joe Thornton JSY/674 5.00 12.00
106 Chris Drury JSY/935 3.00 8.00
107 Jarome Iginla JSY/1183 4.00 10.00
108 Eric Daze JSY/1171 3.00 8.00
109 Milan Hejduk JSY/1183 3.00 8.00
110 Peter Forsberg JSY/685 5.00 12.00
111 Patrick Roy JSY/185 12.00 30.00
112 Joe Sakic JSY/935 6.00 15.00
113 Bill Guerin JSY/1136 4.00 10.00
114 Mike Modano JSY/935 6.00 15.00
115 Marty Turco JSY/685 4.00 10.00
116 Sergei Fedorov JSY/685 6.00 15.00
117 Brendan Shanahan JSY/935 5.00 12.00
118 Steve Yzerman JSY/185 15.00 40.00
119 Mike Comrie JSY/935 3.00 8.00
120 Jason Allison JSY/1176 3.00 8.00
121 Roman Cechmanek JSY/1185 3.00 8.00
122 Zigmund Palffy JSY/1060 4.00 10.00
123 Saku Koivu JSY/935 4.00 10.00
124 Jose Theodore JSY/1185 4.00 10.00
125 Richard Zednik JSY/1185 2.50 6.00
126 David Legwand JSY/1185 3.00 8.00
127 Martin Brodeur JSY/685 8.00 20.00
128 Michael Peca JSY/1185 3.00 8.00
129 Alexei Yashin JSY/1185 3.00 8.00
130 Pavel Bure JSY/935 5.00 12.00
131 Eric Lindros JSY/935 6.00 15.00
132 Daniel Alfredsson JSY/185 6.00 15.00
133 Marian Hossa JSY/185 5.00 12.00
134 Jason Spezza JSY/185 6.00 15.00
135 Tony Amonte JSY/1163 3.00 8.00
136 Jeremy Roenick JSY/1185 4.00 10.00
137 Sean Burke JSY/1185 2.50 6.00
138 Mario Lemieux JSY/305 12.00 30.00
139 Chris Osgood JSY/1185 4.00 10.00
140 Doug Weight JSY/1185 4.00 10.00
141 Nikolai Khabibulin JSY/1125 4.00 10.00
142 Vincent Lecavalier JSY/935 3.00 8.00
143 Martin St. Louis JSY/1185 4.00 10.00
144 Ed Belfour JSY/685 4.00 10.00
145 Mats Sundin JSY/685 4.00 10.00
146 Todd Bertuzzi JSY/935 4.00 10.00
147 Dan Cloutier JSY/1185 3.00 8.00
148 Brendan Morrison JSY/685 3.00 8.00

149 Markus Naslund JSY/185 6.00 15.00
150 Jaromir Jagr JSY/185 15.00 40.00
151 Joffrey Lupul RC 2.50 6.00
152 Patrice Bergeron RC 5.00 12.00
153 Matthew Lombardi RC 1.25 3.00
154 Eric Staal RC 5.00 12.00
155 Nikolai Zherdev RC 2.00 5.00
156 Jiri Hudler RC 2.50 6.00
157 Nathan Horton RC 2.50 6.00
158 Jordin Tootoo RC 2.00 5.00
159 Antoine Vermette RC 2.00 5.00
160 Marc-Andre Fleury RC 6.00 15.00

2003-04 Pacific Prism Blue

*1-100 VETS/325: 1.5X TO 4X BASIC CARDS
*ROOKIES/325: .5X TO 1.2X RC/975
*101-150 JSY/90: .8X TO 2X JSY/300-1185
*101-150 JSY/90: .5X TO 1.2X JSY/185
BLUE ISSUED IN U.S. PACKS ONLY
72 Mark Messier 2.00 5.00

2003-04 Pacific Prism Gold

Inserted at a rate of 6 per retail box, this 100-card set paralleled the base cards of the regular set but carried gold foil highlights and serial-numbering out of 425.
*1-100 VETS/425: 1.2X TO 3X BASIC CARDS
*ROOKIES/425: .4X TO 1X RC/975
72 Mark Messier 1.50 4.00

2003-04 Pacific Prism Patches

*PATCH/50-75: 1X TO 2.5X BASE JERSEYS
118 Steve Yzerman SP 50.00 125.00

2003-04 Pacific Prism Red

*1-100 VETS/260: 2X TO 5X BASIC CARDS
*ROOKIES/260: .6X TO 1.5X RC/975
*101-150 JSY/75: .8X TO 2X JSY/300-1185
*101-150 JSY/75: .5X TO 1.2X JSY/185
ISSUED IN CANADIAN PACKS ONLY
72 Mark Messier 2.50 6.00

2003-04 Pacific Prism Retail Jerseys

This 150-card set mirrored the hobby set except for the jersey cards 101-150 which carried a different foil color and were serial numbered out of 150.
*RETAIL/150: .6X TO 1.5X HOB JSY/300-1185
*RETAIL/150: .4X TO 1X HOB JSY/185

2003-04 Pacific Prism Crease Police

COMPLETE SET (8) 10.00 20.00
STATED ODDS 1:9
1 Jean-Sebastien Giguere 1.50 4.00
2 Patrick Roy 3.00 8.00
3 Marty Turco 1.50 4.00
4 Curtis Joseph 1.50 4.00
5 Jose Theodore 2.00 5.00
6 Martin Brodeur 2.50 6.00
7 Patrick Lalime 1.50 4.00
8 Ed Belfour 1.50 4.00

2003-04 Pacific Prism Paramount Prodigies

COMPLETE SET (20) 15.00 30.00
STATED ODDS 1:3
1 Stanislav Chistov .60 1.50
2 Jean-Sebastien Giguere .60 1.50
3 Dany Heatley 1.00 2.50
4 Ilya Kovalchuk 1.00 2.50
5 Tyler Arnason .60 1.50
6 Rick Nash 1.00 2.50
7 Pavel Datsyuk .75 2.00
8 Henrik Zetterberg 1.25 3.00
9 Mike Comrie .60 1.50
10 Ales Hemsky .60 1.50
11 Jay Bouwmeester .60 1.50
12 Stephen Weiss .60 1.50
13 Alexander Frolov .60 1.50
14 Marian Gaborik 1.00 2.50
15 David Legwand .60 1.50
16 Martin Havlat .60 1.50
17 Marian Hossa .75 2.00
18 Jason Spezza 1.00 2.50
19 Barret Jackman .60 1.50
20 Vincent Lecavalier .60 1.50

2003-04 Pacific Prism Rookie Revolution

COMPLETE SET (12) 8.00 15.00
STATED ODDS 1:5
1 Stanislav Chistov .40 1.00
2 Ales Kotalik .40 1.00
3 Ryan Miller 1.00 2.50
4 Tyler Arnason .40 1.00
5 Rick Nash 1.00 2.50
6 Henrik Zetterberg 1.00 2.50
7 Ales Hemsky .75 2.00
8 Jay Bouwmeester .60 1.50
9 Alexander Frolov .60 1.50
10 Pierre-Marc Bouchard .60 1.50
11 Jason Spezza 1.00 2.50
12 Jonathan Cheechoo .75 2.00

2003-04 Pacific Prism Stat Masters

COMPLETE SET (10) 8.00 15.00
STATED ODDS 1:9
1 Paul Kariya .40 1.00
2 Joe Thornton .50 1.25
3 Peter Forsberg 1.00 2.50
4 Milan Hejduk .40 1.00
5 Mike Modano .60 1.50
6 Steve Yzerman 1.50 4.00
7 Mario Lemieux 2.00 5.00
8 Todd Bertuzzi .40 1.00
9 Markus Naslund .40 1.00
10 Jaromir Jagr .60 1.50

2002-03 Pacific Quest For the Cup

Released in May 2003, this 150-card set featured color player photos on the right side of the card fronts and a silver holographic image of the Stanley Cup on the left. Cards 151-150 were shortprinted to 950 and inserted at 1:5 hobby packs and 1:9 retail packs. Hobby packs contained 6 cards, and retail packs contained 4 cards.
COMP.SET w/o SP's (100) 20.00 40.00
1 Jean-Sebastien Giguere .30 .75
2 Paul Kariya .40 1.00
3 Sandis Ozolinsh .25 .60
4 Dany Heatley .30 .75
5 Ilya Kovalchuk .40 1.00
6 Jeff Hackett .25 .60
7 Glen Murray .25 .60
8 Joe Thornton .40 1.00
9 Martin Biron .25 .60
10 Miroslav Satan .30 .75
11 Chris Drury .30 .75
12 Jarome Iginla .30 .75
13 Roman Turek .30 .75
14 Ron Francis .40 1.00
15 Jeff O'Neill .20 .50
16 Eric Daze .20 .50
17 Theo Fleury .40 1.00
18 Jocelyn Thibault .25 .60
19 Alexei Zhamnov .25 .60
20 Rob Blake .30 .75
21 Peter Forsberg .40 1.00
22 Milan Hejduk .25 .60
23 Patrick Roy .75 2.00
24 Joe Sakic .50 1.25
25 Marc Denis .25 .60
26 Ray Whitney .25 .60
27 Bill Guerin .30 .75
28 Jere Lehtinen .30 .75
29 Mike Modano .50 1.25
30 Marty Turco .30 .75
30AU Marty Turco AU/500 5.00 12.00
31 Pierre Turgeon .30 .75
32 Sergei Fedorov .50 1.25
33 Brett Hull .40 1.00
34 Curtis Joseph .30 .75
35 Nicklas Lidstrom .30 .75
36 Brendan Shanahan .40 1.00
37 Steve Yzerman .60 1.50
38 Mike Comrie .30 .75
39 Tommy Salo .25 .60
40 Ryan Smyth .25 .60
41 Olli Jokinen .30 .75
42 Roberto Luongo .50 1.25
43 Jason Allison .25 .60
44 Zigmund Palffy .30 .75
45 Felix Potvin .50 1.25
46 Pascal Dupuis .20 .50
47 Manny Fernandez .25 .60
48 Marian Gaborik .50 1.25
49 Cliff Ronning .20 .50
50 Saku Koivu .30 .75
51 Yanic Perreault .20 .50
52 Jose Theodore .30 .75
53 Richard Zednik .20 .50
54 David Legwand .25 .60
55 Tomas Vokoun .25 .60
56 Martin Brodeur .60 1.50
57 Patrik Elias .30 .75
58 Jeff Friesen .20 .50
59 Jamie Langenbrunner .25 .60
60 Rick DiPietro .25 .60
61 Michael Peca .25 .60
62 Alexei Yashin .25 .60
63 Pavel Bure .40 1.00
64 Anson Carter .25 .60
65 Alexei Kovalev .30 .75
66 Eric Lindros .50 1.25
67 Mark Messier .50 1.25
68 Daniel Alfredsson .30 .75
69 Radek Bonk .25 .60
70 Martin Havlat .25 .60
71 Marian Hossa .25 .60
72 Patrick Lalime .25 .60
73 Tony Amonte .25 .60
74 Roman Cechmanek .25 .60
75 Simon Gagne .30 .75
76 Sami Kapanen .20 .50
77 Jeremy Roenick .30 .75
78 Sean Burke .20 .50
79 Johan Hedberg .30 .75
80 Mario Lemieux 1.00 2.50
81 Pavol Demitra .40 1.00
82 Brent Johnson .25 .60
83 Cory Stillman .20 .50
84 Keith Tkachuk .30 .75
85 Doug Weight .30 .75
86 Evgeni Nabokov .25 .60
87 Teemu Selanne .60 1.50
88 Nikolai Khabibulin .30 .75
89 Vincent Lecavalier .25 .60
90 Martin St. Louis .30 .75
91 Ed Belfour .30 .75
92 Alexander Mogilny .25 .60
93 Mats Sundin .30 .75
94 Todd Bertuzzi .30 .75
95 Dan Cloutier .25 .60
96 Brendan Morrison .25 .60
97 Markus Naslund .25 .60
98 Jaromir Jagr .75 2.00
99 Olaf Kolzig .30 .75
100 Michael Nylander .20 .50
101 Stanislav Chistov RC .75 2.00
102 Martin Gerber RC 1.25 3.00
103 Kurt Sauer RC .75 2.00
104 Alexei Smirnov RC 1.00 2.50
105 Shaone Morrisonn RC .75 2.00
106 Tim Thomas RC 6.00 15.00
107 Ryan Miller RC 5.00 12.00
108 Chuck Kobasew RC 1.00 2.50
109 Jordan Leopold RC 1.25 3.00
110 Ryan Bayda RC .75 2.00
111 Tomas Malec RC .75 2.00
112 Pascal Leclaire RC 1.00 2.50
113 Rick Nash RC 6.00 15.00
114 Jason Bacashihua RC 1.00 2.50
115 Steve Ott RC 1.50 4.00
116 Dmitri Bykov RC .75 2.00
117 Henrik Zetterberg RC 8.00 20.00
118 Ales Hemsky RC 3.00 8.00
119 Fernando Pisani RC .75 2.00
120 Jay Bouwmeester RC 2.50 6.00
121 Kip Brennan SP .75 2.00
122 Michael Cammalleri RC 2.50 6.00
123 Alexander Frolov RC 1.50 4.00
124 P-M Bouchard RC 1.25 3.00
125 Stephane Veilleux RC .75 2.00
126 Ron Hainsey RC .75 2.00
127 Mike Komisarek RC 1.25 3.00
128 Vernon Fiddler RC 1.00 2.50
129 Adam Hall RC .75 2.00
130 Scottie Upshall RC 1.00 2.50
131 Eric Godard RC .75 2.00
132 Ray Emery RC 2.50 6.00
133 Jason Spezza RC 5.00 12.00
134 Anton Volchenkov RC .75 2.00
135 Dennis Seidenberg RC 1.25 3.00
136 Radovan Somik RC .75 2.00
137 Jim Vandermeer RC .75 2.00
138 Jeff Taffe RC .75 2.00
139 Brooks Orpik RC 1.25 3.00
140 Tomas Surovy RC .75 2.00
141 Dick Tarnstrom RC .75 2.00
142 Curtis Sanford RC 1.25 3.00
143 Matt Walker RC .75 2.00
144 Niko Dimitrakos RC .75 2.00
145 Jim Fahey RC .75 2.00
146 Lynn Loyns RC .75 2.00
147 Alexander Svitov RC .75 2.00
148 Carlo Colaiacovo RC 1.25 3.00
149 Mikael Tellqvist RC .75 2.00
150 Steve Eminger RC .75 2.00

2002-03 Pacific Quest For the Cup Gold

This 150-card set directly paralleled the base set but carried gold foil highlights on the card fronts. Each card was also serial-numbered out of 325 on the card back.
*1-100 VETS/325: 2X TO 5X BASIC CARDS
*101-150 ROOKIES/325: .5X TO 1.2X RC
67 Mark Messier 2.50 6.00

2002-03 Pacific Quest For the Cup Calder Contenders

Inserted at 1:13 hobby and 1:25 retail, this 10-card set featured color player photos on gold foil backgrounds on the card fronts.
COMPLETE SET (10) 8.00 20.00
1 Stanislav Chistov 1.00 2.50
2 Ales Kotalik 1.00 2.50
3 Ryan Miller 1.50 4.00
4 Tyler Arnason 1.00 2.50
5 Pascal Leclaire 1.00 2.50
6 Rick Nash 2.50 6.00
7 Henrik Zetterberg 2.50 6.00
8 Ales Hemsky 1.50 4.00
9 Jay Bouwmeester 1.50 4.00
10 Jason Spezza 2.50 6.00

2002-03 Pacific Quest For the Cup Chasing the Cup

COMPLETE SET (20) 10.00 20.00
STATED ODDS 1:5 HOB, 1:13 RET
1 Paul Kariya .50 1.25
2 Dany Heatley .60 1.50
3 Ilya Kovalchuk .60 1.50
4 Joe Thornton .75 2.00
5 Marty Turco .40 1.00
6 Curtis Joseph .50 1.25
7 Marian Gaborik 1.00 2.50
8 Jose Theodore .50 1.25
9 Alexei Yashin .40 1.00
10 Pavel Bure .50 1.25
11 Eric Lindros .50 1.25
12 Daniel Alfredsson .40 1.00
13 Marian Hossa .50 1.25
14 Jeremy Roenick .50 1.25
15 Teemu Selanne .50 1.25
16 Owen Nolan .40 1.00
17 Mats Sundin .50 1.25
18 Todd Bertuzzi .50 1.25
19 Brendan Morrison .40 1.00
20 Markus Naslund .40 1.00

2002-03 Pacific Quest For the Cup Jerseys

STATED ODDS 1:9 HOB, 1:25 RET
1 Dany Heatley 4.00 10.00
2 Glen Murray 3.00 8.00
3 Joe Thornton 5.00 12.00
4 Rob Blake 3.00 8.00
5 Peter Forsberg 8.00 20.00
6 Patrick Roy 10.00 25.00
7 Mike Modano 5.00 12.00
8 Marty Turco 3.00 8.00
9 Nicklas Lidstrom 4.00 10.00
10 Rick DiPietro 3.00 8.00
11 Mark Messier 4.00 10.00
12 Daniel Alfredsson 3.00 8.00
13 Marian Hossa 4.00 10.00
14 Jason Spezza 8.00 20.00
15 Roman Cechmanek 3.00 8.00
16 Jeremy Roenick 4.00 10.00
17 Mario Lemieux 12.50 30.00
18 Brent Johnson 3.00 8.00
19 Doug Weight 3.00 8.00
20 Martin St. Louis 3.00 8.00
21 Ed Belfour 4.00 10.00
22 Gary Roberts 3.00 8.00
23 Markus Naslund 4.00 10.00
24 Jaromir Jagr 4.00 10.00
25 Olaf Kolzig 3.00 8.00

2002-03 Pacific Quest For the Cup Raising the Cup

COMPLETE SET (12) 15.00 30.00
STATED ODDS 1:9 HOB, 1:13 RET
1 Peter Forsberg 1.50 4.00
2 Patrick Roy 2.50 6.00
3 Joe Sakic 1.00 2.50
4 Mike Modano .75 2.00
5 Sergei Fedorov .75 2.00
6 Brett Hull .75 2.00
7 Brendan Shanahan .60 1.50
8 Steve Yzerman 2.50 6.00
9 Martin Brodeur 2.50 6.00
10 Mark Messier .60 1.50
11 Mario Lemieux 3.00 8.00
12 Jaromir Jagr .75 2.00

2003-04 Pacific Quest for the Cup

This 140-card set consisted of 100 veteran cards and 40 rookie cards (101-140) that were serial-numbered out of 950.
COMP.SET w/o SP's 20.00 40.00
1 Sergei Fedorov .40 1.00
2 Jean-Sebastien Giguere .25 .60
3 Dany Heatley .40 1.00
4 Ilya Kovalchuk .40 1.00
5 Slava Kozlov .15 .40
6 Pasi Nurminen .25 .60
7 Mike Knuble .15 .40
8 Glen Murray .15 .40
9 Andrew Raycroft .25 .60
10 Joe Thornton .40 1.00
11 Daniel Briere .15 .40
12 Ales Kotalik .15 .40
13 Miroslav Satan .25 .60
14 Shean Donovan .15 .40
15 Jarome Iginla .40 1.00
16 Miikka Kiprusoff .25 .60
17 Erik Cole .15 .40
18 Ron Francis .25 .60
19 Tyler Arnason .25 .60
20 Mark Bell .15 .40
21 Kyle Calder .15 .40
22 David Aebischer .25 .60
23 Peter Forsberg .75 2.00
24 Milan Hejduk .30 .75
25 Paul Kariya .30 .75
26 Joe Sakic .60 1.50
27 Teemu Selanne .30 .75
28 Alex Tanguay .25 .60
29 Marc Denis .25 .60
30 Rick Nash .40 1.00
31 Bill Guerin .25 .60
32 Mike Modano .50 1.25
33 Marty Turco .25 .60
34 Pavel Datsyuk .30 .75
35 Kris Draper .15 .40
36 Dominik Hasek .60 1.50
37 Brett Hull .40 1.00
38 Curtis Joseph .30 .75
39 Robert Lang .25 .60
40 Brendan Shanahan .30 .75
41 Steve Yzerman 1.50 4.00
42 Ales Hemsky .25 .60
43 Ryan Smyth .15 .40
44 Raffi Torres .15 .40
45 Jay Bouwmeester .15 .40
46 Valeri Bure .15 .40
47 Olli Jokinen .25 .60
48 Roberto Luongo .40 1.00
49 Roman Cechmanek .25 .60
50 Alexander Frolov .15 .40
51 Ziggy Palffy .25 .60
52 Andrew Brunette .15 .40
53 Alexandre Daigle .15 .40
54 Marian Gaborik .60 1.50
55 Saku Koivu .30 .75
56 Mike Ribeiro .15 .40
57 Michael Ryder .15 .40
58 Sheldon Souray .15 .40
59 Jose Theodore .40 1.00
60 Martin Erat .15 .40
61 Scott Hartnell .15 .40
62 Tomas Vokoun .25 .60
63 Martin Brodeur .75 2.00
64 Patrik Elias .25 .60
65 Scott Stevens .25 .60
66 Rick DiPietro .25 .60
67 Trent Hunter .15 .40
68 Alexei Yashin .15 .40
69 Jaromir Jagr .50 1.25
70 Alex Kovalev .25 .60
71 Eric Lindros .30 .75
72 Daniel Alfredsson .25 .60
73 Peter Bondra .25 .60
74 Martin Havlat .25 .60
75 Marian Hossa .30 .75
76 Patrick Lalime .25 .60
77 Jason Spezza .30 .75
78 Tony Amonte .25 .60
79 Mark Recchi .25 .60
80 Jeremy Roenick .40 1.00
81 Shane Doan .15 .40
82 Ladislav Nagy .15 .40
83 Rico Fata .15 .40
84 Mario Lemieux 2.00 5.00
85 Pavol Demitra .25 .60
86 Keith Tkachuk .30 .75
87 Doug Weight .25 .60
88 Jonathan Cheechoo .20 .50
89 Patrick Marleau .25 .60
90 Evgeni Nabokov .25 .60
91 Nikolai Khabibulin .30 .75
92 Vincent Lecavalier .30 .75
93 Martin St. Louis .25 .60
94 Ed Belfour .30 .75
95 Owen Nolan .25 .60
96 Mats Sundin .30 .75
97 Todd Bertuzzi .30 .75
98 Jason King .15 .40
99 Brendan Morrison .25 .60
100 Markus Naslund .30 .75
101 Joffrey Lupul RC 2.00 5.00
102 Patrice Bergeron RC 4.00 10.00
103 Derek Roy RC 1.50 4.00
104 Brent Krahn RC 1.25 3.00
105 Matthew Lombardi RC 1.25 3.00
106 Eric Staal RC 5.00 12.00
107 Anton Babchuk RC 1.25 3.00
108 Tuomo Ruutu RC 2.00 5.00
109 Pavel Vorobiev RC 1.25 3.00
110 Mikhail Yakubov RC 1.25 3.00
111 Dan Fritsche RC 1.25 3.00
112 Nikolai Zherdev RC 2.50 6.00
113 Antti Miettinen RC 1.25 3.00
114 Darryl Bootland RC 1.25 3.00
115 Jiri Hudler RC 2.00 5.00
116 Nathan Robinson RC 1.25 3.00
117 Tony Salmelainen RC 1.25 3.00
118 Nathan Horton RC 3.00 8.00
119 Dustin Brown RC 1.50 4.00
120 Brent Burns RC 1.25 3.00
121 Christopher Higgins RC 3.00 8.00
122 Dan Hamhuis RC 1.25 3.00
123 Jordin Tootoo RC 3.00 8.00
124 Marek Zidlicky RC 1.25 3.00
125 David Hale RC 1.25 3.00
126 Paul Martin RC 1.25 3.00
127 Dominic Moore RC 1.25 3.00
128 Antoine Vermette RC 1.25 3.00
129 Joni Pitkanen RC 1.25 3.00
130 Fredrik Sjostrom RC 1.25 3.00
131 Marc-Andre Fleury RC 6.00 15.00
132 Ryan Malone RC 2.00 5.00
133 John Pohl RC 1.25 3.00
134 Peter Sejna RC 1.25 3.00
135 Milan Michalek RC 1.25 3.00
136 Matt Stajan RC 2.00 5.00
137 Ryan Kesler RC 2.50 6.00
138 Boyd Gordon RC 1.25 3.00
139 Alexander Semin RC 4.00 10.00
140 Rastislav Stana RC 1.25 3.00

2003-04 Pacific Quest for the Cup Blue

*STARS: 2X TO 5X BASE HI
STATED ODDS 1:25
STATED PRINT RUN 150 SER.#'d SETS

2003-04 Pacific Quest for the Cup Calder Contenders

COMPLETE SET (20) 15.00 30.00
STATED ODDS 1:7
1 Patrice Bergeron 2.50 6.00
2 Andrew Raycroft 2.50 6.00
3 Matthew Lombardi 1.25 3.00
4 Eric Staal 2.00 5.00
5 Tuomo Ruutu 2.00 5.00
6 Philippe Sauve 1.25 3.00
7 Nikolai Zherdev 2.00 5.00
8 Jiri Hudler 1.25 3.00
9 Nathan Horton 1.50 4.00
10 Dustin Brown 1.50 4.00
11 Brent Burns 1.25 3.00
12 Michael Ryder 1.50 4.00
13 Jordin Tootoo 1.50 4.00
14 Trent Hunter 1.25 3.00
15 Antoine Vermette 1.25 3.00
16 Joni Pitkanen 1.25 3.00
17 Marc-Andre Fleury 3.00 8.00
18 Ryan Malone 1.25 3.00
19 Matt Stajan 1.50 4.00
20 Jason King 1.25 3.00

2003-04 Pacific Quest for the Cup Chasing the Cup

COMPLETE SET (9) 6.00 15.00
STATED ODDS 1:16
1 Dany Heatley 1.00 2.50
2 Ilya Kovalchuk 1.00 2.50
3 Joe Thornton 1.00 2.50
4 Paul Kariya .50 1.25
5 Rick Nash .60 1.50
6 Marty Turco .50 1.25
7 Jason Spezza .50 1.25
8 Mats Sundin .50 1.25
9 Todd Bertuzzi .50 1.25

2003-04 Pacific Quest for the Cup Connquest

COMPLETE SET (6) 8.00 15.00
STATED ODDS 1:48
1 Jean-Sebastien Giguere .75 2.00
2 Joe Sakic 1.50 4.00
3 Nicklas Lidstrom .75 2.00
4 Steve Yzerman 2.50 6.00
5 Scott Stevens .75 2.00
6 Mario Lemieux 3.00 8.00

2003-04 Pacific Quest for the Cup Jerseys

STATED ODDS 1:25
1 Ilya Kovalchuk SP 5.00 12.00
2 Joe Thornton 4.00 10.00
3 Jarome Iginla 3.00 8.00
4 Jocelyn Thibault 3.00 8.00
5 David Aebischer SP 4.00 10.00
6 Joe Sakic 5.00 12.00
7 Rick Nash 4.00 10.00
8 Marty Turco 2.50 6.00
9 Steve Yzerman SP 12.00 30.00
10 Ryan Smyth 2.50 6.00
11 Scott Walker 2.50 6.00
12 Patrik Elias 3.00 8.00
13 Jaromir Jagr 4.00 10.00
14 Martin Havlat 2.50 6.00
15 Jeff Hackett 2.50 6.00
16 Mario Lemieux SP 8.00 20.00
17 Nikolai Khabibulin 3.00 8.00
18 Ed Belfour SP 6.00 15.00
19 Dan Cloutier 2.50 6.00

2003-04 Pacific Quest for the Cup Raising the Cup

STATED ODDS 1:9
1 Sergei Fedorov .75 2.00
2 Rob Blake .60 1.50
3 Peter Forsberg 1.50 4.00
4 Milan Hejduk .60 1.50
5 Joe Sakic 1.25 3.00
6 Mike Modano 1.00 2.50
7 Dominik Hasek 1.25 3.00
8 Brett Hull .75 2.00
9 Nicklas Lidstrom .60 1.50
10 Brendan Shanahan .60 1.50
11 Steve Yzerman 2.00 5.00
12 Martin Brodeur 2.00 5.00
13 Scott Stevens .60 1.50
14 Mark Messier .60 1.50
15 Mario Lemieux 2.50 6.00

2003-04 Pacific Supreme

This 140-card set consisted of 100 veteran cards and 40 rookie cards (101-140) serial-numbered to 775 copies each. There were also 14 autographed parallels of rookie players that were seeded randomly and serial-numbered out of 375. These cards are noted below with a "A" suffix which does not appear on the actual cards.
COMP.SET w/o SP's (100) 15.00 40.00
101-140 ROOKIE PRINT RUN 775
ROOKIE AU PRINT RUN 375
1 Sergei Fedorov .40 1.00
2 Jean-Sebastien Giguere .25 .60
3 Petr Sykora .20 .50
4 Dany Heatley .25 .60
5 Ilya Kovalchuk .25 .60
6 Glen Murray .20 .50
7 Sergei Samsonov .20 .50
8 Joe Thornton .30 .75
9 Daniel Briere .25 .60
10 Chris Drury .20 .50
11 Ales Kotalik .15 .40
12 Ryan Miller .25 .60
13 Jarome Iginla .25 .60
14 Chuck Kobasew .15 .40
15 Ron Francis .30 .75
16 Jeff O'Neill .15 .40
17 Radim Vrbata .20 .50
18 Tyler Arnason .15 .40
19 Steve Sullivan .15 .40
20 Jocelyn Thibault .20 .50
21 Peter Forsberg .30 .75
22 Milan Hejduk .20 .50
23 Paul Kariya .30 .75
24 Patrick Roy .60 1.50
25 Joe Sakic .40 1.00
26 Marc Denis .20 .50
27 Rick Nash .25 .60
28 Geoff Sanderson .15 .40
29 Jason Arnott .20 .50
30 Mike Modano .40 1.00
31 Marty Turco .25 .60
32 Dominik Hasek .40 1.00
33 Brett Hull .30 .75
34 Ray Whitney .20 .50
35 Steve Yzerman .60 1.50
36 Henrik Zetterberg .30 .75
37 Mike Comrie .20 .50
38 Ales Hemsky .25 .60
39 Tommy Salo .20 .50
40 Ryan Smyth .20 .50
41 Jay Bouwmeester .25 .60
42 Olli Jokinen .25 .60
43 Roberto Luongo .40 1.00
44 Roman Cechmanek .20 .50
45 Alexander Frolov .20 .50
46 Ziggy Palffy .25 .60
47 Pierre-Marc Bouchard .25 .60
48 Marian Gaborik .40 1.00
49 Dwayne Roloson .20 .50
50 Marcel Hossa .15 .40
51 Saku Koivu .25 .60
52 Jose Theodore .25 .60
53 Richard Zednik .15 .40
54 Andreas Johansson .15 .40
55 David Legwand .20 .50
56 Tomas Vokoun .20 .50
57 Martin Brodeur .50 1.25
58 Patrik Elias .25 .60
59 John Madden .15 .40
60 Jamie Langenbrunner .20 .50
61 Jason Blake .15 .40
62 Rick DiPietro .20 .50
63 Michael Peca .20 .50
64 Alexei Yashin .20 .50
65 Anson Carter .20 .50
66 Alex Kovalev .20 .50
67 Eric Lindros .40 1.00
68 Petr Nedved .15 .40
69 Daniel Alfredsson .25 .60
70 Marian Hossa .20 .50
71 Patrick Lalime .20 .50
72 Jason Spezza .25 .60
73 Tony Amonte .20 .50
74 John LeClair .25 .60
75 Jeremy Roenick .25 .60
76 Sean Burke .15 .40
77 Mike Johnson .15 .40
78 Sebastien Caron .20 .50
79 Mario Lemieux .75 2.00
80 Pavol Demitra .30 .75
81 Barret Jackman .15 .40
82 Chris Pronger .20 .50
83 Keith Tkachuk .25 .60
84 Patrick Marleau .25 .60
85 Evgeni Nabokov .20 .50
86 Marco Sturm .15 .40
87 Nikolai Khabibulin .25 .60
88 Vincent Lecavalier .20 .50
89 Martin St. Louis .25 .60
90 Ed Belfour .25 .60
91 Alexander Mogilny .20 .50
92 Owen Nolan .20 .50
93 Mats Sundin .25 .60
94 Todd Bertuzzi .25 .60
95 Dan Cloutier .20 .50
96 Brendan Morrison .20 .50
97 Markus Naslund .25 .60
98 Peter Bondra .20 .50
99 Jaromir Jagr .60 1.50
100 Olaf Kolzig .25 .60
101 Garrett Burnett RC 1.25 3.00
102 Joffrey Lupul RC 3.00 8.00
102A Joffrey Lupul AU/375 8.00 20.00
103 Joe DiPenta RC 1.50 4.00
104 Patrice Bergeron RC 6.00 15.00
105 Milan Bartovic RC 1.50 4.00
106 Andrew Peters RC 1.50 4.00
107 Brent Krahn RC 1.25 3.00
108 Matthew Lombardi RC 1.50 4.00
109 Eric Staal RC 6.00 15.00
109A Eric Staal AU/375 15.00 40.00
110 Travis Moen RC 1.50 4.00
111 Tuomo Ruutu RC 2.00 5.00
111A Tuomo Ruutu AU/375 5.00 12.00
112 Pavel Vorobiev RC 1.50 4.00
113 Cody McCormick RC 1.50 4.00
114 Dan Fritsche RC 1.25 3.00
115 Kent McDonell RC 1.50 4.00
116 Antti Miettinen RC 2.00 5.00
117 Jiri Hudler RC 3.00 8.00
117A Jiri Hudler AU/375 8.00 20.00
118 Nathan Horton RC 3.00 8.00
118A Nathan Horton AU/375 8.00 20.00
119 Dustin Brown RC 2.50 6.00
119A Dustin Brown AU/375 12.50 30.00
120 Tim Gleason RC 1.50 4.00
121 Esa Pirnes RC 1.25 3.00
122 Brent Burns RC 3.00 8.00
123 Chris Higgins RC 2.50 6.00
123A Chris Higgins AU/375 6.00 15.00
124 Dan Hamhuis RC 1.50 4.00
125 Jordin Tootoo RC 2.50 6.00
125A Jordin Tootoo AU/375 6.00 15.00
126 Marek Zidlicky RC 1.25 3.00
127 David Hale RC 1.25 3.00
128 Paul Martin RC 1.50 4.00
129 Sean Bergenheim RC 1.50 4.00
130 Antoine Vermette RC 2.50 6.00
130A Antoine Vermette AU/375 6.00 15.00
131 Joni Pitkanen RC 2.00 5.00
131A Joni Pitkanen AU/375 5.00 12.00
132 Matthew Spiller RC 1.50 4.00
133 Marc-Andre Fleury RC 8.00 20.00
133A Marc-Andre Fleury AU/375 25.00 50.00
134 Matt Murley RC 1.50 4.00
135 Peter Sejna RC 1.50 4.00
135A Peter Sejna AU/375 4.00 10.00
136 Milan Michalek RC 2.50 6.00
136A Milan Michalek AU/375 6.00 15.00
137 Tom Preissing RC 1.50 4.00
138 Maxim Kondratiev RC 1.25 3.00
139 Matt Stajan RC 2.00 5.00
139A Matt Stajan AU 4.00 10.00
140 Boyd Gordon RC 1.50 4.00

2003-04 Pacific Supreme Blue

*1-100 VETS: 1.2X TO 3X BASIC CARDS
1-100 VET STATED ODDS 1:2
*101-140 ROOKIE/250: .8X TO 2X RC/775
101-140 ROOKIE PRINT RUN 250

2003-04 Pacific Supreme Red

*1-100 VETS: 1.5X TO 4X BASIC CARDS
1-100 VET STATED ODDS 1:3
*101-140 ROOKIE/425: .5X TO 1.2X RC/775
ROOKIE PRINT RUN 425 SER.#'d SETS

2003-04 Pacific Supreme Retail

This 140-card set mirrored the hobby version but carried silver foil highlights in place of the gold foil. Rookie cards were not serial-numbered and were inserted at 1:4.
*1-100 VETS: .4X TO 1X HOBBY GOLD
*101-140 ROOKIES: .25X TO .6X RC/775

2003-04 Pacific Supreme Generations

COMPLETE SET (24) 25.00 50.00
STATED ODDS 1:7
1 R.Francis/R.Vrbata 1.50 4.00
2 P.Roy/D.Aebischer 3.00 8.00
3 G.Sanderson/R.Nash 1.50 4.00
4 S.Yzerman/P.Datysuk 4.00 10.00
5 B.Hull/H.Zetterberg 3.00 8.00
6 D.Alfredsson/J.Spezza 2.50 6.00
7 S.Burke/Z.Bierk 1.25 3.00
8 M.Lemieux/Marc-Andre Fleury 5.00 12.00
9 A.MacInnis/B.Jackman 1.50 4.00
10 V.Damphousse/J.Cheechoo 1.50 4.00
11 M.Sundin/N.Antropov 1.50 4.00
12 M.Naslund/D.Sedin 1.50 4.00

2003-04 Pacific Supreme Jerseys

STATED ODDS 2:10
STATED PRINT RUN 200-500
1 Sergei Fedorov/500 4.00 10.00
2 Ilya Kovalchuk/500 4.00 10.00
3 Joe Thornton/500 5.00 12.00
4 Chris Drury/500 2.50 6.00
5 Miroslav Satan/500 2.50 6.00
6 Jarome Iginla/500 4.00 10.00
7 Eric Daze/500 2.50 6.00
8 Peter Forsberg/200 8.00 20.00
9 Paul Kariya/500 3.00 8.00
10 Patrick Roy/500 10.00 25.00
11 Brett Hull/500 4.00 10.00
12 Steve Yzerman/200 10.00 25.00
13 Mike Comrie/500 2.50 6.00
14 Ryan Smyth/500 2.50 6.00
15 Olli Jokinen/500 2.50 6.00
16 Jose Theodore/500 4.00 10.00
17 Pavel Bure/500 3.00 8.00
18 Eric Lindros/500 3.00 8.00
19 Tony Amonte/500 2.50 6.00
20 Jeremy Roenick/500 4.00 10.00
21 Mario Lemieux/500 10.00 25.00
22 Vincent Lecavalier/500 2.50 6.00
23 Mats Sundin/500 3.00 8.00
24 Markus Naslund/500 3.00 8.00
25 Jaromir Jagr/500 4.00 10.00

2003-04 Pacific Supreme Standing Guard

COMPLETE SET (12) 10.00 25.00
STATED ODDS 1:12
1 Jean-Sebastien Giguere 1.25 3.00
2 Jocelyn Thibault 1.25 3.00
3 Patrick Roy 3.00 8.00
4 Marc Denis 1.25 3.00
5 Marty Turco 1.25 3.00
6 Dominik Hasek 2.00 5.00
7 Roberto Luongo 2.00 5.00
8 Jose Theodore 2.00 5.00
9 Martin Brodeur 2.50 6.00
10 Patrick Lalime 1.25 3.00
11 Sean Burke 1.25 3.00
12 Ed Belfour 1.50 4.00

2003-04 Pacific Supreme Team

COMPLETE SET (10) 8.00 15.00
STATED ODDS 1:12
1 Joe Thornton .50 1.25
2 Peter Forsberg 1.00 2.50
3 Joe Sakic .60 1.50
4 Brett Hull .40 1.00
5 Steve Yzerman 2.00 5.00
6 Marian Gaborik .60 1.50
7 Mario Lemieux 2.50 6.00
8 Todd Bertuzzi .30 .75
9 Markus Naslund .30 .75
10 Jaromir Jagr .50 1.25

2002 Pacific Toronto Fall Expo

Available as a wrapper redemption at the 2002 Toronto Fall Expo, this 10-card set focused on goalies from around the league. One goalie was pictured on each side of the cards and each card was serial-numbered out of 500. A gold parallel was also created and available randomly.
COMPLETE SET (10) 10.00 25.00
*GOLD: 1.5X TO 4X
1 Ed Belfour 2.00 5.00
Curtis Joseph
2 Jose Theodore 4.00 10.00
Patrick Roy
3 Roman Turek .60 1.50
Tommy Salo
4 Patrick Lalime .60 1.50
Dan Cloutier
5 Roberto Luongo 1.25 3.00
Nikolai Khabibulin
6 Martin Brodeur 2.00 5.00
Mike Richter
7 Jean-Sebastien Giguere 3.00 8.00
Felix Potvin
8 Marty Turco 1.25 3.00
Sean Burke
9 Martin Biron .60 1.50
Jocelyn Thibault
10 Brent Johnson .60 1.50
Evgeni Nabokov

2002 Pacific Toronto Spring Expo Rookie Collection

Available as a wrapper redemption at the Pacific booth during the 2002 Spring Expo in Toronto, this 10-card set featured some of the hottest rookies of the year. Each card was serial-numbered out of 500.
COMPLETE SET (10) 10.00 25.00
1 Dany Heatley 2.00 5.00
2 Ilya Kovalchuk 3.00 8.00
3 Mark Bell .75 2.00
4 Radim Vrbata .75 2.00
5 Rostislav Klesla 1.25 3.00
6 Pavel Datsyuk 3.00 8.00
7 Kristian Huselius .75 2.00
8 Raffi Torres .75 2.00
9 Dan Blackburn 1.25 3.00
10 Krystofer Kolanos .75 2.00

2003 Pacific Toronto Spring Expo

Serial-numbered to 499, this 8-card set was available only via wrapper redemption at the Pacific booth during the Toronto Spring Expo. A gold parallel numbered to 99 was also available for the first 99 visitors to open a Pacific box at the booth.
COMPLETE SET (8) 15.00 35.00
*GOLD/99: 1X TO 2.5X BASIC CARDS
1 Stanislav Chistov 1.00 2.50
2 Ryan Miller 1.50 4.00
3 Rick Nash 2.00 5.00
4 Henrik Zetterberg 3.00 8.00
5 Jay Bouwmeester 1.50 4.00
6 Mike Cammalleri 1.00 2.50
7 Jason Spezza 2.00 5.00
8 Carlo Colaiacovo 1.00 2.50

2003 Pacific Toronto Fall Expo

This 6-card set was part of a wrapper redemption during the 2003 Fall Expo. Cards were serial-numbered out of 500 and featured a NHL player on the front and a CFL player on the back.
COMPLETE SET (6) 10.00 20.00
1 Todd Bertuzzi 1.50 4.00
Dave Dickenson
2 Jarome Iginla 2.00 5.00

Marcus Crandell
Ryan Smyth 1.25 3.00
Ricky Ray
Jose Theodore 2.00 5.00
Anthony Calvillo
Marian Hossa 1.25 3.00
Josh Ranek
Ed Belfour 1.50 4.00
Damon Allen

2004 Pacific National Convention

These cards were intended to be issued as part of a wrapper redemption at the 2004 National Sports Collectors Convention in Cleveland, due to circumstances, Pacific did not attend the show and the entire lot was sold on consignment. The cards are serial numbered out of 499. The full bleed borders make them susceptible to chipping.

COMPLETE SET (6) 8.00 20.00
1 Ilya Kovalchuk 2.00 5.00
2 Joe Thornton 2.00 5.00
3 Rick Nash 2.00 5.00
4 Rick DiPietro .75 2.00
5 Marc-Andre Fleury 1.50 4.00
6 Vincent Lecavalier 1.25 3.00

2004 Pacific Toronto Spring Expo

Available only via wrapper redemption at the 2004 Toronto Spring Expo, this 8-card set featured rookies from the 2003-04 season. Each card was serial-numbered out of 499. A gold parallel was also randomly available.

*GOLD/99: .8X TO 2X BASIC CARDS
GOLD PRINT RUN 99 SER.#'d SETS
1 Patrice Bergeron 1.50 4.00
2 Eric Staal .75 2.00
3 Nathan Horton .75 2.00
4 Dustin Brown 1.00 2.50
5 Jordin Tootoo .75 2.00
6 Antoine Vermette .50 1.25
7 Marc-Andre Fleury 2.00 5.00
8 Matt Stajan .60 1.50

2004 Pacific WHA Autographs

These two autographed cards were the only two WHA cards that Pacific produced before the company shut their doors in 2004. Each card was serial-numbered to 1972 and were available only via the Pacific website and various other online dealers for $25US.

1 Bobby Hull 15.00 30.00
2 Andre Lacroix 10.00 20.00

2010-11 Panini All Goalies

COMP.FACT.SET (106) 12.00 30.00
COMPLETE SET (100) 8.00 20.00
1 Jonas Hiller .15 .40
2 Timo Pielmeier .20 .50
3 Dan Ellis .15 .40
4 Ray Emery .15 .40
5 Chris Mason .15 .40
6 Ondrej Pavelec .20 .50
7 Peter Mannino .15 .40
8 Tim Thomas .15 .40
9 Tuukka Rask .20 .50
10 Ryan Miller .20 .50
11 Patrick Lalime .15 .40
12 Jhonas Enroth .20 .50
13 Miikka Kiprusoff .15 .40
14 Henrik Karlsson .15 .40
15 Cam Ward .20 .50
16 Justin Peters .15 .40
17 Corey Crawford .25 .60
18 Marty Turco .20 .50
19 Brian Elliott .15 .40
20 Peter Budaj .15 .40
21 Steve Mason .15 .40
22 Mathieu Garon .15 .40
23 Kari Lehtonen .15 .40
24 Andrew Raycroft .15 .40
25 Richard Bachman .20 .50
26 Chris Osgood .20 .50
27 Jimmy Howard .25 .60
28 Joey MacDonald .15 .40
29 Jordan Pearce .25 .60
30 Thomas McCollum .20 .50
31 Nikolai Khabibulin .15 .40
32 Devan Dubnyk .20 .50
33 Martin Gerber .15 .40
34 Tomas Vokoun .15 .40
35 Jacob Markstrom .25 .60
36 Scott Clemmensen .15 .40
37 Jonathan Bernier .20 .50
38 Jonathan Quick .30 .75
39 Matt Hackett .20 .50
40 Niklas Backstrom .20 .50
41 Jose Theodore .20 .50
42 Anton Khudobin .15 .40
43 Alex Auld .15 .40
44 Carey Price .75 2.00
45 Pekka Rinne .25 .60
46 Anders Lindback .15 .40
47 Mark Dekanich .15 .40
48 Jeff Frazee .25 .60
49 Johan Hedberg .15 .40
50 Martin Brodeur .40 1.00
51 Mike McKenna .15 .40
52 Rick DiPietro .15 .40
53 Nathan Lawson .15 .40
54 Kevin Poulin .20 .50
55 Al Montoya .15 .40
56 Henrik Lundqvist .30 .75
57 Martin Biron .15 .40
58 Craig Anderson .20 .50
59 Pascal Leclaire .15 .40
60 Robin Lehner .30 .75
61 Mike Brodeur .20 .50
62 Curtis McElhinney .15 .40
63 Sergei Bobrovsky .40 1.00
64 Brian Boucher .15 .40
65 Michael Leighton .15 .40
66 Jason LaBarbera .15 .40
67 Ilya Bryzgalov .15 .40
68 Matt Climie .15 .40
69 Marc-Andre Fleury .30 .75
70 Brent Johnson .15 .40
71 Antero Niittymaki .15 .40
72 Antti Niemi .15 .40
73 Alex Stalock .20 .50
74 J.P. Anderson .20 .50
75 Carter Hutton .30 .75
76 Jaroslav Halak .20 .50
77 Ty Conklin .15 .40
78 Ben Bishop .20 .50
79 Dwayne Roloson .15 .40
80 Mike Smith .20 .50
81 Cedrick Desjardins .20 .50
82 James Reimer .20 .50
83 Jean-Sebastien Giguere .15 .40
84 Jonas Gustavsson .25 .60
85 Roberto Luongo .20 .50
86 Cory Schneider .15 .40
87 Semyon Varlamov .20 .50
88 Michal Neuvirth .15 .40
89 Braden Holtby .40 1.00
90 Patrick Roy .50 1.25
91 Tony Esposito .20 .50
92 Ron Hextall .25 .60
93 Gerry Cheevers .20 .50
94 Jim Craig .15 .40
95 Ed Belfour .20 .50
96 Curtis Joseph .25 .60
97 Felix Potvin .30 .75
98 Grant Fuhr .20 .50
99 Richard Brodeur .20 .50
100 Tom Barrasso .20 .50

2010-11 Panini All Goalies Up Close

*UP CLOSE: 2X TO 5X BASE
FIVE PER FACTORY SET
17 Corey Crawford 2.00 5.00
45 Pekka Rinne 2.00 5.00

2010-11 Panini All Goalies Stopper Sweaters

ONE PER FACTORY SET
1 Patrick Roy 10.00 25.00
2 Martin Brodeur 25.00 50.00
3 Roberto Luongo 15.00 30.00
4 Tim Thomas 15.00 30.00
5 Carey Price
6 Craig Anderson 4.00 10.00
7 Henrik Lundqvist 6.00 15.00
8 Pekka Rinne 6.00 15.00
9 Kari Lehtonen 5.00 12.00
10 Cam Ward 4.00 10.00
11 Devan Dubnyk 4.00 10.00
12 Mike Smith 4.00 10.00
13 Ondrej Pavelec 4.00 10.00
14 Cory Schneider 3.00 8.00
15 Andrew Raycroft 3.00 8.00
16 Peter Budaj 3.00 8.00
17 Brian Elliott 3.00 8.00
18 Miikka Kiprusoff 5.00 12.00

2011 Panini Black Friday

8 Steve Stamkos 1.00 2.50
9 Alex Ovechkin 1.00 2.50
10 Sidney Crosby 1.25 3.00
11 Tyler Seguin 1.00 2.50
12 Jeff Skinner .75 2.00
13 Taylor Hall 1.00 2.50

2011 Panini Black Friday Rookies

RC1 Ryan Nugent-Hopkins 8.00 20.00
RC2 Gabriel Landeskog 3.00 8.00
RC3 Adam Larsson 2.00 5.00
RC4 Mark Scheifele 2.50 6.00
RC5 Mika Zibanejad 1.25 3.00

2012 Panini Black Friday

1-23 CRACKED ICE/25: 6X TO 15X BASE HI
24-50 CRACKED ICE/25: 2.5X TO 6X BASE HI
12 Alex Ovechkin .50 1.25
13 Evgeni Malkin .40 1.00
14 Ryan Nugent-Hopkins .60 1.50
15 Gabriel Landeskog .40 1.00
16 Tyler Seguin .40 1.00
17 Jonathan Quick .60 1.50
47 Chris Kreider/599 3.00 8.00

2012 Panini Black Friday Black Holofoil

CRACKED ICE/25: 3X TO 8X BASE HI
18 Alex Ovechkin .60 1.50
19 Sidney Crosby .60 1.50
20 Jonathan Quick .75 2.00

2012 Panini Black Friday Kings

CRACKED ICE/25: 2X TO 5X BASE HI
8 Mark Messier 1.00 2.50
9 Gordie Howe 1.50 4.00
10 Joe Sakic 1.00 2.50

2012 Panini Black Friday Rookie Kings

CRACKED ICE/25: 2X TO 5X BASE HI
9 Chris Kreider .50 1.25

2012 Panini Black Friday Spokesman Jumbo Jerseys

GH Gordie Howe 8.00 20.00

2012 Panini Black Friday Manufactured Patch Autographs

INSERTS IN BLACK FRIDAY PACKS
CK Chris Kreider 50.00 125.00

2013 Panini Black Friday

CRACKED ICE/35: 5X TO 12X BASIC CARDS
LAVA FLOW/150: 2X TO 5X BASIC CARDS
3 Sidney Crosby HK 1.00 2.50
7 Alex Ovechkin HK .60 1.50
11 Steven Stamkos HK .60 1.50
15 Patrick Kane HK .60 1.50
19 Tuukka Rask HK .40 1.00
48 Nathan MacKinnon/299 HK 4.00 10.00
50 Seth Jones/299 HK 1.50 4.00
54 Nail Yakupov JSY/99 HK 2.00 5.00
55 Jonathan Huberdeau JSY/99 HK 1.50 4.00
56 Alex Galchenyuk JSY/99 HK 2.00 5.00

2013 Panini Black Friday Autographs

3 Sidney Crosby
7 Alex Ovechkin
11 Steven Stamkos
15 Patrick Kane
19 Tuukka Rask
48 Nathan MacKinnon
50 Seth Jones
54 Nail Yakupov
55 Jonathan Huberdeau
56 Alex Galchenyuk

2013 Panini Black Friday Collection

CRACKED ICE/35: 4X TO 10X BASIC CARDS
LAVA FLOW/150: 1.5X TO 4X BASIC CARDS
18 Jonathan Toews .60 1.50
19 Nail Yakupov .75 2.00

2013 Panini Black Friday Manufactured Patch Autographs

AG Alex Galchenyuk 20.00 40.00
JQ Jonathan Quick 25.00 50.00

2013 Panini Black Friday Rookie Materials

NM Nathan MacKinnon HK 10.00 25.00

2013 Panini Black Friday VIP

CRACKED ICE/35: 2.5X TO 6X BASIC CARDS
LAVA FLOW/150: 1.2X TO 3X BASIC CARDS
9 Alex Galchenyuk 2.00 5.00
10 Jonathan Huberdeau 1.50 4.00

2014 Panini Black Friday Collection

*CRACKED ICE/25: 4X TO 10X BASIC CARDS
THICK STOCK/50: 1.2X TO 3X BASIC CARDS
19 Mark Messier HK .60 1.50

2014 Panini Black Friday Collection Autographs

ANNOUNCED PRINT RUN 25 OR LESS
19 Mark Messier HK

2010 Panini Century Sports Stamp Autographs

STATED PRINT RUN 5-100
NO PRICING ON QTY 25 OR LESS
18 Mike Bossy/40 15.00 40.00
19 Patrick Roy/18
20 Paul Coffey/50 10.00 25.00
22 Pierre Pilote/75 8.00 20.00
24 Gerry Cheevers/100 6.00 15.00
25 Alex Delvecchio/25
26 Bill Gadsby/75 6.00 15.00
37 Norm Ullman/85 10.00 20.00
38 Cammi Granato/50 20.00 50.00
41 Ray Bourque/52 20.00 50.00
42 Pat LaFontaine/39 40.00 80.00

2010 Panini Century Sports Stamp Materials

STATED PRINT RUN 1-250
NO PRICING ON QTY 25 OR LESS
18 Mike Bossy/250 3.00 8.00
19 Patrick Roy/250 10.00 25.00
22 Pierre Pilote/250 3.00 8.00
25 Alex Delvecchio/250 3.00 8.00
26 Bill Gadsby/99 6.00 15.00
37 Norm Ullman/4
42 Pat LaFontaine/250 4.00 10.00

2010 Panini Century Sports Stamp Materials Autographs

STATED PRINT RUN 2-50
NO PRICING ON QTY 25 OR LESS
37 Norm Ullman/15
42 Pat LaFontaine/15
18 Mike Bossy/10
19 Patrick Roy/7
22 Pierre Pilote/25
25 Alex Delvecchio/15
26 Bill Gadsby/25

2011-12 Panini Contenders

COMP.SET w/o SP's (100) 8.00 20.00
CC STATED PRINT RUN 999
161-200/261-283 ROOK.PRINT RUN 999
195/199/261-283 ISSUED IN ANTHOLOGY
201-260 ROOKIE AU PRINT RUN 763-800
1 Roberto Luongo .40 1.00
2 Duncan Keith .40 1.00
3 Dion Phaneuf .40 1.00
4 Vincent Lecavalier .30 .75
5 Nicklas Lidstrom .40 1.00
6 Shea Weber .30 .75
7 Jeff Carter .40 1.00
8 Teemu Selanne .75 2.00
9 Matt Duchene .40 1.00
10 Corey Perry .40 1.00
11 Daniel Alfredsson .40 1.00
12 Jarome Iginla .40 1.00
13 Pavel Datsyuk .50 1.25
14 Jordan Eberle .40 1.00
15 Dany Heatley .30 .75
16 Andrew Ladd .40 1.00
17 Ryan Kesler .40 1.00
18 Marc Staal .40 1.00
19 Joe Thornton .40 1.00
20 Chris Pronger .30 .75
21 Loui Eriksson .30 .75
22 Dan Boyle .30 .75
23 Dustin Brown .40 1.00
24 Ryan Callahan .40 1.00
25 Chris Stewart .30 .75
26 Martin St. Louis .40 1.00
27 Alex Pietrangelo .30 .75
28 Claude Giroux .40 1.00
29 Marc-Andre Fleury .60 1.50
30 Henrik Lundqvist .50 1.25
31 Carey Price 1.25 3.00
32 Kari Lehtonen .30 .75
33 Zdeno Chara .40 1.00
34 Miikka Kiprusoff .40 1.00
35 Nikolai Khabibulin .30 .75
36 Milan Lucic .40 1.00
37 Mike Smith .40 1.00
38 Jonas Hiller .30 .75
39 Al Montoya .25 .60
40 Henrik Zetterberg .50 1.25
41 Craig Anderson .40 1.00
42 David Backes .40 1.00
43 Tim Thomas .40 1.00
44 Henrik Sedin .40 1.00
45 Jonathan Quick .60 1.50
46 David Krejci .40 1.00
47 Daniel Sedin .40 1.00
48 Danny Briere .40 1.00
49 Joe Pavelski .40 1.00
50 Corey Crawford .50 1.25
51 Jason Spezza .40 1.00
52 Mike Green .40 1.00
53 Jeff Skinner .40 1.00
54 Anze Kopitar .60 1.50
55 Jason Pominville .30 .75
56 Semyon Varlamov .40 1.00
57 Tyler Myers .40 1.00
58 Kris Letang .40 1.00
59 Eric Staal .50 1.25
60 Jose Theodore .40 1.00
61 Rick Nash .40 1.00
62 Patrik Elias .40 1.00
63 Brad Marchand .50 1.25
64 Mike Commodore .30 .75
65 Erik Karlsson .75 2.00
66 Martin Brodeur .75 2.00
67 Max Pacioretty .40 1.00
68 Jaromir Jagr 1.00 2.50
69 Taylor Hall .75 2.00
70 Ryan Miller .40 1.00
71 Evgeni Malkin 1.25 3.00
72 Luke Adam .30 .75
73 Michael Ryder .25 .60
74 T.J. Oshie .60 1.50
75 Brian Gionta .30 .75
76 P.K. Subban .75 2.00
77 Joffrey Lupul .30 .75
78 Marian Gaborik .50 1.25
79 James Reimer .40 1.00
80 Nik Antropov .30 .75
81 Phil Kessel .50 1.25
82 Mike Richards .40 1.00
83 Ales Hemsky .30 .75
84 Mikhail Grabovski .30 .75
85 Jamie Benn .50 1.25
86 Ondrej Pavelec .40 1.00
87 Sidney Crosby 1.50 4.00
88 Patrick Kane .75 2.00
89 Ray Whitney .30 .75
90 Logan Couture .40 1.00
91 Steven Stamkos .75 2.00
92 John Tavares .75 2.00
93 Jimmy Howard .40 1.00
94 Ryan Smyth .30 .75
95 Cam Ward .40 1.00
96 Pierre-Marc Bouchard .40 1.00
97 Ryan Getzlaf .60 1.50
98 Alex Ovechkin 1.50 4.00
99 Jonathan Toews .75 2.00
100 Josh Harding .40 1.00
101 Corey Perry CC 1.50 4.00
102 Ryan Getzlaf CC 2.50 6.00
103 Nathan Horton CC 1.50 4.00
104 Patrice Bergeron CC 2.00 5.00
105 Tim Thomas CC 1.50 4.00
106 Ryan Miller CC 1.50 4.00
107 Jarome Iginla CC 1.50 4.00
108 Jonathan Toews CC 3.00 8.00
109 Matt Duchene CC 1.50 4.00
110 Pavel Datsyuk CC 2.00 5.00
111 Nicklas Lidstrom CC 1.50 4.00
112 Drew Doughty CC 1.50 4.00
113 Anze Kopitar CC 2.50 6.00
114 Dustin Brown CC 1.50 4.00
115 Carey Price CC 5.00 12.00
116 Scott Gomez CC 1.25 3.00
117 John Tavares CC 3.00 8.00
118 Brad Richards CC 1.50 4.00
119 Jaromir Jagr CC 4.00 10.00
120 Claude Giroux CC 1.50 4.00
121 James van Riemsdyk CC 1.50 4.00
122 Danny Briere CC 1.50 4.00
123 Ilya Bryzgalov CC 1.50 4.00
124 Chris Pronger CC 1.25 3.00
125 Shane Doan CC 1.25 3.00
126 Marc-Andre Fleury CC 2.50 6.00
127 Jordan Staal CC 1.50 4.00
128 Sidney Crosby CC 6.00 15.00
129 Kris Letang CC 1.50 4.00
130 James Neal CC 1.50 4.00
131 Evgeni Malkin CC 5.00 12.00
132 Patrick Marleau CC 1.50 4.00
133 Logan Couture CC 1.50 4.00
134 Dan Boyle CC 1.25 3.00
135 Joe Thornton CC 1.50 4.00
136 Martin St. Louis CC 1.50 4.00
137 Vincent Lecavalier CC 1.25 3.00
138 Steven Stamkos CC 3.00 8.00
139 Victor Hedman CC 2.00 5.00
140 Mikhail Grabovski CC 1.25 3.00
141 James Reimer CC 1.50 4.00
142 Phil Kessel CC 2.00 5.00
143 Ryan Kesler CC 1.50 4.00
144 Roberto Luongo CC 1.50 4.00
145 Henrik Sedin CC 1.50 4.00
146 Daniel Sedin CC 1.50 4.00
147 Alexander Semin CC 1.50 4.00
148 Alex Ovechkin CC 6.00 15.00
149 John Carlson CC 2.00 5.00
150 Tomas Vokoun CC 1.25 3.00
151 Steve Yzerman CC 2.50 6.00
152 Denis Savard CC 2.00 5.00
153 Patrick Roy CC 4.00 10.00
154 Mark Messier CC 2.00 5.00
155 Joe Sakic CC 2.50 6.00
156 Brendan Shanahan CC 2.00 5.00
157 Bryan Trottier CC 2.00 5.00
158 Luc Robitaille CC 1.50 4.00
159 Mario Lemieux CC 5.00 12.00
160 Curtis Joseph CC 1.50 4.00
161 Maxime Macenauer RC 1.50 4.00
162 Patrick Maroon RC 1.50 4.00
163 Corey Tropp RC 1.50 4.00
164 Lance Bouma RC 1.50 4.00
165 Cameron Gaunce RC 1.25 3.00
166 Colton Sceviour RC 1.50 4.00
167 Colten Teubert RC 1.50 4.00
168 Chris VandeVelde RC 2.50 6.00
169 Hugh Jessiman RC 1.50 4.00
170 Bracken Kearns RC 1.50 4.00
171 Scott Timmins RC 1.50 4.00
172 Carson McMillan RC 2.00 5.00
173 Drew Bagnall RC 1.50 4.00
174 Frederic St-Denis RC 1.50 4.00
175 Brendon Nash RC 1.50 4.00
176 Mattias Ekholm RC 1.50 4.00
177 Ryan Thang RC 1.25 3.00
178 Keith Kinkaid RC 1.50 4.00
179 Mikko Koskinen RC 2.00 5.00
180 Mark Katic RC 1.50 4.00
181 Shane Sims RC 1.50 4.00
182 Matt Campanale RC 1.50 4.00
183 Dmitry Orlov RC 2.00 5.00
184 Justin DiBenedetto RC 1.25 3.00
185 David Ullstrom RC 1.50 4.00
186 Kevin Marshall RC 1.50 4.00
187 Ben Holmstrom RC 1.50 4.00
188 Brian Strait RC 2.00 5.00
189 Harri Sateri RC 1.50 4.00
190 Todd Ford RC 2.00 5.00
191 Marc-Andre Bourdon RC 3.00 8.00
192 Anders Nilsson RC 1.50 4.00
193 Kris Fredheim RC 1.50 4.00
194 Paul Postma RC 1.50 4.00
195 Tomas Kundratek RC 2.00 5.00
196 Roman Josi RC 2.50 6.00
197 Stefan Elliott RC 1.50 4.00
198 Brayden McNabb RC 1.50 4.00
199 Bill Sweatt RC 1.50 4.00
200 T.J. Brennan RC 1.50 4.00
201 Smith-Pelly AU RC 5.00 12.00
202 Peter Holland AU RC 3.00 8.00
203 Greg Nemisz AU RC 3.00 8.00
204 Roman Horak AU RC 3.00 8.00
205 Justin Faulk AU RC 5.00 12.00
206 Brandon Saad AU RC 8.00 20.00
207 Marcus Kruger AU RC 5.00 12.00
208 G.Landeskog AU RC 12.00 30.00
209 Ryan Johansen AU RC 6.00 15.00
210 Cam Atkinson AU RC 8.00 20.00
211 John Moore AU RC 3.00 8.00
212 David Savard AU RC 3.00 8.00
213 Tomas Kubalik AU RC 3.00 8.00
214 Allen York AU RC 3.00 8.00
215 Tomas Vincour AU RC 3.00 8.00
216 Gustav Nyquist AU RC 12.00 30.00
217 Brendan Smith AU RC 6.00 15.00
218 R.Nugent-Hopkins AU RC 15.00 40.00
219 Carl Hagelin AU/763 RC 12.00 30.00
220 Ryan Ellis AU RC 3.00 8.00
221 Simon Despres AU RC 8.00 20.00
222 Gudbranson AU RC 4.00 10.00
223 Slava Voynov AU RC 3.00 8.00
224 Brett Bulmer AU RC 3.00 8.00
225 Aaron Palushaj AU RC 3.00 8.00
226 Alexei Emelin AU RC 3.00 8.00
227 Raphael Diaz AU RC 3.00 8.00
228 Craig Smith AU RC 4.00 10.00
229 Jonathon Blum AU RC 3.00 8.00
230 Blake Geoffrion AU RC 3.00 8.00
231 Adam Larsson AU RC 4.00 10.00
232 Adam Henrique AU RC 6.00 15.00
233 Tim Erixon AU RC 5.00 12.00
234 Cam Talbot AU RC 8.00 20.00
235 Mika Zibanejad AU RC 8.00 20.00
236 Stephane Da Costa AU RC 3.00 8.00
237 Patrick Wiercioch AU RC 3.00 8.00
238 Colin Greening AU RC 3.00 8.00
239 David Rundblad AU RC 3.00 8.00
240 Erik Condra AU RC 3.00 8.00
241 Sean Couturier AU RC 6.00 15.00
242 Matt Read AU RC 10.00 25.00
243 Zac Rinaldo AU RC 3.00 8.00
244 Erik Gustafsson AU RC 4.00 10.00
245 Calvin de Haan AU RC 3.00 8.00
246 Louis Leblanc AU RC 10.00 25.00
247 Joe Vitale AU RC 5.00 12.00
248 Robert Bortuzzo AU RC 5.00 12.00
249 Brett Connolly AU RC 5.00 12.00
250 Joe Colborne AU RC 5.00 12.00
251 Jake Gardiner AU RC 6.00 15.00
252 Matt Frattin AU RC 6.00 15.00
253 Ben Scrivens AU RC 6.00 15.00
254 Eddie Lack AU RC 6.00 15.00
255 Cody Hodgson AU RC 8.00 20.00
256 Yann Sauve AU RC 3.00 8.00
257 Cody Eakin AU RC 5.00 12.00
258 Carl Klingberg AU RC 3.00 8.00
259 Mark Scheifele AU RC 15.00 40.00
260 Zack Kassian AU RC 6.00 15.00
261 Andrew Shaw RC 5.00 12.00
262 Brad Malone RC 2.50 6.00
263 Cade Fairchild RC 1.25 3.00
264 Dylan Olsen RC 2.50 6.00
265 Gabriel Bourque RC 3.00 8.00
266 Iiro Tarkki RC 2.50 6.00
267 Jeremy Smith RC 3.00 8.00
268 Jimmy Hayes RC 3.00 8.00
269 Leland Irving RC 1.50 4.00
270 Marcus Foligno RC 3.00 8.00
271 Mike Hoffman RC 6.00 15.00
272 Mike Murphy RC 3.00 8.00
273 Riley Nash RC 1.50 4.00
274 Stu Bickel RC 1.50 4.00
275 Matt Fraser RC 2.00 5.00
276 Joakim Andersson RC 3.00 8.00
277 Brian Foster RC 2.50 6.00
278 Andre Petersson RC 2.00 5.00
279 Harry Zolnierczyk RC 1.50 4.00
280 Mark Borowiecki RC 2.00 5.00
281 Andy Miele RC 1.50 4.00
282 Anton Lander RC 1.50 4.00
283 Carl Sneep RC 2.50 6.00

2011-12 Panini Contenders Gold

*VETS 1-100: 2.5X TO 6X BASIC CARDS
*ROOKIES 161-200: .6X TO 1.5X BASIC CARDS
STATED PRINT RUN 100 SER.#'d SETS
50 Corey Crawford 3.00 8.00

2011-12 Panini Contenders Match Ups Booklet Autographs

1 Ovech/Semin/Stl/Mlkn SP
2 Gudbr/Mrkstrm/Conn/Stmk
3 Erixon/Calla/Larsn/Henrq 40.00 80.00
4 Segn/Rask/Kes/Clbrne SP 90.00 150.00
5 Grabv/Rmer/Subn/Price SP 40.00 100.00
6 Frattin/Gard/Grning/Cndra 10.00 25.00
7 Hall/Ebrle/Igin/Giord SP 40.00 100.00
8 Quick/Brwn/Hillr/Perry 40.00 80.00
9 Dats/Hwrd/Tws/Sharp SP
10 Morrow/Leht/Seto/Bckstrm 12.00 30.00
11 Giroux/Read/Call/Stepan 50.00 100.00
12 Doan/Bisn/Kane/Klingbrg 20.00 50.00
13 Johan/Moore/Osh/Pietr 15.00 40.00
14 Smith/Howard/Varla/Land 50.00 120.00
15 Paajrvi/Landr/Karls/Bcklnd 15.00 40.00
16 Atknsn/Svrd/Scheif/Post 12.00 30.00
17 Kesler/Schn/Brown/Bernier 15.00 40.00
18 Jagr/Bryzg/Fleury/Malkin SP 125.00 250.00
19 Staal/Lund/Brdr/Parise SP 175.00 300.00
20 Ctre/Pavel/Selne/Perry SP 40.00 80.00
21 Andrsn/Grning/Eller/Diaz 12.00 30.00
22 Vanek/Miller/Bergrn/Thms 40.00 80.00
23 Sharp/Prngr/Giroux/Toews 75.00 150.00
24 Geof/Smith/Atkin/Jhnsn 12.00 30.00

2011-12 Panini Contenders NHL Ink

*GOLD/25: 1X TO 2.5X BASIC AU
*GOLD/25: .8X TO 2X BASIC AU SP
1 Teemu Selanne SP 20.00 40.00
2 Ray Bourque SP 25.00 60.00
3 Curtis Glencross 2.50 6.00
4 Greg Nemisz 3.00 8.00
5 Mark Giordano 3.00 8.00
6 Jarome Iginla SP 8.00 20.00
7 Roman Horak 3.00 8.00
8 Cam Ward 4.00 10.00
9 Justin Faulk 5.00 12.00
10 Viktor Stalberg 6.00 15.00
11 Marcus Kruger 5.00 12.00
13 John Moore 3.00 8.00
14 Kari Lehtonen SP 8.00 20.00
15 Tomas Vincour 3.00 8.00
16 Cory Emmerton SP 6.00 15.00
17 Jimmy Howard SP 8.00 20.00
18 Steve Yzerman SP 35.00 60.00
20 Teemu Hartikainen 3.00 8.00
21 Evgeny Dadonov 3.00 8.00
22 Anze Kopitar SP 12.00 30.00
23 Drew Doughty SP 8.00 20.00
24 Brett Bulmer 3.00 8.00
25 Nick Johnson 3.00 8.00
26 Cal Clutterbuck 4.00 10.00
27 Cody Almond 2.50 6.00
28 Devin Setoguchi 3.00 8.00
29 Max Pacioretty SP 6.00 15.00
30 Aaron Palushaj 3.00 8.00
31 Colin Wilson SP 4.00 10.00
32 Blake Geoffrion 3.00 8.00
33 Craig Smith 4.00 10.00
34 Adam Larsson 4.00 10.00
35 John Tavares SP 15.00 30.00
36 Derek Stepan SP 5.00 12.00
39 Robin Lehner 3.00 8.00
40 Colin Greening 3.00 8.00
41 David Rundblad 3.00 8.00
42 Erik Gustafsson 5.00 12.00
43 Zac Rinaldo 3.00 8.00
44 James van Riemsdyk SP 6.00 15.00
45 Chris Pronger SP 12.00 30.00
46 Claude Giroux SP 20.00 50.00
48 Jaromir Jagr SP 30.00 60.00
49 Matt Read 8.00 20.00
50 Sean Couturier 15.00 30.00
51 Andy Miele 3.00 8.00
52 Evgeni Malkin SP 25.00 50.00
53 James Neal 6.00 15.00
55 Mario Lemieux SP 50.00 100.00
56 Sidney Crosby SP
57 Patrick Marleau SP 6.00 15.00
58 Alex Pietrangelo 5.00 12.00
59 Matt Frattin 3.00 8.00
60 Dion Phaneuf SP 8.00 20.00
61 James Reimer SP 15.00 30.00
62 Carl Gunnarsson 3.00 8.00
63 Daniel Sedin SP 8.00 20.00
64 Henrik Sedin SP 8.00 20.00
65 Cody Eakin 4.00 10.00
66 Alex Ovechkin SP 30.00 60.00
67 Eric Fehr 4.00 10.00
68 Paul Postma 3.00 8.00
69 Mark Scheifele SP 8.00 20.00
70 Teemu Selanne SP 15.00 40.00

2011-12 Panini Contenders NHL Ink Duals

*GOLD/25: .6X TO 1.5X BASIC INSERTS
1 T.Hall/Nugent-Hopkins SP 40.00 100.00
2 J.Sakic/S.Yzerman SP EXCH 75.00 150.00
3 S.Couturier/M.Read 10.00 25.00
4 Z.Rinaldo/J.Shelley 8.00 20.00
5 B.Scrivens/M.Frattin 8.00 20.00
6 A.Henrique/A.Larsson 15.00 40.00
7 Nugent-Hop/Landeskog SP 40.00 100.00
8 B.Hull/B.Hull SP 60.00 120.00
9 B.Saad/B.Hull SP 30.00 60.00
10 R.McDonagh/T.Erixon 6.00 15.00
11 M.Scheifele/P.Postma 8.00 20.00
12 P.Roy/C.Price SP 90.00 150.00
13 T.Seguin/J.Caron SP 40.00 100.00
14 G.Landeskog/R.O'Reilly 25.00 60.00
15 J.Iginla/C.Glencross SP 12.00 30.00
16 D.Rundblad/Wiercioch 6.00 15.00
17 T.Myers/R.Miller SP 10.00 25.00
18 D.Doughty/J.Johnson SP 15.00 40.00
19 R.Johansen/J.Carter SP 20.00 40.00
20 C.Hodgson/Y.Sauve SP 20.00 40.00

2011-12 Panini Contenders NHL Ink Triples

STATED PRINT RUN 25 SER.#'d SETS
1 Yzerman/Sakic/Trottier 75.00 150.00
2 Hull/Hawerchuk/Selanne 100.00 200.00
3 Sedin/Sedin/Luongo 30.00 60.00
4 Hall/Seguin/Gudbranson 30.00 80.00
5 Price/Subban/Cammalleri 25.00 50.00
6 Hall/Eberle/Schenn 50.00 100.00
7 Carlson/Gardiner/Stepan 40.00 100.00
8 Hedman/Seguin/Landskg 50.00 100.00
9 Tavares/Hall/Nugent-Hop 175.00 300.00
10 Modano/Belfour/Hull 60.00 125.00

2011-12 Panini Contenders Original Six Booklet Autographs

STATED PRINT RUN 25 SER.#'d SETS
1 Chra/Tws/Phn/Lds/Gnt/Clhn 75.00 150.00
2 Yzrm/Svrd/Laf/Clrk/Brqe/Espo 100.00 175.00
3 Roy/Ptv/Chv/Dvdsn/Vch/Espo 200.00 350.00
4 Thm/Stl/Lids/Kne/Price/Kssl 50.00 100.00
5 Colb/Sgn/Stpn/Tatr/Sd/Sbn
6 Bwr/Fhr/Ptvn/Jsph/Blfr/Rmer 250.00 350.00

2011-12 Panini Contenders Patch Autographs

STATED PRINT RUN 9-100
101 Corey Perry/100 15.00 30.00
102 Ryan Getzlaf/100 25.00 60.00
103 Nathan Horton/100 15.00 40.00
104 Patrice Bergeron/100 15.00 40.00
105 Tim Thomas/9
106 Ryan Miller/100 15.00 40.00
107 Jarome Iginla/100 25.00 60.00
108 Jonathan Toews/49 40.00 80.00
109 Matt Duchene/100 15.00 40.00
110 Pavel Datsyuk/100 20.00 50.00
111 Nicklas Lidstrom/100 30.00 60.00
112 Drew Doughty/100 20.00 50.00
113 Anze Kopitar/100 20.00 50.00
114 Dustin Brown/100 15.00 40.00
115 Carey Price/31 60.00 120.00
116 Scott Gomez/100 10.00 25.00
117 John Tavares/100 20.00 50.00
118 Brad Richards/100 15.00 40.00
119 Jaromir Jagr/50 40.00 100.00
120 Claude Giroux/100 25.00 50.00
121 James van Riemsdyk/100 15.00 40.00
122 Danny Briere/100 15.00 40.00
123 Ilya Bryzgalov/78 12.00 30.00
124 Chris Pronger/100 12.00 30.00
125 Shane Doan/100 12.00 30.00
126 Marc-Andre Fleury/100 12.00 30.00
127 Jordan Staal/100 15.00 40.00
128 Sidney Crosby/25 150.00 250.00
129 Kris Letang/100 25.00 50.00
130 James Neal/100 15.00 40.00
131 Evgeni Malkin/25 40.00 80.00
132 Patrick Marleau/100 15.00 40.00
133 Logan Couture/100 15.00 40.00
134 Dan Boyle/100 12.00 30.00
135 Joe Thornton/100 15.00 40.00
136 Martin St. Louis/100 15.00 40.00
137 Vincent Lecavalier/100 12.00 30.00
138 Steven Stamkos/100 30.00 60.00
139 Victor Hedman/100 20.00 50.00
140 Mikhail Grabovski/100 15.00 40.00
141 James Reimer/100 15.00 40.00
142 Phil Kessel/100 20.00 50.00
143 Ryan Kesler/100 15.00 40.00
144 Roberto Luongo/40 30.00 60.00
145 Henrik Sedin/100 10.00 25.00
146 Daniel Sedin/100 12.00 30.00
147 Alexander Semin/100 12.00 30.00
148 Alex Ovechkin/25 100.00 200.00
149 John Carlson/100 20.00 50.00
150 Tomas Vokoun/87 12.00 30.00
151 Steve Yzerman/50 40.00 100.00
152 Denis Savard/100 20.00 50.00
153 Patrick Roy/100 60.00 120.00
154 Mark Messier/25 30.00 60.00
155 Joe Sakic/100 25.00 60.00
156 Brendan Shanahan/25 50.00 100.00
157 Bryan Trottier/50 30.00 60.00
158 Luc Robitaille/90 15.00 40.00
159 Mario Lemieux/25 60.00 120.00
160 Curtis Joseph/100 25.00 50.00
201 Devante Smith-Pelly/100 12.00 30.00
202 Peter Holland/100 12.00 30.00
203 Greg Nemisz/100 8.00 20.00
204 Roman Horak /100 12.00 30.00
205 Justin Faulk/100 15.00 40.00
206 Brandon Saad/100 15.00 40.00
207 Marcus Kruger/100 12.00 30.00
208 Gabriel Landeskog/100 60.00 120.00
209 Ryan Johansen/76 15.00 40.00
210 Cam Atkinson/100 20.00 50.00
211 John Moore/100 8.00 20.00
212 David Savard/100 10.00 25.00
213 Tomas Kubalik/100 8.00 20.00
214 Allen York/100 10.00 25.00
215 Tomas Vincour/100 8.00 20.00
216 Gustav Nyquist/100 20.00 50.00
217 Brendan Smith/100 8.00 20.00
218 R.Nugent-Hopkins/100 75.00 150.00
219 Carl Hagelin/100 25.00 60.00
220 Ryan Ellis/100 8.00 20.00
221 Simon Despres/100 8.00 20.00
222 Erik Gudbranson/100 15.00 40.00
223 Slava Voynov/100 8.00 20.00
224 Brett Bulmer/100 8.00 20.00
225 Aaron Palushaj/100 8.00 20.00
226 Alexei Emelin/100 8.00 20.00
227 Raphael Diaz/100 8.00 20.00
228 Craig Smith/100 20.00 50.00
229 Jonathon Blum /100 8.00 20.00
230 Blake Geoffrion/100 8.00 20.00
231 Adam Larsson/100 30.00 60.00
232 Adam Henrique/100 30.00 80.00
233 Tim Erixon/100 8.00 20.00
234 Cam Talbot/100 20.00 50.00
235 Mika Zibanejad/100 15.00 40.00
236 Stephane Da Costa/100 8.00 20.00
237 Patrick Wiercioch/100 8.00 20.00
238 Colin Greening/100 8.00 20.00
239 David Rundblad/100 8.00 20.00
240 Erik Condra/100 8.00 20.00
241 Sean Couturier/100 15.00 40.00
242 Matt Read/100 12.00 30.00
243 Zac Rinaldo/100 8.00 20.00
244 Erik Gustafsson/100 10.00 25.00
245 Calvin de Haan/100 10.00 25.00
246 Louis Leblanc/100 15.00 40.00
247 Joe Vitale/100 15.00 40.00
248 Robert Bortuzzo/100 12.00 30.00
249 Brett Connolly/100 15.00 40.00
250 Joe Colborne/100 8.00 20.00
251 Jake Gardiner/100 15.00 40.00
252 Matt Frattin/100 8.00 20.00
253 Ben Scrivens/100 15.00 40.00
254 Eddie Lack/100 12.00 30.00
255 Cody Hodgson/100 12.00 30.00
256 Yann Sauve/25 25.00 50.00
257 Cody Eakin/100 15.00 40.00
258 Carl Klingberg/100 15.00 30.00
259 Mark Scheifele/100 40.00 100.00
260 Zack Kassian/100 10.00 25.00

2011-12 Panini Contenders Starting Line Ups Booklet Autographs

STATED PRINT RUN 50
1 Pitt Penguins 125.00 200.00
2 LA Kings
3 Phil.Flyers 50.00 120.00
4 Buffalo Sabres 60.00 120.00
5 NJ Devils 200.00 350.00
6 SJ Sharks 90.00 150.00

2012-13 Panini Contenders Cup Contenders

INSERTS IN 2012-13 ROOKIE ANTHOLOGY
STATED PRINT RUN 999 SER.#'d SETS
1 Teemu Selanne 3.00 8.00
2 Vincent Lecavalier 1.25 3.00
3 Ryan Nugent-Hopkins 1.50 4.00
4 Matt Duchene 1.50 4.00
5 Loui Eriksson 1.25 3.00
6 Joe Thornton 1.50 4.00
7 Patrick Kane 3.00 8.00
8 Rick Nash 1.50 4.00
9 Henrik Sedin 1.50 4.00
10 Ryan Suter 1.00 2.50
11 Zdeno Chara 1.50 4.00
12 Jordan Staal 1.50 4.00
13 Nicklas Backstrom 2.50 6.00
14 Alex Pietrangelo 1.25 3.00
15 Ilya Kovalchuk 1.50 4.00
16 Jason Pominville 1.25 3.00
17 Milan Michalek 1.00 2.50
18 Mike Richards 1.50 4.00
19 Nazem Kadri 1.50 4.00
20 Andrei Markov 1.50 4.00
21 Henrik Zetterberg 2.00 5.00
22 Sidney Crosby 6.00 15.00
23 Evander Kane 1.50 4.00
24 Sean Couturier 1.50 4.00
25 Oliver Ekman-Larsson 1.50 4.00

2012-13 Panini Contenders Hart Contenders

INSERTS IN 2012-13 ROOKIE ANTHOLOGY
STATED PRINT RUN 999 SER.#'d SETS
1 Evgeni Malkin 5.00 12.00
2 Daniel Sedin 1.50 4.00
3 Corey Perry 1.50 4.00
4 Dustin Byfuglien 1.50 4.00
5 Alex Ovechkin 6.00 15.00
6 Claude Giroux 1.50 4.00
7 Patrick Marleau 1.50 4.00
8 Steven Stamkos 3.00 8.00
9 John Tavares 3.00 8.00
10 Jordan Eberle 1.50 4.00
11 Jonathan Toews 3.00 8.00
12 Phil Kessel 2.00 5.00
13 Anze Kopitar 2.50 8.00
14 Tyler Seguin 2.50 6.00
15 Jarome Iginla 1.50 4.00
16 Eric Staal 2.00 5.00
17 Marian Gaborik 1.50 4.00
18 Jaromir Jagr 4.00 10.00
19 Pavel Datsyuk 2.00 5.00
20 Zach Parise 1.50 4.00
21 Shea Weber 1.25 3.00
22 Gabriel Landeskog 1.50 4.00
23 David Backes 1.50 4.00
24 Shane Doan 1.25 3.00
25 Thomas Vanek 1.50 4.00

2012-13 Panini Contenders Legacies

INSERTS IN 2012-13 ROOKIE ANTHOLOGY
STATED PRINT RUN 999 SER.#'d SETS
1 Gordie Howe 4.00 10.00
2 Mark Messier 2.50 6.00
3 Bobby Clarke 2.00 5.00
4 Bobby Hull 2.00 5.00
5 Bernie Parent 2.00 5.00
6 Mario Lemieux 6.00 15.00
7 Stan Mikita 2.50 6.00
8 Eric Lindros 3.00 8.00
9 Larry Robinson 2.00 5.00
10 Cam Neely 2.00 5.00
11 Gilbert Perreault 2.00 5.00
12 Igor Larionov 2.00 5.00
13 Johnny Bower 2.00 5.00
14 Bernie Nicholls 1.50 4.00
15 Patrick Roy 5.00 12.00
16 Steve Yzerman 4.00 10.00
17 Joe Sakic 3.00 8.00
18 Brett Hull 2.00 5.00
19 Doug Gilmour 2.50 6.00
20 Joe Nieuwendyk 2.00 5.00
21 Phil Esposito 3.00 8.00
22 Yvan Cournoyer 2.00 5.00
23 Mike Richter 2.00 5.00
24 Pierre Turgeon 2.00 5.00
25 Curtis Joseph 2.00 5.00

2012-13 Panini Contenders Vezina Contenders

INSERTS IN 2012-13 ROOKIE ANTHOLOGY
STATED PRINT RUN 999 SER.#'d SETS
1 Pekka Rinne 2.00 5.00
2 Jonathan Quick 2.50 6.00
3 Cory Schneider 1.25 3.00
4 Miikka Kiprusoff 1.25 3.00
5 Semyon Varlamov 1.50 4.00
6 Marc-Andre Fleury 2.50 6.00
7 Jonas Hiller 1.25 3.00
8 Mike Smith 1.50 4.00
9 Jimmy Howard 1.50 4.00
10 Tuukka Rask 1.50 4.00
11 Brian Elliott 1.25 3.00
12 Carey Price 5.00 12.00
13 Craig Anderson 1.50 4.00
14 Martin Brodeur 3.00 8.00
15 Ondrej Pavelec 1.50 4.00
16 Ryan Miller 1.50 4.00
17 Devan Dubnyk 1.50 4.00
18 Henrik Lundqvist 2.00 5.00
19 Niklas Backstrom 1.25 3.00
20 Corey Crawford 2.00 5.00
21 Kari Lehtonen 1.25 3.00
22 Anders Lindback 1.00 2.50
23 Sergei Bobrovsky 1.50 4.00
24 Cam Ward 1.50 4.00
25 Ilya Bryzgalov 1.50 4.00

2013-14 Panini Contenders

COMP.SET w/o RC's (100) 10.00 25.00
ROOKE STATED PRINT RUN 600
SP1 ANNCD PRINT RUN 200 OR LESS
SP2 ANNCD PRINT RUN 200-400
RC AU VAR. ANNCD PRINT RUN 50 OR LESS
RC AU SEPIA ANNCD PRINT RUN 25 OR LESS
EXCH EXPIRATION: 12/4/2015
1 Jonathan Toews .75 2.00
2 Marian Hossa .30 .75
3 Patrick Kane .75 2.00
4 Corey Crawford .50 1.25
5 T.J. Oshie .60 1.50
6 Alex Pietrangelo .30 .75
7 Jaroslav Halak .40 1.00
8 Joe Thornton .40 1.00
9 Logan Couture .40 1.00
10 Patrick Marleau .40 1.00
11 Antti Niemi .30 .75
12 Teemu Selanne .75 2.00
13 Ryan Getzlaf .60 1.50
14 Jonas Hiller .30 .75
15 Corey Perry .40 1.00
16 Gabriel Landeskog .30 .75
17 Matt Duchene .40 1.00
18 Semyon Varlamov .40 1.00
19 Shane Doan .30 .75
20 Keith Yandle .40 1.00
21 Mike Smith .40 1.00
22 Zach Parise .40 1.00
23 Ryan Suter .25 .60
24 Josh Harding .40 1.00
25 Dustin Brown .40 1.00
26 Jeff Carter .40 1.00
27 Drew Doughty .40 1.00
28 Jonathan Quick .60 1.50
29 Tuukka Rask .40 1.00
30 Zdeno Chara .40 1.00
31 Patrice Bergeron .50 1.25
32 Jarome Iginla .40 1.00
33 Sidney Crosby 1.50 4.00
34 Evgeni Malkin 1.25 3.00
35 Kris Letang .40 1.00
36 Marc-Andre Fleury .60 1.50
37 Martin St. Louis .40 1.00
38 Steven Stamkos .75 2.00
39 Ben Bishop .40 1.00
40 Phil Kessel .50 1.25
41 Joffrey Lupul .30 .75
42 Jonathan Bernier .40 1.00
43 James Reimer .40 1.00
44 Henrik Zetterberg .50 1.25
45 Pavel Datsyuk .50 1.25
46 Jimmy Howard .40 1.00
47 Daniel Alfredsson .40 1.00
48 Daniel Sedin .40 1.00
49 Henrik Sedin .40 1.00
50 Roberto Luongo .40 1.00
51 Alex Ovechkin 1.50 4.00
52 Nicklas Backstrom .60 1.50
53 Braden Holtby .60 1.50
54 Jamie Benn .50 1.25
55 Kari Lehtonen .30 .75
56 Tyler Seguin .60 1.50
57 Mike Fisher .30 .75
58 Shea Weber .30 .75
59 Pekka Rinne .50 1.25
60 Max Pacioretty .40 1.00
61 Lars Eller .30 .75
62 P.K. Subban .60 1.50
63 Carey Price 1.25 3.00
64 Patrik Elias .40 1.00
65 Martin Brodeur .75 2.00
66 Cory Schneider .30 .75
67 Jaromir Jagr 1.00 2.50
68 Andrew Ladd .40 1.00
69 Zach Bogosian .30 .75
70 Ondrej Pavelec .40 1.00
71 Rick Nash .40 1.00
72 Ryan Callahan .40 1.00
73 Henrik Lundqvist .50 1.25
74 Claude Giroux .40 1.00
75 Sean Couturier .40 1.00
76 Vincent Lecavalier .30 .75
77 Jason Spezza .40 1.00
78 Bobby Ryan .40 1.00
79 Craig Anderson .40 1.00
80 Eric Staal .50 1.25
81 Cam Ward .40 1.00
82 Jordan Staal .40 1.00
83 Marian Gaborik .40 1.00
84 Jack Johnson .25 .60
85 Sergei Bobrovsky .40 1.00
86 John Tavares .75 2.00
87 Kyle Okposo .40 1.00
88 Thomas Vanek .40 1.00
89 Curtis Glencross .25 .60
90 T.J. Brodie .25 .60
91 Mike Cammalleri .30 .75
92 Tim Thomas .40 1.00
93 Brian Campbell .25 .60
94 Brad Boyes .25 .60
95 Jordan Eberle .40 1.00
96 Sam Gagner .30 .75
97 Taylor Hall .75 2.00
98 Drew Stafford .40 1.00
99 Ryan Miller .40 1.00
100 Cody Hodgson .40 1.00
101 Kevan Miller RC 2.50 6.00
102A Ben Hanowski RC 2.50 6.00
102B Ben Hanowski AU 3.00 8.00
103 Damien Brunner RC 2.50 6.00
104 Eric Selleck RC 2.50 6.00
105 Nicolas Blanchard RC 2.50 6.00
106 Sami Aittokallio RC 3.00 8.00
107 Zach Sill RC 3.00 8.00
108 Will Acton RC 2.50 6.00
109 Karl Stollery RC 2.50 6.00
110A Drew LeBlanc RC 2.00 5.00
110B Drew LeBlanc AU 2.50 6.00
111A Michael Latta RC 2.50 6.00
111B Michael Latta AU 3.00 8.00
112 Spencer Abbott RC 2.50 6.00
113 Luke Gazdic RC 2.50 6.00
114 Jean-Gabriel Pageau RC 2.50 6.00
115 Christopher Breen RC 2.50 6.00
116 Brett Bellemore RC 2.50 6.00
117A Ryan Stanton RC 3.00 8.00
117B Ryan Stanton AU 4.00 10.00
118 Patrick Holland RC 5.00 12.00
119A Jesper Fast RC 2.50 6.00
119B Jesper Fast AU 3.00 8.00
120 Eric Gelinas RC 3.00 8.00
121 Connor Carrick RC 2.50 6.00
122 Andrej Sustr RC 2.00 5.00
123A Michael Raffl RC 2.50 6.00
123B Michael Raffl AU 3.00 8.00
124A Matt Tennyson RC 2.00 5.00
124B Matt Tennyson AU 2.50 6.00
125 Carter Bancks RC 2.50 6.00
126A Dave Dziurzynski RC 2.50 6.00
126B Dave Dziurzynski AU SP2 3.00 8.00
127 Anton Belov RC 3.00 8.00
128A Greg Pateryn RC 3.00 8.00
128B Greg Pateryn AU 4.00 10.00
129 Brian Dumoulin RC 3.00 8.00
130 Justin Fontaine RC 3.00 8.00
131 Luke Glendening RC 5.00 12.00
132A Chris Terry RC 2.00 5.00
132B Chris Terry AU 2.50 6.00
133 Adam Almquist RC 2.00 5.00
134 Antti Raanta RC 4.00 10.00
135 Ben Chiarot RC 3.00 8.00
136 Brian Gibbons RC 3.00 8.00
137 Chad Billins RC 2.50 6.00
138 Connor Murphy RC 2.50 6.00
139 Darren Archibald RC 2.50 6.00
140A David Broll RC 3.00 8.00
140B David Broll AU SP2 4.00 10.00
141A Freddie Hamilton RC 3.00 8.00
141B Freddie Hamilton AU 4.00 10.00
142 Jamie Devane RC 2.50 6.00
143A Jayson Megna RC 3.00 8.00
143B Jayson Megna AU 4.00 10.00
144 Joakim Nordstrom RC 2.50 6.00
145 Jordan Szwarz RC 3.00 8.00
146 Linden Vey RC 2.00 5.00
147 Marek Mazanec RC 3.00 8.00
148 Michael Chaput RC 2.00 5.00
149 Nate Schmidt RC 2.50 6.00
150 Olli Maatta RC 5.00 12.00
151 Tyler Johnson AU RC 10.00 25.00
152 Michael Kostka AU RC 3.00 8.00
153 Oliver Lauridsen AU RC 3.00 8.00
154 Anders Lee AU RC 10.00 25.00
155 Taylor Beck AU RC 3.00 8.00
156 Jonathan Rheault AU RC 2.50 6.00
157 Alex Petrovic AU RC 3.00 8.00
158 Chris Brown AU RC 2.50 6.00
159 Joonas Rask AU RC 2.50 6.00
160 Ondrej Palat AU RC 5.00 12.00
161 J.Marchessault AU RC 8.00 20.00
162 Jason Missiaen AU RC 4.00 10.00
163 Victor Bartley AU RC 3.00 8.00
164 Calvin Pickard AU RC 4.00 10.00
165 Steve Oleksy AU RC 4.00 10.00
166 Kevin Henderson AU RC 3.00 8.00
167 Jeff Zatkoff AU RC 4.00 10.00
169 Joe Cannata AU RC 3.00 8.00
170 John Muse AU RC 4.00 10.00
171 Matthew Konan AU RC 4.00 10.00
172 Martin Jones AU RC 10.00 25.00
173 Mark Cundari AU RC 2.50 6.00
174 Harri Pesonen AU RC 3.00 8.00
175 Shawn Lalonde AU RC 4.00 10.00
176 Eric Hartzell AU RC 4.00 10.00
177 Cristopher Nilstorp AU RC 3.00 8.00
178 T.Pearson AU SP2 RC 4.00 10.00
179 Rickard Rakell AU SP2 RC 4.00 10.00
180 Nicklas Jensen AU SP2 RC 3.00 8.00
181 Sami Vatanen AU SP2 RC 4.00 10.00
182 Scott Laughton AU SP2 RC 4.00 10.00
183 Nick Bjugstad AU SP2 RC 5.00 12.00
184 Mark Pysyk AU RC 4.00 10.00
185 Jarred Tinordi AU SP2 RC 4.00 10.00
186 Quinton Howden AU SP2 RC 3.00 8.00
187 Jamie Oleksiak AU SP2 RC 3.00 8.00
188 Frank Corrado AU RC 2.50 6.00
189 Max Reinhart AU RC 4.00 10.00
190 Jared Staal AU RC 4.00 10.00
191 Dmitrij Jaskin AU RC 4.00 10.00
192 Stefan Matteau AU SP2 RC 3.00 8.00
193 Johan Gustafsson AU RC 5.00 12.00
194 Ben Street AU RC 2.50 6.00
195 Michael Caruso AU RC 2.50 6.00
196 Edward Pasquale AU RC 2.50 6.00
197 Carl Soderberg AU RC 4.00 10.00
198 Christian Thomas AU RC 3.00 8.00
199 Ryan Murphy AU RC 4.00 10.00
200 Nick Petrecki AU RC 2.50 6.00
201 Brian Lashoff AU RC 3.00 8.00
202 Anthony Peluso AU RC 2.50 6.00
203 Matt Irwin AU RC 3.00 8.00
204 J.Schroeder AU SP1 RC 4.00 10.00
205 Eric Gryba AU RC 3.00 8.00
206 Michael Sgarbossa AU RC 3.00 8.00
207 Dylan McIlrath AU SP2 RC 2.50 6.00
208 Philipp Grubauer AU RC 4.00 10.00
209 Richard Panik AU RC 4.00 10.00
210 Ryan Spooner AU RC 4.00 10.00
211 Igor Bobkov AU RC 3.00 8.00
212 Antoine Roussel AU RC 4.00 10.00
213 Cody Ceci AU SP2 RC 3.00 8.00
214 Petr Mrazek AU RC 8.00 20.00
215 D.DeKeyser AU SP2 RC 5.00 12.00
216 Drew Shore AU SP2 RC 3.00 8.00
217 Magnus Hellberg AU RC 4.00 10.00
218 John Gibson AU RC 12.00 30.00
219 Nikita Zadorov AU SP2 RC 4.00 10.00
220 J.T. Miller AU SP2 RC 4.00 10.00
221 Kevin Connauton AU RC 3.00 8.00
222 Xavier Ouellet AU SP2 RC 4.00 10.00
223 Tyler Pitlick AU RC 4.00 10.00
224 Darcy Kuemper AU RC EXCH 4.00 10.00
225 Josh Leivo AU RC 4.00 10.00
226A Alex Killorn AU SP2 RC 4.00 10.00
226B Alex Killorn AU/50* 6.00 15.00
227A Austin Watson AU SP2 RC 3.00 8.00
227B Austin Watson AU/50* 5.00 12.00
228A Boone Jenner AU SP2 RC 4.00 10.00
228B Boone Jenner AU/50* 6.00 15.00
229A Brock Nelson AU SP2 RC 4.00 10.00
229B Brock Nelson AU/50* 6.00 15.00
230A Charlie Coyle AU SP2 RC 4.00 10.00
230B Charlie Coyle AU/50* 6.00 15.00
231A E.Lindholm AU SP2 RC 6.00 15.00
231B Elias Lindholm AU/50* 10.00 25.00
232A Emerson Etem AU SP2 RC 4.00 10.00
232B Emerson Etem AU/50* 6.00 15.00
233A Filip Forsberg AU SP2 RC 10.00 25.00
233B Filip Forsberg AU/50* 15.00 40.00
234A Hampus Lindholm AU SP2 RC 6.00 15.00
234B Hampus Lindholm AU/50* 10.00 25.00
235A Jack Campbell AU SP1 RC 3.00 8.00
235B Jack Campbell AU/50* 5.00 12.00
236A Jonas Brodin AU SP1 RC 3.00 8.00
236B Jonas Brodin AU/50* 5.00 12.00
237A Viktor Fasth AU SP2 RC 4.00 10.00
237B Viktor Fasth AU/50* 6.00 15.00
238A Lucas Lessio AU RC 2.50 6.00
238B Lucas Lessio AU/50* 4.00 10.00
239A Mark Arcobello AU RC 4.00 10.00
239B Mark Arcobello AU/50* 6.00 15.00
240A Matt Dumba AU SP2 RC 4.00 10.00
240B Matt Dumba AU/50* 6.00 15.00
241A Johan Larsson AU SP2 RC 3.00 8.00
241B Johan Larsson AU/50* 5.00 12.00
242A Nathan Beaulieu AU SP2 RC 3.00 8.00
242B Nathan Beaulieu AU/50* 5.00 12.00
243A Reto Berra AU RC 4.00 10.00
243B Reto Berra AU/50* 6.00 15.00
245A Ryan Murray AU SP1 RC 6.00 15.00
245B Ryan Murray AU/50* 10.00 25.00
246A Jon Merrill AU SP2 RC 4.00 10.00
246B Jon Merrill AU/50* 6.00 15.00
247A Thomas Hickey AU SP1 RC 3.00 8.00
247B Thomas Hickey AU/50* 5.00 12.00
248A Tye McGinn AU SP2 RC 4.00 10.00
248B Tye McGinn AU/50* 6.00 15.00
249A Tyler Toffoli AU SP2 RC 8.00 20.00
249B Tyler Toffoli AU/50* 12.00 30.00
250A Z.Girgensons AU RC 8.00 20.00
250B Z.Girgensons AU/50* 12.00 30.00
251A F.Andersen AU SP2 RC 6.00 15.00
251B F.Andersen AU/50* 10.00 25.00
251C Frederik Andersen AU SP 20.00 50.00
252A Ryan Strome AU SP1 RC 5.00 12.00
252B Ryan Strome AU/50* 8.00 20.00
252C Ryan Strome AU SP 15.00 40.00
253A D.Hamilton AU SP2 RC 8.00 20.00
253B Dougie Hamilton AU/50* 12.00 30.00
253C Dougie Hamilton AU SP 25.00 60.00
254A M.Grigorenko AU SP1 RC 5.00 12.00
254B M.Grigorenko AU/50* 8.00 20.00
254C M.Grigorenko AU SP 15.00 40.00
255A S.Monahan AU SP2 RC 6.00 15.00
255B Sean Monahan AU/50* 10.00 25.00
255C Sean Monahan AU SP 20.00 50.00
256A N.MacKinnon AU SP1 RC 15.00 40.00
256B N.MacKinnon AU/50* 25.00 60.00
256C N.MacKinnon AU SP 50.00 120.00
257A Alex Chiasson AU SP2 RC 4.00 10.00
257B Alex Chiasson AU/50* 6.00 15.00
257C Alex Chiasson AU SP 12.00 30.00
258A V.Nichushkin AU SP2 C 4.00 10.00
258B Valeri Nichushkin AU/50* 6.00 15.00
258C V.Nichushkin AU SP 12.00 30.00
259A Tomas Jurco AU SP2 RC 6.00 15.00
259B Tomas Jurco AU/50* 10.00 25.00
259C Tomas Jurco AU SP 20.00 50.00
260A Justin Schultz AU SP2 RC 4.00 10.00
260B Justin Schultz AU/50* 6.00 15.00
260C Justin Schultz AU SP 12.00 30.00
261A Nail Yakupov AU SP1 RC 12.00 30.00
261B Nail Yakupov AU/50* 20.00 50.00
261C Nail Yakupov AU SP 40.00 100.00
262A A.Barkov AU SP1 RC 10.00 25.00
262B A.Barkov AU/50* 15.00 40.00
262C A.Barkov AU SP 30.00 80.00
263A J.Huberdeau AU SP1 RC 10.00 25.00
263B J.Huberdeau AU/50* 15.00 40.00
263C J.Huberdeau AU SP 30.00 80.00
264A M.Granlund AU SP1 RC 6.00 15.00
264B Mikael Granlund AU/50* 10.00 25.00
264C Mikael Granlund AU SP 20.00 50.00
265A A.glchenyuk AU SP1 RC 20.00 50.00
265B A.Galchenyuk AU/50* 30.00 80.00
265C Alex Galchenyuk AU SP 60.00 150.00
266A B.Gallagher AU SP2 RC 12.00 30.00
266B B.Gallagher AU/50* 20.00 50.00
266C B.Gallagher AU SP 40.00 100.00
267A Michael Bournival AU SP2 RC 4.00 10.00
267B Michael Bournival AU/50* 6.00 15.00
267C Michael Bournival AU SP 12.00 30.00
268A Seth Jones AU SP1 RC 4.00 10.00
268B Seth Jones AU/50* 6.00 15.00
268C Seth Jones AU SP 12.00 30.00
269A Cory Conacher AU SP2 RC 2.50 6.00
269B Cory Conacher AU/50* 4.00 10.00
269C Cory Conacher AU SP 8.00 20.00
270A Beau Bennett AU SP2 RC 5.00 12.00
270B Beau Bennett AU/50* 8.00 20.00
270C Beau Bennett AU SP 15.00 40.00
271A Tomas Hertl AU SP2 RC 5.00 12.00
271B Tomas Hertl AU/50* 8.00 20.00
271C Tomas Hertl AU SP 15.00 40.00
272A V.Tarasenko AU SP1 RC 15.00 40.00
272B V.Tarasenko AU/50* 25.00 60.00
272C Vladimir Tarasenko AU SP 50.00 125.00
273A Morgan Rielly AU SP2 RC 10.00 25.00
273B Morgan Rielly AU/50* 15.00 40.00
273C Morgan Rielly AU SP 30.00 80.00
274A Jacob Trouba AU SP2 RC 6.00 15.00
274B Jacob Trouba AU/50* 10.00 25.00
274C Jacob Trouba AU SP 20.00 50.00
275A Tom Wilson AU SP2 RC 6.00 15.00
275B Tom Wilson AU/50* 10.00 25.00
275C Tom Wilson AU SP 20.00 50.00
276 Brian Flynn AU RC 3.00 8.00
277 Calvin Heeter AU RC 3.00 8.00
278 Cameron Schilling AU RC 2.50 6.00
279 Chad Ruhwedel AU RC 2.50 6.00
280 Daniel Bang AU RC 3.00 8.00
281 Derek Grant AU RC 3.00 8.00
282 Jamie Tardif AU RC 2.50 6.00
283 Jason Akeson AU RC 3.00 8.00
284 Mark Barberio AU RC 2.50 6.00
285 Sean Collins AU SP2 RC 3.00 8.00
286 Taylor Fedun AU RC 5.00 12.00
287 Zach Redmond AU SP1 RC 3.00 8.00

2013-14 Panini Contenders Gold

*VETS/100: 2.5X TO 6X BASIC CARDS
*ROOKIES/100: .6X TO 1.5X BASIC CARDS/600
*ROOK AU/100: .6X TO 1.5X BASIC CARDS
4 Corey Crawford 3.00 8.00
52 Nicklas Backstrom 4.00 10.00

2013-14 Panini Contenders 3 vs 3 Autographs

33BM Boston Bruins Stars/100 25.00 60.00
33CD Calgary Flames Stars/25 20.00 50.00
33MW Minnesota Wild Stars/25 20.00 50.00
33TB Maple Leafs Stars/25 40.00 100.00
33ALA Anaheim Ducks Stars/100 25.00 60.00

2013-14 Panini Contenders Contending Classes Dual Signatures

CDAM M.Arcobello/S.Monahan 8.00 20.00
CDBD J.Brodin/M.Dumba 5.00 12.00
CDGB B.Gallagher/M.Bournival 10.00 25.00
CDGR A.Galchenyuk/M.Rielly 25.00 60.00
CDHL D.Hamilton/H.Lindholm 10.00 25.00
CDRN A.Roussel/V.Nichushkin 6.00 15.00
CDRT J.Trouba/Z.Redmond 6.00 15.00
CDSJ J.Schultz/S.Jones 6.00 15.00
CDTH T.Hertl/V.Tarasenko 15.00 40.00
CDYM N.Yakupov/N.MacKinnon 30.00 80.00

2013-14 Panini Contenders Cup Contenders

STATED PRINT RUN 499 SER.#'d SETS
CC1 Evgeni Malkin 6.00 15.00
CC2 Teemu Selanne 4.00 10.00
CC3 Patrick Kane 4.00 10.00
CC4 Gabriel Landeskog 1.50 4.00
CC5 Tyler Seguin 3.00 8.00
CC6 Anze Kopitar 3.00 8.00
CC7 Mikhail Grabovski 1.50 4.00
CC8 Joe Thornton 2.00 5.00
CC9 T.J. Oshie 3.00 8.00
CC10 Daniel Sedin 2.00 5.00
CC11 Milan Lucic 2.50 6.00
CC12 Sidney Crosby 4.00 10.00
CC13 Martin St. Louis 2.00 5.00
CC14 James van Riemsdyk 2.00 5.00
CC15 Joffrey Lupul 1.50 4.00
CC16 Niklas Kronwall 1.50 4.00
CC17 Henrik Zetterberg 2.50 6.00
CC18 Max Pacioretty 2.00 5.00
CC19 Erik Karlsson 4.00 10.00
CC20 Patrick Sharp 2.00 5.00
CC21 Logan Couture 2.00 5.00
CC22 Oliver Ekman-Larsson 1.50 4.00
CC23 Zach Parise 2.00 5.00
CC24 Mike Richards 2.00 5.00
CC25 Steven Stamkos 4.00 10.00

2013-14 Panini Contenders Cup Contenders Patch Autographs

STATED PRINT RUN 25 SER.#'d SETS
CCDS Daniel Sedin 12.00 30.00
CCEM Evgeni Malkin 40.00 100.00
CCGL Gabriel Landeskog
CCPK Patrick Kane EXCH 40.00 80.00
CCTS Tyler Seguin 20.00 50.00
CCAKO Anze Kopitar 20.00 50.00
CCJTH Joe Thornton
CCMGR Mikhail Grabovski 12.00 30.00

2013-14 Panini Contenders Eights Autographs

RANDOM INSERTS IN PACKS
C8G Goalie Stars 100.00 200.00
C8C76 1970s Stars 75.00 150.00
C8CPT Canadiens Stars 100.00 200.00
C8FLA Florida Panthers Stars 20.00 50.00
C8NO9 Jersey 9 Stars 100.00 200.00
C8PIT Penguins Stars 75.00 150.00
C8STL St. Louis Blues Stars 25.00 60.00
C8TOR Maple Leafs Stars 100.00 200.00
C8USA USA Stars 50.00 100.00
C8WSH Capitals Stars 50.00 120.00

2013-14 Panini Contenders Eights Autographs Gold

*GOLD/20: .5X TO 1.2X BASIC AU
C8NO9 Hw/Hl/Bk/Gl/Mc/Md/Gv/An 200.00 300.00

2013-14 Panini Contenders Fours Autographs

C4BOS Boston Bruins Stars 15.00 40.00
C4BRO Stall Brothers 25.00 60.00
C4BUF Buffalo Sabres Stars 12.00 30.00
C4CBJ Blue Jackets Stars 8.00 20.00
C4CHI Blackhawks Stars 50.00 100.00
C4COL Avalanche Stars 20.00 50.00
C4HFD Hartford Whalers Stars 12.00 30.00
C4MIN Minnesota Wild Stars 15.00 40.00
C4NYI NY Islanders Stars 40.00 100.00
C4NYR NY Rangers Stars 20.00 50.00
C4RK1 Plso/Rsk/Pckrd/Trba 12.00 30.00
C4RK2 Blieu/Ptrcki/Llnde/Mrrll 10.00 25.00
C4RK3 Rhlt/Pnk/Plt/Brkv 15.00 40.00
C4RK4 Ztkff/Bnntt/Knn/Lghtn 12.00 30.00
C4RK5 Strm/Kllrn/Lndhm/Grgrn 15.00 40.00
C4RK6 Anaheim Ducks Stars 15.00 40.00
C4RK7 Florida Panthers Stars 12.00 30.00
C4SJS San Jose Sharks Stars 15.00 40.00
C4STL St. Louis Blues Stars 30.00 80.00
C4TBL TB Lightning Stars 15.00 40.00

2013-14 Panini Contenders Global Contenders Autographs

GCAN Antti Niemi/25 10.00 25.00
GCCH Carl Hagelin/25 12.00 30.00
GCCP Carey Price/25 40.00 100.00
GCDS Daniel Sedin/25 12.00 30.00
GCEM Evgeni Malkin/25 40.00 100.00
GCGL Gabriel Landeskog/25
GCHL Henrik Lundqvist/25 20.00 50.00
GCJQ Jonathan Quick/25 EXCH 20.00 50.00
GCJT John Tavares/25 20.00 50.00
GCMG Marian Gaborik/25
GCPB Patrice Bergeron 15.00 40.00
(inserted in 2013-14 Panini Prime)
GCPD Pavel Datsyuk/25 15.00 40.00
GCPK Patrick Kane/25 40.00 80.00
GCRM Ryan Miller/25 12.00 30.00
GCZP Zach Parise/25 15.00 40.00
GCJHA Jaroslav Halak/25 15.00 40.00
GCJHI Jonas Hiller/25 10.00 25.00
GCJTO Jonathan Toews/25 40.00 80.00
GCMDU Matt Duchene/25 12.00 30.00
GCOVI Alex Ovechkin/25 30.00 80.00
GCPKE Phil Kessel/25 15.00 40.00
GCSVO Slava Voynov/25
GCTMU Teemu Selanne/25 30.00 80.00

2013-14 Panini Contenders Hart Contenders

STATED PRINT RUN 499 SER.#'d SETS
HC1 Patrice Bergeron 3.00 8.00
HC2 Cody Hodgson 2.50 6.00
HC3 Mike Cammalleri 2.00 5.00
HC4 Eric Staal 3.00 8.00
HC5 Jonathan Toews 5.00 12.00
HC6 Matt Duchene 2.50 6.00
HC7 Jamie Benn 3.00 8.00
HC8 Ryan Nugent-Hopkins 2.50 6.00
HC9 Anze Kopitar 4.00 10.00
HC10 Zach Parise 2.50 6.00
HC11 John Tavares 5.00 12.00
HC12 Claude Giroux 2.50 6.00
HC13 Sidney Crosby 10.00 25.00
HC14 Patrick Marleau 2.50 6.00
HC15 Martin St. Louis 2.50 6.00
HC16 Phil Kessel 3.00 8.00
HC17 Henrik Sedin 2.50 6.00
HC18 Alex Ovechkin 10.00 25.00
HC19 Brad Richards 2.50 6.00
HC20 Evander Kane 2.50 6.00
HC21 Corey Perry 2.50 6.00
HC22 Henrik Zetterberg 3.00 8.00
HC23 Carey Price 8.00 20.00
HC24 Alexander Steen 2.50 6.00
HC25 Keith Yandle 2.50 6.00

2013-14 Panini Contenders Hart Contenders Patch Autographs

STATED PRINT RUN 25 SER.#'d SETS
HCBRI Brad Richards 8.00 20.00
HCCGX Claude Giroux EXCH 15.00 40.00
HCCHO Cody Hodgson 8.00 20.00
HCERS Eric Staal 15.00 40.00
HCEVK Evander Kane 12.00 30.00
HCJT John Tavares 20.00 50.00
HCJTO Jonathan Toews 25.00 60.00
HCMC Mike Cammalleri 10.00 25.00
HCMDU Matt Duchene 12.00 30.00
HCMSL Martin St. Louis 15.00 40.00
HCOVI Alex Ovechkin 50.00 125.00
HCPBE Patrice Bergeron 15.00 40.00
HCPKE Phil Kessel 25.00 60.00
HCPM Patrick Marleau
HCRNH Ryan Nugent-Hopkins 20.00 50.00
HCSC Sidney Crosby EXCH 75.00 150.00
HCZP Zach Parise 20.00 50.00

2013-14 Panini Contenders Legacies

CL1 Eric Lindros 5.00 12.00
CL2 Ron Francis 3.00 8.00
CL3 Stan Mikita 3.00 8.00
CL4 Gordie Howe 5.00 12.00
CL5 Pat LaFontaine 2.50 6.00
CL6 Marcel Dionne 3.00 8.00
CL7 Bobby Clarke 2.50 6.00
CL8 Mario Lemieux 8.00 20.00
CL9 Wendel Clark 2.50 6.00
CL10 Brett Hull 2.50 6.00
CL11 Ray Bourque 4.00 10.00
CL12 Joe Nieuwendyk 2.50 6.00
CL13 Bobby Hull 2.50 6.00
CL14 Joe Sakic 4.00 10.00
CL15 Mike Modano 4.00 10.00
CL16 Steve Yzerman 5.00 12.00
CL17 Jari Kurri 2.50 6.00
CL18 John Vanbiesbrouck 2.50 6.00
CL19 Jean Beliveau 2.50 6.00
CL20 Mike Bossy 2.50 6.00
CL21 Mark Messier 3.00 8.00
CL22 Dave Andreychuk 2.50 6.00
CL23 Johnny Bower 3.00 8.00
CL24 Trevor Linden 2.50 6.00
CL25 Olaf Kolzig 2.50 6.00

2013-14 Panini Contenders Match Ups Booklet Autographs

MAFHM Andr/Fsth/Hlbrg/Mzn/99 10.00 25.00
MBBHH Brkv/Bjg/Hbr/Hwdn/50 20.00 50.00
MBDRT Brdn/Dmb/Rdm/Trba/99 10.00 25.00
MBSSM Bcks/Shk/McDn/Stp/85 10.00 25.00
MCGEG Cmlri/Glncr/Ebrl/Ggn/99 10.00 25.00
MEFRA Etm/Fsth/Rkll/Andr/199 10.00 25.00
MFLVR Rstl/Frsb/Lndh/Vtnn/99 15.00 40.00
MGBBL Brdn/Lndh/Grn/Brkv/99 15.00 40.00
MGPGR Grg/Pysk/Grg/Rstln/99 15.00 40.00
MHBKJ Hbrd/Bjg/Klrn/Jhnsn/99 15.00 40.00
MHZLM Hrtzll/Ztk/Lghtn/McG/99 10.00 25.00
MJMFJ Jnnr/Mrry/Frsbrg/Jnes/99 15.00 40.00
MKSSS Slnne/Koivu/Sdn/Sdn/50 30.00 80.00
MMEBR Mllr/Enrth/Brnr/Rmr/175 10.00 25.00
MMMNH Mttu/Mrrll/Nlsn/Hcky/199 10.00 25.00
MPGTN Prse/Grnl/Tws/Nrds/50 40.00 80.00
MSMHL Stpn/McDn/Hgln/Lndq/25 40.00 80.00
MTJHN Trsnko/Jskn/Hrtl/Nto/99 25.00 60.00
MTNRM Tvrs/Nlsn/Rchrds/Mllr/50
MYAMR Arcb/Rnhrt/Ykv/Mnhn/50 25.00 60.00
MYSSH Sdrb/Hmltn/Schz/Ykv/50 25.00 60.00

2013-14 Panini Contenders NHL Ink

IMT Matt Tennyson 3.00 8.00
(inserted in 2013-14 Panini Prime)
ICC Cory Conacher 2.50 6.00
ICT Christian Thomas 3.00 8.00
IMBA Mikael Backlund 3.00 8.00
IMGB Michael Grabner 3.00 8.00
IMHT Michael Hutchinson 4.00 10.00
IMKO Matthew Konan 2.50 6.00
IMXM Maxime Macenauer 2.50 6.00
INMK Nathan MacKinnon 25.00 60.00
IRLY Morgan Rielly 10.00 25.00
IAB Aleksander Barkov 10.00 25.00
IAG Alex Galchenyuk 20.00 50.00
IAS Andrew Shaw 4.00 10.00
IASH Carter Ashton 2.50 6.00
IBCO Brett Connolly 2.50 6.00
IBJE Boone Jenner 4.00 10.00
IBLA Brian Lashoff 3.00 8.00
IBR Bobby Ryan 4.00 10.00
ICCI Casey Cizikas 2.50 6.00
ICCL Cal Clutterbuck 4.00 10.00
ICGE Chay Genoway 2.50 6.00
ICRU Chad Ruhwedel 2.50 6.00
ICSM Craig Smith 2.50 6.00
ICTE Chris Terry 2.50 6.00
ICWI Colin Wilson 3.00 8.00
IDBA Daniel Bang 3.00 8.00
IDBR Daniel Briere 4.00 10.00
IDDK Danny DeKeyser 5.00 12.00
IDP David Perron 2.50 6.00
IFA Frederik Andersen 6.00 15.00
IGB Gabriel Bourque 3.00 8.00
IGD Gabriel Dumont 2.50 6.00
IIB Igor Bobkov 3.00 8.00
IJAK Jason Akeson 3.00 8.00
IJCN Joe Cannata 3.00 8.00
IJCO Joe Colborne 2.50 6.00
IJFA Jesper Fast 3.00 8.00
IJH Jonathan Huberdeau 10.00 25.00
IJME Jon Merrill 3.00 8.00
IJMI Jason Missiaen 4.00 10.00
IJMU John Muse 3.00 8.00
IJSC Jaden Schwartz 2.50 6.00
IJSI Jakob Silfverberg 3.00 8.00
IJSZ Jordan Szwarz 4.00 10.00
IJTB J.T. Brown 2.50 6.00
IJTR Jacob Trouba 6.00 15.00
IKB Kevin Bieksa 5.00 12.00
IKH Kevin Henderson 3.00 8.00
IKK Keith Kinkaid 2.50 6.00
IMMO Matt Moulson 3.00 8.00
IMSC Mark Scheifele 5.00 12.00
INN Nino Niederreiter 2.50 6.00
INYQ Gustav Nyquist 6.00 15.00
IOL Oliver Lauridsen 3.00 8.00
IOP Ondrej Palat 5.00 12.00
IPCO Philippe Cornet 2.50 6.00
IREL Ryan Ellis 2.50 6.00
IRNA Riley Nash 2.50 6.00
IRSM Reilly Smith 5.00 12.00
ISB Sven Baertschi 2.50 6.00
ISJ Seth Jones 4.00 10.00
ISO Steve Oleksy 4.00 10.00
ISTA Ryan Stanton 2.50 6.00
ISVO Slava Voynov 3.00 8.00
ITBA Tyson Barrie 4.00 10.00
ITHE Tomas Hertl 5.00 12.00
ITK Torey Krug 6.00 15.00
ITT Tyler Toffoli 8.00 20.00
ITW Tom Wilson 6.00 15.00
IDDZ Dave Dziurzynski 3.00 8.00
(inserted in 2013-14 Panini Prime)

2013-14 Panini Contenders NHL Ink Gold

INMK Nathan MacKinnon 30.00 80.00

2013-14 Panini Contenders NHL Ink Duals

STATED PRINT RUN 50 SER.#'d SETS
IDBM S.Baertschi/S.Monahan 10.00 25.00
IDBT D.Byfuglien/J.Trouba 8.00 20.00
IDCH L.Couture/T.Hertl 15.00 40.00
IDCS P.Coffey/J.Schultz 5.00 12.00
IDFF V.Fasth/J.Fast
IDGG B.Gionta/A.Galchenyuk 15.00 40.00
IDGR J.Gardiner/M.Rielly 15.00 40.00
IDGS B.Gallagher/M.St. Louis 15.00 40.00
IDHH D.Hamilton/F.Hamilton 10.00 25.00
IDJJ M.Jones/S.Jones 12.00 30.00
IDJM M.Jones/M.Mazanec 12.00 30.00
IDKH T.Krug/D.Hamilton 10.00 25.00
IDKT N.Kadri/K.Turris 10.00 25.00
IDLL E.Lindholm/H.Lindholm 8.00 20.00
IDRB J.Roenick/B.Bickell 12.00 30.00
IDSM J.Silfverberg/P.Maroon 4.00 10.00
IDTV T.Thomas/J.Vanbiesbrouck 20.00 50.00
IDWJ S.Weber/S.Jones 15.00 40.00

2013-14 Panini Contenders NHL Ink Triples

ITBSH Brodeur/Smith/Hextall 40.00 80.00
ITRSL Richards/St. Louis/Lecavalier 8.00 20.00
ITHNY Hll/Ngnt-Hp/Ykpv/25 75.00 150.00
ITPBS Pietrnglo/Bwmstr/Shtnkrk/25
ITSSS Staal/Staal/Staal/25

2013-14 Panini Contenders Norris Contenders Patch Autographs

STATED PRINT RUN 25 SER.#'d SETS
NCAP Alex Pietrangelo
NCDH Dougie Hamilton 20.00 50.00
NCJB Jonas Brodin
NCKL Kris Letang 20.00 50.00
NCKS Kevin Shattenkirk 10.00 25.00
NCKY Keith Yandle 10.00 25.00
NCSJ Seth Jones 20.00 50.00
NCVH Victor Hedman 12.00 30.00
NCDBO Dan Boyle 8.00 20.00
NCHLI Hampus Lindholm 15.00 40.00
NCJUS Justin Schultz 10.00 25.00
NCMAS Marc Staal 8.00 20.00
NCMGI Mark Giordano 8.00 20.00
NCRJO Roman Josi 12.00 30.00
NCRMR Ryan Murray 10.00 25.00
NCSVO Slava Voynov 20.00 50.00

2013-14 Panini Contenders Patch Autographs

STATED PRINT RUN 49-100
176 Eric Hartzell/100 8.00 20.00
177 Cristopher Nilstorp/100 6.00 15.00
178 Tanner Pearson/100 10.00 25.00
179 Rickard Rakell/100 8.00 20.00
180 Nicklas Jensen/100 10.00 25.00
181 Sami Vatanen/100 10.00 25.00
182 Scott Laughton/100 8.00 20.00
183 Nick Bjugstad/100 10.00 25.00
186 Quinton Howden/100 6.00 15.00
187 Jamie Oleksiak/100 6.00 15.00
188 Frank Corrado/100 5.00 12.00
189 Max Reinhart/100 8.00 20.00
190 Jared Staal/100 8.00 20.00
191 Dmitrij Jaskin/100 8.00 20.00
192 Stefan Matteau/100 8.00 20.00
193 Johan Gustafsson/100 8.00 20.00
194 Ben Street/100 5.00 12.00
195 Michael Caruso/100 10.00 25.00
196 Edward Pasquale/100 6.00 15.00
197 Carl Soderberg/100 8.00 20.00
198 Christian Thomas/100 6.00 15.00
200 Nick Petrecki/100 5.00 12.00
201 Brian Lashoff/100 6.00 15.00
202 Anthony Peluso/100 6.00 15.00
203 Matt Irwin/100 6.00 15.00
204 Jordan Schroeder/100 6.00 15.00
205 Eric Gryba/100 6.00 15.00
206 Michael Sgarbossa/100 6.00 15.00
207 Dylan McIlrath/100 5.00 12.00
208 Philipp Grubauer/100 8.00 20.00
209 Richard Panik/100 8.00 20.00
210 Ryan Spooner/100 8.00 20.00
211 Igor Bobkov/100 6.00 15.00
212 Antoine Roussel/100 12.00 30.00
213 Cody Ceci/100 10.00 25.00
214 Petr Mrazek/100 15.00 40.00
215 Danny DeKeyser/100 10.00 25.00
217 Magnus Hellberg/100 8.00 20.00
218 John Gibson/100 25.00 60.00
219 Nikita Zadorov/100 8.00 20.00
221 Kevin Connauton/100 6.00 15.00
222 Xavier Ouellet/49 12.00 30.00
224 Darcy Kuemper/100
226 Alex Killorn/100 8.00 20.00
227 Austin Watson/100 6.00 15.00
228 Boone Jenner/100 8.00 20.00
229 Brock Nelson/100 8.00 20.00
230 Charlie Coyle/100 12.00 30.00
231 Elias Lindholm/100 12.00 30.00
232 Emerson Etem/100 8.00 20.00
233 Filip Forsberg/100 15.00 40.00
234 Hampus Lindholm/100 12.00 30.00
235 Jack Campbell/100 6.00 15.00
236 Jonas Brodin/100 6.00 15.00
237 Viktor Fasth/100 8.00 20.00
239 Mark Arcobello/100 8.00 20.00
240 Matt Dumba/100 8.00 20.00
242 Nathan Beaulieu/100 6.00 15.00
243 Reto Berra/100 8.00 20.00
245 Ryan Murray/100 12.00 30.00
246 Jon Merrill/100 6.00 15.00
247 Thomas Hickey/100 6.00 15.00
248 Tye McGinn/100 8.00 20.00
249 Tyler Toffoli/100 15.00 40.00
250 Zemgus Girgensons/100 12.00 30.00
251 Frederik Andersen/100 12.00 30.00
252 Ryan Strome/100 10.00 25.00
253 Dougie Hamilton/100 15.00 40.00
254 Mikhail Grigorenko/100 10.00 25.00
255 Sean Monahan/100 12.00 30.00
256 Nathan MacKinnon/100 40.00 100.00
257 Alex Chiasson/100 8.00 20.00
258 Valeri Nichushkin/100 20.00 50.00
259 Tomas Jurco/100 12.00 30.00
260 Justin Schultz/100 8.00 20.00
261 Nail Yakupov/100 15.00 40.00
262 Aleksander Barkov/100 15.00 40.00
263 Jonathan Huberdeau/100 12.00 30.00
264 Mikael Granlund/100 12.00 30.00
265 Alex Galchenyuk/100 40.00 100.00
266 Brendan Gallagher/100 12.00 30.00
267 Michael Bournival/100 6.00 15.00
268 Seth Jones/100 8.00 20.00
269 Cory Conacher/100 8.00 20.00
270 Beau Bennett/100 12.00 30.00
271 Tomas Hertl/100 20.00 50.00
272 Vladimir Tarasenko/100 75.00 150.00
273 Morgan Rielly/100 20.00 50.00
274 Jacob Trouba/100 12.00 30.00
275 Tom Wilson/100 12.00 30.00

2013-14 Panini Contenders Rookie Ticket Recall Autographs

2 John Tavares/25
7 Patrick Kane/25 EXCH 25.00 60.00
8 Jeremy Roenick/25 30.00 60.00
10 Henrik Lundqvist/25 30.00 60.00

2013-14 Panini Contenders Selke Contenders

SC1 Ryan Getzlaf 4.00 10.00
SC2 Patrice Bergeron 3.00 8.00
SC3 Drew Stafford 2.50 6.00
SC4 Curtis Glencross 1.50 4.00
SC5 Jordan Staal 2.50 6.00
SC6 Jonathan Toews 3.00 8.00
SC7 Paul Stastny 2.50 6.00
SC8 Pavel Datsyuk 3.00 8.00
SC9 Dustin Brown 2.50 6.00
SC10 Scottie Upshall 1.50 4.00
SC11 Mike Fisher 2.00 5.00
SC12 Travis Zajac 2.00 5.00
SC13 Brad Richards 2.50 6.00
SC14 Shane Doan 2.00 5.00
SC15 Joe Pavelski 2.50 6.00
SC16 David Backes 2.50 6.00
SC17 Teddy Purcell 2.50 6.00
SC18 David Clarkson 1.50 4.00
SC19 Ryan Kesler 2.50 6.00
SC20 Andrew Ladd 2.50 6.00
SC21 Shawn Horcoff 1.50 4.00
SC22 Mikko Koivu 2.00 5.00
SC23 David Desharnais 2.50 6.00
SC24 Jakub Voracek 2.50 6.00
SC25 Clarke MacArthur 1.50 4.00

2013-14 Panini Contenders Selke Contenders Patch Autographs

STATED PRINT RUN 20-25
SCAL Andrew Ladd/20
SCBRI Brad Richards/25 12.00 30.00
SCCG Curtis Glencross/25 8.00 20.00
SCDB David Backes/25 12.00 30.00
SCDUB Dustin Brown/25 12.00 30.00
SCJOS Jordan Staal/25 12.00 30.00
SCJP Joe Pavelski/25 15.00 40.00
SCJTO Jonathan Toews/25 40.00 80.00
SCMF Mike Fisher/25
SCPB Patrice Bergeron/25 25.00 50.00
SCPD Pavel Datsyuk/25
SCRG Ryan Getzlaf/25 20.00 50.00
SCRK Ryan Kesler/25 12.00 30.00

2013-14 Panini Contenders Sixes Autographs

RANDOM INSERTS IN PACKS
C6G Goalie Stars 125.00 250.00
C6V1 Sln/Sk/Brg/Ov/St.L/Wbr 60.00 120.00
C6BOS Boston Bruins Stars 75.00 150.00
C6DAL Dallas Stars 15.00 40.00
C6EDM Edmonton Oilers Stars 75.00 150.00
C6NSH Nashville Predators Stars 10.00 25.00
C6NYI New York Islanders Stars 30.00 60.00
C6NYR New York Rangers Stars 50.00 100.00
C6OLY Olympic Stars 40.00 80.00

C6OR6 Cnr/Str/Mta/Brq/Yz/Msr 60.00 120.00
C6PHI Philadelphia Flyers Stars 50.00 120.00
C6RK1 Crd/Jns/Sch/Arc/Ptl/Fs 8.00 20.00
C6RK2 Rookie Stars 1 20.00 50.00
C6RK3 Rookie Stars 2 15.00 40.00
C6RUS Russian Stars 75.00 150.00
C6STL St. Louis Blues Stars 20.00 50.00
C6SWE Ert/Sn/Lg/Sn/Sv/Lg 15.00 40.00
C6USG U.S. Goalie Stars 15.00 40.00
C6WIS Jsp/Chs/Hty/Str/Trs/Smt 12.00 30.00
C6WPG Winnipeg Jets Stars 25.00 60.00

2013-14 Panini Contenders Top of the Class Autographs

STATED PRINT RUN 25 SER.#'d SETS
TCD DH/JS/JB/SJ/MR/JT 40.00 80.00
TCF1 NY/JH/AG/NM/SM/TH 60.00 150.00
TCF2 VT/EE/BB/AB/EL/BJ 100.00 175.00
TCF3 BG/AC/MG/MB/VN/ZG 50.00 100.00
TCFDG NY/DH/VF/NM/SJ/RB 150.00 250.00

2013-14 Panini Contenders Vezina Contenders

VC1 Jonas Hiller 2.00 5.00
VC2 Tuukka Rask 2.50 6.00
VC3 Ryan Miller 2.50 6.00
VC4 Semyon Varlamov 2.50 6.00
VC5 Cam Ward 2.50 6.00
VC6 Kari Lehtonen 2.00 5.00
VC7 Jimmy Howard 2.50 6.00
VC8 Jonathan Quick 4.00 10.00
VC9 Niklas Backstrom 2.00 5.00
VC10 Carey Price 8.00 20.00
VC11 Pekka Rinne 3.00 8.00
VC12 Martin Brodeur 5.00 12.00
VC13 Henrik Lundqvist 3.00 8.00
VC14 Craig Anderson 2.50 6.00
VC15 Mike Smith 2.50 6.00
VC16 Marc-Andre Fleury 4.00 10.00
VC17 Antti Niemi 2.00 5.00
VC18 Jaroslav Halak 2.50 6.00
VC19 Jonathan Bernier 2.50 6.00
VC20 Ondrej Pavelec 2.50 6.00
VC21 Sergei Bobrovsky 2.50 6.00
VC22 Corey Crawford 3.00 8.00
VC23 Ben Bishop 2.50 6.00
VC24 Roberto Luongo 2.50 6.00
VC25 Braden Holtby 4.00 10.00

2013-14 Panini Contenders Vezina Contenders Patch Autographs

STATED PRINT RUN 15-25
VCAN Antti Niemi 12.00 30.00
VCCA Craig Anderson
VCCP Carey Price 25.00 50.00
VCHL Henrik Lundqvist 30.00 80.00
VCJQ Jonathan Quick EXCH 25.00 60.00
VCMB Martin Brodeur 50.00 100.00
VCMS Mike Smith 15.00 40.00
VCRM Ryan Miller 12.00 30.00
VCJBE Jonathan Bernier 15.00 40.00
VCJHA Jaroslav Halak 15.00 40.00
VCJHI Jonas Hiller 12.00 30.00
VCJHO Jimmy Howard 15.00 40.00
VCKLE Kari Lehtonen 12.00 30.00
VCMAF Marc-Andre Fleury 25.00 60.00

2013-14 Panini Contenders Winter Classic Contenders Autographs

STATED PRINT RUN 25 SER.#'d SETS
WCNK Nazem Kadri
WCNL Nicklas Lidstrom 15.00 40.00
WCPD Pavel Datsyuk 15.00 40.00
WCSY Steve Yzerman EXCH 30.00 60.00
WCWC Wendel Clark
WCBSM Brendan Smith 10.00 25.00
WCCCH Chris Chelios 12.00 30.00
WCDDK Danny DeKeyser 12.00 30.00
WCDPH Dion Phaneuf 15.00 40.00
WCDSI Darryl Sittler 20.00 50.00
WCJBE Jonathan Bernier
WCJHO Jimmy Howard 12.00 30.00
WCJRE James Reimer EXCH 12.00 30.00
WCPKE Phil Kessel 20.00 50.00
WCRLY Morgan Rielly

2012 Panini Father's Day

RANDOM INSERTS IN FATHER'S DAY PACKS
CRACKED ICE/25: 5X TO 12X BASE HI
23 Henrik Lundqvist .40 1.00
24 Evgeni Malkin .60 1.50
25 Steven Stamkos .60 1.50
26 Alex Ovechkin .60 1.50
27 Tyler Seguin .60 1.50
28 Claude Giroux .50 1.25

2012 Panini Father's Day Elements

RANDOM INSERTS IN FATHERS DAY PACKS
CRACKED ICE/25: 5X TO 12X BASE HI
3 Jaromir Jagr .50 1.25
4 Henrik Lundqvist .40 1.00
5 Alex Ovechkin .60 1.50
6 Tim Thomas .40 1.00
7 Taylor Hall .60 1.50
8 Ryan Ellis .40 1.00

2012 Panini Father's Day Legends

RANDOM INSERTS IN FATHERS DAY PACKS
CRACKED ICE/25: 5X TO 12X BASE HI
1 Gordie Howe 1.00 2.50
2 Mario Lemieux .50 1.25

2012 Panini Father's Day Rookie of the Year Jerseys

RANDOM INSERTS IN FATHERS DAY PACKS
4 Jeff Skinner 4.00 10.00

2012 Panini Father's Day Rookies

STATED PRINT RUN 499 SER.#'d SETS
12 Ryan Nugent-Hopkins 5.00 12.00
13 Gabriel Landeskog 2.00 5.00
14 Adam Henrique 2.00 5.00
15 Cody Hodgson 2.50 6.00
16 Matt Read 1.50 4.00

2012 Panini Father's Day Rookies Cracked Ice

CRACKED ICE/25: 2.5X TO 6X BASE HI
ANNOUNCED PRINT RUN 25

2012 Panini Father's Day Season Highlights

RANDOM INSERTS IN FATHERS DAY PACKS
CRACKED ICE/25: 5X TO 12X BASE HI
10 Marian Gaborik .40 1.00
11 Zdeno Chara .40 1.00
12 Steven Stamkos .60 1.50

2013 Panini Father's Day

CRACKED ICE/25: 4X TO 10X BASIC CARDS
LAVA FLOW/25: 4X TO 10X BASIC CARDS
19 Sidney Crosby 1.00 2.50
20 Alex Ovechkin .60 1.50
21 Steven Stamkos .40 1.00
22 Patrick Kane .50 1.25
35 Jussi Rynnas .50 1.25
36 Sven Baertschi .75 2.00
37 Jaden Schwartz .75 2.00
38 Chris Kreider .75 2.00

2013 Panini Father's Day Team Pinnacle

CRACKED ICE/25: 3X TO 8X BASIC CARDS
LAVA FLOW/25: 3X TO 8X BASIC CARDS
11 Jonathan Quick/Martin Brodeur
14 Chris Kreider/Sven Baertschi 1.00 2.50

2013-14 Panini Father's Day Autographs

TW Tom Wilson 3.00 8.00

2013-14 Panini Father's Day Private Signings

BJ Boone Jenner/25 8.00 20.00
BT Bryan Trottier/25 6.00 15.00
CC Chris Chelios/25 8.00 20.00
CN Cam Neely/25 10.00 25.00
CW Cam Ward/25 4.00 10.00
JH Jonathan Huberdeau/25 5.00 12.00
NM Nathan MacKinnon/25 100.00 200.00
NY Nail Yakupov/25 8.00 20.00
RB1 Ray Bourque/25 20.00 50.00
RM Ryan Murray/25 4.00 10.00
RS Ryan Strome/25 8.00 20.00
SM Sean Monohan/25 5.00 12.00
TH Tomas Hertl/25 40.00 80.00

2014 Panini Father's Day

COMPLETE SET (55) 20.00 50.00
*1-24 THICK STOCK: 1X TO 2.5X BASIC CARDS
*25-55 THICK STOCK: .5X TO 1.2X BASIC CARDS
*1-24 ICE VETS/25: 5X TO 12X BASIC CARDS
*25-55 ICE ROOKIE/25: 2X TO 5X BASIC CARDS/499
13 Sidney Crosby HK 1.00 2.50
14 Alex Ovechkin HK .60 1.50
15 Steven Stamkos HK .40 1.00
16 Teemu Selanne HK .40 1.00
17 Martin Brodeur HK .40 1.00
41 Nathan MacKinnon HK 3.00 8.00
42 Alex Galchenyuk HK 1.50 4.00
43 Nail Yakupov HK 1.50 4.00
44 Sean Monahan HK 1.00 2.50
45 Tomas Hertl HK 1.25 3.00
46 Valeri Nichushkin HK 1.00 2.50

2014 Panini Father's Day Elements

COMPLETE SET (12) 5.00 12.00
*CRACKED ICE/25: 4X TO 10X BASIC CARDS
*THICK STOCK: 1.2X TO 3X BASIC CARDS
8 Jonathan Bernier HK .60 1.50
9 Pavel Datsyuk HK .75 2.00
10 Henrik Lundqvist HK 1.00 2.50

2014 Panini Father's Day Legends

COMPLETE SET (10)
1 Steve Yzerman HK 1.00 2.50
2 Mario Lemieux HK 1.25 3.00

2014 Panini Father's Day Rookie Jerseys

NM Nathan MacKinnon HK 5.00 12.00
TH Tomas Hertl HK 3.00 8.00

2014 Panini Father's Day Rookies

COMPLETE SET (20) 10.00 25.00
*CRACKED ICE/25: 3X TO 8X BASIC CARDS
*THICK STOCK: 1X TO 2.5X BASIC CARDS
R14 Jacob Trouba HK .75 2.00
R15 Tomas Jurco HK .75 2.00
R16 Sean Monahan HK 1.00 2.50
R17 Ryan Strome HK 1.00 2.50
R18 Tomas Hertl HK 1.50 4.00

2012 Panini Golden Age

COMP.SET w/o SP's (146) 15.00 40.00
SP ANNCD PRINT RUN OF 92 PER
143 Gordie Howe 1.00 2.50

2012 Panini Golden Age Mini Broadleaf Blue Ink

*MINI BLUE: 2.5X TO 6X BASIC

2012 Panini Golden Age Mini Broadleaf Brown Ink

*MINI BROWN: .6X TO 1.5X BASIC
APPX.ODDS ONE PER PACK

2012 Panini Golden Age Mini Crofts Candy Blue Ink

*MINI BLUE: 1.5X TO 4X BASIC

2012 Panini Golden Age Mini Crofts Candy Red Ink

*MINI RED: 1.5X TO 4X BASIC
APPX.ODDS 1:8 HOBBY

2012 Panini Golden Age Mini Ty Cobb Tobacco

*MINI COBB: 2.5X TO 6X BASIC

2012 Panini Golden Age Historic Signatures

STATED ODDS 1:24 HOBBY

2013 Panini Golden Age

129 Bobby Hull .50 1.25

2013 Panini Golden Age Mini American Caramel Blue Back

*MINI BLUE: 1.2X TO 3X BASIC

2013 Panini Golden Age Mini American Caramel Red Back

*MINI RED: 2X TO 5X BASIC

2013 Panini Golden Age Mini Carolina Brights Green Back

*MINI GREEN: .75X TO 2X BASIC

2013 Panini Golden Age Mini Carolina Brights Purple Back

*MINI PURPLE: 2X TO 5X BASIC

2013 Panini Golden Age Mini Nadja Caramels Back

*MINI NADJA: 2X TO 5X BASIC

2013 Panini Golden Age White

*WHITE: 3X TO 8X BASIC
NO WHITE SP PRICING AVAILABLE

2013 Panini Golden Age Headlines

COMPLETE SET (15) 8.00 20.00
14 Bobby Hull 1.50 4.00

2013 Panini Golden Age Historic Signatures

EXCHANGE DEADLINE 12/26/2014
BH Bobby Hull 15.00 40.00

2013 Panini Golden Age Museum Age Memorabilia

39 Bobby Hull 15.00 40.00

2014 Panini Golden Age

COMP.SET w/o SP's (150) 12.00 30.00
148 Steve Yzerman .60 1.50

2014 Panini Golden Age First Fifty

*1ST FIFTY: 3X TO 8X BASIC
STATED PRINT RUN 50 SER.#'d SETS

2014 Panini Golden Age Mini Croft's Swiss Milk Cocoa

*MINI CROFTS: 2.5X TO 6X BASIC

2014 Panini Golden Age Mini Hindu Brown Back

*MINI HINDU BROWN: 2X TO 5X BASIC

2014 Panini Golden Age Mini Hindu Red Back

*MINI HINDU RED: 2.5X TO 6X BASIC

2014 Panini Golden Age Mini Mono Brand Blue Back

*MINI MONO BLUE: 1.5X TO 4X BASIC

2014 Panini Golden Age Mini Mono Brand Green Back

*MINI MONO GREEN: 1.5X TO 4X BASIC

2014 Panini Golden Age Mini Smith's Mello Mint

*MINI MELLO: 5X TO 12X BASIC

2014 Panini Golden Age White

*WHITE: 2.5X TO 6X BASIC

2012 Panini Jumbo Materials Toronto Fall Expo

AH Adam Henrique 5.00 12.00
CH Cody Hodgson 5.00 12.00
CK Chris Kreider 6.00 15.00
GH Gordie Howe 8.00 20.00
GL Gabriel Landeskog 5.00 12.00
JG Jake Gardiner 4.00 10.00
RNH Ryan Nugent-Hopkins 6.00 15.00

2012-13 Panini Manufactured Patch Autographs Toronto Fall Expo

CA Carter Ashton
JB Jonathon Blum
JC Joe Colborne
JR Jussi Rynnas
RM Ryan McDonagh
SG Scott Glennie
TT Tomas Tatar

2012 Panini Materials Toronto Fall Expo

1 Chris Kreider 6.00 15.00
2 Jaden Schwartz 4.00 10.00
3 Reilly Smith 5.00 12.00
4 Tyson Barrie 3.00 8.00

2012 Panini National Convention

1-20 CRACKED ICE/25: 5X TO 12X BASE HI
21-40 CRACKED ICE/25: 1.5X TO 4X BASE HI
*HOLO 1-20: 1X TO 2.5X BASIC CARDS
*HOLO 21-40: .6X TO 1.5X BASIC CARDS
*1-20 HOLO LAVA: 2X TO 5X BASE HI
*21-40 HOLO LAVA: 1X TO 2.5X BASE HI
UNPRICED PLATE ANNCD PRINT RUN 5 SETS
9 Pavel Datsyuk .40 1.00
10 Sidney Crosby .75 2.00
11 Steven Stamkos .60 1.50
12 Martin Brodeur .60 1.50
16 Gordie Howe .75 2.00
27 Ryan Nugent-Hopkins/499 4.00 10.00
28 Gabriel Landeskog/499 2.00 5.00
29 Adam Henrique/499 2.00 5.00
30 Cody Hodgson/499 2.00 5.00

2011 Panini National Convention Patch Autographs

BS Brayden Schenn 8.00 20.00
JE Jordan Eberle 10.00 25.00
JM Jacob Markstrom 6.00 15.00
MPS Magnus Paajarvi-Svensson 6.00 15.00
MZA Mats Zuccarello-Aasen 8.00 20.00
RM Ryan McDonagh 6.00 15.00
TH Taylor Hall 12.00 30.00
TS Tyler Seguin 8.00 20.00
ZH Zach Hamill

2012 Panini National Convention Kings VIP

COMPLETE SET (6) 12.00 30.00
3 Ryan Nugent-Hopkins 2.00 5.00

2012 Panini National Convention ROY Materials

1 Gabriel Landeskog 5.00 12.00

2012 Panini National Convention Team Colors Washington

CRACKED ICE/25: 4X TO 10X BASE HI
3 Alex Ovechkin 1.25 3.00

2013 Panini National Convention

1-24 CRACKED ICE/25: 4X TO 10X BASIC CARDS
25-47 CRACKED ICE/25: 2X TO 5X BASIC CARDS
*1-24 LAVA FLOW/99: 2.5X TO 6X BASIC CARDS
*25-47 LAVA FLOW/99: 1.2X TO 3X BASIC CARDS
19 Henrik Zetterberg .50 1.25
20 Patrick Kane .60 1.50
21 Sidney Crosby 1.00 2.50
22 Alex Ovechkin .75 2.00
23 Tuukka Rask .50 1.25
24 John Tavares .60 1.50
33 Nail Yakupov 2.50 6.00
34 Jonathan Huberdeau 2.00 5.00
35 Justin Schultz 1.50 4.00
36 Alex Galchenyuk 2.00 5.00
37 Vladimir Tarasenko 2.50 6.00

2013 Panini National Convention Draft Day Materials

HK1 Nail Yakupov 8.00 20.00
HK2 Stefan Matteau 5.00 12.00
HK3 Tom Wilson 6.00 15.00
HK4 Scott Laughton 5.00 12.00

2013 Panini National Convention Kings

CRACKED ICE/25: 2.5X TO 6X BASIC CARDS
*LAVA FLOW: 1.5X TO 4X BASIC CARDS
R6 Brendan Gallagher .75 2.00

2013 Panini National Convention Rookie Materials

HK1 Dougie Hamilton 5.00 12.00
HK2 Ryan Murphy 4.00 10.00
HK3 Brandon Saad 5.00 12.00

2013 Panini National Convention Team Colors

COMPLETE SET (10) 4.00 10.00
CRACKED ICE/25: 5X TO 12X BASIC CARDS
LAVA FLOW/99: 2.5X TO 6X BASIC CARDS
7 Jonathan Toews .60 1.50
8 Chris Chelios .40 1.00
9 Brandon Saad .50 1.25
10 Drew LeBlanc .40 1.00

2013 Panini National Convention Tools of the Trade Towels

JS Justin Schultz 5.00 12.00
NY Nail Yakupov 8.00 20.00

2013 Panini National Convention VIP

COMPLETE SET (6) 3.00 8.00
2 Nail Yakupov 1.25 3.00

2014 Panini National Convention VIP

PRIZM BLUE VETS/25: 2.5X TO 6X BASIC CARDS
PRIZM BLUE ROOKIES/25: 1.2X TO 3X
43 Gordie Howe HK 1.50 4.00

2013-14 Panini National Treasures

*SILVER/25: .5X TO 1.2X BASIC CARDS/199
EXCH EXPIRATION: 2/27/2016
1 Carey Price 6.00 15.00
2 Jamie Benn 2.50 6.00
3 Phil Kessel 2.50 6.00
4 Taylor Hall 4.00 10.00
5 Denis Potvin 2.00 5.00
6 Shea Weber 1.50 4.00
7 Paul Coffey 2.00 5.00
8 Teemu Selanne 4.00 10.00
9 Gordie Howe 4.00 10.00
10 Guy Lafleur 2.50 6.00
11 Mark Messier 2.50 6.00
12 Yvan Cournoyer 2.00 5.00
13 Pavel Datsyuk 2.50 6.00
14 Zach Parise 2.00 5.00
15 Ryan Getzlaf 3.00 8.00
16 Brett Hull 2.00 5.00
17 Roberto Luongo 2.00 5.00
18 John Tavares 4.00 10.00
19 Steve Yzerman 4.00 10.00
20 Luc Robitaille 2.00 5.00
21 Stan Mikita 2.50 6.00
22 Daniel Sedin 2.00 5.00
23 Evgeni Malkin 6.00 15.00
24 Joe Thornton 2.00 5.00
25 John Vanbiesbrouck 2.00 5.00
26 Jack Johnson 1.25 3.00
27 Cody Hodgson 2.00 5.00
28 Mike Smith 2.00 5.00
29 Alex Ovechkin 8.00 20.00
30 Martin Brodeur 4.00 10.00
31 Curtis Joseph 2.00 5.00
32 Jonathan Quick 3.00 8.00
33 Patrick Roy 5.00 12.00
34 Gilbert Perreault 2.00 5.00
35 Joe Nieuwendyk 2.00 5.00
36 Ron Francis 2.50 6.00
37 Ryan Callahan 2.00 5.00
38 Semyon Varlamov 2.00 5.00
39 Tyler Seguin 3.00 8.00
40 Anze Kopitar 3.00 8.00
41 Craig Anderson 2.00 5.00
42 David Backes 2.00 5.00
43 Corey Perry 2.00 5.00
44 Jonathan Toews 4.00 10.00
45 Pekka Rinne 2.50 6.00
46 Tuukka Rask 2.00 5.00
47 Henrik Lundqvist 2.50 6.00
48 Ed Belfour 2.00 5.00
49 Bobby Clarke 2.00 5.00
50 Marc-Andre Fleury 3.00 8.00
51 Patrick Marleau 2.00 5.00
52 Ryan Miller 2.00 5.00
53 Jeff Skinner 1.50 4.00
54 Henrik Sedin 2.00 5.00
55 Jonas Hiller 1.50 4.00
56 Cam Neely 2.00 5.00
57 Grant Fuhr 2.00 5.00
58 Eric Staal 2.50 6.00
59 Bobby Hull 2.00 5.00
60 Joe Sakic 3.00 8.00
61 Rick Nash 2.00 5.00
62 Henrik Zetterberg 2.50 6.00
63 Mike Modano 3.00 8.00
64 Ryan Nugent-Hopkins 2.00 5.00
65 Erik Karlsson 4.00 10.00
66 Mario Lemieux 6.00 15.00
67 Ryan Suter 1.25 3.00
68 Jaromir Jagr 5.00 12.00
69 Mike Fisher 1.50 4.00
70 Mike Bossy 2.00 5.00
71 Martin St. Louis 2.00 5.00
72 Sergei Bobrovsky 2.00 5.00
73 Jeremy Roenick 2.00 5.00
74 Shane Doan 1.50 4.00
75 Antti Niemi 1.50 4.00
76 P.K. Subban 3.00 8.00
77 Ray Bourque 3.00 8.00
78 Darryl Sittler 2.00 5.00
79 Nicklas Backstrom 3.00 8.00
80 Dustin Byfuglien 2.00 5.00
81 Lanny McDonald 2.00 5.00
82 Jarome Iginla 2.00 5.00
83 Andrew Ladd 2.00 5.00
84 Jordan Eberle 2.00 5.00
85 Claude Giroux 2.00 5.00
86 Matt Duchene 2.00 5.00
87 Sidney Crosby 6.00 15.00
88 Patrick Kane 4.00 10.00
89 Jason Spezza 2.00 5.00
90 Felix Potvin 3.00 8.00
91 Steven Stamkos 4.00 10.00
92 Pat LaFontaine 2.00 5.00
93 Doug Gilmour 2.50 6.00
94 Brendan Shanahan 2.50 6.00
95 Brian Leetch 2.00 5.00
96 Pavel Bure 2.50 6.00
97 Mike Cammalleri 1.50 4.00
98 Ron Hextall 2.00 5.00
99 Marcel Dionne 2.50 6.00
100 Wendel Clark 2.00 5.00
101 Brian Lashoff AU RC 4.00 10.00
102 Mark Arcobello AU RC 5.00 12.00
103 David Broll AU RC 5.00 12.00
104 Freddie Hamilton AU RC 5.00 12.00
105 Harri Pesonen AU RC 4.00 10.00
107 Jason Missiaen AU RC 5.00 12.00
108 Jeff Zatkoff AU RC 5.00 12.00
109 Jesper Fast AU RC 4.00 10.00
110 Joe Cannata AU RC 4.00 10.00
111 Johan Gustafsson AU RC 6.00 15.00
112 Johan Larsson AU RC 4.00 10.00
113 Joonas Rask AU RC 3.00 8.00
114 Jordan Szwarz AU RC 3.00 8.00
115 Michael Kostka AU RC 3.00 8.00
116 Michael Latta AU RC 4.00 10.00
117 Ondrej Palat AU RC 30.00 60.00
118 Patrick Bordeleau AU RC
119 Radko Gudas AU RC 8.00 20.00
120 Rickard Rakell AU RC 5.00 12.00
121 Steve Oleksy AU RC 5.00 12.00
122 Taylor Beck AU RC 4.00 10.00
123 Taylor Fedun AU RC 6.00 15.00
124 Tye McGinn AU RC 5.00 12.00
125 Tyler Johnson AU RC 75.00 125.00
126 A.Barkov JSY AU RC 80.00 200.00
127 Alex Chiasson JSY AU RC 20.00 50.00
128 Alex Galchenyuk JSY AU RC 200.00 400.00
129 Alex Killorn JSY AU RC 20.00 50.00
130 Anthony Peluso JSY AU RC 12.00 30.00
131 Antoine Roussel JSY AU RC 20.00 50.00
132 Austin Watson JSY AU RC 15.00 40.00
133 Beau Bennett JSY AU RC 15.00 40.00
134 Boone Jenner JSY AU RC 30.00 80.00
135 B.Gallagher JSY AU RC 80.00 150.00
136 Brian Flynn JSY AU RC 12.00 30.00
137 Brock Nelson JSY AU RC 25.00 60.00
138 Calvin Pickard JSY AU RC 30.00 80.00
139 Cameron Schilling JSY AU RC 12.00 30.00
140 Carl Soderberg JSY AU RC 15.00 40.00
141 Charlie Coyle JSY AU RC 25.00 60.00
142 Chris Brown JSY AU RC 12.00 30.00
143 Christian Thomas JSY AU RC 12.00 30.00
144 Cody Ceci JSY AU RC 15.00 40.00
145 Cory Conacher JSY AU RC 12.00 30.00
146 Danny DeKeyser JSY AU RC 20.00 50.00
147 Darcy Kuemper JSY AU RC 20.00 50.00
148 Dmitrij Jaskin JSY AU RC 20.00 50.00
149 Dougie Hamilton JSY AU RC 40.00 100.00
150 Dylan McIlrath JSY AU RC 12.00 30.00
151 Edward Pasquale JSY AU RC 12.00 30.00
152 Elias Lindholm JSY AU RC 30.00 80.00
153 Emerson Etem JSY AU RC 12.00 30.00
154 Eric Hartzell JSY AU RC 12.00 30.00
155 Filip Forsberg JSY AU RC 90.00 150.00
156 Frank Corrado JSY AU RC 12.00 30.00
157 Frederik Andersen JSY AU RC 40.00 80.00
158 Hampus Lindholm JSY AU RC 25.00 60.00
159 J.T. Miller JSY AU RC 25.00 60.00
160 Jack Campbell JSY AU RC 15.00 40.00
161 Jacob Trouba JSY AU RC 30.00 80.00
162 Jamie Devane JSY AU RC 15.00 40.00
163 Jamie Oleksiak JSY AU RC 15.00 40.00
164 Jared Staal JSY AU RC 12.00 30.00
165 Jarred Tinordi JSY AU RC 20.00 50.00
166 Jayson Megna JSY AU RC 15.00 40.00
168 Joakim Nordstrom JSY AU RC 15.00 40.00
169 John Gibson JSY AU RC 75.00 150.00
170 Jon Merrill JSY AU RC 15.00 40.00
171 Jonas Brodin JSY AU RC 20.00 50.00
172 J.Huberdeau JSY AU RC 100.00 200.00
173 Jordan Schroeder JSY AU RC 20.00 50.00
174 Justin Schultz JSY AU RC 20.00 50.00
175 Kevin Connauton JSY AU RC 12.00 30.00
176 Lucas Lessio JSY AU RC 15.00 40.00
177 Magnus Hellberg JSY AU RC 20.00 50.00
178 Marek Mazanec JSY AU RC 20.00 50.00
179 Antti Raanta JSY AU RC 25.00 60.00
180 Mark Pysyk JSY AU RC 15.00 40.00
181 Martin Jones JSY AU RC EXCH 50.00 100.00
182 Matt Dumba JSY AU RC 20.00 50.00
183 Matt Nieto JSY AU RC 15.00 40.00
184 M.Bournival JSY AU RC 20.00 50.00
185 Michael Raffl JSY AU RC 15.00 40.00
186 Mikael Granlund JSY AU RC 60.00 120.00
187 M.Grigorenko JSY AU RC 25.00 60.00
188 Morgan Rielly JSY AU RC 50.00 100.00
189 Nail Yakupov JSY AU RC 200.00 400.00
190 Nathan Beaulieu JSY AU RC 15.00 40.00
191 N.MacKinnon JSY AU RC 350.00 600.00
192 Nick Bjugstad JSY AU RC 30.00 80.00
193 Nick Petrecki JSY AU RC 15.00 40.00
194 Nicklas Jensen JSY AU RC 15.00 40.00
196 Nikita Zadorov JSY AU RC 20.00 50.00
197 Olli Maatta JSY AU RC 30.00 80.00
198 Petr Mrazek JSY AU RC 50.00 100.00
199 Philipp Grubauer JSY AU RC 12.00 30.00
200 Quinton Howden JSY AU RC 20.00 50.00
201 R.Ristolainen JSY AU RC 40.00 80.00
203 Reto Berra JSY AU RC 20.00 50.00
204 Richard Panik JSY AU RC 15.00 40.00
205 Ryan Murphy JSY AU RC 20.00 50.00
206 Ryan Murray JSY AU RC 20.00 50.00
207 Ryan Spooner JSY AU RC 20.00 50.00
208 Ryan Strome JSY AU RC 60.00 120.00
209 Sami Vatanen JSY AU RC 40.00 80.00
210 Scott Laughton JSY AU RC 20.00 50.00
211 Sean Monahan JSY AU RC 175.00 300.00
212 Seth Jones JSY AU RC 60.00 150.00
213 Stefan Matteau JSY AU RC 15.00 40.00
214 Tanner Pearson JSY AU RC 50.00 100.00
215 Thomas Hickey JSY AU RC 15.00 40.00
216 Tom Wilson JSY AU RC 30.00 80.00
217 Tomas Hertl JSY AU RC 100.00 200.00
218 Tomas Jurco JSY AU RC 30.00 80.00
219 Tyler Pitlick JSY AU RC 15.00 40.00
220 Tyler Toffoli JSY AU RC 100.00 175.00
221 Valeri Nichushkin JSY AU RC 30.00 80.00
222 Viktor Fasth JSY AU RC 20.00 50.00
224 Xavier Ouellet JSY AU RC 20.00 50.00
225 Z.Girgensons JSY AU RC 50.00 100.00

2013-14 Panini National Treasures Gold

*GOLD AU/25: .6X TO 1.5X BASIC AU/99
125 Tyler Johnson AU 125.00 200.00

2013-14 Panini National Treasures Rainbow

*RAINBOW AU/61-81: .4X TO 1X ROOK AU/99
*RAINBOW AU/30-58: .5X TO 1.2X ROOK AU/99
*RAINBOW AU/15-29: .6X TO 1.5X ROOK AU/99
*RAIN.JSY AU/60-83: .4X TO 1X RK JSY AU/99
*RAIN.JSY AU/30-59: .5X TO 1.2X RK JSY AU/99
*RAIN.JSY AU/15-29: .6X TO 1.5X RK JSY AU/99
126 A.Barkov JSY AU/16 200.00 400.00
128 A.Galchenyuk JSY AU/27 300.00 500.00
149 Dougie Hamilton JSY AU/27 40.00 100.00
169 John Gibson JSY AU/36 60.00 120.00
191 N.MacKinnon JSY AU/29 750.00 1300.00
221 V.Nichushkin JSY AU/43 100.00 200.00

2013-14 Panini National Treasures Silver

*SILVER/25: .8X TO 2X BASIC CARDS/199
79 Nicklas Backstrom 6.00 15.00

2013-14 Panini National Treasures All Star Treasures Autographs

1 Gordie Howe/23 100.00 200.00
2 Ray Bourque/19 40.00 80.00
3 Paul Coffey/15 40.00 80.00
4 Mark Messier/15

2013-14 Panini National Treasures Century Materials Jersey

*PRIME/50: .5X TO 1.2X BASIC JSY/99
*PATCH/25: .6X TO 1.5X BASIC JSY/99
1 Nathan MacKinnon/99 10.00 25.00
2 Pavel Bure/99 6.00 15.00
3 Sidney Crosby/99 12.00 30.00
4 Tomas Hertl/99 3.00 8.00
5 Paul Coffey/99 3.00 8.00
6 Alex Ovechkin/99 12.00 30.00
7 Antti Raanta/99 3.00 8.00
8 Marcel Dionne/99 4.00 10.00
9 Steven Stamkos/99 6.00 15.00
10 Tomas Jurco/99 4.00 10.00
11 Ron Francis/99 4.00 10.00
12 John Tavares/99 6.00 15.00
13 Mikael Granlund/99 4.00 10.00
14 Denis Potvin/99 3.00 8.00
15 Evgeni Malkin/99 6.00 15.00
16 Seth Jones/99 2.50 6.00
17 Steve Yzerman/99 6.00 15.00
18 Jeff Carter/99 3.00 8.00
19 Nail Yakupov/99 5.00 12.00
20 Mario Lemieux/99 10.00 25.00
21 Carey Price/99 10.00 25.00
22 Sean Monahan/99 6.00 15.00
23 Gordie Howe/25 15.00 40.00
24 Martin Brodeur/99 10.00 25.00
25 Morgan Rielly/99 6.00 15.00
26 Jeremy Roenick/99 3.00 8.00
27 Gabriel Landeskog/99 2.50 6.00
28 Valeri Nichushkin/99 2.50 6.00
29 Mike Modano/99 5.00 12.00
30 Patrick Kane/99 6.00 15.00
31 Alex Galchenyuk/99 12.00 30.00
32 Brett Hull/99 6.00 15.00
33 Jason Spezza/99 3.00 8.00
34 Damien Brunner/99 2.50 6.00
35 Joe Sakic/75 10.00 25.00
36 Claude Giroux/99 3.00 8.00
37 Jacob Trouba/99 4.00 10.00
38 Ron Francis/99 4.00 10.00
39 Daniel Sedin/99 3.00 8.00
40 Aleksander Barkov/99 6.00 15.00
41 Yvan Cournoyer/50 4.00 10.00
42 Marian Gaborik/99 3.00 8.00
43 Jonathan Huberdeau/99 6.00 15.00
44 Stan Mikita/99 4.00 10.00
45 Henrik Lundqvist/50 4.00 10.00
46 Elias Lindholm/99 4.00 10.00
47 Phil Esposito/99 5.00 12.00
48 Teemu Selanne/99 6.00 15.00
49 Olli Maatta/99 4.00 10.00
50 Mark Messier/99 6.00 15.00

2013-14 Panini National Treasures Cherry's Treasures Autographs

1 E.Lindros/D.Cherry/49 30.00 60.00
2 J.Tavares/D.Cherry/99 40.00 80.00
3 T.Seguin/D.Cherry/99 30.00 60.00
4 D.Gilmour/D.Cherry/99 30.00 60.00
5 D.Clarkson/D.Cherry/99 12.00 30.00
6 M.Messier/D.Cherry/49 40.00 80.00
7 S.Yzerman/D.Cherry/49 60.00 120.00
8 M.Duchene/D.Cherry/99 12.00 30.00
9 MacKinnon/D.Cherry/99 80.00 150.00
10 C.Neely/D.Cherry/49 30.00 60.00

2013-14 Panini National Treasures Colossal Jerseys

*PRIME/25: .6X TO 1.5X BASIC JSY/50
1 Nathan MacKinnon/50 10.00 25.00
2 Nail Yakupov/50 6.00 15.00
3 Tomas Hertl/50 6.00 15.00
4 Sean Monahan/50 6.00 15.00
5 Valeri Nichushkin/50 6.00 15.00
6 Alex Galchenyuk/50 8.00 20.00
7 Brendan Gallagher/50 6.00 15.00
8 Morgan Rielly/50 8.00 20.00
9 Tom Wilson/50 5.00 12.00
10 Ryan Strome/50 4.00 10.00
11 Tomas Jurco/50 5.00 12.00
12 John Gibson/50 6.00 15.00
13 Tanner Pearson/50 6.00 15.00
14 Boone Jenner/50 3.00 8.00
15 Jon Merrill/50 3.00 8.00
16 Martin Jones/50 4.00 10.00
17 Ryan Spooner/50 3.00 8.00
18 Brock Nelson/50 3.00 8.00
19 Jacob Trouba/50 5.00 12.00
20 Jonathan Huberdeau/25 6.00 15.00
21 Austin Watson/50 2.50 6.00
22 Mikhail Grigorenko/50 4.00 10.00
23 Mikael Granlund/50 5.00 12.00
24 Ryan Murray/50 5.00 12.00
25 Elias Lindholm/50 5.00 12.00
26 Gordie Howe/25 30.00 80.00
27 Jonathan Quick/50 8.00 20.00
28 Adam Henrique/50 4.00 10.00
29 Derek Stepan/50 4.00 10.00
30 Maxime Talbot/50 3.00 8.00
31 Vincent Lecavalier/50 3.00 8.00
32 Tyler Seguin/50 6.00 15.00
33 Jeremy Roenick/50 4.00 10.00
34 Ryan Kesler/50 4.00 10.00
35 Ron Hextall/50 5.00 12.00
36 Reilly Smith/50 4.00 10.00
37 Pierre Turgeon/50 4.00 10.00
38 Pekka Rinne/50 5.00 12.00
39 Paul Coffey/50 5.00 12.00
40 Patrick Marleau/50 4.00 10.00
41 Nazem Kadri/50 4.00 10.00
42 Mikael Backlund/50 3.00 8.00
43 Matt Duchene/50 4.00 10.00
44 Loui Eriksson/50 3.00 8.00
45 Jaromir Jagr/50 8.00 20.00
46 Sean Couturier/50 4.00 10.00
47 Taylor Hall/50 8.00 20.00
48 Steve Yzerman/25 8.00 20.00
49 Torey Krug/50 6.00 15.00
50 Chris Kreider/50 4.00 10.00

2013-14 Panini National Treasures Colossal Jerseys Autograph

1 Nathan MacKinnon/25 60.00 150.00
2 Nail Yakupov/25 20.00 50.00
3 Tomas Hertl/25 15.00 40.00
4 Sean Monahan/25
5 Valeri Nichushkin/25 12.00 30.00
6 Alex Galchenyuk/25 25.00 60.00
7 Brendan Gallagher/25 25.00 60.00
8 Morgan Rielly/25 15.00 40.00
9 Tom Wilson/25 12.00 30.00
10 Ryan Strome/25 10.00 25.00
11 Tomas Jurco/25 12.00 30.00
12 John Gibson/25 12.00 30.00
13 Tanner Pearson/25 8.00 20.00
14 Boone Jenner/25 8.00 20.00
15 Jon Merrill/25 8.00 20.00
16 Martin Jones/25 15.00 40.00
17 Ryan Spooner/25 8.00 20.00
18 Brock Nelson/25 8.00 20.00
19 Jacob Trouba/25 12.00 30.00
20 Jonathan Huberdeau/25 12.00 30.00
21 Austin Watson/25 6.00 15.00
22 Mikhail Grigorenko/25 10.00 25.00
23 Mikael Granlund/25 12.00 30.00
24 Ryan Murray/25 12.00 30.00
25 Elias Lindholm/25 10.00 25.00
27 Jonathan Quick/25 20.00 50.00
28 Adam Henrique/25 12.00 30.00
29 Derek Stepan/25 10.00 25.00
30 Maxime Talbot/25
31 Vincent Lecavalier/25 10.00 25.00
32 Tyler Seguin/25 20.00 50.00
33 Jeremy Roenick/25 20.00 50.00
34 Ryan Kesler/25 12.00 30.00
35 Ron Hextall/25 20.00 50.00
36 Reilly Smith/25 12.00 30.00
37 Pierre Turgeon/25 12.00 30.00
38 Pekka Rinne/25 15.00 40.00
39 Paul Coffey/25 12.00 30.00
40 Patrick Marleau/25
42 Mikael Backlund/25 EXCH 10.00 25.00
43 Matt Duchene/25 12.00 30.00
44 Loui Eriksson/25 10.00 25.00
45 Jaromir Jagr/25 40.00 80.00
46 Sean Couturier/25 12.00 30.00
47 Taylor Hall/25 20.00 50.00
49 Torey Krug/25 15.00 40.00
50 Chris Kreider/25 12.00 30.00

2013-14 Panini National Treasures Crazy 8's Jerseys

*PRIME/25: .6X TO 1.5X BASIC JSY/50
1 Atlantic Division 30.00 80.00
3 Central Division 20.00 50.00
4 Pacific Division 12.00 30.00
5 NHL Stars 12.00 30.00
7 Russian Stars 20.00 50.00
8 NHL Stars 15.00 40.00
9 NHL Stars 20.00 50.00
11 Colorado Stars 25.00 60.00
12 Edmonton Stars 20.00 50.00
13 Anaheim Stars 20.00 50.00
14 NHL Stars 15.00 40.00
15 NHL Stars 15.00 40.00
16 Sidney Crosby 40.00 100.00
MD Metropolitan Division 40.00 100.00
13D 2013 Draft Picks 30.00 80.00
SCF Blackhawks and Bruins 25.00 50.00

2013-14 Panini National Treasures Dual Autographs

*GOLD/15-25:.6X TO 1.5X AU/75-100
3 Silfverberg/R.Rakell/100 6.00 15.00
4 P.Elias/T.Ruutu/100 6.00 15.00
5 A.Peluso/E.Pasquale/100 4.00 10.00
6 C.Ward/E.Staal/100 8.00 20.00
7 R.Panik/V.Filppula/100 8.00 20.00
8 D.Phaneuf/J.Leivo/100 8.00 20.00
9 P.Datsyuk/P.Mrazek/100 12.00 30.00
10 A.Watson/Del Zotto/100 5.00 12.00
12 C.Pickard/C.Pickard/100 6.00 15.00
13 M.Mazanec/P.Mrazek/100 12.00 30.00
14 Markstrom/R.Luongo/100 6.00 15.00
15 B.Schenn/Z.Rinaldo/100 6.00 15.00
17 C.Neely/J.Iginla/100 8.00 20.00
18 J.Howard/P.Mrazek/100 10.00 25.00
20 J.Tavares/N.Yakupov/100 20.00 50.00
21 B.Ryan/J.Silfverberg/100 6.00 15.00
22 M.Foligno/N.Foligno/100 8.00 20.00
23 Galchenyuk/Yakupov/100 20.00 50.00
24 E.Lach/Y.Cournoyer/100 12.00 30.00
25 B.Richards/St. Louis/100 10.00 25.00
27 J.Reimer/J.Bower/100 10.00 25.00
28 J.Iginla/R.Spooner/100 6.00 15.00
29 B.Street/S.Baertschi/100 5.00 12.00
30 J.Johnson/N.Foligno/100 5.00 12.00
31 C.Emmerton/S.Weiss/100 5.00 12.00
32 B.Boyes/J.Rheault/100 4.00 10.00
33 C.Coyle/D.Kuemper/100 10.00 25.00
34 C.Coyle/Z.Parise/100 12.00 30.00
35 B.Gallagher/C.Thomas/75 12.00 30.00
36 Pesonen/S.Matteau/100 5.00 12.00
37 A.Lee/M.Grabner/100 10.00 25.00
38 J.Neal/Z.Rinaldo/100 6.00 15.00
40 M.Kostka/O.Palat/100 8.00 20.00
41 D.Gilmour/W.Clark/100 15.00 40.00
42 M.Naslund/T.Linden/100 12.00 30.00
43 C.Carrick/K.Alzner/100 5.00 12.00
44 M.Konan/T.McGinn/100 6.00 15.00
45 C.Simmer/M.Dionne/100 12.00 30.00

2013-14 Panini National Treasures Dual Memorabilia Autographs

*PRIME/25: .6X TO 1.5X BASIC JSY AU
1 Darcy Kuemper 6.00 15.00
2 Marc Staal 3.00 8.00
3 Cody Hodgson 4.00 10.00
4 Curtis Glencross 2.50 6.00
5 Austin Watson 3.00 8.00
6 Gordie Howe 60.00 120.00
7 Christian Thomas 3.00 8.00
8 Tye McGinn 4.00 10.00
9 Michael Kostka 3.00 8.00
10 Nick Petrecki 2.50 6.00
11 Anthony Peluso 2.50 6.00
12 Xavier Ouellet 4.00 10.00
13 Stefan Matteau 3.00 8.00
14 Anze Kopitar 10.00 25.00
15 Jay Bouwmeester 4.00 10.00
16 Eric Lindros 25.00 50.00
17 Brendan Shanahan 10.00 25.00

18 Dion Phaneuf 4.00 10.00
19 Jerry D'Amigo 4.00 10.00
20 Jason Missiaen 4.00 10.00
21 Mark Messier 20.00 50.00
22 Cam Neely 12.00 30.00
23 Cody Ceci 3.00 8.00
24 Petr Mrazek 8.00 20.00
25 Mark Giordano 3.00 8.00
26 Johan Franzen 4.00 10.00
27 Beau Bennett 5.00 12.00
28 Bryan Trottier 8.00 20.00
29 Mikael Granlund 10.00 25.00
30 Dan Boyle 5.00 12.00
31 Joakim Nordstrom 3.00 8.00
32 Brian Leetch 10.00 25.00
33 Pat LaFontaine 10.00 25.00
34 Magnus Hellberg 4.00 10.00
35 Connor Murphy 3.00 8.00
36 Tyler Ennis 3.00 8.00
37 Rogie Vachon 10.00 25.00
38 Jacob Markstrom 6.00 15.00
39 Stephen Weiss 3.00 8.00
40 Mikael Backlund 6.00 15.00
41 Logan Couture 4.00 10.00
42 Joe Nieuwendyk 8.00 20.00
43 Edward Pasquale 2.50 6.00
44 Max Pacioretty 8.00 20.00
45 David Krejci 10.00 25.00

2013-14 Panini National Treasures Dual Rookie Jumbo Patch Autographs

1 Yakupov/MacKinnon 125.00 250.00
2 Galchenyuk/Gallagher 75.00 150.00
3 A.Barkov/J.Huberdeau 30.00 80.00
4 T.Pearson/T.Toffoli
5 M.Raffl/S.Laughton 15.00 40.00
6 Arcobello/S.Monahan 30.00 80.00
7 H.Lindholm/T.Hertl 30.00 80.00
8 J.Merrill/S.Matteau 15.00 40.00
10 M.Rielly/O.Maatta 40.00 80.00
11 J.Trouba/S.Jones 25.00 60.00
12 Roussel/Nichushkin 25.00 60.00

2013-14 Panini National Treasures Dual Stick Booklet Autographs

1 A.Ovechkin/E.Malkin/25 200.00 300.00
2 C.Joseph/F.Potvin/25 75.00 150.00
5 C.Neely/R.Bourque/20 100.00 200.00
6 T.Seguin/V.Nichushkin/25 40.00 80.00
8 D.Stepan/H.Lundqvist/25
12 E.Lindros/V.Lecavalier/25 60.00 120.00

2013-14 Panini National Treasures Frozen Treasures Jersey Autographs

1 Alex Ovechkin/25 60.00 120.00
2 Sidney Crosby/15
3 John Tavares/35 30.00 80.00
4 Jonathan Toews/35 30.00 80.00
5 Pavel Datsyuk/35 20.00 50.00
6 Henrik Lundqvist/35 20.00 50.00
7 Carey Price/35 50.00 120.00
8 Claude Giroux/35 15.00 40.00
9 Cam Neely/35 15.00 40.00
10 Mario Lemieux/15 90.00 150.00
11 Steve Yzerman/15
12 Jeremy Roenick/35 15.00 40.00
13 Mark Messier/15 50.00 100.00
14 Gabriel Landeskog/35 12.00 30.00
15 Brett Hull/35 30.00 60.00
16 Tyler Seguin/35 25.00 60.00
17 Ryan Getzlaf/35 25.00 60.00
18 Daniel Sedin/35 15.00 40.00
19 Gordie Howe/15
20 Martin Brodeur/35 30.00 80.00
21 Patrick Kane/35 40.00 80.00
22 Phil Kessel/35 20.00 50.00
23 Jonathan Quick/35 25.00 60.00
24 Ryan Miller/35 12.00 30.00
25 Joe Sakic/35 25.00 60.00

2013-14 Panini National Treasures Greatest Signatures

2 Don Cherry/25 60.00 120.00
3 Bobby Clarke/25 15.00 40.00
7 Cam Neely/25 15.00 40.00
9 Tony Esposito/25 40.00 100.00
10 Stan Mikita/25 40.00 80.00
11 Bernie Parent/25 20.00 50.00
12 Joe Sakic/25 25.00 60.00
13 Brett Hull/25 25.00 60.00
14 Bobby Hull/25 40.00 80.00
15 Curtis Joseph/25 15.00 40.00
17 Yvan Cournoyer/25 15.00 40.00
18 Charlie Simmer/25 10.00 25.00
19 Doug Gilmour/25 30.00 60.00
21 Wendel Clark/25 20.00 50.00
22 Milt Schmidt/25 20.00 50.00
23 Johnny Bower/25 20.00 50.00
24 Mike Bossy/25 15.00 40.00
25 Ray Bourque/25 25.00 60.00

2013-14 Panini National Treasures Icy Inscriptions

1 Matt Moulson 6.00 15.00
2 Dylan McIlrath 5.00 12.00
3 John Gibson 15.00 40.00
4 Matt Duchene 12.00 30.00
5 Andrew Ladd 8.00 20.00
6 Jesper Fast 5.00 12.00
7 Sergei Bobrovsky 8.00 20.00
8 Jonathan Toews
9 Henrik Lundqvist 40.00 80.00
10 Sidney Crosby
11 Eric Staal 10.00 25.00
12 Boone Jenner 8.00 20.00
13 Jason Spezza 8.00 20.00
14 Jon Merrill 8.00 20.00
15 Tyler Seguin 30.00 60.00

2013-14 Panini National Treasures Jumbo Jerseys Booklet

*PRIME/25: .6X TO 1.5X BASIC JSY/75-99
1 Tyler Seguin/99 10.00 25.00
2 Alex Ovechkin/99 25.00 60.00
3 Claude Giroux/99 6.00 15.00
4 Taylor Hall/99 12.00 30.00
5 Luc Robitaille/99 6.00 15.00
6 Dion Phaneuf/99 6.00 15.00
7 Sidney Crosby/99 25.00 60.00
8 Steve Yzerman/99 12.00 30.00
9 Jeremy Roenick/99 6.00 15.00
10 Mike Modano/99 10.00 25.00
11 Brad Richards/99 6.00 15.00
12 Evgeni Malkin/99 20.00 50.00
13 Jaromir Jagr/99 12.00 30.00
14 Joe Sakic/99 10.00 25.00
15 John Tavares/99 12.00 30.00
16 Jonathan Quick/99 10.00 25.00
17 Matt Duchene/99 6.00 15.00
18 Jonathan Toews/75 12.00 30.00
19 Patrice Bergeron/99 10.00 25.00
20 Ryan Getzlaf/99 10.00 25.00

2013-14 Panini National Treasures Jumbo Quad Patches Booklet

1 Brkv/Hbrd/Bgstd/Hwdn 50.00 100.00
2 Prry/Crtr/St. Louis/Shrp 25.00 60.00
3 Fwlr/Quick/Ststny/Prse 30.00 60.00
4 McKin/Mnhn/Hrtl/Nchsh 50.00 120.00
5 Glchny/Hbrd/Ykpv/Trsnk 40.00 80.00
6 Andrsn/Bbkv/Gbsn/Hillr 30.00 80.00
7 Alfrds/Khbn/Whtny/Slne
8 Hmltn/Trba/Schltz/Jnes 20.00 50.00
9 Lndq/Erksn/Jhnsn/Bckstr 25.00 60.00

2013-14 Panini National Treasures Jumbo Triple Patches Booklet

1 Hamilton/Bourque/Chara 30.00 60.00
2 Carter/Williams/Richards 25.00 50.00
3 Keith/Karlsson/Subban 30.00 60.00
4 Cogliano/Perry/Bonino 12.00 30.00
5 Yakpv/MacKin/RNH 50.00 120.00
6 Staal/Staal/Staal 12.00 30.00
7 Barkv/Lhtnen/Timon 25.00 60.00
8 MacInnis/Weber/Chara 10.00 25.00
9 Anismv/Dubnsky/Gabrk 25.00 50.00
10 Pysyk/Grigrnko/Grgnsns 25.00 60.00
11 Karlsn/Spzza/Michalek 15.00 40.00
12 Couture/Vlasic/Hertl 30.00 80.00

2013-14 Panini National Treasures Knights in the City Materials

1 J.Sakic/N.MacKinnon 6.00 15.00
2 D.Hamilton/R.Bourque 6.00 15.00
3 L.Robitaille/T.Toffoli 6.00 15.00
4 B.Gainey/B.Gallagher 10.00 25.00
5 Nieuwendyk/Monahan 5.00 12.00
6 M.Modano/V.Nichushkin 5.00 12.00
7 E.Lindholm/R.Francis 5.00 12.00
8 A.Raanta/E.Belfour 4.00 10.00
9 M.Bossy/R.Strome 4.00 10.00
10 Perreault/Girgensons 6.00 15.00
11 Galchenyuk/Cournoyer 8.00 20.00
12 M.Messier/N.Yakupov 10.00 25.00
13 A.Barkov/P.Bure 12.00 30.00
14 B.Clarke/S.Laughton 3.00 8.00
15 O.Maatta/P.Coffey 10.00 25.00
16 B.Hull/V.Tarasenko 12.00 30.00
17 S.Yzerman/T.Jurco 6.00 15.00
18 D.Gilmour/M.Rielly 8.00 20.00
19 M.Gartner/T.Wilson 5.00 12.00
20 M.Dionne/T.Pearson 4.00 10.00
21 B.Bennett/M.Lemieux 10.00 25.00
22 E.Lindros/M.Raffl 8.00 20.00
23 J.Devane/W.Clark 3.00 8.00
24 J.Thornton/T.Hertl 4.00 10.00
25 S.Jones/S.Weber 3.00 8.00

2013-14 Panini National Treasures Matchups Jerseys

*PRIME/25: .8X TO 2X BASIC JSY/99
1 Trouba/MacKinnon/99 8.00 20.00
2 Lemieux/M.Messier/99 10.00 25.00
3 C.Price/J.Quick/99 12.00 30.00
4 A.Raanta/M.Jones/99 6.00 15.00
5 G.Howe/J.Bucyk/25 12.00 30.00
6 Doughty/Karlsson/99 6.00 15.00
7 B.Gallagher/M.Rielly/99 6.00 15.00
8 B.Gainey/B.Clarke/99 6.00 15.00
9 Schneider/R.Luongo/99 6.00 15.00
10 Yakupov/Monahan/99 4.00 10.00
11 D.Potvin/P.Esposito/99 5.00 12.00
12 A.Kopitar/T.Selanne/99 8.00 20.00
13 M.Raffl/O.Maatta/99 6.00 15.00
14 F.Potvin/P.Roy/99 12.00 30.00
15 C.Giroux/E.Malkin/99 10.00 25.00
16 S.Jones/Nichushkin/99 2.50 6.00
17 B.Hull/J.Roenick/99 5.00 12.00
18 P.Kane/T.Oshie/99 6.00 15.00
19 T.Hertl/T.Toffoli/99 8.00 20.00
20 D.Sittler/G.Lafleur/99 6.00 15.00
21 Galchenyuk/Hamilton/99 10.00 25.00
22 B.Leetch/R.Bourque/99 5.00 12.00
23 Ovechkin/S.Stamkos/99 12.00 30.00
24 A.Barkov/S.Vatanen/99 6.00 15.00
25 E.Lindros/S.Yzerman/99 12.00 30.00

2013-14 Panini National Treasures Newfound Treasures Materials Autograph

NTAB Aleksander Barkov 10.00 25.00
NTAG Alex Galchenyuk 30.00 80.00
NTBJ Boone Jenner 6.00 15.00
NTCC Cody Ceci 5.00 12.00
NTEL Elias Lindholm 8.00 20.00
NTHL Hampus Lindholm 8.00 20.00
NTJC Jack Campbell 8.00 20.00
NTJG John Gibson 15.00 40.00
NTJH Jonathan Huberdeau 15.00 40.00
NTJM Jon Merrill 8.00 20.00
NTJT Jacob Trouba 10.00 25.00
NTMJ Martin Jones 12.00 30.00
NTMR Morgan Rielly 15.00 40.00
NTMRA Michael Raffl 10.00 25.00
NTNM Nathan MacKinnon 40.00 100.00
NTNY Nail Yakupov 15.00 40.00
NTOM Olli Maatta 10.00 25.00
NTRS Ryan Spooner 6.00 15.00
NTRST Ryan Strome 8.00 20.00
NTSM Sean Monahan 15.00 40.00
NTTH Tomas Hertl 8.00 20.00
NTTJ Tomas Jurco 15.00 40.00
NTVN Valeri Nichushkin 6.00 15.00
NTZG Zemgus Girgensons 12.00 30.00

2013-14 Panini National Treasures Newfound Treasures Materials Autograph Prime

NTNM Nathan MacKinnon 50.00 120.00

2013-14 Panini National Treasures NHL Gear Autographs

2 Tyler Seguin/50 25.00 50.00
3 Adam Henrique/99 8.00 20.00
4 Alex Ovechkin/25 60.00 120.00
6 Jonathan Toews/50 50.00 100.00
7 Adam Graves/49 10.00 25.00
8 Brendan Shanahan/25
9 Brenden Morrow/99 6.00 15.00
10 Brian Leetch/50 12.00 30.00
11 Cam Neely/50 15.00 40.00
12 Carey Price/50 25.00 60.00
14 Curtis Joseph/50 20.00 50.00
15 Dave Andreychuk/99 8.00 20.00
16 Derek Stepan/99 8.00 20.00
17 Devan Dubnyk/75 EXCH 15.00 30.00
18 Ed Belfour/50 20.00 50.00
19 Mike Modano/50 25.00 50.00
23 Vincent Lecavalier/50 8.00 20.00
24 Ray Bourque/50 30.00 80.00
25 Patrick Roy/25 60.00 120.00
26 Jeremy Roenick/25 25.00 60.00
27 Ryan Getzlaf/50 15.00 40.00
28 Bobby Ryan/50 10.00 25.00
29 Ryan Miller/50 10.00 25.00
30 Ryan Nugent-Hopkins/25 15.00 40.00
31 Jonathan Quick/25 25.00 60.00
32 Joe Thornton/25 20.00 50.00
33 John Tavares/25 25.00 60.00

2013-14 Panini National Treasures NHL Rookie Gear Autographs

1 Nail Yakupov 30.00 80.00
2 Nathan MacKinnon 40.00 100.00
3 Aleksander Barkov 15.00 40.00
4 Jonathan Huberdeau 15.00 40.00
5 Valeri Nichushkin 8.00 20.00
6 Sean Monahan 25.00 50.00
7 Tomas Hertl 20.00 50.00
8 John Gibson 15.00 40.00
9 Elias Lindholm 12.00 30.00
10 Tomas Jurco 12.00 30.00
11 Ryan Strome 10.00 25.00
12 Seth Jones 8.00 20.00
13 Jacob Trouba 12.00 30.00
14 Morgan Rielly 15.00 40.00
15 Michael Raffl 10.00 25.00
16 Tyler Toffoli 15.00 40.00
17 Hampus Lindholm 10.00 25.00
18 Ryan Murray 12.00 30.00
19 Alex Galchenyuk 30.00 60.00
20 Brendan Gallagher 15.00 40.00
21 Nicklas Jensen 6.00 15.00
22 Zemgus Girgensons 15.00 40.00
24 Martin Jones 12.00 30.00
25 Vladimir Tarasenko
26 Matt Dumba 8.00 20.00
27 Dougie Hamilton 15.00 40.00
28 Boone Jenner 8.00 20.00
29 Olli Maatta 20.00 50.00
30 Matt Nieto 8.00 20.00
31 Antoine Roussel 8.00 20.00
32 Mikael Granlund 12.00 30.00
33 Jon Merrill 8.00 20.00
34 Ryan Spooner 8.00 20.00

2013-14 Panini National Treasures Notable Nicknames

1 Ron Hextall/25 20.00 50.00
3 Ed Belfour/25 50.00 100.00
4 Johnny Bower/25 40.00 100.00
6 Pavel Datsyuk/25 25.00 60.00
7 Cam Ward/25 15.00 40.00
8 Tony Esposito/25 20.00 50.00
9 Doug Gilmour/25 20.00 50.00
11 Brett Hull/25
12 Bobby Hull/25 60.00 120.00
13 Jarome Iginla/25 15.00 40.00
14 Curtis Joseph/25 40.00 100.00
16 Henrik Lundqvist/25 25.00 60.00
17 Stan Mikita/25 40.00 80.00
18 Ryan Nugent-Hopkins/25 20.00 50.00
20 Felix Potvin/25 60.00 120.00
21 James Reimer/25 50.00 100.00
22 Luc Robitaille/25 20.00 50.00
23 Jeremy Roenick/25 25.00 60.00
24 Yvan Cournoyer/25
25 John Vanbiesbrouck/25 20.00 50.00

2013-14 Panini National Treasures Numbers Patch

1 Carey Price/31 30.00 80.00
3 Phil Kessel/81 10.00 25.00
15 Ryan Getzlaf/15 15.00 40.00
16 Brett Hull/16 25.00 50.00
18 John Tavares/91 15.00 40.00
19 Steve Yzerman/19 30.00 60.00
20 Luc Robitaille/20 25.00 50.00
21 Stan Mikita/21 25.00 50.00
22 Daniel Sedin/22 12.00 30.00
23 Evgeni Malkin/71 25.00 60.00
24 Joe Thornton/19 12.00 30.00
25 John Vanbiesbrouck/34 10.00 25.00
27 Cody Hodgson/19 12.00 30.00
28 Mike Smith/41 10.00 25.00
30 Martin Brodeur/30 30.00 60.00
31 Curtis Joseph/31 10.00 25.00
32 Jonathan Quick/32 15.00 40.00
33 Patrick Roy/33 20.00 50.00
35 Joe Nieuwendyk/25 12.00 30.00
37 Ryan Callahan/24 12.00 30.00
39 Tyler Seguin/91 12.00 30.00
41 Craig Anderson/41 8.00 20.00
42 David Backes/42 10.00 25.00
44 Jonathan Toews/19 30.00 60.00
45 Pekka Rinne/35 12.00 30.00
46 Tuukka Rask/40 10.00 25.00
47 Henrik Lundqvist/30 12.00 30.00
48 Ed Belfour/20 12.00 30.00
49 Bobby Clarke/16 30.00 60.00
50 Marc-Andre Fleury/29 20.00 50.00
52 Ryan Miller/39 10.00 25.00
53 Jeff Skinner/53 6.00 15.00
54 Henrik Sedin/33 10.00 25.00
57 Grant Fuhr/31 10.00 25.00
60 Joe Sakic/19 15.00 40.00
61 Rick Nash/61 8.00 20.00
62 Henrik Zetterberg/40 10.00 25.00
64 Ryan Nugent-Hopkins/93 8.00 20.00
65 Erik Karlsson/65 6.00 15.00
66 Mario Lemieux/66 25.00 60.00
67 Ryan Suter/20 8.00 20.00
68 Jaromir Jagr/68 20.00 50.00
70 Mike Bossy/22 12.00 30.00
71 Martin St. Louis/26 12.00 30.00
72 Sergei Bobrovsky/72 8.00 20.00
73 Jeremy Roenick/97 6.00 15.00
74 Shane Doan/19 10.00 25.00
75 Antti Niemi/31 8.00 20.00
76 P.K. Subban/76 12.00 30.00
77 Ray Bourque/77 12.00 30.00
78 Darryl Sittler/27 12.00 30.00
79 Nicklas Backstrom/19 20.00 50.00
80 Dustin Byfuglien/33 10.00 25.00
83 Andrew Ladd/16 12.00 30.00
85 Claude Giroux/28 12.00 30.00
87 Sidney Crosby/87 25.00 60.00
88 Patrick Kane/88 15.00 40.00
89 Jason Spezza/19 15.00 40.00
90 Felix Potvin/29 20.00 50.00
92 Pat LaFontaine/16 12.00 30.00
94 Brendan Shanahan/94 10.00 25.00
98 Ron Hextall/27 12.00 30.00
99 Marcel Dionne/16 15.00 40.00
100 Wendel Clark/17 15.00 40.00

2013-14 Panini National Treasures Past and Present Autographs

1 J.Tavares/M.Bossy/99 30.00 60.00
2 E.Staal/K.Primeau/99 15.00 40.00
3 C.Neely/R.Smith/99 12.00 30.00
4 F.Andersen/G.Hebert/99 20.00 50.00
6 C.Kreider/M.Messier/49 30.00 80.00
7 B.Federko/J.Schwartz/99 15.00 40.00
8 E.Lindros/M.Read/99 20.00 50.00
9 H.Lundqvist/M.Richter/99 30.00 80.00
10 C.Price/P.Roy/99 75.00 135.00
11 A.Killorn/D.Andreychuk/99 12.00 30.00
12 G.Howe/P.Datsyuk/49 60.00 120.00
13 C.Joseph/J.Bernier/99 20.00 50.00
14 J.Neal/R.Francis/99 15.00 40.00
15 R.Kesler/T.Linden/99 12.00 30.00

2013-14 Panini National Treasures Past Present and Future Autographs

1 Modano/Seguin/Nichushkin 15.00 40.00
2 Hamilton/Bourque/Krug 40.00 80.00
3 Messier/Yakupov/Hall 30.00 80.00
4 Sakic/Duchene/MacKinnon 60.00 120.00
5 Brown/Robitaille/Toffoli 20.00 50.00
6 Nieuwendyk/Backlund/Monahan 15.00 40.00
7 Tavares/Bossy/Strome 30.00 60.00
8 Giroux/Lindros/Laughton 20.00 50.00
9 Galchenyuk/Pacioretty/Cournoyer 30.00 80.00
10 Phaneuf/Gilmour/Rielly 25.00 60.00

2013-14 Panini National Treasures Phenoms Autographs

PAG Alex Galchenyuk
PEE1 Emerson Etem logo 3.00 8.00
PEE2 Emerson Etem draft 3.00 8.00
PJC1 Jack Campbell Stars 2.50 6.00
PJC2 Jack Campbell Texas SP 2.50 6.00
PMG Mikael Granlund 5.00 12.00
PMR Morgan Rielly SP 15.00 30.00
PNB1 Nathan Beaulieu logo 5.00 12.00
PNB2 Nathan Beaulieu draft 5.00 12.00
PQH1 Quinton Howden Panther 3.00 8.00
PQH2 Q.Howden Panther circle 3.00 8.00
PQH3 Quinton Howden draft 3.00 8.00
PQH4 Q.Howden NHLPA SP 3.00 8.00
PRM1 Ryan Murray logo 5.00 12.00
PRM2 R.Murray war cap SP 5.00 12.00
PRS1 Ryan Strome NYI 4.00 10.00
PRS2 Ryan Strome NHLPA 4.00 10.00
PTW Tom Wilson SP 6.00 15.00

2013-14 Panini National Treasures Quad Autographs

1 Glchn/Gllghr/Lflr/Crnyr/50 60.00 120.00
2 Schn/Rshill/Msn/McGn/50 12.00 30.00
3 Wrd/Sknnr/Jrdn/Gerbe/50 12.00 30.00
4 Prrn/Ebrle/RNH/Gagner/35 12.00 30.00
5 Oats/Chvrs/Lmlin/O'Rlly/35 20.00 50.00
6 Etm/Hbrt/Hllr/Ndrmyer/35 15.00 40.00
7 Sakc/Dchn/Sgrba/Hjdk/50 20.00 50.00
8 Wtsn/Pckrd/Mznc/Fshr/45 10.00 25.00
10 Brsrd/Mre/Diaz/McDngh/50 12.00 30.00
11 Crrck/Alznr/Grbv/Grbr/50 15.00 40.00
12 Hmhs/Mrkst/Cnta/Bksa/50 10.00 25.00
13 Hdgsn/Andrc/Flgn/Trgn/50 12.00 30.00
14 Wrd/Stl/Prmeau/Frncs/50 15.00 40.00
15 Galch/Hbrd/Grnl/Ykpv/20 40.00 100.00

2013-14 Panini National Treasures Retro Phenoms Autographs

RPCSM1 Craig Smith NP Logo SP 4.00 10.00
RPCSM2 Craig Smith tiger 3.00 8.00
RPJSI1 Jakob Silfverberg logo 4.00 10.00
RPJSI2 Jakob Silfverberg circle logo 4.00 10.00
RPJSI3 Jakob Silfverberg draft SP 5.00 12.00
RPJSK1 Jeff Skinner hurricanes 6.00 15.00
RPJSK2 Jeff Skinner Flag 6.00 15.00
RPTC1 Tyler Cuma wolf logo 4.00 10.00
RPTC2 Tyler Cuma circle logo SP 5.00 12.00
RPTC3 Tyler Cuma NHLPA SP 5.00 12.00

2013-14 Panini National Treasures Rookie Jumbo Jerseys Booklet Autographs

1 Nail Yakupov/99 15.00 40.00
2 Nathan MacKinnon/99 40.00 100.00
3 Tomas Hertl/99 15.00 40.00
4 Jonathan Huberdeau/75 12.00 30.00
5 Alex Galchenyuk/99 25.00 60.00
6 Brendan Gallagher/99 20.00 50.00
8 Sean Monahan/99 20.00 50.00
9 Seth Jones/99 8.00 20.00
10 Hampus Lindholm/99 8.00 20.00
11 Jacob Trouba/99 12.00 30.00
12 Morgan Rielly/99 15.00 40.00
13 Tomas Jurco/99 12.00 30.00
14 Jon Merrill/99 8.00 20.00
15 Ryan Strome/99 8.00 20.00
16 Elias Lindholm/99 12.00 30.00
17 Aleksander Barkov/99 12.00 30.00
18 Zemgus Girgensons/99 10.00 25.00
19 Tom Wilson/99 12.00 30.00
20 Ryan Spooner/99 8.00 20.00
21 Ryan Murray/99 12.00 30.00
22 Boone Jenner/99 10.00 25.00
23 Michael Bournival/99 8.00 20.00
24 Magnus Hellberg/99 8.00 20.00
25 Filip Forsberg/99 20.00 50.00
26 Mikael Granlund/99 12.00 30.00
27 Valeri Nichushkin/99 20.00 50.00
28 Darcy Kuemper/99 8.00 20.00
29 Ryan Murphy/99 8.00 20.00
30 Mark Arcobello/99 8.00 20.00
31 Dylan McIlrath/99 8.00 20.00
32 Martin Jones/99 10.00 25.00
33 John Gibson/99 15.00 40.00
34 Brock Nelson/99 12.00 30.00
35 Michael Raffl/99 6.00 15.00
36 Mikhail Grigorenko/99 12.00 30.00

2013-14 Panini National Treasures Rookie Jumbo Jerseys Booklet Autographs Patch

*PATCH/20-25: .6X TO 1.5X BASIC JSY AU/75-99
2 Nathan MacKinnon/25 60.00 150.00

2013-14 Panini National Treasures Rookie Jumbo Jerseys Booklet Autographs Prime

*PRIME/49: .5X TO 1.2X BASIC JSY AU/75-99
2 Nathan MacKinnon 40.00 100.00

2013-14 Panini National Treasures Rookie Riches Autographs

1 Nathan MacKinnon 30.00 80.00
2 Nail Yakupov 15.00 40.00
3 Sean Monahan 12.00 30.00
4 Tomas Hertl 15.00 40.00
5 Alex Galchenyuk 25.00 60.00
6 Jonathan Huberdeau 15.00 40.00
7 Valeri Nichushkin 12.00 30.00
8 Hampus Lindholm 10.00 25.00
9 Jacob Trouba 10.00 25.00
10 Filip Forsberg 20.00 50.00
11 Brendan Gallagher 15.00 40.00
12 Morgan Rielly 12.00 30.00
13 Aleksander Barkov 10.00 25.00
14 Vladimir Tarasenko
15 Martin Jones 12.00 30.00

2013-14 Panini National Treasures Rookie Timeline Jerseys

*PATCH/15-25: .8X TO 2X BASIC JSY/99
*PRIME/50: .5X TO 1.2X BASIC JSY/99
RTAB Aleksander Barkov 6.00 15.00
RTAR Antti Raanta 3.00 8.00
RTBG Brendan Gallagher 8.00 20.00
RTBJ Boone Jenner 2.50 6.00
RTCB Chris Brown 3.00 8.00
RTCC Charlie Coyle 2.50 6.00
RTDH Dougie Hamilton 5.00 12.00
RTDK Darcy Kuemper 4.00 10.00
RTDM Dylan McIlrath 2.50 6.00
RTDS Drew Shore 2.50 6.00
RTEL Elias Lindholm 4.00 10.00
RTEP Edward Pasquale 1.50 4.00
RTFA Frederik Andersen 4.00 10.00
RTJC Jack Campbell 2.00 5.00
RTJG John Gibson 6.00 15.00
RTJM Jon Merrill 3.00 8.00
RTJS Justin Schultz 2.50 6.00
RTJT Jacob Trouba 4.00 10.00
RTLL Lucas Lessio 2.50 6.00
RTMD Matt Dumba 2.50 6.00
RTMG1 Mikael Granlund 4.00 10.00
RTMG2 Mikhail Grigorenko 3.00 8.00
RTMH Magnus Hellberg 2.50 6.00
RTMJ Martin Jones 5.00 12.00
RTMP Mark Pysyk 2.50 6.00
RTMR1 Michael Raffl 2.00 5.00
RTMR2 Morgan Rielly 6.00 15.00
RTNB Nathan Beaulieu 2.00 5.00
RTNJ Nicklas Jensen 3.00 8.00
RTNM Nathan MacKinnon 10.00 25.00
RTNY Nail Yakupov 6.00 15.00
RTNZ Nikita Zadorov 2.50 6.00
RTOM Olli Maatta 6.00 15.00
RTPG Philipp Grubauer 2.50 6.00
RTPM Petr Mrazek 5.00 12.00
RTQH Quinton Howden 2.50 6.00
RTRB Reto Berra 4.00 10.00
RTRM1 Ryan Murphy 2.50 6.00
RTRM2 Ryan Murray 4.00 10.00
RTRS1 Ryan Spooner 5.00 12.00
RTRS2 Ryan Strome 5.00 12.00
RTSJ Seth Jones 2.50 6.00
RTSL Scott Laughton 2.50 6.00
RTSM1 Stefan Matteau 2.00 5.00
RTSM2 Sean Monahan 4.00 10.00
RTTH Tomas Hertl 8.00 20.00
RTTP Tanner Pearson 4.00 10.00
RTTT Tyler Toffoli 5.00 12.00
RTTW Tom Wilson 4.00 10.00
RTVN Valeri Nichushkin 5.00 12.00

2013-14 Panini National Treasures Scratching the Surface Autographs

1 Tomas Jurco
2 Nathan MacKinnon 60.00 120.00
3 Rick Nash

2013-14 Panini National Treasures Six Autographs

1 Russian Stars 50.00 100.00
2 Pittsburgh Stars 60.00 120.00
3 Dallas and Minnesota 20.00 50.00
4 Bruins and Canadiens 20.00 50.00
5 Flames and Oilers 30.00 60.00
6 Wings and Blackhawks 100.00 200.00
7 Penguins and Flyers 50.00 100.00
8 Panthers and Lightning 20.00 50.00
9 Toronto Maple Leafs 75.00 125.00

2013-14 Panini National Treasures Sweeter by the Dozen Jerseys

SDBOS Boston Stars 50.00 100.00
SDBUF Buffalo Stars 30.00 60.00
SDLA Kings/Ducks Stars 40.00 80.00
SDMTL Montreal Stars 75.00 150.00
SDNO1 NHL Stars 40.00 100.00
SDNOS NHL Stars 30.00 60.00
SDNY Devils/Rangers Stars 60.00 120.00
SDOR6 Original 6 Stars 30.00 60.00
SDRD1 1st Round Rookies 40.00 100.00
SDSWE Swedish Stars
SDTOR Toronto Stars 90.00 150.00
SDWC Winter Classic 40.00 80.00

2013-14 Panini National Treasures Timeline Jerseys

*PRIME/35-50: .5X TO 1.2X BASIC JSY/99
*PRIME/25: .6X TO 1.5X BASIC JSY/99
*PRIME/15: 1.5X TO 4X BASIC JSY/99
*PATCH/20-25: .6X TO 1.5X BASIC JSY/99
TAF Adam Foote/99 6.00 15.00
TAM Al MacInnis/99 5.00 12.00
TAO Alex Ovechkin/99 10.00 25.00
TBB Brian Bellows/99 5.00 12.00
TBH Braden Holtby/99 8.00 20.00
TBL Brooks Laich/99 8.00 20.00
TBR Bobby Ryan/99 5.00 12.00
TBS Brendan Shanahan/99 8.00 20.00
TGC Chris Chelios/99 5.00 12.00
TCN Cam Neely/99 6.00 15.00
TCS1 Cory Schneider/99 4.00 10.00
TCS2 Charlie Simmer/99 3.00 8.00
TDC Dan Cloutier/99 4.00 10.00
TDG Doug Gilmour/99 8.00 20.00
TEK Erik Karlsson/99 8.00 20.00
TEL Eric Lindros/99 10.00 25.00
TEM Evgeni Malkin/99 10.00 25.00
TGH Gordie Howe/25 25.00 50.00
TGL1 Guy Lafleur/99 10.00 25.00
TGL2 Gabriel Landeskog/99 4.00 10.00
TGP Gilbert Perreault/99 10.00 25.00
TIL Igor Larionov/99 8.00 20.00
TJB Jamie Benn/99 6.00 15.00
TJS Jordan Staal/99 5.00 12.00
TJV John Vanbiesbrouck/99 8.00 20.00
TKL Ken Linseman/99 6.00 15.00
TLC Logan Couture/99 5.00 12.00
TLM Lanny McDonald/99 6.00 15.00
TMD Marcel Dionne/99 12.00 30.00
TML Milan Lucic/99 5.00 12.00
TNL Nicklas Lidstrom/99 8.00 20.00
TPC Paul Coffey/99 5.00 12.00
TPS1 Patrick Sharp/99 5.00 12.00
TPS2 P.K. Subban/99 8.00 20.00
TRB Rob Blake/99 5.00 12.00
TRF Ron Francis/99 6.00 15.00
TRL Reggie Leach/99 6.00 15.00
TRT Rick Tocchet/99 6.00 15.00
TSC Sidney Crosby/99 12.00 30.00
TSD Shane Doan/99 4.00 10.00
TSM Stan Mikita/99 8.00 20.00
TSS Steven Stamkos/99 6.00 15.00
TSW Shea Weber/99 4.00 10.00
TTB Tom Barrasso/99 12.00 30.00
TTO T.J. Oshie/99 6.00 15.00
TTR Tuukka Rask/99 8.00 20.00
TTS1 Tyler Seguin/99 10.00 25.00
TTS2 Teemu Selanne/99 12.00 30.00
TTT Tim Thomas/99 5.00 12.00
TVL Vincent Lecavalier/99 4.00 10.00

2013-14 Panini National Treasures Treasure Chest Jerseys Booklet

*PRIME/25: .5X TO 1.2X BASIC JSY/50
TCDRC Rookie Stars 80.00 150.00
TCPTS All Time Points Leaders 150.00 250.00
TCWIN 200 Win Goalies 150.00 250.00
TCPHI Philadelphia Stars 75.00 150.00
TCSTR Dallas/Minnesota Stars 75.00 150.00
TCCAN Team Canada 75.00 150.00
TCUSA Team USA 60.00 120.00
TCWJC Junior World Champs 50.00 120.00
TCRKS Rookie Stars 50.00 120.00

2013-14 Panini National Treasures Treasure Hunting Draft Plaques

1 Nathan MacKinnon/25 20.00 50.00
2 Aleksander Barkov/25 12.00 30.00
3 Seth Jones/25 5.00 12.00
4 Elias Lindholm/25 8.00 20.00
5 Sean Monahan/25 12.00 30.00
7 Valeri Nichushkin/25 5.00 12.00

2013-14 Panini National Treasures Treasured Trophies Autographs Art Ross

1 Gordie Howe 50.00 100.00
3 Marcel Dionne 20.00 50.00
4 Jaromir Jagr 50.00 100.00
5 Mario Lemieux 75.00 120.00
6 Martin St. Louis 15.00 40.00
7 Henrik Sedin 15.00 40.00
8 Daniel Sedin 15.00 40.00
9 Sidney Crosby 100.00 200.00

2013-14 Panini National Treasures Treasured Trophies Autographs Calder

1 Jonathan Huberdeau 15.00 40.00
2 Gabriel Landeskog 12.00 30.00
3 Jeff Skinner 12.00 30.00
5 Martin Brodeur 30.00 80.00
6 Ed Belfour 30.00 80.00
7 Brian Leetch 15.00 40.00
8 Joe Nieuwendyk 15.00 40.00
9 Luc Robitaille 15.00 40.00
10 Mario Lemieux 75.00 120.00

2013-14 Panini National Treasures Treasured Trophies Autographs Conn Smythe

2 Jonathan Quick EXCH 30.00 60.00
3 Al MacInnis 15.00 40.00
4 Jonathan Toews 50.00 100.00
5 Evgeni Malkin 50.00 125.00
6 Joe Nieuwendyk 15.00 40.00
7 Brad Richards 15.00 40.00
8 Ron Hextall 30.00 60.00
9 Jean-Sebastien Giguere 12.00 30.00
10 Brian Leetch 15.00 40.00

2013-14 Panini National Treasures Treasured Trophies Autographs Hart

1 Sidney Crosby 100.00 200.00
2 Alex Ovechkin EXCH 20.00 50.00
3 Mark Messier 40.00 80.00
4 Henrik Sedin 15.00 40.00
5 Joe Thornton 15.00 40.00
6 Martin St. Louis 15.00 40.00
7 Joe Sakic 25.00 60.00
8 Jaromir Jagr 50.00 100.00
9 Brett Hull 20.00 50.00
10 Mario Lemieux 75.00 120.00

2013-14 Panini National Treasures Treasured Trophies Autographs Lady Byng

1 Martin St. Louis 15.00 40.00
3 Brad Richards 15.00 40.00
4 Ron Francis 20.00 50.00
5 Joe Sakic 25.00 60.00
6 Pierre Turgeon 20.00 50.00
7 Brett Hull 20.00 50.00
8 Bobby Hull 25.00 60.00
9 Mike Bossy 15.00 40.00
10 Stan Mikita 25.00 60.00

2013-14 Panini National Treasures Treasured Trophies Autographs Norris

1 Nicklas Lidstrom 20.00 50.00
2 Chris Pronger 12.00 30.00
3 Al MacInnis 15.00 40.00
5 Brian Leetch 15.00 40.00
6 Chris Chelios 30.00 80.00
7 Paul Coffey 15.00 40.00
8 Ray Bourque 30.00 80.00
9 Denis Potvin 15.00 40.00
10 Larry Robinson 15.00 40.00

2013-14 Panini National Treasures Treasured Trophies Autographs Selke

1 Jonathan Toews 60.00 120.00
2 Patrice Bergeron EXCH 20.00 50.00
3 Ryan Kesler 20.00 50.00
5 Steve Yzerman 50.00 100.00
6 Ron Francis 20.00 50.00
7 Doug Gilmour 20.00 50.00
8 Bobby Clarke 30.00 80.00
9 Bob Gainey 15.00 40.00
10 Rod Brind'Amour 12.00 30.00

2013-14 Panini National Treasures Treasured Trophies Autographs Vezina

1 Henrik Lundqvist 20.00 50.00
2 Ron Hextall 30.00 60.00
3 Patrick Roy 75.00 150.00
4 Ryan Miller 12.00 30.00
5 Tim Thomas 20.00 50.00
6 Martin Brodeur EXCH 30.00 80.00
7 Ed Belfour 40.00 80.00
8 Grant Fuhr 20.00 50.00
9 John Vanbiesbrouck 50.00 100.00
10 Bernie Parent 20.00 50.00

2013-14 Panini National Treasures Trio Autographs

*GOLD/15-20: .5X TO 1.2X BASIC DUAL AU
1 Kmpr/Zucker/Granlnd/75 15.00 40.00
2 Kostka/Palat/Hedman/75 10.00 25.00
3 Ovchkn/Ykpov/Dtsyk/50 50.00 125.00
4 Yandle/Smith/Doan/60 12.00 30.00
5 Boyes/Shore/Luongo/75 10.00 25.00
6 Lrnov/Ykpov/Tretiak/75 30.00 80.00
7 Glncrss/Cndri/Brtschi/60 8.00 20.00
8 Wtsn/Frsbrg/Maznec/20 15.00 40.00
9 Hnrq/Andry/Matteau/25 12.00 30.00
10 Clarke/Howe/Kerr/50 15.00 40.00
11 Chlios/Rnick/Hebert/50 12.00 30.00
13 Jhnsn/Kessel/Vanek/25 20.00 50.00
14 Coyle/Kmper/Parise/75 12.00 30.00
15 Ptrnglo/Jskin/Reaves/50 12.00 30.00
16 Nchlls/Dghty/Robitlle/35 15.00 40.00
17 Emelin/Rbnsn/Savrd/50 15.00 40.00
18 Ryan/Andrsn/Gryba/50 12.00 30.00
19 Kuempr/Zatkff/Mrazk/75 15.00 40.00
20 Boyle/Irwin/Petrecki/25 12.00 30.00
21 Silfver/Eriksn/Lidstrm/75 12.00 30.00
22 Benn/Bwmstr/Toews/30 20.00 50.00
23 Glchnyk/Gllghr/Thomas/25 30.00 80.00
25 Prout/Johnson/Foligno/75 8.00 20.00

2013-14 Panini National Treasures Triple Memorabilia Autographs

1 Gordie Howe 40.00 100.00
2 Mark Messier 20.00 50.00
3 Joe Sakic 15.00 40.00
4 Alex Ovechkin 60.00 150.00
5 Pavel Datsyuk 20.00 50.00
6 Brendan Shanahan 20.00 50.00
7 Brad Richards 15.00 40.00
8 Cam Neely 12.00 30.00
9 Alex Galchenyuk 20.00 50.00
10 Teemu Selanne 30.00 80.00
11 Patrick Roy 40.00 100.00
12 Carey Price 50.00 120.00
13 Rick Nash 12.00 30.00
14 Bernie Parent 15.00 40.00
15 Bobby Clarke 15.00 40.00
16 Brendan Gallagher 15.00 40.00
17 Taylor Hall 15.00 40.00
18 Jeremy Roenick 15.00 40.00
19 Vladislav Tretiak 20.00 50.00
20 Ron Francis 20.00 50.00
21 Martin Brodeur 30.00 80.00
22 Yvan Cournoyer 12.00 30.00

2012 Panini NHL Draft

COMPLETE SET (8) 7.50 15.00
JJ Jaromir Jagr .60 1.50
ML Mario Lemieux 1.25 3.00
SS Steven Stamkos .75 2.00
TH Taylor Hall .75 2.00
MAF Marc-Andre Fleury .50 1.25
RNH Ryan Nugent-Hopkins 2.50 6.00
SC1 Mario Lemieux SP 2.00 5.00
SC2 Evgeni Malkin SP 1.25 3.00

2013-14 Panini Playbook

1-100 VETS PRINT RUN 249
101-167 JSY AU RC PRINT RUN 199
EXCH EXPIRATION: 10/9/2015
1 Ryan Getzlaf 3.00 8.00
2 Jakob Silfverberg 1.50 4.00
3 Corey Perry 2.00 5.00
4 Cam Fowler 1.50 4.00
5 Patrice Bergeron 2.50 6.00
6 Jarome Iginla 2.00 5.00
7 Zdeno Chara 2.00 5.00
8 Tuukka Rask 2.00 5.00
9 Cody Hodgson 2.00 5.00
10 Ryan Miller 2.00 5.00
11 Curtis Glencross 1.25 3.00
12 Mark Giordano 1.50 4.00
13 Eric Staal 2.50 6.00
14 Jordan Staal 2.00 5.00
15 Patrick Kane 4.00 10.00
16 Jonathan Toews 4.00 10.00
17 Marian Hossa 1.50 4.00
18 Corey Crawford 2.50 6.00
19 Matt Duchene 2.00 5.00
20 Gabriel Landeskog 1.50 4.00
21 Marian Gaborik 2.00 5.00
22 Sergei Bobrovsky 2.00 5.00
23 Tyler Seguin 3.00 8.00
24 Jamie Benn 2.50 6.00
25 Daniel Alfredsson 2.00 5.00
26 Henrik Zetterberg 2.50 6.00
27 Pavel Datsyuk 2.50 6.00
28 Jimmy Howard 2.00 5.00
29 Ryan Nugent-Hopkins 2.00 5.00
30 Taylor Hall 4.00 10.00
31 Jordan Eberle 2.00 5.00
32 Ilya Bryzgalov 2.00 5.00
33 Jacob Markstrom 1.50 4.00
34 Tim Thomas 2.00 5.00
35 Dustin Brown 2.00 5.00
36 Mike Richards 2.00 5.00
37 Drew Doughty 2.00 5.00
38 Jonathan Quick 3.00 8.00
39 Zach Parise 2.00 5.00
40 Ryan Suter 1.25 3.00
41 Max Pacioretty 2.00 5.00
42 Lars Eller 1.50 4.00
43 P.K. Subban 3.00 8.00
44 Carey Price 6.00 15.00
45 Shea Weber 1.50 4.00
46 Pekka Rinne 2.50 6.00
47 Jaromir Jagr 5.00 12.00
48 Martin Brodeur 4.00 10.00
49 John Tavares 4.00 10.00
50 Casey Cizikas 1.25 3.00
51 Derek Stepan 2.00 5.00
52 Rick Nash 2.00 5.00
53 Derick Brassard 2.00 5.00

54 Henrik Lundqvist 2.50 6.00
55 Bobby Ryan 2.00 5.00
56 Jason Spezza 2.00 5.00
57 Claude Giroux 2.00 5.00
58 Vincent Lecavalier 1.50 4.00
59 Shane Doan 1.50 4.00
60 Oliver Ekman-Larsson 1.50 4.00
61 Sidney Crosby 8.00 20.00
62 Evgeni Malkin 6.00 15.00
63 Kris Letang 2.00 5.00
64 Marc-Andre Fleury 3.00 8.00
65 Joe Thornton 2.00 5.00
66 Joe Pavelski 2.00 5.00
67 Logan Couture 2.00 5.00
68 Patrick Marleau 2.00 5.00
69 David Backes 2.00 5.00
70 Alex Pietrangelo 1.50 4.00
71 Steven Stamkos 4.00 10.00
72 Martin St. Louis 2.00 5.00
73 Nazem Kadri 2.00 5.00
74 Phil Kessel 2.50 6.00
75 David Clarkson 1.25 3.00
76 Jonathan Bernier 2.00 5.00
77 Daniel Sedin 2.00 5.00
78 Henrik Sedin 2.00 5.00
79 Ryan Kesler 2.00 5.00
80 Roberto Luongo 2.00 5.00
81 Alex Ovechkin 8.00 20.00
82 Nicklas Backstrom 3.00 8.00
83 Andrew Ladd 2.00 5.00
84 Dustin Byfuglien 2.00 5.00
85 Joe Sakic 3.00 8.00
86 Guy Lafleur 2.50 6.00
87 Mike Modano 3.00 8.00
88 Ed Belfour 2.00 5.00
89 Eric Lindros 3.00 8.00
90 Ron Hextall 2.00 5.00
91 Gordie Howe 4.00 10.00
92 Steve Yzerman 4.00 10.00
93 Pavel Bure 2.50 6.00
94 John Vanbiesbrouck 2.00 5.00
95 Mark Messier 2.50 6.00
96 Mike Richter 2.00 5.00
97 Doug Gilmour 2.50 6.00
98 Felix Potvin 3.00 8.00
99 Ray Bourque 3.00 8.00
100 Patrick Roy 5.00 12.00
101 Sami Vatanen JSY AU RC 8.00 20.00
102 Carl Soderberg JSY AU RC 8.00 20.00
103 M.Grigorenko JSY AU RC 10.00 25.00
104 Max Reinhart JSY AU RC EXCH 8.00 20.00
105 Jared Staal JSY AU RC 8.00 20.00
106 Emerson Etem JSY AU RC 8.00 20.00
107 Antoine Roussel JSY AU RC 8.00 20.00
108 Alex Chiasson JSY AU RC 8.00 20.00
109 Charlie Coyle JSY AU RC 8.00 20.00
110 Danny DeKeyser JSY AU RC 10.00 25.00
111 Petr Mrazek JSY AU RC 15.00 40.00
112 Nick Bjugstad JSY AU RC 10.00 25.00
113 Drew Shore JSY AU RC 6.00 15.00
114 Tanner Pearson JSY AU RC 8.00 20.00
115 Brock Nelson JSY AU RC 8.00 20.00
116 Jonas Brodin JSY AU RC 6.00 15.00
117 Mikael Granlund JSY AU RC 12.00 30.00
118 B.Gallagher JSY AU RC 25.00 60.00
119 Filip Forsberg JSY AU RC 20.00 50.00
120 Stefan Matteau JSY AU RC 6.00 15.00
121 Thomas Hickey JSY AU RC 6.00 15.00
122 J.T. Miller JSY AU RC EXCH 8.00 20.00
123 Viktor Fasth JSY AU RC 8.00 20.00
124 V.Tarasenko JSY AU RC 30.00 80.00
125 Dmitrij Jaskin JSY AU RC 8.00 20.00
126 Alex Killorn JSY AU RC 8.00 20.00
127 Cory Conacher JSY AU RC 5.00 12.00
129 Nicklas Jensen JSY AU RC 6.00 15.00
130 Tom Wilson JSY AU RC 12.00 30.00
131 Nail Yakupov JSY AU RC 15.00 40.00
132 Alex Galchenyuk JSY AU RC 40.00 80.00
133 Dougie Hamilton JSY AU RC 15.00 40.00
134 Justin Schultz JSY AU RC 8.00 20.00
135 Tyler Toffoli JSY AU RC 15.00 40.00
136 J.Huberdeau JSY AU RC 20.00 50.00
137 N.MacKinnon JSY AU RC 30.00 80.00
138 Seth Jones JSY AU RC 8.00 20.00
139 Morgan Rielly JSY AU RC 20.00 50.00
140 Aleksander Barkov JSY AU RC 15.00 40.00
141 Sean Monahan JSY AU RC 20.00 50.00
142 Valeri Nichushkin JSY AU RC 8.00 20.00
143 Ryan Murray JSY AU RC 8.00 20.00
144 Tomas Hertl JSY AU RC 15.00 40.00
145 Elias Lindholm JSY AU RC 12.00 30.00
146 Jacob Trouba JSY AU RC 15.00 40.00
147 Matt Dumba JSY AU RC 8.00 20.00
148 Scott Laughton JSY AU RC 8.00 20.00
149 Beau Bennett JSY AU RC 10.00 25.00
150 Boone Jenner JSY AU RC 8.00 20.00
151 Ryan Murphy JSY AU RC EXCH 8.00 20.00
152 Hampus Lindholm JSY AU RC 12.00 30.00
153 Joakim Nordstrom JSY AU RC 6.00 15.00
154 Olli Maatta JSY AU RC 12.00 30.00
155 Ryan Spooner JSY AU RC 8.00 20.00
156 Jack Campbell JSY AU RC 6.00 15.00
157 Nathan Beaulieu JSY AU RC 6.00 15.00
158 Jamie Oleksiak JSY AU RC 6.00 15.00
159 Z.Girgensons JSY AU RC EXCH 15.00 40.00
160 Jon Merrill JSY AU RC 8.00 20.00
161 John Gibson JSY AU RC 15.00 40.00
162 Matt Nieto JSY AU RC 6.00 15.00
163 Michael Bournival JSY AU RC 8.00 20.00
164 Anthony Peluso JSY AU RC 5.00 12.00
165 R.Strome JSY AU RC EXCH 20.00 40.00
166 Tomas Jurco JSY AU RC 12.00 30.00
167 Dylan McIlrath JSY AU RC 8.00 20.00
168 Lucas Lessio JSY AU RC 5.00 12.00

2013-14 Panini Playbook Gold

*GOLD/25: 1X TO 2.5X BASIC CARDS
18 Corey Crawford 6.00 15.00
82 Nicklas Backstrom 8.00 20.00

2013-14 Panini Playbook Rookie Jerseys Autographs Prime

*PRIME/25: .8X TO 2X BASIC JSY AU/199
135 Tyler Toffoli 40.00 100.00
137 Nathan MacKinnon 300.00 500.00
161 John Gibson 60.00 120.00

2013-14 Panini Playbook Armory

AAH Adam Henrique 20.00 50.00
ABH Brett Hull 20.00 50.00
AIL Igor Larionov 20.00 50.00
AJP Joe Pavelski 20.00 50.00
AMG Marian Gaborik 20.00 50.00
ABRI Brad Richards 20.00 50.00
ADST Derek Stepan 20.00 50.00
AJVR James van Riemsdyk 20.00 50.00
ALUC Luc Robitaille 20.00 50.00
AMHE Milan Hejduk 15.00 40.00
AMRI Mike Richards 20.00 50.00
AOVI Alex Ovechkin 80.00 200.00

2013-14 Panini Playbook AUTObiography

AUAL Andrew Ladd 6.00 15.00
AUAN Antti Niemi 5.00 12.00
AUBH Brett Hull 15.00 30.00
AUBR Bobby Ryan 6.00 15.00
AUBSD Brandon Saad 6.00 15.00
AUCN Cam Neely 12.50 25.00
AUDBR Daniel Briere 6.00 15.00
AUDCI Dino Ciccarelli 6.00 15.00
AUDP David Perron 4.00 10.00
AUDR Derek Roy 5.00 12.00
AUHL Henrik Lundqvist 20.00 40.00
AUJBE Jonathan Bernier 6.00 15.00
AUJCO Joe Colborne 4.00 10.00
AUJI Jarome Iginla 15.00 30.00
AUJM Jacob Markstrom 5.00 12.00
AUJNE James Neal 6.00 15.00
AUJP Joe Pavelski 6.00 15.00
AUJS Joe Sakic 12.00 30.00
AUJTO Jonathan Toews 20.00 50.00
AULE Loui Eriksson 12.00 30.00
AUMB Martin Brodeur 20.00 40.00
AUMS Mike Smith 8.00 20.00
AUMT Marty Turco 6.00 15.00
AUNL Nicklas Lidstrom 8.00 20.00
AUPB Pavel Bure 15.00 30.00
AURB Ray Bourque 20.00 40.00
AURK Ryan Kesler 6.00 15.00
AURNH Ryan Nugent-Hopkins 6.00 15.00
AUTE Tony Esposito 8.00 20.00
AUTL Trevor Linden 8.00 20.00
AUTS Tyler Seguin 12.50 25.00
AUTTH Tim Thomas 10.00 25.00
AUVL Vincent Lecavalier 8.00 20.00
AUYC Yvan Cournoyer 8.00 20.00

2013-14 Panini Playbook Breakout Jerseys

*PRIME/25: .6X TO 1.5X BASIC JSY/180-199
*PRIME/25: .5X TO 1.2X BASIC JSY/25
BAB Aleksander Barkov 6.00 15.00
BAG Alex Galchenyuk 8.00 20.00
BBB Beau Bennett 4.00 10.00
BBG Brendan Gallagher 8.00 20.00
BBJE Boone Jenner 3.00 8.00
BBNE Brock Nelson 3.00 8.00
BCB Chris Brown 2.00 5.00
BCON Cory Conacher 2.00 5.00
BDDK Danny DeKeyser/180 4.00 10.00
BDH Dougie Hamilton 6.00 15.00
BDMI Dylan McIlrath 2.00 5.00
BFA Frederik Andersen 5.00 12.00
BFC Frank Corrado 2.50 6.00
BFF Filip Forsberg/25 10.00 25.00
BJGI John Gibson 10.00 25.00
BJH Jonathan Huberdeau 6.00 15.00
BJME Jon Merrill 5.00 12.00
BJNO Joakim Nordstrom 2.50 6.00
BJTM J.T. Miller 3.00 8.00
BJTR Jacob Trouba 5.00 12.00
BJUS Justin Schultz 3.00 8.00
BMAR Mark Arcobello 3.00 8.00
BMGR Mikael Granlund 5.00 12.00
BMIK Mikhail Grigorenko 4.00 10.00
BNJ Nicklas Jensen 2.50 6.00
BNMK Nathan MacKinnon 10.00 25.00
BNY Nail Yakupov 5.00 12.00
BRBE Reto Berra 3.00 8.00
BRLY Morgan Rielly 6.00 15.00
BRMR Ryan Murray 5.00 12.00
BRS Ryan Strome 4.00 10.00
BSJ Seth Jones 3.00 8.00
BSL Scott Laughton 3.00 8.00
BSMO Sean Monahan 5.00 12.00
BTHE Tomas Hertl 8.00 20.00
BTJU Tomas Jurco 6.00 15.00
BTMG Tye McGinn 3.00 8.00
BTP Tanner Pearson 3.00 8.00
BTW Tom Wilson 5.00 12.00
BVN Valeri Nichushkin 6.00 15.00

2013-14 Panini Playbook Double Rookie Classbook Jerseys

*PRIME/50: .5X TO 1.2X BASIC DUAL
*PATCH/25: .8X TO 2X BASIC DUAL JSY
DRBD N.Beaulieu/J.Devane 8.00 20.00
DRBM B.Bennett/O.Maatta 15.00 40.00
DRCG C.Conacher/Z.Girgensons 12.00 30.00
DRDKR D.DeKeyser/M.Rielly 15.00 40.00
DREN E.Etem/M.Nieto 8.00 20.00
DRFD F.Forsberg/M.Dumba 15.00 40.00
DRGH A.Galchenyuk/T.Hertl 12.00 30.00
DRGM B.Gallagher/S.Monahan 15.00 40.00
DRGN M.Granlund/J.Nordstrom 8.00 20.00
DRGR M.Grigorenko/R.Ristolainen 12.00 30.00
DRHB J.Huberdeau/A.Barkov 12.00 30.00
DRHJ D.Hamilton/S.Jones 10.00 25.00
DRLJ S.Laughton/B.Jenner 8.00 20.00
DRMGS T.McGinn/R.Strome 10.00 25.00
DRMM J.Miller/J.Merrill 8.00 20.00
DRMU R.Murphy/R.Murray 8.00 20.00
DRPC A.Peluso/K.Connauton 6.00 15.00
DRPL T.Pearson/L.Lessio 8.00 20.00
DRSB R.Spooner/M.Bournival 8.00 20.00
DRST J.Schultz/J.Trouba 8.00 20.00
DRTM T.Toffoli/C.Murphy 10.00 25.00
DRTN V.Tarasenko/V.Nichushkin 12.00 30.00
DRTZ J.Tinordi/N.Zadorov 8.00 20.00
DRVL S.Vatanen/H.Lindholm 10.00 25.00
DRWL T.Wilson/E.Lindholm 12.00 30.00
DRYMK N.Yakupov/N.MacKinnon 15.00 40.00

2013-14 Panini Playbook Fabled Fabrics

FFBC Bobby Clarke 5.00 12.00
FFGH Gordie Howe 10.00 25.00
FFMD Marcel Dionne 6.00 15.00
FFPE Phil Esposito 8.00 20.00
FFRV Rogie Vachon 6.00 15.00
FFSM Stan Mikita 6.00 15.00
FFYC Yvan Cournoyer 5.00 12.00
FFBSA Borje Salming 5.00 12.00
FFBSY Mike Bossy 5.00 12.00
FFRMI Rick Middleton 3.00 8.00

2013-14 Panini Playbook First Drafts Signatures

FDZG Zemgus Girgensons 8.00 20.00
FDMG Mikhail Grigorenko 3.00 8.00
(inserted in 2013-14 Panini Prime)
FDJTM J.T. Miller 3.00 8.00
FDAB Aleksander Barkov 8.00 20.00
FDAG Alex Galchenyuk 12.00 30.00
FDAW Austin Watson 2.50 6.00
FDBB Beau Bennett 8.00 20.00
FDBNE Brock Nelson 3.00 8.00
FDCOY Charlie Coyle 5.00 12.00
FDDH Dougie Hamilton 10.00 25.00
FDEE Emerson Etem 3.00 8.00
FDELI Elias Lindholm 5.00 12.00
FDFF Filip Forsberg 12.00 30.00
FDHLI Hampus Lindholm 5.00 12.00
FDJB Jonas Brodin 2.50 6.00
FDJH Jonathan Huberdeau 6.00 15.00
FDJSC Jaden Schwartz 8.00 20.00
FDJT John Tavares 12.50 25.00
FDJTH Joe Thornton 10.00 25.00
FDJTR Jacob Trouba 10.00 25.00
FDMAF Marc-Andre Fleury 12.50 25.00
FDMDB Matt Dumba 3.00 8.00
FDMSC Mark Scheifele 8.00 20.00
FDNBE Nathan Beaulieu 5.00 12.00
FDNJ Nicklas Jensen 2.50 6.00
FDNMK Nathan MacKinnon 30.00 80.00
FDNY Nail Yakupov 10.00 25.00
FDOVI Alex Ovechkin 30.00 60.00
FDPK Patrick Kane 25.00 50.00
FDRLY Morgan Rielly 8.00 20.00
FDRMR Ryan Murray 5.00 12.00
FDRN Rick Nash 6.00 15.00
FDRNH Ryan Nugent-Hopkins 6.00 15.00
FDRSH Riley Sheahan 4.00 10.00
FDSB Sven Baertschi 5.00 12.00
FDSC Sidney Crosby 60.00 120.00
FDSJ Seth Jones 3.00 8.00
FDSL Scott Laughton 3.00 8.00
FDSMA Stefan Matteau 2.50 6.00
FDSMO Sean Monahan 5.00 12.00
FDTH Taylor Hall 12.00 30.00
FDTHE Tomas Hertl 4.00 10.00
FDTW Tom Wilson 6.00 15.00
FDVL Vincent Lecavalier 5.00 12.00
FDVN Valeri Nichushkin 3.00 8.00

2013-14 Panini Playbook First Round Edition Jerseys Autographs

*PRIME/25: .6X TO 1.5X BASIC JSY AU
FRAB Aleksander Barkov 12.00 30.00
FRAG Alex Galchenyuk 25.00 60.00
FRDH Dougie Hamilton 15.00 40.00
FRELI Elias Lindholm 6.00 15.00
FRFF Filip Forsberg 20.00 50.00
FRJH Jonathan Huberdeau 15.00 40.00
FRJTR Jacob Trouba 15.00 40.00
FRMDB Matt Dumba 10.00 25.00
FRMGR Mikael Granlund 12.00 30.00
FRMIK Mikhail Grigorenko 10.00 25.00
FRNMK Nathan MacKinnon 30.00 80.00
FRNY Nail Yakupov 15.00 40.00
FRRLY Morgan Rielly 12.00 30.00
FRRMP Ryan Murphy 8.00 20.00
FRRMR Ryan Murray 12.00 30.00
FRSJ Seth Jones 8.00 20.00
FRSMO Sean Monahan 10.00 25.00
FRTHE Tomas Hertl 15.00 40.00
FRTW Tom Wilson 10.00 25.00
FRVN Valeri Nichushkin 8.00 20.00
FRVT Vladimir Tarasenko 30.00 80.00

2013-14 Panini Playbook Limited Edition Jerseys

*PRIME/25: .6X TO 1.5X BASIC JSY/99
LEAH Adam Henrique 5.00 12.00
LEAP Alex Pietrangelo 4.00 10.00
LEAT Alex Tanguay 5.00 12.00
LEBN Bernie Nicholls 4.00 10.00
LEBR Bobby Ryan 5.00 12.00
LEBW Blake Wheeler 5.00 12.00
LECN Cam Neely 5.00 12.00
LEDS Daniel Sedin 5.00 12.00
LEEL Eric Lindros 8.00 20.00
LEGL Gabriel Landeskog 4.00 10.00
LEJJ Jaromir Jagr 6.00 15.00
LEJR Jeremy Roenick 5.00 12.00
LEJT John Tavares 10.00 25.00
LEMH Marian Hossa 4.00 10.00
LEML Mario Lemieux 8.00 20.00
LEMM Mark Messier 6.00 15.00
LEMO Mike Modano 8.00 20.00
LENL Nicklas Lidstrom 5.00 12.00
LEPB Pavel Bure 6.00 15.00
LEPC Paul Coffey 5.00 12.00
LERF Ron Francis 6.00 15.00
LERM Ryan Miller 5.00 12.00
LERN Rick Nash 5.00 12.00
LESC Sidney Crosby 10.00 25.00
LESK Saku Koivu 5.00 12.00
LESS Steven Stamkos 6.00 15.00
LESW Shea Weber 4.00 10.00
LESY Steve Yzerman 8.00 20.00
LETH Taylor Hall 10.00 25.00
LETS Tyler Seguin 8.00 20.00
LEABU Alexandre Burrows 5.00 12.00
LEAKO Anze Kopitar 8.00 20.00
LEAMI Al MacInnis 5.00 12.00
LEDKR David Krejci 5.00 12.00
LEDST Derek Stepan 5.00 12.00
LEJBE Jonathan Bernier 5.00 12.00
LEJHA Jaroslav Halak 5.00 12.00
LEJOS Jordan Staal 5.00 12.00
LEJTH Joe Thornton 5.00 12.00
LELEL Lars Eller 4.00 10.00
LEMGI Mark Giordano 4.00 10.00
LEMHZ Martin Hanzal 3.00 8.00
LEOVI Alex Ovechkin 20.00 50.00
LEPRI Pekka Rinne 6.00 15.00
LERBL Rob Blake 5.00 12.00
LERNH Ryan Nugent-Hopkins 6.00 15.00
LESJN Matt Stajan 4.00 10.00
LETTH Tim Thomas 5.00 12.00
LEVTR Vladislav Tretiak 10.00 25.00

2013-14 Panini Playbook Nicknames

NBH Brett Hull 20.00 40.00
NJTO Jonathan Toews 50.00 100.00
NJV John Vanbiesbrouck 30.00 80.00
NML Mario Lemieux 30.00 80.00
NOVI Alex Ovechkin 30.00 80.00
NPD Pavel Datsyuk 30.00 60.00
NSS Steven Stamkos 25.00 60.00
NSY Steve Yzerman 25.00 60.00
NTMU Teemu Selanne 40.00 80.00

2013-14 Panini Playbook Signature Jerseys Booklet

*PRIME/25: .8X TO 2X BASIC JSY AU/100
SBDB David Backes/100 10.00 25.00
SBHL Henrik Lundqvist/100 30.00 60.00
SBJE Jordan Eberle/100 10.00 25.00
SBJHO Jimmy Howard/100 12.00 30.00
SBJT John Tavares/100 25.00 50.00
SBJTO Jonathan Toews/100 40.00 100.00
SBLC Logan Couture/100 8.00 20.00
SBMC Mike Cammalleri/100 8.00 20.00
SBMS Mike Smith/100 12.00 30.00
SBPK Patrick Kane/41 50.00 100.00
SBPS Patrick Sharp/100 30.00 60.00
SBRG Ryan Getzlaf/100 12.00 30.00
SBRK Ryan Kesler/100 12.00 30.00
SBSC Sidney Crosby/22 100.00 175.00
SBTS Tyler Seguin/100 30.00 60.00

2013-14 Panini Playbook Split Decisions Jerseys

*PRIME/25: .6X TO 1.5X BASIC JSY
SDBHY Braden Holtby 15.00 40.00
SDCP Carey Price 40.00 100.00
SDDDU Devan Dubnyk 12.00 30.00
SDHL Henrik Lundqvist 15.00 40.00
SDJHI Jonas Hiller 10.00 25.00
SDJQ Jonathan Quick 20.00 50.00
SDKLE Kari Lehtonen 10.00 25.00
SDLU Roberto Luongo
SDPR Patrick Roy 30.00 80.00
SDPRI Pekka Rinne 15.00 40.00
SDRHX Ron Hextall 25.00 50.00
SDSTM Steve Mason 10.00 25.00

2013-14 Panini Playbook Storied Signatures

STAD Alex Delvecchio 8.00 20.00
STBC Bobby Clarke 15.00 40.00
STBP Bernie Parent 15.00 30.00
STBT Bryan Trottier 12.00 30.00
STGH Gordie Howe 60.00 120.00
STLR Larry Robinson 8.00 20.00
STML Mario Lemieux 50.00 100.00
STMM Mark Messier 20.00 40.00
STPE Phil Esposito 15.00 30.00
STPR Patrick Roy 50.00 100.00
STSM Stan Mikita 12.00 30.00
STSY Steve Yzerman 40.00 80.00
STBSY Mike Bossy 15.00 30.00
STBWR Johnny Bower 12.00 30.00
STJET Bobby Hull 20.00 40.00

2013-14 Panini Playbook Then and Now Jerseys

*PRIME/25: .6X TO 1.5X BASIC JSY
TNCA Craig Anderson 12.00 30.00
TNCN Cam Neely 12.00 30.00
TNJFC Jeff Carter 12.00 30.00
TNJS Joe Sakic 20.00 50.00
TNJSG Jean-Sebastien Giguere 15.00 40.00
TNMRI Mike Richards 12.00 30.00
TNPB Pavel Bure 25.00 50.00
TNRB Ray Bourque 20.00 50.00
TNRN Rick Nash 12.00 30.00
TNSVA Semyon Varlamov 15.00 40.00
TNTMU Teemu Selanne 30.00 60.00
TNTS Tyler Seguin 20.00 50.00

2011-12 Panini Player of the Day

COMPLETE SET (5) 7.50 15.00
POD1 Alex Ovechkin 2.50 6.00
POD2 Tim Thomas .60 1.50
POD3 Steven Stamkos 1.25 3.00
POD4 Ryan Nugent-Hopkins 5.00 12.00
POD5 Gabriel Landeskog 1.00 2.50

2011-12 Panini Player of the Day Black Border

COMPLETE SET (9)
PODAH Adam Henrique 1.25 3.00
PODAP Aaron Palushaj .50 1.25
PODBG Blake Geoffrion .50 1.25
PODBS Brandon Saad 1.00 2.50
PODCK Carl Klingberg .50 1.25
PODGN Greg Nemisz .50 1.25
PODJM John Moore .50 1.25
PODMK Marcus Kruger .75 2.00
PODSC Sean Couturier 1.00 2.50
PODPKS P.K. Subban 1.25 3.00

2013-14 Panini Player of the Day

COMPLETE SET (17) 8.00 20.00
*THICK STOCK: .5X TO 1.2X BASIC CARDS
1 John Tavares .75 2.00
2 Steven Stamkos .75 2.00
3 Joe Thornton .40 1.00
4 Jamie Benn .50 1.25
5 Evgeni Malkin 1.25 3.00
6 Corey Crawford .50 1.25
7 Corey Perry .40 1.00
8 Henrik Zetterberg .50 1.25
RC1 Nail Yakupov .75 2.00
RC2 Nathan MacKinnon 1.00 2.50
RC3 Alex Galchenyuk 1.25 3.00
RC4 Sean Monahan .40 1.00
RC5 Jacob Trouba .40 1.00
RC6 Tomas Hertl .30 .75
RC7 Aleksander Barkov .60 1.50
RC8 Morgan Rielly .60 1.50
RC9 Jean-Gabriel Pageau .20 .50

2013-14 Panini Player of the Day Autographs

AK Anze Kopitar
BG Brian Gionta 3.00 8.00
BJ Boone Jenner 4.00 10.00
BR Bobby Ryan
JH Jimmy Howard
JT Jacob Trouba 8.00 20.00
MR Morgan Rielly
NB Nick Bjugstad 3.00 8.00
PM Patrick Marleau 5.00 12.00
RC Ryan Callahan
RL Roberto Luongo
RS Ryan Smyth
SM Sean Monahan 4.00 10.00
SS Steven Stamkos 15.00 40.00

2013-14 Panini Player of the Day Rookie Materials

1 Nicklas Jensen 2.00 5.00
3 Ryan Spooner 2.50 6.00
5 Petr Mrazek 5.00 12.00
9 Ryan Murray 4.00 10.00
AC Alex Chiasson 2.50 6.00
AW Austin Watson 2.00 5.00
JH Jonathan Huberdeau 6.00 15.00
JM J.T. Miller 2.50 6.00
JT Jarred Tinordi 2.50 6.00
NM Nathan MacKinnon 10.00 25.00

2010-11 Panini Preferred Player of the Day Autographs

PODJS Jeff Skinner 8.00 20.00
PODPK Phil Kessel 8.00 20.00

2011-12 Panini Preferred Player of the Day Autographs

PODBR Brad Richards
PODDH Dany Heatley 15.00 40.00
PODGL Gabriel Landeskog
PODJG Jake Gardiner
PODMF Marc-Andre Fleury
PODNL Nicklas Lidstrom
PODRN Ryan Nugent-Hopkins
PODSS Steven Stamkos

2011-12 Panini Prime

1-100 VETERAN PRINT RUN 249
101-150 ROOK.JSY AU PRINT RUN 199
EXCH EXPIRATION: 2/28/2014
1 Bobby Ryan 2.00 5.00
2 Corey Perry 2.00 5.00
3 Ryan Getzlaf 3.00 8.00
4 Cam Neely 2.00 5.00
5 Ray Bourque 3.00 8.00
6 Tim Thomas 2.00 5.00
7 Tyler Seguin 4.00 10.00
8 Gilbert Perreault 2.00 5.00
9 Ryan Miller 2.00 5.00
10 Tyler Myers 2.00 5.00
11 Jarome Iginla 2.00 5.00
12 Michael Cammalleri 1.50 4.00
13 Miikka Kiprusoff 2.00 5.00
14 Cam Ward 2.00 5.00
15 Eric Staal 2.50 6.00
16 Jeff Skinner 2.00 5.00
17 Bobby Hull 2.00 5.00
18 Ed Belfour 2.00 5.00
19 Jonathan Toews 4.00 10.00
20 Patrick Kane 4.00 10.00
21 Patrick Sharp 2.00 5.00
22 Joe Sakic 3.00 8.00
23 Matt Duchene 2.00 5.00
24 Patrick Roy 5.00 12.00
25 Jack Johnson 1.25 3.00
26 Rick Nash 2.00 5.00
27 Brenden Morrow 1.50 4.00
28 Brett Hull 2.50 6.00
29 Jamie Benn 2.50 6.00
30 Kari Lehtonen 1.50 4.00
31 Loui Eriksson 1.50 4.00
32 Gordie Howe 4.00 10.00
33 Henrik Zetterberg 2.50 6.00
34 Pavel Datsyuk 2.50 6.00
35 Steve Yzerman 3.00 8.00
36 Jordan Eberle 2.00 5.00
37 Mark Messier 2.50 6.00
38 Ryan Smyth 1.50 4.00
39 Taylor Hall 4.00 10.00
40 Ed Jovanovski 1.25 3.00
41 Kris Versteeg 1.50 4.00
42 Stephen Weiss 1.50 4.00
43 Anze Kopitar 3.00 8.00
44 Jeff Carter 2.00 5.00
45 Jonathan Quick 3.00 8.00
46 Mike Richards 2.00 5.00
47 Mikko Koivu 1.50 4.00
48 Niklas Backstrom 2.00 5.00
49 Carey Price 6.00 15.00
50 Erik Cole 1.50 4.00
51 Lars Eller 1.50 4.00
52 P.K. Subban 4.00 10.00
53 Pekka Rinne 2.50 6.00
54 Shea Weber 1.50 4.00
55 Ilya Kovalchuk 2.00 5.00
56 Martin Brodeur 4.00 10.00
57 Zach Parise 2.00 5.00
58 Bryan Trottier 2.50 6.00
59 John Tavares 4.00 10.00
60 Brad Richards 2.00 5.00
61 Henrik Lundqvist 2.50 6.00
62 Marian Gaborik 2.50 6.00
63 Daniel Alfredsson 2.00 5.00
64 Erik Karlsson 4.00 10.00
65 Jason Spezza 2.00 5.00
66 Bobby Clarke 2.00 5.00
67 Claude Giroux 2.00 5.00
68 Eric Lindros 3.00 8.00
69 Jaromir Jagr 5.00 12.00
70 Jeremy Roenick 2.00 5.00
71 Mike Smith 2.00 5.00
72 Shane Doan 1.50 4.00
73 Evgeni Malkin 6.00 15.00
74 Kris Letang 2.00 5.00
75 Marc-Andre Fleury 3.00 8.00
76 Mario Lemieux 6.00 15.00
77 Sidney Crosby 8.00 20.00
78 Antti Niemi 1.50 4.00
79 Joe Thornton 2.00 5.00
80 Logan Couture 2.00 5.00
81 Alex Pietrangelo 1.50 4.00
82 Jaroslav Halak 2.00 5.00
83 Martin St. Louis 2.00 5.00
84 Steven Stamkos 4.00 10.00
85 Vincent Lecavalier 1.50 4.00
86 Dion Phaneuf 2.00 5.00
87 Doug Gilmour 2.50 6.00
88 Joffrey Lupul 1.50 4.00
89 Phil Kessel 2.50 6.00
90 Daniel Sedin 2.00 5.00
91 Henrik Sedin 2.00 5.00
92 Roberto Luongo 2.00 5.00
93 Ryan Kesler 2.00 5.00
94 Alex Ovechkin 8.00 20.00
95 Mike Green 2.00 5.00
96 Tomas Vokoun 1.50 4.00
97 Alexander Burmistrov 1.50 4.00
98 Andrew Ladd 2.00 5.00
99 Dustin Byfuglien 2.00 5.00
100 Ondrej Pavelec 2.00 5.00
101 Smith-Pelly JSY AU RC 10.00 25.00
102 Peter Holland JSY AU RC 6.00 15.00
103 Cody Hodgson JSY AU RC 6.00 15.00
104 Roman Horak JSY AU RC 6.00 15.00
105 Greg Nemisz JSY AU RC 6.00 15.00
106 Justin Faulk JSY AU RC 10.00 25.00
107 Brandon Saad JSY AU RC 12.00 30.00
108 Marcus Kruger JSY AU RC 12.00 30.00
109 G.Landeskog JSY AU RC 12.00 30.00
110 C.Gaunce JSY AU RC 5.00 12.00
111 Ryan Johansen JSY AU RC 12.00 30.00
112 Tomas Kubalik JSY AU RC 6.00 15.00
113 John Moore JSY AU RC 6.00 15.00
114 Cam Atkinson JSY AU RC 15.00 40.00
115 Allen York JSY AU RC 8.00 20.00
116 David Savard JSY AU RC 6.00 15.00
117 Tomas Vincour JSY AU RC 6.00 15.00
118 Colton Sceviour JSY AU RC 6.00 15.00
119 Gustav Nyquist JSY AU RC 12.00 30.00
120 Brendan Smith JSY AU RC 6.00 15.00
121 Nug-Hopkins JSY AU RC 30.00 80.00
122 Hartikainen JSY AU RC 6.00 15.00
123 Anton Lander JSY AU RC 6.00 15.00
124 Erik Gudbranson JSY AU RC EXCH 8.00 20.00
125 Slava Voynov JSY AU RC 6.00 15.00
126 Brett Bulmer JSY AU RC 6.00 15.00
127 Louis Leblanc JSY AU RC 6.00 15.00
128 Alexei Emelin JSY AU RC 6.00 15.00
129 Raphael Diaz JSY AU RC 6.00 15.00
130 B.Geoffrion JSY AU RC 6.00 15.00
131 Aaron Palushaj JSY AU RC 6.00 15.00
132 Craig Smith JSY AU RC 8.00 20.00
133 Ryan Ellis JSY AU RC 6.00 15.00
134 Jonathon Blum JSY AU RC 8.00 20.00
135 Adam Henrique JSY AU RC 15.00 40.00
136 Adam Larsson JSY AU RC 8.00 20.00
137 Calvin de Haan JSY AU RC 6.00 15.00
138 Carl Hagelin JSY AU RC 8.00 20.00
139 Tim Erixon JSY AU RC 6.00 15.00
140 Cam Talbot JSY AU RC 15.00 40.00
141 Mika Zibanejad JSY AU RC 10.00 25.00
142 Colin Greening JSY AU RC 6.00 15.00
143 Erik Condra JSY AU RC 6.00 15.00
144 S.Da Costa JSY AU RC 6.00 15.00
145 P.Wiercioch JSY AU RC 6.00 15.00
146 Sean Couturier JSY AU RC 12.00 30.00
147 Matt Read JSY AU RC 12.00 30.00
148 Erik Gustafsson JSY AU RC 8.00 20.00
149 Zac Rinaldo JSY AU RC 6.00 15.00
150 David Rundblad JSY AU RC 6.00 15.00
151 Simon Despres JSY AU RC 6.00 15.00
152 Joe Vitale JSY AU RC 6.00 15.00
153 R.Bortuzzo JSY AU RC 6.00 15.00
154 Harri Sateri JSY AU RC 6.00 15.00
155 Brett Connolly JSY AU RC 6.00 15.00
156 Jake Gardiner JSY AU RC 10.00 25.00
157 Joe Colborne JSY AU RC 6.00 15.00
158 Matt Frattin JSY AU RC 8.00 20.00
159 Ben Scrivens JSY AU RC 10.00 25.00
160 Zack Kassian JSY AU RC 10.00 25.00
161 Eddie Lack JSY AU RC 6.00 15.00
162 Yann Sauve JSY AU RC 6.00 15.00
163 Cody Eakin JSY AU RC 8.00 20.00
164 Dmitry Orlov JSY AU RC 8.00 20.00
165 Mark Scheifele JSY AU RC 15.00 40.00
166 Carl Klingberg JSY AU RC 6.00 15.00

2011-12 Panini Prime Rookies Hologold Patch Autographs

*HOLOGOLD/25: .6X TO 1.5X JSY AU/199
HOLOGOLD JSY AU PRINT RUN 25
121 Ryan Nugent-Hopkins 125.00 250.00

2011-12 Panini Prime Rookies Holosilver Patch Autographs

*HOLOSILVER/50: .5X TO 1.2X JSY AU/199
HOLOSILVER JSY AU PRINT RUN 50

2011-12 Panini Prime Silver

*1-100 VETS/25: 1X TO 2.5X BASIC CARDS
STATED PRINT RUN 25 SER.#'d SETS

2011-12 Panini Prime Colors Patch Horizontal

5 Patrice Bergeron/24 20.00 50.00
6 Ray Bourque/16 25.00 60.00
7 Tim Thomas/18 15.00 40.00
8 Zdeno Chara/16 15.00 40.00
10 Tyler Seguin/19 30.00 80.00
11 Ryan Miller/25 15.00 40.00
12 Derek Roy/15 12.00 30.00
14 Cody Hodgson/15 25.00 60.00
17 Ron Francis/25 20.00 50.00
19 Stan Mikita/15 20.00 50.00
20 Gabriel Landeskog/25 25.00 60.00
21 Matt Duchene/19 15.00 40.00
22 Paul Stastny/22 15.00 40.00
26 Loui Eriksson/18 12.00 30.00
27 Brenden Morrow/20 12.00 30.00
28 Steve Yzerman/18 25.00 60.00
29 Henrik Zetterberg/17 20.00 50.00
30 Ryan Nugent-Hopkins/18 50.00 125.00
32 Ryan Smyth/22 12.00 30.00
35 Dustin Brown/17 15.00 40.00
37 Jonathan Bernier/19 15.00 40.00
40 Cal Clutterbuck/20 15.00 40.00
41 Carey Price/18 50.00 125.00
42 Colin Wilson/20 12.00 30.00
43 Pekka Rinne/25 20.00 50.00
47 Patrik Elias/20 15.00 40.00
48 Scott Niedermayer/20 15.00 40.00
50 Bryan Trottier/15 20.00 50.00
52 Kyle Okposo/24 15.00 40.00
54 Brandon Dubinsky/16 12.00 30.00
65 Danny Briere/16 15.00 40.00
68 Scott Hartnell/22 15.00 40.00
70 Jakub Voracek/18 15.00 40.00
72 Mike Smith/25 15.00 40.00
73 Shane Doan/16 12.00 30.00
74 Jaromir Jagr/16 40.00 100.00
76 Mario Lemieux/16 50.00 125.00
82 Logan Couture/28 15.00 40.00
83 Martin Havlat/16 12.00 30.00
85 Ryane Clowe/16 10.00 25.00
87 Brett Hull/19 20.00 50.00
88 David Backes/16 15.00 40.00
90 Steven Stamkos/18 30.00 80.00
94 Cory Schneider/19 12.00 30.00
95 Daniel Sedin/17 15.00 40.00
96 Henrik Sedin/17 15.00 40.00
98 Karl Alzner/18 10.00 25.00
99 Tomas Vokoun/23 12.00 30.00
100 Ondrej Pavelec/20 15.00 40.00

2011-12 Panini Prime Colors Patch Vertical

STATED PRINT RUN 1-23
8 Zdeno Chara/20 50.00 100.00
9 Tuukka Rask/16 50.00 100.00
18 Patrick Kane/17 225.00 400.00
22 Paul Stastny/17 40.00 100.00
23 Milan Hejduk/18 25.00 60.00
24 Rick Nash/17 60.00 125.00
34 Anze Kopitar/20 40.00 100.00
36 Jeff Carter/18 60.00 120.00
38 Luc Robitaille/18 60.00 125.00
46 Martin Brodeur/16 50.00 100.00
49 Adam Larsson/23 50.00 100.00
60 Jason Spezza/18 30.00 80.00
61 Mika Zibanejad/21 50.00 125.00
63 Chris Pronger/18 25.00 60.00
71 Keith Yandle/20 25.00 60.00
77 Sidney Crosby/22 125.00 250.00
84 Patrick Marleau/16 75.00 150.00
85 Ryane Clowe/21 20.00 50.00
91 Vincent Lecavalier/17 40.00 100.00

2011-12 Panini Prime Combos Jerseys

STATED PRINT RUN 25-225
*PATCH/25: .8X TO 2X DUAL JSY/225
*PRIME/50: .6X TO 1.5X DUAL JSY/225
*PRIME/25: .8X TO 2X DUAL JSY/225
1 B.Ryan/R.Getzlaf/225 8.00 20.00
2 D.Alfredsson/J.Spezza/225 5.00 12.00
3 L.Leblanc/R.Diaz/225 8.00 20.00
4 D.Keith/J.Toews/225 10.00 25.00
5 C.Perry/D.Smith-Pelly/225 6.00 15.00
6 B.Wheeler/M.Scheifele/225 6.00 15.00
7 P.Larsen/T.Vincour/225 4.00 10.00
8 H.Zetterberg/N.Lidstrom/225 8.00 20.00
9 J.Bernier/J.Quick/225 8.00 20.00
10 M.Read/S.Couturier/225 8.00 20.00
11 A.Miele/D.Rundblad/225 4.00 10.00
12 B.Scrivens/M.Frattin/225 4.00 10.00
13 D.Sedin/H.Sedin/225 6.00 15.00
14 M.Neuvirth/T.Vokoun/225 6.00 15.00
15 C.Atkinson/D.Savard/225 10.00 25.00
16 E.Kane/P.Kane/225 10.00 25.00
17 P.Esposito/T.Esposito/25 15.00 40.00
18 A.Ovechkin/A.Semin/225 8.00 20.00
19 C.de Haan/T.Hamonic/225 4.00 10.00
20 J.McBain/J.Faulk/225 6.00 15.00
21 J.Vitale/R.Bortuzzo/225 4.00 10.00
22 B.Schenn/L.Schenn/225 5.00 12.00
23 C.Perry/H.Sedin/225 5.00 12.00
24 B.Elliott/J.Halak/225 6.00 15.00
25 B.Saad/M.Kruger/225 5.00 12.00
26 J.Howard/P.Datsyuk/225 6.00 15.00
27 Y.Sauve/Z.Kassian/225 3.00 8.00
28 G.Nemisz/R.Horak/225 4.00 10.00
29 A.York/T.Kubalik/225 3.00 8.00
30 A.Palushaj/A.Emelin/225 2.50 6.00
31 C.Greening/S.Da Costa/225 4.00 10.00
32 S.Hartnell/Z.Rinaldo/225 5.00 12.00
33 C.Hodgson/Z.Kassian/225 5.00 12.00
34 D.Stafford/J.Pominville/225 5.00 12.00
35 T.Thomas/T.Rask/225 5.00 12.00
36 D.Doughty/S.Voynov/225 5.00 12.00
37 C.Smith/R.Suter/225 6.00 15.00
38 J.Staal/S.Despres/225 5.00 12.00
39 H.Sateri/J.Pavelski/225 5.00 12.00
40 B.Bulmer/D.Setoguchi/225 4.00 10.00
41 J.Moore/R.Johansen/225 5.00 12.00
42 C.Neil/P.Wiercioch/225 4.00 10.00
43 R.Malone/S.Stamkos/225 8.00 20.00
44 C.Joseph/G.Fuhr/225 8.00 20.00
45 B.Holtby/M.Green/225 10.00 25.00
46 C.Klingberg/O.Pavelec/225 5.00 12.00
47 E.Gudbranson/R.Ellis/225 3.00 8.00
48 RNH/S.Couturier/225 8.00 20.00
49 C.Teubert/E.Condra/225 5.00 12.00
50 B.Geoffrion/C.Price/225 6.00 15.00

2011-12 Panini Prime Namesakes Autographs

STATED PRINT RUN 20-75
1 Aaron Palushaj/75 8.00 20.00
2 Adam Henrique/75 20.00 50.00
4 Alex Ovechkin/75 60.00 100.00
5 Anton Lander/75 20.00 50.00
6 Ben Scrivens/75 12.00 30.00
7 Blake Geoffrion/75 8.00 20.00
9 Bobby Ryan/25 20.00 50.00
10 Brandon Saad/25 30.00 60.00
11 Brendan Smith/75 15.00 40.00
12 Brenden Morrow/75 10.00 25.00
13 Brett Connolly/75 8.00 20.00
14 Brian Gionta/75 8.00 20.00
15 Cameron Gaunce/75 6.00 15.00
16 Cody Hodgson/75 20.00 50.00
17 Craig Anderson/75 10.00 25.00
18 Dany Heatley/75 15.00 40.00
19 David Rundblad/75 8.00 20.00
21 Devante Smith-Pelly/75 12.00 30.00
22 Dion Phaneuf/75 15.00 40.00
23 Dustin Brown/75 20.00 50.00
24 Erik Condra/75 8.00 20.00
26 Felix Potvin/75 75.00 150.00
27 Gabriel Landeskog/75 40.00 80.00
30 Harry Zolnierczyk/75 10.00 25.00
31 Jack Johnson/75 15.00 40.00
33 James Neal/25 20.00 50.00
34 James van Riemsdyk/75 12.00 30.00
35 Jarome Iginla/75 25.00 60.00
36 Jaroslav Halak/75 15.00 40.00
38 Jeremy Roenick/75 40.00 100.00
39 Joe Sakic/25 30.00 80.00
40 Jonas Hiller/75 15.00 40.00
41 Jonathan Bernier/75 12.00 30.00
42 Jonathan Quick/75 25.00 60.00
43 Jordan Staal/75 25.00 60.00
44 Jordin Tootoo/75 15.00 40.00
45 Nathan Gerbe/75 10.00 25.00
46 Loui Eriksson/75 12.00 30.00
47 Magnus Paajarvi/75 12.00 30.00
48 Marcus Kruger/75 12.00 30.00
49 Mark Scheifele/75 20.00 50.00
50 Martin Havlat/75 10.00 25.00
51 Matt Duchene/75 10.00 25.00
52 Matt Moulson/75 8.00 20.00
53 Michael Cammalleri/75 12.00 30.00
54 Michael Del Zotto/75 12.00 30.00
56 Nazem Kadri/7 15.00 40.00
57 Nikolai Khabibulin/75 15.00 40.00
58 Patrick Roy/25 75.00 135.00
59 Peter Holland/75 8.00 20.00
60 Ryan Ellis/75 8.00 20.00
61 Ryan Johansen/75 15.00 40.00
62 Ryan Nugent-Hopkins/75 40.00 100.00
63 Sean Couturier/75 25.00 60.00
65 Sidney Crosby/25 100.00 200.00
66 Simon Despres/75 15.00 40.00
67 Slava Voynov/75 8.00 20.00
69 Steve Yzerman/30 60.00 120.00
70 Tim Erixon/75 10.00 25.00
71 Tomas Kubalik/75 8.00 20.00
73 Zac Rinaldo/75 12.00 30.00
74 Zack Kassian/75 10.00 25.00
75 Robin Lehner/75 8.00 20.00
77 Ryan Kesler/75 30.00 60.00
78 Sam Gagner/75 12.00 30.00
79 Alex Pietrangelo/75 15.00 40.00
81 Brad Richards/50 12.00 30.00
82 Carl Hagelin/75 12.00 30.00
83 Carl Klingberg/75 12.00 30.00
84 Colin Greening/75 12.00 30.00
85 Craig Smith/50 12.00 30.00
86 Cody Eakin/50 10.00 25.00
88 Jake Gardiner/50 15.00 40.00
89 Jimmy Hayes/75 10.00 25.00
90 Lance Bouma/75 8.00 20.00
91 Leland Irving/75 8.00 20.00
92 Justin Faulk/85 12.00 30.00
93 Lars Eller/50 10.00 25.00
94 Matt Read/25 30.00 80.00
95 Pekka Rinne/50 15.00 40.00
96 Mark Messier/25 50.00 100.00
97 Louis Leblanc/75 15.00 40.00
98 Mario Lemieux/25 60.00 120.00
99 Gordie Howe/20 75.00 150.00
100 Jaromir Jagr/25 75.00 150.00

2011-12 Panini Prime Prime Time Rookies Jersey Autographs

STATED PRINT RUN 50 SER.#'d SETS
*PRIME/15: .8X TO 2X BASIC AU/50

Card	Low	High
1 Ryan Nugent-Hopkins	20.00	50.00
2 Gabriel Landeskog	15.00	40.00
3 Sean Couturier	10.00	25.00
4 Mark Scheifele	12.00	30.00
5 Adam Henrique	12.00	30.00
6 Matt Read	12.00	30.00
7 Ryan Johansen	10.00	25.00
8 Craig Smith	6.00	15.00
9 Cody Eakin	6.00	15.00
10 Louis Leblanc	5.00	12.00
11 Gustav Nyquist	12.00	30.00
12 Jake Gardiner	12.00	30.00
13 Brett Connolly	8.00	20.00
14 Cody Hodgson	10.00	25.00
15 Zack Kassian	6.00	15.00
16 Carl Hagelin	8.00	20.00
17 Adam Larsson	10.00	25.00
18 Mika Zibanejad	12.00	30.00
19 Joe Colborne		
20 Brandon Saad	10.00	25.00
21 Devante Smith-Pelly	8.00	20.00
22 Tomas Vincour	5.00	12.00
23 Colin Greening	8.00	20.00
24 Brett Bulmer	5.00	12.00
25 Peter Holland	5.00	12.00
26 Marcus Kruger	8.00	20.00
27 David Rundblad	5.00	12.00
28 Tim Erixon	5.00	12.00
29 Brendan Smith	5.00	12.00
30 Matt Frattin EXCH	10.00	25.00
31 John Moore	5.00	12.00
32 Roman Horak	5.00	12.00
33 Aaron Palushaj	5.00	12.00
34 Ryan Ellis	5.00	12.00
36 Slava Voynov	5.00	12.00
37 Harri Sateri	5.00	12.00
38 Simon Despres	5.00	12.00
39 Erik Gudbranson	6.00	15.00
39 Erik Gudbranson		
40 Blake Geoffrion	5.00	12.00
41 Greg Nemisz	5.00	12.00
42 Anton Lander	5.00	12.00
43 Calvin de Haan	5.00	12.00
44 Justin Faulk	8.00	20.00
45 Cam Atkinson	12.00	30.00
46 Ben Scrivens	8.00	20.00
47 Erik Gustafsson	6.00	15.00
48 Eddie Lack	5.00	12.00
49 Carl Klingberg	5.00	12.00
50 Stephane Da Costa	5.00	12.00

2011-12 Panini Prime Prime Time Rookies Jerseys

STATED PRINT RUN 99 SER.#'d SETS
*PRIME/25: .8X TO 2X BASIC JSY/99

Card	Low	High
1 Ryan Nugent-Hopkins	15.00	40.00
2 Gabriel Landeskog	12.00	30.00
3 Sean Couturier	6.00	15.00
4 Mark Scheifele	8.00	20.00
5 Adam Henrique	6.00	15.00
6 Matt Read	6.00	15.00
7 Ryan Johansen	6.00	15.00
8 Craig Smith	4.00	10.00
9 Cody Eakin	4.00	10.00
10 Louis Leblanc	6.00	15.00
11 Gustav Nyquist	6.00	15.00
12 Jake Gardiner	5.00	12.00
13 Brett Connolly	3.00	8.00
14 Cody Hodgson	6.00	15.00
15 Zack Kassian	4.00	10.00
16 Carl Hagelin	6.00	15.00
17 Adam Larsson	5.00	12.00
18 Mika Zibanejad	5.00	12.00
19 Joe Colborne	3.00	8.00
20 Brandon Saad	6.00	15.00
21 Devante Smith-Pelly	5.00	12.00
22 Tomas Vincour	3.00	8.00
23 Colin Greening	3.00	8.00
24 Brett Bulmer	3.00	8.00
25 Peter Holland	3.00	8.00
26 Marcus Kruger	5.00	12.00
27 David Rundblad	3.00	8.00
28 Tim Erixon	3.00	8.00
29 Brendan Smith	3.00	8.00
30 Matt Frattin	3.00	8.00
31 John Moore	3.00	8.00
32 Roman Horak	3.00	8.00
33 Aaron Palushaj	3.00	8.00
34 Ryan Ellis	3.00	8.00
35 Alexei Emelin	3.00	8.00
36 Slava Voynov	3.00	8.00
37 Harri Sateri	3.00	8.00
38 Simon Despres	3.00	8.00
39 Erik Gudbranson	4.00	10.00
40 Blake Geoffrion	3.00	8.00
41 Greg Nemisz	3.00	8.00
42 Anton Lander	3.00	8.00
43 Calvin de Haan	3.00	8.00
44 Justin Faulk	5.00	12.00
45 Cam Atkinson	8.00	20.00
46 Ben Scrivens	5.00	12.00
47 Erik Gustafsson	5.00	12.00
48 Eddie Lack	3.00	8.00
49 Carl Klingberg	3.00	8.00
50 Stephane Da Costa	3.00	8.00

2011-12 Panini Prime Quads Jerseys

STATED PRINT RUN 25-75
*PRIME/15: .6X TO 1.5X BASIC QUAD/75
*PRIME/15: .5X TO 1.2X BASIC QUAD/25

Card	Low	High
1 Prong/Sakic/Mario/Yzermn	25.00	60.00
2 Prust/Boll/Martin/Thornton	6.00	15.00
3 Malkin/Neal/Gabrk/Stamks	12.00	30.00
4 Lndqvst/Quick/Smith/Rinn	12.00	30.00
5 Neil/Dorstt/Rinaldo/Konpk	6.00	15.00
6 Price/Hiller/Kiprsff/Smith	25.00	60.00
7 Richrds/Sakic/StLou/Dats	12.00	30.00
8 Ovech/Sedin/Malkin/Sedin	12.00	30.00
9 Joseph/Belfr/Brodr/Roy	20.00	50.00
10 Hull/Howe/Dion/Espo/25	40.00	100.00
11 Malkn/Zettr/Toews/Thoms	25.00	60.00
12 Jackman/Elliott/Halak/Oshie	12.00	30.00
13 Kunitz/Tangrdi/Vitle/Bortzzo	8.00	20.00
14 Zolnier/Read/Coutr/Rnldo	12.50	30.00
15 deHaan/Nielsn/DiPiet/Hamnc	6.00	15.00
16 Geoffrn/Price/Leblnc/Diaz	25.00	60.00
17 Phanf/Gardnr/Reimr/Schn	10.00	25.00
18 Saad/Toews/Krugr/Kane	10.00	25.00
19 Smith/Nygst/Hwrd/Ldstrm	10.00	25.00
20 Richd/Hgln/Zuccrl/DelZ	12.00	30.00

2011-12 Panini Prime Quads Jerseys Prime

Card	Low	High
1 Pronger/Sakic/Lemieux/Yzerman	40.00	100.00
2 Prust/Boll/Martin/Thornton	12.00	30.00
3 Malkin/Neal/Gaborik/Stamkos	25.00	60.00
4 Lundqvist/Quick/Smith/Rinne	20.00	60.00
5 Neil/Dorsett/Rinaldo/Konopka	12.00	30.00
6 Price/Hiller/Kiprusoff/Smith	40.00	100.00
7 Richards/Sakic/St. Louis/Datsyuk	25.00	60.00
8 Ovechkin/Sedin/Malkin/Sedin	60.00	150.00
9 Joseph/Belfour/Brodeur/Roy	30.00	80.00
10 Hull/Howe/Dionne/Esposito	50.00	120.00
11 Malkin/Zetterberg/Toews/Thomas	40.00	100.00
12 Jackman/Elliott/Halak/Oshie	25.00	60.00
13 Kunitz/Tangradi/Vitale/Bortuzzo	25.00	60.00
14 Zolnierczyk/Read/Couturier/Rinaldo	25.00	60.00
15 de Haan/Nielsen/DiPietro/Hamonic	12.00	30.00
16 Geoffrion/Price/Leblanc/Diaz	40.00	112.00
17 Phaneuf/Gardiner/Reimer/Schenn	15.00	40.00
18 Saad/Toews/Kruger/Kane	20.00	50.00
19 Smith/Nyquist/Howard/Lidstrom	15.00	40.00
20 Richards/Hagelin/Zuccarello/Del Zotto	20.00	50.00

2011-12 Panini Prime Showcase Swatches

STATED PRINT RUN 25 SER.#'d SETS

Card	Low	High
1 Ryan Nugent-Hopkins	30.00	80.00
2 Ryan Ellis	6.00	15.00
3 Adam Henrique	15.00	40.00
4 Greg Nemisz	6.00	15.00
5 Brendan Smith	6.00	15.00
6 Brett Connolly	6.00	15.00
7 Zack Kassian	8.00	20.00
8 Cody Eakin	8.00	20.00
9 Simon Despres	6.00	15.00
10 Joe Colborne	6.00	15.00
11 Gabriel Landeskog	15.00	40.00
12 David Rundblad	6.00	15.00
13 Mika Zibanejad	15.00	40.00
14 Carl Klingberg	6.00	15.00
15 Marcus Kruger	10.00	25.00
16 Tim Erixon	6.00	15.00
17 Justin Faulk	10.00	25.00
18 Jake Gardiner	10.00	25.00
19 Aaron Palushaj	6.00	15.00
20 John Moore	8.00	20.00
21 Erik Gudbranson	8.00	20.00
22 Bobby Ryan	10.00	25.00
23 Corey Perry	10.00	25.00
24 Milan Lucic	10.00	25.00
25 Zdeno Chara	10.00	25.00
26 Cody Hodgson	15.00	40.00
27 Ville Leino	8.00	20.00
28 Miikka Kiprusoff	10.00	25.00
29 Brandon Saad	12.00	30.00
30 Jonathan Toews	15.00	40.00
31 Erik Johnson	6.00	15.00
32 Joe Sakic	15.00	40.00
33 Rick Nash	12.00	30.00
34 Ryan Johansen	12.00	30.00
35 Henrik Zetterberg	12.00	30.00
36 Steve Yzerman	40.00	80.00
37 Anton Lander	6.00	15.00
38 Ryan Nugent-Hopkins	25.00	60.00
39 Taylor Hall	15.00	40.00
40 Erik Gudbranson	8.00	20.00
41 Kris Versteeg	8.00	20.00
42 Jeff Carter	10.00	25.00
43 Jonathan Quick	15.00	40.00
44 Brett Bulmer	8.00	20.00
45 Niklas Backstrom	10.00	25.00
46 Brian Gionta	8.00	20.00
47 Blake Geoffrion	8.00	20.00
48 Louis Leblanc	6.00	15.00
49 Craig Smith	10.00	25.00
50 Jonathon Blum	8.00	20.00
51 Ryan Suter	6.00	15.00
52 Adam Larsson	8.00	20.00
53 Martin Brodeur	20.00	50.00
54 Calvin de Haan	8.00	20.00
55 Henrik Lundqvist	12.00	30.00
56 Ryan Callahan	12.00	30.00
57 Colin Greening	8.00	20.00
58 Daniel Alfredsson	10.00	25.00
59 Erik Karlsson	20.00	50.00
60 Ilya Bryzgalov	12.00	30.00
61 Matt Read	12.00	30.00
62 Scott Hartnell	12.00	30.00
63 Sean Couturier	20.00	50.00
64 Mike Smith	10.00	25.00
65 Mikkel Boedker	6.00	15.00
66 James Neal	12.00	30.00
67 Joe Vitale	8.00	20.00
68 Sidney Crosby	40.00	100.00
69 Joe Pavelski	10.00	25.00
70 Patrick Marleau	10.00	25.00
71 David Backes	10.00	25.00
72 Martin St. Louis	10.00	25.00
73 Ben Scrivens	10.00	25.00
74 Joe Colborne	10.00	25.00
75 Luke Schenn	6.00	15.00
76 Matt Frattin	6.00	15.00
77 Ryan Kesler	12.00	30.00
78 Zack Kassian	8.00	20.00
79 Alex Ovechkin	15.00	40.00
80 Cody Eakin	8.00	20.00
81 Blake Wheeler	15.00	40.00
82 Mark Scheifele	15.00	40.00

2011-12 Panini Prime Showcase Jersey Prime Colors

PRIME COLOR PRINT RUN 35
*PATCH/15: .6X TO 1.5X PRIME COLOR/35

Card	Low	High
1 Ryan Nugent-Hopkins	25.00	60.00
2 Ryan Ellis	5.00	12.00
3 Adam Henrique	10.00	25.00
4 Greg Nemisz	5.00	12.00
5 Brendan Smith	5.00	12.00
6 Brett Connolly	5.00	12.00
7 Zack Kassian	6.00	15.00
8 Cody Eakin	6.00	15.00
9 Simon Despres	5.00	12.00
10 Joe Colborne	5.00	12.00
11 Gabriel Landeskog	15.00	40.00
12 David Rundblad	5.00	12.00
13 Mika Zibanejad	12.00	30.00
14 Carl Klingberg	5.00	12.00
15 Marcus Kruger	8.00	20.00
16 Tim Erixon	5.00	12.00
17 Justin Faulk	8.00	20.00
18 Jake Gardiner	8.00	20.00
19 Aaron Palushaj	5.00	12.00
20 John Moore	5.00	12.00

2011-12 Panini Prime Signatures

*GOLD/50: .5X TO 1.2X BASIC AU/99
*GOLD/50: .4X TO 1X BASIC AU/31
*HOLOSILVER/25: .6X TO 1.5X BASIC AU/99
*HOLOSILVER/25: .5X TO 1.2X BASIC AU/31

Card	Low	High
1 Alex Ovechkin/99	30.00	80.00
2 Gordie Howe/25	50.00	125.00
3 Mario Lemieux/99	40.00	100.00
4 Martin Brodeur/99	25.00	60.00
5 Aaron Palushaj/99	5.00	12.00
6 Sidney Crosby/25	60.00	150.00
8 Brandon Saad/99	10.00	25.00
9 Colten Teubert/99	5.00	12.00
11 Mike Modano/99	10.00	25.00
12 Brendan Smith/30	10.00	25.00
13 Brett Connolly/99	5.00	12.00
14 Cam Ward/99	6.00	15.00
15 Cameron Gaunce/99	4.00	10.00
16 Carl Hagelin/99	8.00	20.00
17 Chris Pronger/99	5.00	12.00
18 Dylan Olsen/31	8.00	20.00
19 Cody Hodgson/99	10.00	25.00
20 Colin Wilson/99	5.00	12.00
20 Colin Wilson	5.00	12.00
(inserted in 2013-14 Panini Prime)		
21 David Rundblad/99	5.00	12.00
22 Craig Anderson/99	6.00	15.00
23 Dale Hawerchuk/99	8.00	20.00
24 Dion Phaneuf/99	6.00	15.00
25 Dustin Brown/99	6.00	15.00
26 Patrick Roy/99	25.00	60.00
27 Gilbert Perreault/99	6.00	15.00
28 Gustav Nyquist/99	12.00	30.00
29 Jack Johnson/99	4.00	10.00
30 Ben Scrivens/99	8.00	20.00
31 Roman Horak/99	5.00	12.00
32 Johnny Bucyk/99	6.00	15.00
34 Jonathon Blum/99	5.00	12.00
35 Matt Read/99	10.00	25.00
36 Devante Smith-Pelly/99	8.00	20.00
37 Marcus Kruger/99	8.00	20.00
38 Leland Irving/99	5.00	12.00
39 Louis Leblanc/99	5.00	12.00
40 Mark Scheifele/99	12.00	30.00
41 Sam Gagner/99	5.00	12.00
42 Martin Havlat/99	5.00	12.00
43 Niklas Backstrom/99	6.00	15.00
45 Pekka Rinne/50	8.00	20.00
46 Peter Holland/99	5.00	12.00
47 Raphael Diaz/99	5.00	12.00
48 Riley Nash/99	5.00	12.00
49 Roberto Luongo/99	6.00	15.00
50 Roman Josi/99	8.00	20.00
51 Ron Hextall/99	8.00	20.00
52 Ryan Ellis/99	5.00	12.00
53 Ryan Kesler/99	6.00	15.00
54 Ryan Smyth/99	5.00	12.00
55 Carl Klingberg/99	5.00	12.00
57 Sean Couturier/99	10.00	25.00
58 Semyon Varlamov/99	6.00	15.00
59 Bill Ranford/99	6.00	15.00
60 Simon Despres/99	5.00	12.00
61 Tim Erixon/99	5.00	12.00
62 Tomas Kubalik	5.00	12.00
(inserted in 2013-14 Panini Prime)		
63 Jimmy Hayes/99	6.00	15.00
64 Anton Lander/99	5.00	12.00
65 Tyler Seguin/99	12.00	30.00
66 Paul Postma/99	5.00	12.00
67 Zach Parise/99	6.00	15.00
68 Zack Kassian/99	6.00	15.00
69 James van Riemsdyk/99	6.00	15.00
70 Peter Stastny/99	6.00	15.00

2011-12 Panini Prime Signatures Duals

STATED PRINT RUN 25 SER.#'d SETS
*GOLD/15: .5X TO 1.2X BASIC DUAL/25

Card	Low	High
2 B.Hull/B.Hull	40.00	80.00
3 C.Price/P.Roy	60.00	120.00
5 E.Lindros/J.Tavares	30.00	60.00
6 C.Neely/P.Esposito		
7 T.Thomas/T.Rask		
8 B.Schenn/L.Schenn		
9 C.Joseph/F.Potvin	30.00	80.00
10 C.Hagelin/T.Erixon	12.00	30.00
11 M.Modano/P.Datsyuk	30.00	60.00
12 J.Roenick/S.Mikita	25.00	60.00
13 R.Luongo/R.Kesler	25.00	60.00
15 D.Briere/C.Pronger	15.00	40.00
16 B.Nicholls/L.Robitaille	15.00	40.00
17 A.Graves/R.Gilbert	12.00	30.00
18 J.Bower/R.Vachon	30.00	80.00
20 K.Letang/S.Despres	60.00	120.00

2011-12 Panini Prime Trios Jerseys

STATED PRINT RUN 25-150
*PATCH/15: .8X TO 2X TRIO/150
*PRIME/25: .6X TO 1.5X TRIO/150
*PRIME/15: .5X TO 1.2X TRIO/25

Card	Low	High
1 Kane/150/Miller/Parise	12.00	30.00
2 Brodr/150/Richrds/Nash	10.00	25.00
3 Alfrdssn/150/Lidstrm/Hrnqvst	6.00	15.00
4 Semin/150/Bryzglv/Datsyk	8.00	20.00
5 Kiprusoff/150/Koivu/Selanne	12.00	30.00
6 Elliott/150/Lundqvist/Quick	10.00	25.00
7 Elliott/150/Quick/Smith	10.00	25.00
8 Burrows/150/Bieksa/Kesler	6.00	15.00
9 Scrivns/150/Phanf/Gstvssn	6.00	15.00
10 Morrow/150/Sceviour/Vincour	5.00	12.00
11 Smith/150/Nyqust/Zettrbrg	10.00	25.00
12 StLouis/150/Stamks/Lecav	8.00	20.00
13 Pietrangelo/150/Crombeen/Oshie	10.00	25.00
14 Nemisz/150/Cammalleri/Horak	5.00	12.00
15 Bryzglv/150/Read/Coutur	10.00	25.00
16 Wheelr/150/Klingbrg/Scheif	12.00	30.00
17 Lander/150/Teubrt/Hartikn	5.00	12.00
18 Bulmer/150/Heatley/Palmieri	5.00	12.00
19 Miele/150/Rundblad/Yandle	6.00	15.00
20 Larssn/150/Greene/Brodr	8.00	20.00
21 Doughty/150/Quick/Voynv	10.00	25.00
22 de Haan/150/Nielsen/DiPietro	5.00	12.00
23 Hagelin/150/Gaborik/Erixon	8.00	20.00
24 Palshj/150/Geoffrn/Leblnc	8.00	20.00
25 Holtby/150/Neuvirth/Vokn	12.00	30.00
26 Gaunce/150/Johnson/Stastny	6.00	15.00
27 Sateri/150/Marleau/Clowe	6.00	15.00
28 Greening/150/Condra/DaCsta	5.00	12.00
29 Emeln/150/Gorges/Diaz	5.00	12.00
30 Sidney Crosby/25	40.00	100.00

2012-13 Panini Prime

Card	Low	High
1 Craig Anderson	2.00	5.00
2 Dave Andreychuk	2.00	5.00
3 Artem Anisimov	1.50	4.00
4 David Backes	2.00	5.00
5 Mikael Backlund	1.50	4.00
6 Niklas Backstrom	1.50	4.00
7 Ed Belfour	2.00	5.00
8 Jamie Benn	2.50	6.00
9 Sergei Bobrovsky	2.00	5.00
10 Ray Bourque	3.00	8.00
11 Martin Brodeur	4.00	10.00
12 Pavel Bure	2.50	6.00
13 Alexander Burmistrov	1.50	4.00
14 Bobby Clarke	2.00	5.00
15 Scott Clemmensen	1.50	4.00
16 Logan Couture	2.00	5.00
17 Sidney Crosby	8.00	20.00
18 Pavel Datsyuk	2.50	6.00
19 Devan Dubnyk	2.00	5.00
20 Matt Duchene	2.00	5.00
21 Jordan Eberle	2.00	5.00
22 Loui Eriksson	1.50	4.00
23 Mike Fisher	1.50	4.00
24 Marc-Andre Fleury	3.00	8.00
25 Ryan Getzlaf	3.00	8.00
26 Doug Gilmour	2.50	6.00
27 Brian Gionta	1.50	4.00
28 Claude Giroux	2.00	5.00
29 Taylor Hall	4.00	10.00
30 Dale Hawerchuk	2.50	6.00
31 Adam Henrique	2.00	5.00
32 Cody Hodgson	2.00	5.00
33 Braden Holtby	3.00	8.00
34 Gordie Howe	4.00	10.00
35 Brett Hull	2.00	5.00
36 Jarome Iginla	2.00	5.00
37 Jaromir Jagr	5.00	12.00
38 Ryan Johansen	2.50	6.00
39 Ed Jovanovski	1.25	3.00
40 Patrick Kane	4.00	10.00
41 Erik Karlsson	4.00	10.00
42 Phil Kessel	2.50	6.00
43 Olaf Kolzig	2.00	5.00
44 Anze Kopitar	3.00	8.00
45 Andrew Ladd	2.00	5.00
46 Pat LaFontaine	2.00	5.00
47 Gabriel Landeskog	2.00	5.00
48 Adam Larsson	2.00	5.00
49 Brian Leetch	2.00	5.00
50 Mario Lemieux	6.00	15.00
51 Anders Lindback	1.25	3.00
52 Eric Lindros	3.00	8.00
53 Henrik Lundqvist	2.50	6.00
54 Al MacInnis	2.00	5.00
55 Evgeni Malkin	6.00	15.00
56 Mark Messier	2.50	6.00
57 Stan Mikita	2.50	6.00
58 Ryan Miller	2.00	5.00
59 Mike Modano	3.00	8.00
60 Matt Moulson	1.50	4.00
61 Kirk Muller	1.50	4.00
62 Rick Nash	2.00	5.00
63 Joe Nieuwendyk	2.00	5.00
64 Owen Nolan	1.50	4.00
65 Ryan Nugent-Hopkins	2.00	5.00
66 Alex Ovechkin	6.00	15.00
67 Max Pacioretty	2.00	5.00
68 Zach Parise	2.00	5.00
69 Ondrej Pavelec	2.00	5.00
70 Joe Pavelski	2.00	5.00
71 Alex Pietrangelo	1.50	4.00
72 Felix Potvin	3.00	8.00
73 Carey Price	6.00	15.00
74 Jonathan Quick	3.00	8.00
75 Tuukka Rask	2.00	5.00
76 Matt Read	1.50	4.00
77 James Reimer	2.00	5.00
78 Mike Richards	2.00	5.00
79 Pekka Rinne	2.50	6.00
80 Luc Robitaille	2.00	5.00
81 Patrick Roy	5.00	12.00
82 Bobby Ryan	2.00	5.00
83 Joe Sakic	3.00	8.00
84 Tyler Seguin	3.00	8.00
85 Teemu Selanne	4.00	10.00
86 Jeff Skinner	2.00	5.00
87 Billy Smith	2.00	5.00
88 Craig Smith	1.25	3.00
89 Mike Smith	2.00	5.00
90 Eric Staal	2.50	6.00
91 Steven Stamkos	4.00	10.00
92 Ryan Suter	1.25	3.00
93 John Tavares	4.00	10.00
94 Joe Thornton	2.00	5.00
95 Jonathan Toews	4.00	10.00
96 Keith Yandle	2.00	5.00
97 Cam Ward	2.00	5.00
98 Steve Yzerman	4.00	10.00
99 Henrik Zetterberg	2.50	6.00
100 Mika Zibanejad	2.00	5.00
101 Mat Clark JSY AU RC	4.00	10.00
102 Max Sauve JSY AU RC	4.00	10.00
103 Michael Hutchinson JSY AU RC	8.00	20.00
104 Torey Krug JSY AU RC	20.00	40.00
105 Carter Camper JSY AU RC	3.00	8.00
106 Lane MacDermid JSY AU RC	4.00	10.00
107 Travis Turnbull JSY AU RC	4.00	10.00
108 Akim Aliu JSY AU RC	4.00	10.00
109 Sven Baertschi JSY AU RC	5.00	12.00
110 Jeremy Welsh JSY AU RC	4.00	10.00
111 Brandon Bollig JSY AU RC	4.00	10.00
112 Mike Connolly JSY AU RC	4.00	10.00
113 Tyson Barrie JSY AU RC	8.00	20.00
114 Andrew Joudrey JSY AU RC	4.00	10.00
115 Cody Goloubef JSY AU RC	4.00	10.00
116 Dalton Prout JSY AU RC	4.00	10.00
117 Shawn Hunwick JSY AU RC	4.00	10.00
118 Brenden Dillon JSY AU RC	6.00	15.00
119 Reilly Smith JSY AU RC	8.00	20.00
120 Ryan Garbutt JSY AU RC	4.00	10.00
121 Scott Glennie JSY AU RC	4.00	10.00
122 Riley Sheahan JSY AU RC	6.00	15.00
123 Philippe Cornet JSY AU RC	4.00	10.00
124 Colby Robak JSY AU RC	4.00	10.00
125 Jordan Nolan JSY AU RC	4.00	10.00
126 Chay Genoway JSY AU RC	4.00	10.00
127 Jason Zucker JSY AU RC	5.00	12.00
128 Kris Foucault JSY AU RC	4.00	10.00
129 Tyler Cuma JSY AU RC	4.00	10.00
130 Gabriel Dumont JSY AU RC	4.00	10.00
131 Robert Mayer JSY AU RC	5.00	12.00
132 Chet Pickard JSY AU RC	4.00	10.00
133 Aaron Ness JSY AU RC	4.00	10.00
134 Casey Cizikas JSY AU RC	4.00	10.00
135 Matt Donovan JSY AU RC	4.00	10.00
136 Matt Watkins JSY AU RC	4.00	10.00
137 Chris Kreider JSY AU RC	8.00	20.00
138 Jakob Silfverberg JSY AU RC	8.00	20.00
139 Mark Stone JSY AU RC	10.00	25.00
140 Brandon Manning JSY AU RC	4.00	10.00
141 Michael Stone JSY AU RC	4.00	10.00
142 Tyson Sexsmith JSY AU RC	4.00	10.00
143 Jaden Schwartz JSY AU RC	8.00	20.00
144 Jake Allen JSY AU RC	12.00	30.00
145 J.T. Brown JSY AU RC	4.00	10.00
146 Carter Ashton JSY AU RC	3.00	8.00
147 Jussi Rynnas JSY AU RC	4.00	10.00
148 Ryan Hamilton JSY AU RC	4.00	10.00

2012-13 Panini Prime Hologold

*101-148 ROOKIES/25: .8X TO 2X BASIC RC

2012-13 Panini Prime Holosilver

*101-148 ROOKIES/50: .6X TO 1.5X BASIC RC

2012-13 Panini Prime Colors Logo

Card	Low	High
1 Adam Foote/23	20.00	50.00
2 Alex Tanguay/26	20.00	50.00
3 Bobby Ryan/17	25.00	60.00
4 Brendan Shanahan/24	60.00	120.00
5 Cam Neely/22	50.00	100.00
6 Chris Chelios/19	40.00	100.00
7 Darryl Sydor/20	15.00	40.00
8 Dave Andreychuk/19	20.00	50.00
9 David Krejci/25	20.00	50.00
10 David Steckel/17	15.00	40.00
11 Dustin Byfuglien/24	20.00	50.00
12 Erik Johnson/17	20.00	50.00
13 Gabriel Landeskog/24	30.00	80.00
15 Jarome Iginla/26	30.00	80.00
16 Jay Bouwmeester/26	20.00	50.00
17 Jeremy Roenick/17	30.00	80.00
18 Jimmy Howard/17	25.00	60.00
19 Joe Sakic/27	50.00	100.00
20 Joe Thornton/21	30.00	80.00
21 Jonathan Quick/16	60.00	120.00
22 Kari Lehtonen/18	20.00	50.00
23 Loui Eriksson/18	25.00	60.00
24 Mario Lemieux/19	100.00	175.00
25 Matt Read/18	25.00	60.00
26 Matt Stajan/27	15.00	40.00
28 Miikka Kiprusoff/25	25.00	60.00
29 Mike Gartner/20	15.00	40.00
30 Milan Hejduk/26	15.00	40.00
31 Milan Lucic/20	30.00	80.00
32 Nathan Horton/22	30.00	80.00
33 Nick Fotiu/16	20.00	50.00
34 Nicklas Backstrom/18	50.00	125.00
35 Pat Falloon/25	20.00	50.00
36 Patrick Sharp/15	50.00	100.00
37 Paul Coffey/16	40.00	100.00
39 Pekka Rinne/18	30.00	80.00
40 Pierre Turgeon/29	15.00	40.00
42 Rod Brind'Amour/25	20.00	50.00
43 Ryan Kesler/29	30.00	80.00
44 Ryan O'Reilly/17	20.00	50.00
46 Shea Weber/18		
47 Steve Downie/24	25.00	60.00
48 Teemu Selanne/17	175.00	300.00
49 Trevor Daley/21	20.00	50.00
50 Tuukka Rask/20	40.00	80.00
51 Tyler Seguin/21	50.00	100.00
52 Wayne Simmonds/18	30.00	80.00
53 Zac Rinaldo/18	25.00	60.00
54 Zach Parise/25	20.00	50.00
55 Zdeno Chara/20	30.00	80.00
56 Al Iafrate/16		
57 Al MacInnis/18	75.00	135.00
58 Alex Ovechkin/20	40.00	100.00
59 Paul Coffey/15	40.00	100.00
60 Rob Blake/20	30.00	80.00
62 Alexandre Burrows/27	30.00	80.00
63 Brian Boyle/16	20.00	50.00
64 Brian Campbell/26	20.00	50.00
65 Brian Gionta/18	25.00	60.00
66 Cory Schneider/23	25.00	60.00
67 Daniel Alfredsson/20	20.00	50.00
68 David Legwand/16	30.00	80.00
69 Duncan Keith/17	50.00	100.00
70 Jason Spezza/21	50.00	100.00
71 Jonathan Toews/17	100.00	175.00
72 Joe Nieuwendyk/23	30.00	80.00
74 John Tavares/21	75.00	135.00
75 Mike Richards/18	60.00	120.00
76 Marian Hossa/23	25.00	60.00
77 Justin Williams/20	30.00	80.00
78 Marc-Edouard Vlasic/22	15.00	30.00
79 Ondrej Pavelec/24	30.00	80.00
80 Paul Bissonnette/22	20.00	50.00
81 Niklas Backstrom/22	20.00	50.00
82 Saku Koivu/20	40.00	80.00
83 Vincent Lecavalier/24	25.00	60.00
84 Tyler Ennis/18	30.00	80.00
85 Thomas Vanek/28	30.00	80.00
86 Stu Grimson/18	25.00	60.00
87 Scott Clemmensen/25	50.00	100.00
89 Grant Fuhr/21	30.00	80.00
90 Evgenii Dadonov/20	25.00	60.00
91 Milan Michalek/22	20.00	50.00
92 Marty McSorley/20	40.00	100.00
93 Chris Neil/23	20.00	50.00
94 Brett Hull/21	50.00	100.00
96 Frans Nielsen/22	20.00	50.00
97 Ray Bourque/17	30.00	80.00
98 Joe Pavelski/20	25.00	60.00
99 Jamie Benn/17	25.00	60.00
100 Curtis Glencross/25	30.00	80.00
101 Chris Kunitz/28	30.00	80.00
102 Derick Brassard/17	30.00	80.00
103 Marc-Andre Fleury/18	40.00	100.00
104 Henrik Lundqvist/15	75.00	125.00
105 Sidney Crosby/17	60.00	120.00
106 Ilya Kovalchuk/22	30.00	80.00
107 Andrei Markov/18	30.00	80.00
108 Keith Yandle/23	20.00	50.00
109 Corey Perry/18	30.00	80.00
110 David Backes/18	40.00	100.00
111 Scott Hartnell/18	20.00	50.00
112 Josh Gorges/15	25.00	60.00
113 Ray Emery/21	30.00	80.00
114 Taylor Hall/20	90.00	150.00
115 Sam Gagner/24	25.00	60.00
116 Jaroslav Halak/20	25.00	60.00
117 Karl Alzner/19	25.00	60.00
118 Kyle Okposo/22	30.00	80.00
119 Jason Pominville/20	30.00	80.00
120 Corey Crawford/23	50.00	120.00

2012-13 Panini Prime Dual Jerseys

*PATCH/25: 1X TO 2.5X BASIC DUAL/200
*PATCH/25: .8X TO 2X BASIC DUAL/100
*PRIME/50: .6X TO 1.5X BASIC DUAL/200
*PRIME/50: .5X TO 1.2X BASIC DUAL/100
*PRIME/25: .8X TO 2X BASIC DUAL/200
*PRIME/25: .6X TO 1.5X BASIC DUAL/50-100

Card	Low	High
1 A.Aliu/S.Baertschi/200	5.00	12.00
2 M.Brodeur/I.Kovalchuk/200	6.00	15.00
3 J.Rynnas/C.Ashton/200	2.50	6.00
4 R.Mayer/C.Price/200	15.00	40.00
5 R.Smith/R.Garbutt/200	5.00	12.00
6 T.Selanne/J.Jagr/100	15.00	40.00
7 J.Brown/S.Stamkos/200	10.00	25.00
8 D.Byfuglien/O.Pavelec/100	6.00	15.00
9 A.Ovechkin/B.Holtby/100	8.00	20.00
10 C.Kreider/D.Stepan/200	5.00	12.00
11 C.Fowler/J.Zucker/200	5.00	12.00
12 C.Goloubef/J.Benn/200	4.00	10.00
13 C.Hodgson/P.Subban/100	10.00	25.00
14 G.Howe/M.Messier/15		
15 R.Hextall/M.Brodeur/200	10.00	25.00
16 J.Quick/W.Mitchell/200	8.00	20.00
17 M.Richards/D.King/100	5.00	12.00
18 R.Nash/M.Gaborik/100	6.00	15.00
19 C.Cizikas/J.Tavares/100	5.00	12.00
20 M.Fleury/C.Kunitz/100	10.00	25.00
21 M.Duchene/M.Connolly/100	6.00	15.00
22 T.Barrie/E.Johnson/200	5.00	12.00
23 T.Bozak/R.Hamilton/200	4.00	10.00
24 J.Zucker/T.Cuma/200	3.00	8.00
25 J.Allen/J.Schwartz/200	8.00	20.00
26 V.Lecavalier/D.Legwand/200	4.00	10.00
27 R.Sheahan/P.Datsyuk/200	6.00	15.00
28 B.Bollig/J.Toews/100	12.00	30.00
29 Sidney Crosby Dual/200	15.00	40.00
30 B.Gainey/P.Roy/100	10.00	25.00
31 P.Roy/J.Vanbiesbrouck/100	10.00	25.00
32 J.Mullen/J.Nieuwendyk/100	6.00	15.00
33 J.Silfverberg/M.Stone/200	5.00	12.00
34 M.Stone/K.Yandle/200	5.00	12.00
35 A.Joudrey/B.Marchand/200	6.00	15.00
36 M.Messier/S.Yzerman/50	12.00	30.00
37 R.Miller/B.Orpik/200	5.00	12.00
38 P.Datsyuk/B.Seabrook/200	6.00	15.00
39 D.Briere/D.Krejci/200	5.00	12.00
40 K.Alzner/C.Kunitz/200	5.00	12.00
41 K.Timonen/M.Staal/200	4.00	10.00
42 M.Watkins/M.Donovan/200	2.50	6.00
43 R.Brind'Amour/A.Hemsky/200	4.00	10.00
44 M.Hossa/M.Hejduk/100	5.00	12.00
45 S.Hunwick/D.Prout/200	2.50	6.00
46 M.Stone/M.Stone/200	5.00	12.00
47 E.Lindros/P.Falloon/200	8.00	20.00
48 M.Lemieux/P.Roy/100	15.00	40.00
49 P.Roy/M.Brodeur/100	15.00	40.00
50 B.Hull/M.Lemieux/100	15.00	40.00

2012-13 Panini Prime Gloves

Card	Low	High
1 Brandon Dubinsky	8.00	20.00
2 Brett Hull	12.00	30.00
3 Claude Giroux	12.00	30.00
4 Dany Heatley	10.00	25.00
5 Derek Stepan	10.00	25.00
6 Igor Larionov	15.00	40.00
7 Ilya Kovalchuk	12.00	30.00
8 James van Riemsdyk	12.00	30.00
9 Jeff Carter	12.00	30.00
10 Joffrey Lupul	10.00	25.00
11 Luc Robitaille	12.00	30.00
12 Matt Read	10.00	25.00
13 Matthew Carle	10.00	25.00
14 Mike Richards	12.00	30.00
15 Milan Hejduk	10.00	25.00
16 Patrick Kane	25.00	60.00
17 Sean Couturier	12.00	30.00
18 Marian Gaborik	12.00	30.00
19 Joe Thornton	12.00	30.00
20 Chris Chelios	12.00	30.00

2012-13 Panini Prime Namesakes Autographs

Card	Low	High
2 Andrew Joudrey/75	6.00	15.00
4 Cal Clutterbuck/75	10.00	25.00
5 Casey Cizikas/75	12.00	30.00
6 Chet Pickard/75	12.00	30.00
7 Chris Kreider/75	12.00	30.00
8 Daniel Carcillo/75	12.00	30.00
9 Gustav Nyquist/75	25.00	50.00
11 Jaden Schwartz/75	12.00	30.00
12 Jakob Silfverberg/75	20.00	40.00
13 James Reimer/75	15.00	40.00
14 James van Riemsdyk/75	15.00	30.00
15 Michael Stone/75	6.00	15.00
16 Raphael Diaz/75	10.00	25.00
18 Roman Josi/75	10.00	25.00
19 Ryan Garbutt/75	6.00	15.00
20 Ryan Hamilton/75	6.00	15.00
21 Scott Glennie/75	6.00	15.00
22 Sven Baertschi/75	8.00	20.00
23 Tyson Barrie/75	12.00	30.00
24 Brayden Schenn/75	15.00	40.00
25 Brett Hull/25	30.00	60.00
26 Cory Emmerton/75	12.00	30.00
27 Derek Roy/75	8.00	20.00
28 Jhonas Enroth/75	10.00	25.00
29 Jimmy Howard/75	25.00	50.00
30 Jordan Nolan/75	15.00	40.00
32 Nazem Kadri/75	25.00	50.00
33 Tony Esposito/75	20.00	40.00
34 Zach Parise/75	25.00	50.00
35 Vincent Lecavalier/75	15.00	30.00
37 Gabriel Dumont/75	12.00	30.00
38 Harri Sateri/75	12.00	30.00
40 J.T. Brown/75	6.00	15.00
41 John Tavares/25	40.00	80.00
42 Mark Stone/75	12.00	30.00
44 Mike Smith/75	15.00	40.00
45 Akim Aliu/75	6.00	15.00
46 Andrew Ladd/75	8.00	20.00
47 Travis Turnbull/75	15.00	40.00
48 Lane MacDermid/75	12.00	30.00

2012-13 Panini Prime Numbersakes Autographs

Card	Low	High
3 Joe Sakic/25	40.00	80.00
4 Chris Kreider/25	40.00	80.00
8 Sven Baertschi/25	15.00	40.00
9 Jakob Silfverberg/25	15.00	40.00
11 John Tavares/25	40.00	80.00
13 Leland Irving/25	12.00	30.00
14 Loui Eriksson/25	15.00	40.00
15 Cory Schneider/25	15.00	40.00
19 Alex Pietrangelo/25	20.00	50.00
21 Pavel Datsyuk/25	25.00	60.00
22 Martin St. Louis/25	20.00	50.00
23 Ben Scrivens/25	15.00	40.00
24 Eric Lindros/25	50.00	100.00
25 Steve Yzerman/25	50.00	100.00
27 Jaden Schwartz/25	30.00	60.00
28 Reilly Smith/25	25.00	50.00
29 John LeClair/25	30.00	60.00
30 Phil Kessel/25	25.00	60.00
31 Ryan Johansen/25	25.00	60.00
32 Brandon Saad/25	30.00	60.00
33 Sean Couturier/25	15.00	40.00
34 Alex Ovechkin/25	50.00	120.00
36 Jordan Eberle/25	40.00	80.00
37 Joe Pavelski/25	20.00	50.00
38 Jake Allen/25	40.00	100.00
40 Mika Zibanejad/25	15.00	40.00
41 Zach Parise/25	20.00	50.00
42 Ryan Garbutt/25	10.00	25.00
43 Ryan Miller/25	20.00	50.00
44 Michael Stone/25	15.00	40.00
45 Mike Smith/25	20.00	40.00
46 Ron Francis/25	25.00	60.00
47 Eric Staal/25	15.00	40.00
48 Tyson Barrie/25	15.00	40.00
49 Brad Boyes/25	12.00	30.00
50 Jordan Nolan/25	15.00	40.00

2012-13 Panini Prime Prime Time Rookies Jersey Autographs

Card	Low	High
1 Ryan Hamilton/50	4.00	10.00
2 Jussi Rynnas/50	4.00	10.00
3 Carter Ashton/50	3.00	8.00
4 J.T. Brown/50	4.00	10.00
5 Jake Allen	12.00	30.00
(inserted in 2013-14 Panini Prime)		
6 Jaden Schwartz/50	8.00	20.00
7 Tyson Sexsmith/50	8.00	20.00
8 Michael Stone/50	4.00	10.00
9 Brandon Manning/50	4.00	10.00
10 Mark Stone/50	8.00	20.00
11 Jakob Silfverberg/50	8.00	20.00
12 Chris Kreider/50	12.50	25.00
13 Matt Watkins/50	4.00	10.00
14 Matt Donovan/50	4.00	10.00
15 Casey Cizikas/50	6.00	15.00
16 Aaron Ness/50	4.00	10.00
18 Robert Mayer/50	5.00	12.00
19 Gabriel Dumont/50	8.00	20.00
20 Tyler Cuma/50	4.00	10.00
21 Kris Foucault/50	4.00	10.00
22 Jason Zucker/50	5.00	12.00
23 Chay Genoway/50	4.00	10.00
24 Jordan Nolan/50	4.00	10.00
25 Colby Robak/50	4.00	10.00
26 Philippe Cornet/50	4.00	10.00
27 Riley Sheahan/50	4.00	10.00
28 Scott Glennie/50	4.00	10.00
29 Ryan Garbutt/50	4.00	10.00
30 Reilly Smith/50	8.00	20.00
31 Brenden Dillon/50	6.00	15.00
32 Shawn Hunwick/50	4.00	10.00
33 Dalton Prout/50	4.00	10.00
34 Cody Goloubef/50	4.00	10.00
35 Andrew Joudrey/50	4.00	10.00
36 Tyson Barrie/50	8.00	20.00
37 Mike Connolly/50	4.00	10.00
39 Jeremy Welsh/50	4.00	10.00
40 Sven Baertschi/50	5.00	12.00
41 Akim Aliu/50	4.00	10.00
42 Travis Turnbull/50	4.00	10.00
43 Lane MacDermid/50	4.00	10.00
44 Carter Camper/50	3.00	8.00
45 Torey Krug/50	20.00	40.00
46 Michael Hutchinson/50	8.00	20.00
47 Max Sauve/50	4.00	10.00
48 Mat Clark/50	4.00	10.00

2012-13 Panini Prime Prime Time Rookies Jerseys

Card	Low	High
1 Ryan Hamilton/99	2.00	5.00
2 Jussi Rynnas/99	2.00	5.00
3 Carter Ashton/99	1.50	4.00
4 J.T. Brown/99	2.00	5.00
5 Jake Allen/99	6.00	15.00
6 Jaden Schwartz/99	4.00	10.00
7 Tyson Sexsmith/99	2.00	5.00
8 Michael Stone/99	2.00	5.00
9 Brandon Manning/99	3.00	8.00
10 Mark Stone/99	4.00	10.00
11 Jakob Silfverberg/99	5.00	12.00
12 Chris Kreider/99	4.00	10.00
13 Matt Watkins/99	2.00	5.00
14 Matt Donovan/99	2.00	5.00
15 Casey Cizikas/99	2.00	5.00
16 Aaron Ness/99	2.00	5.00
17 Chet Pickard/25	3.00	8.00
18 Robert Mayer/99	5.00	12.00
19 Gabriel Dumont/99	3.00	8.00
20 Tyler Cuma/99	2.00	5.00
21 Kris Foucault/99	2.50	6.00
22 Jason Zucker/99	2.50	6.00
23 Chay Genoway/99	2.00	5.00
24 Jordan Nolan/99	2.00	5.00
25 Colby Robak/99	2.00	5.00
26 Philippe Cornet/99	2.00	5.00
27 Riley Sheahan/99	2.00	5.00
28 Scott Glennie/99	2.00	5.00
29 Ryan Garbutt/99	2.00	5.00
30 Reilly Smith/99	4.00	10.00
31 Brenden Dillon/99	2.00	5.00
32 Shawn Hunwick/99	2.00	5.00
33 Dalton Prout/99	2.50	6.00
34 Cody Goloubef/99	2.00	5.00
35 Andrew Joudrey/99	2.00	5.00
36 Tyson Barrie/99	4.00	10.00
37 Mike Connolly/99	2.00	5.00
38 Brandon Bollig/99	3.00	8.00
39 Jeremy Welsh/99	2.00	5.00
40 Sven Baertschi/99	2.50	6.00
41 Akim Aliu/99	2.00	5.00
42 Travis Turnbull/99	2.00	5.00
43 Lane MacDermid/99	2.00	5.00
44 Carter Camper/99	1.50	4.00
45 Torey Krug/99	8.00	20.00
46 Michael Hutchinson/99	4.00	10.00
47 Max Sauve/99	2.00	5.00
48 Mat Clark/99	2.00	5.00

2012-13 Panini Prime Quad Jerseys

STATED PRINT RUN 25-50
*PRIME/15: 1X TO 2.5X BASIC JSY/50
*PRIME/15: .8X TO 2X BASIC JSY/25

Card	Low	High
1 Cmpr/Hmltn/Ryn/Htchn/50	12.00	30.00
2 Howe/Hull/Dnne/Grtnr/25	25.00	50.00
3 Mess/Brque/Coffy/Frncis/50	15.00	40.00
4 Prngr/Tws/Lngo/Mrlau/50	15.00	40.00
5 Rchrd/Brdr/Mrrw/Weber/50	12.00	30.00
6 Ltch/LeClr/LaFn/Mdano/50	10.00	25.00
7 Lemx/Fhr/ulet/Bourque/50	25.00	60.00
8 Clarke/Brbr/Prnt/Leach/50	15.00	40.00
9 Kerr/Hextall/Messr/Fuhr/50	12.00	30.00
10 Lemx/Francis/Jagr/Cofy/50	25.00	60.00
11 Yzer/Shan/Larnv/Lidstrm/50	12.00	30.00
12 Ovech/Mlkn/Staff/Dbnk/50	30.00	80.00
13 Ryan/Price/Kopitar/Staal/50	25.00	60.00
14 Belfr/Gilmr/Hwe/Nieuw/50	10.00	25.00
15 Hull/Leetch/Robit/Yzer/50	15.00	40.00
16 Jdrey/Golbf/Prt/Hnwck/50	6.00	15.00
17 Bchm/Hiller/Getzlf/Seln/50	15.00	40.00
18 Stl/Stl/Schnn/Schenn/50	8.00	20.00
19 Koivu/Koivu/Sdin/Sdin/50	10.00	25.00
20 Piet/Ovech/Brmstv/Tngy/50	30.00	80.00

2012-13 Panini Prime Showcase Jersey Prime Colors

*PATCH/15: .8X TO 2X BASIC JSY/35

Card	Low	High
1 Carter Ashton	3.00	8.00
2 Jake Allen	12.00	30.00
3 Jussi Rynnas	4.00	10.00
4 Scott Glennie	4.00	10.00
5 Reilly Smith	8.00	20.00
6 Chris Kreider	8.00	20.00
7 Tyson Barrie	8.00	20.00
8 Jaden Schwartz	8.00	20.00

2012-13 Panini Prime Showcase Swatches

Chris Kreider/25 8.00 20.00
Jaden Schwartz/25 8.00 20.00
Pat Falloon/25 6.00 15.00
Gordie Howe/10
Alex Ovechkin/25 15.00 40.00
Al Iafrate/25 12.00 30.00
Al MacInnis/25 8.00 20.00
Alex Tanguay/25 6.00 15.00
Andrew Cogliano/25 6.00 15.00
0 Artem Anisimov/25 8.00 20.00
1 Akim Aliu/25 6.00 15.00
2 Anze Kopitar/25 15.00 40.00
3 Barret Jackman/25 8.00 20.00
4 Bernie Nicholls/25 8.00 20.00
5 Bobby Clarke/25 15.00 40.00
6 Bobby Ryan/25 10.00 25.00
7 Zach Parise/25 10.00 25.00
8 Wojtek Wolski/25 6.00 15.00
9 Wayne Simmonds/25 15.00 40.00
20 Wade Redden/25 6.00 15.00
21 Vincent Lecavalier/25 8.00 20.00
22 Valtteri Filppula/25 10.00 25.00
23 Tyson Barrie/25 8.00 20.00
24 Tyler Seguin/25 15.00 40.00
25 Tuukka Rask/25 10.00 25.00
26 Ilya Kovalchuk/25 10.00 25.00
27 Teemu Selanne/25 12.00 30.00
28 Taylor Hall/25 20.00 50.00
29 Stu Grimson/25 10.00 25.00
30 Steven Stamkos/25 20.00 50.00
31 Steve Yzerman/25 30.00 80.00
32 Sidney Crosby/25 40.00 80.00
33 Shea Weber/25 8.00 20.00
34 Shawn Horcoff/25 8.00 20.00
35 Saku Koivu/25 10.00 25.00
36 Ryan Miller/25 10.00 25.00
37 Ryan Kesler/25 10.00 25.00
38 Brandon Bollig/25 8.00 20.00
39 Brandon Prust/25 12.00 30.00
40 Brendan Shanahan/25 12.00 30.00
41 Brian Elliott/25 8.00 20.00
42 Jake Allen/25 12.00 30.00
43 James van Riemsdyk/25 10.00 25.00
44 Jamie Benn/25 12.00 30.00
45 Jonathan Quick/25 15.00 40.00
46 Jussi Rynnas/25 12.00 30.00
47 Luke Schenn/25 6.00 15.00
48 Martin Brodeur/25 20.00 50.00
49 Martin St. Louis/25 10.00 25.00
50 Nicklas Lidstrom/25 15.00 40.00
51 Ondrej Pavelec/25 10.00 25.00
52 Pavel Datsyuk/25 12.00 30.00
53 Ron Francis/25 12.00 30.00
54 Ryan Garbutt/25 6.00 15.00
55 Cal Clutterbuck/25 10.00 25.00
56 Cam Neely/25 10.00 25.00
57 Carey Price/25 30.00 80.00
58 Claude Giroux/25 15.00 40.00
59 Corey Perry/25 10.00 25.00
60 James Neal/25 10.00 25.00
61 Joe Thornton/25 12.00 30.00
62 Jonathan Toews/25 20.00 50.00
63 Sven Baertschi/25 5.00 12.00
64 Casey Cizikas/25 8.00 20.00
65 Brenden Morrow/25 8.00 20.00
66 Dany Heatley/25 8.00 20.00
67 Frans Nielsen/25 6.00 15.00
68 Jeremy Roenick/25 10.00 25.00
69 Joe Sakic/25 15.00 40.00
70 John LeClair/25 10.00 25.00
71 Kari Lehtonen/25 8.00 20.00
72 Matt Stajan/25 8.00 20.00
73 Milan Lucic/25 10.00 25.00
74 Henrik Lundqvist/25 12.00 30.00
75 Nikolai Kulemin/25 8.00 20.00
76 Patrick Marleau/25 10.00 25.00
77 Pekka Rinne/25 12.00 30.00
78 Roberto Luongo/25 10.00 25.00
79 Dustin Brown/25 10.00 25.00
80 Paul Bissonnette/25 12.00 30.00

2012-13 Panini Prime Signatures

*GOLD/25: .5X TO 1.2X BASIC AU/99
1 Adam Henrique/99 6.00 15.00
2 Akim Aliu/99 5.00 12.00
3 Alex Ovechkin/25 30.00 80.00
5 Andrew Joudrey/99 5.00 12.00
6 Andrew Ladd/99 6.00 15.00
7 Bobby Ryan/99 6.00 15.00
8 Brad Richards/50 6.00 15.00
10 Brayden Schenn/99 6.00 15.00
11 Brenden Dillon/99 5.00 12.00
12 Brett Hull/25 25.00 50.00
13 Cal Clutterbuck/99 6.00 15.00
14 Casey Cizikas/99 5.00 12.00
15 Chet Pickard/99 5.00 12.00
16 Chris Chelios/25 10.00 25.00
17 Chris Kreider/99 6.00 15.00
18 Cody Hodgson/99 4.00 10.00
19 Cory Schneider/99 5.00 12.00
20 Craig Smith/99 4.00 10.00
21 Eric Staal/50 8.00 20.00
23 Gabriel Bourque/99
(inserted in 2013-14 Panini Prime)
24 Gordie Howe/10
25 Gustav Nyquist/99 8.00 20.00
26 J.T. Brown/99 4.00 10.00
27 Jaden Schwartz/99 6.00 15.00
28 Jakob Silfverberg/99 6.00 15.00
29 James Neal/99 8.00 20.00
30 Jamie Benn/50 5.00 12.00
(inserted in 2013-14 Panini Prime)
31 Jarome Iginla/50 20.00 40.00
32 Joe Pavelski/99 6.00 15.00
33 Joe Sakic/25 25.00 50.00
34 John LeClair/99 12.00 30.00
35 John Tavares/50 20.00 40.00
36 Jonathan Quick/50 10.00 25.00
37 Jordin Tootoo/99 6.00 15.00
38 Keith Primeau/99 5.00 12.00
39 Keith Yandle/99 6.00 15.00
40 Kyle Turris/99 4.00 10.00
41 Leland Irving/99 5.00 12.00
42 Loui Eriksson/99 3.00 8.00
(inserted in 2013-14 Panini Prime)
43 Marc-Andre Fleury/50 10.00 25.00
44 Mark Messier/25 25.00 60.00
45 Mark Stone/99 10.00 25.00
47 Martin St. Louis/50 6.00 15.00
48 Matt Duchene/50 8.00 20.00
49 Matt Read/99 5.00 12.00
50 Michael Stone/99 5.00 12.00
51 Mika Zibanejad/25 10.00 25.00
52 Michael Hutchinson/99 6.00 15.00
53 Mike Smith/99 6.00 15.00
54 Nazem Kadri/99 6.00 15.00
55 Reilly Smith/99 10.00 25.00
56 Riley Sheahan/99 5.00 12.00
57 Robert Mayer/99 4.00 10.00
58 Ryan Garbutt/99 5.00 12.00
59 Ryan Johansen/99 5.00 12.00
60 Ryan Nugent-Hopkins/99 10.00 25.00
62 Simon Despres/99 5.00 12.00
64 Sven Baertschi/99 4.00 10.00
65 Taylor Hall/50 20.00 40.00
66 Tomas Vokoun/50 12.00 30.00
67 Tony Esposito/50 15.00 40.00
68 Tyson Barrie/99 6.00 15.00
69 Zac Dalpe/99 4.00 10.00
70 Zack Kassian/99 5.00 12.00

2012-13 Panini Prime Signatures Duals

*GOLD/25: .6X TO 1.5X BASIC DUAL/50
1 C.Hagelin/C.Kreider/50 15.00 40.00
2 J.Schwartz/J.Allen/50 10.00 25.00
3 C.Ashton/J.Rynnas/50 8.00 20.00
5 L.Irving/S.Baertschi/50 6.00 15.00
6 C.Cizikas/J.Tavares/50 10.00 25.00
8 M.Richter/B.Leetch/25
9 M.Read/S.Couturier/50 12.00 30.00
11 R.Smith/B.Dillon/50 20.00 50.00
12 T.Barrie/G.Landeskog/50 12.00 30.00
13 J.Rynnas/F.Potvin/50 20.00 50.00
14 R.Nugent-Hopkins/P.Cornet/50 12.00 30.00
16 J.Brown/B.Connolly/50 12.00 30.00
17 K.Foucault/J.Zucker/50 8.00 20.00
18 C.Pickard/P Rinne/50 8.00 20.00
19 A.Kopitar/J.Nolan/50 20.00 50.00
20 J.Neal/M.Fleury/50 12.00 30.00

2012-13 Panini Prime Signatures Trios

1 Kreidr/Slfvrbrg/Btsch/25 25.00 60.00
3 Dilln/Smth/Glennie/25 10.00 25.00
6 Jsph/Ryns/Rmer/25 15.00 40.00
7 Cizikas/Wtkns/Ness/25 8.00 20.00
8 Quick/Brwn/Noln/25 25.00 60.00

2012-13 Panini Prime Skates

1 Adam Henrique 20.00 50.00
2 Igor Larionov 15.00 40.00
3 Joe Nieuwendyk 10.00 25.00
4 Mike Richards 10.00 25.00
5 Zach Parise 10.00 25.00
6 Alex Ovechkin 30.00 80.00
7 Ilya Kovalchuk 10.00 25.00
8 Brad Richards 15.00 40.00
9 Dan Girardi 6.00 15.00
10 Carl Hagelin 12.00 30.00
11 Joe Pavelski 10.00 25.00
12 Marian Gaborik 10.00 25.00

2012-13 Panini Prime Trios Jerseys

*PRIME/15-25: .8X TO 2X BASIC INSERTS/100
1 Sekera/Enroth/Ennis 6.00 15.00
2 Hodgson/Turnbull/Miller 5.00 12.00
3 Clarke/Lindros/Primeau 8.00 20.00
4 Schenn/Manning/Couturier 6.00 15.00
5 Richards/Staal/Lundqvist 6.00 15.00
6 Hagelin/Kreider/Girardi 6.00 15.00
7 Neely/Bourque/Middleton 10.00 25.00
8 Seguin/Rask/Chara 8.00 20.00
9 Hall/Hemsky/Horcoff 12.00 30.00
10 RNH/Cornet/Jones 6.00 15.00
11 Pacioretty/Gorges/Eller 6.00 15.00
12 Gionta/Markov/Dumont 8.00 20.00
13 Mayer/Price/Roy 10.00 25.00
14 Ness/Nielsen/LaFontaine 6.00 15.00
15 Keith/Emery/Crawford 10.00 25.00
16 Tavares/Donovan/Watkins 5.00 12.00
17 Cizikas/Nabokov/Visnovsky 5.00 12.00
18 Lindros/Ovechkin/RNH 10.00 25.00
19 Marleau/Ryan/Seguin 8.00 20.00
20 Toews/Duchene/LaFont 10.00 25.00
21 Miller/Kreider/Kessel 6.00 15.00
22 Eriksson/Landskg/Slfvrbrg 6.00 15.00
23 Hagelin/Alfredsson/Lidstrom 6.00 15.00
24 Allen/Smith/Goloubef 6.00 15.00
25 Barrie/Garbutt/Nolan 6.00 15.00
26 Datsyuk/Bryzglv/Ovechkin 6.00 15.00
27 Malkin/Kovalchuk/Kulemin 8.00 20.00
28 Allen/Schwartz/Jackman 6.00 15.00
29 Koivu/Perry/Clark 6.00 15.00
30 Iafrate/MacInnis/Chara 8.00 20.00

2013-14 Panini Prime

1-100 STATED PRINT RUN 299
101-200 STATED PRINT RUN 199
1 Ryan Getzlaf 3.00 8.00
2 Jakob Silfverberg 1.50 4.00
3 Corey Perry 2.00 5.00
4 Patrice Bergeron 2.50 6.00
5 Jarome Iginla 2.00 5.00
6 Torey Krug 2.50 6.00
7 Tuukka Rask 2.00 5.00
8 Cody Hodgson 2.00 5.00
9 Ryan Miller 2.00 5.00
10 Matt Moulson 1.50 4.00
11 Sven Baertschi 1.50 4.00
12 Mikael Backlund 1.50 4.00
13 Curtis Glencross 1.25 3.00
14 Eric Staal 2.50 6.00
15 Cam Ward 2.00 5.00
16 Nathan Gerbe 1.25 3.00
17 Jonathan Toews 4.00 10.00
18 Patrick Kane 4.00 10.00
19 Brandon Saad 2.00 5.00
20 Corey Crawford 2.50 6.00
21 Gabriel Landeskog 1.50 4.00
22 Matt Duchene 2.00 5.00
23 Patrick Roy 3.00 8.00
24 Joe Sakic 3.00 8.00
25 R.J. Umberger 1.25 3.00
26 Ryan Johansen 2.50 6.00
27 Sergei Bobrovsky 2.00 5.00
28 Tyler Seguin 3.00 8.00
29 Kari Lehtonen 1.50 4.00
30 Mike Modano 3.00 8.00
31 Pavel Datsyuk 2.50 6.00
32 Jimmy Howard 2.00 5.00
33 Gordie Howe 3.00 8.00
34 Steve Yzerman 4.00 10.00
35 Ryan Nugent-Hopkins 2.00 5.00
36 Taylor Hall 4.00 10.00
37 Jordan Eberle 2.00 5.00
38 Tim Thomas 2.00 5.00
39 Scottie Upshall 1.25 3.00
40 Brad Boyes 1.25 3.00
41 Jonathan Quick 3.00 8.00
42 Luc Robitaille 2.00 5.00
43 Anze Kopitar 3.00 8.00
44 Mikko Koivu 1.50 4.00
45 Zach Parise 2.00 5.00
46 Nino Niederreiter 1.25 3.00
47 Carey Price 6.00 15.00
48 Max Pacioretty 2.00 5.00
49 P.K. Subban 3.00 8.00
50 Pekka Rinne 2.50 6.00
51 Shea Weber 1.50 4.00
52 Colin Wilson 1.50 4.00
53 Jaromir Jagr 4.00 10.00
54 Martin Brodeur 4.00 10.00
55 Adam Henrique 2.00 5.00
56 John Tavares 4.00 10.00
57 Casey Cizikas 1.25 3.00
58 Thomas Vanek 2.00 5.00
59 Henrik Lundqvist 2.50 6.00
60 Brad Richards 2.00 5.00
61 Chris Kreider 2.00 5.00
62 Mark Messier 2.50 6.00
63 Bobby Ryan 2.00 5.00
64 Craig Anderson 2.00 5.00
65 Erik Karlsson 4.00 10.00
66 Vincent Lecavalier 1.50 4.00
67 Claude Giroux 2.00 5.00
68 Steve Mason 1.50 4.00
69 Eric Lindros 3.00 8.00
70 Mike Smith 2.00 5.00
71 Michael Stone 1.50 4.00
72 Keith Yandle 2.00 5.00
73 Sidney Crosby 4.00 10.00
74 Evgeni Malkin 6.00 15.00
75 Marc-Andre Fleury 3.00 8.00
76 Mario Lemieux 6.00 15.00
77 Derek Roy 1.50 4.00
78 Jaroslav Halak 2.00 5.00
79 Brett Hull 2.00 5.00
80 Patrick Marleau 2.00 5.00
81 Joe Thornton 2.00 5.00
82 Joe Pavelski 2.00 5.00
83 Antti Niemi 1.50 4.00
84 Martin St. Louis 2.00 5.00
85 Ben Bishop 2.00 5.00
86 Steven Stamkos 4.00 10.00
87 Dion Phaneuf 2.00 5.00
88 Phil Kessel 2.50 6.00
89 Nazem Kadri 2.00 5.00
90 James Reimer 2.00 5.00
91 Pavel Bure 2.50 6.00
92 Roberto Luongo 2.00 5.00
93 Ryan Kesler 2.00 5.00
94 Daniel Sedin 2.00 5.00
95 Alex Ovechkin 8.00 20.00
96 Braden Holtby 3.00 8.00
97 Nicklas Backstrom 3.00 8.00
98 Andrew Ladd 2.00 5.00
99 Dustin Byfuglien 2.00 5.00
100 Mark Scheifele 2.50 6.00
101 Viktor Fasth JSY AU RC 5.00 12.00
102 Jack Campbell JSY AU RC 4.00 10.00
103 Austin Watson JSY AU RC 4.00 10.00
104 Nathan Beaulieu JSY AU RC 4.00 10.00
106 Ryan Spooner JSY AU RC 5.00 12.00
107 Ryan Murphy JSY AU RC 5.00 12.00
108 Charlie Coyle JSY AU RC 5.00 12.00
109 Jordan Schroeder JSY AU RC 5.00 12.00
110 Igor Bobkov JSY AU RC 4.00 10.00
111 Beau Bennett JSY AU RC 6.00 15.00
112 Scott Laughton JSY AU RC 5.00 12.00
113 Emerson Etem JSY AU RC 5.00 12.00
114 Tyler Toffoli JSY AU RC 10.00 25.00
115 Quinton Howden JSY AU RC 4.00 10.00
116 Justin Schultz JSY AU RC 5.00 12.00
117 Alex Galchenyuk JSY AU RC 25.00 60.00
118 Jonathan Huberdeau JSY AU RC 10.00 25.00
119 Dougie Hamilton JSY AU RC 8.00 20.00
120 Nail Yakupov JSY AU RC 15.00 40.00
121 Tom Wilson JSY AU RC 8.00 20.00
122 Nicklas Jensen JSY AU RC 4.00 10.00
123 Leo Komarov JSY AU RC 5.00 12.00
124 Cory Conacher JSY AU RC 3.00 8.00
125 Alex Killorn JSY AU RC 5.00 12.00
126 Dmitrij Jaskin JSY AU RC 5.00 12.00
127 V.Tarasenko JSY AU RC EXCH 25.00 60.00
129 J.T. Miller JSY AU RC 5.00 12.00
130 Thomas Hickey JSY AU RC 4.00 10.00
131 Stefan Matteau JSY AU RC 4.00 10.00
132 Filip Forsberg JSY AU RC 12.00 30.00
133 Brendan Gallagher JSY AU RC 15.00 40.00
134 Mikael Granlund JSY AU RC 8.00 20.00
135 Jonas Brodin JSY AU RC 4.00 10.00
137 Tanner Pearson JSY AU RC 5.00 12.00
138 Drew Shore JSY AU RC 4.00 10.00
139 Nick Bjugstad JSY AU RC 6.00 15.00
140 Petr Mrazek JSY AU RC 10.00 25.00
141 Danny DeKeyser JSY AU RC 6.00 15.00
143 Alex Chiasson JSY AU RC 5.00 12.00
144 Antoine Roussel JSY AU RC 5.00 12.00
145 Tomas Jurco JSY AU RC 8.00 20.00
146 Jared Staal JSY AU RC 5.00 12.00
147 Max Reinhart JSY AU RC 5.00 12.00
148 Mikhail Grigorenko JSY AU RC 5.00 12.00
149 Carl Soderberg JSY AU RC 5.00 12.00
150 Sami Vatanen JSY AU RC 5.00 12.00
151 Jacob Trouba JSY AU RC 8.00 20.00
152 Morgan Rielly JSY AU RC 12.00 30.00
153 Tomas Hertl JSY AU RC 12.00 30.00
154 John Gibson JSY AU RC 10.00 25.00
155 Tye McGinn JSY AU RC 5.00 12.00
156 Michael Raffl JSY AU RC 4.00 10.00
157 Seth Jones JSY AU RC 5.00 12.00
158 Michael Bournival JSY AU RC 5.00 12.00
159 Jamie Oleksiak JSY AU RC 4.00 10.00
160 Matt Dumba JSY AU RC 5.00 12.00
162 Aleksander Barkov JSY AU RC 12.00 30.00
163 Martin Jones JSY AU RC 10.00 25.00
164 Xavier Ouellet JSY AU RC 5.00 12.00
165 Valeri Nichushkin JSY AU RC 8.00 20.00
166 Christian Thomas JSY AU RC 4.00 10.00
167 Boone Jenner JSY AU RC 5.00 12.00
168 Hampus Lindholm JSY AU RC 6.00 15.00
169 Elias Lindholm JSY AU RC 8.00 20.00
170 Ryan Murray JSY AU RC 8.00 20.00
171 Sean Monahan JSY AU RC 8.00 20.00
172 Zemgus Girgensons JSY AU RC 10.00 25.00
173 Joakim Nordstrom JSY AU RC 4.00 10.00
174 Frederik Andersen JSY AU RC 8.00 20.00
176 Anthony Peluso JSY AU RC 3.00 8.00
177 Olli Maatta JSY AU RC 10.00 25.00
178 Nathan MacKinnon JSY AU RC 20.00 50.00
179 Philipp Grubauer JSY AU RC 6.00 15.00
180 Edward Pasquale JSY AU RC 3.00 8.00
181 Frank Corrado JSY AU RC 3.00 8.00
182 Jamie Devane JSY AU RC 4.00 10.00
184 Nikita Zadorov JSY AU RC 5.00 12.00
186 Richard Panik JSY AU RC 5.00 12.00
187 Nick Petrecki JSY AU RC 3.00 8.00
188 Chris Brown JSY AU RC 3.00 8.00
189 Brock Nelson JSY AU RC 5.00 12.00
190 Rickard Rakell JSY AU RC 5.00 12.00
191 Dylan McIlrath JSY AU RC 3.00 8.00
192 Kevin Connauton JSY AU RC 4.00 10.00
193 Magnus Hellberg JSY AU RC 5.00 12.00
194 Mark Arcobello JSY AU RC 5.00 12.00
195 Reto Berra JSY AU RC 5.00 12.00
196 Ryan Strome JSY AU RC 6.00 15.00
197 Cody Ceci JSY AU RC 4.00 10.00
198 Mark Pysyk JSY AU RC 5.00 12.00
199 Jon Merrill JSY AU RC 5.00 12.00

2013-14 Panini Prime Hologold

*101-148 ROOKIES/50: .6X TO 1.5X BASIC RC
178 Nathan MacKinnon JSY AU 50.00 120.00
179 Philipp Grubauer JSY AU 25.00 60.00

2013-14 Panini Prime Holosilver

*VETS/50: .5X TO 1.2X BASIC CARDS
*ROOKIES/50: .5X TO 1.2X BASIC CARDS
20 Corey Crawford 3.00 8.00
97 Nicklas Backstrom 4.00 10.00
117 Alex Galchenyuk JSY AU 75.00 150.00
178 Nathan MacKinnon JSY AU 30.00 80.00
179 Philipp Grubauer JSY AU 20.00 50.00

2013-14 Panini Prime Colors Logo

UNPRICED PRINT RUN 11-14
PCAB Alexandre Burrows/35 15.00 40.00
PCAF Adam Foote/21 30.00 60.00
PCAH Adam Henrique/69 15.00 40.00
PCAM Al MacInnis/23 50.00 100.00
PCAN Antti Niemi/35 15.00 40.00
PCAO Alex Ovechkin/30 40.00 100.00
PCAP Alex Pietrangelo/15 15.00 40.00
PCAT Alex Tanguay/23 12.00 30.00
PCAZ1 Anze Kopitar/31 25.00 60.00
PCAZ2 Anze Kopitar/33 30.00 80.00
PCBBA Bill Barber/16
PCBBE Brian Bellows/34 15.00 40.00
PCBD Brenden Dillon/38 12.00 30.00
PCBHO Braden Holtby/32 25.00 60.00
PCBHU Brett Hull/34 40.00 80.00
PCBLA Brooks Laich/17 12.00 30.00
PCBLI Bryan Little/56 25.00 60.00
PCBT Bryan Trottier/26 20.00 50.00
PCBW Blake Wheeler/36 10.00 25.00
PCCA Craig Anderson/32 12.00 30.00
PCCG Claude Giroux/41 30.00 80.00
PCCH Chris Higgins/31 10.00 25.00
PCCN Cam Neely/40 75.00 150.00
PCCP Carey Price/19 75.00 120.00
PCCSC Cory Schneider/53 12.00 30.00
PCCSM Craig Smith/17 25.00 60.00
PCDA Daniel Alfredsson/15 20.00 50.00
PCDBRO Dustin Brown/54 30.00 80.00
PCDBRU Damien Brunner/22 15.00 40.00
PCDBY Dustin Byfuglien/42 20.00 50.00
PCDD Devan Dubnyk/41 10.00 25.00
PCDH Dan Hamhuis/40 30.00 60.00
PCDKE Duncan Keith/19 50.00 100.00
PCDKR David Krejci/53 12.00 30.00
PCDP Dion Phaneuf/19 20.00 50.00
PCDR Derek Roy/46 15.00 40.00
PCDSED Daniel Sedin/52 25.00 60.00
PCDSET Devin Setoguchi/32 12.00 30.00
PCEC Erik Cole/17 15.00 40.00
PCEF Eric Fehr/21 20.00 50.00
PCEK Erik Karlsson/34 20.00 50.00
PCEM Evgeni Malkin/37 30.00 80.00
PCGB Gabriel Bourque/15 15.00 40.00
PCGC Guy Carbonneau/19 20.00 50.00
PCGF Grant Fuhr/15 75.00 150.00
PCGH Gordie Howe/15 75.00 150.00
PCGP Gilbert Perreault/18 40.00 80.00
PCHZ Henrik Zetterberg/31 40.00 100.00
PCJBA Josh Bailey/23 30.00 60.00
PCJBO Jay Bouwmeester/31 12.00 30.00
PCJE Jordan Eberle/61 20.00 50.00
PCJI Jarome Iginla/52 25.00 60.00
PCJJ Jaromir Jagr/36 40.00 100.00
PDJM Jacob Markstrom/22 15.00 40.00
PCJQ Jonathan Quick/47 25.00 60.00
PCJR2 Jeremy Roenick/80 20.00 50.00
PCJSA Joe Sakic/51 20.00 50.00
PCJSG Jean-Sebastien Giguere/34 30.00 60.00
PCJSP Jason Spezza/57 20.00 50.00
PCJTA John Tavares/22 40.00 100.00
PCJTO Jonathan Toews/30 150.00 250.00
PCJV John Vanbiesbrouck/17 75.00 150.00
PCKLE Kris Letang/40 30.00 80.00
PCKLEH Kari Lehtonen/77 20.00 50.00
PCKO Kyle Okposo/28 25.00 60.00
PCKP Keith Primeau/61 12.00 30.00
PCKV Kris Versteeg/30 20.00 50.00
PCLR1 Luc Robitaille/17 25.00 60.00
PCLR2 Luc Robitaille/39 30.00 60.00
PCLS Luke Schenn/17 12.00 30.00
PCMAF Marc-Andre Fleury/38 25.00 60.00
PCMBA Mikael Backlund/71 12.00 30.00
PCMBO Mikkel Boedker/36 12.00 30.00
PCMBR Martin Brodeur/24 40.00 100.00
PCMDI Marcel Dionne/24 75.00 150.00
PCMDU Matt Duchene/23 40.00 80.00
PCMEV Marc-Edouard Vlasic/43 12.00 30.00
PCMGI Mark Giordano/70 10.00 25.00
PCMGR Mike Green/53 15.00 40.00
PCMHAN Martin Hanzal/39 15.00 40.00
PCMHAV Marty Havlat/15 15.00 40.00
PCML Milan Lucic/32 12.00 30.00
PCMN Michal Neuvirth/17 40.00 80.00
PCMP Max Pacioretty/36 25.00 60.00
PCMS Matt Stajan/25 12.00 30.00
PCMZ Mats Zuccarello/18 25.00 50.00
PCNB Nicklas Backstrom/36 25.00 60.00
PCPAP P.A. Parenteau/22 12.00 30.00
PCPB Patrice Bergeron/42 30.00 80.00
PCPB1 Pavel Bure/21 40.00 80.00
PCPB2 Pavel Bure/23
PCPC Paul Coffey/36 15.00 40.00
PCPK Patrick Kane/25 40.00 80.00
PCPKS P.K. Subban/35 40.00 80.00
PCPR Pekka Rinne/28 20.00 50.00
PCPSS Patrick Sharp/32 100.00 200.00
PCPST Paul Stastny/73 25.00 60.00
PCRB Rob Blake/38 20.00 50.00
PCRF Ron Francis/83 12.00 30.00
PCRH Ron Hextall/20 25.00 60.00
PCRMA Ryan Malone/39 10.00 25.00
PCRMI Ryan Miller/22 20.00 50.00
PCSB Sean Bergenheim/24 20.00 50.00
PCSCL Scott Clemmensen/45 15.00 40.00
PCSCO Sean Couturier/46 60.00 120.00
PCSCR Sidney Crosby/32 50.00 100.00
PCSD Shane Doan/46 15.00 40.00
PCSS Steven Stamkos/21 100.00 200.00
PCST Shawn Thornton/35 25.00 60.00
PCSW Shea Weber/51 25.00 60.00
PCSY Steve Yzerman/16 100.00 200.00
PCTB Tom Barrasso/23 40.00 100.00
PCTJO T.J. Oshie/30 20.00 50.00
PCTKE Tylor Kennedy/31 15.00 40.00
PCTKR Torey Krug/18 25.00 60.00
PCTR Tuukka Rask/27 40.00 80.00
PCTS Tyler Seguin/56 25.00 60.00
PCTSE Teemu Selanne/43 30.00 80.00
PCTV Thomas Vanek/71 20.00 50.00

2013-14 Panini Prime Colors Numbers

UNPRICED PRINT RUN 2-14
PCAF Adam Foote/18 12.00 30.00
PCAK1 Anze Kopitar/15 30.00 60.00
PCAK2 Anze Kopitar/24 40.00 80.00
PCAM Al MacInnis/20 40.00 80.00
PCAT Alex Tanguay/22 12.00 30.00
PCBBE Brian Bellows/32 30.00 60.00
PCBHU Brett Hull/26 50.00 100.00
PCBLA Brooks Laich/15 20.00 40.00
PCBLI Bryan Little/18 12.00 30.00
PCCA Craig Anderson/18 15.00 40.00
PCCG Claude Giroux/35 50.00 100.00
PCCSC Cory Schneider/30 12.00 30.00
PCDBR Dustin Brown/65 25.00 50.00
PCDK David Krejci/47 15.00 40.00
PCDK Duncan Keith/16 20.00 50.00
PCDR Derek Roy/22 15.00 40.00
PCDSED Daniel Sedin/49 15.00 40.00
PCDSET Devin Setoguchi/18 15.00 40.00
PCEF Eric Fehr/19 12.00 30.00
PCEK Erik Karlsson/29 20.00 50.00
PCGF Grant Fuhr/15 30.00 60.00
PCHZ Henrik Zetterberg/51 15.00 40.00
PCJB Jay Bouwmeester/23 20.00 50.00
PCJE Josh Bailey/22 15.00 40.00
PCJE Jordan Eberle/54 25.00 60.00
PCJF Johan Franzen/32 15.00 40.00
PCJI Jarome Iginla/49 20.00 50.00
PCJJ Jaromir Jagr/46 40.00 80.00
PCJQ Jonathan Quick/59 40.00 80.00
PCJR1 Jeremy Roenick/15 40.00 80.00
PCJR2 Jeremy Roenick/31 20.00 50.00
PCJSA Joe Sakic/22
PCJSG Jean-Sebastien Giguere/24 15.00 40.00
PCJSP Jason Spezza/36 15.00 40.00
PCJTA John Tavares/19 40.00 100.00
PCKLEH Kari Lehtonen/82 10.00 25.00
PCKLET Kris Letang/32 25.00 60.00
PCKO Kyle Okposo/20 20.00 50.00
PCKP Keith Primeau/44 10.00 25.00
PCKV Kris Versteeg/24 15.00 40.00
PCLR1 Luc Robitaille/21 20.00 50.00
PCMAF Marc-Andre Fleury/17 30.00 80.00
PCMBA Mikael Backlund/37 12.00 30.00
PCMBO Mikkel Boedker/15 12.00 30.00
PCMBR Martin Brodeur/26 30.00 80.00
PCMD Matt Duchene/16 20.00 50.00
PCMD Marcel Dionne/22 50.00 100.00
PCMEV Marc-Edouard Vlasic/37 15.00 40.00
PCMGI Mark Giordano/24 15.00 40.00
PCMGR Mike Green/34 15.00 40.00
PCMHAV Marty Havlat/16 15.00 40.00
PCML Milan Lucic/26 15.00 40.00
PCMN Michal Neuvirth/15 15.00 40.00
PCMR Mike Richards/44 30.00 80.00
PCMZ Mats Zuccarello/24 15.00 40.00
PCNB Nicklas Backstrom/30 25.00 60.00
PCPAS Paul Stastny/69 12.00 30.00
PCPB Patrice Bergeron/38 40.00 80.00
PCPC Paul Coffey/37 15.00 40.00
PCPK Patrick Kane/57 40.00 80.00
PCPKS P.K. Subban/21 40.00 80.00
PCPR Pekka Rinne/26 20.00 50.00
PCPS Patrick Sharp/27 15.00 40.00
PCRF Ron Francis/64 15.00 40.00
PCRH Ron Hextall/18 25.00 50.00
PCRM Ryan Miller/25 15.00 40.00
PCSC Sean Couturier/26 25.00 60.00
PSCDL Scott Clemmensen/24 15.00 40.00
PCSCR Sidney Crosby/44 50.00 120.00
PCSK Saku Koivu/18 20.00 50.00
PCST Shawn Thornton/26 15.00 40.00
PCSW Shea Weber/32 12.00 30.00
PCTJO T.J. Oshie/20 25.00 50.00
PCTK Tyler Kennedy/32 10.00 25.00
PCTR Tuukka Rask/38 25.00 60.00
PCTSEG Tyler Seguin/58 15.00 40.00
PCTV Thomas Vanek/54 15.00 40.00

2013-14 Panini Prime Colors Patch

UNPRICED PRINT RUN 2-15
PCAB Alexandre Burrows/19
PCAF Adam Foote/38 30.00 60.00
PCAN Antti Niemi/20 15.00 40.00
PCAO Alex Ovechkin/17 75.00 150.00
PCAT Alex Tanguay/19 12.00 30.00
PCBD Brenden Dillon/18 15.00 40.00
PCBHU Brett Hull/18 40.00 80.00
PCBLA Brooks Laich/19 12.00 30.00
PCBW Blake Wheeler/15 20.00 50.00
PCCA Craig Anderson/35 15.00 40.00
PCCSC Cory Schneider/27 12.00 30.00
PCDA Daniel Alfredsson/18 20.00 50.00
PCDB Dustin Byfuglien/20 20.00 50.00
PCDBRO Dustin Brown/15 60.00 120.00
PCDH Dan Hamhuis/20 15.00 40.00
PCDK Duncan Keith/18 20.00 50.00
PCDKR David Krejci/25 30.00 60.00
PCDR Derek Roy/27 12.00 30.00
PCDSED Daniel Sedin/27 30.00 60.00
PCDSET Devin Setoguchi/17 30.00 60.00
PCEF Eric Fehr/22 12.00 30.00
PCEK Erik Karlsson/22 50.00 100.00
PCGC Guy Carbonneau/18 15.00 40.00
PCGL Gabriel Landeskog/22 30.00 60.00
PCJI Jarome Iginla/22 40.00 80.00
PCJJ Jaromir Jagr/15
PCJP Justin Peters/20 15.00 40.00
PCJS Joe Sakic/46
PCJS Jason Spezza/37 25.00 50.00
PCJSG Jean-Sebastien Giguere/15 25.00 50.00
PCJTA John Tavares/17 60.00 120.00
PCJTO Jonathan Toews/15 40.00 100.00
PCKLE Kari Lehtonen/54 15.00 40.00
PCKO Kyle Okposo/18 25.00 50.00
PCKP Keith Primeau/16 15.00 40.00
PCLC Logan Couture/19 30.00 60.00
PCMB Mikael Backlund/29 25.00 60.00
PCMDU Matt Duchene/28 25.00 60.00
PCMEV Marc-Edouard Vlasic/22 20.00 50.00
PCMGI Mark Giordano/17 30.00 60.00
PCMGR Mike Green/31 15.00 40.00
PCMLE Mario Lemieux/27 75.00 150.00
PCNB Nicklas Backstrom/26 25.00 60.00
PCPBE Patrice Bergeron/28 150.00 300.00
PCPC Paul Coffey/18
PCPH Patric Hornqvist/20 15.00 40.00
PCPK Patrick Kane/18 60.00 120.00
PCPR Pekka Rinne/16 30.00 60.00
PCPSH Patrick Sharp/17 40.00 80.00
PCPST Paul Stastny/43 15.00 40.00
PCRB Ray Bourque/17 100.00 200.00
PCRF Ron Francis/37 20.00 50.00
PCRM Ryan Miller/18 40.00 80.00
PCRS Ryan Suter/27 30.00 80.00
PCRW Ray Whitney/19 15.00 40.00
PCSCL Scott Clemmensen/20 15.00 40.00
PCSG Sergei Gonchar/16 20.00 50.00
PCSS Steven Stamkos/16 60.00 120.00
PCSW Shea Weber/25 30.00 60.00
PCTR Tuukka Rask/28 25.00 60.00
PCTSEG Tyler Seguin/28 25.00 60.00
PCTV Thomas Vanek/36 30.00 80.00

2013-14 Panini Prime Coverage

CVAO Alex Ovechkin 30.00 80.00
CVBG Brian Gionta 10.00 25.00
CVBH Brett Hull 15.00 40.00
CVBRI Brad Richards 12.00 30.00
CVCC Chris Chelios 12.00 30.00
CVCG Claude Giroux 20.00 50.00
CVDS Derek Stepan
CVILA Igor Larionov 12.00 30.00
CVJB Jamie Benn 10.00 25.00
CVJLU Joffrey Lupul 10.00 25.00
CVJT Joe Thornton 20.00 50.00
CVJTM J.T. Miller 12.00 30.00
CVKL Kris Letang 40.00 100.00
CVLR Luc Robitaille 12.00 30.00
CVMR Mike Richards 12.00 30.00
CVMT Marty Turco 12.00 30.00
CVPD Pascal Dupuis 8.00 20.00
CVPE Patrik Elias 12.00 30.00
CVPK Patrick Kane 25.00 50.00
CVTS Tyler Seguin

2013-14 Panini Prime Draft Hats

STATED PRINT RUN 4-25
DHAB Aleksander Barkov/25 12.00 30.00
DHEL Elias Lindholm/25 10.00 25.00
DHNM Nathan MacKinnon/25 50.00 120.00
DHNZ Nikita Zadorov/25
DHSJ Seth Jones/25 8.00 20.00
DHVN Valeri Nichushkin/20 8.00 20.00

2013-14 Panini Prime Dual Jerseys

*PATCH/25: 1.2X TO 3X JSY/150-200
*PRIME/50: .5X TO 1.2X JSY/150-200
*PRIME/25: .8X TO 2X JSY/100
DAB F.Andersen/I.Bobkov/200 6.00 15.00
DAP M.Arcobello/M.Pysyk/200 3.00 8.00
DBJ N.Backstrom/N.Jensen/200 6.00 15.00
DBL E.Belfour/R.Luongo/200 4.00 10.00
DBLE B.Bellows/M.Lemieux/200 12.00 30.00
DBM M.Messier/P.Bure/200 8.00 20.00
DCF M.A.Fleury/C.Crawford/200 8.00 20.00
DCG C.Ceci/E.Gryba/200 3.00 8.00
DCK Z.Chara/D.Keith/200 4.00 10.00
DGD M.Granlund/M.Dumba/200 4.00 10.00
DGS B.Gallagher/M.St.Louis/200 6.00 15.00
DHD S.Hartnell/S.Downie/200 4.00 10.00
DHH A.Henrique/T.Hall/200 4.00 10.00
DHHO G.Howe/M.Howe/100 12.00 30.00
DHM E.Hartzell/O.Maatta/200 6.00 15.00
DJH J.Jagr/T.Hertl/200 8.00 20.00
DJL B.Jenner/S.Laughton/200 4.00 10.00
DJO T.Jurco/X.Ouellet/200 4.00 10.00
DJR J.Jagr/J.Roenick/200 10.00 25.00
DKD P.Kessel/P.Datsyuk/150 5.00 12.00
DKG A.Kopitar/R.Getzlaf/200 5.00 12.00
DKM A.Killorn/N.MacKinnon/200 8.00 20.00
DLB H.Lundqvist/M.Brodeur/200 8.00 20.00
DLH H.Lindholm/T.Hertl/200 8.00 20.00
DLJ E.Lindholm/M.Jordan/200 4.00 12.00
DLM S.Laughton/T.McGinn/200 3.00 8.00
DLP E.Lindros/T.Pearson/200 6.00 15.00
DLT I.Larionov/V.Tretiak/200 8.00 20.00
DMJ M.Mazanec/S.Jones/200 5.00 12.00
DML J.Merrill/N.Lidstrom/200 4.00 10.00
DMM R.Murphy/R.Murray/200 3.00 8.00
DMR D.McIlrath/M.Rielly/200 4.00 10.00
DMY C.Murphy/K.Yandle/200 4.00 10.00
DNS B.Nelson/R.Strome/200 5.00 12.00
DON J.Oleksiak/V.Nichushkin/200 4.00 10.00
DOW A.Ovechkin/T.Wilson/200 15.00 40.00
DPT A.Peluso/J.Trouba/200 6.00 15.00
DRD M.Rielly/J.Devane/200 5.00 12.00
DRN A.Raanta/J.Nordstrom/200 5.00 12.00
DSC B.Shanahan/C.Chelios/200 5.00 12.00
DSH J.Sakic/Q.Howden/200 6.00 15.00
DSS D.Sedin/J.Spezza/200 4.00 10.00
DST V.Sobotka/V.Tarasenko/200 6.00 15.00
DSY S.Stamkos/N.Yakupov/200 5.00 12.00
DTC M.Turco/J.Campbell/200 3.00 8.00
DTN J.Tavares/R.Nash/200 8.00 20.00
DTT C.Thomas/J.Tinordi/200 4.00 10.00
DYB N.Yakupov/P.Bure/200 8.00 20.00
DYM S.Yzerman/S.Monahan/200 8.00 20.00

2013-14 Panini Prime Dual Rookie Class '13 Jerseys

13AG Alex Galchenyuk 10.00 25.00
13BB Beau Bennett 8.00 20.00
13BG Brendan Gallagher 6.00 15.00
13DH Dougie Hamilton 5.00 12.00
13EE Emerson Etem 4.00 10.00
13FA Frederik Andersen 4.00 10.00
13FF Filip Forsberg 8.00 20.00
13JH Jonathan Huberdeau 4.00 10.00
13JS Justin Schultz 2.50 6.00
13MG Mikhail Grigorenko 3.00 8.00
13NY Nail Yakupov 4.00 10.00
13RM Ryan Murphy 2.50 6.00
13SL Scott Laughton 2.50 6.00
13TW Tom Wilson 4.00 10.00
13VT Vladimir Tarasenko 5.00 12.00

2013-14 Panini Prime Dual Rookie Class '14 Jerseys

UNLISTED STARS/100 2.50 6.00
14AB Aleksander Barkov 6.00 15.00
14BJ Boone Jenner 2.50 6.00
14EL Elias Lindholm 4.00 10.00
14HL Hampus Lindholm 5.00 12.00
14JT Jacob Trouba 3.00 8.00
14MM Marek Mazanec 2.50 6.00
14MR Morgan Rielly 5.00 12.00
14NM Nathan MacKinnon 10.00 25.00
14OM Olli Maatta 4.00 10.00
14RM Ryan Murray 3.00 8.00
14SJ Seth Jones 2.50 6.00
14SM Sean Monahan 6.00 15.00
14TH Tomas Hertl 3.00 8.00
14VN Valeri Nichushkin 5.00 12.00
14ZG Zemgus Girgensons 5.00 12.00

2013-14 Panini Prime Dual Rookie Class '14 Jerseys Prime

*PRIME/25: .6X TO 1.5X BASIC INSERTS/100
14NM Nathan MacKinnon 15.00 40.00
14OM Olli Maatta 20.00 50.00

2013-14 Panini Prime Gloves

STATED PRINT RUN 50 SER.#'d SETS
PGBD Brandon Dubinsky 3.00 8.00
PGBG Brian Gionta 3.00 8.00
PGBH Brett Hull 6.00 15.00
PGBR Brad Richards 4.00 10.00
PGCC Chris Chelios 6.00 15.00
PGCG Claude Giroux 10.00 25.00
PGCH Dany Heatley 3.00 8.00
PGIL Igor Larionov 4.00 10.00
PGJB Jamie Benn 3.00 8.00
PGJP Joe Pavelski 4.00 10.00
PGJR James van Riemsdyk 4.00 10.00
PGJT Joe Thornton 4.00 10.00
PGLR Luc Robitaille 4.00 10.00
PGMG Marian Gaborik 8.00 20.00
PGMR Mike Richards 4.00 10.00
PGPD Pascal Dupuis 5.00 12.00
PGPE Patrik Elias 4.00 10.00
PGPK Patrick Kane 8.00 20.00
PGSC Sean Couturier 4.00 10.00
PGTS Tyler Seguin 6.00 15.00

2013-14 Panini Prime Namesakes Autographs

STATED PRINT RUN 20-75
NAAB Aleksander Barkov/75 25.00 60.00
NAAG Alex Galchenyuk/75 60.00 120.00
NAAK Alex Killorn/75 10.00 25.00
NAALAD Andrew Ladd/25 15.00 40.00
NAALAR Adam Larsson/75 10.00 25.00
NABB Beau Bennett/75 20.00 50.00
NABH Brett Hull/25 25.00 60.00
NABJ Boone Jenner/75 10.00 25.00
NABS Ben Scrivens/75 12.00 30.00
NADB Derick Brassard/75 15.00 40.00
NADD Danny DeKeyser/75 12.00 30.00
NADG Doug Gilmour/75 25.00 60.00
NADH Dougie Hamilton/75 20.00 50.00
NAEG Erik Gustafsson/75 6.00 15.00
NAELH Elias Lindholm/75 15.00 40.00
NAELR Eric Lindros/75 40.00 80.00
NAFA Frederik Andersen/75 15.00 40.00
NAGB Gabriel Bourque/75 10.00 25.00
NAGH Gordie Howe/20 50.00 125.00
NAHL Hampus Lindholm/75 15.00 40.00
NAJB Jonathan Bernier/75 15.00 40.00
NAJH Jonathan Huberdeau/75 15.00 40.00
NAJN Joe Nieuwendyk/75 12.00 30.00
NAJP Joe Pavelski/75 15.00 40.00
NAJR Jeremy Roenick/75 15.00 40.00
NAJS Justin Schultz/75 10.00 25.00
NAJT Jacob Trouba/75 15.00 40.00
NAMAF Marc-Andre Fleury/25 25.00 60.00
NAMG Michael Grabner/75 30.00 80.00
NAMM Mark Messier/25 25.00 60.00
NAMR Mike Richter/50 15.00 40.00
NANM Nathan MacKinnon/75 30.00 80.00
NANY Nail Yakupov/75 15.00 40.00
NARF Ron Francis/75 15.00 40.00
NARMA Robert Mayer/75 10.00 25.00
NARMU Ryan Murray/75 12.00 30.00
NASE Stefan Elliott/75 8.00 20.00
NASJ Seth Jones/75 15.00 40.00
NASM Sean Monahan/75 20.00 50.00
NATH Tomas Hertl/75 25.00 60.00
NATK Torey Krug/75 20.00 50.00
NAVL Vincent Lecavalier/75 8.00 20.00
NAVN Valeri Nichushkin/75 15.00 40.00
inserted in 2013-14 Panini National Treasures

2013-14 Panini Prime Numbersakes Autographs

NUAB Aleksander Barkov/25 20.00 50.00
NUAG Alex Galchenyuk/25 50.00 125.00
NUAK Alex Killorn/25 10.00 25.00
NUAR Antoine Roussel/25 20.00 50.00
NUBH Brett Hull/25 20.00 40.00
NUBS Brandon Saad/25 15.00 40.00
NUCJ Curtis Joseph/25 30.00 80.00
NUCN Cam Neely/25 12.00 30.00
NUDH Dougie Hamilton/25 20.00 50.00
NUEB Ed Belfour/25 30.00 60.00
NUEE Emerson Etem/25 15.00 40.00
NUEL Elias Lindholm/25 15.00 40.00
NUEM Evgeni Malkin/25 30.00 60.00
NUFP Felix Potvin/25 60.00 120.00
NUGL Gabriel Landeskog/25 15.00 40.00
NUHL Hampus Lindholm/25 15.00 40.00
NUJH Jonathan Huberdeau/25 25.00 60.00
NUJI Jarome Iginla/25 15.00 40.00
NUJJ Jaromir Jagr/25 60.00 120.00
NUJQ Jonathan Quick/25 30.00 80.00
NUJR Jeremy Roenick/25 20.00 50.00
NUJS Joe Sakic/25 30.00 80.00
NUJTO Jonathan Toews/25 30.00 60.00
NUJTR Jacob Trouba/25 30.00 80.00
NUMAF Marc-Andre Fleury/25 25.00 50.00
NUML Mario Lemieux/25 75.00 120.00
NUMME Mark Messier/25 30.00 80.00
NUMMO Mike Modano/25 20.00 50.00
NUMS Mike Smith/25 15.00 40.00
NUMSL Martin St. Louis/25 12.00 30.00
NUNM Nathan MacKinnon/25 60.00 150.00
NUNY Nail Yakupov/25 40.00 80.00
NUPK Phil Kessel/25 15.00 40.00
NUPR Patrick Roy/25 100.00 200.00
NURB Ray Bourque/25 40.00 80.00
NURG Ryan Getzlaf/25 12.00 30.00
NURH Ron Hextall/25 40.00 80.00
NURK Ryan Kesler/25 20.00 50.00
NURNH Ryan Nugent-Hopkins/25 30.00 80.00
NUSJ Seth Jones/25 10.00 25.00
NUTH Tomas Hertl/25 12.00 30.00
NUTL Trevor Linden/25 20.00 40.00
NUTS Tyler Seguin/25 30.00 80.00
NUVL Vincent Lecavalier/25 15.00 30.00

2013-14 Panini Prime Prime Time Rookies Jerseys

RKAB Aleksander Barkov/50 5.00 12.00
RKAC Alex Chiasson/50 3.00 8.00
RKAG Alex Galchenyuk/50 15.00 40.00
RKAK Alex Killorn/50 3.00 8.00
RKAP Anthony Peluso/50 2.00 5.00
RKAR Antoine Roussel/50 3.00 8.00
RKBB Beau Bennett/50 4.00 10.00
RKBG Brendan Gallagher/50 10.00 25.00
RKBJ Boone Jenner/50 3.00 8.00
RKBN Brock Nelson/50 3.00 8.00
RKDH Dougie Hamilton/50 6.00 15.00
RKEE Emerson Etem/50 3.00 8.00
RKEL Elias Lindholm/50 5.00 12.00

RKFA Frederik Andersen/50 5.00 12.00
RKFF Filip Forsberg/50 8.00 20.00
RKHL Hampus Lindholm/50 5.00 12.00
RKJC Jack Campbell/50 2.50 6.00
RKJH Jonathan Huberdeau/50 8.00 20.00
RKJME Jon Merrill/50 3.00 8.00
RKJMI J.T. Miller/50 3.00 8.00
RKJN Joakim Nordstrom/50 2.50 6.00
RKJS Jared Staal/50 3.00 8.00
RKJS Justin Schultz/50 3.00 8.00
RKJT Jacob Trouba/50 5.00 12.00
RKMD Matt Dumba/50 3.00 8.00
RKMGRA Mikael Granlund/50 5.00 12.00
RKMGRI Mikhail Grigorenko/50 4.00 10.00
RKMJ Martin Jones/50 8.00 20.00
RKMN Matt Nieto/50 2.50 6.00
KRMR Michael Raffl/50 2.50 6.00
RKMR Morgan Rielly/50 8.00 20.00
RKNJ Nicklas Jensen/50 2.50 6.00
RKNM Nathan MacKinnon/50 12.00 30.00
RKNY Nail Yakupov/50 10.00 25.00
RKPM Petr Mrazek/50 12.00 30.00
RKRMP Ryan Murphy/50 3.00 8.00
RKRMU Ryan Murray/50 5.00 12.00
RKRS Ryan Strome/50 4.00 10.00
RKSJ Seth Jones/50 3.00 8.00
RKSL Scott Laughton/50 6.00 15.00
RKSM Sean Monahan/50 5.00 12.00
RKTH Tomas Hertl/50 4.00 10.00
RKTJ Tomas Jurco/50 5.00 12.00
RKTP Tanner Pearson/50 3.00 8.00
RKTT Tyler Toffoli/50 6.00 15.00
RKTW Tom Wilson/50 8.00 20.00
RKVN Valeri Nichushkin/50 3.00 8.00
RKVT Vladimir Tarasenko/50 12.00 30.00
RKZG Zemgus Girgensons/50 8.00 20.00

2013-14 Panini Prime Quad Jerseys

QBLMS Brkv/Lndskg/Mrry/Sgn 8.00 20.00
QCBBB Cmpbl/Bgstd/Brgehm/Brkv 6.00 15.00
QEALV Etm/Andrsn/Lndhlm/Vtnn 8.00 20.00
QGGBB Glchnk/Gllgr/Brnvl/Bleu 10.00 25.00
QGGDD Glgski/Gnchr/Dln/Dly 8.00 20.00
QGONS Gtzl/ORlly/NgtHpkns/Strme 8.00 20.00
QHCST Hggns/Crdo/Schrdr/Tnv 5.00 12.00
QHTDG Hbrdu/Tws/Dchne/Glnyk 12.00 30.00
QJLCF Jgr/Lmeux/Cfly/Frncs 15.00 40.00
QJTSK Jhnsn/Tvrs/Stmks/Kne 10.00 25.00
QKHCH Klkv/Hwdn/Clmsn/Hbrdau 6.00 15.00
QLSOL Lmx/St.Ls/Ovchkn/Lndrs 20.00 50.00
QMNHY NgtHpkns/Ykpv/McKnn/Hll 15.00 40.00
QMSSS Mlkn/Sdn/Sdn/StLs 15.00 40.00
QOGPT Ovkn/Glnyk/Ptrnglo/Tngy 10.00 25.00
QPBSG Prry/Bchmn/Slnne/Gtzlf 8.00 20.00
QPTRP Plso/Trba/Rdmnd/Psqle 4.00 10.00
QRDVN Rbtlle/Dnne/Vchn/Nchlls 10.00 25.00
QSSSS Stl/Stl/Stl/Stl 10.00 25.00
QTMMJ Trba/Mrphy/Mller/Jnes 8.00 20.00

2013-14 Panini Prime Rookie Colors Logo

UNPRICED PRINT RUN 1-23
RPCAB Aleksander Barkov/46 50.00 100.00
RPCAR Antti Raanta/23 20.00 50.00
RPCBJ Boone Jenner/27 15.00 40.00
RPCCM Connor Murphy/44 8.00 20.00
RPCDH Dougie Hamilton/28 30.00 80.00
RPCEL Elias Lindholm/48 15.00 40.00
RPCJD Jamie Devane/19 12.00 30.00
RPCJH Jonathan Huberdeau/50 15.00 40.00
RPCJN Joakim Nordstrom/40 20.00 50.00
RPCJT Jacob Trouba/47 12.00 30.00
RPCMD Matt Dumba/48 12.00 30.00
RPCNJ Nicklas Jensen/28 12.00 30.00
RPCNM Nathan MacKinnon/25 60.00 150.00
RPCRMR Ryan Murray/50 20.00 50.00
RPCSJ Seth Jones/39 10.00 25.00
RPCSM Sean Monahan/40 15.00 40.00
RPCTH Tomas Hertl/37 20.00 50.00
RPCTP Tanner Pearson/20 15.00 40.00
RPCTW Tom Wilson/26 25.00 60.00

2013-14 Panini Prime Rookie Showcase Swatches

STATED PRINT RUN 25 SER.#'d SETS
RSAG Alex Galchenyuk 15.00 40.00
RSAW Austin Watson 4.00 10.00
RSBB Beau Bennett 6.00 15.00
RSBG Brendan Gallagher 10.00 25.00
RSBJ Boone Jenner 8.00 20.00
RSBM Brock Nelson
RSCCN Cory Conacher 3.00 8.00
RSCCY Charlie Coyle 5.00 12.00
RSCT Christian Thomas 4.00 10.00
RSDH Dougie Hamilton 10.00 25.00
RSEE Emerson Etem 5.00 12.00
RSJC Jack Campbell 4.00 10.00
RSJH Jonathan Huberdeau 10.00 25.00
RSJM Jon Merrill 8.00 20.00
RSJSR Jordan Schroeder 5.00 12.00
RSJSU Justin Schultz
RSJT Jarred Tinordi 5.00 12.00
RSMDB Matt Dumba
RSMG Mikhail Grigorenko 6.00 15.00
RSMR Morgan Rielly 12.00 30.00
RSNB Nathan Beaulieu 4.00 10.00
RSNM Nathan MacKinnon 20.00 50.00
RSNY Nail Yakupov 10.00 25.00
RSPM Petr Mrazek 10.00 25.00
RSQH Quinton Howden 5.00 12.00
RSRMP Ryan Murphy
RSRMR Ryan Murray 8.00 20.00
RSRS Ryan Spooner
RSSL Scott Laughton 5.00 12.00
RSSM Sean Monahan 8.00 20.00
TSTH Tomas Hertl 10.00 25.00
RSTJ Tomas Jurco 8.00 20.00
RSTP Tanner Pearson 5.00 12.00
RSTT Tyler Toffoli 10.00 25.00
RSTW Tom Wilson 8.00 20.00

2013-14 Panini Prime Showcase Jersey Patches

1 Nail Yakupov 25.00 50.00
2 Alex Galchenyuk 25.00 50.00
3 Justin Schultz 10.00 25.00
4 Scott Laughton 10.00 25.00
5 Emerson Etem 10.00 25.00
6 Morgan Rielly
7 Austin Watson 8.00 20.00
8 Tomas Jurco 12.00 30.00
9 Jack Campbell 8.00 20.00
11 Nathan MacKinnon 40.00 80.00
12 Petr Mrazek 20.00 40.00
13 Mikhail Grigorenko 12.00 30.00
14 Tomas Hertl 15.00 40.00
15 Tom Wilson 15.00 40.00
16 Sean Monahan 15.00 40.00
17 Brendan Gallagher 30.00 60.00
18 Tanner Pearson 30.00 80.00
19 Ryan Murphy
20 Cory Conacher 6.00 15.00
21 Matt Dumba 10.00 25.00
22 Ryan Spooner 10.00 25.00
23 Boone Jenner 10.00 25.00

2013-14 Panini Prime Showcase Swatches

STATED PRINT RUN 5-25
UNPRICED PRINT RUN 5
1 Jordan Eberle/25 10.00 25.00
2 Rene Bourque/25
3 Sean Bergenheim/25
4 Jacob Markstrom/25 8.00 20.00
5 Mike Richards/25 10.00 25.00
6 Derek Stepan/25 10.00 25.00
7 Mark Giordano/25 8.00 20.00
8 Shea Weber/25
9 Dion Phaneuf/25
10 Taylor Hall/25
11 Sidney Crosby/25 40.00 100.00
12 Jeff Carter/25 10.00 25.00
13 Nail Yakupov/25 10.00 25.00
14 Aleksander Barkov/25 8.00 20.00
15 Alex Galchenyuk/25 12.00 30.00
16 Valeri Nichushkin/25 5.00 12.00
17 Sean Monahan/25 8.00 20.00
18 Tomas Hertl/25 10.00 25.00
19 Brendan Gallagher/25 10.00 25.00
20 Nathan MacKinnon/25 20.00 50.00
21 Frederik Andersen/25 8.00 20.00
22 Seth Jones/25 5.00 12.00
23 Danny DeKeyser/25
24 Filip Forsberg/25 12.00 30.00
25 Tom Wilson/25 8.00 20.00
26 Steven Stamkos/25 12.00 30.00
27 John Tavares/25 20.00 50.00
28 Evgeni Malkin/25 30.00 80.00
29 Max Pacioretty/25
30 Dan Cloutier/25 8.00 20.00
31 Jeremy Roenick/25 10.00 25.00
32 Mike Modano/25 15.00 40.00
33 Rob Blake/25 10.00 25.00
34 Tuukka Rask/25 10.00 25.00
35 Tyler Seguin/25 15.00 40.00
36 Jamie Benn/25 12.00 30.00
37 Brooks Laich/25 8.00 20.00
38 Kris Versteeg/25 8.00 20.00
39 Alex Pietrangelo/25 6.00 15.00
40 Steve Yzerman/25 20.00 50.00
41 Sean Couturier/25 10.00 25.00
42 Saku Koivu/25 10.00 25.00
43 Ron Hextall/25 10.00 25.00
44 Pavel Datsyuk/25 12.00 30.00
45 Tanner Pearson/25 6.00 15.00
46 Elias Lindholm/25 8.00 20.00
47 Marek Mazanec/25 5.00 12.00
48 Petr Mrazek/25 15.00 40.00
49 Mikhail Grigorenko/25 6.00 15.00
50 Alex Chiasson/25 5.00 12.00
51 Brian Bellows/25 8.00 20.00
52 Chris Chelios/25 12.00 30.00
53 Eric Lindros/25 25.00 50.00
55 Jean-Sebastien Giguere/25 8.00 20.00
56 Luc Robitaille/25 15.00 40.00
57 Nicklas Lidstrom/25 10.00 25.00
58 Patrick Roy/25 25.00 60.00
59 Brett Hull/25 12.00 30.00
60 Cam Fowler/25 8.00 20.00
61 Joe Thornton/25 10.00 25.00
62 Josh Gorges/25 8.00 20.00
63 Vincent Lecavalier/25
64 Carey Price/25 20.00 50.00
65 Adam Foote/25 6.00 15.00

2013-14 Panini Prime Signatures Duals

STATED PRINT RUN 50 SER.#'d SETS
SDCS C.Chelios/B.Shanahan 25.00 50.00
SDCT J.Campbell/M.Turco 4.00 10.00
SDGJ A.Galchenyuk/S.Jones 12.00 30.00
SDHJ T.Hertl/J.Jagr 30.00 80.00
SDHT D.Hamilton/J.Trouba 8.00 20.00
SDHY G.Howe/S.Yzerman 60.00 120.00
SDLJ S.Laughton/B.Jenner 8.00 20.00
SDLL E.Lindholm/H.Lindholm 6.00 15.00
SDLM G.Landeskog/N.MacKinnon 30.00 80.00
SDMM S.Matteau/S.Matteau 10.00 25.00
SDMY M.Messier/N.Yakupov 15.00 40.00
SDSG M.St.Louis/B.Gallagher 12.00 30.00
SDSS H.Sedin/D.Sedin 10.00 25.00
SDVF V.Fasth/F.Andersen 6.00 15.00
SDYM N.Yakupov/N.MacKinnon 60.00 120.00

2013-14 Panini Prime Signatures Duals Gold

STATED PRINT RUN 25 SER.#'d SETS
SDHY G.Howe/Yzerman EXCH 75.00 150.00
SDMY M.Messier/N.Yakupov 40.00 80.00

2013-14 Panini Prime Signatures Gold

SNM Nathan MacKinnon/25 100.00 250.00

2013-14 Panini Prime Signatures Trios

1 Lemieux/Messier/Howe 175.00 300.00
2 Barkov/McKinn/Hertl 90.00 150.00
3 Yakupov/Glchnyk/Hbrdeau 40.00 100.00
6 Potvin/Reimer/Bernier 40.00 80.00
7 Lindros/LeClair/Hextall 50.00 100.00
8 Glchnyk/Gllaghr/Bournival 40.00 80.00
9 Yakupov/RNH/MacKinnon 75.00 150.00
10 Chiasson/Roussel/Nichushkin 20.00 40.00

2013-14 Panini Prime Skates

STATED PRINT RUN 25-50
PSAC Alex Chiasson/50 4.00 10.00
PSAH Adam Henrique/25 8.00 20.00
PSAH Carl Hagelin/50 5.00 12.00
PSAO Alex Ovechkin/30 20.00 50.00
PSAR Antoine Roussel/50 5.00 12.00
PSBRI Brad Richards/25 8.00 20.00
PSDG Dan Girardi/50 3.00 8.00
PSDS Derek Stepan/50 5.00 12.00
PSIL Igor Larionov/50 5.00 12.00
PSJB Jamie Benn/50 6.00 15.00
PSJM J.T. Miller/40 5.00 12.00
PSJN Joe Nieuwendyk/50 5.00 12.00
PSJP Joe Pavelski/50 5.00 12.00
PSKL Kris Letang/50 12.00 30.00
PSMG Marian Gaborik/50 10.00 25.00
PSMR Mike Richards/50 5.00 12.00
PSPD Pascal Dupuis/50 8.00 20.00
PSRM Ryan McDonagh/50 5.00 12.00
PSZP Zach Parise/50 5.00 12.00

2013-14 Panini Prime Trios Jerseys

*PRIME/25: .6X TO 1.5X BASIC JSY/100
DGTJ Glchnyk/Trba/Jnes 8.00 20.00
EJWS Jagr/Whtny/Slnne 12.00 30.00
RLMD Lndskg/McKnn/Dchne 12.00 30.00
TBCL Brbr/Clrke/Lch 12.00 30.00
TBJS Brra/Jsi/Sbsa 5.00 12.00
TCGY Bcklnd/Mnhn/Nwndyk 6.00 15.00
TCMM Ctre/Mnhn/Mrzk 6.00 15.00
TCON Cmpbll/Olksk/Nchshkn 6.00 15.00
TEDM Schltz/Arcbllo/Ykpv 6.00 15.00
TEJL Ellr/Jnsn/Lrsn 4.00 10.00
TEMH Emry/Msn/Hxtll 6.00 15.00
TGBM Grnlnd/Brkv/Mtta 10.00 25.00
TGGR Grgrnko/Grgnsns/Rstlnn 8.00 20.00
TGJH Gbrk/Jrco/Hssa 8.00 20.00
THBC Hmltn/Brque/Chra 10.00 25.00
THNP Hrtl/Nto/Ptrcki 8.00 20.00
TKNK Kne/Nsh/Kdri 10.00 25.00
TLLF Lndhlm/Lndhlm/Frsbrg 12.00 30.00
TLMM Lndrs/Mrk/Mdno 8.00 20.00
TLPJ Lrssn/Ptrnglo/Jnes 4.00 10.00
TMMP Mrzk/Mznc/Pvlc 10.00 25.00
TNYR Mcllrth/Mllr/Fst 4.00 10.00
TOMN Ovchkn/Mlkn/Nchshkn 20.00 50.00
TPTS Prry/Tvrs/Stmks 5.00 12.00
TQMH Quck/Mllr/Hwrd 8.00 20.00
TRCC Rssl/Chssn/Cnntn 3.00 8.00
TRTP Rnhrt/Tlbt/Pcrtty 5.00 12.00
TSC Sidney Crosby 20.00 50.00
TSTL Roy/Ptrnglo/Trsnko 5.00 12.00
TVLM Vlchnkv/Lrssn/Mrrll 5.00 12.00

2011-12 Panini Private Signings

INSERTS IN '10-11 LUXRY, DOMIN, ZENITH
INSERTS IN VARIOUS '11-12 PANINI BRANDS
AA Artem Anisimov 8.00 20.00
AB Alexandre Burrows 10.00 25.00
AGO Alex Goligoski 8.00 20.00
AH Adam Henrique 30.00 60.00
AO1 Alex Ovechkin white helmet 50.00 100.00
AO2 Alex Ovechkin red helmet 75.00 150.00
AV Antoine Vermette 4.00 10.00
BAI Josh Bailey 6.00 15.00
BC Bobby Clarke 15.00 40.00
BE Brian Elliott 12.50 30.00
BEN Jamie Benn 6.00 15.00
BER Jonathan Bernier 10.00 25.00
BG Blake Geoffrion 8.00 20.00
BH1 Brett Hull Flames 20.00 40.00
BH2 Brett Hull Red Wings 25.00 50.00
BH3 Brett Hull Blues 30.00 60.00
BL1 Brian Leetch Bruins 10.00 25.00
BL2 Brian Leetch Rangers 12.00 30.00
BM Brenden Morrow 6.00 15.00
BOW Drayson Bowman 5.00 12.00
BP1 Brad Park 20.00 40.00
BP2 Brad Park 12.50 30.00
BP3 Bernie Parent 25.00 50.00
BR Brad Richards 6.00 15.00
BS Brendan Shanahan 30.00 80.00
BT1 Bryan Trottier 15.00 30.00
BY Dustin Byfuglien 8.00 20.00
CA Craig Anderson 6.00 15.00
CAR Daniel Carcillo 6.00 15.00
CG Claude Giroux 20.00 40.00
CHF Johnny Bucyk 10.00 25.00
CJ1 Curtis Joseph Oilers 30.00 60.00
CJ2 Curtis Joseph Blues 25.00 50.00
CJ3 Curtis Joseph Leafs 15.00 40.00
CM Chris Mason 6.00 15.00
CN2 Cam Neely 30.00 60.00
CNE Chris Neil 6.00 15.00
CO Colton Orr 25.00 50.00
CP1 Corey Perry 12.00 30.00
CP2 Carey Price 25.00 60.00
CPR Chris Pronger 20.00 50.00
CS Charlie Simmer 8.00 20.00
CSC Cory Schneider 8.00 20.00
DA Daniel Alfredsson 15.00 30.00
DB1 David Backes 6.00 15.00
DB2 Dan Bouchard 8.00 20.00
DBR Dustin Brown 6.00 15.00
DC2 Dino Ciccarelli 8.00 20.00
DD Drew Doughty 10.00 25.00
DE Dan Ellis 5.00 12.00
DG1 Doug Gilmour Leafs 25.00 50.00
DG2 Doug Gilmour Blues 20.00 50.00
DH Dany Heatley 30.00 60.00
DOR Derek Dorsett 5.00 12.00
DP Dustin Penner 4.00 10.00
DR Derek Roy 6.00 15.00
DRO Dwayne Roloson 5.00 12.00
DS Daniel Sedin 20.00 40.00
DS1 Denis Savard Hawks 12.00 30.00
DS2 Denis Savard Canadiens 15.00 40.00
DUC Matt Duchene 10.00 25.00
DYK2 Joe Nieuwendyk 10.00 25.00
EB2 Ed Belfour Stars 30.00 60.00
EB3 Ed Belfour Sharks 30.00 60.00
EG1 Ed Giacomin Red Wings 20.00 50.00
EG2 Ed Giacomin Rangers 15.00 40.00
EK Evander Kane 8.00 20.00
EM Evgeni Malkin 25.00 50.00
ENN Tyler Ennis 8.00 20.00
ES Eric Staal 8.00 20.00
FIS Mike Fisher 6.00 15.00
FN Frans Nielsen 4.00 10.00
FP1 Felix Potvin Leafs 20.00 40.00
FP2 Felix Potvin Canucks 30.00 60.00
GC Gerry Cheevers 15.00 40.00
GF2 Grant Fuhr 30.00 60.00
GH1 Glenn Hall Blackhawks 12.00 30.00
GH2 Glenn Hall Red Wings 12.00 30.00
GH3 Glenn Hall Blues 12.00 30.00
GJ1 Bobby Hull white jersey 15.00 40.00
GJ2 Bobby Hull red jersey 20.00 50.00
GL Guillaume Latendresse 5.00 12.00
GL1 Gabriel Landeskog 25.00 60.00
GL2 Gabriel Landeskog 30.00 60.00
GN Greg Nemisz 6.00 15.00
GP Gilbert Perreault 12.00 30.00
GRE Andy Greene 4.00 10.00
GRP1 Don Cherry Bruins 20.00 50.00
GRP2 Don Cherry Rockies 20.00 50.00
GUY1 Guy Lafleur Habs 15.00 40.00
GUY2 Guy Lafleur Nordiques 15.00 40.00
HAL Taylor Hall 60.00 120.00
HIL Jonas Hiller 6.00 15.00
HL Henrik Lundqvist 25.00 50.00
HR Henri Richard 50.00 100.00
HS Henrik Sedin 15.00 30.00
IB Ilya Bryzgalov
JAN Cam Janssen 4.00 10.00
JB Jean Beliveau 25.00 50.00
JE Jordan Eberle 50.00 100.00
JG Jake Gardiner 12.00 30.00
JH Jimmy Howard 12.00 30.00
JI1 Jarome Iginla red 15.00 40.00
JI2 Jarome Iginla white 12.00 30.00
JN James Neal 12.00 30.00
JP Joe Pavelski 8.00 20.00
JR Jeremy Roenick 50.00 100.00
JS1 Joe Sakic Nordiques 40.00 80.00
JS2 Joe Sakic Avs 40.00 80.00
JT Joe Thornton 12.00 30.00
JVR James van Riemsdyk 8.00 20.00
KH Ken Hodge 15.00 30.00
KL Kari Lehtonen 6.00 15.00
KM Kenndal McArdle 6.00 15.00
KP Keith Primeau 8.00 20.00
KR Kris Russell 4.00 10.00
LAF1 Pat LaFontaine Sabres 25.00 50.00
LAF2 Pat LaFontaine Islanders 15.00 40.00
LE Loui Eriksson 6.00 15.00
LEV Normand Leveille 12.00 30.00
LM Lanny McDonald 15.00 30.00
LR1 Luc Robitaille Red Wings 12.00 30.00
LR2 Luc Robitaille Kings 15.00 40.00
LR3 Luc Robitaille Penguins 12.00 30.00
LS Lee Stempniak 4.00 10.00
MB1 Martin Brodeur white 40.00 80.00
MB2 Martin Brodeur red 50.00 100.00
MC Matt Carkner 6.00 15.00
MC Michael Cammalleri
MD1 Marcel Dionne Red Wings 10.00 25.00
MD2 Marcel Dionne Kings 10.00 25.00
MF1 Marc-Andre Fleury 15.00 30.00
MF2 Michael Frolik 6.00 15.00
MG Marian Gaborik 15.00 40.00
MH Marian Hossa 12.00 30.00
MID Rick Middleton 8.00 20.00
MIK Stan Mikita 12.00 30.00
MK Mike Komisarek 6.00 15.00
ML Mario Lemieux 60.00 120.00
MLE Michael Leighton 8.00 20.00
MO Mike Modano 15.00 40.00
MP Max Pacioretty 8.00 20.00
MR Manon Rheaume 20.00 50.00
MS Mikael Samuelsson 6.00 15.00
MSL Martin St. Louis 20.00 40.00
MT Max Talbot 6.00 15.00
NG Nathan Gerbe 5.00 12.00
NL1 Nicklas Lidstrom 25.00 50.00
OP Ondrej Pavelec 15.00 30.00
PC Paul Coffey 30.00 60.00
PD Pavel Datsyuk 20.00 50.00
PE1 Phil Esposito Bruins 15.00 40.00
PE2 Phil Esposito Rangers 25.00 50.00
PH Patric Hornqvist 6.00 15.00
PK1 Patrick Kane red jersey 25.00 60.00
PK2 Patrick Kane black jersey 20.00 50.00
PKS P.K. Subban 50.00 100.00
PL Pascal Leclaire 6.00 15.00
PM Patrick Marleau 5.00 12.00
POT Denis Potvin 8.00 20.00
PR1 Patrick Roy Avs 50.00 100.00
PR2 Patrick Roy Habs 50.00 100.00
RAP Aaron Palushaj 5.00 12.00
RAY1 Ray Bourque COL 40.00 80.00
RAY2 Ray Bourque BOS 30.00 60.00
BRO Richard Brodeur 12.00 30.00
REG Peter Regin 5.00 12.00
REN Rene Bourque 8.00 20.00
RG Rod Gilbert 8.00 20.00
RIN Pekka Rinne 12.00 30.00
RK Ryan Kesler 15.00 40.00
RM1 Ryan Miller blue 10.00 25.00
RM2 Ryan Miller white 10.00 25.00
RN Rick Nash 15.00 40.00
RRN1 Ryan Nugent-Hopkins 75.00 150.00
RRN2 Ryan Nugent-Hopkins 100.00 200.00
RRN3 Ryan Nugent-Hopkins 50.00 100.00
RR Rick Rypien 15.00 40.00
RS Ryan Smyth 6.00 15.00
RV1 Rogie Vachon Bruins 10.00 25.00
RV2 Rogie Vachon Kings 10.00 25.00
SAN Derek Sanderson 10.00 25.00
SAV Marc Savard 6.00 15.00
SC1 Sidney Crosby white 100.00 200.00
SC2 Sidney Crosby black 100.00 200.00
SC3 Sidney Crosby blue 100.00 200.00
SCH Milt Schmidt 12.00 30.00
SD Shane Doan 6.00 15.00
SEG Tyler Seguin 30.00 80.00
SG Simon Gagne 8.00 20.00
SIT1 Darryl Sittler Flyers 12.00 30.00
SIT2 Darryl Sittler Leafs 12.00 30.00
SM Steve Mason 6.00 15.00
SO Steve Ott 20.00 40.00
SS Steven Stamkos 30.00 60.00
SV Semyon Varlamov 8.00 20.00
SW Shea Weber 6.00 15.00
SY1 Steve Yzerman Wings 75.00 150.00
SY2 Steve Yzerman GM 75.00 150.00
TAV John Tavares 20.00 40.00
TB Tom Barrasso 25.00 50.00
TE1 Tony Esposito Hawks 20.00 50.00
TE2 Tony Esposito Canadiens 30.00 75.00
TEO Jose Theodore 8.00 20.00
TG T.J. Galiardi 5.00 12.00
TL1 Trevor Linden Canucks 15.00 40.00
TL2 Trevor Linden Habs 15.00 40.00
TO Terry O'Reilly 12.00 30.00
TO2 Jonathan Toews 30.00 60.00
TS Teemu Selanne 25.00 50.00
TT Tim Thomas 40.00 80.00
VL Vincent Lecavalier 12.00 30.00
WS Wayne Simmonds 6.00 15.00
WW Wojtek Wolski 4.00 10.00
YC Yvan Cournoyer 30.00 60.00
ZB Zach Boychuk 4.00 10.00
ZP Zach Parise 12.00 30.00
ZS Zack Stortini 6.00 15.00
AO3 Alex Ovechkin blue helmet
BAC Mikael Backlund 4.00 10.00
GET Ryan Getzlaf 10.00 25.00
JAB Justin Abdelkader
LET Kristopher Letang 15.00 40.00
PLL Pierre-Luc Letourneau-Leblond 4.00 10.00
RBC Brett Connolly 10.00 25.00
RBS Brendan Smith 8.00 20.00
RCE Cody Eakin 6.00 15.00
RCK Carl Klingberg 6.00 15.00
RHL Jonathon Huberdeau 4.00 10.00
RJF Justin Faulk 6.00 15.00
RJJ Jack Johnson 5.00 12.00
RJM John Moore 5.00 12.00
RMK Marcus Kruger 8.00 20.00
RMZ Mika Zibanejad 8.00 20.00
RRE Ryan Ellis 5.00 12.00
RSD Simon Despres 6.00 15.00
RST Shawn Thornton 8.00 20.00
RZK Zack Kassian 10.00 25.00
THR Phil Kessel 10.00 25.00
TO1 Jonathan Toews
JCR1 Jim Craig ATL 15.00 40.00
JCR2 Jim Craig BOS 15.00 40.00

2013-14 Panini Private Signings

D ISSUED IN 2013-14 DOMINION
T ISSUED IN 2013-14 TITANIUM
TC ISSUED IN 2013-14 TOTALLY CERT
C ISSUED IN 2013-14 CONTENDERS
PSAC Alex Chiasson D 5.00 12.00
PSAG Alex Galchenyuk D 20.00 50.00
PSAK Alex Killorn T 5.00 12.00
PSAR Antoine Roussel D 5.00 12.00
PSAW Austin Watson C
PSBB Beau Bennett TC 6.00 15.00
PSBG Brendan Gallagher D 20.00 40.00
PSBJ Nick Bjugstad D 6.00 15.00
PSBL Brian Lashoff T 4.00 10.00
PSCC Charlie Coyle TC 5.00 12.00
PSCC Cory Conacher D 3.00 8.00
PSCT Christian Thomas D 4.00 10.00
PSDD Danny DeKeyser D 6.00 15.00
PSDH Dougie Hamilton 10.00 25.00
PSDJ Dmitrij Jaskin T 5.00 12.00
PSDS Drew Shore TC 4.00 10.00
PSFF Filip Forsberg T 12.00 30.00
PSIF Jamie Tardif D 3.00 8.00
PSJB Jonas Brodin C 4.00 10.00
PSJC Jack Campbell D 4.00 10.00
PSJH Jonathan Huberdeau D 12.00 30.00
PSJM J.T. Miller T 5.00 12.00
PSJS Jared Staal T 5.00 12.00
PSJS Jordan Schroeder T 5.00 12.00
PSKO Mikhail Grigorenko D 6.00 15.00
PSMG Mikael Granlund T 8.00 20.00
PSMK Michael Kostka T 4.00 10.00
PSNB Nathan Beaulieu TC 4.00 10.00
PSNJ Nicklas Jensen D 4.00 10.00
PSNY Nail Yakupov T 20.00 40.00
PSOK Jamie Oleksiak D 4.00 10.00
PSPG Philipp Grubauer T 10.00 25.00
PSQH Quinton Howden T 4.00 10.00
PSRM Ryan Murphy TC 5.00 12.00
PSRP Richard Panik T 5.00 12.00
PSRR Rickard Rakell D 5.00 12.00
PSRS Ryan Spooner T 8.00 20.00
PSRZ Petr Mrazek D 10.00 25.00
PSSL Scott Laughton D 5.00 12.00
PSSM Stefan Matteau T 4.00 10.00
PSSO Carl Soderberg D 5.00 12.00
PSSV Sami Vatanen TC 5.00 12.00
PSTH Thomas Hickey T 4.00 10.00
PSTP Tanner Pearson D 5.00 12.00
PSTT Tyler Toffoli T 10.00 25.00
PSTW Tom Wilson D 6.00 15.00
PSVF Viktor Fasth D 5.00 12.00
PSXW Max Reinhart C
PSZR Zach Redmond T 4.00 10.00

2012-13 Panini Prizm

INSERTS IN 2012-13 ROOKIE ANTHOLOGY
1 Teemu Selanne 2.50 6.00
2 Bobby Ryan 1.25 3.00
3 Tyler Seguin 2.00 5.00
4 Tuukka Rask 1.25 3.00
5 Cody Hodgson 1.25 3.00
6 Jarome Iginla 1.25 3.00
7 Eric Staal 1.50 4.00
8 Jordan Staal 1.25 3.00
9 Patrick Kane 2.50 6.00
10 Jonathan Toews 2.50 6.00
11 Gabriel Landeskog 1.25 3.00
12 Matt Duchene 1.25 3.00
13 Ryan Johansen 1.50 4.00
14 Jaromir Jagr 3.00 8.00
15 Loui Eriksson 1.00 2.50
16 Pavel Datsyuk 1.50 4.00
17 Henrik Zetterberg 1.50 4.00
18 Jordan Eberle 1.25 3.00
19 Ryan Nugent-Hopkins 1.25 3.00
20 Stephen Weiss 1.00 2.50
21 Jonathan Quick 2.00 5.00
22 Anze Kopitar 2.00 5.00
23 Zach Parise 1.25 3.00
24 Mikko Koivu 1.00 2.50
25 Carey Price 4.00 10.00
26 Brian Gionta 1.00 2.50
27 Pekka Rinne 1.50 4.00
28 Adam Henrique 1.25 3.00
29 Martin Brodeur 2.50 6.00
30 John Tavares 2.50 6.00
31 Henrik Lundqvist 1.50 4.00
32 Rick Nash 1.25 3.00
33 Jason Spezza 1.25 3.00
34 Daniel Alfredsson 1.25 3.00
35 Claude Giroux 1.25 3.00
36 Sean Couturier 1.25 3.00
37 Mike Smith 1.25 3.00
38 Sidney Crosby 5.00 12.00
39 Marc-Andre Fleury 2.00 5.00
40 Joe Thornton 1.25 3.00
41 Joe Pavelski 1.25 3.00
42 Alex Pietrangelo 1.00 2.50
43 Brian Elliott 1.00 2.50
44 Steven Stamkos 2.50 6.00
45 Vincent Lecavalier 1.00 2.50
46 Phil Kessel 1.50 4.00
47 James Reimer 1.25 3.00
48 Cory Schneider 1.00 2.50
49 Daniel Sedin 1.25 3.00
50 Alex Ovechkin 5.00 12.00
51 Nicklas Backstrom 2.00 5.00
52 Andrew Ladd 1.25 3.00
53 Mat Clark RC 1.50 4.00
54 Carter Camper RC 1.25 3.00
55 Lane MacDermid RC 1.50 4.00
56 Max Sauve RC 1.50 4.00
57 Torey Krug RC 6.00 15.00
58 Michael Hutchinson RC 3.00 8.00
59 Travis Turnbull RC 1.50 4.00
60 Akim Aliu RC 1.50 4.00
61 Jeremy Welsh RC 1.50 4.00
62 Brandon Bollig RC 1.50 4.00
63 Tyson Barrie RC 3.00 8.00
64 Mike Connolly RC 1.50 4.00
65 Andrew Joudrey RC 1.50 4.00
66 Shawn Hunwick RC 1.50 4.00
67 Cody Goloubef RC 1.50 4.00
68 Dalton Prout RC 1.50 4.00
69 Ryan Garbutt RC 1.50 4.00
70 Reilly Smith RC 3.00 8.00
71 Scott Glennie RC 1.50 4.00
72 Brenden Dillon RC 1.50 4.00
73 Riley Sheahan RC 1.50 4.00
74 Philippe Cornet RC 1.50 4.00
75 Colby Robak RC 1.50 4.00
76 Jordan Nolan RC 1.50 4.00
77 Kris Foucault RC 1.50 4.00
78 Tyler Cuma RC 1.50 4.00
79 Chay Genoway RC 1.50 4.00
80 Jason Zucker RC 2.00 5.00
81 Robert Mayer RC 2.00 5.00
82 Gabriel Dumont RC 1.50 4.00
83 Chet Pickard RC 1.50 4.00
84 Aaron Ness RC 1.50 4.00
85 Casey Cizikas RC 1.50 4.00
86 Matt Donovan RC 1.50 4.00
87 Matt Watkins RC 1.50 4.00
88 Jakob Silfverberg RC 3.00 8.00
89 Mark Stone RC 3.00 8.00
90 Brandon Manning RC 1.50 4.00
91 Michael Stone RC 1.50 4.00
92 Tyson Sexsmith RC 1.50 4.00
93 Jake Allen RC 5.00 12.00
94 J.T. Brown RC 1.50 4.00
95 Carter Ashton RC 1.25 3.00
96 Ryan Hamilton RC 1.50 4.00
97 Jussi Rynnas RC 1.50 4.00
98 Sven Baertschi RC 2.00 5.00
99 Chris Kreider RC 3.00 8.00
100 Jaden Schwartz RC 3.00 8.00

2012-13 Panini Prizm Blue

*1-52 VETS/25: 2.5X TO 6X BASIC CARDS
*53-100 ROOKIES/25: 2X TO 5X BASIC RC
INSERTS IN 2012-13 ROOKIE ANTHOLOGY
BLUE PRINT RUN 25 SER.#'d SETS
51 Nicklas Backstrom 12.00 30.00

2012-13 Panini Prizm Pulsar Father's Day

*1-52 VETS: .8X TO 2X BASIC CARDS
*53-100 ROOKIES: .5X TO 1.2X BASIC RC
51 Nicklas Backstrom 4.00 10.00

2012-13 Panini Prizm Rainbow

*1-52 VETS: .8X TO 2X BASIC CARDS
*53-100 ROOKIES: .5X TO 1.2X BASIC RC
INSERTS IN 2012-13 ROOKIE ANTHOLOGY
51 Nicklas Backstrom 4.00 10.00

2012-13 Panini Prizm Red

*1-52 VETS/50: 1.5X TO 4X BASIC CARDS
*53-100 ROOKIES/50: 1.2X TO 3X BASIC RC
INSERTS IN 2012-13 ROOKIE ANTHOLOGY
STATED PRINT RUN 50 SER.#'d SETS
51 Nicklas Backstrom 8.00 20.00

2012-13 Panini Prizm Autographs

INSERTS IN 2012-13 ROOKIE ANTHOLOGY
SP A ANNC'd PRINT RUN 15 OR LESS
SP B ANNC'd PRINT RUN 50 OR LESS
1 Adam Henrique SP B 10.00 25.00
2 Alex Ovechkin SP A 75.00 125.00
3 Paul Postma 4.00 10.00
4 Andrew Shaw 10.00 25.00
5 Brad Richards SP B 15.00 30.00
6 Marcus Kruger 8.00 20.00
7 Brian Elliott 5.00 12.00
8 Alexandre Burrows 15.00 30.00
9 Mikko Koskinen 4.00 10.00
10 Carl Hagelin 6.00 15.00
11 Chris Chelios SP B 15.00 30.00
12 Claude Giroux SP B 40.00 80.00
13 Mike Komisarek 5.00 12.00
14 Robert Bortuzzo 4.00 10.00
15 Colin Greening 5.00 12.00
16 Craig Smith 4.00 10.00
17 Eric Lindros SP A
18 Gabriel Landeskog SP B 20.00 40.00
19 Anders Nilsson 4.00 10.00
20 Gustav Nyquist 8.00 20.00
21 Jack Johnson SP B 4.00 10.00
22 James Neal SP B 10.00 25.00
23 Carey Price SP A 20.00 40.00
24 John Tavares SP B 15.00 30.00
25 Tomas Kubalik 4.00 10.00
26 Jordan Eberle SP B 20.00 40.00
27 Louis Leblanc 8.00 20.00
28 Marcus Foligno 8.00 20.00
29 Matt Read 5.00 12.00
30 Eddie Lack 6.00 15.00
31 Nazem Kadri SP B 10.00 25.00
32 Luke Schenn SP B 8.00 20.00
33 Thomas McCollum 5.00 12.00
34 Pavel Datsyuk SP A 20.00 40.00
35 Rick Nash SP A 30.00 60.00
36 Jonathan Toews SP A 30.00 60.00
37 Matt Calvert 3.00 8.00
38 Ryan Kesler SP B 15.00 30.00
39 Ryan Nugent-Hopkins SP B 40.00 80.00
40 Sidney Crosby SP A 75.00 135.00
41 Simon Despres 4.00 10.00
42 Stephen Weiss 6.00 15.00
43 Lennart Petrell 4.00 10.00
44 Travis Zajac 5.00 12.00
45 Vincent Lecavalier SP A
46 Zack Kassian 8.00 20.00
47 Drew Doughty SP B 20.00 40.00
48 Dion Phaneuf SP B 6.00 15.00
49 Martin Brodeur SP A
50 Alex Pietrangelo 8.00 20.00
51 Zach Parise SP B 8.00 20.00
52 Steve Yzerman SP A
53 Mat Clark 4.00 10.00
54 Carter Camper 3.00 8.00
55 Lane MacDermid SP B 8.00 20.00
56 Max Sauve 4.00 10.00
57 Torey Krug 8.00 20.00
58 Michael Hutchinson 8.00 20.00
59 Travis Turnbull SP B 5.00 12.00
60 Akim Aliu 4.00 10.00
61 Jeremy Welsh SP B 5.00 12.00
62 Brandon Bollig 4.00 10.00
63 Tyson Barrie 8.00 20.00
64 Mike Connolly SP A 12.00 30.00
65 Andrew Joudrey 4.00 10.00
66 Shawn Hunwick SP B 5.00 12.00
67 Cody Goloubef 4.00 10.00
68 Dalton Prout 4.00 10.00
69 Ryan Garbutt SP B 5.00 12.00
70 Reilly Smith 8.00 20.00
71 Scott Glennie 4.00 10.00
72 Brenden Dillon 4.00 10.00
73 Riley Sheahan 4.00 10.00
74 Philippe Cornet 4.00 10.00
75 Colby Robak 4.00 10.00
76 Jordan Nolan 4.00 10.00
77 Kris Foucault 4.00 10.00
78 Tyler Cuma 4.00 10.00
79 Chay Genoway 4.00 10.00
80 Jason Zucker 5.00 12.00
81 Robert Mayer 5.00 12.00
82 Gabriel Dumont SP B 10.00 25.00
83 Chet Pickard SP B 5.00 12.00
84 Aaron Ness 4.00 10.00
85 Casey Cizikas 4.00 10.00
86 Matt Donovan 4.00 10.00
87 Matt Watkins 4.00 10.00
88 Jakob Silfverberg 8.00 20.00
89 Mark Stone 8.00 20.00
90 Brandon Manning 4.00 10.00
91 Michael Stone 4.00 10.00
92 Tyson Sexsmith 4.00 10.00
93 Jake Allen 12.00 30.00
94 J.T. Brown 4.00 10.00
95 Carter Ashton 3.00 8.00
96 Ryan Hamilton 6.00 15.00
97 Jussi Rynnas 8.00 20.00
98 Sven Baertschi 5.00 12.00
99 Chris Kreider 12.00 30.00
100 Jaden Schwartz 8.00 20.00

2013-14 Panini Prizm

ONE ROOKIE PER HOBBY PACK
1 Zdeno Chara .40 1.00
2 Patrice Bergeron .50 1.25
3 Torey Krug .50 1.25
4 Tuukka Rask .40 1.00
5 Brad Marchand .50 1.25
6 Milan Lucic .40 1.00
7 David Krejci .40 1.00
8 Thomas Vanek .40 1.00
9 Ryan Miller .40 1.00
10 Cody Hodgson .40 1.00
11 Steve Ott .30 .75
12 Drew Stafford .40 1.00
13 Tyler Myers .30 .75
14 Eric Staal .50 1.25
15 Jordan Staal .40 1.00
16 Cam Ward .40 1.00
17 Alexander Semin .40 1.00
18 Jiri Tlusty .30 .75
19 Jeff Skinner .30 .75
20 Tuomo Ruutu .30 .75
21 Jack Johnson .25 .60
22 Sergei Bobrovsky .40 1.00
23 Marian Gaborik .40 1.00
24 R.J. Umberger .25 .60
25 Ryan Johansen .50 1.25
26 Brandon Dubinsky .30 .75
27 Henrik Zetterberg .50 1.25
28 Pavel Datsyuk .50 1.25
29 Niklas Kronwall .30 .75
30 Jimmy Howard .40 1.00
31 Johan Franzen .40 1.00
32 Daniel Cleary .40 1.00
33 Jakub Kindl .25 .60
34 Erik Gudbranson .40 1.00
35 Jacob Markstrom .30 .75
36 Brian Campbell .25 .60
37 Ed Jovanovski .25 .60
38 Kris Versteeg .30 .75
39 Max Pacioretty .40 1.00
40 P.K. Subban .60 1.50
41 Carey Price 1.25 3.00
42 Brian Gionta .30 .75
43 Tomas Plekanec .40 1.00
44 Andrei Markov .40 1.00
45 David Desharnais .40 1.00
46 Martin Brodeur .75 2.00
47 Patrik Elias .40 1.00
48 Ilya Kovalchuk .40 1.00
49 Adam Henrique .40 1.00
50 Travis Zajac .30 .75
51 Dainius Zubrus .25 .60
52 Adam Larsson .40 1.00
53 John Tavares .75 2.00
54 Matt Moulson .30 .75
55 Michael Grabner .30 .75
56 Evgeni Nabokov .30 .75
57 Josh Bailey .30 .75
58 Lubomir Visnovsky .25 .60
59 Kyle Okposo .40 1.00
60 Henrik Lundqvist .50 1.25
61 Brad Richards .40 1.00
62 Ryan Callahan .40 1.00
63 Rick Nash .40 1.00
64 Derick Brassard .40 1.00
65 Carl Hagelin .40 1.00
66 Marc Staal .30 .75
67 Derek Stepan .40 1.00
68 Chris Phillips .25 .60
69 Erik Karlsson .75 2.00
70 Craig Anderson .40 1.00
71 Mika Zibanejad .40 1.00
72 Jason Spezza .40 1.00
73 Kyle Turris .25 .60
74 Milan Michalek .25 .60
75 Robin Lehner .30 .75
76 Claude Giroux .40 1.00
77 Steve Mason .30 .75
78 Scott Hartnell .40 1.00
79 Luke Schenn .25 .60
80 Jakub Voracek .40 1.00
81 Sean Couturier .40 1.00
82 Matt Read .25 .60
83 Brayden Schenn .40 1.00
84 Sidney Crosby 1.50 4.00
85 Evgeni Malkin 1.25 3.00
86 Marc-Andre Fleury .60 1.50
87 Kris Letang .40 1.00
88 Tomas Vokoun .30 .75
89 James Neal .40 1.00
90 Chris Kunitz .40 1.00
91 Ben Bishop .40 1.00
92 Martin St. Louis .40 1.00
93 Steven Stamkos .75 2.00
94 Ryan Malone .25 .60
95 Victor Hedman .50 1.25
96 Joffrey Lupul .30 .75
97 Phil Kessel .50 1.25
98 James van Riemsdyk .40 1.00
99 Dion Phaneuf .40 1.00
100 Nazem Kadri .40 1.00
101 James Reimer .40 1.00
102 Jake Gardiner .40 1.00
103 Alex Ovechkin 1.50 4.00
104 Nicklas Backstrom .60 1.50
105 Braden Holtby .60 1.50
106 Brooks Laich .25 .60
107 Mike Green .40 1.00
108 John Carlson .50 1.25
109 Corey Perry .40 1.00
110 Cam Fowler .30 .75
111 Ryan Getzlaf .60 1.50
112 Teemu Selanne .75 2.00
113 Francois Beauchemin .25 .60
114 Saku Koivu .40 1.00
115 Jonas Hiller .30 .75
116 Mike Cammalleri .30 .75
117 Miikka Kiprusoff .30 .75
118 Curtis Glencross .25 .60
119 Dennis Wideman .25 .60
120 Jiri Hudler .30 .75
121 T.J. Brodie .25 .60

122 Jonathan Toews .75 2.00
123 Patrick Kane .75 2.00
124 Duncan Keith .40 1.00
125 Marian Hossa .30 .75
126 Corey Crawford .50 1.25
127 Patrick Sharp .40 1.00
128 Brent Seabrook .40 1.00
129 Gabriel Landeskog .30 .75
130 Milan Hejduk .30 .75
131 Semyon Varlamov .40 1.00
132 Erik Johnson .25 .60
133 Matt Duchene .40 1.00
134 Ryan O'Reilly .40 1.00
135 Jamie Benn .50 1.25
136 Erik Cole .30 .75
137 Kari Lehtonen .30 .75
138 Alex Goligoski .25 .60
139 Ray Whitney .30 .75
140 Taylor Hall .75 2.00
141 Sam Gagner .30 .75
142 Jordan Eberle .40 1.00
143 Devan Dubnyk .40 1.00
144 Ryan Smyth .30 .75
145 Ryan Nugent-Hopkins .40 1.00
146 Nick Schultz .25 .60
147 Ladislav Smid .25 .60
148 Jonathan Quick .60 1.50
149 Dustin Brown .40 1.00
150 Anze Kopitar .60 1.50
151 Drew Doughty .40 1.00
152 Mike Richards .40 1.00
153 Jeff Carter .40 1.00
154 Slava Voynov .30 .75
155 Mikko Koivu .30 .75
156 Zach Parise .40 1.00
157 Jared Spurgeon .25 .60
158 Niklas Backstrom .30 .75
159 Ryan Suter .25 .60
160 Dany Heatley .30 .75
161 Josh Harding .40 1.00
162 Jason Pominville .30 .75
163 Shea Weber .30 .75
164 Pekka Rinne .50 1.25
165 David Legwand .30 .75
166 Mike Fisher .30 .75
167 Roman Josi .40 1.00
168 Shane Doan .30 .75
169 Mike Smith .40 1.00
170 Oliver Ekman-Larsson .30 .75
171 Mikkel Boedker .25 .60
172 Keith Yandle .40 1.00
173 Logan Couture .40 1.00
174 Joe Thornton .40 1.00
175 Joe Pavelski .40 1.00
176 Dan Boyle .30 .75
177 Patrick Marleau .40 1.00
178 Antti Niemi .30 .75
179 Alex Pietrangelo .30 .75
180 T.J. Oshie .60 1.50
181 Kevin Shattenkirk .40 1.00
182 David Backes .40 1.00
183 Jay Bouwmeester .40 1.00
184 Alexander Steen .40 1.00
185 Chris Stewart .30 .75
186 Jake Allen .50 1.25
187 Daniel Sedin .40 1.00
188 Ryan Kesler .40 1.00
189 Alexandre Burrows .40 1.00
190 Chris Higgins .25 .60
191 Henrik Sedin .40 1.00
192 Kevin Bieksa .30 .75
193 Roberto Luongo .40 1.00
194 Mason Raymond .30 .75
195 Andrew Ladd .40 1.00
196 Ondrej Pavelec .40 1.00
197 Evander Kane .40 1.00
198 Mark Scheifele .50 1.25
199 Blake Wheeler .40 1.00
200 Dustin Byfuglien .40 1.00
201 Emerson Etem RC 1.00 2.50
202 Igor Bobkov RC .75 2.00
203 Rickard Rakell RC 1.00 2.50
204 Sami Vatanen RC 1.00 2.50
205 Viktor Fasth RC 1.00 2.50
206 Carl Soderberg RC 1.00 2.50
207 Dougie Hamilton RC 2.00 5.00
208 Ryan Spooner RC 1.00 2.50
209 Brian Flynn RC .75 2.00
210 Chad Ruhwedel RC .60 1.50
211 Johan Larsson RC .75 2.00
212 Mark Pysyk RC 1.00 2.50
213 Mikhail Grigorenko RC 1.25 3.00
214 Ben Hanowski RC .75 2.00
215 Mark Cundari RC .60 1.50
216 Maxwell Reinhart RC 1.00 2.50
217 Roman Cervenka RC .75 2.00
218 Chris Terry RC .60 1.50
219 Jared Staal RC 1.00 2.50
220 Michal Jordan RC .60 1.50
221 Ryan Murphy RC 1.00 2.50
222 Drew LeBlanc RC .60 1.50
223 Ryan Stanton RC 1.00 2.50
224 Calvin Pickard RC 1.00 2.50
225 Michael Sgarbossa RC .75 2.00
226 Patrick Bordeleau RC 1.00 2.50
227 Jonathan Audy-Marchessault RC 2.00 5.00
228 Sean Collins RC .75 2.00
229 Alex Chiasson RC 1.00 2.50
230 Antoine Roussel RC 1.00 2.50
231 Cristopher Nilstorp RC .75 2.00
232 Jack Campbell RC .75 2.00
233 Jamie Oleksiak RC .75 2.00
234 Brian Lashoff RC .75 2.00
235 Damien Brunner RC .75 2.00
236 Danny DeKeyser RC 1.25 3.00
237 Petr Mrazek RC 2.00 5.00
238 Justin Schultz RC 1.00 2.50
239 Mark Arcobello RC 1.00 2.50
240 Nail Yakupov RC 3.00 8.00
241 Alex Petrovic RC .75 2.00
242 Drew Shore RC .75 2.00
243 Jonathan Huberdeau RC 2.50 6.00
244 Nick Bjugstad RC 1.25 3.00
245 Quinton Howden RC .75 2.00
246 Tyler Toffoli RC 2.00 5.00
247 Charlie Coyle RC 1.00 2.50
248 Darcy Kuemper RC 1.00 2.50
249 Jonas Brodin RC .75 2.00
250 Mikael Granlund RC 1.50 4.00
251 Alex Galchenyuk RC 5.00 12.00
252 Brendan Gallagher RC 3.00 8.00
253 Jarred Tinordi RC 1.00 2.50
254 Nathan Beaulieu RC .75 2.00
255 Austin Watson RC .75 2.00
256 Filip Forsberg RC 2.50 6.00
257 Joonas Rask RC .60 1.50
258 Taylor Beck RC .75 2.00
259 Eric Gelinas RC 1.00 2.50
260 Harri Pesonen RC .75 2.00
261 Stefan Matteau RC .75 2.00
262 Anders Lee RC 1.50 4.00
263 Brock Nelson RC 1.00 2.50
264 Thomas Hickey RC .75 2.00
265 Christian Thomas RC .75 2.00
266 J.T. Miller RC 1.00 2.50
267 Cory Conacher RC .60 1.50
268 Dave Dziurzynski RC .75 2.00
269 Eric Gryba RC .75 2.00
270 Jean-Gabriel Pageau RC .75 2.00
271 Jason Akeson RC .75 2.00
272 Oliver Lauridsen RC .75 2.00
273 Scott Laughton RC 1.00 2.50
274 Tye McGinn RC 1.00 2.50
275 Chris Brown RC .60 1.50
276 Beau Bennett RC 1.25 3.00
277 Eric Hartzell RC 1.00 2.50
278 Matt Irwin RC .75 2.00
279 Matt Tennyson RC .60 1.50
280 Nick Petrecki RC .60 1.50
281 Dmitrij Jaskin RC 1.00 2.50
282 Vladimir Tarasenko RC 3.00 8.00
283 Alex Killorn RC 1.00 2.50
284 Ondrej Palat RC 1.25 3.00
285 Radko Gudas RC 1.00 2.50
286 Richard Panik RC 1.00 2.50
287 Tyler Johnson RC 2.50 6.00
288 Leo Komarov RC 1.00 2.50
289 Michael Kostka RC .75 2.00
290 Frank Corrado RC .60 1.50
291 Joe Cannata RC .75 2.00
292 Jordan Schroeder RC 1.00 2.50
293 Nicklas Jensen RC .75 2.00
294 Cameron Schilling RC .60 1.50
295 Philipp Grubauer RC 1.00 2.50
296 Steve Oleksy RC 1.00 2.50
297 Tom Wilson RC 1.50 4.00
298 Anthony Peluso RC .60 1.50
299 Eddie Pasquale RC .60 1.50
300 Zach Redmond RC .75 2.00
301 Loui Eriksson .30 .75
302 Jarome Iginla .40 1.00
303 Reilly Smith .40 1.00
304 Matt Moulson .30 .75
305 Daniel Alfredsson .40 1.00
306 Tim Thomas .40 1.00
307 Daniel Briere .40 1.00
308 Jaromir Jagr 1.00 2.50
309 Cory Schneider .30 .75
310 Thomas Vanek .40 1.00
311 Bobby Ryan .40 1.00
312 Vincent Lecavalier .30 .75
313 Jonathan Bernier .40 1.00
314 David Clarkson .25 .60
315 Mason Raymond .30 .75
316 Tyler Seguin .60 1.50
317 Ilya Bryzgalov .40 1.00
318 David Perron .25 .60
319 Mike Ribeiro .30 .75
320 Devin Setoguchi .30 .75
321 John Gibson RC 3.00 8.00
322 Hampus Lindholm RC 1.50 4.00
323 Kevan Miller RC .75 2.00
324 Jamie Tardif RC .60 1.50
325 Nikita Zadorov RC 1.00 2.50
326 Rasmus Ristolainen RC 1.50 4.00
327 Zemgus Girgensons RC 2.00 5.00
328 Ben Street RC .60 1.50
329 Reto Berra RC 1.00 2.50
330 Sean Monahan RC 1.50 4.00
331 Elias Lindholm RC 1.50 4.00
332 Nathan MacKinnon RC 8.00 20.00
333 John Muse RC 1.00 2.50
334 Antti Raanta RC 1.25 3.00
335 Joakim Nordstrom RC .75 2.00
336 Shawn Lalonde RC 1.00 2.50
337 Boone Jenner RC 1.00 2.50
338 Ryan Murray RC 1.50 4.00
339 Kevin Connauton RC .75 2.00
340 Valeri Nichushkin RC 1.00 2.50
341 Luke Glendening RC 1.50 4.00
342 Tomas Jurco RC 1.50 4.00
343 Xavier Ouellet RC 1.00 2.50
344 Anton Belov RC 1.00 2.50
345 Luke Gazdic RC .75 2.00
346 Martin Marincin RC .75 2.00
347 Taylor Fedun RC 1.25 3.00
348 Tyler Pitlick RC 1.00 2.50
349 Will Acton RC .75 2.00
350 Aleksander Barkov RC 2.50 6.00
351 Jonathan Rheault RC .60 1.50
352 Niklas Svedberg RC 2.00 5.00
353 Linden Vey RC .60 1.50
354 Martin Jones RC 2.50 6.00
355 Tanner Pearson RC 1.00 2.50
356 Erik Haula RC 1.25 3.00
357 Johan Gustafsson RC 1.25 3.00
358 Matt Dumba RC 1.00 2.50
359 Greg Pateryn RC 1.00 2.50
360 Michael Bournival RC 1.00 2.50
361 Patrick Holland RC 1.50 4.00
362 Daniel Bang RC .75 2.00
363 Kevin Henderson RC .75 2.00
364 Magnus Hellberg RC 1.00 2.50
365 Marek Mazanec RC 1.00 2.50
366 Seth Jones RC 1.00 2.50
367 Dylan McIlrath RC .60 1.50
368 Jon Merrill RC 1.00 2.50
369 Reid Boucher RC 1.00 2.50
370 Ryan Strome RC 1.25 3.00
371 Jason Missiaen RC 1.00 2.50
372 Jesper Fast RC .75 2.00
373 Cody Ceci RC .75 2.00
374 Derek Grant RC .75 2.00
375 Calvin Heeter RC .75 2.00
376 Michael Raffl RC .75 2.00
377 Connor Murphy RC .75 2.00
378 Jordan Szwarz RC 1.00 2.50
379 Lucas Lessio RC .60 1.50
380 Brian Dumoulin RC 1.00 2.50
381 Brian Gibbons RC 1.00 2.50
382 Jayson Megna RC 1.00 2.50
383 Jeff Zatkoff RC 1.00 2.50
384 Olli Maatta RC 2.50 6.00
385 Zach Sill RC 1.00 2.50
386 Freddie Hamilton RC 1.00 2.50
387 Matt Nieto RC .75 2.00
388 Tomas Hertl RC 2.50 6.00
389 Mark Barberio RC .60 1.50
390 Nikita Kucherov RC 2.50 6.00
391 David Broll RC 1.00 2.50
392 Jamie Devane RC .75 2.00
393 Jerry D'Amigo RC 1.00 2.50
394 Josh Leivo RC 1.00 2.50
395 Morgan Rielly RC 2.50 6.00
396 Connor Carrick RC .75 2.00
397 Michael Latta RC .75 2.00
398 Patrick Wey RC .75 2.00
399 Jacob Trouba RC 1.50 4.00
400 John Albert RC .75 2.00

2013-14 Panini Prizm Cracked Ice Toronto Fall Expo

*CRACKED ICE: .6X TO 1.5X BASIC RC
RELEASED AT 2013 TORONTO FALL EXPO

2013-14 Panini Prizm Cracked Ice Toronto Fall Expo VIP 30

*1-200 VETS/30: 8X TO 20X BASIC CARDS
*201-300 ROOK/30: 2.5X TO 6X BASIC RC
104 Nicklas Backstrom 12.00 30.00
126 Corey Crawford 10.00 25.00

2013-14 Panini Prizm Prizms

*VETS: 2.5X TO 6X BASIC CARDS
*ROOKIES: 1X TO 2.5X BASIC RC
104 Nicklas Backstrom 4.00 10.00
126 Corey Crawford 3.00 8.00

2013-14 Panini Prizm Prizms Blue

*1-200 VETS: 2.5X TO 6X BASIC CARDS
*201-300 ROOKIES: 1X TO 2.5X BASIC RC
INSERTS IN WAL-MART RETAIL PACKS
104 Nicklas Backstrom 4.00 10.00
126 Corey Crawford 3.00 8.00

2013-14 Panini Prizm Prizms Blue Pulsar

*1-200 VETS: 2X TO 5X BASIC CARDS
*201-300 ROOKIES: .8X TO 2X BASIC RC
THREE PER WAL-MART RACK PACK
104 Nicklas Backstrom 3.00 8.00
126 Corey Crawford 2.50 6.00

2013-14 Panini Prizm Prizms Green

*1-200 VETS: 2.5X TO 6X BASIC CARDS
*201-300 ROOKIES: 1X TO 2.5X BASIC RC
RANDOM INSERTS IN RETAIL PACKS
104 Nicklas Backstrom 4.00 10.00
126 Corey Crawford 3.00 8.00

2013-14 Panini Prizm Prizms Orange Die Cut

*1-200 VETS/50: 6X TO 15X BASIC CARDS
*201-300 ROOKIES/50: 2X TO 5X BASIC RC
104 Nicklas Backstrom 10.00 25.00
126 Corey Crawford 8.00 20.00

2013-14 Panini Prizm Prizms Purple

*ROOKIES: .8X TO 2X BASIC CARDS
ISSUED VIA WRAPPER REDEMPTION

2013-14 Panini Prizm Prizms Red

*1-200 VETS: 2.5X TO 6X BASIC CARDS
*201-300 ROOKIES: 1X TO 2.5X BASIC RC
INSERTS IN TARGET RETAIL PACKS
104 Nicklas Backstrom 4.00 10.00
126 Corey Crawford 3.00 8.00

2013-14 Panini Prizm Prizms Red Pulsar

*1-200 VETS: 2X TO 5X BASIC CARDS
*201-300 ROOKIES: .8X TO 2X BASIC RC
THREE PER TARGET RACK PACK
104 Nicklas Backstrom 3.00 8.00
126 Corey Crawford 2.50 6.00

2013-14 Panini Prizm Autographs

*PRIZM/15-20: .6X TO 1.5X BASIC AU
A1S Eric Staal
AAY Allen York 2.50 6.00
AB4 Jean Beliveau 75.00 135.00
ABB1 Brandon Bollig 4.00 10.00
ABB2 Brett Bulmer 4.00 10.00
ABH Brett Hull 25.00 50.00
ABK Brad Park 5.00 12.00
ABM Basil McRae 3.00 8.00
ABR1 Bill Ranford 6.00 15.00
ABR2 Bobby Ryan 6.00 15.00
ABS Brendan Shanahan 20.00 40.00
ABT Bryan Trottier
ABU Brent Burns 8.00 20.00
ABV Alexander Burmistrov 3.00 8.00
ABZ Tyler Bozak 5.00 12.00
AC7 Chris Chelios 10.00 25.00
ACA Craig Anderson 4.00 10.00
ACD Cedrick Desjardins 3.00 8.00
ACG Chay Genoway 4.00 10.00
ACH Carl Hagelin 4.00 10.00
ACI David Krejci 8.00 20.00
ACK Chris Kreider 8.00 20.00
ACP Carey Price 20.00 40.00
ACS Cory Schneider 6.00 15.00
ACU Tyler Cuma 4.00 10.00
ACW Cam Ward
ADC Daniel Carcillo 4.00 10.00
ADG Doug Gilmour 25.00 50.00
ADP Dalton Prout 3.00 8.00
AEO Jose Theodore 6.00 15.00
AFV Jakob Silfverberg 3.00 8.00
AGC Gerry Cheevers 12.50 25.00
AGF Cody Goloubef 2.50 6.00
AGH Gordie Howe
AGI Mikhail Grabovski 6.00 15.00
AGL Gabriel Landeskog 6.00 15.00
AGS Gary Simmons 20.00 40.00
AGX Claude Giroux 20.00 40.00
AH9 Bobby Hull 30.00 60.00
AHJ Hugh Jessiman 3.00 8.00
AHS Harri Sateri 2.50 6.00
AHY Rich Peverley
AIU Akim Aliu 2.50 6.00
AJA Jake Allen 5.00 12.00
AJB Jamie Benn
AJD Justin DiBenedetto 2.50 6.00
AJE1 Jordan Eberle 15.00 40.00
AJE2 Borje Salming 8.00 20.00
AJF1 Joe Finley 2.50 6.00
AJF2 Johan Franzen
AJG1 Jean-Sebastien Giguere
AJG2 Jonas Gustavsson 5.00 12.00
AJJ Jaromir Jagr 40.00 80.00
AJN1 James Neal 8.00 20.00
AJN2 Jordan Nolan 3.00 8.00
AJQ Jonathan Quick 15.00 30.00
AJS Joe Sakic 20.00 40.00
AJT John Tavares 15.00 30.00
AKF Kris Foucault 2.50 6.00
AKP Keith Primeau
ALC Logan Couture 15.00 30.00
ALE Loui Eriksson 3.00 8.00
ALS Lee Stempniak 4.00 10.00
AM2 Al MacInnis 15.00 30.00
AMC Mat Clark 2.50 6.00
AMG Michael Grabner 6.00 15.00
AMH Matt Hunwick 2.50 6.00
AML Mario Lemieux 40.00 80.00
AMM2 Matt Moulson 4.00 10.00
AMM1 Mark Messier 30.00 60.00
AMS1 Mike Smith 4.00 10.00
AMS2 Michael Stone 3.00 8.00
AN8 Cam Neely 15.00 30.00
ANH Ryan Nugent-Hopkins 10.00 25.00
ANK Nazem Kadri 6.00 15.00
ANO Mark Giordano 3.00 8.00
AOB Jim O'Brien
AOP Ondrej Pavelec 6.00 15.00
AOV Alex Ovechkin 40.00 80.00
APB Pavel Bure 30.00 60.00
APC Patrice Cormier 2.50 6.00
APD Pavel Datsyuk 15.00 30.00
APE Corey Perry 8.00 20.00
APH Peter Holland 2.50 6.00
APK Patrick Kane 25.00 50.00
APP Corey Tropp 4.00 10.00
APR1 Chris Pronger
APR2 Patrick Roy
APS P.K. Subban 20.00 40.00
ARB1 Ray Bourque 20.00 40.00
ARB2 Rene Bourque 6.00 15.00
ARH Ryan Hamilton 6.00 15.00
ARJ Roman Josi 4.00 10.00
ARK1 Rick Kehoe 3.00 8.00
ARK2 Ryan Kesler
ARM Ryan Miller
ARN Rick Nash
ARS Riley Sheahan 5.00 12.00
ASB1 Sven Baertschi 5.00 12.00
ASB2 Sergei Bobrovsky 12.50 25.00
ASC1 Sean Couturier 6.00 15.00
ASC2 Sidney Crosby 3.00 8.00
ASE Stefan Elliott 5.00 12.00
ASG1 Sam Gagner 6.00 15.00
ASG2 Scott Glennie 2.50 6.00
ASI Darryl Sittler
AST Martin St. Louis 6.00 15.00
ASW Shea Weber 5.00 12.00
ASY Steve Yzerman 60.00 100.00
ASZ1 Greg Nemisz 2.50 6.00
ASZ2 Brad Staubitz 2.50 6.00
ATB1 Tyson Barrie 4.00 10.00
ATB2 T.J. Brennan 2.50 6.00
ATO T.J. Oshie 6.00 15.00
ATS Tyler Seguin 25.00 50.00
ATW Jonathan Toews 20.00 50.00
ATZ Jaden Schwartz 5.00 12.00
AUY Jussi Rynnas 5.00 12.00
AVL1 Martin Havlat 6.00 15.00
AVL2 Vincent Lecavalier 8.00 20.00
AVO Tomas Vokoun 6.00 15.00
AWL Drew Bagnall 3.00 8.00
AWN J.T. Brown 2.50 6.00
AYK Colby Robak 2.50 6.00
AZP Zach Parise 8.00 20.00

2013-14 Panini Prizm Cracked Ice Toronto Fall Expo Autographs

RELEASED AT 2013 TORONTO FALL EXPO
201 Emerson Etem 5.00 12.00
207 Dougie Hamilton 12.00 30.00
208 Ryan Spooner 6.00 15.00
232 Jack Campbell 5.00 12.00
237 Petr Mrazek 12.00 30.00
246 Tyler Toffoli 12.00 30.00
247 Charlie Coyle 6.00 15.00
253 Jarred Tinordi 6.00 15.00
254 Nathan Beaulieu 5.00 12.00
263 Brock Nelson 6.00 15.00
265 Christian Thomas 5.00 12.00
273 Scott Laughton 6.00 15.00
276 Beau Bennett 8.00 20.00
293 Nicklas Jensen 5.00 12.00

2013-14 Panini Prizm Endless Impressions

*PRIZM: .6X TO 1.5X BASIC INSERTS
*ORANGE/50: 1.2X TO 3X BASIC INSERTS
EI1 Gordie Howe 3.00 8.00
EI2 Bernie Parent 1.50 4.00
EI3 Johnny Bower 2.00 5.00
EI4 Bobby Hull 1.50 4.00
EI5 Mario Lemieux 5.00 12.00
EI6 Marcel Dionne 2.00 5.00
EI7 Stan Mikita 2.00 5.00
EI8 Johnny Bucyk 1.25 3.00
EI9 Patrick Roy 4.00 10.00
EI10 Mark Messier 2.00 5.00
EI11 Guy Lafleur 2.00 5.00
EI12 Billy Smith 1.50 4.00
EI13 Tony Esposito 1.50 4.00
EI14 Phil Esposito 2.50 6.00
EI15 Steve Yzerman 3.00 8.00

2013-14 Panini Prizm Immortalized

*PRIZM: .6X TO 1.5X BASIC INSERTS
*ORANGE/50: 1.2X TO 3X BASIC INSERTS
1 Sidney Crosby 6.00 15.00
2 Steve Yzerman 3.00 8.00
3 Jonathan Toews 3.00 8.00
4 Teemu Selanne 3.00 8.00
5 Joe Sakic 2.50 6.00
6 Patrick Roy 4.00 10.00
7 Mark Messier 2.00 5.00
8 Mike Richter 1.50 4.00
9 Brett Hull 1.50 4.00
10 Martin Brodeur 3.00 8.00
11 Patrice Bergeron 2.00 5.00
12 Bobby Clarke 1.50 4.00
13 Gordie Howe 3.00 8.00
14 Mike Bossy 1.50 4.00
15 Larry Robinson 1.50 4.00
16 Jonathan Quick 2.50 6.00
17 Martin St. Louis 1.50 4.00
18 Joe Nieuwendyk 1.50 4.00
19 Phil Esposito 2.50 6.00
20 Ray Bourque 2.50 6.00

2013-14 Panini Prizm Initial Impressions

*PRIZM: .8X TO 2X BASIC INSERTS
*ORANGE/50: 1.5X TO 4X BASIC INSERTS
II1 Nail Yakupov 3.00 8.00
II2 Jonathan Huberdeau 2.50 6.00
II3 Vladimir Tarasenko 4.00 10.00
II4 Alex Galchenyuk 5.00 12.00
II5 Dougie Hamilton 2.00 5.00
II6 Ryan Murphy 1.00 2.50
II7 Stefan Matteau .75 2.00
II8 Tyler Toffoli 2.00 5.00
II9 Cory Conacher .60 1.50
II10 Damien Brunner .75 2.00
II11 Viktor Fasth 1.00 2.50
II12 Justin Schultz 1.00 2.50
II13 Emerson Etem 1.00 2.50
II14 Scott Laughton 1.00 2.50
II15 Brendan Gallagher 3.00 8.00

2013-14 Panini Prizm Net Defenders

*PRIZM: .5X TO 1.2X BASIC INSERTS
*ORANGE/50: 1X TO 2.5X BASIC INSERTS
ND1 Henrik Lundqvist 2.50 6.00
ND2 Antti Niemi 1.50 4.00
ND3 Niklas Backstrom 1.50 4.00
ND4 Marc-Andre Fleury 3.00 8.00
ND5 Evgeni Nabokov 1.50 4.00
ND6 Braden Holtby 3.00 8.00
ND7 Sergei Bobrovsky 2.00 5.00
ND8 Jimmy Howard 2.00 5.00
ND9 Carey Price 6.00 15.00
ND10 Ondrej Pavelec 2.00 5.00
ND11 Corey Crawford 2.50 6.00
ND12 Tuukka Rask 2.00 5.00
ND13 James Reimer 2.00 5.00
ND14 Martin Brodeur 4.00 10.00
ND15 Jonathan Quick 3.00 8.00
ND16 Roberto Luongo 2.00 5.00
ND17 Ryan Miller 2.00 5.00
ND18 Jonas Hiller 1.50 4.00
ND19 Pekka Rinne 2.50 6.00
ND20 Mike Smith 2.00 5.00

2013-14 Panini Prizm Pivotal Players

*PRIZM: .6X TO 1.5X BASIC INSERTS
*ORANGE/50: 1.2X TO 3X BASIC INSERTS
PP1 Corey Perry 1.50 4.00
PP2 Patrice Bergeron 2.00 5.00
PP3 Cody Hodgson 1.50 4.00
PP4 Curtis Glencross 1.00 2.50
PP5 Alexander Semin 1.50 4.00
PP6 Patrick Kane 3.00 8.00
PP7 Gabriel Landeskog 1.25 3.00
PP8 Marian Gaborik 1.50 4.00
PP9 Jamie Benn 2.00 5.00
PP10 Henrik Zetterberg 2.00 5.00
PP11 Jordan Eberle 1.50 4.00
PP12 Jonathan Huberdeau 2.00 5.00
PP13 Jeff Carter 1.50 4.00
PP14 Zach Parise 1.50 4.00
PP15 P.K. Subban 2.50 6.00
PP16 Shea Weber 1.25 3.00
PP17 Martin Brodeur 3.00 8.00
PP18 John Tavares 3.00 8.00
PP19 Henrik Lundqvist 2.00 5.00
PP20 Erik Karlsson 3.00 8.00
PP21 Claude Giroux 1.50 4.00
PP22 Oliver Ekman-Larsson 1.25 3.00
PP23 Evgeni Malkin 5.00 12.00
PP24 Logan Couture 1.50 4.00
PP25 David Backes 1.50 4.00
PP26 Steven Stamkos 3.00 8.00
PP27 Nazem Kadri 1.50 4.00
PP28 Roberto Luongo 1.50 4.00
PP29 Alex Ovechkin 6.00 15.00
PP30 Andrew Ladd 1.50 4.00

2013-14 Panini Prizm Rookie Autographs

321 John Gibson 12.00 30.00
322 Hampus Lindholm 6.00 15.00
324 Jamie Tardif 2.50 6.00
325 Nikita Zadorov 4.00 10.00
327 Zemgus Girgensons 8.00 20.00
329 Reto Berra 4.00 10.00
330 Sean Monahan 6.00 15.00
331 Elias Lindholm 6.00 15.00
332 Nathan MacKinnon 40.00 100.00
333 John Muse 4.00 10.00
334 Antti Raanta 5.00 12.00
335 Joakim Nordstrom 3.00 8.00
336 Shawn Lalonde 4.00 10.00
337 Boone Jenner 4.00 10.00
338 Ryan Murray 6.00 15.00
339 Kevin Connauton 3.00 8.00
342 Tomas Jurco 6.00 15.00
347 Taylor Fedun 5.00 12.00
348 Tyler Pitlick 4.00 10.00
350 Aleksander Barkov 10.00 25.00
351 Jonathan Rheault 2.50 6.00
353 Linden Vey 2.50 6.00
354 Martin Jones 10.00 25.00
355 Tanner Pearson 4.00 10.00
358 Matt Dumba 4.00 10.00
359 Greg Pateryn 4.00 10.00
360 Michael Bournival 4.00 10.00
362 Daniel Bang 3.00 8.00
363 Kevin Henderson 3.00 8.00
366 Seth Jones 4.00 10.00
367 Dylan McIlrath 2.50 6.00
368 Jon Merrill 4.00 10.00
370 Ryan Strome 5.00 12.00
372 Jesper Fast 3.00 8.00
375 Calvin Heeter 3.00 8.00
376 Michael Raffl 3.00 8.00
378 Jordan Szwarz 4.00 10.00
379 Lucas Lessio 2.50 6.00
383 Jeff Zatkoff 4.00 10.00
386 Freddie Hamilton 4.00 10.00
387 Matt Nieto 3.00 8.00
388 Tomas Hertl 5.00 12.00
389 Mark Barberio 2.50 6.00
391 David Broll 4.00 10.00
392 Jamie Devane 3.00 8.00
394 Josh Leivo 4.00 10.00
395 Morgan Rielly 10.00 25.00
397 Michael Latta 3.00 8.00
399 Jacob Trouba 6.00 15.00
A2P Calvin Pickard 4.00 10.00
AAC Alex Chiasson 12.00 30.00
AAG Alex Galchenyuk 40.00 100.00
AAK Alex Killorn 4.00 10.00
AAM Jonathan Audy-Marchessault 8.00 20.00
AAR Antoine Roussel 4.00 10.00
AAW Austin Watson 3.00 8.00
ABB Beau Bennett 12.00 30.00
ABJ Nick Bjugstad 5.00 12.00
ABL Brian Lashoff 3.00 8.00
ACC Cory Conacher 2.50 6.00
ACN Cristopher Nilstorp 3.00 8.00
ACT Christian Thomas 3.00 8.00
ADH Dougie Hamilton 15.00 40.00
ADS Drew Shore 3.00 8.00
ADZ Dave Dziurzynski 3.00 8.00
AEE Emerson Etem 4.00 10.00
AEG Eric Gryba 3.00 8.00
AEP Eddie Pasquale 2.50 6.00
AEY Danny DeKeyser 10.00 25.00
AFA Frederik Andersen 6.00 15.00
AFF Filip Forsberg 10.00 25.00
AGA Brendan Gallagher 15.00 40.00
AGO Mikhail Grigorenko 12.00 30.00
AHI Thomas Hickey 3.00 8.00
AHP Harri Pesonen 3.00 8.00
AIJ Dmitrij Jaskin 4.00 10.00
AJC Jack Campbell 6.00 15.00
AJH Jonathan Huberdeau 15.00 40.00
AJL Johan Larsson 3.00 8.00
AJM J.T. Miller 4.00 10.00
AJO Jonas Brodin 3.00 8.00
AKK Michael Kostka 3.00 8.00
ALK Leo Komarov 4.00 10.00
AMA Mark Arcobello 5.00 12.00
AMC Michael Caruso 2.50 6.00
AMG Mikael Granlund 6.00 15.00
AMI Matt Irwin 3.00 8.00
AMJ Michal Jordan 2.50 6.00
ANB Nathan Beaulieu 3.00 8.00
ANJ Nicklas Jensen 3.00 8.00
ANP Nick Petrecki 2.50 6.00
ANY Nail Yakupov 30.00 80.00
ANZ Justin Schultz 4.00 10.00
AOE Jordan Schroeder 4.00 10.00
AOK Jamie Oleksiak 3.00 8.00
AOP Ondrej Palat 5.00 12.00
AOY Charlie Coyle 4.00 10.00
APG Philipp Grubauer 4.00 10.00
APM Petr Mrazek 8.00 20.00
APY Mark Pysyk 4.00 10.00
AQH Quinton Howden 3.00 8.00
ARG Radko Gudas 4.00 10.00
ARM Ryan Murphy 4.00 10.00
ARP Richard Panik 4.00 10.00
ARR Rickard Rakell 4.00 10.00
ASL Scott Laughton 4.00 10.00
ASO Carl Soderberg 5.00 12.00
ASP Ryan Spooner 8.00 20.00
ASV Sami Vatanen 4.00 10.00
ATB Taylor Beck 3.00 8.00
ATI Jarred Tinordi 4.00 10.00
ATM Tye McGinn 4.00 10.00
ATT Tyler Toffoli 10.00 25.00
AU2 Stefan Matteau 3.00 8.00
AUE Darcy Kuemper 6.00 15.00
AVB Victor Bartley 3.00 8.00
AVF Viktor Fasth 4.00 10.00
AVK Roman Cervenka 3.00 8.00
AVT Vladimir Tarasenko 30.00 60.00
AWN Chris Brown 2.50 6.00
AXW Maxwell Reinhart 4.00 10.00
AYP Anthony Peluso 2.50 6.00
AZR Zach Redmond 3.00 8.00

2013-14 Panini Prizm Rookie Autographs Prizms

*PRIZM/15-35: .8X TO 2X BASIC AU
ANY Nail Yakupov/15 125.00 200.00
AVT Vladimir Tarasenko/20 50.00 100.00

2013-14 Panini Prizm Cracked Ice Toronto Spring Expo

*301-320 VETS: 1.5X TO 4X BASIC CARDS
*321-400 ROOKIES: .8X TO 2X BASIC RC

2013-14 Panini Prizm Cracked Ice Toronto Spring Expo Autographs

RELEASED AT 2013 TORONTO SPRING EXPO
321 John Gibson 25.00 50.00
322 Hampus Lindholm 8.00 20.00
324 Jamie Tardif 3.00 8.00
325 Nikita Zadorov 5.00 12.00
329 Reto Berra 5.00 12.00
330 Sean Monahan 8.00 20.00
332 Nathan MacKinnon 125.00 200.00
333 John Muse 5.00 12.00
336 Shawn Lalonde 5.00 12.00
337 Boone Jenner 5.00 12.00
338 Ryan Murray 8.00 20.00
339 Kevin Connauton 4.00 10.00
342 Tomas Jurco 8.00 20.00
347 Taylor Fedun 6.00 15.00
348 Tyler Pitlick 5.00 12.00
350 Aleksander Barkov 12.00 30.00
354 Martin Jones 12.00 30.00
355 Tanner Pearson 5.00 12.00
358 Matt Dumba 5.00 12.00
359 Greg Pateryn 5.00 12.00
360 Michael Bournival 5.00 12.00
362 Daniel Bang 4.00 10.00
365 Marek Mazanec 5.00 12.00
366 Seth Jones 5.00 12.00
367 Dylan McIlrath 3.00 8.00
368 Jon Merrill 5.00 12.00
370 Ryan Strome 6.00 15.00
372 Jesper Fast 4.00 10.00
375 Calvin Heeter 4.00 10.00
378 Jordan Szwarz 5.00 12.00
379 Lucas Lessio 3.00 8.00
383 Jeff Zatkoff 5.00 12.00
386 Freddie Hamilton 5.00 12.00
388 Tomas Hertl 6.00 15.00
389 Mark Barberio 3.00 8.00
391 David Broll 5.00 12.00
392 Jamie Devane 4.00 10.00
394 Josh Leivo 5.00 12.00

2011-12 Panini Rookie Anthology

COMP.SET w/o RC's (100) 10.00 25.00
101-105 ROOKIE JSY AU PRINT RUN 99
116-165 ROOKIE JSY AU PRINT RUN 199
116-165 ROOKIE JSY AU PRINT RUN 499
1 Henrik Sedin .30 .75
2 Phil Kessel .40 1.00
3 Claude Giroux .30 .75
4 Joffrey Lupul .25 .60
5 Daniel Sedin .30 .75
6 Steven Stamkos .60 1.50
7 Marian Hossa .25 .60
8 Evgeni Malkin 1.00 2.50
9 Jordan Eberle .30 .75
10 Jason Pominville .25 .60
11 Pavel Datsyuk .40 1.00
12 Jason Spezza .30 .75
13 Nicklas Backstrom .50 1.25
14 Jonathan Toews .60 1.50
15 Jamie Benn .40 1.00
16 Erik Karlsson .60 1.50
17 Patrick Sharp .30 .75
18 Thomas Vanek .30 .75
19 Teemu Selanne .60 1.50
20 Kris Versteeg .25 .60
21 Loui Eriksson .25 .60
22 Patrik Elias .30 .75
23 Scott Hartnell .30 .75
24 Tyler Seguin .60 1.50
25 Patrick Kane .60 1.50
26 James Neal .30 .75
27 Johan Franzen .30 .75
28 Ray Whitney .25 .60
29 John Tavares .60 1.50
30 Anze Kopitar .50 1.25
31 Corey Perry .30 .75
32 Zach Parise .30 .75
33 Marian Gaborik .40 1.00
34 Tomas Fleischmann .20 .50
35 Ilya Kovalchuk .30 .75
36 Patrice Bergeron .40 1.00
37 Matt Moulson .25 .60
38 Alex Ovechkin 1.25 3.00
39 Jaromir Jagr .75 2.00
40 Jarome Iginla .30 .75
41 Daniel Alfredsson .30 .75
42 Mikko Koivu .25 .60
43 Joe Thornton .30 .75
44 Brad Marchand .40 1.00
45 Ryan Smyth .25 .60
46 Henrik Zetterberg .40 1.00
47 Evander Kane .30 .75
48 Sidney Crosby 1.25 3.00
49 Brad Richards .30 .75
50 Martin St. Louis .30 .75
51 P.K. Subban .60 1.50
52 Erik Cole .25 .60
53 Milan Lucic .30 .75
54 Ryan Kesler .30 .75
55 Shea Weber .25 .60
56 Logan Couture .30 .75
57 Rick Nash .30 .75
58 Taylor Hall .60 1.50
59 David Backes .30 .75
60 Danny Briere .30 .75
61 Ryan O'Reilly .30 .75
62 Eric Staal .40 1.00
63 Milan Michalek .20 .50
64 Dion Phaneuf .30 .75
65 Blake Wheeler .60 1.50
66 Ryan Getzlaf .50 1.25
67 Shane Doan .25 .60
68 Alexander Steen .30 .75
69 Jeff Carter .30 .75
70 Jeff Skinner .30 .75
71 Nicklas Lidstrom .30 .75
72 Pekka Rinne .40 1.00
73 Craig Anderson .30 .75
74 Marc-Andre Fleury .50 1.25
75 Henrik Lundqvist .40 1.00
76 Jonathan Quick .50 1.25
77 Antti Niemi .25 .60
78 Miikka Kiprusoff .30 .75
79 Tim Thomas .30 .75
80 Roberto Luongo .30 .75
81 Mike Smith .30 .75
82 Tomas Vokoun .25 .60
83 Ilya Bryzgalov .30 .75
84 Brian Elliott .25 .60
85 Carey Price 1.00 2.50
86 Kari Lehtonen .25 .60
87 Corey Crawford .40 1.00
88 Ondrej Pavelec .30 .75
89 Jose Theodore .30 .75
90 Semyon Varlamov .30 .75
91 Cam Ward .30 .75
92 Niklas Backstrom .30 .75
93 Martin Brodeur .60 1.50
94 Jonas Gustavsson .30 .75
95 Ryan Miller .30 .75
96 Jonas Hiller .25 .60
97 Tuukka Rask .30 .75
98 Martin Biron .25 .60
99 Cory Schneider .25 .60
100 Jimmy Howard .30 .75
101 Sean Couturier JSY AU RC 15.00 40.00
102 Adam Henrique JSY AU RC 15.00 40.00
103 Nugent-Hopkins JSY AU RC 60.00 120.00
104 C.Hodgson JSY AU RC 50.00 120.00
105 G. Landeskog JSY AU RC 30.00 80.00
106 Brett Connolly JSY AU RC 10.00 25.00
107 Craig Smith JSY AU RC 12.00 30.00
108 Carl Hagelin JSY AU RC 15.00 40.00
109 Adam Larsson JSY AU RC 15.00 40.00
110 Justin Faulk JSY AU RC 15.00 40.00
111 Brendan Smith JSY AU RC 10.00 25.00
112 Louis Leblanc JSY AU RC 10.00 25.00
113 Jake Gardiner JSY AU RC 12.00 30.00
114 Matt Read JSY AU RC 12.00 30.00
115 Mark Scheifele JSY AU RC 20.00 50.00
116 Zack Kassian JSY AU RC 6.00 15.00
117 Tim Erixon JSY AU RC 5.00 12.00
118 S.Despres JSY AU RC 5.00 12.00
119 Cody Eakin JSY AU RC 6.00 15.00
120 Ryan Ellis JSY AU RC 5.00 12.00
121 Greg Nemisz JSY AU RC 5.00 12.00
122 Colin Greening JSY AU RC 5.00 12.00
123 R.Johansen JSY AU RC 10.00 25.00
124 D.Smith-Pelly JSY AU RC 8.00 20.00
125 B.Saad JSY AU RC 12.00 30.00
126 Eddie Lack JSY AU RC 5.00 12.00
127 B.Geoffrion JSY AU RC 5.00 12.00
128 M.Kruger JSY AU RC 8.00 20.00
129 Harri Sateri JSY AU RC 5.00 12.00
130 S.Voynov JSY AU RC 5.00 12.00
131 Cam Atkinson JSY AU RC 12.00 30.00
132 Ben Scrivens JSY AU RC 8.00 20.00
133 Zac Rinaldo JSY AU RC 5.00 12.00
134 Matt Frattin JSY AU RC 5.00 12.00
135 David Savard JSY AU RC 5.00 12.00
136 E.Gudbranson JSY AU RC 8.00 20.00
137 C.de Haan JSY AU RC 5.00 12.00
138 A.Palushaj JSY AU RC 5.00 12.00
139 R.Bortuzzo JSY AU RC 5.00 12.00
140 Erik Condra JSY AU RC 5.00 12.00
141 G.Nyquist JSY AU RC 15.00 40.00
142 P.Wiercioch JSY AU RC 5.00 12.00
143 D.Rundblad JSY AU RC 5.00 12.00
144 J.Blum JSY AU RC 5.00 12.00
145 S.Da Costa JSY AU RC 5.00 12.00
146 T.Vincour JSY AU RC 5.00 12.00
147 Raphael Diaz JSY AU RC 5.00 12.00
148 Carl Klingberg JSY AU RC 5.00 12.00
149 E.Gustafsson JSY AU RC 6.00 15.00
150 M.Macenauer JSY AU RC 5.00 12.00
151 Allen York JSY AU RC 6.00 15.00
152 John Moore JSY AU RC 5.00 12.00
153 Tomas Kubalik JSY AU RC 5.00 12.00
154 Cam Talbot JSY AU RC 6.00 15.00
155 Brian Strait JSY AU RC 6.00 15.00
156 H.Zolnierczyk JSY AU RC 5.00 12.00
157 Joe Vitale JSY AU RC 5.00 12.00
158 Joe Colborne JSY AU RC 6.00 15.00
159 M.Zibanejad JSY AU RC 12.00 30.00
160 Andy Miele JSY AU RC 5.00 12.00
161 Peter Holland JSY AU RC 5.00 12.00
162 T.Hartikainen JSY AU RC 8.00 20.00
163 Brett Bulmer JSY AU RC 5.00 12.00
164 C.Sceviour JSY AU RC 5.00 12.00
165 C.Gaunce JSY AU RC 4.00 10.00

2011-12 Panini Rookie Anthology Draft Year Combo Jerseys

Card	Low	High
1 Selanne/Modano	10.00	25.00
2 Holmstrom/Nabokov	6.00	15.00
3 Datsyuk/Fisher	5.00	12.00
4 Zetterberg/Erat	5.00	12.00
5 D.Sedin/H.Sedin	6.00	15.00
6 Pominville/Spezza	6.00	15.00
7 McElhinney/Nash	4.00	10.00
8 Bergeron/Horton	5.00	12.00
9 A.Kostitsyn/Halak	4.00	10.00
10 M.Richards/Carter	6.00	15.00
11 Howard/Seabrook	4.00	10.00
12 Getzlaf/Perry	5.00	12.00
13 Ovechkin/Green	15.00	40.00
14 Quick/Ryan	6.00	15.00
15 Price/Neal	8.00	20.00
16 Ovechkin/Malkin	10.00	25.00
17 Stastny/Mercier	4.00	10.00
18 Setoguchi/Vlasic	3.00	8.00
19 Toews/J.Staal	8.00	20.00
20 Reimer/Varlamov	5.00	12.00
21 P.Kane/van Riemsdyk	8.00	20.00
22 Stamkos/Doughty	8.00	20.00
23 E.Kane/O'Reilly	6.00	15.00
24 Gagner/Simmonds	5.00	12.00
25 Cogliano/Bass	2.50	6.00
26 Price/M.Staal	12.00	30.00
27 Hossa/Marleau	6.00	15.00
28 Franzen/Olesz	4.00	10.00
29 Fisher/Neil	5.00	12.00
30 Carter/Horton	4.00	10.00
31 Halak/Howard	6.00	15.00
32 Olesz/N.Johnson	3.00	8.00
33 Neal/Cogliano	4.00	10.00
34 Enroth/Varlamov	4.00	10.00
35 Hall/Seguin	20.00	50.00
36 Nugent-Hopkins/Landeskog	12.00	30.00
37 Lecavalier/Legwand	3.00	8.00
38 W.Clark/Nieuwendyk	6.00	15.00
39 Simmonds/Palmieri	5.00	12.00
40 Toews/Frolik	8.00	20.00

2011-12 Panini Rookie Anthology Rookie Rivalry Dual Jerseys

Card	Low	High
1 Smith-Pelly/Voynov	4.00	10.00
2 Kassian/Palushaj	3.00	8.00
3 Geoffrion/B.Smith	5.00	12.00
4 Landeskog/Da Costa	6.00	15.00
5 Nemisz/Zibanejad	6.00	15.00
6 Erixon/de Haan	2.50	6.00
7 Kruger/Nyquist	6.00	15.00
8 Johansen/C.Smith	5.00	12.00
9 Eakin/Connolly	3.00	8.00
10 Gardiner/Palushaj	4.00	10.00
11 Hodgson/Saad	5.00	12.00
12 Gudbranson/Faulk	4.00	10.00
13 Holland/Voynov	2.50	6.00
14 Eakin/Gudbranson	3.00	8.00
15 Horak /Lack	3.00	8.00
16 Rinaldo/Vitale	5.00	12.00
17 Hagelin/Henrique	6.00	15.00
18 Atkinson/Blum	6.00	15.00
19 Larsson/Talbot	6.00	15.00
20 Rundblad/Zibanejad	5.00	12.00
21 Gaunce/Da Costa	2.50	6.00
22 Sceviour/Miele	2.50	6.00
23 Despres/Gustafsson	3.00	8.00
24 Couturier/Talbot	5.00	12.00
25 Leblanc/Scrivens	4.00	10.00
26 Sauve/Bulmer	4.00	10.00
27 Kubalik/Ellis	2.50	6.00
28 Frattin/Wiercioch	2.50	6.00
29 Read/Bortuzzo	5.00	12.00
30 Colborne/Emelin	2.50	6.00
31 Nugent-Hopkins/Hodgson	12.00	30.00
32 Moore/Blum	2.50	6.00
33 Vincour/Sateri	2.50	6.00
34 York/Ellis	3.00	8.00
35 Condra/Diaz	2.50	6.00
36 Jeffrey /Zolnierczyk	2.50	6.00
37 Kassian/Greening	3.00	8.00
38 Saad/Savard	5.00	12.00
39 York/Sateri	3.00	8.00
40 Scrivens/Lack	4.00	10.00
41 York/Talbot	6.00	15.00
42 Henrique/Gustafsson	5.00	12.00
43 Vitale/Read	5.00	12.00
44 Frattin/Rundblad	2.50	6.00
45 Eakin/Bortuzzo	3.00	8.00
46 Hodgson/Kruger	5.00	12.00
47 Hagelin/de Haan	6.00	15.00
48 Colborne/Condra	2.50	6.00
49 Despres/Rinaldo	5.00	12.00
50 Greening/Emelin	2.50	6.00
51 Smith-Pelly/Vincour	4.00	10.00
52 Nugent-Hopkins/Landeskog	12.00	30.00
53 Johansen/Nyquist	6.00	15.00
54 Leblanc/Zibanejad	8.00	20.00
55 C.Smith/Atkinson	6.00	15.00
56 Erixon/Despres	2.50	6.00
57 B.Smith/Read	5.00	12.00
58 Gardiner/Sauve	4.00	10.00
59 Geoffrion/Connolly	2.50	6.00
60 Couturier/Strait	5.00	12.00

2011-12 Panini Rookie Anthology Rookie Treasures Patches

*101-105 PATCH AU/15: .4X TO 1X AU RC/99
*106-115 PTCH AU/15: .5X TO 1.2X AU RC/199
*116-165 PTCH AU/15: 1X TO 2.5X AU RC/499
PATCH AU PRINT RUN 15

2012-13 Panini Rookie Anthology

Card	Low	High
COMP.SET w/o RC's (100)	10.00	25.00
1 Jaromir Jagr	.75	2.00
2 Rick Nash	.30	.75
3 Zach Parise	.30	.75
4 Jordan Staal	.30	.75
5 Colby Armstrong	.20	.50
6 Peter Mueller	.20	.50
7 Anders Lindback	.20	.50
8 Sergei Bobrovsky	.30	.75
9 Alexander Semin	.30	.75
10 Ryan Suter	.20	.50
11 Ruslan Fedotenko	.20	.50
12 Matthew Carle	.25	.60
13 Olli Jokinen	.25	.60
14 Jiri Hudler	.25	.60
15 Sheldon Souray	.20	.50
16 Jordin Tootoo	.25	.60
17 George Parros	.25	.60
18 Guillaume Latendresse	.25	.60
19 Brad Boyes	.20	.50
20 Jonas Gustavsson	.30	.75
21 Teemu Selanne	.60	1.50
22 Evander Kane	.30	.75
23 Tyler Seguin	.50	1.25
24 Alex Ovechkin	1.25	3.00
25 Ryan Miller	.30	.75
26 Henrik Sedin	.30	.75
27 Jarome Iginla	.30	.75
28 Phil Kessel	.40	1.00
29 Eric Staal	.40	1.00
30 Steven Stamkos	.60	1.50
31 Jonathan Toews	.60	1.50
32 Alex Pietrangelo	.25	.60
33 Gabriel Landeskog	.30	.75
34 Joe Thornton	.30	.75
35 Jack Johnson	.20	.50
36 Sidney Crosby	1.25	3.00
37 Loui Eriksson	.25	.60
38 Mike Smith	.30	.75
39 Pavel Datsyuk	.40	1.00
40 Claude Giroux	.30	.75
41 Ryan Nugent-Hopkins	.30	.75
42 Daniel Alfredsson	.30	.75
43 Kris Versteeg	.25	.60
44 Henrik Lundqvist	.40	1.00
45 Jonathan Quick	.50	1.25
46 John Tavares	.60	1.50
47 Niklas Backstrom	.25	.60
48 Martin Brodeur	.60	1.50
49 Carey Price	1.00	2.50
50 Shea Weber	.25	.60
51 Pekka Rinne	.40	1.00
52 Max Pacioretty	.30	.75
53 Ilya Kovalchuk	.30	.75
54 Matt Moulson	.25	.60
55 Dustin Brown	.30	.75
56 Marian Gaborik	.30	.75
57 Scott Clemmensen	.25	.60
58 Jason Spezza	.30	.75
59 Jordan Eberle	.30	.75
60 Ilya Bryzgalov	.30	.75
61 Henrik Zetterberg	.40	1.00
62 Shane Doan	.25	.60
63 Kari Lehtonen	.25	.60
64 Evgeni Malkin	1.00	2.50
65 Ryan Johansen	.40	1.00
66 Logan Couture	.30	.75
67 Matt Duchene	.30	.75
68 Brian Elliott	.25	.60
69 Patrick Kane	.60	1.50
70 Vincent Lecavalier	.25	.60
71 Cam Ward	.30	.75
72 James Reimer	.30	.75
73 Miikka Kiprusoff	.25	.60
74 Ryan Kesler	.30	.75
75 Cody Hodgson	.30	.75
76 Braden Holtby	.50	1.25
77 Tuukka Rask	.30	.75
78 Mark Scheifele	.40	1.00
79 Corey Perry	.30	.75
80 Brayden Schenn	.30	.75
81 Marc-Andre Fleury	.50	1.25
82 Anze Kopitar	.50	1.25
83 Adam Henrique	.30	.75
84 Dion Phaneuf	.30	.75
85 Cory Schneider	.25	.60
86 P.K. Subban	.50	1.25
87 Jimmy Howard	.30	.75
88 Taylor Hall	.60	1.50
89 Brad Richards	.30	.75
90 David Backes	.30	.75
91 Brandon Dubinsky	.25	.60
92 Luke Schenn	.20	.50
93 Eric Tangradi	.20	.50
94 Steve Ott	.25	.60
95 Derek Roy	.25	.60
96 Artem Anisimov	.25	.60
97 James van Riemsdyk	.30	.75
98 Nick Foligno	.25	.60
99 Brandon Sutter	.25	.60
100 Mike Ribeiro	.25	.60
101 M.Clark JSY AU/699 RC	4.00	10.00
102 C.Camper JSY AU/699 RC	3.00	8.00
103 MacDermid JSY AU/699 RC	4.00	10.00
104 M.Sauve JSY AU/499 RC	4.00	10.00
105 T.Krug JSY AU/699 RC	8.00	20.00
106 Hutchinson JSY AU/699 RC	8.00	20.00
107 T.Turnbull JSY AU/699 RC	4.00	10.00
108 A.Aliu JSY AU/499 RC	4.00	10.00
109 J.Welsh JSY AU/699 RC	4.00	10.00
110 B.Bollig JSY AU/499 RC	4.00	10.00
111 T.Barrie JSY AU/699 RC	8.00	20.00
112 M.Connolly JSY AU/699 RC	4.00	10.00
113 A.Joudrey JSY AU/499 RC	4.00	10.00
114 S.Hunwick JSY AU/699 RC	4.00	10.00
115 C.Goloubef JSY AU/699 RC	4.00	10.00
116 D.Prout JSY AU/699 RC	4.00	10.00
117 R.Garbutt JSY AU/699 RC	4.00	10.00
118 R.Smith JSY AU/499 RC	8.00	20.00
119 S.Glennie JSY AU/499 RC	4.00	10.00
120 B.Dillon JSY AU/699 RC	4.00	10.00
121 R.Sheahan JSY AU/499 RC	4.00	10.00
122 P.Cornet JSY AU/699 RC	4.00	10.00
123 C.Robak JSY AU/699 RC	4.00	10.00
124 J.Nolan JSY AU/499 RC	4.00	10.00
125 K.Foucault JSY AU/699 RC	4.00	10.00
126 T.Cuma JSY AU/699 RC	4.00	10.00
127 C.Genoway JSY AU/699 RC	4.00	10.00
128 J.Zucker JSY AU/699 RC	5.00	12.00
129 R.Mayer JSY AU/499 RC	5.00	12.00
130 G.Dumont JSY AU/699 RC	4.00	10.00
131 C.Pickard JSY AU/499 RC	4.00	10.00
132 A.Ness JSY AU/699 RC	4.00	10.00
133 C.Cizikas JSY AU/499 RC	4.00	10.00
134 M.Donovan JSY AU/499 RC	4.00	10.00
135 M.Watkins JSY AU/499 RC	4.00	10.00
136 Silfverberg JSY AU/499 RC	8.00	20.00
137 M.Stone JSY AU/499 RC	8.00	20.00
138 B.Manning JSY AU/699 RC	4.00	10.00
139 M.Stone JSY AU/699 RC	4.00	10.00
140 T.Sexsmith JSY AU/699 RC	4.00	10.00
141 J.Allen JSY AU/499 RC	12.00	30.00
142 J.Brown JSY AU/499 RC	4.00	10.00
143 C.Ashton JSY AU/499 RC	3.00	8.00
144 R.Hamilton JSY AU/499 RC	4.00	10.00
145 J.Rynnas JSY AU/499 RC	4.00	10.00
146 S.Baertschi JSY AU/199 RC	8.00	20.00
147 J.Schwartz JSY AU/199 RC	12.00	30.00
148 C.Kreider JSY AU/199 RC	12.00	30.00

2012-13 Panini Rookie Anthology Rookie Treasures Patches

*PATCH AU/99: .6X TO 1.5X JSY AU/499-699
*PATCH AU/50: .8X TO 2X JSY AU/499-699
*PATCH AU/25: .5X TO 1.2X JSY AU/199

2013-14 Panini Rookie Anthology

Card	Low	High
COMP.SET w/o RC's (100)	10.00	25.00
1 Ryan Getzlaf	.50	1.25
2 Jonas Hiller	.25	.60
3 Corey Perry	.30	.75
4 Teemu Selanne	.60	1.50
5 Patrice Bergeron	.40	1.00
6 Zdeno Chara	.30	.75
7 Jarome Iginla	.30	.75
8 Tuukka Rask	.30	.75
9 Tyler Ennis	.25	.60
10 Drew Stafford	.30	.75
11 Cody Hodgson	.30	.75
12 Mike Cammalleri	.25	.60
13 Mark Giordano	.25	.60
14 Jiri Hudler	.25	.60
15 Jeff Skinner	.25	.60
16 Eric Staal	.40	1.00
17 Cam Ward	.30	.75
18 Corey Crawford	.40	1.00
19 Patrick Kane	.60	1.50
20 Duncan Keith	.30	.75
21 Jonathan Toews	.60	1.50
22 Matt Duchene	.30	.75
23 Gabriel Landeskog	.25	.60
24 Semyon Varlamov	.30	.75
25 Sergei Bobrovsky	.30	.75
26 Marian Gaborik	.30	.75
27 Ryan Johansen	.40	1.00
28 Jamie Benn	.40	1.00
29 Kari Lehtonen	.25	.60
30 Tyler Seguin	.50	1.25
31 Pavel Datsyuk	.40	1.00
32 Jimmy Howard	.30	.75
33 Niklas Kronwall	.25	.60
34 Henrik Zetterberg	.40	1.00
35 Jordan Eberle	.30	.75
36 Taylor Hall	.60	1.50
37 Ryan Nugent-Hopkins	.30	.75
38 Sam Gagner	.25	.60
39 Brian Campbell	.20	.50
40 Roberto Luongo	.30	.75
41 Scottie Upshall	.20	.50
42 Drew Doughty	.30	.75
43 Anze Kopitar	.50	1.25
44 Jonathan Quick	.50	1.25
45 Mike Richards	.30	.75
46 Josh Harding	.30	.75
47 Zach Parise	.30	.75
48 Ryan Suter	.20	.50
49 Max Pacioretty	.30	.75
50 Carey Price	1.00	2.50
51 P.K. Subban	.50	1.25
52 Mike Fisher	.25	.60
53 Pekka Rinne	.40	1.00
54 Shea Weber	.25	.60
55 Martin Brodeur	.60	1.50
56 Jaromir Jagr	.75	2.00
57 Cory Schneider	.25	.60
58 Evgeni Nabokov	.25	.60
59 Kyle Okposo	.30	.75
60 John Tavares	.60	1.50
61 Henrik Lundqvist	.40	1.00
62 Ryan McDonagh	.30	.75
63 Rick Nash	.30	.75
64 Brad Richards	.30	.75
65 Erik Karlsson	.60	1.50
66 Bobby Ryan	.30	.75
67 Jason Spezza	.30	.75
68 Sean Couturier	.30	.75
69 Claude Giroux	.30	.75
70 Vincent Lecavalier	.25	.60
71 Shane Doan	.25	.60
72 Mike Smith	.30	.75
73 Keith Yandle	.30	.75
74 Sidney Crosby	1.25	3.00
75 Marc-Andre Fleury	.50	1.25
76 Kris Letang	.30	.75
77 Evgeni Malkin	1.00	2.50
78 Logan Couture	.30	.75
79 Patrick Marleau	.30	.75
80 Antti Niemi	.25	.60
81 Joe Thornton	.30	.75
82 David Backes	.30	.75
83 Ryan Miller	.30	.75
84 Alexander Steen	.30	.75
85 Ben Bishop	.30	.75
86 Martin St. Louis	.30	.75
87 Steven Stamkos	.60	1.50
88 Jonathan Bernier	.30	.75
89 Phil Kessel	.40	1.00
90 Joffrey Lupul	.25	.60
91 James Reimer	.30	.75
92 Ryan Kesler	.30	.75
93 Daniel Sedin	.30	.75
94 Henrik Sedin	.30	.75
95 Nicklas Backstrom	.50	1.25
96 Braden Holtby	.50	1.25
97 Alex Ovechkin	1.25	3.00
98 Andrew Ladd	.30	.75
99 Ondrej Pavelec	.30	.75
100 Blake Wheeler	.30	.75
101 Sami Vatanen JSY AU RC	4.00	10.00
102 F.Andersen JSY AU RC	6.00	15.00
103 H.Lindholm JSY AU RC	6.00	15.00
104 Emerson Etem JSY AU RC	4.00	10.00
105 Igor Bobkov JSY AU RC	3.00	8.00
106 Viktor Fasth JSY AU RC	4.00	10.00
107 Carl Soderberg JSY AU RC	8.00	20.00
108 Rickard Rakell JSY AU RC	4.00	10.00
109 D.Hamilton JSY AU RC	8.00	20.00
110 Ryan Spooner JSY AU RC	4.00	10.00
111 Mark Pysyk JSY AU RC	4.00	10.00
112 M.Grigorenko JSY AU RC	5.00	12.00
113 Nikita Zadorov JSY AU RC	4.00	10.00
115 Z.Girgensons JSY AU RC	8.00	20.00
116 Reto Berra JSY AU RC	4.00	10.00
117 Sean Monahan JSY AU RC	6.00	15.00
118 Max Reinhart JSY AU RC	4.00	10.00
119 Elias Lindholm JSY AU RC	6.00	15.00
120 Jared Staal JSY AU RC	4.00	10.00
121 Ryan Murphy JSY AU RC	4.00	10.00
122 Martin Jones JSY AU RC	10.00	25.00
123 J.Nordstrom JSY AU RC	3.00	8.00
124 Michael Kostka JSY AU RC	3.00	8.00
125 Calvin Pickard JSY AU RC	4.00	10.00
126 N.MacKinnon JSY AU RC	40.00	100.00
127 Boone Jenner JSY AU RC	4.00	10.00
128 Ryan Murray JSY AU RC	6.00	15.00
129 Alex Chiasson JSY AU RC	4.00	10.00
130 Antoine Roussel JSY AU RC	4.00	10.00
131 Jack Campbell JSY AU RC	3.00	8.00
132 Jamie Oleksiak JSY AU RC	3.00	8.00
133 Kevin Connauton JSY AU RC	3.00	8.00
134 V.Nichushkin JSY AU RC	4.00	10.00
135 Brian Lashoff JSY AU RC	3.00	8.00
136 C.Nilstorp JSY AU RC	3.00	8.00
137 D.DeKeyser JSY AU RC	5.00	12.00
138 Petr Mrazek JSY AU RC	8.00	20.00
139 Xavier Ouellet JSY AU RC	4.00	10.00
140 Justin Schultz JSY AU RC	4.00	10.00
141 Nail Yakupov JSY AU RC	12.00	30.00
142 Connor Murphy JSY AU RC	3.00	8.00
143 Mark Arcobello JSY AU RC	4.00	10.00
144 A.Barkov JSY AU RC	10.00	25.00
145 Drew Shore JSY AU RC	3.00	8.00
146 J.Huberdeau JSY AU RC	8.00	20.00
147 Nick Bjugstad JSY AU RC	5.00	12.00
148 Quinton Howden JSY AU RC	3.00	8.00
149 Tyler Toffoli JSY AU RC	8.00	20.00
150 John Gibson JSY AU RC	15.00	40.00
151 Tanner Pearson JSY AU RC	5.00	12.00
152 Charlie Coyle JSY AU RC	4.00	10.00
153 J.Gustafsson JSY AU RC	5.00	12.00
154 Jonas Brodin JSY AU RC EXCH	3.00	8.00
155 Mikael Granlund JSY AU RC	6.00	15.00
156 Matt Dumba JSY AU RC	4.00	10.00
157 B.Gallagher JSY AU RC	12.00	30.00
158 Michael Bournival JSY AU RC	4.00	10.00
159 Nathan Beaulieu JSY AU RC	3.00	8.00
160 Alex Galchenyuk JSY AU RC	20.00	50.00
162 Austin Watson JSY AU RC	3.00	8.00
163 Christian Thomas JSY AU RC	3.00	8.00
164 F.Forsberg JSY AU/125 RC	15.00	40.00
165 Marek Mazanec JSY AU RC	4.00	10.00
166 Seth Jones JSY AU RC	4.00	10.00
167 Jon Merrill JSY AU RC	4.00	10.00
168 Stefan Matteau JSY AU RC	3.00	8.00
169 Brock Nelson JSY AU RC	4.00	10.00
170 Thomas Hickey JSY AU RC	3.00	8.00
171 Jesper Fast JSY AU RC	3.00	8.00
172 J.T. Miller JSY AU RC	4.00	10.00
173 Cory Conacher JSY AU RC	2.50	6.00
174 Scott Laughton JSY AU RC	4.00	10.00
175 Lucas Lessio JSY AU RC	2.50	6.00
176 Olli Maatta JSY AU RC	6.00	15.00
177 Matt Nieto JSY AU RC	3.00	8.00
178 Eric Hartzell JSY AU RC	4.00	10.00
179 Tomas Hertl JSY AU RC	5.00	12.00
180 V.Tarasenko JSY AU RC	15.00	40.00
181 Alex Killorn JSY AU RC	4.00	10.00
182 Nick Petrecki JSY AU RC	2.50	6.00
184 Jamie Devane JSY AU RC	3.00	8.00
185 Darcy Kuemper JSY AU RC	4.00	10.00
186 Morgan Rielly JSY AU RC	10.00	25.00
188 Frank Corrado JSY AU RC	2.50	6.00
189 J.Schroeder JSY AU RC	4.00	10.00
190 Nicklas Jensen JSY AU RC	3.00	8.00
191 Philipp Grubauer JSY AU RC	4.00	10.00
192 Tom Wilson JSY AU RC	6.00	15.00
193 Jacob Trouba JSY AU RC	6.00	15.00
194 Zach Redmond JSY AU RC	3.00	8.00
195 E.Pasquale JSY AU RC	2.50	6.00
196 Tomas Jurco JSY AU RC	6.00	15.00
197 Ryan Strome JSY AU RC	8.00	20.00
198 Dylan Mcllrath JSY AU RC	2.50	6.00
199 Cody Ceci JSY AU RC	3.00	8.00
200 M.Hellberg JSY AU RC	4.00	10.00

2013-14 Panini Rookie Anthology Gold

*GOLD/100: 4X TO 10X BASIC CARDS

Card	Low	High
18 Corey Crawford	4.00	10.00
95 Nicklas Backstrom	5.00	12.00

2013-14 Panini Rookie Anthology Rookie Patch Autographs

*PATCH/25: 1X TO 2.5X BASIC ROOKIE

Card	Low	High
126 Nathan MacKinnon/25	125.00	225.00

2013-14 Panini Rookie Anthology Rookie Prime Autographs

*PRIME/50: .6X TO 1.5X BASIC ROOKIES
*PRIME/15-25: .8X TO 2X BASIC ROOKIES

Card	Low	High
126 Nathan MacKinnon/50	100.00	200.00

2013-14 Panini Social Signatures

Card	Low	High
SSAK Anze Kopitar TC	8.00	20.00
SSAL Andrew Ladd TC	6.00	15.00
SSAM Andy Miele T	4.00	10.00
SSAO Alex Ovechkin PB	30.00	80.00
SSAS Anthony Stewart PB	4.00	10.00
SSAS Andrew Shaw T	8.00	20.00
SSBBO Brandon Bollig T	5.00	12.00
SSBC Brett Connolly PB	4.00	10.00
SSBE Brian Elliott PB	5.00	12.00
SSBG Brian Gionta PB	6.00	15.00
SSBH Brett Hull PB	60.00	120.00
SSBM Brenden Morrow PB	5.00	12.00
SSBR Brad Richards CR		
SSCG Claude Giroux TC	25.00	60.00
SSCP Carey Price CR	15.00	40.00
SSCT Colten Teubert TC	4.00	10.00
SSDB David Backes PB	6.00	15.00
SSDP David Perron PB	4.00	10.00
SSDR Derek Roy PB	5.00	12.00
SSDS Derek Stepan PP	6.00	15.00
SSEC Erik Condra CR	4.00	10.00
SSEF Eric Fehr TC	4.00	10.00
SSEM Evgeni Malkin PB	30.00	80.00
SSGL Gabriel Landeskog PB	10.00	25.00
SSGP George Parros T	5.00	12.00
SSHL Henrik Lundqvist TC		
SSJB Jamie Benn TC	8.00	20.00
SSJG Jake Gardiner TC	6.00	15.00
SSJHY Jimmy Hayes T	5.00	12.00
SSJL John-Michael Liles PB	8.00	20.00
SSJM Jacob Markstrom CR	5.00	12.00
SSJN James Neal PB	12.00	30.00
SSJQ Jonathan Quick TC	30.00	60.00
SSJR Jeremy Roenick PB		
SSJS Jim Slater PB	4.00	10.00
SSJT John Tavares PB	12.00	30.00
SSJWA Joel Ward T	8.00	20.00
SSKS Kevin Shattenkirk T	6.00	15.00
SSKT Kyle Turris PB	4.00	10.00
SSLA Luke Adam TC	5.00	12.00
SSLC Logan Couture CR	15.00	40.00
SSMB Mikael Backlund PB	5.00	12.00
SSMF Mike Fisher CR	5.00	12.00
SSMG Marian Gaborik PB	12.00	30.00
SSMM Matt Moulson PB	5.00	12.00
SSMT Maxime Talbot CR	5.00	12.00
SSNBO Nick Bonino T	4.00	10.00
SSPK Phil Kessel PB	6.00	15.00
SSPP P.A. Parenteau CR	4.00	10.00
SSRGA Ryan Garbutt T	4.00	10.00
SSRIB Richard Bachman T	6.00	15.00
SSRJ Ryan Johansen TC	8.00	20.00
SSRK Ryan Kesler PB	10.00	25.00
SSRN Ryan Nugent-Hopkins PB	12.00	30.00
SSRT Rick Tocchet PB	10.00	25.00
SSRU R.J. Umberger TC	4.00	10.00
SSSO Steve Ott TC	5.00	12.00
SSSS Sheldon Souray TC	4.00	10.00
SSSU Scottie Upshall CR	4.00	10.00
SSTH Taylor Hall PB	10.00	25.00
SSTO T.J. Oshie CR	12.00	30.00
SSTS Tyler Seguin TC	12.00	30.00
SSVH Victor Hedman TC	8.00	20.00
SSVL Vincent Lecavalier CR		
SSWW Wojtek Wolski PB	4.00	10.00
SSBS1 Brayden Schenn PB	8.00	20.00
SSBS2 Ben Scrivens CR	5.00	12.00
SSCA1 Craig Anderson PB	6.00	15.00
SSCA2 Colby Armstrong CR	4.00	10.00
SSJE1 Jordan Eberle PB	10.00	25.00
SSJE2 Jhonas Enroth PB	6.00	15.00
SSJJ1 Jaromir Jagr PB	20.00	40.00
SSJJ2 Jack Johnson CR	4.00	10.00
SSKA1 Keith Aulie PB	4.00	10.00
SSKA2 Karl Alzner CR	4.00	10.00
SSMC1 Matthew Carle PB	5.00	12.00
SSMC2 Mike Cammalleri PB	5.00	12.00
SSMR1 Mike Rupp CR	4.00	10.00
SSMR2 Matt Read TC	4.00	10.00

2012-13 Panini Stanley Cup Private Signings

Card	Low	High
CW Cam Ward/25		
CW Cam Ward/25		
GF Grant Fuhr/25		
MB Mike Bossy/25		
TS Tyler Seguin/25		

1979 Panini Stickers

This "global" hockey set was produced by Figurine Panini and printed in Italy. Each sticker measures approximately 1 15/16" by 2 3/4". The set also has an album available.

Card	Low	High
COMPLETE SET (400)	30.00	80.00
1 Goal Disallowed	.20	.40
2 Butt-Ending	.10	.20
3 Slow Whistle	.10	.20
4 Hooking	.10	.20
5 Charging	.10	.20
6 Misconduct Penalty	.10	.20
7 Holding	.10	.20
8 High-Sticking	.10	.20
9 Tripping	.10	.20
10 Cross-Checking	.10	.20
11 Elbowing	.10	.20
12 Icing (I)	.10	.20
13 Icing (II)	.10	.20
14 Boarding	.10	.20
15 Kneeing	.10	.20
16 Slashing	.10	.20
17 Excessive Roughness	.10	.20
18 Spearing	.10	.20
19 Interference	.10	.20
20 Poster	.10	.20
21 Czech.-USSR 6-4	.25	.50
22 Czech.-USSR 6-4	.25	.50
23 USSR-Czech. 3-1	.25	.50
24 USSR-Czech. 3-1	.25	.50
25 USSR-Czech. 3-1	.25	.50
26 USSR-Czech. 3-1	.25	.50
27 Can-Sweden 3-2	.25	.50
28 Can-Sweden 3-2	.25	.50
29 USSR-Canada 5-1	.38	.75
30 USSR-Canada 5-1	.38	.75
31 Czech.-Canada 3-2	.25	.50
32 Czech.-Canada 3-2	.25	.50
33 USSR-Sweden 7-1	.25	.50
34 USSR-Sweden 7-1	.25	.50
35 USA-Finland 4-3	.25	.50
36 USA-Finland 4-3	.25	.50
37 Finland-DDR 7-2	.10	.20
38 DDR-BRD 0-0	.10	.20
39 DDR-BRD 0-0	.10	.20
40 Czechoslovakia	.10	.20
41 Poland	.10	.20
42 USSR	.63	1.25
43 USA	.63	1.25
44 Canada	2.50	5.00
45 Deutschland-BRD	.10	.20
46 Finland	.10	.20
47 Sweden	.25	.50
48 Canada Team Picture (upper left)	.50	1.00
49 Canada Team Picture (upper right)	.50	1.00
50 Canada Team Picture (lower left)	.50	1.00
51 Canada Team Picture (lower right)	.50	1.00
52 Denis Herron	1.00	2.00
53 Dan Bouchard	1.00	2.00
54 Rick Hampton	.25	.50
55 Robert Picard	.25	.50
56 Brad Maxwell	.25	.50
57 David Shand	.25	.50
58 Dennis Kearns	.25	.50
59 Tom Lysiak	.50	1.00
60 Dennis Maruk	1.00	2.00
61 Marcel Dionne	3.00	6.00
62 Guy Charron	.50	1.00
63 Glen Sharpley	.25	.50
64 Jean Pronovost	.50	1.00
65 Don Lever	.25	.50
66 Bob MacMillan	.38	.75
67 Wilf Paiement	.50	1.00
68 Pat Hickey	.38	.75
69 Mike Murphy	.25	.50
70 Czechoslovakia Team Picture (upper left)	.25	.50
71 Czechoslovakia Team Picture (upper right)	.25	.50
72 Czechoslovakia Team Picture (lower left)	.25	.50
73 Czechoslovakia Team Picture (lower right)	.25	.50
74 Jiri Holecek	.38	.75
75 Jiri Crha	.50	1.00
76 Jiri Bubla	.38	.75
77 Milan Kajki	.10	.20
78 Miroslav Dvorak	.25	.50
79 Milan Chalupa	.25	.50
80 Frantisek Kaberle	.20	.40
81 Jan Zajicek	.10	.20
82 Jiri Novak	.10	.20
83 Ivan Hlinka	.30	.75
84 Peter Stastny	5.00	10.00
85 Milan Novy	.25	.50
86 Vladimir Martinec	.10	.20
87 Jaroslav Pouzar	.25	.50
88 Pavel Richter	.10	.20
89 Bohuslav Ebermann	.10	.20
90 Marian Stastny	.50	1.00
91 Frantisek Cernick	.20	.40
92 FDR Team Picture (upper left)	.10	.20
93 FDR Team Picture (upper right)	.10	.20
94 FDR Team Picture (lower left)	.10	.20
95 FDR Team Picture (lower right)	.10	.20
96 Erich Weishaupt	.10	.20
97 Bernhard Engelbrecht	.10	.20
98 Ignaz Berndaner	.10	.20
99 Robert Murray	.10	.20
100 Udo Kiessling	.25	.50
101 Klaus Auhuber	.10	.20
102 Horst Kretschmer	.10	.20
103 Erich Kuhnhackl	.25	.50
104 Martin Wild	.10	.20
105 Lorenz Funk, Sr	.10	.20
106 M. Hinterstocker	.10	.20
107 Alois Schloder	.10	.20
108 Rainer Philipp	.10	.20
109 H. Hinterstocker	.10	.20
110 Franz Reindl	.10	.20
111 Walter Koberle	.25	.50
112 Johann Zach	.10	.20
113 Marcus Kuhl	.10	.20
114 Poland Team Picture (upper left)	.10	.20
115 Poland Team Picture (upper right)	.10	.20
116 Poland Team Picture (lower left)	.10	.20
117 Poland Team Picture (lower right)	.10	.20
118 Henryk Wojtynek	.10	.20
119 T. Slowakiewicz	.10	.20
120 Henryk Janiszewski	.10	.20
121 Henryk Gruth	.10	.20
122 Andr. Slowakiewicz	.10	.20
123 Andrzej Eskrzycki	.10	.20
124 Jerzy Potz	.25	.50
125 Marek Marcinczak	.10	.20
126 Jozef Batkiewicz	.10	.20
127 Stefan Chowaniec	.10	.20
128 Andrzej Malysiak	.10	.20
129 Walenty Zietara	.10	.20
130 Henryk Pytel	.10	.20
131 Mieczyslaw Jaskierski	.10	.20
132 Andrezei Zabawa	.10	.20
133 Tadeusz Oboj	.10	.20
134 Jan Piecko	.10	.20
135 Leszek Tokarz	.10	.20
136 USSR Team Picture (upper left)	.38	.75
137 USSR Team Picture (upper right)	.38	.75
138 USSR Team Picture (lower left)	.38	.75
139 USSR Team Picture (lower right)	.38	.75
140 Vladislav Tretiak	5.00	10.00
141 Slava Fetisov	4.00	8.00
142 Vladimir Lutchenko	.50	1.00
143 Vasilij Pervukhin	.38	.75
144 Valeri Vasiliev	1.00	2.00
145 Gennady Tsygankov	.50	1.00
146 Juri Fedorov	.20	.40
147 Vladimir Petrov	2.00	4.00
148 Vladimir Golikov	.20	.40
149 Victor Zhluktov	.25	.50
150 Boris Mikhailov	2.00	4.00
151 Valeri Kharlamov	3.00	6.00
152 Helmut Balderis	.50	1.00
153 Sergej Kapustin	.38	.75
154 Alexander Golikov	.20	.40
155 Alexander Maltsev	2.00	4.00
156 Yuri Lebedev	.38	.75
157 Sergei Makarov	2.50	5.00
158 Finland Team Picture (upper left)	.10	.20
159 Finland Team Picture (upper right)	.10	.20
160 Finland Team Picture (lower left)	.10	.20
161 Finland Team Picture (lower right)	.10	.20
162 Urpo Ylonen	.25	.50
163 Antero Kivela	.10	.20
164 Pekka Rautakallio	.50	1.00
165 Timo Nummelin	.10	.20
166 Risto Siltanen	.50	1.00
167 Pekka Marjamaki	.10	.20
168 Tapio Levo	.20	.40
169 Lasse Litma	.10	.20
170 Esa Peltonen	.10	.20
171 Martti Jarkko	.10	.20
172 Matti Hagman	.25	.50
173 Seppo Repo	.20	.40
174 Pertti Korvulahti	.10	.20
175 Seppo Ahokainen	.10	.20
176 Juhani Tamminen	.20	.40
177 Jukka Porvari	.10	.20
178 Mikko Leinonen	.38	.75
179 Matti Rautiainen	.10	.20
180 Sweden Team Picture (upper left)	.25	.50
181 Sweden Team Picture (upper right)	.25	.50
182 Sweden Team Picture (lower left)	.25	.50
183 Sweden Team Picture (lower right)	.25	.50
184 Goran Hogasta	.20	.40
185 Hardy Astrom	1.00	2.00
186 Stig Ostling	.20	.40
187 Ulf Weinstock	.10	.20
188 Mats Waltin	.10	.20
189 Stig Salming	.25	.50
190 Lars Zetterstrom	.10	.20
191 Lars Lindgren	.25	.50
192 Leif Holmgren	.10	.20
193 Roland Ericksson	.10	.20
194 Rolf Edberg	.10	.20
195 Per-Olov Brasar	.25	.50
196 Mats Ahlberg	.10	.20
197 Bengt Lundholm	.25	.50
198 Lars Gunnar Lundberg	.10	.20
199 Nils-Olov Olsson	.10	.20
200 Kent-Erik Anderson	.38	.75
201 Thomas Gradin	.75	1.50
202 USA Team Picture (upper left)	.38	.75
203 USA Team Picture (upper right)	.38	[illegible]
204 USA Team Picture (lower left)	.38	[illegible]
205 USA Team Picture (lower right)	.38	[illegible]
206 Peter Lopresti	.38	[illegible]
207 Jim Warden	.25	[illegible]
208 Dick Lamby	.25	[illegible]
209 Craig Norwich	.25	[illegible]
210 Glen Patrick	.25	[illegible]
211 Patrick Westrum	.25	[illegible]
212 Don Jackson	.25	[illegible]
213 Mark Johnson	.50	1.00
214 Curt Bennett	.25	[illegible]
215 Dave Debol	.25	[illegible]
216 Bob Collyard	.25	[illegible]
217 Mike Fidler	.25	[illegible]
218 Tom Younghans	.25	.50
219 Harvey Bennett	.25	.50
220 Steve Jensen	.38	.75
221 Jim Warner	.25	.50
222 Mike Eaves	.50	1.00
223 William Gilligan	.25	.50
224 Poster	.25	.50
225 Poland-Rom. 8-6	.10	.20
226 Poland-Rom. 8-6	.10	.20
227 Poland-Rom. 8-6	.10	.20
228 Poland-Rom. 8-6	.10	.20
229 Poland-Hun. 7-2	.10	.20
230 Poland-Hun. 7-2	.10	.20
231 Japan-Yug. 6-1	.10	.20
232 Japan-Yug. 6-1	.10	.20
233 Italy-Yug. 6-1	.10	.20
234 Italy-Yug. 6-1	.10	.20
235 Romania-Italy 5-5	.10	.20
236 Romania-Italy 5-5	.10	.20
237 Poland	.10	.20
238 Poland	.10	.20
239 Deutschland-DDR	.10	.20
240 Hungary	.10	.20
241 Netherland	.10	.20
242 Romania	.10	.20
243 Switzerland	.10	.20
244 Japan	.10	.20
245 Norway	.10	.20
246 Austria	.10	.20
247 DDR	.10	.20
248 DDR	.10	.20
249 Herzig Kraske	.10	.20
250 Simon Peters	.10	.20
251 Frenzel Lempio	.10	.20
252 Fengler Slapke	.10	.20
253 Patschinski Bielas 1	.10	.20
254 Peters Scholz	.10	.20
255 Bogelsack Stasche	.10	.20
256 Switzerland	.10	.20
257 Switzerland	.10	.20
258 Grubauer Anken	.10	.20
259 Zenhausern Meyer	.10	.20
260 Kolliker Locher	.10	.20
261 Mattli Conte	.10	.20
262 Holzer Dellsberger	.10	.20
263 Horisberger Rossetti	.10	.20
264 Berger Schmid	.10	.20
265 Hungary	.10	.20
266 Hungary	.10	.20
267 Balagh Farkas	.10	.20
268 Kovacs Hajzer	.10	.20
269 Flora Kereszty	.10	.20
270 Palla Meszoly	.10	.20
271 Menyhart Havran	.10	.20
272 Poth Muhr	.10	.20
273 Buzas Pek	.10	.20
274 Netherlands	.10	.20
275 Netherlands	.10	.20
276 Van Bilsen Krikke	.10	.20
277 Van Soldt Peternousek	.10	.20
278 Kolijn Van Den Broek	.10	.20
279 Van Wieren Toren	.10	.20
280 Van Onlangs Schaffer	.10	.20
281 Janssen Van Der Griendt	.10	.20
282 De Heer Koopmans	.10	.20
283 Japan	.10	.20
284 Japan	.10	.20
285 Iwamoto Misaw	.10	.20
286 Ito Tonozaki	.10	.20
287 Hori Nakayama	.10	.20
288 Tanaka Kyoya	.10	.20
289 Kawamura Hoshino	.10	.20
290 Misawa Sakurai	.10	.20
291 Honma Hanzawa	.10	.20
292 Norway	.10	.20
293 Norway	.10	.20
294 Walberg Goldstein	.10	.20
295 Martinsen Molberg	.10	.20
296 Nilsen Erevik	.10	.20
297 Lien Roymark	.10	.20

8 Eriksen .10 .20
Ovstedal
9 Johansen .10 .20
Haraldsen
0 Stethereng .10 .20
Throrkildsen
1 Austria .10 .20
2 Austria .10 .20
3 Schilcherl .10 .20
Prohaska
4 Hyytaienen .10 .20
Russ
5 Staribacher .10 .20
Schneider
6 Kotnauer .10 .20
Pok
7 Sadjina .10 .20
Konig
8 Mortl .10 .20
Pepeunig
9 Schilchner .10 .20
Haiszan
10 Romania .10 .20
11 Romania .10 .20
12 Hutan .10 .20
Netedu
13 Antal .10 .20
Gall
14 Lustinian .10 .20
Lonita
15 Hutanu .10 .20
Halauca
16 Tureanu .10 .20
Axinte
17 Nagy .10 .20
Costea
18 Nistor .10 .20
Olenici
19 Poster .10 .20
20 Den.-Net 3-3 .10 .20
21 Den.-Net 3-3 .10 .20
22 Net.-Spain 19-0 .10 .20
23 Net.-Spain 19-0 .10 .20
24 Aus.-Den 7-4 .10 .20
25 Aus.-Den 7-4 .10 .20
26 Net.-Bul. 8-0 .10 .20
27 China-Den. 3-2 .10 .20
28 China-France 8-4 .10 .20
29 Bulgaria .10 .20
30 France .10 .20
31 Italy .10 .20
32 Yugoslavia .10 .20
33 Belgium .10 .20
34 China .10 .20
35 Denmark .10 .20
36 Spain .10 .20
37 Belgium .10 .20
38 Belgium .10 .20
39 Smeets .10 .20
Lauwers
40 Adriaensen .10 .20
Zwikel
41 Cuvelier .10 .20
Sarazin
42 Vermeulen .10 .20
Voskertian
343 Verschraegen .10 .20
Arnould
344 Lejeune .10 .20
Langh
45 Bulgaria .10 .20
346 Bulgaria .10 .20
347 Iliev .10 .20
Lazarov
348 Iliev .10 .20
Krastinov
349 Hristov .10 .20
Petrov
50 Atanasov .10 .20
Nenov
51 Todorov .10 .20
Stoilov
352 Guerasimov .10 .20
Batchvarov
353 China .10 .20
354 China .10 .20
355 Ting Wen .10 .20
Yung Ke
356 Ke .10 .20
Shao Tang
357 Ta Chun .10 .20
Ung Sheng
358 Hsi Kiang .10 .20
Chang Shun
359 Cheng Hsin .10 .20
Te Hsi
360 Shu Ching .10 .20
Sheng Wen
361 Denmark .10 .20
362 Denmark .10 .20
363 Hansen .10 .20
Holten
Moller
364 Andersen .10 .20
Pedersen
365 Henriksen .10 .20
Hviid
366 Nielsen .10 .20
Thomsen
367 Nielsen .10 .20
Kahl
368 Jensen .10 .20
Gjerding
369 Spain .10 .20
370 Spain .10 .20
371 Estrada .10 .20
Lizarraga
372 Gonzalez .10 .20
Munitiz
373 Marin .10 .20
Aguado
374 Raventos .10 .20
Encinas
375 Capillas .10 .20
Sarazirar
376 Labayen .10 .20
Plaza
377 France .10 .20
378 France .10 .20
379 Maric .10 .20
Del Monaco
380 Oprandi .10 .20
Combe
381 Allard .10 .20
Le Blond
382 Vassieux .10 .20
Rey
383 Galiay .10 .20
Le Blond
384 Vinard .10 .20
Smaniotto
385 Italy .10 .20
386 Italy .10 .20
387 Tigliani .10 .20
Gasser
388 Kostner .10 .20
Pasqualotto
389 Lacedelli .10 .20
Polloni
390 Insam .10 .20
De Toni
391 Strohmaier .10 .20
Kasslatter
392 De Marchi .10 .20
Pugliese
393 Yugoslavia .10 .20
394 Yugoslavia .10 .20
395 Zbontar .10 .20
Scap
396 Kumar .10 .20
Kosir
397 Kavec .10 .20
Smolej
398 Kafner .10 .20
Lepsa
399 Poljansek .10 .20
Kosir
400 Klemenc .10 .20
Jan
xx Sticker Album 10.00 20.00

1987-88 Panini Stickers

This set of 396 hockey stickers was produced and distributed by Panini. The sticker number is only on the backing of the sticker. The stickers measure approximately 2 1/8" by 2 11/16". The team logos are foil stickers. On the inside back cover of the sticker album the company offered (via direct mail-order) up to 30 different stickers of your choice for either ten cents each or in trade one-for-one for your unwanted extra stickers plus 1.00 for postage and handling; this is one reason why the values of the most popular players in these sticker sets are somewhat depressed compared to traditional card prices.

COMPLETE SET (396) 14.00 35.00
1 Stanley Cup .02 .10
2 Bruins Action .01 .05
3 Bruins Emblem .01 .05
4 Doug Keans .01 .05
5 Bill Ranford .60 1.50
6 Ray Bourque .40 1.00
7 Reed Larson .01 .05
8 Mike Milbury .01 .05
9 Michael Thelven .01 .05
10 Cam Neely .20 .50
11 Charlie Simmer .01 .05
12 Rick Middleton .01 .05
13 Tom McCarthy .01 .05
14 Keith Crowder .01 .05
15 Steve Kasper .01 .05
16 Ken Linseman .01 .05
17 Dwight Foster .01 .05
18 Jay Miller .01 .05
19 Sabres Action .01 .05
20 Sabres Emblem .01 .05
21 Jacques Cloutier .02 .10
22 Tom Barrasso .02 .10
23 Daren Puppa .02 .10
24 Phil Housley .01 .05
25 Mike Ramsey .01 .05
26 Bill Hajt .01 .05
27 Dave Andreychuk .02 .10
28 Christian Ruuttu .01 .05
29 Mike Foligno .01 .05
30 John Tucker .01 .05
31 Adam Creighton .01 .05
32 Wilf Paiement .01 .05
33 Paul Cyr .01 .05
34 Clark Gillies .01 .05
35 Lindy Ruff .01 .05
36 Whalers Action .01 .05
37 Whalers Emblem .01 .05
38 Mike Liut .02 .10
39 Steve Weeks .01 .05
40 Dave Babych .01 .05
41 Ulf Samuelsson .20 .50
42 Dana Murzyn .01 .05
43 Ron Francis .02 .10
44 Kevin Dineen .01 .05
45 John Anderson .01 .05
46 Ray Ferraro .01 .05
47 Dean Evason .01 .05
48 Paul Lawless .01 .05
49 Stewart Gavin .01 .05
50 Sylvain Turgeon .01 .05
51 Dave Tippett .01 .05
52 Doug Jarvis .01 .05
53 Canadiens Action .01 .05
54 Canadiens Emblem .01 .05
55 Brian Hayward .02 .10
56 Patrick Roy 1.25 3.00
57 Larry Robinson .02 .10
58 Chris Chelios .30 .75
59 Craig Ludwig .01 .05
60 Rick Green .01 .05
61 Mats Naslund .01 .05
62 Bobby Smith .01 .05
63 Claude Lemieux .60 1.50
64 Guy Carbonneau .02 .10
65 Stephane Richer .30 .75
66 Mike McPhee .02 .10
67 Brian Skrudland .01 .05
68 Chris Nilan .01 .05
69 Bob Gainey .02 .10
70 Devils Action .01 .05
71 Devils Emblem .01 .05
72 Craig Billington .02 .10
73 Alain Chevrier .01 .05
74 Bruce Driver .01 .05
75 Joe Cirella .01 .05
76 Ken Daneyko .01 .05
77 Craig Wolanin .01 .05
78 Aaron Broten .01 .05
79 Kirk Muller .02 .10
80 John MacLean .01 .05
81 Pat Verbeek .01 .05
82 Doug Sulliman .01 .05
83 Mark Johnson .01 .05
84 Greg Adams .01 .05
85 Claude Loiselle .01 .05
86 Andy Brickley .01 .05
87 Islanders Action .01 .05
88 Islanders Emblem .01 .05
89 Billy Smith .02 .10
90 Kelly Hrudey .02 .10
91 Denis Potvin .01 .05
92 Tomas Jonsson .01 .05
93 Ken Leiter .01 .05
94 Ken Morrow .01 .05
95 Brian Curran .01 .05
96 Bryan Trottier .02 .10
97 Mike Bossy .20 .50
98 Pat LaFontaine .20 .50
99 Brent Sutter .01 .05
100 Mikko Makela .01 .05
101 Pat Flatley .01 .05
102 Duane Sutter .01 .05
103 Rich Kromm .01 .05
104 Rangers Action .01 .05
105 Rangers Emblem .01 .05
106 John Vanbiesbrouck .75 2.00
107 James Patrick .01 .05
108 Ron Greschner .01 .05
109 Willie Huber .01 .05
110 Curt Giles .01 .05
111 Larry Melnyk .01 .05
112 Walt Poddubny .01 .05
113 Marcel Dionne .20 .50
114 Tomas Sandstrom .01 .05
115 Kelly Kisio .01 .05
116 Pierre Larouche .01 .05
117 Don Maloney .01 .05
118 Tony McKegney .01 .05
119 Ron Duguay .01 .05
120 Jan Erixon .01 .05
121 Flyers Action .01 .05
122 Flyers Emblem .01 .05
123 Ron Hextall .40 1.00
124 Mark Howe .01 .05
125 Doug Crossman .01 .05
126 Brad McCrimmon .01 .05
127 Brad Marsh .01 .05
128 Tim Kerr .01 .05
129 Peter Zezel .01 .05
130 Dave Poulin .01 .05
131 Brian Propp .01 .05
132 Pelle Eklund .01 .05
133 Murray Craven .01 .05
134 Rick Tocchet .40 1.00
135 Derrick Smith .01 .05
136 Ilkka Sinisalo .01 .05
137 Ron Sutter .01 .05
138 Penguins Action .01 .05
139 Penguins Emblem .01 .05
140 Gilles Meloche .02 .10
141 Doug Bodger .01 .05
142 Moe Mantha .01 .05
143 Jim Johnson .01 .05
144 Rod Buskas .01 .05
145 Randy Hillier .01 .05
146 Mario Lemieux 1.25 3.00
147 Dan Quinn .01 .05
148 Randy Cunneyworth .01 .05
149 Craig Simpson .01 .05
150 Terry Ruskowski .01 .05
151 John Chabot .01 .05
152 Bob Errey .01 .05
153 Dan Frawley .01 .05
154 Dave Hannan .01 .05
155 Nordiques Action .01 .05
156 Nordiques Emblem .01 .05
157 Mario Gosselin .02 .10
158 Clint Malarchuk .02 .10
159 Risto Siltanen .01 .05
160 Robert Picard .01 .05
161 Normand Rochefort .01 .05
162 Randy Moller .01 .05
163 Michel Goulet .02 .10
164 Peter Stastny .02 .10
165 John Ogrodnick .01 .05
166 Anton Stastny .01 .05
167 Paul Gillis .01 .05
168 Dale Hunter .01 .05
169 Alain Cote .01 .05
170 Mike Eagles .01 .05
171 Jason Lafreniere .01 .05
172 Capitals Action .01 .05
173 Capitals Emblem .01 .05
174 Pete Peeters .02 .10
175 Bob Mason .02 .10
176 Larry Murphy .20 .50
177 Scott Stevens .02 .10
178 Rod Langway .01 .05
179 Kevin Hatcher .20 .50
180 Mike Gartner .20 .50
181 Mike Ridley .01 .05
182 Craig Laughlin .01 .05
183 Gaetan Duchesne .01 .05
184 Dave Christian .01 .05
185 Greg Adams .01 .05
186 Kelly Miller .01 .05
187 Alan Haworth .01 .05
188 Lou Franceschetti .01 .05
189 Stanley Cup top half .02 .10
190 Stanley Cup bottom half .02 .10
191 Ron Hextall .60 1.50
192 Wayne Gretzky 1.50 4.00
193 Brian Propp .01 .05
194 Mark Messier .40 1.00
195 Flyers/Oilers Action .01 .05
196 Flyers/Oilers Action .01 .05
197 Gretzky Holding Cup .40 1.00
198 Gretzky Holding Cup .40 1.00
199 Gretzky Holding Cup .40 1.00
200 Gretzky Holding Cup .40 1.00
201 Flames Action .01 .05
202 Flames Emblem .01 .05
203 Mike Vernon .60 1.50
204 Rejean Lemelin .02 .10
205 Al MacInnis .20 .50
206 Paul Reinhart .01 .05
207 Gary Suter .02 .10
208 Jamie Macoun .01 .05
209 Neil Sheehy .01 .05
210 Joe Mullen .02 .10
211 Carey Wilson .01 .05
212 Joel Otto .01 .05
213 Jim Peplinski .01 .05
214 Hakan Loob .01 .05
215 Lanny McDonald .01 .05
216 Tim Hunter .01 .05
217 Gary Roberts .02 .10
218 Blackhawks Action .01 .05
219 Blackhawks Emblem .01 .05
220 Bob Sauve .02 .10
221 Murray Bannerman .01 .05
222 Doug Wilson .01 .05
223 Bob Murray .01 .05
224 Gary Nylund .01 .05
225 Denis Savard .02 .10
226 Steve Larmer .02 .10
227 Troy Murray .01 .05
228 Wayne Presley .01 .05
229 Al Secord .01 .05
230 Ed Olczyk .01 .05
231 Curt Fraser .01 .05
232 Bill Watson .01 .05
233 Keith Brown .01 .05
234 Darryl Sutter .01 .05
235 Red Wings Action .01 .05
236 Red Wings Emblem .01 .05
237 Greg Stefan .01 .05
238 Glen Hanlon .02 .10
239 Darren Veitch .01 .05
240 Mike O'Connell .01 .05
241 Harold Snepsts .01 .05
242 Dave Lewis .01 .05
243 Steve Yzerman .75 2.00
244 Brent Ashton .01 .05
245 Gerard Gallant .01 .05
246 Petr Klima .01 .05
247 Shawn Burr .01 .05
248 Adam Oates .02 .10
249 Mel Bridgman .01 .05
250 Tim Higgins .01 .05
251 Joey Kocur .01 .05
252 Oilers Action .01 .05
253 Oilers Emblem .01 .05
254 Grant Fuhr .20 .50
255 Andy Moog .02 .10
256 Paul Coffey .20 .50
257 Kevin Lowe .02 .10
258 Craig Muni .01 .05
259 Steve Smith .01 .05
260 Charlie Huddy .01 .05
261 Wayne Gretzky 1.50 4.00
262 Jari Kurri .20 .50
263 Mark Messier .40 1.00
264 Esa Tikkanen .01 .05
265 Glenn Anderson .02 .10
266 Mike Krushelnyski .01 .05
267 Craig MacTavish .01 .05
268 Dave Hunter .01 .05
269 Kings Action .01 .05
270 Kings Emblem .01 .05
271 Roland Melanson .02 .10
272 Darren Eliot .01 .05
273 Grant Ledyard .01 .05
274 Jay Wells .01 .05
275 Mark Hardy .01 .05
276 Dean Kennedy .01 .05
277 Luc Robitaille 1.00 2.50
278 Bernie Nicholls .02 .10
279 Jimmy Carson .01 .05
280 Dave Taylor .01 .05
281 Jim Fox .01 .05
282 Bryan Erickson .01 .05
283 Tiger Williams .01 .05
284 Sean McKenna .01 .05
285 Phil Sykes .01 .05
286 North Stars Action .01 .05
287 North Stars Emblem .01 .05
288 Kari Takko .02 .10
289 Don Beaupre .02 .10
290 Craig Hartsburg .01 .05
291 Ron Wilson .01 .05
292 Frantisek Musil .01 .05
293 Dino Ciccarelli .02 .10
294 Brian MacLellan .01 .05
295 Dirk Graham .01 .05
296 Brian Bellows .01 .05
297 Neal Broten .01 .05
298 Dennis Maruk .01 .05
299 Keith Acton .01 .05
300 Brian Lawton .01 .05
301 Bob Brooke .01 .05
302 Willi Plett .01 .05
303 Blues Action .01 .05
304 Blues Emblem .01 .05
305 Rick Wamsley .02 .10
306 Rob Ramage .01 .05
307 Ric Nattress .01 .05
308 Bruce Bell .01 .05
309 Charlie Bourgeois .01 .05
310 Jim Pavese .01 .05
311 Doug Gilmour .20 .50
312 Bernie Federko .01 .05
313 Mark Hunter .01 .05
314 Greg Paslawski .01 .05
315 Gino Cavallini .01 .05
316 Rick Meagher .01 .05
317 Ron Flockhart .01 .05
318 Doug Wickenheiser .01 .05
319 Jocelyn Lemieux .01 .05
320 Maple Leafs Action .01 .05
321 Maple Leafs Emblem .01 .05
322 Ken Wregget .02 .10
323 Allan Bester .02 .10
324 Todd Gill .01 .05
325 Al Iafrate .01 .05
326 Borje Salming .01 .05
327 Russ Courtnall .01 .05
328 Rick Vaive .01 .05
329 Steve Thomas .01 .05
330 Wendel Clark .30 .75
331 Gary Leeman .01 .05
332 Tom Fergus .01 .05
333 Vincent Damphousse .20 .50
334 Peter Ihnacak .01 .05
335 Brad Smith .01 .05
336 Miroslav Ihnacak .01 .05
337 Canucks Action .01 .05
338 Canucks Emblem .01 .05
339 Frank Caprice .01 .05
340 Richard Brodeur .01 .05
341 Doug Lidster .01 .05
342 Michel Petit .01 .05
343 Garth Butcher .01 .05
344 Dave Richter .01 .05
345 Tony Tanti .01 .05
346 Barry Pederson .01 .05
347 Petri Skriko .01 .05
348 Patrik Sundstrom .01 .05
349 Stan Smyl .01 .05
350 Rich Sutter .01 .05
351 Steve Tambellini .01 .05
352 Jim Sandlak .01 .05
353 Dave Lowry .01 .05
354 Jets Action .01 .05
355 Jets Emblem .01 .05
356 Daniel Berthiaume .02 .10
357 Pokey Reddick .01 .05
358 Dave Ellett .01 .05
359 Mario Marois .01 .05
360 Randy Carlyle .01 .05
361 Fredrick Olausson .01 .05
362 Jim Kyte .01 .05
363 Dale Hawerchuk .02 .10
364 Paul MacLean .01 .05
365 Thomas Steen .01 .05
366 Gilles Hamel .01 .05
367 Doug Smail .01 .05
368 Laurie Boschman .01 .05
369 Ray Neufeld .01 .05
370 Andrew McBain .01 .05
371 Wayne Gretzky 1.50 4.00
372 Hart Trophy .01 .05
373 Wayne Gretzky 1.50 4.00
374 Art Ross Trophy .01 .05
375 Jennings Trophy .01 .05
376A Brian Hayward .02 .10
376B Patrick Roy 1.25 3.00
377 Vezina Trophy .01 .05
378 Ron Hextall .20 .50
379 Luc Robitaille 1.00 2.50
380 Calder Trophy .01 .05
381 Ray Bourque .20 .50
382 Norris Trophy .01 .05
383 Lady Byng Trophy .01 .05
384 Joe Mullen .02 .10
385 Frank Selke Trophy .01 .05
386 Dave Poulin .01 .05
387 Doug Jarvis .01 .05
388 Masterton Trophy .01 .05
389 Wayne Gretzky 1.50 4.00
390 Emery Edge Award .01 .05
391 Flyers Team Photo .01 .05
(left half)
392 Flyers Team Photo .01 .05
(right half)
393 Prince of Wales .01 .05
Trophy
394 Clarence S. Campbell .01 .05
Bowl
395 Oilers Team Photo .01 .05
(left half
396 Oilers Team Photo .01 .05
(right half
NNO Sticker Album 2.00 5.00

1988-89 Panini Stickers

This set of 408 hockey stickers was produced and distributed by Panini. The sticker number is only on the backing of the sticker. The stickers measure approximately 2 1/8" by 2 11/16". The team picture cards are double stickers with each sticker showing half of the photo; in the checklist below these halves are denoted by LH (left half) and RH (right half). There was an album issued with the set for holding the stickers. On the inside back cover of the sticker album the company offered (via direct mail-order) up to 30 different stickers of your choice for either ten cents each or in trade one-for-one for your unwanted extra stickers plus 1.00 for postage and handling; this is one reason why the values of the most popular players in these sticker sets are somewhat depressed compared to traditional card prices.

COMPLETE SET (408) 12.00 30.00
1 Road to the Cup .01 .05
Stanley Cup
2 Flames Emblem .01 .05
3 Flames Uniform .01 .05
4 Mike Vernon .02 .10
5 Al MacInnis .02 .10
6 Brad McCrimmon .01 .05
7 Gary Suter .02 .10
8 Mike Bullard .01 .05
9 Hakan Loob .01 .05
10 Lanny McDonald .01 .05
11 Joe Mullen .02 .10
12 Joe Nieuwendyk .20 .50
13 Joel Otto .01 .05
14 Jim Peplinski .01 .05
15 Gary Roberts .02 .10
16 Flames Team LH .01 .05
17 Flames Team RH .01 .05
18 Blackhawks Emblem .01 .05
19 Blackhawks Uniform .01 .05
20 Bob Mason .02 .10
21 Darren Pang .02 .10
22 Bob Murray .01 .05
23 Gary Nylund .01 .05
24 Doug Wilson .01 .05
25 Dirk Graham .01 .05
26 Steve Larmer .02 .10
27 Troy Murray .01 .05
28 Brian Noonan .01 .05
29 Denis Savard .02 .10
30 Steve Thomas .01 .05
31 Rick Vaive .01 .05
32 Blackhawks Team LH .01 .05
33 Blackhawks Team RH .01 .05
34 Red Wings Emblem .01 .05
35 Red Wings Uniform .01 .05
36 Glen Hanlon .02 .10
37 Greg Stefan .02 .10
38 Jeff Sharples .01 .05
39 Darren Veitch .01 .05
40 Brent Ashton .01 .05
41 Shawn Burr .01 .05
42 John Chabot .01 .05
43 Gerard Gallant .01 .05
44 Petr Klima .01 .05
45 Adam Oates .02 .10
46 Bob Probert .02 .10
47 Steve Yzerman .60 1.50
48 Red Wings Team LH .01 .05
49 Red Wings Team RH .01 .05
50 Oilers Emblem .01 .05
51 Oilers Uniform .01 .05
52 Grant Fuhr .20 .50
53 Charlie Huddy .01 .05
54 Kevin Lowe .02 .10
55 Steve Smith .01 .05
56 Jeff Beukeboom .01 .05
57 Glenn Anderson .02 .10
58 Wayne Gretzky 1.00 2.50
59 Jari Kurri .20 .50
60 Craig MacTavish .01 .05
61 Mark Messier .30 .75
62 Craig Simpson .01 .05
63 Esa Tikkanen .02 .10
64 Oilers Team LH .01 .05
65 Oilers Team RH .01 .05
66 Kings Emblem .01 .05
67 Kings Uniform .01 .05
68 Glenn Healy .20 .50
69 Roland Melanson .02 .10
70 Steve Duchesne .20 .50
71 Tom Laidlaw .01 .05
72 Jay Wells .01 .05
73 Mike Allison .01 .05
74 Bob Carpenter .01 .05
75 Jimmy Carson .01 .05
76 Jim Fox .01 .05
77 Bernie Nicholls .02 .10
78 Luc Robitaille .20 .50
79 Dave Taylor .01 .05
80 Kings Team LH .01 .05
81 Kings Team RH .01 .05
82 North Stars Emblem .01 .05
83 North Stars Uniform .01 .05
84 Don Beaupre .02 .10
85 Kari Takko .02 .10
86 Craig Hartsburg .01 .05
87 Frantisek Musil .01 .05
88 Dave Archibald .01 .05
89 Brian Bellows .01 .05
90 Scott Bjugstad .01 .05
91 Bob Brooke .01 .05
92 Neal Broten .01 .05
93 Dino Ciccarelli .02 .10
94 Brian Lawton .01 .05
95 Brian MacLellan .01 .05
96 North Stars Team LH .01 .05
97 North Stars Team RH .01 .05
98 Blues Emblem .01 .05
99 Blues Uniform .01 .05
100 Greg Millen .02 .10
101 Brian Benning .01 .05
102 Gordie Roberts .01 .05
103 Gino Cavallini .01 .05
104 Bernie Federko .01 .05
105 Doug Gilmour .20 .50
106 Tony Hrkac .01 .05
107 Brett Hull .20 .50
108 Mark Hunter .01 .05
109 Tony McKegney .01 .05
110 Rick Meagher .01 .05
111 Brian Sutter .01 .05
112 Blues Team LH .01 .05
113 Blues Team RH .01 .05
114 Maple Leafs Emblem .01 .05
115 Maple Leafs Uniform .01 .05
116 Allan Bester .02 .10
117 Ken Wregget .02 .10
118 Al Iafrate .01 .05
119 Luke Richardson .01 .05
120 Borje Salming .01 .05
121 Wendel Clark .02 .10
122 Russ Courtnall .01 .05
123 Vincent Damphousse .02 .10
124 Dan Daoust .01 .05
125 Gary Leeman .01 .05
126 Ed Olczyk .01 .05
127 Mark Osborne .01 .05
128 Maple Leafs Team LH .01 .05
129 Maple Leafs Team RH .01 .05
130 Canucks Emblem .01 .05
131 Canucks Uniform .01 .05
132 Kirk McLean .02 .10
133 Jim Benning .01 .05
134 Garth Butcher .01 .05
135 Doug Lidster .01 .05
136 Greg Adams .01 .05
137 David Bruce .01 .05
138 Barry Pederson .01 .05
139 Jim Sandlak .01 .05
140 Petri Skriko .01 .05
141 Stan Smyl .01 .05
142 Rich Sutter .01 .05
143 Tony Tanti .01 .05
144 Canucks Team LH .01 .05
145 Canucks Team RH .01 .05
146 Jets Emblem .01 .05
147 Jets Uniform .01 .05
148 Daniel Berthiaume .02 .10
149 Randy Carlyle .01 .05
150 Dave Ellett .01 .05
151 Mario Marois .01 .05
152 Peter Taglianetti .01 .05
153 Laurie Boschman .01 .05
154 Iain Duncan .01 .05
155 Dale Hawerchuk .02 .10
156 Paul MacLean .01 .05
157 Andrew McBain .01 .05
158 Doug Smail .01 .05
159 Thomas Steen .01 .05
160 Jets Team LH .01 .05
161 Jets Team RH .01 .05
162 Prince of Wales .01 .05
Trophy
163 Caps/Flyers Action .01 .05
164 Bruins/Canadiens .01 .05
Action
165 Caps/Devils Action .01 .05
166 Bruins/Devils .01 .05
Action LH
167 Bruins/Devils .01 .05
Action RH
168 Flames/Kings Action .01 .05
169 Clarence S. Campbell .01 .05
Bowl
170 Oilers/Flames Action .01 .05
171 Blues/Red Wings Action .01 .05
172 Oilers/Red Wings Action .01 .05
173 Oilers/Red Wings Action .01 .05
174 Oilers Celebrate .01 .05
175 Oilers/Bruins Action .01 .05
176 Stanley Cup .02 .10
(top half)
177 Stanley Cup .02 .10
(bottom half)
178 Wayne Gretzky 1.00 2.50
178 Bruins Action .01 .05
179 Oilers/Bruins Action RH .01 .05
180 Oilers/Bruins Action LH .01 .05
181 Wayne Gretzky 1.00 2.50
182 Conn Smythe Trophy .01 .05
183 Oilers Celebrate UL .01 .05
184 Oilers Celebrate UR .01 .05
185 Oilers Celebrate LL .01 .05
186 Oilers Celebrate LR .01 .05
187 Flames Action .01 .05
188 Grant Fuhr .20 .50
189 Devils Action .01 .05
190 Marcel Dionne .20 .50
191 Cam Neely .20 .50
192 Capitals Action .01 .05
193 Wayne Gretzky 1.00 2.50
194 Jets/Bruins Action .01 .05
195 Bruins/Canadiens Action .01 .05
196 Blues Action .01 .05
197 Caps/Flyers Action .01 .05
198 Islanders Action .01 .05
199 Flames Action .01 .05
200 Penguins Action .01 .05
201 Bruins Emblem .01 .05
202 Bruins Uniform .01 .05
203 Rejean Lemelin .02 .10
204 Ray Bourque .20 .50
205 Gord Kluzak .01 .05
206 Michael Thelven .01 .05
207 Glen Wesley .01 .05
208 Randy Burridge .01 .05
209 Keith Crowder .01 .05
210 Steve Kasper .01 .05
211 Ken Linseman .01 .05
212 Jay Miller .01 .05
214 Bob Sweeney .01 .05
215 Bruins Team LH .01 .05
216 Bruins Team RH .01 .05
217 Sabres Emblem .01 .05
218 Sabres Uniform .01 .05
219 Tom Barrasso .02 .10
220 Phil Housley .01 .05
221 Calle Johansson .01 .05
222 Mike Ramsey .01 .05
223 Dave Andreychuk .02 .10
224 Scott Arniel .01 .05
225 Adam Creighton .01 .05
226 Mike Foligno .01 .05
227 Christian Ruuttu .01 .05
228 Ray Sheppard .20 .50
229 John Tucker .01 .05
230 Pierre Turgeon .20 .50
231 Sabres Team LH .01 .05
232 Sabres Team RH .01 .05
233 Whalers Emblem .01 .05
234 Whalers Uniform .01 .05
235 Mike Liut .02 .10
236 Dave Babych .01 .05
237 Sylvain Cote .01 .05
238 Ulf Samuelsson .01 .05
239 John Anderson .01 .05
240 Kevin Dineen .01 .05
241 Ray Ferraro .01 .05
242 Ron Francis .02 .10
243 Paul MacDermid .01 .05
244 Dave Tippett .01 .05
245 Sylvain Turgeon .01 .05
246 Carey Wilson .01 .05
247 Whalers Team LH .01 .05
248 Whalers Team RH .01 .05
249 Canadiens Emblem .01 .05
250 Canadiens Uniform .01 .05
251 Brian Hayward .02 .10
252 Patrick Roy .75 2.00
253 Chris Chelios .20 .50
254 Craig Ludwig .01 .05
255 Petr Svoboda .01 .05
256 Guy Carbonneau .02 .10
257 Claude Lemieux .20 .50
258 Mike McPhee .01 .05
259 Mats Naslund .01 .05
260 Stephane Richer .02 .10
261 Bobby Smith .01 .05
262 Ryan Walter .01 .05
263 Canadiens Team LH .01 .05
264 Canadiens Team RH .01 .05
265 Devils Emblem .01 .05
266 Devils Uniform .01 .05
267 Sean Burke .20 .50
268 Joe Cirella .01 .05
269 Bruce Driver .01 .05
270 Craig Wolanin .01 .05
271 Aaron Broten .01 .05
272 Doug Brown .01 .05
273 Claude Loiselle .01 .05
274 John MacLean .01 .05
275 Kirk Muller .02 .10
276 Brendan Shanahan .20 .50
277 Patrik Sundstrom .01 .05
278 Pat Verbeek .01 .05
279 Devils Team LH .01 .05
280 Devils Team RH .01 .05
281 Islanders Emblem .01 .05
282 Islanders Uniform .01 .05
283 Kelly Hrudey .02 .10
284 Steve Konroyd .01 .05
285 Ken Morrow .01 .05
286 Pat Flatley .01 .05
287 Greg Gilbert .01 .05
288 Alan Kerr .01 .05
289 Derek King .01 .05
290 Pat LaFontaine .20 .50
291 Mikko Makela .01 .05
292 Brent Sutter .01 .05
293 Bryan Trottier .02 .10
294 Randy Wood .01 .05
295 Islanders Team .01 .05
296 Islanders Team .01 .05
297 Rangers Emblem .01 .05
298 Rangers Uniform .01 .05
299 Bob Froese .02 .10
300 John Vanbiesbrouck .20 .50
301 Brian Leetch .20 .50
302 Norm Maciver .01 .05
303 James Patrick .01 .05
304 Michel Petit .01 .05
305 Ulf Dahlen .01 .05
306 Jan Erixon .01 .05
307 Kelly Kisio .01 .05
308 Don Maloney .01 .05
309 Walt Poddubny .01 .05
310 Tomas Sandstrom .01 .05
311 Rangers Team LH .01 .05
312 Rangers Team RH .01 .05
313 Flyers Emblem .01 .05
314 Flyers Uniform .01 .05
315 Ron Hextall .02 .10
316 Mark Howe .01 .05
317 Kerry Huffman .01 .05
318 Kjell Samuelsson .01 .05
319 Dave Brown .01 .05
320 Murray Craven .01 .05
321 Tim Kerr .01 .05
322 Scott Mellanby .02 .10
323 Dave Poulin .01 .05
324 Brian Propp .01 .05
325 Ilkka Sinisalo .01 .05
326 Rick Tocchet .02 .10
327 Flyers Team LH .01 .05
328 Flyers Team RH .01 .05
329 Penguins Emblem .01 .05
330 Penguins Uniform .01 .05
331 Frank Pietrangelo .02 .10
332 Doug Bodger 01 .05
333 Paul Coffey .20 .50
334 Jim Johnson .01 .05
335 Ville Siren .01 .05
336 Rob Brown .01 .05
337 Randy Cunneyworth .01 .05
338 Dan Frawley .01 .05
339 Dave Hunter .01 .05
340 Mario Lemieux .75 2.00
341 Troy Loney .01 .05
342 Dan Quinn .01 .05
343 Penguins Team LH .01 .05
344 Penguins Team RH .01 .05

345 Nordiques Emblem	.01	.05
346 Nordiques Uniform	.01	.05
347 Mario Gosselin	.02	.10
348 Tommy Albelin	.01	.05
349 Jeff Brown	.01	.05
350 Steven Finn	.01	.05
351 Randy Moller	.01	.05
352 Alain Cote	.01	.05
353 Gaetan Duchesne	.01	.05
354 Mike Eagles	.01	.05
355 Michel Goulet	.02	.10
356 Lane Lambert	.01	.05
357 Anton Stastny	.01	.05
358 Peter Stastny	.02	.10
359 Nordiques Team LH	.01	.05
360 Nordiques Team RH	.01	.05
361 Capitals Emblem	.01	.05
362 Capitals Uniform	.01	.05
363 Clint Malarchuk	.02	.10
364 Pete Peeters	.02	.10
365 Kevin Hatcher	.02	.10
366 Rod Langway	.01	.05
367 Larry Murphy	.02	.10
368 Scott Stevens	.02	.10
369 Dave Christian	.01	.05
370 Mike Gartner	.20	.50
371 Bengt Gustafsson	.01	.05
372 Dale Hunter	.01	.05
373 Kelly Miller	.01	.05
374 Mike Ridley	.01	.05
375 Capitals Team LH	.01	.05
376 Capitals Team RH	.01	.05
377 Hockey Rink Schematic	.01	.05
378 Hockey Rink Schematic	.01	.05
379 Cross-checking	.01	.05
380 Elbowing	.01	.05
381 High-sticking	.01	.05
382 Holding	.01	.05
383 Hooking	.01	.05
384 Interference	.01	.05
385 Spearing	.01	.05
386 Tripping	.01	.05
387 Boarding	.01	.05
388 Charging	.01	.05
389 Delayed Calling of Penalty	.01	.05
390 Kneeing	.01	.05
391 Misconduct	.01	.05
392 Roughing	.01	.05
393 Slashing	.01	.05
394 Unsportsmanlike Conduct	.01	.05
395 Wash-out	.01	.05
396 Icing	.01	.05
397 Off-side	.01	.05
398 Wash-out	.01	.05
399 Bill Masterton Memorial Trophy Bob Bourne	.01	.05
400 Hart Memorial Trophy Mario Lemieux	.20	.50
401 Art Ross Trophy Mario Lemeiux	.20	.50
402 William M. Jennings Trophy Brian Hayward Patrick Roy	.20	.50
403 Vezina Trophy Grant Fuhr	.02	.10
404 Calder Memorial Trophy Joe Nieuwendyk	.02	.10
405 James Norris Memorial Trophy Ray Bourque	.20	.50
406 Lady Byng Trophy Mats Naslund	.02	.10
407 Frank J. Selke Trophy Guy Carbonneau	.02	.10
408 Emery Edge Award Brad McCrimmon	.02	.10
NNO Sticker Album	2.00	5.00

1989-90 Panini Stickers

This set of 384 hockey stickers was produced and distributed by Panini. The stickers are numbered on the back and measure 1 7/8" by 3". The stickers display color action shots of players, teams, arenas, and logos. Some team pictures consist of two stickers, each showing half of the photo; in the checklist below these halves are denoted by LH (left half) and RH (right half), and in the case of a four sticker picture, note the additional prefixes U (upper) and L (lower). A 52-page, full-color glossy album was issued with the set for holding the stickers. The album includes player information and statistics in English and French.

COMPLETE SET (384)	10.00	25.00
1 NHL Logo	.02	.10
2 Playoff schedule	.02	.10
3 Flames/Blackhawks action	.02	.10
4 Flames/Canucks action	.02	.10
5 Kings/Oilers action	.02	.10
6 Vernon goal LH	.02	.10
7 Vernon goal RH	.02	.10
8 Bruins/Sabres action	.02	.10
9 Canadiens/Bruins action	.02	.10
10 Flyers score	.02	.10
11 Canadiens/Flyers action LH	.02	.10
12 Canadiens/Flyers action RH	.02	.10
13 Canadiens/Flames action	.02	.10
14 Canadiens celebration	.02	.10
15 Canadiens/Flames action	.02	.10
16 Canadiens/Flames action	.02	.10
17 Flames celebration	.02	.10
18 Flames/Canadiens action LH	.02	.10
19 Flames/Canadiens action RH	.02	.10
20 Al MacInnis Conn Smythe Trophy	.07	.20
21 Stanley Cup Flames UL	.07	.20
22 Stanley Cup Flames UR	.07	.20
23 Stanley Cup Flames LL	.07	.20
24 Stanley Cup Flames LR	.07	.20
25 Stanley Cup	.07	.20
26 Calgary Flames	.02	.10
27 Joe Mullen	.07	.20
28 Doug Gilmour	.20	.50
29 Joe Nieuwendyk	.07	.20
30 Gary Suter	.07	.20
31 Flames team	.02	.10
32 Al MacInnis	.07	.20
33 Brad McCrimmon	.02	.10
34 Mike Vernon	.07	.20
35 Gary Roberts	.07	.20
36 Colin Patterson	.02	.10
37 Jim Peplinski	.02	.10
38 Jamie Macoun	.02	.10
39 Lanny McDonald	.02	.10
40 Saddledome	.02	.10
41 Chicago Blackhawks	.02	.10
42 Darren Pang	.07	.20
43 Steve Larmer	.07	.20
44 Dirk Graham	.02	.10
45 Doug Wilson	.02	.10
46 Blackhawks/Oilers action (Ed Belfour shown)	.02	.10
47 Dave Manson	.02	.10
48 Troy Murray	.02	.10
49 Denis Savard	.07	.20
50 Steve Thomas	.02	.10
51 Adam Creighton	.02	.10
52 Wayne Presley	.02	.10
53 Trent Yawney	.02	.10
54 Alain Chevrier	.02	.10
55 Chicago Stadium	.02	.10
56 Detroit Red Wings	.02	.10
57 Steve Yzerman	.50	1.25
58 Gerard Gallant	.02	.10
59 Greg Stefan	.07	.20
60 Dave Barr	.02	.10
61 Red Wings Team	.02	.10
62 Steve Chiasson	.02	.10
63 Shawn Burr	.02	.10
64 Rick Zombo	.02	.10
65 Glen Hanlon	.07	.20
66 Jeff Sharples	.02	.10
67 Joey Kocur	.02	.10
68 Lee Norwood	.02	.10
69 Mike O'Connell	.02	.10
70 Joe Louis Arena	.02	.10
71 Edmonton Oilers	.02	.10
72 Jimmy Carson	.02	.10
73 Jari Kurri	.10	.30
74 Mark Messier	.20	.50
75 Craig Simpson	.02	.10
76 Oilers/Flyers action	.02	.10
77 Glenn Anderson	.07	.20
78 Craig MacTavish	.02	.10
79 Kevin Lowe	.07	.20
80 Craig Muni	.02	.10
81 Bill Ranford	.07	.20
82 Charlie Huddy	.02	.10
83 Steve Smith	.02	.10
84 Normand Lacombe	.02	.10
85 Northlands Coliseum	.02	.10
86 L.A. Kings logo	.02	.10
87 Wayne Gretzky	1.00	2.50
88 Bernie Nicholls	.07	.20
89 Kelly Hrudey	.07	.20
90 John Tonelli	.02	.10
91 Oilers/Kings action	.02	.10
92 Steve Kasper	.02	.10
93 Steve Duchesne	.02	.10
94 Mike Krushelnyski	.02	.10
95 Luc Robitaille	.20	.50
96 Ron Duguay	.02	.10
97 Glenn Healy	.07	.20
98 Dave Taylor	.02	.10
99 Marty McSorley	.02	.10
100 The Great Western Forum	.02	.10
101 Minnesota North Stars	.02	.10
102 Kari Takko	.07	.20
103 Dave Gagner	.02	.10
104 Mike Gartner	.10	.30
105 Brian Bellows	.02	.10
106 North Stars Team	.02	.10
107 Neal Broten	.02	.10
108 Larry Murphy	.07	.20
109 Basil McRae	.02	.10
110 Perry Berezan	.02	.10
111 Shawn Chambers	.02	.10
112 Curt Giles	.02	.10
113 Stewart Gavin	.02	.10
114 Jon Casey	.07	.20
115 Metropolitan Sports Center	.02	.10
116 St. Louis Blues	.02	.10
117 Brett Hull	.20	.50
118 Peter Zezel	.02	.10
119 Tony Hrkac	.02	.10
120 Vincent Riendeau	.07	.20
121 Blues/Islanders action	.02	.10
122 Cliff Ronning	.02	.10
123 Gino Cavallini	.02	.10
124 Brian Benning	.02	.10
125 Rick Meagher	.02	.10
126 Steve Tuttle	.02	.10
127 Paul Cavallini	.02	.10
128 Tom Tilley	.02	.10
129 Greg Millen	.07	.20
130 St. Louis Arena	.02	.10
131 Toronto Maple Leafs	.02	.10
132 Ed Olczyk	.02	.10
133 Gary Leeman	.02	.10
134 Vincent Damphousse	.07	.20
135 Tom Fergus	.02	.10
136 Maple Leafs action	.02	.10
137 Daniel Marois	.02	.10
138 Mark Osborne	.02	.10
139 Allan Bester	.07	.20
140 Al Iafrate	.02	.10
141 Brad Marsh	.02	.10
142 Luke Richardson	.02	.10
143 Todd Gill	.02	.10
144 Wendel Clark	.07	.20
145 Maple Leafs Gardens	.02	.10
146 Vancouver Canucks	.02	.10
147 Petri Skriko	.02	.10
148 Trevor Linden	.07	.20
149 Tony Tanti	.02	.10
150 Steve Weeks	.02	.10
151 Canucks/Islanders action	.02	.10
152 Brian Bradley	.02	.10
153 Barry Pederson	.02	.10
154 Greg Adams	.02	.10
155 Kirk McLean	.07	.20
156 Jim Sandlak	.02	.10
157 Rich Sutter	.02	.10
158 Garth Butcher	.02	.10
159 Stan Smyl	.02	.10
160 Pacific Coliseum	.02	.10
161 Winnipeg Jets	.02	.10
162 Dale Hawerchuk	.07	.20
163 Thomas Steen	.02	.10
164 Brent Ashton	.02	.10
165 Pat Elynuik	.02	.10
166 Jets/Islanders action	.02	.10
167 Dave Ellett	.02	.10
168 Randy Carlyle	.02	.10
169 Laurie Boschman	.02	.10
170 Iain Duncan	.02	.10
171 Doug Smail	.02	.10
172 Teppo Numminen	.02	.10
173 Bob Essensa	.07	.20
174 Peter Taglianetti	.02	.10
175 Winnipeg Arena	.02	.10
176 Steve Duchesne AS	.02	.10
177 Luc Robitaille AS	.07	.20
178 Mike Vernon AS	.07	.20
179 Wayne Gretzky AS	.60	1.50
180 Kevin Lowe AS	.07	.20
181 Jari Kurri AS	.10	.30
182 Cam Neely AS	.20	.50
183 Paul Coffey AS	.10	.30
184 Mario Lemieux AS	.40	1.00
185 Sean Burke AS	.07	.20
186 Rob Brown AS	.02	.10
187 Ray Bourque AS	.20	.50
188 Boston Bruins	.02	.10
189 Greg Hawgood	.02	.10
190 Ken Linseman	.02	.10
191 Andy Moog	.07	.20
192 Cam Neely	.20	.50
193 Bruins/Flyers action	.02	.10
194 Andy Brickley	.02	.10
195 Rejean Lemelin	.07	.20
196 Bob Carpenter	.02	.10
197 Randy Burridge	.02	.10
198 Craig Janney	.02	.10
199 Bob Joyce	.02	.10
200 Glen Wesley	.02	.10
201 Ray Bourque	.20	.50
202 Boston Garden	.02	.10
203 Buffalo Sabres	.02	.10
204 Pierre Turgeon	.07	.20
205 Phil Housley	.02	.10
206 Rick Vaive	.02	.10
207 Christian Ruuttu	.02	.10
208 Flyers/Sabres action	.02	.10
209 Doug Bodger	.02	.10
210 Mike Foligno	.02	.10
211 Ray Sheppard	.02	.10
212 John Tucker	.02	.10
213 Scott Arniel	.02	.10
214 Daren Puppa	.07	.20
215 Dave Andreychuk	.07	.20
216 Uwe Krupp	.02	.10
217 Memorial Auditorium	.02	.10
218 Hartford Whalers	.02	.10
219 Kevin Dineen	.02	.10
220 Peter Sidorkiewicz	.07	.20
221 Ron Francis	.07	.20
222 Ray Ferraro	.02	.10
223 Islanders/Whalers action	.02	.10
224 Scott Young	.02	.10
225 Dave Babych	.02	.10
226 Dave Tippett	.02	.10
227 Paul MacDermid	.02	.10
228 Ulf Samuelsson	.02	.10
229 Sylvain Cote	.02	.10
230 Jody Hull	.02	.10
231 Don Maloney	.02	.10
232 Hartford Civic Center	.02	.10
233 Montreal Canadiens	.02	.10
234 Mats Naslund	.02	.10
235 Patrick Roy	.75	2.00
236 Bobby Smith	.02	.10
237 Chris Chelios	.20	.50
238 Flames/Canadiens action	.02	.10
239 Stephane Richer	.07	.20
240 Claude Lemieux	.07	.20
241 Guy Carbonneau	.07	.20
242 Shayne Corson	.02	.10
243 Mike McPhee	.02	.10
244 Petr Svoboda	.02	.10
245 Larry Robinson	.07	.20
246 Brian Hayward	.07	.20
247 Montreal Forum	.02	.10
248 New Jersey Devils	.02	.10
249 John MacLean	.02	.10
250 Patrik Sundstrom	.02	.10
251 Kirk Muller	.07	.20
252 Tom Kurvers	.02	.10
253 Bruins/Devils action	.02	.10
254 Aaron Broten	.02	.10
255 Brendan Shanahan	.20	.50
256 Sean Burke	.07	.20
257 Tommy Albelin	.02	.10
258 Ken Daneyko	.02	.10
259 Randy Velischek	.02	.10
260 Mark Johnson	.02	.10
261 Jim Korn	.02	.10
262 Brendan Byrne Arena	.02	.10
263 New York Islanders	.02	.10
264 Pat LaFontaine	.07	.20
265 Mark Fitzpatrick	.07	.20
266 Brent Sutter	.02	.10
267 David Volek	.02	.10
268 Islanders/Rangers action	.02	.10
269 Bryan Trottier	.07	.20
270 Mikko Makela	.02	.10
271 Derek King	.02	.10
272 Pat Flatley	.02	.10
273 Jeff Norton	.02	.10
274 Gerald Diduck	.02	.10
275 Alan Kerr	.02	.10
276 Jeff Hackett	.07	.20
277 Nassau Veterans Memorial Coliseum	.02	.10
278 New York Rangers	.02	.10
279 Brian Leetch	.10	.30
280 Carey Wilson	.02	.10
281 Tomas Sandstrom	.02	.10
282 John Vanbiesbrouck	.10	.30
283 Oilers/Rangers action	.02	.10
284 Bob Froese	.07	.20
285 Tony Granato	.02	.10
286 Brian Mullen	.02	.10
287 Kelly Kisio	.02	.10
288 Ulf Dahlen	.02	.10
289 James Patrick	.02	.10
290 John Ogrodnick	.02	.10
291 Michel Petit	.02	.10
292 Madison Square Garden	.02	.10
293 Philadelphia Flyers	.02	.10
294 Tim Kerr	.02	.10
295 Rick Tocchet	.07	.20
296 Pelle Eklund	.02	.10
297 Terry Carkner	.02	.10
298 Flyers/Canadiens action	.02	.10
299 Ron Sutter	.02	.10
300 Mark Howe	.02	.10
301 Keith Acton	.02	.10
302 Ron Hextall	.07	.20
303 Gord Murphy	.02	.10
304 Derrick Smith	.02	.10
305 Dave Poulin	.02	.10
306 Brian Propp	.02	.10
307 The Spectrum	.02	.10
308 Pittsburgh Penguins	.02	.10
309 Mario Lemieux	.75	2.00
310 Rob Brown	.02	.10
311 Paul Coffey	.10	.30
312 Tom Barrasso	.07	.20
313 Penguins/Flyers action	.02	.10
314 Dan Quinn	.02	.10
315 Bob Errey	.02	.10
316 John Cullen	.02	.10
317 Phil Bourque	.02	.10
318 Zarley Zalapski	.02	.10
319 Troy Loney	.02	.10
320 Jim Johnson	.02	.10
321 Kevin Stevens	.02	.10
322 Civic Arena	.02	.10
323 Quebec Nordiques	.02	.10
324 Peter Stastny	.07	.20
325 Jeff Brown	.02	.10
326 Michel Goulet	.07	.20
327 Joe Sakic	.20	.50
328 Flyers/Nordiques action	.02	.10
329 Iiro Jarvi	.02	.10
330 Paul Gillis	.02	.10
331 Randy Moller	.02	.10
332 Ron Tugnutt	.07	.20
333 Robert Picard	.02	.10
334 Curtis Leschyshyn	.02	.10
335 Marc Fortier	.02	.10
336 Mario Marois	.02	.10
337 Le Colisee	.02	.10
338 Washington Capitals	.02	.10
339 Mike Ridley	.02	.10
340 Geoff Courtnall	.02	.10
341 Scott Stevens	.07	.20
342 Dino Ciccarelli	.07	.20
343 Capitals/Flames action	.02	.10
344 Bob Mason	.07	.20
345 Dave Christian	.02	.10
346 Dale Hunter	.02	.10
347 Kevin Hatcher	.07	.20
348 Kelly Miller	.02	.10
349 Stephen Leach	.02	.10
350 Rod Langway	.02	.10
351 Bob Rouse	.02	.10
352 Capital Centre	.02	.10
353 Calgary Flames	.02	.10
354 Edmonton Oilers	.02	.10
355 Winnipeg Jets	.02	.10
356 Toronto Maple Leafs	.02	.10
357 Buffalo Sabres	.02	.10
358 Montreal Canadiens	.02	.10
359 Quebec Nordiques	.02	.10
360 New Jersey Devils	.02	.10
361 Boston Bruins	.02	.10
362 Hartford Whalers	.02	.10
363 Vancouver Canucks	.02	.10
364 Minnesota North Stars	.02	.10
365 Los Angeles Kings	.02	.10
366 St. Louis Blues	.02	.10
367 Chicago Blackhawks	.02	.10
368 Detroit Red Wings	.02	.10
369 Pittsburgh Penguins	.02	.10
370 Washington Capitals	.02	.10
371 Philadelphia Flyers	.02	.10
372 New York Rangers	.02	.10
373 New York Islanders	.02	.10
374 Wayne Gretzky	1.00	2.50
375 Mario Lemieux	.75	2.00
376 Patrick Roy	.30	.75
377 Tim Kerr	.02	.10
378 Brian Leetch	.20	.50
379 Chris Chelios	.20	.50
380 Joe Mullen	.07	.20
381 Guy Carbonneau	.07	.20
382 Bryan Trottier	.07	.20
383 Patrick Roy	.75	2.00
384 Joe Mullen	.07	.20
NNO Sticker Album	1.00	2.50

1990-91 Panini Stickers

This set of 351 hockey stickers was produced and distributed by Panini. The stickers are numbered on the back and measure approximately 2 1/16" by 2 15/16". The fronts feature full color action photos of the players. Different color triangles (in one of the team's colors) overlay the upper left corner of the pictures, with the team name in white lettering. A variegated stripe appears below the player photos, with the player's name below. The team logo and conference stickers are in foil. The stickers are arranged according to alphabetical team order.

COMPLETE SET (351)	8.00	20.00
1 Prince of Wales	.01	.05
2 Clarence Campbell	.01	.05
3 Stanley Cup	.02	.10
4 Dave Poulin	.01	.05
5 Brian Propp	.01	.05
6 Glen Wesley	.01	.05
7 Bob Carpenter	.01	.05
8 John Carter	.01	.05
9 Cam Neely	.20	.50
10 Greg Hawgood	.01	.05
11 Andy Moog	.02	.10
12 Boston Bruins logo	.01	.05
13 Rejean Lemelin	.02	.10
14 Craig Janney	.01	.05
15 Bob Sweeney	.01	.05
16 Andy Brickley	.01	.05
17 Ray Bourque	.20	.50
18 Dave Christian	.01	.05
19 Dave Snuggerud	.01	.05
20 Christian Ruuttu	.01	.05
21 Phil Housley	.01	.05
22 Uwe Krupp	.01	.05
23 Rick Vaive	.01	.05
24 Mike Ramsey	.01	.05
25 Mike Foligno	.01	.05
26 Clint Malarchuk	.02	.10
27 Buffalo Sabres logo	.01	.05
28 Pierre Turgeon	.02	.10
29 Dave Andreychuk	.02	.10
30 Scott Arniel	.01	.05
31 Daren Puppa	.02	.10
32 Mike Hartman	.01	.05
33 Doug Bodger	.01	.05
34 Scott Young	.01	.05
35 Todd Krygier	.01	.05
36 Pat Verbeek	.02	.10
37 Dave Tippett	.01	.05
38 Peter Sidorkiewicz	.02	.10
39 Ron Francis	.02	.10
40 Dave Babych	.01	.05
41 Randy Ladouceur	.01	.05
42 Hartford Whalers logo	.01	.05
43 Kevin Dineen	.01	.05
44 Dean Evason	.01	.05
45 Ray Ferraro	.01	.05
46 Mike Tomlak	.01	.05
47 Mikael Andersson	.01	.05
48 Brad Shaw	.01	.05
49 Chris Chelios	.20	.50
50 Petr Svoboda	.01	.05
51 Patrick Roy	.60	1.50
52 Bobby Smith	.01	.05
53 Stephane Richer	.02	.10
54 Shayne Corson	.01	.05
55 Brian Skrudland	.01	.05
56 Russ Courtnall	.01	.05
57 Montreal Canadiens logo	.01	.05
58 Guy Carbonneau	.02	.10
59 Sylvain Lefebvre	.01	.05
60 Mathieu Schneider	.01	.05
61 Brian Hayward	.02	.10
62 Mats Naslund	.01	.05
63 Mike McPhee	.01	.05
64 Brendan Shanahan	.20	.50
65 Patrik Sundstrom	.01	.05
66 Mark Johnson	.01	.05
67 Doug Brown	.01	.05
68 Chris Terreri	.02	.10
69 Bruce Driver	.01	.05
70 Peter Stastny	.02	.10
71 Sylvain Turgeon	.01	.05
72 New Jersey Devils logo	.01	.05
73 Kirk Muller	.02	.10
74 John MacLean	.01	.05
75 Slava Fetisov	.01	.05
76 Tommy Albelin	.01	.05
77 Sean Burke	.02	.10
78 Janne Ojanen	.01	.05
79 Randy Wood	.01	.05
80 Gary Nylund	.01	.05
81 Pat LaFontaine	.20	.50
82 Pat Flatley	.01	.05
83 Bryan Trottier	.02	.10
84 Don Maloney	.01	.05
85 Gerald Diduck	.01	.05
86 Mark Fitzpatrick	.02	.10
87 New York Islanders logo	.01	.05
88 Glenn Healy	.02	.10
89 Alan Kerr	.01	.05
90 Brent Sutter	.01	.05
91 Doug Crossman	.01	.05
92 Hubie McDonough	.01	.05
93 Jeff Norton	.01	.05
94 Kelly Kisio	.01	.05
95 Brian Leetch	.20	.50
96 Brian Mullen	.01	.05
97 James Patrick	.01	.05
98 Mike Richter	.02	.10
99 John Ogrodnick	.01	.05
100 Troy Mallette	.01	.05
101 Mark Janssens	.01	.05
102 New York Rangers logo	.01	.05
103 Mike Gartner	.20	.50
104 Jan Erixon	.01	.05
105 Carey Wilson	.01	.05
106 Bernie Nicholls	.02	.10
107 Darren Turcotte	.02	.10
108 John Vanbiesbrouck	.20	.50
109 Ron Sutter	.01	.05
110 Kjell Samuelsson	.01	.05
111 Ken Linseman	.01	.05
112 Ken Wregget	.02	.10
113 Pelle Eklund	.01	.05
114 Terry Carkner	.01	.05
115 Gord Murphy	.01	.05
116 Murray Craven	.01	.05
117 Philadelphia Flyers logo	.01	.05
118 Ron Hextall	.02	.10
119 Mike Bullard	.01	.05
120 Tim Kerr	.01	.05
121 Rick Tocchet	.02	.10
122 Mark Howe	.01	.05
123 Ilkka Sinisalo	.01	.05
124 Tony Tanti	.01	.05
125 John Cullen	.01	.05
126 Zarley Zalapski	.01	.05
127 Wendell Young	.02	.10
128 Rob Brown	.01	.05
129 Phil Bourque	.01	.05
130 Mark Recchi	.20	.50
131 Kevin Stevens	.01	.05
132 Pittsburgh Penguins logo	.01	.05
133 Bob Errey	.01	.05
134 Tom Barrasso	.02	.10
135 Paul Coffey	.20	.50
136 Mario Lemieux	.60	1.50
137 Randy Hillier	.01	.05
138 Troy Loney	.01	.05
139 Joe Sakic	.20	.50
140 Lucien DeBlois	.01	.05
141 Joe Cirella	.01	.05
142 Ron Tugnutt	.02	.10
143 Paul Gillis	.01	.05
144 Bryan Fogarty	.01	.05
145 Guy Lafleur	.02	.10
146 Tony Hrkac	.01	.05
147 Quebec Nordiques logo	.01	.05
148 Michel Petit	.01	.05
149 Tony McKegney	.01	.05
150 Curtis Leschyshyn	.01	.05
151 Claude Loiselle	.01	.05
152 Mario Brunetta	.01	.05
153 Marc Fortier	.01	.05
154 Michal Pivonka	.01	.05
155 Scott Stevens	.02	.10
156 Kelly Miller	.01	.05
157 John Tucker	.01	.05
158 Don Beaupre	.02	.10
159 Geoff Courtnall	.01	.05
160 Alan May	.01	.05
161 Dino Ciccarelli	.02	.10
162 Washington Capitals logo	.01	.05
163 Mike Ridley	.01	.05
164 Bob Rouse	.01	.05
165 Mike Liut	.02	.10
166 Stephen Leach	.01	.05
167 Kevin Hatcher	.02	.10
168 Dale Hunter	.01	.05
169 Prince of Wales	.01	.05
170 Clarence Campbell	.01	.05
171 Stanley Cup	.02	.10
172 Doug Gilmour	.20	.50
173 Brad McCrimmon	.01	.05
174 Joe Nieuwendyk	.02	.10
175 Mike Vernon	.02	.10
176 Theo Fleury	.20	.50
177 Gary Suter	.02	.10
178 Jamie Macoun	.01	.05
179 Gary Roberts	.02	.10
180 Calgary Flames logo	.01	.05
181 Paul Ranheim	.01	.05
182 Jiri Hrdina	.01	.05
183 Joe Mullen	.02	.10
184 Sergei Makarov	.01	.05
185 Al MacInnis	.02	.10
186 Rick Wamsley	.02	.10
187 Trent Yawney	.01	.05
188 Greg Millen	.02	.10
189 Doug Wilson	.01	.05
190 Jocelyn Lemieux	.01	.05
191 Dirk Graham	.01	.05
192 Keith Brown	.01	.05
193 Adam Creighton	.01	.05
194 Steve Larmer	.02	.10
195 Chicago Blackhawks logo	.01	.05
196 Greg Gilbert	.01	.05
197 Jacques Cloutier	.02	.10
198 Denis Savard	.02	.10
199 Dave Manson	.01	.05
200 Troy Murray	.01	.05
201 Jeremy Roenick	.20	.50
202 Lee Norwood	.01	.05
203 Glen Hanlon	.02	.10
204 Marc Habscheid	.01	.05
205 Gerard Gallant	.01	.05
206 Rick Zombo	.01	.05
207 Steve Chiasson	.01	.05
208 Steve Yzerman	.40	1.00
209 Bernie Federko	.01	.05
210 Detroit Red Wings logo	.01	.05
211 Joey Kocur	.01	.05
212 Tim Cheveldae	.02	.10
213 Shawn Burr	.01	.05
214 Jimmy Carson	.01	.05
215 Mike O'Connell	.01	.05
216 John Chabot	.01	.05
217 Craig Muni	.01	.05
218 Bill Ranford	.02	.10
219 Mark Messier	.20	.50
220 Craig MacTavish	.01	.05
221 Charlie Huddy	.01	.05
222 Jari Kurri	.20	.50
223 Esa Tikkanen	.02	.10
224 Kevin Lowe	.02	.10
225 Edmonton Oilers logo	.01	.05
226 Steve Smith	.01	.05
227 Glenn Anderson	.02	.10
228 Petr Klima	.01	.05
229 Craig Simpson	.01	.05
230 Grant Fuhr	.20	.50
231 Randy Gregg	.01	.05
232 Bob Kudelski	.01	.05
233 Luc Robitaille	.02	.10
234 Marty McSorley	.01	.05
235 John Tonelli	.01	.05
236 Dave Taylor	.01	.05
237 Mikko Makela	.01	.05
238 Steve Kasper	.01	.05
239 Tony Granato	.01	.05
240 Los Angeles Kings logo	.01	.05
241 Steve Duchesne	.01	.05
242 Wayne Gretzky	.75	2.00
243 Tomas Sandstrom	.01	.05
244 Larry Robinson	.02	.10
245 Mike Krushelnyski	.01	.05
246 Kelly Hrudey	.02	.10
247 Aaron Broten	.01	.05
248 Dave Gagner	.01	.05
249 Basil McRae	.01	.05
250 Curt Giles	.01	.05
251 Larry Murphy	.02	.10
252 Shawn Chambers	.01	.05
253 Mike Modano	.20	.50
254 Jon Casey	.02	.10
255 North Stars logo	.01	.05
256 Gaetan Duchesne	.01	.05
257 Brian Bellows	.01	.05
258 Frantisek Musil	.01	.05
259 Don Barber	.01	.05
260 Stewart Gavin	.01	.05
261 Neal Broten	.01	.05
262 Brett Hull	.20	.50
263 Sergio Momesso	.01	.05
264 Peter Zezel	.01	.05
265 Gino Cavallini	.01	.05
266 Rod Brind'Amour	.20	.50
267 Mike Lalor	.01	.05
268 Vincent Riendeau	.02	.10
269 Gordie Roberts	.01	.05
270 St. Louis Blues logo	.01	.05
271 Paul MacLean	.01	.05
272 Curtis Joseph	.20	.50
273 Rick Meagher	.01	.05
274 Jeff Brown	.01	.05
275 Adam Oates	.02	.10
276 Paul Cavallini	.01	.05
277 Brad Marsh	.01	.05
278 Mark Osborne	.01	.05
279 Gary Leeman	.01	.05
280 Rob Ramage	.01	.05
281 Jeff Reese	.02	.10
282 Tom Fergus	.01	.05
283 Ed Olczyk	.01	.05
284 Daniel Marois	.01	.05
285 Maple Leafs logo	.01	.05
286 Wendel Clark	.02	.10
287 Tom Kurvers	.01	.05
288 Gilles Thibaudeau	.01	.05
289 Lou Franceschetti	.01	.05
290 Al Iafrate	.01	.05
291 Vincent Damphousse	.02	.10
292 Stan Smyl	.01	.05
293 Paul Reinhart	.01	.05
294 Igor Larionov	.01	.05
295 Doug Lidster	.01	.05
296 Kirk McLean	.02	.10
297 Andrew McBain	.01	.05
298 Petri Skriko	.01	.05
299 Trevor Linden	.02	.10
300 Vancouver Canucks logo	.01	.05
301 Steve Bozek	.01	.05
302 Brian Bradley	.01	.05
303 Greg Adams	.01	.05
304 Vladimir Krutov	.01	.05
305 Dan Quinn	.01	.05
306 Jim Sandlak	.01	.05
307 Teppo Numminen	.01	.05
308 Doug Smail	.01	.05
309 Greg Paslawski	.01	.05
310 Dave Ellett	.01	.05
311 Bob Essensa	.02	.10
312 Pat Elynuik	.01	.05
313 Paul Fenton	.01	.05
314 Randy Carlyle	.01	.05
315 Winnipeg Jets logo	.01	.05
316 Thomas Steen	.01	.05
317 Dale Hawerchuk	.02	.1
318 Fredrik Olausson	.01	.0
319 Dave McLlwain	.01	.0
320 Laurie Boschman	.01	.0
321 Brent Ashton	.01	.0
322 Ray Bourque	.20	.5
323 Patrick Roy	.60	1.5
324 Paul Coffey	.20	.5
325 Brian Propp	.01	.0
326 Mario Lemieux	.60	1.5
327 Cam Neely	.20	.5
328 Al MacInnis	.02	.1
329 Mike Vernon	.02	.1
330 Kevin Lowe	.02	.1
331 Luc Robitaille	.02	.1
332 Wayne Gretzky	.75	2.0
333 Brett Hull	.20	.5
334 Sergei Makarov	.01	.05
335 Alexei Kasatonov	.01	.05
336 Igor Larionov	.01	.05
337 Vladimir Krutov	.01	.05
338 Alexander Mogilny	.02	.10
339 Slava Fetisov	.01	.05
340 Mike Modano	.20	.50
341 Mark Recchi	.20	.50
342 Paul Ranheim	.01	.05
343 Rod Brind'Amour	.01	.05
344 Brad Shaw	.01	.05
345 Mike Richter	.02	.10
346 Hart Trophy	.01	.05
347 Art Ross Trophy	.01	.05
348 Calder Memorial Trophy	.01	.05
349 Lady Byng Trophy	.01	.05
350 Norris Trophy	.01	.05
351 Vezina Trophy	.01	.05
NNO Sticker Album	1.00	2.50

1991-92 Panini Stickers

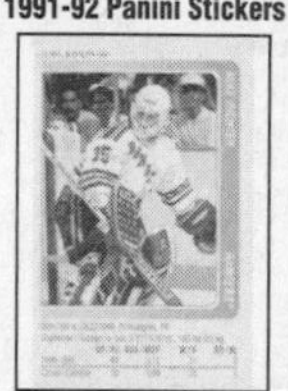

This set of 344 stickers was produced by Panini. They measure approximately 1 7/8" by 2 7/8" and were to be pasted in a 8 1/4" by 10 1/2" bilingual sticker album. The fronts feature color action shots of the players. Pages 2-5 of the album picture highlights of the 1991 Stanley Cup playoffs and finals. Team pages have team colors that highlight player stickers. The NHL 75th Anniversary logo (3-4) and the circular-shaped team logos (148-169) are foil. The stickers are numbered on the back and checklisted below alphabetically according to team.

COMPLETE SET (344)	10.00	25.00
1 NHL Logo	.02	.10
2 NHLPA Logo	.02	.10
3 NHL Logo 75th Anniversary (Left)	.02	.10
4 NHL Logo 75th Anniversary (Right)	.02	.10
5 Clarence Campbell Conference Logo	.02	.10
6 Prince of Wales Conference Logo	.02	.10
7 Stanley Cup Championship Logo	.07	.20
8 Steve Larmer	.07	.20
9 Ed Belfour	.20	.50
10 Chris Chelios	.20	.50
11 Michel Goulet	.07	.20
12 Jeremy Roenick	.20	.50
13 Adam Creighton	.02	.10
14 Steve Thomas	.02	.10
15 Dave Manson	.02	.10
16 Dirk Graham	.02	.10
17 Troy Murray	.02	.10
18 Doug Wilson	.02	.10
19 Wayne Presley	.02	.10
20 Jocelyn Lemieux	.02	.10
21 Keith Brown	.02	.10
22 Curtis Joseph	.20	.50
23 Jeff Brown	.02	.10
24 Gino Cavallini	.02	.10
25 Brett Hull	.20	.50
26 Scott Stevens	.07	.20
27 Dan Quinn	.02	.10
28 Garth Butcher	.02	.10
29 Bob Bassen	.02	.10
30 Rod Brind'Amour	.07	.20
31 Adam Oates	.10	.30
32 Dave Lowry	.02	.10
33 Rich Sutter	.02	.10
34 Ron Wilson	.02	.10
35 Paul Cavallini	.02	.10
36 Trevor Linden	.07	.20
37 Troy Gamble	.02	.10
38 Geoff Courtnall	.02	.10
39 Greg Adams	.02	.10
40 Doug Lidster	.02	.10
41 Dave Capuano	.02	.10
42 Igor Larionov	.07	.20
43 Tom Kurvers	.02	.10
44 Sergio Momesso	.02	.10
45 Kirk McLean	.07	.20
46 Cliff Ronning	.02	.10
47 Robert Kron	.02	.10
48 Steve Bozek	.02	.10
49 Petr Nedved	.07	.20
50 Al MacInnis	.07	.20
51 Theo Fleury	.20	.50
52 Gary Roberts	.07	.20
53 Joe Nieuwendyk	.07	.20
54 Paul Ranheim	.02	.10
55 Mike Vernon	.07	.20
56 Carey Wilson	.02	.10
57 Gary Suter	.07	.20
58 Sergei Makarov	.02	.10
59 Doug Gilmour	.20	.50
60 Joel Otto	.02	.10
61 Jamie Macoun	.02	.10
62 Stephane Matteau	.02	.10
63 Robert Reichel	.02	.10
64 Ed Olczyk	.02	.10
65 Phil Housley	.02	.10

Pat Elynuik .02 .10
Fredrik Olausson .02 .10
Thomas Steen .02 .10
Paul MacDermid .02 .10
Brent Ashton .02 .10
Teppo Numminen .02 .10
Danton Cole .02 .10
Dave McLlwain .02 .10
Scott Arniel .02 .10
Bob Essensa .07 .20
Randy Carlyle .02 .10
Mark Osborne .02 .10
Wayne Gretzky 1.25 3.00
Tomas Sandstrom .02 .10
Steve Duchesne .02 .10
Kelly Hrudey .07 .20
Larry Robinson .07 .20
Tony Granato .02 .10
Marty McSorley .07 .20
Todd Elik .02 .10
Rob Blake .07 .20
Bob Kudelski .02 .10
Steve Kasper .02 .10
Dave Taylor .02 .10
John Tonelli .02 .10
Luc Robitaille .07 .20
Vincent Damphousse .07 .20
Brian Bradley .02 .10
Dave Ellett .02 .10
Daniel Marois .02 .10
Rob Ramage .02 .10
Mike Krushelnyski .02 .10
Michel Petit .02 .10
Peter Ing .02 .10
Lucien DeBlois .02 .10
Bob Rouse .02 .10
2 Wendel Clark .07 .20
3 Peter Zezel .02 .10
4 David Reid .02 .10
5 Aaron Broten .02 .10
6 Brian Hayward .07 .20
7 Neal Broten .07 .20
8 Brian Bellows .02 .10
9 Mark Tinordi .02 .10
Ulf Dahlen .02 .10
Doug Smail .02 .10
2 Dave Gagner .02 .10
3 Bobby Smith .02 .10
4 Brian Glynn .02 .10
5 Brian Propp .02 .10
6 Mike Modano .07 .20
7 Gaetan Duchesne .02 .10
8 Jon Casey .07 .20
9 Basil McRae .02 .10
Glenn Anderson .07 .20
Steve Smith .02 .10
2 Adam Graves .07 .20
3 Esa Tikkanen .07 .20
4 Mark Messier .20 .50
5 Bill Ranford .07 .20
6 Petr Klima .02 .10
7 Anatoli Semenov .02 .10
8 Martin Gelinas .02 .10
9 Charlie Huddy .02 .10
Craig Simpson .02 .10
1 Kevin Lowe .07 .20
2 Craig MacTavish .02 .10
3 Craig Muni .02 .10
4 Steve Yzerman .60 1.50
5 Shawn Burr .02 .10
6 Tim Cheveldae .07 .20
7 Rick Zombo .02 .10
8 Marc Habscheid .02 .10
9 Jimmy Carson .02 .10
Brent Fedyk .02 .10
1 Yves Racine .02 .10
2 Gerard Gallant .02 .10
3 Steve Chiasson .02 .10
4 Johan Garpenlov .02 .10
5 Sergei Fedorov .20 .50
6 Bob Probert .07 .20
7 Rick Green .02 .10
8 Chicago Blackhawks Logo .02 .10
9 Detroit Red Wings Logo .02 .10
Minnesota North Stars Logo .02 .10
1 St. Louis Blues Logo .02 .10
2 Toronto Maple Leafs Logo .02 .10
3 Calgary Flames Logo .02 .10
4 Edmonton Oilers Logo .02 .10
5 Los Angeles Kings Logo .02 .10
6 San Jose Sharks Logo .02 .10
7 Vancouver Canucks Logo .02 .10
8 Winnipeg Jets Logo .02 .10
9 Boston Bruins Logo .02 .10
0 Buffalo Sabres Logo .02 .10
1 Hartford Whalers Logo .02 .10
2 Montreal Canadiens Logo .02 .10
3 Quebec Nordiques Logo .02 .10
4 New Jersey Devils Logo .02 .10
5 New York Islanders Logo .02 .10
6 New York Rangers Logo .02 .10
7 Philadelphia Flyers Logo .02 .10
8 Pittsburgh Penguins Logo .02 .10
9 Washington Capitals Logo .02 .10
0 Craig Janney .02 .10
1 Ray Bourque .20 .50
2 Rejean Lemelin .07 .20
3 Dave Christian .02 .10
4 Randy Burridge .02 .10
5 Garry Galley .02 .10
6 Cam Neely .20 .50
7 Bob Sweeney .02 .10
8 Ken Hodge Jr. .02 .10
9 Andy Moog .07 .20
0 Don Sweeney .02 .10
1 Bob Carpenter .02 .10
2 Glen Wesley .02 .10
3 Chris Nilan .02 .10
4 Patrick Roy 1.00 2.50
5 Petr Svoboda .02 .10
6 Russ Courtnall .02 .10
7 Denis Savard .07 .20
8 Mike McPhee .02 .10

189 Eric Desjardins .07 .20
190 Mike Keane .02 .10
191 Stephan Lebeau .02 .10
192 J.J. Daigneault .02 .10
193 Stephane Richer .07 .20
194 Brian Skrudland .02 .10
195 Mathieu Schneider .02 .10
196 Shayne Corson .02 .10
197 Guy Carbonneau .07 .20
198 Kevin Hatcher .07 .20
199 Mike Ridley .02 .10
200 John Druce .02 .10
201 Don Beaupre .07 .20
202 Kelly Miller .02 .10
203 Dale Hunter .02 .10
204 Nick Kypreos .02 .10
205 Calle Johansson .02 .10
206 Michal Pivonka .02 .10
207 Dino Ciccarelli .07 .20
208 Al Iafrate .07 .20
209 Rod Langway .02 .10
210 Mikhail Tatarinov .02 .10
211 Stephen Leach .02 .10
212 Sean Burke .07 .20
213 John MacLean .02 .10
214 Lee Norwood .02 .10
215 Laurie Boschman .02 .10
216 Alexei Kasatonov .02 .10
217 Patrik Sundstrom .02 .10
218 Ken Daneyko .02 .10
219 Kirk Muller .07 .20
220 Peter Stastny .07 .20
221 Chris Terreri .07 .20
222 Brendan Shanahan .20 .50
223 Eric Weinrich .02 .10
224 Claude Lemieux .07 .20
225 Bruce Driver .02 .10
226 Tim Kerr .02 .10
227 Ron Hextall .07 .20
228 Pelle Eklund .02 .10
229 Rick Tocchet .07 .20
230 Gord Murphy .02 .10
231 Mike Ricci .07 .20
232 Derrick Smith .02 .10
233 Ron Sutter .02 .10
234 Murray Craven .02 .10
235 Terry Carkner .02 .10
236 Ken Wregget .07 .20
237 Keith Acton .02 .10
238 Scott Mellanby .07 .20
239 Kjell Samuelsson .02 .10
240 Jeff Hackett .07 .20
241 David Volek .02 .10
242 Craig Ludwig .02 .10
243 Pat LaFontaine .20 .50
244 Randy Wood .02 .10
245 Pat Flatley .02 .10
246 Brent Sutter .02 .10
247 Derek King .02 .10
248 Jeff Norton .02 .10
249 Glenn Healy .07 .20
250 Ray Ferraro .02 .10
251 Gary Nylund .02 .10
252 Joe Reekie .02 .10
253 Dave Chyzowski .02 .10
254 Mike Hough .02 .10
255 Mats Sundin .07 .20
256 Curtis Leschyshyn .02 .10
257 Joe Sakic .20 .50
258 Stephane Fiset .07 .20
259 Bryan Fogarty .02 .10
260 Alexei Gusarov .02 .10
261 Steven Finn .02 .10
262 Everett Sanipass .02 .10
263 Stephane Morin .02 .10
264 Craig Wolanin .02 .10
265 Randy Velischek .02 .10
266 Owen Nolan .07 .20
267 Ron Tugnutt .07 .20
268 Mario Lemieux 1.00 2.50
269 Kevin Stevens .02 .10
270 Larry Murphy .07 .20
271 Tom Barrasso .07 .20
272 Phil Bourque .02 .10
273 Scott Young .02 .10
274 Paul Stanton .02 .10
275 Jaromir Jagr .20 .50
276 Paul Coffey .20 .50
277 Ulf Samuelsson .02 .10
278 Joe Mullen .07 .20
279 Bob Errey .02 .10
280 Mark Recchi .07 .20
281 Ron Francis .07 .20
282 John Vanbiesbrouck .20 .50
283 Jan Erixon .02 .10
284 Brian Leetch .20 .50
285 Darren Turcotte .07 .20
286 Ray Sheppard .02 .10
287 James Patrick .02 .10
288 Bernie Nicholls .07 .20
289 Brian Mullen .02 .10
290 Mike Richter .07 .20
291 Kelly Kisio .02 .10
292 Mike Gartner .20 .50
293 John Ogrodnick .02 .10
294 David Shaw .02 .10
295 Troy Mallette .02 .10
296 Dale Hawerchuk .07 .20
297 Rick Vaive .02 .10
298 Daren Puppa .07 .20
299 Mike Ramsey .02 .10
300 Benoit Hogue .02 .10
301 Clint Malarchuk .07 .20
302 Mikko Makela .02 .10
303 Pierre Turgeon .07 .20
304 Alexander Mogilny .07 .20
305 Uwe Krupp .02 .10
306 Christian Ruuttu .02 .10
307 Doug Bodger .02 .10
308 Dave Snuggerud .02 .10
309 Dave Andreychuk .07 .20
310 Peter Sidorkiewicz .07 .20
311 Brad Shaw .02 .10
312 Dean Evason .02 .10
313 Pat Verbeek .07 .20
314 John Cullen .02 .10
315 Rob Brown .02 .10
316 Bobby Holik .02 .10
317 Todd Krygier .02 .10
318 Adam Burt .02 .10
319 Mike Tomlak .02 .10
320 Randy Cunneyworth .02 .10
321 Paul Cyr .02 .10
322 Zarley Zalapski .02 .10
323 Kevin Dineen .02 .10
324 Luc Robitaille .07 .20
325 Brett Hull .20 .50
326 All-Star Game Logo .02 .10

327 Wayne Gretzky 1.25 3.00
328 Mike Vernon .07 .20
329 Chris Chelios .20 .50
330 Al MacInnis .07 .20
331 Rick Tocchet .07 .20
332 Cam Neely .20 .50
333 Patrick Roy 1.00 2.50
334 Joe Sakic .20 .50
335 Ray Bourque .20 .50
336 Paul Coffey .20 .50
337 Ed Belfour .20 .50
338 Mike Ricci .07 .20
339 Rob Blake .07 .20
340 Sergei Fedorov .50 1.25
341 Ken Hodge Jr. .02 .10
342 Bobby Holik .02 .10
343 Robert Reichel .02 .10
344 Jaromir Jagr .20 .50
NNO Sticker Album .60 1.50

1992-93 Panini Stickers

This set of 330 stickers was produced by Panini. They measure approximately 2 3/8" by 3 3/8" and were to be pasted in a 9" by 11" album. The fronts have action color player photos with statistics running down the right side in a colored bar. The player's name appears at the top. The team logo is superimposed on the photo at the lower left corner. The backs feature questions and answers that go with the Slap-shot game that is included in the album. The team logos scattered throughout the set are foil. The stickers are numbered on the front on a puck icon at the lower right corner. They are checklisted below alphabetically according to teams in the Campbell and Wales Conferences. Also included are subsets of the 1992 NHL's Top Rookies (270-275), the 1992 All-Star Game (276-289), the European Invasion (290-302), and The Trophies (303-308). Randomly inserted throughout the packs were 22 lettered "Ice-Breaker" stickers, each featuring a star player from each of the 22 NHL teams (minus the new expansion teams, the Tampa Bay Lightning and the Ottawa Senators.

COMPLETE SET (330) 20.00 40.00
*FRENCH: SAME VALUE
1 Stanley Cup .07 .20
2 Blackhawks logo .02 .10
3 Ed Belfour .20 .50
4 Jeremy Roenick .20 .50
5 Steve Larmer .02 .10
6 Michel Goulet .07 .20
7 Dirk Graham .02 .10
8 Jocelyn Lemieux .02 .10
9 Brian Noonan .02 .10
10 Rob Brown .02 .10
11 Chris Chelios .20 .50
12 Steve Smith .02 .10
13 Keith Brown .02 .10
14 St. Louis Blues .02 .10
15 Curtis Joseph .20 .50
16 Brett Hull .30 .75
17 Brendan Shanahan .50 1.25
18 Ron Wilson .02 .10
19 Rich Sutter .02 .10
20 Ron Sutter .07 .20
21 Dave Lowry .02 .10
22 Craig Janney .02 .10
23 Paul Cavallini .02 .10
24 Garth Butcher .02 .10
25 Jeff Brown .02 .10
26 Canucks Logo .02 .10
27 Kirk McLean .07 .20
28 Trevor Linden .07 .20
29 Geoff Courtnall .02 .10
30 Cliff Ronning .02 .10
31 Petr Nedved .07 .20
32 Igor Larionov .07 .20
33 Robert Kron .02 .10
34 Jim Sandlak .02 .10
35 Dave Babych .02 .10
36 Jyrki Lumme .02 .10
37 Doug Lidster .02 .10
38 Flames Logo .02 .10
39 Mike Vernon .07 .20
40 Joe Nieuwendyk .07 .20
41 Gary Leeman .02 .10
42 Robert Reichel .02 .10
43 Joel Otto .02 .10
44 Paul Ranheim .02 .10
45 Gary Roberts .07 .20
46 Theo Fleury .20 .50
47 Sergei Makarov .02 .10
48 Gary Suter .07 .20
49 Al MacInnis .07 .20
50 Jets Logo .02 .10
51 Bob Essensa .07 .20
52 Teppo Numminen .02 .10
53 Thomas Steen .02 .10
54 Pat Elynuik .02 .10
55 Ed Olczyk .02 .10
56 Danton Cole .02 .10
57 Troy Murray .02 .10
58 Darrin Shannon .02 .10
59 Russ Romaniuk .02 .10
60 Fredrik Olausson .02 .10
61 Phil Housley .02 .10
62 Kings Logo .02 .10
63 Kelly Hrudey .07 .20
64 Wayne Gretzky .75 2.00
65 Luc Robitaille .07 .20
66 Jari Kurri .07 .20
67 Tomas Sandstrom .02 .10
68 Tony Granato .02 .10
69 Bob Kudelski .02 .10
70 Corey Millen .02 .10
71 Rob Blake .07 .20
72 Paul Coffey .20 .50
73 Marty McSorley .07 .20
74 Maple Leafs Logo .02 .10
75 Grant Fuhr .07 .20
76 Glenn Anderson .07 .20
77 Doug Gilmour .20 .50
78 Mike Krushelnyski .02 .10
79 Wendel Clark .07 .20
80 Rob Pearson .02 .10
81 Peter Zezel .02 .10
82 Todd Gill .02 .10
83 Dave Ellett .02 .10
84 Mike Foligno .02 .10
85 Ken Baumgartner .02 .10
86 North Stars Logo .02 .10
87 Jon Casey .07 .20
88 Brian Bellows .02 .10
89 Neal Broten .07 .20
90 Dave Gagner .02 .10
91 Mike Modano .30 .75
92 Ulf Dahlen .02 .10
93 Brian Propp .02 .10
94 Jim Johnson .02 .10

95 Mike Craig .02 .10
96 Bobby Smith .02 .10
97 Mark Tinordi .02 .10
98 Oilers Logo .02 .10
99 Bill Ranford .07 .20
100 Joe Murphy .07 .20
101 Craig MacTavish .02 .10
102 Craig Simpson .02 .10
103 Esa Tikkanen .07 .20
104 Vincent Damphousse .07 .20
105 Petr Klima .02 .10
106 Martin Gelinas .02 .10
107 Kevin Lowe .07 .20
108 Dave Manson .02 .10
109 Bernie Nicholls .07 .20
110 Red Wings Logo .02 .10
111 Tim Cheveldae .07 .20
112 Steve Yzerman .75 2.00
113 Sergei Fedorov .50 1.25
114 Jimmy Carson .02 .10
115 Kevin Miller .02 .10
116 Gerard Gallant .02 .10
117 Keith Primeau .07 .20
118 Paul Ysebaert .02 .10
119 Yves Racine .02 .10
120 Steve Chiasson .02 .10
121 Ray Sheppard .02 .10
122 Sharks Logo .02 .10
123 Jeff Hackett .07 .20
124 Kelly Kisio .02 .10
125 Brian Mullen .02 .10
126 David Bruce .02 .10
127 Rob Zettler .02 .10
128 Neil Wilkinson .02 .10
129 Doug Wilson .02 .10
130 Jeff Odgers .02 .10
131 Dean Evason .02 .10
132 Brian Lawton .02 .10
133 Dale Craigwell .02 .10
134 Bruins Logo .02 .10
135 Andy Moog .07 .20
136 Adam Oates 1.00 .30
137 Dave Poulin .02 .10
138 Vladimir Ruzicka .02 .10
139 Jeff Lazaro .02 .10
140 Bob Carpenter .02 .10
141 Peter Douris .02 .10
142 Glen Murray .02 .10
143 Cam Neely .20 .50
144 Ray Bourque .30 .75
145 Glen Wesley .02 .10
146 Canadiens Logo .02 .10
147 Patrick Roy .60 1.50
148 Kirk Muller .07 .20
149 Guy Carbonneau .07 .20
150 Shayne Corson .02 .10
151 Stephan Lebeau .02 .10
152 Denis Savard .07 .20
153 Brent Gilchrist .02 .10
154 Russ Courtnall .02 .10
155 Patrice Brisebois .02 .10
156 Eric Desjardins .07 .20
157 Matt Schneider .02 .10
158 Capitals Logo .02 .10
159 Don Beaupre .07 .20
160 Dino Ciccarelli .07 .20
161 Michal Pivonka .02 .10
162 Mike Ridley .02 .10
163 Randy Burridge .02 .10
164 Peter Bondra .20 .50
165 Dale Hunter .02 .10
166 Kelly Miller .02 .10
167 Kevin Hatcher .07 .20
168 Al Iafrate .07 .20
169 Rod Langway .02 .10
170 Devils Logo .02 .10
171 Chris Terreri .07 .20
172 Claude Lemieux .07 .20
173 Stephane Richer .07 .20
174 Peter Stastny .07 .20
175 Zdeno Ciger .02 .10
176 Alexander Semak .02 .10
177 Valeri Zelepukin .02 .10
178 Bruce Driver .02 .10
179 Scott Niedermayer .07 .20
180 Alexei Kasatonov .02 .10
181 Scott Stevens .07 .20
182 Flyers Logo .02 .10
183 Dominic Roussel .07 .20
184 Mike Ricci .07 .20
185 Mark Recchi .07 .20
186 Kevin Dineen .02 .10
187 Rod Brind'Amour .10 .30
188 Mark Pederson .02 .10
189 Pelle Eklund .07 .20
190 Terry Carkner .02 .10
191 Mark Howe .07 .20
192 Steve Duchesne .02 .10
193 Andrei Lomakin .02 .10
194 Islanders Logo .02 .10
195 Mark Fitzpatrick .07 .20
196 Pierre Turgeon .07 .20
197 Benoit Hogue .02 .10
198 Ray Ferraro .02 .10
199 Derek King .02 .10
200 David Volek .02 .10
201 Patrick Flatley .02 .10
202 Uwe Krupp .02 .10
203 Steve Thomas .02 .10
204 Adam Creighton .02 .10
205 Jeff Norton .02 .10
206 Nordiques Logo .02 .10
207 Stephane Fiset .07 .20
208 Mikhail Tatarinov .02 .10
209 Joe Sakic .50 1.25
210 Owen Nolan .07 .20
211 Mike Hough .02 .10
212 Mats Sundin .20 .50
213 Claude Lapointe .02 .10
214 Stephane Morin .02 .10
215 Alexei Gusarov .02 .10
216 Steven Finn .02 .10
217 Curtis Leschyshyn .02 .10
218 Penguins Logo .02 .10
219 Tom Barrasso .07 .20
220 Mario Lemieux .60 1.50
221 Kevin Stevens .02 .10
222 Shawn McEachern .02 .10
223 Joe Mullen .07 .20
224 Ron Francis .07 .20
225 Phil Bourque .02 .10
226 Rick Tocchet .07 .20
227 Bryan Trottier .07 .20
228 Larry Murphy .07 .20
229 Ulf Samuelsson .02 .10
230 Rangers Logo .02 .10
231 Mike Richter .20 .50
232 John Vanbiesbrouck .20 .50

233 Mark Messier .30 .75
234 Sergei Nemchinov .02 .10
235 Darren Turcotte .07 .20
236 Doug Weight .07 .20
237 Mike Gartner .07 .20
238 Adam Graves .07 .20
239 Brian Leetch .20 .50
240 James Patrick .02 .10
241 Jan Erixon .02 .10
242 Sabres Logo .02 .10
243 Tom Draper .02 .10
244 Grant Ledyard .02 .10
245 Doug Bodger .02 .10
246 Pat LaFontaine .20 .50
247 Dale Hawerchuk .07 .20
248 Alexander Mogilny .07 .20
249 Dave Andreychuk .07 .20
250 Christian Ruuttu .02 .10
251 Randy Wood .02 .10
252 Brad May .07 .20
253 Mike Ramsey .02 .10
254 Whalers Logo .02 .10
255 Kay Whitmore .07 .20
256 Pat Verbeek .07 .20
257 John Cullen .02 .10
258 Mikael Andersson .02 .10
259 Yvon Corriveau .02 .10
260 Randy Cunneyworth .02 .10
261 Robert Holik .02 .10
262 Murray Craven .02 .10
263 Zarley Zalapski .02 .10
264 Adam Burt .02 .10
265 Brad Shaw .02 .10
266 Lightning Logo .02 .10
267 Lightning Jersey .02 .10
268 Senators Logo .02 .10
269 Senators Jersey .02 .10
270 Tony Amonte .07 .20
271 Pavel Bure .60 1.50
272 Gilbert Dionne .07 .20
273 Pat Falloon .07 .20
274 Nicklas Lidstrom .20 .50
275 Kevin Todd .02 .10
276 Prince of Wales Conference Logo .02 .10
277 Patrick Roy AS .60 1.50
278 Paul Coffey AS .20 .50
279 Ray Bourque AS .30 .75
280 Mario Lemieux AS .60 1.50
281 Kevin Stevens AS .02 .10
282 Jaromir Jagr AS .75 2.00
283 Clarence Campbell Conference Logo .02 .10
284 Ed Belfour AS .20 .50
285 Al MacInnis AS .07 .20
286 Chris Chelios AS .20 .50
287 Wayne Gretzky AS .75 2.00
288 Luc Robitaille AS .07 .20
289 Brett Hull AS .20 .50
290 Pavel Bure .60 1.50
291 Sergei Fedorov .50 1.25
292 Dominik Hasek .50 1.25
293 Robert Holik .02 .10
294 Jaromir Jagr .75 2.00
295 Valeri Kamensky .02 .10
296 Alexander Semak .02 .10
297 Igor Kravchuk .02 .10
298 Nicklas Lidstrom .20 .50
299 Alexander Mogilny .07 .20
300 Petr Nedved .07 .20
301 Robert Reichel .02 .10
302 Mats Sundin .20 .50
303 Calder Trophy .02 .10
304 Hart Trophy .02 .10
305 Lady Byng Trophy .02 .10
306 Norris Trophy .02 .10
307 Selke Trophy .02 .10
308 Vezina Trophy .02 .10
A Igor Kravchuk .20 .50
B Nelson Emerson .20 .50
C Pavel Bure 1.00 2.50
D Tomas Forslund .20 .50
E Luciano Borsato .20 .50
F Darryl Sydor .30 .75
G Felix Potvin .60 1.50
H Derian Hatcher .20 .50
I Joseph Beranek .20 .50
J Nicklas Lidstrom .50 1.25
K Pat Falloon .30 .75
L Joe Juneau .30 .75
M Gilbert Dionne .40 1.00
N Dimitri Khristich .20 .50
O Kevin Todd .20 .50
P Eric Lindros .75 2.00
Q Scott Lachance .20 .50
R Valeri Kamensky .20 .50
S Jaromir Jagr .75 2.00
T Tony Amonte .30 .75
U Donald Audette .20 .50
V Geoff Sanderson .30 .75
NNO Sticker Album .60 1.50

1993-94 Panini Stickers

This set of 300 stickers was produced by Panini. They measure approximately 2 3/8" by 3 3/8" and were to be pasted in a 9" by 11" sticker album. The fronts have action color player photos with the player's name and the team name printed to the left side of the photo. The backs promote collecting Panini stickers. Also included are a subset Best of the Best (133-144), and a subset of 24 glitter stickers of Panini's superstars (A-X), one per team. The stickers are numbered on the back. The album also includes players' statistics and a Stanley Cup final review.

COMPLETE SET (300) 25.00 50.00
1 Bruins Logo .02 .10
2 Adam Oates .10 .30
3 Cam Neely .15 .40
4 Dave Poulin .07 .20
5 Steve Leach .02 .10
6 Glen Wesley .02 .10
7 Dmitri Kvartalnov .02 .10
8 Ted Donato .02 .10
9 Andy Moog .07 .20
10 Ray Bourque .30 .75
11 Don Sweeney .02 .10
12 Canadiens Logo .02 .10
13 Vincent Damphousse .10 .30
14 Kirk Muller .07 .20
15 Brian Bellows .07 .20
16 Stephan Lebeau .02 .10
17 Denis Savard .07 .20
18 Gilbert Dionne .02 .10
19 Guy Carbonneau .07 .20
20 Benoit Brunet .02 .10
21 Eric Desjardins .07 .20
22 Mathieu Schneider .02 .10
23 Capitals Logo .02 .10

24 Peter Bondra .10 .30
25 Mike Ridley .02 .10
26 Dale Hunter .07 .20
27 Michal Pivonka .02 .10
28 Dimitri Khristich .02 .10
29 Pat Elynuik .02 .10
30 Kelly Miller .02 .10
31 Calle Johansson .02 .10
32 Al Iafrate .07 .20
33 Don Beaupre .07 .20
34 Devils Logo .02 .10
35 Claude Lemieux .07 .20
36 Alexander Semak .02 .10
37 Stephane Richer .02 .10
38 Valeri Zelepukin .02 .10
39 Bernie Nicholls .07 .20
40 John MacLean .07 .20
41 Peter Stastny .07 .20
42 Scott Niedermayer .10 .30
43 Scott Stevens .07 .20
44 Bruce Driver .02 .10
45 Flyers Logo .02 .10
46 Mark Recchi .07 .20
47 Rod Brind'Amour .10 .30
48 Brent Fedyk .02 .10
49 Kevin Dineen .02 .10
50 Keith Acton .02 .10
51 Pelle Eklund .07 .20
52 Andrei Lomakin .02 .10
53 Garry Galley .02 .10
54 Terry Carkner .02 .10
55 Tommy Soderstrom .02 .10
56 Islanders Logo .02 .10
57 Steve Thomas .02 .10
58 Derek King .02 .10
59 Benoit Hogue .02 .10
60 Patrick Flatley .02 .10
61 Brian Mullen .02 .10
62 Marty McInnis .02 .10
63 Scott Lachance .02 .10
64 Jeff Norton .02 .10
65 Glenn Healy .07 .20
66 Mark Fitzpatrick .02 .10
67 Nordiques Logo .02 .10
68 Mats Sundin .10 .30
69 Mike Ricci .07 .20
70 Owen Nolan .07 .20
71 Andrei Kovalenko .02 .10
72 Valeri Kamensky .02 .10
73 Scott Young .02 .10
74 Martin Rucinsky .02 .10
75 Steven Finn .02 .10
76 Steve Duchesne .07 .20
77 Ron Hextall .15 .40
78 Penguins Logo .02 .10
79 Kevin Stevens .02 .10
80 Rick Tocchet .07 .20
81 Ron Francis .15 .40
82 Jaromir Jagr .30 .75
83 Joe Mullen .07 .20
84 Shawn McEachern .02 .10
85 Dave Tippett .02 .10
86 Larry Murphy .07 .20
87 Ulf Samuelsson .07 .20
88 Tom Barrasso .07 .20
89 Rangers Logo .02 .10
90 Tony Amonte .07 .20
91 Mike Gartner .10 .30
92 Adam Graves .07 .20
93 Sergei Nemchinov .02 .10
94 Darren Turcotte .07 .20
95 Esa Tikkanen .02 .10
96 Brian Leetch .10 .30
97 Kevin Lowe .02 .10
98 John Vanbiesbrouck .10 .30
99 Mike Richter .10 .30
100 Sabres Logo .02 .10
101 Pat LaFontaine .10 .30
102 Dale Hawerchuk .10 .30
103 Donald Audette .07 .20
104 Bob Sweeney .02 .10
105 Randy Wood .02 .10
106 Yuri Khmylev .02 .10
107 Wayne Presley .02 .10
108 Grant Fuhr .20 .50
109 Doug Bodger .02 .10
110 Richard Smehlik .02 .10
111 Senators Logo .02 .10
112 Norm Maciver .02 .10
113 Jamie Baker .02 .10
114 Bob Kudelski .02 .10
115 Jody Hull .02 .10
116 Mike Peluso .02 .10
117 Mark Lamb .02 .10
118 Mark Freer .02 .10
119 Neil Brady .02 .10
120 Brad Shaw .02 .10
121 Peter Sidorkiewicz .02 .10
122 Whalers Logo .02 .10
123 Andrew Cassels .02 .10
124 Pat Verbeek .07 .20
125 Terry Yake .02 .10
126 Patrick Poulin .02 .10
127 Mark Janssens .02 .10
128 Michael Nylander .07 .20
129 Zarley Zalapski .02 .10
130 Eric Weinrich .02 .10
131 Sean Burke .07 .20
132 Frank Pietrangelo .07 .20
133 Phil Housley BB .02 .10
134 Paul Coffey BB .10 .30
135 Larry Murphy BB .07 .20
136 Mario Lemieux BB 1.00 2.50
137 Pat LaFontaine BB .10 .30
138 Adam Oates BB .10 .30
139 Felix Potvin BB .20 .50
140 Ed Belfour BB .15 .40
141 Tom Barrasso BB .07 .20
142 Teemu Selanne BB .20 .50
143 Joe Juneau BB .07 .20
144 Eric Lindros BB .20 .50
145 Blackhawks Logo .02 .10
146 Steve Larmer .07 .20
147 Dirk Graham .02 .10
148 Michel Goulet .02 .10
149 Brian Noonan .02 .10
150 Stephane Matteau .02 .10
151 Brent Sutter .07 .20
152 Jocelyn Lemieux .02 .10
153 Chris Chelios .10 .30
154 Steve Smith .02 .10
155 Ed Belfour .15 .40
156 Blues Logo .02 .10
157 Craig Janney .02 .10
158 Brendan Shanahan .20 .50
159 Nelson Emerson .02 .10
160 Rich Sutter .07 .20
161 Ron Sutter .07 .20

162 Ron Wilson .02 .10
163 Bob Bassen .02 .10
164 Garth Butcher .02 .10
165 Jeff Brown .02 .10
166 Curtis Joseph .20 .50
167 Canucks Logo .02 .10
168 Cliff Ronning .02 .10
169 Murray Craven .02 .10
170 Geoff Courtnall .02 .10
171 Petr Nedved .07 .20
172 Trevor Linden .10 .30
173 Greg Adams .02 .10
174 Anatoli Semenov .02 .10
175 Jyrki Lumme .02 .10
176 Doug Lidster .02 .10
177 Kirk McLean .07 .20
178 Flames Logo .02 .10
179 Theo Fleury .20 .50
180 Robert Reichel .02 .10
181 Gary Roberts .07 .20
182 Joe Nieuwendyk .10 .30
183 Sergei Makarov .02 .10
184 Paul Ranheim .10 .30
185 Joel Otto .02 .10
186 Gary Suter .07 .20
187 Jeff Reese .02 .10
188 Mike Vernon .10 .30
189 Jets Logo .02 .10
190 Alexei Zhamnov .07 .20
191 Thomas Steen .02 .10
192 Darrin Shannon .02 .10
193 Keith Tkachuk .10 .30
194 Evgeny Davydov .02 .10
195 Luciano Borsato .02 .10
196 Phil Housley .02 .10
197 Teppo Numminen .02 .10
198 Fredrik Olausson .02 .10
199 Bob Essensa .07 .20
200 Kings Logo .02 .10
201 Luc Robitaille .10 .30
202 Jari Kurri .15 .40
203 Tony Granato .07 .20
204 Jimmy Carson .02 .10
205 Tomas Sandstrom .02 .10
206 Dave Taylor .02 .10
207 Corey Millen .02 .10
208 Marty McSorley .07 .20
209 Rob Blake .10 .30
210 Kelly Hrudey .07 .20
211 Lightning Logo .02 .10
212 John Tucker .02 .10
213 Chris Kontos .02 .10
214 Rob Zamuner .02 .10
215 Adam Creighton .02 .10
216 Mikael Andersson .02 .10
217 Bob Beers .02 .10
218 Rob DiMaio .02 .10
219 Shawn Chambers .02 .10
220 J.C. Bergeron .02 .10
221 Wendell Young .02 .10
222 Maple Leafs Logo .02 .10
223 Dave Andreychuk .07 .20
224 Nikolai Borschevsky .02 .10
225 Glenn Anderson .07 .20
226 John Cullen .02 .10
227 Wendel Clark .07 .20
228 Mike Foligno .07 .20
229 Mike Krushelnyski .02 .10
230 James Macoun .02 .10
231 Dave Ellett .02 .10
232 Felix Potvin .20 .50
233 Oilers Logo .02 .10
234 Petr Klima .02 .10
235 Doug Weight .07 .20
236 Shayne Corson .02 .10
237 Craig Simpson .02 .10
238 Todd Elik .02 .10
239 Zdeno Ciger .02 .10
240 Craig MacTavish .02 .10
241 Kelly Buchberger .07 .20
242 Dave Manson .02 .10
243 Scott Mellanby .02 .10
244 Red Wings Logo .02 .10
245 Dino Ciccarelli .07 .20
246 Sergei Fedorov .40 1.00
247 Ray Sheppard .02 .10
248 Paul Ysebaert .02 .10
249 Bob Probert .07 .20
250 Keith Primeau .07 .20
251 Steve Chiasson .02 .10
252 Paul Coffey .10 .30
253 Nicklas Lidstrom .20 .50
254 Tim Cheveldae .02 .10
255 Sharks Logo .02 .10
256 Kelly Kisio .02 .10
257 Johan Garpenlov .02 .10
258 Robert Gaudreau .02 .10
259 Dean Evason .02 .10
260 Jeff Odgers .02 .10
261 Ed Courtenay .02 .10
262 Mike Sullivan .02 .10
263 Doug Zmolek .02 .10
264 Doug Wilson .02 .10
265 Brian Hayward .07 .20
266 Stars Logo .02 .10
267 Brian Propp .02 .10
268 Russ Courtnall .07 .20
269 Dave Gagner .07 .20
270 Ulf Dahlen .02 .10
271 Mike Craig .07 .20
272 Neal Broten .07 .20
273 Gaetan Duchesne .02 .10
274 Derian Hatcher .07 .20
275 Mark Tinordi .07 .20
276 Jon Casey .07 .20
A Joe Juneau .30 .75
B Patrick Roy 1.50 4.00
C Kevin Hatcher .20 .50
D Chris Terreri .20 .50
E Eric Lindros .40 1.00
F Pierre Turgeon .30 .75
G Joe Sakic .75 2.00
H Mario Lemieux 1.50 4.00
I Mark Messier .50 1.25
J Alexander Mogilny .30 .75
K Sylvain Turgeon .20 .50
L Geoff Sanderson .20 .50
M Jeremy Roenick .40 1.00
N Brett Hull .50 1.25
O Pavel Bure .50 1.25
P Al MacInnis .30 .75
Q Teemu Selanne .50 1.25
R Wayne Gretzky 2.50 6.00
S Brian Bradley .20 .50

T Doug Gilmour	.40	1.00
U Bill Ranford	.30	.75
V Steve Yzerman	1.00	2.50
W Pat Falloon	.30	.75
X Mike Modano	.40	1.00

1994-95 Panini Stickers

1 Adam Oates	.10	.25
2 Ted Donato	.05	.15
3 Cam Neely	.10	.25
4 Brent Hughes	.05	.15
5 Bruins Logo	.05	.15
6 Glen Wesley	.05	.15
7 Al Iafrate	.05	.15
8 Ray Bourque	.15	.40
9 Jon Casey	.07	.20
10 Guy Carbonneau	.05	.15
11 Pierre Sevigny	.05	.15
12 Kirk Muller	.05	.15
13 Canadiens Logo	.05	.15
14 Vincent Damphousse	.07	.20
15 Gilbert Dionne	.05	.15
16 Mathieu Schneider	.05	.15
17 Eric Desjardins	.07	.20
18 Patrick Roy	.25	.60
19 Joe Juneau	.07	.20
20 Dimitri Khristich	.05	.15
21 Dale Hunter	.05	.15
22 Capitals Logo	.05	.15
23 Mike Ridley	.05	.15
24 Peter Bondra	.07	.20
25 Sylvain Cote	.05	.15
26 Kevin Hatcher	.05	.15
27 Don Beaupre	.07	.20
28 Bernie Nicholls	.07	.20
29 Alexander Semak	.05	.15
30 John MacLean	.07	.20
31 Devils Logo	.05	.15
32 Stephane Richer	.05	.15
33 Valeri Zelepukin	.05	.15
34 Scott Stevens	.10	.25
35 Martin Brodeur	.25	.60
36 Chris Terreri	.07	.20
37 Rod Brind'Amour	.07	.20
38 Eric Lindros	.10	.25
39 Mark Recchi	.12	.30
40 Flyers Logo	.05	.15
41 Kevin Dineen	.05	.15
42 Brent Fedyk	.05	.15
43 Garry Galley	.05	.15
44 Ryan McGill	.05	.15
45 Dominic Roussel	.07	.20
46 Ray Ferraro	.05	.15
47 Benoit Hogue	.05	.15
48 Pierre Turgeon	.07	.20
49 Islanders Logo	.05	.15
50 Patrick Flatley	.05	.15
51 Steve Thomas	.05	.15
52 Darius Kasparaitis	.05	.15
53 Vladimir Malakhov	.05	.15
54 Ron Hextall	.07	.20
55 Mats Sundin	.07	.20
56 Joe Sakic	.20	.50
57 Nordiques Logo	.05	.15
58 Claude Lapointe	.05	.15
59 Scott Young	.05	.15
60 Valeri Kamensky	.07	.20
61 Steven Finn	.05	.15
62 Jocelyn Thibault	.10	.25
63 Stephane Fiset	.07	.20
64 Brian Skrudland	.05	.15
65 Bob Kudelski	.05	.15
66 Jody Hull	.05	.15
67 Scott Mellanby	.07	.20
68 Panthers Logo	.05	.15
69 Dave Lowry	.05	.15
70 Mike Hough	.05	.15
71 Gord Murphy	.05	.15
72 John Vanbiesbrouck	.07	.20
73 Ron Francis	.12	.30
74 Mario Lemieux	.40	1.00
75 Penguins Logo	.05	.15
76 Jaromir Jagr	.25	.60
77 Rick Tocchet	.07	.20
78 Kevin Stevens	.05	.15
79 Ulf Samuelsson	.05	.15
80 Larry Murphy	.07	.20
81 Tom Barrasso	.07	.20
82 Mark Messier	.10	.25
83 Alexei Kovalev	.05	.15
84 Rangers Logo	.05	.15
85 Sergei Nemchinov	.05	.15
86 Steve Larmer	.07	.20
87 Adam Graves	.05	.15
88 Brian Leetch	.10	.25
89 Sergei Zubov	.05	.15
90 Mike Richter	.10	.25
91 Dale Hawerchuk	.12	.30
92 Pat Lafontaine	.10	.25
93 Donald Audette	.05	.15
94 Alexander Mogilny	.07	.20
95 Sabres Logo	.05	.15
96 Yuri Khmylev	.05	.15
97 Brad May	.05	.15
98 Richard Smehlik	.05	.15
99 Dominik Hasek	.20	.50
100 Dave McLlwain	.05	.15
101 Alexandre Daigle	.05	.15
102 David Archibald	.05	.15
103 Senators Logo	.05	.15
104 Troy Murray	.05	.15
105 Sylvain Turgeon	.05	.15
106 Gord Dineen	.05	.15
107 Darren Rumble	.05	.15
108 Craig Billington	.07	.20
109 Geoff Sanderson	.07	.20
110 Andrew Cassels	.05	.15
111 Whalers Logo	.05	.15
112 Pat Verbeek	.07	.20
113 Jim Sandlak	.05	.15
114 Jocelyn Lemieux	.05	.15
115 Brian Propp	.05	.15
116 Frantisek Kucera	.05	.15
117 Sean Burke	.07	.20
118 Anatoli Semenov	.05	.15
119 Stephan Lebeau	.05	.15
120 Mighty Ducks Logo	.05	.15
121 Terry Yake	.05	.15
122 Joe Sacco	.05	.15
123 Todd Ewen	.05	.15
124 Troy Loney	.05	.15
125 Sean Hill	.05	.15
126 Guy Hebert	.07	.20
127 Jeremy Roenick	.20	.50
128 Tony Amonte	.07	.20
129 Joe Murphy	.05	.15
130 BlackHawks Logo	.05	.15
131 Michel Goulet	.05	.15
132 Paul Ysebaert	.05	.15
133 Gary Suter	.05	.15
134 Chris Chelios	.10	.25
135 Ed Belfour	.10	.25
136 Craig Janney	.07	.20
137 Petr Nedved	.07	.20
138 Blues Logo	.05	.15
139 Kevin Miller	.05	.15
140 Brett Hull	.20	.50
141 Brendan Shanahan	.12	.30
142 Phil Housley	.07	.20
143 Steve Duchesne	.05	.15
144 Curtis Joseph	.15	.40
145 Cliff Ronning	.05	.15
146 Pavel Bure	.10	.25
147 Trevor Linden	.07	.20
148 Canucks Logo	.05	.15
149 Geoff Courtnall	.05	.15
150 Gino Odjick	.05	.15
151 Jyrki Lumme	.05	.15
152 Jeff Brown	.05	.15
153 Kirk McLean	.07	.20
154 Robert Reichel	.05	.15
155 Joel Otto	.05	.15
156 Joe Nieuwendyk	.10	.25
157 Flames Logo	.05	.15
158 German Titov	.05	.15
159 Theoren Fleury	.10	.25
160 Gary Roberts	.05	.15
161 Al MacInnis	.07	.20
162 Mike Vernon	.07	.20
163 Alexei Zhamnov	.07	.20
164 Nelson Emerson	.05	.15
165 Jets Logo	.05	.15
166 Teemu Selanne	.20	.50
167 Tie Domi	.07	.20
168 Keith Tkachuk	.10	.25
169 Teppo Numminen	.05	.15
170 Stephane Quintal	.05	.15
171 Tim Cheveldae	.07	.20
172 Wayne Gretzky	.50	1.25
173 Jari Kurri	.07	.20
174 Luc Robitaille	.10	.25
175 Kings Logo	.05	.15
176 Tony Granato	.05	.15
177 Rob Blake	.10	.25
178 Marty McSorley	.05	.15
179 Alexei Zhitnik	.07	.20
180 Kelly Hrudey	.07	.20
181 Denis Savard	.12	.30
182 Brian Bradley	.05	.15
183 Lightning Logo	.05	.15
184 Danton Cole	.05	.15
185 Petr Klima	.05	.15
186 Mikael Andersson	.05	.15
187 Shawn Chambers	.05	.15
188 Roman Hamrlik	.07	.20
189 Daren Puppa	.07	.20
190 Doug Gilmour	.12	.30
191 Mike Gartner	.10	.25
192 Nikolai Borschevsky	.05	.15
193 Maple Leafs Logo	.05	.15
194 Dave Andreychuk	.10	.25
195 Wendel Clark	.07	.20
196 Sylvain Lefebvre	.05	.15
197 Dave Ellett	.05	.15
198 Felix Potvin	.10	.25
199 Doug Weight	.07	.20
200 Zdeno Ciger	.05	.15
201 Kelly Buchberger	.05	.15
202 Shayne Corson	.05	.15
203 Oilers Logo	.05	.15
204 Scott Pearson	.05	.15
205 Igor Kravchuk	.05	.15
206 Luke Richardson	.05	.15
207 Bill Ranford	.07	.20
208 Vyacheslav Kozlov	.07	.20
209 Steve Yzerman	.25	.60
210 Sergei Fedorov	.15	.40
211 Ray Sheppard	.07	.20
212 Red Wings Logo	.05	.15
213 Bob Probert	.05	.15
214 Keith Primeau	.10	.25
215 Paul Coffey	.10	.25
216 Nicklas Lidstrom	.10	.25
217 Igor Larionov	.05	.15
218 Todd Elik	.05	.15
219 Pat Falloon	.05	.15
220 Sharks Logo	.05	.15
221 Ulf Dahlen	.05	.15
222 Sergei Makarov	.05	.15
223 Sandis Ozolinsh	.05	.15
224 Jeff Norton	.05	.15
225 Arturs Irbe	.07	.20
226 Mike Modano	.15	.40
227 Dave Gagner	.07	.20
228 Mike Craig	.05	.15
229 Stars Logo	.05	.15
230 Russ Courtnall	.05	.15
231 Derian Hatcher	.05	.15
232 Mark Tinordi	.05	.15
233 Craig Ludwig	.05	.15
234 Darcy Wakaluk	.07	.20
235 Pavel Bure / Brett Hull	.20	.50
236 Sergei Fedorov / Dave Andreychuk	.15	.40
237 Brendan Shanahan / Ray Sheppard	.12	.30
238 Adam Graves / Cam Neely	.10	.25
239 Mike Modano 50+ Goals	.15	.40
A Bryan Smolinski	.05	.15
B Oleg Petrov	.05	.15
C Pat Peake	.05	.15
D Jaroslav Modry	.05	.15
E Mikael Renberg	.07	.20
F Yan Kaminsky	.05	.15
G Iain Fraser	.05	.15
H Rob Niedermayer	.07	.20
I Markus Naslund	.10	.25
J Alexander Karpovtsev	.05	.15
K Derek Plante	.05	.15
L Alexei Yashin	.10	.25
M Chris Pronger	.10	.25
N Patrik Carnback	.05	.15
O Jeff Shantz	.05	.15
P Vitali Karamnov	.05	.15
Q Nathan Lafayette	.05	.15
R Trevor Kidd	.07	.20
S Dave Tomlinson	.05	.15
T Robert Lang	.05	.15
U Chris Gratton	.05	.15
V Alexei Kudashov	.05	.15
W Jason Arnott	.07	.20
X Chris Osgood	.15	.40
Y Mike Rathje	.05	.15
Z Jarkko Varvio	.05	.15
AA Wayne Gretzky	.50	1.25
BB Sergei Fedorov	.15	.40
CC Adam Oates	.10	.25
DD Mark Recchi	.12	.30
EE Brendan Shanahan	.12	.30
FF Doug Gilmour	.12	.30
GG Pavel Bure	.10	.25
HH Jeremy Roenick	.20	.50
II Jaromir Jagr	.25	.60
JJ Dave Andreychuk	.10	.25

1995-96 Panini Stickers

This popular set of NHL player stickers was distributed primarily in Europe by Panini. The stickers -- which are about half the size of a regulation trading card -- feature action photos on the front, with the card number and licensing logos on the back.

1 Claude Lemieux	.10	.25
2 Claude Lemieux	.10	.25
3 Adam Oates	.10	.25
4 Ted Donato	.05	.15
5 Mariusz Czerkawski	.05	.15
6 Sandy Moger	.05	.15
7 Kevin Stevens	.07	.20
8 Cam Neely	.10	.25
9 Ray Bourque	.15	.40
10 Bruins Logo	.05	.15
11 Don Sweeney	.05	.15
12 Al Iafrate	.07	.20
13 Blaine Lacher	.07	.20
14 Brian Holzinger	.20	.50
15 Pat LaFontaine	.10	.25
16 Derek Plante	.05	.15
17 Yuri Khmylev	.05	.15
18 Jason Dawe	.05	.15
19 Donald Audette	.07	.20
20 Alexei Zhitnik	.05	.15
21 Sabres Logo	.05	.15
22 Richard Smehlik	.07	.20
23 Garry Galley	.05	.15
24 Dominik Hasek	.12	.30
25 Andrew Cassels	.05	.15
26 Jimmy Carson	.07	.20
27 Darren Turcotte	.05	.15
28 Geoff Sanderson	.05	.15
29 Andrei Nikolishin	.05	.15
30 Kevin Smyth	.05	.15
31 Brendan Shanahan	.12	.30
32 Whalers Logo	.05	.15
33 Steven Rice	.05	.15
34 Frantisek Kucera	.05	.15
35 Sean Burke	.05	.15
36 Brian Savage	.05	.15
37 Pierre Turgeon	.10	.25
38 Vincent Damphousse	.07	.20
39 Benoit Brunet	.05	.15
40 Mike Keane	.05	.15
41 Mark Recchi	.12	.30
42 Vladimir Malakhov	.05	.15
43 Canadiens Logo	.05	.15
44 Patrice Brisebois	.05	.15
45 Stephane Quintal	.07	.20
46 Patrick Roy	.25	.60
47 Alexandre Daigle	.05	.15
48 Alexei Yashin	.07	.20
49 Dan Quinn	.07	.20
50 Radek Bonk	.05	.15
51 Scott Levins	.05	.15
52 Sylvain Turgeon	.05	.15
53 Pavol Demitra	.12	.30
54 Senators Logo	.05	.15
55 Steve Larouche	.05	.15
56 Sean Hill	.05	.15
57 Don Beaupre	.07	.20
58 Ron Francis	.12	.30
59 Mario Lemieux	.30	.75
60 Bryan Smolinski	.05	.15
61 Luc Robitaille	.10	.25
62 Tomas Sandstrom	.07	.20
63 Jaromir Jagr	.25	.60
64 Joe Mullen	.07	.20
65 Penguins Logo	.05	.15
66 Ulf Samuelsson	.05	.15
67 Dmitri Mironov	.05	.15
68 Ken Wregget	.07	.20
69 Stu Barnes	.05	.15
70 Jesse Belanger	.05	.15
71 Rob Niedermayer	.07	.20
72 Brian Skrudland	.05	.15
73 Dave Lowry	.05	.15
74 Jody Hull	.05	.15
75 Scott Mellanby	.07	.20
76 Panthers Logo	.05	.15
77 Gord Murphy	.05	.15
78 Magnus Svensson	.07	.20
79 John Vanbiesbrouck	.07	.20
80 Neal Broten	.07	.20
81 Bill Guerin	.07	.20
82 Claude Lemieux	.10	.25
83 John MacLean	.07	.20
84 Randy McKay	.05	.15
85 Stephane Richer	.07	.20
86 Shawn Chambers	.05	.15
87 Devils Logo	.05	.15
88 Scott Niedermayer	.10	.25
89 Scott Stevens	.10	.25
90 Martin Brodeur	.25	.60
91 Kirk Muller	.07	.20
92 Derek King	.07	.20
93 Patrick Flatley	.05	.15
94 Brett Lindros	.05	.15
95 Steve Thomas	.07	.20
96 Darius Kasparaitis	.05	.15
97 Scott Lachance	.05	.15
98 Islanders Logo	.05	.15
99 Mathieu Schneider	.05	.15
100 Dennis Vaske	.05	.15
101 Tommy Salo	.15	.40
102 Mark Messier	.15	.40
103 Ray Ferraro	.05	.15
104 Petr Nedved	.07	.20
105 Adam Graves	.07	.20
106 Alexei Kovalev	.05	.15
107 Steve Larmer	.07	.20
108 Pat Verbeek	.07	.20
109 Rangers Logo	.05	.15
110 Brian Leetch	.10	.25
111 Sergei Zubov	.07	.20
112 Mike Richter	.10	.25
113 Eric Lindros	.15	.40
114 Rod Brind'Amour	.10	.25
115 Joel Otto	.05	.15
116 John LeClair	.10	.25
117 Mikael Renberg	.07	.20
118 Chris Therien	.05	.15
119 Eric Desjardins	.07	.20
120 Flyers Logo	.05	.15
121 Dimitri Yushkevich	.05	.15
122 Karl Dykhuis	.05	.15
123 Ron Hextall	.10	.25
124 Brian Bradley	.07	.20
125 John Tucker	.05	.15
126 Chris Gratton	.05	.15
127 Alexander Semak	.05	.15
128 Brian Bellows	.07	.20
129 Paul Ysebaert	.05	.15
130 Petr Klima	.05	.15
131 Lightning Logo	.05	.15
132 Alexander Selivanov	.07	.20
133 Roman Hamrlik	.05	.15
134 Daren Puppa	.07	.20
135 Dale Hunter	.07	.20
136 Michal Pivonka	.05	.15
137 Steve Konowalchuk	.07	.20
138 Joe Juneau	.07	.20
139 Peter Bondra	.10	.25
140 Keith Jones	.07	.20
141 Sergei Gonchar	.05	.15
142 Capitals Logo	.05	.15
143 Calle Johansson	.05	.15
144 Mark Tinordi	.05	.15
145 Jim Carey	.07	.20
146 Eric Lindros AW	.15	.40
147 Paul Coffey AW	.10	.25
148 Peter Forsberg AW	.25	.60
149 Dominik Hasek AW	.12	.30
150 Jaromir Jagr AW	.25	.60
151 Peter Bondra LL	.10	.25
152 Ron Francis LL	.12	.30
153 Cam Neely LL	.10	.25
154 Dominik Hasek LL	.12	.30
155 Ian Laperriere LL	.05	.15
156 Bernie Nicholls	.05	.15
157 Jeremy Roenick	.12	.30
158 Patrick Poulin	.05	.15
159 Eric Daze	.20	.50
160 Tony Amonte	.07	.20
161 Sergei Krivokrasov	.05	.15
162 Joe Murphy	.05	.15
163 Blackhawks Logo	.05	.15
164 Chris Chelios	.10	.25
165 Gary Suter	.07	.20
166 Ed Belfour	.07	.20
167 Dave Gagner	.05	.15
168 Mike Modano	.15	.40
169 Todd Harvey	.05	.15
170 Mike Donnelly	.05	.15
171 Mike Kennedy	.07	.20
172 Trent Klatt	.05	.15
173 Derian Hatcher	.07	.20
174 Stars Logo	.05	.15
175 Kevin Hatcher	.07	.20
176 Grant Ledyard	.05	.15
177 Andy Moog	.10	.25
178 Sergei Fedorov	.15	.40
179 Steve Yzerman	.12	.30
180 Vyacheslav Kozlov	.07	.20
181 Keith Primeau	.05	.15
182 Dino Ciccarelli	.07	.20
183 Ray Sheppard	.07	.20
184 Paul Coffey	.10	.25
185 Red Wings Logo	.05	.15
186 Nicklas Lidstrom	.10	.25
187 Chris Osgood	.07	.20
188 Mike Vernon	.07	.20
189 Dale Hawerchuk	.12	.30
190 Ian Laperriere	.05	.15
191 David Roberts	.05	.15
192 Esa Tikkanen	.05	.15
193 Geoff Courtnall	.05	.15
194 Brett Hull	.12	.30
195 Steve Duchesne	.05	.15
196 Blues Logo	.05	.15
197 Al MacInnis	.10	.25
198 Chris Pronger	.10	.25
199 Jon Casey	.07	.20
200 Doug Gilmour	.12	.30
201 Mats Sundin	.10	.25
202 Benoit Hogue	.05	.15
203 Dave Andreychuk	.10	.25
204 Mike Gartner	.10	.25
205 Dave Ellett	.05	.15
206 Todd Gill	.05	.15
207 Maple Leafs Logo	.05	.15
208 Kenny Jonsson	.10	.25
209 Larry Murphy	.10	.25
210 Felix Potvin	.10	.25
211 Dallas Drake	.05	.15
212 Alexei Zhamnov	.10	.25
213 Mike Eastwood	.05	.15
214 Keith Tkachuk	.10	.25
215 Igor Korolev	.05	.15
216 Nelson Emerson	.05	.15
217 Teemu Selanne	.20	.50
218 Jets Logo	.05	.15
219 Dave Manson	.05	.15
220 Teppo Numminen	.05	.15
221 Nikolai Khabibulin	.07	.20
222 Steve Rucchin	.07	.20
223 Shaun Van Allen	.05	.15
224 Patrik Carnback	.05	.15
225 Peter Douris	.05	.15
226 Todd Krygier	.05	.15
227 Paul Kariya	.12	.30
228 Bobby Dollas	.05	.15
229 Ducks Logo	.05	.15
230 Milos Holan	.05	.15
231 Oleg Tverdovsky	.10	.25
232 Guy Hebert	.07	.20
233 Joe Nieuwendyk	.10	.25
234 German Titov	.07	.20
235 Paul Kruse	.05	.15
236 Gary Roberts	.05	.15
237 Theo Fleury	.12	.30
238 Ronnie Stern	.05	.15
239 Steve Chiasson	.05	.15
240 Flames Logo	.05	.15
241 Phil Housley	.07	.20
242 Zarley Zalapski	.05	.15
243 Trevor Kidd	.07	.20
244 Peter Forsberg	.25	.60
245 Mike Ricci	.07	.20
246 Joe Sakic	.15	.40
247 Wendel Clark	.10	.25
248 Valeri Kamensky	.07	.20
249 Owen Nolan	.10	.25
250 Scott Young	.05	.15
251 Avalanche Logo	.05	.15
252 Uwe Krupp	.07	.20
253 Curtis Leschyshyn	.05	.15
254 Jocelyn Thibault	.07	.20
255 Jason Arnott	.07	.20
256 Jason Bonsignore	.05	.15
257 Todd Marchant	.05	.15
258 Scott Thornton	.07	.20
259 Doug Weight	.10	.25
260 Shayne Corson	.05	.15
261 Kelly Buchberger	.05	.15
262 Oilers Logo	.05	.15
263 David Oliver	.05	.15
264 Igor Kravchuk	.05	.15
265 Curtis Joseph	.10	.25
266 Wayne Gretzky	.50	1.25
267 Tony Granato	.05	.15
268 Dimitri Khristich	.05	.15
269 John Druce	.07	.20
270 Jari Kurri	.10	.25
271 Rick Tocchet	.07	.20
272 Rob Blake	.07	.20
273 Kings Logo	.05	.15
274 Marty McSorley	.05	.15
275 Darryl Sydor	.07	.20
276 Kelly Hrudey	.07	.20
277 Craig Janney	.05	.15
278 Jeff Friesen	.05	.15
279 Viktor Kozlov	.07	.20
280 Ray Whitney	.07	.20
281 Ulf Dahlen	.05	.15
282 Sergei Makarov	.05	.15
283 Sandis Ozolinsh	.07	.20
284 Sharks Logo	.05	.15
285 Mike Rathje	.07	.20
286 Michal Sykora	.05	.15
287 Arturs Irbe	.07	.20
288 Trevor Linden	.10	.25
289 Mike Ridley	.05	.15
290 Cliff Ronning	.05	.15
291 Josef Beranek	.05	.15
292 Roman Oksiuta	.05	.15
293 Pavel Bure	.12	.30
294 Alexander Mogilny	.07	.20
295 Canucks Logo	.05	.15
296 Russ Courtnall	.05	.15
297 Jeff Brown	.07	.20
298 Kirk McLean	.07	.20
299 Peter Forsberg	.25	.60
300 Paul Kariya	.12	.30
301 Chris Therien	.05	.15
302 Blaine Lacher	.07	.20
303 Jim Carey	.07	.20
304 Jeff Friesen	.05	.15
305 Ian Laperriere	.05	.15
306 Kenny Jonsson	.10	.25

1996-97 Panini Stickers

COMPLETE SET (304)	25.00	50.00
1 Ray Bourque	.15	.40
2 Bill Ranford	.07	.20
3 Cam Neely	.10	.25
4 Adam Oates	.10	.25
5 Kyle McLaren	.05	.15
6 Rick Tocchet	.07	.20
7 Shawn McEachern	.05	.15
8 Boston Logo	.05	.15
9 Jozef Stumpel	.05	.15
10 Ted Donato	.05	.15
11 Dave Reid	.05	.15
12 Donald Audette	.05	.15
13 Garry Galley	.05	.15
14 Dominik Hasek	.15	.40
15 Pat LaFontaine	.10	.25
16 Jason Dawe	.05	.15
17 Alexei Zhitnik	.05	.15
18 Brad May	.05	.15
19 Buffalo Logo	.05	.15
20 Matthew Barnaby	.05	.15
21 Darryl Shannon	.05	.15
22 Derek Plante	.05	.15
23 Geoff Sanderson	.07	.20
24 Sean Burke	.05	.15
25 Nelson Emerson	.05	.15
26 Brendan Shanahan	.12	.30
27 Jeff Brown	.05	.15
28 Andrew Cassels	.05	.15
29 Hartford Logo	.05	.15
30 Jeff O'Neill	.05	.15
31 Robert Kron	.05	.15
32 Andrei Nikolishin	.05	.15
33 Brad McCrimmon	.05	.15
34 Valeri Bure	.05	.15
35 Vincent Damphousse	.07	.20
36 Jocelyn Thibault	.10	.25
37 Saku Koivu	.10	.25
38 Mark Recchi	.12	.30
39 Martin Rucinsky	.05	.15
40 Pierre Turgeon	.10	.25
41 Montreal Logo	.05	.15
42 Andrei Kovalenko	.05	.15
43 Peter Popovic	.05	.15
44 Vladimir Malakhov	.05	.15
45 Alexandre Daigle	.05	.15
46 Daniel Alfredsson	.10	.25
47 Damian Rhodes	.07	.20
48 Alexei Yashin	.07	.20
49 Radek Bonk	.05	.15
50 Steve Duchesne	.05	.15
51 Ottawa Logo	.05	.15
52 Pavol Demitra	.12	.30
53 Antti Tormanen	.05	.15
54 Stanislav Neckar	.05	.15
55 Randy Cunneyworth	.05	.15
56 Petr Nedved	.07	.20
57 Ron Francis	.12	.30
58 Jaromir Jagr	.25	.60
59 Mario Lemieux	.30	.75
60 Tom Barrasso	.07	.20
61 Tomas Sandstrom	.05	.15
62 Bryan Smolinski	.05	.15
63 Pittsburgh Logo	.05	.15
64 Sergei Zubov	.05	.15
65 Dmitri Mironov	.05	.15
66 Kevin Miller	.05	.15
67 Scott Mellanby	.07	.20
68 Ed Jovanovski	.07	.20
69 Ray Sheppard	.07	.20
70 John Vanbiesbrouck	.10	.25
71 Radek Dvorak	.07	.20
72 Rob Niedermayer	.07	.20
73 Florida Logo	.05	.15
74 Robert Svehla	.05	.15
75 Johan Garpenlov	.05	.15
76 Martin Straka	.05	.15
77 Paul Laus	.05	.15
78 Steve Thomas	.05	.15
79 Martin Brodeur	.20	.50
80 Scott Stevens	.10	.25
81 Petr Sykora	.05	.15
82 Dave Andreychuk	.10	.25
83 Bill Guerin	.10	.25
84 New Jersey Logo	.05	.15
85 Phil Housley	.07	.20
86 Scott Niedermayer	.10	.25
87 Valeri Zelepukin	.07	.20
88 John MacLean	.07	.20
89 Todd Bertuzzi	.10	.25
90 Eric Fichaud	.07	.20
91 Zigmund Palffy	.10	.25
92 Travis Green	.07	.20
93 Kenny Jonsson	.05	.15
94 Bryan McCabe	.05	.15
95 Marty McInnis	.05	.15
96 New York Islanders Logo	.05	.15
97 Alexander Semak	.05	.15
98 Niklas Andersson	.05	.15
99 Scott Lachance	.05	.15
100 Adam Graves	.05	.15
101 Mark Messier	.15	.40
102 Brian Leetch	.10	.25
103 Mike Richter	.10	.25
104 Alexei Kovalev	.05	.15
105 Luc Robitaille	.10	.25
106 New York Rangers Logo	.05	.15
107 Ulf Samuelsson	.05	.15
108 Niklas Sundstrom	.05	.15
109 Jari Kurri	.10	.25
110 Sergei Nemchinov	.05	.15
111 Rod Brind'Amour	.10	.25
112 John Leclair	.10	.25
113 Ron Hextall	.07	.20
114 Eric Lindros	.15	.40
115 Eric Desjardins	.07	.20
116 Dale Hawerchuk	.12	.30
117 Philadelphia Logo	.05	.15
118 Mikael Renberg	.07	.20
119 Joel Otto	.05	.15
120 Petr Svoboda	.05	.15
121 Karl Dykhuis	.05	.15
122 Brian Bradley	.05	.15
123 Roman Hamrlik	.07	.20
124 Chris Gratton	.07	.20
125 Daren Puppa	.07	.20
126 Petr Klima	.05	.15
127 Alexander Selivanov	.05	.15
128 Tampa Bay Logo	.05	.15
129 Aaron Gavey	.05	.15
130 Brian Bellows	.07	.20
131 Rob Zamuner	.05	.15
132 Mikael Andersson	.05	.15
133 Peter Bondra	.07	.20
134 Jim Carey	.10	.25
135 Sergei Gonchar	.05	.15
136 Brendan Witt	.05	.15
137 Sylvain Cote	.05	.15
138 Joe Juneau	.05	.15
139 Michal Pivonka	.05	.15
140 Washington Logo	.05	.15
141 Andrew Brunette	.12	.30
142 Calle Johansson	.07	.20
143 Stefan Ustorf	.05	.15
144 Mario Lemieux	.30	.75
145 Ron Francis	.12	.30
146 Ron Hextall	.07	.20
147 Vladimir Konstantinov	.07	.20
148 Brian Leetch	.10	.25
149 Gary Roberts	.05	.15
150 Mario Lemieux	.30	.75
151 Chris Chelios	.10	.25
152 Daniel Alfredsson	.10	.25
153 Paul Kariya	.12	.30
154 Jim Carey	.10	.25
155 Joe Sakic	.15	.40
156 Ed Belfour	.10	.25
157 Chris Chelios	.10	.25
158 Jeremy Roenick	.15	.40
159 Eric Daze	.07	.20
160 Tony Amonte	.07	.20
161 Bernie Nicholls	.05	.15
162 Chicago Logo	.05	.15
163 Gary Suter	.05	.15
164 Denis Savard	.12	.30
165 Brent Sutter	.05	.15
166 Keith Carney	.05	.15
167 Derian Hatcher	.05	.15
168 Mike Modano	.15	.40
169 Joe Nieuwendyk	.10	.25
170 Kevin Hatcher	.05	.15
171 Benoit Hogue	.05	.15
172 Grant Marshall	.05	.15
173 Andy Moog	.10	.25
174 Dallas Logo	.05	.15
175 Jere Lehtinen	.05	.15
176 Greg Adams	.05	.15
177 Brent Gilchrist	.05	.15
178 Sergei Fedorov	.15	.40
179 Paul Coffey	.10	.25
180 Chris Osgood	.10	.25
181 Steve Yzerman	.25	.60
182 Vladimir Konstantinov	.07	.20
183 Slava Kozlov	.05	.15
184 Detroit Logo	.05	.15
185 Nicklas Lidstrom	.12	.30
186 Keith Primeau	.05	.15
187 Viacheslav Fetisov	.05	.15
188 Igor Larionov	.10	.25
189 Nikolai Khabibulin	.07	.20
190 Chad Kilger	.05	.15
191 Keith Tkachuk	.10	.25
192 Oleg Tverdovsky	.07	.20
193 Ed Olczyk	.05	.15
194 Teppo Numminen	.05	.15
195 Phoenix Logo	.05	.15
196 Alexei Zhamnov	.07	.20
197 Dave Manson	.05	.15
198 Craig Janney	.07	.20
199 Igor Korolev	.05	.15
200 Wayne Gretzky	.50	1.25
201 Chris Pronger	.07	.20
202 Brett Hull	.50	1.25
203 Grant Fuhr	.10	.25
204 Shayne Corson	.05	.15
205 Geoff Courtnall	.05	.15
206 St.Louis Logo	.05	.15
207 Al MacInnis	.10	.25
208 Christer Olsson	.05	.15
209 Adam Creighton	.05	.15
210 Tony Twist	.05	.15
211 Felix Potvin	.10	.25
212 Kirk Muller	.05	.15
213 Wendel Clark	.07	.20
214 Doug Gilmour	.12	.30
215 Mike Gartner	.10	.25
216 Larry Murphy	.07	.20
217 Toronto Logo	.05	.15
218 Mats Sundin	.10	.25
219 Dave Gagner	.10	.25
220 Mathieu Schneider	.05	.15
221 Tie Domi	.07	.20
222 Paul Kariya	.12	.30
223 Guy Hebert	.07	.20
224 Roman Oksiuta	.05	.15
225 Teemu Selanne	.20	.50
226 Steve Rucchin	.05	.15
227 Bobby Dollas	.05	[illegible]
228 Anaheim Logo	.05	[illegible]
229 Darren Van Impe	.05	[illegible]
230 Fredrik Olausson	.05	[illegible]
231 Shaun Van Allen	.05	[illegible]
232 Joe Sacco	.12	[illegible]
233 Trevor Kidd	.05	[illegible]
234 Theoren Fleury	.20	[illegible]
235 German Titov	.05	[illegible]
236 James Patrick	.05	[illegible]
237 Michael Nylander	.05	[illegible]
238 Cory Stillman	.05	[illegible]
239 Calgary Logo	.05	[illegible]
240 Gary Roberts	.05	[illegible]
241 Jamie Huscroft	.05	[illegible]
242 Tommy Albelin	.07	[illegible]
243 Zarley Zalapski	.05	[illegible]
244 Peter Forsberg	.15	[illegible]
245 Joe Sakic	.15	[illegible]
246 Claude Lemieux	.05	[illegible]
247 Patrick Roy	.25	[illegible]
248 Valeri Kamensky	.07	[illegible]
249 Uwe Krupp	.05	[illegible]
250 Colorado Logo	.05	[illegible]
251 Sandis Ozolinsh	.05	[illegible]
252 Curtis Leschyshyn	.05	[illegible]
253 Scott Young	.05	[illegible]
254 Alexei Gusarov	.05	[illegible]
255 Curtis Joseph	.10	[illegible]
256 Bryan Marchment	.05	[illegible]
257 Doug Weight	.10	[illegible]
258 Jason Arnott	.07	[illegible]
259 Zdeno Ciger	.05	[illegible]
260 Miroslav Satan	.05	[illegible]
261 Mariusz Czerkawski	.05	[illegible]
262 Edmonton Logo	.05	[illegible]
263 Jiri Slegr	.05	[illegible]
264 Jeff Norton	.07	[illegible]
265 Boris Mironov	.05	[illegible]
266 Vitali Yachmenev	.05	[illegible]
267 Byron Dafoe	.05	[illegible]
268 Rob Blake	.10	[illegible]
269 Ray Ferraro	.05	[illegible]
270 Dimitri Khristich	.05	[illegible]
271 Kevin Todd	.05	[illegible]
272 Yanic Perreault	.05	[illegible]
273 Los Angeles Logo	.05	[illegible]
274 Tony Granato	.05	[illegible]
275 Jaroslav Modry	.05	[illegible]
276 Mattias Norstrom	.05	[illegible]
277 Owen Nolan	.10	[illegible]
278 Jeff Friesen	.05	[illegible]
279 Marcus Ragnarsson	.05	[illegible]
280 Chris Terreri	.07	[illegible]
281 Darren Turcotte	.05	[illegible]
282 Viktor Kozlov	.05	[illegible]
283 Ulf Dahlen	.05	[illegible]
284 San Jose Logo	.05	[illegible]
285 Michal Sykora	.05	[illegible]
286 Ray Whitney	.05	[illegible]
287 Shean Donovan	.05	[illegible]
288 Alexander Mogilny	.07	.20
289 Pavel Bure	.12	.30
290 Trevor Linden	.07	.20
291 Kirk McLean	.07	.20
292 Russ Courtnall	.05	.15
293 Jyrki Lumme	.05	.15
294 Vancouver Logo	.05	.15
295 Cliff Ronning	.05	.15
296 Markus Naslund	.10	.25
297 Esa Tikkanen	.05	.15
298 Josef Beranek	.05	.15
299 Martin Biron	.12	.30
300 Peter Ferraro	.05	.15
301 Jason Bonsignore	.05	.15
302 Jamie Storr	.05	.15
303 Eric Fichaud	.07	.20
304 Andrew Brunette	.12	.30

1997-98 Panini Stickers

COMPLETE SET (252)	30.00	60.00
1 Rob DiMaio	.02	.10
2 Jeff Odgers	.02	.10
3 Jozef Stumpel	.02	.10
4 Ted Donato	.02	.10
5 Mattias Timander	.02	.10
6 Bruins Logo Foil	.10	.30
7 Don Sweeney	.02	.10
8 Jim Carey	.07	.20
9 Ray Bourque	.30	.75
10 Dominik Hasek	.40	1.00
11 Alexei Zhitnik	.02	.10
12 Derek Plante	.07	.20
13 Michael Peca	.07	.20
14 Darryl Shannon	.02	.10
15 Sabres Logo Foil	.10	.30
16 Donald Audette	.07	.20
17 Michal Grosek	.02	.10
18 Miroslav Satan	.07	.20
19 Robert Kron	.02	.10
20 Geoff Sanderson	.07	.20
21 Andrew Cassels	.02	.10
22 Marek Malik	.02	.10
23 Derek King	.02	.10
24 Hurricanes Logo Foil	.10	.30
25 Sami Kapanen	.02	.10
26 Alexander Godynyuk	.02	.10
27 Keith Primeau	.07	.20
28 Saku Koivu	.10	.30
29 Vincent Damphousse	.10	.30
30 Brian Savage	.02	.10
31 Valeri Bure	.02	.10
32 Mark Recchi	.07	.20
33 Canadiens Logo Foil	.10	.30
34 Vladimir Malakhov	.02	.10
35 Peter Popovic	.02	.10
36 Martin Rucinsky	.02	.10
37 Radek Bonk	.07	.20
38 Alexandre Daigle	.10	.30
39 Sergei Zholtok	.02	.10
40 Janne Laukkanen	.02	.10
41 Daniel Alfredsson	.07	.20
42 Senators Lolo Foil	.10	.30
43 Alexei Yashin	.10	.30
44 Frank Musil	.02	.10
45 Steve Duchesne	.07	.20
46 Darius Kasparaitis	.07	.20
47 Jaromir Jagr	.30	.75
48 Roman Oksiuta	.02	.10
49 Kevin Hatcher	.02	.10
50 Ron Francis	.15	.40
51 Penguis Logo Foil	.10	.30
52 Petr Nedved	.07	.20
53 Andreas Johansson	.02	.10
54 Fredrik Olausson	.02	.10
55 Robert Svehla	.02	.10
56 Radek Dvorak	.07	.20
57 Martin Straka	.07	.20

58 Kirk Muller .07 .20
59 Per Gustafsson .02 .10
60 Panthers Logo Foil .10 .30
61 Ray Sheppard .02 .10
62 Johan Garpenlov .02 .10
63 Scott Mellanby .02 .10
64 Martin Brodeur .40 1.00
65 Bobby Holik .02 .10
66 Doug Gilmour .20 .50
67 Valeri Zelepukin .02 .10
68 Petr Sykora .07 .20
69 Devils Logo Foil .10 .30
70 John MacLean .07 .20
71 Dave Andreychuk .07 .20
72 Scott Niedermayer .10 .30
73 Zigmund Palffy .07 .20
74 Tommy Salo .07 .20
75 Niklas Andersson .02 .10
76 Kenny Jonsson .02 .10
77 Robert Reichel .02 .10
78 Islanders Logo Foil .10 .30
79 Travis Green .02 .10
80 Bryan Berard .07 .20
81 Bryan Smolinski .07 .20
82 Wayne Gretzky 1.25 3.00
83 Mark Messier .30 .75
84 Brian Leetch .10 .30
85 Alexei Kovalev .07 .20
86 Esa Tikkanen .02 .10
87 Rangers Logo Foil .10 .30
88 Ulf Samuelsson .07 .20
89 Niklas Sundstrom .02 .10
90 Alexander Karpovtsev .02 .10
91 Ron Hextall .15 .40
92 Eric Lindros .20 .50
93 Rod Brind'Amour .10 .30
94 Janne Niinimaa .02 .10
95 Dainius Zubrus .02 .10
96 Flyers Logo Foil .10 .30
97 Petr Svoboda .02 .10
98 John LeClair .25 .60
99 Mikael Renberg .07 .20
100 Dino Ciccarelli .07 .20
101 Roman Hamrlik .07 .20
102 Alexander Selivanov .02 .10
103 Chris Gratton .07 .20
104 Mikael Andersson .02 .10
105 Lightning Logo Foil .10 .30
106 Igor Ulanov .02 .10
107 John Cullen .02 .10
108 Rob Zamuner .02 .10
109 Peter Bondra .10 .30
110 Bill Ranford .10 .30
111 Michal Pivonka .02 .10
112 Sergei Gonchar .07 .20
113 Calle Johansson .02 .10
114 Capitals Logo Foil .10 .30
115 Dale Hunter .07 .20
116 Adam Oates .10 .30
117 Andrei Nikolishin .02 .10
118 Dominik Hasek Foil .75 2.00
119 Bryan Berard Foil .15 .40
120 Brian Leetch Foil .25 .60
121 Paul Kariya Foil .40 1.00
122 Michael Peca Foil .15 .40
123 Keith Tkachuk Foil .25 .60
124 Martin Brodeur Foil 75.00 2.00
125 John LeClair Foil .50 1.25
126 Miroslav Satan Foil .15 .40
127 Patrick Roy Foil 1.50 4.00
128 Alexei Zhamnov .07 .20
129 Chris Chelios .10 .30
130 Ulf Dahlen .02 .10
131 Tony Amonte .07 .20
132 Michal Sykora .07 .20
133 Blackhawks Logo Foil .10 .30
134 Eric Weinrich .02 .10
135 Sergei Krivokrasov .02 .10
136 Eric Daze .02 .10
137 Pat Verbeek .07 .20
138 Sergei Zubov .07 .20
139 Mike Modano .20 .50
140 Darryl Sydor .07 .20
141 Dave Reid .02 .10
142 Stars Logo Foil .10 .30
143 Benoit Hogue .02 .10
144 Joe Nieuwendyk .10 .30
145 Jere Lehtinen .07 .20
146 Nicklas Lidstrom .20 .50
147 Vladimir Konstantinov .02 .10
148 Sergei Fedorov .40 1.00
149 Steve Yzerman .50 1.25
150 Tomas Sandstrom .02 .10
151 Red Wings Logo Foil .10 .30
152 Igor Larionov .07 .20
153 Vyacheslav Kozlov .07 .20
154 Brendan Shanahan .20 .50
155 Nikolai Khabibulin .10 .30
156 Teppo Numminen .02 .10
157 Jeremy Roenick .20 .50
158 Mike Gartner .10 .30
159 Igor Korolev .02 .10
160 Coyotes Logo Foil .10 .30
161 Craig Janney .02 .10
162 Keith Tkachuk .10 .30
163 Oleg Tverdovsky .02 .10
164 Pierre Turgeon .15 .40
165 Igor Kravchuk .07 .20
166 Robert Petrovicky .02 .10
167 Geoff Courtnall .02 .10
168 Brett Hull .20 .50
169 Blues Logo Foil .10 .30
170 Chris Pronger .10 .30
171 Joe Murphy .02 .10
172 Grant Fuhr .20 .50
173 Dimitri Yushkevich .02 .10
174 Wendel Clark .07 .20
175 Steve Sullivan .02 .10
176 Tie Domi .07 .20
177 Todd Warriner .02 .10
178 Maple Leafs Logo Foil .10 .30
179 Mats Sundin .10 .30
180 Sergei Berezin .02 .10
181 Fredrik Modin .02 .10
182 Dmitri Mironov .02 .10
183 Paul Kariya .20 .50
184 Steve Rucchin .02 .10
185 Darren Van Impe .02 .10
186 Joe Sacco .02 .10
187 Mighty Ducks Logo Foil .10 .30
188 Teemu Selanne .20 .50
189 Jari Kurri .15 .40
190 Brian Bellows .07 .20
191 Dave Gagner .07 .20
192 German Titov .02 .10
193 Marty McInnis .02 .10
194 Jarome Iginla .20 .50
195 Tommy Albelin .02 .10
196 Flames Logo Foil .10 .30
197 Joel Bouchard .02 .10
198 Jonas Hoglund .02 .10
199 Theoren Fleury .20 .50
200 Uwe Krupp .02 .10
201 Peter Forsberg .25 .60
202 Adam Foote .10 .30
203 Valeri Kamensky .02 .10
204 Joe Sakic .30 .75
205 Avalanche Logo Foil .10 .30
206 Sandis Ozolinsh .07 .20
207 Alexei Gusarov .02 .10
208 Patrick Roy .75 2.00
209 Andrei Kovalenko .02 .10
210 Jason Arnott .07 .20
211 Mariusz Czerkawski .02 .10
212 Ryan Smyth .07 .20
213 Mats Lindgren .02 .10
214 Oilers Logo Foil .10 .30
215 Doug Weight .07 .20
216 Boris Mironov .02 .10
217 Petr Klima .02 .10
218 Vladimir Tsyplakov .02 .10
219 Mattias Norstrom .02 .10
220 Rob Blake .10 .30
221 Kai Nurminen .02 .10
222 Vitali Yachmenev .02 .10
223 Kings Logo Foil .10 .30
224 Ray Ferraro .02 .10
225 Kevin Stevens .02 .10
226 Dimitri Khristich .02 .10
227 Tony Granato .07 .20
228 Bernie Nicholls .07 .20
229 Doug Bodger .02 .10
230 Owen Nolan .07 .20
231 Viktor Kozlov .07 .20
232 Sharks Logo Foil .10 .30
233 Jeff Friesen .07 .20
234 Marcus Ragnarsson .02 .10
235 Andrei Nazarov .07 .20
236 Pavel Bure .40 1.00
237 Alexander Mogilny .10 .30
238 Martin Gelinas .02 .10
239 Markus Naslund .07 .20
240 David Roberts .02 .10
241 Canucks Logo Foil .10 .30
242 Trevor Linden .10 .30
243 Mike Ridley .02 .10
244 Jyrki Lumme .02 .10
245 Janne Niinimaa .02 .10
246 Patrick Lalime .02 .10
247 Bryan Berard .07 .20
248 Jim Campbell .02 .10
249 Dainius Zubrus .02 .10
250 Sergei Berezin .02 .10
251 Mats Lindgren .02 .10
252 Jarome Iginla .20 .50

1998-99 Panini Photocards

These postcard-like collectibles were issued in packs of five by Panini for sale primarily in Europe. The fronts featured a full-bleed action photo, while the backs carried the player's name and team. These issues were printed on very thin paper stock, which makes them somewhat condition sensitive.

COMPLETE SET (108) 20.00 40.00
1 Daniel Alfredsson .20 .50
2 Jason Allison .25 .60
3 Tony Amonte .30 .75
4 Jason Arnott .25 .60
5 Tom Barrasso .25 .60
6 Stu Barnes .20 .50
7 Ed Belfour .30 .75
8 Bryan Berard .20 .50
9 Rob Blake .25 .60
10 Peter Bondra .30 .75
11 Ray Bourque .60 1.50
12 Rod Brind'Amour .25 .60
13 Martin Brodeur .75 2.00
14 Andrew Brunette .20 .50
15 Pavel Bure .30 .75
16 Chris Chelios .30 .75
17 Vincent Damphousse .25 .60
18 Eric Daze .20 .50
19 Detroit Red Wings .20 .50
20 Mike Dunham .25 .60
21 Sergei Fedorov .50 1.25
22 Stephane Fiset .20 .50
23 Theo Fleury .30 .75
24 Peter Forsberg .75 2.00
25 Ron Francis .25 .60
26 Jeff Friesen .25 .60
27 Grant Fuhr .25 .60
28 Doug Gilmour .30 .75
29 Adam Graves .25 .60
30 Wayne Gretzky 2.00 5.00
31 Michal Grosek .20 .50
32 Dominik Hasek .60 1.50
33 Kevin Hatcher .20 .50
34 Brett Hull .40 1.00
35 Jaromir Jagr .75 2.00
36 Mike Johnson .20 .50
37 Curtis Joseph .40 1.00
38 Joe Juneau .20 .50
39 Paul Kariya 1.00 2.50
40 Nikolai Khabibulin .25 .60
41 Saku Koivu .25 .60
42 Olaf Kolzig .25 .60
43 Oleg Kvasha .20 .50
44 Vincent Lecavalier .30 .75
45 John LeClair .40 1.00
46 Brian Leetch .25 .60
47 Claude Lemieux .20 .50
48 Trevor Linden .20 .50
49 Eric Lindros .30 .75
50 Al MacInnis .25 .60
51 Mark Messier .30 .75
52 Mike Modano .50 1.25
53 Alexander Mogilny .25 .60
54 Brendan Morrison .20 .50
55 Scott Niedermayer .25 .60
56 Joe Nieuwendyk .25 .60
57 Adam Oates .25 .60
58 Chris Osgood .30 .75
59 Zigmund Palffy .30 .75
60 Mark Parrish .20 .50
61 Michael Peca .20 .50
62 Yanic Perreault .20 .50
63 Felix Potvin .30 .75
64 Keith Primeau .25 .60
65 Chris Pronger .25 .60
66 Daren Puppa .20 .50
67 Mark Recchi .25 .60
68 Mike Richter .30 .75
69 Luc Robitaille .30 .75
70 Jeremy Roenick .30 .75
71 Patrick Roy 1.50 4.00
72 Joe Sakic .60 1.50
73 Tommy Salo .25 .60
74 Sergei Samsonov .25 .60
75 Geoff Sanderson .20 .50
76 Teemu Selanne .60 1.50
77 Brendan Shanahan .30 .75
78 Ryan Smyth .20 .50
79 Garth Snow .25 .60
80 Cory Stillman .20 .50
81 Mats Sundin .30 .75
82 Jocelyn Thibault .25 .60
83 Joe Thornton .30 .75
84 Keith Tkachuk .30 .75
85 Pierre Turgeon .25 .60
86 Oleg Tverdovsky .20 .50
87 John Vanbiesbrouck .30 .75
88 Mike Vernon .25 .60
89 Doug Weight .25 .60
90 Alexei Yashin .25 .60
91 Steve Yzerman 1.25 3.00
92 Steve Yzerman w/CUP 1.25 3.00
93 Rob Blake AW .25 .60
94 Martin Brodeur AW .75 2.00
95 Ron Francis AW .25 .60
96 Dominik Hasek AW .60 1.50
97 Jaromir Jagr AW .75 2.00
98 Sergei Samsonov AW .25 .60
99 Peter Bondra AS .30 .75
100 Ray Bourque AS .60 1.50
101 Peter Forsberg AS .75 2.00
102 Wayne Gretzky AS 2.00 5.00
103 Saku Koivu AS .25 .60
104 Eric Lindros AS .30 .75
105 Mark Messier AS .30 .75
106 Patrick Roy 1.50 4.00
107 Teemu Selanne AS .60 1.50
108 Mats Sundin AS .30 .75

1998-99 Panini Stickers

This set of undersized stickers were issued in packs of five, primarily in Europe. The fronts feature action photos, while the backs display card number and player name.

COMPLETE SET (248) 20.00 50.00
1 Teemu Selanne .30 .75
2 Peter Bondra .20 .50
3 Wayne Gretzky 2.00 5.00
4 Jaromir Jagr .50 1.25
5 Chris Pronger .20 .50
6 Ed Belfour .25 .60
7 Bruins logo .10 .30
8 Dimitri Khristich .10 .30
9 P.J. Axelsson .10 .30
10 Byron Dafoe .15 .40
11 Ted Donato .10 .30
12 Ray Bourque .50 1.25
13 Sergei Samsonov .15 .40
14 Jason Allison .10 .30
15 Sabres logo .10 .30
16 Miroslav Satan .15 .40
17 Donald Audette .15 .40
18 Michal Grosek .10 .30
19 Dominik Hasek .60 1.50
20 Richard Smehlik .10 .30
21 Mike Peca .15 .40
22 Alexei Zhitnik .10 .30
23 Hurricanes logo .10 .30
24 Trevor Kidd .15 .40
25 Nelson Emerson .10 .30
26 Curtis Leschyshyn .10 .30
27 Robert Kron .10 .30
28 Gary Roberts .15 .40
29 Sami Kapanen .10 .30
30 Keith Primeau .15 .40
31 Canadiens logo .10 .30
32 Saku Koivu .20 .50
33 Vladimir Malakhov .10 .30
34 Mark Recchi .15 .40
35 Jocelyn Thibault .15 .40
36 Peter Popovic .10 .30
37 Martin Rucinsky .10 .30
38 Jonas Hoglund .10 .30
39 Senators logo .10 .30
40 Damian Rhodes .15 .40
41 Radek Bonk .15 .40
42 Daniel Alfredsson .15 .40
43 Alexei Yashin .20 .50
44 Magnus Arvedson .15 .40
45 Janne Laukkanen .10 .30
46 Igor Kravchuk .15 .40
47 Penguins logo .10 .30
48 Jaromir Jagr .50 1.25
49 Ron Francis .25 .60
50 Darius Kasparaitis .15 .40
51 Tom Barrasso .15 .40
52 Martin Straka .15 .40
53 Alexei Morozov .15 .40
54 Fredrik Olausson .10 .30
55 Panthers logo .10 .30
56 Radek Dvorak .15 .40
57 Robert Svehla .10 .30
58 Ray Whitney .15 .40
59 Dave Gagner .15 .40
60 John Vanbiesbrouck .20 .50
61 Ed Jovanovski .15 .40
62 Viktor Kozlov .15 .40
63 Devils logo .10 .30
64 Petr Sykora .15 .40
65 Scott Niedermayer .20 .50
66 Dave Andreychuk .15 .40
67 Martin Brodeur .60 1.50
68 Bobby Holik .10 .30
69 Doug Gilmour .30 .75
70 Patrik Elias .20 .50
71 Islanders logo .10 .30
72 Tommy Salo .15 .40
73 Zigmund Palffy .15 .40
74 Bryan Smolinski .15 .40
75 Robert Reichel .10 .30
76 Sergei Nemchinov .10 .30
77 Kenny Jonsson .10 .30
78 Bryan Berard .15 .40
79 Rangers logo .10 .30
80 Wayne Gretzky 2.00 5.00
81 Adam Graves .15 .40
82 Mike Richter .20 .50
83 Brian Leetch .20 .50
84 Alexei Kovalev .15 .40
85 Ulf Samuelsson .15 .40
86 Niklas Sundstrom .10 .30
87 Flyers logo .10 .30
88 John LeClair .40 1.00
89 Petr Svoboda .10 .30
90 Rod Brind'Amour .20 .50
91 Sean Burke .15 .40
92 Dainius Zubrus .10 .30
93 Alexandre Daigle .20 .50
94 Eric Lindros .30 .75
95 Lightning logo .10 .30
96 Mark Fitzpatrick .10 .30
97 Alexander Selivanov .10 .30
98 Mikael Renberg .15 .40
99 Rob Zamuner .10 .30
100 Karl Dykhuis .10 .30
101 Paul Ysebaert .10 .30
102 Mikael Andersson .10 .30
103 Capitals logo .10 .30
104 Peter Bondra .20 .50
105 Sergei Gonchar .15 .40
106 Adam Oates .20 .50
107 Calle Johansson .10 .30
108 Olaf Kolzig .20 .50
109 Esa Tikkanen .10 .30
110 Andrei Nikolishin .10 .30
111 Blackhawks logo .10 .30
112 Alexei Zhamnov .15 .40
113 Eric Daze .10 .30
114 Chris Chelios .20 .50
115 Jeff Hackett .10 .30
116 Gary Suter .15 .40
117 Eric Weinrich .10 .30
118 Tony Amonte .15 .40
119 Stars logo .10 .30
120 Jere Lehtinen .15 .40
121 Joe Nieuwendyk .20 .50
122 Ed Belfour .25 .60
123 Mike Modano .30 .75
124 Sergei Zubov .15 .40
125 Darryl Sydor .15 .40
126 Pat Verbeek .15 .40
127 Red Wings logo .10 .30
128 Chris Osgood .20 .50
129 Sergei Fedorov .60 1.50
130 Stanley Cup .10 .30
131 Igor Larionov .15 .40
132 Slava Kozlov .15 .40
133 Brendan Shanahan .30 .75
134 Nicklas Lidstrom .30 .75
135 Steve Yzerman .75 2.00
136 Predators logo .10 .30
137 Jan Vopat .10 .30
138 Sergei Krivokrasov .10 .30
139 Darren Turcotte .15 .40
140 Tom Fitzgerald .10 .30
141 Joel Bouchard .10 .30
142 Scott Walker .10 .30
143 Coyotes logo .10 .30
144 Keith Tkachuk .20 .50
145 Craig Janney .10 .30
146 Oleg Tverdovsky .10 .30
147 Nikolai Khabibulin .20 .50
148 Teppo Numminen .10 .30
149 Cliff Ronning .10 .30
150 Jeremy Roenick .30 .75
151 Blues logo .10 .30
152 Brett Hull .30 .75
153 Chris Pronger .20 .50
154 Pierre Turgeon .25 .60
155 Grant Fuhr .30 .75
156 Geoff Courtnall .10 .30
157 Pavol Demitra .10 .30
158 Steve Duchesne .15 .40
159 Maple Leafs logo .10 .30
160 Fredrik Modin .10 .30
161 Dimitri Yushkevich .10 .30
162 Tie Domi .15 .40
163 Igor Korolev .10 .30
164 Mats Sundin .20 .50
165 Felix Potvin .30 .75
166 Sergei Berezin .10 .30
167 Mighty Ducks logo .10 .30
168 Guy Hebert .15 .40
169 Teemu Selanne .30 .75
170 Paul Kariya .30 .75
171 Steve Rucchin .10 .30
172 Tomas Sandstrom .10 .30
173 Josef Marha .10 .30
174 Ruslan Salei .10 .30
175 Flames logo .10 .30
176 Theo Fleury .30 .75
177 Michael Nylander .15 .40
178 German Titov .10 .30
179 Rick Tabaracci .15 .40
180 Cory Stillman .10 .30
181 Jarome Iginla .30 .75
182 Tommy Albelin .10 .30
183 Avalanche logo .10 .30
184 Patrick Roy 1.25 3.00
185 Peter Forsberg .40 1.00
186 Alexei Gusarov .10 .30
187 Uwe Krupp .10 .30
188 Valeri Kamensky .10 .30
189 Joe Sakic .50 1.25
190 Sandis Ozolinsh .15 .40
191 Oilers logo .10 .30
192 Boris Mironov .10 .30
193 Mats Lindgren .10 .30
194 Andrei Kovalenko .10 .30
195 Curtis Joseph .30 .75
196 Roman Hamrlik .15 .40
197 Doug Weight .15 .40
198 Janne Niinimaa .10 .30
199 Kings logo .10 .30
200 Stephane Fiset .10 .30
201 Jozef Stumpel .10 .30
202 Aki Berg .10 .30
203 Glen Murray .15 .40
204 Vladimir Tsyplakov .10 .30
205 Rob Blake .20 .50
206 Mattias Norstrom .10 .30
207 Sharks logo .10 .30
208 Marcus Ragnarsson .10 .30
209 Jeff Friesen .15 .40
210 Owen Nolan .15 .40
211 Mike Vernon .20 .50
212 John MacLean .15 .40
213 Andrei Zyuzin .10 .30
214 Marco Sturm .10 .30
215 Canucks logo .10 .30
216 Pavel Bure .60 1.50
217 Alexander Mogilny .20 .50
218 Arturs Irbe .20 .50
219 Mark Messier .50 1.25
220 Markus Naslund .15 .40
221 Mattias Ohlund .10 .30
222 Jyrki Lumme .10 .30
223 Dominik Hasek .60 1.50
224 Rob Blake .20 .50
225 Sergei Samsonov .15 .40
226 Jere Lehtinen .15 .40
227 Ron Francis .25 .60
228 Jamie McLennan .10 .30

1999-00 Panini Stickers

COMPLETE SET (360) 20.00 50.00
1 NHL logo .07 .20
2 NHLPA logo .02 .10
3 Jaromir Jagr .30 .75
4 Chris Drury .07 .20
5 Al MacInnis .10 .30
6 Dominik Hasek .40 1.00
7 Jere Lehtinen .07 .20
8 Joe Nieuwendyk .10 .30
9 Atlanta logo .02 .10
10 Kelly Buchberger .07 .20
11 Johan Garpenlov .02 .10
12 Ray Ferraro .02 .10
13 Nelson Emerson .02 .10
14 Kevin Dean .02 .10
15 Patrik Stefan .02 .10
16 Per Svartvadet .02 .10
17 Damian Rhodes .07 .20
18 Andrew Brunette .07 .20
19 Yannick Tremblay .02 .10
20 Boston logo .02 .10
21 Ray Bourque .30 .75
22 Anson Carter .07 .20
23 Byron Dafoe .07 .20
24 Dave Andreychuk .07 .20
25 Sergei Samsonov .07 .20
26 Joe Thornton .25 .60
27 Jason Allison .02 .10
28 P.J. Axelsson .02 .10
29 Kyle McLaren .02 .10
30 Rob DiMaio .02 .10
31 Buffalo logo .02 .10
32 Dominik Hasek .40 1.00
33 Geoff Sanderson .07 .20
34 Richard Smehlik .02 .10
35 Alexei Zhitnik .02 .10
36 Jason Woolley .02 .10
37 Michael Peca .07 .20
38 Miroslav Satan .07 .20
39 Michal Grosek .02 .10
40 Stu Barnes .07 .20
41 Vaclav Varada .02 .10
42 Carolina logo .02 .10
43 Sami Kapanen .02 .10
44 Ron Francis .15 .40
45 Robert Kron .02 .10
46 Andrei Kovalenko .02 .10
47 Martin Gelinas .02 .10
48 Glen Wesley .02 .10
49 Kent Manderville .02 .10
50 Gary Roberts .07 .20
51 Tommy Westlund .02 .10
52 Bates Battaglia .07 .20
53 Florida logo .02 .10
54 Sean Burke .07 .20
55 Robert Svehla .02 .10
56 Pavel Bure .40 1.00
57 Jaroslav Spacek .02 .10
58 Radek Dvorak .07 .20
59 Rob Niedermayer .10 .30
60 Viktor Kozlov .07 .20
61 Mark Parrish .02 .10
62 Scott Mellanby .02 .10
63 Oleg Kvasha .02 .10
64 Montreal logo .02 .10
65 Saku Koivu .10 .30
66 Trevor Linden .10 .30
67 Brian Savage .02 .10
68 Martin Rucinsky .02 .10
69 Scott Lachance .02 .10
70 Scott Thornton .07 .20
71 Mike Ribeiro .07 .20
72 Jeff Hackett .02 .10
73 Dainius Zubrus .02 .10
74 Eric Weinrich .02 .10
75 New Jersey logo .02 .10
76 Scott Stevens .07 .20
77 Sergei Nemchinov .02 .10
78 Petr Sykora .07 .20
79 Martin Brodeur .40 1.00
80 Claude Lemieux .07 .20
81 Bobby Holik .02 .10
82 Brian Rafalski .02 .10
83 Scott Gomez .10 .30
84 Jason Arnott .07 .20
85 Ken Daneyko .02 .10
86 NY Islanders logo .02 .10
87 Jorgen Jonsson .07 .20
88 Olli Jokinen .07 .20
89 Zdeno Chara .20 .50
90 Mats Lindgren .02 .10
91 Felix Potvin .20 .50
92 Kenny Jonsson .02 .10
93 Tim Connolly .07 .20
94 Mariusz Czerkawski .02 .10
95 Gino Odjick .02 .10
96 Brad Isbister .07 .20
97 NY Rangers logo .02 .10
98 Brian Leetch .10 .30
99 Theo Fleury .20 .50
100 Adam Graves .07 .20
101 Mike Richter .10 .30
102 Kim Johnsson .02 .10
103 Kevin Stevens .02 .10
104 Mathieu Schneider .02 .10
105 Stephane Quintal .02 .10
106 John MacLean .07 .20
107 Kevin Hatcher .02 .10
108 Ottawa logo .02 .10
109 Janne Laukkanen .02 .10
110 Andreas Dackell .02 .10
111 Rob Zamuner .02 .10
112 Daniel Alfredsson .07 .20
113 Shawn McEachern .02 .10
114 Marian Hossa .20 .50
115 Magnus Arvedson .07 .20
116 Radek Bonk .07 .20
117 Ron Tugnutt .10 .30
118 Igor Kravchuk .07 .20
119 Philadelphia logo .02 .10
120 Ulf Samuelsson .07 .20
121 Eric Lindros .20 .50
122 Mikael Renberg .07 .20
123 Valeri Zelepukin .02 .10
124 Rod Brind'Amour .10 .30
125 John LeClair .25 .60
126 Mark Recchi .07 .20
127 Eric Desjardins .07 .20
128 John Vanbiesbrouck .10 .30
129 Simon Gagne .07 .20
130 Pittsburgh logo .02 .10
131 Jaromir Jagr .30 .75
132 Jiri Slegr .02 .10
133 Robert Lang .02 .10
134 Alexei Kovalev .07 .20
135 Darius Kasparaitis .07 .20
136 Alexei Morozov .07 .20
137 Tom Barrasso .07 .20
138 Martin Straka .07 .20
139 German Titov .02 .10
140 Matthew Barnaby .02 .10
141 Tampa Bay logo .02 .10
142 Michael Nylander .07 .20
143 Chris Gratton .07 .20
144 Petr Svoboda .02 .10
145 Stephane Richer .02 .10
146 Pavel Kubina .02 .10
147 Fredrik Modin .02 .10
148 Vincent Lecavalier .20 .50
149 Andrei Zyuzin .02 .10
150 Dan Cloutier .07 .20
151 Darcy Tucker .07 .20
152 Toronto logo .02 .10
153 Mats Sundin .10 .30
154 Steve Thomas .02 .10
155 Alexander Karpovtsev .02 .10
156 Jonas Hoglund .02 .10
157 Curtis Joseph .20 .50
158 Yanic Perreault .07 .20
159 Dimitri Khristich .02 .10
160 Bryan Berard .07 .20
161 Sergei Berezin .02 .10
162 Tie Domi .07 .20
163 Washington logo .02 .10
164 Ulf Dahlen .02 .10
165 Dmitri Mironov .02 .10
166 Adam Oates .10 .30
167 Peter Bondra .10 .30
168 Joe Sacco .02 .10
169 Sergei Gonchar .07 .20
170 Calle Johansson .02 .10
171 Chris Simon .02 .10
172 Richard Zednik .07 .20
173 Andrei Nikolishin .02 .10
174 Anaheim logo .02 .10
175 Paul Kariya .20 .50
176 Teemu Selanne .20 .50
177 Matt Cullen .02 .10
178 Ted Donato .02 .10
179 Niclas Havelid .02 .10
180 Marty McInnis .02 .10
181 Guy Hebert .07 .20
182 Steve Rucchin .02 .10
183 Oleg Tverdovsky .02 .10
184 Pavel Trnka .02 .10
185 Calgary logo .02 .10
186 Grant Fuhr .20 .50
187 Tommy Albelin .02 .10
188 Steve Smith .02 .10
189 Valeri Bure .02 .10
190 Jarome Iginla .20 .50
191 Cory Stillman .02 .10
192 Derek Morris .07 .20
193 Phil Housley .02 .10
194 Marc Savard .07 .20
195 Andrei Nazarov .07 .20
196 Chicago logo .02 .10
197 Bryan McCabe .02 .10
198 Eric Daze .02 .10
199 Anders Eriksson .02 .10
200 Alexei Zhamnov .07 .20
201 Doug Gilmour .20 .50
202 Dean McAmmond .02 .10
203 Tony Amonte .07 .20
204 J-P Dumont .02 .10
205 Wendel Clark .07 .20
206 Bryan Muir .02 .10
207 Colorado logo .02 .10
208 Aelxei Gusarov .02 .10
209 Peter Forsberg .25 .60
210 Joe Sakic .30 .75
211 Patrick Roy .75 2.00
212 Milan Hejduk .20 .50
213 Sandis Ozolinsh .07 .20
214 Adam Deadmarsh .07 .20
215 Chris Drury .07 .20
216 Alex Tanguay .10 .30
217 Adam Foote .10 .30
218 Dallas logo .02 .10
219 Pavel Patera .02 .10
220 Guy Carbonneau .07 .20
221 Sergei Zubov .07 .20
222 Joe Nieuwendyk .10 .30
223 Darryl Sydor .07 .20
224 Derian Hatcher .07 .20
225 Brett Hull .20 .50
226 Mike Modano .20 .50
227 Ed Belfour .15 .40
228 Jamie Langenbrunner .07 .20
229 Detroit logo .02 .10
230 Igor Larionov .07 .20
231 Steve Yzerman .50 1.25
232 Sergei Fedorov .40 1.00
233 Nicklas Lidstrom .20 .50
234 Brendan Shanahan .20 .50
235 Larry Murphy .07 .20
236 Slava Kozlov .07 .20
237 Steve Duchesne .07 .20
238 Chris Chelios .10 .30
239 Chris Osgood .10 .30
240 Edmonton logo .02 .10
241 Tommy Salo .07 .20
242 Tom Poti .02 .10
243 Doug Weight .07 .20
244 Ryan Smyth .07 .20
245 Janne Niinimaa .02 .10
246 Roman Hamrlik .07 .20
247 Bill Guerin .10 .30
248 Todd Marchant .07 .20
249 Mike Grier .07 .20
250 Bill Ranford .10 .30
251 Los Angeles logo .02 .10
252 Rob Blake .10 .30
253 Mattias Norstrom .02 .10
254 Frantisek Kaberle .02 .10
255 Bryan Smolinski .07 .20
256 Stephane Fiset .02 .10
257 Zigmund Palffy .07 .20
258 Luc Robitaille .10 .30
259 Jozef Stumpel .02 .10
260 Garry Galley .02 .10
261 Glen Murray .07 .20
262 Nashville logo .02 .10
263 Ville Peltonen .02 .10
264 Patric Kjellberg .02 .10
265 Kimmo Timonen .02 .10
266 Scott Walker .02 .10
267 Dan Keczmer .02 .10
268 David Legwand .07 .20
269 Cliff Ronning .02 .10
270 Sergei Krivokrasov .02 .10
271 Tom Fitzgerald .02 .10
272 Vitali Yachmenev .02 .10
273 Phoenix logo .02 .10
274 Mika Alatalo .02 .10
275 Juha Ylonen .02 .10
276 Keith Tkachuk .10 .30
277 Travis Green .02 .10
278 Stanislav Neckar .02 .10
279 Jyrki Lumme .02 .10
280 Teppo Numminen .02 .10
281 Jeremy Roenick .20 .50
282 Rick Tocchet .07 .20
283 Shane Doan .07 .20
284 St. Louis logo .02 .10
285 Roman Turek .07 .20
286 Chris Pronger .10 .30
287 Al MacInnis .10 .30
288 Scott Young .02 .10
289 Marc Bergevin .02 .10
290 Jochen Hecht .07 .20
291 Craig Conroy .02 .10
292 Pierre Turgeon .15 .40
293 Pavol Demitra .02 .10
294 Michal Handzus .07 .20
295 San Jose logo .10
296 Jeff Friesen .07 .20
297 Niklas Sundstrom .02 .10
298 Mike Ricci .07 .20
299 Gary Suter .07 .20
300 Owen Nolan .07 .20
301 Patrick Marleau .07 .20
302 Marco Sturm .02 .10
303 Vincent Damphousse .10 .30
304 Brad Stuart .02 .10
305 Mike Vernon .10 .30
306 Vancouver logo .02 .10
307 Mark Messier .30 .75
308 Mattias Ohlund .02 .10
309 Alexander Mogilny .10 .30
310 Markus Naslund .07 .20
311 Andrew Cassels .02 .10
312 Adrian Aucoin .02 .10
313 Steve Kariya .02 .10
314 Peter Schaefer .02 .10
315 Ed Jovanovski .07 .20
316 Garth Snow .02 .10
317 Jaromir Jagr .30 .75
318 Teemu Selanne .20 .50
319 Tony Amonte .07 .20
320 Peter Forsberg .25 .60
321 Paul Kariya .20 .50
322 Alexei Yashin .10 .30
323 Eric Lindros .20 .50
324 Theo Fleury .20 .50
325 John LeClair .25 .60
326 Jason Allison .02 .10
327 Joe Sakic .30 .75
328 Pavol Demitra .02 .10
329 Alexander Karpovtsev .02 .10
330 Dimitri Khristich .02 .10
331 Mark Messier .30 .75
332 Brett Hull .20 .50
333 Scott Pellerin .02 .10
334 Brian Rolston .02 .10
335 Miroslav Satan .07 .20
336 Patrick Roy .75 2.00
337 John Vanbiesbrouck .10 .30
338 Felix Potvin .20 .50
339 Mike Dunham .02 .10
340 Dominic Roussel .02 .10
341 Al MacInnis .10 .30
342 Ray Bourque .30 .75
343 Adrian Aucoin .02 .10
344 Sergei Gonchar .07 .20
345 Phil Housley .02 .10
346 Nicklas Lidstrom .20 .50
347 Martin Brodeur .40 1.00
348 Ron Tugnutt .10 .30
349 Dominik Hasek .40 1.00
350 Guy Hebert .07 .20
351 Byron Dafoe .07 .20
352 Curtis Joseph .20 .50
353 Peter Schaefer .02 .10
354 Scott Gomez .10 .30
355 Alex Tanguay .10 .30
356 Steve Kariya .02 .10
357 Frantisek Kaberle .02 .10
358 Brian Rafalski .02 .10
359 Columbus logo .02 .10
360 Minnesota logo .02 .10

2000-01 Panini Stickers

COMPLETE SET (212) 30.00 60.00
1 NHL logo .05 .10
2 NHLPA logo .05 .10
3 Atlanta logo .05 .10
4 Johan Garpenlov .05 .10
5 Patrik Stefan .05 .10
6 Andrew Brunette .05 .10
7 Andreas Karlsson .05 .10
8 Ray Ferraro .05 .10
9 Petr Buzek .05 .10
10 Boston logo .05 .10
11 Sergei Samsonov .05 .10
12 P.J. Axelsson .05 .10
13 Anson Carter .05 .10
14 Eric Nickulas .05 .10
15 Mikko Eloranta .05 .10
16 Joe Thornton .07 .20
17 Buffalo logo .05 .10
18 Dominik Hasek .07 .20
19 Curtis Brown .05 .10
20 Michael Peca .05 .10
21 Vaclav Varada .05 .10
22 Alexei Zhitnik .05 .10
23 Miroslav Satan .05 .10
24 Carolina logo .05 .10
25 Sami Kapanen .05 .10
26 Paul Coffey .05 .15
27 Marek Malik .05 .10
28 Andrei Kovalenko .05 .10
29 Arturs Irbe .05 .10
30 Ron Francis .05 .15
31 Florida logo .05 .10
32 Scott Mellanby .05 .10
33 Viktor Kozlov .05 .10
34 Jaroslav Spacek .05 .10
35 Ray Whitney .05 .10
36 Robert Svehla .05 .10
37 Pavel Bure .05 .15
38 Montreal logo .05 .10
39 Saku Koivu .05 .15
40 Trevor Linden .05 .15
41 Karl Dykhuis .05 .10
42 Sergei Zholtok .05 .10
43 Martin Rucinsky .05 .10
44 Dainius Zubrus .05 .10
45 New Jersey logo .05 .10
46 Alexander Mogilny .05 .10
47 Petr Sykora .05 .10
48 Martin Brodeur .10 .25
49 Bobby Holik .05 .10
50 Scott Gomez .05 .10
51 Patrik Elias .05 .15
52 NY Islanders logo .05 .10
53 Brad Isbister .05 .10

54 Mariusz Czerkawski .05 .10
55 Mats Lindgren .05 .10
56 Tim Connolly .05 .10
57 Kenny Jonsson .05 .10
58 Olli Jokinen .05 .10
59 NY Rangers logo .05 .10
60 Brian Leetch .05 .15
61 Petr Nedved .05 .10
62 Radek Dvorak .05 .10
63 Valeri Kamensky .05 .10
64 Theo Fleury .05 .15
65 Jan Hlavac .05 .10
66 Ottawa logo .05 .10
67 Magnus Arvedson .05 .10
68 Igor Kravchuk .05 .10
69 Vaclav Prospal .05 .10
70 Daniel Alfredsson .05 .15
71 Shawn McEachern .05 .10
72 Radek Bonk .05 .10
73 Philadelphia logo .05 .10
74 John LeClair .05 .15
75 Eric Lindros .07 .20
76 Mark Recchi .05 .15
77 Daymond Langkow .05 .10
78 Ulf Samuelsson .05 .10
79 Valeri Zelepukin .05 .10
80 Pittsburgh logo .05 .10
81 Jaromir Jagr .12 .30
82 Martin Straka .05 .10
83 Alexei Morozov .05 .10
84 Alexei Kovalev .05 .10
85 Robert Lang .05 .10
86 Darius Kasparaitis .05 .10
87 Tampa Bay logo .05 .10
88 Vincent Lecavalier .05 .10
89 Fredrik Modin .05 .10
90 Jaroslav Svejkovsky .05 .10
91 Mike Johnson .05 .10
92 Pavel Kubina .05 .10
93 Petr Svoboda .05 .10
94 Toronto logo .05 .10
95 Mats Sundin .05 .15
96 Darcy Tucker .05 .10
97 Steve Thomas .05 .10
98 Jonas Hoglund .05 .10
99 Igor Korolev .05 .10
100 Yanic Perreault .05 .10
101 Washington logo .05 .10
102 Peter Bondra .05 .10
103 Sergei Gonchar .05 .10
104 Joe Sacco .05 .10
105 Ulf Dahlen .05 .10
106 Adam Oates .05 .15
107 Calle Johansson .05 .10
108 Anaheim logo .05 .10
109 Paul Kariya .05 .15
110 Guy Hebert .05 .10
111 Teemu Selanne .10 .25
112 Ruslan Salei .05 .10
113 Vitali Vishnevsky .05 .10
114 Oleg Tverdovsky .05 .10
115 Calgary logo .05 .10
116 Valeri Bure .05 .10
117 Jarome Iginla .05 .15
118 Marc Savard .05 .10
119 Andrei Nazarov .05 .10
120 Phil Housley .05 .10
121 Derek Morris .05 .10
122 Chicago logo .05 .10
123 Michael Nylander .05 .10
124 Boris Mironov .05 .10
125 Alexei Zhamnov .05 .10
126 Tony Amonte .05 .10
127 Michal Grosek .05 .10
128 Steve Sullivan .05 .10
129 Colorado logo .05 .10
130 Peter Forsberg .05 .15
131 Patrick Roy .12 .30
132 Joe Sakic .07 .20
133 Stephane Yelle .05 .10
134 Sandis Ozolinsh .05 .10
135 Milan Hejduk .05 .10
136 Columbus logo .05 .10
137 Geoff Sanderson .05 .10
138 Ron Tugnutt .05 .10
139 Radim Bicanek .05 .10
140 Mattias Timander .05 .10
141 Krzsystof Oliwa .05 .10
142 Espen Knutsen .05 .10
143 Dallas logo .05 .10
144 Mike Modano .07 .20
145 Joe Nieuwendyk .05 .15
146 Sergei Zubov .05 .10
147 Richard Matvichuk .05 .10
148 Brett Hull .07 .20
149 Jamie Langenbrunner .05 .10
150 Detroit logo .05 .10
151 Sergei Fedorov .07 .20
152 Brendan Shanahan .05 .15
153 Nicklas Lidstrom .05 .15
154 Slava Kozlov .05 .10
155 Igor Larionov .05 .15
156 Steve Yzerman .15 .40
157 Edmonton logo .05 .10
158 Doug Weight .05 .15
159 German Titov .05 .10
160 Janne Niinimaa .05 .10
161 Roman Hamrlik .05 .10
162 Ryan Smyth .05 .10
163 Alexander Selivanov .05 .10
164 Los Angeles logo .05 .10
165 Rob Blake .05 .15
166 Luc Robitaille .05 .15
167 Ziggy Palffy .05 .15
168 Jozef Stumpel .05 .10
169 Glen Murray .05 .10
170 Mattias Norstrom .05 .10
171 Minnesota logo .05 .10
172 Curtis Leschyshyn .05 .10
173 Sergei Krivokrasov .05 .10
174 Antti Laaksonen .05 .10
175 Pavel Patera .05 .10
176 Sean O'Donnell .05 .10
177 Manny Fernandez .05 .10
178 Nashville logo .05 .10
179 Vitali Yachmenev .05 .10
180 Patric Kjellberg .05 .10
181 Ville Peltonen .05 .10
182 Cliff Ronning .05 .10
183 Greg Johnson .05 .10
184 Kimmo Timonen .05 .10
185 Phoenix logo .05 .10
186 Jeremy Roenick .05 .15
187 Jyrki Lumme .05 .10
188 Travis Green .05 .10
189 Teppo Numminen .05 .10
190 Keith Tkachuk .05 .15
191 Radoslav Suchy .05 .10
192 St. Louis logo .05 .10
193 Chris Pronger .05 .10
194 Pierre Turgeon .05 .15
195 Pavol Demitra .05 .15
196 Roman Turek .05 .10
197 Michal Handzus .05 .10
198 Stephane Richer .05 .10
199 San Jose logo .05 .10
200 Vincent Damphousse .05 .10
201 Niklas Sundstrom .05 .10
202 Stephane Matteau .05 .10
203 Marcus Ragnarsson .05 .10
204 Owen Nolan .05 .15
205 Alexander Korolyuk .05 .10
206 Vancouver logo .02 .10
207 Andrew Cassels .05 .10
208 Artem Chubarov .05 .10
208 Mark Messier .07 .20
210 Mattias Ohlund .05 .10
211 Todd Bertuzzi .05 .10
212 Markus Naslund .05 .10

2003-04 Panini Stickers

112 Mark Messier .15 .40

2005-06 Panini Stickers

COMPLETE SET (390) 30.00 60.00
1 Sidney Crosby 2.50 6.00
2 Alexander Ovechkin 1.25 3.00
3 Mike Richards .30 .75
4 Dion Phaneuf .25 .60
5 Corey Perry .60 1.50
6 Henrik Lundqvist .60 1.50
7 Ilya Kovalchuk .15 .40
8 Marian Hossa .12 .30
9 Bobby Holik .10 .25
10 Kari Lehtonen .12 .30
11 Marc Savard .10 .25
12 Jaroslav Modry .10 .25
13 Thrashers Team Logo .08 .25
14 Thrashers Action Shot A .08 .25
15 Thrashers Action Shot B .08 .25
16 Peter Bondra .12 .30
17 Slava Kozlov .10 .25
18 Patrik Stefan .10 .25
19 Joe Thornton .20 .50
20 Brian Leetch .15 .40
21 Sergei Samsonov .12 .30
22 Patrice Bergeron .20 .50
23 Glen Murray .12 .30
24 Bruins Team Logo .08 .25
25 Bruins Action Shot A .08 .25
26 Bruins Action Shot B .08 .25
27 Andrew Raycroft .12 .30
28 Jiri Slegr .10 .25
29 Shawn McEachern .10 .25
30 P.J. Axelsson .10 .25
31 Sabres Action Shot A .08 .25
32 Sabres Action Shot B .08 .25
33 Chris Drury .12 .30
34 Daniel Briere .15 .40
35 Ryan Miller .15 .40
36 Maxim Afinogenov .10 .25
37 J.P. Dumont .10 .25
38 Sabres Team Logo .08 .25
39 Jochen Hecht .10 .25
40 Thomas Vanek .30 .75
41 Andrew Peters .10 .25
42 Teppo Numminen .12 .30
43 Rod Brind'Amour .15 .40
44 Eric Staal .20 .50
45 Erik Cole .12 .30
46 Justin Williams .12 .30
47 Oleg Tverdovsky .10 .25
48 Hurricanes Action Shot A .08 .25
49 Hurricanes Action Shot B .08 .25
50 Hurricanes Team Logo .08 .25
51 Cory Stillman .08 .25
52 Ray Whitney .12 .30
53 Glen Wesley .10 .25
54 Martin Gerber .12 .30
55 Roberto Luongo .25 .60
56 Olli Jokinen .15 .40
57 Gary Roberts .10 .25
58 Joe Nieuwendyk .15 .40
59 Jay Bouwmeester .15 .40
60 Panthers Action Shot A .08 .25
61 Panthers Action Shot B .08 .25
62 Panthers Team Logo .08 .25
63 Nathan Horton .15 .40
64 Stephen Weiss .10 .25
65 Kristian Huselius .10 .25
66 Jozef Stumpel .10 .25
67 Canadiens Action Shot A .08 .25
68 Canadiens Action Shot B .08 .25
69 Jose Theodore .15 .40
70 Saku Koivu .15 .40
71 Alex Kovalev .12 .30
72 Michael Ryder .12 .30
73 Canadiens Team Logo .08 .25
74 Mike Ribeiro .12 .30
75 Sheldon Souray .10 .25
76 Richard Zednik .10 .25
77 Mathieu Dandenault .10 .25
78 Radek Bonk .10 .25
79 Martin Brodeur .30 .75
80 Scott Gomez .12 .30
81 Alexander Mogilny .12 .30
82 Vladimir Malakhov .10 .25
83 Brian Rafalski .12 .30
84 Jamie Langenbrunner .10 .25
85 Devils Team Logo .08 .25
86 Devils Action Shot A .08 .25
87 Devils Action Shot B .08 .25
88 Brian Gionta .12 .30
89 John Madden .10 .25
90 Zach Parise .40 1.00
91 Alexei Yashin .12 .30
92 Rick DiPietro .12 .30
93 Miroslav Satan .12 .30
94 Jason Blake .10 .25
95 Mark Parrish .10 .25
96 Islanders Action Shot A .08 .25
97 Islanders Action Shot B .08 .25
98 Islanders Team Logo .08 .25
99 Trent Hunter .10 .25
100 Mike York .10 .25
101 Alexei Zhitnik .10 .25
102 Garth Snow .12 .30
103 Jaromir Jagr .40 1.00
104 Michael Nylander .10 .25
105 Martin Straka .10 .25
106 Darius Kasparaitis .10 .25
107 Rangers Action Shot A .08 .25
108 Rangers Action Shot B .08 .25
109 Kevin Weekes .12 .30
110 Tom Poti .10 .25
111 Rangers Team Logo .08 .25
112 Martin Rucinsky .10 .25
113 Steve Rucchin .10 .25
114 Marek Malik .10 .25
115 Dany Heatley .15 .40
116 Jason Spezza .15 .40
117 Dominik Hasek .25 .60
118 Daniel Alfredsson .15 .40
119 Senators Action Shot A .08 .25
120 Senators Action Shot B .08 .25
121 Zdeno Chara .15 .40
122 Martin Havlat .15 .40
123 Senators Team Logo .08 .25
124 Mike Fisher .10 .25
125 Wade Redden .10 .25
126 Chris Phillips .10 .25
127 Flyers Action Shot A .08 .25
128 Flyers Action Shot B .08 .25
129 Peter Forsberg .20 .50
130 Keith Primeau .15 .40
131 Simon Gagne .15 .40
132 Robert Esche .12 .30
133 Joni Pitkanen .10 .25
134 Flyers Team Logo .08 .25
135 Derian Hatcher .10 .25
136 Mike Knuble .10 .25
137 Eric Desjardins .12 .30
138 Jeff Carter .25 .60
139 Sidney Crosby 2.50 6.00
140 Mario Lemieux .50 1.25
141 Mark Recchi .20 .50
142 Zigmund Palffy .15 .40
143 Sergei Gonchar .10 .25
144 Penguins Action Shot A .08 .25
145 Penguins Action Shot B .08 .25
146 Penguins Team Logo .08 .25
147 Marc-Andre Fleury .25 .60
148 John LeClair .15 .40
149 Ryan Malone .10 .25
150 Dick Tarnstrom .10 .25
151 Vincent Lecavalier .12 .30
152 Brad Richards .15 .40
153 Martin St. Louis .15 .40
154 Lightning Action Shot A .08 .25
155 Lightning Action Shot B .08 .25
156 John Grahame .10 .25
157 Fredrik Modin .10 .25
158 Lightning Team Logo .08 .25
159 Ruslan Fedotenko .10 .25
160 Dan Boyle .12 .30
161 Pavel Kubina .10 .25
162 Dave Andreychuk .15 .40
163 Mats Sundin .15 .40
164 Ed Belfour .15 .40
165 Eric Lindros .25 .60
166 Darcy Tucker .12 .30
167 Jeff O'Neill .10 .25
168 Bryan McCabe .10 .25
169 Maple Leafs Team Logo .08 .25
170 Maple Leafs Action Shot A .08 .25
171 Maple Leafs Action Shot B .08 .25
172 Tie Domi .12 .30
173 Tomas Kaberle .10 .25
174 Matt Stajan .12 .30
175 Alexander Ovechkin 1.25 3.00
176 Olaf Kolzig .15 .40
177 Brian Sutherby .10 .25
178 Jeff Halpern .10 .25
179 Danius Zubrus .10 .25
180 Capitals Action Shot A .08 .25
181 Capitals Action Shot B .08 .25
182 Capitals Team Logo .08 .25
183 Brendan Witt .10 .25
184 Andrew Cassels .10 .25
185 Jeff Friesen .10 .25
186 Steve Eminger .10 .25
187 Jean Sebastien Giguere .15 .40
188 Ruslan Salei .10 .25
189 Scott Niedermayer .15 .40
190 Rob Niedermayer .12 .30
191 Sandis Ozolinsh .10 .25
192 Teemu Selanne .30 .75
193 Mighty Ducks Team Logo .08 .25
194 Mighty Ducks Action Shot A .08 .25
195 Mighty Ducks Action Shot B .08 .25
196 Joffrey Lupul .12 .30
197 Petr Sykora .12 .30
198 Ryan Getzlaf .40 1.00
199 Jarome Iginla .15 .40
200 Miikka Kiprusoff .12 .30
201 Shean Donovan .10 .25
202 Roman Hamrlik .12 .30
203 Daymond Langkow .10 .25
204 Steven Reinprecht .10 .25
205 Flames Team Logo .08 .25
206 Flames Action Shot A .08 .25
207 Flames Action Shot B .08 .25
208 Chuck Kobasew .10 .25
209 Jordan Leopold .10 .25
210 Tony Amonte .12 .30
211 Tuomo Ruutu .15 .40
212 Nikolai Khabibulin .15 .40
213 Jassen Cullimore .10 .25
214 Adrian Aucoin .10 .25
215 Tyler Arnason .10 .25
216 Blackhawks Team Logo .08 .25
217 Matthew Barnaby .10 .25
218 Blackhawks Action Shot A .08 .25
219 Blackhawks Action Shot B .08 .25
220 Mark Bell .10 .25
221 Kyle Calder .10 .25
222 Martin Lapointe .10 .25
223 Joe Sakic .25 .60
224 Milan Hejduk .12 .30
225 Rob Blake .15 .40
226 Alex Tanguay .15 .40
227 David Aebischer .12 .30
228 John-Michael Liles .10 .25
229 Avalanche Team Logo .08 .25
230 Avalanche Action Shot A .08 .25
231 Avalanche Action Shot B .08 .25
232 Pierre Turgeon .15 .40
233 Andrew Brunette .10 .25
234 Steve Konowalchuk .10 .25
235 Rick Nash .15 .40
236 Adam Foote .10 .25
237 Marc Denis .12 .30
238 Nikolai Zherdev .10 .25
239 Dan Fritsche .10 .25
240 Manny Malhotra .12 .30
241 Blue Jackets Team Logo .08 .25
242 Blue Jackets Action Shot A .08 .25
243 Blue Jackets Action Shot B .08 .25
244 Bryan Berard .10 .25
245 David Vyborny .10 .25
246 Sergei Federov .25 .60
247 Mike Modano .25 .60
248 Bill Guerin .15 .40
249 Sergei Zubov .12 .30
250 Jere Lehtinen .12 .30
251 Jason Arnott .12 .30
252 Stars Team Logo .08 .25
253 Brenden Morrow .12 .30
254 Stars Action Shot A .08 .25
255 Stars Action Shot B .08 .25
256 Stu Barnes .10 .25
257 Antti Miettinen .10 .25
258 Marty Turco .15 .40
259 Steve Yzerman .40 1.00
260 Brendan Shanahan .20 .50
261 Nicklas Lidstrom .15 .40
262 Kris Draper .20 .50
263 Robert Lang .10 .25
264 Pavel Datsyuk .20 .50
265 Red Wings Team Logo .08 .25
266 Red Wings Action Shot A .08 .25
267 Red Wings Action Shot B .08 .25
268 Chris Osgood .15 .40
269 Chris Chelios .15 .40
270 Henrik Zetterberg .20 .50
271 Ryan Smyth .12 .30
272 Chris Pronger .12 .30
273 Michael Peca .12 .30
274 Ty Conklin .12 .30
275 Georges Laraque .12 .30
276 Oilers Action Shot A .08 .25
277 Oilers Action Shot B .08 .25
278 Oilers Team Logo .08 .25
279 Ales Hemsky .12 .30
280 Jason Smith .08 .25
281 Steve Staios .10 .25
282 Radek Dvorak .10 .25
283 Luc Robitaille .15 .40
284 Jeremy Roenick .12 .30
285 Alexander Frolov .10 .25
286 Pavol Demitra .20 .50
287 Mattias Norstrom .10 .25
288 Kings Team Logo .08 .25
289 Kings Action Shot A .08 .25
290 Kings Action Shot B .08 .25
291 Lubomir Visnovsky .10 .25
292 Eric Belanger .10 .25
293 Mathieu Garon .12 .30
294 Mike Cammalleri .15 .40
295 Marian Gaborik .25 .60
296 Dwayne Roloson .12 .30
297 Marc Chouinard .10 .25
298 Brian Rolston .12 .30
299 Pierre-Marc Bouchard .15 .40
300 Willie Mitchell .10 .25
301 Wild Team Logo .08 .25
302 Wild Action Shot A .08 .25
303 Wild Action Shot B .08 .25
304 Manny Fernandez .12 .30
305 Alexandre Daigle .10 .25
306 Wes Walz .10 .25
307 Paul Kariya .20 .50
308 Steve Sullivan .10 .25
309 Tomas Vokoun .12 .30
310 Kimmo Timonen .10 .25
311 Marek Zidlicky .10 .25
312 Dan Hamuis .12 .30
313 David Legwand .12 .30
314 Predators Team Logo .08 .25
315 Scott Walker .10 .25
316 Predators Action Shot A .08 .25
317 Predators Action Shot B .08 .25
318 Greg Johnson .10 .25
319 Shane Doan .12 .30
320 Geoff Sanderson .10 .25
321 Mike Comrie .12 .30
322 Curtis Joseph .15 .40
323 Mike Ricci .12 .30
324 Paul Mara .10 .25
325 Coyotes Team Logo .08 .25
326 Coyotes Action Shot A .08 .25
327 Coyotes Action Shot B .08 .25
328 Oleg Saprykin .10 .25
329 Petr Nedved .10 .25
330 Derek Morris .10 .25
331 Blues Action Shot A .08 .25
332 Blues Action Shot B .08 .25
333 Doug Weight .15 .40
334 Keith Tkachuk .15 .40
335 Barret Jackman .10 .25
336 Eric Brewer .10 .25
337 Patrick Lalime .12 .30
338 Blues Team Logo .08 .25
339 Dallas Drake .10 .25
340 Scott Young .10 .25
341 Petr Cajanek .10 .25
342 Bryce Salvador .10 .25
343 Evgeni Nabokov .12 .30
344 Patrick Marleau .15 .40
345 Marco Sturm .10 .25
346 Brad Stuart .10 .25
347 Jonathan Cheechoo .15 .40
348 Scott Hannan .10 .25
349 Sharks Team Logo .08 .25
350 Sharks Action Shot A .08 .25
351 Sharks Action Shot B .08 .25
352 Alyn McCauley .10 .25
353 Niko Dimotrakos .10 .25
354 Wayne Primeau .10 .25
355 Markus Naslund .15 .40
356 Brendan Morrison .10 .25
357 Ed Jovanovski .12 .30
358 Todd Bertuzzi .15 .40
359 Dan Cloutier .12 .30
360 Canucks Action Shot A .08 .25
361 Canucks Action Shot B .08 .25
362 Canucks Team Logo .08 .25
363 Trevor Linden .15 .40
364 Daniel Sedin .15 .40
365 Henrik Sedin .15 .40
366 Mattias Ohlund .10 .25
367 Action Shot 1A .08 .25
368 Action Shot 1B .08 .25
369 Action Shot 2A .08 .25
370 Action Shot 2B .08 .25
371 Action Shot 3A .08 .25
372 Action Shot 3B .08 .25
373 Action Shot 4A .08 .25
374 Action Shot 4B .08 .25
375 Action Shot 5A .08 .25
376 Action Shot 5B .08 .25
377 Action Shot 6A .08 .25
378 Action Shot 6B .08 .25
379 Action Shot 7A .08 .25
380 Action Shot 7B .08 .25
381 Action Shot 8A .08 .25
382 Action Shot 8B .08 .25
383 Action Shot 9A .08 .25
384 Action Shot 9B .08 .25
385 Action Shot 10A .08 .25
386 Action Shot 10B .08 .25
387 Action Shot 11A .08 .25
388 Action Shot 11B .08 .25
389 Action Shot 12A .08 .25
390 Action Shot 12B .08 .25

2006-07 Panini Stickers

COMPLETE SET (360) 25.00 60.00
1 Atlanta Thrashers Puzzle Piece .08 .25
2 Atlanta Thrashers Puzzle Piece .08 .25
3 Atlanta Thrashers Team Logo .08 .25
4 Bobby Holik .10 .25
5 Marian Hossa .12 .30
6 Ilya Kovalchuk .15 .40
7 Vyacheslav Kozlov .10 .25
8 Scott Mellanby .10 .25
9 Kari Lehtonen .12 .30
10 Niclas Havelid .10 .25
11 Steve Rucchin .10 .25
12 Andy Sutton .10 .25
13 Boston Bruins Puzzle Piece .08 .25
14 Boston Bruins Puzzle Piece .08 .25
15 Boston Bruins Team Logo .08 .25
16 P.J. Axelsson .10 .25
17 Patrice Bergeron .20 .50
18 Brad Boyes .10 .25
19 Glen Murray .12 .30
20 Marc Savard .10 .25
21 Marco Sturm .10 .25
22 Zdeno Chara .15 .40
23 Brad Stuart .10 .25
24 Paul Mara .10 .25
25 Buffalo Sabres Puzzle Piece .08 .25
26 Buffalo Sabres Puzzle Piece .08 .25
27 Buffalo Sabres Team Logo .08 .25
28 Ryan Miller .15 .40
29 Chris Drury .12 .30
30 Maxim Afinogenov .10 .25
31 Ales Kotalik .10 .25
32 Daniel Briere .15 .40
33 Thomas Vanek .20 .50
34 Derek Roy .10 .25
35 Brian Campbell .12 .30
36 Tim Connolly .10 .25
37 Carolina Hurricanes Puzzle Piece .08 .25
38 Carolina Hurricanes Puzzle Piece .08 .25
39 Carolina Hurricanes Team Logo .08 .25
40 Cam Ward .15 .40
41 Rod Brind'Amour .15 .40
42 Erik Cole .12 .30
43 Eric Staal .20 .50
44 Cory Stillman .10 .25
45 Ray Whitney .12 .30
46 Justin Williams .12 .30
47 Frantisek Kaberle .10 .25
48 Bret Hedican .10 .25
49 Florida Panthers Puzzle Piece .08 .25
50 Florida Panthers Puzzle Piece .08 .25
51 Florida Panthers Team Logo .08 .25
52 Todd Bertuzzi .15 .40
53 Nathan Horton .15 .40
54 Olli Jokinen .15 .40
55 Joe Nieuwendyk .15 .40
56 Rostislav Olesz .10 .25
57 Gary Roberts .10 .25
58 Josef Stumpel .10 .25
59 Jay Bouwmeester .15 .40
60 Ed Belfour .15 .40
61 Montreal Canadiens Puzzle Piece .08 .25
62 Montreal Canadiens Puzzle Piece .08 .25
63 Montreal Canadiens Team Logo .08 .25
64 Saku Koivu .15 .40
65 Alexei Kovalev .12 .30
66 Chris Higgins .10 .25
67 Mike Ribeiro .12 .30
68 Michael Ryder .10 .25
69 Sergei Samsonov .12 .30
70 Andrei Markov .15 .40
71 Sheldon Souray .10 .25
72 Cristobal Huet .12 .30
73 New Jersey Devils Puzzle Piece .08 .25
74 New Jersey Devils Puzzle Piece .08 .25
75 New Jersey Devils Team Logo .08 .25
76 Martin Brodeur .30 .75
77 Brian Gionta .12 .30
78 Patrik Elias .15 .40
79 Scott Gomez .12 .30
80 Brian Rafalski .12 .30
81 Colin White .10 .25
82 Jamie Langenbrunner .10 .25
83 John Madden .10 .25
84 Zach Parise .20 .50
85 New York Islanders Puzzle Piece .08 .25
86 New York Islanders Puzzle Piece .08 .25
87 New York Islanders Team Logo .08 .25
88 Rick DiPietro .12 .30
89 Miroslav Satan .12 .30
90 Alexei Yashin .12 .30
91 Mike York .10 .25
92 Jason Blake .10 .25
93 Brendan Witt .10 .25
94 Alexei Zhitnik .10 .25
95 Mike Sillinger .10 .25
96 Trent Hunter .10 .25
97 New York Rangers Puzzle Piece .08 .25
98 New York Rangers Puzzle Piece .08 .25
99 New York Rangers Team Logo .08 .25
100 Jaromir Jagr .40 1.00
101 Brendan Shanahan .20 .50
102 Henrik Lundqvist .30 .75
103 Marek Malik .10 .25
104 Michal Rozsival .10 .25
105 Petr Prucha .12 .30
106 Martin Straka .10 .25
107 Michael Nylander .10 .25
108 Darius Kasparaitis .10 .25
109 Ottawa Senators Puzzle Piece .08 .25
110 Ottawa Senators Puzzle Piece .08 .25
111 Ottawa Senators Team Logo .08 .25
112 Daniel Alfredsson .15 .40
113 Jason Spezza .15 .40
114 Dany Heatley .15 .40
115 Mike Fisher .10 .25
116 Patrick Eaves .10 .25
117 Chris Phillips .10 .25
118 Wade Redden .10 .25
119 Martin Gerber .12 .30
120 Ray Emery .12 .30
121 Philadelphia Flyers Puzzle Piece .08 .25
122 Philadelphia Flyers Puzzle Piece .08 .25
123 Philadelphia Flyers Team Logo .08 .25
124 Peter Forsberg .20 .50
125 Kyle Calder .10 .25
126 Simon Gagne .15 .40
127 Petr Nedved
128 Derian Hatcher .10 .25
129 Joni Pitkanen .10 .25
130 Robert Esche .12 .30
131 Mike Knuble .10 .25
132 Jeff Carter .15 .40
133 Pittsburgh Penguins Puzzle Piece .08 .25
134 Pittsburgh Penguins Puzzle Piece .08 .25
135 Pittsburgh Penguins Team Logo .08 .25
136 Sidney Crosby 1.00 2.50
137 Mark Recchi .20 .50
138 Marc-Andre Fleury .25 .60
139 Sergei Gonchar .10 .25
140 Ronald Petrovicky
141 John LeClair .15 .40
142 Ryan Malone .10 .25
143 Ryan Whitney .12 .30
144 Nils Ekman .10 .25
145 Tampa Bay Lightning Puzzle Piece .08 .25
146 Tampa Bay Lightning Puzzle Piece .08 .25
147 Tampa Bay Lightning Team Logo .08 .25
148 Marc Denis .12 .30
149 Vincent Lecavalier .12 .30
150 Brad Richards .15 .40
151 Vaclav Prospal .10 .25
152 Dan Boyle .12 .30
153 Martin St. Louis .15 .40
154 Filip Kuba .10 .25
155 Ruslan Fedotenko .10 .25
156 Cory Sarich .10 .25
157 Toronto Maple Leafs Puzzle Piece .08 .25
158 Toronto Maple Leafs Puzzle Piece .08 .25
159 Toronto Maple Leafs Team Logo .08 .25
160 Andrew Raycroft .12 .30
161 Mats Sundin .15 .40
162 Pavel Kubina
163 Michael Peca .12 .30
164 Darcy Tucker .12 .30
165 Tomas Kaberle .10 .25
166 Bryan McCabe .10 .25
167 Jeff O'Neill .10 .25
168 Alexander Steen .15 .40
169 Washington Capitals Puzzle Piece .08 .25
170 Washington Capitals Puzzle Piece .08 .25
171 Washington Capitals Team Logo .08 .25
172 Alexander Ovechkin .60 1.50
173 Richard Zednik .10 .25
174 Dainius Zubrus .10 .25
175 Olaf Kolzig .15 .40
176 Chris Clark .10 .25
177 Matt Pettinger .12 .30
178 Ben Clymer .10 .25
179 Brian Sutherby .10 .25
180 Brian Pothier .10 .25
181 Anaheim Ducks Puzzle Piece .08 .25
182 Anaheim Ducks Puzzle Piece .08 .25
183 Anaheim Ducks Team Logo .08 .25
184 Chris Pronger .12 .30
185 Scott Niedermayer .15 .40
186 Jean-Sebastien Giguere .15 .40
187 Teemu Selanne .30 .75
188 Andy McDonald .12 .30
189 Rob Niedermayer .12 .30
190 Ilya Bryzgalov .15 .40
191 Ryan Getzlaf .25 .60
192 Chris Kunitz .15 .40
193 Calgary Flames Puzzle Piece .08 .25
194 Calgary Flames Puzzle Piece .08 .25
195 Calgary Flames Team Logo .08 .25
196 Jarome Iginla .15 .40
197 Miikka Kiprusoff .12 .30
198 Alex Tanguay .10 .25
199 Dion Phaneuf .15 .40
200 Tony Amonte .12 .30
201 Robyn Regehr .10 .25
202 Rhett Warrener
203 Daymond Langkow .10 .25
204 Kristian Huselius .10 .25
205 Chicago Blackhawks Puzzle Piece .08 .25
206 Chicago Blackhawks Puzzle Piece .08 .25
207 Chicago Blackhawks Team Logo .08 .25
208 Nikolai Khabibulin .15 .40
209 Martin Havlat .10 .25
210 Tuomo Ruutu .15 .40
211 Michal Handzus .12 .30
212 Radim Vrbata .12 .30
213 Bryan Smolinski .10 .25
214 Patrick Sharp .15 .40
215 Adrian Aucoin .10 .25
216 Martin Lapointe .10 .25
217 Colorado Avalanche Puzzle Piece .08 .25
218 Colorado Avalanche Puzzle Piece .08 .25
219 Colorado Avalanche Team Logo .08 .25
220 Jose Theodore .15 .40
221 Joe Sakic .25 .60
222 Milan Hejduk .12 .30
223 Marek Svatos .10 .25
224 Pierre Turgeon .15 .40
225 Andrew Brunette .10 .25
226 Steve Konowalchuk
227 John-Michael Liles .10 .25
228 Ian Laperriere .10 .25
229 Columbus Blue Jackets Puzzle Piece.08 .25
230 Columbus Blue Jackets Puzzle Piece.08 .25
231 Columbus Blue Jackets Team Logo.08 .25
232 Rick Nash .15 .40
233 Sergei Fedorov .25 .60
234 Fredrik Modin .10 .25
235 David Vyborny .10 .25
236 Adam Foote .10 .25
237 Rostislav Klesla .10 .25
238 Pascal Leclaire .12 .30
239 Nikolai Zherdev .10 .25
240 Jason Chimera .10 .25
241 Dallas Stars Puzzle Piece .08 .25
242 Dallas Stars Puzzle Piece .08 .25
243 Dallas Stars Team Logo .08 .25
244 Marty Turco .15 .40
245 Mike Modano .25 .60
246 Eric Lindros .25 .60
247 Sergei Zubov .12 .30
248 Jere Lehtinen .10 .25
249 Brenden Morrow .12 .30
250 Jaroslav Modry .10 .25
251 Stu Barnes .10 .25
252 Phillipe Boucher .10 .25
253 Detroit Red Wings Puzzle Piece .08 .25
254 Detroit Red Wings Puzzle Piece .08 .25
255 Detroit Red Wings Team Logo .08 .25
256 Dominik Hasek .20 .50
257 Pavel Datsyuk .20 .50
258 Chris Chelios .15 .40
259 Nicklas Lidstrom .15 .40
260 Henrik Zetterberg .20 .50
261 Robert Lang .10 .25
262 Mathieu Schneider .10 .25
263 Kris Draper .10 .25
264 Tomas Holmstrom .12 .30
265 Edmonton Oilers Puzzle Piece .08 .25
266 Edmonton Oilers Puzzle Piece .08 .25
267 Edmonton Oilers Team Logo .08 .25
268 Dwayne Roloson .12 .30
269 Ryan Smyth .12 .30
270 Jason Smith .10 .25
271 Joffrey Lupul .12 .30
272 Ales Hemsky .12 .30
273 Fernando Pisani .10 .25
274 Raffi Torres .10 .25
275 Shawn Horcoff .10 .25
276 Jarret Stoll .12 .30
277 Los Angeles Kings Puzzle Piece .08 .25
278 Los Angeles Kings Puzzle Piece .08 .25
279 Los Angeles Kings Team Logo .08 .25
280 Alexander Frolov .10 .25
281 Rob Blake .15 .40
282 Dan Cloutier .12 .30
283 Mattias Norstrom .10 .25
284 Lubomir Visnovsky .10 .25
285 Craig Conroy .10 .25
286 Sean Avery .10 .25
287 Mike Cammalleri .10 .25
288 Dustin Brown .15 .40
289 Minnesota Wild Puzzle Piece .08 .25
290 Minnesota Wild Puzzle Piece .08 .25
291 Minnesota Wild Team Logo .08 .25
292 Manny Fernandez .12 .30
293 Marian Gaborik .20 .50
294 Mark Parrish .10 .25
295 Pavol Demitra .20 .50
296 Brian Rolston .12 .30
297 Wes Walz .10 .25
298 Pierre-Marc Bouchard .15 .40
299 Todd White .10 .25
300 Martin Skoula
301 Nashville Predators Puzzle Piece .08 .25
302 Nashville Predators Puzzle Piece .08 .25
303 Nashville Predators Team Logo .08 .25
304 Paul Kariya .20 .50
305 Jason Arnott .12 .30
306 Steve Sullivan .10 .25
307 Tomas Vokoun .12 .30
308 Marek Zidlicky .10 .25
309 David Legwand .12 .30
310 Martin Erat .10 .25
311 Kimmo Timonen .10 .25
312 Scott Hartnell .15 .40
313 Phoenix Coyotes Puzzle Piece .08 .25
314 Phoenix Coyotes Puzzle Piece .08 .25
315 Phoenix Coyotes Team Logo .08 .25
316 Ed Jovanovski .12 .30
317 Jeremy Roenick .15 .40
318 Curtis Joseph .15 .40
319 Shane Doan .12 .30
320 Mike Comrie .12 .30
321 Ladislav Nagy .10 .25
322 Nick Boynton .10 .25
323 Derek Morris .10 .25
324 Steve Reinprecht .10 .25
325 San Jose Sharks Puzzle Piece .08 .25
326 San Jose Sharks Puzzle Piece .08 .25
327 San Jose Sharks Team Logo .08 .25
328 Vesa Toskala .12 .30
329 Evgeni Nabokov .12 .30
330 Joe Thornton .20 .50
331 Jonathan Cheechoo .15 .40
332 Mark Bell .10 .25
333 Patrick Marleau .15 .40
334 Steve Bernier .10 .25
335 Scott Hannan .10 .25
336 Milan Michalek .10 .25
337 St. Louis Blues Puzzle Piece .08 .25
338 St. Louis Blues Puzzle Piece .08 .25
339 St. Louis Blues Team Logo .08 .25
340 Doug Weight .15 .40
341 Bill Guerin .15 .40
342 Martin Rucinsky .10 .25
343 Jay McKee .10 .25
344 Barret Jackman .10 .25
345 Eric Brewer .10 .25
346 Keith Tkachuk .15 .40
347 Manny Legace .12 .30
348 Petr Cajanek .10 .25
349 Vancouver Canucks Puzzle Piece .08 .25
350 Vancouver Canucks Puzzle Piece .08 .25
351 Vancouver Canucks Team Logo .08 .25
352 Roberto Luongo .25 .60
353 Jan Bulis .10 .25
354 Markus Naslund .12 .30
355 Brendan Morrison .10 .25
356 Daniel Sedin .15 .40
357 Henrik Sedin .15 .40
358 Mattias Ohlund .10 .25
359 Sami Salo .10 .25
360 Matt Cooke .10 .25

2008-09 Panini Stickers

COMPLETE SET (270) 40.00 80.00
1 Atlanta Thrashers Logo .08 .25
2 Kari Lehtonen .12 .30
3 Vyacheslav Kozlov .08 .25
4 Colby Armstrong .10 .25
5 Garnet Exelby .10 .25
6 Niclas Havelid .10 .25
7 Ilya Kovalchuk .15 .40
8 Todd White .10 .25
9 Tobias Enstrom .10 .25
10 Boston Bruins Logo .08 .25
11 Tim Thomas .15 .40
12 Zdeno Chara .15 .40
13 Patrice Bergeron .20 .50
14 Phil Kessel .20 .50
15 Dennis Wideman .10 .25
16 Marc Savard .10 .25
17 Marco Sturm .10 .25
18 Milan Lucic .25 .60
19 Buffalo Sabres Logo .08 .25
20 Ryan Miller .15 .40
21 Jason Pominville .15 .40
22 Derek Roy .10 .25
23 Tim Connolly .10 .25
24 Jaroslav Spacek .10 .25
25 Thomas Vanek .15 .40
26 Henrik Tallinder .10 .25
27 Drew Stafford .12 .30
28 Carolina Hurricanes Logo .08 .25
29 Cam Ward .15 .40
30 Frantisek Kaberle .10 .25
31 Joni Pitkanen .10 .25
32 Rod Brind'Amour .15 .40
33 Justin Williams .12 .30
34 Eric Staal .20 .50
35 Ray Whitney .12 .30

Card	Low	High
Patrick Eaves	.10	.25
Florida Panthers Logo	.08	.25
Tomas Vokoun	.12	.30
Stephen Weiss	.10	.25
Rostislav Olesz	.10	.25
David Booth	.10	.25
Jay Bouwmeester	.15	.40
Nathan Horton	.12	.30
Bryan Allen	.10	.25
Shawn Matthias	.15	.40
Montreal Canadiens Logo	.08	.25
Carey Price	.60	1.50
Saku Koivu	.15	.40
Andrei Markov	.15	.40
Tomas Plekanec	.15	.40
Christopher Higgins	.10	.25
Alex Kovalev	.12	.30
Mike Komisarek	.10	.25
Andrei Kostitsyn	.12	.30
New Jersey Devils Logo	.08	.25
Martin Brodeur	.30	.75
Paul Martin	.10	.25
John Madden	.10	.25
Patrik Elias	.15	.40
Brian Gionta	.12	.30
Zach Parise	.15	.40
John Oduya	.12	.30
Travis Zajac	.12	.30
New York Islanders Logo	.08	.25
Rick DiPietro	.12	.30
Bill Guerin	.15	.40
Chris Campoli	.10	.25
Brendan Witt	.10	.25
Mike Sillinger	.10	.25
Mike Comrie	.12	.30
Trent Hunter	.10	.25
Kyle Okposo	.15	.40
New York Rangers Logo	.08	.25
Henrik Lundqvist	.20	.50
Chris Drury	.12	.30
Markus Naslund	.12	.30
Marc Staal	.15	.40
Michal Rozsival	.10	.25
Scott Gomez	.12	.30
Colton Orr	.10	.25
Brandon Dubinsky	.12	.30
Ottawa Senators Logo	.08	.25
Martin Gerber	.12	.30
Dany Heatley	.15	.40
Jason Spezza	.15	.40
Mike Fisher	.10	.25
Chris Phillips	.10	.25
Daniel Alfredsson	.15	.40
Filip Kuba	.10	.25
Nick Foligno	.15	.40
Philadelphia Flyers Logo	.08	.25
Martin Biron	.12	.30
Mike Richards	.15	.40
Simon Gagne	.15	.40
Jeff Carter	.15	.40
Kimmo Timonen	.10	.25
Danny Briere	.15	.40
Braydon Coburn	.10	.25
Claude Giroux	.30	.75
0 Pittsburgh Penguins Logo	.08	.25
1 Marc-Andre Fleury	.25	.60
2 Evgeni Malkin	.50	1.25
3 Petr Sykora	.12	.30
4 Sergei Gonchar	.10	.25
5 Jordan Staal	.15	.40
6 Sidney Crosby	.60	1.50
7 Ryan Whitney	.15	.40
8 Kris Letang	.15	.40
9 Tampa Bay Lightning Logo	.08	.25
0 Mike Smith	.15	.40
1 Vaclav Prospal	.10	.25
2 Martin St-Louis	.15	.40
3 Ryan Malone	.10	.25
4 Paul Ranger	.10	.25
5 Vincent Lecavalier	.12	.30
6 Andrej Meszaros	.08	.25
7 Steven Stamkos	1.00	2.50
8 Toronto Maple Leafs Logo	.08	.25
9 Vesa Toskala	.12	.30
0 Jason Blake	.10	.25
1 Alex Steen	.15	.40
2 Matt Stajan	.12	.30
3 Tomas Kaberle	.10	.25
4 Nik Antropov	.12	.30
5 Pavel Kubina	.10	.25
6 Jiri Tlusty	.12	.30
7 Washington Capitals Logo	.08	.25
8 Jose Theodore	.15	.40
9 Mike Green	.15	.40
0 Alexander Semin	.15	.40
1 Sergei Fedorov	.25	.60
2 Tom Poti	.10	.25
3 Alex Ovechkin	.60	1.50
4 Brooks Laich	.10	.25
5 Nicklas Backstrom	.25	.60
6 Anaheim Ducks Logo	.08	.25
7 Jean-Sebastien Giguere	.15	.40
8 Chris Pronger	.12	.30
9 Corey Perry	.15	.40
0 Chris Kunitz	.15	.40
1 Scott Niedermayer	.15	.40
2 Ryan Getzlaf	.25	.60
3 George Parros	.10	.25
4 Bobby Ryan	.15	.40
5 Calgary Flames Logo	.08	.25
6 Miikka Kiprusoff	.12	.30
7 Dion Phaneuf	.15	.40
8 Robyn Regehr	.10	.25
9 Daymond Langkow	.10	.25
0 Mike Cammalleri	.12	.30
1 Jarome Iginla	.15	.40
2 Matthew Lombardi	.10	.25
3 Dustin Boyd	.10	.25
4 Chicago Blackhawks Logo	.08	.25
5 Cristobal Huet	.12	.30
6 Brian Campbell	.12	.30
7 Martin Havlat	.15	.40
8 Duncan Keith	.15	.40
9 Patrick Sharp	.15	.40
0 Jonathan Toews	.40	1.00
1 Dustin Byfuglien	.15	.40
2 Patrick Kane	.30	.75
3 Colorado Avalanche Logo	.08	.25
4 Peter Budaj	.12	.30
5 Paul Stastny	.15	.40
6 Ryan Smyth	.12	.30
7 Milan Hejduk	.12	.30
8 John-Michael Liles	.10	.25
9 Joe Sakic	.25	.60
70 Adam Foote	.10	.25
71 T.J. Hensick	.12	.30
72 Columbus Blue Jackets Logo	.08	.25
73 Pascal Leclaire	.12	.30
174 Fredrik Modin	.10	.25
175 Rostislav Klesla	.10	.25
176 Kris Russell	.10	.25
177 Michael Peca	.12	.30
178 Rick Nash	.15	.40
179 Manny Malhotra	.10	.25
180 Derick Brassard	.12	.30
181 Dallas Stars Logo	.08	.25
182 Marty Turco	.15	.40
183 Brenden Morrow	.12	.30
184 Mike Modano	.25	.60
185 Sean Avery	.10	.25
186 Philippe Boucher	.10	.25
187 Mike Ribeiro	.12	.30
188 Sergei Zubov	.12	.30
189 Matt Niskanen	.12	.30
190 Detroit Red Wings Logo	.08	.25
191 Chris Osgood	.15	.40
192 Nicklas Lidstrom	.15	.40
193 Marian Hossa	.12	.30
194 Pavel Datsyuk	.20	.50
195 Brian Rafalski	.12	.30
196 Henrik Zetterberg	.20	.50
197 Johan Franzen	.15	.40
198 Valtteri Filppula	.15	.40
199 Edmonton Oilers Logo	.08	.25
200 Mathieu Garon	.12	.30
201 Sheldon Souray	.10	.25
202 Shawn Horcoff	.10	.25
203 Andrew Cogliano	.12	.30
204 Dustin Penner	.12	.30
205 Ales Hemsky	.12	.30
206 Lubomir Visnovsky	.10	.25
207 Sam Gagner	.12	.30
208 Los Angeles Kings Logo	.08	.25
209 Jason Labarbera	.12	.30
210 Dustin Brown	.15	.40
211 Tom Preissing	.10	.25
212 Jack Johnson	.10	.25
213 Alexander Frolov	.10	.25
214 Anze Kopitar	.25	.60
215 Patrick O'Sullivan	.12	.30
216 Jonathan Bernier	.20	.50
217 Minnesota Wild Logo	.08	.25
218 Niklas Backstrom	.15	.40
219 Brent Burns	.20	.50
220 Pierre-Marc Bouchard	.15	.40
221 Mikko Koivu	.12	.30
222 Nick Schultz	.10	.25
223 Marian Gaborik	.20	.50
224 Derek Boogaard	.10	.25
225 James Sheppard	.10	.25
226 Nashville Predators Logo	.08	.25
227 Dan Ellis	.10	.25
228 J.P. Dumont	.10	.25
229 Martin Erat	.10	.25
230 David Legwand	.12	.30
231 Shea Weber	.12	.30
232 Jason Arnott	.12	.30
233 Ryan Suter	.12	.30
234 Ville Koistinen	.12	.30
235 Phoenix Coyotes Logo	.08	.25
236 Ilya Bryzgalov	.12	.30
237 Olli Jokinen	.12	.30
238 Peter Mueller	.12	.30
239 Daniel Carcillo	.10	.25
240 Ed Jovanovski	.12	.30
241 Shane Doan	.12	.30
242 Derek Morris	.10	.25
243 Kyle Turris	.25	.60
244 San Jose Sharks Logo	.08	.25
245 Evgeni Nabokov	.12	.30
246 Jonathan Cheechoo	.15	.40
247 Patrick Marleau	.15	.40
248 Milan Michalek	.10	.25
249 Marc-Edouard Vlasic	.10	.25
250 Joe Thornton	.20	.50
251 Christian Ehrhoff	.10	.25
252 Devin Setoguchi	.12	.30
253 St. Louis Blues Logo	.08	.25
254 Manny Legace	.15	.40
255 Keith Tkachuk	.15	.40
256 Andy McDonald	.12	.30
257 Brad Boyes	.10	.25
258 Eric Brewer	.10	.25
259 Paul Kariya	.20	.50
260 Erik Johnson	.12	.30
261 David Perron	.12	.30
262 Vancouver Canucks Logo	.08	.25
263 Roberto Luongo	.20	.50
264 Mattias Ohlund	.10	.25
265 Kevin Bieksa	.12	.30
266 Daniel Sedin	.15	.40
267 Henrik Sedin	.15	.40
268 Ryan Kesler	.20	.50
269 Pavol Demitra	.20	.50
270 Alexander Edler	.10	.25

2009-10 Panini Stickers

Card	Low	High
COMPLETE SET (364)	50.00	100.00
1 NHLPA Logo	.08	.25
2 NHL Logo	.08	.25
3 EASTERN CONFERENCE Logo	.08	.25
4 WESTERN CONFERENCE Logo	.08	.25
5 Central Division CHAMPION	.08	.25
6 Northwest Division Champion	.08	.25
7 Pacific Division Champion	.08	.25
8 Atlantic Division Champion	.08	.25
9 Northeast Division Champion	.08	.25
10 Southeast Division Champion	.08	.25
11 Atlanta Thrashers Logo	.08	.25
12 Kari Lehtonen	.12	.30
13 Slava Kozlov	.10	.25
14 Tobias Enstrom	.15	.40
15 Colby Armstrong	.10	.25
16 Chris Thorburn	.10	.25
17 Zach Bogosian	.12	.30
18 Ilya Kovalchuk SS	.15	.40
19 Todd White	.10	.25
20 Bryan Little	.15	.40
21 Boston Bruins Logo	.08	.25
22 Tim Thomas	.15	.40
23 Zdeno Chara	.15	.40
24 Milan Lucic	.12	.30
25 Patrice Bergeron	.20	.50
26 Michael Ryder	.10	.25
27 Dennis Wideman	.10	.25
28 Marc Savard SS	.10	.25
29 David Krejci	.15	.40
30 Blake Wheeler	.15	.40
31 Buffalo Sabres Logo	.08	.25
32 Ryan Miller	.15	.40
33 Derek Roy	.12	.30
34 Jason Pominville	.15	.40
35 Thomas Vanek SS	.15	.40
36 Tim ConnOlly	.10	.25
37 Craig Rivet	.10	.25
38 Drew Stafford	.15	.40
39 Henrik Tallinder	.10	.25
40 Patrick Kaleta	.10	.25
41 Carolina Hurricanes Logo	.08	.25
42 Cam Ward	.15	.40
43 Rod Brindâ•™Amour	.15	.40
44 Joni Pitkanen	.12	.30
45 Joe Corvo	.10	.25
46 Chad LaRose	.10	.25
47 Erik Cole	.12	.30
48 Eric Staal SS	.20	.50
49 Ray Whitney	.12	.30
50 Tuomo Ruutu	.10	.25
51 Florida Panthers Logo	.08	.25
52 Tomas Vokoun	.12	.30
53 Stephen Weiss	.10	.25
54 Nathan Horton SS	.15	.40
55 Rostislav Olesz	.10	.25
56 David Booth	.10	.25
57 Keith Ballard	.10	.25
58 Bryan McCabe	.12	.30
59 Cory Stillman	.10	.25
60 Michael Frolik	.12	.30
61 Montreal Canadiens Logo	.08	.25
62 Carey PRICE	.60	1.50
63 Scott Gomez SS	.12	.30
64 Andrei MARKOV	.15	.40
65 Andrei KOSTITSYN	.12	.30
66 Tomas PLEKANEC	.15	.40
67 Maxim Lapierre	.10	.25
68 Guillaume Latendresse	.12	.30
69 Roman Hamrlik	.10	.25
70 Mike Cammalleri	.12	.30
71 New Jersey Devils Logo	.08	.25
72 Martin Brodeur	.30	.75
73 Zach Parise SS	.15	.40
74 Brian Rolston	.12	.30
75 Patrik Elias	.15	.40
76 Jamie Langenbrunner	.10	.25
77 Travis Zajac	.12	.30
78 Paul Martin	.10	.25
79 Johnny Oduya	.12	.30
80 David Clarkson	.12	.30
81 New York Islanders Logo	.08	.25
82 Rick DiPietro	.12	.30
83 Kyle Okposo	.15	.40
84 Brendan Witt	.10	.25
85 Josh Bailey	.12	.30
86 Trent Hunter	.10	.25
87 Jeff Tambellini	.10	.25
88 Mark Streit	.10	.25
89 Sean Bergenheim	.10	.25
90 Doug Weight	.15	.40
91 New York Rangers Logo	.08	.25
92 Henrik Lundqvist SS	.25	.60
93 Brandon Dubinsky	.12	.30
94 Marian Gaborik	.20	.50
95 Chris Drury	.12	.30
96 Marc Staal	.15	.40
97 Sean Avery	.12	.30
98 Ryan Callahan	.15	.40
99 Wade Redden	.10	.25
100 Michal Rozsival	.10	.25
101 Ottawa Senators Logo	.08	.25
102 Pascal LeClaire	.15	.40
103 Alex Kovalev	.15	.40
104 Daniel Alfredsson SS	.15	.40
105 Chris Kelly	.12	.30
106 Jason Spezza	.15	.40
107 Mike Fisher	.10	.25
108 Chris Phillips	.10	.25
109 Filip Kuba	.10	.25
110 Nick Foligno	.12	.30
111 Philadelphia Flyers Logo	.08	.25
112 Ray Emery	.12	.30
113 Daniel Briere	.15	.40
114 Simon Gagne	.15	.40
115 Mike Richards	.15	.40
116 Jeff Carter	.15	.40
117 Claude Giroux	.15	.40
118 Kimmo Timonen	.12	.30
119 Braydon Coburn	.10	.25
120 Scott Hartnell	.15	.40
121 Pittsburgh Penguins Logo	.08	.25
122 Marc-Andre Fleury	.25	.60
123 Evgeni Malkin	.50	1.25
124 Tyler Kennedy	.12	.30
125 Sidney Crosby SS	.60	1.50
126 Jordan Staal	.15	.40
127 Kris Letang	.15	.40
128 Sergei Gonchar	.10	.25
129 Maxime Talbot	.15	.40
130 Brooks Orpik	.12	.30
131 Tampa Bay Lightning Logo	.08	.25
132 Mike Smith	.15	.40
133 Martin St. Louis	.15	.40
134 Vincent Lecavalier SS	.12	.30
135 Steven Stamkos	.30	.75
136 Alex Tanguay	.10	.25
137 Ryan Malone	.10	.25
138 Paul Ranger	.10	.25
139 Andrej Meszaros	.10	.25
140 Jeff HALPERN	.10	.25
141 Toronto Maple Leafs Logo	.08	.25
142 Vesa Toskala	.15	.40
143 Jason Blake	.10	.25
144 Luke Schenn SS	.12	.30
145 Niklas Hagman	.10	.25
146 Nikolai Kulemin	.12	.30
147 Tomas Kaberle	.10	.25
148 Mike Komisarek	.12	.30
149 Matt STAJAN	.12	.30
150 John Mitchell	.10	.25
151 Washington Capitals Logo	.08	.25
152 Semyon Varlamov	.15	.40
153 Mike Green	.15	.40
154 Nicklas Backstrom	.25	.60
155 Alexander Semin	.15	.40
156 Chris Clark	.10	.25
157 David Steckel	.10	.25
158 Alex Ovechkin SS	.60	1.50
159 John Erskine	.10	.25
160 Brooks Laich	.15	.40
161 Anaheim Ducks Logo	.08	.25
162 Jonas Hiller	.12	.30
163 Ryan Whitney	.10	.25
164 Corey Perry	.15	.40
165 Ryan Getzlaf SS	.25	.60
166 Scott Niedermayer	.15	.40
167 Bobby Ryan	.15	.40
168 George Parros	.10	.25
169 Teemu Selanne	.30	.75
170 Andrew Ebbett	.10	.25
171 Calgary Flames Logo	.08	.25
172 Miikka Kiprusoff	.12	.30
173 Dion Phaneuf	.20	.50
174 Jarome Iginla SS	.15	.40
175 Robyn Regehr	.12	.30
176 Daymond Langkow	.10	.25
177 Rene Bourque	.10	.25
178 Olli Jokinen	.12	.30
179 Dustin Boyd	.10	.25
180 Craig Conroy	.10	.25
181 Chicago Blackhawks Logo	.08	.25
182 Cristobal Huet	.15	.40
183 Jonathan Toews SS	.30	.75
184 Patrick Kane	.30	.75
185 Brian Campbell	.12	.30
186 Marian Hossa	.12	.30
187 Duncan Keith	.15	.40
188 Patrick Sharp	.15	.40
189 Dustin Byfuglien	.15	.40
190 Brent Seabrook	.12	.30
191 Colorado Avalanche Logo	.08	.25
192 Peter Budaj	.12	.30
193 Chris Stewart	.12	.30
194 Scott Hannan	.10	.25
195 John-Michael Liles	.10	.25
196 Paul Stastny SS	.15	.40
197 Milan Hejduk	.12	.30
198 Wojtek Wolski	.10	.25
199 Adam Foote	.10	.25
200 Marek Svatos	.10	.25
201 Columbus Blue Jackets Logo	.08	.25
202 Steve Mason	.12	.30
203 Kristian Huselius	.10	.25
204 Derick Brassard	.15	.40
205 Rick Nash SS	.12	.30
206 Rustislav Klesla	.15	.40
207 Mike Commodore	.10	.25
208 Nikita Filatov	.12	.30
209 Jakub Voracek	.15	.40
210 R.J. Umberger	.12	.30
211 Dallas Stars Logo	.08	.25
212 Marty Turco	.15	.40
213 Mike Modano	.25	.60
214 James Neal	.15	.40
215 Brenden Morrow SS	.12	.30
216 Mike Ribeiro	.12	.30
217 Loui Eriksson	.12	.30
218 Fabian Brunnstrom	.12	.30
219 Matt Niskanen	.12	.30
220 Brad Richards	.15	.40
221 Detroit Red Wings Logo	.08	.25
222 Chris Osgood	.15	.40
223 Nicklas Lidstrom	.15	.40
224 Pavel Datsyuk SS	.20	.50
225 Henrik Zetterberg	.20	.50
226 Dan Cleary	.15	.40
227 Brian Rafalski	.10	.25
228 Valterri Filppula	.15	.40
229 Johan Franzen	.15	.40
230 Tomas Holmstrom	.12	.30
231 Edmonton Oilers Logo	.08	.25
232 Nikolai Khabibulin	.15	.40
233 Ales Hemsky SS	.12	.30
234 Sam Gagner	.12	.30
235 Sheldon Souray	.10	.25
236 Shawn Horcoff	.10	.25
237 Andrew Cogliano	.12	.30
238 Patrick O'Sullivan	.12	.30
239 Tom Gilbert	.10	.25
240 Ethan Moreau	.10	.25
241 Los Anglese Kings Logo	.08	.25
242 Erik Ersberg	.12	.30
243 Dustin Brown	.12	.30
244 Justin Williams	.12	.30
245 Jack Johnson	.10	.25
246 Drew Doughty	.20	.50
247 Alexander Frolov	.12	.30
248 Ryan Smyth	.12	.30
249 Anze Kopitar SS	.25	.60
250 Wayne Simmonds	.20	.50
251 Minnesota Wild Logo	.08	.25
252 Niklas Backstrom	.15	.40
253 Martin Havlat	.12	.30
254 Brent Burns	.20	.50
255 Pierre-Marc Bouchard	.15	.40
256 Andrew Brunette	.10	.25
257 Derek Boogaard	.10	.25
258 Mikko Koivu SS	.15	.40
259 Nick Schultz	.10	.25
260 Cal Clutterbuck	.10	.25
261 Nashville Predators Logo	.08	.25
262 Pekka Rinne	.20	.50
263 Jason Arnott	.12	.30
264 J.P. Dumont	.10	.25
265 Jordin Tootoo	.15	.40
266 David Legwand	.12	.30
267 Ryan Suter	.15	.40
268 Shea Weber SS	.12	.30
269 Dan Hamhuis	.12	.30
270 Martin Erat	.10	.25
271 Phoenix Coyotes Logo	.08	.25
272 Ilya Bryzgalov	.12	.30
273 Peter Mueller	.12	.30
274 Kyle Turris	.15	.40
275 Ed Jovanovski	.10	.25
276 Martin Hanzal	.12	.30
277 Mikkel Boedker	.10	.25
278 Zbynek Michalek	.10	.25
279 Shane Doan SS	.12	.30
280 Viktor Tikhonov	.12	.30
281 San Jose Sharks Logo	.08	.25
282 Evgeni Nabokov	.12	.30
283 Joe Pavelski	.15	.40
284 Patrick Marleau	.15	.40
285 Milan Michalek	.10	.25
286 Joe Thornton SS	.15	.40
287 Devin Setoguchi	.12	.30
288 Ryane Clowe	.12	.30
289 Rob Blake	.15	.40
290 Dan Boyle	.12	.30
291 St Louis Blues Logo	.08	.25
292 Chris Mason	.12	.30
293 Paul Kariya	.20	.50
294 T.J. Oshie	.25	.60
295 Brad Boyes SS	.10	.25
296 Andy McDonald	.12	.30
297 Keith Tkachuk	.15	.40
290 Erik Johnson	.12	.30
299 Barret Jackman	.10	.25
300 David Backes	.15	.40
301 Vancouver Canucks Logo	.08	.25
302 Roberto Luongo SS	.20	.50
303 Ryan Kesler	.15	.40
304 Alexander Edler	.10	.25
305 Mason Raymond	.15	.40
306 Kevin Bieksa	.12	.30
307 Daniel Sedin	.15	.40
308 Henrik Sedin	.15	.40
309 Alexandre Burrows	.15	.40
310 Pavol Demitra	.20	.50
311 James van Riemsdyk	.30	.75
312 John Tavares	.75	2.00
313 Ville Leino	.12	.30
314 Michael Del Zotto	.15	.40
315 Benn Ferriero	.15	.40
316 Victor Hedman	.30	.75
317 Matt Duchene	.30	.75
318 Erik Karlsson	.50	1.25
319 Ryan O'Reilly	.25	.60
320 Evander Kane	.30	.75
321 Viktor Stalberg	.15	.40
322 Jamie Benn	.50	1.25
323 Tyler Myers	.25	.60
324 Sergei Shirokov	.10	.25
325 Matt Gilroy	.15	.40
326 Dmitry Kulikov	.15	.40
327 James Wright	.15	.40
328 Artem Anisimov	.15	.40
329 Matt Halischuk	.12	.30
330 Peter Regin	.12	.30
331 Byron Bitz	.12	.30
332 Mikael Backlund	.15	.40
333 Kris Chucko	.12	.30
334 Taylor Chorney	.15	.40
335 Alec Martinez	.20	.50
336 Yannick Weber	.15	.40
337 Luca Caputi	.15	.40
338 Teemu Laakso	.10	.25
339 Jonas Gustavsson	.20	.50
340 Jason Demers	.25	.60
341 Season Opener	.08	.25
342 Season Opener	.08	.25
343 Winter Classic	.08	.25
344 Winter Classic	.08	.25
345 Winter Classic	.08	.25
346 Winter Classic	.08	.25
347 Alexander Ovechkin AW	.60	1.50
348 Alexander Ovechkin AW	.60	1.50
349 Martin Brodeur AW	.30	.75
350 Martin Brodeur AW	.30	.75
351 Martin Brodeur AW	.30	.75
352 Martin Brodeur AW	.30	.75
353 Pittsburgh Penguins East.Champs	.08	.25
354 Detroit Red Wings West Champs	.08	.25
355 Stanley Cup	.08	.25
356 Stanley Cup	.08	.25
357 Stanley Cup	.08	.25
358 Stanley Cup	.08	.25
359 Alexander Ovechkin AW	.60	1.50
360 Zdeno Chara AW	.15	.40
361 Tim Thomas AW	.15	.40
362 Evgeni Malkin AW	.50	1.25
363 Steve Mason AW	.12	.30
364 Pavel Datsyuk AW	.20	.50

2010-11 Panini Stickers

Card	Low	High
COMPLETE SET (364)	60.00	120.00
1 NHL Logo Foil	.15	.40
2 NHLPA Logo Foil	.15	.40
3 Stanley Cup Foil	.15	.40
4 Western Conference Logo Foil	.15	.40
5 Western Conference Logo Foil	.15	.40
6 Eastern Conference Logo Foil	.15	.40
7 Atlanta Thrashers Foil	.15	.40
8 Nik Antropov Foil	.15	.40
9 Evander Kane	.20	.50
10 Zach Bogosian	.15	.40
11 Tobias Ensrom	.12	.30
12 Ondrej Pavelec	.20	.50
13 Rich Peverley	.20	.50
14 Ron Hainsey	.12	.30
15 Johnny Oduya	.15	.40
16 Niclas Bergfors	.15	.40
17 Boston Bruins Foil	.15	.40
18 Marc Savard Foil	.12	.30
19 Zdeno Chara	.15	.40
20 Patrice Bergeron	.25	.60
21 David Krejci	.20	.50
22 Tuukka Rask	.20	.50
23 Milan Lucic	.20	.50
24 Dennis Seidenberg	.15	.40
25 Marco Sturm	.12	.30
26 Shawn Thornton	.12	.30
27 Buffalo Sabres Foil	.15	.40
28 Ryan Miller Foil	.20	.50
29 Thomas Vanek	.20	.50
30 Derek Roy	.20	.50
31 Jason Pominville	.20	.50
32 Tyler Myers	.20	.50
33 Craig Rivet	.12	.30
34 Tyler Ennis	.15	.40
35 Patrick Kaleta	.12	.30
36 Tim Connolly	.12	.30
37 Carolina Hurricanes Foil	.15	.40
38 Eric Staal Foil	.25	.60
39 Cam Ward	.20	.50
40 Tim Gleason	.12	.30
41 Joni Pitkanen	.15	.40
42 Tuomu Ruutu	.15	.40
43 Chad LaRose	.12	.30
44 Brandon Sutter	.15	.40
45 Jussi Jokinen	.12	.30
46 Sergei Samsonov	.15	.40
47 Florida Panthers Foil	.15	.40
48 Stephen Weiss Foil	.15	.40
49 Rostislav Olesz	.12	.30
50 David Booth	.12	.30
51 Tomas Vokoun	.15	.40
52 Bryan McCabe	.12	.30
53 Shawn Matthias	.12	.30
54 Cory Stillman	.12	.30
55 Michael Frolik	.12	.30
56 Dmitry Kulikov	.15	.40
57 Montreal Canadiens Foil	.15	.40
58 Michael Cammalleri Foil	.20	.50
59 Scott Gomez	.15	.40
60 Brian Gionta	.15	.40
61 Tomas Plekanec	.20	.50
62 Josh Gorges	.12	.30
63 Andrei Markov	.20	.50
64 Hal Gill	.12	.30
65 Carey Price	.75	2.00
66 Travis Moen	.12	.30
67 New Jersey Devils Foil	.15	.40
68 Zach Parise Foil	.20	.50
69 Martin Brodeur	.40	1.00
70 Travis Zajac	.15	.40
71 Jamie Langenbrunner	.12	.30
72 David Clarkson	.12	.30
73 Andy Greene	.12	.30
74 Colin White	.12	.30
75 Patrik Elias	.20	.50
76 Dainius Zubrus	.12	.30
77 New York Islanders Foil	.15	.40
78 John Tavares Foil	.40	1.00
79 Kyle Okposo	.20	.50
80 Mark Streit	.12	.30
81 Matt Moulson	.15	.40
82 Dwayne Roloson	.15	.40
83 Rick DiPietro	.15	.40
84 Trent Hunter	.12	.30
85 Josh Bailey	.15	.40
86 Blake Comeau	.12	.30
87 New York Rangers Foil	.15	.40
88 Marian Gaborik Foil	.25	.60
89 Henrik Lundqvist	.30	.75
90 Marc Staal	.20	.50
91 Daniel Girardi	.12	.30
92 Brandon Dubinsky	.15	.40
93 Ryan Callahan	.20	.50
94 Sean Avery	.15	.40
95 Michael Del Zotto	.15	.40
96 Chris Drury	.15	.40
97 Ottawa Senators Foil	.15	.40
98 Daniel Alfredsson Foil	.20	.50
99 Jason Spezza	.12	.30
100 Mike Fisher	.20	.50
101 Milan Michalek	.12	.30
102 Chris Phillips	.12	.30
103 Erik Karlsson	.40	1.00
104 Brian Elliot	.15	.40
105 Alex Kovalev	.20	.50
106 Jarkko Ruutu	.12	.30
107 Philadelphia Flyers Foil	.15	.40
108 Mike Richards Foil	.20	.50
109 Jeff Carter	.20	.50
110 Daniel Briere	.20	.50
111 Claude Giroux	.20	.50
112 Chris Pronger	.15	.40
113 Kimmo Timonen	.12	.30
114 Brian Boucher	.15	.40
115 James van Riemsdyk	.30	.75
116 Ville Leino	.15	.40
117 Pittsburgh Penguins Foil	.15	.40
118 Sidney Crosby Foil	1.25	3.00
119 Evgeni Malkin	.60	1.50
120 Marc-Andre Fleury	.30	.75
121 Jordan Staal	.20	.50
122 Kris Letang	.20	.50
123 Matt Cooke	.12	.30
124 Maxime Talbot	.20	.50
125 Brooks Orpik	.15	.40
126 Chris Kunitz	.20	.50
127 Tampa Bay Lightning Foil	.15	.40
128 Steven Stamkos Foil	.60	1.50
129 Vincent Lecavalier	.15	.40
130 Martin St. Louis	.20	.50
131 Victor Hedman	.25	.60
132 Steve Downie	.12	.30
133 Nate Thompson	.12	.30
134 Mike Smith	.20	.50
135 Ryan Malone	.12	.30
136 Mattias Ohlund	.12	.30
137 Toronto Maple Leafs Foil	.15	.40
138 Phil Kessel Foil	.25	.60
139 Dion Phaneuf	.20	.50
140 Jonas Gustavsson	.25	.60
141 Jean-Sebastien Giguere	.15	.40
142 Luke Schenn	.15	.40
143 Tyler Bozak	.20	.50
144 Mike Komisarek	.12	.30
145 Colton Orr	.12	.30
146 Mikhail Grabovski	.15	.40
147 Washington Capitals Foil	.15	.40
148 Alex Ovechkin Foil	1.25	3.00
149 Alex Semin	.20	.50
150 Nicklas Backstrom	.30	.75
151 Mike Green	.20	.50
152 Brooks Laich	.12	.30
153 Jeff Schultz	.12	.30
154 Semyon Varlamov	.20	.50
155 Mike Knuble	.12	.30
156 John Carlson	.25	.60
157 Anaheim Ducks Foil	.15	.40
158 Ryan Getzlaf Foil	.30	.75
159 Corey Perry	.20	.50
160 Jonas Hiller	.15	.40
161 Bobby Ryan	.20	.50
162 Lubomir Visnovsky	.12	.30
163 George Parros	.15	.40
164 Jason Blake	.12	.30
165 Joffrey Lupul	.15	.40
166 Teemu Selanne	.40	1.00
167 Calgary Flames Foil	.15	.40
168 Jarome Iginla Foil	.20	.50
169 Miikka Kiprusoff	.15	.40
170 Jay Bouwmeester	.25	.60
171 Matt Stajan	.15	.40
172 Rene Bourque	.12	.30
173 Robyn Regehr	.12	.30
174 Mark Giordano	.15	.40
175 Daymond Langkow	.12	.30
176 Mikael Backlund	.12	.30
177 Chicago Blackhawks Foil	.15	.40
178 Jonathan Toews Foil	.40	1.00
179 Patrick Kane	.40	1.00
180 Tomas Kopecky	.15	.40
181 Marian Hossa	.15	.40
182 Duncan Keith	.20	.50
183 Brent Seabrook	.20	.50
184 Dave Bolland	.15	.40
185 Bryan Bickell	.12	.30
186 Patrick Sharp	.20	.50
187 Colorado Avalanche Foil	.15	.40
188 Paul Stastny Foil	.20	.50
189 Matt Duchene	.20	.50
190 Craig Anderson	.20	.50
191 Ryan O'Reilly	.20	.50
192 Milan Hejduk	.15	.40
193 Chris Stewart	.15	.40
194 Scott Hannan	.12	.30
195 John-Michael Liles	.12	.30
196 T.J. Galiardi	.15	.40
197 Columbus Blue Jackets Foil	.15	.40
198 Rick Nash Foil	.20	.50
199 Kristian Huselius	.12	.30
200 Steve Mason	.15	.40
201 Jakub Voracek	.20	.50
202 Antoine Vermette	.12	.30
203 Kris Russell	.12	.30
204 Mike Commodore	.12	.30
205 R.J. Umberger	.12	.30
206 Derick Brassard	.20	.50
207 Dallas Stars Foil	.15	.40
208 Brad Richards Foil	.20	.50
209 Brenden Morrow	.15	.40
210 Mike Ribeiro	.15	.40
211 Loui Eriksson	.15	.40
212 James Neal	.20	.50
213 Jamie Benn	.25	.60
214 Stephane Robidas	.12	.30
215 Steve Ott	.15	.40
216 Kari Lehtonen	.15	.40
217 Detroit Red Wings Foil	.15	.40
218 Pavel Datsyuk Foil	.25	.60
219 Henrik Zetterberg	.25	.60
220 Nicklas Lidstrom	.20	.50
221 Brian Rafalski	.12	.30
222 Jimmy Howard	.25	.60
223 Johan Franzen	.20	.50
224 Valtteri Filppula	.20	.50
225 Tomas Holmstrom	.12	.30
226 Niklas Kronwall	.12	.30
227 Edmonton Oilers Foil	.15	.40
228 Ales Hemsky Foil	.15	.40
229 Dustin Penner	.12	.30
230 Sam Gagner	.15	.40
231 Ryan Whitney	.12	.30
232 Andrew Cogliano	.12	.30
233 Tom Gilbert	.12	.30
234 Shawn Horcoff	.12	.30
235 Jeff Deslauriers	.12	.30
236 Zach Stortini	.12	.30
237 Los Angeles Kings Foil	.15	.40
238 Drew Doughty Foil	.20	.50
239 Anze Kopitar	.30	.75
240 Ryan Smyth	.15	.40
241 Dustin Brown	.20	.50
242 Jonathan Quick	.30	.75
243 Jack Johnson	.12	.30
244 Wayne Simmonds	.25	.60
245 Jarret Stoll	.15	.40
246 Matt Greene	.12	.30
247 Minnesota Wild Foil	.15	.40
248 Mikko Koivu Foil	.20	.50
249 Niklas Backstrom	.20	.50
250 Martin Havlat	.15	.40
251 Brent Burns	.25	.60
252 Marek Zidlicky	.12	.30
253 Cal Clutterbuck	.20	.50
254 Guillaume Latendresse	.15	.40
255 Andrew Brunette	.12	.30
256 Pierre-Marc Bouchard	.20	.50
257 Nashville Predators Foil	.15	.40
258 Shea Weber Foil	.15	.40
259 Pekka Rinne	.25	.60
260 Ryan Suter	.12	.30
261 Martin Erat	.12	.30
262 Patric Hornqvist	.15	.40
263 David Legwand	.15	.40
264 Colin Wilson	.15	.40
265 Steve Sullivan	.12	.30
266 Jordin Tootoo	.15	.40
267 Phoenix Coyotes Foil	.15	.40
268 Shane Doan Foil	.15	.40
269 Radim Vrbata	.15	.40
270 Vernon Fiddler	.12	.30
271 Ilya Bryzgalov	.15	.40
272 Ed Jovanovski	.12	.30
273 Keith Yandle	.20	.50
274 Wojtek Wolski	.12	.30
275 Martin Hanzal	.12	.30
276 Daniel Winnik	.12	.30
277 San Jose Sharks Foil	.15	.40
278 Joe Thornton Foil	.20	.50
279 Dany Heatley	.15	.40
280 Dan Boyle	.15	.40
281 Joe Pavelski	.20	.50
282 Devin Setoguchi	.15	.40
283 Ryane Clowe	.12	.30
284 Logan Couture	.20	.50
285 Douglas Murray	.12	.30
286 Thomas Greiss	.12	.30
287 St Louis Blues Foil	.15	.40
288 Erik Johnson Foil	.12	.30
289 T.J. Oshie	.30	.75
290 Brad Boyes	.12	.30
291 David Backes	.20	.50
292 Andy McDonald	.15	.40
293 Barret Jackman	.12	.30
294 Ty Conklin	.15	.40
295 Alex Pietrangelo	.15	.40
296 Jay McClement	.12	.30
297 Vancouver Canucks Foil	.15	.40
298 Henrik Sedin Foil	.20	.50
299 Daniel Sedin	.20	.50
300 Roberto Luongo	.20	.50
301 Ryan Kesler	.20	.50
302 Alex Burrows	.20	.50
303 Kevin Bieksa	.15	.40
304 Alexander Edler	.12	.30
305 Mikael Samuelsson	.12	.30
306 Mason Raymond	.15	.40
307 Season Première 1	.12	.30
308 Season Premiere 1	.12	.30
309 Season premiere 2	.12	.30
310 Season premiere 2	.12	.30
311 Martin Brodeur	.40	1.00
312 Martin Brodeur	.40	1.00
313 Winter Classic	.12	.30
314 Winter Classic	.12	.30
315 Capitals' President Cup Winners	.12	.30
316 Capitals' President Cup Winners	.12	.30
317 Western Conf.Champs	.12	.30
318 Western Conf.Champs	.12	.30
319 Eastern Conf.Champs	.12	.30
320 Eastern Conf.Champs	.12	.30
321 Stanley Cup Champs	.12	.30
322 Stanley Cup Champs	.12	.30
323 Henrik Sedin ROSS	.20	.50
324 Ryan Miller VEZINA	.20	.50
325 Duncan Keith NORRIS	.20	.50
326 Tyler Myers CALDER	.20	.50
327 Pavel Datsyuk SELKE	.25	.60
328 Martin St. Louis BING	.20	.50
329 Sidney Crosby MESSIER	.75	2.00
330 Jose Theodore MASTERSON	.20	.50
331 Dave Tippett ADAMS	.12	.30
332 Jonathan Toews CONN	.40	1.00
333 Shane Doan CLANCY	.15	.40
334 Alexander Ovechkin LINDSAY	.75	2.00
335 Nick Palmieri	.15	.40
336 Zach Hamill	.15	.40
337 Jamie McBain	.15	.40
338 Justin Mercier	.15	.40
339 Brayden Irwin	.15	.40
340 Nick Bonino	.20	.50
341 Philip Larsen	.15	.40
342 Bobby Butler	.15	.40
343 Maxim Noreau	.12	.30
344 Nick Johnson	.12	.30
345 Brock Trotter	.30	.75
346 Matt Martin	.25	.60
347 Jerome Samson	.15	.40
348 Arturs Kulda	.15	.40
349 Ryan Wilson	.15	.40
350 Casey Wellman	.15	.40
351 Evgeny dadonov	.20	.50
352 P.K. Subban	.50	1.25
353 Nick Spaling	.15	.40
354 Kyle Wilson	.20	.50
355 James Wyman	.15	.40

356 Dylan Reese .15 .40
357 Carter Hutton .30 .75
358 Jared Cowen .15 .40
359 Cody Almond .15 .40
360 Eric Tangradi .15 .40
361 Andrew Bodnarchuk .15 .40
362 Dustin Tokarski .15 .40
363 Nazem Kadri .50 1.25
364 Anton Klementyev .15 .40

2011-12 Panini Stickers

COMPLETE SET (384) 40.00 80.00
1 NHL Logo .08 .25
2 NHLPA Logo .08 .25
3 Stanley Cup .08 .25
4 Stanley Cup Champions Bruins .08 .25
5 Western Conference Logo .08 .25
6 Chicago Blackhawks .08 .25
7 Columbus Blue Jackets .08 .25
8 Detroit Red Wings .08 .25
9 Nashville Predators .08 .25
10 St. Louis Blues .08 .25
11 Calgary Flames .08 .25
12 Colorado Avalanche .08 .25
13 Edmonton Oilers .08 .25
14 Minnesota Wild .08 .25
15 Vancouver Canucks .08 .25
16 Anaheim Ducks .08 .25
17 Dallas Stars .08 .25
18 Los Angeles Kings .08 .25
19 Phoenix Coyotes .08 .25
20 San Jose Sharks .08 .25
21 Eastern Conference Logo .08 .25
22 New Jersey Devils .08 .25
23 New York Islanders .08 .25
24 New York Rangers .08 .25
25 Philadelphia Flyers .08 .25
26 Pittsburgh Penguins .08 .25
27 Boston Bruins .08 .25
28 Buffalo Sabres .08 .25
29 Montreal Canadiens .08 .25
30 Ottawa Senators .08 .25
31 Toronto Maple Leafs .08 .25
32 Carolina Hurricanes .08 .25
33 Florida Panthers .08 .25
34 Tampa Bay Lightning .08 .25
35 Washington Capitals .08 .25
36 Winnipeg Jets .08 .25
37 Boston Bruins .08 .25
38 Tim Thomas .15 .40
39 Brad Marchand .20 .50
40 David Krejci .15 .40
41 Dennis Seidenberg .12 .30
42 Milan Lucic .15 .40
43 Nathan Horton .15 .40
44 Patrice Bergeron .20 .50
45 Tyler Seguin .30 .75
46 Zdeno Chara .15 .40
47 Buffalo Sabres .08 .25
48 Ryan Miller .15 .40
49 Brad Boyes .10 .25
50 Derek Roy .12 .30
51 Drew Stafford .15 .40
52 Jason Pominville .12 .30
53 Jochen Hecht .10 .25
54 Nathan Gerbe .10 .25
55 Thomas Vanek .15 .40
56 Tyler Myers .15 .40
57 Carolina Hurricanes .08 .25
58 Eric Staal .20 .50
59 Brandon Sutter .12 .30
60 Cam Ward .15 .40
61 Jamie McBain .10 .25
62 Jeff Skinner .15 .40
63 Tim Gleason .10 .25
64 Tuomo Ruutu .12 .30
65 Jussi Jokinen .10 .25
66 Chad Larose .10 .25
67 Florida Panthers .08 .25
68 Stephen Weiss .12 .30
69 David Booth .10 .25
70 Dmitry Kulikov .10 .25
71 Evgeny Dadonov .12 .30
72 Jacob Markstrom .15 .40
73 Jason Garrison .10 .25
74 Mike Santorelli .10 .25
75 Mike Weaver .10 .25
76 Jack Skille .12 .30
77 Montreal Canadiens .08 .25
78 Carey Price .50 1.25
79 Andrei Kostitsyn .12 .30
80 Brian Gionta .12 .30
81 David Deshardnais .08 .25
82 Lars Eller .12 .30
83 Michael Cammalleri .12 .30
84 P.K. Subban .30 .75
85 Scott Gomez .12 .30
86 Tomas Plekanec .15 .40
87 New Jersey Devils .08 .25
88 Martin Brodeur .30 .75
89 Andy Greene .10 .25
90 Dainius Zubrus .10 .25
91 David Clarkson .10 .25
92 David Steckel .10 .25
93 Ilya Kovalchuk .15 .40
94 Mattias Tedenby .10 .25
95 Patrik Elias .15 .40
96 Travis Zajac .12 .30
97 New York Islanders .08 .25
98 John Tavares .30 .75
99 Frans Nielsen .10 .25
100 Kyle Okposo .15 .40
101 Mark Streit .10 .25
102 Matt Moulson .12 .30
103 Michael Grabner .12 .30
104 P.A. Parenteau .10 .25
105 Rick DiPietro .12 .30
106 Travis Hamonic .12 .30
107 New York Rangers .08 .25
108 Henrik Lundqvist .20 .50
109 Artem Anisimov .12 .30
110 Brandon Dubinsky .12 .30
111 Dan Girardi .10 .25
112 Derek Stepan .15 .40
113 Marc Staal .15 .40
114 Marian Gaborik .20 .50
115 Ryan Callahan .15 .40
116 Sean Avery .12 .30
117 Ottawa Senators .08 .25
118 Daniel Alfredsson .15 .40
119 Chris Neil .10 .25
120 Chris Phillips .10 .25
121 Craig Anderson .15 .40
122 Erik Karlsson .30 .75
123 Jason Spezza .15 .40
124 Milan Michalek .10 .25
125 Nick Foligno .12 .30
126 Sergei Gonchar .10 .25
127 Philadelphia Flyers .08 .25
128 Claude Giroux .15 .40
129 Blair Betts .10 .25
130 Chris Pronger .12 .30
131 Danny Briere .15 .40
132 James van Riemsdyk .15 .40
133 Kimmo Timonen .10 .25
134 Scott Hartnell .15 .40
135 Sergei Bobrovsky .15 .40
136 Jaromir Jagr .40 1.00
137 Pittsburgh Penguins .08 .25
138 Sidney Crosby .60 1.50
139 Brooks Orpik .12 .30
140 Chris Kunitz .15 .40
141 Evgeni Malkin .50 1.25
142 James Neal .15 .40
143 Jordan Staal .15 .40
144 Kris Letang .15 .40
145 Marc-Andre Fleury .25 .60
146 Mark Letestu .12 .30
147 Tampa Bay Lightning .08 .25
148 Steven Stamkos .30 .75
149 Martin St. Louis .15 .40
150 Mattias Ohlund .10 .25
151 Ryan Malone .10 .25
152 Dwayne Roloson .12 .30
153 Steve Downie .10 .25
154 Teddy Purcell .15 .40
155 Victor Hedman .20 .50
156 Vincent Lecavalier .12 .30
157 Toronto Maple Leafs .08 .25
158 James Reimer .15 .40
159 Colby Armstrong .10 .25
160 Dion Phaneuf .15 .40
161 Joffrey Lupul .12 .30
162 Luke Schenn .12 .30
163 Mikhail Grabovski .12 .30
164 Nikolai Kulemin .15 .40
165 Phil Kessel .20 .50
166 Tyler Bozak .15 .40
167 Washington Capitals .08 .25
168 Alex Ovechkin .60 1.50
169 Alexander Semin .15 .40
170 Brooks Laich .10 .25
171 Tomas Vokoun .12 .30
172 John Carlson .20 .50
173 Michal Neuvirth .12 .30
174 Mike Green .15 .40
175 Mike Knuble .10 .25
176 Nicklas Backstrom .25 .60
177 Winnipeg Jets .08 .25
178 Dustin Byfuglien .15 .40
179 Andrew Ladd .15 .40
180 Blake Wheeler .30 .75
181 Bryan Little .15 .40
182 Evander Kane .15 .40
183 Nik Antropov .12 .30
184 Ondrej Pavelec .15 .40
185 Tobias Enstrom .10 .25
186 Zach Bogosian .12 .30
187 Anaheim Ducks .08 .25
188 Corey Perry .15 .40
189 Bobby Ryan .15 .40
190 Cam Fowler .12 .30
191 Jonas Hiller .12 .30
192 Lubomir Visnovsky .10 .25
193 Luca Sbisa .12 .30
194 Saku Koivu .15 .40
195 George Parros .12 .30
196 Ryan Getzlaf .25 .60
197 Calgary Flames .08 .25
198 Jarome Iginla .15 .40
199 Alex Tanguay .10 .25
200 David Moss .10 .25
201 Daymond Langkow .10 .25
202 Jay Bouwmeester .15 .40
203 Mark Giordano .12 .30
204 Miikka Kiprusoff .15 .40
205 Olli Jokinen .12 .30
206 Rene Bourque .10 .25
207 Chicago Blackhawks .08 .25
208 Jonathan Toews .30 .75
209 Brent Seabrook .15 .40
210 Corey Crawford .20 .50
211 Dave Bolland .12 .30
212 Duncan Keith .15 .40
213 Marian Hossa .12 .30
214 Niklas Hjalmarsson .10 .25
215 Patrick Kane .30 .75
216 Patrick Sharp .15 .40
217 Colorado Avalanche .08 .25
218 Matt Duchene .15 .40
219 Daniel Winnik .10 .25
220 David Jones .10 .25
221 Erik Johnson .10 .25
222 Milan Hejduk .12 .30
223 Paul Stastny .15 .40
224 Ryan O'Reilly .15 .40
225 Brandon Yip .10 .25
226 Semyon Varlamov .15 .40
227 Columbus Blue Jackets .08 .25
228 Rick Nash .15 .40
229 Antoine Vermette .10 .25
230 Derick Brassard .15 .40
231 Matt Calvert .12 .30
232 Kris Russell .10 .25
233 Kristian Huselius .10 .25
234 Marc Methot .10 .25
235 R.J. Umberger .10 .25
236 Steve Mason .12 .30
237 Dallas Stars .08 .25
238 Loui Ericksson .12 .30
239 Alex Goligoski .12 .30
240 Brenden Morrow .12 .30
241 Jamie Benn .20 .50
242 Kari Lehtonen .12 .30
243 Mike Ribeiro .12 .30
244 Stephane Robidas .10 .25
245 Steve Ott .12 .30
246 Tom Wandell .10 .25
247 Detroit Red Wings .08 .25
248 Pavel Datsyuk .20 .50
249 Danny Cleary .15 .40
250 Henrik Zetterberg .20 .50
251 Jimmy Howard .15 .40
252 Johan Franzen .15 .40
253 Nicklas Lidstrom .15 .40
254 Niklas Kronwall .12 .30
255 Tomas Holmstrom .10 .25
256 Valtteri Filppula .15 .40
257 Edmonton Oilers .08 .25
258 Jordan Eberle .15 .40
259 Ales Hemsky .12 .30
260 Nikolai Khabibulin .12 .30
261 Ryan Jones .12 .30
262 Ryan Whitney .10 .25
263 Sam Gagner .12 .30
264 Shawn Horcoff .10 .25
265 Taylor Hall .30 .75
266 Tom Gilbert .10 .25
267 Los Angeles Kings .08 .25
268 Drew Doughty .15 .40
269 Anze Kopitar .25 .60
270 Dustin Brown .15 .40
271 Jack Johnson .10 .25
272 Jarret Stoll .12 .30
273 Jonathan Quick .25 .60
274 Justin Williams .12 .30
275 Kyle Clifford .10 .25
276 Mike Richards .15 .40
277 Minnesota Wild .08 .25
278 Mikko Koivu .12 .30
279 Nick Schultz .10 .25
280 Cal Clutterbuck .15 .40
281 Kyle Brodziak .10 .25
282 Marek Zidicky .10 .25
283 Matt Cullen .10 .25
284 Niklas Backstrom .15 .40
285 Pierre-Marc Bouchard .15 .40
286 Dany Heatley .12 .30
287 Nashville Predators .08 .25
288 Pekka Rinne .20 .50
289 Colin Wilson .12 .30
290 David Legwand .12 .30
291 Martin Erat .10 .25
292 Mike Fisher .15 .40
293 Patric Hornqvist .12 .30
294 Ryan Suter .10 .25
295 Sergei Kostitsyn .10 .25
296 Shea Weber .12 .30
297 Phoenix Coyotes .08 .25
298 Shane Doan .12 .30
299 Derek Morris .10 .25
300 Keith Yandle .15 .40
301 Lauri Korpikoski .10 .25
302 Lee Stempniak .10 .25
303 Martin Hanzal .10 .25
304 Mikkel Boedker .10 .25
305 Ray Whitney .12 .30
306 Taylor Pyatt .10 .25
307 San Jose Sharks .08 .25
308 Joe Thornton .15 .40
309 Antti Niemi .12 .30
310 Dan Boyle .12 .30
311 Joe Pavelski .15 .40
312 Logan Couture .15 .40
313 Marc-Edouard Vlasic .10 .25
314 Patrick Marleau .15 .40
315 Ryane Clowe .10 .25
316 Torrey Mitchell .10 .25
317 St. Louis Blues .08 .25
318 Jaroslav Halak .15 .40
319 Alex Pietrangelo .12 .30
320 Alexander Steen .15 .40
321 Andy McDonald .12 .30
322 T.J. Oshie .25 .60
323 Chris Stewart .12 .30
324 David Backes .15 .40
325 David Perron .10 .25
326 Patrik Berglund .12 .30
327 Vancouver Canucks .08 .25
328 Daniel Sedin .15 .40
329 Alexandre Burrows .15 .40
330 Kevin Bieksa .12 .30
331 Dan Hamhuis .12 .30
332 Henrik Sedin .15 .40
333 Mason Raymond .12 .30
334 Mikael Samuelsson .10 .25
335 Roberto Luongo .15 .40
336 Ryan Kesler .15 .40
337 Carey Price HC .50 1.25
338 Jarome Iginla HC .15 .40
339 Sidney Crosby WC .60 1.50
340 Alex Ovechkin WC .60 1.50
341 Eric Staal H .20 .50
342 Mikko Koivu H .12 .30
343 Prague .08 .25
344 Prague 2 .08 .25
345 R.Nash/J.Thornton S .15 .40
346 Stockholm .08 .25
347 Boston Bruins .08 .25
348 Boston Bruins 2 .08 .25
349 Vancouver Canucks .08 .25
350 Vancouver Canucks 2 .08 .25
351 Zdeno Chara SC .15 .40
352 Boston Bruins 3 .08 .25
353 Boston Bruins 4 .08 .25
354 Boston Bruins 5 .08 .25
355 Patrick Kane AS FOIL .50 1.25
356 Martin St. Louis AS FOIL .25 .60
357 Steven Stamkos AS FOIL .50 1.25
358 Henrik Sedin AS FOIL .25 .60
359 Jonathan Toews AS FOIL .50 1.25
360 Matt Duchene AS FOIL .25 .60
361 Nicklas Lidstrom AS FOIL .25 .60
362 Tim Thomas AS FOIL .25 .60
363 Eric Staal AS FOIL .30 .75
364 Jeff Skinner AS FOIL .25 .60
365 Daniel Sedin AS FOIL .25 .60
366 Alex Ovechkin AS FOIL 1.00 2.50
367 Claude Giroux AS FOIL .25 .60
368 Corey Perry AS FOIL .25 .60
369 Zdeno Chara AS FOIL .25 .60
370 Cam Ward AS FOIL .25 .60
371 Henrik Lundqvist AS FOIL .30 .75
372 Carey Price AS FOIL .75 2.00
373 Alexander Burmistrov YS FOIL .20 .50
374 Tyler Ennis YS FOIL .20 .50
375 Linus Omark YS FOIL .25 .60
376 Magnus Paajarvi YS FOIL .20 .50
377 Mats Zuccarello YS FOIL .25 .60
378 Nazem Kadri YS FOIL .40 1.00
379 Joe Colborne R FOIL .20 .50
380 Cody Hodgson R FOIL .40 1.00
381 Aaron Palushaj R FOIL .20 .50
382 Marcus Kruger R FOIL .30 .75
383 Stephane Da Costa R FOIL .20 .50
384 Tomas Vincour R FOIL .20 .50

2012-13 Panini Stickers

1 NHL Logo .08 .25
2 NHLPA Logo .08 .25
3 Stanley Cup Champions Logo .08 .25
4 Eastern Conference .08 .25
5 Stanley Cup Logo .08 .25
6 Western Conference .08 .25
7 Rangers Division Champs .08 .25
8 Rangers Division Champs .08 .25
9 Devils Conference Champs .08 .25
10 Devils Conference Champs .08 .25
11 Bruins Division Champs .08 .25
12 Bruins Division Champs .08 .25
13 2011 Premier Sabres vs. Kings .08 .25
14 2011 Premier Sabres vs. Kings .08 .25
15 Panthers Division Champs .08 .25
16 Panthers Division Champs .08 .25
17 Cup Playoffs Panthers vs. Devils .08 .25
18 Cup Playoffs Panthers vs. Devils .08 .25
19 Blues Division Champs .08 .25
20 Blues Division Champs .08 .25
21 Cup Playoffs Coyotes vs. Predators .08 .25
22 Cup Playoffs Coyotes vs. Predators .08 .25
23 Canucks Division Champs .08 .25
24 Canucks Division Champs .08 .25
25 Heritage Classic Canadiens vs. Flames .08 .25
26 Heritage Classic Canadiens vs. Flames .08 .25
27 Kings Stanley Cup Champs .08 .25
28 Kings Stanley Cup Champs .08 .25
29 Sharks Division Champs .08 .25
30 Sharks Division Champs .08 .25
31 Zdeno Chara .15 .40
32 Brad Marchand .20 .50
33 David Krejci .15 .40
34 Milan Lucic .15 .40
35 Nathan Horton .15 .40
36 Patrice Bergeron .20 .50
37 Dennis Seidenberg .12 .30
38 Tuukka Rask .15 .40
39 Tyler Seguin .25 .60
40 Ryan Miller .15 .40
41 Steve Ott .12 .30
42 Drew Stafford .15 .40
43 Jhonas Enroth .15 .40
44 Nathan Gerbe .10 .25
45 Jason Pominville .12 .30
46 Thomas Vanek .15 .40
47 Tyler Ennis .12 .30
48 Tyler Myers .12 .30
49 Eric Staal .20 .50
50 Jordan Staal .15 .40
51 Cam Ward .15 .40
52 Chad LaRose .10 .25
53 Jamie McBain .10 .25
54 Jeff Skinner .15 .40
55 Jiri Tlusty .12 .30
56 Jussi Jokinen .10 .25
57 Alexander Semin .15 .40
58 Brian Campbell .10 .25
59 Jose Theodore .15 .40
60 Tomas Kopecky .12 .30
61 Stephen Weiss .12 .30
62 Sean Bergenheim .10 .25
63 Jacob Markstrom .15 .40
64 Kris Versteeg .12 .30
65 George Parros .12 .30
66 Tomas Fleischmann .10 .25
67 Carey Price .50 1.25
68 David Desharnais .15 .40
69 Erik Cole .12 .30
70 Lars Eller .12 .30
71 Max Pacioretty .15 .40
72 P.K. Subban .25 .60
73 Rene Bourque .10 .25
74 Brian Gionta .12 .30
75 Tomas Plekanec .15 .40
76 Martin Brodeur .30 .75
77 Adam Henrique .15 .40
78 Adam Larsson .15 .40
79 Dainius Zubrus .10 .25
80 David Clarkson .10 .25
81 Ilya Kovalchuk .15 .40
82 Patrik Elias .15 .40
83 Travis Zajac .12 .30
84 Petr Sykora .12 .30
85 John Tavares .30 .75
86 Frans Nielsen .10 .25
87 Kyle Okposo .15 .40
88 Mark Streit .10 .25
89 Matt Moulson .12 .30
90 Michael Grabner .12 .30
91 Nino Neiderreiter .10 .25
92 Rick DiPietro .12 .30
93 Travis Hamonic .12 .30
94 Henrik Lundqvist .20 .50
95 Dan Girardi .10 .25
96 Brad Richards .15 .40
97 Rick Nash .15 .40
98 Carl Hagelin .15 .40
99 Derek Stepan .15 .40
100 Marian Gaborik .15 .40
101 Michael Del Zotto .10 .25
102 Ryan Callahan .15 .40
103 Daniel Alfredsson .15 .40
104 Chris Neil .10 .25
105 Colin Greening .10 .25
106 Craig Anderson .15 .40
107 Erik Karlsson .30 .75
108 Jason Spezza .15 .40
109 Milan Michalek .10 .25
110 Guilliaume Latendresse .12 .30
111 Mika Zibanejad .15 .40
112 Claude Giroux .15 .40
113 Chris Pronger .12 .30
114 Danny Briere .15 .40
115 Ilya Bryzgalov .15 .40
116 Luke Schenn .10 .25
117 Kimmo Timonen .10 .25
118 Matt Read .12 .30
119 Scott Hartnell .15 .40
120 Wayne Simmonds .20 .50
121 Sidney Crosby .60 1.50
122 Brooks Orpik .12 .30
123 Chris Kunitz .15 .40
124 James Neal .15 .40
125 Brandon Sutter .12 .30
126 Kris Letang .15 .40
127 Marc-Andre Fleury .25 .60
128 Pascal Dupuis .10 .25
129 Evgeni Malkin .50 1.25
130 Steven Stamkos .30 .75
131 Mathieu Garon .12 .30
132 Anders Lindback .10 .25
133 Marc-Andre Bergeron .10 .25
134 Martin St. Louis .15 .40
135 Ryan Malone .10 .25
136 Teddy Purcell .15 .40
137 Victor Hedman .20 .50
138 Vincent Lecavalier .12 .30
139 Phil Kessel .20 .50
140 James van Riemsdyk .15 .40
141 Dion Phaneuf .15 .40
142 James Reimer .15 .40
143 Joffrey Lupul .12 .30
144 Ben Scrivens .15 .40
145 Mikhail Grabovski .12 .30
146 Jake Gardiner .15 .40
147 Tyler Bozak .12 .30
148 Alex Ovechkin .60 1.50
149 Karl Alzner .10 .25
150 Brooks Laich .10 .25
151 John Carlson .20 .50
152 Marcus Johansson .12 .30
153 Mike Ribeiro .12 .30
154 Mike Green .15 .40
155 Nicklas Backstrom .25 .60
156 Braden Holtby .25 .60
157 Evander Kane .15 .40
158 Alexander Burmistrov .12 .30
159 Andrew Ladd .15 .40
160 Blake Wheeler .15 .40
161 Bryan Little .15 .40
162 Dustin Byfuglien .15 .40
163 Olli Jokinen .12 .30
164 Ondrej Pavelec .15 .40
165 Tobias Enstrom .10 .25
166 Corey Perry .15 .40
167 Andrew Cogliano .10 .25
168 Bobby Ryan .15 .40
169 Cam Fowler .12 .30
170 Teemu Selanne .30 .75
171 Jonas Hiller .12 .30
172 Sheldon Souray .10 .25
173 Ryan Getzlaf .25 .60
174 Saku Koivu .15 .40
175 Jarome Iginla .15 .40
176 Alex Tanguay .10 .25
177 Curtis Glencross .10 .25
178 Jay Bouwmeester .15 .40
179 Dennis Wideman .10 .25
180 Mark Giordano .12 .30
181 Michael Cammalleri .12 .30
182 Miikka Kiprusoff .12 .30
183 Jiri Hudler .12 .30
184 Jonathan Toews FOIL .30 .75
185 Marcus Kruger .20 .50
186 Corey Crawford .20 .50
187 Viktor Stalberg .10 .25
188 Dave Bolland .12 .30
189 Duncan Keith .15 .40
190 Marian Hossa .12 .30
191 Patrick Kane .30 .75
192 Patrick Sharp .15 .40
193 Matt Duchene .15 .40
194 David Jones .10 .25
195 P.A. Parenteau .10 .25
196 Gabriel Landeskog .15 .40
197 Jean-Sebastien Giguere .12 .30
198 Milan Hejduk .12 .30
199 Paul Stastny .15 .40
200 Ryan O'Reilly .15 .40
201 Semyon Varlamov .15 .40
202 Vinny Prospal .10 .25
203 Derek Dorsett .10 .25
204 Derick Brassard .15 .40
205 Sergei Bobrovsky .15 .40
206 Nick Foligno .12 .30
207 R.J. Umberger .10 .25
208 Ryan Johansen .20 .50
209 Steve Mason .12 .30
210 Jack Johnson .10 .25
211 Jamie Benn .20 .50
212 Richard Bachman .12 .30
213 Brenden Morrow .12 .30
214 Kari Lehtonen .12 .30
215 Loui Eriksson .12 .30
216 Derek Roy .12 .30
217 Jaromir Jagr .40 1.00
218 Ray Whitney .12 .30
219 Trevor Daley .10 .25
220 Pavel Datsyuk .20 .50
221 Danny Cleary .15 .40
222 Henrik Zetterberg .20 .50
223 Jimmy Howard .15 .40
224 Johan Franzen .15 .40
225 Jonas Gustavsson .15 .40
226 Niklas Kronwall .12 .30
227 Tomas Holmstrom .10 .25
228 Valtteri Filppula .15 .40
229 Jordan Eberle .15 .40
230 Ales Hemsky .12 .30
231 Nikolai Khabibulin .15 .40
232 Devan Dubnyk .15 .40
233 Ryan Nugent-Hopkins .15 .40
234 Ryan Smyth .12 .30
235 Sam Gagner .12 .30
236 Shawn Horcoff .10 .25
237 Taylor Hall .30 .75
238 Anze Kopitar .25 .60
239 Jeff Carter .15 .40
240 Jonathan Bernier .15 .40
241 Drew Doughty .15 .40
242 Dustin Brown .15 .40
243 Jarret Stoll .12 .30
244 Jonathan Quick .25 .60
245 Justin Williams .12 .30
246 Mike Richards .15 .40
247 Dany Heatley .12 .30
248 Ryan Suter .10 .25
249 Mikko Koivu .12 .30
250 Devin Setoguchi .12 .30
251 Josh Harding .15 .40
252 Kyle Brodziak .10 .25
253 Matt Cullen .10 .25
254 Niklas Backstrom .12 .30
255 Zach Parise .15 .40
256 Shea Weber .12 .30
257 David Legwand .12 .30
258 Craig Smith .10 .25
259 Martin Erat .10 .25
260 Mike Fisher .12 .30
261 Pekka Rinne .20 .50
262 Chris Mason .12 .30
263 Sergei Kostitsyn .10 .25
264 Patric Hornqvist .12 .30
265 Shane Doan .12 .30
266 Radim Vrbata .12 .30
267 Keith Yandle .15 .40
268 Lauri Korpikoski .10 .25
269 Martin Hanzal .10 .25
270 Mike Smith .15 .40
271 Mikkel Boedker .10 .25
272 Oliver Ekman-Larsson .15 .40
273 Paul Bissonnette .10 .25
274 Joe Thornton .15 .40
275 Antti Niemi .12 .30
276 Dan Boyle .12 .30
277 Joe Pavelski .15 .40
278 Logan Couture .15 .40
279 Martin Havlat .12 .30
280 Patrick Marleau .15 .40
281 Ryane Clowe .10 .25
282 Adam Burish .10 .25
283 David Backes .15 .40
284 Alex Pietrangelo .12 .30
285 Brian Elliott .12 .30
286 Chris Stewart .12 .30
287 David Perron .10 .25
288 Kevin Shattenkirk .15 .40
289 Patrik Berglund .10 .25
290 T.J. Oshie .25 .60
291 Jaroslav Halak .15 .40
292 Daniel Sedin .15 .40
293 Alexandre Burrows .15 .40
294 Cory Schneider .12 .30
295 Kevin Bieksa .12 .30
296 David Booth .10 .25
297 Henrik Sedin .15 .40
298 Alexander Edler .10 .25
299 Roberto Luongo .15 .40
300 Ryan Kesler .15 .40
301 Andrew Shaw YS .15 .40
302 Luke Adam YS .12 .30
303 Slava Voynov YS .15 .40
304 Cody Hodgson YS .15 .40
305 Gustav Nyquist YS .15 .40
306 Sean Couturier YS .15 .40
307 Carter Ashton .10 .25
308 Sven Baertschi .15 .40
309 Jaden Schwartz .25 .60
310 Brandon Bollig .12 .30
311 Jakob Silfverberg .25 .60
312 Chris Kreider .25 .60
313 Dion Phaneuf AS .15 .40
314 Erik Karlsson AS .30 .75
315 Carey Price AS .50 1.25
316 Claude Giroux AS .15 .40
317 Corey Perry AS .15 .40
318 Daniel Sedin AS .15 .40
319 Evgeni Malkin AS .50 1.25
320 Henrik Lundqvist AS .20 .50
321 Henrik Sedin AS .15 .40
322 Jarome Iginla AS .15 .40
323 John Tavares AS .30 .75
324 Tyler Seguin AS .25 .60
325 Kris Letang AS .15 .40
326 Patrick Kane AS .30 .75
327 Pavel Datsyuk AS .20 .50
328 Steven Stamkos AS .30 .75
329 Tim Thomas AS .15 .40
330 Zdeno Chara AS .15 .40

2012-13 Panini Stickers Team Logo Foils

A1 New Jersey Devils .30 .75
A2 New York Islanders .30 .75
A3 New York Rangers .30 .75
A4 Philadephia Flyers .30 .75
A5 Pittsburgh Penguins .30 .75
A6 Boston Bruins .30 .75
A7 Buffalo Sabres .30 .75
A8 Montreal Canadiens .30 .75
A9 Ottawa Senators .30 .75
A10 Toronto Maple Leafs .30 .75
A11 Carolina Hurricanes .30 .75
A12 Florida Panthers .30 .75
A13 Tampa Bay Lightning .30 .75
A14 Washington Capitals .30 .75
A15 Winnipeg Jets .30 .75
A16 Chicago Blackhawks .30 .75
A17 Columbus Blue Jackets .30 .75
A18 Detroit Red Wings .30 .75
A19 Nashville Predators .30 .75
A20 St. Louis Blues .30 .75
A21 Calgary Flames .30 .75
A22 Colorado Avalanche .30 .75
A23 Edmonton Oilers .30 .75
A24 Minnesota Wild .30 .75
A25 Vancouver Canucks .30 .75
A26 Anaheim Ducks .30 .75
A27 Dallas Stars .30 .75
A28 Los Angeles Kings .30 .75
A29 Phoenix Coyotes .30 .75
A30 San Jose Sharks .30 .75
A31 Boston Bruins .30 .75
A32 Buffalo Sabres .30 .75
A33 Carolina Hurricanes .30 .75
A34 Florida Panthers .30 .75
A35 Montreal Canadiens .30 .75
A36 New Jersey Devils .30 .75
A37 New York Islanders .30 .75
A38 New York Rangers .30 .75
A39 Ottawa Senators .30 .75
A40 Philadephia Flyers .30 .75
A41 Pittsburgh Penguins .30 .75
A42 Tampa Bay Lightning .30 .75
A43 Toronto Maple Leafs .30 .75
A44 Washington Capitals .30 .75
A45 Winnipeg Jets .30 .75
A46 Anaheim Ducks .30 .75
A47 Calgary Flames .30 .75
A48 Chicago Blackhawks .30 .75
A49 Colorado Avalanche .30 .75
A50 Columbus Blue Jackets .30 .75
A51 Dallas Stars .30 .75
A52 Detroit Red Wings .30 .75
A53 Edmonton Oilers .30 .75
A54 Los Angeles Kings .30 .75
A55 Minnesota Wild .30 .75
A56 Nashville Predators .30 .75
A57 Phoenix Coyotes .30 .75
A58 San Jose Sharks .30 .75
A59 St. Louis Blues .30 .75
A60 Vancouver Canucks .30 .75

2013-14 Panini Stickers

1 NHL Logo .08 .25
2 NHLPA Logo .08 .25
3 Stanley Cup Championship Logo .08 .25
4 Eastern Conference Logo .08 .25
5 Stanley Cup Logo .08 .25
6 Western Conference Logo .08 .25
7 Eastern Conference Action Puzzle .08 .25
8 Eastern Conference Action Puzzle .08 .25
9 Eastern Conference Action Puzzle .08 .25
10 Eastern Conference Action Puzzle .08 .25
11 Eastern Conference Action Puzzle .08 .25
12 Eastern Conference Action Puzzle .08 .25
13 Boston Bruins Eastern Conference Champs .08 .25
14 Boston Bruins Eastern Conference Champs .08 .25
15 Western Conference Action Puzzle .08 .25
16 Western Conference Action Puzzle .08 .25
17 Western Conference Action Puzzle .08 .25
18 Western Conference Action Puzzle .08 .25
19 Western Conference Action Puzzle .08 .25
20 Western Conference Action Puzzle .08 .25
21 Chicago Blackhawks Team Western Conference Champs Puzzle .08 .25
22 Chicago Blackhawks Team Western Conference Champs Puzzle .08 .25
23 Stanley Cup Finals Action Puzzle .08 .25
24 Stanley Cup Finals Action Puzzle .08 .25
25 Stanley Cup Finals Action Puzzle .08 .25
26 Stanley Cup Finals Action Puzzle .08 .25
27 Chicago Blackhawks Team Stanley Cup Champs Puzzle .08 .25
28 Chicago Blackhawks Team Stanley Cup Champs Puzzle .08 .25
29 Tuukka Rask .15 .40
30 Torey Krug .20 .50
31 Zdeno Chara FOIL .25 .60
32 Dennis Seidenberg .12 .30
33 Brad Marchand .20 .50
34 Milan Lucic .15 .40
35 Jarome Iginila .15 .40
36 David Krejci .15 .40
37 Patrice Bergeron .20 .50
38 Ryan Miller FOIL .25 .60
39 Christian Ehrhoff .10 .25
40 Tyler Myers .12 .30
41 Thomas Vanek .15 .40
42 Nathan Gerbe .10 .25
43 Drew Stafford .15 .40
44 Steve Ott .12 .30
45 Tyler Ennis .12 .30
46 Cody Hodgson .15 .40
47 Cam Ward .15 .40
48 Justin Faulk .10 .25
49 Jeff Skinner .12 .30
50 Alexander Semin .15 .40
51 Chad LaRose .10 .25
52 Eric Staal .20 .50
53 Tuomo Ruutu .12 .30
54 Jiri Tlusty .12 .30
55 Jordan Staal .15 .40
56 Sergei Bobrovsky .15 .40
57 Jack Johnson .10 .25
58 Tim Erixon .10 .25
59 R.J. Umberger .10 .25
60 Marian Gaborik FOIL .25 .60
61 Cam Atkinson .15 .40
62 Brandon Dubinsky .12 .30
63 Mark Letestu .12 .30
64 Ryan Johansen .20 .50
65 Jimmy Howard .15 .40
66 Niklas Kronwall .12 .30
67 Kyle Quincey .10 .25
68 Henrik Zetterberg .20 .50
69 Justin Abdelkader .12 .30
70 Danny Cleary .15 .40
71 Johan Franzen .15 .40
72 Daniel Alfredsson .15 .40
73 Pavel Datsyuk FOIL .30 .75
74 Jacob Markstrom .12 .30
75 Erik Gudbranson .15 .40
76 Ed Jovanovski .10 .25
77 Dmitry Kulikov .10 .25
78 Brian Campbell FOIL .15 .40
79 Tomas Fleischmann .10 .25
80 Tomas Kopecky .12 .30
81 Kris Versteeg .12 .30
82 Peter Mueller .10 .25
83 Carey Price FOIL .75 2.00
84 Andrei Markov .15 .40
85 P.K. Subban .25 .60
86 Max Pacioretty .15 .40
87 Rene Bourque .10 .25
88 Brian Gionta .12 .30
89 David Desharnais .15 .40
90 Lars Eller .12 .30
91 Tomas Plekanec .15 .40
92 Martin Brodeur FOIL .50 1.25
93 Cory Schneider .12 .30
94 Adam Larsson .15 .40
95 Bryce Salvador .10 .25
96 Ryan Carter .10 .25
97 Patrik Elias .15 .40
98 Dainus Zubrus .10 .25
99 Adam Henrique .15 .40
100 Travis Zajac .12 .30
101 Evgeni Nabokov .12 .30
102 Travis Hamonic .10 .25
103 Lubomir Visnovsky .10 .25
104 Matt Moulson .12 .30
105 Kyle Okposo .15 .40
106 Michael Grabner .12 .30
107 John Tavares FOIL .50 1.25
108 Frans Nielsen .10 .25
109 Josh Bailey .12 .30
110 Henrik Lundqvist FOIL .30 .75
111 Marc Staal .12 .30
112 Michael Del Zotto .10 .25
113 Carl Hagelin .15 .40
114 Rick Nash .15 .40
115 Ryan Callahan .15 .40
116 Brian Boyle .10 .25
117 Derick Brassard .15 .40
118 Derek Stepan .15 .40
119 Craig Anderson FOIL .25 .60
120 Erik Karlsson .30 .75
121 Chris Phillips .10 .25
122 Milan Michalek .10 .25
123 Colin Greening .10 .25
124 Chris Neil .10 .25
125 Kyle Turris .10 .25
126 Jason Spezza .15 .40
127 Mika Zibanejad .15 .40
128 Steve Mason .12 .30
129 Braydon Coburn .10 .25
130 Kimmo Timonen .10 .25
131 Scott Hartnell .15 .40
132 Claude Giroux FOIL .25 .60
133 Matt Read .10 .25
134 Wayne Simmonds .20 .50
135 Vincent Lecavalier .12 .30
136 Sean Couturier .15 .40
137 Tomas Vokoun .12 .30
138 Marc-Andre Fleury .25 .60
139 Brooks Orpik .12 .30
140 Kris Letang .15 .40
141 Chris Kunitz .15 .40
142 James Neal .15 .40
143 Pascal Dupuis .10 .25
144 Sidney Crosby FOIL 1.00 2.50
145 Evgeni Malkin .50 1.25
146 Ben Bishop .15 .40
147 Anders Lindback .10 .25
148 Victor Hedman .20 .50
149 Ryan Malone .10 .25
150 Teddy Purcell .15 .40
151 B.J. Crombeen .10 .25
152 Martin St. Louis .15 .40

3 Steven Stamkos FOIL .50 1.25
4 Valtteri Filppula .15 .40
5 James Reimer .15 .40
6 Jonathan Bernier .15 .40
7 Dion Phaneuf .15 .40
8 Jake Gardiner .15 .40
9 James van Riemsdyk .15 .40
0 Joffrey Lupul .12 .30
1 Phil Kessel FOIL .30 .75
2 Tyler Bozak .12 .30
3 Nazem Kadri .15 .40
4 Michal Neuvirth .12 .30
5 Braden Holtby .25 .60
6 John Carlson .20 .50
7 Mike Green .15 .40
8 Karl Alzner .10 .25
9 Alex Ovechkin FOIL 1.00 2.50
0 Martin Erat .10 .25
1 Nicklas Backstrom .25 .60
2 Brooks Laich .10 .25
3 Jonas Hiller .12 .30
4 Cam Fowler .12 .30
5 Francois Beauchemin .10 .25
6 Corey Perry FOIL .25 .60
7 Teemu Selanne .30 .75
8 Nick Bonino .10 .25
9 Saku Koivu .15 .40
0 Andrew Cogliano .10 .25
1 Ryan Getzlaf .25 .60
2 Mark Giordano .12 .30
3 Dennis Wideman .10 .25
4 Curtis Glencross .10 .25
5 Sven Baertschi .12 .30
6 David Jones .10 .25
7 Lee Stempniak .10 .25
8 Michael Cammalleri FOIL .20 .50
9 Mikael Backlund .12 .30
0 Jiri Hudler .12 .30
1 Corey Crawford .20 .50
2 Duncan Keith .15 .40
3 Brent Seabrook .15 .40
4 Patrick Sharp .15 .40
5 Brandon Saad .15 .40
6 Bryan Bickell .10 .25
7 Marian Hossa .12 .30
8 Patrick Kane .30 .75
9 Jonathan Toews FOIL .50 1.25
0 Semyon Varlamov .15 .40
1 Erik Johnson .10 .25
2 Gabriel Landeskog FOIL .20 .50
3 Alex Tanguay .10 .25
4 P.A. Parenteau .10 .25
5 Milan Hejduk .12 .30
6 Paul Stastny .15 .40
7 Ryan O'Reilly .15 .40
8 Matt Duchene .15 .40
9 Richard Bachman .12 .30
0 Kari Lehtonen .12 .30
1 Alex Goligoski .10 .25
2 Brenden Dillon .12 .30
3 Erik Cole .12 .30
4 Jamie Benn FOIL .30 .75
5 Tyler Seguin .25 .60
6 Ryan Garbutt .10 .25
7 Cody Eakin .10 .25
8 Devan Dubnyk .15 .40
9 Nick Schultz .10 .25
0 Ladislav Smid .10 .25
1 Taylor Hall FOIL .50 1.25
2 Ryan Smyth .12 .30
3 Jordan Eberle .15 .40
4 Ales Hemsky .10 .25
5 Sam Gagner .12 .30
6 Ryan Nugent-Hopkins .15 .40
7 Jonathan Quick FOIL .40 1.00
8 Slava Voynov .12 .30
9 Drew Doughty .15 .40
0 Justin Williams .12 .30
1 Dustin Brown .15 .40
2 Jarret Stoll .12 .30
3 Anze Kopitar .25 .60
4 Jeff Carter .15 .40
5 Mike Richards .15 .40
6 Josh Harding .15 .40
7 Nicklas Backstrom .25 .60
8 Ryan Suter .10 .25
9 Jared Spurgeon .10 .25
0 Dany Heatley .12 .30
1 Zach Parise FOIL .25 .60
2 Jason Pominville .12 .30
3 Torrey Mitchell .10 .25
4 Mikko Koivu .12 .30
5 Pekka Rinne FOIL .30 .75
6 Chris Mason .12 .30
7 Roman Josi .15 .40
8 Shea Weber .12 .30
9 Sergei Kostitsyn .10 .25
0 Gabriel Bourque .12 .30
1 David Legwand .12 .30
2 Craig Smith .10 .25
3 Mike Fisher .12 .30
4 Mike Smith .15 .40
5 Oliver Ekman-Larsson .12 .30
6 Keith Yandle .15 .40
7 Lauri Korpikoski .10 .25
8 Mikkel Boedker .10 .25
9 Shane Doan FOIL .20 .50
0 Radim Vrbata .12 .30
1 Martin Hanzal .10 .25
2 Antoine Vermette .10 .25
3 Antti Niemi .12 .30
4 Dan Boyle .12 .30
5 Brent Burns .20 .50
6 Marc-Edouard Vlasic .10 .25
7 Patrick Marleau .15 .40
8 Logan Couture FOIL .25 .60
9 Tommy Wingels .10 .25
0 Joe Thornton .15 .40
1 Joe Pavelski .15 .40
2 Brian Elliott .12 .30
3 Jaroslav Halak .15 .40
4 Jay Bouwmeester .15 .40
5 Alex Pietrangelo FOIL .20 .50
6 David Perron .10 .25
7 Alexander Steen .15 .40
8 T.J. Oshie .25 .60
9 Chris Stewart .12 .30
0 David Backes .15 .40
1 Roberto Luongo .15 .40
2 Alexander Edler .10 .25
3 Kevin Bieksa .12 .30
4 Jason Garrison .10 .25
5 Chris Higgins .10 .25
6 Daniel Sedin FOIL .25 .60
7 Alexandre Burrows .15 .40
8 Ryan Kesler .15 .40
9 Henrik Sedin .15 .40
0 Ondrej Pavelec .15 .40

291 Dustin Byfuglien .15 .40
292 Zach Bogosian .12 .30
293 Tobias Enstrom .10 .25
294 Evander Kane .15 .40
295 Andrew Ladd .15 .40
296 Blake Wheeler .15 .40
297 Nik Antropov .12 .30
298 Bryan Little .15 .40
299 Beau Bennett .20 .50
300 Jonas Brodin .12 .30
301 Damien Brunner .12 .30
302 Alex Chiasson .15 .40
303 Cory Conacher .10 .25
304 Emerson Etem .15 .40
305 Filip Forsberg .40 1.00
306 Alex Galchenyuk .75 2.00
307 Brendan Gallagher .50 1.25
308 Mikael Granlund .25 .60
309 Mikhail Grigorenko .20 .50
310 Dougie Hamilton .30 .75
311 Thomas Hickey .12 .30
312 Jonathan Huberdeau .40 1.00
313 Alex Killorn .15 .40
314 Danny DeKeyser .20 .50
315 Scott Laughton .15 .40
316 Ryan Murphy .15 .40
317 Jean-Gabriel Pageau .12 .30
318 Justin Schultz .15 .40
319 Vladimir Tarasenko .60 1.50
320 Tyler Toffoli .30 .75
321 Tom Wilson .25 .60
322 Nail Yakupov .50 1.25
323 Alex Ovechkin TW .60 1.50
324 Sergei Bobrovsky TW .15 .40
325 P.K. Subban TW .25 .60
326 Jonathan Huberdeau TW .40 1.00
327 Martin St. Louis TW .10 .25
328 Alex Ovechkin TW .60 1.50

2013-14 Panini Stickers Team Logo Foils

A1 Boston Bruins/A2. Buffalo Sabres .30 .75
A3 Detroit Red Wings/A4. Florida Panthers .30 .75
A5 Montreal Canadiens/A6. Ottawa Senators .30 .75
A7 Tampa Bay Lightning/A8. Toronto Maple Leafs .30 .75
A9 Carolina Hurricanes/A10. Columbus Blue Jackets .30 .75
A11 New Jersey Devils/A12. NY Islanders .30 .75
A13 NY Rangers/A14. Philadelphia Flyers .30 .75
A15 Pittsburgh Penguins/A16. Washington Capitals .30 .75
A17 Anaheim Ducks/A18. Calgary Flames .30 .75
A19 Edmonton Oilers/A20. L.A Kings .30 .75
A21 Phoenix Coyotes/A22. San Jose Sharks .30 .75
A23 Vancouver Canucks/A24. Chicago Blackhawks .30 .75
A25 Colorado Avalanche/A26. Dallas Stars .30 .75
A27 Minnesota Wild/A28. Nashville Predators .30 .75
A29 St. Louis Blues/A30. Winnipeg Jets .30 .75
A31 Boston Bruins/A32. Buffalo Sabres .30 .75
A33 Carolina Hurricanes/A34. Columbus Blue Jackets .30 .75
A35 Detroit Red Wings/A36. Florida Panthers .30 .75
A37 Montreal Canadiens/A38. New Jersey Devils .30 .75
A39 NY Islanders/A40. NY Rangers .30 .75
A41 Ottawa Senators/A42. Philadelphia Flyers .30 .75
A43 Pittsburgh Penguins/A44. Tampa Bay Lightning .30 .75
A45 Toronto Maple Leafs/A46. Washington Capitals .30 .75
A47 Anaheim Ducks/A48. Calgary Flames .30 .75
A49 Chicago Blackhawks/A50. Colorado Avalanche .30 .75
A51 Dallas Stars/A52. Edmonton Oilers .30 .75
A53 L.A Kings/A54. Minnesota Wild .30 .75
A55 Nashville Predators/A56. Phoenix Coyotes .30 .75
A57 San Jose Sharks/A58. St. Louis Blues .30 .75
A59 Vancouver Canucks/A60. Winnipeg Jets .30 .75

2014-15 Panini Stickers

1 NHL Logo FOIL .30 .75
2 Panini Logo FOIL .30 .75
3 NHLPA Logo FOIL .30 .75
4 Boston Bruins Home Jersey .08 .25
5 Boston Bruins Away Jersey .08 .25
6 Patrice Bergeron FOIL .30 .75
7 Boston Bruins Team Logo .08 .25
8 Tuukka Rask FOIL .25 .60
9 Tuukka Rask .15 .40
10 Zdeno Chara .15 .40
11 Dougie Hamilton .15 .40
12 Torey Krug .15 .40
13 Patrice Bergeron .20 .50
14 David Krejci .15 .40
15 Milan Lucic .15 .40
16 Brad Marchand .20 .50
17 Reilly Smith .15 .40
18 Buffalo Sabres Home Jersey .08 .25
19 Buffalo Sabres Away Jersey .08 .25
20 Matt Moulson FOIL .20 .50
21 Buffalo Sabres Team Logo .08 .25
22 Tyler Ennis FOIL .20 .50
23 Jhonas Enroth .15 .40
24 Michal Neuvirth .12 .30
25 Tyler Myers .12 .30
26 Tyler Ennis .12 .30
27 Brian Gionta .12 .30
28 Zemgus Girgensons .15 .40
29 Cody Hodgson .15 .40
30 Matt Moulson .12 .30
31 Drew Stafford .15 .40
32 Carolina Hurricanes Home Jersey .08 .25
33 Carolina Hurricans Away Jersey .08 .25
34 Eric Staal FOIL .30 .75
35 Carolina Hurricanes Team Logo .08 .25
36 Jeff Skinner FOIL .25 .60
37 Cam Ward .15 .40
38 Justin Faulk .10 .25
39 Nathan Gerbe .10 .25
40 Elias Lindholm .15 .40
41 Alexander Semin .15 .40
42 Jeff Skinner .15 .40
43 Eric Staal .20 .50
44 Jordan Staal .15 .40
45 Jiri Tlusty .12 .30
46 Columbus Blue Jackets Home Jersey .08 .25
47 Columbus Blue Jackets Away Jersey .08 .25
48 Sergei Bobrovsky FOIL .25 .60
49 Columbus Blue Jackets Team Logo .08 .25
50 Ryan Johansen FOIL .30 .75
51 Sergei Bobrovsky .15 .40
52 Jack Johnson .10 .25
53 Ryan Murray .10 .25
54 James Wisniewski .10 .25
55 Brandon Dubinsky .12 .30
56 Nick Foligno .12 .30
57 Scott Hartnell .15 .40
58 Boone Jenner .10 .25
59 Ryan Johansen .20 .50
60 Detroit Red Wings Home Jersey .08 .25
61 Detroit Red Wings Away Jersey .08 .25
62 Pavel Datsyuk FOIL .30 .75
63 Detroit Red Wings Team Logo .08 .25
64 Henrik Zetterberg FOIL .30 .75
65 Jimmy Howard .08 .25
66 Jonas Gustavsson .12 .30
67 Danny DeKeyser .08 .25
68 Niklas Kronwall .12 .30
69 Pavel Datsyuk .20 .50
70 Johan Franzen .15 .40
71 Gustav Nyquist .12 .30
72 Tomas Tatar .12 .30
73 Henrik Zetterberg .20 .50
74 Florida Panthers Home Team .08 .25
75 Florida Panthers Away Team .08 .25
76 Brian Campbell FOIL .15 .40
77 Florida Panthers Logo .08 .25
78 Roberto Luongo FOIL .25 .60
79 Roberto Luongo .15 .40
80 Brian Campbell .10 .25
81 Erik Gudbranson .15 .40
82 Aleksander Barkov .15 .40
83 Nick Bjugstad .12 .30
84 Tomas Fleischmann .10 .25
85 Jonathan Huberdeau .15 .40
86 Jussi Jokinen .10 .25
87 Scottie Upshall .10 .25
88 Montreal Canadiens Home Jersey .08 .25
89 Montreal Canadiens Away Jersey .08 .25
90 P.K. Subban FOIL .40 1.00
91 Montreal Canadiens Team Logo .08 .25
92 Carey Price FOIL .75 2.00
93 Carey Price .50 1.25
94 Andrei Markov .15 .40
95 P K Subban .08 .25
96 David Desharnais .15 .40
97 Lars Eller .12 .30
98 Alex Galchenyuk .25 .60
99 Brendan Gallagher .15 .40
100 Max Pacioretty .15 .40
101 Tomas Plekanec .15 .40
102 New Jersey Devils Home Jersey .08 .25
103 New Jersey Devils Away Jersey .08 .25
104 Jaromir Jagr FOIL .60 1.50
105 New Jersey Devils Team Logo .08 .25
106 Cory Schneider FOIL .20 .50
107 Cory Schneider .12 .30
108 Marek Zidlicky .10 .25
109 Andy Greene .10 .25
110 Damien Brunner .10 .25
111 Mike Cammalleri .12 .30
112 Patrik Elias .15 .40
113 Adam Henrique .15 .40
114 Jaromir Jagr .40 1.00
115 Travis Zajac .12 .30
116 New York Islanders Home Jersey .08 .25
117 New York Islanders Away Jersey .08 .25
118 Kyle Okposo FOIL .25 .60
119 New York Islanders Logo .08 .25
120 John Tavares FOIL .50 1.25
121 Jaroslav Halak .12 .30
122 Travis Hamonic .10 .25
123 Thomas Hickey .10 .25
124 Josh Bailey .12 .30
125 Michael Grabner .12 .30
126 Frans Nielsen .10 .25
127 Kyle Okposo .15 .40
128 Ryan Strome .12 .30
129 John Tavares .30 .75
130 New York Rangers Home Jersey .08 .25
131 New York Rangers Away Jersey .08 .25
132 Mats Zuccarello-Aasen FOIL .25 .60
133 New York Rangers Team Logo .08 .25
134 Henrik Lundqvist FOIL .30 .75
135 Henrik Lundqvist .20 .50
136 Ryan McDonagh .15 .40
137 Marc Staal .12 .30
138 Derick Brassard .15 .40
139 Carl Hagelin .15 .40
140 Rick Nash .15 .40
141 Martin St. Louis .15 .40
142 Derek Stepan .15 .40
143 Mats Zuccarello-Aasen .15 .40
144 Ottawa Senators Home Jersey .08 .25
145 Ottawa Senators Away Jersey .08 .25
146 Bobby Ryan FOIL .25 .60
147 Ottawa Senators Team Logo .08 .25
148 Erik Karlsson FOIL .50 1.25
149 Craig Anderson .15 .40
150 Cody Ceci .10 .25
151 Erik Karlsson .30 .75
152 Alex Chiasson .12 .30
153 Clarke MacArthur .10 .25
154 Milan Michalek .10 .25
155 Bobby Ryan .15 .40
156 Kyle Turris .15 .40
157 Mika Zibanejad .15 .40
158 Philadelphia Flyers Home Team .08 .25
159 Philadelphia Flyers Away Team .08 .25
160 Wayne Simmonds FOIL .30 .75
161 Philadelphia Flyers Logo .08 .25
162 Claude Giroux FOIL .25 .60
163 Steve Mason .12 .30
164 Luke Schenn .10 .25
165 Braydon Coburn .10 .25
166 Sean Couturier .15 .40
167 Claude Giroux .15 .40
168 Vincent Lecavalier .12 .30
169 Brayden Schenn .15 .40
170 Wayne Simmonds .20 .50
171 Jakub Voracek .15 .40
172 Pittsburgh Penguins Home Jersey .08 .25
173 Pittsburgh Penguins Away Jersey .08 .25
174 Marc-Andre Fleury FOIL .40 1.00
175 Pittsburgh Penguins Logo .08 .25
176 Sidney Crosby FOIL 1.00 2.50
177 Marc-Andre Fleury .25 .60
178 Kris Letang .15 .40
179 Olli Maatta .15 .40
180 Beau Bennett .10 .25
181 Sidney Crosby .60 1.50
182 Pascal Dupuis .10 .25
183 Patric Hornqvist .12 .30
184 Chris Kunitz .15 .40
185 Evgeni Malkin .50 1.25
186 Tampa Bay Lightning Home Jersey .08 .25
187 Tampa Bay Lightning Away Jersey .08 .25
188 Ben Bishop FOIL .25 .60
189 Tampa Bay Lightning Team Logo .08 .25
190 Steven Stamkos FOIL .50 1.25
191 Ben Bishop .15 .40
192 Mathieu Carle .10 .25
193 Victor Hedman .20 .50
194 Brian Boyle .10 .25
195 Ryan Callahan .15 .40
196 Valtteri Filppula .15 .40
197 Tyler Johnson .15 .40
198 Ondrej Palat .12 .30
199 Steven Stamkos .30 .75
200 Toronto Maple Leafs Home Jersey .08 .25
201 Toronto Maple Leafs Away Jersey .08 .25
202 Phil Kessel FOIL .30 .75
203 Toronto Maple Leafs Logo .08 .25
204 James van Riemsdyk FOIL .25 .60
205 Jonathan Bernier .15 .40
206 James Reimer .15 .40
207 Jake Gardiner .15 .40
208 Dion Phaneuf .15 .40
209 David Clarkson .10 .25
210 Nazem Kadri .15 .40
211 Phil Kessel .20 .50
212 Joffrey Lupul .12 .30
213 James van Riemsdyk .15 .40
214 Washington Capitals Home Jersey .08 .25
215 Washington Capitals Away Jersey .08 .25
216 Nicklas Backstrom FOIL .40 1.00
217 Washington Capitals Team Logo .08 .25
218 Alex Ovechkin FOIL 1.00 2.50
219 Braden Holtby .25 .60
220 Karl Alzner .10 .25
221 John Carlson .20 .50
222 Mike Green .15 .40
223 Nicklas Backstrom .25 .60
224 Troy Brouwer .12 .30
225 Brooks Laich .10 .25
226 Alex Ovechkin .60 1.50
227 Joel Ward .10 .25
228 Anaheim Ducks Home Jersey .08 .25
229 Anaheim Ducks Away Jersey .08 .25
230 Corey Perry FOIL .25 .60
231 Anaheim Ducks Team Logo .08 .25
232 Ryan Getzlaf FOIL .40 1.00
233 Frederik Andersen .12 .30
234 Cam Fowler .12 .30
235 Hampus Lindholm .12 .30
236 Andrew Cogliano .10 .25
237 Ryan Getzlaf .25 .60
238 Ryan Kesler .15 .40
239 Kyle Palmieri .12 .30
240 Corey Perry .15 .40
241 Jakob Silfverberg .12 .30
242 Arizona Coyotes Home Jersey .08 .25
243 Arizona Coyotes Away Jersey .08 .25
244 Keith Yandle FOIL .25 .60
245 Arizona Coyotes Team Logo .08 .25
246 Mike Smith FOIL .25 .60
247 Mike Smith .15 .40
248 Oliver Ekman-Larsson .12 .30
249 Keith Yandle .15 .40
250 Mikkel Boedker .10 .25
251 Shane Doan .12 .30
252 Sam Gagner .12 .30
253 Martin Hanzal .10 .25
254 Lauri Korpikoski .10 .25
255 Antoine Vermette .10 .25
256 Calgary Flames Home Jersey .08 .25
257 Calgary Flames Away Jersey .08 .25
258 Jiri Hudler FOIL .20 .50
259 Calgary Flames Team Logo .08 .25
260 Mark Giordano FOIL .20 .50
261 Jonas Hiller .12 .30
262 T.J. Brodie .10 .25
263 Mark Giordano .12 .30
264 Dennis Wideman .10 .25
265 Mikael Backlund .12 .30
266 Curtis Glencross .10 .25
267 Jiri Hudler .12 .30
268 Sean Monahan .15 .40
269 Mason Raymond .12 .30
270 Chicago Blackhawks Home Jersey .08 .25
271 Chicago Blackhawks Away Jersey .08 .25
272 Jonathan Toews FOIL .50 1.25
273 Chicago Blackhawks Logo .08 .25
274 Patrick Kane FOIL .50 1.25
275 Corey Crawford .20 .50
276 Duncan Keith .15 .40
277 Brent Seabrook .15 .40
278 Marian Hossa .12 .30
279 Patrick Kane .30 .75
280 Brad Richards .15 .40
281 Patrick Sharp .15 .40
282 Andrew Shaw .15 .40
283 Jonathan Toews .30 .75
284 Colorado Avalanche Home Jersey .08 .25
285 Colorado Avalanche Away Jersey .08 .25
286 Nathan MacKinnon FOIL .50 1.25
287 Colorado Avalanche Team Logo .08 .25
288 Semyon Varlamov FOIL .25 .60
289 Semyon Varlamov .15 .40
290 Erik Johnson .10 .25
291 Tyson Barrie .15 .40
292 Matt Duchene .15 .40
293 Jarome Iginla .15 .40
294 Gabriel Landeskog .12 .30
295 Nathan MacKinnon .30 .75
296 Jamie McGinn .10 .25
297 Ryan O'Reilly .15 .40
298 Dallas Stars Home Jersey .08 .25
299 Dallas Stars Away Jersey .08 .25
300 Jamie Benn FOIL .30 .75
301 Dallas Stars Team Logo .08 .25
302 Tyler Seguin FOIL .40 1.00
303 Kari Lehtonen .12 .30
304 Brenden Dillon .10 .25
305 Alex Goligoski .10 .25
306 Jamie Benn .20 .50
307 Erik Cole .12 .30
308 Valeri Nichushkin .12 .30
309 Antoine Roussel .10 .25
310 Tyler Seguin .25 .60
311 Jason Spezza .15 .40
312 Edmonton Oilers Home Jersey .08 .25
313 Edmonton Oilers Away Jersey .08 .25
314 Jordan Eberle FOIL .25 .60
315 Edmonton Oilers Team Logo .08 .25
316 Taylor Hall FOIL .50 1.25
317 Ben Scrivens .12 .30
318 Andrew Ference .10 .25
319 Justin Schultz .12 .30
320 Jordan Eberle .15 .40
321 Taylor Hall .30 .75
322 Ryan Nugent-Hopkins .15 .40
323 David Perron .10 .25
324 Teddy Purcell .15 .40
325 Nail Yakupov .12 .30
326 Los Angeles Kings Home Jersey .08 .25
327 Los Angeles Kings Away Jersey .08 .25
328 Drew Doughty FOIL .25 .60
329 Los Angeles Kings Logo .08 .25
330 Anze Kopitar FOIL .40 1.00
331 Jonathan Quick .25 .60
332 Drew Doughty .15 .40
333 Slava Voynov .15 .40
334 Dustin Brown .12 .30
335 Jeff Carter .15 .40
336 Marian Gaborik .15 .40
337 Anze Kopitar .25 .60
338 Mike Richards .15 .40
339 Justin Williams .12 .30
340 Minnesota Wild Home Jersey .08 .25
341 Minnesota Wild Away Jersey .08 .25
342 Mikael Granlund FOIL .20 .50
343 Minnesota Wild Team Logo .08 .25
344 Zach Parise FOIL .25 .60
345 Nicklas Backstrom .25 .60
346 Josh Harding .12 .30
347 Ryan Suter .15 .40
348 Charlie Coyle .12 .30
349 Mikael Granlund .12 .30
350 Mikko Koivu .12 .30
351 Zach Parise .15 .40
352 Jason Pominville .12 .30
353 Thomas Vanek .15 .40
354 Nashville Predators Home Jersey .08 .25
355 Nashville Predators Away Jersey .08 .25
356 Pekka Rinne FOIL .30 .75
357 Nashville Predators Team Logo .08 .25
358 Shea Weber FOIL .20 .50
359 Pekka Rinne .20 .50
360 Seth Jones .12 .30
361 Roman Josi .15 .40
362 Shea Weber .12 .30
363 Mike Fisher .12 .30
364 James Neal .15 .40
365 Mike Ribeiro .12 .30
366 Craig Smith .10 .25
367 Colin Wilson .10 .25
368 San Jose Sharks Home Jersey .08 .25
369 San Jose Sharks Away Jersey .08 .25
370 Brent Burns FOIL .30 .75
371 San Jose Sharks Logo .08 .25
372 Joe Pavelski FOIL .25 .60
373 Antti Niemi .12 .30
374 Brent Burns .20 .50
375 Marc-Edouard Vlasic .10 .25
376 Logan Couture .15 .40
377 Tomas Hertl .15 .40
378 Patrick Marleau .15 .40
379 Joe Pavelski .15 .40
380 Joe Thornton .15 .40
381 Tommy Wingels .10 .25
382 St Louis Blues Home Jersey .08 .25
383 St Louis Blues Away Jersey .08 .25
384 David Backes FOIL .25 .60
385 St Louis Blues Team Logo .08 .25
386 T.J. Oshie FOIL .40 1.00
387 Brian Elliott .12 .30
388 Jay Bouwmeester .15 .40
389 Alex Pietrangelo .12 .30
390 Kevin Shattenkirk .15 .40
391 David Backes .15 .40
392 T.J. Oshie .25 .60
393 Jaden Schwartz .20 .50
394 Alexander Steen .15 .40
395 Vladimir Tarasenko .25 .60
396 Vancouver Cannucks Home Jersey .08 .25
397 Vancouver Cannucks Away Jersey .08 .25
398 Daniel Sedin FOIL .25 .60
399 Vancouver Cannucks Team Logo .08 .25
400 Henrik Sedin FOIL .25 .60
401 Ryan Miller .15 .40
402 Kevin Bieksa .12 .30
403 Alexander Edler .10 .25
404 Alexandre Burrows .15 .40
405 Jannik Hansen .12 .30
406 Chris Higgins .10 .25
407 Daniel Sedin .15 .40
408 Henrik Sedin .15 .40
409 Radim Vrbata .12 .30
410 Winnipeg Jets Home Jersey .08 .25
411 Winnipeg Jets Away Jersey .08 .25
412 Dustin Byfuglien FOIL .25 .60
413 Winnipeg Jets Team Logo .08 .25
414 Blake Wheeler FOIL .25 .60
415 Ondrej Pavelec .15 .40
416 Zach Bogosian .12 .30
417 Jacob Trouba .12 .30
418 Dustin Byfuglien .15 .40
419 Evander Kane .15 .40
420 Andrew Ladd .15 .40
421 Bryan Little .15 .40
422 Mark Scheifele .20 .50
423 Blake Wheeler .15 .40
424 Jake Allen RR .20 .50
425 John Gibson RR .20 .50
426 Johnny Gaudreau RR .50 1.25
427 Brandon Gormley RR .15 .40
428 Evgeny Kuznetsov RR .60 1.50
429 Calle Jarnkrok RR .15 .40
430 Tanner Pearson RR .10 .25
431 Nikita Zadorov RR .12 .30
432 Teuvo Teravainen RR .25 .60
433 2014 Winter Classic Logo .08 .25
434 Winter Classic Maple Leafs .08 .25
435 Winter Classic Lineup .08 .25
436 Winter Classic Jimmy Howard .08 .25
437 Winter Classic Jonathan Bernier .08 .25
438 Winter Classic Faceoff .08 .25
439 Winter Classic Goal .08 .25
440 Heritage Classic Logo .08 .25
441 Heritage Classic Ottawa Senators .08 .25
442 Heritage Classic Cannucks Lockers .08 .25
443 Heritage Classic Vancouver Cannucks .08 .25
444 Heritage Classic Save .08 .25
445 Heritage Classic 2 on 1 .08 .25
446 Heritage Classic Ottawa Wins .08 .25
447 Stadium Series Ducks vs. Kings .08 .25
448 Stadium Series Ducks Win .08 .25
449 Stadium Series Rangers vs. Devils .08 .25
450 Stadium Series Rangers Win .08 .25
451 Stadium Series Rangers vs. Islanders .08 .25
452 Stadium Series Rangers Win .08 .25
453 Stadium Series Penguins vs. Blackhawks .08 .25
454 Stadium Series Blackhawks Win .08 .25
455 Western Conference Final .08 .25
456 Western Conference First Round .08 .25
457 Western Conference Second Round .08 .25
458 Western Conference Second Round .08 .25
459 Western Conference First Round .08 .25
460 Western Conference First Round .08 .25
461 Western Conference First Round .08 .25
462 Eastern Conference Final .08 .25
463 Eastern Conference Second Round .08 .25
464 Eastern Conference Second Round .08 .25
465 Eastern Conference First Round .08 .25
466 Eastern Conference First Round .08 .25
467 Eastern Conference First Round .08 .25
468 Eastern Conference First Round .08 .25
469 Stanley Cup Finals Rangers 2; Kings 3 .08 .25
470 Stanley Cup Finals Rangers 4; Kings 5 .08 .25
471 Stanley Cup Finals Kings 3; Rangers 0 .08 .25
472 Stanley Cup Finals Kings 1; Rangers 0 .08 .25
473 Stanley Cup Finals Rangers 2; Kings 3 .08 .25
474 Stanley Cup MVP .08 .25
475 Stanley Cup Kings 1 .08 .25
476 Stanley Cup Kings 2 .08 .25
477 Art Ross Trophy .08 .25
478 Sidney Crosby Art Ross Winner .60 1.50
479 Rocket Richard Trophy .08 .25
480 Alex Ovechkin Rocket Richard Winner .60 1.50
481 Selke Trophy .08 .25
482 Patrice Bergeron Selke Trophy Winner .20 .50
483 Masterton Trophy .08 .25
484 Masterton Trophy Winner .08 .25
485 Hart Trophy .08 .25
486 Sidney Crosby Hart Trophy Winner .60 1.50
487 Vezina Trophy .08 .25
488 Tuukka Rask Vezina Winner .15 .40
489 Norris Trophy .08 .25
490 Duncan Keith Norris Trophy Winner .15 .40
491 Lady Byng Trophy .08 .25
492 Ryan O'Reilly Lady Byng Winner .15 .40
493 Calder Trophy .08 .25
494 Nathan MacKinnon Calder Winner .30 .75
495 Stanley Cup Puzzle A .08 .25
496 Stanley Cup Puzzle B .08 .25
497 Stanley Cup Puzzle C .08 .25
498 Stanley Cup Puzzle D .08 .25
499 Stanley Cup Puzzle E .08 .25
500 Stanley Cup Puzzle F .08 .25

2015-16 Panini Stickers

COMPLETE SET (516)
1 Florida Panthers Washington Capitals Shootout SH .10 .25
2 Martin Brodeur SH .30 .75
3 Andrew Hammond SH .50 1.25
4 Jaromir Jagr SH .40 1.00
5 Jamie Benn SH .20 .50
6 Johnny Gaudreau Matt Stone SH .25 .60
7 Devan Dubnyk SH .15 .40
8 Carey Price SH .50 1.25
9 Winnipeg Jets SH .10 .25
10 Bruins Jerseys .10 .25
11 Boston Bruins Logo .10 .25
12 Tuukka Rask FOIL .25 .60
13 Patrice Bergeron FOIL .30 .75
14 Zdeno Chara FOIL .25 .60
15 Tuukka Rask .15 .40
16 Zdeno Chara .15 .40
17 Torey Krug .15 .40
18 Patrice Bergeron .20 .50
19 Loui Eriksson .12 .30
20 David Krejci .12 .30
21 Brad Marchand .20 .50
22 David Pastrnak .25 .60
23 Dennis Seidenberg .12 .30
24 Sabres Jerseys .10 .25
25 Buffalo Sabres Logo .10 .25
26 Matt Moulson FOIL .20 .50
27 Tyler Ennis FOIL .20 .50
28 Zemgus Girgensons FOIL .20 .50
29 Robin Lehner .12 .30
30 Zach Bogosian .12 .30
31 Rasmus Ristolainen .12 .30
32 Tyler Ennis .12 .30
33 Marcus Foligno .10 .25
34 Brian Gionta .12 .30
35 Zemgus Girgensons .12 .30
36 Matt Moulson .12 .30
37 Ryan O'Reilly .15 .40
38 Hurricanes Jerseys .10 .25
39 Carolina Hurricanes Logo .10 .25
40 Eric Staal FOIL .30 .75
41 Justin Faulk FOIL .25 .60
42 Jeff Skinner FOIL .20 .50
43 Cam Ward .15 .40
44 Justin Faulk .15 .40
45 James Wisniewski .10 .25
46 Nathan Gerbe .10 .25
47 Elias Lindholm .10 .25
48 Victor Rask .10 .25
49 Jeff Skinner .12 .30
50 Eric Staal .20 .50
51 Jordan Staal .15 .40
52 Blue Jackets Jerseys .10 .25
53 Columbus Blue Jackets Logo .10 .25
54 Nick Foligno FOIL .20 .50
55 Jack Johnson FOIL .15 .40
56 Ryan Johansen FOIL .30 .75
57 Sergei Bobrovsky .15 .40
58 Jack Johnson .10 .25
59 David Savard .10 .25
60 Cam Atkinson .15 .40
61 Brandon Dubinsky .12 .30
62 Nick Foligno .12 .30
63 Scott Hartnell .15 .40
64 Boone Jenner .10 .25
65 Ryan Johansen .20 .50
66 Red Wings Jerseys .10 .25
67 Detroit Red Wings Logo .10 .25
68 Pavel Datsyuk FOIL .30 .75
69 Niklas Kronwall FOIL .20 .50
70 Henrik Zetterberg FOIL .30 .75
71 Jimmy Howard .15 .40
72 Petr Mrazek .20 .50
73 Danny DeKeyser .12 .30
74 Niklas Kronwall .12 .30
75 Justin Abdelkader .12 .30
76 Pavel Datsyuk .20 .50
77 Gustav Nyquist .15 .40
78 Tomas Tatar .12 .30
79 Henrik Zetterberg .20 .50
80 Panthers Jerseys .10 .25
81 Florida Panthers Logo .10 .25
82 Aaron Ekblad FOIL .25 .60
83 Jaromir Jagr FOIL .60 1.50
84 Roberto Luongo FOIL .25 .60
85 Roberto Luongo .15 .40
86 Brian Campbell .10 .25
87 Aaron Ekblad .15 .40
88 Aleksander Barkov .15 .40
89 Nick Bjugstad .12 .30
90 Jonathan Huberdeau .15 .40
91 Jaromir Jagr .40 1.00
92 Jussi Jokinen .10 .25
93 Brandon Pirri .10 .25
94 Canadiens Jerseys .10 .25
95 Montreal Canadiens Logo .10 .25
96 Carey Price FOIL .75 2.00
97 Max Pacioretty FOIL .25 .60
98 P.K. Subban FOIL .40 1.00
99 Carey Price .50 1.25
100 Andrei Markov .15 .40
101 P.K. Subban .25 .60
102 David Desharnais .12 .30
103 Lars Eller .12 .30
104 Alex Galchenyuk .20 .50
105 Brendan Gallagher .20 .50
106 Max Pacioretty .15 .40
107 Tomas Plekanec .15 .40
108 Devils Jerseys .10 .25
109 New Jersey Devils Logo .10 .25
110 Cory Schneider FOIL .20 .50
111 Mike Cammalleri FOIL .20 .50
112 Adam Henrique FOIL .25 .60
113 Cory Schneider .12 .30
114 Eric Gelinas .10 .25
115 Andy Greene .10 .25
116 Adam Larsson .15 .40
117 Jon Merrill .10 .25
118 Mike Cammalleri .12 .30
119 Patrik Elias .15 .40
120 Adam Henrique .15 .40
121 Travis Zajac .12 .30
122 Islanders Jerseys .10 .25
123 New York Islanders Logo .10 .25
124 John Tavares FOIL .50 1.25
125 Jaroslav Halak FOIL .20 .50
126 Kyle Okposo FOIL .25 .60
127 Jaroslav Halak .12 .30
128 Johnny Boychuk .10 .25
129 Travis Hamonic .10 .25
130 Nick Leddy .10 .25
131 Brock Nelson .12 .30
132 Frans Nielsen .10 .25
133 Kyle Okposo .15 .40
134 Ryan Strome .12 .30
135 John Tavares .30 .75
136 Rangers Jerseys .10 .25
137 New York Rangers Logo .10 .25
138 Henrik Lundqvist FOIL .30 .75
139 Derick Brassard FOIL .25 .60
140 Rick Nash FOIL .25 .60
141 Henrik Lundqvist .20 .50
142 Ryan McDonagh .12 .30
143 Keith Yandle .15 .40
144 Derick Brassard .15 .40
145 Chris Kreider .15 .40
146 J.T. Miller .10 .25
147 Rick Nash .15 .40
148 Derek Stepan .15 .40
149 Mats Zuccarello .12 .30
150 Senators Jerseys .10 .25
151 Ottawa Senators Logo .10 .25
152 Erik Karlsson FOIL .50 1.25
153 Mike Hoffman FOIL .20 .50
154 Mark Stone FOIL .20 .50
155 Craig Anderson .15 .40
156 Andrew Hammond .50 1.25
157 Cody Ceci .10 .25
158 Erik Karlsson .30 .75
159 Mike Hoffman .12 .30
160 Bobby Ryan .12 .30
161 Mark Stone .12 .30
162 Kyle Turris .12 .30
163 Mika Zibanejad .15 .40
164 Flyers Jerseys .10 .25
165 Philadelphia Flyers Logo .10 .25
166 Claude Giroux FOIL .25 .60
167 Steve Mason FOIL .20 .50
168 Jakub Voracek FOIL .25 .60
169 Steve Mason .12 .30
170 Luke Schenn .10 .25
171 Mark Streit .10 .25
172 Sean Couturier .15 .40
173 Claude Giroux .15 .40
174 Vincent Lecavalier .12 .30
175 Brayden Schenn .15 .40
176 Wayne Simmonds .20 .50
177 Jakub Voracek .15 .40
178 Penguins Jerseys .10 .25
179 Pittsburgh Penguins Logo .10 .25
180 Sidney Crosby FOIL 1.00 2.50
181 Marc-Andre Fleury FOIL .40 1.00
182 Evgeni Malkin FOIL .75 2.00
183 Marc-Andre Fleury .25 .60
184 Kris Letang .15 .40
185 Phil Kessel .25 .60
186 David Perron .10 .25
187 Sidney Crosby .60 1.50
188 Patric Hornqvist .12 .30
189 Chris Kunitz .15 .40
190 Evgeni Malkin .50 1.25
191 Rob Scuderi .10 .25
192 Lightning Jerseys .10 .25
193 Tampa Bay Lightning Logo .10 .25
194 Steven Stamkos FOIL .50 1.25
195 Ben Bishop FOIL .25 .60
196 Tyler Johnson FOIL .20 .50
197 Ben Bishop .15 .40
198 Victor Hedman .20 .50
199 Anton Stralman .10 .25
200 Ryan Callahan .15 .40
201 Valtteri Filppula .12 .30
202 Tyler Johnson .12 .30
203 Nikita Kucherov .25 .60
204 Ondrej Palat .12 .30
205 Steven Stamkos .30 .75
206 Maple Leafs Jerseys .10 .25
207 Toronto Maple Leafs Logo .10 .25
208 Tyler Bozak FOIL .20 .50
209 Morgan Rielly FOIL .20 .50
210 James van Riemsdyk FOIL .25 .60
211 Jonathan Bernier .15 .40
212 James Reimer .15 .40
213 Dion Phaneuf .15 .40

214 Morgan Rielly .12 .30
215 Tyler Bozak .12 .30
216 Nazem Kadri .12 .30
217 Jake Gardiner .15 .40
218 Joffrey Lupul .12 .30
219 James van Riemsdyk .15 .40
220 Capitals Jerseys .10 .25
221 Washington Capitals Logo .10 .25
222 Alex Ovechkin FOIL 1.00 2.50
223 Braden Holtby FOIL .40 1.00
224 Nicklas Backstrom FOIL .40 1.00
225 Braden Holtby .25 .60
226 Karl Alzner .10 .25
227 John Carlson .20 .50
228 Nicklas Backstrom .25 .60
229 T.J. Oshie .25 .60
230 Andre Burakovsky .12 .30
231 Marcus Johansson .12 .30
232 Evgeny Kuznetsov .25 .60
233 Alex Ovechkin .60 1.50
234 Ducks Jerseys .10 .25
235 Anaheim Ducks Logo .10 .25
236 Corey Perry FOIL .25 .60
237 Ryan Getzlaf FOIL .40 1.00
238 Ryan Kesler FOIL .25 .60
239 Frederik Andersen .12 .30
240 Cam Fowler .12 .30
241 Hampus Lindholm .12 .30
242 Sami Vatanen .10 .25
243 Ryan Getzlaf .25 .60
244 Ryan Kesler .15 .40
245 Patrick Maroon .10 .25
246 Corey Perry .15 .40
247 Jakob Silfverberg .12 .30
248 Coyotes Jerseys .10 .25
249 Arizona Coyotes Logo .10 .25
250 Oliver Ekman-Larsson FOIL .20 .50
251 Shane Doan FOIL .20 .50
252 Martin Hanzal FOIL .15 .40
253 Mike Smith .15 .40
254 Oliver Ekman-Larsson .12 .30
255 Boyd Gordon .10 .25
256 Michael Stone .10 .25
257 Mikkel Boedker .10 .25
258 Shane Doan .12 .30
259 Martin Hanzal .10 .25
260 Antoine Vermette .10 .25
261 Tobias Rieder .10 .25
262 Flames Jerseys .10 .25
263 Calgary Flames Logo .10 .25
264 Johnny Gaudreau FOIL .40 1.00
265 Jiri Hudler FOIL .20 .50
266 Sean Monahan FOIL .25 .60
267 Jonas Hiller .12 .30
268 T.J. Brodie .10 .25
269 Mark Giordano .15 .40
270 Dennis Wideman .10 .25
271 Mikael Backlund .12 .30
272 Lance Bouma .10 .25
273 Johnny Gaudreau .25 .60
274 Jiri Hudler .12 .30
275 Sean Monahan .15 .40
276 Blackhawks Jerseys .10 .25
277 Chicago Blackhawks Logo .10 .25
278 Jonathan Toews FOIL .50 1.25
279 Marian Hossa FOIL .20 .50
280 Patrick Kane FOIL .50 1.25
281 Corey Crawford .20 .50
282 Duncan Keith .15 .40
283 Brent Seabrook .15 .40
284 Marian Hossa .12 .30
285 Patrick Kane .30 .75
286 Niklas Hjalmarsson .10 .25
287 Teuvo Teravainen .15 .40
288 Andrew Shaw .15 .40
289 Jonathan Toews .30 .75
290 Avalanche Jerseys .10 .25
291 Colorado Avalanche Logo .10 .25
292 Gabriel Landeskog FOIL .25 .60
293 Semyon Varlamov FOIL .25 .60
294 Jarome Iginla FOIL .25 .60
295 Semyon Varlamov .15 .40
296 Tyson Barrie .15 .40
297 Erik Johnson .10 .25
298 Matt Duchene .15 .40
299 Jarome Iginla .15 .40
300 Gabriel Landeskog .15 .40
301 Nathan MacKinnon .30 .75
302 Carl Soderberg .12 .30
303 Alex Tanguay .10 .25
304 Stars Jerseys .10 .25
305 Dallas Stars Logo .10 .25
306 Jamie Benn FOIL .30 .75
307 John Klingberg FOIL .20 .50
308 Tyler Seguin FOIL .40 1.00
309 Antti Niemi .12 .30
310 Kari Lehtonen .12 .30
311 Alex Goligoski .10 .25
312 John Klingberg .12 .30
313 Jamie Benn .20 .50
314 Cody Eakin .10 .25
315 Patrick Sharp .15 .40
316 Tyler Seguin .25 .60
317 Jason Spezza .12 .30
318 Oilers Jerseys .10 .25
319 Edmonton Oilers Logo .10 .25
320 Jordan Eberle FOIL .25 .60
321 Ryan Nugent-Hopkins FOIL .25 .60
322 Taylor Hall FOIL .50 1.25
323 Ben Scrivens .12 .30
324 Cam Talbot .20 .50
325 Justin Schultz .12 .30
326 Jordan Eberle .15 .40
327 Taylor Hall .30 .75
328 Ryan Nugent-Hopkins .15 .40
329 Benoit Pouliot .10 .25
330 Teddy Purcell .15 .40
331 Nail Yakupov .12 .30
332 Kings Jerseys .10 .25
333 Los Angeles Kings Logo .10 .25
334 Drew Doughty FOIL .25 .60
335 Jeff Carter FOIL .25 .60
336 Anze Kopitar FOIL .40 1.00
337 Jonathan Quick .25 .60
338 Drew Doughty .15 .40
339 Jake Muzzin .10 .25
340 Dustin Brown .12 .30
341 Jeff Carter .15 .40
342 Marian Gaborik .15 .40
343 Anze Kopitar .25 .60
344 Milan Lucic .12 .30
345 Tyler Toffoli .15 .40
346 Wild Jerseys .10 .25
347 Minnesota Wild Logo .10 .25
348 Zach Parise FOIL .25 .60
349 Devan Dubnyk FOIL .25 .60
350 Ryan Suter FOIL .15 .40
351 Devan Dubnyk .15 .40
352 Jonas Brodin .12 .30
353 Matt Dumba .12 .30
354 Ryan Suter .10 .25
355 Mikael Granlund .12 .30
356 Mikko Koivu .12 .30
357 Zach Parise .15 .40
358 Jason Pominville .12 .30
359 Thomas Vanek .15 .40
360 Predators Jerseys .10 .25
361 Nashville Predators Logo .10 .25
362 Filip Forsberg FOIL .30 .75
363 Pekka Rinne FOIL .30 .75
364 Roman Josi FOIL .25 .60
365 Pekka Rinne .20 .50
366 Seth Jones .12 .30
367 Roman Josi .15 .40
368 Shea Weber .12 .30
369 Mike Fisher .12 .30
370 Filip Forsberg .20 .50
371 James Neal .15 .40
372 Craig Smith .10 .25
373 Colin Wilson .10 .25
374 Sharks Jerseys .10 .25
375 San Jose Sharks Logo .10 .25
376 Joe Pavelski FOIL .25 .60
377 Brent Burns FOIL .30 .75
378 Logan Couture FOIL .25 .60
379 Martin Jones .15 .40
380 Brent Burns .20 .50
381 Marc-Edouard Vlasic .10 .25
382 Logan Couture .15 .40
383 Tomas Hertl .15 .40
384 Patrick Marleau .15 .40
385 Joe Pavelski .15 .40
386 Joe Thornton .15 .40
387 Tommy Wingels .10 .25
388 Blues Jerseys .10 .25
389 St. Louis Blues Logo .10 .25
390 Vladimir Tarasenko FOIL .40 1.00
391 Kevin Shattenkirk FOIL .20 .50
392 Alexander Steen FOIL .25 .60
393 Jake Allen .20 .50
394 Brian Elliott .12 .30
395 Alex Pietrangelo .12 .30
396 Kevin Shattenkirk .12 .30
397 David Backes .15 .40
398 Paul Stastny .15 .40
399 Jaden Schwartz .20 .50
400 Alexander Steen .15 .40
401 Vladimir Tarasenko .25 .60
402 Canucks Jerseys .10 .25
403 Vancouver Canucks Logo .10 .25
404 Daniel Sedin FOIL .25 .60
405 Henrik Sedin FOIL .25 .60
406 Radim Vrbata FOIL .20 .50
407 Ryan Miller .15 .40
408 Jannik Hansen .10 .25
409 Alexander Edler .10 .25
410 Christopher Tanev .12 .30
411 Chris Higgins .10 .25
412 Alexandre Burrows .12 .30
413 Daniel Sedin .15 .40
414 Henrik Sedin .15 .40
415 Radim Vrbata .12 .30
416 Jets Jerseys .10 .25
417 Winnipeg Jets Logo .10 .25
418 Andrew Ladd FOIL .25 .60
419 Mark Scheifele FOIL .30 .75
420 Blake Wheeler FOIL .25 .60
421 Michael Hutchinson .15 .40
422 Ondrej Pavelec .15 .40
423 Dustin Byfuglien .15 .40
424 Tyler Myers .12 .30
425 Jacob Trouba .12 .30
426 Andrew Ladd .15 .40
427 Bryan Little .12 .30
428 Mark Scheifele .20 .50
429 Blake Wheeler .15 .40
430 Winter Classic 1 .10 .25
431 Winter Classic 2 .10 .25
432 Winter Classic 3 .10 .25
433 2015 Winter Classic Logo .10 .25
434 Winter Classic 4 .10 .25
435 Stadium Series 1 .10 .25
436 Stadium Series Kings Win .15 .40
(Logan Couture))
437 Stadium Series 3 .10 .25
438 2015 Stadium Series Logo .10 .25
439 Stadium Series 4 .10 .25
440 Jonathan Drouin AS .20 .50
441 2015-16 All Star Game Logo .10 .25
442 Patrick Kane AS .30 .75
443 Ryan Johansen AS .30 .75
444 Shea Weber AS .20 .50
445 Jonathan Toews AS .30 .75
446 Ryan Johansen AS MVP .20 .50
447 Nick Foligno AS .12 .30
448 Corey Crawford AS .20 .50
449 Aaron Ekblad AS .15 .40
450 Mark Giordano AS .15 .40
451 Patrice Bergeron AS .20 .50
452 Rick Nash AS .15 .40
453 Tyler Seguin AS .25 .60
454 Vladimir Tarasenko AS .25 .60
455 John Tavares AS .30 .75
456 Jakub Voracek AS .15 .40
457 Carey Price AS .50 1.25
458 Brent Burns AS .20 .50
459 Kevin Shattenkirk AS .12 .30
460 Zemgus Girgensons AS .12 .30
461 Claude Giroux AS .15 .40
462 Alex Ovechkin AS .60 1.50
463 Bobby Ryan AS .12 .30
464 Steven Stamkos AS .30 .75
465 Radim Vrbata AS .12 .30
466 Western Conference First Round .10 .25
467 Western Conference First Round .10 .25
468 Western Conference First Round .15 .40
469 Western Conference First Round .10 .25
470 Western Conference Second Round .10 .25
471 Western Conference Second Round .10 .25
472 Western Conference Finals .10 .25
473 Eastern Conference Finals .10 .25
474 Eastern Conference Second Round .10 .25
475 Eastern Conference Second Round .10 .25
476 Eastern Conference First Round .10 .25
477 Eastern Conference First Round .10 .25
478 Eastern Conference First Round .10 .25
479 Eastern Conference First Round .10 .25
480 Stanley Cup Finals .10 .25
Blackhawks 2; Lightning 1
481 Stanley Cup Finals .10 .25
Blackhawks 3; Lightning 4
482 Stanley Cup Finals .10 .25
Lightning 3; Blackhawks 2
483 Stanley Cup Finals .10 .25
Lightning 1; Blackhawks 2
484 Stanley Cup Finals .10 .25
Blackhawks 2; Lightning 1
485 Stanley Cup Finals .10 .25
Lightning 0; Blackhawks 2
486 Conn Smythe Trophy FOIL .10 .50
487 Duncan Keith .15 .40
Conn Smythe Winner
488 Stanley Cup FOIL .10 .50
489 Blackhawks Champions 1 .10 .40
490 Blackhawks Champions 2 .10 .40
491 Blackhawks Champs Logo 1 .10 .40
(half team and Cup logo)
492 Blackhawks Champs Logo 2 .10 .40
(half team and Cup logo)
493 Carey Price .50 1.25
Hart Trophy Winner
494 Jamie Benn .20 .50
Art Ross Trophy Winner
495 Alex Ovechkin .60 1.50
Rocket Richard Winner
496 Carey Price .50 1.25
Vezina Trophy Winner
497 Erik Karlsson .30 .75
Norris Trophy Winner
498 Patrice Bergeron .20 .50
Selke Trophy Winner
499 Aaron Ekblad .15 .40
Calder Trophy Winner
500 Jiri Hudler .12 .30
Lady Bing Trophy Winner
501 Devan Dubnyk .15 .40
Masterton Trophy Winner
502 Sam Bennett RR .20 .50
503 Kevin Fiala RR .15 .40
504 Darnell Nurse RR .15 .40
505 Matt Puempel RR .12 .30
506 Rated Rookie Logo .10 .25
507 Ty Rattie RR .12 .30
508 Griffin Reinhart RR .12 .30
509 Sam Reinhart RR .15 .40
510 Andrei Vasilevskiy RR .20 .50
511 Stanley Cup Puzzle A .10 .25
512 Stanley Cup Puzzle B .10 .25
513 Stanley Cup Puzzle C .10 .25
514 Stanley Cup Puzzle D .10 .25
515 Stanley Cup Puzzle E .10 .25
516 Stanley Cup Puzzle F .10 .25

2017-18 Panini Stickers

1 Connor McDavid .60 1.50
Hart Trophy Winner FOIL
2 Connor McDavid .60 1.50
Art Ross Trophy Winner FOIL
3 Sidney Crosby .60 1.50
Rocket Richard Trophy Winner FOIL
4 Sergei Bobrovsky .15 .40
Vezina Trophy Winner FOIL
5 Brent Burns .20 .50
Norris Trophy Winner FOIL
6 Patrice Bergeron .20 .50
Selke Trophy Winner FOIL
7 Auston Matthews .60 1.50
Calder Trophy Winner FOIL
8 Johnny Gaudreau .25 .60
Lady Byng Trophy Winner FOIL
9 Craig Anderson .12 .30
Masterton Trophy Winner
10 Boston Bruins Team Logo FOIL .10 .25
11 Zdeno Chara ILL .15 .40
12 David Pastrnak STAR .25 .60
13 Tuukka Rask STAR .15 .40
14 Brad Marchand STAR .20 .50
15 Tuukka Rask .15 .40
16 Brandon Carlo .12 .30
17 Zdeno Chara .15 .40
18 Torey Krug .15 .40
19 David Backes .12 .30
20 Patrice Bergeron .20 .50
21 David Krejci .12 .30
22 Brad Marchand .20 .50
23 David Pastrnak .25 .60
24 Buffalo Sabres Team Logo FOIL .10 .25
25 Evander Kane ILL .15 .40
26 Rasmus Ristolainen STAR .15 .40
27 Jack Eichel STAR .25 .60
28 Kyle Okposo STAR .12 .30
29 Robin Lehner .10 .25
30 Zach Bogosian .12 .30
31 Rasmus Ristolainen .15 .40
32 Jack Eichel .25 .60
33 Evander Kane .15 .40
34 Matt Moulson .10 .25
35 Kyle Okposo .12 .30
36 Ryan O'Reilly .15 .40
37 Sam Reinhart .12 .30
38 Carolina Hurricanes Team Logo FOIL .10 .25
39 Justin Faulk ILL .12 .30
40 Jeff Skinner STAR .12 .30
41 Cam Ward STAR .12 .30
42 Sebastian Aho STAR .15 .40
43 Cam Ward .12 .30
44 Justin Faulk .12 .30
45 Noah Hanifin .15 .40
46 Justin Williams .12 .30
47 Sebastian Aho .15 .40
48 Elias Lindholm .12 .30
49 Victor Rask .15 .40
50 Jeff Skinner .12 .30
51 Jordan Staal .15 .40
52 Columbus Blue Jackets .10 .25
Team Logo FOIL
53 Seth Jones ILL .12 .30
54 Zach Werenski STAR .15 .40
55 Sergei Bobrovsky STAR .15 .40
56 Cam Atkinson STAR .15 .40
57 Sergei Bobrovsky .15 .40
58 Seth Jones .12 .30
59 Zach Werenski .15 .40
60 Cam Atkinson .15 .40
61 Brandon Dubinsky .12 .30
62 Nick Foligno .12 .30
63 Boone Jenner .12 .30
64 Artemi Panarin .15 .40
65 Alexander Wennberg .12 .30
66 Detroit Red Wings Team Logo FOIL .10 .25
67 Anthony Mantha ILL .15 .40
68 Henrik Zetterberg STAR .15 .40
69 Dylan Larkin STAR .15 .40
70 Mike Green STAR .12 .30
71 Jimmy Howard .10 .25
72 Petr Mrazek .15 .40
73 Mike Green .12 .30
74 Niklas Kronwall .12 .30
75 Andreas Athanasiou .15 .40
76 Dylan Larkin .15 .40
77 Anthony Mantha .15 .40
78 Frans Nielsen .12 .30
79 Henrik Zetterberg .15 .40
80 Florida Panthers Team Logo FOIL .10 .25
81 Vincent Trocheck ILL .12 .30
82 Keith Yandle STAR .10 .25
83 Aleksander Barkov STAR .15 .40
84 Jonathan Huberdeau STAR .12 .30
85 Roberto Luongo .15 .40
86 James Reimer .15 .40
87 Aaron Ekblad .15 .40
88 Keith Yandle .10 .25
89 Aleksander Barkov .15 .40
90 Jonathan Huberdeau .12 .30
91 Radim Vrbata .10 .25
92 Nick Bjugstad .12 .30
93 Vincent Trocheck .12 .30
94 Montreal Canadiens Team Logo FOIL .10 .25
95 Max Pacioretty ILL .15 .40
96 Shea Weber STAR .12 .30
97 Alex Galchenyuk STAR .20 .50
98 Carey Price STAR .50 1.25
99 Carey Price .50 1.25
100 Andrew Shaw .12 .30
101 Jeff Petry .10 .25
102 Shea Weber .12 .30
103 Alex Galchenyuk .20 .50
104 Brendan Gallagher .15 .40
105 Max Pacioretty .15 .40
106 Tomas Plekanec .12 .30
107 Jonathan Drouin .15 .40
108 New Jersey Devils Team Logo FOIL .10 .25
109 Cory Schneider ILL .12 .30
110 Taylor Hall STAR .30 .75
111 Kyle Palmieri STAR .12 .30
112 Travis Zajac STAR .10 .25
113 Cory Schneider .12 .30
114 Andy Greene .10 .25
115 John Moore .12 .30
116 Brian Boyle .10 .25
117 Marcus Johansson .12 .30
118 Taylor Hall .30 .75
119 Adam Henrique .12 .30
120 Kyle Palmieri .12 .30
121 Travis Zajac .10 .25
122 New York Islanders Team Logo FOIL .10 .25
123 Anders Lee ILL .15 .40
124 Nick Leddy STAR .10 .25
125 John Tavares STAR .30 .75
126 Thomas Greiss STAR .12 .30
127 Thomas Greiss .12 .30
128 Johnny Boychuk .12 .30
129 Nick Leddy .10 .25
130 Jordan Eberle .15 .40
131 Josh Bailey .12 .30
132 Andrew Ladd .15 .40
133 Anders Lee .15 .40
134 Brock Nelson .12 .30
135 John Tavares .30 .75
136 New York Rangers Team Logo FOIL .10 .25
137 Henrik Lundqvist ILL .25 .60
138 Ryan McDonagh STAR .12 .30
139 Chris Kreider STAR .15 .40
140 J.T. Miller STAR .12 .30
141 Henrik Lundqvist .25 .60
142 Ryan McDonagh .12 .30
143 Brady Skjei .12 .30
144 Kevin Hayes .12 .30
145 Chris Kreider .15 .40
146 J.T. Miller .12 .30
147 Rick Nash .15 .40
148 Kevin Shattenkirk .15 .40
149 Mats Zuccarello .15 .40
150 Ottawa Senators Team Logo FOIL .10 .25
151 Erik Karlsson ILL .20 .50
152 Kyle Turris STAR .15 .40
153 Mark Stone STAR .15 .40
154 Mike Hoffman STAR .12 .30
155 Craig Anderson .12 .30
156 Erik Karlsson .20 .50
157 Jean-Gabriel Pageau .10 .25
158 Dion Phaneuf .12 .30
159 Derick Brassard .15 .40
160 Mike Hoffman .12 .30
161 Bobby Ryan .12 .30
162 Mark Stone .15 .40
163 Kyle Turris .15 .40
164 Philadelphia Flyers Team Logo FOIL .10 .25
165 Jakub Voracek ILL .15 .40
166 Shayne Gostisbehere STAR .15 .40
167 Claude Giroux STAR .15 .40
168 Wayne Simmonds STAR .20 .50
169 Brian Elliott .12 .30
170 Michal Neuvirth .12 .30
171 Shayne Gostisbehere .15 .40
172 Ivan Provorov .15 .40
173 Sean Couturier .12 .30
174 Claude Giroux .15 .40
175 Jori Lehtera .10 .25
176 Wayne Simmonds .20 .50
177 Jakub Voracek .15 .40
178 Pittsburgh Penguins Team Logo FOIL .10 .25
179 Evgeni Malkin ILL .50 1.25
180 Phil Kessel STAR .20 .50
181 Sidney Crosby STAR .60 1.50
182 Conor Sheary STAR .15 .40
183 Matt Murray .25 .60
184 Kris Letang .15 .40
185 Justin Schultz .15 .40
186 Jake Guentzel .20 .50
187 Sidney Crosby .60 1.50
188 Patric Hornqvist .12 .30
189 Phil Kessel .20 .50
190 Evgeni Malkin .50 1.25
191 Conor Sheary .15 .40
192 Tampa Bay Lightning .10 .25
Team Logo FOIL
193 Nikita Kucherov ILL .25 .60
194 Victor Hedman STAR .20 .50
195 Tyler Johnson STAR .12 .30
196 Steven Stamkos STAR .30 .75
197 Andrei Vasilevskiy .20 .50
198 Victor Hedman .20 .50
199 Anton Stralman .12 .30
200 Ryan Callahan .12 .30
201 Alex Killorn .12 .30
202 Tyler Johnson .12 .30
203 Nikita Kucherov .25 .60
204 Brayden Point .15 .40
205 Steven Stamkos .30 .75
206 Toronto Maple Leafs Team Logo FOIL .10 .25
207 Frederik Andersen ILL .12 .30
208 Auston Matthews STAR .60 1.50
209 Nazem Kadri STAR .12 .30
210 Mitch Marner STAR .25 .60
211 Frederik Andersen .12 .30
212 Jake Gardiner .12 .30
213 Morgan Rielly .15 .40
214 Tyler Bozak .12 .30
215 Nazem Kadri .12 .30
216 Mitch Marner .25 .60
217 Auston Matthews .60 1.50
218 William Nylander .25 .60
219 James van Riemsdyk .15 .40
220 Washington Capitals Team Logo FOIL .10 .25
221 Braden Holtby ILL .25 .60
222 Evgeny Kuznetsov STAR .25 .60
223 Nicklas Backstrom STAR .25 .60
224 Alex Ovechkin STAR .60 1.50
225 Braden Holtby .25 .60
226 John Carlson .20 .50
227 Matt Niskanen .12 .30
228 Nicklas Backstrom .25 .60
229 Andre Burakovsky .12 .30
230 Dmitry Orlov .12 .30
231 Evgeny Kuznetsov .25 .60
232 T.J. Oshie .25 .60
233 Alex Ovechkin .60 1.50
234 Anaheim Ducks Team Logo FOIL .10 .25
235 Ryan Kesler ILL .15 .40
236 Corey Perry STAR .15 .40
237 Rickard Rakell STAR .12 .30
238 Ryan Getzlaf STAR .15 .40
239 John Gibson .15 .40
240 Cam Fowler .12 .30
241 Hampus Lindholm .12 .30
242 Sami Vatanen .10 .25
243 Ryan Getzlaf .15 .40
244 Ryan Kesler .15 .40
245 Corey Perry .15 .40
246 Rickard Rakell .12 .30
247 Jakob Silfverberg .12 .30
248 Arizona Coyotes Team Logo FOIL .10 .25
249 Oliver Ekman-Larsson ILL .15 .40
250 Tobias Rieder STAR .10 .25
251 Alex Goligoski STAR .12 .30
252 Max Domi STAR .15 .40
253 Louis Domingue .10 .25
254 Antti Raanta .15 .40
255 Oliver Ekman-Larsson .15 .40
256 Alex Goligoski .12 .30
257 Jakob Chychrun .12 .30
258 Max Domi .15 .40
259 Christian Dvorak .12 .30
260 Derek Stepan .12 .30
261 Tobias Rieder .10 .25
262 Calgary Flames Team Logo FOIL .10 .25
263 Sean Monahan ILL .15 .40
264 Mikael Backlund STAR .10 .25
265 Mark Giordano STAR .12 .30
266 Johnny Gaudreau STAR .25 .60
267 Mike Smith .15 .40
268 TJ Brodie .12 .30
269 Mark Giordano .12 .30
270 Dougie Hamilton .12 .30
271 Mikael Backlund .10 .25
272 Troy Brouwer .12 .30
273 Johnny Gaudreau .25 .60
274 Sean Monahan .15 .40
275 Matthew Tkachuk .15 .40
276 Chicago Blackhawks Team Logo FOIL .10 .25
277 Duncan Keith ILL .15 .40
278 Jonathan Toews STAR .30 .75
279 Patrick Kane STAR .30 .75
280 Corey Crawford STAR .20 .50
281 Corey Crawford .20 .50
282 Duncan Keith .15 .40
283 Brent Seabrook .12 .30
284 Artem Anisimov .12 .30
285 Ryan Hartman .15 .40
286 Patrick Kane .30 .75
287 Brandon Saad .15 .40
288 Richard Panik .12 .30
289 Jonathan Toews .30 .75
290 Colorado Avalanche Team Logo FOIL .10 .25
291 Mikko Rantanen ILL .15 .40
292 Nathan MacKinnon STAR .30 .75
293 Gabriel Landeskog STAR .12 .30
294 Matt Duchene STAR .15 .40
295 Semyon Varlamov .15 .40
296 Jonathan Bernier .12 .30
297 Tyson Barrie .15 .40
298 Francois Beauchemin .10 .25
299 Erik Johnson .12 .30
300 Matt Duchene .15 .40
301 Gabriel Landeskog .12 .30
302 Nathan MacKinnon .30 .75
303 Mikko Rantanen .15 .40
304 Dallas Stars Team Logo FOIL .10 .25
305 John Klingberg ILL .12 .30
306 Tyler Seguin STAR .25 .60
307 Jason Spezza STAR .15 .40
308 Jamie Benn STAR .20 .50
309 Ben Bishop .15 .40
310 Kari Lehtonen .12 .30
311 Alexander Radulov .15 .40
312 John Klingberg .12 .30
313 Jamie Benn .20 .50
314 Marc Methot .10 .25
315 Antoine Roussel .12 .30
316 Tyler Seguin .25 .60
317 Jason Spezza .15 .40
318 Edmonton Oilers Team Logo FOIL .10 .25
319 Connor McDavid ILL .60 1.50
320 Leon Draisaitl STAR .25 .60
321 Oscar Klefbom STAR .12 .30
322 Cam Talbot STAR .15 .40
323 Cam Talbot .15 .40
324 Oscar Klefbom .12 .30
325 Adam Larsson .15 .40
326 Andrej Sekera .10 .25
327 Leon Draisaitl .25 .60
328 Ryan Nugent-Hopkins .15 .40
329 Milan Lucic .15 .40
330 Connor McDavid .60 1.50
331 Patrick Maroon .12 .30
332 Los Angeles Kings Team Logo FOIL .10 .25
333 Drew Doughty ILL .15 .40
334 Jeff Carter STAR .15 .40
335 Tyler Toffoli STAR .12 .30
336 Tanner Pearson STAR .12 .30
337 Jonathan Quick .25 .60
338 Drew Doughty .15 .40
339 Alec Martinez .10 .25
340 Jake Muzzin .12 .30
341 Dustin Brown .12 .30
342 Jeff Carter .15 .40
343 Anze Kopitar .25 .60
344 Tanner Pearson .12 .30
345 Tyler Toffoli .12 .30
346 Minnesota Wild Team Logo FOIL .10 .25
347 Mikael Granlund ILL .15 .40
348 Ryan Suter STAR .10 .25
349 Devan Dubnyk STAR .15 .40
350 Zach Parise STAR .15 .40
351 Devan Dubnyk .15 .40
352 Jared Spurgeon .10 .25
353 Ryan Suter .10 .25
354 Mikael Granlund .15 .40
355 Mikko Koivu .12 .30
356 Nino Niederreiter .12 .30
357 Zach Parise .15 .40
358 Eric Staal .20 .50
359 Jason Zucker .12 .30
360 Nashville Predators Team Logo FOIL .10 .25
361 Roman Josi ILL .15 .40
362 P.K. Subban STAR .15 .40
363 Viktor Arvidsson STAR .12 .30
364 Filip Forsberg STAR .20 .50
365 Pekka Rinne .20 .50
366 Ryan Ellis .12 .30
367 Roman Josi .15 .40
368 P.K. Subban .15 .40
369 Viktor Arvidsson .12 .30
370 Calle Jarnkrok .12 .30
371 Filip Forsberg .20 .50
372 Ryan Johansen .15 .40
373 Mattias Ekholm .10 .25
374 San Jose Sharks Team Logo FOIL .10 .25
375 Martin Jones ILL .15 .40
376 Brent Burns STAR .20 .50
377 Joe Pavelski STAR .15 .40
378 Logan Couture STAR .15 .40
379 Martin Jones .15 .40
380 Brent Burns .20 .50
381 Marc-Edouard Vlasic .10 .25
382 Logan Couture .15 .40
383 Tomas Hertl .15 .40
384 Melker Karlsson .10 .25
385 Joe Pavelski .15 .40
386 Joe Thornton .15 .40
387 Joel Ward .12 .30
388 St. Louis Blues Team Logo FOIL .10 .25
389 Alex Pietrangelo ILL .12 .30
390 Vladimir Tarasenko STAR .25 .60
391 Jaden Schwartz STAR .20 .50
392 Jake Allen STAR .20 .50
393 Jake Allen .20 .50
394 Jay Bouwmeester .15 .40
395 Colton Parayko .15 .40
396 Alex Pietrangelo .12 .30
397 Robby Fabbri .15 .40
398 Jaden Schwartz .20 .50
399 Paul Stastny .15 .40
400 Alexander Steen .15 .40
401 Vladimir Tarasenko .25 .60
402 Vancouver Canucks Team Logo FOIL .10 .25
403 Henrik Sedin ILL .15 .40
404 Daniel Sedin STAR .15 .40
405 Bo Horvat STAR .15 .40
406 Alexander Edler STAR .10 .25
407 Jacob Markstrom .10 .25
408 Alexander Edler .10 .25
409 Christopher Tanev .10 .25
410 Sven Baertschi .10 .25
411 Loui Eriksson .12 .30
412 Bo Horvat .15 .40
413 Daniel Sedin .15 .40
414 Henrik Sedin .15 .40
415 Brandon Sutter .12 .30
416 Vegas Golden Knights .10 .25
Team Logo FOIL
417 James Neal ILL .12 .30
418 Reilly Smith STAR .15 .40
419 Marc-Andre Fleury STAR .25 .60
420 Jonathan Marchessault STAR .15 .40
421 Marc-Andre Fleury .25 .60
422 Shea Theodore .12 .30
423 Jason Garrison .10 .25
424 Cody Eakin .12 .30
425 Oscar Lindberg .12 .30
426 Jonathan Marchessault .15 .40
427 James Neal .12 .30
428 David Perron .15 .40
429 Reilly Smith .15 .40
430 Winnipeg Jets Team Logo FOIL .10 .25
431 Jacob Trouba ILL .12 .30
432 Mark Scheifele STAR .20 .50
433 Blake Wheeler STAR .15 .40
434 Patrik Laine STAR .25 .60
435 Steve Mason .12 .30
436 Dustin Byfuglien .15 .40
437 Jacob Trouba .12 .30
438 Nikolaj Ehlers .15 .40
439 Patrik Laine .25 .60
440 Bryan Little .12 .30
441 Mathieu Perreault .12 .30
442 Mark Scheifele .20 .50
443 Blake Wheeler .15 .40
444 Centennial Classic .60 1.50
Auston Matthews
445 Centennial Classic Photo .10 .25
puzzle 1
446 Centennial Classic Photo .10 .25
puzzle 2
447 Winter Classic Photo .10 .25
puzzle 1
448 Winter Classic Photo .10 .25
puzzle 2
449 Winter Classic .25 .60
Vladimir Tarasenko
450 Stadium Series .20 .50
Jake Guentzel
451 Stadium Series Photo .10 .25
puzzle 1
452 Stadium Series Photo .10 .25
puzzle 2
453 Connor McDavid .60 1.50
Fastest Skater
'17 ASG
454 2017 NHL All-Star Game Logo .10 .25
455 Four Line Challenge Winner .10 .25
Pacific Division
456 Sidney Crosby .60 1.50
Most Accurate Shooter
457 Wayne Simmonds .20 .50
All-Star MVP
458 Shea Weber .12 .30
Hardest Shot
459 Patrik Laine .25 .60
460 P.K. Subban .15 .40
461 Tyler Seguin .25 .60
462 Vladimir Tarasenko .25 .60
463 Jonathan Toews .30 .75
464 Jeff Carter .15 .40
465 Johnny Gaudreau .25 .60
466 Bo Horvat .15 .40
467 Connor McDavid .60 1.50
468 Joe Pavelski .15 .40
469 Erik Karlsson .20 .50
470 Carey Price .50 1.25
471 Nikita Kucherov .25 .60
472 Auston Matthews .60 1.50
473 Vincent Trocheck .12 .30
474 Cam Atkinson .15 .40
475 Justin Faulk .12 .30
476 Braden Holtby .25 .60
477 Sidney Crosby .60 1.50
478 John Tavares .30 .75
479 Chicago Blackhawks vs. .10 .25
Nashville Predators
480 Minnesota Wild vs. St. Louis Blues .10 .25
481 Anaheim Ducks vs. Calgary Flames .10 .25
482 Edmonton Oilers vs. San Jose Sharks .10 .25
483 St. Louis Blues vs. .10 .25
Nashville Predators
484 Anaheim Ducks vs. Edmonton Oilers .10 .25
485 Anaheim Ducks vs. .10 .25
Nashville Predators
486 Pittsburgh Penguins vs. .10 .25
Ottawa Senators
487 Ottawa Senators vs. .10 .25
New York Rangers
488 Washington Capitals vs. .10 .25
Pittsburgh Penguins
489 Montreal Canadiens vs. .10 .25
New York Rangers
490 Ottawa Senators vs. Boston Bruins .10 .25
491 Washington Capitals vs. .10 .25
Toronto Maple Leafs
492 Pittsburgh Penguins vs. .10 .25
Columbus Blue Jackets
493 Game 1 .10 .25
494 Game 2 .10 .25
495 Game 3 .10 .25
496 Game 4 .10 .25
497 Game 5 .10 .25
498 Game 6 .10 .25
499 Conn Smythe Trophy .10 .25
500 Sidney Crosby .60 1.50
Conn Smythe Trophy Winner
501 Stanley Cup .10 .25
502 2017 Stanley Cup Champions Logo .10 .25
Left Side
503 2017 Stanley Cup Champions Logo .10 .25
Right Side
504 Pittsburgh Penguins Team Photo .10 .25
Left Side
505 Pittsburgh Penguins Team Photo .10 .25
Right Side
506 NHL 100th Anniversary Logo .10 .25
Top Left
507 NHL 100th Anniversary Logo .10 .25
Top Right
508 NHL 100th Anniversary Logo .10 .25
Bottom Left
509 NHL 100th Anniversary Logo .10 .25
Bottom Right

2011 Panini Team Colors National Convention

TC7 Jonathan Toews 1.25 3.00
TC8 Patrick Kane 1.25 3.00

2011-12 Panini Team Colors Toronto Fall Expo

1 Phil Kessel 1.50 4.00
2 Dion Phaneuf 1.25 3.00

2011-12 Panini Titanium

101-200 ROOKIE PRINT RUN 1-93
ROOKIES PRINTED ON THICK HOLOFOIL STOCK
1 Jonathan Toews .75 2.00
2 Rick Nash .40 1.00
3 Jimmy Howard .40 1.00
4 Taylor Hall .75 2.00
5 Carey Price 1.25 3.00
6 Zach Parise .40 1.00
7 Claude Giroux .40 1.00
8 Alex Ovechkin 1.50 4.00
9 Marc-Andre Fleury .60 1.50
10 Brian Elliott .30 .75
11 Phil Kessel .50 1.25
12 Henrik Sedin .40 1.00
13 Teemu Selanne .75 2.00
14 Patrick Kane .75 2.00
15 Ryan Miller .40 1.00
16 Jose Theodore .40 1.00
17 Tyler Seguin .75 2.00
18 Loui Eriksson .30 .75
19 Anze Kopitar .60 1.50
20 Cal Clutterbuck .40 1.00
21 Dustin Byfuglien .40 1.00
22 Brad Richards .40 1.00
23 Al Montoya .25 .60
24 Luke Adam .30 .75
25 Cam Ward .40 1.00
26 Shane Doan .30 .75
27 Patrick Marleau .40 1.00
28 Dion Phaneuf .40 1.00
29 Ray Emery .30 .75
30 Milan Hejduk .30 .75
31 Zdeno Chara .40 1.00
32 Miikka Kiprusoff .40 1.00
33 Jason Pominville .30 .75
34 Johan Franzen .40 1.00
35 Jordan Eberle .40 1.00
36 Mikko Koivu .30 .75
37 Marian Gaborik .50 1.25
38 Jaromir Jagr 1.00 2.50
39 Stephen Weiss .30 .75
40 Logan Couture .40 1.00
41 Jonathan Quick .60 1.50
42 Nicklas Lidstrom .40 1.00
43 Evander Kane .40 1.00
44 Daniel Sedin .40 1.00
45 Martin Brodeur .75 2.00
46 Shea Weber .30 .75
47 Kris Versteeg .30 .75
48 Joffrey Lupul .30 .75
49 Blake Wheeler .75 2.00
50 Nicklas Backstrom .60 1.50
51 Patrick Sharp .40 1.00
52 Kari Lehtonen .30 .75
53 Tim Thomas .40 1.00
54 Corey Perry .40 1.00
55 Ryan O'Reilly .40 1.00
56 Daniel Alfredsson .40 1.00
57 Kris Letang .40 1.00
58 Jonas Gustavsson .40 1.00
59 Tomas Vokoun .30 .75
60 Jarome Iginla .40 1.00
61 Jeff Skinner .40 1.00
62 Matt Duchene .40 1.00
63 Matt Moulson .30 .75
64 Vincent Lecavalier .30 .75
65 Henrik Lundqvist .50 1.25
66 Dany Heatley .30 .75
67 Henrik Zetterberg .50 1.25
68 Milan Lucic .40 1.00
69 Ondrej Pavelec .40 1.00
70 Jamie Benn .50 1.25
71 Evgeni Malkin 1.25 3.00

72 Derek Stepan .40 1.00
73 Ilya Bryzgalov .40 1.00
74 Michael Cammalleri .30 .75
75 Nikolai Khabibulin .30 .75
76 P.K. Subban .75 2.00
77 Thomas Vanek .40 1.00
78 Marian Hossa .30 .75
79 Ryan Kesler .40 1.00
80 Joe Thornton .40 1.00
81 Ryan Getzlaf .60 1.50
82 Ilya Kovalchuk .40 1.00
83 James Neal .40 1.00
84 John Tavares .75 2.00
85 Pavel Datsyuk .50 1.25
86 Patrice Bergeron .50 1.25
87 Roberto Luongo .40 1.00
88 Josh Harding .40 1.00
89 Jeff Carter .40 1.00
90 Eric Staal .50 1.25
91 Steven Stamkos .75 2.00
92 Jean-Sebastien Giguere .30 .75
93 Ales Hemsky .30 .75
94 Mike Smith .40 1.00
95 T.J. Oshie .60 1.50
96 Jason Spezza .40 1.00
97 Pekka Rinne .50 1.25
98 Rene Bourque .25 .60
99 Martin St. Louis .40 1.00
100 Sidney Crosby 1.50 4.00
101 Mika Zibanejad/93 RC 30.00 80.00
102 Ryan Nugent-Hopkins/93 RC 100.00 200.00
103 Gabriel Landeskog/92 RC 60.00 120.00
104 Cade Fairchild/82 RC 10.00 25.00
105 Tomas Vincour/81 RC 12.00 30.00
106 Dmitry Orlov/81 RC 15.00 40.00
107 Cam Talbot/81 RC 30.00 80.00
108 Brayden McNabb/81 RC 12.00 30.00
109 Corey Tropp/78 RC 12.00 30.00
110 Devante Smith-Pelly/77 RC 20.00 50.00
111 Scott Timmins/75 RC 20.00 40.00
112 Peter Holland/74 RC 12.00 30.00
113 Alexei Emelin/74 RC 12.00 30.00
114 Louis Leblanc/71 RC 20.00 50.00
115 Mike Murphy/70 RC 15.00 40.00
116 Mike Hoffman/68 RC 30.00 60.00
117 Joakim Andersson/63 RC 12.00 30.00
118 Carl Hagelin/62 RC 90.00 150.00
119 Frederic St-Denis/62 RC 12.00 30.00
120 Raphael Diaz/61 RC 12.00 30.00
121 Aaron Palushaj/60 RC 12.00 30.00
122 Roman Josi/59 RC 25.00 60.00
123 Kris Fredheim/59 RC 15.00 40.00
124 Carl Sneep/59 RC 15.00 40.00
125 David Savard/58 RC 15.00 40.00
126 Anton Lander/57 RC 15.00 40.00
127 Gabriel Bourque/57 RC 15.00 40.00
128 Teemu Hartikainen/56 RC 15.00 40.00
129 Mark Scheifele/55 RC 50.00 100.00
130 Zack Kassian/54 RC 20.00 50.00
131 Tim Erixon/53 RC 15.00 40.00
132 Roman Horak/51 RC 15.00 40.00
133 Jake Gardiner/51 RC 25.00 60.00
134 Cody Eakin/50 RC 20.00 50.00
135 Ryan Ellis/49 RC 15.00 40.00
136 Greg Nemisz/48 RC 15.00 40.00
137 Carl Klingberg/48 RC 15.00 40.00
138 Brendon Nash/47 RC 15.00 40.00
139 Yann Sauve/47 RC 30.00 60.00
140 Simon Despres/47 RC 15.00 40.00
141 Stefan Elliott/46 RC 20.00 50.00
142 Joe Vitale/46 RC 15.00 40.00
143 Patrick Wiercioch/46 RC 15.00 40.00
144 Kevin Marshall/45 RC 15.00 40.00
145 Anders Nilsson/45 RC 15.00 40.00
146 Erik Gudbranson/44 RC 20.00 50.00
147 Calvin de Haan/44 RC 15.00 40.00
148 Marc-Andre Bourdon/43 RC 15.00 40.00
149 Brandon Saad/43 RC 50.00 100.00
150 Bill Sweatt/41 RC 15.00 40.00
151 Brad Malone/42 RC 15.00 40.00
152 Stu Bickel/41 RC 15.00 40.00
153 David Ullstrom/41 RC 15.00 40.00
154 Robert Bortuzzo/41 RC 15.00 40.00
155 Allen York/41 RC 20.00 50.00
156 Matt Frattin/39 RC 20.00 50.00
157 Paul Postma/38 RC 15.00 40.00
158 Brian Strait/37 RC 20.00 50.00
159 Leland Irving/37 RC 15.00 40.00
160 Jimmy Hayes/39 RC 20.00 50.00
161 Zac Rinaldo/36 RC 15.00 40.00
162 Keith Kinkaid/35 RC 20.00 50.00
163 Harri Sateri/35 RC 40.00 80.00
164 David McIntyre/34 RC 20.00 50.00
165 Tomas Kubalik/33 RC 25.00 60.00
166 T.J. Brennan/33 RC 20.00 50.00
167 Colten Teubert/33 RC 20.00 50.00
168 Joe Colborne/32 RC 60.00 100.00
169 Eddie Lack/31 RC 20.00 50.00
170 Ben Scrivens/30 RC 40.00 80.00
171 Harry Zolnierczyk/29 RC 20.00 50.00
172 Justin Faulk/28 RC 30.00 80.00
173 Hugh Jessiman/28 RC 15.00 40.00
174 Slava Voynov/26 RC 75.00 150.00
175 Erik Gustafsson/26 RC 30.00 80.00
176 Stephane Da Costa/24 RC
177 Cameron Gaunce/24 RC
178 Matt Read/24 RC 125.00 200.00
179 Erik Condra/22 RC 40.00 80.00
180 Colton Sceviour/22 RC 20.00 50.00
181 Ben Holmstrom/22 RC 75.00 150.00
182 Andy Miele/21 RC 30.00 60.00
183 Brett Bulmer/19 RC 30.00 60.00
184 Ryan Johansen/19 RC 50.00 100.00
185 Marcus Kruger/16 RC 40.00 80.00
186 Craig Smith/15 RC 30.00 60.00
187 Blake Geoffrion/15 RC 60.00 120.00
188 Colin Greening/14 RC
189 Adam Henrique/14 RC
190 Sean Couturier/14 RC
191 Brett Connolly/14 RC
192 Gustav Nyquist/14 RC
193 Cam Atkinson/13 RC
194 Cody Hodgson/19 RC 200.00 350.00
195 Jonathon Blum/7 RC
196 David Rundblad/7 RC
197 Adam Larsson/5 RC
198 John Moore/4 RC
199 Brendan Smith/2 RC
200 Mikko Koskinen/1 RC

2011-12 Panini Titanium Spectrum Ruby

*RUBY/99: 5X TO 12X BASIC CARDS
RUBY PRINT RUN 99 SER.#'d SETS
50 Nicklas Backstrom 6.00 15.00

2011-12 Panini Titanium Spectrum

1-100 UNPRICED VET PRINT RUN 10
VETS PRINTED ON SPECTRUM GOLD CARD STOCK
101-200 ROOKIE PRINT RUN 1-100
ROOKIES PRINTED ON BASIC CARD STOCK
104 Cade Fairchild/96 6.00 15.00
105 Tomas Vincour/100 8.00 20.00
106 Dmitry Orlov/55 12.00 30.00
107 Cam Talbot/100 20.00 50.00
108 Brayden McNabb/66 10.00 25.00
109 Corey Tropp/89 8.00 20.00
110 Devante Smith-Pelly/42 15.00 40.00
111 Scott Timmins/100 8.00 20.00
112 Peter Holland/15 15.00 40.00
113 Alexei Emelin/84 8.00 20.00
114 Louis Leblanc/18 60.00 120.00
115 Mike Murphy/100 8.00 20.00
116 Mike Hoffman/100 30.00 80.00
117 Joakim Andersson/88 8.00 20.00
118 Carl Hagelin/100 12.00 30.00
119 Frederic St-Denis/100 8.00 20.00
120 Raphael Diaz/100 8.00 20.00
121 Aaron Palushaj/44 10.00 25.00
122 Roman Josi/38 15.00 40.00
123 Kris Fredheim/100 8.00 20.00
124 Carl Sneep/32 10.00 25.00
125 David Savard/94 8.00 20.00
126 Anton Lander/40 10.00 25.00
127 Gabriel Bourque/100 8.00 20.00
128 Teemu Hartikainen/100 8.00 20.00
131 Tim Erixon/23 12.00 30.00
132 Roman Horak/100 10.00 25.00
133 Jake Gardiner/17 25.00 60.00
134 Cody Eakin/85 25.00 50.00
136 Greg Nemisz/25 12.00 30.00
137 Carl Klingberg/34 10.00 25.00
138 Brendon Nash/100 8.00 20.00
139 Yann Sauve/41 10.00 25.00
140 Simon Despres/30 10.00 25.00
141 Stefan Elliott/49 10.00 25.00
142 Joe Vitale/100 8.00 20.00
143 Patrick Wiercioch/42 10.00 25.00
144 Kevin Marshall/41 15.00 40.00
145 Anders Nilsson/62 8.00 20.00
148 Marc-Andre Bourdon/67 8.00 20.00
149 Brandon Saad/43 25.00 60.00
150 Bill Sweatt/38 10.00 25.00
151 Brad Malone/100 8.00 20.00
152 Stu Bickel/100 8.00 20.00
153 David Ullstrom/100 8.00 20.00
154 Robert Bortuzzo/78 8.00 20.00
155 Allen York/100 10.00 25.00
156 Matt Frattin/99 8.00 20.00
157 Paul Postma/100 8.00 20.00
158 Brian Strait/65 10.00 25.00
159 Leland Irving/26 12.00 30.00
160 Jimmy Hayes/60 10.00 25.00
161 Zac Rinaldo/100 8.00 20.00
162 Keith Kinkaid/100 8.00 20.00
163 Harri Sateri/100 10.00 25.00
164 David McIntyre/100 8.00 20.00
165 Tomas Kubalik/100 8.00 20.00
166 T.J. Brennan/31 10.00 25.00
168 Joe Colborne/16 15.00 40.00
169 Eddie Lack/100 8.00 20.00
170 Ben Scrivens/100 12.00 30.00
171 Harry Zolnierczyk/100 8.00 20.00
172 Justin Faulk/37 15.00 40.00
174 Slava Voynov/32 10.00 25.00
175 Erik Gustafsson/100 10.00 25.00
176 Stephane Da Costa/100 8.00 20.00
177 Cameron Gaunce/50 8.00 20.00
178 Matt Read/100 15.00 40.00
179 Erik Condra/100 8.00 20.00
180 Colton Sceviour/100 8.00 20.00
181 Ben Holmstrom/100 8.00 20.00
182 Andy Miele/100 8.00 20.00
183 Brett Bulmer/39 10.00 25.00
185 Marcus Kruger/100 12.00 30.00
186 Craig Smith/98 10.00 25.00
187 Blake Geoffrion/56 10.00 25.00
188 Colin Greening/100 8.00 20.00
189 Adam Henrique/82 20.00 50.00
192 Gustav Nyquist/100 20.00 50.00
193 Cam Atkinson/100 20.00 50.00
195 Jonathon Blum/23 12.00 30.00
196 David Rundblad/17 15.00 40.00
198 John Moore/21 12.00 30.00
199 Brendan Smith/27 40.00 80.00
200 Mikko Koskinen/31 12.00 30.00

2011-12 Panini Titanium Draft Day Autographs

STATED PRINT RUN 8-99
1 Ryan Nugent-Hopkins/25 75.00 150.00
2 Gabriel Landeskog/25 20.00 50.00
3 Adam Larsson/99 12.00 30.00
4 Mika Zibanejad/99 12.00 30.00
5 Mark Scheifele/99 15.00 40.00
6 Sean Couturier/99 12.00 30.00
7 Brandon Saad/99 12.00 30.00
8 Taylor Hall/25 25.00 60.00
9 Tyler Seguin/25 60.00 120.00
10 Erik Gudbranson/99 8.00 20.00
11 Ryan Johansen/99 12.00 30.00
12 Brett Connolly/99 6.00 15.00
13 Ian Cole/8
14 Alexander Burmistrov/99 8.00 20.00
15 Justin Faulk/99 10.00 25.00
16 Brett Bulmer/99 6.00 15.00
17 Devante Smith-Pelly/99 10.00 25.00
18 John Tavares/25 40.00 80.00
19 Victor Hedman/99 8.00 20.00
20 Matt Duchene/99 10.00 25.00
21 Evander Kane/99 10.00 25.00
22 Brayden Schenn/99 10.00 25.00
23 Oliver Ekman-Larsson/99 10.00 25.00
24 Nazem Kadri/99 15.00 40.00
25 Magnus Paajarvi/25 12.00 30.00
26 Calvin de Haan/99 8.00 20.00
27 Zack Kassian/99 8.00 20.00
28 Peter Holland/99 6.00 15.00
29 David Rundblad/99 8.00 20.00
30 Louis Leblanc/99 12.00 30.00
31 John Moore/99 6.00 15.00
32 Tim Erixon/99 6.00 15.00
33 Jordan Caron/99 10.00 25.00
34 Simon Despres/99 15.00 40.00
35 Steven Stamkos/25 30.00 80.00
36 Drew Doughty/25 25.00 50.00
37 Alex Pietrangelo/99 12.00 30.00
38 Luke Schenn/99 10.00 25.00
39 Cody Hodgson/25 40.00 80.00
40 Tyler Myers/99 10.00 25.00
41 Colten Teubert/99 6.00 15.00
42 Joe Colborne/99 6.00 15.00
43 Jake Gardiner/99 10.00 25.00
44 Jordan Eberle/25 40.00 80.00
45 Mattias Tedenby/99 6.00 15.00
46 Greg Nemisz/99 6.00 15.00
47 Tyler Ennis/99 8.00 20.00
48 Thomas McCollum/99 10.00 25.00
50 James van Riemsdyk/99 10.00 25.00

2011-12 Panini Titanium Four Star Memorabilia

STATED PRINT RUN 25-75
*PRIME/25: .6X TO 1.5X BASIC JSY/75
1 Prry/Selan/Gtzlf/Fowlr/25 15.00 40.00
2 Lndqvst/Rchrds/Gbrk/Staal 10.00 25.00
3 Miller/Pminvlle/Adam/Vanek 8.00 20.00
4 Koptr/Rchrds/Dghty/Cliffrd 15.00 40.00
5 Datsk/Zetter/Hwrd/Hlmstrm 10.00 25.00
6 Brvsky/Prngr/Brre/vanRiems 8.00 20.00
7 Mrchnd/Thoms/Char/Lucic 12.00 30.00
8 Malkn/Fleury/Kendy/Letng 25.00 60.00
9 Reimr/Kessl/Phanf/Grbvsk 10.00 25.00
10 Ovchk/Nvirth/Semn/Jhasn 30.00 80.00
11 Toews/Sharp/Seabrk/Hoss 15.00 40.00
12 RNH/Ebrle/Khabi/Hmsky 15.00 40.00
13 Karlsn/Alfrdsn/Spezz/Folg 10.00 25.00
14 Iginla/Glncrs/Grdno/Bwmster 8.00 20.00
15 Dorsett/Prust/Neil/Ott 6.00 15.00
16 Parise/Pavlski/Kslr/Callhn 10.00 25.00
17 Kiprsff/Rinne/Bckstrm/Rask 10.00 25.00
20 RNH/Lndskg/Larsn/Ziban 15.00 40.00

2011-12 Panini Titanium Game Worn Gear

*PATCH/15-25: 1X TO 2.5X BASIC JSY
1 Vincent Lecavalier 3.00 8.00
2 Tyler Myers 4.00 10.00
3 Tyler Kennedy 2.50 6.00
4 Tuukka Rask 4.00 10.00
5 Trevor Daley 2.50 6.00
6 Tobias Enstrom 2.50 6.00
7 Tim Thomas 4.00 10.00
8 Thomas Vanek 4.00 10.00
9 Teemu Selanne 8.00 20.00
10 T.J. Galiardi 3.00 8.00
11 Steve Ott 3.00 8.00
12 Sidney Crosby 15.00 40.00
13 Shea Weber 3.00 8.00
14 Shawn Horcoff 2.50 6.00
15 Shane Doan 3.00 8.00
16 Sergei Bobrovsky 5.00 12.00
17 Sean Avery 4.00 10.00
18 Scott Gomez 3.00 8.00
19 Sam Gagner 3.00 8.00
20 Ryane Clowe 4.00 10.00
21 Ryan O'Reilly 4.00 10.00
22 Calvin de Haan 3.00 8.00
23 Ryan Miller 4.00 10.00
24 Ryan Kesler 4.00 10.00
25 Ryan Getzlaf 6.00 15.00
26 Rick Nash 4.00 10.00
27 Philip Larsen 2.50 6.00
28 Phil Kessel 5.00 12.00
29 Peter Regin 2.50 6.00
30 Pekka Rinne 5.00 12.00
31 Pavel Datsyuk 5.00 12.00
32 Paul Stastny 4.00 10.00
33 Paul Gaustad 2.50 6.00
34 Patrik Elias 4.00 10.00
35 Patrick Sharp 4.00 10.00
36 Patrick Kane 8.00 20.00
37 Patrice Bergeron 5.00 12.00
38 Nikolai Kulemin 4.00 10.00
39 Niklas Backstrom 4.00 10.00
40 Nicklas Backstrom 6.00 15.00
41 Nick Spaling 2.50 6.00
42 Nick Bonino 2.50 6.00
43 Nathan Horton 4.00 10.00
44 Milan Michalek 2.50 6.00
45 Milan Hejduk 3.00 8.00
46 Mikko Koivu 3.00 8.00
47 Mike Richards 4.00 10.00
48 Mike Green 4.00 10.00
49 Matt Duchene 4.00 10.00
50 Mats Zuccarello 4.00 10.00
51 Mark Giordano 3.00 8.00
52 Marian Gaborik 5.00 12.00
53 Marc-Andre Fleury 5.00 12.00
54 Loui Eriksson 3.00 8.00
56 Lars Eller 3.00 8.00
57 Kyle Okposo 4.00 10.00
58 Kris Letang SP 10.00 25.00
59 Keith Yandle 4.00 10.00
60 Kari Lehtonen 3.00 8.00
61 Jordan Staal 4.00 10.00
62 Jordan Eberle 5.00 12.00
63 Jonathan Toews SP 40.00 80.00
64 Jonathan Quick 5.00 12.00
65 Jonathan Bernier 4.00 10.00
66 Jonas Hiller 3.00 8.00
67 Jonas Gustavsson 4.00 10.00
68 Johan Franzen 4.00 10.00
69 Joe Thornton 4.00 10.00
70 Joe Pavelski 4.00 10.00
71 Jody Shelley 3.00 8.00
72 Jimmy Howard 4.00 10.00
73 Jason Spezza 4.00 10.00
74 Jamie Benn 5.00 12.00
75 James van Riemsdyk 4.00 10.00
76 James Neal 4.00 10.00
77 Henrik Lundqvist 5.00 12.00
78 Evgeni Malkin 12.00 30.00
79 Derek Stepan 4.00 10.00
80 Danny Briere 5.00 12.00
81 Corey Perry 4.00 10.00
82 Carey Price 12.00 30.00
83 Brent Seabrook 4.00 10.00
84 Brenden Morrow 3.00 8.00
85 Brad Richards 4.00 10.00
86 Brad Marchand 5.00 12.00
87 Anze Kopitar 6.00 15.00
88 Alex Ovechkin 15.00 40.00
89 Alexander Semin 4.00 10.00
90 Ales Hemsky 3.00 8.00
91 Alex Pietrangelo 3.00 8.00
92 Andrew Ladd 5.00 12.00
93 Brandon Dubinsky 3.00 8.00
94 Craig Anderson 4.00 10.00
95 David Backes 4.00 10.00
96 Jay Bouwmeester 4.00 10.00
97 Jeff Deslauriers 2.50 6.00
98 Joe Mullen 3.00 8.00
99 Nick Palmieri 3.00 8.00
100 Ryan McDonagh 4.00 10.00

2011-12 Panini Titanium Game Worn Gear Prime

*PRIME/50: .6X TO 1.5X BASIC INSERTS
*PRIME/25: .8X TO 2X BASIC INSERTS
30 Pekka Rinne/50 8.00 20.00
63 Jonathan Toews/50 12.00 30.00

2011-12 Panini Titanium Game Worn Gear Autographs

AUTO STATED PRINT RUN 10-100
*PRIME/50: .6X TO 1.5X JSY AU/75-100
*PRIME/50: .5X TO 1.2X JSY AU/50
*PRIME/50: .4X TO 1X JSY AU/25
*PRIME/25: .8X TO 2X JSY AU/75-100
*PRIME/20-25: .6X TO 1.5X JSY AU/35-51
*PRIME/20-25: .5X TO 1.2X JSY AU/25
1 Vincent Lecavalier/50 8.00 20.00
4 Tuukka Rask/100 8.00 20.00
7 Tim Thomas/25 15.00 40.00
8 Thomas Vanek/50 10.00 25.00
12 Sidney Crosby/10
13 Shea Weber/100 8.00 20.00
16 Sergei Bobrovsky/85 8.00 20.00
18 Scott Gomez/100 6.00 15.00
19 Sam Gagner/100 8.00 20.00
21 Ryan O'Reilly/50 10.00 25.00
22 Calvin de Haan/100 6.00 15.00
23 Ryan Miller/50 10.00 25.00
24 Ryan Kesler/50 12.00 30.00
27 Philip Larsen/100 5.00 12.00
28 Phil Kessel/75 10.00 25.00
30 Pekka Rinne/25 15.00 40.00
31 Pavel Datsyuk/100 10.00 25.00
34 Patrik Elias/25 12.00 30.00
38 Nikolai Kulemin/100 8.00 20.00
39 Niklas Backstrom/25 10.00 25.00
43 Nathan Horton/50 10.00 25.00
49 Matt Duchene/25 12.00 30.00
50 Mats Zuccarello/100 8.00 20.00
51 Mark Giordano/100 6.00 15.00
52 Marian Gaborik/25 15.00 40.00
54 Loui Eriksson/49 8.00 20.00
56 Lars Eller/100 6.00 15.00
57 Kyle Okposo/75 8.00 20.00
58 Kris Letang/50 12.00 30.00
61 Jordan Staal/100 6.00 15.00
62 Jordan Eberle/75 8.00 20.00
65 Jonathan Bernier/100 6.00 15.00
66 Jonas Hiller/75 6.00 15.00
67 Jonas Gustavsson/75 8.00 20.00
71 Jody Shelley/50 12.00 30.00
72 Jimmy Howard/100 12.00 30.00
74 Jamie Benn/25 15.00 40.00
75 James van Riemsdyk/100 8.00 20.00
76 James Neal/50 10.00 25.00
77 Henrik Lundqvist/25 15.00 40.00
79 Derek Stepan/25 12.00 30.00
80 Danny Briere/50 10.00 25.00
81 Corey Perry/50 10.00 25.00
82 Carey Price/50 30.00 80.00
84 Brenden Morrow/75 5.00 12.00
86 Brad Marchand/75 10.00 25.00
88 Alex Ovechkin/25 30.00 80.00
90 Ales Hemsky/100 6.00 15.00
91 Alex Pietrangelo/100 6.00 15.00
92 Andrew Ladd/32 10.00 25.00
93 Brandon Dubinsky/100 6.00 15.00
94 Craig Anderson/51 10.00 25.00
95 David Backes/42 10.00 25.00
96 Jay Bouwmeester/35 8.00 20.00
97 Jeff Deslauriers/100 5.00 12.00
98 Joe Mullen/100 6.00 15.00
99 Nick Palmieri/100 6.00 15.00
100 Ryan McDonagh/100 8.00 20.00

2011-12 Panini Titanium Game Worn Gear Autographs Patch

*PATCH AU/15: 1X TO 2.5X JSY AU/75-100
*PATCH AU/15: .8X TO 2X JSY AU/35-51
*PATCH AU/15: .6X TO 1.5X JSY AU/25
PATCH AU PRINT RUN 5-15
69 Joe Thornton/15 30.00 60.00
78 Evgeni Malkin/15 40.00 80.00

2011-12 Panini Titanium Game Worn Gear Dual Memorabilia

STATED PRINT RUN 50-300
*PATCH/15: 1X TO 2.5X BASIC DUAL
*PATCH/15: .8X TO 2X DUAL/50
*PRIME/37-50: .8X TO 2X DUAL/100-300
*PRIME/25: 1X TO 2.5X DUAL/100-300
*PRIME/25: .8X TO 2X DUAL/50
1 B.Ryan/C.Fowler/300 5.00 12.00
2 T.Selanne/S.Koivu/50 10.00 25.00
3 M.Lucic/S.Thornton/150 5.00 12.00
4 L.Adam/P.Kaleta/300 4.00 10.00
5 D.Stafford/T.Vanek/300 5.00 12.00
6 M.Kiprusoff/J.Bouwmeester/300 5.00 12.00
7 D.Keith/B.Seabrook/50 6.00 15.00
8 E.Johnson/B.Yip/300 3.00 8.00
9 D.Brassard/D.Dorsett/300 5.00 12.00
10 B.Holtby/M.Neuvirth/300 10.00 25.00
11 R.Malone/B.Connolly/300 4.00 10.00
12 B.Prust/B.Boyle/300 3.00 8.00
13 E.Karlsson/N.Foligno/300 10.00 25.00
14 T.Wandell/P.Larsen/300 3.00 8.00
15 R.O'Reilly/B.Yip/300 5.00 12.00
16 M.Grabovski/N.Kulemin/300 5.00 12.00
17 I.Kovalchuk/T.Zajac/300 5.00 12.00
18 J.Staal/T.Kennedy/300 6.00 15.00
19 B.Laich/M.Knuble/300 3.00 8.00
20 A.Burrows/K.Bieksa/300 5.00 12.00
21 V.Lecavalier/D.Tyrell/300 4.00 10.00
22 P.Marleau/T.Mitchell/300 5.00 12.00
23 M.Boedker/K.Yandle/300 5.00 12.00
24 D.Briere/K.Timonen/300 3.00 8.00
25 D.Doughty/J.Johnson/300 5.00 12.00
26 H.Lundqvist/C.Crawford 8.00 20.00
27 R.Miller/J.Quick/300 6.00 15.00
28 M.Brodeur/J.Reimer/300 10.00 25.00
29 M.Kiprusoff/T.Rask/300 5.00 12.00
30 N.Khabibulin/S.Varlamov/300 5.00 12.00
31 C.Neil/D.Dorsett/300 3.00 8.00
32 Z.Chara/T.Myers/300 5.00 12.00
33 G.Parros/C.Perry/300 5.00 12.00
34 P.Sharp/M.Hossa/100 5.00 12.00
35 G.Landeskog/P.Mueller/300 4.00 10.00
36 T.Enstrom/A.Kulda/300 5.00 12.00
37 B.Hull/B.Smith/300 6.00 15.00
38 J.Pominville/J.Leopold/300 4.00 10.00
39 J.Nieuwendyk/J.Hedberg/300 4.00 10.00
40 S.Varlamov/M.Neuvirth/300 6.00 15.00
41 D.Krejci/P.Bergeron/300 6.00 15.00
42 J.Thornton/M.Vlasic/300 5.00 12.00
43 D.Kulikov/E.Gudbranson/300 4.00 10.00
44 J.Blum/C.Wilson/300 4.00 10.00
45 B.Wheeler/B.Little/300 10.00 25.00
46 J.Eberle/R.Whitney/100 6.00 15.00
47 L.Eller/J.Gorges/300 4.00 10.00
48 G.Campbell/M.Bartkowski/300 3.00 8.00
49 K.Lehtonen/E.Belfour/300 5.00 12.00
50 C.de Haan/T.Hamonic/300 4.00 10.00

2011-12 Panini Titanium Game Worn Gear Dual Memorabilia Prime

11 R.Malone/B.Connolly/50 8.00 20.00

2011-12 Panini Titanium Hat Tricks Memorabilia

STATED PRINT RUN 199 SER.#'d SETS
*PATCH/15: .6X TO 2X BASIC JSY/199
*PRIME/15-25: .6X TO 1.5X BASIC JSY/199
1 Gaborik/Anisimov/Avery 8.00 20.00
2 Kopitar/Johnson/Brown 10.00 25.00
3 Burmistrov/Enstrom/Bogosian 8.00 20.00
4 Vokoun/Green/Backstrom 10.00 25.00
5 Sedin/Raymond/Hansen 6.00 15.00
6 Kiprusoff/Nemisz/Karlsson 6.00 15.00
7 Duchene/Yip/Galiardi 6.00 15.00
8 Johansen/Dorsett/Brassard 6.00 15.00
9 Koivu/Backstrom/Clttrbck 6.00 15.00
10 Cammalleri/Gorges/Gomez 5.00 12.00
11 Weber/Suter/Fisher 6.00 15.00
12 Lindros/Brodeur/Jagr 15.00 40.00
13 Price/Lundqvist/Thomas 20.00 50.00
14 Hull/Modano/Belfour 10.00 25.00
15 de Haan/DiPietro/Okposo 6.00 15.00
16 Daugavins/Spezza/Alfredsson 6.00 15.00
17 Pronger/Hartnell/van Riems 6.00 15.00
18 Stamkos/Tyrell/Connolly 8.00 20.00
19 Staal/Despres/Neal 6.00 15.00
20 Richards/Dubinsky/Staal 6.00 15.00
21 Shanahan/Howard/Datsyuk 15.00 40.00
22 Henrique/Kruger/Palushaj 6.00 15.00
23 Joseph/Fuhr/Giguere 10.00 25.00
24 Neely/Middleton/Vachon 10.00 25.00
25 Boychuk/McBain/Faulk 8.00 20.00
26 Lehtonen/Eriksson/Wandell 5.00 12.00
27 Messier/Del Zotto/Erixon 8.00 20.00
28 Kessel/Schenn/Orr 8.00 20.00
29 Yzerman/Zetterbrg/Lidstrm 10.00 25.00
30 Nugnt-Hop/de Hn/Johnsn 10.00 25.00

2011-12 Panini Titanium Hat Tricks Memorabilia Prime

4 Vokoun/Green/Backstrom 15.00 40.00
18 Stamkos/Tyrell/Connolly 12.00 30.00

2011-12 Panini Titanium Hat Tricks Memorabilia Patch

4 Vokoun/Green/Backstrom 20.00 50.00

2011-12 Panini Titanium Home Sweaters Memorabilia Autographs

STATED PRINT RUN 40-100
*PRIME/25: .6X TO 1.5X BASIC JSY AU
1 Bobby Ryan/100 10.00 25.00
2 Brad Marchand/100 20.00 50.00
3 Nathan Gerbe/100 6.00 15.00
4 Henrik Karlsson/78 8.00 20.00
5 Jamie McBain/100 6.00 15.00
6 Denis Savard/100 15.00 40.00
7 Erik Johnson/100 6.00 15.00
9 John Moore/100 8.00 20.00
10 Ryan Johansen/100 10.00 25.00
11 Philip Larsen/100 8.00 20.00
12 Luc Robitaille/100 15.00 40.00
13 Pavel Datsyuk/100 15.00 40.00
14 Adam Graves/100 10.00 25.00
15 Nikolai Khabibulin/100 10.00 25.00
16 Grant Fuhr/100 12.00 30.00
17 Ryan Ellis/100 10.00 25.00
18 Adam Larsson/100 10.00 25.00
19 Travis Zajac/75 10.00 25.00
20 Calvin de Haan/100 10.00 25.00
21 Henrik Lundqvist/100 20.00 40.00
22 David Rundblad/100 8.00 20.00
23 Mika Zibanejad/100 20.00 50.00
24 Jakub Voracek/40 12.00 30.00
25 Vincent Lecavalier/100 10.00 25.00
26 Michal Neuvirth/100 10.00 25.00
28 Cody Hodgson/100 15.00 40.00
29 Gabriel Landeskog/100 15.00 40.00
30 Ryan Nugent-Hopkins/100 30.00 80.00

2011-12 Panini Titanium Marks of Honour Autographs

STATED PRINT RUN 2-25
3 Stan Mikita/25 15.00 40.00
4 Scott Niedermayer/25 12.00 30.00
5 Ron Francis/25 15.00 40.00
6 Phil Esposito/25 20.00 40.00
7 Peter Stastny/25 12.00 30.00
9 Pat LaFontaine/25 15.00 40.00
10 Mike Bossy/25 12.00 30.00
11 Markus Naslund/25
15 Joe Sakic/25 30.00 60.00
16 Jean Beliveau/25 25.00 50.00
18 Felix Potvin/25 25.00 50.00
20 Curtis Joseph/25 15.00 40.00

2011-12 Panini Titanium New Wave Autographs

1 Drayson Bowman 4.00 10.00
2 Adam Henrique 10.00 25.00
3 Adam McQuaid 4.00 10.00
4 Craig Smith 6.00 15.00
5 Cody Eakin 5.00 12.00
6 Alex Urbom 4.00 10.00
7 Ben Scrivens 6.00 15.00
8 Blake Geoffrion 4.00 10.00
9 Louis Leblanc 4.00 10.00
10 Anders Lindback 5.00 12.00
11 Brandon Yip 4.00 10.00
12 Raphael Diaz 4.00 10.00
13 Slava Voynov 4.00 10.00
14 Zack Kassian 5.00 12.00
15 Carl Gunnarsson 4.00 10.00
16 Chris Vande Velde 5.00 12.00
17 Dale Weise 5.00 12.00
18 Dwight King 4.00 10.00
19 Adam Larsson SP 8.00 20.00
20 Justin Faulk 6.00 15.00
21 Mark Scheifele 10.00 25.00
22 Jared Cowen 5.00 12.00
23 Ryan Nugent-Hopkins 60.00 120.00
24 Gabriel Landeskog SP 20.00 50.00
25 Jay Rosehill 4.00 10.00
26 Taylor Hall 10.00 25.00
27 Timo Pielmeier 5.00 12.00
28 Travis Hamonic 5.00 12.00
29 Aaron Palushaj 4.00 10.00
30 Joe Vitale 4.00 10.00
31 Nick Bonino 4.00 10.00
32 David Rundblad 4.00 10.00
33 Robert Bortuzzo 4.00 10.00
34 Joe Colborne 4.00 10.00
35 Justin DiBenedetto 4.00 10.00
36 Justin Falk 4.00 10.00
37 Ryan McDonagh 5.00 12.00
38 Viktor Stalberg 4.00 10.00
39 J.P. Anderson 5.00 12.00
40 Tyler Seguin SP 40.00 80.00
41 Cody Hodgson 8.00 20.00
42 Brendon Nash 4.00 10.00
43 Calvin de Haan 4.00 10.00
44 Jonas Gustavsson 5.00 12.00
45 John McCarthy 4.00 10.00
46 Brad Marchand SP 15.00 30.00
47 Cameron Gaunce 3.00 8.00
48 Brandon Saad 12.00 30.00
49 Jonathon Blum 4.00 10.00
50 Cory Emmerton 5.00 12.00

2011-12 Panini Titanium Quad Memorabilia

STATED PRINT RUN 10-25
1 Ryan Callahan/25 15.00 40.00
2 Milan Michalek/15 10.00 25.00
3 Milan Lucic/25 15.00 40.00
4 Ilya Kovalchuk/25 15.00 40.00
5 Shea Weber/25 12.00 30.00
6 Derek Roy/25 12.00 30.00
7 David Legwand/25 12.00 30.00
8 Shawn Horcoff/25 10.00 25.00
9 Ryan O'Reilly/25 15.00 40.00
10 Tim Thomas/25 15.00 40.00
11 Henrik Zetterberg/25 20.00 50.00
12 Dmitry Kulikov/25 10.00 25.00
13 John Carlson/25 20.00 50.00
14 Michael Cammalleri/25 12.00 30.00
15 Johan Franzen/25 15.00 40.00
16 Erik Johnson/25 10.00 25.00
17 Miikka Kiprusoff/25 15.00 40.00
18 Tyler Myers/25 15.00 40.00
19 Zdeno Chara/25 15.00 40.00
20 Kris Letang/25 15.00 40.00
21 Joe Pavelski/25 15.00 40.00
24 Phil Kessel/25 20.00 50.00
25 Ryan Kesler/25 15.00 40.00
26 Michal Neuvirth/25 12.00 30.00
27 Teemu Selanne/10
28 Cam Ward/10
29 Nicklas Lidstrom/25 15.00 40.00
30 Mike Richards/25 15.00 40.00
31 Brad Richards/25 15.00 40.00
32 Tuukka Rask/25 15.00 40.00
33 Jason Pominville/25 12.00 30.00
34 T.J. Galiardi/25 12.00 30.00
35 Jamie Benn/25 20.00 50.00
36 Kyle Okposo/25 15.00 40.00
37 Adam Larsson/25 15.00 40.00
38 Jason Spezza/25 15.00 40.00
39 Chris Pronger/25 12.00 30.00
40 Shane Doan/25 12.00 30.00
41 Patrick Marleau/25 15.00 40.00
42 Ryan Malone/25 10.00 25.00
43 Luke Adam/10
44 Daniel Alfredsson/25 15.00 40.00
45 James van Riemsdyk/25 15.00 40.00
46 Drew Doughty/25 15.00 40.00
47 Nicklas Backstrom/25 25.00 60.00
49 Antti Niemi/25 12.00 30.00
50 Jonathan Quick/25 25.00 60.00

2011-12 Panini Titanium Reserve Autographs

1 Adam Henrique 12.00 30.00
2 Brandon Yip 4.00 10.00
3 Antoine Vermette 4.00 10.00
4 Anze Kopitar 10.00 25.00
5 Bobby Clarke 20.00 40.00
6 Manon Rheaume 20.00 40.00
7 Grant Clitsome 4.00 10.00
8 Brayden Schenn 6.00 15.00
9 Brenden Morrow 5.00 12.00
10 Cam Fowler 5.00 12.00
11 Cam Ward 6.00 15.00
12 Carey Price 15.00 30.00
13 Cody Hodgson 12.00 30.00
14 Corey Perry 6.00 15.00
15 Craig Anderson 6.00 15.00
16 Alex Ovechkin 30.00 80.00
17 Curtis Joseph 12.00 30.00
18 Daniel Sedin 6.00 15.00
19 Dany Heatley 5.00 12.00
20 David Backes 6.00 15.00
21 David Krejci 10.00 25.00
22 Devin Setoguchi 5.00 12.00
23 Dustin Brown 6.00 15.00
24 Gabriel Landeskog 12.00 30.00
25 James van Riemsdyk 6.00 15.00
26 Jonas Hiller 5.00 12.00
27 Marty Turco 6.00 15.00
28 Kevin Dineen 6.00 15.00
29 Marian Gaborik 8.00 20.00
30 Mario Lemieux SP
31 Mark Messier SP 20.00 50.00
32 Martin Brodeur 40.00 80.00
33 Matt Hackett 5.00 12.00
34 Nathan Horton 6.00 15.00
35 Nazem Kadri 10.00 25.00
36 Nikolai Khabibulin 8.00 20.00
37 P.K. Subban 12.00 30.00
38 Patrice Bergeron SP 20.00 40.00
39 Patrick Wiercioch 5.00 12.00
40 Ryan Nugent-Hopkins 25.00 60.00
41 Sam Gagner 6.00 15.00
42 Sean Couturier 10.00 25.00
43 Steve Ott 5.00 12.00
44 Steven Stamkos SP 30.00 60.00
45 Mike Bossy 10.00 25.00
46 Teddy Purcell 6.00 15.00
47 Tuukka Rask 10.00 25.00
48 Kris Russell 6.00 15.00
49 Tyler Seguin SP 40.00 80.00
50 Zack Kassian 5.00 12.00

2011-12 Panini Titanium Road Sweaters Memorabilia Autographs

STATED PRINT RUN 10-50
*PRIME/15: .6X TO 1.5X BASIC AU/50
*PRIME/15: .5X TO 1.2X BASIC AU/25
1 Alexander Burmistrov/50 10.00 25.00
2 Brandon Dubinsky/50 10.00 25.00
3 Cam Fowler/50 10.00 25.00
5 David Backes/50 12.00 30.00
6 Drew Doughty/50 10.00 25.00
7 Dustin Brown/50 15.00 40.00
8 Jaroslav Halak/50 12.00 30.00
9 Joe Vitale/50 10.00 25.00
10 Jonas Hiller/50 10.00 25.00
11 Jonathan Bernier/50 12.00 30.00
12 Loui Eriksson/10
13 Marc Staal/50 12.00 30.00
14 Marian Gaborik/50 15.00 40.00
15 Mason Raymond/50 10.00 25.00
16 Matt Frattin/50 10.00 25.00
17 Matt Read/50 15.00 40.00
18 Michael Cammalleri/50 10.00 25.00
20 Michael Del Zotto/25 10.00 25.00
21 Nicklas Lidstrom/50 15.00 40.00
22 Carey Price/25 50.00 120.00
23 Patrick Marleau/50 12.00 30.00
24 Rick Nash/50 12.00 30.00
25 Ryan Ellis/50 12.00 30.00
26 Ryan Miller/50 15.00 40.00
27 Sean Couturier/50 15.00 40.00
28 Thomas Vanek/50 8.00 20.00
29 Zac Dalpe/25 10.00 25.00
30 Zack Kassian/50 15.00 40.00

2011-12 Panini Titanium Rookie Dual Signatures

STATED PRINT RUN 50 SER.#'d SETS
1 Nugent-Hopkins/A.Lander 50.00 120.00
2 G.Landeskog/S.Elliott 25.00 50.00
3 S.Couturier/H.Zolnierczyk 20.00 50.00
4 M.Read/Z.Rinaldo EXCH 15.00 40.00
5 D.Smith-Pelly/P.Holland 12.00 30.00
6 Z.Kassian/B.McNabb 10.00 25.00
7 G.Nemisz/R.Horak 8.00 20.00
8 B.Saad/M.Kruger 15.00 40.00
9 R.Johansen/C.Atkinson 20.00 50.00
10 T.Vincour/C.Sceviour 10.00 25.00
11 Nugent-Hopkins/C.Teubert 40.00 100.00
12 E.Gudbranson/S.Timmins 10.00 25.00
14 L.Leblanc/A.Emelin 8.00 20.00
15 C.Smith/J.Blum 10.00 25.00
16 B.Geoffrion/R.Josi 10.00 25.00
17 A.Henrique/A.Larsson 20.00 40.00
19 C.Hagelin/T.Erixon 15.00 40.00
20 M.Zibanejad/C.Greening 20.00 50.00
21 A.Miele/D.Rundblad 10.00 25.00
22 B.Scrivens/B.Holmstrom 10.00 25.00
23 S.Despres/J.Vitale 15.00 40.00
24 J.Colborne/M.Frattin 8.00 20.00
25 C.Hodgson/G.Landeskog 25.00 50.00
26 D.Orlov/C.Eakin 10.00 25.00
27 M.Scheifele/C.Klingberg 10.00 25.00
28 J.Gardiner/S.Voynov 12.00 30.00
29 R.Diaz/A.Palushaj 8.00 20.00
30 B.Smith/G.Nyquist 15.00 40.00

2011-12 Panini Titanium Rookie Reserve Dual Memorabilia Autographs

STATED PRINT RUN 90-100
*PATCH AU/15: 1X TO 2.5X JSY AU/90-100
*PRIME AU/21-25: .8X TO 2X JSY AU/90-100
1 Ryan Nugent-Hopkins/100 25.00 60.00
2 Sean Couturier/100 15.00 40.00
3 Adam Henrique/100 25.00 50.00
4 Craig Smith/100 10.00 25.00
5 Matt Read/100 15.00 40.00
6 Adam Larsson/100 12.00 30.00
7 Marcus Kruger/90 12.00 30.00
8 Gabriel Landeskog/100 20.00 50.00
9 Ryan Johansen/100 12.00 30.00
10 Cody Hodgson/100 10.00 25.00
11 Jake Gardiner/100 12.00 30.00
12 Brett Connolly/100 8.00 20.00
13 Zack Kassian/100 12.50 30.00
14 Simon Despres/100 8.00 20.00
15 Brendan Smith/100 8.00 20.00
16 Joe Colborne/100 12.00 30.00
17 Calvin de Haan/100 8.00 20.00
18 Greg Nemisz/100 8.00 20.00
19 Tim Erixon/100 8.00 20.00
20 David Rundblad/100 10.00 25.00
21 Louis Leblanc/100 15.00 40.00
22 Devante Smith-Pelly/100 12.00 30.00
23 Ben Scrivens/100 12.00 30.00
24 Cody Eakin/100 10.00 25.00
25 Erik Gudbranson/100 6.00 15.00

2011-12 Panini Titanium Six Star Memorabilia

STATED PRINT RUN 10-25
1 Anze Kopitar/25 30.00 80.00
2 Ryan Miller/25 20.00 50.00
3 Henrik Lundqvist/25 25.00 60.00
4 Henrik Zetterberg/25 25.00 60.00
5 Corey Perry/25 20.00 50.00
6 Derek Stepan/25 20.00 50.00
7 Zdeno Chara/25 20.00 50.00
8 Nicklas Backstrom/25 30.00 80.00
9 Sidney Crosby/25 50.00 120.00
10 Ryan Getzlaf/25 30.00 80.00
11 Corey Crawford/10
12 Paul Stastny/25 20.00 50.00
13 Ed Belfour/25 20.00 50.00
14 Nicklas Lidstrom/25 20.00 50.00
15 Sam Gagner/25 15.00 40.00
16 Bernie Nicholls/25 20.00 50.00
17 Ilya Kovalchuk/10
18 Travis Hamonic/25 40.00 100.00
19 Jimmy Howard/25 20.00 50.00
20 Mario Lemieux/25 60.00 120.00
21 Steven Stamkos/25 40.00 100.00
22 Daniel Sedin/25 20.00 50.00
23 Mike Green/25 20.00 50.00
24 Steve Yzerman/25 30.00 80.00
25 Joe Pavelski/25 20.00 50.00

2011-12 Panini Titanium Third Sweaters Memorabilia Autographs

STATED PRINT RUN 13-25
1 Sidney Crosby/25 75.00 150.00
2 Henrik Lundqvist/25 30.00 60.00
3 Tim Thomas/25 25.00 50.00
4 Alex Ovechkin/25 40.00 100.00
5 Joe Thornton/25 15.00 40.00
8 Saku Koivu/25 20.00 50.00
9 Martin St. Louis/24 15.00 40.00
10 Jarome Iginla/25 20.00 40.00
11 Evgeni Malkin/13
12 Steven Stamkos/25 40.00 80.00
13 Ryan Miller/25 25.00 50.00
14 Ryan Nugent-Hopkins/25 75.00 150.00
15 Henrik Sedin/25 15.00 40.00

2012-13 Panini Titanium Game Worn Gear

*PATCH/25: 1X TO 2.5X BASIC JSY
*PRIME/50: .8X TO 2X BASIC JSY
*PRIME/20-25: 1X TO 2.5X BASIC JSY
INSERTS IN 2012-13 ROOKIE ANTHOLOGY
GGAA Artem Anisimov 3.00 8.00
GGAB Alexander Burmistrov SP 4.00 10.00
GGAC Andrew Cogliano 2.50 6.00
GGAK Andrei Kostitsyn 3.00 8.00
GGAM Andrei Markov 4.00 10.00

GGAM1 Al MacInnis 4.00 10.00
GGAM2 Alec Martinez 2.50 6.00
GGAN Antti Niemi 3.00 8.00
GGAO Alex Ovechkin 15.00 40.00
GGBB Brent Burns 5.00 12.00
GGBB1 Brian Boucher 3.00 8.00
GGBB2 Brian Boyle 2.50 6.00
GGBD Brandon Dubinsky 3.00 8.00
GGBE1 Ben Eager 2.50 6.00
GGBE2 Brian Elliott 3.00 8.00
GGBH Brett Hull 4.00 10.00
GGBJ Barret Jackman 2.50 6.00
GGBP Brandon Prust 3.00 8.00
GGBR Brad Richards 4.00 10.00
GGBS Brendan Shanahan 5.00 12.00
GGCA1 Colby Armstrong 3.00 8.00
GGCA2 Craig Anderson 4.00 10.00
GGCC Chris Chelios 4.00 10.00
GGCM Chris Mason 3.00 8.00
GGCS1 Chris Stewart 3.00 8.00
GGCS2 Cory Schneider 3.00 8.00
GGDA Daniel Alfredsson 4.00 10.00
GGDB1 Danny Briere 4.00 10.00
GGDB2 David Backes 4.00 10.00
GGDD Drew Doughty 4.00 10.00
GGDG Dan Girardi 2.50 6.00
GGDL David Legwand 3.00 8.00
GGDP1 Dion Phaneuf 4.00 10.00
GGDP2 Dustin Penner 3.00 8.00
GGDR Derek Roy 3.00 8.00
GGDS1 Daniel Sedin 4.00 10.00
GGDS2 Derek Stepan 4.00 10.00
GGDS3 Drew Stafford 4.00 10.00
GGDT Dana Tyrell 2.50 6.00
GGED Evgeny Dadonov 3.00 8.00
GGEK1 Erik Karlsson 8.00 20.00
GGEK2 Evander Kane 4.00 10.00
GGEL Eric Lindros 5.00 12.00
GGGH1 Gordie Howe SP 10.00 25.00
GGGL Gabriel Landeskog SP 5.00 12.00
GGGP George Parros 3.00 8.00
GGHL Henrik Lundqvist 5.00 12.00
GGHZ Henrik Zetterberg 5.00 12.00
GGJB Jamie Benn 5.00 12.00
GGJC Jeff Carter 4.00 10.00
GGJH Jaroslav Halak 4.00 10.00
GGJH1 Jimmy Howard 4.00 10.00
GGJH2 Johan Hedberg 3.00 8.00
GGJJ Jaromir Jagr 10.00 25.00
GGJM Jay McClement 2.50 6.00
GGJN1 James Neal 4.00 10.00
GGJN2 Joe Nieuwendyk 4.00 10.00
GGJP Jason Pominville 3.00 8.00
GGJQ Jonathan Quick 6.00 15.00
GGRE James Reimer 4.00 10.00
GGJS Jordan Staal 4.00 10.00
GGJS1 Jarret Stoll 3.00 8.00
GGJS2 Jason Spezza 4.00 10.00
GGJT Joe Thornton 4.00 10.00
GGJV James van Riemsdyk 4.00 10.00
GGJW Justin Williams 3.00 8.00
GGKP Keith Primeau 3.00 8.00
GGKT Kimmo Timonen 2.50 6.00
GGKY Keith Yandle 4.00 10.00
GGLR Luc Robitaille 4.00 10.00
GGMG1 Marian Gaborik 4.00 10.00
GGMG2 Mikhail Grabovski 4.00 10.00
GGMH Marian Hossa 3.00 8.00
GGMK Mikko Koivu 3.00 8.00
GGML1 Michael Leighton 3.00 8.00
GGML2 Milan Lucic 4.00 10.00
GGMM1 Milan Michalek 2.50 6.00
GGMM2 Matt Moulson 3.00 8.00
GGRD Matt Read SP 4.00 10.00
GGMR2 Mike Richards 4.00 10.00
GGMS Marc Staal 3.00 8.00
GGNB Nicklas Backstrom 6.00 15.00
GGNK Nikolai Khabibulin 4.00 10.00
GGPB Paul Bissonnette 3.00 8.00
GGPD Pavel Datsyuk 5.00 12.00
GGPM Peter Mueller 2.50 6.00
GGRI Brad Richards 4.00 10.00
GGRL Roberto Luongo 4.00 10.00
GGRN2 Rick Nash 4.00 10.00
GGRR Robyn Regehr 2.50 6.00
GGRV Rogie Vachon SP 8.00 20.00
GGRW Ryan Whitney 2.50 6.00
GGSC1 Sidney Crosby 8.00 20.00
GGCO Sean Couturier SP 5.00 12.00
GGSH Scott Hartnell 4.00 10.00
GGSS Steven Stamkos 8.00 20.00
GGSW Shea Weber 3.00 8.00
GGTM Torrey Mitchell 2.50 6.00
GGTS Tyler Seguin 5.00 12.00
GGTV Tomas Vokoun 3.00 8.00
GGTZ Travis Zajac 3.00 8.00

2012-13 Panini Titanium Metallic Marks

GOLD ANNC'D PRINT RUN 25 OR LESS
INSERTS IN 2012-13 ROOKIE ANTHOLOGY
2 Andrew Desjardins B 2.50 6.00
3 Andrew Shaw B 8.00 20.00
4 Brandon Mashinter B 2.50 6.00
5 Brandon McMillan B 2.50 6.00
6 Brayden McNabb B 4.00 10.00
8 Brett Connolly B 3.00 8.00
9 Brett MacLean B 2.50 6.00
10 Cameron Gaunce B 2.50 6.00
11 Carl Hagelin B 5.00 12.00
12 Cody Eakin B 4.00 10.00
13 Colby Cohen B 2.50 6.00
14 Colten Teubert B 2.50 6.00
15 Colton Sceviour B 2.50 6.00
16 Corey Tropp B 3.00 8.00
17 Dana Tyrell B 2.50 6.00
18 David Rundblad B 3.00 8.00
19 Derick Brassard B 4.00 10.00
20 Gabriel Bourque B 3.00 8.00
22 Gustav Nyquist B 4.00 10.00
24 Harry Zolnierczyk B 2.50 6.00
25 Jacob Markstrom B 4.00 10.00
26 Jake Gardiner B SP 6.00 15.00
27 Jeff Skinner B SP 8.00 20.00
29 John McCarthy B 2.50 6.00
30 John Moore B 2.50 6.00
31 Jon Matsumoto B 2.50 6.00
33 Jonathan Bernier B 4.00 10.00
34 Jordan Caron B 4.00 10.00
35 Justin DiBenedetto B 2.50 6.00
36 Justin Falk B 2.50 6.00
37 Keith Aulie B 2.50 6.00
38 Lance Bouma B 2.50 6.00
39 Louis Leblanc B SP 5.00 12.00
40 Luca Caputi B 2.50 6.00
41 Magnus Paajarvi B 3.00 8.00
42 Matt Bartkowski B 2.50 6.00
44 Nino Niederreiter B 2.50 6.00
45 Oliver Ekman-Larsson B 4.00 10.00
46 Raphael Diaz B 2.50 6.00
48 Roman Josi B 4.00 10.00
49 Ryan Ellis B 2.50 6.00
50 Scott Timmins B 2.50 6.00
51 Slava Voynov B 4.00 10.00
52 Stefan Elliott B 3.00 8.00
53 T.J. Brennan B 2.50 6.00
54 Tim Erixon B 2.50 6.00
55 Tomas Kubalik B 2.50 6.00
57 Tommy Wingels B 2.50 6.00
58 Tyler Bozak B 3.00 8.00
59 Zac Dalpe B 2.50 6.00
61 Jean Beliveau S 30.00 60.00
62 Teemu Selanne S 20.00 40.00
63 Don Cherry S SP
64 Al Secord S 4.00 10.00
65 Steve Mason S 4.00 10.00
66 Brad Richards S
67 Brenden Morrow S 4.00 10.00
68 Corey Perry S 6.00 15.00
69 Henrik Sedin S 5.00 12.00
70 Victor Hedman S 6.00 15.00
71 Joe Thornton S
72 Kris Letang S
73 Logan Couture S 8.00 20.00
75 Niklas Backstrom S 10.00 25.00
76 P.K. Subban S 10.00 25.00
77 Rick Nash S 10.00 25.00
78 Roberto Luongo S SP 10.00 25.00
79 Ryan Miller S 8.00 20.00
80 Sam Gagner S SP
81 Tim Thomas S SP 8.00 20.00
82 Tyler Seguin S 20.00 40.00
83 Vincent Lecavalier S
84 Zach Parise S 8.00 20.00
85 Martin St. Louis S
86 Brendan Shanahan G
87 Joe Sakic G 25.00 50.00
88 John Tavares G
89 Patrick Roy G 40.00 80.00
90 Bobby Hull G 25.00 60.00
91 Martin Brodeur G 40.00 80.00
92 Ray Bourque G 25.00 50.00
94 Nicklas Lidstrom G 25.00 50.00
95 Eric Lindros G 30.00 60.00

2012-13 Panini Titanium Rookies

INSERTS IN 2012-13 ROOKIE ANTHOLOGY
STATED PRINT RUN 4-74
1 Max Sauve/74 6.00 15.00
2 Mat Clark/73 6.00 15.00
3 Kris Foucault/72 6.00 15.00
4 Jordan Nolan/71 6.00 15.00
5 Michael Hutchinson/70 10.00 25.00
6 Robert Mayer/65 12.00 30.00
7 Travis Turnbull/65 6.00 15.00
8 Tyler Cuma/65 6.00 15.00
9 Lane MacDermid/64 6.00 15.00
10 Mark Stone/60 12.00 30.00
11 Carter Camper/58 5.00 12.00
12 Aaron Ness/55 6.00 15.00
13 Casey Cizikas/53 6.00 15.00
14 Brandon Bollig/52 6.00 15.00
15 Philippe Cornet/51 6.00 15.00
16 Cody Goloubef/48 10.00 25.00
17 Ryan Hamilton/48 8.00 20.00
18 Chay Genoway/47 10.00 25.00
19 Colby Robak/47 10.00 25.00
20 Dalton Prout/47 10.00 25.00
21 Sven Baertschi/47 12.00 30.00
22 Torey Krug/47 30.00 80.00
23 Matt Donovan/46 10.00 25.00
24 Tyson Barrie/41 20.00 50.00
25 Jussi Rynnas/40 10.00 25.00
26 Ryan Garbutt/40 10.00 25.00
27 Carter Ashton/37 8.00 20.00
28 Chet Pickard/37 10.00 25.00
29 Gabriel Dumont/37 10.00 25.00
30 Matt Watkins/50 6.00 15.00
31 Tyson Sexsmith/37 10.00 25.00
32 Jake Allen/34 30.00 80.00
33 Jakob Silfverberg/33 20.00 50.00
34 Shawn Hunwick/31 10.00 25.00
35 Akim Aliu/29 12.00 30.00
36 Andrew Joudrey/23 12.00 30.00
37 Michael Stone/29 12.00 30.00
38 Brandon Manning/23 12.00 30.00
39 Jeremy Welsh/23 12.00 30.00
40 Chris Kreider/20 75.00 150.00
41 J.T. Brown/19 12.00 30.00
42 Mike Connolly/18 12.00 30.00
43 Reilly Smith/18 25.00 60.00
44 Jason Zucker/16 15.00 40.00
45 Riley Sheahan/15 12.00 30.00
46 Scott Glennie/15 12.00 30.00

2012-13 Panini Titanium Rookies Gold

1 Max Sauve/47 10.00 25.00
2 Mat Clark/37 10.00 25.00
3 Kris Foucault/100 5.00 12.00
4 Jordan Nolan/100 5.00 12.00
5 Michael Hutchinson/100 10.00 25.00
6 Robert Mayer/100 12.00 30.00
7 Travis Turnbull/100 5.00 12.00
8 Tyler Cuma/23 12.00 30.00
9 Lane MacDermid/100 5.00 12.00
10 Mark Stone/100 10.00 25.00
11 Carter Camper/100 4.00 10.00
12 Aaron Ness/40 10.00 25.00
13 Casey Cizikas/92 5.00 12.00
14 Brandon Bollig/100 5.00 12.00
15 Philippe Cornet/100 5.00 12.00
16 Cody Goloubef/37 10.00 25.00
17 Ryan Hamilton/100 5.00 12.00
18 Chay Genoway/100 5.00 12.00
19 Colby Robak/46 10.00 25.00
20 Dalton Prout/100 5.00 12.00
22 Torey Krug/100 50.00 120.00
23 Matt Donovan/96 5.00 12.00
24 Tyson Barrie/64 12.00 30.00
25 Jussi Rynnas/100 5.00 12.00
26 Ryan Garbutt/100 5.00 12.00
27 Carter Ashton/29 10.00 25.00
28 Chet Pickard/18 12.00 30.00
29 Gabriel Dumont/100 5.00 12.00
30 Matt Watkins/100 5.00 12.00
31 Tyson Sexsmith/91 5.00 12.00
32 Jake Allen/34 30.00 80.00
33 Jakob Silfverberg/39 20.00 50.00
34 Shawn Hunwick/100 5.00 12.00
35 Akim Aliu/56 6.00 15.00
36 Andrew Joudrey/100 5.00 12.00
37 Michael Stone/69 6.00 15.00
38 Brandon Manning/100 5.00 12.00
39 Jeremy Welsh/100 5.00 12.00
40 Chris Kreider/19 75.00 150.00
41 J.T. Brown/100 5.00 12.00
42 Mike Connolly/100 5.00 12.00
43 Reilly Smith/69 12.00 30.00
44 Jason Zucker/59 8.00 20.00
45 Riley Sheahan/21 12.00 30.00
48 Brenden Dillon/100 5.00 12.00

2013-14 Panini Titanium

1 Adam Henrique .40 1.00
2 Alex Ovechkin 1.50 4.00
3 Alex Pietrangelo .30 .75
4 Andrew Ladd .40 1.00
5 Anze Kopitar .60 1.50
6 Ben Bishop .40 1.00
7 Bobby Ryan .40 1.00
8 Braden Holtby .60 1.50
9 Brayden Schenn .40 1.00
10 Brian Elliott .30 .75
11 Cal Clutterbuck .40 1.00
12 Cam Ward .40 1.00
13 Carey Price 1.25 3.00
14 Clarke MacArthur .25 .60
15 Claude Giroux .40 1.00
16 Cody Hodgson .40 1.00
17 Corey Crawford .50 1.25
18 Corey Perry .40 1.00
19 Cory Schneider .30 .75
20 Craig Anderson .40 1.00
21 Daniel Alfredsson .40 1.00
22 Daniel Sedin .40 1.00
23 David Backes .40 1.00
24 David Perron .25 .60
25 Derick Brassard .40 1.00
26 Devin Setoguchi .30 .75
27 Dion Phaneuf .40 1.00
28 Drew Doughty .40 1.00
29 Duncan Keith .40 1.00
30 Dustin Brown .40 1.00
31 Dustin Byfuglien .40 1.00
32 Ed Jovanovski .25 .60
33 Eric Staal .50 1.25
34 Erik Karlsson .75 2.00
35 Evgeni Malkin 1.25 3.00
36 Gabriel Landeskog .30 .75
37 Henrik Lundqvist .50 1.25
38 Henrik Sedin .40 1.00
39 Henrik Zetterberg .50 1.25
40 Jacob Markstrom .30 .75
41 Jakob Silfverberg .30 .75
42 James van Riemsdyk .40 1.00
43 Jamie Benn .50 1.25
44 Jarome Iginla .40 1.00
45 Jaromir Jagr 1.00 2.50
46 Jason Spezza .40 1.00
47 Jeff Skinner .30 .75
48 Joe Pavelski .40 1.00
49 Joe Thornton .40 1.00
50 John Tavares .75 2.00
51 Jonas Hiller .30 .75
52 Jonathan Bernier .40 1.00
53 Jonathan Quick .60 1.50
54 Jonathan Toews .75 2.00
55 Jordan Eberle .40 1.00
56 Kari Lehtonen .30 .75
57 Kris Versteeg .30 .75
58 Logan Couture .40 1.00
59 Loui Eriksson .30 .75
60 Marc-Andre Fleury .60 1.50
61 Marcus Foligno .25 .60
62 Marian Gaborik .40 1.00
63 Martin Brodeur .75 2.00
64 Matt Duchene .40 1.00
65 Matt Stajan .30 .75
66 Max Pacioretty .40 1.00
67 Michael Grabner .30 .75
68 Karri Ramo .30 .75
69 Mikael Backlund .30 .75
70 Mike Fisher .30 .75
71 Mike Smith .40 1.00
72 Nathan Horton .40 1.00
73 Nicklas Backstrom .60 1.50
74 Niklas Backstrom .30 .75
75 Oliver Ekman-Larsson .30 .75
76 P.K. Subban .60 1.50
77 Patrick Kane .75 2.00
78 Pavel Datsyuk .50 1.25
79 Pekka Rinne .50 1.25
80 Phil Kessel .50 1.25
81 Rick Nash .40 1.00
82 Roberto Luongo .40 1.00
83 Ryan Getzlaf .60 1.50
84 Ryan Miller .40 1.00
85 Ryan Nugent-Hopkins .40 1.00
86 Ryan Suter .25 .60
87 Semyon Varlamov .40 1.00
88 Sergei Bobrovsky .40 1.00
89 Shane Doan .30 .75
90 Shea Weber .30 .75
91 Sidney Crosby 1.50 4.00
92 Stephen Weiss .30 .75
93 Steven Stamkos .75 2.00
94 Taylor Hall .75 2.00
95 Tuukka Rask .40 1.00
96 Tyler Seguin .60 1.50
97 Valtteri Filppula .40 1.00
98 Vincent Lecavalier .30 .75
99 Zach Parise .40 1.00
100 Zdeno Chara .40 1.00
101 Vladimir Tarasenko/91 RC 40.00 80.00
102 Cory Conacher/89 RC 4.00 10.00
103 John Muse/80 RC 6.00 15.00
104 Matt Tennyson/80 RC 4.00 10.00
105 Eric Selleck/76 RC 5.00 12.00
106 Radko Gudas/75 RC 6.00 15.00
107 Ondrej Palat/74 RC 8.00 20.00
108 Brett Bellemore/73 RC 5.00 12.00
109 Tyler Toffoli/73 RC 12.00 30.00
110 Igor Bobkov/72 RC 5.00 12.00
111 Nicolas Blanchard/72 RC 5.00 12.00
112 Alex Petrovic/72 RC 5.00 12.00
113 Joonas Rask/72 RC 4.00 10.00
114 Richard Panik/71 RC 6.00 15.00
115 Tanner Pearson/70 RC 6.00 15.00
116 Jamie Tardif/68 RC 4.00 10.00
117 Rickard Rakell/67 RC 6.00 15.00
118 Emerson Etem/65 RC 6.00 15.00
119 Brian Flynn/65 RC 5.00 12.00
120 Danny DeKeyser/65 RC 8.00 20.00
121 Nail Yakupov/64 RC 50.00 100.00
122 Mikael Granlund/64 RC 10.00 25.00
123 Greg Pateryn/64 RC 6.00 15.00
124 Victor Bartley/64 RC 5.00 12.00
125 Charlie Coyle/63 RC 6.00 15.00
126 Tyler Johnson/63 RC 30.00 60.00
127 Mark Arcobello/62 RC 6.00 15.00
128 Michael Caruso/62 RC 4.00 10.00
129 Eric Gryba/62 RC 5.00 12.00
130 Andrej Sustr/62 RC 4.00 10.00
131 Steve Oleksy/61 RC 6.00 15.00
132 Max Reinhart/59 RC 8.00 20.00
133 Dave Dziurzynski/59 RC 6.00 15.00
134 Ben Hanowski/58 RC 6.00 15.00
135 Chris Terry/58 RC 5.00 12.00
136 Patrick Bordeleau/58 RC 8.00 20.00
137 Christian Thomas/58 RC 6.00 15.00
138 Derek Grant/57 RC 6.00 15.00
139 Taylor Beck/56 RC 6.00 15.00
140 Ryan Stanton/18 RC
141 Nick Petrecki/54 RC 5.00 12.00
142 Mark Pysyk/53 RC 8.00 20.00
144 Jonathan Rheault/52 RC 5.00 12.00
145 Austin Watson/52 RC 6.00 15.00
146 Matt Irwin/52 RC 6.00 15.00
147 Ryan Spooner/51 RC 15.00 40.00
148 Daniel Bang/50 RC 6.00 15.00
149 Michal Jordan/47 RC 5.00 12.00
150 Johan Larsson/22 RC
152 Leo Komarov/47 RC 8.00 20.00
153 Carter Bancks/46 RC 6.00 15.00
154 Kevin Henderson/46 RC 6.00 15.00
155 Nicklas Jensen/46 RC 6.00 15.00
156 Sami Vatanen/45 RC 8.00 20.00
157 Jordan Schroeder/45 RC 8.00 20.00
158 Cameron Schilling/45 RC 6.00 15.00
159 Jean-Gabriel Pageau/44 RC 6.00 15.00
160 Chris Brown/44 RC 5.00 12.00
161 Michael Sgarbossa/43 RC 6.00 15.00
162 Sean Collins/43 RC 6.00 15.00
163 Tom Wilson/43 RC 12.00 30.00
164 Mark Cundari/42 RC 5.00 12.00
165 Shawn Lalonde/42 RC 8.00 20.00
166 Quinton Howden/42 RC 6.00 15.00
167 Jarred Tinordi/42 RC 8.00 20.00
168 Jason Akeson/42 RC 6.00 15.00
169 Cristopher Nilstorp/41 RC 6.00 15.00
170 Nathan Beaulieu/40 RC 6.00 15.00
171 Ben Street/38 RC 5.00 12.00
172 Oliver Lauridsen/38 RC 6.00 15.00
173 Jonathan Marchessault/36 RC 15.00 40.00
174 Jeff Zatkoff/36 RC 8.00 20.00
175 Darcy Kuemper/35 RC 12.00 30.00
176 Calvin Heeter/35 RC 12.00 30.00
177 Carl Soderberg/34 RC 25.00 50.00
178 Petr Mrazek/34 RC 20.00 50.00
179 Matthew Konan/34 RC 10.00 25.00
180 Eric Gelinas/32 RC 10.00 25.00
181 Edward Pasquale/32 RC 6.00 15.00
182 Frederik Andersen/31 RC 15.00 40.00
183 Calvin Pickard/31 RC 10.00 25.00
184 Eric Hartzell/31 RC 10.00 25.00
185 Philipp Grubauer/31 RC 10.00 25.00
186 Viktor Fasth/30 RC 10.00 25.00
187 Sami Aittokallio/30 RC 12.00 30.00
188 Joe Cannata/30 RC 8.00 20.00
189 Brock Nelson/29 RC 10.00 25.00
190 Dougie Hamilton/27 RC 75.00 135.00
191 Nick Bjugstad/27 RC 12.00 30.00
192 Alex Galchenyuk/27 RC 150.00 300.00
193 Anders Lee/27 RC 15.00 40.00
194 Dmitrij Jaskin/26 RC 10.00 25.00
195 Frank Corrado/26 RC 8.00 20.00
196 Mikhail Grigorenko/25 RC 30.00 60.00
197 Jonas Brodin/25 RC 8.00 20.00
198 Zach Redmond/25 RC 8.00 20.00
200 Brian Lashoff/23 RC
201 Scott Laughton/21 RC
202 Antoine Roussel/21 RC
203 Justin Schultz/19 RC 25.00 50.00
204 Beau Bennett/19 RC
205 Alex Killorn/17 RC
206 Harri Pesonen/15 RC
207 Drew Shore/15 RC
208 Stefan Matteau/15 RC
209 Tye McGinn/15 RC
227 Anton Belov/77 RC 8.00 20.00
228 Will Acton/41 RC 8.00 20.00
229 Luke Gazdic/20 RC 10.00 25.00
230 Joakim Nordstrom/42 RC 8.00 20.00
231 Connor Carrick/58 RC 25.00 60.00
232 Michael Latta/46 RC 20.00 50.00
233 Nathan MacKinnon/29 RC 450.00 800.00
234 Zemgus Girgensons/28 RC
235 Rasmus Ristolainen/55 RC 15.00 40.00
237 Sean Monahan/23 RC 90.00 150.00
239 Justin Fontaine/52 RC 10.00 25.00
240 Aleksander Barkov/16 RC
241 Valeri Nichushkin/43 RC 100.00 175.00
242 Jesper Fast/31 RC 10.00 25.00
243 Lucas Lessio/51 RC 6.00 15.00
244 Matt Nieto/83 RC 6.00 15.00
245 Tomas Hertl/48 RC 100.00 200.00
246 Boone Jenner/38 RC 10.00 25.00
247 Ryan Murray/27 RC
248 Morgan Rielly/44 RC 25.00 60.00
249 Matt Dumba/55 RC 10.00 25.00
250 Hampus Lindholm/47 RC 15.00 40.00
251 Alex Grant/51 RC 8.00 20.00
252 Kevan Miller/86 RC 6.00 15.00
253 Nikita Zadorov/61 RC 8.00 20.00
254 Christopher Breen/43 RC 6.00 15.00
255 Reto Berra/20 RC 15.00 40.00
256 Chad Billins/41 RC 8.00 20.00
257 Antti Raanta/31 RC 15.00 40.00
258 Michael Chaput/39 RC 6.00 15.00
259 Kevin Connauton/23 RC
260 Xavier Ouellet/61 RC 8.00 20.00
261 Luke Glendening/41 RC 15.00 40.00
262 Adam Almquist/53 RC 6.00 15.00
263 Tyler Pitlick/68 RC 8.00 20.00
264 Taylor Fedun/81 RC 8.00 20.00
265 Martin Marincin/85 RC 6.00 15.00
266 Linden Vey/57 RC 6.00 15.00
267 Martin Jones/31 RC 30.00 80.00
268 Erik Haula/56 RC 12.00 30.00
269 Johan Gustafsson/31 RC 15.00 40.00
270 Patrick Holland/82 RC 12.00 30.00
271 Michael Bournival/49 RC 10.00 25.00
272 Magnus Hellberg/45 RC 10.00 25.00
273 Marek Mazanec/39 RC 10.00 25.00
274 Jon Merrill/34 RC 12.00 30.00
276 Jason Missiaen/31 RC 12.00 30.00
278 Jordan Szwarz/29 RC 12.00 30.00
280 Jayson Megna/59 RC 10.00 25.00
281 Zach Sill/38 RC 10.00 25.00
282 Brian Gibbons/49 RC 10.00 25.00
283 Freddie Hamilton/75 RC 8.00 20.00
284 Dmitry Korobov/24 RC
285 Nikita Kucherov/86 RC 30.00 60.00
286 Spencer Abbott/56 RC 8.00 20.00
287 Josh Leivo/32 RC
288 David Broll/46 RC 10.00 25.00
289 Jamie Devane/59 RC 6.00 15.00
290 Jerry D'Amigo/29 RC 12.00 30.00
292 Darren Archibald/49 RC 8.00 20.00
293 Nate Schmidt/88 RC 6.00 15.00
294 Patrick Wey/56 RC 8.00 20.00
295 Ben Chiarot/63 RC 8.00 20.00
296 John Albert/70 RC 4.00 10.00
297 Kent Simpson/40 RC 8.00 20.00
299 Dylan McIlrath/42 RC 10.00 25.00
300 Ryan Strome/18 RC 50.00 100.00
301 Brian Dumoulin/8 RC
302 Tomas Jurco/26 RC 20.00 50.00
303 Philip Samuelsson/55 RC 6.00 15.00
304 Eric O'Dell/58 RC 6.00 15.00
305 Craig Cunningham/61 RC 6.00 15.00
306 David Warsofsky/79 RC 8.00 20.00
307 Niklas Svedberg/72 RC 10.00 25.00
308 Zach Trotman/42 RC 10.00 25.00
309 Conor Allen/37 RC 8.00 20.00
310 Joacim Eriksson/30 RC 12.00 30.00
311 Julian Melchiori/71 RC 5.00 12.00
312 Eriah Hayes/76 RC 8.00 20.00
313 Brad Hunt/59 RC 15.00 40.00
314 Alexey Marchenko/47 RC 8.00 20.00
315 Justin Florek/57 RC 25.00 60.00
316 Mike Sislo/9 RC
317 John Gibson/36 RC 30.00 80.00
318 Karl Stollery/3 RC

2013-14 Panini Titanium Draft Position

*1-100 VETS/62-100: 4X TO 10X BASIC CARD
*1-100 VETS/39-57: 5X TO 12X BASIC CARD
*1-100 VETS/20-33: 6X TO 15X BASIC CARD
*1-100 VETS/10-19: 8X TO 20X BASIC CARD
17 Corey Crawford/52 6.00 15.00
102 Cory Conacher/100 4.00 10.00
109 Tyler Toffoli/47 15.00 40.00
120 Danny DeKeyser/100 8.00 20.00
123 Greg Pateryn/100 6.00 15.00
126 Tyler Johnson/100 30.00 60.00
127 Mark Arcobello/100 6.00 15.00
147 Ryan Spooner/45 8.00 20.00
152 Leo Komarov/100 6.00 15.00
174 Jeff Zatkoff/74 6.00 15.00
175 Darcy Kuemper/100 8.00 20.00
177 Carl Soderberg/49 8.00 20.00
178 Petr Mrazek/100 12.00 30.00
182 Frederik Andersen/87 10.00 25.00
185 Philipp Grubauer/100 6.00 15.00
186 Viktor Fasth/100 6.00 15.00
194 Dmitrij Jaskin/41 8.00 20.00
203 Justin Schultz/43 8.00 20.00
215 Alex Chiasson/38 8.00 20.00
218 Brendan Gallagher/100 20.00 50.00
232 Michael Latta/72 10.00 25.00
239 Justin Fontaine/100 6.00 15.00
242 Jesper Fast/100 5.00 12.00
244 Matt Nieto/47 6.00 15.00

2013-14 Panini Titanium Jersey Number

*1-100 VETS/61-93: 4X TO 10X BASIC CARD
*1-100 VETS/39-57: 5X TO 12X BASIC CARD
*1-100 VETS/20-35: 6X TO 15X BASIC CARD
*1-100 VETS/10-19: 8X TO 20X BASIC CARD
17 Corey Crawford/50 6.00 15.00
73 Nicklas Backstrom/19 12.00 30.00

2013-14 Panini Titanium Four Star Memorabilia

4SBY Brandon Yip/25 6.00 15.00
4SDK Duncan Keith/25 15.00 40.00
4SEM Evgeni Malkin/25 30.00 80.00
4SHZ Henrik Zetterberg/25 12.00 30.00
4SJG Josh Gorges/25 8.00 20.00
4SJT John Tavares/25 20.00 50.00
4SKS Kevin Shattenkirk/25 8.00 20.00
4SMM Mark Messier/25 12.00 30.00
4SPK Patrick Kane/25 15.00 40.00
4SRG Ryan Getzlaf/25 15.00 40.00
4SSG Sam Gagner/25
4SST Shawn Thornton/25 8.00 20.00
4SSW Shea Weber/25 8.00 20.00
4SAHE Ales Hemsky/25 6.00 15.00
4SAKO Anze Kopitar/25 12.00 30.00
4SCST Chris Stewart/25 8.00 20.00
4SDKR David Krejci/25 10.00 25.00
4SJEN Jhonas Enroth/25
4SJMC Jay McClement/25
4SJSP Jason Spezza/25 10.00 25.00
4SKTI Kimmo Timonen/25 8.00 20.00
4SOPV Ondrej Pavelec/25 10.00 25.00
4SPBG Patrik Berglund/15 6.00 15.00
4SRBL Rob Blake/25

2013-14 Panini Titanium Game Worn Gear

*PATCH/25: .8X TO 2X BASIC JSY
*PATCH/25: .6X TO 1.5X BASIC JSY SP
*PRIME/50: .6X TO 1.5X BASIC JSY
*PRIME/30-50: .5X TO 1.2X BASIC JSY SP
GGAAN Artem Anisimov 3.00 8.00
GGAF Adam Foote 2.50 6.00
GGASE Alexander Semin 4.00 10.00
GGAV Antoine Vermette 2.50 6.00
GGBCA Brian Campbell SP 3.00 8.00
GGBDU Brandon Dubinsky 3.00 8.00
GGBJ Barret Jackman 2.50 6.00
GGBM Brenden Morrow 3.00 8.00
GGBR Bobby Ryan 4.00 10.00
GGBS Brendan Shanahan 5.00 12.00
GGBSE Brent Seabrook 4.00 10.00
GGCF Cam Fowler 3.00 8.00
GGCGX Claude Giroux SP 5.00 12.00
GGCP Carey Price 12.00 30.00
GGCSM Craig Smith 2.50 6.00
GGDA Dave Andreychuk 4.00 10.00
GGDBR Daniel Briere 4.00 10.00
GGDBY Dustin Byfuglien 4.00 10.00
GGDL David Legwand 3.00 8.00
GGDP David Perron 2.50 6.00
GGDRS Drew Stafford 4.00 10.00
GGDS Daniel Sedin 4.00 10.00
GGDSM Derek Smith 2.50 6.00
GGDST Derek Stepan 4.00 10.00
GGDSY Darryl Sydor 2.50 6.00
GGEK Erik Karlsson 8.00 20.00
GGET Eric Tangradi 3.00 8.00
GGFB Francois Beauchemin 2.50 6.00
GGGH Gordie Howe SP
GGHL Henrik Lundqvist 5.00 12.00
GGHS Henrik Sedin 4.00 10.00
GGJBA Josh Bailey 3.00 8.00
GGJLC John LeClair 4.00 10.00
GGJLU Joffrey Lupul SP 4.00 10.00
GGJPO Jason Pominville 3.00 8.00
GGJRE James Reimer 4.00 10.00
GGJS Joe Sakic SP 6.00 15.00
GGJTO Jonathan Toews SP 10.00 25.00
GGJVR James van Riemsdyk 4.00 10.00
GGKC Kyle Clifford 2.50 6.00
GGKD Kaspars Daugavins 4.00 10.00
GGKJS Kjell Samuelsson 2.50 6.00
GGKL Kari Lehtonen 3.00 8.00
GGKO Kyle Okposo 4.00 10.00
GGKP Keith Primeau 3.00 8.00
GGKS Kevin Shattenkirk 4.00 10.00
GGLAI Brooks Laich 2.50 6.00
GGLE Loui Eriksson 3.00 8.00
GGLEI Michael Leighton 3.00 8.00
GGLU Roberto Luongo SP 5.00 12.00
GGMB Martin Brodeur SP 10.00 25.00
GGMBA Mikael Backlund 3.00 8.00
GGMBI Martin Biron 3.00 8.00
GGMDZ Michael Del Zotto 2.50 6.00
GGMEV Marc-Edouard Vlasic 2.50 6.00
GGMHZ Martin Hanzal 2.50 6.00
GGMK Miikka Kiprusoff 3.00 8.00
GGMLO Matthew Lombardi 2.50 6.00
GGMM Mark Messier SP 6.00 15.00
GGMMS Marty McSorley 3.00 8.00
GGMN Michal Neuvirth 3.00 8.00
GGMRI Mike Richards SP 5.00 12.00
GGMSA Mikael Samuelsson 2.50 6.00
GGMSL Martin St. Louis 4.00 10.00
GGNKU Nikolai Kulemin SP 4.00 10.00
GGNL Nicklas Lidstrom 4.00 10.00
GGOPV Ondrej Pavelec 4.00 10.00
GGOVI Alex Ovechkin SP 6.00 15.00
GGPAS Paul Stastny 4.00 10.00
GGPBG Patrik Berglund 2.50 6.00
GGPC Paul Coffey 4.00 10.00
GGPF Pat Falloon 2.50 6.00
GGPM Patrick Marleau 4.00 10.00
GGPR Patrick Roy SP 12.00 30.00
GGPS Patrick Sharp 4.00 10.00
GGPT Pierre Turgeon 4.00 10.00
GGRBL Rob Blake 4.00 10.00
GGRE Ray Emery 3.00 8.00
GGRF Ron Francis 5.00 12.00
GGRM Ryan Miller 4.00 10.00
GGROR Ryan O'Reilly 4.00 10.00
GGSBE Steve Bernier 2.50 6.00
GGSC Sidney Crosby 8.00 20.00
GGSCL Scott Clemmensen 3.00 8.00
GGSD Shane Doan 3.00 8.00
GGSGR Stu Grimson 2.50 6.00
GGSH Shawn Horcoff 2.50 6.00
GGSK Saku Koivu 4.00 10.00
GGSS Steven Stamkos SP 5.00 12.00
GGSVA Semyon Varlamov 4.00 10.00
GGSW Shea Weber 3.00 8.00
GGSY Steve Yzerman SP 6.00 15.00
GGTD Trevor Daley 2.50 6.00
GGTJO T.J. Oshie 6.00 15.00
GGTM Torrey Mitchell 2.50 6.00
GGTR Tuukka Rask 4.00 10.00
GGTZ Travis Zajac 3.00 8.00
GGZP Zach Parise 4.00 10.00
GGVLE Ville Leino 3.00 8.00
GGZRI Zac Rinaldo 3.00 8.00

2013-14 Panini Titanium Game Worn Gear Autographs

*PRIME/25: .8X TO 2X JSY AU/75-100
*PRIME/25: .6X TO 1.5X JSY AU/50
GADB David Backes/100 8.00 20.00
GADD Drew Doughty/50 12.00 30.00
GADS Daniel Sedin/50 10.00 25.00
GAEL Eric Lindros/15
GAGL Gabriel Landeskog/50 8.00 20.00
GAJJ Jaromir Jagr/15 30.00 80.00
GAJQ Jonathan Quick/50 15.00 40.00
GAJR Jeremy Roenick/25
GAMP Max Pacioretty /100 8.00 20.00
GANG Nathan Gerbe/75 5.00 12.00
GANH Nathan Horton/75 8.00 20.00
GAPB Pavel Bure/15
GAPM Patrick Marleau/50
GASK Saku Koivu/50 10.00 25.00
GATZ Travis Zajac/100 6.00 15.00
GAVH Victor Hedman/50 8.00 20.00
GAVL Vincent Lecavalier/25 20.00 40.00
GAZC Zdeno Chara/50 10.00 25.00
GAAMI Al MacInnis/50 10.00 25.00
GACGX Claude Giroux/50 12.00 30.00
GACPR Chris Pronger/100 6.00 15.00
GACSM Craig Smith/50 10.00 25.00
GACWI Colin Wilson/100 6.00 15.00
GADDU Devan Dubnyk /100 8.00 20.00
GADKR David Krejci/75
GADPH Dion Phaneuf/50 10.00 25.00
GADRS Drew Stafford/100 8.00 20.00
GADUB Dustin Brown/50 10.00 25.00
GAEVK Evander Kane/100 8.00 20.00
GAJBE Jonathan Bernier/100 8.00 20.00
GAJHA Jaroslav Halak/50 10.00 25.00
GAJHI Jonas Hiller/100 6.00 15.00
GAJHO Jimmy Howard/50 10.00 25.00
GAJSG Jean-Sebastien Giguere/50 8.00 20.00
GAJTO Jonathan Toews/25
GAJVI Joe Vitale/100 5.00 12.00
GAJVR James van Riemsdyk/100 10.00 25.00
GAMBO Mikkel Boedker/100 5.00 12.00
GAMRE Matt Read/100 6.00 15.00
GANBA Niklas Backstrom/100 10.00 25.00
GAOVI Alex Ovechkin/15
GAPBE Patrice Bergeron/50 12.00 30.00
GAPEL Patrik Elias/50 10.00 25.00
GAPRI Pekka Rinne/50
GARBA Rod Brind'Amour/50 8.00 20.00
GARIB Richard Bachman/100 6.00 15.00
GARNH Ryan Nugent-Hopkins/50 10.00 25.00
GASVA Semyon Varlamov/100 10.00 25.00
GATEN Tyler Ennis/100 6.00 15.00
GATVA Thomas Vanek/75

2013-14 Panini Titanium Game Worn Gear Dual Memorabilia

*PATCH/15: 1X TO 2.5X DUAL JSY/300
*PRIME/50: .6X TO 1.5X DUAL JSY/300
*PRIME/25: .8X TO 2X DUAL JSY/300
*PRIME/25: .6X TO 1.5X DUAL JSY/100
GDAS K.Alzner/M.Staal/300 3.00 8.00
GDBB Berglund/Backstrom/300 6.00 15.00
GDBF D.Byfuglien/E.Fehr/300 4.00 10.00
GDBK Burrows/R.Kesler/300 4.00 10.00
GDBL Bobrovsky/Lundqvist/300 5.00 12.00
GDBM P.Bure/M.Messier/100 6.00 15.00
GDBR M.Boedker/D.Roy/300 3.00 8.00
GDBS Brodeur/Schneider/300 8.00 20.00
GDCO Clutterbuck/Okposo/300 4.00 10.00
GDCR J.Carter/M.Richards/300 4.00 10.00
GDCV S.Voynov/P.Coffey/300 4.00 10.00
GDDG Dubinsky/M.Gaborik/300 3.00 8.00
GDEL B.Laich/M.Erat/300 2.50 6.00
GDEM L.Eller/A.Markov/300 4.00 10.00
GDES L.Eriksson/T.Seguin/300 6.00 15.00
GDFM Falloon/P.Marleau/300 4.00 10.00
GDGL Getzlaf/Lombardi/300 6.00 15.00
GDGS Glencross/Stajan/300 3.00 8.00
GDHE R.Hextall/R.Emery/300 5.00 12.00
GDHH M.Howe/G.Howe/15
GDHJ Holtby/M.Johansson/300 6.00 15.00
GDHS M.Hossa/P.Sharp/300 6.00 15.00
GDIP A.Iafrate/D.Phaneuf/300 4.00 10.00
GDJH R.Jones/A.Hemsky/300 3.00 8.00
GDJJ E.Johnson/J.Johnsn/300 2.50 6.00
GDJL Josefson/A.Larsson/300 4.00 10.00
GDKH T.Kerr/S.Hartnell/300 4.00 10.00
GDKH Kronwall/Hedman/300 5.00 12.00
GDLD M.Lucic/M.Duchene/300 4.00 10.00
GDLH P.Larsen/S.Horcoff/300 3.00 8.00
GDMA R.Miller/L.Adam/300 4.00 10.00
GDMD E.Malkin/P.Datsyuk/300 12.00 30.00
GDMS MacInnis/Shattnkrk/300 4.00 10.00
GDNYR B.Boyle/McDonagh/300 4.00 10.00
GDOD R.O'Reilly/S.Downie/300 4.00 10.00
GDOT Ovechkin/J.Tavares/100 20.00 50.00
GDPB Primeau/Brind'Amour/300 3.00 8.00
GDPC C.Price/C.Crawford/300 12.00 30.00
GDPS Z.Parise/D.Stepan/300 4.00 10.00
GDQH J.Quick/J.Howard/300 6.00 15.00
GDRC C.Crawford/T.Rask/300 5.00 12.00
GDRJ Reaves/B.Jackman/300 3.00 8.00
GDSF N.Spaling/M.Fisher/300 3.00 8.00
GDSG J.Sakic/M.Goulet/300 6.00 15.00
GDSK M.St. Louis/P.Kane/300 8.00 20.00
GDSS P.Subban/R.Suter/100 8.00 20.00
GDTB P.Bergeron/J.Toews/100 10.00 25.00
GDVN Varlamov/Nabokov/300 4.00 10.00
GDYH K.Yandle/M.Hanzal/300 4.00 10.00
GDZA Zetterberg/Alfredsson/300 5.00 12.00

2013-14 Panini Titanium Home Sweaters Memorabilia Autographs

*PRIME/15-25: .8X TO 2X JSY AU/75-100
*PRIME/15-25: .6X TO 1.5X JSY AU/50
HSAG Alex Galchenyuk/100 20.00 50.00
HSAH Adam Henrique/100 8.00 20.00
HSAK Alex Killorn/100 8.00 20.00
HSANP Anthony Peluso/100 8.00 20.00
HSBE Brian Elliott/100 8.00 20.00
HSBG Brendan Gallagher/100 15.00 40.00
HSBRI Brad Richards/50 10.00 25.00
HSBSC Brayden Schenn/50 12.00 30.00
HSCB Chris Brown/100 5.00 12.00
HSCC Cory Conacher/100 5.00 12.00
HSJE Jordan Eberle/50 10.00 25.00
HSJH Jonathan Huberdeau/100 12.00 30.00
HSJRE James Reimer/50 10.00 25.00
HSJSD Jordan Schroeder/100 8.00 20.00
HSMAR Mark Arcobello/100 8.00 20.00
HSMGR Mikael Granlund/100 8.00 20.00
HSMH Marian Hossa/75 20.00 40.00
HSPK Patrick Kane/50 30.00 60.00
HSRM Ryan Miller/50 10.00 25.00
HSSCO Sean Couturier/100 8.00 20.00
HSSMA Stefan Matteau/100 6.00 15.00
HSTP Tanner Pearson/100 10.00 25.00

2013-14 Panini Titanium Metallic Marks

SILVER ANNC'D PRINT RUN 100 OR LESS
SILVER SP ANNC'D PRINT RUN 25 OR LESS
UNPRICED GOLD ANNC'D PRINT RUN 10
UNPRICED PLATINUM ANNC'D PRINT RUN 5
MM1 Ben Holmstrom B 2.50 6.00
MM2 Jaden Schwartz B 5.00 12.00
MM3 Justin DiBenedetto B 2.50 6.00
MM4 Chris Kreider B SP 5.00 12.00
MM5 Brandon Manning B 2.50 6.00
MM6 David Rundblad B 3.00 8.00
MM7 Stefan Elliott B 3.00 8.00
MM8 Teddy Purcell B 4.00 10.00
MM9 Daniel Cleary B SP 5.00 12.00
MM10 Philip McRae B 2.50 6.00
MM11 Evan Brophey B 2.50 6.00
MM12 Scott Timmins B 2.50 6.00
MM13 Sven Baertschi B 3.00 8.00
MM14 Valtteri Filppula B SP 6.00 15.00
MM15 Jakob Silfverberg B 3.00 8.00
MM16 Mike Connolly B 3.00 8.00
MM17 Troy Brouwer B 3.00 8.00
MM18 Antoine Vermette B 2.50 6.00
MM19 Nino Niederreiter B 2.50 6.00
MM20 Akim Aliu B 2.50 6.00
MM23 Roman Josi B 4.00 10.00
MM25 Reilly Smith B 10.00 25.00
MM26 Mikhail Grabovski B SP 10.00 25.00
MM28 Riley Sheahan B 2.50 6.00
MM29 Corey Tropp B 2.50 6.00
MM30 Colten Teubert B 2.50 6.00
MM31 Joe Finley B 2.50 6.00
MM33 Chay Genoway B 4.00 10.00
MM34 Jason Zucker B 3.00 8.00
MM35 Tyson Barrie B 4.00 10.00
MM36 Marcus Kruger B SP 5.00 12.00
MM37 Max Sauve B 2.50 6.00
MM39 Maxime Macenauer B 2.50 6.00
MM41 Anders Nilsson B 2.50 6.00
MM42 Philippe Cornet B 2.50 6.00
MM43 Lane MacDermid B 3.00 8.00
MM44 Brayden McNabb B 2.50 6.00
MM45 Riley Nash B 2.50 6.00
MM46 Matt Donovan B 2.50 6.00
MM47 Mark Stone B 3.00 8.00
MM48 Matt Fraser B SP 4.00 10.00
MM49 Brenden Dillon B 3.00 8.00
MM50 Zac Rinaldo B 4.00 10.00
MM51 Ryan Hamilton B 3.00 8.00
MM52 Shawn Hunwick B 2.50 6.00
MM54 Cory Emmerton B 2.50 6.00
MM55 Colin Wilson B 3.00 8.00
MM57 Tim Erixon B 2.50 6.00
MM59 Carter Camper B 2.50 6.00
MM61 Jay Bouwmeester S/100* 5.00 12.00
MM62 Dany Heatley S/100* 4.00 10.00
MM63 Dan Boyle S/100* 4.00 10.00
MM64 Vincent Lecavalier S/25* 10.00 25.00
MM65 Dion Phaneuf S/100* 5.00 12.00
MM66 Semyon Varlamov S/100* 12.00 30.00
MM67 Chris Pronger S/100* 8.00 20.00
MM68 Daniel Briere S/100* 10.00 25.00
MM69 Brandon Dubinsky S/100* 4.00 10.00
MM70 Joe Thornton S/25*
MM71 Tyler Ennis S/100* 4.00 10.00
MM72 Chris Chelios S/100* 8.00 20.00
MM73 Bill Ranford S/100* 6.00 15.00
MM74 Jamie Benn S/100* 6.00 15.00
MM75 Eric Staal S/100* 6.00 15.00
MM76 Matt Moulson S/100* 4.00 10.00
MM77 Bobby Ryan S/100* 5.00 12.00
MM78 Jonathan Bernier S/100* 12.00 30.00
MM79 Taylor Hall S/100* 10.00 25.00

181 Nick Foligno S/100* 4.00 10.00
182 Brandon Saad S/100* 8.00 20.00
183 Matt Duchene S/100*
184 Michael Grabner S/100* 4.00 10.00
185 Phil Kessel S/100* 12.00 30.00

2013-14 Panini Titanium Milestone Goal Scorer Jerseys

IME/15-25: .6X TO 1.5X BASIC JSY/50-100
H Brett Hull/25
N Bernie Nicholls/50 5.00 12.00
S Brendan Shanahan/100 6.00 15.00
SY Mike Bossy/75 5.00 12.00
N Cam Neely/100 5.00 12.00
PE Corey Perry/100 5.00 12.00
M Dennis Maruk/75 5.00 12.00
M Evgeni Malkin/100 6.00 15.00
I Jarome Iginla/100 8.00 20.00
J Jaromir Jagr/75 10.00 25.00
N Joe Nieuwendyk/100 5.00 12.00
R Jeremy Roenick/100 5.00 12.00
S Joe Sakic/100 8.00 20.00
M Lanny McDonald/75 5.00 12.00
R Luc Robitaille/75 5.00 12.00
HE Milan Hejduk/100 6.00 15.00
L Mario Lemieux/25 12.00 30.00
O Mike Modano/100 8.00 20.00
V Alex Ovechkin/75 20.00 50.00
B Pavel Bure/75 8.00 20.00
C Sidney Crosby/100 20.00 50.00
S Steven Stamkos/75 10.00 25.00
Y Steve Yzerman/75 10.00 25.00
MU Teemu Selanne/50 12.00 30.00
L Vincent Lecavalier/100 4.00 10.00

2013-14 Panini Titanium Road Sweaters Memorabilia Autographs

IME/15: .6X TO 1.5X JSY AU/50
IME/15: .5X TO 1.2X JSY AU/25
R Antoine Roussel/50 15.00 30.00
W Austin Watson/50 8.00 20.00
N Brock Nelson/50 6.00 15.00
A Frederik Andersen/50 10.00 25.00
S Henrik Sedin/25 12.00 30.00
P Joe Pavelski/50 10.00 25.00
Q Jonathan Quick/25
B Martin Brodeur/15
Y Nail Yakupov/25 25.00 60.00
D Pavel Datsyuk/25 25.00 50.00
H Quinton Howden/50 8.00 20.00
W Tom Wilson/50 12.00 30.00
F Viktor Fasth/50 6.00 15.00
GX Claude Giroux/25 15.00 40.00
PE Corey Perry/25
DK Danny DeKeyser/50 8.00 20.00
TO Jonathan Toews/25 40.00 80.00
IK Mikhail Grigorenko/50 12.00 30.00
RX Max Reinhart/50 8.00 20.00
VI Alex Ovechkin/15
KS P.K. Subban/50 20.00 40.00
HI Thomas Hickey/50 8.00 20.00
MG Tye McGinn/50 10.00 25.00

2013-14 Panini Titanium Rookie Dual Signatures

OS C.Soderberg/D.Hamilton 15.00 40.00
UF M.Pysyk/M.Grigorenko 10.00 25.00
BJ S.Collins/J.Marchessault
GY M.Reinhart/B.Street 6.00 15.00
OL M.Sgarbossa/C.Pickard 8.00 20.00
AL J.Campbell/C.Nilstorp 6.00 15.00
ET D.DeKeyser/P.Mrazek 15.00 40.00
UK S.Vatanen/V.Fasth 8.00 20.00
LA M.Caruso/J.Huberdeau 12.00 30.00
LY S.Laughton/T.McGinn 8.00 20.00
AK T.Pearson/T.Toffoli 15.00 40.00
JD H.Pesonen/S.Matteau 6.00 15.00
SH A.Watson/F.Forsberg 20.00 50.00
TT C.Conacher/E.Gryba
AN N.Bjugstad/Q.Howden 10.00 25.00
HI J.Akeson/O.Lauridsen 8.00 20.00
JS M.Irwin/N.Petrecki 6.00 15.00
TR A.Chiasson/A.Roussel 8.00 20.00
BL R.Panik/R.Gudas 8.00 20.00
LD M.Granlund/D.Kuemper 12.00 30.00
PG Z.Redmond/A.Peluso 6.00 15.00
SH T.Wilson/P.Grubauer 15.00 40.00

2013-14 Panini Titanium Rookie Four Star Memorabilia

B Aleksander Barkov/25
G Alex Galchenyuk/25
B Beau Bennett/25 10.00 25.00
G Brendan Gallagher/25 25.00 50.00
C Cory Conacher/25
H Dougie Hamilton/25 12.00 30.00
E Emerson Etem/25
F Filip Forsberg/25 15.00 40.00
H Jonathan Huberdeau/25 15.00 40.00
O Jamie Oleksiak/25 6.00 15.00
SD Jordan Schroeder/25 10.00 25.00
US Justin Schultz/25
IK Mikhail Grigorenko/25
MK Nathan MacKinnon/25 30.00 80.00
Y Nail Yakupov/25 20.00 50.00
MP Ryan Murphy/25 8.00 20.00
J Seth Jones/25 12.00 30.00
M Sean Monahan/25 12.00 30.00
MA Stefan Matteau/25 5.00 12.00
MG Tye McGinn/25
P Tanner Pearson/25
W Tom Wilson/25 25.00 60.00
N Valeri Nichushkin/25 25.00 60.00
T Vladimir Tarasenko/25

2013-14 Panini Titanium Rookie Gear

B Aleksander Barkov 5.00 12.00
G Alex Galchenyuk 6.00 15.00
R Antoine Roussel 2.00 5.00
G Brendan Gallagher 5.00 12.00
C Cody Ceci 1.50 4.00
M Connor Murphy 1.50 4.00
H Dougie Hamilton 4.00 10.00
A Frederik Andersen 3.00 8.00
C Frank Corrado 1.25 3.00
H Jonathan Huberdeau 5.00 12.00
J Nicklas Jensen 1.50 4.00
Y Nail Yakupov 5.00 12.00
Z Nikita Zadorov 2.00 5.00
M Olli Maatta 3.00 8.00
G Philipp Grubauer 4.00 10.00
S Ryan Strome 2.50 6.00
J Seth Jones 3.00 8.00
L Scott Laughton 2.00 5.00
P Tanner Pearson 2.00 5.00
T Tyler Toffoli 4.00 10.00
W Tom Wilson 3.00 8.00
N Valeri Nichushkin 4.00 10.00

RGVT Vladimir Tarasenko 8.00 20.00
RGZG Zemgus Girgensons 4.00 10.00
RGBJE Boone Jenner 2.00 5.00
RGBNE Brock Nelson 2.00 5.00
RGDMI Dylan McIlrath 1.25 3.00
RGELI Elias Lindholm 3.00 8.00
RGHLI Hampus Lindholm 3.00 8.00
RGJAS Jared Staal 2.00 5.00
RGJME Jon Merrill 2.00 5.00
RGJNO Joakim Nordstrom 1.50 4.00
RGJTM J.T. Miller 2.00 5.00
RGJTR Jacob Trouba 5.00 12.00
RGJUS Justin Schultz 2.00 5.00
RGMDB Matt Dumba 2.00 5.00
RGMIG Mikael Granlund 3.00 8.00
RGMKK Michael Kostka 1.50 4.00
RGMMZ Marek Mazanec 2.00 5.00
RGNMK Nathan MacKinnon 8.00 20.00
RGRBE Reto Berra 2.00 5.00
RGRLY Morgan Rielly 5.00 12.00
RGRMP Ryan Murphy 2.00 5.00
RGRMR Ryan Murray 3.00 8.00
RGRSP Ryan Spooner 2.00 5.00
RGSMA Stefan Matteau 1.50 4.00
RGSMO Sean Monahan 5.00 12.00
RGTHE Tomas Hertl 2.50 6.00
RGTJU Tomas Jurco 3.00 8.00

2013-14 Panini Titanium Rookie Gear Patch

RANMK Nathan MacKinnon 40.00 80.00

2013-14 Panini Titanium Rookie Gear Autographs

*PRIME AU/25: .6X TO 1.5X JSY AU/100
*PATCH AU/15: .8X TO 2X JSY AU/100
RAAB Aleksander Barkov 12.00 30.00
RAAG Alex Galchenyuk 20.00 50.00
RAAR Antoine Roussel 5.00 12.00
RABG Brendan Gallagher 15.00 40.00
RABJE Boone Jenner 5.00 12.00
RABNE Brock Nelson 5.00 12.00
RACM Connor Murphy 4.00 10.00
RADH Dougie Hamilton 10.00 25.00
RADMI Dylan McIlrath 3.00 8.00
RAELI Elias Lindholm 8.00 20.00
RAFA Frederik Andersen 8.00 20.00
RAFC Frank Corrado 3.00 8.00
RAHLI Hampus Lindholm 8.00 20.00
RAJAS Jared Staal 5.00 12.00
RAJH Jonathan Huberdeau 12.00 30.00
RAJME Jon Merrill 5.00 12.00
RAJNO Joakim Nordstrom 4.00 10.00
RAJTR Jacob Trouba 8.00 20.00
RAJUS Justin Schultz 5.00 12.00
RAMDB Matt Dumba 5.00 12.00
RAMIG Mikael Granlund 8.00 20.00
RAMKK Michael Kostka 4.00 10.00
RAMMZ Marek Mazanec 5.00 12.00
RANJ Nicklas Jensen 4.00 10.00
RANMK Nathan MacKinnon 50.00 100.00
RANY Nail Yakupov 12.00 30.00
RANZ Nikita Zadorov 5.00 12.00
RAOM Olli Maatta 10.00 25.00
RAPG Philipp Grubauer 5.00 12.00
RARBE Reto Berra 5.00 12.00
RARLY Morgan Rielly 12.00 30.00
RARMR Ryan Murray 8.00 20.00
RARS Ryan Strome 6.00 15.00
RARSP Ryan Spooner 5.00 12.00
RASJ Seth Jones 5.00 12.00
RASL Scott Laughton 5.00 12.00
RASMA Stefan Matteau 4.00 10.00
RASMO Sean Monahan 8.00 20.00
RATHE Tomas Hertl 6.00 15.00
RATJU Tomas Jurco 8.00 20.00
RATP Tanner Pearson 5.00 12.00
RATT Tyler Toffoli 10.00 25.00
RATW Tom Wilson 8.00 20.00

2013-14 Panini Titanium Rookie Reserve Memorabilia Autographs

RRAG Alex Galchenyuk/50 20.00 50.00
RRAW Austin Watson/100 3.00 8.00
RRBG Brendan Gallagher/100 12.00 30.00
RRDH Dougie Hamilton/50 8.00 20.00
RRJB Jonas Brodin/100 3.00 8.00
RRJC Jack Campbell/100 3.00 8.00
RRJH Jonathan Huberdeau/50 10.00 25.00
RRNM Nathan MacKinnon/100 15.00 40.00
RRNY Nail Yakupov/50 12.00 30.00
RRSJ Seth Jones/100 4.00 10.00
RRSM Sean Monahan/100 6.00 15.00
RRTP Tanner Pearson/100 4.00 10.00
RRTW Tom Wilson/100 6.00 15.00
RRVN Valeri Nichushkin/100 4.00 10.00
RRANP Anthony Peluso/100 2.50 6.00
RRCSO Carl Soderberg/100 4.00 10.00
RRDDK Danny DeKeyser/100 5.00 12.00
RRDSH Drew Shore/100 3.00 8.00
RRJTM J.T. Miller/100 4.00 10.00
RRMGR Mikael Granlund/100 6.00 15.00
RRMIK Mikhail Grigorenko/100 5.00 12.00
RRSMA Stefan Matteau/100 3.00 8.00
RRTHI Thomas Hickey/100 3.00 8.00

2013-14 Panini Titanium Rookie Six Star Memorabilia

STATED PRINT RUN 25 SER.#'d SETS
R4CSO Carl Soderberg 12.00 30.00
R6AB Aleksander Barkov 20.00 50.00
R6AG Alex Galchenyuk 40.00 100.00
R6AK Alex Killorn 8.00 20.00
R6AR Antoine Roussel 8.00 20.00
R6AW Austin Watson 6.00 15.00
R6BF Brian Flynn 6.00 15.00
R6BLA Brian Lashoff 8.00 20.00
R6COY Charlie Coyle 8.00 20.00
R6IB Igor Bobkov 6.00 15.00
R6JH Jonathan Huberdeau 20.00 50.00
R6JTI Jarrod Tinordi 8.00 20.00
R6MI Matt Irwin 10.00 25.00
R6MIK Mikhail Grigorenko 10.00 25.00
R6NMK Nathan MacKinnon 30.00 80.00
R6NY Nail Yakupov 25.00 60.00
R6PG Philipp Grubauer 15.00 40.00
R6RCV Roman Cervenka 6.00 15.00
R6RMP Ryan Murphy 8.00 20.00
R6RR Rickard Rakell 8.00 20.00
R6SJ Seth Jones 8.00 20.00
R6SM Sean Monahan 12.00 30.00
R6TH Tomas Hertl 10.00 25.00
R6VN Valeri Nichushkin 8.00 20.00
R6VT Vladimir Tarasenko 30.00 80.00

2013-14 Panini Titanium Rookie Trio Signatures

RTANA Fsth/Bobkv/Andersn/25 15.00 40.00
RTDAL Chson/Oleksk/Cmpbll/25 10.00 25.00
RTDET Lshff/DeKey/Mrazek/25 12.00 30.00
RTFLA Huber/Shore/Hwdn/25 20.00 50.00
RTMTL Galch/Gllghr/Beaul/20
RTRK1 Gllghr/Hberd/Grigrnk/25 20.00 50.00

2013-14 Panini Titanium Rookie Jumbos

J1 Nathan MacKinnon 5.00 12.00
J2 Seth Jones 1.25 3.00
J3 Aleksander Barkov 3.00 8.00
J4 Nail Yakupov 5.00 12.00
J5 Alex Galchenyuk 5.00 12.00
J6 Jonathan Huberdeau 3.00 8.00
J7 Vladimir Tarasenko 5.00 12.00
J8 Dougie Hamilton 2.50 6.00
J9 Brendan Gallagher 4.00 10.00
J10 Filip Forsberg 2.00 5.00

2013-14 Panini Titanium Six Star Memorabilia

6SBEN Jamie Benn/25 20.00 50.00
6SBSE Brent Seabrook/25 15.00 40.00
6SCKU Chris Kunitz/25 15.00 40.00
6SCPE Corey Perry/25 15.00 40.00
6SGF Grant Fuhr/25
6SGRN Mike Green/25 15.00 40.00
6SHL Henrik Lundqvist/25 20.00 50.00
6SIL Igor Larionov/25 20.00 50.00
6SJE Jordan Eberle/25 15.00 40.00
6SJFC Jeff Carter/25 15.00 40.00
6SJQ Jonathan Quick/25 25.00 60.00
6SJS Joe Sakic/25 25.00 60.00
6SMBA Mikael Backlund/25
6SML Mario Lemieux/25 50.00 125.00
6SMRI Mike Richards/25 15.00 40.00
6SPAS Paul Stastny/25 15.00 40.00
6SPS Patrick Sharp/25 15.00 40.00
6SRB Ray Bourque/15 30.00 80.00
6SRC Ryan Callahan/25 15.00 40.00
6SRN Rick Nash/25 15.00 40.00
6SSC Sidney Crosby/25 60.00 150.00
6SSHA Scott Hartnell/25 15.00 40.00
6STPL Tomas Plekanec/25 12.00 30.00
6STR Tuukka Rask/25 20.00 50.00
6SZC Zdeno Chara/25

2013-14 Panini Titanium Team Building Quad Jerseys

*PRIME/25: .6X TO 1.5X QUAD JSY/100
TBANA Perry/Fwlr/Etem/Rakll 6.00 15.00
TBBOS Brgrn/Luc/Hmiltn/Spnr 8.00 20.00
TBBUF Enrth/Grig/Adam/Ennis 8.00 20.00
TBCHI Keith/Crwfd/Tws/Kane 12.00 30.00
TBCOL Ststny/Dchn/Lnds/Pck 6.00 15.00
TBDAL Ben/Olksk/Cmpbl/Dley 10.00 25.00
TBDET Frnzn/Hwrd/Dtsyk/Ztrb 6.00 15.00
TBEDM Dbnk/Hall/RNH/Yakpv 12.00 30.00
TBFLA Bjgstd/Hwd/Hbrd/Shre 6.00 15.00
TBLAK Qck/Toff/Prsn/Dghty 10.00 25.00
TBMON Prce/Sbn/Gllgh/Glchn 12.00 30.00
TBNJD Brdr/Lrsn/Mtteau/Zajc 12.00 30.00
TBNSH Hrnqst/Rne/Wtsn/Lgw 8.00 20.00
TBNYI Nlsn/Bley/Tvres/Okpso 12.00 30.00
TBNYR Lndqvt/Staal/Stpn/Mllr 8.00 20.00
TBOTT Gryba/Krlsn/Spzz/Neil 12.00 30.00
TBPHI Ctrier/Rnldo/Girx/Lghtn 8.00 20.00
TBPHX Bdkr/Brwn/Doan/Hnzl 5.00 12.00
TBPIT Dsprs/Mlkn/Flry/Bnnt 12.00 30.00
TBSJS Ptrck/Mrlu/Vlsic/Pvlski 8.00 20.00
TBSTL Bcks/Osh/Trsnk/Jckm 15.00 40.00
TBTBL Kllrn/Stmks/Panik/Tyrll 8.00 20.00
TBVAN Edler/Sedins/Schroeder 6.00 15.00
TBWPG Lttl/E.Kne/Rdmnd/Psql 6.00 15.00
TBWSH Jhnsn/Ovch/Wlsn/Grbr 15.00 40.00

2013-14 Panini Titanium Third Sweaters Memorabilia Autographs

TSDH Dougie Hamilton/25
TSDJ Dmitrij Jaskin/25
TSGL Gabriel Landeskog/25 12.00 30.00
TSIB Igor Bobkov/25 12.00 30.00
TSKL Kris Letang/25 40.00 80.00
TSNM Nathan MacKinnon/25
TSNP Nick Petrecki/25 10.00 25.00
TSPM Patrick Marleau/25 15.00 40.00
TSRK Ryan Kesler/25 15.00 40.00
TSSV Sami Vatanen/25 15.00 40.00
TSTH Taylor Hall/25
TSCVP Calvin Pickard/25 12.00 30.00
TSJEN Jhonas Enroth/25 15.00 40.00
TSJTM J.T. Miller/25 12.00 30.00
TSMAF Marc-Andre Fleury/25 25.00 60.00
TSMDU Matt Duchene/25
TSRNH Ryan Nugent-Hopkins/25 12.00 30.00
TSRSP Ryan Spooner/25
TSSVA Semyon Varlamov/25

2013-14 Panini Titanium Three Star Selections Autographs

3GHL Henrik Lundqvist/25 20.00 50.00
3GJHO Jimmy Howard/50 12.00 30.00
3GJQ Jonathan Quick/50 12.00 30.00
3GJRE James Reimer/50 10.00 25.00
3GMB Martin Brodeur/25 30.00 60.00
3GMS Mike Smith/50 10.00 25.00
3GPRI Pekka Rinne/50 10.00 25.00
3GRM Ryan Miller/50 12.00 30.00
3RAG Alex Galchenyuk/50 15.00 40.00
3RBG Brendan Gallagher/100 10.00 25.00
3RDDK Danny DeKeyser/100 8.00 20.00
3RDH Dougie Hamilton/100 12.00 30.00
3RFF Filip Forsberg/100 12.00 30.00
3RJB Jonas Brodin/15
3RMGR Mikael Granlund/100 8.00 15.00
3RNY Nail Yakupov/50 15.00 40.00
3RTW Tom Wilson/100 12.00 30.00
3SAH Adam Henrique/50 12.00 30.00
3SGL Gabriel Landeskog/50 10.00 25.00
3SJI Jarome Iginla/50 12.00 30.00
3SJP Joe Pavelski/25 15.00 40.00
3SJT John Tavares/50 25.00 60.00
3SLE Loui Eriksson/50 10.00 25.00
3SOVI Alex Ovechkin/25
3SPD Pavel Datsyuk/50 25.00 50.00
3SRNH Ryan Nugent-Hopkins/50 15.00 40.00
3STS Tyler Seguin/50 20.00 50.00

2013-14 Panini Titanium Retail

COMP.SET w/o RC's (100) 12.00 30.00
*1-100 VETS: .3X TO .8X HOBBY
17 Corey Crawford .40 1.00
73 Nicklas Backstrom .50 1.25
101 Vladimir Tarasenko RC 12.00 30.00
102 Cory Conacher RC 2.00 5.00
103 John Muse RC 3.00 8.00
104 Matt Tennyson RC 2.00 5.00
105 Eric Selleck RC 2.50 6.00
106 Radko Gudas RC 3.00 8.00
107 Ondrej Palat RC 4.00 10.00
108 Brett Bellemore RC 2.50 6.00
109 Tyler Toffoli RC 8.00 20.00
110 Igor Bobkov RC 2.50 6.00
111 Nicolas Blanchard RC 2.50 6.00
112 Alex Petrovic RC 2.50 6.00
113 Joonas Rask RC 2.00 5.00
114 Richard Panik RC 3.00 8.00
115 Tanner Pearson RC 3.00 8.00
116 Jamie Tardif RC 2.00 5.00
117 Rickard Rakell RC 3.00 8.00
118 Emerson Etem RC 3.00 8.00
119 Brian Flynn RC 2.50 6.00
120 Danny DeKeyser RC 4.00 10.00
121 Nail Yakupov RC 10.00 25.00
122 Mikael Granlund RC 5.00 12.00
123 Greg Pateryn RC 3.00 8.00
124 Victor Bartley RC 2.50 6.00
125 Charlie Coyle RC 3.00 8.00
126 Tyler Johnson RC 8.00 20.00
127 Mark Arcobello RC 3.00 8.00
128 Michael Caruso RC 2.00 5.00
129 Eric Gryba RC 2.50 6.00
130 Andrej Sustr RC 2.00 5.00
131 Steve Oleksy RC 3.00 8.00
132 Max Reinhart RC 3.00 8.00
133 Dave Dziurzynski RC 2.50 6.00
134 Ben Hanowski RC 2.50 6.00
135 Chris Terry RC 2.00 5.00
136 Patrick Bordeleau RC 3.00 8.00
137 Christian Thomas RC 2.50 6.00
138 Derek Grant RC 2.50 6.00
139 Taylor Beck RC 2.50 6.00
140 Ryan Stanton RC 3.00 8.00
141 Nick Petrecki RC 2.00 5.00
142 Mark Pysyk RC 3.00 8.00
143 Michael Kostka RC 2.50 6.00
144 Jonathan Rheault RC 2.00 5.00
145 Austin Watson RC 2.50 6.00
146 Matt Irwin RC 2.50 6.00
147 Ryan Spooner RC 3.00 8.00
148 Daniel Bang RC 2.50 6.00
149 Michal Jordan RC 2.00 5.00
150 Johan Larsson RC 2.50 6.00
151 J.T. Miller RC 3.00 8.00
152 Leo Komarov RC 3.00 8.00
153 Carter Bancks RC 2.50 6.00
154 Kevin Henderson RC 2.50 6.00
155 Nicklas Jensen RC 2.50 6.00
156 Sami Vatanen RC 3.00 8.00
157 Jordan Schroeder RC 3.00 8.00
158 Cameron Schilling RC 2.00 5.00
159 Jean-Gabriel Pageau RC 2.50 6.00
160 Chris Brown RC 2.00 5.00
161 Michael Sgarbossa RC 2.50 6.00
162 Sean Collins RC 2.50 6.00
163 Tom Wilson RC 5.00 12.00
164 Mark Cundari RC 2.00 5.00
165 Shawn Lalonde RC 3.00 8.00
166 Quinton Howden RC 2.50 6.00
167 Jarred Tinordi RC 3.00 8.00
168 Jason Akeson RC 2.50 6.00
169 Cristopher Nilstorp RC 2.50 6.00
170 Nathan Beaulieu RC 2.50 6.00
171 Ben Street RC 2.00 5.00
172 Oliver Lauridsen RC 2.50 6.00
173 Jonathan Marchessault RC 6.00 15.00
174 Jeff Zatkoff RC 3.00 8.00
175 Darcy Kuemper RC 4.00 10.00
176 Calvin Heeter RC 2.50 6.00
177 Carl Soderberg RC 3.00 8.00
178 Petr Mrazek RC 6.00 15.00
179 Matthew Konan RC 3.00 8.00
180 Eric Gelinas RC 3.00 8.00
181 Edward Pasquale RC 2.00 5.00
182 Frederik Andersen RC 5.00 12.00
183 Calvin Pickard RC 3.00 8.00
184 Eric Hartzell RC 3.00 8.00
185 Philipp Grubauer RC 3.00 8.00
186 Viktor Fasth RC 3.00 8.00
187 Sami Aittokallio RC 3.00 8.00
188 Joe Cannata RC 2.50 6.00
189 Brock Nelson RC 3.00 8.00
190 Dougie Hamilton RC 6.00 15.00
191 Nick Bjugstad RC 4.00 10.00
192 Alex Galchenyuk RC 15.00 40.00
193 Anders Lee RC 5.00 12.00
194 Dmitrij Jaskin RC 3.00 8.00
195 Frank Corrado RC 2.00 5.00
196 Mikhail Grigorenko RC 4.00 10.00
197 Jonas Brodin RC 2.50 6.00
198 Zach Redmond RC 2.50 6.00
199 Damien Brunner RC 2.50 6.00
200 Brian Lashoff RC 2.50 6.00
201 Scott Laughton RC 3.00 8.00
202 Antoine Roussel RC 3.00 8.00
203 Justin Schultz RC 3.00 8.00
204 Beau Bennett RC 4.00 10.00
205 Alex Killorn RC 3.00 8.00
206 Harri Pesonen RC 2.50 6.00
207 Drew Shore RC 2.50 6.00
208 Stefan Matteau RC 2.50 6.00
209 Tye McGinn RC 3.00 8.00
210 Drew LeBlanc RC 2.00 5.00
211 Thomas Hickey RC 2.50 6.00
212 Anthony Peluso RC 2.00 5.00
213 Jared Staal RC 3.00 8.00
214 Steven Pinizzotto RC 3.00 8.00
215 Alex Chiasson RC 3.00 8.00
216 Matt Anderson RC 2.00 5.00
217 Jonathan Huberdeau RC 8.00 20.00
218 Brendan Gallagher RC 10.00 25.00
219 Roman Cervenka RC 2.50 6.00
220 Filip Forsberg RC 8.00 20.00
221 Mark Barberio RC 2.00 5.00
222 Ryan Murphy RC 3.00 8.00
223 Chad Ruhwedel RC 2.00 5.00
224 Jamie Oleksiak RC 2.50 6.00
225 Jack Campbell RC 2.50 6.00
226 Jacob Trouba RC 8.00 20.00
227 Anton Belov RC 3.00 8.00
228 Will Acton RC 2.50 6.00
229 Luke Gazdic RC 2.50 6.00
230 Joakim Nordstrom RC 2.50 6.00
231 Connor Carrick RC 2.50 6.00
232 Michael Latta RC 2.50 6.00
233 Nathan MacKinnon RC 12.00 30.00
234 Zemgus Girgensons RC 6.00 15.00
235 Rasmus Ristolainen RC 5.00 12.00
236 Seth Jones RC 3.00 8.00
237 Sean Monahan RC 5.00 12.00
238 Olli Maatta RC 5.00 12.00
239 Justin Fontaine RC 3.00 8.00
240 Aleksander Barkov RC 8.00 20.00
241 Valeri Nichushkin RC 3.00 8.00
242 Jesper Fast RC 2.50 6.00
243 Lucas Lessio RC 2.00 5.00
244 Matt Nieto RC 2.50 6.00
245 Tomas Hertl RC 4.00 10.00
246 Boone Jenner RC 3.00 8.00
247 Ryan Murray RC 3.00 8.00
248 Morgan Rielly RC 8.00 20.00
249 Matt Dumba RC 3.00 8.00
250 Hampus Lindholm RC 5.00 12.00

2013-14 Panini Titanium Retail Red

*1-100 VETS/199: 2.5X TO 6X RETAIL
*101-250 ROOKIE/99: .6X TO 1.5X RETAIL/299
17 Corey Crawford 2.50 6.00
73 Nicklas Backstrom 3.00 8.00

2013-14 Panini Titanium Titanium Reserve Autographs

TRAA Akim Aliu 2.50 6.00
TRAJO Andrew Joudrey 2.50 6.00
TRAK Alex Killorn 4.00 10.00
TRANE Aaron Ness 2.50 6.00
TRANL Anton Lander 3.00 8.00
TRANP Anthony Peluso 2.50 6.00
TRAP Alex Pietrangelo SP 4.00 10.00
TRBES Ben Smith 4.00 10.00
TRBL Brian Leetch SP 6.00 15.00
TRBM Brenden Morrow SP 5.00 12.00
TRBMA Brandon Manning 2.50 6.00
TRBN Bernie Nicholls SP 8.00 20.00
TRBSM Brendan Smith 3.00 8.00
TRBWR Johnny Bower SP 8.00 20.00
TRCB Chris Brown 2.50 6.00
TRCCI Casey Cizikas
TRCGR Colin Greening SP 4.00 10.00
TRCJ Curtis Joseph SP
TRCK Chris Kreider SP
TRCNI Cristopher Nilstorp 3.00 8.00
TRCP Carey Price SP 15.00 30.00
TRCS Cory Schneider SP 5.00 12.00
TRCSO Carl Soderberg 4.00 10.00
TRDGR Derek Grant 3.00 8.00
TRDR Derek Roy SP 5.00 12.00
TREH Eric Hartzell 4.00 10.00
TRERS Eric Staal SP 8.00 20.00
TRFA Frederik Andersen 6.00 15.00
TRFF Filip Forsberg 10.00 25.00
TRFP Felix Potvin SP 15.00 30.00
TRGH Gordie Howe SP
TRGL Gabriel Landeskog SP 8.00 20.00
TRHP Harri Pesonen 3.00 8.00
TRJAM Jonathan Marchessault 8.00 20.00
TRJAS Jared Staal 4.00 10.00
TRJB Jonas Brodin 3.00 8.00
TRJHY Jimmy Hayes 3.00 8.00
TRJMO Jeremy Morin 3.00 8.00
TRJO Jamie Oleksiak 3.00 8.00
TRJS Joe Sakic SP 30.00 60.00
TRJSD Jordan Schroeder 4.00 10.00
TRJVR James van Riemsdyk SP 8.00 20.00
TRLE Loui Eriksson SP 6.00 15.00
TRLP Lennart Petrell 3.00 8.00
TRMAS Marc Staal SP 5.00 12.00
TRML Mario Lemieux SP 30.00 60.00
TRMPY Mark Pysyk 4.00 10.00
TRMXR Max Reinhart 4.00 10.00
TRMXT Maxime Talbot SP 5.00 12.00
TRNP Nick Petrecki 2.50 6.00
TROVI Alex Ovechkin SP 25.00 60.00
TRRCL Ryane Clowe SP 4.00 10.00
TRRH Ryan Hamilton 4.00 10.00
TRRIB Richard Bachman 3.00 8.00
TRRJO Roman Josi 4.00 10.00
TRRNH Ryan Nugent-Hopkins SP 6.00 15.00
TRRR Rickard Rakell 4.00 10.00
TRSE Stefan Elliott 3.00 8.00
TRSGO Scott Gomez SP 5.00 12.00
TRSTM Steve Mason SP 5.00 12.00
TRSV Sami Vatanen 4.00 10.00
TRTMG Tye McGinn 4.00 10.00
TRTVA Thomas Vanek SP 6.00 15.00
TRZK Zack Kassian 3.00 8.00

2012-13 Panini Tools of the Trade Materials Kreider Promos

1 Chris Kreider Black Friday
C Chris Kreider Fall Expo

2011-12 Panini Toronto Fall Expo

1 Alex Ovechkin 2.50 6.00
2 Steven Stamkos 1.25 3.00
3 Tim Thomas .60 1.50
4 Sidney Crosby 2.50 6.00
5 Nicklas Lidstrom .60 1.50
6 Corey Perry .60 1.50
7 Ryan Nugent-Hopkins 8.00 20.00
8 Gabriel Landeskog 1.25 3.00
9 Adam Larsson .75 2.00
HOF1 Doug Gilmour 1.00 2.50
HOF2 Joe Nieuwendyk .75 2.00
HOF3 Ed Belfour .75 2.00

2012-13 Panini Toronto Fall Expo

COMPLETE SET (25)
COMP.SET w/o RC's (15)
STATED RC PRINT RUN 399
1 Sidney Crosby .75 2.00
2 Alex Ovechkin .75 2.00
3 Tyler Seguin .60 1.50
4 Martin Brodeur .75 2.00
5 Phil Kessel .75 2.00
6 Carey Price .75 2.00
7 Jarome Iginla .60 1.50
8 Henrik Sedin .60 1.50
9 Daniel Sedin .60 1.50
10 Steven Stamkos .75 2.00
11 Claude Giroux .75 2.00
12 Ryan Nugent-Hopkins 1.00 2.50
13 Gabriel Landeskog .75 2.00
14 Adam Henrique .60 1.50
15 John Tavares .75 2.00
16 Jakob Silfverberg RR 1.00 2.50
17 Tyson Barrie RR 1.00 2.50
18 Jordan Nolan RR 1.00 2.50
19 Cartor Ashton RR 1.25 3.00
20 Sven Baertschi RR 1.25 3.00
21 Jaden Schwartz RR 1.25 3.00
22 Reilly Smith RR 1.00 2.50
23 Chet Pickard RR 1.00 2.50
24 Chris Kreider RR 2.00 5.00
25 Jake Allen RR 1.00 2.50

2012-13 Panini Toronto Fall Expo Cracked Ice

STATED PRINT RUN 25

2013-14 Panini Toronto Fall Expo

*LAVA FLOW: 1X TO 2.5X BASIC CARDS
1 Sidney Crosby 1.50 4.00
2 Nazem Kadri .40 1.00
3 Tuukka Rask .40 1.00
4 Taylor Hall .75 2.00
5 Patrick Kane .75 2.00
6 Carey Price 1.25 3.00
7 John Tavares .75 2.00
8 Pavel Datsyuk .50 1.25
9 Alex Ovechkin 1.50 4.00
10 Chris Chelios .40 1.00
11 Scott Niedermayer .40 1.00
12 Brendan Shanahan .50 1.25
13 Nail Yakupov 3.00 8.00
14 Tyler Toffoli 2.00 5.00
15 Jonathan Huberdeau 2.50 6.00
16 Alex Galchenyuk 5.00 12.00
17 Brendan Gallagher 3.00 8.00
18 Jean-Gabriel Pageau .75 2.00
19 Vladimir Tarasenko 4.00 10.00
20 Alex Chiasson 1.00 2.50
21 Emerson Etem 1.00 2.50
22 Anthony Bennett 1.50 4.00
23 EJ Manuel 2.50 6.00
24 Yasiel Puig 5.00 12.00
25 Morgan Rielly 2.50 6.00
26 Nathan MacKinnon 4.00 10.00
27 Aleksander Barkov 2.50 6.00
28 Sean Monahan 1.50 4.00
29 Seth Jones 1.00 2.50
30 Valeri Nichushkin 1.00 2.50

2013-14 Panini Toronto Fall Expo Hot Rookies

*LAVA FLOW: 1.2X TO 3X BASIC INSERTS
HK1 Austin Watson .40 1.00
HK2 Brock Nelson .50 1.25
HK3 Jamie Oleksiak .40 1.00
HK4 Beau Bennett .60 1.50
HK5 Charlie Coyle .50 1.25
HK6 Ryan Spooner .50 1.25
HK7 Ryan Murphy .50 1.25
HK8 Scott Laughton .50 1.25
HK9 Mikhail Grigorenko .60 1.50
HK10 Christian Thomas .40 1.00
HK11 Cory Conacher .30 .75
HK12 Nicklas Jensen .40 1.00
HK13 Petr Mrazek 1.00 2.50
HK14 Tanner Pearson .50 1.25
HK15 Tom Wilson .75 2.00
HK16 Justin Schultz .50 1.25

2011-12 Panini Toronto Spring Expo

COMPLETE SET (10) 12.50 25.00
1 Tim Thomas .60 1.50
2 Evgeni Malkin 2.00 5.00
3 Phil Kessel .75 2.00
4 Henrik Lundqvist .75 2.00
5 Steven Stamkos 1.25 3.00
6 Claude Giroux .60 1.50
7 Pavel Datsyuk .75 2.00
8 Jonathan Toews 1.25 3.00
9 Alex Ovechkin SP 6.00 15.00
10 Sidney Crosby SP 6.00 15.00

2011-12 Panini Toronto Spring Expo Legends

COMPLETE SET (4) 4.00 10.00
MVP1 Gordie Howe 1.50 4.00
MVP2 Ray Bourque 1.25 3.00
MVP3 Joe Sakic 1.25 3.00
MVP4 Brett Hull 1.00 2.50

2011-12 Panini Toronto Spring Expo Rookie Patch Autographs

BS Brendan Smith/50* 12.50 25.00
EG Erik Gudbranson/50* 6.00 15.00
JB Jonathon Blum/24* 6.00 15.00
RE Ryan Ellis/25* 15.00 30.00
RJ Ryan Johansen/50* 8.00 20.00
SD Simon Despres/25* 15.00 30.00
ZK Zack Kassian/79* 6.00 15.00
CDH Calvin de Haan/50* 6.00 15.00

2011-12 Panini Toronto Spring Expo Rookies

COMPLETE SET (8) 20.00 50.00
RC1 Ryan Nugent-Hopkins 8.00 20.00
RC2 Gabriel Landeskog 2.00 5.00
RC3 Adam Larsson 1.25 3.00
RC4 Adam Henrique 2.50 6.00
RC5 Jake Gardiner 1.50 4.00
RC6 Sean Couturier 2.00 5.00
RC7 Matt Read 2.00 5.00
RC8 Cody Hodgson 2.00 5.00

2011-12 Panini Toronto Spring Expo Tools of the Trade

COMPLETE SET (5) 25.00 50.00
AS Daniel Sedin 4.00 10.00
BC Alex Ovechkin 6.00 15.00
FS Michael Grabner 3.00 8.00
HS Zdeno Chara 4.00 10.00
MVP Patrick Sharp 4.00 10.00

2013-14 Panini Toronto Spring Expo Autographs

BR Brad Richards
BS Brendan Shanahan 8.00 20.00
CC Connor Carrick 10.00 25.00
DP Dion Phaneuf
GH Gordie Howe
HL Hampus Lindholm
JB Jay Bouwmeester
JC Jack Campbell 3.00 8.00
JG John Gibson
JH Jonathon Huberdeau
JS Joe Sakic
JT Jacob Trouba
LC Logan Couture
LM Lanny McDonald 5.00 12.00
MB Martin Brodeur
MH Magnus Hellberg
MM Mark Messier 12.00 30.00
MP Max Paclorelly 5.00 12.00
MR Michael Raffl
MS Mike Smith
NM Nathan MacKinnon
PR Patrick Roy 30.00 60.00
RF Ron Francis
RL Roberto Luongo 4.00 10.00
SM Sean Monahan
TJ Tomas Jurco
VT Vladislav Tretiak

2013-14 Panini Toronto Spring Expo Priority Signings 5x7

RS Ryan Strome 4.00 10.00
SM Sean Monahan 4.00 10.00

1993-94 Panthers Team Issue

These eight blank-backed cards were printed on thin stock and measure approximately 3 3/4" by 7". They feature on their white-bordered fronts black-and-white action shots framed by a thin red line. The player's uniform number (in large red characters), his name and position, and the Panthers' logo are printed across the top. The cards are unnumbered and checklisted below in alphabetical order.

COMPLETE SET (8) 4.80 12.00
1 Joe Cirella .60 1.50
2 Tom Fitzgerald .60 1.50
3 Mike Foligno .60 1.50
4 Paul Laus .75 2.00
5 Bill Lindsay .60 1.50
6 Andrei Lomakin .60 1.50
7 Scott Mellanby .75 2.00
8 Brent Severyn .60 1.50

1994-95 Panthers Boston Market

COMPLETE SET (28) 4.00 10.00
1 Stu Barnes .20 .50
2 Jesse Belanger .20 .50
3 Brian Benning .20 .50
4 Keith Brown .20 .50
5 Joe Cirella .20 .50
6 Jeff Daniels .20 .50
7 Tom Fitzgerald .20 .50
8 Mark Fitzpatrick .20 .50
9 Mike Hough .20 .50
10 Jody Hull .20 .50
11 Bob Kudelski .20 .50
12 Paul Laus .20 .50
13 Bill Lindsay .20 .50
14 Andrei Lomakin .20 .50
15 Dave Lowry .20 .50
16 Scott Mellanby .20 .50
17 Randy Moller .20 .50
18 Gord Murphy .20 .50
19 Rob Niedermayer .20 .50
20 Brent Severyn .20 .50
21 Brian Skrudland .20 .50
22 Geoff Smith .20 .50
23 John Vanbiesbrouck .30 .75
24 Roger Neilson .20 .50
25 Craig Ramsay .20 .50
26 Lindy Ruff .20 .50
27 Billy Smith .20 .50
28 The Panther .08 .25

1994-95 Panthers Pop-ups

Issued by Health Plan of Florida, these cards measure 4" x 10". They were given away at five different home games throughout the season. Back has biographical information.

COMPLETE SET (5) 4.00 10.00
1 Brian Skrudland .60 1.50
2 John Vanbiesbrouck 1.25 3.00
3 Scott Mellanby .60 1.50
4 Stu Barnes .60 1.50
5 Jesse Belanger .60 1.50

1995-96 Panthers Boston Market

COMPLETE SET (32) 4.00 10.00
1 Stu Barnes .20 .50
2 Jesse Belanger .20 .50
3 Terry Carkner .20 .50
4 Radek Dvorak .20 .50
5 Tom Fitzgerald .20 .50
6 Mark Fitzpatrick .20 .50
7 Johan Garpenlov .20 .50
8 Mike Hough .20 .50
9 Jody Hull .20 .50
10 Ed Jovanovski .20 .50
11 Bob Kudelski .20 .50
12 Paul Laus .20 .50
13 Bill Lindsay .20 .50
14 Dave Lowry .20 .50
15 Scott Mellanby .20 .50
16 Gord Murphy .20 .50
17 David Nemirovsky .20 .50
18 Rob Niedermayer .20 .50
19 Brian Skrudland .20 .50
20 Geoff Smith .20 .50
21 Robert Svehla .20 .50
22 Magnus Svensson .20 .50
23 John Vanbiesbrouck .30 .75
24 Rhett Warrener .20 .50
25 Jason Woolley .20 .50
26 Doug MacLean .20 .50
27 Lindy Ruff .20 .50
28 Duane Sutter .20 .50
29 Billy Smith .20 .50
30 Boston Market .08 .25
31 Stanley C. Panther .08 .25
32 Boston Market .08 .25

1999-00 Panthers Cigna

COMPLETE SET (36) 6.00 15.00
1 Dan Boyle .40 1.00
2 Pavel Bure 2.00 5.00
3 Radek Dvorak .20 .50
4 Dwayne Hay .20 .50
5 Bret Hedican .20 .50
6 John Jakopin .20 .50
7 Ryan Johnson .20 .50
8 Trevor Kidd .30 .75
9 Viktor Kozlov .30 .75
10 Filip Kuba .20 .50
11 Oleg Kvasha .20 .50
12 Paul Laus .20 .50
13 Scott Mellanby .20 .50
14 Rob Niedermayer .30 .75
15 Ivan Novoseltsev .20 .50
16 Mark Parrish .40 1.00
17 Lance Pitlick .20 .50
18 Ray Sheppard .30 .75
19 Mikhail Shtalenkov .20 .50
20 Denis Shvidki .20 .50
21 Todd Simpson .20 .50
22 Jaroslav Spacek .20 .50
23 Cam Stewart .20 .50
24 Robert Svehla .20 .50
25 Chris Wells .20 .50
26 Ray Whitney .40 1.00
27 Mike Wilson .20 .50
28 Peter Worrell .20 .50
29 Terry Murray CO .08 .25
30 Slavomir Lener ACO .08 .25
31 Billy Smith ACO .08 .25
32 Bryan Murray GM .08 .25
33 2000 Schedule .08 .25
34 Chuck Fletcher AGM .08 .25

35 Stanley C. Panther .08 .25
36 William Torrey PRES .08 .25

2000-01 Panthers Team Issue

This set features the Panthers of the NHL. The cards were issued as a promotional giveaway. The perforated card sheets were stapled into a booklet with four cards per page.

COMPLETE SET (32) 10.00 25.00
1 Bill Torrey CO .04 .10
2 Chuck Fletcher GM .04 .10
3 Duane Sutter CO .10 .25
4 Panther MASCOT .04 .10
5 Slavomir Lener TR .04 .10
6 Billy Smith CO .40 1.00
7 Roberto Luongo 2.00 5.00
8 Lance Pitlick .20 .50
9 Paul Laus .40 1.00
10 Bret Hedican .20 .50
11 Mike Wilson .20 .50
12 Peter Worrell .60 1.50
13 Len Barrie .20 .50
14 Pavel Bure 2.00 5.00
15 Olli Jokinen .30 .75
16 Vaclav Prospal .20 .50
17 Ray Whitney .20 .50
18 John Jakopin .20 .50
19 Mike Sillinger .20 .50
20 Greg Adams .20 .50
21 Marcus Nilsson .20 .50
22 Serge Payer .20 .50
23 Todd Simpson .20 .50
24 Robert Svehla .20 .50
25 Viktor Kozlov .30 .75
26 Dan Boyle .20 .50
27 Scott Mellanby .20 .50
28 Anders Eriksson .20 .50
29 Trevor Kidd .30 .75
30 Ivan Novoseltsev .30 .75
31 Rob Niedermayer .20 .50
32 Lance Ward .20 .50

2003-04 Panthers Team Issue

These cards are oversized and were distributed by the team at club events. It's likely this checklist is incomplete. Additional information can be forwarded to hockeymag@beckett.com.

COMPLETE SET (18) 8.00 20.00
1 Mathieu Biron .20 .50
2 Jay Bouwmeester .40 1.00
3 Valeri Bure .20 .50
4 Matt Cullen .20 .50
5 Niklas Hagman .20 .50
6 Darcy Hordichuk .40 1.00
7 Nathan Horton 1.50 4.00
8 Kristian Huselius .30 .75
9 Olli Jokinen .40 1.00
10 Viktor Kozlov .20 .50
11 Roberto Luongo 1.25 3.00
12 Eric Messier .20 .50
13 Branislav Mezei .20 .50
14 Lyle Odelein .20 .50
15 Mikael Samuelsson .20 .50
16 Pavel Trnka .20 .50
17 Mike Van Ryn .20 .50
18 Stephen Weiss .40 1.00

1943-48 Parade Sportive

These blank-backed photo sheets of sports figures from the Montreal area around 1945 measure approximately 5" by 8 1/4". They were issued to promote a couple of Montreal radio stations that used to broadcast interviews with some of the pictured athletes. The sheets feature white-bordered black-and-white player photos, some of them crudely retouched. The player's name appears in the bottom white margin and also as a facsimile autograph across the photo. The sheets are unnumbered and are checklisted below in alphabetical order within sport as follows: hockey (1-75), baseball (76-95) and various other sports (96-101). Additions to this checklist are appreciated. Many players are known to appear with two different poses. Since the values are the same for both poses, we have put a (2) next to the players name but have placed a value on only one of the photos.

COMPLETE SET 1250.00 2500.00
1 George Allen 12.50 25.00
2 Aldege(Bazz) Bastien 12.50 25.00
3 Bobby Bauer 25.00 50.00
Milt Schmidt
Woody Dumart
4 Joe Benoit 12.50 25.00
5 Paul Bibeault 12.50 25.00
6 Emile(Butch) Bouchard (2) 20.00 40.00
7 Butch Bouchard 20.00 40.00
Leo Lamoureux
Bill Durnan
8 Toe Blake 25.00 50.00
9 Lionel Bouvrette (2) 12.50 25.00
10 Frank Brimsek 20.00 40.00
11 Turk Broda (2) 25.00 50.00
12 Eddie Bruneteau 12.50 25.00
13 Modere Bruneteau (2) 12.50 25.00
14 Jean Claude Campeau 12.50 25.00
15 J.P. Campeau 12.50 25.00
16 Bob Carse 12.50 25.00
17 Joe Carveth 20.00 40.00
18 Denys Casavant (2) 12.50 25.00
19 Murph Chamberlain 12.50 25.00
20 Bill Cowley 12.50 25.00
21 Floyd Curry 12.50 25.00
22 Tony Demers (2) 12.50 25.00
23 Connie Dion 12.50 25.00
24 Bill Durnan (2) 20.00 40.00
25 Normand Dussault (2) 12.50 25.00
26 Frank Eddolls 12.50 25.00
27 Johnny Gagnon 12.50 25.00
28 Bob Fillion (2) 12.50 25.00
29 Johnny Gagnon 12.50 25.00
Aurel Joliat
Howie Morenz
30 Armand Gaudreault (2) 12.50 25.00
31 Fernand Gauthier (2) 12.50 25.00
32 Fernand Gauthier 12.50 25.00
Buddy O'Connor
Dutch Hiller
33 Jean-Paul Gladu (2) 12.50 25.00
34 Leo Gravelle 12.50 25.00
35 Glen Harmon (2) 12.50 25.00
36 Doug Harvey 20.00 40.00
37 Jerry Heffernan 12.50 25.00
Buddy O'Connor
Pete Morin
38 (Sugar) Jim Henry 15.00 30.00
39 Dutch Hiller (2) 12.50 25.00
40 Rosario Joanette 12.50 25.00
41 Michael Karakas (2) 12.50 25.00
42 Elmer Lach 25.00 50.00
43 Ernest Laforce 12.50 25.00
44 Leo Lamoureux 12.50 25.00
45 Edgar Laprade 12.50 25.00
46 Hal Laycoe 12.50 25.00
47 Roger Leger 12.50 25.00
48 Jacques Locas (2) 12.50 25.00
49 Harry Lumley 20.00 40.00
50 Fernand Mageau 12.50 25.00
51 Georges Mantha (2) 12.50 25.00
52 Jean Marois 12.50 25.00
53 Mike McMahon 12.50 25.00
54 Gerry McNeil 12.50 25.00
55 Pierre(Pete) Morin 12.50 25.00
56 Ken Mosdell 12.50 25.00
57 Bill Mosienko 20.00 40.00
Max Bentley
Doug Bentley
58 Buddy O'Connor 12.50 25.00
59 Gerry Plamondon 12.50 25.00
60 Robert(Bob) Pepin 12.50 25.00
61 Jimmy Peters 12.50 25.00
62 Jerry Plamondon 12.50 25.00
63 Paul Raymond 12.50 25.00
64 Billy Reay 15.00 30.00
65 John Quilty 12.50 25.00
66 Kenny Reardon 15.00 30.00
67 Maurice Richard (2) 37.50 75.00
68 Maurice Richard 25.00 50.00
Elmer Lach
Toe Blake
69 Howie(Rip) Riopelle 12.50 25.00
70 Gaye Stewart 12.50 25.00
71 Phil Watson 15.00 30.00
72 Montreal Canadiens 12.50 25.00
Team Photo 1943-44
73 Montreal Canadiens 12.50 25.00
{Team Photo 1944-45
74 Montreal Canadiens 12.50 25.00
{Team Photo 1945-46
75 Montreal Canadiens 12.50 25.00
{Team Photo 1946-47

1997-98 Paramount

The 1997-98 Pacific Paramount set was issued in one series totalling 200 cards and distributed in five-card packs. The fronts feature color action player photos with holographic gold foil highlights. The backs carry another action player photo and player information.

1 Guy Hebert .12 .30
2 Paul Kariya .20 .50
3 Espen Knutsen RC .15 .40
4 Dmitri Mironov .12 .30
5 Steve Rucchin .12 .30
6 Tomas Sandstrom .10 .25
7 Teemu Selanne .30 .75
8 Scott Young .12 .30
9 Ray Bourque .25 .60
10 Jim Carey .10 .25
11 Anson Carter .10 .25
12 Ted Donato .10 .25
13 Dave Ellett .10 .25
14 Dimitri Khristich .12 .30
15 Sergei Samsonov .10 .25
16 Joe Thornton .15 .40
17 Matthew Barnaby .12 .30
18 Jason Dawe .12 .30
19 Dominik Hasek .25 .60
20 Brian Holzinger .12 .30
21 Michael Peca .12 .30
22 Derek Plante .12 .30
23 Erik Rasmussen .12 .30
24 Miroslav Satan .10 .25
25 Steve Begin RC .10 .25
26 Andrew Cassels .10 .25
27 Chris Dingman RC .15 .40
28 Theo Fleury .20 .50
29 Jonas Hoglund .12 .30
30 Jarome Iginla .15 .40
31 Rick Tabaracci .12 .30
32 German Titov .10 .25
33 Kevin Dineen .12 .30
34 Nelson Emerson .12 .30
35 Trevor Kidd .10 .25
36 Stephen Leach .10 .25
37 Keith Primeau .12 .30
38 Steven Rice .12 .30
39 Gary Roberts .12 .30
40 Tony Amonte .12 .30
41 Chris Chelios .15 .40
42 Daniel Cleary .12 .30
43 Eric Daze .10 .25
44 Jeff Hackett .10 .25
45 Sergei Krivokrasov .10 .25
46 Ethan Moreau .10 .25
47 Alexei Zhamnov .10 .25
48 Adam Deadmarsh .10 .25
49 Peter Forsberg .20 .50
50 Valeri Kamensky .12 .30
51 Jari Kurri .15 .40
52 Claude Lemieux .12 .30
53 Sandis Ozolinsh .12 .30
54 Patrick Roy .40 1.00
55 Joe Sakic .25 .60
56 Ed Belfour .15 .40
57 Derian Hatcher .12 .30
58 Jamie Langenbrunner .12 .30
59 Jere Lehtinen .12 .30
60 Mike Modano .25 .60
61 Joe Nieuwendyk .15 .40
62 Darryl Sydor .10 .25
63 Pat Verbeek .12 .30
64 Anders Eriksson .12 .30
65 Sergei Fedorov .25 .60
66 Vyacheslav Kozlov .12 .30
67 Nicklas Lidstrom .15 .40
68 Darren McCarty .12 .30
69 Chris Osgood .15 .40
70 Brendan Shanahan .20 .50
71 Steve Yzerman .30 .75
72 Jason Arnott .12 .30
73 Boyd Devereaux .12 .30
74 Mike Grier .12 .30
75 Curtis Joseph .15 .40
76 Andrei Kovalenko .10 .25
77 Ryan Smyth .12 .30
78 Doug Weight .15 .40
79 Dave Gagner .10 .25
80 Ed Jovanovski .10 .25
81 Scott Mellanby .12 .30
82 Kirk Muller .10 .25
83 Rob Niedermayer .10 .25
84 Ray Sheppard .12 .30
85 Esa Tikkanen .10 .25
86 John Vanbiesbrouck .15 .40
87 Rob Blake .15 .40
88 Stephane Fiset .12 .30
89 Garry Galley .10 .25
90 Olli Jokinen RC .20 .50
91 Luc Robitaille .15 .40
92 Jozef Stumpel .12 .30
93 Shayne Corson .10 .25
94 Vincent Damphousse .12 .30
95 Saku Koivu .15 .40
96 Andy Moog .15 .40
97 Mark Recchi .20 .50
98 Stephane Richer .10 .25
99 Brian Savage .10 .25
100 Dave Andreychuk .15 .40
101 Martin Brodeur .30 .75
102 Doug Gilmour .20 .50
103 Bobby Holik .10 .25
104 John MacLean .10 .25
105 Brian Rolston .12 .30
106 Bryan Berard .10 .25
107 Todd Bertuzzi .15 .40
108 Travis Green .12 .30
109 Zigmund Palffy .15 .40
110 Robert Reichel .12 .30
111 Tommy Salo .10 .25
112 Bryan Smolinski .12 .30
113 Christian Dube .12 .30
114 Adam Graves .10 .25
115 Wayne Gretzky .75 2.00
116 Alexei Kovalev .10 .25
117 Pat LaFontaine .15 .40
118 Brian Leetch .15 .40
119 Mike Richter .15 .40
120 Brian Skrudland .10 .25
121 Kevin Stevens .10 .25
122 Daniel Alfredsson .15 .40
123 Radek Bonk .10 .25
124 Alexandre Daigle .10 .25
125 Marian Hossa RC .20 .50
126 Igor Kravchuk .10 .25
127 Chris Phillips .12 .30
128 Damian Rhodes .12 .30
129 Alexei Yashin .12 .30
130 Rod Brind'Amour .15 .40
131 Chris Gratton .10 .25
132 Ron Hextall .15 .40
133 John LeClair .15 .40
134 Eric Lindros .25 .60
135 Janne Niinimaa .12 .30
136 Vaclav Prospal RC .12 .30
137 Garth Snow .12 .30
138 Dainius Zubrus .12 .30
139 Mike Gartner .15 .40
140 Brad Isbister .12 .30
141 Nikolai Khabibulin .15 .40
142 Jeremy Roenick .20 .50
143 Cliff Ronning .10 .25
144 Keith Tkachuk .15 .40
145 Rick Tocchet .10 .25
146 Oleg Tverdovsky .12 .30
147 Tom Barrasso .12 .30
148 Ron Francis .20 .50
149 Kevin Hatcher .10 .25
150 Jaromir Jagr .40 1.00
151 Darius Kasparaitis .12 .30
152 Alexei Morozov .12 .30
153 Petr Nedved .15 .40
154 Ed Olczyk .10 .25
155 Jim Campbell .10 .25
156 Kelly Chase .10 .25
157 Geoff Courtnall .10 .25
158 Grant Fuhr .15 .40
159 Brett Hull .20 .50
160 Joe Murphy .12 .30
161 Pierre Turgeon .15 .40
162 Tony Twist .12 .30
163 Shawn Burr .10 .25
164 Jeff Friesen .12 .30
165 Tony Granato .12 .30
166 Viktor Kozlov .12 .30
167 Patrick Marleau .20 .50
168 Stephane Matteau .10 .25
169 Owen Nolan .15 .40
170 Mike Vernon .12 .30
171 Dino Ciccarelli .15 .40
172 Karl Dykhuis .10 .25
173 Roman Hamrlik .12 .30
174 Daymond Langkow .10 .25
175 Mikael Renberg .12 .30
176 Alexander Selivanov .10 .25
177 Paul Ysebaert .12 .30
178 Sergei Berezin .12 .30
179 Wendel Clark .15 .40
180 Glenn Healy .10 .25
181 Derek King .12 .30
182 Alyn McCauley .12 .30
183 Felix Potvin .15 .40
184 Martin Prochazka RC .12 .30
185 Mats Sundin .15 .40
186 Pavel Bure .20 .50
187 Martin Gelinas .10 .25
188 Trevor Linden .12 .30
189 Kirk McLean .12 .30
190 Mark Messier .25 .60
191 Lubomir Vaic RC .12 .30
192 Mattias Ohlund .12 .30
193 Peter Bondra .12 .30
194 Dale Hunter .12 .30
195 Joe Juneau .12 .30
196 Olaf Kolzig .12 .30
197 Steve Konowalchuk .12 .30
198 Adam Oates .15 .40
199 Bill Ranford .12 .30
200 Jaroslav Svejkovsky .12 .30
P60 Mike Modano PROMO .25 .60

1997-98 Paramount Copper

*COPPER: 1X TO 2.5X BASIC CARDS
*COPPER ROOKIE STAR: .4X TO 1X RC
STATED ODDS 1:1 HOBBY

1997-98 Paramount Dark Gray

*DARK GRAY: 1X TO 2.5X BASIC CARDS
*GRAY ROOKIE STAR: .4X TO 1X RC
STATED ODDS 1:1 HOBBY

1997-98 Paramount Emerald Green

*GREEN: 1X TO 2.5X BASIC CARDS
*GREEN ROOKIE STAR: .4X TO 1X RC
STATED ODDS 1:1 CANADIAN PACKS

1997-98 Paramount Ice Blue

*ICE BLUE: 12X TO 30X BASIC CARDS
*ICE BLUE ROOKIE STAR: 5X TO 12X RC
STATED ODDS 1:73

1997-98 Paramount Red

*RED: 1X TO 2.5X BASIC CARDS
*RED ROOKIE STAR: .4X TO 1X RC
STATED ODDS 1:1 TREAT PACK

1997-98 Paramount Silver

*SILVER: 1X TO 2.5X BASIC CARDS
*SILVER ROOKIE STAR: .4X TO 1X RC
STATED ODDS 1:1 RETAIL

1997-98 Paramount Big Numbers Die-Cuts

Randomly inserted in packs at the rate of 1:37, this 20-card set features die-cut textured cards in the shape of the players jersey number. The backs carry a small player head photo and player information in a newspaper story design.

COMPLETE SET (20) 25.00 50.00
1 Paul Kariya .75 2.00
2 Teemu Selanne .75 2.00
3 Joe Thornton 2.00 5.00
4 Dominik Hasek 1.50 4.00
5 Peter Forsberg 2.00 5.00
6 Patrick Roy 4.00 10.00
7 Joe Sakic 2.00 5.00
8 Sergei Fedorov 1.25 3.00
9 Brendan Shanahan .75 2.00
10 Steve Yzerman 4.00 10.00
11 John Vanbiesbrouck .60 1.50
12 Martin Brodeur 2.50 6.00
13 Doug Gilmour .75 2.00
14 Wayne Gretzky 5.00 12.00
15 Eric Lindros 1.25 3.00
16 Keith Tkachuk .75 2.00
17 Jaromir Jagr 1.25 3.00
18 Brett Hull 1.00 2.50
19 Pavel Bure 1.00 2.50
20 Mark Messier .75 2.00

1997-98 Paramount Canadian Greats

Randomly inserted at 2:48 Canadian retail packs only, this 12-card set features color photos of star players. The backs carry player information.

COMPLETE SET (12) 15.00 30.00
1 Paul Kariya .60 1.50
2 Joe Thornton 1.50 4.00
3 Jarome Iginla .75 2.00
4 Patrick Roy 4.00 10.00
5 Joe Sakic 1.25 3.00
6 Brendan Shanahan .60 1.50
7 Steve Yzerman 3.00 8.00
8 Ryan Smyth .50 1.25
9 Martin Brodeur 2.50 6.00
10 Wayne Gretzky 5.00 12.00
11 Eric Lindros 1.00 2.50
12 Mark Messier .60 1.50

1997-98 Paramount Glove Side Laser Cuts

Randomly inserted in packs at the rate of 1:73, this 20-card set features color photos of top goalies printed on a die-cut card in the shape of the goalie's glove.

COMPLETE SET (20) 25.00 60.00
1 Guy Hebert 2.00 5.00
2 Dominik Hasek 4.00 10.00
3 Trevor Kidd 2.00 5.00
4 Jeff Hackett 2.00 5.00
5 Patrick Roy 10.00 25.00
6 Ed Belfour 2.50 6.00
7 Chris Osgood 2.00 5.00
8 Curtis Joseph 2.50 6.00
9 John Vanbiesbrouck 2.00 5.00
10 Andy Moog 2.00 5.00
11 Martin Brodeur 6.00 15.00
12 Tommy Salo 2.00 5.00
13 Mike Richter 2.50 6.00
14 Ron Hextall 2.00 5.00
15 Garth Snow 2.00 5.00
16 Nikolai Khabibulin 2.00 5.00
17 Tom Barrasso 2.00 5.00
18 Grant Fuhr 2.00 5.00
19 Mike Vernon 2.00 5.00
20 Felix Potvin 3.00 8.00

1997-98 Paramount Photoengravings

Randomly inserted in packs at the rate of 2:37, this 20-card set features color images of top stars using photoengraving technology and printed with a textured paper stock finish.

COMPLETE SET (20) 8.00 20.00
1 Paul Kariya .60 1.50
2 Teemu Selanne .60 1.50
3 Joe Thornton 1.50 4.00
4 Dominik Hasek 1.25 3.00
5 Peter Forsberg 1.50 4.00
6 Patrick Roy 3.00 8.00
7 Joe Sakic 1.25 3.00
8 Mike Modano 1.00 2.50
9 Brendan Shanahan .60 1.50
10 Steve Yzerman 3.00 8.00
11 John Vanbiesbrouck .50 1.25
12 Saku Koivu .60 1.50
13 Wayne Gretzky 4.00 10.00
14 John LeClair .60 1.50
15 Eric Lindros .60 1.50
16 Keith Tkachuk .60 1.50
17 Jaromir Jagr 1.00 2.50
18 Brett Hull .75 2.00
19 Pavel Bure .60 1.50
20 Mark Messier .60 1.50

1998-99 Paramount

The 1998-99 Pacific Paramount set consists of 250 standard-size cards. The fronts feature full bleed action photos with the player's name and team logo on holographic gold foil. The flipside offers the player's statistics. Each pack contains six cards. The cards were released around October, 1998.

COMPLETE SET (250) 15.00 30.00
1 Travis Green .02 .10
2 Guy Hebert .08 .25
3 Paul Kariya .02 .10
4 Josef Marha .02 .10
5 Steve Rucchin .02 .10
6 Tomas Sandstrom .02 .10
7 Teemu Selanne .10 .30
8 Jason Allison .02 .10
9 Per Axelsson .02 .10
10 Ray Bourque .20 .50
11 Anson Carter .08 .25
12 Byron Dafoe .08 .25
13 Ted Donato .02 .10
14 Dave Ellett .02 .10
15 Dimitri Khristich .02 .10
16 Sergei Samsonov .08 .25
17 Matthew Barnaby .02 .10
18 Michal Grosek .02 .10
19 Dominik Hasek .25 .60
20 Brian Holzinger .02 .10
21 Michael Peca .02 .10
22 Miroslav Satan .08 .25
23 Vaclav Varada .02 .10
24 Dixon Ward .02 .10
25 Alexei Zhitnik .02 .10
26 Andrew Cassels .02 .10
27 Theo Fleury .02 .10
28 Jarome Iginla .15 .40
29 Marty McInnis .02 .10
30 Derek Morris .02 .10
31 Michael Nylander .02 .10
32 Cory Stillman .02 .10
33 Rick Tabaracci .02 .10
34 Kevin Dineen .02 .10
35 Nelson Emerson .02 .10
36 Martin Gelinas .02 .10
37 Sami Kapanen .02 .10
38 Trevor Kidd .08 .25
39 Robert Kron .02 .10
40 Jeff O'Neill .02 .10
41 Keith Primeau .02 .10
42 Gary Roberts .02 .10
43 Tony Amonte .08 .25
44 Chris Chelios .10 .30
45 Paul Coffey .10 .30
46 Eric Daze .08 .25
47 Doug Gilmour .08 .25
48 Jeff Hackett .08 .25
49 Jean-Yves Leroux .02 .10
50 Eric Weinrich .02 .10
51 Alexei Zhamnov .02 .10
52 Craig Billington .08 .25
53 Adam Deadmarsh .02 .10
54 Adam Foote .02 .10
55 Peter Forsberg .30 .75
56 Valeri Kamensky .02 .10
57 Claude Lemieux .02 .10
58 Eric Messier .02 .10
59 Sandis Ozolinsh .02 .10
60 Patrick Roy .60 1.50
61 Joe Sakic .30 .75
62 Ed Belfour .10 .30
63 Derian Hatcher .02 .10
64 Brett Hull .15 .40
65 Jamie Langenbrunner .02 .10
66 Jere Lehtinen .02 .10
67 Juha Lind .02 .10
68 Mike Modano .20 .50
69 Joe Nieuwendyk .08 .25
70 Darryl Sydor .02 .10
71 Roman Turek .08 .25
72 Sergei Zubov .02 .10
73 Anders Eriksson .02 .10
74 Sergei Fedorov .20 .50
75 Kevin Hodson .08 .25
76 Vyacheslav Kozlov .08 .25
77 Igor Larionov .02 .10
78 Nicklas Lidstrom .10 .30
79 Darren McCarty .02 .10
80 Larry Murphy .08 .25
81 Chris Osgood .08 .25
82 Brendan Shanahan .10 .30
83 Steve Yzerman .75 2.00
84 Kelly Buchberger .02 .10
85 Mike Grier .02 .10
86 Bill Guerin .08 .25
87 Roman Hamrlik .02 .10
88 Todd Marchant .02 .10
89 Dean McAmmond .02 .10
90 Boris Mironov .02 .10
91 Janne Niinimaa .02 .10
92 Ryan Smyth .08 .25
93 Doug Weight .08 .25
94 Dino Ciccarelli .08 .25
95 Dave Gagner .02 .10
96 Ed Jovanovski .02 .10
97 Viktor Kozlov .02 .10
98 Paul Laus .02 .10
99 Scott Mellanby .02 .10
100 Robert Svehla .02 .10
101 Ray Whitney .02 .10
102 Rob Blake .08 .25
103 Russ Courtnall .02 .10
104 Stephane Fiset .08 .25
105 Glen Murray .02 .10
106 Yanic Perreault .02 .10
107 Luc Robitaille .08 .25
108 Jamie Storr .08 .25
109 Jozef Stumpel .08 .25
110 Vladimir Tsyplakov .02 .10
111 Shayne Corson .02 .10
112 Vincent Damphousse .02 .10
113 Saku Koivu .10 .30
114 Vladimir Malakhov .02 .10
115 Dave Manson .02 .10
116 Mark Recchi .08 .25
117 Martin Rucinsky .02 .10
118 Brian Savage .02 .10
119 Jocelyn Thibault .08 .25
120 Blair Atcheynum .02 .10
121 Andrew Brunette .08 .25
122 Mike Dunham .08 .25
123 Tom Fitzgerald .02 .10
124 Sergei Krivokrasov .02 .10
125 Denny Lambert .02 .10
126 Jay More .02 .10
127 Mikhail Shtalenkov .02 .10
128 Darren Turcotte .02 .10
129 Scott Walker .02 .10
130 Dave Andreychuk .08 .25
131 Jason Arnott .02 .10
132 Martin Brodeur .50 1.25
133 Patrik Elias .08 .25
134 Bobby Holik .02 .10
135 Randy McKay .02 .10
136 Scott Niedermayer .02 .10
137 Krzysztof Oliwa .02 .10
138 Sheldon Souray RC .40 1.00
139 Scott Stevens .08 .25
140 Bryan Berard .08 .25
141 Mariusz Czerkawski .02 .10
142 Jason Dawe .02 .10
143 Kenny Jonsson .02 .10
144 Trevor Linden .08 .25
145 Zigmund Palffy .08 .25
146 Rich Pilon .02 .10
147 Robert Reichel .02 .10
148 Tommy Salo .08 .25
149 Bryan Smolinski .02 .10
150 Dan Cloutier .02 .10
151 Adam Graves .02 .10
152 Wayne Gretzky 1.25 3.00
153 Alexei Kovalev .02 .10
154 Pat LaFontaine .10 .30
155 Brian Leetch .10 .30
156 Mike Richter .10 .30
157 Ulf Samuelsson .02 .10
158 Kevin Stevens .02 .10
159 Niklas Sundstrom .02 .10
160 Daniel Alfredsson .08 .25
161 Magnus Arvedson .02 .10
162 Andreas Dackell .02 .10
163 Igor Kravchuk .02 .10
164 Shawn McEachern .02 .10
165 Chris Phillips .02 .10
166 Damian Rhodes .08 .25
167 Ron Tugnutt .08 .25
168 Alexei Yashin .02 .10
169 Rod Brind'Amour .08 .25
170 Alexandre Daigle .02 .10
171 Eric Desjardins .08 .25
172 Colin Forbes .02 .10
173 Chris Gratton .08 .25
174 Ron Hextall .08 .25
175 Trent Klatt .02 .10
176 John LeClair .10 .30
177 Eric Lindros .10 .30
178 John Vanbiesbrouck .08 .25
179 Dainius Zubrus .02 .10
180 Dallas Drake .02 .10
181 Brad Isbister .02 .10
182 Nikolai Khabibulin .08 .25
183 Teppo Numminen .02 .10
184 Jeremy Roenick .20 .50
185 Cliff Ronning .02 .10
186 Keith Tkachuk .10 .30
187 Rick Tocchet .08 .25
188 Oleg Tverdovsky .02 .10
189 Stu Barnes .02 .10
190 Tom Barrasso .08 .25
191 Kevin Hatcher .02 .10
192 Jaromir Jagr .20 .50
193 Darius Kasparaitis .02 .10
194 Alexei Morozov .02 .10
195 Fredrik Olausson .02 .10
196 Jiri Slegr .02 .10
197 Martin Straka .02 .10
198 Jim Campbell .02 .10
199 Kelly Chase .02 .10
200 Craig Conroy .02 .10
201 Geoff Courtnall .02 .10
202 Pavol Demitra .08 .25
203 Grant Fuhr .08 .25
204 Al MacInnis .08 .25
205 Jamie McLennan .08 .25
206 Chris Pronger .08 .25
207 Pierre Turgeon .08 .25
208 Tony Twist .02 .10
209 Jeff Friesen .02 .10
210 Tony Granato .02 .10
211 Patrick Marleau .08 .20
212 Stephane Matteau .02 .10
213 Marty McSorley .02 .10
214 Owen Nolan .08 .25
215 Marco Sturm .08 .25
216 Mike Vernon .08 .25
217 Karl Dykhuis .02 .10
218 Sandy McCarty .02 .10
219 Mikael Renberg .08 .25
220 Stephane Richer .08 .25
221 Alexander Selivanov .02 .10
222 Paul Ysebaert .02 .10
223 Rob Zamuner .02 .10
224 Sergei Berezin .08 .25
225 Tie Domi .08 .25
226 Mike Johnson .02 .10
227 Curtis Joseph .10 .30
228 Derek King .02 .10
229 Igor Korolev .02 .10
230 Mathieu Schneider .02 .10
231 Mats Sundin .10 .30
232 Todd Bertuzzi .10 .30
233 Donald Brashear .02 .10
234 Pavel Bure .10 .30
235 Arturs Irbe .08 .25
236 Mark Messier .10 .30
237 Alexander Mogilny .08 .25
238 Mattias Ohlund .08 .25
239 Dave Scatchard .02 .10
240 Garth Snow .08 .25
241 Brian Bellows .02 .10
242 Peter Bondra .08 .25
243 Jeff Brown .02 .10
244 Sergei Gonchar .02 .10
245 Calle Johansson .02 .10
246 Joe Juneau .08 .25
247 Olaf Kolzig .08 .25
248 Steve Konowalchuk .02 .10
249 Adam Oates .08 .25
250 Richard Zednik .02 .10
NNO Martin Brodeur SAMPLE .60 1.50

1998-99 Paramount Copper

*COPPER: 2.5X TO 6X BASIC CARDS
STATED ODDS 1:1 US HOBBY

1998-99 Paramount Emerald

*EMERALD: 2.5X TO 6X BASIC CARDS
STATED ODDS 1:1 CANADIAN HOBBY

1998-99 Paramount HoloElectric

This 250-card parallel set carried a holographic silver foil and gold foil impression. Cards were numbered out of 99.

*HOLOELECTRIC: 20X TO 50X BASIC CARDS

1998-99 Paramount Ice Blu

*ICE BLUE: 6X TO 15X BASIC CARDS
ICE BLUE STATED ODDS 1:73

1998-99 Paramount Silver

*SILVER: 3X TO 8X BASIC CARDS
SILVER STATED ODDS 1:1 RETAIL

1998-99 Paramount Glove Sid Laser Cuts

The 1998-99 Pacific Paramount Glove Side Laser C set consists of 20 cards and is an insert of the regu Pacific Paramount base set. The cards are randoml inserted in packs at a rate of 1:73. The cards featur superstar goalies delivered on one of the most unic designs.

COMPLETE SET (20) 40.00 80
1 Guy Hebert 2.00 5
2 Byron Dafoe 2.00 5
3 Dominik Hasek 5.00 12
4 Trevor Kidd 2.00 5
5 Jeff Hackett 2.00 5
6 Patrick Roy 12.50 30
7 Ed Belfour 2.50 6
8 Chris Osgood 2.00 5
9 Mike Dunham 2.00 5
10 Martin Brodeur 6.00 15
11 Tommy Salo 2.00 5
12 Mike Richter 2.00 5
13 Damian Rhodes 2.00 5
14 Ron Hextall 2.00 5
15 Nikolai Khabibulin 2.00 5
16 Tom Barrasso 2.00 5
17 Grant Fuhr 2.00 5
18 Mike Vernon 2.00 5
19 Curtis Joseph 2.50 6
20 Olaf Kolzig 2.00 5

1998-99 Paramount Hall of Far Bound

This 10-card set was inserted in packs at a rate of 1:361. The cards honor 10 NHL superstars on a full foiled and etched card. A proof parallel was also created and randomly inserted in packs. Each parall card is limited to only 20 copies.

COMPLETE SET (10) 100.00 200
*PACIFIC PROOF/20: 2.5X TO 6X BASIC INSERTS
1 Teemu Selanne 5.00 12
2 Dominik Hasek 8.00 20
3 Peter Forsberg 10.00 25
4 Patrick Roy 15.00 40
5 Steve Yzerman 15.00 40
6 Martin Brodeur 12.50 30
7 Wayne Gretzky 20.00 50
8 Eric Lindros 5.00 12
9 Jaromir Jagr 6.00 15
10 Mark Messier 5.00 12

1998-99 Paramount Ice Galax

Randomly inserted into Canadian retail packs only a rate of 1:97, this 10-card set features action color player photos with bronze foil highlights. Only 140 were made. A silver foil parallel set was also produc Only 50 of these sets were made. A very limited gol foil parallel set was produced with a print run of onl 10 sets.

COMPLETE SET (10) 100.00 200
SILVER/50: .8X TO 2X BRONZE/140*
1 Paul Kariya 6.00 15
2 Peter Forsberg 8.00 20
3 Patrick Roy 15.00 40
4 Joe Sakic 6.00 15
5 Steve Yzerman 15.00 40
6 Martin Brodeur 10.00 25
7 Wayne Gretzky 25.00 60
8 Alexei Yashin 4.00 10
9 Eric Lindros 8.00 20
10 Curtis Joseph 6.00 15

1998-99 Paramount Special Delivery Die-Cuts

This 20-card set was inserted in packs at a rate of 1

COMPLETE SET (20) 20.00 40
1 Paul Kariya .25
2 Teemu Selanne .75 2
3 Sergei Samsonov .60 1
4 Peter Forsberg 2.00 5
5 Joe Sakic 1.50 4
6 Mike Modano 1.25 3
7 Sergei Fedorov 1.25 3
8 Brendan Shanahan .75 2
9 Steve Yzerman 4.00 10
10 Saku Koivu .75 2
11 Zigmund Palffy .60 1
12 Wayne Gretzky 5.00 12
13 John LeClair .75 2
14 Eric Lindros .75 2
15 Keith Tkachuk .75 2
16 Jaromir Jagr 1.25 3
17 Mats Sundin .75 2
18 Pavel Bure .75 2
19 Mark Messier .75 2
20 Peter Bondra .60 1

1998-99 Paramount Team Checklists Die-Cuts

This 27-card set was inserted in packs at a rate of 2 The set included the league's 1998-99 expansion franchise, the Nashville Predators.

COMPLETE SET (27) 20.00 40
1 Teemu Selanne .60 1
2 Sergei Samsonov .50 1
3 Dominik Hasek 1.25 3
4 Theo Fleury .20
5 Keith Primeau .20
6 Chris Chelios .60 1
7 Patrick Roy 3.00 8
8 Mike Modano 1.00 2
9 Steve Yzerman 3.00 8
10 Ryan Smyth .50 1
11 Dino Ciccarelli .50 1
12 Rob Blake .50 1
13 Saku Koivu .60 1
14 Tom Fitzgerald .20
15 Martin Brodeur 1.50 4
16 Zigmund Palffy .50 1
17 Wayne Gretzky 4.00 10
18 Alexei Yashin .20
19 Eric Lindros .60 1
20 Keith Tkachuk .60 1
21 Jaromir Jagr 1.00 2
22 Grant Fuhr .50 1
23 Patrick Marleau .20
24 Rob Zamuner .20
25 Mats Sundin .60 1
26 Mark Messier .60 1
27 Peter Bondra .50 1

1999-00 Paramount

leased as a 251-card set, Paramount featured white
rdered base cards with color action photography and
ver foil highlights. Paramount was packaged in 36-
ck boxes with packs containing six cards and carried
SRP of $1.49. Cards #251-269 were not found in
cks. They were available only as stadium giveaways
part of an NHL/NHLPA trading card promotion. They
not included in the complete set price and are not
und in any of the parallel versions. Reportedly, cards
62 and #265 were not issued.

)MPLETE SET (251) 15.00 30.00
Matt Cullen .02 .10
Guy Hebert .08 .25
Paul Kariya .10 .30
Marty McInnis .02 .10
Fredrik Olausson .02 .10
Steve Rucchin .08 .25
Ruslan Salei .02 .10
Teemu Selanne .10 .30
Jason Botterill .02 .10
Andrew Brunette .08 .25
Kelly Buchberger .02 .10
Matt Johnson .02 .10
Norm Maracle .08 .25
Damian Rhodes .08 .25
Steve Staios .02 .10
Jason Allison .02 .10
Ray Bourque .20 .50
Anson Carter .08 .25
Byron Dafoe .08 .25
Jonathan Girard .02 .10
Steve Heinze .02 .10
Dimitri Khristich .02 .10
Sergei Samsonov .08 .25
Joe Thornton .20 .50
Stu Barnes .02 .10
Curtis Brown .02 .10
Michal Grosek .02 .10
Dominik Hasek .25 .60
Michael Peca .08 .25
Geoff Sanderson .08 .25
Miroslav Satan .08 .25
Dixon Ward .02 .10
Jason Woolley .02 .10
Alexei Zhitnik .02 .10
Valeri Bure .02 .10
Rene Corbet .02 .10
Rico Fata .02 .10
Jean-Sebastien Giguere .08 .25
Phil Housley .08 .25
Jarome Iginla .15 .40
Derek Morris .02 .10
Steve Smith .02 .10
Cory Stillman .02 .10
Ron Francis .08 .25
Martin Gelinas .02 .10
Arturs Irbe .08 .25
Sami Kapanen .02 .10
Jeff O'Neill .02 .10
Keith Primeau .02 .10
Gary Roberts .02 .10
Shane Willis .02 .10
Tony Amonte .08 .25
Eric Daze .08 .25
J-P Dumont .08 .25
Doug Gilmour .08 .25
Dean McAmmond .02 .10
Boris Mironov .02 .10
Jocelyn Thibault .08 .25
Alexei Zhamnov .08 .25
Adam Deadmarsh .02 .10
Marc Denis .08 .25
Chris Drury .08 .25
Peter Forsberg .30 .75
Milan Hejduk .10 .30
Claude Lemieux .02 .10
Sandis Ozolinsh .02 .10
Patrick Roy .60 1.50
Joe Sakic .25 .60
Ed Belfour .10 .30
Guy Carbonneau .02 .10
Derian Hatcher .02 .10
Brett Hull .15 .40
Jamie Langenbrunner .02 .10
Jere Lehtinen .08 .25
Mike Modano .20 .50
Joe Nieuwendyk .08 .25
Darryl Sydor .08 .25
Sergei Zubov .08 .25
Chris Chelios .10 .30
Sergei Fedorov .20 .50
Vyacheslav Kozlov .08 .25
Igor Larionov .02 .10
Nicklas Lidstrom .10 .30
Darren McCarty .02 .10
Larry Murphy .08 .25
Chris Osgood .08 .25
Brendan Shanahan .10 .30
Steve Yzerman .60 1.50
Josef Beranek .02 .10
Pat Falloon .02 .10
Mike Grier .08 .25
Bill Guerin .02 .10
Rem Murray .02 .10
Tom Poti .02 .10
Tommy Salo .08 .25
Ryan Smyth .08 .25
Doug Weight .08 .25
Pavel Bure .10 .30
Sean Burke .08 .25
Viktor Kozlov .02 .10
Oleg Kvasha .08 .25
Scott Mellanby .02 .10
Rob Niedermayer .02 .10
Marcus Nilsson .02 .10
Mark Parrish .02 .10
Ray Whitney .08 .25
Donald Audette .02 .10
Rob Blake .08 .25
Stephane Fiset .08 .25
Glen Murray .02 .10
Zigmund Palffy .08 .25
Jamie Storr .08 .25
Jozef Stumpel .08 .25
Benoit Brunet .02 .10
Shayne Corson .02 .10
Jeff Hackett .08 .25
Saku Koivu .10 .30
Trevor Linden .08 .25
Vladimir Malakhov .02 .10
Martin Rucinsky .02 .10
Igor Ulanov .02 .10
Dainius Zubrus .08 .25
Mike Dunham .08 .25
Tom Fitzgerald .02 .10
Greg Johnson .02 .10
Sergei Krivokrasov .02 .10
127 David Legwand .08 .25
128 Cliff Ronning .08 .25
129 Scott Walker .02 .10
130 Jason Arnott .02 .10
131 Martin Brodeur .30 .75
132 Patrik Elias .08 .25
133 Bobby Holik .02 .10
134 John Madden RC .25 .60
135 Randy McKay .02 .10
136 Brendan Morrison .08 .25
137 Scott Niedermayer .02 .10
138 Brian Rolston .02 .10
139 Petr Sykora .02 .10
140 Eric Brewer .02 .10
141 Mariusz Czerkawski .02 .10
142 Kenny Jonsson .02 .10
143 Claude Lapointe .02 .10
144 Mats Lindgren .02 .10
145 Vladimir Orszagh RC .02 .10
146 Felix Potvin .10 .30
147 Mike Watt .02 .10
148 Theo Fleury .02 .10
149 Adam Graves .02 .10
150 Todd Harvey .08 .25
151 Valeri Kamensky .08 .25
152 Brian Leetch .10 .30
153 John MacLean .02 .10
154 Manny Malhotra .08 .25
155 Petr Nedved .02 .10
156 Mike Richter .10 .30
157 Kevin Stevens .08 .25
158 Daniel Alfredsson .08 .25
159 Magnus Arvedson .02 .10
160 Radek Bonk .02 .10
161 Andreas Dackell .02 .10
162 Marian Hossa .10 .30
163 Shawn McEachern .02 .10
164 Wade Redden .02 .10
165 Sami Salo .08 .25
166 Ron Tugnutt .08 .25
167 Alexei Yashin .02 .10
168 Rod Brind'Amour .08 .25
169 Eric Desjardins .08 .25
170 Keith Jones .02 .10
171 Daymond Langkow .08 .25
172 John LeClair .10 .30
173 Eric Lindros .10 .30
174 Mark Recchi .02 .10
175 Mikael Renberg .02 .10
176 John Vanbiesbrouck .08 .25
177 Greg Adams .02 .10
178 Dallas Drake .02 .10
179 Nikolai Khabibulin .08 .25
180 Jyrki Lumme .02 .10
181 Teppo Numminen .08 .25
182 Jeremy Roenick .15 .40
183 Mike Sullivan .02 .10
184 Keith Tkachuk .10 .30
185 Rick Tocchet .08 .25
186 Matthew Barnaby .08 .25
187 Tom Barrasso .08 .25
188 Jan Hrdina .02 .10
189 Jaromir Jagr .20 .50
190 Alexei Kovalev .02 .10
191 Ian Moran .02 .10
192 Martin Straka .02 .10
193 German Titov .02 .10
194 Craig Conroy .02 .10
195 Pavol Demitra .08 .25
196 Grant Fuhr .08 .25
197 Jochen Hecht RC .50 1.25
198 Al MacInnis .08 .25
199 Ricard Persson .02 .10
200 Chris Pronger .08 .25
201 Pierre Turgeon .08 .25
202 Scott Young .02 .10
203 Vincent Damphousse .02 .10
204 Jeff Friesen .02 .10
205 Alexander Korolyuk .02 .10
206 Patrick Marleau .08 .25
207 Owen Nolan .08 .25
208 Mike Ricci .08 .25
209 Steve Shields .08 .25
210 Marco Sturm .08 .25
211 Ron Sutter .02 .10
212 Mike Vernon .08 .25
213 Karel Betik RC .02 .10
214 Dan Cloutier .08 .25
215 Jassen Cullimore .02 .10
216 Colin Forbes .02 .10
217 Chris Gratton .08 .25
218 Pavel Kubina .08 .25
219 Vincent Lecavalier .10 .30
220 Darcy Tucker .02 .10
221 Bryan Berard .08 .25
222 Sergei Berezin .08 .25
223 Tie Domi .08 .25
224 Mike Johnson .02 .10
225 Curtis Joseph .10 .30
226 Derek King .02 .10
227 Igor Korolev .02 .10
228 Yanic Perreault .02 .10
229 Steve Sullivan .02 .10
230 Mats Sundin .10 .30
231 Steve Thomas .02 .10
232 Adrian Aucoin .02 .10
233 Donald Brashear .08 .25
234 Ed Jovanovski .02 .10
235 Mark Messier .10 .30
236 Alexander Mogilny .08 .25
237 Bill Muckalt .08 .25
238 Markus Naslund .10 .30
239 Mattias Ohlund .08 .25
240 Garth Snow .08 .25
241 Brian Bellows .02 .10
242 Peter Bondra .08 .25
243 Jan Bulis .02 .10
244 Sergei Gonchar .02 .10
245 Olaf Kolzig .08 .25
246 Steve Konowalchuk .02 .10
247 Andrei Nikolishin .02 .10
248 Adam Oates .08 .25
249 Alexei Tezikov RC .02 .10
250 Richard Zednik .02 .10
251 Patrik Stefan RC .60 4.00
252 Jonathan Girard AG
253 Maxim Afinogenov AG
254 Byron Ritchie AG
255 Alex Tanguay AG
256 Brenden Morrow AG
257 Yuri Butsayev AG
258 Ivan Novoseltsev AG
259 Frantisek Kaberle AG
260 Richard Lintner AG
261 Tim Connolly AG
263 Jason Doig AG
264 Mike Fisher AG
266 Stan Neckar AG
267 Andrew Ference AG
268 Paul Mara AG
269 Steve Kariya AG

1999-00 Paramount Copper

*COPPER: 2X TO 5X BASIC CARDS
COPPER STATED ODDS 1:1 HOBBY

1999-00 Paramount Emerald

*EMERALD: 2X TO 5X BASIC CARDS
EMERALD STATED ODDS 1:1 CANADIAN

1999-00 Paramount Gold

*GOLD: 2.5X TO 6X BASIC CARDS
GOLD STATED ODDS 1:1 RETAIL

1999-00 Paramount Holographic Emerald

Randomly inserted in Canadian 7-11 packs, this 251-card set parallels the base Paramount set and is enhanced with green foil highlights. Each card is serial numbered out of 99.
*HOLO.EMERALD: 25X TO 60X BASIC CARDS

1999-00 Paramount Holographic Gold

*HOLO.GOLD: 10X TO 25X BASIC CARDS
HOLO.GOLD PRINT RUN 199 SER.#'d SETS

1999-00 Paramount Holographic Silver

*HOLO.SILVER: 20X TO 50X BASIC CARDS
STATED PRINT RUN 99 SER.#'d SETS

1999-00 Paramount Ice Blue

*ICE BLUE: 15X TO 40X BASIC CARDS
ICE BLUE STATED ODDS 1:73

1999-00 Paramount Premiere Date

*PREM.DATE: 30X TO 80X BASIC CARDS
PREM.DATE/50 ODDS 1:37 HOBBY

1999-00 Paramount Red

Randomly inserted in Jewel Boxes, this 251-card set parallels the base Paramount set and is enhanced with red foil highlights.
*RED: .6X TO 1.5X BASIC CARDS

1999-00 Paramount Glove Side Net Fusions

Randomly inserted in packs at the rate of 1:73, this 20-card set features circular goalie portraits on a die cut card in the shape of a goalie's glove with actual netting.

COMPLETE SET (20) 50.00 100.00
1 Guy Hebert 2.00 5.00
2 Byron Dafoe 2.00 5.00
3 Dominik Hasek 5.00 12.00
4 Arturs Irbe 2.00 5.00
5 Jocelyn Thibault 2.00 5.00
6 Patrick Roy 12.50 30.00
7 Ed Belfour 2.50 6.00
8 Chris Osgood 2.00 5.00
9 Tommy Salo 2.00 5.00
10 Jeff Hackett 2.00 5.00
11 Martin Brodeur 6.00 15.00
12 Felix Potvin 2.50 6.00
13 Mike Richter 2.50 6.00
14 Ron Tugnutt 2.00 5.00
15 John Vanbiesbrouck 2.00 5.00
16 Nikolai Khabibulin 2.00 5.00
17 Tom Barrasso 2.00 5.00
18 Grant Fuhr 2.00 5.00
19 Curtis Joseph 2.50 6.00
20 Olaf Kolzig 2.00 5.00

1999-00 Paramount Hall of Fame Bound

Randomly inserted in packs at the rate of 1:361, this 10-card set features future NHL-hall of famers. Card fronts contain action player photos and the respective player's team logo on a "mesh jersey" card stock. A proof parallel was also created and inserted randomly. Proof were serial numbered to just 35 and their value can be determined by using the multiplier below.

COMPLETE SET (10) 75.00 150.00
*PROOFS/35: 1.2X TO 3X BASIC INSERTS
1 Paul Kariya 5.00 12.00
2 Ray Bourque 8.00 20.00
3 Dominik Hasek 8.00 20.00
4 Peter Forsberg 10.00 25.00
5 Patrick Roy 15.00 40.00
6 Steve Yzerman 15.00 40.00
7 Martin Brodeur 12.50 30.00
8 Eric Lindros 5.00 12.00
9 Jaromir Jagr 6.00 15.00
10 Mark Messier 5.00 12.00

1999-00 Paramount Ice Advantage

Randomly inserted in Canadian packs at the rate of 2:25, this 20-card set featured top NHL players. A proof parallel was also created and randomly inserted Canadian 7-11 retail packs. Proofs were numbered to just 10 and are not priced due to scarcity.

COMPLETE SET (20) 20.00 40.00
1 Paul Kariya .60 1.50
2 Teemu Selanne .60 1.50
3 Dominik Hasek 1.25 3.00
4 Jarome Iginla .75 2.00
5 Peter Forsberg 1.50 4.00
6 Patrick Roy 3.00 8.00
7 Joe Sakic 1.25 3.00
8 Joe Nieuwendyk .50 1.25
9 Brendan Shanahan .60 1.50
10 Steve Yzerman 3.00 8.00
11 Doug Weight .50 1.25
12 Pavel Bure .60 1.50
13 Jeff Hackett .50 1.25
14 Martin Brodeur 1.50 4.00
15 Marian Hossa .60 1.50
16 Eric Lindros .60 1.50
17 Jaromir Jagr 1.00 2.50
18 Curtis Joseph .60 1.50
19 Mats Sundin .60 1.50
20 Mark Messier .60 1.50

1999-00 Paramount Ice Alliance

Randomly inserted in packs at the rate of 2:37, this 28-card set features NHL team leader portraits with their team's logo in gold foil.

COMPLETE SET (28) 20.00 40.00
1 Paul Kariya .60 1.50
2 Damian Rhodes .50 1.25
3 Ray Bourque 1.00 2.50
4 Dominik Hasek 1.50 4.00
5 Jarome Iginla .75 2.00
6 Keith Primeau .50 1.25
7 Tony Amonte .50 1.25
8 Patrick Roy 3.00 8.00
9 Mike Modano 1.00 2.50
10 Steve Yzerman 3.00 8.00
11 Bill Guerin .50 1.25
12 Pavel Bure .60 1.50
13 Luc Robitaille .50 1.25
14 Jeff Hackett .50 1.25
15 Cliff Ronning .50 1.25
16 Martin Brodeur 1.50 4.00
17 Felix Potvin .60 1.50
18 Brian Leetch .50 1.25
19 Alexei Yashin .50 1.25
20 Eric Lindros .60 1.50
21 Keith Tkachuk .60 1.50
22 Jaromir Jagr 1.00 2.50
23 Pierre Turgeon .50 1.25
24 Vincent Damphousse .50 1.25
25 Vincent Lecavalier .60 1.50
26 Curtis Joseph .60 1.50
27 Mark Messier .60 1.50
28 Peter Bondra .50 1.25

1999-00 Paramount Personal Best

Randomly inserted in packs at the rate of 1:37, this 36-card set features color portraits set against a blue background with silver foil highlights of some of the NHL's marquee players.

COMPLETE SET (36) 30.00 60.00
1 Paul Kariya .75 2.00
2 Teemu Selanne .75 2.00
3 Ray Bourque 1.25 3.00
4 Sergei Samsonov .40 1.00
5 Dominik Hasek 1.50 4.00
6 Michael Peca .40 1.00
7 Tony Amonte .40 1.00
8 Chris Drury .40 1.00
9 Peter Forsberg 2.00 5.00
10 Patrick Roy 4.00 10.00
11 Joe Sakic 1.50 4.00
12 Ed Belfour .75 2.00
13 Brett Hull 1.00 2.50
14 Mike Modano 1.25 3.00
15 Joe Nieuwendyk .40 1.00
16 Sergei Fedorov 1.50 4.00
17 Brendan Shanahan .75 2.00
18 Steve Yzerman 4.00 10.00
19 Pavel Bure .75 2.00
20 Saku Koivu .75 2.00
21 Martin Brodeur 2.00 5.00
22 Theo Fleury .40 1.00
23 Mike Richter .75 2.00
24 Alexei Yashin .40 1.00
25 John LeClair .75 2.00
26 Eric Lindros .75 2.00
27 Mark Recchi .40 1.00
28 John Vanbiesbrouck .40 1.00
29 Jeremy Roenick 1.00 2.50
30 Keith Tkachuk .75 2.00
31 Jaromir Jagr 1.25 3.00
32 Pavol Demitra .40 1.00
33 Vincent Lecavalier .75 2.00
34 Curtis Joseph .75 2.00
35 Mats Sundin .75 2.00
36 Mark Messier .75 2.00

2000-01 Paramount

Released as a 252-card set, Paramount features a white bordered card stock with full color player action photography centered on the card. The featured player's team name is in gold and is overlaid with the player's name in silver foil. Paramount was packaged in 36-pack boxes with each pack containing six cards.

COMPLETE SET (252) 20.00 40.00
1 Antti Aalto .10 .25
2 Maxim Balmochnyk .10 .25
3 Matt Cullen .10 .25
4 Guy Hebert .12 .30
5 Paul Kariya .20 .50
6 Steve Rucchin .10 .25
7 Teemu Selanne .30 .75
8 Oleg Tverdovsky .10 .25
9 Donald Audette .12 .30
10 Andrew Brunette .10 .25
11 Shean Donovan .10 .25
12 Scott Fankhouser .10 .25
13 Ray Ferraro .10 .25
14 Damian Rhodes .10 .25

2000-01 Paramount

Released as a 252-card set, Paramount features a white bordered card stock with full color player action photography centered on the card. The featured player's team name is in gold and is overlaid with the player's name in silver foil. Paramount was packaged in 36-pack boxes with each pack containing six cards.

15 Patrik Stefan .12 .30
16 Jason Allison .12 .30
17 Anson Carter .12 .30
18 Byron Dafoe .12 .30
19 John Grahame .10 .25
20 Brian Rolston .12 .30
21 Sergei Samsonov .12 .30
22 Don Sweeney .10 .25
23 Joe Thornton .25 .60
24 Maxim Afinogenov .10 .25
25 Stu Barnes .12 .30
26 Martin Biron .12 .30
27 Curtis Brown .10 .25
28 Doug Gilmour .20 .50
29 Chris Gratton .10 .25
30 Dominik Hasek .25 .60
31 Michael Peca .12 .30
32 Miroslav Satan .10 .25
33 Fred Brathwaite .12 .30
34 Valeri Bure .12 .30
35 Phil Housley .12 .30
36 Jarome Iginla .15 .40
37 Oleg Saprykin .10 .25
38 Marc Savard .12 .30
39 Cory Stillman .10 .25
40 Clarke Wilm .10 .25
41 Rod Brind'Amour .15 .40
42 Ron Francis .20 .50
43 Arturs Irbe .12 .30
44 Sami Kapanen .10 .25
45 Jeff O'Neill .12 .30
46 Dave Tanabe .10 .25
47 Glen Wesley .10 .25
48 Tony Amonte .12 .30
49 Michal Grosek .10 .25
50 Dean McAmmond .10 .25
51 Boris Mironov .10 .25
52 Michael Nylander .10 .25
53 Steve Sullivan .10 .25
54 Jocelyn Thibault .12 .30
55 Alexei Zhamnov .12 .30
56 Ray Bourque .25 .60
57 Adam Deadmarsh .12 .30
58 Chris Drury .12 .30
59 Adam Foote .12 .30
60 Peter Forsberg .20 .50
61 Milan Hejduk .12 .30
62 Patrick Roy .40 1.00
63 Joe Sakic .25 .60
64 Martin Skoula .12 .30
65 Alex Tanguay .12 .30
66 Kevyn Adams .10 .25
67 Serge Aubin RC .12 .30
68 Marc Denis .12 .30
69 Ted Drury .10 .25
70 Steve Heinze .10 .25
71 Lyle Odelein .10 .25
72 Ron Tugnutt .12 .30
73 Ed Belfour .15 .40
74 Derian Hatcher .12 .30
75 Brett Hull .25 .60
76 Jamie Langenbrunner .12 .30
77 Jere Lehtinen .12 .30
78 Roman Lyashenko .10 .25
79 Mike Modano .25 .60
80 Brenden Morrow .12 .30
81 Joe Nieuwendyk .15 .40
82 Sergei Zubov .12 .30
83 Chris Chelios .15 .40
84 Mathieu Dandenault .10 .25
85 Sergei Fedorov .25 .60
86 Martin Lapointe .12 .30
87 Nicklas Lidstrom .15 .40
88 Chris Osgood .15 .40
89 Brendan Shanahan .20 .50
90 Pat Verbeek .12 .30
91 Jesse Wallin .10 .25
92 Ken Wregget .12 .30
93 Steve Yzerman .50 1.25
94 Mike Grier .10 .25
95 Bill Guerin .15 .40
96 Todd Marchant .10 .25
97 Tom Poti .10 .25
98 Tommy Salo .12 .30
99 Alexander Selivanov .10 .25
100 Ryan Smyth .12 .30
101 Doug Weight .15 .40
102 Pavel Bure .20 .50
103 Brad Ference .10 .25
104 Trevor Kidd .10 .25
105 Viktor Kozlov .12 .30
106 Scott Mellanby .10 .25
107 Ivan Novoseltsev .10 .25
108 Robert Svehla .10 .25
109 Ray Whitney .12 .30
110 Rob Blake .15 .40
111 Stephane Fiset .10 .25
112 Glen Murray .10 .25
113 Zigmund Palffy .15 .40
114 Luc Robitaille .15 .40
115 Bryan Smolinski .12 .30
116 Jamie Storr .12 .30
117 Jozef Stumpel .10 .25
118 Manny Fernandez .12 .30
119 Sergei Krivokrasov .10 .25
120 Jamie McLennan .10 .25
121 Jeff Nielsen .10 .25
122 Sean O'Donnell .10 .25
123 Jeff Odgers .10 .25
124 Scott Pellerin .10 .25
125 Jeff Hackett .10 .25
126 Saku Koivu .15 .40
127 Trevor Linden .15 .40
128 Patrick Poulin .10 .25
129 Mike Ribeiro .12 .30
130 Martin Rucinsky .10 .25
131 Brian Savage .10 .25
132 Jose Theodore .20 .50
133 Dainius Zubrus .10 .25
134 Mike Dunham .10 .25
135 Greg Johnson .10 .25
136 David Legwand .15 .40
137 Cliff Ronning .10 .25
138 Rob Valicevic .10 .25
139 Tomas Vokoun .12 .30
140 Vitali Yachmenev .10 .25
141 Jason Arnott .12 .30
142 Martin Brodeur .30 .75
143 Patrik Elias .15 .40
144 Scott Gomez .12 .30
145 John Madden .12 .30
146 Alexander Mogilny .12 .30
147 Scott Niedermayer .15 .40
148 Brian Rafalski .10 .25
149 Scott Stevens .15 .40
150 Petr Sykora .12 .30
151 Colin White RC .10 .25
152 Tim Connolly .10 .25
153 Mariusz Czerkawski .10 .25
154 Brad Isbister .10 .25
155 Jason Krog .10 .25
156 Claude Lapointe .10 .25
157 Bill Muckalt .10 .25
158 Steve Valiquette RC .12 .30
159 Radek Dvorak .12 .30
160 Theo Fleury .20 .50
161 Adam Graves .12 .30
162 Jan Hlavac .10 .25
163 Brian Leetch .15 .40
164 Sylvain Lefebvre .10 .25
165 Mark Messier .25 .60
166 Petr Nedved .12 .30
167 Mike Richter .15 .40
168 Mike York .10 .25
169 Daniel Alfredsson .15 .40
170 Magnus Arvedson .10 .25
171 Radek Bonk .12 .30
172 Marian Hossa .12 .30
173 Jani Hurme RC .60 1.50
174 Patrick Lalime .12 .30
175 Shawn McEachern .10 .25
176 Vaclav Prospal .10 .25
177 Brian Boucher .12 .30
178 Andy Delmore .10 .25
179 Eric Desjardins .12 .30
180 Simon Gagne .15 .40
181 Daymond Langkow .10 .25
182 John LeClair .15 .40
183 Eric Lindros .25 .60
184 Keith Primeau .12 .30
185 Mark Recchi .20 .50
186 Rick Tocchet .12 .30
187 Shane Doan .12 .30
188 Robert Esche .10 .25
189 Travis Green .10 .25
190 Trevor Letowski .10 .25
191 Stanislav Neckar .10 .25
192 Teppo Numminen .10 .25
193 Jeremy Roenick .15 .40
194 Keith Tkachuk .15 .40
195 Jean-Sebastien Aubin .12 .30
196 Matthew Barnaby .12 .30
197 Jan Hrdina .10 .25
198 Jaromir Jagr .40 1.00
199 Alexei Kovalev .12 .30
200 Robert Lang .10 .25
201 John Slaney .10 .25
202 Martin Straka .12 .30
203 Lubos Dartecko .10 .25
204 Pavol Demitra .20 .50
205 Michal Handzus .10 .25
206 Al MacInnis .15 .40
207 Jamal Mayers .10 .25
208 Chris Pronger .12 .30
209 Roman Turek .12 .30
210 Pierre Turgeon .15 .40
211 Scott Young .10 .25
212 Vincent Damphousse .12 .30
213 Jeff Friesen .10 .25
214 Patrick Marleau .15 .40
215 Owen Nolan .15 .40
216 Mike Ricci .12 .30
217 Steve Shields .10 .25
218 Brad Stuart .12 .30
219 Dan Cloutier .12 .30
220 Brian Holzinger .10 .25
221 Mike Johnson .10 .25
222 Vincent Lecavalier .12 .30
223 Fredrik Modin .10 .25
224 Petr Svoboda .10 .25
225 Todd Warriner .10 .25
226 Nikolai Antropov .12 .30
227 Sergei Berezin .10 .25
228 Tie Domi .25 .60
229 Jeff Farkas .10 .25
230 Curtis Joseph .20 .50
231 Tomas Kaberle .10 .25
232 Yanic Perreault .10 .25
233 Mats Sundin .15 .40
234 Steve Thomas .10 .25
235 Darcy Tucker .10 .25
236 Todd Bertuzzi .12 .30
237 Andrew Cassels .10 .25
238 Ed Jovanovski .12 .30
239 Steve Kariya .10 .25
240 Markus Naslund .12 .30
241 Mattias Ohlund .10 .25
242 Felix Potvin .25 .60
243 Peter Bondra .12 .30
244 Sergei Gonchar .10 .25
245 Jeff Halpern .10 .25
246 Olaf Kolzig .15 .40
247 Steve Konowalchuk .10 .25
248 Adam Oates .15 .40
249 Chris Simon .10 .25
250 Richard Zednik .10 .25
251 Daniel Sedin .30 .75
252 Henrik Sedin .25 .60

2000-01 Paramount Copper

*VETS: 1.5X TO 4X BASIC CARDS
STATED ODDS 1:1 HOBBY
165 Mark Messier 1.00 2.50

2000-01 Paramount Gold

*GOLD: 2X TO 5X BASIC CARDS
STATED ODDS 1:1 RETAIL
165 Mark Messier 1.50 4.00

2000-01 Paramount HoloGold

Randomly inserted in Retail packs at the rate of 2:37, this 252-card set parallels the base set enhanced with a holographic gold foil shift from the base set silver on the player's name. Each card is sequentially numbered to 74.
*HOLOGOLD/74: 10X TO 25X BASIC CARDS
165 Mark Messier 8.00 20.00

2000-01 Paramount HoloSilver

Randomly inserted in Hobby packs, this 252-card set parallels the base set enhanced with a holographic silver foil shift from the base set silver on the player's name. Each card is sequentially numbered to 74.
*HOLOSILVER/74: 10X TO 25X BASIC CARDS
165 Mark Messier 8.00 20.00

2000-01 Paramount Ice Blue

*BLUE/50: 15X TO 40X BASIC CARDS
STATED PRINT RUN 50 SER.#'d SETS
STATED ODDS 1:73 HOBBY
165 Mark Messier 12.00 30.00

2000-01 Paramount Premiere Date

*PREM.DATE/45: 20X TO 50X BASIC CARDS
STATED PRINT RUN 45 SER.#'d SETS
RANDOM INSERTS IN HOBBY PACKS
165 Mark Messier 15.00 40.00

2000-01 Paramount Epic Scope

This 20-card set was inserted at a rate of 2:37.

COMPLETE SET (20) 30.00 60.00
1 Paul Kariya 1.00 2.50
2 Teemu Selanne 1.00 2.50
3 Dominik Hasek 2.00 5.00
4 Ray Bourque 2.00 5.00
5 Peter Forsberg 2.50 6.00
6 Patrick Roy 5.00 12.00
7 Joe Sakic 2.00 5.00
8 Brett Hull 1.25 3.00
9 Mike Modano 1.50 4.00
10 Brendan Shanahan 1.00 2.50
11 Steve Yzerman 5.00 12.00
12 Pavel Bure 1.00 2.50
13 Martin Brodeur 2.50 6.00
14 Scott Gomez .75 2.00
15 Brian Boucher .75 2.00
16 John LeClair 1.00 2.50
17 Jaromir Jagr 1.50 4.00
18 Vincent Lecavalier 1.00 2.50
19 Curtis Joseph 1.00 2.50
20 Mats Sundin 1.00 2.50

2000-01 Paramount Freeze Frame

Randomly inserted in packs at the rate of 1:37, this 36-card set features full color player action shots and a filmstrip border along the top and bottom of the card. Cards are highlighted with copper foil.

COMPLETE SET (36) 50.00 100.00
1 Paul Kariya 1.25 3.00
2 Teemu Selanne 1.25 3.00
3 Doug Gilmour 1.00 2.50
4 Dominik Hasek 2.50 6.00
5 Valeri Bure .40 1.00
6 Tony Amonte 1.00 2.50
7 Ray Bourque 2.50 6.00
8 Peter Forsberg 3.00 8.00
9 Joe Sakic 2.50 6.00
10 Patrick Roy 6.00 15.00
11 Ed Belfour 1.25 3.00
12 Brett Hull 1.50 4.00
13 Mike Modano 2.00 5.00
14 Sergei Fedorov 2.50 6.00
15 Brendan Shanahan 1.25 3.00
16 Steve Yzerman 6.00 15.00
17 Doug Weight 1.00 2.50
18 Pavel Bure 1.25 3.00
19 Luc Robitaille 1.00 2.50
20 Saku Koivu 1.25 3.00
21 Martin Brodeur 3.00 8.00
22 Scott Gomez .40 1.00
23 Tim Connolly .40 1.00
24 Marian Hossa 1.25 3.00
25 Brian Boucher 1.25 3.00
26 John LeClair 1.25 3.00
27 Mark Recchi 1.00 2.50
28 Jaromir Jagr 2.00 5.00
29 Jeremy Roenick 1.50 4.00
30 Chris Pronger 1.00 2.50
31 Roman Turek 1.00 2.50
32 Owen Nolan 1.00 2.50
33 Vincent Lecavalier 1.25 3.00
34 Mats Sundin 1.25 3.00
35 Curtis Joseph 1.25 3.00
36 Olaf Kolzig 1.00 2.50

2000-01 Paramount Game Used Sticks

Randomly inserted in packs, this 17-card set features player action photography on a horizontal design front coupled with an oval swatch of a game used stick. Each card is individually serial numbered in a gold foil box in the lower right hand corner of the card front.

1 Ron Francis/165 10.00 25.00
2 Ray Bourque/190 12.00 30.00
3 Adam Deadmarsh/200 10.00 25.00
4 Chris Drury/205 10.00 25.00
5 Joe Sakic/190 10.00 25.00
6 Martin Skoula/200 10.00 25.00
7 Alex Tanguay/200 10.00 25.00
8 Ed Belfour/205 15.00 40.00
9 Chris Chelios/165 12.50 30.00
10 Chris Osgood/205 10.00 25.00
11 Doug Weight/165 10.00 25.00
12 Luc Robitaille/185 10.00 25.00
13 Alexander Mogilny/155 8.00 20.00
14 Theo Fleury/190 10.00 25.00
15 Eric Lindros/190 12.50 30.00
16 Al MacInnis/165 10.00 25.00
17 Curtis Joseph/150 12.50 30.00

2000-01 Paramount Jersey and Patches

Randomly inserted in Hobby packs, this 10-card set features full color action photography coupled with a swatch of a game worn jersey on the card front and a game worn jersey patch on the back. Each card is sequentially numbered to 30.

1 Jarome Iginla 60.00 125.00
2 Tony Amonte 40.00 100.00
3 Ray Bourque 75.00 150.00
4 Joe Sakic 60.00 125.00
5 Darryl Sydor 40.00 100.00
6 Saku Koivu 25.00 60.00
7 John Vanbiesbrouck 50.00 100.00
8 Eric Desjardins 40.00 100.00
9 Shane Doan 40.00 100.00
10 Olaf Kolzig 40.00 100.00

2000-01 Paramount Glove Side Net Fusions

Randomly seeded in packs at the rate of 1:73, this 20-card set features a close-up of a goalie glove on the left side, player action shots on the right, and a die cut goal in the background with goal "netting." A platinum parallel numbered to just 25 was also created and inserted randomly.

COMPLETE SET (20) 50.00 100.00
*PLATINUM/25: 2.5X TO 6X BASIC INSERTS
1 Byron Dafoe 2.00 5.00
2 Martin Biron 2.00 5.00
3 Dominik Hasek 5.00 12.00
4 Fred Brathwaite 2.00 5.00
5 Arturs Irbe 2.00 5.00
6 Jocelyn Thibault 2.00 5.00
7 Patrick Roy 12.50 30.00
8 Ed Belfour 2.50 6.00
9 Chris Osgood 2.00 5.00
10 Tommy Salo 2.00 5.00
11 Jose Theodore 3.00 8.00
12 Martin Brodeur 6.00 15.00
13 Mike Richter 2.50 6.00
14 Brian Boucher 2.00 5.00
15 Jean-Sebastien Aubin 2.00 5.00
16 Roman Turek 2.00 5.00
17 Steve Shields 2.00 5.00
18 Curtis Joseph 2.50 6.00
19 Felix Potvin 2.50 6.00
20 Olaf Kolzig 2.00 5.00

2000-01 Paramount Hall of Fame Bound

Randomly inserted in packs at the rate of 1:361, this 10-card set features embossed oval portraits of top NHL players and a banner bearing the line "Hall of Fame Bound." Two different proof parallels were also created. Regular proofs were randomly inserted and numbered to just 25, canvas proofs were randomly Inserted and numbered 1/1.

COMPLETE SET (10) 75.00 150.00
*PROOF/25: 1.2X TO 3X BASIC INSERTS
1 Paul Kariya 5.00 12.00
2 Dominik Hasek 8.00 20.00
3 Ray Bourque 8.00 20.00
4 Patrick Roy 15.00 40.00
5 Brett Hull 10.00 25.00
6 Steve Yzerman 15.00 40.00
7 Pavel Bure 6.00 15.00
8 Martin Brodeur 12.50 30.00
9 John LeClair 5.00 12.00
10 Jaromir Jagr 6.00 15.00

2000-01 Paramount Sub Zero

Randomly inserted in Canadian Retail packs at the rate of 1:49, this 10-card set features top NHL players on a card enhanced with silver foil highlights. Each card is sequentially numbered to 159. A gold parallel was also created and numbered to 99.

*GOLD/99: .8X TO 2X BASIC INSERTS

Card	Low	High
1 Paul Kariya	4.00	10.00
2 Peter Forsberg	6.00	15.00
3 Patrick Roy	15.00	40.00
4 Brendan Shanahan	4.00	10.00
5 Steve Yzerman	12.00	30.00
6 Pavel Bure	4.00	10.00
7 Martin Brodeur	10.00	25.00
8 Jaromir Jagr	6.00	15.00
9 Curtis Joseph	4.00	10.00
10 Mats Sundin	4.00	10.00

1951-52 Parkhurst

The 1951-52 Parkhurst set contains 105 small cards in crude color. Cards are 1 3/4" by 2 1/2". The player's name, team, card number, and 1950-51 statistics all appear on the front of the card. The backs of the cards are blank. Unopened wax packs, though rarely seen, consist of five cards. The cards feature players from each of the six NHL teams. The set numbering is basically according to teams, i.e., Montreal Canadiens (1-18), Boston Bruins (19-35), Chicago Blackhawks (36-51 and 53), Detroit Red Wings (54-69), Toronto Maple Leafs (70-88), and New York Rangers (89-105). Card #52 features a photo of one of the most famous goals in hockey history as Bill Barilko scored the Stanley Cup winning goal and then went flying into the air. The set features the first cards of hockey greats Gordie Howe and Maurice Richard. Please be alert when purchasing cards of Maurice Richard, Gordie Howe and Terry Sawchuk as counterfeits are known to exist of these players.

Card	Low	High
COMPLETE SET (105)	6000.00	12000.00
1 Elmer Lach	350.00	500.00
2 Paul Meger RC	40.00	60.00
3 Butch Bouchard RC	75.00	200.00
4 Maurice Richard RC	1200.00	1800.00
5 Bert Olmstead RC	75.00	125.00
6 Bud MacPherson RC	40.00	60.00
7 Tom Johnson RC	75.00	125.00
8 Paul Masnick RC	40.00	60.00
9 Calum Mackay RC	40.00	60.00
10 Doug Harvey RC	400.00	600.00
11 Ken Mosdell RC	50.00	80.00
12 Floyd Curry RC	50.00	80.00
13 Billy Reay RC	50.00	80.00
14 Bernie Geoffrion RC	400.00	600.00
15 Gerry McNeil RC	175.00	300.00
16 Dick Gamble RC	50.00	80.00
17 Gerry Couture RC	40.00	60.00
18 Ross Robert Lowe RC	40.00	60.00
19 Jim Henry RC	90.00	150.00
20 Victor Ivan Lynn RC	40.00	60.00
21 Walter Kyle RC	40.00	60.00
22 Ed Sandford RC	40.00	60.00
23 John Henderson RC	40.00	60.00
24 Dunc Fisher RC	40.00	60.00
25 Hal Laycoe RC	50.00	80.00
26 Bill Quackenbush RC	75.00	125.00
27 George Sullivan RC	50.00	80.00
28 Woody Dumart	60.00	100.00
29 Milt Schmidt	100.00	150.00
30 Adam Brown RC	40.00	60.00
31 Pentti Lund RC	50.00	80.00
32 Ray Barry RC	40.00	60.00
33 Ed Kryznowski UER RC	40.00	60.00
34 Johnny Peirson RC	50.00	80.00
35 Lorne Ferguson RC	40.00	60.00
36 Clare Raglan RC	40.00	60.00
37 Bill Gadsby RC	75.00	125.00
38 Al Dewsbury RC	40.00	60.00
39 George Clare Martin RC	40.00	60.00
40 Gus Bodnar RC	50.00	80.00
41 Jim Peters RC	40.00	60.00
42 Bep Guidolin RC	50.00	80.00
43 George Gee RC	40.00	60.00
44 Jim McFadden RC	40.00	60.00
45 Fred Hucul RC	40.00	60.00
46 Lee Fogolin RC	40.00	60.00
47 Harry Lumley RC	100.00	175.00
48 Doug Bentley RC	75.00	125.00
49 Bill Mosienko RC	75.00	125.00
50 Roy Conacher	50.00	80.00
51 Pete Babando RC	40.00	60.00
52 B.Barilko/G.McNeil IA	250.00	500.00
53 Jack Stewart	50.00	80.00
54 Marty Pavelich RC	40.00	60.00
55 Red Kelly RC	200.00	300.00
56 Ted Lindsay RC	200.00	300.00
57 Glen Skov RC	40.00	60.00
58 Benny Woit RC	40.00	60.00
59 Tony Leswick RC	50.00	80.00
60 Fred Glover RC	40.00	60.00
61 Terry Sawchuk RC	800.00	1200.00
62 Vic Stasiuk RC	50.00	80.00
63 Alex Delvecchio RC	300.00	500.00
64 Sid Abel	60.00	100.00
65 Metro Prystai RC	40.00	60.00
66 Gordie Howe RC	2000.00	3000.00
67 Bob Goldham RC	40.00	60.00
68 Marcel Pronovost RC	60.00	125.00
69 Leo Reise Jr. RC	40.00	60.00
70 Harry Watson RC	60.00	125.00
71 Danny Lewicki RC	40.00	60.00
72 Howie Meeker RC	90.00	150.00
73 Gus Mortson RC	50.00	80.00
74 Joe Klukay RC	40.00	60.00
75 Turk Broda	125.00	200.00
76 Al Rollins RC	75.00	150.00
77 Bill Juzda RC	40.00	60.00
78 Ray Timgren RC	40.00	60.00
79 Hugh Bolton RC	40.00	60.00
80 Fern Flaman RC	75.00	125.00
81 Max Bentley	60.00	100.00
82 Jim Thomson RC	40.00	60.00
83 Fleming Mackell RC	50.00	80.00
84 Sid Smith RC	75.00	125.00
85 Cal Gardner RC	50.00	80.00
86 Teeder Kennedy RC	175.00	275.00
87 Tod Sloan RC	50.00	80.00
88 Bob Solinger RC	40.00	60.00
89 Frank Eddolls RC	40.00	60.00
90 Jack Evans RC	60.00	100.00
91 Hy Buller RC	40.00	60.00
92 Steve Kraftcheck RC	40.00	60.00
93 Don Raleigh RC	40.00	60.00
94 Allan Stanley RC	90.00	150.00
95 Paul Ronty RC	40.00	60.00
96 Edgar Laprade RC	60.00	100.00
97 Nick Mickoski RC	40.00	60.00
98 Jack McLeod RC	40.00	60.00
99 Gaye Stewart RC	40.00	60.00
100 Wally Hergesheimer RC	50.00	80.00
101 Ed Kullman RC	40.00	60.00
102 Ed Slowinski RC	40.00	60.00
103 Reg Sinclair RC	40.00	60.00
104 Chuck Rayner RC	75.00	125.00
105 Jim Conacher RC	100.00	200.00

1952-53 Parkhurst

The 1952-53 Parkhurst set contains 105 color, line-drawing cards. Cards are approximately 1 15/16" by 2 15/16". The obverse contains a facsimile autograph of the player pictured while the backs contain a short biography in English and 1951-52 statistics. The backs also contain the card number and a special album (for holding a set of cards) offer. The cards feature players from each of the Original Six NHL teams. The set numbering is roughly according to teams, i.e., Montreal Canadiens (1-15, 52, 93), Boston Bruins (68-85), Chicago Blackhawks (16-17, 26-27, 29-33, 35-41, 55-56), Detroit Red Wings (53, 60-67, 86-92, 104), Toronto Maple Leafs (28, 34, 42-48, 50-51, 54, 58-59, 94-96, 105), and New York Rangers (18-25, 49, 57, 97-103). The key Rookie Cards in this set are George Armstrong, Tim Horton, and Dickie Moore.

Card	Low	High
COMPLETE SET (105)	4500.00	7000.00
1 Maurice Richard	800.00	1200.00
2 Billy Reay	25.00	40.00
3 Boom Boom Geoffrion UER	150.00	250.00
4 Paul Meger	18.00	30.00
5 Dick Gamble	25.00	40.00
6 Elmer Lach	50.00	80.00
7 Floyd Curry	25.00	40.00
8 Ken Mosdell	25.00	40.00
9 Tom Johnson	25.00	40.00
10 Dickie Moore RC	150.00	250.00
11 Bud MacPherson	18.00	30.00
12 Gerry McNeil	60.00	100.00
13 Butch Bouchard	25.00	40.00
14 Doug Harvey	150.00	250.00
15 John McCormack RC	18.00	30.00
16 Pete Babando	18.00	30.00
17 Al Dewsbury	18.00	30.00
18 Ed Kullman	18.00	30.00
19 Ed Slowinski	18.00	30.00
20 Wally Hergesheimer	25.00	40.00
21 Allan Stanley	50.00	80.00
22 Chuck Rayner	40.00	60.00
23 Steve Kraftcheck	18.00	30.00
24 Paul Ronty	18.00	30.00
25 Gaye Stewart	18.00	30.00
26 Fred Hucul	18.00	30.00
27 Bill Mosienko	30.00	50.00
28 Jim Morrison RC	18.00	30.00
29 Ed Kryznowski	18.00	30.00
30 Cal Gardner	25.00	40.00
31 Al Rollins	40.00	60.00
32 Enio Sclisizzi RC	18.00	30.00
33 Pete Conacher RC	25.00	40.00
34 Leo Boivin RC	40.00	60.00
35 Jim Peters	18.00	30.00
36 George Gee	18.00	30.00
37 Gus Bodnar	25.00	40.00
38 Jim McFadden	18.00	30.00
39 Gus Mortson	25.00	40.00
40 Fred Glover	18.00	30.00
41 Gerry Couture	18.00	30.00
42 Howie Meeker	50.00	80.00
43 Jim Thomson	18.00	30.00
44 Teeder Kennedy	60.00	100.00
45 Sid Smith	25.00	40.00
46 Harry Watson	30.00	50.00
47 Fern Flaman	25.00	40.00
48 Tod Sloan	25.00	40.00
49 Leo Reise Jr.	18.00	30.00
50 Bob Solinger	18.00	30.00
51 George Armstrong RC	150.00	250.00
52 Dollard St.Laurent RC	25.00	40.00
53 Alex Delvecchio	90.00	150.00
54 Gord Hannigan RC	18.00	30.00
55 Lee Fogolin	18.00	30.00
56 Bill Gadsby	30.00	50.00
57 Herb Dickenson RC	18.00	30.00
58 Tim Horton RC	500.00	700.00
59 Harry Lumley	60.00	100.00
60 Metro Prystai	18.00	30.00
61 Marcel Pronovost	25.00	40.00
62 Benny Woit	18.00	30.00
63 Glen Skov	18.00	30.00
64 Bob Goldham	18.00	30.00
65 Tony Leswick	18.00	30.00
66 Marty Pavelich	18.00	30.00
67 Red Kelly	90.00	150.00
68 Bill Quackenbush	30.00	50.00
69 Ed Sandford	18.00	30.00
70 Milt Schmidt	40.00	60.00
71 Hal Laycoe	25.00	40.00
72 Woody Dumart	25.00	40.00
73 Zellio Toppazzini RC	18.00	30.00
74 Jim Henry	25.00	40.00
75 Joe Klukay	18.00	30.00
76 Dave Creighton RC	25.00	40.00
77 Jack McIntyre RC	18.00	30.00
78 Johnny Peirson	18.00	30.00
79 George Sullivan	25.00	40.00
80 Real Chevrefils RC	25.00	40.00
81 Leo Labine RC	30.00	50.00
82 Fleming Mackell	25.00	40.00
83 Pentti Lund	18.00	30.00
84 Bob Armstrong RC	18.00	30.00
85 Warren Godfrey RC	18.00	30.00
86 Terry Sawchuk	300.00	500.00
87 Ted Lindsay	90.00	150.00
88 Gordie Howe	600.00	1000.00
89 Johnny Wilson RC	25.00	40.00
90 Vic Stasiuk	25.00	40.00
91 Larry Zeidel RC	18.00	30.00
92 Larry Wilson RC	18.00	30.00
93 Bert Olmstead	25.00	40.00
94 Ron Stewart RC	25.00	40.00
95 Max Bentley	30.00	50.00
96 Rudy Migay RC	18.00	30.00
97 Jack Stoddard RC	18.00	30.00
98 Hy Buller	18.00	30.00
99 Don Raleigh UER	18.00	30.00
100 Edgar Laprade	25.00	40.00
101 Nick Mickoski	18.00	30.00
102 Jack McLeod UER (Robert on back)	18.00	30.00
103 Jim Conacher	25.00	40.00
104 Reg Sinclair	18.00	30.00
105 Bob Hassard RC	75.00	125.00

1953-54 Parkhurst

The 1953-54 Parkhurst set contains 100 cards in full color. Cards measure approximately 2 1/2" by 3 5/8". The cards were sold in five-cent wax packs each containing four cards and gum. The size of the card increased from the previous year, and the picture and color show marked improvement. A facsimile autograph of the player is found on the front. The backs contain the card number, 1952-53 statistics, a short biography, and an album offer. The back data is presented in both English and French. The cards feature players from each of the six NHL teams. The set numbering is basically according to teams, i.e., Toronto Maple Leafs (1-17), Montreal Canadiens (18-35), Detroit Red Wings (36-52), New York Rangers (53-68), Chicago Blackhawks (69-84), and Boston Bruins (85-100). The key Rookie Cards in this set are Al Arbour, Andy Bathgate, Jean Beliveau, Harry Howell, and Gump Worsley.

Card	Low	High
COMPLETE SET (100)	3000.00	4500.00
1 Harry Lumley	175.00	300.00
2 Sid Smith	20.00	40.00
3 Gord Hannigan	20.00	40.00
4 Bob Hassard	20.00	40.00
5 Tod Sloan	20.00	40.00
6 Leo Boivin	20.00	40.00
7 Teeder Kennedy	40.00	80.00
8 Jim Thomson	20.00	40.00
9 Ron Stewart	20.00	40.00
10 Eric Nesterenko RC	40.00	80.00
11 George Armstrong	60.00	100.00
12 Harry Watson	30.00	60.00
13 Tim Horton	175.00	300.00
14 Fern Flaman	25.00	50.00
15 Jim Morrison	20.00	40.00
16 Bob Solinger	20.00	40.00
17 Rudy Migay	20.00	40.00
18 Dick Gamble	20.00	40.00
19 Bert Olmstead	25.00	50.00
20 Eddie Mazur RC	20.00	40.00
21 Paul Meger	20.00	40.00
22 Bud MacPherson	20.00	40.00
23 Dollard St.Laurent	20.00	40.00
24 Maurice Richard	300.00	500.00
25 Gerry McNeil	50.00	80.00
26 Doug Harvey	125.00	200.00
27 Jean Beliveau RC	600.00	1000.00
28 Dickie Moore UER	75.00	125.00
29 Bernie Geoffrion	125.00	200.00
30 E.Lach/M.Richard	125.00	200.00
31 Elmer Lach	40.00	80.00
32 Butch Bouchard	25.00	50.00
33 Ken Mosdell	20.00	40.00
34 John McCormack	20.00	40.00
35 Floyd Curry	20.00	40.00
36 Earl Reibel RC	20.00	40.00
37 Bill Dineen UER RC	40.00	80.00
38 Al Arbour RC UER	60.00	100.00
39 Vic Stasiuk	20.00	40.00
40 Red Kelly	60.00	100.00
41 Marcel Pronovost	25.00	50.00
42 Metro Prystai	20.00	40.00
43 Tony Leswick	20.00	40.00
44 Marty Pavelich	20.00	40.00
45 Benny Woit	20.00	40.00
46 Terry Sawchuk	200.00	350.00
47 Alex Delvecchio	60.00	100.00
48 Glen Skov	20.00	40.00
49 Bob Goldham	20.00	40.00
50 Gordie Howe	500.00	800.00
51 Johnny Wilson	20.00	40.00
52 Ted Lindsay	60.00	100.00
53 Gump Worsley RC	275.00	400.00
54 Jack Evans	20.00	40.00
55 Max Bentley	30.00	60.00
56 Andy Bathgate RC	90.00	150.00
57 Harry Howell RC	90.00	150.00
58 Hy Buller	20.00	40.00
59 Chuck Rayner	25.00	50.00
60 Jack Stoddard	20.00	40.00
61 Ed Kullman	25.00	50.00
62 Nick Mickoski	20.00	40.00
63 Paul Ronty	20.00	40.00
64 Allan Stanley	30.00	60.00
65 Leo Reise Jr.	20.00	40.00
66 Aldo Guidolin RC	20.00	40.00
67 Wally Hergesheimer	20.00	40.00
68 Don Raleigh	20.00	40.00
69 Jim Peters	20.00	40.00
70 Pete Conacher	20.00	40.00
71 Fred Hucul	20.00	40.00
72 Lee Fogolin	20.00	40.00
73 Larry Zeidel	20.00	40.00
74 Larry Wilson	20.00	40.00
75 Gus Bodnar	20.00	40.00
76 Bill Gadsby	30.00	60.00
77 Jim McFadden	20.00	40.00
78 Al Dewsbury	20.00	40.00
79 Clare Raglan	20.00	40.00
80 Bill Mosienko	30.00	60.00
81 Gus Mortson	20.00	40.00
82 Al Rollins	25.00	50.00
83 George Gee	20.00	40.00
84 Gerry Couture	20.00	40.00
85 Dave Creighton	20.00	40.00
86 Jim Henry	25.00	50.00
87 Hal Laycoe	20.00	40.00
88 Johnny Peirson UER	25.00	50.00
89 Real Chevrefils	20.00	40.00
90 Ed Sandford	20.00	40.00
91A Fleming Mackell No Bio	25.00	50.00
91B Fleming Mackell Full Bio	250.00	400.00
92 Milt Schmidt	40.00	80.00
93 Leo Labine	20.00	40.00
94 Joe Klukay	20.00	40.00
95 Warren Godfrey	20.00	40.00
96 Woody Dumart	25.00	50.00
97 Frank Martin RC	20.00	40.00
98 Jerry Toppazzini RC	25.00	50.00
99 Cal Gardner	20.00	40.00
100 Bill Quackenbush	75.00	150.00

1954-55 Parkhurst

The 1954-55 Parkhurst set contains 100 cards in full color with both the card number and a facsimile autograph on the fronts. Cards in the set measure approximately 2 1/2" by 3 5/8". Unopened wax packs consisted of four cards. The backs, in both English and French, contain 1953-54 statistics, a short player biography, and an album offer (contained only on cards 1-88). Cards 1-88 feature players from each of the six NHL teams and the remaining cards are action scenes. Cards 1-88 were available with either a stat or a premium back. The cards with the statistics on the back are generally more desirable. The player/set numbering is basically according to teams, i.e., Montreal Canadiens (1-15), Toronto Maple Leafs (16-32), Detroit Red Wings (33-48), Boston Bruins (49-64), New York Rangers (65-76), and Chicago Blackhawks (77-88), and All-Star selections from the previous season are noted discreetly on the card front by a red star (first team selection) or blue star (second team). The key Rookie Card in this set is Johnny Bower, although there are several Action Scene cards featuring Jacques Plante in the year before his regular Rookie Card.

Card	Low	High
COMPLETE SET (100)	2500.00	4000.00
*1-88 PREMIUM BACK: SAME VALUE		
1 Gerry McNeil	75.00	150.00
2 Dickie Moore	50.00	80.00
3 Jean Beliveau	200.00	300.00
4 Eddie Mazur	15.00	25.00
5 Bert Olmstead	18.00	30.00
6 Butch Bouchard	25.00	40.00
7 Maurice Richard	275.00	400.00
8 Bernie Geoffrion	75.00	125.00
9 John McCormack	15.00	25.00
10 Tom Johnson	18.00	30.00
11 Calum Mackay	18.00	30.00
12 Ken Mosdell	18.00	30.00
13 Paul Masnick	18.00	30.00
14 Doug Harvey	75.00	125.00
15 Floyd Curry	15.00	25.00
16 Harry Lumley	25.00	40.00
17 Harry Watson	25.00	40.00
18 Jim Morrison	18.00	30.00
19 Eric Nesterenko	18.00	30.00
20 Fern Flaman	18.00	30.00
21 Rudy Migay	15.00	25.00
22 Sid Smith	15.00	25.00
23 Ron Stewart	18.00	30.00
24 George Armstrong	50.00	80.00
25 Earl Balfour RC	18.00	30.00
26 Leo Boivin	15.00	25.00
27 Gord Hannigan	18.00	30.00
28 Bob Bailey RC	18.00	30.00
29 Teeder Kennedy	30.00	50.00
30 Tod Sloan	15.00	25.00
31 Tim Horton	150.00	250.00
32 Jim Thomson	18.00	30.00
33 Terry Sawchuk	150.00	250.00
34 Marcel Pronovost	18.00	30.00
35 Metro Prystai	15.00	25.00
36 Alex Delvecchio	50.00	80.00
37 Earl Reibel	15.00	25.00
38 Benny Woit	15.00	25.00
39 Bob Goldham	15.00	25.00
40 Glen Skov	18.00	30.00
41 Gordie Howe	400.00	600.00
42 Red Kelly	50.00	80.00
43 Marty Pavelich	15.00	25.00
44 Johnny Wilson	15.00	25.00
45 Tony Leswick	15.00	25.00
46 Ted Lindsay	50.00	80.00
47 Keith Allen RC	18.00	30.00
48 Bill Dineen	15.00	25.00
49 Jim Henry	25.00	40.00
50 Fleming Mackell	18.00	30.00
51 Bill Quackenbush	25.00	40.00
52 Hal Laycoe	15.00	25.00
53 Cal Gardner	15.00	25.00
54 Joe Klukay	15.00	25.00
55 Bob Armstrong	15.00	25.00
56 Warren Godfrey	18.00	30.00
57 Doug Mohns RC	25.00	40.00
58 Dave Creighton	30.00	50.00
59 Milt Schmidt	30.00	50.00
60 Johnny Peirson	15.00	25.00
61 Leo Labine	18.00	30.00
62 Gus Bodnar	15.00	25.00
63 Real Chevrefils	15.00	25.00
64 Ed Sandford	18.00	30.00
65 Johnny Bower UER RC	300.00	500.00
66 Paul Ronty	15.00	25.00
67 Leo Reise Jr.	15.00	25.00
68 Don Raleigh	18.00	30.00
69 Bob Chrystal RC	15.00	25.00
70 Harry Howell	35.00	60.00
71 Wally Hergesheimer	15.00	25.00
72 Jack Evans	15.00	25.00
73 Camille Henry RC	18.00	30.00
74 Dean Prentice RC	25.00	40.00
75 Nick Mickoski	15.00	25.00
76 Ron Murphy RC	15.00	25.00
77 Al Rollins	25.00	40.00
78 Al Dewsbury	15.00	25.00
79 Lou Jankowski RC	15.00	25.00
80 George Gee	15.00	25.00
81 Gus Mortson	15.00	25.00
82 Fred Saskamoose RC	75.00	125.00
83 Ike Hildebrand RC	15.00	25.00
84 Lee Fogolin	15.00	25.00
85 Larry Wilson	15.00	25.00
86 Pete Conacher	15.00	25.00
87 Bill Gadsby	25.00	40.00
88 Jack McIntyre	15.00	25.00
89 Floyd Curry	15.00	25.00
90 Alex Delvecchio	18.00	30.00
91 R.Kelly/H.Lumley	25.00	40.00
92 Lumley/Howe/Stewart	60.00	100.00
93 H.Lumley/R.Murphy	15.00	25.00
94 P.Meger/J.Morrison	15.00	25.00
95 D.Harvey/E.Nesterenko	30.00	50.00
96 T.Sawchuk/T.Kennedy	60.00	100.00
97 Plante/B.Bouchard/Reibel	60.00	100.00
98 J.Plante/Harvey/Sloan	60.00	100.00
99 J.Plante/T.Kennedy	60.00	100.00
100 T.Sawchuk/B.Geoffrion	125.00	200.00

1955-56 Parkhurst

The 1955-56 Parkhurst set contains 79 cards in full color with the number and team insignia on the fronts. Cards in the set measure approximately 2 1/2" by 3 9/16". The set features players from Montreal and Toronto as well as Old-Time Greats. The Old-Time Great selections are numbers 21-32 and 55-66. The backs, printed in red ink, in both English and French, contain 1954-55 statistics, a short biography, a "Do You Know" information section, and an album offer. The key Rookie Card in this set is Jacques Plante. The same 79 cards can also be found with Quaker Oats backs, i.e., green printing on back. The Quaker Oats version is much tougher to locate. Reportedly, cards #1, 33 and 37 are extremely difficult to acquire in the Quaker Oats version, and can often sell for much more than the suggested multipliers.

Card	Low	High
COMPLETE SET (79)	2800.00	5000.00
1 Harry Lumley	200.00	300.00
2 Sid Smith	15.00	30.00
3A Tim Horton COR	150.00	250.00
3B Tim Horton ERR		
4 George Armstrong	50.00	80.00
5 Ron Stewart	15.00	30.00
6 Joe Klukay	12.00	20.00
7 Marc Reaume RC	12.00	20.00
8 Jim Morrison	12.00	20.00
9 Parker MacDonald RC	12.00	20.00
10 Tod Sloan	12.00	20.00
11 Jim Thomson	12.00	20.00
12 Rudy Migay	12.00	20.00
13 Brian Cullen RC	15.00	30.00
14 Hugh Bolton	12.00	20.00
15 Eric Nesterenko	15.00	30.00
16 Larry Cahan RC	12.00	20.00
17 Willie Marshall RC	12.00	20.00
18 Dick Duff RC	50.00	100.00
19 Jack Caffery RC	12.00	20.00
20 Billy Harris RC	15.00	30.00
21 Lorne Chabot OTG	15.00	30.00
22 Harvey Jackson OTG	30.00	50.00
23 Turk Broda OTG	60.00	100.00
24 Joe Primeau OTG	25.00	40.00
25 Gordie Drillon OTG	15.00	30.00
26 Chuck Conacher OTG	25.00	40.00
27 Sweeney Schriner OTG	15.00	30.00
28 Syl Apps OTG	25.00	40.00
29 Teeder Kennedy OTG	30.00	50.00
30 Ace Bailey OTG	40.00	60.00
31 Babe Pratt OTG	15.00	30.00
32 Harold Cotton OTG	15.00	30.00
33 King Clancy CO	60.00	100.00
34 Hap Day	15.00	30.00
35 Don Marshall RC	30.00	50.00
36 Jackie LeClair RC	15.00	30.00
37 Maurice Richard	275.00	400.00
38 Dickie Moore	50.00	80.00
39 Ken Mosdell	15.00	30.00
40 Floyd Curry	12.00	20.00
41 Calum Mackay	12.00	20.00
42 Bert Olmstead	15.00	30.00
43 Bernie Geoffrion	75.00	125.00
44 Jean Beliveau	250.00	350.00
45 Doug Harvey	75.00	125.00
46 Butch Bouchard	15.00	30.00
47 Bud MacPherson	12.00	20.00
48 Dollard St.Laurent	12.00	20.00
49 Tom Johnson	15.00	30.00
50 Jacques Plante RC	800.00	1200.00
51 Paul Meger	12.00	20.00
52 Gerry McNeil	25.00	40.00
53 Jean-Guy Talbot RC	15.00	30.00
54 Bob Turner RC	12.00	20.00
55 Newsy Lalonde OTG	40.00	60.00
56 Georges Vezina OTG	75.00	125.00
57 Howie Morenz OTG	60.00	100.00
58 Aurel Joliat OTG	40.00	60.00
59 George Hainsworth OTG	60.00	100.00
60 Sylvio Mantha OTG	15.00	30.00
61 Battleship Leduc OTG	15.00	30.00
62 Babe Siebert OTG UER	25.00	40.00
63 Bill Durnan OTG RC	40.00	60.00
64 Ken Reardon OTG	40.00	60.00
65 Johnny Gagnon OTG	15.00	30.00
66 Billy Reay OTG	15.00	30.00
67 Toe Blake CO	30.00	50.00
68 Frank Selke MG	18.00	30.00
69 Hugh Beats Hodge	18.00	30.00
70 Lumley Stops BoomBoom	40.00	60.00
71 J.Plante Is Protected	50.00	80.00
72 Rocket Roars Through	50.00	80.00
73 Richard Tests Lumley	50.00	80.00
74 Beliveau Bats Puck	40.00	60.00
75 Nesterenko/Smith/Plante	50.00	80.00
76 Curry/Lumley/Morrison	15.00	30.00
77 Sloan/MacD/Harvey/Beliv	50.00	80.00
78 Montreal Forum	150.00	300.00
79 Maple Leaf Gardens	150.00	300.00

1955-56 Parkhurst Quaker Oats

Card	Low	High
1 Harry Lumley	400.00	700.00
2 Sid Smith	20.00	60.00
3 Tim Horton	350.00	600.00
4 George Armstrong	75.00	200.00
5 Ron Stewart	15.00	40.00
6 Joe Klukay	15.00	40.00
7 Marc Reaume RC	15.00	40.00
8 Jim Morrison	15.00	40.00
9 Parker MacDonald RC	15.00	40.00
10 Tod Sloan	20.00	60.00
11 Jim Thomson	15.00	40.00
12 Rudy Migay	15.00	40.00
13 Brian Cullen RC	30.00	80.00
14 Hugh Bolton	15.00	40.00
15 Eric Nesterenko	20.00	60.00
16 Larry Cahan RC	20.00	60.00
17 Willie Marshall RC	15.00	40.00
18 Dick Duff RC	150.00	300.00
19 Jack Caffery RC	15.00	40.00
20 Billy Harris RC	30.00	80.00
21 Lorne Chabot OTG	40.00	100.00
22 Harvey Jackson OTG	60.00	150.00
23 Turk Broda OTG	150.00	300.00
24 Joe Primeau OTG	30.00	80.00
25 Gordie Drillon OTG	30.00	80.00
26 Chuck Conacher OTG	30.00	80.00
27 Sweeney Schriner OTG	30.00	80.00
28 Syl Apps OTG	30.00	80.00
29 Teeder Kennedy OTG	40.00	100.00
30 Ace Bailey OTG	50.00	125.00
31 Babe Pratt OTG	20.00	60.00
32 Harold Cotton OTG	20.00	60.00
33 King Clancy CO	75.00	200.00
34 Hap Day	30.00	80.00
35 Don Marshall RC	40.00	100.00
36 Jackie LeClair RC	20.00	60.00
37 Maurice Richard	500.00	750.00
38 Dickie Moore	60.00	150.00
39 Ken Mosdell	20.00	60.00
40 Floyd Curry	20.00	60.00
41 Calum Mackay	15.00	40.00
42 Bert Olmstead	20.00	60.00
43 Boom Boom Geoffrion	125.00	250.00
44 Jean Beliveau	400.00	700.00
45 Doug Harvey	125.00	250.00
46 Butch Bouchard	20.00	60.00
47 Bud MacPherson	15.00	40.00
48 Dollard St.Laurent	20.00	60.00
49 Tom Johnson	30.00	80.00
50 Jacques Plante RC	2000.00	3500.00
51 Paul Meger	20.00	60.00
52 Gerry McNeil	40.00	100.00
53 Jean-Guy Talbot RC	30.00	80.00
54 Bob Turner RC	15.00	40.00
55 Newsy Lalonde OTG	50.00	125.00
56 Georges Vezina OTG	150.00	300.00
57 Howie Morenz OTG	150.00	300.00
58 Aurel Joliat OTG	50.00	125.00
59 George Hainsworth OTG	125.00	250.00
60 Sylvio Mantha OTG	20.00	60.00
61 Battleship Leduc OTG	20.00	60.00
62 Babe Siebert OTG UER (Misspelled Seibert on both sides	30.00	80.00
63 Bill Durnan OTG RC	50.00	125.00
64 Ken Reardon OTG	50.00	125.00
65 Johnny Gagnon OTG	20.00	60.00
66 Billy Reay OTG	20.00	60.00
67 Toe Blake CO	40.00	100.00
68 Frank Selke MG	20.00	60.00
69 Hugh Beats Hodge	20.00	60.00
70 Lum Stops BoomBoom	50.00	125.00
71 J.Plante Is Protected	75.00	200.00
72 Rocket Roars Through	75.00	200.00
73 Richard Tests Lumley	75.00	200.00
74 Beliveau Bats Puck	60.00	150.00
75 Nester Smith Plante	75.00	200.00
76 Curry Lumley Morrison	30.00	80.00
77 Sloan MacDonald Harvey Beliveau	60.00	150.00
78 Montreal Forum	500.00	750.00
79 Maple Leaf Gardens	500.00	750.00

1957-58 Parkhurst

The 1957-58 Parkhurst set contains 50 color cards featuring Montreal and Toronto players. Cards are approximately 2 7/16" by 3 5/8". There are card numbers 1 to 25 for Montreal (M prefix in checklist) and card numbers 1 to 25 for Toronto (T prefix in checklist). The cards are numbered on the fronts and the backs feature resumes in both French and English. The card number, the player's name, and his position appear in a red rectangle on the front. The backs are printed in blue ink. The key Rookie Cards in this set are Frank Mahovlich and Henri Richard. There was no Parkhurst hockey set in 1956-57 reportedly due to market re-evaluation.

Card	Low	High
COMPLETE SET (50)	2000.00	3500.00
M1 Doug Harvey	150.00	275.00
M2 Bernie Geoffrion	80.00	150.00
M3 Jean Beliveau	200.00	300.00
M4 Henri Richard RC	400.00	600.00
M5 Maurice Richard	300.00	400.00
M6 Tom Johnson	15.00	25.00
M7 Andre Pronovost RC	20.00	40.00
M8 Don Marshall	12.00	20.00
M9 Jean-Guy Talbot	12.00	20.00
M10 Dollard St.Laurent	12.00	20.00
M11 Phil Goyette RC	25.00	40.00
M12 Claude Provost RC	25.00	40.00
M13 Bob Turner	12.00	20.00
M14 Dickie Moore	35.00	60.00
M15 Jacques Plante	250.00	400.00
M16 Toe Blake CO	25.00	40.00
M17 Charlie Hodge RC	50.00	80.00
M18 Marcel Bonin	15.00	25.00
M19 Bert Olmstead	15.00	25.00
M20 Floyd Curry	12.00	20.00
M21 Len Broderick IA RC	25.00	40.00
M22 Brian Cullen scores	12.00	20.00
M23 Broderick/Harvey IA	25.00	40.00
M24 Geoffrion/Chadwick IA	30.00	50.00
M25 Olmstead/Chadwick IA	20.00	40.00
T1 George Armstrong	60.00	100.00
T2 Ed Chadwick RC	100.00	175.00
T3 Dick Duff	15.00	25.00
T4 Bob Pulford RC	90.00	150.00
T5 Tod Sloan	18.00	30.00
T6 Rudy Migay	12.00	20.00
T7 Ron Stewart	12.00	20.00
T8 Gerry James RC	15.00	25.00
T9 Brian Cullen	12.00	20.00
T10 Sid Smith	12.00	20.00
T11 Jim Morrison	12.00	20.00
T12 Marc Reaume	12.00	20.00
T13 Hugh Bolton	12.00	20.00
T14 Pete Conacher		
T15 Billy Harris	12.00	20.00
T16 Mike Nykoluk RC		
T17 Frank Mahovlich RC	300.00	500.00
T18 Ken Girard RC		
T19 Al MacNeil RC		
T20 Bob Baun RC	60.00	100.00
T21 Barry Cullen RC		
T22 Tim Horton	100.00	175.00
T23 Gary Collins RC		
T24 Gary Aldcorn RC	12.00	20.00
T25 Billy Reay CO	18.00	30.00

1958-59 Parkhurst

The 1958-59 Parkhurst set contains 50 color cards of Montreal and Toronto players. Cards are approximately 2 7/16" by 3 5/8". In contrast to the 1957-58 Parkhurst set, the cards, numbered on the fronts, are numbered continuously from 1 to 50. Resumes on the backs of the cards are in both French and English. The player's name and the team logo appears in a yellow rectangle at the bottom on the front. The number, position, and (usually) a hockey stick appear on the front at the upper left. The backs are printed in black ink. The key Rookie Card in this set is Ralph Backstrom.

Card	Low	High
COMPLETE SET (50)	1200.00	1800.00
1 Bob Pulford IA	30.00	50.00
2 Henri Richard	125.00	200.00
3 Andre Pronovost	10.00	15.00
4 Billy Harris	12.00	20.00
5 Albert Langlois RC	10.00	15.00
6 Noel Price RC	10.00	15.00
7 G.Armstrong/Johnson IA	15.00	25.00
8 Dickie Moore	25.00	40.00
9 Toe Blake CO	15.00	25.00
10 Tom Johnson	12.00	20.00
11 J.Plante/G.Armstrong	35.00	50.00
12 Ed Chadwick	25.00	40.00
13 Bob Nevin RC	15.00	25.00
14 Ron Stewart	12.00	18.00
15 Bob Baun	25.00	40.00
16 Ralph Backstrom RC	30.00	50.00
17 Charlie Hodge	25.00	40.00
18 Gary Aldcorn	10.00	15.00
19 Willie Marshall	10.00	15.00
20 Marc Reaume	10.00	15.00
21 Jacques Plante IA	40.00	60.00
22 Jacques Plante	200.00	300.00
23 Allan Stanley UER	15.00	25.00
24 Ian Cushenan RC	12.00	18.00
25 Billy Reay CO	12.00	18.00
26 Jacques Plante IA	40.00	60.00
27 Bert Olmstead	12.00	18.00
28 Bernie Geoffrion	50.00	80.00
29 Dick Duff	12.00	18.00
30 Ab McDonald RC	10.00	15.00
31 Barry Cullen	10.00	15.00
32 Marcel Bonin	10.00	15.00
33 Frank Mahovlich	125.00	200.00
34 Jean Beliveau	125.00	200.00
35 Jacques Plante IA	40.00	60.00
36 Brian Cullen Shoots	12.00	18.00
37 Steve Kraftcheck	10.00	15.00
38 Maurice Richard	200.00	300.00
39 Jacques Plante IA	40.00	60.00
40 Bob Turner	10.00	15.00
41 Jean-Guy Talbot	12.00	18.00
42 Tim Horton	75.00	125.00
43 Claude Provost	12.00	18.00
44 Don Marshall	12.00	18.00
45 Bob Pulford	15.00	25.00
46 Johnny Bower UER	90.00	150.00
47 Phil Goyette	12.00	18.00
48 George Armstrong	25.00	40.0
49 Doug Harvey	50.00	80.0
50 Brian Cullen	20.00	40.0

1959-60 Parkhurst

The 1959-60 Parkhurst set contains 50 color cards o[f] Montreal and Toronto players. Cards are approximate[ly] 2 7/16" by 3 5/8". The cards are numbered on the fronts. The backs, which contain 1958-59 statistics, a short biography, and a Hockey Gum contest ad, are written in both French and English. The key Rookie Cards in this set are Carl Brewer and Punch Imlach.

Card	Low	High
COMPLETE SET (50)	700.00	1400.0
1 Canadiens On Guard Jacques Plante Tom Johnson Phil Goyette	75.00	150.0
2 Maurice Richard	150.00	300.0
3 Carl Brewer RC	40.00	80.0
4 Phil Goyette	12.00	30.0
5 Ed Chadwick	15.00	40.0
6 Jean Beliveau	75.00	150.0
7 George Armstrong	15.00	40.0
8 Doug Harvey	40.00	80.0
9 Billy Harris	12.00	30.0
10 Tom Johnson	12.00	30.0
11 Marc Reaume	12.00	30.0
12 Marcel Bonin	12.00	30.0
13 Johnny Wilson	12.00	30.0
14 Dickie Moore	20.00	50.0
15 Punch Imlach CO RC	20.00	50.0
16 Charlie Hodge	15.00	40.0
17 Larry Regan	12.00	30.0
18 Claude Provost	12.00	30.0
19 Gerry Ehman RC	12.00	30.0
20 Ab McDonald	12.00	30.0
21 Bob Baun	12.00	30.0
22 Ken Reardon VP	12.00	30.0
23 Tim Horton	65.00	120.0
24 Frank Mahovlich	75.00	150.0
25 Johnny Bower IA	20.00	50.0
26 Ron Stewart	12.00	30.0
27 Toe Blake CO	12.00	30.0
28 Bob Pulford	12.00	30.0
29 Ralph Backstrom	12.00	30.0
30 Action Around the Net	15.00	40.0
31 Bill Hicke RC	15.00	40.0
32 Johnny Bower	60.00	120.0
33 Bernie Geoffrion	40.00	80.0
34 Ted Hampson RC	12.00	30.0
35 Andre Pronovost	12.00	30.0
36 Stafford Smythe CHC	12.00	30.0
37 Don Marshall	12.00	30.0
38 Dick Duff	12.00	30.0
39 Henri Richard	75.00	150.0
40 Bert Olmstead	12.00	30.0
41 Jacques Plante	125.00	250.0
42 Noel Price	12.00	30.0
43 Bob Turner	12.00	30.0
44 Allan Stanley	20.00	50.0
45 Albert Langlois	12.00	30.0
46 Officials Intervene	12.00	30.0
47 Frank Selke MD	12.00	30.0
48 Gary Edmundson RC	12.00	30.0
49 Jean-Guy Talbot	12.00	30.0
50 King Clancy AGM	50.00	100.0

1960-61 Parkhurst

The 1960-61 Parkhurst set of 61 color cards, numbered on the fronts, contains players from Montreal, Toronto, and Detroit. The numbering of th[e] players in the set is basically by teams, i.e., Toronto Maple Leafs (1-19), Detroit Red Wings (20-37), and Montreal Canadiens (38-55). Cards in the set are 2 7/16" by 3 5/8". The backs, in both French and English, are printed in blue ink and contain NHL lifetime records, vital statistics, and biographical dat[a] of the player. This set contains the last card of Mauri[ce] "Rocket" Richard. The key Rookie Card in this set is John McKenzie.

Card	Low	High
COMPLETE SET (61)	1100.00	1700.0
1 Tim Horton	75.00	150.0
2 Frank Mahovlich	50.00	100.0
3 Johnny Bower	40.00	80.0
4 Bert Olmstead	8.00	20.0
5 Gary Edmundson	6.00	15.0
6 Ron Stewart	6.00	15.0
7 Gerry James	6.00	15.0
8 Gerry Ehman	6.00	15.0
9 Red Kelly	15.00	30.0
10 Dave Creighton	6.00	15.0
11 Bob Baun	8.00	20.0
12 Dick Duff	8.00	20.0
13 Larry Regan	6.00	15.0
14 Johnny Wilson	6.00	15.0
15 Billy Harris	6.00	15.0
16 Allan Stanley	12.00	25.0
17 George Armstrong	12.00	25.0
18 Carl Brewer	8.00	20.0
19 Bob Pulford	8.00	20.0
20 Gordie Howe	200.00	350.0
21 Val Fonteyne RC	6.00	15.0
22 Murray Oliver RC	12.00	25.0
23 Sid Abel CO	12.00	25.0
24 Jack McIntyre	6.00	15.0
25 Marc Reaume	6.00	15.0
26 Norm Ullman	20.00	50.0
27 Brian Smith RC	6.00	15.0
28 Gerry Melnyk UER RC	6.00	15.0
29 Marcel Pronovost	8.00	20.0
30 Warren Godfrey	6.00	15.0
31 Terry Sawchuk	75.00	150.0
32 Barry Cullen	6.00	15.0
33 Gary Aldcorn	6.00	15.0
34 Pete Goegan	6.00	15.0
35 Len Lunde	6.00	15.0
36 Alex Delvecchio	15.00	30.0
37 John McKenzie RC	12.00	25.0
38 Dickie Moore	12.00	25.0
39 Albert Langlois	6.00	15.0
40 Bill Hicke	6.00	15.0
41 Ralph Backstrom	6.00	15.0
42 Don Marshall	6.00	15.0
43 Bob Turner	6.00	15.0
44 Tom Johnson	8.00	20.0
45 Maurice Richard	100.00	200.0
46 Bernie Geoffrion	20.00	50.0
47 Henri Richard	50.00	100.0
48 Doug Harvey	20.00	50.0
49 Jean Beliveau	50.00	100.0
50 Phil Goyette	6.00	15.0
51 Marcel Bonin	6.00	15.0
52 Jean-Guy Talbot	8.00	20.0
53 Jacques Plante	125.00	200.0
54 Claude Provost	6.00	15.0
55 Andre Pronovost	6.00	15.0
56 Hicke/McDonald/Backstrom	12.00	25.0
57 Marsh/H.Richard/Moore	20.00	50.0
58 Provost/Pronovost/Goyette	12.00	25.0
59 Boom/Marshall/Beliveau	40.00	80.0
60 Ab McDonald	6.00	15.0
61 Jim Morrison	50.00	100.0

1961-62 Parkhurst

e 1961-62 Parkhurst set contains 51 cards in full or, numbered on the fronts. Cards are 2 7/16" by 3 ". The backs contain 1960-61 statistics and a oon; the punch line for which could be seen by bing the card with a coin. The cards contain players n Montreal, Toronto, and Detroit. The numbering of players in the set is basically by teams, i.e., onto Maple Leafs (1-18), Detroit Red Wings (19- , and Montreal Canadiens (35-51). The backs are in h French and English. The key Rookie Card in this is Dave Keon.

MPLETE SET (51) 1000.00 1600.00
m Horton 100.00 200.00
rank Mahovlich 40.00 80.00
ohnny Bower 30.00 60.00
ert Olmstead 10.00 20.00
ave Keon RC 250.00 400.00
on Stewart 10.00 20.00
ddie Shack 50.00 100.00
ob Pulford 10.00 20.00
ed Kelly 12.00 25.00
Bob Nevin 10.00 20.00
Bob Baun 10.00 20.00
Dick Duff 10.00 20.00
Larry Keenan RC 7.50 15.00
Larry Hillman 10.00 20.00
Billy Harris 7.50 15.00
Allan Stanley 12.00 25.00
George Armstrong 12.00 25.00
Carl Brewer 10.00 20.00
Howie Glover RC 7.50 15.00
Gordie Howe 150.00 250.00
Val Fonteyne 7.50 15.00
Al Johnson RC 7.50 15.00
Pete Goegan 7.50 15.00
Len Lunde 7.50 15.00
Alex Delvecchio 12.00 25.00
Norm Ullman 20.00 40.00
Bill Gadsby 7.50 15.00
Ed Litzenberger 7.50 15.00
Marcel Pronovost 10.00 20.00
Warren Godfrey 7.50 15.00
Terry Sawchuk 75.00 125.00
Vic Stasiuk 7.50 15.00
Leo Labine 7.50 15.00
John McKenzie 12.00 25.00
Bernie Geoffrion 25.00 50.00
Dickie Moore 12.00 25.00
Albert Langlois 7.50 15.00
Bill Hicke 7.50 15.00
Ralph Backstrom 10.00 20.00
Don Marshall 10.00 20.00
Bob Turner 7.50 15.00
Tom Johnson 10.00 20.00
Henri Richard 40.00 80.00
Wayne Connelly RC 12.00 25.00
Jean Beliveau 40.00 80.00
Phil Goyette 7.50 15.00
Marcel Bonin 7.50 15.00
Jean-Guy Talbot 10.00 20.00
Jacques Plante 100.00 175.00
Claude Provost 10.00 20.00
Andre Pronovost UER 20.00 40.00

1962-63 Parkhurst

1962-63 Parkhurst set contains 55 cards in full r, with the card number and, on some cards, a imile autograph on the front. There is also one umbered checklist which is part of the complete set e. An unnumbered game or tally card, which is also rred to as the "Zip" card, is not part of the set. Both ese are considered rather difficult to obtain. Cards approximately 2 7/16" by 3 5/8". The backs, in both ich and English, contain player lifetime statistics player vital statistics in paragraph form. There are eral different styles or designs within this set ending on card number, e.g., some cards have a t puck as background for their photo on the front. er cards have the player's team logo as kground. The numbering of the players in the set is cally by teams, i.e., Toronto Maple Leafs (1-18), oit Red Wings (19-36), and Montreal Canadiens 54). The notable Rookie Cards in this set are by Rousseau, Gilles Tremblay, and J.C.Tremblay.

MPLETE SET (55) 1200.00 2000.00
lly Harris 25.00 40.00
ck Duff 9.00 15.00
b Baun 9.00 15.00
ank Mahovlich 50.00 80.00
d Kelly 18.00 30.00
n Stewart 7.00 12.00
m Horton 60.00 100.00
rl Brewer 9.00 15.00
lan Stanley 10.00 20.00
Bob Nevin 9.00 15.00
Bob Pulford 9.00 15.00
Ed Litzenberger 7.00 12.00
George Armstrong 10.00 20.00
Eddie Shack 35.00 60.00
Dave Keon 60.00 100.00
Johnny Bower 30.00 50.00
Larry Hillman 9.00 15.00
Frank Mahovlich 40.00 70.00
Hank Bassen RC 9.00 15.00
Gerry Odrowski RC 7.00 12.00
Norm Ullman 18.00 30.00
Vic Stasiuk 7.00 12.00
Bruce MacGregor RC 7.00 12.00
Claude Laforge 7.00 12.00
Bill Gadsby 7.00 12.00
Leo Labine 7.00 12.00
Val Fonteyne 7.00 12.00
Howie Glover 7.00 12.00
Marc Boileau RC 7.00 12.00
Gordie Howe 150.00 250.00
Gordie Howe 150.00 250.00
Alex Delvecchio 15.00 25.00
Marcel Pronovost 9.00 15.00
Sid Abel CO 9.00 15.00
Len Lunde 7.00 12.00
Warren Godfrey 7.00 12.00
Phil Goyette 7.00 12.00
Henri Richard 50.00 80.00
Jean Beliveau 50.00 80.00
Bill Hicke 7.00 12.00
Claude Provost 7.00 12.00
Dickie Moore 10.00 20.00
Don Marshall 9.00 15.00
Ralph Backstrom 9.00 15.00
Marcel Bonin 7.00 12.00
Gilles Tremblay RC 20.00 40.00
Bobby Rousseau RC 15.00 25.00
Bernie Geoffrion 25.00 40.00
Jacques Plante 75.00 125.00
Tom Johnson 9.00 15.00
Jean-Guy Talbot 9.00 15.00
Lou Fontinato 9.00 15.00
Bernie Geoffrion 25.00 40.00
54 J.C.Tremblay RC 40.00 60.00
NNO Zip Entry Game Card 125.00 250.00
NNO Checklist Card 250.00 400.00

1963-64 Parkhurst

The 1963-64 Parkhurst set contains 99 color cards. The cards measure approximately 2 7/16" by 3 5/8". The fronts of the cards feature the player with a varying background depending upon whether the player is on Detroit (American flag), Toronto (Canadian Red Ensign), or Montreal (multi-color striped background). The numbering of the players in the set is basically by teams, i.e., Toronto Maple Leafs (1-20 and 61-79), Detroit Red Wings (41-60), and Montreal Canadiens (21-40 and 80-99). The backs, in both French and English, contain the card number, player lifetime NHL statistics, player biography, and a Stanley Cup replica offer. The set includes two different cards of each Montreal and Toronto player and only one of each Detroit player (with the following exceptions, numbers 15, 20, and 75 (single card Maple Leafs). Each Toronto player's double is obtained by adding 60, e.g., 1 and 61, 2 and 62, 3 and 63, etc., are the same player. Each Montreal player's double is obtained by adding 59, e.g., 21 and 80, 22 and 81, 23 and 82, etc., are the same player. The key Rookie Cards in the set are Red Berenson, Alex Faulkner, John Ferguson, Jacques Laperriere, and Cesare Maniago. Maniago is the last card in the set and is not often found in top condition.

COMPLETE SET (99) 1500.00 2500.00
1 Allan Stanley 25.00 40.00
2 Don Simmons 9.00 15.00
3 Red Kelly 12.00 25.00
4 Dick Duff 9.00 15.00
5 Johnny Bower 30.00 50.00
6 Ed Litzenberger 7.00 12.00
7 Kent Douglas RC 7.00 12.00
8 Carl Brewer 9.00 15.00
9 Eddie Shack 40.00 80.00
10 Bob Nevin 9.00 15.00
11 Billy Harris 7.00 12.00
12 Bob Pulford 9.00 15.00
13 George Armstrong 10.00 20.00
14 Ron Stewart 7.00 12.00
15 John McMillan RC 7.00 12.00
16 Tim Horton 50.00 100.00
17 Frank Mahovlich 40.00 60.00
18 Bob Baun 9.00 15.00
19 Punch Imlach ACO/GM 12.00 25.00
20 King Clancy ACO 18.00 30.00
21 Gilles Tremblay 9.00 15.00
22 Jean-Guy Talbot 9.00 15.00
23 Henri Richard 40.00 60.00
24 Ralph Backstrom 9.00 15.00
25 Bill Hicke 7.00 12.00
26 Red Berenson RC 25.00 40.00
27 Jacques Laperriere RC 30.00 50.00
28 Jean Gauthier RC 7.00 12.00
29 Bernie Geoffrion 25.00 40.00
30 Jean Beliveau 45.00 80.00
31 J.C.Tremblay 9.00 15.00
32 Terry Harper RC 18.00 30.00
33 John Ferguson RC 50.00 80.00
34 Toe Blake CO 12.00 25.00
35 Bobby Rousseau 9.00 15.00
36 Claude Provost 7.00 12.00
37 Marc Reaume 7.00 12.00
38 Dave Balon 7.00 12.00
39 Gump Worsley 25.00 40.00
40 Cesare Maniago RC 25.00 50.00
41 Bruce MacGregor 7.00 12.00
42 Alex Faulkner RC 90.00 150.00
43 Pete Goegan 7.00 12.00
44 Parker MacDonald 7.00 12.00
45 Andre Pronovost 7.00 12.00
46 Marcel Pronovost 9.00 15.00
47 Bob Dillabough RC 7.00 12.00
48 Larry Jeffrey RC 7.00 12.00
49 Ian Cushenan 7.00 12.00
50 Alex Delvecchio 12.00 25.00
51 Hank Ciesla 7.00 12.00
52 Norm Ullman 18.00 30.00
53 Terry Sawchuk 70.00 110.00
54 Ron Ingram RC 7.00 12.00
55 Gordie Howe 300.00 450.00
56 Billy McNeil 7.00 12.00
57 Floyd Smith RC 7.00 12.00
58 Vic Stasiuk 7.00 12.00
59 Bill Gadsby 7.00 12.00
60 Doug Barkley RC 7.00 12.00
61 Allan Stanley 10.00 20.00
62 Don Simmons 9.00 15.00
63 Red Kelly 12.00 25.00
64 Dick Duff 9.00 15.00
65 Johnny Bower 30.00 50.00
66 Ed Litzenberger 7.00 12.00
67 Kent Douglas 7.00 12.00
68 Carl Brewer 9.00 15.00
69 Eddie Shack 30.00 50.00
70 Bob Nevin 9.00 15.00
71 Billy Harris 7.00 12.00
72 Bob Pulford 9.00 15.00
73 George Armstrong 10.00 20.00
74 Ron Stewart 7.00 12.00
75 Dave Keon 50.00 80.00
76 Tim Horton 50.00 80.00
77 Frank Mahovlich 40.00 60.00
78 Bob Baun 9.00 15.00
79 Punch Imlach ACO/GM 12.00 25.00
80 Gilles Tremblay 9.00 15.00
81 Jean-Guy Talbot 7.00 12.00
82 Henri Richard 40.00 60.00
83 Ralph Backstrom 9.00 15.00
84 Bill Hicke 7.00 12.00
85 Red Berenson RC 25.00 40.00
86 Jacques Laperriere RC 25.00 40.00
87 Jean Gauthier RC 7.00 12.00
88 Bernie Geoffrion 25.00 40.00
89 Jean Beliveau 50.00 80.00
90 J.C.Tremblay 9.00 15.00
91 Terry Harper RC 20.00 30.00
92 John Ferguson RC 50.00 80.00
93 Toe Blake CO 12.00 25.00
94 Bobby Rousseau 9.00 15.00
95 Claude Provost 7.00 12.00
96 Marc Reaume 7.00 12.00
97 Dave Balon 7.00 12.00
98 Gump Worsley 25.00 40.00
99 Cesare Maniago RC 100.00 175.00

1991-92 Parkhurst

The 1991-92 Parkhurst hockey set marks Pro Set's resurrection of this venerable hockey card brand. The set was primarily released in two series. Both series contain 225 standard-size cards and five (four in the second series) special PHC collectible cards randomly inserted into foil packs. First and second series production quantities were each reported to be 15,000 numbered ten-box foil cases, including 2,500 cases that were translated into French and distributed predominantly to Quebec. The fronts feature full-bleed glossy color photos, bordered on the left by a dark brown marbled border stripe. The player's name appears in the stripe; Parkhurst's teal oval-shaped logo in the lower left corner rounds out the card face. The backs carry a color head shot, with biography, career statistics, and player profile all on a bronze background. The NNO Santa Claus card was randomly inserted in first series packs. A special promotion offer for a 25-card Final Update set was included on Parkhurst Series II packs. It is estimated that less than 15,000 of these sets exist.

*FRENCH: .5X TO 1.25X PARKHURST
1 Matt DelGuidice RC .15 .40
2 Ken Hodge Jr. .15 .40
3 Vladimir Ruzicka .12 .30
4 Craig Janney .12 .30
5 Glen Wesley .12 .30
6 Stephen Leach .12 .30
7 Garry Galley .12 .30
8 Andy Moog .12 .30
9 Ray Bourque .25 .60
10 Brad May .12 .30
11 Donald Audette .12 .30
12 Alexander Mogilny .12 .30
13 Randy Wood .12 .30
14 Daren Puppa .12 .30
15 Doug Bodger .12 .30
16 Pat LaFontaine .15 .40
17 Dave Andreychuk .15 .40
18 Dale Hawerchuk .20 .50
19 Mike Ramsey .12 .30
20 Tomas Forslund RC .15 .40
21 Robert Reichel .30 .75
22 Theo Fleury .12 .30
23 Joe Nieuwendyk .12 .30
24 Gary Roberts .12 .30
25 Gary Suter .12 .30
26 Doug Gilmour .30 .75
27 Mike Vernon .12 .30
28 Al MacInnis .12 .30
29 Jeremy Roenick .40 1.00
30 Ed Belfour .40 1.00
31 Steve Smith .15 .40
32 Chris Chelios .15 .40
33 Dirk Graham .12 .30
34 Steve Larmer .12 .30
35 Brent Sutter .12 .30
36 Michel Goulet .12 .30
37 Nicklas Lidstrom RC .60 1.50
38 Sergei Fedorov .25 .60
39 Tim Cheveldae .12 .30
40 Kevin Miller .12 .30
41 Ray Sheppard .12 .30
42 Paul Ysebaert .12 .30
43 Jimmy Carson .12 .30
44 Steve Yzerman .50 1.25
45 Shawn Burr .12 .30
46 Vladimir Konstantinov RC .40 1.00
47 Josef Beranek RC .15 .40
48 Vincent Damphousse .12 .30
49 Dave Manson .12 .30
50 Scott Mellanby .12 .30
51 Kevin Lowe .12 .30
52 Joe Murphy .12 .30
53 Bill Ranford .12 .30
54 Craig Simpson .10 .25
55 Esa Tikkanen .12 .30
56 Michel Picard RC .15 .40
57 Geoff Sanderson RC .15 .40
58 Kay Whitmore .12 .30
59 John Cullen .12 .30
60 Rob Brown .12 .30
61 Zarley Zalapski .12 .30
62 Brad Shaw .10 .25
63 Mikael Andersson .12 .30
64 Pat Verbeek .12 .30
65 Peter Ahola RC .15 .40
66 Tony Granato .12 .30
67 Dave Taylor .12 .30
68 Luc Robitaille .12 .30
69 Marty McSorley .12 .30
70 Tomas Sandstrom .12 .30
71 Kelly Hrudey .12 .30
72 Jari Kurri .12 .30
73 Wayne Gretzky .75 2.00
74 Larry Robinson .10 .25
75 Derian Hatcher .12 .30
76 Ulf Dahlen .12 .30
77 Jon Casey .12 .30
78 Dave Gagner .12 .30
79 Brian Bellows .12 .30
80 Neal Broten .12 .30
81 Mike Modano .30 .75
82 Brian Propp .12 .30
83 Bobby Smith .12 .30
84 John LeClair RC .40 1.00
85 Eric Desjardins .15 .40
86 Shayne Corson .12 .30
87 Stephan Lebeau .12 .30
88 Mathieu Schneider .12 .30
89 Kirk Muller .10 .25
90 Patrick Roy .40 1.00
91 Sylvain Turgeon .12 .30
92 Guy Carbonneau .12 .30
93 Denis Savard .20 .50
94 Scott Niedermayer .15 .40
95 Tom Chorske .12 .30
96 Slava Fetisov .12 .30
97 Kevin Todd RC .15 .40
98 Chris Terreri .12 .30
99 David Maley .12 .30
100 Stephane Richer .12 .30
101 Claude Lemieux .12 .30
102 Scott Stevens .15 .40
103 Peter Stastny .12 .30
104 David Volek .12 .30
105 Steve Thomas .12 .30
106 Pierre Turgeon .12 .30
107 Glenn Healy .15 .40
108 Derek King .10 .25
109 Uwe Krupp .12 .30
110 Ray Ferraro .12 .30
111 Pat Flatley .12 .30
112 Tom Kurvers .12 .30
113 Adam Creighton .12 .30
114 Tony Amonte RC .40 1.00
115 John Ogrodnick .12 .30
116 Doug Weight RC .40 1.00
117 Mike Richter .15 .40
118 Darren Turcotte .12 .30
119 Brian Leetch .12 .30
120 James Patrick .12 .30
121 Mark Messier .40 1.00
122 Mike Gartner .12 .30
123 Mike Ricci .15 .40
124 Rod Brind'Amour .12 .30
125 Steve Duchesne .10 .25
126 Ron Hextall .15 .40
127 Brad Jones .12 .30
128 Pelle Eklund .12 .30
129 Rick Tocchet .12 .30
130 Mark Howe .15 .40
131 Andrei Lomakin .12 .30
132 Jaromir Jagr .40 1.00
133 Jim Paek RC .15 .40
134 Mark Recchi .20 .50
135 Kevin Stevens .12 .30
136 Phil Bourque .12 .30
137 Mario Lemieux .60 1.50
138 Bob Errey .12 .30
139 Tom Barrasso .12 .30
140 Paul Coffey .12 .30
141 Joe Mullen .12 .30
142 Kip Miller .12 .30
143 Owen Nolan .15 .40
144 Mats Sundin .15 .40
145 Mikhail Tatarinov .12 .30
146 Bryan Fogarty .12 .30
147 Stephane Morin .12 .30
148 Joe Sakic .50 1.25
149 Ron Tugnutt .12 .30
150 Mike Hough .12 .30
151 Nelson Emerson .12 .30
152 Curtis Joseph .12 .30
153 Brendan Shanahan .20 .50
154 Paul Cavallini .12 .30
155 Adam Oates .15 .40
156 Jeff Brown .12 .30
157 Brett Hull .25 .60
158 Ron Sutter .12 .30
159 Dave Christian .12 .30
160 Pat Falloon .12 .30
161 Pat MacLeod RC .15 .40
162 Jarmo Myllys .12 .30
163 Wayne Presley .12 .30
164 Perry Anderson .12 .30
165 Kelly Kisio .12 .30
166 Brian Mullen .12 .30
167 Brian Lawton .12 .30
168 Doug Wilson .12 .30
169 Rob Pearson RC .15 .40
170 Wendel Clark .15 .40
171 Brian Bradley .12 .30
172 Dave Ellett .12 .30
173 Gary Leeman .12 .30
174 Peter Zezel .10 .25
175 Grant Fuhr .15 .40
176 Bob Rouse .12 .30
177 Glenn Anderson .15 .40
178 Petr Nedved .12 .30
179 Trevor Linden .12 .30
180 Jyrki Lumme .12 .30
181 Kirk McLean .12 .30
182 Cliff Ronning .12 .30
183 Greg Adams .12 .30
184 Doug Lidster .12 .30
185 Sergio Momesso .12 .30
186 Geoff Courtnall .12 .30
187 Dave Babych .12 .30
188 Peter Bondra .12 .30
189 Dimitri Khristich .12 .30
190 Randy Burridge .12 .30
191 Kevin Hatcher .12 .30
192 Mike Ridley .12 .30
193 Dino Ciccarelli .12 .30
194 Al Iafrate .12 .30
195 Dale Hunter .12 .30
196 Mike Liut .12 .30
197 Rod Langway .12 .30
198 Russell Romaniuk RC .15 .40
199 Bob Essensa .12 .30
200 Teppo Numminen .12 .30
201 Darrin Shannon .12 .30
202 Pat Elynuik .12 .30
203 Fredrik Olausson .12 .30
204 Ed Olczyk .12 .30
205 Phil Housley .12 .30
206 Troy Murray .12 .30
207 Wayne Gretzky 1000 .75 2.00
208 Bryan Trottier 1000 .20 .50
209 Peter Stastny 1000 .12 .30
210 Jari Kurri 1000 .12 .30
211 Denis Savard 1000 .20 .50
212 Paul Coffey 1000 .12 .30
213 Mark Messier 1000 .40 1.00
214 Dave Taylor 1000 .12 .30
215 Michel Goulet 1000 .12 .30
216 Dale Hawerchuk 1000 .20 .50
217 Bobby Smith 1000 .12 .30
218 Ed Belfour LL .40 1.00
219 Brett Hull LL .25 .60
220 Patrick Roy AS .40 1.00
221 Ray Bourque AS .25 .60
222 Wayne Gretzky AS .75 2.00
223 Jari Kurri AS .12 .30
224 Luc Robitaille AS .12 .30
225 Paul Coffey AS .12 .30
226 Bob Carpenter .12 .30
227 Gord Murphy .12 .30
228 Don Sweeney .12 .30
229 Glen Murray RC .15 .40
230 Ted Donato RC .15 .40
231 Jozef Stumpel RC .15 .40
232 Stephen Heinze RC .15 .40
233 Adam Oates .15 .40
234 Joe Juneau RC .15 .40
235 Gord Hynes RC .15 .40
236 Tony Tanti .12 .30
237 Petr Svoboda .12 .30
238 Bob Corkum .10 .25
239 Ken Sutton RC .15 .40
240 Tom Draper RC .15 .40
241 Grant Ledyard .12 .30
242 Christian Ruuttu .12 .30
243 Brad Miller .12 .30
244 Clint Malarchuk .12 .30
245 Trent Yawney .12 .30
246 Craig Berube .12 .30
247 Sergei Makarov .12 .30
248 Alexander Godynyuk RC .15 .40
249 Paul Ranheim .15 .40
250 Jeff Reese .12 .30
251 Chris Lindberg RC .15 .40
252 Michel Petit .12 .30
253 Joel Otto .12 .30
254 Gary Leeman .12 .30
255 Ray LeBlanc RC .15 .40
256 Jocelyn Lemieux .12 .30
257 Igor Kravchuk RC .15 .40
258 Rob Brown .12 .30
259 Stephane Matteau .12 .30
260 Mike Hudson .12 .30
261 Keith Brown .12 .30
262 Karl Dykhuis .12 .30
263 Dominik Hasek RC 1.50 4.00
264 Brian Noonan .10 .25
265 Yves Racine .12 .30
266 Slava Kozlov RC .15 .40
267 Martin Lapointe .12 .30
268 Steve Chiasson .12 .30
269 Gerard Gallant .10 .25
270 Brent Fedyk .12 .30
271 Brad McCrimmon .12 .30
272 Bob Probert .12 .30
273 Alan Kerr .12 .30
274 Luke Richardson .12 .30
275 Kelly Buchberger .12 .30
276 Craig MacTavish .12 .30
277 Ron Tugnutt .12 .30
278 Bernie Nicholls .12 .30
279 Anatoli Semenov .12 .30
280 Petr Klima .12 .30
281 Louie DeBrusk RC .15 .40
282 Norm Maciver RC .15 .40
283 Martin Gelinas .12 .30
284 Randy Cunneyworth .12 .30
285 Andrew Cassels .12 .30
286 Peter Sidorkiewicz .12 .30
287 Steve Konroyd .12 .30
288 Murray Craven .12 .30
289 Randy Ladouceur .12 .30
290 Bobby Holik .15 .40
291 Adam Burt .12 .30
292 Corey Millen RC .15 .40
293 Rob Blake .15 .40
294 Mike Donnelly RC .15 .40
295 Kyosti Karjalainen RC .15 .40
296 John McIntyre .12 .30
297 Paul Coffey .12 .30
298 Charlie Huddy .12 .30
299 Bob Kudelski .10 .25
300 Todd Elik .12 .30
301 Mike Craig .12 .30
302 Marc Bureau .12 .30
303 Jim Johnson .12 .30
304 Mark Tinordi .12 .30
305 Gaetan Duchesne .10 .25
306 Darcy Wakaluk RC .15 .40
307 Sylvain Lefebvre .12 .30
308 Russ Courtnall .12 .30
309 Patrice Brisebois .10 .25
310 Mike McPhee .12 .30
311 Mike Keane .10 .25
312 J.J. Daigneault .10 .25
313 Gilbert Dionne RC .15 .40
314 Brian Skrudland .12 .30
315 Brent Gilchrist .12 .30
316 Laurie Boschman .12 .30
317 Ken Daneyko .12 .30
318 Eric Weinrich .15 .40
319 Alexei Kasatonov .10 .25
320 Craig Billington RC .15 .40
321 Claude Vilgrain .12 .30
322 Bruce Driver .12 .30
323 Alexander Semak RC .15 .40
324 Valeri Zelepukin RC .15 .40
325 Rob DiMaio .12 .30
326 Scott Lachance RC .15 .40
327 Marty McInnis RC .15 .40
328 Joe Reekie .12 .30
329 Daniel Marois .12 .30
330 Wayne McBean .10 .25
331 Jeff Norton .12 .30
332 Benoit Hogue .12 .30
333 Tie Domi .12 .30
334 Sergei Nemchinov .12 .30
335 Randy Gilhen .12 .30
336 Paul Broten .10 .25
337 Kris King .12 .30
338 John Vanbiesbrouck .12 .30
339 Adam Graves .12 .30
340 Joe Cirella .12 .30
341 Jeff Beukeboom .12 .30
342 Terry Carkner .12 .30
343 Mark Freer RC .15 .40
344 Corey Foster RC .15 .40
345 Mark Pederson .12 .30
346 Kimbi Daniels RC .15 .40
347 Mark Recchi .20 .50
348 Kevin Dineen .12 .30
349 Kerry Huffman .10 .25
350 Garry Galley .12 .30
351 Dan Quinn .12 .30
352 Troy Loney .10 .25
353 Ron Francis .20 .50
354 Rick Tocchet .12 .30
355 Shawn McEachern RC .40 1.00
356 Kjell Samuelsson .12 .30
357 Ken Wreggett .12 .30
358 Larry Murphy .12 .30
359 Ken Priestlay .12 .30
360 Bryan Trottier .20 .50
361 Ulf Samuelsson .12 .30
362 Valeri Kamensky RC .40 1.00
363 Stephane Fiset .10 .25
364 Alexei Gusarov RC .12 .30
365 Greg Paslawski .12 .30
366 Martin Rucinsky RC .12 .30
367 Curtis Leschyshyn .12 .30
368 Jacques Cloutier .12 .30
369 Craig Wolanin .12 .30
370 Claude Lapointe RC .12 .30
371 Adam Foote RC .30 .75
372 Rich Sutter .12 .30
373 Lee Norwood .10 .25
374 Garth Butcher .12 .30
375 Philippe Bozon RC .15 .40
376 Dave Lowry .12 .30
377 Darin Kimble .12 .30
378 Craig Janney .12 .30
379 Bob Bassen .12 .30
380 Rick Zombo .12 .30
381 Perry Berezan .12 .30
382 Neil Wilkinson .12 .30
383 Mike Sullivan RC .15 .40
384 David Bruce RC .15 .40
385 Johan Garpenlov .12 .30
386 Jeff Odgers RC .15 .40
387 Jay More RC .15 .40
388 Dean Evason .12 .30
389 Dale Craigwell .10 .25
390 Darryl Shannon RC .15 .40
391 Dimitri Mironov .12 .30
392 Kent Manderville .10 .25
393 Todd Gill .12 .30
394 Rick Wamsley .10 .25
395 Joe Sacco RC .15 .40
396 Doug Gilmour .30 .75
397 Mike Bullard .12 .30
398 Felix Potvin .30 .75
399 Guy Larose RC .15 .40
400 Tom Fergus .12 .30
401 Ryan Walter .12 .30
402 Troy Gamble .10 .25
403 Robert Dirk .12 .30
404 Pavel Bure .12 .30
405 Jim Sandlak .12 .30
406 Igor Larionov .12 .30
407 Gerald Diduck .12 .30
408 Todd Krygier .12 .30
409 Tim Bergland .12 .30
410 Calle Johansson .12 .30
411 Nick Kypreos .12 .30
412 Michal Pivonka .12 .30
413 Brad Schlegel RC .15 .40
414 Kelly Miller .12 .30
415 John Druce .12 .30
416 Don Beaupre .12 .30
417 Alan May .12 .30
418 Randy Carlyle .12 .30
419 Stu Barnes .12 .30
420 Mike Eagles .12 .30
421 Igor Ulanov RC .15 .40
422 Evgeny Davydov RC .15 .40
423 Shawn Cronin .12 .30
424 Keith Tkachuk RC .15 .40
425 Luciano Borsato RC .15 .40
426 Stephane Beauregard .10 .25
427 Mike Lalor .12 .30
428 Michel Goulet 500 .12 .30
429 Wayne Gretzky 500 .75 2.00
430 Mike Gartner 500 .12 .30
431 Bryan Trottier 500 .20 .50
432 Brett Hull LL .25 .60
433 Wayne Gretzky LL 3.00 8.00
434 Steve Yzerman LL .50 1.25
435 Paul Ysebaert LL .12 .30
436 Gary Roberts LL .12 .30
437 Dave Andreychuk LL .15 .40
438 Brian Leetch LL .12 .30
439 Jeremy Roenick LL .40 1.00
440 Kirk McLean LL .12 .30
441 Tim Cheveldae LL .12 .30
442 Patrick Roy LL .40 1.00
443 Tony Amonte RL .40 1.00
444 Kevin Todd RL .15 .40
445 Nicklas Lidstrom RL .60 1.50
446 Pavel Bure RL .12 .30
447 Gilbert Dionne RL .15 .40
448 Tom Draper RL .15 .40
449 Dominik Hasek RL .50 1.25
450 Dominic Roussel RL RC .15 .40
451 Checklist .12 .30
452 Trent Klatt XRC 1.25 3.00
453 Bill Guerin XRC 3.00 8.00
454 Ray Whitney XRC 2.00 5.00
455 Boston/Adams winner .12 .30
456 Pittsburgh/Patrick .12 .30
457 Chicago/Norris .12 .30
458 Edmonton/Smythe .12 .30
459 Pittsburgh/Wales .60 1.50
460 Chicago/Capbell .12 .30
461 Pittsburgh/Stanley Cup .40 1.00
462 Pavel Bure AW .12 .30
463 Patrick Roy AW .40 1.00
464 Brian Leetch AW .12 .30
465 Wayne Gretzky AW .75 2.00
466 Guy Carbonneau AW .12 .30
467 Mario Lemieux AW 5.00 12.00
468 Mark Messier AW 3.00 8.00
469 Ray Bourque AW 3.00 8.00
470 Patrick Roy AS 3.00 8.00
471 Brian Leetch AS 2.00 5.00
472 Ray Bourque AS 2.50 6.00
473 Kevin Stevens AS 2.00 5.00
474 Brett Hull AS 4.00 10.00
475 Mark Messier AS .40 1.00
SC Santa Claus .60 1.50
P1 Doug Gilmour PROMO 1.25 3.00
P2 Robert Reichel PROMO 1.25 3.00

1991-92 Parkhurst PHC

This nine card standard-size set was randomly inserted in packs of 1991-92 Parkhurst hockey cards with cards 1-5 being in the first series and 6-9 in the second series, which featured award winners. PHC stands for Parkhurst Collectibles. The cards are numbered with a "PHC" prefix. A French version of these cards exist and are valued the same.

*FRENCH: .5X TO 1.25X BASIC INSERTS
PHC1 Gordie Howe 1.00 2.50
PHC2 Alex Delvecchio .30 .75
PHC3 Ken Hodge Jr. .30 .75
PHC4 Robert Kron .25 .60
PHC5 Sergei Fedorov .50 1.25
PHC6 Brett Hull .50 1.25
PHC7 Mario Lemieux 1.25 3.00
PHC8 Brian Leetch .75 2.00
Mark Messier
PHC9 Terry Sawchuk .25 .60

1992-93 Parkhurst Previews

Randomly inserted in 1992-93 Pro Set foil packs, these five preview standard-size cards were issued to show the design of the 1992-93 Parkhurst issue. The fronts feature color action player photos that are full-bleed except for one edge that is bordered by a dark blue-green marbleized stripe. The player's name is printed vertically in this stripe. The Parkhurst logo overlays the stripe. The backs have a bluish-green background and carry small close-up shots, biography, statistics, and career highlights in French and English. The cards are numbered on the back with a "PV" prefix.

PV1 Paul Ysebaert .60 1.50
PV2 Sean Burke .75 2.00
PV3 Gilbert Dionne .60 1.50
PV4 Ken Hammond .60 1.50
PV5 Grant Fuhr .75 2.00

1992-93 Parkhurst

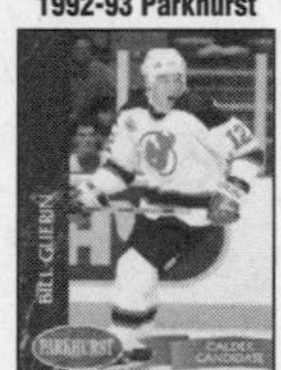

The 1992-93 Parkhurst set consists of 480 standard-size cards plus a 30-card update set. The set was released in two series of 240. The final 30 cards were issued in set form only and are slightly more difficult to obtain. The fronts feature color action player photos that are full-bleed except for one edge that is bordered by a dark blue-green marbleized stripe. The Parkhurst logo overlays the stripe. The backs have a bluish green background and carry small close-up shots, biographies, statistics, and career highlights in French and English. The second series featured traded players in their new uniforms as well as 35 Calder Candidates. The cards are checklisted alphabetically according to teams.

1 Ray Bourque .15 .40
2 Joe Juneau .05 .15
3 Andy Moog .07 .20
4 Adam Oates .10 .25
5 Vladimir Ruzicka .05 .15
6 Glen Wesley .05 .15
7 Dmitri Kvartalnov RC .05 .15
8 Ted Donato .05 .15
9 Glen Murray .05 .15
10 Dave Andreychuk .10 .25
11 Dale Hawerchuk .12 .30
12 Pat LaFontaine .10 .25
13 Alexander Mogilny .07 .20
14 Richard Smehlik RC .05 .15
15 Keith Carney RC .20 .50
16 Philippe Boucher .05 .15
17 Viktor Gordijuk RC .05 .15
18 Donald Audette .07 .20
19 Theo Fleury .15 .40
20 Al MacInnis .07 .20
21 Joe Nieuwendyk .07 .20
22 Gary Roberts .05 .15
23 Gary Suter .05 .15
24 Mike Vernon .07 .20
25 Sergei Makarov .05 .15
26 Robert Reichel .05 .15
27 Chris Lindberg .05 .15
28 Ed Belfour .10 .25
29 Chris Chelios .10 .25
30 Steve Larmer .05 .15
31 Jeremy Roenick .15 .40
32 Steve Smith .05 .15
33 Brent Sutter .05 .15
34 Christian Ruuttu .05 .15
35 Igor Kravchuk .05 .15
36 Sergei Krivokrasov .05 .15
37 Tim Cheveldae .05 .15
38 Mike Sillinger .05 .15
39 Sergei Fedorov .15 .40
40 Slava Kozlov .07 .20
41 Bob Probert .07 .20
42 Nicklas Lidstrom .07 .20
43 Paul Ysebaert .05 .15
44 Steve Yzerman .25 .60
45 Dino Ciccarelli .07 .20
46 Esa Tikkanen .05 .15
47 Dave Manson .05 .15
48 Craig MacTavish .05 .15
49 Bernie Nicholls .05 .15
50 Bill Ranford .07 .20
51 Craig Simpson .05 .15
52 Scott Mellanby .05 .15
53 Shayne Corson .05 .15
54 Petr Klima .05 .15
55 Murray Craven .05 .15
56 Eric Weinrich .05 .15
57 Sean Burke .07 .20
58 Pat Verbeek .05 .15
59 Zarley Zalapski .05 .15
60 Patrick Poulin .05 .15
61 Robert Petrovicky RC .05 .15
62 Geoff Sanderson .07 .20
63 Paul Coffey .10 .25
64 Robert Lang RC .05 .15
65 Wayne Gretzky .50 1.25
66 Kelly Hrudey .07 .20
67 Jari Kurri .10 .25
68 Luc Robitaille .07 .20
69 Darryl Sydor .05 .15
70 Jim Hiller RC .05 .15
71 Alexei Zhitnik .05 .15
72 Derian Hatcher .05 .15
73 Jon Casey .05 .15
74 Richard Matvichuk RC .07 .20
75 Mike Modano .25 .60
76 Mark Tinordi .05 .15
77 Todd Elik .05 .15
78 Russ Courtnall .05 .15
79 Tommy Sjodin RC .05 .15
80 Eric Desjardins .07 .20
81 Gilbert Dionne .05 .15
82 Stephan Lebeau .05 .15
83 Kirk Muller .05 .15
84 Patrick Roy .25 .60
85 Denis Savard .12 .30
86 Vincent Damphousse .07 .20
87 Brian Bellows .07 .20
88 Ed Ronan RC .05 .15
89 Claude Lemieux .05 .15
90 John MacLean .07 .20
91 Stephane Richer .07 .20
92 Scott Stevens .10 .25
93 Chris Terreri .07 .20
94 Kevin Todd .05 .15
95 Scott Niedermayer .10 .25
96 Bobby Holik .07 .20
97 Bill Guerin RC .20 .50
98 Ray Ferraro .05 .15
99 Mark Fitzpatrick .07 .20
100 Derek King .05 .15
101 Uwe Krupp .05 .15
102 Darius Kasparaitis .05 .15
103 Pierre Turgeon .07 .20
104 Benoit Hogue .05 .15
105 Scott Lachance .05 .15
106 Marty McInnis .05 .15
107 Tony Amonte .07 .20
108 Mike Gartner .07 .20
109 Alexei Kovalev .07 .20
110 Brian Leetch .07 .20
111 Mark Messier .15 .40
112 Mike Richter .10 .25
113 James Patrick .05 .15
114 Sergei Nemchinov .05 .15
115 Doug Weight .20 .50
116 Mark Lamb .05 .15
117 Norm Maciver .05 .15
118 Mike Peluso .07 .20
119 Jody Hull .05 .15
120 Peter Sidorkiewicz .05 .15
121 Sylvain Turgeon .05 .15
122 Laurie Boschman .05 .15
123 Brad Marsh .07 .20
124 Neil Brady .05 .15
125 Brian Benning .05 .15
126 Rod Brind'Amour .05 .15
127 Kevin Dineen .05 .15
128 Eric Lindros .30 .75
129 Dominic Roussel .07 .20
130 Mark Recchi .12 .30
131 Brent Fedyk .05 .15
132 Greg Paslawski .05 .15
133 Dimitri Yushkevich RC .05 .15
134 Tom Barrasso .07 .20
135 Jaromir Jagr .25 .60
136 Mario Lemieux .40 1.00
137 Larry Murphy .07 .20
138 Kevin Stevens .05 .15
139 Rick Tocchet .07 .20
140 Martin Straka RC .20 .50
141 Ron Francis .12 .30
142 Shawn McEachern .05 .15
143 Steve Duchesne .05 .15
144 Ron Hextall .07 .20
145 Owen Nolan .05 .15
146 Mike Ricci .07 .20
147 Joe Sakic .25 .60
148 Mats Sundin .10 .25
149 Martin Rucinsky .05 .15

1992-93 Parkhurst

150 Andrei Kovalenko RC .15 .40
151 Dave Karpa RC .05 .15
152 Nelson Emerson .05 .15
153 Brett Hull .15 .40
154 Craig Janney .07 .20
155 Curtis Joseph .10 .25
156 Brendan Shanahan .12 .30
157 Vitali Prokhorov RC .05 .15
158 Igor Korolev RC .05 .15
159 Philippe Bozon .05 .15
160 Ray Whitney RC .15 .40
161 Pat Falloon .05 .15
162 Jeff Hackett .07 .20
163 Brian Lawton .07 .20
164 Sandis Ozolinsh .05 .15
165 Neil Wilkinson .05 .15
166 Kelly Kisio .07 .20
167 Doug Wilson .07 .20
168 Dale Craigwell .05 .15
169 Mikael Andersson .05 .15
170 Wendell Young .07 .20
171 Rob Zamuner RC .07 .20
172 Adam Creighton .05 .15
173 Roman Hamrlik RC .20 .50
174 Brian Bradley .05 .15
175 Rob Ramage .05 .15
176 Chris Kontos RC .05 .15
177 Stan Drulia RC .05 .15
178 Glenn Anderson .10 .25
179 Wendel Clark .07 .20
180 John Cullen .05 .15
181 Dave Ellett .05 .15
182 Grant Fuhr .10 .25
183 Doug Gilmour .12 .30
184 Kent Manderville .05 .15
185 Joe Sacco .05 .15
186 Nikolai Borschevsky RC .05 .15
187 Felix Potvin .20 .50
188 Pavel Bure .20 .50
189 Geoff Courtnall .05 .15
190 Trevor Linden .07 .20
191 Jyrki Lumme .05 .15
192 Kirk McLean .05 .15
193 Cliff Ronning .05 .15
194 Dixon Ward RC .07 .20
195 Greg Adams .05 .15
196 Jiri Slegr .05 .15
197 Don Beaupre .07 .20
198 Kevin Hatcher .05 .15
199 Brad Schlegel .05 .15
200 Mike Ridley .05 .15
201 Calle Johansson .05 .15
202 Steve Konowalchuk RC .07 .20
203 Al Iafrate .07 .20
204 Peter Bondra .07 .20
205 Pat Elynuik .05 .15
206 Keith Tkachuk .10 .25
207 Bob Essensa .07 .20
208 Phil Housley .05 .15
209 Teemu Selanne .20 .50
210 Alexei Zhamnov .07 .20
211 Evgeny Davydov .05 .15
212 Fredrik Olausson .05 .15
213 Ed Olczyk .05 .15
214 Thomas Steen .05 .15
215 Darius Kasparaitis .05 .15
216 Nikolai Borschevsky IRS .05 .15
217 Teemu Selanne IRS .20 .50
218 Alexander Mogilny IRS .07 .20
219 Sergei Fedorov IRS .15 .40
220 Jaromir Jagr IRS .25 .60
221 Mats Sundin IRS .10 .25
222 Dmitri Kvartalnov IRS .05 .15
223 Andrei Kovalenko IRS .15 .40
224 Tommy Sjodin IRS .05 .15
225 Alexei Kovalev IRS .07 .20
226 Evgeny Davydov .05 .15
227 Robert Lang IRS .05 .15
228 Valeri Zelepukin SPH .05 .15
229 Doug Weight .20 .50
230 Valeri Kamensky SPH .05 .15
231 Donald Audette .07 .20
232 Nelson Emerson SPH .05 .15
233 Pat Falloon SPH .05 .15
234 Pavel Bure SPH .20 .50
235 Tony Amonte SPH .07 .20
236 Sergei Nemchinov SPH .05 .15
237 Gilbert Dionne SPH .05 .15
238 Kevin Todd .05 .15
239 Nicklas Lidstrom SPH .07 .20
240 Brad May .05 .15
241 Stephen Leach .05 .15
242 Dave Poulin .05 .15
243 Grigori Panteleyev RC .05 .15
244 Don Sweeney .05 .15
245 John Blue RC .07 .20
246 C.J.Young RC .05 .15
247 Stephen Heinze .05 .15
248 Cam Neely .10 .25
249 David Reid .05 .15
250 Grant Fuhr .10 .25
251 Bob Sweeney .05 .15
252 Rob Ray .07 .20
253 Doug Bodger .05 .15
254 Ken Sutton .05 .15
255 Yuri Khmylev RC .05 .15
256 Mike Ramsey .05 .15
257 Brad May .05 .15
258 Brent Ashton .05 .15
259 Joel Otto .05 .15
260 Paul Ranheim .05 .15
261 Kevin Dahl RC .05 .15
262 Trent Yawney .07 .20
263 Roger Johansson .07 .20
264 Jeff Reese .05 .15
265 Ron Stern .07 .20
266 Brian Skrudland .07 .20
267 Bryan Marchment .07 .20
268 Stephane Matteau .05 .15
269 Frantisek Kucera .07 .20
270 Jim Waite .07 .20
271 Dirk Graham .05 .15
272 Michel Goulet .07 .20
273 Joe Murphy .05 .15
274 Keith Brown .07 .20
275 Jocelyn Lemieux .05 .15
276 Paul Coffey .10 .25
277 Keith Primeau .07 .20
278 Vincent Riendeau .07 .20
279 Mark Howe .10 .25
280 Ray Sheppard .05 .15
281 Jim Hiller .05 .15
282 Steve Chiasson .05 .15
283 Vladimir Konstantinov .10 .25
284 Brian Benning .05 .15
285 Kevin Todd .05 .15
286 Zdeno Ciger .05 .15
287 Brian Glynn .05 .15
288 Shaun Van Allen .07 .20
289 Brad Werenka RC .07 .20
290 Ron Tugnutt .07 .20
291 Igor Kravchuk .05 .15
292 Todd Elik .05 .15
293 Terry Yake .05 .15
294 Michael Nylander RC .05 .15
295 Yvon Corriveau .05 .15
296 Frank Pietrangelo .07 .20
297 Nick Kypreos .05 .15
298 Andrew Cassels .05 .15
299 Steve Konroyd .07 .20
300 Allen Pedersen .07 .20
301 Tony Granato .05 .15
302 Rob Blake .07 .20
303 Robb Stauber .07 .20
304 Marty McSorley .05 .15
305 Lonnie Loach RC .05 .15
306 Corey Millen .05 .15
307 Dave Taylor .07 .20
308 Jimmy Carson .05 .15
309 Warren Rychel RC .05 .15
310 Ulf Dahlen .05 .15
311 Dave Gagner .07 .20
312 Brad Berry RC .07 .20
313 Neal Broten .07 .20
314 Mike Craig .05 .15
315 Darcy Wakaluk .07 .20
316 Shane Churla .07 .20
317 Trent Klatt RC .07 .20
318 Mike Keane .05 .15
319 Mathieu Schneider .05 .15
320 Patrice Brisebois .05 .15
321 Andre Racicot .07 .20
322 Mario Roberge .07 .20
323 Gary Leeman .05 .15
324 Jean-Jacques Daigneault .05 .15
325 Lyle Odelein .07 .20
326 John LeClair .15 .40
327 Valeri Zelepukin .05 .15
328 Bernie Nicholls .05 .15
329 Alexander Semak .05 .15
330 Craig Billington .07 .20
331 Randy McKay .07 .20
332 Ken Daneyko .05 .15
333 Bruce Driver .05 .15
334 Slava Fetisov .05 .15
335 Dennis Vaske .05 .15
336 Brad Dalgarno .07 .20
337 Jeff Norton .07 .20
338 Steve Thomas .07 .20
339 Vladimir Malakhov .05 .15
340 David Volek .05 .15
341 Glenn Healy .07 .20
342 Patrick Flatley .07 .20
343 Travis Green RC .07 .20
344 Corey Hirsch RC .10 .25
345 Darren Turcotte .05 .15
346 Adam Graves .05 .15
347 Steven King RC .05 .15
348 Kevin Lowe .07 .20
349 John Vanbiesbrouck .07 .20
350 Ed Olczyk .05 .15
351 Sergei Zubov RC .15 .40
352 Brad Shaw .05 .15
353 Jamie Baker .05 .15
354 Mark Freer .05 .15
355 Darcy Loewen .05 .15
356 Darren Rumble RC .05 .15
357 Bob Kudelski .07 .20
358 Ken Hammond .07 .20
359 Daniel Berthiaume .07 .20
360 Josef Beranek .05 .15
361 Greg Hawgood .05 .15
362 Terry Carkner .07 .20
363 Vyatcheslav Butsayev RC .05 .15
364 Garry Galley .05 .15
365 Andre Faust RC .07 .20
366 Ryan McGill RC .05 .15
367 Tommy Soderstrom RC .07 .20
368 Joe Mullen .07 .20
369 Ulf Samuelsson .05 .15
370 Mike Needham RC .05 .15
371 Ken Wregget .07 .20
372 Dave Tippett .07 .20
373 Kjell Samuelsson .07 .20
374 Bob Errey .07 .20
375 Jim Paek .07 .20
376 Bill Lindsay RC .05 .15
377 Valeri Kamensky .05 .15
378 Stephane Fiset .05 .15
379 Steven Finn .05 .15
380 Mike Hough .07 .20
381 Scott Pearson .07 .20
382 Kerry Huffman .05 .15
383 Scott Young .05 .15
384 Stephane Quintal .05 .15
385 Bret Hedican RC .07 .20
386 Guy Hebert RC .15 .40
387 Vitali Karamnov RC .05 .15
388 Doug Crossman .07 .20
389 Ron Sutter .05 .15
390 Garth Butcher .07 .20
391 Basil McRae .07 .20
392 Dean Evason .05 .15
393 Doug Zmolek RC .05 .15
394 Jay More .05 .15
395 Mike Sullivan .05 .15
396 Arturs Irbe .07 .20
397 Johan Garpenlov .05 .15
398 Jeff Odgers .05 .15
399 Jaroslav Otevrel RC .07 .20
400 Marc Bureau .07 .20
401 Bob Beers .07 .20
402 Rob DiMaio .05 .15
403 Steve Kasper .07 .20
404 Pat Jablonski .07 .20
405 John Tucker .05 .15
406 Shawn Chambers .05 .15
407 Mike Hartman .05 .15
408 Danton Cole .07 .20
409 Dave Andreychuk .10 .25
410 Peter Zezel .05 .15
411 Mike Krushelnyski .05 .15
412 Daren Puppa .07 .20
413 Ken Baumgartner .07 .20
414 Rob Pearson .05 .15
415 Mike Foligno .07 .20
416 Sylvain Lefebvre .05 .15
417 Dimitri Mironov .05 .15
418 Petr Nedved .07 .20
419 Gerald Diduck .07 .20
420 Anatoli Semenov .05 .15
421 Sergio Momesso .05 .15
422 Gino Odjick .07 .20
423 Kay Whitmore .07 .20
424 Dave Babych .07 .20
425 Robert Dirk .07 .20
426 Reggie Savage .05 .15
427 Keith Jones RC .10 .25
428 Dimitri Khristich .05 .15
429 Jason Woolley RC .05 .15
430 Jim Hrivnak .07 .20
431 Sylvain Cote .07 .20
432 Michal Pivonka .05 .15
433 Rod Langway .07 .20
434 Tie Domi .10 .25
435 Sergei Bautin RC .05 .15
436 Darrin Shannon .05 .15
437 John Druce .05 .15
438 Teppo Numminen .05 .15
439 Luciano Borsato .05 .15
440 Igor Ulanov .05 .15
441 Mike O'Neill RC .07 .20
442 Kris King .05 .15
443 Roman Hamrlik IRS .20 .50
444 Steve Smith .05 .15
445 Jari Kurri .10 .25
446 Ulf Samuelsson .05 .15
447 Sergei Nemchinov IRS .05 .15
448 Tommy Soderstrom IRS .07 .20
449 Petr Nedved IRS .07 .20
450 Peter Sidorkiewicz .05 .15
451 Nicklas Lidstrom IRS .07 .20
452 Philippe Bozon IRS .05 .15
453 Uwe Krupp .05 .15
454 Steve Thomas .07 .20
455 Owen Nolan IRS .05 .15
456 Steve Yzerman AS .25 .60
457 Chris Chelios .10 .25
458 Paul Coffey AS .10 .25
459 Brett Hull AS .15 .40
460 Pavel Bure AS .20 .50
461 Ed Belfour AS .10 .25
462 Mario Lemieux AS .40 1.00
463 Patrick Roy AS .25 .60
464 Ray Bourque AS .15 .40
465 Jaromir Jagr AS .25 .60
466 Kevin Stevens AS .05 .15
467 Brian Leetch AS .07 .20
468 Bobby Clarke FLYER .07 .20
469 Bill Barber .07 .20
470 Bernie Parent FLYER .07 .20
471 Reggie Leach .07 .20
472 Rick MacLeish .07 .20
473 Dave Schultz .07 .20
474 Joe Watson .07 .20
475 Bobby Taylor .07 .20
476 Orest Kindrachuk .07 .20
477 Bob Kelly .07 .20
478 Bill Clement .07 .20
479 Ed Van Impe .07 .20
480 Fred Shero .07 .20
481 Bryan Smolinski RC .07 .20
482 Sergei Zholtok .07 .20
483 Matthew Barnaby RC .07 .20
484 Gary Shuchuk .07 .20
485 Guy Carbonneau .07 .20
486 Oleg Petrov RC .05 .15
487 Sean Hill RC .05 .15
488 Jesse Belanger RC .07 .20
489 Paul DiPietro .05 .15
490 Rich Pilon .05 .15
491 Greg Parks .07 .20
492 Jeff Daniels .05 .15
493 Denny Felsner RC .07 .20
494 Mike Eastwood RC .07 .20
495 Murray Craven .05 .15
496 Vincent Damphousse .07 .20
497 Grant Fuhr .10 .25
498 Mario Lemieux SCP .40 1.00
499 Ray Ferraro .05 .15
500 Teemu Selanne SCP .20 .50
501 Luc Robitaille SCP .07 .20
502 Doug Gilmour SCP .12 .30
503 Curtis Joseph SCP .10 .25
504 Kirk Muller .05 .15
505 Glenn Healy .07 .20
506 Pavel Bure SCP .20 .50
507 Felix Potvin SCP .20 .50
508 Guy Carbonneau .07 .20
509 Wayne Gretzky SCP .50 1.25
510 Patrick Roy SCP .25 .60

1992-93 Parkhurst Emerald Ice

The 1992-93 Parkhurst Emerald Ice set consists of 480 cards and a 30 card update set. This parallel set version can be differentiated from its basic set counterpart by the company's use of an "emerald green" embossed-foil Parkhurst logo on the lower left of the card. Cards 1-240 were inserted one per foil pack, two per jumbo pack in series one product; likewise for cards 241-480 in series two product. Cards 481-510 were available in Update set form only, and are slightly more difficult to obtain.

COMPLETE SET (480) 60.00 120.00
COMP.SERIES 1 (240) 30.00 80.00
COMP.SERIES 2 (240) 40.00 80.00
COMP.FINAL UPDATE (30) 12.50 25.00
*VETS: 2X TO 5X BASIC CARDS
*ROOKIES: 1.2X TO 3X BASIC CARDS
*UPDATE: 1.2X TO 3X BASIC CARDS

1992-93 Parkhurst Cherry Picks

Randomly inserted in second series Parkhurst foil packs, this 21-card standard-size set features Don Cherry's "Cherry Picks" as selected by the ex-coach and host of "Coach's Corner" on Hockey Night in Canada. The cards feature full-bleed, color action player photos. The player's name is printed in gold foil near the bottom of the card along with the Cherry Picks logo. The backs have a dark blue-gray and black stripe background. Set at an angle on this background is a hockey arena graphic design that carries comments from Don Cherry in French and English. Overlapping the arena design is a small, action player photo. The cards are numbered on the backs with a "CP" prefix. The cover card carries a message from Don Cherry. The Doug Gilmour card (CP 1993) was randomly inserted in Final Update sets.

COMPLETE SET (21) 25.00 50.00
CP1 Doug Gilmour 1.50 4.00
CP2 Jeremy Roenick 2.50 6.00
CP3 Brent Sutter 1.00 2.50
CP4 Mark Messier 1.50 4.00
CP5 Kirk Muller 1.25 3.00
CP6 Eric Lindros 2.00 5.00
CP7 Dale Hunter 1.00 2.50
CP8 Gary Roberts 1.00 2.50
CP9 Bob Probert 1.25 3.00
CP10 Brendan Shanahan 2.00 5.00
CP11 Wendel Clark 1.25 3.00
CP12 Rick Tocchet 1.00 2.50
CP13 Owen Nolan 1.25 3.00
CP14 Cam Neely 1.50 4.00
CP15 Dave Manson 1.00 2.50
CP16 Chris Chelios 1.50 4.00
CP17 Marty McSorley UER 1.25 3.00
CP18 Scott Stevens 1.25 3.00
CP19 John Blue 1.00 2.50
CP20 Ron Hextall 1.50 4.00
CP1993 Doug Gilmour 5.00 12.00
AU Don Cherry AU 40.00 80.00
CL Don Cherry CL 8.00 20.00
NNO Don Cherry RDMP 1.50 4.00

1992-93 Parkhurst Cherry Picks Sheet

This approximately 11" by 8 1/2" sheet displays the cards of the 1992-93 Parkhurst Cherry Picks insert set. The sheet could be obtained by collectors in exchange for four Don Cherry redemption cards, which were randomly inserted in 1992-93 Parkhurst series II packs. The sheet pictures the fronts of the cards from the 1992-93 Cherry Picks set with Don Cherry's card in the middle. The words "1993 Cherry Picks Promo" are printed in a pink to purple shaded bar at the top of the sheet. The back is blank and the sheet is unnumbered.

1 Dale Hunter 4.00 10.00
Dave Manson
Doug Gilmour
Gary Roberts
Chris Chelios
Jeremy Roenick
Bob Probert
Marty McSorley
B.Sutter
Brenden Shanahan
Don Cherry
Mark Messier
Wendel Clark
Kirk Muller
Rick Tocchet
Scott Stevens
Eric Lindros
Owen Nolan
John Blue
Ron Hextall

1992-93 Parkhurst Parkie Reprints

This set of 36 cards was issued in four separate series. The cards are reprints of cards from the 1950s. Capturing eight goalies from the 1950's Parkhurst collections, the first set was inserted into first series 12-card foil packs. The second eight cards showcase defensemen; these cards were randomly inserted in series 1 jumbo packs. Forwards (17-24) were inserted in second series foil with the remaining forwards (25-32) inserted in second series jumbo packs. The cover cards, which reproduce Parkhurst wrappers on their fronts (1953-54 and 1955-56), have a checklist on their backs. The fronts vary in design but all carry a color shot of the featured player. The players' names are on the fronts, some in print, some in signature form. The backs carry the information from the original card. The print varies from red to black to a combination. The Turk Broda and Terry Sawchuk cards are blank on the back as the originals are. Only Canadian cases included a newly created 1954-55 Don Cherry Parkie 101 card. The Parkie Reprints set is considered complete without it.

COMPLETE SET (36) 75.00 150.00
*PROMO: .4X TO 1X BASIC INSERT
PR1 Jacques Plante 3.00 8.00
PR2 Terry Sawchuk 3.00 8.00
PR3 Johnny Bower 2.50 6.00
PR4 Gump Worsley 2.50 6.00
PR5 Harry Lumley 2.50 6.00
PR6 Turk Broda 2.50 6.00
PR7 Jim Henry 1.50 4.00
PR8 Al Rollins 2.00 5.00
PR9 Bill Gadsby 2.00 5.00
PR10 Red Kelly 2.00 5.00
PR11 Allan Stanley 1.50 4.00
PR12 Bob Baun 2.00 5.00
PR13 Carl Brewer 1.50 4.00
PR14 Doug Harvey 2.50 6.00
PR15 Harry Howell 2.00 5.00
PR16 Tim Horton 2.00 5.00
PR17 George Armstrong 1.50 4.00
PR18 Ralph Backstrom 1.50 4.00
PR19 Alex Delvecchio 2.50 6.00
PR20 Bill Mosienko 1.50 4.00
PR21 Dave Keon 2.00 5.00
PR22 Andy Bathgate 2.00 5.00
PR23 Milt Schmidt 2.00 5.00
PR24 Dick Duff 2.00 5.00
PR25 Norm Ullman 2.00 5.00
PR26 Dickie Moore 2.00 5.00
PR27 Jerry Toppazzini 1.50 4.00
PR28 Henri Richard 2.50 6.00
PR29 Frank Mahovlich 2.50 6.00
PR30 Jean Beliveau 3.00 8.00
PR31 Ted Lindsay 2.50 6.00
PR32 Bernie Geoffrion 2.50 6.00
CL1 Parkies Checklist 1 1.50 4.00
CL2 Parkies Checklist 2 1.50 4.00
CL3 Parkies Checklist 3 1.50 4.00
CL4 Parkies Checklist 4 1.50 4.00
AU Don Cherry Parkie AU 50.00 100.00
NNO D.Cherry Parkie 101 2.50 6.00

1992-93 Parkhurst Arena Tour Sheets

Each sheet in this set of eight measures approximately 11" by 8 1/2" and commemorates a stop on the Canadian Arena Tour. The fronts feature color photos of 1992-93 Parkhurst hockey cards against a blue-green background that shades from dark to light. A thin metallic gold line frames the cards, and the word "Commemorative" is printed in large white letters on this line at the top of the sheet. Near the center are the words "Canadian Arena Tour" and a specific arena name along with the date the sheet was distributed. The team logo is printed above this text. Each sheet carries a serial number and the production run (noted beside the dates below). The backs are blank. The sheets are unnumbered and checklisted below in chronological order. The Montreal sheet was not distributed at the Forum; reportedly because the sheet was not bilingual.

1 Calgary Flames 2.50 6.00
Olympic
2 Edmonton Oilers 2.50 6.00
Northla
3 Quebec Nordiques 2.50 6.00
Colisee de Quebec, April 6 1993
Bill Lindsay
Ron Hextall
Valeri Kamensky
Kerry Huffman
Mats Sundin
Joe Sakic
4 Vancouver Canucks 4.00 10.00
Pacif
5 Montreal Canadiens 6.00 15.00
The
6 Toronto Maple Leafs 5.00 12.00
Maple Leaf Gardens
April 13&
7 Ottawa Senators 2.50 6.00
Ottawa
8 Winnipeg Jets 2.50 6.00
Winnipeg

1992-93 Parkhurst Parkie Sheets

These five commemorative sheets measure approximately 8 1/2" by 11". The sheets are individually numbered; the announced production quantities are listed in the checklist below. The sheets were distributed one per case as an insert with the various series of 1992-93 Parkhurst hockey cards. The players pictured are the players in that respective Parkie reprint series. The Stanley Cup Commemorative Update sheet was issued one per case of Final Update. A promo version of each sheet was also issued but not serial numbered.

1 Goalies 6.00 15.00
(7000 sheets issued)
2 Defensemen 8.00 20.00
(3000 sheets issued)
3 Forwards 6.00 15.00
Wingers
(7000 sheets issued)
4 Forwards 8.00 20.00
Centers
(3000 sheets issued)
5 Stanley Cup Update/(1000 sheets issued) 8.00
20.00

1992-93 Parkhurst Parkie Sheets Promo

These 11" by 8 1/2" sheets were promos of the 1992-93 Parkhurst Limited Edition Commemorative Sheets. The fronts feature color photos of actual Parkhurst Parkies. The cards are set against a dark green marbleized background. A thin metallic gold line frames the cards. The words "Commemorative Sheet" are printed in white over the gold line near the top of the Parkie Reprint sheets. Above this, are the words "1992-93 Parkhurst Limited Edition" printed in metallic gold. A gold or white oval at the bottom right corner carries the word "Promo." The backs are blank. The sheets are unnumbered.

*1-5 PROMO SHEET: .2X TO .5X NUMBERED SHEET
6 Maple Leafs vs. Canadiens 3.00 8.00

1993-94 Parkhurst

Issued in two series, these 540 standard-size cards feature color player action shots on their fronts. They are borderless, except on the right, where black and green stripes set off by a silver-foil line carry the player's name in white lettering; and at the lower left, where a black and green corner backs up the silver-foil-stamped Parkhurst logo. The player's team name appears near the right edge in vertical silver-foil lettering. The horizontal back carries another color player action shot on the right. On the left are the player's team name, position, biography, career highlights, and statistics. Card numbers 398 and 498 were not issued.

1 Steven King .05 .15
2 Sean Hill .05 .15
3 Anatoli Semenov .05 .15
4 Garry Valk .05 .15
5 Todd Ewen .05 .15
6 Bob Corkum .05 .15
7 Tim Sweeney .05 .15
8 Patrick Carnback RC .10 .25
9 Troy Loney .05 .15
10 Cam Neely .10 .25
11 Adam Oates .10 .25
12 Jon Casey .07 .20
13 Don Sweeney .05 .15
14 Ray Bourque .15 .40
15 Jozef Stumpel .05 .15
16 Glen Murray .05 .15
17 Glen Wesley .05 .15
18 Fred Knipscheer RC .05 .15
19 Craig Simpson .05 .15
20 Richard Smehlik .05 .15
21 Alexander Mogilny .07 .20
22 Grant Fuhr .10 .25
23 Dale Hawerchuk .12 .30
24 Philippe Boucher .05 .15
25 Scott Thomas RC .10 .25
26 Donald Audette .05 .15
27 Brad May .07 .20
28 Theo Fleury .05 .15
29 Andrei Trefilov .05 .15
30 Sandy McCarthy .05 .15
31 Joe Nieuwendyk .07 .20
32 Paul Ranheim .05 .15
33 Kelly Kisio .05 .15
34 Joel Otto .05 .15
35 Ted Drury .05 .15
36 Al MacInnis .07 .20
37 Kevin Todd .05 .15
38 Joe Murphy .05 .15
39 Christian Ruuttu .05 .15
40 Steve Dubinsky RC .10 .25
41 Stephane Matteau .05 .15
42 Ivan Droppa RC .05 .15
43 Jocelyn Lemieux .05 .15
44 Ed Belfour .10 .25
45 Chris Chelios .10 .25
46 Derian Hatcher .05 .15
47 Andy Moog .10 .25
48 Trent Klatt .05 .15
49 Mike Modano .15 .40
50 Paul Cavallini .05 .15
51 Mike McPhee .05 .15
52 Brent Gilchrist .05 .15
53 Russ Courtnall .05 .15
54 Neal Broten .07 .20
55 Steve Chiasson .05 .15
56 Paul Coffey .10 .25
57 Slava Kozlov .07 .20
58 Sergei Fedorov .15 .40
59 Tim Cheveldae .07 .20
60 Dino Ciccarelli .07 .20
61 Dallas Drake RC .10 .25
62 Nicklas Lidstrom .10 .25
63 Martin Lapointe .05 .15
64 Dean McAmmond .05 .15
65 Igor Kravchuk .05 .15
66 Shjon Podein RC .10 .25
67 Bill Ranford .07 .20
68 Brad Werenka .05 .15
69 Doug Weight .07 .20
70 Ian Herbers RC .05 .15
71 Todd Elik .05 .15
72 Steven Rice .05 .15
73 John Vanbiesbrouck .07 .20
74 Alexander Godynyuk .05 .15
75 Brian Skrudland .05 .15
76 Jody Hull .05 .15
77 Brent Severyn RC .10 .25
78 Evegny Davydov .05 .15
79 Dave Lowry .05 .15
80 Scott Levins RC .10 .25
81 Scott Mellanby .07 .20
82 Dan Keczmer .05 .15
83 Michael Nylander .05 .15
84 Jim Sandlak .05 .15
85 Brian Propp .05 .15
86 Geoff Sanderson .07 .20
87 Mike Lenarduzzi RC .05 .15
88 Zarley Zalapski .05 .15
89 Robert Petrovicky .05 .15
90 Robert Kron .05 .15
91 Luc Robitaille .07 .20
92 Alexei Zhitnik .05 .15
93 Tony Granato .05 .15
94 Rob Blake .07 .20
95 Gary Shuchuk .05 .15
96 Darryl Sydor .05 .15
97 Kelly Hrudey .07 .20
98 Warren Rychel .05 .15
99 Wayne Gretzky .50 1.25
100 Patrick Roy .25 .60
101 Gilbert Dionne .05 .15
102 Eric Desjardins .07 .20
103 Peter Popovic RC .10 .25
104 Vincent Damphousse .07 .20
105 Patrice Brisebois .05 .15
106 Pierre Sevigny .05 .15
107 John LeClair .10 .25
108 Paul DiPietro .05 .15
109 Alexander Semak .05 .15
110 Claude Lemieux .05 .15
111 Scott Niedermayer .10 .25
112 Chris Terreri .07 .20
113 Stephane Richer .07 .20
114 Scott Stevens .10 .25
115 John MacLean .07 .20
116 Scott Pellerin RC .10 .25
117 Bernie Nicholls .05 .15
118 Ron Hextall .07 .20
119 Derek King .05 .15
120 Scott Lachance .05 .15
121 Scott Scissons .05 .15
122 Darius Kasparaitis .05 .15
123 Ray Ferraro .05 .15
124 Steve Thomas .05 .15
125 Vladimir Malakhov .05 .15
126 Travis Green .07 .20
127 Mark Messier .10 .25
128 Sergei Nemchinov .05 .15
129 Mike Richter .10 .25
130 Alexei Kovalev .07 .20
131 Brian Leetch .10 .25
132 Tony Amonte .07 .20
133 Sergei Zubov .05 .15
134 Adam Graves .05 .15
135 Esa Tikkanen .05 .15
136 Sylvain Turgeon .05 .15
137 Norm Maciver .05 .15
138 Craig Billington .07 .20
139 Dmitri Filiminov .05 .15
140 Pavol Demitra .12 .30
141 Brian Glynn .05 .15
142 Darrin Madeley RC .10 .25
143 Radek Hamr RC .10 .25
144 Robert Burakovsky RC .10 .25
145 Dimitri Yushkevich .05 .15
146 Claude Boivin .05 .15
147 Pelle Eklund .05 .15
148 Brent Fedyk .05 .15
149 Mark Recchi .12 .30
150 Tommy Soderstrom .07 .20
151 Vyacheslav Butsayev .05 .15
152 Rod Brind'Amour .07 .20
153 Josef Beranek .05 .15
154 Jaromir Jagr .25 .60
155 Ulf Samuelsson .05 .15
156 Martin Straka .05 .15
157 Tom Barrasso .07 .20
158 Kevin Stevens .05 .15
159 Joe Mullen .07 .20
160 Ron Francis .12 .30
161 Marty McSorley .05 .15
162 Larry Murphy .07 .20
163 Owen Nolan .07 .20
164 Stephane Fiset .07 .20
165 Dave Karpa .05 .15
166 Martin Gelinas .05 .15
167 Andrei Kovalenko .05 .15
168 Steve Duchesne .05 .15
169 Joe Sakic .25 .60
170 Martin Rucinsky .05 .15
171 Chris Simon RC .10 .25
172 Brendan Shanahan .12 .30
173 Jeff Brown .05 .15
174 Phil Housley .07 .20
175 Curtis Joseph .10 .25
176 Jim Montgomery RC .10 .25
177 Bret Hedican .05 .15
178 Kevin Miller .05 .15
179 Philippe Bozon .05 .15
180 Brett Hull .15 .40
181 Jimmy Waite .07 .20
182 Ray Whitney .05 .15
183 Pat Falloon .05 .15
184 Tom Pederson .05 .15
185 Igor Larionov .05 .15
186 Dody Wood RC .10 .25
187 Sandis Ozolinsh .05 .15
188 Sergei Makarov .05 .15
189 Rob Gaudreau RC .10 .25
190 Roman Hamrlik .05 .15
191 Stan Drulia .05 .15
192 Pat Jablonski .05 .15
193 Denis Savard .12 .30
194 Rob Zamuner .05 .15
195 Petr Klima .05 .15
196 Rob Dimiao .05 .15
197 Chris Kontos .05 .15
198 Mikael Andersson .05 .15
199 Drake Berehowsky .05 .15
200 Dave Andreychuk .10 .25
201 Glenn Anderson .10 .25
202 Felix Potvin .20 .50
203 Nikolai Borschevsky .05 .15
204 Kent Manderville .05 .15
205 Dave Ellett .05 .15
206 Peter Zezel .05 .15
207 Ken Baumgartner .05 .15
208 Murray Craven .05 .15
209 Dixon Ward .05 .15
210 Cliff Ronning .05 .15
211 Pavel Bure .10 .25
212 Sergio Momesso .05
213 Kirk McLean .07
214 Jiri Slegr .05
215 Trevor Linden .07
216 Geoff Courtnall .05
217 Al Iafrate .05
218 Mike Ridley .05
219 Enrico Ciccone .05
220 Dimitri Khristich .05
221 Kevin Hatcher .05
222 Peter Bondra .07
223 Steve Konowalchuk .05
224 Pat Elynuik .05
225 Don Beaupre .07
226 Stu Barnes .05
227 Fredrik Olausson .05
228 Keith Tkachuk .10
229 Mike Eagles .05
230 Tie Domi .05
231 Teppo Numminen .05
232 Arto Blomsten .05
233 Teemu Selanne .20
234 Bob Essensa .07
235 Teemu Selanne SPH .20
236 Eric Lindros SPH .30
237 Felix Potvin SPH .20
238 Alexei Kovalev SPH .07
239 Vladimir Malakhov SPH .05
240 Scott Niedermayer SPH .10
241 Joe Juneau SPH .07
242 Shawn McEachern SPH .05
243 Alexei Zhamnov SPH .07
244 Alexandre Daigle PKP .05
245 Markus Naslund PKP .10
246 Rob Niedermayer PKP .07
247 Jocelyn Thibault RC .10
248 Brent Gretzky PKP RC .10
249 Chris Pronger PKP .10
250 Chris Gratton PKP .07
251 Mikael Renberg PKP .10
252 Jarkko Varvio PKP .05
253 Micah Aivazoff PKP RC .10
254 Alexei Yashin PKP .07
255 German Titov PKP RC .10
256 Mattias Norstrom PKP RC .10
257 Michal Sykora PKP RC .10
258 Roman Oksiuta PKP RC .10
259 Bryan Smolinski PKP .05
260 Alexei Kudashov PKP RC .10
261 Jason Arnott PKP RC .20
262 Aaron Ward PKP RC .10
263 Vesa Vitakoski PKP RC .10
264 Boris Mironov PKP .05
265 Darren McCarty PKP RC .15
266 Vlastimil Kroupa PKP RC .10
267 Denny Felsner PKP .05
268 Milos Holan PKP RC .10
269 Alex Karpovtsev PKP .05
270 Greg Johnson PKP .05
271 Terry Yake .05
272 Bill Houlder .05
273 Joe Sacco .05
274 Myles O'Connor .05
275 Mark Ferner RC .05
276 Alexei Kasatanov .05
277 Stu Grimson .05
278 Shaun Van Allen .05
279 Guy Hebert .07
280 Joe Juneau .07
281 Sergei Zholtok .05
282 Daniel Marois .05
283 Ted Donato .05
284 Cam Stewart RC .10
285 Stephen Leach .05
286 Darren Banks .05
287 Dmitri Kvartalnov .05
288 Paul Stanton .05
289 Pat LaFontaine .10
290 Bob Sweeney .05
291 Craig Muni .05
292 Sergei Petrenko .05
293 Derek Plante RC .10
294 Wayne Presley .05
295 Mark Astley RC .10
296 Matthew Barnaby .07
297 Randy Wood .05
298 Kevin Dahl .05
299 Gary Suter .05
300 Robert Reichel .05
301 Mike Vernon .07
302 Gary Roberts .05
303 Ronnie Stern .05
304 Michel Petit .05
305 Wes Walz .05
306 Brad Miller RC .05
307 Patrick Poulin .05
308 Brent Sutter .05
309 Jeremy Roenick .15
310 Steve Smith .05
311 Eric Weinrich .05
312 Jeff Hackett .05
313 Michel Goulet .05
314 Jeff Shantz RC .05
315 Neil Wilkinson .05
316 Shane Churla .05
317 Dave Gagner .07
318 Chris Tancill .05
319 Dean Evason .05
320 Mark Tinordi .05
321 Grant Ledyard .05
322 Ulf Dahlen .05
323 Mike Craig .05
324 Paul Broten .05
325 Vladimir Konstantinov .07
326 Steve Yzerman .25
327 Keith Primeau .05
328 Shawn Burr .05
329 Chris Osgood RC .60
330 Ray Sheppard .07
331 Mike Sillinger .05
332 Terry Carkner .05
333 Bob Probert .07
334 Adam Bennett .10
335 Dave Manson .05
336 Zdeno Ciger .05
337 Louie DeBrusk .05
338 Shayne Corson .05
339 Vladimir Vujtek .05
340 Tyler Wright .05
341 Ilya Byakin RC .05
342 Craig MacTavish .05
343 Brian Benning .05
344 Mark Fitzpatrick .05
345 Gord Murphy .05
346 Jesse Belanger .05
347 Joe Cirella .05
348 Tom Fitzgerald .05
349 Andrei Lomakin .05
350 Bill Lindsay .05
351 Len Barrie .05
352 Frank Pietrangelo .07

3 Pat Verbeek .05 .15
4 Jim Storm .05 .15
5 Mark Janssens .05 .15
6 Darren Turcotte .05 .15
7 Jim McKenzie .05 .15
8 Brad McCrimmon .05 .15
9 Andrew Cassels .05 .15
0 James Patrick .05 .15
1 Bob Jay RC .10 .25
2 Tomas Sandstrom .05 .15
3 Pat Conacher .05 .15
4 Shawn McEachern .05 .15
5 Jari Kurri .10 .25
6 Dominic Lavoie .05 .15
7 Dave Taylor .05 .15
8 Jimmy Carson .05 .15
9 Mike Donnelly .05 .15
0 Lyle Odelein .05 .15
1 Brian Bellows .07 .20
2 Guy Carbonneau .05 .15
3 Mathieu Schneider .05 .15
4 Stephan Lebeau .05 .15
5 Benoit Brunet .05 .15
6 Kevin Haller .05 .15
7 J.J. Daigneault .05 .15
8 Kirk Muller .05 .15
9 Jason Smith RC .05 .15
0 Martin Brodeur .25 .60
1 Corey Millen .05 .15
2 Bill Guerin .05 .15
3 Valeri Zelepukin .05 .15
4 Tom Chorske .05 .15
5 Bobby Holik .05 .15
6 Jaroslav Modry RC .10 .25
7 Ken Daneyko .05 .15
8 Uwe Krupp .05 .15
9 Pierre Turgeon .07 .20
0 Marty McInnis .05 .15
1 Patrick Flatley .05 .15
2 Tom Kurvers .05 .15
3 Brad Dalgarno .05 .15
4 Steve Junker RC .10 .25
5 David Volek .05 .15
6 Benoit Hogue .05 .15
7 Zigmund Palffy .05 .15
9 Joby Messier RC .10 .25
0 Mike Gartner .07 .20
1 Joey Kocur .05 .15
2 Ed Olczyk .05 .15
3 Doug Lidster .05 .15
4A Greg Gilbert .05 .15
4B Steve Larmer UER .07 .20
Should be 398)
5 Glenn Healy .07 .20
6 Dennis Vial .05 .15
7 Darcy Loewen .05 .15
8 Bob Kudelski .05 .15
9 Hank Lammens RC .05 .15
0 Jarmo Kekalainen .05 .15
1 Darren Rumble .05 .15
2 Francois Leroux .05 .15
3 Troy Mallette .05 .15
4 Bill Huard RC .10 .25
5 Ryan McGill .05 .15
6 Eric Lindros .30 .75
7 Dominic Roussel .07 .20
8 Jason Bowen RC .10 .25
9 Andre Faust .05 .15
0 Stewart Malgunas RC .10 .25
1 Kevin Dineen .05 .15
2 Yves Racine .05 .15
3 Garry Galley .05 .15
4 Doug Brown .05 .15
5 Mario Lemieux .40 1.00
6 Ladislav Karabin RC .10 .25
7 Grant Jennings .05 .15
8 Rick Tocchet .07 .20
9 Jeff Daniels .05 .15
0 Peter Taglianetti .05 .15
1 Bryan Trottier .12 .30
2 Kjell Samuelsson .05 .15
3 Rene Corbet RC .10 .25
4 Iain Fraser RC .10 .25
5 Mats Sundin .07 .20
6 Curtis Leschyshyn .05 .15
7 Claude LaPointe .05 .15
8 Valeri Kamensky .07 .20
9 Mike Ricci .05 .15
0 Chris Lindberg .05 .15
Alexei Gusarov .05 .15
2 Tom Tilley .05 .15
3 Craig Janney .07 .20
4 Vitali Karamnov .05 .15
5 Bob Bassen .05 .15
6 Igor Korolev .05 .15
7 Kevin Miehm .05 .15
8 Tony Hrkac .05 .15
9 Garth Butcher .05 .15
0 Vitali Prokhorov .05 .15
Arturs Irbe .07 .20
2 Jay More .05 .15
3 Bob Errey .05 .15
4 Mike Sullivan .05 .15
5 Jeff Norton .05 .15
6 Gaeten Duchesne .05 .15
7 Doug Zmolek .05 .15
8 Mike Rathje .05 .15
9 Jamie Baker .05 .15
0 Joe Reekie .05 .15
Mark Bureau .05 .15
2 John Tucker .05 .15
3 Bill McDougall RC .10 .25
4 Danton Cole .05 .15
5 Brian Bradley .05 .15
6 Jason Lafreniere .05 .15
7 Donald Dufresne .05 .15
8 Daren Puppa .05 .15
9 Doug Gilmour .12 .30
0 Damian Rhodes RC .10 .25
Matt Martin RC .10 .25
Bill Berg .05 .15
John Cullen .05 .15
Rob Pearson .05 .15
Wendel Clark .07 .20
Mark Osborne .05 .15
Dmitri Mironov .05 .15
A Kay Whitmore .05 .15
B Kris King UER .05 .15
Should be 498)
Shawn Antoski .05 .15
Greg Adams .05 .15
Dave Babych .05 .15
John McIntyre .05 .15
Jyrki Lumme .05 .15
Jose Charbonneau RC .10 .25
Gino Odjick .05 .15
Dana Murzyn .05 .15
Michal Pivonka .05 .15
Dave Poulin .05 .15
Sylvain Cote .05 .15
Pat Peake .05 .15
491 Kelly Miller .05 .15
492 Randy Burridge .05 .15
493 Kevin Kaminski RC .05 .15
494 John Slaney .05 .15
495 Keith Jones .05 .15
496 Harijs Vitolinsh .05 .15
497 Nelson Emerson .05 .15
499 Darrin Shannon .05 .15
500 Stephane Quintal .05 .15
501 Luciano Borsato .05 .15
502 Thomas Steen .05 .15
503 Alexei Zhamnov .07 .20
504 Paul Ysebaert .05 .15
505 Jeff Friesen RC .10 .25
506 Niklas Sundstrom .05 .15
507 Nick Stajduhar RC .10 .25
508 Jamie Storr RC .10 .25
509 Valeri Bure RC .10 .25
510 Jason Bonsignore RC .10 .25
511 Mats Lindgren RC .10 .25
512 Yanick Dube RC .10 .25
513 Todd Harvey RC .10 .25
514 Ladislav Prokupek RC .05 .15
515 Tomas Vlasak RC .05 .15
516 Josef Marha RC .05 .15
517 Tomas Blazek RC .05 .15
518 Zdenek Nedved RC .05 .15
519 Jaroslav Miklenda RC .10 .25
520 Janne Niinimaa RC .05 .15
521 Saku Koivu .10 .25
522 Tommi Miettinen RC .05 .15
523 Tuomas Gronman .05 .15
524 Jani Nikko RC .05 .15
525 Jouni Vauhkonen .05 .15
526 Nikolai Tsulygin .05 .15
527 Vadim Sharifjanov .07 .20
528 Valeri Bure RC .10 .25
529 Alex Kharlamov RC .05 .15
530 Nikolai Zavarukhin RC .05 .15
531 Oleg Tverdovsky RC .10 .25
532 Sergei Kondrashkin RC .05 .15
533 Evgeni Riabchikov RC .05 .15
534 Mats Lindgren RC .10 .25
535 Kenny Jonsson .05 .15
536 Edvin Frylen RC .10 .25
537 Mathias Johansson RC .05 .15
538 Johan Davidsson RC .05 .15
539 Mikael Hakansson RC .05 .15
540 Anders Eriksson RC .05 .15

1993-94 Parkhurst Emerald Ice

The 540 cards in this parallel set can be found one per foil pack and two per jumbo pack. The Parkhurst logo, team name, and vertical strip near the right edge of the card are adorned with green foil, as opposed to the silver foil used for the basic card set.
*VETS: 2.5X TO 6X BASIC CARDS
*ROOKIES: 1.5X TO 4X BASIC CARDS

1993-94 Parkhurst Calder Candidates

The silver trade card randomly inserted in '93-94 Parkhurst packs was redeemable for this Calder Candidates insert set.This set was also randomly inserted in U.S. Series 2 retail packs. The gold trade card was redeemable for a gold foil-enhanced edition; multipliers can be found below to determine values for these. The expiration date for both trade cards was July 31st, 1994.
*GOLD: .6X TO 1.5X SILVER INSERTS
C1 Alexandre Daigle .40 1.00
C2 Chris Pronger 1.50 4.00
C3 Chris Gratton .40 1.00
C4 Rob Niedermayer .40 1.00
C5 Markus Naslund .40 1.00
C6 Jason Arnott 1.00 2.50
C7 Pierre Sevigny .40 1.00
C8 Jarkko Varvio .40 1.00
C9 Dean McAmmond .40 1.00
C10 Alexei Yashin .40 1.00
C11 Philippe Boucher .40 1.00
C12 Mikael Renberg .40 1.00
C13 Chris Simon .40 1.00
C14 Brent Gretzky .40 1.00
C15 Jesse Belanger .40 1.00
C16 Jocelyn Thibault .75 2.00
C17 Chris Osgood .40 1.00
C18 Derek Plante .40 1.00
C19 Iain Fraser .40 1.00
C20 Vesa Viitakoski .40 1.00

1993-94 Parkhurst Cherry's Playoff Heroes

Randomly inserted in Canadian second-series foil packs, these twenty different cards feature color player action shots on their fronts and a photo of Machiavellian TV personality Don Cherry -- who chose the players to be featured in this set based on his unique set of standards -- on the back. The cards are numbered with a "D" prefix.
COMPLETE SET (20) 15.00 40.00
D1 Wayne Gretzky 3.00 8.00
D2 Mario Lemieux 2.50 6.00
D3 Al MacInnis .40 1.00
D4 Mark Messier .60 1.50
D5 Dino Ciccarelli .40 1.00
D6 Dale Hunter .40 1.00
D7 Grant Fuhr .75 2.00
D8 Paul Coffey .60 1.50
D9 Doug Gilmour .50 1.25
D10 Patrick Roy 6.00 10.00
D11 Alexandre Daigle .40 1.00
D12 Chris Gratton .40 1.00
D13 Chris Pronger .50 1.25
D14 Felix Potvin 1.00 2.50
D15 Eric Lindros .75 2.00
D16 Maurice Richard 2.50 6.00
D17 Gordie Howe 2.00 5.00
D18 Henri Richard .50 1.25
D19 Reggie Leach .40 1.00
D20 Don Cherry CL 1.00 2.50

1993-94 Parkhurst East/West Stars

Randomly inserted in U.S. second-series hobby packs, these cards feature color player action shots on their fronts. The first ten cards feature Eastern Conference stars, numbered with an "E" prefix, while the last ten cards present Western Conference stars, numbered with a "W" prefix.
COMPLETE SET (20) 15.00 35.00
COMP.EAST SERIES (10) 6.00 15.00
COMP.WEST SERIES (10) 8.00 20.00
E1 Eric Lindros .60 1.50
E2 Mario Lemieux 2.50 6.00
E3 Alexandre Daigle .20 .50
E4 Patrick Roy 2.50 6.00
E5 Rob Niedermayer .30 .75
E6 Chris Gratton .30 .75
E7 Alexei Yashin .20 .50
E8 Pat LaFontaine .40 1.00
E9 Joe Sakic 1.00 2.50
E10 Pierre Turgeon .30 .75
W1 Wayne Gretzky 3.00 8.00
W2 Pavel Bure .60 1.50
W3 Teemu Selanne .60 1.50
W4 Doug Gilmour .30 .75
W5 Steve Yzerman 2.50 6.00
W6 Jeremy Roenick .60 1.50
W7 Brett Hull .60 1.50
W8 Jason Arnott .60 1.50
W9 Felix Potvin 1.00 2.50
W10 Sergei Fedorov .75 2.00

1993-94 Parkhurst First Overall

Randomly inserted in Canadian Series I retail foil packs, this ten-card set featured color action shots of players drafted first overall in the annual NHL Entry Draft over the past decade. The cards are numbered on the back with an "F" prefix.
COMPLETE SET (10) 8.00 20.00
F1 Alexandre Daigle .30 .75
F2 Roman Hamrlik .50 1.25
F3 Eric Lindros .75 2.00
F4 Owen Nolan .50 1.25
F5 Mats Sundin .75 2.00
F6 Mike Modano 1.25 3.00
F7 Pierre Turgeon .50 1.25
F8 Joe Murphy .30 .75
F9 Wendel Clark .50 1.25
F10 Mario Lemieux 4.00 10.00

1993-94 Parkhurst Parkie Reprints

A continuation of the '92-93 Parkie Reprints set, these 40 (numbered 33-68, plus four checklists) cards measure the standard-size. The first ten cards (33-41, plus checklist (5) were randomly inserted in '93-94 Parkhurst series I foil packs. The second series (42-50, plus checklist (6) were random inserts in Parkhurst series one jumbo packs only. The third series (51-59, plus checklist (7) were random inserts in all series two Parkhurst packs. The fourth Parkie Reprints series (60-68, plus checklist (8) were random inserts in Parkhurst series two jumbo packs. The fronts are that of 1951-64 Parkhurst styles, but all carry a color player photo. The backs carry the information from the original card. The print varies from red to black to a combination. The cards are numbered on the back with a "PR" prefix. A hobby exclusive Parkie Reprints bonus pack was included in every series one and series two case.
COMPLETE SET (40) 25.00 60.00
PR33 Gordie Howe 2.50 6.00
PR34 Tim Horton 1.25 3.00
PR35 B.Barilko/McNeil 1.25 3.00
PR36 E.Lach/M.Richard 2.00 5.00
PR37 Terry Sawchuk 1.50 4.00
PR38 George Armstrong 1.00 2.50
PR39 William Harris 1.00 2.50
PR40 Doug Harvey 1.25 3.00
PR41 Gump Worsley 1.25 3.00
PR42 Gordie Howe 2.50 6.00
PR43 Jacques Plante 1.25 3.00
PR44 Frank Mahovlich 1.25 3.00
PR45 Fern Flaman 1.00 2.50
PR46 Bernie Geoffrion 1.50 4.00
PR47 Toe Blake CO 1.00 2.50
PR48 Maurice Richard 1.50 4.00
PR49 Ted Lindsay 1.00 2.50
PR50 Camille Henry 1.00 2.50
PR51 Gordie Howe 2.50 6.00
PR52 Jean-Guy Talbot 1.00 2.50
PR53 Terry Sawchuk 1.50 4.00
PR54 Warren Godfrey 1.00 2.50
PR55 Tom Johnson 1.00 2.50
PR56 Bert Olmstead 1.00 2.50
PR57 Cal Gardner 1.00 2.50
PR58 Red Kelly 1.25 3.00
PR59 Phil Goyette 1.00 2.50
PR60 Gordie Howe 2.50 6.00
PR61 Lou Fontinato 1.00 2.50
PR62 Bill Dineen 1.00 2.50
PR63 Maurice Richard 1.25 3.00
PR64 Vic Stasiuk 1.00 2.50
PR65 Marcel Pronovost 1.00 2.50
PR66 Ed Litzenberger 1.00 2.50
PR67 Dave Keon 1.25 3.00
PR68 Dollard St. Laurent 1.00 2.50
CL5 Parkies Checklist 5 .75 2.00
CL6 Parkies Checklist 6 .75 2.00
CL7 Parkies Checklist 7 .75 2.00
CL8 Parkies Checklist 8 .75 2.00

1993-94 Parkhurst Parkie Reprints Case Inserts

These sets were inserted one per hobby case. Cards 1-6 were found in series I cases, while 7-12 were inserted in series II cases. Parkhurst selected vintage cards from its past to reprint in this 12-card standard-size set. The cards are coated on both sides and are easily recognizable as reprints. The cards are numbered on the back with the prefix "DPR".
COMPLETE SET (12) 25.00 60.00
COMP.SERIES 1 SET (6) 12.50 30.00
COMP.SERIES 2 SET (6) 12.50 30.00
DPR1 Gordie Howe 6.00 15.00
DPR2 Milt Schmidt 2.50 6.00
DPR3 Tim Horton 3.00 8.00
DPR4 Al Rollins 2.50 6.00
DPR5 Maurice Richard 4.00 10.00
DPR6 Harry Howell 2.50 6.00
DPR7 Gordie Howe 6.00 15.00
DPR8 Johnny Bower 4.00 10.00
DPR9 Dean Prentice 2.50 6.00
DPR10 Leo Labine 2.50 6.00
DPR11 Harry Watson 3.00 8.00
DPR12 Dickie Moore 3.00 8.00

1993-94 Parkhurst USA/Canada Gold

Randomly inserted at the rate of 1:30 U.S. Series I foil packs, this 10-card set depicted the 10 best NHL players form both the U.S. and Canada. Accordingly, cards 1-5 are USA Gold while cards 6-10 are Canadian Gold. The cards are numbered on the back with a "G" prefix.
COMPLETE SET (10) 10.00 25.00
G1 Wayne Gretzky 3.00 8.00
G2 Mario Lemieux 2.50 6.00
G3 Eric Lindros .50 1.25
G4 Brett Hull .60 1.50
G5 Rob Niedermayer .30 .75
G6 Alexandre Daigle .20 .50
G7 Pavel Bure .50 1.25
G8 Teemu Selanne .50 1.25
G9 Patrick Roy 2.50 6.00
G10 Doug Gilmour .30 .75

1994 Parkhurst Missing Link

This 180-card set attempts to capture what a Parkhurst set might have looked like had one been produced for the 1956-57 NHL campaign. Although the inclusion of all six original teams may seem somewhat anachronistic (keeping in mind that Parkhurst, at that time, issued cards featuring Canadian-based players only) the set does capture the old-time flavor. The simple design includes an isolated player photo (taken during the 1955-56 season) over a cream colored background. A black bar runs along the left side of the card front, and contains the player name and team logo. Card backs include stats for the 1955-56 season and biographical information in both French and English. Subsets include All-Stars (135-146), Trophy Winners (147-152), Action Shots (153-168), Team Leaders (169-174) and Playoffs (175-178). The set was issued in 10-card wax packs and production was limited to 1956 numbered cases for each of the Canadian and American markets.
COMPLETE SET (180) 20.00 35.00
1 Jerry Toppazzini .02 .10
2 Fern Flaman .15 .40
3 Fleming MacKell .02 .10
4 Leo Labine .07 .20
5 John Peirson .05 .15
6 Don McKenney .05 .15
7 Bob Armstrong .02 .10
8 Real Chevrefils .02 .10
9 Vic Stasiuk .05 .15
10 Cal Gardner .02 .10
11 Leo Boivin .15 .40
12 Jack Caffery .02 .10
13 Bob Beckett RC .02 .10
14 Jack Bionda .02 .10
15 Claude Pronovost RC .15 .40
16 Larry Regan .02 .10
17 Terry Sawchuk 1.00 2.50
18 Doug Mohns .07 .20
19 Marcel Bonin .05 .15
20 Allan Stanley .20 .50
21 Milt Schmidt CO .20 .50
22 Al Dewsbury .02 .10
23 Glen Skov .05 .15
24 Ed Litzenberger .05 .15
25 Nick Mickoski .02 .10
26 Walter Hergesheimer .02 .10
27 Jack McIntyre .02 .10
28 Al Rollins .20 .50
29 Hank Ciesla .02 .10
30 Gus Mortson .02 .10
31 Elmer Vasko .05 .15
32 Pierre Pilote .20 .50
33 Ron Ingram .02 .10
34 Frank Martin .02 .10
35 Forbes Kennedy .07 .20
36 Harry Watson .05 .15
37 Eddie Kachur RC .02 .10
38 Hec Lalande .02 .10
39 Eric Nesterenko .07 .20
40 Ben Woit .02 .10
41 Ken Mosdell .05 .15
42 Tommy Ivan CO RC .15 .40
43 Gordie Howe 1.50 4.00
44 Ted Lindsay .20 .50
45 Norm Ullman .20 .50
46 Glenn Hall .40 1.00
47 Billy Dea .02 .10
48 Bill McNeill .02 .10
49 Earl Reibel .05 .15
50 Bill Dineen .07 .20
51 Warren Godfrey .05 .15
52 Red Kelly .20 .50
53 Marty Pavelich .02 .10
54 Lorne Ferguson .02 .10
55 Larry Hillman .05 .15
56 John Bucyk .20 .50
57 Metro Prystai .02 .10
58 Marcel Pronovost .20 .50
59 Alex Delvecchio .20 .50
60 Murray Costello RC .02 .10
61 Al Arbour .20 .50
62 Bucky Hollingworth .02 .10
63 Jim Skinner CO RC .02 .10
64 Jean Beliveau .75 2.00
65 Maurice Richard 1.00 2.50
66 Henri Richard .20 .50
67 Doug Harvey .20 .50
68 BoomBoom Geoffrion .30 .75
69 Dollard St. Laurent .08 .25
70 Dickie Moore .20 .50
71 Bert Olmstead .08 .25
72 Jacques Plante 1.00 2.50
73 Claude Provost .15 .40
74 Phil Goyette .05 .15
75 Andre Pronovost .05 .15
76 Don Marshall .08 .25
77 Ralph Backstrom .07 .20
78 Floyd Curry .07 .20
79 Tom Johnson .20 .50
80 Jean Guy Talbot .07 .20
81 Bob Turner .02 .10
82 Connie Broden RC .02 .10
83 Jackie Leclair .02 .10
84 Toe Blake CO .30 .75
85 Frank Selke MD .20 .50
86 George Sullivan .02 .10
87 Larry Cahan .02 .10
88 Jean Guy Gendron .02 .10
89 Bill Gadsby .20 .50
90 Andy Bathgate .20 .50
91 Dean Prentice .02 .10
92 Gump Worsley .40 1.00
93 Lou Fontinato .05 .15
94 Gerry Foley .02 .10
95 Larry Popein .05 .15
96 Harry Howell .20 .50
97 Andy Hebenton .02 .10
98 Danny Lewicki .02 .10
99 Dave Creighton .02 .10
100 Camille Henry .02 .10
101 Jack Evans .02 .10
102 Ron Murphy .02 .10
103 Johnny Bower .30 .75
104 Parker MacDonald .02 .10
105 Bronco Horvath .07 .20
106 Bruce Cline RC .02 .10
107 Ivan Irwin .02 .10
108 Phil Watson CO .02 .10
109 Sid Smith .02 .10
110 Ron Stewart .02 .10
111 Rudy Migay .02 .10
112 Tod Sloan .05 .15
113 Bob Pulford .20 .50
114 Marc Reaume .05 .15
115 Jim Morrison .05 .15
116 Ted Kennedy .20 .50
117 Gerry James .07 .20
118 Brian Cullen .08 .25
119 Jim Thomson .02 .10
120 Barry Cullen .02 .10
121 Al MacNeil .05 .15
122 Gary Aldcorn .02 .10
123 Bob Baun .20 .50
124 Hugh Bolton .02 .10
125 George Armstrong .20 .50
126 Dick Duff .20 .50
127 Tim Horton .75 2.00
128 Ed Chadwick .20 .50
129 Billy Harris .15 .40
130 Mike Nykoluk .02 .10
131 Noel Price .02 .10
132 Ken Girard .02 .10
133 Howie Meeker .20 .50
134 Hap Day CO .08 .25
135 Jacques Plante AS .40 1.00
136 Doug Harvey AS .20 .50
137 Bill Gadsby AS .20 .50
138 Jean Beliveau AS .30 .75
139 Maurice Richard AS .40 1.00
140 Ted Lindsay AS .15 .40
141 Glenn Hall AS .20 .50
142 Red Kelly AS .20 .50
143 Tom Johnson AS .20 .50
144 Tod Sloan AS .05 .15
145 Gordie Howe AS .60 1.50
146 Bert Olmstead AS .08 .25
147 Earl Reibel AW .02 .10
Lady Byng
148 Doug Harvey AW .20 .50
Norris
149 Jean Beliveau AW .30 .75
150 Jean Beliveau AW .30 .75
151 Jacques Plante AW .40 1.00
152 Glenn Hall AW .20 .50
153 Sawchuk Picks Pocket .40 1.00
154 Action Shot .08 .25
155 Action Shot .08 .25
156 Beliveau Draws Crowd .30 .75
157 Beliveau in Close .30 .75
158 Leafs Besiege Hall .08 .25
159 Hall Makes The Save .08 .25
160 Howe Notches Another .60 1.50
161 Plante Stands Guard .40 1.00
162 Howe Outhustles Habs .60 1.50
163 Plante's Flying Save .40 1.00
164 Canadien's Big Line .08 .25
165 Gump Stops Leafs .08 .25
166 Action Shot .08 .25
167 Sawchuk Foils Duff .40 1.00
168 Sawchuk In Action .40 1.00
169 Vic Stasiuk SL .05 .15
170 George Sullivan SL .05 .15
171 Gordie Howe SL .60 1.50
172 Jean Beliveau SL .30 .75
173 Andy Bathgate SL .20 .50
174 Tod Sloan SL .05 .15
175 Stanley Cup .08 .25
176 Stanley Cup .08 .25
177 Stanley Cup .08 .25
178 Stanley Cup .08 .25
179 Checklist 1 .02 .10
180 Checklist 2 .02 .10

1994 Parkhurst Missing Link Autographs

The 1994 Parkhurst Missing Link Autograph set is comprised of six Hall of Famers. Randomly inserted in Missing Link packs, the cards are autographed on the front and numbered "X of 956" on the back. The cards are also numbered for set purposes A1-A6. The design is different from those found in the Missing Link issue. Card fronts are color, but do not contain the player's name (except for autograph) or team name. The backs provide a congratulatory note to the collector.
1 Gordie Howe 75.00 150.00
2 Maurice Richard 100.00 200.00
3 Bernie Geoffrion 40.00 80.00
4 Gump Worsley 40.00 100.00
5 Jean Beliveau 75.00 150.00
6 Frank Mahovlich 25.00 60.00

1994 Parkhurst Missing Link Future Stars

The six cards in this set were randomly inserted in both US and Canadian product and featured well-known players who had yet to make their mark in the league by the 1956-57 season, the year which is represented in this set. Cards are numbered with an "FS" prefix.
COMPLETE SET (6) 30.00 70.00
RANDOM INSERTS IN PACKS
FS1 Carl Brewer 3.00 8.00
FS2 Dave Keon 5.00 12.00
FS3 Stan Mikita 6.00 15.00
FS4 Eddie Shack 5.00 12.00
FS5 Frank Mahovlich 6.00 15.00
FS6 Charlie Hodge 5.00 12.00

1994 Parkhurst Missing Link Pop-Ups

These 12 die-cut cards were randomly inserted over two distribution channels: cards 1-6 in Canadian cases and 7-12 in American product. The cards feature the heroes of hockey's past in a design which approximates the style made famous by the 1936-37 O-Pee-Chee V304D set. The cards are created in such a way that they may be popped open for a 3-D effect; collectors are strongly urged not to follow this course of action unless you're not concerned about the card's value. Card backs contain brief personal information, as well as a wrap-up of career statistics. The cards are numbered with a P prefix in the top left corner. Only 1,000 of each card were circulated.
COMPLETE SET (12) 125.00 200.00
RANDOM INSERTS IN US PACKS
P1 Howie Morenz 20.00 50.00
P2 George Hainsworth 12.00 30.00
P3 Georges Vezina 20.00 50.00
P4 King Clancy 15.00 40.00
P5 Syl Apps 12.00 30.00
P6 Turk Broda 12.00 30.00
P7 Eddie Shore 25.00 50.00
P8 Bill Cook 10.00 25.00
P9 Woody Dumart 10.00 25.00
P10 Lester Patrick 12.00 30.00
P11 Doug Bentley 10.00 25.00
P12 Earl Seibert 10.00 25.00

1994 Parkhurst Tall Boys

This 180-card set recreates what might have been had the Parkhurst company issued a set of NHL player cards for the 1964-65 season. As the title suggests, the card size matches that of the 1964-65 Topps Tall Boys set (2 1/2" by 4 11/16"). Announced production was 1,964 cases for each of the US and Canadian hobby markets.
COMPLETE SET (180) 10.00 12.00
1 John Bucyk .15 .40
2 Murray Oliver .02 .10
3 Ted Green .05 .15
4 Tom Williams .02 .10
5 Dean Prentice .02 .10
6 Ed Westfall .02 .10
7 Orland Kurtenbach .02 .10
8 Reg Fleming .02 .10
9 Leo Boivin .05 .15
10 Bob McCord .02 .10
11 Bob Leiter .02 .10
12 Tom Johnson .08 .25
13 Bob Woytowich .02 .10
14 Ab McDonald .02 .10
15 Ed Johnston .08 .25
16 Forbes Kennedy .05 .15
17 Murray Balfour .02 .10
18 Wayne Cashman .05 .15
19 Don Awrey .02 .10
20 Gary Dornhoefer .05 .15
21 Ron Schock .02 .10
22 Milt Schmidt .20 .50
23 Ken Wharram .05 .15
24 Chico Maki .02 .10
25 Bobby Hull .75 2.00
26 Stan Mikita .30 .75
27 Doug Mohns .05 .15
28 Denis DeJordy .07 .20
29 Phil Esposito .20 .50
30 Elmer Vasko .02 .10
31 Pierre Pilote .08 .25
32 Glenn Hall .30 .75
33 Eric Nesterenko .02 .10
34 Doug Robinson .02 .10
35 Matt Ravlich .02 .10
36 John McKenzie .05 .15
37 Fred Stanfield .02 .10
38 Doug Jarrett .02 .10
39 Dennis Hull .07 .20
40 Al MacNeil .02 .10
41 Wayne Hillman .02 .10
42 Bill Hay .02 .10
43 Billy Reay .02 .10
44 Parker MacDonald .02 .10
45 Floyd Smith .02 .10
46 Gordie Howe 1.00 2.50
47 Bruce MacGregor .02 .10
48 Ron Murphy .02 .10
49 Doug Barkley .02 .10
50 Paul Henderson .05 .15
51 Pit Martin .05 .15
52 Al Langlois .02 .10
53 Roger Crozier .08 .25
54 Bill Gadsby .08 .25
55 Marcel Pronovost .15 .40
56 Alex Delvecchio .15 .40
57 Gary Bergman .02 .10
58 Norm Ullman .15 .40
59 Larry Jeffrey .02 .10
60 Lowell MacDonald .02 .10
61 Pete Goegan .02 .10
62 Andre Pronovost .05 .15
63 Warren Godfrey .02 .10
64 Ted Lindsay .15 .40
65 Sid Abel .15 .40
66 John Ferguson .05 .15
67 Henri Richard .20 .50
68 Dave Balon .02 .10
69 Noel Picard .02 .10
70 Claude Provost .05 .15
71 Claude Larose .02 .10
72 Jacques Laperriere .08 .25
73 Ralph Backstrom .05 .15
74 J.C. Tremblay .05 .15
75 Yvan Cournoyer .15 .40
76 Jean-Guy Talbot .05 .15
77 Gilles Tremblay .02 .10
78 Ted Harris .02 .10
79 Jim Roberts .02 .10
80 Red Berenson .05 .15
81 Gump Worsley .30 .75
82 Charlie Hodge .08 .25
83 Terry Harper .02 .10
84 Bobby Rousseau .02 .10
85 Jean Beliveau .60 1.50
86 Bill Hicke .02 .10
87 Toe Blake .20 .50
88 Don Marshall .05 .15
89 Jean Ratelle .15 .40
90 Vic Hadfield .02 .10
91 Earl Ingarfield .02 .10
92 Harry Howell .15 .40
93 Rod Seiling .02 .10
94 Dave Richardson .02 .10
95 Val Fonteyne .02 .10
96 Lou Angotti .02 .10
97 Arnie Brown .02 .10
98 Don Johns .02 .10
99 Jim Mikol .02 .10
100 Jacques Plante .75 2.00
101 Marcel Paille .05 .15
102 Jim Neilson .02 .10
103 Bob Nevin .02 .10
104 Rod Gilbert .15 .40
105 Phil Goyette .02 .10
106 Dick Duff .08 .25
107 Camille Henry .02 .10
108 Red Sullivan .02 .10
109 Kent Douglas .02 .10
110 Bob Pulford .05 .15
111 Dave Keon .20 .50
112 Don McKenney .02 .10
113 Pete Stemkowski .02 .10
114 Carl Brewer .05 .15
115 Allan Stanley .08 .25
116 Dickie Moore .15 .40
117 Eddie Shack .20 .50
118 Larry Hillman .02 .10
119 Terry Sawchuk .75 2.00
120 Bob Baun .08 .25
121 Brit Selby .02 .10
122 George Armstrong .20 .50
123 Jim Pappin .02 .10
124 Andy Bathgate .15 .40
125 Ron Ellis .02 .10
126 Billy Harris .02 .10
127 Red Kelly .07 .20
128 Ron Stewart .02 .10
129 Johnny Bower .20 .50
130 Frank Mahovlich .20 .50
131 Tim Horton .60 1.50
132 King Clancy .15 .40
133 Glenn Hall AS .20 .50
134 Pierre Pilote AS .08 .25
135 Tim Horton AS .30 .75
136 Bobby Hull AS .40 1.00
137 Ken Wharram AS .05 .15
138 Stan Mikita AS .20 .50
139 Charlie Hodge AS .05 .15
140 Jacques Laperriere AS .05 .15
141 Elmer Vasko AS .02 .10
142 Jean Beliveau AS .30 .75
143 Frank Mahovlich AS .15 .40
144 Gordie Howe AS .60 1.50
145 Pierre Pilote .08 .25
146 Jean Beliveau TW .30 .75
147 Stan Mikita TW .15 .40
148 Charlie Hodge .08 .25
149 Jacques Laperriere .08 .25
150 Ken Wharram .05 .15
151 1964 All Star Game .05 .15
152 Ratelle Invades Crease .08 .25
153 Center Ice Action .05 .15
154 G.Howe .60 1.50
T.Sawchuk IA
155 All Eyes on the Puck .05 .15
156 Terry Sawchuk IA .40 1.00
157 Crozier Makes The .05 .15
Stretch
158 Crozier Plays .08 .25
Center Field
159 Jean Beliveau IA .30 .75
160 Montreal's Speedy .05 .15
Rookie
161 Laperriere Wins Race .05 .15
162 Ellis Robbed by Habs .05 .15
163 Terry Sawchuk IA .40 1.00
164 Eddie Shack IA .15 .40
165 G.Hall .20 .50
R.Kelly IA
166 Hall Holds His .15 .40
Ground
167 Johnston Freezes .05 .15
Action
168 Ellis Robbed By .05 .15
Johnston
169 Murray Oliver LL .02 .10
170 Stan Mikita LL .20 .50
171 Gordie Howe LL .60 1.50
172 Jean Beliveau LL .30 .75
173 Phil Goyette LL .02 .10
174 Andy Bathgate LL .08 .25
175 Stanley Cup .02 .10
Semi-Finals
176 Stanley Cup .02 .10
Semi-Finals
177 G.Howe .60 1.50
T.Sawchuk SCF
178 Stanley Cup .08 .25
179 Checklist 1 .02 .10
180 Checklist 2 .02 .10

1994 Parkhurst Tall Boys Autographs

This 6-card set was randomly inserted throughout the production run of 1994 Parkhurst Tall Boys. The player's autograph appears in a white, oblong box along the bottom. A congratulatory note appears on the back. The cards are serially numbered out of 964 on the back.
COMPLETE SET (6) 350.00 500.00
A1 Rod Gilbert 25.00 50.00
A2 Yvan Cournoyer 40.00 60.00
A3 Bobby Hull 40.00 100.00
A4 Phil Esposito 60.00 100.00
A5 Gordie Howe 75.00 150.00
A6 Dave Keon 50.00 80.00

1994 Parkhurst Tall Boys Future Stars

The six cards in this set were randomly inserted in both US and Canadian product and featured well-known players who had yet to make their mark in the league by the 1964-65 season, the year which is represented in this set. Card backs include 1963-64 amateur stats, a report on the player's prospects in both French and English, and a merchandise offer. Cards are numbered with an "FS" prefix.
COMPLETE SET (6) 40.00 80.00
FS1 Jacques Lemaire 7.50 15.00
FS2 Gerry Cheevers 12.00 25.00
FS3 Ken Hodge 4.00 10.00
FS4 Bernie Parent 6.00 15.00
FS5 Rogatien Vachon 7.50 15.00
FS6 Derek Sanderson 10.00 20.00

1994 Parkhurst Tall Boys Greats

The 12 cards in this set were split over two distribution channels: cards 1-6 were randomly inserted in Canadian wax, while 7-12 were inserted in American. The cards feature legendary greats from the game's past. These oddly designed cards were the same size as the regular Tall Boys if maintained intact. A large, beige border surrounded the "real card", which approximates the appearance and size of the smaller 1951-52 Parkhurst issue. Although the cards are scored so that they may be punched out from the larger background, collectors are strongly advised against doing this. Card backs are blank. 1,000 copies of each of these cards were circulated.
COMPLETE SET (12) 175.00 250.00
1 Ace Bailey 15.00 30.00
2 Alex Levinsky 6.00 15.00
3 Babe Pratt 6.00 15.00
4 Elmer Lach 6.00 15.00
5 Maurice Richard 25.00 40.00
6 Bill Durnan 15.00 30.00
7 Frank Brimsek 15.00 30.00
8 Dit Clapper 8.00 20.00
9 Tiny Thompson 15.00 30.00
10 Bun Cook 6.00 15.00
11 Ching Johnson 8.00 20.00
12 Lionel Conacher 15.00 30.00

1994 Parkhurst Tall Boys Mail-Ins

Available through a mail-in offer, the cards in these three six-card sets measure 2 1/2" by 4 3/4". To obtain one of the sets, the collector sent in 10 "Tall Boy" wrappers and a check or money order for 12.95. The fronts feature color action cutouts on team color-coded backgrounds. The information on the beige backs varies depending on the particular series. At the bottom, each card carries its serial number out of a total of 1,964. The cards are arranged below as follows: All-Stars, Scoring Leaders, and Trophy Winners.
COMPLETE SET (18) 20.00 50.00
AS1 Roger Crozier 1.00 2.50
AS2 Pierre Pilote .75 2.00
AS3 Jacques Laperriere .75 2.00
AS4 Norm Ullman 1.00 2.50
AS5 Bobby Hull 4.00 10.00
AS6 Claude Provost .40 1.00
SL1 John Bucyk 1.00 2.50
SL2 Stan Mikita 1.50 4.00
SL3 Norm Ullman 1.00 2.50
SL4 Claude Provost .40 1.00
SL5 Rod Gilbert 1.00 2.50
SL6 Frank Mahovlich 1.50 4.00
TW1 Pierre Pilote .75 2.00

TW2 Bobby Hull 4.00 10.00
TW3 Stan Mikita 1.50 4.00
TW4 Terry Sawchuk 3.00 8.00
Johnny Bo
TW5 Roger Crozier 1.00 2.50
TW6 Bobby Hull 4.00 10.00

1994-95 Parkhurst

This 315-card set was issued in one series. Due to the NHL lockout, series two was not released; therefore, this set does not have a comprehensive player selection. Ten card packs retailed for 99 cents in 36 pack boxes. Sixteen-card jumbo packs also were produced. The design features a nearly full-bleed front, broken only in the lower right corner where a small gray bar features a silver foil hockey player icon. The green Parkhurst logo appears in an upper corner with player name running down either side. Card backs are unique in that they have full career stats and a player photo. Subsets included Rookie Standouts (270-294) and Parkie's Best (295-315). This set is noteworthy for being the last product domestically released by Upper Deck using the Parkhurst name. Although no second series was domestically released, a European-only product - Parkhurst SE - appears to have been the remnants of that planned issue. Prices for that set appear elsewhere.

*GOLD: 3X TO 8X BASIC CARDS
1 Anatoli Semenov .05 .15
2 Stephan Lebeau .05 .15
3 Stu Grimson .05 .15
4 Mikhail Shtalenkov RC .05 .15
5 Troy Loney .05 .15
6 Sean Hill .05 .15
7 Patrik Carnback .05 .15
8 John Lilley .05 .15
9 Tim Sweeney .05 .15
10 Maxim Bets .05 .15
11 Cam Neely .10 .25
12 Bryan Smolinski .05 .15
13 Ray Bourque .15 .40
14 Vincent Riendeau .05 .15
15 Al Iafrate .05 .15
16 Andrew McKim RC .05 .15
17 Glen Wesley .05 .15
18 Daniel Marois .05 .15
19 Jozef Stumpel .05 .15
20 Mariusz Czerkawski RC .10 .25
21 Alexander Mogilny .07 .20
22 Yuri Khmylev .05 .15
23 Donald Audette .05 .15
24 Dominik Hasek .20 .50
25 Randy Wood .05 .15
26 Brad May .05 .15
27 Wayne Presley .05 .15
28 Richard Smehlik .05 .15
29 Dale Hawerchuk .12 .30
30 Rob Ray .05 .15
31 Zarley Zalapski .05 .15
32 Michael Nylander .07 .20
33 Joe Nieuwendyk .10 .25
34 Robert Reichel .05 .15
35 Al MacInnis .07 .20
36 Andrei Trefilov .05 .15
37 Guy Larose .05 .15
38 Wes Walz .05 .15
39 Michel Petit .05 .15
40 James Patrick .05 .15
41 Ed Belfour .10 .25
42 Christian Ruuttu .05 .15
43 Eric Weinrich .05 .15
44 Joe Murphy .05 .15
45 Chris Chelios .10 .25
46 Jeff Shantz .05 .15
47 Gary Suter .05 .15
48 Paul Ysebaert .05 .15
49 Ivan Droppa .05 .15
50 Keith Carney .05 .15
51 Andy Moog .10 .25
52 Russ Courtnall .05 .15
53 Neal Broten .07 .20
54 Mike Craig .05 .15
55 Brent Gilchrist .05 .15
56 Pelle Eklund .05 .15
57 Richard Matvichuk .05 .15
58 Dave Gagner .07 .20
59 Mark Tinordi .05 .15
60 Paul Broten .05 .15
61 Nicklas Lidstrom .10 .25
62 Shawn Burr .05 .15
63 Paul Coffey .10 .25
64 Bob Essensa .05 .15
65 Dino Ciccarelli .07 .20
66 Slava Kozlov .07 .20
67 Keith Primeau .10 .25
68 Steve Chiasson .05 .15
69 Terry Carkner .05 .15
70 Martin Lapointe .05 .15
71 Bob Probert .05 .15
72 Bill Ranford .07 .20
73 Scott Thornton .05 .15
74 Doug Weight .07 .20
75 Shayne Corson .05 .15
76 Zdeno Ciger .05 .15
77 Adam Bennett .05 .15
78 Scott Pearson .05 .15
79 Brent Grieve RC .05 .15
80 Gordon Mark RC .05 .15
81 Shjon Podein .05 .15
82 Geoff Smith .05 .15
83 Bob Kudelski .05 .15
84 Andrei Lomakin .05 .15
85 Scott Mellanby .07 .20
86 Jesse Belanger .05 .15
87 Mark Fitzpatrick .07 .20
88 Peter Andersson .05 .15
89 Jody Hull .05 .15
90 Brent Severyn .05 .15
91 Jim Sandlak .05 .15
92 Pat Verbeek .07 .20
93 Ted Crowley .05 .15
94 Robert Petrovicky .05 .15
95 Geoff Sanderson .07 .20
96 Ted Drury .05 .15
97 Andrew Cassels .05 .15
98 Igor Chibirev .05 .15
99 Kevin Smyth .05 .15
100 Alexander Godynyuk .05 .15
101 Alexei Zhitnik .07 .20
102 Dixon Ward .05 .15
103 Wayne Gretzky .50 1.25
104 Jari Kurri .07 .20
105 Rob Blake .10 .25
106 Marty McSorley .05 .15
107 Pat Conacher .05 .15
108 Kevin Todd .05 .15
109 Robb Stauber .05 .15
110 Keith Redmond .07 .20
111 John LeClair .10 .25
112 Brian Bellows .07 .20
113 Patrick Roy .25 .60
114 Les Kuntar RC .05 .15
115 Vincent Damphousse .07 .20
116 Patrice Brisebois .05 .15
117 Pierre Sevigny .05 .15
118 Eric Desjardins .07 .20
119 Oleg Petrov .05 .15
120 Kevin Haller .05 .15
121 Christian Proulx RC .05 .15
122 Corey Millen .05 .15
123 Jaroslav Modry .05 .15
124 Valeri Zelepukin .05 .15
125 John MacLean .07 .20
126 Martin Brodeur .25 .60
127 Bill Guerin .07 .20
128 Bobby Holik .05 .15
129 Claude Lemieux .10 .25
130 Jason Smith .07 .20
131 Ken Daneyko .05 .15
132 Derek King .05 .15
133 Darius Kasparaitis .05 .15
134 Ray Ferraro .05 .15
135 Pierre Turgeon .07 .20
136 Ron Hextall .07 .20
137 Travis Green .07 .20
138 Joe Day .05 .15
139 David Volek .05 .15
140 Scott Lachance .05 .15
141 Dennis Vaske .05 .15
142 Alexei Kovalev .05 .15
143 Brian Noonan .05 .15
144 Sergei Zubov .05 .15
145 Craig MacTavish .05 .15
146 Steve Larmer .07 .20
147 Adam Graves .05 .15
148 Jeff Beukeboom .05 .15
149 Corey Hirsch .07 .20
150 Stephane Matteau .05 .15
151 Brian Leetch .10 .25
152 Mattias Norstrom .05 .15
153 Sylvain Turgeon .05 .15
154 Norm Maciver .05 .15
155 Scott Levins .05 .15
156 Derek Mayer .05 .15
157 Dave McLlwain .05 .15
158 Craig Billington .07 .20
159 Claude Boivin .05 .15
160 Troy Mallette .05 .15
161 Evgeny Davydov .05 .15
162 Dmitri Filimonov .05 .15
163 Dimitri Yushkevich .05 .15
164 Rob Zettler .05 .15
165 Mark Recchi .12 .30
166 Josef Beranek .05 .15
167 Rod Brind'Amour .07 .20
168 Yves Racine .05 .15
169 Dominic Roussel .07 .20
170 Brent Fedyk .05 .15
171 Bob Wilkie RC .05 .15
172 Kevin Dineen .05 .15
173 Shawn McEachern .05 .15
174 Jaromir Jagr .25 .60
175 Tomas Sandstrom .05 .15
176 Ron Francis .12 .30
177 Kevin Stevens .05 .15
178 Jim McKenzie .05 .15
179 Larry Murphy .07 .20
180 Joe Mullen .07 .20
181 Greg Hawgood .05 .15
182 Tom Barrasso .07 .20
183 Ulf Samuelsson .05 .15
184 Bob Bassen .05 .15
185 Mats Sundin .07 .20
186 Mike Ricci .05 .15
187 Iain Fraser .05 .15
188 Garth Butcher .07 .20
189 Jocelyn Thibault .10 .25
190 Valeri Kamensky .07 .20
191 Martin Rucinsky .05 .15
192 Ron Sutter .05 .15
193 Rene Corbet .05 .15
194 Reggie Savage .05 .15
195 Alexei Kasatonov .05 .15
196 Brendan Shanahan .12 .30
197 Phil Housley .07 .20
198 Jim Montgomery .05 .15
199 Curtis Joseph .15 .40
200 Craig Janney .07 .20
201 David Roberts .07 .20
202 Dave Mackey .05 .15
203 Peter Stastny .07 .20
204 Terry Hollinger RC .07 .20
205 Steve Duchesne .05 .15
206 Vitali Prokhorov .05 .15
207 Rob Gaudreau .05 .15
208 Sandis Ozolinsh .05 .15
209 Johan Garpenlov .05 .15
210 Todd Elik .05 .15
211 Sergei Makarov .05 .15
212 Jean-Francois Quintin .05 .15
213 Vyacheslav Butsayev .05 .15
214 Jimmy Waite .05 .15
215 Ulf Dahlen .05 .15
216 Andrei Nazarov .05 .15
217 Denis Savard .12 .30
218 Brent Gretzky .05 .15
219 Petr Klima .05 .15
220 Chris Gratton .05 .15
221 Brian Bradley .05 .15
222 Adam Creighton .05 .15
223 Shawn Chambers .05 .15
224 Rob Zamuner .05 .15
225 Daren Puppa .07 .20
226 Mikael Andersson .05 .15
227 Dave Ellett .05 .15
228 Mike Gartner .10 .25
229 Felix Potvin .10 .25
230 Yanic Perreault .05 .15
231 Nikolai Borschevsky .05 .15
232 Dmitri Mironov .05 .15
233 Todd Gill .05 .15
234 Eric Lacroix RC .10 .25
235 Kent Manderville .05 .15
236 Chris Govedaris .05 .15
237 Frank Bialowas RC .05 .15
238 Kirk McLean .07 .20
239 Jimmy Carson .05 .15
240 Geoff Courtnall .05 .15
241 Trevor Linden .07 .20
242 Murray Craven .05 .15
243 Bret Hedican .05 .15
244 Jeff Brown .05 .15
245 Mike Peca .07 .20
246 Yevgeny Namestnikov .05 .15
247 Nathan Lafayette .05 .15
248 Shawn Antoski .05 .15
249 Sergio Momesso .10 .25
250 Mike Ridley .05 .15
251 Peter Bondra .07 .20
252 Dimitri Khristich .05 .15
253 Dave Poulin .05 .15
254 Dale Hunter .05 .15
255 Rick Tabaracci .07 .20
256 Kelly Miller .05 .15
257 John Slaney .05 .15
258 Todd Krygier .05 .15
259 Kevin Hatcher .05 .15
260 Alexei Zhamnov .07 .20
261 Dallas Drake .05 .15
262 Dave Manson .05 .15
263 Thomas Steen .05 .15
264 Keith Tkachuk .10 .25
265 Russ Romaniuk .05 .15
266 Michal Grosek RC .05 .15
267 Nelson Emerson .05 .15
268 Michael O'Neill RC .05 .15
269 Kris King .05 .15
270 Teppo Numminen .05 .15
271 Jason Arnott RS .07 .20
272 Mikael Renberg RS .07 .20
273 Alexei Yashin RS .10 .25
274 Chris Pronger RS .10 .25
275 Jocelyn Thibault RS .10 .25
276 Bryan Smolinski RS .05 .15
277 Derek Plante RS .05 .15
278 Martin Brodeur RS .25 .60
279 Jim Dowd .05 .15
280 Iain Fraser .05 .15
281 Pat Peake .05 .15
282 Chris Gratton RS .05 .15
283 Chris Osgood RS .15 .40
284 Jesse Belanger .05 .15
285 Alexandre Daigle RS .05 .15
286 Robert Lang .05 .15
287 Markus Naslund .10 .25
288 Trevor Kidd .07 .20
289 Jeff Shantz .05 .15
290 Jaroslav Modry .05 .15
291 Oleg Petrov .05 .15
292 Scott Levins .05 .15
293 Jozef Stumpel .05 .15
294 Rob Niedermayer RS .07 .20
295 Brent Gretzky .05 .15
296 Mario Lemieux PB .40 1.00
297 Pavel Bure PB .10 .25
298 Brendan Shanahan PB .12 .30
299 Steve Yzerman PB .25 .60
300 Teemu Selanne PB .20 .50
301 Eric Lindros PB .10 .25
302 Jeremy Roenick PB .20 .50
303 Dave Andreychuk .10 .25
304 Ray Bourque PB .15 .40
305 Sergei Fedorov PB .15 .40
306 Wayne Gretzky PB .50 1.25
307 Adam Graves PB .05 .15
308 Mike Modano PB .15 .40
309 Brett Hull PB .20 .50
310 Pat LaFontaine PB .10 .25
311 Adam Oates PB .10 .25
312 Patrick Roy PB .25 .60
313 Doug Gilmour PB .12 .30
314 Jaromir Jagr PB .25 .60
315 Mark Recchi PB .12 .30

1994-95 Parkhurst Gold

The 315 cards in this parallel version of the '94-95 Parkhurst set were issued 1:47 packs. A gold foil hockey player icon and the addition of the word "Parkie", written in gold foil distinguish this set from the regular Parkhurst set. The Rookie Standout and Parkie's Best subset gold cards were made available for the European marketplace by means other than normal pack distribution, and a sufficient amount of product made its way back into the North American marketplace.

*GOLD: 6X TO 15X BASIC CARDS

1994-95 Parkhurst Crash the Game Green

The 28 cards in this set were randomly inserted into Parkhurst product at a rate of 1:23 packs. There were three variations of each card in this set. Each of the three foil logo colors reflected the different distribution method. Red foil indicated Canadian packaging, blue foil U.S. retail and green foil U.S. hobby. The cards were numbered on the back with a corresponding prefix of C, R, or H. Since the cards were created to be used as an interactive game, the backs contain the rules in extremely fine-print legalese in both English and French, as well as two game dates. If the team featured on the front won on one or both of those dates, the card could be redeemed for a specially foiled set. Unfortunately, the NHL lockout of 1994 prevented the games from being played. As a result, Upper Deck declared all cards winners, enabling each to be redeemed for a 28-card gold-foil version of the set by mail. The expiration date for the exchange was June 30th, 1995.

COMPLETE SET (28) 20.00 40.00
*GOLD: .2X TO .5X GREEN
*BLUE: .4X TO 1X GREEN
*RED: .4X TO 1X GREEN
H1 Stephan Lebeau .25 .60
H2 Ray Bourque .60 1.50
H3 Pat LaFontaine .40 1.00
H4 Joe Nieuwendyk .30 .75
H5 Jeremy Roenick .40 1.00
H6 Mike Modano .50 1.25
H7 Sergei Fedorov .75 2.00
H8 Jason Arnott .30 .75
H9 John Vanbiesbrouck .40 1.00
H10 Geoff Sanderson .25 .60
H11 Wayne Gretzky 2.50 6.00
H12 Patrick Roy 2.00 5.00
H13 Scott Stevens .30 .75
H14 Pierre Turgeon .30 .75
H15 Adam Graves .30 .75
H16 Alexei Yashin .30 .75
H17 Eric Lindros .75 2.00
H18 Mario Lemieux 2.00 5.00
H19 Joe Sakic .75 2.00
H20 Brett Hull .50 1.25
H21 Sandis Ozolinsh .30 .75
H22 Chris Gratton .25 .60
H23 Doug Gilmour .40 1.00
H24 Pavel Bure 1.00 2.50
H25 Joe Juneau .30 .75
H26 Teemu Selanne .40 1.00
H27 Mark Messier 1.25 3.00
Eastern
H28 Wayne Gretzky 4.00 10.00
Western

1994-95 Parkhurst Vintage

The 90 cards in this set were included one per Parkhurst pack and two per jumbo pack. They are printed on heavy white card stock with a design that hearkens back to the style of Parkhurst issues of the '50s and '60s. The player photo is cut out and placed on a white and tan background. The player's name appears in a black bar on the lower portion of the card, alongside the set logo. The card backs are an unfinished cardboard and feature professional statistics, biography and a "Did You Know" section containing interesting trivia. This trivia did not apply to the player pictured. The cards were numbered with a "V" prefix.

V1 Dominik Hasek .30 .75
V2 Mike Modano .25 .60
V3 Shayne Corson .10 .25
V4 Kirk Muller .10 .25
V5 Mike Richter .15 .40
V6 Mario Lemieux .60 1.50
V7 Sandis Ozolinsh .10 .25
V8 Dave Ellett .10 .25
V9 Dave Manson .10 .25
V10 Terry Yake .10 .25
V11 Craig Simpson .10 .25
V12 Paul Cavallini .10 .25
V13 John Vanbiesbrouck .12 .30
V14 Gilbert Dionne .10 .25
V15 Brian Leetch .15 .40
V16 Martin Straka .10 .25
V17 Curtis Joseph .25 .60
V18 Pavel Bure .15 .40
V19 Garry Valk .10 .25
V20 Theo Fleury .15 .40
V21 Brent Gilchrist .10 .25
V22 Rob Niedermayer .12 .30
V23 Vincent Damphousse .12 .30
V24 Alexei Kovalev .10 .25
V25 Rick Tocchet .12 .30
V26 Steve Duchesne .10 .25
V27 Jiri Slegr .10 .25
V28 Patrick Carnback .10 .25
V29 Gary Roberts .10 .25
V30 Derian Hatcher .10 .25
V31 Jesse Belanger .10 .25
V32 Mathieu Schneider .10 .25
V33 Mark Messier .15 .40
V34 Joe Sakic .30 .75
V35 Brett Hull .30 .75
V36 Martin Gelinas .10 .25
V37 Maxim Bets .10 .25
V38 Joel Otto .10 .25
V39 Sergei Fedorov .25 .60
V40 Chris Pronger .15 .40
V41 Scott Stevens .15 .40
V42 Alexandre Daigle .10 .25
V43 Owen Nolan .15 .40
V44 Petr Nedved .12 .30
V45 Jeff Brown .10 .25
V46 Adam Oates .15 .40
V47 Robert Reichel .10 .25
V48 Slava Kozlov .12 .30
V49 Geoff Sanderson .12 .30
V50 Stephane Richer .12 .30
V51 Sylvain Turgeon .10 .25
V52 Mike Ricci .10 .25
V53 Roman Hamrlik .12 .30
V54 Kevin Hatcher .10 .25
V55 Mariusz Czerkawski .15 .40
V56 Tony Amonte .12 .30
V57 Steve Yzerman .40 1.00
V58 Andrew Cassels .10 .25
V59 Claude Lemieux .15 .40
V60 Derek Mayer .10 .25
V61 Jocelyn Thibault .15 .40
V62 Brent Gretzky .10 .25
V63 Pat Peake .10 .25
V64 Cam Neely .15 .40
V65 Jeremy Roenick .30 .75
V66 Keith Primeau .15 .40
V67 Luc Robitaille .15 .40
V68 Steve Thomas .10 .25
V69 Eric Lindros .15 .40
V70 Pat Falloon .10 .25
V71 Brian Bradley .10 .25
V72 Kelly Miller .10 .25
V73 Pat LaFontaine .15 .40
V74 Gary Suter .10 .25
V75 Bill Ranford .12 .30
V76 Tony Granato .10 .25
V77 Vladimir Malakhov .10 .25
V78 Mikael Renberg .12 .30
V79 Arturs Irbe .12 .30
V80 Doug Gilmour .20 .50
V81 Teemu Selanne .30 .75
V82 Dale Hawerchuk .20 .50
V83 Eric Weinrich .10 .25
V84 Jason Arnott .12 .30
V85 Rob Blake .15 .40
V86 Ray Ferraro .10 .25
V87 Garry Galley .10 .25
V88 Igor Larionov .10 .25
V89 Dave Andreychuk .15 .40
V90 Dallas Drake .10 .25

1996 Parkhurst Beehive Promos

These cards were available as part of a card show wrapper redemption offer. The five Howe cards were available at the 1996 National in Anaheim in exchange for Parkhurst '66-67 wrappers. The Orr promos were available at several major shows.

COMMON BOBBY ORR 4.00 10.00
COMMON GORDIE HOWE 3.00 8.00

2001-02 Parkhurst

Printed on green foil stock, this 400-card set was originally released in late-November 2001 as a 300 card base set with 50 short prints. Cards 301-400 were available in packs of BAP Update. Cards 251-300 were serial-numbered to 500 copies each.

COMP.SERIES 1 w/o SP's (250) 20.00 50.00
1 Paul Kariya .30 .75
2 Patrik Stefan .20 .50
3 Jeremy Roenick .25 .60
4 Patrick Roy .60 1.50
5 Jarome Iginla .25 .60
6 Jeff O'Neill .15 .40
7 Sergei Samsonov .20 .50
8 Peter Forsberg .30 .75
9 Scott Gomez .20 .50
10 Mike Modano .40 1.00
11 Brendan Shanahan .30 .75
12 Jean-Sebastien Giguere .20 .50
13 Pavel Bure .30 .75
14 Zigmund Palffy .25 .60
15 Marian Gaborik .40 1.00
16 Pavol Demitra .30 .75
17 Alexei Kovalev .20 .50
18 Patrik Elias .25 .60
19 Keith Tkachuk .25 .60
20 Mats Sundin .25 .60
21 Marian Hossa .20 .50
22 Mark Recchi .30 .75
23 John Madden .20 .50
24 Mario Lemieux .75 2.00
25 Teemu Selanne .50 1.25
26 Joe Sakic .40 1.00
27 Brad Richards .25 .60
28 Brian Leetch .25 .60
29 Markus Naslund .25 .60
30 Peter Bondra .25 .60
31 Steve Yzerman .75 2.00
32 Michael Peca .20 .50
33 Bill Guerin .25 .60
34 Jaromir Jagr .60 1.50
35 Alexei Yashin .20 .50
36 Theo Fleury .30 .75
37 Al MacInnis .25 .60
38 Milan Hejduk .20 .50
39 Martin Biron .20 .50
40 Brad Isbister .15 .40
41 Nicklas Lidstrom .25 .60
42 Rick DiPietro .20 .50
43 Roberto Luongo .40 1.00
44 Tim Connolly .15 .40
45 Manny Fernandez .20 .50
46 Scott Niedermayer .25 .60
47 David Legwand .20 .50
48 Petr Sykora .15 .40
49 Ryan Smyth .20 .50
50 Mark Messier .40 1.00
51 Dave Tanabe .15 .40
52 Keith Primeau .20 .50
53 Teppo Numminen .15 .40
54 Milan Kraft .15 .40
55 Owen Nolan .25 .60
56 Alexander Mogilny .20 .50
57 Brent Johnson .20 .50
58 Curtis Joseph .25 .60
59 Felix Potvin .40 1.00
60 Olaf Kolzig .25 .60
61 Eric Lindros .40 1.00
62 Pierre Turgeon .25 .60
63 Martin Straka .15 .40
64 Maxim Afinogenov .15 .40
65 Oleg Saprykin .15 .40
66 Shane Willis .15 .40
67 Brett Hull .30 .75
68 Alex Tanguay .20 .50
69 Marc Denis .20 .50
70 Ed Belfour .25 .60
71 Roman Cechmanek .20 .50
72 Tommy Salo .20 .50
73 Rob Blake .25 .60
74 Jose Theodore .25 .60
75 Henrik Sedin .25 .60
76 Tony Amonte .20 .50
77 Scott Hartnell .25 .60
78 Brian Rafalski .15 .40
79 Joe Thornton .30 .75
80 Patrick Marleau .25 .60
81 Daniel Alfredsson .25 .60
82 Simon Gagne .25 .60
83 Patrick Lalime .20 .50
84 Johan Hedberg .20 .50
85 Adam Oates .25 .60
86 Chris Pronger .20 .50
87 Vincent Lecavalier .20 .50
88 Tomas Kaberle .15 .40
89 Daniel Sedin .25 .60
90 Martin Lapointe .15 .40
91 Chris Drury .20 .50
92 Dominik Hasek .40 1.00
93 Evgeni Nabokov .20 .50
94 Ed Jovanovski .20 .50
95 John LeClair .25 .60
96 Sergei Fedorov .40 1.00
97 Martin Havlat .20 .50
98 Martin Brodeur .50 1.25
99 Jason Arnott .20 .50
100 Mike Comrie .20 .50
101 Petr Nedved .20 .50
102 Ray Ferraro .15 .40
103 Miroslav Satan .20 .50
104 Rod Brind'Amour .25 .60
105 Ron Tugnutt .20 .50
106 Oleg Tverdovsky .15 .40
107 Anson Carter .20 .50
108 Wes Walz .15 .40
109 Andrei Markov .25 .60
110 Mike Dunham .20 .50
111 Eric Desjardins .20 .50
112 Radek Dvorak .20 .50
113 Pavel Kubina .15 .40
114 Gary Roberts .15 .40
115 Andrew Cassels .15 .40
116 Vitali Vishnevski .15 .40
117 Byron Dafoe .20 .50
118 Chris Gratton .15 .40
119 Marc Savard .15 .40
120 Shawn McEachern .15 .40
121 Jocelyn Thibault .20 .50
122 Joe Nieuwendyk .25 .60
123 Janne Niinimaa .15 .40
124 Shane Doan .20 .50
125 Willie Mitchell .15 .40
126 Glen Murray .20 .50
127 Scott Walker .15 .40
128 Geoff Sanderson .15 .40
129 Kenny Jonsson .15 .40
130 Radek Bonk .15 .40
131 Brad Stuart .15 .40
132 Scott Young .15 .40
133 Brendan Morrison .20 .50
134 Sergei Gonchar .15 .40
135 Jonathan Girard .15 .40
136 Arturs Irbe .20 .50
137 Chris Herperger .15 .40
138 Brenden Morrow .20 .50
139 Sergei Zubov .20 .50
140 Lubomir Visnovsky .15 .40
141 Aaron Miller .15 .40
142 Ossi Vaananen .15 .40
143 Saku Koivu .25 .60
144 Sean Burke .15 .40
145 Darryl Sydor .15 .40
146 Chris Chelios .25 .60
147 Brian Savage .15 .40
148 Wade Redden .15 .40
149 Derian Hatcher .15 .40
150 Igor Larionov .25 .60
151 Steve Sullivan .15 .40
152 Michal Handzus .15 .40
153 Ron Francis .30 .75
154 David Vyborny .15 .40
155 Manny Legace .20 .50
156 Jeff Friesen .15 .40
157 Jeff Hackett .20 .50
158 Marian Cisar .15 .40
159 Mike York .15 .40
160 Nikolai Antropov .15 .40
161 Trevor Linden .25 .60
162 Bryan Smolinski .15 .40
163 Janne Laukkanen .15 .40
164 Dan Cloutier .20 .50
165 Scott Stevens .25 .60
166 Jani Hurme .20 .50
167 Fredrik Modin .15 .40
168 Steven Reinprecht .15 .40
169 Kevyn Adams .15 .40
170 Richard Zednik .20 .50
171 Viktor Kozlov .15 .40
172 Cliff Ronning .15 .40
173 Mariusz Czerkawski .15 .40
174 Todd Bertuzzi .25 .60
175 Vincent Damphousse .20 .50
176 Roman Hamrlik .15 .40
177 Sandis Ozolinsh .15 .40
178 Mike Richter .25 .60
179 Stu Barnes .20 .50
180 Patric Kjellberg .15 .40
181 Tomas Holmstrom .15 .40
182 Sergei Brylin .15 .40
183 Magnus Arvedson .15 .40
184 Sami Kapanen .15 .40
185 Niklas Sundstrom .20 .50
186 Todd Marchant .15 .40
187 Mark Parrish .15 .40
188 Adam Foote .20 .50
189 Peter Schaefer .15 .40
190 Mike Ricci .20 .50
191 Alexei Zhamnov .20 .50
192 Dainius Zubrus .15 .40
193 Espen Knutsen .15 .40
194 Shean Donovan .15 .40
195 Bobby Holik .15 .40
196 Tom Poti .15 .40
197 Marcus Ragnarsson .15 .40
198 Jozef Stumpel .15 .40
199 Martin Rucinsky .15 .40
200 Matt Davidson RC .15 .40
201 Jan Bulis .15 .40
202 Matt Pettinger .15 .40
203 Rob Zamuner .15 .40
204 Chris Osgood .25 .60
205 Dan Hinote .15 .40
206 Travis Green .15 .40
207 Joe Juneau .20 .50
208 Mikael Renberg .15 .40
209 Zdeno Ciger .15 .40
210 Jochen Hecht .15 .40
211 Jan Hlavac .15 .40
212 Jeff Halpern .15 .40
213 Tom Barrasso .20 .50
214 Bill Muckalt .15 .40
215 Luc Robitaille .25 .60
216 Jason Wiemer .15 .40
217 Deron Quint .15 .40
218 Jyrki Lumme .15 .40
219 Andreas Dackell .15 .40
220 Tomi Kallio .15 .40
221 Roman Turek .20 .50
222 Taylor Pyatt .15 .40
223 Richard Jackman .20 .50
224 Michael Nylander .15 .40
225 Brian Pothier RC .15 .40
226 Slava Kozlov .20 .50
227 Kim Johnsson .15 .40
228 J-P Dumont .15 .40
229 Marty Reasoner .15 .40
230 Dimitri Kalinin .15 .40
231 Damian Rhodes .20 .50
232 Jason Allison .20 .50
233 Doug Weight .25 .60
234 Yanic Perreault .15 .40
235 Eric Daze .20 .50
236 Brian Campbell .15 .40
237 Valeri Bure .15 .40
238 Adam Deadmarsh .20 .50
239 Robert Reichel .15 .40
240 Anders Eriksson .15 .40
241 Nikolai Khabibulin .25 .60
242 Sean O'Donnell .15 .40
243 Bob Essensa .20 .50
244 Josef Vasicek .15 .40
245 Donald Audette .15 .40
246 Steve Heinze .15 .40
247 Bryan Berard .20 .50
248 Ville Nieminen .15 .40
249 Eric Weinrich .15 .40
250 Adam Graves .20 .50
251 Jesse Boulerice 2.00 5.00
252 Marko Kiprusoff 2.00 5.00
253 Ivan Ciernik RC 2.00 5.00
254 Pavel Datsyuk RC 20.00 40.00
255 Jaroslav Bednar RC 2.00 5.00
256 Andreas Salomonsson RC 2.00 5.00
257 Mike Ribeiro 2.50 6.00
258 Darcy Hordichuk 2.00 5.00
259 Chris Neil RC 2.50 6.00
260 Rostislav Klesla 2.00 5.00
261 Kristian Huselius RC 3.00 8.00
262 Brian Sutherby RC 2.00 5.00
263 Jiri Dopita RC 2.00 5.00
264 Radek Martinek RC 2.00 5.00
265 Barrett Heisten 2.00 5.00
266 Krystofer Kolanos RC 2.00 5.00
267 Pascal Dupuis RC 3.00 8.00
268 Andreas Lilja 2.00 5.00
269 Chris Mason 2.00 5.00
270 Mathieu Garon 2.50 6.00
271 Andrew Raycroft 2.50 6.00
272 Jeff Jillson RC 2.00 5.00
273 Jiri Bicek 2.00 5.00
274 Niklas Hagman RC 2.50 6.00
275 Pavel Brendl 2.00 5.00
276 Stephen Peat 2.00 5.00
277 Sascha Goc 2.00 5.00
278 Nick Boynton 2.00 5.00
279 Timo Parssinen RC 2.50 6.00
280 Mika Noronen 2.00 5.00
281 Scott Clemmensen RC 2.00 5.00
282 Dan Blackburn RC 2.50 6.00
283 Nikita Alexeev RC 2.00 5.00
284 Vaclav Nedorost RC 2.00 5.00
285 Ilja Bryzgalov RC 5.00 12.00
286 Dany Heatley 3.00 8.00
287 Niko Kapanen RC 3.00 8.00
288 Rick Berry 2.00 5.00
289 Mark Bell 2.00 5.00
290 Kamil Piros RC 2.00 5.00
291 Maxime Ouellet 3.00 8.00
292 Kris Beech 2.00 5.00
293 Miikka Kiprusoff 3.00 8.00
294 Martti Jarventie 2.00 5.00
295 Ilya Kovalchuk RC 15.00 40.00
296 Nick Schultz RC 2.00 5.00
297 Bryan Allen 2.00 5.00
298 Josef Boumedienne RC 2.00 5.00
299 Jason Williams 2.00 5.00
300 Daniel Tjarnqvist 2.00 5.00
301 Frederic Cassivi RC .60 1.50
302 Mark Hartigan RC .60 1.50
303 Pasi Nurminen RC .60 1.50
304 Ivan Huml RC .60 1.50
305 Zdenek Kutlak RC .60 1.50
306 Ales Kotalik RC 1.25 3.00
307 Jukka Hentunen RC .60 1.50
308 Erik Cole RC 1.25 3.00
309 Tyler Arnason RC .75 2.00
310 Jaroslav Obsut RC .60 1.50
311 Riku Hahl RC .60 1.50
312 Martin Spanhel RC .60 1.50
313 Andrej Nedorost RC .60 1.50
314 Ty Conklin RC 1.00 2.50
315 Jason Chimera RC .60 1.5
316 Kyle Rossiter RC .60 1.5
317 Lukas Krajicek RC .60 1.5
318 Stephen Weiss RC 1.50 4.0
319 Tony Virta RC .60 1.5
320 Marcel Hossa RC 1.00 2.5
321 Olivier Michaud RC 1.00 2.5
322 Henrik Tallinder RC .60 1.5
323 Martin Erat RC 1.00 2.5
324 Nathan Perrott RC .60 1.5
325 Pavel Skrbek RC .60 1.5
326 Robert Schnabel RC .60 1.5
327 Christian Berglund .75 2.0
328 Stanislav Gron RC .60 1.5
329 Raffi Torres RC 1.00 2.5
330 Mikael Samuelsson RC .75 2.0
331 Chris Bala RC .60 1.5
332 Josh Langfeld RC .60 1.5
333 Martin Prusek RC .60 1.5
334 Sean Avery RC .60 1.5
335 Neil Little RC .60 1.5
336 Tomas Divisek RC .75 2.0
337 Vaclav Pletka RC .60 1.5
338 Guillaume Lefebvre RC .60 1.5
339 Branko Radivojevic RC .60 1.5
340 Trent Hunter RC 1.25 3.0
341 Jan Lasak RC .60 1.5
342 Tom Kostopoulos RC .60 1.5
343 Hannes Hyvonen RC .60 1.5
344 Shane Endicott RC .60 1.5
345 Evgeny Konstantinov RC .60 1.5
346 Martin Cibak RC .60 1.5
347 Karel Pilar RC .60 1.5
348 Sebastien Centomo RC .60 1.5
349 Mike Farrell RC .60 1.5
350 Sebastien Charpentier RC .60 1.5
351 Radim Vrbata .20 .5
352 Andy McDonald .20 .5
353 J.P. Vigier .20 .5
354 Donald Brashear .20 .5
355 Adrian Aucoin .20 .5
356 Stephane Richer .20 .5
357 Byron Ritchie .20 .5
358 Sergei Berezin .20 .5
359 Cliff Ronning .20 .5
360 Tony Hrkac .20 .5
361 Andre Roy .20 .5
362 Shjon Podein .20 .5
363 Andrei Nazarov .20 .5
364 Marty McInnis .25 .6
365 Petr Tenkrat .20 .5
366 Trevor Letowski .20 .5
367 Randy Robitaille .20 .5
368 Kim Johnsson .20 .5
369 Jozef Stumpel .20 .5
370 P.J. Stock .20 .5
371 Dean McAmmond .20 .5
372 Steve Thomas .20 .5
373 Darius Kasparaitis .20 .5
374 Mike Sillinger .20 .5
375 Jason Arnott .25 .6
376 Alex Auld .20 .5
377 Mike York .20 .5
378 Pierre Dagenais .20 .5
379 Andrew Brunette .20 .5
380 Sergei Zholtok .20 .5
381 Donald Audette .20 .5
382 Doug Gilmour .40 1.0
383 Andy Delmore .20 .5
384 Martin Rucinsky .20 .5
385 Jamie Langenbrunner .20 .5
386 Joe Nieuwendyk .30 .7
387 John Vanbiesbrouck .30 .7
388 Shawn Bates .20 .5
389 Matthew Barnaby .20 .5
390 Pavel Bure .40 1.0
391 Tom Poti .20 .5
392 Zdeno Chara .30 .7
393 Adam Oates .30 .7
394 Marty Murray .20 .5
395 Brian Savage .20 .5
396 Daniil Markov .20 .5
397 Tom Barrasso .25 .6
398 Jan Hlavac .20 .5
399 Trevor Linden .30 .7
400 Ivan Ciernik .20 .5

2001-02 Parkhurst Gold

This 300-card set paralleled the base 250 cards but carried gold foil in place of the silver. Cards were numbered out of 50 on the card backs.

*GOLD/50: 4X TO 10X BASIC CARDS

2001-02 Parkhurst Silver

This 300-card set paralleled the first 100 base cards but carried silver foil in place of the silver. Cards were numbered out of 500 on the card backs.

*SILVER/500: 1.5X TO 4X BASIC CARDS
50 Mark Messier 2.00 5.0

2001-02 Parkhurst Autographs

This 59-card set featured autographs of retired greats. Each card was green in color with a full-color player photo in the center of the card. Underneath the photo was a light area that the featured player signed. Print runs are listed below for each card and cards with less than 25 copies are not priced due to scarcity. Cards PA41-PA59 were only available in BAP Update packs.

PA1 Frank Mahovlich/20 30.00 80.0
PA2 Glenn Hall/90 15.00 40.0
PA3 Jean Beliveau/60 30.00 80.0
PA4 Frank Mahovlich/20 30.00 80.0
PA5 Henri Richard/90 12.00 30.0
PA6 Jean Beliveau/60 25.00 60.0
PA7 Milt Schmidt/90 12.00 30.0
PA8 Elmer Lach/90 12.00 30.0
PA9 Woody Dumart/20 75.00 150.0
PA10 Chuck Rayner/90 25.00 60.0
PA11 Henri Richard/90 15.00 40.0
PA12 Gordie Howe/20 150.00 300.0
PA13 Phil Esposito/60 20.00 50.0
PA14 Bernie Geoffrion/60 25.00 60.0
PA15 Dollard St.Laurent/90 12.00 30.0
PA16 Dickie Moore/90 15.00 40.0
PA17 Jean-Guy Talbot/90 12.00 30.0
PA18 Bill Gadsby/90 15.00 40.0
PA19 Lanny McDonald/80 12.00 30.0
PA20 Gilbert Perreault/60 20.00 50.0
PA21 Johnny Bucyk/90 12.00 30.0
PA22 Dale Hawerchuk/80 12.00 30.0
PA23 Mike Gartner/80 12.00 30.0
PA24 Johnny Bower/90 15.00 40.0
PA25 Butch Bouchard/90 15.00 40.0
PA26 Gordie Howe/20 125.00 250.0
PA27 Jean Beliveau/60 40.00 100.0
PA28 Guy Lafleur/60 40.00 100.0
PA29 Mike Bossy/80 15.00 40.0
PA30 Bryan Trottier/80 12.00 30.0
PA31 Marcel Dionne/60 12.00 30.0
PA32 Jari Kurri/80 30.00 80.0
PA33 Gerry Cheevers/90 15.00 40.0
PA34 Dino Ciccarelli/90 12.00 30.0

35 Stan Mikita/60 25.00 60.00
36 Gordie Howe/20 200.00 300.00
37 Tony Esposito/60 25.00 60.00
38 Gump Worsley/90 15.00 40.00
39 Ted Lindsay/90 12.00 30.00
40 Red Kelly/90 15.00 40.00
41 Joe Watson/90 12.00 30.00
42 Bobby Clarke/90 15.00 40.00
43 Dave Schultz/90 12.00 30.00
44 Tiger Williams/90 12.00 30.00
45 Serge Savard/90 12.00 30.00
46 Jacques Laperriere/90 12.00 30.00
47 Peter Mahovlich/90 12.00 30.00
48 Denis Potvin/90 10.00 25.00
49 Cam Neely/90 15.00 40.00
50 Ron Hextall/90 12.00 30.00
51 Steve Shutt/90 12.00 30.00
52 Yvan Cournoyer/90 15.00 40.00
53 Bill Barber/90 10.00 25.00
54 Reggie Leach/90 10.00 25.00
55 Dennis Hull/90 12.00 30.00
56 Bernie Parent/90 15.00 40.00
57 Bob Nystrom/90 10.00 25.00
58 Guy Lapointe/90 12.00 30.00
59 Larry Robinson/90 12.00 30.00

2001-02 Parkhurst 500 Goal Scorers

is 27-card set featured players who hit the milestone 500 goals in their career. Each card featured an ion photo of the given player alongside a game-rn swatch of his jersey on the card front. Print runs listed below. The Shanahan and Francis cards were ilable in random packs of BAP Update only.

S1 Bobby Hull/30 50.00 120.00
S2 Gordie Howe/30 125.00 250.00
S3 Marcel Dionne/30 25.00 60.00
S4 Phil Esposito/30 25.00 60.00
S5 Mike Gartner/80 12.00 30.00
S6 Mark Messier/30 40.00 100.00
S7 Steve Yzerman/30 100.00 200.00
S8 Brett Hull/30 30.00 80.00
S9 Mario Lemieux/30 125.00 250.00
S10 Dino Ciccarelli/80 10.00 25.00
S11 Jari Kurri/80 10.00 25.00
S12 Luc Robitaille/30 25.00 60.00
S13 Mike Bossy/30 25.00 60.00
S14 Dave Andreychuk/80 10.00 25.00
S15 Guy Lafleur/30 30.00 80.00
S16 John Bucyk/80 10.00 25.00
S17 Maurice Richard/80 100.00 250.00
S18 Stan Mikita/80 10.00 25.00
S19 Frank Mahovlich/80 20.00 50.00
S20 Bryan Trottier/80 12.50 30.00
S21 Dale Hawerchuk/80 10.00 25.00
S22 Gilbert Perreault/80 10.00 25.00
S23 Jean Beliveau/80 50.00 120.00
S24 Pat Verbeek/80 10.00 25.00
S25 Michel Goulet/80 8.00 20.00
S26 Joe Mullen/80 10.00 25.00
S27 Lanny McDonald/80 12.50 30.00
0 Brendan Shanahan/25 25.00 60.00
0 Ron Francis/25 25.00 60.00

001-02 Parkhurst He Shoots He Scores Points

erted one per pack, these cards carried a value of 1, r 3 points. The points could be redeemed for special morabilia cards. The cards are unnumbered and are ed below in alphabetical order by point value. The emption program ended November 31, 2002.

ean Beliveau 1 pt. .20 .50
oug Harvey 1 pt. .20 .50
m Horton 1 pt. .20 .50
obby Hull 1 pt. .30 .75
ed Lindsay 1 pt. .20 .50
tan Mikita 1 pt. .30 .75
acques Plante 1 pt. .25 .60
hris Pronger 1 pt. .20 .50
erry Sawchuk 1 pt. .25 .60
Mats Sundin 1 pt. .20 .50
Martin Brodeur 2 pt. .50 1.25
Peter Forsberg 2 pt. .40 1.00
Patrick Roy 2 pt. 1.00 2.50
Joe Sakic 2 pt. .40 1.00
Steve Yzerman 2 pt. .75 2.00
Paul Kariya 2 pt. .25 .60
Pavel Bure 3 pt. .25 .60
Gordie Howe 3 pt. .75 2.00
Mario Lemieux 3 pt. 1.00 2.50
Rocket Richard 3 pt. .30 .75

001-02 Parkhurst Heroes Dual Jerseys

s 16-card set featured game-worn jersey swatches he two players featured on each card. Each card ured both players, the modern player in color and vintage player in opaque. Cards from this set were ited to 40 copies each.

J.Beliveau/V.Lecavalier 20.00 50.00
G.Howe/S.Yzerman 40.00 100.00
T.Sawchuk/P.Roy 25.00 60.00
R.Richard/P.Bure 30.00 80.00
P.Esposito/J.Thornton 15.00 40.00
G.Lafleur/P.Kariya 25.00 60.00
D.Harvey/B.Leetch 15.00 40.00
S.Mikita/J.Sakic 20.00 50.00
J.Plante/M.Brodeur 25.00 60.00
T.Lindsay/O.Nolan 20.00 50.00
V.Tretiak/E.Belfour 30.00 80.00
T.Horton/S.Stevens 15.00 40.00
Bo.Hull/Br.Hull 25.00 60.00
G.Perreault/M.Lemieux 25.00 60.00
H.Richard/S.Gomez 15.00 40.00
B.Gadsby/C.Pronger 15.00 40.00

2001-02 Parkhurst Jerseys

ds from this 60-card set featured swatches of ne-worn jersey from the featured player. Each card ied a player photo and the swatch on a multi-ered card front which included part of the kground from the action photo. Cards in this set e limited to 90 copies each.

Mario Lemieux 25.00 60.00
Milan Hejduk 6.00 15.00
Vincent Lecavalier 6.00 15.00
Mats Sundin 8.00 20.00
Mark Recchi 6.00 15.00
PJ6 Mark Messier 8.00 20.00
PJ7 Peter Bondra 8.00 20.00
PJ8 Jeff Friesen 6.00 15.00
PJ9 Scott Gomez 6.00 15.00
PJ10 Daniel Alfredsson 6.00 15.00
PJ11 Nicklas Lidstrom 8.00 20.00
PJ12 Daniel Sedin 6.00 15.00
PJ13 Peter Forsberg 10.00 25.00
PJ14 Ron Francis 6.00 15.00
PJ15 Joe Sakic 15.00 40.00
PJ16 Mike Modano 12.00 30.00
PJ17 Patrik Stefan 6.00 15.00
PJ18 Steve Yzerman 20.00 50.00
PJ19 Pavel Bure 8.00 20.00
PJ20 Al MacInnis 6.00 15.00
PJ21 Joe Thornton 12.00 30.00
PJ22 John LeClair 8.00 20.00
PJ23 Owen Nolan 6.00 15.00
PJ24 Paul Kariya 8.00 20.00
PJ25 Tony Amonte 6.00 15.00
PJ26 Zigmund Palffy 6.00 15.00
PJ27 Brian Leetch 6.00 15.00
PJ28 Scott Stevens 6.00 15.00
PJ29 Sergei Gonchar 6.00 15.00
PJ30 Chris Drury 6.00 15.00
PJ31 Fredrik Modin 6.00 15.00
PJ32 Alexei Zhamnov 6.00 15.00
PJ33 Curtis Joseph 6.00 15.00
PJ34 Patrik Elias 6.00 15.00
PJ35 Roberto Luongo 8.00 20.00
PJ36 Darren McCarty 6.00 15.00
PJ37 Saku Koivu 8.00 20.00
PJ38 Patrick Roy 20.00 50.00
PJ39 Brendan Shanahan 8.00 20.00
PJ40 Chris Pronger 6.00 15.00
PJ41 Martin Straka 6.00 15.00
PJ42 Chris Chelios 8.00 20.00
PJ43 Theo Fleury 6.00 15.00
PJ44 Roman Cechmanek 6.00 15.00
PJ45 Viktor Kozlov 6.00 15.00
PJ46 Martin Brodeur 20.00 50.00
PJ47 Radek Bonk 6.00 15.00
PJ48 Byron Dafoe 6.00 15.00
PJ49 Adam Foote 6.00 15.00
PJ50 Eric Daze 6.00 15.00
PJ51 Ed Belfour 8.00 20.00
PJ52 Milan Kraft 6.00 15.00
PJ53 Arturs Irbe 6.00 15.00
PJ54 Alex Tanguay 6.00 15.00
PJ55 Sergei Fedorov 8.00 20.00
PJ56 Mike Richter 8.00 20.00
PJ57 Marian Hossa 8.00 20.00
PJ58 Joe Nieuwendyk 6.00 15.00
PJ59 Keith Primeau 6.00 15.00
PJ60 Olaf Kolzig 6.00 15.00

2001-02 Parkhurst Jersey and Stick

This set partially paralleled the jersey set but each card carried a jersey swatch and a stick piece from the featured player. Cards in this set were limited to just 70 copies each.

PSJ1 Steve Yzerman 25.00 60.00
PSJ2 Pavel Bure 10.00 25.00
PSJ3 Mats Sundin 10.00 25.00
PSJ4 Paul Kariya 10.00 25.00
PSJ5 Patrick Roy 30.00 80.00
PSJ6 Chris Pronger 8.00 20.00
PSJ7 Ed Belfour 10.00 25.00
PSJ8 Martin Brodeur 25.00 60.00
PSJ9 Sergei Fedorov 10.00 25.00
PSJ10 Marian Hossa 10.00 25.00
PSJ11 Olaf Kolzig 8.00 20.00
PSJ12 Vincent Lecavalier 8.00 20.00
PSJ13 Joe Sakic 20.00 50.00
PSJ14 Peter Forsberg 20.00 50.00
PSJ15 Mark Recchi 8.00 20.00
PSJ16 Al MacInnis 8.00 20.00
PSJ17 Roman Cechmanek 8.00 20.00
PSJ18 John LeClair 10.00 25.00
PSJ19 Byron Dafoe 8.00 20.00
PSJ20 Joe Thornton 15.00 40.00

2001-02 Parkhurst Milestones

This 56-card set featured players who hit the various milestones in their career. Each card featured an action photo of the given player alongside a game-worn swatch of his jersey on the card front. Cards M1-M22 were limited to just 50 cards each. Cards M19U-M52 were limited to just 90 copies each and were available in random BAP Update packs. Due to a printing error, card numbers M19-M22 were used for two different cards each, a "U" suffix is used below to denote the cards available in BAP Update packs.

M1 Chris Osgood 6.00 15.00
M2 Martin Brodeur 15.00 40.00
M3 Jaromir Jagr 10.00 25.00
M4 Jaromir Jagr 10.00 25.00
M5 Ed Belfour 6.00 15.00
M6 Brian Leetch 6.00 15.00
M7 Luc Robitaille 6.00 15.00
M8 Jaromir Jagr 10.00 25.00
M9 Mark Recchi 6.00 15.00
M10 Curtis Joseph 8.00 20.00
M11 Dominik Hasek 12.00 30.00
M12 Mark Messier 12.00 30.00
M13 Scott Stevens 6.00 15.00
M14 Steve Yzerman 20.00 50.00
M15 Doug Gilmour 6.00 15.00
M16 Martin Brodeur 15.00 40.00
M17 Steve Yzerman 20.00 50.00
M18 Patrick Roy 20.00 50.00
M19 Ray Bourque 12.00 30.00
M19U Luc Robitaille 8.00 20.00
M20 Mario Lemieux 15.00 40.00
M20U Brett Hull 8.00 20.00
M21 Ray Bourque 12.00 30.00
M21U Mario Lemieux 15.00 40.00
M22 Jeremy Roenick 10.00 25.00
M22U Steve Yzerman 15.00 40.00
M23 Joe Nieuwendyk 6.00 15.00
M24 Ron Francis 5.00 12.00
M25 Brendan Shanahan 8.00 20.00
M26 Pavel Bure 8.00 20.00
M27 Alexander Mogilny 5.00 12.00
M28 Peter Bondra 5.00 12.00
M29 Mats Sundin 5.00 12.00
M30 Mark Recchi 5.00 12.00
M31 Mike Modano 10.00 25.00
M32 Teemu Selanne 8.00 20.00
M33 Steve Yzerman 15.00 40.00
M34 Adam Oates 5.00 12.00
M35 Mark Messier 8.00 20.00
M36 Mario Lemieux 20.00 50.00
M37 Patrick Roy 15.00 40.00
M38 Dominik Hasek 10.00 25.00
M39 Patrick Roy 20.00 50.00
M40 Ed Belfour 6.00 15.00
M41 Curtis Joseph 8.00 20.00
M42 Mike Richter 6.00 15.00
M43 Martin Brodeur 20.00 50.00
M44 Ron Francis 5.00 12.00
M45 Adam Oates 5.00 12.00
M46 Brett Hull 10.00 25.00
M47 Joe Sakic 12.00 30.00
M48 Al MacInnis 5.00 12.00
M49 Jaromir Jagr 8.00 20.00
M50 Theo Fleury 8.00 20.00
M51 Brendan Shanahan 6.00 15.00
M52 Jeremy Roenick 8.00 20.00

2001-02 Parkhurst Reprints

This 150-card set featured reprints of vintage Parkhurst cards. Of the 150 cards, 57 were printed intentionally with blank backs as part of the Parkie Back Checking Contest (labeled with BC in our checklist). Collector's who received one of these blank backed card could answer a question from the BAP website that could be answered by reading the back of the original card, write the answer on the blank back card and send it to BAP. They would then receive a returned card complete with a printed back. Cards #1, 18, 27, 36, 45, 54, 63, 72, 81, 90, 99, and 108 were originally issued as blank backs in 1951-52 and, therefore, are also blank backs in this insert set but were not included in the Beck Checking redemption program.

1 Gordie Howe 4.00 10.00
2 Maurice Richard 2.50 6.00
3 Bernie Geoffrion BC 2.50 6.00
4 Bill Mosienko BC 1.50 4.00
5 Terry Sawchuk 2.50 6.00
6 Woody Dumart BC 1.50 4.00
7 Doug Harvey 2.00 5.00
8 Frank Mahovlich BC 2.50 6.00
9 Jean Beliveau BC 3.00 8.00
10 Jacques Plante 2.50 6.00
11 Jean-Guy Talbot 2.00 5.00
12 Gordie Howe BC 4.00 10.00
13 Terry Sawchuk BC 2.50 6.00
14 Maurice Richard 2.50 6.00
15 Harry Lumley 2.00 5.00
16 Jean Beliveau 3.00 8.00
17 Red Kelly BC 2.00 5.00
18 Bernie Geoffrion 2.50 6.00
19 Dickie Moore 2.00 5.00
20 Dollard St. Laurent 1.50 4.00
21 Terry Sawchuk BC 2.50 6.00
22 Harry Lumley BC 2.00 5.00
23 Woody Dumart 1.50 4.00
24 Tim Horton 2.00 5.00
25 George Hainsworth 2.00 5.00
26 Johnny Bower BC 2.50 6.00
27 Doug Harvey 2.00 5.00
28 Bill Gadsby 2.00 5.00
29 Dickie Moore 2.00 5.00
30 Gordie Howe BC 4.00 10.00
31 Red Kelly BC 2.00 5.00
32 Bernie Geoffrion 2.50 6.00
33 Jean Beliveau BC 3.00 8.00
34 Jacques Plante 2.50 6.00
35 Henri Richard BC 2.50 6.00
36 Chuck Rayner 1.50 4.00
37 Henri Richard 2.50 6.00
38 Frank Mahovlich 2.50 6.00
39 Bill Gadsby BC 2.00 5.00
40 Bernie Geoffrion BC 2.50 6.00
41 Doug Harvey 2.00 5.00
42 Maurice Richard BC 2.50 6.00
43 Georges Vezina 2.50 6.00
44 Jean-Guy Talbot BC 2.00 5.00
45 Terry Sawchuk 2.50 6.00
46 Terry Sawchuk 2.50 6.00
47 Jacques Plante 2.50 6.00
48 Frank Mahovlich BC 2.50 6.00
49 Bill Gadsby BC 2.00 5.00
50 Butch Bouchard 1.50 4.00
51 Bernie Geoffrion BC 2.50 6.00
52 Dollard St. Laurent 1.50 4.00
53 Red Kelly BC 2.00 5.00
54 Red Kelly 2.00 5.00
55 Johnny Bower 2.50 6.00
56 Henri Richard 2.50 6.00
57 Bernie Geoffrion BC 2.50 6.00
58 Gordie Howe 3.00 8.00
Harry Lumley BC
59 Chuck Rayner 1.50 4.00
60 Red Kelly BC 2.00 5.00
61 Dickie Moore 2.00 5.00
62 Bernie Geoffrion BC 2.50 6.00
63 Butch Bouchard 1.50 4.00
64 Frank Mahovlich 2.50 6.00
65 Doug Harvey 2.00 5.00
66 Jacques Plante 2.50 6.00
67 Tim Horton BC 2.00 5.00
68 Dollard St. Laurent 1.50 4.00
69 Bernie Geoffrion 2.50 6.00
70 Butch Bouchard 1.50 4.00
71 Gordie Howe 4.00 10.00
72 Milt Schmidt 2.00 5.00
73 Butch Bouchard BC 1.50 4.00
74 Henri Richard 2.50 6.00
75 Tim Horton 2.00 5.00
76 Gordie Howe 4.00 10.00
77 Dickie Moore 2.00 5.00
78 Elmer Lach BC 2.00 5.00
79 Bernie Geoffrion 2.50 6.00
80 Jean Beliveau BC 3.00 8.00
81 Bill Gadsby 2.00 5.00
82 Jean Beliveau BC 3.00 8.00
83 Bill Gadsby BC 2.00 5.00
84 Henri Richard BC 2.50 6.00
85 Jacques Plante 2.50 6.00
Ted Sloan
86 Frank Mahovlich 2.50 6.00
87 Terry Sawchuk BC 2.50 6.00
88 Maurice Richard 2.50 6.00
89 Tim Horton 2.00 5.00
90 Ted Lindsay 2.50 6.00
91 Johnny Bower BC 2.50 6.00
92 Maurice Richard 2.50 6.00
93 Red Kelly 2.00 5.00
94 Dickie Moore BC 2.00 5.00
95 Bill Gadsby 2.00 5.00
96 Ted Lindsay BC 2.50 6.00
97 Tim Horton BC 2.00 5.00
98 Bernie Geoffrion 2.50 6.00
99 Woody Dumart 1.50 4.00
100 Doug Harvey 2.00 5.00
101 Frank Mahovlich 2.50 6.00
102 Dickie Moore 2.00 5.00
103 Tim Horton BC 2.00 5.00
104 Harry Lumley 2.00 5.00
105 Butch Bouchard BC 1.50 4.00
106 Turk Broda 2.00 5.00
107 Jean Beliveau 4.00 10.00
108 Maurice Richard 2.50 6.00
109 Red Kelly BC 2.00 5.00
110 Jean Beliveau BC 3.00 8.00
111 Jean-Guy Talbot 2.00 5.00
112 Terry Sawchuk 2.50 6.00
Bernie Geoffrion BC
113 Tim Horton 2.00 5.00
114 Dollard St. Laurent BC 1.50 4.00
115 Doug Harvey 2.00 5.00
116 Gump Worsley 2.50 6.00
117 Milt Schmidt 2.00 5.00
118 Jean Beliveau BC 3.00 8.00
119 Tim Horton BC 2.00 5.00
120 Dickie Moore BC 2.00 5.00
121 Doug Harvey 2.00 5.00
122 Henri Richard 2.50 6.00
123 Milt Schmidt BC 2.00 5.00
124 Frank Mahovlich 2.50 6.00
125 Johnny Bower 2.50 6.00
126 Ted Lindsay 2.50 6.00
127 Tim Horton BC 2.00 5.00
128 Jacques Plante 2.50 6.00
129 Jean-Guy Talbot 2.00 5.00
130 Jean Beliveau 3.00 8.00
131 Doug Harvey 2.00 5.00
132 Gump Worsley BC 2.50 6.00
133 Terry Sawchuk 2.50 6.00
134 Frank Mahovlich 2.50 6.00
135 Bill Mosienko 1.50 4.00
136 Jean Beliveau BC 3.00 8.00
137 Tim Horton BC 2.00 5.00
138 Jacques Plante 2.50 6.00
139 Johnny Bower 2.50 6.00
140 Gordie Howe 4.00 10.00
141 Chuck Rayner BC 1.50 4.00
142 Henri Richard 2.50 6.00
143 Gump Worsley BC 2.50 6.00
144 Red Kelly 2.00 5.00
145 Dickie Moore 2.00 5.00
146 Frank Mahovlich 2.50 6.00
147 Henri Richard BC 2.50 6.00
148 Johnny Bower 2.50 6.00
149 Red Kelly 2.00 5.00
150 Bill Gadsby BC 2.00 5.00

2001-02 Parkhurst Sticks

This 70-card set featured pieces of game-used sticks from the featured players alongside color player photos. Cards in this set were limited to 90 copies each.

PS1 Mario Lemieux 30.00 80.00
PS2 Milan Hejduk 8.00 20.00
PS3 Vincent Lecavalier 8.00 20.00
PS4 Mats Sundin 8.00 20.00
PS5 Mark Recchi 6.00 15.00
PS6 Mark Messier 8.00 20.00
PS7 Peter Bondra 6.00 15.00
PS8 Jeff Friesen 6.00 15.00
PS9 Scott Gomez 6.00 15.00
PS10 Daniel Alfredsson 6.00 15.00
PS11 Nicklas Lidstrom 8.00 20.00
PS12 Daniel Sedin 6.00 15.00
PS13 Peter Forsberg 15.00 40.00
PS14 Ron Francis 6.00 15.00
PS15 Joe Sakic 15.00 40.00
PS16 Mike Modano 12.50 30.00
PS17 Patrik Stefan 6.00 15.00
PS18 Steve Yzerman 25.00 60.00
PS19 Pavel Bure 8.00 20.00
PS20 Al MacInnis 6.00 15.00
PS21 Joe Thornton 12.50 30.00
PS22 John LeClair 8.00 20.00
PS23 Owen Nolan 6.00 15.00
PS24 Paul Kariya 8.00 20.00
PS25 Tony Amonte 8.00 20.00
PS26 Zigmund Palffy 6.00 15.00
PS27 Brian Leetch 8.00 20.00
PS28 Scott Stevens 6.00 15.00
PS29 Sergei Gonchar 6.00 15.00
PS30 Chris Drury 6.00 15.00
PS31 Martin Brodeur 20.00 50.00
PS32 Chris Chelios 6.00 15.00
PS33 Rob Blake 6.00 15.00
PS34 Teemu Selanne 8.00 20.00
PS35 Pavol Demitra 6.00 15.00
PS36 Markus Naslund 8.00 20.00
PS37 Alex Tanguay 6.00 15.00
PS38 Keith Primeau 6.00 15.00
PS39 Olaf Kolzig 6.00 15.00
PS40 Sergei Fedorov 12.50 30.00
PS41 Brad Richards 6.00 15.00
PS42 Adam Oates 6.00 15.00
PS43 Darren McCarty 10.00 25.00
PS44 Adam Foote 6.00 15.00
PS45 Sandis Ozolinsh 6.00 15.00
PS46 Chris Pronger 6.00 15.00
PS47 Jason Arnott 6.00 15.00
PS48 Keith Tkachuk 8.00 20.00
PS49 Sergei Samsonov 6.00 15.00
PS50 Kenny Jonsson 6.00 15.00
PS51 Gary Roberts 6.00 15.00
PS52 Marian Hossa 8.00 20.00
PS53 Brendan Shanahan 8.00 20.00
PS54 Patrick Roy 20.00 50.00
PS55 Pierre Turgeon 6.00 15.00
PS56 Roman Turek 6.00 15.00
PS57 Doug Weight 6.00 15.00
PS58 Jaromir Jagr 12.50 30.00
PS59 Brett Hull 10.00 25.00
PS60 Dominik Hasek 15.00 40.00
PS61 Luc Robitaille 6.00 15.00
PS62 Eric Lindros 8.00 20.00
PS63 Stan Mikita 15.00 40.00
PS64 Guy Lafleur 12.00 30.00
PS65 Lanny McDonald 12.50 30.00
PS66 Jari Kurri 15.00 40.00
PS67 Jeremy Roenick 10.00 25.00
PS68 Rick DiPietro 6.00 15.00
PS69 Joe Nieuwendyk 6.00 15.00
PS70 Alexander Mogilny 6.00 15.00

2001-02 Parkhurst Teammates

Cards in this 28-card set featured three swatches of game-worn jerseys from the three teammates pictured on the card front. The cards were produced vertically, and the swatches were affixed parallel to a photo of each player. Cards T1-T18 were available in random packs of Parkhurst and were limited to 30 copies each. Cards T19-T28 were available in random packs of BAP Update and were limited to 80 copies each.

T1 Shanahan/Yzerman/Lidstrom 75.00 150.00
T2 Kraft/Aubin/Lemieux 20.00 50.00
T3 Fleury/Messier/Leetch 20.00 50.00
T4 Dafoe/Thornton/Allison 15.00 40.00
T5 Foote/Sakic/Drury 20.00 50.00
T6 Kolzig/Gonchar/Bondra 20.00 50.00
T7 Joseph/Sundin/Kaberle 20.00 50.00
T8 Roy/Forsberg/Hejduk 40.00 100.00
T9 Thibault/Amonte/Daze 12.00 30.00
T10 Luongo/Bure/Kozlov 20.00 50.00
T11 Biron/Satan/ Zhitnik 12.00 30.00
T12 Belfour/Modano/Sydor 15.00 40.00
T13 Cechmanek/Recchi/LeClair 12.00 30.00
T14 Brodeur/Stevens/Elias 30.00 80.00
T15 Holik/Gomez/Arnott 12.00 30.00
T16 Hossa/Alfredsson/Bonk 12.00 30.00
T17 D.Sedin/Naslund/Bertuzzi 15.00 40.00
T18 Francis/Irbe/Ozolinsh 15.00 40.00
T19 Samsonov/Thornton/Guerin 15.00 40.00
T20 Ozolinsh/V.Bure/Luongo 10.00 25.00
T21 Turco/Modano/Belfour 20.00 50.00
T22 Sakic/Roy/Drury 20.00 50.00
T23 Yzerman/Shanahan/Hasek 30.00 80.00
T24 Lindros/Leetch/Messier 15.00 40.00
T25 Selanne/Hurme/Kapanen 10.00 25.00
T26 Sundin/Salo/Naslund 10.00 25.00
T27 Jagr/Hasek/Kaberle 25.00 60.00
T28 Yzerman/Lemieux/Brodeur 40.00 100.00

2001-02 Parkhurst Vintage Memorabilia

Cards from this 30-card set featured reprints of vintage Parkhurst cards with a piece of game-used memorabilia attached to the card front. Production quantities varied and are listed below beside the card descriptions.

PV1 Rocket Richard GJ/90 60.00 150.00
PV2 Rocket Richard Number/5
PV3 Rocket Richard Emblem/5
PV4 Jacques Plante GJ/90 30.00 80.00
PV5 Jacques Plante Glove/90 30.00 80.00
PV6 Jacques Plante Emblem/5
PV7 Jacques Plante Number/5
PV8 Jacques Plante Stick/90 30.00 80.00
PV9 Bill Gadsby Glove/90 15.00 40.00
PV10 Doug Harvey GJ/90 15.00 40.00
PV11 Doug Harvey Emblem/5
PV12 Doug Harvey Number/5
PV13 Gordie Howe GJ/40 50.00 120.00
PV14 Gordie Howe Emblem/5
PV15 Gordie Howe Number/5
PV16 Bill Mosienko Pants/90 15.00 40.00
PV17 Jean Beliveau GJ/90 30.00 60.00
PV18 Jean Beliveau Number/5
PV19 Jean Beliveau Emblem/5
PV20 Turk Broda Glove/90 25.00 60.00
PV21 Tim Horton Pants/90 20.00 50.00
PV22 Henri Richard GJ/90 15.00 40.00
PV23 Henri Richard Emblem/5
PV24 Chuck Rayner Glove/90 30.00 80.00
PV25 Terry Sawchuk Glove/90 30.00 80.00
PV26 Terry Sawchuk Pad/90 30.00 80.00
PV27 Terry Sawchuk GJ/90 30.00 80.00
PV28 Ted Lindsay GJ/90 15.00 40.00
PV29 Ted Lindsay Emblem/5
PV30 Johnny Bower Pad/90 12.00 30.00

2001-02 Parkhurst World Class Jerseys

This 8-card set featured player photos and game-worn jersey swatches over a background of the national flag of the given player. Each card in this set was limited to just 80 copies each.

*EMBLEM/20: 1X TO 2.5X JSY/80
EMBLEM PRINT RUN 20 SETS
*NUMBER/20: 1X TO 2.5X JSY/80
NUMBER PRINT RUN 20 SETS
WCJ1 Steve Yzerman 25.00 60.00
WCJ2 Teemu Selanne 8.00 20.00
WCJ3 Olaf Kolzig 10.00 25.00
WCJ4 Zigmund Palffy 10.00 25.00
WCJ5 Peter Forsberg 15.00 40.00
WCJ6 Mike Modano 12.50 30.00
WCJ7 Jaromir Jagr 15.00 40.00
WCJ8 Alexei Yashin 10.00 25.00

2001-02 Parkhurst Waving the Flag

Inspired by the 1963-64 Parkhurst Design, this set featured a portrait shot of the player with his native flag in the background. Card backs summarize each player's international experience in tournaments. The cards were printed on 20-point foilboard stock and the print run was limited to 2,002 sets. Each set was accompanied by a sequentially-numbered header card to enhance collectibility. The set was available by mail via the Be a Player website.

1 Mario Lemieux 6.00 15.00
2 Joe Sakic 2.00 5.00
3 Steve Yzerman 5.00 12.00
4 Paul Kariya 1.00 2.50
5 Curtis Joseph 1.00 2.50
6 Martin Brodeur 2.50 6.00
7 Eric Lindros 1.00 2.50
8 Chris Pronger .75 2.00
9 Jaromir Jagr 1.50 4.00
10 Milan Hejduk 1.00 2.50
11 Dominik Hasek 2.00 5.00
12 Martin Havlat .75 2.00
13 Teemu Selanne 1.00 2.50
14 Jani Hurme .75 2.00
15 Miikka Kiprusoff .75 2.00
16 Sami Kapanen .75 2.00
17 Mats Sundin 1.00 2.50
18 Nicklas Lidstrom 1.00 2.50
19 Tommy Salo .75 2.00
20 Kristian Huselius .75 2.00
21 Jeremy Roenick 1.25 3.00
22 Doug Weight .75 2.00
23 Tony Amonte .75 2.00
24 Brian Leetch .75 2.00
25 Mike Modano 1.50 4.00
26 Brett Hull 1.25 3.00
27 John LeClair 1.00 2.50
28 Keith Tkachuk 1.00 2.50
29 Alexei Yashin .75 2.00
30 Pavel Bure 1.00 2.50
31 Nikolai Khabibulin 1.00 2.50
32 Darius Kasparaitis .75 2.00

2001-02 Parkhurst Beckett Promos

Inserted into issues of Beckett Hockey collector, this 50-card set paralleled the base Parkhurst set but carried a "Beckett" stamp on the card backs.

*PROMO: .4X TO 1X BASIC CARDS

2002-03 Parkhurst

Released in late February, this 250-card set consisted of 200 veteran cards and 50 shortprinted rookie cards serial-numbered out of 500.

COMP.SET w/o SP's (200) 15.00 40.00
1 Rod Brind'Amour .30 .75
2 Alexei Kovalev .30 .75
3 Brad Richards .30 .75
4 Milan Hnilicka .25 .60
5 Arturs Irbe .25 .60
6 Al MacInnis .30 .75
7 Pavel Bure .40 1.00
8 Patrick Lalime .25 .60
9 Vincent Damphousse .25 .60
10 Bates Battaglia .20 .50
11 Evgeni Nabokov .25 .60
12 Glen Murray .25 .60
13 Chris Osgood .30 .75
14 Pierre Turgeon .30 .75
15 Scott Stevens .30 .75
16 Daniel Briere .25 .60
17 Patrik Stefan .25 .60
18 Pavol Demitra .40 1.00
19 Mark Parrish .20 .50
20 Jason Allison .25 .60
21 Jaromir Jagr .75 2.00
22 Mike Modano .50 1.25
23 Mark Messier .50 1.25
24 Ilya Kovalchuk .40 1.00
25 Teemu Selanne .60 1.50
26 Marty Turco .30 .75
27 Keith Tkachuk .30 .75
28 Simon Gagne .30 .75
29 Brent Johnson .25 .60
30 Anson Carter .25 .60
31 Jeff Jillson .20 .50
32 Gary Roberts .20 .50
33 Mike Richter .30 .75
34 Martin Lapointe .25 .60
35 Todd Bertuzzi .30 .75
36 Valeri Bure .25 .60
37 Marian Hossa .25 .60
38 Eric Daze .20 .50
39 Nikolai Khabibulin .30 .75
40 Miikka Kiprusoff .25 .60
41 Kevin Weekes .25 .60
42 Mark Recchi .40 1.00
43 Dan Cloutier .25 .60
44 Keith Primeau .30 .75
45 Alex Tanguay .25 .60
46 Ed Jovanovski .25 .60
47 Roberto Luongo .50 1.25
48 Saku Koivu .30 .75
49 Chris Drury .30 .75
50 Olaf Kolzig .30 .75
51 Dan Blackburn .25 .60
52 Erik Cole .25 .60
53 Darcy Tucker .20 .50
54 Chris Chelios .30 .75
55 Pavel Datsyuk .40 1.00
56 Mike Comrie .30 .75
57 Paul Kariya .40 1.00
58 Eric Lindros .50 1.25
59 Martin Havlat .25 .60
60 Scott Niedermayer .30 .75
61 Krys Kolanos .20 .50
62 Rostislav Klesla .20 .50
63 Jocelyn Thibault .25 .60
64 Mike Dunham .25 .60
65 Shane Doan .25 .60
66 John LeClair .30 .75
67 Tommy Salo .25 .60
68 Doug Gilmour .40 1.00
69 Johan Hedberg .30 .75
70 Brett Hull .40 1.00
71 Alexander Mogilny .25 .60
72 Chris Pronger .25 .60
73 Sergei Fedorov .50 1.25
74 David Legwand .25 .60
75 Kristian Huselius .20 .50
76 Manny Fernandez .25 .60
77 Vincent Lecavalier .25 .60
78 Rick DiPietro .25 .60
79 Mike Peca .25 .60
80 Ryan Smyth .25 .60
81 Brian Rolston .25 .60
82 Brian Leetch .30 .75
83 Steve Sullivan .20 .50
84 Scott Gomez .25 .60
85 Adam Foote .20 .50
86 Scott Hartnell .30 .75
87 Alexei Zhamnov .25 .60
88 Marc Denis .25 .60
89 Joe Nieuwendyk .30 .75
90 Brad Stuart .20 .50
91 Patrik Elias .30 .75
92 Mats Sundin .30 .75
93 Jose Theodore .30 .75
94 Brendan Shanahan .40 1.00
95 Daniel Alfredsson .30 .75
96 Martin Brodeur .60 1.50
97 Jarome Iginla .30 .75
98 Peter Bondra .30 .75
99 Peter Forsberg .40 1.00
100 Steve Yzerman .60 1.50
101 Alexei Yashin .25 .60
102 Patrick Roy .75 2.00
103 Markus Naslund .25 .60
104 Jeremy Roenick .30 .75
105 Darius Kasparaitis .20 .50
106 Curtis Joseph .30 .75
107 Marian Gaborik .50 1.25
108 Bill Guerin .30 .75
109 Joe Sakic .50 1.25
110 Adam Oates .30 .75
111 Owen Nolan .30 .75
112 Rob Blake .30 .75
113 Nicklas Lidstrom .30 .75
114 Joe Thornton .40 1.00
115 Mario Lemieux 1.00 2.50
116 Sergei Gonchar .25 .60
117 Bobby Holik .20 .50
118 Sandis Ozolinsh .25 .60
119 Steven Reinprecht .20 .50
120 Jeff O'Neill .20 .50
121 Radek Bonk .25 .60
122 Milan Hejduk .25 .60
123 Zigmund Palffy .30 .75
124 Luc Robitaille .30 .75
125 Dany Heatley .30 .75
126 Doug Weight .30 .75
127 Fredrik Modin .20 .50
128 Ron Francis .40 1.00
129 Roman Turek .30 .75
130 Adam Deadmarsh .25 .60
131 Sami Kapanen .20 .50
132 Sergei Samsonov .25 .60
133 Jeff Friesen .20 .50
134 Martin St. Louis .30 .75
135 Phil Housley .25 .60
136 Mark Bell .20 .50
137 Felix Potvin .50 1.25
138 Ed Belfour .30 .75
139 Martin Biron .25 .60
140 Alyn McCauley .20 .50
141 Miroslav Satan .30 .75
142 Jan Hrdina .20 .50
143 Ron Tugnutt .25 .60
144 Steve Shields .25 .60
145 Cliff Ronning .20 .50
146 Wade Redden .20 .50
147 Patrick Marleau .30 .75
148 Tony Amonte .25 .60
149 Byron Dafoe .25 .60
150 Roman Cechmanek .25 .60
151 Martin Straka .25 .60
152 Sergei Zubov .25 .60
153 Maxim Afinogenov .20 .50
154 Brian Boucher .25 .60
155 Jason Arnott .25 .60
156 Oleg Tverdovsky .20 .50
157 Daymond Langkow .25 .60
158 Andrew Brunette .20 .50
159 Brian Rafalski .20 .50
160 Mike York .20 .50
161 Richard Zednik .20 .50
162 Radim Vrbata .25 .60
163 Tim Connolly .20 .50
164 Jamie Storr .25 .60
165 Henrik Sedin .30 .75
166 Sean Burke .20 .50
167 Daniel Sedin .30 .75
168 Jason Smith .20 .50
169 Stephen Weiss .30 .75
170 Bryan McCabe .20 .50
171 Theo Fleury .40 1.00
172 Jean-Sebastien Giguere .30 .75
173 Espen Knutsen .20 .50
174 Mika Noronen .25 .60
175 Michael Nylander .20 .50
176 Yanic Perreault .20 .50
177 Donald Brashear .20 .50
178 Denis Arkhipov .20 .50
179 Adrian Aucoin .20 .50
180 Tie Domi .25 .60
181 Andrew Cassels .20 .50
182 Eric Brewer .20 .50
183 Trevor Linden .30 .75
184 Brendan Witt .20 .50
185 Robert Lang .20 .50
186 Brendan Morrison .25 .60
187 Mike Fisher .20 .50
188 Alexei Morozov .20 .50
189 Martin Erat .20 .50
190 Jeff Hackett .25 .60
191 Mariusz Czerkawski .20 .50
192 Olli Jokinen .30 .75
193 Brad Isbister .20 .50
194 Niklas Hagman .20 .50
195 Jere Lehtinen .30 .75
196 Igor Larionov .30 .75
197 Curtis Brown .20 .50
198 Ray Whitney .25 .60
199 Grant Marshall .20 .50
200 Craig Conroy .20 .50
201 P-M Bouchard RC 2.50 6.00
202 Rick Nash RC 12.00 30.00
203 Dennis Seidenberg RC 2.50 6.00
204 Jay Bouwmeester RC 5.00 12.00
205 Stanislav Chistov RC 1.50 4.00
206 Jared Aulin RC 1.50 4.00
207 Ivan Majesky RC 1.50 4.00
208 Chuck Kobasew RC 2.00 5.00
209 Jordan Leopold RC 2.50 6.00
210 Ryan Miller RC 10.00 25.00
211 Ales Hemsky RC 6.00 15.00
212 Patrick Sharp RC 5.00 12.00
213 Kari Haakana RC 1.50 4.00
214 Dmitri Bykov RC 1.50 4.00
215 Pascal Leclaire RC 2.00 5.00
216 Henrik Zetterberg RC 10.00 25.00
217 Alexander Frolov RC 3.00 8.00
218 Steve Eminger RC 1.50 4.00
219 Scottie Upshall RC 2.00 5.00
220 Tom Koivisto RC 1.50 4.00
221 Shaone Morrisonn RC 1.50 4.00
222 Ron Hainsey RC 1.50 4.00
223 Martin Gerber RC 2.50 6.00
224 Adam Hall RC 1.50 4.00
225 Lasse Pirjeta RC 1.50 4.00
226 Anton Volchenkov RC 1.50 4.00
227 Craig Andersson RC 5.00 12.00
228 Rickard Wallin RC 1.50 4.00
229 Alexander Svitov RC 1.50 4.00
230 Alexei Smirnov RC 2.00 5.00
231 Jeff Taffe RC 1.50 4.00
232 Mikael Tellqvist RC 1.50 4.00
233 Radovan Somik RC 1.50 4.00
234 Dick Tarnstrom RC 1.50 4.00
235 Steve Ott RC 3.00 8.00
236 Brooks Orpik RC 2.50 6.00
237 Eric Bertrand RC 1.50 4.00
238 Sylvain Blouin RC 1.50 4.00
239 Greg Koehler RC 1.50 4.00
240 Stephane Veilleux RC 1.50 4.00
241 Curtis Sanford RC 2.50 6.00
242 Carlo Colaiacovo RC 2.50 6.00
243 Patrick Boileau RC 1.50 4.00
244 Tim Thomas RC 6.00 15.00
245 Mike Cammalleri RC 5.00 12.00
246 Levente Szuper RC 2.50 6.00
247 Jason Spezza RC 10.00 25.00
248 Cody Rudkowsky RC 1.50 4.00
249 Eric Godard RC 1.50 4.00
250 Valeri Kharlamov RC 5.00 12.00

2002-03 Parkhurst Bronze

This 250-card parallel set was serial-numbered to just 100 sets.

*1-200 VETS/100: 4X TO 10X BASIC CARDS
*201-250 ROOKIE/100: .5X TO 1.2X BASIC RC
23 Mark Messier 5.00 12.00

2002-03 Parkhurst Silver

This 250-card parallel set was serial-numbered to just 50 sets.

*1-200 VETS/50: 6X TO 15X BASIC CARDS
*201-250 ROOKIE/50: .8X TO 2X BASIC RC

2002-03 Parkhurst College Ranks

This 18-card set featured players who played in the NCAA. Cards were limited to 100 copies each.

CR1 Chris Drury 2.50 6.00
CR2 Erik Cole 2.50 6.00
CR3 Keith Tkachuk 3.00 8.00
CR4 Rick DiPietro 3.00 8.00
CR5 Rob Blake 2.50 6.00
CR6 Adam Oates 2.50 6.00
CR7 Chris Chelios 3.00 8.00
CR8 Brett Hull 3.00 8.00
CR9 Paul Kariya 2.50 6.00
CR10 Tony Amonte 2.50 6.00
CR11 Doug Weight 2.50 6.00
CR12 Dany Heatley 4.00 10.00
CR13 Steven Reinprecht 1.50 4.00
CR14 Curtis Joseph 3.00 8.00
CR15 Anson Carter 1.50 4.00
CR16 Mike Dunham 1.50 4.00
CR17 Mike Richter 3.00 8.00
CR18 Ed Belfour 3.00 8.00

2002-03 Parkhurst College Ranks Jerseys

This 18-card set paralleled the regular set with the addition of jersey swatches. Cards were limited to 60 copies each.

CRM1 Chris Drury 8.00 20.00
CRM2 Erik Cole 6.00 15.00
CRM3 Keith Tkachuk 8.00 20.00
CRM4 Rick DiPietro 8.00 20.00
CRM5 Rob Blake 6.00 15.00
CRM6 Adam Oates 8.00 20.00
CRM7 Chris Chelios 8.00 20.00
CRM8 Brett Hull 10.00 25.00
CRM9 Paul Kariya 8.00 20.00
CRM10 Tony Amonte 8.00 20.00
CRM11 Doug Weight 6.00 15.00
CRM12 Dany Heatley 8.00 20.00
CRM13 Steven Reinprecht 5.00 12.00
CRM14 Curtis Joseph 8.00 20.00
CRM15 Anson Carter 5.00 12.00
CRM16 Mike Dunham 5.00 12.00
CRM17 Mike Richter 8.00 20.00
CRM18 Ed Belfour 8.00 20.00

2002-03 Parkhurst Franchise Players Jerseys

Limited to just 50 copies each, this 30-card set featured game jersey swatches from team leaders.

FP1 Paul Kariya 8.00 20.00
FP2 Ilya Kovalchuk 12.50 30.00
FP3 Joe Thornton 15.00 40.00
FP4 Miroslav Satan 8.00 20.00
FP5 Jarome Iginla 15.00 40.00
FP6 Jeff O'Neill 8.00 20.00
FP7 Eric Daze 8.00 20.00
FP8 Patrick Roy 25.00 60.00
FP9 Rostislav Klesla 8.00 20.00
FP10 Mike Modano 10.00 25.00
FP11 Steve Yzerman 20.00 50.00
FP12 Mike Comrie 8.00 20.00
FP13 Roberto Luongo 10.00 25.00
FP14 Zigmund Palffy 8.00 20.00
FP15 Marian Gaborik 15.00 40.00
FP16 Jose Theodore 12.50 30.00
FP17 Scott Hartnell 8.00 20.00
FP18 Martin Brodeur 20.00 50.00
FP19 Alexei Yashin 8.00 20.00
FP20 Pavel Bure 8.00 20.00
FP21 Marian Hossa 8.00 20.00
FP22 Simon Gagne 8.00 20.00
FP23 Daniel Briere 8.00 20.00
FP24 Mario Lemieux 25.00 60.00
FP25 Chris Pronger 8.00 20.00
FP26 Owen Nolan 8.00 20.00
FP27 Nikolai Khabibulin 8.00 20.00
FP28 Mats Sundin 8.00 20.00
FP29 Markus Naslund 8.00 20.00
FP30 Jaromir Jagr 12.50 30.00

2002-03 Parkhurst Hardware

These cards were part of a redemption program launched by BAP focusing on the annual NHL awards. Each NHL trophy category was represented by 9 hopefuls and a Wild Card. Collectors had the choice of keeping their redemption cards (announced print run of just 100 copies of each inserted into packs), or sending them in for a random chance to win a memorabilia card serial numbered to just 10. Collectors had to send in the card of the eventual trophy winner in order to be eligible for the random drawing. Adjusted print run numbers below correlate to the amount of cards not mailed in according to In the Game.

COMMON CARD 1.50 4.00
A1 Eric Lindros/96 2.00 5.00
A2 Jarome Iginla/95 2.50 6.00
A3 Jaromir Jagr/98 2.00 5.00
A4 Joe Sakic/97 2.00 5.00
A5 Markus Naslund/82 1.50 4.00
A6 Pavel Bure/94 2.00 5.00
A7 Peter Forsberg/83 2.00 5.00
A8 Mario Lemieux/88 5.00 12.00
A9 Mats Sundin/98 2.00 5.00
A10 Wild card/87 1.50 4.00
C1 Chuck Kobasew/95 1.50 4.00
C2 Henrik Zetterberg/78 4.00 10.00
C3 Alexander Svitov/94 1.50 4.00
C4 Jay Bouwmeester/92 2.00 5.00
C5 Jordan Leopold/95 1.50 4.00
C6 Ron Hainsey/96 1.50 4.00
C7 Rick Nash/81 4.00 10.00
C8 Stanislav Chistov/94 1.50 4.00
C9 Stephen Weiss/96 1.50 4.00
C10 Wild card/85 1.50 4.00
H1 Eric Lindros/92 2.00 5.00
H2 Jarome Iginla/88 2.50 6.00
H3 Jaromir Jagr/85 2.00 5.00
H4 Joe Sakic/82 2.00 5.00
H5 Jose Theodore/91 2.00 5.00
H6 Markus Naslund/78 1.50 4.00
H7 Pavel Bure/91 2.00 5.00
H8 Peter Forsberg/73 4.00 10.00
H9 Mario Lemieux/92 5.00 12.00
H10 Wildcard/85 1.50 4.00
N1 Nicklas Lidstrom/85 3.00 8.00
N2 Sergei Gonchar/95 1.50 4.00
N3 Rob Blake/93 1.50 4.00
N4 Ed Jovanovski/96 1.50 4.00
N5 Brian Rafalski/99 1.50 4.00
N6 Bryan McCabe/98 1.50 4.00
N7 Chris Chelios/95 2.00 5.00
N8 Adrian Aucoin/97 1.50 4.00
N9 Brian Leetch/96 2.00 5.00
N10 Wild card/77 1.50 4.00
P1 Eric Lindros/94 2.00 5.00
P2 Jarome Iginla/96 2.50 6.00
P3 Jaromir Jagr/88 2.00 5.00
P4 Joe Sakic/89 2.00 5.00
P5 Markus Naslund/79 3.00 8.00
P6 Pavel Bure/98 2.00 5.00
P7 Peter Forsberg/81 4.00 10.00
P8 Mario Lemieux/88 5.00 12.00
P9 Mats Sundin/93 2.00 5.00
P10 Wild card/77 1.50 4.00
V1 Curtis Joseph/96 2.00 5.00
V2 Evgeni Nabokov/95 1.50 4.00
V3 Jose Theodore/95 2.00 5.00
V4 Martin Brodeur/72 4.00 10.00
V5 Mike Richter/97 2.00 5.00
V6 Patrick Lalime/93 2.00 5.00
V7 Patrick Roy/86 4.00 10.00
V8 Roberto Luongo/97 2.50 6.00
V9 Olaf Kolzig/98 2.00 5.00
V10 Wildcard/86 1.50 4.00
AW1 Peter Forsberg Hart
AW2 Barret Jackman Calder
AW3 Martin Brodeur Vezina
AW4 Peter Forsberg Art Ross
AW5 Nicklas Lidstrom Norris
AW6 Markus Naslund Pearson

2002-03 Parkhurst Heroes Jerseys

Limited to 25 sets, this 12-card set featured swatches of game jerseys from modern era players and their idols.

NH1 I.Kovalchuk/V.Kharlamov 15.00 40.00
NH2 J.Thornton/S.Yzerman 15.00 40.00
NH3 J.Iginla/M.Messier 15.00 40.00
NH4 S.Yzerman/B.Trottier 30.00 60.00
NH5 S.Gagne/M.Lemieux 25.00 50.00
NH6 E.Lindros/M.Messier 15.00 40.00
NH7 M.Lemieux/G.Lafleur 30.00 60.00
NH8 R.Nash/M.Sundin 20.00 50.00
NH9 C.Pronger/A.MacInnis 12.00 30.00
NH10 J.Bouwmeester/S.Yzerman 25.00 50.00
NH11 D.Heatley/B.Hull 15.00 40.00
NH12 S.Weiss/P.Forsberg 15.00 40.00

2002-03 Parkhurst He Shoots He Scores Points

Inserted one per pack, these cards carried a value of 1, 2 or 3 points. The points could be redeemed for special memorabilia cards. The cards are unnumbered and are listed below in alphabetical order by point value. The redemption program ended January 31, 2004.

1 Martin Brodeur 1pt. .40 1.00
2 Peter Forsberg 1pt. .40 1.00
3 Mark Messier 1pt. .40 1.00
4 Owen Nolan 1 pt. .40 1.00
5 Jeremy Roenick 1 pt. .40 1.00
6 Patrick Roy 1 pt. .40 1.00
7 Joe Sakic 1 pt. .40 1.00
8 Brendan Shanahan 1 pt. .40 1.00
9 Mats Sundin 1 pt. .40 1.00
10 Jose Theodore 1 pt. .40 1.00
11 Joe Thornton 1 pt. .40 1.00
12 Pavel Bure 2 pt. .40 1.00
13 Jaromir Jagr 2 pt. .40 1.00
14 Paul Kariya 2 pt. .40 1.00
15 Eric Lindros 2 pt. .40 1.00
16 Mike Modano 2 pt. .40 1.00
17 Steve Yzerman 2 pt. .40 1.00
18 Jarome Iginla 3 pt. .40 1.00
19 Ilya Kovalchuk 3 pt. .40 1.00
20 Mario Lemieux 3 pt. .40 1.00

2002-03 Parkhurst Jerseys

STATED PRINT RUN 90 SETS

GJ1 Mario Lemieux 15.00 40.00
GJ2 Jose Theodore 8.00 20.00
GJ3 Brian Leetch 6.00 15.00
GJ4 Jaromir Jagr 10.00 25.00
GJ5 Steve Yzerman 15.00 40.00
GJ6 Eric Daze 6.00 15.00
GJ7 Saku Koivu 8.00 20.00
GJ8 John LeClair 8.00 20.00
GJ9 Jeff O'Neill 5.00 12.00
GJ10 Gary Roberts 6.00 15.00
GJ11 Al MacInnis 6.00 15.00
GJ12 Marian Gaborik 8.00 20.00
GJ13 Teemu Selanne 8.00 20.00
GJ14 Alexander Mogilny 6.00 15.00
GJ15 Eric Lindros 10.00 25.00
GJ16 Milan Hejduk 8.00 20.00
GJ17 Zigmund Palffy 6.00 15.00
GJ18 Luc Robitaille 6.00 15.00
GJ19 Ilya Kovalchuk 8.00 20.00
GJ20 Rostislav Klesla 6.00 15.00
GJ21 Mark Messier 8.00 20.00
GJ22 Ron Francis 6.00 15.00
GJ23 Chris Pronger 6.00 15.00
GJ24 Dany Heatley 8.00 20.00
GJ25 Mark Recchi 6.00 15.00
GJ26 Doug Weight 6.00 15.00
GJ27 Alex Tanguay 6.00 15.00
GJ28 Sergei Fedorov 10.00 25.00
GJ29 Todd Bertuzzi 6.00 15.00
GJ30 Sami Kapanen 5.00 12.00
GJ31 Sergei Samsonov 6.00 15.00
GJ32 Jeremy Roenick 10.00 25.00
GJ33 Mike Modano 8.00 20.00
GJ34 Joe Sakic 12.50 30.00
GJ35 Pavel Bure 10.00 25.00
GJ36 Paul Kariya 8.00 20.00
GJ37 Owen Nolan 6.00 15.00
GJ38 Rob Blake 6.00 15.00
GJ39 Nicklas Lidstrom 10.00 25.00
GJ40 Joe Thornton 8.00 20.00
GJ41 Brendan Shanahan 8.00 20.00
GJ42 Daniel Alfredsson 6.00 15.00
GJ43 Martin Brodeur 15.00 40.00
GJ44 Jarome Iginla 8.00 20.00
GJ45 Peter Bondra 6.00 15.00
GJ46 Peter Forsberg 8.00 20.00
GJ47 Mats Sundin 8.00 20.00
GJ48 Alexei Yashin 6.00 15.00
GJ49 Patrick Roy 15.00 40.00
GJ50 Markus Naslund 6.00 15.00
GJ51 Jay Bouwmeester 6.00 15.00
GJ52 Jason Spezza 8.00 20.00
GJ53 Stephen Weiss 5.00 12.00
GJ54 Ron Hainsey 6.00 15.00
GJ55 Jordan Leopold 5.00 12.00
GJ56 Chuck Kobasew 5.00 12.00
GJ57 Rick Nash 12.50 30.00
GJ58 Scottie Upshall 6.00 15.00

2002-03 Parkhurst Magnificent Inserts

This 10-card set featured game-used equipment from the career of Mario Lemieux. Cards MI1-MI5 had a print run of 40 copies each and cards MI6-MI10 were limited to just 10 copies each. Cards MI6-MI10 are not priced due to scarcity.

MI1 2000-01 Season Jersey 30.00 80.00
MI2 1985-86 Season Jersey 30.00 80.00
MI3 2002 All-Star Game Jersey 30.00 80.00
MI4 1987 Canada Cup Jersey 30.00 80.00
MI5 Dual Jersey 50.00 125.00
MI6 Number
MI7 Emblem
MI8 Triple Jersey
MI9 Quad Jersey
MI10 Complete Package

2002-03 Parkhurst Mario's Mates

Limited to 25 sets, this 10-card set carried dual jersey swatches of Mario Lemieux and other top players.

MM1 M.Lemieux/P.Roy 50.00 120.00
MM2 M.Lemieux/S.Yzerman 25.00 60.00
MM3 M.Lemieux/J.Jagr 30.00 80.00
MM4 M.Lemieux/M.Brodeur 50.00 120.00
MM5 M.Lemieux/E.Lindros 40.00 100.00
MM6 M.Lemieux/R.Francis 30.00 80.00
MM7 M.Lemieux/M.Sundin 25.00 60.00
MM8 M.Lemieux/J.Sakic 60.00 150.00
MM9 M.Lemieux/P.Kariya 30.00 80.00
MM10 M.Lemieux/J.Theodore 25.00 60.00

2002-03 Parkhurst Milestones

This 11-card set honored career highlights of several veteran players. Cards were limited to 60 copies each (except for the Roy card).

MS1 Jeremy Roenick 12.50 30.00
MS2 Martin Brodeur 15.00 40.00
MS3 Ed Belfour 10.00 25.00
MS4 Mike Richter 10.00 25.00
MS5 Jaromir Jagr 12.50 30.00
MS6 Vincent Damphousse 10.00 25.00
MS7 Ron Francis 10.00 25.00
MS8 Mats Sundin 10.00 25.00
MS9 Peter Forsberg 12.50 35.00
MS10 Pavel Bure 10.00 25.00
MS11 Patrick Roy/33 30.00 80.00

2002-03 Parkhurst Patented Power Jerseys

ANNOUNCED PRINT RUN 20 SETS

PP1 M.Lemieux/B.Shanahan 25.00 60.00
PP2 S.Yzerman/M.Sundin 40.00 100.00
PP3 J. Jagr/T.Selanne 25.00 60.00
PP4 P.Kariya/J.Roenick 15.00 40.00
PP5 J.Sakic/M.Modano 15.00 40.00
PP6 P.Bure/D.Heatley 15.00 40.00
PP7 P.Forsberg/S.Fedorov 20.00 50.00
PP8 E.Lindros/T.Bertuzzi 20.00 50.00
PP9 I.Kovalchuk/M.Messier 20.00 50.00
PP10 B.Hull/J.Thornton 15.00 40.00

2002-03 Parkhurst Reprints

This 150-card set of Parkhurst reprints picks up the numbering where the 2001-02 reprint set left off.

151 Floyd Curry 1.50 4.00
152 Billy Reay 1.50 4.00
153 Jim Henry 1.50 4.00
154 Ed Sandford 1.50 4.00
155 Pentti Lund 1.50 4.00
156 Al Dewsbury 1.50 4.00
157 Gerry McNeil 2.00 5.00
158 Jack Stewart 1.50 4.00
159 Alex Delvecchio 2.50 6.00
160 Sid Abel 2.00 5.00
161 Ray Timgren 2.00 5.00
162 Ed Kullman 1.50 4.00
163 Billy Reay 1.50 4.00
164 Floyd Curry 1.50 4.00
165 Al Dewsbury 1.50 4.00
166 Allan Stanley 2.00 5.00
167 Paul Ronty 1.50 4.00
168 Gaye Stewart 1.50 4.00
169 Al Rollins 2.00 5.00
170 Leo Boivin 2.00 5.00
171 George Gee 2.00 5.00
172 Ted Kennedy 2.50 6.00
173 Alex Delvecchio 2.50 6.00
174 Marcel Pronovost 2.00 5.00
175 Leo Boivin 2.00 5.00
176 Ted Kennedy 2.50 6.00
177 Ron Stewart 2.00 5.00
178 Bud MacPherson 1.50 4.00
179 Marcel Pronovost 2.00 5.00
180 Alex Delvecchio 2.50 6.00
181 Max Bentley 2.00 5.00
182 Andy Bathgate 2.00 5.00
183 Harry Howell 2.00 5.00
184 Allan Stanley 2.00 5.00
185 Ed Sandford 1.50 4.00
186 Bill Quackenbush 2.00 5.00
187 Eddie Mazur 1.50 4.00
188 Floyd Curry 1.50 4.00
189 Eric Nesterenko 1.50 4.00
190 Ron Stewart 2.00 5.00
191 Leo Boivin 2.00 5.00
192 Ted Kennedy 2.50 6.00
193 Alex Delvecchio 2.50 6.00
194 Bob Armstrong 2.00 5.00
195 Paul Ronty 1.50 4.00
196 Camille Henry 1.50 4.00
197 Al Rollins 2.00 5.00
198 Al Dewsbury 1.50 4.00
199 Netminders nightmare 2.00 5.00
200 Ron Stewart 2.00 5.00
201 Dick Duff 2.00 5.00
202 Lorne Chabot 2.00 5.00
203 Busher Jackson 2.00 5.00
204 Joe Primeau 2.00 5.00
205 Harold Cotton 1.50 4.00
206 King Clancy 2.00 5.00
207 Hap Day 2.00 5.00
208 Newsy Lalonde 2.00 5.00
209 Albert Leduc 1.50 4.00
210 Babe Siebert 1.50 4.00
211 Toe Blake 2.00 5.00
212 Claude Provost 2.00 5.00
213 Toe Blake 2.00 5.00
214 Charlie Hodge 2.00 5.00
215 Floyd Curry 1.50 4.00
216 Len Broderick 1.50 4.00
217 Ed Chadwick 2.00 5.00
218 George Armstrong 2.00 5.00
219 Dick Duff 2.00 5.00
220 Ron Stewart 2.00 5.00
221 Billy Harris 1.50 4.00
222 Bob Baun 2.00 5.00
223 Billy Reay 1.50 4.00
224 Billy Harris 1.50 4.00
225 Toe Blake 2.00 5.00
226 Bob Nevin 1.50 4.00
227 Bob Baun 2.00 5.00
228 Charlie Hodge 2.00 5.00
229 Allan Stanley 2.00 5.00
230 Billy Reay 1.50 4.00
231 Dick Duff 2.00 5.00
232 Marcel Bonin 1.50 4.00
233 Claude Provost 2.00 5.00
234 Canadiens on guard 2.00 5.00
235 Elmer Lach Maurice Richard 2.50 6.00
236 Billy Harris 1.50 4.00
237 Punch Imlach 2.00 5.00
238 Charlie Hodge 2.00 5.00
239 Bob Baun 2.00 5.00
240 Ron Stewart 2.00 5.00
241 Toe Blake 2.00 5.00
242 Action around the net 1.50 4.00
243 Officials intervene 2.00 5.00
244 Frank Selke 2.00 5.00
245 King Clancy 2.00 5.00
246 Ron Stewart 2.00 5.00
247 Bob Baun 2.00 5.00
248 Dick Duff 2.00 5.00
249 Billy Harris 1.50 4.00
250 Allan Stanley 2.00 5.00
251 Jacques Plante 2.50 6.00
252 Sid Abel 2.00 5.00
253 Norm Ullman 2.50 6.00
254 Marcel Pronovost 2.00 5.00
255 Alex Delvecchio 2.50 6.00
256 Marcel Bonin 1.50 4.00
257 Claude Provost 2.00 5.00
258 Ron Stewart 2.00 5.00
259 Bob Nevin 1.50 4.00
260 Bob Baun 2.00 5.00
261 Dick Duff 2.00 5.00
262 Billy Harris 1.50 4.00
263 Allan Stanley 2.00 5.00
264 Maurice Richard 3.00 8.00
265 Alex Delvecchio 2.50 6.00
266 Norm Ullman 2.50 6.00
267 Ed Litzenberger 1.50 4.00
268 Marcel Pronovost 2.00 5.00
269 Marcel Bonin 1.50 4.00
270 Billy Harris 1.50 4.00
271 Dick Duff 2.00 5.00
272 Bob Baun 2.00 5.00
273 Maurice Richard 3.00 8.00
274 Allan Stanley 2.00 5.00
275 Bob Nevin 1.50 4.00
276 Ed Litzenberger 1.50 4.00
277 Norm Ullman 2.50 6.00
278 Alex Delvecchio 2.50 6.00
279 Marcel Pronovost 2.00 5.00
280 Sid Abel 2.00 5.00
281 Claude Provost 2.00 5.00
282 J.C. Tremblay 2.00 5.00
283 Allan Stanley 2.00 5.00
284 Ed Litzenberger 1.50 4.00
285 Rocket Roars Through 2.50 6.00
286 Bob Nevin 1.50 4.00
287 Jacques Laperriere 2.00 5.00
288 J.C. Tremblay 2.00 5.00
289 John Ferguson 1.50 4.00
290 Toe Blake 2.00 5.00
291 Marcel Pronovost 2.00 5.00
292 Alex Delvecchio 2.50 6.00
293 Allan Stanley 2.00 5.00
294 Dick Duff 2.00 5.00
295 Maurice Richard 3.00 8.00
296 Ron Stewart 2.00 5.00
297 J.C. Tremblay 2.00 5.00
298 John Ferguson 1.50 4.00
299 Toe Blake 2.00 5.00
300 Bill Quackenbush 2.00 5.00

2002-03 Parkhurst Stick and Jerseys

*STK/JSY: .5X TO 1.25X JSY HI
STATED PRINT RUN 90 SETS

2002-03 Parkhurst Teammates

This 20-card set featured three swatches of game jersey from players who were with the same club. Cards were limited to just 60 copies each.

TT1 Lindros/Leetch/Bure 12.50 30.00
TT2 LeClair/Recchi/Gagne 12.50 30.00
TT3 Sundin/Mogilny/Roberts 12.50 30.00
TT4 Yzerman/Shanahan/Fedorov 40.00 100.00
TT5 Brodeur/Stevens/Elias 20.00 50.00
TT6 Potvin/Palffy/Allison 15.00 40.00
TT7 Koivu/Theodore/Rivet 12.50 30.00
TT8 Thornton/Samsonov/McLaren 12.50 30.00
TT9 Kovalchuk/Heatley/Stefan 15.00 40.00
TT10 Dunham/Legwand/Hartnell 12.50 30.00
TT11 Alfredsson/Havlat/Hossa 15.00 40.00
TT12 Satan/Connolly/Dumont 12.50 30.00
TT13 Daze/Thibault/Zhamnov 12.50 30.00
TT14 Lemieux/Hedberg/Kovalev 30.00 80.00
TT15 Nolan/Selanne/Nabokov 12.50 30.00
TT16 Pronger/MacInnis/Weight 12.50 30.00
TT17 Jagr/Kolzig/Bondra 15.00 40.00
TT18 Cloutier/Bertuzzi/Naslund 12.50 30.00
TT19 Forsberg/Sakic/Roy 25.00 60.00
TT20 Burke/Briere/Numminen 12.50 30.00

2002-03 Parkhurst Vintage Memorabilia

This 20-card set featured pieces of game-used equipment. Each card was limited to just 20 copies each.

VM1 John Bucyk 12.00 30.00
VM2 Gilbert Perreault 15.00 40.00
VM3 Bobby Hull 20.00 50.00
VM4 Stan Mikita 20.00 50.00
VM5 Marcel Dionne
VM6 Jari Kurri 12.00 30.00
VM7 Jean Beliveau 25.00 50.00
VM8 Doug Harvey 12.00 30.00
VM9 Guy Lafleur 12.00 30.00
VM10 Frank Mahovlich 15.00 40.00
VM11 Henri Richard 15.00 40.00
VM12 Maurice Richard 30.00 80.00
VM13 Tiny Thompson 15.00 40.00
VM14 Bernie Parent 30.00 80.00
VM15 Tim Horton 15.00 40.00
VM16 Terry Sawchuk
VM17 Vladislav Tretiak 25.00 60.00
VM18 Gerry Cheevers 15.00 40.00
VM19 Ted Kennedy 20.00 50.00
VM20 Bill Gadsby 15.00 40.00

2002-03 Parkhurst Vintage Teammates

Limited to just 20 sets, this 20-card set featured dual game jersey swatches from retired greats who played for the same club.

VT1 B.Hull/D.Hull 20.00 50.00
VT2 P.Esposito/Giacomin 15.00 40.00
VT3 Bucyk/G.Cheevers 15.00 40.00
VT4 Savard/Robinson 30.00 60.00
VT5 T.Esposito/Mikita 30.00 60.00
VT6 Sawchuk/S.Abel 20.00 40.00
VT7 Mahovlich/Mahovlich 20.00 40.00
VT8 Beliveau/D.Harvey 20.00 50.00
VT9 Lafleur/H.Richard 20.00 50.00
VT10 Trottier/M.Bossy 20.00 50.00
VT11 Potvin/B.Nystrom 15.00 40.00
VT12 Clarke/B.Barber 15.00 40.00
VT13 Parent/D.Schultz 25.00 60.00
VT14 T.Horton/R.Kelly 40.00 100.00
VT15 Kharlamov/Tretiak 50.00 100.00
VT16 Mosienko/H.Lumley 15.00 40.00
VT17 Delvecchio/Crozier 15.00 40.00
VT18 Bailey/K.Clancy 20.00 50.00
VT19 Shore/Thompson 20.00 50.00
VT20 McDonald/Williams 15.00 40.00

2005-06 Parkhurst

This 700-card set was issued into the hobby in six-card packs, with a $1.59 SRP, which came 36 packs to a box and 20 boxes to a case. Cards numbered 1-499 feature a mix of veterans and Rookie Cards in team alphabetical order while cards 501-530 honor team captains and cards 531-560 are team cards. Cards 561-585 is a Northern Stars subset while cards 586-600 are highlight cards. The set concludes with two more subsets: Rookies (601-670) and Team Checklists (671-700)

COMPLETE SET (700) 60.00 120.00
1 Andy McDonald .25 .60
2 Teemu Selanne .60 1.50
3 Scott Niedermayer .30 .75
4 Joffrey Lupul .25 .60
5 Todd Marchant .20 .50
6 Chris Kunitz .30 .75
7 Jean-Sebastien Giguere .30 .75
8 Samuel Pahlsson .20 .50
9 Jonathan Hedstrom .20 .50
10 Ilja Bryzgalov .30 .75
11 Jeff Friesen .20 .50
12 Rob Niedermayer .25 .60
13 Francois Beauchemin .20 .50
14 Vitaly Vishnevski .20 .50
15 Ruslan Salei .20 .50
16 Todd Fedoruk .20 .50
17 Dustin Penner RC 1.00 2.50
18 Ilya Kovalchuk .30 .75
19 Marc Savard .20 .50
20 Marian Hossa .25 .60
21 Vyacheslav Kozlov .20 .50
22 Peter Bondra .25 .60
23 Jaroslav Modry .20 .50
24 Greg de Vries .20 .50
25 Niclas Havelid .20 .50
26 Patrik Stefan .20 .50
27 Serge Aubin .20 .50
28 Andy Sutton .20 .50
29 Kari Lehtonen .25 .60
30 Garnet Exelby .20 .50
31 Michael Garnett .20 .50
32 Bobby Holik .20 .50
33 Scott Mellanby .20 .50
34 Patrice Bergeron .40 1.00
35 Brad Boyes .25 .60
36 Tim Thomas .30 .75
37 Glen Murray .25 .60
38 Marco Sturm .20 .50
39 Wayne Primeau .20 .50
40 Brad Stuart .20 .50
41 Andrew Raycroft .25 .60
42 P.J. Axelsson .20 .50
43 Brian Leetch .30 .75
44 Travis Green .20 .50
45 David Tanabe .20 .50
46 Nick Boynton .20 .50
47 Hal Gill .20 .50
48 Josh Langfeld .20 .50
49 Tom Fitzgerald .20 .50
50 Ales Kotalik .20 .50
51 Maxim Afinogenov .20 .50
52 Chris Drury .25 .60
53 Tim Connolly .20 .50
54 Ryan Miller .30 .75
55 Brian Campbell .25 .60
56 Jochen Hecht .20 .50
57 Teppo Numminen .25 .60
58 Martin Biron .25 .60
59 Derek Roy .20 .50
60 Mike Grier .20 .50
61 Paul Gaustad .20 .50
62 Daniel Briere .30 .75
63 Jason Pominville .30 .75
64 Jay McKee .20 .50
65 J.P. Dumont .20 .50
66 Henrik Tallinder .20 .50
67 Jarome Iginla .30 .75
68 Daymond Langkow .20 .50
69 Kristian Huselius .20 .50
70 Tony Amonte .25 .60
71 Andrew Ference .20 .50
72 Chuck Kobasew .20 .50
73 Miikka Kiprusoff .25 .60
74 Robyn Regehr .20 .50
75 Roman Hamrlik .25 .60
76 Darren McCarty .20 .50
77 Stephane Yelle .20 .50
78 Chris Simon .20 .50
79 Jordan Leopold .20 .50
80 Rhett Warrener .20 .50
81 Shean Donovan .20 .50
82 Marcus Nilson .20 .50
83 Mike LeClerc .20 .50
84 Eric Staal .40 1.00
85 Cory Stillman .25 .60
86 Erik Cole .25 .60
87 Justin Williams .25 .60
88 Rod Brind`Amour .30 .75
89 Martin Gerber .25 .60
90 Doug Weight .30 .75
91 Ray Whitney .25 .60
92 Matt Cullen .20 .50
93 Frantisek Kaberle .20 .50
94 Bret Hedican .20 .50
95 Oleg Tverdovsky .20 .50
96 Kevyn Adams .20 .50
97 Aaron Ward .20 .50
98 Mark Recchi .40 1.00
99 Glen Wesley .20 .50
100 Josef Vasicek .20 .50
101 Brandon Bochenski RC 1.00 2.50
102 Kyle Calder .20 .50
103 Mark Bell .20 .50
104 Martin Lapointe .20 .50
105 Pavel Vorobiev .20 .50
106 Nikolai Khabibulin .30 .75
107 Craig Anderson .30 .75
108 Matthew Barnaby .20 .50
109 Radim Vrbata .25 .60
110 Rene Bourque RC 1.00 2.50
111 Eric Daze .25 .60
112 Tuomo Ruutu .30 .75
113 Adrian Aucoin .20 .50
114 Jim Vandermeer .20 .50
115 Milan Bartovic .20 .50
116 Curtis Brown .20 .50
117 Alex Tanguay .30 .75
118 Joe Sakic .50 1.25
119 Marek Svatos .25 .60
120 Jose Theodore .30 .75
121 Andrew Brunette .20 .50
122 Milan Hejduk .25 .60
123 John-Michael Liles .20 .50
124 Rob Blake .30 .75
125 Pierre Turgeon .30 .75
126 Ian Laperriere .20 .50
127 Antti Laaksonen .20 .50
128 Patrice Brisebois .20 .50
129 Brett Clark .20 .50
130 Karlis Skrastins .20 .50
131 Brett McLean .20 .50
132 Dan Hinote .20 .50
133 Steve Konowalchuk .20 .50
134 David Vyborny .20 .50
135 Nikolai Zherdev .20 .50
136 Bryan Berard .20 .50
137 Rick Nash .30 .75
138 Sergei Fedorov .50 1.25
139 Jan Hrdina .20 .50
140 Duvie Westcott .20 .50
141 Manny Malhotra .25 .60
142 Marc Denis .25 .60
143 Jason Chimera .20 .50
144 Trevor Letowski .20 .50
145 Adam Foote .20 .50
146 Rostislav Klesla .20 .50
147 Dan Fritsche .20 .50
148 Pascal LeClaire .25 .60
149 Jody Shelley .20 .50
150 Jaroslav Balastik RC .60 1.50
151 Johan Hedberg .25 .60
152 Trevor Daley .20 .50
153 Jon Klemm .20 .50
154 Willie Mitchell .20 .50
155 Steve Ott .25 .60
156 Antti Miettinen .20 .50
157 Niko Kapanen .20 .50
158 Stu Barnes .20 .50
159 Philippe Boucher .20 .50
160 Bill Guerin .30 .75
161 Jason Arnott .25 .60
162 Mike Modano .50 1.25
163 Marty Turco .30 .75
164 Brenden Morrow .25 .60
165 Sergei Zubov .25 .60
166 Jere Lehtinen .25 .60
167 Pavel Datsyuk .40 1.00
168 Henrik Zetterberg .40 1.00
169 Manny Legace .30 .75
170 Nicklas Lidstrom .30 .75
171 Brendan Shanahan .40 1.00
172 Jason Williams .20 .50
173 Steve Yzerman .75 2.00
174 Mathieu Schneider .20 .50
175 Robert Lang .20 .50
176 Tomas Holmstrom .25 .60
177 Mikael Samuelsson .20 .50
178 Chris Osgood .30 .75
179 Kris Draper .40 1.00
180 Kirk Maltby .20 .50
181 Chris Chelios .30 .75
182 Johan Franzen RC 1.50 4.00
183 Brett Lebda RC .60 1.50
184 Jiri Fischer .20 .50
185 Shawn Horcoff .20 .50
186 Ty Conklin .25 .60
187 Ales Hemsky .25 .60
188 Jarret Stoll .25 .60
189 Ryan Smyth .25 .60
190 Chris Pronger .25 .60
191 Jaroslav Spacek .20 .50
192 Raffi Torres .20 .50
193 Jussi Markkanen .20 .50
194 Marc-Andre Bergeron .20 .50
195 Fernando Pisani .20 .50
196 Michael Peca .25 .60
197 Jason Smith .20 .50
198 Dwayne Roloson .25 .60
199 Georges Laraque .25 .60
200 Sergei Samsonov .25 .60
201 Olli Jokinen .30 .75
202 Roberto Luongo .50 1.25
203 Nathan Horton .30 .75
204 Joe Nieuwendyk .30 .75
205 Jozef Stumpel .20 .50
206 Jay Bouwmeester .30 .75
207 Gary Roberts .20 .50
208 Chris Gratton .20 .50
209 Martin Gelinas .20 .50
210 Stephen Weiss .20 .50
211 Mike Van Ryn .20 .50
212 Jamie McLennan .20 .50
213 Lukas Krajicek .20 .50
214 Jon Sim .20 .50
215 Sean Hill .20 .50
216 Juraj Kolnik .20 .50
217 Pavol Demitra .40 1.00
218 Mathieu Garon .25 .60
219 Lubomir Visnovsky .20 .50
220 Craig Conroy .20 .50
221 Alexander Frolov .20 .50
222 Mike Cammalleri .30 .75
223 Derek Armstrong .20 .50
224 Joe Corvo .20 .50
225 Eric Belanger .20 .50
226 Sean Avery .20 .50
227 Luc Robitaille .30 .75
228 Dustin Brown .30 .75
229 Jeremy Roenick .30 .75
230 Jason Labarbera .25 .60
231 Mattias Norstrom .20 .50
232 Mark Parrish .20 .50
233 Brian Rolston .25 .60
234 Pierre-Marc Bouchard .30 .75
235 Manny Fernandez .25 .60
236 Marian Gaborik .50 1.25
237 Randy Robitaille .20 .50
238 Todd White .20 .50
239 Alexandre Daigle .20 .50
240 Wes Walz .20 .50
241 Marc Chouinard .20 .50
242 Martin Skoula .20 .50
243 Filip Kuba .20 .50
244 Nick Schultz .20 .50
245 Kurtis Foster .20 .50
246 Derek Boogaard RC 1.25 3.00
247 Brent Burns .40 1.00
248 Pascal Dupuis .20 .50
249 Saku Koivu .30 .75
250 David Aebischer .25 .60
251 Alex Kovalev .25 .60
252 Michael Ryder .25 .60
253 Mike Ribeiro .25 .60
254 Andrei Markov .30 .75
255 Jan Bulis .20 .50
256 Craig Rivet .20 .50
257 Steve Begin .20 .50
258 Sheldon Souray .20 .50
259 Tomas Plekanec .30 .75
260 Richard Zednik .20 .50
261 Cristobal Huet .25 .60
262 Francis Bouillon .20 .50
263 Chris Higgins .20 .50
264 Radek Bonk .20 .50
265 Niklas Sundstrom .20 .50
266 Pierre Dagenais .20 .50
267 Mathieu Dandenault .20 .50
268 Paul Kariya .40
269 Tomas Vokoun .25
270 Steve Sullivan .20
271 Yanic Perreault .20
272 Mike Sillinger .20
273 Kimmo Timonen .20
274 Marek Zidlicky .20
275 Scott Hartnell .30
276 Martin Erat .20
277 Dan Hamhuis .25
278 Adam Hall .20
279 Scottie Upshall .20
280 David Legwand .25
281 Darcy Hordichuk .20
282 Vernon Fiddler .20
283 Scott Walker .20
284 Brendan Witt .20
285 Brian Gionta .25
286 Scott Gomez .25
287 Martin Brodeur .60
288 Jamie Langenbrunner .20
289 Brian Rafalski .25
290 Sergei Brylin .20
291 Patrik Elias .30
292 John Madden .20
293 Viktor Kozlov .20
294 Scott Clemmensen .20
295 Grant Marshall .20
296 Jay Pandolfo .20
297 Richard Matvichuk .20
298 Erik Rasmussen .20
299 Colin White .20
300 Paul Martin .20
301 Alexei Yashin .25
302 Miroslav Satan .25
303 Mike York .20
304 Jason Blake .20
305 Robert Nilsson RC 1.00
306 Trent Hunter .20
307 Alexei Zhitnik .20
308 Eric Godard .20
309 Rick DiPietro .25
310 Arron Asham .20
311 Denis Grebeshkov .20
312 John Erskine .20
313 Radek Martinek .20
314 Garth Snow .25
315 Shawn Bates .20
316 Sean Bergenheim .20
317 Jaromir Jagr .75
318 Martin Straka .20
319 Michael Nylander .20
320 Martin Rucinsky .20
321 Kevin Weekes .25
322 Petr Sykora .25
323 Steve Rucchin .20
324 Jason Ward .20
325 Michal Rozsival .20
326 Fedor Tyutin .20
327 Marek Malik .20
328 Tom Poti .20
329 Dominic Moore .20
330 Darius Kasparaitis .20
331 Jed Ortmeyer .20
332 Marcel Hossa .20
333 Dominik Hasek .50
334 Daniel Alfredsson .30
335 Dany Heatley .30
336 Jason Spezza .30
337 Wade Redden .20
338 Peter Schaefer .20
339 Bryan Smolinski .20
340 Mike Fisher .20
341 Zdeno Chara .30
342 Chris Neil .20
343 Antoine Vermette .25
344 Ray Emery .30
345 Patrick Eaves RC 1.00
346 Vaclav Varada .20
347 Martin Havlat .30
348 Chris Phillips .20
349 Tyler Arnason .20
350 Antero Niittymaki .25
351 Simon Gagne .30
352 Peter Forsberg .40
353 Mike Knuble .20
354 Michal Handzus .25
355 Joni Pitkanen .20
356 Sami Kapanen .20
357 Kim Johnsson .20
358 Mike Rathje .20
359 Eric Desjardins .25
360 Derian Hatcher .20
361 Robert Esche .25
362 Brian Savage .20
363 Chris Therien .20
364 Keith Primeau .30
365 Petr Nedved .20
366 Donald Brashear .20
367 Curtis Joseph .30
368 Ladislav Nagy .20
369 Shane Doan .25
370 Mike Comrie .25
371 Mike Johnson .20
372 Paul Mara .20
373 Geoff Sanderson .20
374 Steven Reinprecht .20
375 Dave Scatchard .20
376 Oleg Saprykin .20
377 Zbynek Michalek .20
378 Boyd Devereaux .20
379 Fredrik Sjostrom .20
380 Mike Ricci .25
381 Tyson Nash .20
382 Derek Morris .20
383 Niklas Nordgren RC 1.00
384 Sergei Gonchar .20
385 Marc-Andre Fleury .50
386 John LeClair .30
387 Richard Jackman .20
388 Ryan Malone .20
389 Sebastien Caron .20
390 Mario Lemieux 1.00
391 Brooks Orpik .25
392 Konstantin Koltsov .20
393 Erik Christensen RC .60
394 Josef Melichar .20
395 Jocelyn Thibault .25
396 Tomas Surovy .20
397 Andre Roy .20
398 Jani Rita .20
399 Vesa Toskala .25
400 Joe Thornton .40
401 Patrick Marleau .30
402 Jonathan Cheechoo .30
403 Evgeni Nabokov .25
404 Nils Ekman .20
405 Tom Preissing .20
406 Milan Michalek .20
407 Alyn McCauley .20
408 Scott Thornton .20

Card	Low	High
Kyle McLaren	.20	.50
Scott Hannan	.20	.50
Marcel Goc	.25	.60
Grant Stevenson RC	.60	1.50
Christian Ehrhoff	.20	.50
Mark Smith	.20	.50
Scott Young	.20	.50
Petr Cajanek	.20	.50
Dean McAmmond	.20	.50
Curtis Sanford	.25	.60
Keith Tkachuk	.30	.75
Dallas Drake	.20	.50
Jamal Mayers	.20	.50
Jeff Hoggan RC	.60	1.50
Christian Backman	.20	.50
Barret Jackman	.20	.50
Mark Rycroft	.20	.50
Jay McClement RC	.60	1.50
Patrick Lalime	.25	.60
Kevin Dallman RC	.75	2.00
Dennis Wideman RC	.60	1.50
Brad Richards	.30	.75
Vaclav Prospal	.20	.50
John Grahame	.20	.50
Vincent Lecavalier	.25	.60
Martin St. Louis	.30	.75
Dan Boyle	.25	.60
Fredrik Modin	.20	.50
Ruslan Fedotenko	.20	.50
Pavel Kubina	.20	.50
Darryl Sydor	.20	.50
Sean Burke	.20	.50
Tim Taylor	.20	.50
Cory Sarich	.20	.50
Nolan Pratt	.20	.50
Rob DiMaio	.20	.50
Paul Ranger RC	.60	1.50
Ryan Craig RC	.60	1.50
Mats Sundin	.30	.75
Ed Belfour	.30	.75
Bryan McCabe	.20	.50
Jason Allison	.25	.60
Tomas Kaberle	.20	.50
Darcy Tucker	.25	.60
Kyle Wellwood	.25	.60
Jeff O'Neill	.20	.50
Alexei Ponikarovsky	.20	.50
Eric Lindros	.50	1.25
Chad Kilger	.20	.50
Mikael Tellqvist	.25	.60
Staffan Kronwall RC	.60	1.50
Nik Antropov	.25	.60
Matt Stajan	.25	.60
Tie Domi	.25	.60
Luke Richardson	.20	.50
Alexander Khavanov	.20	.50
Markus Naslund	.30	.75
Daniel Sedin	.30	.75
Henrik Sedin	.30	.75
Todd Bertuzzi	.30	.75
Alexander Auld	.20	.50
Brendan Morrison	.20	.50
Anson Carter	.25	.60
Sami Salo	.20	.50
Ed Jovanovski	.25	.60
Nolan Baumgartner	.20	.50
Mattias Ohlund	.20	.50
Dan Cloutier	.25	.60
Jarkko Ruutu	.20	.50
Bryan Allen	.20	.50
Ryan Kesler	.40	1.00
Matt Cooke	.20	.50
Trevor Linden	.30	.75
Mika Noronen	.25	.60
Brooks Laich	.20	.50
Dainius Zubrus	.20	.50
Olaf Kolzig	.30	.75
Matt Pettinger	.20	.50
Jeff Halpern	.20	.50
Brian Willsie	.20	.50
Brent Johnson	.20	.50
Chris Clark	.20	.50
Brian Sutherby	.20	.50
Jamie Heward	.20	.50
Ben Clymer	.20	.50
Bryan Muir	.20	.50
Mathieu Biron	.20	.50
Shaone Morrisonn	.20	.50
Matt Bradley	.20	.50
Mike Green RC	1.25	3.00
Rico Fata	.20	.50
Gordie Howe	1.00	2.50
Scott Niedermayer CPT	.30	.75
Scott Mellanby CPT	.20	.50
Vincent Lecavalier CPT	.25	.60
Chris Drury CPT	.25	.60
Jarome Iginla CPT	.30	.75
Rod Brind`Amour CPT	.30	.75
Adrian Aucoin CPT	.20	.50
Joe Sakic CPT	.50	1.25
Adam Foote CPT	.20	.50
Mike Modano CPT	.50	1.25
Steve Yzerman CPT	.75	2.00
Jason Smith CPT	.20	.50
Olli Jokinen CPT	.30	.75
Mattias Norstrom CPT	.20	.50
Saku Koivu CPT	.30	.75
Greg Johnson CPT	.20	.50
Alexei Yashin CPT	.25	.60
Daniel Alfredsson CPT	.30	.75
Keith Primeau CPT	.30	.75
Shane Doan CPT	.25	.60
Patrick Marleau CPT	.30	.75
Dallas Drake CPT	.20	.50
Mats Sundin CPT	.30	.75
Markus Naslund CPT	.30	.75
Jeff Halpern CPT	.20	.50
Sidney Crosby CPT	2.50	6.00
Brian Leetch CPT	.30	.75
Jaromir Jagr CPT	.75	2.00
Wes Walz CPT	.20	.50
Patrik Elias CPT	.30	.75
Anaheim Mighty Ducks	.20	.50
Atlanta Thrashers	.20	.50
Boston Bruins	.20	.50
Buffalo Sabres	.20	.50
Calgary Flames	.20	.50
Carolina Hurricanes	.20	.50
Chicago Blackhawks	.20	.50
Colorado Colorado Avalanche	.20	.50
Columbus Blue Jackets	.20	.50
Dallas Stars	.20	.50
Detroit Red Wings	.20	.50
Edmonton Oilers	.20	.50
Florida Panthers	.20	.50
Los Angeles Kings	.20	.50
Minnesota Wild	.20	.50
Montreal Canadiens	.20	.50
Nashville Predators	.20	.50
New Jersey Devils	.20	.50
New York Islanders	.20	.50
550 New York Rangers	.20	.50
551 Ottawa Senators	.20	.50
552 Philadelphia Flyers	.20	.50
553 Phoenix Coyotes	.20	.50
554 Pittsburgh Penguins	.20	.50
555 San Jose Sharks	.20	.50
556 St. Louis Blues	.20	.50
557 Tampa Bay Lightning	.20	.50
558 Toronto Maple Leafs	.20	.50
559 Vancouver Canucks	.20	.50
560 Washington Capitals	.20	.50
561 Martin Brodeur NS	1.50	4.00
562 Roberto Luongo NS	.50	1.25
563 Marty Turco NS	.30	.75
564 Rob Blake NS	.30	.75
565 Adam Foote NS	.20	.50
566 Chris Pronger NS	.25	.60
567 Wade Redden NS	.20	.50
568 Robyn Regehr NS	.20	.50
569 Todd Bertuzzi NS	.30	.75
570 Shane Doan NS	.25	.60
571 Kris Draper NS	.40	1.00
572 Simon Gagne NS	.30	.75
573 Dany Heatley NS	.30	.75
574 Jarome Iginla NS	.30	.75
575 Vincent Lecavalier NS	.25	.60
576 Rick Nash NS	.30	.75
577 Brad Richards NS	.30	.75
578 Joe Sakic NS	.50	1.25
579 Ryan Smyth NS	.25	.60
580 Martin St. Louis NS	.30	.75
581 Joe Thornton NS	.40	1.00
582 Jay Bouwmeester NS	.30	.75
583 Bryan McCabe NS	.20	.50
584 Ed Jovanovski NS	.25	.60
585 Scott Niedermayer NS	.30	.75
586 Sidney Crosby HL	2.50	6.00
587 Sidney Crosby HL	2.50	6.00
588 Alexander Ovechkin HL	2.50	6.00
589 Ed Belfour HL	.30	.75
590 Mario Lemieux HL	1.00	2.50
591 Joe Thornton HL	.40	1.00
592 Teemu Selanne HL	.60	1.50
593 Sidney Crosby HL	2.50	6.00
594 Jaromir Jagr HL	.75	2.00
595 Luc Robitaille HL	.30	.75
596 Manny Legace HL	.30	.75
597 Alexander Ovechkin HL	2.50	6.00
598 Daniel Alfredsson HL	.30	.75
599 Henrik Lundqvist HL	2.00	5.00
600 Alexander Ovechkin HL	2.50	6.00
601 Ryan Getzlaf RC	2.50	6.00
602 Corey Perry RC	4.00	10.00
603 Braydon Coburn RC	1.00	2.50
604 Jim Slater RC	.75	2.00
605 Andrew Alberts RC	.60	1.50
606 Hannu Toivonen RC	1.00	2.50
607 Milan Jurcina RC	.75	2.00
608 Jordan Sigalet RC	.60	1.50
609 Ben Walter RC	.60	1.50
610 Thomas Vanek RC	2.00	5.00
611 Daniel Paille RC	1.00	2.50
612 Dion Phaneuf RC	1.50	4.00
613 Eric Nystrom RC	.75	2.00
614 Cam Ward RC	1.50	4.00
615 Andrew Ladd RC	1.25	3.00
616 Brent Seabrook RC	2.00	5.00
617 Cam Barker RC	.75	2.00
618 Corey Crawford RC	3.00	8.00
619 Peter Budaj RC	1.25	3.00
620 Wojtek Wolski RC	.75	2.00
621 Brad Richardson RC	1.00	2.50
622 Gilbert Brule RC	1.00	2.50
623 Alexandre Picard RC	.60	1.50
624 Jussi Jokinen RC	1.00	2.50
625 Jim Howard RC	2.50	6.00
626 Kyle Quincey RC	.75	2.00
627 Valtteri Filppula RC	1.25	3.00
628 Matt Greene RC	.60	1.50
629 Jean-Francois Jacques RC	.60	1.50
630 Rostislav Olesz RC	.75	2.00
631 Anthony Stewart RC	.75	2.00
632 Rob Globke RC	.60	1.50
633 George Parros RC	.60	1.50
634 Mikko Koivu RC	1.25	3.00
635 Yann Danis RC	.75	2.00
636 Alexander Perezhogin RC	.75	2.00
637 Maxim Lapierre RC	1.00	2.50
638 Andrei Kostitsyn RC	1.25	3.00
639 Ryan Suter RC	1.25	3.00
640 Zach Parise RC	2.50	6.00
641 Barry Tallackson RC	.75	2.00
642 Jeff Tambellini RC	.60	1.50
643 Chris Campoli RC	.60	1.50
644 Jeremy Colliton RC	.60	1.50
645 Bruno Gervais RC	.60	1.50
646 Henrik Lundqvist RC	4.00	10.00
647 Petr Prucha RC	1.00	2.50
648 Al Montoya RC	1.00	2.50
649 Patrick Eaves	1.00	2.50
650 Andrej Meszaros RC	.75	2.00
651 Christoph Schubert RC	.60	1.50
652 Mike Richards RC	2.00	5.00
653 Jeff Carter RC	1.50	4.00
654 R.J. Umberger RC	1.00	2.50
655 Ben Eager RC	.75	2.00
656 Keith Ballard RC	.75	2.00
657 Sidney Crosby RC	12.00	30.00
658 Maxime Talbot RC	1.00	2.50
659 Ryan Whitney RC	1.00	2.50
660 Colby Armstrong RC	1.00	2.50
661 Ryane Clowe RC	1.25	3.00
662 Steve Bernier RC	1.00	2.50
663 Dimitri Patzold RC	.60	1.50
664 Lee Stempniak RC	1.00	2.50
665 Evgeny Artyukhin RC	.75	2.00
666 Jay Harrison RC	.75	2.00
667 Alexander Steen RC	2.00	5.00
668 Kevin Bieksa RC	1.25	3.00
669 Alexander Ovechkin RC	8.00	20.00
670 Tomas Fleischmann RC	1.00	2.50
671 Jean-Sebastien Giguere TC	.30	.75
672 Ilya Kovalchuk TC	.30	.75
673 Patrice Bergeron TC	.40	1.00
674 Ryan Miller TC	.30	.75
675 Jarome Iginla TC	.30	.75
676 Eric Staal TC	.40	1.00
677 Nikolai Khabibulin TC	.30	.75
678 Joe Sakic TC	.50	1.25
679 Rick Nash TC	.30	.75
680 Mike Modano TC	.50	1.25
681 Steve Yzerman TC	.75	2.00
682 Chris Pronger TC	.25	.60
683 Roberto Luongo TC	.50	1.25
684 Luc Robitaille TC	.30	.75
685 Marian Gaborik TC	.50	1.25
686 Saku Koivu TC	.30	.75
687 Paul Kariya TC	.40	1.00
688 Martin Brodeur TC	.60	1.50
689 Alexei Yashin TC	.25	.60
690 Jaromir Jagr TC	.75	2.00
691 Dominik Hasek TC	.50	1.25
692 Peter Forsberg TC	.40	1.00
693 Shane Doan TC	.25	.60
694 Sidney Crosby TC	2.50	6.00
695 Joe Thornton TC	.40	1.00
696 Keith Tkachuk TC	.30	.75
697 Vincent Lecavalier TC	.25	.60
698 Mats Sundin TC	.30	.75
699 Markus Naslund TC	.30	.75
700 Alexander Ovechkin TC	2.50	6.00

2005-06 Parkhurst Facsimile Auto Parallel

PRINT RUN 100 SER.#'d SETS

Card	Low	High
526 Sidney Crosby CPT	25.00	60.00
586 Sidney Crosby HL	25.00	60.00
587 Sidney Crosby HL	25.00	60.00
593 Sidney Crosby HL	25.00	60.00
652 Mike Richards	10.00	25.00
657 Sidney Crosby	60.00	120.00
669 Alexander Ovechkin	25.00	60.00
694 Sidney Crosby TC	25.00	60.00

2005-06 Parkhurst Signatures

STATED ODDS 1:36

Card	Low	High
AL Andrew Alberts	5.00	12.00
AB Adam Berkhoel	5.00	12.00
AK Andrei Kostitsyn	6.00	15.00
AL Andrew Ladd	8.00	20.00
AM Andrei Meszaros	3.00	8.00
AM Al Montoya	6.00	15.00
AN Antero Niittymaki	8.00	20.00
AO Alexander Ovechkin SP	150.00	300.00
AP Alexandre Picard SP	6.00	15.00
BA Milan Bartovic	3.00	8.00
BB Brad Boyes	3.00	8.00
BC Braydon Coburn	5.00	12.00
BE Ben Eager	5.00	12.00
BL Brett Lebda	5.00	12.00
BO Brandon Bochenski	5.00	12.00
BS Brent Seabrook	6.00	15.00
BT Barry Tallackson	5.00	12.00
BU Peter Budaj	6.00	15.00
BW Ben Walter	3.00	8.00
CC Chris Campoli	3.00	8.00
CK Chuck Kobasew	3.00	8.00
CS Christoph Schubert	3.00	8.00
CT Chris Thorburn	3.00	8.00
DB Daniel Briere	6.00	15.00
DE Derek Boogaard	6.00	15.00
DK Duncan Keith	12.50	25.00
DL David Leneveu	5.00	12.00
DP Dimitri Patzold	5.00	12.00
DW Dwayne Roloson	6.00	15.00
EA Evgeny Artyukhin	3.00	8.00
FP Fernando Pisani	6.00	15.00
GP George Parros	3.00	8.00
HO Marcel Hossa SP	10.00	25.00
JF Johan Franzen	12.00	30.00
JH Jim Howard	10.00	25.00
JH Jeff Halpern	3.00	8.00
JI Jarome Iginla SP	30.00	60.00
JJ Jussi Jokinen SP	10.00	25.00
JL Jason Labarbera	3.00	8.00
JS Jordan Sigalet	6.00	15.00
JS Jim Slater	5.00	12.00
JT Jeff Tambellini	3.00	8.00
JV Josef Vasicek	3.00	8.00
JW Jeff Woywitka	3.00	8.00
KC Kyle Calder	3.00	8.00
KN Kevin Nastiuk	5.00	12.00
KO Mikko Koivu	6.00	15.00
KQ Kyle Quincey	3.00	8.00
IL Ian Laperriere	5.00	12.00
LI John-Michael Liles	6.00	15.00
LS Lee Stempniak SP	8.00	20.00
MA Maxim Afinogenov SP	12.00	30.00
MB Martin Biron	6.00	15.00
MC Mike Cammalleri	8.00	20.00
MG Marian Gaborik SP	30.00	60.00
MH Michal Handzus	12.00	30.00
MJ Milan Jurcina SP	8.00	20.00
ML Maxim Lapierre	6.00	15.00
MM Milan Michalek SP	8.00	20.00
MR Mike Richards SP	30.00	60.00
MS Marc Savard	3.00	8.00
MT Mikael Tellqvist	6.00	15.00
NA Nik Antropov SP	10.00	25.00
NN Niklas Nordgren	3.00	8.00
OJ Olli Jokinen SP	10.00	25.00
OK Olaf Kolzig	6.00	15.00
OK Ole-Kristian Tollefson	3.00	8.00
PB Pierre-Marc Bouchard	3.00	8.00
PE Patrick Eaves	6.00	15.00
PN Petteri Nokelainen	3.00	8.00
PP Petr Prucha SP	10.00	25.00
PS Philippe Sauve	4.00	10.00
RC Ryan Craig	5.00	12.00
RE Robert Esche SP	10.00	25.00
RF Ruslan Fedotenko	3.00	8.00
RG Ryan Getzlaf SP	25.00	50.00
RH Ryan Hollweg	5.00	12.00
RM Ryan Malone	6.00	15.00
RN Robert Nilsson	5.00	12.00
RO Rostislav Olesz	5.00	12.00
SB Steve Bernier	6.00	15.00
SC Sidney Crosby SP	600.00	900.00
SH Scott Hartnell	3.00	8.00
TB Todd Bertuzzi SP	25.00	50.00
TC Ty Conklin	3.00	8.00
TF Tomas Fleischmann	5.00	12.00
TG Tim Gleason	3.00	8.00
TS Timofei Shishkanov	3.00	8.00
WI Brad Winchester	5.00	12.00
YD Yann Danis	6.00	15.00
ZM Zbynek Michalek	3.00	8.00
ZP Zach Parise	12.00	30.00

2005-06 Parkhurst True Colors

STATED ODDS 1:432

Card	Low	High
TCANA Anaheim Ducks	30.00	80.00
TCATL Atlanta Thrashers	30.00	80.00
TCBOS Boston Bruins	30.00	80.00
TCBUF Buffalo Sabres	25.00	60.00
TCCAR Carolina Hurricanes	25.00	60.00
TCCGY Calgary Flames	40.00	100.00
TCCHI Chicago Blackhawks	30.00	80.00
TCCLB Columbus Blue Jackets	40.00	100.00
TCCOL Colorado Avalanche	20.00	50.00
TCDAL Dallas Stars	25.00	60.00
TCDET Detroit Red Wings	40.00	100.00
TCEDM Edmonton Oilers	40.00	100.00
TCFLA Florida Panthers	25.00	60.00
TCLAK Los Angeles Kings	25.00	60.00
TCMIN Minnesota Wild	30.00	80.00
TCMTL Montreal Canadiens	30.00	80.00
TCNJD New Jersey Devils	40.00	100.00
TCNSH Nashville Predators	30.00	80.00
TCNYI New York Islanders SP	75.00	150.00
TCNYR New York Rangers	30.00	80.00
TCOTT Ottawa Senators	30.00	80.00
TCPHI Philadelphia Flyers	40.00	100.00
TCPHX Phoenix Coyotes	25.00	60.00
TCPIT Pittsburgh Penguins	40.00	100.00
TCSJS San Jose Sharks	30.00	80.00
TCSTL St. Louis Blues	20.00	50.00
TCTBL Tampa Bay Lightning	25.00	60.00
TCTOR Toronto Maple Leafs	30.00	80.00
TCVAN Vancouver Canucks	25.00	60.00
TCWAS Washington Capitals	30.00	80.00
TCCHDE Detroit/Chicago	40.00	100.00
TCDECO Colorado/Detroit	50.00	100.00
TCEDCA Edmonton/Calgary	40.00	100.00
TCFLTB Tampa Bay/Florida	30.00	80.00
TCMIDA Dallas/Minnesota	30.00	80.00
TCMOBO Boston/Montreal	40.00	100.00
TCNJNY Rangers/New Jersey	40.00	100.00
TCNYNY Rangers/Islanders	40.00	100.00
TCOTTO Ottawa/Toronto	40.00	100.00
TCPHPI Philadelphia/Pittsburgh	75.00	125.00
TCSJLA Los Angeles/San Jose	40.00	100.00
TCTOMO Toronto/Montreal	25.00	40.00

2006-07 Parkhurst

Card	Low	High
COMPLETE SET (250)	75.00	200.00
COMP.SET w/o SPs (160)	10.00	25.00
ENFORCE/CAPT PRINT RUN 3999		
1 Ron MacLean	.30	.75
2 John Anderson	.20	.50
3 Al Arbour	.25	.60
4 Lou Fontinato	.20	.50
5 Grant Fuhr	.30	.75
6 Bill Gadsby	.30	.75
7 Danny Gare	.20	.50
8 Ed Giacomin	.50	1.25
9 Andy Bathgate	.25	.60
10 Bob Baun	.25	.60
11 Don Beaupre	.25	.60
12 Barry Beck	.20	.50
13 Jean Beliveau	.30	.75
14 Rod Gilbert	.25	.60
15 Clark Gillies	.30	.75
16 Doug Gilmour	.40	1.00
17 Danny Grant	.20	.50
18 Ron Greschner	.20	.50
19 Bob Bourne	.20	.50
20 Mike Bossy	.30	.75
21 Johnny Bower	.50	1.25
22 Scotty Bowman	.60	1.50
23 Stu Grimson	.20	.50
24 Richard Brodeur	.25	.60
25 Aaron Broten	.20	.50
26 Neal Broten	.20	.50
27 Dale Hawerchuk	.40	1.00
28 Johnny Bucyk	.30	.75
29 Paul Henderson	.25	.60
30 Ron Hextall	.50	1.25
31 Rejean Houle	.20	.50
32 Harry Howell	.25	.60
33 Gerry Cheevers	.30	.75
34 Don Cherry	1.00	2.50
35 Kelly Hrudey	.25	.60
36 Bobby Hull	.50	1.25
37 Dino Ciccarelli	.30	.75
38 Wendel Clark	.30	.75
39 Bobby Clarke	.30	.75
40 Dale Hunter	.25	.60
41 Dick Irvin	.20	.50
42 Tom Johnson	.25	.60
43 Mike Keenan	.20	.50
44 J.P. Kelly	.20	.50
45 Red Kelly	.25	.60
46 John Davidson	.30	.75
47 Kelly Kisio	.20	.50
48 Marcel Dionne	.40	1.00
49 Joey Kocur	.20	.50
50 Kevin Dineen	.20	.50
51 Jari Kurri	.30	.75
52 Elmer Lach	.30	.75
53 Ron Duguay	.25	.60
54 Ron Ellis	.20	.50
55 Guy Lafleur	.40	1.00
56 Phil Esposito	.50	1.25
57 Tony Esposito	.30	.75
58 Bernie Federko	.25	.60
59 Rod Langway	.25	.60
60 Edgar Laprade	.20	.50
61 Pierre Larouche	.20	.50
62 Mike Foligno	.20	.50
63 Reed Larson	.20	.50
64 Reggie Leach	.20	.50
65 Rejean Lemelin	.25	.60
66 Ted Lindsay	.25	.60
67 Mike Liut	.25	.60
68 Al MacInnis	.30	.75
69 Clint Malarchuk	.25	.60
70 Cesare Maniago	.25	.60
71 Butch Bouchard	.25	.60
72 Brian McFarlane	.20	.50
73 Marty McSorley	.25	.60
74 Howie Meeker	.20	.50
75 Gilles Meloche	.30	.75
76 Barry Melrose	.25	.60
77 Ray Bourque	.50	1.25
78 Brian Mullen	.20	.50
79 Joe Mullen	.25	.60
80 Cam Neely	.30	.75
81 Eric Nesterenko	.20	.50
82 Bernie Nicholls	.25	.60
83 Kent Nilsson	.20	.50
84 Ulf Nilsson	.20	.50
85 Adam Oates	.30	.75
86 John Ogrodnick	.20	.50
87 Willie O'Ree	.30	.75
88 Terry O'Reilly	.20	.50
89 Bobby Orr	1.00	2.50
90 Greg Millen	.25	.60
91 Jim Pappin	.20	.50
92 Bernie Parent	.30	.75
93 Brad Park	.25	.60
94 Jim Peplinski	.20	.50
95 Gilbert Perreault	.30	.75
96 Pete Peeters	.25	.60
97 Pierre Pilote	.25	.60
98 Willi Plett	.20	.50
99 Wayne Cashman	.20	.50
100 Denis Potvin	.30	.75
101 Bob Probert	.25	.60
102 Marcel Pronovost	.25	.60
103 Rob Ramage	.20	.50
104 Mike Krushelnyski	.20	.50
105 Pokey Reddick	.25	.60
106 Larry Robinson	.30	.75
107 Reijo Ruotsalainen	.20	.50
108 Jim Rutherford	.25	.60
109 Borje Salming	.30	.75
110 Milt Schmidt	.30	.75
111 Jim Schoenfeld	.20	.50
112 Dave Schultz	.25	.60
113 Dave Semenko	.20	.50
114 Eddie Shack	.25	.60
115 Claude Lemieux	.25	.60
116 Darryl Sittler	.30	.75
117 Dickie Moore	.20	.50
118 Bobby Smith	.20	.50
119 Clint Smith	.25	.60
120 Anton Stastny	.20	.50
121 Marian Stastny	.20	.50
122 Peter Stastny	.30	.75
123 Thomas Steen	.20	.50
124 Scott Stevens	.30	.75
125 Brent Sutter	.20	.50
126 Duane Sutter	.20	.50
127 Darryl Sutter	.20	.50
128 J.P. Parise	.20	.50
129 Ron Sutter	.30	.75
130 Brian Sutter	.20	.50
131 Walt Tkaczuk	.20	.50
132 Denis Savard	.40	1.00
133 Frank Udvari	.20	.50
134 Gump Worsley	.30	.75
135 Doug Jarvis	.20	.50
136 Jacques Lemaire	.25	.60
137 Peter McNab	.20	.50
138 Rick Middleton	.25	.60
139 Mike Rogers	.20	.50
140 Mats Naslund	.20	.50
141 Jim Neilson	.20	.50
142 Don Metz	.20	.50
143 Pat LaFontaine	.30	.75
144 Gordie Howe	1.00	2.50
145 Patrick Roy	.75	2.00
146 Garry Unger	.20	.50
147 Larry Murphy	.25	.60
148 Rick Vaive	.20	.50
149 Tiger Williams	.25	.60
150 Mario Lemieux	1.00	2.50
151 Michel Dion	.25	.60
152 Bill Dineen	.20	.50
153 Gary Dornhoefer	.20	.50
154 Hakan Loob	.20	.50
155 Craig MacTavish	.25	.60
156 Allan Stanley	.20	.50
157 Marc Tardif	.20	.50
158 Ryan Walter	.20	.50
159 Zigmund Palffy	.30	.75
160 Wilf Paiement	.20	.50
161 Milt Schmidt	1.50	4.00
162 Johnny Bucyk	1.50	4.00
163 Ray Bourque	2.50	6.00
164 Terry O'Reilly	1.00	2.50
165 Jim Schoenfeld	1.00	2.50
166 Danny Gare	.60	1.50
167 Gilbert Perreault	1.00	2.50
168 Mike Foligno	.60	1.50
169 Jim Peplinski	.60	1.50
170 Pierre Pilote	.75	2.00
171 Darryl Sutter	.60	1.50
172 Denis Savard	1.25	3.00
173 Bill Gadsby	1.00	2.50
174 Marc Tardif	.60	1.50
175 Peter Stastny	1.00	2.50
176 J.P. Parise	.60	1.50
177 Ted Lindsay	.75	2.00
178 Red Kelly	.75	2.00
179 Gordie Howe	2.50	6.00
180 Danny Grant	.60	1.50
181 Reed Larson	.60	1.50
182 Wayne Cashman	.60	1.50
183 Craig MacTavish	.75	2.00
184 Doug Wilson	.75	2.00
185 Marcel Dionne	1.25	3.00
186 Butch Bouchard	.75	2.00
187 Jean Beliveau	1.00	2.50
188 Wilf Paiement	.60	1.50
189 Scott Stevens	1.00	2.50
190 Clark Gillies	1.00	2.50
191 Denis Potvin	1.00	2.50
192 Brent Sutter	.60	1.50
193 Allan Stanley	.60	1.50
194 Andy Bathgate	.75	2.00
195 Brad Park	.75	2.00
196 Phil Esposito	1.50	4.00
197 Barry Beck	.60	1.50
198 Ron Greschner	.60	1.50
199 Kelly Kisio	.60	1.50
200 Bobby Clarke	1.00	2.50
201 Ron Sutter	1.00	2.50
202 Dale Hawerchuk	1.25	3.00
203 Thomas Steen	.60	1.50
204 Mario Lemieux	2.50	6.00
205 Al Arbour	.75	2.00
206 Brian Sutter	.60	1.50
207 Bernie Federko	.75	2.00
208 Scott Stevens	1.00	2.50
209 Darryl Sittler	1.00	2.50
210 Rick Vaive	.60	1.50
211 Rob Ramage	.60	1.50
212 Wendel Clark	1.00	2.50
213 Doug Gilmour	1.25	3.00
214 Kevin Dineen	.60	1.50
215 Rod Langway	.75	2.00
216 Dale Hunter	.75	2.00
217 Adam Oates	1.00	2.50
218 Walt Tkaczuk	.60	1.50
219 Harry Howell	.75	2.00
220 Rob Ramage	.60	1.50
221 Clint Smith	.75	2.00
222 Doug Gilmour	1.25	3.00
223 Mike Rogers	.60	1.50
224 Pat LaFontaine	1.00	2.50
225 Neal Broten	.60	1.50
226 Al MacInnis	1.00	2.50
227 Kevin Dineen	.60	1.50
228 Joey Kocur	.60	1.50
229 Tiger Williams	.75	2.00
230 Tiger Williams	.75	2.00
231 Dale Hunter	.75	2.00
232 Marty McSorley	.75	2.00
233 Bob Probert	.75	2.00
234 Stu Grimson	.60	1.50
235 Dave Schultz	.75	2.00
236 Bill Gadsby	1.00	2.50
237 Lou Fontinato	.60	1.50
238 Joey Kocur	.60	1.50
239 Ted Lindsay	.75	2.00
240 Dave Semenko	.60	1.50
241 Gary Dornhoefer	.60	1.50
242 Pierre Pilote	.75	2.00
243 Clark Gillies	1.00	2.50
244 Terry O'Reilly	.60	1.50
245 Wendel Clark	1.00	2.50
246 Willi Plett	.60	1.50
247 Wilf Paiement	.60	1.50
248 Tiger Williams	.75	2.00
249 Marty McSorley	.75	2.00
250 Bob Probert	.75	2.00

2006-07 Parkhurst Autographs

Card	Low	High
2 John Anderson	8.00	20.00
3 Al Arbour	8.00	20.00
4 Lou Fontinato	10.00	25.00
5 Grant Fuhr	10.00	25.00
6 Bill Gadsby	12.00	30.00
7 Danny Gare SP	12.00	30.00
8 Ed Giacomin	8.00	20.00
9 Andy Bathgate	6.00	15.00
10 Bob Baun	15.00	40.00
11 Don Beaupre	6.00	15.00
12 Barry Beck	4.00	10.00
13 Jean Beliveau SP	200.00	300.00
14 Rod Gilbert SP	60.00	100.00
15 Clark Gillies	8.00	20.00
16 Doug Gilmour	60.00	120.00
17 Danny Grant	6.00	15.00
18 Ron Greschner	6.00	15.00
19 Bob Bourne	4.00	10.00
20 Mike Bossy	30.00	75.00
21 Johnny Bower	20.00	50.00
22 Scotty Bowman SP	150.00	250.00
23 Stu Grimson	5.00	12.00
24 Richard Brodeur	4.00	10.00
25 Aaron Broten	4.00	10.00
26 Neal Broten	8.00	20.00
27 Dale Hawerchuk	10.00	25.00
28 Johnny Bucyk SP	60.00	120.00
29 Paul Henderson	10.00	25.00
30 Ron Hextall	12.00	30.00
31 Rejean Houle	8.00	20.00
32 Harry Howell	5.00	12.00
33 Gerry Cheevers	8.00	20.00
34 Don Cherry	15.00	40.00
35 Kelly Hrudey	5.00	12.00
36 Bobby Hull	30.00	80.00
37 Dino Ciccarelli	8.00	20.00
38 Wendel Clark	20.00	40.00
39 Bobby Clarke	12.00	30.00
40 Dale Hunter	10.00	25.00
41 Dick Irvin	8.00	20.00
42 Tom Johnson	30.00	80.00
43 Mike Keenan	8.00	20.00
44 J.P. Kelly	12.00	30.00
45 Red Kelly	6.00	15.00
46 John Davidson	8.00	20.00
47 Kelly Kisio	6.00	15.00
48 Marcel Dionne	10.00	25.00
49 Joey Kocur	30.00	80.00
50 Kevin Dineen	8.00	20.00
51 Jari Kurri	8.00	20.00
52 Elmer Lach	15.00	40.00
53 Ron Duguay	6.00	15.00
54 Ron Ellis	8.00	20.00
55 Guy Lafleur	15.00	40.00
56 Phil Esposito	25.00	60.00
57 Tony Esposito	20.00	50.00
58 Bernie Federko	5.00	12.00
59 Rod Langway	4.00	10.00
60 Edgar Laprade	20.00	50.00
61 Pierre Larouche	6.00	15.00
62 Mike Foligno	4.00	10.00
63 Reed Larson	8.00	20.00
64 Reggie Leach	8.00	20.00
66 Ted Lindsay	8.00	20.00
67 Mike Liut	6.00	15.00
68 Al MacInnis	6.00	15.00
69 Clint Malarchuk	8.00	20.00
70 Cesare Maniago	10.00	25.00
71 Butch Bouchard	30.00	80.00
72 Brian McFarlane	6.00	15.00
73 Marty McSorley	6.00	15.00
74 Howie Meeker	10.00	25.00
75 Gilles Meloche	5.00	12.00
76 Barry Melrose	6.00	15.00
77 Ray Bourque SP	60.00	100.00
78 Brian Mullen	4.00	10.00
79 Joe Mullen	5.00	12.00
80 Cam Neely	12.00	30.00
81 Eric Nesterenko	10.00	25.00
82 Bernie Nicholls	4.00	10.00
84 Ulf Nilsson	6.00	15.00
85 Adam Oates	8.00	20.00
86 John Ogrodnick	5.00	12.00
87 Willie O'Ree	10.00	25.00
88 Terry O'Reilly	15.00	40.00
89 Bobby Orr	60.00	120.00
90 Greg Millen	5.00	12.00
91 Jim Pappin	10.00	25.00
92 Bernie Parent	10.00	25.00
93 Brad Park	5.00	12.00
94 Jim Peplinski	10.00	25.00
95 Gilbert Perreault	12.00	30.00
96 Pete Peeters	6.00	15.00
97 Pierre Pilote	8.00	20.00
98 Willi Plett	4.00	10.00
100 Denis Potvin	6.00	15.00
101 Bob Probert	15.00	40.00
102 Marcel Pronovost	10.00	25.00
103 Rob Ramage	4.00	10.00
104 Mike Krushelnyski	4.00	10.00
106 Larry Robinson	10.00	25.00
107 Reijo Ruotsalainen	4.00	10.00
108 Jim Rutherford	10.00	25.00
109 Borje Salming	10.00	25.00
110 Milt Schmidt	12.00	30.00
111 Jim Schoenfeld	6.00	15.00
112 Dave Schultz	6.00	15.00
113 Dave Semenko	15.00	40.00
114 Eddie Shack	8.00	20.00
115 Claude Lemieux	8.00	20.00
116 Darryl Sittler	15.00	40.00
118 Bobby Smith	5.00	12.00
119 Clint Smith	30.00	60.00
120 Anton Stastny	6.00	15.00
121 Marian Stastny	6.00	15.00
122 Peter Stastny	10.00	25.00
123 Thomas Steen	4.00	10.00
124 Scott Stevens	30.00	60.00
125 Brent Sutter	4.00	10.00
126 Duane Sutter	5.00	12.00
127 Darryl Sutter	5.00	12.00
128 J.P. Parise	4.00	10.00
130 Brian Sutter	8.00	20.00
131 Walt Tkaczuk	6.00	15.00
132 Denis Savard SP	30.00	60.00
133 Frank Udvari	8.00	20.00
135 Doug Jarvis	8.00	20.00
136 Jacques Lemaire	8.00	20.00
137 Peter McNab	10.00	25.00
138 Rick Middleton	10.00	25.00
139 Mike Rogers	5.00	12.00
140 Mats Naslund	6.00	15.00
141 Jim Neilson	6.00	15.00
143 Pat LaFontaine	8.00	20.00
144 Gordie Howe	60.00	120.00
145 Patrick Roy SP		
146 Garry Unger	12.00	30.00
148 Rick Vaive	6.00	15.00
149 Tiger Williams	12.00	30.00
150 Mario Lemieux SP	600.00	1000.00
151 Michel Dion	25.00	50.00
152 Bill Dineen	12.00	30.00
153 Gary Dornhoefer	4.00	10.00
154 Hakan Loob	5.00	12.00
155 Craig MacTavish	6.00	15.00
156 Allan Stanley	10.00	25.00
157 Marc Tardif	12.00	30.00
158 Ryan Walter	4.00	10.00
160 Wilf Paiement	4.00	10.00
161 Milt Schmidt CAP	12.00	30.00
162 Johnny Bucyk CAP SP	125.00	250.00
163 Ray Bourque CAP SP	100.00	175.00
164 Terry O'Reilly CAP	12.00	30.00
165 Jim Schoenfeld CAP	8.00	20.00
166 Danny Gare CAP	12.00	30.00
167 Gilbert Perreault CAP	15.00	40.00
168 Mike Foligno CAP	4.00	10.00
169 Jim Peplinski CAP	12.00	30.00
170 Pierre Pilote CAP	15.00	40.00
171 Darryl Sutter CAP	15.00	40.00
172 Denis Savard CAP	50.00	100.00
173 Bill Gadsby CAP	12.00	30.00
174 Marc Tardif CAP	10.00	25.00
175 Peter Stastny CAP	25.00	60.00
176 J.P. Parise CAP	10.00	25.00
177 Ted Lindsay CAP	12.00	30.00
178 Red Kelly CAP	12.00	30.00
179 Gordie Howe CAP	100.00	175.00
180 Danny Grant CAP	8.00	20.00
181 Reed Larson CAP	6.00	15.00
183 Craig MacTavish CAP	5.00	12.00
185 Marcel Dionne CAP	40.00	70.00
186 Butch Bouchard CAP	25.00	60.00
187 Jean Beliveau CAP SP	25.00	50.00
188 Wilf Paiement CAP	12.00	30.00
189 Scott Stevens CAP	15.00	40.00
190 Clark Gillies CAP	10.00	25.00
191 Denis Potvin CAP	12.00	30.00
192 Brent Sutter CAP	10.00	25.00
193 Allan Stanley CAP	12.00	30.00
194 Andy Bathgate CAP	8.00	20.00
195 Brad Park CAP	8.00	20.00
196 Phil Esposito CAP	25.00	60.00
197 Barry Beck CAP	10.00	25.00
198 Ron Greschner CAP	8.00	20.00
199 Kelly Kisio CAP	12.00	30.00
200 Bobby Clarke CAP	30.00	60.00
201 Ron Sutter CAP	10.00	25.00
202 Dale Hawerchuk CAP	20.00	50.00
203 Thomas Steen CAP	10.00	25.00
204 Mario Lemieux CAP SP		
205 Al Arbour CAP	12.00	30.00
206 Brian Sutter CAP	6.00	15.00
207 Bernie Federko CAP	10.00	25.00
208 Scott Stevens CAP SP	25.00	60.00
209 Darryl Sittler CAP	25.00	60.00
210 Rick Vaive CAP	25.00	50.00
211 Rob Ramage CAP	10.00	25.00
212 Wendel Clark CAP	50.00	100.00
213 Doug Gilmour CAP	12.00	30.00
214 Kevin Dineen CAP		
215 Rod Langway CAP	10.00	25.00
216 Dale Hunter CAP	8.00	20.00
217 Adam Oates CAP	12.00	30.00
219 Harry Howell CAP	20.00	40.00
220 Rob Ramage CAP		
221 Clint Smith CAP	25.00	60.00
222 Doug Gilmour CAP EXCH	15.00	40.00
223 Mike Rogers CAP	20.00	50.00
224 Pat LaFontaine CAP		
225 Neal Broten CAP	12.00	30.00
226 Al MacInnis CAP	20.00	50.00
227 Kevin Dineen CAP	15.00	40.00
228 Joey Kocur ENF	20.00	50.00
229 Tiger Williams ENF EXCH	12.00	30.00
230 Tiger Williams ENF	25.00	50.00
231 Dale Hunter ENF	12.00	30.00
232 Marty McSorley ENF	25.00	50.00
233 Bob Probert ENF	30.00	60.00
234 Stu Grimson ENF	10.00	25.00
235 Dave Schultz ENF	20.00	50.00
236 Bill Gadsby ENF	20.00	50.00
237 Lou Fontinato ENF		
238 Joey Kocur ENF	20.00	50.00
239 Ted Lindsay ENF	15.00	40.00
240 Dave Semenko ENF	15.00	40.00
241 Gary Dornhoefer ENF	15.00	30.00
242 Pierre Pilote ENF	20.00	40.00
243 Clark Gillies ENF	6.00	15.00
244 Terry O'Reilly ENF	20.00	50.00
245 Wendel Clark ENF	12.00	30.00
246 Willi Plett ENF	8.00	20.00
247 Wilf Paiement ENF	15.00	40.00
248 Tiger Williams ENF	15.00	40.00
249 Marty McSorley ENF	25.00	50.00
250 Bob Probert ENF	20.00	50.00

2006-07 Parkhurst Autographs Dual

Card	Low	High
DAAB A.Arbour/S.Bowman SP	60.00	100.00
DABB N.Broten/A.Broten	60.00	125.00
DABG M.Bossy/C.Gillies	40.00	80.00
DABL B.Bouchard/E.Lach	75.00	150.00
DABM J.Beliveau/D.Moore SP	150.00	300.00
DABO G.Cheevers/B.Park	50.00	100.00
DACL B.Clarke/R.Leach	90.00	150.00
DACP B.Clarke/B.Parent	50.00	100.00
DADN M.Dionne/B.Nicholls	25.00	60.00
DADR D.Savard/R.Vaive	25.00	60.00
DAEB P.Esposito/J.Bucyk	60.00	125.00
DAEE P.Esposito/T.Esposito	30.00	80.00
DAES R.Ellis/E.Shack	25.00	60.00
DAFG L.Fontinato/B.Gadsby		
DAFM B.Federko/J.Mullen	30.00	80.00
DAGB R.Greschner/B.Beck	30.00	80.00
DAGC G.Fuhr/C.MacTavish	50.00	125.00
DAHE B.Hull/T.Esposito	50.00	100.00
DAHL G.Howe/T.Lindsay SP	100.00	200.00
DAHP B.Hull/J.Pappin	25.00	60.00
DAHS D.Hawerchuk/T.Steen		
DAIM D.Irvin/B.McFarlane	15.00	40.00
DALD M.Liut/K.Dineen	40.00	80.00
DALK T.Lindsay/R.Kelly	50.00	100.00
DALL G.Lafleur/J.Lemaire	75.00	150.00
DALS P.LaFontaine/B.Sutter		
DAMB G.Meloche/D.Beaupre	75.00	150.00
DAMM J.Mullen/B.Mullen	40.00	80.00
DAMP M.McSorley/B.Probert	100.00	175.00
DANO C.Neely/A.Oates	25.00	60.00
DAOB B.Orr/R.Bourque SP	250.00	400.00
DAOE B.Orr/P.Esposito SP		
DAOL J.Ogrodnick/R.Larson	40.00	80.00
DAOM T.O'Reilly/P.McNab	20.00	50.00

2006-07 Parkhurst Autographs Dual

DAPF G.Perreault/M.Foligno 25.00 60.00
DAPG G.Perreault/D.Gare 75.00 150.00
DAPK B.Probert/J.Kocur 25.00 60.00
DAPM P.Peeters/R.Middleton 20.00 50.00
DAPP J.Peplinski/W.Plett 25.00 60.00
DARP L.Robinson/D.Potvin 25.00 60.00
DASB M.Schmidt/J.Bucyk 60.00 100.00
DASD D.Schultz/G.Dornhoefer 40.00 80.00
DAST1 P.Stastny/A.Stastny 40.00 100.00
DAST2 P.Stastny/M.Stastny 25.00 60.00
DASU1 D.Sutter/D.Sutter 25.00 60.00
DASU2 B.Sutter/B.Sutter
DASV D.Sittler/R.Vaive 40.00 80.00
DATB T.Williams/R.Brodeur 40.00 80.00
DAWS T.Williams/D.Semenko 75.00 125.00

1995-96 Parkhurst '66-67 Prototypes

This five-card set was issued to promote the third installment of the Missing Link trilogy. The cards mirror the corresponding regular versions, save for the word PROTOTYPE stamped on the back, and a statement which reveals these cards were limited to 1966 copies.

COMPLETE SET (5) 6.00 15.00
16 Gerry Cheevers 1.25 3.00
42 Gordie Howe 4.00 10.00
125 Jean Beliveau 1.50 4.00
Stan Mikita AS
128 Jacques Laperriere .30 .75
Norris Trophy Winner
144 Bob Nevin .30 .75

1995-96 Parkhurst '66-67

This 150-card set lovingly speculates on what might have been had Parkhurst, the venerable Canadian card manufacturer, been active during Bobby Orr's rookie card season. 2500 numbered 16-box cases were produced of the eight-card packs. The cards utilized period photos and a design element consistent with the time. There were two five-card insert sets honoring "Super Rookie" Orr and "Mr. Hockey" Gordie Howe. Orr and Howe autographed 500 of each card in their respective sets. The five promo cards were issued in set form. They are identical to the regular versions of the cards, save for the bold notation on the back which proclaims them to be prototypes limited to 1966 copies.

COMPLETE SET (150) 12.50 25.00
1 Pit Martin .05 .15
2 Ron Stewart .05 .15
3 Joe Watson .02 .10
4 Ed Westfall .02 .10
5 John Bucyk .08 .25
6 Ted Green .05 .15
7 Bobby Orr 2.50 5.00
8 Bob Woytowich .02 .10
9 Murray Oliver .02 .10
10 John McKenzie .05 .15
11 Tom Williams .02 .10
12 Don Awrey .02 .10
13 Ron Schock .02 .10
14 Bernie Parent .40 1.00
15 Ron Murphy .02 .10
16 Gerry Cheevers .40 1.00
17 Gilles Marotte .02 .10
18 Ed Johnston .05 .15
19 Derek Sanderson .40 1.00
20 Wayne Connelly .02 .10
21 Bobby Hull 1.25 3.00
22 Matt Ravlich .02 .10
23 Ken Hodge .05 .15
24 Stan Mikita .60 1.50
25 Fred Stanfield .02 .10
26 Eric Nesterenko .05 .15
27 Doug Jarrett .02 .10
28 Lou Angotti .02 .10
29 Ken Wharram .02 .10
30 Bill Hay .02 .10
31 Glenn Hall .60 1.50
32 Chico Maki .02 .10
33 Phil Esposito .60 1.50
34 Pierre Pilote .08 .25
35 Doug Mohns .02 .10
36 Ed Van Impe .02 .10
37 Dennis Hull .05 .15
38 Pat Stapleton .02 .10
39 Denis DeJordy .02 .10
40 Paul Henderson .20 .50
41 Gary Bergman .02 .10
42 Gordie Howe 1.50 4.00
43 Bob McCord .02 .10
44 Andy Bathgate .08 .25
45 Norm Ullman .08 .25
46 Peter Mahovlich .05 .15
47 Ted Hampson .02 .10
48 Leo Boivin .08 .25
49 Bruce MacGregor .02 .10
50 Ab McDonald .05 .15
51 Dean Prentice .02 .10
52 Floyd Smith .02 .10
53 Alex Delvecchio .08 .25
54 Pete Goegan .02 .10
55 Parker MacDonald .02 .10
56 Roger Crozier .05 .15
57 Val Fonteyne .02 .10
58 Henri Richard .40 1.00
59 John Ferguson .05 .15
60 Yvan Cournoyer .08 .25
61 Claude Provost .05 .15
62 Dave Balon .02 .10
63 Ted Harris .02 .10
64 Ralph Backstrom .05 .15
65 Jacques Laperriere .08 .25
66 Terry Harper .05 .15
67 J.C. Tremblay .05 .15
68 Jean Guy Talbot .05 .15
69 Claude Larose .05 .15
70 Charlie Hodge .05 .15
71 Gilles Tremblay .02 .10
72 Jim Roberts .02 .10
73 Jean Beliveau .60 1.50
74 Serge Savard .10 .25
75 Rogatien Vachon .30 .75
76 Lorne Worsley .60 1.50
77 Bobby Rousseau .05 .15
78 Dick Duff .05 .15
79 Rod Gilbert .08 .25
80 Harry Howell .08 .25
81 Jim Neilson .02 .10
82 Don Marshall .02 .10
83 Reg Fleming .02 .10
84 Wayne Hillman .02 .10
85 Bob Nevin .02 .10
86 Arnie Brown .02 .10
87 Earl Ingarfield .02 .10
88 Jean Ratelle .08 .25
89 Bernie Geoffrion .40 1.00
90 Orland Kurtenbach .02 .10
91 Bill Hicke .02 .10
92 Red Berenson .05 .15
93 Ed Giacomin .08 .25
94 Al MacNeil .02 .10
95 Rod Seiling .02 .10
96 Doug Robinson .02 .10
97 Cesare Maniago .05 .15
98 Vic Hadfield .02 .10
99 Phil Goyette .02 .10
100 Dave Keon .08 .25
101 Mike Walton .02 .10
102 Frank Mahovlich .60 1.50
103 Tim Horton .60 1.50
104 Larry Hillman .02 .10
105 Kent Douglas .02 .10
106 Ron Ellis .02 .10
107 Jim Pappin .02 .10
108 Marcel Pronovost .08 .25
109 Red Kelly .08 .25
110 Allan Stanley .08 .25
111 Brit Selby .02 .10
112 Pete Stemkowski .02 .10
113 Eddie Shack .40 1.00
114 Bob Pulford .08 .25
115 Larry Jeffrey .02 .10
116 George Armstrong .08 .25
117 Bob Baun .10 .25
118 Bruce Gamble .02 .10
119 Johnny Bower .60 1.50
120 Terry Sawchuk .75 2.00
121 Hall/Worsley AS .30 .75
122 Laperriere/Stanley AS .05 .15
123 Pilote/Stapleton AS .05 .15
124 Hull/Mahovlich AS .40 1.00
125 Mikita/Beliveau AS .30 .75
126 Howe/Rousseau AS .60 1.50
127 Alex Delvecchio TW .05 .15
128 Jacques Laperriere TW .05 .15
129 Bobby Hull TW .60 1.50
130 Bobby Hull TW .60 1.50
131 Worsley/Hodge TW .20 .50
132 Brit Selby .02 .10
133 Action Card .05 .15
134 Action Card .05 .15
135 Action Card .05 .15
136 Action Card .05 .15
137 Action Card .05 .15
138 Action Card .05 .15
139 Action Card .05 .15
140 Murray Oliver L .02 .10
141 Bobby Hull LL .60 1.50
142 Gordie Howe LL .75 2.00
143 Bobby Rousseau L .02 .10
144 Bob Nevin L .02 .10
145 Mahovlich .08 .25
Pulford L
146 Stanley Cup Playoffs Semifinals .05 .15
147 Stanley Cup Playoffs Semifinals .05 .15
148 Stanley Cup Playoffs Finals .05 .15
149 Checklist .02 .10
150 Checklist .02 .10

1995-96 Parkhurst '66-67 Bobby Orr Super Rookie

COMMON ORR (SR1-SR5) 5.00 12.00
COMMON ORR AU/500 100.00 200.00
COMMON ORR JUMBO 6.00 15.00

1995-96 Parkhurst '66-67 Coins

In tip of the hat fashion, this 120-coin insert set recreates the popular Shirriff coins of the 1960s. The plastic coins were team color coded, and were inserted one per pack. The coins measure about 1 3/8" in diameter. They are numbered in identical fashion to the card set as the same players are featured. Parkhurst officials, say no coin was printed in shorter quantity than any other. There also were five black coins randomly inserted honoring Bobby Orr and Gordie Howe. These are not numbered on the coins. We have done so for classification purposes.

COMPLETE SET (120) 90.00 175.00
1 Pit Martin .40 1.00
2 Ron Stewart .40 1.00
3 Joe Watson .25 .60
4 Ed Westfall .25 .60
5 John Bucyk .60 1.50
6 Ted Green .40 1.00
7 Bobby Orr 5.00 10.00
8 Bob Woytowich .25 .60
9 Murray Oliver .25 .60
10 John McKenzie .40 1.00
11 Tom Williams .25 .60
12 Don Awrey .25 .60
13 Ron Schock .25 .60
14 Bernie Parent 1.25 3.00
15 Ron Murphy .25 .60
16 Gerry Cheevers 1.25 3.00
17 Gilles Marotte .25 .60
18 Ed Johnston .40 1.00
19 Derek Sanderson 1.25 3.00
20 Wayne Connelly .25 .60
21 Bobby Hull 3.00 6.00
22 Matt Ravlich .25 .60
23 Ken Hodge .40 1.00
24 Stan Mikita 1.50 4.00
25 Fred Stanfield .25 .60
26 Eric Nesterenko .40 1.00
27 Doug Jarrett .25 .60
28 Lou Angotti .25 .60
29 Ken Wharram .25 .60
30 Bill Hay .25 .60
31 Glenn Hall 1.50 4.00
32 Chico Maki .25 .60
33 Phil Esposito 1.50 4.00
34 Pierre Pilote .60 1.50
35 Doug Mohns .25 .60
36 Ed Van Impe .25 .60
37 Dennis Hull .40 1.00
38 Pat Stapleton .25 .60
39 Denis DeJordy .25 .60
40 Paul Henderson 5.00 10.00
41 Gary Bergman .25 .60
42 Gordie Howe 4.00 8.00
43 Bob McCord .25 .60
44 Andy Bathgate .60 1.50
45 Norm Ullman .60 1.50
46 Peter Mahovlich .40 1.00
47 Ted Hampson .25 .60
48 Leo Boivin .60 1.50
49 Bruce MacGregor .25 .60
50 Ab McDonald .40 1.00
51 Dean Prentice .25 .60
52 Floyd Smith .25 .60
53 Alex Delvecchio .60 1.50
54 Pete Goegan .25 .60
55 Parker MacDonald .25 .60
56 Roger Crozier .40 1.00
57 Val Fonteyne .25 .60
58 Henri Richard 1.25 3.00
59 John Ferguson .40 1.00
60 Yvan Cournoyer .60 1.50
61 Claude Provost .40 1.00
62 Dave Balon .25 .60
63 Ted Harris .25 .60
64 Ralph Backstrom .40 1.00
65 Jacques Laperriere .60 1.50
66 Terry Harper .40 1.00
67 J.C. Tremblay .40 1.00
68 Jean Guy Talbot .40 1.00
69 Claude Larose .40 1.00
70 Charlie Hodge .40 1.00
71 Gilles Tremblay .25 .60
72 Jim Roberts .25 .60
73 Jean Beliveau 1.50 4.00
74 Serge Savard .60 1.50
75 Rogatien Vachon 1.25 3.00
76 Lorne Worsley 1.50 4.00
77 Bobby Rousseau .40 1.00
78 Dick Duff .40 1.00
79 Rod Gilbert .60 1.50
80 Harry Howell .60 1.50
81 Jim Neilson .25 .60
82 Don Marshall .25 .60
83 Reg Fleming .25 .60
84 Wayne Hillman .25 .60
85 Bob Nevin .25 .60
86 Arnie Brown .25 .60
87 Earl Ingarfield .25 .60
88 Jean Ratelle .60 1.50
89 Bernie Geoffrion 1.25 3.00
90 Orland Kurtenbach .25 .60
91 Bill Hicke .25 .60
92 Red Berenson .40 1.00
93 Ed Giacomin .60 1.50
94 Al MacNeil .25 .60
95 Rod Seiling .25 .60
96 Doug Robinson .25 .60
97 Cesare Maniago .40 1.00
98 Vic Hadfield .25 .60
99 Phil Goyette .25 .60
100 Dave Keon .60 1.50
101 Mike Walton .25 .60
102 Frank Mahovlich 1.50 4.00
103 Tim Horton 1.50 4.00
104 Larry Hillman .25 .60
105 Kent Douglas .25 .60
106 Ron Ellis .25 .60
107 Jim Pappin .25 .60
108 Marcel Pronovost .60 1.50
109 Red Kelly .60 1.50
110 Allan Stanley .60 1.50
111 Brit Selby .25 .60
112 Pete Stemkowski .25 .60
113 Eddie Shack 1.25 3.00
114 Bob Pulford .60 1.50
115 Larry Jeffrey .25 .60
116 George Armstrong .60 1.50
117 Bob Baun .40 1.00
118 Bruce Gamble .25 .60
119 Johnny Bower 1.50 4.00
120 Terry Sawchuk 2.50 5.00
BO1 Bobby Orr Black Coin 4.00 10.00
BO2 Bobby Orr Black Coin 4.00 10.00
BO3 Bobby Orr Black Coin 4.00 10.00
BO4 Bobby Orr Black Coin 4.00 10.00
BO5 Bobby Orr Black Coin 4.00 10.00
GH1 Gordie Howe Black Coin 3.00 8.00
GH2 Gordie Howe Black Coin 3.00 8.00
GH3 Gordie Howe Black Coin 3.00 8.00
GH4 Gordie Howe Black Coin 3.00 8.00
GH5 Gordie Howe Black Coin 3.00 8.00

1995-96 Parkhurst '66-67 Gordie Howe Mr. Hockey

COMMON HOWE 5.00 12.00
COMMON HOWE AU/500 50.00 100.00
COMMON HOWE JUMBO 6.00 15.00

2011-12 Parkhurst Champions

COMPLETE SET (160) 50.00 120.00
COMP.SET w/o SPs (100) 12.00 30.00
WIRE STATED ODDS 1:5
DUAL WIRE STATED ODDS 1:20
RENDITIONS STATED ODDS 1:8
B&W RENDITIONS STATED ODDS 1:32
1 Wayne Gretzky 1.25 3.00
2 Gordie Howe .50 1.25
3 Bobby Orr .75 2.00
4 Mario Lemieux .75 2.00
5 Patrick Roy .60 1.50
6 Bobby Hull .25 .60
7 Jean Beliveau .25 .60
8 Mark Messier .30 .75
9 Guy Lafleur .30 .75
10 Ray Bourque .40 1.00
11 Phil Esposito .40 1.00
12 Stan Mikita .30 .75
13 Mike Bossy .25 .60
14 Denis Potvin .25 .60
15 Ted Lindsay .25 .60
16 Bobby Clarke .25 .60
17 Brett Hull .30 .75
18 Red Kelly .20 .50
19 Larry Robinson .25 .60
20 Jari Kurri .25 .60
21 Marcel Dionne .30 .75
22 Johnny Bucyk .25 .60
23 Gilbert Perreault .25 .60
24 Eric Lindros .40 1.00
25 Joe Sakic .40 1.00
26 Peter Stastny .25 .60
27 Grant Fuhr .25 .60
28 Andy Bathgate .25 .60
29 Cam Neely .25 .60
30 Claude Lemieux .20 .50
31 Tony Esposito .25 .60
32 Luc Robitaille .25 .60
33 Denis Savard .30 .75
34 Darryl Sittler .25 .60
35 Steve Shutt .25 .60
36 Borje Salming .25 .60
37 Ron Francis .30 .75
38 Milt Schmidt .20 .50
39 Dale Hawerchuk .30 .75
40 Doug Gilmour .30 .75
41 Dino Ciccarelli .25 .60
42 Johnny Bower .25 .60
43 Glenn Anderson .25 .60
44 Adam Oates .25 .60
45 Clark Gillies .25 .60
46 Guy Carbonneau .25 .60
47 Ron Hextall .30 .75
48 Igor Larionov .25 .60
49 Rogie Vachon .30 .75
50 Alex Delvecchio .20 .50
51 Wendel Clark .25 .60
52 Neal Broten .20 .50
53 Joe Mullen .20 .50
54 Brad Park .20 .50
55 Richard Brodeur .25 .60
56 Bill Ranford .25 .60
57 Reggie Leach .20 .50
58 Bernie Federko .20 .50
59 Terry O'Reilly .20 .50
60 Harry Howell .20 .50
61 Bill Barber .25 .60
62 Anton Stastny .15 .40
63 Rick MacLeish .20 .50
64 Ken Morrow .15 .40
65 Tony Twist .15 .40
66 Wilf Paiement .20 .50
67 Doug Wilson .20 .50
68 Dave Schultz .25 .60
69 Ken Hodge .20 .50
70 Thomas Steen .15 .40
71 Duane Sutter .15 .40
72 Mike Liut .20 .50
73 Bernie Nicholls .25 .60
74 Brent Sutter .15 .40
75 Dave Taylor .20 .50
76 Ron Sutter .20 .50
77 Rejean Lemelin .30 .75
78 Steve Larmer .20 .50
79 Don Beaupre .20 .50
80 Darryl Sutter .20 .50
81 Mark Howe .25 .60
82 Russ Courtnall .15 .40
83 Tony Tanti .15 .40
84 Tim Kerr .20 .50
85 Mike Foligno .20 .50
86 Marty McSorley .25 .60
87 Danny Gare .20 .50
88 Basil McRae .20 .50
89 Brian Sutter .20 .50
90 Rich Sutter .20 .50
91 Stan Smyl .15 .40
92 Al Iafrate .20 .50
93 Jim Neilson .15 .40
94 Pat Stapleton .15 .40
95 Mike Gartner .25 .60
96 Rick Middleton .40 1.00
97 Willi Plett .20 .50
98 Gilles Villemure .20 .50
99 Wayne Gretzky 1.25 3.00
100 Gordie Howe .50 1.25
101 Wayne Gretzky WIRE 2.50 6.00
102 Mario Lemieux WIRE 1.50 4.00
103 Gordie Howe WIRE 1.00 2.50
104 Bobby Orr WIRE 1.50 4.00
105 Brett Hull WIRE .60 1.50
106 Mark Messier WIRE .60 1.50
107 Patrick Roy WIRE 1.25 3.00
108 Luc Robitaille WIRE .50 1.25
109 Marcel Dionne WIRE .60 1.50
110 Bobby Clarke WIRE .50 1.25
111 Ray Bourque WIRE .75 2.00
112 Denis Potvin WIRE .50 1.25
113 Red Kelly WIRE .40 1.00
114 Phil Esposito WIRE .75 2.00
115 Johnny Bower WIRE .50 1.25
116 Mike Bossy WIRE .50 1.25
117 Ted Lindsay WIRE .50 1.25
118 Larry Robinson WIRE .50 1.25
119 Jean Beliveau WIRE .50 1.25
120 Wendel Clark WIRE .50 1.25
121 Robnsn/Hawrchk WIRE 1.25 3.00
122 B.Park/B.Barber WIRE 1.00 2.50
123 W.Gretzky/G.Howe WIRE 5.00 12.00
124 M.Messier/J.Kurri WIRE 1.25 3.00
125 G.Howe/J.Bower WIRE 2.00 5.00
126 B.Hull/S.Mikita WIRE 1.25 3.00
127 T.Lindsay/G.Howe WIRE 2.00 5.00
128 T.Esposito/B.Orr WIRE 3.00 8.00
129 Esposito/Clarke/Orr WIRE 3.00 8.00
130 Esposito/Bucyk/Orr WIRE 3.00 8.00
131 Wayne Gretzky R 3.00 8.00
132 Bobby Orr R 2.00 5.00
133 Gordie Howe R 1.25 3.00
134 Mario Lemieux R 2.00 5.00
135 Brett Hull R .75 2.00
136 Patrick Roy R 1.50 4.00
137 Mark Messier R .75 2.00
138 Guy Lafleur R .75 2.00
139 Stan Mikita R .75 2.00
140 Mike Bossy R .60 1.50
141 Bobby Hull R .60 1.50
142 Bobby Clarke R .60 1.50
143 Ray Bourque R 1.00 2.50
144 Dale Hawerchuk R .75 2.00
145 Cam Neely R .60 1.50
146 Rogie Vachon R .75 2.00
147 Peter Stastny R .60 1.50
148 Darryl Sittler R .60 1.50
149 Eric Lindros R 1.00 2.50
150 Gilbert Perreault R .60 1.50
151 Patrick Roy R BW 4.00 10.00
152 Bobby Orr R BW 5.00 12.00
153 Guy Lafleur R BW 2.00 5.00
154 Phil Esposito R BW 2.50 6.00
155 Mark Messier R BW 2.00 5.00
156 Jean Beliveau R BW 1.50 4.00
157 Bobby Hull R BW 1.50 4.00
158 Gordie Howe R BW 3.00 8.00
159 Mario Lemieux R BW 5.00 12.00
160 Wayne Gretzky R BW 8.00 20.00

2011-12 Parkhurst Champions Autographs

(1-100) OVERALL ODDS 1:14
(1-100) GROUP A ODDS 1:696
(1-100) GROUP B ODDS 1:523
(1-100) GROUP C ODDS 1:206
(1-100) GROUP D ODDS 1:110
(1-100) GROUP E ODDS 1:56
(1-100) GROUP F ODDS 1:28
(101-120) WIRE PHOTO ODDS 1:354
(101-120) GROUP G ODDS 1:2145
(101-120) GROUP H ODDS 1:1247
(101-120) GROUP I ODDS 1:642
(121-130) DUAL WIRE PHOTO ODDS 1:2093
(121-130) GROUP J ODDS 1:24,000
(121-130) GROUP K ODDS 1:2293
(131-150) RENDITIONS ODDS 1:614
(131-150) GROUP L ODDS 1:11,993
(131-150) GROUP M ODDS 1:1353
(131-150) GROUP N ODDS 1:1241
(151-160) BW RENDITIONS ODDS 1:3214
LINDROS AU ISSUED IN 2011-12 BLACK DIAMOND
1 Wayne Gretzky C EXCH 200.00 300.00
2 Gordie Howe C 75.00 150.00
3 Bobby Orr D 60.00 120.00
4 Mario Lemieux A 150.00 250.00
5 Patrick Roy A 150.00 250.00
6 Bobby Hull A 60.00 100.00
7 Jean Beliveau A 150.00 250.00
8 Mark Messier A 75.00 135.00
9 Guy Lafleur A 40.00 80.00
10 Ray Bourque A 125.00 200.00
11 Phil Esposito A 125.00 200.00
12 Stan Mikita A 75.00 135.00
13 Mike Bossy A 100.00 175.00
14 Denis Potvin B 15.00 40.00
15 Ted Lindsay C 10.00 25.00
16 Bobby Clarke C 30.00 60.00
17 Brett Hull A 175.00 300.00
18 Red Kelly B 25.00 50.00
19 Larry Robinson B 20.00 40.00
20 Jari Kurri C 15.00 30.00
21 Marcel Dionne B 25.00 50.00
22 Johnny Bucyk B 30.00 60.00
23 Gilbert Perreault C 25.00 50.00
24 Eric Lindros A
25 Joe Sakic A 75.00 150.00
26 Peter Stastny C 10.00 25.00
27 Grant Fuhr A 60.00 100.00
28 Andy Bathgate B 10.00 25.00
29 Cam Neely B 15.00 40.00
30 Claude Lemieux D 5.00 12.00
31 Tony Esposito A 60.00 100.00
32 Luc Robitaille B 30.00 60.00
33 Denis Savard B 15.00 30.00
34 Darryl Sittler C 12.00 30.00
35 Steve Shutt B 30.00 60.00
36 Borje Salming B 12.00 30.00
37 Ron Francis A 125.00 225.00
38 Milt Schmidt E 5.00 12.00
39 Dale Hawerchuk C 12.00 30.00
40 Doug Gilmour C 8.00 20.00
41 Dino Ciccarelli C 12.50 30.00
42 Johnny Bower C 15.00 40.00
43 Glenn Anderson B 6.00 15.00
44 Adam Oates E 6.00 15.00
45 Clark Gillies C 6.00 15.00
46 Guy Carbonneau E 6.00 15.00
47 Ron Hextall B 25.00 60.00
48 Igor Larionov A 125.00 200.00
49 Rogie Vachon A 30.00 60.00
50 Alex Delvecchio D 8.00 20.00
51 Wendel Clark A 90.00 150.00
52 Neal Broten C 10.00 25.00
53 Joe Mullen B 5.00 12.00
54 Brad Park C 5.00 12.00
55 Richard Brodeur D 6.00 15.00
56 Bill Ranford D 6.00 15.00
57 Reggie Leach F 5.00 12.00
58 Bernie Federko C 10.00 25.00
59 Terry O'Reilly C 12.00 30.00
60 Harry Howell D 5.00 12.00
61 Bill Barber F 6.00 15.00
62 Anton Stastny C 4.00 10.00
63 Rick MacLeish F 5.00 12.00
64 Ken Morrow D 4.00 10.00
65 Tony Twist F 6.00 15.00
66 Wilf Paiement E 5.00 12.00
67 Doug Wilson F 5.00 12.00
68 Dave Schultz C 12.00 30.00
69 Ken Hodge F 5.00 12.00
70 Thomas Steen D 4.00 10.00
71 Duane Sutter E 4.00 10.00
72 Mike Liut D 6.00 15.00
73 Bernie Nicholls F 6.00 15.00
74 Brent Sutter E 4.00 10.00
75 Dave Taylor D 5.00 12.00
76 Ron Sutter E 5.00 12.00
77 Rejean Lemelin F 8.00 20.00
78 Steve Larmer D 6.00 15.00
79 Don Beaupre F 5.00 12.00
80 Darryl Sutter E 5.00 12.00
81 Mark Howe F 6.00 15.00
82 Russ Courtnall F 6.00 15.00
83 Tony Tanti C 12.00 30.00
84 Tim Kerr F 5.00 12.00
85 Mike Foligno E 5.00 12.00
86 Marty McSorley D 6.00 15.00
87 Danny Gare F 5.00 12.00
88 Basil McRae F 5.00 12.00
89 Brian Sutter E 5.00 12.00
90 Rich Sutter E 5.00 12.00
91 Stan Smyl E EXCH 4.00 10.00
92 Al Iafrate F 5.00 12.00
93 Jim Neilson E 4.00 10.00
94 Pat Stapleton F 4.00 10.00
95 Mike Gartner F 6.00 15.00
96 Rick Middleton A 60.00 120.00
97 Willi Plett D 5.00 12.00
98 Gilles Villemure F 5.00 12.00
99 Wayne Gretzky A EXCH 200.00 350.00
100 Gordie Howe A 100.00 200.00
101 Wayne Gretzky H WIRE 250.00 400.00
102 Mario Lemieux G WIRE 125.00 250.00
103 Gordie Howe I WIRE 100.00 175.00
104 Bobby Orr I WIRE 100.00 200.00
105 Brett Hull G WIRE 50.00 100.00
106 Mark Messier G WIRE 75.00 150.00
107 Patrick Roy G WIRE 125.00 250.00
108 Luc Robitaille I WIRE 30.00 80.00
109 Marcel Dionne H WIRE 40.00 80.00
110 Bobby Clarke I WIRE 40.00 80.00
111 Ray Bourque H WIRE 40.00 100.00
112 Denis Potvin H WIRE 50.00 100.00
113 Red Kelly I WIRE 25.00 60.00
114 Phil Esposito G WIRE 40.00 80.00
115 Johnny Bower I WIRE 40.00 80.00
116 Mike Bossy H WIRE 40.00 100.00
117 Ted Lindsay I WIRE 30.00 60.00
118 Larry Robinson H WIRE 30.00 60.00
119 Jean Beliveau G WIRE 150.00 250.00
120 Wendel Clark WIRE EXCH 50.00 100.00
121 Rbnsn/Hawer WIRE K EX
122 B.Park/B.Barber WIRE K 125.00 250.00
123 Gretzky/Howe WIRE K EX 400.00 700.00
124 Messier/Kurri WIRE K EX 200.00 400.00
125 G.Howe/J.Bower WIRE K 200.00 400.00
126 B.Hull/S.Mikita WIRE K 100.00 200.00
127 Lindsay/G.Howe WIRE K 200.00 400.00
128 T.Esposito/B.Orr WIRE K 250.00 500.00
129 Espsto/Clrke/Orr WIRE J
130 Esposito/Bucyk/Orr WIRE J 250.00 400.00
131 Wayne Gretzky R M EXCH 250.00 400.00
132 Bobby Orr R N 150.00 300.00
133 Gordie Howe R M
134 Mario Lemieux R L 125.00 200.00
135 Brett Hull R L 50.00 100.00
136 Patrick Roy R M 100.00 175.00
137 Mark Messier R M 60.00 120.00
138 Guy Lafleur R M 50.00 100.00
139 Stan Mikita R M 40.00 80.00
140 Mike Bossy R M 30.00 60.00
141 Bobby Hull R M 30.00 60.00
142 Bobby Clarke R M 30.00 60.00
143 Ray Bourque R M 40.00 80.00
144 Dale Hawerchuk R N 25.00 50.00
145 Cam Neely R M 25.00 50.00
146 Rogie Vachon R N 12.00 30.00
147 Peter Stastny R N 25.00 60.00
148 Darryl Sittler R N 15.00 40.00
149 Eric Lindros R N 150.00 250.00
150 Gilbert Perreault R N 15.00 40.00
151 Patrick Roy R BW 175.00 300.00
152 Bobby Orr R BW 175.00 300.00
153 Guy Lafleur R BW
154 Phil Esposito R BW 200.00 350.00
155 Mark Messier R BW
156 Jean Beliveau R BW 150.00 250.00
157 Bobby Hull R BW 100.00 175.00
158 Gordie Howe R BW 175.00 300.00
159 Mario Lemieux R BW
160 Wayne Gretzky R BW 300.00 400.00

2011-12 Parkhurst Champions Champ's Fossils and Artifacts

STATED ODDS 1:1280
NNO Redemption Card 75.00 135.00

2011-12 Parkhurst Champions Champ's Mini

COMPLETE SET (57) 40.00 100.00
COMP.SET w/o SPs (45) 12.00 30.00
CHAMPS BASE CARDS 1 PER PACK
SP STATED ODDS 1:20
*1-45 GREEN BACK: 1.2X TO 3X BASIC INSERT
*46-57 GREEN BACK: .6X TO 1.5X BASIC SP
*1-45 PARKHURST: 8X TO 20X BASIC INSERTS
46-57 PARHURST SPs NOT PRICED
1 Georges Vezina .30 .75
2 Denis Savard .40 1.00
3 Stan Mikita .40 1.00
4 Adam Oates .30 .75
5 Alex Delvecchio .25 .60
6 Eric Lindros .50 1.25
7 Gump Worsley .30 .75
8 Don Cherry .30 .75
9 Andy Bathgate .30 .75
10 Borje Salming .30 .75
11 Clark Gillies .30 .75
12 Dale Hawerchuk .40 1.00
13 Denis Potvin .30 .75
14 Howie Morenz .25 .60
15 Duane Sutter .20 .50
16 Gilbert Perreault .30 .75
17 Jari Kurri .30 .75
18 Cam Neely .30 .75
19 Larry Robinson .30 .75
20 Marcel Dionne .40 1.00
21 Red Kelly .25 .60
22 Scotty Bowman .30 .75
23 Rogie Vachon .40 1.00
24 Ted Lindsay .30 .75
25 Terry O'Reilly .25 .60
26 Doug Gilmour .40 1.00
27 Johnny Bucyk .30 .75
28 Luc Robitaille .30 .75
29 Tony Esposito .30 .75
30 Steve Shutt .30 .75
31 King Clancy .30 .75
32 Mark Howe .30 .75
33 Darryl Sittler .30 .75
34 Eddie Shore .25 .60
35 Igor Larionov .30 .75
36 Ron Francis .40 1.00
37 Willie O'Ree .25 .60
38 Wendel Clark .30 .75
39 Ron Hextall .40 1.00
40 Glenn Anderson .30 .75
41 Joe Sakic .50 1.25
42 Ray Bourque .50 1.25
43 Peter Stastny .30 .75
44 Johnny Bower .30 .75
45 Grant Fuhr .30 .75
46 Bobby Hull SP 2.50 6.00
47 Patrick Roy SP 6.00 15.00
48 Mark Messier SP 3.00 8.00
49 Brett Hull SP 3.00 8.00
50 Bobby Orr SP 8.00 20.00
51 Phil Esposito SP 4.00 10.00
52 Bobby Clarke SP 2.50 6.00
53 Mario Lemieux SP 8.00 20.00
54 Guy Lafleur SP 3.00 8.00
55 Mike Bossy SP 2.50 6.00
56 Gordie Howe SP 5.00 12.00
57 Wayne Gretzky SP 8.00 20.00

2011-12 Parkhurst Champions Champ's Mini Gold Rainbow

STATED PRINT RUN 11 SER.#'d SETS

2011-12 Parkhurst Champions Champ's Mini Signatures

STATED ODDS 1:90
SP STATED ODDS 1:1300
LINDROS AU ISSUED IN 2011-12 BLACK DIAMOND
2 Denis Savard 15.00 40.00
3 Stan Mikita 15.00 30.00
4 Adam Oates 6.00 15.00
5 Alex Delvecchio 6.00 15.00
6 Eric Lindros
8 Don Cherry 12.00 30.00
9 Andy Bathgate 12.00 30.00
10 Borje Salming 12.00 30.00
11 Clark Gillies 6.00 15.00
12 Dale Hawerchuk 8.00 20.00
13 Denis Potvin 6.00 15.00
15 Duane Sutter 4.00 10.00
16 Gilbert Perreault 6.00 15.00
17 Jari Kurri 6.00 15.00
18 Cam Neely 6.00 15.00
19 Larry Robinson 6.00 15.00
20 Marcel Dionne 10.00 25.00
21 Red Kelly 5.00 12.00
22 Scotty Bowman 25.00 50.00
23 Rogie Vachon 8.00 20.00
24 Ted Lindsay 8.00 20.00
25 Terry O'Reilly 5.00 12.00
26 Doug Gilmour 20.00 40.00
27 Johnny Bucyk 6.00 15.00
28 Luc Robitaille 15.00 30.00
29 Tony Esposito 30.00 60.00
30 Steve Shutt 10.00 25.00
32 Mark Howe 6.00 15.00
33 Darryl Sittler 10.00 25.00
35 Igor Larionov 50.00 100.00
36 Ron Francis 15.00 40.00
37 Willie O'Ree 8.00 20.00
38 Wendel Clark EXCH 6.00 15.00
39 Ron Hextall 12.00 30.00
40 Glenn Anderson 6.00 15.00
41 Joe Sakic 40.00 80.00
42 Ray Bourque 40.00 80.00
43 Peter Stastny 6.00 15.00
44 Johnny Bower 10.00 25.00
45 Grant Fuhr EXCH 40.00 80.00
46 Bobby Hull SP
47 Patrick Roy SP 75.00 125.00
48 Mark Messier SP 75.00 125.00
49 Brett Hull SP 75.00 125.00
50 Bobby Orr SP 100.00 200.00
51 Phil Esposito SP 30.00 60.00
52 Bobby Clarke SP 30.00 60.00
53 Mario Lemieux SP 75.00 150.00
54 Guy Lafleur SP 60.00 120.00
55 Mike Bossy SP 20.00 40.00
56 Gordie Howe SP 90.00 150.00
57 Wayne Gretzky SP EXCH 150.00 300.00

1995-96 Parkhurst International

This two-series issue was produced by Parkhurst in Canada for release in eleven European countries. Interest in the cards, which featured NHL players and were licensed by both the NHL and NHLPA, was suc[h] that they became widely available throughout North America. The first series was produced in larger quantities than the second series, which by some estimates was limited to around 900 cases. Each bo[x] included 48 14-card packs. The second series is notable for including the first card of Wayne Gretzky [in] a St. Louis Blues uniform. Two different players autographed cards for insertion in each series: Teem[u] Selanne and Mikael Renberg each signed 2,500 card[s] for series 1, while Martin Brodeur and Saku Koivu inked up 2,500 each for series 2. One jumbo Saku Koivu card was inserted in each series 2 box; autographed copies of this jumbo card were random[ly] inserted as well.

1 Patrik Carnback .05
2 Milos Holan .05
3 Paul Kariya .12
4 Guy Hebert .07
5 Garry Valk .05
6 Mikhail Shtalenkov .05
7 Randy Ladouceur .05
8 Shaun Van Allen .05
9 Oleg Tverdovsky .10
10 Kevin Stevens .07
11 Ray Bourque .15
12 Cam Neely .10
13 Jozef Stumpel .05
14 Blaine Lacher .07
15 Alexei Kasatonov .05
16 Adam Oates .10
17 Ted Donato .05
18 Mariusz Czerkawski .05
19 Alexei Zhitnik .05
20 Pat LaFontaine .10
21 Garry Galley .05
22 Scott Pearson .05
23 Yuri Khmylev .05
24 Jason Dawe .05
25 Robb Stauber .05
26 Wayne Primeau .05
27 Brian Holzinger XRC .20
28 German Titov .07
29 Theo Fleury .12
30 Phil Housley .07
31 Zarley Zalapski .05
32 Rick Tabaracci .07
33 Joe Nieuwendyk .10
34 Michael Nylander .05
35 Trevor Kidd .07
36 Dean Evason .05
37 Bernie Nicholls .05
38 Chris Chelios .10
39 Gary Suter .07
40 Denis Savard .12
41 Ed Belfour .07
42 Patrick Poulin .05
43 Steve Smith .05
44 Jeff Hackett .07
45 Eric Daze .20
46 Joe Sakic .15
47 John Slaney .05
48 Valeri Kamensky .07
49 Owen Nolan .10
50 Uwe Krupp .07
51 Andrei Kovalenko .05
52 Janne Laukkanen .05
53 Jocelyn Thibault .07
54 Adam Deadmarsh .05
55 Mike Modano .15
56 Kevin Hatcher .07
57 Mike Donnelly .05
58 Derian Hatcher .07
59 Andy Moog .10
60 Jamie Langenbrunner .05
61 Shane Churla .05
62 Todd Harvey .05
63 Manny Fernandez .07
64 Nicklas Lidstrom .10
65 Vyacheslav Kozlov .07
66 Paul Coffey .10
67 Chris Osgood .07
68 Slava Fetisov .07
69 Vladimir Konstantinov .07
70 Steve Yzerman .12
71 Aaron Ward .05
72 Keith Primeau .05
73 Jason Arnott .07
74 Igor Kravchuk .05
75 Boris Mironov .05
76 David Oliver .05
77 Kelly Buchberger .05
78 Bill Ranford .07
79 Zdeno Ciger .07
80 Jason Bonsignore .05
81 Louie DeBrusk .07
82 Rob Niedermayer .07
83 Magnus Svensson .07
84 Robert Svehla .05
85 John Vanbiesbrouck .07
86 Stu Barnes .05
87 Jesse Belanger .05
88 Mark Fitzpatrick .07
89 Jason Woolley .05
90 Johan Garpenlov .05
91 Geoff Sanderson .05
92 Robert Kron .05
93 Darren Turcotte .05
94 Andrei Nikolishin .05
95 Steven Rice .05
96 Sean Burke .05
97 Brendan Shanahan .12
98 Glen Wesley .05
99 Marek Malik .05
100 Wayne Gretzky .50 1.
101 Robert Lang .05
102 Jari Kurri .10
103 Kelly Hrudey .07
104 Jamie Storr .07
105 Marty McSorley .05
106 Rob Blake .07
107 Eric LaCroix .05
108 Dimitri Khristich .05

Card	Low	High
09 Pierre Turgeon	.10	.25
10 Vincent Damphousse	.07	.20
11 Peter Popovic	.05	.15
12 Brian Savage	.05	.15
13 Patrick Roy	.25	.60
14 Valeri Bure	.05	.15
15 Vladimir Malakhov	.05	.15
16 Benoit Brunet	.05	.15
17 Stephane Quintal	.07	.20
18 Stephane Richer	.07	.20
19 Sergei Brylin	.05	.15
20 Neal Broten	.07	.20
21 Scott Stevens	.10	.25
22 Martin Brodeur	.25	.60
23 John MacLean	.07	.20
24 Bill Guerin	.07	.20
25 Bobby Holik	.05	.15
26 Tommy Albelin	.05	.15
27 Tommy Soderstrom	.07	.20
28 Tommy Salo	.15	.40
29 Kirk Muller	.07	.20
30 Mathieu Schneider	.05	.15
31 Zigmund Palffy	.10	.25
32 Derek King	.07	.20
33 Brett Lindros	.05	.15
34 Marty McInnis	.05	.15
35 Alexander Semak	.05	.15
36 Mark Messier	.15	.40
37 Adam Graves	.07	.20
38 Mike Richter	.10	.25
39 Alexei Kovalev	.05	.15
40 Luc Robitaille	.10	.25
41 Sergei Nemchinov	.05	.15
42 Alexander Karpovtsev	.05	.15
43 Mattias Norstrom	.07	.20
44 Brian Leetch	.10	.25
45 Martin Straka	.05	.15
46 Sylvain Turgeon	.05	.15
47 Radek Bonk	.05	.15
48 Stanislav Neckar	.05	.15
49 Pavol Demitra	.12	.30
50 Alexandre Daigle	.05	.15
51 Alexei Yashin	.07	.20
52 Don Beaupre	.07	.20
53 Steve Duchesne	.05	.15
54 Eric Lindros	.15	.40
55 Kjell Samuelsson	.05	.15
56 Chris Therien	.05	.15
57 John LeClair	.10	.25
58 Rod Brind'Amour	.10	.25
59 Ron Hextall	.10	.25
60 Patrik Juhlin	.05	.15
61 Mikael Renberg	.07	.20
62 Joel Otto	.05	.15
63 Markus Naslund	.10	.25
64 Ron Francis	.12	.30
65 Jaromir Jagr	.25	.60
66 Tomas Sandstrom	.07	.20
67 Ken Wregget	.07	.20
68 Bryan Smolinski	.05	.15
69 Richard Park	.10	.25
70 Mario Lemieux	.30	.75
71 Norm Maciver	.07	.20
72 Brett Hull	.12	.30
73 Esa Tikkanen	.05	.15
74 Shayne Corson	.05	.15
75 Chris Pronger	.10	.25
76 Ian Laperriere	.05	.15
77 Jon Casey	.07	.20
78 Al MacInnis	.10	.25
79 David Roberts	.05	.15
80 Dale Hawerchuk	.12	.30
81 Michal Sykora	.05	.15
82 Jeff Friesen	.05	.15
83 Ray Whitney	.07	.20
84 Igor Larionov	.05	.15
85 Sandis Ozolinsh	.07	.20
86 Andrei Nazarov	.07	.20
87 Viktor Kozlov	.07	.20
88 Arturs Irbe	.07	.20
89 Wade Flaherty	.07	.20
90 Brian Bradley	.07	.20
91 Paul Ysebaert	.05	.15
92 John Tucker	.05	.15
93 Jason Wiemer	.05	.15
94 Alexander Selivanov	.07	.20
95 Daren Puppa	.07	.20
96 Mikael Andersson	.07	.20
97 Petr Klima	.05	.15
98 Roman Hamrlik	.05	.15
99 Doug Gilmour	.12	.30
00 Damian Rhodes	.07	.20
01 Mats Sundin	.10	.25
02 Todd Gill	.05	.15
03 Kenny Jonsson	.10	.25
04 Felix Potvin	.10	.25
05 Tie Domi	.07	.20
06 Mike Gartner	.10	.25
07 Larry Murphy	.10	.25
08 Josef Beranek	.05	.15
09 Trevor Linden	.10	.25
10 Russ Courtnall	.05	.15
11 Roman Oksiuta	.05	.15
12 Alexander Mogilny	.07	.20
13 Kirk McLean	.07	.20
14 Mike Ridley	.05	.15
15 Jyrki Lumme	.05	.15
16 Bret Hedican	.05	.15
17 Keith Jones	.07	.20
18 Calle Johansson	.05	.15
19 Kelly Miller	.05	.15
20 Olaf Kolzig	.07	.20
21 Joe Juneau	.07	.20
22 Sylvain Cote	.05	.15
23 Dale Hunter	.07	.20
24 Mark Tinordi	.05	.15
25 Sergei Gonchar	.05	.15
26 Alexei Zhamnov	.10	.25
27 Igor Korolev	.05	.15
28 Teppo Numminen	.05	.15
29 Craig Martin	.05	.15
30 Nikolai Khabibulin	.07	.20
31 Michal Grosek	.05	.15
32 Teemu Selanne	.20	.50
33 Dave Manson	.05	.15
34 Tim Cheveldae	.07	.20
35 Esa Tikkanen	.05	.15
36 Dominik Hasek II	.12	.30
37 Peter Forsberg II	.25	.60
38 Sergei Fedorov II	.15	.40
39 Jari Kurri	.10	.25
40 Tommy Soderstrom	.07	.20
41 Alexei Zhamnov II	.10	.25
42 Alexei Yashin II	.07	.20
43 Mikael Renberg II	.07	.20
44 Jaromir Jagr II	.25	.60
45 Ulf Dahlen	.05	.15
46 Alexander Mogilny II	.07	.20
47 Mats Sundin II	.10	.25
48 Pavel Bure II	.12	.30
49 Slava Fetisov	.07	.20
250 Teemu Selanne II	.20	.50
251 Arturs Irbe	.07	.20
252 Nicklas Lidstrom	.10	.25
253 Aki Berg	.10	.25
254 Zdenek Nedved	.05	.15
255 Chad Kilger	.10	.25
256 Bryan McCabe	.10	.25
257 Daniel Alfredsson XRC	.50	1.25
258 Brendan Witt	.10	.25
259 Jeff O'Neill	.10	.25
260 Radek Dvorak	.12	.30
261 Niklas Sundstrom	.10	.25
262 Kyle McLaren	.05	.15
263 Saku Koivu	.10	.25
264 Todd Bertuzzi	.12	.30
265 Jere Lehtinen	.07	.20
266 Vitali Yachmenev	.10	.25
267 Shane Doan	.30	.75
268 Marko Kiprusoff	.07	.20
269 Deron Quint	.07	.20
270 Daymond Langkow XRC	.10	.25
271 Alex Hicks	.05	.15
272 Steve Rucchin	.07	.20
273 David Karpa	.05	.15
274 Mike Sillinger	.05	.15
275 Teemu Selanne	.20	.50
276 Todd Krygier	.05	.15
277 Valeri Karpov	.05	.15
278 Peter Douris	.05	.15
279 Team Checklist	.05	.15
280 Shawn McEachern	.05	.15
281 Dave Reid	.05	.15
282 Bill Ranford	.07	.20
283 Don Sweeney	.05	.15
284 Stephen Leach	.05	.15
285 Craig Billington	.07	.20
286 Clayton Beddoes	.07	.20
287 Rick Tocchet	.07	.20
288 Team Checklist	.05	.15
289 Brad May	.05	.15
290 Mike Peca	.07	.20
291 Dominik Hasek	.12	.30
292 Donald Audette	.07	.20
293 Randy Burridge	.05	.15
294 Derek Plante	.05	.15
295 Martin Biron XRC	.20	.50
296 Andrei Trefilov	.05	.15
297 Team Checklist	.05	.15
298 Steve Chiasson	.05	.15
299 Cory Stillman	.05	.15
300 Mike Sullivan	.07	.20
301 Gary Roberts	.05	.15
302 Pavel Torgajev	.05	.15
303 James Patrick	.05	.15
304 Corey Millen	.05	.15
305 Ed Ward	.07	.20
306 Team Checklist	.05	.15
307 Jeremy Roenick	.12	.30
308 Mike Prokopec	.05	.15
309 Joe Murphy	.05	.15
310 Eric Weinrich	.05	.15
311 Tony Amonte	.07	.20
312 Bob Probert	.07	.20
313 Murray Craven	.05	.15
314 Sergei Krivokrasov	.05	.15
315 Team Checklist	.05	.15
316 Peter Forsberg	.25	.60
317 Stephane Fiset	.07	.20
318 Mike Ricci	.07	.20
319 Claude Lemieux	.10	.25
320 Sandis Ozolinsh	.07	.20
321 Sylvain Lefebvre	.05	.15
322 Scott Young	.05	.15
323 Patrick Roy	.25	.60
324 Team Checklist	.05	.15
325 Brent Fedyk	.05	.15
326 Brent Gilchrist	.05	.15
327 Greg Adams	.05	.15
328 Richard Matvichuk	.07	.20
329 Joe Nieuwendyk	.10	.25
330 Benoit Hogue	.05	.15
331 Darcy Wakaluk	.05	.15
332 Guy Carbonneau	.10	.25
333 Team Checklist	.05	.15
334 Mike Vernon	.07	.20
335 Mathieu Dandenault	.20	.50
336 Igor Larionov	.05	.15
337 Sergei Fedorov	.15	.40
338 Greg Johnson	.05	.15
339 Dino Ciccarelli	.07	.20
340 Martin Lapointe	.05	.15
341 Darren McCarty	.05	.15
342 Team Checklist	.05	.15
343 Joaquin Gage	.07	.20
344 Jiri Slegr	.05	.15
345 Mariusz Czerkawski	.05	.15
346 Doug Weight	.10	.25
347 Todd Marchant	.05	.15
348 Miroslav Satan XRC	.12	.30
349 Jeff Norton	.05	.15
350 Curtis Joseph	.10	.25
351 Team Checklist	.05	.15
352 Tom Fitzgerald	.05	.15
353 Jody Hull	.05	.15
354 Terry Carkner	.05	.15
355 Scott Mellanby	.07	.20
356 Bill Lindsay	.05	.15
357 Gord Murphy	.05	.15
358 Brian Skrudland	.05	.15
359 David Nemirovsky	.07	.20
360 Team Checklist	.05	.15
361 Paul Ranheim	.05	.15
362 Jason Muzzatti	.07	.20
363 Glen Featherstone	.05	.15
364 Andrew Cassels	.05	.15
365 Jeff Brown	.07	.20
366 Kevin Dineen	.07	.20
367 Nelson Emerson	.05	.15
368 Gerald Diduck	.05	.15
369 Team Checklist	.05	.15
370 Kevin Stevens	.07	.20
371 Darryl Sydor	.07	.20
372 Yanic Perreault	.05	.15
373 Arto Blomsten	.05	.15
374 Kevin Todd	.05	.15
375 Byron Dafoe	.07	.20
376 Tony Granato	.05	.15
377 Vladimir Tsyplakov XRC	.20	.50
378 Team Checklist	.05	.15
379 Martin Rucinsky	.05	.15
380 Patrice Brisebois	.05	.15
381 Lyle Odelein	.05	.15
382 Andrei Kovalenko	.05	.15
383 Mark Recchi	.12	.30
384 Jocelyn Thibault	.07	.20
385 Turner Stevenson	.05	.15
386 Pat Jablonski	.05	.15
387 Team Checklist	.05	.15
388 Scott Niedermayer	.10	.25
389 Corey Schwab XRC	.20	.50
390 Steve Thomas	.07	.20
391 Valeri Zelepukin	.05	.15
392 Shawn Chambers	.05	.15
393 Jocelyn Lemieux	.07	.20
394 Brian Rolston	.05	.15
395 Denis Pederson	.05	.15
396 Team Checklist	.05	.15
397 Martin Straka	.05	.15
398 Niclas Andersson	.07	.20
399 Wendel Clark	.10	.25
400 Travis Green	.07	.20
401 Chris Marinucci	.07	.20
402 Darius Kasparaitis	.05	.15
403 Patrick Flatley	.05	.15
404 Jamie McLennan	.05	.15
405 Team Checklist	.05	.15
406 Glenn Healy	.07	.20
407 Pat Verbeek	.07	.20
408 Ian Laperriere	.05	.15
409 Ray Ferraro	.05	.15
410 Jeff Beukeboom	.05	.15
411 Ulf Samuelsson	.05	.15
412 Doug Lidster	.05	.15
413 Bruce Driver	.05	.15
414 Team Checklist	.05	.15
415 Antti Tormanen	.05	.15
416 Sean Hill	.05	.15
417 Damian Rhodes	.07	.20
418 Jaroslav Modry	.05	.15
419 Mike Bales	.05	.15
420 Trent McCleary	.07	.20
421 Randy Cunneyworth	.05	.15
422 Ted Drury	.05	.15
423 Team Checklist	.05	.15
424 Pat Falloon	.05	.15
425 Garth Snow	.07	.20
426 Shjon Podein	.05	.15
427 Petr Svoboda	.05	.15
428 Eric Desjardins	.07	.20
429 Anatoli Semenov	.07	.20
430 Kevin Haller	.05	.15
431 Rob Dimaio	.05	.15
432 Team Checklist	.05	.15
433 Chris Joseph	.05	.15
434 Sergei Zubov	.07	.20
435 Tom Barrasso	.07	.20
436 Chris Tamer	.05	.15
437 Dmitri Mironov	.05	.15
438 Petr Nedved	.07	.20
439 Neil Wilkinson	.05	.15
440 Glen Murray	.05	.15
441 Team Checklist	.05	.15
442 J.J. Daigneault	.05	.15
443 Grant Fuhr	.10	.25
444 Adam Creighton	.05	.15
445 Brian Noonan	.05	.15
446 Stephane Matteau	.05	.15
447 Roman Vopat	.05	.15
448 Geoff Courtnall	.05	.15
449 Wayne Gretzky	.50	1.25
450 Team Checklist	.05	.15
451 Chris Terreri	.07	.20
452 Ulf Dahlen	.05	.15
453 Owen Nolan	.10	.25
454 Doug Bodger	.05	.15
455 Craig Janney	.05	.15
456 Ville Peltonen	.05	.15
457 Ray Sheppard	.07	.20
458 Shean Donovan	.05	.15
459 Team Checklist	.05	.15
460 Jeff Reese	.05	.15
461 Shawn Burr	.05	.15
462 Chris Gratton	.05	.15
463 John Cullen	.05	.15
464 Bill Houlder	.05	.15
465 J.C. Bergeron	.07	.20
466 Brian Bellows	.07	.20
467 Drew Bannister	.07	.20
468 Team Checklist	.05	.15
469 Dimitri Yushkevich	.05	.15
470 Dave Andreychuk	.10	.25
471 Dave Gagner	.05	.15
472 Todd Warriner	.07	.20
473 Sergio Momesso	.05	.15
474 Kirk Muller	.07	.20
475 Dave Ellett	.05	.15
476 Ken Baumgartner	.05	.15
477 Team Checklist	.05	.15
478 Esa Tikkanen	.05	.15
479 Cliff Ronning	.05	.15
480 Martin Gelinas	.05	.15
481 Brian Loney	.05	.15
482 Pavel Bure	.12	.30
483 Corey Hirsch	.07	.20
484 Scott Walker	.05	.15
485 Jim Dowd	.05	.15
486 Team Checklist	.05	.15
487 Michal Pivonka	.05	.15
488 Pat Peake	.05	.15
489 Martin Gendron	.07	.20
490 Peter Bondra	.10	.25
491 Nolan Baumgartner	.05	.15
492 Jim Carey	.07	.20
493 Steve Konowalchuk	.07	.20
494 Jason Allison	.07	.20
495 Team Checklist	.05	.15
496 Oleg Tverdovsky	.10	.25
497 Craig Mills	.05	.15
498 Darren Turcotte	.05	.15
499 Norm Maciver	.07	.20
500 Chad Kilger PN	.10	.25
501 Keith Tkachuk	.10	.25
502 Kris King	.05	.15
503 Dallas Drake	.05	.15
504 Team Checklist	.05	.15
505 Saku Koivu PN	.10	.25
506 Vitali Yachmenev PN	.10	.25
507 Daniel Alfredsson PN	.50	1.25
508 Radek Dvorak	.12	.30
509 Miroslav Satan	.12	.30
510 Aki Berg PN	.10	.25
511 Valeri Bure	.05	.15
512 Petr Sykora PN	.25	.60
513 Andrei Vasilyev PN	.05	.15
514 Niklas Sundstrom	.10	.25
515 Viktor Kozlov	.07	.20
516 Sami Kapanen	.07	.20
517 Anders Myrvold	.07	.20
518 Jere Lehtinen	.07	.20
519 Marcus Ragnarsson XRC	.12	.30
520 Stefan Ustorf	.05	.15
521 Ville Peltonen	.05	.15
522 Antti Tormanen PN	.05	.15
523 Petr Sykora	.25	.60
524 Scott Bailey XRC	.12	.30
525 Kevin Hodson XRC	.20	.50
526 Landon Wilson	.05	.15
527 Aaron Gavey	.05	.15
528 Darren Langdon XRC	.20	.50
529 Jason Doig	.10	.25
530 Marty Murray	.10	.25
531 Marcus Ragnarsson	.12	.30
532 Peter Ferraro	.07	.20
533 Grant Marshall	.05	.15
534 Mike Wilson XRC	.20	.50
535 Rory Fitzpatrick	.07	.20
536 Ed Jovanovski	.10	.25
537 Eric Fichaud	.07	.20
538 Stefan Ustorf	.05	.15
539 Stephane Yelle	.07	.20
540 Ethan Moreau XRC	.20	.50
NNO1 M.Renberg AU/2500	5.00	12.00
NNO2 T.Selanne AU/2500	30.00	80.00
NNO3 M.Brodeur AU/1500	25.00	60.00
NNO4 S.Koivu AU/1500	12.00	30.00
NNO5 Saku Koivu Jumbo	1.50	4.00
NNO6 Saku Koivu Jumbo AU	10.00	25.00

1995-96 Parkhurst International Emerald Ice

This 540-card set was issued as a parallel to the regular Parkhurst International series. The cards feature the standard card player photo superimposed on brilliant emerald green foil. The cards were inserted at a rate of 1:3 packs.
*1-270 VETS: 2X TO 5X BASIC CARDS
*1-270 XRCs: 1.5X TO 4X BASIC XRC
*271-540 VETS: 2X TO 5X BASIC CARDS
*271-540 XRCs: 1.5X TO 4X BASIC XRC

1995-96 Parkhurst International All-Stars

These six two-sided cards feature the best foreign-born stars in the NHL at each position. The cards were randomly inserted at a rate of 1:96 first series packs.

Card	Low	High
COMPLETE SET (6)	6.00	15.00
1 D.Hasek/A.Irbe	1.00	2.50
2 N.Lidstrom/S.Ozolinsh	3.00	8.00
3 S.Zubov/A.Zhitnik	.40	1.00
4 S.Fedorov/P.Forsberg	1.25	3.00
5 J.Jagr/T.Selanne	1.00	2.50
6 M.Sundin/M.Renberg	3.00	8.00

1995-96 Parkhurst International Crown Collection Silver Series 1

This sixteen-card set features some of the most popular players in the game on an attractive silver etched foil background. The cards were inserted 1:16 series 1 packs and feature a black colored border. A gold parallel version of this set exists as well. These cards were significantly tougher, coming out of 1:96 series 1 packs.

Card	Low	High
COMPLETE SET (16)	12.00	30.00
*GOLD: 1.2X TO 3X SILVER		
1 Eric Lindros	.50	1.25
2 Felix Potvin	.50	1.25
3 Mario Lemieux	2.50	6.00
4 Paul Kariya	.50	1.25
5 Pavel Bure	.50	1.25
6 Wayne Gretzky	4.00	10.00
7 Mikael Renberg	.30	.75
8 Paul Coffey	.50	1.25
9 Teemu Selanne	.50	1.25
10 Brett Hull	.60	1.50
11 Martin Brodeur	1.25	3.00
12 Doug Gilmour	.30	.75
13 Peter Forsberg	1.25	3.00
14 Sergei Fedorov	.75	2.00
15 Saku Koivu	.50	1.25
16 Jim Carey	.30	.75

1995-96 Parkhurst International Crown Collection Silver Series 2

This 16-card set of the NHL's top stars was randomly inserted in series 2 packs. Although this set echoes the theme of the series 1 Crown Collection, the numbering again is 1-16, but the cards feature a purple colored border. There also are several players who make return appearances in this set. As with series one, the silver version come 1:16 packs, while the gold are found 1:96 packs.

Card	Low	High
COMPLETE SET (16)	10.00	25.00
*GOLD: 1.2X TO 3X SILVER		
1 Jaromir Jagr	.75	2.00
2 Patrick Roy	2.50	6.00
3 Alexander Mogilny	.30	.75
4 Paul Kariya	.50	1.25
5 Dominik Hasek	1.00	2.50
6 Peter Forsberg	1.25	3.00
7 Mark Messier	.50	1.25
8 Mats Sundin	.50	1.25
9 Ray Bourque	.75	2.00
10 Wayne Gretzky	4.00	10.00
11 Eric Lindros	.50	1.25
12 John Vanbiesbrouck	.30	.75
13 Chris Chelios	.50	1.25
14 Brian Leetch	.30	.75
15 Daniel Alfredsson	1.25	3.00
16 Eric Daze	.30	.75

1995-96 Parkhurst International Goal Patrol

This 12-card, horizontally-oriented set salutes the top netminders in the NHL. The cards feature an embossed photo in the Action Packed style, and were inserted 1:24 series 1 packs.

Card	Low	High
COMPLETE SET (12)	10.00	25.00
1 Martin Brodeur	3.00	8.00
2 Felix Potvin	1.25	3.00
3 Patrick Roy	4.00	10.00
4 Dominik Hasek	2.50	6.00
5 Jim Carey	.75	2.00
6 Ed Belfour	1.25	3.00
7 John Vanbiesbrouck	.75	2.00
8 Trevor Kidd	.75	2.00
9 Bill Ranford	.75	2.00
10 Arturs Irbe	.75	2.00
11 Kirk McLean	.75	2.00
12 Mike Richter	1.25	3.00

1995-96 Parkhurst International NHL All-Stars

These six, two-sided cards feature the NHL's top players by position. The cards were randomly inserted in series 2 packs at a rate of 1:96.

Card	Low	High
COMPLETE SET (6)	10.00	25.00
1 M.Lemieux/W.Gretzky	6.00	15.00
2 J.Jagr/B.Hull	1.25	3.00
3 B.Shanahan/P.Bure	2.50	6.00
4 S.Stevens/C.Chelios	2.50	6.00
5 R.Bourque/P.Coffey	1.50	4.00
6 M.Brodeur/E.Belfour	3.00	8.00

1995-96 Parkhurst International Parkie's Trophy Picks

This 54-card set illustrates Parkhurst's choices for the key individual awards for the 1995-96 NHL season. The cards were noted as being one of 1,000 produced, but were not individually numbered. The odds of pulling one from a second series pack were 1:48.

Card	Low	High
COMPLETE SET (54)	40.00	80.00
PP1 Eric Lindros	1.25	3.00
PP2 Mario Lemieux	3.00	8.00
PP3 Sergei Fedorov	1.25	3.00
PP4 Peter Forsberg	1.50	4.00
PP5 John Vanbiesbrouck	.75	2.00
PP6 Mark Messier	1.00	2.50
PP7 Jaromir Jagr	1.50	4.00
PP8 Joe Sakic	2.00	5.00
PP9 Grant Fuhr	.75	2.00
PP10 Eric Lindros	1.25	3.00
PP11 Mario Lemieux	3.00	8.00
PP12 Mark Messier	1.00	2.50
PP13 Peter Forsberg	1.50	4.00
PP14 Jaromir Jagr	1.50	4.00
PP15 Paul Kariya	1.00	2.50
PP16 Joe Sakic	4.00	10.00
PP17 Teemu Selanne	1.00	2.50
PP18 Alexander Mogilny	.60	1.50
PP19 Paul Coffey	1.00	2.50
PP20 Chris Chelios	1.00	2.50
PP21 Brian Leetch	.60	1.50
PP22 Ray Bourque	1.00	2.50
PP23 Larry Murphy	.40	1.00
PP24 Nicklas Lidstrom	1.00	2.50
PP25 Roman Hamrlik	.40	1.00
PP26 Gary Suter	.40	1.00
PP27 Sergei Zubov	.40	1.00
PP28 Dominik Hasek	1.50	4.00
PP29 John Vanbiesbrouck	.75	2.00
PP30 Chris Osgood	.60	1.50
PP31 Mike Richter	1.00	2.50
PP32 Martin Brodeur	2.00	5.00
PP33 Ron Hextall	.75	2.00
PP34 Grant Fuhr	1.00	2.50
PP35 Patrick Roy	3.00	8.00
PP36 Jim Carey	.40	1.00
PP37 Vitali Yachmenev	.40	1.00
PP38 Daniel Alfredsson	.60	1.50
PP39 Saku Koivu	1.00	2.50
PP40 Eric Daze	.40	1.00
PP41 Marcus Ragnarsson	.40	1.00
PP42 Ed Jovanovski	.40	1.00
PP43 Petr Sykora	.40	1.00
PP44 Todd Bertuzzi	1.00	2.50
PP45 Radek Dvorak	.40	1.00
PP46 Paul Kariya	1.00	2.50
PP47 Ron Francis	.60	1.50
PP48 Alexander Mogilny	.60	1.50
PP49 Pat LaFontaine	1.00	2.50
PP50 Pierre Turgeon	.40	1.00
PP51 Teemu Selanne	1.00	2.50
PP52 Sergei Fedorov	1.25	3.00
PP53 Adam Oates	.60	1.50
PP54 Brett Hull	1.25	3.00

1995-96 Parkhurst International Trophy Winners

This six-card set recognizes the winners of the key individual trophies from the 1994-95 season. The cards were inserted at a rate of 1:24 series one packs.

Card	Low	High
COMPLETE SET (6)	3.00	8.00
1 Eric Lindros	.50	1.25
2 Jaromir Jagr	.75	2.00
3 Peter Forsberg	1.25	3.00
4 Paul Coffey	.50	1.25
5 Dominik Hasek	1.00	2.50
6 Ron Francis	.30	.75

2003-04 Parkhurst Original Six Boston

This 100-card set featured players from one of the Original Six teams in the NHL, Boston. The set was produced as a stand alone product.

Card	Low	High
COMPLETE SET (100)	15.00	40.00
1 P. J. Axelsson	.15	.40
2 Michal Grosek	.15	.40
3 Nick Boynton	.15	.40
4 Jeff Jillson	.15	.40
5 Felix Potvin	.40	1.00
6 Patrick Leahy XRC	.40	1.00
7 Joe Thornton	.60	1.50
8 Ted Donato	.15	.40
9 Hal Gill	.15	.40
10 Jonathan Girard	.15	.40
11 Rob Zamuner	.15	.40
12 Shoane Morrisonn	.15	.40
13 Martin Samuelsson	.15	.40
14 Doug Doull XRC	.15	.40
15 Ivan Huml	.15	.40
16 Mike Knuble	.15	.40
17 Kris Vernarsky	.15	.40
18 Patrice Bergeron XRC	3.00	8.00
19 Sergei Zinovjev XRC	.40	1.00
20 Martin Lapointe	.15	.40
21 Dan McGillis	.15	.40
22 Sandy McCarthy	.15	.40
23 Glen Murray	.15	.40
24 P.J. Stock	.15	.40
25 Sean O'Donnell	.15	.40
26 Andrew Raycroft	.40	1.00
27 Brian Rolston	.15	.40
28 Sergei Samsonov	.40	1.00
29 Ian Moran	.15	.40
30 Travis Green	.15	.40
31 Adam Oates	.40	1.00
32 Cam Neely	.75	2.00
33 Jason Allison	.15	.40
34 Dit Clapper	.40	1.00
35 Fern Flaman	.15	.40
36 John Bucyk	.40	1.00
37 Milt Schmidt	.40	1.00
38 Brad Park	.40	1.00
39 Terry O'Reilly	.40	1.00
40 Wayne Cashman	.40	1.00
41 Ray Bourque	.75	2.00
42 Allan Stanley	.15	.40
43 Bernie Parent	.60	1.50
44 Derek Sanderson	.40	1.00
45 Bobby Orr	1.50	4.00
46 Tiny Thompson	.60	1.50
47 Eddie Shore	1.00	2.50
48 Frank Brimsek	.40	1.00
49 Jean Ratelle	.40	1.00
50 Ken Hodge	.40	1.00
51 Lionel Hitchman	.15	.40
52 Phil Esposito	.60	1.50
53 Rick Middleton	.40	1.00
54 Terry Sawchuk	.60	1.50
55 Woody Dumart	.15	.40
56 Gerry Cheevers	.60	1.50
57 Andy Moog	.40	1.00
58 Byron Dafoe	.40	1.00
59 Anson Carter	.15	.40
60 Bill Guerin	.40	1.00
61 Frank Brimsek	.40	1.00
62 Bobby Orr	1.50	4.00
63 Eddie Shore	1.00	2.50
64 Dit Clapper	.40	1.00
65 Cam Neely	.75	2.00
66 Phil Esposito	.60	1.50
67 Milt Schmidt	.40	1.00
68 Johnny Bucyk	.40	1.00
69 Woody Dumart	.15	.40
70 Ray Bourque	.75	2.00
71 Joe Thornton	.60	1.50
72 Dit Clapper	.40	1.00
73 Ray Bourque	.75	2.00
74 Fern Flaman	.15	.40
75 Johnny Bucyk	.40	1.00
76 Milt Schmidt	.40	1.00
77 Rick Middleton	.40	1.00
78 Terry O'Reilly	.40	1.00
79 Wayne Cashman	.40	1.00
80 Lionel Hitchman	.15	.40
81 Bobby Orr	1.50	4.00
82 Johnny Bucyk	.40	1.00
83 Phil Esposito	.60	1.50
84 Frank Brimsek	.40	1.00
85 Fern Flaman	.15	.40
86 Gerry Cheevers	.60	1.50
87 Dit Clapper	.40	1.00
88 Woody Dumart	.15	.40
89 Eddie Shore	1.00	2.50
90 Milt Schmidt	.40	1.00
91 Bobby Orr	1.50	4.00
92 Johnny Bucyk	.40	1.00
93 Terry O'Reilly	.40	1.00
94 Ray Bourque	.75	2.00
95 Cam Neely	.75	2.00
96 Phil Esposito	.60	1.50
97 Bobby Orr	1.50	4.00
98 Cam Neely	.75	2.00
99 Phil Esposito	.60	1.50
100 Ray Bourque	.75	2.00

2003-04 Parkhurst Original Six Boston Autographs

This 18-card set featured certified autographs of past Bruins greats. Print runs are listed below.

Card	Low	High
1 Ray Bourque/30	75.00	175.00
2 Johnny Bucyk/90	25.00	60.00
3 Wayne Cashman/85	25.00	60.00
4 Gerry Cheevers/90	50.00	125.00
5 Phil Esposito/55	75.00	175.00
6 Fern Flaman/85	30.00	80.00
7 Ken Hodge/90	25.00	60.00
8 Stan Jonathan/85	20.00	50.00
9 Rick Middleton/90	20.00	50.00
10 Andy Moog/90	25.00	60.00
11 Cam Neely/90	40.00	80.00
12 Terry O'Reilly/95	50.00	100.00
13 Bobby Orr/30	350.00	600.00
14 Bernie Parent/90	20.00	50.00
15 Brad Park/90	25.00	50.00
16 Jean Ratelle/90	30.00	60.00
17 Derek Sanderson/90	40.00	80.00
18 Milt Schmidt/85	30.00	80.00

2003-04 Parkhurst Original Six Boston Inserts

Card	Low	High
COMPLETE SET (17)	30.00	60.00
STATED ODDS 1:6		
B1 Eddie Shore	2.00	5.00
B2 Milt Schmidt	1.25	3.00
B3 Dit Clapper	1.25	3.00
B4 Phil Esposito	2.00	5.00
B5 Johnny Bucyk	1.25	3.00
B6 Bobby Orr	3.00	8.00
B7 Eddie Shore	2.00	5.00
B8 Phil Esposito	2.00	5.00
B9 Milt Schmidt	1.25	3.00
B10 Phil Esposito	2.00	5.00
B11 Bobby Orr	3.00	8.00
B12 Ray Bourque	2.50	6.00
B13 Derek Sanderson	1.25	3.00
B14 Tiny Thompson	2.00	5.00
B15 Frank Brimsek	1.25	3.00
B16 Joe Thornton	2.00	5.00
B17 Ray Bourque	2.50	6.00

2003-04 Parkhurst Original Six Boston Memorabilia

This 67-card set featured memorabilia from past and present Bruins players. Cards BM1-13 and BM61-62 were single jerseys and were limited to 100 copies sets. Cards BM14-18 and BM63 were jersey/stick combos and were limited to 80 sets. Cards BM19-20 were game gear inserts and print runs are listed below. Cards BM21-26, BM58 and BM64 were vintage memorabilia cards and print runs are listed below. Cards BM27-34, BM57 and BM65-67 were vintage jersey cards and were limited to 50 copies each. Cards BM35-39 and BM59 were vintage stick cards and print runs are listed below. Cards BM39-40 and BM60 are retired numbers cards and were limited to 20 copies. Cards BM51-56 were grouped into a subset known as Original Six Shooters, players who have scored high career totals against original six teams. The shooters cards were limited to 100 copies each. Cards BM51-56 were dual-jersey cards and were limited to 100 copies each.

Card	Low	High
BM1 Brian Rolston	8.00	20.00
BM2 Sergei Samsonov	6.00	15.00
BM3 Martin Lapointe	6.00	15.00
BM4 Don Sweeny	6.00	15.00
BM5 Nick Boynton	6.00	15.00
BM6 Joe Thornton	20.00	50.00
BM7 Jeff Hackett	6.00	15.00
BM8 Ivan Huml	6.00	15.00
BM9 Steve Shields	8.00	20.00
BM10 Glen Murray	6.00	15.00
BM11 Shaone Morrisonn	6.00	15.00
BM12 Bryan Berard	8.00	20.00
BM13 Mike Knuble	6.00	15.00
BM14 Bryan Berard J/S	12.00	30.00
BM15 Sergei Samsonov J/S	15.00	40.00
BM16 Joe Thornton J/S/50	30.00	80.00
BM17 Jeff Hackett J/S	8.00	20.00
BM18 Steve Shields J/S	15.00	40.00
BM19 Joe Thornton/20		
BM20 S.Samsonov/50 Glove	12.00	30.00
BM21 Tiny Thompson/20		
BM22 Gilles Gilbert/50	15.00	40.00
BM23 Gerry Cheevers/50 Pad	30.00	80.00
BM24 Eddie Shore/20 Glove		
BM25 Eddie Shore/60 Pants	20.00	50.00
BM26 Frank Brimsek/20		
BM27 John Bucyk J	20.00	50.00
BM28 Gerry Cheevers J	20.00	50.00
BM29 Andy Moog J	20.00	50.00
BM30 Gilles Gilbert J	20.00	50.00
BM31 Jason Allison J	15.00	40.00
BM32 Cam Neely J	30.00	80.00
BM33 Phil Esposito J	20.00	50.00
BM34 Adam Oates J	25.00	60.00
BM35 Phil Esposito/30 S	20.00	50.00
BM36 Ray Bourque/50 S	30.00	80.00
BM37 John Bucyk/20 S		
BM38 Gerry Cheevers/50 S	15.00	40.00
BM39 Eddie Shore/20 RN J		
BM40 Cam Neely/20 RN J	75.00	150.00
BM41 Mario Lemieux SS	15.00	40.00
BM42 Ron Francis SS	6.00	15.00
BM43 Joe Sakic SS	12.50	30.00
BM44 Brett Hull SS	8.00	20.00
BM45 Jaromir Jagr SS	8.00	20.00
BM46 Mike Modano SS	8.00	20.00
BM47 Teemu Selanne SS	10.00	25.00
BM48 Pavel Bure SS	6.00	15.00
BM49 Paul Kariya SS	8.00	20.00
BM50 Peter Forsberg SS	10.00	25.00
BM51 G.Cheevers/F.Potvin	20.00	50.00
BM52 P.Esposito/J.Thornton	25.00	60.00
BM53 B.Orr/R.Bourque	75.00	150.00
BM54 J.Bucyk/G.Murray	20.00	50.00
BM55 T.O'Reilly/C.Neely	25.00	60.00
BM56 T.Thompson/B.Parent	30.00	80.00
BM57 Bobby Orr J	100.00	200.00
BM58 Bobby Orr/50	100.00	200.00
BM59 Bobby Orr/50 S	100.00	200.00
BM60 Bobby Orr/20 RN J		
BM61 Felix Potvin	12.00	30.00
BM62 Andrew Raycroft	15.00	40.00
BM63 Felix Potvin J/S	25.00	60.00
BM64 Ray Bourque/50	15.00	40.00
BM65 Brad Park/50 J	20.00	50.00
BM66 Ray Bourque/50 J	20.00	50.00
BM67 Terry O'Reilly/50 J	20.00	50.00

2003-04 Parkhurst Original Six Chicago

This 100-card set featured players from one of the Original Six teams in the NHL, Chicago. The set was produced as a stand alone product.

Card	Low	High
COMPLETE SET	15.00	40.00
1 Tyler Arnason	.40	1.00
2 Mark Bell	.15	.40
3 Deron Quint	.15	.40
4 Kyle Calder	.15	.40
5 Bryan Berard	.15	.40
6 Eric Daze	.40	1.00
7 Jason Strudwick	.15	.40
8 Nathan Dempsey	.15	.40
9 Jon Klemm	.15	.40
10 Igor Korolev	.15	.40
11 Pavel Vorobiev XRC	.75	2.00
12 Scott Nichol	.15	.40
13 Alexander Karpovtsev	.15	.40
14 Tuomo Ruutu XRC	1.25	3.00
15 Ville Nieminen	.15	.40
16 Steve McCarthy	.15	.40
17 Igor Radulov	.15	.40
18 Alexei Zhamnov	.15	.40
19 Burke Henry	.15	.40
20 Craig Andersson	.40	1.00
21 Steve Passmore	.40	1.00
22 Lasse Kukkonen XRC	.75	2.00
23 Steve Poapst	.15	.40
24 Michael Leighton	.40	1.00
25 Shawn Thornton	.15	.40
26 Brett McLean	.15	.40
27 Steve Sullivan	.15	.40
28 Jocelyn Thibault	.40	1.00
29 Travis Moen XRC	.75	2.00
30 Ryan Vandenbussche	.15	.40
31 Chris Chelios	.50	1.25
32 Dominik Hasek	.75	2.00
33 Jeremy Roenick	.60	1.50
34 Ed Belfour	.50	1.25
35 Doug Gilmour	.40	1.00
36 Charlie Gardiner	.40	1.00
37 Howie Morenz	.60	1.50
38 Steve Larmer	.40	1.00
39 Dirk Graham	.15	.40
40 Ken Wharram	.40	1.00
41 Pat Stapleton	.15	.40
42 Pierre Pilote	.40	1.00
43 Bobby Hull	1.25	3.00
44 Tony Amonte	.40	1.00
45 Stan Mikita	.60	1.50
46 Dennis Hull	.60	1.50
47 Denis Savard	.75	2.00
48 Doug Wilson	.15	.40
49 Bobby Orr	1.50	3.50
50 Glenn Hall	.75	2.00
51 Harry Lumley	.50	1.25
52 Bill Mosienko	.50	1.25
53 Ken Hodge	.40	1.00
54 Michel Goulet	.50	1.25
55 Keith Magnuson	.75	2.00
56 Ted Lindsay	.50	1.25
57 Bill Gadsby	.40	1.00
58 Darren Pang	.50	1.25
59 Tony Esposito	.75	2.00
60 Phil Esposito	.75	2.00
61 Glenn Hall	.75	2.00
62 Ed Belfour	.50	1.25
63 Charlie Gardiner	.40	1.00
64 Tony Esposito	.75	2.00
65 Stan Mikita	.60	1.50
66 Bobby Hull	1.25	3.00
67 Pierre Pilote	.40	1.00
68 Doug Wilson	.15	.40
69 Chris Chelios	.50	1.25
70 Ken Wharram	.40	1.00
71 Alexei Zhamnov	.15	.40
72 Chris Chelios	.50	1.25
73 Doug Gilmour	.40	1.00
74 Bill Gadsby	.40	1.00
75 Denis Savard	.75	2.00
76 Tony Amonte	.40	1.00
77 Dirk Graham	.15	.40
78 Stan Mikita	.60	1.50
79 Ed Litzenberger	.40	1.00
80 Pierre Pilote	.40	1.00
81 Denis Savard	.75	2.00
82 Johnny Bower	.40	1.00
83 Stan Mikita	.60	1.50
84 Bill Mosienko	.50	1.25
85 Glenn Hall	.75	2.00
86 Bobby Hull	1.25	3.00
87 Phil Esposito	.75	2.00
88 Tony Esposito	.75	2.00
89 Bill Gadsby	.40	1.00
90 Michel Goulet	.50	1.25
91 Bobby Hull	1.25	3.00
92 Stan Mikita	.60	1.50
93 Stan Mikita	.60	1.50
94 Tony Esposito	.75	2.00
95 Bobby Hull	1.25	3.00
96 Denis Savard	.75	2.00
97 Tony Esposito	1.25	3.00
98 Ed Belfour	.50	1.25
99 Chris Chelios	.50	1.25
100 Steve Larmer	.40	1.00

2003-04 Parkhurst Original Six Chicago Autographs

This 18-card set featured certified autographs of past Blackhawks greats. Print runs are listed below.

Card	Low	High
1 Phil Esposito/55	50.00	100.00
2 Tony Esposito/85	30.00	60.00
3 Michel Goulet/90	20.00	50.00
4 Dirk Graham/90	15.00	40.00
5 Glenn Hall/85	50.00	125.00
6 Ken Hodge/89	20.00	50.00
7 Bobby Hull/75	50.00	100.00
8 Steve Larmer/85	40.00	80.00

9 Ted Lindsay/90 25.00 60.00
10 Eddie Litzenberger/90 20.00 50.00
11 Keith Magnuson/99 40.00 80.00
12 Stan Mikita/80 20.00 50.00
13 Darren Pang/99 15.00 40.00
14 Pierre Pilote/85 20.00 50.00
15 Denis Savard/90 25.00 60.00
16 Ken Wharram/90 25.00 60.00
17 Doug Wilson/90 25.00 60.00

2003-04 Parkhurst Original Six Chicago Inserts

COMPLETE SET (16) 30.00 60.00
C1 Stan Mikita 2.00 5.00
C2 Bobby Hull 2.00 5.00
C3 Tony Esposito 2.00 5.00
C4 Glenn Hall 1.50 4.00
C5 Denis Savard 1.50 4.00
C6 Bobby Hull 2.00 5.00
C7 Ed Belfour 1.50 4.00
C8 Tony Esposito 2.00 5.00
C9 Glenn Hall 1.50 4.00
C10 Tony Esposito 2.00 5.00
C11 Stan Mikita 2.00 5.00
C12 Bobby Hull 2.00 5.00
C13 Pierre Pilote 1.50 4.00
C14 Charlie Gardiner 1.50 4.00
C15 Jeremy Roenick 2.00 5.00
C16 Denis Savard 1.50 4.00

2003-04 Parkhurst Original Six Chicago Memorabilia

This 62-card set featured memorabilia from past and present Blackhawks players. Cards CM1-9 were single jerseys and were limited to 100 copies sets. Cards CM10-13 were jersey/stick combos and were limited to 80 sets. Cards CM15-18 were vintage memorabilia cards and were limited to 20 copies each. Cards CM19-30 and CM59-62 were vintage jersey cards and print runs are listed below. Cards CM31-36 were vintage stick cards and print runs are listed below. Cards CM37-40 were retired numbers cards and were limited to 20 copies. Cards CM41-50 were grouped into a subset known as Original Six Shooters; players who have scored high career totals against original six teams. The shooters cards were limited to 100 copies each. Cards CM51-58 were dual-jersey cards and were limited to 100 copies each.

CM1 Jocelyn Thibault/100* 10.00 25.00
CM2 Steve Sullivan/100* 10.00 25.00
CM3 Eric Daze/100* 6.00 15.00
CM4 Alexei Zhamnov/100* 6.00 15.00
CM5 Mark Bell/100* 6.00 15.00
CM6 Steve McCarthy/100* 6.00 15.00
CM7 Tyler Arnason/100* 6.00 15.00
CM8 Steve Passmore/100* 10.00 25.00
CM9 Ryan Vandenbussche/100* 6.00 15.00
CM10 Jocelyn Thibault/80* J/S 20.00 50.00
CM11 Steve Sullivan/80* J/S 15.00 40.00
CM12 Eric Daze/80* J/S 12.50 30.00
CM13 Alexei Zhamnov/80* J/S 12.50 30.00
CM14 Jocelyn Thibault/50 30.00 80.00
CM15 Tony Esposito/20* Pad
CM16 Bill Mosienko/20* Pants 15.00 40.00
CM17 Chuck Gardiner/20* Pad 20.00 40.00
CM18 Harry Lumley/20* 30.00 60.00
CM19 Frank Brimsek/20* J
CM20 Ed Belfour/100* J 15.00 40.00
CM21 Jeremy Roenick/100* J 12.50 30.00
CM22 Tony Amonte/100* J 12.50 30.00
CM23 Bill Mosienko/60* J 25.00 60.00
CM24 Michel Goulet/100* J 12.50 30.00
CM25 Bobby Hull/50* J 25.00 60.00
CM26 Dennis Hull/60* J 15.00 40.00
CM27 Glenn Hall/50* J 20.00 50.00
CM28 Tony Esposito/50* J 25.00 60.00
CM29 Harry Lumley/50* J 20.00 50.00
CM30 Stan Mikita/50* J 25.00 60.00
CM31 Bobby Hull/50* S 25.00 60.00
CM32 Tony Esposito/60* S 25.00 60.00
CM33 Glenn Hall/60* S 15.00 40.00
CM34 Michel Goulet/70* S 10.00 25.00
CM35 Tony Amonte/70* S 10.00 25.00
CM36 Jeremy Roenick/70* S 10.00 25.00
CM37 Stan Mikita/20* RN 25.00 50.00
CM38 Bobby Hull/20* RN 60.00 120.00
CM39 Tony Esposito/20* RN
CM40 Glenn Hall/20* RN
CM41 Mario Lemieux/100* SS 15.00 40.00
CM42 Ron Francis/100* SS 8.00 20.00
CM43 Joe Sakic/100* SS 8.00 20.00
CM44 Brett Hull/100* SS 8.00 20.00
CM45 Jaromir Jagr/100* SS 8.00 20.00
CM46 Mike Modano/100* SS 8.00 20.00
CM47 Teemu Selanne/100* SS 10.00 25.00
CM48 Pavel Bure/100* SS 6.00 15.00
CM49 Paul Kariya/100* SS 8.00 20.00
CM50 Peter Forsberg/100* SS 10.00 25.00
CM51 G.Hall/T.Esposito/100* 12.50 30.00
CM52 B.Hull/J.Roenick/100* 20.00 50.00
CM53 S.Mikita/T.Amonte/100* 15.00 40.00
CM54 H.Lumley/J.Thibault/100* 12.50 30.00
CM55 M.Goulet/E.Daze/100* 15.00 40.00
CM56 B.Mosienko/S.Sullivan/100* 12.50 30.00
CM57 F.Brimsek/E.Belfour/100* 12.50 30.00
CM58 D.Hull/A.Zhamnov/100* 15.00 40.00
CM59 Chris Chelios/100* J 15.00 40.00
CM60 Jeff Hackett/100* J 15.00 40.00
CM61 Bob Probert/100* J 20.00 50.00
CM62 Denis Savard/100* J 20.00 50.00

2003-04 Parkhurst Original Six Detroit

This 100-card set featured players from one of the Original Six teams in the NHL, Detroit. The set was produced as a stand alone product.

COMPLETE SET (100) 15.00 40.00
1 Mathieu Schneider .15 .40
2 Chris Chelios .40 1.00
3 Mathieu Dandenault .15 .40
4 Pavel Datsyuk .60 1.50
5 Boyd Devereaux .15 .40
6 Kris Draper .15 .40
7 Jason Woolley .15 .40
8 Mark Mowers .15 .40
9 Ray Whitney .15 .40
10 Jiri Fischer .15 .40
11 Tomas Holmstrom .15 .40
12 Brett Hull .60 1.50
13 Curtis Joseph .50 1.25
14 Jamie Rivers .15 .40
15 Dominik Hasek .75 2.00
16 Henrik Zetterberg .60 1.50
17 Steve Thomas .15 .40
18 Manny Legace .40 1.00
19 Nicklas Lidstrom .60 1.50
20 Kirk Maltby .15 .40
21 Darren McCarty .15 .40
22 Jiri Hudler XRC 1.50 4.00
23 Brendan Shanahan .50 1.25
24 Marc Lamothe .40 1.00
25 Derian Hatcher .15 .40
26 Jason Williams .30 .75
27 Steve Yzerman 2.00 4.00
28 Michel Picard .15 .40
29 Derek King .15 .40
30 Dmitri Bykov .15 .40
31 Bob Probert .40 1.00
32 Chris Osgood .40 1.00
33 Mike Vernon .40 1.00
34 Adam Oates .40 1.00
35 Terry Sawchuk .50 1.25
36 Alex Delvecchio .50 1.25
37 Danny Gare .15 .40
38 Marcel Dionne .50 1.25
39 Mickey Redmond .40 1.00
40 Ted Lindsay .40 1.00
41 Sid Abel .40 1.00
42 Red Kelly .40 1.00
43 Reed Larson .15 .40
44 Ebbie Goodfellow .15 .40
45 Bill Gadsby .40 1.00
46 Dino Ciccarelli .40 1.00
47 Glenn Hall .50 1.25
48 John Bucyk .50 1.25
49 Brad Smith .40 1.00
50 Norm Ullman .40 1.00
51 Marcel Pronovost .15 .40
52 Roger Crozier .50 1.25
53 Brad Park .50 1.25
54 Keith Primeau .40 1.00
55 Adam Graves .40 1.00
56 Ed Giacomin .50 1.25
57 Pat Verbeek .40 1.00
58 Harry Lumley .40 1.00
59 Gary Bergman .15 .40
60 Gerard Gallant .15 .40
61 Terry Sawchuk AS .50 1.25
62 Glenn Hall AS .50 1.25
63 Red Kelly AS .40 1.00
64 Nicklas Lidstrom AS .60 1.50
65 Marcel Pronovost AS .15 .40
66 Ted Lindsay AS .40 1.00
67 Sid Abel AS .40 1.00
68 Steve Yzerman AS .75 2.00
69 Brendan Shanahan AS .50 1.25
70 Alex Delvecchio AS .50 1.25
71 Steve Yzerman C .75 2.00
72 Alex Delvecchio C .50 1.25
73 Danny Gare C .15 .40
74 Marcel Dionne C .50 1.25
75 Mickey Redmond C .40 1.00
76 Ted Lindsay C .40 1.00
77 Sid Abel C .40 1.00
78 Red Kelly C .40 1.00
79 Reed Larson C .15 .40
80 Ebbie Goodfellow C .15 .40
81 Sid Abel E .40 1.00
82 Alex Delvecchio E .50 1.25
83 Ed Giacomin E .50 1.25
84 Red Kelly E .40 1.00
85 Ted Lindsay E .40 1.00
86 Marcel Pronovost E .15 .40
87 Terry Sawchuk E .50 1.25
88 Norm Ullman E .40 1.00
89 Bill Gadsby E .40 1.00
90 Glenn Hall E .50 1.25
91 Steve Yzerman FL .75 2.00
92 Steve Yzerman FL .75 2.00
93 Steve Yzerman FL .75 2.00
94 Terry Sawchuk FL .50 1.25
95 Terry Sawchuk FL .50 1.25
96 Steve Yzerman FL .75 2.00
97 Sergei Fedorov FL .30 .75
98 Nicklas Lidstrom FL .60 1.50
99 Marcel Dionne FL .50 1.25
100 Alex Delvecchio FL .50 1.25

2003-04 Parkhurst Original Six Detroit Autographs

This 18-card set featured certified autographs of past Red Wings greats. Print runs are listed below.

OSDC Dino Ciccarelli/85 20.00 50.00
OSAD Alex Delvecchio/90 25.00 60.00
OSMD Marcel Dionne/75 15.00 40.00
OSGH Glenn Hall/80 30.00 80.00
OSGG Gerard Gallant/90 15.00 40.00
OSRK Red Kelly/80 25.00 60.00
OSTL Ted Lindsay/90 25.00 60.00
OSJB John Bucyk/80 25.00 60.00
OSNU Norm Ullman/85 15.00 40.00
OSMP Marcel Pronovost/88 20.00 50.00
OSDG Danny Gare/90 15.00 40.00
OSRL Reed Larson/98 15.00 40.00
OSBG Bill Gadsby/90 15.00 40.00
OSBS Brad Smith/90 15.00 40.00

2003-04 Parkhurst Original Six Detroit Inserts

COMPLETE SET (18) 30.00 60.00
STATED ODDS 1:6
D1 Terry Sawchuk 2.00 5.00
D2 Ted Lindsay 1.50 4.00
D3 Alex Delvecchio 2.00 5.00
D4 Sid Abel 1.50 4.00
D5 Ted Lindsay 1.50 4.00
D6 Sid Abel 1.50 4.00
D7 Terry Sawchuk 2.00 5.00
D8 Red Kelly 1.50 4.00
D9 Glenn Hall 2.00 5.00
D10 Roger Crozier 2.00 5.00
D11 Alex Delvecchio 2.00 5.00
D12 Red Kelly 1.50 4.00
D13 Nicklas Lidstrom 2.00 5.00
D14 Steve Yzerman 3.00 8.00
D15 Steve Yzerman 3.00 8.00
D16 Keith Primeau 1.50 4.00
D17 Marcel Dionne 2.00 5.00
D18 Martin Lapointe 1.50 4.00

2003-04 Parkhurst Original Six Detroit Memorabilia

This 63-card set featured memorabilia from past and present Red Wings players. Cards DM1-13 amd DM57-59 were single jerseys and were limited to 100 copies sets. Cards DM14-19 and DM60-62 were jersey/stick combos and were limited to 80 sets. Cards DM20-25 were memorabilia cards and were limited to 20 copies each. Cards DM26-33 were vintage jersey cards and print runs are listed below. Cards DM34-36 were vintage stick cards and print runs are listed below. Cards DM37-40 were retired numbers cards and were limited to 20 copies. Cards DM41-50 were grouped into a subset known as Original Six Shooters; players who have scored high career totals against original six teams. The shooters cards were limited to 100 copies each. Cards DM51-56 were dual-jersey . cards and were limited to 100 copies each.

DM1 Nicklas Lidstrom 10.00 25.00
DM2 Brendan Shanahan 10.00 25.00
DM3 Sergei Fedorov 15.00 40.00
DM4 Luc Robitaille 12.00 30.00
DM5 Steve Yzerman 20.00 50.00
DM6 Manny Legace 10.00 25.00
DM7 Mathieu Dandenault 6.00 15.00
DM8 Jiri Fischer 10.00 25.00
DM9 Darren McCarty 12.00 30.00
DM10 Pavel Datsyuk 15.00 40.00
DM11 Brett Hull 12.00 30.00
DM12 Igor Larionov 15.00 40.00
DM13 Chris Chelios 12.00 30.00
DM14 Nicklas Lidstrom J/S 15.00 40.00
DM15 Steve Yzerman J/S 40.00 80.00
DM16 Luc Robitaille J/S 15.00 40.00
DM17 Brendan Shanahan J/S 15.00 40.00
DM18 Sergei Fedorov J/S 20.00 50.00
DM19 Brett Hull J/S 15.00 40.00
DM20 Sergei Fedorov Glove 60.00 120.00
DM21 Henrik Zetterberg Skate
DM22 Pavel Datsyuk Skate
DM23 Bill Gadsby/50 Glove
DM24 Roger Crozier/20 Pad 100.00 200.00
DM25 Terry Sawchuk/20 Glove
DM26 Sid Abel/40 J 40.00 100.00
DM27 Dino Ciccarelli/60 J 20.00 50.00
DM28 Alex Delvecchio/60 J 12.00 30.00
DM29 Terry Sawchuk/20 J
DM30 Ted Lindsay/20 J 20.00 40.00
DM31 Chris Osgood/80 J 12.50 30.00
DM32 Keith Primeau/80 J 12.50 30.00
DM33 Roger Crozier/50 J 12.50 30.00
DM34 Terry Sawchuk/20 S
DM35 Dino Ciccarelli/60 S 12.00 30.00
DM36 Ed Giacomin/60 S 25.00 60.00
DM37 T.Sawchuk/20 RN J
DM38 A.Delvecchio/20 RN J 75.00 150.00
DM39 S.Abel/20 RN J
DM40 T.Lindsay/20 RN J
DM41 Mario Lemieux SS 15.00 40.00
DM42 Ron Francis SS 6.00 15.00
DM43 Joe Sakic SS 10.00 25.00
DM44 Brett Hull SS 10.00 25.00
DM45 Jaromir Jagr SS 8.00 20.00
DM46 Mike Modano SS 8.00 20.00
DM47 Teemu Selanne SS 8.00 20.00
DM48 Pavel Bure SS 6.00 15.00
DM49 Paul Kariya SS 8.00 20.00
DM50 Peter Forsberg SS 10.00 25.00
DM51 T.Lindsay/B.Hull 15.00 40.00
DM52 T.Sawchuk/D.Hasek 30.00 80.00
DM53 S.Abel/S.Yzerman 25.00 60.00
DM54 A.Delvecchio/B.Shanahan 20.00 50.00
DM55 D.Ciccarelli/P.Datsyuk 20.00 50.00
DM56 R.Crozier/C.Osgood 15.00 40.00
DM57 Henrik Zetterberg 10.00 25.00
DM58 Dominik Hasek 15.00 40.00
DM59 Manny Legace 12.50 30.00
DM60 Henrik Zetterberg J/S 25.00 60.00
DM61 Pavel Datsyuk J/S 25.00 60.00
DM62 Dominik Hasek J/S 20.00 50.00
DM63 Mike Vernon/100 J 15.00 40.00

2003-04 Parkhurst Original Six Montreal

This 100-card set featured players from one of the Original Six teams in the NHL, Montreal. The set was produced as a stand alone product.

COMPLETE SET (100) 15.00 40.00
COMP. SET w/o SP's
1 Tomas Plekanec XRC .15 .40
2 Jose Theodore .50 .13
3 Ron Hainsey .15 .40
4 Patrice Brisebois .15 .40
5 Jan Bulis .15 .40
6 Niklas Sundstrom .15 .40
7 Steve Begin .15 .40
8 Andreas Dackell .15 .40
9 Karl Dykhuis .15 .40
10 Michael Ryder .50 1.25
11 Jason Ward .15 .40
12 Benoit Gratton .15 .40
13 Chistopher Higgins XRC .40 1.00
14 Craig Rivet .15 .40
15 Marcel Hossa .30 .75
16 Joe Juneau .15 .40
17 Chad Kilger .15 .40
18 Saku Koivu .50 1.25
19 Sheldon Souray .15 .40
20 Andrei Markov .15 .40
21 Olivier Michaud .15 .40
22 Mathieu Garon .15 .40
23 Yanic Perreault .15 .40
24 Francis Bouillon .15 .40
25 Mike Ribeiro .15 .40
26 Stephane Quintal .15 .40
27 Richard Zednik .15 .40
28 Darren Langdon .15 .40
29 Mike Komisarek .15 .40
30 Pierre Dagenais .15 .40
31 Chris Chelios .50 1.25
32 John LeClair .50 1.25
33 Mark Recchi .40 1.00
34 Rejean Houle .15 .40
35 Howie Morenz .40 1.00
36 Jacques Laperriere .15 .40
37 Elmer Lach .40 1.00
38 Yvan Cournoyer .50 1.25
39 Larry Robinson .50 1.25
40 Serge Savard .50 1.25
41 Butch Bouchard .15 .40
42 Guy Lafleur 1.00 2.50
43 Henri Richard .50 1.25
44 Jean Beliveau .50 1.25
45 Maurice Richard 1.50 4.00
46 Toe Blake .50 1.25
47 Guy Lapointe .15 .40
48 Gump Worsley .75 2.00
49 Patrick Roy 1.50 4.00
50 Rogie Vachon .40 1.00
51 Bill Durnan .40 1.00
52 John Ferguson .40 1.00
53 Georges Vezina 1.25 3.00
54 Denis Savard .40 1.00
55 Dollard St-Laurent .15 .40
56 Jean-Guy Talbot .15 .40
57 Steve Shutt .40 1.00
58 Frank Mahovlich .50 1.25
59 Jacques Plante 1.00 2.50
60 Dickie Moore .40 1.00
61 Howie Morenz .40 1.00
62 Maurice Richard 1.50 4.00
63 Jean Beliveau .50 1.25
64 Elmer Lach .40 1.00
65 Henri Richard .50 1.25
66 Doug Harvey .50 1.25
67 Jacques Plante 1.00 2.50
68 Larry Robinson .50 1.25
69 Patrick Roy 1.50 4.00
70 Guy Lafleur 1.00 2.50
71 Saku Koivu .50 1.25
72 Butch Bouchard .15 .40
73 Vincent Damphousse .15 .40
74 Henri Richard .50 1.25
75 Jean Beliveau .50 1.25
76 Maurice Richard 1.50 4.00
77 Newsy Lalonde .15 .40
78 Yvan Cournoyer .50 1.25
79 Doug Harvey .50 1.25
80 Serge Savard .50 1.25
81 Howie Morenz .40 1.00
82 Georges Vezina 1.25 3.00
83 Elmer Lach .40 1.00
84 Maurice Richard 1.50 4.00
85 Jean Beliveau .50 1.25
86 Yvan Cournoyer .50 1.25
87 Doug Harvey .50 1.25
88 Guy Lafleur 1.00 2.50
89 Larry Robinson .50 1.25
90 Henri Richard .40 1.00
91 Henri Richard .40 1.00
92 Maurice Richard 1.50 4.00
93 Guy Lafleur 1.00 2.50
94 Guy Lafleur 1.00 2.50
95 Jacques Plante 1.00 2.50
96 Steve Shutt .40 1.00
97 Jean Beliveau .50 1.25
98 Larry Robinson .50 1.25
99 Patrick Roy 2.00 5.00
100 Maurice Richard 1.50 4.00

2003-04 Parkhurst Original Six Montreal Autographs

This 18-card set featured certified autographs of past Canadiens greats. Print runs are listed below.

1 Jean Beliveau/85 75.00 125.00
2 Butch Bouchard/85 20.00 50.00
3 Yvan Cournoyer/85 25.00 60.00
4 John Ferguson/90 20.00 50.00
5 Charlie Hodge/85 25.00 60.00
6 Rejean Houle/85 20.00 50.00
7 Elmer Lach/90 25.00 60.00
8 Guy Lafleur/85 40.00 80.00
9 Jacques Laperriere/85 20.00 50.00
10 Frank Mahovlich/90 25.00 60.00
11 Dickie Moore/85 20.00 50.00
12 Henri Richard/85 25.00 60.00
13 Larry Robinson/85 40.00 100.00
14 Denis Savard/90 20.00 50.00
15 Serge Savard/85 25.00 60.00
16 Steve Shutt/85 20.00 50.00
17 Jean-Guy Talbot/85 20.00 50.00
18 Gump Worsley/40 75.00 150.00

2003-04 Parkhurst Original Six Montreal Inserts

COMPLETE SET (16) 25.00 50.00
STATED ODDS 1:6
M1 Jacques Plante 2.00 5.00
M2 Doug Harvey 1.50 4.00
M3 Jean Beliveau 1.50 4.00
M4 Maurice Richard 3.00 8.00
M5 Henri Richard 1.50 4.00
M6 Howie Morenz 1.50 4.00
M7 Guy Lafleur 2.00 5.00
M8 Jean Beliveau 2.00 5.00
M9 Jacques Plante 2.00 5.00
M10 Howie Morenz 1.50 4.00
M11 Doug Harvey 1.50 4.00
M12 Elmer Lach 1.50 4.00
M13 Bill Durnan 1.50 4.00
M14 Patrick Roy 3.00 8.00
M15 Saku Koivu 1.50 4.00
M16 Guy Lafleur 2.00 5.00

2003-04 Parkhurst Original Six Montreal Memorabilia

This 63-card set featured memorabilia from past and present Canadiens players. Cards MM1-10 amd MM57-58 were single jerseys and were limited to 100 copies sets. Cards MM11-13 were jersey/stick combos and were limited to 80 sets. Cards MM15-21 were vintage memorabilia cards and print runs are listed below. Cards MM16-30 and MM59-63 were vintage jersey cards and print runs are listed below. Cards MM31-35 were vintage stick cards and print runs are listed below. Cards MM35-40 were retired numbers cards and were limited to 20 copies. Cards MM41-50 were grouped into a subset known as Original Six Shooters; players who have scored high career totals against original six teams. The shooters cards were limited to 100 copies each. Cards MM51-56 were dual-jersey cards and were limited to 100 copies each.

JSY PRINT RUN 100 SETS
JSY/STK PRINT RUN 80 SETS
RET.NMBRS PRINT RUN 20 SETS
SIX SHOOT.PRINT RUN 100 SETS
TIMELINE PRINT RUN 100 SETS
MM1 Jose Theodore 12.50 30.00
MM2 Niklas Sundstrom 6.00 15.00
MM3 Stephane Quintal 6.00 15.00
MM4 Jan Bulis 6.00 15.00
MM5 Saku Koivu 10.00 25.00
MM6 Craig Rivet 6.00 15.00
MM7 Mathieu Garon 10.00 25.00
MM8 Yanic Perreault 8.00 20.00
MM9 Chad Kilger 8.00 20.00
MM10 Marcel Hossa 10.00 25.00
MM11 Jose Theodore J/S 25.00 60.00
MM12 Stephane Quintal J/S 12.50 30.00
MM13 Saku Koivu J/S 25.00 60.00
MM14 Jose Theodore/80 20.00 50.00
MM15 Patrick Roy/80 Pad 25.00 60.00
MM16 Dickie Moore/70 J 30.00 80.00
MM17 Jacques Plante/20
MM18 Guy Lafleur/80 30.00 80.00
MM19 Doug Harvey/60 20.00 50.00
MM20 Charlie Hodge/50 Glove 20.00 50.00
MM21 Newsy Lalonde/60 30.00 80.00
MM22 Aurel Joliat/50 J 30.00 80.00
MM23 Henri Richard/60 J 20.00 50.00
MM24 Jean Beliveau/60 J 20.00 50.00
MM25 Doug Harvey/60 J 20.00 50.00
MM26 Guy Lafleur/50 J 20.00 50.00
MM27 Gump Worsley/70 J 20.00 50.00
MM28 George Hainsworth/20 J
MM29 Maurice Richard/20 J
MM30 Patrick Roy/80 J 25.00 60.00
MM31 Maurice Richard/20 S
MM32 Jean Beliveau/60 S 25.00 60.00
MM33 Guy Lafleur/50 S 30.00 80.00
MM34 Jacques Plante/60 S 30.00 80.00
MM35 Georges Vezina/20 RN J
MM36 Jacques Plante/20 RN J
MM37 Maurice Richard/20 RN J
MM38 Jean Beliveau/20 RN J
MM39 Guy Lafleur/20 RN J
MM40 Doug Harvey/20 RN J
MM41 Mario Lemieux SS 15.00 40.00
MM42 Ron Francis SS 6.00 15.00
MM43 Joe Sakic SS 12.50 30.00
MM44 Brett Hull SS 10.00 25.00
MM45 Jaromir Jagr SS 8.00 20.00
MM46 Mike Modano SS 8.00 20.00
MM47 Teemu Selanne SS 6.00 15.00
MM48 Pavel Bure SS 6.00 15.00
MM49 Paul Kariya SS 8.00 20.00
MM50 Peter Forsberg SS 10.00 25.00
MM51 J.Plante/P.Roy 50.00 120.00
MM52 H.Richard/S.Koivu 30.00 80.00
MM53 D.Harvey/L.Robinson 15.00 40.00
MM54 G.Worsley/J.Theodore 40.00 100.00
MM55 J.Beliveau/J.LeClair 15.00 40.00
MM56 A.Joliat/G.Lafleur 50.00 100.00
MM57 Mike Komisarek/100 J 10.00 25.00
MM58 Ron Hainsey/100 J 10.00 25.00
MM59 Guy Lapointe/80 J 20.00 50.00
MM60 Serge Savard/100 J 20.00 50.00
MM61 Steve Shutt/100 J 20.00 50.00
MM62 Peter Mahovlich/100 J 20.00 50.00
MM63 Jacques Plante/100 J 30.00 60.00

2003-04 Parkhurst Original Six New York

This 100-card set featured players from one of the Original Six teams in the NHL, New York. The set was produced as a stand alone product.

COMPLETE SET (100) 15.00 40.00
1 Matthew Barnaby .15 .40
2 Alex Kovalev .40 1.00
3 Dan Blackburn .40 1.00
4 Pavel Bure .50 1.25
5 Anson Carter .40 1.00
6 Jussi Markkanen .40 1.00
7 Jamie Lundmark .15 .40
8 Boris Mironov .15 .40
9 Joel Bouchard .15 .40
10 Dale Purinton .15 .40
11 Bobby Holik .15 .40
12 Dan Lacouture .15 .40
13 Mike Dunham .40 1.00
14 Greg de Vries .15 .40
15 Darius Kasparaitis .15 .40
16 Dominic Moore XRC .15 .40
17 Martin Rucinsky .15 .40
18 Brian Leetch .75 2.00
19 Pascal Rheaume .15 .40
20 Eric Lindros .50 1.25
21 Jan Hlavac .15 .40
22 Chris Simon .15 .40
23 Vladimir Malakhov .15 .40
24 Jed Ortmeyer XRC .15 .40
25 Mark Messier 1.50 4.00
26 Jason Labarbera .15 .40
27 Phil Osaer XRC .15 .40
28 Petr Nedved .15 .40
29 Tom Poti .15 .40
30 Jason MacDonald XRC .15 .40
31 Adam Graves .15 .40
32 Doug Weight .40 1.00
33 Tony Amonte .40 1.00
34 Ed Giacomin .60 1.50
35 Mike Gartner 1.50 3.00
36 Phil Esposito 1.50 4.00
37 Dan Cloutier .40 1.00
38 Ron Greschner .40 1.00
39 Luc Robitaille .40 1.00
40 Andy Bathgate .40 1.00
41 Frank Boucher .40 1.00
42 Brad Park .50 1.25
43 Ron Duguay .40 1.00
44 Bill Gadsby .40 1.00
45 Harry Howell .40 1.00
46 Ching Johnson .40 1.00
47 Doug Harvey .50 1.25
48 Guy Lafleur 1.50 3.00
49 John Davidson .60 1.50
50 Jean Ratelle .50 1.25
51 Mike Richter .75 2.00
52 John Vanbiesbrouck .40 1.00
53 Chuck Rayner .40 1.00
54 Lou Fontinato .15 .40
55 Rod Gilbert .50 1.25
56 Lester Patrick .50 1.25
57 Vic Hadfield .50 1.25
58 Walt Tkaczuk .15 .40
59 Gump Worsley .75 2.00
60 Bun Cook .40 1.00
61 Mark Messier 1.50 4.00
62 Brian Leetch .75 2.00
63 Phil Esposito 1.50 4.00
64 Ed Giacomin .60 1.50
65 Brad Park .50 1.25
66 Jean Ratelle .50 1.25
67 Pat Verbeek .15 .40
68 Barry Beck .15 .40
69 Rod Gilbert .50 1.25
70 Chuck Rayner .40 1.00
71 Mark Messier 1.50 4.00
72 Brian Leetch .75 2.00
73 Vic Hadfield .50 1.25
74 Phil Esposito 1.50 4.00
75 Ron Greschner .40 1.00
76 Walt Tkaczuk .15 .40
77 Harry Howell .40 1.00
78 Andy Bathgate .40 1.00
79 Barry Beck .15 .40
80 Brad Park .50 1.25
81 Brad Park .50 1.25
82 Ed Giacomin .60 1.50
83 Jean Ratelle .50 1.25
84 Phil Esposito 1.50 4.00
85 Rod Gilbert .50 1.25
86 Harry Howell .40 1.00
87 Chuck Rayner .40 1.00
88 Ching Johnson .40 1.00
89 Bill Cook .75 2.00
90 Andy Bathgate .40 1.00
91 Rod Gilbert .50 1.25
92 Harry Howell .40 1.00
93 Brian Leetch .75 2.00
94 Mike Richter .75 2.00
95 Ed Giacomin .60 1.50
96 Jean Ratelle .50 1.25
97 Brad Park .50 1.25
98 Mark Messier 1.50 4.00
99 Brian Leetch .75 2.00
100 Adam Graves .15 .40

2003-04 Parkhurst Original Six New York Autographs

This 18-card set featured certified autographs of past Rangers greats. Print runs are listed below.

1 Andy Bathgate/80 20.00 50.00
2 John Davidson/90 15.00 40.00
3 Ron Duguay/90 15.00 40.00
4 Phil Esposito/55 25.00 60.00
5 Lou Fontinato/95 15.00 40.00
6 Ed Giacomin/90 30.00 80.00
7 Rod Gilbert/85 30.00 80.00
8 Ron Greschner/95 15.00 40.00
9 Vic Hadfield/90 15.00 40.00
10 Harry Howell/95 15.00 40.00
11 Guy Lafleur/80 30.00 80.00
12 Brad Park/90 20.00 50.00
13 Jean Ratelle/90 20.00 50.00
14 Allan Stanley/85 20.00 50.00
15 Walt Tkaczuk/90 15.00 40.00
16 Gump Worsley/80 25.00 60.00

2003-04 Parkhurst Original Six New York Inserts

COMPLETE SET (16) 25.00 60.00
STATED ODDS 1:6
N1 Rod Gilbert 1.50 4.00
N2 Ed Giacomin 2.00 5.00
N3 Frank Boucher 1.50 4.00
N4 Rod Gilbert 1.50 4.00
N5 Phil Esposito 3.00 8.00
N6 Gump Worsley 2.00 5.00
N7 Ed Giacomin 2.00 5.00
N8 Doug Harvey 1.50 4.00
N9 Mark Messier 3.00 8.00
N10 Jean Ratelle 1.50 4.00
N11 Andy Bathgate 1.50 4.00
N12 Brian Leetch 2.00 5.00
N13 Chuck Rayner 1.50 4.00
N14 Brian Leetch 1.50 4.00
N15 Alex Kovalev 1.50 4.00
N16 Brad Park 1.50 4.00

2003-04 Parkhurst Original Six New York Memorabilia

This 63-card set featured memorabilia from past and present Rangers players. Cards NM1-12 and NM56-58 were single jerseys and were limited to 100 copies sets. Cards NM13-19 and NM57 were jersey/stick combos and were limited to 80 sets. Cards NM21-26 were vintage memorabilia cards and were limited to 20 copies each. Cards NM27-33 and NM62-63 were vintage jersey cards and print runs are listed below. Cards NM34-38 and NM59-61 were vintage stick cards and print runs are listed below. Cards NM39-40 were retired numbers cards and were limited to 20 copies. Cards NM411-50 were grouped into a subset known as Original Six Shooters; players who have scored high career totals against original six teams. The shooters cards were limited to 100 copies each. Cards NM51-55 were dual-jersey cards and were limited to 100 copies each.

JSY PRINT RUN 100 SETS
JSY/STK PRINT RUN 80 SETS
VIN.MEM PRINT RUN 20 SETS
RET.NMBRS PRINT RUN 20 SETS
SIX SHOOT.PRINT RUN 100 SETS
TIMELINE PRINT RUN 100 SETS
NM1 Mike Dunham/100* 10.00 25.00
NM2 Brian Leetch/100* 15.00 40.00
NM3 Eric Lindros/100* 10.00 25.00
NM4 Mark Messier 10.00 25.00
NM5 Tom Poti/100* 6.00 15.00
NM6 Pavel Bure/100* 10.00 25.00
NM7 Mike Richter/100* 12.50 30.00
NM8 Dan Blackburn/100* 6.00 15.00
NM9 Darius Kasparaitis/100* 6.00 15.00
NM10 Bobby Holik/100* 6.00 15.00
NM11 Vladimir Malakhov/100* 6.00 15.00
NM12 Jamie Lundmark/100* 6.00 15.00
NM13 Brian Leetch J-S/80* 15.00 40.00
NM14 Eric Lindros J-S/80* 15.00 40.00
NM15 Mark Messier J-S/80* 30.00 80.00
NM16 Mike Richter J-S/80* 20.00 50.00
NM17 Pavel Bure J-S/80* 15.00 40.00
NM18 Dan Blackburn J-S/80* 12.50 30.00
NM19 Mike Dunham J-S/80* 15.00 40.00
NM20 Eric Lindros/30* 15.00 40.00
NM21 Terry Sawchuk/20* 40.00 80.00
NM22 Jacques Plante/20* 40.00 80.00
NM23 Bill Gadsby/20* 25.00 50.00
NM24 Doug Harvey/20* 40.00 80.00
NM25 Chuck Rayner/20*
NM26 Ed Giacomin/20*
NM27 Theo Fleury/50* J 10.00 25.00
NM28 Bryan Berard/60* J 10.00 25.00
NM29 Marcel Dionne/60* J 12.50 30.00
NM30 Ed Giacomin/50* J 30.00 80.00
NM31 Phil Esposito/50* J 15.00 40.00
NM32 Rod Gilbert/50* J 25.00 60.00
NM33 Jean Ratelle/50* J 25.00 60.00
NM34 Emile Francis/60* S 15.00 40.00
NM35 Gilles Villemure/60* S 15.00 40.00
NM36 Ed Giacomin/20* S 50.00 100.00
NM37 Phil Esposito/20* S 40.00 80.00
NM38 Johnny Bower/20* S 75.00 150.00
NM39 Ed Giacomin/20* RN
NM40 Rod Gilbert/20* RN
NM41 Mario Lemieux SS/100* 15.00 40.00
NM42 Ron Francis SS/100* 6.00 15.00
NM43 Joe Sakic SS/100* 10.00 25.00
NM44 Brett Hull SS/100* 8.00 20.00
NM45 Jaromir Jagr SS/100* 8.00 20.00
NM46 Mike Modano SS/100* 8.00 20.00
NM47 Teemu Selanne SS/100* 10.00 25.00
NM48 Pavel Bure SS/100* 6.00 15.00
NM49 Paul Kariya SS/100* 8.00 20.00
NM50 Peter Forsberg SS/100* 10.00 25.00
NM51 E.Giacomin/D.Blackburn 30.00 80.00
NM52 P.Esposito/E.Lindros 20.00 50.00
NM53 M.Dionne/A.Kovalev 12.50 30.00
NM54 J.Ratelle/M.Messier 40.00 100.00
NM55 R.Gilbert/P.Bure 12.50 30.00
NM56 Alex Kovalev/100 J 12.50 30.00
NM57 Alex Kovalev/100 J/S 12.50 30.00
NM58 Anson Carter/100 J 12.50 30.00
NM59 John Davidson/100 S 15.00 40.00
NM60 Marcel Dionne/100 S 12.50 30.00
NM61 Adam Graves/100 S 8.00 20.00
NM62 Sergei Zubov/100 J 8.00 20.00
NM63 Dan Cloutier/100 J 12.50 30.00

2003-04 Parkhurst Original Six Toronto

This 100-card set featured players from one of the Original Six teams in the NHL, Toronto. The set was produced as a stand alone product.

COMPLETE SET (100) 15.00 40.00
1 Nikolai Antropov .15 .40
2 Wade Belak .30 .75
3 Ed Belfour .40 1.00
4 Aki Berg .15 .40
5 Maxim Kondratiev XRC 1.25 3.00
6 Owen Nolan .30 .75
7 Nathan Perrott .15 .40
8 Tie Domi .40 1.00
9 Matt Stajan XRC 1.50 4.00
10 Ken Klee .15 .40
11 Bryan Marchment .15 .40
12 Jamie Hodson .15 .40
13 Carlo Colaiacovo .15 .40
14 Tomas Kaberle .15 .40
15 Joe Nieuwendyk .40 1.00
16 Bryan McCabe .15 .40
17 Ric Jackman .15 .40
18 Alexander Mogilny .40 1.00
19 Karel Pilar .15 .40
20 Alexei Ponikarovsky .15 .40
21 Robert Reichel .15 .40
22 Mikael Renberg .15 .40
23 Gary Roberts .15 .40
24 Mats Sundin .40 1.00
25 Mikael Tellqvist .30 .75
26 Darcy Tucker .15 .40
27 Aaron Gavey .15 .40
28 Josh Holden .15 .40
29 Trevor Kidd .40 1.00
30 Tom Fitzgerald .15 .40
31 Charlie Conacher .40 1.00
32 Doug Gilmour .40 1.00
33 Felix Potvin .40 1.00
34 Vincent Damphousse .40 1.00
35 Terry Sawchuk .75 2.00
36 Tiger Williams .75 2.00
37 Wendel Clark .60 1.50
38 Teeder Kennedy .40 1.00
39 Syl Apps .40 1.00
40 Hap Day .15 .40
41 Rick Vaive .15 .40
42 Curtis Joseph .40 1.00
43 Darryl Sittler .40 1.00
44 Bill Barilko .60 1.50
45 Bobby Baun .40 1.00
46 Borje Salming .40 1.00
47 Harry Lumley .40 1.00
48 Dick Duff .40 1.00
49 Mike Palmateer 1.00 2.50
50 Norm Ullman .40 1.00
51 Frank Mahovlich .40 1.00
52 Red Kelly .40 1.00
53 Sid Smith .40 1.00
54 Mike Gartner .60 1.50
55 Dave Andreychuk .15 .40
56 Johnny Bower 1.50 4.00
57 Turk Broda .60 1.50
58 Tim Horton 1.25 3.50
59 King Clancy .40 1.00
60 Ace Bailey .60 1.50
61 Mats Sundin .40 1.00
62 Doug Gilmour .40 1.00
63 Borje Salming .40 1.00
64 Lanny McDonald .40 1.00
65 Darryl Sittler .60 2.00
66 King Clancy .40 1.00
67 Turk Broda .60 1.50
68 Felix Potvin .40 1.00
69 Tim Horton 1.25 3.50
70 Sid Smith .40 1.00
71 Mats Sundin .40 1.00
72 Doug Gilmour .40 1.00
73 Wendel Clark .60 1.50
74 Teeder Kennedy .40 1.00
75 Syl Apps .40 1.00
76 Hap Day .15 .40
77 Rick Vaive .15 .40
78 Charlie Conacher .40 1.00
79 Darryl Sittler .60 2.00
80 Sid Smith .40 1.00
81 Ace Bailey .60 1.50
82 Johnny Bower 1.50 4.00
83 Turk Broda .60 1.50
84 Tim Horton 1.25 3.50
85 Red Kelly .40 1.00
86 Frank Mahovlich .40 1.00
87 Borje Salming .40 1.00
88 Marcel Pronovost .75 2.00
89 King Clancy .40 1.00
90 Syl Apps .40 1.00
91 Darryl Sittler .60 2.00
92 Tim Horton 1.25 3.50
93 Darryl Sittler .60 2.00
94 Borje Salming .40 1.00
95 Turk Broda .60 1.50
96 Rick Vaive .15 .40
97 Doug Gilmour .40 1.00
98 Frank Mahovlich .40 1.00
99 Wendel Clark .60 1.50
100 Ed Belfour .40 1.00

2003-04 Parkhurst Original Six Toronto Autographs

This 18-card set featured certified autographs of past Maple Leafs greats. Print runs are listed below.

COMMON CARD (1-16) 20.00 50.00
1 Bobby Baun/85 30.00 80.00
2 Johnny Bower/90 25.00 60.00
3 Wendel Clark/90 30.00 80.00
4 Dick Duff/85 25.00 60.00
5 Red Kelly/90 25.00 60.00
6 Ted Kennedy/85 25.00 60.00
7 Frank Mahovlich/85 25.00 60.00
8 Eddie Shack/85 25.00 60.00
9 Darryl Sittler/95 25.00 60.00
10 Sid Smith/95 40.00 100.00
11 Ron Stewart/85 25.00 60.00
12 Rick Vaive/95 20.00 50.00
13 Tiger Williams/90 20.00 50.00

4 Mike Palmateer/95 25.00 60.00
5 Mike Gartner/85 25.00 60.00
6 Borje Salming/85 30.00 80.00

2003-04 Parkhurst Original Six Toronto Inserts

OMPLETE SET (17) 30.00 60.00
TATED ODDS 1:6
1 Bill Barilko 2.00 5.00
2 Ace Bailey 2.00 5.00
3 Tim Horton 3.00 8.00
4 Syl Apps 1.50 4.00
5 Ted Kennedy 2.00 5.00
6 Frank Mahovlich 3.00 8.00
7 Ted Kennedy 2.00 5.00
8 Red Kelly 2.00 5.00
9 Ace Bailey 2.00 5.00
10 Charlie Conacher 2.00 5.00
11 Syl Apps 1.50 4.00
12 Turk Broda 2.00 5.00
13 Terry Sawchuk 2.00 5.00
14 Johnny Bower 2.50 6.00
15 Darryl Sittler 1.50 4.00
16 Wendel Clark 3.00 8.00
17 Lanny McDonald 1.50 4.00

2003-04 Parkhurst Original Six Toronto Memorabilia

his 63-card set featured memorabilia from past and resent Maple Leafs players. Cards TM1-13 were ingle jerseys and were limited to 100 copies sets. ards TM14-19 were jersey/stick combos and were mitod to 80 sets. Cards TM20-27 were vintage nemorabilia cards and print runs are listed below. ards TM28-32 and TM59-62 were vintage jersey ards and print runs are listed below. Cards TM33-35 nd TM63 were vintage stick cards and print runs are sted below. Cards TM37-40 were retired numbers ards and were limited to 20 copies. Cards TM41-50 ere grouped into a subset known as Original Six hooters; players who have scored high career totals gainst original six teams. The shooters cards were mited to 100 copies each. Cards tM51-58 were dual-rsey cards and were limited to 100 copies each.

M1 Mats Sundin 15.00 40.00
M2 Gary Roberts 10.00 25.00
M3 Bryan McCabe 8.00 20.00
M4 Darcy Tucker 10.00 25.00
M5 Nik Antropov 10.00 25.00
M6 Tomas Kaberle 10.00 25.00
M7 Alexander Mogilny 10.00 25.00
M8 Tie Domi 10.00 25.00
M9 Ed Belfour 12.50 30.00
M10 Owen Nolan 8.00 20.00
M11 Carlo Colaiacovo 6.00 15.00
M12 Robert Svehla 6.00 15.00
M13 Trevor Kidd 10.00 25.00
M14 Mats Sundin J/S 15.00 40.00
M15 Alexander Mogilny J/S 12.50 30.00
M16 Darcy Tucker J/S 12.50 30.00
M17 Bryan McCabe J/S 12.50 30.00
M18 Tomas Kaberle J/S 15.00 40.00
M19 Gary Roberts J/S 12.50 30.00
M20 Johnny Bower/20 Glove
M21 Terry Sawchuk/20 Glove
M22 Ted Kennedy/20 Glove
M23 Charlie Conacher/20
M24 Tim Horton/60 Pants 40.00 100.00
M25 Wendel Clark/30 20.00 50.00
M26 Bill Barilko/20
M27 Borje Salming/80 15.00 40.00
M28 Tim Horton/20 J
M29 Red Kelly/20 J
M30 Lanny McDonald/60 J 20.00 50.00
M31 Tiger Williams/60 J 15.00 40.00
M32 Curtis Joseph/60 J 20.00 50.00
M33 Frank Mahovlich/50 S 25.00 60.00
M34 Johnny Bower/50 S 25.00 60.00
M35 Turk Broda/20 S
M36 Mats Sundin/50 25.00 50.00
M37 Johnny Bower/20 RN J
M38 T.Kennedy/20 RN Glove
M39 Ace Bailey/20 RN Glove
M40 Tim Horton/20 RN Pants
M41 Mario Lemieux SS 15.00 40.00
M42 Ron Francis SS 6.00 15.00
M43 Joe Sakic SS 10.00 25.00
M44 Brett Hull SS 8.00 20.00
M45 Jaromir Jagr SS 8.00 20.00
M46 Mike Modano SS 8.00 20.00
M47 Teemu Selanne SS 8.00 20.00
M48 Pavel Bure SS 6.00 15.00
M49 Paul Kariya SS 8.00 20.00
M50 Peter Forsberg SS 10.00 25.00
M51 T.Horton/W.Clark 30.00 80.00
M52 R.Kelly/O.Nolan 15.00 40.00
M53 L.McDonald/A.Mogilny 15.00 40.00
M54 T.Williams/T.Domi 20.00 50.00
M55 D.Sittler/M.Sundin 30.00 80.00
M56 M.Gartner/G.Roberts 15.00 40.00
M57 B.Salming/B.McCabe 15.00 40.00
M58 R.Vaive/D.Tucker 15.00 40.00
M59 Felix Potvin/100 J 15.00 40.00
M60 Wendel Clark/100 J 20.00 50.00
M61 Mike Gartner/100 J 15.00 40.00
M62 Rick Vaive/100 J 15.00 40.00
M63 Mike Gartner/80 S 15.00 40.00

2002-03 Parkhurst Retro

leased in mid-April, this 250-card set payed tribute the look and feel of the 1951-52 Parkhurst set. Card cks were blank. The set consisted of 200 veterans d 50 shorprinted rookies. Rookie cards were serial-mbered to 300 copies each.

MP.SET w/o SP's (200) 20.00 50.00
Mario Lemieux 1.00 2.50
arome Iginla .30 .75
aromir Jagr .75 2.00
lexei Kovalev .30 .75
odd Bertuzzi .30 .75
oe Thornton .40 1.00
ason Allison .25 .60
Markus Naslund .25 .60
ric Lindros .50 1.25
Keith Tkachuk .30 .75
Adam Oates .30 .75
Mike Modano .50 1.25
Pavel Bure .40 1.00
Ron Francis .40 1.00
Joe Sakic .50 1.25
Brendan Shanahan .40 1.00
Alexei Yashin .25 .60
Patrick Roy .75 2.00
Dwayne Roloson .20 .50
Pavol Demitra .40 1.00
Sergei Samsonov .25 .60
Steve Yzerman .60 1.50
Mats Sundin .30 .75
Peter Bondra .30 .75
Daniel Alfredsson .30 .75
Jeremy Roenick .30 .75
Zigmund Palffy .30 .75
28 Ray Whitney .25 .60
29 Sami Kapanen .20 .50
30 Alexei Zhamnov .25 .60
31 Radek Bonk .25 .60
32 Eric Daze .20 .50
33 Tommy Salo .25 .60
34 Marian Gaborik .50 1.25
35 Alexander Mogilny .25 .60
36 Glen Murray .25 .60
37 Patrik Elias .30 .75
38 Simon Gagne .30 .75
39 Ryan Smyth .25 .60
40 Bill Guerin .30 .75
41 Jeff Oneill .20 .50
42 Miroslav Satan .30 .75
43 Adam Deadmarsh .25 .60
44 Sergei Fedorov .50 1.25
45 Owen Nolan .30 .75
46 Tony Amonte .25 .60
47 Doug Weight .30 .75
48 Marian Hossa .25 .60
49 Mark Parrish .20 .50
50 Theo Fleury .40 1.00
51 Steven Reinprecht .20 .50
52 Dany Heatley .30 .75
53 Sergei Gonchar .25 .60
54 Ilya Kovalchuk .40 1.00
55 Brett Hull .40 1.00
56 Daniel Briere .25 .60
57 Brad Richards .30 .75
58 Brendan Morrison .25 .60
59 Steve Sullivan .20 .50
60 Mike York .20 .50
61 Nicklas Lidstrom .30 .75
62 Michael Peca .25 .60
63 Mark Recchi .40 1.00
64 Daymond Langkow .25 .60
65 Tyler Arnason .30 .75
66 Rob Blake .30 .75
67 Mike Comrie .30 .75
68 Felix Potvin .50 1.25
69 Brian Rolston .25 .60
70 Martin Brodeur .60 1.50
71 Anson Carter .25 .60
72 Roberto Luongo .50 1.25
73 Joe Nieuwendyk .30 .75
74 Dean McAmmond .20 .50
75 Niko Kapanen .25 .60
76 Jan Hrdina .20 .50
77 Vincent Damphousse .25 .60
78 Jozef Stumpel .20 .50
79 Milan Hejduk .25 .60
80 Stu Barnes .20 .50
81 Pierre Turgeon .30 .75
82 Marty Turco .30 .75
83 Bryan McCabe .20 .50
84 Gary Roberts .20 .50
85 Martin Havlat .25 .60
86 Kyle Calder .20 .50
87 Paul Kariya .40 1.00
88 Martin Straka .25 .60
89 Yanic Perreault .20 .50
90 Brian Boucher .25 .60
91 Darcy Tucker .20 .50
92 Mike Ricci .25 .60
93 Keith Primeau .30 .75
94 Bobby Holik .20 .50
95 Chris Osgood .30 .75
96 Brian Leetch .30 .75
97 Teemu Selanne .60 1.50
98 Alex Tanguay .25 .60
99 Rod Brind'Amour .30 .75
100 Petr Sykora .25 .60
101 Jere Lehtinen .30 .75
102 Kevin Weekes .25 .60
103 Jason Arnott .25 .60
104 Al MacInnis .30 .75
105 Scott Gomez .25 .60
106 Byron Dafoe .25 .60
107 Evgeni Nabokov .25 .60
108 Sandis Ozolinsh .25 .60
109 John LeClair .30 .75
110 Mike Dunham .25 .60
111 Manny Fernandez .25 .60
112 Johan Hedberg .30 .75
113 Chris Pronger .25 .60
114 Fredrik Modin .20 .50
115 Rostislav Klesla .20 .50
116 Manny Legace .30 .75
117 Teppo Numminen .25 .60
118 Shane Doan .25 .60
119 Martin Biron .25 .60
120 Luc Robitaille .30 .75
121 Igor Larionov .30 .75
122 Doug Gilmour .40 1.00
123 Roman Cechmanek .25 .60
124 Marc Savard .20 .50
125 Scott Stevens .30 .75
126 Steve Rucchin .20 .50
127 Olaf Kolzig .30 .75
128 Ed Jovanovski .25 .60
129 Petr Nedved .20 .50
130 Valeri Bure .25 .60
131 J-P Dumont .20 .50
132 Jocelyn Thibault .25 .60
133 Martin Lapointe .25 .60
134 Tomas Kaberle .20 .50
135 Jose Theodore .30 .75
136 Bates Battaglia .20 .50
137 Chris Drury .30 .75
138 Patrick Lalime .25 .60
139 Derek Morris .20 .50
140 Sean Burke .20 .50
141 Radek Dvorak .25 .60
142 Ladislav Nagy .20 .50
143 Oleg Petrov .20 .50
144 Kristian Huselius .20 .50
145 Mark Messier .50 1.25
146 Curtis Joseph .30 .75
147 Tim Connolly .20 .50
148 Arturs Irbe .25 .60
149 Espen Knutsen .20 .50
150 Ed Belfour .30 .75
151 Jaroslav Modry .20 .50
152 Dan Cloutier .25 .60
153 Jeff Friesen .20 .50
154 Janne Niinimaa .20 .50
155 Nikolai Khabibulin .30 .75
156 Justin Williams .25 .60
157 Kyle McLaren .20 .50
158 Sergei Zubov .25 .60
159 Brian Savage .20 .50
160 Chris Chelios .30 .75
161 Roman Hamrlik .20 .50
162 Scott Niedermayer .30 .75
163 Danny Markov .20 .50
164 Marc Denis .25 .60
165 Scott Hartnell .30 .75
166 Roman Turek .30 .75
107 Brenden Morrow .25 .60
168 David Legwand .25 .60
169 Henrik Sedin .30 .75
170 Oleg Tverdovsky .20 .50
171 Peter Forsberg .40 1.00
172 Vincent Lecavalier .25 .60
173 Pavel Datsyuk .40 1.00
174 Dan Blackburn .25 .60
175 Adam Foote .20 .50
176 Joe Juneau .25 .60
177 Mike Richter .30 .75
178 Shawn Bates .20 .50
179 Erik Cole .25 .60
180 Jean-Sebastien Giguere .30 .75
181 Saku Koivu .30 .75
182 Zdeno Chara .30 .75
183 Stephen Weiss .30 .75
184 Robert Svehla .20 .50
185 Patrick Stefan .25 .60
186 Robert Lang .20 .50
187 Olli Jokinen .30 .75
188 Pavel Brendl .20 .50
189 Brent Johnson .25 .60
190 Boris Mironov .20 .50
191 Tomas Vokoun .25 .60
192 Darius Kasparaitis .20 .50
193 Martin St. Louis .30 .75
194 Radim Vrbata .25 .60
195 Jeff Hackett .25 .60
196 Nik Antropov .25 .60
197 Craig Conroy .20 .50
198 Nick Boynton .20 .50
199 Richard Zednik .20 .50
200 Vaclav Prospal .20 .50
201 P-M Bouchard RC 3.00 8.00
202 Rick Nash RC 15.00 40.00
203 Dennis Seidenberg RC 3.00 8.00
204 Jay Bouwmeester RC 6.00 15.00
205 Stanislav Chistov RC 2.00 5.00
206 Pascal Leclaire RC 2.50 6.00
207 Jared Aulin RC 2.00 5.00
208 Chuck Kobasew RC 2.50 6.00
209 Jordan Leopold RC 3.00 8.00
210 Steve Ott RC 4.00 10.00
211 Ales Hemsky RC 8.00 20.00
212 Matt Walker RC 2.00 5.00
213 Tomas Malec RC 2.00 5.00
214 Dmitri Bykov RC 2.00 5.00
215 Michael Leighton RC 3.00 8.00
216 Henrik Zetterberg RC 20.00 50.00
217 Alexander Frolov RC 4.00 10.00
218 Steve Eminger RC 2.00 5.00
219 Scottie Upshall RC 2.50 6.00
220 Rickard Wallin RC 2.00 5.00
221 Alexei Semenov RC 2.00 5.00
222 Ron Hainsey RC 2.00 5.00
223 Martin Gerber RC 3.00 8.00
224 Adam Hall RC 2.00 5.00
225 Ray Emery RC 6.00 15.00
226 Anton Volchenkov RC 2.00 5.00
227 Levente Szuper RC 3.00 8.00
228 Carlo Colaiacovo RC 3.00 8.00
229 Alexander Svitov RC 2.00 5.00
230 Alexei Smirnov RC 2.50 6.00
231 Jeff Taffe RC 2.00 5.00
232 Mikael Tellqvist RC 2.00 5.00
233 Ari Ahonen RC 2.00 5.00
234 Martin Samuelsson RC 2.00 5.00
235 Shaone Morrisonn RC 2.00 5.00
236 Craig Andersson RC 8.00 20.00
237 Jim Fahey RC 2.00 5.00
238 Brooks Orpik RC 3.00 8.00
239 Mike Komisarek RC 3.00 8.00
240 Frederic Cloutier RC 2.00 5.00
241 Curtis Sanford RC 3.00 8.00
242 Jim Vandermeer RC 2.00 5.00
243 Paul Manning RC 2.00 5.00
244 Kris Vernarsky RC 2.00 5.00
245 Dany Sabourin RC 2.00 5.00
246 Mike Cammalleri RC 6.00 15.00
247 Jason Spezza RC 12.00 30.00
248 Cristobal Huet RC 4.00 10.00
249 Ryan Miller RC 12.00 30.00
250 Dick Tarnstrom RC 2.00 5.00

2002-03 Parkhurst Retro Minis

A throwback to the 1951-52 Parkhurst cards, this 250-card set paralleled the base set on cards approximately 2 1/2" X 1 1/2". Cards 201-250 were shortprinted, but no print run was made public.

*1-200 VETS: 1.2X TO 3X BASIC CARDS
*201-250 ROOKIE: .3X TO .8X BASIC RC
145 Mark Messier 1.50 4.00

2002-03 Parkhurst Retro Back In Time

This 15-card set put Mario Lemieux on cards fashioned after Parkhurst designs of the past. Cards carried a swatch of game jersey and were limited to 30 copies each.

1 1951-52 Parkhurst 25.00 60.00
2 1952-53 Parkhurst 25.00 60.00
3 1953-54 Parkhurst 25.00 60.00
4 1954-55 Parkhurst 25.00 60.00
5 1955-56 Parkhurst 25.00 60.00
6 1957-58 Parkhurst 25.00 60.00
7 1958-89 Parkhurst 25.00 60.00
8 1959-60 Parkhurst 25.00 60.00
9 1960-61 Parkhurst 25.00 60.00
10 1961-62 Parkhurst 25.00 60.00
11 1962-63 Parkhurst 25.00 60.00
12 1962-63 Parkhurst 25.00 60.00
13 1962-63 Parkhurst 25.00 60.00
14 1963-64 Parkhurst 25.00 60.00
15 1963-64 Parkhurst 25.00 60.00

2002-03 Parkhurst Retro Franchise Players Jerseys

Limited to just 60 copies each, this 30-card set featured game jersey swatches from team leaders.

RF1 Paul Kariya 8.00 20.00
RF2 Dany Heatley 10.00 25.00
RF3 Joe Thornton 12.50 30.00
RF4 Miroslav Satan 8.00 20.00
RF5 Jarome Iginla 12.50 30.00
RF6 Ron Francis 8.00 20.00
RF7 Jocelyn Thibault 8.00 20.00
RF8 Rick Nash 12.50 30.00
RF9 Joe Sakic 15.00 40.00
RF10 Mike Modano 10.00 25.00
RF11 Steve Yzerman 15.00 40.00
RF12 Mike Comrie 8.00 20.00
RF13 Roberto Luongo 12.50 30.00
RF14 Jason Allison 8.00 20.00
RF15 Marian Gaborik 12.50 30.00
RF16 Jose Theodore 12.50 30.00
RF17 David Legwand 8.00 20.00
RF18 Martin Brodeur 15.00 40.00
RF19 Mike Peca 8.00 20.00
RF20 Pavel Bure 8.00 20.00
RF21 Marian Hossa 8.00 20.00
RF22 Jeremy Roenick 10.00 25.00
RF23 Daniel Briere 8.00 20.00
RF24 Mario Lemieux 20.00 50.00
RF25 Teemu Selanne 8.00 20.00
RF26 Chris Pronger 8.00 20.00
RF27 Vincent Lecavalier 8.00 20.00
RF28 Mats Sundin 8.00 20.00
RF29 Markus Naslund 8.00 20.00
RF30 Jaromir Jagr 12.50 30.00

2002-03 Parkhurst Retro He Shoots He Scores Points

Inserted one per pack, these cards carried a value of 1, 2 or 3 points. The points could be redeemed for special memorabilia cards. The cards are unnumbered and are listed below in alphabetical order by point value. The redemption program ended March 31, 2004.

1 Marian Gaborik 1 pt. .20 .50
2 Dany Heatley 1 pt. .20 .50
3 Marian Hossa 1 pt. .20 .50
4 Mike Modano 1 pt. .20 .50
5 Rick Nash 1 pt. .20 .50
6 Brendan Shanahan 1 pt. .20 .50
7 Joe Thornton 1 pt. .20 .50
8 Marty Turco 1 pt. .20 .50
9 Ed Belfour 2 pts. .20 .50
10 Martin Brodeur 2 pts. .20 .50
11 Pavel Bure 2 pts. .20 .50
12 Peter Forsberg 2 pts. .20 .50
13 Jaromir Jagr 2 pts. .20 .50
14 Paul Kariya 2 pts. .20 .50
15 Ilya Kovalchuk 2 pts. .20 .50
16 Eric Lindros 2 pts. .20 .50
17 Joe Sakic 2 pts. .20 .50
18 Mario Lemieux 3 pts. .20 .50
19 Patrick Roy 3 pts. .20 .50
20 Steve Yzerman 3 pts. .20 .50

2002-03 Parkhurst Retro Hopefuls

Limited to just 30 copies each, this 40-card set featured players who were considered contenders for the Calder, Hart, Norris, Richard, or Vezina awards. Each card carried a swatch of game jersey.

CH1 Tyler Arnason 12.50 30.00
CH2 Rick Nash 25.00 60.00
CH3 Ryan Miller 15.00 40.00
CH4 Niko Kapanen 10.00 25.00
CH5 Alexander Frolov 12.50 30.00
CH6 Stanislav Chistov 12.50 30.00
CH7 Barret Jackman 12.50 30.00
CH8 Jay Bouwmeester 12.50 30.00
HH1 Mario Lemieux 25.00 60.00
HH2 Joe Thornton 12.50 30.00
HH3 Markus Naslund 12.50 30.00
HH4 Marty Turco 12.50 30.00
HH5 Nicklas Lidstrom 12.50 30.00
HH6 Marian Gaborik 15.00 40.00
HH7 Marian Hossa 12.50 30.00
HH8 Jaromir Jagr 15.00 40.00
NH1 Nicklas Lidstrom 12.50 30.00
NH2 Rob Blake 12.50 30.00
NH3 Adam Foote 12.50 30.00
NH4 Al MacInnis 12.50 30.00
NH5 Sergei Zubov 10.00 25.00
NH6 Ed Jovanovski 10.00 25.00
NH7 Tomas Kaberle 10.00 25.00
NH8 Derian Hatcher 10.00 25.00
RR1 Jaromir Jagr 15.00 40.00
RR2 Marian Hossa 12.50 30.00
RR3 Mats Sundin 12.50 30.00
RR4 Marian Gaborik 15.00 40.00
RR5 Markus Naslund 10.00 25.00
RR6 Ilya Kovalchuk 20.00 50.00
RR7 Joe Thornton 12.50 30.00
RR8 Milan Hejduk 10.00 25.00
VH1 Ed Belfour 15.00 40.00
VH2 Marty Turco 10.00 25.00
VH3 Martin Brodeur 20.00 50.00
VH4 Patrick Lalime 10.00 25.00
VH5 Jean-Sebastien Giguere 10.00 25.00
VH6 Jocelyn Thibault 10.00 25.00
VH7 Patrick Roy 20.00 50.00
VH8 Nikolai Khabibulin 10.00 25.00

2002-03 Parkhurst Retro Jerseys

RJ1 Patrick Roy 12.00 30.00
RJ2 Mike Modano 8.00 20.00
RJ3 Peter Forsberg 10.00 25.00
RJ4 Mark Messier 8.00 20.00
RJ5 Brett Hull 10.00 25.00
RJ6 Martin Brodeur 12.50 30.00
RJ7 Joe Thornton 10.00 25.00
RJ8 Ed Belfour 8.00 20.00
RJ9 Pavel Bure 8.00 20.00
RJ10 Rick Nash 12.50 30.00
RJ11 Marty Turco 6.00 15.00
RJ12 Jay Bouwmeester 6.00 15.00
RJ13 Jason Spezza 10.00 30.00
RJ14 Jaromir Jagr 8.00 20.00
RJ15 Mario Lemieux 15.00 40.00
RJ16 Markus Naslund 8.00 20.00
RJ17 Brendan Shanahan 8.00 20.00
RJ18 Paul Kariya 8.00 20.00
RJ19 Roberto Luongo 10.00 25.00
RJ20 Joe Sakic 12.50 30.00
RJ21 Mats Sundin 8.00 20.00
RJ22 Steve Yzerman 12.50 30.00
RJ23 Dany Heatley 8.00 20.00
RJ24 Jose Theodore 8.00 20.00
RJ25 John LeClair 8.00 20.00
RJ26 Marian Hossa 8.00 20.00
RJ27 Eric Lindros 8.00 20.00
RJ28 Sergei Fedorov 8.00 20.00
RJ29 Todd Bertuzzi 8.00 20.00
RJ30 Sergei Samsonov 6.00 15.00
RJ31 Jeremy Roenick 8.00 20.00
RJ32 Nicklas Lidstrom 8.00 20.00
RJ33 Bill Guerin 6.00 15.00
RJ34 Chris Pronger 6.00 15.00
RJ35 Saku Koivu 8.00 20.00
RJ36 Marian Gaborik 8.00 20.00
RJ37 Ilya Kovalchuk 8.00 20.00
RJ38 Jocelyn Thibault 6.00 15.00
RJ39 Vincent Lecavalier 6.00 15.00
RJ40 Teemu Selanne 8.00 20.00

2002-03 Parkhurst Retro Jersey and Sticks

*JSY/STK: .6X TO 1.5X JSY CARD HI
STATED PRINT RUN 60 SETS

2002-03 Parkhurst Retro Magnificent Inserts

This 10-card set featured game-used equipment from the career of Mario Lemieux. Cards MI1-MI5 had a print run of 40 copies each and cards MI6-MI10 were limited to just 10 copies each. Cards MI6-MI10 are not priced due to scarcity.

MI1 Mario Lemieux 2000-01 Season 30.00 80.00
MI2 Mario Lemieux 1985-86 Season 30.00 80.00
MI3 Mario Lemieux 2002 All-Star 30.00 80.00
MI4 Mario Lemieux 1987 Canada Cup 30.00 80.00
MI5 Mario Lemieux Dual Jersey 50.00 125.00
MI6 Mario Lemieux Number
MI7 Mario Lemieux Emblem
MI8 Mario Lemieux Triple Jersey
MI9 Mario Lemieux Quad Jersey
MI10 Mario Lemieux Complete Package

2002-03 Parkhurst Retro Memorabilia

This 30-card set featured swatches of game-used equipment. Print runs for each card are listed below.

RM1 Mario Lemieux/50 15.00 40.00
RM2 Joe Sakic/50 12.50 30.00
RM3 Joe Thornton/60 12.50 30.00
RM4 Marian Hossa/50 10.00 25.00
RM5 Nicklas Lidstrom/50 10.00 25.00
RM6 Patrick Roy/50 15.00 40.00
RM7 Jose Theodore/50 12.50 30.00
RM8 Mario Lemieux/30 25.00 60.00
RM9 Martin Brodeur/50 15.00 40.00
RM10 Dany Heatley/50 12.50 30.00
RM11 Ilya Kovalchuk/60 12.50 30.00
RM12 Marty Turco/50 10.00 25.00
RM13 Sergei Fedorov/50 10.00 25.00
RM14 Steve Yzerman/50 20.00 50.00
RM15 Jason Spezza/60 12.50 30.00
RM16 Pavel Bure/50 10.00 25.00
RM17 Peter Forsberg/50 12.50 30.00
RM18 Brendan Shanahan/50 10.00 25.00
RM19 Joe Thornton/30 15.00 40.00
RM20 Mike Modano/60 10.00 25.00
RM21 Nikolai Khabibulin/30 10.00 25.00
RM22 Jaromir Jagr/60 10.00 25.00
RM23 Joe Sakic/50 12.50 30.00
RM24 Mats Sundin/50 10.00 25.00
RM25 Saku Koivu/60 10.00 25.00
RM26 Jay Bouwmeester/60 12.50 30.00
RM27 Paul Kariya/60 10.00 25.00
RM28 Rick Nash/50 12.50 30.00
RM29 Mario Lemieux/50 15.00 40.00
RM30 Brett Hull/30 12.50 30.00

2002-03 Parkhurst Retro Nicknames

This 30-card set featured game-used memorabilia swatches of the given player on the card fronts beside their "nickname". Individual print runs are listed below.

ANNOUNCED PRINT RUN 20-65
RN1 Frank Brimsek/35* 25.00 50.00
RN2 Henri Richard/40* 20.00 50.00
RN3 Ed Giacomin/40* 20.00 50.00
RN4 Bobby Hull/35* 20.00 50.00
RN5 Bernie Geoffrion/20* 30.00 80.00
RN6 Gerry Cheevers/50* 12.00 30.00
RN7 Johnny Bucyk/40* 20.00 50.00
RN8 Johnny Bower/40* 20.00 50.00
RN9 Gump Worsley/40* 30.00 80.00
RN10 Glenn Hall/40* 15.00 40.00
RN11 Red Kelly/40* 15.00 40.00
RN12 F.Mahvlch/P.Mahvlch/40* 40.00 80.00
RN13 Ace Bailey/20* 60.00 120.00
RN14 King Clancy/20* 30.00 60.00
RN15 Roy Worters/20* 15.00 40.00
RN16 Stan Mikita/50* 15.00 40.00
RN17 Rocket Richard/20* 50.00 100.00
RN18 Turk Broda/20* 12.00 30.00
RN19 Tony Esposito/35* 20.00 50.00
RN20 Jean Beliveau/35* 40.00 80.00
RN21 Jacques Plante/35* 30.00 80.00
RN22 Steve Yzerman/65* 15.00 40.00
RN23 Brett Hull/65* 15.00 40.00
RN24 Patrick Roy/65* 20.00 50.00
RN25 Felix Potvin/65* 15.00 40.00
RN26 Teemu Selanne/65* 12.00 30.00
RN27 Olaf Kolzig/65* 12.00 30.00
RN28 Pavel Bure/65* 12.00 30.00
RN29 Eric Lindros/65* 12.00 30.00
RN30 Mario Lemieux/65* 30.00 80.00

2003-04 Parkhurst Rookie

This 200-card set consisted of 60-vetaran cards; 18-dual prospect cards; 52-single prospect cards; 25-prospect jersey cards; 30-autographed prospect cards and 25 jersey/autograph prospect cards. Cards 61-130 were serial-numbered out of 500; cards 131-155 were numbered out of 180; cards 156-175 were numbered out of 120 and cards 176-200 were numbered to 100.

1 Steve Yzerman 4.00 10.00
2 Joe Sakic 2.50 6.00
3 Jeremy Roenick 1.50 4.00
4 Brian Leetch 1.50 4.00
5 Andrew Raycroft 1.25 3.00
6 Dan Cloutier 1.25 3.00
7 Marty Turco 1.50 4.00
8 Owen Nolan 1.25 3.00
9 Joe Thornton 2.00 5.00
10 Marian Gaborik 2.50 6.00
11 Mario Lemieux 5.00 12.00
12 Zigmund Palffy 1.50 4.00
13 Vincent Lecavalier 1.25 3.00
14 Sean Burke 1.00 2.50
15 Miikka Kiprusoff 1.25 3.00
16 Dominik Hasek 2.50 6.00
17 Nikolai Khabibulin 1.50 4.00
18 Ed Belfour 1.50 4.00
19 Ilya Kovalchuk 1.50 4.00
20 Marian Hossa 1.25 3.00
21 Tommy Salo 1.25 3.00
22 Keith Tkachuk 1.50 4.00
23 Alex Kovalev 1.25 3.00
24 Michael Ryder 1.25 3.00
25 Steve Sullivan 1.00 2.50
26 Martin St-Louis 1.50 4.00
27 Al MacInnis 1.50 4.00
28 Sergei Gonchar 1.00 2.50
29 Jaromir Jagr 4.00 10.00
30 Ron Francis 2.00 5.00
31 Henrik Zetterberg 2.00 5.00
32 Paul Kariya 2.00 5.00
33 Robert Lang 1.00 2.50
34 Nicklas Lidstrom 1.50 4.00
35 Sergei Fedorov 2.50 6.00
36 Jarome Iginla 1.50 4.00
37 Bill Guerin 1.50 4.00
38 Jose Theodore 1.50 4.00
39 Roberto Luongo 2.50 6.00
40 Alex Tanguay 1.25 3.00
41 Peter Forsberg 2.00 5.00
42 Mike Modano 2.50 6.00
43 Dwayne Roloson 1.25 3.00
44 Martin Brodeur 3.00 8.00
45 Dany Heatley 1.50 4.00
46 Rick Nash 1.50 4.00
47 Jason Spezza 1.50 4.00
48 Chris Pronger 1.25 3.00
49 Brett Hull 2.00 5.00
50 Markus Naslund 1.50 4.00
51 Curtis Joseph 1.50 4.00
52 Olaf Kolzig 1.50 4.00
53 Peter Bondra 1.25 3.00
54 Eric Lindros 2.50 6.00
55 Mats Sundin 1.50 4.00
56 Patrick Roy 4.00 10.00
57 Ray Bourque 4.00 10.00
58 Terry Sawchuk 3.00 8.00
59 Maurice Richard 5.00 12.00
60 Bobby Orr 8.00 20.00
61 Bartovic RC/Pominville RC 6.00 15.00
62 McDonell RC/A.Johnson RC 3.00 8.00
63 Hutchinson RC/L.Pivko RC 2.50 6.00
64 Gernander RC/P.Osaer RC 2.50 6.00
65 R.Mrozik RC/J.Pollock RC 2.50 6.00
66 S.Meyer RC/D.Verot RC 3.00 8.00
67 M.Yeats RC/D.Zinger RC 2.50 6.00
68 J.DiPenta RC/[J. Olson RC 3.00 8.00
69 Rourke RC/J.MacMillan RC 3.00 8.00
70 Underhill RC/D.Salficky RC 3.00 8.00
71 Vauclair RC/Z.Michalek RC 2.50 6.00
72 M.Hussey RC/M.Stutzel RC 2.50 6.00
73 B.Lampman RC/T.Pock RC 3.00 8.00
74 G.Mink RC/R.Tvrdon RC 2.50 6.00
75 MacDonald RC/Morrison RC 3.00 8.00
76 Pandolfo RC/G.Mauldin RC 3.00 8.00
77 J.Yablonski RC/C.Larose RC 3.00 8.00
78 C.Brandner RC/E.Perrin RC 3.00 8.00
79 Michal Barinka RC 2.50 6.00
80 Erik Westrum RC 2.50 6.00
81 Gavin Morgan RC 3.00 8.00
82 Matt Ellison RC 2.50 6.00
83 Seamus Kotyk RC 2.50 6.00
84 Andy Chiodo RC 2.50 6.00
85 Mikko Luoma RC 2.50 6.00
86 Jed Ortmeyer RC 2.50 6.00
87 Brad Boyes RC 4.00 10.00
88 Robert Scuderi RC 3.00 8.00
89 Nolan Schaefer RC 2.50 6.00
90 Colton Orr RC 3.00 8.00
91 Travis Moen RC 3.00 8.00
92 Fred Meyer RC 2.50 6.00
93 Joe Motzko RC 2.50 6.00
94 Ryan Barnes RC 2.50 6.00
95 Rob Skrlac RC 2.50 6.00
96 Quintin Laing RC 2.50 6.00
97 Mikhail Kuleshov RC 2.50 6.00
98 Adam Munro RC 2.50 6.00
99 Wade Dubielewicz RC 2.50 6.00
100 Matt Keith RC 2.50 6.00
101 Steve McLaren RC 2.50 6.00
102 Tim Jackman RC 3.00 8.00
103 Doug Doull RC 2.50 6.00
104 Lawrence Nycholat RC 3.00 8.00
105 Aleksander Suglobov RC 2.50 6.00
106 Martin Strbak RC 3.00 8.00
107 Lasse Kukkonen RC 2.50 6.00
108 Gregory Campbell RC 2.50 6.00
109 Tony Martensson RC 2.50 6.00
110 Carl Corazzini RC 2.50 6.00
111 Mike Green RC 3.00 8.00
112 Nathan Robinson RC 2.50 6.00
113 Brent Krahn RC 2.50 6.00
114 Mike Smith RC 8.00 20.00
115 Mike Stuart RC 2.50 6.00
116 Karl Stewart RC 2.50 6.00
117 Jason MacDonald RC 2.50 6.00
118 Brooks Laich RC 4.00 10.00
119 Tom Preissing RC 3.00 8.00
120 Mikhail Yakubov RC 2.50 6.00
121 Benoit Dusablon RC 2.50 6.00
122 Nathan Smith RC 2.50 6.00
123 Goran Bezina RC 2.50 6.00
124 Dan Ellis RC 3.00 8.00
125 Pat Rissmiller RC 3.00 8.00
126 Owen Fussey RC 2.50 6.00
127 Mike Bishai RC 2.50 6.00
128 Matt Murley RC 3.00 8.00
129 Wade Brookbank RC 3.00 8.00
130 Randy Jones RC 2.50 6.00
131 Fedor Tyutin JSY RC 4.00 10.00
132 Niklas Kronwall JSY RC 8.00 20.00
133 Boyd Kane JSY RC 4.00 10.00
134 Sergei Zinovjev JSY RC 4.00 10.00
135 Mark Popovic JSY RC 5.00 12.00
136 Sean Bergenheim JSY RC 5.00 12.00
137 Ryan Kesler JSY RC 15.00 40.00
138 Christian Ehrhoff JSY RC 5.00 12.00
139 Peter Sejna JSY RC 5.00 12.00
140 Denis Grebeshkov JSY RC 4.00 10.00
141 Tuomas Pihlman JSY RC 5.00 12.00
142 A. Niittymaki JSY RC 10.00 25.00
143 Patrick Leahy JSY RC 5.00 12.00
144 Rastislav Stana JSY RC 6.00 15.00
145 Grant McNeill JSY RC 4.00 10.00
146 Cody McCormick JSY RC 5.00 12.00
147 Boyd Gordon JSY RC 5.00 12.00
148 Garth Murray JSY RC 5.00 12.00
149 Trevor Daley JSY RC 6.00 15.00
150 M. Svatos JSY RC 8.00 20.00
151 Esa Pirnes JSY RC 4.00 10.00
152 Garrett Burnett JSY RC 4.00 10.00
153 Tony Salmelainen JSY RC 4.00 10.00
154 John Pohl JSY RC 4.00 10.00
155 Dominic Moore JSY RC 4.00 10.00
156 Fredrik Sjostrom AU RC 10.00 25.00
157 Jozef Balej AU RC 6.00 15.00
158 Jiri Hudler AU RC 15.00 40.00
159 Joffrey Lupul AU RC 15.00 40.00
160 Tomas Plekanec AU RC 20.00 50.00
161 Kyle Wellwood AU RC 10.00 25.00
162 Peter Sarno AU RC 6.00 15.00
163 Pavel Vorobiev AU RC 8.00 20.00
164 Andrew Peters AU RC 8.00 20.00
165 Jeff Hamilton AU RC 6.00 15.00
166 Darryl Bootland AU RC 8.00 20.00
167 Noah Clarke AU RC 6.00 15.00
168 Matthew Spiller AU RC 8.00 20.00
169 Milan Michalek AU RC 12.00 30.00
170 Doug Lynch AU RC 6.00 15.00
171 Timofei Shishkanov AU RC 6.00 15.00
172 Maxim Kondratiev AU RC 6.00 15.00
173 Chris Kunitz AU RC 12.00 30.00
174 Jordin Tootoo AU RC 12.00 30.00
175 Anton Babchuk AU RC 6.00 15.00
176 Eric Staal JSY AU RC 40.00 100.00
177 Dan Fritsche JSY AU RC 10.00 25.00
178 J. Pitkanen JSY AU RC 15.00 40.00
179 Tim Gleason JSY AU RC 12.00 30.00
180 C. Higgins JSY AU RC 20.00 50.00
181 N.Horton JSY AU RC 25.00 60.00
182 Marek Zidlicky JSY AU RC 10.00 25.00
183 Antti Miettinen JSY AU RC 15.00 40.00
184 P.Bergeron JSY AU RC 60.00 125.00
185 R. Malone JSY AU RC 20.00 50.00
186 M. Lombardi JSY AU RC 12.00 30.00
107 Dan Hamhuis JSY AU RC 12.00 30.00
188 J-M Liles JSY AU RC 12.00 30.00
189 David Hale JSY AU RC 10.00 25.00
190 T.Ruutu JSY AU RC 15.00 40.00
191 Derek Roy JSY AU RC 15.00 40.00
192 Paul Martin JSY AU RC 12.00 30.00
193 K.Lehtonen JSY AU RC 60.00 150.00
194 Dustin Brown JSY AU RC 25.00 60.00
195 A. Vermette JSY AU RC 20.00 50.00
196 A. Semin JSY AU RC 25.00 60.00
197 Brent Burns JSY AU RC 25.00 60.00
198 Matt Stajan JSY AU RC 15.00 40.00
199 Nik Zherdev JSY AU RC 20.00 50.00
200 M.Fleury JSY AU RC 75.00 175.00

2003-04 Parkhurst Rookie All-Rookie Jerseys

PRINT RUN 60 SETS
ART1 Andrew Raycroft 6.00 15.00
ART2 Paul Martin 6.00 15.00
ART3 Joni Pitkanen 6.00 15.00
ART4 Eric Staal 10.00 25.00
ART5 Michael Ryder 10.00 25.00
ART6 Ryan Malone 6.00 15.00
ART7 Philippe Sauve 6.00 15.00
ART8 Dan Hamhuis 6.00 15.00
ART9 John-Michael Liles 6.00 15.00
ART10 Tuomo Ruutu 6.00 15.00
ART11 Nikolai Zherdev 8.00 20.00
ART12 Joffrey Lupul 6.00 15.00

2003-04 Parkhurst Rookie Before the Mask

PRINT RUN 40 SETS
BTM1 Roy Worters 12.50 30.00
BTM2 Frank Brimsek 12.50 30.00
BTM3 Harry Lumley 12.50 30.00
BTM4 Gump Worsley 12.50 30.00
BTM5 Johnny Bower 12.50 30.00
BTM6 Jacques Plante 20.00 50.00
BTM7 Tiny Thompson 12.50 30.00
BTM8 Charlie Gardiner 12.50 30.00
BTM9 Bill Durnan 12.50 30.00
BTM10 George Hainsworth 20.00 50.00
BTM11 Terry Sawchuk 20.00 50.00
BTM12 Glenn Hall 12.50 30.00
BTM13 Ed Giacomin 12.50 30.00
BTM14 Roger Crozier 12.50 30.00
BTM15 Chuck Rayner 12.50 30.00
BTM16 Turk Broda 15.00 40.00

2003-04 Parkhurst Rookie Calder Candidates

PRINT RUN 50 SETS
CMC1 Eric Staal 8.00 20.00
CMC2 Michael Ryder 8.00 20.00
CMC3 Marc-Andre Fleury 12.50 30.00
CMC4 Patrice Bergeron 8.00 20.00
CMC5 Ryan Malone 6.00 15.00
CMC6 Joffrey Lupul 6.00 15.00
CMC7 Andrew Raycroft 6.00 15.00
CMC8 Mathew Lombardi 6.00 15.00
CMC9 Joni Pitkanen 6.00 15.00
CMC10 Nikolai Zherdev 6.00 15.00
CMC11 Jordin Tootoo 8.00 20.00
CMC12 Matt Stajan 6.00 15.00
CMC13 Nathan Horton 8.00 20.00
CMC14 Tuomo Ruutu 6.00 15.00
CMC15 Derek Roy 6.00 15.00

2003-04 Parkhurst Rookie High Expectations Jerseys

PRINT RUN 40 SETS
HE1 Ilya Kovalchuk 10.00 25.00
HE2 Rick Nash 10.00 25.00
HE3 Wendel Clark 10.00 25.00
HE4 Mario Lemieux 15.00 40.00
HE5 Guy Lafleur 8.00 20.00
HE6 Gilbert Perreault 10.00 25.00
HE7 Denis Potvin 8.00 20.00
HE8 Mike Modano 10.00 25.00
HE9 Mats Sundin 8.00 20.00
HE10 Joe Thornton 12.50 30.00
HE11 Rick DiPietro 8.00 20.00
HE12 Marc-Andre Fleury 12.50 30.00
HE13 Vincent Lecavalier 8.00 20.00
HE14 Owen Nolan 8.00 20.00

2003-04 Parkhurst Rookie Jerseys

ANNOUNCED PRINT RUN 70 SETS
GJ1 Mario Lemieux 15.00 40.00
GJ2 Ilya Kovalchuk 10.00 25.00
GJ3 Joe Thornton 12.00 30.00
GJ4 Bill Guerin 6.00 15.00
GJ5 Jason Spezza 6.00 15.00
GJ6 Peter Forsberg 10.00 25.00
GJ7 Brian Leetch 6.00 15.00
GJ8 Milan Hejduk 6.00 15.00
GJ9 Evgeni Nabokov 6.00 15.00
GJ10 Martin St. Louis 6.00 15.00
GJ11 Rick Nash 6.00 15.00
GJ12 Steve Yzerman 15.00 40.00
GJ13 Pavel Datsyuk 6.00 15.00
GJ14 Henrik Zetterberg 8.00 20.00
GJ15 Joe Sakic 12.00 30.00
GJ16 Jeremy Roenick 10.00 25.00
GJ17 Martin Brodeur 15.00 40.00
GJ18 Mats Sundin 6.00 15.00
GJ19 Keith Tkachuk 6.00 15.00
GJ20 Mike Modano 10.00 25.00
GJ21 Dany Heatley 8.00 20.00
GJ22 Roberto Luongo 10.00 25.00
GJ23 Markus Naslund 6.00 15.00
GJ24 Jose Theodore 8.00 20.00
GJ25 Dominik Hasek 12.00 30.00
GJ26 Paul Kariya 6.00 15.00
GJ27 Teemu Selanne 8.00 20.00
GJ28 Marian Hossa 6.00 15.00
GJ29 Marian Gaborik 10.00 25.00
GJ30 Sergei Fedorov 8.00 20.00
GJ31 Mark Messier 12.50 30.00
GJ32 Jarome Iginla 10.00 25.00
GJ33 Brendan Shanahan 8.00 20.00
GJ34 Ed Belfour 8.00 20.00
GJ35 Curtis Joseph 8.00 20.00
GJ36 Zdeno Chara 8.00 20.00
GJ37 Vincent Lecavalier 8.00 20.00
GJ38 Brett Hull 10.00 25.00

GJ39 Nicklas Lidstrom 8.00 20.00
GJ40 Marty Turco 6.00 15.00
GJ41 Patrick Roy 15.00 40.00
GJ42 Bobby Clarke 10.00 25.00
GJ43 Lanny McDonald 6.00 15.00
GJ44 Marcel Dionne 6.00 15.00
GJ45 Gilbert Perreault 8.00 20.00
GJ46 Ray Bourque 12.00 30.00
GJ47 Mike Bossy 6.00 15.00
GJ48 Vladislav Tretiak 20.00 50.00
GJ49 Bobby Orr 40.00 100.00
GJ50 Cam Neely 8.00 20.00

2003-04 Parkhurst Rookie Jersey and Sticks

*JSY/STKS: .6X TO 1.5X JSY
PRINT RUN 80 SETS
SJ6 Marc-Andre Fleury 20.00 50.00
SJ7 Eric Lindros 12.50 30.00
SJ15 Chris Pronger 10.00 25.00
SJ21 Andrew Raycroft 12.50 30.00

2003-04 Parkhurst Rookie Records Jerseys

PRINT RUN 40 SETS
RRE1 Teemu Selanne 8.00 20.00
RRE2 Teemu Selanne 8.00 20.00
RRE3 Luc Robitaille 8.00 20.00
RRE4 Joe Nieuwendyk 8.00 20.00
RRE5 Brian Leetch 8.00 20.00
RRE6 Tony Esposito 12.50 30.00
RRE7 Patrick Lalime 8.00 20.00
RRE8 Terry Sawchuk 20.00 40.00

2003-04 Parkhurst Rookie Retro Rookies

PRINT RUN 70 SETS
RR1 Mike Modano 10.00 25.00
RR2 Peter Forsberg 12.50 30.00
RR3 Joe Sakic 12.50 30.00
RR4 Patrick Roy 20.00 40.00
RR5 Jaromir Jagr 10.00 25.00
RR6 Rob Blake 8.00 20.00
RR7 Brett Hull 10.00 25.00
RR8 Roberto Luongo 10.00 25.00
RR9 Brian Leetch 8.00 20.00
RR10 Jeremy Roenick 10.00 25.00
RR11 Mats Sundin 8.00 20.00
RR12 Ed Belfour 8.00 20.00
RR13 Curtis Joseph 8.00 20.00
RR14 Sergei Fedorov 10.00 25.00
RR15 Paul Kariya 8.00 20.00
RR16 Mark Messier 10.00 25.00
RR17 Al MacInnis 8.00 20.00
RR18 Felix Potvin 12.00 30.00
RR19 Eric Lindros 10.00 25.00
RR20 Teemu Selanne 15.00 40.00

2003-04 Parkhurst Rookie Road to the NHL Jerseys

PRINT RUN 40 SETS
EMBLEM PRINT RUN 9 SETS
GOLD EMBLEM 1/1's EXIST
RNJ1 Nick Schultz 6.00 15.00
RNJ2 Jason Spezza 12.50 30.00
RNJ3 Rick Nash 12.50 30.00
RNJ4 Dustin Brown 6.00 15.00
RNJ5 Jay Bouwmeester 6.00 15.00
RNJ6 Jose Theodore 10.00 25.00
RNJ7 Barret Jackman 6.00 15.00
RNJ8 Dany Heatley 10.00 25.00
RNJ9 Eric Staal 12.50 30.00
RNJ10 Scottie Upshall 6.00 15.00
RNJ11 Derek Roy 6.00 15.00
RNJ12 Dan Blackburn 6.00 15.00
RNJ13 Tim Gleason 6.00 15.00
RNJ14 Ron Hainsey 6.00 15.00
RNJ15 Mathieu Garon 6.00 15.00
RNJ16 Steve Ott 8.00 20.00
RNJ17 Dan Hamhuis 6.00 15.00

2003-04 Parkhurst Rookie Rookie Emblems

This 50-card set paralleled the Rookie Jerseys set. Cards were limited to just 19 copies each and gold 1/1's were also created.
RE1 Patrice Bergeron 15.00 40.00
RE2 Fedor Tyutin 3.00 8.00
RE3 Joffrey Lupul 8.00 20.00
RE4 Antti Miettinen 5.00 12.00
RE5 Nathan Horton 8.00 20.00
RE6 Dustin Brown 6.00 15.00
RE7 Tim Gleason 4.00 10.00
RE8 Chris Higgins 6.00 15.00
RE9 Jordin Tootoo 6.00 15.00
RE10 Dan Hamhuis 4.00 10.00
RE11 David Hale 3.00 8.00
RE12 Garth Murray 4.00 10.00
RE13 Paul Martin 4.00 10.00
RE14 Sean Bergenheim 4.00 10.00
RE15 Joni Pitkanen 5.00 12.00
RE16 John Pohl 3.00 8.00
RE17 Libor Pivko 3.00 8.00
RE18 Marek Svatos 6.00 15.00
RE19 Dan Fritsche 3.00 8.00
RE20 Denis Grebeshkov 3.00 8.00
RE21 Antero Niittymaki 8.00 20.00
RE22 Tuomo Ruutu 5.00 12.00
RE23 Kari Lehtonen 15.00 40.00
RE24 Dominic Moore 3.00 8.00
RE25 Tony Salmelainen 3.00 8.00
RE26 Christian Ehrhoff 4.00 10.00
RE27 Trevor Daley 5.00 12.00
RE28 Nikolai Zherdev 6.00 15.00
RE29 Mark Popovic 4.00 10.00
RE30 Peter Sejna 4.00 10.00
RE31 Derek Roy 5.00 12.00
RE32 Trent Hunter 3.00 8.00
RE33 Cody McCormick 4.00 10.00
RE34 John-Michael Liles 4.00 10.00
RE35 Matthew Lombardi 4.00 10.00
RE36 Marek Zidlicky 3.00 8.00
RE37 Ryan Malone 6.00 15.00
RE38 Niklas Kronwall 6.00 15.00
RE39 Rastislav Stana 5.00 12.00
RE40 Andrew Raycroft 4.00 10.00
RE41 Alexander Semin 10.00 25.00
RE42 Andrew Peters 4.00 10.00
RE43 Brent Burns 8.00 20.00
RE44 Matt Stajan 5.00 12.00
RE45 Antoine Vermette 6.00 15.00
RE46 Michael Ryder 4.00 10.00
RE47 Ryan Kesler 15.00 40.00
RE48 Eric Staal 15.00 40.00
RE49 Patrick Leahy 4.00 10.00
RE50 Marc-Andre Fleury 20.00 50.00

2003-04 Parkhurst Rookie Rookie Jerseys

PRINT RUN 90 SETS
RJ1 Patrice Bergeron 10.00 25.00
RJ2 Fedor Tyutin 6.00 15.00
RJ3 Joffrey Lupul 6.00 15.00
RJ4 Antti Miettinen 6.00 15.00
RJ5 Nathan Horton 8.00 20.00
RJ6 Dustin Brown 8.00 20.00
RJ7 Tim Gleason 6.00 15.00
RJ8 Chris Higgins 6.00 15.00
RJ9 Jordin Tootoo 8.00 20.00
RJ10 Dan Hamhuis 6.00 15.00
RJ11 David Hale 6.00 15.00
RJ12 Garth Murray 6.00 15.00
RJ13 Paul Martin 6.00 15.00
RJ14 Sean Bergenheim 6.00 15.00
RJ15 Joni Pitkanen 6.00 15.00
RJ16 John Pohl 6.00 15.00
RJ17 Libor Pivko 6.00 15.00
RJ18 Marek Svatos 6.00 15.00
RJ19 Dan Fritsche 6.00 15.00
RJ20 Denis Grebeshkov 6.00 15.00
RJ21 Antero Niittymaki 8.00 20.00
RJ22 Tuomo Ruutu 6.00 15.00
RJ23 Kari Lehtonen 10.00 25.00
RJ24 Dominic Moore 6.00 15.00
RJ25 Tony Salmelainen 6.00 15.00
RJ26 Christian Ehrhoff 6.00 15.00
RJ27 Trevor Daley 6.00 15.00
RJ28 Nikolai Zherdev 8.00 20.00
RJ29 Mark Popovic 6.00 15.00
RJ30 Peter Sejna 6.00 15.00
RJ31 Derek Roy 6.00 15.00
RJ32 Trent Hunter 6.00 15.00
RJ33 Cody McCormick 6.00 15.00
RJ34 John-Michael Liles 6.00 15.00
RJ35 Matthew Lombardi 6.00 15.00
RJ36 Marek Zidlicky 6.00 15.00
RJ37 Ryan Malone 6.00 15.00
RJ38 Niklas Kronwall 8.00 20.00
RJ39 Rastislav Stana 6.00 15.00
RJ40 Andrew Raycroft 8.00 20.00
RJ41 Alexander Semin 8.00 20.00
RJ42 Andrew Peters 6.00 15.00
RJ43 Brent Burns 6.00 15.00
RJ44 Matt Stajan 6.00 15.00
RJ45 Antoine Vermette 6.00 15.00
RJ46 Michael Ryder 8.00 20.00
RJ47 Ryan Kesler 6.00 15.00
RJ48 Eric Staal 10.00 25.00
RJ49 Patrick Leahy 6.00 15.00
RJ50 Marc-Andre Fleury 12.50 30.00

2003-04 Parkhurst Rookie ROYalty Jerseys

PRINT RUN 50 SETS
VR1 Dany Heatley 12.50 30.00
VR2 Martin Brodeur 20.00 50.00
VR3 Peter Forsberg 15.00 40.00
VR4 Daniel Alfredsson 10.00 25.00
VR5 Teemu Selanne 10.00 25.00
VR6 Sergei Samsonov 10.00 25.00
VR7 Ray Bourque 15.00 40.00
VR8 Brian Leetch 10.00 25.00
VR9 Mario Lemieux 25.00 60.00
VR10 Bobby Orr 30.00 80.00
VR11 Terry Sawchuk 15.00 40.00
VR12 Jacques Laperriere 10.00 25.00
VR13 Gilbert Perreault 10.00 25.00
VR14 Bryan Trottier 10.00 25.00
VR15 Denis Potvin 10.00 25.00
VR16 Roger Crozier 10.00 25.00
VR17 Pavel Bure 10.00 25.00
VR18 Ed Belfour 10.00 25.00
VR19 Glenn Hall 10.00 25.00
VR20 Evgeni Nabokov 10.00 25.00
VR21 Frank Brimsek 10.00 25.00
VR22 Mike Bossy 12.50 30.00
VR23 Luc Robitaille 10.00 25.00
VR24 Scott Gomez 10.00 25.00
VR25 Bernie Geoffrion 12.50 30.00
VR26 Gump Worsley 10.00 25.00
VR27 Joe Nieuwendyk 10.00 25.00
VR28 Tony Esposito 12.50 30.00

2003-04 Parkhurst Rookie Teammates Jerseys

PRINT RUN 60 SETS
RT1 M.Lemieux/M.Fleury 15.00 40.00
RT2 S.Fedorov/J.Lupul 10.00 25.00
RT3 M.Sundin/M.Stajan 12.50 30.00
RT4 R.Nash/N.Zherdev 12.50 30.00
RT5 M.Modano/T.Daley 8.00 20.00
RT6 J.Bouwmeester/N.Horton 10.00 25.00
RT7 A.Frolov/D.Brown 8.00 20.00
RT8 J.Spezza/A.Vermette 10.00 25.00
RT9 J.Roenick/J.Pitkanen 8.00 20.00
RT10 J.Sakic/C.McCormick 10.00 25.00
RT11 J.Thornton/P.Bergeron 12.50 30.00
RT12 P.Forsberg/M.Svatos 12.50 30.00
RT13 D.Legwand/J.Tootoo 10.00 25.00
RT14 K.Tkachuk/P.Sejna 8.00 20.00
RT15 S.Stevens/P.Martin 8.00 20.00
RT16 J.Theodore/M.Ryder 12.50 30.00
RT17 R.Blake/J.Michael Liles 8.00 20.00
RT18 J.Iginla/M.Lombardi 10.00 25.00
RT19 M.Satan/D.Roy 8.00 20.00
RT20 S.Koivu/C.Higgins 8.00 20.00
RT21 M.Messier/D.Moore 12.50 30.00
RT22 J.Thibault/T.Ruutu 8.00 20.00

1994-95 Parkhurst SE

This 270-card set apparently was designed to serve as the second series to the 1994-95 Parkhurst product. In the wake of the NHL lockout of that year, licensing regulations were relaxed, and Upper Deck chose to release the SP line instead. This product subsequently was issued in eleven European countries. However, large quantities eventually made their way to North America. The basic cards have the same design as Parkhurst. Although essentially a companion issue to Parkhurst, this set is numbered from 1-270, with an SE prefix. Subsets include World Junior Championships (206-250) and CAHA Program of Excellence (251-270). Although this set contains the first year cards of many players, they are not recognized as Rookie Cards because of the European-only distribution. A 4" X 6" blowup version of 1994-95 Upper Deck #226, which commemorates Wayne Gretzky's 802 career goals, is inserted at the top of each box.
*GOLD: 1X TO 2.5X BASIC INSERTS
SE1 Guy Hebert .07 .20
SE2 Bob Corkum .05 .15
SE3 Randy Ladouceur .07 .20
SE4 Tom Kurvers .05 .15
SE5 Joe Sacco .05 .15
SE6 Valeri Karpov .05 .15
SE7 Garry Valk .05 .15
SE8 Paul Kariya .12 .30
SE9 Alexei Kasatonov .05 .15
SE10 Sergei Zholtok .05 .15
SE11 Glen Murray .05 .15
SE12 David Reid .05 .15
SE13 Adam Oates .10 .25
SE14 Ted Donato .05 .15
SE15 Don Sweeney .05 .15
SE16 Philippe Boucher .05 .15
SE17 Bob Sweeney .05 .15
SE18 Pat LaFontaine .10 .25
SE19 Derek Plante .05 .15
SE20 Jason Dawe .05 .15
SE21 Petr Svoboda .05 .15
SE22 Craig Simpson .05 .15
SE23 Viktor Gordiouk .07 .20
SE24 Trevor Kidd .07 .20
SE25 Todd Hlushko .07 .20
SE26 German Titov .05 .15
SE27 Gary Roberts .05 .15
SE28 Theo Fleury .10 .25
SE29 Cory Stillman .05 .15
SE30 Phil Housley .07 .20
SE31 Joel Otto .05 .15
SE32 Patrick Poulin .05 .15
SE33 Christian Soucy .07 .20
SE34 Kari Dykhuis .07 .20
SE35 Jeremy Roenick .20 .50
SE36 Tony Amonte .07 .20
SE37 Sergei Krivokrasov .05 .15
SE38 Bernie Nicholls .07 .20
SE39 Todd Harvey .05 .15
SE40 Jarkko Varvio .05 .15
SE41 Shane Churla .05 .15
SE42 Paul Cavallini .05 .15
SE43 Trent Klatt .05 .15
SE44 Darcy Wakaluk .07 .20
SE45 Derian Hatcher .05 .15
SE46 Dean Evason .05 .15
SE47 Mike Modano .15 .40
SE48 Greg Johnson .05 .15
SE49 Ray Sheppard .07 .20
SE50 Sergei Fedorov .15 .40
SE51 Bob Rouse .05 .15
SE52 Mike Vernon .07 .20
SE53 Vladimir Konstantinov .07 .20
SE54 Chris Osgood .15 .40
SE55 Steve Yzerman .25 .60
SE56 Jason York .05 .15
SE57 Boris Mironov .05 .15
SE58 Igor Kravchuk .05 .15
SE59 Jason Arnott .07 .20
SE60 David Oliver .05 .15
SE61 Todd Marchant .05 .15
SE62 Dean McAmmond .05 .15
SE63 Brian Skrudland .05 .15
SE64 Tom Fitzgerald .05 .15
SE65 Brian Benning .05 .15
SE66 Stu Barnes .05 .15
SE67 John Vanbiesbrouck .07 .20
SE68 Rob Niedermayer .07 .20
SE69 Jimmy Carson .05 .15
SE70 Mark Janssens .05 .15
SE71 Sean Burke .07 .20
SE72 Andrei Nikolishin .05 .15
SE73 Chris Pronger .10 .25
SE74 Jeff Reese .05 .15
SE75 Darren Turcotte .05 .15
SE76 Robert Kron .05 .15
SE77 Kevin Brown .10 .25
SE78 Robert Lang .05 .15
SE79 Rick Tocchet .07 .20
SE80 Jamie Storr .07 .20
SE81 Kelly Hrudey .07 .20
SE82 Darryl Sydor .05 .15
SE83 Tony Granato .05 .15
SE84 Warren Rychel .05 .15
SE85 Gary Shuchuk .07 .20
SE86 Peter Popovic .05 .15
SE87 Valeri Bure .05 .15
SE88 Kirk Muller .05 .15
SE89 Lyle Odelein .07 .20
SE90 Brian Savage .05 .15
SE91 Gilbert Dionne .05 .15
SE92 Mathieu Schneider .05 .15
SE93 Jim Montgomery .05 .15
SE94 Chris Terreri .07 .20
SE95 Scott Niedermayer .10 .25
SE96 Bob Carpenter .05 .15
SE97 Scott Stevens .10 .25
SE98 Jim Dowd .05 .15
SE99 Brian Rolston .05 .15
SE100 Stephane Richer .07 .20
SE101 Mick Vukota .07 .20
SE102 Steve Thomas .05 .15
SE103 Patrick Flatley .05 .15
SE104 Marty McInnis .05 .15
SE105 Rich Pilon .07 .20
SE106 Benoit Hogue .05 .15
SE107 Zigmund Palffy .07 .20
SE108 Vladimir Malakhov .05 .15
SE109 Brett Lindros .05 .15
SE110 Mike Richter .10 .25
SE111 Greg Gilbert .05 .15
SE112 Kevin Lowe .05 .15
SE113 Mark Messier .10 .25
SE114 Alexander Karpovtsev .05 .15
SE115 Sergei Nemchinov .05 .15
SE116 Petr Nedved .07 .20
SE117 Glenn Healy .07 .20
SE118 Dave Archibald .05 .15
SE119 Alexandre Daigle .05 .15
SE120 Darrin Madeley .05 .15
SE121 Pavol Demitra .12 .30
SE122 Brad Shaw .05 .15
SE123 Alexei Yashin .10 .25
SE124 Sean Hill .05 .15
SE125 Vladislav Boulin .10 .25
SE126 Kevin Haller .05 .15
SE127 Chris Therien .05 .15
SE128 Garry Galley .05 .15
SE129 Mikael Renberg .07 .20
SE130 Ron Hextall .07 .20
SE131 Eric Lindros .10 .25
SE132 Craig MacTavish .05 .15
SE133 Patrik Juhlin .05 .15
SE134 Martin Straka .05 .15
SE135 Doug Brown .05 .15
SE136 Markus Naslund .10 .25
SE137 Luc Robitaille .10 .25
SE138 Kjell Samuelsson .05 .15
SE139 Ken Wregget .07 .20
SE140 John Cullen .05 .15
SE141 Peter Taglianetti .05 .15
SE142 Janne Laukkanen .07 .20
SE143 Owen Nolan .10 .25
SE144 Adam Deadmarsh .05 .15
SE145 Dave Karpa .05 .15
SE146 Wendel Clark .07 .20
SE147 Joe Sakic .20 .50
SE148 Alexei Gusarov .07 .20
SE149 Peter Forsberg .25 .60
SE150 Kevin Miller .05 .15
SE151 Denny Felsner .05 .15
SE152 Al MacInnis .07 .20
SE153 Philippe Bozon .07 .20
SE154 Brett Hull .20 .50
SE155 Guy Carbonneau .05 .15
SE156 Igor Korolev .05 .15
SE157 Esa Tikkanen .05 .15
SE158 Jon Casey .07 .20
SE159 Viktor Kozlov .05 .15
SE160 Mike Rathje .05 .15
SE161 Bob Errey .05 .15
SE162 Arturs Irbe .07 .20
SE163 Ray Whitney .05 .15
SE164 Igor Larionov .05 .15
SE165 Pat Falloon .05 .15
SE166 Jeff Friesen .05 .15
SE167 Vlastimil Kroupa .05 .15
SE168 Chris Joseph .05 .15
SE169 Danton Cole .05 .15
SE170 John Tucker .05 .15
SE171 Roman Hamrlik .07 .20
SE172 Jason Wiemer .05 .15
SE173 Kenny Jonsson .05 .15
SE174 Eric Fichaud XRC .10 .25
SE175 Mats Sundin .07 .20
SE176 Doug Gilmour .12 .30
SE177 Drake Berehowsky .05 .15
SE178 Mike Ridley .05 .15
SE179 Jamie Macoun .05 .15
SE180 Alexei Kudashov .05 .15
SE181 Bill Berg .05 .15
SE182 Dave Andreychuk .10 .25
SE183 Mike Eastwood .05 .15
SE184 Martin Gelinas .05 .15
SE185 Greg Adams .05 .15
SE186 Gino Odjick .05 .15
SE187 Pavel Bure .10 .25
SE188 Cliff Ronning .05 .15
SE189 Jiri Slegr .05 .15
SE190 Jyrki Lumme .05 .15
SE191 Jassen Cullimore .05 .15
SE192 Steve Konowalchuk .05 .15
SE193 Sylvain Cote .05 .15
SE194 Jason Allison .07 .20
SE195 Sergei Gonchar .05 .15
SE196 Pat Peake .05 .15
SE197 Calle Johansson .05 .15
SE198 Joe Juneau .07 .20
SE199 Jeff Nelson .05 .15
SE200 Luciano Borsato .05 .15
SE201 Teemu Selanne .20 .50
SE202 Tie Domi .07 .20
SE203 Tim Cheveldae .07 .20
SE204 Darrin Shannon .05 .15
SE205 Ravil Gusmanov .05 .15
SE206 Todd Harvey .05 .15
SE207 Ed Jovanovski XRC .15 .40
SE208 Jason Allison .07 .20
SE209 Bryan McCabe .05 .15
SE210 Dan Cloutier XRC .15 .40
SE211 Ladislav Kohn XRC .10 .25
SE212 Marek Malik XRC .05 .15
SE213 Jan Hlavac XRC .15 .40
SE214 Petr Cajanek XRC .15 .40
SE215 Jussi Markkanen XRC .75 2.00
SE216 Jere Karalahti XRC .10 .25
SE217 Janne Niinimaa .10 .25
SE218 Kimmo Timonen .07 .20
SE219 Mikko Helisten XRC .10 .25
SE220 Niko Halttunen XRC .10 .25
SE221 Tommi Miettinen .07 .20
SE222 Veli-Pekka Nutikka XRC .10 .25
SE223 Timo Salonen XRC .10 .25
SE224 Tommi Sova XRC .10 .25
SE225 Jussi Tarvainen XRC .10 .25
SE226 Tommi Rajamaki XRC .07 .20
SE227 Antti Aalto XRC .07 .20
SE228 Alexander Korolyuk XRC .10 .25
SE229 Vitali Yachmenev .10 .25
SE230 Nicolai Zavaroukhine .10 .25
SE231 Vadim Epantchinsev .07 .20
SE232 Dmitri Klevakin .07 .20
SE233 Anders Eriksson .07 .20
SE234 Anders Soderberg .07 .20
SE235 Per Svartvadet XRC .10 .25
SE236 Johan Davidsson .10 .25
SE237 Niklas Sundstrom .10 .25
SE238 J. Andersson-Junkka XRC .10 .25
SE239 Dick Tarnstrom XRC .10 .25
SE240 P.J. Axelsson XRC .10 .25
SE241 Frederik Johansson .10 .25
SE242 Peter Strom .10 .25
SE243 Mattias Ohlund .15 .40
SE244 Jesper Mattsson .07 .20
SE245 Jonas Forsberg .07 .20
SE246 Adam Deadmarsh .05 .15
SE247 Deron Quint .05 .15
SE248 Jamie Langenbrunner .07 .20
SE249 Richard Park .05 .15
SE250 Bryan Berard XRC .15 .40
SE251 David Belitski XRC .10 .25
SE252 Mike McBain XRC .10 .25
SE253 Hugh Hamilton XRC .10 .25
SE254 Jason Doig XRC .10 .25
SE255 Xavier Delisle XRC .10 .25
SE256 Wade Redden XRC .15 .40
SE257 Jeff Ware XRC .10 .25
SE258 Christian Dube XRC .10 .25
SE259 Louis-Phil.Sevigny XRC .10 .25
SE260 Jarome Iginla XRC 4.00 10.00
SE261 Daniel Briere XRC 4.00 10.00
SE262 Justin Kurtz XRC .10 .25
SE263 Marc Savard XRC .10 .25
SE264 Alyn McCauley XRC .10 .25
SE265 Brad Mehalko XRC .10 .25
SE266 Jeffrey Ambrosio XRC .10 .25
SE267 Todd Norman XRC .10 .25
SE268 Brian Scott XRC .10 .25
SE269 Brad Larsen XRC .10 .25
SE270 J-S Giguere XRC 2.50 6.00
NNO Wayne Gretzky Large .50 1.25

1994-95 Parkhurst SE Euro-Stars

The 20 cards in this set were randomly inserted in Parkhurst SE product at an approximate rate of 1:8 packs. The set has some of the top European-born talent in the NHL. The cards feature a horizontal design with an action photo on the right and set logo and European map elements on the left. Card numbers have an "ES" prefix.
COMPLETE SET (20) 8.00 20.00
ES1 Peter Forsberg 2.50 6.00
ES2 Mats Sundin .60 1.50
ES3 Mikael Renberg .30 .75
ES4 Niklas Lidstrom .60 1.50
ES5 Mariusz Czerkawski .15 .40
ES6 Ulf Dahlen .15 .40
ES7 Kjell Samuelsson .15 .40
ES8 Jyrki Lumme .15 .40
ES9 Jari Kurri .30 .75
ES10 Teppo Numminen .15 .40
ES11 Esa Tikkanen .15 .40
ES12 Christian Ruuttu .15 .40
ES13 Teemu Selanne .60 1.50
ES14 Alexander Mogilny .30 .75
ES15 Pavel Bure .60 1.50
ES16 Sergei Fedorov 1.00 2.50
ES17 Arturs Irbe .30 .75
ES18 Alexei Kovalev .15 .40
ES19 Dominik Hasek 1.25 3.00
ES20 Jaromir Jagr 1.00 2.50

1994-95 Parkhurst SE Vintage

This 45-card standard-size was inserted in Parkhurst SE packs at approximately the rate of 1:6. They are printed on heavy white card stock with a design that hearkens back to the style of Parkhurst issues of the 1950s and 1960s. The player photo is cut out and placed on a white-and-tan background. The player's name appears in a black bar on the lower portion of the card, alongside the set logo. The card backs are an unfinished cardboard and feature professional statistics, biography and a "Did You Know" section containing interesting trivia, which did not apply to the player pictured. The cards were numbered with a "seV" prefix.
COMPLETE SET (45) 15.00 40.00
1 Paul Kariya .60 1.50
2 Dino Ciccarelli .20 .50
3 Patrick Roy 3.00 8.00
4 Markus Naslund .60 1.50
5 Trevor Linden .40 1.00
6 Valeri Karpov .20 .50
7 Pat Verbeek .20 .50
8 Martin Brodeur 1.50 4.00
9 Kevin Stevens .20 .50
10 Kirk McLean .40 1.00
11 Stephan Lebeau .20 .50
12 Scott Niedermayer .20 .50
13 Peter Bondra .40 1.00
14 Ed Belfour .60 1.50
15 Paul Coffey .60 1.50
16 Chris Gratton .20 .50
17 Joe Juneau .40 1.00
18 Ray Bourque .60 1.50
19 Sergei Krivokrasov .20 .50
20 Wayne Gretzky 4.00 10.00
21 Alexei Yashin .20 .50
22 Al Iafrate .20 .50
23 Doug Weight .40 1.00
24 Jari Kurri .20 .50
25 Rod Brind'Amour .40 1.00
26 Bryan Smolinski .20 .50
27 Darius Kasparaitis .20 .50
28 Mark Recchi .20 .50
29 Mike Gartner .40 1.00
30 Russ Courtnall .20 .50
31 Pierre Turgeon .40 1.00
32 Felix Potvin .60 1.50
33 Nelson Emerson .20 .50
34 Alexander Mogilny .40 1.00
35 Bob Kudelski .20 .50
36 Brett Lindros .20 .50
37 Mats Sundin .60 1.50
38 Keith Tkachuk .60 1.50
39 Derek Plante .20 .50
40 Oleg Petrov .20 .50
41 Adam Graves .20 .50
42 Jaromir Jagr 1.00 2.50
43 Viktor Kozlov .20 .50
44 Nathan Lafayette .20 .50
45 Alexei Zhamnov .40 1.00

2003-04 Parkhurst Toronto Spring Expo Rookie Preview

Inserted one in each "Super Box" available at the Toronto Spring Expo, this 20 -card set featured promising prospects and swatches of game-used jerseys.
PRP1 Marc-Andre Fleury 40.00 100.00
PRP2 Jordin Tootoo 15.00 40.00
PRP3 Joni Pitkanen 10.00 25.00
PRP4 Fedor Tyutin 8.00 20.00
PRP5 Derek Roy 15.00 40.00
PRP6 Nathan Horton 15.00 40.00
PRP7 Eric Staal 25.00 60.00
PRP8 Patrice Bergeron 25.00 60.00
PRP9 Dustin Brown 10.00 25.00
PRP10 Dan Hamhuis 10.00 25.00
PRP11 Tim Gleason 8.00 20.00
PRP12 Rastislav Stana 8.00 20.00
PRP13 Matt Stajan 15.00 40.00
PRP14 Matthew Lombardi 8.00 20.00
PRP15 Nikolai Zherdev 20.00 50.00
PRP16 Tuomo Ruutu 20.00 50.00
PRP17 Ryan Malone 15.00 40.00
PRP18 Antoine Vermette 8.00 20.00
PRP19 Kari Lehtonen 30.00 80.00
PRP20 Alexander Semin 20.00 50.00

2016-17 Parkhurst

1 Corey Perry .25 .60
2 Ryan Kesler .25 .60
3 John Gibson .25 .60
4 Jakob Silfverberg .25 .60
5 Sami Vatanen .20 .50
6 Cam Fowler .20 .50
7 Rickard Rakell .25 .60
8 Jonathan Bernier .25 .60
9 Hampus Lindholm .15 .40
10 Ryan Getzlaf .40 1.00
11 Nick Ritchie .20 .50
12 Oliver Ekman-Larsson .20 .50
13 Anthony Duclair .25 .60
14 Max Domi .30 .75
15 Connor Murphy .15 .40
16 Tobias Rieder .15 .40
17 Martin Hanzal .20 .50
18 Mike Smith .25 .60
19 Alex Goligoski .15 .40
20 Shane Doan .20 .50
21 Jamie McGinn .20 .50
22 Jordan Martinook .15 .40
23 David Krejci .25 .60
24 David Backes .25 .60
25 Brad Marchand .30 .75
26 Zdeno Chara .25 .60
27 Ryan Spooner .20 .50
28 Torey Krug .25 .60
29 Matt Beleskey .20 .50
30 Patrice Bergeron .30 .75
31 Tuukka Rask .25 .60
32 David Pastrnak .40 1.00
33 Jimmy Hayes .15 .40
34 Ryan O'Reilly .25 .60
35 Sam Reinhart .20 .50
36 Brian Gionta .20 .50
37 Evander Kane .25 .60
38 Zemgus Girgensons .20 .50
39 Rasmus Ristolainen .20 .50
40 Jack Eichel .50 1.25
41 Tyler Ennis .20 .50
42 Cody Franson .15 .40
43 Matt Moulson .20 .50
44 Kyle Okposo .25 .60
45 Sean Monahan .25 .60
46 Mark Giordano .20 .50
47 Mikael Backlund .20 .50
48 T.J. Brodie .20 .50
49 Dougie Hamilton .25 .60
50 Johnny Gaudreau .40 1.00
51 Dennis Wideman .15 .40
52 Sam Bennett .30 .75
53 Brian Elliott .20 .50
54 Alex Chiasson .20 .50
55 Troy Brouwer .20 .50
56 Victor Rask .20 .50
57 Elias Lindholm .25 .60
58 Noah Hanifin .25 .60
59 Justin Faulk .20 .50
60 Jeff Skinner .25 .60
61 Joakim Nordstrom .15 .40
62 Ron Hainsey .20 .50
63 Cam Ward .25 .60
64 Jay McClement .15 .40
65 Andrej Nestrasil .20 .50
66 Teuvo Teravainen .25 .60
67 Artem Anisimov .20 .50
68 Artemi Panarin .30 .75
69 Duncan Keith .25 .60
70 Patrick Kane .50 1.25
71 Brent Seabrook .20 .50
72 Corey Crawford .30 .75
73 Niklas Hjalmarsson .20 .50
74 Marian Hossa .20 .50
75 Jonathan Toews .50 1.25
76 Marcus Kruger .25 .60
77 Brian Campbell .20 .50
78 Matt Duchene .25 .60
79 Gabriel Landeskog .20 .50
80 Nathan MacKinnon .50 1.25
81 Carl Soderberg .15 .40
82 Tyson Barrie .25 .60
83 Jarome Iginla .25 .60
84 Francois Beauchemin .20 .50
85 Mikhail Grigorenko .15 .40
86 Semyon Varlamov .25 .60
87 Erik Johnson .15 .40
88 Blake Comeau .15 .40
89 Cam Atkinson .25 .60
90 Brandon Saad .25 .60
91 Brandon Dubinsky .25 .60
92 Scott Hartnell .25 .60
93 Alexander Wennberg .20 .50
94 Nick Foligno .20 .50
95 Seth Jones .20 .50
96 Ryan Murray .15 .40
97 Boone Jenner .25 .60
98 Sergei Bobrovsky .25 .60
99 Jack Johnson .15 .40
100 Jamie Benn .30 .75
101 Jason Spezza .25 .60
102 John Klingberg .25 .60
103 Patrick Sharp .20 .50
104 Valeri Nichushkin .20 .50
105 Antoine Roussel .15 .40
106 Ales Hemsky .20 .50
107 Johnny Oduya .20 .50
108 Antti Niemi .20 .50
109 Kari Lehtonen .20 .50
110 Tyler Seguin .40 1.00
111 Henrik Zetterberg .30 .75
112 Mike Green .25 .60
113 Gustav Nyquist .25 .60
114 Justin Abdelkader .20 .50
115 Andreas Athanasiou .25 .60
116 Tomas Tatar .20 .50
117 Frans Nielsen .20 .50
118 Niklas Kronwall .15 .40
119 Petr Mrazek .25 .60
120 Dylan Larkin .40 1.00
121 Danny DeKeyser .15 .40
122 Leon Draisaitl .30 .75
123 Jordan Eberle .25 .60
124 Ryan Nugent-Hopkins .25 .60
125 Connor McDavid 1.25 3.00
126 Andrej Sekera .15 .40
127 Oscar Klefbom .40 1.00
128 Nail Yakupov .20 .50
129 Adam Larsson .25 .60
130 Milan Lucic .20 .50
131 Benoit Pouliot .20 .50
132 Cam Talbot .30 .75
133 Aaron Ekblad .25 .60
134 Aleksander Barkov .25 .60
135 Jonathan Huberdeau .25 .60
136 Jussi Jokinen .25 .60
137 Vincent Trocheck .25 .60
138 Reilly Smith .25 .60
139 Alex Petrovic .15 .40
140 Jaromir Jagr .60 1.50
141 Nick Bjugstad .20 .50
142 Roberto Luongo .25 .60
143 Keith Yandle .25 .60
144 Anze Kopitar .40 1.00
145 Jeff Carter .25 .60
146 Tyler Toffoli .25 .60
147 Jake Muzzin .20 .50
148 Dustin Brown .20 .50
149 Drew Doughty .25 .60
150 Jonathan Quick .40 1.00
151 Marian Gaborik .25 .60
152 Alec Martinez .15 .40
153 Nick Shore .20 .50
154 Tanner Pearson .20 .50
155 Mikko Koivu .20 .50
156 Ryan Suter .20 .50
157 Charlie Coyle .20 .50
158 Jason Pominville .20 .50
159 Jason Zucker .20 .50
160 Zach Parise .25 .60
161 Mikael Granlund .20 .50
162 Eric Staal .30 .75
163 Nino Niederreiter .25 .60
164 Jonas Brodin .15 .40
165 Devan Dubnyk .25 .60
166 Max Pacioretty .25 .60
167 Alex Galchenyuk .30 .75
168 Tomas Plekanec .25 .60
169 Brendan Gallagher .30 .75
170 Andrei Markov .25 .60
171 Nathan Beaulieu .15 .40
172 David Desharnais .20 .50
173 Sven Andrighetto .20 .50
174 Andrew Shaw .25 .60
175 Carey Price .75 2.00
176 Shea Weber .20 .50
177 Filip Forsberg .30 .75
178 Roman Josi .25 .60
179 James Neal .20 .50
180 Calle Jarnkrok .20 .50
181 Mike Ribeiro .20 .50
182 Ryan Johansen .30 .75
183 Colin Wilson .25 .60
184 Craig Smith .15 .40
185 P.K. Subban .40 1.00
186 Mattias Ekholm .15 .40
187 Pekka Rinne .30 .75
188 Kyle Palmieri .20 .50
189 Adam Henrique .25 .60
190 Cory Schneider .20 .50
191 Travis Zajac .20 .50
192 Michael Cammalleri .20 .50
193 Taylor Hall .50 1.25
194 Damon Severson .20 .50
195 Reid Boucher .15 .40
196 Devante Smith-Pelly .20 .50
197 Jon Merrill .20 .50
198 Sergei Kalinin .20 .50
199 Nick Leddy .15 .40
200 John Tavares .50 1.25
201 Anders Lee .25 .60
202 Johnny Boychuk .25 .60
203 Brock Nelson .20 .50
204 Jason Chimera .15 .40
205 Casey Cizikas .15 .40
206 Cal Clutterbuck .15 .40
207 Thomas Greiss .20 .50
208 Andrew Ladd .25 .60
209 Jaroslav Halak .25 .60
210 Henrik Lundqvist .25 .60
211 Mats Zuccarello .25 .60
212 Marc Staal .15 .40
213 Derek Stepan .20 .50
214 J.T. Miller .20 .50
215 Chris Kreider .25 .60
216 Ryan McDonagh .20 .50
217 Oscar Lindberg .15 .40
218 Mika Zibanejad .25 .60
219 Kevin Hayes .20 .50
220 Rick Nash .25 .60
221 Mark Stone .25 .60
222 Bobby Ryan .20 .50
223 Mike Hoffman .20 .50
224 Chris Wideman .20 .50
225 Jean-Gabriel Pageau .20 .50
226 Kyle Turris .20 .50
227 Cody Ceci .20 .50
228 Erik Karlsson .50 1.25
229 Derick Brassard .25 .60
230 Craig Anderson .25 .60
231 Dion Phaneuf .25 .60
232 Wayne Simmonds .30 .75
233 Brayden Schenn .25 .60
234 Jakub Voracek .25 .60
235 Sean Couturier .25 .60
236 Shayne Gostisbehere .30 .75
237 Michael Raffl .15 .40
238 Radko Gudas .15 .40
239 Matt Read .20 .50
240 Steve Mason .20 .50
241 Claude Giroux .25 .60
242 Michal Neuvirth .20 .50
243 Evgeni Malkin .75 2.00
244 Phil Kessel .30 .75
245 Patric Hornqvist .20 .50
246 Nick Bonino .15 .40
247 Chris Kunitz .25 .60
248 Olli Maatta .25 .60
249 Trevor Daley .20 .50
250 Carl Hagelin .25 .60
251 Sidney Crosby 1.00 2.50
252 Matt Murray .40 1.00
253 Kris Letang .25 .60
254 Brent Burns .30 .75
255 Joe Pavelski .25 .60
256 Patrick Marleau .25 .60
257 Tomas Hertl .25 .60
258 Joel Ward .20 .50
259 Logan Couture .25 .60
260 Joe Thornton .25 .60
261 Mikkel Boedker .20 .50
262 Marc-Edouard Vlasic .15 .40
263 Martin Jones .25 .60
264 Joonas Donskoi .20 .50
265 Kevin Shattenkirk .20 .50
266 Jaden Schwartz .30 .75
267 David Perron .20 .50
268 Alexander Steen .25 .60
269 Alex Pietrangelo .20 .50
270 Robby Fabbri .25 .60
271 Paul Stastny .25 .60
272 Jori Lehtera .20 .50
273 Colton Parayko .25 .60
274 Jake Allen .30 .75
275 Vladimir Tarasenko .40 1.00
276 Tyler Johnson .20 .50
277 Jonathan Drouin .30 .75
278 Alex Killorn .15 .40
279 Victor Hedman .30 .75
280 Steven Stamkos .50 1.25
281 Ondrej Palat .20 .50
282 Vladislav Namestnikov .15 .40
283 Nikita Kucherov .40 1.00
284 Ryan Callahan .25 .60
285 Ben Bishop .25 .60
286 Anton Stralman .20 .50
287 Nazem Kadri .20 .50
288 Colin Greening .20 .50
289 Leo Komarov .25 .60
290 James van Riemsdyk .25 .60
291 Morgan Rielly .20 .50
292 Jake Gardiner .25 .60
293 Tyler Bozak .20 .50
294 Matt Martin .20 .50
295 Roman Polak .15 .40
296 Frederik Andersen .20 .50
297 Milan Michalek .15 .40
298 Daniel Sedin .25 .60
299 Bo Horvat .40 1.00
300 Henrik Sedin .25 .60
301 Alexandre Burrows .20 .50
302 Jannik Hansen .15 .40
303 Sven Baertschi .15 .40
304 Ben Hutton .25 .60
305 Jake Virtanen .30 .75
306 Erik Gudbranson .25 .60
307 Ryan Miller .25 .60
308 Loui Eriksson .25 .60
309 John Carlson .30 .75
310 Alexander Ovechkin 1.00 2.50
311 T.J. Oshie .40 1.00
312 Nicklas Backstrom .40 1.00
313 Evgeny Kuznetsov .40 1.00
314 Justin Williams .20 .50
315 Andre Burakovsky .20 .50
316 Matt Niskanen .20 .50

17 Lars Eller .20 .50
18 Karl Alzner .15 .40
19 Braden Holtby .40 1.00
20 Jacob Trouba .20 .50
21 Mark Scheifele .30 .75
22 Drew Stafford .20 .50
23 Nikolaj Ehlers .25 .60
24 Bryan Little .20 .50
25 Blake Wheeler .25 .60
26 Tyler Myers .20 .50
27 Marko Dano .20 .50
28 Adam Lowry .15 .40
29 Connor Hellebuyck .40 1.00
30 Dustin Byfuglien .25 .60
31 Brendan Leipsic RC 1.25 3.00
32 Ryan Pulock RC 1.25 3.00
33 Tom Kuhnhackl RC 1.00 2.50
34 Tobias Lindberg RC 2.00 5.00
35 Alan Quine RC 1.25 3.00
36 Chase De Leo RC 1.25 3.00
37 Pontus Aberg RC 1.50 4.00
38 Steven Santini RC 1.00 2.50
39 Nikita Soshnikov RC .75 2.00
40 Kasperi Kapanen RC 2.50 6.00
41 Oliver Kylington RC 1.00 2.50
42 Miles Wood RC 1.00 2.50
43 Jason Dickinson RC 1.00 2.50
44 Josh Morrissey RC 1.50 4.00
45 Charlie Lindgren RC 2.50 6.00
46 Justin Bailey RC 1.25 3.00
47 Connor Brown RC 2.00 5.00
48 Nic Dowd RC 1.25 3.00
49 Trevor Carrick RC 1.25 3.00
50 William Nylander RC 5.00 12.00
51 Oliver Bjorkstrand RC 1.00 2.50
52 Stephen Johns RC 1.00 2.50
53 Nick Paul RC 1.50 4.00
54 Sergey Tolchinsky RC 1.00 2.50
55 Chris Bigras RC 1.00 2.50
56 Mike Reilly RC 1.00 2.50
57 J.C. Lipon RC 1.25 3.00
58 Dominik Simon RC 1.25 3.00
59 Frederik Gauthier RC 1.00 2.50
60 Sonny Milano RC 1.50 4.00
61 Hudson Fasching RC 1.25 3.00
62 Michael Matheson RC 1.25 3.00
63 Zach Hyman RC 1.50 4.00
64 Evan Rodrigues RC 1.50 4.00
65 Anthony Mantha RC 3.00 8.00
66 Pavel Zacha RC 1.50 4.00
67 Ivan Provorov RC 2.50 6.00
68 Nick Sorensen RC 1.25 3.00
69 Artturi Lehkonen RC 1.25 3.00
70 Auston Matthews RC 8.00 20.00
71 Tyler Motte RC 1.25 3.00
72 Brayden Point RC 3.00 8.00
73 Zach Werenski RC 2.50 6.00
74 Travis Konecny RC 2.50 6.00
75 Patrik Laine RC 5.00 12.00
76 Pavel Buchnevich RC 2.00 5.00
77 Nick Schmaltz RC 1.25 3.00
78 Danton Heinen RC 2.00 5.00
79 Thomas Chabot RC 2.50 6.00
80 Mikhail Sergachev RC 2.50 6.00
81 Jimmy Vesey RC 2.50 6.00
82 Anthony Beauvillier RC 1.25 3.00
83 Christian Dvorak RC 1.25 3.00
84 Jesse Puljujarvi RC 3.00 8.00
85 Matthew Tkachuk RC 4.00 10.00
86 Sebastian Aho RC 2.50 6.00
87 Mathew Barzal RC 4.00 10.00
88 Jakob Chychrun RC 1.25 3.00
89 Lawson Crouse RC 1.00 2.50
90 Mitch Marner RC 6.00 15.00
91 Brandon Carlo RC 1.25 3.00
92 Zach Sanford RC 1.25 3.00
93 Joel Eriksson Ek RC 1.25 3.00
94 Gustav Forsling RC 1.25 3.00
95 Dylan Strome RC 2.50 6.00
96 Kyle Connor RC 3.00 8.00
97 Jamie Benn CL .50 1.25
98 Connor McDavid CL 2.00 5.00
99 Sidney Crosby CL 1.50 4.00
100 Auston Matthews CL 2.50 6.00

2016-17 Parkhurst Black

VETS: 1.25X TO 3X BASIC CARDS
ROOKIES: 1.5X TO 4X BASIC CARDS
2 Corey Crawford 2.00 5.00
7 Jonathan Drouin 2.00 5.00
2 Nicklas Backstrom 2.50 6.00
3 Evgeny Kuznetsov 2.50 6.00
70 Auston Matthews 80.00 150.00

2016-17 Parkhurst All Star Favorites

S1 Sidney Crosby 8.00 20.00
S2 Patrick Kane 4.00 10.00
S3 Jamie Benn 2.50 6.00
S4 Erik Karlsson 4.00 10.00
S5 Brent Burns 2.50 6.00
S6 Drew Doughty 2.00 5.00
S7 Vladimir Tarasenko 3.00 8.00
S8 John Tavares 4.00 10.00
S9 Claude Giroux 2.00 5.00
S10 Alexander Ovechkin 8.00 20.00

2016-17 Parkhurst Letter On The Sweater

S1 Henrik Zetterberg 2.50 6.00
S2 Zdeno Chara 2.00 5.00
S3 Shane Doan 1.50 4.00
S4 Jonathan Toews 4.00 10.00
S5 Henrik Sedin 2.00 5.00
S6 Sidney Crosby 8.00 20.00
S7 Alexander Ovechkin 8.00 20.00
S8 Jamie Benn 2.50 6.00

2016-17 Parkhurst Protectors Of The Net

N1 Carey Price 6.00 15.00
N2 Braden Holtby 3.00 8.00
N3 Jonathan Quick 3.00 8.00
N4 Cory Schneider 1.50 4.00
N5 Henrik Lundqvist 2.00 5.00
N6 Corey Crawford 2.50 6.00
N7 Tuukka Rask 2.00 5.00
N8 Pekka Rinne 2.50 6.00

2016-17 Parkhurst Rookie Parade

P1 William Nylander 20.00 50.00
P2 Pavel Zacha 6.00 15.00
P3 Justin Bailey 5.00 12.00
P4 Sonny Milano 6.00 15.00
P5 Anthony Mantha 12.00 30.00
P6 Kasperi Kapanen 10.00 25.00
P7 Miles Wood 4.00 10.00
P8 Josh Morrissey 6.00 15.00
P9 Jason Dickinson 4.00 10.00
P10 Brendan Leipsic 5.00 12.00
P11 Charlie Lindgren 10.00 25.00
RP12 Hudson Fasching 5.00 12.00
RP13 Connor Brown 8.00 20.00
RP14 Oliver Kylington 4.00 10.00
RP15 Ryan Pulock 5.00 12.00
RP16 Daniel Altshuller 4.00 10.00
RP17 Trevor Carrick 5.00 12.00
RP18 Sergey Tolchinsky 4.00 10.00
RP19 Michael Matheson 5.00 12.00
RP20 Tom Kuhnhackl 4.00 10.00
RP21 Dylan Strome 10.00 25.00
RP22 Ivan Provorov 10.00 25.00
RP23 Matthew Tkachuk 15.00 40.00
RP24 Jimmy Vesey 10.00 25.00
RP25 Patrik Laine 20.00 50.00
RP26 Travis Konecny 10.00 25.00
RP27 Kyle Connor 12.00 30.00
RP28 Zach Werenski 10.00 25.00
RP29 Mikhail Sergachev 10.00 25.00
RP30 Jesse Puljujarvi 12.00 30.00
RP31 Mathew Barzal 15.00 40.00
RP32 Mitch Marner 25.00 60.00
RP33 Auston Matthews 30.00 80.00

2016-17 Parkhurst Rookie Parade Blue

RP20 Tom Kuhnhackl AU E 20.00 50.00

2016-17 Parkhurst Tis The Season

TS1 Carey Price 25.00 60.00
TS2 John Tavares 15.00 40.00
TS3 Steven Stamkos 15.00 40.00
TS4 Jonathan Toews 15.00 40.00
TS5 Henrik Lundqvist 8.00 20.00
TS6 Henrik Zetterberg 10.00 25.00
TS7 Connor McDavid 40.00 100.00
TS8 Sidney Crosby 30.00 80.00
TS9 Drew Doughty 8.00 20.00
TS10 Patrice Bergeron 10.00 25.00
TS11 Henrik Sedin 8.00 20.00
TS12 Alex Ovechkin 30.00 80.00
TS13 Mark Messier 10.00 25.00
TS14 Mike Bossy 8.00 20.00
TS15 Patrick Roy 20.00 50.00
TS16 Doug Gilmour 10.00 25.00
TS17 Bobby Orr 25.00 60.00
TS18 Wayne Gretzky 40.00 100.00

2016-17 Parkhurst Top 25

TOP1 Jonathan Toews 4.00 10.00
TOP2 Henrik Zetterberg 2.50 6.00
TOP3 Brent Burns 2.50 6.00
TOP4 Alexander Ovechkin 8.00 20.00
TOP5 Evgeni Malkin 6.00 15.00
TOP6 Nikita Kucherov 3.00 8.00
TOP7 David Krejci 2.00 5.00
TOP8 Drew Doughty 2.00 5.00
TOP9 John Tavares 4.00 10.00
TOP10 Sidney Crosby 8.00 20.00
TOP11 Carey Price 6.00 15.00
TOP12 Jamie Benn 2.50 6.00
TOP13 Anze Kopitar 3.00 8.00
TOP14 Corey Perry 2.00 5.00
TOP15 Pekka Rinne 2.50 6.00
TOP16 Patrick Kane 4.00 10.00
TOP17 Joe Pavelski 2.00 5.00
TOP18 Nathan MacKinnon 4.00 10.00
TOP19 Steven Stamkos 4.00 10.00
TOP20 Max Pacioretty 2.00 5.00
TOP21 Connor McDavid 10.00 25.00
TOP22 Erik Karlsson 4.00 10.00
TOP23 Ryan Getzlaf 3.00 8.00
TOP24 Vladimir Tarasenko 3.00 8.00
TOP25 Tyler Seguin 3.00 8.00

2017-18 Parkhurst Priority Signings

PSAB Anders Bjork/50
PSAD Alex DeBrincat/50
PSAF Alex Formenton/50
PSAK Adrian Kempe/75 12.00 30.00
PSAK Alex Kerfoot/50
PSAL Artturi Lehkonen/75 8.00 20.00
PSAN Alexander Nylander/50 15.00 40.00
PSAR Alexander Radulov/15
PSAT Alex Tuch/40
PSBB Brock Boeser/50 50.00 120.00
PSBG Brendan Gallagher/15
PSBL Brendan Lemieux/75
PSBR Bobby Ryan/25 8.00 20.00
PSBS Brady Skjei/25 8.00 20.00
PSBU Will Butcher/50
PSCA Cam Atkinson/25 10.00 25.00
PSCD Chris DiDomenico/75
PSCF Christian Fischer/50 12.00 30.00
PSCH Carl Hagelin/25 10.00 25.00
PSCH Chris Kreider/15
PSCK Clayton Keller/75
PSCW Colin White/50 10.00 25.00
PSDB David Backes/25 8.00 20.00
PSDG Denis Gurianov/75
PSDK David Krejci/15
PSEC J.T. Compher/50 12.00 30.00
PSEK Evander Kane/25 10.00 25.00
PSES Evgeny Svechnikov/75 20.00 50.00
PSJB Jesper Bratt/50
PSJG Jon Gillies/75 10.00 25.00
PSJH Josh Ho-Sang/50 12.00 30.00
PSJM Josh Morrissey/25 6.00 15.00
PSJM Jake Muzzin/50
PSJR Jack Roslovic/50 12.00 30.00
PSKT Kyle Turris/25 10.00 25.00
PSKY Kailer Yamamoto/50
PSLE Anders Lee/25 10.00 25.00
PSLK Luke Kunin/50
PSMA Jacob Markstrom/25 15.00 40.00
PSMB Madison Bowey/75
PSMG Mikael Granlund/50 10.00 25.00
PSMJ Martin Jones/15
PSMJ Martin Jones/15
PSMM Mitch Marner/25 50.00 120.00
PSMP Max Pacioretty/15
PSMS Mark Stone/25 10.00 25.00
PSMV Mike Vecchione/75 8.00 20.00
PSNE Nikolaj Ehlers/25 10.00 25.00
PSNS Nikita Scherbak/50 20.00 50.00
PSOM Olli Maatta/25
PSPD Phillip Danault/50 6.00 15.00
PSPD Pierre-Luc Dubois/50
PSRH Robert Hagg/50
PSRN Ryan Nugent-Hopkins/25 10.00 25.00
PSSB Sam Bennett/15
PSST Shea Theodore/25
PSTH Tage Thompson/50
PSTJ Tyson Jost/50 20.00 50.00
PSTP Tucker Poolman/75
PSTS Troy Stecher/25 15.00 40.00
PSTS Travis Sanheim/50
PSTT Teuvo Teravainen/25
PSVH Ville Husso/75
PSVM Victor Mete/50
PSVS Vadim Shipachyov/75
PSWN William Nylander/25 15.00 40.00

2017-18 Parkhurst

*RED.VET: 1X TO 2.5X BASIC CARDS
*RED.RC: .6X TO 1.5X BASIC CARDS
OVERALL STATED ODDS 1:3
*BLACK.VET: 1.5X TO 4X BASIC CARDS
*BLACK.RC: 1X TO 2.5X BASIC CARDS
OVERALL STATED ODDS 1:12
1 Ryan Getzlaf .25 .60
2 Corey Perry .25 .60
3 Ryan Kesler .25 .60
4 Jakob Silfverberg .20 .50
5 Cam Fowler .20 .50
6 Sami Vatanen .15 .40
7 John Gibson .25 .60
8 Rickard Rakell .20 .50
9 Derek Stepan .20 .50
10 Oliver Ekman-Larsson .25 .60
11 Max Domi .25 .60
12 Christian Dvorak .20 .50
13 Jakob Chychrun .20 .50
14 Antti Raanta .25 .60
15 Alex Goligoski .20 .50
16 Dylan Strome .25 .60
17 David Backes .20 .50
18 Brad Marchand .30 .75
19 David Krejci .20 .50
20 Patrice Bergeron .30 .75
21 Torey Krug .25 .60
22 Tuukka Rask .25 .60
23 David Pastrnak .40 1.00
24 Zdeno Chara .25 .60
25 Jack Eichel .40 1.00
26 Rasmus Ristolainen .25 .60
27 Sam Reinhart .20 .50
28 Jason Pominville .20 .50
29 Kyle Okposo .20 .50
30 Ryan O'Reilly .25 .60
31 Evander Kane .25 .60
32 Robin Lehner .15 .40
33 Sean Monahan .25 .60
34 Dougie Hamilton .20 .50
35 Mike Smith .25 .60
36 Matthew Tkachuk .25 .60
37 Travis Hamonic .20 .50
38 Mark Giordano .20 .50
39 Mikael Backlund .15 .40
40 Johnny Gaudreau .40 1.00
41 Jeff Skinner .20 .50
42 Victor Rask .25 .60
43 Jordan Staal .25 .60
44 Justin Williams .20 .50
45 Noah Hanifin .25 .60
46 Sebastian Aho .25 .60
47 Justin Faulk .20 .50
48 Scott Darling .20 .50
49 Duncan Keith .25 .60
50 Patrick Sharp .20 .50
51 Jonathan Toews .50 1.25
52 Artem Anisimov .20 .50
53 Brent Seabrook .20 .50
54 Brandon Saad .25 .60
55 Corey Crawford .30 .75
56 Patrick Kane .50 1.25
57 Tyson Barrie .25 .60
58 Gabriel Landeskog .20 .50
59 Mikko Rantanen .25 .60
60 Nathan MacKinnon .50 1.25
61 Semyon Varlamov .25 .60
62 Erik Johnson .20 .50
63 Nail Yakupov .20 .50
64 Blake Comeau .15 .40
65 Artemi Panarin .25 .60
66 Zach Werenski .25 .60
67 Alexander Wennberg .20 .50
68 Nick Foligno .20 .50
69 Sergei Bobrovsky .25 .60
70 Cam Atkinson .25 .60
71 Seth Jones .20 .50
72 Boone Jenner .20 .50
73 Martin Hanzal .20 .50
74 Jason Spezza .25 .60
75 Jamie Benn .30 .75
76 Radek Faksa .20 .50
77 Alexander Radulov .25 .60
78 Ben Bishop .25 .60
79 Marc Methot .15 .40
80 Tyler Seguin .40 1.00
81 Anthony Mantha .25 .60
82 Andreas Athanasiou .25 .60
83 Dylan Larkin .25 .60
84 Trevor Daley .20 .50
85 Henrik Zetterberg .25 .60
86 Gustav Nyquist .25 .60
87 Tomas Tatar .25 .60
88 Jim Howard .15 .40
89 Leon Draisaitl .40 1.00
90 Connor McDavid 1.00 2.50
91 Ryan Nugent-Hopkins .25 .60
92 Milan Lucic .25 .60
93 Oscar Klefbom .20 .50
94 Andrej Sekera .15 .40
95 Patrick Maroon .20 .50
96 Cam Talbot .25 .60
97 Aleksander Barkov .25 .60
98 Jonathan Huberdeau .20 .50
99 Roberto Luongo .25 .60
100 Checklist Card .15 .40
101 Aaron Ekblad .25 .60
102 Vincent Trocheck .20 .50
103 Keith Yandle .15 .40
104 Jason Demers .15 .40
105 Radim Vrbata .15 .40
106 Anze Kopitar .40 1.00
107 Tanner Pearson .20 .50
108 Jeff Carter .25 .60
109 Jonathan Quick .40 1.00
110 Drew Doughty .25 .60
111 Dustin Brown .20 .50
112 Tyler Toffoli .20 .50
113 Alec Martinez .15 .40
114 Mikael Granlund .25 .60
115 Ryan Suter .15 .40
116 Eric Staal .30 .75
117 Charlie Coyle .20 .50
118 Nino Niederreiter .20 .50
119 Mikko Koivu .20 .50
120 Devan Dubnyk .25 .60
121 Zach Parise .25 .60
122 Max Pacioretty .25 .60
123 Shea Weber .20 .50
124 Jonathan Drouin .25 .60
125 Carey Price .75 2.00
126 Paul Byron .20 .50
127 Jeff Petry .15 .40
128 Alex Galchenyuk .30 .75
129 Karl Alzner .15 .40
130 P.K. Subban .25 .60
131 Filip Forsberg .30 .75
132 Roman Josi .25 .60
133 Pekka Rinne .30 .75
134 Ryan Johansen .25 .60
135 Viktor Arvidsson .20 .50
136 Ryan Ellis .20 .50
137 Mattias Ekholm .15 .40
138 Nick Bonino .20 .50
139 Cory Schneider .20 .50
140 Marcus Johansson .20 .50
141 Taylor Hall .50 1.25
142 Adam Henrique .20 .50
143 Andy Greene .15 .40
144 Kyle Palmieri .20 .50
145 Pavel Zacha .25 .60
146 Travis Zajac .15 .40
147 Josh Bailey .20 .50
148 Anders Lee .25 .60
149 Nick Leddy .15 .40
150 John Tavares .50 1.25
151 Jordan Eberle .25 .60
152 Andrew Ladd .25 .60
153 Thomas Greiss .20 .50
154 Brock Nelson .20 .50
155 Mats Zuccarello .25 .60
156 J.T. Miller .20 .50
157 Chris Kreider .25 .60
158 Ryan McDonagh .20 .50
159 Brady Skjei .20 .50
160 Henrik Lundqvist .40 1.00
161 Kevin Shattenkirk .25 .60
162 Rick Nash .25 .60
163 Mike Hoffman .20 .50
164 Dion Phaneuf .20 .50
165 Kyle Turris .25 .60
166 Mark Stone .25 .60
167 Jean-Gabriel Pageau .15 .40
168 Bobby Ryan .20 .50
169 Craig Anderson .25 .60
170 Erik Karlsson .30 .75
171 Wayne Simmonds .30 .75
172 Shayne Gostisbehere .25 .60
173 Ivan Provorov .25 .60
174 Jakub Voracek .25 .60
175 Sean Couturier .20 .50
176 Claude Giroux .25 .60
177 Travis Konecny .25 .60
178 Brian Elliott .20 .50
179 Evgeni Malkin .75 2.00
180 Sidney Crosby 1.00 2.50
181 Matt Murray .40 1.00
182 Jake Guentzel .30 .75
183 Phil Kessel .30 .75
184 Kris Letang .25 .60
185 Justin Schultz .25 .60
186 Patric Hornqvist .20 .50
187 Conor Sheary .25 .60
188 Joe Thornton .25 .60
189 Joe Pavelski .25 .60
190 Brent Burns .30 .75
191 Martin Jones .25 .60
192 Logan Couture .25 .60
193 Marc-Edouard Vlasic .15 .40
194 Tomas Hertl .25 .60
195 Joel Ward .20 .50
196 Colton Parayko .25 .60
197 Jake Allen .30 .75
198 Alexander Steen .25 .60
199 Jaden Schwartz .30 .75
200 Checklist Card .15 .40
201 Paul Stastny .25 .60
202 Vladimir Tarasenko .40 1.00
203 Alex Pietrangelo .20 .50
204 Robby Fabbri .25 .60
205 Alex Killorn .20 .50
206 Andrei Vasilevskiy .30 .75
207 Nikita Kucherov .40 1.00
208 Victor Hedman .30 .75
209 Ondrej Palat .25 .60
210 Steven Stamkos .50 1.25
211 Brayden Point .25 .60
212 Tyler Johnson .20 .50
213 Patrick Marleau .25 .60
214 William Nylander .40 1.00
215 Frederik Andersen .20 .50
216 Mitch Marner .40 1.00
217 Nazem Kadri .20 .50
218 Morgan Rielly .25 .60
219 James van Riemsdyk .25 .60
220 Auston Matthews 1.00 2.50
221 Troy Stecher .20 .50
222 Henrik Sedin .25 .60
223 Jacob Markstrom .15 .40
224 Bo Horvat .25 .60
225 Daniel Sedin .25 .60
226 Sven Baertschi .15 .40
227 Sam Gagner .20 .50
228 Loui Eriksson .20 .50
229 Jonathan Marchessault .25 .60
230 Marc-Andre Fleury .40 1.00
231 James Neal .20 .50
232 Reilly Smith .25 .60
233 Oscar Lindberg .20 .50
234 Shea Theodore .20 .50
235 David Perron .25 .60
236 Nate Schmidt .20 .50
237 T.J. Oshie .40 1.00
238 Nicklas Backstrom .40 1.00
239 Braden Holtby .40 1.00
240 Alexander Ovechkin 1.00 2.50
241 Evgeny Kuznetsov .40 1.00
242 John Carlson .30 .75
243 Matt Niskanen .20 .50
244 Andre Burakovsky .20 .50
245 Bryan Little .20 .50
246 Blake Wheeler .25 .60
247 Dustin Byfuglien .25 .60
248 Steve Mason .20 .50
249 Jacob Trouba .20 .50
250 Mark Scheifele .30 .75
251 Nikolaj Ehlers .25 .60
252 Patrik Laine .40 1.00
253 Alexander Nylander RC 1.25 3.00
254 Josh Ho-Sang RC 1.00 2.50
255 Adrian Kempe RC 1.00 2.50
256 Ivan Barbashev RC .75 2.00
257 Christian Fischer RC 1.00 2.50
258 Tyson Jost RC 1.50 4.00
259 Colin White RC .75 2.00
260 Jon Gillies RC .75 2.00
261 J.T. Compher RC 1.00 2.50
262 Mike Vecchione RC .60 1.50
263 Nikita Scherbak RC 1.50 4.00
264 Riley Barber RC .60 1.50
265 Jonny Brodzinski RC .75 2.00
266 Jordan Schmaltz RC 1.00 2.50
267 Vladislav Kamenev RC 1.25 3.00
268 Jakob Forsbacka-Karlsson RC .75 2.00
269 Gabriel Carlsson RC .60 1.50
270 Brock Boeser RC 4.00 10.00
271 Denis Gurianov RC .75 2.00
272 Alex Tuch RC 2.00 5.00
273 Jack Roslovic RC 1.00 2.50
274 Charlie McAvoy RC 2.50 6.00
275 Clayton Keller RC 2.00 5.00
276 Nicolas Kerdiles RC .75 2.00
277 Eric Comrie RC .60 1.50
278 Marcus Sorensen RC .60 1.50
279 Jake Dotchin RC .60 1.50
280 Evgeny Svechnikov RC 1.50 4.00
281 Carter Rowney RC .60 1.50
282 Jesper Bratt RC 1.25 3.00
283 Will Butcher RC 1.00 2.50
284 Nathan Walker RC .75 2.00
285 Nolan Patrick RC 1.50 4.00
286 Kailer Yamamoto RC 2.00 5.00
287 Anders Bjork RC 1.00 2.50
288 Alex DeBrincat RC 2.00 5.00
289 Owen Tippett RC 1.50 4.00
290 Nico Hischier RC 2.50 6.00
291 Filip Chytil RC .75 2.00
292 Martin Necas RC .75 2.00
293 Jake DeBrusk RC 1.25 3.00
294 Victor Mete RC .75 2.00
295 Pierre-Luc Dubois RC 1.50 4.00
296 Calle Rosen RC .75 2.00
297 Logan Brown RC .75 2.00
298 Luke Kunin RC .75 2.00
299 Vadim Shipachyov RC 2.50 6.00
300 Checklist Card RC .15 .40

2017-18 Parkhurst Blow The Horn

BH1 Connor McDavid 2.00 5.00
BH2 Evgeni Malkin 1.50 4.00
BH3 Patrick Kane 1.00 2.50
BH4 Vladimir Tarasenko .75 2.00
BH5 Alexander Ovechkin 2.00 5.00
BH6 Auston Matthews 2.00 5.00
BH7 Patrik Laine .75 2.00
BH8 Nikita Kucherov .75 2.00
BH9 Brad Marchand .60 1.50
SH10 Sidney Crosby 2.00 5.00

2017-18 Parkhurst East Vs. West

E1 Sidney Crosby 2.50 6.00
E2 Auston Matthews 2.50 6.00
E3 Victor Hedman .75 2.00
E4 Erik Karlsson .75 2.00
E5 Alexander Ovechkin 2.50 6.00
E6 Brad Marchand .75 2.00
E7 Evgeni Malkin 2.00 5.00
E8 Carey Price 2.00 5.00
W1 Connor McDavid 2.50 6.00
W2 Patrick Kane 1.25 3.00
W3 Brent Burns .75 2.00
W4 P.K. Subban .60 1.50
W5 Patrik Laine 1.00 2.50
W6 Drew Doughty .60 1.50
W7 Jonathan Toews 1.25 3.00
W8 Vladimir Tarasenko 1.00 2.50

2017-18 Parkhurst Parkhurst International

PI1 Sidney Crosby 1.50 4.00
PI2 Connor McDavid 1.50 4.00
PI3 Wayne Gretzky 2.00 5.00
PI4 Patrick Kane .75 2.00
PI5 Auston Matthews 1.50 4.00
PI6 Mike Modano .60 1.50
PI7 Evgeni Malkin 1.25 3.00
PI8 Alexander Ovechkin 1.50 4.00
PI9 Pavel Bure .40 1.00
PI10 Erik Karlsson .50 1.25
PI11 Henrik Zetterberg .40 1.00
PI12 Nicklas Lidstrom .30 .75
PI13 Mikael Granlund .40 1.00
PI14 Pekka Rinne .50 1.25
PI15 Teemu Selanne .50 1.25
PI16 Jakub Voracek .40 1.00
PI17 David Krejci .30 .75
PI18 Dominik Hasek .40 1.00
PI19 Leon Draisaitl .60 1.50
PI20 Thomas Greiss .30 .75
PI21 Dennis Seidenberg .25 .60
PI22 Roman Josi .40 1.00
PI23 Nino Niederreiter .30 .75
PI24 Mark Streit .30 .75

2017-18 Parkhurst Prominent Prospects

*GREEN/399: .75X TO 2X BASIC INSERTS
STATED PRINT RUN 399 SER.#'d SETS
*RED/199: 1.25X TO 3X BASIC INSERTS
STATED PRINT RUN 199 SER.#'d SETS
*GOLD/99: 2X TO 5X BASIC INSERTS
STATED PRINT RUN 99 SER.#'d SETS
PP1 Brock Boeser 3.00 8.00
PP2 Nikita Scherbak 1.25 3.00
PP3 Colin White .60 1.50
PP4 Christian Fischer .75 2.00
PP5 Josh Ho-Sang .75 2.00
PP6 Alexander Nylander 1.00 2.50
PP7 Evgeny Svechnikov 1.25 3.00
PP8 Jack Roslovic .75 2.00
PP9 Ivan Barbashev .60 1.50
PP10 Clayton Keller 1.50 4.00
PP11 Tyson Jost 1.25 3.00
PP12 Jon Gillies .60 1.50
PP13 Adrian Kempe .75 2.00
PP14 Alex Tuch 1.50 4.00
PP15 Charlie McAvoy 2.00 5.00
PP16 Nico Hischier 2.00 5.00
PP17 Alex DeBrincat 1.50 4.00
PP18 Kailer Yamamoto 1.50 4.00
PP19 Owen Tippett 1.25 3.00
PP20 Pierre-Luc Dubois 1.25 3.00
PP21 Filip Chytil .60 1.50
PP22 Logan Brown .60 1.50
PP23 Vadim Shipachyov 2.00 5.00
PP24 Will Butcher .75 2.00
PP25 Nolan Patrick 1.25 3.00

2017-18 Parkhurst Seeing Stars

*RED: .75X TO 2X BASIC INSERTS
OVERALL STATED ODDS 1:3
*BLUE: 1.5X TO 4X BASIC INSERTS
OVERALL STATED ODDS 1:10
SS1 Sidney Crosby 1.50 4.00
SS2 Patrick Kane .75 2.00
SS3 Henrik Zetterberg .40 1.00
SS4 Brad Marchand .50 1.25
SS5 Auston Matthews 1.50 4.00
SS6 Carey Price 1.25 3.00
SS7 Henrik Lundqvist .60 1.50
SS8 Evgeni Malkin 1.25 3.00
SS9 Alexander Ovechkin 1.50 4.00
SS10 Connor McDavid 1.50 4.00

1971-72 Penguins Postcards

This 22-card set (measuring approximately 3 1/2" by 5 1/2") features full-bleed posed action color player photos. The cards originally came bound together in a flip book, but had perforations at the card top to allow them to be removed. The backs carry the player's name and biography in blue print on a white background. Only the Red Kelly card has a career summary on its back. The cards are unnumbered and checklisted below in alphabetical order. The set is dated by the inclusion of Roy Edwards, whose only season with the Penguins was 1971-72.

COMPLETE SET (22) 20.00 40.00
1 Syl Apps 1.25 2.50
2 Les Binkley 1.25 2.50
3 Dave Burrows 1.00 2.00
4 Darryl Edestrand .75 1.50
5 Roy Edwards 1.00 2.00
6 Val Fonteyne .75 1.50
7 Nick Harbaruk .75 1.50
8 Bryan Hextall 2.00 4.00
9 Sheldon Kannegiesser .75 1.50
10 Red Kelly CO 2.00 4.00
11 Bob Leiter .75 1.50
12 Keith McCreary .75 1.50
13 Joe Noris .75 1.50
14 Greg Polis .75 1.50
15 Jean Pronovost 2.00 4.00
16 Rene Robert 1.25 2.50
17 Jim Rutherford 1.25 2.50
18 Ken Schinkel .75 1.50
19 Ron Schock 1.00 2.00
20 Bryan Watson 1.00 2.00
21 Bob Woytowich .75 1.50
22 Title Card .75 1.50

1974-75 Penguins Postcards

This 22-card set features full-bleed black and white action pictures by photographer Paul Salva. The player's autograph is inscribed across the bottom of the picture. The cards are in the postcard format and measure approximately 3 1/2" by 5 1/2". The horizontal backs are blank. The cards are unnumbered and checklisted below in alphabetical order. The set is dated by the fact that Nelson Debenedet was only with the Penguins during the 1974-75 season. Pierre Larouche appears in this set prior to his Rookie Card appearance.

COMPLETE SET (22) 15.00 30.00
1 Syl Apps 1.25 2.50
2 Chuck Arnason .75 1.50
3 Dave Burrows 1.00 2.00
4 Colin Campbell 1.25 2.50
5 Nelson Debenedet .75 1.50
6 Steve Durbano .75 1.50
7 Vic Hadfield 1.00 2.00
8 Gary Inness 1.00 2.00
9 Bob(B.J.) Johnson .75 1.50
10 Rick Kehoe 1.25 2.50
11 Bob Kelly .75 1.50
12 Jean-Guy Lagace .75 1.50
13 Ron Lalonde .75 1.50
14 Pierre Larouche 2.50 5.00
15 Lowell MacDonald 1.00 2.00
16 Dennis Owchar .75 1.50
17 Bob Paradise .75 1.50
18 Kelly Pratt .75 1.50
19 Jean Pronovost 1.00 2.00
20 Ron Schock 1.00 2.00
21 Ron Stackhouse 1.00 2.00
22 Barry Williams .75 1.50

1977-78 Penguins Puck Bucks

This 18-card set of Pittsburgh Penguins was sponsored by McDonald's restaurants, whose company logo appears at the top of the card face. The cards measure approximately 1 15/16" by 3 1/2" and are perforated so that the bottom tab (measuring 1 15/16" by 1") may be removed. The front of the top portion features a color head shot of the player, with a white border on a mustard-colored background. The back of the top portion has "Hockey Talk," in which a hockey term is explained. The front side of the tab portion shows a hockey puck on an orange background. Its back states that the "puck bucks" are coupons worth 1.00 toward the purchase of any 7.50 Penguins game ticket. These coupons had to be redeemed no later than December 31, 1977.

COMPLETE SET (18) 12.50 25.00
1 Denis Herron 1.50 3.00
3 Ron Stackhouse 1.00 2.00
4 Dave Burrows .75 1.50
6 Colin Campbell 1.25 2.50
7 Russ Anderson .75 1.50
9 Blair Chapman .75 1.50
10 Pierre Larouche 1.50 3.00
12 Greg Malone 1.00 2.00
14 Wayne Bianchin .75 1.50
17 Rick Kehoe 1.50 3.00
18 Lowell MacDonald 1.00 2.00
19 Jean Pronovost 1.25 2.50
23 Jim Hamilton .75 1.50
25 Dennis Owchar .75 1.50
26 Syl Apps 1.00 2.00
27 Mike Corrigan .75 1.50
29 Dunc Wilson 1.00 2.00
NNO Johnny Wilson CO .50 1.00

1983-84 Penguins Coke

This 19-card set of the Pittsburgh Penguins measures approximately 5" by 7". The fronts feature black-and-white player portraits framed in white with the player's name, team name, team logo, and the words "Coke is it!" printed in black in the wide white bottom border. The backs are blank. The cards are unnumbered and checklisted below in alphabetical order. The card of Marty McSorley appears four years before his rookie card.

COMPLETE SET (19) 10.00 25.00
1 Pat Boutette .60 1.50
2 Andy Brickley .40 1.00
3 Mike Bullard .75 2.00
4 Ted Bulley .40 1.00
5 Rod Buskas .40 1.00
6 Randy Carlyle .75 2.00
7 Michel Dion .75 2.00
8 Bob Errey .75 2.00
9 Ron Flockhart .60 1.50
10 Steve Gatzos .40 1.00
11 Jim Hamilton .40 1.00
12 Dave Hannan .40 1.00
13 Denis Herron 1.00 2.50
14 Troy Loney .40 1.00
15 Bryan Maxwell .40 1.00
16 Marty McSorley 2.00 5.00
17 Norm Schmidt .40 1.00
18 Mark Taylor .40 1.00
19 Greg Tebbutt .40 1.00

1983-84 Penguins Heinz Photos

This Pittsburgh Penguins "Photo Pak" was sponsored by Heinz. The cards are unnumbered and checklisted below in alphabetical order. They were giveaways at Pittsburgh Penguins home games. Each photo measures approximately 6" by 9" and they were produced on one large folded sheet.

COMPLETE SET (22) 10.00 25.00
1 Paul Baxter .60 1.50
2 Pat Boutette .60 1.50
3 Randy Boyd .40 1.00
4 Mike Bullard .75 2.00
5 Randy Carlyle .75 2.00
6 Marc Chorney .40 1.00
7 Michel Dion .75 2.00
8 Bill Gardner .40 1.00
9 Pat Graham .40 1.00
10 Anders Hakansson .40 1.00
11 Dave Hannan .40 1.00
12 Denis Herron 1.00 2.50
13 Greg Hotham .40 1.00
14 Stan Jonathan .60 1.50
15 Rick Kehoe 1.00 2.50
16 Peter Lee .75 2.00
17 Greg Malone .60 1.50
18 Kevin McClelland .40 1.00
19 Ron Meighan .40 1.00
20 Doug Shedden .40 1.00
21 Andre St. Laurent .40 1.00
22 Rich Sutter .60 1.50

1984-85 Penguins Heinz Photos

This Pittsburgh Penguins "Photo Pak" was sponsored by Heinz. The cards are unnumbered and checklisted below in alphabetical order. They were giveaways at Pittsburgh Penguins home games. Each photo measures approximately 6" by 9" and they were produced on one large folded sheet.

COMPLETE SET (22) 10.00 25.00
1 Pat Boutette .60 1.50
2 Andy Brickley .40 1.00
3 Mike Bullard .75 2.00
4 Rod Buskas .40 1.00
5 Randy Carlyle .75 2.00
6 Michel Dion .75 2.00
7 Bob Errey .60 1.50
8 Ron Flockhart .40 1.00
9 Greg Fox .40 1.00
10 Steve Gatzos .40 1.00
11 Denis Herron 1.00 2.50
12 Greg Hotham .40 1.00
13 Rick Kehoe .75 2.00
14 Bryan Maxwell .60 1.50
15 Marty McSorley 2.00 5.00
16 Tom O'Regan .40 1.00
17 Gary Rissling .40 1.00
18 Roberto Romano .60 1.50
19 Tom Roulston .40 1.00
20 Rocky Saganiuk .40 1.00
21 Doug Shedden .60 1.50
22 Mark Taylor .40 1.00

1986-87 Penguins Kodak

The 1986-87 Pittsburgh Penguins Team Photo Album was sponsored by Kodak and commemorates the team's 20 years in the NHL. It consists of three large sheets, each measuring approximately 11" by 8 1/4", joined together to form one continuous sheet. The first panel has a team photo of the 1967 Pittsburgh Penguins. The second panel presents three rows of five cards each. The third panel presents two rows of five cards, with five Kodak coupons completing the left over portion of the panel. After perforation, the cards measure approximately 2 3/16" by 2 1/2". They feature color posed photos bordered in yellow, with player information below the picture. A Kodak film box serving as a logo completes the card face. The back has biographical and statistical information in a horizontal format. We have checklisted the names below in alphabetical order, with the uniform number to the right of the name.

COMPLETE SET (26) 20.00 50.00
1 Bob Berry CO .20 .50
2 Mike Blaisdell 26 .40 1.00
3 Doug Bodger 3 .40 1.00
4 Rod Buskas 7 .30 .75
5 John Chabot 9 .30 .75
6 Randy Cunneyworth 15 .30 .75
7 Ron Duguay 10 .40 1.00
8 Bob Errey 12 .40 1.00
9 Dan Frawley 28 .30 .75
10 Dave Hannan 32 .30 .75
11 Randy Hillier 23 .30 .75
12 Jim Johnson 6 .30 .75
13 Kevin Lavallee 16 .30 .75
14 Mario Lemieux 66 12.00 30.00
15 Willy Lindstrom 19 .30 .75
16 Moe Mantha 20 .30 .75
17 Gilles Meloche 27 .40 1.00
18 Dan Quinn 14 .40 1.00
19 Jim Roberts CO .20 .50
20 Roberto Romano 30 .40 1.00
21 Terry Ruskowski 8 .40 1.00
22 Norm Schmidt 25 .30 .75
23 Craig Simpson 18 .60 1.50
24 Ville Siren 5 .30 .75
25 Warren Young 35 .40 1.00
NNO Team Photo .75 2.00

1987-88 Penguins Masks

These masks were issued by KDKA and Eagle Food Stores. Mask fronts show top of players head, and backs feature name, stats, and sponsors logos. These masks are unnumbered and checklisted below in alphabetical order.

COMPLETE SET (10) 8.00 20.00
1 Doug Bodger .40 1.00
2 Randy Cunneyworth .40 1.00
3 Bob Errey .40 1.00
4 Dan Frawley .40 1.00
5 Jim Johnson .40 1.00
6 Mario Lemieux 4.00 10.00
7 Gilles Meloche .75 2.00
8 Dan Quinn .40 1.00
9 Craig Simpson .75 2.00
10 Ville Siren .40 1.00

1987-88 Penguins Kodak

The 1987-88 Pittsburgh Penguins Team Photo Album was sponsored by Kodak. It consists of three large sheets, each measuring approximately 11" by 8 1/4", joined together to form one continuous sheet. The first panel has a team photo, with the players' names listed according to rows below the picture. The second panel presents three rows of five cards each. The third panel presents two rows of five cards, with five Kodak coupons completing the left over portion of the panel. After perforation, the cards measure approximately 2 3/16" by 2 1/2". A Kodak film box serves as a logo in the upper right hand corner of the card face. The front features a color head shot inside a thin black border. The picture is set on a Kodak "yellow" background, with white stripes traversing the top of the card. The player's name, number, and position are printed in black lettering below the picture. The back has biographical information and career statistics in a horizontal format. We have checklisted the cards below in alphabetical order, with the player's number to the right of his name.

COMPLETE SET (26) 14.00 35.00
1 Doug Bodger 3 .30 .75
2 Rob Brown 44 .40 1.00

3 Rod Buskas 7 .30 .75
4 Jock Callander 36 .30 .75
5 Paul Coffey 77 .75 2.00
6 Randy Cunneyworth 15 .30 .75
7 Chris Dahlquist 4 .30 .75
8 Bob Errey 12 .30 .75
9 Dan Frawley 28 .30 .75
10 Steve Guenette 30 .40 1.00
11 Randy Hillier 23 .30 .75
12 Dave Hunter 20 .30 .75
13 Jim Johnson 6 .30 .75
14 Mark Kachowski 26 .30 .75
15 Chris Kontos 14 .30 .75
16 Mario Lemieux 66 6.00 15.00
17 Troy Loney 24 .30 .75
18 Dwight Mathiasen 34 .30 .75
19 Dave McLlwain 19 .30 .75
20 Gilles Meloche 27 .40 1.00
21 Dan Quinn 10 .40 1.00
22 Pat Riggin 1 .40 1.00
23 Charlie Simmer 16 .40 1.00
24 Ville Siren 5 .30 .75
25 Wayne Van Dorp .30 .75
NNO Large Team Photo 1.50 4.00

1989-90 Penguins Coke/Elby's

This set measures approximately 4" by 6" and features color action player photos bordered in white with player information at the top and sponsor logos in the bottom margin. The backs are blank except for a coupon for free burger and fries at participating Elby's Big Boy restaurants. The cards are unnumbered and checklisted below in alphabetical order.

COMPLETE SET (5) 4.80 12.00
1 Phil Bourque .20 .50
2 Rob Brown .30 .75
3 Mario Lemieux 4.00 10.00
4 Kevin Stevens .75 2.00
5 Zarley Zalapski .30 .75

1989-90 Penguins Foodland

This 15-card set was sponsored by Foodland in conjunction with the Pittsburgh Penguins and the Crime Prevention Officers of Western Pennsylvania. The Foodland company logo appears on the top and back of each card. The cards measure approximately 2 9/16" by 4 1/8" and could be collected from police officers. The front features a color action photo with a thin black border on white card stock. The player information below the picture is sandwiched between the Penguin and the Crime Dog McGruff logos. The back is dated and presents a Penguins tip and a safety tip (both illustrated with cartoons) in a horizontal format. There were two late issue cards distributed after trades. They are rather scarce and not typically considered part of the complete set.

COMPLETE SET (15) 8.00 20.00
1 Rob Brown .30 .75
2 Jim Johnson .20 .50
3 Zarley Zalapski .30 .75
4 Paul Coffey .75 2.00
5 Phil Bourque .20 .50
6A Dan Quinn .30 .75
6B Gilbert Delorme SP .75 2.00
7 Kevin Stevens .75 2.00
8 Bob Errey .20 .50
9 John Cullen .30 .75
10 Mario Lemieux 4.00 10.00
11 Randy Hillier .20 .50
12 Jay Caufield .20 .50
13A Andrew McBain .20 .50
13B Troy Loney SP .75 2.00
14 Wendell Young .30 .75
15 Tom Barrasso .40 1.00

1990-91 Penguins Foodland

This 15-card set was sponsored by Foodland in conjunction with the Pittsburgh Penguins and the Crime Prevention Officers of Western Pennsylvania. The Foodland company logo appears at the bottom of the card front and the top of the horizontally oriented back. The cards measure approximately 2 11/16" by 4 1/8" and could be collected from police officers. The front features a color action photo with a thin black border surrounded by wide yellow margins on three sides. The team name is printed in white block lettering, running the length of the card on the left side of the picture. The back presents a Penguins tip and a safety tip (both illustrated with cartoons). The set features the appearance of three Penguins, Jaromir Jagr, Mark Recchi, and Kevin Stevens, in their Rookie Card year.

COMPLETE SET (15) 12.00 30.00
1 Phil Bourque 29 .08 .25
2 Paul Coffey 77 .40 1.00
3 Randy Hillier 23 .08 .25
4 Barry Pederson 10 .15 .40
5 Tom Barrasso 35 .30 .75
6 Mark Recchi 8 .75 2.00
7 Bob Johnson CO .75 2.00
8 Joe Mullen 7 .30 .75
9 Kevin Stevens 25 .60 1.50
10 John Cullen 11 .15 .40
11 Jaromir Jagr 68 10.00 25.00
12 Zarley Zalapski 33 .15 .40
13 Mario Lemieux 66 3.00 8.00
14 Tony Tanti 9 .08 .25
15 Bryan Trottier 19 .30 .75

1991-92 Penguins Coke/Elby's

This 24-card set was sponsored by Cola-Cola in conjunction with Elby's Big Boy restaurants. The cards measure approximately 4" by 6" and are printed on thin card stock. The headline "1990-91 Stanley Cup Champions" adorns the top of each front. Immediately below appears the uniform number, player's name, and a twenty-fifth anniversary team logo. The color action player photos are bordered in white, with the two sponsor logos appearing in the bottom white border. The backs are blank. The cards are skip-numbered by uniform number and checklisted below accordingly.

COMPLETE SET (24) 10.00 25.00
1 Wendell Young .30 .75
2 Jim Paek .20 .50
3 Grant Jennings .20 .50
5 Ulf Samuelsson .40 1.00
7 Joe Mullen .40 1.00
8 Mark Recchi .75 2.00
10 Ron Francis 1.00 2.50
16 Jay Caufield .20 .50
18 Ken Priestlay .20 .50
19 Bryan Trottier .40 1.00
20 Jamie Leach .20 .50
22 Paul Stanton .20 .50
24 Troy Loney .20 .50
25 Kevin Stevens .40 1.00
28 Gord Roberts .20 .50
29 Phil Bourque .20 .50
32 Peter Taglianetti .20 .50
40 Frank Pietrangelo .30 .75
43 Jeff Daniels .20 .50
55 Larry Murphy .40 1.00
66 Mario Lemieux 2.50 6.00
68 Jaromir Jagr 3.00 8.00
NNO Scotty Bowman CO .40 1.00

1991-92 Penguins Foodland

This 15-card standard-size set was sponsored by Foodland in conjunction with the Pittsburgh Penguins and the Crime Prevention Officers of Western Pennsylvania. The Foodland logo and McGruff the Crime Dog appear at the bottom of the card face, while a 25th year anniversary emblem appears at the top center. The fronts feature color action player photos on an orangish-yellow card face. The player's name, uniform number, and his position appear in the top silver stripe; the words "1991 Stanley Cup Champions" appears in another silver stripe beneath the picture. The horizontally oriented backs have a "Penguins Tip" and a "Safety Tip," each of which is illustrated by a cartoon.

COMPLETE SET (15) 8.00 20.00
1 Jim Paek .20 .50
2 Ulf Samuelsson .30 .75
3 Ron Francis .75 2.00
4 Mario Lemieux 3.00 8.00
5 Rick Tocchet .40 1.00
6 Joe Mullen .40 1.00
7 Troy Loney .20 .50
8 Kevin Stevens .30 .75
9 Tom Barrasso .40 1.00
10 Larry Murphy .30 .75
11 Jaromir Jagr 3.00 8.00
12 Bryan Trottier .40 1.00
13 Paul Stanton .20 .50
14 Peter Taglianetti .20 .50
15 Phil Bourque .20 .50

1991-92 Penguins Foodland Coupon Stickers

This set of twelve stickers is the result of a unique cross-promotion with Topps and the Foodland stores of Pittsburgh. The stickers, issued in a 3-sticker sheet over a four week period, mimic the 1991-92 Topps card of a Penguin player on the front, with a coupon for Foodland on the peel-off backs. Most feature the player's regular card front; exceptions are Jaromir Jagr (Super Rookie), Mario Lemieux (Award Winner) and Kevin Stevens (All-Star). The stickers are unnumbered, but are listed below in issue of order, top to bottom, per week.

COMPLETE SET (12) 6.00 15.00
1 Bryan Trottier .30 .75
2 Joe Mullen .30 .75
3 Larry Murphy .30 .75
4 Tom Barrasso .30 .75
5 Ron Francis .60 1.50
6 Ulf Samuelsson .30 .75
7 Jaromir Jagr 2.50 6.00
8 Mario Lemieux 2.50 6.00
9 Kevin Stevens .30 .75
10 Mark Recchi .40 1.00
11 Paul Coffey .60 1.50
12 Frank Pietrangelo .30 .75

1992-93 Penguins Coke/Clark

This 26-card set was sponsored by Cola-Cola and Clark. These cards followed the same concept as Coke/Elby's sets of the previous years, i.e., large autograph cards issued to the players for use in personal appearances. The cards measure approximately 4" by 6" and were printed on thin card stock. The backs are blank. The cards are unnumbered and checklisted below in alphabetical order.

COMPLETE SET (26) 10.00 25.00
1 Tom Barrasso .40 1.00
2 Scotty Bowman CO .60 1.50
3 Jay Caufield .20 .50
4 Jeff Daniels .20 .50
5 Bob Errey .20 .50
6 Bryan Fogarty .20 .50
7 Ron Francis .75 2.00
8 Jaromir Jagr 2.50 6.00
9 Grant Jennings .20 .50
10 Mario Lemieux 2.50 6.00
11 Troy Loney .20 .50
12 Shawn McEachern .40 1.00
13 Joe Mullen .40 1.00
14 Larry Murphy .40 1.00
15 Mike Needham .20 .50
16 Jim Paek .20 .50
17 Kjell Samuelsson .20 .50
18 Ulf Samuelsson .30 .75
19 Paul Stanton .20 .50
20 Mike Stapleton .20 .50
21 Kevin Stevens .30 .75
22 Martin Straka .40 1.00
23 Dave Tippett .20 .50
24 Rick Tocchet .50 1.25
25 Ken Wregget .50 1.25
26 Penguins Mascot .08 .25

1992-93 Penguins Foodland

This 18-card standard-size set was sponsored by Foodland in conjunction with the Pittsburgh Penguins and the Crime Prevention Officers of Western Pennsylvania. The cards feature color action player photos with orange-yellow borders on a black card face. The player's name is printed in an orange-yellow stripe below the photo. The words "1991 and 1992 Stanley Cup Champions" are on an orange-yellow bar that overlaps the top of the picture. The Foodland logo and McGruff the Crime Dog appear at the bottom. The horizontal backs have a "Penguins Tip" and a "Safety Tip," each illustrated with a cartoon.

COMPLETE SET (18) 6.00 15.00
1 Mario Lemieux 2.00 5.00
2 Bob Errey .20 .50
3 Jaromir Jagr 1.25 3.00
4 Rick Tocchet .40 1.00
5 Tom Barrasso .40 1.00
6 Joe Mullen .30 .75
7 Ron Francis .75 2.00
8 Troy Loney .20 .50
9 Shawn McEachern .20 .50
10 Larry Murphy .30 .75
11 Jim Paek .20 .50
12 Ulf Samuelsson .20 .50
13 Paul Stanton .20 .50
14 Kjell Samuelsson .20 .50
15 Kevin Stevens .30 .75
16 Dave Tippett .20 .50
17 Martin Straka .40 1.00
18 Penguins Mascot .08 .25

1992-93 Penguins Foodland Coupon Stickers

Sponsored by Foodland and issued in four three-sticker vertical strips, this 12-sticker set features white-bordered color player action photos, with the peel-away backs doubling as manufacturer coupons for different products. Each sticker measures the standard size. The player's name and uniform number appear in a yellow bar under the photo and the words "Back to Back Champs" are printed in a bar alongside the left. The team logo also appears on the front. The strips are numbered as Week 1-4; the stickers themselves are unnumbered. The players are listed below in alphabetical order; W1 to W4 indicates the week the stickers were issued.

COMPLETE SET (12) 6.00 15.00
1 Tom Barrasso W2 .40 1.00
2 Ron Francis W1 .60 1.50
3 Jaromir Jagr W4 2.00 5.00
4 Mario Lemieux W2 2.50 6.00
5 Troy Loney W2 .20 .50
6 Shawn McEachern W4 .20 .50
7 Joe Mullen W3 .30 .75
8 Larry Murphy W4 .30 .75
9 Jim Paek W1 .20 .50
10 Ulf Samuelsson W3 .20 .50
11 Kevin Stevens W1 .30 .75
12 Rick Tocchet W3 .40 1.00

1993-94 Penguins Foodland

Sponsored by Foodland, this 25-card standard-size set features the 1993-94 Pittsburgh Penguins. The fronts have color action player photos with black borders on gray backgrounds. The team name appears in the top part of the card, while the player's name, number and position are printed under the photo. The sponsor's logo on the bottom rounds out the front. The horizontal backs have a "Penguin Tip" and a "Safety Tip," each illustrated with a cartoon.

COMPLETE SET (25) 6.00 15.00
1 Mario Lemieux 1.50 4.00
2 Grant Jennings .15 .40
3 Ulf Samuelsson .20 .50
4 Rick Tocchet .30 .75
5 Marty McSorley .30 .75
6 Rick Kehoe ACO .08 .25
7 Doug Brown .15 .40
8 Martin Straka .30 .75
9 Jim Paek .15 .40
10 Ken Wregget .30 .75
11 Jeff Daniels .15 .40
12 Bryan Trottier .20 .50
13 Larry Murphy .20 .50
14 Ron Francis .40 1.00
15 Mike Needham .15 .40
16 Mike Ramsey .15 .40
17 Kevin Stevens .20 .50
18 Kjell Samuelsson .15 .40
19 Ed Johnston .08 .25
20 Markus Naslund .20 .50
21 Mike Stapleton .15 .40
22 Peter Taglianetti .15 .40
23 Jaromir Jagr .75 2.00
24 Tom Barrasso .20 .50
25 Joe Mullen .20 .50

1994-95 Penguins Foodland

Sponsored by Foodland, this 25-card standard-size set features the 1994-1995 Pittsburgh Penguins. The fronts have color action player photos with gray borders on marbleized gray backgrounds. The team name across the top part of the card, while the player's name, number, position, and the team logo are printed under the picture. The horizontal backs carry a "Penguin Tip" and a "Safety Tip", each illustrated with a cartoon.

COMPLETE SET (25) 4.80 12.00
1 Grant Jennings .10 .30
2 Greg Hawgood .10 .30
3 Shawn McEachern .20 .50
4 Len Barrie .10 .30
5 Ulf Samuelsson .20 .50
6 Joe Mullen .20 .50
7 John Cullen .10 .30
8 Mike Hudson .10 .30
9 Ron Francis .40 1.00
10 Tomas Sandstrom .20 .50
11 Eddie Johnston CO .08 .25
12 Chris Tamer .10 .30
13 Francois Leroux .10 .30
14 Luc Robitaille .40 1.00
15 Markus Naslund .20 .50
16 Ken Wregget .20 .50
17 Chris Joseph .10 .30
18 Peter Taglianetti .10 .30
19 Kevin Stevens .20 .50
20 Jim McKenzie .10 .30
21 Kjell Samuelsson .10 .30
22 Tom Barrasso .20 .50
23 Jaromir Jagr 1.50 4.00
24 Larry Murphy .20 .50
25 Martin Straka .10 .30

1995-96 Penguins Foodland

This 25-card set maintains the string of issues released by Foodland, a Pittsburgh-area grocery chain, to honor the hometown Penguins. The cards feature action player photos surrounded by an icy blue border on the front. The backs have two Penguin tips, and the card number. Card number 24 erroneously pictures Ian Moran instead of Bryan Smolinski. The error is not believed to have been corrected.

COMPLETE SET (25) 4.00 10.00
1 Ron Francis .40 1.00
2 Glen Murray .08 .25
3 Chris Wells .08 .25
4 Markus Naslund .10 .30
5 Jaromir Jagr 1.25 3.00
6 Francois Leroux .08 .25
7 Richard Park .08 .25
8 Norm Maciver .08 .25
9 Ken Wregget .20 .50
10 Tom Barrasso .20 .50
11 Rick Kehoe .08 .25
12 Sergei Zubov .20 .50
13 Joe Dziedzic .08 .25
14 Ed Patterson .08 .25
15 Tomas Sandstrom .10 .30
16 Dave Roche .08 .25
17 Petr Nedved .20 .50
18 Chris Tamer .08 .25
19 Chris Joseph .08 .25
20 Ian Moran .08 .25
21 Iceburgh (Mascot) .02 .10
22 Ed Johnston CO .08 .25
23 Mario Lemieux 1.50 4.00
24 Bryan Smolinski .10 .30
25 Dmitri Mironov .10 .30

1996-97 Penguins Tribune-Review

These oversized 5" x 7" thick stock cards were distributed as inserts in the Penguins game programs to honor the club's two Cup championships of the early '90s. As issued, the cards were folded in half, with the first two "pages" explaining the promotion, the third page actually containing the card/photo, and the fourth page offering biographical info and stats from one of the two seasons.

COMPLETE SET (8) 12.00 30.00
1 Ron Francis 1.50 4.00
2 Joe Mullen .75 2.00
3 Ulf Samuelsson .75 2.00
4 Bryan Trottier 1.25 3.00
5 Tom Barrasso .75 2.00
6 Kevin Stevens 1.25 3.00
7 Jaromir Jagr 3.00 8.00
8 Mario Lemieux 4.00 10.00

1997-98 Penguins USPS Lineup Cards

These oversized issues were inserted in Penguins programs and were sponsored by the post office. The front featured a glossy player photo, while the back listed that night's lineups. This obviously is not a complete listing. Anyone who can help fill it in is encouraged to write hockeymag@beckett.com.

COMPLETE SET (?) 3.00 8.00
NNO Darius Kasparaitis .75 2.00
NNO Jaromir Jagr 2.00 5.00
NNO Ron Francis .75 2.00

1980-81 Pepsi-Cola Caps

This set of 140 bottle caps features 20 players from each of the seven Canadian hockey teams. The bottle caps are written in French and English. There are two sizes of caps depending on whether the cap was from a small or large bottle. The top of the cap displays the Pepsi logo in the familiar red, white, and blue. The sides of the cap were done in blue and white lettering on a pink background. On the inside of the cap is a "black and aluminum" head shot of the player, with his name and the city (from which the team hails) below. We have checklisted the caps in alphabetical order of the teams as follows: Calgary Flames (1-20), Edmonton Oilers (21-40), Montreal Canadiens (41-60), Quebec Nordiques (61-80), Toronto Maple Leafs (81-100), Vancouver Canucks (101-120), and Winnipeg Jets (121-140). Also the players' names have been alphabetized within their teams. Also available through a mail-in offer -- in either English or French -- was a white plastic circular display plaque (approximately 24" by 24") for the caps. The French version sometimes sells for a slight premium. There also are reports that two different size variations exist: a 10 ounce and a 26 ounce size. There does not appear to be a premium on either size cap at this time.

COMPLETE SET (140) 100.00 200.00
1 Dan Bouchard .75 2.00
2 Guy Chouinard .75 2.00
3 Bill Clement .75 2.00
4 Randy Holt .60 1.50
5 Ken Houston .60 1.50
6 Kevin Lavallee .60 1.50
7 Don Lever .60 1.50
8 Bob MacMillan .60 1.50
9 Brad Marsh 1.00 2.50
10 Bob Murdoch .60 1.50
11 Kent Nilsson .75 2.00
12 Willi Plett .75 2.00
13 Jim Peplinski .75 2.00
14 Pekka Rautakillio .60 1.50
15 Paul Reinhart .75 2.00
16 Pat Riggin .75 2.00
17 Phil Russell .60 1.50
18 Brad Smith .60 1.50
19 Eric Vail .60 1.50
20 Bert Wilson .60 1.50
21 Glenn Anderson 1.50 4.00
22 Curt Brackenbury .60 1.50
23 Brett Callighen .60 1.50
24 Paul Coffey 7.50 15.00
25 Lee Fogolin .60 1.50
26 Matti Hagman .60 1.50
27 John Hughes .60 1.50
28 Dave Hunter .60 1.50
29 Jari Kurri 4.00 8.00
30 Ron Low .75 2.00
31 Kevin Lowe 1.00 2.50
32 Dave Lumley .60 1.50
33 Blair MacDonald .60 1.50
34 Mark Messier 12.50 25.00
35 Ed Mio .75 2.00
36 Don Murdoch .60 1.50
37 Pat Price .60 1.50
38 Dave Semenko .75 2.00
39 Risto Siltanen .60 1.50
40 Stan Weir .60 1.50
41 Keith Acton .60 1.50
42 Brian Engblom .60 1.50
43 Bob Gainey 1.25 3.00
44 Gaston Gingras .60 1.50
45 Denis Herron .75 2.00
46 Rejean Houle .60 1.50
47 Doug Jarvis .60 1.50
48 Yvon Lambert .60 1.50
49 Rod Langway 1.25 3.00
50 Guy Lapointe .75 2.00
51 Pierre Larouche 1.00 2.50
52 Pierre Mondou .60 1.50
53 Mark Napier .75 2.00
54 Chris Nilan 1.00 2.50
55 Doug Risebrough .60 1.50
56 Larry Robinson 1.50 4.00
57 Serge Savard .75 2.00
58 Steve Shutt 1.25 3.00
59 Mario Tremblay .75 2.00
60 Doug Wickenheiser .60 1.50
61 Serge Bernier .60 1.50
62 Kim Clackson .75 2.00
63 Real Cloutier .60 1.50
64 Andre Dupont .60 1.50
65 Robbie Ftorek .75 2.00
66 Michel Goulet 2.50 5.00
67 Jamie Hislop .60 1.50
68 Dale Hoganson .60 1.50
69 Dale Hunter 1.50 4.00
70 Pierre Lacroix .60 1.50
71 Garry Lariviere .60 1.50
72 Rich Leduc .60 1.50
73 John Paddock .75 2.00
74 Michel Plasse .75 2.00
75 Jacques Richard .60 1.50
76 Anton Stastny .75 2.00
77 Peter Stastny 3.00 6.00
78 Mark Tardif .75 2.00
79 Wally Weir .60 1.50
80 John Wensink .75 2.00
81 John Anderson .60 1.50
82 Laurie Boschman .60 1.50
83 Jiri Crha .75 2.00
84 Bill Derlago .60 1.50
85 Vitezslav Duris .60 1.50
86 Ron Ellis .75 2.00
87 Dave Farrish .60 1.50
88 Stewart Gavin .75 2.00
89 Pat Hickey .60 1.50
90 Dan Maloney .75 2.00
91 Terry Martin .60 1.50
92 Barry Melrose .75 2.00
93 Wilf Paiement .75 2.00
94 Robert Picard .60 1.50
95 Jim Rutherford 1.00 2.50
96 Rocky Saganiuk .60 1.50
97 Borje Salming 1.25 3.00
98 David Shand .60 1.50
99 Ian Turnbull .75 2.00
100 Rick Vaive 1.00 2.50
101 Brent Ashton .60 1.50
102 Ivan Boldirev .60 1.50
103 Per-Olov Brasar .60 1.50
104 Richard Brodeur 1.00 2.50
105 Jerry Butler .60 1.50
106 Colin Campbell .75 2.00
107 Curt Fraser .60 1.50
108 Thomas Gradin .75 2.00
109 Dennis Kearns .60 1.50
110 Rick Lanz .60 1.50
111 Lars Lindgren .60 1.50
112 Dave Logan .60 1.50
113 Mario Marois .60 1.50
114 Kevin McCarthy .60 1.50
115 Gerald Minor .60 1.50
116 Darcy Rota .60 1.50
117 Bobby Schmautz .60 1.50
118 Stan Smyl .75 2.00
119 Harold Snepsts 1.00 2.50
120 Tiger Williams 1.00 2.50
121 Dave Babych .75 2.00
122 Al Cameron .60 1.50
123 Scott Campbell .60 1.50
124 Dave Christian .75 2.00
125 Jude Drouin .60 1.50
126 Norm Dupont .60 1.50
127 Dan Geoffrion .60 1.50
128 Pierre Hamel .60 1.50
129 Barry Legge .60 1.50
130 Willy Lindstrom .60 1.50
131 Barry Long .60 1.50
132 Kris Manery .60 1.50
133 Jimmy Mann .75 2.00
134 Moe Mantha .60 1.50
135 Markus Mattsson .75 2.00
136 Doug Smail .75 2.00
137 Don Spring .60 1.50
138 Anders Steen .60 1.50
139 Peter Sullivan .60 1.50
140 Ron Wilson .60 1.50
NNO Plastic Circular Display 40.00 80.00

2007-08 Pepsi

COMPLETE SET (32) 25.00 50.00
AVAIL. ON CDN PEPSI PACKAGES
1 Sidney Crosby 4.00 10.00
2 Joe Sakic 1.50 4.00
3 Nicklas Lidstrom 1.25 3.00
4 Saku Koivu 1.25 3.00
5 Daniel Alfredsson 1.25 3.00
6 Vincent Lecavalier 1.00 2.50
7 Mats Sundin 1.25 3.00
8 Patrice Bergeron 1.50 4.00
9 Rick Nash 1.25 3.00
10 Marian Gaborik 1.50 4.00
11 Jaromir Jagr 3.00 8.00
12 Simon Gagne 1.25 3.00
13 Doug Weight 1.25 3.00
14 Duncan Keith 1.25 3.00
15 Jay Bouwmeester 1.25 3.00
16 Rob Blake 1.25 3.00
17 Shea Weber 1.00 2.50
18 Ed Jovanovski 1.00 2.50
19 Ryan Miller 1.25 3.00
20 Miikka Kiprusoff 1.00 2.50
21 Marty Turco 1.25 3.00
22 Dwayne Roloson 1.00 2.50
23 Martin Brodeur 2.00 5.00
24 Rick DiPietro 1.00 2.50
25 Roberto Luongo 1.50 4.00
26 Jean-Sebastien Giguere 1.25 3.00
27 Ilya Kovalchuk 1.25 3.00
28 Cam Ward 1.25 3.00
29 Evgeni Malkin 3.00 8.00
30 Joe Thornton 1.50 4.00
31 Alexander Ovechkin 4.00 10.00
32 Sidney Crosby 4.00 10.00

2007-08 Pepsi 3x5 Stanley Cup Champion

COMPLETE SET (7) 6.00 15.00
1 Jean-Sebastien Giguere 1.00 2.50
2 Patrik Elias 1.00 2.50
3 Nicklas Lidstrom 1.00 2.50
4 Rob Brind' Amour 1.00 2.50
5 Chris Drury .75 2.00
6 Ryan Getzlaf 1.50 4.00
7 Mark Messier 1.50 4.00

1972-73 Philadelphia Blazers

These postcard-like issues feature the short-lived Blazers of the WHA. While we have confirmed just three cards, it is believed that many more exist. The cards are unnumbered and checklisted below in alphabetical order.

COMPLETE SET (3) 15.00 30.00
1 Danny Lawson 5.00 10.00
2 Bernie Parent 10.00 20.00
3 Ron Plumb 5.00 10.00

1992 Philadelphia Daily News

This nine-card set, which is aptly subtitled "Great Moments in Philadelphia Sports," was sponsored by the Philadelphia Daily News. The fronts of the standard-size cards have red borders and feature miniature reproductions of newspaper front pages with famous headlines and memorable photos. Each card captures a great moment in the history of Philadelphia sports. Sports represented are baseball, (cards 1 and 7-8) hockey, (2) basketball, (3-4) football, (5-6) and boxing (9). The backs are printed in gray, black and white and provide text relating to the event commemorated on the card.

COMPLETE SET (9) 1.40 3.50
2 God Bless the Flyers .10 .25
Flyers win Stanley Cup

1981-82 Philip Morris

This 18-card standard-size set was included in the Champions of American Sport program and features major stars from a variety of sports. The program was issued in conjunction with a traveling exhibition organized by the National Portrait Gallery and the Smithsonian Institution and sponsored by Philip Morris and Miller Brewing Company. The cards are either reproductions of works of art (paintings) or famous photographs of the time. The cards are frequently found with a perforated edge on at least one side. The cards were actually obtained from two perforated pages in the program. There is no notation anywhere on the cards indicating the manufacturer or sponsor.

COMPLETE SET (18) 40.00 100.00
6 Bobby Hull 4.00 10.00

1974-75 Phoenix Roadrunners WHA Pins

These pins feature color head shots and measure 3 1/2" in diameter. Player name and team name are featured in a black rectangle at the bottom of the pin. Pins are checklisted below in alphabetical order.

COMPLETE SET (9) 20.00 40.00
1 Bob Barlow 2.00 4.00
2 Cam Connor 2.00 4.00
3 Michel Cormier 2.00 4.00
4 Robbie Ftorek 6.00 12.00
5 Dave Gorman 2.00 4.00
6 John Hughes 2.00 4.00
7 Murray Koegan 2.00 4.00
8 Dennis Sobchuk 2.00 4.00
9 Howie Young 2.00 4.00

1975-76 Phoenix Roadrunners WHA

This 22-card set features players of the WHA Phoenix Roadrunners. The cards measure approximately 3" by 4" and the backs are blank. The front features a poor quality black and white head-and-shoulders shot of the player with a white border. The cards are numbered by the uniform number on the front and we have checklisted them below accordingly. The player's position and weight are also given.

COMPLETE SET (22) 25.00 50.00
1 Serge Beaudoin 1.00 2.00
2 Jim Boyd 1.00 2.00
3 Jim Clarke 1.00 2.00
4 Cam Connors 1.00 2.00
5 Michel Cormier 1.00 2.00
6 Barry Dean 1.00 2.00
7 Robbie Ftorek 7.50 15.00
8 Dave Gorman 1.50 3.00
9 John Gray 1.00 2.00
10 Del Hall 1.00 2.00
11 Ron Huston 1.00 2.00
12 Murray Keogan 1.00 2.00
13 Gary Kurt 1.00 2.00
14 Garry Lariviere 1.00 2.00
15 Al McLeod 1.00 2.00
16 Peter NcNamee 1.00 2.00
17 John Migneault 1.00 2.00
18 Lauri Mononen 1.00 2.00
19 Jim Niekamp 1.00 2.00
20 Jack Norris 1.00 2.00
21 Pekka Rautakallio 2.00 4.00
22 Ron Serafini 1.00 2.00

1976-77 Phoenix Roadrunners WHA

This 18-card set features players of the WHA Phoenix Roadrunners. Each card measures approximately 3 3/8" by 4 5/16". The front features a black and white head shot of the player, enframed by an aqua blue border on white card stock. The top and bottom inner borders are curved, creating space for the basic biographical information as well as the team and league logos that surround the picture. The backs are blank. The cards are unnumbered and we have checklisted them below in alphabetical order.

COMPLETE SET (18) 25.00 50.00
1 Serge Beaudoin 1.00 2.00
2 Michel Cormier 1.00 2.00
3 Robbie Ftorek 7.50 15.00
4 Del Hall 1.00 2.00
5 Clay Hebenton 1.00 2.00
6 Andre Hinse 1.00 2.00
7 Mike Hobin 1.00 2.00
8 Frank Hughes 1.00 2.00
9 Ron Huston 1.00 2.00
10 Gary Kurt 1.00 2.00
11 Garry Lariviere 1.00 2.00
12 Bob Liddington 1.00 2.00
13 Lauri Mononen 1.00 2.00
14 Jim Niekamp 1.00 2.00
15 Pekka Rautakallio 2.00 4.00
16 Seppo Repo 2.00 4.00
17 Jerry Rollins 1.00 2.00
18 Juhani Tamminen 2.00 4.00

1991-92 Pinnacle

The 1991-92 (Score) Pinnacle Hockey set was issued in English and French editions; each set consists of 420 standard-size cards. The front design of the veteran player cards features two color photos, an action photo and a head shot, on a black background with white borders. The card backs have a color action shot silhouetted against a black background. The rookie cards have the same design, except with green background on the front, and black-and-white head shots rather than action shots on the back. The backs of the veteran player cards include biography, player profile, and statistics, while those of the rookie cards only have a player profile. Rookie Cards include Tony Amonte, Valeri Kamensky, John LeClair, Nicklas Lidstrom, Geoff Sanderson and Doug Weight.

COMPLETE SET (420) 10.00 25.00
1 Mario Lemieux .60 1.50
2 Trevor Linden .12 .30
3 Kirk Muller .10 .25
4 Phil Housley .07 .20
5 Mike Modano .30 .75
6 Adam Oates .15 .40
7 Tom Kurvers .12 .30
8 Doug Bodger .12 .30
9 Rod Brind'Amour .12 .30
10 Mats Sundin .15 .40
11 Gary Suter .12 .30
12 Glenn Anderson .15 .40
13 Doug Wilson .12 .30
14 Stephane Richer .12 .30
15 Ray Bourque .25 .60
16 Adam Graves .12 .30
17 Luc Robitaille .12 .30
18 Steve Smith .15 .40
19 Uwe Krupp .12 .30
20 Rick Tocchet .12 .30
21 Tim Cheveldae .12 .30
22 Kay Whitmore .12 .30
23 Kelly Miller .12 .30
24 Esa Tikkanen .12 .30
25 Pat LaFontaine .15 .40
26 James Patrick .12 .30
27 Daniel Marois .12 .30
28 Denis Savard .20 .50
29 Steve Larmer .12 .30
30 Pierre Turgeon .12 .30
31 Gary Leeman .12 .30
32 Mike Ricci .15 .4
33 Troy Murray .12 .3
34 Sergio Momesso .12 .3
35 Marty McSorley .12 .3
36 Paul Ysebaert .12 .3
37 Gary Roberts .12 .3
38 Mike Hudson .12 .3
39 Kelly Hrudey .12 .3
40 Dale Hunter .12 .3
41 Brendan Shanahan .20 .5
42 Steve Duchesne .10 .2
43 Pat Verbeek .12 .3
44 Tom Barrasso .12 .3
45 Scott Mellanby .12 .3
46 Stephen Leach .12 .3
47 Darren Turcotte .12 .3
48 Jari Kurri .12 .3
49 Michel Petit .12 .3
50 Mark Messier .40 1.0
51 Terry Carkner .12 .3
52 Tim Kerr .12 .3
53 Jaromir Jagr .40 1.0
54 Joe Nieuwendyk .12 .3
55 Randy Burridge .12 .3
56 Robert Reichel .30 .7
57 Craig Janney .12 .3
58 Chris Chelios .15 .4
59 Bryan Fogarty .12 .3
60 Christian Ruuttu .12 .3
61 Steve Bozek .12 .3
62 Dave Manson .12 .3
63 Bruce Driver .12 .3
64 Mike Ramsey .12 .3
65 Bobby Holik .15 .4
66 Bob Essensa .12 .3
67 Pat Flatley .12 .3
68 Wayne Presley .12 .3
69 Mike Bullard .12 .3
70 Claude Lemieux .12 .3
71 Dave Gagner .12 .3
72 Jeff Brown .12 .3
73 Eric Desjardins .15 .4
74 Fredrik Olausson .12 .3
75 Steve Yzerman .50 1.2
76 Tony Granato .12 .3
77 Adam Burt .12 .3
78 Cam Neely .15 .4
79 Brent Sutter .12 .3
80 Dale Hawerchuk .20 .5
81 Scott Stevens .15 .4
82 Adam Creighton .12 .3
83 Brian Hayward .12 .3
84 Dan Quinn .12 .3
85 Garth Butcher .12 .3
86 Shawn Burr .12 .3
87 Peter Bondra .12 .3
88 Brad Shaw .10 .2
89 Eric Weinrich .15 .4
90 Brian Bradley .12 .3
91 Vincent Damphousse .12 .3
92 Doug Gilmour .30 .7
93 Martin Gelinas .12 .3
94 Mike Ridley .12 .3
95 Ron Sutter .12 .3
96 Mark Osborne .12 .3
97 Mikhail Tatarinov .12 .3
98 Bob McGill .12 .3
99 Bob Carpenter .12 .3
100 Wayne Gretzky .75 2.0
101 Slava Fetisov .12 .3
102 Shayne Corson .12 .3
103 Clint Malarchuk .12 .3
104 Randy Wood .12 .3
105 Curtis Joseph .12 .3
106 Cliff Ronning .12 .3
107 Derek King .10 .2
108 Neil Wilkinson .12 .3
109 Michel Goulet .12 .3
110 Zarley Zalapski .12 .3
111 Dave Ellett .12 .3
112 Glen Wesley .12 .3
113 Bob Kudelski .10 .2
114 Jamie Macoun .12 .3
115 John MacLean .12 .3
116 Steve Thomas .12 .3
117 Pat Elynuik .12 .3
118 Ron Hextall .15 .4
119 Jeff Hackett .12 .3
120 Jeremy Roenick .40 1.0
121 John Vanbiesbrouck .12 .3
122 Dave Andreychuk .15 .4
123 Ray Ferraro .12 .3
124 Ron Tugnutt .12 .3
125 John Cullen .12 .3
126 Andy Moog .12 .3
127 Ed Belfour .40 1.0
128 Dino Ciccarelli .12 .3
129 Brian Bellows .12 .3
130 Guy Carbonneau .12 .3
131 Kevin Hatcher .12 .3
132 Mike Vernon .12 .3
133 Kevin Miller .12 .3
134 Pelle Eklund .12 .3
135 Brian Mullen .12 .3
136 Brian Leetch .12 .3
137 Daren Puppa .12 .3
138 Steven Finn .12 .3
139 Stephan Lebeau .12 .3
140 Gord Murphy .12 .3
141 Rob Brown .12 .3
142 Ken Daneyko .12 .3
143 Larry Murphy .12 .3
144 Jon Casey .12 .3
145 John Ogrodnick .12 .3
146 Benoit Hogue .12 .3
147 Mike McPhee .12 .3
148 Don Beaupre .12 .3
149 Kjell Samuelsson .12 .3
150 Joe Sakic .50 1.2
151 Mark Recchi .20 .5
152 Ulf Dahlen .12 .3
153 Dean Evason .12 .3
154 Keith Brown .12 .3
155 Ray Sheppard .12 .3
156 Owen Nolan .15 .4
157 Sergei Fedorov .25 .6
158 Kirk McLean .12 .3
159 Petr Klima .12 .3
160 Brian Skrudland .12 .3
161 Neal Broten .12 .3
162 Dimitri Khristich .12 .3
163 Alexander Mogilny .12 .3
164 Mike Richter .15 .4
165 Daniel Berthiaume .12 .3
166 Teppo Numminen .12 .3
167 Ron Francis .20 .5
168 Grant Fuhr .15 .4
169 Mike Liut .12 .3
170 Bill Ranford .12 .3
171 Garry Galley .12 .3
172 Jeff Norton .12 .3

173 Jimmy Carson .12 .30
174 Peter Zezel .10 .25
175 Patrick Roy .40 1.00
176 Joe Mullen .12 .30
177 Murray Craven .12 .30
178 Tomas Sandstrom .12 .30
179 Joel Otto .12 .30
180 Steve Konroyd .12 .30
181 Vladimir Ruzicka .12 .30
182 Paul Cavallini .12 .30
183 Bob Probert .12 .30
184 Brian Propp .12 .30
185 Glenn Healy .15 .40
186 Paul Coffey .12 .30
187 Jan Erixon .12 .30
188 Kevin Lowe .12 .30
189 Doug Lidster .12 .30
190 Theo Fleury .12 .30
191 Kevin Stevens .12 .30
192 Petr Nedved .12 .30
193 Ed Olczyk .12 .30
194 Mike Hough .12 .30
195 Rod Langway .12 .30
196 Craig Simpson .10 .25
197 Petr Svoboda .12 .30
198 David Volek .12 .30
199 Mark Tinordi .12 .30
200 Brett Hull .25 .60
201 Rob Blake .15 .40
202 Mike Gartner .12 .30
203 Ken Hodge Jr. .15 .40
204 Murray Baron .12 .30
205 Gerard Gallant .10 .25
206 Joe Murphy .12 .30
207 Al Iafrate .12 .30
208 Larry Robinson .10 .25
209 Mathieu Schneider .12 .30
210 Bobby Smith .12 .30
211 Gerald Diduck .12 .30
212 Luke Richardson .12 .30
213 Rob Zettler .12 .30
214 Brad McCrimmon .12 .30
215 Craig MacTavish .12 .30
216 Gino Cavallini .12 .30
217 Craig Wolanin .12 .30
218 Greg Adams .12 .30
219 Mike Craig .12 .30
220 Al MacInnis .12 .30
221 Sylvain Cote .12 .30
222 Bob Sweeney .12 .30
223 Dave Snuggerud .10 .25
224 Randy Ladouceur .12 .30
225 Charlie Huddy .12 .30
226 Sylvain Turgeon .12 .30
227 Phil Bourque .12 .30
228 Rob Ramage .12 .30
229 Jeff Beukeboom .12 .30
230 Alexei Gusarov RC .12 .30
231 Kelly Kisio .12 .30
232 Calle Johansson .12 .30
233 Yves Racine .12 .30
234 Peter Sidorkiewicz .12 .30
235 Jim Johnson .12 .30
236 Brent Gilchrist .12 .30
237 Jyrki Lumme .12 .30
238 Randy Gilhen .12 .30
239 Ken Baumgartner .12 .30
240 Joey Kocur .12 .30
241 Bryan Trottier .20 .50
242 Todd Krygier .12 .30
243 Darrin Shannon .12 .30
244 Dave Christian .12 .30
245 Stephane Morin .12 .30
246 Kevin Dineen .12 .30
247 Chris Terreri .12 .30
248 Craig Ludwig .12 .30
249 Dave Taylor .12 .30
250 Wendel Clark .15 .40
251 David Shaw .12 .30
252 Paul Ranheim .15 .40
253 Mark Hunter .12 .30
254 Russ Courtnall .12 .30
255 Alexei Kasatonov .10 .25
256 Randy Moller .12 .30
257 Bob Errey .12 .30
258 Curtis Leschyshyn .12 .30
259 Rick Zombo .12 .30
260 Dana Murzyn .12 .30
261 Dirk Graham .12 .30
262 Craig Muni .12 .30
263 Geoff Courtnall .12 .30
264 Todd Elik .12 .30
265 Mike Keane .10 .25
266 Peter Stastny .12 .30
267 Ulf Samuelsson .12 .30
268 Rich Sutter .12 .30
269 Mike Krushelnyski .12 .30
270 Dave Babych .12 .30
271 Sergei Makarov .12 .30
272 David Maley .12 .30
273 Normand Rochefort .12 .30
274 Gordie Roberts .12 .30
275 Thomas Steen .12 .30
276 Dave Lowry .12 .30
277 Michal Pivonka .12 .30
278 Todd Gill .12 .30
279 Paul MacDermid .12 .30
280 Brent Ashton .12 .30
281 Randy Hillier .12 .30
282 Frank Musil .12 .30
283 Geoff Smith .12 .30
284 John Tonelli .12 .30
285 Joe Reekie .12 .30
286 Greg Paslawski .12 .30
287 Perry Berezan .12 .30
288 Randy Carlyle .12 .30
289 Chris Nilan .12 .30
290 Patrik Sundstrom .12 .30
291 Garry Valk .12 .30
292 Mike Foligno .15 .40
293 Igor Larionov .12 .30
294 Jim Sandlak .12 .30
295 Tom Chorske .12 .30
296 Claude Loiselle .12 .30
297 Mark Howe .15 .40
298 Steve Chiasson .12 .30
299 Mike Donnelly RC .15 .40
300 Bernie Nicholls .12 .30
301 Tony Amonte RC .40 1.00
302 Brad May .12 .30
303 Josef Beranek RC .15 .40
304 Rob Pearson RC .15 .40
305 Andrei Lomakin .12 .30
306 Kip Miller .12 .30
307 Kevin Haller RC .15 .40
308 Kevin Todd RC .15 .40
309 Geoff Sanderson RC .15 .40
310 Doug Weight RC .40 1.00
311 Vladimir Konstantinov RC .40 1.00
312 Peter Ahola RC .15 .40
313 Claude Lapointe RC .12 .30
314 Nelson Emerson .12 .30
315 Pavel Bure .12 .30
316 Jim Waite .12 .30
317 Sergei Nemchinov .12 .30
318 Alexander Godynyuk RC .15 .40
319 Stu Barnes .12 .30
320 Nicklas Lidstrom RC 1.00 2.50
321 Darryl Sydor .12 .30
322 John LeClair RC .40 1.00
323 Arturs Irbe .12 .30
324 Russ Romaniuk RC .15 .40
325 Ken Sutton RC .15 .40
326 Bob Beers .12 .30
327 Michel Picard RC .15 .40
328 Derian Hatcher .12 .30
329 Pat Falloon .12 .30
330 Donald Audette .12 .30
331 Pat Jablonski RC .12 .30
332 Corey Foster RC .15 .40
333 Tomas Forslund RC .15 .40
334 Steven Rice .12 .30
335 Marc Bureau .12 .30
336 Kimbi Daniels RC .15 .40
337 Adam Foote RC .30 .75
338 Dan Kordic RC .12 .30
339 Link Gaetz .12 .30
340 Valeri Kamensky RC .40 1.00
341 Tom Draper RC .15 .40
342 Jayson More RC .15 .40
343 Dominic Roussel RC .15 .40
344 Jim Paek RC .15 .40
345 Felix Potvin .30 .75
346 Dan Lambert RC .12 .30
347 Louie DeBrusk RC .15 .40
348 Jamie Baker RC .12 .30
349 Scott Niedermayer .15 .40
350 Paul DiPietro RC .12 .30
351 Chris Winnes RC .12 .30
352 Mark Greig .12 .30
353 Luciano Borsato RC .15 .40
354 Valeri Zelepukin RC .15 .40
355 Martin Lapointe .12 .30
356 Brett Hull GW .25 .60
357 Steve Larmer GW .12 .30
358 Theo Fleury GW .12 .30
359 Jeremy Roenick GW .40 1.00
360 Mark Recchi GW .20 .50
361 Brad Marsh .15 .40
362 Kris King .12 .30
363 Doug Brown .12 .30
364 Carey Wilson .12 .30
365 Eric Lindros .12 .30
366 Kevin Dineen GG .12 .30
367 John Vanbiesbrouck GG .12 .30
368 Ray Bourque GG .25 .60
369 Doug Wilson GG .12 .30
370 Keith Brown GG .12 .30
371 Kevin Lowe GG .12 .30
372 Kelly Miller GG .12 .30
373 Dave Taylor GG .12 .30
374 Guy Carbonneau GG .12 .30
375 Tim Hunter GG .12 .30
376 Brett Hull TECH .25 .60
377 Paul Coffey TECH .12 .30
378 Adam Oates TECH .15 .40
379 Andy Moog TECH .12 .30
380 Mario Lemieux TECH .60 1.50
381 J.Sakic/W.Gretzky .75 2.00
382 R.Blake/L.Robinson .15 .40
383 D.Weight/S.Yzerman .50 1.25
384 M.Richter/B.Parent .15 .40
385 L.Robitaille/M.Dionne .20 .50
386 E.Olczyk/B.Clarke .12 .30
387 P.Roy/R.Vachon .40 1.00
388 E.Belfour/T.Esposito .40 1.00
389 M.Sundin/M.Naslund .15 .40
390 T.Amonte/M.Messier .40 1.00
391 J.Cullen/R.Cullen .12 .30
392 G.Suter/B.Orr .60 1.50
393 R.Zombo/G.Resch .12 .30
394 T.Krygier/G.Perreault .12 .30
395 J.Druce/B.Gainey .12 .30
396 Bob Carpenter SL .12 .30
397 Clint Malarchuk SL .12 .30
398 Jim Kyte SL .12 .30
399 Al MacInnis SL .12 .30
400 Ed Belfour SL .40 1.00
401 Brad Marsh SL .15 .40
402 Brian Benning SL .12 .30
403 Larry Robinson SL .10 .25
404 Craig Ludwig SL .12 .30
405 Pat Flatley SL .12 .30
406 Gary Nylund SL .12 .30
407 Kjell Samuelsson SL .12 .30
408 Dan Quinn SL .12 .30
409 Garth Butcher SL .12 .30
410 Rick Zombo SL .12 .30
411 Paul Cavallini SL .12 .30
412 Link Gaetz SL .12 .30
413 Dave Hannan SL .12 .30
414 Peter Zezel SL .10 .25
415 Randy Gregg SL .12 .30
416 Pat Elynuik SL .12 .30
417 Rod Buskas SL .12 .30
418 Mark Howe SL .15 .40
419 Don Sweeney .12 .30
420 Mark Hardy .12 .30

1991-92 Pinnacle French

COMPLETE SET (420) 15.00 30.00
*FRENCH: .4X TO 1X BASIC PINNACLE

1991-92 Pinnacle B

This 12-card standard-size set presents the starting lineup from the 1991 All-Star Game. It features six players each from the Wales Conference (B1-B6) and the Campbell Conference (B7-B12). The cards were inserted into Pinnacle French and English foil packs. The French version has a red name plate, while the English version has a blue name plate. The fronts feature black-and-white head shots, with black borders on three sides and a thicker white border at the bottom. The words "Team Pinnacle" appear in the top black border, while the player's name and team affiliation are listed in the bottom white border. The border design on the back is similar and frames a player profile. The cards are numbered on the back with a "B" prefix.

COMPLETE SET (12) 60.00 120.00
*FRENCH: SAME VALUE
B1 Patrick Roy 8.00 20.00
B2 Ray Bourque 6.00 15.00
B3 Brian Leetch 4.00 10.00
B4 Kevin Stevens 2.50 6.00
B5 Mario Lemieux 15.00 30.00
B6 Cam Neely 4.00 10.00
B7 Bill Ranford 3.00 8.00
B8 Al MacInnis 3.00 8.00
B9 Chris Chelios 4.00 10.00
B10 Luc Robitaille 3.00 8.00
B11 Wayne Gretzky 12.00 30.00
B12 Brett Hull 5.00 12.00

1992-93 Pinnacle American Promo Panel

This promo sheet features six standard-size cards and was issued to promote the U.S. edition of Pinnacle hockey cards. The cards feature color action photos with the players extending beyond the picture background. The card face is black and a thin white line forms a frame around the picture. The player's name appears in a gradated bar at the bottom that matches the team colors. The horizontal backs feature the player's name in a gradated turquoise bar at the top. Close-up player photos are surrounded by biography, statistics, and career highlights on a black background. The backs have white borders. This sheet was intended to remain uncut and the disclaimers "Not For Resale" and "For Promotional Use Only" are printed in the white borders between the rows of cards. The cards are numbered on the back and listed as they appear on the sheet from left to right.

1 Promo Sheet 1.25 3.00
91 Andy Moog
Boston Bruins/36 Nelso

1992-93 Pinnacle Canadian Promo Panels

These three promo panels were issued to preview the design of the Canadian version of the 1992-93 Pinnacle hockey series. Measuring approximately 5" by 7", each panel consists of four standard-size cards. The fronts display glossy color action photos framed by black borders. The horizontal backs feature the player's name in a gradated burgundy bar at the top. Close-up photos are surrounded by biography, statistics, and career highlights on a black background. The sheet was intended to remain uncut and the disclaimers "Not For Resale" and "For Promotional Use Only" are printed in the white borders between the rows of cards. The cards on the panels are listed below alphabetically according to player's last name.

COMPLETE SET (3) 2.50 6.00
1 Promo Panel 1.25 3.00
Bure
Iafrate
Recchi
S.Stevens
2 Promo Panel .75 2.00
Brian Bradley
Tampa Bay Lightning#
3 Promo Panel .75 2.00
Doug Gilmour
Toronto Maple Leafs/

1992-93 Pinnacle

The 1992-93 Pinnacle Hockey set was issued in U.S. and Canadian bilingual editions; each set consists of 420 cards. While card numbers 1-220 and 271-390 have different front photography in the U.S. and Canadian versions, the subset cards (221-270) depict the same photos. Rookie Cards in the set include Roman Hamrlik, Andrei Kovalenko, and Martin Straka.

*FRENCH: .4X TO 1X BASIC CARDS
1 Mark Messier .15 .40
2 Ray Bourque .15 .40
3 Gary Roberts .05 .15
4 Bill Ranford .07 .20
5 Gilbert Dionne .05 .15
6 Owen Nolan .05 .15
7 Pat LaFontaine .10 .25
8 Nicklas Lidstrom .07 .20
9 Pat Falloon .05 .15
10 Jeremy Roenick .15 .40
11 Kevin Hatcher .05 .15
12 Cliff Ronning .05 .15
13 Jeff Brown .07 .20
14 Kevin Dineen .05 .15
15 Brian Leetch .07 .20
16 Eric Desjardins .07 .20
17 Derek King .05 .15
18 Mark Tinordi .05 .15
19 Kelly Hrudey .07 .20
20 Sergei Fedorov .15 .40
21 Mike Ramsey .05 .15
22 Michel Goulet .07 .20
23 Joe Murphy .05 .15
24 Mark Fitzpatrick .07 .20
25 Cam Neely .10 .25
26 Rod Brind'Amour .05 .15
27 Neil Wilkinson .05 .15
28 Greg Adams .05 .15
29 Thomas Steen .05 .15
30 Calle Johansson .05 .15
31 Joe Nieuwendyk .07 .20
32 Rob Blake .07 .20
33 Darren Turcotte .05 .15
34 Derian Hatcher .05 .15
35 Mikhail Tatarinov .05 .15
36 Nelson Emerson .05 .15
37 Tim Cheveldae .05 .15
38 Donald Audette .07 .20
39 Brent Sutter .05 .15
40 Adam Oates .10 .25
41 Luke Richardson .07 .20
42 Jon Casey .05 .15
43 Guy Carbonneau .07 .20
44 Patrick Flatley .07 .20
45 Brian Benning .05 .15
46 Curtis Leschyshyn .07 .20
47 Trevor Linden .07 .20
48 Don Beaupre .07 .20
49 Troy Murray .05 .15
50 Paul Coffey .10 .25
51 Frank Musil .07 .20
52 Doug Wilson .07 .20
53 Pat Elynuik .05 .15
54 Curtis Joseph .10 .25
55 Tony Amonte .07 .20
56 Bob Probert .07 .20
57 Steve Smith .05 .15
58 Dave Andreychuk .10 .25
59 Vladimir Ruzicka .05 .15
60 Jari Kurri .10 .25
61 Denis Savard .12 .30
62 Benoit Hogue .05 .15
63 Terry Carkner .07 .20
64 Valeri Kamensky .05 .15
65 Jyrki Lumme .05 .15
66 Al Iafrate .07 .20
67 Paul Ranheim .05 .15
68 Ulf Dahlen .05 .15
69 Tony Granato .05 .15
70 Phil Housley .05 .15
71 Brian Lawton .07 .20
72 Garth Butcher .07 .20
73 Steve Leach .05 .15
74 Steve Larmer .05 .15
75 Mike Richter .10 .25
76 Vladimir Konstantinov .10 .25
77 Alexander Mogilny .07 .20
78 Craig MacTavish .05 .15
79 Mathieu Schneider .05 .15
80 Mark Recchi .12 .30
81 Gerald Diduck .07 .20
82 Peter Bondra .07 .20
83 Al MacInnis .07 .20
84 Bob Kudelski .07 .20
85 Dave Gagner .07 .20
86 Uwe Krupp .05 .15
87 Randy Carlyle .07 .20
88 Eric Lindros .30 .75
89 Rob Zettler .05 .15
90 Mats Sundin .10 .25
91 Andy Moog .07 .20
92 Keith Brown .07 .20
93 Paul Ysebaert .05 .15
94 Mike Gartner .07 .20
95 Kelly Buchberger .05 .15
96 Dominic Roussel .07 .20
97 Doug Bodger .05 .15
98 Mike Donnelly .05 .15
99 Mike Craig .05 .15
100 Brett Hull .15 .40
101 Robert Reichel .05 .15
102 Jeff Norton .07 .20
103 Garry Galley .05 .15
104 Dale Hunter .07 .20
105 Jeff Hackett .07 .20
106 Darrin Shannon .05 .15
107 Craig Wolanin .05 .15
108 Adam Graves .05 .15
109 Chris Chelios .10 .25
110 Pavel Bure .20 .50
111 Kirk Muller .05 .15
112 Jeff Beukeboom .05 .15
113 Mike Hough .07 .20
114 Brendan Shanahan .12 .30
115 Randy Burridge .05 .15
116 Dave Poulin .05 .15
117 Petr Svoboda .07 .20
118 Ed Belfour .10 .25
119 Ray Sheppard .05 .15
120 Bernie Nicholls .05 .15
121 Glenn Healy .07 .20
122 Johan Garpenlov .05 .15
123 Mike Lalor .07 .20
124 Brad McCrimmon .05 .15
125 Theo Fleury .15 .40
126 Randy Gilhen .05 .15
127 Petr Nedved .07 .20
128 Steve Thomas .07 .20
129 Rick Zombo .05 .15
130 Patrick Roy .25 .60
131 Rod Langway .07 .20
132 Gord Murphy .07 .20
133 Randy Wood .05 .15
134 Mike Hudson .05 .15
135 Gerard Gallant .05 .15
136 Brian Glynn .05 .15
137 Jim Johnson .07 .20
138 Corey Millen .05 .15
139 Daniel Marois .05 .15
140 James Patrick .05 .15
141 Claude Lapointe .05 .15
142 Bobby Smith .07 .20
143 Charlie Huddy .07 .20
144 Murray Baron .05 .15
145 Ed Olczyk .05 .15
146 Dimitri Khristich .05 .15
147 Doug Lidster .07 .20
148 Perry Berezan .05 .15
149 Pelle Eklund .07 .20
150 Joe Sakic .25 .60
151 Michal Pivonka .05 .15
152 Joey Kocur .07 .20
153 Patrice Brisebois .05 .15
154 Ray Ferraro .05 .15
155 Mike Modano .25 .60
156 Marty McSorley .05 .15
157 Norm Maciver .05 .15
158 Sergei Nemchinov .05 .15
159 David Bruce .05 .15
160 Kelly Miller .05 .15
161 Alexei Gusarov .05 .15
162 Andrei Lomakin .05 .15
163 Sergio Momesso .05 .15
164 Mike Keane .05 .15
165 Pierre Turgeon .07 .20
166 Martin Gelinas .05 .15
167 Chris Dahlquist .07 .20
168 Kris King .05 .15
169 Dean Evason .05 .15
170 Mike Ridley .05 .15
171 Shawn Burr .05 .15
172 Dana Murzyn .05 .15
173 Dirk Graham .05 .15
174 Trent Yawney .07 .20
175 Luc Robitaille .07 .20
176 Randy Moller .05 .15
177 Vincent Riendeau .07 .20
178 Brian Propp .05 .15
179 Don Sweeney .05 .15
180 Stephane Matteau .05 .15
181 Garry Valk .05 .15
182 Sylvain Cote .07 .20
183 Dave Snuggerud .05 .15
184 Gary Leeman .05 .15
185 John Druce .05 .15
186 John Vanbiesbrouck .07 .20
187 Geoff Courtnall .05 .15
188 David Volek .05 .15
189 Doug Weight .20 .50
190 Bob Essensa .07 .20
191 Jan Erixon .07 .20
192 Geoff Smith .05 .15
193 Dave Christian .05 .15
194 Brian Noonan .05 .15
195 Gary Suter .05 .15
196 Craig Janney .07 .20
197 Brad May .05 .15
198 Gaetan Duchesne .05 .15
199 Adam Creighton .05 .15
200 Wayne Gretzky .50 1.25
201 Dave Babych .07 .20
202 Fredrik Olausson .05 .15
203 Bob Bassen .05 .15
204 Todd Krygier .07 .20
205 Grant Ledyard .05 .15
206 Michel Petit .05 .15
207 Todd Elik .05 .15
208 Josef Beranek .05 .15
209 Neal Broten .07 .20
210 Jim Sandlak .05 .15
211 Kevin Haller .05 .15
212 Paul Broten .05 .15
213 Mark Pederson .05 .15
214 John McIntyre .05 .15
215 Teppo Numminen .05 .15
216 Ken Sutton .05 .15
217 Ronnie Stern .07 .20
218 Luciano Borsato .05 .15
219 Claude Loiselle .05 .15
220 Mark Hardy .07 .20
221 Joe Juneau .05 .15
222 Keith Tkachuk .10 .25
223 Scott Lachance .05 .15
224 Glen Murray .05 .15
225 Igor Kravchuk .05 .15
226 Evgeny Davydov .05 .15
227 Ray Whitney RC .15 .40
228 Bret Hedican RC .07 .20
229 Keith Carney RC .20 .50
230 Slava Kozlov .07 .20
231 Drake Berehowsky .05 .15
232 Cam Neely SL .10 .25
233 Doug Gilmour SL .12 .30
234 Randy Wood SL .05 .15
235 Luke Richardson SL .07 .20
236 Eric Lindros SL .30 .75
237 Dale Hunter SL .07 .20
238 Pat Falloon SL .05 .15
239 Dean Kennedy SL .07 .20
240 Uwe Krupp SL .05 .15
241 S.Niedermayer/S.Yzerman .25 .60
242 Gary Roberts IDOL .05 .15
(Lanny McDonald)
243 Peter Ahola IDOL .10 .25
(Jari Kurri)
244 Scott Lachance IDOL .10 .25
(Mark Howe)
245 R.Pearson/M.Bossy .05 .15
246 Kirk McLean IDOL .07 .20
(Bernie Parent)
247 Dmitri Mironov IDOL .05 .15
(Viacheslav Fetisov)
248 Brendan Shanahan IDOL .12 .30
(Darryl Sittler)
249 P.Nedved/W.Gretzky .50 1.25
250 Todd Ewen IDOL .10 .25
(Clark Gillies
251 Luc Robitaille GG .07 .20
252 Mark Tinordi GG .05 .15
253 Kris King GG .05 .15
254 Pat LaFontaine GG .10 .25
255 Ryan Walter GG .07 .20
256 Jeremy Roenick GW .15 .40
257 Brett Hull GW .15 .40
258 Steve Yzerman GW .25 .60
259 Claude Lemieux GW .05 .15
260 Mike Modano GW .25 .60
261 Vincent Damphousse GW .07 .20
262 Tony Granato GW .05 .15
263 Andy Moog MASK .07 .20
264 Curtis Joseph MASK .10 .25
265 Ed Belfour MASK .10 .25
266 Brian Hayward MASK .05 .15
267 Grant Fuhr MASK .10 .25
268 Don Beaupre MASK .07 .20
269 Tim Cheveldae MASK .05 .15
270 Mike Richter MASK .10 .25
271 Zarley Zalapski .05 .15
272 Kevin Todd .05 .15
273 Dave Ellett .05 .15
274 Chris Terreri .07 .20
275 Jaromir Jagr .25 .60
276 Wendel Clark .07 .20
277 Bobby Holik .07 .20
278 Bruce Driver .05 .15
279 Doug Gilmour .12 .30
280 Scott Stevens .10 .25
281 Murray Craven .05 .15
282 Rick Tocchet .07 .20
283 Peter Zezel .05 .15
284 Claude Lemieux .05 .15
285 John Cullen .05 .15
286 Valeri Zelepukin .05 .15
287 Rob Pearson .05 .15
288 Kevin Stevens .05 .15
289 Alexei Kasatonov .05 .15
290 Todd Gill .05 .15
291 Randy Ladouceur .05 .15
292 Larry Murphy .07 .20
293 Tom Chorske .07 .20
294 Jamie Macoun .07 .20
295 Sean Burke .07 .20
296 Ulf Samuelsson .05 .15
297 Eric Weinrich .05 .15
298 Tom Barrasso .07 .20
299 Slava Fetisov .05 .15
300 Mario Lemieux .40 1.00
301 Grant Fuhr .10 .25
302 Zdeno Ciger .05 .15
303 Ron Francis .12 .30
304 Scott Niedermayer .10 .25
305 Mark Osborne .05 .15
306 Kjell Samuelsson .07 .20
307 Geoff Sanderson .07 .20
308 Paul Stanton .05 .15
309 Frank Pietrangelo .07 .20
310 Bob Errey .07 .20
311 Dino Ciccarelli .07 .20
312 Gordie Roberts .07 .20
313 Kevin Miller .05 .15
314 Mike Ricci .07 .20
315 Bob Carpenter .05 .15
316 Dale Hawerchuk .12 .30
317 Christian Ruuttu .05 .15
318 Mike Vernon .07 .20
319 Paul Cavallini .05 .15
320 Steve Duchesne .05 .15
321 Craig Simpson .05 .15
322 Mark Howe .10 .25
323 Shayne Corson .05 .15
324 Tom Kurvers .05 .15
325 Brian Bellows .07 .20
326 Glen Wesley .05 .15
327 Daren Puppa .07 .20
328 Joel Otto .05 .15
329 Jimmy Carson .05 .15
330 Kirk McLean .05 .15
331 Rob Brown .05 .15
332 Yves Racine .05 .15
333 Brian Mullen .05 .15
334 Dave Manson .05 .15
335 Sergei Makarov .05 .15
336 Esa Tikkanen .05 .15
337 Russ Courtnall .05 .15
338 Kevin Lowe .07 .20
339 Steve Chiasson .05 .15
340 Ron Hextall .07 .20
341 Stephan Lebeau .05 .15
342 Mike McPhee .05 .15
343 David Shaw .07 .20
344 Petr Klima .05 .15
345 Tomas Sandstrom .07 .20
346 Scott Mellanby .05 .15
347 Brian Skrudland .07 .20
348 Pat Verbeek .05 .15
349 Vincent Damphousse .07 .20
350 Steve Yzerman .25 .60
351 John MacLean .07 .20
352 Steve Konroyd .07 .20
353 Phil Bourque .05 .15
354 Ken Daneyko .05 .15
355 Glenn Anderson .10 .25
356 Ken Wregget .07 .20
357 Brent Gilchrist .05 .15
358 Bob Rouse .07 .20
359 Peter Stastny .07 .20
360 Joe Mullen .07 .20
361 Stephane Richer .07 .20
362 Kelly Kisio .07 .20
363 Keith Acton .07 .20
364 Felix Potvin .20 .50
365 Martin Lapointe .05 .15
366 Ron Tugnutt .07 .20
367 Dave Taylor .07 .20
368 Tim Kerr .05 .15
369 Carey Wilson .07 .20
370 Greg Paslawski .05 .15
371 Peter Sidorkiewicz .05 .15
372 Brad Shaw .05 .15
373 Sylvain Turgeon .05 .15
374 Mark Lamb .05 .15
375 Laurie Boschman .05 .15
376 Mark Osiecki .07 .20
377 Doug Smail .05 .15
378 Brad Marsh .07 .20
379 Mike Peluso .07 .20
380 Steve Weeks .05 .15
381 Wendell Young .07 .20
382 Joe Reekie .05 .15
383 Peter Taglianetti .07 .20
384 Mikael Andersson .05 .15
385 Marc Bergevin .07 .20
386 Anatoli Semenov .05 .15
387 Brian Bradley .05 .15
388 Michel Mongeau .07 .20
389 Rob Ramage .05 .15
390 Ken Hodge Jr. .05 .15
391 Richard Matvichuk RC .07 .20
392 Alexei Zhitnik .05 .15
393 Richard Smehlik RC .05 .15
394 Dimitri Yushkevich RC .05 .15
395 Andrei Kovalenko RC .15 .40
396 Vladimir Vujtek RC .05 .15
397 Nikolai Borschevsky RC .05 .15
398 Vitali Karamnov RC .05 .15
399 Jim Hiller RC .05 .15
400 Michael Nylander RC .05 .15
401 Tommy Sjodin RC .05 .15
402 Robert Petrovicky RC .05 .15
403 Alexei Kovalev .07 .20
404 Vitali Prokhorov RC .05 .15
405 Dmitri Kvartalnov RC .05 .15
406 Teemu Selanne .20 .50
407 Darius Kasparaitis .05 .15
408 Roman Hamrlik RC .20 .50
409 Vladimir Malakhov .05 .15
410 Sergei Krivokrasov .05 .15
411 Robert Lang RC .05 .15
412 Jozef Stumpel .05 .15
413 Denny Felsner RC .07 .20
414 Rob Zamuner RC .07 .20
415 Jason Woolley RC .05 .15
416 Alexei Zhamnov .07 .20
417 Igor Korolev RC .05 .15
418 Patrick Poulin .05 .15
419 Dmitri Mironov .05 .15
420 Shawn McEachern .05 .15

1992-93 Pinnacle Team 2000

Inserted two per 27-card super pack, these 30 standard-size cards feature players who Pinnacle predicts will be stars in the NHL in the year 2000. The U.S. version features glossy color action photos that are full-bleed on the top and right and edged by black wedged-shaped borders on the left and bottom. In a gold-foil edged circle, the team logo appears in the lower left corner at the intersection of these two stripes. In gold-foil lettering, the words "Team 2000" are printed vertically in the left stripe while the player's name appears in the bottom stripe. The Canadian version offers different player photos and has a maple leaf following the Team 2000 insignia. The horizontal backs have a black panel with bilingual player profile on the left half and a full-bleed color close-up photo on the right.

*FRENCH: 1X TO 1.25X BASIC CARDS
1 Eric Lindros .60 1.50
2 Mike Modano .50 1.25
3 Nicklas Lidstrom .15 .40
4 Tony Amonte .15 .40
5 Felix Potvin .40 1.00
6 Scott Lachance .12 .30
7 Mats Sundin .20 .50
8 Pavel Bure .40 1.00
9 Eric Desjardins .15 .40
10 Owen Nolan .12 .30
11 Dominic Roussel .15 .40
12 Scott Niedermayer .20 .50
13 Slava Kozlov .15 .40
14 Patrick Poulin .12 .30
15 Jaromir Jagr .50 1.25
16 Rob Blake .15 .40
17 Pierre Turgeon .15 .40
18 Rod Brind'Amour .12 .30
19 Joe Juneau .12 .30
20 Tim Cheveldae .12 .30
21 Joe Sakic .50 1.25
22 Kevin Todd .12 .30
23 Rob Pearson .12 .30
24 Trevor Linden .15 .40
25 Dimitri Khristich .12 .30
26 Pat Falloon .12 .30
27 Jeremy Roenick .30 .75
28 Alexander Mogilny .15 .40
29 Gilbert Dionne .12 .30
30 Sergei Fedorov .30 .75

1992-93 Pinnacle Team Pinnacle

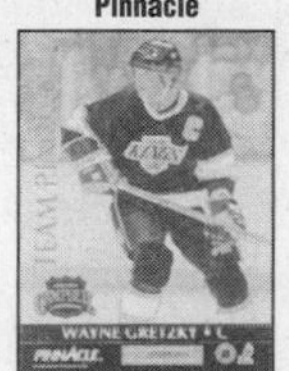

Randomly inserted in 1992-93 Pinnacle foil packs, these six double-sided cards feature a top player from the Campbell Conference with his Wales Conference counterpart on the other side. According to Score, the odds of finding a card are not less than 1:125 packs. Painted by Score artist Christopher Greco, the pictures are full-bleed on three sides but edged on the bottom by a gold-foil stripe that features the player's name and position. A black stripe immediately below completes the card face. The words "Team Pinnacle" are printed in turquoise (pink in the Canadian version) vertically near the left edge of both sides of the card, and the conference logo appears below it. The backs of these cards may be distinguished from the fronts by the card number in the lower right corner.

*FRENCH: .4X TO 1X BASIC INSERTS
1 M.Richter/E.Belfour 2.50 6.00
2 R.Bourque/C.Chelios 2.00 5.00
3 B.Leeth/P.Coffey 3.00 8.00
4 K.Stevens/P.Bure 2.50 6.00
5 E.Lindros/W.Gretzky 4.00 10.00
6 J.Jagr/B.Hull 3.00 8.00

1992-93 Pinnacle Eric Lindros

This 30-card boxed standard-size set features posed and action color photos of Eric Lindros as he has progressed from the junior leagues to the NHL. The set begins when Eric Lindros first received attention as a 14-year-old with the St. Michael's Buzzers and ends with his playing for the Philadelphia Flyers. According to Pinnacle, 3,750 numbered cases were produced. The cards have black borders, and his name is printed in gold foil at the top. The backs display a vertical, color photo and Eric's comments about a particular phase of his career.

COMPLETE SET (30) 4.80 12.00
1 St. Michael's Buzzers .30 .75
2 Detroit Compuware .20 .50
3 Oshawa Generals .20 .50
(Skatin
4 Oshawa Generals .20 .50
(Red je
5 Oshawa Generals .20 .50
(Passin
6 Oshawa Generals .20 .50
(Slidin
7 Memorial Cup .20 .50
8 World Junior .20 .50
Championsh
9 World Junior .20 .50
Championsh
10 World Junior .40 1.00
Championship
11 Canada Cup .40 1.00
12 Canada Cup .20 .50
13 Canadian National .40 1.00
Team (In action&
black eye vis
14 Canadian National .40 1.00
Team (White jersey&
arms raise
15 Canadian National .20 .50
Team
16 Canadian National .20 .50
Team
17 First-Round Draft Pick .20 .50
18 Trade To Philadelphia .20 .50
19 Happy Flyer .20 .50
20 Preseason Action .20 .50
(White
21 Preseason Action .20 .50
(Black
22 Regular Season Debut .20 .50
23 First NHL Goal .20 .50
24 Winning Home Debut .20 .50
25 First NHL Hat Trick .20 .50
26 Playing Golf .20 .50
27 Backyard Fun .20 .50
28 Fan Favorite .20 .50
29 Welcome To Philly .20 .50
30 Philly Hero .40 1.00

1993 Pinnacle Power

This card was given to dealers who attended the Pinnacle Brands factory tour during the 1993 SCAI Convention. It measures approximately 3 1/2" by 5", and came in a hard plastic holder with a black velvet case that carries the word "Pinnacle" in yellow letters. According to Score, only 200 cards exist, the remainder of the print run having been shredded following distribution of the gift. The horizontal front features color head shots of Pinnacle spokesmen, Alexander Daigle, Franco Harris, and Eric Lindros, on a red background with a thin gold border, and a slightly thicker black border around it. The words "Pinnacle Power" on a red bar on the bottom of the card complete the front. On a shaded red to black background, the horizontal back carries biographical information about all three players.

1 Alexandre Daigle/200 60.00 150.00
Franco Harris
Eric Lindros

1993-94 Pinnacle I Samples

These six cards were distributed to dealers and media during the summer of 1993 to show the style of the upcoming Pinnacle hockey cards for the 1993-94 season. The cards can be differentiated from regular issues by the presence of dashes rather than stats in the tables on the reverse.

COMPLETE SET (6) 1.50 4.00
1 Tony Amonte .10 .30
2 Tom Barrasso .02 .10
3 Joe Juneau .08 .25
4 Eric Lindros .75 2.00
5 Teemu Selanne .60 1.50
6 Mats Sundin .20 .50

1993-94 Pinnacle II Samples

This 11-card hobby sample set was enclosed in a cello pack. With the exception of the Mogilny "Nifty 50" card, the top right corners of each card have been cut off, apparently to indicate that these are promo cards. The disclaimer "SAMPLE" is stamped across the photo on the back of the Mogilny, WJC card, and the Lindros redemption card.

COMPLETE SEALED SET (11) 4.00 10.00
275 Brian Leetch .01 .05
280 Guy Carbonneau .01 .05
300 Pat LaFontaine .01 .05
320 Pavel Bure .08 .25
340 Terry Yake .01 .05
341 Brian Benning .01 .05
0 World Jr. Championship .30 .75
NF9 Alexander Mogilny 1.25 3.00
SR1 Alexandre Daigle .20 .50
NNO Ad Card .20 .50
NNO Winner Card .60 1.50

1993-94 Pinnacle

Issued in two series of 236 and 275 cards, respectively, the 1993-94 Pinnacle hockey set consists of 511 standard-size cards. On a black background with a thin white border, the fronts feature color action player photos. Both series were offered in a U.S. version as well as a Canadian, bilingual version. Former prospect Brett Lindros is featured on a pair of cards with his talented brother Eric. Inserted at a rate of 1:100 packs, the cards are similar, but feature different photos for the U.S. and Canadian versions; the Canadian card also features bilingual text. A card honoring Wayne Gretzky's 802nd career goal was included in second series jumbo packs. Because of its distribution, the card (No. 512) is not considered part of the set. Rookie Cards include Jason Arnott, Jeff Friesen, Todd Harvey, Chris Osgood, Jamie Storr, Jocelyn Thibault and Oleg Tverdovsky.

Card		
1 Eric Lindros	.50	1.25
2 Mats Sundin	.12	.30
3 Tom Barrasso	.12	.30
4 Teemu Selanne	.30	.75
5 Joe Juneau	.12	.30
6 Tony Amonte	.12	.30
7 Bob Probert	.12	.30
8 Chris Kontos	.10	.25
9 Geoff Sanderson	.12	.30
10 Alexander Mogilny	.12	.30
11 Kevin Lowe	.10	.25
12 Nikolai Borschevsky	.10	.25
13 Dale Hunter	.10	.25
14 Gary Suter	.10	.25
15 Curtis Joseph	.15	.40
16 Mark Tinordi	.10	.25
17 Doug Weight	.12	.30
18 Benoit Hogue	.10	.25
19 Tommy Soderstrom	.12	.30
20 Pat Falloon	.10	.25
21 Jyrki Lumme	.10	.25
22 Brian Bellows	.12	.30
23 Alexei Zhitnik	.10	.25
24 Dirk Graham	.10	.25
25 Scott Stevens	.15	.40
26 Adam Foote	.10	.25
27 Mike Gartner	.12	.30
28 Dallas Drake RC	.15	.40
29 Ulf Samuelsson	.10	.25
30 Cam Neely	.15	.40
31 Sean Burke	.10	.25
32 Petr Svoboda	.10	.25
33 Keith Tkachuk	.15	.40
34 Roman Hamrlik	.10	.25
35 Robert Reichel	.10	.25
36 Igor Kravchuk	.10	.25
37 Mathieu Schneider	.10	.25
38 Bob Kudelski	.10	.25
39 Jeff Brown	.10	.25
40 Mike Modano	.25	.60
41 Rob Gaudreau RC	.15	.40
42 Dave Andreychuk	.15	.40
43 Trevor Linden	.12	.30
44 Dimitri Khristich	.10	.25
45 Joe Murphy	.10	.25
46 Rob Blake	.12	.30
47 Alexander Semak	.10	.25
48 Ray Ferraro	.10	.25
49 Curtis Leschyshyn	.10	.25
50 Mark Recchi	.20	.50
51 Sergei Nemchinov	.10	.25
52 Larry Murphy	.12	.30
53 Steve Heinze	.10	.25
54 Sergei Fedorov	.25	.60
55 Gary Roberts	.10	.25
56 Alexei Zhamnov	.12	.30
57 Derian Hatcher	.10	.25
58 Kelly Buchberger	.10	.25
59 Eric Desjardins	.12	.30
60 Brian Bradley	.10	.25
61 Patrick Poulin	.10	.25
62 Scott Lachance	.10	.25
63 Johan Garpenlov	.10	.25
64 Sylvain Turgeon	.10	.25
65 Grant Fuhr	.15	.40
66 Garth Butcher	.10	.25
67 Michal Pivonka	.10	.25
68 Todd Gill	.10	.25
69 Cliff Ronning	.10	.25
70 Steve Smith	.10	.25
71 Bobby Holik	.10	.25
72 Garry Galley	.10	.25
73 Steve Leach	.10	.25
74 Ron Francis	.20	.50
75 Jari Kurri	.15	.40
76 Alexei Kovalev	.12	.30
77 Dave Gagner	.12	.30
78 Steve Duchesne	.10	.25
79 Theo Fleury	.10	.25
80 Paul Coffey	.15	.40
81 Bill Ranford	.12	.30
82 Doug Bodger	.10	.25
83 Nick Kypreos	.10	.25
84 Darius Kasparaitis	.10	.25
85 Vincent Damphousse	.12	.30
86 Arturs Irbe	.12	.30
87 Shawn Chambers	.10	.25
88 Murray Craven	.10	.25
89 Rob Pearson	.10	.25
90 Kevin Hatcher	.10	.25
91 Brent Sutter	.10	.25
92 Teppo Numminen	.10	.25
93 Shawn Burr	.10	.25
94 Valeri Zelepukin	.10	.25
95 Ron Sutter	.10	.25
96 Craig MacTavish	.10	.25
97 Dominic Roussel	.12	.30
98 Nicklas Lidstrom	.15	.40
99 Adam Graves	.10	.25
100 Doug Gilmour	.20	.50
101 Frank Musil	.10	.25
102 Ted Donato	.10	.25
103 Andrew Cassels	.10	.25
104 Vladimir Malakhov	.10	.25
105 Shawn McEachern	.10	.25
106 Petr Nedved	.10	.25
107 Calle Johansson	.10	.25
108 Rich Sutter	.10	.25
109 Evgeny Davydov	.10	.25
110 Mike Ricci	.10	.25
111 Scott Niedermayer	.15	.40
112 John LeClair	.15	.40
113 Darryl Sydor	.10	.25
114 Paul DiPietro	.10	.25
115 Stephane Fiset	.12	.30
116 Christian Ruuttu	.10	.25
117 Doug Zmolek	.10	.25
118 Bob Sweeney	.10	.25
119 Brent Fedyk	.10	.25
120 Norm Maciver	.10	.25
121 Rob Zamuner	.10	.25
122 Brian Mullen	.10	.25
123 Trent Yawney	.10	.25
124 David Shaw	.10	.25
125 Mark Messier	.15	.40
126 Kevin Miller	.10	.25
127 Dino Ciccarelli	.12	.30
128 Derek King	.10	.25
129 Scott Young	.10	.25
130 Craig Janney	.12	.30
131 Jamie Macoun	.10	.25
132 Geoff Courtnall	.10	.25
133 Bob Essensa	.12	.30
134 Ken Daneyko	.10	.25
135 Mike Ridley	.10	.25
136 Stephan Lebeau	.10	.25
137 Tony Granato	.10	.25
138 Kay Whitmore	.10	.25
139 Luke Richardson	.10	.25
140 Jeremy Roenick	.25	.60
141 Brad May	.12	.30
142 Sandis Ozolinsh	.10	.25
143 Stephane Richer	.12	.30
144 John Tucker	.10	.25
145 Luc Robitaille	.12	.30
146 Dimitri Yushkevich	.10	.25
147 Sean Hill	.10	.25
148 John Vanbiesbrouck	.12	.30
149 Kevin Stevens	.10	.25
150 Patrick Roy	.40	1.00
151 Owen Nolan	.12	.30
152 Richard Smehlik	.10	.25
153 Ray Sheppard	.12	.30
154 Ed Olczyk	.10	.25
155 Al MacInnis	.12	.30
156 Sergei Zubov	.10	.25
157 Wendel Clark	.12	.30
158 Kirk McLean	.12	.30
159 Thomas Steen	.10	.25
160 Pierre Turgeon	.12	.30
161 Dmitri Kvartalnov	.10	.25
162 Brian Noonan	.10	.25
163 Mike McPhee	.10	.25
164 Peter Bondra	.12	.30
165 Bernie Nicholls	.10	.25
166 Michael Nylander	.10	.25
167 Guy Hebert	.12	.30
168 Scott Mellanby	.12	.30
169 Bob Bassen	.10	.25
170 Rod Brind'Amour	.12	.30
171 Andrei Kovalenko	.10	.25
172 Mike Donnelly	.10	.25
173 Steve Thomas	.10	.25
174 Rick Tocchet	.12	.30
175 Steve Yzerman	.40	1.00
176 Dixon Ward	.10	.25
177 Randy Wood	.10	.25
178 Dean Kennedy	.10	.25
179 Joel Otto	.10	.25
180 Kirk Muller	.10	.25
181 Chris Chelios	.15	.40
182 Richard Matvichuk	.10	.25
183 John MacLean	.12	.30
184 Joe Kocur	.10	.25
185 Adam Oates	.15	.40
186 Bob Beers	.10	.25
187 Ron Tugnutt	.12	.30
188 Brian Skrudland	.10	.25
189 Al Iafrate	.10	.25
190 Felix Potvin	.30	.75
191 David Reid	.10	.25
192 Jim Johnson	.10	.25
193 Kevin Haller	.10	.25
194 Steve Chiasson	.10	.25
195 Jaromir Jagr	.40	1.00
196 Martin Rucinsky	.10	.25
197 Sergei Bautin	.10	.25
198 Joe Nieuwendyk	.12	.30
199 Gilbert Dionne	.10	.25
200 Brett Hull	.25	.60
201 Yuri Khmylev	.10	.25
202 Todd Elik	.10	.25
203 Patrick Flatley	.10	.25
204 Martin Straka	.10	.25
205 Brendan Shanahan	.20	.50
206 Mark Beaufait RC	.15	.40
207 Mike Lenarduzzi RC	.10	.25
208 Chris LiPuma	.10	.25
209 Andre Faust	.10	.25
210 Ben Hankinson RC	.10	.25
211 Darrin Madeley RC	.15	.40
212 Oleg Petrov	.10	.25
213 Philippe Boucher	.10	.25
214 Tyler Wright	.10	.25
215 Jason Bowen RC	.15	.40
216 Matthew Barnaby	.12	.30
217 Bryan Smolinski	.10	.25
218 Dan Keczmer	.10	.25
219 Chris Simon RC	.15	.40
220 Corey Hirsch	.12	.30
221 Mario Lemieux AW	.60	1.50
222 Teemu Selanne AW	.30	.75
223 Chris Chelios AW	.15	.40
224 Ed Belfour AW	.15	.40
225 Pierre Turgeon AW	.12	.30
226 Doug Gilmour AW	.20	.50
227 Ed Belfour AW	.15	.40
228 Patrick Roy AW	.40	1.00
229 Dave Poulin AW	.10	.25
230 Mario Lemieux AW	.60	1.50
231 Mike Vernon HH	.12	.30
232 Vincent Damphousse HH	.12	.30
233 Chris Chelios HH	.15	.40
234 Cliff Ronning HH	.10	.25
235 Mark Howe HH	.15	.40
236 Alexandre Daigle	.10	.25
237 Wayne Gretzky NT	.75	2.00
238 Mark Messier NT	.15	.40
239 Dino Ciccarelli	.12	.30
240 Joe Mullen	.12	.30
241 Mike Gartner	.12	.30
242 Mike Richter	.15	.40
243 Pat Verbeek	.10	.25
244 Valeri Kamensky	.12	.30
245 Nelson Emerson	.10	.25
246 James Patrick	.10	.25
247 Greg Adams	.10	.25
248 Ulf Dahlen	.10	.25
249 Shayne Corson	.10	.25
250 Ray Bourque	.25	.60
251 Claude Lemieux	.10	.25
252 Kelly Hrudey	.12	.30
253 Patrice Brisebois	.10	.25
254 Mark Howe	.15	.40
255 Ed Belfour	.15	.40
256 Pelle Eklund	.10	.25
257 Zarley Zalapski	.10	.25
258 Sylvain Cote	.10	.25
259 Uwe Krupp	.10	.25
260 Dale Hawerchuk	.20	.50
261 Alexei Gusarov	.10	.25
262 Dave Ellett	.10	.25
263 Tomas Sandstrom	.10	.25
264 Vladimir Konstantinov	.12	.30
265 Paul Ranheim	.10	.25
266 Darrin Shannon	.10	.25
267 Chris Terreri	.12	.30
268 Russ Courtnall	.10	.25
269 Don Sweeney	.10	.25
270 Kevin Todd	.10	.25
271 Brad Shaw	.10	.25
272 Adam Creighton	.10	.25
273 Dana Murzyn	.10	.25
274 Donald Audette	.10	.25
275 Brian Leetch	.15	.40
276 Kevin Dineen	.10	.25
277 Bruce Driver	.10	.25
278 Jim Paek	.10	.25
279 Esa Tikkanen	.10	.25
280 Guy Carbonneau	.10	.25
281 Eric Weinrich	.10	.25
282 Tim Cheveldae	.12	.30
283 Bryan Marchment	.10	.25
284 Kelly Miller	.10	.25
285 Jimmy Carson	.10	.25
286 Terry Carkner	.10	.25
287 Mike Sullivan	.10	.25
288 Joe Reekie	.10	.25
289 Bob Rouse	.10	.25
290 Joe Sakic	.40	1.00
291 Gerald Diduck	.10	.25
292 Don Beaupre	.12	.30
293 Kjell Samuelsson	.10	.25
294 Claude Lapointe	.10	.25
295 Tie Domi	.10	.25
296 Charlie Huddy	.10	.25
297 Peter Zezel	.10	.25
298 Craig Muni	.10	.25
299 Rick Tabaracci	.10	.25
300 Pat LaFontaine	.15	.40
301 Lyle Odelein	.10	.25
302 Jocelyn Lemieux	.10	.25
303 Craig Ludwig	.10	.25
304 Marc Bergevin	.10	.25
305 Bill Guerin	.10	.25
306 Rick Zombo	.10	.25
307 Steven Finn	.10	.25
308 Gino Odjick	.10	.25
309 Jeff Beukeboom	.10	.25
310 Mario Lemieux	.60	1.50
311 J.J. Daigneault	.10	.25
312 Vincent Riendeau	.10	.25
313 Adam Burt	.10	.25
314 Mike Craig	.10	.25
315 Bret Hedican	.10	.25
316 Kris King	.10	.25
317 Sylvain Lefebvre	.10	.25
318 Troy Murray	.10	.25
319 Gordie Roberts	.10	.25
320 Pavel Bure	.15	.40
321 Marc Bureau	.10	.25
322 Randy McKay	.10	.25
323 Mark Lamb	.10	.25
324 Brian Mullen	.10	.25
325 Ken Wregget	.10	.25
326 Stephane Quintal	.10	.25
327 Robert Dirk	.10	.25
328 Mike Krushelnyski	.10	.25
329 Mikael Andersson	.10	.25
330 Paul Stanton	.10	.25
331 Phil Bourque	.10	.25
332 Andre Racicot	.10	.25
333 Brad Dalgarno	.10	.25
334 Neal Broten	.12	.30
335 John Blue	.12	.30
336 Ken Sutton	.10	.25
337 Greg Paslawski	.10	.25
338 Robb Stauber	.10	.25
339 Mike Keane	.10	.25
340 Terry Yake	.10	.25
341 Brian Benning	.10	.25
342 Brian Propp	.10	.25
343 Frank Pietrangelo	.12	.30
344 Stephane Matteau	.10	.25
345 Steven King	.10	.25
346 Joe Cirella	.10	.25
347 Andy Moog	.15	.40
348 Paul Ysebaert	.10	.25
349 Petr Klima	.10	.25
350 Corey Millen	.10	.25
351 Phil Housley	.12	.30
352 Craig Billington	.12	.30
353 Jeff Norton	.10	.25
354 Neil Wilkinson	.10	.25
355 Doug Lidster	.10	.25
356 Steve Larmer	.12	.30
357 Jon Casey	.12	.30
358 Brad McCrimmon	.10	.25
359 Alexei Kasatonov	.10	.25
360 Andrei Lomakin	.10	.25
361 Daren Puppa	.10	.25
362 Sergei Makarov	.10	.25
363 Dave Manson	.10	.25
364 Jim Sandlak	.10	.25
365 Glenn Healy	.12	.30
366 Martin Gelinas	.10	.25
367 Igor Larionov	.10	.25
368 Anatoli Semenov	.10	.25
369 Mark Fitzpatrick	.10	.25
370 Paul Cavallini	.10	.25
371 Jimmy Waite	.12	.30
372 Yves Racine	.10	.25
373 Jeff Hackett	.10	.25
374 Marty McSorley	.10	.25
375 Scott Pearson	.10	.25
376 Ron Hextall	.12	.30
377 Gaetan Duchesne	.10	.25
378 Jamie Baker	.10	.25
379 Troy Loney	.10	.25
380 Gord Murphy	.10	.25
381 Peter Sidorkiewicz	.10	.25
382 Pat Elynuik	.10	.25
383 Glen Wesley	.10	.25
384 Dean Evason	.10	.25
385 Mike Peluso	.10	.25
386 Darren Turcotte	.10	.25
387 Dave Poulin	.10	.25
388 John Cullen	.10	.25
389 Randy Ladouceur	.10	.25
390 Tom Fitzgerald	.10	.25
391 Denis Savard	.20	.50
392 Fredrik Olausson	.10	.25
393 Sergio Momesso	.10	.25
394 Mike Ramsey	.10	.25
395 Kelly Kisio	.10	.25
396 Craig Simpson	.10	.25
397 Slava Fetisov	.10	.25
398 Glenn Anderson	.15	.40
399 Michel Goulet	.10	.25
400 Wayne Gretzky	.75	2.00
401 Stu Grimson	.10	.25
402 Mike Hough	.10	.25
403 Dominik Hasek	.30	.75
404 Gerard Gallant	.10	.25
405 Greg Gilbert	.10	.25
406 Vladimir Ruzicka	.10	.25
407 Jim Hrivnak	.10	.25
408 Dave Lowry	.10	.25
409 Todd Ewen	.10	.25
410 Bob Errey	.10	.25
411 Bryan Trottier	.20	.50
412 Dave Taylor	.10	.25
413 Grant Ledyard	.10	.25
414 Chris Dahlquist	.10	.25
415 Brent Gilchrist	.10	.25
416 Geoff Smith	.10	.25
417 Jiri Slegr	.10	.25
418 Randy Burridge	.10	.25
419 Sergei Krivokrasov	.10	.25
420 Keith Primeau	.10	.25
421 Robert Kron	.10	.25
422 Keith Brown	.10	.25
423 David Volek	.10	.25
424 Josef Beranek	.10	.25
425 Wayne Presley	.10	.25
426 Stu Barnes	.10	.25
427 Milos Holan RC	.15	.40
428 Jeff Shantz	.10	.25
429 Brent Gretzky RC	.15	.40
430 Jarkko Varvio	.10	.25
431 Chris Osgood RC	1.00	2.50
432 Aaron Ward RC	.15	.40
433 Jason Smith RC	.10	.25
434 Cam Stewart RC	.15	.40
435 Derek Plante RC	.15	.40
436 Pat Peake	.10	.25
437 Alexander Karpovtsev	.10	.25
438 Jim Montgomery RC	.15	.40
439 Rob Niedermayer	.12	.30
440 Jocelyn Thibault RC	.15	.40
441 Jason Arnott RC	.30	.75
442 Mike Rathje	.10	.25
443 Chris Gratton	.12	.30
444 Vesa Viitakoski RC	.15	.40
445 Alexei Kudashov RC	.15	.40
446 Pavol Demitra	.20	.50
447 Ted Drury	.10	.25
448 Rene Corbet RC	.15	.40
449 Markus Naslund	.15	.40
450 Dmitri Filimonov	.10	.25
451 Roman Oksiuta RC	.15	.40
452 Michal Sykora RC	.15	.40
453 Greg Johnson	.10	.25
454 Mikael Renberg	.15	.40
455 Alexei Yashin	.12	.30
456 Chris Pronger	.15	.40
457 Manny Fernandez RC	.15	.40
458 Jamie Storr RC	.15	.40
459 Chris Armstrong RC	.15	.40
460 Drew Bannister RC	.10	.25
461 Joel Bouchard RC	.15	.40
462 Bryan McCabe RC	.15	.40
463 Nick Stajduhar RC	.15	.40
464 Brent Tully	.12	.30
465 Brendan Witt RC	.15	.40
466 Jason Allison RC	.15	.40
467 Jason Botterill RC	.15	.40
468 Curtis Bowen RC	.15	.40
469 Anson Carter RC	.15	.40
470 Brandon Convery RC	.15	.40
471 Yanick Dube RC	.15	.40
472 Jeff Friesen RC	.15	.40
473 Aaron Gavey RC	.15	.40
474 Martin Gendron RC	.12	.30
475 Rick Girard RC	.15	.40
476 Todd Harvey RC	.15	.40
477 Marty Murray RC	.15	.40
478 Mike Peca RC	.15	.40
479 Aaron Ellis RC	.15	.40
480 Toby Kvalevog RC	.15	.40
481 Jon Coleman RC	.15	.40
482 Ashlin Halfnight RC	.10	.25
483 Jason McBain RC	.15	.40
484 Chris O'Sullivan RC	.15	.40
485 Deron Quint RC	.15	.40
486 Blake Sloan RC	.10	.25
487 David Wilkie RC	.15	.40
488 Kevyn Adams RC	.15	.40
489 Jason Bonsignore RC	.15	.40
490 Andy Brink RC	.10	.25
491 Adam Deadmarsh	.10	.25
492 John Emmons	.10	.25
493 Kevin Hilton RC	.15	.40
494 Jason Karmanos RC	.10	.25
495 Bob Lachance RC	.15	.40
496 Jam.Langenbrunner RC	.15	.40
497 Jay Pandolfo RC	.15	.40
498 Richard Park RC	.15	.40
499 Ryan Sittler	.10	.25
500 John Varga RC	.15	.40
501 Valeri Bure RC	.15	.40
502 Maxim Bets RC	.10	.25
503 Vadim Sharifjanov	.12	.30
504 Alex.Kharlamov RC	.10	.25
505 Pavel Desyatkov RC	.10	.25
506 Oleg Tverdovsky RC	.15	.40
507 Nikolai Tsulygin	.10	.25
508 Evgeni Ryabchikov RC	.10	.25
509 Sergei Brylin RC	.15	.40
510 Maxim Sushinski RC	.10	.25
511 Sergei Kondrashkin RC	.10	.25
512 Wayne Gretzky HL SP	.75	2.00
AU1 Alexandre Daigle AU	12.00	30.00
AU2 Eric Lindros AU	12.00	30.00
NNO Eric/Brett Lindros	1.50	4.00
NNO Lindros Redempt.Exp.	.50	1.25

1993-94 Pinnacle Canadian

COMPLETE SET (511)	12.00	30.00
COMP.SERIES 1 (236)	6.00	15.00
COMP.SERIES 2 (275)	6.00	15.00

*CANADIAN: .4X TO 1X BASIC CARDS

Card		
1 Eric Lindros	1.00	2.50
2 Mats Sundin	.15	.40
3 Tom Barrasso	.05	.15
4 Teemu Selanne	.40	1.00
5 Joe Juneau	.15	.40
6 Tony Amonte	.02	.10
7 Bob Probert	.02	.10
8 Chris Kontos	.04	.10
9 Geoff Sanderson	.02	.10
10 Alexander Mogilny	.15	.40
11 Kevin Lowe	.04	.10
12 Nikolai Borschevsky	.04	.10
13 Dale Hunter	.02	.10
14 Gary Suter	.02	.10
15 Curtis Joseph	.10	.30
16 Mark Tinordi	.04	.10
17 Doug Weight	.02	.10
18 Benoit Hogue	.04	.10
19 Tommy Soderstrom	.02	.10
20 Pat Falloon	.04	.10
21 Jyrki Lumme	.04	.10
22 Brian Bellows	.02	.10
23 Alexei Zhitnik	.02	.10
24 Dirk Graham	.04	.10
25 Scott Stevens	.02	.10
26 Adam Foote	.04	.10
27 Mike Gartner	.05	.15
28 Dallas Drake RC	.07	.20
29 Ulf Samuelsson	.04	.10
30 Cam Neely	.10	.30
31 Sean Burke	.05	.15
32 Petr Svoboda	.04	.10
33 Keith Tkachuk	.15	.40
34 Roman Hamrlik	.02	.10
35 Robert Reichel	.02	.10
36 Igor Kravchuk	.04	.10
37 Mathieu Schneider	.04	.10
38 Bob Kudelski	.04	.10
39 Jeff Brown	.02	.10
40 Mike Modano	.10	.30
41 Rob Gaudreau RC	.04	.10
42 Dave Andreychuk	.05	.15
43 Trevor Linden	.05	.15
44 Dimitri Khristich	.04	.10
45 Joe Murphy	.02	.10
47 Alexander Semak	.04	.10
48 Ray Ferraro	.02	.10
49 Curtis Leschyshyn	.04	.10
50 Mark Recchi	.08	.25
51 Sergei Nemchinov	.04	.10
52 Larry Murphy	.05	.15
53 Steve Heinze	.04	.10
54 Sergei Fedorov	.40	1.00
55 Gary Roberts	.02	.10
56 Alexei Zhamnov	.20	.50
57 Derian Hatcher	.04	.10
58 Kelly Buchberger	.04	.10
60 Brian Bradley	.04	.10
61 Patrick Poulin	.04	.10
62 Scott Lachance	.04	.10
63 Johan Garpenlov	.04	.10
64 Sylvain Turgeon	.04	.10
65 Grant Fuhr	.05	.15
66 Garth Butcher	.04	.10
67 Michal Pivonka	.04	.10
68 Todd Gill	.04	.10
69 Cliff Ronning	.04	.10
70 Steve Smith	.04	.10
71 Bobby Holik	.04	.10
72 Garry Galley	.04	.10
73 Steve Leach	.04	.10
74 Ron Francis	.05	.15
75 Jari Kurri	.05	.15
76 Alexei Kovalev	.15	.40
77 Dave Gagner	.02	.10
78 Steve Duchesne	.02	.10
79 Theo Fleury	.05	.15
80 Paul Coffey	.07	.20
81 Bill Ranford	.05	.15
82 Doug Bodger	.04	.10
83 Nick Kypreos	.04	.10
84 Darius Kasparaitis	.04	.10
85 Vincent Damphousse	.02	.10
86 Arturs Irbe	.20	.50
87 Shawn Chambers	.04	.10
88 Murray Craven	.04	.10
89 Rob Pearson	.04	.10
90 Kevin Hatcher	.02	.10
91 Brent Sutter	.02	.10
92 Teppo Numminen	.04	.10
93 Shawn Burr	.04	.10
94 Valeri Zelepukin	.04	.10
95 Ron Sutter	.04	.10
96 Craig MacTavish	.04	.10
97 Dominic Roussel	.02	.10
98 Nicklas Lidstrom	.02	.10
99 Adam Graves	.08	.25
100 Doug Gilmour	.10	.30
101 Frank Musil	.04	.10
102 Ted Donato	.04	.10
103 Andrew Cassels	.04	.10
104 Vladimir Malakhov	.02	.10
105 Shawn McEachern	.04	.10
106 Petr Nedved	.02	.10
107 Calle Johansson	.04	.10
108 Rich Sutter	.04	.10
109 Evgeny Davydov	.04	.10
110 Mike Ricci	.02	.10
111 Scott Niedermayer	.02	.10
112 John LeClair	.15	.40
113 Darryl Sydor	.04	.10
114 Paul DiPietro	.04	.10
115 Stephane Fiset	.05	.15
116 Christian Ruuttu	.04	.10
117 Doug Zmolek	.04	.10
118 Bob Sweeney	.04	.10
119 Brent Fedyk	.04	.10
120 Norm Maciver	.04	.10
121 Rob Zamuner	.04	.10
122 Brian Mullen	.05	.15
123 Trent Yawney	.04	.10
124 David Shaw	.04	.10
125 Mark Messier	.07	.20
126 Kevin Miller	.04	.10
127 Dino Ciccarelli	.05	.15
128 Derek King	.04	.10
129 Scott Young	.04	.10
130 Craig Janney	.02	.10
131 Jamie Macoun	.04	.10
132 Geoff Courtnall	.02	.10
133 Bob Essensa	.02	.10
134 Ken Daneyko	.04	.10
135 Mike Ridley	.02	.10
136 Stephan Lebeau	.04	.10
137 Tony Granato	.04	.10
138 Kay Whitmore	.02	.10
139 Luke Richardson	.04	.10
140 Jeremy Roenick	.30	.75
141 Brad May	.04	.10
142 Sandis Ozolinsh	.02	.10
143 Stephane Richer	.02	.10
144 John Tucker	.04	.10
145 Luc Robitaille	.07	.20
146 Dimitri Yushkevich	.04	.10
147 Sean Hill	.04	.10
148 John Vanbiesbrouck	.05	.15
149 Kevin Stevens	.08	.25
150 Patrick Roy	.40	1.00
151 Owen Nolan	.02	.10
152 Richard Smehlik	.04	.10
153 Ray Sheppard	.02	.10
154 Ed Olczyk	.04	.10
155 Al MacInnis	.05	.15
156 Sergei Zubov	.20	.50
157 Wendel Clark	.05	.15
158 Kirk McLean	.05	.15
159 Thomas Steen	.04	.10
160 Pierre Turgeon	.10	.30
161 Dmitri Kvartalnov	.04	.10
162 Brian Noonan	.04	.10
163 Mike McPhee	.04	.10
164 Peter Bondra	.02	.10
165 Bernie Nicholls	.05	.15
166 Michael Nylander	.04	.10
167 Guy Hebert	.07	.20
168 Scott Mellanby	.04	.10
169 Bob Bassen	.04	.10
170 Rod Brind'Amour	.05	.15
171 Andrei Kovalenko	.04	.10
172 Mike Donnelly	.04	.10
173 Steve Thomas	.02	.10
174 Rick Tocchet	.05	.15
175 Steve Yzerman	.20	.50
176 Dixon Ward	.04	.10
177 Randy Wood	.04	.10
178 Dean Kennedy	.04	.10
179 Joel Otto	.04	.10
180 Kirk Muller	.02	.10
181 Chris Chelios	.05	.15
182 Richard Matvichuk	.04	.10
183 John MacLean	.02	.10
184 Joe Kocur	.04	.10
185 Adam Oates	.07	.20
186 Bob Beers	.04	.10
187 Ron Tugnutt	.02	.10
188 Brian Skrudland	.04	.10
189 Al Iafrate	.02	.10
190 Felix Potvin	.40	1.00
191 David Reid	.04	.10
192 Jim Johnson	.04	.10
193 Kevin Haller	.04	.10
194 Steve Chiasson	.04	.10
195 Jaromir Jagr	.40	1.00
196 Martin Rucinsky	.04	.10
197 Sergei Bautin	.04	.10
198 Joe Nieuwendyk	.05	.15
199 Gilbert Dionne	.04	.10
200 Brett Hull	.30	.75
201 Yuri Khmylev	.04	.10
202 Todd Elik	.04	.10
203 Patrick Flatley	.04	.10
204 Martin Straka	.02	.10
205 Brendan Shanahan	.15	.40
206 Mark Beaufait RC	.04	.10
207 Mike Lenarduzzi RC	.02	.10
208 Chris LiPuma	.04	.10
209 Andre Faust	.04	.10
210 Ben Hankinson RC	.04	.10
211 Darrin Madeley RC	.02	.10
212 Oleg Petrov	.04	.10
213 Philippe Boucher	.04	.10
214 Tyler Wright	.04	.10
215 Jason Bowen RC	.04	.10
216 Matthew Barnaby	.04	.10
217 Bryan Smolinski	.15	.40
218 Dan Keczmer	.04	.10
219 Chris Simon RC	.07	.20
220 Corey Hirsch	.02	.10
221 Mario Lemieux AW	.15	.40
222 Teemu Selanne AW	.15	.40
223 Chris Chelios AW	.02	.10
224 Ed Belfour AW	.05	.15
225 Pierre Turgeon AW	.05	.15
226 Doug Gilmour AW	.07	.20
227 Ed Belfour AW	.05	.15
228 Patrick Roy AW	.15	.40
229 Dave Poulin AW	.04	.10
230 Mario Lemieux AW	.15	.40
231 Mike Vernon HH	.02	.10
232 Vincent Damphousse HH	.02	.10
233 Chris Chelios HH	.02	.10
234 Cliff Ronning HH	.04	.10
235 Mark Howe HH	.02	.10
236 Alexandre Daigle	.20	.50
237 Wayne Gretzky NT	.60	1.50
238 Mark Messier NT	.08	.25
239 Dino Ciccarelli	.04	.10
240 Joe Mullen	.05	.15
241 Mike Gartner	.05	.15
242 Mike Richter	.08	.25
243 Pat Verbeek	.02	.10
244 Valeri Kamensky	.04	.10
245 Nelson Emerson	.04	.10
246 James Patrick	.04	.10
247 Greg Adams	.04	.10
248 Ulf Dahlen	.04	.10
249 Shayne Corson	.02	.10
250 Ray Bourque	.07	.20
251 Claude Lemieux	.02	.10
252 Kelly Hrudey	.05	.15
253 Patrice Brisebois	.04	.10
254 Mark Howe	.02	.10
255 Ed Belfour	.15	.40
256 Pelle Eklund	.04	.10
257 Zarley Zalapski	.04	.10
258 Sylvain Cote	.04	.10
259 Uwe Krupp	.04	.10
260 Dale Hawerchuk	.05	.15
261 Alexei Gusarov	.04	.10
262 Dave Ellett	.04	.10
263 Tomas Sandstrom	.02	.10
264 Vladimir Konstantinov	.04	.10
265 Paul Ranheim	.04	.10
266 Darrin Shannon	.04	.10
267 Chris Terreri	.02	.10
268 Russ Courtnall	.02	.10
269 Don Sweeney	.04	.10
270 Kevin Todd	.04	.10
271 Brad Shaw	.04	.10
272 Adam Creighton	.04	.10
273 Dana Murzyn	.04	.10
274 Donald Audette	.04	.10
275 Brian Leetch	.08	.25
276 Kevin Dineen	.04	.10
277 Bruce Driver	.04	.10
278 Jim Paek	.04	.10
279 Esa Tikkanen	.02	.10
280 Guy Carbonneau	.02	.10
281 Eric Weinrich	.04	.10
282 Tim Cheveldae	.02	.10
283 Bryan Marchment	.04	.10
284 Kelly Miller	.04	.10
285 Jimmy Carson	.04	.10
286 Terry Carkner	.04	.10
287 Mike Sullivan	.04	.10
288 Joe Reekie	.04	.10
289 Bob Rouse	.04	.10
290 Joe Sakic	.15	.40
291 Gerald Diduck	.04	.10
292 Don Beaupre	.02	.10
293 Kjell Samuelsson	.04	.10
294 Claude Lapointe	.04	.10
296 Charlie Huddy	.04	.10
297 Peter Zezel	.04	.10
298 Craig Muni	.04	.10
299 Rick Tabaracci	.02	.10
300 Pat LaFontaine	.07	.20
301 Lyle Odelein	.04	.10
302 Jocelyn Lemieux	.04	.10
303 Craig Ludwig	.04	.10
304 Marc Bergevin	.04	.10
305 Bill Guerin	.04	.10
306 Rick Zombo	.04	.10
307 Steven Finn	.04	.10
308 Gino Odjick	.04	.10
309 Jeff Beukeboom	.04	.10
310 Mario Lemieux	.40	1.00
311 J.J. Daigneault	.04	.10
312 Vincent Riendeau	.02	.10
313 Adam Burt	.04	.10
314 Mike Craig	.04	.10
315 Bret Hedican	.04	.10
316 Kris King	.04	.10
317 Sylvain Lefebvre	.04	.10
318 Troy Murray	.04	.10
319 Gordie Roberts	.04	.10
320 Pavel Bure	.60	1.50
321 Marc Bureau	.04	.10
322 Randy McKay	.04	.10
323 Mark Lamb	.04	.10
324 Brian Mullen	.02	.10
325 Ken Wregget	.02	.10
326 Stephane Quintal	.04	.10
327 Robert Dirk	.04	.10
328 Mike Krushelnyski	.04	.10
329 Mikael Andersson	.04	.10
330 Paul Stanton	.04	.10
331 Phil Bourque	.04	.10
332 Andre Racicot	.02	.10
333 Brad Dalgarno	.04	.10
334 Neal Broten	.02	.10
335 John Blue	.02	.10
336 Ken Sutton	.04	.10
337 Greg Paslawski	.04	.10
338 Robb Stauber	.02	.10
339 Mike Keane	.04	.10
340 Terry Yake	.04	.10
341 Brian Benning	.04	.10
342 Brian Propp	.02	.10
343 Frank Pietrangelo	.02	.10
344 Stephane Matteau	.04	.10
345 Steven King	.04	.10
346 Joe Cirella	.04	.10
347 Andy Moog	.05	.15
348 Paul Ysebaert	.04	.10
349 Petr Klima	.04	.10
350 Corey Millen	.04	.10
351 Phil Housley	.02	.10
352 Craig Billington	.02	.10
353 Jeff Norton	.04	.10
354 Neil Wilkinson	.04	.10
355 Doug Lidster	.04	.10
356 Steve Larmer	.05	.15
357 Jon Casey	.02	.10
358 Brad McCrimmon	.04	.10
359 Alexei Kasatonov	.04	.10
360 Andrei Lomakin	.04	.10
361 Daren Puppa	.05	.15
362 Sergei Makarov	.05	.15
363 Dave Manson	.04	.10
364 Jim Sandlak	.04	.10
365 Glenn Healy	.02	.10
366 Martin Gelinas	.04	.10
367 Igor Larionov	.02	.10
368 Anatoli Semenov	.04	.10
369 Mark Fitzpatrick	.02	.10
370 Paul Cavallini	.04	.10
371 Jimmy Waite	.02	.10
372 Yves Racine	.04	.10
373 Jeff Hackett	.02	.10
374 Marty McSorley	.02	.10
375 Scott Pearson	.04	.10
376 Ron Hextall	.02	.10
377 Gaetan Duchesne	.04	.10
378 Jamie Baker	.04	.10
379 Troy Loney	.04	.10
380 Gord Murphy	.04	.10
381 Peter Sidorkiewicz	.02	.10
382 Pat Elynuik	.04	.10
383 Glen Wesley	.04	.10
384 Dean Evason	.04	.10
385 Mike Peluso	.04	.10
386 Darren Turcotte	.04	.10
387 Dave Poulin	.04	.10
388 John Cullen	.04	.10
389 Randy Ladouceur	.04	.10
390 Tom Fitzgerald	.04	.10
391 Denis Savard	.05	.15
392 Fredrik Olausson	.04	.10
393 Sergio Momesso	.04	.10
394 Mike Ramsey	.04	.10
395 Kelly Kisio	.04	.10
396 Craig Simpson	.04	.10
397 Slava Fetisov	.02	.10
398 Glenn Anderson	.02	.10
399 Michel Goulet	.05	.15
400 Wayne Gretzky	.75	2.00
401 Stu Grimson	.04	.10
402 Mike Hough	.04	.10
403 Dominik Hasek	.20	.50
404 Gerard Gallant	.04	.10
405 Greg Gilbert	.04	.10
406 Vladimir Ruzicka	.04	.10
407 Jim Hrivnak	.02	.10
408 Dave Lowry	.04	.10
409 Todd Ewen	.04	.10
410 Bob Errey	.04	.10
411 Bryan Trottier	.05	.15
412 Dave Taylor	.05	.15
413 Grant Ledyard	.04	.10
414 Chris Dahlquist	.04	.10
415 Brent Gilchrist	.04	.10
416 Geoff Smith	.04	.10
417 Jiri Slegr	.04	.10
418 Randy Burridge	.04	.10
419 Sergei Krivokrasov	.02	.10
420 Keith Primeau	.05	.15
421 Robert Kron	.04	.10
422 Keith Brown	.04	.10
423 David Volek	.04	.10
424 Josef Beranek	.04	.10
425 Wayne Presley	.04	.10
426 Stu Barnes	.04	.10
427 Milos Holan RC	.07	.20
428 Jeff Shantz	.04	.10
429 Brent Gretzky RC	.10	.30
430 Jarkko Varvio	.04	.10
431 Chris Osgood RC	.25	.60
432 Aaron Ward RC	.04	.10
433 Jason Smith RC	.04	.10
434 Cam Stewart RC	.04	.10
435 Derek Plante RC	.08	.25
436 Pat Peake	.04	.10
437 Alexander Karpovtsev	.04	.10
438 Jim Montgomery RC	.04	.10
439 Rob Niedermayer	.15	.40
440 Jocelyn Thibault RC	.30	.75
441 Jason Arnott RC	.75	2.00
442 Mike Rathje	.04	.10
443 Chris Gratton	.15	.40
444 Vesa Viitakoski RC	.04	.10
445 Alexei Kudashov RC	.04	.10
447 Ted Drury	.04	.10
448 Rene Corbet RC	.04	.10
449 Markus Naslund	.04	.10
450 Dmitri Filimonov	.04	.10
451 Roman Oksiuta RC	.08	.25
452 Michal Sykora RC	.07	.20
453 Greg Johnson	.04	.10
454 Mikael Renberg	.30	.75
456 Chris Pronger	.15	.40
457 Emmanuel Fernandez RC	.25	.60
458 Jamie Storr RC	.75	2.00
459 Chris Armstrong RC	.05	.15
460 Drew Bannister RC	.05	.15
461 Joel Bouchard RC	.05	.15
462 Bryan McCabe RC	.15	.40
463 Nick Stajduhar RC	.10	.30
464 Brent Tully	.05	.15
465 Brendan Witt RC	.15	.40
466 Jason Allison RC	.30	.75
467 Jason Botterill RC	.15	.40

468 Curtis Bowen RC	.05	.15
469 Anson Carter RC	.08	.25
470 Brandon Convery RC	.08	.25
471 Yanick Dube RC	.15	.40
472 Jeff Friesen RC	1.00	2.50
473 Aaron Gavey RC	.20	.50
474 Martin Gendron RC	.15	.40
475 Rick Girard RC	.05	.15
476 Todd Harvey RC	.50	1.25
477 Marty Murray RC	.30	.75
478 Mike Peca RC	.15	.40
479 Aaron Ellis RC	.05	.15
480 Toby Kvalevog RC	.05	.15
481 Jon Coleman RC	.05	.15
482 Ashlin Halfnight RC	.05	.15
483 Jason McBain RC	.05	.15
484 Chris O'Sullivan RC	.07	.20
485 Deron Quint RC	.15	.40
486 Blake Sloan RC	.05	.15
487 David Wilkie RC	.15	.40
488 Kevyn Adams RC	.20	.50
489 Jason Bonsignore RC	.30	.75
490 Andy Brink RC	.05	.15
491 Adam Deadmarsh	.15	.40
492 John Emmons	.05	.15
493 Kevin Hilton RC	.15	.40
494 Jason Karmanos RC	.05	.15
495 Bob Lachance RC	.05	.15
496 Jamie Langenbrunner RC	.20	.50
497 Jay Pandolfo RC	.05	.15
498 Richard Park RC	.30	.75
499 Ryan Sittler	.05	.15
500 John Varga RC	.15	.40
501 Valeri Bure RC	.40	1.00
502 Maxim Bets RC	.08	.25
503 Vadim Sharifjanov	.08	.25
504 Alexander Kharlamov RC	.25	.60
505 Pavel Desyatkov RC	.05	.15
506 Oleg Tverdovsky RC	.50	1.25
507 Nikolai Tsulygin	.05	.15
508 Evgeni Ryabchikov RC	.15	.40
509 Sergei Brylin RC	.15	.40
510 Maxim Sushinski RC	.05	.15
511 Sergei Kondrashkin RC	.07	.20
NNO Brett/Eric Lindros CDN	3.00	8.00

1993-94 Pinnacle All-Stars

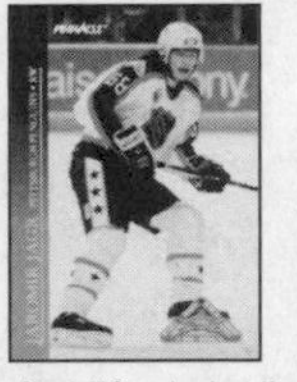

One bonus Pinnacle All-Star card was inserted in every U.S. and Canadian pack of '93-94 Score series 1 hockey cards. The wrappers from those packs carried a mail-away offer for cards 46-50. These cards feature on their fronts color action shots of players in their All-Star uniforms. The photos of Canadian and U.S. cards differ.

COMPLETE INSERT SET (45)	5.00	10.00
COMP.MAIL-IN SET (5)	10.00	25.00
1 Craig Billington	.07	.20
2 Zarley Zalapski	.05	.15
3 Kevin Lowe	.05	.15
4 Scott Stevens	.08	.25
5 Pierre Turgeon	.08	.25
6 Mark Recchi	.08	.25
7 Kirk Muller	.05	.15
8 Mike Gartner	.08	.25
9 Adam Oates	.08	.25
10 Brad Marsh	.05	.15
11 Pat LaFontaine	.08	.25
12 Peter Bondra	.08	.25
13 Joe Sakic	.20	.50
14 Rick Tocchet	.08	.25
15 Kevin Stevens	.08	.25
16 Steve Duchesne	.05	.15
17 Peter Sidorkiewicz	.08	.25
18 Patrick Roy	.50	1.25
19 Al Iafrate	.05	.15
20 Jaromir Jagr	.15	.40
21 Ray Bourque	.08	.25
22 Alexander Mogilny	.08	.25
23 Steve Chiasson	.05	.15
24 Garth Butcher	.05	.15
25 Phil Housley	.07	.20
26 Chris Chelios	.08	.25
27 Randy Carlyle	.05	.15
28 Mike Modano	.15	.40
29 Gary Roberts	.05	.15
30 Kelly Kisio	.05	.15
31 Pavel Bure	.08	.25
32 Teemu Selanne	.08	.25
33 Brian Bradley	.05	.15
34 Brett Hull	.10	.30
35 Jari Kurri	.08	.25
36 Steve Yzerman	.50	1.25
37 Luc Robitaille	.08	.25
38 Dave Manson	.05	.15
39 Jeremy Roenick	.10	.30
40 Mike Vernon	.08	.25
41 Jon Casey	.08	.25
42 Ed Belfour	.08	.25
43 Paul Coffey	.08	.25
44 Doug Gilmour	.08	.25
45 Wayne Gretzky	.60	1.50
46 Mike Gartner	1.50	4.00
47 Al Iafrate	1.50	4.00
48 Ray Bourque	6.00	15.00
49 Jon Casey	1.50	4.00
50 Campbell Conf.	2.00	5.00

1993-94 Pinnacle Captains

Randomly inserted in second-series jumbo packs at a rate of 1:4, these 27 standard-size cards feature on their fronts two photos of each NHL team captain. The photos of the Canadian and U.S. versions differ. The large borderless photo is a ghosted colour action shot; the smaller image in the center overlays the larger and is a full-contrast color head shot. The player's name in gold-foil lettering appears above the smaller photo. The grayish back carries a color action cutout on the left and a player profile in English (bilingual for the Canadian version) on the right. The cards are numbered on the back with a "CA" prefix.

COMPLETE SET (27)	40.00	100.00
*CANADIAN: .4X TO 1X BASIC INSERTS		
1 Troy Loney	.75	2.00
2 Ray Bourque	2.50	6.00
3 Pat LaFontaine	1.25	3.00
4 Joe Nieuwendyk	1.25	3.00
5 Dirk Graham	.75	2.00
6 Mark Tinordi	.75	2.00
7 Steve Yzerman	6.00	15.00
8 Craig MacTavish	.75	2.00
9 Brian Skrudland	.75	2.00
10 Pat Verbeek	.75	2.00
11 Wayne Gretzky	10.00	25.00
12 Guy Carbonneau	.75	2.00
13 Scott Stevens	.75	2.00
14 Pat Flatley	.75	2.00
15 Mark Messier	2.50	6.00
16 Mark Lamb	.75	2.00
17 Kevin Dineen	.75	2.00
18 Mario Lemieux	8.00	20.00
19 Joe Sakic	5.00	12.00
20 Brett Hull	2.50	6.00
21 Bob Errey	.75	2.00
22 M.Bergevin D.Savard	.75	2.00
23 Wendel Clark	1.25	3.00
24 Trevor Linden	1.25	3.00
25 Kevin Hatcher	.75	2.00
26 Keith Tkachuk	1.25	3.00
27 Checklist Card	2.00	5.00

1993-94 Pinnacle Expansion

Inserted one per series 1 hobby box, this six-card set measures the standard size. One side features a color action shot of a player from the Anaheim Mighty Ducks; the other, his counterpart at that position from the Florida Panthers. Each player's name and position, along with his team's logo, appear in a team color-coded bar below the photo. The cards are numbered on both sides as "X of 6."

COMPLETE SET (6)	5.00	10.00
1 J.Vanbiesbrouck G.Hebert	1.25	3.00
2 G.Murphy R.Ladouceur	.75	2.00
3 J.Cirella S.Hill	.75	2.00
4 D.Lowry T.Loney	.75	2.00
5 B.Skrudland T.Yake	.75	2.00
6 S.Mellanby S.King	.75	2.00

1993-94 Pinnacle Masks

Randomly inserted in first-series packs at a rate of 1:24 packs, this 10-card standard-size set showcases some of the elaborate masks NHL goalies wear. The cards are numbered on the back as "X of 10."

COMPLETE SET (10)	30.00	80.00
1 Grant Fuhr	4.00	10.00
2 Mike Vernon	4.00	10.00
3 Robb Stauber	4.00	10.00
4 Dominic Roussel	4.00	10.00
5 Pat Jablonski	4.00	10.00
6 Stephane Fiset	4.00	10.00
7 Wendell Young	4.00	10.00
8 Ron Hextall	4.00	10.00
9 John Vanbiesbrouck	4.00	10.00
10 Peter Sidorkiewicz	4.00	10.00

1993-94 Pinnacle Nifty Fifty

Randomly inserted in second-series foil packs at a rate of 1:36 and featuring Pinnacle's Dufex process, this 15-card standard-size set spotlights players who scored 50 or more goals. The borderless fronts feature metallic color head shots with a gold-foil Nifty Fifty logo at the lower left. The cards are numbered on the back as "X of 15."

1 Introductory CL	2.00	5.00
2 Alexander Mogilny	.50	1.25
3 Teemu Selanne	1.00	2.50
4 Mario Lemieux	4.00	10.00
5 Luc Robitaille	.50	1.25
6 Pavel Bure	1.25	3.00
7 Pierre Turgeon	.50	1.25
8 Steve Yzerman	3.00	8.00
9 Kevin Stevens	.30	.75
10 Brett Hull	2.00	5.00
11 Dave Andreychuk	.50	1.25
12 Pat LaFontaine	1.00	2.50
13 Mark Recchi	.50	1.25
14 Brendan Shanahan	1.00	2.50
15 Jeremy Roenick	1.00	2.50

1993-94 Pinnacle Super Rookies

Randomly inserted in second-series hobby foil packs at a rate of 1:36, this nine-card standard-size set spotlights players who were rookies in 1993-94. The fronts feature color action player shots on darkened backgrounds. The player's name in gold-foil lettering appears at the lower right. On a dark red background, the horizontal backs carry a color player cutout on the left, with career highlights to the right. The set was issued in Canadian and U.S. versions. Each version carries its own front photos and the backs of the Canadian cards are bilingual. The cards are numbered on the back with an "SR" prefix.

COMPLETE SET (9)	2.00	5.00
*CANADIAN: .4X TO 1X BASIC INSERTS		
1 Alexandre Daigle	.20	.50
2 Chris Pronger	.60	1.50
3 Chris Gratton	.20	.50
4 Rob Niedermayer	.20	.50
5 Alexei Yashin	.20	.50
6 Mikael Renberg	.20	.50
7 Jason Arnott	.60	1.50
8 Markus Naslund	.40	1.00
9 Pat Peake	.20	.50

1993-94 Pinnacle Team Pinnacle

Randomly inserted in packs at a rate of 1:90, this 12-card set measures the standard size. On the U.S. version, one side features a black-bordered color drawing of a player from the Eastern Conference, the other, one of a player from the Western Conference. The Canadian version carries color photos instead of color drawings. The cards are numbered on both sides as "X of 12."

COMPLETE SET (12)	50.00	100.00
COMP.SERIES 1 (6)	30.00	60.00
COMP.SERIES 2 (6)	20.00	40.00
*CANADIAN: .5X TO 1.2X BASIC INSERTS		
1 P.Roy/E.Belfour	8.00	20.00
2 B.Leetch/C.Chelios	8.00	20.00
3 S.Stevens/A.MacInnis	4.00	10.00
4 K.Stevens/L.Robitaille	4.00	10.00
5 M.Lemieux/W.Gretzky	12.00	30.00
6 J.Jagr/B.Hull	5.00	12.00
7 T.Barrasso/K.McLean	5.00	12.00
8 R.Bourque/P.Coffey	4.00	10.00
9 A.Iafrate/P.Housley	4.00	10.00
10 V.Damphousse/P.Bure	4.00	10.00
11 E.Lindros/J.Roenick	5.00	12.00
12 A.Mogilny/T.Selanne	5.00	12.00

1993-94 Pinnacle Team 2001

Inserted one per first-series jumbo pack, this 30-card set measures the standard size. The fronts feature color action player photos. The words "Team 2001" are printed in gold foil inside a black bar on the left, while the player's name in gold foil appears in a black bar on the bottom, along with the team logo. The horizontal backs carry a color head shot on the right. On a black background to the left of the photo are the player's name in gold foil and career highlights. The Canadian version carries color player drawings instead of photos. The cards are numbered on the back as "X of 30."

COMPLETE SET (30)	12.00	30.00
*CANADIAN: .4X TO 1X BASIC INSERTS		
1 Eric Lindros	.75	2.00
2 Alexander Mogilny	.60	1.50
3 Pavel Bure	.75	2.00
4 Joe Juneau	.50	1.25
5 Felix Potvin	.75	2.00
6 Nicklas Lidstrom	.75	2.00
7 Alexei Kovalev	.50	1.25
8 Patrick Poulin	.40	1.00
9 Shawn McEachern	.40	1.00
10 Teemu Selanne	.75	2.00
11 Rod Brind'Amour	.60	1.50
12 Jaromir Jagr	1.50	4.00
13 Pierre Turgeon	.50	1.25
14 Scott Niedermayer	.50	1.25
15 Mats Sundin	.60	1.50
16 Trevor Linden	.60	1.50
17 Mike Modano	1.25	2.00
18 Roman Hamrlik	.50	1.25
19 Tony Amonte	.50	1.25
20 Jeremy Roenick	1.25	2.00
21 Scott Lachance	.40	1.00
22 Mike Ricci	.50	1.25
23 Dimitri Khristich	.40	1.00
24 Sergei Fedorov	1.25	3.00
25 Joe Sakic	2.00	5.00
26 Pat Falloon	.50	1.25
27 Mathieu Schneider	.40	1.00
28 Owen Nolan	.50	1.25
29 Brendan Shanahan	.60	1.50
30 Mark Recchi	.50	1.25

1993-94 Pinnacle Daigle Entry Draft

To commemorate Daigle's signing with Score as a spokesperson, Score issued this standard-size card and distributed it to the news media and others who attended the 1993 NHL Draft in Quebec on June 26. The card was also distributed to media at the 1993 National Sports Collectors Convention in Chicago. The front features a color close-up photo with white borders. Daigle is pictured wearing a jersey with "Score" emblazoned across it. The back has a full-bleed action shot with Daigle wearing a "Pinnacle" jersey. A black stripe at the bottom carries the player's name and the anti-counterfeiting device. The card is unnumbered.

1 Alexandre Daigle	4.00	10.00

1994-95 Pinnacle I Hobby Samples

These standard-size cards were issued in a sealed ten-card pack to preview the 1994-95 Pinnacle I regular series. They are identical to the regular issue counterparts, except that the upper right corner has been cut off, and the printing of the names on front is done in the style of Rink Collection, rather than regular, cards. The cards are numbered on the back.

COMPLETE SEALED SET (10)	1.00	2.50
1 Eric Lindros Philadelph	.40	1.00
2 Alexandre Daigle Ottawa	.07	.20
3 Mike Modano Dallas Star	.20	.50
4 Vincent Damphousse Mont	.02	.10
5 Dave Andreychuk Toronto	.02	.10
6 Curtis Joseph St. Louis	.10	.30
7 Joe Juneau Washington C	.02	.10
246 Mariusz Czerkawski Bost	.01	.05
BR1 Al Iafrate Boston Bruin	.08	.25
NNO Title Card	.20	.50

1994-95 Pinnacle

This 540-card standard-size set was issued in two series of 270 cards. Cards were distributed in 14-card U.S. and Canadian packs, and 17-card jumbo packs. Series 1 packs had exclusive Canadian and U.S. inserts, series 2 did not. Members of the St. Louis Blues and Calgary Flames are posed in front of a locker which displays their newly designed sweaters. Rookie Cards include Mariusz Czerkawski, Eric Daze, Eric Fichaud, Ed Jovanovski, Jeff O'Neill and Wade Redden. A one-per-case (360 packs) insert card was produced for Canadian, and U.S. series 1 packs. Pavel Bure is numbered MVPC, while Dominik Hasek is MVPU. Both cards have MVP printed at top front and utilize a silver Dufex design. The backs feature dual photos over a silver reflective background.

1 Eric Lindros	.10	.25
2 Alexandre Daigle	.05	.15
3 Mike Modano	.15	.40
4 Vincent Damphousse	.07	.20
5 Dave Andreychuk	.10	.25
6 Curtis Joseph	.15	.40
7 Joe Juneau	.07	.20
8 Trevor Linden	.07	.20
9 Rob Blake	.10	.25
10 Mike Richter	.10	.25
11 Chris Pronger	.10	.25
12 Robert Reichel	.05	.15
13 Bryan Smolinski	.05	.15
14 Ray Sheppard	.07	.20
15 Guy Hebert	.07	.20
16 Tony Amonte	.07	.20
17 Richard Smehlik	.05	.15
18 Doug Weight	.07	.20
19 Chris Gratton	.05	.15
20 Tom Barrasso	.07	.20
21 Brian Skrudland	.05	.15
22 Sandis Ozolinsh	.05	.15
23 Bill Guerin	.07	.20
24 Curtis Leschyshyn	.05	.15
25 Teemu Selanne	.20	.50
26 Darius Kasparaitis	.05	.15
27 Garry Galley	.05	.15
28 Alexei Yashin	.10	.25
29 Mark Tinordi	.05	.15
30 Patrick Roy	.25	.60
31 Mike Gartner	.10	.25
32 Brendan Shanahan	.12	.30
33 Sylvain Cote	.05	.15
34 Jeff Brown	.05	.15
35 Jari Kurri	.07	.20
36 Sergei Zubov	.05	.15
37 Pat Verbeek	.07	.20
38 Theo Fleury	.10	.25
39 Al Iafrate	.05	.15
40 Keith Primeau	.10	.25
41 Bobby Dollas	.05	.15
42 Ed Belfour	.10	.25
43 Dale Hawerchuk	.12	.30
44 Shayne Corson	.05	.15
45 Danton Cole	.05	.15
46 Ulf Samuelsson	.05	.15
47 Stu Barnes	.05	.15
48 Ulf Dahlen	.05	.15
49 Valeri Zelepukin	.05	.15
50 Joe Sakic	.20	.50
51 Dave Manson	.05	.15
52 Steve Thomas	.05	.15
53 Mark Recchi	.12	.30
54 Dave McLlwain	.05	.15
55 Derian Hatcher	.05	.15
56 Mathieu Schneider	.05	.15
57 Bill Berg	.05	.15
58 Petr Nedved	.07	.20
59 Dimitri Khristich	.05	.15
60 Kirk McLean	.07	.20
61 Marty McSorley	.05	.15
62 Adam Graves	.05	.15
63 Geoff Sanderson	.07	.20
64 Frank Musil	.05	.15
65 Cam Neely	.10	.25
66 Nicklas Lidstrom	.10	.25
67 Stephan Lebeau	.05	.15
68 Joe Murphy	.05	.15
69 Yuri Khmylev	.05	.15
70 Zdeno Ciger	.05	.15
71 Daren Puppa	.07	.20
72 Ron Francis	.12	.30
73 Scott Mellanby	.07	.20
74 Igor Larionov	.05	.15
75 Scott Niedermayer	.10	.25
76 Owen Nolan	.10	.25
77 Teppo Numminen	.05	.15
78 Pierre Turgeon	.07	.20
79 Mikael Renberg	.07	.20
80 Norm Maciver	.05	.15
81 Paul Cavallini	.05	.15
82 Kirk Muller	.05	.15
83 Felix Potvin	.10	.25
84 Craig Janney	.07	.20
85 Dale Hunter	.05	.15
86 Jyrki Lumme	.05	.15
87 Alexei Zhitnik	.07	.20
88 Steve Larmer	.07	.20
89 Jocelyn Lemieux	.05	.15
90 Joe Nieuwendyk	.10	.25
91 Don Sweeney	.05	.15
92 Slava Kozlov	.07	.20
93 Tim Sweeney	.05	.15
94 Chris Chelios	.10	.25
95 Derek Plante	.05	.15
96 Igor Kravchuk	.05	.15
97 Shawn Chambers	.05	.15
98 Jaromir Jagr	.25	.60
99 Jeff Norton	.05	.15
100 John Vanbiesbrouck	.07	.20
101 John MacLean	.07	.20
102 Stephane Fiset	.07	.20
103 Keith Tkachuk	.10	.25
104 Vladimir Malakhov	.05	.15
105 Mike McPhee	.05	.15
106 Eric Desjardins	.07	.20
107 Alexei Kovalev	.05	.15
108 Steve Duchesne	.05	.15
109 Peter Zezel	.05	.15
110 Randy Burridge	.05	.15
111 Jason Bowen	.05	.15
112 Phil Bourque	.05	.15
113 Cliff Ronning	.05	.15
114 Sean Burke	.07	.20
115 Gary Roberts	.05	.15
116 Vladimir Konstantinov	.07	.20
117 Brent Sutter	.07	.20
118 Tony Granato	.05	.15
119 Garry Valk	.05	.15
120 Adam Oates	.10	.25
121 Arturs Irbe	.07	.20
122 Jesse Belanger	.05	.15
123 Roman Hamrlik	.07	.20
124 Jason Arnott	.07	.20
125 Alexander Mogilny	.07	.20
126 Bruce Driver	.05	.15
127 Shawn McEachern	.05	.15
128 Andrei Kovalenko	.05	.15
129 Benoit Hogue	.05	.15
130 Tim Cheveldae	.07	.20
131 Brian Noonan	.05	.15
132 Lyle Odelein	.07	.20
133 Russ Courtnall	.05	.15
134 Peter Stastny	.07	.20
135 Doug Gilmour	.12	.30
136 Pat Peake	.05	.15
137 Gary Suter	.05	.15
138 Paul Ranheim	.05	.15
139 Troy Murray	.05	.15
140 Pavel Bure	.10	.25
141 Gord Murphy	.05	.15
142 Michael Nylander	.07	.20
143 Craig Muni	.05	.15
144 Bob Corkum	.05	.15
145 Martin Brodeur	.25	.60
146 Ted Donato	.05	.15
147 Alexei Zhamnov	.07	.20
148 Josef Beranek	.05	.15
149 Joe Mullen	.07	.20
150 Sergei Fedorov	.15	.40
151 Mike Keane	.05	.15
152 Sergei Makarov	.05	.15
153 Marty McInnis	.05	.15
154 Steven Rice	.05	.15
155 Brian Leetch	.10	.25
156 Chris Joseph	.05	.15
157 Darcy Wakaluk	.07	.20
158 Kelly Miller	.05	.15
159 Jim Montgomery	.05	.15
160 Nikolai Borschevsky	.05	.15
161 Darren Turcotte	.05	.15
162 Brad Shaw	.05	.15
163 Mark Lamb	.05	.15
164 Alexei Gusarov	.07	.20
165 Jeremy Roenick	.20	.50
166 Stephane Richer	.07	.20
167 German Titov	.05	.15
168 Rob Niedermayer	.07	.20
169 Glen Murray	.05	.15
170 Mario Lemieux	.40	1.00
171 Thomas Steen	.05	.15
172 Ron Tugnutt	.07	.20
173 Pat Falloon	.05	.15
174 Esa Tikkanen	.05	.15
175 Dominik Hasek	.20	.50
176 Patrick Flatley	.05	.15
177 Gino Odjick	.05	.15
178 Charlie Huddy	.05	.15
179 Dave Poulin	.05	.15
180 Darren McCarty	.05	.15
181 Todd Gill	.05	.15
182 Tom Chorske	.05	.15
183 Marc Bergevin	.05	.15
184 Dave Lowry	.05	.15
185 Brent Gilchrist	.05	.15
186 Eric Weinrich	.05	.15
187 Ted Drury	.05	.15
188 Boris Mironov	.05	.15
189 Patrik Carnback	.05	.15
190 Ray Bourque	.15	.40
191 Patrice Brisebois	.05	.15
192 Bob Errey	.05	.15
193 Scott Lachance	.05	.15
194 Brad May	.05	.15
195 Jeff Beukeboom	.05	.15
196 James Patrick	.05	.15
197 Doug Brown	.05	.15
198 Dana Murzyn	.05	.15
199 Chris Osgood	.15	.40
200 Wayne Gretzky	.50	1.25
201 Bob Carpenter	.05	.15
202 Evgeny Davydov	.05	.15
203 Oleg Petrov	.05	.15
204 Grant Ledyard	.05	.15
205 Jocelyn Thibault	.10	.25
206 Bill Houlder	.05	.15
207 Tom Fitzgerald	.05	.15
208 Dominic Roussel	.07	.20
209 Dave Ellett	.05	.15
210 Frank Kucera	.05	.15
211 Steve Smith	.05	.15
212 Vincent Riendeau	.05	.15
213 Scull Pearson	.05	.15
214 John Slaney	.05	.15
215 Larry Murphy	.07	.20
216 Travis Green	.07	.20
217 Joel Otto	.05	.15
218 Randy Wood	.05	.15
219 Gaetan Duchesne	.05	.15
220 Sergei Nemchinov	.05	.15
221 Terry Carkner	.05	.15
222 Randy McKay	.05	.15
223 Mike Donnelly	.05	.15
224 J.J. Daigneault	.05	.15
225 Dallas Drake	.05	.15
226 John Tucker	.05	.15
227 Dimitri Yushkevich	.05	.15
228 Mike Stapleton	.07	.20
229 Dmitri Mironov	.05	.15
230 Ken Wregget	.07	.20
231 Claude Lapointe	.05	.15
232 Joe Sacco	.05	.15
233 Craig Ludwig	.05	.15
234 David Reid	.05	.15
235 Rich Sutter	.05	.15
236 Mark Fitzpatrick	.07	.20
237 Jim Storm	.07	.20
238 Brad Dalgarno	.05	.15
239 Dixon Ward	.05	.15
240 Greg Adams	.05	.15
241 Dino Ciccarelli	.07	.20
242 Vlastimil Kroupa	.05	.15
243 Joe Kocur	.05	.15
244 Donald Audette	.05	.15
245 Trent Yawney	.05	.15
246 Mariusz Czerkawski RC	.10	.25
247 Jason Allison	.07	.20
248 Brian Savage	.05	.15
249 Fred Knipscheer	.05	.15
250 Jamie McLennan	.07	.20
251 Aaron Gavey	.05	.15
252 Jeff Friesen	.05	.15
253 Adam Deadmarsh	.05	.15
254 Jamie Storr	.07	.20
255 Brian Rolston	.05	.15
256 Zigmund Palffy	.07	.20
257 Brett Lindros	.05	.15
258 Denis Tsygurov RC	.10	.25
259 Chris Tamer RC	.05	.15
260 Mike Peca	.07	.20
261 Oleg Tverdovsky	.07	.20
262 Todd Harvey	.05	.15
263 Yan Kaminsky	.05	.15
264 Kenny Jonsson	.05	.15
265 Paul Kariya	.12	.30
266 Peter Forsberg	.25	.60
267 Atlantic Division Checklist	.05	.15
268 Northeast Division Checklist	.05	.15
269 Central Division Checklist	.05	.15
270 Pacific Division Checklist	.05	.15
271 Steve Yzerman	.25	.60
272 John LeClair	.10	.25
273 Rod Brind'Amour	.07	.20
274 Ron Hextall	.07	.20
275 Todd Elik	.05	.15
276 Geoff Courtnall	.05	.15
277 Kjell Samuelsson	.05	.15
278 Brian Bradley	.05	.15
279 Darrin Shannon	.05	.15
280 Mike Ricci	.05	.15
281 Peter Bondra	.07	.20
282 Terry Yake	.05	.15
283 Patrick Poulin	.05	.15
284 Bob Kudelski	.05	.15
285 Bill Ranford	.07	.20
286 Alexander Godynyuk	.05	.15
287 Claude Lemieux	.10	.25
288 S.Turgeon/P. Kane	15.00	40.00
289 Kevin Miller	.05	.15
290 Brian Bellows	.07	.20
291 Murray Craven	.05	.15
292 Kelly Hrudey	.07	.20
293 Neal Broten	.07	.20
294 Craig Simpson	.05	.15
295 Mark Howe	.10	.25
296 Johan Garpenlov	.05	.15
297 Jamie Macoun	.05	.15
298 Steve Leach	.05	.15
299 Kevin Stevens	.05	.15
300 Mark Messier	.10	.25
301 Paul Ysebaert	.05	.15
302 Derek King	.05	.15
303 Fredrik Olausson	.05	.15
304 John Druce	.07	.20
305 Calle Johansson	.05	.15
306 Kelly Kisio	.05	.15
307 Sergio Momesso	.10	.25
308 Joe Cirella	.05	.15
309 Tommy Soderstrom	.07	.20
310 Scott Stevens	.10	.25
311 Petr Klima	.05	.15
312 Steven Finn	.05	.15
313 Tomas Sandstrom	.05	.15
314 Ray Ferraro	.05	.15
315 Andy Moog	.10	.25
316 Ray Whitney	.05	.15
317 Dirk Graham	.05	.15
318 Shawn Burr	.05	.15
319 Andrew Cassels	.05	.15
320 Craig Billington	.07	.20
321 Wayne Presley	.05	.15
322 Anatoli Semenov	.05	.15
323 Michal Pivonka	.07	.20
324 Martin Gelinas	.05	.15
325 Nelson Emerson	.05	.15
326 Brent Fedyk	.05	.15
327 Bob Bassen	.05	.15
328 Darryl Sydor	.05	.15
329 Stephane Matteau	.05	.15
330 Ken Daneyko	.05	.15
331 Mikhail Shtalenkov RC	.05	.15
332 Kelly Buchberger	.05	.15
333 Mike Hough	.05	.15
334 Dave Gagner	.07	.20
335 Chris Terreri	.07	.20
336 Robert Kron	.05	.15
337 Andrei Lomakin	.05	.15
338 Kevin Lowe	.05	.15
339 Steve Konroyd	.05	.15
340 Denis Savard	.12	.30
341 Steve Heinze	.05	.15
342 Zarley Zalapski	.05	.15
343 Valeri Kamensky	.07	.20
344 Tie Domi	.07	.20
345 Kevin Hatcher	.05	.15
346 Dean Evason	.05	.15
347 Bobby Holik	.05	.15
348 Steve Konowalchuk	.05	.15
349 Rob Gaudreau	.05	.15
350 Pat LaFontaine	.10	.25
351 Joe Reekie	.05	.15
352 Martin Straka	.05	.15
353 Dave Babych	.05	.15
354 Geoff Smith	.05	.15
355 Don Beaupre	.07	.20
356 Adam Burt	.05	.15
357 Doug Bodger	.05	.15
358 Dean McAmmond	.05	.15
359 Gerald Diduck	.05	.15
360 Rob DiMaio	.05	.15
361 Scott Young	.05	.15
362 Alexander Semak	.05	.15
363 Mike Rathje	.05	.15
364 Alexander Karpovtsev	.05	.15
365 Trevor Kidd	.07	.20
366 Jason Dawe	.05	.15
367 Vitali Prokhorov	.05	.15
368 Keith Brown	.05	.15
369 Bret Hedican	.05	.15
370 Markus Naslund	.10	.25
371 Rick Tocchet	.07	.20
372 Guy Carbonneau	.05	.15
373 Kevin Haller	.05	.15
374 Bob Rouse	.05	.15
375 Rob Pearson	.05	.15
376 Steve Chiasson	.05	.15
377 Mike Vernon	.07	.20
378 Keith Jones	.05	.15
379 Sylvain Lefebvre	.05	.15
380 Tom Kurvers	.05	.15
381 Pat Elynuik	.05	.15
382 Uwe Krupp	.05	.15
383 Ron Sutter	.05	.15
384 Mike Ridley	.05	.15
385 Wendel Clark	.07	.20
386 Mats Sundin	.07	.20
387 Al MacInnis	.07	.20
388 Glen Wesley	.05	.15
389 Jim Paek	.05	.15
390 Rudy Poeschek	.07	.20
391 Yves Racine	.05	.15
392 Craig MacTavish	.05	.15
393 Jon Casey	.07	.20
394 Garth Butcher	.07	.20
395 Sean Hill	.05	.15
396 Troy Loney	.05	.15
397 John Cullen	.05	.15
398 Alexei Kasatonov	.05	.15
399 Mike Craig	.05	.15
400 Luc Robitaille	.10	.25
401 Randy Moller	.05	.15
402 Chris Dahlquist	.05	.15
403 Pat Conacher	.05	.15
404 Bob Probert	.05	.15
405 Robert Dirk	.05	.15
406 Randy Cunneyworth	.05	.15
407 Bryan Marchment	.07	.20
408 Nick Kypreos	.05	.15
409 Doug Lidster	.05	.15
410 Phil Housley	.07	.20
411 Bob Sweeney	.05	.15
412 Mike Ramsey	.05	.15
413 Robert Lang	.05	.15
414 Brian Benning	.05	.15
415 Greg Gilbert	.05	.15
416 Martin Rucinsky	.05	.15
417 Jason Smith	.07	.20
418 Jozef Stumpel	.05	.15
419 Bob Beers	.07	.20
420 Ed Olczyk	.05	.15
421 Grant Fuhr	.10	.25
422 Gilbert Dionne	.05	.15
423 Mike Peluso	.05	.15
424 Petr Svoboda	.05	.15
425 Corey Millen	.05	.15
426 Kevin Dineen	.05	.15
427 Brad McCrimmon	.05	.15
428 Bob Essensa	.05	.15
429 Paul Coffey	.10	.25
430 Glenn Healy	.07	.20
431 Luke Richardson	.05	.15
432 Adam Foote	.05	.15
433 Paul Broten	.05	.15
434 Christian Ruuttu	.05	.15
435 David Shaw	.05	.15
436 Jimmy Carson	.05	.15
437 Ken Sutton	.05	.15
438 Kay Whitmore	.05	.15
439 Jim Dowd	.05	.15
440 Jim Johnson	.05	.15
441 Kirk Maltby	.05	.15
442 Trent Klatt	.05	.15
443 Paul DiPietro	.05	.15
444 Rick Tabaracci	.07	.20
445 Craig Wolanin	.05	.15
446 Dave Hannan	.05	.15
447 Rick Zombo	.05	.15
448 Tom Pederson	.05	.15
449 Martin LaPointe	.05	.15
450 Brett Hull	.20	.50
451 Mikael Andersson	.05	.15
452 Benoit Brunet	.05	.15
453 Nathan Lafayette	.05	.15
454 Kent Manderville	.05	.15
455 Todd Krygier	.05	.15
456 Dennis Vaske	.05	.15
457 Peter Popovic	.05	.15
458 Jeff Shantz	.05	.15
459 Darrin Madeley	.05	.15
460 Rene Corbet	.05	.15
461 Alexandre Daigle IB	.05	.15
462 Martin Brodeur IB	.25	.60
463 Jason Arnott IB	.07	.20
464 Mikael Renberg IB	.07	.20
465 Alexei Yashin IB	.10	.25
466 Chris Pronger IB	.10	.25
467 Mariusz Czerkawski IB	.10	.25
468 Chris Gratton IB	.05	.15
469 Rob Niedermayer IB	.07	.20
470 Bryan Smolinski IB	.05	.15
471 Chris Osgood IB	.15	.40
472 Derek Plante IB	.05	.15
473 Brian Rolston IB	.05	.15
474 Jason Allison IB	.07	.20
475 Jamie Storr IB	.07	.20
476 Kenny Jonsson IB	.05	.15
477 Viktor Kozlov IB	.05	.15
478 Brett Lindros IB	.05	.15
479 Peter Forsberg IB	.25	.60
480 Paul Kariya IB	.12	.30
481 Viktor Kozlov	.05	.15
482 Michal Grosek RC	.05	.15
483 Maxim Bets	.05	.15
484 Jason Wiemer RC	.05	.15
485 Janne Laukkanen	.07	.20
486 Valeri Karpov RC	.05	.15
487 Andrei Nikolishhin	.05	.15
488 Dan Plante RC	.05	.15
489 Mattias Norstrom	.05	.15
490 David Oliver RC	.05	.15
491 Todd Simon RC	.05	.15
492 Valeri Bure	.05	.15
493 Eric Fichaud RC	.10	.25
494 Cory Stillman RC	.05	.15
495 Chris Therien	.05	.15
496 Matt Johnson RC	.05	.15
497 Joby Messier	.05	.15
498 Slava Butsayev	.05	.15
499 Bernie Nicholls	.07	.20
500 Mark Osborne	.05	.15
501 Stephane Quintal	.05	.15
502 Jamie Baker	.05	.15
503 Todd Ewen	.05	.15
504 Dan Quinn	.07	.20
505 Peter Taglianetti	.05	.15
506 Chris Simon	.05	.15
507 Jay Wells	.05	.15
508 Tommy Albelin	.05	.15
509 Warren Rychel	.05	.15
510 Brent Hughes	.05	.15
511 Greg Johnson	.05	.15
512 Stu Grimson	.05	.15
513 Iain Fraser	.05	.15
514 Rob Ray	.05	.15
515 Craig Berube	.05	.15
516 Shane Churla	.05	.15
517 Checklist	.05	.15
518 Checklist	.05	.15
519 Checklist	.05	.15
520 Checklist	.05	.15
521 Jamie Storr	.07	.20
522 Dan Cloutier RC	.15	.40
523 Bryan McCabe	.05	.15
524 Ed Jovanovski RC	.15	.40
525 Nolan Baumgartner RC	.10	.25
526 Jamie Rivers RC	.10	.25
527 Wade Redden RC	.15	.40
528 Lee Sorochan RC	.10	.25
529 Eric Daze RC	.15	.40
530 Jason Allison	.07	.20
531 Alexandre Daigle	.05	.15
532 Jeff Friesen	.05	.15
533 Todd Harvey	.05	.15
534 Jeff O'Neill RC	.07	.20
535 Ryan Smyth RC	.30	.75
536 Marty Murray	.07	.20
537 Darcy Tucker RC	.15	.40
538 Denis Pederson RC	.07	.20
539 Shean Donovan RC	.10	.25
540 Larry Courville RC	.10	.25
MVPC Pavel Bure	12.00	30.00
MVPU Dominik Hasek	8.00	20.00

1994-95 Pinnacle Artist's Proofs

This set is a parallel version of the standard set. The difference is a reflective gold foil Artist's Proof logo on the front. Series 1 cards also featured an Artist's Proof logo on the back; this logo did not appear on series 2 card backs. The Pinnacle and player name bearing icon, which is gold on normal cards, is printed with a more reflective gold foil on these inserts. Series two production made this feature more bold than in series 1. Cards were inserted at a rate of 1:36 packs in both series 1 and 2, 14 card packs. There are no Artist's Proof versions of the first series checklists, however, there is an Artist's Proof version of the second series checklists. Estimated production of these cards varies; one press release suggests "less than 700 sets", while wrappers state "less than 500".

*VETS: 12X TO 30X BASIC CARDS		
*ROOKIES: 4X TO 10X BASIC CARDS		
200 Wayne Gretzky	60.00	150.00
288 S. Turgeon/P. Kane	20.00	50.00

1994-95 Pinnacle Rink Collection

This set is a parallel to the Pinnacle set. The cards were inserted in packs at a rate of 1:4. The fronts have a full-color action photo with the player's last name on the left surrounded by the chain for a gold medallion at the bottom. The background consists of silver-foil sunrays. The backs have a color photo with player information and statistics. The bottom has the words "Rink Collection" and the Pinnacle emblem.

*VETS: 4X TO 10X BASIC CARDS		
*ROOKIES: 2X TO 5X BASIC CARDS		
288 S. Turgeon/P. Kane	30.00	80.00

1994-95 Pinnacle Boomers

This 18 card set could be found randomly inserted at a rate of 1:24 U.S. series 1 hobby packs. These horizontally-oriented cards are notable for their design, which utilizes two-thirds of the space for an action shot of the featured player shooting the puck. The remaining third featured a ghosted goalie image. The player's last name is printed in gold foil down the left side of the card. "Boomers" is written in blue and red on the bottom left portion. The backs are occupied mostly with a player photo, while text assumes the remaining third. Cards are numbered with a "BR" prefix.

COMPLETE SET (18)	15.00	40.00
BR1 Al Iafrate	.60	1.50
BR2 Vladimir Malakhov	.60	1.50

BR3 Al MacInnis 1.00 2.50
BR4 Chris Chelios 2.00 5.00
BR5 Mike Modano 3.00 8.00
BR6 Brendan Shanahan 2.00 5.00
BR7 Ray Bourque 3.00 8.00
BR8 Geoff Sanderson 1.00 2.50
BR9 Brett Hull 2.50 6.00
BR10 Rob Blake 1.00 2.50
BR11 Steve Thomas .60 1.50
BR12 Cam Neely 2.00 5.00
BR13 Pavel Bure 2.00 5.00
BR14 Stephane Richer 1.00 2.50
BR15 Teemu Selanne 2.00 5.00
BR16 Eric Lindros 2.00 5.00
BR17 Alexander Mogilny 1.00 2.50
BR18 Rick Tocchet 1.00 2.50

1994-95 Pinnacle Gamers

This 18-card set was randomly inserted 1:18 packs of all Pinnacle series 2 product. The cards are enhanced by the Dufex printing technology. Each card is color-coded to the team colors of the player. The player is pictured inside a shape which approximates the design of his team's emblem. The backs are reflective colored, with a photo and paragraph of information. Cards are numbered with a "GR" prefix.

COMPLETE SET (18) 20.00 50.00
GR1 Teemu Selanne 2.00 5.00
GR2 Pat LaFontaine 1.25 3.00
GR3 Sergei Fedorov 2.00 5.00
GR4 Pavel Bure 2.00 5.00
GR5 Jaromir Jagr 3.00 8.00
GR6 Alexandre Daigle .75 2.00
GR7 Kirk Muller .75 2.00
GR8 Mike Modano 2.00 5.00
GR9 Mark Messier 2.00 5.00
GR10 Brendan Shanahan 2.00 5.00
GR11 Doug Gilmour .75 2.00
GR12 Rick Tocchet .75 2.00
GR13 Wendel Clark .75 2.00
GR14 Jeremy Roenick 2.00 5.00
GR15 Adam Graves .75 2.00
GR16 Eric Lindros 2.00 5.00
GR17 Cam Neely 2.00 5.00
GR18 Keith Tkachuk 1.25 3.00

1994-95 Pinnacle Goaltending Greats

Any one of the 18 cards in this set could be found randomly inserted at a rate of 1:9 Pinnacle series 2 jumbo packs. This horizontal set has a full-bleed photo design, with the set logo and player name in gold foil on the left side of the card. Vertical backs have a crowded design, with a small player photo on the lower left, personal information and statistics. Cards are numbered with a "GT" prefix.

COMPLETE SET (18) 40.00 80.00
GT1 Dominik Hasek 5.00 10.00
GT2 Mike Richter 2.50 6.00
GT3 John Vanbiesbrouck 1.50 4.00
GT4 Ed Belfour 3.00 8.00
GT5 Patrick Roy 8.00 20.00
GT6 Bill Ranford 1.50 4.00
GT7 Martin Brodeur 5.00 12.00
GT8 Felix Potvin 3.00 8.00
GT9 Arturs Irbe 1.50 4.00
GT10 Mike Vernon 1.50 4.00
GT11 Kirk McLean 1.50 4.00
GT12 Sean Burke 1.50 4.00
GT13 Curtis Joseph 2.50 6.00
GT14 Andy Moog 1.50 4.00
GT15 Daren Puppa 1.50 4.00
GT16 Chris Osgood 1.50 4.00
GT17 Tom Barrasso 1.50 4.00
GT18 Jocelyn Thibault 1.50 4.00

1994-95 Pinnacle Masks

This popular ten-card insert set was inserted in Canadian series 1 product at the rate of 1:90 packs. The cards feature a photo of a goaltender's mask over a metallic blue Dufex background. No team or player name appears on the front. Backs feature dual photos on a mirror finish and the player and team names. Cards are numbered with an "MA" prefix.

COMPLETE SET (10) 100.00 200.00
MA1 Patrick Roy 25.00 50.00
MA2 John Vanbiesbrouck 10.00 25.00
MA3 Kelly Hrudey 10.00 25.00
MA4 Guy Hebert 8.00 20.00
MA5 Rick Tabaracci 8.00 20.00
MA6 Ron Hextall 10.00 25.00
MA7 Trevor Kidd 8.00 20.00
MA8 Andy Moog 10.00 25.00
MA9 Jimmy Waite 8.00 20.00
MA10 Curtis Joseph 10.00 25.00

1994-95 Pinnacle Northern Lights

This 18-card insert set was randomly inserted 1:24 Canadian series 1 hobby packs. The series highlights the top players from Canadian-based teams. The fronts have a player photo which fades into a sky design with a northern lights image on the left side. The player name is stamped in gold foil above the word "Canada", written in yellow. The horizontal backs have a photo on the left, with some personal information printed over another interpretation of the famous northern lights. Cards are numbered with an "NL" prefix in a red maple leaf.

COMPLETE SET (18) 15.00 40.00
NL1 Patrick Roy 5.00 12.00
NL2 Kirk Muller .75 2.00
NL3 Vincent Damphousse .75 2.00
NL4 Joe Sakic 2.50 6.00
NL5 Wendel Clark 1.25 3.00
NL6 Alexandre Daigle .75 2.00
NL7 Alexei Yashin .75 2.00
NL8 Doug Gilmour 1.25 3.00
NL9 Felix Potvin 2.50 6.00
NL10 Mats Sundin 1.50 4.00
NL11 Teemu Selanne 1.50 4.00
NL12 Keith Tkachuk 1.25 3.00
NL13 Bill Ranford 1.25 3.00
NL14 Jason Arnott .75 2.00
NL15 Theo Fleury .75 2.00
NL16 Gary Roberts .75 2.00
NL17 Pavel Bure 1.50 4.00
NL18 Trevor Linden 1.25 3.00

1994-95 Pinnacle Rookie Team Pinnacle

The 12 cards in this set, featuring a player from each conference on either side, were inserted in Pinnacle series two product at the rate of 1:90 packs. The set focuses on 24 top rookies in the league. Cards are printed using the Gold-line foil technology; either side could be found with the Gold-line foil finish. The cards feature a cutout player photo on a striped background of reds and yellows. The player name is printed on a black border on the top of the card. One side has the card number with an "RTP" prefix and the Pinnacle anti-counterfeiting device.

COMPLETE SET (12) 15.00 40.00
1 C.Hirsch/J.Storr 1.00 2.50
2 M.Norstrom/O.Tverdovsky 1.00 2.50
3 D.Tsygurov/J.Laukkanen 1.00 2.50
4 C.Tamer/K.Jonsson 1.00 2.50
5 Z.Palffy/V.Kozlov 2.00 5.00
6 R.Corbet/M.Bets 1.00 2.50
7 J.Allison/J.Friesen 2.00 5.00
8 B.Rolston/M.Peca 2.00 5.00
9 P.Forsberg/P.Kariya 8.00 20.00
10 B.Savage/T.Harvey 1.00 2.50
11 B.Lindros/V.Karpov 1.00 2.50
12 M.Czerkawski/S.Krivokrasov 1.00 2.50

1994-95 Pinnacle Team Pinnacle

This 12-card set features 24 top players in the league, 12 per conference (one player on either side of the card). These were inserted in series 1 U.S. product at the rate of 1:90 packs. Cards have full-bleed photos on each side. Either side could be found with the Dufex technology, while the other has a mirror finish. The words "Team Pinnacle '94-95" are printed in gold on both sides. The player's last name is printed in an ovoid sphere along the bottom.

COMPLETE SET (12) 75.00 150.00
*DUFEX BACK: .4X TO 1X BASIC INSERTS
TP1 F.Potvin/P.Roy 8.00 20.00
TP2 C.Joseph/M.Richter 5.00 12.00
TP3 C.Chelios/R.Bourque 4.00 10.00
TP4 B.Leetch/R.Blake 6.00 15.00
TP5 S.Stevens/P.Coffey 6.00 15.00
TP6 B.Shanahan/A.Graves 10.00 25.00
TP7 L.Robitaille/K.Stevens 4.00 10.00
TP8 S.Fedorov/E.Lindros 8.00 20.00
TP9 W.Gretzky/M.Messier 10.00 25.00
TP10 D.Gilmour/M.Lemieux 8.00 20.00
TP11 B.Hull/J.Jagr 5.00 12.00
TP12 P.Bure/C.Neely 8.00 20.00

1994-95 Pinnacle World Edition

The 18 cards in this set were randomly inserted at a rate of 1:18 Pinnacle series 2 hobby packs. The cards feature a player photo with his native country's flag as a background. The World Edition logo is stamped in gold foil on the upper left corner. Horizontal backs have a small player photo on the left and a paragraph of information. The cards are numbered with a "WE" prefix. The Pinnacle anti-counterfeiting device also appears on the back.

COMPLETE SET (18) 15.00 40.00
WE1 Teemu Selanne 1.00 2.50
WE2 Doug Gilmour .60 1.50
WE3 Jeremy Roenick 1.00 2.50
WE4 Ulf Dahlen .40 1.00
WE5 Sergei Fedorov 1.00 2.50
WE6 Dominik Hasek 2.00 5.00
WE7 Jari Kurri .60 1.50
WE8 Mario Lemieux 4.00 10.00
WE9 Mike Modano 1.00 2.50
WE10 Mikael Renberg .40 1.00
WE11 Sandis Ozolinsh .40 1.00
WE12 Alexei Kovalev .40 1.00
WE13 Robert Reichel .40 1.00
WE14 Eric Lindros 1.00 2.50
WE15 Brian Leetch 1.00 2.50
WE16 Nicklas Lidstrom 1.00 2.50
WE17 Alexei Yashin .40 1.00
WE18 Petr Nedved .40 1.00

1995-96 Pinnacle

This single-series issue of 225 cards was left incomplete when Pinnacle decided to release the Summit brand in the place of Pinnacle series 2. Nevertheless, most major stars are included. The highlight of the set is a large rookies subset, extending from card #201-220. However, there are no key Rookie Cards in this set.

1 Pavel Bure .12 .30
2 Paul Kariya .12 .30
3 Adam Oates .10 .25
4 Garry Galley .05 .15
5 Mark Messier .15 .40
6 Theo Fleury .12 .30
7 Alexandre Daigle .05 .15
8 Joe Murphy .05 .15
9 Eric Lindros .15 .40
10 Kevin Hatcher .07 .20
11 Jaromir Jagr .25 .60
12 Owen Nolan .10 .25
13 Ulf Dahlen .05 .15
14 Paul Coffey .10 .25
15 Brett Hull .12 .30
16 Jason Arnott .07 .20
17 Paul Ysebaert .05 .15
18 Jesse Belanger .05 .15
19 Mats Sundin .10 .25
20 Darren Turcotte .05 .15
21 Dale Hunter .07 .20
22 Jari Kurri .10 .25
23 Alexei Zhamnov .10 .25
24 Mark Recchi .12 .30
25 Dallas Drake .05 .15
26 John MacLean .07 .20
27 Keith Jones .07 .20
28 Mathieu Schneider .05 .15
29 Jeff Brown .07 .20
30 Patrick Flatley .05 .15
31 Dave Andreychuk .10 .25
32 Bill Guerin .07 .20
33 Chris Gratton .05 .15
34 Pierre Turgeon .10 .25
35 Stephane Richer .07 .20
36 Marty McSorley .05 .15
37 Craig Janney .05 .15
38 Geoff Sanderson .05 .15
39 Ron Francis .12 .30
40 Stu Barnes .05 .15
41 Mikael Renberg .07 .20
42 David Oliver .05 .15
43 Radek Bonk .05 .15
44 Sergei Fedorov .15 .40
45 Adam Graves .07 .20
46 Uwe Krupp .07 .20
47 Mike Richter .10 .25
48 Todd Harvey .05 .15
49 Stanislav Neckar .05 .15
50 Chris Chelios .10 .25
51 John LeClair .10 .25
52 German Titov .07 .20
53 Garth Butcher .05 .15
54 Pat LaFontaine .10 .25
55 Jeff Friesen .05 .15
56 Ray Bourque .15 .40
57 Esa Tikkanen .05 .15
58 Steve Rucchin .07 .20
59 Roman Hamrlik .05 .15
60 Oleg Tverdovsky .10 .25
61 Doug Gilmour .12 .30
62 Jocelyn Lemieux .07 .20
63 Roman Oksiuta .05 .15
64 Alexei Zhitnik .05 .15
65 Sylvain Cote .05 .15
66 Paul Kruse .05 .15
67 Teppo Numminen .05 .15
68 Gary Suter .07 .20
69 Darrin Shannon .05 .15
70 Derian Hatcher .07 .20
71 Sergei Gonchar .05 .15
72 Adam Deadmarsh .05 .15
73 Jyrki Lumme .05 .15
74 Dino Ciccarelli .07 .20
75 Mike Gartner .10 .25
76 Todd Marchant .05 .15
77 Jason Wiemer .05 .15
78 Scott Mellanby .07 .20
79 Al MacInnis .10 .25
80 Glen Wesley .05 .15
81 Igor Larionov .05 .15
82 Eric Lacroix .05 .15
83 Mike Keane .05 .15
84 Vincent Damphousse .07 .20
85 Robert Kron .05 .15
86 Scott Stevens .10 .25
87 Don Beaupre .07 .20
88 Zigmund Palffy .10 .25
89 Kevin Lowe .07 .20
90 Tommy Soderstrom .07 .20
91 Glenn Healy .07 .20
92 Randy McKay .05 .15
93 Sean Hill .05 .15
94 Brian Savage .05 .15
95 Ron Hextall .10 .25
96 Darryl Sydor .07 .20
97 Tom Barrasso .07 .20
98 Andrei Nikolishin .05 .15
99 Viktor Kozlov .07 .20
100 Rob Niedermayer .07 .20
101 Wayne Gretzky .50 1.25
102 Shaun Van Allen .05 .15
103 Dave Manson .05 .15
104 Donald Audette .07 .20
105 Daren Puppa .07 .20
106 Jeremy Roenick .12 .30
107 Ken Wregget .07 .20
108 Mike Modano .15 .40
109 Rod Brind'Amour .10 .25
110 Eric Desjardins .07 .20
111 Pat Verbeek .07 .20
112 Jeff Beukeboom .05 .15
113 John Druce .07 .20
114 Andy Moog .10 .25
115 Turner Stevenson .05 .15
116 Alexander Selivanov .07 .20
117 Neal Broten .07 .20
118 Nikolai Khabibulin .07 .20
119 Claude Lemieux .10 .25
120 Sergei Brylin .05 .15
121 Bob Corkum .05 .15
122 Kelly Hrudey .07 .20
123 Jason Dawe .05 .15
124 Sean Burke .05 .15
125 Dave Gagner .05 .15
126 Kirk Maltby .07 .20
127 Ian Laperriere .05 .15
128 Slava Kozlov .07 .20
129 Vladimir Konstantinov .07 .20
130 Kenny Jonsson .10 .25
131 Sylvain Lefebvre .05 .15
132 Kirk McLean .07 .20
133 Brian Leetch .10 .25
134 Olaf Kolzig .07 .20
135 Patrick Poulin .05 .15
136 Tim Cheveldae .07 .20
137 Gary Roberts .05 .15
138 Jim Carey .07 .20
139 Dominik Hasek .12 .30
140 Josef Beranek .05 .15
141 Don Sweeney .05 .15
142 Felix Potvin .10 .25
143 Guy Hebert .07 .20
144 Guy Carbonneau .10 .25
145 Mikhail Shtalenkov .05 .15
146 Kevin Miller .07 .20
147 Blaine Lacher .07 .20
148 Craig MacTavish .05 .15
149 Derek Plante .05 .15
150 Kevin Dineen .07 .20
151 Trevor Kidd .07 .20
152 Sergei Nemchinov .05 .15
153 Ed Belfour .07 .20
154 Sergei Krivokrasov .05 .15
155 Mike Rathje .07 .20
156 Mike Donnelly .05 .15
157 David Roberts .05 .15
158 Jocelyn Thibault .07 .20
159 Tie Domi .07 .20
160 Chris Osgood .07 .20
161 Martin Gelinas .05 .15
162 Scott Thornton .07 .20
163 Bob Rouse .05 .15
164 Randy Wood .05 .15
165 Chris Therien .05 .15
166 Steven Rice .05 .15
167 Scott Lachance .05 .15
168 Petr Svoboda .05 .15
169 Patrick Roy .25 .60
170 Norm Maciver .07 .20
171 Todd Gill .05 .15
172 Brian Rolston .05 .15
173 Wade Flaherty RC .07 .20
174 Valeri Bure .05 .15
175 Mark Fitzpatrick .07 .20
176 Darren McCarty .05 .15
177 Ken Daneyko .05 .15
178 Yves Racine .05 .15
179 Murray Craven .05 .15
180 Nicklas Lidstrom .10 .25
181 Gord Murphy .05 .15
182 Eric Weinrich .05 .15
183 Todd Krygier .05 .15
184 Cliff Ronning .05 .15
185 Mariusz Czerkawski .05 .15
186 Benoit Hogue .05 .15
187 Richard Smehlik .07 .20
188 Jeff Norton .05 .15
189 Steve Chiasson .05 .15
190 Andrei Nazarov .07 .20
191 Steve Smith .05 .15
192 Mario Lemieux .30 .75
193 Trent Klatt .05 .15
194 Valeri Zelepukin .05 .15
195 Adam Foote .07 .20
196 Lyle Odelein .05 .15
197 Keith Primeau .05 .15
198 Rob Blake .07 .20
199 Dave Lowry .05 .15
200 Adam Burt .05 .15
201 Martin Gendron .07 .20
202 Tommy Salo RC .15 .40
203 Eric Daze .20 .50
204 Ryan Smyth .07 .20
205 Brian Holzinger RC .20 .50
206 Chris Marinucci RC .07 .20
207 Jason Bonsignore .05 .15
208 Craig Johnson .05 .15
209 Steve Larouche RC .05 .15
210 Chris McAlpine RC .07 .20
211 Shean Donovan .05 .15
212 Cory Stillman .05 .15
213 Craig Darby .05 .15
214 Philippe DeRouville .07 .20
215 Kevin Brown .07 .20
216 Manny Fernandez .07 .20
217 Radim Bicanek .07 .20
218 Craig Conroy RC .07 .20
219 Todd Warriner .07 .20
220 Richard Park .10 .25
221 Checklist .05 .15
222 Checklist .05 .15
223 Checklist .05 .15
224 Checklist .05 .15
225 Checklist .05 .15

1995-96 Pinnacle Artist's Proofs

This 225-card set is a high-end parallel of the standard Pinnacle issue. The cards utilize the same Dufex technology as the Rink Collection cards, but have the Artist's Proof logo embossed on, typically in the lower right corner. On some cards, this can be very difficult to detect: collectors should double check all dufexed cards before buying or selling to ensure which type they are. These cards were inserted at a rate of 1:48 packs.

*VETS: 12X TO 30X BASIC CARDS
*ROOKIES: 4X TO 10X BASIC CARDS

1995-96 Pinnacle Rink Collection

These 225 cards form a low-end parallel version of the Pinnacle set. The cards, which utilize the Dufex process, are difficult to distinguish from the very similar, but much more expensive Artist's Proof cards. Collectors are advised to carefully look for the embossed AP symbol in the lower right corner before buying or selling the 1995-96 Dufexed cards. The Rink Collection cards were inserted at a rate of 1:4 packs.

*VETS: 4X TO 10X BASIC CARDS
*ROOKIES: 2X TO 5X BASIC CARDS

1995-96 Pinnacle Clear Shots

Fifteen veteran superstars are recognized in this set which is distinguished by its use of a clear plastic rainbow holographic printing technology. The cards were inserted at a rate of 1:60 hobby and retail packs.

1 Martin Brodeur 5.00 12.00
2 Brett Hull 2.50 6.00
3 Paul Kariya 2.50 6.00
4 Eric Lindros 3.00 8.00
5 Cam Neely 2.00 5.00
6 Doug Gilmour 2.50 6.00
7 Sergei Fedorov 3.00 8.00
8 Peter Forsberg 5.00 12.00
9 Wayne Gretzky 10.00 25.00
10 Patrick Roy 5.00 12.00
11 Jaromir Jagr 5.00 12.00
12 Pavel Bure 2.50 6.00
13 Mario Lemieux 6.00 15.00
14 Pierre Turgeon 2.00 5.00
15 Dominik Hasek 2.50 6.00

1995-96 Pinnacle First Strike

This 15-card set focusing on game breaking players is enhanced by the use of spot micro-etch technology. The cards were randomly inserted at a rate of 1:24 retail packs only.

COMPLETE SET (15) 10.00 20.00
1 Mark Messier .40 1.00
2 Wayne Gretzky 2.50 6.00
3 Doug Gilmour .20 .50
4 Patrick Roy 2.00 5.00
5 Cam Neely .40 1.00
6 Brian Leetch .20 .50
7 Ed Belfour .40 1.00
8 Wendel Clark .20 .50
9 Chris Chelios .40 1.00
10 Claude Lemieux .10 .30
11 Peter Forsberg .75 2.00
12 Brett Hull .50 1.25
13 Mario Lemieux 2.00 5.00
14 Dominik Hasek .75 2.00
15 Theo Fleury .10 .30

1995-96 Pinnacle Full Contact

This 12-card set used the spot micro-etch technology to bring out the best of the NHL's top bangers and bruisers. The cards were randomly inserted 1:9 retail jumbo packs.

COMPLETE SET (12) 5.00 12.00
1 Cam Neely .30 .75
2 Scott Stevens .30 .75
3 Owen Nolan .20 .50
4 Jeremy Roenick .50 1.25
5 Brendan Shanahan .20 .50
6 Chris Chelios .30 .75
7 Brett Lindros .20 .50
8 Jason Arnott .20 .50
9 Tie Domi .20 .50
10 Mark Tinordi .20 .50
11 Keith Tkachuk .30 .75
12 Mark Messier .40 1.00

1995-96 Pinnacle Global Gold

These 25 cards set were randomly inserted into Pinnacle International boxes at a rate of 1:6 packs. These cards are identical to the ones found in the Pinnacle U.S. basic set, save for the circular gold-foil stamp on the front that reads, "Global Gold", and the numbering on the back reading "X of 25" instead of the regular card number.

1 Pavel Bure 2.50 6.00
2 Jaromir Jagr 3.00 8.00
3 Mats Sundin 1.00 2.50
4 Jari Kurri .75 2.00
5 Mikael Renberg .75 2.00
6 Radek Bonk .20 .50
7 Sergei Fedorov 2.00 5.00
8 Uwe Krupp .20 .50
9 German Titov .20 .50
10 Esa Tikkanen .75 2.00
11 Oleg Tverdovsky .20 .50
12 Teppo Numminen .20 .50
13 Jyrki Lumme .20 .50
14 Zigmund Palffy 1.00 2.50
15 Tommy Soderstrom .75 2.00
16 Viktor Kozlov .75 2.00
17 Alexander Selivanov .20 .50
18 Sergei Brylin .20 .50
19 Dominik Hasek 2.00 5.00
20 Sergei Nemchinov .20 .50
21 Petr Svoboda .20 .50
22 Valeri Bure .75 2.00
23 Nicklas Lidstrom 1.00 2.50
24 Mariusz Czerkawski .75 2.00
25 Valeri Zelepukin .20 .50

1995-96 Pinnacle Masks

This popular Dufex set returns for the third year to spotlight the unique and colorful world of protection NHL style. No team or player names appear on the front. The cards were randomly inserted at the rate of 1:90 retail and hobby packs.

COMPLETE SET (10) 60.00 120.00
1 Blaine Lacher 4.00 10.00
2 Martin Brodeur 15.00 40.00
3 Jim Carey 4.00 10.00
4 Felix Potvin 10.00 25.00
5 Andy Moog 4.00 10.00
6 Mike Vernon 5.00 12.00
7 Mark Fitzpatrick 8.00 20.00
8 Ron Hextall 6.00 15.00
9 Sean Burke 5.00 12.00
10 Jocelyn Thibault 10.00 25.00

1995-96 Pinnacle Roaring 20s

This 20-card set highlights the young guns of the NHL. The cards benefit from the use of the spot micro-etch technology and were randomly inserted in 1:19 hobby packs.

COMPLETE SET (20) 20.00 50.00
1 Eric Lindros 1.25 3.00
2 Paul Kariya 1.00 2.50
3 Martin Brodeur 3.00 8.00
4 Jeremy Roenick 1.50 4.00
5 Mike Modano 1.50 4.00
6 Sergei Fedorov 1.50 4.00
7 Mats Sundin 1.00 2.50
8 Pavel Bure 1.25 3.00
9 Jim Carey .60 1.50
10 Felix Potvin 2.50 6.00
11 Alexei Zhamnov .60 1.50
12 Mikael Renberg .60 1.50
13 Jaromir Jagr 2.00 5.00
14 Peter Bondra .60 1.50
15 Peter Forsberg 2.00 5.00
16 John LeClair .60 1.50
17 Joe Sakic 2.50 6.00
18 Brendan Shanahan 1.25 3.00
19 Teemu Selanne 1.25 3.00
20 Pierre Turgeon .60 1.50

1995-96 Pinnacle FANtasy

This 30-card set was distributed as a promotional item at the 1996 All-Star FanFest in Boston and features players from that game as well as four extra Boston Bruins. The cards were available in 2-card packs, free for the asking. Pinnacle later handed out remaining packs at several large sports card conventions in Canada and the U.S. Card #31 features Bobby Orr and injured collegiate player Travis Roy. This tribute card was short printed, and the set is considered complete without it.

COMPLETE SET (30) 15.00 40.00
1 Cam Neely .40 1.00
2 Ray Bourque 1.25 3.00
3 Alexandre Daigle .10 .30
4 Mariusz Czerkawski .10 .25
5 Adam Oates .40 1.00
6 Brendan Shanahan .75 2.00
7 Arturs Irbe .40 1.00
8 Mario Lemieux 3.00 8.00
9 Theo Fleury .40 1.00
10 Patrick Roy 3.00 8.00
11 Roman Hamrlik .20 .50
12 Pavel Bure 1.25 3.00
13 Wayne Gretzky 4.00 10.00
14 Mike Modano .75 2.00
15 Teemu Selanne .75 2.00
16 John Vanbiesbrouck .40 1.00
17 Dominik Hasek .75 2.00
18 Mark Messier .75 2.00
19 Martin Brodeur 1.25 3.00
20 Jim Carey .20 .50
21 Wendel Clark .20 .50
22 Jason Arnott .20 .50
23 Jeremy Roenick .60 1.50
24 Brett Hult .75 2.00
25 Peter Forsberg 1.25 3.00
26 Paul Kariya 2.00 5.00
27 Eric Lindros 1.25 3.00
28 Kevin Stevens .10 .30
29 Felix Potvin .40 1.00
30 Sergei Fedorov .75 2.00
31 Travis Roy 8.00 20.00
Bobby Orr SP

1996-97 Pinnacle

This 250-card set was distributed in 10-card packs with a suggested retail price of $2.49. The set featured color action player photos with player statistics and included a rookie subset plus three numerical checklist cards. Rookies of note include Ethan Moreau and Kevin Hodson.

1 Wayne Gretzky .50 1.25
2 Mark Messier .15 .40
3 Kevin Hatcher .05 .15
4 Scott Stevens .10 .25
5 Derek Plante .05 .15
6 Theo Fleury .20 .50
7 Brian Rolston .07 .20
8 Teppo Numminen .05 .15
9 Adam Graves .05 .15
10 Jason Dawe .05 .15
11 Sergei Nemchinov .05 .15
12 Jeff Brown .05 .15
13 Alexei Zhamnov .07 .20
14 Paul Coffey .10 .25
15 Kevin Miller .05 .15
16 Mike Vernon .07 .20
17 Brian Bradley .05 .15
18 Jeff Friesen .05 .15
19 Phil Housley .07 .20
20 Ray Whitney .05 .15
21 Sergei Fedorov .15 .40
22 Pierre Turgeon .10 .25
23 Rick Tocchet .07 .20
24 Uwe Krupp .05 .15
25 Steve Yzerman .25 .60
26 Tom Chorske .05 .15
27 Pat LaFontaine .10 .25
28 Nicklas Lidstrom .12 .30
29 Ray Ferraro .05 .15
30 Brian Noonan .05 .15
31 Dino Ciccarelli .10 .25
32 Rob Niedermayer .07 .20
33 Stephane Richer .07 .20
34 Chris Chelios .10 .25
35 Mike Gartner .10 .25
36 German Titov .05 .15
37 Sean Burke .05 .15
38 Robert Svehla .05 .15
39 Dave Gagner .10 .25
40 Sergei Gonchar .05 .15
41 Bernie Nicholls .05 .15
42 Yanic Perreault .05 .15
43 Adam Deadmarsh .05 .15
44 Dale Hawerchuk .12 .30
45 Alexei Kovalev .05 .15
46 Esa Tikkanen .05 .15
47 Valeri Kamensky .07 .20
48 Craig Janney .07 .20
49 John LeClair .10 .25
50 Radek Bonk .05 .15
51 David Oliver .05 .15
52 Todd Harvey .05 .15
53 Steve Thomas .05 .15
54 Tony Amonte .07 .20
55 Mikael Renberg .07 .20
56 Brendan Shanahan .12 .30
57 Tom Fitzgerald .05 .15
58 Chris Pronger .07 .20
59 Donald Audette .05 .15
60 Nelson Emerson .05 .15
61 Joe Mullen .07 .20
62 Marty McInnis .05 .15
63 Martin Rucinsky .05 .15
64 Mark Recchi .12 .30
65 Vladimir Konstantinov .07 .20
66 Rick Tabaracci .07 .20
67 Marty McSorley .05 .15
68 Pat Verbeek .05 .15
69 Garry Galley .05 .15
70 Travis Green .07 .20
71 Chris Tancill .05 .15
72 Vincent Damphousse .07 .20
73 Benoit Hogue .05 .15
74 Igor Larionov .10 .25
75 Russ Courtnall .05 .15
76 Mike Hough .05 .15
77 Alexander Selivanov .05 .15
78 Peter Forsberg .15 .40
79 Petr Klima .05 .15
80 Adam Creighton .05 .15
81 Dave Lowry .05 .15
82 Andrew Cassels .05 .15
83 Martin Gelinas .05 .15
84 Bob Probert .07 .20
85 Calle Johansson .07 .20
86 Mario Lemieux .30 .75
87 Alexander Mogilny .07 .20
88 Guy Hebert .07 .20
89 Bill Ranford .07 .20
90 Kirk McLean .07 .20
91 Kenny Jonsson .05 .15
92 Martin Brodeur .20 .50
93 Keith Jones .05 .15
94 Ed Belfour .10 .25
95 Tom Barrasso .07 .20
96 Felix Potvin .10 .25
97 Daren Puppa .07 .20
98 Jeremy Roenick .15 .40
99 Chris Osgood UER .10 .25
100 Zigmund Palffy .10 .25
101 Ron Hextall .07 .20
102 Jaromir Jagr .25 .60
103 Chris Terreri .07 .20
104 Shayne Corson .05 .15
105 Jim Carey .10 .25
106 Dominik Hasek .15 .40
107 Eric Lindros .15 .40
108 Petr Nedved .07 .20
109 Peter Bondra .07 .20
110 Jeff Hackett .07 .20
111 Trevor Linden .07 .20
112 Mike Richter .10 .25
113 Claude Lemieux .05 .15
114 Keith Tkachuk .10 .25
115 Pat Falloon .05 .15
116 Brent Fedyk .05 .15
117 Todd Marchant .05 .15
118 Jason Arnott .07 .20
119 Zarley Zalapski .05 .15
120 Kelly Hrudey .07 .20
121 Alexei Yashin .07 .20
122 Sergei Zubov .05 .15
123 Rod Brind'Amour .10 .25
124 Mathieu Schneider .05 .15
125 Bryan Smolinski .05 .15
126 Scott Mellanby .07 .20
127 Doug Gilmour .12 .30
128 Brett Hull .50 1.25
129 Vyacheslav Kozlov .05 .15
130 Adam Oates .10 .25
131 Steve Konowalchuk .05 .15
132 Robert Kron .05 .15
133 Alexandre Daigle .05 .15
134 Brian Savage .05 .15
135 Stu Barnes .05 .15
136 Cam Neely .10 .25
137 Steve Rucchin .05 .15
138 Patrick Roy .25 .60
139 Roman Oksiuta .05 .15
140 Greg Johnson .05 .15
141 Chris Gratton .07 .20
142 Jocelyn Thibault .10 .25
143 Ron Francis .12 .30
144 Mats Sundin .10 .25
145 Oleg Tverdovsky .07 .20
146 Geoff Courtnall .05 .15
147 Kirk Muller .05 .15
148 Zdeno Ciger .05 .15
149 John MacLean .07 .20
150 Damian Rhodes .07 .20
151 Michael Nylander .05 .15
152 Andrei Kovalenko .05 .15
153 Al MacInnis .10 .25
154 Mike Modano .15 .40
155 Teemu Selanne .20 .50
156 Tomas Sandstrom .05 .15
157 Bobby Dollas .05 .15
158 Doug Weight .10 .25
159 Sandis Ozolinsh .05 .15
160 Joe Juneau .05 .15
161 Nikolai Khabibulin .07 .20
162 Murray Craven .05 .15
163 Cliff Ronning .05 .15
164 Curtis Joseph .10 .25
165 Darren Turcotte .05 .15
166 Andy Moog .10 .25
167 Mariusz Czerkawski .05 .15
168 Keith Primeau .05 .15
169 Eric Desjardins .07 .20
170 Bill Guerin .10 .25
171 Glenn Anderson .10 .25
172 Mike Ridley .05 .15
173 Michal Pivonka .05 .15
174 Trevor Kidd .05 .15
175 Pavel Bure .12 .30
176 Todd Gill .07 .20
177 Dave Andreychuk .10 .25
178 Roman Hamrlik .07 .20
179 Andrei Nikolishin .05 .15
180 Alexei Zhitnik .05 .15
181 Grant Fuhr .10 .25
182 Dave Reid .05 .15
183 Joe Nieuwendyk .10 .25
184 Paul Kariya .12 .30
185 Jyrki Lumme .05 .15
186 Owen Nolan .10 .25
187 Geoff Sanderson .07 .20
188 Alexander Semak .05 .15
189 Larry Murphy .07 .20
190 Dimitri Khristich .05 .15
191 Shane Churla .05 .15
192 Bill Lindsay .05 .15
193 Brian Leetch .10 .25
194 Greg Adams .05 .15
195 Gary Suter .05 .15
196 Wendel Clark .07 .20
197 Scott Young .05 .15
198 Randy Burridge .05 .15
199 Ray Bourque .15 .40
200 Joe Murphy .05 .15
201 Joe Sakic .15 .40
202 Saku Koivu .10 .25
203 John Vanbiesbrouck .10 .25
204 Ed Jovanovski .07 .20
205 Daniel Alfredsson .10 .25
206 Vitali Yachmenev .05 .15
207 Marcus Ragnarsson .05 .15
208 Todd Bertuzzi .10 .25
209 Valeri Bure .05 .15
210 Jeff O'Neill .05 .15
211 Corey Hirsch .07 .20
212 Eric Daze .07 .20
213 David Sacco .05 .15
214 Jan Vopat .05 .15
215 Scott Bailey .05 .15
216 Jamie Rivers .05 .15
217 Jose Theodore .12 .30
218 Peter Ferraro .05 .15
219 Anders Eriksson .05 .15
220 Wayne Primeau .05 .15
221 Denis Pederson .05 .15
222 Jay McKee RC .05 .15
223 Sean Pronger .05 .15
224 Martin Biron RC .12 .30
225 Marek Malik .05 .15
226 Steve Sullivan RC .07 .20
227 Curtis Brown .05 .15
228 Eric Fichaud .07 .20
229 Jan Caloun RC .10 .25
230 Niklas Sundblad .05 .15
231 Steve Staios RC .10 .25
232 Steve Washburn RC .10 .25
233 Chris Ferraro .05 .15
234 Marko Kiprusoff .05 .15
235 Larry Courville .05 .15
236 David Nemirovsky .05 .15
237 Ralph Intranuovo .05 .15
238 Kevin Hodson RC .10 .25
239 Ethan Moreau RC .10 .25
240 Daymond Langkow .07 .20
241 Brandon Convery .05 .15
242 Cale Hulse .05 .15
243 Zdenek Nedved .05 .15
244 Tommy Salo .07 .20
245 Nolan Baumgartner .05 .15
246 Patrick Labrecque .05 .15
247 Jamie Langenbrunner .05 .15
248 Pavel Bure CL .12 .30
249 Peter Forsberg CL .15 .40
250 Teemu Selanne CL .20 .50

1996-97 Pinnacle Artist's Proofs

Randomly inserted in packs at a rate of 1:47 hobby packs and 1:67 magazine packs, this 250-card parallel set was distinguishable from the regular set by the inclusion of a special holographic foil-stamped Artist's Proof logo.

*VETS: 12X TO 30X BASIC CARDS
*ROOKIES: 4X TO 10X

1996-97 Pinnacle Foil

ndomly inserted in retail packs, this set parallels the base set with special foil highlights.

*VETS: .6X TO 1.5X BASIC CARDS
*ROOKIES: .2X TO .5X
2 Mark Messier .25 .60

1996-97 Pinnacle Premium Stock

This set parallels the base Pinnacle issue of that season, but unlike most parallels, this was a stand-alone brand, rather than an insert. As the name suggests, the cards were printed on 24 pt. premium card stock and utilized micro-etched silver foil to distinguish them from the other parallels from that season.

*VETS: 1.2X TO 3X BASIC CARDS
*ROOKIES: .4X TO 1X BASIC CARDS
2 Mark Messier .50 1.25

1996-97 Pinnacle Rink Collection

Randomly inserted in packs at a rate of 1:7, this 250-card parallel set was distinguished from the regular set through the use of the all-foil Dufex print technology. A Rink Collection logo is also found on the back of each card.

*VETS: 4X TO 10X BASIC CARDS
*ROOKIES: 2X TO 5X

1996-97 Pinnacle By The Numbers

Randomly inserted in packs at a rate of 1:23, this 15-card, die-cut set honored the league's top statistical standouts. The etched metal, Dufex insert pictured the player with a likeness of his jersey serving as the background. The backs carried the reason for his selection to this insert set. The three confirmed promos were not die-cut like the rest of the set. This design mirrored that which would later be used in the Premium Stock parallel version of this issue inserted at a rate of 1:8 premium stock packs. They are notable for

e word PROMO written on the back.
OMPLETE SET (15) 25.00 50.00
PREM.STOCK: 1X TO 2.5X BASIC INSERTS
Teemu Selanne 1.50 4.00
Brendan Shanahan 1.50 4.00
Sergei Fedorov 2.00 5.00
Ed Jovanovski 1.00 2.50
Doug Weight 1.00 2.50
Brett Hull 2.00 5.00
Doug Gilmour 1.00 2.50
Jaromir Jagr 2.50 6.00
Wayne Gretzky 10.00 25.00
0 Daniel Alfredsson 1.50 4.00
1 Eric Daze 1.00 2.50
2 Mark Messier 1.50 4.00
3 Jocelyn Thibault 1.50 4.00
4 Eric Lindros 2.00 5.00
5 Pavel Bure 1.50 4.00
1 Teemu Selanne PROMO 1.50 4.00
11 Eric Daze PROMO 1.50 4.00
16 Brett Hull PROMO 2.00 5.00

1996-97 Pinnacle Masks

andomly inserted in packs at a rate of 1:90, this 10-ard set spotlighted the most colorful protective eadgear worn in the NHL. A die-cut parallel was also reated and inserted at a rate of 1:300 hobby packs.

OMPLETE SET (10) 60.00 125.00
DIE CUTS: .6X TO 1.5X BASIC CARDS
Patrick Roy 15.00 40.00
Jim Carey 6.00 15.00
John Vanbiesbrouck 8.00 20.00
Martin Brodeur 10.00 25.00
Jocelyn Thibault 5.00 12.00
Ron Hextall 6.00 15.00
Nikolai Khabibulin 6.00 15.00
Stephane Fiset 5.00 12.00
Mike Richter 6.00 15.00
0 Kelly Hrudey 5.00 12.00

1996-97 Pinnacle Team Pinnacle

andomly inserted in packs at a rate of 1:90 hobby acks and 1:127 magazine packs, this 10-card set eatured a double-front card design which showcased op players by position from both the Eastern and Vestern Conferences, back to back. One player from ach conference was displayed on opposite sides of he cards, with one side also being enhanced with Dufex technology. Although a small premium might be ttached to the card depending upon which side was Dufexed, this premium was not universally applied.

W.Gretzky/J.Sakic 8.00 20.00
M.Lemieux/P.Forsberg 6.00 15.00
E.Lindros/J.Roenick 4.00 10.00
M.Messier/D.Weight 4.00 10.00
B.Shanahan/P.Kariya 4.00 10.00
J.Jagr/B.Hull 5.00 12.00
E.Jovanovski/P.Coffey 4.00 10.00
J.Vanbiesbrouck/P.Roy 6.00 15.00
M.Brodeur/C.Osgood 5.00 12.00
0 S.Koivu/E.Daze 4.00 10.00

1996-97 Pinnacle Trophies

andomly inserted only in prepriced magazine packs at rate of 1:33, this 10-card set featured NHL trophies vith the previous season's winners on the card backs. Card fronts were printed with Dufex technology and eatured the trophy itself. The card backs featured the ecipients.

OMPLETE SET (10) 30.00 80.00
Mario Lemieux 12.00 30.00
Paul Kariya 10.00 25.00
Sergei Fedorov 5.00 12.00
Daniel Alfredsson 3.00 8.00
Jim Carey 1.50 4.00
C.Osgood 6.00 15.00
M.Vernon
Kris King 1.50 4.00
Chris Chelios 3.00 8.00
Joe Sakic 8.00 20.00
10 Colorado Avalanche 6.00 15.00

1997-98 Pinnacle

The 1997-98 Pinnacle set was issued in one series totaling 200 cards and was distributed in packs and collectible Mask tins. The fronts feature color action player photos. The backs carry player information.

1 Espen Knutsen RC .15 .40
2 Juha Lind RC .15 .40
3 Erik Rasmussen .12 .30
4 Olli Jokinen RC .20 .50
5 Chris Phillips .12 .30
6 Alexei Morozov .12 .30
7 Chris Dingman RC .15 .40
8 Mattias Ohlund .12 .30
9 Sergei Samsonov .10 .25
10 Daniel Cleary .12 .30
11 Terry Ryan .10 .25
12 Patrick Marleau .20 .50
13 Boyd Devereaux .12 .30
14 Donald MacLean .15 .40
15 Marc Savard .10 .25
16 Magnus Arvedson .15 .40
17 Marian Hossa RC .20 .50
18 Alyn McCauley .12 .30
19 Vaclav Prospal RC .12 .30
20 Brad Isbister .12 .30
21 Robert Dome RC .10 .25
22 Kevyn Adams .10 .25
23 Joe Thornton .15 .40
24 Jan Bulis RC .15 .40
25 Jaroslav Svejkovsky .12 .30
26 Saku Koivu .15 .40
27 Mark Messier .25 .60
28 Dominik Hasek .25 .60
29 Patrick Roy .40 1.00
30 Jaromir Jagr .40 1.00
31 Jarome Iginla .15 .40
32 Joe Sakic .25 .60
33 Jeremy Roenick .20 .50
34 Chris Osgood .15 .40
35 Brett Hull .20 .50
36 Mike Vernon .12 .30
37 John Vanbiesbrouck .15 .40
38 Ray Bourque .25 .60
39 Doug Gilmour .20 .50
40 Keith Tkachuk .15 .40
41 Pavel Bure .20 .50
42 Sean Burke .10 .25
43 Martin Brodeur .30 .75
44 Damian Rhodes .12 .30
45 Geoff Sanderson .12 .30
46 Bill Ranford .12 .30
47 Kevin Hodson .12 .30
48 Eric Lindros .25 .60
49 Owen Nolan .15 .40
50 Mats Sundin .15 .40
51 Ed Belfour .15 .40
52 Stephane Fiset .12 .30
53 Paul Kariya .20 .50
54 Doug Weight .15 .40
55 Mike Richter .15 .40
56 Zigmund Palffy .15 .40
57 John LeClair .15 .40
58 Alexander Mogilny .12 .30
59 Tommy Salo .10 .25
60 Trevor Kidd .10 .25
61 Jason Arnott .12 .30
62 Adam Oates .15 .40
63 Garth Snow .12 .30
64 Rob Blake .15 .40
65 Chris Chelios .15 .40
66 Eric Fichaud .12 .30
67 Wayne Gretzky .75 2.00
68 Dino Ciccarelli .15 .40
69 Pat LaFontaine .15 .40
70 Andy Moog .15 .40
71 Steve Yzerman .30 .75
72 Jeff Hackett .10 .25
73 Peter Forsberg .20 .50
74 Arturs Irbe .12 .30
75 Pierre Turgeon .15 .40
76 Tom Barrasso .12 .30
77 Sergei Fedorov .25 .60
78 Ron Francis .20 .50
79 Mike Dunham .12 .30
80 Brendan Shanahan .20 .50
81 Grant Fuhr .15 .40
82 Jamie Storr .12 .30
83 Jim Carey .10 .25
84 Daren Puppa .12 .30
85 Vincent Damphousse .12 .30
86 Teemu Selanne .30 .75
87 Dwayne Roloson .12 .30
88 Kirk McLean .12 .30
89 Olaf Kolzig .12 .30
90 Guy Hebert .12 .30
91 Mike Modano .25 .60
92 Brian Leetch .15 .40
93 Curtis Joseph .15 .40
94 Nikolai Khabibulin .15 .40
95 Felix Potvin .15 .40
96 Ken Wregget .10 .25
97 Steve Shields RC .15 .40
98 Jocelyn Thibault .10 .25
99 Ron Tugnutt .15 .40
100 Ron Hextall .15 .40
101 Mike Peca .12 .30
102 Donald Audette .12 .30
103 Theo Fleury .20 .50
104 Mark Recchi .20 .50
105 Dainius Zubrus .12 .30
106 Trevor Linden .12 .30
107 Joe Juneau .12 .30
108 Matthew Barnaby .12 .30
109 Keith Primeau .12 .30
110 Joe Nieuwendyk .15 .40
111 Rod Brind'Amour .15 .40
112 Daymond Langkow .10 .25
113 Ed Jovanovski .10 .25
114 Adam Deadmarsh .10 .25
115 Scott Niedermayer .15 .40
116 Al MacInnis .15 .40
117 Slava Kozlov .12 .30
118 Jere Lehtinen .12 .30
119 Jeff Friesen .12 .30
120 Alexei Kovalev .10 .25
121 Eric Daze .10 .25
122 Mariusz Czerkawski .10 .25
123 Alexei Zhamnov .10 .25
124 Petr Nedved .15 .40
125 Dmitri Mironov .12 .30
126 Alexei Yashin .12 .30
127 Todd Marchant .12 .30
128 Sandis Ozolinsh .12 .30
129 Igor Larionov .10 .25
130 Jim Campbell .10 .25
131 Dave Andreychuk .15 .40
132 Glen Wesley .10 .25
133 Rem Murray .10 .25
134 Steve Sullivan .12 .30
135 Miroslav Satan .10 .25
136 Bill Guerin .15 .40
137 Mike Gartner .15 .40
138 Jozef Stumpel .12 .30
139 Darryl Sydor .10 .25
140 Darcy Tucker .15 .40
141 Robert Svehla .12 .30
142 Steve Duchesne .10 .25
143 Kevin Stevens .10 .25
144 Mikael Renberg .12 .30
145 Bryan Berard .10 .25
146 Ray Ferraro .10 .25
147 Jason Allison .12 .30
148 Tony Amonte .12 .30
149 Luc Robitaille .15 .40
150 Mathieu Schneider .12 .30
151 Steve Rucchin .12 .30
152 Brian Savage .10 .25
153 Paul Coffey .15 .40
154 Jeff O'Neill .12 .30
155 Daniel Alfredsson .15 .40
156 Dave Gagner .10 .25
157 Rob Niedermayer .10 .25
158 Scott Stevens .15 .40
159 Alexandre Daigle .10 .25
160 Stephane Richer .10 .25
161 Harry York .12 .30
162 Sergei Berezin .12 .30
163 Claude Lemieux .12 .30
164 Ray Sheppard .12 .30
165 Bernie Nicholls .12 .30
166 Oleg Tverdovsky .12 .30
167 Travis Green .12 .30
168 Martin Gelinas .10 .25
169 Derek Plante .12 .30
170 Gary Roberts .12 .30
171 Kevin Hatcher .10 .25
172 Martin Rucinsky .12 .30
173 Pat Verbeek .12 .30
174 Adam Graves .10 .25
175 Roman Hamrlik .12 .30
176 Darren McCarty .12 .30
177 Mike Grier .12 .30
178 Andrew Cassels .10 .25
179 Dimitri Khristich .12 .30
180 Tomas Sandstrom .10 .25
181 Peter Bondra .12 .30
182 Derian Hatcher .12 .30
183 Chris Gratton .10 .25
184 John MacLean .10 .25
185 Wendel Clark .15 .40
186 Valeri Kamensky .12 .30
187 Tony Granato .12 .30
188 Vladimir Vorobiev RC .15 .40
189 Ethan Moreau .10 .25
190 Kirk Muller .10 .25
191 Peter Forsberg SM .20 .50
192 Wayne Gretzky SM .75 2.00
193 Jaromir Jagr SM .40 1.00
194 Mark Messier SM .25 .60
195 Brian Leetch SM .15 .40
196 John LeClair SM .15 .40
197 Jeremy Roenick SM .20 .50
198 Checklist .02 .10
199 Checklist .02 .10
200 Checklist .02 .10
NNO John Vanbiesbrouck 3x5 PROMO .15 .40
NNO Paul Kariya 3x5 PROMO .15 .40

1997-98 Pinnacle Artist's Proofs

Randomly inserted in packs at the rate of 1:39 and in tins at the rate of one in 13, this 100-card set is a partial parallel version of the base set. The fronts display the "Artist's Proof" seal.

*ART.PROOF: 12X TO 30X BASIC CARDS

1997-98 Pinnacle Rink Collection

Randomly inserted in packs at the rate of 1:7, this 100-card set is a partial parallel version of the 1997-98 Pinnacle base set printed using Dufex Technology.

*RINK COLL.: 4X TO 10X BASIC CARDS

1997-98 Pinnacle Epix Game Orange

This 24-card set was inserted in various Pinnacle products at the following odds: Certified 1:15; Score 1:121; Pinnacle 1:21 and Zenith 1:11. The set was printed in progressively-scarce three color versions: orange, purple, and emerald and prices for those parallels can be found by using the multipliers below.

COMPLETE SET (24) 40.00 100.00
1-6 INSERTED IN SCORE PACKS
7-12 INSERTED IN PIN.CERT.PACKS
13-18 INSERTED IN ZENITH PACKS
19-24 INSERTED IN PINNACLE PACKS
*PURPLE: .6X TO 1.5X ORANGE
*EMERALD: 1.2X TO 3X ORANGE
PURPLE/EMERALD OVERALL ODDS 1:19
1 Wayne Gretzky 8.00 20.00
2 John Vanbiesbrouck .75 2.00
3 Joe Sakic 2.00 5.00
4 Alexei Yashin .75 2.00
5 Sergei Fedorov 1.50 4.00
6 Keith Tkachuk .75 2.00
7 Patrick Roy 6.00 15.00
8 Martin Brodeur 3.00 8.00
9 Steve Yzerman 6.00 15.00
10 Saku Koivu .75 2.00
11 Felix Potvin .75 2.00
12 Mark Messier 1.25 3.00
13 Eric Lindros 1.25 3.00
14 Peter Forsberg 2.50 6.00
15 Teemu Selanne 1.25 3.00
16 Brendan Shanahan 1.25 3.00
17 Curtis Joseph 1.25 3.00
18 Brett Hull 1.50 4.00
19 Paul Kariya 1.25 3.00
20 Jaromir Jagr 2.00 5.00
21 Pavel Bure 1.25 3.00
22 Dominik Hasek 2.00 5.00
23 John LeClair .75 2.00
24 Doug Gilmour .75 2.00

1997-98 Pinnacle Epix Moment Orange

This 24-card set was inserted in various Pinnacle products at the following odds: Certified 1:15; Score 1:121; Pinnacle 1:21 and Zenith 1:11. The set was printed in progressively-scarce three color versions: orange, purple, and emerald.

COMPLETE SET (24) 100.00 200.00
1-6 INSERTED IN ZENITH PACKS
7-12 INSERTED IN PINNACLE PACKS
13-18 INSERTED IN SCORE PACKS
19-24 INSERTED IN PIN.CERT.PACKS
*PURPLE: .6X TO 1.5X ORANGE
PURPLE STATED ODDS 1:19
*EMERALD: 1.2X TO 3X ORANGE
EMERALD ANNC'D PRINT RUN 30 OR LESS
1 Wayne Gretzky 20.00 50.00
2 John Vanbiesbrouck 2.00 5.00
3 Joe Sakic 6.00 15.00
4 Alexei Yashin 2.00 5.00
5 Sergei Fedorov 4.00 10.00
6 Keith Tkachuk 2.00 5.00
7 Patrick Roy 15.00 40.00
8 Martin Brodeur 10.00 25.00
9 Steve Yzerman 12.00 30.00
10 Saku Koivu 3.00 8.00
11 Felix Potvin 3.00 8.00
12 Mark Messier 3.00 8.00
13 Eric Lindros 3.00 8.00
14 Peter Forsberg 8.00 20.00
15 Teemu Selanne 3.00 8.00
16 Brendan Shanahan 3.00 8.00
17 Curtis Joseph 3.00 8.00
18 Brett Hull 4.00 10.00
19 Paul Kariya 3.00 8.00
20 Jaromir Jagr 5.00 12.00
21 Pavel Bure 3.00 8.00
22 Dominik Hasek 6.00 15.00
23 John LeClair 2.00 5.00
24 Doug Gilmour 2.00 5.00

1997-98 Pinnacle Epix Play Orange

This 24-card set was inserted in various Pinnacle products at the following odds: Certified 1:15; Score 1:121; Pinnacle 1:21 and Zenith 1:11. The set was printed in progressively-scarce three color versions: orange, purple, and emerald and prices for those parallels can be found by using the multipliers below.

COMPLETE SET (24) 40.00 80.00
1-6 INSERTED IN PIN.CERT.PACKS
7-12 INSERTED IN ZENITH PACKS
13-18 INSERTED IN PINNACLE PACKS
19-24 INSERTED IN SCORE PACKS
*PURPLE: .6X TO 1.5X ORANGE
*EMERALD: 1.2X TO 3X ORANGE
PURPLE/EMERALD OVERALL ODDS 1:19
1 Wayne Gretzky 8.00 20.00
2 John Vanbiesbrouck .60 1.50
3 Joe Sakic 1.50 4.00
4 Alexei Yashin .60 1.50
5 Sergei Fedorov 1.25 3.00
6 Keith Tkachuk .75 2.00
7 Patrick Roy 4.00 10.00
8 Martin Brodeur 2.00 5.00
9 Steve Yzerman 4.00 10.00
10 Saku Koivu .75 2.00
11 Felix Potvin .75 2.00
12 Mark Messier .75 2.00
13 Eric Lindros .75 2.00
14 Peter Forsberg 2.00 5.00
15 Teemu Selanne .75 2.00
16 Brendan Shanahan .75 2.00
17 Curtis Joseph .75 2.00
18 Brett Hull 1.00 2.50
19 Paul Kariya .75 2.00
20 Jaromir Jagr 1.25 3.00
21 Pavel Bure .75 2.00
22 Dominik Hasek 1.50 4.00
23 John LeClair .75 2.00
24 Doug Gilmour .60 1.50

1997-98 Pinnacle Epix Season Orange

This 24-card set was inserted in various Pinnacle products at the following odds: Certified 1:15; Score 1:121; Pinnacle 1:21 and Zenith 1:11.

COMPLETE SET (24) 75.00 150.00
1-6 INSERTED IN PINNACLE PACKS
7-12 INSERTED IN SCORE PACKS
13-18 INSERTED IN PIN.CERT.PACKS
19-24 INSERTED IN ZENITH PACKS
*PURPLE: .6X TO 1.5X ORANGE
*EMERALD: 1.2X TO 3X ORANGE
ANNC'D EMERALD PRINT RUN 50 OR LESS
1 Wayne Gretzky 10.00 25.00
2 John Vanbiesbrouck 1.50 4.00
3 Joe Sakic 5.00 12.00
4 Alexei Yashin 1.50 4.00
5 Sergei Fedorov 3.00 8.00
6 Keith Tkachuk 1.50 4.00
7 Patrick Roy 8.00 20.00
8 Martin Brodeur 7.50 15.00
9 Steve Yzerman 8.00 20.00
10 Saku Koivu 2.50 6.00
11 Felix Potvin 3.00 8.00
12 Mark Messier 2.50 6.00
13 Eric Lindros 2.50 6.00
14 Peter Forsberg 6.00 15.00
15 Teemu Selanne 2.50 6.00
16 Brendan Shanahan 2.50 6.00
17 Curtis Joseph 2.50 6.00
18 Brett Hull 3.00 8.00
19 Paul Kariya 2.50 6.00
20 Jaromir Jagr 4.00 10.00
21 Pavel Bure 3.00 8.00
22 Dominik Hasek 4.00 10.00
23 John LeClair 1.50 4.00
24 Doug Gilmour 1.50 4.00

1997-98 Pinnacle Masks

Randomly inserted in packs at the rate of 1:89 and in tins at the rate of 1:30, this ten-card features color photos of masks worn by the NHL's elite goalies printed on Dufex technology. A die-cut parallel was also produced and inserted at a rate of 1:299 packs and 1:100 tins.

COMPLETE SET (10) 75.00 150.00
*JUMBOS: .4X TO 1X BASIC INSERTS
*PROMOS: .15X TO .4X BASIC INSERTS
1 John Vanbiesbrouck 6.00 15.00
2 Mike Richter 5.00 12.00
3 Martin Brodeur 10.00 25.00
4 Curtis Joseph 5.00 12.00
5 Patrick Roy 10.00 25.00
6 Guy Hebert 5.00 12.00
7 Jeff Hackett 5.00 12.00
8 Garth Snow 5.00 12.00
9 Nikolai Khabibulin 5.00 12.00
10 Grant Fuhr 6.00 15.00

1997-98 Pinnacle Masks Die Cuts

Randomly inserted into hobby packs only at a rate of 1:299 packs and 1:100 tins, this ten-card set is a parallel version of the Pinnacle Masks regular set and features a die-cut design, with all other features being the same as their regular counterparts.

*DIE CUT: .5X TO 1.2X BASIC INSERTS

1997-98 Pinnacle Team Pinnacle

Randomly inserted in packs at the rate of 1:99 and in tins at the rate of 1:33, this 10-card set features color action photos of the game's biggest stars as voted by Hockey fans and printed on double-sided cards with Mylar technology on just one side. A parallel of each card was produced with this special printing on the other side. Finally, mirror parallels were also created of each version (making a total of four different versions of each card) and inserted randomly.

COMPLETE SET (10) 40.00 80.00
*WHITE FRONT PARALLEL: .4X TO 1X
*MIRRORS: 3X TO 8X BASIC INSERTS
1 M.Brodeur/P.Roy 8.00 20.00
2 D.Hasek/C.Joseph 4.00 10.00
3 B.Leetch/C.Chelios 5.00 12.00
4 W.Gretzky/P.Kariya 8.00 20.00
5 E.Lindros/M.Messier 5.00 12.00
6 J.Jagr/K.Tkachuk 5.00 12.00
7 S.Koivu/P.Forsberg 4.00 10.00
8 J.LeClair/B.Shanahan 2.50 6.00
9 D.Gilmour/S.Yzerman 6.00 15.00
10 J.Vanbiesbrouck/C.Osgood 5.00 12.00

2010-11 Pinnacle

COMP.SET w/o RC's (200) 10.00 25.00
201-250 ROOKIE ODDS 1:6
251-270 ROOKIE AU PRINT RUN 199-299
1 Nicklas Backstrom .40 1.00
2 Mike Green .25 .60
3 Michal Neuvirth .20 .50
4 Karl Alzner .15 .40
5 David Steckel .15 .40
6 Eric Fehr .15 .40
7 Alex Ovechkin 1.00 2.50
8 Ryan Kesler .25 .60
9 Roberto Luongo .25 .60
10 Mason Raymond .20 .50
11 Henrik Sedin .25 .60
12 Dan Hamhuis .20 .50
13 Daniel Sedin .25 .60
14 Alexandre Burrows .25 .60
15 Tyler Bozak .25 .60
16 Tomas Kaberle .15 .40
17 Phil Kessel .30 .75
18 Nikolai Kulemin .20 .50
19 Kris Versteeg .20 .50
20 Jonas Gustavsson .30 .75
21 Dion Phaneuf .25 .60
22 Vincent Lecavalier .20 .50
23 Victor Hedman .30 .75
24 Steven Stamkos .50 1.25
25 Simon Gagne .25 .60
26 Martin St. Louis .25 .60
27 Dan Ellis .20 .50
28 T.J. Oshie .40 1.00
29 Jaroslav Halak .25 .60
30 David Perron .15 .40
31 David Backes .25 .60
32 Cam Janssen .15 .40
33 B.J. Crombeen .15 .40
34 Torrey Mitchell .15 .40
35 Ryane Clowe .15 .40
36 Patrick Marleau .25 .60
37 Joe Thornton .25 .60
38 Joe Pavelski .25 .60
39 Dany Heatley .20 .50
40 Antero Niittymaki .20 .50
41 Zbynek Michalek .15 .40
42 Sidney Crosby 1.00 2.50
43 Max Talbot .25 .60
44 Marc-Andre Fleury .40 1.00
45 Jordan Staal .25 .60
46 Evgeni Malkin .75 2.00
47 Vernon Fiddler .15 .40
48 Shane Doan .20 .50
49 Scottie Upshall .15 .40
50 Ray Whitney .20 .50
51 Paul Bissonnette .15 .40
52 Lee Stempniak .15 .40
53 Ilya Bryzgalov .20 .50
54 Ville Leino .20 .50
55 Sean O'Donnell .15 .40
56 Mike Richards .25 .60
57 Jeff Carter .25 .60
58 Danny Briere .25 .60
59 Claude Giroux .25 .60
60 Chris Pronger .20 .50
61 Sergei Gonchar .15 .40
62 Pascal Leclaire .20 .50
63 Nick Foligno .20 .50
64 Jason Spezza .15 .40
65 Daniel Alfredsson .25 .60
66 Brian Elliott .20 .50
67 Alex Kovalev .25 .60
68 Sean Avery .20 .50
69 Ryan Callahan .25 .60
70 Michael Del Zotto .20 .50
71 Martin Biron .20 .50
72 Marian Gaborik .30 .75
73 Henrik Lundqvist .40 1.00
74 Matt Moulson .20 .50
75 Kyle Okposo .25 .60
76 Josh Bailey .20 .50
77 John Tavares .50 1.25
78 Dwayne Roloson .20 .50
79 Zach Parise .25 .60
80 Travis Zajac .20 .50
81 Patrik Elias .25 .60
82 Martin Brodeur .50 1.25
83 Ilya Kovalchuk .25 .60
84 Steve Sullivan .15 .40
85 Shea Weber .20 .50
86 Pekka Rinne .30 .75
87 Patric Hornqvist .20 .50
88 Matthew Lombardi .15 .40
89 Joel Ward .15 .40
90 Cody Franson .15 .40
91 Tomas Plekanec .25 .60
92 Scott Gomez .20 .50
93 Michael Cammalleri .25 .60
94 Josh Gorges .15 .40
95 Carey Price 1.00 2.50
96 Brian Gionta .20 .50
97 Andrei Kostitsyn .20 .50
98 Niklas Backstrom .25 .60
99 Mikko Koivu .25 .60
100 Matt Cullen .15 .40
101 Jose Theodore .25 .60
102 Pierre-Marc Bouchard .25 .60
103 Andrew Brunette .15 .40
104 Brent Burns .30 .75
105 Wayne Simmonds .30 .75
106 Ryan Smyth .20 .50
107 Jonathan Quick .40 1.00
108 Jack Johnson .15 .40
109 Dustin Brown .25 .60
110 Drew Doughty .25 .60
111 Anze Kopitar .40 1.00
112 Tomas Vokoun .20 .50
113 Steve Bernier .15 .40
114 Radek Dvorak .15 .40
115 Keaton Ellerby .15 .40
116 David Booth .15 .40
117 Bryan McCabe .15 .40
118 Shawn Horcoff .15 .40
119 Sam Gagner .20 .50
120 Ryan Whitney .15 .40
121 Nikolai Khabibulin .20 .50
122 Kurtis Foster .15 .40
123 Dustin Penner .15 .40
124 Ales Hemsky .20 .50
125 Todd Bertuzzi .20 .50
126 Pavel Datsyuk .30 .75
127 Nicklas Lidstrom .25 .60
128 Mike Modano .40 1.00
129 Johan Franzen .25 .60
130 Jimmy Howard .30 .75
131 Henrik Zetterberg .30 .75
132 Tom Wandell .15 .40
133 Steve Ott .20 .50
134 Kari Lehtonen .20 .50
135 Loui Eriksson .20 .50
136 James Neal .25 .60
137 Brenden Morrow .20 .50
138 Adam Burish .15 .40
139 Mathieu Garon .20 .50
140 Rick Nash .25 .60
141 R.J. Umberger .15 .40
142 Nikita Filatov .15 .40
143 Jakub Voracek .25 .60
144 Derek Dorsett .15 .40
145 Antoine Vermette .15 .40
146 T.J. Galiardi .20 .50
147 Paul Stastny .25 .60
148 Milan Hejduk .20 .50
149 Matt Duchene .25 .60
150 John-Michael Liles .15 .40
151 Craig Anderson .25 .60
152 Chris Stewart .20 .50
153 Patrick Sharp .25 .60
154 Patrick Kane .50 1.25
155 Niklas Hjalmarsson .15 .40
156 Marian Hossa .20 .50
157 Jonathan Toews .50 1.25
158 Duncan Keith .25 .60
159 Corey Crawford .30 .75
160 Tuomo Ruutu .20 .50
161 Tim Gleason .15 .40
162 Jussi Jokinen .15 .40
163 Eric Staal .30 .75
164 Cam Ward .25 .60
165 Brandon Sutter .20 .50
166 Rene Bourque .15 .40
167 Olli Jokinen .20 .50
168 Niklas Hagman .15 .40
169 Miikka Kiprusoff .20 .50
170 Jay Bouwmeester .30 .75
171 Jarome Iginla .25 .60
172 Alex Tanguay .15 .40
173 Tyler Myers .25 .60
174 Tyler Ennis .20 .50
175 Tim Connolly .15 .40
176 Thomas Vanek .25 .60
177 Ryan Miller .25 .60
178 Nathan Gerbe .15 .40
179 Derek Roy .25 .60
180 Tim Thomas .20 .50
181 Shawn Thornton .15 .40
182 Patrice Bergeron .30 .75
183 Nathan Horton .20 .50
184 Milan Lucic .25 .60
185 Mark Recchi .30 .75
186 Marc Savard .15 .40
187 Tobias Enstrom .15 .40
188 Ondrej Pavelec .25 .60
189 Nik Antropov .20 .50
190 Nicklas Bergfors .20 .50
191 Evander Kane .25 .60
192 Dustin Byfuglien .25 .60
193 Chris Mason .20 .50
194 Teemu Selanne .50 1.25
195 Saku Koivu .25 .60
196 Ryan Getzlaf .40 1.00
197 Lubomir Visnovsky .15 .40
198 George Parros .20 .50
199 Corey Perry .25 .60
200 Bobby Ryan .25 .60
201 Jordan Eberle RC 3.00 8.00
202 Nazem Kadri RC 4.00 10.00
203 Tyler Seguin RC 5.00 12.00
204 Brayden Schenn RC 2.00 5.00
205 Travis Hamonic RC 1.50 4.00
206 Sergei Bobrovsky RC 3.00 8.00
207 Alexander Burmistrov RC 1.25 3.00
208 Nino Niederreiter RC 1.50 4.00
209 Nick Leddy RC 1.25 3.00
210 Luke Adam RC 1.25 3.00
211 Jordan Caron RC 2.00 5.00
212 Taylor Hall RC 5.00 12.00
213 Jacob Josefson RC 1.25 3.00
214 Kyle Clifford RC 1.25 3.00
215 Jared Spurgeon RC 1.25 3.00
216 Patrice Cormier RC 1.50 4.00
217 Steven Kampfer RC 2.00 5.00
218 P.K. Subban RC 4.00 10.00
219 Magnus Paajarvi RC 1.50 4.00
220 Evan Brophey RC 1.25 3.00
221 Kevin Poulin RC 1.50 4.00
222 Linus Omark RC 3.00 8.00
223 Jeff Skinner RC 2.50 6.00
224 Nathan Lawson RC 1.25 3.00
225 Marcus Johansson RC 2.00 5.00
226 Brandon Pirri RC 1.25 3.00
227 Brandon McMillan RC 1.25 3.00
228 Nick Holden RC 1.25 3.00
229 Richard Bachman RC 1.50 4.00
230 Anders Lindback RC 1.25 3.00
231 Alexander Vasyunov RC 1.25 3.00
232 Cam Fowler RC 1.50 4.00
233 Ben Smith RC 1.25 3.00
234 Dana Tyrell RC 1.25 3.00
235 Ryan Reaves RC 1.50 4.00
236 Alex Urbom RC 1.25 3.00
237 Kyle Palmieri RC 2.50 6.00
238 Mark Dekanich RC 1.25 3.00
239 Matt Kassian RC 1.25 3.00
240 Jonas Holos RC 1.25 3.00
241 Rob Klinkhammer RC 1.25 3.00
242 Jamie Arniel RC 1.25 3.00
243 Justin Braun RC 1.25 3.00
244 Keith Aulie RC 1.25 3.00
245 Kevin Shattenkirk RC 2.50 6.00
246 Johan Harju RC 1.25 3.00
247 Stefan Della Rovere RC 1.25 3.00
248 Evgeny Grachev RC 1.25 3.00
249 Eric Wellwood RC 1.50 4.00
250 Jeremy Morin RC 1.25 3.00
251 Mattias Tedenby AU RC 3.00 8.00
252 Brayden Irwin AU RC 4.00 10.00
253 Bobby Butler AU RC 4.00 10.00
254 Ian Cole AU RC 4.00 10.00
255 Derek Stepan AU/199 RC 12.00 30.00
256 Jake Muzzin AU RC 4.00 10.00
257 Jared Cowen AU RC 4.00 10.00
258 John McCarthy AU RC 4.00 10.00
259 Dustin Tokarski AU RC 4.00 10.00
260 Nick Bonino AU RC 5.00 12.00
261 Justin Mercier AU RC 4.00 10.00
262 Maxim Noreau AU RC 3.00 8.00
263 Mats Zuccarello AU RC 12.00 30.00
264 Jacob Markstrom AU RC 20.00 40.00
265 Robin Lehner AU RC 8.00 20.00
266 Jamie McBain AU RC 4.00 10.00
267 Ryan McDonagh AU RC 15.00 30.00
268 Tomas Tatar AU RC 8.00 20.00
269 Zach Hamill AU RC 4.00 10.00
270 Philip Larsen AU RC 4.00 10.00

2010-11 Pinnacle Artists Proofs

*1-200 VETS: 4X TO 10X BASIC CARDS
*201-250 ROOKIES: .6X TO 1.5X BASE
STATED ODDS 1:24
159 Corey Crawford 3.00 8.00
218 P.K. Subban 15.00 40.00
223 Jeff Skinner 15.00 40.00

2010-11 Pinnacle Rink Collection

*1-200 VETS: 2.5X TO 6X BASIC CARDS
*201-250 ROOKIES: .5X TO 1.2X
STATED ODDS 1:6
159 Corey Crawford 2.00 5.00
212 Taylor Hall 12.00 30.00
218 P.K. Subban 12.00 30.00
223 Jeff Skinner 12.00 30.00

2010-11 Pinnacle Chemistry On Canvas

COMPLETE SET (18) 40.00 80.00
1 A.Ovechkin/N.Backstrom 8.00 20.00
2 R.Getzlaf/C.Perry 3.00 8.00
3 S.Stamkos/M.St. Louis 4.00 10.00
4 D.Krejci/M.Lucic 2.00 5.00
5 N.Lidstrom/B.Rafalski 2.00 5.00
6 H.Sedin/D.Sedin 2.00 5.00
7 P.Stastny/C.Stewart 2.00 5.00
8 J.Thornton/D.Heatley 2.00 5.00
9 B.Richards/L.Eriksson 2.00 5.00
10 T.Selanne/S.Koivu 4.00 10.00
11 D.Alfredsson/J.Spezza 2.00 5.00
12 D.Keith/B.Seabrook 2.00 5.00
13 H.Zetterberg/P.Datsyuk 2.50 6.00
14 M.Richards/C.Giroux 2.00 5.00
15 M.Koivu/A.Brunette 2.00 5.00
16 J.Tavares/M.Moulson 4.00 10.00
17 B.Gionta/S.Gomez 1.50 4.00
18 A.Kopitar/R.Smyth 3.00 8.00

2010-11 Pinnacle City Lights Materials

STATED PRINT RUN 99-499
*PRIME/25: .5X TO 1.2X BASIC JSY
1 Sidney Crosby 10.00 25.00
2 Brian Elliott 4.00 10.00
3 Zdeno Chara 4.00 10.00
4 Anze Kopitar 8.00 20.00
5 Christian Hanson 3.00 8.00
6 Jordan Staal 5.00 12.00
7 Dustin Penner 3.00 8.00
8 Peter Regin 4.00 10.00
9 Miikka Kiprusoff 4.00 10.00
10 Tobias Enstrom 3.00 8.00
11 Ryan Malone 3.00 8.00
12 Paul Stastny 5.00 12.00
13 Daniel Sedin 5.00 12.00
14 Mikael Samuelsson 3.00 8.00
15 Zach Bogosian 4.00 10.00
16 Jarome Iginla 5.00 12.00
17 Mason Raymond
18 Nik Antropov 4.00 10.00
19 Jeff Deslauriers 3.00 8.00
20 Tuukka Rask 5.00 12.00
21 Steve Ott 4.00 10.00
22 Chris Pronger 4.00 10.00
23 Ryan Suter 3.00 8.00
24 Tomas Vokoun 4.00 10.00
25 Ryan Smyth 4.00 10.00
26 Stephen Weiss 4.00 10.00
27 Jonas Gustavsson 6.00 15.00
28 Mike Green 5.00 12.00
29 Rene Bourque 3.00 8.00
30 Darcy Hordichuk 3.00 8.00
31 Erik Karlsson 10.00 25.00
32 Mike Smith 5.00 12.00
33 Loui Eriksson 4.00 10.00
34 Pekka Rinne 6.00 15.00
35 Cory Schneider 4.00 10.00
36 Vincent Lecavalier 4.00 10.00
37 James van Riemsdyk 8.00 20.00
38 Mike Fisher 5.00 12.00
39 Fredrik Sjostrom 3.00 8.00
40 Martin St. Louis 5.00 12.00
41 Alex Tanguay 3.00 8.00
42 Andrew Bodnarchuk 4.00 10.00
43 Ilya Kovalchuk 5.00 12.00
44 Brad Richards 5.00 12.00
45 Mikael Backlund 3.00 8.00
46 Patric Hornqvist 4.00 10.00
47 Roberto Luongo 8.00 20.00
48 Steve Downie 3.00 8.00
49 Cody Bass 4.00 10.00
50 Jannik Hansen 4.00 10.00
51 Matt Zaba 5.00 12.00
52 Henrik Zetterberg/299 6.00 15.00
53 Victor Hedman 6.00 15.00
54 Wade Belak 4.00 10.00
55 Martin Erat 3.00 8.00
56 Shawn Thornton 3.00 8.00
57 Nicklas Bergfors/199
58 Evander Kane 5.00 12.00
59 Evan Oberg 5.00 12.00
60 Jamie Langenbrunner/399 3.00 8.00
61 Mike Brodeur 5.00 12.00
62 Karl Alzner 3.00 8.00
63 Maxim Lapierre 3.00 8.00
64 Ilya Bryzgalov 4.00 10.00
65 Travis Zajac/99 4.00 10.00
66 Milan Hejduk 4.00 10.00
67 Jason Spezza/399 3.00 8.00
68 Jamie Benn 6.00 15.00
69 Wayne Simmonds/99 6.00 15.00
70 Joe Thornton 5.00 12.00
71 James Neal 5.00 12.00
72 Evgeni Malkin 6.00 15.00
73 Craig Anderson 5.00 12.00
74 Marian Gaborik 6.00 15.00
75 Steve Mason/399 4.00 10.00
76 Jordin Tootoo/99 4.00 10.00
77 John Tavares/99 6.00 15.00
78 Mikkel Boedker 3.00 8.00
79 Luke Schenn 4.00 10.00
80 Jeff Carter 5.00 12.00
81 Jared Cowen 3.00 8.00
82 Zach Hamill 3.00 8.00
83 Nazem Kadri 5.00 12.00
84 Kevin Shattenkirk 6.00 15.00
85 Jeff Skinner 8.00 20.00
86 Magnus Paajarvi 4.00 10.00
87 Tyler Seguin 8.00 20.00
88 Taylor Hall 12.00 30.00
89 Jordan Eberle/499 10.00 25.00
90 Brayden Schenn 4.00 10.00
91 Ryan Getzlaf/99 8.00 20.00
92 Kari Lehtonen 4.00 10.00
93 Marc Staal 5.00 12.00
94 Shane Doan/99 4.00 10.00
95 Matt Moulson/99 4.00 10.00
96 Henrik Sedin/499 5.00 12.00
97 Scott Hartnell 5.00 12.00
98 Shea Weber 4.00 10.00
99 Andy Greene/99
100 Colton Orr 3.00 8.00

2010-11 Pinnacle City Lights Signatures

STATED PRINT RUN 35-100
1 Sidney Crosby/35 60.00 120.00
2 Brian Elliott/100 6.00 15.00
3 Zdeno Chara/100 10.00 25.00
4 Anze Kopitar/100 12.00 30.00
5 Christian Hanson/100 5.00 12.00
6 Jordan Staal/100 8.00 20.00
7 Dustin Penner/100 5.00 12.00
8 Peter Regin/100 6.00 15.00
11 Ryan Malone/100 5.00 12.00
12 Paul Stastny/100 8.00 20.00
13 Daniel Sedin/100 8.00 20.00
14 Mikael Samuelsson/100 5.00 12.00
15 Zach Bogosian/100 6.00 15.00
16 Jarome Iginla/100 8.00 20.00
17 Mason Raymond/100 6.00 15.00
19 Jeff Deslauriers/100 8.00 20.00
20 Tuukka Rask/100 8.00 20.00
21 Steve Ott/100 6.00 15.00
22 Chris Pronger/100 6.00 15.00
23 Ryan Suter/100 5.00 12.00
24 Tomas Vokoun/100 6.00 15.00
25 Ryan Smyth/100 6.00 15.00
26 Stephen Weiss/100 6.00 15.00
27 Jonas Gustavsson/100 8.00 20.00
28 Mike Green/100 8.00 20.00
29 Rene Bourque/100 10.00 25.00
31 Erik Karlsson/100 10.00 25.00
32 Mike Smith/100 8.00 20.00
33 Loui Eriksson/100 6.00 15.00
34 Pekka Rinne/100 10.00 25.00
35 Cory Schneider/100 6.00 15.00
36 Vincent Lecavalier/100 6.00 15.00
37 James van Riemsdyk/100 12.00 30.00
38 Mike Fisher/60
40 Martin St. Louis/100 8.00 20.00
41 Alex Tanguay/100 5.00 12.00
43 Ilya Kovalchuk/100 8.00 20.00
44 Brad Richards/100 8.00 20.00
45 Mikael Backlund/100 5.00 12.00
46 Patric Hornqvist/100 6.00 15.00
48 Steve Downie/100 8.00 20.00
54 Wade Belak/100 8.00 20.00
56 Shawn Thornton/100 8.00 20.00
58 Evander Kane/100 8.00 20.00
61 Mike Brodeur/100 8.00 20.00
62 Karl Alzner/100 5.00 12.00
64 Ilya Bryzgalov/50 6.00 15.00

65 Travis Zajac/100 6.00 15.00
66 Milan Hejduk/100 6.00 15.00
67 Jason Spezza/100 5.00 12.00
68 Jamie Benn/100 10.00 25.00
69 Wayne Simmonds/100 10.00 25.00
70 Joe Thornton/97 6.00 15.00
71 James Neal/100 5.00 12.00
72 Evgeni Malkin/100 25.00 60.00
73 Craig Anderson/100 8.00 20.00
74 Marian Gaborik/100 10.00 25.00
75 Steve Mason/100 6.00 15.00
76 Jordin Tootoo/100 6.00 15.00
77 John Tavares/100 15.00 40.00
78 Mikkel Boedker/100
79 Luke Schenn/100 6.00 15.00
80 Jeff Carter/100 8.00 20.00
81 Jared Cowen/100 5.00 12.00
82 Zach Hamill/100 8.00 20.00
83 Nazem Kadri/100 15.00 40.00
84 Kevin Shattenkirk/100 10.00 25.00
85 Jeff Skinner/100 25.00 60.00
86 Magnus Paajarvi/100 8.00 20.00
87 Tyler Seguin/100 25.00 60.00
88 Taylor Hall/100 30.00 80.00
89 Jordan Eberle/100 30.00 60.00
90 Brayden Schenn/100 8.00 20.00
91 Ryan Getzlaf/100 12.00 30.00
92 Kari Lehtonen/100 6.00 15.00
93 Marc Staal/100 8.00 20.00
94 Shane Doan/100 6.00 15.00
95 Matt Moulson/100 6.00 15.00
96 Henrik Sedin/75 8.00 20.00
98 Shea Weber/100 6.00 15.00
99 Andy Greene/95
100 Colton Orr/100 5.00 12.00

2010-11 Pinnacle Fans of the Game

COMPLETE SET (3) 4.00 10.00
1 Noureen DeWulf 1.50 4.00
2 Sam Bradford 2.50 6.00
3 Duff Goldman 1.50 4.00

2010-11 Pinnacle Fans of the Game Autographs

1 Noureen DeWulf 8.00 20.00
2 Sam Bradford 40.00 80.00
3 Duff Goldman 8.00 20.00

2010-11 Pinnacle Pantheon

STATED ODDS 1:288 HOB
1 Pavel Datsyuk 8.00 20.00
2 Daniel Alfredsson 6.00 15.00
3 Jonathan Toews 10.00 25.00
4 Nicklas Lidstrom 6.00 15.00
5 Zach Parise 6.00 15.00
6 Martin St. Louis 6.00 15.00
7 Patrick Marleau 6.00 15.00
8 Henrik Sedin 8.00 20.00
9 Mikko Koivu 6.00 15.00
10 Jean Beliveau 6.00 15.00
11 Joe Nieuwendyk 6.00 15.00
12 Joe Sakic 8.00 20.00
13 Rick Middleton 8.00 20.00
14 Brian Leetch 6.00 15.00
15 Dale Hawerchuk 8.00 20.00
16 Ed Giacomin 8.00 20.00
17 Denis Savard 8.00 20.00
18 Gilbert Perreault 8.00 20.00

2010-11 Pinnacle Pencraft

STATED PRINT RUN 50-100
1 Jaroslav Halak/100 8.00 20.00
2 Martin Brodeur/50 20.00 50.00
3 Mike Richards/50 10.00 25.00
4 Marian Gaborik/50 12.00 30.00
5 Ryan Miller/50 10.00 25.00
6 Ryan Getzlaf/50 15.00 40.00
7 Sidney Crosby/50 75.00 150.00
8 Teemu Selanne/50
9 Chris Pronger/50 8.00 20.00
10 Cam Janssen/100 8.00 20.00
11 Brandon Sutter/100
12 Artem Anisimov/100 6.00 15.00
13 Jeff Carter/50 10.00 25.00
14 Patrick Kane/50 20.00 50.00
15 John Tavares/50 20.00 50.00
16 Shane Doan/100
17 Thomas Vanek/100 6.00 15.00
18 Rich Peverley/100 8.00 20.00
19 Tomas Vokoun/50 8.00 20.00
20 Marc-Andre Fleury/50 15.00 40.00
21 Joe Thornton/50 10.00 25.00
22 Kari Lehtonen/50 8.00 20.00
23 Jonathan Quick/100 15.00 35.00
24 Dion Phaneuf/50 10.00 25.00
25 Doug Gilmour/50 15.00 40.00
26 Derek Sanderson/50 8.00 20.00
27 Brian Leetch/50 10.00 25.00
28 Bobby Hull/50 10.00 25.00
29 Stan Mikita/50 12.00 30.00
30 Yvan Cournoyer/50 10.00 25.00
31 Richard Brodeur/100 8.00 20.00
32 Reggie Lemelin/50
33 Ken Linseman/100 8.00 20.00
34 Jean Beliveau/50 30.00 60.00
35 Keith Primeau/50 10.00 25.00

2010-11 Pinnacle Rookie Team Pinnacle Signatures

STATED PRINT RUN 50 SER.#'d SETS
1 T.Hall/T.Seguin 100.00 200.00
2 J.Eberle/M.Paajarvi 50.00 100.00
3 J.Skinner/N.Kadri 50.00 100.00
4 C.Fowler/N.Leddy 20.00 40.00
5 P.Subban/O.Ekman-Larsson 60.00 150.00
6 R.Lehner/S.Bobrovsky 20.00 50.00

2010-11 Pinnacle Saving Face

COMPLETE SET (13) 20.00 50.00
1 Curtis McElhinney 1.50 4.00
2 Ondrej Pavelec 2.00 5.00
3 Tim Thomas 1.50 4.00
5 Cam Ward 2.00 5.00
6 Corey Crawford 2.50 6.00
9 Jonathan Quick 3.00 8.00
10 Jose Theodore 2.00 5.00
11 Carey Price 8.00 20.00
12 Martin Brodeur 4.00 10.00
14 Marc-Andre Fleury 3.00 8.00
15 Cory Schneider 1.50 4.00
16 Michal Neuvirth 1.50 4.00
18 Nikolai Khabibulin 1.50 4.00

2010-11 Pinnacle Team Pinnacle

COMPLETE SET (12) 50.00 100.00
1 M.Richards/P.Datsyuk 8.00 20.00
2 A.Ovechkin/D.Sedin 12.00 30.00
3 M.Gaborik/P.Kane 6.00 15.00
4 M.Green/D.Keith 3.00 8.00
5 C.Pronger/D.Doughty 3.00 8.00
6 R.Miller/I.Bryzgalov 3.00 8.00
7 H.Sedin/S.Stamkos 6.00 15.00
8 H.Zetterberg/M.Lucic 4.00 10.00
9 C.Perry/M.St. Louis 3.00 8.00
10 N.Lidstrom/T.Myers 3.00 8.00
11 S.Weber/Z.Chara 2.50 6.00
12 M.Brodeur/J.Quick 6.00 15.00

2010-11 Pinnacle Threads

STATED PRINT RUN 15-499
*PRIME/25: .5X TO 1.2X BASIC/499
*PRIME/25: .4X TO 1X BASIC/50
AA Artem Anisimov 4.00 10.00
AH Ales Hemsky 4.00 10.00
AK Andrei Kostitsyn 4.00 10.00
AK Anze Kopitar/50 10.00 25.00
AV Antoine Vermette 3.00 8.00
BC Blake Comeau 3.00 8.00
BER Nicklas Bergfors 4.00 10.00
BL Bryan Little/50 6.00 15.00
BM Brenden Morrow 4.00 10.00
BP Benoit Pouliot 3.00 8.00
BR Bobby Ryan 5.00 12.00
BS Brayden Schenn 4.00 10.00
CA Craig Anderson 5.00 12.00
CC Cal Clutterbuck 5.00 12.00
CE Christian Ehrhoff 3.00 8.00
CG Claude Giroux 5.00 12.00
CP Corey Perry/50 6.00 15.00
CW Colin Wilson/15
DB Dustin Brown 5.00 12.00
DB Danny Briere 5.00 12.00
DK Dmitry Kulikov 4.00 10.00
DK Duncan Keith 5.00 12.00
DK David Krejci 5.00 12.00
DR Derek Roy 5.00 12.00
DWN Steve Downie 3.00 8.00
EF Eric Fehr 3.00 8.00
HL Henrik Lundqvist/50 10.00 25.00
HZ Henrik Zetterberg/50 8.00 20.00
IB Ilya Bryzgalov 4.00 10.00
JB Jay Bouwmeester 5.00 12.00
JB Jamie Benn 6.00 15.00
JE Jordan Eberle 6.00 15.00
JI Jarome Iginla 5.00 12.00
JP Joe Pavelski/400 5.00 12.00
JR James van Riemsdyk 8.00 20.00
JS Jordan Staal 5.00 12.00
JS Jason Spezza 3.00 8.00
JS Jeff Skinner 8.00 20.00
JT Jordin Tootoo 4.00 10.00
JT Joe Thornton/50 6.00 15.00
KA Karl Alzner 3.00 8.00
KL Kristopher Letang 5.00 12.00
KO Kyle Okposo 5.00 12.00
LE Loui Eriksson 4.00 10.00
MD Michael Del Zotto 4.00 10.00
MF Mike Fisher 3.00 8.00
MF Michael Frolik 3.00 8.00
MF Marc-Andre Fleury/50 10.00 25.00
MG Marian Gaborik/50 8.00 20.00
MK Miikka Kiprusoff/50 5.00 12.00
ML Milan Lucic 5.00 12.00
MM Matt Moulson 4.00 10.00
MP Magnus Paajarvi/50 3.00 8.00
MR Mason Raymond 4.00 10.00
MS Marc Staal 5.00 12.00
MZ Mats Zuccarello 20.00 50.00
NA Nik Antropov 4.00 10.00
NB Niklas Backstrom 5.00 12.00
NK Nikolai Kulemin 4.00 10.00
PA Pascal Leclaire 4.00 10.00
PB Patrice Bergeron 6.00 15.00
PD Pavel Datsyuk/50 8.00 20.00
PE Patrik Elias 5.00 12.00
PLL Pierre-Luc Letourneau-Leblond 3.00 8.00
PM Patrick Marleau/50
PM Peter Mueller 4.00 10.00
PR Pekka Rinne/50 8.00 20.00
PS Paul Stastny/50 6.00 15.00
PS Patrick Sharp 5.00 12.00
RB Rene Bourque 3.00 8.00
RC Ryan Callahan 5.00 12.00
RG Ryan Getzlaf 8.00 20.00
RM Ryan Malone 3.00 8.00
RM Ryan Miller 5.00 12.00
RO Ryan O'Reilly/50 8.00 20.00
RS Ryan Smyth 4.00 10.00
SC Sidney Crosby/50 25.00 60.00
SD Shane Doan 4.00 10.00
SG Sam Gagner 4.00 10.00
SM Steve Mason 4.00 10.00
SO Steve Ott/50 5.00 12.00
SU Ryan Suter 3.00 8.00
SW Shea Weber/50 5.00 12.00
TB Tyler Bozak/50 6.00 15.00
TE Tobias Enstrom 3.00 8.00
TG T.J. Galiardi 4.00 10.00
THO Tomas Holmstrom 3.00 8.00
TH Taylor Hall/50 10.00 25.00
TR Tuukka Rask/50 12.00 30.00
TS Tyler Seguin/50 10.00 25.00
TT Tim Thomas 6.00 15.00
TV Tomas Vokoun 4.00 10.00
TZ Travis Zajac 4.00 10.00
VL Vincent Lecavalier 4.00 10.00
VO Jakub Voracek 5.00 12.00
WS Wayne Simmonds 6.00 15.00

2010-11 Pinnacle Tough Times

COMPLETE SET (12) 10.00 25.00
STATED ODDS 1:24
BK Bob Kelly 1.50 4.00
AD Andre Dupont 2.00 5.00
BS Bobby Schmautz 1.25 3.00
BW Bryan Watson 1.50 4.00
DP Dennis Polonich 1.25 3.00
DS Dave Schultz 1.50 4.00
JK Jerry Korab 2.50 6.00
JW John Wensink 2.50 6.00
NF Nick Fotiu 2.00 5.00
TO Terry O'Reilly 1.25 3.00
TW Tiger Williams 1.25 3.00
WP Willi Plett 1.25 3.00

2010-11 Pinnacle Tough Times Autographs

STATED PRINT RUN 250 SER.#'d SETS
BK Bob Kelly 10.00 25.00
AD Andre Dupont 12.00 30.00
BS Bobby Schmautz 8.00 20.00
BW Bryan Watson 12.00 30.00
DP Dennis Polonich 8.00 20.00
DS Dave Schultz 10.00 25.00
JK Jerry Korab 15.00 40.00
JW John Wensink 15.00 40.00
NF Nick Fotiu 12.00 30.00
TO Terry O'Reilly 12.00 30.00
TW Tiger Williams 8.00 20.00
WP Willi Plett 8.00 20.00

2011-12 Pinnacle

COMP.SET w/o RC's (250) 20.00 40.00
251-280 ROOKIE ODDS 1:6 HOB
281-290 ROOKIE AU ODDS 1:288 HOB
291-330 INSERTED IN ANTHOLOGY
1 Roberto Luongo .25 .60
2 Dan Hamhuis .20 .50
3 Kevin Bieksa .20 .50
4 Taylor Hall .50 1.25
5 Nicklas Lidstrom .25 .60
6 Shea Weber .25 .60
7 Jeff Carter .25 .60
8 Alex Ovechkin 1.00 2.50
9 Zach Parise .25 .60
10 Corey Perry .25 .60
11 Saku Koivu .25 .60
12 Jarome Iginla .25 .60
13 Pavel Datsyuk .30 .75
14 Alexandre Burrows .25 .60
15 Ryan Getzlaf .40 1.00
16 Derick Brassard .25 .60
17 Milan Lucic .25 .60
18 Nathan Horton .25 .60
19 Tyler Seguin .50 1.25
20 Chris Pronger .25 .60
21 James van Riemsdyk .25 .60
22 Daniel Sedin .25 .60
23 Milan Hejduk .25 .60
24 Martin Havlat .20 .50
25 Chris Stewart .20 .50
26 Martin St. Louis .25 .60
27 Alex Pietrangelo .25 .60
28 Claude Giroux .25 .60
29 Steve Ott .20 .50
30 Tim Thomas .25 .60
31 Carey Price .75 2.00
32 Niklas Backstrom .25 .60
33 Zdeno Chara .25 .60
34 Miikka Kiprusoff .25 .60
35 Jimmy Howard .25 .60
36 Dave Bolland .20 .50
37 Patrice Bergeron .30 .75
38 Derek Roy .20 .50
39 Logan Couture .25 .60
40 Henrik Zetterberg .30 .75
41 Jaroslav Halak .25 .60
42 David Backes .25 .60
43 Kyle Clifford .15 .40
44 Mark Letestu .20 .50
45 Jonathan Bernier .20 .50
46 David Krejci .25 .60
47 Andrei Kostitsyn .20 .50
48 Danny Briere .25 .60
49 Rich Peverley .20 .50
50 Corey Crawford .30 .75
51 Valtteri Filppula .20 .50
52 Mike Green .25 .60
53 Jeff Skinner .25 .60
54 David Jones .15 .40
55 Nick Schultz .15 .40
56 Nicklas Backstrom .40 1.00
57 Tyler Myers .25 .60
58 Kris Letang .25 .60
59 Tomas Vokoun .20 .50
60 Jose Theodore .20 .50
61 Rick Nash .25 .60
62 Michal Neuvirth .20 .50
63 Brad Marchand .30 .75
64 Joffrey Lupul .20 .50
65 Brad Richards .25 .60
66 Rene Bourque .15 .40
67 Mattias Tedenby .15 .40
68 Jaromir Jagr .60 1.50
69 Magnus Paajarvi .20 .50
70 Mikko Koivu .20 .50
71 Evgeni Malkin .75 2.00
72 Ilya Bryzgalov .25 .60
73 Curtis Glencross .15 .40
74 Sergei Kostitsyn .15 .40
75 Jay Bouwmeester .25 .60
76 P.K. Subban .50 1.25
77 Victor Hedman .30 .75
78 Mike Richards .25 .60
79 Andrei Markov .25 .60
80 Nik Antropov .15 .40
81 Phil Kessel .30 .75
82 Anze Kopitar .40 1.00
83 Karl Alzner .15 .40
84 Mikhail Grabovski .20 .50
85 Jason Pominville .20 .50
86 Daymond Langkow .15 .40
87 Sidney Crosby 1.00 2.50
88 Patrick Kane .50 1.25
89 Danny Cleary .25 .60
90 Ian White .15 .40
91 Steven Stamkos .50 1.25
92 Andy McDonald .20 .50
93 Johan Franzen .25 .60
94 Ryan Smyth .20 .50
95 Justin Williams .20 .50
96 Pierre-Marc Bouchard .25 .60
97 Drew Doughty .25 .60
98 Brandon Dubinsky .20 .50
99 Derek Stepan .25 .60
100 Ville Leino .20 .50
101 Steve Mason .20 .50
102 Duncan Keith .25 .60
103 Marc Methot .15 .40
104 Vincent Lecavalier .25 .60
105 Mark Giordano .20 .50
106 Andy Greene .15 .40
107 Paul Martin .15 .40
108 Teemu Selanne .50 1.25
109 Matt Duchene .25 .60
110 Patrick Sharp .25 .60
111 Daniel Alfredsson .25 .60
112 Eric Staal .30 .75
113 Daniel Carcillo .15 .40
114 Jordan Eberle .25 .60
115 Andrew Brunette .15 .40
116 Eric Fehr .15 .40
117 Ilya Kovalchuk .25 .60
118 R.J. Umberger .15 .40
119 Joe Thornton .25 .60
120 Alexander Steen .25 .60
121 Brooks Laich .15 .40
122 Cal Clutterbuck .25 .60
123 Dustin Brown .25 .60
124 Ryan Callahan .25 .60
125 Chris Neil .15 .40
126 Patrik Elias .25 .60
127 Manny Malhotra .20 .50
128 Alexander Semin .25 .60
129 Marc-Andre Fleury .40 1.00
130 Martin Brodeur .50 1.25
131 Antti Niemi .20 .50
132 Kari Lehtonen .20 .50
133 Henrik Sedin .25 .60
134 James Reimer .25 .60
135 Nikolai Khabibulin .20 .50
136 Drew Stafford .20 .50
137 Ryan O'Reilly .25 .60
138 Brayden Schenn .25 .60
139 Matt Beleskey .15 .40
140 Alex Tanguay .15 .40
141 Jakub Voracek .25 .60
142 Steve Sullivan .15 .40
143 David Steckel .15 .40
144 Evgeni Nabokov .25 .60
145 Wayne Simmonds .30 .75
146 John-Michael Liles .15 .40
147 Cam Janssen .15 .40
148 Matthew Lombardi .15 .40
149 Travis Zajac .20 .50
150 Antoine Vermette .15 .40
151 Brian Campbell .15 .40
152 Shawn Horcoff .15 .40
153 Erik Cole .20 .50
154 Joe Corvo .15 .40
155 Ed Jovanovski .15 .40
156 James Wisniewski .15 .40
157 Devin Setoguchi .20 .50
158 David Desharnais .30 .75
159 Patrick Berglund .20 .50
160 Marc Staal .25 .60
161 Mike Ribeiro .20 .50
162 Tomas Fleischmann .15 .40
163 Tyler Ennis .20 .50
164 Kris Versteeg .20 .50
165 Steve Downie .15 .40
166 Jason Spezza .25 .60
167 Anthony Stewart .15 .40
168 Shane Doan .20 .50
169 Cam Ward .25 .60
170 Ray Whitney .20 .50
171 Nick Foligno .20 .50
172 Henrik Lundqvist .30 .75
173 Brenden Morrow .20 .50
174 T.J. Oshie .40 1.00
175 Scottie Upshall .15 .40
176 Ryan Malone .15 .40
177 Milan Michalek .15 .40
178 Tuomo Ruutu .30 .75
179 Martin Hanzal .15 .40
180 Andrew Ladd .25 .60
181 Marian Hossa .25 .60
182 Paul Stastny .20 .50
183 Mike Fisher .25 .60
184 Matt Moulson .20 .50
185 Jamie Benn .30 .75
186 David Booth .20 .50
187 Semyon Varlamov .25 .60
188 Brent Burns .30 .75
189 Mike Santorelli .15 .40
190 Zack Smith .15 .40
191 Brandon Sutter .20 .50
192 Radim Vrbata .15 .40
193 Evander Kane .25 .60
194 Jean-Sebastien Giguere .25 .60
195 Jordin Tootoo .20 .50
196 John Tavares .50 1.25
197 Michael Ryder .15 .40
198 Craig Anderson .25 .60
199 Tomas Kaberle .15 .40
200 Kyle Turris .15 .40
201 Jonas Hiller .20 .50
202 Mark Streit .15 .40
203 Dion Phaneuf .25 .60
204 Cam Fowler .20 .50
205 Dan Girardi .15 .40
206 Ryan Whitney .15 .40
207 Matt Cullen .15 .40
208 Joe Pavelski .25 .60
209 Bobby Ryan .25 .60
210 Marian Gaborik .30 .75
211 Jordan Staal .25 .60
212 Patrick Marleau .25 .60
213 Michael Cammalleri .25 .60
214 Tomas Plekanec .25 .60
215 Dany Heatley .25 .60
216 Teddy Purcell .25 .60
217 Ryan Kesler .25 .60
218 James Neal .25 .60
219 Jonathan Toews .50 1.25
220 Ryan Suter .15 .40
221 Brian Gionta .20 .50
222 Dan Boyle .20 .50
223 Linus Omark .25 .60
224 Blake Wheeler .25 .60
225 Pekka Rinne .30 .75
226 Thomas Vanek .25 .60
227 Rick DiPietro .20 .50
228 Mike Smith .25 .60
229 Ryane Clowe .25 .60
230 Ryan Miller .25 .60
231 Ondrej Pavelec .25 .60
232 Josh Bailey .20 .50
233 Dustin Byfuglien .25 .60
234 Matt Hallschuk .15 .40
235 Dwayne Roloson .20 .50
236 Sheldon Souray .15 .40
237 Alexander Burmistrov .20 .50
238 Keith Yandle .20 .50
239 Matt Carkner .20 .50
240 Michael Grabner .20 .50
241 Bryan Little .20 .50
242 Kyle Okposo .25 .60
243 Tim Gleason .15 .40
244 Erik Johnson .15 .40
245 Raffi Torres .15 .40
246 Al Montoya .15 .40
247 Jack Johnson .15 .40
248 Martin Erat .15 .40
249 Loui Eriksson .20 .50
250 Tim Thomas .25 .60
251 Blake Geoffrion RC 1.00 2.50
252 Ben Scrivens RC 1.50 4.00
253 Patrick Wiercioch RC 1.00 2.50
254 Matt Fraitin RC 1.00 2.50
255 Brett Connolly RC 1.00 2.50
256 Tomas Vincour RC 1.00 2.50
257 Brendon Nash RC 1.00 2.50
258 Erik Condra RC 1.00 2.50
259 Zac Rinaldo RC 1.00 2.50
260 Devante Smith-Pelly RC 1.50 4.00
261 David Savard RC 1.00 2.50
262 Brandon Saad RC 2.00 5.00
263 Erik Gudbranson RC 1.25 3.00
264 Raphael Diaz RC 1.00 2.50
265 Jonathon Blum RC 1.00 2.50
266 Adam Henrique RC 2.50 6.00
267 Maxime Macenauer RC 1.00 2.50
268 Justin Faulk RC 1.50 4.00
269 Cam Atkinson RC 2.50 6.00
270 Roman Horak RC 1.00 2.50
271 Anton Lander RC 1.00 2.50
272 Brett Bulmer RC 1.00 2.50
273 Alexei Emelin RC 1.00 2.50
274 Craig Smith RC 1.25 3.00
275 Adam Larsson RC 1.25 3.00
276 Stephane Da Costa RC 1.00 2.50
277 Colin Greening RC 1.00 2.50
278 Matt Read RC 3.00 8.00
279 Joe Vitale RC 1.00 2.50
280 Harri Sateri RC 1.00 2.50
281 Tim Erixon AU RC 8.00 20.00
282 Cody Hodgson AU RC 10.00 25.00
283 Joe Colborne AU RC 6.00 15.00
284 Nugent-Hopkins AU SP RC 20.00 50.00
285 Gabriel Landeskog AU RC 15.00 40.00
286 Mika Zibanejad AU RC 10.00 25.00
287 Mark Scheifele AU RC 15.00 40.00
288 Ryan Johansen AU RC 8.00 20.00
289 Sean Couturier AU RC 12.00 30.00
290 Jake Gardiner AU RC 8.00 20.00
291 Iiro Tarkki RC 1.50 4.00
292 Jeremy Smith RC 1.50 4.00
293 Pierre-Cedric Labrie RC 1.25 3.00
294 Dylan Olsen RC 1.50 4.00
295 Andrew Shaw RC 3.00 8.00
296 Colten Teubert RC 1.25 3.00
297 Greg Rallo RC 1.50 4.00
298 Jarod Palmer RC 1.25 3.00
299 Joe Finley RC 1.25 3.00
300 Stu Bickel RC 1.25 3.00
301 John Moore RC 1.25 3.00
302 Anders Nilsson RC 1.25 3.00
303 Brayden McNabb RC 1.25 3.00
304 David Ullstrom RC 1.25 3.00
305 Eddie Lack RC 1.25 3.00
306 Brian Foster RC 1.50 4.00
307 David McIntyre RC 1.25 3.00
308 Roman Josi RC 2.00 5.00
309 Keith Kinkaid RC 1.25 3.00
310 Peter Holland RC 1.25 3.00
311 Chad Rau RC 1.25 3.00
312 Kevin Marshall RC 1.25 3.00
313 Marc-Andre Bourdon RC 1.25 3.00
314 T.J. Brennan RC 1.25 3.00
315 Stefan Elliott RC 1.25 3.00
316 Corey Tropp RC 1.25 3.00
317 Brendan Smith RC 1.25 3.00
318 Slava Voynov RC 1.50 4.00
319 Dmitry Orlov RC 1.50 4.00
320 Matt Fraser RC 1.50 4.00
321 Allen York RC 1.25 3.00
322 Leland Irving RC 1.25 3.00
323 Harry Zolnierczyk RC 1.25 3.00
324 Frederic St-Denis RC 1.25 3.00
325 Gabriel Bourque RC 1.25 3.00
326 Jimmy Hayes RC 1.25 3.00
327 Riley Nash RC 1.25 3.00
328 Mike Murphy RC 1.25 3.00
329 Carl Sneep RC 1.25 3.00
330 Ryan Ellis RC 1.50 4.00
331 David Rundblad RC 1.25 3.00
332 Cody Eakin RC 1.50 4.00
333 Zack Kassian RC 1.50 4.00
334 Louis Leblanc RC 1.50 4.00
335 Andy Miele RC 1.25 3.00
336 Marcus Foligno RC 2.00 5.00
337 Joakim Andersson RC 1.25 3.00
338 Gustav Nyquist RC 3.00 8.00
339 Carl Hagelin RC 2.00 5.00
340 Calvin de Haan RC 1.25 3.00
341 Jordie Benn RC 1.25 3.00
342 Brad Malone RC 1.25 3.00
343 Derek Whitmore RC 1.25 3.00
344 Greg Nemisz RC 1.25 3.00
345 Ryan Russell RC 1.50 4.00
346 Lennart Petrell RC 1.50 4.00
347 Mark Borowiecki RC 1.50 4.00
348 Cade Fairchild RC 1.00 2.50
349 Mike Angelidis RC 1.25 3.00
350 Yann Sauve RC 1.25 3.00
351 Carl Klingberg RC 1.25 3.00
352 Tomas Kundratek RC 1.25 3.00
353 Andre Petersson RC 1.25 3.00
354 Simon Despres RC 1.25 3.00
355 Erik Gustafsson RC 1.25 3.00
356 Robert Bortuzzo RC 1.25 3.00
357 Mike Hoffman RC 5.00 12.00
358 Bill Sweatt RC 1.25 3.00
359 Paul Postma RC 1.25 3.00
360 Marcus Kruger RC 2.00 5.00
361 Lance Bouma RC 1.25 3.00
362 Warren Peters RC 1.50 4.00
363 Aaron Palushaj RC 1.25 3.00
364 Milan Kytnar RC 1.50 4.00
365 Kris Fredheim RC 1.25 3.00

2011-12 Pinnacle Rink Collection

*1-250 VETS: 2.5X TO 6X BASIC CARDS
STATED ODDS 1:24 HOB
50 Corey Crawford 2.00 5.00
56 Nicklas Backstrom 2.50 6.00

2011-12 Pinnacle Black

STATED ODDS 1:288 HOB
1 Sidney Crosby 25.00 60.00
2 Steven Stamkos 12.00 30.00
3 Alex Ovechkin 25.00 60.00
4 Carey Price 12.00 30.00
5 Tim Thomas 8.00 20.00
6 Martin Brodeur 10.00 25.00
7 Jonathan Toews 10.00 25.00
8 Roberto Luongo 6.00 15.00
9 Jeff Skinner 6.00 15.00
10 Joe Sakic 10.00 25.00
11 Patrick Roy 15.00 40.00
12 Mario Lemieux 20.00 50.00
13 Mark Messier 10.00 25.00
14 Steve Yzerman 12.00 30.00

2011-12 Pinnacle Breakthrough

COMPLETE SET (20) 15.00 30.00
STATED ODDS 1:8 HOB
1 Ryan Kesler 1.00 2.50
2 Corey Perry 1.00 2.50
3 Claude Giroux 1.00 2.50
4 Corey Crawford 1.25 3.00
5 Jeff Skinner 1.00 2.50
6 David Backes 1.00 2.50
7 Ryane Clowe .60 1.50
8 Clarke MacArthur .60 1.50
9 Keith Yandle .60 1.50
10 Milan Lucic 1.00 2.50
11 Nikolai Kulemin 1.00 2.50
12 Jamie Benn 1.25 3.00
13 Logan Couture 1.00 2.50
14 James van Riemsdyk 1.00 2.50
15 Brad Marchand 1.25 3.00
16 Andrew Ladd 1.00 2.50
17 David Krejci 1.00 2.50
18 Michael Grabner .75 2.00
19 James Reimer 1.25 3.00
20 Loui Eriksson .75 2.00

2011-12 Pinnacle Canvas Creations

1 Sidney Crosby 8.00 20.00
2 Martin Brodeur 4.00 10.00
3 Patrick Kane 4.00 10.00
4 Pavel Datsyuk 2.50 6.00
5 Alex Ovechkin 8.00 20.00
6 Carey Price 6.00 15.00
7 Claude Giroux 2.00 5.00
8 Jordan Eberle 2.00 5.00
9 Roberto Luongo 2.00 5.00
10 Tim Thomas 2.00 5.00
11 Evgeni Malkin 6.00 15.00
12 Rick Nash 2.00 5.00
13 James Reimer 2.50 6.00
14 Mike Richards 2.00 5.00
15 Marian Gaborik 2.50 6.00
16 Steven Stamkos 4.00 10.00
17 Logan Couture 2.00 5.00
18 Jarome Iginla 2.00 5.00

2011-12 Pinnacle Captains

1 Jonathan Toews 5.00 12.00
2 Nicklas Lidstrom 2.50 6.00
3 Joe Thornton 2.50 6.00
4 Alex Ovechkin 10.00 25.00
5 Henrik Sedin 2.50 6.00
6 Zdeno Chara 2.50 6.00
7 Sidney Crosby 10.00 25.00
8 Daniel Alfredsson 2.50 6.00
9 Dion Phaneuf 2.50 6.00
10 Vincent Lecavalier 2.00 5.00
11 Brian Gionta 2.00 5.00
12 Shane Doan 2.00 5.00
13 Andrew Ladd 2.50 6.00
14 Rick Nash 2.50 6.00
15 Shea Weber 2.00 5.00
16 Eric Staal 3.00 8.00
17 Jarome Iginla 2.50 6.00
18 Ryan Getzlaf 4.00 10.00
19 Mikko Koivu 2.00 5.00
20 Shawn Horcoff 1.50 4.00

2011-12 Pinnacle Fans of the Game

1 Michelle Beadle 1.50 4.00
2 Heidi Androl 1.50 4.00
3 Dave Hanson 2.00 5.00
4 Jeff Carlson 1.50 4.00
5 Steve Carlson 1.50 4.00
6 Jonathan Davis 1.50 4.00
7 Alyssa Milano 1.50 4.00
8 Jaime Pressly 1.50 4.00

2011-12 Pinnacle Fans of the Game Autographs

1 Michelle Beadle 15.00 40.00
2 Heidi Androl 12.00 30.00
3 Dave Hanson 10.00 25.00
4 Jeff Carlson 10.00 25.00
5 Steve Carlson 12.00 30.00
6 Jonathan Davis 15.00 40.00
7 Alyssa Milano 40.00 100.00
8 Jaime Pressly

2011-12 Pinnacle Foundation Tandems East

1 T.Seguin/T.Thomas 1.50 4.00
2 R.Miller/T.Ennis .75 2.00
3 E.Staal/J.Skinner 1.25 3.00
4 C.Price/P.Subban 3.00 8.00
5 M.Brodeur/Z.Parise 2.00 5.00
6 H.Lundqvist/D.Stepan 1.25 3.00
7 C.Giroux/B.Schenn 1.00 2.50
8 S.Crosby/M.Letestu 4.00 10.00
9 S.Stamkos/V.Lecavalier 2.00 5.00
10 J.Carlson/A.Ovechkin 3.00 8.00

2011-12 Pinnacle Foundation Tandems West

1 C.Fowler/R.Getzlaf 1.25 3.00
2 J.Toews/M.Kruger 1.50 4.00
3 P.Stastny/M.Duchene .75 2.00
4 R.Nash/J.Moore .75 2.00
5 P.Datsyuk/T.Tatar 1.00 2.50
6 J.Eberle/T.Hall 1.50 4.00
7 A.Pietrangelo/J.Halak .75 2.00
8 J.Thornton/L.Couture .75 2.00
9 C.Hodgson/R.Luongo .75 2.00
10 G.Nemisz/J.Iginla .75 2.00

2011-12 Pinnacle Game Night Materials

STATED ODDS 1:24 HOB
*PRIME/30-50: .6X TO 1.5X BASIC JSY
1 Sidney Crosby 8.00 20.00
2 Alex Ovechkin 8.00 20.00
3 Carey Price 12.00 30.00
4 Zdeno Chara 4.00 10.00
5 Bobby Butler 3.00 8.00
6 Tyler Seguin 8.00 20.00
7 Matt Carkner 3.00 8.00
8 Tim Thomas 4.00 10.00
9 Tyler Myers 4.00 10.00
10 Jarome Iginla 4.00 10.00
11 Patrick Kane 8.00 20.00
12 Pavel Datsyuk 5.00 12.00
13 Jeff Carter 4.00 10.00
14 Bobby Ryan 4.00 10.00
15 Nathan Horton 4.00 10.00
16 Anze Kopitar 6.00 15.00
17 Curtis Glencross 2.50 6.00
18 Marian Gaborik 5.00 12.00
19 Kevin Bieksa 3.00 8.00
20 Corey Perry 4.00 10.00
21 Stephane Da Costa 3.00 8.00
22 Ryan Kesler 4.00 10.00
23 David Backes 4.00 10.00
24 Taylor Hall 8.00 20.00
25 Shawn Thornton 3.00 8.00
26 Jamie Benn 5.00 12.00
27 Ondrej Pavelec 4.00 10.00
28 Scott Hartnell 4.00 10.00
29 Cam Fowler 3.00 8.00
30 Pekka Rinne 5.00 12.00
31 Logan Couture 4.00 10.00
32 P.K. Subban 8.00 20.00
33 Ryan Suter 2.50 6.00
34 Niklas Backstrom 4.00 10.00
35 Drew Doughty 4.00 10.00
36 Dustin Byfuglien 4.00 10.00
37 Henrik Sedin 4.00 10.00
38 Claude Giroux 4.00 10.00
39 Marc-Andre Fleury 6.00 15.00
40 Dany Heatley 3.00 8.00
41 Henrik Lundqvist 4.00 10.00
42 Jeff Skinner 4.00 10.00
43 Mike Richards 4.00 10.00
44 Dion Phaneuf 4.00 10.00
45 Ryan Smyth 4.00 10.00
46 Zac Dalpe 2.50 6.00
47 Patrick Marleau 4.00 10.00
48 Paul Stastny 4.00 10.00
49 Vincent Lecavalier 3.00 8.00
50 Martin St. Louis 4.00 10.00

2011-12 Pinnacle Game Night Signatures

ANNOUNCED PRINT RUN 5-75
1 Sidney Crosby/25* 60.00 120.00
2 Alex Ovechkin/50* 30.00 80.00
3 Carey Price/25* 15.00 40.00
5 Bobby Butler/75* 6.00 15.00
6 Tyler Seguin/25* 30.00 60.00
7 Matt Carkner/10*
8 Tim Thomas/25* 15.00 30.00
9 Tyler Myers/35* 10.00 25.00
10 Jarome Iginla/75* 8.00 20.00
11 Patrick Kane/75* 20.00 40.00
12 Pavel Datsyuk/50* 10.00 25.00
13 Jeff Carter/50* 8.00 20.00
14 Bobby Ryan/75* 8.00 20.00
15 Nathan Horton/50* 8.00 20.00
17 Curtis Glencross/75* 5.00 12.00
20 Corey Perry/75* 8.00 20.00
21 Stephane Da Costa/75* 6.00 15.00
22 Ryan Kesler/50* 12.00 30.00
23 David Backes/50*
24 Taylor Hall/25*
25 Shawn Thornton/20* 25.00 50.00
26 Jamie Benn/75* 10.00 25.00
27 Ondrej Pavelec/75* 8.00 20.00
29 Cam Fowler/75* 6.00 15.00
30 Pekka Rinne/75*
31 Logan Couture/75* 8.00 20.00
32 P.K. Subban/75* 15.00 40.00
34 Niklas Backstrom/75* 8.00 20.00
35 Drew Doughty/35* 10.00 25.00
36 Dustin Byfuglien/75*
37 Henrik Sedin/25* 10.00 25.00
38 Claude Giroux/50* 8.00 20.00
39 Marc-Andre Fleury/75* 15.00 30.00
40 Dany Heatley/25*
41 Henrik Lundqvist/50* 15.00 30.00
42 Jeff Skinner/75* 8.00 20.00
44 Dion Phaneuf/25* 12.00 30.00
45 Ryan Smyth/75* 6.00 15.00
46 Zac Dalpe/75*
47 Patrick Marleau/75* 8.00 20.00
48 Paul Stastny/75*
49 Vincent Lecavalier/35* 8.00 20.00
50 Martin St. Louis/50*

2011-12 Pinnacle Ice Breakers Autographs

RANDOM INSERTS IN ANTHOLOGY PACKS
302 Anders Nilsson 6.00 15.00
305 Eddie Lack 6.00 15.00
308 Roman Josi 10.00 25.00
310 Peter Holland 6.00 15.00
317 Brendan Smith 6.00 15.00
318 Slava Voynov 6.00 15.00
323 Harry Zolnierczyk 6.00 15.00
326 Jimmy Hayes 8.00 20.00
330 Ryan Ellis 6.00 15.00
331 David Rundblad 6.00 15.00
332 Cody Eakin 8.00 20.00
333 Zack Kassian 8.00 20.00
334 Louis Leblanc
335 Andy Miele 6.00 15.00
338 Gustav Nyquist 15.00 40.00
339 Carl Hagelin 10.00 25.00
340 Calvin de Haan 6.00 15.00
344 Greg Nemisz 6.00 15.00
351 Carl Klingberg 6.00 15.00
354 Simon Despres 6.00 15.00
361 Lance Bouma 6.00 15.00

2011-12 Pinnacle Pantheon

1 Steven Stamkos 12.00 30.00
2 Tim Thomas 10.00 25.00
3 Alex Ovechkin 25.00 60.00
4 Corey Perry 6.00 15.00
5 Daniel Sedin 6.00 15.00
6 Sidney Crosby 25.00 60.00
7 Carey Price 20.00 50.00
8 Henrik Zetterberg
9 Jarome Iginla 6.00 15.00
10 Claude Giroux 6.00 15.00

2011-12 Pinnacle Revolution

1 P.K. Subban 3.00 8.00
2 Jeff Skinner 1.50 4.00
3 Alex Ovechkin 6.00 15.00
4 Steven Stamkos 3.00 8.00
5 Sidney Crosby 6.00 15.00
6 Milan Lucic 1.50 4.00
7 Dustin Byfuglien 1.50 4.00
8 Tyler Ennis 1.25 3.00
9 James Reimer 1.50 4.00
10 Henrik Lundqvist 2.00 5.00

2011-12 Pinnacle Starting Six Threads

1-10 STATED PRINT RUN 199
*1-10 PRIME/50: .6X TO 1.5X BASIC JSY/199
11-40 INSERTED IN ANTHOLOGY
11-40 NNOUNCED PRINT RUN 25-200
1 Thms/Chr/Brg/Lcic/Hrtn/Brtk 20.00 40.00
2 Hmh/Sdin/Ehr/Sdn/Brrw/Lng 12.00 30.00
3 Mrkv/Gnta/Kst/Prc/Cam/Sbn 10.00 25.00
4 Kln/Rmr/Phnf/Kssl/Grbv/Sch 12.00 30.00
5 Flry/Mlkn/Stl/Neal/Letng/Strt 12.00 30.00
6 Alzn/Smn/Ovc/Bck/Crls/Nsh 15.00 40.00
7 Lpld/Mlr/Pmvl/Ry/Myrs/Ennis 8.00 20.00
8 Gbrt/Wlt/Khb/Hmsk/Hll/Ebrl 10.00 25.00
9 Mrl/Clwe/Thrn/Byle/Nml/Brns 10.00 25.00
10 Dbn/Stl/Gbrk/Clfn/DlZt/Lndq 10.00 25.00
11 Predators/137* 6.00 15.00
12 Kings/200* 10.00 25.00
13 Ducks/200* 12.00 30.00
14 Blackhawks/25* 40.00 80.00
15 Avalanche/200* 12.00 30.00
16 Stars/50* 15.00 30.00
17 Oilers/200* 10.00 25.00
18 Wild/200* 10.00 25.00
19 Devils/200* 15.00 40.00
20 Senators/200* 12.00 30.00
21 Flyers/100* 20.00 40.00
22 Red Wings/200* 8.00 20.00
23 Hurricanes/100* 10.00 25.00
24 Blue Jackets/200* 15.00 40.00
25 Islanders/200* 8.00 20.00
26 Tws/Grx/Ebr/Kth/Prn/Prc/100* 12.00 30.00

27 Bck/Kne/Rch/Str/Yndl/Thm 15.00 40.00
28 Sdn Br./Alfrd/Krlsn/Lds/Lnd 12.00 30.00
29 Kvu/Slne/Flpp/Tim/Kth/Kip 15.00 40.00
30 Jgr/Ert/Mclk/Krjc/Kbrl/Nvr 12.00 30.00
31 Dtsk/Ov/Kvl/Gnch/Voy/Khb 12.00 30.00
32 Nl/Spz/Kss/Piet/Dn/Hwrd 12.00 30.00
33 Hrtn/Stm/StL/Dgty/Zot/Nie 12.00 30.00
34 Ctr/Hnrg/Smt/Jhn/Emln/Yrk 10.00 25.00
35 Jhn/Smt/Krg/Sav/Emln/Scr 12.00 30.00
36 Adm/RNH/Ctr/Voy/Els/Scr 12.00 30.00
37 Lnd/Hnrg/Rd/Grd/Flk/Yrk 12.00 30.00
38 Hag/Grn/Frt/Dz/Lrsn/Yrk 6.00 15.00
39 Hnrg/Rd/Grn/Svr/Grd/Scr 10.00 25.00
40 RNH/Lnd/Hds/Voy/Els/Yrk 8.00 20.00

2011-12 Pinnacle Team Pinnacle

1 H.Sedin/S.Stamkos 4.00 10.00
2 M.St. Louis/C.Perry 2.00 5.00
3 D.Sedin/A.Ovechkin 8.00 20.00
4 Z.Chara/N.Lidstrom 2.50 6.00
5 T.Thomas/R.Luongo 2.00 5.00
6 S.Crosby/J.Toews 5.00 12.00
7 J.Iginla/C.Giroux 2.00 5.00
8 M.Lucic/H.Zetterberg 2.50 6.00
9 S.Weber/P.Subban 4.00 10.00
10 P.Rinne/C.Price 6.00 15.00

2011-12 Pinnacle Threads

STATED ODDS 1:24 HOB
*PATCH/15-25: .8X TO 2X BASIC JSY
*PRIME/50: .6X TO 1.5X BASIC JSY
1 Corey Perry 4.00 10.00
2 Eric Staal 5.00 12.00
3 Thomas Vanek 4.00 10.00
4 Mark Giordano 3.00 8.00
5 Sidney Crosby 15.00 40.00
6 Alex Ovechkin 10.00 25.00
7 Anze Kopitar 6.00 15.00
8 Martin St. Louis 4.00 10.00
9 Daniel Alfredsson 4.00 10.00
10 John Tavares 8.00 20.00
11 Patrick Roy 10.00 25.00
12 Dion Phaneuf 4.00 10.00
13 Joe Thornton 4.00 10.00
14 Matt Duchene 4.00 10.00
15 Nicklas Lidstrom 4.00 10.00
16 Ryan Getzlaf 6.00 15.00
17 Jason Spezza 4.00 10.00
18 Henrik Zetterberg 5.00 12.00
19 Jonathan Toews 8.00 20.00
20 Milan Lucic 4.00 10.00
21 Alexandre Burrows 4.00 10.00
22 Nazem Kadri 6.00 15.00
23 Sergei Kostitsyn 2.50 6.00
24 Mike Green 4.00 10.00
25 Steve Ott 3.00 8.00
26 Jonas Gustavsson 4.00 10.00
27 Rene Bourque 2.50 6.00
28 Kris Letang 4.00 10.00
29 Rick DiPietro 3.00 8.00
30 Taylor Hall 8.00 20.00
31 Trevor Daley 2.50 6.00
32 Ales Hemsky 3.00 8.00
33 Andrei Markov 4.00 10.00
34 Antti Niemi 3.00 8.00
35 Barret Jackman 2.50 6.00
36 Brad Marchand 5.00 12.00
37 Brandon McMillan 2.50 6.00
38 Marc-Andre Fleury 6.00 15.00
39 Magnus Paajarvi 3.00 8.00
40 Luke Schenn 3.00 8.00
41 Loui Eriksson 3.00 8.00
42 Linus Omark 4.00 10.00
43 Kris Versteeg 3.00 8.00
44 Keith Yandle 4.00 10.00
45 Tim Thomas 4.00 10.00
46 Tom Wandell 2.50 6.00
47 Tomas Tatar 3.00 8.00
48 Zdeno Chara 4.00 10.00
49 Cal Clutterbuck 4.00 10.00
50 Brian Gionta 3.00 8.00
51 Brian Boyle 2.50 6.00
52 Brent Seabrook 4.00 10.00
53 Colin Wilson 3.00 8.00
54 Shea Weber 3.00 8.00
55 Derek Stepan 4.00 10.00
56 Erik Johnson 2.50 6.00
57 Evgeni Malkin 12.00 30.00
58 Devan Dubnyk 4.00 10.00
59 Drew Doughty 4.00 10.00
60 Dustin Tokarski 4.00 10.00
61 Mattias Tedenby 2.50 6.00
62 Ryan McDonagh 4.00 10.00
63 Rick Nash 4.00 10.00
64 Henrik Lundqvist 5.00 12.00
65 Alexander Burmistrov 3.00 8.00
66 Jamie McBain 2.50 6.00
67 Jordan Leopold 2.50 6.00
68 Milan Michalek 2.50 6.00
69 Nathan Gerbe 2.50 6.00
70 Jordan Staal 4.00 10.00
71 Niklas Backstrom 4.00 10.00
72 Patrik Elias 4.00 10.00
73 Scott Gomez 3.00 8.00
74 Tomas Vokoun 3.00 8.00
75 Travis Zajac 3.00 8.00
76 Zach Hamill 3.00 8.00
77 Duncan Keith 4.00 10.00
78 Dustin Brown 4.00 10.00
79 Craig Anderson 4.00 10.00
80 Claude Giroux 4.00 10.00
81 Carey Price 12.00 30.00
82 Chris Pronger 3.00 8.00
83 George Parros 3.00 8.00
84 Henrik Sedin 6.00 15.00
85 Ilya Kovalchuk 4.00 10.00
86 James Neal 4.00 10.00
87 Jason Pominville 3.00 8.00
88 Logan Couture 4.00 10.00
89 Marc Staal 4.00 10.00
90 P.K. Subban 6.00 15.00

2011-12 Pinnacle Tough Times

STATED ODDS 1:12 HOB
1 Wendel Clark 1.50 4.00
3 Rob Ray 1.25 3.00
4 Bruce Shoebottom 1.00 2.50
5 Marty McSorley 1.50 4.00
8 Gino Odjick 1.00 2.50
10 Shane Churla 1.00 2.50

2011-12 Pinnacle Tough Times Autographs

1 Wendel Clark 15.00 40.00
3 Rob Ray 6.00 15.00
4 Bruce Shoebottom 5.00 12.00
5 Marty McSorley 8.00 20.00
8 Gino Odjick SP 12.00 30.00
10 Shane Churla 5.00 12.00

2011-12 Pinnacle Winter Classic

Cards from this set were issued in special packs for release at the 2012 Winter Classic game. All of the cards feature the Winter Classic logo on the fronts and the five Great Outdoors cards were a non-foil glossy stock version of the same three 2010-11 Contenders cards with the addition of a Pinnacle logo on the front instead of Contenders.

INSERTS IN WINTER CLASSIC PACKS
1 Ryan Miller GO 1.25 3.00
2 Jonathan Toews GO 2.50 6.00
3 Marian Hossa GO 1.00 2.50
4 Alex Ovechkin GO 5.00 12.00
5 Tim Thomas GO 1.25 3.00
PF1 Chris Pronger 1.00 2.50
PF2 Claude Giroux 1.25 3.00
PF3 Ilya Bryzgalov 1.25 3.00
PF4 Jaromir Jagr 3.00 8.00
PF5 Sean Couturier 3.00 8.00
WC1 Tim Thomas 1.25 3.00
WC2 Gabriel Landeskog 3.00 8.00
WC3 Ryan Nugent-Hopkins 12.50 30.00
WC4 Steven Stamkos 2.50 6.00
WC5 Alex Ovechkin 5.00 12.00
NYR1 Brad Richards 1.25 3.00
NYR2 Derek Stepan 1.25 3.00
NYR3 Henrik Lundqvist 1.50 4.00
NYR4 Marian Gaborik 1.50 4.00
NYR5 Tim Erixon 1.00 2.50

2011-12 Pinnacle All Star Game

COMPLETE SET (10) 10.00 20.00
1 Daniel Alfredsson .40 1.00
2 Nicklas Lidstrom .40 1.00
3 Jaromir Jagr .40 1.00
4 Alex Ovechkin 1.25 3.00
5 Sidney Crosby 1.50 3.50
6 Tim Thomas .75 2.00
7 Ryan Nugent-Hopkins 1.50 4.00
8 Mika Zibanejad 1.25 3.00
9 Gabriel Landeskog 1.50 3.50
ML Mario Lemieux 1.00 2.50

1997-98 Pinnacle Collector's Club Team Pinnacle

This set was available with membership to Pinnacle's Collector's Club. Promo cards carried the player's name across the top of the card not the side like the regular cards.

COMPLETE SET (10) 40.00 80.00
H1 Wayne Gretzky 8.00 20.00
H2 Patrick Roy 6.00 15.00
H3 Eric Lindros 3.00 8.00
H4 Paul Kariya 5.00 12.00
H5 Peter Forsberg 5.00 12.00
H6 John Vanbiesbrouck 2.00 5.00
H7 Martin Brodeur 6.00 15.00
H8 Steve Yzerman 6.00 15.00
H9 Jaromir Jagr 4.00 10.00
H10 Mark Messier 3.00 8.00
NNO Wayne Gretzky PROMO 10.00 25.00
NNO Peter Forsberg PROMO 6.00 15.00

1997-98 Pinnacle Certified

The 1997-98 Pinnacle Certified set was issued in one series totaling 130 cards and was distributed in five-card hobby packs only with a suggested retail price of $4.99. The fronts feature borderless color action player photos. The backs carry player information.

1 Dominik Hasek .30 .75
2 Patrick Roy .50 1.25
3 Martin Brodeur .40 1.00
4 Chris Osgood .20 .50
5 Andy Moog .20 .50
6 John Vanbiesbrouck .20 .50
7 Steve Shields RC .20 .50
8 Mike Vernon .15 .40
9 Ed Belfour .20 .50
10 Grant Fuhr .20 .50
11 Felix Potvin .20 .50
12 Bill Ranford .15 .40
13 Mike Richter .20 .50
14 Stephane Fiset .15 .40
15 Jim Carey .12 .30
16 Nikolai Khabibulin .20 .50
17 Ken Wregget .12 .30
18 Curtis Joseph .20 .50
19 Guy Hebert .15 .40
20 Damian Rhodes .15 .40
21 Trevor Kidd .12 .30
22 Daren Puppa .15 .40
23 Patrick Lalime .15 .40
24 Tommy Salo .12 .30
25 Sean Burke .12 .30
26 Jocelyn Thibault .12 .30
27 Kirk McLean .15 .40
28 Garth Snow .15 .40
29 Ron Tugnutt .20 .50
30 Jeff Hackett .12 .30
31 Eric Lindros .30 .75
32 Peter Forsberg .25 .60
33 Mike Modano .30 .75
34 Paul Kariya .25 .60
35 Jaromir Jagr .50 1.25
36 Brian Leetch .20 .50
37 Keith Tkachuk .20 .50
38 Steve Yzerman .40 1.00
39 Teemu Selanne .40 1.00
40 Bryan Berard .12 .30
41 Ray Bourque .30 .75
42 Theo Fleury .25 .60
43 Mark Messier .30 .75
44 Saku Koivu .20 .50
45 Pavel Bure .25 .60
46 Peter Bondra .15 .40
47 Dave Gagner .12 .30
48 Ed Jovanovski .12 .30
49 Adam Oates .20 .50
50 Joe Sakic .30 .75
51 Doug Gilmour .25 .60
52 Jim Campbell .12 .30
53 Mats Sundin .20 .50
54 Derian Hatcher .15 .40
55 Jarome Iginla .20 .50
56 Sergei Fedorov .30 .75
57 Keith Primeau .15 .40
58 Mark Recchi .25 .60
59 Owen Nolan .20 .50
60 Alexander Mogilny .15 .40
61 Brendan Shanahan .25 .60
62 Pierre Turgeon .20 .50
63 Joe Juneau .15 .40
64 Steve Rucchin .15 .40
65 Jeremy Roenick .25 .60
66 Doug Weight .20 .50
67 Valeri Kamensky .15 .40
68 Tony Amonte .15 .40
69 Dave Andreychuk .20 .50
70 Brett Hull .25 .60
71 Wendel Clark .20 .50
72 Vincent Damphousse .15 .40
73 Mike Grier .15 .40
74 Chris Chelios .20 .50
75 Nicklas Lidstrom .20 .50
76 Joe Nieuwendyk .20 .50
77 Rob Blake .20 .50
78 Alexei Yashin .15 .40
79 Ryan Smyth .15 .40
80 Pat LaFontaine .20 .50
81 Jeff Friesen .15 .40
82 Ray Ferraro .12 .30
83 Steve Sullivan .15 .40
84 Chris Gratton .12 .30
85 Mike Gartner .20 .50
86 Kevin Hatcher .12 .30
87 Ted Donato .12 .30
88 German Titov .12 .30
89 Sandis Ozolinsh .15 .40
90 Ray Sheppard .15 .40
91 John MacLean .12 .30
92 Luc Robitaille .20 .50
93 Rod Brind'Amour .20 .50
94 Zigmund Palffy .20 .50
95 Petr Nedved .20 .50
96 Adam Graves .12 .30
97 Jozef Stumpel .15 .40
98 Alexandre Daigle .12 .30
99 Mike Peca .15 .40
100 Wayne Gretzky 1.00 2.50
101 Alexei Zhamnov .12 .30
102 Paul Coffey .20 .50
103 Oleg Tverdovsky .15 .40
104 Trevor Linden .15 .40
105 Dino Ciccarelli .20 .50
106 Andrei Kovalenko .12 .30
107 Scott Mellanby .15 .40
108 Bryan Smolinski .15 .40
109 Bernie Nicholls .15 .40
110 Derek Plante .15 .40
111 Pat Verbeek .15 .40
112 Adam Deadmarsh .12 .30
113 Martin Gelinas .12 .30
114 Daniel Alfredsson .20 .50
115 Scott Stevens .20 .50
116 Dainius Zubrus .15 .40
117 Kirk Muller .12 .30
118 Brian Holzinger .15 .40
119 John LeClair .20 .50
120 Al MacInnis .20 .50
121 Ron Francis .25 .60
122 Eric Daze .12 .30
123 Travis Green .15 .40
124 Jason Arnott .15 .40
125 Geoff Sanderson .15 .40
126 Dimitri Khristich .15 .40
127 Sergei Berezin .15 .40
128 Jeff O'Neill .15 .40
129 Claude Lemieux .15 .40
130 Andrew Cassels .12 .30
NNO CHECKLIST 1 .07 .20
NNO CHECKLIST 2 .07 .20

1997-98 Pinnacle Certified Red

Randomly inserted in packs at the rate of 1:5, this 130-card set is parallel to the Pinnacle Certified base set and is distinguished by the red treatment of the mirror Mylar regular cards.

*RED: 1.2X TO 3X BASIC CARDS

1997-98 Pinnacle Certified Mirror Blue

Randomly inserted in packs at the rate of 1:199, this 130-card set is parallel to the Pinnacle Certified base set. The difference is found in the blue design element on holographic foil.

*MIRROR BLUE: 6X TO 15X BASIC CARDS

1997-98 Pinnacle Certified Mirror Gold

Randomly inserted in packs at the rate of 1:299, this 130-card set is parallel to the Pinnacle Certified base set. The difference is found in the golden holographic mirror Mylar highlights of the set.

*MIRROR GOLD: 12X TO 30X BASIC CARDS
100 Wayne Gretzky 75.00 150.00

1997-98 Pinnacle Certified Mirror Red

Randomly inserted in packs at the rate of 1:99, this 130-card set is parallel to the Pinnacle Certified base set. The difference is found in the holographic red foil design of the set.

*MIRROR RED: 4X TO 10X BASIC CARDS

1997-98 Pinnacle Certified Team

Randomly inserted in packs at the rate of 1:19, this 20-card set features color action photos of 10 Eastern Conference megastars matched with 10 Western Conference superstar counterparts and printed on mirror Mylar all-foil card stock. A gold parallel was also created and randomly inserted at a rate of 1:129. These parallels are distinctive because of the added gold accents and foil stamping. Only 300 of this set were produced and are sequentially numbered.

COMPLETE SET (20) 75.00 150.00
*GOLD TEAM/300: 2X TO 5X BASIC INSERTS
*GT PROMOS: .2X TO .5X BASIC INSERTS
1 Martin Brodeur 5.00 12.00
2 Patrick Roy 10.00 25.00
3 John Vanbiesbrouck 1.25 3.00
4 Dominik Hasek 4.00 10.00
5 Chris Chelios 2.00 5.00
6 Brian Leetch 2.00 5.00
7 Wayne Gretzky 12.50 30.00
8 Eric Lindros 2.00 5.00
9 Paul Kariya 2.00 5.00
10 Peter Forsberg 5.00 12.00
11 Keith Tkachuk 2.00 5.00
12 Mark Messier 2.00 5.00
13 Steve Yzerman 10.00 25.00
14 Jaromir Jagr 3.00 8.00
15 Mats Sundin 2.00 5.00
16 Teemu Selanne 2.00 5.00
17 Brendan Shanahan 2.00 5.00
18 Saku Koivu 2.00 5.00
19 Brett Hull 2.50 6.00
20 John LeClair 2.00 5.00

1997-98 Pinnacle Certified Rookie Redemption

Randomly inserted in packs at the rate of 1:19, this 12-card set was obtained through the mail with the redemption card and features color action player photos printed on super-premium 24-point card stock with an exclusive authenticator bar to protect the set from counterfeiting. Gold and Mirror Gold versions of these cards were also available via redemption. Gold parallels were inserted at a rate of 1:259 and were limited to 250 sets.

COMPLETE SET (12) 25.00 50.00
*GOLD: 2X TO 5X BASIC INSERTS
*MIRROR GOLD: 8X TO 20X BASIC INSERTS
A Joe Thornton 5.00 12.00
B Chris Phillips 1.50 4.00
C Patrick Marleau 4.00 10.00
D Sergei Samsonov 1.50 4.00
E Daniel Cleary 1.50 4.00
F Olli Jokinen 2.50 6.00
G Alyn McCauley 1.50 4.00
H Alexei Morozov 1.50 4.00
I Brad Isbister 1.50 4.00
J Boyd Devereaux 1.50 4.00
K Espen Knutsen 1.50 4.00
L Marc Savard 1.50 4.00

1997-98 Pinnacle Certified Summit Silver

Randomly inserted in packs at the rate of 1:29, this five card set features color action renditions of Paul Henderson by artist Daniel Parry printed on mirror Mylar. The set commemorates Paul Henderson's winning goal at the 1972 Canada-Russia Summit Series. Only 1,000 of each card were produced.

COMMON CARD (1-5) 4.00 10.00
NNO P.Henderson SIL AU/200 30.00 80.00
NNO P.Henderson BLK AU/700 20.00 50.00
NNO P.Henderson GLD AU/100 75.00 200.00

1996-97 Pinnacle Fantasy

This 20-card set was made available to attendees of the All-Star FanFest held in San Jose in January, 1997. The cards were distributed in three-card packs, and featured an action photo with a blue foil shark bite design along the top. A 21st card featuring Sharks netminder Kelly Hrudey was available through a redemption card which was randomly inserted in packs. The card had to be redeemed at a San Jose-area card shop. There were, in fact, two variations of the Hrudey card, the more difficult of which featured a refractor-like gloss. Collectors may also run across what appears to be a non-gloss parallel version of this set. The cards are smaller and are in playing card form, with black along the top and a uniform black back with a Pinnacle logo. These were used for a promotion at the show and were not licensed by the NHL or NHLPA. Therefore, these cards will not be listed in the annual.

FC1 Ray Bourque 1.00 2.50
FC2 Paul Coffey .40 1.00
FC3 Eric Lindros 1.50 4.00
FC4 Mario Lemieux 3.00 8.00
FC5 Wayne Gretzky 4.00 10.00
FC6 Mark Messier 1.00 2.50
FC7 Jaromir Jagr 1.50 4.00
FC8 Brendan Shanahan 1.50 4.00
FC9 John Vanbiesbrouck .60 1.50
FC10 Mike Richter .60 1.50
FC11 Chris Chelios .60 1.50
FC12 Nicklas Lidstrom .20 .50
FC13 Sergei Fedorov 1.50 4.00
FC14 Pavel Bure 1.50 4.00
FC15 Peter Forsberg 2.50 6.00
FC16 Brett Hull 1.00 2.50
FC17 Joe Sakic 1.50 4.00
FC18 Owen Nolan .40 1.00
FC19 Patrick Roy 3.00 8.00
FC20 Ed Belfour .60 1.50
NNO1 Kelly Hrudey 10.00 25.00
NNO2 Kelly Hrudey FOIL 15.00 40.00
NNO3 Kelly Hrudey Offer Card 4.00 10.00

1997-98 Pinnacle Inside

The 1997-98 Pinnacle Inside set was issued in one series totaling 190 cards and was distributed inside 24 different collectible player cans with ten cards to a can. The fronts feature color action player photos printed on 20 pt. card stock. The backs carry player information.

COMPLETE SET (190) 20.00 40.00
1 Brendan Shanahan .25 .60
2 Dominik Hasek .50 1.25
3 Wayne Gretzky 1.50 4.00
4 Eric Lindros .25 .60
5 Keith Tkachuk .25 .60
6 Jaromir Jagr .40 1.00
7 Martin Brodeur .60 1.50
8 Peter Forsberg .60 1.50
9 Chris Osgood .20 .50
10 Paul Kariya .25 .60
11 Pavel Bure .25 .60
12 Brett Hull .30 .75
13 Saku Koivu .25 .60
14 Zigmund Palffy .20 .50
15 Mike Modano .40 1.00
16 Ray Bourque .40 1.00
17 Jarome Iginla .30 .75
18 Chris Chelios .25 .60
19 John Vanbiesbrouck .20 .50
20 Brian Leetch .25 .60
21 Mats Sundin .25 .60
22 Ron Hextall .20 .50
23 Stephane Fiset .20 .50
24 Steve Yzerman 1.25 3.00
25 Curtis Joseph .25 .60
26 Daniel Alfredsson .20 .50
27 Owen Nolan .20 .50
28 Adam Oates .20 .50
29 Corey Hirsch .20 .50
30 Sean Burke .20 .50
31 Eric Fichaud .20 .50
32 Ken Wregget .20 .50
33 Dainius Zubrus .25 .60
34 Alexander Mogilny .20 .50
35 Bill Ranford .20 .50
36 Vincent Damphousse .07 .20
37 Patrick Roy 1.25 3.00
38 Teemu Selanne .25 .60
39 Pat LaFontaine .25 .60
40 Theo Fleury .07 .20
41 Jeff Hackett .20 .50
42 Sergei Fedorov .40 1.00
43 Jocelyn Thibault .20 .50
44 Nikolai Khabibulin .20 .50
45 Daren Puppa .20 .50
46 Felix Potvin .25 .60
47 Andy Moog .20 .50
48 Doug Weight .20 .50
49 Tommy Salo .20 .50
50 Mark Messier .25 .60
51 Grant Fuhr .20 .50
52 Ron Francis .20 .50
53 Tony Amonte .20 .50
54 Joe Sakic .50 1.25
55 Jason Arnott .07 .20
56 Jose Theodore .30 .75
57 Alexei Yashin .07 .20
58 John LeClair .25 .60
59 Jeremy Roenick .30 .75
60 Kirk McLean .20 .50
61 Arturs Irbe .20 .50
62 Jim Carey .20 .50
63 Jean-Sebastien Giguere .20 .50
64 Marc Denis .20 .50
65 Damian Rhodes .20 .50
66 Jim Campbell .07 .20
67 Patrick Lalime .20 .50
68 Garth Snow .20 .50
69 Marcel Cousineau .20 .50
70 Guy Hebert .20 .50
71 Rob Blake .20 .50
72 Tomas Vokoun RC .25 .60
73 Doug Gilmour .20 .50
74 Ed Belfour .25 .60
75 Parris Duffus RC .07 .20
76 Mike Fountain .07 .20
77 Steve Shields RC .25 .60
78 Geoff Sanderson .20 .50
79 Roman Turek .20 .50
80 Bryan Berard .20 .50
81 Mike Richter .25 .60
82 Ron Tugnutt .20 .50
83 Peter Bondra .20 .50
84 Mike Vernon .20 .50
85 Mike Grier .07 .20
86 Ed Jovanovski .20 .50
87 Trevor Kidd .20 .50
88 Eric Daze .20 .50
89 Wendel Clark .20 .50
90 Checklist (1-190) .07 .20
91 Nicklas Lidstrom .25 .60
92 Rod Brind'Amour .20 .50
93 Hnat Domenichelli .07 .20
94 Rem Murray .07 .20
95 Scott Niedermayer .07 .20
96 Martin Rucinsky .07 .20
97 Mike Gartner .20 .50
98 Kevin Hatcher .07 .20
99 Daymond Langkow .20 .50
100 Jamie Langenbrunner .07 .20
101 Ted Donato .07 .20
102 Steve Sullivan .07 .20
103 Martin Gelinas .07 .20
104 Adam Graves .07 .20
105 Donald Audette .07 .20
106 Andrew Cassels .07 .20
107 Alexei Zhamnov .07 .20
108 Kirk Muller .07 .20
109 Alexandre Daigle .07 .20
110 Chris Gratton .20 .50
111 Andrew Brunette .20 .50
112 Mark Recchi .20 .50
113 Jari Kurri .20 .50
114 Valeri Kamensky .20 .50
115 Joe Nieuwendyk .20 .50
116 Slava Kozlov .07 .20
117 Steve Kelly .07 .20
118 Dave Andreychuk .07 .20
119 Mikael Renberg .20 .50
120 Sergei Berezin .07 .20
121 Jeff Friesen .07 .20
122 Pierre Turgeon .20 .50
123 Vladimir Vorobiev RC .07 .20
124 Dimitri Khristich .07 .20
125 Jaroslav Svejkovsky .20 .50
126 Vladimir Konstantinov .20 .50
127 Jozef Stumpel .20 .50
128 Mike Peca .07 .20
129 Jonas Hoglund .07 .20
130 Travis Green .07 .20
131 Bill Guerin .20 .50
132 Oleg Tverdovsky .07 .20
133 Petr Nedved .20 .50
134 Dino Ciccarelli .07 .20
135 Brian Savage .07 .20
136 Steve Duchesne .07 .20
137 Sandis Ozolinsh .07 .20
138 Derian Hatcher .07 .20
139 Ray Sheppard .07 .20
140 Brian Bellows .07 .20
141 Paul Brousseau .07 .20
142 Tony Granato .07 .20
143 Vaclav Prospal RC .25 .60
144 Vitali Yachmenev .07 .20
145 John MacLean .07 .20
146 Igor Larionov .07 .20
147 Jason Allison .07 .20
148 Derek Plante .07 .20
149 Jeff O'Neill .07 .20
150 Trevor Linden .20 .50
151 Joe Juneau .20 .50
152 Brandon Convery .07 .20
153 Kevin Stevens .20 .50
154 Scott Stevens .20 .50
155 Niklas Sundstrom .07 .20
156 Claude Lemieux .07 .20
157 Pat Verbeek .07 .20
158 Mariusz Czerkawski .07 .20
159 Robert Svehla .07 .20
160 Paul Coffey .25 .60
161 Al MacInnis .20 .50
162 Roman Hamrlik .20 .50
163 Brian Holzinger .07 .20
164 Cory Stillman .07 .20
165 Scott Mellanby .07 .20
166 Todd Warriner .07 .20
167 Terry Ryan .07 .20
168 Luc Robitaille .20 .50
169 Ed Olczyk .07 .20
170 Adam Deadmarsh .07 .20
171 Anson Carter .20 .50
172 Mike Knuble RC .07 .20
173 Cliff Ronning .07 .20
174 Rick Tocchet .20 .50
175 Chris Pronger .20 .50
176 Matthew Barnaby .07 .20
177 Andrei Kovalenko .07 .20
178 Bryan Smolinski .07 .20
179 Janne Niinimaa .20 .50
180 Ray Ferraro .07 .20
181 Dave Gagner .07 .20
182 Rob Niedermayer .07 .20
183 Vadim Sharifijanov .07 .20
184 Ethan Moreau .07 .20
185 Bernie Nicholls .07 .20
186 Jean-Yves Leroux RC .07 .20
187 Jere Lehtinen .07 .20
188 Steve Rucchin .07 .20
189 Keith Primeau .07 .20
190 Red Wings Champs CL .20 .50
4 Eric Lindros PROMO
10 Paul Kariya PROMO
70 Guy Hebert PROMO

1997-98 Pinnacle Inside Coach's Collection

Randomly inserted in cans at the rate of 1:7, this 90-card set is a partial parallel version of the base set and highlights some of the NHL's top impact players. The cards are printed entirely on silver foil with bronze foil stamped accents.

*COACH COLL.: 3X TO 8X BASIC CARDS

1997-98 Pinnacle Inside Executive Collection

Randomly inserted in cans at the rate of 1:57, this 90-card set is a partial parallel version of the base set printed on full prismatic foil with foil stamped treatments and an external die-cut card design.

*EXEC.COLL.: 8X TO 20X BASIC CARDS

1997-98 Pinnacle Inside Stand Up Guys

Inserted one per mask can, this 20-card set features color action photos of top goalies on one side with close-up photos of their masks on the flipsides.

COMPLETE SET (20) 15.00 30.00
*PROMOS: .4X TO 1X BASIC INSERTS
1A/B M.Vernon/T.Barasso .60 1.50
1C/D M.Vernon/T.Barasso .60 1.50
2A/B J.Vanbiesbrck./M.Brodeur 2.00 5.00
2C/D J.Vanbiesbrck./M.Brodeur 2.00 5.00
3A/B J.Thibault/J.Carey .60 1.50
3C/D J.Thibault/J.Carey .60 1.50
4A/B G.Snow/M.Cousineau .60 1.50
4C/D G.Snow/M.Cousineau .60 1.50
5A/B P.Roy/E.Fichaud 4.00 10.00
5C/D P.Roy/E.Fichaud 4.00 10.00
6A/B P.Lalime/G.Fuhr .60 1.50
6C/D P.Lalime/G.Fuhr .60 1.50
7A/B O.Kolzig/J.Hackett .60 1.50
7C/D O.Kolzig/J.Hackett .60 1.50
8A/B T.Kidd/G.Hebert .60 1.50
8C/D T.Kidd/G.Hebert .60 1.50
9A/B N.Khabibulin/C.Hirsch .60 1.50
9C/D N.Khabibulin/C.Hirsch .60 1.50
10A/B C.Joseph/K.Hrudey .60 1.50
10C/D C.Joseph/K.Hrudey .60 1.50

1997-98 Pinnacle Inside Stoppers

Randomly inserted in cans at the rate of 1:7, this 24-card set features color action photos of the NHL's top goal tenders printed on circular die-cut card stock in 3-D.

COMPLETE SET (24) 30.00 60.00
1 Patrick Roy 8.00 20.00
2 John Vanbiesbrouck 1.00 2.50
3 Dominik Hasek 3.00 8.00
4 Martin Brodeur 4.00 10.00
5 Mike Richter 1.50 4.00
6 Guy Hebert 1.00 2.50
7 Jim Carey 1.00 2.50
8 Jeff Hackett 1.00 2.50
9 Roman Turek 1.00 2.50
10 Kevin Hodson 1.00 2.50
11 Mike Vernon 1.00 2.50
12 Curtis Joseph 1.50 4.00
13 Jean-Sebastien Giguere 1.00 2.50
14 Jose Theodore 2.00 5.00
15 Jocelyn Thibault 1.00 2.50
16 Nikolai Khabibulin 1.00 2.50
17 Garth Snow 1.00 2.50
18 Ron Hextall 1.00 2.50
19 Steve Shields 1.00 2.50
20 Grant Fuhr 1.00 2.50
21 Felix Potvin 1.50 4.00
22 Marcel Cousineau 1.00 2.50
23 Bill Ranford 1.00 2.50
24 Ed Belfour 1.50 4.00

1997-98 Pinnacle Inside Track

Randomly inserted in cans at the rate of 1:19, this 30-card set features color action photos of some of the game's elite stars with information as to how they became the best players in the NHL.

COMPLETE SET (30) 75.00 200.00
1 Wayne Gretzky 10.00 25.00
2 Patrick Roy 10.00 25.00
3 Eric Lindros 3.00 8.00
4 Paul Kariya 3.00 8.00
5 Peter Forsberg 4.00 10.00
6 Martin Brodeur 6.00 15.00
7 John Vanbiesbrouck 2.00 5.00
8 Joe Sakic 5.00 12.00
9 Steve Yzerman 10.00 25.00
10 Jaromir Jagr 4.00 10.00
11 Teemu Selanne 3.00 8.00
12 Pavel Bure 3.00 8.00
13 Sergei Fedorov 3.00 8.00
14 Brendan Shanahan 3.00 8.00
15 Dominik Hasek 5.00 12.00
16 Saku Koivu 2.00 5.00
17 Jocelyn Thibault 1.00 2.50
18 Mark Messier 2.00 5.00
19 Brett Hull 4.00 10.00
20 Felix Potvin 4.00 10.00
21 Curtis Joseph 3.00 8.00
22 Zigmund Palffy 2.00 5.00
23 Mats Sundin 3.00 8.00
24 Keith Tkachuk 3.00 8.00
25 John LeClair 3.00 8.00
26 Mike Richter 3.00 8.00
27 Alexander Mogilny 2.00 5.00
28 Jarome Iginla 4.00 10.00
29 Mike Grier 1.00 2.50
30 Dainius Zubrus 1.00 2.50

1997-98 Pinnacle Inside Cans

This 24-can set features eight of the most distinctive goalie masks in the game and photos of 16 of the hottest superstars reproduced on the can labels and painted directly on the metal.

COMPLETE SET (24) 8.00 20.00
*GOLD CANS: 2.5X TO 6X BASIC CAN
1 Brendan Shanahan .15 .40
2 Jaromir Jagr .30 .75
3 Saku Koivu .15 .40
4 Mats Sundin .15 .40
5 Mike Vernon .20 .50
6 John LeClair .15 .40
7 Keith Tkachuk .15 .40
8 Joe Sakic .30 .75
9 Steve Yzerman .60 1.50
10 Eric Lindros .15 .40
11 Guy Hebert .20 .50
12 Patrick Roy .75 2.00
13 Pavel Bure .15 .40
14 Jocelyn Thibault .20 .50
15 Paul Kariya .40 1.00
16 Peter Forsberg .40 1.00
17 Martin Brodeur .40 1.00
18 Wayne Gretzky 1.00 2.50
19 Teemu Selanne .30 .75
20 John Vanbiesbrouck .20 .50
21 Mark Messier .15 .40
22 Mike Richter .15 .40
23 Brett Hull .20 .50
24 Curtis Joseph .15 .40

1997-98 Pinnacle Inside Promos

COMPLETE SET
1 Brendan Shanahan PROMO .40 1.00
7 Martin Brodeur/250 .75 2.00
8 Peter Forsberg PROMO .75 2.00
10 Paul Kariya/250 .75 2.00
70 Guy Hebert PROMO .40 1.00
84 Mike Vernon PROMO .40 1.00

1997 Pinnacle Mario's Moments

The Pinnacle Mario Lemieux "Moments" set was issued in one series totaling 18 cards. The set was a Pittsburgh area regional set and was sold over a period of six weeks in three-card packs at Giant Eagle grocery stores. A folder to hold the set, which pictured Lemieux, was available for 99 cents during the first week of the promotion. A gold parallel version of the set also can be found. These cards, issued at a rate of one per ten packs, featured gold foil lettering of Lemieux's name. Authentic autographed cards also were randomly inserted into packs. Reports from the manufacturer suggest approximately 700 of these were available.

COMPLETE SET (18) 10.00 25.00
COMMON CARD (1-18) .60 1.50
*GOLD: 2X to 5X BASIC CARDS
NNO Mario Lemieux AUTO 60.00 120.00

1996-97 Pinnacle Mint

The 1996-97 Pinnacle Mint set was issued in one series totaling 30 cards and was distributed in packs of three cards and two coins for a suggested retail price of $3.99. The challenge was to fit the coins with the die-cut cards that pictured the same player on the minted coin. The fronts feature color action player images on a sepia player portrait background with a cut-out area for the matching coin. Eric Lindros was featured on two promo cards, issued to dealers along with their ordering forms. The cards are identical to the regular die-cut and bronze cards except for the word "promo" written on the right hand side of the card back.

COMP.DIE CUT SET (30) 10.00 25.00
1 Mario Lemieux 1.00 2.50
2 Dominik Hasek .50 1.25
3 Eric Lindros .50 1.25
4 Jaromir Jagr .75 2.00
5 Paul Kariya .40 1.00
6 Peter Forsberg .50 1.25
7 Pavel Bure .40 1.00
8 Sergei Fedorov .50 1.25
9 Saku Koivu .30 .75
10 Daniel Alfredsson .30 .75
11 Joe Sakic .50 1.25
12 Steve Yzerman .75 2.00
13 Teemu Selanne .60 1.50
14 Brett Hull 1.50 4.00
15 Jeremy Roenick .50 1.25
16 Mark Messier .50 1.25
17 Mats Sundin .30 .75
18 Brendan Shanahan .40 1.00
19 Keith Tkachuk .30 .75
20 Paul Coffey .30 .75
21 Patrick Roy .75 2.00
22 Chris Chelios .30 .75
23 Martin Brodeur .60 1.50
24 Felix Potvin .30 .75
25 Chris Osgood .30 .75
26 John Vanbiesbrouck .30 .75
27 Jocelyn Thibault .30 .75
28 Jim Carey .30 .75
29 Jarome Iginla .40 1.00
30 Jim Campbell .20 .50
P3A Eric Lindros Bronze Promo 1.50 4.00
P3B Eric Lindros Die-Cut Promo .50 1.25

1996-97 Pinnacle Mint Bronze

This 30-card version of the 1996-97 Pinnacle Mint set features color action player images on a sepia player portrait background with a bronze foil stamp instead of the die-cut area.

*BRONZE: 1X TO 2X BASIC CARDS
ONE PARALLEL PER PACK

1996-97 Pinnacle Mint Gold

Randomly inserted in packs at a rate of 1:48 (and 1:72 magazine packs), this 30-card set parallels the regular issue version and is distinguished by the use of full Gold-foil Dufex print technologies.

*GOLD: 8X TO 20X BASIC CARDS

1996-97 Pinnacle Mint Silver

Randomly inserted in packs at a rate of 1:15 (and 1:23 magazine packs), this 30-card set is a parallel to the 1996-97 Pinnacle Mint set and features color action player images on a sepia player portrait background with a silver foil stamp instead of the die-cut area.

*SILVER: 4X TO 10X BASIC CARDS

1996-97 Pinnacle Mint Coins Brass

This 30-coin set features embossed brass coins designed to be inserted into a die-cut card of the player who is pictured on the coin. Additional quantities of the Eric Lindros coin were mailed out to dealers with their order forms.

COMP.BRASS SET (30) 12.00 30.00
*NICKEL: 2X TO 5X BRASS
*GOLD PLATED: 5X TO 12X BRASS
1 Mario Lemieux 1.50 4.00
2 Dominik Hasek .60 1.50
3 Eric Lindros .75 2.00
4 Jaromir Jagr 1.00 2.50
5 Paul Kariya 1.25 3.00
6 Peter Forsberg .75 2.00
7 Pavel Bure .75 2.00
8 Sergei Fedorov .60 1.50
9 Saku Koivu .30 .75
10 Daniel Alfredsson .25 .60
11 Joe Sakic .60 1.50
12 Steve Yzerman 1.00 2.50
13 Teemu Selanne .60 1.50
14 Brett Hull .40 1.00
15 Jeremy Roenick .30 .75
16 Mark Messier .40 1.00
17 Mats Sundin .30 .75
18 Brendan Shanahan .50 1.25
19 Keith Tkachuk .30 .75
20 Paul Coffey .30 .75
21 Patrick Roy 1.50 4.00
22 Chris Chelios .30 .75
23 Martin Brodeur .75 2.00
24 Felix Potvin .30 .75
25 Chris Osgood .30 .75
26 John Vanbiesbrouck .30 .75
27 Jocelyn Thibault .25 .60
28 Jim Carey .25 .60
29 Jarome Iginla .25 .60
30 Jim Campbell .25 .60

1997-98 Pinnacle Mint

The 1997-98 Pinnacle Mint set was issued in one series totaling 30 cards and was distributed in packs of three cards and two coins with a suggested retail price of $3.99. The challenge was to fit the coins with the die-cut cards that pictured the same player on the minted coin. The fronts feature color player photos with a cut-out area for the matching coin.

1 Eric Lindros .15 .40
2 Paul Kariya .15 .40
3 Peter Forsberg .40 1.00
4 John Vanbiesbrouck .10 .30
5 Steve Yzerman .75 2.00
6 Brendan Shanahan .15 .40
7 Teemu Selanne .15 .40
8 Dominik Hasek .30 .75
9 Jarome Iginla .20 .50
10 Mats Sundin .15 .40
11 Patrick Roy .75 2.00
12 Joe Sakic .30 .75
13 Mark Messier .15 .40
14 Sergei Fedorov .25 .60
15 Saku Koivu .15 .40
16 Martin Brodeur .40 1.00
17 Pavel Bure .15 .40
18 Wayne Gretzky 1.00 2.50
19 Brian Leetch .10 .30
20 John LeClair .15 .40
21 Keith Tkachuk .15 .40
22 Jaromir Jagr .25 .60
23 Brett Hull .20 .50
24 Curtis Joseph .15 .40
25 Jaroslav Svejkovsky .07 .20
26 Sergei Samsonov .10 .30
27 Alexei Morozov .07 .20
28 Alyn McCauley .07 .20
29 Joe Thornton .25 .60
30 Vaclav Prospal RC .10 .30
P3 Peter Forsberg PROMO 3.00 8.00

1997-98 Pinnacle Mint Bronze

This 30-card set is parallel to the base set and is similar in design. The difference is found in the bronze foil stamp instead of the die-cut area. They were inserted at 1:1 hobby and 2:1 retail.
*BRONZE: .8X TO 2X BASIC CARDS

1997-98 Pinnacle Mint Gold Team

Randomly inserted in packs, this 30-card set is parallel version of the Pinnacle Mint base set printed on full gold foil card stock. They were inserted at 1:31 hobby and 1:71 retail.
*GOLD TEAM: 10X TO 25X BASIC CARDS

1997-98 Pinnacle Mint Silver Team

Randomly inserted in packs, this 30-card set is parallel version of the Pinnacle Mint base set printed on full silver foil card stock. They were inserted at 1:15 hobby and 1:23 retail.
*SILVER TEAM: 5X TO 12X BASIC CARDS

1997-98 Pinnacle Mint Coins Brass

Randomly inserted in packs at overall rates of 2:1 hobby and 1:1 retail, this 30-coin set features embossed brass coins designed to be inserted into a die-cut card of the player who is pictured on the coin. A number of parallels were also created and inserted randomly.

COMP.BRASS SET (30) 30.00 60.00
*BRASS PROOF/500: 6X TO 15X BRASS
*NICKEL SILVER: 2X TO 5X BRASS
NICKEL STATED ODDS 1:41 HOB/RET
*NICKEL PROOF: 10X TO 25X BRASS
NICKEL PROOF PRINT RUN 250
*GOLD PLATED: 10X TO 25X BRASS
GOLD PLATED ODDS 1:199 HOB/RET
*GOLD PLT PROOF/100: 25X TO 60X BRASS
GOLD PLATED PROOF PRINT RUN 100
SOLID SILVER TOO SCARCE TO PRICE
1 Eric Lindros .75 2.00
2 Paul Kariya 1.25 3.00
3 Peter Forsberg .75 2.00
4 John Vanbiesbrouck .30 .75
5 Steve Yzerman 1.00 2.50
6 Brendan Shanahan .50 1.25
7 Teemu Selanne .60 1.50
8 Dominik Hasek .60 1.50
9 Jarome Iginla .25 .60
10 Mats Sundin .30 .75
11 Patrick Roy 1.50 4.00
12 Joe Sakic .60 1.50
13 Mark Messier .40 1.00
14 Sergei Fedorov .60 1.50
15 Saku Koivu .30 .75
16 Martin Brodeur .75 2.00
17 Pavel Bure .75 2.00
18 Wayne Gretzky 2.50 5.00
19 Brian Leetch .30 .75
20 John LeClair .50 1.25
21 Keith Tkachuk .30 .75
22 Jaromir Jagr 1.00 2.50
23 Brett Hull .40 1.00
24 Curtis Joseph .40 1.00
25 Jaroslav Svejkovsky .25 .60
26 Sergei Samsonov .30 .75
27 Alexei Morozov .25 .60
28 Alyn McCauley .25 .60
29 Joe Thornton .30 .75
30 Vaclav Prospal .25 .60

1997-98 Pinnacle Mint Minternational

Randomly inserted in hobby packs at the rate of 1:31 and retail packs at the rate of 1:47, this six-card set commemorates the Winter Olympic games with color photos of one player from each nation printed on full silver foil card stock.

COMPLETE SET (6) 15.00 30.00
1 Eric Lindros 6.00 15.00
2 Peter Forsberg 4.00 10.00
3 Brett Hull 2.00 5.00
4 Teemu Selanne 2.50 6.00
5 Dominik Hasek 3.00 8.00
6 Pavel Bure 2.50 6.00

1997-98 Pinnacle Mint Minternational Coins

Randomly inserted in hobby packs only at the rate of 1:31, this six-coin set is parallel to the 1997-98 Pinnacle Mint Minternational set and features the six players on double-sized embossed coins.

COMPLETE SET (6) 30.00 60.00
1 Eric Lindros 8.00 20.00
2 Peter Forsberg 8.00 20.00
3 Brett Hull 3.00 8.00
4 Teemu Selanne 5.00 12.00
5 Dominik Hasek 5.00 12.00
6 Pavel Bure 6.00 12.00

2011 Pinnacle NHL Draft

This sealed 6 card set was issued at the 2011 NHL Draft as part of a wrapper redemption program.

COMPLETE SET (6) 8.00 20.00
1 Alex Ovechkin 1.00 2.50
2 Steven Stamkos 1.00 2.50
3 Sidney Crosby 3.00
4 Tyler Seguin 1.25 3.00
5 Mario Lemieux .75 2.00
6 Mark Messier .75 2.00

2011 Pinnacle NHL Draft Minnesota

This sealed 6 card set was issued at the 2011 NHL Draft as part of a wrapper redemption program.

COMPLETE SET (6) 6.00 12.00
1 Martin Havlat .75 2.00
2 Mikko Koivu .75 2.00
3 Niklas Backstrom 1.00 2.50
4 Cal Clutterbuck 1.00 2.50
5 Mike Modano 1.25 3.00
6 Dino Ciccarelli 1.00 2.50

2012 Pinnacle NHL Draft Pittsburgh

COMPLETE SET (7) 6.00 12.00
1 Sidney Crosby 2.00 5.00
2 Evgeni Malkin 1.00 2.50
3 Marc-Andre Fleury .60 1.50
4 James Neal .50 1.25
5 Kris Letang .50 1.25
6 Jordan Staal .50 1.25
7 Simon Despres .50 1.25
NNO Checklist .30 .75

1996 Pinnacle Bobby Orr Autograph

This extremely rare card was produced as a giveaway at a Dallas golf tournament run by Pinnacle. It is believed that fewer than 25 copies of this card exist. The card is an all gold foil laser-etched design using the basic card design from 1996-97 Pinnacle.

NNO Bobby Orr 100.00 200.00

1997-98 Pinnacle Power Pack Blow-Ups

Randomly inserted in packs, this 24-card set features color action photos of some of the hottest players in the NHL printed on 3" X 5" cards.

1 Eric Lindros 1.00 2.50
2 Paul Kariya 1.25 3.00
3 Joe Thornton .40 1.00
4 Dominik Hasek .60 1.50
5 Patrick Roy 1.50 4.00
6 Keith Tkachuk .30 .75
7 Martin Brodeur .75 2.00
8 Brett Hull .40 1.00
9 Mark Messier .40 1.00
10 Saku Koivu .30 .75
11 Jaromir Jagr 1.00 2.50
12 Joe Sakic .60 1.50
13 John Vanbiesbrouck .30 .75
14 Pavel Bure .75 2.00
15 Jarome Iginla .40 1.00
16 Mats Sundin .30 .75
17 Wayne Gretzky 2.00 5.00
18 Steve Yzerman 1.00 2.50
19 Peter Forsberg .75 2.00
20 Brendan Shanahan .60 1.50
21 Sergei Fedorov .60 1.50
22 Curtis Joseph .40 1.00
23 John LeClair .40 1.00
24 Teemu Selanne .60 1.50
P2 Paul Kariya PROMO 1.25 3.00
P13 John Vanbiesbrouck PROMO .60 1.50

1998 Pinnacle Team Pinnacle Collector's Club Promos

This four-card set originally to have been issued to members of the Pinnacle Collector's Club. Ultimately the cards were released after the company's bankruptcy. Each card reads "Team Pinnacle" at the bottom of the cardfront with the player's name above the image on the front.

COMPLETE SET (4) 15.00 30.00
4 Eric Lindros 2.00 5.00

1997-98 Pinnacle Tins

This set features photos of some of the most distinctive goalie masks in the game printed on collectible tins. Each tin contains 30 cards from the 1997-98 Pinnacle Hockey base set as well as insert sets. The tins are unnumbered and checklisted below in alphabetical order.

COMPLETE SET (10) 6.00 15.00
1 Martin Brodeur 1.25 3.00
2 Grant Fuhr .40 1.00
3 Jeff Hackett .40 1.00
4 Guy Hebert .40 1.00
5 Curtis Joseph .40 1.00
6 Nikolai Khabibulin .40 1.00
7 Mike Richter .50 1.25
8 Patrick Roy 2.00 5.00
9 Garth Snow .40 1.00
10 John Vanbiesbrouck .75 2.00

1997-98 Pinnacle Totally Certified Platinum Blue

Inserted one in every pack, this 130-card set is parallel to the Totally Certified Platinum Gold and Platinum Red sets. The difference is found in the platinum blue micro-etched holographic foil and foil stamping. Only 2599 goalie cards and 3099 skater cards were printed.
*PLAT.BLUE: .8X TO 2X PLAT.RED

1997-98 Pinnacle Totally Certified Platinum Gold

Randomly inserted in packs at the rate of 1:79, this 130-card set is parallel to the Totally Certified Platinum Blue and Platinum Red sets. The difference is found in the platinum gold micro-etched holographic foil and foil stamping. Only 59 serially numbered goalie cards and 69 serially numbered skater cards were printed. A mirror gold parallel to the gold set was also created and randomly inserted.
*PLAT.GOLD: 6X TO 15X PLAT.RED

1997-98 Pinnacle Totally Certified Platinum Red

Inserted in packs at the rate of two to a pack, this 130-card set was distributed in three card packs with a suggested retail price of $7.99 and featured color player photos printed on 24 pt. card stock with micro-etched holographic foil and platinum red foil stamping. Only 4299 goalie cards and 6199 skater cards were printed and serially numbered.

COMPLETE SET (130) 100.00 250.00
1 Dominik Hasek 5.00 10.00
2 Patrick Roy 12.50 25.00
3 Martin Brodeur 6.00 12.00
4 Chris Osgood 1.50 4.00
5 Andy Moog 1.50 4.00
6 John Vanbiesbrouck 1.50 4.00
7 Steve Shields RC 2.00 5.00
8 Mike Vernon 1.50 4.00
9 Ed Belfour 2.00 5.00
10 Grant Fuhr 1.50 4.00
11 Felix Potvin 2.00 5.00
12 Bill Ranford 1.50 4.00
13 Mike Richter 2.00 5.00
14 Stephane Fiset 1.25 3.00
15 Jim Carey 1.50 4.00
16 Nikolai Khabibulin 1.50 4.00
17 Ken Wregget 1.25 3.00
18 Curtis Joseph 2.00 5.00
19 Guy Hebert 1.50 4.00
20 Damian Rhodes 1.50 4.00
21 Trevor Kidd 1.50 4.00
22 Daren Puppa 1.25 3.00
23 Patrick Lalime 1.50 4.00
24 Tommy Salo 1.50 4.00
25 Sean Burke 1.25 3.00
26 Jocelyn Thibault 1.50 4.00
27 Kirk McLean 1.50 4.00
28 Garth Snow 1.50 4.00
29 Ron Tugnutt 1.50 4.00
30 Jeff Hackett 1.25 3.00
31 Eric Lindros 1.50 4.00
32 Peter Forsberg 5.00 10.00
33 Mike Modano 3.00 6.00
34 Paul Kariya 1.50 4.00
35 Jaromir Jagr 2.50 6.00
36 Brian Leetch 1.50 4.00
37 Keith Tkachuk 1.50 4.00
38 Steve Yzerman 10.00 20.00
39 Teemu Selanne 1.50 4.00
40 Bryan Berard 1.25 3.00
41 Ray Bourque 2.50 5.00
42 Theo Fleury .75 2.00
43 Mark Messier 2.00 5.00
44 Saku Koivu 1.50 4.00
45 Pavel Bure 2.00 5.00
46 Peter Bondra 1.25 3.00
47 Dave Gagner .75 2.00
48 Ed Jovanovski 1.25 3.00
49 Adam Oates 1.25 3.00
50 Joe Sakic 4.00 8.00
51 Doug Gilmour 1.25 3.00
52 Jim Campbell .75 2.00
53 Mats Sundin 1.50 4.00
54 Derian Hatcher .75 2.00
55 Jarome Iginla 2.00 5.00
56 Sergei Fedorov 2.50 6.00
57 Keith Primeau .75 2.00
58 Mark Recchi 1.25 3.00
59 Owen Nolan 1.25 3.00
60 Alexander Mogilny 1.25 3.00
61 Brendan Shanahan 2.00 5.00
62 Pierre Turgeon 1.25 3.00
63 Joe Juneau 1.25 3.00
64 Steve Rucchin .75 2.00
65 Jeremy Roenick 2.00 5.00
66 Doug Weight 1.25 3.00
67 Valeri Kamensky 1.25 3.00
68 Tony Amonte 1.25 3.00
69 Dave Andreychuk .75 2.00
70 Brett Hull 2.50 5.00
71 Wendel Clark 1.25 3.00
72 Vincent Damphousse .75 2.00
73 Mike Grier .75 2.00
74 Chris Chelios 1.50 4.00
75 Nicklas Lidstrom 1.50 4.00
76 Joe Nieuwendyk 1.25 3.00
77 Rob Blake 1.25 3.00
78 Alexei Yashin .75 2.00
79 Ryan Smyth .75 2.00
80 Pat Lafontaine 1.50 4.00
81 Jeff Friesen .75 2.00
82 Ray Ferraro .75 2.00
83 Steve Sullivan .75 2.00
84 Chris Gratton 1.25 3.00
85 Mike Gartner 1.25 3.00
86 Kevin Hatcher .75 2.00
87 Ted Donato .75 2.00
88 German Titov .75 2.00
89 Sandis Ozolinsh .75 2.00
90 Ray Sheppard .75 2.00
91 John MacLean .75 2.00
92 Luc Robitaille 1.25 3.00
93 Rod Brind'Amour 1.25 3.00
94 Zigmund Palffy 1.25 3.00
95 Petr Nedved 1.25 3.00
96 Adam Graves .75 2.00
97 Jozef Stumpel 1.25 3.00
98 Alexandre Daigle .75 2.00
99 Mike Peca .75 2.00
100 Wayne Gretzky 12.50 25.00
101 Alexei Zhamnov .75 2.00
102 Paul Coffey 1.50 4.00
103 Oleg Tverdovsky .75 2.00
104 Trevor Linden 1.25 3.00
105 Dino Ciccarelli .75 2.00
106 Andrei Kovalenko .75 2.00
107 Scott Mellanby .75 2.00
108 Bryan Smolinski .75 2.00
109 Bernie Nicholls .75 2.00
110 Derek Plante .75 2.00
111 Pat Verbeek .75 2.00
112 Adam Deadmarsh .75 2.00
113 Martin Gelinas .75 2.00
114 Daniel Alfredsson 1.25 3.00
115 Scott Stevens .75 2.00
116 Dainius Zubrus 2.50 6.00
117 Kirk Muller .75 2.00
118 Brian Holzinger .75 2.00
119 John LeClair 2.00 5.00
120 Al MacInnis 1.25 3.00
121 Ron Francis 1.25 3.00
122 Eric Daze 1.25 3.00
123 Travis Green .75 2.00
124 Jason Arnott .75 2.00
125 Geoff Sanderson 1.25 3.00
126 Dimitri Khristich .75 2.00
127 Sergei Berezin .75 2.00
128 Jeff O'Neill .75 2.00
129 Claude Lemieux .75 2.00
130 Andrew Cassels .75 2.00
82P Ray Ferraro PROMO .40 1.00
106P Andrei Kovalenko PROMO .40 1.00

1997-98 Pinnacle Totally Certified Platinum Gold Mirror

Randomly inserted in packs, this 130-card set is a parallel version of the 1997-98 Pinnacle Totally Certified base set and is printed on super-premium 24-point, micro-etched holographic Mylar foil card stock with gold foil stamping.
*MIRROR GOLD/25: 12X TO 30X PLAT.RED

1997-98 Pinnacle Hockey Night in Canada

These cards feature the top on-air personalities from the only hockey broadcast that matters. The cards were produced by Pinnacle, and were given away at autograph signings and other personal appearances.

COMPLETE SET (13) 30.00 75.00
1 Steve Armitage 1.25 3.00
2 Don Cherry 20.00 50.00
3 Bob Cole 2.00 5.00
4 Chris Cuthbert 1.25 3.00
5 John Garrett 2.00 5.00
6 Dick 1rvin, Jr. 4.00 10.00
7 Ron Maclean 4.00 10.00
8 Greg Millen 1.25 3.00
9 Harry Neale 2.00 5.00
10 Scott Oake 1.25 3.00
11 Scott Russell 1.25 3.00
12 John Shannon .75 2.00
13 Don Whittman 1.25 3.00

1995-96 Playoff One on One

The 1995-96 Playoff One on One Hockey Challenge is a set of 330 cards which can be used to play a fantasy game. The cards could be found in four different card types: Common (1-110), Uncommon (111-220), Rare, Ultra Rare (found in Booster Packs) and Ultra Rare (found in Starter Packs). The scarcer the card, the higher the point values that can be used during the game. Fifty-card starter decks, including three dice and a rule book, were available for $9.95 ea. Game players could add to the power of their decks by purchasing booster packs for $2.50 ea. Ultra rare cards are designated with suffixes below. URS cards were found in starter packs, while URB were hidden in booster packs.

1 Guy Hebert .12 .30
2 Paul Kariya .20 .50
3 Mike Sillinger .10 .25
4 Oleg Tverdovsky .15 .40
5 Ray Bourque .25 .60
6 Alexei Kasatonov .10 .25
7 Blaine Lacher .12 .30
8 Cam Neely .15 .40
9 Adam Oates .15 .40
10 Kevin Stevens .12 .30
11 Donald Audette .12 .30
12 Dominik Hasek .20 .50
13 Pat LaFontaine .15 .40
14 Alexei Zhitnik .10 .25
15 Steve Chiasson .10 .25
16 Theo Fleury .20 .50
17 Phil Housley .12 .30
18 Joe Nieuwendyk .15 .40
19 Gary Roberts .10 .25
20 German Titov .12 .30
21 Ed Belfour .12 .30
22 Chris Chelios .15 .40
23 Bernie Nicholls .10 .25
24 Jeremy Roenick .20 .50
25 Peter Forsberg .40 1.00
26 Sylvain Lefebvre .10 .25
27 Owen Nolan .15 .40
28 Joe Sakic .25 .60
29 Jocelyn Thibault .12 .30
30 Dave Gagner .10 .25
31 Mike Modano .25 .60
32 Andy Moog .15 .40
33 Paul Coffey .15 .40
34 Sergei Fedorov .25 .60
35 Keith Primeau .10 .25
36 Ray Sheppard .12 .30
37 Jason Arnott .12 .30
38 David Oliver .10 .25
39 Mike Stapleton .10 .25
40 Jesse Belanger .10 .25
41 Paul Laus .10 .25
42 Rob Niedermayer .12 .30
43 Brian Skrudland .10 .25
44 John Vanbiesbrouck .12 .30
45 Sean Burke .10 .25
46 Andrew Cassels .10 .25
47 Brendan Shanahan .20 .50
48 Rob Blake .12 .30
49 Tony Granato .10 .25
50 Wayne Gretzky .75 2.00
51 Marty McSorley .10 .25
52 Jamie Storr .12 .30
53 Vincent Damphousse .12 .30
54 Mark Recchi .20 .50
55 Patrick Roy .40 1.00
56 Pierre Turgeon .15 .40
57 Martin Brodeur .40 1.00
58 Bill Guerin .12 .30
59 Scott Niedermayer .15 .40
60 Stephane Richer .12 .30
61 Scott Stevens .15 .40
62 Patrick Flatley .10 .25
63 Brett Lindros .10 .25
64 Mathieu Schneider .10 .25
65 Kirk Muller .12 .30
66 Adam Graves .12 .30
67 Alexei Kovalev .10 .25
68 Brian Leetch .15 .40
69 Mike Richter .15 .40
70 Pat Verbeek .12 .30
71 Luc Robitaille .15 .40
72 Radek Bonk .10 .25
73 Alexandre Daigle .10 .25
74 Alexei Yashin .12 .30
75 Eric Desjardins .12 .30
76 Eric Lindros .25 .60
77 Ron Francis .20 .50
78 Jaromir Jagr .40 1.00
79 Mario Lemieux .50 1.25
80 Ken Wregget .12 .30
81 Francois Leroux .10 .25
82 Pat Falloon .10 .25
83 Jeff Friesen .10 .25
84 Arturs Irbe .12 .30
85 Igor Larionov .10 .25
86 Shayne Corson .10 .25
87 Geoff Courtnall .10 .25
88 Steve Duchesne .10 .25
89 Brett Hull .20 .50
90 Al MacInnis .15 .40
91 Brian Bellows .12 .30
92 Chris Gratton .10 .25
93 Dave Andreychuk .15 .40
94 Tie Domi .12 .30
95 Mike Gartner .15 .40
96 Doug Gilmour .20 .50
97 Larry Murphy .15 .40
98 Felix Potvin .15 .40
99 Mats Sundin .15 .40
100 Pavel Bure .20 .50
101 Kirk McLean .12 .30
102 Alexander Mogilny .12 .30
103 Christian Ruuttu .12 .30
104 Jim Carey .12 .30
105 Joe Juneau .12 .30
106 Jason Allison .12 .30
107 Teppo Numminen .10 .25
108 Teemu Selanne .30 .75
109 Keith Tkachuk .15 .40
110 Alexei Zhamnov .15 .40
111 Patrik Carnback .10 .25
112 Bobby Dollas .10 .25
113 Guy Hebert .12 .30
114 Paul Kariya .20 .50
115 Shaun Van Allen .10 .25
116 Ray Bourque .25 .60
117 Mariusz Czerkawski .10 .25
118 Todd Elik .10 .25
119 Blaine Lacher .12 .30
120 Cam Neely .15 .40
121 Adam Oates .15 .40
122 Dave Reid .10 .25
123 Kevin Stevens .12 .30
124 Garry Galley .10 .25
125 Dominik Hasek .20 .50
126 Brian Holzinger .30 .75
127 Pat LaFontaine .15 .40
128 Mike Peca .12 .30
129 Phil Housley .12 .30
130 Paul Kruse .10 .25
131 Ronnie Stern .10 .25
132 Zarley Zalapski .10 .25
133 Patrick Poulin .10 .25
134 Bob Probert .12 .30
135 Jeremy Roenick .20 .50
136 Adam Deadmarsh .10 .25
137 Peter Forsberg .40 1.00
138 Andrei Kovalenko .10 .25
139 Joe Sakic .25 .60
140 Derian Hatcher .12 .30
141 Grant Ledyard .10 .25
142 Mike Modano .25 .60
143 Paul Coffey .15 .40
144 Sergei Fedorov .25 .60
145 Vladimir Konstantinov .12 .30
146 Nicklas Lidstrom .15 .40
147 Steve Yzerman .20 .50
148 Igor Kravchuk .10 .25
149 Kirk Maltby .12 .30
150 Boris Mironov .10 .25
151 Bill Ranford .12 .30
152 Stu Barnes .10 .25
153 Jesse Belanger .10 .25
154 Scott Mellanby .12 .30
155 Adam Burt .10 .25
156 Steven Rice .10 .25
157 Brendan Shanahan .20 .50
158 Glen Wesley .10 .25
159 Wayne Gretzky .50 1.25
160 Darryl Sydor .12 .30
161 Rick Tocchet .12 .30
162 Benoit Brunet .10 .25
163 J.J. Daigneault .10 .25
164 Saku Koivu .15 .40
165 Lyle Odelein .10 .25
166 Patrick Roy .40 1.00
167 Scott Stevens .15 .40
168 Valeri Zelepukin .10 .25
169 Steve Thomas .12 .30
170 Dennis Vaske .10 .25
171 Brett Lindros .10 .25
172 Zigmund Palffy .15 .40
173 Ray Ferraro .10 .25
174 Brian Leetch .15 .40
175 Mark Messier .25 .60
176 Ulf Samuelsson .10 .25
177 Don Beaupre .12 .30
178 Alexandre Daigle .10 .25
179 Steve Larouche .10 .25
180 Scott Levins .10 .25
181 Ron Hextall .15 .40
182 Eric Lindros .25 .60
183 Mikael Renberg .12 .30
184 Kjell Samuelsson .10 .25
185 Jaromir Jagr .40 1.00
186 Mario Lemieux .50 1.25
187 Sergei Zubov .12 .30
188 Bryan Smolinski .10 .25
189 Dmitri Mironov .10 .25
190 Ulf Dahlen .10 .25
191 Arturs Irbe .12 .30
192 Craig Janney .10 .25
193 Sandis Ozolinsh .12 .30
194 Jon Casey .12 .30
195 Brett Hull .20 .50
196 Esa Tikkanen .10 .25
197 Brian Bradley .12 .30
198 Daren Puppa .12 .30
199 Alexander Selivanov .12 .30
200 Rob Zamuner .10 .25
201 Ken Baumgartner .10 .25
202 Doug Gilmour .20 .50
203 Kenny Jonsson .15 .40
204 Felix Potvin .15 .40
205 Randy Wood .10 .25
206 Jeff Brown .12 .30
207 Pavel Bure .20 .50
208 Trevor Linden .15 .40
209 Alexander Mogilny .12 .30
210 Roman Oksiuta .10 .25
211 Cliff Ronning .10 .25
212 Peter Bondra .15 .40
213 Jim Carey .12 .30
214 Pat Peake .10 .25
215 Mark Tinordi .10 .25
216 Mike Eastwood .10 .25
217 Nelson Emerson .10 .25
218 Dave Manson .10 .25
219 Teemu Selanne .30 .75
220 Keith Tkachuk .15 .40
221 Bob Corkum R .10 .25
222 Peter Douris R .10 .25
223 Paul Kariya URB .20 .50
224 Todd Krygier URS .10 .25
225 Mike Sillinger R .10 .25
226 Ray Bourque URB .25 .60
227 Fred Knipscheer R .10 .25
228 Cam Neely URB .15 .40
229 Adam Oates URB .15 .40
230 Jason Dawe R .10 .25
231 Yuri Khmylev R .10 .25
232 Bob Sweeney URS .10 .25
233 Trevor Kidd R .12 .30
234 Eric Daze R .30 .75
235 Tony Amonte R .12 .30
236 Jeremy Roenick URB .20 .50
237 Denis Savard R .20 .50
238 Gary Suter R .12 .30
239 Peter Forsberg URS .40 1.00
240 Curtis Leschyshyn R .10 .25
241 Owen Nolan URB .15 .40
242 Joe Sakic URS .25 .60
243 Valeri Kamensky R .12 .30
244 Claude Lemieux R .15 .40
245 Bob Bassen R .10 .25
246 Shane Churla R .10 .25
247 Todd Harvey R .10 .25
248 Kevin Hatcher URS .12 .30
249 Richard Matvichuk R .12 .30
250 Mike Modano URB .25 .60
251 Dino Ciccarelli R .12 .30
252 Paul Coffey URS .15 .40
253 Sergei Fedorov URS .25 .60
254 Vyacheslav Kozlov R .12 .30
255 Mike Vernon R .12 .30
256 Jason Bonsignore R .10 .25
257 Dean McAmmond R .10 .25
258 Bill Ranford R .12 .30
259 Doug Weight URB .15 .40
260 Bob Kudelski R .10 .25
261 Dave Lowry R .10 .25
262 Gord Murphy R .10 .25
263 Rob Niedermayer URS .12 .30
264 Frantisek Kucera R .10 .25
265 Paul Ranheim R .10 .25
266 Geoff Sanderson URS .10 .25
267 Darren Turcotte R .10 .25
268 Pat Conacher R .10 .25
269 Wayne Gretzky URB .75 2.00
270 Kelly Hrudey R .12 .30
271 Jari Kurri R .15 .40
272 Patrice Brisebois R .10 .25
273 Vladimir Malakhov R .10 .25
274 Patrick Roy URB .40 1.00
275 Martin Brodeur URB .40 1.00
276 Neal Broten R .12 .30
277 Sergei Brylin R .10 .25
278 John MacLean R .12 .30
279 Wendel Clark R .15 .40
280 Travis Green R .12 .30
281 Scott Lachance URS .10 .25
282 Tommy Salo R .25 .60
283 Brian Leetch URB .15 .40
284 Mark Messier URB .25 .60
285 Sergei Nemchinov R .10 .25
286 Luc Robitaille URS .15 .40
287 Sean Hill R .10 .25
288 Jim Paek URS .10 .25
289 Martin Straka R .10 .25
290 Sylvain Turgeon R .10 .25
291 Rod Brind'Amour URS .15 .40
292 Kevin Haller R .10 .25
293 John LeClair R .15 .40
294 Eric Lindros URB .25 .60
295 Joel Otto R .10 .25
296 Chris Therien R .10 .25
297 Jaromir Jagr URS .40 1.00
298 Mario Lemieux URB .50 1.25
299 Glen Murray R .10 .25
300 Petr Nedved R .12 .30
301 Jamie Baker R .10 .25
302 Arturs Irbe URB .12 .30
303 Jayson More R .10 .25
304 Ray Whitney R .12 .30
305 Geoff Courtnall URS .10 .25
306 Dale Hawerchuk R .20 .50
307 Brett Hull URB .20 .50
308 Ian Laperriere R .10 .25
309 Chris Pronger R .15 .40
310 Roman Hamrlik R .10 .25
311 Petr Klima URS .10 .25
312 John Tucker R .10 .25
313 Paul Ysebaert URB .10 .25
314 Ken Baumgartner R .10 .25
315 Doug Gilmour URB .20 .50
316 Pavel Bure URB .20 .50
317 Bret Hedican R .10 .25
318 Alexander Mogilny URS .12 .30
319 Mike Ridley R .10 .25
320 Peter Bondra R .15 .40
321 Sylvain Cote R .10 .25
322 Dale Hunter R .12 .30
323 Keith Jones URS .12 .30
324 Kelly Miller R .10 .25
325 Tim Cheveldae R .12 .30
326 Dallas Drake R .10 .25
327 Igor Korolev R .10 .25
328 Teppo Numminen R .10 .25
329 Teemu Selanne URB .30 .75
330 Alexei Zhamnov URS .15 .40

1996-97 Playoff One on One

This 110-card set serves as a follow-up to the '95-96 game set of the same name, allowing collectors/players to expand their playing experience. As with the previous set, the cards were available in varying degrees of difficulty. The suffixes below indicate how difficult each is to obtain: C is common, UC is uncommon, R is rare and UR is ultra rare. The cards can also be differentiated quickly be referring to the background color: commons are green, uncommons are violet, rares are silver and ultra rares are gold.

COMPLETE SET (110) 80.00 200.00
331 Mike Sillinger C .02 .10
332 Oleg Tverdovsky C .07 .20
333 Kevin Stevens C .02 .10
334 Joe Nieuwendyk C .07 .20
335 Owen Nolan C .08 .25
336 Jocelyn Thibault C .07 .20
337 Dave Gagner C .02 .10
338 Ray Sheppard C .02 .10
339 Jesse Belanger C .02 .10
340 Tony Granato C .02 .10
341 Daniel Alfredsson C .07 .20
342 Stephane Richer C .02 .10
343 Mathieu Schneider C .02 .10
344 Kirk Muller C .02 .10
345 Arturs Irbe C .08 .25
346 Igor Larionov C .02 .10
347 Steve Duchesne C .02 .10
348 Dave Andreychuk C .02 .10
349 Mike Gartner C .07 .20
350 Teppo Numminen C .02 .10
351 Keith Tkachuk C .20 .50
352 Mike Modano C .20 .50
353 Paul Kariya C .30 .75
354 German Titov C .02 .10
355 Bernie Nicholls C .02 .10
356 Doug Gilmour C .20 .50
357 Peter Forsberg C .30 .75
358 David Oliver C .02 .10
359 Pat Verbeek C .02 .10
360 Ron Francis C .07 .20
361 Pat Falloon C .02 .10
362 Jeff Friesen C .07 .20
363 Todd Krygier C .02 .10
364 Felix Potvin C .20 .50
365 Shane Churla C .02 .10
366 Steve Yzerman C .40 1.00
367 Kelly Hrudey C .02 .10
368 Mariusz Czerkawski U .07 .20
369 Patrick Poulin U .05 .15
370 Chris Chelios U .40 1.00
371 Ray Bourque U .75 2.00
372 Igor Kravchuk U .05 .15
373 Kirk Maltby U .05 .15
374 Bill Ranford U .07 .20
375 Darryl Sydor U .05 .15
376 Rick Tocchet U .07 .20
377 J.J. Daigneault U .05 .15
378 Chris Osgood U .40 1.00
379 Zigmund Palffy U .20 .50
380 Ray Ferraro U .05 .15
381 Don Beaupre U .07 .20
382 Andy Moog U .20 .50
383 Sergei Zubov U .07 .20
384 Craig Janney U .05 .15
385 Sandis Ozolinsh U .07 .20
386 Dave Reid U .05 .15
387 Scott Mellanby U .07 .20
388 Saku Koivu U .40 1.00
389 Bryan Smolinski U .07 .20
390 Alexander Selivanov U .05 .15
391 Peter Bondra U .20 .50
392 Esa Tikkanen U .07 .20
393 Ken Baumgartner U .05 .15
394 Ed Belfour U .40 1.00
395 Randy Wood U .05 .15
396 Jeff Brown U .05 .15
397 Roman Oksiuta U .05 .15
398 Cliff Ronning U .05 .15
399 Mike Eastwood U .05 .15
400 Nelson Emerson U .05 .15
401 Dave Manson U .05 .15
402 Jamie Baker U .05 .15
403 Ian Laperriere U .05 .15
404 Petr Klima U .05 .15
405 Dallas Drake R .07 .20
406 Tim Cheveldae R .20 .50
407 Igor Korolev R .07 .20
408 Kevin Hatcher R .07 .20
409 Dale Hawerchuk R .40 1.00
410 Martin Straka R .30 .75
411 Wendel Clark R .75 2.00
412 Jari Kurri R .75 2.00
413 Darren Turcotte R .07 .20
414 Yuri Khmylev R .07 .20
415 Bob Corkum R .07 .20
416 Roman Hamrlik R .30 .75
417 Jayson More R .07 .20
418 Travis Green R .30 .75
419 Dean McAmmond R .07 .20
420 Valeri Kamensky R .20 .50
421 Jason Dawe R .07 .20
422 Alexander Mogilny R .75 2.00
423 Keith Jones R .07 .20
424 Mark Messier R 3.00 8.00
425 John Vanbiesbrouck R 2.00 5.00
426 Jim Carey R .40 1.00
427 Brett Hull R 4.00 10.00
428 Teemu Selanne UR 6.00 15.00
429 Phil Housley UR 2.00 5.00
430 Wayne Gretzky UR 20.00 50.00
431 Patrick Roy UR 15.00 40.00
432 Joe Sakic UR 8.00 20.00
433 Jaromir Jagr UR 8.00 20.00
434 Doug Weight UR 2.00 5.00
435 Rob Niedermayer UR 2.00 5.00
436 Mario Lemieux UR 15.00 40.00
437 Sergei Fedorov UR 6.00 15.00
438 Pavel Bure UR 6.00 15.00
439 Eric Lindros UR 6.00 15.00
440 Martin Brodeur UR 8.00 20.00

2010-11 Playoff Contenders

COMP.SET w/o SPs (100) 10.00 25.00
1 Corey Perry .40 1.00
2 Nicklas Bergfors .30 .75
3 Derek Roy .40 1.00
4 Eric Staal .50 1.25
5 Patrick Kane .75 2.00
6 Mathieu Garon .30 .75
7 Pavel Datsyuk .50 1.25
8 Ryan Whitney .25 .60
9 Drew Doughty .40 1.00
10 Matt Cullen .25 .60
11 Matthew Lombardi .25 .60
12 John Tavares .75 2.00
13 Sean Avery .30 .75
14 Claude Giroux .40 1.00
15 Kristopher Letang .40 1.00
16 Patrick Marleau .40 1.00
17 David Backes .40 1.00
18 Vincent Lecavalier .30 .75
19 Phil Kessel .50 1.25
20 Henrik Sedin .40 1.00
21 Ryan Getzlaf .60 1.50
22 Tim Thomas .30 .75
23 Thomas Vanek .40 1.00
24 Brandon Sutter .30 .75
25 Matt Duchene .40 1.00
26 Brad Richards .40 1.00
27 Nicklas Lidstrom .40 1.00
28 Ales Hemsky .30 .75
29 Jonathan Quick .60 1.50
30 Carey Price 1.50 4.00
31 Ilya Kovalchuk .40 1.00
32 Dwayne Roloson .30 .75
33 Jason Spezza .25 .60
34 Jeff Carter .40 1.00
35 Evgeni Malkin 1.25 3.00
36 Joe Thornton .40 1.00
37 Jaroslav Halak .40 1.00
38 Mike Smith .40 1.00
39 Roberto Luongo .40 1.00
40 Alex Ovechkin 1.50 4.00
41 Teemu Selanne .75 2.00
42 Milan Lucic .40 1.00
43 Jarome Iginla .40 1.00
44 Cam Ward .40 1.00
45 Chris Stewart .30 .75
46 Loui Eriksson .30 .75
47 Henrik Zetterberg .50 1.25
48 David Booth .25 .60
49 Ryan Smyth .30 .75
50 Tomas Plekanec .40 1.00
51 Zach Parise .40 1.00
52 Brandon Dubinsky .30 .75
53 Daniel Alfredsson .40 1.00
54 Mike Richards .40 1.00
55 Brent Johnson .30 .75
56 Joe Pavelski .40 1.00
57 T.J. Oshie .60 1.50
58 Jean-Sebastien Giguere .30 .75
59 Alexandre Burrows .40 1.00
60 John Carlson .50 1.25
61 Andrew Ladd .40 1.00

62 Nathan Horton .30 .75
63 Miikka Kiprusoff .30 .75
64 Duncan Keith .40 1.00
65 Derick Brassard .40 1.00
66 Steve Ott .30 .75
67 Jimmy Howard .50 1.25
68 Tomas Vokoun .30 .75
69 Mikko Koivu .40 1.00
70 Michael Cammalleri .40 1.00
71 Martin Brodeur .75 2.00
72 Henrik Lundqvist .60 1.50
73 Chris Neil .25 .60
74 Ville Leino .30 .75
75 Sidney Crosby 1.50 4.00
76 Dany Heatley .30 .75
77 Martin St. Louis .40 1.00
78 Jonas Gustavsson .50 1.25
79 Cory Schneider .30 .75
80 Michal Neuvirth .30 .75
81 Evander Kane .40 1.00
82 Ryan Miller .40 1.00
83 Rene Bourque .25 .60
84 Jonathan Toews .75 2.00
85 Rick Nash .40 1.00
86 Todd Bertuzzi .30 .75
87 Nikolai Khabibulin .30 .75
88 Anze Kopitar .60 1.50
89 Niklas Backstrom .40 1.00
90 Pekka Rinne .50 1.25
91 Josh Bailey .30 .75
92 Ryan Callahan .40 1.00
93 Chris Pronger .30 .75
94 Zbynek Michalek .25 .60
95 Ryane Clowe .25 .60
96 Alex Steen .40 1.00
97 Steven Stamkos .75 2.00
98 Mikhail Grabovski .30 .75
99 Daniel Sedin .40 1.00
100 Nicklas Backstrom .60 1.50
101 Paul Coffey 1.50 4.00
102 Stan Mikita 2.00 5.00
103 Trevor Linden 1.50 4.00
104 Darryl Sittler 1.25 3.00
105 Rod Gilbert 1.50 4.00
106 Reggie Lemelin 2.00 5.00
107 Patrick Roy 4.00 10.00
108 Mario Lemieux 5.00 12.00
109 Luc Robitaille 1.50 4.00
110 Joe Sakic 2.50 6.00
111 Kelly Hrudey 1.25 3.00
112 Steve Yzerman 4.00 10.00
113 Johnny Bower 2.00 5.00
114 Joe Nieuwendyk 1.50 4.00
115 Gerry Cheevers 1.50 4.00
116 Cam Fowler AU SP RC EXCH 5.00 12.00
117 Kyle Palmieri AU RC 8.00 20.00
118 Alexander Burmistrov AU RC 4.00 10.00
119 Jordan Caron AU RC 6.00 15.00
120 Tyler Seguin AU SP RC 25.00 60.00
121 Zach Hamill AU RC 4.00 10.00
122 Luke Adam AU RC 4.00 10.00
123 T.J. Brodie AU RC 5.00 12.00
124 Henrik Karlsson AU RC 4.00 10.00
125 Zac Dalpe AU RC 4.00 10.00
126 Jeff Skinner AU SP RC 8.00 20.00
127 Nick Leddy AU RC 4.00 10.00
128 Jeremy Morin AU RC 4.00 10.00
129 Evan Brophey AU RC 4.00 10.00
130 Brandon Yip AU RC 4.00 10.00
131 Mark Olver AU RC 4.00 10.00
132 Philip McRae AU RC 4.00 10.00
133 Kevin Shattenkirk AU RC 8.00 20.00
134 Jeff Penner AU SP RC 6.00 15.00
135 Taylor Hall AU SP RC 15.00 40.00
136 Magnus Paajarvi AU SP RC 20.00 50.00
137 Jordan Eberle AU SP RC 10.00 25.00
138 Jake Muzzin AU RC 4.00 10.00
139 Kyle Clifford AU RC 4.00 10.00
140 Brayden Schenn AU SP RC 6.00 15.00
141 Matt Kassian AU RC 4.00 10.00
142 P.K. Subban AU SP RC 20.00 50.00
143 Anders Lindback AU RC 4.00 10.00
144 Mark Dekanich AU RC 4.00 10.00
145 Jeff Frazee AU RC 6.00 15.00
146 Linus Omark AU RC 10.00 25.00
147 Matt Taormina AU RC 4.00 10.00
148 Jacob Josefson AU RC 4.00 10.00
149 Alexander Vasyunov AU RC 4.00 10.00
150 Nino Niederreiter AU RC 5.00 12.00
151 Derek Stepan AU RC 8.00 20.00
152 Evgeny Grachev AU RC 4.00 10.00
153 Robin Lehner AU RC 8.00 20.00
154 Sergei Bobrovsky AU RC 10.00 25.00
155 Eric Wellwood AU RC 5.00 12.00
156 Oliver Ekman-Larsson AU RC 10.00 25.00
157 Eric Tangradi AU RC 4.00 10.00
158 Mike Moore AU RC 4.00 10.00
159 Tommy Wingels AU RC 4.00 10.00
160 Ryan Reaves AU RC 5.00 12.00
161 Ian Cole AU RC 4.00 10.00
162 Dana Tyrell AU RC 4.00 10.00
163 Nazem Kadri AU SP RC 10.00 25.00
164 Korbinian Holzer AU RC 4.00 10.00
165 M.Johansson AU RC 6.00 15.00

2010-11 Playoff Contenders Playoff Tickets

*1-100 PLAYOFF TIX: 2X TO 5X BASE
*101-115 PLAYOFF TIX: .6X TO 1.5X BASE
*116-165 PLAYOFF TIX: .2X TO .5X BASE
STATED PRINT RUN 100 SER.#'d SETS
100 Nicklas Backstrom 4.00 10.00
120 Tyler Seguin 12.00 30.00
121 Zach Hamill 5.00 12.00
126 Jeff Skinner 12.00 30.00
135 Taylor Hall 10.00 25.00
136 Magnus Paajarvi 3.00 8.00
137 Jordan Eberle 12.00 30.00
140 Brayden Schenn 4.00 10.00
142 P.K. Subban 15.00 40.00
157 Eric Tangradi 5.00 12.00
163 Nazem Kadri 6.00 15.00

2010-11 Playoff Contenders Against The Glass

COMPLETE SET (18) 15.00 40.00
1 Alex Ovechkin 6.00 15.00
2 Ryan Callahan 1.50 4.00
3 Dustin Brown 1.50 4.00
4 Troy Brouwer 1.50 4.00
5 Luke Schenn 1.25 3.00
6 Shea Weber 1.25 3.00
7 Ryan Getzlaf 2.50 6.00
8 Tuomo Ruutu 1.25 3.00
9 Steve Ott 1.25 3.00
10 Chris Neil 1.00 2.50
11 Michael Del Zotto 1.25 3.00
12 Dustin Byfuglien 1.50 4.00
13 Evander Kane 1.50 4.00
14 Drew Doughty 1.50 4.00
15 Jarome Iginla 1.50 4.00
16 James Neal 1.50 4.00
17 Tyler Myers 1.50 4.00
18 Bobby Ryan 1.50 4.00

2010-11 Playoff Contenders Against The Glass Autographs

STATED PRINT RUN 25-50
1 Alex Ovechkin/25 30.00 80.00
2 Ryan Callahan 8.00 20.00
3 Dustin Brown 8.00 20.00
4 Troy Brouwer 8.00 20.00
5 Luke Schenn 6.00 15.00
6 Shea Weber 6.00 15.00
7 Ryan Getzlaf 12.00 30.00
8 Tuomo Ruutu 6.00 15.00
9 Steve Ott 6.00 15.00
10 Chris Neil 5.00 12.00
11 Michael Del Zotto 6.00 15.00
12 Dustin Byfuglien 8.00 20.00
13 Evander Kane 8.00 20.00
14 Drew Doughty 8.00 20.00
15 Jarome Iginla 8.00 20.00
16 James Neal 8.00 20.00
17 Tyler Myers 8.00 20.00
18 Bobby Ryan 8.00 20.00

2010-11 Playoff Contenders Awards Contenders

COMPLETE SET (20) 25.00 60.00
*GREEN/50: .6X TO 1.5X BASIC
*PURPLF/100: .5X TO 1.2X BASIC
1 Tim Thomas 1.25 3.00
2 Carey Price 6.00 15.00
3 Jimmy Howard 2.00 5.00
4 Jonathan Quick 2.50 6.00
5 Ondrej Pavelec 1.50 4.00
6 Nicklas Lidstrom 1.50 4.00
7 Drew Doughty 1.50 4.00
8 Kristopher Letang 1.50 4.00
9 John-Michael Liles 1.00 2.50
10 Zdeno Chara 1.25 3.00
11 Sidney Crosby 6.00 15.00
12 Patrick Sharp 1.50 4.00
13 Steven Stamkos 3.00 8.00
14 Daniel Sedin 1.50 4.00
15 Alex Ovechkin 6.00 15.00
16 Sidney Crosby 6.00 15.00
17 Steven Stamkos 3.00 8.00
18 Alexander Semin 1.50 4.00
19 Alex Ovechkin 6.00 15.00
20 Henrik Sedin 1.50 4.00

2010-11 Playoff Contenders Awards Contenders Autographs

STATED PRINT RUN 10-50
1 Tim Thomas/50 20.00 50.00
2 Carey Price/50 25.00 60.00
3 Jimmy Howard/50 10.00 25.00
4 Jonathan Quick/50 12.00 30.00
5 Ondrej Pavelec/50 10.00 25.00
6 Nicklas Lidstrom/50 12.00 30.00
7 Drew Doughty/50 8.00 20.00
8 Kristopher Letang/50 25.00 60.00
9 John-Michael Liles/50 8.00 20.00
10 Zdeno Chara/50 10.00 25.00
11 Sidney Crosby/10
12 Patrick Sharp/50 12.00 30.00
13 Steven Stamkos/25 30.00 60.00
14 Daniel Sedin/50 12.00 30.00
15 Alex Ovechkin/10
16 Sidney Crosby/10
17 Steven Stamkos/25 25.00 60.00
18 Alexander Semin/50 8.00 20.00
19 Alex Ovechkin/10
20 Henrik Sedin/50 8.00 20.00

2010-11 Playoff Contenders Classic Tickets Autographs

STATED PRINT RUN 10-50
101 Paul Coffey/25 12.00 30.00
102 Stan Mikita 15.00 40.00
103 Trevor Linden/25 25.00 60.00
104 Darryl Sittler 20.00 50.00
105 Rod Gilbert 15.00 40.00
106 Reggie Lemelin 12.00 30.00
107 Patrick Roy/10
108 Mario Lemieux/10
109 Luc Robitaille/25
110 Joe Sakic/19
111 Kelly Hrudey /50 6.00 15.00
112 Steve Yzerman/19
113 Johnny Bower/25 20.00 50.00
114 Joe Nieuwendyk 8.00 20.00
115 Gerry Cheevers/25 15.00 40.00

2010-11 Playoff Contenders Draft Tandems

COMPLETE SET (20) 25.00 60.00
*GREEN/50: .6X TO 1.5X BASIC
*PURPLE/100: .5X TO 1.2X BASIC
1 M.Messier/R.Bourque 2.50 6.00
2 P.Coffey/D.Savard 2.00 5.00
3 G.Fuhr/D.Hawerchuk 2.00 5.00
4 P.LaFontaine/S.Yzerman 4.00 10.00
5 P.Roy/M.Lemieux 5.00 12.00
6 B.Leetch/A.Graves 1.50 4.00
7 B.Shanahan/J.Sakic 2.50 6.00
8 M.Modano/T.Linden 2.50 6.00
9 F.Potvin/M.Brodeur 3.00 8.00
10 R.Smyth/T.Holmstrom 1.25 3.00
11 J.Iginla/S.Doan 1.50 4.00
12 P.Marleau/J.Thornton 1.50 4.00
13 S.Gagne/V.Lecavalier 1.50 4.00
14 H.Sedin/D.Sedin 1.50 4.00
15 D.Roy/A.Hemsky 1.50 4.00
16 R.Nash/K.Lehtonen 1.50 4.00
17 M.Fleury/E.Staal 2.50 6.00
18 E.Malkin/A.Ovechkin 6.00 15.00
19 B.Ryan/J.Johnson 1.50 4.00
20 J.Toews/J.Staal 3.00 8.00

2010-11 Playoff Contenders Draft Tandems Autographs

STATED PRINT RUN 10-25
1 M.Messier/R.Bourque/10
2 P.Coffey/D.Savard 15.00 40.00
3 G.Fuhr/D.Hawerchuk 15.00 40.00
4 P.LaFontaine/S.Yzerman 40.00 100.00
5 P.Roy/M.Lemieux/10
6 B.Leetch/A.Graves 12.00 30.00
7 B.Shanahan/J.Sakic 60.00 120.00
8 M.Modano/T.Linden 60.00 120.00
9 F.Potvin/M.Brodeur 50.00 100.00
10 R.Smyth/T.Holmstrom 25.00 50.00
11 J.Iginla/S.Doan 12.00 30.00
12 P.Marleau/J.Thornton 12.00 30.00
13 S.Gagne/V.Lecavalier 12.00 30.00
14 H.Sedin/D.Sedin 20.00 50.00
15 D.Roy/A.Hemsky 12.00 30.00
16 R.Nash/K.Lehtonen 15.00 40.00
17 M.Fleury/E.Staal 25.00 60.00
18 E.Malkin/A.Ovechkin 100.00 200.00
19 B.Ryan/J.Johnson 12.00 30.00
20 J.Toews/J.Staal 25.00 60.00

2010-11 Playoff Contenders Leather Larceny

COMPLETE SET (18) 20.00 50.00
1 Cam Ward 2.00 5.00
2 Carey Price 8.00 20.00
3 Chris Mason 1.50 4.00
4 Craig Anderson 2.00 5.00
5 Dwayne Roloson 1.50 4.00
6 Henrik Lundqvist 3.00 8.00
7 Jaroslav Halak 2.00 5.00
8 Jonas Gustavsson 2.50 6.00
9 Jonas Hiller 1.50 4.00
10 Kari Lehtonen 1.50 4.00
11 Marc-Andre Fleury 3.00 8.00
12 Martin Brodeur 4.00 10.00
13 Mike Smith 2.00 5.00
14 Niklas Backstrom 2.00 5.00
15 Pekka Rinne 2.50 6.00
16 Ryan Miller 2.00 5.00
17 Steve Mason 1.50 4.00
18 Tim Thomas 1.50 4.00

2010-11 Playoff Contenders Leather Larceny Autographs

STATED PRINT RUN 10-50
1 Cam Ward 15.00 40.00
2 Carey Price 15.00 40.00
3 Chris Mason 8.00 20.00
4 Craig Anderson 10.00 25.00
5 Dwayne Roloson 12.00 30.00
6 Henrik Lundqvist 15.00 40.00
7 Jaroslav Halak 15.00 40.00
8 Jonas Gustavsson 12.00 30.00
9 Jonas Hiller 8.00 20.00
10 Kari Lehtonen 8.00 20.00
11 Marc-Andre Fleury 15.00 40.00
12 Martin Brodeur/10
13 Mike Smith 10.00 25.00
14 Niklas Backstrom 10.00 25.00
15 Pekka Rinne 10.00 25.00
16 Ryan Miller 15.00 40.00
17 Steve Mason 8.00 20.00
18 Tim Thomas 20.00 50.00

2010-11 Playoff Contenders Legendary Contenders

COMPLETE SET (20) 20.00 50.00
*GREEN/50: .6X TO 1.5X BASIC
*PURPLE/100: .5X TO 1.2X BASIC
1 Yvan Cournoyer 1.50 4.00
2 Phil Esposito 2.50 6.00
3 Rogie Vachon 2.00 5.00
4 Mike Bossy 1.50 4.00
5 Richard Brodeur 1.50 4.00
6 Mario Lemieux 5.00 12.00
7 Ken Hodge 1.25 3.00
8 Johnny Bucyk 1.50 4.00
9 Guy Lafleur 2.00 5.00
10 Charlie Hodge 1.25 3.00
11 Bryan Trottier 2.00 5.00
12 Bobby Clarke 1.50 4.00
13 Brett Hull 2.50 6.00
14 Bernie Parent 1.50 4.00
15 Glenn Hall 1.50 4.00
16 Henri Richard 1.50 4.00
17 Jeremy Roenick 1.50 4.00
18 Grant Fuhr 1.50 4.00
19 Tony Esposito 1.50 4.00
20 Terry O'Reilly 1.25 3.00

2010-11 Playoff Contenders Legendary Contenders Autographs

STATED PRINT RUN 25 SER.#'d SETS
1 Yvan Cournoyer 15.00 40.00
2 Phil Esposito 12.00 30.00
3 Rogie Vachon 6.00 15.00
4 Mike Bossy 8.00 20.00
5 Richard Brodeur 8.00 20.00
6 Mario Lemieux 40.00 80.00
7 Ken Hodge 6.00 15.00
8 Johnny Bucyk 8.00 20.00
9 Guy Lafleur 40.00 80.00
10 Charlie Hodge 6.00 15.00
11 Bryan Trottier 10.00 25.00
12 Bobby Clarke 8.00 20.00
13 Brett Hull 15.00 40.00
14 Bernie Parent 12.00 30.00
15 Glenn Hall
16 Henri Richard
17 Jeremy Roenick 12.00 30.00
18 Grant Fuhr 15.00 40.00
19 Tony Esposito 12.00 30.00
20 Terry O'Reilly 6.00 15.00

2010-11 Playoff Contenders Lottery Winners

COMPLETE SET (15) 20.00 50.00
*GREEN/50: .6X TO 1.5X BASIC
*PURPLE/100: .5X TO 1.2X BASIC
1 Alex Ovechkin 6.00 15.00
2 Jonathan Toews 3.00 8.00
3 Patrick Kane 3.00 8.00
4 Sidney Crosby 6.00 15.00
5 John Tavares 3.00 8.00
6 Steven Stamkos 3.00 8.00
7 Matt Duchene 1.50 4.00
8 Evander Kane 1.50 4.00
9 Jordan Staal 1.50 4.00
10 Zach Bogosian 1.25 3.00
11 Sam Gagner 1.25 3.00
12 James van Riemsdyk 2.50 6.00
13 Drew Doughty 1.50 4.00
14 Carey Price 6.00 15.00
15 Bobby Ryan 1.50 4.00

2010-11 Playoff Contenders Lottery Winners Autographs

STATED PRINT RUN 25-50
1 Alex Ovechkin/25 40.00 100.00
2 Jonathan Toews 25.00 50.00
3 Patrick Kane 15.00 40.00
4 Sidney Crosby/25 100.00 200.00
5 John Tavares 15.00 40.00
6 Steven Stamkos 20.00 50.00
7 Matt Duchene 8.00 20.00
8 Evander Kane 8.00 20.00
9 Jordan Staal 10.00 25.00
10 Zach Bogosian 6.00 15.00
11 Sam Gagner 6.00 15.00
12 James van Riemsdyk 8.00 20.00
13 Drew Doughty 8.00 20.00
14 Carey Price 15.00 40.00
15 Bobby Ryan 8.00 20.00

2010-11 Playoff Contenders Perennial Contenders

COMPLETE SET (20) 25.00 60.00
*GREEN/50: .6X TO 1.5X BASIC
*PURPLE/100: .5X TO 1.2X BASIC
1 Nicklas Lidstrom 1.50 4.00
2 Joe Thornton 1.50 4.00
3 Roberto Luongo 1.50 4.00
4 Drew Doughty 1.50 4.00
5 Dany Heatley 1.25 3.00
6 Patrick Kane 3.00 8.00
7 Henrik Sedin 1.50 4.00
8 Jonathan Toews 3.00 8.00
9 Henrik Zetterberg 2.00 5.00
10 Jonathan Quick 2.50 6.00
11 Sidney Crosby 6.00 15.00
12 Mike Richards 1.50 4.00
13 Tomas Holmstrom 1.00 2.50
14 Alex Ovechkin 6.00 15.00
15 Zach Parise 1.50 4.00
16 Marc-Andre Fleury 2.50 6.00
17 Carey Price 6.00 15.00
18 Chris Pronger 1.25 3.00
19 Claude Giroux 1.50 4.00
20 Jordan Staal 1.50 4.00

2010-11 Playoff Contenders Perennial Contenders Autographs

STATED PRINT RUN 25 SER.#'d SETS
1 Nicklas Lidstrom 12.00 30.00
2 Joe Thornton 8.00 20.00
4 Drew Doughty 8.00 20.00
5 Dany Heatley 6.00 15.00
6 Patrick Kane 15.00 40.00
7 Henrik Sedin 8.00 20.00
8 Jonathan Toews 15.00 40.00
10 Jonathan Quick 15.00 30.00
11 Sidney Crosby 75.00 150.00
12 Mike Richards 25.00 60.00
13 Tomas Holmstrom 12.00 30.00
14 Alex Ovechkin 40.00 100.00
15 Zach Parise 10.00 25.00
16 Marc-Andre Fleury 15.00 40.00
17 Carey Price 20.00 50.00
18 Chris Pronger 6.00 15.00
19 Claude Giroux 15.00 40.00
20 Jordan Staal 8.00 20.00

2010-11 Playoff Contenders Rookie of the Year Contenders

COMPLETE SET (15) 20.00 50.00
*GREEN/50: .6X TO 1.5X BASIC
*PURPLE/100: .5X TO 1.2X BASIC
1 Jeff Skinner 2.50 6.00
2 Derek Stepan 2.50 6.00
3 Jordan Eberle 3.00 8.00
4 Logan Couture 1.50 4.00
5 Tyler Ennis 1.25 3.00
6 Taylor Hall 5.00 12.00
7 John Carlson 2.00 5.00
8 Cam Fowler 1.50 4.00
9 Kevin Shattenkirk 2.50 6.00
10 Sergei Bobrovsky 3.00 8.00
11 Michal Neuvirth 1.25 3.00
12 Tyler Seguin 5.00 12.00
13 P.K. Subban 4.00 10.00
14 Mattias Tedenby 1.00 2.50
15 Jake Dowell 1.25 3.00

2010-11 Playoff Contenders Rookie of the Year Contenders Autographs

STATED PRINT RUN 50 SER.#'d SETS
1 Jeff Skinner 20.00 50.00
2 Derek Stepan 10.00 25.00
3 Jordan Eberle 15.00 40.00
4 Logan Couture 15.00 40.00
5 Tyler Ennis 6.00 15.00
6 Taylor Hall 25.00 60.00
7 John Carlson 10.00 25.00
8 Cam Fowler 8.00 20.00
9 Kevin Shattenkirk 12.00 30.00
10 Sergei Bobrovsky
11 Michal Neuvirth 6.00 15.00
12 Tyler Seguin 25.00 60.00
13 P.K. Subban 30.00 80.00
14 Mattias Tedenby 5.00 12.00
15 Jake Dowell EXCH 6.00 15.00

2010-11 Playoff Contenders The Great Outdoors

COMPLETE SET (18) 20.00 50.00
1 Jose Theodore 1.50 4.00
2 Ryan Smyth 1.25 3.00
3 Sidney Crosby 6.00 15.00
4 Ryan Miller 1.50 4.00
5 Derek Roy 1.50 4.00
6 Jordan Staal 1.50 4.00
7 Pavel Datsyuk 2.00 5.00
8 Jonathan Toews 3.00 8.00
9 Marian Hossa 1.25 3.00
10 Dustin Byfuglien 1.50 4.00
11 Tim Thomas 1.25 3.00
12 Mark Recchi 2.00 5.00
13 Shawn Thornton 1.00 2.50
14 Michael Leighton 1.25 3.00
15 Jeff Carter 1.50 4.00
16 Evgeni Malkin 5.00 12.00
17 Alex Ovechkin 6.00 15.00
18 Mario Lemieux 5.00 12.00

2010-11 Playoff Contenders The Great Outdoors Autographs

STATED PRINT RUN 25-50
1 Jose Theodore 8.00 20.00
2 Ryan Smyth 10.00 25.00
3 Sidney Crosby/25 100.00 200.00
4 Ryan Miller 12.00 30.00
5 Derek Roy 8.00 20.00
6 Jordan Staal 12.00 30.00
7 Pavel Datsyuk 15.00 40.00
8 Jonathan Toews 25.00 50.00
9 Marian Hossa 6.00 15.00
10 Dustin Byfuglien 8.00 20.00
11 Tim Thomas 20.00 50.00
12 Mark Recchi 15.00 40.00
13 Shawn Thornton 20.00 50.00
14 Evgeni Malkin 25.00 60.00
15 Jeff Carter 12.00 30.00
17 Alex Ovechkin/25 75.00 150.00
16 Michael Leighton 6.00 15.00
18 Mario Lemieux/25 75.00 150.00

1975-76 Popsicle

This 18-card set presents the teams of the NHL. The cards measure approximately 3 3/8" by 2 1/8" and are printed in the "credit card format", only slightly thinner than an actual credit card. The front has the NHL logo in the upper left hand corner, and the city and team names in the black bar across the top. A colorful team logo appears on the left side of the card face, while a color action shot of the teams' players appears on the right side. The back provides a brief history of the team. The set was issued in two versions (English and bilingual). We have checklisted the cards below in alphabetical order of the team nicknames.

COMPLETE SET (18) 15.00 30.00
1 Chicago Blackhawks 1.50 3.00
2 St. Louis Blues 1.00 2.00
3 Boston Bruins 1.50 3.00
4 Montreal Canadiens 1.50 3.00
5 Vancouver Canucks 1.00 2.00
6 Washington Capitals 1.00 2.00
7 Atlanta Flames 1.50 3.00
8 Philadelphia Flyers 1.00 2.00
9 California Golden Seals 1.50 3.00
10 New York Islanders 1.00 2.00
11 Los Angeles Kings 1.00 2.00
12 Toronto Maple Leafs 1.50 3.00
13 Minnesota North Stars 1.00 2.00
14 Pittsburgh Penguins 1.00 2.00
15 New York Rangers 1.50 3.00
16 Detroit Red Wings 1.50 3.00
17 Buffalo Sabres 1.00 2.00
18 Kansas City Scouts 1.50 3.00

1976-77 Popsicle

This 18-card set presents the teams of the NHL. The cards measure approximately 3 3/8" by 2 1/8" and are printed in the "credit card format", only slightly thinner than an actual credit card. The front has the NHL logo in the upper left hand corner, and the city and team names in the black bar across the top. A colorful team logo appears on the left side of the card face, while a color action shot of the teams' players appears on the right side. The back provides a brief history of the team. The set was issued in two versions (English and bilingual); a bilingual membership card is known to exist. We have checklisted the cards below in alphabetical order of the team nicknames.

COMPLETE SET (19) 20.00 40.00
1 Cleveland Barons 1.50 3.00
2 Chicago Blackhawks 1.50 3.00
3 St. Louis Blues 1.00 2.00
4 Boston Bruins 1.50 3.00
5 Montreal Canadiens 1.50 3.00
6 Vancouver Canucks 1.00 2.00
7 Washington Capitals 1.00 2.00
8 Atlanta Flames 1.50 3.00
9 Philadelphia Flyers 1.00 2.00
10 New York Islanders 1.00 2.00
11 Los Angeles Kings 1.00 2.00
12 Toronto Maple Leafs 1.50 3.00
13 Minnesota North Stars 1.00 2.00
14 Pittsburgh Penguins 1.00 2.00
15 New York Rangers 1.50 3.00
16 Detroit Red Wings 1.50 3.00
17 Colorado Rockies 1.50 3.00
18 Buffalo Sabres 1.00 2.00
19 Membership Card 1.50 3.00

1966-67 Post Cereal Box Backs

These three box backs seem to vary from the 1967-68 set, so we have listed them seperately. The backs picture Pulford and Hall in All-Star uniforms and Worsely in his Canadiens uniform with a notation that Montreal won the Stanley Cup in 1965-66. A "hockey tip" was printed below the pictures in both English and French, though often the picture was cut from the box without the writing underneath.

1 Gump Worsley 15.00 40.00
2 Bob Pulford 15.00 40.00
3 Glenn Hall 15.00 40.00

1967-68 Post Cereal Box Backs

These photo premiums were issued on the back of Post cereal boxes. They measure approximately 6 1/2 by 7 1/2 and are blank backed. They are unnumbered and so are listed below in alphabetical order.

COMPLETE SET (13)
1 Gordie Howe 25.00 50.00
(net in background
2 Gordie Howe 25.00 50.00
(no net
3 Harry Howell 10.00 20.00
(passing
4 Harry Howell 10.00 20.00
(kneeling
5 Jacques Laperriere 10.00 20.00
(net in background
6 Jacques Laperriere 10.00 20.00
(no net
7 Stan Mikita 15.00 30.00
(red jersey
8 Stan Mikita 15.00 30.00
(white jersey
9 Bobby Orr 25.00 50.00
(posed
10 Bobby Orr 25.00 50.00
(in action
11 Henri Richard 12.50 25.00
(with puck
12 Henri Richard 12.50 25.00
(no puck
13 Checklist 25.00 50.00

1967-68 Post Flip Books

This 1967-68 Post set consists of 12 flip books. They display a Montreal player on one side of the page and a Toronto player on the other side. In the listing below, the Montreal player is listed first.

COMPLETE SET (12) 100.00 200.00
1 Gump Worsley 15.00 30.00
Johnny Bower
2 Rogatien Vachon 17.50 35.00
Johnny Bower
3 J.C. Tremblay 12.50 25.00
Tim Horton
4 Jacques Laperriere 7.50 15.00
Marcel Pronovost
5 Henri Richard 12.50 25.00
Frank Mahovlich
6 Dick Duff 10.00 20.00
Dave Keon
7 Jean Beliveau 15.00 30.00
Jim Pappin
8 Jean Beliveau 15.00 30.00
Ron Ellis
9 Gilles Tremblay 10.00 20.00
George Armstrong
10 J.C. Tremblay 5.00 10.00
Pete Stemkowski
11 Ralph Backstrom 7.50 15.00
Bob Pulford
12 Bobby Rousseau 5.00 10.00
Wayne Hillman

1968-69 Post Marbles

This set of 30 marbles was issued by Post Cereal in Canada and features players of the Montreal Canadiens (MC) and the Toronto Maple Leafs (TML). Also produced was an attractive game board which is rather difficult to find and not included in the complete set price below.

COMPLETE SET (30) 250.00 500.00
1 Ralph Backstrom MC 4.00 8.00
2 Jean Beliveau MC 20.00 40.00
3 Johnny Bower TML 7.50 15.00
4 Wayne Carleton TML 4.00 8.00
5 Yvan Cournoyer MC 10.00 20.00
6 Ron Ellis TML 4.00 8.00
7 John Ferguson MC 4.00 8.00
8 Bruce Gamble TML 4.00 8.00
9 Terry Harper MC 4.00 8.00
10 Ted Harris MC 4.00 8.00
11 Paul Henderson TML 5.00 10.00
12 Tim Horton TML 20.00 40.00
13 Dave Keon TML 12.50 25.00
14 Jacques Laperriere MC 5.00 10.00
15 Jacques Lemaire MC 12.50 25.00
16 Murray Oliver TML 4.00 8.00
17 Mike Pelyk TML 4.00 8.00
18 Pierre Pilote TML 5.00 10.00
19 Marcel Pronovost TML 5.00 10.00
20 Bob Pulford TML 5.00 10.00
21 Henri Richard MC 10.00 20.00
22 Bobby Rousseau MC 4.00 8.00
23 Serge Savard MC 5.00 10.00
24 Floyd Smith TML 4.00 8.00
25 Gilles Tremblay MC 4.00 8.00
26 J.C. Tremblay MC 4.00 8.00
27 Norm Ullman TML 5.00 10.00
28 Rogatien Vachon MC 15.00 30.00
29 Mike Walton TML 4.00 8.00
30 Gump Worsley MC 10.00 20.00
xx Game Board 87.50 175.00

1970-71 Post Shooters

This set of 16 shooters was intended to be used with the hockey game that Post had advertised as a premium. The shooter consists of a plastic figure with a colorful adhesive decal sheet, with stickers that could be applied to the shooter for identification. All players come with home and away, i.e., red or blue shoulders. The figures measure approximately 3 1/2" by 4 1/2". Players are featured in their NHLPA uniform. They are unnumbered and hence are listed below in alphabetical order.

COMPLETE SET (16) 150.00 300.00
1 Johnny Bucyk 7.50 15.00
2 Ron Ellis 5.00 10.00
3 Ed Giacomin 10.00 20.00
4 Paul Henderson 7.50 15.00
5 Ken Hodge 6.25 12.50
6 Dennis Hull 6.25 12.50
7 Orland Kurtenbach 5.00 10.00
8 Jacques Laperriere 6.25 12.50
9 Jacques Lemaire 7.50 15.00
10 Frank Mahovlich 7.50 15.00
11 Peter Mahovlich 6.25 12.50
12 Bobby Orr 50.00 100.00
13 Jacques Plante 20.00 40.00
14 Jean Ratelle 7.50 15.00
15 Dale Tallon 5.00 10.00
16 J.C. Tremblay 6.25 12.50

1972-73 Post Action Transfers

These 12 cards feature two players on each transfer. Each card depicts an important facet of the game. We are listing the players first and then the English title of the card afterwards.

COMPLETE SET (12) 125.00 250.00
1 Garry Unger 30.00 60.00
Bobby Orr
Defense
2 Red Berenson 7.50 15.00
Dale Tallon
In the Corner
3 Gary Dornhoeffer 7.50 15.00
Wayne Cashman
Face Off
4 Jim McKenny 10.00 20.00
Ed Giacomin
Power Save
5 Pat Quinn 7.50 15.00
Keith Magnuson
Power Play Goal
6 Paul Shmyr 7.50 15.00
Rod Seiling
Break Away
7 Danny Grant 10.00 20.00
Jacques Plante
Slap Shot
8 Syl Apps Jr. 10.00 20.00
Serge Savard
Rebound
9 Gump Worsley 12.50 25.00
Gary Bergman
Wrist Shot
10 Roger Crozier 10.00 20.00
Ed Westfall
Last Minute
11 Dennis Hull 7.50 15.00
Orland Kurtenbach
Goalmouth Scramble
12 Rogatien Vachon 15.00 30.00
Yvan Cournoyer
Chest Save

1981-82 Post Standups

Each thick card in this 28-card set measures approximately 2 13/16" by 3 3/4" and consists of three panels joined together at one end. The front of the first panel has the logos of Post, the NHL, the NHLPA, and a NHL team, with the title NHL Stars in Action in English and French. The back of the first panel has a full color action photo of a player from the NHL team featured on the card. The second panel is blank backed and features a standup of the player, with his signature at the bottom of the standup. The front of the third panel has the player's name and statistics (from the 1980-81 regular season) in English and French for that player as well as for his entire team, with instructions on the card back in both languages for creating the standup. These three dimensional cards were issued in cellophane packs with one card per specially marked box of Post Sugar-Crisp, Honeycomb, or Alpha-Bits. The set is composed of two players from each Canadian team and one player from each American NHL team. The promotion included a mail-in offer for an official NHL fact chart, which featured the new NHL divisional alignment. Also available, but hard to find, is a two-piece display box; the cover has logos of all NHL teams with two slots inside for cards and space to display one "opened" card.

COMPLETE SET (28) 20.00 50.00
1 Ray Bourque 3.00 8.00
2 Gilbert Perreault 1.00 2.50
3 Denis Savard 1.50 4.00
4 Dale McCourt .40 1.00
5 Bobby Smith .60 1.50
6 Mike Bossy 2.50 6.00
7 Bobby Clarke 1.50 4.00
8 Randy Carlyle .40 1.00
9 Mike Palmateer .75 2.00
10 Tiger Williams .60 1.50
11 Mark Howe .75 2.00
12 Marcel Dionne 1.25 3.00
13 Mike Liut .60 1.50
14 Barry Beck .40 1.00
15 Mark Messier 5.00 12.00
16 Larry Robinson 1.25 3.00
17 Real Cloutier .40 1.00
18 Borje Salming .75 2.00
19 Morris Lukowich .40 1.00
20 Brett Callighen .40 1.00
21 Rob Ramage .60 1.50
22 Wilf Paiement .40 1.00
23 Mario Tremblay .60 1.50
24 Robbie Ftorek .40 1.00
25 Stan Smyl .60 1.50
26 Dave Babych .40 1.00
27 Willi Plett .40 1.00
28 Kent Nilsson .75 2.00
xx Display Box 8.00 20.00

1982-83 Post Cereal Panels

This set is composed of panels of 16 mini playing cards, each measuring approximately 1 1/4" by 2" after perforation. The cards were issued in panel form in a cellophane wrapper inside specially marked packages of Post Cereal. The front of each individual card has an action color photo of the player, with uniform number in the upper left-hand corner, and the player's name and uniform number beneath the picture. The back is done in the team's colors and includes the logos of the team, the sponsor (Post), the NHL, and the NHLPA. There were 21 panels produced, one for each NHL team. Game instructions were included in each box so that one could play Shut-out, Face Off, or Hockey Match with the set of 16 hockey playing cards. By mailing in the UPC code or a reasonable hand drawn facsimile, one could enter the sweepstakes for the grand prize of a trip for two to a Stanley Cup Final playoff game. The complete set was available for a limited time through a mail-in offer. Apparently, a salesman's promo kit was produced in conjunction with this offer, which included six oversized sample cards (Dale Hawerchuk, Real Cloutier, Kent Nilsson, Glenn Anderson, Bob Gainey and Rick Vaive).

COMPLETE SET (21) 30.00 80.00
1 Bruins 2.50 6.00
Rogie Vachon
Ray Bourque
Peter McNab
Steve Kasper
Wayne Cashman
Mike Gillis
Rick Middleton
Stan Jonathan
Mike O'Connell
Brad Park
Terry O'Reilly
Mike Milbury
Tom Fergus
Brad McCrimmon
Bruce Crowder
Larry Melnyk
2 Sabres 2.00 5.00
Don Edwards
Richie Dunn
John Van Boxmeer
Mike Ramsey
Dale McCourt
Tony McKegney
Craig Ramsay
Gilbert Perreault
Andre Savard
Yvon Lambert
Ric Seiling
Mike Foligno
J.Francois Sauve
Lindy Ruff
Bill Hajt
Larry Playfair
3 Flames 2.00 5.00
Mel Bridgman
Guy Chouinard
Denis Cyr
Jamie Hislop
Ken Houston
Kevin Lavallee
Gary McAdam
Lanny McDonald
Bob Murdoch
Kent Nilsson
Jim Peplinski
Jim Peplinski
Willi Plett
Paul Reinhart
Pat Riggin
Phil Russell
4 Blackhawks 2.50 6.00
Greg Fox
Dave Hutchison
Terry Ruskowski
Reg Kerr
Tom Lysiak
Bill Gardner
Tim Higgins
Rich Preston
Denis Savard
Al Secord
Grant Mulvey
Doug Crossman
Doug Wilson
Rick Paterson
Ted Bulley
Tony Esposito
5 Red Wings 1.50 4.00
Jim Schoenfeld
John Barrett
Greg Smith
Willie Huber
Walt McKechnie
Paul Woods
Mark Kirton
Danny Gare
Vaclav Nedomansky
Mike Blaisdell
Greg Joly
Mark Osborne
Derek Smith
John Ogrodnick
Reed Larson
Bob Sauve

6 Oilers 8.00 20.00
Grant Fuhr
Lee Fogolin
Kevin Lowe
Garry Lariviere
Paul Coffey
Risto Siltanen
Glenn Anderson
Matti Hagman
Mark Messier
Dave Hunter
Pat Hughes
Jari Kurri
Brett Callighen
Dave Lumley
Dave Semenko
Wayne Gretzky
7 Whalers 2.00 5.00
Paul Shmyr
Ron Francis
Mark Howe
Blake Wesley
Garry Howatt
Jordy Douglas
Dave Keon
George Lyle
Blaine Stoughton
Doug Sulliman
Chris Kotsopoulos
Don Nachbaur
Warren Miller
Pierre Larouche
Greg Millen
8 Kings 2.00 5.00
Mario Lessard
Rick Chartraw
Jerry Korab
Larry Murphy
Charlie Simmer
Dean Hopkins
Marcel Dionne
John P.Kelly
Dave Taylor
Jim Fox
Mark Hardy
Steve Jensen
Doug Smith
Jay Wells
Dave Lewis
Steve Bozek
9 North Stars 1.50 4.00
Curt Giles
Fred Barrett
Craig Hartsburg
Brad Maxwell
K.E. Anderson
Gord Roberts
Tom McCarthy
Brad Palmer
Bobby Smith
Tim Young
Dino Ciccarelli
Gary Sargent
Al MacAdam
Steve Payne
Gilles Meloche
Steve Christoff
10 Canadiens 3.00 8.00
Brian Engblom
Pierre Mondou
Doug Risebrough
Guy Lafleur
Keith Acton
Mario Tremblay
Rod Langway
Larry Robinson
Mark Hunter
Doug Jarvis
Steve Shutt
Bob Gainey
Robert Picard
Craig Laughlin
Mark Napier
Richard Sevigny
11 Rockies 1.50 4.00
Brent Ashton
Dave Cameron
Joe Cirella
Dwight Foster
Mike Kitchen
Don Lever
Bob Lorimer
Bob MacMillan
Merlin Malinowski
Kevin Maxwell
Joe Micheletti
Joe Micheletti
Bobby Miller
Glenn Resch
Steve Tambellini
John Wensink
12 Islanders 3.00 8.00
Mike McEwen
Tomas Jonsson
Denis Potvin
Ken Morrow
Stefan Persson
Clark Gillies
Wayne Merrick
Bob Bourne
Bryan Trottier
Mike Bossy
Bob Nystrom
Dave Langevin
John Tonelli
Anders Kallur
Billy Smith
Butch Goring
13 Rangers 1.50 4.00
Tom Laidlaw
Barry Beck
Ron Greschner
Steve Vickers
Ron Duguay
Don Maloney
Mike Allison
Ed Johnstone
Nick Fotiu
Dave Maloney
Mike Rogers
Reijo Ruotsalainen
Steve Weeks
Andre Dore
Robbie Ftorek
Mark Pavelich
14 Flyers 2.50 6.00
Behn Wilson
Fred Arthur
Bill Barber
Brad Marsh
Reid Bailey
Darryl Sittler
Tim Kerr
Kenny Linseman
Bobby Clarke
Paul Holmgren
Jimmy Watson
Ilkka Sinisalo
Brian Propp
Reggie Leach
Glen Cochrane
Pete Peeters
15 Penguins 1.50 4.00
Pat Price
Ron Stackhouse
Paul Baxter
Peter Lee
George Ferguson
Greg Malone
Doug Shedden
Pat Boutette
Marc Chorney
Rick Kehoe
Gregg Sheppard
Paul Gardner
Mike Bullard
Pat Graham
Randy Carlyle
Michel Dion
16 Nordiques 2.00 5.00
John Garrett
Wally Weir
Normand Rochefort
Marc Tardif
Real Cloutier
Jere Gillis
Michel Goulet
Marian Stastny
Alain Cote
Anton Stastny
Mario Marois
Jacques Richard
Peter Stastny
Wilf Paiement
Andre Dupont
Dale Hunter
17 Blues 1.50 4.00
Mike Liut
Guy Lapointe
Larry Patey
Perry Turnbull
Wayne Babych
Brian Sutter
Jack Brownschidle
Ed Kea
Rick Lapointe
Blake Dunlop
Mike Zuke
Jorgen Pettersson
Bernie Federko
Bill Baker
Mike Crombeen
Jim Payese
18 Maple Leafs 2.00 5.00
Michel Larocque
Bob Manno
Bob McGill
Rocky Saganiuk
John Anderson
Fred Boimistruck
Walt Poddubny
Miroslav Frycer
Jim Benning
Stewart Gavin
Bill Derlago
Borje Salming
Rick Vaive
Normand Aubin
Terry Martin
Barry Melrose
19 Canucks 1.50 4.00
Doug Halward
Gary Lupul
Ivan Boldirev
Stan Smyl
Lars Lindgren
Darcy Rota
Ron Delorme
Ivan Hlinka
Tiger Williams
Thomas Gradin
Curt Fraser
Kevin McCarthy
Lars Molin
Harold Snepsts
Marc Crawford
Richard Brodeur
20 Capitals 2.00 5.00
Doug Hicks
Randy Holt
Rick Green
Darren Veitch
Ryan Walter
Bob Carpenter
Mike Gartner
Glen Currie
Gaetan Duchesne
Bengt Gustafsson
Greg Theberge
Dennis Maruk
Bob Gould
Terry Murray
Chris Valentine
Al Jensen
21 Jets 2.00 5.00
Bryan Maxwell
Tim Watters
Dale Hawerchuk
Scott Arniel
Morris Lukowich
Dave Christian
Tim Trimper
Paul MacLean
Serge Savard
Willy Lindstrom
Bengt Lundholm
Lucien DeBlois
Don Spring
Norm Dupont
Ed Staniowski
Dave Babych

1994-95 Post Box Backs

This set of 25 jumbo player cards was issued one per box on the backs of Post Honeycomb and Sugar-Crisp and Alpha-Bits cereals sold in Canada. Each jumbo card measures 8 3/4" by 12 1/4". Inside the box was information on a mail-in offer whereby the collector could receive a complete set by mailing in 4 UPC symbols and 8.00. The offer was valid while supplies lasted, and in no event extended beyond September 30, 1995. The fronts feature posed color photos framed by a black-and-red border design. The player's name and his number are printed vertically along the lower left edge, while the team's city is printed beneath the picture. On a ghosted version of the front photo, the bilingual backs present biography, statistics, and player profile. The prices below are for cut backs; complete, unopened cereal boxes sell for a premium of about two times the prices listed below. The box backs are unnumbered and checklisted below in alphabetical order.

COMPLETE SET (25) 16.00 40.00
1 Tony Amonte .75 2.00
Chicago Bla
2 Jason Arnott .60 1.50
Edmonton O
3 Ray Bourque 1.25 3.00
Boston
4 Martin Brodeur 1.25 3.00
New Jers
5 Pavel Bure 1.25 3.00
Vancouver Ca
6 Chris Chelios .75 2.00
Chicago B
7 Geoff Courtnall .60 1.50
Vancouv
8 Russ Courtnall .60 1.50
Dallas S
9 Steve Duchesne .60 1.50
St. Loui
10 Sergei Fedorov 1.25 3.00
Detroit
11 Theo Fleury .75 2.00
Calgary
12 Doug Gilmour .75 2.00
Toronto Ma
13 Wayne Gretzky 4.00 10.00
Los Angel
14 Jari Kurri .60 1.50
Los Angeles
15 Eric Lindros 1.25 3.00
Philadelph
16 Marty McSorley .60 1.50
Los Ange
17 Alexander Mogilny .60 1.50
Buffa
18 Kirk Muller .60 1.50
Montreal Ca
19 Rob Niedermayer .60 1.50
20 Felix Potvin .75 2.00
Toronto Ma
21 Luc Robitaille .75 2.00
Pittsbur
22 Joe Sakic 1.50 4.00
Quebec Nordiq
23 Teemu Selanne 1.25 3.00
Winnipeg
24 Alexei Yashin .60 1.50
Ottawa Se
25 Title Card .40 1.00

1995-96 Post Upper Deck

This 24-card set features color action photos on the front with the player's name in a black bar at the top. The backs carry a color player portrait, biographical information, and statistics. The cards were inserted one per specially marked box of Post cereals in Canada. Collectors also could get the cards through the mail in complete set form with proofs of purchase and a small charge. These factory sets included the NNO title and checklist cards. Cards still in the original cellophane wrapper from the cereal boxes are somewhat more desirable and can carry a slight premium of up to 1.5X the basic card. There were only 500 copies of the Wayne Gretzky autographed cards randomly inserted into Post cereal boxes. Lucky collectors who found this card could call a toll-free number to have their find certified by Upper Deck. The set is considered complete without the signed card.

COMPLETE FACTORY SET (26) 14.00 35.00
COMPLETE CELLO. BOX SET (24) 20.00 50.00
1 Ray Bourque .75 2.00
2 Martin Brodeur 1.50 4.00
3 Steve Duchesne .08 .25
4 Vincent Damphousse .20 .50
5 Eric Desjardins .08 .25
6 Eric Lindros 2.00 5.00
7 Joe Juneau .20 .50
8 Luc Robitaille .20 .50
9 Mark Recchi .20 .50
10 Patrick Roy 3.00 8.00
11 Brendan Shanahan 1.25 3.00
12 Scott Stevens .08 .25
13 Jason Arnott .20 .50
14 Trevor Linden .08 .25
15 Chris Chelios .60 1.50
16 Paul Coffey .60 1.50
17 Wayne Gretzky 4.00 10.00
18 Doug Gilmour .60 1.50
19 Kelly Hrudey .08 .25
20 Paul Kariya 2.50 6.00
21 Larry Murphy .08 .25
22 Felix Potvin .75 2.00
23 Keith Tkachuk .60 1.50
24 Rob Blake .08 .25
AU17 Wayne Gretzky AUTO (500) 200.00 400.00
NNO Title card .08 .25
NNO Checklist .08 .25

1996-97 Post Upper Deck

This 24-card set marks the third consecutive season for Post's collaboration with the NHLPA, and second with Upper Deck. The cards feature action photography on the fronts, with all players pictured in NHLPA togs. The cards were issued one per specially marked box of Post Cereals during the mid-part of the '96-97 season. Unlike the '95-96 product, these cards were actually inserted into the cereal bag itself, making theft from stores more difficult. Because this factor was negated, fewer complete sets hit the market, hence the slightly higher values. The player's name and the logos of Upper Deck and Post also are prominently featured, the latter in the blue or purple border which defines the right side of the card. The backs are noteworthy for including a childhood photo of the player, as well as '95-96 and career totals. The cards are unnumbered, and are listed below in alphabetical order.

COMPLETE SET (24) 18.00 45.00
1 Ray Bourque .50 1.25
2 Chris Chelios .30 .75
3 Paul Coffey .30 .75
4 Vincent Damphousse .25 .60
5 Steve Duchesne .20 .50
6 Theo Fleury .60 1.50
7 Doug Gilmour .40 1.00
8 Wayne Gretzky 1.50 4.00
9 Curtis Joseph .30 .75
10 Ed Jovanovski .25 .60
11 Paul Kariya .40 1.00
12 Eric Lindros .50 1.25
13 Al MacInnis .30 .75
14 Felix Potvin .30 .75
15 Mark Recchi .40 1.00
16 Luc Robitaille .30 .75
17 Jeremy Roenick .50 1.25
18 Patrick Roy .75 2.00
19 Joe Sakic .50 1.25
20 Mathieu Schneider .20 .50
21 Brendan Shanahan .40 1.00
22 Scott Stevens .30 .75
23 John Vanbiesbrouck .30 .75
24 Alexei Yashin .25 .60

1997 Post Pinnacle

Card fronts feature full color photos on the front with jersey number and their country of origin flag also prominently displayed. Backs feature biographical information and 96-97 season stats.

COMPLETE SET (24) 12.00 30.00
1 Eric Lindros 1.00 2.50
2 Patrick Roy 1.50 4.00
3 Joe Sakic .60 1.50
4 Brian Leetch .30 .75
5 Mark Messier .40 1.00
6 Jason Arnott .25 .60
7 Paul Kariya 1.25 3.00
8 Martin Brodeur .75 2.00
9 Vincent Damphousse .25 .60
10 Steve Yzerman 1.00 2.50
11 Brett Hull .40 1.00
12 Chris Chelios .30 .75
13 Sergei Fedorov .60 1.50
14 Nicklas Lidstrom .25 .60
15 Sergei Berezin .15 .40
16 Dominik Hasek .60 1.50
17 Pavel Bure .75 2.00
18 Saku Koivu .30 .75
19 Teemu Selanne .60 1.50
20 Peter Forsberg .75 2.00
21 Jaromir Jagr 1.00 2.50
22 Peter Bondra .30 .75
23 Alexei Yashin .15 .40
24 Slava Fetisov .15 .40
NNO Eric Lindros AUTO/888 25.00 50.00

1998-99 Post

1 Wayne Gretzky 2.00 5.00
2 Martin Brodeur .75 2.00
3 Joe Nieuwendyk .20 .50
4 Rick Tocchet .20 .50
5 Theoren Fleury .20 .50
6 Adam Oates .20 .50
7 Mark Recchi .20 .50
8 Eric Lindros .30 .75
9 Steve Yzerman 1.00 2.50
10 Wade Redden .20 .50
11 Glen Murray .20 .50
12 Mike Johnson .20 .50
13 Kelly Buchberger .20 .50
14 Joe Sakic .75 2.00
15 Mark Messier .40 1.00
16 Keith Primeau .20 .50
17 Mike Vernon .20 .50
18 Chris Pronger .20 .50
19 Mike Peca .20 .50
20 Dave Gagner .20 .50
21 Rob Zamuner .20 .50
22 Doug Gilmour .40 1.00
G1 Wayne Gretzky 2.00 5.00
G2 Wayne Gretzky 2.00 5.00
G3 Wayne Gretzky 2.00 5.00
G4 Wayne Gretzky 2.00 5.00
G5 Wayne Gretzky 2.00 5.00
G6 Wayne Gretzky 2.00 5.00

1999-00 Post Wayne Gretzky

These cards were included one per specially marked box of Post Cereals in Canada. The cards were wrapped in cellophane and often sell for slightly less if removed from that original packaging.

COMPLETE SET (14) 12.00 30.00
COMMON CARD (1-14) 1.25 3.00

2012-13 Post Cereal CHL Goalies

COMPLETE SET (24)
1 Jordan Binnington
2 Corbin Boes
3 Francois Brassard
4 Laurent Brossoit
5 Eric Comrie
6 Jordon Cooke
7 Andrew D'Agostini
8 Chris Driedger
9 Zachary Fucale
10 John Gibson
11 Domenic Graham
12 Robin Gusse
13 Maxime Lagace
14 Matt Mahalak
15 Andrey Makarov
16 Etienne Marcoux
17 Matt Murray .50 1.25
18 Jake Paterson
19 Mackenzie Skapski
20 Garret Sparks .75 2.00
21 Malcolm Subban
22 Francois Tremblay
23 Brandon Whitney

2013-14 Post Cereal CHL

COMPLETE SET (24) 8.00 20.00
1 Madison Bowey .50 1.25
2 William Carrier .40 1.00
3 Laurent Dauphin .30 .75
4 Jean-Sebastien Dea .40 1.00
5 Mathew Dumba .50 1.25
6 Aaron Ekblad 1.00 2.50
7 Adam Erne .50 1.25
8 Brendan Gaunce .40 1.00
9 Frederik Gauthier .50 1.25
10 Bo Horvat 1.00 2.50
11 Morgan Klimchuk .40 1.00
12 Curtis Lazar .60 1.50
13 Connor McDavid 5.00 12.00
14 Sean Monahan .75 2.00
15 Josh Morrissey .40 1.00
16 Darnell Nurse .50 1.25
17 Marc-Olivier Roy .50 1.25
18 Gabryel Paquin-Boudreau .40 1.00
19 Emile Poirier .50 1.25
20 Derrick Pouliot .60 1.50
21 Ryan Pulock .50 1.25
22 Nick Ritchie .50 1.25
23 Hunter Shinkaruk .60 1.50
24 Tom Wilson .75 2.00

2014-15 Post Cereal CHL

COMPLETE SET (24) 8.00 20.00
1 Aaron Ekblad 2.00 5.00
2 Alexis Vanier .30 .75
3 Anthony DeLuca .40 1.00
4 Brayden Point .50 1.25
5 Brendan Perlini .75 2.00
6 Brycen Martin .50 1.25
7 Connor McDavid 4.00 10.00
8 Daniel Sprong .75 2.00
9 Haydn Fleury .50 1.25
10 Ivan Barbashev .50 1.25
11 Jake Virtanen .60 1.50
12 Jayce Hawryluk .30 .75
13 Jeremy Roy .50 1.25
14 Joe Hicketts .40 1.00
15 Josh Ho-Sang .60 1.50
16 Michael Dal Colle .60 1.50
17 Nathan Noel .60 1.50
18 Nicolas Petan .50 1.25
19 Nicolas Roy .50 1.25
20 Nikolaj Ehlers 1.00 2.50
21 Sam Bennett .75 2.00
22 Spencer Martin .60 1.50
23 Travis Konecny .75 2.00
24 Tristan Jarry .40 1.00

1993-94 PowerPlay

This 520-card set measures 2 1/2" by 4 3/4". The fronts feature color action shots set within a blended team-colored border. The team name and the player's name appear in team-colored lettering below the photo. The backs carry color player photos at the upper left. The player's name appears above; his number, position, and a short biography are displayed alongside. Statistics are shown below. The cards are checklisted alphabetically according to teams. Rookie Cards include Jason Arnott, Chris Osgood, Damian Rhodes, and Jocelyn Thibault.

1 Stu Grimson .05 .15
2 Guy Hebert .07 .20
3 Sean Hill .05 .15
4 Bill Houlder .05 .15
5 Alexei Kasatonov .05 .15
6 Steven King .05 .15
7 Lonnie Loach .05 .15
8 Troy Loney .05 .15
9 Joe Sacco .05 .15
10 Anatoli Semenov .05 .15
11 Jarrod Skalde .05 .15
12 Tim Sweeney .05 .15
13 Ron Tugnutt .07 .20
14 Terry Yake .05 .15
15 Shaun Van Allen .05 .15
16 Ray Bourque .15 .40
17 Jon Casey .07 .20
18 Ted Donato .05 .15
19 Joe Juneau .07 .20
20 Dmitri Kvartalnov .05 .15
21 Steve Leach .05 .15
22 Cam Neely .10 .25
23 Adam Oates .10 .25
24 Don Sweeney .05 .15
25 Glen Wesley .05 .15
26 Doug Bodger .05 .15
27 Grant Fuhr .10 .25
28 Viktor Gordiouk .05 .15
29 Dale Hawerchuk .12 .30
30 Yuri Khmylev .05 .15
31 Pat LaFontaine .10 .25
32 Alexander Mogilny .07 .20
33 Richard Smehlik .05 .15
34 Bob Sweeney .05 .15
35 Randy Wood .05 .15
36 Theo Fleury .05 .15
37 Kelly Kisio .05 .15
38 Al MacInnis .07 .20
39 Joe Nieuwendyk .07 .20
40 Joel Otto .05 .15
41 Robert Reichel .05 .15
42 Gary Roberts .05 .15
43 Ronnie Stern .05 .15
44 Gary Suter .05 .15
45 Mike Vernon .07 .20
46 Ed Belfour .10 .25
47 Chris Chelios .10 .25
48 Karl Dykhuis .05 .15
49 Michel Goulet .05 .15
50 Dirk Graham .05 .15
51 Sergei Krivokrasov .05 .15
52 Steve Larmer .07 .20
53 Joe Murphy .05 .15
54 Jeremy Roenick .15 .40
55 Steve Smith .05 .15
56 Brent Sutter .05 .15
57 Neal Broten .07 .20
58 Russ Courtnall .05 .15
59 Ulf Dahlen .05 .15
60 Dave Gagner .07 .20
61 Derian Hatcher .05 .15
62 Trent Klatt .05 .15
63 Mike Modano .15 .40
64 Andy Moog .10 .25
65 Tommy Sjodin .05 .15
66 Mark Tinordi .05 .15
67 Tim Cheveldae .07 .20
68 Steve Chiasson .05 .15
69 Dino Ciccarelli .07 .20
70 Paul Coffey .10 .25
71 Dallas Drake RC .10 .25
72 Sergei Fedorov .15 .40
73 Vladimir Konstantinov .07 .20
74 Nicklas Lidstrom .10 .25
75 Keith Primeau .05 .15
76 Ray Sheppard .07 .20
77 Steve Yzerman .25 .60
78 Zdeno Ciger .05 .15
79 Shayne Corson .05 .15
80 Todd Elik .05 .15
81 Igor Kravchuk .05 .15
82 Craig MacTavish .05 .15
83 Dave Manson .05 .15
84 Shjon Podein RC .10 .25
85 Bill Ranford .07 .20
86 Steven Rice .05 .15
87 Doug Weight .07 .20
88 Doug Barrault RC .05 .15
89 Jesse Belanger .05 .15
90 Brian Benning .05 .15
91 Joe Cirella .05 .15
92 Mark Fitzpatrick .05 .15
93 Randy Gilhen .05 .15
94 Mike Hough .05 .15
95 Bill Lindsay .05 .15
96 Andrei Lomakin .05 .15
97 Dave Lowry .05 .15
98 Scott Mellanby .07 .20
99 Gord Murphy .05 .15
100 Brian Skrudland .05 .15
101 Milan Tichy RC .05 .15
102 John Vanbiesbrouck .07 .20
103 Sean Burke .05 .15
104 Andrew Cassels .05 .15
105 Nick Kypreos .05 .15
106 Michael Nylander .05 .15
107 Robert Petrovicky .05 .15
108 Patrick Poulin .05 .15
109 Geoff Sanderson .07 .20
110 Pat Verbeek .05 .15
111 Eric Weinrich .05 .15
112 Zarley Zalapski .05 .15
113 Rob Blake .07 .20
114 Jimmy Carson .05 .15
115 Tony Granato .05 .15
116 Wayne Gretzky .50 1.25
117 Kelly Hrudey .07 .20
118 Jari Kurri .10 .25
119 Shawn McEachern .05 .15
120 Luc Robitaille .07 .20
121 Tomas Sandstrom .05 .15
122 Darryl Sydor .05 .15
123 Alexei Zhitnik .05 .15
124 Brian Bellows .07 .20
125 Patrice Brisebois .05 .15
126 Guy Carbonneau .05 .15
127 Vincent Damphousse .07 .20
128 Eric Desjardins .07 .20
129 Mike Keane .05 .15
130 Stephan Lebeau .05 .15
131 Kirk Muller .05 .15
132 Lyle Odelein .05 .15
133 Patrick Roy .25 .60
134 Mathieu Schneider .05 .15
135 Bruce Driver .05 .15
136 Slava Fetisov .05 .15
137 Claude Lemieux .05 .15
138 John MacLean .07 .20
139 Bernie Nicholls .05 .15
140 Scott Niedermayer .10 .25
141 Stephane Richer .07 .20
142 Alexander Semak .05 .15
143 Scott Stevens .10 .25
144 Chris Terreri .07 .20
145 Valeri Zelepukin .05 .15
146 Patrick Flatley .05 .15
147 Ron Hextall .07 .20
148 Benoit Hogue .05 .15
149 Darius Kasparaitis .05 .15
150 Derek King .05 .15
151 Uwe Krupp .05 .15
152 Scott Lachance .05 .15
153 Vladimir Malakhov .05 .15
154 Steve Thomas .05 .15
155 Pierre Turgeon .07 .20
156 Tony Amonte .07 .20
157 Mike Gartner .07 .20
158 Adam Graves .05 .15
159 Alexei Kovalev .07 .20
160 Brian Leetch .10 .25
161 Joby Messier RC .10 .25
162 Mark Messier .10 .25
163 Sergei Nemchinov .05 .15
164 James Patrick .05 .15
165 Mike Richter .10 .25
166 Darren Turcotte .05 .15
167 Sergei Zubov .05 .15
168 Dave Archibald .05 .15
169 Craig Billington .07 .20
170 Bob Kudelski .05 .15
171 Mark Lamb .05 .15
172 Norm Maciver .05 .15
173 Darren Rumble .05 .15
174 Vladimir Ruzicka .05 .15
175 Brad Shaw .05 .15
176 Sylvain Turgeon .05 .15
177 Josef Beranek .05 .15
178 Rod Brind'Amour .07 .20
179 Kevin Dineen .05 .15
180 Pelle Eklund .05 .15
181 Brent Fedyk .05 .15
182 Garry Galley .05 .15
183 Eric Lindros .30 .75
184 Mark Recchi .12 .30
185 Tommy Soderstrom .07 .20
186 Dimitri Yushkevich .05 .15
187 Tom Barrasso .07 .20
188 Ron Francis .12 .30
189 Jaromir Jagr .25 .60
190 Mario Lemieux .40 1.00
191 Marty McSorley .05 .15
192 Joe Mullen .07 .20
193 Larry Murphy .07 .20
194 Ulf Samuelsson .05 .15
195 Kevin Stevens .05 .15
196 Rick Tocchet .07 .20
197 Steve Duchesne .05 .15
198 Stephane Fiset .07 .20
199 Valeri Kamensky .07 .20
200 Andrei Kovalenko .05 .15
201 Owen Nolan .07 .20
202 Mike Ricci .05 .15
203 Martin Rucinsky .05 .15
204 Joe Sakic .25 .60
205 Mats Sundin .07 .20
206 Scott Young .05 .15
207 Jeff Brown .05 .15
208 Garth Butcher .05 .15
209 Nelson Emerson .05 .15
210 Bret Hedican .05 .15
211 Brett Hull .15 .40
212 Craig Janney .07 .20
213 Curtis Joseph .10 .25
214 Igor Korolev .05 .15
215 Kevin Miller .05 .15
216 Brendan Shanahan .12 .30
217 Ed Courtenay .05 .15
218 Pat Falloon .05 .15
219 Johan Garpenlov .05 .15
220 Rob Gaudreau RC .10 .25
221 Arturs Irbe .07 .20
222 Sergei Makarov .05 .15
223 Jeff Norton .05 .15
224 Jeff Odgers .05 .15
225 Sandis Ozolinsh .05 .15
226 Tom Pederson .05 .15
227 Bob Beers .05 .15
228 Brian Bradley .05 .15
229 Shawn Chambers .05 .15
230 Gerard Gallant .05 .15
231 Roman Hamrlik .05 .15
232 Petr Klima .05 .15
233 Chris Kontos .05 .15
234 Daren Puppa .05 .15
235 John Tucker .05 .15
236 Rob Zamuner .05 .15
237 Glenn Anderson .10 .25
238 Dave Andreychuk .10 .25
239 Drake Berehowsky .05 .15
240 Nikolai Borschevsky .05 .15
241 Wendel Clark .07 .20
242 John Cullen .05 .15
243 Dave Ellett .05 .15
244 Doug Gilmour .12 .30
245 Dimitri Mironov .05 .15
246 Felix Potvin .20 .50
247 Greg Adams .05 .15
248 Pavel Bure .10 .25
249 Geoff Courtnall .05 .15
250 Gerald Diduck .05 .15
251 Trevor Linden .07 .20
252 Jyrki Lumme .05 .15
253 Kirk McLean .07 .20
254 Petr Nedved .05 .15
255 Cliff Ronning .05 .15
256 Jiri Slegr .05 .15
257 Dixon Ward .05 .15
258 Peter Bondra .07 .20
259 Sylvain Cote .05 .15
260 Pat Elynuik .05 .15
261 Kevin Hatcher .05 .15
262 Dale Hunter .05 .15
263 Al Iafrate .05 .15
264 Dimitri Khristich .05 .15
265 Michal Pivonka .05 .15
266 Mike Ridley .05 .15
267 Rick Tabaracci .05 .15
268 Sergei Bautin .05 .15
269 Evgeny Davydov .05 .15
270 Bob Essensa .07 .20
271 Phil Housley .07 .20
272 Teppo Numminen .05 .15
273 Fredrik Olausson .05 .15
274 Teemu Selanne .20 .50
275 Thomas Steen .05 .15
276 Keith Tkachuk .10 .25
277 Paul Ysebaert .05 .15
278 Alexei Zhamnov .07 .20
279 Checklist .05 .15
280 Checklist .05 .15
281 Patrick Carnback RC .10 .25
282 Bob Corkum .05 .15
283 Bobby Dollas .05 .15
284 Peter Douris .05 .15
285 Todd Ewen .05 .15
286 Garry Valk .05 .15
287 John Blue .07 .20
288 Glen Featherstone .05 .15
289 Steve Heinze .05 .15
290 David Reid .05 .15
291 Bryan Smolinski .05 .15
292 Cam Stewart RC .10 .25
293 Jozef Stumpel .05 .15
294 Sergei Zholtok .05 .15
295 Donald Audette .05 .15
296 Philippe Boucher .05 .15
297 Dominik Hasek .20 .50
298 Brad May .07 .20
299 Craig Muni .05 .15
300 Derek Plante RC .10 .25
301 Craig Simpson .05 .15
302 Scott Thomas RC .10 .25
303 Ted Drury .05 .15
304 Dan Keczmer RC .05 .15
305 Trevor Kidd .07 .20
306 Sandy McCarthy .05 .15
307 Frank Musil .05 .15
308 Michel Petit .05 .15
309 Paul Ranheim .05 .15
310 German Titov RC .10 .25
311 Andrei Trefilov .05 .15
312 Jeff Hackett .05 .15
313 Stephane Matteau .05 .15
314 Brian Noonan .05 .15
315 Patrick Poulin .05 .15
316 Jeff Shantz RC .05 .15
317 Rich Sutter .05 .15
318 Kevin Todd .05 .15
319 Eric Weinrich .05 .15
320 Dave Barr .05 .15
321 Paul Cavallini .05 .15
322 Mike Craig .05 .15
323 Dean Evason .05 .15
324 Brent Gilchrist .05 .15
325 Grant Ledyard .05 .15
326 Mike McPhee .05 .15
327 Darcy Wakaluk .05 .15
328 Terry Carkner .05 .15
329 Mark Howe .10 .25
330 Greg Johnson .05 .15
331 Slava Kozlov .07 .20
332 Martin Lapointe .05 .15
333 Darren McCarty RC .15 .40
334 Chris Osgood RC .60 1.50
335 Bob Probert .07 .20
336 Mike Sillinger .05 .15
337 Jason Arnott RC .20 .50
338 Bob Beers .05 .15
339 Fred Brathwaite RC .10 .25
340 Kelly Buchberger .05 .15
341 Ilya Byakin RC .05 .15
342 Fredrik Olausson .05 .15
343 Vladimir Vujtek .05 .15
344 Peter White RC .05 .15
345 Stu Barnes .05 .15
346 Mike Foligno .05 .15
347 Greg Hawgood .05 .15
348 Bob Kudelski .05 .15
349 Rob Niedermayer .07 .20
350 Igor Chibirev RC .05 .15
351 Robert Kron .05 .15
352 Bryan Marchment .05 .15
353 James Patrick .05 .15
354 Chris Pronger .10 .25
355 Jeff Reese .05 .15
356 Jim Storm RC .05 .15
357 Darren Turcotte .05 .15
358 Pat Conacher .05 .15
359 Mike Donnelly .05 .15
360 John Druce .05 .15
361 Charlie Huddy .05 .15
362 Warren Rychel .05 .15
363 Robb Stauber .05 .15
364 Dave Taylor .05 .15
365 Dixon Ward .05 .15
366 Benoit Brunet .05 .15
367 J.J. Daigneault .05 .15
368 Gilbert Dionne .05 .15
369 Paul DiPietro .05 .15
370 Kevin Haller .05 .15
371 Oleg Petrov .05 .15
372 Peter Popovic RC .10 .25
373 Ron Wilson .05 .15
374 Martin Brodeur .25 .60
375 Tom Chorske .05 .15
376 Jim Dowd RC .10 .25
377 David Emma .05 .15
378 Bobby Holik .05 .15
379 Corey Millen .05 .15
380 Jaroslav Modry RC .10 .25
381 Jason Smith RC .05 .15

482 Ray Ferraro .05 .15
483 Travis Green .07 .20
484 Tom Kurvers .05 .15
485 Marty McInnis .05 .15
486 Jamie McLennan RC .05 .15
487 Dennis Vaske .05 .15
488 Dave Volek .05 .15
489 Jeff Beukeboom .05 .15
490 Glenn Healy .07 .20
491 Alexander Karpovtsev .05 .15
492 Steve Larmer .07 .20
493 Kevin Lowe .05 .15
494 Ed Olczyk .05 .15
495 Esa Tikkanen .05 .15
496 Alexandre Daigle .05 .15
497 Evgeny Davydov .05 .15
498 Dmitri Filimonov .05 .15
499 Brian Glynn .05 .15
400 Darrin Madeley RC .10 .25
401 Troy Mallette .05 .15
402 Dave McLlwain .05 .15
403 Alexei Yashin .07 .20
404 Jason Bowen RC .10 .25
405 Jeff Finley .05 .15
406 Yves Racine .05 .15
407 Rob Ramage .05 .15
408 Mikael Renberg .10 .25
409 Dominic Roussel .07 .20
410 Dave Tippett .05 .15
411 Doug Brown .05 .15
412 Markus Naslund .10 .25
413 Pat Neaton RC .10 .25
414 Kjell Samuelsson .05 .15
415 Martin Straka .05 .15
416 Bryan Trottier .12 .30
417 Ken Wregget .05 .15
418 Adam Foote .05 .15
419 Iain Fraser RC .10 .25
420 Alexei Gusarov .05 .15
421 Dave Karpa .05 .15
422 Claude Lapointe .05 .15
423 Curtis Leschyshyn .05 .15
424 Mike McKee RC .05 .15
425 Garth Snow RC .05 .15
426 Jocelyn Thibault RC .10 .25
427 Phil Housley .07 .20
428 Jim Hrivnak .05 .15
429 Vitali Karamnov .05 .15
430 Basil McRae .05 .20
431 Jim Montgomery RC .10 .25
432 Vitali Prokhorov .05 .15
433 Gaetan Duchesne .05 .15
434 Todd Elik .05 .15
435 Bob Errey .05 .15
436 Igor Larionov .05 .15
437 Mike Rathje .05 .15
438 Jim Waite .07 .20
439 Ray Whitney .05 .15
440 Mikael Anderson .05 .15
441 Danton Cole .05 .15
442 Pat Elynuik .05 .15
443 Chris Gratton .07 .20
444 Pat Jablonski .05 .15
445 Chris Joseph .05 .15
446 Chris LiPuma RC .05 .15
447 Denis Savard .12 .30
448 Ken Baumgartner .05 .15
449 Todd Gill .05 .15
450 Sylvain Lefebvre .05 .15
451 Jamie Macoun .05 .15
452 Mark Osborne .05 .15
453 Rob Pearson .05 .15
454 Damian Rhodes RC .10 .25
455 Peter Zezel .05 .15
456 Dave Babych .05 .15
457 Jose Charbonneau RC .10 .25
458 Murray Craven .05 .15
459 Neil Eisenhut RC .10 .25
460 Dan Kesa RC .10 .25
461 Gino Odjick .05 .15
462 Kay Whitmore .05 .15
463 Don Beaupre .07 .20
464 Randy Burridge .05 .15
465 Calle Johansson .05 .15
466 Keith Jones .05 .15
467 Todd Krygier .05 .15
468 Kelly Miller .05 .15
469 Pat Peake .05 .15
470 Dave Poulin .05 .15
471 Luciano Borsato .05 .15
472 Nelson Emerson .05 .15
473 Randy Gilhen .05 .15
474 Boris Mironov .05 .15
475 Stephane Quintal .05 .15
476 Thomas Steen .05 .15
477 Igor Ulanov .07 .20
478 Adrian Aucoin RC .10 .25
479 Todd Brost RC .10 .25
480 Martin Gendron RC .07 .20
481 David Harlock .07 .20
482 Corey Hirsch .07 .20
483 Todd Hlushko RC .07 .20
484 Fabian Joseph RC .07 .20
485 Paul Kariya .40 1.00
486 Brett Lindros RC .15 .40
487 Ken Lovsin RC .07 .20
488 Jason Marshall .07 .20
489 Derek Mayer RC .05 .15
490 Petr Nedved .05 .15
491 Dwayne Norris RC .05 .15
492 Russ Romaniuk .05 .15
493 Brian Savage RC .10 .25
494 Trevor Sim RC .10 .25
495 Chris Therien RC .10 .25
496 Todd Warriner RC .10 .25
497 Craig Woodcroft RC .10 .25
498 Mark Beaufait RC .10 .25
499 Jim Campbell .07 .20
500 Ted Crowley RC .10 .25
501 Mike Dunham .07 .20
502 Chris Ferraro RC .07 .20
503 Peter Ferraro .07 .20
504 Brett Hauer RC .07 .20
505 Darby Hendrickson RC .07 .20
506 Chris Imes RC .07 .20
507 Craig Johnson RC .07 .20
508 Peter Lavinlette RC .07 .20
509 Jeff Lazaro .07 .20
510 John Lilley RC .07 .20
511 Todd Marchant .07 .20
512 Ian Moran RC .07 .20
513 Travis Richards RC .07 .20
514 Barry Richter RC .07 .20
515 David Roberts RC .07 .20
516 Brian Rolston .07 .20
517 David Sacco RC .07 .20
518 Checklist .05 .15
519 Checklist .05 .15
520 Checklist .05 .15

1993-94 PowerPlay Gamebreakers

Randomly inserted in series two packs at 1:4, this ten-card set measures 2 1/2" by 4 3/4". The fronts feature color action cutouts on a borderless marbleized background. The player's name in gold foil appears at the lower right, while the word "Gamebreakers" is printed vertically in pastel-colored lettering on the left side. On the same marbleized background, the backs carry another color photo, with the player's name displayed above and career highlights shown below. The cards are numbered on the back as "X of 10."

COMPLETE SET (10) 10.00 20.00
1 Sergei Fedorov .60 1.50
2 Doug Gilmour .20 .50
3 Wayne Gretzky 2.50 6.00
4 Curtis Joseph .40 1.00
5 Mario Lemieux 2.00 5.00
6 Eric Lindros .40 1.00
7 Felix Potvin .40 1.00
8 Jeremy Roenick .50 1.25
9 Patrick Roy 2.00 5.00
10 Steve Yzerman 2.00 5.00

1993-94 PowerPlay Global Greats

Randomly inserted in series two packs at 1:4, this 10-card set measures 2 1/2" by 4 3/4". The borderless fronts feature color action cutouts superimposed on the player's national flag. The player's name and the Global Greats logo in gold foil appear at the bottom. On the same national flag background, the backs carry another color photo with the player's name above and career highlights below. The cards are numbered on the back as "X of 10."

COMPLETE SET (10) 3.00 8.00
1 Pavel Bure .50 1.25
2 Sergei Fedorov .50 1.25
3 Jaromir Jagr .75 2.00
4 Jari Kurri .40 1.00
5 Alexander Mogilny .25 .60
6 Mikael Renberg .10 .30
7 Teemu Selanne .50 1.25
8 Mats Sundin .50 1.25
9 Esa Tikkanen .10 .30
10 Alexei Yashin .10 .30

1993-94 PowerPlay Netminders

Randomly inserted at a rate of 1:8 series one packs, this eight-card set measures 2 1/2" by 4 3/4". On a blue marbleized background, the fronts feature color action photos with the goalie's name in blue-foil lettering under the photo.

COMPLETE SET (8) 10.00 25.00
1 Tom Barrasso .75 2.00
2 Ed Belfour 1.50 4.00
3 Grant Fuhr .75 2.00
4 Curtis Joseph 1.50 4.00
5 Felix Potvin 1.50 4.00
6 Bill Ranford .75 2.00
7 Patrick Roy 4.00 10.00
8 Tommy Soderstrom .75 2.00

1993-94 PowerPlay Point Leaders

Randomly inserted at a rate of 1:2 series one packs, this 20-card set measures 2 1/2" by 4 3/4". The yellow-bordered fronts feature color action cutouts against a yellow-tinted background. The player's name in silver foil appears under the photo. On a yellow background, the backs carry another color photo with the player's name in silver foil above the photo, and career highlights below. The cards are numbered on the back as "X of 20."

COMPLETE SET (20) 8.00 20.00
1 Pavel Bure .40 1.00
2 Doug Gilmour .20 .50
3 Wayne Gretzky 2.00 5.00
4 Brett Hull .50 1.25
5 Jaromir Jagr .60 1.50
6 Joe Juneau .10 .30
7 Pat LaFontaine .20 .50
8 Mario Lemieux 1.50 4.00
9 Mark Messier .40 1.00
10 Alexander Mogilny .20 .50
11 Adam Oates .20 .50
12 Mark Recchi .20 .50
13 Luc Robitaille .20 .50
14 Jeremy Roenick .50 1.25
15 Joe Sakic .75 2.00
16 Teemu Selanne .40 1.00
17 Kevin Stevens .10 .30
18 Mats Sundin .40 1.00
19 Pierre Turgeon .20 .50
20 Steve Yzerman 1.50 4.00

1993-94 PowerPlay Rising Stars

Randomly inserted in series two packs at 1:10, this ten-card set measures 2 1/2" by 4 3/4". Each borderless front features a color action cutout, highlighted with a yellow "aura" and yellow radial lines, set on a stellar background. The player's name and the words "Rising Star" in silver foil appear in a top corner. On a similar background, the borderless horizontal back carries another color cutout on the left, with the player's name and career highlights to the right. The cards are numbered on the back as "X of 10."

COMPLETE SET (10) 4.00 10.00
1 Arturs Irbe .30 .75
2 Slava Kozlov .30 .75
3 Felix Potvin 2.00 5.00
4 Keith Primeau .30 .75
5 Robert Reichel .30 .75
6 Geoff Sanderson .30 .75
7 Martin Straka .30 .75
8 Keith Tkachuk .75 2.00
9 Alexei Zhamnov .30 .75
10 Sergei Zubov .40 1.00

1993-94 PowerPlay Rookie Standouts

Randomly inserted in series two packs at 1:5, this 16-card set measures 2 1/2" by 4 3/4". The borderless fronts feature color player action shots on grainy and ghosted backgrounds. The player's name and the words "Rookie Standouts" in gold foil are printed atop ghosted bars to the right of the player. The cards are numbered on the back as "X of 16."

COMPLETE SET (16) 3.00 8.00
1 Jason Arnott .40 1.00
2 Jesse Belanger .10 .30
3 Alexandre Daigle .10 .30
4 Iain Fraser .10 .30
5 Chris Gratton .10 .30
6 Boris Mironov .10 .30
7 Jaroslav Modry .10 .30
8 Rob Niedermayer .25 .60
9 Chris Osgood .75 2.00
10 Pat Peake .10 .30
11 Derek Plante .10 .30
12 Chris Pronger .75 2.00
13 Mikael Renberg .10 .30
14 Bryan Smolinski .10 .30
15 Jocelyn Thibault .40 1.00
16 Alexei Yashin .10 .30

1993-94 PowerPlay Second Year Stars

Randomly inserted at a rate of 1:3 series one packs, this 12-card set measures 2 1/2" by 4 3/4". The fronts feature color action photos with light blue metallic borders. The player's name in gold foil appears on the bottom, while the words "2nd Year Stars" are printed in gold foil in an upper corner. The cards are numbered on the back as "X of 12."

COMPLETE SET (12) 6.00 12.00
1 Rob Gaudreau .10 .25
2 Joe Juneau .20 .50
3 Darius Kasparaitis .10 .25
4 Dmitri Kvartalnov .10 .25
5 Eric Lindros .60 1.50
6 Vladimir Malakhov .10 .25
7 Shawn McEachern .10 .25
8 Felix Potvin .60 1.50
9 Patrick Poulin .10 .25
10 Teemu Selanne .60 1.50
11 Tommy Soderstrom .20 .50
12 Alexei Zhamnov .20 .50

1993-94 PowerPlay Slapshot Artists

Randomly inserted in series two packs at 1:10, this ten-card set measures 2 1/2" by 4 3/4". On a team-colored tinted background, the fronts feature color action cutouts with a smaller tinted head shot in an upper corner. The player's name and the Slapshot Artist logo in gold foil appear at the bottom. The cards are numbered on the back as "X of 10."

COMPLETE SET (10) 8.00 20.00
1 Dave Andreychuk .40 1.00
2 Ray Bourque 1.50 4.00
3 Sergei Fedorov 1.25 3.00
4 Brett Hull 1.25 3.00
5 Al Iafrate .40 1.00
6 Brian Leetch .60 1.50
7 Al MacInnis .60 1.50
8 Mike Modano 1.50 4.00
9 Teemu Selanne 1.25 3.00
10 Brendan Shanahan 1.25 3.00

1998-99 Predators Team Issue

This set features the Predators of the NHL. The cards were issued on six card sheets at Nashville-area Wendy's restaurants. Each sheet featured five cards and one ad card.

COMPLETE SET (25) 8.00 20.00
1 Blair Atcheynum .30 .75
2 Drake Berehowsky .30 .75
3 Sebastien Bordeleau .30 .75
4 Joel Bouchard .30 .75
5 Bob Boughner .40 1.00
6 Andrew Brunette .40 1.00
7 Patrick Cote .40 1.00
8 Mike Dunham .75 2.00
9 Eric Fichaud .40 1.00
10 Tom Fitzgerald .30 .75
11 Jamie Heward .30 .75
12 Greg Johnson .30 .75
13 Patric Kjellberg .30 .75
14 Sergei Krivokrasov .30 .75
15 Denny Lambert .30 .75
16 Jayson More .30 .75
17 Ville Peltonen .40 1.00
18 Cliff Ronning .40 1.00
19 John Slaney .30 .75
20 Kimmo Timonen .30 .75
21 Darren Turcotte .30 .75
22 Tomas Vokoun .60 1.50
23 Jan Vopat .30 .75
24 Scott Walker .40 1.00
25 Vitali Yachmenev .30 .75

2002-03 Predators Team Issue

These oversized (8X10) blank-backed collectibles were issued by the Predators. It's believed they may have been offered as game program inserts, but that has not been confirmed. We have only listed the cards we have physically confirmed below. Any additional information regarding distribution or checklist should be sent to hockeymag@beckett.com.

COMPLETE SET
1 Brent Gilchrist 1.25 3.00
2 Scott Hartnell 2.50 6.00
3 Greg Johnson 1.50 4.00
4 Domenic Pittis 1.25 3.00
5 Kimmo Timonen 1.50 4.00
6 Vitali Yachmenev 1.25 3.00

2010-11 Prestige Player of the Day

COMPLETE SET (7) 10.00 20.00
*GOLD/160: .6X TO 1.5X BASIC CARDS
PODAO Alex Ovechkin 2.50 6.00
PODJS Jeff Skinner 1.00 2.50
PODRM Ryan Miller .60 1.50
PODSC Sidney Crosby 2.50 6.00
PODSS Steven Stamkos 1.25 3.00
PODTH Taylor Hall 2.00 5.00
PODTS Tyler Seguin 2.00 5.00

2000-01 Private Stock

Released in mid January 2001 as a 152-card set, Pacific Private Stock features 101 base card and 51 Short Prints, card numbers 101-151. Base cards feature a white background with gold highlights. SP's are sequentially numbered to 155. Private Stock came packaged with one memorabilia card per pack and carried a suggested retail price of $14.99.

COMP.SET w/o SP's (101) 25.00 50.00
101-151 SP ODDS 1:10 HOB, 1:49 RET
101-151 SP STATED PRINT RUN 155
1 Guy Hebert .15 .40
2 Paul Kariya .25 .60
3 Teemu Selanne .40 1.00
4 Ray Ferraro .12 .30
5 Damian Rhodes .12 .30
6 Patrik Stefan .15 .40
7 Byron Dafoe .15 .40
8 Sergei Samsonov .15 .40
9 Joe Thornton .30 .75
10 Maxim Afinogenov .12 .30
11 Doug Gilmour .25 .60
12 Dominik Hasek .30 .75
13 Miroslav Satan .12 .30
14 Fred Brathwaite .15 .40
15 Valeri Bure .15 .40
16 Ron Francis .25 .60
17 Arturs Irbe .15 .40
18 Sami Kapanen .12 .30
19 Tony Amonte .15 .40
20 Jocelyn Thibault .15 .40
21 Alexei Zhamnov .15 .40
22 Ray Bourque .30 .75
23 Peter Forsberg .25 .60
24 Milan Hejduk .15 .40
25 Patrick Roy .50 1.25
26 Joe Sakic .30 .75
27 Marc Denis .15 .40
28 Ted Drury .12 .30
29 Geoff Sanderson .15 .40
30 Ed Belfour .20 .50
31 Brett Hull .30 .75
32 Mike Modano .30 .75
33 Brenden Morrow .15 .40
34 Joe Nieuwendyk .20 .50
35 Sergei Fedorov .30 .75
36 Chris Osgood .20 .50
37 Brendan Shanahan .25 .60
38 Steve Yzerman .60 1.50
39 Tommy Salo .15 .40
40 Ryan Smyth .15 .40
41 Doug Weight .20 .50
42 Pavel Bure .25 .60
43 Trevor Kidd .12 .30
44 Viktor Kozlov .15 .40
45 Stephane Fiset .12 .30
46 Zigmund Palffy .20 .50
47 Luc Robitaille .20 .50
48 Manny Fernandez .15 .40
49 Sergei Krivokrasov .12 .30
50 Stacy Roest .12 .30
51 Saku Koivu .20 .50
52 Trevor Linden .20 .50
53 Jose Theodore .25 .60
54 Mike Dunham .12 .30
55 David Legwand .20 .50
56 Jason Arnott .15 .40
57 Martin Brodeur .40 1.00
58 Patrik Elias .20 .50
59 Scott Gomez .15 .40
60 Petr Sykora .15 .40
61 Tim Connolly .12 .30
62 Mariusz Czerkawski .12 .30
63 John Vanbiesbrouck .15 .40
64 Theo Fleury .25 .60
65 Brian Leetch .20 .50
66 Mark Messier .30 .75
67 Mike Richter .20 .50
68 Daniel Alfredsson .20 .50
69 Radek Bonk .15 .40
70 Marian Hossa .15 .40
71 Brian Boucher .15 .40
72 Simon Gagne .20 .50
73 John LeClair .20 .50
74 Eric Lindros .30 .75
75 Nikolai Khabibulin .30 .75
76 Jeremy Roenick .20 .50
77 Keith Tkachuk .20 .50
78 Jean-Sebastien Aubin .15 .40
79 Jan Hrdina .12 .30
80 Jaromir Jagr .50 1.25
81 Martin Straka .15 .40
82 Pavol Demitra .25 .60
83 Al MacInnis .20 .50
84 Chris Pronger .15 .40
85 Roman Turek .15 .40
86 Pierre Turgeon .20 .50
87 Vincent Damphousse .15 .40
88 Jeff Friesen .12 .30
89 Owen Nolan .20 .50
90 Dan Cloutier .15 .40
91 Vincent Lecavalier .15 .40
92 Nikolai Antropov .15 .40
93 Curtis Joseph .25 .60
94 Mats Sundin .20 .50
95 Steve Kariya .12 .30
96 Markus Naslund .15 .40
97 Felix Potvin .30 .75
98 Jeff Halpern .12 .30
99 Olaf Kolzig .20 .50
100 Adam Oates .20 .50
101 Jonas Ronnqvist RC 6.00 15.00
102 Samuel Pahlsson 2.50 6.00
103 Andrew Raycroft RC 15.00 40.00
104 Eric Boulton RC 6.00 15.00
105 Dimitri Kalinin 2.50 6.00
106 Mika Noronen 2.50 6.00
107 Oleg Saprykin 2.50 6.00
108 Josef Vasicek RC 15.00 40.00
109 Shane Willis 2.50 6.00
110 Steven McCarthy 2.50 6.00
111 David Aebischer RC 12.00 30.00
112 Serge Aubin RC 8.00 20.00
113 Rostislav Klesla RC 15.00 40.00
114 David Vyborny 2.50 6.00
115 Tyler Bouck RC 6.00 15.00
116 Richard Jackman 2.50 6.00
117 Marty Turco RC 20.00 50.00
118 Dan Lacouture 2.50 6.00
119 Brian Swanson RC 6.00 15.00
120 Denis Shvidki 2.50 6.00
121 Eric Belanger RC 8.00 20.00
122 Steven Reinprecht RC 10.00 25.00
123 Lubomir Visnovsky RC 12.00 30.00
124 Manny Fernandez 3.00 8.00
125 Marian Gaborik RC 30.00 80.00
126 Filip Kuba 2.50 6.00
127 Maxim Sushinski 2.50 6.00
128 Andrei Markov 5.00 12.00
129 Scott Hartnell RC 12.00 30.00
130 Colin White RC 6.00 15.00
131 Taylor Pyatt 2.50 6.00
132 Martin Havlat RC 30.00 60.00
133 Jani Hurme RC 6.00 15.00
134 Karel Rachunek 2.50 6.00
135 Maxime Ouellet 4.00 10.00
136 Justin Williams RC 12.00 30.00
137 Robert Esche 2.50 6.00
138 Wyatt Smith 2.50 6.00
139 Ossi Vaananen RC 8.00 20.00
140 Brent Johnson 3.00 8.00
141 Ladislav Nagy 2.50 6.00
142 Mike Van Ryn 2.50 6.00
143 Bryce Salvador RC 8.00 20.00
144 Evgeni Nabokov 3.00 8.00
145 Alexander Kharitonov RC 6.00 15.00
146 Brad Richards 4.00 10.00
147 Petr Svoboda RC 8.00 20.00
148 Daniel Sedin 8.00 20.00
149 Henrik Sedin 6.00 15.00
150 Kris Beech 2.50 6.00
151 Rick DiPietro RC 20.00 50.00
152 Mario Lemieux 2.50 6.00

2000-01 Private Stock Gold

Randomly inserted in Hobby packs, this 152-card set parallels the base set enhanced with a gold border and gold foil highlights. Each card is sequentially numbered to 75.

*1-100 VETS/75: 6X TO 15X BASIC CARDS
*101-152 SP VET/75 101-151: .5X TO 1.2X SP/155
*101-152 ROOK/75: .3X TO .8X SP RC/155
66 Mark Messier 6.00 15.00

2000-01 Private Stock Premiere Date

Randomly inserted in Hobby packs at the rate of 2:21, this 152-card set parallels the base Private Stock Set enhanced with a foil premiere date box in which cards are sequentially numbered to 60.

*1-100 VETS/60: 8X TO 20X BASIC CARDS
*101-152 SP VET/60 101-151: .6X TO 1.5X SP/155
*101-152 ROOK/60: .4X TO 1X SP RC/155
66 Mark Messier 8.00 20.00

2000-01 Private Stock Retail

This 152-card retail set mirrored the hobby set except that base cards featured silver highlights. SP's were sequentially numbered to 230 and were inserted at a rate of 1:49. Retail packs did not contain memorabilia cards in every pack, and carried an SRP of $2.99.

*1-100 VETS: .4X TO 1X BASIC CARDS
*101-150 SP/230: .25X TO .6X SP/155
66 Mark Messier .40 1.00

2000-01 Private Stock Silver

Randomly inserted in Retail packs at the rate of three in 25, this 152-card set parallels the main set enhanced with silver borders and silver foil highlights. Each card is sequentially numbered to 120.

*1-100 VETS/120: 5X TO 12X BASIC CARDS
*101-152 SP VET/120 101-151: .4X TO 1X SP/155
*101-152 ROOK/120: .3X TO .8X SP RC/155
66 Mark Messier 5.00 12.00

2000-01 Private Stock Artist's Canvas

Randomly inserted in Hobby packs at the rate of 1:21 and retail packs at the rate of 1:49, this 20-card set features base card artwork on a card printed on canvas stock.

COMPLETE SET (20) 50.00 100.00
1 Paul Kariya 2.00 5.00
2 Teemu Selanne 2.00 5.00
3 Joe Thornton 3.00 8.00
4 Maxim Afinogenov 1.50 4.00
5 Dominik Hasek 4.00 10.00
6 Peter Forsberg 5.00 12.00
7 Patrick Roy 10.00 25.00
8 Joe Sakic 4.00 10.00
9 Brett Hull 2.50 6.00
10 Mike Modano 3.00 8.00
11 Brendan Shanahan 3.00 8.00
12 Steve Yzerman 10.00 25.00
13 Pavel Bure 2.00 5.00
14 Martin Brodeur 5.00 12.00
15 Mark Messier 2.50 6.00
16 John LeClair 2.50 6.00
17 Jeremy Roenick 2.50 6.00
18 Jaromir Jagr 3.00 8.00
19 Vincent Lecavalier 2.00 5.00
20 Curtis Joseph 2.00 5.00

2000-01 Private Stock Extreme Action

Randomly inserted in packs at the rate of 2:21, this 20-card set features full color panoramic photography of game action. Cards are enhanced with a colored border along the bottom of the card containing the featured player's name with gold foil highlights.

COMPLETE SET (20) 20.00 40.00
1 Paul Kariya .75 2.00
2 Teemu Selanne .75 2.00
3 Dominik Hasek 1.50 4.00
4 Patrick Roy 4.00 10.00
5 Joe Sakic 1.50 4.00
6 Ed Belfour .75 2.00
7 Brett Hull 1.00 2.50
8 Mike Modano 1.25 3.00
9 Steve Yzerman 4.00 10.00
10 Luc Robitaille .60 1.50
11 Trevor Linden .50 1.25
12 Petr Sykora .50 1.25
13 Martin Brodeur 2.00 5.00
14 Tim Connolly .50 1.25
15 John LeClair 1.00 2.50
16 Eric Lindros 1.25 3.00
17 Jeremy Roenick 1.00 2.50
18 Jaromir Jagr 1.25 3.00
19 Vincent Lecavalier .75 2.00
20 Curtis Joseph .75 2.00

2000-01 Private Stock Game Gear

Inserted one per hobby and 1:49 retail packs, this 105-card set features one or two swatches of game used memorabilia. Included on cards are jersey swatches, stick swatches, or jersey/stick combos. Cards feature a full color action photograph and a circular memorabilia swatch.

1 Guy Hebert J 4.00 10.00
2 Marty McInnis J 3.00 8.00
3 Teemu Selanne J 5.00 12.00
4 Shawn Bates J 3.00 8.00
5 Paul Coffey S 8.00 20.00
6 Paul Coffey J/S 20.00 50.00
7 Bill Guerin S 6.00 15.00
8 Sergei Samsonov J 4.00 10.00
9 Dominik Hasek S 20.00 50.00
10 Jay McKee J 3.00 8.00
11 Jarome Iginla J 6.00 15.00
12 Rod Brind'Amour S 6.00 15.00
13 Kevin Hatcher S 5.00 12.00
14 Sandis Ozolinsh S 5.00 12.00
15 Tony Amonte J 4.00 10.00
16 Eric Daze J 3.00 8.00
17 Alexei Zhamnov J 3.00 8.00
18 Ray Bourque J 15.00 40.00
19 Ray Bourque S 12.00 30.00
20 Greg DeVries J 3.00 8.00
21 Chris Dingman J 3.00 8.00
22 Chris Drury S 6.00 15.00
23 Adam Foote S 5.00 12.00
24 Peter Forsberg S 15.00 40.00
25 Peter Forsberg J/S 15.00 40.00
26 Eric Messier J 3.00 8.00
27 Aaron Miller J 3.00 8.00
28 Patrick Roy S 12.00 30.00
29 Joe Sakic J/S 15.00 40.00
30 Joe Sakic J 10.00 25.00
31 Martin Skoula S 5.00 12.00
32 Alex Tanguay S 6.00 15.00
33 Marc Denis S 6.00 15.00
34 Ed Belfour S 8.00 20.00
35 Derian Hatcher J 3.00 8.00
36 Derian Hatcher J 3.00 8.00
37 Jamie Langenbrunner J 3.00 8.00
38 Jere Lehtinen J 3.00 8.00
39 Mike Modano J 6.00 15.00
40 Darryl Sydor J 3.00 8.00
41 Darryl Sydor J 3.00 8.00
42 Sergei Zubov J 3.00 8.00
43 Chris Chelios S 8.00 20.00
44 Sergei Fedorov J 8.00 20.00
45 Nicklas Lidstrom J 4.00 10.00
46 Chris Osgood J 4.00 10.00
47 Brendan Shanahan J 5.00 12.00
48 Anson Carter J 3.00 8.00
49 Tommy Salo S 5.00 12.00
50 Doug Weight J 4.00 10.00
51 Olli Jokinen S 5.00 12.00
52 Roberto Luongo J 6.00 15.00
53 Scott Mellanby S 5.00 12.00
54 Rob Blake S 6.00 15.00
55 Zigmund Palffy S 6.00 15.00
56 Jeff Hackett J 4.00 10.00
57 Saku Koivu J 5.00 12.00
58 Trevor Linden S 5.00 12.00
59 Brian Savage S 5.00 12.00
60 Eric Weinrich S 5.00 12.00
61 Dainius Zubrus J 3.00 8.00
62 Cliff Ronning S 5.00 12.00
63 Bobby Holik J 3.00 8.00
64 Scott Niedermayer J 3.00 8.00
65 Petr Sykora J 3.00 8.00
66 Chris Terreri J 4.00 10.00
67 Zdeno Chara J 3.00 8.00
68 Tim Connolly S 5.00 12.00
69 Mariusz Czerkawski J 3.00 8.00
70 Claude LaPointe J 3.00 8.00
71 Mats Lindgren J 3.00 8.00
72 John Vanbiesbrouck J 4.00 10.00
73 Adam Graves S 5.00 12.00
74 Valeri Kamensky S 5.00 12.00
75 Brian Leetch J 4.00 10.00
76 Brian Leetch J/S 20.00 50.00
77 Mark Messier J 5.00 12.00
78 Mike Richter J 5.00 12.00
79 Mike Richter J 5.00 12.00
80 Andreas Dackell J 3.00 8.00
81 Eric Desjardins J 3.00 8.00
82 Daymond Langkow J 3.00 8.00
83 John LeClair J 4.00 10.00
84 Eric Lindros J 5.00 12.00
85 Eric Lindros S 12.50 30.00
86 Rick Tocchet S 6.00 15.00
87 Shane Doan J 3.00 8.00
88 Radoslav Suchy J 3.00 8.00
89 Jaromir Jagr J 6.00 15.00
90 Dallas Drake J 3.00 8.00
91 Vincent Damphousse J 3.00 8.00
92 Vincent Damphousse J/S 15.00 40.00
93 Vincent Lecavalier S 8.00 20.00
94 Petr Svoboda J 3.00 8.00
95 Shayne Corson J 3.00 8.00
96 Curtis Joseph S 5.00 12.00
97 Yanic Perreault S 5.00 12.00
98 Gary Roberts S 5.00 12.00
99 Mats Sundin J 5.00 12.00
100 Craig Berube S 5.00 12.00
101 Peter Bondra J 5.00 12.00
102 Sylvain Cote S 5.00 12.00
103 Ulf Dahlen J 3.00 8.00
104 Olaf Kolzig J/S 15.00 40.00
105 Adam Oates S 6.00 15.00

2000-01 Private Stock Game Gear Patches

Randomly inserted in packs, this 62-card set parallels only the jersey portion of the Game Gear insert set. Each card is sequentially numbered and contains a premium swatch of a game jersey emblem or numbers. Card 81 is not priced due to scarcity.

1 Guy Hebert/164 12.50 30.00
2 Marty McInnis/156 10.00 25.00
3 Teemu Selanne/202 15.00 40.00
4 Shawn Bates/156 10.00 25.00
8 Sergei Samsonov/101 15.00 40.00
10 Jay McKee/161 10.00 25.00
11 Jarome Iginla/94 15.00 40.00
15 Tony Amonte/134 12.50 30.00
16 Eric Daze/177 12.50 30.00
17 Alexei Zhamnov/142 10.00 25.00
18 Ray Bourque/39 75.00 200.00
20 Greg DeVries/184 10.00 25.00
21 Chris Dingman/163 10.00 25.00
26 Eric Messier/121 10.00 25.00
27 Aaron Miller/202 10.00 25.00
35 Derian Hatcher/172 10.00 25.00
36 Derian Hatcher/184 10.00 25.00
37 Jamie Langenbrunner/178 10.00 25.00
38 Jere Lehtinen/151 10.00 25.00
39 Mike Modano/417 12.00 30.00
40 Darryl Sydor/40 10.00 25.00
41 Darryl Sydor/88 12.50 30.00
42 Sergei Zubov/220 10.00 25.00
44 Sergei Fedorov/175 15.00 40.00
45 Nicklas Lidstrom/193 15.00 40.00
46 Chris Osgood/143 12.50 30.00
47 Brendan Shanahan/17 150.00 300.00
48 Anson Carter/190 10.00 25.00
50 Doug Weight/162 12.50 30.00
52 Roberto Luongo/183 12.00 30.00
56 Jeff Hackett/149 10.00 25.00
57 Saku Koivu/28 60.00 120.00
61 Dainius Zubrus/172 10.00 25.00
63 Bobby Holik/144 10.00 25.00
64 Scott Niedermayer/119 10.00 25.00
65 Petr Sykora/247 10.00 25.00
66 Chris Terreri/149 10.00 25.00
67 Zdeno Chara/149 10.00 25.00
69 Mariusz Czerkawski/169 10.00 25.00
70 Claude LaPointe/137 10.00 25.00
71 Mats Lindgren/166 10.00 25.00
72 John Vanbiesbrouck/108 12.50 30.00
75 Brian Leetch/122 12.50 30.00
77 Mark Messier/67 20.00 50.00
78 Mike Richter/184 15.00 40.00
79 Mike Richter/193 15.00 40.00
80 Andreas Dackell/175 10.00 25.00
81 Eric Desjardins/20
82 Daymond Langkow/77 12.50 30.00
83 John LeClair/158 15.00 40.00
84 Eric Lindros 15.00 40.00
87 Shane Doan/92 10.00 25.00
88 Radoslav Suchy/125 10.00 25.00
89 Jaromir Jagr/388 12.00 30.00
90 Dallas Drake/180 10.00 25.00
94 Petr Svoboda/227 10.00 25.00
95 Shayne Corson/165 10.00 25.00
99 Mats Sundin/103 15.00 40.00
101 Peter Bondra/190 15.00 40.00
103 Ulf Dahlen/183 10.00 25.00

2000-01 Private Stock PS-2001 Action

Inserted two per pack, this 60-mini card set features top NHL players in action where cards are enhanced with gold foil highlights.

COMPLETE SET (60) 15.00 30.00
1 Paul Kariya .40 1.00
2 Teemu Selanne .40 1.00
3 Sergei Samsonov .30 .75
4 Joe Thornton .60 1.50
5 Maxim Afinogenov .30 .75
6 Doug Gilmour .30 .75
7 Dominik Hasek .75 2.00
8 Ray Bourque .75 2.00
9 Chris Drury .30 .75
10 Peter Forsberg 1.00 2.50
11 Milan Hejduk .40 1.00
12 Patrick Roy 2.00 5.00
13 Joe Sakic .75 2.00
14 Alex Tanguay .30 .75
15 Marc Denis .30 .75
16 Ed Belfour .40 1.00
17 Brett Hull .50 1.25
18 Mike Modano .60 1.50
19 Chris Chelios .40 1.00
20 Sergei Fedorov .75 2.00
21 Chris Osgood .30 .75
22 Brendan Shanahan .60 1.50
23 Steve Yzerman 2.00 5.00
24 Doug Weight .30 .75
25 Pavel Bure .50 1.25
26 Zigmund Palffy .30 .75
27 Luc Robitaille .30 .75
28 Saku Koivu .40 1.00
29 Jose Theodore .50 1.25
30 David Legwand .30 .75
31 Martin Brodeur 1.00 2.50
32 Patrik Elias .30 .75
33 Scott Gomez .30 .75
34 Petr Sykora .30 .75
35 Tim Connolly .30 .75
36 Theo Fleury .30 .75
37 Brian Leetch .30 .75
38 Mark Messier .50 1.25
39 Mike Richter .40 1.00
40 Marian Hossa .40 1.00
41 Brian Boucher .40 1.00
42 John LeClair .50 1.25
43 Eric Lindros .60 1.50
44 Jeremy Roenick .50 1.25
45 Keith Tkachuk .40 1.00
46 Jan Hrdina .30 .75
47 Jaromir Jagr .60 1.50
48 Martin Straka .30 .75
49 Jeff Friesen .30 .75
50 Owen Nolan .30 .75
51 Pavol Demitra .30 .75
52 Chris Pronger .30 .75
53 Pierre Turgeon .30 .75
54 Vincent Lecavalier .40 1.00
55 Curtis Joseph .40 1.00
56 Mats Sundin .40 1.00
57 Steve Kariya .30 .75
58 Markus Naslund .40 1.00
59 Peter Bondra .40 1.00
60 Olaf Kolzig .30 .75

2000-01 Private Stock PS-2001 New Wave

Randomly inserted at the rate of 2 per Hobby case and 1 per Retail case, this 25-card set features mini player cards with player action photograph and bronze foil highlights. Each card is sequentially numbered to 70.

COMPLETE SET (26) 60.00 150.00
1 Patrik Stefan 2.50 6.00
2 Joe Thornton 8.00 20.00
3 Maxim Afinogenov 3.00 8.00
4 Sami Kapanen 2.50 6.00
5 Valeri Bure 2.50 6.00
6 Oleg Saprykin 2.50 6.00
7 Jocelyn Thibault 3.00 8.00
8 Milan Hejduk 4.00 10.00
9 Marc Denis 3.00 8.00
10 Brenden Morrow 4.00 10.00
11 Jose Theodore 5.00 12.00
12 David Legwand 2.50 6.00
13 Patrik Elias 4.00 10.00
14 Scott Gomez 4.00 10.00
15 Tim Connolly 3.00 8.00
16 Marian Hossa 6.00 15.00
17 Brian Boucher 2.50 6.00
18 Simon Gagne 5.00 12.00
19 Jean-Sebastien Aubin 2.50 6.00
20 Roman Turek 2.50 6.00
21 Jeff Friesen 2.50 6.00
22 Dan Cloutier 3.00 8.00
23 Vincent Lecavalier 6.00 15.00
24 Nikolai Antropov 2.50 6.00
25 Steve Kariya 2.50 6.00
26 Rick DiPietro 10.00 25.00

2000-01 Private Stock PS-2001 Rookies

Randomly inserted in packs at the rate of one per Hobby and Retail cases, this 26-card set is comprised of mini cards that feature some of the NHL's brightest prospects. Cards are enhanced with silver foil highlights and are sequentially numbered to 45

1 Samuel Pahlsson 3.00 8.00
2 Andrew Raycroft 12.00 30.00
3 Dimitri Kalinin 3.00 8.00
4 Oleg Saprykin 5.00 12.00
5 Josef Vasicek 5.00 12.00
6 David Aebischer 15.00 40.00
7 David Vyborny 5.00 12.00
8 Marty Turco 20.00 50.00
9 Eric Belanger 3.00 8.00
10 Steven Reinprecht 4.00 10.00
11 Marian Gaborik 30.00 80.00
12 Andrei Markov 6.00 15.00
13 Colin White 3.00 8.00
14 Martin Havlat 20.00 50.00
15 Maxime Ouellet 5.00 12.00
16 Justin Williams 15.00 40.00
17 Wyatt Smith 3.00 8.00
18 Ossi Vaananen 3.00 8.00
19 Brent Johnson 5.00 12.00
20 Ladislav Nagy 4.00 10.00
21 Evegeni Nabokov 15.00 40.00
22 Alexander Kharitonov 3.00 8.00
23 Brad Richards 12.00 30.00
24 Daniel Sedin 15.00 40.00
25 Henrik Sedin 15.00 40.00
26 Rick DiPietro 20.00 50.00

2000-01 Private Stock PS-2001 Stars

Randomly inserted in packs at the rate of three per Hobby case and two per Retail case, this 25-card set features mini cards. Each card is features a portrait style photograph and cards are sequentially numbered to 105.

COMPLETE SET (25) 150.00 300.00
1 Paul Kariya 3.00 8.00
2 Teemu Selanne 3.00 8.00
3 Sergei Samsonov 2.50 6.00
4 Dominik Hasek 8.00 20.00
5 Ray Bourque 8.00 20.00
6 Peter Forsberg 10.00 25.00
7 Patrick Roy 20.00 50.00
8 Joe Sakic 10.00 25.00
9 Brett Hull 4.00 10.00
10 Mike Modano 5.00 12.00
11 Sergei Fedorov 8.00 20.00
12 Brendan Shanahan 6.00 15.00

13 Steve Yzerman 20.00 50.00
14 Pavel Bure 5.00 12.00
15 Luc Robitaille 2.50 6.00
16 Saku Koivu 3.00 8.00
17 Martin Brodeur 12.00 30.00
18 Mark Messier 6.00 15.00
19 John LeClair 4.00 10.00
20 Eric Lindros 5.00 12.00
21 Jeremy Roenick 4.00 10.00
22 Jaromir Jagr 6.00 15.00
23 Pierre Turgeon 2.50 6.00
24 Curtis Joseph 3.00 8.00
25 Mats Sundin 3.00 8.00

2000-01 Private Stock Reserve

Randomly inserted in Hobby packs at the rate of 1:21, this 20-card set features a framed oval portrait style photos of players accented with gold foil highlights.

COMPLETE SET (20) 40.00 80.00
1 Paul Kariya 2.00 5.00
2 Teemu Selanne 3.00 8.00
3 Patrik Stefan 1.25 3.00
4 Dominik Hasek 2.50 6.00
5 Peter Forsberg 2.00 5.00
6 Patrick Roy 4.00 10.00
7 Joe Sakic 2.50 6.00
8 Mike Modano 2.50 6.00
9 Brendan Shanahan 2.00 5.00
10 Steve Yzerman 5.00 12.00
11 Pavel Bure 2.00 5.00
12 Saku Koivu 1.50 4.00
13 Scott Gomez 1.25 3.00
14 Martin Brodeur 3.00 8.00
15 Mark Messier 2.50 6.00
16 John LeClair 1.50 4.00
17 Eric Lindros 2.50 6.00
18 Jaromir Jagr 4.00 10.00
19 Vincent Lecavalier 1.25 3.00
20 Curtis Joseph 2.00 5.00

2001-02 Private Stock

This 140-card set featured player action photos on mat-like finish card fronts with red foil highlights and white borders. Cards were 101-117 were short-printed and inserted at a rate of 1:17, while cards 111-140 were serial-numbered to 414 copies each.

1 Jeff Friesen .12 .30
2 Paul Kariya .25 .60
3 Milan Hnilicka .15 .40
4 Patrik Stefan .15 .40
5 Bill Guerin .20 .50
6 Sergei Samsonov .15 .40
7 Joe Thornton .25 .60
8 Martin Biron .15 .40
9 Tim Connolly .12 .30
10 J-P Dumont .12 .30
11 Jarome Iginla .20 .50
12 Marc Savard .12 .30
13 Roman Turek .15 .40
14 Ron Francis .25 .60
15 Arturs Irbe .15 .40
16 Jeff O'Neill .12 .30
17 Tony Amonte .15 .40
18 Steve Sullivan .12 .30
19 Jocelyn Thibault .15 .40
20 Rob Blake .20 .50
21 Chris Drury .15 .40
22 Milan Hejduk .15 .40
23 Patrick Roy .50 1.25
24 Joe Sakic .30 .75
25 Alex Tanguay .15 .40
26 Espen Knutsen .12 .30
27 Ron Tugnutt .15 .40
28 Ed Belfour .20 .50
29 Mike Modano .30 .75
30 Joe Nieuwendyk .20 .50
31 Pierre Turgeon .20 .50
32 Sergei Fedorov .30 .75
33 Dominik Hasek .30 .75
34 Brett Hull .25 .60
35 Nicklas Lidstrom .20 .50
36 Luc Robitaille .20 .50
37 Brendan Shanahan .25 .60
38 Steve Yzerman .60 1.50
39 Mike Comrie .15 .40
40 Tommy Salo .15 .40
41 Ryan Smyth .15 .40
42 Pavel Bure .25 .60
43 Roberto Luongo .30 .75
44 Jason Allison .15 .40
45 Zigmund Palffy .20 .50
46 Felix Potvin .30 .75
47 Manny Fernandez .15 .40
48 Marian Gaborik .30 .75
49 Yanic Perreault .12 .30
50 Brian Savage .12 .30
51 Jose Theodore .20 .50
52 Mike Dunham .15 .40
53 David Legwand .15 .40
54 Jason Arnott .15 .40
55 Martin Brodeur .40 1.00
56 Patrik Elias .20 .50
57 Scott Gomez .15 .40
58 Chris Osgood .20 .50
59 Michael Peca .15 .40
60 Alexei Yashin .15 .40
61 Theo Fleury .25 .60
62 Brian Leetch .20 .50
63 Eric Lindros .30 .75
64 Mark Messier .30 .75
65 Mike Richter .20 .50
66 Daniel Alfredsson .20 .50
67 Martin Havlat .15 .40
68 Marian Hossa .15 .40
69 Patrick Lalime .15 .40
70 Roman Cechmanek .15 .40
71 Simon Gagne .20 .50
72 John LeClair .20 .50
73 Mark Recchi .25 .60
74 Jeremy Roenick .20 .50
75 Sean Burke .12 .30
76 Daymond Langkow .15 .40
77 Alexei Kovalev .15 .40
78 Mario Lemieux .60 1.50
79 Martin Straka .12 .30
80 Brent Johnson .15 .40
81 Chris Pronger .15 .40
82 Keith Tkachuk .20 .50
83 Doug Weight .20 .50
84 Patrick Marleau .20 .50
85 Evgeni Nabokov .15 .40
86 Owen Nolan .20 .50
87 Teemu Selanne .40 1.00
88 Vincent Lecavalier .15 .40
89 Brad Richards .20 .50
90 Curtis Joseph .20 .50
91 Alexander Mogilny .15 .40
92 Mats Sundin .20 .50
93 Dan Cloutier .15 .40
94 Markus Naslund .20 .50
95 Daniel Sedin .20 .50
96 Henrik Sedin .20 .50
97 Peter Bondra .20 .50
98 Jaromir Jagr .50 1.25
99 Olaf Kolzig .20 .50
100 Adam Oates .20 .50
101 Dany Heatley SP 4.00 10.00
102 Mark Bell SP 2.50 6.00
103 Rostislav Klesla SP 2.50 6.00
104 Jason Williams SP 2.50 6.00
105 Rick DiPietro SP 3.00 8.00
106 Pavel Brendl SP 2.50 6.00
107 Kris Beech SP 2.50 6.00
108 Johan Hedberg SP 3.00 8.00
109 Miikka Kiprusoff SP 4.00 10.00
110 Bryan Allen SP 2.50 6.00
111 Ilja Bryzgalov RC 6.00 15.00
112 Timo Parssinen RC 3.00 8.00
113 Ilya Kovalchuk RC 12.00 30.00
114 Kamil Piros RC 2.50 6.00
115 Brian Pothier RC 2.50 6.00
116 Jukka Hentunen RC 2.50 6.00
117 Erik Cole RC 5.00 12.00
118 Vaclav Nedorost RC 2.50 6.00
119 Niko Kapanen RC 4.00 10.00
120 Pavel Datsyuk RC 15.00 40.00
121 Jason Chimera RC 2.50 6.00
122 Niklas Hagman RC 3.00 8.00
123 Kristian Huselius RC 4.00 10.00
124 Jaroslav Bednar RC 2.50 6.00
125 Pascal Dupuis RC 4.00 10.00
126 Nick Schultz RC 2.50 6.00
127 Francis Belanger RC 3.00 8.00
128 Martin Erat RC 4.00 10.00
129 Scott Clemmensen RC 2.50 6.00
130 Radek Martinek RC 2.50 6.00
131 Dan Blackburn RC 3.00 8.00
132 Peter Smrek RC 2.50 6.00
133 Chris Neil RC 3.00 8.00
134 Jiri Dopita RC 2.50 6.00
135 David Cullen RC 2.50 6.00
136 Krystofer Kolanos RC 2.50 6.00
137 Jeff Jillson RC 2.50 6.00
138 Mark Rycroft RC 3.00 8.00
139 Nikita Alexeev RC 2.50 6.00
140 Brian Sutherby RC 2.50 6.00

2001-02 Private Stock Gold

This 140-card hobby only set paralleled the base set but featured gold foil highlights in place of the red. Cards were serial-numbered out of 106.

*1-100 VETS/106: 5X TO 12X BASIC CARDS
*101-110 VETS/106: .5X TO 1.2X BASIC SP
*111-140 ROOKIE/106: .3X TO .8X RC

2001-02 Private Stock Premiere Date

This 140-card hobby only set paralleled the base set but featured a premiere date stamp on the card front. Cards were serial-numbered on the card front out of 100.

*1-100 VETS/100: 5X TO 12X BASIC CARDS
*101-110 VETS/100: .5X TO 1.2X SP
*111-140 ROOKIES/100: .4X TO 1X RC

2001-02 Private Stock Retail

This 140-card retail set mirrored the hobby set but featured blue foil highlights in place of the red. Cards 111-140 were serial numbered to 450.

*1-100 VETS: .4X TO 1X HOBBY
*101-110 VETS: .3X TO .8X SP
*111-140 ROOKIE/450: .4X TO 1X HOB

2001-02 Private Stock Silver

This 140-card retail only set paralleled the base set but featured silver foil highlights in place of the red. Cards were serial-numbered on the card front out of 108.

*1-100 VETS/108: 5X TO 12X BASIC CARDS
*101-100 VETS/108: .5X TO 1.2X SP
*111-140 ROOKIES/108: .4X TO 1X RC

2001-02 Private Stock Game Gear

Inserted at one per pack hobby and four per case retail, this 100-card set featured pieces of game-used jerseys or sticks. Stick cards were serial-numbered out of 200. Cards with significantly shorter print runs are noted below with an SP tag. Please note that cards #58, 65 and 72 were not produced in jersey form.

1 Jean-Sebastien Giguere 5.00 12.00
2 Paul Kariya 5.00 12.00
3 Mike Leclerc SP 3.00 8.00
4 Steve Rucchin 3.00 8.00
5 Oleg Tverdovsky 3.00 8.00
6 Ilya Kovalchuk STK/200 15.00 40.00
7 P.J. Axelsson 3.00 8.00
8 Byron Dafoe 5.00 12.00
9 Stu Barnes SP 3.00 8.00
10 J-P Dumont 3.00 8.00
11 Jay McKee SP 3.00 8.00
12 Rob Ray 3.00 8.00
13 Richard Smehlik SP 3.00 8.00
14 Craig Conroy 3.00 8.00
15 Jarome Iginla 6.00 15.00
16 Marc Savard 3.00 8.00
17 Roman Turek 5.00 12.00
18 Rod Brind'Amour STK/200 10.00 25.00
19 Jeff O'Neill STK/200 10.00 25.00
20 Tony Amonte 5.00 12.00
21 Kyle Calder 3.00 8.00
22 Eric Daze SP 3.00 8.00
23 Boris Mironov 3.00 8.00
24 Michael Nylander 3.00 8.00
25 Steve Sullivan 3.00 8.00
26 Jocelyn Thibault 5.00 12.00
27 Alexei Zhamnov 3.00 8.00
28 Chris Drury STK/200 10.00 25.00
29 Peter Forsberg SP 12.50 30.00
30 Patrick Roy SP 12.50 30.00
31 Joe Sakic 8.00 20.00
32 Grant Marshall SP 3.00 8.00
33 Blake Sloan SP 3.00 8.00
34 Ed Belfour 5.00 12.00
35 Derian Hatcher 3.00 8.00
36 Jamie Langenbrunner 3.00 8.00
37 Mike Modano 8.00 20.00
38 Joe Nieuwendyk 5.00 12.00
39 Darryl Sydor 3.00 8.00
40 Pierre Turgeon 5.00 12.00
41 Sergei Zubov 3.00 8.00
42 Dominik Hasek SP 12.50 30.00
43 Brett Hull SP 10.00 25.00
44 Brendan Shanahan 5.00 12.00
45 Steve Yzerman 10.00 25.00
46 Anson Carter SP 5.00 12.00
47 Jochen Hecht 3.00 8.00
48 Ryan Smyth SP 3.00 8.00
49 Valeri Bure SP 3.00 8.00
50 Robert Svehla 3.00 8.00
51 Aaron Miller 3.00 8.00
52 Felix Potvin SP 6.00 15.00
53 Jamie McLennan 3.00 8.00
54 Saku Koivu SP 5.00 12.00
55 Jose Theodore 6.00 15.00
56 Mike Dunham 5.00 12.00
57 Tom Fitzgerald 3.00 8.00
59 Cliff Ronning 3.00 8.00
60 Bobby Holik 3.00 8.00
61 Shawn Bates 3.00 8.00
62 Mariusz Czerkawski 3.00 8.00
63 Kenny Jonsson SP 3.00 8.00
64 Chris Osgood 5.00 12.00
66 Rico Fata 3.00 8.00
67 Eric Lindros SP 5.00 12.00
68 Petr Nedved 3.00 8.00
69 Mike Richter 5.00 12.00
70 Pavel Brendl 5.00 12.00
71 John LeClair SP 5.00 12.00
73 Sean Burke 5.00 12.00
74 Shane Doan 3.00 8.00
75 Jean-Sebastien Aubin 5.00 12.00
76 Jan Hrdina 3.00 8.00
77 Alexei Kovalev 5.00 12.00
78 Milan Kraft 5.00 12.00
79 Mario Lemieux SP 12.00 30.00
80 Ian Moran 3.00 8.00
81 Alexei Morozov 3.00 8.00
82 Wayne Primeau SP 3.00 8.00
83 Michal Rozsival 3.00 8.00
84 Kevin Stevens 3.00 8.00
85 Martin Straka 3.00 8.00
86 Fred Brathwaite 5.00 12.00
87 Mike Eastwood 3.00 8.00
88 Cory Stillman 3.00 8.00
89 Doug Weight SP 5.00 12.00
90 Scott Young 3.00 8.00
91 Vincent Damphousse SP 3.00 8.00
92 Teemu Selanne 5.00 12.00
93 Vincent Lecavalier SP 5.00 12.00
94 Tie Domi 5.00 12.00
95 Curtis Joseph SP 8.00 20.00
96 Robert Reichel STK/200 10.00 25.00
97 Mats Sundin 5.00 12.00
98 Andrew Cassels 3.00 8.00
99 Peter Bondra 5.00 12.00
100 Jaromir Jagr 8.00 20.00

2001-02 Private Stock Game Gear Patches

This 88-card set paralleled the jerseys in the Game Gear set but carried swatches of patches. The set was skip numbered.

*PATCH: .6X TO 1.5X BSIC JERSEY
58 David Legwand 10.00 20.00
65 Alexei Yashin 6.00 15.00
72 Jeremy Roenick 12.50 25.00

2001-02 Private Stock Moments in Time

This 10-card hobby only set featured a color action photo combined with a larger silhouette and a blurred effect on the card front. Each card was serial-numbered out of 85.

1 Dany Heatley 15.00 40.00
2 Ilya Kovalchuk 20.00 50.00
3 Vaclav Nedorost 15.00 40.00
4 Rostislav Klesla 10.00 25.00
5 Jaroslav Bednar 10.00 25.00
6 Rick DiPietro 10.00 25.00
7 Dan Blackburn 6.00 15.00
8 Pavel Brendl 10.00 25.00
9 Krystofer Kolanos 10.00 25.00
10 Johan Hedberg 10.00 25.00

2001-02 Private Stock PS-2002

This 102-card set featured small retro styled mini-cards. Card fronts carried a player photo, name, and birthplace. Card backs resembled vintage "tobacco" cards with single color printing. Cards 1-92 were inserted at 2 per pack and cards 93-102 were serial numbered out of 50 and inserted into hobby packs only. Cards 1-92 had red backs and cards 93-102 had blue backs.

1 Paul Kariya .40 1.00
2 Steve Shields .20 .50
3 Ray Ferraro .20 .50
4 Jason Allison .20 .50
5 Byron DaFoe .30 .75
6 Joe Thornton .60 1.50
7 Stu Barnes .20 .50
8 Martin Biron .30 .75
9 Miroslav Satan .30 .75
10 Jarome Iginla .50 1.25
11 Derek Morris .20 .50
12 Sami Kapanen .20 .50
13 Jeff O'Neill .20 .50
14 Eric Daze .30 .75
15 Jocelyn Thibault .30 .75
16 David Aebischer .30 .75
17 Chris Drury .30 .75
18 Peter Forsberg 1.00 2.50
19 Patrick Roy 2.00 5.00
20 Joe Sakic .75 2.00
21 Marc Denis .30 .75
22 Geoff Sanderson .20 .50
23 Ed Belfour .40 1.00
24 Mike Modano .60 1.50
25 Marty Turco .30 .75
26 Pat Verbeek .20 .50
27 Dominik Hasek .75 2.00
28 Brett Hull .50 1.25
29 Brendan Shanahan .60 1.50
30 Steve Yzerman 2.00 5.00
31 Mike Comrie .30 .75
32 Tommy Salo .30 .75
33 Ryan Smyth .20 .50
34 Pavel Bure .60 1.50
35 Roberto Luongo .50 1.25
36 Zigmund Palffy .30 .75
37 Felix Potvin .40 1.00
38 Marian Gaborik .75 2.00
39 Doug Gilmour .30 .75
40 Jeff Hackett .30 .75
41 Joe Juneau .20 .50
42 Cliff Ronning .20 .50
43 Jason Arnott .20 .50
44 Martin Brodeur 1.00 2.50
45 Michael Peca .20 .50
46 Alexei Yashin .20 .50
47 Zdeno Ciger .20 .50
48 Eric Lindros .60 1.50
49 Mark Messier .50 1.25
50 Petr Nedved .20 .50
51 Radek Bonk .20 .50
52 Martin Havlat .30 .75
53 Roman Cechmanek .30 .75
54 John LeClair .50 1.25
55 Jeremy Roenick .50 1.25
56 Sean Burke .30 .75
57 Shane Doan .20 .50
58 Robert Lang .20 .50
59 Mario Lemieux 2.50 6.00
60 Fred Brathwaite .30 .75
61 Chris Pronger .30 .75
62 Keith Tkachuk .40 1.00
63 Doug Weight .30 .75
64 Evgeni Nabokov .30 .75
65 Owen Nolan .30 .75
66 Teemu Selanne .40 1.00
67 Nikolai Khabibulin .40 1.00
68 Vincent Lecavalier .40 1.00
69 Brad Richards .30 .75
70 Curtis Joseph .40 1.00
71 Mats Sundin .40 1.00
72 Andrew Cassels .20 .50
73 Brendan Morrison .30 .75
74 Peter Bondra .40 1.00
75 Jaromir Jagr .60 1.50
76 Ilja Bryzgalov .30 .75
77 Timo Parssinen .20 .50
78 Erik Cole .50 1.25
79 Mark Bell .20 .50
80 Pavel Datsyuk 8.00 20.00
81 Jason Williams .20 .50
82 Jaroslav Bednar .20 .50
83 Scott Clemmensen .30 .75
84 Pavel Brendl .30 .75
85 Jiri Dopita .20 .50
86 Kris Beech .20 .50
87 Mark Rycroft .20 .50
88 Jeff Jillson .20 .50
89 Miikka Kiprusoff .30 .75
90 Nikita Alexeev .20 .50
91 Bryan Allen .20 .50
92 Brian Sutherby .20 .50
93 Dany Heatley SP 12.50 30.00
94 Ilya Kovalchuk SP 25.00 60.00
95 Vaclav Nedorost SP 12.50 30.00
96 Rostislav Klesla SP 12.50 30.00
97 Kristian Huselius SP 12.50 30.00
98 Martin Erat SP 12.50 30.00
99 Rick DiPietro SP 12.50 30.00
100 Dan Blackburn SP 12.50 30.00
101 Krystofer Kolanos SP 12.50 30.00
102 Johan Hedberg SP 12.50 30.00

2001-02 Private Stock Reserve

This 40-card set consisted of 3 different subsets; goalies, superstars, and rookies. Goalies and rookies were inserted into packs at a rate of 1:4 boxes for hobby and 1:8 boxes for retail. Superstar cards were inserted at 1:2 boxes for hobby and 1:4 boxes retail. The prefix before each number below is for checklisting only, the letters do not appear on the cards themselves.

G1 Martin Biron 1.50 4.00
G2 Patrick Roy 8.00 20.00
G3 Ed Belfour 2.00 5.00
G4 Dominik Hasek 4.00 10.00
G5 Tommy Salo 1.50 4.00
G6 Roberto Luongo 3.00 8.00
G7 Martin Brodeur 5.00 12.00
G8 Roman Cechmanek 1.50 4.00
G9 Evgeni Nabokov 1.50 4.00
G10 Curtis Joseph 2.00 5.00
R1 Dany Heatley 6.00 15.00
R2 Ilya Kovalchuk 12.00 30.00
R3 Vaclav Nedorost 1.50 4.00
R4 Pavel Datsyuk 8.00 20.00
R5 Jaroslav Bednar 1.50 4.00
R6 Dan Blackburn 1.50 4.00
R7 Pavel Brendl 1.50 4.00
R8 Krys Kolanos 1.50 4.00
R9 Kris Beech 1.50 4.00
R10 Nikita Alexeev 1.50 4.00
S1 Paul Kariya 2.00 5.00
S2 Joe Thornton 3.00 8.00
S3 Joe Sakic 4.00 10.00
S4 Brendan Shanahan 2.00 5.00
S5 Steve Yzerman 8.00 20.00
S6 Mike Comrie 1.00 2.50
S7 Pavel Bure 2.50 6.00
S8 Zigmund Palffy 1.00 2.50
S9 Marian Gaborik 3.00 8.00
S10 Alexei Yashin 1.00 2.50
S11 Eric Lindros 2.00 5.00
S12 Martin Havlat 1.00 2.50
S13 John LeClair 1.00 2.50
S14 Jeremy Roenick 2.50 6.00
S15 Mario Lemieux 12.00 30.00
S16 Keith Tkachuk 1.00 2.50
S17 Teemu Selanne 2.00 5.00
S18 Vincent Lecavalier 2.00 5.00
S19 Mats Sundin 2.00 5.00
S20 Jaromir Jagr 3.00 8.00

2002-03 Private Stock Reserve

This 185-card set featured full-color player photos on white borderless card fronts accented with gold foil highlights. Cards 101-150 also carried swatches of game-worn jerseys on the card fronts. Cards 151-185 were serial-numbered to just 99 copies each.

COMP.SET w/o SP's (100) 15.00 40.00
1 Jean-Sebastien Giguere .30 .75
2 Paul Kariya .40 1.00
3 Petr Sykora .25 .60
4 Milan Hnilicka .25 .60
5 Patrik Stefan .25 .60
6 Glen Murray .25 .60
7 Brian Rolston .25 .60
8 Sergei Samsonov .25 .60
9 Steve Shields .25 .60
10 Martin Biron .25 .60
11 Tim Connolly .20 .50
12 J-P Dumont .20 .50
13 Craig Conroy .20 .50
14 Chris Drury .30 .75
15 Rod Brind'Amour .30 .75
16 Erik Cole .25 .60
17 Arturs Irbe .25 .60
18 Jeff O'Neill .20 .50
19 Mark Bell .20 .50
20 Eric Daze .20 .50
21 Jocelyn Thibault .25 .60
22 Alexei Zhamnov .25 .60
23 Rob Blake .30 .75
24 Peter Forsberg .40 1.00
25 Milan Hejduk .25 .60
26 Dean McAmmond .20 .50
27 Steven Reinprecht .20 .50
28 Alex Tanguay .25 .60
29 Radim Vrbata .25 .60
30 Andrew Cassels .20 .50
31 Espen Knutsen .20 .50
32 Ray Whitney .25 .60
33 Marty Turco .30 .75
34 Pierre Turgeon .30 .75
35 Chris Chelios .30 .75
36 Brett Hull .40 1.00
37 Brendan Shanahan .40 1.00
38 Anson Carter .25 .60
39 Ryan Smyth .25 .60
40 Mike York .20 .50
41 Valeri Bure .25 .60
42 Kristian Huselius .20 .50
43 Stephen Weiss .30 .75
44 Jason Allison .25 .60
45 Adam Deadmarsh .25 .60
46 Zigmund Palffy .30 .75
47 Bryan Smolinski .25 .60
48 Andrew Brunette .20 .50
49 Manny Fernandez .25 .60
50 Cliff Ronning .20 .50
51 Mariusz Czerkawski .20 .50
52 Marcel Hossa .20 .50
53 Saku Koivu .30 .75
54 Yanic Perreault .20 .50
55 Richard Zednik .20 .50
56 Denis Arkhipov .20 .50
57 Mike Dunham .25 .60
58 Scott Hartnell .30 .75
59 Greg Johnson .20 .50
60 Christian Berglund .20 .50
61 Jeff Friesen .20 .50
62 Joe Nieuwendyk .30 .75
63 Chris Osgood .30 .75
64 Mark Parrish .20 .50
65 Dan Blackburn .25 .60
66 Pavel Bure .40 1.00
67 Bobby Holik .20 .50
68 Brian Leetch .30 .75
69 Mike Richter .30 .75
70 Daniel Alfredsson .30 .75
71 Radek Bonk .25 .60
72 Martin Havlat .25 .60
73 Patrick Lalime .25 .60
74 John LeClair .30 .75
75 Jeremy Roenick .30 .75
76 Tony Amonte .25 .60
77 Daniel Briere .25 .60
78 Sean Burke .20 .50
79 Johan Hedberg .30 .75
80 Alexei Kovalev .30 .75
81 Alexei Morozov .20 .50
82 Pavol Demitra .40 1.00
83 Barret Jackman .25 .60
84 Brent Johnson .25 .60
85 Doug Weight .30 .75
86 Vincent Damphousse .25 .60
87 Patrick Marleau .30 .75
88 Teemu Selanne .60 1.50
89 Scott Thornton .20 .50
90 Dave Andreychuk .30 .75
91 Vincent Lecavalier .25 .60
92 Alexander Mogilny .25 .60
93 Gary Roberts .20 .50
94 Darcy Tucker .20 .50
95 Dan Cloutier .25 .60
96 Brendan Morrison .25 .60
97 Markus Naslund .25 .60
98 Sergei Gonchar .25 .60
99 Olaf Kolzig .30 .75
100 Dainius Zubrus .20 .50
101 Adam Oates JSY/1225 4.00 10.00
102 Dany Heatley JSY/975 4.00 10.00
103 Ilya Kovalchuk JSY/725 5.00 12.00
104 Joe Thornton JSY/1475 5.00 12.00
105 Miroslav Satan JSY/510 4.00 10.00
106 Jarome Iginla JSY/1000 8.00 20.00
107 Roman Turek JSY/1475 4.00 10.00
108 Ron Francis JSY/1175 5.00 12.00
109 Theo Fleury JSY/1100 5.00 12.00
110 Patrick Roy JSY/475 10.00 25.00
111 Joe Sakic JSY/975 8.00 20.00
112 Marc Denis JSY/1175 3.00 8.00
113 Jason Arnott JSY/1475 3.00 8.00
114 Bill Guerin JSY/875 4.00 10.00
115 Mike Modano JSY/975 6.00 15.00
116 Sergei Fedorov JSY 6.00 15.00
117 Dominik Hasek JSY/1475 6.00 15.00
118 Curtis Joseph JSY/1475 4.00 10.00
119 Nicklas Lidstrom JSY/1475 4.00 10.00
120 Luc Robitaille JSY/1475 4.00 10.00
121 Steve Yzerman JSY/730 8.00 20.00
122 Mike Comrie JSY/1475 4.00 10.00
123 Tommy Salo JSY/1475 3.00 8.00
124 Roberto Luongo JSY/1475 6.00 15.00
125 Felix Potvin JSY/1250 6.00 15.00
126 Marian Gaborik JSY/1175 8.00 20.00
127 Jose Theodore JSY/1475 4.00 10.00
128 David Legwand JSY/1475 3.00 8.00
129 Martin Brodeur JSY/975 8.00 20.00
130 Patrik Elias JSY/1475 4.00 10.00
131 Michael Peca JSY/1475 3.00 8.00
132 Alexei Yashin JSY/1475 3.00 8.00
133 Eric Lindros JSY/1475 6.00 15.00
134 Marian Hossa JSY/1100 3.00 8.00
135 Roman Cechmanek JSY/1475 3.00 8.00
136 Simon Gagne JSY/1475 4.00 10.00
137 Daymond Langkow JSY/1175 3.00 8.00
138 Mario Lemieux JSY/531 12.00 30.00
139 Chris Pronger JSY/1475 3.00 8.00
140 Keith Tkachuk JSY/1475 4.00 10.00
141 Evgeni Nabokov JSY/1475 3.00 8.00
142 Owen Nolan JSY/1475 4.00 10.00
143 Nikolai Khabibulin JSY/1475 4.00 10.00
144 Brad Richards JSY/1475 4.00 10.00
145 Ed Belfour JSY/865 4.00 10.00
146 Mats Sundin JSY 8.00 20.00
147 Todd Bertuzzi JSY/1475 4.00 10.00
148 Peter Bondra JSY/1475 4.00 10.00
149 Jaromir Jagr JSY/1475 8.00 20.00
150 Robert Lang JSY/1475 2.50 6.00
151 Stanislav Chistov RC 8.00 20.00
152 Martin Gerber RC 12.00 30.00
153 Alexei Smirnov RC 10.00 25.00
154 Tim Thomas RC 40.00 80.00
155 Chuck Kobasew RC 10.00 25.00
156 Jordan Leopold RC 12.00 30.00
157 Rick Nash RC 75.00 150.00
158 Lasse Pirjeta RC 8.00 20.00
159 Dmitri Bykov RC 8.00 20.00
160 Henrik Zetterberg RC 60.00 120.00
161 Kari Haakana RC 8.00 20.00
162 Ales Hemsky RC 30.00 80.00
163 Jay Bouwmeester RC 25.00 60.00
164 Alexander Frolov RC 15.00 40.00
165 P-M Bouchard RC 12.00 30.00
166 Stephane Veilleux RC 8.00 20.00
167 Sylvain Blouin RC 8.00 20.00
168 Ron Hainsey RC 8.00 20.00
169 Adam Hall RC 8.00 20.00
170 Scottie Upshall RC 10.00 25.00
171 Ray Schultz RC 8.00 20.00
172 Mattias Weinhandl 8.00 20.00
173 Jason Spezza RC 75.00 150.00
174 Anton Volchenkov RC 8.00 20.00
175 Dennis Seidenberg RC 12.00 30.00
176 Patrick Sharp RC 25.00 50.00
177 Radovan Somik RC 8.00 20.00
178 Jeff Taffe RC 8.00 20.00
179 Dick Tarnstrom RC 8.00 20.00
180 Tom Koivisto RC 8.00 20.00
181 Curtis Sanford RC 12.00 30.00
182 Alexander Svitov RC 8.00 20.00
183 Carlo Colaiacovo RC 12.00 30.00
184 Steve Eminger RC 8.00 20.00
185 Alex Henry RC 10.00 25.00

2002-03 Private Stock Reserve Blue

This 135-card set paralleled the base set without the jersey card subset. Each card carried blue foil highlights. Cards 1-100 were serial-numbered to 499 and cards 151-185 were serial-numbered to 250.

*1-100 VETS/499: 1.2X TO 3X BASIC CARDS
*151-185 ROOKIE/250: .05X TO .15X HOB

2002-03 Private Stock Reserve Red

This hobby-only set paralled the base set but was accented with red foil. Cards were serial-numbered to just 50.

*1-100 VETS/50: 6X TO 15X BASIC CARDS
*101-150 JSY/50: .8X TO 2X BASIC JSY
*151-185 ROOKIE/50: .2X TO .5X BASIC RC

2002-03 Private Stock Reserve Retail

This 185-card set mirrored the hobby version but with silver foil highlights. Shortprints (151-185) were serial-numbered to 1550.

*1-100 VETS: .4X TO 1X BASIC CARDS
*101-150 JSY: .3X TO .8X BASIC JSY
COMMON ROOKIE/1550 1.00 2.50
ROOK.SEMISTARS/1550 1.25 3.00
ROOK.UNL.STARS/1550 1.50 4.00
154 Tim Thomas RC 4.00 10.00
157 Rick Nash RC 8.00 20.00
160 Henrik Zetterberg RC 10.00 25.00
162 Ales Hemsky RC 4.00 10.00
163 Jay Bouwmeester RC 3.00 8.00
164 Alexander Frolov RC 2.00 5.00
173 Jason Spezza RC 6.00 15.00
176 Patrick Sharp RC 3.00 8.00

2002-03 Private Stock Reserve Class Act

COMPLETE SET (10) 15.00 40.00
STATED ODDS 1:9 HBBY/1:49 RETAIL
1 Stanislav Chistov 1.50 4.00
2 Alexei Smirnov 1.50 4.00
3 Ivan Huml 1.50 4.00
4 Chuck Kobasew 2.00 5.00
5 Tyler Arnason 1.50 4.00
6 Rick Nash 6.00 15.00
7 Henrik Zetterberg 6.00 15.00
8 Jay Bouwmeester 4.00 10.00
9 Stephen Weiss 2.00 5.00
10 Barret Jackman 1.50 4.00

2002-03 Private Stock Reserve Elite

COMPLETE SET (6) 15.00 40.00
STATED ODDS 1:17 HBBY/1:49 RETAIL
1 Ilya Kovalchuk 2.50 6.00
2 Peter Forsberg 4.00 10.00
3 Patrick Roy 5.00 12.00
4 Steve Yzerman 5.00 12.00
5 Mario Lemieux 5.00 12.00
6 Jaromir Jagr 2.50 6.00

2002-03 Private Stock Reserve InCrease Security

COMPLETE SET (20) 15.00 30.00
STATED ODDS 1:3 HBBY/1:25 RETAIL
1 Jean-Sebastien Giguere .75 2.00
2 Roman Turek .75 2.00
3 Arturs Irbe .75 2.00
4 Jocelyn Thibault .75 2.00
5 Patrick Roy 3.00 8.00
6 Marc Denis .75 2.00
7 Marty Turco .75 2.00
8 Curtis Joseph 1.25 3.00
9 Tommy Salo .75 2.00
10 Roberto Luongo 2.00 5.00
11 Felix Potvin .75 2.00
12 Jose Theodore 2.00 5.00
13 Martin Brodeur 2.50 6.00
14 Chris Osgood .75 2.00
15 Mike Richter 1.25 3.00
16 Roman Cechmanek .75 2.00
17 Sean Burke .75 2.00
18 Brent Johnson .75 2.00
19 Evgeni Nabokov .75 2.00
20 Ed Belfour 1.50 4.00

2002-03 Private Stock Reserve Moments in Time

COMPLETE SET (8) 10.00 25.00
STATED ODDS 1:9 HBBY/1:49 RETAIL
1 Chuck Kobasew 2.00 5.00
2 Rick Nash 6.00 15.00
3 Jay Bouwmeester 3.00 8.00
4 Stephen Weiss 2.00 5.00
5 Alexander Frolov 2.00 5.00
6 Jamie Lundmark 1.50 4.00
7 Barret Jackman 1.50 4.00
8 Alexander Svitov 2.00 5.00

2002-03 Private Stock Reserve Patches

This 39-card hobby only set partially paralleled the jersey cards in the base set but were affixed with jersey patches. Each card was serial-numbered individually. Lower print runs are not priced due to scarcity.

102 Dany Heatley/50 20.00 50.00
103 Ilya Kovalchuk/50 25.00 60.00
104 Joe Thornton/275 12.50 30.00
105 Miroslav Satan/275 10.00 25.00
106 Jarome Iginla/70 15.00 40.00
107 Roman Turek/90 10.00 25.00
109 Theo Fleury/275 10.00 25.00
112 Marc Denis/250 10.00 25.00
113 Jason Arnott/250 10.00 25.00
114 Bill Guerin/100 10.00 25.00
115 Mike Modano/150 15.00 40.00
116 Sergei Fedorov/150 15.00 40.00
119 Nicklas Lidstrom/275 12.50 30.00
121 Steve Yzerman/15
122 Mike Comrie/125 10.00 25.00
123 Tommy Salo/275 10.00 25.00
124 Roberto Luongo/150 15.00 40.00
125 Felix Potvin/250 12.50 30.00
126 Marian Gaborik/100 15.00 40.00
127 Jose Theodore/50 15.00 40.00
128 David Legwand/250 10.00 25.00
129 Martin Brodeur/150 15.00 40.00
130 Patrik Elias/150 10.00 25.00
131 Michael Peca/250 10.00 25.00
133 Eric Lindros/250 12.50 30.00
134 Marian Hossa/250 12.50 30.00
135 Roman Cechmanek/250 10.00 25.00
136 Simon Gagne/200 12.50 30.00
137 Daymond Langkow/150 10.00 25.00
139 Chris Pronger/250 10.00 25.00
140 Keith Tkachuk/150 12.50 30.00
141 Evgeni Nabokov/200 10.00 25.00
142 Owen Nolan/250 10.00 25.00
143 Nikolai Khabibulin/275 12.50 30.00
144 Brad Richards/275 10.00 25.00
145 Ed Belfour/245 12.50 30.00
147 Todd Bertuzzi/275 12.50 30.00
148 Peter Bondra/275 10.00 25.00
150 Robert Lang/250 10.00 25.00

2003-04 Private Stock Reserve

This 212-card set was released in late-January and consisted of 100 base veteran cards; 40 short-printed rookie cards (numbered to 99) and 72 jersey cards with varying print runs. Hobby cards were printed with gold foil highlights and retail silver foil. Overall jerseys were inserted one per pack.

COMP.SET w/o SP's (100) 15.00 40.00
1 Stanislav Chistov .20 .50
2 Jean-Sebastien Giguere .30 .75
3 Vaclav Prospal .20 .50
4 Petr Sykora .25 .60
5 Byron Dafoe .25 .60
6 Slava Kozlov .25 .60
7 Pasi Nurminen .25 .60
8 Marc Savard .25 .60
9 Mike Knuble .20 .50
10 Felix Potvin .50 1.25
11 Sergei Samsonov .25 .60
12 Daniel Briere .30 .75
13 Ales Kotalik .20 .50
14 Ryan Miller .30 .75
15 Blair Betts .20 .50
16 Chuck Kobasew .20 .50
17 Jordan Leopold .20 .50
18 Ron Francis .40 1.00
19 Jeff O'Neill .20 .50
20 Kevin Weekes .25 .60
21 Igor Radulov .20 .50
22 Jocelyn Thibault .25 .60
23 Alexei Zhamnov .25 .60
24 David Aebischer .25 .60
25 Rob Blake .30 .75
26 Andrew Cassels .20 .50
27 Rick Nash .30 .75
28 Geoff Sanderson .20 .50
29 Niko Kapanen .20 .50
30 Jere Lehtinen .25 .60
31 Steve Ott .25 .60
32 Pavel Datsyuk .40 1.00
33 Nicklas Lidstrom .30 .75
34 Dominik Hasek .50 1.25
35 Henrik Zetterberg .40 1.00
36 Ales Hemsky .30 .75
37 Georges Laraque .25 .60
38 Tommy Salo .25 .60
39 Mike York .20 .50
40 Jay Bouwmeester .30 .75
41 Valeri Bure .20 .50
42 Viktor Kozlov .20 .50
43 Roberto Luongo .50 1.25
44 Stephen Weiss .20 .50
45 Roman Cechmanek .25 .60
46 Adam Deadmarsh .25 .60
47 Alexander Frolov .25 .60
48 Pierre-Marc Bouchard .30 .75
49 Andrew Brunette .20 .50
50 Marian Gaborik .50 1.25
51 Dwayne Roloson .25 .60
52 Mathieu Garon .20 .50
53 Marcel Hossa .20 .50
54 Yanic Perreault .20 .50
55 Mike Ribeiro .25 .60
56 Andreas Johansson .20 .50
57 Scottie Upshall .25 .60
58 Scott Walker .20 .50
59 Patrik Elias .30 .75
60 Jeff Friesen .20 .50
61 Jamie Langenbrunner .25 .60
62 Scott Stevens .30 .75
63 Jason Blake .20 .50
64 Oleg Kvasha .20 .50
65 Mark Parrish .20 .50
66 Garth Snow .25 .60
67 Mattias Weinhandl .20 .50
68 Mike Dunham .25 .60
69 Alex Kovalev .25 .60
70 Brian Leetch .30 .75
71 Mark Messier .50 1.25
72 Radek Bonk .25 .60
73 Vaclav Varada .20 .50
74 Todd White .20 .50
75 Simon Gagne .30 .75
76 John LeClair .30 .75
77 Mark Recchi .40 1.00
78 Shane Doan .25 .60
79 Mike Johnson .20 .50
80 Daymond Langkow .20 .50
81 Ladislav Nagy .20 .50
82 Sebastien Caron .25 .60
83 Alexei Morozov .20 .50
84 Brent Johnson .25 .60
85 Al MacInnis .30 .75
86 Chris Pronger .25 .60
87 Keith Tkachuk .30 .75
88 Jonathan Cheechoo .25 .60
89 Vincent Damphousse .25 .60
90 Patrick Marleau .30 .75
91 Evgeni Nabokov .25 .60
92 Dave Andreychuk .30 .75
93 Dan Boyle .25 .60
94 Alexander Mogilny .25 .60
95 Owen Nolan .25 .60
96 Darcy Tucker .25 .60
97 Ed Jovanovski .25 .60
98 Trevor Linden .30 .75
99 Sergei Gonchar .20 .50
100 Olaf Kolzig .30 .75
101 Garrett Burnett RC 6.00 15.00
102 Joffrey Lupul RC 15.00 40.00

103 Joe DiPenta RC 8.00 20.00
104 Patrice Bergeron RC 30.00 80.00
105 Milan Bartovic RC 8.00 20.00
106 Andrew Peters RC 8.00 20.00
107 Brent Krahn RC 6.00 15.00
108 Eric Staal RC 30.00 80.00
109 Lasse Kukkonen RC 6.00 15.00
110 Travis Moen RC 8.00 20.00
111 Tuomo Ruutu RC 10.00 25.00
112 Pavel Vorobiev RC 8.00 20.00
113 Cody McCormick RC 8.00 20.00
114 Dan Fritsche RC 6.00 15.00
115 Kent McDonell RC 8.00 20.00
116 Trevor Daley RC 10.00 25.00
117 Antti Miettinen RC 10.00 25.00
118 Jiri Hudler RC 15.00 40.00
119 Nathan Horton RC 15.00 40.00
120 Dustin Brown RC 12.00 30.00
121 Tim Gleason RC 8.00 20.00
122 Esa Pirnes RC 6.00 15.00
123 Brent Burns RC 15.00 40.00
124 Chris Higgins RC 12.00 30.00
125 Dan Hamhuis RC 8.00 20.00
126 Jordin Tootoo RC 12.00 30.00
127 Marek Zidlicky RC 6.00 15.00
128 David Hale RC 6.00 15.00
129 Paul Martin RC 8.00 20.00
130 Sean Bergenheim RC 8.00 20.00
131 Antoine Vermette RC 12.00 30.00
132 Joni Pitkanen RC 10.00 25.00
133 Matthew Spiller RC 8.00 20.00
134 Marc-Andre Fleury RC 50.00 100.00
135 Matt Murley RC 8.00 20.00
136 Peter Sejna RC 8.00 20.00
137 Milan Michalek RC 12.00 30.00
138 Maxim Kondratiev RC 6.00 15.00
139 Matt Stajan RC 10.00 25.00
140 Boyd Gordon RC 8.00 20.00
141 Sergei Fedorov JSY 6.00 15.00
142 Dany Heatley JSY/700 4.00 10.00
143 Ilya Kovalchuk JSY/900 4.00 10.00
144 Glen Murray JSY 3.00 8.00
145 Joe Thornton JSY/900 5.00 12.00
146 Martin Biron JSY/1000 3.00 8.00
147 Chris Drury JSY 3.00 8.00
148 Miroslav Satan JSY/1000 3.00 8.00
149 Craig Conroy JSY 2.50 6.00
150 Jarome Iginla JSY 4.00 10.00
151 Erik Cole JSY 3.00 8.00
152 Eric Daze JSY 3.00 8.00
153 Theo Fleury JSY 5.00 12.00
154 Peter Forsberg JSY 5.00 12.00
155 Milan Hejduk JSY 3.00 8.00
156 Paul Kariya JSY 5.00 12.00
157 Patrick Roy JSY/99 15.00 40.00
158 Joe Sakic JSY/975 6.00 15.00
159 Teemu Selanne JSY 8.00 20.00
160 Marc Denis JSY 3.00 8.00
161 Rostislav Klesla JSY 2.50 6.00
162 Bill Guerin JSY 4.00 10.00
163 Mike Modano JSY/1000 6.00 15.00
164 Marty Turco JSY 4.00 10.00
165 Brett Hull JSY/750 5.00 12.00
166 Steve Yzerman JSY/900 10.00 25.00
167 Mike Comrie JSY 3.00 8.00
168 Ryan Smyth JSY 3.00 8.00
169 Olli Jokinen JSY/1000 4.00 10.00
170 Jason Allison JSY 3.00 8.00
171 Zigmund Palffy JSY/1000 4.00 10.00
172 Filip Kuba JSY/99 8.00 20.00
173 Saku Koivu JSY/1000 4.00 10.00
174 Jose Theodore JSY 4.00 10.00
175 Richard Zednik JSY/1000 2.50 6.00
176 David Legwand JSY 3.00 8.00
177 Tomas Vokoun JSY 3.00 8.00
178 Martin Brodeur JSY/750 8.00 20.00
179 Rick DiPietro JSY/900 3.00 8.00
180 Michael Peca JSY/900 3.00 8.00
181 Alexei Yashin JSY/750 3.00 8.00
182 Pavel Bure JSY/750 5.00 12.00
183 Eric Lindros JSY 6.00 15.00
184 Mike Richter JSY/99
185 Daniel Alfredsson JSY 4.00 10.00
186 Marian Hossa JSY 3.00 8.00
187 Patrick Lalime JSY 3.00 8.00
188 Bryan Smolinski JSY 2.50 6.00
189 Jason Spezza JSY/750 4.00 10.00
190 Tony Amonte JSY 3.00 8.00
191 Jeff Hackett JSY/1000 3.00 8.00
192 Jeremy Roenick JSY/500 4.00 10.00
193 Sean Burke JSY 2.50 6.00
194 Mario Lemieux JSY/99 10.00 25.00
195 Martin Straka JSY 2.50 6.00
196 Pavol Demitra JSY 5.00 12.00
197 Chris Osgood JSY 4.00 10.00
198 Doug Weight JSY 4.00 10.00
199 Nikolai Khabibulin JSY 4.00 10.00
200 Vincent Lecavalier JSY/500 3.00 8.00
201 Fredrik Modin JSY/600 2.50 6.00
202 Brad Richards JSY/750 4.00 10.00
203 Martin St. Louis JSY 4.00 10.00
204 Cory Stillman JSY/99 8.00 20.00
205 Ed Belfour JSY 4.00 10.00
206 Mats Sundin JSY 4.00 10.00
207 Todd Bertuzzi JSY 4.00 10.00
208 Dan Cloutier JSY 3.00 8.00
209 Brendan Morrison JSY/750 3.00 8.00
210 Markus Naslund JSY/950 4.00 10.00
211 Jaromir Jagr JSY 10.00 25.00
212 Robert Lang JSY/425 2.50 6.00

2003-04 Private Stock Reserve Blue

*1-100 VETS/350: 1.5X TO 4X BASIC CARDS
*101-140 ROOKIE/250: .1X TO .3X RC/99
*JERSEY/25: 1.2X TO 3X BASIC JSY
*JERSEY/25: .8X TO 2X JSY/99
71 Mark Messier 2.00 5.00

2003-04 Private Stock Reserve Patches

This 68-card set paralleled the jerseys of the base set but included patch swatches. Please note that cards #151,159 and 161 do not exist. Cards with print runs under 25 were not priced due to scarcity. Known shortprints are listed below.
*PATCHES: 1.25X TO 3X BASE JSY
141 Sergei Fedorov 15.00 40.00
142 Dany Heatley/50 15.00 40.00
143 Ilya Kovalchuk/25 50.00 120.00
144 Glen Murray 10.00 25.00
145 Joe Thornton/50 20.00 50.00
146 Martin Biron 15.00 30.00
147 Chris Drury 15.00 30.00
148 Miroslav Satan 15.00 30.00
150 Jarome Iginla 12.50 30.00
152 Eric Daze 12.50 40.00
153 Theo Fleury 10.00 25.00
154 Peter Forsberg/70 20.00 50.00
155 Milan Hejduk 12.50 30.00
156 Paul Kariya 12.50 30.00
157 Patrick Roy 15.00 40.00
158 Joe Sakic 15.00 40.00
159 Teemu Selanne/10
160 Marc Denis 15.00 30.00
162 Bill Guerin 12.50 40.00
163 Mike Modano 15.00 40.00
164 Marty Turco/50 12.50 40.00
165 Brett Hull 15.00 40.00
166 Steve Yzerman/19
167 Mike Comrie/25 30.00 80.00
168 Ryan Smyth/25 15.00 40.00
169 Olli Jokinen 12.50 40.00
170 Jason Allison 10.00 25.00
171 Zigmund Palffy 15.00 30.00
172 Filip Kuba 12.50 30.00
173 Saku Koivu 12.50 30.00
174 Jose Theodore 15.00 40.00
175 Richard Zednik 10.00 25.00
176 David Legwand 12.50 40.00
177 Tomas Vokoun 15.00 30.00
178 Martin Brodeur 30.00 80.00
179 Rick DiPietro/200 15.00 40.00
180 Michael Peca 10.00 25.00
181 Alexei Yashin 10.00 25.00
182 Pavel Bure 12.50 30.00
183 Eric Lindros 12.50 30.00
184 Mike Richter
185 Daniel Alfredsson 15.00 40.00
186 Marian Hossa 12.50 30.00
187 Patrick Lalime 12.50 40.00
188 Bryan Smolinski/20
189 Jason Spezza/25 15.00 40.00
190 Tony Amonte 10.00 25.00
191 Jeff Hackett 15.00 30.00
192 Jeremy Roenick 15.00 40.00
193 Sean Burke/65 15.00 40.00
194 Mario Lemieux 25.00 60.00
195 Martin Straka 10.00 25.00
197 Chris Osgood 15.00 40.00
198 Doug Weight 15.00 40.00
199 Nikolai Khabibulin 12.50 30.00
200 Vincent Lecavalier 12.50 30.00
201 Fredrik Modin 12.50 30.00
202 Brad Richards/25 25.00 60.00
203 Martin St. Louis 15.00 40.00
204 Cory Stillman 8.00 20.00
205 Ed Belfour 12.50 30.00
206 Mats Sundin/50 10.00 30.00
207 Todd Bertuzzi 12.50 30.00
208 Dan Cloutier 15.00 30.00
209 Brendan Morrison 12.50 40.00
210 Markus Naslund/75 12.50 30.00
211 Jaromir Jagr 20.00 50.00
212 Robert Lang 10.00 25.00

2003-04 Private Stock Reserve Red

*1-100 VETS/199: 2.5X TO 6X BASIC CARDS
*101-140 ROOKIE/225: .1X TO .3X RC/99
*JERSEY/50: .8X TO 2X BASIC JSY
*JERSEY/50: .5X TO 1.2X BASIC JSY/99
71 Mark Messier 3.00 8.00

2003-04 Private Stock Reserve Retail

The retail version of this set carried silver foil highlights. Rookies were serial-numbered out of 1299.
*1-100 VETS: .4X TO 1X HOBBY
*101-140 ROOKIE/1299: .08X TO .2X HOBBY/99
*141-212 JERSEY: .6X TO 1.5X HOBBY
*141-212 JERSEY: .4X TO 1X JSY/99
71 Mark Messier .50 1.25

2003-04 Private Stock Reserve Class Act

COMPLETE SET (12) 15.00 30.00
STATED ODDS 1:9
1 Joffrey Lupul .60 1.50
2 Eric Staal 1.25 3.00
3 Tuomo Ruutu .60 1.50
4 Nathan Horton 1.00 2.50
5 Dustin Brown .60 1.50
6 Chris Higgins .40 1.00
7 Jordin Tootoo 1.00 2.50
8 Joni Pitkanen .60 1.50
9 Marc-Andre Fleury 2.00 5.00
10 Peter Sejna .40 1.00
11 Milan Michalek .40 1.00
12 Matt Stajan .40 1.00

2003-04 Private Stock Reserve Increase Security

COMPLETE SET (16) 10.00 25.00
STATED ODDS 1:5
1 Jean-Sebastien Giguere .75 2.00
2 Felix Potvin .75 2.00
3 Ryan Miller 1.00 2.50
4 Jocelyn Thibault .75 2.00
5 David Aebischer .75 2.00
6 Marty Turco .75 2.00
7 Dominik Hasek 1.50 4.00
8 Jose Theodore 1.00 2.50
9 Martin Brodeur 2.50 6.00
10 Rick DiPietro .75 2.00
11 Patrick Lalime .75 2.00
12 Sean Burke .75 2.00
13 Marc-Andre Fleury 2.50 6.00
14 Evgeni Nabokov .75 2.00
15 Nikolai Khabibulin .75 2.00
16 Ed Belfour .75 2.00

2003-04 Private Stock Reserve Moments in Time

COMPLETE SET (10) 20.00 40.00
UNLISTED STARS 1.00 2.50
STATED ODDS 1:17
1 Sergei Fedorov 1.00 2.50
2 Joe Thornton 1.25 3.00
3 Peter Forsberg 1.50 4.00
4 Paul Kariya 1.25 3.00
5 Joe Sakic 1.50 4.00
6 Mike Modano 1.25 3.00
7 Brett Hull 1.00 2.50
8 Steve Yzerman 2.00 5.00
9 Mario Lemieux 2.50 6.00
10 Todd Bertuzzi .75 2.00

2003-04 Private Stock Reserve Rising Stock

COMPLETE SET (12) 10.00 20.00
STATED ODDS 1:9
1 Ilya Kovalchuk 1.00 2.50
2 Ales Kotalik .40 1.00
3 Ryan Miller .75 2.00
4 Chuck Kobasew .40 1.00
5 Rick Nash .75 2.00
6 Henrik Zetterberg .75 2.00
7 Ales Hemsky .50 1.25
8 Jay Bouwmeester .40 1.00
9 Pierre-Marc Bouchard .40 1.00
10 Marcel Hossa .40 1.00
11 Jason Spezza 1.00 2.50
12 Barret Jackman .40 1.00

1995-96 Pro Magnets

This set of 130 magnets was produced by Chris Martin Enterprises. Each magnet featured a color photo of the player on front, along with his name and team. The backs were simply a black magnetic surface.
COMPLETE SET (130) 30.00 75.00
1 Ed Belfour 1.00 2.50
2 Chris Chelios 1.00 2.50
3 Joe Murphy .50 1.25
4 Jeremy Roenick 1.00 2.50
5 Bernie Nicholls .50 1.25
6 Brett Hull 1.00 2.50
7 Esa Tikkanen .50 1.25
8 Chris Pronger .50 1.25
9 Al MacInnis .50 1.25
10 Geoff Courtnall .50 1.25
11 Ray Bourque 1.50 4.00
12 Blaine Lacher .60 1.50
13 Cam Neely .75 2.00
14 Adam Oates .75 2.00
15 Kevin Stevens .50 1.25
16 Vincent Damphousse .60 1.50
17 Mark Recchi .75 2.00
18 Pierre Turgeon .60 1.50
19 Valeri Bure .50 1.25
20 Patrick Roy 3.00 8.00
21 Pavel Bure 1.50 4.00
22 Alexander Mogilny .60 1.50
23 Trevor Linden .75 2.00
24 Kirk McLean .60 1.50
25 Cliff Ronning .50 1.25
26 Jim Carey .60 1.50
27 Dale Hunter .50 1.25
28 Joe Juneau .50 1.25
29 Jason Allison .50 1.25
30 Brendan Witt .50 1.25
31 John MacLean .50 1.25
32 Scott Niedermayer .50 1.25
33 Martin Brodeur 1.50 4.00
34 Stephane Richer .50 1.25
35 Scott Stevens .50 1.25
36 Patrik Carnback .50 1.25
37 Guy Hebert .60 1.50
38 Oleg Tverdovsky .50 1.25
39 Paul Kariya 2.00 5.00
40 Garry Valk .50 1.25
41 Theo Fleury .75 2.00
42 German Titov .50 1.25
43 Joe Nieuwendyk .60 1.50
44 Gary Roberts .50 1.25
45 Trevor Kidd .50 1.25
46 Rod Brind'Amour .50 1.25
47 Eric Lindros 1.50 4.00
48 Ron Hextall .60 1.50
49 John LeClair 1.00 2.50
50 Mikael Renberg .50 1.25
51 Patrick Flatley .50 1.25
52 Kirk Muller .50 1.25
53 Mathieu Schneider .50 1.25
54 Wendel Clark .50 1.25
55 Brett Lindros .50 1.25
56 Tim Cheveldae .50 1.25
57 Dallas Drake .50 1.25
58 Teemu Selanne 1.25 3.00
59 Keith Tkachuk .75 2.00
60 Alexei Zhamnov .50 1.25
61 Rob Blake .75 2.00
62 Wayne Gretzky 5.00 12.00
63 Jari Kurri .50 1.25
64 Jamie Storr .50 1.25
65 Rick Tocchet .50 1.25
66 Brian Bradley .50 1.25
67 Roman Hamrlik .50 1.25
68 Rob Zamuner .50 1.25
69 Paul Ysebaert .50 1.25
70 Chris Gratton .50 1.25
71 Dave Andreychuk .50 1.25
72 Kenny Jonsson .50 1.25
73 Doug Gilmour .75 2.00
74 Felix Potvin 1.00 2.50
75 Mats Sundin .75 2.00
76 Claude Lemieux .50 1.25
77 Peter Forsberg 1.00 2.50
78 Mike Ricci .50 1.25
79 Stephane Fiset .60 1.50
80 Joe Sakic 1.50 4.00
81 Jason Arnott .60 1.50
82 Jason Bonsignore .50 1.25
83 Doug Weight .50 1.25
84 Todd Marchant .50 1.25
85 Bill Ranford .50 1.25
86 Rob Niedermayer .50 1.25
87 Jody Hull .50 1.25
88 Bob Kudelski .50 1.25
89 Scott Mellanby .50 1.25
90 John Vanbiesbrouck .75 2.00
91 Bryan Smolinski .50 1.25
92 Mario Lemieux 3.00 8.00
93 Jaromir Jagr 1.50 4.00
94 Sergei Zubov .50 1.25
95 Ron Francis .60 1.50
96 Adam Graves .50 1.25
97 Brian Leetch .75 2.00
98 Mark Messier 1.00 2.50
99 Mike Richter .75 2.00
100 Luc Robitaille .60 1.50
101 Paul Coffey .60 1.50
102 Sergei Fedorov 1.50 4.00
103 Nicklas Lidstrom 1.00 2.50
104 Ray Sheppard .50 1.25
105 Steve Yzerman 3.00 8.00
106 Dominik Hasek 1.50 4.00
107 Alexei Zhitnik .50 1.25
108 Yuri Khmylev .50 1.25
109 Pat LaFontaine .50 1.25
110 Donald Audette .50 1.25
111 Radek Bonk .50 1.25
112 Alexandre Daigle .50 1.25
113 Steve Larouche .50 1.25
114 Martin Straka .50 1.25
115 Randy Cunneyworth .50 1.25
116 Jeff Friesen .50 1.25
117 Arturs Irbe .60 1.50
118 Ulf Dahlen .50 1.25
119 Craig Janney .50 1.25
120 Pat Falloon .50 1.25
121 Shane Churla .50 1.25
122 Todd Harvey .50 1.25
123 Derian Hatcher .50 1.25
124 Mike Modano 1.00 2.50
125 Andy Moog .60 1.50
126 Sean Burke .50 1.25
127 Andrew Cassels .50 1.25
128 Darren Turcotte .50 1.25
129 Geoff Courtnall .50 1.25
130 Brendan Shanahan 1.25 3.00

1995-96 Pro Magnets Iron Curtain

IC1 Ed Belfour 2.50 6.00
IC2 Martin Brodeur 3.00 8.00
IC3 Arturs Irbe 2.00 5.00
IC4 Mike Richter 2.00 5.00
IC5 Mike Vernon 2.00 5.00
IC6 Ron Hextall 2.50 6.00

1990-91 Pro Set

The inaugural Pro Set issue contains 705 cards measuring the standard size, with the first series containing 405 cards followed by a 300 card second series. The fronts feature a color action photo, banded above and below in the team's colors. The horizontally oriented backs have a head shot of each player and player information sandwiched between color stripes in the team's colors. Many grammatical, statistical and factual errors punctuated this issue.
COMPLETE SET (705) 10.00 25.00
COMP.SERIES 1 (405) 5.00 12.00
COMP.SERIES 2 (300) 5.00 12.00
1A Brett Hull Promo 1.00 2.50
1B Ray Bourque ERR .15 .40
1C Ray Bourque COR .15 .40
2 Randy Burridge .07 .20
3 Lyndon Byers RC .07 .20
4 Bob Carpenter .07 .20
5 John Carter RC .07 .20
6 Dave Christian .07 .20
7A Garry Galley ERR RC .05 .15
7B Garry Galley COR RC .05 .15
8 Craig Janney .10 .25
9 Rejean Lemelin .07 .20
10 Andy Moog .10 .25
11 Cam Neely .10 .25
12 Allen Pedersen .07 .20
13 Dave Poulin .10 .25
14 Brian Propp .10 .25
15 Bob Sweeney .05 .15
16 Glen Wesley .07 .20
17A Dave Andreychuk ERR .10 .25
17B Dave Andreychuk COR .10 .25
18A Scott Arniel ERR .05 .15
18B Scott Arniel COR .05 .15
19 Doug Bodger .07 .20
20 Mike Foligno .07 .20
21A Phil Housley ERR .07 .20
21B Phil Housley COR .07 .20
22 Dean Kennedy RC .05 .15
23 Uwe Krupp .10 .25
24 Grant Ledyard RC .10 .25
25 Clint Malarchuk .07 .20
26 Alexander Mogilny RC .30 .75
27 Daren Puppa .07 .20
28 Mike Ramsey .05 .15
29 Christian Ruuttu .07 .20
30 Dave Snuggerud RC .07 .20
31 Pierre Turgeon .07 .20
32 Rick Vaive .07 .20
33 Theo Fleury .12 .30
34 Doug Gilmour .12 .30
35 Al MacInnis .07 .20
36 Brian MacLellan .07 .20
37 Jamie Macoun .07 .20
38 Sergei Makarov RC .20 .50
39A Brad McCrimmon ERR .10 .25
39B Brad McCrimmon COR .10 .25
40A Joe Mullen ERR .07 .20
40B Joe Mullen COR .07 .20
41 Dana Murzyn .10 .25
42A Joe Nieuwendyk ERR .05 .15
42B Joe Nieuwendyk COR .05 .15
43 Joel Otto .07 .20
44 Paul Ranheim RC .10 .25
45 Gary Roberts .10 .25
46 Gary Suter .10 .25
47 Mike Vernon .10 .25
48 Rick Wamsley .10 .25
49 Keith Brown .07 .20
50 Adam Creighton .05 .15
51 Dirk Graham .07 .20
52 Steve Konroyd .05 .15
53A Steve Larmer ERR .07 .20
53B Steve Larmer COR .07 .20
54A Dave Manson ERR .10 .25
54B Dave Manson COR .10 .25
55A Bob McGill ERR .05 .15
55B Bob McGill COR .05 .15
56 Greg Millen .07 .20
57A Troy Murray .07 .20
57B Troy Murray .07 .20
58 Jeremy Roenick RC .30 .75
59A Denis Savard .12 .30
59B Denis Savard .12 .30
60A Al Secord ERR .05 .15
60B Al Secord COR .05 .15
61A Duane Sutter ERR .07 .20
61B Duane Sutter COR .07 .20
62 Steve Thomas .05 .15
63A Doug Wilson ERR .10 .25
63B Doug Wilson COR .10 .25
64 Trent Yawney .10 .25
65 Dave Barr .10 .25
66 Shawn Burr .07 .20
67 Jimmy Carson .07 .20
68 John Chabot .10 .25
69 Steve Chiasson .05 .15
70 Bernie Federko .07 .20
71 Gerard Gallant .05 .15
72 Glen Hanlon .07 .20
73 Joey Kocur RC .20 .50
74 Lee Norwood .07 .20
75 Mike O'Connell .07 .20
76 Bob Probert .10 .25
77 Torrie Robertson .05 .15
78 Daniel Shank RC .10 .25
79 Steve Yzerman .30 .75
80 Rick Zombo RC .10 .25
81 Glenn Anderson .10 .25
82 Grant Fuhr .10 .25
83 Martin Gelinas RC .20 .50
84 Adam Graves RC .20 .50
85 Charlie Huddy .07 .20
86 Petr Klima .05 .15
87A Jari Kurri ERR .12 .30
87B Jari Kurri COR .12 .30
88 Mark Lamb .10 .25
89 Kevin Lowe .10 .25
90 Craig MacTavish .07 .20
91 Mark Messier .20 .50
92 Craig Muni .07 .20
93 Joe Murphy RC .07 .20
94 Bill Ranford .07 .20
95 Craig Simpson .07 .20
96 Steve Smith .07 .20
97 Esa Tikkanen .07 .20
98 Mikael Andersson .10 .25
99 Dave Babych .05 .15
100 Yvon Corriveau RC .07 .20
101 Randy Cunneyworth .07 .20
102 Kevin Dineen .10 .25
103 Dean Evason .07 .20
104 Ray Ferraro .07 .20
105 Ron Francis .12 .30
106 Grant Jennings RC .10 .25
107 Todd Krygier RC .07 .20
108 Randy Ladouceur .10 .25
109 Ulf Samuelsson .10 .25
110 Brad Shaw RC .07 .20
111 Dave Tippett .07 .20
112 Pat Verbeek .07 .20
113 Scott Young .05 .15
114 Brian Benning .07 .20
115 Steve Duchesne .05 .15
116 Todd Elik RC .10 .25
117 Tony Granato .07 .20
118 Wayne Gretzky .50 1.25
119 Kelly Hrudey .05 .15
120 Steve Kasper .07 .20
121A Mike Kushelnyski ERR .10 .25
121B Mike Kushelnyski COR .10 .25
122 Bob Kudelski RC .07 .20
123 Tom Laidlaw .10 .25
124 Marty McSorley .10 .25
125 Larry Robinson .07 .20
126 Luc Robitaille .10 .25
127 Tomas Sandstrom .10 .25
128 Dave Taylor .10 .25
129A John Tonelli ERR .07 .20
129B John Tonelli COR .07 .20
130A Brian Bellows ERR .07 .20
130B Brian Bellows COR .07 .20
ERR
131 Aaron Broten .07 .20
132 Neal Broten .05 .15
133 Jon Casey .10 .25
134 Shawn Chambers .07 .20
135 Shane Churla RC .05 .15
136 Ulf Dahlen .10 .25
137 Gaetan Duchesne .10 .25
138 Dave Gagner .10 .25
139 Stewart Gavin .10 .25
140 Curt Giles .07 .20
141 Basil McRae .07 .20
142 Mike Modano RC .30 .75
143 Larry Murphy .07 .20
144 Ville Siren RC .07 .20
145 Mark Tinordi RC .05 .15
146 Guy Carbonneau .05 .15
147A Chris Chelios ERR .10 .25
147B Chris Chelios COR .10 .25
148 Shayne Corson .07 .20
149 Russ Courtnall .10 .25
150 Brian Hayward .10 .25
151 Mike Keane RC .05 .15
152 Stephan Lebeau RC .07 .20
153 Claude Lemieux .05 .15
154 Craig Ludwig .10 .25
155 Mike McPhee .07 .20
156 Stephane Richer .10 .25
157 Patrick Roy .25 .60
158 Mathieu Schneider RC .07 .20
159 Brian Skrudland .07 .20
160 Bobby Smith .07 .20
161 Petr Svoboda .07 .20
162 Tommy Albelin .05 .15
163 Doug Brown .07 .20
164 Sean Burke .07 .20
165 Ken Daneyko .05 .15
166 Bruce Driver .10 .25
167A Slava Fetisov ERR RC .20 .50
167B Slava Fetisov COR RC .20 .50
168 Mark Johnson .07 .20
169 Alexei Kasatonov RC .10 .25
170 John MacLean .07 .20
171A David Maley ERR RC .10 .25
171B David Maley COR RC .10 .25
172 Kirk Muller .07 .20
173 Janne Ojanen RC .10 .25
174 Brendan Shanahan .12 .30
175A Peter Stastny ERR .07 .20
175B Peter Stastny COR .07 .20
176A Patrik Sundstrom ERR .10 .25
176B Patrik Sundstrom COR .10 .25
177 Sylvain Turgeon .07 .20
178 Ken Baumgartner RC .10 .25
179 Doug Crossman .07 .20
180 Gerald Diduck .07 .20
181 Mark Fitzpatrick RC .07 .20
182 Pat Flatley .10 .25
183 Glenn Healy RC .20 .50
184 Alan Kerr .07 .20
185 Derek King .10 .25
186 Pat LaFontaine .10 .25
187 Don Maloney .10 .25
188 Hubie McDonough RC .07 .20
189 Jeff Norton .10 .25
190 Gary Nylund .07 .20
191 Brent Sutter .07 .20
192 Bryan Trottier .12 .30
193 David Volek .10 .25
194 Randy Wood .05 .15
195 Jan Erixon .10 .25
196 Mike Gartner .10 .25
197 Ron Greschner .05 .15
198A Miloslav Horava ERR RC .07 .20
198B Miloslav Horava COR RC .07 .20
199 Mark Janssens RC .10 .25
200 Kelly Kisio .07 .20
201 Brian Leetch .12 .30
202 Randy Moller .10 .25
203 Brian Mullen .10 .25
204 Bernie Nicholls .10 .25
205A Chris Nilan ERR .05 .15
205B Chris Nilan COR .05 .15
206 John Ogrodnick .10 .25
207 James Patrick .10 .25
208 Darren Turcotte RC .07 .20
209 John Vanbiesbrouck .07 .20
210 Carey Wilson .07 .20
211 Mike Bullard .07 .20
212 Terry Carkner .07 .20
213 Jeff Chychrun RC .07 .20
214 Murray Craven .10 .25
215 Pelle Eklund .05 .15
216 Ron Hextall .07 .20
217 Mark Howe .10 .25
218 Tim Kerr .10 .25
219 Ken Linseman .07 .20
220 Scott Mellanby .10 .25
221 Gord Murphy .10 .25
222 Kjell Samuelsson .07 .20
223 Ilkka Sinisalo .07 .20
224 Ron Sutter .07 .20
225 Rick Tocchet .10 .25
226 Ken Wregget .10 .25
227 Tom Barrasso .07 .20
228A Phil Bourque ERR .07 .20
228B Phil Bourque COR .07 .20
229 Rob Brown .20 .50
230 Alain Chevrier .07 .20
231 Paul Coffey .10 .25
232 John Cullen .10 .25
233 Gord Dineen .07 .20
234 Bob Errey .07 .20
235 Jim Johnson .05 .15
236 Mario Lemieux .40 1.00
237 Troy Loney RC .10 .25
238 Barry Pederson .07 .20
239 Mark Recchi RC .30 .75
240 Kevin Stevens RC .20 .50
241 Tony Tanti .07 .20
242 Zarley Zalapski .07 .20
243 Joe Cirella .05 .15
244 Lucien DeBlois .07 .20
245A Marc Fortier ERR .07 .20
245B Marc Fortier COR .07 .20
246A P.Gillis ERR bloody nose 60.00 150.00
246B Paul Gillis COR .07 .20
247 Mike Hough .07 .20
248 Tony Hrkac .05 .15
249 Jeff Johnson RC .05 .15
250 Guy Lafleur .12 .30
251 Curtis Leschyshyn RC .07 .20
252 Claude Loiselle RC .05 .15
253 Mario Marois .07 .20
254 Tony McKegney .05 .15
255 Ken McRae RC .10 .25
256A Michel Petit ERR .07 .20
256B Michel Petit COR .07 .20
257 Joe Sakic .30 .75
258 Ron Tugnutt .07 .20
259 Rod Brind'Amour RC .20 .50
260 Jeff Brown .10 .25
261 Gino Cavallini .10 .25
262 Paul Cavallini .07 .20
263 Brett Hull .20 .50
264 Mike Lalor RC .07 .20
265 Dave Lowry RC .07 .20
266 Paul MacLean .07 .20
267 Rick Meagher .07 .20
268 Sergio Momesso RC .07 .20
269 Adam Oates .10 .25
270 Vincent Riendeau RC .10 .25
271 Gordie Roberts .05 .15
272 Rich Sutter .10 .25
273 Steve Tuttle .07 .20
274 Peter Zezel .10 .25
275A Allan Bester ERR .10 .25
275B Allan Bester COR .10 .25
276 Wendel Clark .10 .25
277 Brian Curran .05 .15
278 Vin Damphousse .07 .20
279A Tom Fergus ERR .07 .20
279B Tom Fergus COR .07 .20
280 Lou Franceschetti RC .10 .25
281 Al Iafrate .05 .15
282 Tom Kurvers .10 .25
283 Gary Leeman .07 .20
284 Daniel Marois .07 .20
285 Brad Marsh .07 .20
286 Ed Olczyk .10 .25
287 Mark Osborne .07 .20
288 Rob Ramage .10 .25
289 Luke Richardson .07 .20
290 Gilles Thibaudeau RC .05 .15
291 Greg Adams .05 .15
292 Jim Benning .05 .15
293 Steve Bozek .07 .20
294 Brian Bradley .07 .20
295 Garth Butcher .07 .20
296 Vladimir Krutov RC .20 .50
297 Igor Larionov RC .20 .50
298 Doug Lidster .10 .25
299 Trevor Linden .07 .20
300 Jyrki Lumme RC .05 .15
301A Andrew McBain ERR .07 .20
301B Andrew McBain COR .07 .20
302 Kirk McLean .05 .15
303 Dan Quinn .07 .20
304 Paul Reinhart .10 .25
305 Jim Sandlak .10 .25
306 Petri Skriko .10 .25
307 Don Beaupre .05 .15
308 Dino Ciccarelli .10 .25
309 Geoff Courtnall .07 .20
310 John Druce RC .10 .25
311 Kevin Hatcher .07 .20
312 Dale Hunter .10 .25
313 Calle Johansson .10 .25
314 Rod Langway .10 .25
315 Stephen Leach .07 .20
316 Mike Liut .07 .20
317 Alan May RC .05 .15
318 Kelly Miller .05 .15
319 Michal Pivonka RC .07 .20
320A Mike Ridley ERR .05 .15
320B Mike Ridley COR .05 .15
321 Scott Stevens .10 .25
322 John Tucker .07 .20
323 Brent Ashton .10 .25
324 Laurie Boschman .07 .20
325 Randy Carlyle .07 .20
326 Dave Ellett .05 .15
327 Pat Elynuik .07 .20
328 Bob Essensa RC .15 .40
329 Paul Fenton .10 .25
330A Dale Hawerchuk ERR .12 .30
330B Dale Hawerchuk COR .12 .30
331 Paul MacDermid .07 .20
332 Moe Mantha .10 .25
333 Dave McLlwain .10 .25
334 Teppo Numminen RC .20 .50
335A Fredrik Olausson ERR .07 .20
335B Fredrik Olausson COR .07 .20
336 Greg Paslawski .07 .20
337 Al MacInnis AS .07 .20
338 Mike Vernon AS .10 .25
339 Kevin Lowe AS .10 .25
340 Wayne Gretzky AS .50 1.25
341 Luc Robitaille AS .10 .25
342 Brett Hull AS .20 .50
343 Joe Mullen AS .07 .20
344 Joe Nieuwendyk AS .05 .15
345 Steve Larmer AS .07 .20
346 Doug Wilson AS .10 .25
347 Steve Yzerman AS .30 .75
348A Jari Kurri AS ERR .12 .30
348B Jari Kurri AS COR .12 .30
(includes "Signed With")
349 Mark Messier AS .20 .50
350 Steve Duchesne AS .05 .15
351 Mike Gartner AS .10 .25
352 Bernie Nicholls AS .10 .25
353 Paul Cavallini AS .07 .20
354 Al Iafrate AS .05 .15
355 Kirk McLean AS .05 .15
356 Thomas Steen AS .07 .20
357 Ray Bourque AS .15 .40
358 Cam Neely AS .10 .25
359 Patrick Roy AS .25 .60
360 Brian Propp AS .10 .25
361 Paul Coffey AS .10 .25
362 Mario Lemieux AS .40 1.00
363 Dave Andreychuk AS .10 .25
364 Phil Housley AS .07 .20
365 Daren Puppa AS .07 .20
366 Pierre Turgeon AS .07 .20
367 Ron Francis AS .12 .30
368 Chris Chelios AS .10 .25
369A Shayne Corson AS ERR .07 .20
369B Shayne Corson AS COR .07 .20
370 Stephane Richer AS .10 .25
371 Kirk Muller AS .07 .20
372 Pat LaFontaine AS .10 .25
373 Brian Leetch AS .12 .30
374 Rick Tocchet AS .10 .25
375 Joe Sakic AS .30 .75
376 Kevin Hatcher AS .07 .20
377 Bob Murdoch Adams .05 .15
378 Brett Hull Byng .20 .50
379 Sergei Makarov Calder .20 .50
380 Kevin Lowe Clancy .10 .25
381 Mark Messier Hart .20 .50
382 Moog .10 .25
Lemelin Jennings
383 Gord Kluzak Mast .07 .20
384 Ray Bourque Norris .15 .40
385A Len Ceglarski Patrick ERR .05 .15
385B Len Ceglarski Patrick COR .05 .15
386 Mark Messier Pearson .20 .50
387 Boston Bruins .05 .15
388 Wayne Gretzky Ross .50 1.25
389 Rick Meagher Selke .07 .20
390 Bill Ranford Smythe .07 .20
391 Patrick Roy Vezina .25 .60
392 Edmonton Oilers .05 .15
393 Boston Bruins .05 .15
394 Wayne Gretzky LL .50 1.25
395 Brett Hull LL UER .20 .50
396 Sergei Makarov ROY .20 .50
397 Mark Messier MVP .20 .50
398 Mike Richter RLL .30 .75
399 Patrick Roy LL .25 .60
400 Darren Turcotte RLL .07 .20
401 Owen Nolan RC .30 .75
402 Petr Nedved RC .10 .25
403 Phil Esposito HOF .15 .40
404 Darryl Sittler HOF .10 .25
405 Stan Mikita HOF .12 .30
406 Andy Brickley .05 .15
407 Peter Douris RC .10 .25
408 Nevin Markwart .05 .15
409 Chris Nilan .05 .15
410 Stephane Quintal RC .05 .15
411 Bruce Shoebottom RC .05 .15
412 Don Sweeney RC .05 .15
413 Jim Wiemer RC .10 .25
414 Mike Hartman RC .10 .25
415 Dale Hawerchuk .12 .30
416 Benoit Hogue .10 .25
417 Bill Houlder RC .10 .25
418 Mikko Makela .07 .20
419 Robert Ray RC .10 .25
420 John Tucker .07 .20
421 Jiri Hrdina RC .07 .20
422 Mark Hunter .05 .15
423 Tim Hunter RC .07 .20
424 Roger Johansson RC .10 .25
425 Frank Musil .05 .15
426 Ric Nattress .05 .15
427 Chris Chelios .10 .25
428 Jacques Cloutier RC .07 .20
429 Greg Gilbert .05 .15
430 Michel Goulet UER .05 .15
(White position and number on front, not black)
431 Mike Hudson RC .07 .20
432 Jocelyn Lemieux RC .07 .20
433 Brian Noonan .10 .25
434 Wayne Presley .05 .15
435 Brent Fedyk RC .10 .25
436 Rick Green .10 .25
437 Marc Habscheid .07 .20
438 Brad McCrimmon .10 .25
439 Jeff Beukeboom RC .07 .20
440 Dave Brown RC .05 .15
441 Kelly Buchberger RC .05 .15
442 Greg Hawgood .07 .20
443 Chris Joseph RC .05 .15
444 Ken Linseman .07 .20
445 Eldon Reddick RC .20 .50
446 Geoff Smith RC .10 .25
447 Adam Burt RC .07 .20
448 Sylvain Cote .05 .15
449 Paul Cyr .05 .15
450 Ed Kastelic RC .10 .25
451 Peter Sidorkiewicz .10 .25
452 Mike Tomlak RC .10 .25
453 Carey Wilson .07 .20
454 Daniel Berthiaume .07 .20
455 Scott Bjugstad .05 .15
456 Rod Buskas RC .10 .25
457 John McIntyre .07 .20
458 Tim Watters .05 .15
459 Perry Berezan RC .10 .25
460 Brian Propp .10 .25
461 Ilkka Sinisalo .07 .20
462 Doug Smail .07 .20
463 Bobby Smith .07 .20
464 Chris Dahlquist RC .10 .25
465 Neil Wilkinson RC .07 .20
466 J.J. Daigneault RC .05 .15
467 Eric Desjardins RC .20 .50
468 Gerald Diduck .07 .20
469 Donald Dufresne RC .05 .15
470A Todd Ewen ERR RC .05 .15
470B Todd Ewen COR RC .05 .15
471 Brent Gilchrist RC .07 .20
472 Sylvain Lefebvre RC .07 .20
473 Denis Savard .12 .30
474 Sylvain Turgeon .07 .20
475 Ryan Walter .10 .25
476 Laurie Boschman .07 .20
477 Pat Conacher RC .05 .15
478 Claude Lemieux .05 .15
479 Walt Poddubny .07 .20
480 Alan Stewart RC .10 .25
481 Chris Terreri RC .20 .50
482 Brad Dalgarno .05 .15
483 Dave Chyzowski RC .07 .20
484 Craig Ludwig .10 .25
485 Wayne McBean RC .05 .15
486 Rich Pilon RC .05 .15
487 Joe Reekie RC .05 .15
488 Mick Vukota RC .10 .25
489 Mark Hardy .05 .15
490 Jody Hull RC .10 .25
491 Kris King RC .10 .25
492 Troy Mallette RC .07 .20
493 Kevin Miller RC .10 .25
494 Normand Rochefort .05 .15
495 David Shaw .10 .25

496 Ray Sheppard .05 .15
497 Keith Acton .10 .25
498 Craig Berube RC .05 .15
499 Tony Horacek RC .05 .15
500 Normand Lacombe RC .05 .15
501 Jiri Latal RC .10 .25
502 Pete Peeters .05 .15
503 Derrick Smith RC .07 .20
504 Jay Caufield RC .05 .15
505 Peter Taglianetti .07 .20
506 Randy Gilhen RC .05 .15
507 Randy Hillier .10 .25
508 Joe Mullen .07 .20
509 Frank Pietrangelo RC .05 .15
510 Gordie Roberts .05 .15
511 Bryan Trottier .12 .30
512 Wendell Young RC .10 .25
513 Shawn Anderson RC .05 .15
514 Steven Finn RC .05 .15
515 Bryan Fogarty RC .05 .15
516 Mike Hough .07 .20
517 Darin Kimble .20 .50
518 Randy Velischek .05 .15
519 Craig Wolanin RC .07 .20
520 Bob Bassen RC .05 .15
521 Geoff Courtnall .07 .20
522 Robert Dirk RC .05 .15
523 Glen Featherstone RC .07 .20
524 Mario Marois .07 .20
525 Herb Raglan RC .05 .15
526 Cliff Ronning .05 .15
527 Harold Snepsts .05 .15
528 Scott Stevens .10 .25
529 Ron Wilson .05 .15
530 Aaron Broten .07 .20
531 Lucien DeBlois .07 .20
532 Dave Ellett .05 .15
533A Paul Fenton ERR .10 .25
533B Paul Fenton COR .10 .25
534 Todd Gill RC .05 .15
535 Dave Hannan .05 .15
536 John Kordic .20 .50
537 Mike Krushelnyski .10 .25
538 Kevin Maguire RC .05 .15
539 Michel Petit .07 .20
540 Jeff Reese RC .10 .25
541 David Reid RC .10 .25
542 Doug Shedden .05 .15
543 Dave Capuano RC .10 .25
544 Craig Coxe RC .07 .20
545 Kevan Guy RC .05 .15
546 Rob Murphy RC .10 .25
547 Robert Nordmark RC .07 .20
548 Stan Smyl .05 .15
549 Ronnie Stern RC .05 .15
550 Tim Bergland RC .07 .20
551 Nick Kypreos RC .10 .25
552 Mike Lalor RC .07 .20
553 Rob Murray RC .05 .15
554 Bob Rouse .05 .15
555 Dave Tippett .07 .20
556 Peter Zezel .10 .25
557 Scott Arniel .05 .15
558 Don Barber .07 .20
559 Shawn Cronin RC .05 .15
560 Gord Donnelly RC .05 .15
561 Doug Evans RC .10 .25
562 Phil Housley .07 .20
563 Ed Olczyk .10 .25
564 Mark Osborne .07 .20
565 Thomas Steen .07 .20
566 Boston Bruins Logo .05 .15
567 Buffalo Sabres Logo .05 .15
568 Calgary Flames Logo .05 .15
569 Chicago Blackhawks Logo .05 .15
570 Detroit Red Wings Logo .05 .15
571 Edmonton Oilers Logo .05 .15
572 Hartford Whalers Logo .05 .15
573A Los Angeles Kings Logo ERR .05 .15
573B Los Angeles Kings Logo COR .05 .15
574 Minn. North Stars Logo .05 .15
575 Montreal Canadiens Logo .10 .25
576 New Jersey Devils Logo .05 .15
577 New York Islanders Logo .05 .15
578 New York Rangers Logo .05 .15
579 Philadelphia Flyers Logo .05 .15
580 Pittsburgh Penguins Logo .05 .15
581 Quebec Nordiques Logo .05 .15
582 St. Louis Blues Logo .05 .15
583 Toronto Maple Leafs Logo .08 .20
584 Vancouver Canucks Logo .05 .15
585 Washington Capitals Logo .05 .15
586 Winnipeg Jets Logo .05 .15
587 Ken Hodge Jr. RC .05 .15
588 Vladimir Ruzicka RC .10 .25
589 Wes Walz RC .10 .25
590 Greg Brown RC .10 .25
591 Brad Miller .05 .15
592 Darrin Shannon RC .10 .25
593 Stephane Matteau RC .10 .25
594 Sergei Priakin RC .05 .15
595 Robert Reichel RC .10 .25
596 Ken Sabourin RC .05 .15
597 Tim Sweeney RC .05 .15
598 Ed Belfour RC .30 .75
599 Frantisek Kucera RC .10 .25
600 Mike McNeil .05 .15
601 Mike Peluso RC .05 .15
602 Tim Cheveldae RC .07 .20
603 Per Djoos RC .05 .15
604 Sergei Fedorov RC .20 .50
605 Johan Garpenlov RC .10 .25
606 Keith Primeau RC .15 .40
607 Paul Ysebaert RC .07 .20
608 Anatoli Semenov RC .07 .20
609 Bobby Holik RC .07 .20
610 Kay Whitmore RC .10 .25
611 Rob Blake RC .15 .40
612 Francois Breault RC .05 .15
613 Mike Craig RC .10 .25
614 Jean-Claude Bergeron RC .10 .25
615 Andrew Cassels RC .05 .15
616 Tom Chorske RC .07 .20
617 Lyle Odelein RC .05 .15
618 Mark Pederson RC .10 .25
619 Zdeno Ciger .10 .25
620 Troy Crowder RC .05 .15
621 Jon Morris RC .05 .15
622 Eric Weinrich RC .10 .25
623 David Marcinyshyn RC .10 .25
624 Jeff Hackett RC .15 .40
625 Rob DiMaio RC .10 .25
626 Steven Rice RC .10 .25
627 Mike Richter RC .30 .75
628 Dennis Vial RC .07 .20
629 Martin Hostak RC .10 .25
630 Pat Murray RC .10 .25
631 Mike Ricci RC .10 .25
632A Jaromir Jagr RC ERR .60 1.50
632B Jaromir Jagr RC COR .60 1.50
633 Paul Stanton RC .10 .25
634 Scott Gordon RC .05 .15
635 Owen Nolan .30 .75
636 Mats Sundin RC .10 .25
637 John Tanner RC .10 .25
638 Curtis Joseph RC .30 .75
639 Peter Ing RC .10 .25
640 Scott Thornton RC .05 .15
641 Troy Gamble RC .10 .25
642 Robert Kron RC .10 .25
643 Petr Nedved .10 .25
644 Adrien Plavsic RC .10 .25
645 Peter Bondra RC .15 .40
646 Jim Hrivnak RC .10 .25
647 Mikhail Tatarinov RC .10 .25
648 Stephane Beauregard RC .07 .20
649 Rick Tabaracci RC .05 .15
650 Mike Bossy CPL .05 .15
651 Bobby Clarke CPL .10 .25
652 Alex Delvecchio CPL .05 .15
653 Marcel Dionne CPL .12 .30
654 Gordie Howe CPL .30 .75
655 Stan Mikita CPL .12 .30
656 Denis Potvin CPL .05 .15
657 Bobby Clarke HOF .10 .25
658 Alex Delvecchio HOF .05 .15
659 Tony Esposito HOF .05 .15
660 Gordie Howe HOF .30 .75
661 Mike Milbury CO .05 .15
662 Rick Dudley CO .05 .15
663 Doug Risebrough CO .05 .15
664 Bryan Murray CO RC .05 .15
665 John Muckler CO RC .05 .15
666 Rick Ley CO .05 .15
667 Tom Webster CO .05 .15
668 Bob Gainey CO .05 .15
669 Pat Burns CO RC .20 .50
670 John Cunniff CO RC .05 .15
671 Al Arbour CO .05 .15
672 Roger Neilson CO RC .20 .50
673 Paul Holmgren CO .05 .15
674 Bob Johnson CO RC .20 .50
675 Dave Chambers CO RC .05 .15
676 Brian Sutter CO .05 .15
677 Tom Watt CO RC .05 .15
678 Bob McCammon CO .05 .15
679 Terry Murray CO .05 .15
680 Bob Murdoch CO .10 .25
681 Ron Asselstine OFF .05 .15
682 Wayne Bonney OFF .05 .15
683 Kevin Collins OFF .05 .15
684 Pat Dapuzzo OFF .05 .15
685 Ron Finn OFF .05 .15
686 Kerry Fraser OFF .05 .15
687 Gerard Gauthier OFF .05 .15
688 Terry Gregson OFF .05 .15
689 Bob Hodges OFF .05 .15
690 Ron Hoggarth OFF .05 .15
691 Dan Koharski OFF .05 .15
692 Dan Marouelli OFF .05 .15
693 Danny McCourt OFF .05 .15
694 Bill McCreary OFF .05 .15
695 Denis Morel OFF .05 .15
696 Jerry Pateman OFF .05 .15
697 Ray Scapinello OFF .05 .15
698 Rob Shick OFF .05 .15
699 Paul Stewart OFF .05 .15
700 Leon Stickle OFF .05 .15
701 Andy van Hellemond OFF .05 .15
702 Mark Vines OFF .05 .15
703 Wayne Gretzky 2000th .50 1.25
704 Stanley Cup Champs .05 .15
705 The Puck-La Rondelle .05 .15
NNO Stanley Cup Hologram 100.00 200.00

1990-91 Pro Set Player of the Month

This four-card set features the NHL player of the month for four consecutive months (the month for which the player won the award is listed below his name). All cards feature the basic 1990-91 Pro Set design, and say NHL Pro Set Player of the Month and the date at the bottom of each obverse. The cards are numbered on the back; note that the Peeters card has no number. The cards were issued in the home rink of the winner each month after announcement of the winner. Pro Set sponsored the Player of the Week/Month/Year Awards for the NHL. Reportedly less than 25,000 of each POM card were produced.

COMPLETE SET (4) 8.00 20.00
P1 Tom Barrasso 1.50 4.00
POM December 1990
P2 Wayne Gretzky 4.00 10.00
POM January 1991
P3 Brett Hull 2.50 6.00
POM February 1991
NNO Pete Peeters 1.50 4.00
POM November 1990

1991-92 Pro Set Preview

This six-card standard-size set was given to dealers to show what the 1991-92 Pro Set hockey set would look like. There is really not that much interest in the set due to the egregiously poor player selection, i.e., no superstars in the set. The setup of the text on the card backs of these preview cards is different from the regular issue cards; cards are labeled "Promo" on the back where the card number is in the regular issue cards. The David Reid card has an entirely different photo. Even though the cards are unnumbered, they are assigned reference numbers below according to their numbers in the 1991-92 Pro Set regular issue.

COMPLETE SET (6) .60 1.50
151 Randy Wood NNO .08 .25
107 Gord Murphy NNO .08 .25
203 Craig Wolanin NNO .08 .25
229 David Reid NNO .08 .25
266 Bob Essensa NNO .08 .25
NNO Title Card .02 .10

1991-92 Pro Set

The Pro Set hockey issue contains 615 numbered cards. The set was released in two series of 345 and 270 cards, respectively. Pro Set also issued a French version which carries the same value. French wax boxes contained randomly inserted Patrick Roy personally autographed cards signed and numbered on the back; 1,000 of card number 125 (first series) and 1,000 of card number 599 numbered 1001 to 2000 (second series). Roy also signed 500 cards for distribution in Canadian collector's kits. Randomly inserted in U.S. packs were a limited quantity of Kirk McLean autographed cards. Ten thousand hand-numbered 3-D hologram cards were inserted in second series foil packs to commemorate the NHL's Diamond Anniversary.

COMPLETE SET (615) 7.50 15.00
COMP.SERIES 1 (345) 3.00 8.00
COMP.SERIES 2 (270) 3.00 8.00
1 Glen Wesley .07 .20
2 Craig Janney .07 .20
3 Ken Hodge Jr. .10 .25
4 Randy Burridge .07 .20
5 Cam Neely .10 .25
6 Bob Sweeney .07 .20
7 Garry Galley .07 .20
8 Petri Skriko .05 .15
9 Ray Bourque .15 .40
10 Andy Moog UER .07 .20
11 Dave Christian .07 .20
12 Dave Poulin .07 .20
13 Jeff Lazaro RC .07 .20
14 Darrin Shannon .07 .20
15 Pierre Turgeon UER .07 .20
16 Alexander Mogilny .07 .20
17 Benoit Hogue UER .07 .20
(Stats show two seasons with Winnipeg)
18 Dave Snuggerud .05 .15
19 Doug Bodger UER .07 .20
20 Uwe Krupp .07 .20
21 Daren Puppa .07 .20
22 Christian Ruuttu .07 .20
23 Dave Andreychuk .10 .25
24 Dale Hawerchuk .12 .30
25 Mike Ramsey .07 .20
26 Rick Vaive .05 .15
27 Stephane Matteau .07 .20
28 Theo Fleury .07 .20
29 Joe Nieuwendyk .07 .20
30 Gary Roberts .07 .20
31 Paul Ranheim .10 .25
32 Gary Suter .07 .20
33 Al MacInnis .07 .20
34 Doug Gilmour .20 .50
35 Mike Vernon .07 .20
36 Carey Wilson .05 .15
37 Joel Otto .07 .20
38 Jamie Macoun .07 .20
39 Sergei Makarov .07 .20
40 Jeremy Roenick .25 .60
41 Dave Manson .07 .20
42 Adam Creighton .07 .20
43 Ed Belfour .25 .60
44 Wayne Presley .07 .20
45 Steve Thomas .07 .20
46 Troy Murray .07 .20
47 Bob McGill .07 .20
48 Chris Chelios .10 .25
49 Steve Larmer .07 .20
50 Michel Goulet .07 .20
51 Dirk Graham .07 .20
52 Doug Wilson .07 .20
53 Sergei Fedorov .15 .40
54 Yves Racine .07 .20
55 Jimmy Carson .07 .20
56 Johan Garpenlov .07 .20
57 Tim Cheveldae .07 .20
58 Shawn Burr .07 .20
59 Paul Ysebaert .07 .20
60 Kevin Miller .07 .20
61 Bob Probert .07 .20
62 Steve Yzerman .30 .75
63 Gerard Gallant .05 .15
64 Rick Zombo .07 .20
65 Dave Barr .07 .20
66 Martin Gelinas .07 .20
67 Adam Graves UER .07 .20
68 Joe Murphy .07 .20
69 Craig Simpson .05 .15
70 Bill Ranford .07 .20
71 Esa Tikkanen .07 .20
72 Petr Klima .07 .20
73 Steve Smith .10 .25
74 Mark Messier .25 .60
75 Glenn Anderson .10 .25
76 Kevin Lowe .07 .20
77 Craig MacTavish .07 .20
78 Grant Fuhr .10 .25
79 Bobby Holik .10 .25
80 Rob Brown .07 .20
81 Doug Houda .07 .20
82 Sylvain Cote .07 .20
83 Todd Krygier .07 .20
84 Dean Evason .07 .20
85 John Cullen .07 .20
86 Pat Verbeek .07 .20
87 Brad Shaw .05 .15
88 Paul Cyr UER .07 .20
89 Kevin Dineen .07 .20
90 Peter Sidorkiewicz .07 .20
91 Zarley Zalapski .07 .20
92 Rob Blake .10 .25
93 Jari Kurri UER .07 .20
94 Todd Elik .07 .20
95 Luc Robitaille .07 .20
96 Steve Duchesne .05 .15
97 Tomas Sandstrom .07 .20
98 Tony Granato .07 .20
99 Bob Kudelski .05 .15
100 Marty McSorley .07 .20
101 Wayne Gretzky .50 1.25
102 Kelly Hrudey .07 .20
103 Dave Taylor .07 .20
104 Larry Robinson .05 .15
105 Mike Modano .20 .50
106 Ulf Dahlen .07 .20
107 Mark Tinordi .07 .20
108 Dave Gagner .07 .20
109 Brian Bellows .07 .20
110 Gaetan Duchesne .05 .15
111 Jon Casey .07 .20
112 Neal Broten .07 .20
113 Brian Propp .07 .20
114 Curt Giles .10 .25
115 Bobby Smith .07 .20
116 Jim Johnson .07 .20
117 Doug Smail .07 .20
118 Eric Desjardins .10 .25
119 Mathieu Schneider .07 .20
120 Stephan Lebeau .07 .20
121 Mike Keane .05 .15
122 Stephane Richer .07 .20
123 Petr Svoboda .07 .20
124 J.J. Daigneault .07 .20
125 Patrick Roy .25 .60
126 Russ Courtnall .07 .20
127 Brian Skrudland .07 .20
128 Denis Savard .12 .30
129 Mike McPhee .07 .20
130 Guy Carbonneau .07 .20
131 Brendan Shanahan .12 .30
132 Sean Burke .10 .25
133 Eric Weinrich .10 .25
134 Kirk Muller .05 .15
135 Claude Lemieux .07 .20
136 John MacLean .07 .20
137 Chris Terreri .07 .20
138 Doug Brown .07 .20
139 Ken Daneyko .07 .20
140 Bruce Driver .07 .20
141 Patrik Sundstrom .07 .20
142 Slava Fetisov .07 .20
143 Peter Stastny .07 .20
144 Wayne McBean .05 .15
145 Bill Berg .07 .20
146 Derek King .07 .20
147 David Volek .07 .20
148 Jeff Norton .07 .20
149 Pat LaFontaine .10 .25
150 Gary Nylund .07 .20
151 Randy Wood .07 .20
152 Pat Flatley .07 .20
153 Glenn Healy .10 .25
154 Brent Sutter .07 .20
155 Craig Ludwig .07 .20
156 Ray Ferraro .07 .20
157 Troy Mallette .07 .20
158 Mark Janssens .07 .20
159 Brian Leetch UER .07 .20
160 Darren Turcotte .07 .20
161 Mike Richter .10 .25
162 Ray Sheppard .07 .20
163 Randy Moller .07 .20
164 James Patrick .07 .20
165 Brian Mullen UER .07 .20
166 Bernie Nicholls .07 .20
167 Mike Gartner .07 .20
168 Kelly Kisio UER .07 .20
169 John Ogrodnick .07 .20
170 Mike Ricci .10 .25
171 Gord Murphy .07 .20
172 Scott Mellanby .07 .20
173 Terry Carkner .07 .20
174 Derrick Smith .07 .20
175 Murray Craven .07 .20
176 Ron Hextall .10 .25
177 Rick Tocchet .07 .20
178 Ron Sutter .07 .20
179 Pelle Eklund .07 .20
180 Tim Kerr UER .07 .20
181 Kjell Samuelsson .07 .20
182 Mark Howe .10 .25
183 Jaromir Jagr .25 .60
184 Mark Recchi .12 .30
185 Kevin Stevens .07 .20
186 Tom Barrasso .07 .20
187 Bob Errey .07 .20
188 Ron Francis .12 .30
189 Phil Bourque .07 .20
190 Paul Coffey .07 .20
191 Joe Mullen .07 .20
192 Bryan Trottier .07 .20
193 Larry Murphy .07 .20
194 Mario Lemieux .40 1.00
195 Scott Young .07 .20
196 Owen Nolan .10 .25
197 Mats Sundin .10 .25
198 Curtis Leschyshyn .07 .20
199 Joe Sakic .30 .75
200 Bryan Fogarty .07 .20
201 Stephane Morin .07 .20
202 Ron Tugnutt .07 .20
203 Craig Wolanin .07 .20
204 Steven Finn .07 .20
205 Tony Hrkac .07 .20
206 Randy Velischek .07 .20
207 Alexei Gusarov RC .07 .20
208 Scott Pearson .07 .20
209 Dan Quinn .07 .20
210 Garth Butcher .07 .20
211 Rod Brind'Amour UER .07 .20
212 Jeff Brown .07 .20
213 Vincent Riendeau .07 .20
214 Paul Cavallini .07 .20
215 Brett Hull .15 .40
216 Scott Stevens .10 .25
217 Rich Sutter .07 .20
218 Gino Cavallini .07 .20
219 Adam Oates UER .10 .25
220 Ron Wilson .07 .20
221 Bob Bassen .07 .20
222 Peter Ing .07 .20
223 Daniel Marois .07 .20
224 Vincent Damphousse .07 .20
225 Wendel Clark .10 .25
226 Todd Gill .07 .20
227 Peter Zezel .05 .15
228 Bob Rouse .05 .15
229 David Reid .05 .15
230 Dave Ellett .07 .20
231 Gary Leeman .07 .20
232 Rob Ramage .07 .20
233 Mike Krushelnyski .10 .25
234 Tom Fergus .07 .20
235 Petr Nedved .07 .20
236 Trevor Linden .07 .20
237 Dave Capuano .07 .20
238 Troy Gamble .05 .15
239 Robert Kron UER .07 .20
240 Jyrki Lumme .07 .20
241 Cliff Ronning .07 .20
242 Sergio Momesso .07 .20
243 Greg Adams .07 .20
244 Tom Kurvers .07 .20
245 Geoff Courtnall .07 .20
246 Igor Larionov .07 .20
247 Doug Lidster UER .07 .20
248 Calle Johansson .07 .20
249 Kevin Hatcher .07 .20
250 Al Iafrate .07 .20
251 John Druce .07 .20
252 Michal Pivonka .07 .20
253 Stephen Leach .07 .20
254 Mike Ridley .07 .20
255 Mike Lalor .07 .20
256 Kelly Miller .07 .20
257 Don Beaupre .07 .20
258 Dino Ciccarelli .07 .20
259 Rod Langway .07 .20
260 Dimitri Khristich .07 .20
261 Teppo Numminen .07 .20
262 Pat Elynuik .07 .20
263 Danton Cole .05 .15
264 Fredrik Olausson UER .07 .20
265 Ed Olczyk .07 .20
266 Bob Essensa .07 .20
267 Phil Housley .07 .20
268 Shawn Cronin .07 .20
269 Paul MacDermid .07 .20
270 Mark Osborne .07 .20
271 Thomas Steen .07 .20
272 Brent Ashton .07 .20
273 Randy Carlyle .07 .20
274 Theo Fleury AS .07 .20
275 Al MacInnis AS .05 .15
276 Gary Suter AS .07 .20
277 Mike Vernon AS .07 .20
278 Chris Chelios AS .10 .25
279 Steve Larmer AS .07 .20
280 Jeremy Roenick AS .25 .60
281 Steve Yzerman AS .30 .75
282 Mark Messier AS .25 .60
283 Bill Ranford AS .07 .20
284 Steve Smith AS .10 .25
285 Wayne Gretzky AS .50 1.25
286 Luc Robitaille AS .07 .20
287 Tomas Sandstrom AS .05 .15
288 Dave Gagner AS .07 .20
289 Bobby Smith AS .07 .20
290 Brett Hull AS .15 .40
291 Adam Oates AS .10 .25
292 Scott Stevens AS .10 .25
293 Vincent Damphousse AS .07 .20
294 Trevor Linden AS .07 .20
295 Phil Housley AS .07 .20
296 Ray Bourque AS .15 .40
297 Dave Christian AS .07 .20
298 Garry Galley AS .07 .20
299 Andy Moog AS .07 .20
300 Cam Neely AS .10 .25
301 Uwe Krupp AS .07 .20
302 John Cullen AS .10 .25
303 Pat Verbeek AS .07 .20
304 Patrick Roy AS .25 .60
305 Denis Savard AS .12 .30
306 Brian Skrudland AS .07 .20
307 John MacLean AS .07 .20
308 Pat LaFontaine AS .10 .25
309 Brian Leetch AS .07 .20
310 Darren Turcotte AS .07 .20
311 Rick Tocchet AS .07 .20
312 Paul Coffey AS .07 .20
313 Mark Recchi AS .12 .30
314 Kevin Stevens AS .07 .20
315 Joe Sakic AS .30 .75
316 Kevin Hatcher AS .07 .20
317 Guy Lafleur AS .10 .25
318 Mario Lemieux Smythe .40 1.00
319 Pittsburgh Penguins UER .25 .60
320 Brett Hull Hart .15 .40
321 Ed Belfour Jennings .25 .60
Vezina
322 Ray Bourque .15 .40
Norris
323 Dirk Graham .07 .20
Selke
324 W.Gretzky Ross/Byng .50 1.25
325 Dave Taylor .07 .20
King Clancy Trophy
326 Brett Hull PS-POY .15 .40
327 Brian Hayward .07 .20
328 Neil Wilkinson UER .07 .20
329 Craig Coxe .05 .15
330 Rob Zettler .07 .20
331 Jeff Hackett .40 1.00
332 Joe Malone .07 .20
333 Georges Vezina .07 .20
334 The Modern Arena .05 .15
335 Ace Bailey Benefit .07 .20
336 Howie Morenz .07 .20
337 The Punch Line .07 .20
338 The Kid Line .07 .20
339 Before the Zamboni .05 .15
340 Bill Barilko .07 .20
341 Jacques Plante .07 .20
342 Arena Designs .05 .15
343 Terry Sawchuk .07 .20
344 Gordie Howe .30 .75
345 Guy Carbonneau .07 .20
346 Stephen Leach .07 .20
347 Peter Douris .07 .20
348 David Reid .05 .15
349 Bob Carpenter .07 .20
350 Stephane Quintal .07 .20
351 Barry Pederson .07 .20
352 Brent Ashton .07 .20
353 Vladimir Ruzicka .10 .25
354 Brad Miller .07 .20
355 Robert Ray .07 .20
356 Colin Patterson .07 .20
357 Gord Donnelly .07 .20
358 Pat LaFontaine .10 .25
359 Randy Wood .07 .20
360 Randy Hillier .07 .20
361 Robert Reichel .20 .50
362 Ronnie Stern .07 .20
363 Ric Nattress .07 .20
364 Tim Sweeney .05 .15
365 Marc Habscheid .07 .20
366 Tim Hunter .05 .15
367 Rick Wamsley .05 .15
368 Frank Musil .07 .20
369 Mike Hudson .07 .20
370 Steve Smith .10 .25
371 Keith Brown .07 .20
372 Greg Gilbert .07 .20
373 John Tonelli .07 .20
374 Brent Sutter .07 .20
375 Brad Lauer .07 .20
376 Alan Kerr .07 .20
377 Brad McCrimmon .07 .20
378 Brad Marsh .10 .25
379 Brent Fedyk .07 .20
380 Ray Sheppard .07 .20
381 Vincent Damphousse .07 .20
382 Craig Muni .07 .20
383 Scott Mellanby .07 .20
384 Geoff Smith .07 .20
385 Kelly Buchberger .07 .20
386 Bernie Nicholls .07 .20
387 Luke Richardson .07 .20
388 Peter Ing .07 .20
389 Dave Manson .07 .20
390 Mark Hunter .07 .20
391 Jim McKenzie RC .10 .25
392 Randy Cunneyworth .07 .20
393 Murray Craven .07 .20
394 Mikael Andersson .07 .20
395 Andrew Cassels .07 .20
396 Randy Ladouceur .07 .20
397 Marc Bergevin .07 .20
398 Brian Benning .07 .20
399 Mike Donnelly RC .10 .25
400 Charlie Huddy .07 .20
401 John McIntyre .07 .20
402 Jay Miller .07 .20
403 Randy Gilhen .07 .20
404 Stewart Gavin .07 .20
405 Mike Craig .07 .20
406 Brian Glynn .07 .20
407 Rob Ramage .07 .20
408 Chris Dahlquist .07 .20
409 Basil McRae .07 .20
410 Todd Elik .07 .20
411 Craig Ludwig .07 .20
412 Kirk Muller .05 .15
413 Shayne Corson .07 .20
414 Brent Gilchrist .07 .20
415 Mario Roberge .07 .20
416 Sylvain Turgeon .07 .20
417 Alain Cote .07 .20
418 Donald Dufresne .07 .20
419 Todd Ewen .07 .20
420 Stephane Richer .07 .20
421 David Maley .07 .20
422 Randy McKay .07 .20
423 Scott Stevens .10 .25
424 Jon Morris .07 .20
425 Claude Vilgrain .07 .20
426 Laurie Boschman .07 .20
427 Pat Conacher .07 .20
428 Tom Kurvers .07 .20
429 Joe Reekie .07 .20
430 Rob DiMaio .07 .20
431 Tom Fitzgerald .07 .20
432 Ken Baumgartner .07 .20
433 Pierre Turgeon .15 .40
434 Dave McLlwain .07 .20
435 Benoit Hogue .07 .20
436 Uwe Krupp .07 .20
437 Adam Creighton .07 .20
438 Steve Thomas .07 .20
439 Mark Messier .25 .60
440 Tie Domi .07 .20
441 Sergei Nemchinov .07 .20
442 Mark Hardy .07 .20
443 Adam Graves .07 .20
444 Jeff Beukeboom .07 .20
445 Kris King .07 .20
446 Tim Kerr .07 .20
447 John Vanbiesbrouck .07 .20
448 Steve Duchesne .05 .15
449 Steve Kasper .07 .20
450 Ken Wregget .07 .20
451 Kevin Dineen .07 .20
452 Dave Brown .07 .20
453 Rod Brind'Amour .07 .20
454 Jiri Latal .05 .15
455 Tony Horacek .07 .20
456 Brad Jones .07 .20
457 Paul Stanton .07 .20
458 Gordie Roberts .07 .20
459 Ulf Samuelsson .07 .20
460 Ken Priestlay .07 .20
461 Jiri Hrdina .07 .20
462 Mikhail Tatarinov .07 .20
463 Mike Hough .07 .20
464 Don Barber .07 .20
465 Greg Smyth RC .07 .20
466 Doug Smail .07 .20
467 Mike McNeill .07 .20
468 John Kordic .07 .20
469 Greg Paslawski .07 .20
470 Herb Raglan .07 .20
471 Dave Christian .07 .20
472 Murray Baron .07 .20
473 Curtis Joseph .07 .20
474 Rick Zombo .07 .20
475 Brendan Shanahan .12 .30
476 Ron Sutter .07 .20
477 Mario Marois .07 .20
478 Doug Wilson .07 .20
479 Kelly Kisio .07 .20
480 Bob McGill .07 .20
481 Perry Anderson .07 .20
482 Brian Lawton .07 .20
483 Neil Wilkinson .07 .20
484 Ken Hammond RC .07 .20
485 David Bruce RC .10 .25
486 Steve Bozek .07 .20
487 Perry Berezan .07 .20
488 Wayne Presley .07 .20
489 Brian Bradley .07 .20
490 Darryl Shannon .10 .25
491 Lucien DeBlois .07 .20
492 Michel Petit .07 .20
493 Claude Loiselle .07 .20
494 Grant Fuhr .10 .25
495 Craig Berube .07 .20
496 Mike Bullard .07 .20
497 Jim Sandlak .07 .20
498 Dana Murzyn .07 .20
499 Garry Valk .07 .20
500 Andrew McBain .07 .20
501 Kirk McLean .07 .20
502 Gerald Diduck .07 .20
503 Dave Babych .07 .20
504 Ryan Walter .07 .20
505 Gino Odjick .07 .20
506 Dale Hunter .07 .20
507 Tim Bergland .07 .20
508 Alan May .07 .20
509 Jim Hrivnak .07 .20
510 Randy Burridge .07 .20
511 Peter Bondra .07 .20
512 Sylvain Cote .07 .20
513 Nick Kypreos .07 .20
514 Troy Murray .07 .20
515 Darrin Shannon .07 .20
516 Bryan Erickson .07 .20
517 Petri Skriko .05 .15
518 Mike Eagles .07 .20
519 Mike Hartman .07 .20
520 Bob Beers .07 .20
521 Mat DelGuidice RC .10 .25
522 Chris Winnes .07 .20
523 Brad May .07 .20
524 Donald Audette .07 .20
525 Kevin Haller RC .10 .25
526 Martin Simard .07 .20
527 Tomas Forslund RC .10 .25
528 Mark Osiecki .07 .20
529 Dominik Hasek RC .30 .75
530 Jimmy Waite .07 .20
531 Nicklas Lidstrom RC .40 1.00
532 Martin Lapointe .07 .20
533 Vladimir Konstantinov RC .25 .60
534 Josef Beranek RC .10 .25
535 Louie DeBrusk RC .10 .25
536 Geoff Sanderson RC .10 .25
537 Mark Greig .07 .20
538 Michel Picard RC .10 .25
539 Chris Tancill RC .07 .20
540 Peter Ahola RC .10 .25
541 Francois Breault .07 .20
542 Darryl Sydor .07 .20
543 Derian Hatcher .07 .20
544 Marc Bureau .07 .20
545 John LeClair RC .25 .60
546 Paul DiPietro RC .10 .25
547 Scott Niedermayer .10 .25
548 Kevin Todd RC .10 .25
549 Doug Weight RC .25 .60
550 Tony Amonte RC .25 .60
551 Corey Foster RC .10 .25
552 Dominic Roussel RC .10 .25
553 Dan Kordic RC .07 .20
554 Jim Paek RC .10 .25
555 Kip Miller .07 .20
556 Claude Lapointe RC .07 .20
557 Nelson Emerson .07 .20
558 Pat Falloon .07 .20
559 Pat MacLeod RC .10 .25
560 Rick Lessard RC .07 .20
561 Link Gaetz .07 .20
562 Rob Pearson RC .10 .25
563 Alexander Godynyuk RC .10 .25
564 Pavel Bure .07 .20
565 Russell Romaniuk RC .10 .25
566 Stu Barnes .07 .20
567 Ray Bourque CAP .15 .40
568 Mike Ramsey CAP .07 .20
569 Joe Nieuwendyk CAP .07 .20
570 Dirk Graham CAP .07 .20
571 Steve Yzerman CAP .30 .75
572 Kevin Lowe CAP .07 .20
573 Randy Ladouceur CAP .07 .20
574 Wayne Gretzky CAP .50 1.25
575 Mark Tinordi CAP .07 .20
576 Guy Carbonneau CAP .07 .20
577 Bruce Driver CAP .07 .20
578 Pat Flatley CAP .07 .20
579 Mark Messier CAP .25 .60
580 Rick Tocchet CAP .07 .20
581 Mario Lemieux CAP .40 1.00
582 Mike Hough CAP .07 .20
583 Garth Butcher CAP .07 .20
584 Doug Wilson CAP .07 .20
585 Wendel Clark CAP .10 .25
586 Trevor Linden CAP .07 .20
587 Rod Langway CAP .07 .20
588 Troy Murray CAP .07 .20
589 Practicing Outdoors .05 .15
590 Shape Up .05 .15
591 Boston Bruins Cartoon .05 .15
592 Opening Night .05 .15
593 Rod Gilbert .07 .20
594 Phil Esposito .15 .40
595 Dale Tallon .07 .20
596 Gilbert Perreault .10 .25
597 Bernie Federko .07 .20
598 All-Star Game .05 .15
599 Patrick Roy LL .25 .60
600 Ed Belfour LL .25 .60
601 Don Beaupre LL .07 .20
602 Bob Essensa LL .07 .20
603 Kirk McLean UER LL .07 .20
604 Mike Gartner LL .07 .20
605 Jeremy Roenick LL .25 .60
606 Rob Brown LL .07 .20
607 Ulf Dahlen LL .07 .20
608 Paul Ysebaert LL .07 .20
609 Brad McCrimmon LL .07 .20
610 Nicklas Lidstrom LL .40 1.00
611 Kelly Miller LL .07 .20
612 Jim Kyte SMART .07 .20
613 Patrick Roy SMART .25 .60
614 Alan May SMART .07 .20
615 Kelly Miller SMART .07 .20
AU125 Patrick Roy AU/1000 40.00 100.00
AU501 Kirk McLean AU/500 20.00 50.00
AU599 Patrick Roy LL AU/1000 40.00 100.00
NNO 75th Anniv.HOLO/10,000 20.00 50.00

1991-92 Pro Set French

COMPLETE SET (615) 6.00 15.00
COMP.SERIES 1 (345) 3.00 8.00
COMP.SERIES 2 (270) 3.00 8.00
*FRENCH: .4X TO 1X BASIC PRO SET

1991-92 Pro Set CC

These standard-size cards were issued as random inserts in French and English Pro Set 15-card foil packs. The first four were in the first series and the last five were inserted in with the second series. The Pat Falloon and Scott Niedermayer cards were withdrawn early in the first series print run. This was due to the cards being released prior to the players having appeared in an NHL game; a contravention of licensing regulations. The cards are numbered on the back with a "CC" prefix.

COMPLETE SET (9) 6.00 15.00
*FRENCH: .5X TO 1.2X BASIC INSERTS
CC1 Entry Draft .40 1.00
CC2 The Mask 2.00 5.00
CC3 Pat Falloon SP 3.00 8.00
CC4 Scott Niedermayer SP 3.00 8.00
CC5 Wayne Gretzky 2.00 5.00
CC6 Brett Hull .60 1.50
CC7 Adam Oates .50 1.25
CC8 Mark Recchi .60 1.50
CC9 John Cullen .40 1.00

1991-92 Pro Set Gazette

These standard-size cards were issued in cello packs.The front of card number 2 had the words "Pro Set Gazette" in the upper left corner and the player's name in a blue stripe near the bottom of the card. The SC1 Roy card has his name appearing in a red stripe at the bottom with the words "Goalie of the Year" in a blue stripe. The card is numbered "Special Collectible 1" on the back.

COMPLETE SET (2) 2.00 5.00
2 Patrick Roy 1.25 3.00
(Gazette Collectible)
SC1 Patrick Roy 1.25 3.00
(Special Collectible 1)

1991-92 Pro Set HOF Induction

This 14-card set was issued by Pro Set to commemorate the 1991 Hockey Hall of Fame Induction Dinner and Ceremonies in September, 1991 held in Ottawa. The standard-size cards feature borderless glossy sepia-toned player or team photos on the fronts. A colorful insignia with the words "Hockey Hall of Fame and Museum" appears on the front of each card. The team cards represent the past Ottawa Stanley Cup winning teams.

COMPLETE SET (14) 30.00 75.00
1 Mike Bossy/1991 HOF Inductee 6.00 15.00
2 Denis Potvin/1991 HOF Inductee 5.00 12.00
3 Bob Pulford/1991 HOF Inductee 3.00 8.00
4 William Scott Bowman 6.00 15.00
1991 HOF Inductee
5 Neil P. Armstrong/1991 HOF Inductee 2.50 6.00
6 Clint Smith/1991 HOF Inductee 2.50 6.00
7 1903-04 Ottawa Silver 2.00 5.00
Seven
8 1905 Ottawa Silver 2.00 5.00
Seven
9 1909 Ottawa Senators 2.00 5.00
10 1911 Ottawa Senators 2.00 5.00
11 1920-21 Ottawa 2.00 5.00
Senators
12 1923 Ottawa Senators 2.00 5.00

3 1927 Ottawa Senators 2.00 5.00
4 Title Card 2.00 5.00
1991 Hockey Hall of Fame

1991-92 Pro Set Awards Special

This 17-card standard-size set features NHL players who were All-Stars, nominees, or winners of prestigious trophies. The fronts feature a borderless color action photo, with the team logo in the lower left corner, and the player's name in the black wedge below the logo. The backs present player information and the award which the player won or was nominated for, on a white and gray hockey puck background. The cards are numbered on the back and also have a star logo with the words "A Celebration of Excellence". The cards have the 1991-92 Pro Set style of design.

AC1 Ed Belfour 12.00 30.00
AC2 Mike Richter 12.00 30.00
AC3 Patrick Roy 75.00 200.00
AC4 Wayne Gretzky 125.00 300.00
AC5 Joe Sakic 30.00 75.00
AC6 Brett Hull 25.00 60.00
AC7 Ray Bourque 25.00 60.00
AC8 Al MacInnis 6.00 15.00
AC9 Luc Robitaille 10.00 25.00
AC10 Sergei Fedorov 40.00 100.00
AC11 Ken Hodge Jr. .75 2.00
AC12 Dirk Graham .75 2.00
AC13 Steve Larmer 2.00 5.00
AC14 Esa Tikkanen 4.00 10.00
AC15 Chris Chelios 15.00 40.00
AC16 Dave Taylor 1.50 4.00
NNO Title Card .40 1.00

1991-92 Pro Set NHL Sponsor Awards

This eight-card standard-size set is numbered as an extension of the 1991-92 Pro Set NHL Awards Special. The cards feature the same glossy color player photos as does the regular issue. The fronts differ in having the name of the award inscribed across the bottom of the card face. Also the backs differ in that they omit the head and shoulders photo and have only a player profile. The cards were distributed at The Hockey News Sponsor Awards luncheon in Toronto on June 6, 1991.

AC17 Kevin Dineen 2.50 6.00
Bud Light
NHL Man
of the Year Award
AC18 Brett Hull 25.00 60.00
NHL Pro Set Player
of the Year Award
AC19 Ed Belfour 10.00 25.00
Trico Goaltender Award
AC20 Theo Fleury 10.00 25.00
Alka-Seltzer
Plus Award
AC21 Marty McSorley 2.50 6.00
Alka-Seltzer
Plus Award
AC22 Mike Ilitch 1.50 4.00
Detroit Red Wings OWN
Lester Patrick Award
AC23 Rod Gilbert 2.50 6.00
Lester Patrick Award
NNO Title Card .40 1.00
1990-91 NHL
Sponsor Awards

1991-92 Pro Set Opening Night

This six-card promo set was issued by Pro Set to commemorate the opening night of the 1991-92 NHL season. The standard-size player cards are the same as the regular issue, with borderless glossy color player photos on the fronts, and a color headshot and player information on the backs. Four (different each time) regular issue cards were included in each promo pack.

COMPLETE SET (2) 3.00 8.00
NNO NHL 75th Anniversary 1.50 4.00
Opening Night
NNO 1991-92 Opening Night 1.50 4.00

1991-92 Pro Set Platinum

The 1991-92 Pro Set Platinum hockey set was released in two series of 150 standard-size cards. The front design features full-bleed glossy color action player photos, with the Pro Set Platinum icon superimposed at the lower right corner. Player names do not appear on the front.

COMPLETE SET (300) 3.00 8.00
COMP.SERIES 1 (150) 1.50 4.00
COMP.SERIES 2 (150) 1.50 4.00
1 Cam Neely .07 .20
2 Ray Bourque .15 .40
3 Craig Janney .02 .10
4 Andy Moog .07 .20
5 Dave Poulin .01 .05
6 Ken Hodge Jr. .01 .05
7 Glen Wesley .01 .05
8 Dave Andreychuk .02 .10
9 Daren Puppa .02 .10
10 Pierre Turgeon .02 .10
11 Dale Hawerchuk .02 .10
12 Doug Bodger .01 .05
13 Mike Ramsey .01 .05
14 Alexander Mogilny .07 .20
15 Sergei Makarov .01 .05
16 Theo Fleury .01 .05
17 Joel Otto .01 .05
18 Joe Nieuwendyk .02 .10
19 Al MacInnis .02 .10
20 Gary Suter .01 .05
21 Mike Vernon .02 .10
22 John Tonelli .01 .05
23 Dirk Graham .01 .05
24 Jeremy Roenick .15 .40
25 Chris Chelios .07 .20
26 Ed Belfour .20 .50
27 Steve Smith .01 .05
28 Steve Larmer .02 .10
29 Johan Garpenlov .01 .05
30 Sergei Fedorov .15 .40
31 Tim Cheveldae .02 .10
32 Steve Yzerman .40 1.00
33 Jimmy Carson .01 .05
34 Bob Probert .02 .10
35 Vincent Damphousse .01 .05
36 Bill Ranford .02 .10
37 Petr Klima .01 .05
38 Kevin Lowe .02 .10
39 Esa Tikkanen .01 .05
40 Craig Simpson .01 .05
41 Peter Ing .01 .05
42 Rob Brown .01 .05
43 Bobby Holik .02 .10
44 Pat Verbeek .01 .05
45 Brad Shaw .01 .05
46 Kevin Dineen .01 .05
47 Zarley Zalapski .01 .05
48 Jari Kurri .07 .20
49 Tony Granato .01 .05
50 Luc Robitaille .02 .10
51 Rob Blake .02 .10
52 Wayne Gretzky .50 1.25
53 Tomas Sandstrom .01 .05
54 Kelly Hrudey .02 .10
55 Mike Modano .20 .50
56 Jon Casey .02 .10
57 Todd Elik .01 .05
58 Mark Tinordi .01 .05
59 Brian Bellows .01 .05
60 Dave Gagner .01 .05
61 Patrick Roy .40 1.00
62 Russ Courtnall .01 .05
63 Guy Carbonneau .02 .10
64 Denis Savard .02 .10
65 Petr Svoboda .01 .05
66 Kirk Muller .01 .05
67 Stephane Richer .02 .10
68 Chris Terreri .02 .10
69 Bruce Driver .01 .05
70 John MacLean .02 .10
71 Patrik Sundstrom .01 .05
72 Scott Stevens .02 .10
73 Glenn Healy .02 .10
74 Brent Sutter .01 .05
75 David Volek .01 .05
76 Ray Ferraro .01 .05
77 Pat Flatley .01 .05
78 Jeff Norton .01 .05
79 Brian Leetch .07 .20
80 Tim Kerr .01 .05
81 Mark Messier .07 .20
82 James Patrick .01 .05
83 Mike Richter .07 .20
84 Mike Gartner .02 .10
85 Mike Ricci .07 .20
86 Steve Duchesne .01 .05
87 Ron Hextall .02 .10
88 Rick Tocchet .02 .10
89 Pelle Eklund .01 .05
90 Rod Brind'Amour .07 .20
91 Mario Lemieux .40 1.00
92 Jaromir Jagr .15 .40
93 Kevin Stevens .01 .05
94 Paul Coffey .07 .20
95 Ulf Samuelsson .01 .05
96 Tom Barrasso .02 .10
97 Mark Recchi .07 .20
98 Ron Tugnutt .02 .10
99 Mats Sundin .07 .20
100 Stephane Morin .01 .05
101 Owen Nolan .07 .20
102 Joe Sakic .20 .50
103 Bryan Fogarty .01 .05
104 Kelly Kisio .01 .05
105 Tony Hrkac .01 .05
106 Brian Mullen .01 .05
107 Doug Wilson .02 .10
108 Rich Sutter .01 .05
109 Brett Hull .15 .40
110 Dave Christian .01 .05
111 Brendan Shanahan .07 .20
112 Vincent Riendeau .02 .10
113 Adam Oates .02 .10
114 Jeff Brown .01 .05
115 Gary Leeman .01 .05
116 Dave Ellett .01 .05
117 Grant Fuhr .07 .20
118 Daniel Marois .01 .05
119 Mike Krushelnyski .01 .05
120 Wendel Clark .02 .10
121 Troy Gamble .02 .10
122 Robert Kron .01 .05
123 Geoff Courtnall .02 .10
124 Trevor Linden .02 .10
125 Greg Adams .01 .05
126 Igor Larionov .01 .05
127 Kevin Hatcher .02 .10
128 Mike Ridley .01 .05
129 John Druce .01 .05
130 Al Iafrate .02 .10
131 Dino Ciccarelli .02 .10
132 Michal Pivonka .01 .05
133 Fredrik Olausson .01 .05
134 Ed Olczyk .01 .05
135 Bob Essensa .02 .10
136 Pat Elynuik .01 .05
137 Phil Housley .02 .10
138 Thomas Steen .01 .05
139 Don Beaupre .02 .10
140 Boston Bruins .01 .05
141 Chicago Blackhawks .01 .05
142 Kings (Gretzky back) .01 .05
143 Minnesota North Stars .01 .05
144 Pittsburgh Penguins .01 .05
145 Boston Bruins .01 .05
146 Chicago Blackhawks .01 .05
147 Detroit Red Wings .01 .05
148 Montreal Canadiens .01 .05
149 New York Rangers .01 .05
150 Toronto Maple Leafs .01 .05
151 Stephen Leach .01 .05
152 Vladimir Ruzicka .01 .05
153 Don Sweeney .01 .05
154 Bob Carpenter .01 .05
155 Brent Ashton .01 .05
156 Gord Murphy .01 .05
157 Pat LaFontaine .07 .20
158 Randy Hillier .01 .05
159 Clint Malarchuk .02 .10
160 Randy Wood .01 .05
161 Gary Roberts .02 .10
162 Gary Leeman .01 .05
163 Robert Reichel .01 .05
164 Brent Sutter .01 .05
165 Brian Noonan .01 .05
166 Michel Goulet UER .01 .05
167 Paul Ysebaert .01 .05
168 Kevin Miller .01 .05
169 Ray Sheppard .01 .05
170 Brad McCrimmon .01 .05
171 Joe Murphy .01 .05
172 Dave Manson .01 .05
173 Scott Mellanby .01 .05
174 Bernie Nicholls .02 .10
175 John Cullen .01 .05
176 Marc Bergevin .01 .05
177 Steve Konroyd .01 .05
178 Kay Whitmore .02 .10
179 Murray Craven .01 .05
180 Mikael Andersson .01 .05
181 Bob Kudelski .01 .05
182 Brian Benning .01 .05
183 Mike Donnelly .01 .05
184 Marty McSorley .01 .05
185 Corey Millen RC .01 .05
186 Ulf Dahlen .01 .05
187 Brian Propp .01 .05
188 Neal Broten .02 .10
189 Mike Craig .01 .05
190 Stephan Lebeau .01 .05
191 Mike Keane .01 .05
192 Brent Gilchrist .01 .05
193 Eric Desjardins .02 .10
194 Peter Stastny .02 .10
195 Claude Vilgrain .01 .05
196 Claude Lemieux .01 .05
197 Craig Billington RC .02 .10
198 Alexei Kasatonov .01 .05
199 Slava Fetisov .01 .05
200 Benoit Hogue .01 .05
201 Derek King .01 .05
202 Uwe Krupp .01 .05
203 Steve Thomas .01 .05
204 John Ogrodnick .01 .05
205 Sergei Nemchinov .01 .05
206 Jeff Beukeboom .01 .05
207 Adam Graves .02 .10
208 Andrei Lomakin .01 .05
209 Dan Quinn .01 .05
210 Ken Wreggett .02 .10
211 Garry Galley .01 .05
212 Terry Carkner .01 .05
213 Larry Murphy .02 .10
214 Ron Francis .02 .10
215 Bob Errey .01 .05
216 Bryan Trottier .07 .20
217 Mike Hough .01 .05
218 Mikhail Tatarinov .01 .05
219 Jacques Cloutier .02 .10
220 Greg Paslawski .01 .05
221 Alexei Gusarov RC .02 .10
222 Ron Sutter .01 .05
223 Garth Butcher .01 .05
224 Paul Cavallini .01 .05
225 Curtis Joseph .07 .20
226 Jeff Hackett .07 .20
227 David Bruce RC .01 .05
228 Wayne Presley .01 .05
229 Neil Wilkinson .01 .05
230 Dean Evason .01 .05
231 Brian Bradley .01 .05
232 Peter Zezel .01 .05
233 Mike Bullard .01 .05
234 Doug Gilmour .02 .10
235 Jamie Macoun .01 .05
236 Cliff Ronning .01 .05
237 Jyrki Lumme .01 .05
238 Tom Fergus .01 .05
239 Kirk McLean .02 .10
240 Sergio Momesso .01 .05
241 Randy Burridge .01 .05
242 Dimitri Khristich .01 .05
243 Calle Johansson .01 .05
244 Peter Bondra .02 .10
245 Dale Hunter .01 .05
246 Darrin Shannon .01 .05
247 Troy Murray .01 .05
248 Teppo Numminen .02 .10
249 Donald Audette .01 .05
250 Kevin Haller RC .01 .05
251 Alexander Godynyuk .01 .05
252 Dominik Hasek RC 1.00 2.50
253 Nicklas Lidstrom RC .50 1.25
254 Vladimir Konstantinov RC .25 .60
255 Josef Beranek RC .01 .05
256 Geoff Sanderson RC .02 .10
257 Peter Ahola RC .01 .05
258 Derian Hatcher .02 .10
259 John LeClair RC .50 1.25
260 Kevin Todd RC .01 .05
261 Valeri Zelepukin RC .01 .05
262 Tony Amonte RC .50 1.25
263 Doug Weight RC .40 1.00
264 Claude Boivin RC .01 .05
265 Corey Foster RC .01 .05
266 Jim Paek RC .01 .05
267 Claude Lapointe RC .01 .05
268 Adam Foote RC .08 .25
269 Nelson Emerson .01 .05
270 Arturs Irbe .07 .20
271 Pat Falloon .01 .05
272 Pavel Bure .07 .20
273 Stu Barnes .01 .05
274 Russ Romaniuk RC .01 .05
275 Luciano Borsato RC .01 .05
276 Al MacInnis AS .01 .05
277 Sergei Fedorov AS .07 .20
278 Ray Bourque AS .07 .20
279 Mike Richter AS .02 .10
280 Campbell Conference .01 .05
281 Wales Conference .01 .05
282 Brett Hull PP .07 .20
283 Alexander Mogilny PP .02 .10
284 Brian Leetch PP .02 .10
285 Bob Essensa PP .01 .05
286 Derek King PP .01 .05
287 Steve Larmer PP .01 .05
288 Chris Terreri PP .02 .10
289 Terry O'Reilly CAP .01 .05
290 Burton Cummings CAP .01 .05
291 Marv Albert CAP .01 .05
292 Larry King CAP .01 .05
293 Jim Kelly CAP .07 .20
294 David Wheaton CAP .01 .05
295 Ralph Macchio CAP .01 .05
296 Rick Hansen CAP .01 .05
297 Fred Rogers CAP .01 .05
298 Gaetan Boucher CAP .01 .05
299 Susan Saint James CAP .01 .05
300 James Belushi CAP .01 .05

1991-92 Pro Set Platinum PC

The 1991-92 Pro Set Platinum PC set consists of 20 standard size cards randomly inserted in Platinum foil packs. The first series inserts were a ten-card Platinum Collectibles subset featuring Players of the Month (PC1-PC6) and Sensational Sophomores (PC7-PC10). The second series inserts were subtitled Platinum Milestones (PC11-PC20).

COMPLETE SET (20) 12.50 25.00
PC1 John Vanbiesbrouck .50 1.25
PC2 Pete Peeters .30 .75
PC3 Tom Barrasso .30 .75
PC4 Wayne Gretzky 2.00 5.00
PC5 Brett Hull .75 2.00
PC6 Kelly Hrudey .30 .75
PC7 Sergei Fedorov .75 2.00
PC8 Rob Blake .30 .75
PC9 Ken Hodge Jr. .20 .50
PC10 Eric Weinrich .20 .50
PC11 Mike Gartner .30 .75
PC12 Paul Coffey .50 1.25
PC13 Bobby Smith .30 .75
PC14 Wayne Gretzky 2.00 5.00
PC15 Michel Goulet .40 1.00
PC16 Mike Liut .30 .75
PC17 Brian Propp .20 .50
PC18 Denis Savard .30 .75
PC19 Bryan Trottier .40 1.00
PC20 Mark Messier .60 1.50

1991-92 Pro Set Platinum HOF 75th

This eight-card standard-size set was issued in a cello pack to pay tribute to the NHL's 75th Anniversary. The set includes the Original Six team cards (indistinguishable from cards 145-150 in the regular set) from the 1991-92 Pro Set Platinum hockey set and two special cards. The Hockey Hall of Fame Collectible features on the front a full-bleed sepia-toned picture of Exhibition Place, where the Hockey Hall of Fame has been located since 1961. In addition to commentary, the back features a small color picture of BCE Place, its new location beginning in the fall of 1992. On a black background, the title card features the Hockey Hall of Fame and Museum logo at the top as well as the NHL and Pro Set logos at the bottom. The title card has a blank back. The actual numbering of the cards is reflected in the listing below.

COMPLETE SET (8) 3.00 8.00
145 Boston Bruins .02 .10
146 Chicago Blackhawks .02 .10
147 Detroit Red Wings .02 .10
148 Montreal Canadiens .02 .10
149 New York Rangers .02 .10
150 Toronto Maple Leafs .02 .10
NNO Title Card 1.25 3.00
(Blank back)
HHOF1 Hockey Hall of Fame 2.00 5.00

1991-92 Pro Set Player of the Month

This six-card set was issued by Pro Set to honor hockey players for their outstanding performances during the season. The cards were distributed to all ticket holders at home games the evening of the presentation. Another feature of the presentation was a $1200 donation on behalf of the winning player to the youth hockey organization of his choice. Measuring the standard 2 1/2" by 3 1/2", card fronts feature borderless four-color action photographs. The player's team emblem appears in the lower left corner while the player's name is reversed-out white in a black wedge. On a screened hockey puck design, the horizontally oriented backs have a head shot in a circular format, biography, career statistics, and a summary of the outstanding achievement. The card number and team position appears in the upper right corner.

COMPLETE SET (6) 28.00 70.00
P1 Kirk McLean 2.00 5.00
P2 Kevin Stevens 2.00 5.00
P3 Mario Lemieux 12.00 30.00
P4 Andy Moog 4.00 10.00
P5 Pat LaFontaine 4.00 10.00
P6 Luc Robitaille 4.00 10.00

1991-92 Pro Set Puck Candy Promos

This set of three standard-size hockey cards was distributed in a cello pack to show the design of the upcoming Puck cards. The fronts of the promos are identical to the regular issue. Their backs differ in two respects: 1) instead of a card number, the promos have the words "Prototype For Review Only" in an aqua box; and 2) The "Puck Note" on the promos differs from that found on the regular cards. The cards are unnumbered and checklisted below in alphabetical order.

COMPLETE SET (3) 1.50 4.00
1 Kirk McLean .40 1.00
2 Andy Moog .75 2.00
3 Pat Verbeek .40 1.00

1991-92 Pro Set Puck Candy

This set of thirty standard-size hockey cards was created for a new product, the NHL Pro Set Puck, a combination chocolate, peanut vanilla nougat, and caramel confection. This test product was available in all U.S. NHL and Northeast markets, and each candy package contained three Puck hockey cards. The fronts feature a borderless four-color action player photo with the Pro Set logo and player's name in the bottom border. The horizontally oriented backs have a head shot, biography, and a "Puck Note" that consists of personal information about the player. Pro Set advertised this 30-card set as Series 1; however no Series 2 was ever issued.

COMPLETE SET (30) 16.00 40.00
1 Ray Bourque .75 2.00
2 Andy Moog .30 .75
3 Doug Bodger .15 .40
4 Theo Fleury .30 .75
5 Al MacInnis .30 .75
6 Jeremy Roenick .60 1.50
7 Tim Cheveldae .15 .40
8 Steve Yzerman 1.50 4.00
9 Craig Simpson .15 .40
10 Pat Verbeek .15 .40
11 Wayne Gretzky 15.00 30.00
12 Luc Robitaille .30 .75
13 Brian Bellows .15 .40
14 Patrick Roy 3.00 8.00
15 Guy Carbonneau .15 .40
16 Peter Stastny .30 .75
17 Adam Creighton .15 .40
18 Glenn Healy .30 .75
19 Mark Messier .75 2.00
20 Rod Brind'Amour .30 .75
21 Paul Coffey .60 1.50
22 Tom Barasso .30 .75
23 Joe Sakic 1.25 3.00
24 Brett Hull .75 2.00
25 Adam Oates .30 .75
26 Kelly Kisio .15 .40
27 Grant Fuhr .30 .75
28 Kirk McLean .30 .75
29 Kevin Hatcher .15 .40
30 Phil Housley .15 .40

1991-92 Pro Set Rink Rat

These standard-size cards were produced by Pro Set to promote education. On card number 2 the front cartoon portrays the Rink Rat shooting the puck through a defenseman's legs right toward the viewer of the card; on a screen design with miniature hockey pucks, the horizontally oriented back has another circular-shaped cartoon picture of the Rink Rat reading and a "stay in school/study hard" message.

COMPLETE SET (2) 3.00 8.00
RR1 Rink Rat 1.50 4.00
RR2 Rink Rat 1.50 4.00

1991-92 Pro Set St. Louis Midwest

This four-card standard-size set was available at the Midwest Sports Collectors Show in St. Louis in November 1991. The cards were a special issue for the card show; in fact, Pro Set did not even issue a Meagher card in its regular set. All four cards show explicitly on the front that they were a special issue from this show. The fronts of these cards differ from the regular issue in two respects: 1) a royal blue border stripe runs the length of the card on the right side; and 2) the cards are numbered in the stripe "X of Four Midwest Collectors Show". The card backs are the same as the regular issue cards.

COMPLETE SET (4) 4.00 10.00
1 Adam Oates 1.25 3.00
2 Paul Cavallini .40 1.00
3 Rick Meagher .40 1.00
4 Brett Hull 3.00 8.00

1992-93 Pro Set

The 1992-93 Pro Set hockey set consists of 270 cards. The production run was 8,000 numbered 20-box foil cases and 2,000 20-box jumbo cases. One thousand Kirk McLean autographed cards were randomly inserted. The McLean cards have No. 239 on the back; his regular card is #193. The most noteworthy Rookie Card in the set is Bill Guerin.

1 Mario Lemieux PS-POY .40 1.00
2 Patrick Roy THN-POY .25 .60
3 Adam Oates .10 .25
4 Ray Bourque .15 .40
5 Vladimir Ruzicka .05 .15
6 Stephen Leach .05 .15
7 Andy Moog .07 .20
8 Cam Neely .10 .25
9 Dave Poulin .05 .15
10 Glen Wesley .05 .15
11 Gord Murphy .07 .20
12 Dale Hawerchuk .12 .30
13 Pat LaFontaine .10 .25
14 Tom Draper .05 .15
15 Dave Andreychuk .10 .25
16 Petr Svoboda .07 .20
17 Doug Bodger .05 .15
18 Donald Audette .07 .20
19 Alexander Mogilny .07 .20
20 Randy Wood .05 .15
21 Gary Roberts .05 .15
22 Al MacInnis .07 .20
23 Theo Fleury .15 .40
24 Sergei Makarov .05 .15
25 Mike Vernon .07 .20
26 Joe Nieuwendyk .07 .20
27 Gary Suter .05 .15
28 Joel Otto .05 .15
29 Paul Ranheim .05 .15
30 Jeremy Roenick .15 .40
31 Steve Larmer .05 .15
32 Michel Goulet .07 .20
33 Ed Belfour .10 .25
34 Chris Chelios .10 .25
35 Igor Kravchuk .05 .15
36 Brent Sutter .05 .15
37 Steve Smith .05 .15
38 Dirk Graham .05 .15
39 Steve Yzerman .25 .60
40 Sergei Fedorov .15 .40
41 Paul Ysebaert .05 .15
42 Nicklas Lidstrom .07 .20
43 Tim Cheveldae .05 .15
44 Vladimir Konstantinov .10 .25
45 Shawn Burr .05 .15
46 Bob Probert .07 .20
47 Ray Sheppard .05 .15
48 Kelly Buchberger .05 .15
49 Joe Murphy .05 .15
50 Norm Maciver .05 .15
51 Bill Ranford .07 .20
52 Bernie Nicholls .05 .15
53 Esa Tikkanen .05 .15
54 Scott Mellanby .05 .15
55 Dave Manson .05 .15
56 Craig Simpson .05 .15
57 John Cullen .05 .15
58 Pat Verbeek .05 .15
59 Zarley Zalapski .05 .15
60 Murray Craven .05 .15
61 Bobby Holik .07 .20
62 Steve Konroyd .07 .20
63 Geoff Sanderson .07 .20
64 Frank Pietrangelo .07 .20
65 Mikael Andersson UER .05 .15
66 Wayne Gretzky .50 1.25
67 Rob Blake .07 .20
68 Jari Kurri .10 .25
69 Marty McSorley .05 .15
70 Kelly Hrudey .07 .20
71 Paul Coffey .10 .25
72 Luc Robitaille .07 .20
73 Peter Ahola .05 .15
74 Tony Granato .05 .15
75 Derian Hatcher .05 .15
76 Mike Modano .25 .60
77 Dave Gagner .07 .20
78 Mark Tinordi .05 .15
79 Craig Ludwig .07 .20
80 Ulf Dahlen .05 .15
81 Bobby Smith .07 .20
82 Jon Casey .05 .15
83 Jim Johnson .07 .20
84 Denis Savard .12 .30
85 Patrick Roy .25 .60
86 Eric Desjardins .07 .20
87 Kirk Muller .05 .15
88 Guy Carbonneau .07 .20
89 Shayne Corson .05 .15
90 Brent Gilchrist .05 .15
91 Mathieu Schneider UER .05 .15
92 Gilbert Dionne .05 .15
93 Stephane Richer .07 .20
94 Kevin Todd .05 .15
95 Scott Stevens .10 .25
96 Slava Fetisov .05 .15
97 Chris Terreri .07 .20
98 Claude Lemieux .05 .15
99 Bruce Driver .05 .15
100 Peter Stastny .07 .20
101 Alexei Kasatonov .05 .15
102 Patrick Flatley .07 .20
103 Adam Creighton UER .05 .15
104 Pierre Turgeon .07 .20
105 Ray Ferraro .05 .15
106 Steve Thomas .07 .20
107 Mark Fitzpatrick .07 .20
108 Benoit Hogue .05 .15
109 Uwe Krupp .05 .15
110 Derek King .05 .15
111 Mark Messier .15 .40
112 Brian Leetch .07 .20
113 Mike Gartner .07 .20
114 Darren Turcotte .05 .15
115 Adam Graves .05 .15
116 Mike Richter .10 .25
117 Sergei Nemchinov .05 .15
118 Tony Amonte .07 .20
119 James Patrick .05 .15
120 Andrew McBain .07 .20
121 Rob Murphy .05 .15
122 Mike Peluso .07 .20
123 Sylvain Turgeon .05 .15
124 Brad Shaw .05 .15
125 Peter Sidorkiewicz .05 .15
126 Brad Marsh .07 .20
127 Mark Freer .05 .15
128 Marc Fortier .05 .15
129 Ron Hextall .07 .20
130 Claude Boivin .05 .15
131 Mark Recchi .12 .30
132 Rod Brind'Amour .05 .15
133 Mike Ricci .07 .20
134 Kevin Dineen .05 .15
135 Brian Benning .05 .15
136 Kerry Huffman .05 .15
137 Steve Duchesne .05 .15
138 Rick Tocchet .07 .20
139 Mario Lemieux .40 1.00
140 Kevin Stevens .05 .15
141 Jaromir Jagr .25 .60
142 Joe Mullen .07 .20
143 Ulf Samuelsson .05 .15
144 Ron Francis .12 .30
145 Tom Barrasso .07 .20
146 Larry Murphy .07 .20
147 Alexei Gusarov .05 .15
148 Valeri Kamensky .05 .15
149 Mats Sundin .10 .25
150 Joe Sakic .25 .60
151 Claude Lapointe .05 .15
152 Stephane Fiset .05 .15
153 Owen Nolan .05 .15
154 Mike Hough .07 .20
155 Greg Paslawski .05 .15
156 Brett Hull .15 .40
157 Craig Janney .07 .20
158 Jeff Brown .07 .20
159 Paul Cavallini .05 .15
160 Garth Butcher .07 .20
161 Nelson Emerson .05 .15
162 Ron Sutter .05 .15
163 Brendan Shanahan .12 .30
164 Curtis Joseph .10 .25
165 Doug Wilson .07 .20
166 Pat Falloon .05 .15
167 Kelly Kisio .07 .20
168 Neil Wilkinson .05 .15
169 Jay More .05 .15
170 David Bruce .05 .15
171 Jeff Hackett .07 .20
172 David Williams RC .05 .15
173 Brian Lawton .07 .20
174 Brian Bradley .05 .15
175 Jock Callander RC .07 .20
176 Basil McRae .07 .20
177 Rob Ramage .05 .15
178 Pat Jablonski .07 .20
179 Joe Reekie .05 .15
180 Doug Crossman .07 .20
181 Jim Benning .07 .20
182 Ken Hodge Jr. .05 .15
183 Grant Fuhr .10 .25
184 Doug Gilmour .12 .30
185 Glenn Anderson .10 .25
186 Dave Ellett .05 .15
187 Peter Zezel .05 .15
188 Jamie Macoun .05 .15
189 Wendel Clark .07 .20
190 Bob Halkidis .07 .20
191 Rob Pearson .05 .15
192 Pavel Bure .20 .50
193 Kirk McLean .05 .15
194 Sergio Momesso .05 .15
195 Cliff Ronning .05 .15
196 Jyrki Lumme .05 .15
197 Trevor Linden .07 .20
198 Geoff Courtnall .05 .15
199 Doug Lidster .05 .15
200 Dave Babych .07 .20
201 Michal Pivonka .07 .20
202 Dale Hunter .05 .15
203 Calle Johansson .05 .15
204 Kevin Hatcher .05 .15
205 Al Iafrate .07 .20
206 Don Beaupre .05 .15
207 Randy Burridge .05 .15
208 Dimitri Khristich .07 .20
209 Peter Bondra .07 .20
210 Teppo Numminen .05 .15
211 Bob Essensa .07 .20
212 Phil Housley .07 .20
213 Ed Olczyk .05 .15
214 Pat Elynuik .05 .15
215 Troy Murray .05 .15
216 Igor Ulanov .05 .15
217 Thomas Steen .05 .15
218 Darrin Shannon .05 .15
219 Joe Juneau .05 .15
220 Steve Heinze .05 .15
221 Ted Donato .05 .15
222 Glen Murray .05 .15
223 Keith Carney RC .20 .50
224 Dean McAmmond RC .05 .15
225 Slava Kozlov .07 .20
226 Martin Lapointe .05 .15
227 Patrick Poulin .05 .15
228 Darryl Sydor .05 .15
229 Trent Klatt RC .07 .20
230 Bill Guerin RC .20 .50
231 Jarrod Skalde .05 .15
232 Scott Niedermayer .10 .25
233 Marty McInnis .05 .15
234 Scott Lachance .05 .15
235 Dominic Roussel .07 .20
236 Eric Lindros .30 .75
237 Shawn McEachern .05 .15
238 Martin Rucinsky .05 .15
239 Bill Lindsay RC .05 .15
240 Bret Hedican RC .07 .20
241 Ray Whitney RC .15 .40
242 Felix Potvin .20 .50
243 Keith Tkachuk .10 .25
244 Evgeny Davydov .05 .15
245 Brett Hull LL .15 .40
246 Wayne Gretzky LL .50 1.25
247 Steve Yzerman LL .25 .60
248 Paul Ysebaert SL .05 .15
249 Dave Andreychuk SL .10 .25
250 Kirk McLean LL .05 .15
251 Tim Cheveldae SL .05 .15
252 Jeremy Roenick LL .15 .40
253 NHL Pro Set NR .05 .15
254 NHL Pro Set NR .05 .15
255 NHL Pro Set NR .05 .15
256 Mike Gartner MS .07 .20
257 Brian Propp MS .05 .15
258 Dave Taylor MS .07 .20
259 Bobby Smith MS .07 .20
260 Denis Savard MS .12 .30
261 Ray Bourque MS .15 .40
262 Joe Mullen MS .07 .20
263 John Tonelli MS .07 .20
264 Brad Marsh MS .07 .20
265 Randy Carlyle MS .07 .20
266 Mike Hough PS .07 .20
267 Bob Essensa PS .07 .20
268 Mike Lalor PS .07 .20
269 Terry Carkner PS .07 .20
270 Todd Krygier PS .07 .20
AU239 Kirk McLean AU/100 15.00 40.00

1992-93 Pro Set Award Winners

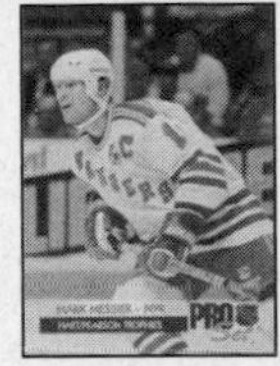

Randomly inserted in 1992-93 Pro Set packs, these five standard-size cards capture five NHL players who were honored with trophies for their outstanding play. The fronts feature full-bleed color action player photos. A gold-foil stamped "Award Winner" emblem is superimposed at the upper right corner. The player's name, team name, and trophy awarded appear in two bars toward the bottom of the picture. The backs carry a color headshot and a career summary.

COMPLETE SET (5) 8.00 15.00
CC1 Mark Messier 1.00 2.50
CC2 Patrick Roy 4.00 10.00
CC3 Pavel Bure 1.00 2.50
CC4 Brian Leetch 1.00 2.50
CC5 Guy Carbonneau .40 1.00

1992-93 Pro Set Gold Team Leaders

Inserted one per jumbo pack, this 15-card standard-size set spotlights team scoring leaders from the Campbell Conference. The color action player photos on the fronts are full-bleed with "1991-92 Team Leader" gold foil stamped on the picture at the upper right corner. Toward the bottom of the picture the player's name appears on a rust-colored bar that overlays a jagged design. Bordered by a dark brown screened background with Campbell Conference logos, the back carries career summary on a rust-colored panel. The cards are numbered on the back "X of 15."

COMPLETE SET (15) 10.00 25.00
1 Gary Roberts .20 .50
2 Jeremy Roenick 1.25 3.00
3 Steve Yzerman 2.00 5.00
4 Nicklas Lidstrom .75 2.00
5 Vincent Damphousse .40 1.00
6 Wayne Gretzky 3.00 8.00
7 Mike Modano 1.25 3.00
8 Brett Hull 1.25 3.00
9 Nelson Emerson .20 .50
10 Pat Falloon .20 .50
11 Doug Gilmour .40 1.00
12 Trevor Linden .40 1.00
13 Pavel Bure .75 2.00
14 Phil Housley .40 1.00
15 Luciano Borsato .20 .50

1992-93 Pro Set Rookie Goal Leaders

This 12-card Rookie Goal Leader standard-size set features the top rookie goal scorers from the 1991-92 season. The cards were randomly inserted in 1992-93 Pro Set packs. The player's name appears in a white bar above the picture, while the words "1991-92 Rookie Goal Leader" are gold foil-stamped across the bottom of the picture.

COMPLETE SET (12) 2.50 6.00
1 Tony Amonte .40 1.00
2 Pavel Bure 1.25 3.00
3 Donald Audette .20 .50
4 Pat Falloon .20 .50
5 Nelson Emerson .20 .50
6 Gilbert Dionne .20 .50
7 Kevin Todd .20 .50
8 Luciano Borsato .20 .50
9 Rob Pearson .20 .50
10 Valeri Zelepukin .20 .50
11 Geoff Sanderson .40 1.00
12 Claude Lapointe .20 .50

1991 Pro Stars Posters

These three posters were folded, cello wrapped, and inserted in Pro Stars cereal boxes. Through an offer on the side panel of the box, the collector could receive another poster by sending in three Pro Stars UPC symbols and 1.00 for postage and handling. In the cello packs, the posters measure approximately 4 1/2" by 4"; they unfold to a narrow poster that measures approximately 4 1/2" by 24". On a background of blue, purple, and bright yellow stars, a cartoon drawing portrays the athlete in an action pose. At the bottom of each poster appears a player profile in English and French. The backsides of all three posters combine to form a composite poster featuring all three players. The posters are unnumbered and listed below alphabetically.

COMPLETE SET (3) 4.00 10.00
3 Wayne Gretzky 1.60 4.00

1987 Pro-Sport All-Stars

Issued in Canadian retail packs that included an LCD quartz watch, each of these red, white, and blue oversized cards measures approximately 11 3/4" by 10 1/2" when unfolded and features a color player action shot at the lower right. The player's name, along with his career highlights in English and French, are shown at the lower left. A middle section is cut away to accommodate the watch. The cards are numbered on the front with a "CW" prefix. These cards are priced below without the watches. Number 4 was apparently not issued.

COMPLETE SET (17) 20.00 50.00
1 Larry Robinson 1.25 3.00
2 Guy Carbonneau .75 2.00
3 Chris Chelios 2.00 5.00
5 Mario Lemieux 6.00 15.00
6 Mike Bossy 1.50 4.00
7 Dale Hawerchuk 1.25 3.00

8 Joe Mullen 1.25 3.00
9 Rick Vaive .75 2.00
10 Wendel Clark 1.50 4.00
11 Michel Goulet 1.25 3.00
12 Peter Stastny 1.25 3.00
13 Mark Messier 2.50 6.00
14 Paul Coffey 2.00 5.00
15 Tony Tanti .75 2.00
16 Borje Salming 1.25 3.00
17 Chris Nilan .75 2.00
18 Mats Naslund 1.25 3.00

1983-84 Puffy Stickers

This set of 150 puffy stickers was issued in panels of six stickers each. The panels measure approximately 3 1/2" by 6". There are 21 player panels and four logo panels. The NHL and NHLPA logos appear in the center of each panel. The stickers are oval-shaped and measure approximately 1 1/4" by 1 3/4". In the top portion of the oval they feature a color head shot of the player, with the team name above the head and the player name below the picture in a white box. The sticker background is wood-grain in design. The 21 player panels are numbered and we have checklisted them below accordingly. The logo panels are unnumbered and they are listed after the player panels. The backs are blank. There was also an album produced for this set; the album is not included in the complete set price below.

COMPLETE SET (25) 30.00 75.00
1 Doug Risebrough 6.00 15.00
Wayne Gretzky
Mats Naslund
Bill Derlago
Richard Brodeur
Dave Babych
2 Glenn Anderson 1.50 4.00
Larry Robinson
Rick Vaive
Stan Smyl
Scott Arniel
Don Edwards
3 Ryan Walter 1.25 3.00
Peter Ihnacak
Thomas Gradin
Morris Lukowich
Kent Nilsson
Paul Coffey
4 John Anderson 2.50 6.00
Tiger Williams
Brian Mullen
Steve Tambellini
Mark Messier
Guy Lafleur
5 Darcy Rota 1.25 3.00
Dale Hawerchuk
Paul Reinhart
Jari Kurri
Mario Tremblay
Mike Palmateer
6 Paul MacLean 1.50 4.00
Lanny McDonald
Ken Linseman
Steve Shutt
Borje Salming
Kevin McCarthy
7 Barry Pederson 1.25 3.00
Mike Foligno
Jim Fox
Don Lever
Bobby Clarke
Greg Malone
8 Gilbert Perreault 1.25 3.00
Charlie Simmer
Hector Marini
Mark Howe
Rick Kehoe
Jim Schoenfeld
9 Larry Murphy 1.25 3.00
Phil Russell
Bill Barber
Mike Bullard
Pete Peeters
John Van Boxmeer
10 Tapio Levo 1.50 4.00
Darryl Sittler
Paul Gardner
Rick Middleton
Real Cloutier
Bernie Nicholls
11 Brian Propp 1.50 4.00
Michel Dion
Ray Bourque
Dale McCourt
Marcel Dionne
Bob MacMillan
12 Randy Carlyle 1.25 3.00
Terry O'Reilly
Phil Housley
Dave Taylor
Glenn Resch
Behn Wilson
13 Tony Esposito 1.50 4.00
Ron Duguay
Pierre Larouche
Neal Broten
Peter Stastny
Blake Dunlop
14 Walt McKechnie 1.00 2.50
Risto Siltanen
Bobby Smith
Anton Stastny
Mike Liut
Doug Wilson
15 Blaine Stoughton 1.25 3.00
Dino Ciccarelli
Michel Goulet
Jorgen Pettersson
Tom Lysiak
Brad Park
16 Craig Hartsburg 1.00 2.50
Marian Stastny
Rob Ramage
Al Secord
John Ogrodnick
Greg Millen
17 Tony McKegney 1.00 2.50
Brian Sutter
Steve Larmer
Danny Gare
Mark Johnson
Brian Bellows
18 Bernie Federko 1.25 3.00
Denis Savard
Reed Larson
Ron Francis
Dennis Maruk
Dan Bouchard
19 Mike Bossy 1.50 4.00
Anders Hedberg
Rod Langway
Billy Smith
Reijo Ruotsalainen
Milan Novy
20 Barry Beck 1.25 3.00
Bob Carpenter
Clark Gillies
Rob McClanahan
Brian Engblom
Denis Potvin
21 Mike Gartner 1.50 4.00
John Tonelli
Willie Huber
Pat Riggin
Bryan Trottier
Don Maloney
22 Norris Division 2.00 5.00
Blackhawks logo
Red Wings logo
North Stars logo
Blues logo
Maple Leafs logo
NHL logo
23 Patrick Division 2.00 5.00
Devils logo
Islanders logo
Rangers logo
Flyers logo
Penguins logo
Capitals logo
24 Adams Division 2.00 5.00
Bruins logo
Sabres logo
Whalers logo
Canadiens logo
Nordiques logo
NHL logo
25 Smythe Division 2.00 5.00
Flames logo
Oilers logo
Kings logo
Canucks logo
Jets logo
NHL logo
xx Album 10.00 25.00

1938-39 Quaker Oats Photos

This 30-card set of Toronto Maple Leafs and Montreal Canadiens was sponsored by Quaker Oats. The photos were obtainable by mail with the redemption of proofs of purchase. These oversized cards (approximately 6 1/4" by 7 3/8") are unnumbered and hence are listed below alphabetically. Facsimile autographs are printed in white on the fronts of these blank-backed cards.

COMPLETE SET (30) 750.00 1500.00
1 Syl Apps 62.50 125.00
2 Toe Blake 125.00 250.00
3 Buzz Boll 25.00 50.00
4 Turk Broda 87.50 175.00
5 Walter Buswell 25.00 50.00
6 Herb Cain 30.00 60.00
7 Murph Chamberlain 25.00 50.00
8 Wilf Cude 30.00 60.00
9 Bob Davidson 25.00 50.00
10 Gordie Drillon 50.00 100.00
11 Paul Drouin 25.00 50.00
12 Stew Evans 25.00 50.00
13 James Fowler 25.00 50.00
14 Johnny Gagnon 25.00 50.00
15 Robert Gracie 25.00 50.00
16 Reg Hamilton 25.00 50.00
17 Paul Haynes 25.00 50.00
18 Foster Hewitt 50.00 100.00
19 Red Horner 50.00 100.00
20 Harvey(Busher) Jackson 75.00 125.00
21 Bingo Kampman 25.00 50.00
22 Pep Kelly 25.00 50.00
23 Rod Lorrain 25.00 50.00
24 George Mantha 25.00 50.00
25 Nick Metz 25.00 50.00
26 George Parsons 25.00 50.00
27 Babe Siebert 50.00 100.00
28 Bill Thoms 25.00 50.00
29 James Ward 25.00 50.00
30 Cy Wentworth 30.00 60.00

1945-54 Quaker Oats Photos

Quaker Oats of Canada continued its tradition of redeeming proofs of purchase for photos of Montreal Canadiens and Toronto Maple Leafs in this nine-year series. Many players are featured in multiple versions, as their photos were updated over the years. The photos themselves are black and white with a thin white border and measure 8" X 10". Because of the numerous variations and the potential for more to be unearthed, no complete set price is listed below. Currently, 113 players are featured on 200 different photos. Anyone with information regarding other photos or variations is encouraged to contact Beckett Publications. The photos are blank-backed and unnumbered and are listed below in alphabetical order within their team (Toronto first, then Montreal).

1A Syl Apps/Home Still, CJS Apps auto. 15.00 30.00
1B Syl Apps/Home Still, Syl Apps auto. 12.50 25.00
1C Syl Apps/Away With Stanley Cup 75.00 150.00
2 George Armstrong/Home Action 12.50 25.00
3 Doug Baldwin/Home Still 50.00 100.00
4A Bill Barilko/Home Action auto. 1/4-inch from border 12.50 25.00
4B Bill Barilko/Home Action auto. 3/4-inch from border 12.50 25.00
4C Bill Barilko/Away Action 12.50 25.00
5 Baz Bastien/Home Still 62.50 125.00
6 Gordon Bell/Home Still 62.50 125.00
7A Max Bentley/Home Still 10.00 20.00
7B Max Bentley/Home Dressing Room 75.00 150.00
7C Max Bentley/Away Action 10.00 20.00
8 Gus Bodnar/Home Still 20.00 40.00
9A Garth Boesch/Home Still closed B in auto. 7.50 15.00
9B Garth Boesch/Home Still open B in auto. 7.50 15.00
9C Garth Boesch/Away Action 50.00 100.00
10 Hugh Bolton/Home Action 6.00 12.00
11 Leo Boivin/Home Action 15.00 30.00
12A Turk Broda/Away Splits, W.E. auto. 25.00 50.00
12B Turk Broda/Away Splits, Turk auto. 20.00 40.00
12C Turk Broda/Away Action 20.00 40.00
13 Lorne Carr/Home Still 15.00 30.00
14 Les Costello/Home Still 15.00 30.00
15 Bob Davidson/Home Still 12.50 25.00
16A Bill Ezinicki/cropped William auto., blue tint 10.00 20.00
16B Bill Ezinicki/entire William auto. 6.00 12.00
16C Bill Ezinicki/Home Still, Bill auto. 6.00 12.00
16D Bill Ezinicki/Away Action 6.00 12.00
17 Fernie Flaman/Home Action 7.50 15.00
18A Cal Gardner/Home Still 6.00 12.00
18B Cal Gardner/Away Action 6.00 12.00
19A Bob Goldham/sweeping G in auto. 6.00 12.00
19B Bob Goldham/normal G, entire blade 6.00 12.00
19C Bob Goldham/normal G blade cropped 75.00 150.00
20 Gord Hannigan/Home Action 15.00 30.00
21 Bob Hassard/Away Action 25.00 50.00
22 Mel Hill/Home Still 40.00 80.00
23 Tim Horton/Home Action 50.00 100.00
24A Bill Judza/Home Still 6.00 12.00
24B Bill Judza/Away Action 6.00 12.00
25A Ted Kennedy/Home Still blade in corner 25.00 50.00
25B Ted Kennedy/Home Still 25.00 50.00
25C Ted Kennedy/Home Still 50.00 100.00
25D Ted Kennedy/Home Still, C on jersey 10.00 20.00
25E Ted Kennedy/Home With Stanley Cup 87.50 175.00
25F Ted Kennedy/Away Action 10.00 20.00
26A Joe Klukay/Home Still 6.00 12.00
26B Joe Klukay/Away Action 6.00 12.00
27 Danny Lewicki/Home Action 7.50 15.00
28 Harry Lumley/Home Action 30.00 60.00
29A Vic Lynn/Home Still/head 3/8-inch from border 6.00 12.00
29B Vic Lynn/Home Still/head 1/8-inch from border 15.00 30.00
29C Vic Lynn/Away Action 6.00 12.00
30A Fleming Mackell/Home Still 6.00 12.00
30B Fleming Mackell/Away Action 7.50 15.00
31 Phil Maloney/Home Action 40.00 80.00
32 Frank Mathers/Home Still 20.00 40.00
33 Frank McCool/Home Still 62.50 125.00
34 John McCormick/Away Action 15.00 30.00
35A Howie Meeker/Home Still large image 10.00 20.00
35B Howie Meeker/Home Still small image 10.00 20.00
35C Howie Meeker/Away Action 10.00 20.00
36A Don Metz/Home, posed to right 6.00 12.00
36B Don Metz/Home, center pose, b&w tint 12.50 25.00
36C Don Metz/Home, center pose, blue tint 40.00 80.00
37A Nick Metz/Home Still, original stick 6.00 12.00
37B Nick Metz/Home Still 12.50 25.00
37C Nick Metz/Home Still 25.00 50.00
38 Rudy Migay/Home Action 30.00 60.00
39 Elwyn Morris/Home Still 40.00 80.00
40 Jim Morrison/Home Action 6.00 12.00
41A Gus Mortson/Home Still 6.00 12.00
41B Gus Mortson/Away Action 6.00 12.00
42 Eric Nesterenko/Home Action 40.00 80.00
43 Bud Poile/Home Still 15.00 30.00
44 Babe Pratt/Home Still 50.00 100.00
45 Al Rollins/Home Action 12.50 25.00
46 Dave Schriner/Home Still 30.00 60.00
47A Tod Sloan/Home Still 12.50 25.00
47B Tod Sloan/Home Action 6.00 12.00
48A Sid Smith/Home Still 12.50 25.00
48B Sid Smith/Away Action 6.00 12.00
49 Bob Solinger 15.00 30.00
50A Wally Stanowski/Home Still entire blade 12.50 25.00
50B Wally Stanowski/Home Still blade cropped 6.00 12.00
51A Gaye Stewart/Home Still 50.00 100.00
51B Gaye Stewart/Home Still, blue tint 6.00 12.00
52 Ron Stewart/Home Action 50.00 100.00
53 Harry Taylor/Home Still 7.50 15.00
54 Billy Taylor/Home Still 25.00 50.00
55 Cy Thomas/Home Still 25.00 50.00
56A Jim Thomson/Home Still stick cropped 30.00 60.00
56B Jim Thomson/Home Still stick touching border 6.00 12.00
56C Jim Thomson/Home Still stick away from border 30.00 60.00
56D Jim Thomson/Away Action 6.00 12.00
57A Ray Timgren/Home Still 7.50 15.00
57B Ray Timgren/Away Action 6.00 12.00
58A Harry Watson/Home Still tape on stick 6.00 12.00
58B Harry Watson/Home Still no tape visible 6.00 12.00
58C Harry Watson/Away Action 6.00 12.00
59 1947-49 Toronto Team Picture 30.00 60.00
60A Leafs Attack McNeil 87.50 175.00
60B Gardner attacks Harvey 100.00 200.00
60C Rollins, Judza stop Curry 100.00 200.00
60D McNeil Saves on Gardner 100.00 200.00
61 George Allen/Home Still 6.00 12.00
62 Jean Beliveau/Home Action 87.50 175.00
63 Joe Benoit/Home Still 10.00 20.00
64A Toe Blake/Hector Toe Blake auto. 75.00 150.00
64B Toe Blake/Toe Blake auto. above skates 10.00 20.00
64C Toe Blake/Toe Blake auto. below skate 10.00 20.00
65A Butch Bouchard/Home Still entire skate 6.00 12.00
65B Butch Bouchard/Home Still skate cropped 6.00 12.00
65C Butch Bouchard/Home Action 7.50 15.00
66 Todd Campeau/Home Still 6.00 12.00
67 Bob Carse/Home Still 6.00 12.00
68 Joe Carveth/Home Portrait 6.00 12.00
69A Murph Chamberlain/facing sideways, entire skates 10.00 20.00
69B Murph Chamberlain/Home Still 10.00 20.00
69C Murph Chamberlain/Home Still, facing forward 15.00 30.00
70 Gerry Couture/Away Action 6.00 12.00
71A Floyd Curry/Home Still 62.50 125.00
71B Floyd Curry/Home Action 6.00 12.00
72 Ed Dorohoy/Home Action 6.00 12.00
73A Bill Durnan/Home Still stick handle cropped 12.50 25.00
73B Bill Durnan/Home Still 25.00 50.00
73C Bill Durnan/Home Still 87.50 175.00
73D Bill Durnan/Home Action 15.00 30.00
74A Norm Dussault/Home Portrait 6.00 12.00
74B Norm Dussault/Home Action 15.00 30.00
75 Frank Eddolls/Home Still 10.00 20.00
76A Bob Fillion/Home Still/small image 25.00 50.00
76B Bob Fillion/Home Still 6.00 12.00
76C Bob Fillion/Home Still/test 12.50 25.00
76D Bob Fillion/Home Action teststesttees/testst 6.00 12.00
77 Dick Gamble/Away Action 10.00 20.00
78 Bernie Geoffrion/Home Action 15.00 30.00
79A Leo Gravelle/Home Still 6.00 12.00
79B Leo Gravelle/Away Still 25.00 50.00
79C Leo Gravelle/Home Action 6.00 12.00
80A Glen Harmon/Home Still, entire puck 6.00 12.00
80B Glen Harmon/Home Still, no puck 6.00 12.00
80C Glen Harmon/Home Action 12.50 25.00
81A Doug Harvey/Home Still 12.50 25.00
81B Doug Harvey/Home Action 10.00 20.00
82 Dutch Hiller/Home Still 10.00 20.00
83 Bert Hirschfield/Home Action Testtestestsetstset 10.00 20.00
84 Tom Johnson/Home Action/sdfsdfsdfsdfsdfsdfsdf 10.00 20.00
85 Vern Kaiser/Home Action 10.00 20.00
86A Elmer Lach/Home Still stick in corner 10.00 20.00
86B Elmer Lach/Home Still, stick cropped 10.00 20.00
86C Elmer Lach/Home Still stick 1/2-inch up from corner 40.00 80.00
86D Elmer Lach/Home Action 10.00 20.00
87A Leo Lamoureaux/Home Still entire blade 12.50 25.00
87B Leo Lamoureaux/Home Still blade cropped 10.00 20.00
88A Hal Laycoe/Home Portrait 50.00 100.00
88B Hal Laycoe/Home Action 6.00 12.00
89A Roger Leger/Home Still light background 6.00 12.00
89B Roger Leger/Home Still dark background 6.00 12.00
89C Roger Leger/Home Action 25.00 50.00
90 Jacques Locas/Home Still 10.00 20.00
91 Ross Lowe/Away Action 10.00 20.00
92 Callum MacKay/Home Action 6.00 12.00
93 Murdo MacKay/Home Portrait 6.00 12.00
94 James MacPherson/Home Action 6.00 12.00
95 Paul Masnick/Home Action 6.00 12.00
96A John McCormick/Home Action, vertical 50.00 100.00
96B John McCormick/Home Action, horizontal 30.00 60.00
97 Mike McMahon/Home Still 50.00 100.00
98 Gerry McNeil/Home Action 12.50 25.00
99 Paul Meger/Home Action 7.50 15.00
100 Dickie Moore/Home Action 15.00 30.00
101A Ken Mosdell/Home Still, small image 6.00 12.00
101B Ken Mosdell/Home Still, large image/auto. croppe 25.00 50.00
101C Ken Mosdell/Home Still large image/auto. not cr 25.00 50.00
101D Ken Mosdell/Home Action 6.00 12.00
102A Buddy O'Connor/Home Still entire blade 20.00 40.00
102B Buddy O'Connor/Home Still blade cropped 10.00 20.00
103 Bert Olmstead/Home Action 12.50 25.00
104A Jim Peters/Home Still, large image 6.00 12.00
104B Jim Peters/Home Still, small image 6.00 12.00
105 Gerry Plamondon/Home Action 7.50 15.00
106 Johnny Quilty/Home Portrait 7.50 15.00
107A Ken Reardon/Home Still large image 10.00 20.00
107B Ken Reardon/Home Still small image 15.00 30.00
107C Kenny Reardon/Home Action 10.00 20.00
108A Billy Reay/Home Still large image/stick touchin 6.00 12.00
108B Billy Reay/Home Still large image/stick away fr 6.00 12.00
108C Billy Reay/Home Still, small image 62.50 125.00
108D Billy Reay/Home Action 6.00 12.00
109A Maurice Richard/Home screen background 150.00 300.00
109B Maurice Richard/Home large image/auto. cropped 15.00 30.00
109C Maurice Richard/Home large image/entire auto. 15.00 30.00
109D Maurice Richard/Home Action 30.00 60.00
110A Howie Riopelle/Home Still 10.00 20.00
110B Howie Riopelle/Home Action 10.00 20.00
111 George Robertson/Home Action 20.00 40.00
112 Dollard St. Laurent/Home Action 30.00 60.00
113 Grant Warwick/Home Action 40.00 80.00

1972-73 Whalers New England WHA

This 17-photo card set measures 3 3/4" by 5". The fronts feature black-and-white posed player photographs. The backs are blank. The cards are unnumbered and checklisted below in alphabetical order.

COMPLETE SET (15) 20.00 40.00
1 Mike Byers 1.00 2.00
2 Terry Caffery 1.00 2.00
3 John Cunniff 1.50 3.00
4 John Danby 1.00 2.00
5 Jim Dorey 1.50 3.00
6 Tom Earl 1.00 2.00
7 John French 1.00 2.00
8 Ted Green 2.50 5.00
9 Ric Jordan 1.00 2.00
10 Bruce Landon 1.00 2.00
11 Rick Ley 2.50 5.00
12 Larry Pleau 2.00 4.00
13 Brad Selwood 1.00 2.00
14 Tim Sheehy 1.00 2.00
15 Al Smith 2.50 5.00
16 Tom Webster 2.50 5.00
17 Tom Williams 2.00 4.00

1973-74 Quaker Oats WHA

This set of 50 cards features players of the World Hockey Association. The cards were issued in strips (panels) of five in Quaker Oats products. The cards measure approximately 2 1/4" by 3 1/4" and are numbered on the back. The information on the card backs is written in English and French. The value of unseparated panels would be approximately 20 percent greater than the sum of the individual values listed below.

COMPLETE SET (50) 137.50 275.00
1 Jim Wiste 2.50 5.00
2 Al Smith 3.00 6.00
3 Rosaire Paiement 2.50 5.00
4 Ted Hampson 2.00 4.00
5 Gavin Kirk 2.00 4.00
6 Andre Lacroix 3.00 6.00
7 John Schella 2.00 4.00
8 Gerry Cheevers 10.00 20.00
9 Norm Beaudin 2.00 4.00
10 Jim Harrison 2.00 4.00
11 Gerry Pinder 2.50 5.00
12 Bob Sicinski 2.00 4.00
13 Bryan Campbell 2.00 4.00
14 Murray Hall 2.00 4.00
15 Chris Bordeleau 2.50 5.00
16 Al Hamilton 3.00 6.00
17 Jimmy McLeod 2.00 4.00
18 Larry Pleau 2.50 5.00
19 Larry Lund 2.00 4.00
20 Bobby Sheehan 2.50 5.00
21 Jan Popiel 2.00 4.00
22 Andre Gaudette 2.00 4.00
23 Bob Charlebois 2.00 4.00
24 Gene Peacosh 2.00 4.00
25 Rick Ley 2.50 5.00
26 Larry Hornung 2.00 4.00
27 Gary Jarrett 2.00 4.00
28 Ted Taylor 2.00 4.00
29 Pete Donnelly 2.00 4.00
30 J.C. Tremblay 3.00 6.00
31 Jim Cardiff 2.00 4.00
32 Gary Veneruzzo 2.00 4.00
33 John French 2.00 4.00
34 Ron Ward 2.50 5.00
35 Wayne Connelly 2.50 5.00
36 Ron Buchanan 2.00 4.00
37 Ken Block 2.00 4.00
38 Alain Caron 2.00 4.00
39 Brit Selby 2.50 5.00
40 Guy Trottier 2.00 4.00
41 Ernie Wakely 3.00 6.00
42 J.P. LeBlanc 2.00 4.00
43 Michel Parizeau 2.00 4.00
44 Wayne Rivers 2.00 4.00
45 Reg Fleming 2.50 5.00
46 Don Herriman 2.00 4.00
47 Jim Dorey 2.00 4.00
48 Danny Lawson 3.00 6.00
49 Dick Paradise 2.00 4.00
50 Bobby Hull 30.00 60.00

1954 Quaker Sports Oddities

This 27-card set features strange moments in sports and was issued as an insert inside Quaker Puffed Rice cereal boxes. Fronts of the cards are drawings depicting the person or the event. In a stripe at the top of the card face appear the words "Sports Oddities." Two colorful drawings fill the remaining space: the left half is a portrait, while the right half is action-oriented. A variety of sports are included. The cards measure approximately 2 1/4" by 3 1/2" and have rounded corners. The last line on the back of each card declares, "It's Odd but True." A person could also buy the complete set for fifteen cents and two box tops from Quaker Puffed Wheat or Quaker Rice. If a collector did send in their material to Quaker Oats the set came back in a specially marked box with the cards in cellophane wrapping. Sets in original wrapping are valued at 1.25x to 1.5X the high column listings in our checklist.

COMPLETE SET (27) 125.00 250.00
10 Chicago Blackhawks 7.50 15.00

1950 R423

Many numbers of these small and unattractive cards may be yet unknown for this issue of the early 1950s. The cards are printed on thin stock and measure 5/8" by 3/4"; sometimes they are found as a long horizontal strip of 13 cards connected by a perforation. Complete strips intact are worth 50 percent more than the sum of the individual players on the strip. The cards were available with a variety of back colors, red, green, blue, or purple, with the red and blue being the rarest of the varieties. The cards on the strip are in no apparent order, numerically or alphabetically. The producer's numbering of the cards in the set is very close to alphabetical order. Cards are so small they are sometimes lost. These strips were premiums or prizes in one-cent bubblegum machines; they were folded accordion style and held together by a small metal clip.

1 Taffy Abel 12.50 25.00
2 George Allen 10.00 20.00
3 Syl Apps 12.50 25.00
4 Pete Backor 10.00 20.00
5 Baz Bastien 10.00 20.00
6 Bobby Bauer 10.00 20.00
7 Gordie Bell 10.00 20.00
8 Lin Bend 10.00 20.00
9 Paul Bibeault 10.00 20.00
10 Garth Boesch 10.00 20.00
11 Butch Bouchard 12.50 25.00
12 Frank Boucher 12.50 25.00
13 Adam Brown 10.00 20.00
14 Hal Brown 10.00 20.00
15 Mud Bruneteau 10.00 20.00
16 Frank Bull 10.00 20.00
17 Scotty Cameron 10.00 20.00
18 Joe Carveth 10.00 20.00
19 Murph Chamberlain 10.00 20.00
20 Dit Clapper 12.50 25.00
21 Mac Colville 10.00 20.00
22 Lionel Conacher 15.00 30.00
23 Bun Cook 10.00 20.00
24 Ernie Dickens 10.00 20.00
25 Cecil Dillon 10.00 20.00
26 Connie Dion 10.00 20.00
27 Gordie Drillon 10.00 20.00
28 Bill Ezinicki 10.00 20.00
29 Wilfy Field 10.00 20.00
30 Bob Fillion 10.00 20.00
31 Chuck Gardiner 10.00 20.00
32 George Gee 10.00 20.00
33 Gus Giesebrecht 10.00 20.00
34 Bob Goldham 10.00 20.00
35 Dutch Hiller 10.00 20.00
36 Dick Irvin 10.00 20.00
37 Aurel Joliat 12.50 25.00
38 Alex Kaleta 10.00 20.00
39 Mike Karakas 10.00 20.00
40 Ted Kennedy 15.00 30.00
41 Dave Kerr 12.50 25.00
42 Roger Leger 10.00 20.00
43 Carl Liscombe 10.00 20.00
44 Vic Lynn 10.00 20.00
45 Kilby MacDonald 10.00 20.00
46 Bucko McDonald 10.00 20.00
47 Howie Morenz 20.00 35.00
48 Gus Mortson 10.00 20.00
49 Ken Mosdell 10.00 20.00
50 Frank Nighbor 12.50 25.00
51 Lynn Patrick 12.50 25.00
52 Billy Reay 10.00 20.00
53 Leo Reise 10.00 20.00
54 Earl Babe Seibert 12.50 25.00
55 Clint Smith 10.00 20.00
56 Wally Stanowski 10.00 20.00
57 Gaye Stewart 10.00 20.00
58 Tiny Thompson 15.00 30.00
59 Roy Worters 12.50 25.00

1989-90 Rangers Marine Midland Bank

This 30-card set of New York Rangers was sponsored by Marine Midland Bank; the card backs have the bank's logo and name at the bottom. The cards measure approximately 2 5/8" by 3 5/8". The fronts feature color action photos of the players, with a thin red border on the left and bottom of the picture. Outside the red border appears a blue margin, with the player's name, position, and jersey number printed at right angles to one another. The Rangers' logo in the lower right hand corner completes the face of the card. The back has biographical information and career statistics. The cards have been listed below according to sweater number. The key cards in the set are early cards of Brian Leetch and Mike Richter.

COMPLETE SET (30) 14.00 35.00
2 Brian Leetch 3.00 8.00
3 James Patrick .30 .75
4 Ron Greschner .40 1.00
5 Normand Rochefort .20 .50
6 Miloslav Horava .20 .50
8 Darren Turcotte .30 .75
9 Bernie Nicholls .40 1.00
11 Kelly Kisio .30 .75
12 Kris King .40 1.00
14 Mark Hardy .20 .50
15 Mark Janssens .20 .50
16 Ulf Dahlen .30 .75
17 Carey Wilson .20 .50
19 Brian Mullen .30 .75
20 Jan Erixon .20 .50
21 David Shaw .20 .50
23 Corey Millen .20 .50
24 Randy Moller .20 .50
25 John Ogrodnick .40 1.00
26 Troy Mallette .20 .50
29 Rudy Poeschek .40 1.00
30 Chris Nilan .40 1.00
33 Bob Froese .40 1.00
34 John Vanbiesbrouck 1.50 4.00
35 Mike Richter 3.00 8.00
37 Paul Broten .20 .50
38 Jeff Bloemberg .20 .50
44 Lindy Ruff .20 .50
NNO Roger Neilson CO .20 .50
NNO Rangers MasterCard .02 .10

2002-03 Rangers Team Issue

This unusual team issue features two different sizes. The player cards measure 6 X 9.5, while the coach cards measure approx. 5 X 6. The fronts feature different designs, but the backs are similar. Information on distribution and any additional cards in the checklist can be forwarded to hockeymag@beckett.com.

1 Matthew Barnaby .60 1.50
2 Dan Blackburn .60 1.50
3 Pavel Bure 2.00 5.00
4 Ted Green ACO .20 .50
5 Bobby Holik .40 1.00
6 Dave Karpa .40 1.00
7 Darius Kasparaitis .40 1.00
8 Sylvain Lefebvre .40 1.00
9 Vladimir Malakhov .40 1.00
10 Sandy McCarthy .60 1.50
11 Mark Messier 2.00 5.00
12 Terry O'Reilly ACO .40 1.00
13 Mike Richter .75 2.00
14 Jim Schoenfeld ACO .20 .50

2003-04 Rangers Team Issue

These oversized cards measure 6x9 and were available only at team events. This checklist is possibly incomplete. Please forward additional information to hockeymag@beckett.com.

COMPLETE SET (24) 15.00 30.00
1 Matthew Barnaby .75 2.00
2 Dan Blackburn .60 1.50
3 Anson Carter .60 1.50
4 Greg deVries .40 1.00
5 Mike Dunham .60 1.50
6 Jan Hlavac .40 1.00
7 Bobby Holik .40 1.00
8 Darius Kasparaitis .40 1.00
9 Alexei Kovalev .40 1.00
10 Dan Lacouture .40 1.00
11 Brian Leetch .75 2.00
12 Eric Lindros 1.25 3.00
13 Jamie Lundmark .40 1.00
14 Vladimir Malakhov .40 1.00
15 Jussi Markkanen .75 2.00
16 Mark Messier .75 2.00
17 Boris Mironov .40 1.00
18 Petr Nedved .40 1.00
19 Tom Poti .40 1.00
20 Dale Purinton .75 2.00
21 Martin Rucinsky .40 1.00
22 Glen Sather HCO .20 .50
23 Chris Simon .60 1.50
24 Glen Sather .20 .50
Tom Renney
Terry O'Reilly
Ted Green

1970-71 Red Wings Volpe Marathon Oil

This 11-card (artistic) portrait set of Detroit Red Wings was part of a (Pro Star Portraits) promotion by Marathon Oil. The cards measure approximately 7 1/2" by 14"; the bottom portion, which measures 7 1/2" by 4 1/16", was a tear-off postcard in the form of a credit card application. The front features a full color portrait by Nicholas Volpe, with a facsimile autograph of the player inscribed across the bottom of the painting. The back included an offer for other sports memorabilia on the upper portion.

COMPLETE SET (11) 40.00 80.00
1 Gary Bergman 2.50 5.00
2 Wayne Connelly 2.00 4.00
3 Alex Delvecchio 5.00 10.00
4 Roy Edwards 2.50 5.00
5 Gordie Howe 25.00 50.00
6 Bruce MacGregor 2.00 4.00
7 Frank Mahovlich 6.00 12.00
8 Dale Rolfe 2.00 4.00
9 Jim Rutherford 3.00 6.00
10 Garry Unger 2.50 5.00
11 Tom Webster 2.50 5.00

1971 Red Wings Citgo Tumblers

These tumblers were available at Citgo gas stations and measure approximately 8" high. Tumblers feature color head shots, a facsimile autograph, and a color artwork action shot. They are made by Cinemac Inc, and feature a copyright of 1971.

COMPLETE SET 100.00 200.00
1 Wayne Connelly 12.50 25.00
2 Alex Delvecchio 20.00 40.00
3 Don Edwards 10.00 20.00
4 Garry Unger 10.00 20.00
5 Gordie Howe 37.50 75.00
6 Frank Mahovlich 15.00 30.00

1973-74 Red Wings Team Issue

Cards measure 8 3/4" x 10 3/4". Fronts feature color photos, and backs are blank. Cards are unnumbered and checklisted below in alphabetical order.

COMPLETE SET (18) 50.00 100.00
1 Ace Bailey 2.50 5.00
2 Red Berenson 4.00 8.00
3 Gary Bergman 2.50 5.00
4 Thommie Bergman 4.00 8.00
5 Guy Charron 2.50 5.00
6 Bill Collins 2.50 5.00
7 Denis Dejordy 4.00 8.00
8 Alex Delvecchio 7.50 15.00
9 Marcel Dionne 7.50 15.00
10 Gary Doak 2.50 5.00
11 Tim Ecclestone 2.50 5.00
12 Larry Johnston 2.50 5.00
13 Al Karlander 2.50 5.00
14 Brian Lavender 2.50 5.00
15 Nick Libett 2.50 5.00
16 Ken Murphy 2.50 5.00
17 Mickey Redmond 7.50 15.00
18 Ron Stackhouse 2.50 5.00

1973-75 Red Wings McCarthy Postcards

Measuring approximately 3 1/4" by 5 1/2", these postcards display color posed action shots on their fronts. The backs are blank. Since there is no Marcel Dionne or Alex Delvecchio (the latter played 11 games in 1973-74 before coaching), it is doubtful that this is a complete set. The date is established by two players: Brent Hughes (1973-74 was his only season with the Red Wings) and Tom Mellor (1974-75). The cards are unnumbered and checklisted below in alphabetical order. The photos and cards were produced by noted photographer J.D. McCarthy.

COMPLETE SET (15) 12.50 25.00
1 Garnet Bailey 1.00 2.00
2 Thommie Bergman 1.00 2.00
3 Henry Boucha 1.25 2.50
4 Guy Charron 1.00 2.00
5 Bill Collins 1.00 2.00
6 Doug Grant 1.00 2.00
7 Ted Harris 1.00 2.00
8 Bill Hogaboam 1.00 2.00
9 Brent Hughes 1.00 2.00
10 Pierre Jarry 1.00 2.00
11 Larry Johnston 1.00 2.00
12 Nick Libett 1.00 2.00
13 Tom Mellor 1.00 2.00
14 Doug Roberts 1.00 2.00
15 Ron Stackhouse 1.00 2.00

1979 Red Wings Postcards

This set features borderless color fronts and was issued by the Red Wings during the 1979 season.

COMPLETE SET (18) 7.50 15.00
1 Thommie Bergman .38 .75
2 Dan Bolduc .38 .75
3 Mike Foligno .38 .75
4 Jean Hamel .38 .75
5 Glen Hicks .38 .75
6 Greg Joly .38 .75
7 Willie Huber .38 .75
8 Jim Korn .38 .75
9 Dan Labraaten .38 .75
10 Barry Long .38 .75
11 Reed Larson .38 .75
12 Dale McCourt .38 .75
13 Vaclav Nedomansky .38 .75
14 Jim Rutherford .38 .75
15 Dennis Polonich .38 .75
16 Errol Thompson .38 .75
17 Rogie Vachon .38 .75
18 Paul Woods .38 .75

1981-82 Red Wings Oldtimers

This set of slightly undersized cards features black and white head shots of former players with the Detroit Red Wings. The backs are blank. It is not known how these were distributed. Any additional information can be forwarded to hockeymag@beckett.com.

COMPLETE SET (24) 10.00 25.00
1 Bob Johnson .40 1.00
2 Ed Giacomin .75 2.00
3 Gary Bergman .40 1.00
4 Bill Gadsby .40 1.00
5 Larry Johnston .40 1.00
6 Jim Peters .40 1.00
7 Bobby Kromm .40 1.00
8 Marcel Pronovost .75 2.00
9 Gerry Abel .40 1.00
10 Bill Collins .40 1.00
11 Billy Dea .40 1.00
12 Nelson DeBenedet .40 1.00
13 Alex Delvecchio .75 2.00
14 Dennis Hextall .60 1.50
15 Nick Libett .40 1.00
16 Mickey Redmond 1.25 3.00
17 John Wilson .40 1.00
18 Joe Klukay .40 1.00
19 Art Skov .40 1.00
20 Art Bouge .40 1.00
21 Rollie Roulston .40 1.00
22 Gordie Howe 2.00 5.00
23 Dr.C Boone .40 1.00
24 Checklist .40 1.00

1987-88 Red Wings Little Caesars

This 30-card set was sponsored by Little Caesars Pizza and measures approximately 3 3/4" by 6". The fronts have color action player photos with white borders. The player's name appears below the photo, along with the team and sponsor logos. The backs are blank. The cards are unnumbered and checklisted below in alphabetical order.

COMPLETE SET (30) 18.00 45.00
1 Brent Ashton .40 1.00
2 Dave Barr .40 1.00
3 Mel Bridgman .40 1.00
4 Shawn Burr .40 1.00
5 John Chabot .40 1.00
6 Steve Chiasson .60 1.50
7 Gilbert Delorme .40 1.00
8 Jacques Demers CO .75 2.00
9 Ron Duguay .40 1.00
10 Dwight Foster .40 1.00
11 Gerard Gallant .40 1.00
12 Adam Graves 1.50 4.00
13 Doug Halward .40 1.00
14 Glen Hanlon .60 1.50
15 Tim Higgins .40 1.00
16 Petr Klima .60 1.50
17 Joe Kocur .75 2.00
18 Lane Lambert .40 1.00
19 Joe Murphy .40 1.00
20 Lee Norwood .40 1.00
21 Adam Oates 4.00 10.00
22 Mike O'Connell .40 1.00
23 John Ogrodnick .60 1.50
24 Bob Probert 2.00 5.00
25 Jeff Sharples .40 1.00
26 Greg Smith .40 1.00
27 Greg Stefan .60 1.50
28 Darren Veitch .40 1.00
29 Steve Yzerman 5.00 12.00
30 Rick Zombo .40 1.00

1988-89 Red Wings Little Caesars

Set features color action photos with a white border. Players name and team logo are also visible on the front. Cards are blank backed and checklisted below in alphabetical order.

COMPLETE SET (24) 10.00 25.00
1 David Barr .40 1.00
2 Shawn Burr .40 1.00
3 John Chabot .40 1.00
4 Steve Chiasson .75 2.00
5 Gilbert Delorme .40 1.00
6 Jacques Demers .40 1.00
7 Gerard Gallant .40 1.00
8 Adam Graves .75 2.00
9 Doug Houda .40 1.00
10 Glen Hanlon .60 1.50
11 Kris King .40 1.00
12 Petr Klima .40 1.00
13 Joe Kocur .60 1.50
14 Paul Maclean .40 1.00
15 Jim Nill .40 1.00
16 Lee Norwood .40 1.00
17 Adam Oates 1.25 3.00
18 Mike O'Connell .40 1.00
19 Jim Pavese .40 1.00
20 Bob Probert .75 2.00
21 Jeff Sharples .40 1.00
22 Greg Stefan .60 1.50
23 Steve Yzerman 2.50 6.00
24 Rick Zombo .40 1.00

1989-90 Red Wings Little Caesars

This elongated postcard-sized set features color action photos with a white border. Players name and team logo are also visible on the front. Cards are blank backed and are checklisted below in alphabetical order, save for the recently confirmed team personnel cards that are lumped in at the end.

COMPLETE SET (24) 10.00 25.00
1 Dave Barr .40 1.00
2 Shawn Burr .40 1.00
3 Jim Carson .40 1.00
4 John Chabot .40 1.00
5 Steve Chiasson .40 1.00
6 Bernie Federko .40 1.00
7 Gerard Gallant .40 1.00
8 Marc Habscheid .40 1.00
9 Glen Hanlon .40 1.00
10 Doug Houda .40 1.00
11 Joey Kocur .40 1.00
12 Kevin McLelland .40 1.00
13 Lee Norwood .40 1.00
14 Mike O'Connell .40 1.00
15 Borje Salming .40 1.00
16 Greg Stefan .40 1.00
17 Steve Yzerman .40 1.00
18 Rick Zombo .40 1.00
19 Jacques Demers CO .40 1.00
20 Team Photo .40 1.00
21 Mickey Redmond .20 .50
22 Dave Lewis .20 .50
Phil Myre
Jacques Demers
Colin Campbell
23 Bruce Martin .20 .50
Paul Woods
24 Dave Strader .20 .50
Mickey Redmond

1990-91 Red Wings Little Caesars

Set features color action photos with a white border. Players name and team logo are also visible on the front. Cards are blank backed and checklisted below in alphabetical order.

COMPLETE SET (20) 16.00 40.00
1 Dave Barr .40 1.00
2 Shawn Burr .40 1.00
3 John Chabot .40 1.00
4 Tim Cheveldae .60 1.50
5 Per Djoos .40 1.00
6 Bobby Dollas .40 1.00
7 Sergei Fedorov 4.00 10.00
8 Brent Fedyk .40 1.00
9 Johan Garpenlov .40 1.00
10 Rick Green .40 1.00
11 Sheldon Kennedy .75 2.00
12 Kevin McClelland .40 1.00
13 Brad McCrimmon .40 1.00
14 Randy McKay .40 1.00
15 Keith Primeau 1.50 4.00
16 Bob Probert 1.25 3.00
17 Steve Yzerman 2.00 5.00
18 Rick Zombo .40 1.00
19 Bryan Murray CO .40 1.00
20 Team Photo .75 2.00

1991-92 Red Wings Little Caesars

Sponsored by Little Caesars, this 19-card set measures approximately 8 1/2" by 3 5/8" and features a color, action player photo on the left half of the card. The right half displays the player's name, position, biographical information, early career history, and jersey number, along with a close-up player photo. The backs are blank. The cards are unnumbered and checklisted below in alphabetical order.

COMPLETE SET (19) 16.00 40.00
1 Shawn Burr .40 1.00
2 Jimmy Carson .40 1.00
3 Steve Chiasson .40 1.00
4 Sergei Fedorov 3.00 8.00
5 Gerard Gallant .40 1.00
6 Johan Garpenlov .40 1.00
7 Rick Green .40 1.00
8 Marc Habscheid .40 1.00
9 Sheldon Kennedy .40 1.00
10 Martin Lapointe .75 2.00
11 Nicklas Lidstrom 1.25 3.00
12 Brad McCrimmon .40 1.00
13 Bryan Murray CO .20 .50
MG
14 Keith Primeau .60 1.50
15 Bob Probert 1.25 3.00
16 Dennis Vial .40 1.00
17 Paul Ysebaert .40 1.00
18 Steve Yzerman 4.00 10.00
19 Team Card .75 2.00

1996-97 Red Wings Detroit News/Free Press

These five posters were issued one per week in the Sunday editions of the Detroit News/Free Press. They measure approximately 12 by 18 inches and feature a full color photo on the front. The backs feature an ad for the issuing paper.

COMPLETE SET (5) 8.00 20.00
1 D.McCarty 1.50 4.00
K.Draper
K.Maltby
J.Kocur
2 Sergei Fedorov 2.50 6.00
3 Mike Vernon 1.50 4.00
4 Mike Vernon 1.50 4.00
5 Sergei Fedorov 2.50 6.00

1932 Reemstma Olympia

This colorful set was produced by Reemstma for the 1932 winter Olympics. Cards measure approximately 6 3/4 by 4 3/4 and are in full color. Backs are in German. Smaller versions of the cards also exist and are in black and white.

188 Dutch hockey player 10.00 20.00
191 USA vs. Canada 25.00 50.00

1936 Reemstma Olympia

This group of cards may or may not make up a complete set of Reemstma Olympia. These undersized issues picture international hockey players and matches from the early 1930s. It is believed they were issued as some sort of premium -- perhaps with cigarettes -- and it's likely that they were issued in Germany.

30 Team Canada 20.00 40.00
(6 3/4 x 4 3/4
31 Ice Hockey Spectators 20.00 40.00
32 Hockey Action Photo 20.00 40.00
33 Goalie making sliding save 20.00 40.00
34 Hockey Action Photo 20.00 40.00
35 Hockey Action Photo 20.00 40.00
Canada player in crease
36 Team Canada Photo 20.00 40.00
37 Team USA Photo 20.00 40.00
38 Gustav Jaenecke 20.00 40.00
39 Teiji Homna 20.00 40.00
Japan Goalie
40 Clearing the Ice 20.00 40.00

1997-98 Revolution

The 1997-98 Pacific Revolution set was issued in one series totaling 150 cards and distributed in three-card packs. The fronts feature color player images printed with etched gold and holographic silver foils on the circular design background. The backs carry another player photo and career statistics.

COMPLETE SET (150) 30.00 60.00
1 Guy Hebert .30 .75
2 Paul Kariya .40 1.00
3 Dmitri Mironov .20 .50
4 Ruslan Salei .20 .50
5 Teemu Selanne .40 1.00
6 Jason Allison .20 .50
7 Ray Bourque .75 2.00
8 Byron Dafoe .30 .75
9 Ted Donato .20 .50
10 Dimitri Khristich .20 .50
11 Joe Thornton .60 1.50
12 Matthew Barnaby .20 .50
13 Jason Dawe .20 .50
14 Dominik Hasek .75 2.00
15 Michael Peca .20 .50
16 Miroslav Satan .20 .50
17 Theo Fleury .20 .50
18 Jarome Iginla .50 1.25
19 Marty McInnis .20 .50
20 Cory Stillman .20 .50
21 Rick Tabaracci .30 .75
22 Martin Gelinas .20 .50
23 Sami Kapanen .20 .50
24 Trevor Kidd .30 .75
25 Keith Primeau .20 .50
26 Gary Roberts .20 .50
27 Tony Amonte .30 .75
28 Chris Chelios .40 1.00
29 Eric Daze .30 .75
30 Jeff Hackett .30 .75
31 Dmitri Nabokov .20 .50
32 Peter Forsberg 1.00 2.50
33 Valeri Kamensky .30 .75
34 Jari Kurri .30 .75
35 Claude Lemieux .20 .50
36 Eric Messier RC .30 .75
37 Sandis Ozolinsh .20 .50
38 Patrick Roy 1.50 4.00
39 Joe Sakic .75 2.00
40 Ed Belfour .40 1.00
41 Jamie Langenbrunner .20 .50
42 Jere Lehtinen .20 .50
43 Mike Modano .60 1.50
44 Joe Nieuwendyk .30 .75
45 Sergei Zubov .20 .50
46 Slava Fetisov .20 .50
47 Nicklas Lidstrom .40 1.00
48 Darren McCarty .20 .50
49 Larry Murphy .20 .50
50 Chris Osgood .30 .75
51 Brendan Shanahan .40 1.00
52 Steve Yzerman 1.50 4.00
53 Roman Hamrlik .30 .75
54 Bill Guerin .30 .75
55 Curtis Joseph .40 1.00
56 Ryan Smyth .30 .75
57 Doug Weight .30 .75
58 Dino Ciccarelli .20 .50
59 Dave Gagner .20 .50
60 Ed Jovanovski .30 .75
61 Paul Laus .20 .50
62 John Vanbiesbrouck .30 .75
63 Ray Whitney .20 .50
64 Russ Courtnall .20 .50
65 Yanic Perreault .20 .50
66 Luc Robitaille .30 .75
67 Jozef Stumpel .30 .75
68 Vladimir Tsyplakov .20 .50
69 Shayne Corson .20 .50
70 Vincent Damphousse .20 .50
71 Saku Koivu .40 1.00
72 Andy Moog .30 .75
73 Mark Recchi .30 .75
74 Jocelyn Thibault .30 .75
75 Martin Brodeur 1.00 2.50
76 Patrik Elias RC 2.00 5.00
77 Doug Gilmour .30 .75
78 Bobby Holik .20 .50
79 Scott Niedermayer .20 .50
80 Bryan Berard .30 .75
81 Travis Green .20 .50
82 Zigmund Palffy .30 .75
83 Robert Reichel .20 .50
84 Tommy Salo .30 .75
85 Dan Cloutier .20 .50
86 Adam Graves .20 .50
87 Wayne Gretzky 2.00 5.00
88 Pat LaFontaine .40 1.00
89 Brian Leetch .40 1.00
90 Mike Richter .40 1.00
91 Kevin Stevens .30 .75
92 Daniel Alfredsson .30 .75
93 Shawn McEachern .20 .50
94 Damian Rhodes .30 .75
95 Ron Tugnutt .30 .75
96 Alexei Yashin .20 .50
97 Rod Brind'Amour .30 .75
98 Paul Coffey .40 1.00
99 Alexandre Daigle .20 .50
100 Chris Gratton .30 .75
101 Ron Hextall .30 .75
102 John LeClair .40 1.00
103 Eric Lindros .40 1.00
104 Dainius Zubrus .40 1.00
105 Mike Gartner .30 .75
106 Craig Janney .20 .50
107 Nikolai Khabibulin .30 .75
108 Jeremy Roenick .50 1.25
109 Keith Tkachuk .40 1.00
110 Stu Barnes .20 .50
111 Tom Barrasso .30 .75
112 Ron Francis .30 .75
113 Jaromir Jagr .60 1.50
114 Peter Skudra RC .20 .50
115 Martin Straka .20 .50
116 Blair Atcheynum RC .20 .50
117 Jim Campbell .20 .50
118 Geoff Courtnall .20 .50
119 Steve Duchesne .20 .50
120 Grant Fuhr .30 .75
121 Brett Hull .50 1.25
122 Pierre Turgeon .30 .75
123 Jeff Friesen .20 .50
124 John MacLean .20 .50
125 Patrick Marleau .30 .75
126 Owen Nolan .30 .75
127 Marco Sturm RC 1.00 2.50
128 Mike Vernon .30 .75
129 Daren Puppa .30 .75
130 Mikael Renberg .30 .75
131 Paul Ysebaert .20 .50
132 Rob Zamuner .20 .50
133 Wendel Clark .30 .75
134 Tie Domi .30 .75
135 Igor Korolev .20 .50
136 Felix Potvin .40 1.00
137 Mats Sundin .40 1.00
138 Donald Brashear .20 .50
139 Pavel Bure .40 1.00
140 Sean Burke .30 .75
141 Trevor Linden .30 .75
142 Mark Messier .40 1.00
143 Alexander Mogilny .30 .75
144 Mattias Ohlund .30 .75
145 Peter Bondra .30 .75
146 Phil Housley .20 .50
147 Dale Hunter .20 .50
148 Joe Juneau .30 .75
149 Olaf Kolzig .30 .75
150 Adam Oates .30 .75

1997-98 Revolution Copper

*VETS: 2X TO 8X BASIC CARDS
*ROOKIES: 1.5X TO 4X BASIC CARDS
STATED ODDS 2:25 HOBBY

1997-98 Revolution Emerald

*VETS: 3X TO 8X BASIC CARDS
*ROOKIES: 1.5X TO 4X BASIC CARDS
STATED ODDS 2:25 CANADIAN

1997-98 Revolution Ice Blue

*VETS: 5X TO 12X BASIC CARDS
*ROOKIES: 2X TO 4X BASIC CARDS
STATED ODDS 1:49

1997-98 Revolution Red

Randomly inserted in special Treat Entertainment retail and hobby packs at the rate of two in 25, this 150-card set is parallel to the base set and is similar in design. The difference is seen in the red foil design element.

*VETS: 3X TO 8X BASIC CARDS
*ROOKIES: 2X TO 4X BASIC CARDS
STATED ODDS 2:25 SPECIAL RETAIL
1 Guy Hebert 2.50 6.00
2 Paul Kariya 3.00 8.00
3 Dmitri Mironov 1.50 4.00
4 Ruslan Salei 1.50 4.00
5 Teemu Selanne 3.00 8.00
6 Jason Allison 1.50 4.00
7 Ray Bourque 6.00 15.00
8 Byron Dafoe 2.50 6.00
9 Ted Donato 1.50 4.00
10 Dimitri Khristich 1.50 4.00
11 Joe Thornton 5.00 12.00
12 Matthew Barnaby 1.50 4.00
13 Jason Dawe 1.50 4.00
14 Dominik Hasek 6.00 15.00
15 Michael Peca 1.50 4.00
16 Miroslav Satan 1.50 4.00
17 Theoren Fleury 1.50 4.00
18 Jarome Iginla 4.00 10.00
19 Marty McInnis 1.50 4.00
20 Cory Stillman 1.50 4.00
21 Rick Tabaracci 2.50 6.00
22 Martin Gelinas 1.50 4.00
23 Sami Kapanen 1.50 4.00
24 Trevor Kidd 2.50 6.00
25 Keith Primeau 1.50 4.00
26 Gary Roberts 1.50 4.00
27 Tony Amonte 2.50 6.00
28 Chris Chelios 3.00 8.00
29 Eric Daze 2.50 6.00
30 Jeff Hackett 2.50 6.00
31 Dmitri Nabokov 1.50 4.00
32 Peter Forsberg 8.00 20.00
33 Valeri Kamensky 2.50 6.00
34 Jari Kurri 2.50 6.00
35 Claude Lemieux 1.50 4.00
36 Eric Messier 2.00 5.00
37 Sandis Ozolinsh 1.50 4.00
38 Patrick Roy 12.00 30.00
39 Joe Sakic 6.00 15.00
40 Ed Belfour 3.00 8.00
41 Jamie Langenbrunner 1.50 4.00
42 Jere Lehtinen 1.50 4.00
43 Mike Modano 5.00 12.00
44 Joe Nieuwendyk 2.50 6.00
45 Sergei Zubov 1.50 4.00
46 Viacheslav Fetisov 1.50 4.00
47 Nicklas Lidstrom 3.00 8.00
48 Darren McCarty 1.50 4.00
49 Larry Murphy 1.50 4.00
50 Chris Osgood 2.50 6.00
51 Brendan Shanahan 3.00 8.00
52 Steve Yzerman 12.00 30.00
53 Roman Hamrlik 2.50 6.00
54 Bill Guerin 2.50 6.00
55 Curtis Joseph 3.00 8.00
56 Ryan Smyth 2.50 6.00
57 Doug Weight 2.50 6.00
58 Dino Ciccarelli 1.50 4.00
59 Dave Gagner 1.50 4.00
60 Ed Jovanovski 2.50 6.00
61 Paul Laus 1.50 4.00
62 John Vanbiesbrouck 2.50 6.00
63 Ray Whitney 1.50 4.00
64 Russ Courtnall 1.50 4.00
65 Yanic Perreault 1.50 4.00
66 Luc Robitaille 2.50 6.00
67 Jozef Stumpel 2.50 6.00
68 Vladimir Tsyplakov 1.50 4.00
69 Shayne Corson 1.50 4.00
70 Vincent Damphousse 1.50 4.00
71 Saku Koivu 3.00 8.00
72 Andy Moog 2.50 6.00
73 Mark Recchi 2.50 6.00
74 Jocelyn Thibault 2.50 6.00
75 Martin Brodeur 8.00 20.00
76 Patrik Elias 12.00 30.00
77 Doug Gilmour 2.50 6.00
78 Bobby Holik 1.50 4.00
79 Scott Niedermayer 1.50 4.00
80 Bryan Berard 2.50 6.00
81 Travis Green 1.50 4.00
82 Zigmund Palffy 2.50 6.00
83 Robert Reichel 1.50 4.00
84 Tommy Salo 2.50 6.00
85 Dan Cloutier 1.50 4.00
86 Adam Graves 1.50 4.00
87 Wayne Gretzky 15.00 40.00
88 Pat LaFontaine 3.00 8.00
89 Brian Leetch 3.00 8.00
90 Mike Richter 3.00 8.00
91 Kevin Stevens 2.50 6.00
92 Daniel Alfredsson 2.50 6.00
93 Shawn McEachern 1.50 4.00
94 Damian Rhodes 2.50 6.00
95 Ron Tugnutt 2.50 6.00
96 Alexei Yashin 1.50 4.00
97 Rod Brind'Amour 2.50 6.00
98 Paul Coffey 3.00 8.00
99 Alexandre Daigle 1.50 4.00
100 Chris Gratton 2.50 6.00
101 Ron Hextall 2.50 6.00
102 John LeClair 3.00 8.00
103 Eric Lindros 3.00 8.00
104 Dainius Zubrus 3.00 8.00
105 Mike Gartner 2.50 6.00
106 Craig Janney 1.50 4.00
107 Nikolai Khabibulin 2.50 6.00
108 Jeremy Roenick 4.00 10.00
109 Keith Tkachuk 3.00 8.00
110 Stu Barnes 1.50 4.00
111 Tom Barrasso 2.50 6.00
112 Ron Francis 2.50 6.00
113 Jaromir Jagr 5.00 12.00
114 Peter Skudra 1.25 3.00
115 Martin Straka 1.50 4.00
116 Blair Atcheynum 1.25 3.00
117 Jim Campbell 1.50 4.00
118 Geoff Courtnall 1.50 4.00
119 Steve Duchesne 1.50 4.00
120 Grant Fuhr 2.50 6.00
121 Brett Hull 4.00 10.00
122 Pierre Turgeon 2.50 6.00
123 Jeff Friesen 1.50 4.00
124 John MacLean 1.50 4.00
125 Patrick Marleau 2.50 6.00
126 Owen Nolan 2.50 6.00
127 Marco Sturm 6.00 15.00
128 Mike Vernon 2.50 6.00
129 Daren Puppa 2.50 6.00
130 Mikael Renberg 2.50 6.00
131 Paul Ysebaert 1.50 4.00
132 Rob Zamuner 1.50 4.00
133 Wendel Clark 2.50 6.00
134 Tie Domi 2.50 6.00
135 Igor Korolev 1.50 4.00
136 Felix Potvin 3.00 8.00
137 Mats Sundin 3.00 8.00
138 Donald Brashear 1.50 4.00
139 Pavel Bure 3.00 8.00
140 Sean Burke 2.50 6.00
141 Trevor Linden 2.50 6.00
142 Mark Messier 3.00 8.00
143 Alexander Mogilny 2.50 6.00
144 Mattias Ohlund 2.50 6.00
145 Peter Bondra 2.50 6.00
146 Phil Housley 1.50 4.00
147 Dale Hunter 1.50 4.00
148 Joe Juneau 2.50 6.00
149 Olaf Kolzig 2.50 6.00
150 Adam Oates 2.50 6.00

1997-98 Revolution Silver

*VETS: 3X TO 8X BASIC CARDS
*ROOKIES: 1.5X TO 4X BASIC CARDS
STATED ODDS 2:25 RETAIL

1997-98 Revolution 1998 All-Star Game Die-Cuts

Randomly inserted in packs at the rate of 1:49, this 20-card set features color photos of the hottest players named to the 1998 NHL All-Star game printed on a die-cut star-background card and appearing in their All-Star uniform from the game in Vancouver.

COMPLETE SET (20) 40.00 80.00
1 Teemu Selanne 1.50 4.00
2 Ray Bourque 3.00 8.00
3 Dominik Hasek 3.00 8.00
4 Theo Fleury 1.25 3.00
5 Chris Chelios 1.50 4.00
6 Peter Forsberg 4.00 10.00
7 Patrick Roy 6.00 15.00
8 Joe Sakic 4.00 10.00
9 Ed Belfour 1.50 4.00
10 Mike Modano 2.50 6.00
11 Brendan Shanahan 1.50 4.00
12 Saku Koivu 1.50 4.00
13 Martin Brodeur 4.00 10.00
14 Wayne Gretzky 10.00 25.00
15 John LeClair 1.50 4.00
16 Eric Lindros 1.50 4.00
17 Jaromir Jagr 2.50 6.00
18 Pavel Bure 1.50 4.00
19 Mark Messier 1.50 4.00
20 Peter Bondra 1.25 3.00

1997-98 Revolution NHL Icons

Randomly inserted in packs at the rate of 1:121, this 10-card set features color photos of today's living legends of hockey printed on a die-cut card.

COMPLETE SET (10) 30.00 60.00
1 Paul Kariya 1.50 4.00
2 Teemu Selanne 1.50 4.00
3 Peter Forsberg 4.00 10.00
4 Patrick Roy 6.00 15.00
5 Steve Yzerman 6.00 15.00
6 Martin Brodeur 4.00 10.00
7 Wayne Gretzky 8.00 20.00
8 Eric Lindros 1.50 4.00
9 Jaromir Jagr 2.50 6.00
10 Pavel Bure 1.50 4.00

1997-98 Revolution Return to Sender Die-Cuts

Randomly inserted in packs at the rate of 1:25, this 20-card set features color photos of the top goalies printed on a postage stamp shaped die-cut card.

COMPLETE SET (20) 15.00 40.00
1 Guy Hebert 1.00 2.50
2 Byron Dafoe 1.00 2.50
3 Dominik Hasek 2.50 6.00
4 Jeff Hackett 1.00 2.50
5 Patrick Roy 5.00 12.00
6 Ed Belfour 1.25 3.00
7 Chris Osgood 1.00 2.50
8 Curtis Joseph 1.25 3.00
9 John Vanbiesbrouck 1.00 2.50
10 Andy Moog 1.00 2.50
11 Martin Brodeur 3.00 8.00
12 Tommy Salo 1.00 2.50
13 Mike Richter 1.25 3.00
14 Ron Hextall 1.00 2.50
15 Nikolai Khabibulin 1.00 2.50
16 Tom Barrasso 1.00 2.50
17 Grant Fuhr 1.00 2.50
18 Mike Vernon 1.00 2.50
19 Felix Potvin 1.25 3.00
20 Olaf Kolzig 1.00 2.50

1997-98 Revolution Team Checklist Laser Cuts

Randomly inserted in packs at the rate of 1:25, this 26-card set features color action photos of top players with his laser-cut team logo beside the player image. The backs carry a Revolution main set checklist.

COMPLETE SET (26) 40.00 80.00
1 Paul Kariya 1.25 3.00
2 Joe Thornton 2.00 5.00
3 Michael Peca .60 1.50
4 Theo Fleury .60 1.50
5 Keith Primeau .60 1.50
6 Chris Chelios 1.25 3.00
7 Patrick Roy 5.00 12.00
8 Mike Modano 2.00 5.00
9 Steve Yzerman 4.00 10.00
10 Ryan Smyth 1.00 2.50
11 John Vanbiesbrouck 1.00 2.50
12 Jozef Stumpel 1.00 2.50
13 Saku Koivu 1.25 3.00
14 Martin Brodeur 3.00 8.00
15 Zigmund Palffy 1.00 2.50
16 Wayne Gretzky 6.00 15.00
17 Daniel Alfredsson 1.00 2.50
18 Eric Lindros 1.25 3.00
19 Keith Tkachuk 1.25 3.00
20 Jaromir Jagr 2.00 5.00
21 Brett Hull 1.50 4.00
22 Mike Vernon 1.00 2.50
23 Rob Zamuner .60 1.50
24 Mats Sundin 1.25 3.00
25 Pavel Bure 1.25 3.00
26 Peter Bondra 1.00 2.50

1998-99 Revolution

The 1998-99 Pacific Revolution set was issued in one series totaling 150 cards and distributed in three-card packs with a suggested retail price of $3.99. The set features color action player photos on dual-foiled, etched and embossed cards. The backs carry another player photos, biographical information, and career statistics.

COMPLETE SET (150) 50.00 100.00
1 Guy Hebert .30 .75
2 Paul Kariya .40 1.00
3 Marty McInnis .20 .50
4 Steve Rucchin .20 .50
5 Teemu Selanne .40 1.00
6 Jason Allison .20 .50
7 Ray Bourque .75 2.00
8 Anson Carter .30 .75
9 Byron Dafoe .30 .75
10 Dimitri Khristich .20 .50
11 Sergei Samsonov .30 .75
12 Matthew Barnaby .20 .50
13 Michal Grosek .20 .50
14 Dominik Hasek .75 2.00
15 Michael Peca .20 .50
16 Miroslav Satan .30 .75
17 Dixon Ward .20 .50
18 Theo Fleury .20 .50
19 Jean-Sebastien Giguere .30 .75
20 Jarome Iginla .50 1.25
21 Tyler Moss .20 .50
22 Cory Stillman .20 .50
23 Ron Francis .30 .75
24 Arturs Irbe .30 .75
25 Trevor Kidd .30 .75
26 Keith Primeau .20 .50
27 Ray Sheppard .20 .50
28 Tony Amonte .30 .75
29 Chris Chelios .40 1.00
30 Eric Daze .30 .75
31 Doug Gilmour .30 .75
32 Jocelyn Thibault .30 .75
33 Adam Deadmarsh .20 .50
34 Chris Drury .30 .75
35 Peter Forsberg 1.00 2.50
36 Milan Hejduk RC 2.00 5.00
37 Claude Lemieux .20 .50
38 Patrick Roy 1.50 4.00
39 Joe Sakic .75 2.00
40 Ed Belfour .40 1.00
41 Brett Hull .50 1.25
42 Jamie Langenbrunner .20 .50
43 Jere Lehtinen .20 .50
44 Mike Modano .60 1.50
45 Joe Nieuwendyk .30 .75
46 Darryl Sydor .20 .50
47 Sergei Fedorov .50 1.25
48 Nicklas Lidstrom .40 1.00
49 Norm Maracle RC .40 1.00
50 Darren McCarty .20 .50
51 Chris Osgood .30 .75
52 Brendan Shanahan .40 1.00
53 Steve Yzerman 1.25 3.00
54 Bill Guerin .30 .75
55 Andrei Kovalenko .20 .50
56 Mikhail Shtalenkov .20 .50
57 Ryan Smyth .30 .75
58 Doug Weight .30 .75
59 Pavel Bure .40 1.00
60 Sean Burke .20 .50
61 Dino Ciccarelli .30 .75
62 Viktor Kozlov .20 .50
63 Rob Niedermayer .20 .50
64 Mark Parrish RC .40 1.00
65 Rob Blake .30 .75
66 Stephane Fiset .30 .75
67 Olli Jokinen .30 .75
68 Luc Robitaille .30 .75
69 Pavel Rosa RC .20 .50
70 Jozef Stumpel .30 .75
71 Shayne Corson .20 .50
72 Vincent Damphousse .20 .50
73 Jeff Hackett .30 .75
74 Saku Koivu .40 1.00
75 Mark Recchi .30 .75
76 Brian Savage .20 .50
77 Andrew Brunette .30 .75
78 Mike Dunham .30 .75
79 Sergei Krivokrasov .20 .50
80 Cliff Ronning .20 .50
81 Tomas Vokoun .20 .50
82 Jason Arnott .20 .50
83 Martin Brodeur 1.00 2.50
84 Patrik Elias .30 .75
85 Bobby Holik .20 .50
86 Brendan Morrison .30 .75
87 Felix Potvin .40 1.00
88 Trevor Linden .30 .75
89 Zigmund Palffy .30 .75
90 Tommy Salo .30 .75
91 Mike Watt .20 .50
92 Wayne Gretzky 2.00 5.00
93 Todd Harvey .20 .50
94 Brian Leetch .40 1.00
95 Manny Malhotra .30 .75
96 Petr Nedved .30 .75
97 Mike Richter .40 1.00
98 Daniel Alfredsson .30 .75
99 Marian Hossa .40 1.00
100 Shawn McEachern .20 .50
101 Damian Rhodes .30 .75
102 Alexei Yashin .20 .50
103 Rod Brind'Amour .30 .75
104 Ron Hextall .30 .75
105 John LeClair .40 1.00
106 Eric Lindros .40 1.00
107 John Vanbiesbrouck .30 .75
108 Dainius Zubrus .20 .50
109 Daniel Briere .20 .50
110 Nikolai Khabibulin .30 .75
111 Jeremy Roenick .50 1.25
112 Keith Tkachuk .40 1.00
113 Rick Tocchet .30 .75
114 Jim Waite .30 .75
115 Jean-Sebastien Aubin RC .40 1.00
116 Stu Barnes .20 .50
117 Tom Barrasso .30 .75
118 Jaromir Jagr .60 1.50
119 Alexei Kovalev .20 .50
120 Martin Straka .20 .50
121 Pavol Demitra .30 .75
122 Grant Fuhr .30 .75
123 Al MacInnis .30 .75
124 Chris Pronger .30 .75
125 Pierre Turgeon .30 .75
126 Jeff Friesen .20 .50
127 Patrick Marleau .20 .50
128 Owen Nolan .30 .75
129 Marco Sturm .20 .50
130 Mike Vernon .30 .75
131 Wendel Clark .30 .75
132 Daren Puppa .30 .75
133 Vincent Lecavalier .40 1.00
134 Stephane Richer .30 .75
135 Rob Zamuner .20 .50
136 Tie Domi .30 .75
137 Mike Johnson .20 .50
138 Curtis Joseph .40 1.00
139 Tomas Kaberle RC .75 2.00
140 Mats Sundin .40 1.00
141 Mark Messier .40 1.00
142 Alexander Mogilny .30 .75
143 Bill Muckalt RC .20 .50
144 Mattias Ohlund .30 .75
145 Garth Snow .30 .75
146 Peter Bondra .30 .75
147 Joe Juneau .30 .75
148 Olaf Kolzig .30 .75
149 Adam Oates .30 .75
150 Richard Zednik .20 .50
NNO Martin Brodeur SAMPLE .20 .50

1998-99 Revolution Ice Shadow

Randomly inserted into hobby packs only, this 150-card set is a limited blue foil hobby parallel version of the base set. Only 99 serial-numbered sets were made.

*VETERANS: 6X TO 15X BASIC CARDS
*ROOKIES: 1.5X TO 4X BASIC CARDS

1998-99 Revolution Red

*VETERANS: 2.5X TO 6X BASIC CARDS
*ROOKIES: 1.5X TO 4X BASIC CARDS
RED PRINT RUN 299 SER.#'d SETS

1998-99 Revolution All-Star Die Cuts

Randomly inserted in packs at the rate of 1:25, this 30-card set features color images of players from the 1999 World and North America All-Star teams printed on full-foil die-cut cards with a jagged star design at the top.

COMPLETE SET (30) 30.00 80.00
1 Tony Amonte .75 2.00
2 Ed Belfour 1.25 3.00
3 Peter Bondra .75 2.00
4 Ray Bourque 2.00 5.00
5 Martin Brodeur 3.00 8.00
6 Theo Fleury .75 2.00
7 Peter Forsberg 2.50 6.00
8 Wayne Gretzky 6.00 15.00
9 Dominik Hasek 2.50 6.00
10 Bobby Holik .40 1.00
11 Arturs Irbe .75 2.00
12 Jaromir Jagr 2.00 5.00
13 Paul Kariya 1.25 3.00
14 Nikolai Khabibulin 1.25 3.00
15 Sergei Krivokrasov .40 1.00
16 John LeClair .40 1.00
17 Nicklas Lidstrom .75 2.00
18 Eric Lindros 1.25 3.00
19 Al MacInnis .75 2.00
20 Mike Modano 2.00 5.00
21 Mattias Ohlund .40 1.00
22 Keith Primeau .75 2.00
23 Chris Pronger .75 2.00
24 Mark Recchi .75 2.00
25 Jeremy Roenick 1.50 4.00
26 Teemu Selanne 1.25 3.00
27 Brendan Shanahan 1.25 3.00
28 Mats Sundin 1.25 3.00
29 Keith Tkachuk .75 2.00
30 Alexei Yashin .40 1.00

1998-99 Revolution Chalk Talk Laser-Cuts

Randomly inserted into packs at the rate of 1:49, this 20-card set features color action player photos printed on full-foil horizontal cards alongside plays diagramed on a laser cut chalkboard.

COMPLETE SET (20) 40.00 80.00
1 Paul Kariya 1.50 4.00
2 Teemu Selanne 1.50 4.00
3 Theo Fleury .75 2.00
4 Peter Forsberg 4.00 10.00
5 Joe Sakic 3.00 8.00
6 Brett Hull 2.00 5.00
7 Mike Modano 2.50 6.00
8 Sergei Fedorov 2.00 5.00
9 Brendan Shanahan 1.50 4.00
10 Steve Yzerman 6.00 15.00
11 Wayne Gretzky 8.00 20.00
12 Alexei Yashin .75 2.00
13 John LeClair 1.50 4.00
14 Eric Lindros 1.50 4.00
15 Keith Tkachuk 1.50 4.00
16 Jaromir Jagr 2.50 6.00
17 Vincent Lecavalier 1.50 4.00
18 Mats Sundin 1.50 4.00
19 Mark Messier 1.50 4.00
20 Peter Bondra 1.25 3.00

1998-99 Revolution NHL Icons

Randomly inserted into packs at the rate of 1:121, this 10-card set features color images of some of the most renown players in hockey printed on die-cut silver foil cards.

COMPLETE SET (10) 30.00 60.00
1 Paul Kariya 1.50 4.00
2 Dominik Hasek 3.00 8.00
3 Peter Forsberg 4.00 10.00
4 Patrick Roy 6.00 15.00
5 Mike Modano 2.50 6.00
6 Steve Yzerman 6.00 15.00
7 Martin Brodeur 4.00 10.00
8 Wayne Gretzky 8.00 20.00
9 Eric Lindros 1.50 4.00
10 Jaromir Jagr 2.50 6.00

1998-99 Revolution Showstoppers

Randomly inserted into packs at the rate of 2:25, this 36-card set features color action photos of players known for their game-winning heroics printed on holographic silver foil cards.

COMPLETE SET (36) 10.00 25.00
1 Paul Kariya 1.00 2.50
2 Teemu Selanne 1.00 2.50
3 Ray Bourque 1.25 3.00
4 Dominik Hasek 2.00 5.00
5 Michael Peca .40 1.00
6 Theo Fleury .40 1.00
7 Tony Amonte .60 1.50
8 Chris Chelios .60 1.50
9 Doug Gilmour .60 1.50
10 Peter Forsberg 1.50 4.00
11 Patrick Roy 3.00 8.00
12 Joe Sakic 2.00 5.00
13 Ed Belfour 1.00 2.50
14 Brett Hull 1.25 3.00
15 Mike Modano 1.25 3.00
16 Sergei Fedorov 1.25 3.00
17 Brendan Shanahan 1.00 2.50
18 Steve Yzerman 3.00 8.00
19 Mark Parrish .40 1.00
20 Saku Koivu 1.00 2.50
21 Martin Brodeur 2.50 6.00
22 Zigmund Palffy .60 1.50
23 Wayne Gretzky 4.00 10.00
24 Alexei Yashin .40 1.00
25 John LeClair .60 1.50
26 Eric Lindros 1.00 2.50
27 John Vanbiesbrouck .60 1.50
28 Nikolai Khabibulin .60 1.50
29 Jeremy Roenick 1.25 3.00
30 Keith Tkachuk .60 1.50
31 Jaromir Jagr 1.50 4.00
32 Vincent Lecavalier 1.00 2.50
33 Curtis Joseph 1.00 2.50
34 Mats Sundin 1.00 2.50
35 Mark Messier 1.25 3.00
36 Peter Bondra .60 1.50

1998-99 Revolution Three Pronged Attack

Randomly inserted into hobby packs only at the rate of 4:25, this 30-card set features color action photos of some of the NHL's top players. A parallel version of this set was also produced and inserted only in hobby packs. The parallel consists of three separate tiers of 10 cards each with each tier serially numbered in varying amounts. Only 99 serial-numbered Tier 1 (cards #1-10) sets were made; 199 Tier 2 (11-20) serial-numbered sets were made; and 299 serial-numbered Tier 3 (21-30) sets were produced.

COMPLETE SET (30) 15.00 30.00
*1-10 PARALLEL/99: 5X TO 12X BASIC INSERT
*11-20 PARALLEL/199: 3X TO 8X BASIC INSERT
*21-30 PARALLEL/299: 2X TO 5X BASIC INSERT
1 Matthew Barnaby .30 .75
2 Theo Fleury .30 .75
3 Chris Chelios .50 1.25
4 Darren McCarty .30 .75
5 Brendan Shanahan .50 1.25
6 Eric Lindros .50 1.25
7 Keith Tkachuk .50 1.25
8 Tony Twist .30 .75
9 Tie Domi .30 .75
10 Donald Brashear .30 .75
11 Dominik Hasek .75 2.00
12 Patrick Roy 1.25 3.00
13 Ed Belfour .50 1.25
14 Chris Osgood .40 1.00
15 Martin Brodeur 1.00 2.50
16 Mike Richter .50 1.25
17 John Vanbiesbrouck .40 1.00
18 Nikolai Khabibulin .40 1.00
19 Curtis Joseph .50 1.25
20 Olaf Kolzig .40 1.00
21 Paul Kariya .50 1.25
22 Teemu Selanne .50 1.25
23 Peter Forsberg 1.00 2.50
24 Joe Sakic .75 2.00
25 Mike Modano .30 .75
26 Steve Yzerman 1.25 3.00
27 Wayne Gretzky 1.50 4.00
28 John LeClair .50 1.25
29 Jaromir Jagr .60 1.50
30 Pavel Bure .50 1.25

1999-00 Revolution

Released as a 150-card set, Revolution features holographic foil base cards with gold foil highlights. Packaged in 24-pack boxes, each pack contained three cards and carried a suggested retail price of $3.99.

COMPLETE SET (150) 40.00 80.00
1 Guy Hebert .30 .75
2 Paul Kariya .40 1.00
3 Marty McInnis .20 .50
4 Teemu Selanne .40 1.00
5 Steve Rucchin .30 .75
6 Kelly Buchberger .20 .50
7 Ray Ferraro .20 .50
8 Damian Rhodes .20 .50
9 Johan Garpenlov .20 .50

10 Jason Allison .20 .50
11 Ray Bourque .75 2.00
12 Anson Carter .30 .75
13 Byron Dafoe .30 .75
14 Sergei Samsonov .30 .75
15 Joe Thornton .60 1.50
16 Martin Biron .30 .75
17 Curtis Brown .20 .50
18 Dominik Hasek .75 2.00
19 Michael Peca .30 .75
20 Miroslav Satan .30 .75
21 Dixon Ward .20 .50
22 Valeri Bure .20 .50
23 Fred Brathwaite .30 .75
24 Phil Housley .30 .75
25 Jarome Iginla .50 1.25
26 Cory Stillman .20 .50
27 Ron Francis .30 .75
28 Arturs Irbe .30 .75
29 Sami Kapanen .20 .50
30 Keith Primeau .20 .50
31 Gary Roberts .20 .50
32 Tony Amonte .30 .75
33 J-P Dumont .30 .75
34 Doug Gilmour .30 .75
35 Jocelyn Thibault .30 .75
36 Alexei Zhamnov .20 .50
37 Adam Deadmarsh .20 .50
38 Chris Drury .30 .75
39 Peter Forsberg 1.00 2.50
40 Milan Hejduk .40 1.00
41 Claude Lemieux .20 .50
42 Patrick Roy 1.00 2.50
43 Joe Sakic .75 2.00
44 Ed Belfour .40 1.00
45 Brett Hull .50 1.25
46 Jamie Langenbrunner .20 .50
47 Jere Lehtinen .30 .75
48 Mike Modano .60 1.50
49 Joe Nieuwendyk .30 .75
50 Chris Chelios .40 1.00
51 Sergei Fedorov .50 1.25
52 Vyacheslav Kozlov .30 .75
53 Nicklas Lidstrom .40 1.00
54 Chris Osgood .30 .75
55 Brendan Shanahan .40 1.00
56 Steve Yzerman 1.50 4.00
57 Mike Grier .30 .75
58 Bill Guerin .20 .50
59 Tommy Salo .30 .75
60 Ryan Smyth .30 .75
61 Doug Weight .30 .75
62 Pavel Bure .40 1.00
63 Sean Burke .30 .75
64 Viktor Kozlov .20 .50
65 Mark Parrish .20 .50
66 Ray Whitney .30 .75
67 Donald Audette .20 .50
68 Rob Blake .30 .75
69 Stephane Fiset .30 .75
70 Zigmund Palffy .30 .75
71 Luc Robitaille .30 .75
72 Jamie Storr .30 .75
73 Shayne Corson .20 .50
74 Jeff Hackett .30 .75
75 Saku Koivu .40 1.00
76 Vladimir Malakhov .20 .50
77 Martin Rucinsky .20 .50
78 Mike Dunham .30 .75
79 Greg Johnson .20 .50
80 Sergei Krivokrasov .20 .50
81 Cliff Ronning .30 .75
82 Scott Walker .20 .50
83 Jason Arnott .20 .50
84 Martin Brodeur 1.00 2.50
85 Patrik Elias .30 .75
86 Bobby Holik .20 .50
87 Brendan Morrison .30 .75
88 Scott Niedermayer .20 .50
89 Petr Sykora .20 .50
90 Mariusz Czerkawski .20 .50
91 Kenny Jonsson .20 .50
92 Mats Lindgren .20 .50
93 Felix Potvin .40 1.00
94 Mike Watt .20 .50
95 Theo Fleury .20 .50
96 Adam Graves .20 .50
97 Brian Leetch .40 1.00
98 John MacLean .20 .50
99 Petr Nedved .30 .75
100 Mike Richter .40 1.00
101 Magnus Arvedson .20 .50
102 Marian Hossa .40 1.00
103 Shawn McEachern .20 .50
104 Ron Tugnutt .30 .75
105 Alexei Yashin .20 .50
106 Rod Brind'Amour .30 .75
107 Eric Lindros .40 1.00
108 John LeClair .40 1.00
109 Mark Recchi .30 .75
110 John Vanbiesbrouck .30 .75
111 Nikolai Khabibulin .30 .75
112 Teppo Numminen .20 .50
113 Jeremy Roenick .50 1.25
114 Keith Tkachuk .40 1.00
115 Rick Tocchet .30 .75
116 Tom Barrasso .30 .75
117 Jan Hrdina .20 .50
118 Jaromir Jagr .60 1.50
119 Alexei Kovalev .20 .50
120 Martin Straka .20 .50
121 Pavol Demitra .30 .75
122 Jochen Hecht RC .75 2.00
123 Al MacInnis .30 .75
124 Chris Pronger .30 .75
125 Pierre Turgeon .30 .75
126 Vincent Damphousse .20 .50
127 Jeff Friesen .20 .50
128 Patrick Marleau .30 .75
129 Steve Shields .30 .75
130 Mike Vernon .30 .75
131 Chris Gratton .20 .50
132 Colin Forbes .20 .50
133 Vincent Lecavalier .40 1.00
134 Darcy Tucker .20 .50
135 Sergei Berezin .30 .75
136 Tie Domi .30 .75
137 Mike Johnson .30 .75
138 Curtis Joseph .40 1.00
139 Derek King .20 .50
140 Mats Sundin .40 1.00
141 Steve Thomas .20 .50
142 Mark Messier .40 1.00
143 Bill Muckalt .30 .75
144 Markus Naslund .40 1.00
145 Mattias Ohlund .30 .75
146 Garth Snow .30 .75
147 Peter Bondra .30 .75
148 Sergei Gonchar .20 .50
149 Olaf Kolzig .30 .75
150 Adam Oates .30 .75

1999-00 Revolution Premiere Date

Randomly inserted in Hobby packs at 1:25, this 150-card set parallels the base Revolution set with a foil Premier Date stamp. Each card is sequentially numbered to 42.
*PREM.DATE: 15X TO 40X BASIC CARDS

1999-00 Revolution Red

Randomly inserted in retail packs, this 150-card set parallels the base Revolution set in a red foil version. Each card is sequentially numbered to 299.
*RED: 4X TO 10X BASIC CARDS

1999-00 Revolution Shadow Series

Randomly inserted in Hobby packs, this 150-card set parallels the base Revolution set. Each card has a Shadow Series stamp and is sequentially numbered to 99.
*SHADOWS: 10X TO 25X BASIC CARDS

1999-00 Revolution Ice Sculptures

Randomly inserted in packs at the rate of 1:49, this 10-card set features top NHL players on an embossed silver foil card giving the effect of an ice carving.
COMPLETE SET (10) 50.00 100.00
1 Paul Kariya 2.00 5.00
2 Dominik Hasek 4.00 10.00
3 Patrick Roy 10.00 25.00
4 Joe Sakic 4.00 10.00
5 Steve Yzerman 10.00 25.00
6 Pavel Bure 2.50 6.00
7 Martin Brodeur 5.00 12.00
8 Theo Fleury 2.00 5.00
9 Eric Lindros 3.00 8.00
10 Jaromir Jagr 3.00 8.00

1999-00 Revolution NHL Icons

Randomly inserted in packs at the rate of 1:121, this 20-card set features close up action photography on a die cut card stock.
COMPLETE SET (20) 30.00 80.00
1 Teemu Selanne 1.50 4.00
2 Ray Bourque 3.00 8.00
3 Dominik Hasek 3.00 8.00
4 Doug Gilmour 1.25 3.00
5 Peter Forsberg 4.00 10.00
6 Patrick Roy 6.00 15.00
7 Joe Sakic 3.00 8.00
8 Brett Hull 2.00 5.00
9 Mike Modano 2.50 6.00
10 Brendan Shanahan 1.50 4.00
11 Steve Yzerman 6.00 15.00
12 Martin Brodeur 4.00 10.00
13 John LeClair 1.50 4.00
14 Eric Lindros 1.50 4.00
15 John Vanbiesbrouck 1.25 3.00
16 Keith Tkachuk 1.50 4.00
17 Jaromir Jagr 2.50 6.00
18 Curtis Joseph 1.50 4.00
19 Mats Sundin 1.50 4.00
20 Mark Messier 1.50 4.00

1999-00 Revolution Ornaments

Randomly seeded in packs at the rate of 1:25, this 20-card set features color player photos on a die-cut Christmas tree ornament.
COMPLETE SET (20) 40.00 80.00
1 Paul Kariya 1.25 3.00
2 Teemu Selanne 1.50 4.00
3 Sergei Samsonov 1.00 2.50
4 Dominik Hasek 3.00 8.00
5 Jarome Iginla 1.50 4.00
6 Peter Forsberg 3.00 8.00
7 Patrick Roy 5.00 12.00
8 Ed Belfour 1.25 3.00
9 Mike Modano 2.50 6.00
10 Brendan Shanahan 1.25 3.00
11 Steve Yzerman 6.00 15.00
12 Pavel Bure 2.50 6.00
13 Martin Brodeur 4.00 10.00
14 John LeClair 1.25 3.00
15 Eric Lindros 2.50 6.00
16 Jaromir Jagr 2.50 6.00
17 Vincent Lecavalier 1.25 3.00
18 Curtis Joseph 1.25 3.00
19 Mats Sundin 1.25 3.00
20 Mark Messier 1.25 3.00

1999-00 Revolution Showstoppers

Randomly seeded in packs at the rate of 2:25, this 36-card set features top NHL players on an all foil insert card.
COMPLETE SET (36) 30.00 70.00
1 Paul Kariya 1.00 2.50
2 Teemu Selanne 1.00 2.50
3 Ray Bourque 1.50 4.00
4 Byron Dafoe .40 1.00
5 Dominik Hasek 1.50 4.00
6 Michael Peca .40 1.00
7 Tony Amonte .75 2.00
8 Chris Drury .75 2.00
9 Peter Forsberg 1.50 4.00
10 Patrick Roy 4.00 10.00
11 Joe Sakic 2.00 5.00
12 Ed Belfour 1.00 2.50
13 Brett Hull 1.00 2.50
14 Mike Modano 1.00 2.50
15 Joe Nieuwendyk .75 2.00
16 Sergei Fedorov 1.00 2.50
17 Brendan Shanahan 1.00 2.50
18 Doug Weight .40 1.00
19 Pavel Bure 1.00 2.50
20 Mark Parrish .40 1.00
21 Martin Brodeur 2.50 6.00
22 Felix Potvin 1.00 2.50
23 Mike Richter 1.00 2.50
24 Marian Hossa .75 2.00
25 Alexei Yashin .40 1.00
26 John LeClair .75 2.00
27 John Vanbiesbrouck 1.25 3.00
28 Jeremy Roenick 1.00 2.50
29 Keith Tkachuk .75 2.00
30 Pavol Demitra .40 1.00
31 Patrick Marleau .75 2.00
32 Vincent Lecavalier 1.00 2.50
33 Curtis Joseph 1.00 2.50
34 Mats Sundin .75 2.00
35 Mark Messier 1.00 2.50
36 Peter Bondra .40 1.00

1999-00 Revolution Top of the Line

Randomly inserted in packs, this 30-card set was released as a three tier issue. Card numbers 1-10 are serial numbered out of 99, card numbers 11-20 are serial numbered out of 199, and card numbers 21-30 are serial numbered out of 299.
1 Paul Kariya/99 12.00 30.00
2 Sergei Samsonov/99 10.00 25.00
3 Brendan Shanahan/99 12.00 30.00
4 Pavel Bure/99 12.00 30.00
5 Luc Robitaille/99 10.00 25.00
6 Marian Hossa/99 10.00 25.00
7 John LeClair/99 8.00 20.00
8 Keith Tkachuk/99 12.00 30.00
9 Pavol Demitra/99 8.00 20.00
10 Jeff Friesen/99 8.00 20.00
11 Chris Drury/199 4.00 10.00
12 Peter Forsberg/199 12.00 30.00
13 Joe Sakic/199 12.00 30.00
14 Steve Yzerman/199 25.00 60.00
15 Mike Modano/199 10.00 25.00
16 Joe Nieuwendyk/199 6.00 15.00
17 Alexei Yashin/199 4.00 10.00
18 Eric Lindros/199 5.00 12.00
19 Mats Sundin/199 6.00 15.00
20 Mark Messier/199 6.00 15.00
21 Teemu Selanne/299 4.00 10.00
22 Miroslav Satan/299 3.00 8.00
23 Jarome Iginla/299 6.00 15.00
24 Tony Amonte/299 3.00 8.00
25 Milan Hejduk/299 3.00 8.00
26 Brett Hull/299 6.00 15.00
27 Theo Fleury/299 3.00 8.00
28 Mark Recchi/299 3.00 8.00
29 Jaromir Jagr/299 8.00 20.00
30 Peter Bondra/299 3.00 8.00

1999-00 Revolution CSC Silver

These cards were not available in packs nor in boxed form. They were only available to dealers who dealt with Continental Sports Cards, a distributor in Canada. The checklist parallels the copper set.
*CSC SILVER: 20X TO 50X BASIC CARDS

2000-01 Revolution

Released as a 150-card set in late September 2000, Revolution base cards featured a centered player action photo set against holographic and gold foil accented blue card stock. Revolution was packaged in 24-pack boxes with each pack contained three cards.
COMPLETE SET (150) 50.00 100.00
1 Guy Hebert .30 .75
2 Paul Kariya .50 1.25
3 Steve Rucchin .25 .60
4 Teemu Selanne .75 2.00
5 Andrew Brunette .25 .60
6 Ray Ferraro .25 .60
7 Damian Rhodes .25 .60
8 Patrik Stefan .30 .75
9 Anson Carter .30 .75
10 Byron Dafoe .30 .75
11 John Grahame .25 .60
12 Sergei Samsonov .30 .75
13 Joe Thornton .60 1.50
14 Maxim Afinogenov .25 .60
15 Martin Biron .30 .75
16 Doug Gilmour .50 1.25
17 Dominik Hasek .60 1.50
18 Michael Peca .30 .75
19 Miroslav Satan .25 .60
20 Fred Brathwaite .30 .75
21 Valeri Bure .30 .75
22 Phil Housley .30 .75
23 Jarome Iginla .40 1.00
24 Oleg Saprykin .25 .60
25 Rod Brind'Amour .40 1.00
26 Ron Francis .50 1.25
27 Arturs Irbe .30 .75
28 Sami Kapanen .25 .60
29 Tony Amonte .30 .75
30 Michal Grosek .25 .60
31 Steve Sullivan .25 .60
32 Jocelyn Thibault .30 .75
33 Alexei Zhamnov .30 .75
34 Ray Bourque .60 1.50
35 Chris Drury .30 .75
36 Peter Forsberg .50 1.25
37 Milan Hejduk .30 .75
38 Patrick Roy 1.00 2.50
39 Joe Sakic .60 1.50
40 Alex Tanguay .30 .75
41 Kevyn Adams .25 .60
42 Marc Denis .30 .75
43 Krzysztof Oliwa .25 .60
44 Geoff Sanderson .30 .75
45 Ed Belfour .40 1.00
46 Brett Hull .60 1.50
47 Mike Modano .60 1.50
48 Brenden Morrow .30 .75
49 Joe Nieuwendyk .40 1.00
50 Chris Chelios .40 1.00
51 Sergei Fedorov .60 1.50
52 Nicklas Lidstrom .40 1.00
53 Chris Osgood .40 1.00
54 Brendan Shanahan .50 1.25
55 Steve Yzerman 1.25 3.00
56 Bill Guerin .40 1.00
57 Todd Marchant .25 .60
58 Tommy Salo .30 .75
59 Ryan Smyth .30 .75
60 Doug Weight .40 1.00
61 Pavel Bure .50 1.25
62 Trevor Kidd .25 .60
63 Viktor Kozlov .30 .75
64 Scott Mellanby .25 .60
65 Ray Whitney .30 .75
66 Rob Blake .40 1.00
67 Stephane Fiset .25 .60
68 Zigmund Palffy .40 1.00
69 Luc Robitaille .40 1.00
70 Jamie Storr .30 .75
71 Manny Fernandez .30 .75
72 Jamie McLennan .25 .60
73 Sean O'Donnell .25 .60
74 Stacy Roest .25 .60
75 Jeff Hackett .25 .60
76 Saku Koivu .40 1.00
77 Trevor Linden .40 1.00
78 Martin Rucinsky .25 .60
79 Jose Theodore .50 1.25
80 Mike Dunham .25 .60
81 David Gosselin RC .30 .75
82 David Legwand .40 1.00
83 Cliff Ronning .25 .60
84 Jason Arnott .30 .75
85 Martin Brodeur .75 2.00
86 Patrik Elias .40 1.00
87 Scott Gomez .30 .75
88 Scott Stevens .40 1.00
89 Petr Sykora .30 .75
90 Tim Connolly .25 .60
91 Mariusz Czerkawski .25 .60
92 Brad Isbister .25 .60
93 Steve Valiquette RC .30 .75
94 Theo Fleury .50 1.25
95 Adam Graves .30 .75
96 Brian Leetch .40 1.00
97 Mark Messier .60 1.50
98 Petr Nedved .30 .75
99 Mike Richter .40 1.00
100 Mike York .25 .60
101 Daniel Alfredsson .40 1.00
102 Radek Bonk .30 .75
103 Marian Hossa .30 .75
104 Patrick Lalime .30 .75
105 Shawn McEachern .25 .60
106 Brian Boucher .30 .75
107 Eric Desjardins .30 .75
108 Simon Gagne .40 1.00
109 John LeClair .40 1.00
110 Eric Lindros .60 1.50
111 Mark Recchi .50 1.25
112 Shane Doan .30 .75
113 Nikolai Khabibulin .60 1.50
114 Jeremy Roenick .40 1.00
115 Keith Tkachuk .40 1.00
116 Jean-Sebastien Aubin .30 .75
117 Jan Hrdina .25 .60
118 Jaromir Jagr 1.00 2.50
119 Alexei Kovalev .30 .75
120 Martin Straka .30 .75
121 Pavol Demitra .50 1.25
122 Michal Handzus .25 .60
123 Al MacInnis .40 1.00
124 Chris Pronger .30 .75
125 Roman Turek .30 .75
126 Pierre Turgeon .40 1.00
127 Vincent Damphousse .30 .75
128 Jeff Friesen .25 .60
129 Patrick Marleau .40 1.00
130 Owen Nolan .40 1.00
131 Steve Shields .25 .60
132 Dan Cloutier .30 .75
133 Mike Johnson .25 .60
134 Dieter Kochan RC .25 .60
135 Vincent Lecavalier .30 .75
136 Nikolai Antropov .30 .75
137 Tie Domi .60 1.50
138 Jeff Farkas .25 .60
139 Curtis Joseph .50 1.25
140 Mats Sundin .40 1.00
141 Darcy Tucker .25 .60
142 Todd Bertuzzi .30 .75
143 Steve Kariya .25 .60
144 Markus Naslund .30 .75
145 Felix Potvin .60 1.50
146 Peter Bondra .30 .75
147 Jeff Halpern .25 .60
148 Olaf Kolzig .40 1.00
149 Adam Oates .40 1.00
150 Chris Simon .25 .60

2000-01 Revolution Blue

Randomly inserted in Hobby packs, this 150-card set parallels the base set with an embossed stamp in the middle of the card, and each card is sequentially numbered to 85.
*BLUE/85: 4X TO 10X BASIC CARDS
97 Mark Messier 8.00 20.00

2000-01 Revolution Premiere Date

Randomly inserted in Hobby packs, this 150-card set parallels the base set where each card is sequentially numbered to 60.
*PREM.DATE/60: 5X TO 12X BASIC CARDS
97 Mark Messier 10.00 25.00

2000-01 Revolution Red

Randomly inserted in Retail packs, this 150-card set parallels the base set enhanced with red highlights where each card is sequentially numbered to 99.
*RED/99: 4X TO 10X BASIC CARDS
97 Mark Messier 8.00 20.00

2000-01 Revolution Game-Worn Jerseys

Randomly inserted in packs, this 10-card set features a player action photo on the right side of the card front with circular swatches of game worn jerseys on the left. A gold foil serial number box appears right below the jersey swatch, and each card is sequentially numbered to 400.
*PATCH/50: 1.2X TO 3X BSIC JSY
1 Marty McInnis 4.00 10.00
2 Anson Carter 6.00 15.00
3 Jarome Iginla 10.00 25.00
4 Tony Amonte 6.00 15.00
5 Jamie Langenbrunner 4.00 10.00
6 Saku Koivu 8.00 20.00
7 Zdeno Chara 6.00 15.00
8 Brian Leetch 6.00 15.00
9 Andreas Dackell 4.00 10.00
10 Petr Svoboda 4.00 10.00

2000-01 Revolution HD NHL

This 36-card set was randomly inserted in packs at the rate of 2:25.
COMPLETE SET (36) 30.00 60.00
1 Paul Kariya 1.00 2.50
2 Teemu Selanne 1.00 2.50
3 Patrik Stefan .50 1.25
4 Joe Thornton 1.50 4.00
5 Dominik Hasek 2.00 5.00
6 Jarome Iginla 1.25 3.00
7 Tony Amonte .75 2.00
8 Peter Forsberg 2.50 6.00
9 Milan Hejduk 1.00 2.50
10 Joe Sakic 2.00 5.00
11 Patrick Roy 5.00 12.00
12 Ed Belfour 1.00 2.50
13 Brett Hull 1.25 3.00
14 Sergei Fedorov 1.50 4.00
15 Brendan Shanahan 1.00 2.50
16 Pavel Bure 1.00 2.50
17 Zigmund Palffy .75 2.00
18 Luc Robitaille .75 2.00
19 Saku Koivu 1.00 2.50
20 Martin Brodeur 2.50 6.00
21 Patrik Elias .75 2.00
22 Scott Gomez .50 1.25
23 Marian Hossa 1.00 2.50
24 Brian Boucher 1.00 2.50
25 John LeClair 1.00 2.50
26 Mark Recchi .75 2.00
27 Jeremy Roenick 1.25 3.00
28 Keith Tkachuk 1.00 2.50
29 Chris Pronger .75 2.00
30 Roman Turek .75 2.00
31 Owen Nolan .75 2.00
32 Vincent Lecavalier 1.00 2.50
33 Nikolai Antropov .50 1.25
34 Mats Sundin 1.00 2.50
35 Curtis Joseph 1.00 2.50
36 Olaf Kolzig .75 2.00

2000-01 Revolution Ice Immortals

Randomly inserted in packs at the rate of 1:25, this 20-card set features gray borders and a "snow" effect in front of player action photography on a blue and white background.
COMPLETE SET (20) 30.00 60.00
1 Paul Kariya 1.25 3.00
2 Teemu Selanne 1.25 3.00
3 Dominik Hasek 2.50 6.00
4 Ray Bourque 2.50 6.00
5 Peter Forsberg 3.00 8.00
6 Patrick Roy 6.00 15.00
7 Ed Belfour 1.25 3.00
8 Brett Hull 1.50 4.00
9 Mike Modano 2.00 5.00
10 Brendan Shanahan 1.25 3.00
11 Steve Yzerman 6.00 15.00
12 Pavel Bure 1.25 3.00
13 Martin Brodeur 3.00 8.00
14 Scott Gomez .60 1.50
15 John LeClair 1.25 3.00
16 Mark Recchi 1.00 2.50
17 Jeremy Roenick 1.50 4.00
18 Jaromir Jagr 2.00 5.00
19 Curtis Joseph 1.25 3.00
20 Olaf Kolzig 1.00 2.50

2000-01 Revolution NHL Game Gear

Randomly inserted in packs, this 10-card set features swatches of game worn jerseys and game used sticks. A player photo appears on the right side of the card front while two circular swatches of memorabilia, jersey on top and stick on bottom are separated by a gold serial number box. Each card is sequentially numbered to 200.
1 Peter Forsberg 15.00 40.00
2 Joe Sakic 15.00 40.00
3 Mike Modano 12.50 30.00
4 Sergei Fedorov 12.50 30.00
5 Nicklas Lidstrom 8.00 20.00
6 Steve Yzerman 20.00 50.00
7 Mark Messier 8.00 20.00
8 Nikolai Khabibulin 8.00 20.00
9 Jaromir Jagr 12.50 30.00
10 Peter Bondra 6.00 15.00

2000-01 Revolution NHL Icons

Randomly inserted in packs at the rate of 1:121, this 20-card set features a die-cut card stock in the shape of the NHL logo. Each card features gray borders around full color player photography.
COMPLETE SET (20) 50.00 100.00
1 Paul Kariya 1.50 4.00
2 Teemu Selanne 1.50 4.00
3 Doug Gilmour 1.25 3.00
4 Dominik Hasek 3.00 8.00
5 Ray Bourque 3.00 8.00
6 Peter Forsberg 4.00 10.00
7 Patrick Roy 6.00 15.00
8 Joe Sakic 3.00 8.00
9 Brett Hull 2.00 5.00
10 Mike Modano 2.50 6.00
11 Brendan Shanahan 1.50 4.00
12 Steve Yzerman 8.00 20.00
13 Pavel Bure 1.50 4.00
14 Luc Robitaille 1.25 3.00
15 Martin Brodeur 4.00 10.00
16 John LeClair 1.50 4.00
17 Jaromir Jagr 2.50 6.00
18 Curtis Joseph 1.50 4.00
19 Mats Sundin 1.50 4.00
20 Olaf Kolzig 1.25 3.00

2000-01 Revolution Stat Masters

Randomly inserted in packs, this 30-card set is a three tier issue. Tier one features top goal scorers and cards are sequentially numbered to 99, tier two features the NHL's leaders in shutouts and cards are sequentially numbered to 199, and tier three features assist leaders and cards are sequentially numbered to 299.
COMPLETE SET (30) 100.00 200.00
1 Teemu Selanne/99 6.00 15.00
2 Tony Amonte/99 5.00 12.00
3 Milan Hejduk/99 5.00 12.00
4 Brett Hull/99 6.00 15.00
5 Brendan Shanahan/99 5.00 12.00
6 Pavel Bure/99 5.00 12.00
7 Luc Robitaille/99 5.00 12.00
8 John LeClair/99 5.00 12.00
9 Jaromir Jagr/99 10.00 25.00
10 Owen Nolan/99 5.00 12.00
11 Martin Biron/199 2.50 6.00
12 Dominik Hasek/199 6.00 15.00
13 Patrick Roy/199 10.00 25.00
14 Ed Belfour/199 2.50 6.00
15 Jose Theodore/199 3.00 8.00
16 Martin Brodeur/199 6.00 15.00
17 Brian Boucher/199 2.50 6.00
18 Roman Turek/199 2.50 6.00
19 Curtis Joseph/199 2.50 6.00
20 Olaf Kolzig/199 2.50 6.00
21 Paul Kariya/299 5.00 12.00
22 Doug Gilmour/299 2.00 5.00
23 Ray Bourque/299 4.00 10.00
24 Joe Sakic/299 4.00 10.00
25 Mike Modano/299 3.00 8.00
26 Steve Yzerman/299 8.00 20.00
27 Scott Gomez/299 2.00 5.00
28 Mark Recchi/299 2.00 5.00
29 Mats Sundin/299 2.00 5.00
30 Adam Oates/299 2.00 5.00

2006-07 Rochester Americans

COMPLETE SET (25) 10.00 18.00
1 Craig Anderson .30 .75
2 David Booth .20 .50
3 Mike Card .20 .50
4 Adam Dennis .40 1.00
5 Mike Funk .20 .50
6 Rob Globke .40 1.00
7 Dylan Hunter .40 1.00
8 Greg Jacina .20 .50
9 Patrick Kaleta .20 .50
10 Kamil Kreps .20 .50
11 Drew Larman .20 .50
12 Martin Lojek .20 .50
13 Clarke MacArthur .40 1.00
14 Mark Mancari .40 1.00
15 Stefan Meyer .20 .50
16 Daniel Paille .40 1.00
17 Michael Ryan .40 1.00
18 Andrej Sekera .20 .50
19 Brandon Smith .20 .50
20 Janis Sprukts .20 .50
21 Drew Stafford .75 2.00
22 Anthony Stewart .30 .75
23 Marek Zagrapan .30 .75
24 Coaches .10 .25
NNO Cover Card .01 .01

1976-77 Rockies Puck Bucks

This 20-card set measures approximately 2 9/16" by 2 1/8" (after perforation) and features members of the then-expansion Colorado Rockies team. The set was issued in the Greater Denver area as part of a regional promotion for the Rockies. The cards feature a horizontal format on the front which has the player's photo. The cards were issued two to a panel (they could be separated, but then one couldn't compete in contest). Left side and right side in the rules refers to the two different cards that were joined: an action scene on the left side and a posed head shot in a circle on the right side). If the same player appeared in the action scene and in the circle, and if the ticket values and the color bars below both pictures matched, the contestant became an instant winner of two Colorado Rockies' hockey tickets, whose value is shown in the color bar. One could also save all player pictures until one had the same player appearing in the action scene and in the circle both with matching ticket values and matching color bars. The color bars at the bottom appeared in four different colors (yellow, blue, green, or orange). The cards feature either a "Play Puck Bucks" logo on the back, which also features a skeletal-like picture of a player, or a rules definition. Winners had to claim prizes by February 20, 1977. Since there is no numerical designation for the cards, they are checklisted alphabetically below.
COMPLETE SET (20) 37.50 75.00
1 Ron Andruff 2.00 4.00
2 Chuck Arnason 2.00 4.00
3 Henry Boucha 2.50 5.00
4 Colin Campbell 3.00 6.00
5 Gary Croteau 2.00 4.00
6 Guy Delparte 2.00 4.00
7 Steve Durbano 2.50 5.00
8 Tom Edur 2.00 4.00
9 Doug Favell 3.00 6.00
10 Dave Hudson 2.00 4.00
11 Bryan Lefley 2.00 4.00
12 Roger Lemelin 2.00 4.00
13 Simon Nolet 2.00 4.00
14 Wilf Paiement 2.50 5.00
15 Michel Plasse 3.00 6.00
16 Tracy Pratt 2.00 4.00
17 Nelson Pyatt 2.00 4.00
18 Phil Roberto 2.00 4.00
19 Sean Shanahan 2.00 4.00
20 Larry Skinner 2.00 4.00

1979-80 Rockies Team Issue

This 23-card set of the Colorado Rockies measures approximately 4" by 6". The fronts feature black-and-white action player photos. The backs are blank. The cards are unnumbered and checklisted below in alphabetical order.
COMPLETE SET (23) 20.00 40.00
1 Hardy Astrom 1.50 3.00
2 Doug Berry .75 1.50
3 Nick Beverley 1.00 2.00
4 Mike Christie .75 1.50
5 Gary Croteau 1.00 2.00
6 Lucien Deblois 1.00 2.00
7 Ron Delorme .75 1.50
8 Mike Gillis .75 1.50
9 Trevor Johansen .75 1.50
10 Mike Kitchen .75 1.50
11 Lanny McDonald 2.50 5.00
12 Mike McEwen .75 1.50
13 Bill McKenzie .75 1.50
14 Kevin Morrison .75 1.50
15 Bill Olesehuk .75 1.50
16 Randy Pierce .75 1.50
17 Michel Plasse 1.50 3.00
18 Joel Quenneville 1.00 2.00
19 Rob Ramage 2.50 5.00
20 Rene Robert 1.00 2.00
21 Don Saleski 1.00 2.00
22 Barry Smith 1.00 2.00
23 Jack Valiquette .75 1.50

1981-82 Rockies Postcards

This 30-card postcard set measures 3 1/2" by 5 1/2" and features borderless black-and-white action player photos of the Colorado Rockies. The backs have the standard white postcard design with the player's name and biographical information in the upper left corner. The team emblem is printed in light gray on the left side. The cards are unnumbered and checklisted below in alphabetical order.
COMPLETE SET (30) 14.00 35.00
1 Brent Ashton .75 2.00
2 Aaron Broten .40 1.00
3 Dave Cameron .40 1.00
4 Joe Cirella .75 2.00
5 Dwight Foster .40 1.00
6 Paul Gagne .40 1.00
7 Marshall Johnston CO .40 1.00
8 Veli-Pekka Ketola .60 1.50
9 Mike Kitchen .40 1.00
10 Rick Laferriere .40 1.00
11 Don Lever .60 1.50
12 Tapio Levo .40 1.00
13 Bob Lorimer .40 1.00
14 Bill MacMillan .40 1.00
15 Bob MacMillan VP .60 1.50
16 Merlin Malinowski .60 1.50
17 Bert Marshall GM .40 1.00
18 Kevin Maxwell .40 1.00
19 Joe Micheletti .75 2.00
20 Bobby Miller .40 1.00
21 Phil Myre .75 2.00
22 Graeme Nicolson .40 1.00
23 Jukka Porvari .40 1.00
24 Joel Quenneville .60 1.50
25 Rob Ramage 1.25 3.00
26 Glenn Resch 1.25 3.00
27 Steve Tambellini .60 1.50
28 Yvon Vautour .40 1.00
29 John Wensink .60 1.50
30 Title Card (Team logo) .75 2.00

1930 Rogers Peet

The Rogers Peet Department Store in New York released this set in early 1930. The cards were given out four at time to employees at the store for enrolling boys in Ropeco (the store's magazine club). Employees who completed the set, and pasted them in the album designed to house the cards, were eligible to win prizes. The blankbacked cards measure roughly 1 3/4" by 2 1/2" and feature a black and white photo of the famous athlete with his name and card number below the picture. Additions to this list are appreciated.
10 Lionel Conacher HK 62.50 125.00
22 Frank Boucher HK 50.00 75.00
29 Ching Johnson HK 62.50 125.00
42 Bill Burch HK 35.00 50.00

2010-11 Rookies and Stars Toronto Fall Expo Autographs

BS Brayden Schenn
JE Jordan Eberle
JS Jeff Skinner
MP Magnus Paajarvi
TH Taylor Hall 175.00 250.00
TS Tyler Seguin
ZH Zach Hamill

1952 Royal Desserts

The 1952 Royal Desserts Hockey set contains eight cards. The cards measure approximately 2 5/8" by 3 1/4". The set is cataloged as F219-2. The cards formed the backs of Royal Desserts packages of the period; consequently many cards are found with uneven edges stemming from the method of cutting the cards off the box. Each card has its number and the statement "Royal Stars of Hockey" in a red rectangle at the top. The blue tinted picture also features a facsimile autograph of the player. An album was presumably available as it is advertised on the card. The exact year (or years) of issue of these cards is not verified at this time.
COMPLETE SET (8) 6500.00 13000.00
1 Tony Leswick 300.00 750.00
2 Chuck Rayner 400.00 800.00
3 Edgar Laprade 300.00 750.00
4 Sid Abel 600.00 1200.00
5 Ted Lindsay 600.00 1200.00
6 Leo Reise Jr. 300.00 750.00
7 Red Kelly 600.00 1200.00
8 Gordie Howe 3000.00 6000.00

1971-72 Sabres Postcards

These standard-sized postcards feature borderless color photos. The backs feature player name, position, uniform number, and biographical information. These postcards were issued in bound form, with perforated top edges so as to be separated if necessary. The postcards are numbered in a long code format (for example, Punch Imlach is 82269-C). For space reasons, the 822 prefix and -C suffix have been deleted in the checklist below. Thanks to collector Edward Morse for updating the information seen below.
COMPLETE SET (22) 15.00 30.00
69 Punch Imlach CO 1.25 3.00
70 Roger Crozier 1.50 4.00
71 Jim Watson .75 2.00
72 Mike Robitaille .75 2.00
73 Tracy Pratt .75 2.00
74 Doug Barrie .75 2.00
75 Al Hamilton .75 2.00
76 Richard Martin 1.50 4.00
77 Dick Duff .75 2.00
78 Danny Lawson .75 2.00
79 Phil Goyette .75 2.00
80 Gil Perreault 3.00 6.00
81 Rod Zaine .75 2.00
82 Gerry Meehan .75 2.00
83 Ron Anderson .75 2.00
84 Floyd Smith .75 2.00
85 Kevin O'Shea .75 2.00
86 Steve Atkinson .75 2.00
87 Don Luce .75 2.00
88 Ray McKay .75 2.00
89 Eddie Shack 1.25 3.00
90 Dave Dryden 1.25 3.00

1972-73 Sabres Pepsi Pinback Buttons

These smallish buttons were apparently given away with the purchase of Pepsi products in the Buffalo area. The photos are black and white and feature early heroes of the Sabres history.
COMPLETE SET (9) 25.00 50.00
1 Roger Crozier 2.50 5.00
2 Don Luce 2.00 4.00
3 Rick Martin (action) 2.50 5.00
4 Rick Martin (head) 2.50 5.00
5 Gilbert Perreault (action) 5.00 10.00
6 Gilbert Perreault (head) 5.00 10.00
7 Gilbert Perreault (action) 2.50 5.00
8 Jim Schoenfeld 2.50 5.00
9 French Connection 5.00 10.00

1972-73 Sabres Postcards

This set of color postcards was issued by the team in response to autograph requests. It is not known whether they were actually sold in set form at any point, but given the difficulty in completing a set, it seems unlikely.
COMPLETE SET (20) 30.00 60.00
1 Steve Atkinson 1.00 2.00
2 Larry Carriere 1.00 2.00
3 Roger Crozier 4.00 8.00
4 Butch Deadmarsh 1.00 2.00
5 Dave Dryden 1.50 3.00
6 Larry Hillman 1.00 2.00
7 Tim Horton 5.00 10.00
8 Jim Lorentz 1.00 2.00
9 Don Luce 1.50 3.00
10 Richard Martin 3.00 6.00
11 Gerry Meehan 1.50 3.00
12 Larry Mickey 1.00 2.00
13 Gilbert Perreault 5.00 10.00
14 Tracy Pratt 1.50 3.00
15 Craig Ramsay 1.50 3.00
16 Rene Robert 1.50 3.00
17 Mike Robitaille 1.00 2.00
18 Jim Schoenfeld 3.00 6.00
19 Paul Terbenche 1.00 2.00
20 Randy Wyrozub 1.00 2.00

1973-74 Sabres Bells

This set of four photos of Buffalo Sabres players was sponsored by Bells Markets. The photos measure approximately 3 15/16" by 5 1/2" and were sold for 10 cents each. The front has a color action photo. These blank-backed cards are unnumbered and listed alphabetically in the checklist below. The team card was issued and cost 50 cents apiece.
COMPLETE SET (4) 15.00 30.00
1 Roger Crozier 4.00 8.00
2 Jim Lorentz 2.50 5.00

ichard Martin 4.00 8.00
ilbert Perreault 6.00 12.00
eam Photo

1973-74 Sabres Postcards

s 13-card set was published by Robert B. Shaver of
ımore, New York. The cards are in the postcard
mat and measure approximately 3 1/2" by 5 1/2".
e fronts feature a black-and-white action shot with
ite borders. The backs carry the player's name,
sition, and team name at the upper left and are
ided in the middle. The set is dated by the inclusion
loe Norris, who played with the Sabres only during
1973-74 season. The cards are unnumbered and
ecklisted below in alphabetical order.

MPLETE SET (13) 20.00 40.00
Roger Crozier 2.00 4.00
Dave Dryden 2.00 4.00
im Horton 5.00 10.00
im Lorentz 1.00 2.00
Don Luce 1.25 2.50
Rick Martin 2.00 4.00
Gerry Meehan 1.50 3.00
Larry Mickey 1.00 2.00
loe Noris 1.00 2.00
Gilbert Perreault 4.00 8.00
Mike Robitaille 1.00 2.00
Jim Schoenfeld 2.00 4.00
Paul Terbenche 1.00 2.00

1974-75 Sabres Postcards

s set of color postcards was issued by the team in
sponse to autograph requests. It is not known
ether they were actually sold in set form at any
int, but given the difficulty in completing a set, it
ems unlikely.

MPLETE SET (21) 30.00 60.00
Gary Bromley 2.00 4.00
Larry Carriere 1.00 2.00
Roger Crozier 4.00 8.00
Rick Dudley 2.00 4.00
Rocky Farr 1.00 2.00
Lee Fogolin 2.00 4.00
Danny Gare 2.00 4.00
Norm Gratton 1.00 2.00
Jocelyn Guevremont 1.00 2.00
Bill Hajt 1.00 2.00
Jerry Korab 2.00 4.00
Jim Lorentz 1.00 2.00
Don Luce 1.25 2.50
Richard Martin 2.00 4.00
Peter McNab 1.25 2.50
Larry Mickey 1.00 2.00
Gilbert Perreault 4.00 8.00
Craig Ramsay 1.50 3.00
Rene Robert 1.50 3.00
Jim Schoenfeld 2.00 4.00
Brian Spencer 2.50 5.00

1975-76 Sabres Linnett

oduced by Linnett Studios, this 12-card set featured
ffalos Sabres players ftom the 1975-76 season.

MPLETE SET (12) 15.00 30.00
Roger Crozier 2.00 4.00
Gerry Desjardins 1.50 3.00
Dave Dryden 1.50 3.00
Jim Lorentz 1.00 2.00
Don Luce 1.25 2.50
Richard Martin 2.00 4.00
Peter McNab 1.25 2.50
Gerry Meehan 1.00 2.00
Gilbert Perreault 4.00 8.00
Rene Robert 1.50 3.00
Jim Schoenfeld 2.00 4.00
Fred Stanfield 1.50 3.00

1976-77 Sabres Glasses

asses feature a black and white portrait of the player.
asses were available at Your Host restaurants.

MPLETE SET (4) 12.50 25.00
Jerry Korab 3.00 6.00
Rick Martin 3.00 6.00
Gilbert Perreault 3.00 6.00
Jim Schoenfeld 3.00 6.00

1979-80 Sabres Bells

is set of nine photos of Buffalo Sabres players was
onsored by Bells Markets. The photos measure
proximately 7 5/8" by 10". The front has a color
tion photo, with the player's name and team name in
e white border at the lower right hand corner. The
ck is printed in blue and has the Sabres' logo, a
ad shot of the player, biographical information, and
reer statistics.

MPLETE SET (9) 10.00 20.00
Don Edwards 2.00 4.00
Danny Gare 1.25 2.50
Jerry Korab 1.00 2.00
Richard Martin 2.00 4.00
Tony McKegney 1.25 2.50
Craig Ramsay 1.00 2.00
Bob Sauve 2.00 4.00
Jim Schoenfeld 1.50 3.00
John Van Boxmeer 1.00 2.00

1979-80 Sabres Milk Panels

is set of four confirmed panels feature singles that
e approximately 3 1/2 by 1 1/2. The top portion
atures a blue-toned head shot, while the bottom
cludes player bio information. The backs are blank.

MPLETE SET (4) 3.00 6.00
Don Edwards .50 1.00
Ric Seiling .50 1.00
Jerry Korab .50 1.00
Gil Perreault .50 1.00

1980-81 Sabres Milk Panels

is set of Buffalo Sabres was issued on the side of
alf gallon milk cartons. After cutting, the panels
easure approximately 3 3/4" by 7 1/2", with two
ayers per panel. The picture and text of the player
anels are printed in red; the set can also be found in
ue print. The top of the panel reads "Kids, Collect a
omplete Set of Buffalo Sabres Players". Arranged
ongside each other, the panel features for each player
head shot, biographical information, and player
ofile. The panels are subtly dated and numbered
elow the photo area in the following way,
erreault/Seiling is M325-80-4H (M325 is the product
ode, the number 80 gives the last two digits of the
ear, and 4 is the card number perhaps also indicating
elease week).

OMPLETE SET (2) 15.00 30.00
Gilbert Perreault 10.00 20.00
Ric Seiling
Bob Sauve 6.00 12.00
Richard Martin

1981-82 Sabres Milk Panels

his sixteen-panel set of Buffalo Sabres was issued by
Wilson Farms Dairy on the side of 2 percent milk fat
nd homogenized Vitamin D half gallon milk cartons.
fter cutting, the panels measure approximately 3 3/4"
y 7 1/2". Although the 2 percent milk fat cartons have
some lime green lettering and a lime green stripe, the picture and text of the player panels are printed in red on both cartons. The top of the panel reads "Kids, Collect Action Photos of the 1981-82 Buffalo Sabres." Inside a red broken border, the panel has a action player photo, with player information and career summary beneath the picture. The panels are subtly dated and numbered below the photo area in the following way, Gilbert Perreault is M325-81-4H (M325 is the product code, the number 81 gives the last two digits of year, and 4 is the card number perhaps also indicating release week). The set can also be found in blue print.

COMPLETE SET (17) 60.00 150.00
1 Craig Ramsay 4.00 10.00
2 John Van Boxmeer 4.00 10.00
3 Don Edwards 5.00 12.00
4 Gilbert Perreault 8.00 20.00
5 Alan Haworth 4.00 10.00
6 Jim Schoenfeld 6.00 15.00
7 Richie Dunn 4.00 10.00
8 Bob Sauve 5.00 12.00
9 Bill Hajt 4.00 10.00
10 Larry Playfair 4.00 10.00
11 Tony McKegney 5.00 12.00
12 Mike Ramsey 5.00 12.00
13 Andre Savard 4.00 10.00
14 Derek Smith 4.00 10.00
15 Ric Seiling 4.00 10.00
16 Yvon Lambert 4.00 10.00
17 Dale McCourt 4.00 10.00

1982-83 Sabres Milk Panels

This seventeen-panel set of Buffalo Sabres was issued on the side of half gallon milk cartons. After cutting, the panels measure approximately 3 3/4" by 7 1/2". The picture and text of the player panels are printed in blue. The top of the panel reads "Kids, Clip and Save Exciting Tips and Pictures of Buffalo Sabres." Inside a blue broken border, the panel has a posed head and shoulders shot, with the player's name, position, and a hockey tip beneath the picture. The panels are subtly dated and numbered below the photo area in the following way, Gilbert Perreault is M325-82-7H. Phil Housley's card predates his Rookie Card.

COMPLETE SET (17) 60.00 150.00
2 1982-83 Home Schedule 6.00 15.00
3 Craig Ramsay 4.00 10.00
4 John Van Boxmeer 4.00 10.00
5 Lindy Ruff 4.00 10.00
6 Bob Sauve 5.00 12.00
7 Gilbert Perreault 8.00 20.00
8 Ric Seiling 4.00 10.00
9 Jacques Cloutier 5.00 12.00
10 Larry Playfair 4.00 10.00
11 Phil Housley 8.00 20.00
12 Mike Foligno 5.00 12.00
13 Tony McKegney 5.00 12.00
14 Dale McCourt 4.00 10.00
15 Mike Ramsey 4.00 10.00
16 Hannu Virta 4.00 10.00
17 Brent Peterson 4.00 10.00
18 Scott Bowman GM 8.00 20.00

1984-85 Sabres Blue Shield

This 21-card set was issued by the Buffalo Sabres in conjunction with Blue Shield of Western New York. The cards measure approximately 2 1/2" by 3 3/4". It has been reported that only 500 sets were printed as a test for future issues. The fronts feature a head and shoulders color photo with player information below the picture. The card backs have the Blue Shield logo and the words "The Caring Card -- The Blue Shield of Western New York, Inc." We have checklisted the cards below in alphabetical order. Dave Andreychuk and Tom Barrasso appear in their Rookie Card year.

COMPLETE SET (21) 40.00 100.00
1 Dave Andreychuk 8.00 20.00
2 Tom Barrasso 8.00 20.00
3 Adam Creighton 2.00 5.00
4 Paul Cyr 1.25 3.00
5 Malcolm Davis 1.25 3.00
6 Mike Foligno 2.00 5.00
7 Bill Hajt 1.25 3.00
8 Gilles Hamel 1.25 3.00
9 Phil Housley 4.00 10.00
10 Sean McKenna 1.25 3.00
11 Mike Moller 1.25 3.00
12 Gilbert Perreault 6.00 15.00
13 Brent Peterson 1.25 3.00
14 Larry Playfair 1.25 3.00
15 Craig Ramsay 2.00 5.00
16 Mike Ramsey 2.00 5.00
17 Lindy Ruff 2.00 5.00
18 Bob Sauve 2.00 5.00
19 Ric Seiling 1.25 3.00
20 John Tucker 2.00 5.00
21 Hannu Virta 1.25 3.00

1985-86 Sabres Blue Shield

This 28-card set was issued by the Buffalo Sabres in conjunction with Blue Shield of Western New York. The cards were printed in two different sizes: large (4" by 6" with postcard backs) and small (2 1/2" by 3 1/2"). Both sizes have the Blue Shield logo on the backs. Though both sizes are scarce, the small cards are considered harder to obtain. The front of the large card features a color action photo of the player, with his name as well as biographical and statistical information below the picture. The front of the small card is identical except for the omission of the statistical information. The firing of Sabres' coach Jim Schoenfeld at the time the cards were issued makes his card rare as he was removed from the set. The set is priced below as complete without the Schoenfeld card. Daren Puppa's card predates his Rookie Card by three years.

COMPLETE SET (27) 16.00 40.00
1 Mikael Andersson .40 1.00
2 Dave Andreychuk 2.00 5.00
3 Tom Barrasso 1.25 3.00
4 Adam Creighton .40 1.00
5 Paul Cyr .40 1.00
6 Malcolm Davis .40 1.00
7 Steve Dykstra .40 1.00
8 Dave Fenyves .40 1.00
9 Mike Foligno .40 1.00
10 Bill Hajt .40 1.00
11 Bob Halkidis .40 1.00
12 Gilles Hamel .40 1.00
13 Phil Housley 1.25 3.00
14 Pat Hughes .40 1.00
15 Normand Lacombe .40 1.00
16 Chris Langevin .40 1.00
17 Sean McKenna .40 1.00
18 Gates Orlando .75 2.00
19 Gilbert Perreault 2.00 5.00
20 Larry Playfair .40 1.00
21 Daren Puppa 1.00 2.50
22 Craig Ramsay ACO .20 .50
23 Mike Ramsey .40 1.00
24 Lindy Ruff .40 1.00
25 Jim Schoenfeld CO SP 6.00 15.00
26 Ric Seiling .40 1.00
27 John Tucker .60 1.50
28 Hannu Virta .40 1.00

1985-86 Sabres Blue Shield Small

This set is the same as the regular Sabres Blue Shield set, only in a smaller format.

COMPLETE SET (27) 16.00 40.00
1 Mikael Andersson .40 1.00
2 Dave Andreychuk 1.50 4.00
3 Tom Barrasso .75 2.00
4 Adam Creighton .40 1.00
5 Paul Cyr .40 1.00
6 Malcolm Davis .40 1.00
7 Steve Dykstra .40 1.00
8 Dave Fenyves .40 1.00
9 Mike Foligno .40 1.00
10 Bill Hajt .40 1.00
11 Bob Halkidis .40 1.00
12 Gilles Hamel .40 1.00
13 Phil Housley .75 2.00
14 Pat Hughes .40 1.00
15 Normand Lacombe .40 1.00
16 Chris Langevin .40 1.00
17 Sean McKenna .40 1.00
18 Gates Orlando .60 1.50
19 Gilbert Perreault 1.50 4.00
20 Larry Playfair .40 1.00
21 Daren Puppa .75 2.00
22 Craig Ramsay ACO .20 .50
23 Mike Ramsey .40 1.00
24 Lindy Ruff .40 1.00
25 Jim Schoenfeld CO SP 4.00 10.00
26 Ric Seiling .40 1.00
27 John Tucker .60 1.50
28 Hannu Virta .40 1.00

1986-87 Sabres Blue Shield

This 28-card set was issued by the Buffalo Sabres in conjunction with Blue Shield of Western New York. In contrast to the previous year's issue, the cards were printed only in one size, the approximately 4" by 6" postcard type with the Blue Shield logo on the backs. The front of the cards can be distinguished from the previous year's issue by the addition of the player's uniform number (inadvertently omitted on the Creighton and Fenyves cards) and updated statistics.

COMPLETE SET (28) 12.00 30.00
1 Shawn Anderson .30 .75
2 Dave Andreychuk 2.50 6.00
3 Scott Arniel .30 .75
4 Tom Barrasso 1.25 3.00
5 Jacques Cloutier .40 1.00
6 Adam Creighton .40 1.00
7 Paul Cyr .30 .75
8 Steve Dykstra .30 .75
9 Dave Fenyves .30 .75
10 Mike Foligno .60 1.50
11 Clark Gillies .75 2.00
12 Bill Hajt .30 .75
13 Bob Halkidis .30 .75
14 Jim Hofford .30 .75
15 Phil Housley 1.00 2.50
16 Jim Korn .30 .75
17 Uwe Krupp .60 1.50
18 Tom Kurvers .30 .75
19 Norm Lacombe .30 .75
20 Gates Orlando .30 .75
21 Wilf Paiement .40 1.00
22 Gilbert Perreault 2.00 5.00
23 Daren Puppa 1.25 3.00
24 Mike Ramsey .40 1.00
25 Lindy Ruff .30 .75
26 Christian Ruuttu .30 .75
27 Doug Smith .30 .75
28 John Tucker .40 1.00

1986-87 Sabres Blue Shield Small

Same as the regular Sabres Shield set only in a smaller format.

COMPLETE SET (28) 14.00 35.00
1 Shawn Anderson .30 .75
2 Dave Andreychuk 2.50 6.00
3 Scott Arniel .30 .75
4 Tom Barrasso 1.25 3.00
5 Jacques Cloutier .40 1.00
6 Adam Creighton .40 1.00
7 Paul Cyr .30 .75
8 Steve Dykstra .30 .75
9 Dave Fenyves .30 .75
10 Mike Foligno .60 1.50
11 Clark Gillies .75 2.00
12 Bill Hajt .30 .75
13 Bob Halkidis .30 .75
14 Jim Hofford .30 .75
15 Phil Housley 1.25 3.00
16 Jim Korn .30 .75
17 Uwe Krupp .60 1.50
18 Tom Kurvers .30 .75
19 Norm Lacombe .30 .75
20 Gates Orlando .30 .75
21 Wilf Paiement .40 1.00
22 Gilbert Perreault 2.00 5.00
23 Daren Puppa 1.25 3.00
24 Mike Ramsey .40 1.00
25 Lindy Ruff .30 .75
26 Christian Ruuttu .30 .75
27 Doug Smith .30 .75
28 John Tucker .40 1.00

1987-88 Sabres Blue Shield

This 28-card set was issued by the Buffalo Sabres in conjunction with Blue Shield of Western New York. In contrast to the previous year's issue, the cards are a different size, approximately 4" by 5", again in the postcard format with the Blue Shield logo on the backs. The front of the cards feature a color action photo of the player, with the player's name, team name, and team logo in a yellow stripe at the top. The player's number and a facsimile autograph appear in blue at the bottom on the front. Supposedly there exists a rare variation on the Phil Housley card which has his last name misspelled "Housley". The card of Pierre Turgeon predates his Rookie Card by one year.

COMPLETE SET (28) 10.00 25.00
1 Mikael Andersson 14 .30 .75
2 Dave Andreychuk 25 1.25 3.00
3 Scott Arniel 9 .30 .75
4 Tom Barrasso 30 .60 1.50
5 Jacques Cloutier 1 .40 1.00
6 Adam Creighton 38 .40 1.00
7 Mike Donnelly 16 .30 .75
8 Mike Foligno 17 .40 1.00
9 Clark Gillies 90 .40 1.00
10 Bob Halkidis 18 .30 .75
11 Mike Hartman 20 .30 .75
12 Ed Hospodar 24 .30 .75
13 Phil Housley 6 .60 1.50
14 Calle Johansson 3 .40 1.00
15 Uwe Krupp 40 .40 1.00
16 Jan Ludvig 36 .30 .75
17 Kevin Maguire 19 .30 .75
18 Mark Napier 65 .30 .75
19 Ken Priestlay 12 .30 .75
20 Daren Puppa 35 .60 1.50
21 Mike Ramsey 5 .40 1.00
22 Joe Reekie 27 .30 .75
23 Lindy Ruff 22 .30 .75
24 Christian Ruuttu 21 .40 1.00
25 Ray Sheppard 23 1.25 3.00
26 Doug Smith 15 .30 .75
27 John Tucker 7 .40 1.00
28 Pierre Turgeon 77 4.00 10.00

1987-88 Sabres Wonder Bread/Hostess

The 1987-88 Buffalo Sabres Team Photo Album was sponsored by Wonder Bread and Hostess Cakes. It consists of three large sheets, each measuring approximately 13 1/2" by 10 1/4" and joined together to form one continuous sheet. The first panel has a team photo of the Buffalo Sabres. The second and third panels present three rows of five cards each. After perforation, the cards measure approximately 2 5/8" by 3 3/8". They feature color posed photos bordered in various color dots, with player information below the picture sandwiched between the Sabres' and sponsors' logos. The back has biographical and statistical information in a horizontal format. We have checklisted the names below in alphabetical order, with the uniform number to the right of the name. The set features an early card of Pierre Turgeon pre-dating his Rookie Cards by one year.

COMPLETE SET (31) 8.00 20.00
1 Mikael Andersson 14 .20 .50
2 Shawn Anderson 37 .20 .50
3 Dave Andreychuk 25 1.00 2.50
4 Scott Arniel 9 .20 .50
5 Tom Barrasso 30 .75 2.00
6 Jacques Cloutier 1 .30 .75
7 Adam Creighton 38 .30 .75
8 Steve Dykstra 4 .20 .50
9 Mike Foligno 17 .30 .75
10 Clark Gillies 90 .30 .75
11 Ed Hospodar 24 .20 .50
12 Phil Housley 6 .50 1.25
13 Calle Johansson 3 .30 .75
14 Uwe Krupp 40 .30 .75
15 Don Lever CO .20 .50
16 Bob Logan 26 .20 .50
17 Jan Ludvig 36 .20 .50
18 Kevin Maguire 19 .20 .50
19 Mark Napier 65 .30 .75
20 Daren Puppa 31 .60 1.50
21 Mike Ramsey 5 .30 .75
22 Joe Reekie 27 .30 .75
23 Lindy Ruff 22 .20 .50
24 Christian Ruuttu 21 .30 .75
25 Ted Sator CO .20 .50
26 Ray Sheppard 23 .75 2.00
27 Barry Smith CO .20 .50
28 Doug Smith 15 .20 .50
29 John Tucker 7 .30 .75
30 Pierre Turgeon 77 3.00 8.00
NNO Large Team Photo 1.25 3.00

1988-89 Sabres Blue Shield

This 28-card set was issued by the Buffalo Sabres in conjunction with Blue Shield of Western New York. The cards measure approximately 4" by 6" and are in the postcard format, with the Blue Shield logo on the backs. The fronts feature a color action photo of the player. The picture is sandwiched between yellow stripes, with team logo and player's name above, and player information below. The cards are unnumbered and we have checklisted them below in alphabetical order, with the uniform number next to the player's name. The cards of Benoit Hogue, Jan Ludvig, Mark Napier, and Joe Reekie were apparently late additions to the set; they are marked as SP in the checklist below.

COMPLETE SET (28) 10.00 25.00
1 Mikael Andersson 14 .20 .50
2 Dave Andreychuk 25 .60 1.50
3 Scott Arniel 9 .08 .25
4 Doug Bodger 8 .30 .75
5 Jacques Cloutier 1 .30 .75
6 Mike Donnelly 16 .20 .50
7 Mike Foligno 17 .30 .75
8 Bob Halkidis 18 .08 .25
9 Mike Hartman 20 .08 .25
10 Benoit Hogue 33 SP 1.25 3.00
11 Phil Housley 6 .40 1.00
12 Calle Johansson 3 .30 .75
13 Uwe Krupp 4 .30 .75
14 Jan Ludvig 36 SP .75 2.00
15 Kevin Maguire 19 .08 .25
16 Mark Napier 65 SP .75 2.00
17 Jeff Parker 29 .08 .25
18 Larry Playfair 27 .08 .25
19 Daren Puppa 31 .75 2.00
20 Mike Ramsey 5 .20 .50
21 Joe Reekie 55 SP .75 2.00
22 Lindy Ruff 22 .08 .25
23 Christian Ruuttu 21 .20 .50
24 Sabretooth Mascot .08 .25
25 Ray Sheppard 23 .60 1.50
26 John Tucker 7 .20 .50
27 Pierre Turgeon 77 2.50 6.00
28 Rick Vaive 12 .30 .75

1988-89 Sabres Wonder Bread/Hostess

The 1988-89 Buffalo Sabres Team Photo Album was sponsored by Wonder Bread and Hostess Cakes. It consists of three large sheets, each measuring approximately 13 1/2" by 10 1/4" and joined together to form one continuous sheet. The first panel has a team photo of the Sabres in civilian clothing. The second and third panels present three rows of five cards each. After perforation, the cards measure approximately 2 5/8" by 3 3/8". They feature color posed photos on white card stock. The top half has thin diagonal blue lines traversing the white background. Player information appears below the picture, between the Sabres' and sponsors' logos. The back has biographical and statistical information in a horizontal format. The cards are unnumbered and we have checklisted them below in alphabetical order, with the uniform number to the right of the player's name.

COMPLETE SET (31) 8.00 20.00
1 Mikael Andersson 14 .20 .50
2 Dave Andreychuk 25 .60 1.50
3 Scott Arniel 9 .20 .50
4 Doug Bodger 8 .30 .75
5 Jacques Cloutier 1 .30 .75
6 Adam Creighton 38 .25 .60
7 Mike Foligno 17 .30 .75
8 Bob Halkidis 18 .20 .50
9 Mike Hartman 20 .20 .50
10 Benoit Hogue 33 .40 1.00
11 Phil Housley 6 .40 1.00
12 Calle Johansson 3 .30 .75
13 Uwe Krupp 4 .30 .75
14 Don Lever CO .20 .50
15 Jan Ludvig 36 .20 .50
16 Kevin Maguire 19 .20 .50
17 Brad Miller 44 .20 .50
18 Mark Napier 65 .20 .50
19 Jeff Parker 29 .20 .50
20 Larry Playfair 27 .20 .50
21 Daren Puppa 31 .75 2.00
22 Mike Ramsey 5 .20 .50
23 Joe Reekie 55 .20 .50
24 Lindy Ruff 22 .20 .50
25 Christian Ruuttu 21 .20 .50
26 Ted Sator CO .20 .50
27 Ray Sheppard 23 .60 1.50
28 Barry Smith CO .20 .50
29 John Tucker 7 .20 .50
30 Pierre Turgeon 77 2.50 6.00
xx Large Team Photo .40 1.00

1989-90 Sabres Blue Shield

This 24-card set was issued by the Buffalo Sabres in conjunction with Blue Shield of Western New York. The cards measure approximately 4" by 6" and are in the postcard format, with the Blue Shield logo on the backs. The fronts feature a color action photo of the player. The picture is sandwiched between yellow stripes, with team logo and player's name above, and player information below. The cards are unnumbered and we have checklisted them below in alphabetical order, with the uniform number next to the player's name. The card of Alexander Mogilny predates his Rookie Card by one year.

COMPLETE SET (24) 8.00 20.00
1 Dave Andreychuk 25 .60 1.50
2 Scott Arniel 9 .20 .50
3 Doug Bodger 8 .20 .50
4 Mike Foligno 17 .30 .75
5 Mike Hartman 20 .20 .50
6 Benoit Hogue 33 .40 1.00
7 Phil Housley 6 .40 1.00
8 Dean Kennedy 26 .20 .50
9 Uwe Krupp 4 .30 .75
10 Grant Ledyard 3 .20 .50
11 Kevin Maguire 19 .20 .50
12 Clint Malarchuk 30 .30 .75
13 Alexander Mogilny 89 2.00 5.00
14 Jeff Parker 29 .20 .50
15 Larry Playfair 27 .20 .50
16 Ken Priestlay 56 .20 .50
17 Daren Puppa 31 .60 1.50
18 Mike Ramsey 5 .20 .50
19 Christian Ruuttu 21 .20 .50
20 Ray Sheppard 23 .40 1.00
21 Dave Snuggerud 18 .20 .50
22 Sabretooth Mascot .08 .25
23 Pierre Turgeon 77 1.25 3.00
24 Rick Vaive 22 .30 .75

1989-90 Sabres Campbell's

The 1989-90 Buffalo Sabres Team Photo Album was sponsored by Campbell's and commemorates 20 years in the NHL. It consists of three large sheets (the first two measuring approximately 10" by 13 1/2" and the third smaller), all joined together to form one continuous sheet. The first panel has three color action shots superimposed on a large black and white picture of the Sabres. While the second panel presents four rows of four cards each (16 player cards), the third panel presents four rows of three cards each (11 player cards and a 20th year card). After perforation, the cards measure approximately 2 1/2" by 3 3/8". They feature color posed photos bordered in yellow (on three sides), on a dark blue background interspersed with Sabres' logos in light blue. Player information appears below the picture in a yellow diamond, sandwiched between the Sabres' and the Franco-American logos. The back has biographical and statistical information in a horizontal format. We have checklisted the names below in alphabetical order, with the uniform number to the right of the name. The card of Alexander Mogilny predates his Rookie Card by one year.

COMPLETE SET (28) 8.00 20.00
1 Shawn Anderson 37 .20 .50
2 Dave Andreychuk 25 .60 1.50
3 Scott Arniel 9 .20 .50
4 Doug Bodger 8 .20 .50
5 Rick Dudley CO .30 .75
6 Mike Foligno 17 .30 .75
7 Mike Hartman 20 .20 .50
8 Benoit Hogue 33 .40 1.00
9 Phil Housley 6 .40 1.00
10 Dean Kennedy 26 .20 .50
11 Uwe Krupp 4 .30 .75
12 Grant Ledyard 3 .20 .50
13 Kevin Maguire 19 .20 .50
14 Clint Malarchuk 39 .30 .75
15 Alexander Mogilny 89 2.00 5.00
16 Mark Napier 65 .20 .50
17 Jeff Parker 29 .20 .50
18 Larry Playfair 27 .20 .50
19 Daren Puppa 31 .60 1.50
20 Mike Ramsey 5 .20 .50
21 Robert Ray 32 .40 1.00
22 Christian Ruuttu 21 .20 .50
23 Ray Sheppard 23 .40 1.00
24 Dave Snuggerud 18 .20 .50
25 John Tortorella CO .20 .50
26 Pierre Turgeon 77 1.25 3.00
27 Rick Vaive 22 .30 .75
xx Large Team Photo .40 1.00

1990-91 Sabres Blue Shield

This 26-card set was issued by the Buffalo Sabres in conjunction with Blue Shield of Western New York. The cards measure approximately 4" by 6" and are in the postcard format, with the Blue Shield logo on the backs. The fronts feature a color action photo of the player. The picture is sandwiched between yellow stripes, with team logo and player's name above, and player information below. These cards may be distinguished from the previous year's issue by the "medical shield logo" in the upper right corner. The cards are unnumbered and we have checklisted them below in alphabetical order, with the uniform number next to the player's name.

COMPLETE SET (26) 6.00 15.00
1 Dave Andreychuk 25 .30 .75
2 Donald Audette 28 .40 1.00
3 Doug Bodger 8 .20 .50
4 Greg Brown 9 .20 .50
5 Brian Curran 39 .20 .50
6 Lou Franceschetti 15 .20 .50
7 Mike Hartman 20 .20 .50
8 Dale Hawerchuk 10 .40 1.00
9 Benoit Hogue 33 .25 .60
10 Dean Kennedy 26 .20 .50
11 Uwe Krupp 4 .30 .75
12 Grant Ledyard 3 .20 .50
13 Mikkn Makela 42 .20 .50
14 Clint Malarchuk 30 .30 .75
15 Alexander Mogilny 89 1.25 3.00
16 Daren Puppa 31 .40 1.00
17 Mike Ramsey 5 .20 .50
18 Robert Ray 32 .30 .75
19 Christian Ruuttu 21 .20 .50
20 Sabretooth Mascot .08 .25
21 Jiri Sejba 23 .20 .50
22 Dave Snuggerud 18 .20 .50
23 John Tucker 7 .20 .50
24 Pierre Turgeon 77 .60 1.50
25 Rick Vaive 22 .20 .50
26 Jay Wells 24 .20 .50

1990-91 Sabres Campbell's

The 1990-91 Buffalo Sabres Team Photo Album was sponsored by Campbell's. It consists of three large sheets, each measuring approximately 10" by 13 1/2" and joined together to form one continuous sheet. The first panel has a team photo of the Sabres in street clothing. The second and third panels present four rows of four cards each (31 player cards plus a Sabres' logo card). After perforation, the cards measure approximately 2 1/2" by 3 3/8". They feature color posed photos bordered in white, on a dark blue background. The player's name is given above the picture, with the Sabres' logo, uniform number, and Franco-American logo below the picture. The back has biographical and statistical information in a horizontal format. We have checklisted the names below in alphabetical order, with the uniform number to the right of the name.

COMPLETE SET (32) 6.00 15.00
1 Dave Andreychuk 25 .30 .75
2 Donald Audette 28 .40 1.00
3 Doug Bodger 8 .20 .50
4 Greg Brown 9 .20 .50
5 Bob Corkum 19 .20 .50
6 Rick Dudley CO .08 .25
7 Mike Foligno 17 .30 .75
8 Mike Hartman 20 .20 .50
9 Dale Hawerchuk 10 .40 1.00
10 Benoit Hogue 33 .25 .60
11 Dean Kennedy 26 .20 .50
12 Uwe Krupp 4 .30 .75
13 Grant Ledyard 3 .20 .50
14 Darcy Loewen 36 .20 .50
15 Mikko Makela 42 .20 .50
16 Clint Malarchuk 30 .30 .75
17 Brad Miller 44 .20 .50
18 Alexander Mogilny 89 1.25 3.00
19 Daren Puppa 31 .40 1.00
20 Mike Ramsey 5 .20 .50
21 Robert Ray 32 .30 .75
22 Christian Ruuttu 21 .20 .50
23 Jiri Sejba 23 .20 .50
24 Darrin Shannon 16 .20 .50
25 Dave Snuggerud 18 .20 .50
26 John Tortorella CO .08 .25
27 John Tucker 7 .20 .50
28 Pierre Turgeon 77 .60 1.50
29 Rick Vaive 22 .20 .50
30 John Van Boxmeer CO .08 .25
31 Jay Wells 24 .20 .50
xx Large Team Photo .40 1.00
(In street clothes)

1991-92 Sabres Blue Shield

This 26-card postcard set of Buffalo Sabres measuring approximately 4" by 6" features an action photograph enclosed in white and blue borders. The player's name, date, and team name appear in blue lettering on a gold background and are flanked on the right and left by the team logo and Blue Shield of Western New York's logo. Biographical information and the player's jersey number appear in blue over gold within a blue border at the bottom. Card backs carry a large Blue Shield logo and motto on the left side. The cards are unnumbered and checklisted below in alphabetical order, with the jersey number to the right of the name.

COMPLETE SET (26) 6.00 15.00
1 Dave Andreychuk 25 .40 1.00
2 Donald Audette 28 .30 .75
3 Doug Bodger 8 .25 .60
4 Gord Donnelly 34 .20 .50
5 Tom Draper 35 .25 .60
6 Kevin Haller 7 .20 .50
7 Dale Hawerchuk 10 .60 1.50
8 Randy Hillier 23 .20 .50
9 Pat LaFontaine 16 1.25 3.00
10 Grant Ledyard 3 .20 .50
11 Clint Malarchuk 30 .30 .75
12 Brad May 27 .40 1.00
13 Brad Miller 44 .20 .50
14 Alexander Mogilny 89 .75 2.00
15 Colin Patterson 17 .20 .50
16 Daren Puppa 31 .40 1.00
17 Mike Ramsey 5 .20 .50
18 Robert Ray 32 .30 .75
19 Christian Ruuttu 21 .20 .50
20 Dave Snuggerud 18 .20 .50
21 Ken Sutton 41 .20 .50
22 Tony Tanti 19 .20 .50
23 Rick Vaive 22 .25 .60
24 Jay Wells 24 .20 .50
25 Randy Wood 15 .20 .50
26 Sabretooth (Mascot) .08 .25

1991-92 Sabres Pepsi/Campbell's

The 1991-92 Buffalo Sabres Team Photo Album was sponsored in two different varieties. One version was sponsored by Pepsi in conjunction with the Sheriff's Office of Erie County. The Pepsi logo appears on both sides of each card. A second version was sponsored by Campbell's; the card fronts have the Campbell's Chunky soup logo and the flipside carries the Franco-American emblem. The set consists of three large sheets, joined together to form one continuous sheet. The first panel has a team photo of the Sabres in street clothing, superimposed over lightning streaks on the left side. The second (10" by 13") and third (7 1/2" by 13") panels present 28 cards; after perforation, the cards measure 2 1/2" by 3 1/4". The color action photos are full-bleed on three sides; the blue border running down their right side carries the jersey number, team logo, player's name (on a gold band which jets out into the photo), and the Pepsi logo. The backs list biographical and statistical information. The cards are unnumbered and checklisted below in alphabetical order, with the jersey number to the right of the name.

COMPLETE SET (29) 6.00 15.00
1 Dave Andreychuk 25 .40 1.00
2 Donald Audette 28 .30 .75
3 Doug Bodger 8 .25 .60
4 Gord Donnelly 34 .20 .50
5 Tom Draper 35 .25 .60
6 Kevin Haller 7 .20 .50
7 Dale Hawerchuk 10 .60 1.50
8 Randy Hillier 23 .20 .50
9 Pat LaFontaine 16 .75 2.00
10 Grant Ledyard 3 .20 .50
11 Clint Malarchuk 30 .30 .75
12 Brad May 27 .40 1.00
13 Brad Miller 44 .20 .50
14 Alexander Mogilny 89 1.25 3.00
15 Colin Patterson 17 .20 .50
16 Daren Puppa 31 .40 1.00
17 Mike Ramsey 5 .20 .50
18 Robert Ray 32 .30 .75
19 Christian Ruuttu 21 .20 .50
20 Dave Snuggerud 18 .20 .50
21 Ken Sutton 41 .20 .50
22 Tony Tanti 19 .20 .50
23 Rick Vaive 22 .20 .50
24 Jay Wells 24 .20 .50
25 Randy Wood 15 .20 .50
26 Sabretooth (Mascot) .08 .25
27 Team Logo .08 .25
28 NHL Logo .08 .25
xx Large Team Photo .40 1.00
(In street clothes)

1992-93 Sabres Blue Shield

Sponsored by Blue Shield of Western New York, this 26-card postcard set measures approximately 4" by 6" and features color action player photos. In a mustard-colored box at the top are printed the player's name, the year and team name, and the team and sponsor logos. In a mustard-colored box at the bottom is biographical information. These boxes and the photo are outlined by a thin royal blue line. The horizontal backs have a light blue postcard design with the sponsor logo and a "Wellness Goal." The cards are unnumbered and checklisted below in alphabetical order.

COMPLETE SET (26) 6.00 15.00
1 Dave Andreychuk .30 .75
2 Donald Audette .30 .75
3 Doug Bodger .15 .40
4 Bob Corkum .15 .40
5 Gord Donnelly .15 .40
6 Dave Hannan .15 .40
7 Dominik Hasek 2.50 6.00
8 Dale Hawerchuk .40 1.00
9 Yuri Khmylev .15 .40
10 Pat LaFontaine .60 1.50
11 Grant Ledyard .15 .40
12 Brad May .20 .50
13 Alexander Mogilny .60 1.50
14 Randy Moller .15 .40
15 John Muckler CO .15 .40
16 Colin Patterson .15 .40
17 Wayne Presley .15 .40
18 Daren Puppa .30 .75
19 Mike Ramsey .15 .40
20 Rob Ray .30 .75
21 Richard Smehlik .15 .40
22 Ken Sutton .15 .40
23 Petr Svoboda .20 .50
24 Bob Sweeney .15 .40
25 Randy Wood .15 .40
26 Sabretooth (Mascot) .02 .10

1992-93 Sabres Jubilee Foods

Printed on thin white stock, the cards of this set, which are subtitled "Junior Fan Club," measure approximately 4" by 7" and feature color action shots of Sabres players on their fronts. These photos are borderless, except across the bottom, where a half-inch wide, mustard-colored stripe carries the sponsor's name. A thin blue stripe edges the card at the very bottom. The player's name appears vertically in blue lettering down one side. The Junior Fan Club logo in the lower left straddles the bottom of the photo and the two stripes. The backs have the player's name and biography in the upper left and the Sabres logo in the upper right. Beneath are highlights and stats from the 1991-92 season. The Stanley Cup logo at the bottom rounds out the card. The cards are unnumbered and checklisted below in alphabetical order.

COMPLETE SET (16) 4.80 12.00
1 Dave Andreychuk .30 .75
2 Doug Bodger .15 .40
3 Gord Donnelly .40 1.00
Rob Ray
4 Dominik Hasek 2.50 6.00
Daren Puppa
5 Dale Hawerchuk .40 1.00
6 Yuri Khmylev .15 .40
Viktor Gordijuk
7 Pat LaFontaine .60 1.50
8 Brad May .30 .75
9 Alexander Mogilny .60 1.50
10 Randy Moller .15 .40
Ken Sutton
11 Wayne Presley .30 .75
Donald Audette
12 Mike Ramsey .15 .40
13 Richard Smehlik .15 .40
Bob Corkum
14 Petr Svoboda .20 .50
15 Bob Sweeney .15 .40
16 Randy Wood .15 .40

1993-94 Sabres Limited Edition Team Issue

Given out one per fan at a Sabres home game during the 93-94 season, these blank back cards with color action photos on the front are limited to 5,000 sets. There is a yellow stripe at the bottom of the card with the players name, and Sabres logo. Cards are unnumbered and checklisted below in alphabetical order.

COMPLETE SET (4) 4.00 10.00
1 Doug Bodger .40 1.00
2 Dominik Hasek 2.00 5.00
3 Dale Hawerchuk .75 2.00
4 Alexander Mogilny 1.25 3.00

1993-94 Sabres Noco

Subtitled Sabres Stars and issued in five-card perforated strips, these 20 standard-size cards feature on their fronts white-bordered color player action shots framed by a yellow line. The player's name and the team logo appear in the white margin below the photo. The white back carries the player's name and number at the top, followed below by statistics and career highlights. The logo for the set's sponsor, Noco Express Shop, rounds out the card at the bottom. The cards are unnumbered and checklisted below in alphabetical order.

COMPLETE SET (20) 4.80 12.00
1 Roger Crozier .25 .60
2 Rick Dudley .20 .50
3 Mike Foligno .20 .50
4 Grant Fuhr .40 1.00
5 Danny Gare .20 .50
6 Dominik Hasek 2.00 5.00
7 Dale Hawerchuk .30 .75
8 Tim Horton .75 2.00
9 Pat LaFontaine .50 1.25
10 Don Luce .20 .50
11 Rick Martin .30 .75

12 Brad May .25 .60
13 Alexander Mogilny .50 1.25
14 Gilbert Perreault .40 1.00
15 Craig Ramsay .20 .50
16 Mike Ramsey .20 .50
17 Rene Robert .25 .60
18 Sabretooth Mascot .15 .40
19 Jim Schoenfeld .30 .75
20 Knoxes Unveil .15 .40
Sabres Uniform
Northrup Knox
Punc

2002-03 Sabres Team Issue

This oversized (5X7) set features action photos on the front and blank backs. It was printed on very thin stock. The cards likely were handed out as promotional items at signing appearances. It's possible the checklist is not complete. Internal documents revealed that just 500 copies were printed for Mair, Hecht, Noronen, Patrick and Campbell. 1,000 copies of each were printed of the remaining players.

COMPLETE SET (14) 10.00 20.00
1 Stu Barnes .75 2.00
2 Martin Biron .75 2.00
3 Eric Boulton .75 2.00
4 Brian Campbell .75 2.00
5 Tim Connolly .40 1.00
6 Jochen Hecht .75 2.00
7 Dmitri Kalinin .40 1.00
8 Adam Mair .75 2.00
9 Jay McKee .40 1.00
10 Mika Noronen .75 2.00
11 James Patrick .75 2.00
12 Taylor Pyatt .40 1.00
13 Rob Ray .75 2.00
14 Rhett Warrener .40 1.00

1974-75 San Diego Mariners WHA

Sponsored by Dean's Photo Service Inc., this set of seven photos measured approximately 5 3/8" by 8 1/2" and featured black-and-white action pictures against a white background on thin paper stock. The player's name appeared in the white margin below the photo along with the team and sponsor logos. The backs featured biographical information, career highlights, and statistics. The cards came in a light blue paper "picture pack" with the team and sponsor logos and game dates suggested for acquiring autographs. The cards were unnumbered and checklisted below in alphabetical order. This set may be incomplete; additions to the checklist would be welcome.

COMPLETE SET (7) 20.00 40.00
1 Andre Lacroix 5.00 10.00
2 Mike Laughton 2.50 5.00
3 Brian Morenz 2.50 5.00
4 Kevin Morrison 2.50 5.00
5 Gene Peacosh 2.50 5.00
6 Ron Plumb 4.00 8.00
7 Craig Reichmuth 2.50 5.00

1976-77 San Diego Mariners WHA

These cards measure 5" x 8" and were issued in two sheets of seven players each. Card fronts feature black and white photos with a white border. Backs feature player statistics. Cards are unnumbered and checklisted below alphabetically. Prices below are for individual cards.

COMPLETE SET (14) 20.00 40.00
1 Kevin Devine 1.25 2.50
2 Bob Dobek 1.25 2.50
3 Norm Ferguson 1.25 2.50
4 Brent Hughes 1.25 2.50
5 Randy Legge 1.25 2.50
6 Ken Lockett 1.25 2.50
7 Kevin Morrison 1.25 2.50
8 Joe Norris 1.25 2.50
9 Gerry Pinder 2.00 4.00
10 Brad Rhiness 1.25 2.50
11 Wayne Rivers 2.00 4.00
12 Paul Shmyr 1.50 3.00
13 Gary Veneruzzo 1.50 3.00
14 Ernie Wakely 2.50 5.00

1932 Sanella Margarine

The cards in this set measure approximately 2 3/4" by 4 1/8" and feature color images of famous athletes printed on thin stock. The cards were created in Germany and originally designed to be pasted into an album called "Handbook of Sports." The Ruth, and possibly the other cards in the set, was created in four versions with slight differences being found on the cardbacks.

2 Ice Hockey 25.00 50.00

1994 Santa Fe Hotel and Casino Manon Rheaume Postcard

Card is full color, and measures 3" x 5". Was given out as promotional piece for the Santa Fe Hotel and Casino in Las Vegas. Item is limited to 10,000 pieces.

NNO Manon Rheaume 2.00 5.00

1970-71 Sargent Promotions Stamps

This set consists of 224 total stamps, 16 for each NHL team. Individual stamps measure approximately 2" by 2 1/2". The set could be put into a album featuring Bobby Orr on the cover. Stamp fronts feature a full-color head shot of the player, player's name, and team. The stamp number is located in the upper left corner. The 1970-71 set features one-time appearances in Eddie Sargent Promotions sets by Hall of Famers Gordie Howe, Jean Beliveau, Andy Bathgate. The set also features first appearances of Gil Perreault, Brad Park, and Bobby Clarke. The three have Rookie Cards in both Topps and O-Pee-Chee for the same year.

COMPLETE SET (224) 325.00 650.00
1 Bobby Orr 62.50 125.00
2 Don Awrey .50 1.00
3 Derek Sanderson 5.00 10.00
4 Ted Green .63 1.25
5 Eddie Johnston 1.25 2.50
6 Wayne Carleton .50 1.00
7 Ed Westfall .75 1.50
8 Johnny Bucyk 2.50 5.00
9 John McKenzie .50 1.00
10 Ken Hodge 1.00 2.00
11 Rick Smith .50 1.00
12 Fred Stanfield .50 1.00
13 Garnet Bailey .50 1.00
14 Phil Esposito 10.00 20.00
15 Gerry Cheevers 5.00 10.00
16 Dallas Smith .50 1.00
17 Joe Daley 1.00 2.00
18 Ron Anderson .50 1.00
19 Tracy Pratt .50 1.00
20 Gerry Meehan .75 1.50
21 Reg Fleming .50 1.00
22 Al Hamilton .63 1.25
23 Gil Perreault 12.50 25.00
24 Skip Krake .50 1.00
25 Kevin O'Shea .50 1.00
26 Roger Crozier 1.50 3.00
27 Bill Inglis .50 1.00
28 Mike McMahon .50 1.00
29 Cliff Schmautz .50 1.00
30 Floyd Smith .50 1.00
31 Randy Wyrozub .50 1.00
32 Jim Watson .50 1.00
33 Tony Esposito 15.00 30.00
34 Doug Jarrett .50 1.00
35 Keith Magnuson .63 1.25
36 Dennis Hull 1.00 2.00
37 Cliff Koroll .50 1.00
38 Eric Nesterenko .75 1.50
39 Pit Martin .63 1.25
40 Lou Angotti .50 1.00
41 Jim Pappin .63 1.25
42 Gerry Pinder .63 1.25
43 Bobby Hull 25.00 50.00
44 Pat Stapleton .63 1.25
45 Gerry Desjardins 1.00 2.00
46 Chico Maki .63 1.25
47 Doug Mohns .63 1.25
48 Stan Mikita 10.00 20.00
49 Gary Bergman .63 1.25
50 Pete Stemkowski .63 1.25
51 Bruce MacGregor .50 1.00
52 Ron Harris .50 1.00
53 Billy Dea .50 1.00
54 Wayne Connelly .50 1.00
55 Dale Rolfe .50 1.00
56 Gordie Howe 40.00 80.00
57 Tom Webster .63 1.25
58 Al Karlander .50 1.00
59 Alex Delvecchio 2.50 5.00
60 Nick Libett .63 1.25
61 Garry Unger 1.00 2.00
62 Roy Edwards 1.00 2.00
63 Frank Mahovlich 5.00 10.00
64 Bob Baun 1.25 2.50
65 Dick Duff 1.00 2.00
66 Ross Lonsberry .50 1.00
67 Ed Joyal .50 1.00
68 Dale Hoganson .50 1.00
69 Eddie Shack 2.50 5.00
70 Real Lemieux .50 1.00
71 Matt Ravlich .50 1.00
72 Bob Pulford 1.50 3.00
73 Denis DeJordy 1.25 2.50
74 Larry Mickey .50 1.00
75 Bill Flett .50 1.00
76 Juha Widing .75 1.50
77 Jim Peters .63 1.25
78 Gilles Marotte .63 1.25
79 Larry Cahan .50 1.00
80 Howie Hughes .50 1.00
81 Cesare Maniago 1.25 2.50
82 Ted Harris .50 1.00
83 Tom Williams .50 1.00
84 Gump Worsley 5.00 10.00
85 Tom Reid .50 1.00
86 Murray Oliver .50 1.00
87 Charlie Burns .50 1.00
88 Jude Drouin .50 1.00
89 Walt McKechnie .50 1.00
90 Danny O'Shea .50 1.00
91 Barry Gibbs .50 1.00
92 Danny Grant .63 1.25
93 Bob Barlow .50 1.00
94 J.P. Parise .63 1.25
95 Bill Goldsworthy .75 1.50
96 Bobby Rousseau .63 1.25
97 Jacques Laperriere 1.00 2.00
98 Henri Richard 5.00 10.00
99 J.C. Tremblay .75 1.50
100 Rogie Vachon 4.00 8.00
101 Claude Larose .50 1.00
102 Pete Mahovlich .75 1.50
103 Jacques Lemaire 4.00 8.00
104 Bill Collins .50 1.00
105 Guy Lapointe 1.50 3.00
106 Mickey Redmond 2.50 5.00
107 Larry Pleau .63 1.25
108 Jean Beliveau 12.50 25.00
109 Yvan Cournoyer 4.00 8.00
110 Serge Savard 4.00 8.00
111 Terry Harper .63 1.25
112 Phil Myre 1.00 2.00
113 Syl Apps .63 1.25
114 Ted Irvine .50 1.00
115 Ed Giacomin 5.00 10.00
116 Arnie Brown .50 1.00
117 Walt Tkaczuk .63 1.25
118 Jean Ratelle 2.50 5.00
119 Dave Balon .50 1.00
120 Ron Stewart .50 1.00
121 Jim Neilson .50 1.00
122 Rod Gilbert 2.50 5.00
123 Bill Fairbairn .50 1.00
124 Brad Park 10.00 20.00
125 Tim Horton 7.50 15.00
126 Vic Hadfield .75 1.50
127 Bob Nevin .50 1.00
128 Rod Seiling .50 1.00
129 Gary Smith 1.25 2.50
130 Carol Vadnais .50 1.00
131 Bert Marshall .50 1.00
132 Earl Ingarfield .50 1.00
133 Dennis Hextall .63 1.25
134 Harry Howell 1.50 3.00
135 Wayne Muloin .50 1.00
136 Mike Laughton .50 1.00
137 Ted Hampson .50 1.00
138 Doug Roberts .50 1.00
139 Dick Mattiussi .50 1.00
140 Gary Jarrett .50 1.00
141 Gary Croteau .50 1.00
142 Norm Ferguson .50 1.00
143 Bill Hicke .50 1.00
144 Gerry Ehman .50 1.00
145 Ralph McSweyn .50 1.00
146 Bernie Parent 7.50 15.00
147 Brent Hughes .50 1.00
148 Bobby Clarke 20.00 40.00
149 Gary Dornhoefer .63 1.25
150 Simon Nolet .50 1.00
151 Garry Peters .50 1.00
152 Doug Favell 1.25 2.50
153 Jim Johnson .50 1.00
154 Andre Lacroix .75 1.50
155 Larry Hale .50 1.00
156 Joe Watson .50 1.00
157 Jean-Guy Gendron .50 1.00
158 Larry Hillman .50 1.00
159 Ed Van Impe .50 1.00
160 Wayne Hillman .50 1.00
161 Al Smith 1.00 2.00
162 Jean Pronovost .63 1.25
163 Bob Woytowich .50 1.00
164 Bryan Watson .63 1.25
165 Dean Prentice .75 1.50
166 Duane Rupp .50 1.00
167 Glen Sather 1.00 2.00
168 Keith McCreary .50 1.00
169 Jim Morrison .50 1.00
170 Ron Schock .50 1.00
171 Wally Boyer .50 1.00
172 Nick Harbaruk .50 1.00
173 Andy Bathgate 2.50 5.00
174 Ken Schinkel .50 1.00
175 Les Binkley 1.00 2.00
176 Val Fonteyne .50 1.00
177 Red Berenson .75 1.50
178 Ab McDonald .50 1.00
179 Jim Roberts .50 1.00
180 Frank St. Marseille .50 1.00
181 Ernie Wakely 1.25 2.50
182 Terry Crisp .63 1.25
183 Bob Plager .75 1.50
184 Barclay Plager .75 1.50
185 Chris Bordeleau .50 1.00
186 Gary Sabourin .50 1.00
187 Bill Plager .63 1.25
188 Tim Ecclestone .50 1.00
189 Jean-Guy Talbot .75 1.50
190 Noel Picard .50 1.00
191 Bob Wall .50 1.00
192 Jim Lorentz .50 1.00
193 Bruce Gamble 1.50 3.00
194 Jim Harrison .50 1.00
195 Paul Henderson 1.50 3.00
196 Brian Glennie .50 1.00
197 Jim Dorey .50 1.00
198 Rick Ley .63 1.25
199 Jacques Plante 12.50 25.00
200 Ron Ellis .75 1.50
201 Jim McKenny .50 1.00
202 Brit Selby .50 1.00
203 Mike Pelyk .50 1.00
204 Norm Ullman 2.50 5.00
205 Bill MacMillan .50 1.00
206 Mike Walton .63 1.25
207 Garry Monahan .50 1.00
208 Dave Keon 2.50 5.00
209 Pat Quinn 1.00 2.00
210 Wayne Maki .50 1.00
211 Charlie Hodge 1.25 2.50
212 Orland Kurtenbach .63 1.25
213 Paul Popiel .63 1.25
214 Dan Johnson .50 1.00
215 Dale Tallon .63 1.25
216 Ray Cullen .63 1.25
217 Bob Dillabough .50 1.00
218 Gary Doak .50 1.00
219 Andre Boudrias .75 1.50
220 Rosaire Paiement .63 1.25
221 Darryl Sly .50 1.00
222 George Gardner .50 1.00
223 Jim Wiste .50 1.00
224 Murray Hall .50 1.00
NNO Stamp Album 17.50 35.00
(Bobby Orr on cover)

1971-72 Sargent Promotions Stamps

Issued by Eddie Sargent Promotions in a series of 16 ten-cent sheets of 14 NHL players each, this 224-stamp set featured posed color photos of players in their NHLPA jerseys. The pictures are framed on their tops and sides in different color borders with the players' names and teams appearing along the bottom. Each sheet measured approximately 7 7/8" by 10" and was divided into four rows, with four 2" by 2 1/2" stamps per row. Two of these 16 sections gave the series number (e.g., Series 1), resulting in a total of 14 players per sheet. The sections are perforated and the backs are blank. There was a stamp album (approximately 9 1/2" by 13") which featured information on the team history and individual players. The stamps are numbered in the upper left corner and they are grouped into 14 teams of 16 players each as follows: Boston Bruins (1-16), Buffalo Sabres (17-32), Chicago Blackhawks (33-48), Detroit Red Wings (49-64), Los Angeles Kings (65-80), Minnesota North Stars (81-96), Montreal Canadiens (97-112), New York Rangers (113-128), California Golden Seals (129-144), Philadelphia Flyers (145-160), Pittsburgh Penguins (161-176), St. Louis Blues (177-192), Toronto Maple Leafs (193-208), and Vancouver Canucks (209-224).

COMPLETE SET (224) 225.00 450.00
1 Fred Stanfield .50 1.00
2 Ed Westfall .75 1.50
3 John McKenzie .50 1.00
4 Derek Sanderson 4.00 8.00
5 Rick Smith .50 1.00
6 Teddy Green .63 1.25
7 Phil Esposito 7.50 15.00
8 Ken Hodge 1.00 2.00
9 Johnny Bucyk 4.00 8.00
10 Bobby Orr 50.00 100.00
11 Dallas Smith .50 1.00
12 Mike Walton .63 1.25
13 Don Awrey .50 1.00
14 Unknown .50 1.00
15 Eddie Johnston 1.00 2.00
16 Gerry Cheevers 4.00 8.00
17 Gerry Meehan .75 1.50
18 Ron Anderson .50 1.00
19 Gilbert Perreault 6.00 12.00
20 Eddie Shack 2.00 4.00
21 Jim Watson .50 1.00
22 Kevin O'Shea .50 1.00
23 Al Hamilton .50 1.00
24 Dick Duff .75 1.50
25 Tracy Pratt .50 1.00
26 Don Luce .50 1.00
27 Roger Crozier 1.00 2.00
28 Doug Barrie .50 1.00
29 Mike Robitaille .50 1.00
30 Phil Goyette .50 1.00
31 Larry Keenan .50 1.00
32 Dave Dryden 1.00 2.00
33 Stan Mikita 6.00 12.00
34 Bobby Hull 20.00 40.00
35 Cliff Koroll .50 1.00
36 Chico Maki .63 1.25
37 Danny O'Shea .50 1.00
38 Lou Angotti .50 1.00
39 Andre Lacroix .63 1.25
40 Jim Pappin .50 1.00
41 Doug Jarrett .50 1.00
42 Pit Martin .63 1.25
43 Gary Smith 1.00 2.00
44 Tony Esposito 7.50 15.00
45 Pat Stapleton .50 1.00
46 Dennis Hull 1.00 2.00
47 Bill White .50 1.00
48 Keith Magnuson .63 1.25
49 Bill Collins .50 1.00
50 Bob Wall .50 1.00
51 Red Berenson .75 1.50
52 Mickey Redmond 1.50 3.00
53 Nick Libett .50 1.00
54 Gary Bergman .63 1.25
55 Alex Delvecchio 2.50 5.00
56 Tim Ecclestone .50 1.00
57 Arnie Brown .50 1.00
58 Ron Harris .50 1.00
59 Ab McDonald .50 1.00
60 Guy Charron .63 1.25
61 Al Smith 1.00 2.00
62 Joe Daley 1.00 2.00
63 Leon Rochefort .50 1.00
64 Ron Stackhouse .50 1.00
65A Larry Johnston .75 1.50
65B Juha Widing .50 1.00
66 Bob Pulford 1.00 2.00
67 Bill Flett .50 1.00
68 Rogie Vachon 2.50 5.00
69 Ross Lonsberry .50 1.00
70 Gilles Marotte .50 1.00
71 Harry Howell 1.00 2.00
72 Real Lemieux .50 1.00
73 Butch Goring .50 1.00
74 Ed Joyal .50 1.00
75 Larry Hillman .50 1.00
76 Lucien Grenier .50 1.00
77 Paul Curtis .50 1.00
78 Unknown .50 1.00
79 Unknown .50 1.00
80 Unknown .50 1.00
81 Jude Drouin .50 1.00
82 Tom Reid .50 1.00
83 J.P. Parise .63 1.25
84 Doug Mohns .63 1.25
85 Danny Grant .63 1.25
86 Bill Goldsworthy .75 1.50
87 Charlie Burns .50 1.00
88 Murray Oliver .50 1.00
89 Dean Prentice .75 1.50
90 Bob Nevin .63 1.25
91 Ted Harris .63 1.25
92 Cesare Maniago 1.00 2.00
93 Lou Nanne .63 1.25
94 Ted Hampton .50 1.00
95 Barry Gibbs .50 1.00
96 Gump Worsley 4.00 8.00
97 J.C. Tremblay .75 1.50
98 Guy Lapointe 1.00 2.00
99 Pete Mahovlich .75 1.50
100 Larry Pleau .63 1.25
101 Phil Myre 1.00 2.00
102 Yvan Cournoyer 2.50 5.00
103 Henri Richard 5.00 10.00
104 Frank Mahovlich 5.00 10.00
105 Jacques Lemaire 2.00 4.00
106 Claude Larose .50 1.00
107 Terry Harper .63 1.25
108 Jacques Laperriere 1.00 2.00
109 Phil Roberto .50 1.00
110 Serge Savard 2.00 4.00
111 Marc Tardif .63 1.25
112 Pierre Bouchard .63 1.25
113 Rod Gilbert 2.50 5.00
114 Jean Ratelle 2.50 5.00
115 Pete Stemkowski .50 1.00
116 Brad Park 4.00 8.00
117 Bobby Rousseau .50 1.00
118 Dale Rolfe .50 1.00
119 Rod Seiling .50 1.00
120 Walt Tkaczuk .50 1.00
121 Vic Hadfield .63 1.25
122 Jim Neilson .50 1.00
123 Bill Fairbairn .50 1.00
124 Bruce MacGregor .50 1.00
125 Dave Balon .50 1.00
126 Ted Irvine .50 1.00
127 Gilles Villemure 1.00 2.00
128 Ed Giacomin 4.00 8.00
129 Walt McKechnie .50 1.00
130 Tom Williams .50 1.00
131 Wayne Carleton .63 1.25
132 Gerry Pinder .50 1.00
133 Gary Croteau .50 1.00
134 Bert Marshall .50 1.00
135 Tom Webster .50 1.00
136 Norm Ferguson .50 1.00
137 Carol Vadnais .50 1.00
138 Gary Jarrett .50 1.00
139 Ernie Hicke .50 1.00
140 Paul Shmyr .50 1.00
141 Marshall Johnston .50 1.00
142 Don O'Donoghue .50 1.00
143 Joey Johnston .50 1.00
144 Dick Redmond .50 1.00
145 Simon Nolet .50 1.00
146 Wayne Hillman .50 1.00
147 Brent Hughes .50 1.00
148 Jim Johnson .50 1.00
149 Larry Mickey .50 1.00
150 Ed Van Impe .50 1.00
151 Gary Dornhoefer .63 1.25
152 Bobby Clarke 12.50 25.00
153 Jean-Guy Gendron .50 1.00
154 Larry Hale .50 1.00
155 Serge Bernier .50 1.00
156 Doug Favell 1.00 2.00
157 Bob Kelly .50 1.00
158 Joe Watson .50 1.00
159 Larry Brown .50 1.00
160 Bruce Gamble 1.00 2.00
161 Syl Apps .63 1.25
162 Ken Schinkel .50 1.00
163 Val Fonteyne .50 1.00
164 Bryan Watson .75 1.50
165 Bob Woytowich .50 1.00
166 Les Binkley 1.00 2.00
167 Roy Edwards 1.00 2.00
168 Jean Pronovost .63 1.25
169 Tim Horton 6.00 12.00
170 Ron Schock .50 1.00
171 Nick Harbaruk .50 1.00
172 Greg Polis .50 1.00
173 Bryan Hextall .63 1.25
174 Keith McCreary .50 1.00
175 Bill Hicke .50 1.00
176 Jim Rutherford 1.00 2.00
177 Gary Sabourin .50 1.00
178 Garry Unger 1.00 2.00
179 Terry Crisp .63 1.25
180 Noel Picard .50 1.00
181 Jim Roberts .50 1.00
182 Barclay Plager .75 1.50
183 Brit Selby .50 1.00
184 Frank St. Marseille .50 1.00
185 Ernie Wakely 1.00 2.00
186 Wayne Connelly .50 1.00
187 Chris Bordeleau .50 1.00
188 Bill Sutherland .50 1.00
189 Bob Plager .75 1.50
190 Bill Plager .63 1.25
191 George Morrison .50 1.00
192 Jim Lorentz .50 1.00
193 Norm Ullman 2.50 5.00
194 Jim McKenny .50 1.00
195 Rick Ley .50 1.00
196 Bob Baun 1.00 2.00
197 Mike Pelyk .50 1.00
198 Bill MacMillan .50 1.00
199 Garry Monahan .50 1.00
200 Paul Henderson 1.50 3.00
201 Jim Dorey .50 1.00
202 Jim Harrison .50 1.00
203 Ron Ellis .75 1.50
204 Darryl Sittler 3.00 6.00
205 Bernie Parent 2.50 5.00
206 Dave Keon 2.50 5.00
207 Brad Selwood .50 1.00
208 Don Marshall .50 1.00
209 Dale Tallon .63 1.25
210 Dan Johnson .50 1.00
211 Murray Hall .50 1.00
212 Paul Popiel .63 1.25
213 George Gardner .50 1.00
214 Gary Doak .50 1.00
215 Andre Boudrias .63 1.25
216 Orland Kurtenbach .63 1.25
217 Wayne Maki .50 1.00
218 Rosaire Paiement .63 1.25
219 Pat Quinn 1.00 2.00
220 Fred Speck .50 1.00
221 Barry Wilkins .50 1.00
222 Dune Wilson 1.00 2.00
223 Ted Taylor .50 1.00
224 Mike Corrigan .50 1.00
NNO Stamp Album 12.50 25.00
(Bobby Orr on cover)

1972-73 Sargent Promotions Stamps

During the 1972-73 hockey season, Eddie Sargent Promotions produced a set of 224 stamps. They were issued in cello packages in a series of 16 sheets and, at that time, sold for ten cents per sheet with one sheet being available each week of the promotion. Each sheet measures approximately 7 7/8" by 10" and was divided into four rows, with four 2" by 2 1/2" sections per row. Since two of the 16 sections gave the series number (e.g., Series 1), color photos of fourteen-NHL players were featured in each series. The set features 224 players from sixteen NHL teams. The pictures were numbered in the upper left hand corner and are checklisted below accordingly. The pictures are framed on their top and sides in different color borders, with the player's name and the team's city name given below. There are two sticker albums (approximately 11 1/4" by 12") available for the set, both of which are bilingual. After a general introduction, the album is divided into team sections, with two pages devoted to each team. A brief history of each team is presented, followed by 14 numbered sticker slots. Biographical information and career summary appear below each stamp slot on the page itself. The typically found album has Bobby Orr on the cover. Another album is the more difficult Paul Henderson Team Canada cover. The toughest of the three is the Richard Martin cover. The stamps are numbered on the front and checklisted below alphabetically according to teams as follows: Atlanta Flames (1-14), Boston Bruins (15-28), Buffalo Sabres (29-42), California Seals (43-56), Chicago Blackhawks (57-70), Detroit Red Wings (71-84), Los Angeles Kings (85-98), Minnesota North Stars (99-112), Montreal Canadiens (113-126), New York Islanders (127-140), New York Rangers (141-154), Philadelphia Flyers (155-168), Pittsburgh Penguins (169-182), St. Louis Blues (183-196), Toronto Maple Leafs (197-210), and Vancouver Canucks (211-224).

COMPLETE SET (224) 112.50 225.00
1 Lucien Grenier .25 .50
2 Phil Myre .50 1.00
3 Ernie Hicke .25 .50
4 Keith McCreary .25 .50
5 Bill MacMillan .25 .50
6 Pat Quinn .50 1.00
7 Bill Plager .38 .75
8 Noel Price .25 .50
9 Bob Leiter .25 .50
10 Randy Manery .25 .50
11 Bob Paradise .25 .50
12 Larry Romanchych .25 .50
13 Lew Morrison .25 .50
14 Dan Bouchard .50 1.00
15 Fred Stanfield .25 .50
16 Johnny Bucyk 1.50 3.00
17 Bobby Orr 20.00 40.00
18 Wayne Cashman .38 .75
19 Dallas Smith .25 .50
20 Ed Johnston .75 1.50
21 Phil Esposito 5.00 10.00
22 Ken Hodge .50 1.00
23 Don Awrey .25 .50
24 Mike Walton .25 .50
25 Carol Vadnais .25 .50
26 Doug Roberts .25 .50
27 Don Marcotte .25 .50
28 Garnet Bailey .25 .50
29 Gerry Meehan .25 .50
30 Tracy Pratt .25 .50
31 Gilbert Perreault 2.00 4.00
32 Roger Crozier 1.00 2.00
33 Don Luce .25 .50
34 Dave Dryden .50 1.00
35 Richard Martin .50 1.00
36 Jim Lorentz .25 .50
37 Tim Horton 4.00 8.00
38 Craig Ramsay .25 .50
39 Larry Hillman .25 .50
40 Steve Atkinson .25 .50
41 Jim Schoenfeld .38 .75
42 Rene Robert .38 .75
43 Walt McKechnie .25 .50
44 Marshall Johnston .25 .50
45 Joey Johnston .25 .50
46 Dick Redmond .25 .50
47 Bert Marshall .25 .50
48 Gary Croteau .25 .50
49 Marv Edwards .50 1.00
50 Gilles Meloche .50 1.00
51 Ivan Boldirev .25 .50
52 Stan Gilbertson .25 .50
53 Peter Laframboise .25 .50
54 Reggie Leach .50 1.00
55 Craig Patrick .50 1.00
56 Bob Stewart .25 .50
57 Keith Magnuson .38 .75
58 Doug Jarrett .25 .50
59 Cliff Koroll .25 .50
60 Chico Maki .25 .50
61 Gary Smith .50 1.00
62 Bill White .25 .50
63 Stan Mikita 3.00 6.00
64 Jim Pappin .25 .50
65 Lou Angotti .25 .50
66 Tony Esposito 4.00 8.00
67 Dennis Hull .50 1.00
68 Pit Martin .25 .50
69 Pat Stapleton .25 .50
70 Dan Maloney .25 .50
71 Bill Collins .25 .50
72 Arnie Brown .25 .50
73 Red Berenson .38 .75
74 Mickey Redmond 1.00 2.00
75 Nick Libett .25 .50
76 Alex Delvecchio 1.25 2.50
77 Ron Stackhouse .25 .50
78 Tim Ecclestone .25 .50
79 Gary Bergman .25 .50
80 Guy Charron .25 .50
81 Leon Rochefort .25 .50
82 Larry Johnston .25 .50
83 Andy Brown .25 .50
84 Henry Boucha .38 .75
85 Paul Curtis .25 .50
86 Jim Stanfield .25 .50
87 Rogatien Vachon 1.50 3.00
88 Ralph Backstrom .38 .75
89 Gilles Marotte .25 .50
90 Harry Howell .75 1.50
91 Real Lemieux .25 .50
92 Butch Goring .38 .75
93 Juha Widing .25 .50
94 Mike Corrigan .25 .50
95 Larry Brown .25 .50
96 Terry Harper .38 .75
97 Serge Bernier .25 .50
98 Bob Berry .25 .50
99 Tom Reid .25 .50
100 Jude Drouin .25 .50
101 Jean-Paul Parise .38 .75
102 Doug Mohns .38 .75
103 Danny Grant .38 .75
104 Bill Goldsworthy .50 1.00
105 Gump Worsley 2.50 5.00
106 Charlie Burns .25 .50
107 Murray Oliver .25 .50
108 Barry Gibbs .25 .50
109 Ted Harris .25 .50
110 Cesare Maniago 1.00 2.00
111 Lou Nanne .38 .75
112 Bob Nevin .25 .50
113 Guy Lapointe .75 1.50
114 Peter Mahovlich .38 .75
115 Jacques Lemaire 1.00 2.00
116 Pierre Bouchard .25 .50
117 Yvan Cournoyer 1.25 2.50
118 Marc Tardif .25 .50
119 Henri Richard 2.50 5.00
120 Frank Mahovlich 2.50 5.00
121 Jacques Laperriere .75 1.50
122 Claude Larose .25 .50
123 Serge Savard 1.00 2.00
124 Ken Dryden 10.00 20.00
125 Rejean Houle .38 .75
126 Jim Roberts .25 .50
127 Ed Westfall .38 .75
128 Terry Crisp .38 .75
129 Gerry Desjardins .50 1.00
130 Denis DeJordy .75 1.50
131 Billy Harris .25 .50
132 Brian Spencer .50 1.00
133 Germaine Gagnon UER .25 .50
134 David Hedson .25 .50
135 Lorne Henning .25 .50
136 Brian Marchinko .25 .50
137 Tom Miller .25 .50
138 Gerry Hart .25 .50
139 Bryan Lefley .25 .50
140 James Mair .25 .50
141 Rod Gilbert 1.25 2.50
142 Jean Ratelle 1.25 2.50
143 Pete Stemkowski .25 .50
144 Brad Park 1.50 3.00
145 Bobby Rousseau .25 .50
146 Dale Rolfe .25 .50
147 Ed Giacomin 1.50 3.00
148 Rod Seiling .25 .50
149 Walt Tkaczuk .25 .50
150 Bill Fairbairn .25 .50
151 Vic Hadfield .38 .75
152 Ted Irvine .25 .50
153 Bruce MacGregor .25 .50
154 Jim Neilson .25 .50
155 Brent Hughes .25 .50
156 Wayne Hillman .25 .50
157 Doug Favell .75 1.50
158 Simon Nolet .25 .50
159 Joe Watson .25 .50
160 Ed Van Impe .25 .50
161 Gary Dornhoefer .38 .75
162 Bobby Clarke 5.00 10.00
163 Bob Kelly .25 .50
164 Bill Flett .25 .50
165 Rick Foley .25 .50
166 Ross Lonsberry .25 .50
167 Rick MacLeish .50 1.00
168 Bill Clement .50 1.00
169 Syl Apps .38 .75
170 Ken Schinkel .25 .50
171 Nick Harbaruk .25 .50
172 Bryan Watson .38 .75
173 Bryan Hextall .38 .75
174 Roy Edwards .50 1.00
175 Jim Rutherford .75 1.50
176 Jean Pronovost .38 .75
177 Rick Kessell .25 .50
178 Greg Polis .25 .50
179 Ron Schock .25 .50
180 Duane Rupp .25 .50
181 Darryl Edestrand .25 .50
182 Dave Burrows .25 .50
183 Gary Sabourin .25 .50
184 Garry Unger .50 1.00
185 Noel Picard .25 .50
186 Bob Plager .38 .75
187 Barclay Plager .38 .75
188 Frank St. Marseille .25 .50
189 Danny O'Shea .25 .50
190 Kevin O'Shea .25 .50
191 Wayne Stephenson .50 1.00
192 Chris Evans .25 .50
193 Jacques Caron .25
194 Andre Dupont .25
195 Mike Murphy .25
196 Jack Egers .25
197 Norm Ullman 1.25 2.
198 Jim McKenny .25
199 Bob Baun .50 1.
200 Mike Pelyk .25
201 Ron Ellis .38
202 Garry Monahan .25
203 Paul Henderson 1.00 2.
204 Darryl Sittler 1.75 3.
205 Brian Glennie .25
206 Dave Keon 1.25 2.
207 Jacques Plante 5.00 10.
208 Pierre Jarry .25
209 Rick Kehoe .38
210 Denis Dupere .25
211 Dale Tallon .38
212 Murray Hall .25
213 Dunc Wilson .50 1.
214 Andre Boudrias .38
215 Orland Kurtenbach .38
216 Wayne Maki .25
217 Barry Wilkins .25
218 Richard Lemieux .25
219 Bobby Schmautz .25
220 Dave Balon .25
221 Robert Lalonde .25
222 Jocelyn Guevremont .25
223 Gregg Boddy .25
224 Dennis Kearns .25
NNO1 Stamp Album 17.50 35.0
(Paul Hende
NNO2 Stamp Album 25.00 50.0
Richard Martin
NNO3 Stamp Album 10.00 20.0
(Bobby Orr

1990 Score Rookie/Traded

The standard-size 110-card 1990 Score Rookie and Traded set marked the third consecutive year Score h issued an end of the year set to note trades and give rookies early cards. The set was issued through hobb accounts and only in factory set form. The first 66 cards are traded players while the last 44 cards are rookie cards. Hockey star Eric Lindros is included in this set. Rookie Cards in the set include Derek Bell, Todd Hundley and Ray Lankford.

COMP.FACT.SET (110) 1.25 3.0
100T Eric Lindros .40 1.0

1990-91 Score Promos

The 1990-91 Score Promo set contains six different player standard-size cards. The promos were issued i both a Canadian and an American version. Three (10 Patrick Roy, 40 Gary Leeman, and 100 Mark Messier) were distributed as Canadian promos and the other three were given to U.S. card dealer accounts. Thoug all these promo versions have the same numbering as the regular issues, several of them are easily distinguished from their regular issue counterparts. The Roy and Messier promos have different player photos on their fronts (Roy promo also has a different photo on its back). The photo on the front of the Roenick promo is cropped differently, and the blurb o its back is also slightly different. Even for those promos that appear to be otherwise identical with the regular cards, close inspection reveals the following distinguishing marks: 1) on the backs, the promos have the registered mark (circle R) by the Score logo, whereas the regular issues have instead the trademark (TM); and 2) on the back, the NHL logo is slightly larger on the promos and the text around it is only in English (the regular issues also have a French translation).

1A Wayne Gretzky ERR 25.00 60.0
(Catches left in cardback bio)
1B Wayne Gretzky COR 10.00 25.0
(Shoots left in cardback bio)
10 Patrick Roy 8.00 20.0
(kick save photo on front)
40 Gary Leeman .30 .75
100A Mark Messier ERR 6.00 15.0
(Won Smythe in 1990)
100B Mark Messier COR 2.50 6.0
(Won Smythe in 1984)
179 Jeremy Roenick 2.00 5.0
200 Ray Bourque 2.50 6.0

1990-91 Score

The 1990-91 Score hockey set contains 440 standard-size cards. The fronts feature a color action photo, superimposed over blue and red stripes on a white background. The team logo appears in the upper left hand corner, while an image of a hockey player (in various colors) appears in the lower right hand corner. The backs are outlined in a blue border and show a head shot of the player on the upper half. The career statistics and highlights on the lower half are printed on a pale yellow background. The complete factory set price includes the five Eric Lindros bonus cards (B1-B5) that were only available in the factory sets sold to hobby dealers.

COMPLETE SET (440) 10.00 25.00
COMP.FACT.SET (445) 12.00 30.00
BEWARE LINDROS RC COUNTERFEITS
1 Wayne Gretzky .75 2.00
2 Mario Lemieux .60 1.50
3 Steve Yzerman .50 1.25
4 Cam Neely .15 .40
5 Al MacInnis .12 .30
6 Paul Coffey .15 .40
7 Brian Bellows .12 .30
8 Joe Sakic .50 1.25
9 Bernie Nicholls .15 .40
10 Patrick Roy .40 1.00
11 Doug Houda RC .15 .40
12 David Volek .15 .40
13 Esa Tikkanen .12 .30
14 Thomas Steen .12 .30
15 Chris Chelios .15 .40
16 Bob Carpenter .12 .30
17 Dirk Graham .12 .30
18 Garth Butcher .12 .30
19 Patrik Sundstrom .15 .40
20 Rod Langway .15 .40
21 Scott Young .10 .25
22 Ulf Dahlen .15 .40
23 Mike Ramsey .10 .25
24 Peter Zezel .15 .40
25 Ron Hextall .12 .30
26 Steve Duchesne .10 .25
27 Allan Bester .15 .40
28 Everett Sanipass RC .12 .30
29 Steve Konroyd .10 .25
30A Joe Nieuwendyk ERR .10 .25
30B Joe Nieuwendyk COR .10 .25
31A Brent Ashton ERR .15 .40
(No position on card front)
31B Brent Ashton COR .15 .40
(LW on card front)

Trevor Linden .12 .30
Mike Ridley .10 .25
Sean Burke .12 .30
Pat Verbeek .12 .30
Rob Ramage .15 .40
Kelly Kisio .12 .30
Craig Muni .12 .30
Brent Sutter .12 .30
Gary Leeman .12 .30
Jeff Brown .15 .40
Greg Millen .12 .30
Alexander Mogilny RC .50 1.25
Dale Hunter .15 .40
Randy Moller .15 .40
Peter Sidorkiewicz .15 .40
Terry Carkner .12 .30
Tony Granato .12 .30
Shawn Burr .12 .30
Dale Hawerchuk .20 .50
A Don Sweeney RC .10 .25
Mike Vernon UER .15 .40
Kevin Stevens RC .30 .75
Bryan Fogarty RC .10 .25
Dan Quinn .12 .30
Murray Craven .15 .40
Shawn Chambers .12 .30
Craig Simpson .12 .30
Doug Crossman .12 .30
Daren Puppa .12 .30
Bobby Smith .12 .30
Slava Fetisov RC .30 .75
Gino Cavallini .15 .40
Jimmy Carson .12 .30
Dave Ellett .10 .25
Steve Thomas .10 .25
Mike Lalor RC .12 .30
Mike Liut .12 .30
Tom Laidlaw .15 .40
Ron Francis .20 .50
Sergei Makarov RC .30 .75
Randy Burridge .12 .30
Doug Lidster .15 .40
Mike Richter RC .50 1.25
Stephane Richer .15 .40
Randy Hillier .15 .40
Christian Ruuttu .12 .30
Marc Fortier .12 .30
Bill Ranford .12 .30
Rick Tocchet .15 .40
Fredrik Olausson .12 .30
Adam Creighton .10 .25
Sylvain Cote .10 .25
Brian Mullen .15 .40
Adam Oates .15 .40
Gary Nylund .12 .30
Tim Cheveldae RC .12 .30
Gary Suter .15 .40
John Tonelli .12 .30
Kevin Hatcher .12 .30
Guy Carbonneau .10 .25
Curtis Leschyshyn RC .12 .30
Kirk McLean .10 .25
Curt Giles .12 .30
Vincent Damphousse .12 .30
Peter Stastny .12 .30
Glen Wesley .12 .30
David Shaw .15 .40
Brad Shaw RC .12 .30
00 Mark Messier .30 .75
01 Rick Zombo RC .15 .40
02A Mark Fitzpatrick ERR RC .12 .30
02B Mark Fitzpatrick COR RC .12 .30
03 Rick Vaive .12 .30
04 Mark Osborne .12 .30
05 Rob Brown .30 .75
06 Gary Roberts .15 .40
07 Vincent Riendeau RC .15 .40
08 Dave Gagner .15 .40
09 Bruce Driver .15 .40
10 Pierre Turgeon .12 .30
11 Claude Lemieux .10 .25
12 Bob Essensa RC .25 .60
13 John Ogrodnick .15 .40
14 Glenn Anderson .15 .40
15 Kelly Hrudey .10 .25
16 Sylvain Turgeon .12 .30
17 Gord Murphy RC .15 .40
18 Craig Janney .15 .40
19 Randy Wood .10 .25
20 Mike Modano RC .50 1.25
21 Tom Barrasso .12 .30
22 Daniel Marois .12 .30
23 Igor Larionov RC .30 .75
24 Geoff Courtnall .12 .30
25 Denis Savard .20 .50
26 Ron Tugnutt .12 .30
27 Mathieu Schneider RC .12 .30
28 Joel Otto .12 .30
29 Steve Smith .12 .30
30 Mike Gartner .15 .40
31 Rod Brind'Amour RC .30 .75
32 Jyrki Lumme RC .10 .25
33 Mike Foligno .12 .30
34 Ray Ferraro .12 .30
35 Steve Larmer .12 .30
36 Randy Carlyle .12 .30
37 Tony Tanti .12 .30
38 Jeff Chychrun RC .12 .30
39 Gerald Diduck .12 .30
40 Andy Moog .15 .40
41 Paul Gillis .12 .30
42 Tom Kurvers .15 .40
43 Bob Probert .15 .40
44 Neal Broten .10 .25
45 Phil Housley .12 .30
46 Brendan Shanahan .20 .50
47 Bob Rouse .10 .25
48 Russ Courtnall .15 .40
49 Normand Rochefort UER .10 .25
(RW, should be D)
50 Luc Robitaille .15 .40
51 Curtis Joseph RC .50 1.25
52 Ulf Samuelsson .15 .40
53 Ron Sutter .12 .30
54 Petri Skriko .15 .40
55 Doug Gilmour .20 .50
56 Paul Fenton .15 .40
57 Jeff Norton .15 .40
58 Jari Kurri .20 .50
59 Rejean Lemelin .12 .30
60 Kirk Muller .12 .30
61 Keith Brown .12 .30
62 Aaron Broten UER .12 .30
63 Adam Graves RC .30 .75
64 v .15 .40
65 Craig Ludwig .15 .40
66 Dave Taylor .15 .40
67 Craig Wolanin RC .12 .30
68 Kelly Miller .10 .25
69 Uwe Krupp .15 .40
70 Kevin Lowe .15 .40

171 Wendel Clark .15 .40
172 Dave Babych .10 .25
173 Paul Reinhart .15 .40
174 Pat Flatley .15 .40
175 John Vanbiesbrouck .12 .30
176 Teppo Numminen RC .30 .75
177 Tim Kerr .15 .40
178 Ken Daneyko .10 .25
179 Jeremy Roenick RC .50 1.25
180 Gerard Gallant .10 .25
181 Allen Pederson .12 .30
182 Jon Casey .15 .40
183 Tomas Sandstrom .15 .40
184 Brad McCrimmon .15 .40
185 Paul Cavallini .12 .30
186 Mark Recchi RC .50 1.25
187 Michel Petit .12 .30
188 Scott Stevens .15 .40
189 Dave Andreychuk .15 .40
190 John MacLean .12 .30
191 Petr Svoboda .12 .30
192 Dave Tippett .12 .30
193 Dave Manson .15 .40
194 James Patrick .15 .40
195 Al Iafrate .10 .25
196 Doug Smail .12 .30
197 Kjell Samuelsson .12 .30
198 Brian Bradley .12 .30
199 Charlie Huddy .12 .30
200 Ray Bourque .25 .60
201 Joey Kocur RC .30 .75
202 Jim Johnson UER .10 .25
203 Paul MacLean .12 .30
204 Tim Watters .10 .25
205 Pat Elynuik .12 .30
206 Larry Murphy .12 .30
207 Claude Loiselle RC .10 .25
208 Joe Mullen .12 .30
209 Alexei Kasatonov RC .15 .40
210 Ed Olczyk .15 .40
211 Doug Bodger .12 .30
212 Kevin Dineen .15 .40
213 Shayne Corson .12 .30
214 Steve Chiasson .10 .25
215 Don Beaupre .10 .25
216 Jamie Macoun .12 .30
217 Dave Poulin .15 .40
218 Zarley Zalapski .12 .30
219 Brad Marsh .12 .30
220 Mark Howe .15 .40
221 Michel Goulet .10 .25
222 Hubie McDonough RC .12 .30
223 Frank Musil .10 .25
224 Sergio Momesso RC .12 .30
225 Brian Leetch .20 .50
226 Theo Fleury .20 .50
227 Mike Krushelnyski .15 .40
228 Glen Hanlon .12 .30
229 Mario Marois .12 .30
230 Dino Ciccarelli .15 .40
231A Dave McLlwain ERR .15 .40
(Shoots right)
231B Dave McLlwain COR .15 .40
(Shoots left)
232 Petr Klima .10 .25
233 Grant Ledyard RC .15 .40
234 Phil Bourque .12 .30
235 Rob Sweeney .10 .25
236 Luke Richardson .12 .30
237 Todd Krygier RC .12 .30
238 Brian Skrudland .12 .30
239 Chris Terreri RC .30 .75
240 Greg Adams .10 .25
241 Darren Turcotte RC .12 .30
242 Scott Mellanby .15 .40
243 Troy Murray .12 .30
244 Stewart Gavin .15 .40
245 Gordie Roberts .10 .25
246 John Druce RC .15 .40
247 Steve Kasper .12 .30
248 Paul Ranheim RC .15 .40
249 Greg Paslawski .12 .30
250 Pat LaFontaine .15 .40
251 Scott Arniel .10 .25
252 Bernie Federko .12 .30
253 Garry Galley RC .10 .25
254 Carey Wilson .12 .30
255 Bob Errey .12 .30
256 Tony Hrkac .10 .25
257 Andrew McBain .12 .30
258 Craig MacTavish .12 .30
259A Dean Evason ERR .12 .30
(Reversed negative)
259B Dean Evason COR .12 .30
(photo is correct)
260 Larry Robinson .12 .30
261 Basil McRae .12 .30
262 Stephan Lebeau RC .12 .30
263 Ken Wregget .15 .40
264 Greg Gilbert .10 .25
265 Ken Baumgartner RC .15 .40
266 Lou Franceschetti RC .15 .40
267 Rick Meagher .12 .30
268 Michal Pivonka RC .12 .30
269 Brian Propp .15 .40
270 Bryan Trottier .20 .50
271 Marty McSorley .15 .40
272 Jan Erixon .15 .40
273 Vladimir Krutov RC .30 .75
274 Dana Murzyn .15 .40
275 Grant Fuhr .15 .40
276 Randy Cunneyworth .12 .30
277 John Chabot .15 .40
278 Walt Poddubny .12 .30
279 Stephen Leach .12 .30
280 Doug Wilson .15 .40
281 Rich Sutter .15 .40
282 Stephane Beauregard RC .12 .30
283 John Carter RC .12 .30
284 Don Barber RC .12 .30
285 Tom Fergus .12 .30
286 Ilkka Sinisalo .12 .30
287 Kevin McClelland UER .12 .30
288 Troy Mallette RC .12 .30
289 Clint Malarchuk UER .12 .30
290 Guy Lafleur .20 .50
291 Bob Joyce .12 .30
292 Trent Yawney .15 .40
293 Joe Murphy RC .12 .30
294 Glenn Healy RC .30 .75
295 Dave Christian .12 .30
296 Paul MacDermid .12 .30
297 Todd Elik RC .15 .40
298 Wendell Young RC .15 .40
299 Dean Kennedy RC .10 .25
300 Brett Hull .30 .75
301 Keith Acton .15 .40
302 Yvon Corriveau RC .12 .30
303 Don Maloney .15 .40
304 Mark Tinordi RC .10 .25
305 Bob Kudelski RC .12 .30

306 Brian Benning .12 .30
307 Alan Kerr .12 .30
308 Pelle Eklund .10 .25
309 Calle Johansson .15 .40
310 David Maley RC .15 .40
311 Chris Nilan .10 .25
312 Patrick Roy AS1 .40 1.00
313 Ray Bourque AS1 .25 .60
314 Al MacInnis AS1 .12 .30
315 Mark Messier AS1 .30 .75
316 Luc Robitaille AS1 .15 .40
317 Brett Hull AS1 .30 .75
318 Daren Puppa AS2 .12 .30
319 Paul Coffey AS2 .15 .40
320 Doug Wilson AS2 .15 .40
321 Wayne Gretzky AS2 .75 2.00
322 Brian Bellows AS2 .12 .30
323 Cam Neely AS2 .15 .40
324 Bob Essensa ART .25 .60
325 Brad Shaw ART .12 .30
326 Geoff Smith ART .15 .40
327 Mike Modano ART .50 1.25
328 Rod Brind'Amour ART .30 .75
329 Sergei Makarov ART .30 .75
330A Kip Miller Hob ERR RC .12 .30
(Score logo missing on front)
330B Kip Miller Hob COR RC .12 .30
(Score logo appears on front)
331 Edmonton Oilers Champs .30 .75
332 Paul Coffey Speed .15 .40
333 Mike Gartner Speed .15 .40
334 Al Iafrate Blaster .10 .25
335 Al MacInnis Blaster .12 .30
336 Wayne Gretzky Sniper .75 2.00
337 Mario Lemieux Sniper .60 1.50
338 Wayne Gretzky Magic .75 2.00
339 Steve Yzerman Magic .50 1.25
340 Cam Neely Banger .15 .40
341 Scott Stevens Banger .15 .40
342 Esa Tikkanen Shadow .12 .30
343 Jan Erixon Shadow .15 .40
344 Patrick Roy Stopper .40 1.00
345 Bill Ranford Stopper .12 .30
346 Brett Hull RB .30 .75
347 Wayne Gretzky RB .75 2.00
348 Jari Kurri LL .20 .50
349 Paul Cavallini LL .12 .30
350 Sergei Makarov RLL .30 .75
351 Brett Hull LL .30 .75
352 Wayne Gretzky LL .75 2.00
353 Wayne Gretzky LL .75 2.00
354 P.Roy/Liut LL .40 1.00
355 Gilbert Perreault HOF .15 .40
356 Bill Barber HOF .12 .30
357 Fern Flaman HOF .12 .30
358 Bill Ranford Smythe .12 .30
359 Rick Meagher Selke .12 .30
360 Mark Messier Hart .30 .75
361 Wayne Gretzky Ross .75 2.00
362 Sergei Makarov Calder .30 .75
363 Ray Bourque Norris .25 .60
364 Patrick Roy Vezina .40 1.00
365 Andy Moog .15 .40
Reggie Lemelin
Jennings
366 Brett Hull Byng .30 .75
367 Gord Kluzak Mast .12 .30
368 Boston/Washington UER .25 .60
369 Edmonton .12 .30
Chicago
370 Adam Burt RC .12 .30
371 Troy Loney RC .15 .40
372 Dave Chyzowski RC .12 .30
373 Geoff Smith RC .15 .40
374 Stan Smyl .10 .25
375 Gaetan Duchesne .15 .40
376 Bob Murray .12 .30
377 Daniel Shank RC .15 .40
378 Tommy Albelin .10 .25
379 Perry Berezan RC .15 .40
380 Ken Linseman .12 .30
381 Stephane Matteau RC .15 .40
382 Mario Thyer RC .12 .30
383 Nelson Emerson RC .12 .30
384 Kory Kocur RC .12 .30
385 Bob Beers RC .12 .30
386 Jim Hrivnak RC .15 .40
387 Mark Pederson RC .15 .40
388 Jeff Hackett RC .25 .60
389 Eric Weinrich RC .15 .40
390 Steven Rice RC .15 .40
391 Stu Barnes RC .12 .30
392 Olaf Kolzig RC UER .12 .30
393 Francois Leroux RC .12 .30
394 Adrien Plavsic RC .15 .40
395 Michel Mongeau RC .12 .30
396 Rick Corriveau RC .12 .30
397 Wayne Doucet RC .12 .30
398 Mats Sundin RC .15 .40
399 Murray Baron RC .12 .30
400 Rick Bennett RC .10 .25
401 Jon Morris RC .10 .25
402 Kay Whitmore RC .12 .30
403 Peter Lappin RC .12 .30
404 Kris Draper RC .12 .30
405 Shayne Stevenson RC .12 .30
406 Paul Ysebaert RC .12 .30
407A Jim Waite ERR RC .15 .40
407B Jim Waite COR RC .15 .40
408 Cam Russell RC .12 .30
409 Kim Issel RC .12 .30
410 Darrin Shannon RC .15 .40
411 Link Gaetz RC .15 .40
412 Craig Fisher RC .15 .40
413 Bruce Hoffort RC .15 .40
414 Peter Ing RC .15 .40
415 Stephane Fiset RC .30 .75
416 Dominic Lavoie RC .12 .30
417 Steve Maltais RC .12 .30
418 Wes Walz RC .15 .40
419 Terry Yake RC .12 .30
420 Jamie Leach RC .12 .30
421 Rob Blake RC .25 .60
422 Andrew Cassels RC .10 .25
423 Marc Bureau RC .12 .30
424 Scott Allison RC .12 .30
425 Darryl Sydor RC .15 .40
426 Turner Stevenson RC .12 .30
427 Brad May RC .12 .30
428 Jaromir Jagr RC 1.50 4.00
429 Shawn Antoski RC .12 .30
430 Derian Hatcher RC .12 .30
431 Mark Greig RC .12 .30
432 Scott Scissons RC .12 .30
433 Mike Ricci RC .15 .40
434 Drake Berehowsky RC .12 .30
435 Owen Nolan RC .50 1.25
436 Keith Primeau RC .25 .60
437 Karl Dykhuis RC .12 .30
438 Trevor Kidd RC .12 .30
439 Martin Brodeur RC 4.00 10.00

440 Eric Lindros RC 2.00 5.00
B1 Eric Lindros 1.00 2.50
Junior B Team
B2 Eric Lindros 1.00 2.50
Regular Junior OHL
B3 Eric Lindros 1.00 2.50
OHL All-Star
B4 Eric Lindros 1.00 2.50
Oshawa Generals
(Non-action pose;
head shot with his
gloves over his mouth)
B5 Eric Lindros 1.00 2.50
Oshawa Generals
(Non-action pose;
shot from waist up&
arms draped over hockey
stick across his back)

1990-91 Score Canadian

COMPLETE SET (440) 8.00 20.00
COMP.FACT.SET (445) 10.00 25.00
LINDROS B1-B5 IN FACTORY SET ONLY
BEWARE LINDROS COUNTERFEITS
*CANADIAN: .4X TO 1X BASIC SCORE

1990-91 Score Hottest/Rising Stars

This 100-card standard-size set was released along with a special book. The book provided further information about the players. The fronts of the cards have the same photos as the regular Score issue but the numbers are different on the back.

1 Wayne Gretzky .50 1.25
2 Craig Simpson .07 .20
3 Brian Bellows .07 .20
4 Steve Yzerman .30 .75
5 Bernie Nicholls .10 .25
6 Esa Tikkanen .07 .20
7 Joe Sakic .30 .75
8 Thomas Steen .07 .20
9 Chris Chelios .10 .25
10 Patrik Sundstrom .10 .25
11 Rod Langway .10 .25
12 Scott Young .05 .15
13 Mike Ramsey .05 .15
14 Ron Hextall .07 .20
15 Steve Duchesne .05 .15
16 Trevor Linden .07 .20
17 Sean Burke .07 .20
18 Pat Verbeek .07 .20
19 Brent Sutter .07 .20
20 Gary Leeman .07 .20
21 Shawn Burr .07 .20
22 Dale Hawerchuk .12 .30
23 Mike Vernon .10 .25
24 Dan Quinn .07 .20
25 Patrick Roy .25 .60
26 Daren Puppa .07 .20
27 Gino Cavallini .10 .25
28 Jimmy Carson .07 .20
29 Dave Ellett .05 .15
30 Steve Thomas .05 .15
31 Jeremy Roenick .30 .75
32 Mike Liut .07 .20
33 Mark Messier .20 .50
34 Mario Lemieux .40 1.00
35 Ray Bourque .15 .40
36 Al MacInnis .07 .20
37 Ron Francis .12 .30
38 Stephane Richer .10 .25
39 Bill Ranford .07 .20
40 Rick Tocchet .10 .25
41 Adam Oates .10 .25
42 Kevin Hatcher .07 .20
43 Guy Carbonneau .05 .15
44 Curtis Leschyshyn .07 .20
45 Joe Nieuwendyk .05 .15
46 Kirk McLean .05 .15
47 Vincent Damphousse .07 .20
48 Peter Stastny .07 .20
49 Rick Zombo .10 .25
50 Mark Fitzpatrick .07 .20
51 Rob Brown .20 .50
52 Dave Gagner .10 .25
53 Pierre Turgeon .07 .20
54 Glenn Anderson .10 .25
55 Kelly Hrudey .05 .15
56 Gord Murphy .10 .25
57 Glen Wesley .07 .20
58 Craig Janney .10 .25
59 Denis Savard .12 .30
60 Mike Gartner .10 .25
61 Steve Larmer .07 .20
62 Andy Moog .10 .25
63 Phil Housley .07 .20
64 Ulf Samuelsson .10 .25
65 Paul Coffey .10 .25
66 Luc Robitaille .10 .25
67 Cam Neely .10 .25
68 Doug Wilson .10 .25
69 Doug Gilmour .12 .30
70 Jeff Norton .10 .25
71 Kirk Muller .07 .20
72 Aaron Broten .07 .20
73 John Cullen .10 .25
74 Craig Ludwig .10 .25
75 Kevin Lowe .10 .25
76 John Vanbiesbrouck .07 .20
77 Tim Kerr .10 .25
78 Gerard Gallant .05 .15
79 Tomas Sandstrom .10 .25
80 Jon Casey .10 .25
81 Mark Recchi .30 .75
82 Scott Stevens .10 .25
83 John MacLean .07 .20
84 James Patrick .10 .25
85 Al Iafrate .05 .15
86 Pat Elyniuk .07 .20
87 Dave Andreychuk .10 .25
88 Joe Mullen .07 .20
89 Ed Olczyk .10 .25
90 Kevin Dineen .10 .25
91 Shayne Corson .07 .20
92 Mark Howe .10 .25
93 Brian Leetch .12 .30
94 Dino Ciccarelli .10 .25
95 Pat LaFontaine .10 .25
96 Guy Lafleur .12 .30
97 Mike Modano .30 .75
98 Rod Brind'Amour .20 .50
99 Sergei Makarov .20 .50
100 Brett Hull .20 .50

1990-91 Score Rookie Traded

The 1990-91 Score Rookie and Traded hockey set contains 110 standard-size cards. The cards were issued as a complete set in a factory box. The fronts feature a color action photo, superimposed over blue and red stripes on a white background. The team logo appears in the upper left hand corner, while an image of a hockey player (in various colors) appears in the lower right hand corner. Yellow strips appear at the top and bottom of the card front. The backs are outlined in a yellow border and show a head shot of the player on the upper half. The career statistics and highlights on the lower half are printed on a pale blue background. Rookie Cards include Ed Belfour, Peter Bondra, Sergei Fedorov, Petr Nedved and Robert Reichel. The back of the set's custom box contains the set checklist. The cards are numbered with a "T" suffix.

COMP. FACT SET (110) 6.00 15.00
1T Denis Savard .12 .30
2T Dale Hawerchuk .12 .30
3T Phil Housley .07 .20
4T Chris Chelios .10 .25
5T Geoff Courtnall .07 .20
6T Peter Zezel .10 .25
7T Joe Mullen .07 .20
8T Craig Ludwig .10 .25
9T Claude Lemieux .05 .15
10T Bobby Holik RC .10 .25
11T Peter Ing .10 .25
12T Rod Buskas RC .10 .25
13T Tim Sweeney RC .10 .25
14T Don Barber .07 .20
15T Ray Ferraro .07 .20
16T Peter Taglianetti .07 .20
17T Johan Garpenlov RC .10 .25
18T Kevin Miller RC .10 .25
19T Frank Musil .05 .15
20T Sergei Fedorov RC .60 1.50
21T Aaron Broten .07 .20
22T Chris Nilan .05 .15
23T Gerald Diduck .07 .20
24T Marc Habscheid .07 .20
25T Glen Featherstone RC .07 .20
26T Mikko Makela .07 .20
27T Paul Stanton .10 .25
28T Mark Osborne .07 .20
29T Dave Tippett .07 .20
30T Robert Reichel RC .10 .25
31T Grant Jennings RC .10 .25
32T Troy Gamble .10 .25
33T Mark Janssens .10 .25
34T Brian Propp .10 .25
35T Donald Dufresne RC .05 .15
36T Martin Hostak RC .10 .25
37T Brad McCrimmon .10 .25
38T Dave Lowry RC .07 .20
39T Anatoli Semenov RC .07 .20
40T Scott Stevens .10 .25
41T Paul Broten .07 .20
42T Carey Wilson .07 .20
43T Troy Crowder RC .05 .15
44T Vladimir Ruzicka RC .10 .25
45T Rich Pilon .05 .15
46T John McIntyre RC .07 .20
47T Mike Krushelnyski .10 .25
48T Dave Snuggerud .07 .20
49T Bob McGill .05 .15
50T Petr Nedved RC .50 1.25
51T Ed Olczyk .10 .25
52T Doug Crossman .07 .20
53T Mikhail Tatarinov RC .05 .15
54T Michel Petit .07 .20
55T Frank Pietrangelo RC .05 .15
56T Brian MacLellan .07 .20
57T Paul Fenton .10 .25
58T Eric Desjardins RC .25 .60
59T Mike Craig RC .10 .25
60T Mike Ricci .10 .25
61T Harold Snepsts .05 .15
62T John Byce .07 .20
63T Laurie Boschman .07 .20
64T Randy Velischek .05 .15
65T Robert Kron .10 .25
66T Jocelyn Lemieux .07 .20
67T Dave Ellett .05 .15
68T Scott Arniel .05 .15
69T Doug Smail .07 .20
70T Jaromir Jagr 3.00 8.00
71T Peter Bondra RC .40 1.00
72T Paul Cyr .05 .15
73T Daniel Berthiaume .07 .20
74T Lee Norwood .07 .20
75T Bobby Smith .07 .20
76T Kris King RC .10 .25
77T Mark Hunter .05 .15
78T Brian Hayward .10 .25
79T Greg Hawgood .07 .20
80T Owen Nolan .30 .75
81T Cliff Ronning .05 .15
82T Zdeno Ciger RC .10 .25
83T Gordie Roberts .05 .15
84T Rick Green .10 .25
85T Ken Hodge Jr. RC .05 .15
86T Derek King .10 .25
87T Brent Gilchrist RC .07 .20
88T Eric Lindros .75 2.00
89T Steve Bozek .07 .20
90T Keith Primeau .15 .40
91T Roger Johansson RC .10 .25
92T Wayne Presley .05 .15
93T Ilkka Sinisalo .07 .20
94T Mario Marois .07 .20
95T Ken Linseman .07 .20
96T Greg Brown RC .10 .25
97T Ray Sheppard .05 .15
98T Mike Lalor .07 .20
99T Normand Lacombe .05 .15
100T Mats Sundin .40 1.00
101T Jergus Baca RC .07 .20
102T Mike Keane RC .05 .15
103T Ed Belfour RC .30 .75
104T Mark Hardy .05 .15
105T Dave Capuano RC .10 .25
106T Bryan Trottier .12 .30
107T Per Djoos RC .10 .25
108T Sylvain Turgeon .07 .20
109T David Reid .10 .25
110T W.Gretzky 2000th .50 1.25

1990-91 Score Young Superstars

This 40-card standard-size set was issued by Score to honor some of the leading young players active in hockey. The set has a glossy sheen to it with an action shot of the player, while the back of the card has a portrait color shot on the back along with biographical and statistical information. The set was available only in this special box format. The set was also available direct to collectors through an offer detailed on certain wax wrappers.

1 Pierre Turgeon .07 .20
2 Brian Leetch .12 .30
3 Daniel Marois .07 .20
4 Peter Sidorkiewicz .10 .25
5 Rob Brown .20 .50
6 Theo Fleury .12 .30
7 Mats Sundin .10 .25
8 Glen Wesley .07 .20
9 Sergei Fedorov .20 .50
10 Joe Sakic .30 .75
11 Sean Burke .07 .20
12 Dave Chyzowski .07 .20
13 Gord Murphy .10 .25
14 Scott Young .05 .15
15 Curtis Joseph .30 .75
16 Darren Turcotte .07 .20
17 Kevin Stevens .20 .50
18 Mathieu Schneider .07 .20
19 Trevor Linden .07 .20
20 Mike Modano .30 .75
21 Martin Gelinas .20 .50
22 Stephane Fiset .20 .50
23 Brendan Shanahan .12 .30
24 Jeremy Roenick .30 .75
25 John Druce .10 .25
26 Alexander Mogilny .30 .75
27 Mike Richter .30 .75
28 Pat Elyniuk .07 .20
29 Robert Reichel .10 .25
30 Craig Janney .10 .25
31 Rod Brind'Amour .20 .50
32 Mark Fitzpatrick .07 .20
33 Tony Granato .07 .20
34 Bobby Holik .10 .25
35 Mark Recchi .30 .75
36 Owen Nolan .30 .75
37 Petr Nedved .10 .25
38 Keith Primeau .15 .40
39 Mike Ricci .10 .25
40 Eric Lindros 3.00 8.00

1991 Score National Convention

This ten-card standard-size set features outstanding hockey players. The cards were given out as a cello wrapped complete set by Score at the National Sports Collectors Convention in Anaheim, at the Fanfest in Toronto, and at the National Candy Wholesalers Convention in St. Louis. Some dealers have reported selling the cards with the NCWA imprint and no imprint (FanFest) for a premium above the prices listed below. The front has an action photo of the player, bounded by diagonal green borders above and below the picture. The player's name and team name appear in the top green border. The light blue background shows through above and below the green borders, and it is decorated with hockey pucks and player icons. The back presents player information and career summary in a diagonal format similar to the design of the front. Some dealers have reported getting premiums of 2-3 times the values below for the Toronto FanFest versions.

COMPLETE SET (10) 6.00 15.00
*NCWA BACK: .4X TO 1X NATIONAL
1 Wayne Gretzky 2.00 5.00
2 Brett Hull .60 1.50
3 Ray Bourque .60 1.50
4 Al MacInnis .40 1.00
5 Luc Robitaille .40 1.00
6 Ed Belfour .60 1.50
7 Steve Yzerman 1.25 3.00
8 Cam Neely .40 1.00
9 Paul Coffey .40 1.00
10 Patrick Roy 1.50 4.00

1991 Score Fanfest

COMPLETE SET (10) 12.00 30.00
1 Wayne Gretzky 4.00 10.00
2 Brett Hull .75 2.00
3 Ray Bourque .75 2.00
4 Al MacInnis .60 1.50
5 Luc Robitaille .60 1.50
6 Ed Belfour .75 2.00
7 Steve Yzerman 2.00 5.00
8 Cam Neely .60 1.50
9 Paul Coffey .60 1.50
10 Patrick Roy 2.50 6.00

1991-92 Score American

The 1991-92 Score American hockey set features 440 standard-size cards. As one moves down the card face, the card's borders shade from purple to white. The color action player photo is enclosed by an thin red border, with a shadow border on the right and below. At the card top, the player's name is written over a hockey puck, and the team name is printed below the picture in the lower right corner. A purple border stripe at the bottom completes the front. In a horizontal format, the backs have biography, statistics, player profile, and a color close-up photo.

COMPLETE SET (440) 4.00 10.00
COMP.FACT.SET (440) 4.00 10.00
1 Brett Hull .25 .60
2 Al MacInnis .12 .30
3 Luc Robitaille .12 .30
4 Pierre Turgeon .12 .30
5 Brian Leetch .12 .30
6 Cam Neely .15 .40
7 John Cullen .12 .30
8 Trevor Linden .12 .30
9 Rick Tocchet .12 .30
10 John Vanbiesbrouck .12 .30
11 Steve Smith .15 .40
12 Doug Smail .12 .30
13 Craig Ludwig .12 .30
14 Paul Fenton .12 .30
15 Dirk Graham .12 .30
16 Brad McCrimmon .12 .30
17 Dean Evason .12 .30
18 Fredrik Olausson .12 .30
19 Guy Carbonneau .12 .30
20 Kevin Hatcher .12 .30
21 Paul Ranheim .15 .40
22 Claude Lemieux .12 .30
23 Vincent Riendeau .12 .30
24 Garth Butcher .12 .30
25 Joe Sakic .50 1.25
26 Rick Vaive .10 .25
27 Rob Blake .15 .40
28 Mike Ricci .15 .40
29 Pat Flatley .12 .30
30 Bill Ranford .12 .30
31 Larry Murphy .12 .30
32 Bobby Smith .12 .30
33 Mike Krushelnyski .12 .30
34 Gerard Gallant .10 .25
35 Doug Wilson .12 .30
36 John Ogrodnick .12 .30
37 Mikhail Tatarinov .12 .30
38 Doug Crossman .12 .30
39 Mark Osborne .12 .30
40 Scott Stevens .15 .40
41 Ron Tugnutt .12 .30
42 Russ Courtnall .12 .30
43 Gord Murphy .12 .30
44 Greg Adams .12 .30
45 Christian Ruuttu .12 .30
46 Ken Daneyko .12 .30
47 Glenn Anderson .15 .40
48 Ray Ferraro .12 .30
49 Tony Tanti .12 .30
50 Ray Bourque .25 .60
51 Sergei Makarov .12 .30
52 Jim Johnson .12 .30
53 Troy Murray .12 .30
54 Shawn Burr .12 .30
55 Peter Ing .12 .30
56 Dale Hunter .12 .30
57 Tony Granato .12 .30
58 Curtis Leschyshyn .12 .30
59 Brian Mullen .12 .30
60 Ed Olczyk .12 .30
61 Mike Ramsey .12 .30
62 Dan Quinn .12 .30
63 Rich Sutter .12 .30
64 Terry Carkner .12 .30
65 Shayne Corson .12 .30
66 Peter Stastny .12 .30
67 Craig Muni .12 .30
68 Glenn Healy .15 .40
69 Phil Bourque .12 .30
70 Pat Verbeek .12 .30
71 Garry Galley .12 .30
72 Dave Gagner .12 .30
73 Bob Probert .12 .30
74 Craig Wolanin .12 .30
75 Patrick Roy .40 1.00
76 Keith Brown .12 .30
77 Gary Leeman .12 .30
78 Brent Ashton .12 .30
79 Randy Moller .12 .30
80 Mike Vernon .12 .30
81 Kelly Miller .12 .30
82 Ulf Samuelsson .12 .30
83 Todd Elik .12 .30
84 Uwe Krupp .12 .30
85 Rod Brind'Amour .12 .30
86 Dave Capuano .12 .30
87 Geoff Smith .12 .30
88 David Volek .12 .30
89 Bruce Driver .12 .30
90 Andy Moog .12 .30
91 Pelle Eklund .12 .30
92 Joey Kocur .12 .30
93 Mark Tinordi .12 .30
94 Steve Thomas .12 .30
95 Petr Svoboda .12 .30
96 Joel Otto .12 .30
97 Todd Krygier .12 .30
98 Jaromir Jagr .40 1.00
99 Mike Liut .12 .30
100 Wayne Gretzky .75 2.00
101 Teppo Numminen .12 .30
102 Randy Burridge .12 .30
103 Michel Petit .12 .30
104 Tony McKegney .12 .30
105 Mathieu Schneider .12 .30
106 Daren Puppa .12 .30
107 Paul Cavallini .12 .30
108 Tim Kerr .12 .30
109 Kevin Lowe .12 .30
110 Kirk Muller .10 .25
111 Zarley Zalapski .12 .30
112 Mike Hough .12 .30
113 Ken Hodge Jr. .15 .40
114 Grant Fuhr .15 .40
115 Paul Coffey .12 .30
116 Wendel Clark .15 .40
117 Patrik Sundstrom .12 .30
118 Kevin Dineen .12 .30
119 Eric Desjardins .15 .40
120 Mike Richter .15 .40
121 Sergio Momesso .12 .30
122 Tony Hrkac .12 .30
123 Joe Reekie .12 .30
124 Petr Nedved .12 .30
125 Randy Carlyle .12 .30
126 Kevin Miller .12 .30
127 Rejean Lemelin .12 .30
128 Dino Ciccarelli .12 .30
129 Sylvain Cote .12 .30
130 Mats Sundin .15 .40
131 Eric Weinrich .15 .40
132 Daniel Berthiaume .12 .30
133 Keith Acton .12 .30
134 Benoit Hogue .12 .30
135 Mike Gartner .12 .30
136 Petr Klima .12 .30
137 Curt Giles .15 .40
138 Scott Pearson .12 .30
139 Luke Richardson .12 .30
140 Steve Larmer .12 .30
141 Ken Wregget .12 .30
142 Frank Musil .12 .30
143 Owen Nolan .15 .40
144 Keith Primeau .12 .30
145 Mark Recchi .20 .50
146 Don Sweeney .12 .30
147 Mike McPhee .12 .30
148 Ken Baumgartner .12 .30
149 Dave Lowry .12 .30
150 Geoff Courtnall .12 .30
151 Chris Terreri .12 .30
152 Dave Manson .12 .30
153 Bobby Holik .15 .40
154 Bob Kudelski .10 .25
155 Calle Johansson .12 .30
156 Mark Hunter .12 .30
157 Randy Gilhen .12 .30
158 Yves Racine .12 .30
159 Martin Gelinas .12 .30
160 Brian Bellows .12 .30
161 David Shaw .12 .30
162 Bob Carpenter .12 .30
163 Doug Brown .12 .30
164 Ulf Dahlen .12 .30
165 Denis Savard .20 .50
166 Paul Ysebaert .12 .30
167 Derek King .10 .25
168 Igor Larionov .12 .30
169 Bob Errey .12 .30
170 Joe Nieuwendyk .12 .30
171 Normand Rochefort .12 .30
172 John Tonelli .12 .30
173 David Reid .10 .25
174 Tom Kurvers .12 .30
175 Dimitri Khristich .12 .30
176 Bob Sweeney .12 .30
177 Rick Zombo .12 .30
178 Troy Mallette .12 .30
179 Bob Bassen .12 .30
180 John Druce .12 .30
181 Mike Craig .12 .30
182 John McIntyre .12 .30
183 Murray Baron .12 .30
184 Slava Fetisov .12 .30
185 Don Beaupre .12 .30
186 Brian Benning .12 .30
187 Dave Barr .12 .30
188 Petri Skriko .10 .25
189 Steve Konroyd .12 .30
190 Steve Yzerman .50 1.25
191 Jon Casey .12 .30
192 Gary Nylund .12 .30

193 Michal Pivonka .12 .30
194 Alexei Kasatonov .10 .25
195 Garry Valk .12 .30
196 Darren Turcotte .12 .30
197 Chris Nilan .12 .30
198 Thomas Steen .12 .30
199 Gary Roberts .12 .30
200 Mario Lemieux .60 1.50
201 Michel Goulet .12 .30
202 Craig MacTavish .12 .30
203 Peter Sidorkiewicz .12 .30
204 Johan Garpenlov .12 .30
205 Steve Duchesne .10 .25
206 Dave Snuggerud .10 .25
207 Kjell Samuelsson .12 .30
208 Sylvain Turgeon .12 .30
209 Al Iafrate .12 .30
210 John MacLean .12 .30
211 Brian Hayward .12 .30
212 Cliff Ronning .12 .30
213 Ray Sheppard .12 .30
214 Dave Taylor .12 .30
215 Doug Lidster .12 .30
216 Peter Bondra .12 .30
217 Marty McSorley .12 .30
218 Doug Gilmour .30 .75
219 Paul MacDermid .12 .30
220 Jeremy Roenick .40 1.00
221 Wayne Presley .12 .30
222 Jeff Norton .12 .30
223 Brian Propp .12 .30
224 Jimmy Carson .12 .30
225 Tom Barrasso .12 .30
226 Theo Fleury .12 .30
227 Carey Wilson .12 .30
228 Rod Langway .12 .30
229 Bryan Trottier .20 .50
230 James Patrick .12 .30
231 Kelly Hrudey .12 .30
232 Dave Poulin .12 .30
233 Rob Ramage .12 .30
234 Stephane Richer .12 .30
235 Chris Chelios .15 .40
236 Alexander Mogilny .12 .30
237 Bryan Fogarty .12 .30
238 Adam Oates .15 .40
239 Ron Hextall .15 .40
240 Bernie Nicholls .12 .30
241 Esa Tikkanen .12 .30
242 Jyrki Lumme .12 .30
243 Brent Sutter .12 .30
244 Gary Suter .12 .30
245 Sean Burke .15 .40
246 Rob Brown .12 .30
247 Mike Modano .30 .75
248 Kevin Stevens .12 .30
249 Mike Lalor .12 .30
250 Sergei Fedorov .25 .60
251 Bob Essensa .12 .30
252 Mark Howe .15 .40
253 Craig Janney .12 .30
254 Daniel Marois .12 .30
255 Craig Simpson .10 .25
256 Steve Kasper .12 .30
257 Randy Velischek .12 .30
258 Gino Cavallini .12 .30
259 Dale Hawerchuk .20 .50
260 Pat LaFontaine .15 .40
261 Kirk McLean .12 .30
262 Murray Craven .12 .30
263 Robert Reichel .30 .75
264 Jan Erixon .12 .30
265 Adam Creighton .12 .30
266 Mark Fitzpatrick .12 .30
267 Ron Francis .20 .50
268 Joe Mullen .12 .30
269 Peter Zezel .10 .25
270 Tomas Sandstrom .12 .30
271 Phil Housley .12 .30
272 Tim Cheveldae .12 .30
273 Glen Wesley .12 .30
274 Stephan Lebeau .12 .30
275 Dave Ellett .12 .30
276 Jeff Brown .12 .30
277 Dave Andreychuk .15 .40
278 Steven Finn .12 .30
279 Scott Mellanby .12 .30
280 Neal Broten .12 .30
281 Randy Wood .12 .30
282 Troy Gamble .10 .25
283 Mike Ridley .12 .30
284 Jamie Macoun .12 .30
285 Mark Messier .40 1.00
286 Brendan Shanahan .20 .50
287 Scott Young .12 .30
288 Kelly Kisio .12 .30
289 Brad Shaw .10 .25
290 Ed Belfour .40 1.00
291 Larry Robinson .10 .25
292 Dave Christian .12 .30
293 Steve Chiasson .12 .30
294 Brian Skrudland .12 .30
295 Pat Elynuik .12 .30
296 Curtis Joseph .12 .30
297 Doug Bodger .12 .30
298 Ron Sutter .12 .30
299 Joe Murphy .12 .30
300 Vincent Damphousse .12 .30
301 Cam Neely CC .15 .40
302 Rick Tocchet CC .12 .30
303 Scott Stevens CC .15 .40
304 Ulf Samuelsson CC .12 .30
305 Jeremy Roenick CC .40 1.00
306 The Hunter Brothers .12 .30
Dale Hunter
Mark Hunter
307 The Broten Brothers .12 .30
Aaron Broten
Neal Broten
308 The Cavallini Brothers .12 .30
Gino Cavallini
Paul Cavallini
309 The Miller Brothers .12 .30
Kelly Miller
Kevin Miller
310 Dennis Vaske TP .12 .30
311 Rob Pearson RC .15 .40
312 Jason Miller TP .12 .30
313 John LeClair RC .40 1.00
314 Bryan Marchment TP RC .12 .30
315 Gary Shuchuk TP .12 .30
316 Dominik Hasek RC .50 1.25
317 Michel Picard TP RC .15 .40
318 Corey Millen RC .15 .40
319 Joe Sacco RC .15 .40
320 Reggie Savage RC .12 .30
321 Pat Murray TP .12 .30
322 Myles O'Connor TP .12 .30
323 Shawn Antoski TP .12 .30
324 Geoff Sanderson RC .15 .40
325 Chris Govedaris TP .12 .30
326 Alexei Gusarov RC .12 .30
327 Mike Sillinger TP .12 .30
328 Bob Wilkie TP .12 .30
329 Pat Jablonski RC .12 .30
330 David Emma RC .12 .30
331 Kirk Muller FP .10 .25
332 Pat LaFontaine FP .15 .40
333 Brian Leetch FP .12 .30
334 Rick Tocchet FP .12 .30
335 Mario Lemieux FP .60 1.50
336 Joe Sakic FP .50 1.25
337 Brett Hull FP .25 .60
338 Vincent Damphousse FP .12 .30
339 Trevor Linden FP .12 .30
340 Kevin Hatcher FP .12 .30
341 Pat Elynuik FP .12 .30
342 Patrick Roy DT .40 1.00
343 Brian Leetch DT .12 .30
344 Ray Bourque DT .25 .60
345 Luc Robitaille DT .12 .30
346 Wayne Gretzky DT .75 2.00
347 Brett Hull DT .25 .60
348 Ed Belfour ART .40 1.00
349 Rob Blake ART .15 .40
350 Eric Weinrich ART .15 .40
351 Jaromir Jagr ART .40 1.00
352 Sergei Fedorov ART .25 .60
353 Ken Hodge Jr. ART .15 .40
354 Eric Lindros ART .12 .30
355 Eric Lindros Awards .12 .30
356 Eric Lindros Number 1 .12 .30
357 Dana Murzyn .12 .30
358 Adam Graves .12 .30
359 Ken Linseman .12 .30
360 Mike Keane .10 .25
361 Stephane Morin .12 .30
362 Grant Ledyard .12 .30
363 Kris King .12 .30
364 Paul Gillis .12 .30
365 Chris Dahlquist .12 .30
366 Paul Stanton .12 .30
367 Jeff Hackett .12 .30
368 Bob McGill .12 .30
369 Neil Wilkinson .12 .30
370 Rob Zettler .12 .30
371 Brett Hull MOY .25 .60
372 Paul Coffey 1000 .12 .30
373 Mark Messier 1000 .40 1.00
374 Dave Taylor 1000 .12 .30
375 Michel Goulet 1000 .12 .30
376 Dale Hawerchuk 1000 .20 .50
377 The Turgeon Brothers .12 .30
Pierre Turgeon
Sylvain Turgeon
378 The Sutter Brothers .12 .30
Rich Sutter
Brian Sutter
Ron Sutter
379 The Mullen Brothers .12 .30
Brian Mullen
Joe Mullen
380 The Courtnall Brothers .12 .30
Geoff Courtnall
Russ Courtnall
381 Trevor Kidd TP .12 .30
382 Patrice Brisebois TP .10 .25
383 Mark Greig TP .12 .30
384 Kip Miller TP .12 .30
385 Drake Berehowsky TP .12 .30
386 Kevin Haller RC .15 .40
387 Dave Gagnon TP .12 .30
388 Jason Marshall TP .12 .30
389 Donald Audette TP .12 .30
390 Patrick Lebeau RC .12 .30
391 Alexander Godynyuk TP .15 .40
392 Jarrod Skalde TP RC .12 .30
393 Ken Sutton RC .15 .40
394 Sergei Kharin TP .12 .30
395 Andre Racicot TP RC .12 .30
396 Doug Weight RC .40 1.00
397 Kevin Todd RC .15 .40
398 Tony Amonte TP RC .40 1.00
399 Kimbi Daniels TP .15 .40
400 Jeff Daniels RC .12 .30
401 Guy Lafleur .20 .50
402 Guy Lafleur .20 .50
403 Guy Lafleur .20 .50
404 Brett Hull SL .25 .60
405 Wayne Gretzky SL .75 2.00
406 Wayne Gretzky SL .75 2.00
407 Theo Fleury SL .12 .30
Marty McSorley SL
408 Sergei Fedorov SL .25 .60
409 Al MacInnis SL .12 .30
410 Ed Belfour SL .40 1.00
411 Ed Belfour SL .40 1.00
412 Brett Hull 50/50 .25 .60
413 Wayne Gretzky 700th .75 2.00
414 San Jose Sharks Logo .10 .25
415 Ray Bourque FP .25 .60
416 Pierre Turgeon FP .12 .30
417 Al MacInnis FP .12 .30
418 Jeremy Roenick FP .40 1.00
419 Steve Yzerman FP .50 1.25
420 Mark Messier FP .40 1.00
421 John Cullen FP .12 .30
422 Wayne Gretzky FP .75 2.00
423 Mike Modano FP .30 .75
424 Patrick Roy FP .40 1.00
425 Stanley Cup Champs .60 1.50
426 Mario Lemieux Smythe .60 1.50
427 Wayne Gretzky Ross .75 2.00
428 Brett Hull Hart .25 .60
429 Ray Bourque Norris .25 .60
430 Ed Belfour Calder .40 1.00
431 Ed Belfour Vezina .40 1.00
432 Dirk Graham Selke .12 .30
433 Ed Belfour Jennings .40 1.00
434 Wayne Gretzky Byng .75 2.00
435 Dave Taylor Masterton Tr. .12 .30
436 Randy Ladouceur .12 .30
437 Dave Tippett .12 .30
438 Clint Malarchuk .12 .30
439 Gordie Roberts .12 .30
440 Frank Pietrangelo .12 .30

1991-92 Score Canadian Bilingual

The 1991-92 Score Canadian hockey set features 660 standard-size cards. The set was released in two series of 330 cards each. The borders on the front of first series cards shade from red to white, top to bottom. The fronts of the second series cards shade from bright blue to white. The two series also differ in that first series cards have the player enclosed by a thin purple border and second series cards have a red border. At the top, the player's name is written over a hockey puck and the team name is printed below the picture in the lower right corner. A red border stripe at the bottom completes the front. In a horizontal format, the bilingual backs have biography, statistics, player profile, and a color close-up photo. An identical version (Score Canadian English) to this set exists, with the difference being that the text on each card is strictly in English.

1 Brett Hull .15 .40
2 Al MacInnis .07 .20
3 Luc Robitaille .07 .20
4 Pierre Turgeon .07 .20
5 Brian Leetch .07 .20
6 Cam Neely .10 .25
7 John Cullen .07 .20
8 Trevor Linden .07 .20
9 Rick Tocchet .07 .20
10 John Vanbiesbrouck .07 .20
11 Steve Smith .10 .25
12 Doug Smail .07 .20
13 Craig Ludwig .07 .20
14 Paul Fenton .07 .20
15 Dirk Graham .07 .20
16 Brad McCrimmon .07 .20
17 Dean Evason .07 .20
18 Fredrik Olausson .07 .20
19 Guy Carbonneau .07 .20
20 Kevin Hatcher .07 .20
21 Paul Ranheim .10 .25
22 Claude Lemieux .07 .20
23 Vincent Riendeau .07 .20
24 Garth Butcher .07 .20
25 Joe Sakic .30 .75
26 Rick Vaive .05 .15
27 Rob Blake .10 .25
28 Mike Ricci .10 .25
29 Pat Flatley .07 .20
30 Bill Ranford .07 .20
31 Larry Murphy .07 .20
32 Bobby Smith .07 .20
33 Mike Krushelnyski .07 .20
34 Gerard Gallant .05 .15
35 Doug Wilson .07 .20
36 John Ogrodnick .07 .20
37 Mikhail Tatarinov .07 .20
38 Doug Crossman .07 .20
39 Mark Osborne .07 .20
40 Scott Stevens .10 .25
41 Ron Tugnutt .07 .20
42 Russ Courtnall .07 .20
43 Gord Murphy .07 .20
44 Greg Adams .07 .20
45 Christian Ruuttu .07 .20
46 Ken Daneyko .07 .20
47 Glenn Anderson .10 .25
48 Ray Ferraro .07 .20
49 Tony Tanti .07 .20
50 Ray Bourque .15 .40
51 Sergei Makarov .07 .20
52 Jim Johnson .07 .20
53 Troy Murray .07 .20
54 Shawn Burr .07 .20
55 Peter Ing .07 .20
56 Dale Hunter .07 .20
57 Tony Granato .07 .20
58 Curtis Leschyshyn .07 .20
59 Brian Mullen .07 .20
60 Ed Olczyk .07 .20
61 Mike Ramsey .07 .20
62 Dan Quinn .07 .20
63 Rich Sutter .07 .20
64 Terry Carkner .07 .20
65 Shayne Corson .07 .20
66 Peter Stastny .07 .20
67 Craig Muni .07 .20
68 Glenn Healy .10 .25
69 Phil Bourque .07 .20
70 Pat Verbeek .07 .20
71 Garry Galley .07 .20
72 Dave Gagner .07 .20
73 Bob Probert .07 .20
74 Craig Wolanin .07 .20
75 Patrick Roy .25 .60
76 Keith Brown .07 .20
77 Gary Leeman .07 .20
78 Brent Ashton .07 .20
79 Randy Moller .07 .20
80 Mike Vernon .07 .20
81 Kelly Miller .07 .20
82 Ulf Samuelsson .07 .20
83 Todd Elik .07 .20
84 Uwe Krupp .07 .20
85 Rod Brind'Amour .07 .20
86 Dave Capuano .07 .20
87 Geoff Smith .07 .20
88 David Volek .07 .20
89 Bruce Driver .07 .20
90 Andy Moog .07 .20
91 Pelle Eklund .07 .20
92 Joey Kocur .07 .20
93 Mark Tinordi .07 .20
94 Steve Thomas .07 .20
95 Petr Svoboda .07 .20
96 Joel Otto .07 .20
97 Todd Krygier .07 .20
98 Jaromir Jagr .25 .60
99 Mike Liut .07 .20
100 Wayne Gretzky 1.00 2.50
101 Teppo Numminen .07 .20
102 Randy Burridge .07 .20
103 Michel Petit .07 .20
104 Tony McKegney .07 .20
105 Mathieu Schneider .07 .20
106 Daren Puppa .07 .20
107 Paul Cavallini .07 .20
108 Tim Kerr .07 .20
109 Kevin Lowe .07 .20
110 Kirk Muller .05 .15
111 Zarley Zalapski .07 .20
112 Mike Hough .07 .20
113 Ken Hodge Jr. .10 .25
114 Grant Fuhr .10 .25
115 Paul Coffey .07 .20
116 Wendel Clark .10 .25
117 Patrik Sundstrom .07 .20
118 Kevin Dineen .07 .20
119 Eric Desjardins .10 .25
120 Mike Richter .10 .25
121 Sergio Momesso .07 .20
122 Tony Hrkac .07 .20
123 Joe Reekie .07 .20
124 Petr Nedved .07 .20
125 Randy Carlyle .07 .20
126 Kevin Miller .07 .20
127 Rejean Lemelin .07 .20
128 Dino Ciccarelli .07 .20
129 Sylvain Cote .07 .20
130 Mats Sundin .10 .25
131 Eric Weinrich .10 .25
132 Daniel Berthiaume .07 .20
133 Keith Acton .07 .20
134 Benoit Hogue .07 .20
135 Mike Gartner .07 .20
136 Petr Klima .07 .20
137 Curt Giles .10 .25
138 Scott Pearson .07 .20
139 Luke Richardson .07 .20
140 Steve Larmer .07 .20
141 Ken Wregget .07 .20
142 Frank Musil .07 .20
143 Owen Nolan .10 .25
144 Keith Primeau .07 .20
145 Mark Recchi .12 .30
146 Don Sweeney .07 .20
147 Mike McPhee .07 .20
148 Ken Baumgartner .07 .20
149 Dave Lowry .07 .20
150 Geoff Courtnall .07 .20
151 Chris Terreri .07 .20
152 Dave Manson .07 .20
153 Bobby Holik .10 .25
154 Bob Kudelski .05 .15
155 Calle Johansson .07 .20
156 Mark Hunter .07 .20
157 Randy Gilhen .07 .20
158 Yves Racine .07 .20
159 Martin Gelinas .07 .20
160 Brian Bellows .07 .20
161 David Shaw .07 .20
162 Bob Carpenter .07 .20
163 Doug Brown .07 .20
164 Ulf Dahlen .07 .20
165 Denis Savard .12 .30
166 Paul Ysebaert .07 .20
167 Derek King .05 .15
168 Igor Larionov .07 .20
169 Bob Errey .07 .20
170 Joe Nieuwendyk .07 .20
171 Normand Rochefort .07 .20
172 John Tonelli .07 .20
173 David Reid .05 .15
174 Tom Kurvers .07 .20
175 Dimitri Khristich .07 .20
176 Bob Sweeney .07 .20
177 Rick Zombo .07 .20
178 Troy Mallette .07 .20
179 Bob Bassen .07 .20
180 John Druce .07 .20
181 Mike Craig .07 .20
182 John McIntyre .07 .20
183 Murray Baron .07 .20
184 Slava Fetisov .07 .20
185 Don Beaupre .07 .20
186 Brian Benning .07 .20
187 Dave Barr .07 .20
188 Petri Skriko .05 .15
189 Steve Konroyd .07 .20
190 Steve Yzerman .30 .75
191 Jon Casey .07 .20
192 Gary Nylund .07 .20
193 Michal Pivonka .07 .20
194 Alexei Kasatonov .05 .15
195 Garry Valk .07 .20
196 Darren Turcotte .07 .20
197 Chris Nilan .07 .20
198 Thomas Steen .07 .20
199 Gary Roberts .07 .20
200 Mario Lemieux .40 1.00
201 Michel Goulet .07 .20
202 Craig MacTavish .07 .20
203 Peter Sidorkiewicz .07 .20
204 Johan Garpenlov .07 .20
205 Steve Duchesne .05 .15
206 Dave Snuggerud .05 .15
207 Kjell Samuelsson .07 .20
208 Sylvain Turgeon .07 .20
209 Al Iafrate .07 .20
210 John MacLean .07 .20
211 Brian Hayward .07 .20
212 Cliff Ronning .07 .20
213 Ray Sheppard .07 .20
214 Dave Taylor .07 .20
215 Doug Lidster .07 .20
216 Peter Bondra .07 .20
217 Marty McSorley .07 .20
218 Doug Gilmour .20 .50
219 Paul MacDermid .07 .20
220 Jeremy Roenick .25 .60
221 Wayne Presley .07 .20
222 Jeff Norton .07 .20
223 Brian Propp .07 .20
224 Jimmy Carson .07 .20
225 Tom Barrasso .07 .20
226 Theo Fleury .07 .20
227 Carey Wilson .07 .20
228 Rod Langway .07 .20
229 Bryan Trottier .12 .30
230 James Patrick .07 .20
231 Dana Murzyn .07 .20
232 Rick Wamsley .05 .15
233 Dave McLlwain .07 .20
234 Tom Fergus .07 .20
235 Adam Graves .07 .20
236 Jacques Cloutier .07 .20
237 Gino Odjick .07 .20
238 Andrew Cassels .07 .20
239 Ken Linseman .07 .20
240 Danton Cole .05 .15
241 Dave Hannan .07 .20
242 Stephane Matteau .07 .20
243 Gerald Diduck .07 .20
244 Rick Tabaracci .07 .20
245 Sylvain Lefebvre .07 .20
246 Bob Rouse .07 .20
247 Charlie Huddy .07 .20
248 Mike Foligno .10 .25
249 Ric Nattress .07 .20
250 Aaron Broten .07 .20
251 Mike Keane .05 .15
252 Steve Bozek .07 .20
253 Jeff Beukeboom .07 .20
254 Stephane Morin .07 .20
255 Brian Bradley .07 .20
256 Scott Arniel .07 .20
257 Robert Kron .07 .20
258 Anatoli Semenov .07 .20
259 Brent Gilchrist .07 .20
260 Jim Sandlak .07 .20
261 Brett Hull MOY .15 .40
262 Paul Coffey 1000 PTS .07 .20
263 Mark Messier 1000 PTS .25 .60
264 Dave Taylor 1000 PTS .07 .20
265 Michel Goulet 1000 PTS .07 .20
266 Dale Hawerchuk 1000 PTS .12 .30
267 Turgeon Bros. .07 .20
268 Sutter Bros. .07 .20
269 Mullen Bros. .07 .20
270 Courtnall Bros. .07 .20
271 Trevor Kidd TP .07 .20
272 Patrice Brisebois TP .05 .15
273 Mark Greig TP .07 .20
274 Kip Miller TP .07 .20
275 Drake Berehowsky TP .07 .20
276 Kevin Haller RC .10 .25
277 Dave Gagnon TP .07 .20
278 Jason Marshall TP .07 .20
279 Donald Audette TP .07 .20
280 Patrick Lebeau RC .07 .20
281 Alexander Godynyuk TP .10 .25
282 Jarrod Skalde TP RC .07 .20
283 Ken Sutton RC .10 .25
284 Sergei Kharin TP .07 .20
285 Andre Racicot TP RC .07 .20
286 Doug Weight RC .25 .60
287 Kevin Todd RC .10 .25
288 Tony Amonte TP RC .25 .60
289 Kimbi Daniels TP .10 .25
290 Jeff Daniels RC .07 .20
291 Guy Lafleur .12 .30
292 Guy Lafleur .12 .30
293 Guy Lafleur .12 .30
294 Brett Hull SL .15 .40
295 Wayne Gretzky SL 1.00 2.50
296 Wayne Gretzky SL .60 2.50
297 Theo Fleury .07 .20
Marty McSorley SL
298 Sergei Fedorov SL .15 .40
299 Al MacInnis SL .07 .20
300 Ed Belfour SL .25 .60
301 Ed Belfour SL .25 .60
302 Brett Hull 50/50 .15 .40
303 Wayne Gretzky 700th .60 2.50
304 San Jose Sharks Logo .05 .15
305 Cam Neely Crunch .10 .25
306 Rick Tocchet Crunch .07 .20
307 Scott Stevens Crunch .10 .25
308 Ulf Samuelsson Crunch .07 .20
309 Jeremy Roenick Crunch .25 .60
310 Mark Messier FRAN .25 .60
311 John Cullen FRAN .07 .20
312 Wayne Gretzky FRAN .60 2.50
313 Mike Modano FRAN .20 .50
314 Patrick Roy FRAN .25 .60
315 Stanley Cup Champs .40 1.00
316 Mario Lemieux Smythe .40 1.00
317 Wayne Gretzky Ross .60 2.50
318 Brett Hull Hart .15 .40
319 Ray Bourque Norris .15 .40
320 Ed Belfour Calder .25 .60
321 Ed Belfour Vezina .25 .60
322 Dirk Graham Selke .07 .20
323 Ed Belfour Jennings .25 .60
324 Wayne Gretzky Byng .60 2.50
325 Dave Taylor Masterton .07 .20
326 Jeff Hackett .07 .20
327 Bob McGill .07 .20
328 Neil Wilkinson .07 .20
329 Eric Lindros Draft .07 .20
330 Eric Lindros Medals .07 .20
331 Ray Bourque FP .15 .40
332 Pierre Turgeon FP .07 .20
333 Al MacInnis FP .07 .20
334 Jeremy Roenick FP .25 .60
335 Steve Yzerman FP .30 .75
336 Hunter Bros. .07 .20
337 Broten Bros. .07 .20
338 Cavallini Bros. .07 .20
339 Miller Bros. .07 .20
340 Dennis Vaske TP .07 .20
341 Rob Pearson RC .10 .25
342 Jason Miller TP .07 .20
343 John LeClair RC .25 .60
344 Bryan Marchment TP RC .07 .20
345 Gary Shuchuk TP .07 .20
346 Dominik Hasek RC .30 .75
347 Michel Picard TP RC .10 .25
348 Corey Millen RC .10 .25
349 Joe Sacco RC .10 .25
350 Reggie Savage RC .07 .20
351 Pat Murray TP .07 .20
352 Myles O'Connor TP .07 .20
353 Shawn Antoski TP .07 .20
354 Geoff Sanderson RC .10 .25
355 Chris Govedaris TP .07 .20
356 Alexei Gusarov RC .07 .20
357 Mike Sillinger TP .07 .20
358 Bob Wilkie TP .07 .20
359 Pat Jablonski RC .07 .20
360 Memorial Cup .05 .14
Spokane Chiefs
361 Kirk Muller FP .05 .15
362 Pat LaFontaine FP .10 .25
363 Brian Leetch FP .07 .20
364 Rick Tocchet FP .07 .20
365 Mario Lemieux FP .40 1.00
366 Joe Sakic FP .30 .75
367 Brett Hull FP .15 .40
368 Vincent Damphousse FP .07 .20
369 Trevor Linden FP .07 .20
370 Kevin Hatcher FP .07 .20
371 Pat Elynuik FP .07 .20
372 Patrick Roy DT .25 .60
373 Brian Leetch DT .07 .20
374 Ray Bourque DT .15 .40
375 Luc Robitaille DT .07 .20
376 Wayne Gretzky DT 1.00 2.50
377 Brett Hull DT .15 .40
378 Ed Belfour ART .25 .60
379 Rob Blake ART .10 .25
380 Eric Weinrich ART .10 .25
381 Jaromir Jagr ART .25 .60
382 Sergei Fedorov ART .15 .40
383 Ken Hodge Jr. ART .10 .25
384 Eric Lindros Art .07 .20
385 E.Lindros/R.Pearson .10 .25
386 Ottawa/Tampa Bay .07 .20
387 Mick Vukota .07 .20
388 Lou Franceschetti .07 .20
389 Mike Hudson .07 .20
390 Frantisek Kucera .07 .20
391 Basil McRae .07 .20
392 Donald Dufresne .07 .20
393 Tommy Albelin .05 .15
394 Normand Lacombe .07 .20
395 Lucien DeBlois .07 .20
396 Tony Twist RC .05 .15
397 Rob Murphy .05 .15
398 Ken Sabourin .07 .20
399 Doug Evans .05 .15
400 Walt Poddubny .05 .15
401 Grant Ledyard .07 .20
402 Kris King .07 .20
403 Paul Gillis .07 .20
404 Chris Dahlquist .07 .20
405 Zdeno Ciger .07 .20
406 Paul Stanton .07 .20
407 Randy Ladouceur .07 .20
408 Ronnie Stern .07 .20
409 Dave Tippett .07 .20
410 Jeff Reese .07 .20
411 Vladimir Ruzicka .07 .20
412 Brent Fedyk .07 .20
413 Paul Cyr .07 .20
414 Mike Eagles .07 .20
415 Chris Joseph .07 .20
416 Brad Marsh .10 .25
417 Rich Pilon .07 .20
418 Jiri Hrdina .07 .20
419 Clint Malarchuk .07 .20
420 Steven Rice .07 .20
421 Mark Janssens .07 .20
422 Gordie Roberts .07 .20
423 Shawn Cronin .07 .20
424 Randy Cunneyworth .07 .20
425 Frank Pietrangelo .07 .20
426 David Maley .07 .20
427 Rod Buskas .07 .20
428 Dennis Vial .05 .15
429 Kelly Buchberger .07 .20
430 Wes Walz .07 .20
431 Dean Kennedy .07 .20
432 Nick Kypreos .07 .20
433 Stewart Gavin .07 .20
434 Norm Maciver RC .10 .25
435 Mark Pederson .07 .20
436 Laurie Boschman .07 .20
437 Stephane Quintal .07 .20
438 Darrin Shannon .07 .20
439 Trent Yawney .07 .20
440 Gaetan Duchesne .05 .15
441 Joe Cirella .07 .20
442 Doug Houda .07 .20
443 Dave Chyzowski .05 .15
444 Derrick Smith .07 .20
445 Jeff Lazaro .07 .20
446 Brian Glynn .07 .20
447 Jocelyn Lemieux .07 .20
448 Peter Taglianetti .05 .15
449 Adam Burt .07 .20
450 Hubie McDonough .07 .20
451 Kelly Hrudey .07 .20
452 Dave Poulin .07 .20
453 Mark Hardy .07 .20
454 Mike Hartman .07 .20
455 Chris Chelios .10 .25
456 Alexander Mogilny .07 .20
457 Bryan Fogarty .07 .20
458 Adam Oates .10 .25
459 Ron Hextall .10 .25
460 Bernie Nicholls .07 .20
461 Esa Tikkanen .07 .20
462 Jyrki Lumme .07 .20
463 Brent Sutter .07 .20
464 Gary Suter .07 .20
465 Sean Burke .10 .25
466 Rob Brown .07 .20
467 Mike Modano .20 .50
468 Kevin Stevens .07 .20
469 Mike Lalor .07 .20
470 Sergei Fedorov .15 .40
471 Bob Essensa .07 .20
472 Mark Howe .10 .25
473 Craig Janney .07 .20
474 Daniel Marois .07 .20
475 Craig Simpson .05 .15
476 Marc Bureau .07 .20
477 Randy Velischek .07 .20
478 Gino Cavallini .07 .20
479 Dale Hawerchuk .12 .30
480 Pat LaFontaine .10 .25
481 Kirk McLean .07 .20
482 Murray Craven .07 .20
483 Robert Reichel .20 .50
484 Jan Erixon .07 .20
485 Adam Creighton .07 .20
486 Mark Fitzpatrick .07 .20
487 Ron Francis .12 .30
488 Joe Mullen .07 .20
489 Peter Zezel .05 .15
490 Tomas Sandstrom .07 .20
491 Phil Housley .07 .20
492 Tim Cheveldae .07 .20
493 Glen Wesley .07 .20
494 Stephan Lebeau .07 .20
495 Dave Ellett .07 .20
496 Jeff Brown .07 .20
497 Dave Andreychuk .10 .25
498 Steven Finn .07 .20
499 Mike Donnelly RC .10 .25
500 Neal Broten .07 .20
501 Randy Wood .07 .20
502 Troy Gamble .05 .15
503 Mike Ridley .07 .20
504 Jamie Macoun .07 .20
505 Mark Messier .25 .60
506 Moe Mantha .07 .20
507 Scott Young .07 .20
508 Robert Dirk .07 .20
509 Brad Shaw .05 .15
510 Ed Belfour .25 .60
511 Larry Robinson .05 .15
512 Dale Kushner .07 .20
513 Steve Chiasson .07 .20
514 Brian Skrudland .07 .20
515 Pat Elynuik .07 .20
516 Curtis Joseph .07 .20
517 Doug Bodger .07 .20
518 Greg Brown .05 .15
519 Joe Murphy .07 .20
520 J.J. Daigneault .05 .15
521 Todd Gill .07 .20
522 Troy Loney .05 .15
523 Tim Watters .05 .15
524 Jody Hull .05 .15
525 Colin Patterson .07 .20
526 Darin Kimble .07 .20
527 Perry Berezan .07 .20
528 Lee Norwood .05 .15
529 Mike Peluso .07 .20
530 Wayne McBean .05 .15
531 Grant Jennings .07 .20
532 Claude Loiselle .07 .20
533 Ron Wilson .07 .20
534 Phil Sykes .07 .20
535 Jim Wiemer .07 .20
536 Herb Raglan .07 .20
537 Tim Hunter .07 .20
538 Mike Tomlak .07 .20
539 Greg Gilbert .07 .20
540 Jiri Latal .05 .15
541 Bill Berg .07 .20
542 Shane Churla .05 .15
543 Jay Miller .07 .20
544 Pete Peeters .05 .15
545 Alan May .07 .20
546 Mario Marois .07 .20
547 Jim Kyte .07 .20
548 Jon Morris .07 .20
549 Mikko Makela .07 .20
550 Nelson Emerson .07 .20
551 Doug Wilson .07 .20
552 Brian Mullen .07 .20
553 Kelly Kisio .07 .20
554 Brian Hayward .07 .20
555 Tony Hrkac .07 .20
556 Steve Bozek .07 .20
557 John Carter .07 .25
558 Neil Wilkinson .07 .20
559 Wayne Presley .07 .20
560 Bob McGill .07 .20
561 Craig Ludwig .07 .20
562 Mikhail Tatarinov .07 .20
563 Todd Elik .07 .20
564 Randy Burridge .07 .20
565 Tim Kerr .07 .20
566 Randy Gilhen .07 .20
567 John Tonelli .07 .20
568 Tom Kurvers .07 .20
569 Steve Duchesne .05 .15
570 Charlie Huddy .07 .20
571 Alan Kerr .07 .20
572 Shawn Chambers .05 .15
573 Rob Ramage .07 .20
574 Steve Kasper .07 .20
575 Scott Mellanby .07 .20
576 Stephen Leach .07 .20
577 Scott Niedermayer .10 .25
578 Craig Berube .07 .20
579 Greg Paslawski .07 .20
580 Randy Hillier .07 .20
581 Stephane Richer .07 .20
582 Brian MacLellan .07 .20
583 Marc Habscheid .07 .20
584 Dave Babych .07 .20
585 Troy Murray .07 .20
586 Ray Sheppard .07 .20
587 Glen Featherstone .05 .15
588 Brendan Shanahan .12 .30
589 Dave Christian .07 .20
590 Mike Bullard .07 .20
591 Ryan Walter .07 .20
592 Doug Smail .07 .20
593 Paul Fenton .07 .20
594 Adam Graves .07 .20
595 Scott Stevens .10 .25
596 Sylvain Cote .07 .20
597 Dave Barr .07 .20
598 Randy Gregg .07 .20
599 Allen Pedersen .07 .20
600 Jari Kurri .07 .20
601 Troy Mallette .07 .20
602 Troy Crowder .07 .20
603 Brad Jones .07 .20
604 Randy McKay .07 .20
605 Scott Thornton .07 .20
606 Bryan Marchment RC .07 .20
607 Andrew Cassels .07 .20
608 Grant Fuhr .10 .25
609 Vincent Damphousse .07 .20
610 Robert Ray .07 .20
611 Glenn Anderson .10 .25
612 Peter Ing .07 .20
613 Tom Chorske .07 .20
614 Kirk Muller .05 .15
615 Dan Quinn .07 .20
616 Murray Baron .07 .20
617 Sergei Nemchinov .07 .20
618 Rod Brind'Amour .07 .20
619 Ron Sutter .07 .20
620 Luke Richardson .07 .20
621 Nicklas Lidstrom RC .40 1.00
622 Ken Linseman .07 .20
623 Steve Smith .10 .25
624 Dave Manson .07 .20
625 Kay Whitmore .07 .20
626 Jeff Chychrun .05 .15
627 Russ Romaniuk RC .10 .25
628 Brad May .07 .20
629 Tomas Forslund RC .10 .25
630 Stu Barnes .07 .20
631 Darryl Sydor .07 .20
632 Jimmy Waite .07 .20
633 Peter Douris .07 .20
634 Dave Brown .07 .20
635 Mark Messier .25 .60
636 Neil Sheehy .07 .20
637 Todd Krygier .07 .20
638 Stephane Beauregard .05 .15
639 Barry Pederson .07 .20
640 Pat Falloon .07 .20
641 Dean Evason .07 .20
642 Jeff Hackett .07 .20
643 Rob Zettler .07 .20
644 David Bruce RC .10 .25
645 Pat MacLeod RC .10 .25
646 Craig Coxe .05 .15
647 Ken Hammond RC .07 .20
648 Brian Lawton .07 .20
649 Perry Anderson .07 .20
650 Kevin Evans .05 .15
651 Mike McHugh .07 .20
652 Mark Lamb .05 .15
653 Darcy Wakaluk RC .10 .25
654 Pat Conacher .07 .20
655 Martin Lapointe .07 .20
656 Derian Hatcher .07 .20
657 Bryan Erickson .07 .20
658 Ken Priestlay .07 .20
659 Vladimir Konstantinov RC .25 .60
660 Andrei Lomakin .07 .20

1991-92 Score Canadian English

*CANADIAN ENGLISH: .4X TO 1X BASIC CARDS

1991-92 Score Bobby Orr

This six-card standard-size set highlights the career of Bobby Orr, one of hockey's all-time greats. The cards were inserted in 1991-92 Score hockey poly packs. Cards 1 and 2 were inserted in both American and Canadian editions. Cards 3 and 4 were inserted in Canadian packs, while cards 5 and 6 were inserted in American packs. On a black card face, the fronts feature color player photos enclosed by a thin red border and accented by yellow borders on three sides. The backs carry a close-up color photo and biographical comments on Orr's career. The cards are not numbered on the back. It is claimed that 270,000 of these Orr cards were produced, and that Orr personally signed 2,500 of each of these cards. The personally autographed cards are autographed on the card back. They are slightly different in design.

COMPLETE SET (6) 20.00 40.00
COMMON ORR (1-6) 3.00 8.00
AU Bobby Orr AU/2500* 80.00 200.00

1991-92 Score Eric Lindros

This three-card standard-size set was produced by Score and distributed in a cello pack with the first printing of Eric Lindros' autobiography "Fire on Ice". The cards feature on the fronts color photos that capture three different moments in Lindros' life (childhood, adolescence, and NHL Entry Draft). The pictures are bordered on all sides by light blue, with the player's name in block lettering between two red stripes at the card top. A red stripe at the bottom separates the picture from its title line. The backs have relevant biographical comments as well as a second color photo. The cards are unnumbered and checklisted below in chronological order.

COMPLETE SET (3) 6.00 15.00
COMMON LINDROS (1-3) 2.00 5.00

1991-92 Score Hot Cards

The 1991-92 Score Hot cards were inserted in American and Canadian English 100-card blister packs at a rate of one per pack. The standard size cards feature on the fronts color action player photos bordered in bright red. Thin yellow stripes accent the photos, and the player's name appears beneath the picture in a purple stripe. The back design reflects the same three colors as the front and features a color head shot, team logo, and player profile. The cards are numbered on the back. Hot Cards differ in design, photos, and text from the regular issues.

1 Eric Lindros .60 1.50
2 Wayne Gretzky 3.00 8.00
3 Brett Hull 1.00 2.50
4 Sergei Fedorov .60 1.50
5 Mario Lemieux 2.50 6.00
6 Adam Oates .60 1.50
7 Theo Fleury .40 1.00
8 Jaromir Jagr 2.00 5.00
9 Ed Belfour .60 1.50
10 Jeremy Roenick .60 1.50

1991-92 Score Rookie Traded

The 1991-92 Score Rookie and Traded hockey set contains 110 standard-size cards. It was issued only as a factory set. As one moves down the card face, the fronts shade from dark green to white. The color action player photo is enclosed by an thin red border, with a shadow border on the right and below. At the card top, the player's name is written over a hockey puck, and the team name is printed below the picture in the lower right corner. A dark green border stripe at the bottom rounds out the front. In a horizontal format, the backs present biography, statistics, player profile, and a color close-up photo. The cards are numbered on the back with a "T" suffix. The set includes Eric Lindros pictured in his World Junior uniform. The back of the set's custom box contains the set checklist. The key Rookie Cards in this set are Valeri Kamensky and Nicklas Lidstrom.

1T Doug Wilson .12 .30
2T Brian Mullen .12 .30
3T Kelly Kisio .12 .30
4T Brian Hayward .12 .30
5T Tony Hrkac .12 .30
6T Steve Bozek .12 .30
7T John Carter .12 .30
8T Neil Wilkinson .12 .30
9T Wayne Presley .12 .30
10T Bob McGill .12 .30
11T Craig Ludwig .12 .30
12T Mikhail Tatarinov .12 .30
13T Todd Elik .12 .30
14T Randy Burridge .12 .30
15T Tim Kerr .12 .30
16T Randy Gilhen .12 .30
17T John Tonelli .12 .30
18T Tom Kurvers .12 .30
19T Steve Duchesne .10 .25
20T Charlie Huddy .12 .30
21T Adam Creighton .12 .30
22T Brent Ashton .12 .30
23T Rob Ramage .12 .30
24T Steve Kasper .12 .30
25T Scott Mellanby .12 .30
26T Stephen Leach .12 .30
27T Scott Niedermayer .15 .40
28T Craig Berube .12 .30
29T Greg Paslawski .12 .30
30T Randy Hillier .12 .30
31T Stephane Richer .12 .30
32T Brian MacLellan .12 .30
33T Marc Habscheid .12 .30
34T Dave Babych .12 .30
35T Troy Murray .12 .30
36T Ray Sheppard .12 .30
37T Glen Featherstone .10 .25
38T Brendan Shanahan .20 .50
39T Dave Christian .12 .30
40T Mike Bullard .12 .30
41T Ryan Walter .12 .30
42T Randy Wood .12 .30
43T Vincent Riendeau .12 .30
44T Adam Graves .12 .30
45T Scott Stevens .15 .40
46T Sylvain Cote .12 .30
47T Dave Barr .12 .30
48T Randy Gregg .12 .30
49T Pavel Bure .12 .30
50T Jari Kurri .12 .30
51T Steve Thomas .12 .30
52T Troy Crowder .12 .30
53T Brad Jones .12 .30
54T Randy McKay .12 .30
55T Scott Thornton .12 .30
56T Bryan Marchment .12 .30
57T Andrew Cassels .12 .30
58T Grant Fuhr .15 .40
59T Vincent Damphousse .12 .30
60T Rick Zombo .12 .30
61T Glenn Anderson .15 .40
62T Peter Ing .12 .30
63T Tom Chorske .12 .30
64T Kirk Muller .10 .25
65T Dan Quinn .12 .30
66T Murray Baron .12 .30
67T Sergei Nemchinov .12 .30
68T Rod Brind'Amour .12 .30
69T Ron Sutter .12 .30
70T Luke Richardson .12 .30
71T Nicklas Lidstrom RC .60 1.50
72T Petri Skriko .10 .25
73T Steve Smith .15 .40
74T Dave Manson .12 .30
75T Kay Whitmore .12 .30
76T Valeri Kamensky RC .40 1.00
77T Russ Romaniuk RC .15 .40
78T Brad May .12 .30
79T Tomas Forslund RC .15 .40
80T Stu Barnes .12 .30
81T Darryl Sydor .12 .30
82T Jimmy Waite .12 .30
83T Vladimir Ruzicka .12 .30
84T Dave Brown .12 .30
85T Mark Messier .40 1.00
86T Neil Sheehy .12 .30
87T Todd Krygier .12 .30
88T Eric Lindros .12 .30
89T Nelson Emerson .12 .30
90T Pat Falloon .12 .30
91T Dean Evason .12 .30
92T Jeff Hackett .12 .30
93T Rob Zettler .12 .30
94T Perry Berezan .12 .30
95T Pat MacLeod RC .15 .40
96T Craig Coxe .10 .25
97T Ken Hammond RC .12 .30
98T Brian Lawton .12 .30
99T Perry Anderson .12 .30
100T Pat LaFontaine .15 .40
101T Pierre Turgeon .12 .30
102T Dave McLlwain .12 .30
103T Brent Sutter .12 .30
104T Uwe Krupp .12 .30
105T Martin Lapointe .12 .30
106T Derian Hatcher .12 .30
107T Darrin Shannon .12 .30
108T Benoit Hogue .12 .30
109T Vladimir Konstantinov RC .40 1.00
110T Andrei Lomakin .12 .30

1991-92 Score Kellogg's

This 24-card standard-size set was produced by Score as a promotion for Kellogg's Canada. Two-card foil packs were inserted in specially marked 675-gram Kellogg's Corn Flakes cereals. The side panel of the cereal boxes presented a mail-in offer for the complete set and a card binder for 5.99 plus three proof of purchase tokens (one token featured per side panel). Card fronts have player action photos enclosed in a small red border, player's name in white reverse-out lettering, and team logo in bottom portion of the purple border. Card backs, also in purple, red, and white, carry the card number, Kellogg's Limited Edition Collector's Set logo, biography, statistics, and player profile in English and French.

COMPLETE SET (24) 14.00 35.00
1 Patrick Roy 3.00 8.00
2 Rick Tocchet .40 1.00
3 Wendel Clark .40 1.00
4 Mike Modano .75 2.00
5 Jeremy Roenick .60 1.50
6 Pierre Turgeon .40 1.00
7 Kevin Hatcher .20 .50
8 Brian Leetch .60 1.50
9 Mark Recchi .40 1.00
10 Andy Moog .40 1.00
11 Kevin Dineen .20 .50
12 Joe Sakic 1.25 3.00
13 John MacLean .20 .50
14 Steve Yzerman 2.00 5.00
15 Pat LaFontaine .40 1.00
16 Al MacInnis .40 1.00
17 Petr Klima .20 .50
18 Ed Olczyk .20 .50
19 Doug Wilson .20 .50
20 Trevor Linden .20 .50
21 Brett Hull .75 2.00
22 Rob Blake .20 .50
23 Dave Ellett .20 .50
24 Cornelius Rooster SP .75 2.00
Kellogg's mascot
NNO Card Binder 2.00 5.00

1991-92 Score Young Superstars

This 40-card standard-size set was issued by Score to showcase some of the leading young hockey players. The color action player photos on the fronts are framed in green on a card face consisting of blended diagonal taupe stripes. In a horizontal format, the backs have a color head shot on the left half while the right half carries biography, "Rink Report," and career statistics.

1 Sergei Fedorov .25 .60
2 Mike Richter .15 .40
3 Mats Sundin .15 .40
4 Theo Fleury .12 .30
5 John Cullen .12 .30
6 Dimitri Khristich .12 .30
7 Stephan Lebeau .12 .30
8 Rob Blake .15 .40
9 Ken Hodge Jr. .15 .40
10 Mike Ricci .15 .40
11 Trevor Linden .12 .30
12 Peter Ing .12 .30
13 Alexander Mogilny .12 .30
14 Martin Gelinas .12 .30
15 Chris Terreri .12 .30
16 Jeff Norton .12 .30
17 Bob Essensa .12 .30
18 Mark Tinordi .12 .30
19 Curtis Joseph .12 .30
20 Joe Sakic .50 1.25
21 Jeremy Roenick .40 1.00
22 Mark Recchi .20 .50
23 Eric Desjardins .15 .40
24 Robert Reichel .30 .75
25 Tim Cheveldae .12 .30
26 Eric Weinrich .15 .40
27 Murray Baron .12 .30
28 Darren Turcotte .12 .30
29 Troy Gamble .10 .25
30 Eric Lindros .12 .30
31 Benoit Hogue .12 .30
32 Ed Belfour .40 1.00
33 Ron Tugnutt .12 .30
34 Pat Elynuik .12 .30
35 Mike Modano .30 .75
36 Bobby Holik .15 .40
37 Yves Racine .12 .30
38 Jaromir Jagr .40 1.00
39 Stephane Morin .12 .30
40 Kevin Miller .12 .30

1992-93 Score Canadian Promo Sheets

These two 5" by 7" promotional sheets each feature four uncut cards. If the cards were cut, they would measure the standard size. The fronts feature color action player photos bordered at the top and bottom by black stripes containing the player's name and position. The outer borders are metallic-blue with diagonal stripes formed by an alternating matte and glossy finish. The backs have the disclaimers "For Promotional Purposes Only" and "Not For Resale" overprinted in magenta. They show a white background with a narrow color player photo running along the left edge. Biography and career highlights are contained in a graded blue panel with black borders. Statistical information appears at the bottom. The cards are numbered on the back and are listed below as the appear on the sheets from left to right starting with the top row.

COMPLETE SET (2) 2.00 5.00
1 Promo Sheet 1 .75 2.00
6. Pat LaFontaine
25. Kevin Stevens
2. Chris Chelios
16. Esa Tikkanen
2 Promo Sheet 2 1.50 4.00
5. Mike Richter
14. Pavel Bure
6. Pat LaFontaine
25. Kevin Stevens

1992-93 Score

The 1992-93 Score hockey set contains 550 standard-size cards. The American and Canadian sets are identical in terms of player selection (except for card numbers 548-549) but feature different insert subsets (USA Greats in the American and Canadian Olympic Heroes in the Canadian). Moreover, the player photos and card design differ in each set. In the American set, the color action photos on the fronts have two-toned borders on three sides (icy gray diagonal stripes accented by either red, blue, or black); in the Canadian, the front borders are metallic blue with diagonally varnished stripes. The American backs are horizontally oriented and include biography, statistics, career summary, and a close-up photo; the Canadian backs are vertically oriented, bilingual, and have the same features in a different layout. A special Eric Lindros card, unnumbered and featuring his first photo in a Philadelphia Flyers uniform, was randomly inserted into packs. Reportedly more than 500 of these special Lindros "Press Conference" cards were given away to news media, members of the Flyers organization, and other guests attending the July 15 news conference which marked Lindros' signing with the Flyers. It is claimed that the odds of finding one of these cards are no less than one in 500 packs. Rookie Cards include Guy Hebert and Yanic Perrault.

*CANADIAN: .4X TO 1X SCORE US
1 Wayne Gretzky .50 1.25
2 Chris Chelios .10 .25
3 Joe Mullen .07 .20
4 Russ Courtnall .05 .15
5 Mike Richter .10 .25
6 Pat LaFontaine .10 .25
7 Mark Tinordi .05 .15
8 Claude Lemieux .05 .15
9 Jimmy Carson .05 .15
10 Cam Neely .10 .25
11 Al Iafrate .07 .20
12 Steve Thomas .07 .20
13 Fredrik Olausson .05 .15
14 Pavel Bure .20 .50
15 Doug Wilson .07 .20
16 Esa Tikkanen .05 .15
17 Gary Suter .05 .15
18 Murray Craven .05 .15
19 Garry Galley .05 .15
20 Grant Fuhr .10 .25
21 Craig Wolanin .05 .15
22 Paul Cavallini .05 .15
23 Eric Desjardins .07 .20
24 Joey Kocur .07 .20
25 Kevin Stevens .05 .15
26 Marty McSorley .05 .15
27 Dirk Graham .05 .15
28 Mike Ramsey .05 .15
29 Gord Murphy .07 .20
30 John MacLean .07 .20
31 Vladimir Konstantinov .10 .25
32 Neal Broten .07 .20
33 Dimitri Khristich .05 .15
34 Gerald Diduck .07 .20
35 Ken Baumgartner .07 .20
36 Darrin Shannon .05 .15
37 Steve Bozek .05 .15
38 Michel Petit .05 .15
39 Kevin Lowe .07 .20
40 Doug Gilmour .12 .30
41 Peter Sidorkiewicz .05 .15
42 Gino Cavallini .05 .15
43 Dan Quinn .07 .20
44 Steven Finn .05 .15
45 Larry Murphy .07 .20
46 Brent Gilchrist .05 .15
47 Daren Puppa .07 .20
48 Steve Smith .05 .15
49 Dave Taylor .07 .20
50 Mike Gartner .07 .20
51 Derian Hatcher .05 .15
52 Bob Probert .07 .20
53 Ken Daneyko .05 .15
54 Steve Leach .05 .15
55 Kelly Miller .05 .15
56 Jeff Norton .07 .20
57 Kelly Kisio .07 .20
58 Igor Larionov .05 .15
59 Paul MacDermid .07 .20
60 Mike Vernon .07 .20
61 Randy Ladouceur .05 .15
62 Luke Richardson .07 .20
63 Daniel Marois .05 .15
64 Miko Hough .07 .20
65 Garth Butcher .07 .20
66 Terry Carkner .07 .20
67 Mike Donnelly .05 .15
68 Keith Brown .07 .20
69 Mathieu Schneider .05 .15
70 Tom Barrasso .07 .20
71 Adam Graves .05 .15
72 Brian Propp .05 .15
73 Randy Wood .05 .15
74 Yves Racine .05 .15
75 Scott Stevens .10 .25
76 Chris Nilan .05 .15
77 Uwe Krupp .05 .15
78 Sylvain Cote .07 .20
79 Sergio Momesso .05 .15
80 Thomas Steen .05 .15
81 Craig Muni .07 .20
82 Jeff Hackett .07 .20
83 Frank Musil .07 .20
84 Mike Ricci .07 .20
85 Brad Shaw .05 .15
86 Ron Sutter .05 .15
87 Curtis Leschyshyn .07 .20
88 Jamie Macoun .07 .20
89 Brian Noonan .05 .15
90 Ulf Samuelsson .05 .15
91 Mike McPhee .05 .15
92 Charlie Huddy .07 .20
93 Tim Kerr .05 .15
94 Craig Ludwig .07 .20
95 Paul Ysebaert .05 .15
96 Brad May .05 .15
97 Slava Fetisov .05 .15
98 Todd Krygier .07 .20
99 Patrick Flatley .07 .20
100 Ray Bourque .15 .40
101 Petr Nedved .07 .20
102 Teppo Numminen .05 .15
103 Dean Evason .05 .15
104 Ron Hextall .07 .20
105 Josef Beranek .05 .15
106 Robert Reichel .05 .15
107 Mikhail Tatarinov .05 .15
108 Geoff Sanderson .07 .20
109 Dave Lowry .07 .20
110 Wendel Clark .07 .20
111 Corey Millen UER .05 .15
112 Brent Sutter .05 .15
113 Jaromir Jagr .25 .60
114 Petr Svoboda .07 .20
115 Sergei Nemchinov .05 .15
116 Tony Tanti .05 .15
117 Stewart Gavin .05 .15
118 Doug Brown .07 .20
119 Gerard Gallant .05 .15
120 Andy Moog .07 .20
121 John Druce .05 .15
122 Dave McLlwain .05 .15
123 Bob Essensa .07 .20
124 Doug Lidster .07 .20
125 Pat Falloon .05 .15
126 Kelly Buchberger .05 .15
127 Carey Wilson .07 .20
128 Bobby Holik .07 .20
129 Andrei Lomakin .05 .15
130 Bob Rouse .07 .20
131 Adam Foote .07 .20
132 Bob Bassen .05 .15
133 Brian Benning .05 .15
134 Greg Gilbert .07 .20
135 Paul Stanton .05 .15
136 Brian Skrudland .07 .20
137 Jeff Beukeboom .05 .15
138 Clint Malarchuk .05 .15
139 Mike Modano .25 .60
140 Stephane Richer .07 .20
141 Brad McCrimmon .05 .15
142 Bob Carpenter .05 .15
143 Rod Langway .07 .20
144 Adam Creighton .05 .15
145 Ed Olczyk .05 .15
146 Greg Adams .05 .15
147 Jay More .05 .15
148 Scott Mellanby .05 .15
149 Paul Ranheim .05 .15
150 John Cullen .05 .15
151 Steve Duchesne .05 .15
152 Dave Ellett .05 .15
153 Mats Sundin .10 .25
154 Rick Zombo .05 .15
155 Kelly Hrudey .07 .20
156 Mike Hudson .05 .15
157 Bryan Trottier .12 .30
158 Shayne Corson .05 .15
159 Kevin Haller .05 .15
160 John Vanbiesbrouck .07 .20
161 Jim Johnson .07 .20
162 Kevin Todd .05 .15
163 Ray Sheppard .05 .15
164 Brent Ashton .05 .15
165 Peter Bondra .07 .20
166 David Volek .05 .15
167 Randy Carlyle .07 .20
168 Dana Murzyn .05 .15
169 Perry Berezan .05 .15
170 Vincent Damphousse .07 .20
171 Gary Leeman .05 .15
172 Steve Konroyd .07 .20
173 Pelle Eklund .07 .20
174 Peter Zezel .05 .15
175 Greg Paslawski .05 .15
176 Murray Baron .05 .15
177 Rob Blake .07 .20
178 Ed Belfour .10 .25
179 Mike Keane .05 .15
180 Mark Recchi .12 .30
181 Kris King .05 .15
182 Dave Snuggerud .05 .15
183 David Shaw .07 .20
184 Tom Chorske .07 .20
185 Steve Chiasson .05 .15
186 Don Sweeney .05 .15
187 Mike Ridley .05 .15
188 Glenn Healy .07 .20
189 Troy Murray .05 .15
190 Tom Fergus .07 .20
191 Rob Zettler .05 .15
192 Geoff Smith .05 .15
193 Joe Nieuwendyk .07 .20
194 Mark Hunter .07 .20
195 Kjell Samuelsson .07 .20
196 Todd Gill .05 .15
197 Doug Smail .05 .15
198 Dave Christian .05 .15
199 Tomas Sandstrom .07 .20
200 Jeremy Roenick .15 .40
201 Gordie Roberts .07 .20
202 Denis Savard .12 .30
203 James Patrick .05 .15
204 Dave Andreychuk .10 .25
205 Bobby Smith .07 .20
206 Valeri Zelepukin .05 .15
207 Shawn Burr .05 .15
208 Vladimir Ruzicka .05 .15
209 Calle Johansson .05 .15
210 Mark Fitzpatrick .07 .20
211 Dean Kennedy .07 .20
212 Dave Babych .07 .20
213 Wayne Presley .05 .15
214 Dave Manson .05 .15
215 Mikael Andersson .05 .15
216 Trent Yawney .07 .20
217 Mark Howe .10 .25
218 Mike Bullard .07 .20
219 Claude Lapointe .05 .15
220 Jeff Brown .07 .20
221 Bob Kudelski .07 .20
222 Michel Goulet .07 .20
223 Phil Bourque .05 .15
224 Darren Turcotte .05 .15
225 Kirk Muller .05 .15
226 Doug Bodger .05 .15
227 Dave Gagner .07 .20
228 Craig Billington .07 .20
229 Kevin Miller .05 .15
230 Glen Wesley .05 .15
231 Dale Hunter .07 .20
232 Tom Kurvers .05 .15
233 Pat Elynuik .05 .15
234 Geoff Courtnall .05 .15
235 Neil Wilkinson .05 .15
236 Bill Ranford .07 .20
237 Ronnie Stern .07 .20
238 Zarley Zalapski .05 .15
239 Kerry Huffman .05 .15
240 Joe Sakic .25 .60
241 Glenn Anderson .10 .25
242 Stephane Quintal .05 .15
243 Tony Granato .05 .15
244 Rob Brown .05 .15
245 Rick Tocchet .07 .20
246 Stephan Lebeau .05 .15
247 Mark Hardy .07 .20
248 Alexander Mogilny .07 .20
249 Jon Casey .05 .15
250 Adam Oates .10 .25
251 Bruce Driver .05 .15
252 Sergei Fedorov .15 .40
253 Michal Pivonka .05 .15
254 Cliff Ronning .05 .15
255 Derek King .05 .15
256 Luciano Borsato .05 .15
257 Paul Fenton .07 .20
258 Craig Berube .05 .15
259 Brian Bradley .05 .15
260 Craig Simpson .05 .15
261 Adam Burt .05 .15
262 Curtis Joseph .10 .25
263 Mark Pederson .05 .15
264 Alexei Gusarov .05 .15
265 Paul Coffey .10 .25
266 Steve Larmer .05 .15
267 Ron Francis .12 .30
268 Randy Gilhen .05 .15
269 Guy Carbonneau .07 .20
270 Chris Terreri .07 .20
271 Mike Craig .05 .15
272 Dale Hawerchuk .12 .30
273 Kevin Hatcher .05 .15
274 Ken Hodge Jr. .05 .15
275 Tim Cheveldae .05 .15
276 Benoit Hogue .05 .15
277 Mark Osborne .05 .15
278 Brian Mullen .05 .15
279 Robert Dirk .07 .20
280 Theo Fleury .15 .40
281 Martin Gelinas .05 .15
282 Pat Verbeek .05 .15
283 Mike Krushelnyski .05 .15
284 Kevin Dineen .05 .15
285 Craig Janney .07 .20
286 Owen Nolan .05 .15
287 Bob Errey .07 .20
288 Bryan Marchment .07 .20
289 Randy Moller .05 .15
290 Luc Robitaille .07 .20
291 Peter Stastny .07 .20
292 Ken Sutton .05 .15
293 Brad Marsh .07 .20
294 Chris Dahlquist .07 .20
295 Patrick Roy .25 .60
296 Andy Brickley .07 .20
297 Randy Burridge .05 .15
298 Ray Ferraro .05 .15
299 Phil Housley .05 .15
300 Mark Messier .15 .40
301 David Bruce .05 .15
302 Al MacInnis .07 .20
303 Craig MacTavish .05 .15
304 Kay Whitmore .07 .20
305 Trevor Linden .07 .20
306 Steve Kasper .07 .20
307 Todd Elik .05 .15
308 Eric Weinrich .05 .15
309 Jocelyn Lemieux .05 .15
310 Peter Ahola .05 .15
311 J.J. Daigneault .05 .15
312 Colin Patterson .07 .20
313 Darcy Wakaluk .07 .20
314 Doug Weight .20 .50
315 Dave Barr .05 .15
316 Keith Primeau .07 .20
317 Bob Sweeney .05 .15
318 Jyrki Lumme .05 .15
319 Stu Barnes .05 .15
320 Don Beaupre .07 .20
321 Joe Murphy .05 .15
322 Gary Roberts .05 .15
323 Andrew Cassels .05 .15
324 Rod Brind'Amour .05 .15
325 Pierre Turgeon .07 .20
326 Claude Vilgrain .07 .20
327 Rich Sutter .05 .15
328 Claude Loiselle .05 .15
329 John Ogrodnick .05 .15
330 Ulf Dahlen .05 .15
331 Gilbert Dionne .05 .15
332 Joel Otto .05 .15
333 Rob Pearson .05 .15
334 Christian Ruuttu .05 .15
335 Brian Bellows .07 .20
336 Anatoli Semenov .05 .15
337 Brent Fedyk .05 .15
338 Gaetan Duchesne .05 .15
339 Randy McKay .07 .20
340 Bernie Nicholls .05 .15
341 Keith Acton .07 .20
342 John Tonelli .07 .20
343 Brian Lawton .07 .20
344 Ric Nattress .07 .20
345 Mike Eagles .05 .15
346 Frantisek Kucera .07 .20
347 John McIntyre .05 .15
348 Troy Loney .05 .15
349 Norm Maciver .05 .15
350 Brett Hull .15 .40
351 Rob Ramage .05 .15
352 Claude Boivin .05 .15
353 Paul Broten .05 .15
354 Stephane Fiset .05 .15
355 Garry Valk .05 .15
356 Basil McRae .07 .20
357 Alan May .05 .15
358 Grant Ledyard .05 .15
359 Dave Poulin .05 .15
360 Valeri Kamensky .05 .15
361 Brian Glynn .05 .15
362 Jan Erixon .07 .20
363 Mike Lalor .07 .20
364 Jeff Chychrun .05 .15
365 Ron Wilson .07 .20
366 Shawn Cronin .05 .15
367 Sylvain Turgeon .05 .15
368 Mike Liut .05 .15
369 Joe Cirella .07 .20
370 David Maley .05 .15
371 Lucien Deblois .05 .15
372 Per Djoos .07 .20
373 Dominik Hasek .20 .50
374 Laurie Boschman .05 .15
375 Brian Leetch .07 .20
376 Nelson Emerson .05 .15
377 Normand Rochefort .05 .15
378 Jacques Cloutier .07 .20
379 Jim Sandlak .05 .15
380 David Reid .05 .15
381 Gary Nylund .05 .15
382 Sergei Makarov .05 .15
383 Petr Klima .05 .15
384 Peter Douris .05 .15
385 Kirk McLean .05 .15
386 Bob McGill .05 .15
387 Ron Tugnutt .07 .20
388 Patrice Brisebois .05 .15
389 Tony Amonte .07 .20
390 Mario Lemieux .40 1.00
391 Nicklas Lidstrom .07 .20
392 Brendan Shanahan .12 .30
393 Donald Audette .07 .20
394 Alexei Kasatonov .05 .15
395 Dino Ciccarelli .07 .20
396 Vincent Riendeau .07 .20
397 Joe Reekie .05 .15
398 Jari Kurri .10 .25
399 Ken Wregget .07 .20
400 Steve Yzerman .25 .60
401 Scott Niedermayer .10 .25
402 Stephane Beauregard .07 .20
403 Tim Hunter .05 .15
404 Marc Bergevin .07 .20
405 Sylvain Lefebvre .05 .15
406 Johan Garpenlov .05 .15
407 Tony Hrkac .05 .15
408 Tie Domi .10 .25
409 Martin Lapointe .05 .15
410 Darryl Sydor .05 .15
411 Brett Hull SL .15 .40
412 Wayne Gretzky SL .50 1.25
413 Mario Lemieux SL .40 1.00
414 Paul Ysebaert SL .05 .15
415 Tony Amonte SL .07 .20
416 Brian Leetch SL .07 .20
417 Tim Cheveldae SL .05 .15
418 Patrick Roy SL .25 .60
419 Ray Bourque FP .15 .40
420 Pat LaFontaine FP .10 .25
421 Al MacInnis FP .07 .20
422 Jeremy Roenick FP .15 .40
423 Steve Yzerman FP .25 .60
424 Bill Ranford FP .07 .20
425 John Cullen FP .05 .15
426 Wayne Gretzky FP .50 1.25
427 Mike Modano FP .25 .60
428 Patrick Roy FP .25 .60
429 Scott Stevens FP .10 .25
430 Pierre Turgeon FP .07 .20
431 Mark Messier FP .15 .40
432 Eric Lindros FP .30 .75
433 Mario Lemieux FP .40 1.00
434 Joe Sakic FP .25 .60
435 Brett Hull FP .15 .40
436 Pat Falloon FP .05 .15
437 Grant Fuhr FP .10 .25
438 Trevor Linden FP .07 .20
439 Kevin Hatcher FP .05 .15
440 Phil Housley FP .05 .15
441 Paul Coffey SH .10 .25
442 Brett Hull HL .15 .40
443 Mike Gartner SH .07 .20
444 Michel Goulet SH .07 .20
445 Mike Gartner SH .07 .20
446 Bobby Smith SH .07 .20
447 Ray Bourque SH .15 .40
448 Mario Lemieux HL .40 1.00
449 Scott Lachance TP .05 .15
450 Keith Tkachuk .10 .25
451 Alexander Semak TP .05 .15
452 John Tanner TP .05 .15
453 Joe Juneau TP .05 .15
454 Igor Kravchuk TP .05 .15
455 Brent Thompson TP .07 .20
456 Evgeny Davydov TP .05 .15
457 Arturs Irbe TP .07 .20
458 Kent Manderville TP .05 .15
459 Shawn McEachern TP .05 .15
460 Guy Hebert RC .15 .40
461 Keith Carney TP RC .20 .50
462 Karl Dykhuis TP .05 .15
463 Bill Lindsay TP RC .05 .15
464 Dominic Roussel TP .07 .20
465 Marty McInnis TP .05 .15
466 Dale Craigwell TP .05 .15
467 Igor Ulanov TP .05 .15
468 Dmitri Mironov TP .05 .15
469 Dean McAmmond TP RC .05 .15
470 Bill Guerin TP RC .20 .50
471 Bret Hedican TP RC .07 .20
472 Felix Potvin .20 .50
473 Slava Kozlov TP .07 .20
474 Martin Rucinsky TP .05 .15
475 Ray Whitney TP RC .15 .40
476 Steve Heinze TP .05 .15
477 Brad Schlegel TP .05 .15
478 Patrick Poulin TP .05 .15
479 Ted Donato TP .05 .15
480 Martin Brodeur .25 .60
481 Denny Felsner TP RC .07 .20
482 Trent Klatt TP RC .07 .20
483 Gord Hynes TP .05 .15
484 Glen Murray TP .05 .15
485 Chris Lindberg TP .05 .15
486 Ray LeBlanc TP .07 .20
487 Yanic Perreault TP RC .25 .60
488 J.F.Quintin TP RC .05 .15
489 Patrick Roy DT .25 .60
490 Ray Bourque DT .15 .40
491 Brian Leetch DT .07 .20
492 Kevin Stevens DT .05 .15
493 Mark Messier DT .15 .40
494 Jaromir Jagr DT .25 .60
495 Bill Ranford DT .07 .20
496 Al MacInnis DT .07 .20
497 Chris Chelios DT .10 .25
498 Luc Robitaille DT .07 .20
499 Jeremy Roenick DT .15 .40
500 Brett Hull DT .15 .40
501 Felix Potvin DT .20 .50
502 Nicklas Lidstrom DT .07 .20
503 Vladimir Konstantinov .10 .25
504 Pavel Bure DT .20 .50
505 Nelson Emerson DT .05 .15
506 Tony Amonte DT .07 .20
507 T.B.Lightning Logo .05 .15
508 Shawn Chambers .05 .15
509 Basil McRae .07 .20
510 Joe Reekie .05 .15
511 Wendell Young .07 .20
512 Ottawa Senators Logo .05 .15
513 Laurie Boschman .05 .15
514 Mark Lamb .05 .15
515 Peter Sidorkiewicz .05 .15
516 Sylvain Turgeon .05 .15
517 Bill Dineen .05 .15
Kevin Dineen
518 Stanley Cup .12 .30
Champions
519 Mario Lemieux AW .40 1.00
520 Ray Bourque AW .15 .40
521 Mark Messier AW .15 .40
522 Brian Leetch AW .07 .20
523 Pavel Bure AW .20 .50
524 Guy Carbonneau AW .07 .20
525 Wayne Gretzky AW .50 1.25
526 Mark Fitzpatrick AW .07 .20
527 Patrick Roy AW .25 .60
528 Memorial Cup Kamloops .05 .15
529 Rick Tabaracci .05 .15
530 Tom Draper .05 .15
531 Adrien Plavsic .05 .15
532 Joe Sacco .05 .15
533 Mike Sullivan .05 .15
534 Zdeno Ciger .05 .15
535 Frank Pietrangelo .07 .20
536 Mike Peluso .07 .20
537 Jim Paek .07 .20
538 Dave Hannan .05 .15
539 David Williams RC .05 .15
540 Gino Odjick .07 .20
541 Yvon Corriveau .05 .15
542 Grant Jennings .05 .15
543 Stephane Matteau .05 .15
544 Pat Conacher .05 .15
545 Steven Rice .05 .15
546 Marc Habscheid .05 .15
547 Steve Weeks .05 .15
548A Jay Wells USA .10 .25
548C Maurice Richard CAN .10 .25
549A Mick Vukota USA .10 .25
549C Maurice Richard CAN .10 .25
550 Eric Lindros .30 .75
NNO E.Lindros Press Conf. 5.00 12.00

1992-93 Score Canadian Olympians

This 13-card standard-size set showcases Canadian hockey players who participated in the '92 Olympics in Albertville, France. The cards were randomly inserted at the rate of 1:24 '92-93 Score Canadian hockey packs. The color action photos on the fronts are highlighted by a red border with a diagonal white stripe. The year appears in a maple leaf at the upper left. The player's name and position are printed in the borders above and below the picture respectively. The backs feature the same red border design as the front with a player profile printed on a ghosted photo of the Canadian flag. The cards are numbered on the back. Not part of the set, but inserted in Canadian foil packs are two Maurice Richard cards and one autographed card of The Rocket.

COMPLETE SET (13) 15.00 40.00
1 Eric Lindros 2.50 5.00
2 Joe Juneau 1.00 2.50
3 Dave Archibald 1.00 2.50
4 Randy Smith 1.00 2.50
5 Gord Hynes 1.00 2.50
6 Chris Lindberg 1.00 2.50
7 Jason Woolley 1.00 2.50
8 Fabian Joseph 1.00 2.50
9 Brad Schlegel 1.00 2.50
10 Kent Manderville 1.00 2.50
11 Adrien Plavsic 1.00 2.50
12 Trevor Kidd 1.00 2.50
13 Sean Burke 1.00 2.50
NNO1 Maurice Richard 2.00 5.00
NNO2 Maurice Richard 2.00 5.00
AU1 Maurice Richard AU/1250 80.00 150.00
AU2 Maurice Richard AU AP/10

1992-93 Score Sharp Shooters

This 30-card standard-size set showcases the most accurate shooters during the 1991-92 season. Two cards were inserted in each 1992-93 Score jumbo pack. The cards feature full-bleed color action photos. A black border at the bottom contains the player's name in red and the words "Sharp Shooters" in gold foil lettering. A puck and target icon fills out the card front at the lower left corner. The horizontal backs carry close-up player photos with statistics and the team logo on either side against a gray background. A black border, nearly identical to the front, runs across the bottom. The cards are numbered on the back and arranged in descending order of 1991-92 shooting percentage ranking.

COMPLETE SET (30) 5.00 12.00
*CANADIAN: .4X TO 1X US INSERTS
1 Gary Roberts .08 .25
2 Sergei Makarov .08 .25
3 Ray Ferraro .08 .25
4 Dale Hunter .40 1.00
5 Sergei Nemchinov .08 .25
6 Mike Ridley .08 .25
7 Gilbert Dionne .08 .25
8 Pat LaFontaine .50 1.25
9 Jimmy Carson .08 .25
10 Jeremy Roenick .60 1.50
11 Kelly Buchberger .08 .25
12 Owen Nolan .40 1.00
13 Igor Larionov .08 .25
14 Claude Vilgrain .08 .25
15 Derek King .08 .25
16 Greg Paslawski .08 .25
17 Bob Probert .40 1.00
18 Mark Recchi .40 1.00
19 Donald Audette .08 .25
20 Ray Sheppard .08 .25
21 Benoit Hogue .08 .25
22 Rob Brown .08 .25
23 Pat Elyniuk .08 .25
24 Petr Klima .08 .25
25 Pierre Turgeon .40 1.00
26 Corey Millen .08 .25
27 Dimitri Khristich .08 .25
28 Anatoli Semenov .08 .25
29 Kirk Muller .08 .25
30 Craig Simpson .08 .25

1992-93 Score USA Greats

This 15-card set showcases outstanding United States-born players. The standard-size cards were randomly inserted at the rate of 1:24 '92-93 Score American hockey packs. The color action photos on the fronts are full-bleed on the right side only and framed on the other three sides by a red foil stripe and a blue outer border. The backs feature a close-up photo and a player profile.

COMPLETE SET (15) 15.00 40.00
1 Pat LaFontaine 1.50 4.00
2 Chris Chelios 1.50 4.00
3 Jeremy Roenick 1.50 4.00
4 Tony Granato 1.00 2.50
5 Mike Modano 2.00 5.00

6 Mike Richter 1.50 4.00
7 John Vanbiesbrouck 1.50 4.00
8 Brian Leetch 1.50 4.00
9 Joe Mullen 1.00 2.50
10 Kevin Stevens 1.00 2.50
11 Craig Janney 1.00 2.50
12 Brian Mullen 1.00 2.50
13 Kevin Hatcher 1.00 2.50
14 Kelly Miller 1.00 2.50
15 Ed Olczyk 1.00 2.50

1992-93 Score Young Superstars

This 40-card, boxed standard-size set was issued to showcase some of the leading young hockey players. The fronts feature glossy color player photos with white and bluish-gray streaked borders. The player's team name is printed in the top border, while the player's name is printed in the bottom border. The horizontal backs carry a close-up color photo, biography, "Rink Report," and statistics.

COMP.FACT SET (40) 3.00 8.00
1 Eric Lindros 1.00 2.50
2 Tony Amonte .10 .30
3 Mats Sundin .20 .50
4 Jaromir Jagr 1.00 2.50
5 Sergei Fedorov .60 1.50
6 Gilbert Dionne .02 .10
7 Mark Recchi .10 .30
8 Alexander Mogilny .10 .30
9 Mike Richter .20 .50
10 Jeremy Roenick .20 .50
11 Nicklas Lidstrom .20 .50
12 Scott Lachance .02 .10
13 Nelson Emerson .02 .10
14 Pat Falloon .02 .10
15 Dimitri Khristich .02 .10
16 Trevor Linden .10 .30
17 Curtis Joseph .40 1.00
18 Rob Pearson .02 .10
19 Kevin Todd .02 .10
20 Joe Sakic .60 1.50
21 Tim Cheveldae .10 .30
22 Joe Juneau .10 .30
23 Vladimir Konstantinov .10 .30
24 Valeri Kamensky .10 .30
25 Ed Belfour .20 .50
26 Rod Brind'Amour .10 .30
27 Pierre Turgeon .10 .30
28 Eric Desjardins .10 .30
29 Keith Tkachuk .20 .50
30 Pavel Bure .75 2.00
31 Patrick Poulin .02 .10
32 Viacheslav Kozlov .10 .30
33 Scott Niedermayer .10 .30
34 Jyrki Lumme .02 .10
35 Paul Ysebaert .02 .10
36 Dominic Roussel .10 .30
37 Owen Nolan .10 .30
38 Rob Blake .10 .30
39 Felix Potvin .20 .50
40 Mike Modano .20 .50

1993-94 Score Promo Panel

This promo panel was issued to promote the second series of the 1993-94 Score hockey series. Measuring approximately 5" by 2 1/2", the panel is actually the size of two standard-size cards. The left front features a Gold Rush version of the Alexandre Daigle card. On a purple foil background, the right front presents an advertisement for the second series. The reverse of the left front is the expected card back as with a regular card; the reverse of the right front is the front of the regular issue Daigle card.

587 Alexandre Daigle .75 2.00
(Gold

1993-94 Score Samples

This six-card standard-size set was issued by Score as a preview of the design of the 1993-94 Score hockey set. The fronts display color action shots within a white border. The team name is printed on a team color-coded stripe along the left side. The player's position and name is printed across the bottom of the picture. The backs have team color-coded backgrounds with a head shot on the upper half and biography, statistics, and player profile. The words "sample card" are printed in the lower right corner.

COMPLETE SET (6) 1.50 4.00
1 Eric Lindros .75 2.00
2 Mike Gartner .20 .50
3 Steve Larmer .08 .25
4 Brian Bellows .08 .25
5 Felix Potvin .40 1.00
6 Pierre Turgeon .30 .75

1993-94 Score

The 1993-94 Score hockey set consists of 661 standard-size cards. The first series contains 495 cards and the second series 166. The fronts of the first series feature white-bordered color player action shots. The player's name and position appear at the bottom, with his team name displayed vertically on the left within a team color-coded stripe. The second series was redesigned and consists of traded players in new uniforms, rookies and individual highlights. Blue borders surround the card with player name and team logo at the bottom. Card 496, Alexandre Daigle, is the card received after mailing in the unnumbered Daigle redemption card. The set is considered complete without it. The redemption card was randomly inserted in first series packs. An Eric Lindros All-Star card was the SP insert in series two, at a rate of 1:360 packs.

*CANADIAN: .4X TO 1X BASIC CARDS
1 Eric Lindros .30 .75
2 Mike Gartner .07 .20
3 Steve Larmer .07 .20
4 Brian Bellows .07 .20
5 Felix Potvin .20 .50
6 Pierre Turgeon .07 .20
7 Joe Mullen .07 .20
8 Craig MacTavish .05 .15
9 Mats Sundin .07 .20
10 Pat Verbeek .05 .15
11 Andy Moog .10 .25
12 Dirk Graham .05 .15
13 Gary Suter .05 .15
14 Brent Fedyk .05 .15
15 Brad Shaw .05 .15
16 Benoit Hogue .05 .15
17 Cliff Ronning .05 .15
18 Mathieu Schneider .05 .15
19 Bernie Nicholls .05 .15
20 Vladimir Konstantinov .07 .20
21 Doug Bodger .05 .15
22 Peter Stastny .05 .15
23 Larry Murphy .07 .20
24 Darren Turcotte .05 .15
25 Doug Crossman .05 .15
26 Bob Essensa .07 .20
27 Kelly Kisio .05 .15
28 Nelson Emerson .05 .15
29 Ray Bourque .15 .40
30 Kelly Miller .05 .15
31 Peter Zezel .05 .15
32 Owen Nolan .07 .20
33 Sergei Makarov .05 .15
34 Stephane Richer .07 .20
35 Adam Graves .05 .15
36 Rob Ramage .05 .15
37 Ed Olczyk .05 .15
38 Jeff Hackett .05 .15
39 Ron Sutter .05 .15
40 Dale Hunter .05 .15
41 Nikolai Borschevsky .05 .15
42 Curtis Leschyshyn .05 .15
43 Mike Vernon .07 .20
44 Brent Sutter .05 .15
45 Rod Brind'Amour .07 .20
46 Sylvain Turgeon .05 .15
47 Kirk McLean .07 .20
48 Derek King .05 .15
49 Murray Craven .05 .15
50 Jaromir Jagr .25 .60
51 Guy Carbonneau .05 .15
52 Tony Granato .05 .15
53 Mark Tinordi .05 .15
54 Brad McCrimmon .05 .15
55 Randy Wood .05 .15
56 Scott Young .05 .15
57 Jamie Baker .05 .15
58 Don Beaupre .07 .20
59 Bob Probert .07 .20
60 Ray Ferraro .05 .15
61 Alexei Kasatonov .05 .15
62 Corey Millen .05 .15
63 Scott Mellanby .07 .20
64 Brian Benning .05 .15
65 Doug Lidster .05 .15
66 Doug Gilmour .12 .30
67 Shawn McEachern .05 .15
68 Tim Cheveldae .07 .20
69 Jeff Norton .05 .15
70 Ed Belfour .10 .25
71 Thomas Steen .05 .15
72 Stephan Lebeau .05 .15
73 James Patrick .05 .15
74 Joel Otto .05 .15
75 Grant Fuhr .10 .25
76 Calle Johansson .05 .15
77 Donald Audette .05 .15
78 Geoff Courtnall .05 .15
79 Fredrik Olausson .05 .15
80 Dimitri Khristich .05 .15
81 John MacLean .07 .20
82 Dominic Roussel .07 .20
83 Ray Sheppard .07 .20
84 Christian Ruuttu .05 .15
85 Mike McPhee .05 .15
86 Adam Creighton .05 .15
87 Uwe Krupp .05 .15
88 Steve Leach .05 .15
89 Kevin Miller .05 .15
90 Charlie Huddy .05 .15
91 Mark Howe .10 .25
92 Sylvain Cote .05 .15
93 Anatoli Semenov .05 .15
94 Jeff Beukeboom .05 .15
95 Gord Murphy .05 .15
96 Rob Pearson .05 .15
97 Esa Tikkanen .05 .15
98 Dave Gagner .07 .20
99 Mike Richter .10 .25
100 Jari Kurri .10 .25
101 Chris Chelios .10 .25
102 Peter Sidorkiewicz .05 .15
103 Scott Lachance .05 .15
104 Zarley Zalapski .05 .15
105 Denis Savard .12 .30
106 Paul Coffey .10 .25
107 Ulf Dahlen .05 .15
108 Shayne Corson .05 .15
109 Jimmy Carson .05 .15
110 Petr Svoboda .05 .15
111 Scott Stevens .10 .25
112 Kevin Lowe .05 .15
113 Chris Kontos .05 .15
114 Evgeny Davydov .05 .15
115 Doug Wilson .05 .15
116 Curtis Joseph .10 .25
117 Trevor Linden .07 .20
118 Michal Pivonka .05 .15
119 Dave Ellett .05 .15
120 Mike Ricci .05 .15
121 Al MacInnis .07 .20
122 Kevin Dineen .05 .15
123 Norm Maciver .05 .15
124 Darius Kasparaitis .05 .15
125 Adam Oates .10 .25
126 Sean Burke .05 .15
127 Dave Manson .05 .15
128 Eric Desjardins .07 .20
129 Tomas Sandstrom .05 .15
130 Russ Courtnall .05 .15
131 Roman Hamrlik .05 .15
132 Teppo Numminen .05 .15
133 Pat Falloon .05 .15
134 Jyrki Lumme .05 .15
135 Joe Sakic .25 .60
136 Kevin Hatcher .05 .15
137 Wendel Clark .07 .20
138 Neil Wilkinson .05 .15
139 Craig Simpson .05 .15
140 Kelly Hrudey .07 .20
141 Steve Thomas .05 .15
142 Mike Modano .15 .40
143 Garry Galley .05 .15
144 Jim Johnson .05 .15
145 Rod Langway .05 .15
146 Bob Sweeney .05 .15
147 Gary Leeman .05 .15
148 Alexei Zhitnik .05 .15
149 Adam Foote .05 .15
150 Mark Recchi .12 .30
151 Ron Francis .12 .30
152 Ron Hextall .07 .20
153 Michel Goulet .05 .15
154 Vladimir Ruzicka .05 .15
155 Bill Ranford .07 .20
156 Mike Craig .05 .15
157 Vladimir Malakhov .05 .15
158 Nicklas Lidstrom .10 .25
159 Dale Hawerchuk .12 .30
160 Claude Lemieux .05 .15
161 Ulf Samuelsson .05 .15
162 John Vanbiesbrouck .07 .20
163 Patrice Brisebois .05 .15
164 Andrew Cassels .05 .15
165 Paul Ranheim .05 .15
166 Neal Broten .07 .20
167 Joe Reekie .05 .15
168 Derian Hatcher .05 .15
169 Don Sweeney .05 .15
170 Mike Keane .05 .15
171 Mark Fitzpatrick .05 .15
172 Paul Cavallini .05 .15
173 Garth Butcher .05 .15
174 Andrei Kovalenko .05 .15
175 Shawn Burr .05 .15
176 Mike Donnelly .05 .15
177 Glenn Healy .07 .20
178 Gilbert Dionne .05 .15
179 Mike Ramsey .05 .15
180 Glenn Anderson .10 .25
181 Pelle Eklund .05 .15
182 Kerry Huffman .05 .15
183 Johan Garpenlov .05 .15
184 Kjell Samuelsson .05 .15
185 Todd Elik .05 .15
186 Craig Janney .07 .20
187 Dmitri Kvartalnov .05 .15
188 Al Iafrate .05 .15
189 John Cullen .05 .15
190 Steve Duchesne .05 .15
191 Theo Fleury .05 .15
192 Steve Smith .05 .15
193 Jon Casey .07 .20
194 Jeff Brown .05 .15
195 Keith Tkachuk .10 .25
196 Greg Adams .05 .15
197 Mike Ridley .05 .15
198 Bobby Holik .05 .15
199 Joe Nieuwendyk .07 .20
200 Mark Messier .10 .25
201 Jim Hrivnak .05 .15
202 Patrick Poulin .05 .15
203 Alexei Kovalev .07 .20
204 Robert Reichel .05 .15
205 David Shaw .05 .15
206 Brent Gilchrist .05 .15
207 Craig Billington .07 .20
208 Bob Errey .05 .15
209 Dmitri Mironov .05 .15
210 Dixon Ward .05 .15
211 Rick Zombo .05 .15
212 Marty McSorley .05 .15
213 Geoff Sanderson .07 .20
214 Dino Ciccarelli .07 .20
215 Tony Amonte .07 .20
216 Dimitri Yushkevich .05 .15
217 Scott Niedermayer .10 .25
218 Sergei Nemchinov .05 .15
219 Steve Konroyd .05 .15
220 Patrick Flatley .05 .15
221 Steve Chiasson .05 .15
222 Alexander Mogilny .07 .20
223 Pat Elynuik .05 .15
224 Jamie Macoun .05 .15
225 Tom Barrasso .07 .20
226 Gaetan Duchesne .05 .15
227 Eric Weinrich .05 .15
228 Dave Poulin .05 .15
229 Slava Fetisov .05 .15
230 Brian Bradley .05 .15
231 Petr Nedved .05 .15
232 Phil Housley .07 .20
233 Terry Carkner .05 .15
234 Kirk Muller .05 .15
235 Brian Leetch .10 .25
236 Rob Blake .07 .20
237 Chris Terreri .07 .20
238 Brendan Shanahan .12 .30
239 Paul Ysebaert .05 .15
240 Jeremy Roenick .15 .40
241 Gary Roberts .05 .15
242 Petr Klima .05 .15
243 Glen Wesley .05 .15
244 Vincent Damphousse .07 .20
245 Luc Robitaille .07 .20
246 Dallas Drake RC .10 .25
247 Rob Gaudreau RC .10 .25
248 Tommy Sjodin .05 .15
249 Richard Smehlik .05 .15
250 Sergei Fedorov .15 .40
251 Steve Heinze .05 .15
252 Luke Richardson .05 .15
253 Doug Weight .07 .20
254 Martin Rucinsky .05 .15
255 Sergio Momesso .05 .15
256 Alexei Zhamnov .07 .20
257 Bob Kudelski .05 .15
258 Brian Skrudland .05 .15
259 Terry Yake .05 .15
260 Alexei Gusarov .05 .15
261 Sandis Ozolinsh .05 .15
262 Ted Donato .05 .15
263 Bruce Driver .05 .15
264 Yves Racine .05 .15
265 Mike Peluso .05 .15
266 Craig Muni .05 .15
267 Bob Carpenter .05 .15
268 Kevin Haller .05 .15
269 Brad May .07 .20
270 Joe Kocur .05 .15
271 Igor Korolev .05 .15
272 Troy Murray .05 .15
273 Daren Puppa .05 .15
274 Gordie Roberts .05 .15
275 Michel Petit .05 .15
276 Vincent Riendeau .05 .15
277 Robert Petrovicky .05 .15
278 Valeri Zelepukin .05 .15
279 Bob Bassen .05 .15
280 Darrin Shannon .05 .15
281 Dominik Hasek .20 .50
282 Craig Ludwig .05 .15
283 Lyle Odelein .05 .15
284 Alexander Semak .05 .15
285 Richard Matvichuk .05 .15
286 Ken Daneyko .05 .15
287 Jan Erixon .05 .15
288 Robert Dirk .05 .15
289 Laurie Boschman .05 .15
290 Greg Paslawski .05 .15
291 Rob Zamuner .05 .15
292 Todd Gill .05 .15
293 Neil Brady .05 .15
294 Murray Baron .05 .15
295 Peter Taglianetti .05 .15
296 Wayne Presley .05 .15
297 Paul Broten .05 .15
298 Dana Murzyn .05 .15
299 J.J. Daigneault .05 .15
300 Wayne Gretzky .50 1.25
301 Keith Acton .05 .15
302 Yuri Khmylev .05 .15
303 Frank Musil .05 .15
304 Bob Rouse .05 .15
305 Greg Gilbert .05 .15
306 Geoff Smith .05 .15
307 Adam Burt .05 .15
308 Phil Bourque .05 .15
309 Igor Kravchuk .05 .15
310 Steve Yzerman .25 .60
311 Darryl Sydor .05 .15
312 Tie Domi .05 .15
313 Sergei Zubov .05 .15
314 Chris Dahlquist .05 .15
315 Patrick Roy .25 .60
316 Mark Osborne .05 .15
317 Kelly Buchberger .05 .15
318 John LeClair .10 .25
319 Randy McKay .05 .15
320 Jody Hull .05 .15
321 Paul Stanton .05 .15
322 Steven Finn .05 .15
323 Rich Sutter .05 .15
324 Ray Whitney .05 .15
325 Kevin Stevens .05 .15
326 Valeri Kamensky .07 .20
327 Doug Zmolek .05 .15
328 Mikhail Tatarinov .05 .15
329 Ken Wregget .05 .15
330 Joe Juneau .07 .20
331 Teemu Selanne .20 .50
332 Trent Yawney .05 .15
333 Pavel Bure .10 .25
334 Jim Paek .05 .15
335 Brett Hull .15 .40
336 Tommy Soderstrom .07 .20
337 Grigori Panteleyev .05 .15
338 Kevin Todd .05 .15
339 Mark Janssens .05 .15
340 Rick Tocchet .07 .20
341 Wendell Young .05 .15
342 Cam Neely .10 .25
343 Dave Andreychuk .10 .25
344 Peter Bondra .07 .20
345 Pat LaFontaine .10 .25
346 Robb Stauber .05 .15
347 Brian Mullen .05 .15
348 Joe Murphy .05 .15
349 Pat Jablonski .05 .15
350 Mario Lemieux .40 1.00
351 Sergei Bautin .05 .15
352 Claude Lapointe .05 .15
353 Dean Evason .05 .15
354 John Tucker .05 .15
355 Drake Berehowsky .05 .15
356 Gerald Diduck .05 .15
357 Todd Krygier .05 .15
358 Adrien Plavsic .05 .15
359 Sylvain Lefebvre .05 .15
360 Kay Whitmore .05 .15
361 Sheldon Kennedy .05 .15
362 Kris King .05 .15
363 Marc Bergevin .05 .15
364 Keith Primeau .05 .15
365 Jimmy Waite .07 .20
366 Dean Kennedy .05 .15
367 Mike Krushelnyski .05 .15
368 Ron Tugnutt .07 .20
369 Bob Beers .05 .15
370 Randy Burridge .05 .15
371 David Reid .05 .15
372 Frantisek Kucera .05 .15
373 Scott Pellerin RC .10 .25
374 Brad Dalgarno .05 .15
375 Martin Straka .05 .15
376 Scott Pearson .05 .15
377 Arturs Irbe .07 .20
378 Jiri Slegr .05 .15
379 Stephane Fiset .07 .20
380 Stu Barnes .05 .15
381 Ric Nattress .05 .15
382 Steven King .05 .15
383 Michael Nylander .05 .15
384 Keith Brown .05 .15
385 Gino Odjick .05 .15
386 Bryan Marchment .05 .15
387 Mike Foligno .05 .15
388 Zdeno Ciger .05 .15
389 Dave Taylor .05 .15
390 Mike Sullivan .05 .15
391 Shawn Chambers .05 .15
392 Brad Marsh .05 .15
393 Mike Hough .05 .15
394 Jeff Reese .05 .15
395 Bill Guerin .05 .15
396 Greg Hawgood .05 .15
397 Jim Sandlak .05 .15
398 Stephane Matteau .05 .15
399 John Blue .07 .20
400 Tony Twist .05 .15
401 Luciano Borsato .05 .15
402 Gerard Gallant .05 .15
403 Rick Tabaracci .05 .15
404 Nick Kypreos .05 .15
405 Marty McInnis .05 .15
406 Craig Wolanin .05 .15
407 Mark Lamb .05 .15
408 Martin Gelinas .05 .15
409 Ronnie Stern .05 .15
410 Ken Sutton .05 .15
411 Brian Noonan .05 .15
412 Stephane Quintal .05 .15
413 Rob Zettler .05 .15
414 Gino Cavallini .05 .15
415 Mark Hardy .05 .15
416 Jay Wells .05 .15
417 Keith Jones .05 .15
418 Dave McLlwain .05 .15
419 Frank Pietrangelo .07 .20
420 Jocelyn Lemieux .05 .15
421 Slava Kozlov .07 .20
422 Randy Moller .05 .15
423 Kevin Dahl .05 .15
424 Shjon Podein RC .10 .25
425 Shane Churla .05 .15
426 Guy Hebert .07 .20
427 Mikael Andersson .05 .15
428 Robert Kron .05 .15
429 Mike Eagles .05 .15
430 Alan May .05 .15
431 Ron Wilson .05 .15
432 Darcy Wakaluk .05 .15
433 Rob Ray .05 .15
434 Brent Ashton .05 .15
435 Jason Woolley .05 .15
436 Basil McRae .07 .20
437 Andre Racicot .05 .15
438 Brad Werenka .05 .15
439 Josef Beranek .05 .15
440 Dave Christian .05 .15
441 Theo Fleury LBM .05 .15
442 Mark Recchi LBM .12 .30
443 Cliff Ronning LBM .05 .15
444 Tony Granato LBM .05 .15
445 John Vanbiesbrouck LBM .07 .20
446 Jari Kurri HL .10 .25
447 Mike Gartner HL .07 .20
448 Steve Yzerman HL .25 .60
449 Glenn Anderson HL .10 .25
450 Iafrate .05 .15
Cote
Hatcher
451 Luc Robitaille HL .07 .20
452 Pittsburgh Penguins HL .05 .15
17-Game Winning Streak
453 Corey Hirsch TR .07 .20
454 Jesse Belanger TR .05 .15
455 Philippe Boucher TR .05 .15
456 Robert Lang TR .07 .20
457 Doug Barrault TR RC .05 .15
458 Steve Konowalchuk TR .05 .15
459 Oleg Petrov TR .05 .15
460 Niclas Andersson TR .05 .15
461 Milan Tichy RC .05 .15
462 Darrin Madeley TR RC .10 .25
463 Tyler Wright TR .05 .15
464 Sergei Krivokrasov TR .05 .15
465 Vladimir Vujtek .05 .15
466 Rick Knickle RC .07 .20
467 Gord Kruppke RC .07 .20
468 David Emma .05 .15
469 Scott Thomas RC .10 .25
470 Shawn Rivers RC .07 .20
471 Jason Bowen TR RC .10 .25
472 Bryan Smolinski TR .05 .15
473 Chris Simon TR RC .10 .25
474 Peter Ciavaglia RC .07 .20
475 Sergei Zholtok TR .05 .15
476 Radek Hamr RC .10 .25
477 T.Selanne .20 .50
A.Mogilny SL
478 Adam Oates SL .10 .25
479 Mario Lemieux SL .40 1.00
480 Mario Lemieux SL .40 1.00
481 Dave Andreychuk SL .10 .25
482 Phil Housley SL .07 .20
483 Tom Barrasso SL .07 .20
484 Felix Potvin SL .20 .50
485 Ed Belfour SL .10 .25
486 S.S.Marie Mem. Cup .05 .15
487 Canadiens Stanley Cup .05 .15
488 Mighty Ducks Logo .05 .15
489 Guy Hebert .07 .20
490 Sean Hill Ducks .05 .15
491 Florida Panthers Logo .05 .15
492 J.Vanbiesbrouck Panthers .07 .20
493 Tom Fitzgerald Panthers .05 .15
494 Paul DiPietro .05 .15
495 David Volek .05 .15
496 Alexandre Daigle SP .05 .15
497 Shawn McEachern .05 .15
498 Rich Sutter .05 .15
499 Evgeny Davydov .05 .15
500 Sean Hill .05 .15
501 John Vanbiesbrouck .07 .20
502 Guy Hebert .07 .20
503 Scott Mellanby .07 .20
504 Ron Tugnutt .07 .20
505 Brian Skrudland .05 .15
506 Nelson Emerson .05 .15
507 Kevin Todd .05 .15
508 Terry Carkner .05 .15
509 Stephane Quintal .05 .15
510 Paul Stanton .05 .15
511 Terry Yake .05 .15
512 Brian Benning .05 .15
513 Brian Propp .05 .15
514 Steven King .05 .15
515 Joe Cirella .05 .15
516 Andy Moog .10 .25
517 Paul Ysebaert .05 .15
518 Petr Klima .05 .15
519 Corey Millen .05 .15
520 Phil Housley .07 .20
521 Craig Billington .07 .20
522 Jeff Norton .05 .15
523 Neil Wilkinson .05 .15
524 Doug Lidster .05 .15
525 Steve Larmer .07 .20
526 Jon Casey .07 .20
527 Brad McCrimmon .05 .15
528 Alexei Kasatonov .05 .15
529 Andrei Lomakin .05 .15
530 Daren Puppa .05 .15
531 Sergei Makarov .05 .15
532 Jim Sandlak .05 .15
533 Glenn Healy .07 .20
534 Martin Gelinas .05 .15
535 Igor Larionov .05 .15
536 Anatoli Semenov .05 .15
537 Mark Fitzpatrick .05 .15
538 Paul Cavallini .05 .15
539 Jimmy Waite .07 .20
540 Yves Racine .05 .15
541 Jeff Hackett .05 .15
542 Marty McSorley .05 .15
543 Scott Pearson .05 .15
544 Ron Hextall .07 .20
545 Gaetan Duchesne .05 .15
546 Jamie Baker .05 .15
547 Troy Loney .05 .15
548 Gord Murphy .05 .15
549 Bob Kudelski .05 .15
550 Dean Evason .05 .15
551 Mike Peluso .05 .15
552 Dave Poulin .05 .15
553 Randy Ladouceur .05 .15
554 Tom Fitzgerald .05 .15
555 Denis Savard .12 .30
556 Kelly Kisio .05 .15
557 Craig Simpson .05 .15
558 Stu Grimson .05 .15
559 Mike Hough .05 .15
560 Gerard Gallant .05 .15
561 Greg Gilbert .05 .15
562 Vladimir Ruzicka .05 .15
563 Jim Hrivnak .05 .15
564 Dave Lowry .05 .15
565 Todd Ewen .05 .15
566 Bob Errey .05 .15
567 Bryan Trottier .12 .30
568 Grant Ledyard .05 .15
569 Keith Brown .05 .15
570 Darren Turcotte .05 .15
571 Patrick Poulin .05 .15
572 Jimmy Carson .05 .15
573 Eric Weinrich .05 .15
574 James Patrick .05 .15
575 Bob Beers .05 .15
576 Chris Joseph .05 .15
577 Bryan Marchment .05 .15
578 Bob Carpenter .05 .15
579 Craig Muni .05 .15
580 Pat Elynuik .05 .15
581 Todd Elik .05 .15
582 Doug Brown .05 .15
583 Dave McLlwain .05 .15
584 Dave Tippett .05 .15
585 Jesse Belanger .05 .15
586 Chris Pronger .10 .25
587 Alexandre Daigle .05 .15
588 Cam Stewart RC .10 .25
589 Derek Plante RC .10 .25
590 Pat Peake .05 .15
591 Alexander Karpovtsev .05 .15
592 Rob Niedermayer .07 .20
593 Jocelyn Thibault RC .10 .25
594 Jason Arnott RC .20 .50
595 Mike Rathje .05 .15
596 Chris Gratton .07 .20
597 Markus Naslund .10 .25
598 Dmitri Filimonov .05 .15
599 Andrei Trefilov .05 .15
600 Michal Sykora RC .10 .25
601 Greg Johnson .05 .15
602 Mikael Renberg .10 .25
603 Alexei Yashin .07 .20
604 Damian Rhodes RC .10 .25
605 Jeff Shantz RC .05 .15
606 Brent Gretzky RC .10 .25
607 Boris Mironov .05 .15
608 Ted Drury .05 .15
609 Chris Osgood RC .60 1.50
610 Jim Storm RC .05 .15
611 Dave Karpa .05 .15
612 Stewart Malgunas RC .10 .25
613 Jason Smith RC .05 .15
614 German Titov RC .10 .25
615 Patrick Carnback RC .10 .25
616 Jaroslav Modry RC .10 .25
617 Scott Levins RC .10 .25
618 Fred Brathwaite RC .10 .25
619 Ilya Byakin RC .05 .15
620 Jarkko Varvio .05 .15
621 Jim Montgomery RC .10 .25
622 Vesa Viitakoski RC .10 .25
623 Alexei Kudashov RC .10 .25
624 Pavol Demitra .12 .30
625 Iain Fraser RC .10 .25
626 Peter Popovic RC .10 .25
627 Kirk Maltby RC .10 .25
628 Garth Snow RC .05 .15
629 Peter White RC .05 .15
630 Mike McKee RC .05 .15
631 Darren McCarty RC .15 .40
632 Pat Neaton RC .10 .25
633 Sandy McCarthy .05 .15
634 Pierre Sevigny .05 .15
635 Matt Martin RC .10 .25
636 John Slaney .05 .15
637 Bob Corkum .05 .15
638 Mike Stapleton RC .07 .20
639 Bill Houlder .05 .15
640 Warren Rychel .05 .15
641 Garry Valk .05 .15
642 Greg Hawgood .05 .15
643 Randy Gilhen .05 .15
644 Stu Barnes .05 .15
645 Fredrik Olausson .05 .15
646 Geoff Smith .05 .15
647 Mike Foligno .05 .15
648 Martin Brodeur .25 .60
649 Ryan McGill .05 .15
650 Jeff Reese .05 .15
651 Mike Sillinger .05 .15
652 Brent Severyn RC .10 .25
653 Rob Ramage .05 .15
654 Dixon Ward .05 .15
655 Danton Cole .05 .15
656 Viacheslav Butsayev .05 .15
657 Ron Wilson .05 .15
658 Paul Broten .05 .15
659 Mike Hudson .07 .20
660 Trevor Kidd .07 .20
661 Travis Green .07 .20
662 Wayne Gretzky 802 .50 1.25
NNO A.Daigle Redemption .05 .15
NNO Eric Lindros AS SP 4.00 10.00

1993-94 Score Gold Rush

The 1993-94 Score Gold Rush set consists of 166 standard-size cards. The fronts are identical in design with the regular second-series Score cards, except for the metallic finish and gold marbleized borders. The backs are nearly identical to the regular issue cards, the Gold Rush logo at the top being the only difference. No Gold Rush parallels were produced for first series cards.

COMPLETE SET (166) 15.00 40.00
*VETS: 2.5X TO 6X BASIC CARDS
*ROOKIES: 1.2X TO 3X BASIC CARDS

1993-94 Score Canadian Gold

COMPLETE SET (166) 15.00 40.00
*ROOKIES: 1.2X TO 3X BASIC CARDS
*VETS: 2.5X TO 6X BASIC CARDS
ONE GOLD PER SER.2 FOIL PACK

1993-94 Score Dream Team

Randomly inserted at the rate of 1:24 first series Canadian packs, this 24 card standard-size set features Score's Dream Team selections. Horizontal fronts feature an action photo and a head shot at lower right. The player's name and position appear in beneath the large photo. The backs contain career highlights and are numbered "X of 24".

COMPLETE SET (24) 30.00 80.00
1 Tom Barrasso .75 2.00
2 Patrick Roy 8.00 20.00
3 Chris Chelios 1.50 4.00
4 Al MacInnis .75 2.00
5 Scott Stevens .75 2.00
6 Brian Leetch 1.50 4.00
7 Ray Bourque 2.50 6.00
8 Paul Coffey 1.50 4.00
9 Al Iafrate .40 1.00
10 Mario Lemieux 8.00 20.00
11 Wayne Gretzky 10.00 25.00
12 Eric Lindros 1.50 4.00
13 Pat LaFontaine 1.50 4.00
14 Joe Sakic 3.00 8.00
15 Pierre Turgeon .75 2.00
16 Steve Yzerman 8.00 20.00
17 Adam Oates .75 2.00
18 Brett Hull 2.00 5.00
19 Pavel Bure 1.50 4.00
20 Alexander Mogilny .75 2.00
21 Teemu Selanne 1.50 4.00
22 Steve Larmer .75 2.00
23 Kevin Stevens .40 1.00
24 Luc Robitaille .75 2.00

1993-94 Score Dynamic Duos Canadian

Randomly inserted at a rate of 1:48 Canadian second-series packs, this nine-card standard-size set highlights two team members on each card. Both the front and back of each card features a color player action shot. The player's name appears in red lettering within the team-colored bottom margin. The words "Dynamic Duos" appears in gold foil along the right side. A red maple leaf is placed at the upper left. The cards are numbered on the back with a "DD" prefix.

COMPLETE SET (9) 20.00 50.00
1 D.Gilmour/D.Andreychuk 2.00 5.00
2 T.Selanne/A.Zhamnov 2.50 6.00
3 A.Daigle/A.Yashin 1.50 4.00
4 G.Roberts/J.Nieuwendyk 2.00 5.00
5 J.Sakic/M.Sundin 5.00 12.00
6 B.Bellows/K.Muller 1.50 4.00
7 S.Corson/J.Arnott 1.50 4.00
8 M.Lemieux/K.Stevens 6.00 15.00
9 P.Turgeon/Derek King 1.50 4.00

1993-94 Score Dynamic Duos U.S.

Randomly inserted at a rate of 1:48 U.S. second series packs, this nine-card standard-size set highlights two team members on each card. Both the front and back of each card features a color player action shot. The player's name appears in red lettering within the team-colored bottom margin. The words "Dynamic Duos" appear in gold foil along the right side. A blue star is placed at the upper left. The cards are numbered on the back with a "DD" prefix.

COMPLETE SET (9) 25.00 60.00
DD1 M.Recchi/E.Lindros 3.00 8.00
DD2 LaFontaine/A.Mogilny 2.00 5.00
DD3 A.Oates/C.Neely 2.50 6.00
DD4 B.Hull/C.Janney 3.00 8.00
DD5 M.Messier/A.Graves 3.00 8.00
DD6 J.Roenick/J.Murphy 2.50 6.00
DD7 J.Kurri/W.Gretzky 6.00 15.00
DD8 S.Makarov/I.Larionov 2.00 5.00
DD9 S.Yzerman/S.Fedorov 5.00 12.00

1993-94 Score Franchise

Randomly inserted at a rate of 1:24 U.S. first series packs, this 24-card set features borderless color player action shots on the fronts, the backgrounds of which are ghosted and darkened. The cards are numbered "X of 24" on the back.

COMPLETE SET (24) 40.00 80.00
1 Ray Bourque 2.50 6.00
2 Pat Lafontaine 1.50 4.00
3 Al MacInnis .75 2.00
4 Jeremy Roenick 2.00 5.00
5 Mike Modano 2.00 5.00
6 Steve Yzerman 5.00 12.00
7 Bill Ranford .75 2.00
8 Sean Burke .75 2.00
9 Wayne Gretzky 6.00 15.00
10 Patrick Roy 6.00 15.00
11 Scott Stevens .75 2.00
12 Pierre Turgeon .75 2.00
13 Brian Leetch 1.50 4.00
14 Peter Sidorkiewicz .75 2.00
15 Eric Lindros 1.50 4.00
16 Mario Lemieux 6.00 15.00
17 Joe Sakic 3.00 8.00
18 Brett Hull 2.00 5.00
19 Pat Falloon .40 1.00
20 Brian Bradley .40 1.00
21 Doug Gilmour .75 2.00
22 Pavel Bure 1.50 4.00
23 Kevin Hatcher .40 1.00
24 Teemu Selanne 1.50 4.00

1993-94 Score International Stars

Inserted one per series one jumbo pack, this 22-card standard-size set highlights some of the NHL's hottest international stars. The fronts feature full-bleed color action shots, with the player's name and nationality appearing in a banner at the bottom that bears the colors of his national flag. The words "International Stars" in gold foil are printed at the top. On purplish backgrounds, the backs carry a color headshot at the upper left, with the player's national flag to the right and his name and country in his flag's colors below. Career highlights at the bottom round out the card. The cards are numbered on the back as "X of 22." Multipliers to determine values for the French version can be found in the header below.

COMPLETE SET (22) 8.00 20.00
*CANADIAN: .4X TO 1X BASIC INSERTS
1 Pavel Bure .75 2.00
2 Teemu Selanne .75 2.00
3 Sergei Fedorov 1.25 3.00
4 Peter Bondra .40 1.00
5 Tommy Soderstrom .20 .50
6 Robert Reichel .20 .50
7 Jari Kurri .75 2.00
8 Alexander Mogilny .40 1.00
9 Jaromir Jagr 1.25 3.00
10 Mats Sundin .75 2.00
11 Uwe Krupp .20 .50
12 Nikolai Borschevsky .20 .50
13 Ulf Dahlen .20 .50
14 Alexander Semak .20 .50
15 Michal Pivonka .20 .50
16 Sergei Nemchinov .20 .50
17 Darius Kasparaitis .20 .50
18 Sandis Ozolinsh .20 .50
19 Alexei Kovalev .40 1.00
20 Dimitri Khristich .20 .50
21 Tomas Sandstrom .20 .50
22 Petr Nedved .20 .50

1994-95 Score Samples

Issued in packs of 12, the 1994 Score hockey Hobby Sample cards measure the standard-size and preview the 1994 Score hockey issue. The top right and left corners have been cut off of some cards. The fronts feature color action player photos with white borders, and a small headshot in the left bottom corner. The player's name appears in colorful letters at the bottom of the picture. The horizontal backs carry another player photo on the left, along with the player's name, biography, career highlights and stats on the right.

COMPLETE SEALED SET (12) 1.50 4.00
1 Eric Lindros .20 .50
Philadelph
2 Pat LaFontaine .01 .05
Buffalo
3 Wendel Clark .01 .05
Toronto Ma
4 Cam Neely .01 .05
5 Larry Murphy .01 .05
Pittsburgh
6 Patrick Poulin .01 .05
Chicago
7 Bob Beers .01 .05
Edmonton Oile
254 Jason Arnott .02 .10
Edmonton Oilers
Young Stars
CI3 Darius Kasparaitis .75 2.00
New
TF16 Alexandre Daigle .40 1.00
Ottawa
NNO Pro Debut Rookie .20 .50
Redemp
NNO Title Card .01 .05

1994-95 Score

is 275-card standard-size set was issued in one ries and does not have a comprehensive player lection. Due to the NHL lock-out, series two was placed on the production schedule by Select; erefore many stars such as Patrick Roy and Wayne etzky were not featured in this set. The unique design tures a full color player photo, surrounded by a ite border. The Score logo appears in the top right rner, while a player head shot and team logo minate the lower left. The upper right corner displays e globes; player name appears in a multi-hued strip ong the card bottom. Cards were issued in 14-card S. and Canadian packs that included one Gold Line rallel card. Retail jumbo packs contained 30 cards d two Gold Line cards for $1.79. Subsets include orld Junior Championships (201-215), Season ghlights (241-247), Young Stars (248-262), and am Checklists (263-275). The only Rookie Card of te in the set is Mariusz Czerkawski.

OMPLETE SET (275) 6.00 15.00
Eric Lindros .10 .25
Pat LaFontaine .10 .25
Wendel Clark .07 .20
Cam Neely .10 .25
Larry Murphy .07 .20
Patrick Poulin .05 .15
Bob Beers .07 .20
James Patrick .05 .15
Gino Odjick .05 .15
Arturs Irbe .07 .20
Darius Kasparaitis .05 .15
Peter Bondra .07 .20
Garth Butcher .07 .20
Sergei Nemchinov .05 .15
Doug Brown .05 .15
Anatoli Semenov .05 .15
Mike McPhee .05 .15
Joel Otto .05 .15
Dino Ciccarelli .07 .20
Marty McSorley .05 .15
Ron Tugnutt .07 .20
Scott Niedermayer .10 .25
John Tucker .05 .15
Norm Maciver .05 .15
Kevin Miller .05 .15
Garry Galley .05 .15
Ted Donato .05 .15
Bob Kudelski .05 .15
Craig Muni .05 .15
Nikolai Borschevsky .05 .15
Tom Barrasso .07 .20
Brent Sutter .07 .20
Igor Kravchuk .05 .15
Andrew Cassels .05 .15
Jyrki Lumme .05 .15
Sandis Ozolinsh .05 .15
Steve Thomas .05 .15
Dave Poulin .05 .15
Andrei Kovalenko .05 .15
Steve Larmer .07 .20
Nelson Emerson .05 .15
Guy Hebert .07 .20
Russ Courtnall .05 .15
Gary Suter .05 .15
Steve Chiasson .05 .15
Guy Carbonneau .05 .15
Rob Blake .10 .25
Roman Hamrlik .07 .20
Valeri Zelepukin .05 .15
Mark Recchi .12 .30
Darrin Madeley .05 .15
Steve Duchesne .05 .15
Brian Skrudland .05 .15
Craig Simpson .05 .15
Todd Gill .05 .15
Dirk Graham .05 .15
Joe Mullen .07 .20
Doug Weight .07 .20
Michael Nylander .07 .20
Kirk McLean .07 .20
Igor Larionov .05 .15
Vladimir Malakhov .05 .15
Kelly Miller .05 .15
Curtis Leschyshyn .05 .15
Thomas Steen .05 .15
Jeff Beukeboom .05 .15
Troy Loney .05 .15
Mark Tinordi .05 .15
Theo Fleury .10 .25
Slava Kozlov .07 .20
Tony Granato .05 .15
Daren Puppa .07 .20
Brian Bellows .07 .20
Bernie Nicholls .07 .20
Rick Zombo .05 .15
Brad Shaw .05 .15
Josef Beranek .05 .15
Dominik Hasek .20 .50
Steve Leach .05 .15
David Reid .05 .15
Dave Lowry .05 .15
Martin Straka .05 .15
Dave Ellett .05 .15
Sean Burke .07 .20
Craig MacTavish .05 .15
Cliff Ronning .05 .15
Bob Errey .05 .15
Marty McInnis .05 .15
Mats Sundin .07 .20
Randy Burridge .05 .15
Teppo Numminen .05 .15
Tony Amonte .07 .20
Terry Yake .05 .15
Paul Cavallini .05 .15
German Titov .05 .15
Vladimir Konstantinov .07 .20
Darryl Sydor .05 .15
Chris Joseph .05 .15
Corey Millen .05 .15
Brett Hull .20 .50
Don Sweeney .05 .15
Scott Mellanby .07 .20
Mathieu Schneider .05 .15
Brad May .05 .15
Dominic Roussel .07 .20
Jamie Macoun .05 .15
Bryan Marchment .07 .20
Shawn McEachern .05 .15
Murray Craven .05 .15
Eric Desjardins .07 .20
Jon Casey .07 .20
Mike Gartner .10 .25
Neal Broten .07 .20
Jari Kurri .07 .20
Bruce Driver .05 .15
Patrick Flatley .05 .15
Gord Murphy .05 .15
Dimitri Khristich .05 .15
Nicklas Lidstrom .10 .25
120 Al MacInnis .07 .20
121 Steve Smith .05 .15
122 Zdeno Ciger .05 .15
123 Tie Domi .07 .20
124 Joe Juneau .07 .20
125 Todd Elik .05 .15
126 Stephane Fiset .07 .20
127 Craig Janney .07 .20
128 Stephan Lebeau .05 .15
129 Richard Smehlik .05 .15
130 Mike Richter .10 .25
131 Danton Cole .05 .15
132 Rod Brind'Amour .07 .20
133 Dave Archibald .05 .15
134 Dana Murzyn .05 .15
135 Jaromir Jagr .25 .60
136 Esa Tikkanen .05 .15
137 Rob Pearson .05 .15
138 Stu Barnes .05 .15
139 Frank Musil .05 .15
140 Ron Hextall .07 .20
141 Adam Oates .10 .25
142 Ken Daneyko .05 .15
143 Dale Hunter .05 .15
144 Geoff Sanderson .07 .20
145 Kelly Hrudey .07 .20
146 Kirk Muller .05 .15
147 Fredrik Olausson .05 .15
148 Derian Hatcher .05 .15
149 Ed Belfour .10 .25
150 Steve Yzerman .25 .60
151 Adam Foote .05 .15
152 Pat Falloon .05 .15
153 Shawn Chambers .05 .15
154 Alexei Zhamnov .07 .20
155 Brendan Shanahan .12 .30
156 Ulf Samuelsson .05 .15
157 Donald Audette .05 .15
158 Bob Corkum .05 .15
159 Joe Nieuwendyk .10 .25
160 Felix Potvin .10 .25
161 Geoff Courtnall .05 .15
162 Yves Racine .05 .15
163 Tom Fitzgerald .05 .15
164 Adam Graves .05 .15
165 Vincent Damphousse .07 .20
166 Pierre Turgeon .07 .20
167 Craig Billington .07 .20
168 Al Iafrate .05 .15
169 Darren Turcotte .05 .15
170 Joe Murphy .05 .15
171 Alexei Zhitnik .07 .20
172 John MacLean .07 .20
173 Andy Moog .10 .25
174 Shayne Corson .05 .15
175 Ray Sheppard .07 .20
176 Johan Garpenlov .05 .15
177 Ron Sutter .05 .15
178 Teemu Selanne .20 .50
179 Brian Bradley .05 .15
180 Ray Bourque .15 .40
181 Curtis Joseph .15 .40
182 Kevin Stevens .05 .15
183 Alexei Kasatonov .05 .15
184 Brian Leetch .10 .25
185 Doug Gilmour .12 .30
186 Gary Roberts .05 .15
187 Mike Keane .05 .15
188 Mike Modano .15 .40
189 Chris Chelios .10 .25
190 Pavel Bure .10 .25
191 Bob Essensa .05 .15
192 Dale Hawerchuk .12 .30
193 Scott Stevens .10 .25
194 Claude Lapointe .05 .15
195 Scott Lachance .05 .15
196 Gaetan Duchesne .05 .15
197 Kevin Dineen .05 .15
198 Doug Bodger .05 .15
199 Mike Ridley .05 .15
200 Alexander Mogilny .07 .20
201 Jamie Storr .07 .20
202 Jason Botterill .07 .20
203 Jeff Friesen .05 .15
204 Todd Harvey .05 .15
205 Brendan Witt .05 .15
206 Jason Allison .07 .20
207 Aaron Gavey .05 .15
208 Deron Quint .05 .15
209 Jason Bonsignore .10 .25
210 Richard Park .05 .15
211 Jamie Langenbrunner .07 .20
212 Vadim Sharifjanov .05 .15
213 Alexander Kharlamov .05 .15
214 Oleg Tverdovsky .07 .20
215 Valeri Bure .05 .15
216 Dane Jackson RC .05 .15
217 Josef Cierny RC .05 .15
218 Yevgeny Namestnikov .05 .15
219 Daniel Laperriere .05 .15
220 Fred Knipscheer .05 .15
221 Yan Kaminsky .05 .15
222 David Roberts .07 .20
223 Derek Mayer .05 .15
224 Jamie McLennan .07 .20
225 Kevin Smyth .05 .15
226 Todd Marchant .05 .15
227 Mariusz Czerkawski RC .10 .25
228 John Lilley .05 .15
229 Aaron Ward .05 .15
230 Brian Savage .05 .15
231 Jason Allison .07 .20
232 Maxim Bets .05 .15
233 Ted Crowley .05 .15
234 Todd Simon RC .05 .15
235 Zigmund Palffy .07 .20
236 Rene Corbet .05 .15
237 Mike Peca .07 .20
238 Dwayne Norris .05 .15
239 Andrei Nazarov .05 .15
240 David Sacco .05 .15
241 Wayne Gretzky HL .50 1.25
242 Mike Gartner .10 .25
243 Dino Ciccarelli .07 .20
244 Ron Francis .12 .30
245 Bernie Nicholls .07 .20
246 Dino Ciccarelli .07 .20
247 Brian Propp .05 .15
248 Alexandre Daigle YS .05 .15
249 Mikael Renberg YS .07 .20
250 Jocelyn Thibault YS .10 .25
251 Derek Plante YS .05 .15
252 Chris Pronger YS .10 .25
253 Alexei Yashin YS .10 .25
254 Jason Arnott YS .07 .20
255 Boris Mironov .05 .15
256 Chris Osgood YS .15 .40
257 Jesse Belanger .05 .15
258 Darren McCarty .05 .15
259 Trevor Kidd .07 .20
260 Oleg Petrov .05 .15
261 Mike Rathje .05 .15
262 John Slaney .05 .15
263 Anaheim Mighty Ducks .05 .15
Boston Bruins CL
264 Buffalo Sabres .05 .15
Calgary Flames CL
265 Chicago Blackhawks .05 .15
Dallas Stars CL
266 Detroit Red Wings .05 .15
Edmonton Oilers CL
267 Florida Panthers .05 .15
Hartford Whalers CL
268 Los Angeles Kings .05 .15
Montreal Canadiens CL
269 New Jersey Devils .05 .15
New York Islanders CL
270 New York Rangers .05 .15
Ottawa Senators CL
271 Philadelphia Flyers .05 .15
Pittsburgh Penguins CL
272 Quebec Nordiques .05 .15
St.Louis Blues CL
273 San Jose Sharks .05 .15
Tampa Bay Lightning CL
274 Toronto Maple Leafs .05 .15
Vancouver Canucks CL
275 Washington Capitals .05 .15
Winnipeg Jets CL

1994-95 Score Gold Line

These parallel cards were issued one per regular or jumbo pack. These differ from the basic cards through the usage of a gold foil coating. In a unique offer designed to promote set building, Score offered collectors who submitted complete team sets a limited Platinum foil team set in return. Redeemed gold cards were returned with a Pinnacle brand logo hole-punched through them.

*VETS: 4X TO 10X BASIC CARDS
*ROOKIES: 2.5X TO 6X BASIC CARDS
*HOLE PUNCHED: .8X TO 2X BASIC GOLD

1994-95 Score Platinum

This set was a partial parallel set to Score. Platinum cards could only be obtained through a mail-in offer via the trading of complete Score Gold Line team sets. The cards feature a platinum reflective mirror finish. Because the cards are almost invariably traded in complete team set form, that is how they are listed below. Score reportedly made 1,994 of each team set available for redemption. Pinnacle officials report very few sets were redeemed.

COMP.BLACKHAWKS (9) 15.00 30.00
COMP.BLUES (10) 15.00 30.00
COMP.BRUINS (11) 12.50 25.00
COMP.CANADIENS (10) 12.50 25.00
COMP.CANUCKS (11) 20.00 40.00
COMP.CAPITALS (10) 7.50 15.00
COMP.DEVILS (9) 7.50 15.00
COMP.FLAMES (10) 12.50 25.00
COMP.FLYERS (9) 30.00 60.00
COMP.ISLANDERS (11) 7.50 15.00
COMP.JETS (6) 12.50 25.00
COMP.KINGS (8) 50.00 75.00
COMP.LIGHTNING (7) 7.50 15.00
COMP.MAPLE LEAFS (11) 15.00 30.00
COMP.MIGHTY DUCKS (8) 7.50 15.00
COMP.NORDIQUES (11) 15.00 30.00
COMP.OILERS (10) 12.50 25.00
COMP.PANTHERS (8) 7.50 15.00
COMP.PENGUINS (10) 17.50 35.00
COMP.RANGERS (8) 15.00 30.00
COMP.RED WINGS (13) 20.00 40.00
COMP.SABRES (12) 10.00 20.00
COMP.SENATORS (8) 7.50 15.00
COMP.SHARKS (10) 10.00 20.00
COMP.STARS (8) 7.50 15.00
COMP.WHALERS (9) 7.50 15.00
*VETS: 20X TO 40X BASIC CARDS
*ROOKIES: 10X TO 20X BASIC CARDS

1994-95 Score Check It

The 18 cards in this set were randomly inserted into Score Canadian hobby product at the rate of 1:72 packs.

COMPLETE SET (18) 75.00 175.00
CI1 Eric Lindros 15.00 40.00
CI2 Scott Stevens 5.00 12.00
CI3 Darius Kasparaitis 3.00 8.00
CI4 Kevin Stevens 3.00 8.00
CI5 Brendan Shanahan 8.00 20.00
CI6 Jeremy Roenick 8.00 20.00
CI7 Ulf Samuelsson 3.00 8.00
CI8 Cam Neely 8.00 20.00
CI9 Adam Graves 10.00 25.00
CI10 Kirk Muller 3.00 8.00
CI11 Rick Tocchet 3.00 8.00
CI12 Gary Roberts 3.00 8.00
CI13 Wendel Clark 8.00 20.00
CI14 Keith Tkachuk 5.00 12.00
CI15 Theo Fleury 5.00 12.00
CI16 Claude Lemieux 4.00 10.00
CI17 Chris Chelios 4.00 10.00
CI18 Pat Verbeek 3.00 8.00

1994-95 Score Dream Team

The 24 cards in this set were randomly inserted into all Score U.S. product at the rate of 1:36 packs. The cards feature a holographic image on the front which must be angled properly in the light, along with player name and the 1994 Dream Team logo. A full color photo and player information appear on the back. The cards are numbered with an "DT" prefix.

COMPLETE SET (24) 50.00 100.00
DT1 Patrick Roy 8.00 20.00
DT2 Felix Potvin 2.50 6.00
DT3 Ray Bourque 2.50 6.00
DT4 Brian Leetch 2.00 5.00
DT5 Scott Stevens 1.50 4.00
DT6 Paul Coffey 2.00 5.00
DT7 Al MacInnis 1.50 4.00
DT8 Chris Chelios 2.00 5.00
DT9 Adam Graves 1.50 4.00
DT10 Luc Robitaille 1.00 2.50
DT11 Dave Andreychuk 1.00 2.50
DT12 Sergei Fedorov 2.50 6.00
DT13 Doug Gilmour 1.50 4.00
DT14 Wayne Gretzky 8.00 20.00
DT15 Mario Lemieux 6.00 15.00
DT16 Mark Messier 2.50 6.00
DT17 Mike Modano 2.50 6.00
DT18 Jeremy Roenick 2.50 6.00
DT19 Eric Lindros 3.00 8.00
DT20 Steve Yzerman 5.00 12.00
DT21 Alexandre Daigle 1.00 2.50
DT22 Brett Hull 2.50 6.00
DT23 Cam Neely 2.00 5.00
DT24 Pavel Bure 2.50 6.00

1994-95 Score Franchise

The 26 cards in this set were randomly inserted into Score U.S. hobby product at the rate of 1:72 packs. The cards feature red printing and gold foil on the card face. A largely black and white action shot, with the player's head and torso punched out in full color, dominates the card front. Cards are numbered with a TF prefix on the back. The backs also feature a color photo with text information.

COMPLETE SET (26) 75.00 200.00
TF1 Guy Hebert 4.00 10.00
TF2 Cam Neely 4.00 10.00
TF3 Pat LaFontaine 4.00 10.00
TF4 Theo Fleury 2.00 5.00
TF5 Jeremy Roenick 4.00 10.00
TF6 Mike Modano 4.00 10.00
TF7 Sergei Fedorov 5.00 12.00
TF8 Jason Arnott 2.00 5.00
TF9 John Vanbiesbrouck 2.00 5.00
TF10 Geoff Sanderson 2.00 5.00
TF11 Wayne Gretzky 15.00 40.00
TF12 Patrick Roy 10.00 25.00
TF13 Scott Stevens 2.00 5.00
TF14 Pierre Turgeon 2.00 5.00
TF15 Mark Messier 4.00 10.00
TF16 Alexandre Daigle 2.00 5.00
TF17 Eric Lindros 4.00 10.00
TF18 Mario Lemieux 10.00 25.00
TF19 Joe Sakic 6.00 15.00
TF20 Brett Hull 5.00 12.00
TF21 Arturs Irbe 2.00 5.00
TF22 Daren Puppa 2.00 5.00
TF23 Doug Gilmour 2.00 5.00
TF24 Pavel Bure 4.00 10.00
TF25 Joe Juneau 2.00 5.00
TF26 Teemu Selanne 4.00 10.00

1994-95 Score 90 Plus Club

The 21 cards in this set were randomly inserted into Score retail jumbo packs at the rate of 1:4. The set features all players who tallied more than 90 points in the previous season. The cards have a full tan border. A simple round set logo is on the lower portion of the card. The player name is in gold foil. The backs are team color coordinated, with a player photo, and short text information. The cards are numbered with an "NP" prefix.

COMPLETE SET (21) 30.00 60.00
1 Wayne Gretzky 8.00 20.00
2 Sergei Fedorov 2.00 5.00
3 Adam Oates 1.00 2.50
4 Doug Gilmour 1.00 2.50
5 Pavel Bure 1.50 4.00
6 Jeremy Roenick 2.00 5.00
7 Mark Recchi 1.00 2.50
8 Brendan Shanahan 1.50 4.00
9 Jaromir Jagr 3.00 8.00
10 Dave Andreyckuk .40 1.00
11 Brett Hull 2.00 5.00
12 Eric Lindros 1.50 4.00
13 Rod Brind'Amour 1.00 2.50
14 Pierre Turgeon 1.00 2.50
15 Ray Sheppard .40 1.00
16 Mike Modano 2.00 5.00
17 Robert Reichel .40 1.00
18 Ron Francis 1.00 2.50
19 Joe Sakic 4.00 10.00
20 Vincent Damphousse .40 1.00
21 Ray Bourque 2.00 5.00

1994-95 Score Team Canada

The 24 cards in this set were randomly inserted into Score Canadian retail and hobby product at the rate of 1:36 packs. The cards feature a holographic player photo front with a background that reads Lillehammer. The set highlights players from the Canadian Olympic team which took home the silver in the 1994 Games. Although included in this set, Brett Lindros actually did not play in Norway due to an injury. The backs have a full color player portrait over a maple leaf background. The cards are numbered with a CT prefix.

COMPLETE SET (24) 30.00 60.00
CT1 Paul Kariya 5.00 12.00
CT2 Petr Nedved 1.50 4.00
CT3 Todd Warriner 1.25 3.00
CT4 Corey Hirsch 1.50 4.00
CT5 Greg Johnson 1.25 3.00
CT6 Chris Kontos 1.25 3.00
CT7 Dwayne Norris 1.25 3.00
CT8 Brian Savage 1.50 4.00
CT9 Todd Hlushko 1.25 3.00
CT10 Fabian Joseph 1.25 3.00
CT11 Greg Parks 1.25 3.00
CT12 Jean Yves Roy 1.25 3.00
CT13 Mark Astley 1.25 3.00
CT14 Adrian Aucoin 1.25 3.00
CT15 David Harlock 1.25 3.00
CT16 Ken Lovsin 1.25 3.00
CT17 Derek Mayer 1.25 3.00
CT18 Brad Schlegel 1.25 3.00
CT19 Chris Therien 1.50 4.00
CT20 Manny Legace 2.00 5.00
CT21 Brad Werenka 1.25 3.00
CT22 Wally Schreiber 1.25 3.00
CT23 Allain Roy 1.25 3.00
CT24 Brett Lindros 1.25 3.00

1994-95 Score Top Rookie Redemption

The 10 cards in this set were available only through a redemption card offer. Redemption cards were inserted at the rate of 1:48 Score packs. The redemption cards were individually numbered 1-10, but do not mention the player for whom they are redeemable. The mail-in offer expired April 1, 1995. These redemption cards are priced in the header below. Top Rookie redeemed cards have a cut-out photo of the player over a silver foil background. The Top Rookie logo runs down the right side of the card; the player name, position and team logo are on the bottom of the card. The back has a color photo with text information and is numbered with a "TR" prefix.

COMPLETE SET (10) 20.00 40.00
1 Paul Kariya 8.00 20.00
2 Peter Forsberg 8.00 20.00
3 Brett Lindros 1.25 3.00
4 Oleg Tverdovsky 1.25 3.00
5 Jamie Storr 1.25 3.00
6 Kenny Jonsson 1.25 3.00
7 Brian Rolston 1.25 3.00
8 Jeff Friesen 1.25 3.00
9 Todd Harvey 1.25 3.00
10 Viktor Kozlov 1.25 3.00

1995-96 Score Promos

Enclosed in a cello pack, this nine-card standard-size set was issued to preview the 1995-96 Score hockey series. The cards are identical in design to their regular issue counterparts, save for the way the player's name is presented on the back and the hole punched into the upper right corner. On the promos, it is last name only, while the regular cards include Christian name as well.

COMPLETE SEALED SET (9) .75 2.00
3 Chris Chelios .08 .25
8 Jason Arnott .02 .10
10 Mark Recchi .05 .15
19 Trevor Kidd .05 .15
25 Martin Brodeur .20 .50
33 Keith Tkachuk .15 .40
313 Jamie Linden .01 .05
3 Cam Neely .40 1.00
Border Battle
NNO Ad Card .01 .05

1995-96 Score

This 330-card standard-size set was issued in one series in packs of 12-card hobby, 12-card retail and 24-card retail jumbo. Canadian packs of 5-cards each also were available. These packs also held chase cards, but because of the pack size, the odds were considerably more difficult. The fronts feature a full-color action photo on a white background with the player's last name at the bottom and the team name at the top both in team colors. The backs have a color photo with the player's name at the top. Player information, statistics and the team emblem are also on the back of the card. Subsets are Rookies (291-315) and Stoppers (316-325). The Ron Hextall Contest Winner card (#AD4) was awarded to collectors who correctly spotted four errors in a photograph in a contest sponsored by Score. The card back approximates the standard Score issue, but the front uses a silver prismatic foil background.

1 Jaromir Jagr .25 .60
2 Adam Graves .07 .20
3 Chris Chelios .10 .25
4 Felix Potvin .10 .25
5 Joe Sakic .15 .40
6 Chris Pronger .10 .25
7 Teemu Selanne .20 .50
8 Jason Arnott .07 .20
9 John LeClair .10 .25
10 Mark Recchi .12 .30
11 Rob Blake .07 .20
12 Kevin Hatcher .07 .20
13 Shawn Burr .05 .15
14 Brett Lindros .05 .15
15 Craig Janney .05 .15
16 Oleg Tverdovsky .10 .25
17 Blaine Lacher .07 .20
18 Alexandre Daigle .05 .15
19 Trevor Kidd .07 .20
20 Brendan Shanahan .12 .30
21 Alexander Mogilny .07 .20
22 Stu Barnes .05 .15
23 Jeff Brown .07 .20
24 Paul Coffey .10 .25
25 Martin Brodeur .25 .60
26 Darryl Sydor .07 .20
27 Steve Smith .05 .15
28 Ted Donato .05 .15
29 Bernie Nicholls .05 .15
30 Kenny Jonsson .10 .25
31 Peter Forsberg .25 .60
32 Sean Burke .05 .15
33 Keith Tkachuk .10 .25
34 Todd Marchant .05 .15
35 Mikael Renberg .07 .20
36 Vincent Damphousse .07 .20
37 Rick Tocchet .07 .20
38 Todd Harvey .05 .15
39 Chris Gratton .05 .15
40 Darius Kasparaitis .05 .15
41 Sergei Nemchinov .05 .15
42 Bob Corkum .05 .15
43 Bryan Smolinski .05 .15
44 Kevin Stevens .07 .20
45 Phil Housley .07 .20
46 Al MacInnis .10 .25
47 Alexei Zhitnik .05 .15
48 Rob Niedermayer .07 .20
49 Kirk McLean .07 .20
50 Mark Messier .15 .40
51 Nicklas Lidstrom .10 .25
52 Scott Niedermayer .10 .25
53 Peter Bondra .10 .25
54 Luc Robitaille .10 .25
55 Jeremy Roenick .12 .30
56 Mats Sundin .10 .25
57 Wendel Clark .10 .25
58 Todd Elik .05 .15
59 Dave Manson .05 .15
60 David Oliver .05 .15
61 Yuri Khmylev .05 .15
62 Sergei Krivokrasov .05 .15
63 Randy Wood .05 .15
64 Andy Moog .10 .25
65 Petr Klima .05 .15
66 Ray Ferraro .05 .15
67 Sandis Ozolinsh .07 .20
68 Joe Sacco .05 .15
69 Zarley Zalapski .05 .15
70 Ron Tugnutt .07 .20
71 German Titov .07 .20
72 Ian Laperriere .05 .15
73 Doug Gilmour .12 .30
74 Brian Skrudland .05 .15
75 Cliff Ronning .05 .15
76 Brian Savage .05 .15
77 John MacLean .07 .20
78 Jim Carey .07 .20
79 Alexei Kovalev .05 .15
80 Brian Rolston .05 .15
81 Shawn McEachern .05 .15
82 Gary Suter .07 .20
83 Owen Nolan .10 .25
84 Ray Whitney .07 .20
85 Alexei Zhamnov .10 .25
86 Shawn Chambers .05 .15
87 Ed Belfour .07 .20
88 Patrice Tardif .07 .20
89 Greg Adams .05 .15
90 Pierre Turgeon .10 .25
91 Jeff Friesen .05 .15
92 Marty McSorley .05 .15
93 Dave Gagner .05 .15
94 Guy Hebert .07 .20
95 Keith Jones .07 .20
96 Kirk Muller .07 .20
97 Gary Roberts .05 .15
98 Chris Therien .05 .15
99 Steve Duchesne .05 .15
100 Sergei Fedorov .15 .40
101 Donald Audette .07 .20
102 Jyrki Lumme .05 .15
103 Darrin Shannon .05 .15
104 Gord Murphy .05 .15
105 John Cullen .05 .15
106 Bill Guerin .07 .20
107 Dale Hunter .07 .20
108 Uwe Krupp .07 .20
109 Dave Andreychuk .10 .25
110 Joe Murphy .05 .15
111 Geoff Sanderson .05 .15
112 Garry Galley .05 .15
113 Ron Sutter .07 .20
114 Viktor Kozlov .07 .20
115 Jari Kurri .10 .25
116 Paul Ysebaert .05 .15
117 Vladimir Malakhov .05 .15
118 Josef Beranek .05 .15
119 Adam Oates .10 .25
120 Mike Modano .15 .40
121 Theo Fleury .12 .30
122 Pat Verbeek .07 .20
123 Esa Tikkanen .05 .15
124 Brian Leetch .10 .25
125 Paul Kariya .12 .30
126 Ken Wregget .07 .20
127 Ray Sheppard .07 .20
128 Jason Allison .07 .20
129 Dave Ellett .05 .15
130 Stephane Richer .07 .20
131 Jocelyn Thibault .07 .20
132 Martin Straka .05 .15
133 Tony Amonte .07 .20
134 Scott Mellanby .07 .20
135 Pavel Bure .12 .30
136 Andrew Cassels .05 .15
137 Ulf Dahlen .05 .15
138 Valeri Bure .05 .15
139 Teppo Numminen .05 .15
140 Mike Richter .10 .25
141 Rob Gaudreau .05 .15
142 Nikolai Khabibulin .07 .20
143 Mariusz Czerkawski .05 .15
144 Mark Tinordi .05 .15
145 Patrick Roy .25 .60
146 Steve Chiasson .05 .15
147 Mike Donnelly .05 .15
148 Patrice Brisebois .05 .15
149 Jason Wiemer .05 .15
150 Eric Lindros .15 .40
151 Dimitri Khristich .05 .15
152 Tom Barrasso .07 .20
153 Curtis Leschyshyn .05 .15
154 Robert Kron .05 .15
155 Jesse Belanger .05 .15
156 Brian Noonan .05 .15
157 Mike Peca .07 .20
158 Patrick Poulin .05 .15
159 Sergei Makarov .05 .15
160 Scott Stevens .10 .25
161 Sergio Momesso .05 .15
162 Todd Gill .05 .15
163 Don Sweeney .05 .15
164 Randy Burridge .05 .15
165 Slava Kozlov .07 .20
166 Shaun Van Allen .05 .15
167 Steven Rice .05 .15
168 Adam Deadmarsh .05 .15
169 Andrei Nikolishin .05 .15
170 Valeri Karpov .05 .15
171 Doug Bodger .05 .15
172 Corey Millen .05 .15
173 Mark Fitzpatrick .07 .20
174 Bob Errey .05 .15
175 Dan Quinn .07 .20
176 Vladimir Konstantinov .07 .20
177 Scott Lachance .05 .15
178 Jeff Norton .05 .15
179 Valeri Zelepukin .05 .15
180 Dmitri Mironov .05 .15
181 Pat Peake .05 .15
182 Dominic Roussel .05 .15
183 Sylvain Cote .05 .15
184 Pat Falloon .05 .15
185 Roman Hamrlik .07 .20
186 Joel Otto .05 .15
187 Ron Francis .12 .30
188 Sergei Zubov .07 .20
189 Arturs Irbe .07 .20
190 Radek Bonk .05 .15
191 John Tucker .05 .15
192 Sylvain Lefebvre .05 .15
193 Doug Brown .05 .15
194 Glen Wesley .05 .15
195 Ron Hextall .10 .25
196 Patrick Flatley .05 .15
197 Darcy Wakaluk .05 .15
198 Kelly Hrudey .07 .20
199 Ray Bourque .15 .40
200 Dominik Hasek .12 .30
201 Pat LaFontaine .10 .25
202 Chris Osgood .07 .20
203 Ulf Samuelsson .05 .15
204 Mike Gartner .10 .25
205 Stephane Fiset .07 .20
206 Mathieu Schneider .05 .15
207 Eric Desjardins .07 .20
208 Trevor Linden .10 .25
209 Cam Neely .10 .25
210 Daren Puppa .07 .20
211 Steve Larmer .07 .20
212 Tim Cheveldae .07 .20
213 Derek Plante .05 .15
214 Murray Craven .05 .15
215 Tommy Soderstrom .07 .20
216 Bob Bassen .05 .15
217 Marty McInnis .05 .15
218 Dave Lowry .05 .15
219 Mike Vernon .07 .20
220 Petr Nedved .07 .20
221 Yves Racine .05 .15
222 Dale Hawerchuk .12 .30
223 Wayne Presley .05 .15
224 Darren Turcotte .10 .25
225 Derian Hatcher .07 .20
226 Steve Thomas .07 .20
227 Stephane Matteau .05 .15
228 Grant Fuhr .10 .25
229 Joe Nieuwendyk .10 .25
230 Alexei Yashin .07 .20
231 Brian Bellows .07 .20
232 Brian Bradley .07 .20
233 Tony Granato .05 .15
234 Mike Ricci .07 .20
235 Brett Hull .12 .30
236 Mike Ridley .05 .15
237 Al Iafrate .07 .20
238 Derek King .07 .20
239 Bill Ranford .07 .20
240 Steve Yzerman .12 .30
241 John Vanbiesbrouck .07 .20
242 Russ Courtnall .05 .15
243 Chris Terreri .07 .20
244 Rod Brind'Amour .10 .25
245 Shayne Corson .05 .15
246 Don Beaupre .07 .20
247 Dino Ciccarelli .07 .20
248 Kevin Lowe .07 .20
249 Craig MacTavish .05 .15
250 Wayne Gretzky .50 1.25
251 Curtis Joseph .10 .25
252 Joe Mullen .07 .20
253 Andrei Kovalenko .05 .15
254 Igor Larionov .05 .15
255 Geoff Courtnall .05 .15
256 Joe Juneau .07 .20
257 Bruce Driver .05 .15
258 Michal Pivonka .05 .15
259 Nelson Emerson .05 .15
260 Larry Murphy .10 .25
261 Brent Gilchrist .05 .15
262 Benoit Hogue .05 .15
263 Doug Weight .10 .25
264 Keith Primeau .05 .15
265 Neal Broten .07 .20
266 Mike Keane .07 .20
267 Zigmund Palffy .10 .25
268 Valeri Kamensky .07 .20
269 Claude Lemieux .10 .25
270 Bryan Marchment .05 .15
271 Kelly Miller .05 .15
272 Brent Sutter .05 .15
273 Glenn Healy .07 .20
274 Sergei Brylin .05 .15
275 Tie Domi .07 .20
276 Norm Maciver .07 .20
277 Kevin Dineen .07 .20
278 Scott Young .05 .15
279 Tomas Sandstrom .07 .20
280 Guy Carbonneau .10 .25
281 Denis Savard .12 .30
282 Ed Olczyk .05 .15
283 Adam Creighton .05 .15
284 Tom Chorske .05 .15
285 Roman Oksiuta .05 .15
286 David Roberts .05 .15
287 Petr Svoboda .05 .15
288 Brad May .05 .15
289 Michael Nylander .05 .15
290 Jon Casey .07 .20
291 Philippe DeRouville .07 .20
292 Craig Johnson .05 .15
293 Chris McAlpine RC .07 .20
294 Ralph Intranuovo .05 .15
295 Richard Park .10 .25
296 Todd Warriner .07 .20
297 Craig Conroy RC .07 .20
298 Marek Malik .05 .15
299 Manny Fernandez .07 .20
300 Cory Stillman .05 .15
301 Kevin Brown .07 .20
302 Steve Larouche RC .05 .15
303 Chris Taylor .07 .20
304 Ryan Smyth .07 .20
305 Craig Darby .05 .15
306 Radim Bicanek .07 .20
307 Shean Donovan .05 .15
308 Jason Bonsignore .05 .15
309 Chris Marinucci RC .07 .20
310 Brian Holzinger RC .20 .50
311 Mike Torchia RC .07 .20
312 Eric Daze .20 .50
313 Jamie Linden .07 .20
314 Tommy Salo RC .15 .40
315 Martin Gendron .07 .20
316 Felix Potvin ST .10 .25
317 Jim Carey ST .07 .20
318 Ed Belfour ST .07 .20
319 Mike Vernon ST .07 .20
320 Sean Burke ST .05 .15
321 Mike Richter ST .10 .25
322 John Vanbiesbrouck ST .07 .20
323 Martin Brodeur ST .25 .60
324 Patrick Roy ST .25 .60
325 Dominik Hasek ST .12 .30
326 Checklist .05 .15
Pacific Division
327 Checklist .05 .15
Central Division
328 Checklist .05 .15
Atlantic Division
329 Checklist .05 .15
Northeast Division
330 Checklist - Chase .05 .15
AD4 Ron Hextall Contest Winner 2.50 5.00

1995-96 Score Black Ice Artist's Proofs

This 330-card set is a high-end parallel of the basic Score issue. The cards can be differentiated from the standard issue by a black foil background with the words "Artist's Proof" written throughout. The cards were randomly inserted 1:36 packs.

*VETS: 40X TO 100X BASIC CARDS

1995-96 Score Black Ice

This 330-card set is a parallel version of the basic set. Card fronts differ in that they feature a silver, metallic background surrounded by a grayish border. The words "Black Ice" are stamped on the back in a gray block. They were inserted one in every three packs.

*VETS: 4X TO 12X BASIC CARDS

1995-96 Score Border Battle

This 15-card standard-size set was inserted in 12-card hobby and retail packs at a rate of one in 12 and retail jumbos at a rate of one in 9. The set features the top players from different countries. The fronts have a color action photo with the background in the color of the player's home country. The left side of the card has a gold foil triangle jutting out with a red circle in it that has the words "Border Battle" and the country's flag. The backs have a color head shot and an action photo tinted in the color of the player's country. The backs also state the player's home country and have information on him. The cards are numbered "X of 15" at the bottom.

COMPLETE SET (15) 10.00 20.00
1 Pierre Turgeon .25 .60
2 Wayne Gretzky 3.00 8.00
3 Cam Neely .50 1.25
4 Joe Sakic 1.00 2.50
5 Doug Gilmour .25 .60
6 Brett Hull .60 1.50
7 Pat LaFontaine .50 1.25
8 Joe Mullen .25 .60
9 Mike Modano .75 2.00
10 Jeremy Roenick .60 1.50
11 Pavel Bure .50 1.25
12 Alexei Zhamnov .25 .60
13 Sergei Fedorov .75 2.00
14 Jaromir Jagr .75 2.00
15 Mats Sundin .50 1.25

1995-96 Score Check It

This 12-card standard-size set was inserted in 12-card retail packs at a rate of 1:36, and in 1:86 Canadian packs. Cards were numbered "X of 12" at the topof the card backs..

COMPLETE SET (12) 20.00 40.00
1 Eric Lindros 6.00 15.00
2 Owen Nolan .75 2.00
3 Brett Lindros .75 2.00
4 Chris Gratton .75 2.00
5 Chris Pronger 2.00 5.00
6 Adam Deadmarsh .75 2.00
7 Peter Forsberg 6.00 15.00
8 Derian Hatcher .75 2.00
9 Rob Blake .75 2.00
10 Jeff Friesen .75 2.00
11 Keith Tkachuk 1.50 4.00
12 Mike Ricci .75 2.00

1995-96 Score Dream Team

This 12-card standard-size set was inserted in 12-card hobby and retail packs at a rate of 1:72. The cards are numbered "X of 12" at the top.

COMPLETE SET (12) 25.00 50.00
1 Wayne Gretzky 10.00 25.00
2 Sergei Fedorov 1.25 3.00
3 Eric Lindros 1.00 2.50
4 Mark Messier 1.25 3.00
5 Peter Forsberg 3.00 8.00
6 Doug Gilmour .60 1.50
7 Paul Kariya 1.00 2.50
8 Jaromir Jagr 2.00 5.00
9 Brett Hull 1.25 3.00
10 Pavel Bure 1.00 2.50
11 Patrick Roy 6.00 15.00
12 Jim Carey .60 1.50

1995-96 Score Golden Blades

This 20-card set was randomly inserted in 1:18 retail jumbo packs. The cards, which feature the fastest skaters in the game, are printed on gold prismatic foil.

COMPLETE SET (20) 25.00 50.00
1 Joe Sakic 5.00 12.00
2 Teemu Selanne 1.50 4.00
3 Alexander Mogilny .75 2.00
4 Peter Bondra .40 1.00
5 Paul Coffey .75 2.00
6 Mike Modano 2.00 5.00
7 Alexei Yashin .40 1.00
8 Pat LaFontaine .75 2.00
9 Paul Kariya 2.00 5.00
10 Peter Forsberg 3.00 8.00
11 Jeff Friesen .40 1.00
12 Steve Yzerman 6.00 15.00
13 Theo Fleury 1.50 4.00
14 Stephane Richer .40 1.00
15 Mark Messier 2.00 5.00
16 Mats Sundin 1.50 4.00
17 Brendan Shanahan 1.50 4.00
18 Mark Recchi .75 2.00
19 Jeremy Roenick 1.50 4.00
20 Jason Arnott .40 1.00

1995-96 Score Lamplighters

This 15-card standard-size set was inserted in 12-card hobby packs at a rate of 1:36. The cards, which feature the top goal scorers in the game, are printed on a silver prismatic foil card stock.

COMPLETE SET (15) 25.00 50.00
1 Wayne Gretzky 8.00 20.00
2 Pavel Bure 1.25 3.00
3 Cam Neely 1.25 3.00
4 Owen Nolan .60 1.50
5 Sergei Fedorov 1.25 3.00
6 Pierre Turgeon .60 1.50
7 Peter Bondra .60 1.50
8 Mikael Renberg .60 1.50
9 Luc Robitaille .60 1.50
10 Alexei Zhamnov .60 1.50
11 Brett Hull 1.50 3.00
12 Jaromir Jagr 2.00 5.00
13 Theo Fleury .60 1.50
14 Teemu Selanne 1.25 3.00
15 Eric Lindros 1.25 3.00

1996-97 Score Samples

This eight-card set features samples of the 1996-97 Score hockey issue. Interestingly, all samples mirror the linen-stock Golden Blades parallel set rather than the basic issue. The cards are identical in design to their regular counterparts with the exception of the word "sample" printed on the backs at the bottom. The cards are listed below according to their regular issue numbers.

COMPLETE SET (8) 3.00 8.00
1 Patrick Roy 1.00 2.50
10W Martin Brodeur WINNER .50 1.25
10GBW Martin Brodeur .50 1.25
{ Golden Blades WINNER
10 Martin Brodeur .50 1.25
16 Alexander Mogilny .20 .50
19 Brett Hull .25 .60
63 John Vanbiesbrouck .30 .75
77 Sergei Fedorov .40 1.00
236 Eric Daze .20 .50
238 Saku Koivu .20 .50

1996-97 Score

The 1996-97 Score set -- the first release of that season -- was issued in one series totaling 275 cards. The 10-card packs retailed for $.99 each. The cards featured action photography on the front complemented by simple white borders, while the backs were highlighted by another photograph and complete career stats. The only rookie of note is Ethan Moreau.

COMPLETE SET (275) 6.00 15.00
1 Patrick Roy .07 .20
2 Brendan Shanahan .05 .10
3 Rob Niedermayer .01 .05
4 Jeff Friesen .01 .05
5 Teppo Numminen .01 .05
6 Mario Lemieux .10 .25
7 Eric Lindros .05 .10
8 Paul Kariya .05 .10
9 Joe Sakic .05 .10
10 Martin Brodeur .05 .15
11 Mark Tinordi .01 .05
12 Theo Fleury .05 .15
13 Guy Hebert .01 .05
14 Dave Gagner .05 .10
15 Travis Green .01 .05
16 Alexander Mogilny .01 .05
17 Stephane Fiset .01 .05
18 Dominik Hasek .05 .10
19 Brett Hull .15 .40
20 Zdeno Ciger .01 .05
21 Pat Falloon .01 .05
22 Jyrki Lumme .01 .05
23 Rick Tabaracci .01 .05
24 Mark Messier .05 .10
25 Yanic Perreault .01 .05
26 Mark Recchi .05 .10
27 Alexander Selivanov .01 .05
28 Chris Terreri .01 .05
29 Jaromir Jagr .07 .20
30 Ted Donato .01 .05
31 Scott Mellanby .01 .05
32 Geoff Courtnall .01 .05
33 Michal Pivonka .01 .05
34 Glenn Healy .01 .05
35 Pavel Bure .05 .10
36 Chris Chelios .05 .10
37 Nelson Emerson .01 .05
38 Petr Nedved .01 .05
39 Greg Adams .01 .05
40 Bill Ranford .01 .05
41 Wayne Gretzky .15 .40
42 Wendel Clark .01 .05
43 Sandis Ozolinsh .01 .05
44 Dave Andreychuk .05 .10
45 Brian Bradley .01 .05
46 Sean Burke .01 .05
47 Keith Tkachuk .05 .10
48 Brad May .01 .05
49 Brent Gilchrist .01 .05
50 Vincent Damphousse .01 .05
51 Dale Hawerchuk .05 .10
52 Randy Burridge .01 .05
53 Ray Bourque .05 .10
54 Keith Primeau .01 .05
55 Jason Arnott .01 .05
56 Ron Francis .05 .10
57 Craig Janney .01 .05
58 Trevor Kidd .01 .05
59 Jason Dawe .01 .05
60 Steve Yzerman .07 .20
61 Alexei Kovalev .01 .05
62 Steve Duchesne .01 .05
63 John Vanbiesbrouck .05 .10
64 Steve Thomas .01 .05
65 Bernie Nicholls .01 .05
66 Alexandre Daigle .01 .05
67 Pat Peake .01 .05
68 Kelly Hrudey .01 .05
69 Owen Nolan .05 .10
70 Alexei Zhitnik .01 .05
71 Pierre Turgeon .05 .10
72 Mike Modano .05 .10
73 Slava Fetisov .01 .05
74 Jim Carey .05 .10
75 Larry Murphy .01 .05
76 Roman Oksiuta .01 .05
77 Sergei Fedorov .05 .10
78 Shayne Corson .01 .05
79 Michael Nylander .01 .05
80 Ron Hextall .01 .05
81 Adam Graves .01 .05
82 Tommy Soderstrom .01 .05
83 Robert Svehla .01 .05
84 Vladimir Konstantinov .01 .05
85 Jeff Hackett .01 .05
86 Todd Harvey .01 .05
87 Jeff Brown .01 .05
88 Bryan Smolinski .01 .05
89 Oleg Tverdovsky .01 .05
90 Curtis Joseph .05 .10
91 Grant Fuhr .05 .10
92 Rick Tocchet .01 .05
93 Adam Deadmarsh .01 .05
94 Pat Verbeek .01 .05
95 Doug Gilmour .05 .10
96 Jocelyn Thibault .05 .10
97 Radek Bonk .01 .05
98 Martin Gelinas .01 .05
99 Peter Forsberg .05 .10
100 Joe Murphy .01 .05
101 Dino Ciccarelli .05 .10
102 Rod Brind'Amour .05 .10
103 Kirk Muller .01 .05
104 Andy Moog .05 .10
105 Nikolai Khabibulin .01 .05
106 Mike Ricci .01 .05
107 Ray Ferraro .01 .05
108 Scott Niedermayer .05 .10
109 Russ Courtnall .01 .05
110 Dale Hunter .01 .05
111 Cam Neely .05 .10
112 Ray Sheppard .01 .05
113 Luc Robitaille .05 .10
114 Al MacInnis .05 .10
115 Mathieu Schneider .01 .05
116 Claude Lemieux .01 .05
117 Kevin Hatcher .01 .05
118 Daren Puppa .01 .05
119 Geoff Sanderson .01 .05
120 Zigmund Palffy .05 .10
121 Denis Savard .05 .10
122 Dimitri Khristich .01 .05
123 Ed Belfour .05 .10
124 Tom Barrasso .01 .05
125 Bob Rouse
126 Tomas Sandstrom .01 .05
127 Roman Hamrlik .01 .05
128 Alexei Zhamnov .01 .05
129 Chris Osgood .05 .10
130 Rob Blake .05 .10
131 Garry Galley .01 .05
132 Greg Johnson .01 .05
133 Brian Skrudland .01 .05
134 Martin Rucinsky .01 .05
135 Steve Konowalchuk .01 .05
136 Damian Rhodes .01 .05
137 Jeremy Roenick .05 .10
138 Scott Stevens .05 .10
139 Pat LaFontaine .05 .10
140 Scott Young .01 .05
141 Benoit Hogue .01 .05
142 Paul Coffey .05 .10
143 John MacLean .01 .05
144 Joe Juneau .01 .05
145 Teemu Selanne .05 .15
146 Andrew Cassels .01 .05
147 Brian Savage .01 .05
148 Chris Gratton .01 .05
149 Corey Hirsch .01 .05
150 Mike Richter .05 .10
151 Shawn McEachern .01 .05
152 Joe Nieuwendyk .05 .10
153 Phil Housley .01 .05
154 Mike Gartner .05 .10
155 Kirk McLean .01 .05
156 Bob Probert .01 .05
157 Valeri Kamensky .01 .05
158 Vyacheslav Kozlov .01 .05
159 Eric Desjardins .01 .05
160 Mats Sundin .05 .10
161 John LeClair .05 .10
162 Adam Oates .05 .10
163 Cliff Ronning .01 .05
164 Mike Vernon .01 .05
165 German Titov .01 .05
166 Chris Pronger .01 .05
167 Norm MacIver .01 .05
168 Kenny Jonsson .01 .05
169 Tony Amonte .01 .05
170 Doug Weight .05 .10
171 Sergei Zubov .01 .05
172 Felix Potvin .05 .10
173 Trevor Linden .01 .05
174 Derek Plante .01 .05
175 Uwe Krupp .01 .05
176 Nicklas Lidstrom .05 .10
177 Mikael Renberg .01 .05
178 Igor Larionov .05 .10
179 Brian Leetch .05 .10
180 Stu Barnes .01 .05
181 Alexei Yashin .01 .05
182 Gary Suter .01 .05
183 Ken Wregget .01 .05
184 Mike Ridley .01 .05
185 Peter Bondra .01 .05
186 Steve Rucchin .01 .05
187 Jozef Stumpel .01 .05
188 Matthew Barnaby .01 .05
189 James Patrick .01 .05
190 Chris Simon .01 .05
191 Brent Fedyk .01 .05
192 Kris Draper .01 .05
193 David Oliver .01 .05
194 Dave Lowry .01 .05
195 Robert Kron .01 .05
196 Andrei Kovalenko .01 .05
197 Bill Guerin .05 .10
198 Ed Olczyk .01 .05
199 Yuri Khmylev .01 .05
200 Rob Ray .05 .10
201 Joe Mullen .01 .05
202 Petr Klima .01 .05
203 Todd Krygier .01 .05
204 Garth Snow .01 .05
205 Zarley Zalapski .01 .05
206 Ken Baumgartner .01 .05
207 Tony Twist .01 .05
208 Todd Gill .01 .05
209 Mike Peca .01 .05
210 Darcy Wakaluk
211 Milos Holan .01 .05
212 Alexander Semak .01 .05
213 Jeff Reese .01 .05
214 Jon Casey .01 .05
215 Sandy McCarthy .01 .05
216 Curtis Leschyshyn .01 .05
217 Todd Marchant .01 .05
218 Bob Bassen .01 .05
219 Darren Turcotte .01 .05
220 David Reid .01 .05
221 Brian Bellows .01 .05
222 Jesse Belanger .01 .05
223 Bill Lindsay .01 .05
224 Lyle Odelein .01 .05
225 Keith Jones .01 .05
226 Sylvain Lefebvre .01 .05
227 Shaun Van Allen .01 .05
228 Dan Quinn .01 .05
229 Richard Matvichuk .01 .05
230 Craig MacTavish .01 .05
231 Craig Billington
232 Stephane Richer .01 .05
233 Donald Audette .01 .05
234 Ulf Dahlen .01 .05
235 Steve Chiasson .01 .05
236 Eric Daze .01 .05
237 Petr Sykora .01 .05
238 Saku Koivu .05 .10
239 Ed Jovanovski .01 .05
240 Daniel Alfredsson .05 .10
241 Vitali Yachmenev .01 .05
242 Marcus Ragnarsson .01 .05
243 Cory Stillman .01 .05
244 Todd Bertuzzi .05 .10
245 Valeri Bure .01 .05
246 Jere Lehtinen .01 .05
247 Radek Dvorak .01 .05
248 Niclas Andersson .01 .05
249 Miroslav Satan .01 .05
250 Jeff O'Neill .01 .05
251 Nolan Baumgartner .01 .05
252 Roman Vopat .01 .05
253 Bryan McCabe .01 .05
254 Jamie Langenbrunner .01 .05
255 Chad Kilger .01 .05
256 Eric Fichaud .01 .05
257 Landon Wilson .01 .05
258 Kyle McLaren .01 .05
259 Aaron Gavey .01 .05
260 Byron Dafoe .01 .05
261 Grant Marshall .01 .05
262 Shane Doan .01 .05
263 Ralph Intranuovo .01 .05
264 Aki Berg .01 .05
265 Antti Tormanen .01 .05
266 Brian Holzinger .01 .05
267 Jose Theodore .05 .10
268 Ethan Moreau RC .05 .10
269 Niklas Sundstrom .01 .05
270 Brendan Witt .01 .05
271 Checklist (1-70) .01 .05
272 Checklist (71-140) .01 .05
273 Checklist (141-210) .01 .05
274 Checklist (211-275) .01 .05
275 Checklist (Chase Program) .01 .05

1996-97 Score Artist's Proofs

This 275-card parallel of the 1996-97 Score set could be differentiated from the regular cards by the bronze foil circular Artist's Proof logo on the card front. These chase cards were inserted 1:55 hobby and retail packs, and 1:27 magazine packs.

*SINGLES: 30X TO 80X BASIC CARDS

1996-97 Score Dealer's Choice Artist's Proofs

Another parallel to the Score set, these cards were sent to dealers whose customers pulled winning Golden Blades cards. The dealer mailed in the winning card and was given two cards in exchange. The customer received the Special Artist Proof while the dealer received this version. Identical to regular Artist Proofs, only the words 'Dealers Choice' were added around the circular AP logo.

*SINGLES: 50X TO 100X BASIC CARDS
TWO PER MAIL REDEMPTION

1996-97 Score Special Artist's Proofs

A parallel to the Score set, these cards were redemptions of winning Golden Blades cards, which had blacked out boxes readable only with a special lens available at hobby shops. Customers received a Special Artist Proof card while the dealers who sent in the cards for the customers received similar versions called Dealer's Choice Artist Proofs. The only difference is on the Artist Proof logo, which adds the word 'Special' on these versions.

*SINGLES: 60X TO 120X BASIC CARDS
ISSUED ONE PER GOLDEN BLADE EXCH

1996-97 Score Check It

Randomly inserted in magazine packs at a rate of 1:35, this 16-card set features some of the toughest hitters in the game.

COMPLETE SET (16) 15.00 30.00
1 Eric Lindros 2.00 5.00
2 Peter Forsberg 2.00 5.00
3 Keith Tkachuk 1.00 2.50
4 Cam Neely 2.50 6.00
5 Jeremy Roenick 1.50 4.00
6 Brendan Shanahan 1.50 4.00
7 Wendel Clark 1.50 4.00
8 Owen Nolan .60 1.50
9 Doug Gilmour .60 1.50
10 Trevor Linden .75 2.00
11 Saku Koivu .60 1.50
12 Ed Jovanovski .60 1.50
13 Theo Fleury .75 2.00
14 Doug Weight .60 1.50
15 Chris Chelios .60 1.50
16 Eric Daze .60 1.50

1996-97 Score Golden Blades

This 275-card set was a parallel to the basic issue. The cards were inserted at rates of 1:7 hobby and retail packs, and 1:3 magazine packs. The cards were printed on linen stock and featured the Golden Blades logo superimposed over the stat package on the card backs. Each Golden Blades card has a rectangular box within the player's picture on the back which to the naked eye, resembles television snow. But placing a special Pinnacle device over the rectangle revealed (for one out of every eight Golden Blades) the words "Special Artist's Proof". These cards were eligible to be redeemed for two more parallel cards: a Special Artist's Proof for the collector and a Dealer's Choice Artist Proof for the redeeming hobby store owner. These SAP winner cards were inserted at approximately the same rate as standard Artist Proof cards, but because of the limited redemption period, are in somewhat shorter supply. This checklist represents the Score Golden Blades cards that have Sorry Try Again in the decoder window and were not redeemable for Special Artist Proofs.

COMPLETE SET (275) 100.00 200.00
*SINGLES: 4X TO 10X BASIC CARDS

1996-97 Score Golden Blades Winners

This checklist represents the Score Golden Blades cards that are noted as Special Artist Proof winners in the decoder box. These cards were eligible to be redeemed for two more parallel cards: a Special Artist's Proof for the collector and a Dealer's Choice Artist Proof for the redeeming hobby store owner. These Special Artist Proof winner cards were inserted at approximately the same rate as standard Artist Proof cards, but because of the limited redemption period, are in somewhat shorter supply.

*SINGLES: 5X TO 12X BASIC CARDS
ISSUED VIA MAIL REDEMPTION

1996-97 Score Golden Blades Winners Punched

This checklist represents the version of the card that was sent back to collectors once they were redeemed for the Platinum version. Pinnacle punched their logo into the card over the Score logo to indicate the card has already been redeemed.

*SINGLES: 5X TO 12X BASIC CARDS
ISSUED VIA MAIL REDEMPTION

1996-97 Score Dream Team

Randomly inserted in packs at a rate of 1:71 hobby and retail packs, this 12-card set features the top players at each position in the NHL today on an all-rainbow holographic foil card stock.

COMPLETE SET (12) 12.50 30.00
1 Eric Lindros .60 1.50
2 Paul Kariya .60 1.50
3 Joe Sakic 1.25 3.00
4 Peter Forsberg 1.50 4.00
5 Mark Messier .60 1.50
6 Mario Lemieux 3.00 8.00
7 Jaromir Jagr 1.00 2.50
8 Wayne Gretzky 4.00 10.00
9 Alexander Mogilny .25 .60
10 Pavel Bure .60 1.50
11 Sergei Fedorov .75 2.00
12 Patrick Roy 3.00 8.00

1996-97 Score Net Worth

Inserted exclusively into retail packs at a rate of 1:35, these cards feature the top netminders in the NHL today. Two photos grace the front of each card, with one being a black and silver metallic image.

COMPLETE SET (18) 10.00 20.00
1 Patrick Roy 2.00 5.00
2 Martin Brodeur 2.00 5.00
3 Jim Carey .40 1.00
4 Dominik Hasek 1.25 3.00
5 Ed Belfour .40 1.00
6 Chris Osgood .40 1.00
7 Curtis Joseph .40 1.00
8 John Vanbiesbrouck .40 1.00
9 Jocelyn Thibault .40 1.00
10 Stephane Fiset .40 1.00
11 Ron Hextall .40 1.00
12 Tom Barrasso .40 1.00
13 Daren Puppa .40 1.00
14 Mike Vernon .40 1.00
15 Bill Ranford .40 1.00
16 Corey Hirsch .40 1.00
17 Damian Rhodes .40 1.00
18 Nikolai Khabibulin .40 1.00

1996-97 Score Sudden Death

Randomly inserted in hobby packs only at a rate of 1:35, this 15-card holofoil set features two action photos simulating matchups of some of the deadliest snipers against the stingiest netminders.

COMPLETE SET (15) 12.00 25.00
1 M.Brodeur/P.Turgeon .75 2.00
2 J.Carey/S.Yzerman 1.00 2.50
3 D.Hasek/B.Shanahan .40 1.00
4 E.Belfour/B.Hull .40 1.00
5 C.Osgood/J.Roenick .40 1.00
6 C.Joseph/P.Bure .40 1.00
7 J.Vanbiesbrouck/M.Lemieux 3.00 8.00
8 J.Thibault/A.Mogilny .40 1.00
9 M.Richter/J.Jagr .40 1.00
10 T.Barrasso/M.Messier .40 1.00
11 D.Puppa/J.Sakic .75 2.00
12 F.Potvin/W.Gretzky 4.00 10.00
13 C.Hirsch/P.Kariya .40 1.00
14 R.Hextall/S.Fedorov .40 1.00
15 N.Khabibulin/T.Selanne .40 1.00

1996-97 Score Superstitions

The 13-cards in this set (note the foolhardy use of this unlucky number!) highlight some of the unusual pre-game rituals and neuroses of some of the NHL's most successful players. The cards were randomly inserted 1:19 hobby and retail packs and 1:10 magazine packs.

COMPLETE SET (13) 3.00 8.00
1 Teemu Selanne .30 .75
2 Doug Weight .25 .60
3 Mats Sundin .30 .75
4 Mike Modano .40 1.00
5 Felix Potvin .30 .75
6 Paul Coffey .30 .75
7 Ray Bourque .50 1.25
8 Chris Chelios .30 .75
9 Ron Hextall .25 .60
10 Alexander Selivanov .25 .60
11 Brett Hull .40 1.00
12 Mike Richter .30 .75
13 Scott Mellanby .25 .60

1997-98 Score

The 1997-98 Score set was issued in one series totaling 270 cards and was distributed in packs with a suggested retail price of $.99. The fronts feature color player photos in white borders. The backs carry player information.

COMPLETE SET (270) 7.50 15.00
1 Sean Burke .05 .15
2 Chris Osgood .05 .15
3 Garth Snow .05 .15
4 Mike Vernon .05 .15
5 Grant Fuhr .05 .15
6 Guy Hebert .05 .15
7 Arturs Irbe .05 .15
8 Andy Moog .05 .15
9 Tommy Salo .05 .15
10 Nikolai Khabibulin .05 .15
11 Mike Richter .08 .25
12 Corey Hirsch .05 .15
13 Bill Ranford .05 .15
14 Jim Carey .05 .15
15 Jeff Hackett .05 .15
16 Damian Rhodes .05 .15
17 Tom Barrasso .05 .15
18 Daren Puppa .05 .15
19 Craig Billington .05 .15
20 Ed Belfour .08 .25
21 Mikhail Shtalenkov .01 .05
22 Glenn Healy .05 .15
23 Marcel Cousineau .05 .15
24 Kevin Hodson .05 .15
25 Olaf Kolzig .05 .15
26 Eric Fichaud .05 .15
27 Ron Hextall .05 .15
28 Rick Tabaracci .05 .15
29 Felix Potvin .08 .25
30 Martin Brodeur .25 .60
31 Curtis Joseph .08 .25
32 Ken Wregget .05 .15
33 Patrick Roy .50 1.25
34 John Vanbiesbrouck PROMO 1.00 2.50
34 John Vanbiesbrouck .05 .15
35 Stephane Fiset .05 .15
36 Roman Turek .05 .15
37 Trevor Kidd .05 .15
38 Dwayne Roloson .01 .05
39 Dominik Hasek .20 .50
40 Patrick Lalime .05 .15
41 Jocelyn Thibault .05 .15
42 Jose Theodore .10 .30
43 Kirk McLean .05 .15
44 Steve Shields RC .15 .40
45 Mike Dunham .05 .15
46 Jamie Storr .05 .15
47 Byron Dafoe .05 .15
48 Chris Terreri .05 .15
49 Ron Tugnutt .05 .15
50 Kelly Hrudey .05 .15
51 Vaclav Prospal RC .08 .25
52 Alyn McCauley .05 .15
53 Jaroslav Svejkovsky .05 .15
54 Joe Thornton .25 .60
55 Chris Dingman RC .01 .05
56 Vadim Sharifijanov .01 .05
57 Larry Courville .01 .05
58 Erik Rasmussen .01 .05
59 Sergei Samsonov .05 .15
60 Kevyn Adams .01 .05
61 Daniel Cleary .05 .15
62 Martin Prochazka RC .01 .05
63 Mattias Ohlund .05 .15
64 Juha Lind RC .01 .05
65 Olli Jokinen RC .30 .75
66 Espen Knutsen RC .20 .50
67 Marc Savard .05 .15
68 Hnat Domenichelli .01 .05
69 Warren Luhning RC .01 .05
70 Magnus Arvedson RC .01 .05
71 Chris Phillips .01 .05
72 Brad Isbister .01 .05
73 Boyd Devereaux .01 .05
74 Alexei Morozov .05 .15
75 Vladimir Vorobiev RC .01 .05
76 Steven Rice .01 .05
77 Tony Granato .01 .05
78 Lonny Bohonos .01 .05
79 Dave Gagner .01 .05
80 Brendan Shanahan .08 .25
81 Brett Hull .10 .30
82 Jaromir Jagr .15 .40
83 Peter Forsberg .25 .60
84 Paul Kariya .08 .25
85 Mark Messier .08 .25
86 Steve Yzerman .50 1.25
87 Keith Tkachuk .08 .25
88 Eric Lindros .08 .25
89 Ray Bourque .15 .40
90 Chris Chelios .08 .25
91 Sergei Fedorov .15 .40
92 Mike Modano .15 .40
93 Doug Gilmour .05 .15
94 Saku Koivu .08 .25
95 Mats Sundin .08 .25
96 Pavel Bure .08 .25
97 Theo Fleury .01 .05
98 Keith Primeau .01 .05
99 Wayne Gretzky .50 1.25
100 Doug Weight .05 .15
101 Alexandre Daigle .01 .05
102 Owen Nolan .05 .15
103 Peter Bondra .05 .15
104 Pat LaFontaine .08 .25
105 Kirk Muller .01 .05
106 Zigmund Palffy .05 .15
107 Jeremy Roenick .10 .30
108 John LeClair .08 .25
109 Derek Plante .01 .05
110 Geoff Sanderson .05 .15
111 Dimitri Khristich .01 .05
112 Vincent Damphousse .01 .05
113 Teemu Selanne .08 .25
114 Tony Amonte .05 .15
115 Dave Andreychuk .01 .05
116 Alexei Yashin .01 .05
117 Adam Oates .05 .15
118 Pierre Turgeon .05 .15
119 Dino Ciccarelli .01 .05
120 Ryan Smyth .05 .15
121 Ray Sheppard .01 .05
122 Jozef Stumpel .05 .15
123 Jarome Iginla .10 .30
124 Pat Verbeek .01 .05
125 Joe Sakic .20 .50
126 Brian Leetch .08 .25
127 Rod Brind'Amour .05 .15
128 Wendel Clark .05 .15
129 Alexander Mogilny .05 .15
130 Mark Recchi .05 .15
131 Daniel Alfredsson .05 .15
132 Ron Francis .05 .15
133 Martin Gelinas .01 .05
134 Andrew Cassels .01 .05
135 Joe Nieuwendyk .05 .15
136 Jason Arnott .01 .05
137 Bryan Berard .05 .15
138 Mikael Renberg .05 .15
139 Mike Gartner .05 .15
140 Joe Juneau .05 .15
141 John MacLean .01 .05
142 Adam Graves .01 .05
143 Petr Nedved .05 .15
144 Trevor Linden .05 .15
145 Sergei Berezin .01 .05
146 Adam Deadmarsh .01 .05
147 Jeff O'Neill .01 .05
148 Rob Blake .05 .15
149 Luc Robitaille .05 .15
150 Markus Naslund .08 .25
151 Ethan Moreau .01 .05
152 Martin Rucinsky .01 .05
153 Mike Grier .01 .05
154 Craig Janney .01 .05
155 John Cullen .01 .05
156 Alexei Kovalev .01 .05
157 Tony Twist .05 .15
158 Claude Lemieux .01 .05
159 Kevin Stevens .05 .15
160 Mathieu Schneider .01 .05
161 Randy Cunneyworth .01 .05
162 Darius Kasparaitis .01 .05
163 Joe Murphy .01 .05
164 Brandon Convery .01 .05
165 Janne Niinimaa .05 .15
166 Paul Coffey .08 .25
167 Daymond Langkow .05 .15
168 Chris Gratton .05 .15
169 Ray Ferraro .01 .05
170 Jeff Friesen .01 .05
171 Ted Donato .01 .05
172 Brian Holzinger .01 .05
173 Travis Green .01 .05
174 Sandis Ozolinsh .01 .05
175 Alexei Zhamnov .01 .05
176 Steve Rucchin .01 .05
177 Scott Mellanby .01 .05
178 Andrei Kovalenko .01 .05
179 Donald Audette .01 .05
180 Bernie Nicholls .01 .05
181 Jonas Hoglund .01 .05
182 Nicklas Lidstrom .08 .25
183 Bobby Holik .01 .05
184 Geoff Courtnall .01 .05
185 Steve Sullivan .01 .05
186 Valeri Kamensky .05 .15
187 Mike Peca .01 .05
188 Jere Lehtinen .01 .05
189 Robert Svehla .01 .05
190 Darren McCarty .01 .05
191 Brian Savage .01 .05
192 Harry York .01 .05
193 Eric Daze .05 .15
194 Niklas Sundstrom .01 .05
195 Oleg Tverdovsky .01 .05
196 Eric Desjardins .05 .15
197 German Titov .01 .05
198 Derian Hatcher .01 .05
199 Bill Guerin .05 .15
200 Rob Zamuner .01 .05
201 Dale Hunter .01 .05
202 Darcy Tucker .01 .05
203 Andreas Dackell .01 .05
204 Jason Dawe .01 .05
205 Brian Rolston .01 .05
206 Ed Olczyk .01 .05
207 Todd Warriner .01 .05
208 Mariusz Czerkawski .01 .05
209 Slava Kozlov .01 .05
210 Marty McInnis .01 .05
211 Jamie Langenbrunner .01 .05
212 Vitali Yachmenev .01 .05
213 Stephane Richer .01 .05
214 Roman Hamrlik .05 .15
215 Jim Campbell .01 .05
216 Matthew Barnaby .01 .05
217 Benoit Hogue .01 .05
218 Robert Reichel .01 .05
219 Tie Domi .05 .15
220 Steve Konowalchuk .01 .05
221 Radek Dvorak .01 .05
222 Kevin Hatcher .01 .05
223 Viktor Kozlov .01 .05
224 Scott Stevens .05 .15
225 Cory Stillman .01 .05
226 Anson Carter .05 .15
227 Rem Murray .01 .05
228 Vladimir Konstantinov .05 .15
229 Scott Niedermayer .01 .05
230 Steve Duchesne .01 .05
231 Valeri Bure .01 .05
232 Miroslav Satan .01 .0
233 Jason Allison .01 .0
234 Mark Fitzpatrick .05 .1
235 Ed Jovanovski .05 .1
236 Esa Tikkanen .01 .0
237 Stu Barnes .01 .0
238 Darryl Sydor .01 .0
239 Ulf Samuelsson .01 .0
240 Dmitri Mironov .01 .0
241 Bryan Smolinski .01 .0
242 Rob Ray .01 .0
243 Todd Marchant .01 .0
244 Cliff Ronning .01 .0
245 Alexander Selivanov .01 .0
246 Rick Tocchet .05 .1
247 Vladimir Malakhov .01 .0
248 Al MacInnis .05 .1
249 Dainius Zubrus .08 .2
250 Keith Jones .01 .0
251 Darren Turcotte .01 .0
252 Ulf Dahlen .01 .0
253 Rob Niedermayer .01 .0
254 J.J. Daigneault .01 .0
255 Michal Grosek .01 .0
256 Chris Therien .01 .0
257 Adam Foote .01 .0
258 Tomas Sandstrom .01 .0
259 Scott Lachance .01 .0
260 Paul Kariya SM .08 .2
261 Pavel Bure SM .08 .2
262 Mike Modano SM .08 .2
263 Steve Yzerman SM .08 .2
264 Sergei Fedorov SM .08 .2
265 Eric Lindros SM .08 .2
266 Dominik Hasek CL (1-66) .05 .15
267 Bryan Berard CL (67-132) .01 .05
268 Mike Peca CL (133-201) .01 .05
269 M.Brodeur .01 .05
M.Dunham CL (202-270)
270 Paul Kariya CL (inserts) .08 .25
82 Jaromir Jagr PROMO 1.00 2.50
83 Peter Forsberg PROMO 1.25 3.00
84 Paul Kariya PROMO 1.25 3.00
86 Steve Yzerman PROMO 1.50 4.00
88 Eric Lindros PROMO 1.25 3.00

1997-98 Score Artist's Proofs

Randomly inserted in packs at the rate of 1:35, this 160-card set is a partial parallel version of the base set and is printed on prismatic foil board with the "Artist's Proof" seal on the front.

*ART.PROOF: 25X TO 60X BASIC CARDS

1997-98 Score Golden Blades

Randomly inserted in packs at the rate of 1:7, this 160-card set is a partial parallel version of the base set printed on silver gloss foil board.

*GOLDEN BLADES: 1.2X TO 3X BASIC CARDS

1997-98 Score Check It

Randomly inserted in packs at the rate of 1:18, this 18-card set features action color photos of some of the toughest hitters in the game.

COMPLETE SET (18) 5.00 12.00
COMMON CARD (1-18) .20 .50
SEMISTARS .15 .40
UNLISTED STARS .30 .75
STATED ODDS 1:18
1 Eric Lindros .75 2.00
2 Mark Recchi .20 .50
3 Brendan Shanahan .60 1.50
4 Keith Tkachuk .30 .75
5 John LeClair .30 .75
6 Doug Gilmour .20 .50
7 Jarome Iginla .50 1.25
8 Ryan Smyth .20 .50
9 Chris Chelios .30 .75
10 Mike Grier .10 .25
11 Vincent Damphousse .10 .25
12 Bryan Berard .20 .50
13 Jaromir Jagr .75 2.00
14 Mike Peca .10 .25
15 Dino Ciccarelli .10 .25
16 Rod Brind'Amour .20 .50
17 Owen Nolan .20 .50
18 Pat Verbeek .20 .50

1997-98 Score Net Worth

Randomly inserted in packs at the rate of 1:35, this 18-card set features color action photos of the NHL's best goalies.

COMPLETE SET (18) 8.00 15.00
1 Guy Hebert .25 .60
2 Jim Carey .25 .60
3 Trevor Kidd .25 .60
4 Chris Osgood .25 .60
5 Curtis Joseph .40 1.00
6 Mike Richter .40 1.00
7 Damian Rhodes .25 .60
8 Garth Snow .25 .60
9 Nikolai Khabibulin .25 .60
10 Grant Fuhr .25 .60
11 Jocelyn Thibault .25 .60
12 Tommy Salo .25 .60
13 Patrick Roy 2.00 5.00
14 Martin Brodeur 1.00 2.50
15 John Vanbiesbrouck .25 .60
16 Felix Potvin .40 1.00
17 Dominik Hasek .75 2.00
18 Ed Belfour .40 1.00

1997-98 Score Avalanche

This 20-card team set of the Colorado Avalanche was produced by Pinnacle and features bordered color action player photos. The backs carry player information.

COMPLETE SET (20) 4.00 10.00
*PLATINUM: 1.2X TO 3X BASIC CARDS
*PREMIER: 3X TO 8X BASIC CARDS
1 Patrick Roy 1.50 4.00
2 Craig Billington .25 .60
3 Marc Denis .25 .60
4 Peter Forsberg 1.00 2.50
5 Jari Kurri .25 .60
6 Sandis Ozolinsh .25 .60
7 Valeri Kamensky .25 .60
8 Adam Deadmarsh .25 .60
9 Keith Jones .10 .30
10 Josef Marha .08 .25

Claude Lemieux .25 .60
Adam Foote .10 .30
Eric Lacroix .08 .25
Rene Corbet .08 .25
Uwe Krupp .08 .25
Sylvain Lefebvre .08 .25
Mike Ricci .25 .60
Joe Sakic .75 2.00
Stephane Yelle .08 .25
Yves Sarault .08 .25

1997-98 Score Blues

is 20-card team set of the St. Louis Blues was oduced by Pinnacle and features bordered color tion player photos. The backs carry player formation.

OMPLETE SET (20) 3.00 8.00
LATINUM: 1.2X TO 3X BASIC CARDS
REMIER: 3X TO 8X BASIC CARDS
Brett Hull .40 1.00
Pierre Turgeon .25 .60
Joe Murphy .08 .25
Jim Campbell .08 .25
Harry York .08 .25
Al MacInnis .25 .60
Chris Pronger .25 .60
Darren Turcotte .08 .25
Robert Petrovicky .08 .25
Tony Twist .30 .75
Grant Fuhr .25 .60
Scott Pellerin .08 .25
Jamie Rivers .10 .25
Chris McAlpine .08 .25
Geoff Courtnall .25 .60
Steve Duchesne .20 .50
Libor Zabransky .08 .25
Pavol Demitra .25 .60
Marc Bergevin .08 .25
Jamie McLennan .08 .25

1997-98 Score Bruins

is 20-card team set of the Boston Bruins was oduced by Pinnacle and features bordered color tion player photos. The backs carry player formation.

OMPLETE SET (20) 2.50 6.00
LATINUM: 1.2X TO 3X BASIC CARDS
REMIER: 3X TO 8X BASIC CARDS
Shawn Bates .08 .25
Jim Carey .15 .40
Rob Tallas .08 .25
Ray Bourque .30 .75
Dimitri Khristich .08 .25
Ted Donato .08 .25
Jason Allison .25 .60
Anson Carter .15 .40
Rob Dimaio .08 .25
Steve Heinze .08 .25
Jean Yves Roy .08 .25
Randy Robitaille .08 .25
Byron Dafoe .30 .75
Sergei Samsonov .75 2.00
Ken Baumgartner .08 .25
Dave Ellett .08 .25
Joe Thornton .75 2.00
Jeff Odgers .08 .25
Kyle McLaren .08 .25
Don Sweeney .08 .25

1997-98 Score Canadiens

is 20-card team set of the Montreal Canadiens was oduced by Pinnacle and features bordered color tion player photos. The backs carry player formation.

OMPLETE SET (20) 3.00 8.00
LATINUM: 1.2X TO 3X BASIC CARDS
REMIER: 3X TO 8X BASIC CARDS
Andy Moog .25 .60
Jocelyn Thibault .25 .60
Jose Theodore .25 .60
Vincent Damphousse .25 .60
Mark Recchi .25 .60
Brian Savage .08 .25
Saku Koivu .60 1.50
Stephane Richer .25 .60
Martin Rucinsky .08 .25
Valeri Bure .08 .25
Vladimir Malakhov .08 .25
Shayne Corson .25 .60
Darcy Tucker .08 .25
Sebastien Bordeleau .08 .25
Terry Ryan .08 .25
David Ling .08 .25
Dave Manson .08 .25
Benoit Brunet .08 .25
Marc Bureau .08 .25
Patrice Brisebois .08 .25

1997-98 Score Canucks

is 20-card team set of the Vancouver Canucks was oduced by Pinnacle and features bordered color tion player photos. The backs carry player formation.

OMPLETE SET (20) 3.00 8.00
LATINUM: 1.2X TO 3X BASIC CARDS
REMIER: 3X TO 8X BASIC CARDS
Pavel Bure .60 1.50
Alexander Mogilny .25 .60
Mark Messier .40 1.00
Trevor Linden .25 .60
Martin Gelinas .08 .25
Mattias Ohlund .15 .40
Markus Naslund .08 .25
Jyrki Lumme .08 .25
Lonny Bohonos .08 .25
Kirk McLean .25 .60
Corey Hirsch .25 .60
Arturs Irbe .25 .60
Larry Courville .08 .25
Adrian Aucoin .08 .25
Grant Ledyard .08 .25
Gino Odjick .08 .25
Donald Brashear .08 .25
Brian Noonan .08 .25
David Roberts .08 .25
Dave Babych .08 .25

1997-98 Score Devils

is 20-card team set of the New Jersey Devils was oduced by Pinnacle and features bordered color tion player photos. The backs carry player formation.

OMPLETE SET (20) 3.00 8.00
LATINUM: 1.2X TO 3X BASIC CARDS
REMIER: 3X TO 8X BASIC CARDS
Doug Gilmour .30 .75
Bobby Holik .08 .25
Dave Andreychuk .25 .60
John MacLean .08 .25
Bill Guerin .08 .25
Brian Rolston .08 .25
Scott Niedermayer .08 .25
Scott Stevens .08 .25
9 Valeri Zelepukin .08 .25
10 Steve Thomas .08 .25
11 Denis Pederson .08 .25
12 Randy McKay .08 .25
13 Mike Dunham .25 .60
14 Petr Sykora .15 .40
15 Lyle Odelein .08 .25
16 Martin Brodeur .75 2.00
17 Vadim Sharifijanov .08 .25
18 Bob Carpenter .08 .25
19 Sergei Brylin .08 .25
20 Ken Daneyko .08 .25

1997-98 Score Flyers

This 20-card team set of the Philadelphia Flyers was produced by Pinnacle and features bordered color action player photos. The backs carry player information.

COMPLETE SET (20) 4.00 10.00
*PLATINUM: 1.2X TO 3X BASIC CARDS
*PREMIER: 3X TO 8X BASIC CARDS
1 Ron Hextall .25 .60
2 Garth Snow .25 .60
3 Eric Lindros 1.25 3.00
4 John LeClair .60 1.50
5 Rod Brind'Amour .25 .60
6 Chris Gratton .15 .40
7 Eric Desjardins .08 .25
8 Trent Klatt .08 .25
9 Janne Niinimaa .25 .60
10 Luke Richardson .08 .25
11 Paul Coffey .30 .75
12 Dainius Zubrus .30 .75
13 Shjon Podein .08 .25
14 Joel Otto .08 .25
15 Chris Therien .08 .25
16 Pat Falloon .08 .25
17 Petr Svoboda .08 .25
18 Vaclav Prospal .30 .75
19 John Druce .08 .25
20 Daniel Lacroix .08 .25

1997-98 Score Maple Leafs

This 20-card team set of the Toronto Maple Leafs was produced by Pinnacle and features bordered color action player photos. The backs carry player information.

COMPLETE SET (20) 3.00 8.00
*PLATINUM: 1.2X TO 3X BASIC CARDS
*PREMIER: 3X TO 8X BASIC CARDS
1 Felix Potvin .30 .75
2 Glenn Healy .25 .60
3 Marcel Cousineau .25 .60
4 Mats Sundin .30 .75
5 Wendel Clark .25 .60
6 Sergei Berezin .25 .60
7 Steve Sullivan .08 .25
8 Tie Domi .10 .30
9 Todd Warriner .08 .25
10 Mathieu Schneider .08 .25
11 Mike Craig .08 .25
12 Darby Hendrickson .08 .25
13 Fredrik Modin .08 .25
14 Brandon Convery .08 .25
15 Kevyn Adams .08 .25
16 Dimitri Yushkevich .08 .25
17 Alyn McCauley .08 .25
18 Derek King .08 .25
19 Jamie Baker .08 .25
20 Martin Prochazka .08 .25

1997-98 Score Mighty Ducks

This 20-card team set of the Mighty Ducks of Anaheim was produced by Pinnacle and features bordered color action player photos. The backs carry player information.

COMPLETE SET (20) 4.00 10.00
*PLATINUM: 1.2X TO 3X BASIC CARDS
*PREMIER: 3X TO 8X BASIC CARDS
1 Paul Kariya 1.25 3.00
2 Teemu Selanne .75 2.00
3 Steve Rucchin .08 .25
4 Dmitri Mironov .08 .25
5 Matt Cullen .08 .25
6 Kevin Todd .08 .25
7 Joe Sacco .08 .25
8 J.J. Daigneault .08 .25
9 Darren Van Impe .08 .25
10 Scott Young .08 .25
11 Ted Drury .08 .25
12 Tomas Sandstrom .08 .25
13 Warren Rychel .08 .25
14 Guy Hebert .25 .60
15 Shawn Antoski .08 .25
16 Mikhail Shtalenkov .25 .60
17 Peter Leboutillier .08 .25
18 Sean Pronger .08 .25
19 Dave Karpa .08 .25
20 Espen Knutsen .20 .50

1997-98 Score Penguins

This 20-card team set of the Pittsburgh Penguins was produced by Pinnacle and features bordered color action player photos. The backs carry player information.

COMPLETE SET (20) 3.60 9.00
*PLATINUM: 1.2X TO 3X BASIC CARDS
*PREMIER: 3X TO 8X BASIC CARDS
1 Tom Barrasso .08 .25
2 Ken Wregget .25 .60
3 Patrick Lalime .25 .60
4 Jaromir Jagr 1.00 2.50
5 Ron Francis .25 .60
6 Petr Nedved .25 .60
7 Ed Olczyk .08 .25
8 Kevin Hatcher .08 .25
9 Stu Barnes .08 .25
10 Darius Kasparaitis .08 .25
11 Greg Johnson .08 .25
12 Garry Valk .08 .25
13 Roman Oksiuta .08 .25
14 Dan Quinn .08 .25
15 Alex Hicks .08 .25
16 Robert Dome .08 .25
17 Dave Roche .08 .25
18 Alexei Morozov .25 .60
19 Rob Brown .08 .25
20 Domenic Pittis .08 .25

1997-98 Score Rangers

This 20-card team set of the New York Rangers was produced by Pinnacle and features bordered color action player photos. The backs carry player information.

COMPLETE SET (20) 4.00 10.00
*PLATINUM: 1.2X TO 3X BASIC CARDS
*PREMIER: 3X TO 8X BASIC CARDS
1 Wayne Gretzky 2.00 5.00
2 Brian Leetch .30 .75
3 Mike Keane .08 .25
4 Adam Graves .25 .60
5 Niklas Sundstrom .08 .25
6 Kevin Stevens .08 .25
7 Alexei Kovalev .08 .25
8 Alexander Karpovtsev .08 .25
9 Bill Berg .08 .25
10 Pat Lafontaine .25 .60
11 Bruce Driver .08 .25
12 Pat Flatley .08 .25
13 Vladimir Vorobiev .08 .25
14 Christian Dube .08 .25
15 Ulf Samuelsson .08 .25
16 Mike Richter .30 .75
17 Jason Muzzatti .08 .25
18 Daniel Goneau .08 .25
19 Marc Savard .08 .25
20 Jeff Beukeboom .08 .25

1997-98 Score Red Wings

This 20-card team set of the Detroit Red Wings was produced by Pinnacle and features bordered color action player photos. The backs carry player information.

COMPLETE SET (20) 4.00 10.00
*PLATINUM: 1.2X TO 3X BASIC CARDS
*PREMIER: 3X TO 8X BASIC CARDS
1 Brendan Shanahan .60 1.50
2 Steve Yzerman 1.00 2.50
3 Sergei Fedorov .60 1.50
4 Nicklas Lidstrom .25 .60
5 Igor Larionov .15 .40
6 Darren McCarty .25 .60
7 Slava Kozlov .25 .60
8 Larry Murphy .25 .60
9 Vladimir Konstantinov .25 .60
10 Martin Lapointe .10 .30
11 Slava Fetisov .10 .30
12 Kris Draper .10 .30
13 Doug Brown .08 .25
14 Brent Gilchrist .08 .25
15 Kirk Maltby .08 .25
16 Tomas Holmstrom .08 .25
17 Chris Osgood .30 .75
18 Kevin Hodson .30 .75
19 Jamie Pushor .08 .25
20 Mike Knuble .25 .60

1997-98 Score Sabres

This 20-card team set of the Buffalo Sabres was produced by Pinnacle and features bordered color action player photos. The backs carry player information.

COMPLETE SET (20) 3.00 8.00
*PLATINUM: 1.2X TO 3X BASIC CARDS
*PREMIER: 3X TO 8X BASIC CARDS
1 Dominik Hasek .75 2.00
2 Steve Shields .25 .60
3 Dixon Ward .08 .25
4 Donald Audette .08 .25
5 Matthew Barnaby .08 .25
6 Randy Burridge .08 .25
7 Jason Dawe .08 .25
8 Michael Grosek .08 .25
9 Brian Holzinger .25 .60
10 Brad May .08 .25
11 Mike Peca .30 .75
12 Derek Plante .08 .25
13 Wayne Primeau .08 .25
14 Rob Ray .25 .60
15 Miroslav Satan .25 .60
16 Erik Rasmussen .08 .25
17 Jason Woolley .08 .25
18 Alexei Zhitnik .08 .25
19 Darryl Shannon .08 .25
20 Mike Wilson .08 .25

2010-11 Score

COMP.SET w/o SSPs (550) 40.00 80.00
COMP.SET w/o SPs (500) 15.00 40.00
COMP.R/T.FACT.SET (105) 20.00 40.00
COMP.ROOK/TRD SET (99) 12.00 30.00
501-550 ROOKIE ODDS 1:2
1 Joe Sakic banner HL .30 .75
2 Elmer Lach banner HL .15 .40
3 Emile Bouchard banner HL .20 .50
4 Phil Kessel HL .25 .60
5 Josh Bailey HL .15 .40
6 Cristobal Huet HL .20 .50
7 NHL heads overseas HL .20 .50
Nicklas Lidstrom
8 Martin Brodeur HL .40 1.00
9 B.Pouliot/G.Latendresse .15 .40
10 Michael Cammalleri HL .20 .50
11 Martin Brodeur HL .40 1.00
12 Marco Sturm HL .12 .30
13 Tim Thomas HL .15 .40
14 Roberto Luongo HL .20 .50
15 Ryan Miller HL .20 .50
16 Jonathan Toews HL .40 1.00
17 Chris Chelios HL .20 .50
18 Dion Phaneuf HL .20 .50
19 Ilya Kovalchuk HL .20 .50
20 Alex Ovechkin HL .75 2.00
21 Shane Doan HL .15 .40
Vern Fiddler
22 Claude Giroux HL .20 .50
23 Keith Tkachuk HL .20 .50
24 Bobby Orr Statue HL .60 1.50
25 Sidney Crosby HL .75 2.00
26 Steven Stamkos HL .40 1.00
27 I.Bryzgalov/J.Quick .15 .40
28 Henrik Sedin HL .20 .50
29 Jordan Staal HL .20 .50
30 Marian Hossa HL .15 .40
31 Hawks capture Cup HL .40 1.00
32 Jonathan Toews HL .40 1.00
33 Brent Sopel HL .12 .30
34 Rob Blake HL .20 .50
35 Scott Niedermayer HL .20 .50
36 Corey Perry .20 .50
37 Ryan Getzlaf .30 .75
38 Joffrey Lupul .15 .40
39 Saku Koivu .20 .50
40 George Parros .15 .40
41 Dan Sexton .15 .40
42 Ryan Carter .12 .30
43 Troy Bodie .12 .30
44 Matt Beleskey .15 .40
45 Teemu Selanne .40 1.00
46 Bobby Ryan .20 .50
47 Lubomir Visnovsky .12 .30
48 Luca Sbisa .15 .40
49 Jonas Hiller .15 .40
50 Curtis McElhinney .15 .40
51 Nik Antropov .15 .40
52 Evander Kane .20 .50
53 Todd White .12 .30
54 Dustin Byfuglien .20 .50
55 Bryan Little .20 .50
56 Niclas Bergfors .15 .40
57 Rich Peverley .20 .50
58 Chris Thorburn .12 .30
59 Ben Eager .12 .30
60 Ron Hainsey .12 .30
61 Tobias Enstrom .12 .30
62 Zach Bogosian .15 .40
63 Johnny Oduya .15 .40
64 Chris Mason .15 .40
65 Ondrej Pavelec .20 .50
66 Marc Savard .12 .30
67 Patrice Bergeron .25 .60
68 David Krejci .20 .50
69 Marco Sturm .12 .30
70 Milan Lucic .20 .50
71 Nathan Horton .15 .40
72 Mark Recchi .25 .60
73 Blake Wheeler .20 .50
74 Matt Hunwick .12 .30
75 Johnny Boychuk .12 .30
76 Zdeno Chara .15 .40
77 Mark Stuart .12 .30
78 Shawn Thornton .12 .30
79 Tuukka Rask .20 .50
80 Tim Thomas .15 .40
81 Thomas Vanek .20 .50
82 Jason Pominville .20 .50
83 Tim Connolly .12 .30
84 Derek Roy .20 .50
85 Jochen Hecht .12 .30
86 Paul Gaustad .12 .30
87 Drew Stafford .20 .50
88 Tyler Ennis .15 .40
89 Nathan Gerbe .12 .30
90 Patrick Kaleta .12 .30
91 Craig Rivet .12 .30
92 Tyler Myers .20 .50
93 Chris Butler .12 .30
94 Ryan Miller .20 .50
95 Jhonas Enroth .20 .50
96 Jarome Iginla .20 .50
97 Daymond Langkow .12 .30
98 Rene Bourque .12 .30
99 David Moss .12 .30
100 Curtis Glencross .12 .30
101 Niklas Hagman .12 .30
102 Olli Jokinen .15 .40
103 Matt Stajan .15 .40
104 Mikael Backlund .12 .30
105 Jay Bouwmeester .25 .60
106 Robyn Regehr .12 .30
107 Cory Sarich .12 .30
108 Mark Giordano .15 .40
109 Alex Tanguay .12 .30
110 Miikka Kiprusoff .15 .40
111 Eric Staal .25 .60
112 Tuomo Ruutu .15 .40
113 Erik Cole .15 .40
114 Sergei Samsonov .15 .40
115 Jussi Jokinen .12 .30
116 Chad LaRose .12 .30
117 Brandon Sutter .15 .40
118 Drayson Bowman .15 .40
119 Jiri Tlusty .15 .40
120 Tom Kostopoulos .12 .30
121 Zach Boychuk .15 .40
122 Joni Pitkanen .15 .40
123 Tim Gleason .12 .30
124 Cam Ward .20 .50
125 Justin Peters .15 .40
126 Marian Hossa .15 .40
127 Patrick Sharp .20 .50
128 Patrick Kane .40 1.00
129 Jonathan Toews .40 1.00
130 Dave Bolland .15 .40
131 Troy Brouwer .20 .50
132 Viktor Stalberg .15 .40
133 Jack Skille .15 .40
134 Brent Seabrook .20 .50
135 Duncan Keith .20 .50
136 Niklas Hjalmarsson .12 .30
137 Jordan Hendry .12 .30
138 Brian Campbell .12 .30
139 Tomas Kopecky .15 .40
140 Marty Turco .20 .50
141 Paul Stastny .20 .50
142 Milan Hejduk .15 .40
143 Matt Duchene .20 .50
144 Peter Mueller .15 .40
145 Ryan O'Reilly .20 .50
146 T.J. Galiardi .15 .40
147 Adam Foote .12 .30
148 Chris Stewart .15 .40
149 Ryan Stoa .12 .30
150 Cody McLeod .12 .30
151 David Jones .12 .30
152 Scott Hannan .12 .30
153 Kyle Cumiskey .12 .30
154 Peter Budaj .15 .40
155 Craig Anderson .20 .50
156 Rick Nash .20 .50
157 Kristian Huselius .12 .30
158 R.J. Umberger .12 .30
159 Antoine Vermette .12 .30
160 Samuel Pahlsson .12 .30
161 Chris Clark .12 .30
162 Jakub Voracek .20 .50
163 Derick Brassard .20 .50
164 Derek Dorsett .12 .30
165 Mike Commodore .12 .30
166 Kris Russell .12 .30
167 Marc Methot .12 .30
168 Jan Hejda .12 .30
169 Steve Mason .15 .40
170 Mathieu Garon .15 .40
171 Brad Richards .20 .50
172 Brenden Morrow .15 .40
173 Loui Eriksson .15 .40
174 Steve Ott .15 .40
175 Jamie Benn .25 .60
176 James Neal .20 .50
177 Tom Wandell .12 .30
178 Brandon Segal .12 .30
179 Krys Barch .12 .30
180 Trevor Daley .12 .30
181 Stephane Robidas .12 .30
182 Mark Fistric .12 .30
183 Nicklas Grossman .12 .30
184 Raymond Sawada .12 .30
185 Kari Lehtonen .15 .40
186 Pavel Datsyuk .25 .60
187 Henrik Zetterberg .25 .60
188 Tomas Holmstrom .12 .30
189 Johan Franzen .20 .50
190 Valtteri Filppula .20 .50
191 Daniel Cleary .20 .50
192 Justin Abdelkader .15 .40
193 Mattias Ritola .12 .30
194 Drew Miller .12 .30
195 Mike Modano .30 .75
196 Nicklas Lidstrom .20 .50
197 Brian Rafalski .12 .30
198 Niklas Kronwall .12 .30
199 Jimmy Howard .25 .60
200 Chris Osgood .20 .50
201 Dustin Penner .12 .30
202 Sam Gagner .15 .40
203 Ales Hemsky .15 .40
204 Shawn Horcoff .12 .30
205 Zack Stortini .12 .30
206 Gilbert Brule .20 .50
207 Andrew Cogliano .12 .30
208 J-F Jacques .12 .30
209 Alex Plante .15 .40
210 Kurtis Foster .12 .30
211 Tom Gilbert .12 .30
212 Ryan Whitney .12 .30
213 Taylor Chorney .15 .40
214 Nikolai Khabibulin .15 .40
215 Jeff Deslauriers .12 .30
216 Stephen Weiss .15 .40
217 David Booth .12 .30
218 Cory Stillman .12 .30
219 Rostislav Olesz .12 .30
220 Michael Frolik .12 .30
221 Steve Reinprecht .12 .30
222 Michal Repik .12 .30
223 Shawn Matthias .12 .30
224 Byron Bitz .12 .30
225 Radek Dvorak .12 .30
226 Dmitry Kulikov .15 .40
227 Keaton Ellerby .12 .30
228 Dennis Wideman .12 .30
229 Tomas Vokoun .15 .40
230 Tyler Plante .12 .30
231 Anze Kopitar .30 .75
232 Ryan Smyth .15 .40
233 Dustin Brown .20 .50
234 Jarret Stoll .15 .40
235 Justin Williams .15 .40
236 Michal Handzus .15 .40
237 Wayne Simmonds .25 .60
238 Oscar Moller .15 .40
239 Alexei Ponikarovsky .12 .30
240 Matt Greene .12 .30
241 Drew Doughty .20 .50
242 Davis Drewiske .12 .30
243 Jack Johnson .12 .30
244 Jonathan Quick .30 .75
245 Jonathan Bernier .20 .50
246 Mikko Koivu .20 .50
247 Martin Havlat .15 .40
248 Pierre-Marc Bouchard .20 .50
249 Andrew Brunette .12 .30
250 Antti Miettinen .12 .30
251 Chuck Kobasew .12 .30
252 James Sheppard .12 .30
253 Cal Clutterbuck .20 .50
254 Guillaume Latendresse .15 .40
255 Colton Gillies .12 .30
256 Brent Burns .25 .60
257 Nick Schultz .12 .30
258 Greg Zanon .12 .30
259 Cam Barker .12 .30
260 Niklas Backstrom .20 .50
261 Scott Gomez .15 .40
262 Michael Cammalleri .20 .50
263 Brian Gionta .15 .40
264 Benoit Pouliot .12 .30
265 Andrei Kostitsyn .15 .40
266 Travis Moen .12 .30
267 Max Pacioretty .20 .50
268 Tom Pyatt .12 .30
269 Maxim Lapierre .12 .30
270 Josh Gorges .12 .30
271 Tomas Plekanec .20 .50
272 Lars Eller .15 .40
273 Hal Gill .12 .30
274 Andrei Markov .20 .50
275 Carey Price .75 2.00
276 Martin Erat .12 .30
277 Patric Hornqvist .15 .40
278 Colin Wilson .15 .40
279 Jordin Tootoo .15 .40
280 J.P. Dumont .12 .30
281 Steve Sullivan .12 .30
282 Joel Ward .12 .30
283 David Legwand .15 .40
284 Matthew Lombardi .12 .30
285 Shea Weber .15 .40
286 Ryan Suter .12 .30
287 Kevin Klein .12 .30
288 Cody Franson .12 .30
289 Pekka Rinne .25 .60
290 Matt Halischuk .15 .40
291 Ilya Kovalchuk .20 .50
292 Zach Parise .20 .50
293 Travis Zajac .15 .40
294 Jamie Langenbrunner .12 .30
295 Patrik Elias .20 .50
296 Brian Rolston .15 .40
297 Dainius Zubrus .12 .30
298 Pierre-Luc Letourneau-Leblond .12 .30
299 Andrew Peters .12 .30
300 Jason Arnott .15 .40
301 Colin White .12 .30
302 Bryce Salvador .12 .30
303 Andy Greene .12 .30
304 David Clarkson .12 .30
305 Martin Brodeur .40 1.00
306 John Tavares .40 1.00
307 Matt Moulson .15 .40
308 Rob Schremp .12 .30
309 Trent Hunter .12 .30
310 Josh Bailey .15 .40
311 Kyle Okposo .20 .50
312 Doug Weight .20 .50
313 Blake Comeau .12 .30
314 Zenon Konopka .15 .40
315 Frans Nielsen .12 .30
316 Mark Streit .12 .30
317 Bruno Gervais .12 .30
318 Jack Hillen .12 .30
319 Dwayne Roloson .15 .40
320 Rick DiPietro .15 .40
321 Marian Gaborik .25 .60
322 Alexander Frolov .12 .30
323 Chris Drury .15 .40
324 Ryan Callahan .20 .50
325 Sean Avery .15 .40
326 Brandon Dubinsky .15 .40
327 Artem Anisimov .15 .40
328 Brian Boyle .12 .30
329 Wade Redden .12 .30
330 Matt Gilroy .12 .30
331 Michael Del Zotto .15 .40
332 Daniel Girardi .12 .30
333 Marc Staal .20 .50
334 Brandon Prust .12 .30
335 Henrik Lundqvist .30 .75
336 Jason Spezza .12 .30
337 Daniel Alfredsson .20 .50
338 Milan Michalek .12 .30
339 Mike Fisher .20 .50
340 Chris Neil .12 .30
341 Chris Kelly .15 .40
342 Alex Kovalev .20 .50
343 Nick Foligno .15 .40
344 Peter Regin .15 .40
345 Sergei Gonchar .12 .30
346 Chris Phillips .12 .30
347 Erik Karlsson .40 1.00
348 Matt Carkner .15 .40
349 Pascal Leclaire .15 .40
350 Brian Elliott .15 .40
351 Mike Richards .20 .50
352 Jeff Carter .20 .50
353 Nikolai Zherdev .12 .30
354 James van Riemsdyk .30 .75
355 Daniel Carcillo .12 .30
356 Kimmo Timonen .12 .30
357 Daniel Briere .20 .50
358 Scott Hartnell .20 .50
359 Claude Giroux .20 .50
360 Ville Leino .15 .40
361 Matt Carle .15 .40
362 Braydon Coburn .12 .30
363 Chris Pronger .15 .40
364 Brian Boucher .15 .40
365 Michael Leighton .15 .40
366 Wojtek Wolski .12 .30
367 Shane Doan .15 .40
368 Ray Whitney .15 .40
369 Radim Vrbata .15 .40
370 Scottie Upshall .12 .30
371 Vernon Fiddler .12 .30
372 Petr Prucha .12 .30
373 Martin Hanzal .12 .30
374 Mikkel Boedker .12 .30
375 Lee Stempniak .12 .30
376 Kurt Sauer .12 .30
377 Keith Yandle .20 .50
378 Ed Jovanovski .12 .30
379 Jason LaBarbera .15 .40
380 Ilya Bryzgalov .15 .40
381 Evgeni Malkin .60 1.50
382 Sidney Crosby .75 2.00
383 Jordan Staal .20 .50
384 Chris Kunitz .20 .50
385 Pascal Dupuis .12 .30
386 Max Talbot .20 .50
387 Mike Rupp .12 .30
388 Tyler Kennedy .12 .30
389 Matt Cooke .12 .30
390 Brooks Orpik .15 .40
391 Alex Goligoski .15 .40
392 Kristopher Letang .20 .50
393 Marc-Andre Fleury .30 .75
394 Brent Johnson .15 .40
395 Paul Martin .12 .30
396 Joe Thornton .20 .50
397 Joe Pavelski .20 .50
398 Patrick Marleau .20 .50
399 Dany Heatley .15 .40
400 Ryane Clowe .12 .30
401 Devin Setoguchi .15 .40
402 Logan Couture .20 .50
403 Torrey Mitchell .12 .30
404 Marc-Edouard Vlasic .12 .30
405 Douglas Murray .12 .30
406 Dan Boyle .15 .40
407 Kent Huskins .12 .30
408 Jason Demers .12 .30
409 Antero Niittymaki .15 .40
410 Antti Niemi .15 .40
411 T.J. Oshie .30 .75
412 Patrik Berglund .12 .30
413 Andy McDonald .15 .40
414 Brad Boyes .12 .30
415 David Backes .20 .50
416 Alex Steen .20 .50
417 Jay McClement .12 .30
418 David Perron .12 .30
419 Matt D'Agostini .12 .30
420 Cam Janssen .12 .30
421 Erik Johnson .12 .30
422 Barret Jackman .12 .30
423 Alex Pietrangelo .15 .40
424 Jaroslav Halak .20 .50
425 Ty Conklin .15 .40
426 Vincent Lecavalier .15 .40
427 Steven Stamkos .40 1.00
428 Martin St. Louis .20 .50
429 Ryan Malone .12 .30
430 Steve Downie .12 .30
431 Blair Jones .12 .30
432 Teddy Purcell .20 .50
433 James Wright .12 .30
434 Dan Ellis .15 .40
435 Pavel Kubina .12 .30
436 Mattias Ohlund .12 .30
437 Victor Hedman .25 .60
438 Simon Gagne .20 .50
439 Matt Smaby .12 .30
440 Mike Smith .20 .50
441 Phil Kessel .25 .60
442 Tyler Bozak .20 .50
443 Mikhail Grabovski .15 .40
444 Colton Orr .12 .30
445 Kris Versteeg .15 .40
446 Christian Hanson .12 .30
447 Fredrik Sjostrom .12 .30
448 Luca Caputi .15 .40
449 Colby Armstrong .12 .30
450 Mike Komisarek .12 .30
451 Francois Beauchemin .12 .30
452 Dion Phaneuf .20 .50
453 Luke Schenn .15 .40
454 Jonas Gustavsson .25 .60
455 Jean-Sebastien Giguere .15 .40
456 Henrik Sedin .20 .50
457 Daniel Sedin .20 .50
458 Alexandre Burrows .20 .50
459 Mason Raymond .15 .40
460 Ryan Kesler .20 .50
461 Mikael Samuelsson .12 .30
462 Rick Rypien .20 .50
463 Sergei Shirokov .15 .40
464 Christian Ehrhoff .12 .30
465 Sami Salo .12 .30
466 Dan Hamhuis .15 .40
467 Darcy Hordichuk .12 .30
468 Keith Ballard .12 .30
469 Cory Schneider .15 .40
470 Roberto Luongo .20 .50
471 Alex Ovechkin .75 2.00
472 Alexander Semin .20 .50
473 Nicklas Backstrom .30 .75
474 Mike Knuble .12 .30
475 Brooks Laich .12 .30
476 Eric Fehr .12 .30
477 David Steckel .12 .30
478 Tomas Fleischmann .12 .30
479 Mathieu Perreault .15 .40
480 Mike Green .20 .50
481 Jeff Schultz .12 .30
482 John Carlson .25 .60
483 Karl Alzner .12 .30
484 Michal Neuvirth .15 .40
485 Semyon Varlamov .20 .50
486 Jaroslav Halak .20 .50
487 Brian Boucher .15 .40
488 Tuukka Rask .20 .50
489 Sidney Crosby .75 2.00
490 Joe Pavelski .20 .50
491 Marian Hossa .15 .40
492 Alexandre Burrows .20 .50
493 Jimmy Howard .25 .60
494 Jaroslav Halak .20 .50
495 Simon Gagne .20 .50
496 Patrick Marleau .20 .50
497 Dustin Byfuglien .20 .50
498 Michael Leighton .15 .40
499 Antti Niemi .15 .40
500 Jonathan Toews .40 1.00
501 Nazem Kadri HR RC 2.00 5.00
502 Nick Johnson HR RC .50 1.25
503 Matt Martin HR RC 1.00 2.50
504 Jamie McBain HR RC .60 1.50
505 Nick Palmieri HR RC .60 1.50
506 Derek Smith HR RC .60 1.50
507 Brandon Yip HR RC .60 1.50
508 Justin Mercier HR RC .60 1.50
509 Evgeny Dadonov HR RC .75 2.00
510 Brad Thiessen HR RC .75 2.00
511 A.Pechurskiy HR RC .75 2.00
512 Dustin Kohn HR RC .60 1.50
513 Tomas Kana HR RC .60 1.50
514 Dustin Tokarski HR RC .60 1.50
515 Jerome Samson HR RC .60 1.50
516 Kyle Wilson HR RC .75 2.00
517 Arturs Kulda HR RC .60 1.50
518 Matt Zaba HR RC .75 2.00
519 P.K. Subban HR RC 5.00 12.00
520 Casey Wellman HR RC .60 1.50
521 Justin Falk HR RC .50 1.25
522 Cody Almond HR RC .60 1.50
523 Nick Bonino HR RC .75 2.00
524 Anton Klementyev HR RC .60 1.50
525 Nick Spaling HR RC .60 1.50
526 Brayden Irwin HR RC .60 1.50
527 Bobby Butler HR RC .60 1.50
528 Jeremy Duchesne HR RC .75 2.00
529 Andrew Bodnarchuk HR RC .60 1.50
530 J.Philippe Levasseur HR RC .60 1.50
531 Trevor Frischmon HR RC .60 1.50
532 Carter Hutton HR RC 1.25 3.00
533 Dylan Reese HR RC .60 1.50
534 Philip Larsen HR RC .60 1.50
535 Jared Cowen HR RC .60 1.50
536 Maxim Noreau HR RC .50 1.25
537 Jeff Penner HR RC 1.00 2.50
538 Eric Tangradi HR RC .60 1.50
539 Zach Hamill HR RC .60 1.50
540 James Wyman HR RC .60 1.50
541 Brock Trotter HR RC 1.25 3.00
542 Corey Elkins HR RC .50 1.25
543 Rich Clune HR RC .75 2.00
544 Evan Oberg HR RC .75 2.00
545 Bryan Pitton HR RC .75 2.00
546 John McCarthy HR RC .60 1.50
547 Marc-Andre Cliche HR RC .50 1.25
548 Maxime Fortunus HR RC .50 1.25
549 Adam McQuaid HR RC .75 2.00
550 Scott Jackson HR RC .60 1.50
551 Cam Fowler HR RC 8.00 20.00
552 Derek Stepan HR RC 8.00 20.00
553 Nino Niederreiter HR RC 12.00 30.00
554 Tyler Seguin HR RC 12.00 30.00
555 Magnus Paajarvi HR RC 8.00 20.00
556 Jordan Eberle HR RC 20.00 50.00
557 Brayden Schenn HR RC 12.00 30.00
558 Jeff Skinner HR RC 6.00 15.00
559 Taylor Hall HR RC 15.00 40.00
560 Taylor Hall 2.00 5.00
561 Tyler Seguin 2.00 5.00
562 Cam Fowler .60 1.50
563 Brayden Schenn .75 2.00
564 Jeff Skinner 1.00 2.50
565 Derek Stepan 1.00 2.50
566 Jordan Eberle 1.25 3.00
567 Magnus Paajarvi .60 1.50
568 Nino Niederreiter .60 1.50
569 Dustin Penner .12 .30
570 Jason Arnott .15 .40
571 Erik Johnson .12 .30
572 Chris Stewart .15 .40
573 Blake Wheeler .20 .50
574 Rich Peverley .20 .50
575 Craig Anderson .20 .50
576 Brian Elliott .15 .40
577 Peter Forsberg .25 .60
578 Tomas Kaberle .12 .30
579 Ray Emery .15 .40
580 Dennis Wideman .12 .30
581 Bryan McCabe .12 .30
582 Mike Fisher .20 .50
583 Marco Sturm .12 .30
584 Alex Kovalev .20 .50
585 James Neal .20 .50
586 Kris Versteeg .15 .40
587 Michael Frolik .12 .30
588 Al Montoya .15 .40
589 Tomas Fleischmann .12 .30
590 Dwayne Roloson .15 .40
591 Joffrey Lupul .15 .40
592 James Wisniewski .12 .30
593 Michael Grabner .15 .40
594 Justin Braun RC .50 1.25
595 Zac Dalpe RC .50 1.25
596 Evgeny Dadonov .60 1.50
597 Jonas Holos RC .50 1.25
598 Jordan Caron RC .75 2.00
599 Alexander Burmistrov RC .50 1.25
600 Nick Leddy RC .50 1.25
601 Kevin Shattenkirk RC 1.00 2.50
602 Tomas Tatar RC 1.00 2.50
603 Anders Lindback RC .50 1.25
604 Andreas Engqvist RC .75 2.00
605 Luke Adam RC .50 1.25
606 Cory Emmerton RC .60 1.50
607 Linus Omark RC 1.25 3.00
608 Kyle Clifford RC .50 1.25
609 Jacob Markstrom RC .75 2.00
610 Mats Zuccarello RC .75 2.00
611 Jordan Pearce RC .75 2.00
612 Matt Calvert RC .75 2.00
613 Mattias Tedenby RC .40 1.00
614 Kevin Poulin RC .60 1.50
615 Patrice Cormier RC .60 1.50
616 Philip McRae RC .50 1.25
617 Sergei Bobrovsky RC 1.25 3.00

618 Travis Hamonic RC .60 1.50
619 Thomas McCollum RC .60 1.50
620 Jeff Frazee RC .75 2.00
621 Henrik Karlsson RC .50 1.25
622 Jan Mursak RC 1.00 2.50
623 Eric Wellwood RC .60 1.50
624 Jamie Arniel RC .50 1.25
625 Alex Stalock RC .60 1.50
626 Evgeny Grachev RC .50 1.25
627 Jacob Josefson RC .50 1.25
628 Jim O'Brien RC .60 1.50
629 Keith Aulie RC .50 1.25
630 Steven Kampfer RC .75 2.00
631 Robin Lehner RC 1.00 2.50
632 Ryan McDonagh RC 1.25 3.00
633 Jeremy Morin RC .50 1.25
634 Brandon McMillan RC .50 1.25
635 Chris Mueller RC .50 1.25
636 Richard Bachman RC .60 1.50
637 Stefan Della Rovere RC .50 1.25
638 Rhett Rakhshani RC .50 1.25
639 Oliver Ekman-Larsson RC .75 2.00
640 Matt Taormina RC .50 1.25
641 Marcus Johansson RC .75 2.00
642 Mike Moore RC .50 1.25
643 Dana Tyrell RC .50 1.25
644 Cedrick Desjardins RC .60 1.50
645 Chris Summers RC .50 1.25
646 Alexander Vasyunov RC .50 1.25
647 Ian Cole RC .50 1.25
648 Jake Muzzin RC .50 1.25
649 Marcel Mueller RC .60 1.50
650 Mark Dekanich RC .50 1.25
651 Brandon Pirri RC .50 1.25
652 Evan Brophey RC .50 1.25
653 Kyle Palmieri RC 1.00 2.50
654 Matt Bartkowski RC .60 1.50
655 Timo Pielmeier RC .60 1.50
656 Tommy Wingels RC .50 1.25
657 Paul Byron RC .60 1.50
658 Jeff Petry RC .60 1.50
659 Taro Tsujimoto SP 10.00 25.00

2010-11 Score Anniversary

*ANNIVERSARY 35-500: 5X TO 12X BASE
*ANN.ROOKIES 501-550: 1.2X TO 3X BASE
APPROX.ODDS 1:36
473 Nicklas Backstrom 4.00 10.00

2010-11 Score Glossy

*GLOSSY 1-500: 2X TO 5X BASE
*GLOSSY ROOKIES 501-550: .5X TO 1.2X BASE
APPROX.ODDS 1 PER PACK
473 Nicklas Backstrom 1.50 4.00

2010-11 Score Gold

*GOLD TRADED: 2.5X TO 6X BASE
*GOLD ROOKIES: .8X TO 2X BASE
FIVE GOLDS PER FACTORY SET
659 Taro Tsujimoto/25*

2010-11 Score Canadian Greats

COMPLETE SET (20) 40.00 80.00
1 Sidney Crosby 6.00 15.00
2 Jonathan Toews 3.00 8.00
3 Mike Richards 1.50 4.00
4 Jarome Iginla 1.50 4.00
5 Martin Brodeur 3.00 8.00
6 Carey Price 6.00 15.00
7 Dany Heatley 1.25 3.00
8 Steve Yzerman 4.00 10.00
9 Corey Perry 1.50 4.00
10 Drew Doughty 1.50 4.00
11 Duncan Keith 1.50 4.00
12 John Tavares 3.00 8.00
13 Patrice Bergeron 2.00 5.00
14 Patrick Roy 4.00 10.00
15 Roberto Luongo 1.50 4.00
16 Ryan Smyth 1.25 3.00
17 Mario Lemieux 5.00 12.00
18 Scott Niedermayer 1.50 4.00
19 Vincent Lecavalier 1.25 3.00
20 Ryan Getzlaf 2.50 6.00

2010-11 Score Franchise

COMPLETE SET (30) 25.00 60.00
APPROX.ODDS 1:36
1 Ryan Getzlaf 2.00 5.00
2 Zach Bogosian 1.00 2.50
3 Tuukka Rask 1.25 3.00
4 Ryan Miller 1.25 3.00
5 Jarome Iginla 1.25 3.00
6 Eric Staal 1.50 4.00
7 Jonathan Toews 2.50 6.00
8 Matt Duchene 1.25 3.00
9 Rick Nash 1.25 3.00
10 James Neal 1.25 3.00
11 Pavel Datsyuk 1.50 4.00
12 Ales Hemsky 1.00 2.50
13 Tomas Vokoun 1.00 2.50
14 Drew Doughty 1.25 3.00
15 Mikko Koivu 1.25 3.00
16 Carey Price 5.00 12.00
17 Shea Weber 1.00 2.50
18 Zach Parise 1.25 3.00
19 Henrik Lundqvist 2.00 5.00
20 John Tavares 2.50 6.00
21 Daniel Alfredsson 1.25 3.00
22 Mike Richards 1.25 3.00
23 Ilya Bryzgalov 1.00 2.50
24 Sidney Crosby 5.00 12.00
25 Joe Thornton 1.25 3.00
26 Erik Johnson .75 2.00
27 Steven Stamkos 2.50 6.00
28 Jonas Gustavsson 1.50 4.00
29 H.Sedin/D.Sedin 1.25 3.00
30 Alex Ovechkin 5.00 12.00

2010-11 Score Net Cam

COMPLETE SET (20) 10.00 25.00
APPROX.ODDS 1:12
1 Ryan Miller 1.00 2.50
2 Martin Brodeur 2.00 5.00
3 Tuukka Rask 1.00 2.50
4 Roberto Luongo 1.00 2.50
5 Jimmy Howard 1.25 3.00
6 Jonas Gustavsson 1.25 3.00
7 Carey Price 4.00 10.00
8 Marc-Andre Fleury 1.50 4.00
9 Steve Mason .75 2.00
10 Cam Ward 1.00 2.50
11 Miikka Kiprusoff .75 2.00
12 Ilya Bryzgalov .75 2.00
13 Michael Leighton .75 2.00
14 Craig Anderson 1.00 2.50
15 Jonathan Quick 1.50 4.00
16 Pekka Rinne 1.25 3.00
17 Niklas Backstrom 1.00 2.50
18 Tomas Vokoun .75 2.00
19 Henrik Lundqvist 1.50 4.00
20 Antti Niemi .75 2.00

2010-11 Score Playoff Heroes

COMPLETE SET (25) 6.00 15.00
APPROX.ODDS 1:6
1 Joe Pavelski .60 1.50
2 Tuukka Rask .60 1.50
3 Michael Cammalleri .60 1.50
4 Sidney Crosby 2.50 6.00
5 Johan Franzen .60 1.50
6 Mike Richards .60 1.50
7 Jaroslav Halak .60 1.50
8 Joe Thornton .60 1.50
9 Antti Niemi .50 1.25
10 Michael Leighton .50 1.25
11 Simon Gagne .60 1.50
12 Daniel Briere .60 1.50
13 Mikael Samuelsson .40 1.00
14 Claude Giroux .60 1.50
15 Henrik Zetterberg .75 2.00
16 P.K. Subban 1.50 4.00
17 Marian Hossa .50 1.25
18 Ville Leino .50 1.25
19 Dustin Byfuglien .60 1.50
20 Brian Gionta .50 1.25
21 Mark Recchi .75 2.00
22 Chris Pronger .50 1.25
23 Duncan Keith .60 1.50
24 Patrick Kane 1.25 3.00
25 Jonathan Toews 1.25 3.00

2010-11 Score Signatures

PANINI ANNCD PRINT RUNS BELOW
560-657 R/T AU 1 PER FACT.SET
49 Jonas Hiller/25* 6.00 15.00
54 Dustin Byfuglien/25* 8.00 20.00
57 Rich Peverley/25* 8.00 20.00
62 Zach Bogosian/25* 6.00 15.00
74 Matt Hunwick/25*
88 Tyler Ennis/25* 6.00 15.00
89 Nathan Gerbe/25* 5.00 12.00
94 Ryan Miller/25* 8.00 20.00
96 Jarome Iginla/25* 20.00 50.00
105 Jay Bouwmeester/25* 10.00 25.00
121 Zach Boychuk/25* 6.00 15.00
141 Paul Stastny/25* 12.00 30.00
143 Matt Duchene/25* 8.00 20.00
155 Craig Anderson/25* 8.00 20.00
159 Antoine Vermette/25* 5.00 12.00
172 Brenden Morrow/25* 6.00 15.00
179 Krys Barch/25* 5.00 12.00
185 Kari Lehtonen/25* 6.00 15.00
189 Johan Franzen/25* 8.00 20.00
205 Zack Stortini/25* 5.00 12.00
220 Michael Frolik/25* 8.00 20.00
232 Ryan Smyth/25* 6.00 15.00
245 Jonathan Bernier/25* 8.00 20.00
254 Guillaume Latendresse/25* 6.00 15.00
258 Greg Zanon/25*
262 Michael Cammalleri/25* 8.00 20.00
263 Brian Gionta/25* 6.00 15.00
267 Max Pacioretty/25* 8.00 20.00
275 Carey Price/25* 40.00 80.00
277 Patric Hornqvist/25* 6.00 15.00
278 Colin Wilson/25* 10.00 25.00
293 Travis Zajac/25* 8.00 20.00
298 Pierre-Luc Letourneau-Leblond/25* 5.00 12.00
303 Andy Greene/25* 5.00 12.00
306 John Tavares/25* 15.00 40.00
307 Matt Moulson/25* 6.00 15.00
310 Josh Bailey/25* 6.00 15.00
321 Marian Gaborik/25* 10.00 25.00
327 Artem Anisimov/25* 6.00 15.00
337 Daniel Alfredsson/25* EXCH 10.00 25.00
339 Mike Fisher/25* 8.00 20.00
348 Matt Carkner/25* 6.00 15.00
350 Brian Elliott/25* 6.00 15.00
359 Claude Giroux/25* 8.00 20.00
364 Brian Boucher/25* 8.00 20.00
365 Michael Leighton/25*
377 Keith Yandle/25* 8.00 20.00
383 Jordan Staal/25* 8.00 20.00
397 Joe Pavelski/25* 8.00 20.00
398 Patrick Marleau/25* 8.00 20.00
415 David Backes/25* 8.00 20.00
420 Cam Janssen/25* 15.00 40.00
428 Martin St. Louis/25* 8.00 20.00
430 Steve Downie/25* 12.00 30.00
438 Simon Gagne/25* 10.00 25.00
440 Mike Smith/25* 8.00 20.00
444 Colton Orr/25* 5.00 12.00
457 Daniel Sedin/25*
460 Ryan Kesler/25* 25.00 50.00
482 John Carlson/25* 10.00 25.00
501 Nazem Kadri 40.00 100.00
505 Nick Palmieri SP 6.00 15.00
507 Brandon Yip 4.00 10.00
508 Justin Mercier 4.00 10.00
510 Brad Thiessen 5.00 12.00
519 P.K. Subban/50* 40.00 100.00
523 Nick Bonino SP 8.00 20.00
525 Nick Spaling 4.00 10.00
526 Brayden Irwin 4.00 10.00
527 Bobby Butler SP 6.00 15.00
530 Jean Philippe Levasseur/20*
534 Philip Larsen SP 6.00 15.00
535 Jared Cowen SP 6.00 15.00
538 Eric Tangradi 4.00 10.00
539 Zach Hamill SP 6.00 15.00
540 James Wyman 4.00 10.00
549 Adam McQuaid SP 8.00 20.00
551 Cam Fowler 15.00 40.00
552 Derek Stepan 40.00 80.00
553 Nino Niederreiter 5.00 12.00
554 Tyler Seguin 30.00 80.00
555 Magnus Paajarvi 5.00 12.00
556 Jordan Eberle 50.00 120.00
557 Brayden Schenn 30.00 60.00
558 Jeff Skinner 20.00 50.00
559 Taylor Hall 50.00 120.00
560 Taylor Hall 75.00 150.00
561 Tyler Seguin 50.00 100.00
564 Jeff Skinner
568 Nino Niederreiter 6.00 15.00
595 Zac Dalpe 5.00 12.00
597 Jonas Holos 15.00 40.00
598 Jordan Caron 8.00 20.00
600 Nick Leddy
601 Kevin Shattenkirk 10.00 25.00
606 Cory Emmerton 6.00 15.00
607 Linus Omark 8.00 20.00
609 Jacob Markstrom 12.00 30.00
612 Matt Calvert 8.00 20.00
613 Mattias Tedenby 4.00 10.00
617 Sergei Bobrovsky 12.00 30.00
618 Travis Hamonic 6.00 15.00
620 Jeff Frazee 10.00 25.00
622 Jan Mursak 15.00 40.00
631 Robin Lehner 10.00 25.00
632 Ryan McDonagh 8.00 20.00
635 Chris Mueller 5.00 12.00
638 Rhett Rakhshani 6.00 15.00
640 Matt Taormina 5.00 12.00
647 Ian Cole 5.00 12.00
649 Marcel Mueller 8.00 20.00
650 Mark Dekanich 6.00 15.00
651 Brandon Pirri 5.00 12.00
654 Matt Bartkowski 6.00 15.00
657 Paul Byron 8.00 20.00

2010-11 Score Snow Globe Die Cuts

COMPLETE SET (13) 15.00 40.00
APPROX.ODDS 1:36
1 Henrik Sedin 1.25 3.00
2 Alex Ovechkin 5.00 12.00
3 Martin Brodeur 2.50 6.00
4 Patrick Kane 2.50 6.00
5 Joe Thornton 1.25 3.00
6 Steven Stamkos 2.50 6.00
7 Henrik Zetterberg 1.50 4.00
8 Jarome Iginla 1.25 3.00
9 Roberto Luongo 1.25 3.00
10 Antti Niemi 1.00 2.50
11 Mike Richards 1.25 3.00
12 John Tavares 2.50 6.00
13 Jonas Gustavsson 1.50 4.00

2010-11 Score Sudden Death

COMPLETE SET (12) 15.00 40.00
APPROX.ODDS 1:36
1 Sidney Crosby 5.00 12.00
2 Jonathan Toews 2.50 6.00
3 Mike Modano 2.00 5.00
4 Anze Kopitar 2.00 5.00
5 Scott Niedermayer 1.25 3.00
6 Teemu Selanne 2.50 6.00
7 Zach Parise 1.25 3.00
8 Nicklas Backstrom 2.00 5.00
9 Steven Stamkos 2.50 6.00
10 Claude Giroux 1.25 3.00
11 Alex Ovechkin 5.00 12.00
12 Drew Doughty 1.25 3.00

2010-11 Score USA Greats

COMPLETE SET (20) 20.00 50.00
1 Patrick Kane 3.00 8.00
2 Zach Parise 1.50 4.00
3 Ryan Kesler 1.50 4.00
4 Scott Gomez 1.25 3.00
5 Paul Stastny 1.50 4.00
6 Erik Johnson 1.00 2.50
7 Brett Hull 2.50 6.00
8 Ryan Miller 1.50 4.00
9 Joe Pavelski 1.50 4.00
10 Jonathan Quick 2.50 6.00
11 Phil Kessel 2.00 5.00
12 Jack Johnson 1.00 2.50
13 Mike Modano 2.50 6.00
14 Peter Mueller 1.25 3.00
15 Craig Anderson 1.50 4.00
16 T.J. Oshie 2.50 6.00
17 Kyle Okposo 1.50 4.00
18 John Carlson 2.00 5.00
19 Pat LaFontaine 1.50 4.00
20 Bill Guerin 1.50 4.00

2010-11 Score All Star Game

1 Eric Staal 2.50 6.00
2 Alexander Ovechkin 8.00 20.00
3 Sidney Crosby 8.00 20.00
4 Steven Stamkos 4.00 10.00
5 Ryan Miller 2.00 5.00
6 Jeff Skinner HR 3.00 8.00
7 Taylor Hall HR 6.00 15.00
JS Jeff Skinner HL 3.00 8.00
SC Cam Ward HL 2.00 5.00

2010-11 Score Franchise All Star Game

ES Eric Staal 3.00 8.00

2010-11 Score Net Cam All Star Game

CW Cam Ward 2.50 6.00

2010-11 Score USA Greats All Star Game

PM Peter Mueller 2.00 5.00

2011-12 Score

COMP.SET w/o SP's (500) 15.00 40.00
501-546 ROOKIE ODDS 1:2
551-570 ROOKIE SP ODDS 1:36
1 Taylor Hall SH .40 1.00
2 Jason Pominville SH .15 .40
3 Brandon Sutter SH .15 .40
4 Antti Niemi SH .15 .40
5 Radim Vrbata SH .15 .40
6 Daniel Alfredsson SH .20 .50
7 Nicklas Lidstrom SH .20 .50
8 Steven Stamkos SH .40 1.00
9 Sidney Crosby SH .75 2.00
10 Mario Lemieux SH .60 1.50
11 Eric Fehr SH .12 .30
12 Patrick Marleau SH .20 .50
13 Eric Staal SH .25 .60
14 P.K. Subban SH .40 1.00
15 Zdeno Chara SH .20 .50
16 Matt Duchene SH .20 .50
17 Tim Thomas SH .20 .50
18 Logan Couture SH .20 .50
19 Rod Brind'Amour SH .15 .40
20 Shane Doan SH .15 .40
21 Martin Brodeur SH .40 1.00
22 Lanny McDonald SH .20 .50
23 Miikka Kiprusoff SH .20 .50
24 Roberto Luongo SH .20 .50
25 Henrik Lundqvist SH .25 .60
26 Corey Perry SH .20 .50
27 Tim Stapleton SH .12 .30
28 Daniel Sedin SH .20 .50
29 Ryan Kesler SH .20 .50
30 Tim Thomas SH .20 .50
31 Joel Ward SH .12 .30
32 Mark Recchi SH .25 .60
33 Peter Forsberg SH .20 .50
34 Doug Weight SH .20 .50
35 Brian Rafalski SH .12 .30
36 Bobby Ryan .20 .50
37 Corey Perry .20 .50
38 George Parros .15 .40
39 Ryan Getzlaf .30 .75
40 Saku Koivu .20 .50
41 Teemu Selanne .40 1.00
42 Jason Blake .12 .30
43 Brandon McMillan .12 .30
44 Matt Beleskey .12 .30
45 Cam Fowler .15 .40
46 Francois Beauchemin .12 .30
47 Lubomir Visnovsky .12 .30
48 Luca Sbisa .15 .40
49 Jonas Hiller .15 .40
50 Dan Ellis .15 .40
51 Brad Marchand .25 .60
52 Chris Kelly .15 .40
53 David Krejci .20 .50
54 Gregory Campbell .12 .30
55 Milan Lucic .20 .50
56 Nathan Horton .20 .50
57 Patrice Bergeron .25 .60
58 Tyler Seguin .40 1.00
59 Daniel Paille .12 .30
60 Shawn Thornton .15 .40
61 Zdeno Chara .20 .50
62 Dennis Seidenberg .15 .40
63 Johnny Boychuk .12 .30
64 Tim Thomas .20 .50
65 Tuukka Rask .20 .50
66 Brad Boyes .12 .30
67 Derek Roy .15 .40
68 Drew Stafford .20 .50
69 Jason Pominville .15 .40
70 Jochen Hecht .12 .30
71 Nathan Gerbe .12 .30
72 Patrick Kaleta .12 .30
73 Paul Gaustad .12 .30
74 Thomas Vanek .20 .50
75 Tyler Ennis .15 .40
76 Shaone Morrisonn .12 .30
77 Jordan Leopold .12 .30
78 Tyler Myers .20 .50
79 Ryan Miller .20 .50
80 Jhonas Enroth .20 .50
81 Alex Tanguay .12 .30
82 Curtis Glencross .12 .30
83 Jarome Iginla .20 .50
84 Matt Stajan .15 .40
85 Mikael Backlund .20 .50
86 Olli Jokinen .15 .40
87 David Moss .12 .30
88 Rene Bourque .12 .30
89 Tom Kostopoulos .12 .30
90 Tim Jackman .12 .30
91 Cory Sarich .12 .30
92 Jay Bouwmeester .20 .50
93 Mark Giordano .15 .40
94 Miikka Kiprusoff .20 .50
95 Henrik Karlsson .15 .40
96 Brandon Sutter .15 .40
97 Eric Staal .25 .60
98 Jeff Skinner .20 .50
99 Tuomo Ruutu .15 .40
100 Jussi Jokinen .12 .30
101 Chad LaRose .12 .30
102 Patrick Dwyer .12 .30
103 Drayson Bowman .12 .30
104 Jerome Samson .12 .30
105 Jiri Tlusty .15 .40
106 Tim Gleason .12 .30
107 Tomas Kaberle .12 .30
108 Jamie McBain .12 .30
109 Cam Ward .20 .50
110 Justin Peters .12 .30
111 Dave Bolland .15 .40
112 Jonathan Toews .40 1.00
113 Marian Hossa .15 .40
114 Michael Frolik .12 .30
115 Patrick Kane .40 1.00
116 Patrick Sharp .20 .50
117 Bryan Bickell .12 .30
118 John Scott .12 .30
119 Andrew Brunette .12 .30
120 Rostislav Olesz .12 .30
121 Nick Leddy .12 .30
122 Duncan Keith .20 .50
123 Brent Seabrook .20 .50
124 Niklas Hjalmarsson .12 .30
125 Corey Crawford .25 .60
126 Matt Duchene .20 .50
127 Paul Stastny .20 .50
128 Ryan O'Reilly .20 .50
129 Milan Hejduk .15 .40
130 David Jones .12 .30
131 Daniel Winnik .12 .30
132 Jay McClement .12 .30
133 Cody McLeod .12 .30
134 Brandon Yip .12 .30
135 T.J. Galiardi .15 .40
136 Ryan O'Byrne .12 .30
137 Erik Johnson .12 .30
138 Kyle Quincey .12 .30
139 Semyon Varlamov .20 .50
140 Jean-Sebastien Giguere .15 .40
141 Antoine Vermette .12 .30
142 Derick Brassard .20 .50
143 Jeff Carter .20 .50
144 Matt Calvert .15 .40
145 R.J. Umberger .12 .30
146 Rick Nash .20 .50
147 Samuel Pahlsson .12 .30
148 Kristian Huselius .12 .30
149 James Wisniewski .12 .30
150 Grant Clitsome .12 .30
151 Marc Methot .12 .30
152 Fedor Tyutin .12 .30
153 Kris Russell .12 .30
154 Steve Mason .15 .40
155 Mark Dekanich .12 .30
156 Adam Burish .12 .30
157 Brenden Morrow .15 .40
158 Jamie Benn .25 .60
159 Loui Eriksson .15 .40
160 Steve Ott .15 .40
161 Tom Wandell .12 .30
162 Mike Ribeiro .15 .40
163 Krys Barch .12 .30
164 Michael Ryder .12 .30
165 Sheldon Souray .12 .30
166 Alex Goligoski .15 .40
167 Stephane Robidas .12 .30
168 Nicklas Grossman .12 .30
169 Kari Lehtonen .15 .40
170 Andrew Raycroft .15 .40
171 Pavel Datsyuk .25 .60
172 Henrik Zetterberg .25 .60
173 Johan Franzen .20 .50
174 Valtteri Filppula .20 .50
175 Daniel Cleary .20 .50
176 Jiri Hudler .15 .40
177 Todd Bertuzzi .15 .40
178 Tomas Holmstrom .12 .30
179 Darren Helm .15 .40
180 Justin Abdelkader .15 .40
181 Niklas Kronwall .15 .40
182 Brad Stuart .12 .30
183 Jakub Kindl .12 .30
184 Nicklas Lidstrom .20 .50
185 Jimmy Howard .20 .50
186 Ales Hemsky .15 .40
187 Shawn Horcoff .12 .30
188 Taylor Hall .40 1.00
189 Sam Gagner .15 .40
190 Gilbert Brule .20 .50
191 Jordan Eberle .20 .50
192 Magnus Paajarvi .15 .40
193 Linus Omark .20 .50
194 Ryan Jones .15 .40
195 Ryan Smyth .15 .40
196 Tom Gilbert .12 .30
197 Ryan Whitney .12 .30
198 Ladislav Smid .12 .30
199 Nikolai Khabibulin .15 .40
200 Devan Dubnyk .20 .50
201 David Booth .12 .30
202 Michal Repik .12 .30
203 Stephen Weiss .15 .40
204 Evgeny Dadonov .15 .40
205 Jack Skille .15 .40
206 Tomas Fleischmann .12 .30
207 Kris Versteeg .15 .40
208 Scottie Upshall .12 .30
209 Ed Jovanovski .12 .30
210 Brian Campbell .12 .30
211 Dmitry Kulikov .12 .30
212 Mike Weaver .12 .30
213 Jason Garrison .12 .30
214 Jacob Markstrom .20 .50
215 Scott Clemmensen .15 .40
216 Anze Kopitar .30 .75
217 Simon Gagne .20 .50
218 Dustin Penner .15 .40
219 Jarret Stoll .15 .40
220 Justin Williams .15 .40
221 Dustin Brown .20 .50
222 Kevin Westgarth .12 .30
223 Kyle Clifford .12 .30
224 Mike Richards .20 .50
225 Scott Parse .12 .30
226 Drew Doughty .20 .50
227 Jack Johnson .12 .30
228 Matt Greene .12 .30
229 Jonathan Bernier .20 .50
230 Jonathan Quick .30 .75
231 Dany Heatley .15 .40
232 Pierre-Marc Bouchard .20 .50
233 Mikko Koivu .15 .40
234 Matt Cullen .12 .30
235 Guillaume Latendresse .15 .40
236 Eric Nystrom .12 .30
237 Cal Clutterbuck .20 .50
238 Kyle Brodziak .12 .30
239 Brad Staubitz .12 .30
240 Devin Setoguchi .15 .40
241 Nick Schultz .12 .30
242 Greg Zanon .12 .30
243 Marek Zidlicky .12 .30
244 Niklas Backstrom .20 .50
245 Josh Harding .20 .50
246 Scott Gomez .15 .40
247 Mike Cammalleri .15 .40
248 Brian Gionta .15 .40
249 Tomas Plekanec .20 .50
250 Travis Moen .12 .30
251 Lars Eller .15 .40
252 David Desharnais .25 .60
253 Andrei Kostitsyn .15 .40
254 Max Pacioretty .20 .50
255 Andrei Markov .20 .50
256 P.K. Subban .40 1.00
257 Jaroslav Spacek .12 .30
258 Hal Gill .12 .30
259 Carey Price .60 1.50
260 Peter Budaj .15 .40
261 Colin Wilson .15 .40
262 Martin Erat .12 .30
263 Mike Fisher .20 .50
264 David Legwand .15 .40
265 Sergei Kostitsyn .12 .30
266 Nick Spaling .12 .30
267 Patric Hornqvist .15 .40
268 Jordin Tootoo .15 .40
269 Jerred Smithson .12 .30
270 Shea Weber .15 .40
271 Ryan Suter .12 .30
272 Kevin Klein .12 .30
273 Francis Bouillon .12 .30
274 Pekka Rinne .25 .60
275 Anders Lindback .15 .40
276 Ilya Kovalchuk .20 .50
277 Patrik Elias .20 .50
278 Travis Zajac .15 .40
279 Dainius Zubrus .12 .30
280 David Clarkson .12 .30
281 David Steckel .12 .30
282 Jacob Josefson .12 .30
283 Mattias Tedenby .12 .30
284 Rod Pelley .12 .30
285 Zach Parise .20 .50
286 Andy Greene .12 .30
287 Anton Volchenkov .12 .30
288 Colin White .12 .30
289 Martin Brodeur .40 1.00
290 Johan Hedberg .15 .40
291 John Tavares .40 1.00
292 Matt Moulson .15 .40
293 Blake Comeau .12 .30
294 Pierre Parenteau .12 .30
295 Frans Nielsen .12 .30
296 Kyle Okposo .20 .50
297 Trevor Gillies .12 .30
298 Michael Grabner .15 .40
299 Josh Bailey .15 .40
300 Andrew MacDonald .12 .30
301 Mark Streit .12 .30
302 Mark Katic .15 .40
303 Travis Hamonic .15 .40
304 Al Montoya .12 .30
305 Rick DiPietro .15 .40
306 Marian Gaborik .25 .60
307 Wojtek Wolski .12 .30
308 Brad Richards .20 .50
309 Sean Avery .15 .40
310 Ruslan Fedotenko .12 .30
311 Derek Stepan .20 .50
312 Brandon Prust .12 .30
313 Mats Zuccarello-Aasen .20 .50
314 Erik Christensen .12 .30
315 Brandon Dubinsky .15 .40
316 Marc Staal .20 .50
317 Daniel Girardi .12 .30
318 Ryan McDonagh .20 .50
319 Henrik Lundqvist .25 .60
320 Martin Biron .15 .40
321 Jason Spezza .20 .50
322 Daniel Alfredsson .20 .50
323 Milan Michalek .12 .30
324 Chris Neil .12 .30
325 Nick Foligno .15 .40
326 Zack Smith .12 .30
327 Peter Regin .12 .30
328 Jesse Winchester .12 .30
329 Brian Lee .15 .40
330 Sergei Gonchar .12 .30
331 Erik Karlsson .40 1.00
332 Chris Phillips .12 .30
333 Matt Carkner .15 .40
334 Craig Anderson .20 .50
335 Alex Auld .15 .40
336 Daniel Briere .20 .50
337 Brayden Schenn .20 .50
338 Wayne Simmonds .25 .60
339 Scott Hartnell .20 .50
340 Andreas Nodl .12 .30
341 James van Riemsdyk .20 .50
342 Jakub Voracek .20 .50
343 Jody Shelley .15 .40
344 Claude Giroux .20 .50
345 Blair Betts .12 .30
346 Jaromir Jagr .50 1.25
347 Chris Pronger .15 .40
348 Kimmo Timonen .12 .30
349 Sergei Bobrovsky .20 .50
350 Ilya Bryzgalov .20 .50
351 Shane Doan .15 .40
352 Ray Whitney .15 .40
353 Lee Stempniak .12 .30
354 Martin Hanzal .12 .30
355 Taylor Pyatt .12 .30
356 Paul Bissonnette .12 .30
357 Mikkel Boedker .12 .30
358 Radim Vrbata .15 .40
359 Kyle Turris .12 .30
360 Keith Yandle .20 .50
361 Derek Morris .12 .30
362 Rostislav Klesla .12 .30
363 David Schlemko .12 .30
364 Mike Smith .20 .50
365 Jason LaBarbera .15 .40
366 Sidney Crosby .75 2.00
367 Evgeni Malkin .60 1.50
368 Jordan Staal .20 .50
369 Chris Kunitz .20 .50
370 James Neal .20 .50
371 Matt Cooke .12 .30
372 Mark Letestu .15 .40
373 Pascal Dupuis .12 .30
374 Tyler Kennedy .12 .30
375 Kristopher Letang .20 .50
376 Brooks Orpik .15 .40
377 Paul Martin .12 .30
378 Ben Lovejoy .12 .30
379 Marc-Andre Fleury .30 .75
380 Brent Johnson .15 .40
381 Joe Pavelski .20 .50
382 Martin Havlat .15 .40
383 Patrick Marleau .20 .50
384 Ryane Clowe .12 .30
385 Joe Thornton .20 .50
386 Logan Couture .20 .50
387 Torrey Mitchell .12 .30
388 Benn Ferriero .12 .30
389 Brent Burns .25 .60
390 Dan Boyle .15 .40
391 Marc-Edouard Vlasic .12 .30
392 Doug Murray .12 .30
393 Jason Demers .12 .30
394 Antero Niittymaki .15 .40
395 Antti Niemi .15 .40
396 Andy McDonald .15 .40
397 Alexander Steen .20 .50
398 Chris Stewart .15 .40
399 David Backes .20 .50
400 David Perron .12 .30
401 Patrik Berglund .15 .40
402 Vladimir Sobotka .12 .30
403 T.J. Oshie .30 .75
404 B.J. Crombeen .12 .30
405 Alex Pietrangelo .15 .40
406 Carlo Colaiacovo .12 .30
407 Barret Jackman .12 .30
408 Kevin Shattenkirk .15 .40
409 Jaroslav Halak .20 .50
410 Ben Bishop .20 .50
411 Vincent Lecavalier .15 .40
412 Martin St. Louis .20 .50
413 Steven Stamkos .40 1.00
414 Teddy Purcell .20 .50
415 Adam Hall .12 .30
416 Steve Downie .12 .30
417 Ryan Malone .12 .30
418 Nate Thompson .12 .30
419 Dominic Moore .12 .30
420 Dana Tyrell .12 .30
421 Pavel Kubina .12 .30
422 Mattias Ohlund .12 .30
423 Victor Hedman .25 .60
424 Eric Brewer .12 .30
425 Dwayne Roloson .15 .40
426 Mathieu Garon .15 .40
427 Phil Kessel .25 .60
428 Joffrey Lupul .15 .40
429 Tyler Bozak .20 .50
430 Colby Armstrong .12 .30
431 Nazem Kadri .30 .75
432 Nikolai Kulemin .20 .50
433 Mikhail Grabovski .15 .40
434 Colton Orr .12 .30
435 Clarke MacArthur .12 .30
436 Dion Phaneuf .20 .50
437 Luke Schenn .15 .40
438 Keith Aulie .15 .40
439 Jonas Gustavsson .20 .50
440 James Reimer .20 .50
441 Daniel Sedin .20 .50
442 Henrik Sedin .20 .50
443 Ryan Kesler .20 .50
444 Mason Raymond .15 .40
445 Mikael Samuelsson .12 .30
446 Manny Malhotra .15 .40
447 Alexandre Burrows .20 .50
448 Maxim Lapierre .12 .30
449 Kevin Bieksa .15 .40
450 Dan Hamhuis .15 .40
451 Keith Ballard .12 .30
452 Sami Salo .12 .30
453 Alexander Edler .12 .30
454 Cory Schneider .15 .40
455 Roberto Luongo .20 .50
456 Alexander Ovechkin .75 2.00
457 Alexander Semin .20 .50
458 Marcus Johansson .15 .40
459 Nicklas Backstrom .30 .75
460 Brooks Laich .12 .30
461 Jay Beagle .15 .40
462 Jason Chimera .12 .30
463 Mike Knuble .12 .30
464 Matt Hendricks .12 .30
465 Mike Green .20 .50
466 Karl Alzner .12 .3
467 John Carlson .25 .6
468 Jeff Schultz .12 .3
469 Michal Neuvirth .15 .4
470 Braden Holtby .40 1.0
471 Alexander Burmistrov .15 .4
472 Andrew Ladd .20 .5
473 Blake Wheeler .40 1.0
474 Bryan Little .20 .5
475 Evander Kane .20 .5
476 Nik Antropov .15 .4
477 Patrice Cormier .12 .3
478 Chris Thorburn .12 .3
479 Jim Slater .12 .3
480 Tobias Enstrom .12 .3
481 Dustin Byfuglien .20 .5
482 Johnny Oduya .15 .4
483 Zach Bogosian .15 .4
484 Ondrej Pavelec .20 .5
485 Chris Mason .15 .4
486 Dwayne Roloson HL .15 .4
487 Michael Ryder HL .12 .3
488 Alexander Ovechkin HL .75 2.0
489 James van Riemsdyk HL .20 .5
490 Pekka Rinne HL .25 .6
491 Alexandre Burrows HL .20 .5
492 Pavel Datsyuk HL .25 .6
493 Joe Thornton HL .20 .5
494 Milan Lucic HL .20 .5
495 Vincent Lecavalier HL .15 .4
496 Antti Niemi HL .15 .4
497 Ryan Kesler HL .20 .5
498 Nathan Horton HL .20 .5
499 Daniel Sedin HL .20 .5
500 Brad Marchand HL .25 .6
501 Paul Postma HR RC .60 1.5
502 Lance Bouma HR RC .60 1.5
503 Greg Nemisz HR RC .60 1.5
504 Marcus Kruger HR RC 1.00 2.5
505 Cameron Gaunce HR RC .50 1.2
506 John Moore HR RC .60 1.5
507 Tomas Kubalik HR RC .60 1.5
508 Colton Sceviour HR RC .60 1.5
509 Tomas Vincour HR RC .60 1.5
510 Chris Vande Velde HR RC 1.00 2.5
511 Teemu Hartikainen HR RC .60 1.5
512 Scott Timmins HR RC .60 1.5
513 Hugh Jessiman HR RC .60 1.5
514 Carson McMillan HR RC .75 2.0
515 Brendon Nash HR RC .60 1.5
516 Aaron Palushaj HR RC .60 1.5
517 Jonathon Blum HR RC .60 1.5
518 Blake Geoffrion HR RC .60 1.5
519 Mark Katic HR RC .60 1.5
520 Mikko Koskinen HR RC .75 2.0
521 Matt Campanale HR RC .60 1.5
522 Justin DiBenedetto HR RC .50 1.2
523 Colin Greening HR RC .60 1.5
524 Erik Condra HR RC .60 1.5
525 Andre Benoit HR RC .75 2.0
526 Roman Wick HR RC .75 2.0
527 Stephane Da Costa HR RC .60 1.5
528 Patrick Wiercioch HR RC .60 1.5
529 Erik Gustafsson HR RC .75 2.0
530 Ben Holmstrom HR RC .60 1.5
531 Brian Strait HR RC .75 2.0
532 Joe Vitale HR RC .60 1.5
533 Cody Hodgson HR RC 1.25 3.0
534 Yann Sauve HR RC .60 1.5
535 Cam Talbot HR RC 1.50 4.0
536 Carl Klingberg HR RC .60 1.5
537 Todd Ford HR RC .75 2.0
538 Ben Scrivens HR RC 1.00 2.5
539 Andrey Zubarev HR RC .75 2.0
540 Joe Colborne HR RC .60 1.5
541 Zac Rinaldo HR RC .60 1.5
542 Matt Frattin HR RC .60 1.5
543 Adam Henrique HR RC 1.50 4.0
544 Jamie Doornbosch HR RC .60 1.5
545 Shane Sims HR RC .60 1.5
546 Drew Bagnall HR RC .60 1.5
551 Nugent-Hopkins HR SP RC 10.00 25.0
552 Mika Zibanejad HR SP RC 8.00 20.0
553 G.Landeskog HR SP RC 8.00 20.0
554 Devante Smith-Pelly HR SP RC 5.00 12.0
555 Brandon Saad HR SP RC 6.00 15.0
556 Mark Scheifele HR SP RC 8.00 20.0
557 Sean Couturier HR SP RC 6.00 15.0
558 Brett Connolly HR SP RC 3.00 8.0
559 Tim Erixon HR SP RC 3.00 8.0
560 Jake Gardiner HR SP RC 5.00 12.0
561 Ryan Johansen HR SP RC 6.00 15.0
562 Adam Larsson HR SP RC 4.00 10.0
563 Justin Faulk HR SP RC 5.00 12.0
564 Erik Gudbranson HR SP RC 4.00 10.0
565 Matt Read HR SP RC 6.00 15.0
566 Alexei Emelin HR SP RC 5.00 12.0
567 Roman Horak HR SP RC 10.00 25.0
568 Craig Smith HR SP RC 6.00 15.0
569 Harri Sateri HR SP RC 10.00 25.0
570 Cam Atkinson HR SP RC 12.00 30.0
NNO Bruins Champs SP 40.00 80.0

2011-12 Score Black

*BLACK: 20X TO 50X BASE
STATED ODDS 1:720
125 Corey Crawford 12.00 30.0
459 Nicklas Backstrom 15.00 40.0

2011-12 Score Glossy

Inserted one per pack, these cards feature a high glossy surface on the front of the cards. The cardback feature the the title "glossy" near the card number on all cards except for a few select rookies and most of th Boston Bruins.
COMPLETE SET (500) 40.00 100.0
*GLOSSY: 1.2X TO 3X BASE
STATED ODDS 1 PER PACK
125 Corey Crawford .75 2.0
459 Nicklas Backstrom 1.00 2.5

2011-12 Score Gold

*1-500 VETERANS: 4X TO 10X BASIC CARDS
STATED ODDS 1:36
125 Corey Crawford 3.00 8.0
459 Nicklas Backstrom 4.00 10.0

2011-12 Score B

COMPLETE SET (10) 15.00 40.0
1 Marc-Andre Fleury 2.50 6.0
2 Martin Brodeur 3.00 8.0
3 Roberto Luongo 1.50 4.0
4 Carey Price 5.00 12.0
5 Alexander Ovechkin 6.00 15.0
6 Daniel Sedin 1.50 4.0
7 Steven Stamkos 3.00 8.0
8 Corey Perry 1.50 4.0
9 Taylor Hall 3.00 8.0
10 Sidney Crosby 6.00 15.0

2011-12 Score First Goal

Card	Low	High
OMPLETE SET (15)	15.00	40.00
Jeff Skinner	1.00	2.50
Taylor Hall	2.00	5.00
Erik Condra	.75	2.00
Derek Stepan	1.00	2.50
Jordan Eberle	1.00	2.50
Cam Fowler	.75	2.00
P.K. Subban	2.00	5.00
Blake Geoffrion	.75	2.00
Cody Hodgson	1.50	4.00
0 David Desharnais	1.25	3.00
1 Linus Omark	1.00	2.50
2 Brad Marchand	1.25	3.00
3 Nino Niederreiter	.60	1.50
4 Tomas Tatar	.75	2.00
5 Marcus Johansson	.75	2.00

2011-12 Score Franchise

Card	Low	High
OMP.SET wo SPs (30)	40.00	100.00
Corey Perry	1.25	3.00
Dustin Byfuglien	1.25	3.00
Tim Thomas	1.25	3.00
Ryan Miller	1.25	3.00
Jarome Iginla	1.25	3.00
Jeff Skinner	1.25	3.00
Patrick Kane	2.50	6.00
Matt Duchene	1.25	3.00
Rick Nash	1.25	3.00
0 Jamie Benn	1.50	4.00
1 Nicklas Lidstrom	1.25	3.00
2 Taylor Hall	2.50	6.00
3 Jacob Markstrom	1.25	3.00
4 Anze Kopitar	2.00	5.00
5 Mikko Koivu	1.00	2.50
6 Carey Price	4.00	10.00
7 Pekka Rinne	1.50	4.00
8 Martin Brodeur	2.50	6.00
9 John Tavares	2.50	6.00
0 Henrik Lundqvist	1.50	4.00
1 Daniel Alfredsson	1.25	3.00
2 Claude Giroux	1.25	3.00
3 Shane Doan	1.00	2.50
4 Sidney Crosby	5.00	12.00
5 Joe Thornton	1.25	3.00
6 David Backes	1.25	3.00
7 Steven Stamkos	2.50	6.00
8 Dion Phaneuf	1.25	3.00
9 Roberto Luongo	1.25	3.00
0 Alexander Ovechkin	5.00	12.00
1 Guy Lafleur SP	15.00	40.00
2 Mario Lemieux SP	20.00	40.00
3 Steve Yzerman SP	20.00	40.00
4 Dale Hawerchuk SP	20.00	40.00
5 Joe Sakic SP	12.50	25.00
6 Mark Messier SP	12.50	25.00

2011-12 Score Making An Entrance

Card	Low	High
OMPLETE SET (10)	10.00	25.00
Jamie Benn	1.25	3.00
Joe Thornton	1.00	2.50
Jordan Eberle	1.00	2.50
Alexander Ovechkin	4.00	10.00
Marc-Andre Fleury	1.50	4.00
Patrick Kane	2.00	5.00
Martin St. Louis	1.00	2.50
Nicklas Lidstrom	1.00	2.50
Carey Price	3.00	8.00
0 Miikka Kiprusoff	1.00	2.50

2011-12 Score Net Cam

Card	Low	High
OMPLETE SET (15)	12.00	30.00
Tim Thomas	1.00	2.50
Pekka Rinne	1.25	3.00
Roberto Luongo	1.00	2.50
Cam Ward	1.00	2.50
Carey Price	3.00	8.00
Miikka Kiprusoff	1.00	2.50
Jimmy Howard	1.00	2.50
Henrik Lundqvist	1.25	3.00
Ryan Miller	1.00	2.50
0 Michal Neuvirth	.75	2.00
1 Antti Niemi	.75	2.00
2 Martin Brodeur	2.00	5.00
3 Corey Crawford	1.25	3.00
4 James Reimer	1.00	2.50
5 Jonathan Quick	1.50	4.00

2011-12 Score NHL Shield Die Cuts

Card	Low	High
OMPLETE SET (10)	15.00	40.00
Pekka Rinne	1.50	4.00
Henrik Lundqvist	1.50	4.00
Nicklas Lidstrom	1.25	3.00
P.K. Subban	2.50	6.00
Jarome Iginla	1.25	3.00
Sidney Crosby	5.00	12.00
Alexander Ovechkin	5.00	12.00
Henrik Sedin	1.25	3.00
Steven Stamkos	2.50	6.00
0 Eric Staal	1.50	4.00

2011-12 Score Playoff Heroes

Card	Low	High
OMPLETE SET (10)	10.00	25.00
Michael Ryder	.75	2.00
Joe Thornton	1.25	3.00
Alexandre Burrows	1.25	3.00
Kevin Bieksa	1.00	2.50
Nathan Horton	1.25	3.00
Ryan Kesler	1.25	3.00
Dwayne Roloson	1.00	2.50
Teddy Purcell	1.25	3.00
Patrice Bergeron	1.50	4.00
0 Roberto Luongo	1.25	3.00

2011-12 Score Signatures

Card	Low	High
7 Corey Perry		
8 George Parros	6.00	15.00
9 Jonas Hiller	6.00	15.00
0 Dan Ellis	6.00	15.00
6 Nathan Horton	8.00	20.00
8 Tyler Seguin	25.00	60.00
0 Shawn Thornton		
4 Tim Thomas EXCH	10.00	25.00
5 Tuukka Rask	12.00	25.00
7 Derek Roy		
4 Thomas Vanek	10.00	25.00
5 Tyler Ennis		
8 Tyler Myers		
9 Ryan Miller		
3 Jarome Iginla	20.00	40.00
5 Mikael Backlund		
8 Rene Bourque	10.00	25.00
2 Jay Bouwmeester		
5 Henrik Karlsson		
6 Brandon Sutter		
7 Eric Staal	10.00	25.00
8 Jeff Skinner	15.00	40.00
9 Tuomo Ruutu	6.00	15.00
03 Drayson Bowman	5.00	12.00
04 Jerome Samson		
09 Cam Ward		
112 Jonathan Toews		
113 Marian Hossa		
115 Patrick Kane		
116 Patrick Sharp		
126 Matt Duchene		
127 Paul Stastny		
134 Brandon Yip	5.00	12.00
135 T.J. Galiardi	6.00	15.00
137 Erik Johnson	5.00	12.00
139 Semyon Varlamov	8.00	20.00
141 Antoine Vermette		
144 Matt Calvert	6.00	15.00
146 Rick Nash	12.00	30.00
153 Kris Russell		
154 Steve Mason	12.00	30.00
157 Brenden Morrow		
158 Jamie Benn	10.00	25.00
159 Loui Eriksson	12.00	25.00
160 Steve Ott	6.00	15.00
163 Krys Barch	5.00	12.00
173 Johan Franzen		
178 Tomas Holmstrom		
180 Justin Abdelkader	6.00	15.00
184 Nicklas Lidstrom		
185 Jimmy Howard	10.00	25.00
188 Taylor Hall	20.00	40.00
191 Jordan Eberle		
192 Magnus Paajarvi	8.00	20.00
193 Linus Omark		
195 Ryan Smyth		
199 Nikolai Khabibulin		
203 Stephen Weiss		
216 Anze Kopitar	20.00	40.00
217 Simon Gagne	10.00	25.00
218 Dustin Penner		
221 Dustin Brown		
224 Mike Richards	12.00	30.00
226 Drew Doughty		
229 Jonathan Bernier		
230 Jonathan Quick		
235 Guillaume Latendresse		
237 Cal Clutterbuck		
239 Brad Staubitz	8.00	20.00
242 Greg Zanon		
246 Scott Gomez		
254 Max Pacioretty	10.00	25.00
256 P.K. Subban	25.00	60.00
259 Carey Price	25.00	60.00
261 Colin Wilson	6.00	15.00
263 Mike Fisher	8.00	20.00
267 Patric Hornqvist		
268 Jordin Tootoo		
270 Shea Weber		
274 Pekka Rinne		
285 Zach Parise		
286 Andy Greene	5.00	12.00
289 Martin Brodeur	40.00	80.00
292 Matt Moulson	5.00	12.00
295 Frans Nielsen		
297 Trevor Gillies	5.00	12.00
299 Josh Bailey		
306 Marian Gaborik	10.00	25.00
307 Wojtek Wolski		
311 Derek Stepan	8.00	20.00
316 Marc Staal	8.00	20.00
319 Henrik Lundqvist		
324 Chris Neil		
331 Erik Karlsson	15.00	40.00
333 Matt Carkner	6.00	15.00
334 Craig Anderson		
337 Brayden Schenn	8.00	20.00
338 Wayne Simmonds	10.00	25.00
341 James van Riemsdyk		
342 Jakub Voracek	8.00	20.00
344 Claude Giroux	8.00	20.00
347 Chris Pronger	8.00	20.00
351 Shane Doan		
353 Lee Stempniak		
357 Mikkel Boedker		
360 Keith Yandle		
364 Mike Smith		
366 Sidney Crosby	60.00	120.00
367 Evgeni Malkin	20.00	40.00
368 Jordan Staal		
379 Marc-Andre Fleury		
381 Joe Pavelski		
383 Patrick Marleau		
385 Joe Thornton	10.00	25.00
386 Logan Couture		
389 Brent Burns	10.00	25.00
390 Dan Boyle	6.00	15.00
395 Antti Niemi	6.00	15.00
398 Chris Stewart	6.00	15.00
399 David Backes	8.00	20.00
400 David Perron		
403 T.J. Oshie	12.00	30.00
409 Jaroslav Halak		
411 Vincent Lecavalier	25.00	50.00
412 Martin St. Louis		
413 Steven Stamkos	20.00	50.00
416 Steve Downie	8.00	20.00
420 Dana Tyrell		
425 Dwayne Roloson	6.00	15.00
429 Tyler Bozak		
431 Nazem Kadri		
434 Colton Orr	12.00	30.00
435 Carl Gunnarsson		
436 Dion Phaneuf	8.00	20.00
437 Luke Schenn		
439 Jonas Gustavsson		
441 Daniel Sedin	15.00	40.00
442 Henrik Sedin		
445 Mikael Samuelsson	6.00	15.00
447 Alexandre Burrows	8.00	20.00
450 Dan Hamhuis	6.00	15.00
454 Cory Schneider	6.00	15.00
455 Roberto Luongo		
456 Alexander Ovechkin		
457 Alexander Semin		
467 John Carlson	12.00	30.00
475 Evander Kane	8.00	20.00
481 Dustin Byfuglien	8.00	20.00
485 Chris Mason		
501 Paul Postma HR	6.00	15.00
502 Lance Bouma HR		
503 Greg Nemisz HR	6.00	15.00
504 Marcus Kruger HR	10.00	25.00
505 Cameron Gaunce HR	5.00	12.00
506 John Moore HR	8.00	20.00
507 Tomas Kubalik HR	6.00	15.00
508 Colton Sceviour HR	6.00	15.00
509 Tomas Vincour HR	6.00	15.00
510 Chris Vande Velde HR		
511 Teemu Hartikainen HR	6.00	15.00
512 Scott Timmins HR	6.00	15.00
513 Hugh Jessiman HR	6.00	15.00
514 Carson McMillan HR		
515 Brendon Nash HR		
516 Aaron Palushaj HR	6.00	15.00
517 Jonathon Blum HR	8.00	20.00
518 Blake Geoffrion HR	8.00	15.00
519 Mark Katic HR	6.00	15.00
520 Mikko Koskinen HR	8.00	20.00
522 Justin DiBenedetto HR	8.00	20.00
523 Colin Greening HR	6.00	15.00
524 Erik Condra HR	6.00	15.00
527 Stephane Da Costa HR	6.00	15.00
528 Patrick Wiercioch HR	6.00	15.00
529 Erik Gustafsson HR	8.00	20.00
530 Ben Holmstrom HR	6.00	15.00
531 Brian Strait HR	8.00	20.00
532 Joe Vitale HR	6.00	15.00
533 Cody Hodgson HR	15.00	40.00
534 Yann Sauve HR	6.00	15.00
535 Cam Talbot HR	15.00	40.00
536 Carl Klingberg HR	6.00	15.00
538 Ben Scrivens HR	10.00	25.00
540 Joe Colborne HR	20.00	50.00
541 Zac Rinaldo HR	6.00	15.00
542 Matt Frattin HR	6.00	15.00
543 Adam Henrique HR	30.00	60.00
546 Drew Bagnall HR	6.00	15.00
551 Ryan Nugent-Hopkins HR	200.00	400.00
552 Mika Zibanejad HR	15.00	40.00
553 Gabriel Landeskog HR		
554 Devante Smith-Pelly HR	10.00	25.00
555 Brandon Saad HR	15.00	40.00
556 Mark Scheifele HR	50.00	100.00
557 Sean Couturier HR	30.00	60.00
558 Brett Connolly HR	12.00	30.00
559 Tim Erixon HR	15.00	40.00
560 Jake Gardiner HR	20.00	50.00
561 Ryan Johansen HR	12.00	30.00
562 Adam Larsson HR	15.00	40.00
563 Justin Faulk HR		
564 Erik Gudbranson HR		
565 Matt Read HR	20.00	50.00

2011-12 Score Snow Globe Die Cuts

Card	Low	High
COMPLETE SET (10)	15.00	40.00
1 Daniel Sedin	2.00	5.00
2 Sidney Crosby	8.00	20.00
3 Ryan Kesler	2.00	5.00
4 Thomas Vanek	2.00	5.00
5 Anze Kopitar	3.00	8.00
6 Patrick Sharp	2.00	5.00
7 Matt Duchene	2.00	5.00
8 Jeff Skinner	2.00	5.00
9 Mikko Koivu	1.50	4.00
10 Logan Couture	2.00	5.00

2011-12 Score Sudden Death

Card	Low	High
COMPLETE SET (25)	15.00	40.00
1 Linus Omark	1.00	2.50
2 Alexander Ovechkin	4.00	10.00
3 Simon Gagne	1.00	2.50
4 Ryane Clowe	.60	1.50
5 Patrick Marleau	1.00	2.50
6 P.K. Subban	2.00	5.00
7 Nazem Kadri	1.50	4.00
8 Mats Zuccarello-Aasen	1.00	2.50
9 Alexandre Burrows	1.00	2.50
10 Shea Weber	.75	2.00
11 Ilya Kovalchuk	1.00	2.50
12 Lubomir Visnovsky	.60	1.50
13 Bobby Ryan	1.00	2.50
14 Brandon Sutter	.75	2.00
15 Ryan Callahan	1.00	2.50
16 Henrik Zetterberg	1.25	3.00
17 Alexander Steen	1.00	2.50
18 Jason Chimera	.60	1.50
19 Tyler Ennis	.75	2.00
20 John Tavares	2.00	5.00
21 Corey Perry	1.00	2.50
22 Steven Stamkos	2.00	5.00
23 Martin St. Louis	1.00	2.50
24 Jarome Iginla	1.00	2.50
25 Matt Duchene	1.00	2.50

2011-12 Score Supreme Team

Card	Low	High
COMPLETE SET (20)	25.00	60.00
1 Sidney Crosby	8.00	20.00
2 Steven Stamkos	4.00	10.00
3 Henrik Sedin	2.00	5.00
4 Jonathan Toews	4.00	10.00
5 Jeff Skinner	2.00	5.00
6 Pavel Datsyuk	2.50	6.00
7 Daniel Sedin	2.00	5.00
8 Alexander Ovechkin	8.00	20.00
9 Henrik Zetterberg	2.50	6.00
10 Milan Lucic	2.00	5.00
11 Corey Perry	2.00	5.00
12 Martin St. Louis	2.00	5.00
13 Claude Giroux	2.00	5.00
14 Patrick Kane	4.00	10.00
15 Nicklas Lidstrom	2.00	5.00
16 P.K. Subban	4.00	10.00
17 Drew Doughty	2.00	5.00
18 Tim Thomas	2.00	5.00
19 Roberto Luongo	2.00	5.00
20 Carey Price	6.00	15.00

2012 Score Hot Rookies Toronto Fall Expo

CRACKED ICE/25: 1.5X TO 4X BASE HI

Card	Low	High
1 Chris Kreider	3.00	8.00
2 Carter Ashton	1.00	2.50
3 Jussi Rynnas	.75	2.00
4 Max Sauve	.75	2.00
5 J.T. Brown	.75	2.00
6 Sven Baertschi	1.50	4.00

2012-13 Score

COMP.SET w/o RC's (500) 25.00 60.00
501-548 ROOKIE ODDS 1:2

Card	Low	High
1 Ryan Nugent-Hopkins SH	.15	.40
2 Thomas Vanek SH	.15	.40
3 Anze Kopitar SH	.25	.60
4 Bobby Ryan SH	.15	.40
5 Luke Adam SH	.12	.30
6 Bernie Parent SH	.15	.40
7 Mark Messier SH	.20	.50
8 Henrik Lundqvist SH	.20	.50
9 Brayden Schenn SH	.15	.40
10 Pavel Datsyuk SH	.20	.50
11 Carl Hagelin SH	.15	.40
12 Patrick Kane SH	.30	.75
13 Jamie Benn SH	.20	.50
14 Zdeno Chara SH	.15	.40
15 Steven Stamkos SH	.30	.75
16 Marian Gaborik SH	.15	.40
17 Tim Thomas SH	.15	.40
18 Teemu Selanne SH	.30	.75
19 Jaromir Jagr SH	.40	1.00
20 Ray Whitney SH	.12	.30
21 Cam Ward SH	.15	.40
22 Miikka Kiprusoff SH	.12	.30
23 Daniel Alfredsson SH	.15	.40
24 Marian Hossa SH	.12	.30
25 Ilya Kovalchuk SH	.15	.40
26 Jarome Iginla SH	.15	.40
27 Evgeni Malkin SH	.50	1.25
28 Steven Stamkos SH	.30	.75
29 Henrik Lundqvist SH	.20	.50
30 Martin Brodeur SH	.30	.75
31 Sam Gagner SH	.12	.30
32 Jimmy Howard SH	.15	.40
33 Nicklas Lidstrom SH	.15	.40
34 Stephen Weiss SH	.12	.30
35 Sidney Crosby SH	.60	1.50
36 Cam Ward SH	.15	.40
37 Nik Antropov SH	.12	.30
38 Scott Niedermayer SH	.15	.40
39 Steven Stamkos SH	.30	.75
40 Shane Doan SH	.12	.30
41 Corey Perry	.20	.50
42 Teemu Selanne	.40	1.00
43 Saku Koivu	.20	.50
44 Ryan Getzlaf	.30	.75
45 Bobby Ryan	.20	.50
46 Andrew Cogliano	.12	.30
47 Jonas Hiller	.15	.40
48 Cam Fowler	.15	.40
49 Devante Smith-Pelly	.15	.40
50 Sheldon Souray	.12	.30
51 Francois Beauchemin	.12	.30
52 Niklas Hagman	.12	.30
53 Luca Sbisa	.15	.40
54 Dan Ellis	.15	.40
55 Nick Bonino	.12	.30
56 Tyler Seguin	.30	.75
57 Tim Thomas	.20	.50
58 Zdeno Chara	.20	.50
59 Patrice Bergeron	.25	.60
60 David Krejci	.20	.50
61 Milan Lucic	.20	.50
62 Brad Marchand	.25	.60
63 Rich Peverley	.20	.50
64 Tuukka Rask	.20	.50
65 Shawn Thornton	.15	.40
66 Nathan Horton	.20	.50
67 Johnny Boychuk	.12	.30
68 Chris Kelly	.15	.40
69 Benoit Pouliot	.12	.30
70 Gregory Campbell	.12	.30
71 Ryan Miller	.20	.50
72 Jason Pominville	.15	.40
73 Drew Stafford	.20	.50
74 Thomas Vanek	.20	.50
75 Steve Ott	.15	.40
76 Cody Hodgson	.20	.50
77 Tyler Myers	.15	.40
78 Tyler Ennis	.15	.40
79 Jhonas Enroth	.20	.50
80 Christian Ehrhoff	.12	.30
81 Nathan Gerbe	.12	.30
82 Luke Adam	.15	.40
83 Corey Tropp	.15	.40
84 Marcus Foligno	.15	.40
85 Brayden McNabb	.20	.50
86 Jarome Iginla	.20	.50
87 Jay Bouwmeester	.20	.50
88 Miikka Kiprusoff	.15	.40
89 Jiri Hudler	.15	.40
90 Alex Tanguay	.12	.30
91 Curtis Glencross	.12	.30
92 Lee Stempniak	.12	.30
93 Michael Cammalleri	.15	.40
94 Matt Stajan	.15	.40
95 Leland Irving	.15	.40
96 Blake Comeau	.12	.30
97 Mark Giordano	.15	.40
98 Mikael Backlund	.15	.40
99 Greg Nemisz	.12	.30
100 Tim Jackman	.12	.30
101 Eric Staal	.25	.60
102 Jordan Staal	.20	.50
103 Tim Gleason	.12	.30
104 Cam Ward	.20	.50
105 Jussi Jokinen	.12	.30
106 Jeff Skinner	.20	.50
107 Jiri Tlusty	.15	.40
108 Tuomo Ruutu	.15	.40
109 Chad LaRose	.12	.30
110 Justin Faulk	.12	.30
111 Joe Corvo	.12	.30
112 Jamie McBain	.12	.30
113 Riley Nash	.15	.40
114 Zach Boychuk	.12	.30
115 Brian Boucher	.15	.40
116 Jonathan Toews	.40	1.00
117 Patrick Sharp	.20	.50
118 Duncan Keith	.20	.50
119 Patrick Kane	.40	1.00
120 Marian Hossa	.15	.40
121 Corey Crawford	.25	.60
122 Viktor Stalberg	.12	.30
123 Dave Bolland	.15	.40
124 Brandon Saad	.20	.50
125 Brent Seabrook	.20	.50
126 Nick Leddy	.12	.30
127 Andrew Shaw	.20	.50
128 Marcus Kruger	.25	.60
129 Ray Emery	.15	.40
130 Bryan Bickell	.12	.30
131 Gabriel Landeskog	.20	.50
132 Paul Stastny	.20	.50
133 Milan Hejduk	.15	.40
134 Matt Duchene	.20	.50
135 Ryan O'Reilly	.20	.50
136 David Jones	.12	.30
137 Semyon Varlamov	.20	.50
138 Erik Johnson	.12	.30
139 Steve Downie	.12	.30
140 P.A. Parenteau	.12	.30
141 Cameron Gaunce	.12	.30
142 Jamie McGinn	.12	.30
143 Jean-Sebastien Giguere	.15	.40
144 Peter Mueller	.12	.30
145 Ryan Wilson	.15	.40
146 Ryan Johansen	.25	.60
147 Rick Nash	.20	.50
148 Vinny Prospal	.12	.30
149 R.J. Umberger	.12	.30
150 Derick Brassard	.20	.50
151 Derek Dorsett	.12	.30
152 James Wisniewski	.12	.30
153 Jack Johnson	.12	.30
154 Nick Foligno	.15	.40
155 Steve Mason	.15	.40
156 John Moore	.12	.30
157 Mark Letestu	.15	.40
158 Sergei Bobrovsky	.20	.50
159 Jared Boll	.12	.30
160 Cam Atkinson	.20	.50
161 Loui Eriksson	.15	.40
162 Brenden Morrow	.15	.40
163 Derek Roy	.15	.40
164 Stephane Robidas	.12	.30
165 Kari Lehtonen	.15	.40
166 Jamie Benn	.25	.60
167 Cody Eakin	.15	.40
168 Richard Bachman	.15	.40
169 Jaromir Jagr	.50	1.25
170 Ray Whitney	.15	.40
171 Alex Goligoski	.12	.30
172 Trevor Daley	.12	.30
173 Tomas Vincour	.12	.30
174 Michael Ryder	.12	.30
175 Colton Sceviour	.12	.30
176 Pavel Datsyuk	.25	.60
177 Nicklas Lidstrom	.20	.50
178 Henrik Zetterberg	.25	.60
179 Niklas Kronwall	.15	.40
180 Jimmy Howard	.20	.50
181 Valtteri Filppula	.20	.50
182 Johan Franzen	.20	.50
183 Jordin Tootoo	.15	.40
184 Todd Bertuzzi	.15	.40
185 Danny Cleary	.20	.50
186 Brendan Smith	.15	.40
187 Drew Miller	.12	.30
188 Tomas Holmstrom	.12	.30
189 Justin Abdelkader	.15	.40
190 Gustav Nyquist	.20	.50
191 Ryan Nugent-Hopkins	.20	.50
192 Taylor Hall	.40	1.00
193 Jordan Eberle	.20	.50
194 Shawn Horcoff	.12	.30
195 Ales Hemsky	.15	.40
196 Ryan Whitney	.12	.30
197 Sam Gagner	.15	.40
198 Ryan Smyth	.15	.40
199 Devan Dubnyk	.20	.50
200 Nikolai Khabibulin	.20	.50
201 Ryan Jones	.15	.40
202 Ben Eager	.12	.30
203 Magnus Paajarvi	.15	.40
204 Anton Lander	.15	.40
205 Teemu Hartikainen	.15	.40
206 Stephen Weiss	.15	.40
207 Brian Campbell	.12	.30
208 Tomas Kopecky	.15	.40
209 Ed Jovanovski	.12	.30
210 Jose Theodore	.20	.50
211 Tomas Fleischmann	.12	.30
212 Kris Versteeg	.15	.40
213 Jacob Markstrom	.20	.50
214 Sean Bergenheim	.12	.30
215 Erik Gudbranson	.20	.50
216 Dmitry Kulikov	.12	.30
217 George Parros	.15	.40
218 Krys Barch	.12	.30
219 Wojtek Wolski	.12	.30
220 Scott Clemmensen	.15	.40
221 Anze Kopitar	.30	.75
222 Dustin Brown	.20	.50
223 Matt Greene	.12	.30
224 Jonathan Quick	.30	.75
225 Drew Doughty	.20	.50
226 Justin Williams	.15	.40
227 Mike Richards	.20	.50
228 Simon Gagne	.20	.50
229 Jeff Carter	.20	.50
230 Jarret Stoll	.15	.40
231 Jonathan Bernier	.20	.50
232 Dustin Penner	.15	.40
233 Slava Voynov	.20	.50
234 Kyle Clifford	.12	.30
235 Willie Mitchell	.12	.30
236 Mikko Koivu	.15	.40
237 Dany Heatley	.15	.40
238 Matt Cullen	.12	.30
239 Cal Clutterbuck	.20	.50
240 Kyle Brodziak	.12	.30
241 Devin Setoguchi	.15	.40
242 Nick Johnson	.15	.40
243 Niklas Backstrom	.15	.40
244 Zach Parise	.20	.50
245 Josh Harding	.20	.50
246 Pierre-Marc Bouchard	.20	.50
247 Ryan Suter	.12	.30
248 Zenon Konopka	.15	.40
249 Torrey Mitchell	.12	.30
250 Matt Kassian	.12	.30
251 Carey Price	.60	1.50
252 Andrei Markov	.20	.50
253 Brian Gionta	.15	.40
254 Max Pacioretty	.20	.50
255 Erik Cole	.15	.40
256 David Desharnais	.20	.50
257 P.K. Subban	.30	.75
258 Tomas Plekanec	.20	.50
259 Lars Eller	.15	.40
260 Louis Leblanc	.20	.50
261 Blake Geoffrion	.20	.50
262 Brandon Prust	.12	.30
263 Colby Armstrong	.12	.30
264 Yannick Weber	.15	.40
265 Alexei Emelin	.20	.50
266 Pekka Rinne	.25	.60
267 Chris Mason	.15	.40
268 Shea Weber	.15	.40
269 Martin Erat	.12	.30
270 David Legwand	.15	.40
271 Mike Fisher	.15	.40
272 Sergei Kostitsyn	.12	.30
273 Patric Hornqvist	.15	.40
274 Ryan Ellis	.12	.30
275 Craig Smith	.12	.30
276 Nick Spaling	.12	.30
277 Colin Wilson	.15	.40
278 Andrei Kostitsyn	.15	.40
279 Gabriel Bourque	.15	.40
280 Roman Josi	.20	.50
281 Martin Brodeur	.40	1.00
282 Anton Volchenkov	.12	.30
283 Patrik Elias	.20	.50
284 Ilya Kovalchuk	.20	.50
285 Adam Henrique	.20	.50
286 David Clarkson	.12	.30
287 Petr Sykora	.15	.40
288 Dainius Zubrus	.12	.30
289 Johan Hedberg	.15	.40
290 Adam Larsson	.20	.50
291 Alexei Ponikarovsky	.12	.30
292 Mark Fayne	.12	.30
293 Andy Greene	.12	.30
294 Travis Zajac	.15	.40
295 Jacob Josefson	.12	.30
296 John Tavares	.40	1.00
297 Mark Streit	.12	.30
298 Kyle Okposo	.20	.50
299 Steve Staios	.12	.30
300 Matt Moulson	.15	.40
301 Anders Nilsson	.12	.30
302 Frans Nielsen	.12	.30
303 Michael Grabner	.15	.40
304 Josh Bailey	.15	.40
305 Evgeni Nabokov	.15	.40
306 Travis Hamonic	.15	.40
307 Eric Boulton	.12	.30
308 Andrew MacDonald	.12	.30
309 Calvin de Haan	.15	.40
310 Rick DiPietro	.15	.40
311 Henrik Lundqvist	.25	.60
312 Ryan Callahan	.20	.50
313 Brad Richards	.20	.50
314 Marian Gaborik	.20	.50
315 Derek Stepan	.20	.50
316 Michael Del Zotto	.12	.30
317 Carl Hagelin	.20	.50
318 Marc Staal	.15	.40
319 Artem Anisimov	.15	.40
320 Brandon Dubinsky	.15	.40
321 Ryan McDonagh	.20	.50
322 Dan Girardi	.12	.30
323 Brian Boyle	.12	.30
324 Taylor Pyatt	.12	.30
325 Martin Biron	.15	.40
326 Daniel Alfredsson	.20	.50
327 Jason Spezza	.20	.50
328 Erik Karlsson	.40	1.00
329 Chris Phillips	.12	.30
330 Craig Anderson	.20	.50
331 Milan Michalek	.12	.30
332 Guillaume Latendresse	.15	.40
333 Sergei Gonchar	.12	.30
334 Colin Greening	.12	.30
335 Mika Zibanejad	.20	.50
336 Kyle Turris	.12	.30
337 Jared Cowen	.20	.50
338 Chris Neil	.12	.30
339 Erik Condra	.12	.30
340 Zack Smith	.12	.30
341 Claude Giroux	.20	.50
342 Scott Hartnell	.20	.50
343 Brayden Schenn	.20	.50
344 Danny Briere	.20	.50
345 Jakub Voracek	.20	.50
346 Wayne Simmonds	.25	.60
347 Matt Read	.15	.40
348 Chris Pronger	.15	.40
349 Ilya Bryzgalov	.20	.50
350 Sean Couturier	.20	.50
351 Luke Schenn	.12	.30
352 Zac Rinaldo	.15	.40
353 Kimmo Timonen	.12	.30
354 Max Talbot	.15	.40
355 Eric Wellwood	.12	.30
356 Shane Doan	.15	.40
357 Keith Yandle	.20	.50
358 Paul Bissonnette	.12	.30
359 Martin Hanzal	.12	.30
360 Mikkel Boedker	.12	.30
361 Mike Smith	.20	.50
362 Radim Vrbata	.15	.40
363 David Rundblad	.15	.40
364 Oliver Ekman-Larsson	.20	.50
365 Rostislav Klesla	.12	.30
366 Raffi Torres	.12	.30
367 Antoine Vermette	.12	.30
368 Daymond Langkow	.12	.30
369 Andy Miele	.12	.30
370 Michal Rozsival	.12	.30
371 Sidney Crosby	.75	2.00
372 Evgeni Malkin	.60	1.50
373 Brandon Sutter	.15	.40
374 Marc-Andre Fleury	.30	.75
375 Kris Letang	.20	.50
376 James Neal	.20	.50
377 Brooks Orpik	.15	.40
378 Chris Kunitz	.20	.50
379 Pascal Dupuis	.12	.30
380 Steve Sullivan	.12	.30
381 Tyler Kennedy	.12	.30
382 Matt Cooke	.12	.30
383 Joe Vitale	.12	.30
384 Simon Despres	.15	.40
385 Paul Martin	.12	.30
386 Joe Thornton	.20	.50
387 Patrick Marleau	.20	.50
388 Dan Boyle	.15	.40
389 Ryane Clowe	.12	.30
390 Logan Couture	.20	.50
391 Joe Pavelski	.20	.50
392 Antti Niemi	.15	.40
393 Brent Burns	.25	.60
394 Martin Havlat	.15	.40
395 Michal Handzus	.12	.30
396 Adam Burish	.12	.30
397 Marc-Edouard Vlasic	.12	.30
398 Brad Winchester	.12	.30
399 Andrew Desjardins	.12	.30
400 T.J. Galiardi	.15	.40
401 David Backes	.20	.50
402 Alexander Steen	.20	.50
403 Andy McDonald	.15	.40
404 Brian Elliott	.15	.40
405 Jaroslav Halak	.20	.50
406 Alex Pietrangelo	.15	.40
407 T.J. Oshie	.30	.75
408 Barret Jackman	.12	.30
409 Jamie Langenbrunner	.12	.30
410 Kevin Shattenkirk	.20	.50
411 David Perron	.12	.30
412 Patrik Berglund	.12	.30
413 Jason Arnott	.15	.40
414 Chris Stewart	.15	.40
415 Vladimir Sobotka	.12	.30
416 Steven Stamkos	.40	1.00
417 Martin St. Louis	.20	.50
418 Vincent Lecavalier	.15	.40
419 Eric Brewer	.12	.30
420 Mattias Ohlund	.12	.30
421 Teddy Purcell	.20	.50
422 Ryan Malone	.12	.30
423 Brett Connolly	.15	.40
424 Victor Hedman	.25	.60
425 Dwayne Roloson	.15	.40
426 Anders Lindback	.12	.30
427 Tom Pyatt	.12	.30
428 J.T. Wyman	.12	.30
429 Marc-Andre Bergeron	.12	.30
430 Dana Tyrell	.12	.30
431 Phil Kessel	.25	.60
432 Dion Phaneuf	.20	.50
433 Mikhail Grabovski	.15	.40
434 Mike Komisarek	.15	.40
435 Jake Gardiner	.20	.50
436 Joffrey Lupul	.15	.40
437 Tyler Bozak	.15	.40
438 James van Riemsdyk	.20	.50
439 James Reimer	.20	.50
440 Cody Franson	.12	.30
441 Clarke MacArthur	.12	.30
442 Joe Colborne	.15	.40
443 Tim Connolly	.12	.30
444 Nazem Kadri	.20	.50
445 Matt Frattin	.15	.40
446 Henrik Sedin	.20	.50
447 Daniel Sedin	.20	.50
448 Ryan Kesler	.20	.50
449 Cory Schneider	.15	.40
450 Alexandre Burrows	.20	.50
451 Kevin Bieksa	.15	.40
452 Manny Malhotra	.15	.40
453 Roberto Luongo	.20	.50
454 Alexander Edler	.12	.30
455 Zack Kassian	.15	.40
456 Jannik Hansen	.15	.40
457 Dan Hamhuis	.15	.40
458 Maxim Lapierre	.12	.30
459 Dale Weise	.15	.40
460 Chris Higgins	.12	.30
461 Alex Ovechkin	.75	2.00
462 Nicklas Backstrom	.30	.75
463 Brooks Laich	.12	.30
464 Troy Brouwer	.15	.40
465 Mike Knuble	.12	.30
466 Alexander Semin	.20	.50
467 Braden Holtby	.30	.75
468 Mike Green	.20	.50
469 Dmitry Orlov	.20	.50
470 Marcus Johansson	.15	.40
471 Mike Ribeiro	.15	.40
472 Joel Ward	.12	.30
473 John Carlson	.25	.60
474 Mathieu Perreault	.15	.40
475 Michal Neuvirth	.15	.40
476 Evander Kane	.20	.50
477 Dustin Byfuglien	.20	.50
478 Blake Wheeler	.20	.50
479 Andrew Ladd	.20	.50
480 Mark Scheifele	.25	.60
481 Tobias Enstrom	.12	.30
482 Al Montoya	.12	.30
483 Alexander Burmistrov	.15	.40
484 Olli Jokinen	.15	.40
485 Bryan Little	.20	.50
486 Nik Antropov	.15	.40
487 Zach Bogosian	.15	.40
488 Ondrej Pavelec	.20	.50
489 Kyle Wellwood	.15	.40
490 Mark Stuart	.12	.30
491 Evgeni Malkin AW	.50	1.25
492 Evgeni Malkin AW	.50	1.25
493 Henrik Lundqvist AW	.20	.50
494 Gabriel Landeskog AW	.15	.40
495 Steven Stamkos AW	.30	.75
496 Erik Karlsson AW	.30	.75
497 Brian Campbell AW	.10	.25
498 Patrice Bergeron AW	.20	.50
499 Jonathan Quick AW	.25	.60
500 Jonathan Quick AW	.25	.60
501 Philippe Cornet HR RC	.60	1.50
502 Andrew Joudrey HR RC	.60	1.50
503 Tyson Sexsmith HR RC	.60	1.50
504 Jakob Silfverberg HR RC	1.25	3.00
505 Tyson Barrie HR RC	1.25	3.00
506 Mike Connolly HR RC	.60	1.50
507 Aaron Ness HR RC	.60	1.50
508 Jordan Nolan HR RC	.60	1.50
509 Colby Robak HR RC	.60	1.50
510 Kristopher Foucault HR RC	.60	1.50
511 Ryan Garbutt HR RC	.60	1.50
512 Michael Stone HR RC	.60	1.50
513 Carter Camper HR RC	.50	1.25
514 Casey Cizikas HR RC	.60	1.50
515 Brandon Bollig HR RC	.60	1.50
516 Lane MacDermid HR RC	.60	1.50
517 Carter Ashton HR RC	.50	1.25
518 Sven Baertschi HR RC	.75	2.00
519 Brandon Manning HR RC	.60	1.50
520 Maxime Sauve HR RC	.60	1.50
521 Jaden Schwartz HR RC	1.25	3.00
522 Travis Turnbull HR RC	.60	1.50
523 Ryan Hamilton HR RC	.60	1.50
524 Jussi Rynnas HR RC	.60	1.50
525 Shawn Hunwick HR RC	.60	1.50
526 Reilly Smith HR RC	1.25	3.00
527 Cody Goloubef HR RC	.60	1.50
528 J.T. Brown HR RC	.60	1.50
529 Mat Clark HR RC	.60	1.50
530 Dalton Prout HR RC	.60	1.50
531 Torey Krug HR RC	2.50	6.00
532 Matt Donovan HR RC	.60	1.50
533 Robert Mayer HR RC	.75	2.00
534 Gabriel Dumont HR RC	.60	1.50
535 Akim Aliu HR RC	.60	1.50
536 Tyler Cuma HR RC	.60	1.50
537 Chet Pickard HR RC	.60	1.50
538 Riley Sheahan HR RC	.60	1.50
539 Jeremy Welsh HR RC	.60	1.50
540 Chay Genoway HR RC	.60	1.50
541 Scott Glennie HR RC	.60	1.50
542 Brenden Dillon HR RC	.60	1.50
543 Chris Kreider HR RC	1.25	3.00
544 Jake Allen HR RC	2.00	5.00
545 Jason Zucker HR RC	.75	2.00
546 Matt Watkins HR RC	.60	1.50
547 Michael Hutchinson HR RC	1.25	3.00
548 Mark Stone HR RC	1.25	3.00

2012-13 Score Black Ice

*VETS 1-500: 15X TO 40X BASIC CARDS
*ROOKIES 501-548: 4X TO 10X BASIC CARDS

Card	Low	High
121 Corey Crawford	10.00	25.00
462 Nicklas Backstrom	12.00	30.00

2012-13 Score Gold Rush

*VETS 1-500: 1.2X TO 3X BASIC CARDS
*ROOKIES 101-548: .6X TO 1.5X BASIC RC
ONE GOLD RUSH PER PACK
501-548 ROOKIE GOLD ODDS 1:36

Card	Low	High
121 Corey Crawford	.75	2.00
462 Nicklas Backstrom	1.00	2.50

2012-13 Score Check It

Card	Low	High
C1 Cal Clutterbuck	4.00	10.00
C2 Zdeno Chara	4.00	10.00
C3 Alex Ovechkin	15.00	40.00
C4 Dion Phaneuf	4.00	10.00
C5 Jeremy Roenick	4.00	10.00
C6 Cam Neely	10.00	20.00
C7 Chris Pronger	3.00	8.00
C8 Dustin Brown	4.00	10.00
C9 Milan Lucic	4.00	10.00
C10 Niklas Kronwall	3.00	8.00
C11 Eric Lindros	4.00	10.00
C12 Steve Ott	3.00	8.00
C13 Ryan Callahan	4.00	10.00
C14 Matt Martin	2.50	6.00
C15 David Backes	4.00	10.00
C16 Luke Schenn	6.00	15.00
C17 Brendan Shanahan	5.00	12.00
C18 Dustin Byfuglien	4.00	10.00
C19 Wendel Clark	4.00	10.00
C20 Chris Neil	2.50	6.00

2012-13 Score First Goal
FG1 Matt Read .75 2.00
FG2 Gabriel Landeskog 1.00 2.50
FG3 Andrew Shaw 1.00 2.50
FG4 Ryan Nugent-Hopkins 1.00 2.50
FG5 Chris Kreider 1.50 4.00
FG6 Adam Henrique 1.00 2.50
FG7 Carl Hagelin 1.00 2.50
FG8 Craig Smith .60 1.50
FG9 Sean Couturier 1.00 2.50
FG10 Marcus Kruger 1.25 3.00
FG11 Ryan Johansen 1.25 3.00
FG12 Mark Scheifele 1.25 3.00
FG13 Sven Baertschi 1.00 2.50
FG14 Jake Gardiner 1.00 2.50
FG15 Slava Voynov 1.00 2.50
FG16 Brayden Schenn 1.00 2.50
FG17 Justin Faulk .60 1.50
FG18 Matt Frattin .75 2.00
FG19 Gabriel Bourque .75 2.00
FG20 Devante Smith-Pelly .75 2.00
FG21 Cam Atkinson 1.00 2.50
FG22 Marcus Foligno .75 2.00
FG23 Jared Cowen 1.00 2.50
FG24 Roman Josi 1.00 2.50

2012-13 Score Franchise
F1 Corey Perry 1.25 3.00
F2 Tyler Seguin 2.00 5.00
F3 Ryan Miller 1.25 3.00
F4 Jarome Iginla 1.25 3.00
F5 Eric Staal 1.50 4.00
F6 Jonathan Toews 2.50 6.00
F7 Matt Duchene 1.25 3.00
F8 Rick Nash 1.25 3.00
F9 Loui Eriksson 1.00 2.50
F10 Pavel Datsyuk 1.50 4.00
F11 Jordan Eberle 1.25 3.00
F12 Stephen Weiss 1.00 2.50
F13 Jonathan Quick 2.00 5.00
F14 Dany Heatley 1.00 2.50
F15 Max Pacioretty 1.25 3.00
F16 Pekka Rinne 1.50 4.00
F17 Ilya Kovalchuk 1.25 3.00
F18 John Tavares 2.50 6.00
F19 Henrik Lundqvist 1.50 4.00
F20 Jason Spezza 1.25 3.00
F21 Claude Giroux 1.25 3.00
F22 Keith Yandle 1.25 3.00
F23 Sidney Crosby 5.00 12.00
F24 Joe Thornton 1.25 3.00
F25 David Backes 1.25 3.00
F26 Steven Stamkos 2.50 6.00
F27 Phil Kessel 1.50 4.00
F28 Henrik Sedin 1.25 3.00
F29 Alex Ovechkin 5.00 12.00
F30 Dustin Byfuglien 1.25 3.00

2012-13 Score Franchise Original Six
RANDOM INSERTS IN RETAIL PACKS
OS1 Johnny Bucyk .75 2.00
OS2 Gordie Howe 2.00 5.00
OS3 Johnny Bower 1.00 2.50
OS4 Jean Beliveau 1.00 2.50
OS5 Ed Giacomin 1.00 2.50
OS6 Bobby Hull 1.00 2.50
FCL1 Hull/Howe/Bower 10.00 25.00
FCL2 Giac/Beliv/Bucyk 10.00 25.00

2012-13 Score Net Cam
COMPLETE SET (20) 12.50 25.00
NC1 Jonathan Quick 1.50 4.00
NC2 Henrik Lundqvist 1.25 3.00
NC3 Corey Crawford 1.25 3.00
NC4 Jimmy Howard 1.00 2.50
NC5 Brian Elliott .75 2.00
NC6 Tim Thomas 1.00 2.50
NC7 Carey Price 3.00 8.00
NC8 Mike Smith 1.00 2.50
NC9 Kari Lehtonen .75 2.00
NC10 Marc-Andre Fleury 1.50 4.00
NC11 Pekka Rinne 1.25 3.00
NC12 Roberto Luongo 1.00 2.50
NC13 Martin Brodeur 2.00 5.00
NC14 Antti Niemi .75 2.00
NC15 Cory Schneider .75 2.00
NC16 Jose Theodore 1.00 2.50
NC17 Ilya Bryzgalov 1.00 2.50
NC18 Braden Holtby 1.50 4.00
NC19 Ryan Miller 1.00 2.50
NC20 Miikka Kiprusoff .75 2.00

2012-13 Score Hot Rookie Autographs
503 Tyson Sexsmith 8.00 20.00
506 Mike Connolly 8.00 20.00
508 Jordan Nolan 15.00 40.00
515 Brandon Bollig 8.00 20.00
517 Carter Ashton 6.00 15.00
518 Sven Baertschi 10.00 25.00
520 Maxime Sauve 8.00 20.00
521 Jaden Schwartz 15.00 40.00
524 Jussi Rynnas 25.00 50.00
533 Robert Mayer 10.00 25.00
537 Chet Pickard 8.00 20.00
541 Scott Glennie 8.00 20.00
543 Chris Kreider 150.00 250.00
544 Jake Allen 25.00 60.00
548 Mark Stone 15.00 40.00

2012-13 Score Signatures
SSAA Artem Anisimov 5.00 12.00
SSAB Alexander Burmistrov 5.00 12.00
SSAE Andreas Engqvist 5.00 12.00
SSAL Anton Lander 5.00 12.00
SSAM Andy Miele 4.00 10.00
SSAO Alex Ovechkin SP
SSAS Alex Stalock 5.00 12.00
SSBB Bobby Butler 5.00 12.00
SSBHO Ben Holmstrom 6.00 15.00
SSBY Brandon Yip 4.00 10.00
SSCAR Daniel Carcillo 4.00 10.00
SSCC Cal Clutterbuck 6.00 15.00
SSCDH Calvin de Haan 5.00 12.00
SSCE Cody Eakin 5.00 12.00
SSCF Cam Fowler 5.00 12.00
SSCGR Colin Greening 4.00 10.00
SSCM Chris Mason 5.00 12.00
SSCOW Jared Cowen 6.00 15.00
SSCSM Craig Smith 4.00 10.00
SSDD Derek Dorsett 4.00 10.00
SSDR Dwayne Roloson 5.00 12.00
SSEME Alexei Emelin 6.00 15.00
SSFAU Justin Faulk 4.00 10.00
SSFRO Michael Frolik 6.00 15.00
SSGN Gustav Nyquist 8.00 20.00
SSGRA Michael Grabner 5.00 12.00
SSHAG Carl Hagelin
SSHAY Jimmy Hayes 5.00 12.00
SSHOW Jimmy Howard SP
SSHS Henrik Sedin
SSJAB Justin Abdelkader 5.00 12.00
SSJAG Jaromir Jagr SP 40.00 80.00
SSJB Justin Braun 5.00 12.00
SSJC Jeff Carter 6.00 15.00
SSJI Jarome Iginla SP
SSJOS Roman Josi 6.00 15.00
SSKM Kenndal McArdle 4.00 10.00
SSLAC Eddie Lack 6.00 15.00
SSLAN Gabriel Landeskog SP 15.00 40.00
SSLAR Adam Larsson 6.00 15.00
SSLI Leland Irving SP 8.00 20.00
SSLID Nicklas Lidstrom SP 75.00 135.00
SSLL Louis Leblanc 6.00 15.00
SSMAC Clarke MacArthur 6.00 15.00
SSMAF Marc-Andre Fleury 10.00 25.00
SSMB Martin Brodeur SP
SSMCN Brayden McNabb 6.00 15.00
SSMF Marcus Foligno 12.00 30.00
SSMG Mikhail Grabovski 5.00 12.00
SSMIT Torrey Mitchell 4.00 10.00
SSML Michael Leighton 6.00 15.00
SSMOU Matt Moulson 5.00 12.00
SSMP Max Pacioretty 6.00 15.00
SSNA Nik Antropov 5.00 12.00
SSNB Nick Bonino 4.00 10.00
SSNP Nick Palmieri 5.00 12.00
SSOE Oliver Ekman-Larsson 6.00 15.00
SSOP Ondrej Pavelec 6.00 15.00
SSORL Dmitry Orlov 6.00 15.00
SSOTT Steve Ott 5.00 12.00
SSPER David Perron 4.00 10.00
SSPHO Peter Holland 4.00 10.00
SSPK Phil Kessel 8.00 20.00
SSPL Philip Larsen 4.00 10.00
SSRBZ Robert Bortuzzo 4.00 10.00
SSRH Roman Horak 5.00 12.00
SSSAT Harri Sateri 5.00 12.00
SSSAV David Savard 4.00 10.00
SSSD Steve Downie 4.00 10.00
SSSED Daniel Sedin
SSSW Stephen Weiss 5.00 12.00
SSTB Troy Brouwer 5.00 12.00
SSTG T.J. Galiardi 5.00 12.00
SSTOE Jonathan Toews SP 25.00 50.00
SSTRO Corey Tropp 5.00 12.00
SSTT Tim Thomas SP
SSVAR Semyon Varlamov 6.00 15.00
SSYS Yann Sauve 4.00 10.00
SSZB Zach Boychuk 4.00 10.00

2012-13 Score Team Future
TF1 Gabriel Landeskog 1.50 4.00
TF2 Ryan Nugent-Hopkins 1.50 4.00
TF3 Sean Couturier 1.50 4.00
TF4 Jake Gardiner 1.50 4.00
TF5 Adam Larsson 1.50 4.00
TF6 Richard Bachman 1.25 3.00
TF7 Carl Hagelin 1.50 4.00
TF8 Adam Henrique 1.50 4.00
TF9 Andrew Shaw 1.50 4.00
TF10 Ryan Ellis 1.00 2.50
TF11 Justin Faulk 1.00 2.50
TF12 Jake Allen 4.00 10.00

2012-13 Score Team Score
COMPLETE SET (12) 8.00 20.00
TS1 Pavel Datsyuk 1.25 3.00
TS2 Evgeni Malkin 3.00 8.00
TS3 Claude Giroux 1.00 2.50
TS4 Erik Karlsson 2.00 5.00
TS5 Zdeno Chara 1.00 2.50
TS6 Henrik Lundqvist 1.25 3.00
TS7 Daniel Sedin 1.00 2.50
TS8 Steven Stamkos 2.00 5.00
TS9 Phil Kessel 1.25 3.00
TS10 Shea Weber .75 2.00
TS11 Keith Yandle 1.00 2.50
TS12 Jonathan Quick 1.50 4.00

2013-14 Score
COMPLETE SET (750) 60.00 120.00
HR ODDS 2:1 HOB JUM, 1:1.5 RET
651-750 INSERTED IN 13-14 ANTHOLOGY
1 Bobby Ryan .20 .50
2 Jonas Hiller .15 .40
3 Ryan Getzlaf .30 .75
4 Corey Perry .20 .50
5 Teemu Selanne .40 1.00
6 Cam Fowler .15 .40
7 Francois Beauchemin .12 .30
8 Sheldon Souray .12 .30
9 Saku Koivu .20 .50
10 Andrew Cogliano .12 .30
11 Luca Sbisa .15 .40
12 Daniel Winnik .12 .30
13 Kyle Palmieri .15 .40
14 Devante Smith-Pelly .15 .40
15 Bryan Allen .12 .30
16 Matt Beleskey .12 .30
17 Nick Bonino .12 .30
18 Matthew Lombardi .12 .30
19 Tyler Seguin .30 .75
20 Patrice Bergeron .25 .60
21 Zdeno Chara .20 .50
22 Milan Lucic .20 .50
23 Brad Marchand .25 .60
24 Tuukka Rask .20 .50
25 Nathan Horton .20 .50
26 David Krejci .20 .50
27 Rich Peverley .20 .50
28 Shawn Thornton .15 .40
29 Gregory Campbell .12 .30
30 Anton Khudobin .15 .40
31 Jaromir Jagr .50 1.25
32 Dennis Seidenberg .15 .40
33 Johnny Boychuk .12 .30
34 Daniel Paille .12 .30
35 Chris Kelly .15 .40
36 Adam McQuaid .12 .30
37 Andrew Ference .12 .30
38 Torey Krug .25 .60
39 Ryan Miller .20 .50
40 Thomas Vanek .20 .50
41 Drew Stafford .20 .50
42 Tyler Myers .15 .40
43 Cody Hodgson .20 .50
44 Nathan Gerbe .12 .30
45 Christian Ehrhoff .12 .30
46 Steve Ott .15 .40
47 Tyler Ennis .15 .40
48 Jhonas Enroth .20 .50
49 Ville Leino .15 .40
50 Patrick Kaleta .12 .30
51 Marcus Foligno .12 .30
52 Jochen Hecht .12 .30
53 Luke Adam .15 .40
54 John Scott .12 .30
55 Andrej Sekera .12 .30
56 Curtis Glencross .12 .30
57 Miikka Kiprusoff .15 .40
58 Mike Cammalleri .15 .40
59 Mikael Backlund .15 .40
60 Akim Aliu .12 .30
61 Alex Tanguay .12 .30
62 Sven Baertschi .15 .40
63 Roman Horak .15 .40
64 Mark Giordano .15 .40
65 Lee Stempniak .12 .30
66 Jiri Hudler .15 .40
67 Matt Stajan .15 .40
68 Dennis Wideman .12 .30
69 Cory Sarich .12 .30
70 Chris Butler .12 .30
71 T.J. Brodie .12 .30
72 Leland Irving .15 .40
73 Tim Jackman .12 .30
74 Eric Staal .25 .60
75 Cam Ward .20 .50
76 Chad LaRose .12 .30
77 Jeff Skinner .15 .40
78 Tuomo Ruutu .15 .40
79 Jordan Staal .20 .50
80 Alexander Semin .20 .50
81 Justin Faulk .12 .30
82 Jamie McBain .12 .30
83 Jeremy Welsh .12 .30
84 Joni Pitkanen .15 .40
85 Tim Gleason .12 .30
86 Jay Harrison .12 .30
87 Jiri Tlusty .15 .40
88 Joe Corvo .12 .30
89 Zac Dalpe .12 .30
90 Dan Ellis .15 .40
91 Jonathan Toews .40 1.00
92 Patrick Kane .40 1.00
93 Patrick Sharp .20 .50
94 Duncan Keith .20 .50
95 Marian Hossa .15 .40
96 Brent Seabrook .20 .50
97 Corey Crawford .25 .60
98 Nick Leddy .12 .30
99 Michael Frolik .12 .30
100 Viktor Stalberg .12 .30
101 Niklas Hjalmarsson .12 .30
102 Dave Bolland .12 .30
103 Brandon Saad .20 .50
104 Marcus Kruger .20 .50
105 Andrew Shaw .20 .50
106 Johnny Oduya .15 .40
107 Bryan Bickell .12 .30
108 Brandon Bollig .15 .40
109 Gabriel Landeskog .15 .40
110 Milan Hejduk .15 .40
111 Matt Duchene .20 .50
112 Paul Stastny .20 .50
113 Semyon Varlamov .20 .50
114 Erik Johnson .12 .30
115 David Jones .12 .30
116 P.A. Parenteau .12 .30
117 Greg Zanon .12 .30
118 Cody McLeod .12 .30
119 Jan Hejda .12 .30
120 Shane O'Brien .12 .30
121 Jamie McGinn .12 .30
122 Matt Hunwick .12 .30
123 Jean-Sebastien Giguere .15 .40
124 John Mitchell .12 .30
125 Mike Connolly .15 .40
126 Tyson Barrie .20 .50
127 Ryan O'Reilly .20 .50
128 R.J. Umberger .12 .30
129 Ryan Johansen .25 .60
130 Marian Gaborik .20 .50
131 Jack Johnson .12 .30
132 Vinny Prospal .12 .30
133 James Wisniewski .12 .30
134 Brandon Dubinsky .15 .40
135 Cam Atkinson .20 .50
136 Fedor Tyutin .12 .30
137 Nick Foligno .15 .40
138 Nikita Nikitin .12 .30
139 Artem Anisimov .15 .40
140 Tim Erixon .12 .30
141 Mark Letestu .15 .40
142 Michael Leighton .15 .40
143 Jared Boll .12 .30
144 Sergei Bobrovsky .20 .50
145 Loui Eriksson .15 .40
146 Ryan Garbutt .12 .30
147 Kari Lehtonen .15 .40
148 Jamie Benn .25 .60
149 Stephane Robidas .12 .30
150 Cody Eakin .12 .30
151 Alex Goligoski .12 .30
152 Lane MacDermid .15 .40
153 Trevor Daley .12 .30
154 Scott Glennie .12 .30
155 Philip Larsen .12 .30
156 Reilly Smith .20 .50
157 Brenden Dillon .15 .40
158 Ray Whitney .15 .40
159 Erik Cole .15 .40
160 Aaron Rome .12 .30
161 Jordie Benn .15 .40
162 Tom Wandell .12 .30
163 Pavel Datsyuk .25 .60
164 Henrik Zetterberg .25 .60
165 Jimmy Howard .20 .50
166 Niklas Kronwall .15 .40
167 Johan Franzen .20 .50
168 Valtteri Filppula .20 .50
169 Todd Bertuzzi .15 .40
170 Justin Abdelkader .15 .40
171 Jonathan Ericsson .15 .40
172 Daniel Cleary .20 .50
173 Mikael Samuelsson .12 .30
174 Kyle Quincey .12 .30
175 Ian White .15 .40
176 Damien Brunner RC .40 1.00
177 Jonas Gustavsson .15 .40
178 Patrick Eaves .12 .30
179 Brendan Smith .15 .40
180 Jordin Tootoo .15 .40
181 Jordan Eberle .20 .50
182 Taylor Hall .40 1.00
183 Ryan Nugent-Hopkins .20 .50
184 Ryan Smyth .15 .40
185 Shawn Horcoff .12 .30
186 Sam Gagner .15 .40
187 Ryan Whitney .12 .30
188 Ales Hemsky .12 .30
189 Ladislav Smid .12 .30
190 Nick Schultz .12 .30
191 Devan Dubnyk .20 .50
192 Jeff Petry .15 .40
193 Eric Belanger .12 .30
194 Ben Eager .12 .30
195 Ryan Jones .15 .40
196 Mark Fistric .12 .30
197 Teemu Hartikainen .15 .40
198 Magnus Paajarvi .20 .50
199 Ed Jovanovski .12 .30
200 Brian Campbell .12 .30
201 Stephen Weiss .15 .40
202 Tomas Fleischmann .12 .30
203 Filip Kuba .12 .30
204 Kris Versteeg .15 .40
205 Dmitry Kulikov .12 .30
206 Peter Mueller .12 .30
207 Tomas Kopecky .15 .40
208 Mike Weaver .12 .30
209 Scottie Upshall .12 .30
210 George Parros .15 .40
211 Shawn Matthias .12 .30
212 Erik Gudbranson .20 .50
213 Marcel Goc .15 .40
214 Jack Skille .15 .40
215 Scott Clemmensen .15 .40
216 Jose Theodore .20 .50
217 Anze Kopitar .30 .75
218 Dustin Brown .20 .50
219 Jonathan Quick .30 .75
220 Drew Doughty .20 .50
221 Mike Richards .20 .50
222 Jeff Carter .20 .50
223 Justin Williams .15 .40
224 Rob Scuderi .12 .30
225 Jarret Stoll .15 .40
226 Jonathan Bernier .20 .50
227 Matt Greene .12 .30
228 Jordan Nolan .15 .40
229 Slava Voynov .15 .40
230 Dustin Penner .15 .40
231 Alec Martinez .12 .30
232 Trevor Lewis .12 .30
233 Kyle Clifford .12 .30
234 Keaton Ellerby .12 .30
235 Zach Parise .20 .50
236 Dany Heatley .15 .40
237 Mikko Koivu .15 .40
238 Ryan Suter .12 .30
239 Niklas Backstrom .15 .40
240 Pierre-Marc Bouchard .20 .50
241 Matt Cullen .12 .30
242 Tom Gilbert .12 .30
243 Devin Setoguchi .15 .40
244 Jared Spurgeon .12 .30
245 Cal Clutterbuck .20 .50
246 Kyle Brodziak .12 .30
247 Josh Harding .20 .50
248 Clayton Stoner .12 .30
249 Torrey Mitchell .12 .30
250 Zenon Konopka .15 .40
251 Mike Rupp .12 .30
252 Jason Pominville .15 .40
253 Carey Price .60 1.50
254 Max Pacioretty .20 .50
255 Tomas Plekanec .20 .50
256 Andrei Markov .20 .50
257 Michael Ryder .12 .30
258 Brian Gionta .15 .40
259 P.K. Subban .30 .75
260 Raphael Diaz .12 .30
261 Rene Bourque .12 .30
262 David Desharnais .20 .50
263 Josh Gorges .15 .40
264 Ryan White .12 .30
265 Travis Moen .12 .30
266 Francis Bouillon .12 .30
267 Lars Eller .15 .40
268 Alexei Emelin .15 .40
269 Brandon Prust .12 .30
270 Tomas Kaberle .12 .30
271 Peter Budaj .15 .40
272 Shea Weber .15 .40
273 Pekka Rinne .25 .60
274 Mike Fisher .15 .40
275 Craig Smith .12 .30
276 Roman Josi .20 .50
277 Patric Hornqvist .15 .40
278 David Legwand .15 .40
279 Sergei Kostitsyn .12 .30
280 Kevin Klein .12 .30
281 Jonathon Blum .15 .40
282 Nick Spaling .12 .30
283 Colin Wilson .15 .40
284 Chris Mason .15 .40
285 Brandon Yip .12 .30
286 Paul Gaustad .12 .30
287 Hal Gill .12 .30
288 Gabriel Bourque .15 .40
289 Rich Clune .12 .30
290 Ilya Kovalchuk .20 .50
291 Adam Henrique .20 .50
292 Martin Brodeur .40 1.00
293 Patrik Elias .20 .50
294 Travis Zajac .15 .40
295 Adam Larsson .20 .50
296 Dainius Zubrus .12 .30
297 Anton Volchenkov .12 .30
298 Andy Greene .12 .30
299 Johan Hedberg .15 .40
300 David Clarkson .12 .30
301 Bryce Salvador .12 .30
302 Jacob Josefson .12 .30
303 Stephen Gionta .12 .30
304 Marek Zidlicky .12 .30
305 Henrik Tallinder .12 .30
306 Ryan Carter .12 .30
307 Steve Bernier .12 .30
308 John Tavares .40 1.00
309 Matt Moulson .15 .40
310 Kyle Okposo .20 .50
311 Josh Bailey .15 .40
312 Michael Grabner .15 .40
313 Rick DiPietro .15 .40
314 Andrew MacDonald .12 .30
315 Frans Nielsen .12 .30
316 Travis Hamonic .12 .30
317 Evgeni Nabokov .15 .40
318 Mark Streit .12 .30
319 Brad Boyes .12 .30
320 David Ullstrom .12 .30
321 Lubomir Visnovsky .12 .30
322 Brian Strait .12 .30
323 Matt Martin .12 .30
324 Matt Carkner .12 .30
325 Colin McDonald .15 .40
326 Henrik Lundqvist .25 .60
327 Ryane Clowe .12 .30
328 Brad Richards .20 .50
329 Rick Nash .20 .50
330 Ryan Callahan .20 .50
331 Marc Staal .15 .40
332 Ryan McDonagh .20 .50
333 Carl Hagelin .20 .50
334 Martin Biron .15 .40
335 Dan Girardi .12 .30
336 Derek Stepan .20 .50
337 Michael Del Zotto .12 .30
338 Chris Kreider .20 .50
339 Brian Boyle .12 .30
340 Derick Brassard .20 .50
341 Taylor Pyatt .12 .30
342 Darroll Powe .12 .30
343 Matt Gilroy .12 .30
344 Anton Stralman .12 .30
345 Erik Karlsson .40 1.00
346 Daniel Alfredsson .20 .50
347 Jason Spezza .20 .50
348 Craig Anderson .20 .50
349 Milan Michalek .12 .30
350 Kyle Turris .12 .30
351 Sergei Gonchar .12 .30
352 Colin Greening .12 .30
353 Chris Neil .12 .30
354 Chris Phillips .12 .30
355 Erik Condra .12 .30
356 Zack Smith .12 .30
357 Marc Methot .12 .30
358 Mika Zibanejad .20 .50
359 Jakob Silfverberg .15 .40
360 Guillaume Latendresse .15 .40
361 Robin Lehner .15 .40
362 Jim O'Brien .12 .30
363 Claude Giroux .20 .50
364 Danny Briere .20 .50
365 Sean Couturier .20 .50
366 Kimmo Timonen .12 .30
367 Braydon Coburn .12 .30
368 Scott Hartnell .20 .50
369 Maxime Talbot .15 .40
370 Luke Schenn .12 .30
371 Wayne Simmonds .25 .60
372 Brayden Schenn .20 .50
373 Andrej Meszaros .12 .30
374 Jakub Voracek .20 .50
375 Ilya Bryzgalov .20 .50
376 Matt Read .12 .30
377 Nicklas Grossmann .12 .30
378 Steve Mason .15 .40
379 Ruslan Fedotenko .12 .30
380 Simon Gagne .20 .50
381 Shane Doan .15 .40
382 Keith Yandle .20 .50
383 Martin Hanzal .12 .30
384 Mike Smith .20 .50
385 Derek Morris .12 .30
386 Antoine Vermette .12 .30
387 Mikkel Boedker .12 .30
388 Radim Vrbata .15 .40
389 Zbynek Michalek .12 .30
390 Michael Stone .15 .40
391 Jason LaBarbera .15 .40
392 Boyd Gordon .12 .30
393 Oliver Ekman-Larsson .15 .40
394 Lauri Korpikoski .12 .30
395 Rostislav Klesla .12 .30
396 David Moss .12 .30
397 Paul Bissonnette .12 .30
398 Kyle Chipchura .12 .30
399 Sidney Crosby .75 2.00
400 Evgeni Malkin .60 1.50
401 Marc-Andre Fleury .30 .75
402 James Neal .20 .50
403 Kris Letang .20 .50
404 Pascal Dupuis .12 .30
405 Chris Kunitz .20 .50
406 Brooks Orpik .15 .40
407 Tyler Kennedy .12 .30
408 Jarome Iginla .20 .50
409 Tomas Vokoun .15 .40
410 Brandon Sutter .15 .40
411 Matt Niskanen .15 .40
412 Craig Adams .12 .30
413 Matt Cooke .12 .30
414 Brenden Morrow .15 .40
415 Tanner Glass .12 .30
416 Simon Despres .15 .40
417 Joe Thornton .20 .50
418 Patrick Marleau .20 .50
419 Logan Couture .20 .50
420 Joe Pavelski .20 .50
421 Dan Boyle .15 .40
422 Antti Niemi .15 .40
423 Brent Burns .25 .60
424 Scott Hannan .12 .30
425 James Sheppard .12 .30
426 Martin Havlat .15 .40
427 Marc-Edouard Vlasic .12 .30
428 Adam Burish .12 .30
429 Brad Stuart .12 .30
430 Tommy Wingels .12 .30
431 T.J. Galiardi .15 .40
432 Scott Gomez .15 .40
433 Jason Demers .12 .30
434 Justin Braun .12 .30
435 Andrew Desjardins .12 .30
436 Thomas Greiss .15 .40
437 David Backes .20 .50
438 Alex Pietrangelo .15 .40
439 T.J. Oshie .30 .75
440 Kevin Shattenkirk .20 .50
441 Jake Allen .25 .60
442 Jaroslav Halak .20 .50
443 Alexander Steen .20 .50
444 Barret Jackman .12 .30
445 David Perron .12 .30
446 Patrik Berglund .12 .30
447 Andy McDonald .15 .40
448 Roman Polak .12 .30
449 Chris Stewart .15 .40
450 Vladimir Sobotka .12 .30
451 Kris Russell .12 .30
452 Jaden Schwartz .25 .60
453 Ryan Reaves .12 .30
454 Ian Cole .12 .30
455 Jay Bouwmeester .20 .50
456 Steven Stamkos .40 1.00
457 Vincent Lecavalier .15 .40
458 Martin St. Louis .20 .50
459 Victor Hedman .25 .60
460 Ryan Malone .12 .30
461 Anders Lindback .12 .30
462 Ondrej Palat RC .60 1.50
463 Ben Bishop .20 .50
464 Teddy Purcell .20 .50
465 Sami Salo .12 .30
466 Tom Pyatt .12 .30
467 Nate Thompson .12 .30
468 Eric Brewer .12 .30
469 Benoit Pouliot .12 .30
470 Matthew Carle .15 .40
471 B.J. Crombeen .12 .30
472 Keith Aulie .12 .30
473 Dana Tyrell .12 .30
474 Mathieu Garon .15 .40
475 Dion Phaneuf .20 .50
476 Phil Kessel .25 .60
477 Joffrey Lupul .15 .40
478 James van Riemsdyk .20 .50
479 Tyler Bozak .15 .40
480 Clarke MacArthur .12 .30
481 Mikhail Grabovski .15 .40
482 Carl Gunnarsson .12 .30
483 Nikolai Kulemin .15 .40
484 Korbinian Holzer .12 .30
485 James Reimer .20 .50
486 Ben Scrivens .15 .40
487 John-Michael Liles .12 .30
488 Jay McClement .12 .30
489 Nazem Kadri .20 .50
490 Jake Gardiner .20 .50
491 Matt Frattin .15 .40
492 Cody Franson .12 .30
493 Colton Orr .12 .30
494 Henrik Sedin .20 .50
495 Daniel Sedin .20 .50
496 Ryan Kesler .20 .50
497 Alexandre Burrows .20 .50
498 Roberto Luongo .20 .50
499 Kevin Bieksa .15 .40
500 Cory Schneider .15 .40
501 Manny Malhotra .15 .40
502 Mason Raymond .15 .40
503 Dan Hamhuis .15 .40
504 Zack Kassian .15 .40
505 Keith Ballard .12 .30
506 Jannik Hansen .15 .40
507 Chris Higgins .12 .30
508 Alexander Edler .12 .30
509 Maxim Lapierre .12 .30
510 Jason Garrison .12 .30
511 David Booth .12 .30
512 Chris Tanev .15 .40
513 Derek Roy .15 .40
514 Alex Ovechkin .75 2.00
515 Mike Green .20 .50
516 Brooks Laich .12 .30
517 Nicklas Backstrom .30 .75
518 Marcus Johansson .15 .40
519 John Carlson .25 .60
520 Braden Holtby .30 .75
521 Mike Ribeiro .15 .40
522 Michal Neuvirth .15 .40
523 Karl Alzner .12 .30
524 Troy Brouwer .15 .40
525 Joel Ward .12 .30
526 Jason Chimera .12 .30
527 Jay Beagle .15 .40
528 Dmitry Orlov .20 .50
529 Eric Fehr .12 .30
530 Wojtek Wolski .12 .30
531 Tomas Kundratek .15 .40
532 Martin Erat .12 .30
533 Dustin Byfuglien .20 .50
534 Andrew Ladd .20 .50
535 Ondrej Pavelec .20 .50
536 Nik Antropov .15 .40
537 Evander Kane .20 .50
538 Zach Bogosian .15 .40
539 Blake Wheeler .20 .50
540 Mark Scheifele .25 .60
541 Bryan Little .20 .50
542 Olli Jokinen .15 .40
543 Alexander Burmistrov .15 .40
544 Tobias Enstrom .12 .30
545 Chris Thorburn .12 .30
546 Ron Hainsey .12 .30
547 Kyle Wellwood .15 .40
548 Al Montoya .12 .30
549 Jim Slater .12 .30
550 Mark Stuart .12 .30
551 Gtzlf/Prry/Prry/Fsth .30 .75
552 Rask/Mrchnd/Krjci/Lucic .25 .60
553 Vanek/Ott/Miller/Ennis .20 .50
554 Kprusff/Glncrss/Stmpnk/Jckmn .15 .40
555 Ward/Tlusty/Staal/Staal .25 .60
556 Toews/Kane/Bollig/Crwfrd .40 1.00
557 Varlamov/McLd/Prnteau/Duchne .20 .50
558 Letestu/Tyutin/Boll/Bbrvsky .20 .50
559 Lhtnen/Gligski/Roussel/Erikssn .20 .50
560 Dtsyk/Zttrbrg/Tootoo/Howard .25 .60
561 Dubnyk/Hall/Brown/Yakupov .30 .75
562 Flschmnn/Parros/Mrkstrm/Kpcky .15 .40
563 Quick/Crtr/Kopitar/Ellerby .30 .75
564 Parise/Suter/Knpka/Backstrom .20 .50
565 Price/Sbbn/Prust/Ryder .60 1.50
566 Weber/Clune/Rinne/Legwand .25 .60
567 Clarksn/Elias/Clarksn/Brodeur .40 1.00
568 Nabkv/Tavares/Mulsn/Martin .40 1.00
569 Lndqvst/Nash/Stepan/Clowe .25 .60
570 Turris/Gnchar/Neil/Andersn .20 .50
571 Voracek/Giroux/Rinaldo/Bryzglv .20 .50
572 Smith/Doan/Ekmn-Lrssn/Yandle .20 .50
573 Fleury/Kunitz/Crsby/Glass .75 2.00
574 Couture/Thrntn/Desjrdins/Niemi .20 .50
575 Stwrt/Reaves/Ellitt/Backes .20 .50
576 Bishp/Stamks/St. Louis/Crmbeen .40 1.00
577 Kessel/Orr/Reimer/Kessel .25 .60
578 Burrws/Sedin/Schneider/Sestito .20 .50
579 Hltby/Ovechkn/Backstrm/Hndrcks .75 2.00
580 Ladd/Kane/Pavelec/Wheeler .20 .50
581 Los Angeles Kings SH .10 .30
582 Chicago Blackhawks SH .10 .30
583 Patrick Marleau SH .20 .50
584 Vincent Lecavalier SH .15 .40
585 Milan Hejduk SH .15 .40
586 Marian Hossa SH .15 .40
587 Jaromir Jagr SH .50 1.25
588 Martin Brodeur SH .40 1.00
589 Sidney Crosby SH .75 2.00
590 Teemu Selanne SH .40 1.00
591 Alex Killorn HR RC .75 2.00
592 Sean Collins HR RC .60 1.50
593 Dave Dziurzynski HR RC .60 1.50
594 Derek Grant HR RC .60 1.50
595 Christian Thomas HR RC .60 1.50
596 Eddie Pasquale HR RC .50 1.25
597 Beau Bennett HR RC 1.00 2.50
598 Tyler Toffoli HR RC 1.50 4.00
599 Calvin Pickard HR RC .75 2.00
600 Michal Jordan HR RC .50 1.25
601 Darcy Kuemper HR RC .75 2.00
602 Anthony Peluso HR RC .50 1.25
603 Richard Panik HR RC .75 2.00
604 Nathan Beaulieu HR RC .60 1.50
605 Ryan Murphy HR RC .75 2.00
606 Mark Arcobello HR RC .75 2.00
607 Ryan Spooner HR RC .75 2.00
608 J.T. Miller HR RC .75 2.00
609 Charlie Coyle HR RC .75 2.00
610 Zach Redmond HR RC .60 1.50
611 Jonas Brodin HR RC .60 1.50
612 Jack Campbell HR RC .60 1.50
613 Jamie Tardif HR RC .50 1.25
614 Jamie Oleksiak HR RC .60 1.50
615 Sami Vatanen HR RC .75 2.00
616 Michael Sgarbossa HR RC .60 1.50
617 Antoine Roussel HR RC .75 2.00
618 Matt Irwin HR RC .60 1.50
619 Philipp Grubauer HR RC .75 2.00
620 Patrick Bordeleau HR RC .75 2.00
621 Cory Conacher HR RC .50 1.25
622 Rickard Rakell HR RC .75 2.00
623 Roman Cervenka HR RC .60 1.50
624 Brendan Gallagher HR RC 2.50 6.00
625 Viktor Fasth HR RC .75 2.00
626 Tye McGinn HR RC .75 2.00
627 Petr Mrazek HR RC 1.50 4.00
628 Michael Kostka HR RC .60 1.50
629 Jarred Tinordi HR RC .75 2.00
630 Filip Forsberg HR RC 2.00 5.00
631 Eric Gryba HR RC .60 1.50
632 Thomas Hickey HR RC .60 1.50
633 Drew Shore HR RC .60 1.50
634 Nick Petrecki HR RC .50 1.25
635 Brian Lashoff HR RC .60 1.50
636 Christopher Nilstorp HR RC .60 1.50
637 Jordan Schroeder HR RC .75 2.00
638 Leo Komarov HR RC .75 2.00
639 Emerson Etem HR RC .75 2.00
640 Stefan Matteau HR RC .60 1.50
641 Quinton Howden HR RC .60 1.50
642 Justin Schultz HR RC .75 2.00
643 Mikhail Grigorenko HR RC 1.00 2.50
644 Scott Laughton HR RC .75 2.00
645 Alex Galchenyuk HR RC 4.00 10.00
646 Dougie Hamilton HR RC 1.50 4.00
647 Vladimir Tarasenko HR RC 3.00 8.00
648 Jonathan Huberdeau HR RC 2.00 5.00
649 Mikael Granlund HR RC 1.25 3.00
650 Nail Yakupov HR RC 2.50 6.00
651 Jakob Silfverberg .40 1.00
652 Loui Eriksson .40 1.00
653 Matt Moulson .40 1.00
654 Jarome Iginla .50 1.25
655 Karri Ramo .40 1.00
656 Nathan Gerbe .30 .75
657 Kris Versteeg .40 1.00
658 Maxime Talbot .40 1.00
659 Tyler Seguin .75 2.00
660 Shawn Horcoff .30 .75
661 Daniel Alfredsson .50 1.25
662 Stephen Weiss .40 1.00
663 David Perron .30 .75
664 Ilya Bryzgalov .50 1.25
665 Tim Thomas .50 1.25
666 Jacob Markstrom .40 1.00
667 Ben Scrivens .40 1.00
668 Daniel Briere .50 1.25
669 Jaromir Jagr 1.25 3.00
670 Cory Schneider .40 1.00
671 Thomas Vanek .50 1.25
672 Mats Zuccarello .40 1.00
673 Bobby Ryan .50 1.25
674 Clarke MacArthur .30 .75
675 Steve Downie .30 .75
676 Vincent Lecavalier .40 1.00
677 Mike Ribeiro .40 1.00
678 Jussi Jokinen .30 .75
679 Derek Roy .40 1.00
680 Valtteri Filppula .50 1.25
681 Dave Bolland .30 .75
682 Jonathan Bernier .50 1.25
683 Mason Raymond .40 1.00
684 David Clarkson .30 .75
685 Mikhail Grabovski .40 1.00
686 Nathan MacKinnon HR RC 3.00 8.00
687 Aleksander Barkov HR RC 2.00 5.00
688 Seth Jones HR RC .75 2.00
689 Elias Lindholm HR RC 1.25 3.00
690 Sean Monahan HR RC 1.25 3.00
691 Valeri Nichushkin HR RC .75 2.00
692 Rasmus Ristolainen HR RC 1.25 3.00
693 Nikita Zadorov HR RC .75 2.00
694 Ryan Murray HR RC 1.25 3.00
695 Morgan Rielly HR RC 2.00 5.00
696 Hampus Lindholm HR RC 1.25 3.00
697 Matt Dumba HR RC .75 2.00
698 Jacob Trouba HR RC 1.25 3.00
699 Zemgus Girgensons HR RC 1.50 4.00
700 Tomas Hertl HR RC 1.00 2.50
701 Olli Maatta HR RC 1.25 3.00
702 Boone Jenner HR RC .75 2.00
703 Jon Merrill HR RC .75 2.00
704 Matt Nieto HR RC .60 1.50
705 Nikita Kucherov HR RC 2.00 5.00
706 Reto Berra HR RC .75 2.00
707 Joakim Nordstrom HR RC .60 1.50
708 Michael Bournival HR RC .75 2.00
709 Kevin Connauton HR RC .60 1.50
710 Xavier Ouellet HR RC .75 2.00
711 Magnus Hellberg HR RC .75 2.00
712 Marek Mazanec HR RC .75 2.00
713 Cody Ceci HR RC .60 1.50
714 Jesper Fast HR RC .60 1.50
715 Lucas Lessio HR RC .50 1.25
716 Ryan Strome HR RC 1.00 2.50
717 Josh Leivo HR RC .75 2.00
718 Nicklas Jensen HR RC .60 1.50
719 Brock Nelson HR RC .75 2.00
720 Austin Watson HR RC .60 1.50
721 Frederik Andersen HR RC 1.25 3.00
722 Igor Bobkov HR RC .60 1.50
723 Alex Chiasson HR RC .75 2.00
724 Drew LeBlanc HR RC .50 1.25
725 John Gibson HR RC 2.50 6.00
726 Johan Larsson HR RC .60 1.50
727 Max Reinhart HR RC .75 2.00
728 Mark Cundari HR RC .50 1.25
729 Danny DeKeyser HR RC 1.00 2.50
730 Tyler Pitlick HR RC .75 2.00
731 Nick Bjugstad HR RC 1.00 2.50
732 Tanner Pearson HR RC .75 2.00
733 Tom Wilson HR RC 1.25 3.00
734 Jared Staal HR RC .75 2.00
735 Chris Brown HR RC .50 1.25
736 Eric Hartzell HR RC .75 2.00
737 Taylor Beck HR RC .60 1.50
738 Anders Lee HR RC 1.25 3.00
739 Antti Raanta HR RC 1.00 2.50
740 Alex Petrovic HR RC .60 1.50
741 Mark Pysyk HR RC .75 2.00
742 Frank Corrado HR RC .50 1.25
743 Joonas Rask HR RC .50 1.25
744 Tomas Jurco HR RC 1.25 3.00
745 Radko Gudas HR RC .75 2.00
746 Jonathan Marchessault HR RC 1.50 4.00
747 Victor Bartley HR RC .60 1.50
748 Johan Gustafsson HR RC 1.00 2.50
749 Ben Street HR RC .50 1.25
750 Cameron Schilling HR RC .50 1.25

2013-14 Score Black
*VETS: 12X TO 30X BASIC CARDS
*ROOKIES: 8X TO 20X BASIC RC
*591-650 ROOKIES: 3X TO 8X BASIC RC
RANDOM INSERTS IN HOBBY JUMBO
97 Corey Crawford 8.00 20.00
517 Nicklas Backstrom 10.00 25.00

2013-14 Score Gold
'ETS: 1.2X TO 3X BASIC CARDS
OOKIE: 1X TO 2.5X BASIC RC
91-650 ROOKIE: .6X TO 1.5X BASIC RC
'ATED ODDS 2:1 HOB JUM, 1:1 RET
Corey Crawford .75 2.00
7 Nicklas Backstrom 1.00 2.50

2013-14 Score Red Back
-590 VETS: 15X TO 40X BASIC CARDS
-590 ROOKIES: 10X TO 25X BASIC RC
91-650 ROOKIES: 4X TO 10X BASIC RC
NDOM INSERTS IN HOBBY JUMBO
Corey Crawford 10.00 25.00
7 Nicklas Backstrom 12.00 30.00

2013-14 Score Red Border
-590 VETS: 2X TO 5X BASIC CARDS
-590 ROOKIE: 1.5X TO 4X BASIC RC
91-650 ROOKIE: 1.5X TO 4X BASIC RC
VO PER RACK PACK
Corey Crawford 1.25 3.00
7 Nicklas Backstrom 1.50 4.00

2013-14 Score Check It
NDOM INSERTS IN PACKS
Brenden Dillon 2.50 6.00
Leo Komarov 3.00 8.00
Mark Fraser 2.00 5.00
Zac Rinaldo 2.50 6.00
Dougie Hamilton 5.00 12.00
Alexei Emelin 2.50 6.00
Ed Jovanovski 2.00 5.00
Milan Lucic 3.00 8.00
Brian Boyle 2.00 5.00
Steve Ott 2.50 6.00
Luke Schenn 2.00 5.00
Evander Kane 3.00 8.00
Shane Doan 2.50 6.00
Zdeno Chara 3.00 8.00
Chris Kunitz 3.00 8.00
Zack Kassian 2.50 6.00
Colin Greening 2.00 5.00
Matt Martin 2.00 5.00
Anton Volchenkov 2.00 5.00
Alex Ovechkin 12.00 30.00
Rob Blake 3.00 8.00
Denis Potvin 3.00 8.00
Cam Neely 3.00 8.00
Eric Lindros 5.00 12.00
Derian Hatcher 2.00 5.00

2013-14 Score First Goal
Nail Yakupov 4.00 10.00
Mikael Granlund 1.50 4.00
Vladimir Tarasenko 2.50 6.00
Jonathan Huberdeau 2.50 6.00
Mikhail Grigorenko 1.25 3.00
Mika Zibanejad 1.25 3.00
Alex Galchenyuk 4.00 10.00
Damien Brunner .75 2.00
Alex Killorn 1.00 2.50
Justin Schultz 1.00 2.50
Dougie Hamilton 2.00 5.00
Jason Zucker .75 2.00
Stefan Matteau 1.00 2.50
J.T. Miller 1.00 2.50
Brandon Saad 1.25 3.00
Brendan Gallagher 2.50 6.00
Drew Shore .75 2.00
Tye McGinn 1.00 2.50
Leo Komarov 1.00 2.50
Jordan Schroeder 1.25 3.00

2013-14 Score Franchise
NDOM INSERTS IN PACKS
Ryan Getzlaf 2.00 5.00
Zdeno Chara 1.25 3.00
Thomas Vanek 1.25 3.00
Miikka Kiprusoff 1.00 2.50
Jeff Skinner 1.00 2.50
Patrick Kane 2.50 6.00
Gabriel Landeskog 1.00 2.50
Jack Johnson .75 2.00
Kari Lehtonen 1.00 2.50
Henrik Zetterberg 1.50 4.00
Taylor Hall 2.50 6.00
Ed Jovanovski .75 2.00
Dustin Brown 1.25 3.00
Zach Parise 1.25 3.00
Carey Price 4.00 10.00
Shea Weber 1.00 2.50
Martin Brodeur 2.50 6.00
John Tavares 2.50 6.00
Rick Nash 1.25 3.00
Erik Karlsson 2.50 6.00
Sean Couturier 1.25 3.00
Mike Smith 1.25 3.00
Evgeni Malkin 4.00 10.00
Patrick Marleau 1.25 3.00
Alex Pietrangelo 1.00 2.50
Steven Stamkos 2.50 6.00
Dion Phaneuf 1.25 3.00
Daniel Sedin 1.25 3.00
Alex Ovechkin 5.00 12.00
Evander Kane 1.25 3.00

013-14 Score Future Franchise
NDOM INSERTS IN PACKS
Nail Yakupov 5.00 12.00
Dougie Hamilton 3.00 8.00
Mikael Granlund 2.50 6.00
Jonathan Huberdeau 4.00 10.00
Vladimir Tarasenko 6.00 15.00
Alex Galchenyuk 8.00 20.00
Mikhail Grigorenko 2.00 5.00
Damien Brunner 1.25 3.00
Alex Killorn 1.50 4.00
Emerson Etem 1.50 4.00

2013-14 Score Hot Rookie Signatures
2 ANNC'D PRINT RUN 100 OR LESS
6-750 INSERTED IN 13-14 ANTHOLOGY
1 Alex Killorn 5.00 12.00
2 Sean Collins 4.00 10.00
3 Dave Dziurzynski 4.00 10.00
4 Derek Grant 4.00 10.00
5 Christian Thomas 4.00 10.00
6 Eddie Pasquale 3.00 8.00
7 Beau Bennett 8.00 20.00
8 Tyler Toffoli 6.00 15.00
9 Calvin Pickard 5.00 12.00
0 Michal Jordan 3.00 8.00
1 Darcy Kuemper 5.00 12.00
2 Anthony Peluso 3.00 8.00
3 Richard Panik 5.00 12.00
4 Nathan Beaulieu 4.00 10.00
5 Ryan Murphy SP 8.00 20.00
6 Mark Arcobello 5.00 12.00
7 Ryan Spooner 5.00 12.00
8 J.T. Miller SP 8.00 20.00
9 Charlie Coyle 5.00 12.00

610 Zach Redmond 4.00 10.00
611 Jonas Brodin SP 6.00 15.00
612 Jack Campbell SP 6.00 15.00
613 Jamie Tardif 3.00 8.00
614 Jamie Oleksiak 4.00 10.00
615 Sami Vatanen 5.00 12.00
616 Michael Sgarbossa 4.00 10.00
617 Antoine Roussel 5.00 12.00
618 Matt Irwin 4.00 10.00
619 Philipp Grubauer 5.00 12.00
620 Patrick Bordeleau 5.00 12.00
621 Cory Conacher 3.00 8.00
622 Rickard Rakell 5.00 12.00
623 Roman Cervenka 4.00 10.00
624 Brendan Gallagher SP 25.00 60.00
625 Viktor Fasth 5.00 12.00
626 Tye McGinn 5.00 12.00
627 Petr Mrazek 10.00 25.00
628 Michael Kostka 4.00 10.00
629 Jarred Tinordi 6.00 15.00
631 Eric Gryba 4.00 10.00
632 Thomas Hickey SP 6.00 15.00
633 Drew Shore 4.00 10.00
634 Nick Petrecki 3.00 8.00
635 Brian Lashoff 4.00 10.00
636 Christopher Nilstorp 4.00 10.00
637 Jordan Schroeder 5.00 12.00
638 Leo Komarov 5.00 12.00
639 Emerson Etem SP 10.00 25.00
640 Stefan Matteau SP 6.00 15.00
641 Quinton Howden 4.00 10.00
642 Justin Schultz SP 8.00 20.00
643 Mikhail Grigorenko SP 8.00 20.00
644 Scott Laughton 5.00 12.00
646 Dougie Hamilton SP 8.00 20.00
647 Vladimir Tarasenko SP 50.00 125.00
686 Nathan MacKinnon 50.00 125.00
687 Aleksander Barkov 12.00 30.00
688 Seth Jones 5.00 12.00
689 Elias Lindholm 8.00 20.00
690 Sean Monahan 8.00 20.00
691 Valeri Nichushkin 5.00 12.00
693 Nikita Zadorov 5.00 12.00
694 Ryan Murray 8.00 20.00
695 Morgan Rielly 12.00 30.00
696 Hampus Lindholm 8.00 20.00
697 Matt Dumba 5.00 12.00
698 Jacob Trouba 8.00 20.00
699 Zemgus Girgensons 10.00 25.00
700 Tomas Hertl 8.00 20.00
701 Olli Maatta 8.00 20.00
702 Boone Jenner 5.00 12.00
703 Jon Merrill 5.00 12.00
704 Matt Nieto 4.00 10.00
706 Reto Berra 5.00 12.00
708 Michael Bournival 5.00 12.00
709 Kevin Connauton 4.00 10.00
710 Xavier Ouellet 5.00 12.00
711 Magnus Hellberg 5.00 12.00
712 Marek Mazanec 5.00 12.00
713 Cody Ceci 4.00 10.00
714 Jesper Fast 4.00 10.00
715 Lucas Lessio 3.00 8.00
716 Ryan Strome 6.00 15.00
717 Josh Leivo 5.00 12.00
718 Nicklas Jensen 4.00 10.00
719 Brock Nelson 5.00 12.00
720 Austin Watson 4.00 10.00
721 Frederik Andersen 8.00 20.00
722 Igor Bobkov 4.00 10.00
723 Alex Chiasson 5.00 12.00
724 Drew LeBlanc 3.00 8.00
725 Carl Soderberg 5.00 12.00
726 Johan Larsson 4.00 10.00
727 Max Reinhart 5.00 12.00
728 Mark Cundari 3.00 8.00
729 Danny DeKeyser 6.00 15.00
730 Tyler Pitlick 5.00 12.00
731 Nick Bjugstad 6.00 15.00
732 Tanner Pearson 5.00 12.00
733 Tom Wilson 8.00 20.00
734 Jared Staal 5.00 12.00
735 Chris Brown 3.00 8.00
736 Eric Hartzell 5.00 12.00
737 Taylor Beck 4.00 10.00
738 Anders Lee 8.00 20.00
739 Antti Raanta 6.00 15.00
740 Alex Petrovic 4.00 10.00
741 Mark Pysyk 5.00 12.00
742 Frank Corrado 3.00 8.00
743 Joonas Rask 3.00 8.00
744 Tomas Jurco 8.00 20.00
745 Radko Gudas 5.00 12.00
746 Jonathan Marchessault 10.00 25.00
747 Victor Bartley 4.00 10.00
748 Johan Gustafsson 6.00 15.00
749 Ben Street 3.00 8.00
750 Cameron Schilling 3.00 8.00

2013-14 Score Net Cams
1 Anders Lindback .60 1.50
2 Devan Dubnyk 1.00 2.50
3 Henrik Lundqvist 1.25 3.00
4 Semyon Varlamov 1.00 2.50
5 Ondrej Pavelec 1.00 2.50
6 Corey Crawford 1.25 3.00
7 Tuukka Rask 1.00 2.50
8 James Reimer 1.00 2.50
9 Cory Schneider .75 2.00
10 Jonathan Quick 1.50 4.00
11 Michal Neuvirth .75 2.00
12 Carey Price 3.00 8.00
13 Ryan Miller 1.00 2.50
14 Craig Anderson 1.00 2.50
15 Ilya Bryzgalov 1.00 2.50
16 Niklas Backstrom .75 2.00
17 Pekka Rinne 1.25 3.00
18 Patrick Roy 2.50 6.00
19 Mike Richter 1.00 2.50
20 Martin Brodeur 2.00 5.00

2013-14 Score Signatures
RANDOM INSERTS IN PACKS
SSAA Aaron Ness 3.00 8.00
SSAM Andy Miele 3.00 8.00
SSAMC Andy McDonald 4.00 10.00
SSAN Anders Nilsson 4.00 10.00
SSBM Braydon McNabb 3.00 8.00
SSBS Ben Scrivens 4.00 10.00
SSCC Carter Camper 4.00 10.00
SSCCL Cal Clutterbuck 5.00 12.00
SSCDH Calvin de Haan 3.00 8.00
SSCG Claude Giroux 15.00 40.00
SSCS Chris Summers SP 4.00 10.00
SSCT Colten Teubert 3.00 8.00
SSCW Casey Wellman 3.00 8.00
SSDC Daniel Cleary 5.00 12.00
SSDO Dmitry Orlov 5.00 12.00
SSDS David Savard 3.00 8.00
SSDT Dana Tyrell SP 4.00 10.00
SSEL Eddie Lack 4.00 10.00
SSGB Gabriel Bourque 4.00 10.00
SSGN Gustav Nyquist 4.00 10.00
SSGP George Parros 4.00 10.00
SSHZ Harry Zolnierczyk 3.00 8.00
SSJA Jamie Arniel 4.00 10.00
SSJB Jonathan Bernier 5.00 12.00
SSJC Jordan Caron 12.00 30.00
SSJD Jeremy Duchesne 4.00 10.00
SSJF Justin Falk SP 4.00 10.00
SSJG Jonas Gustavsson 4.00 10.00
SSJH Jimmy Hayes 5.00 12.00
SSJI Jarome Iginla 6.00 15.00
SSJJ Jaromir Jagr 25.00 60.00
SSJM Jamie McBain 3.00 8.00
SSJS Jaden Schwartz 6.00 15.00
SSJZ Jason Zucker 4.00 10.00
SSKA Keith Aulie SP 4.00 10.00
SSLC Luca Caputi SP 4.00 10.00
SSLK Linus Klasen 3.00 8.00
SSMC John McCarthy 3.00 8.00
SSMD Matt Donovan 3.00 8.00
SSMF Marcus Foligno 3.00 8.00
SSMFT Matt Frattin 4.00 10.00
SSMO Mark Olver 3.00 8.00
SSMR Mason Raymond 4.00 10.00
SSMS Mikael Samuelsson SP 5.00 12.00
SSNK Nazem Kadri 5.00 12.00
SSNKU Nikolai Kulemin 4.00 10.00
SSNP Nick Palmieri 5.00 12.00
SSPK Patrick Kane 20.00 50.00
SSPL Pascal Leclaire SP 5.00 12.00
SSPR Peter Regin SP 5.00 12.00
SSRB Robert Bortuzzo 3.00 8.00
SSRC Ryane Clowe 3.00 8.00
SSRH Roman Horak 4.00 10.00
SSRJ Ryan Johansen 4.00 10.00
SSRS Reilly Smith 5.00 12.00
SSRSM Ryan Smyth 4.00 10.00
SSSC Sean Couturier 5.00 12.00
SSSE Stefan Elliott 4.00 10.00
SSSG Stephen Gionta 3.00 8.00
SSSGO Scott Gomez 4.00 10.00
SSSGR Stu Grimson 5.00 12.00
SSSV Semyon Varlamov 8.00 20.00
SSTB Tyson Barrie 5.00 12.00
SSTE Tim Erixon 3.00 8.00
SSTH Travis Hamonic 3.00 8.00
SSTK Tomas Kubalik 5.00 12.00
SSTM Travis Morin 3.00 8.00
SSTR Torey Krug 10.00 25.00
SSTS Tyler Seguin 12.00 30.00
SSTSE Tyson Sexsmith 3.00 8.00
SSTT Tim Thomas 8.00 20.00
SSVS Viktor Stalberg 3.00 8.00
SSYS Yann Sauve 3.00 8.00
SSZH Zach Hamill SP 5.00 12.00

2013-14 Score Team Future
RANDOM INSERTS IN PACKS
1 Nail Yakupov 5.00 12.00
2 Chris Kreider 1.50 4.00
3 Alex Galchenyuk 5.00 12.00
4 Emerson Etem 1.50 4.00
5 Dougie Hamilton 2.00 5.00
6 Justin Schultz 1.00 2.50
7 Jack Campbell 1.25 3.00
8 Ryan Murphy 1.50 4.00
9 Jaden Schwartz 2.00 5.00
10 Quinton Howden 1.25 3.00
11 Scott Laughton 1.50 4.00
12 Tyler Toffoli 3.00 8.00
13 Jamie Oleksiak 1.25 3.00
14 Charlie Coyle 1.50 4.00
15 Beau Bennett 2.00 5.00

2013-14 Score Team Score
RANDOM INSERTS IN PACKS
1 Sidney Crosby 5.00 12.00
2 Jonathan Toews 2.50 6.00
3 Rick Nash 1.25 3.00
4 Claude Giroux 1.25 3.00
5 Alex Ovechkin 5.00 12.00
6 Henrik Zetterberg 1.50 4.00
7 Alex Pietrangelo 1.00 2.50
8 Erik Karlsson 2.50 6.00
9 Martin Brodeur 2.50 6.00
10 Jonathan Quick 2.00 5.00

2013-14 Score Team 8s Jerseys
ONE PER HOBBY JUMBO
ALB Flames/Oilers SP 15.00 40.00
ANA Anaheim Ducks 10.00 25.00
ATL Atlantic Division 12.00 30.00
ATL2 Atlantic Division 15.00 40.00
AVS Colorado Avalanche 10.00 25.00
BLU St. Louis Blues 10.00 25.00
BOMO Bruins/Canadiens 15.00 40.00
BOS Boston Bruins 12.00 30.00
CAL Calgary Flames 10.00 25.00
CAP Washington Capitals 10.00 25.00
CEN Central Division 15.00 40.00
CHI Chicago Blackhawks SP 15.00 40.00
DAL Dallas Stars 10.00 25.00
DAMI Stars/Wild 12.00 30.00
DET Detroit Red Wings SP 15.00 40.00
DEV New Jersey Devils SP 15.00 40.00
FLA Panthers/Lightning SP 12.00 30.00
FLY Philadelphia Flyers 15.00 40.00
FRW Ducks/Kings 12.00 30.00
HAB Montreal Canadiens 20.00 50.00
JET Winnipeg Jets SP 15.00 40.00
KNG Los Angeles Kings 10.00 25.00
LAK Los Angeles Kings SP 15.00 40.00
MIN Minnesota Wild 10.00 25.00
NAS Nashville Predators SP 15.00 40.00
NE Northeast Division 15.00 40.00
NJNY Devils/Rangers 12.00 30.00
NYI New York Islanders 10.00 25.00
NYR New York Rangers 10.00 25.00
OIL Edmonton Oilers 15.00 40.00
PA Flyers/Penguins 15.00 40.00
PAC Pacific Division 12.00 30.00
PICA Penguins/Capitals SP 15.00 40.00
PIT Pittsburgh Penguins SP 40.00 100.00
RAG New York Rangers 15.00 40.00
RK Rookies/Yak/Galch 20.00 50.00
RK2 Rookies/Laugh/Spoon 15.00 40.00
RVL Leafs/Canadiens SP 20.00 50.00
SAB Buffalo Sabres SP 15.00 40.00
SEN Ottawa Senators 10.00 25.00
SJS San Jose Sharks SP 15.00 40.00
SJVA Sharks/Canucks 12.00 30.00
STL St. Louis Blues 12.00 30.00
STNA Blues/Predators SP 12.00 30.00
STP Blues/Coyotes 12.00 30.00
TBL Tampa Bay Lightning SP 12.00 30.00
TOR Toronto Maple Leafs 15.00 40.00
VAN Vancouver Canucks SP

2013-14 Score Stadium Series
HL Henrik Lundqvist
MB Martin Brodeur
RN Rick Nash
SC Sidney Crosby
TS Teemu Selanne
JT1 John Tavares
JT2 Jonathan Toews

2013-14 Score NHL Draft
COMPLETE SET (6) 5.00 10.00
1 Sidney Crosby 2.50 6.00
2 John Tavares 1.25 3.00
3 Henrik Lundqvist .75 2.00
4 Tyler Seguin 1.00 2.50
5 Alex Ovechkin 2.50 6.00
6 Eric Lindros 1.00 2.50

1967-68 Seals Team Issue
Produced as a first year team issue of the expansion Oakland Seals, this 19-piece set features 8x10 individual player cards on thin cardboard stock. They are not numbered and are listed below in alphabetical order.
1 Bobby Baun 10.00 20.00
2 Ron Boehm 2.00 4.00
3 Wally Boyer 3.00 6.00
4 Charlie Burns 4.00 8.00
5 Larry Cahan 2.00 4.00
6 Alain Caron 2.00 4.00
7 Terry Clancy 2.00 4.00
8 Kent Douglas 4.00 8.00
9 Gerry Ehman 3.00 6.00
10 Autry Erickson 3.00 6.00
11 Billy Harris 3.00 6.00
12 Ron Harris 3.00 6.00
13 Bill Hicke 3.00 6.00
14 Charlie Hodge 7.50 15.00
15 Mike Laughton 2.00 4.00
16 Bob Lemieux 2.00 4.00
17 Gary Smith 6.00 12.00
18 George Swarbrick 3.00 6.00
19 Joe Szura 3.00 6.00

1992-93 Seasons Patches
Each measuring approximately 3 1/8" by 4 1/4", these 70 patches were licensed by the NHL/NHLPA and feature color action player photos on black fabric. The player's team appears above the photo and his name, position, and sweater number are below. An embroidered border in the team color edges the patch. The patches come in a poly-wrap sleeve attached to a teal cardboard rack display. These displays were pegged on team customized counter display easels, showcasing four different players (six patches per player), for a total of 24 patches per team display. Two versions are available. The bilingual version has both French and English printed on the package. The other version is printed in English only. A checklist of 71 patches is printed on the back of the display. In the checklist, patch 22, an unnamed prototype, features ex-NHL star and Seasons President Grant Mulvey. Mulvey's patch was only available through him as a handout and could not be purchased by the public; it is not considered part of the complete set.
COMPLETE SET (70) 60.00 150.00
1 Jeremy Roenick 1.25 3.00
2 Steve Larmer 1.00 2.50
3 Ed Belfour 1.25 3.00
4 Chris Chelios 1.25 3.00
5 Sergei Fedorov 1.25 3.00
6 Steve Yzerman 2.00 5.00
7 Tim Cheveldae .40 1.00
8 Bob Probert 1.00 2.50
9 Wayne Gretzky 4.00 10.00
10 Luc Robitaille 1.00 2.50
11 Tony Granato .40 1.00
12 Kelly Hrudey 1.00 2.50
13 Brett Hull 1.25 3.00
14 Curtis Joseph 1.25 3.00
15 Brendan Shanahan 1.25 3.00
16 Nelson Emerson .40 1.00
17 Ray Bourque 1.25 3.00
18 Joe Juneau 1.00 2.50
19 Andy Moog 1.00 2.50
20 Adam Oates 1.00 2.50
21 Patrick Roy 3.00 8.00
22 Grant Mulvey PROMO 8.00 20.00
23 Denis Savard 1.00 2.50
24 Gilbert Dionne .40 1.00
25 Kirk Muller 1.00 2.50
26 Mark Messier 1.25 3.00
27 Tony Amonte 1.00 2.50
28 Brian Leetch 1.25 3.00
29 Mike Richter 1.25 3.00
30 Trevor Linden 1.00 2.50
31 Pavel Bure 1.25 3.00
32 Cliff Ronning .40 1.00
33 Russ Courtnall .40 1.00
34 Mario Lemieux 3.00 8.00
35 Jaromir Jagr 2.00 5.00
36 Tom Barrasso 1.00 2.50
37 Rick Tocchet 1.00 2.50
38 Eric Lindros 2.00 5.00
39 Rod Brind'Amour 1.00 2.50
40 Dominic Roussel .40 1.00
41 Mark Recchi 1.00 2.50
42 Pat LaFontaine 1.00 2.50
43 Donald Audette .40 1.00
44 Pat Verbeek 1.00 2.50
45 John Cullen .40 1.00
46 Owen Nolan 1.00 2.50
47 Joe Sakic 1.25 3.00
Quebec Nordiq
48 Kevin Hatcher .40 1.00
49 Don Beaupre .40 1.00
50 Scott Stevens 1.00 2.50
51 Chris Terreri .40 1.00
52 Scott Lachance .40 1.00
53 Pierre Turgeon 1.00 2.50
54 Grant Fuhr 1.00 2.50
55 Doug Gilmour 1.25 3.00
56 Dave Manson .40 1.00
57 Bill Ranford 1.00 2.50
58 Troy Murray .40 1.00
59 Phil Housley .40 1.00
60 Al MacInnis 1.00 2.50
61 Mike Vernon 1.00 2.50
62 Pat Falloon .40 1.00
63 Doug Wilson 1.00 2.50
64 Jon Casey .40 1.00
65 Mike Modano 1.25 3.00
66 Kevin Stevens .40 1.00
67 Al Iafrate .40 1.00
68 Dale Hawerchuk 1.00 2.50
69 Igor Kravchuk .40 1.00
70 Wendel Clark 1.00 2.50
71 Kirk McLean 1.00 2.50

1993-94 Seasons Patches
Each measuring approximately 3 1/8" by 4 1/4", these 20 patches were licensed by the NHL/NHLPA and feature color action player photos on black fabric. The player's team appears above the photo and his name, position, and jersey number are below. An embroidered border in the team color edges the patch. The team logo and year of issue in the lower right corner round out the front. The patches were encased in a hard plastic sleeve attached to a black cardboard rack display. A checklist was printed on the back of the display. The patches are unnumbered but are checklisted below according to the numbering of the checklist card.
COMPLETE SET (20) 24.00 60.00
1 Ed Belfour .60 1.50
2 Pavel Bure 1.25 3.00
3 Paul Coffey .60 1.50
4 Doug Gilmour .60 1.50
5 Wayne Gretzky 4.00 10.00
6 Brett Hull .75 2.00
7 Jaromir Jagr 2.00 5.00
8 Joe Juneau .40 1.00
9 Mario Lemieux 3.00 8.00
10 Eric Lindros 2.00 5.00
11 Shawn McEachern .40 1.00
12 Alexander Mogilny .50 1.25
13 Adam Oates .50 1.25
14 Felix Potvin 1.50 4.00
15 Jeremy Roenick .60 1.50
16 Patrick Roy 3.00 8.00
17 Joe Sakic 1.25 3.00
18 Teemu Selanne 1.25 3.00
19 Kevin Stevens .40 1.00
20 Steve Yzerman 2.00 5.00

1994-95 Select Promos
These nine standard-size cards were issued to herald the release of the 1994-95 Select hockey series. The fronts feature borderless color action player photos. The player's last name and position, the team logo and a small, sepia-toned player portrait appear on gold-foil background in the lower left corner. The backs carry another color action player photo with player biography, profile and stats next to it. The top right corner of these cards has been cut off to mark them as sample cards. The Jamie Storr YE1 card is a sample of the Youth Explosion insert set.
COMPLETE SEALED SET (9) .40 1.00
7 John Vanbiesbrouck .05 .15
Flor
90 Felix Potvin .05 .15
Toronto Ma
108 Stephane Richer .01 .05
New Jer
118 Dino Ciccarelli .01 .05
Detroit
128 Sylvain Cote .01 .05
Washington
142 Kevin Dineen .01 .05
Philadelph
194 Mattias Norstrom .01 .05
New Yo
YE1 Jamie Storr .40 1.00
Los Angeles
NNO Title Card .02 .10

1994-95 Select
This 200-card set had an announced print run of 3,950, 24-box hobby-only cases. The design resembled a modernized version of the 1984-85 OPC set with a main action shot complemented by a corner head shot. The set is notable for the inclusion of 20 cards of players who competed in the 1994 Mexico Cup for 17-year-olds. One 4" by 6" bonus Mike Modano card featuring Sportflics technology was included in every box.
1 Mark Messier .10 .25
2 Rick Tocchet .07 .20
3 Alexandre Daigle .05 .15
4 Owen Nolan .10 .25
5 Bill Ranford .07 .20
6 Dave Gagner .07 .20
7 John Vanbiesbrouck .07 .20
8 Sergei Makarov .05 .15
9 Derek King .05 .15
10 Sergei Fedorov .15 .40
11 Trevor Linden .07 .20
12 Don Beaupre .07 .20
13 Dave Manson .05 .15
14 Sergei Zubov .05 .15
15 Keith Primeau .10 .25
16 Joe Mullen .07 .20
17 Bernie Nicholls .07 .20
18 Ray Bourque .15 .40
19 Mike Ridley .05 .15
20 Wendel Clark .07 .20
21 Mats Sundin .07 .20
22 Alexander Mogilny .07 .20
23 Mathieu Schneider .05 .15
24 Brian Leetch .10 .25
25 Rob Niedermayer .07 .20
26 Donald Audette .05 .15
27 Doug Weight .07 .20
28 Al MacInnis .07 .20
29 Jeremy Roenick .20 .50
30 Mark Recchi .12 .30
31 Chris Chelios .10 .25
32 Luc Robitaille .10 .25
33 Dale Hunter .05 .15
34 Kelly Hrudey .07 .20
35 Steve Yzerman .25 .60
36 Martin Straka .05 .15
37 Arturs Irbe .07 .20
38 Mike Modano .15 .40
39 Cam Neely .10 .25
40 Igor Larionov .05 .15
41 Ray Ferraro .05 .15
42 Dale Hawerchuk .12 .30
43 Brian Bradley .05 .15
44 Joe Murphy .05 .15
45 Daren Puppa .07 .20
46 Pierre Turgeon .07 .20
47 Shayne Corson .05 .15
48 Adam Graves .05 .15
49 Craig Billington .07 .20
50 Derian Hatcher .05 .15
51 Alexei Zhamnov .07 .20
52 Dominik Hasek .20 .50
53 Ed Belfour .10 .25
54 Mike Vernon .07 .20
55 Bob Kudelski .05 .15
56 Ray Sheppard .07 .20
57 Pat LaFontaine .10 .25
58 Adam Oates .10 .25
59 Vincent Damphousse .07 .20
60 Jaromir Jagr .25 .60
61 Mikael Renberg .07 .20
62 Joe Sakic .20 .50
63 Sandis Ozolinsh .05 .15
64 Kirk McLean .07 .20
65 Stephan Lebeau .05 .15
66 Alexei Kovalev .05 .15
67 Ron Hextall .07 .20
68 Geoff Sanderson .07 .20
69 Doug Gilmour .12 .30
70 Russ Courtnall .05 .15
71 Jari Kurri .07 .20
72 Paul Coffey .10 .25
73 Claude Lemieux .10 .25
74 Teemu Selanne .20 .50
75 Keith Tkachuk .10 .25
76 Pat Verbeek .07 .20
77 Chris Gratton .05 .15
78 Martin Brodeur .25 .60
79 Guy Hebert .07 .20
80 Al Iafrate .05 .15
81 Glen Wesley .05 .15
82 Scott Stevens .10 .25
83 Wayne Gretzky .50 1.25
84 Ron Francis .12 .30
85 Scott Mellanby .07 .20
86 Joe Juneau .07 .20
87 Jason Arnott .07 .20
88 Tom Barrasso .07 .20
89 Peter Bondra .07 .20
90 Felix Potvin .10 .25
91 Brian Bellows .07 .20
92 Pavel Bure .10 .25
93 Grant Fuhr .10 .25
94 Andy Moog .10 .25
95 Mike Gartner .10 .25
96 Patrick Roy .25 .60
97 Brett Hull .20 .50
98 Rob Blake .10 .25
99 Dave Andreychuk .10 .25
100 Eric Lindros .10 .25
101 Scott Niedermayer .10 .25
102 Tim Cheveldae .07 .20
103 Slava Kozlov .07 .20
104 Dimitri Khristich .05 .15
105 Steve Thomas .05 .15
106 Kevin Stevens .05 .15
107 Kirk Muller .05 .15
108 Stephane Richer .07 .20
109 Theo Fleury .10 .25
110 Jeff Brown .05 .15
111 Chris Pronger .10 .25
112 Steve Larmer .07 .20
113 Eric Desjardins .07 .20
114 Mike Ricci .05 .15
115 Tony Amonte .07 .20
116 Pat Falloon .05 .15
117 Garry Galley .05 .15
118 Dino Ciccarelli .07 .20
119 Rod Brind'Amour .07 .20
120 Petr Nedved .07 .20
121 Curtis Joseph .15 .40
122 Cliff Ronning .05 .15
123 Ulf Dahlen .05 .15
124 Marty McSorley .05 .15
125 Nelson Emerson .05 .15
126 Brian Skrudland .05 .15
127 Sean Burke .07 .20
128 Sylvain Cote .05 .15
129 Brendan Shanahan .12 .30
130 Benoit Hogue .05 .15
131 Joe Nieuwendyk .10 .25
132 Bryan Smolinski .05 .15
133 Mike Richter .10 .25
134 Nicklas Lidstrom .10 .25
135 Alexei Yashin .10 .25
136 John MacLean .07 .20
137 Geoff Courtnall .05 .15
138 Robert Reichel .05 .15
139 Craig Janney .07 .20
140 Zarley Zalapski .05 .15
141 Andrew Cassels .05 .15
142 Kevin Dineen .05 .15
143 Larry Murphy .07 .20
144 Valeri Kamensky .07 .20
145 Steve Duchesne .05 .15
146 Phil Housley .07 .20
147 Gary Roberts .05 .15
148 Kevin Hatcher .05 .15
149 Bryan Berard RC .15 .40
150 Marty Reasoner RC .10 .25
151 Andrew Berenzweig RC .10 .25
152 Erik Rasmussen RC .10 .25
153 Luke Curtin RC .10 .25
154 Dan Lacouture RC .10 .25
155 Brian Boucher RC .10 .25
156 Wyatt Smith RC .10 .25
157 Maxim Kuznetsov RC .10 .25
158 Alexei Morozov RC .10 .25
159 Dmitri Nabokov RC .10 .25
160 Wade Redden RC .15 .40
161 Jason Doig RC .10 .25
162 Alyn McCauley RC .10 .25
163 Jeff Ware RC .10 .25
164 Brad Larsen RC .10 .25
165 Jarome Iginla RC 3.00 8.00
166 Christian Dube RC .10 .25
167 Mike McBain RC .10 .25
168 Todd Norman RC .10 .25
169 Oleg Tverdovsky .07 .20
170 Jamie Storr .07 .20
171 Jason Wiemer RC .05 .15
172 Kenny Jonsson .05 .15
173 Paul Kariya .12 .30
174 Viktor Kozlov .05 .15
175 Peter Forsberg .25 .60
176 Jeff Friesen .05 .15
177 Brian Rolston .05 .15
178 Brett Lindros .05 .15
179 Adam Deadmarsh .05 .15
180 Aaron Gavey .05 .15
181 Janne Laukkanen .07 .20
182 Todd Harvey .05 .15
183 Valeri Karpov RC .05 .15
184 Andrei Nikolishin .05 .15
185 Pavol Demitra .12 .30
186 Radek Bonk RC .05 .15
187 Valeri Bure .05 .15
188 Eric Fichaud RC .10 .25
189 Jamie McLennan .07 .20
190 Mariusz Czerkawski RC .10 .25
191 John Lilley .05 .15
192 Brian Savage .05 .15
193 Jason Allison .07 .20
194 Mattias Norstrom .05 .15
195 Todd Simon RC .05 .15
196 Zigmund Palffy .07 .20
197 Rene Corbet .05 .15
198 Mike Peca .07 .20
199 Checklist (1-100) .05 .15
200 Checklist (101-198) .05 .15
NNO Mike Modano Large .15 .40

1994-95 Select Gold
This 200-card set is a parallel version of the regular Select issue. These cards feature a gold foil printing process on the front, as well as a Certified Gold logo printed on the back. These were inserted at a rate of 1:3 packs.
COMPLETE SET (200) 25.00 60.00
*VETS: 1X TO 2.5X BASIC CARDS
*ROOKIES: .75X TO 2X BASIC CARDS

1994-95 Select First Line
The 12 cards in this set utilize the Dufex printing technology and were inserted at a rate of 1:48 packs. The player's name, team affiliation and "1st Line" logo appear along the left card front. Cards are numbered with an "FL" prefix.
COMPLETE SET (12) 15.00 30.00
FL1 Patrick Roy 5.00 12.00
FL2 Ray Bourque 1.50 4.00
FL3 Brian Leetch .75 2.00
FL4 Brendan Shanahan .75 2.00
FL5 Eric Lindros .75 2.00
FL6 Pavel Bure .75 2.00
FL7 Mike Richter .75 2.00
FL8 Scott Stevens .50 1.25
FL9 Chris Chelios .75 2.00
FL10 Luc Robitaille .50 1.25
FL11 Wayne Gretzky 6.00 15.00
FL12 Brett Hull 1.25 3.00

1994-95 Select Youth Explosion
The 12 cards in this set were randomly inserted in Select product at the rate of 1:24 packs. The striking design benefits from the use of a special holographic silver foil printing. The borders are blue and silver with player name and position above the set title located near the bottom. The cards are numbered with a "YE" prefix.
COMPLETE SET (12) 8.00 15.00
YE1 Jamie Storr .50 1.25
YE2 Oleg Tverdovsky .50 1.25
YE3 Janne Laukkanen .20 .50
YE4 Kenny Jonsson .20 .50
YE5 Paul Kariya .50 1.25
YE6 Viktor Kozlov .50 1.25
YE7 Peter Forsberg 2.50 6.00
YE8 Jason Allison .60 1.50
YE9 Jeff Friesen .20 .50
YE10 Brian Rolston .50 1.25
YE11 Mariusz Czerkawski .60 1.50
YE12 Brett Lindros .30 .75

1995-96 Select Certified Promos
These cards are samples of the 1995-96 Select Certified series. Their description is the same as the regular series with the exception of the word "Sample" printed on the back of each one. The cards are listed below according to their number in their regular series. The Pavel Bure card is from the Gold Team insert series. It is identical to the expensive insert save for the word "sample" written on the card back.
COMPLETE SET (9) 12.00 30.00
5 Pavel Bure 6.00 15.00
12 Jim Carey .60 1.50
13 Paul Kariya 4.00 10.00
17 Mike Modano 1.25 3.00
19 Owen Nolan .75 2.00
43 Alexander Mogilny .75 2.00
68 Peter Forsberg 3.00 8.00
69 Felix Potvin .75 2.00
NNO Title Card .08 .25

1995-96 Select Certified
The 1995-96 Select Certified set was issued in one series totaling 144 cards. The 6-card packs retailed for $4.99. The cards featured a smart, silver mirror finish, which was protected from routine scratching by a "Pinnacle Peel", which collectors could remove if they so wished. Although collectors are free to do so, cards without the foil may be slightly harder to resell, although they will be more sightly. The card stock was 24-point, double that of a normal card. Rookie Cards in this set include Daniel Alfredsson and Petr Sykora.
1 Mario Lemieux .50 1.25
2 Chris Chelios .15 .40
3 Scott Mellanby .12 .30
4 Brett Hull .20 .50
5 Theo Fleury .20 .50
6 Alexei Zhamnov .15 .40
7 Mats Sundin .15 .40
8 Mathieu Schneider .10 .25
9 Jason Arnott .12 .30
10 Mark Recchi .20 .50
11 Adam Oates .15 .40
12 Jim Carey .12 .30
13 Paul Kariya .20 .50
14 Mark Messier .25 .60
15 Eric Lindros .25 .60
16 Pavel Bure .20 .50
17 Mike Modano .25 .60
18 Pat LaFontaine .15 .40
19 Owen Nolan .15 .40
20 Roman Hamrlik .10 .25
21 Paul Coffey .15 .40
22 Alexandre Daigle .10 .25
23 Wayne Gretzky .75 2.00
24 Martin Brodeur .40 1.00
25 Ulf Dahlen .10 .25
26 Geoff Sanderson .10 .25
27 Brian Leetch .15 .40
28 Dave Andreychuk .15 .40
29 Sergei Fedorov .25 .60
30 Jocelyn Thibault .12 .30
31 Mikael Renberg .12 .30
32 Joe Nieuwendyk .15 .40
33 Craig Janney .10 .25
34 Ray Bourque .25 .60
35 Jari Kurri .15 .40
36 Alexei Yashin .12 .30
37 Keith Tkachuk .15 .40
38 Jaromir Jagr .40 1.00
39 Stephane Richer .12 .30
40 Trevor Kidd .12 .30
41 Kevin Hatcher .12 .30
42 Mike Vernon .12 .30
43 Alexander Mogilny .12 .30
44 John LeClair .15 .40
45 Joe Sakic .25 .60
46 Kevin Stevens .12 .30
47 Adam Graves .12 .30
48 Doug Gilmour .20 .50
49 Pierre Turgeon .15 .40
50 Joe Murphy .10 .25
51 Peter Bondra .15 .40
52 Ron Francis .20 .50
53 Luc Robitaille .15 .40
54 Mike Gartner .15 .40
55 Bill Ranford .12 .30

56 Jeff Friesen .10 .25
57 Cam Neely .15 .40
58 Daren Puppa .12 .30
59 Rod Brind'Amour .15 .40
60 Jeremy Roenick .20 .50
61 Brett Lindros .10 .25
62 Todd Harvey .10 .25
63 Kirk McLean .12 .30
64 Brendan Shanahan .20 .50
65 Kelly Hrudey .12 .30
66 Scott Stevens .15 .40
67 Sergei Zubov .12 .30
68 Peter Forsberg .40 1.00
69 Felix Potvin .15 .40
70 Scott Niedermayer .15 .40
71 Keith Primeau .10 .25
72 Al MacInnis .15 .40
73 Mike Richter .15 .40
74 Rob Blake .12 .30
75 Vincent Damphousse .12 .30
76 Teemu Selanne .30 .75
77 Andy Moog .15 .40
78 Ron Hextall .15 .40
79 Oleg Tverdovsky .15 .40
80 Joe Juneau .12 .30
81 Patrick Roy .40 1.00
82 Wendel Clark .15 .40
83 Brian Bradley .12 .30
84 Curtis Joseph .15 .40
85 John Vanbiesbrouck .12 .30
86 Phil Housley .12 .30
87 Trevor Linden .15 .40
88 Alexei Kovalev .10 .25
89 Dominik Hasek .20 .50
90 Larry Murphy .15 .40
91 Arturs Irbe .12 .30
92 John MacLean .12 .30
93 Ed Belfour .12 .30
94 Steve Yzerman .20 .50
95 Tom Barrasso .12 .30
96 Rob Niedermayer .12 .30
97 Dale Hawerchuk .20 .50
98 Rick Tocchet .12 .30
99 Claude Lemieux .15 .40
100 Sean Burke .10 .25
101 Shayne Corson .10 .25
102 Dino Ciccarelli .12 .30
103 Kirk Muller .12 .30
104 Don Beaupre .12 .30
105 Valeri Kamensky .12 .30
106 Markus Naslund .15 .40
107 Tomas Sandstrom .12 .30
108 Pat Verbeek .12 .30
109 Doug Weight .15 .40
110 Brian Holzinger RC .30 .75
111 Antti Tormanen .10 .25
112 Tommy Salo RC .25 .60
113 Jason Bonsignore .10 .25
114 Shane Doan RC .50 1.25
115 Robert Svehla RC .10 .25
116 Chad Kilger RC .15 .40
117 Saku Koivu .15 .40
118 Jeff O'Neill .15 .40
119 Brendan Witt .15 .40
120 Byron Dafoe .12 .30
121 Ryan Smyth .12 .30
122 Daniel Alfredsson RC .75 2.00
123 Todd Bertuzzi RC .20 .50
124 Daymond Langkow RC .15 .40
125 Miroslav Satan RC .20 .50
126 Bryan McCabe .15 .40
127 Aki Berg RC .15 .40
128 Cory Stillman .10 .25
129 Deron Quint .12 .30
130 Vitali Yachmenev .15 .40
131 Valeri Bure .10 .25
132 Eric Daze .30 .75
133 Radek Dvorak RC .20 .50
134 Landon Wilson RC .10 .25
135 Niklas Sundstrom .15 .40
136 Jamie Storr .12 .30
137 Ed Jovanovski .15 .40
138 Marcus Ragnarsson RC .20 .50
139 Kyle McLaren RC .10 .25
140 Sandy Moger .10 .25
141 Marty Murray .15 .40
142 Darby Hendrickson .10 .25
143 Corey Hirsch .12 .30
144 Petr Sykora RC .40 1.00

1995-96 Select Certified Mirror Gold

The cards from this high-end parallel set of the base Select Certified issue were randomly inserted 1:5 packs. Instead of the typical silver finish, these, as the title suggests, had a golden background.
*VETS: 2X TO 5X BASIC CARDS
*ROOKIES: .8X TO 2X

1995-96 Select Certified Double Strike

Randomly inserted in packs at a rate of 1:32, this 20-card set shines the spotlight on players whose abilities make them an imposing threat both offensively and defensively. The cards feature a rainbow silver foil background on the front, while the backs contain a note stating that no more than 1,975 complete sets were produced. There also was a Gold version of this set, with singles issued in black packs as inserts in roughly every 3.5 boxes. The fronts are essentially the same, save for the use of a gold foil background. The backs contain a small box reading "Case Chase" and "No more than 903 sets produced."
COMPLETE SET (20) 15.00 40.00
*GOLD: 1X TO 2.5X BASIC INSERTS
1 Doug Gilmour .75 2.00
2 Ron Francis .75 2.00
3 Ray Bourque 1.50 4.00
4 Chris Chelios 1.25 3.00
5 Adam Oates .75 2.00
6 Mike Ricci .75 2.00
7 Jeremy Roenick 1.25 3.00
8 Jason Arnott .75 2.00
9 Brendan Shanahan 1.25 3.00
10 Joe Nieuwendyk .75 2.00
11 Trevor Linden .75 2.00
12 Mikael Renberg .75 2.00
13 Theo Fleury .75 2.00
14 Sergei Fedorov 1.50 4.00
15 Mark Messier 1.50 4.00
16 Keith Primeau .75 2.00
17 Keith Tkachuk 1.25 3.00
18 Scott Stevens .75 2.00
19 Claude Lemieux .75 2.00
20 Alexei Zhamnov .75 2.00

1995-96 Select Certified Future

Randomly inserted in packs at a rate of 1:19, this 10-card set features some of the league's brightest future stars in silver rainbow holographic foil print technology.
COMPLETE SET (10) 15.00 30.00
1 Peter Forsberg 6.00 15.00
2 Jim Carey .75 2.00
3 Paul Kariya 2.00 5.00
4 Jocelyn Thibault 1.25 3.00
5 Saku Koivu 2.00 5.00
6 Brian Holzinger .75 2.00
7 Todd Harvey .75 2.00
8 Jeff O'Neill .75 2.00
9 Oleg Tverdovsky .75 2.00
10 Ed Jovanovski .75 2.00

1995-96 Select Certified Gold Team

Randomly inserted in packs at a rate of 1:41, this 10-card set honors some of the league's top players, bestowing best-of-the-best honors with a Dufexed gold-foil design element. The presence of a Pavel Bure Gold Team sample card in the Promo set led to some softening of demand for the insert version of the card found in this set.
COMPLETE SET (10) 50.00 125.00
1 Eric Lindros 3.00 8.00
2 Wayne Gretzky 12.00 30.00
3 Mario Lemieux 10.00 25.00
4 Jaromir Jagr 4.00 10.00
5 Pavel Bure 3.00 8.00
6 Brett Hull 3.00 8.00
7 Cam Neely 3.00 8.00
8 Joe Sakic 6.00 15.00
9 Martin Brodeur 6.00 15.00
10 Patrick Roy 10.00 25.00

1996-97 Select Certified

The 1996-97 Select Certified set was issued in one series totaling 120 cards. The cards featured a silver mirror-like background with player names scripted horizontally in gold foil on the front and complete stats on the reverse against each opposing team.
COMPLETE SET (120) 15.00 40.00
1 Eric Lindros .25 .60
2 Mike Modano .25 .60
3 Jocelyn Thibault .15 .40
4 Wayne Gretzky .75 2.00
5 Ray Bourque .25 .60
6 Martin Brodeur .30 .75
7 Rob Niedermayer .12 .30
8 Stephane Fiset .12 .30
9 Pat LaFontaine .15 .40
10 Mario Lemieux .50 1.25
11 Ed Belfour .15 .40
12 Ron Francis .20 .50
13 Luc Robitaille .15 .40
14 Paul Kariya .20 .50
15 Doug Gilmour .20 .50
16 Joe Sakic .25 .60
17 Nikolai Khabibulin .12 .30
18 Valeri Bure .10 .25
19 Brett Hull .75 2.00
20 Chris Osgood .15 .40
21 Trevor Kidd .10 .25
22 Kirk McLean .12 .30
23 Zigmund Palffy .15 .40
24 Keith Tkachuk .15 .40
25 Andy Moog .15 .40
26 Bill Guerin .15 .40
27 Chris Chelios .15 .40
28 Damian Rhodes .12 .30
29 Jim Carey .15 .40
30 Ed Jovanovski .12 .30
31 Felix Potvin .15 .40
32 Teemu Selanne .30 .75
33 John LeClair .15 .40
34 Pavel Bure .20 .50
35 Grant Fuhr .15 .40
36 Mark Messier .25 .60
37 Vincent Damphousse .12 .30
38 Jason Arnott .12 .30
39 Mike Richter .15 .40
40 Keith Primeau .10 .25
41 Steve Yzerman .40 1.00
42 Trevor Linden .12 .30
43 Jaromir Jagr .40 1.00
44 Sean Burke .10 .25
45 Alexei Zhitnik .10 .25
46 Dimitri Khristich .10 .25
47 Daniel Alfredsson .15 .40
48 Roman Hamrlik .12 .30
49 Pat Verbeek .10 .25
50 Doug Weight .15 .40
51 Adam Graves .10 .25
52 Michal Pivonka .10 .25
53 Claude Lemieux .10 .25
54 Scott Stevens .15 .40
55 Sergei Fedorov .25 .60
56 Owen Nolan .15 .40
57 Niklas Andersson .10 .25
58 Cory Stillman .10 .25
59 John Vanbiesbrouck .15 .40
60 Craig Janney .12 .30
61 Jeff Friesen .10 .25
62 Igor Larionov .15 .40
63 Ron Hextall .12 .30
64 Saku Koivu .15 .40
65 Wendel Clark .12 .30
66 Curtis Joseph .15 .40
67 Valeri Kamensky .12 .30
68 Adam Oates .15 .40
69 Daren Puppa .12 .30
70 Alexander Mogilny .12 .30
71 Corey Hirsch .12 .30
72 Brendan Shanahan .20 .50
73 Shayne Corson .10 .25
74 Dominik Hasek .25 .60
75 Theo Fleury .30 .75
76 Brian Leetch .15 .40
77 Jeremy Roenick .25 .60
78 Peter Bondra .12 .30
79 Eric Daze .12 .30
80 Todd Bertuzzi .15 .40
81 Patrick Roy .40 1.00
82 Pierre Turgeon .15 .40
83 Alexei Yashin .12 .30
84 Scott Mellanby .12 .30
85 Mats Sundin .15 .40
86 Jari Kurri .15 .40
87 Kelly Hrudey .12 .30
88 Joe Nieuwendyk .15 .40
89 Paul Coffey .15 .40
90 Jeff O'Neill .10 .25
91 Kai Nurminen RC .15 .40
92 Anders Eriksson .10 .25
93 Jarome Iginla .20 .50
94 Anson Carter .12 .30
95 Christian Dube .10 .25
96 Harry York RC .15 .40
97 Tomas Holmstrom RC .50 1.25
98 Sergei Berezin RC .25 .60
99 Mattias Timander RC .15 .40
100 Wade Redden .10 .25
101 Mike Grier RC .20 .50
102 Jonas Hoglund .10 .25
103 Eric Fichaud .12 .30
104 Janne Niinimaa .15 .40
105 Tuomas Gronman .10 .25
106 Jim Campbell .10 .25
107 Daniel Goneau RC .15 .40
108 Patrick Lalime RC 1.25 3.00
109 Ruslan Salei RC .15 .40
110 Richard Zednik RC .20 .50
111 Chris O'Sullivan .10 .25
112 Fredrik Modin RC .40 1.00
113 Brad Smyth RC .12 .30
114 Bryan Berard .15 .40
115 Jamie Langenbrunner .10 .25
116 Ethan Moreau RC .15 .40
117 Daymond Langkow .12 .30
118 Andreas Dackell RC .15 .40
119 Rem Murray RC .15 .40
120 Dainius Zubrus RC .20 .50
48P Roman Hamrlik PROMO .12 .30
60P Craig Janney PROMO .12 .30
65P Wendel Clark PROMO .12 .30

1996-97 Select Certified Artist's Proofs

Inserted 1:48 packs, this insert parallels the base set. The cards can be distinguished by an Artist Proof logo stamped on the front of the card. Although the cards suggest that 500 were printed, there were, in fact, just 150 of each card made.
*VETS: 3X TO 8X BASIC CARDS
*ROOKIES: 1.5X TO 4X
36 Mark Messier 4.00 10.00
P60 Craig Janney PROMO 2.00 5.00
P65 Wendel Clark PROMO 2.00 5.00

1996-97 Select Certified Blue

Inserted at 1:50 packs, these cards can be differentiated from the base cards by the blue foil background on the front of the card.
*VETS: 3X TO 8X BASIC CARDS
*ROOKIES: 1.5X TO 4X

1996-97 Select Certified Mirror Blue

Inserted at 1:200 packs, these cards are differentiated by a blue holographic foil background on the front of the card and the words 'Mirror Blue' on the reverse. Though the actual number of cards printed is not known, sources estimate that only 36 copies of each Mirror Blue card exists.
*VETS: 8X TO 20X BASIC CARDS
*ROOKIES: 4X TO 10X

1996-97 Select Certified Mirror Gold

Inserted at 1:300, this 120-card parallel set could be differentiated from the base set by a gold holographic foil background on the front of the card and the words 'Mirror Gold' on the reverse. Though the actual number of cards printed is not known, sources estimate that only 24 copies of each Mirror Gold card exists.
*VETS: 12X TO 30X BASIC CARDS
*ROOKIES: 6X TO 15X

1996-97 Select Certified Mirror Red

Inserted at 1:100 packs, these cards can be differentiated from the base set by a red holographic foil background on the front of the card and the words 'Mirror Red' on the reverse. Though the actual number of cards printed is not known, sources estimate that just 72 copies of each Mirror Red card exists.
*VETS: 4X TO 10X BASIC CARDS
*ROOKIES: 2X TO 5X
36 Mark Messier 4.00 10.00

1996-97 Select Certified Red

A 1:8 pack parallel insert, these cards are differentiated from those in the base set by a red foil background on the front of the card.
*VETS: 2.5X TO 6X BASIC CARDS
*ROOKIES: 1.2X TO 3X

1996-97 Select Certified Cornerstones

Randomly inserted in packs at a rate of 1:38, these cards feature a player photo framed in silver and black etched metal Dufex foil. The text on the card backs describe why each of the 15 players is considered his team's cornerstone player.
COMPLETE SET (15) 30.00 80.00
1 Eric Lindros 2.50 6.00
2 Mario Lemieux 6.00 15.00
3 Jaromir Jagr 3.00 8.00
4 Wayne Gretzky 8.00 20.00
5 Mark Messier 2.50 6.00
6 Brett Hull 2.50 6.00
7 Pavel Bure 2.50 6.00
8 Saku Koivu 2.00 5.00
9 Joe Sakic 4.00 10.00
10 Keith Tkachuk 2.00 5.00
11 Paul Kariya 2.50 6.00
12 Teemu Selanne 2.50 6.00
13 Sergei Fedorov 2.50 6.00
14 Steve Yzerman 6.00 15.00
15 Peter Forsberg 3.00 8.00

1996-97 Select Certified Freezers

Randomly inserted in packs at a rate of 1:41, this set features silver holofoil cards of 15 highly regarded NHL goaltenders.
COMPLETE SET (15) 40.00 100.00
1 Martin Brodeur 6.00 15.00
2 Patrick Roy 10.00 25.00
3 Jim Carey 2.00 5.00
4 John Vanbiesbrouck 2.50 6.00
5 Dominik Hasek 4.00 10.00
6 Ed Belfour 2.50 6.00
7 Curtis Joseph 2.50 6.00
8 Felix Potvin 3.00 8.00
9 Daren Puppa 2.00 5.00
10 Chris Osgood 2.50 6.00
11 Mike Richter 2.50 6.00
12 Jocelyn Thibault 2.00 5.00
13 Ron Hextall 2.00 5.00
14 Nikolai Khabibulin 2.00 5.00
15 Damian Rhodes 2.00 5.00

2013-14 Select

1 Patrick Kane .75 2.00
2 Jonathan Toews .75 2.00
3 Corey Crawford .50 1.25
4 Duncan Keith .40 1.00
5 Marian Hossa .30 .75
6 Sidney Crosby 1.50 4.00
7 Evgeni Malkin 1.25 3.00
8 Kris Letang .40 1.00
9 James Neal .40 1.00
10 Marc-Andre Fleury .60 1.50
11 Corey Perry .40 1.00
12 Ryan Getzlaf .60 1.50
13 Saku Koivu .40 1.00
14 Jonas Hiller .30 .75
15 Cam Fowler .30 .75
16 Max Pacioretty .40 1.00
17 Carey Price 1.25 3.00
18 P.K. Subban .60 1.50
19 Brian Gionta .30 .75
20 David Desharnais .40 1.00
21 Patrice Bergeron .50 1.25
22 Jarome Iginla .40 1.00
23 Zdeno Chara .40 1.00
24 Milan Lucic .40 1.00
25 Tuukka Rask .40 1.00
26 Alex Pietrangelo .30 .75
27 T.J. Oshie .60 1.50
28 David Backes .40 1.00
29 Jaroslav Halak .40 1.00
30 Alexander Steen .40 1.00
31 Jonathan Quick .60 1.50
32 Dustin Brown .40 1.00
33 Anze Kopitar .60 1.50
34 Drew Doughty .40 1.00
35 Mike Richards .40 1.00
36 Henrik Sedin .40 1.00
37 Daniel Sedin .40 1.00
38 Roberto Luongo .40 1.00
39 Ryan Kesler .40 1.00
40 Alexandre Burrows .40 1.00
41 Joffrey Lupul .30 .75
42 James Reimer .40 1.00
43 Dion Phaneuf .40 1.00
44 Phil Kessel .50 1.25
45 Nazem Kadri .40 1.00
46 Alex Ovechkin 1.50 4.00
47 Braden Holtby .60 1.50
48 Mike Green .40 1.00
49 Nicklas Backstrom .60 1.50
50 Brooks Laich .25 .60
51 Logan Couture .40 1.00
52 Patrick Marleau .40 1.00
53 Joe Thornton .40 1.00
54 Antti Niemi .30 .75
55 Dan Boyle .30 .75
56 Henrik Lundqvist .50 1.25
57 Rick Nash .40 1.00
58 Ryan Callahan .40 1.00
59 Derick Brassard .40 1.00
60 Marc Staal .30 .75
61 Jimmy Howard .40 1.00
62 Pavel Datsyuk .50 1.25
63 Henrik Zetterberg .50 1.25
64 Johan Franzen .40 1.00
65 Niklas Kronwall .30 .75
66 Craig Anderson .40 1.00
67 Jason Spezza .40 1.00
68 Erik Karlsson .75 2.00
69 Bobby Ryan .40 1.00
70 Mika Zibanejad .40 1.00
71 Zach Parise .40 1.00
72 Dany Heatley .30 .75
73 Mikko Koivu .30 .75
74 Ryan Suter .25 .60
75 Niklas Backstrom .30 .75
76 John Tavares .75 2.00
77 Matt Moulson .30 .75
78 Evgeni Nabokov .30 .75
79 Travis Hamonic .25 .60
80 Michael Grabner .30 .75
81 Sergei Bobrovsky .40 1.00
82 Marian Gaborik .40 1.00
83 Jack Johnson .25 .60
84 Brandon Dubinsky .30 .75
85 Ryan Johansen .50 1.25
86 Ondrej Pavelec .40 1.00
87 Dustin Byfuglien .40 1.00
88 Andrew Ladd .40 1.00
89 Evander Kane .40 1.00
90 Blake Wheeler .40 1.00
91 Mike Smith .40 1.00
92 Shane Doan .30 .75
93 Keith Yandle .40 1.00
94 Mikkel Boedker .25 .60
95 Oliver Ekman-Larsson .30 .75
96 Claude Giroux .40 1.00
97 Vincent Lecavalier .30 .75
98 Sean Couturier .40 1.00
99 Luke Schenn .25 .60
100 Steve Mason .30 .75
101 Jamie Benn .50 1.25
102 Tyler Seguin .60 1.50
103 Kari Lehtonen .30 .75
104 Brenden Dillon .30 .75
105 Erik Cole .30 .75
106 Martin Brodeur .75 2.00
107 Adam Larsson .40 1.00
108 Adam Henrique .40 1.00
109 Patrik Elias .40 1.00
110 Cory Schneider .30 .75
111 Cody Hodgson .40 1.00
112 Thomas Vanek .40 1.00
113 Ryan Miller .40 1.00
114 Steve Ott .30 .75
115 Christian Ehrhoff .25 .60
116 Sam Gagner .30 .75
117 Taylor Hall .75 2.00
118 Ryan Nugent-Hopkins .40 1.00
119 Jordan Eberle .40 1.00
120 Devan Dubnyk .40 1.00
121 Jiri Hudler .30 .75
122 Mike Cammalleri .30 .75
123 Curtis Glencross .25 .60
124 Miikka Kiprusoff .30 .75
125 Mark Giordano .30 .75
126 Cam Ward .40 1.00
127 Eric Staal .50 1.25
128 Alexander Semin .40 1.00
129 Jiri Tlusty .30 .75
130 Jordan Staal .40 1.00
131 Shea Weber .30 .75
132 Pekka Rinne .50 1.25
133 Mike Fisher .30 .75
134 Patric Hornqvist .30 .75
135 Colin Wilson .30 .75
136 Martin St. Louis .40 1.00
137 Steven Stamkos .75 2.00
138 Anders Lindback .25 .60
139 Victor Hedman .50 1.25
140 Ben Bishop .40 1.00
141 Matt Duchene .40 1.00
142 Gabriel Landeskog .30 .75
143 Erik Johnson .25 .60
144 Semyon Varlamov .40 1.00
145 P.A. Parenteau .25 .60
146 Jacob Markstrom .30 .75
147 Tomas Fleischmann .25 .60
148 Brian Campbell .25 .60
149 Kris Versteeg .30 .75
150 Erik Gudbranson .40 1.00
151 Mario Lemieux 1.25 3.00
152 Mark Messier .50 1.25
153 Brett Hull .40 1.00
154 Bobby Hull .40 1.00
155 Joe Sakic .60 1.50
156 Patrick Roy 1.00 2.50
157 Guy Lafleur .50 1.25
158 Pat LaFontaine .40 1.00
159 Al MacInnis .40 1.00
160 Stan Mikita .50 1.25
161 Bobby Clarke .40 1.00
162 Brendan Shanahan .50 1.25
163 Brian Leetch .40 1.00
164 Bryan Trottier .50 1.25
165 Cam Neely .40 1.00
166 Chris Chelios .40 1.00
167 Ray Bourque .60 1.50
168 Darryl Sittler .40 1.00
169 Mike Richter .40 1.00
170 Bernie Parent .40 1.00
171 Steve Yzerman .75 2.00
172 Gordie Howe .75 2.00
173 Grant Fuhr .40 1.00
174 Guy Carbonneau .40 1.00
175 Igor Larionov .40 1.00
176 Jari Kurri .40 1.00
177 Jeremy Roenick .40 1.00
178 Trevor Linden .40 1.00
179 Luc Robitaille .40 1.00
180 Pavel Bure .50 1.25
181 Mike Bossy .40 1.00
182 Mike Modano .60 1.50
183 Paul Coffey .40 1.00
184 Peter Stastny .30 .75
185 Phil Esposito .60 1.50
186 Andrej Sustr RC .75 2.00
187 Steve Oleksy RC 1.25 3.00
188 Steven Pinizzotto RC 1.25 3.00
189 Anders Lee RC 2.00 5.00
190 Ben Hanowski RC 1.00 2.50
191 Drew LeBlanc RC .75 2.00
192 Daniel Bang RC 1.00 2.50
193 Chad Ruhwedel RC .75 2.00
194 Cameron Schilling RC .75 2.00
195 John Muse RC 1.25 3.00
196 Jean-Gabriel Pageau RC 1.00 2.50
197 Carter Bancks RC 1.00 2.50
198 Jason Akeson RC 1.00 2.50
199 Nicolas Blanchard RC 1.00 2.50
200 Matthew Konan RC 1.25 3.00
201 Jamie Tardif AU/399 RC 2.00 5.00
202 Brian Flynn AU/399 RC 2.50 6.00
203 Mark Cundari AU/399 RC 2.00 5.00
204 Michal Jordan AU/399 RC 2.00 5.00
205 Chris Terry AU/399 RC 2.00 5.00
206 Shawn Lalonde AU/399 RC 3.00 8.00
207 Ryan Stanton AU/399 RC 3.00 8.00
208 Drew Shore AU/399 RC 2.50 6.00
209 Greg Pateryn AU/399 RC 3.00 8.00
210 J.Rheault AU/399 RC 2.00 5.00
211 Oliver Lauridsen AU/399 RC 2.50 6.00
212 Jeff Zatkoff AU/399 RC 3.00 8.00
213 Matt Tennyson AU/399 RC 2.00 5.00
214 Tyler Johnson AU/399 RC 15.00 30.00
215 Ben Street AU/399 RC 2.00 5.00
216 P.Bordeleau AU/399 RC 3.00 8.00
217 M.Sgarbossa AU/399 RC 2.50 6.00
218 Sean Collins AU/399 RC 2.50 6.00
219 Brian Lashoff AU/99 RC 4.00 10.00
220 Mark Arcobello AU/399 RC 3.00 8.00
221 Michael Caruso AU/399 RC 2.00 5.00
222 Petr Mrazek AU/399 RC 6.00 15.00
223 D.Dziurzynski AU/399 RC 2.50 6.00
224 Harri Pesonen AU/399 RC 2.50 6.00
225 Victor Bartley AU/399 RC 2.50 6.00
226 Darcy Kuemper AU/399 RC 3.00 8.00
227 Richard Panik AU/399 RC 3.00 8.00
228 Derek Grant AU/399 RC 2.50 6.00
229 J.Marchessault AU/399 RC 6.00 15.00
230 M.Reinhart AU/399 RC 3.00 8.00
231 Taylor Beck AU/399 RC 2.50 6.00
232 Tye McGinn AU/399 RC 3.00 8.00
233 Antoine Roussel AU/399 RC 3.00 8.00
234 Eric Gryba AU/399 RC 2.50 6.00
235 Matt Irwin AU/399 RC 2.50 6.00
236 Ondrej Palat AU/399 RC 4.00 10.00
237 J.Schroeder AU/399 RC 3.00 8.00
238 Philipp Grubauer AU/399 RC 3.00 8.00
239 Zach Redmond AU/399 RC 2.50 6.00
240 Radko Gudas AU/399 RC 3.00 8.00
241 Viktor Fasth AU/399 RC 3.00 8.00
242 Carl Soderberg AU/399 RC 3.00 8.00
243 Mark Pysyk AU/399 RC 3.00 8.00
244 R.Cervenka AU/199 RC 4.00 10.00
245 Calvin Pickard AU/399 RC 3.00 8.00
246 Alex Petrovic AU/399 RC 2.50 6.00
247 Johan Larsson AU/399 RC 2.50 6.00
248 Joonas Rask AU/399 RC 2.00 5.00
249 Chris Brown AU/399 RC 2.00 5.00
250 Nick Petrecki AU/399 RC 2.00 5.00
251 Dmitrij Jaskin AU/399 RC 3.00 8.00
252 Alex Killorn AU/399 RC 3.00 8.00
253 Frank Corrado AU/399 RC 2.00 5.00
254 Anthony Peluso AU/399 RC 2.00 5.00
255 Stefan Matteau AU/399 RC 2.50 6.00
256 Thomas Hickey AU/399 RC 2.50 6.00
257 D.DeKeyser AU/399 RC 4.00 10.00
258 E.Pasquale AU/399 RC 2.00 5.00
259 C.Thomas AU/399 RC 2.50 6.00
260 Eric Hartzell AU/399 RC 3.00 8.00
261 Rickard Rakell AU/399 RC 3.00 8.00
262 Leo Komarov AU/299 RC 3.00 8.00
263 Sami Vatanen AU/399 RC 3.00 8.00
264 C.Nilstorp AU/399 RC 2.50 6.00
265 Mathew Dumba AU/399 RC 3.00 8.00
266 Jonas Brodin AU/399 RC 2.50 6.00
267 Michael Kostka AU/399 RC 2.50 6.00
268 Nicklas Jensen AU/399 RC 2.50 6.00
269 Emerson Etem AU/399 RC 3.00 8.00
270 Ryan Spooner AU/399 RC EXCH 3.00 8.00
271 Jamie Oleksiak AU/399 RC 2.50 6.00
272 Q.Howden AU/199 RC 4.00 10.00
273 Ryan Murphy AU/199 RC 5.00 12.00
274 Charlie Coyle AU/399 RC 3.00 8.00
275 Jarred Tinordi AU/399 RC 3.00 8.00
276 Austin Watson AU/399 RC 2.50 6.00
277 Brock Nelson AU/399 RC 3.00 8.00
278 Scott Laughton AU/99 RC 5.00 12.00
279 Beau Bennett AU/399 RC 4.00 10.00
280 F.Andersen AU/399 RC 5.00 12.00
281 Nathan Beaulieu AU/99 RC 4.00 10.00
282 J.T. Miller AU/399 RC 3.00 8.00
283 M.Grigorenko AU/399 RC 4.00 10.00
284 Nick Bjugstad AU/399 RC 4.00 10.00
285 Tanner Pearson AU/399 RC 3.00 8.00
286 Jared Staal AU/399 RC 3.00 8.00
287 Tom Wilson AU/399 RC 5.00 12.00
288 M.Granlund AU/399 RC 5.00 12.00
289 Justin Schultz AU/399 RC 3.00 8.00
290 Tyler Toffoli AU/399 RC 6.00 15.00
291 Jack Campbell AU/399 RC 2.50 6.00
292 Filip Forsberg AU/399 RC 8.00 20.00
293 Dougie Hamilton AU/399 RC 6.00 15.00
294 Alex Chiasson AU/399 RC 3.00 8.00
295 B.Gallagher AU/399 RC 10.00 25.00
296 Cory Conacher AU/399 RC 2.00 5.00
297 V.Tarasenko AU/399 RC 40.00 80.00
298 A.Galchenyuk AU/399 RC 15.00 40.00
299 J.Huberdeau AU/199 RC 12.00 30.00
300 Nail Yakupov AU/399 RC 10.00 25.00
301 N.MacKinnon AU/399 RC 25.00 60.00
302 Seth Jones AU/399 RC 3.00 8.00
303 V.Nichushkin AU/399 RC 3.00 8.00
304 Sean Monahan AU/399 RC 5.00 12.00
305 Tomas Hertl AU/399 RC 4.00 10.00
306 Boone Jenner AU/399 RC 3.00 8.00
307 Ryan Murray AU/399 RC 5.00 12.00
308 Morgan Rielly AU/399 RC 8.00 20.00
309 Jason Missiaen JSY AU RC 5.00 12.00
310 Michael Raffl JSY AU RC 4.00 10.00
311 Cody Ceci JSY AU RC 4.00 10.00
312 Johan Gustafsson JSY AU RC 6.00 15.00
313 Jacob Trouba JSY AU RC 8.00 20.00
314 Hampus Lindholm JSY AU RC 8.00 20.00
315 Zemgus Girgensons JSY AU RC 10.00 25.00
317 Nikita Zadorov JSY AU RC 5.00 12.00
318 Reto Berra JSY AU RC 5.00 12.00
319 Elias Lindholm JSY AU RC 8.00 20.00
320 Joakim Nordstrom JSY AU RC 4.00 10.00
321 Xavier Ouellet JSY AU RC 5.00 12.00
322 Aleksander Barkov JSY AU RC 8.00 20.00
323 Michael Bournival JSY AU RC 5.00 12.00
324 Marek Mazanec JSY AU RC 5.00 12.00
325 Jon Merrill JSY AU RC 5.00 12.00
326 Tomas Jurco JSY AU RC 8.00 20.00
327 Olli Maatta JSY AU RC 12.00 30.00
328 Matt Nieto JSY AU RC 4.00 10.00
329 Martin Jones JSY AU RC 12.00 30.00
331 Kevin Connauton JSY AU RC 3.00 8.00
332 Connor Murphy JSY AU RC 3.00 8.00
333 Ryan Strome JSY AU RC 6.00 15.00
334 Dylan McIlrath JSY AU RC 3.00 8.00
335 Jesper Fast JSY AU RC 4.00 10.00
336 Magnus Hellberg JSY AU RC 4.00 10.00
337 Lucas Lessio JSY AU RC 3.00 8.00
338 John Gibson JSY AU RC 12.00 30.00
339 Josh Leivo AU/299 RC 3.00 8.00
340 Joe Cannata AU/299 RC 2.50 6.00
341 Linden Vey AU/299 RC 2.00 5.00
342 Taylor Fedun AU/299 RC 4.00 10.00
343 Calvin Heeter AU/299 RC 2.50 6.00
344 Jordan Szwarz AU/299 RC 3.00 8.00
345 Mark Barberio AU/299 RC 2.00 5.00
346 Michael Latta AU/299 RC 2.50 6.00
347 Jamie Devane AU/299 RC 2.50 6.00
348 Freddie Hamilton AU/299 RC 3.00 8.00
349 Tyler Pitlick AU/299 RC 3.00 8.00
350 Jayson Megna AU/299 RC 3.00 8.00
351 Darcy Kuemper AU/299 RC 3.00 8.00
352 Kevin Henderson AU/299 RC 2.50 6.00
353 David Broll AU/299 RC 3.00 8.00
355 Antti Raanta AU/299 RC 4.00 10.00
356 Karl Stollery RC 1.00 2.50
357 Kevan Miller RC 1.00 2.50
358 Christopher Breen RC 1.00 2.50
359 Chad Billins RC 1.00 2.50
360 Brett Bellemore RC 1.00 2.50
361 Sami Aittokallio RC 1.25 3.00
362 Michael Chaput RC .75 2.00
363 Luke Glendening RC 2.00 5.00
364 Luke Gazdic RC 1.00 2.50
365 Anton Belov RC 1.25 3.00
366 Will Acton RC 1.00 2.50
367 Eric Selleck RC 1.00 2.50
368 Justin Fontaine RC 1.25 3.00
369 Patrick Holland RC 2.00 5.00
370 Matt Anderson RC .75 2.00
371 David Warsofsky RC 1.25 3.00
372 Zach Sill RC 1.25 3.00
373 Brian Gibbons RC 1.25 3.00
374 Dmitry Korobov RC 1.25 3.00
375 Spencer Abbott RC 1.00 2.50
376 Darren Archibald RC 1.00 2.50
377 Connor Carrick RC 1.00 2.50
378 Alex Grant RC .75 2.00
379 Antti Raanta RC 1.50 4.00
380 Eric Gelinas RC 1.25 3.00
381 Julian Melchiori RC .75 2.00
382 Nate Schmidt RC 1.00 2.50
383 Nicolas Blanchard RC 1.00 2.50
384 Ben Chiarot RC 1.25 3.00
385 Reid Boucher RC 1.25 3.00
386 Kent Simpson RC .75 2.00
387 Martin Marincin RC 1.00 2.50
388 Patrick Wey RC 1.00 2.50
389 John Albert RC 1.00 2.50
390 Erik Haula RC 1.50 4.00
391 Adam Almquist RC .75 2.00
392 Craig Cunningham RC 1.00 2.50
393 Eric O'Dell RC .75 2.00
394 Philip Samuelsson RC .75 2.00
395 Brian Dumoulin RC 1.25 3.00
396 Conor Allen RC 1.00 2.50
397 Joacim Eriksson RC 1.25 3.00
398 Zach Trotman RC 1.25 3.00
399 Niklas Svedberg RC 2.50 6.00
400 Brad Hunt RC 1.00 2.50
401 Alexey Marchenko RC 1.00 2.50
402 Justin Florek RC 3.00 8.00
403 Mike Sislo RC 1.25 3.00
404 Eriah Hayes RC 1.25 3.00
405 Kevin Klein .25 .60
406 Devan Dubnyk .40 1.00
407 Matt Hendricks .25 .60
408 Derek Roy .30 .75
409 Mats Zuccarello .30 .75
410 Andrew Ference .25 .60
411 Mike Santorelli .30 .75
412 Michael Ryder .25 .60
413 Tim Gleason .25 .60
414 Maxim Lapierre .25 .60
415 Ray Emery .30 .75
416 Michael Del Zotto .25 .60
417 Zac Dalpe .25 .60
418 Mathieu Perreault .25 .60
419 Cal Clutterbuck .40 1.00
420 Taylor Pyatt .25 .60
421 Daniel Briere .40 1.00
422 Jonathan Bernier .40 1.00
423 Mike Ribeiro .30 .75
424 Manny Malhotra .30 .75
425 Kris Versteeg .30 .75
426 Dustin Penner .30 .75
427 Tyler Kennedy .25 .60
428 Thomas Vanek .40 1.00
429 Loui Eriksson .30 .75
430 Brenden Morrow .30 .75
431 Ben Scrivens .30 .75
432 Mason Raymond .30 .75
433 Mikhail Grabovski .30 .75
434 Daniel Carcillo .25 .60
435 Tim Thomas .40 1.00
436 Maxime Talbot .30 .75
437 Daniel Alfredsson .40 1.00
438 Shawn Horcoff .25 .60
439 Ryane Clowe .25 .60
440 Valtteri Filppula .40 1.00
441 David Clarkson .25 .60
442 Ilya Bryzgalov .40 1.00
443 Nathan Gerbe .25 .60
444 Karri Ramo .30 .75
445 Reilly Smith .40 1.00
446 Nino Niederreiter .25 .60
447 Steve Downie .25 .60
448 Matt Moulson .30 .75
449 Stephen Weiss .30 .75
450 Nathan Horton .40 1.00
451 Devin Setoguchi .30 .75
452 David Perron .25 .60
453 Jaromir Jagr 2.00 5.00
454 Clarke MacArthur .25 .60
455 Jakob Silfverberg .30 .75

2013-14 Select Cracked Ice Toronto Spring Expo

*405-455 VETS: 1.2X TO 3X BASIC CARDS
*356-404 ROOKIES: .5X TO 1.2X BASIC RC

2013-14 Select Prizms

*VETS: 1.2X TO 3X BASIC CARDS
*ROOKIES: .5X TO 1.2X BASIC RC
*ROOK.AU/99: .5X TO 1.2X AU RC/299-399
*ROOK.AU/99: .4X TO 1X AU RC/99-199
49 Nicklas Backstrom 2.00 5.00
297 Vladimir Tarasenko AU 50.00 100.00

2013-14 Select Prizms Green

*1-185 VETS/25: 4X TO 10X BASIC CARDS
*186-200 ROOKIES/25: 1.2X TO 3X BASIC RC
49 Nicklas Backstrom 6.00 15.00
265 Mathew Dumba AU/15 15.00 40.00
300 Nail Yakupov AU/15
301 Nathan MacKinnon AU/15 125.00 250.00
302 Seth Jones AU/15 20.00 50.00
303 Valeri Nichushkin AU/15
304 Sean Monahan AU/15
305 Tomas Hertl AU/15 20.00 50.00
306 Boone Jenner AU/15 15.00 40.00
307 Ryan Murray AU/15
308 Morgan Rielly AU/15 40.00 100.00

2013-14 Select Prizms Red

*1-185 VETS/35: 3X TO 8X BASIC CARDS
*186-200 ROOKIES/35: 1X TO 2.5X BASIC RC
49 Nicklas Backstrom 5.00 12.00

2013-14 Select Cornerstone

*PRIZM/25: 1.5X TO 4X BASIC INSERTS
C1 Sidney Crosby 6.00 15.00
C2 Alex Ovechkin 6.00 15.00
C3 Claude Giroux 1.50 4.00
C4 Milan Lucic 1.50 4.00
C5 Taylor Hall 3.00 8.00
C6 Nazem Kadri 1.50 4.00
C7 Steven Stamkos 3.00 8.00
C8 Pavel Datsyuk 2.00 5.00
C9 Jonathan Toews 3.00 8.00
C10 Gabriel Landeskog 1.25 3.00
C11 Oliver Ekman-Larsson 1.25 3.00
C12 Adam Henrique 1.50 4.00
C13 Eric Staal 2.00 5.00
C14 John Tavares 3.00 8.00
C15 Erik Karlsson 3.00 8.00
C16 Alex Pietrangelo 1.25 3.00
C17 Henrik Sedin 1.50 4.00
C18 Ryan Getzlaf 2.50 6.00
C19 Anze Kopitar 2.50 6.00
C20 Patrick Marleau 1.50 4.00
C21 Evander Kane 1.50 4.00
C22 Zach Parise 1.50 4.00
C23 Jonathan Huberdeau 2.00 5.00
C24 Max Pacioretty 1.50 4.00
C25 Thomas Vanek 1.50 4.00

2013-14 Select Double Strike

*PRIZM/25: .8X TO 2X BASIC INSERTS
DS1 David Backes 3.00 8.00
DS2 Patrice Bergeron 4.00 10.00
DS3 Dustin Brown 3.00 8.00
DS4 Ryan Callahan 3.00 8.00
DS5 Pavel Datsyuk 4.00 10.00
DS6 Marian Hossa 2.50 6.00
DS7 Jonathan Toews 6.00 15.00
DS8 Ryan Kesler 4.00 10.00
DS9 Doug Gilmour 4.00 10.00
DS10 Steve Yzerman 6.00 15.00
DS11 Zdeno Chara 3.00 8.00
DS12 Erik Karlsson 6.00 15.00
DS13 Duncan Keith 3.00 8.00
DS14 Niklas Kronwall 2.50 6.00
DS15 Kris Letang 3.00 8.00
DS16 Alex Pietrangelo 2.50 6.00
DS17 P.K. Subban 5.00 12.00
DS18 Shea Weber 2.50 6.00
DS19 Nicklas Lidstrom 3.00 8.00
DS20 Al MacInnis 3.00 8.00
DS21 Martin Brodeur 6.00 15.00
DS22 Mike Smith 3.00 8.00
DS23 Ed Belfour 3.00 8.00
DS24 Ron Hextall 3.00 8.00
DS25 Marty Turco 3.00 8.00

2013-14 Select Fire on Ice Rookies

*BLUE: .4X TO 1X BASIC INSERTS
*FALL EXPO/35: 1X TO 2.5X BASIC INSERTS
*PRIZM/35: 1X TO 2.5X BASIC INSERTS
*PRIZM BLUE/25: 1.2X TO 3X BASIC INSERTS
*PRIZM GREEN/25: 1.2X TO 3X BASIC INSERTS
*PRIZM RED/25: 1.2X TO 3X BASIC INSERTS
FR1 Emerson Etem 1.25 3.00
FR2 Viktor Fasth 1.25 3.00
FR3 Dougie Hamilton 2.50 6.00
FR4 Mikhail Grigorenko 1.50 4.00
FR5 Mark Cundari .75 2.00
FR6 Ryan Murphy 1.25 3.00
FR7 Calvin Pickard 1.25 3.00
FR8 Alex Chiasson 1.25 3.00
FR9 Jack Campbell 1.00 2.50
FR10 Damien Brunner 1.00 2.50
FR11 Danny DeKeyser 1.50 4.00
FR12 Justin Schultz 1.25 3.00
FR13 Nail Yakupov 4.00 10.00
FR14 Jonathan Huberdeau 3.00 8.00
FR15 Drew Shore 1.00 2.50
FR16 Nick Bjugstad 1.50 4.00
FR17 Tyler Toffoli 2.50 6.00
FR18 Jonas Brodin 1.00 2.50
FR19 Mikael Granlund 2.00 5.00
FR20 Alex Galchenyuk 6.00 15.00
FR21 Brendan Gallagher 4.00 10.00
FR22 Jarred Tinordi 1.25 3.00
FR23 Nathan Beaulieu 1.00 2.50
FR24 Austin Watson 1.00 2.50

:5 Filip Forsberg 3.00 8.00
:6 Thomas Hickey 1.00 2.50
:7 J.T. Miller 1.25 3.00
:8 Jean-Gabriel Pageau 1.00 2.50
:9 Cory Conacher .75 2.00
:0 Scott Laughton 1.25 3.00
:1 Tye McGinn 1.25 3.00
:2 Beau Bennett 1.50 4.00
:3 Matt Irwin 1.00 2.50
:4 Vladimir Tarasenko 5.00 12.00
:5 Radko Gudas 1.25 3.00
:6 Alex Killorn 1.25 3.00
:7 Leo Komarov 1.25 3.00
:8 Jordan Schroeder 1.25 3.00
:9 Tom Wilson 2.00 5.00
:0 Zach Redmond 1.00 2.50

013-14 Select Fire on Ice Stars

UE: .4X TO 1X BASIC INSERTS
IZM/35: 1X TO 2.5X BASIC INSERTS
IZM BLUE/25: 1.2X TO 3X BASIC INSERTS
IZM GREEN/25: 1.2X TO 3X BASIC INSERTS
LL EXPO/35: 1X TO 2.5X BASIC INSERTS
IZM RED/25: 1.2X TO 3X BASIC INSERTS
Corey Perry 2.00 5.00
Teemu Selanne 4.00 10.00
Patrice Bergeron 2.50 6.00
Tuukka Rask 2.00 5.00
Zdeno Chara 2.00 5.00
Ryan Miller 2.00 5.00
Mike Cammalleri 1.50 4.00
Eric Staal 2.50 6.00
Jonathan Toews 4.00 10.00
0 Patrick Kane 4.00 10.00
1 Gabriel Landeskog 1.50 4.00
2 Henrik Zetterberg 2.50 6.00
3 Pavel Datsyuk 2.50 6.00
4 Sam Gagner 1.50 4.00
5 Taylor Hall 4.00 10.00
6 Jonathan Quick 3.00 8.00
7 Anze Kopitar 3.00 8.00
8 Zach Parise 2.00 5.00
9 Carey Price 6.00 15.00
0 P.K. Subban 3.00 8.00
1 Shea Weber 1.50 4.00
2 Pekka Rinne 2.50 6.00
3 Martin Brodeur 4.00 10.00
4 John Tavares 4.00 10.00
5 Henrik Lundqvist 2.50 6.00
6 Erik Karlsson 4.00 10.00
7 Claude Giroux 2.00 5.00
8 Sidney Crosby 8.00 20.00
9 Evgeni Malkin 6.00 15.00
0 Logan Couture 2.00 5.00
1 Alex Pietrangelo 1.50 4.00
2 Steven Stamkos 4.00 10.00
3 Martin St. Louis 2.00 5.00
4 Vincent Lecavalier 1.50 4.00
5 Phil Kessel 2.50 6.00
6 Joffrey Lupul 1.50 4.00
7 Henrik Sedin 2.00 5.00
8 Daniel Sedin 2.00 5.00
9 Alex Ovechkin 8.00 20.00
0 Andrew Ladd 2.00 5.00

2013-14 Select Freezers

IZM/25: 1.2X TO 3X BASIC INSERTS
Mike Richter 2.00 5.00
Curtis Joseph 2.00 5.00
Patrick Roy 5.00 12.00
Ron Hextall 2.00 5.00
John Vanbiesbrouck 2.00 5.00
Martin Brodeur 4.00 10.00
Jonathan Quick 3.00 8.00
Jimmy Howard 2.00 5.00
Henrik Lundqvist 2.50 6.00
James Reimer 2.00 5.00
Tuukka Rask 2.00 5.00
Cam Ward 2.00 5.00
Pekka Rinne 2.50 6.00
Ryan Miller 2.00 5.00
Carey Price 6.00 15.00
Marc-Andre Fleury 3.00 8.00
Corey Crawford 2.50 6.00
Cory Schneider 1.50 4.00
Sergei Bobrovsky 2.00 5.00
Jacob Markstrom 1.50 4.00
Jake Allen 2.50 6.00
Darcy Kuemper 2.00 5.00
Petr Mrazek 4.00 10.00
Jack Campbell 1.50 4.00
Viktor Fasth 2.00 5.00

2013-14 Select Future

IZM/25: 1.2X TO 3X BASIC INSERTS
Nazem Kadri 2.00 5.00
Alex Killorn 2.00 5.00
Jake Allen 2.50 6.00
Vladimir Tarasenko 4.00 10.00
Mika Zibanejad 2.00 5.00
Jean-Gabriel Pageau 1.50 4.00
Emerson Etem 2.00 5.00
Cory Conacher 1.25 3.00
Alex Galchenyuk 5.00 12.00
0 Brendan Gallagher 3.00 8.00
1 Mikael Granlund 1.50 4.00
2 Tyler Toffoli 2.00 5.00
3 Jonathan Huberdeau 2.50 6.00
4 Danny DeKeyser 1.25 3.00
5 J.T. Miller 1.00 2.50
6 Nail Yakupov 3.00 8.00
7 Justin Schultz 1.00 2.50
8 Alex Chiasson 1.00 2.50
9 Jack Campbell 1.50 4.00
0 Gabriel Landeskog 1.50 4.00
1 Brandon Saad 2.00 5.00
2 Filip Forsberg 2.50 6.00
3 Mikhail Grigorenko 1.25 3.00
4 Dougie Hamilton 2.00 5.00
5 Mark Scheifele 2.50 6.00

2013-14 Select Honored Selections

ZM/25: 1.2X TO 3X BASIC INSERTS
L EXPO/35: 1X TO 2.5X BASIC INSERTS
Phil Esposito 3.00 8.00
Lanny McDonald 2.00 5.00
Bobby Hull 2.00 5.00
Stan Mikita 2.50 6.00
Joe Sakic 3.00 8.00
Gordie Howe 4.00 10.00
Steve Yzerman 4.00 10.00
Mark Messier 2.50 6.00
Jari Kurri 2.50 6.00
0 Marcel Dionne 2.50 6.00
1 Jean Beliveau 2.00 5.00
2 Guy Lafleur 2.50 6.00
3 Patrick Roy 5.00 12.00
4 Mike Bossy 2.00 5.00
5 Denis Potvin 2.00 5.00
6 Bobby Clarke 2.00 5.00
7 Mario Lemieux 6.00 15.00

HS18 Brett Hull 2.00 5.00
HS19 Darryl Sittler 2.00 5.00
HS20 Pavel Bure 2.50 6.00

2013-14 Select Rookies Jersey Autographs

*PRIME/50: .8X TO 2X JSY AU/199
*PRIME/50: .6X TO 1.5X JSY AU/99
*PRIME PRZM/25: 1X TO 2.5X JSY AU/199
*PRIME PRZM/25: .8X TO 2X JSY AU/99
*PRIZM/99: .5X TO 1.2X JSY AU/199
*PRIZM/99: .4X TO 1X JSY AU/99
201 Jamie Tardif/199 3.00 8.00
202 Brian Flynn/199 4.00 10.00
204 Michal Jordan/199 3.00 8.00
208 Drew Shore/199 4.00 10.00
215 Ben Street/199 3.00 8.00
217 Michael Sgarbossa/199 4.00 10.00
219 Brian Lashoff/199 4.00 10.00
220 Mark Arcobello/199 5.00 12.00
221 Michael Caruso/199 3.00 8.00
222 Petr Mrazek/199 10.00 25.00
227 Richard Panik/199 5.00 12.00
230 Maxwell Reinhart/199 5.00 12.00
232 Tye McGinn/199 5.00 12.00
233 Antoine Roussel/199 5.00 12.00
234 Eric Gryba/199 4.00 10.00
235 Matt Irwin/199 4.00 10.00
237 Jordan Schroeder/199 5.00 12.00
238 Philipp Grubauer/199 5.00 12.00
239 Zach Redmond/199 4.00 10.00
241 Viktor Fasth/199 5.00 12.00
242 Carl Soderberg/199 10.00 25.00
244 Roman Cervenka/199 4.00 10.00
245 Calvin Pickard/199 5.00 12.00
247 Johan Larsson/199 4.00 10.00
249 Chris Brown/199 3.00 8.00
250 Nick Petrecki/199 3.00 8.00
251 Dmitrij Jaskin/199 5.00 12.00
252 Alex Killorn/199 5.00 12.00
254 Anthony Peluso/199 3.00 8.00
255 Stefan Matteau/199 4.00 10.00
256 Thomas Hickey/199 4.00 10.00
257 Danny DeKeyser/199 6.00 15.00
258 Edward Pasquale/199 3.00 8.00
259 Christian Thomas/199 4.00 10.00
260 Eric Hartzell/199 5.00 12.00
261 Rickard Rakell/199 5.00 12.00
262 Leo Komarov/199 5.00 12.00
263 Sami Vatanen/199 5.00 12.00
264 Cristopher Nilstorp/199 4.00 10.00
265 Mathew Dumba/199 5.00 12.00
266 Jonas Brodin/199 4.00 10.00
267 Michael Kostka/199 4.00 10.00
268 Nicklas Jensen/199 4.00 10.00
269 Emerson Etem/199 5.00 12.00
270 Ryan Spooner/199 5.00 12.00
271 Jamie Oleksiak/199 4.00 10.00
272 Quinton Howden/199 4.00 10.00
273 Ryan Murphy/199 8.00 20.00
274 Charlie Coyle/199 5.00 12.00
275 Jarred Tinordi/199 5.00 12.00
276 Austin Watson/199 6.00 15.00
277 Brock Nelson/199 8.00 20.00
278 Scott Laughton/199 5.00 12.00
279 Beau Bennett/199 6.00 15.00
280 Frederik Andersen/199 8.00 20.00
281 Nathan Beaulieu/199 4.00 10.00
282 J.T. Miller/199 5.00 12.00
283 Mikhail Grigorenko/199 10.00 25.00
284 Nick Bjugstad/199 6.00 15.00
285 Tanner Pearson/199 5.00 12.00
286 Jared Staal/199 5.00 12.00
287 Tom Wilson/199 8.00 20.00
288 Mikael Granlund/199 8.00 20.00
289 Justin Schultz/199 5.00 12.00
290 Tyler Toffoli/199 10.00 25.00
291 Jack Campbell/199 4.00 10.00
292 Filip Forsberg/199 12.00 30.00
293 Dougie Hamilton/199 12.00 30.00
294 Alex Chiasson/199 5.00 12.00
295 Brendan Gallagher/199 12.00 30.00
296 Cory Conacher/199 3.00 8.00
297 Vladimir Tarasenko/99 50.00 100.00
298 Alex Galchenyuk/199 20.00 50.00
299 Jonathan Huberdeau/199 15.00 30.00
300 Nail Yakupov/199 15.00 40.00
301 Nathan MacKinnon/199 60.00 120.00
302 Seth Jones/199 20.00 40.00
303 Valeri Nichuskin/199 5.00 12.00
304 Sean Monahan/199 25.00 50.00
305 Tomas Hertl/199 6.00 15.00
306 Boone Jenner/199 5.00 12.00
307 Ryan Murray/199 6.00 15.00
308 Morgan Rielly/199 12.00 30.00

2013-14 Select Signatures

*PRIZM/25: .6X TO 1.5X BASIC AU
*PRIZM/25: .5X TO 1.2X BASIC AU SP
SIBB Brad Boyes SP 3.00 8.00
SIBS Brandon Saad SP 6.00 15.00
SICG Cameron Gaunce 2.50 6.00
SICV Chris Vande Velde 2.50 6.00
SIDO Dylan Olsen SP 3.00 8.00
SIDR Dwayne Roloson 2.50 6.00
SIDW Steve Downie SP 3.00 8.00
SIFY Jeff Petry 3.00 8.00
SIGO Gino Odjick SP 4.00 10.00
SIHM Ben Holmstrom 2.50 6.00
SIJC John Carlson 5.00 12.00
SILM Lane MacDermid EXCH 3.00 8.00
SIMH Matt Hackett 2.50 6.00
SIML Mark Letestu 3.00 8.00
SIMM Maxime Macenauer SP
SIMS Mike Santorelli 3.00 8.00
SIMX Max Sauve 2.50 6.00
SIOJ Ondrej Pavelec SP
SION Brendon Nash 3.00 8.00
SIOR Ryan O'Reilly 5.00 12.00
SIPH Patric Hornqvist 3.00 8.00
SIRC Roman Cervenka SP 8.00 20.00
SIRL Robin Lehner SP 4.00 10.00
SIRS Ryan Stoa 2.50 6.00
SITC Tyler Cuma SP 5.00 12.00
SITI Scott Timmins 2.50 6.00
SITK Torey Krug 10.00 25.00
SITP Timo Pielmeier 2.50 6.00
SITR Travis Turnbull 3.00 8.00
SIUM Thomas McCollum 3.00 8.00
SIWI Colin Wilson SP 4.00 10.00
SIYS Yann Sauve 3.00 8.00

2013-14 Select Stars Jersey Autographs

*PRIZM/20: .4X TO 1X JSY AU/25
STAG Alex Galchenyuk/25 25.00 50.00
STAM Al MacInnis/25 15.00 40.00
STAN Antti Niemi/25 12.00 30.00
STBB Beau Bennett/25 12.00 30.00
STBG Brendan Gallagher/25 25.00 50.00
STBH Brett Hull/25 30.00 60.00
STBR Bobby Ryan/25
STCA Craig Anderson/25 15.00 40.00
STCI David Krejci/25 15.00 40.00
STCP Carey Price/25 30.00 60.00
STCS Cory Schneider/25 12.00 30.00
STDB David Backes/25 15.00 40.00
STDH Dougie Hamilton/25 20.00 50.00
STDZ Michael Del Zotto/25 10.00 25.00
STFP Felix Potvin/25 15.00 40.00
STGL Gabriel Landeskog/25 12.00 30.00
STGX Claude Giroux/25
STHL Henrik Lundqvist/25 15.00 40.00
STIK Marian Gaborik/25 15.00 40.00
STJB Jonas Brodin/25 10.00 25.00
STJE Borje Salming/25
STJH Jonathan Huberdeau/25 30.00 60.00
STJJ Jaromir Jagr/15 40.00 80.00
STJS Joe Sakic/25 40.00 80.00
STJT John Tavares/25 15.00 40.00
STKP Keith Primeau/25 12.00 30.00
STLC Logan Couture/25 12.00 30.00
STMB Martin Brodeur/25 40.00 80.00
STML Mario Lemieux/15
STNY Nail Yakupov/25
STOS Chris Chelios/25 15.00 40.00
STOV Alex Ovechkin/25 30.00 60.00
STPK Patrick Kane/25
STSO Carl Soderberg/25
STST Martin St. Louis/25 15.00 40.00
STSX Marc Staal/25 12.00 30.00
STSZ Justin Schultz/25 15.00 40.00
STTT Tyler Toffoli/25 20.00 50.00
STUD Marcel Dionne/25 12.00 30.00
STVR James van Riemsdyk/25 12.00 30.00
STVT Vladimir Tarasenko/25 75.00 125.00
STWS Jonathan Toews/25 25.00 50.00
STXB Jamie Benn/25 12.00 30.00
STXE Jhonas Enroth/25 15.00 40.00

2013-14 Select Youth Explosion Autographs

*PRIZM/25: .6X TO 1.5X BASIC AU
YEAK Alex Killorn SP 4.00 10.00
YEAL Anders Lee 8.00 20.00
YEAS Andrew Shaw EXCH 6.00 15.00
YECC Cory Conacher SP 3.00 8.00
YECO Colby Cohen 3.00 8.00
YECT Colten Teubert SP 3.00 8.00
YEDV Matt Donovan SP 3.00 8.00
YEFR Matt Fraser 3.00 8.00
YEHT Michael Hutchinson SP 5.00 12.00
YEJD Justin DiBenedetto 3.00 8.00
YEJS Jaden Schwartz SP 6.00 15.00
YEKK Keith Kinkaid SP
YEKO Mikhail Grigorenko SP 6.00 15.00
YELB Lance Bouma 3.00 8.00
YELI Leland Irving SP 4.00 10.00
YEMC Mike Connolly 4.00 10.00
YEMZ Mika Zibanejad SP
YENH Ryan Nugent-Hopkins SP 10.00 25.00
YEPC Philippe Cornet SP
YEPI Chet Pickard SP 5.00 12.00
YEPM Patrick Maroon
YERD Raphael Diaz SP 3.00 8.00
YERG Ryan Garbutt 3.00 8.00
YERH Ryan Hamilton 3.00 8.00
YESE Stefan Elliott 4.00 10.00
YETJ Tyler Johnson 20.00 40.00
YEWN J.T. Brown 3.00 8.00
YEZD Zac Dalpe 3.00 8.00

1992-93 Senators Team Issue

This 15-postcard set commemorates the inaugural season of the Ottawa Senators. The postcards feature full-bleed action photography, along with the logos of the set's two sponsors, CFRA Radio and Colonial Furniture. There is no indication of the player's identity anywhere on the card, so knowledge of obscure expansion draft-caliber players is a must to truly appreciate this set. The backs are blank. The cards are unnumbered, and are listed below alphabetically.

COMPLETE SET (15) 6.00 15.00
1 Jamie Baker .40 1.00
2 Daniel Berthiaume .60 1.50
3 Neil Brady .40 1.00
4 Ken Hammond .40 1.00
5 Dave Hannan .40 1.00
6 Jody Hull .40 1.00
7 Mark Lamb .40 1.00
8 Darcy Loewen .40 1.00
9 Norm Maciver .40 1.00
10 Brad Marsh .60 1.50
11 Andrew McBain .40 1.00
12 Mike Peluso .50 1.25
13 Darren Rumble .40 1.00
14 Brad Shaw .40 1.00
15 Sylvain Turgeon .40 1.00

1993-94 Senators Kraft Sheets

These 27 blank-backed photo sheets of the 1993-94 Ottawa Senators measure approximately 8 1/2" by 11" and feature color player action shots bordered in team colors (red, white, and gold). The player's name and uniform number, along with the Senators' logo, appear near the top. The logo for Kraft appears at the lower right; the logo for Loeb appears at the lower left. The production number out of the total produced for each sheet is shown within the white rectangle immediately above the Kraft logo. The sheets were produced in differing quantities. These production figures are shown in the checklist below. A special storage album was also available for the sheets. The sheets are unnumbered and checklisted below in alphabetical order.

COMPLETE SET (27) 60.00 150.00
1 Dave Archibald/3500 2.00 5.00
2 Craig Billington/6500 2.50 6.00
3 Rick Bowness CO/6500 2.00 5.00
4 Robert Burakovsky/1500 3.00 8.00
5 Alexandre Daigle/6500 2.00 5.00
6 Pavol Demitra/1500 4.00 10.00
7 Gord Dineen/3500 2.00 5.00
8 Dmitri Filimonov/1500 3.00 8.00
9 Brian Glynn/1500 3.00 8.00
10 Bill Huard/1500 3.00 8.00
11 Jarmo Kekalainen/1500 3.00 8.00
12 Bob Kudelski/1500 3.00 8.00
13 Mark Lamb/1500 3.00 8.00
14 Darcy Loewen/3500 2.00 5.00
15 Norm Maciver/3500 2.00 5.00
16 Darrin Madeley/1500 3.00 8.00
17 Troy Mallette/3500 2.00 5.00
18 Brad Marsh/6500 3.00 8.00
19 Dave McLlwain/3500 2.00 5.00
20 Darren Rumble/1500 3.00 8.00
21 Vladimir Ruzicka/1500 3.00 8.00
22 Brad Shaw/6500 2.00 5.00
23 Graeme Townshend/1500 3.00 8.00
24 Sylvain Turgeon/6500 2.50 6.00
25 Dennis Vial/1500 3.00 8.00
26 Alexei Yashin/6500 2.00 5.00
27 Team Photo/12500 2.00 5.00
ALB Album 6.00 15.00
NNO Team Photo 2.00 5.00

1994-95 Senators Team Issue

Sponsored by Bell Mobility, this 28-card sets measures approximately 4" by 6" and features members of the 1994-95 Ottawa Senators. The fronts have full-bleed color action player photos with a fading team color-coded inside border. The player's name appears alongside the left, while his uniform number is on the bottom. The team logo in the upper right corner and sponsor logos in English and French on the bottom round out the card face. The backs are blank. The cards are unnumbered and checklisted below in alphabetical order.

COMPLETE SET (28) 6.00 15.00
1 Dave Archibald .20 .50
2 Don Beaupre .30 .75
3 Radim Bicanek .20 .50
4 Craig Billington .30 .75
5 Claude Boivin .20 .50
6 Radek Bonk .40 1.00
7 Phil Bourque .20 .50
8 Rick Bowness CO .20 .50
9 Randy Cunneyworth .20 .50
10 Chris Dahlquist .20 .50
11 Alexandre Daigle .40 1.00
12 Pat Elynuik .20 .50
13 Rob Gaudreau .20 .50
14 Sean Hill .20 .50
15 Bill Huard .20 .50
16 Kerry Huffman .20 .50
17 Scott Levins .20 .50
18 Norm Maciver .20 .50
19 Darrin Madeley .30 .75
20 Troy Mallette .20 .50
21 Brad Marsh CO .30 .75
22 Dave McLlwain .20 .50
23 Troy Murray .20 .50
24 Stanislav Neckar .25 .60
25 Jim Paek .20 .50
26 Sylvain Turgeon .20 .50
27 Dennis Vial .20 .50
28 Alexei Yashin .75 2.00

1995-96 Senators Team Issue

This 24-postcard set was produced by the Senators as a promotional giveaway. The cards feature full-bleed action photography with the club's name in both English and French inscribed along three borders. The fourth border displays the player's name. The backs are blank. As the cards are unnumbered, they are listed below in alphabetical order.

COMPLETE SET (24) 6.00 15.00
1 Daniel Alfredsson 1.25 3.00
2 Dave Archibald .20 .50
3 Mike Bales .25 .60
4 Don Beaupre .30 .75
5 Radek Bonk .25 .60
6 Tom Chorske .20 .50
7 Randy Cunneyworth .20 .50
8 Alexandre Daigle .20 .50
9 Ted Drury .20 .50
10 Steve Duchesne .25 .60
11 Rob Gaudreau .20 .50
12 Sean Hill .20 .50
13 Kerry Huffman .20 .50
14 Scott Levins .20 .50
15 Troy Mallette .20 .50
16 Brad Marsh .40 1.00
17 Trent McCleary .20 .50
18 Jaroslav Modry .20 .50
19 Frank Musil .20 .50
20 Stan Neckar .25 .60
21 Martin Straka .40 1.00
22 Antti Tormanen .20 .50
23 Dennis Vial .20 .50
24 Alexei Yashin .40 1.00

1996-97 Senators Pizza Hut

This 30-card set of the Ottawa Senators was produced in conjunction with Pizza Hut as a promotional giveaway. This standard postcard size set features glossy fronts and full-bleed action photography, with the player's name on the right side, and the Pizza Hut Canada logo in the bottom left corner. The backs are blank. As the cards are unnumbered, they are listed below in alphabetical order.

COMPLETE SET (32) 6.00 15.00
1 Daniel Alfredsson .75 2.00
2 Radek Bonk .30 .75
3 Tom Chorske .20 .50
4 Randy Cunneyworth .20 .50
5 Andreas Dackell .20 .50
6 Alexandre Daigle .20 .50
7 Steve Duchesne .30 .75
8 Bruce Gardiner .20 .50
9 Dave Hannan .20 .50
10 Sean Hill .20 .50
11 Denny Lambert .20 .50
12 Janne Laukkanen .30 .75
13 Jacques Martin CO .08 .25
14 Shawn Mceachern .20 .50
15 Frank Musil .20 .50
16 Phil Myre .20 .50
17 Stan Neckar .20 .50
18 Christer Olsson .20 .50
19 Perry Pearn ACO .08 .25
20 Lance Pitlick .20 .50
21 Craig Ramsay .20 .50
22 Wade Redden .40 1.00
23 Damian Rhodes .40 1.00
24 Ron Tugnutt .40 1.00
25 Shaun Van Allen .20 .50
26 Dennis Vial .20 .50
27 Alexei Yashin .40 1.00
28 Jason York .20 .50
29 Jason Zent .20 .50
30 Sergei Zholtok .20 .50

1998-99 Senators Team Issue

This set features the Senators of the NHL. These oversized cards were sold in set form by the team at home games. The backs are blank and the cards unnumbered. Therefore, they are listed in alphabetical order.

COMPLETE SET (26) 6.00 15.00
1 Daniel Alfredsson .40 1.00
2 Magnus Arvedson .20 .50
3 Bill Berg .20 .50
4 Radek Bonk .20 .50
5 Andreas Dackell .20 .50
6 Bruce Gardiner .20 .50
7 Marian Hossa .75 2.00
8 Andreas Johansson .20 .50
9 Igor Kravchuk .20 .50
10 Janne Laukkanen .20 .50
11 Jacques Martin CO .20 .50
12 Steve Martins .20 .50
13 Shawn McEachern .20 .50
14 Chris Murray .20 .50
15 Chris Phillips .20 .50
16 Lance Pitlick .20 .50
17 Vaclav Prospal .20 .50
18 Wade Redden .40 1.00
19 Damian Rhodes .30 .75
20 Sami Salo .20 .50
21 Patrick Traverse .20 .50
22 Ron Tugnutt .40 1.00
23 Shaun Van Allen .20 .50
24 Alexei Yashin .20 .50
25 Ottawa Senators .20 .50
26 Spartacat MASCOT .08 .25

1999-00 Senators Team Issue

This team-issued set measures approximately 4 1/2" x 8 1/2". The cards carry an action photo of each player on the front accompanied by their jersey number, the CCM logo and the team logo. The back of each card carries the Senators 1999-00 game schedule. The card are not numbered and are listed below in alphabetical order.

COMPLETE SET (26) 8.00 20.00
1 Daniel Alfredsson .40 1.00
2 Magnus Arvedson .20 .50
3 Radek Bonk .30 .75
4 Andreas Dackell .20 .50
5 Kevin Dineen .20 .50
6 Mike Fisher .40 1.00
7 Bruce Gardiner .20 .50
8 Marian Hossa 2.00 5.00
9 Joe Juneau .20 .50
10 Igor Kravchuk .20 .50
11 Patrick Lalime .60 1.50
12 Janne Laukkanen .20 .50
13 Shawn McEachern .30 .75
14 Chris Phillips .30 .75
15 Vaclav Prospal .20 .50
16 Wade Redden .40 1.00
17 Andre Roy .20 .50
18 Sami Salo .20 .50
19 Patrick Traverse .20 .50
20 Ron Tugnutt .40 1.00
21 Shaun Van Allen .20 .50
22 Jason York .20 .50
23 Rob Zamuner .20 .50
24 Jacques Martin HCO .08 .25
25 Spartacat MASCOT .02 .10
26 Team Photo .20 .50

2000-01 Senators Team Issue

This set features the Senators of the NHL. The slightly oversized cards were issued as a promotional giveaway early in the season. The cards feature an action photo on the front and a complete season schedule on the back.

COMPLETE SET (26)
1 Daniel Alfredsson .40 1.00
2 Magnus Arvedson .20 .50
3 Radek Bonk .30 .75
4 Andreas Dackell .20 .50
5 Mike Fisher .30 .75
6 Colin Forbes .20 .50
7 Martin Havlat 1.60 4.00
8 Marian Hossa 2.00 5.00
9 Jani Hurme .60 1.50
10 Patrick Lalime .60 1.50
11 Jacques Martin CO .10 .25
12 Shawn McEachern .20 .50
13 Roger Neilson ACO .10 .25
14 Perry Pearn ACO .10 .25
15 Ricard Persson .20 .50
16 Chris Phillips .20 .50
17 Vaclav Prospal .20 .50
18 Karel Rachunek .20 .50
19 Wade Redden .30 .75
20 Jamie Rivers .20 .50
21 Andre Roy .30 .75
22 Sami Salo .20 .50
23 Spartacat MASCOT .04 .10
24 Alexei Yashin .40 1.00
25 Jason York .20 .50
26 Rob Zamuner .20 .50
27 Team Photo

2001-02 Senators Team Issue

This 29-card set was issued by the NHL Senators. The cards measure and oversized 3 X 5 inches, and feature a stylized color photo on the front, with a black and white team schedule on the back. It is not known how they were distributed, but evidence suggests they were a giveaway of some kind. The cards are not numbered, so are listed below alphabetically. Note: the autograph card is not signed: it is a blank front with room for autographs.

COMPLETE SET (29) 5.00 12.00
1 Daniel Alfredsson .60 1.50
2 Magnus Arvedson .20 .50
3 Radek Bonk .20 .50
4 Zdeno Chara .60 1.50
5 Ivan Ciernik .30 .75
6 Mike Fisher .30 .75
7 Martin Havlat 1.25 3.00
8 Chris Herperger .20 .50
9 Shane Hnidy .20 .50
10 Marian Hossa .75 2.00
11 Jani Hurme .60 1.50
12 Don Jackson ACO .04 .10
13 Patrick Lalime .40 1.00
14 Curtis Leschyshyn .20 .50
15 Jacques Martin CO .04 .10
16 Shawn McEachern .20 .50
17 Bill Muckalt .20 .50
18 Chris Neil .40 1.00
19 Roger Neilson ACO .04 .10
20 Perry Pearn ACO .04 .10
21 Ricard Persson .20 .50
22 Chris Phillips .20 .50
23 Karel Rachunek .20 .50
24 Wade Redden .30 .75
25 Andre Roy .30 .75
26 Sami Salo .20 .50
27 Todd White .20 .50
28 SpartaCat .04 .10
29 Autograph Card .04 .10

2002-03 Senators Team Issue

This 15-card set was issued by the team and given away as promotions. The cards measured approximately 3 1/2" X 4 1/2". Card backs carried the 02-03 schedule.

COMPLETE SET (15) 12.00 20.00
1 Daniel Alfredsson .75 2.00
2 Magnus Arvedson .40 1.00
3 Radek Bonk .40 1.00
4 Zdeno Chara .60 1.50
5 Mike Fisher .60 1.50
6 Martin Havlat 1.25 3.00
7 Marian Hossa 1.25 3.00
8 Jody Hull .40 1.00
9 Patrick Lalime .60 1.50
10 Curtis Leschyshyn .40 1.00
11 Chris Neil .40 1.00
12 Chris Phillips .40 1.00
13 Martin Prusek .60 1.50
14 Wade Redden .60 1.50
15 Anton Volchenkov .40 1.00

2003-04 Senators Postcards

COMPLETE SET (28) 10.00 20.00
1 Brian Pothier .20 .50
2 Zdeno Chara .40 1.00
3 Chris Phillips .20 .50
4 Wade Redden .40 1.00
5 Curtis Leschyshyn .20 .50
6 Martin Havlat .60 1.50
7 Daniel Alfredsson .75 2.00
8 Mike Fisher .40 1.00
9 Radek Bonk .20 .50
10 Peter Schaefer .20 .50
11 Jody Hull .20 .50
12 Marian Hossa .60 1.50
13 Petr Schastlivy .20 .50
14 Bryan Smolinski .20 .50
15 Shaun Van Allen .20 .50
16 Karel Rachunek .20 .50
17 Anton Volchenkov .20 .50
18 Chris Neil .20 .50
19 Vaclav Varada .20 .50
20 Todd White .20 .50
21 Martin Prusek .30 .75
22 Shane Hnidy .20 .50
23 Jason Spezza 1.25 3.00
24 Patrick Lalime .40 1.00
25 Jacques Martin CO .10 .25
26 Don Jackson ACO .10 .25
27 Perry Pearn ACO .10 .25
28 Spartacat MASCOT .04 .10

2006-07 Senators Postcards

This listing is believed to be incomplete. If you can confirm other singles within this set, please email us at hockeymag@beckett.com.

3 Daniel Alfredsson 1.25 3.00
4 Joe Corvo .40 1.00
5 Denis Hamel .40 1.00
6 Dany Heatley 1.25 3.00
7 Chris Kelly .40 1.00
8 Brian McGrattan .75 2.00
9 Andrei Meszaros .40 1.00
10 Chris Phillips .40 1.00
11 Jason Spezza 1.25 3.00
12 Peter Schaefer .40 1.00
13 Christoph Schubert .40 1.00
14 Wade Redden .75 2.00
15 Logo Card .10 .25

1972-73 7-Eleven Slurpee Cups WHA

This 20-cup set features a color head shot and facsimile autograph on the front, and a 7-11 logo, team logo, players name, and biographical information on the back. Cups are unnumbered and checklisted below alphabetically.

COMPLETE SET (20) 125.00 250.00
1 Norm Beaudin 5.00 10.00
2 Chris Bordeleau 5.00 10.00
3 Carl Brewer 5.00 10.00
4 Wayne Carleton 6.00 12.00
5 Gerry Cheevers 12.50 25.00
6 Wayne Connelly 7.50 15.00
7 Jean-Guy Gendron 5.00 10.00
8 Ted Green 5.00 10.00
9 Al Hamilton 5.00 10.00
10 Jim Harrison 5.00 10.00
11 Bobby Hull 25.00 50.00
12 Andre Lacroix 6.00 12.00
13 Danny Lawson 5.00 10.00
14 John McKenzie 5.00 10.00
15 Jim Mcleod 5.00 10.00
16 Jack Norris 5.00 10.00
17 John Schella 5.00 10.00
18 J.C. Tremblay 7.50 15.00
19 Ron Ward 5.00 10.00
20 Jim Watson 5.00 10.00

1984-85 7-Eleven Discs

This set of 60 discs was sponsored by 7-Eleven. Each disc or coin measures approximately 2" in diameter and features an alternating portrait of the player and the team's logo. The coins are quite colorful and have adhesive backing. We have checklisted the coins below in alphabetical order of team name. Also the player's names have been alphabetized within their teams, and their uniform numbers placed to the right of their names. In addition, 7-Eleven also issued a large 4 1/2" diameter Wayne Gretzky disc which is not considered an essential part of the complete set. There is also a paper checklist sheet produced which pictured (in red, white, and blue) some of the coins and listed the players in the set.

COMPLETE SET (60) 50.00 125.00
1 Ray Bourque 7 2.00 5.00
2 Rick Middleton 16 .60 1.50
3 Tom Barrasso 30 1.00 2.50
4 Gilbert Perreault 11 .75 2.00
5 Rejean Lemelin 31 .60 1.50
6 Lanny McDonald 9 1.00 2.50
7 Paul Reinhart 23 .40 1.00
8 Doug Risebrough 8 .40 1.00
9 Denis Savard 18 1.00 2.50
10 Al Secord 20 .40 1.00
11 Steve Yzerman 19 6.00 15.00
12 Tiger Williams 55 .60 1.50
13 Glenn Anderson 9 .75 2.00
14 Paul Coffey 7 2.00 5.00
15 Michel Goulet 16 .75 2.00
16 Wayne Gretzky 99 8.00 20.00
17 Charlie Huddy 22 .40 1.00
18 Pat Hughes 16 .40 1.00
19 Jari Kurri 17 1.25 3.00
20 Kevin Lowe 4 .40 1.00
21 Mark Messier 11 3.00 8.00
22 Ron Francis 10 1.50 4.00
23 Sylvain Turgeon 16 .40 1.00
24 Marcel Dionne 16 .75 2.00
25 Dave Taylor 18 .60 1.50
26 Brian Bellows 23 .40 1.00
27 Dino Ciccarelli 20 .60 1.50
28 Harold Snepsts 28 .60 1.50
29 Bob Gainey 23 .75 2.00
30 Larry Robinson 19 1.00 2.50
31 Mel Bridgman 18 .40 1.00
32 Chico Resch 1 .60 1.50
33 Mike Bossy 22 1.25 3.00
34 Bryan Trottier 19 1.00 2.50
35 Barry Beck 5 .40 1.00
36 Don Maloney 12 .40 1.00
37 Tim Kerr 12 .60 1.50
38 Darryl Sittler 27 1.00 2.50
39 Mike Bullard 22 .40 1.00
40 Rick Kehoe 17 .60 1.50
41 Peter Stastny 26 1.25 3.00
42 Bernie Federko 24 .60 1.50
43 Rob Ramage 5 .40 1.00
44 John Anderson 10 .40 1.00
45 Bill Derlago 19 .40 1.00
46 Gary Nylund 2 .40 1.00
47 Rick Vaive 22 .40 1.00
48 Richard Brodeur 35 .60 1.50
49 Gary Lupul 7 .40 1.00
50 Darcy Rota 18 .40 1.00
51 Stan Smyl 12 .60 1.50
52 Tony Tanti 9 .40 1.00
53 Mike Gartner 11 1.25 3.00
54 Rod Langway 5 .40 1.00
55 Scott Arniel 11 .40 1.00
56 Dave Babych 44 .40 1.00
57 Laurie Boschman 16 .40 1.00
58 Dale Hawerchuk 10 1.00 2.50
59 Paul MacLean 15 .40 1.00
60 Brian Mullen 19 .40 1.00
NNO Wayne Gretzky Large 10.00 25.00
NNO Paper Checklist Sheet 2.00 5.00

1985-86 7-Eleven Credit Cards

This 25-card set was sponsored by 7-Eleven. The cards measure approximately 3 3/8" by 2 1/8" and were issued in the "credit card" format. The front features color head and shoulder shots of two players from the same NHL team. These pictures are enframed by a black background, with the player's name, position, and uniform number in blue lettering below the photo. The information on the card back is framed in red boxes. In the smaller box on the left appears the 7-Eleven logo, card number, and the team logo. The right-hand box gives a brief history of the team. The key card in the set is Mario Lemieux, shown during his Rookie Card year.

COMPLETE SET (25) 14.00 35.00
1 Ray Bourque and Rick Middleton .75 2.00
2 Tom Barrasso Gilbert Perreault .60 1.50
3 Paul Reinhart Lanny McDonald .40 1.00
4 Denis Savard Doug Wilson .60 1.50
5 Ron Duguay Steve Yzerman 3.00 8.00
6 Paul Coffey Jari Kurri 1.00 2.50
7 Ron Francis Mike Liut .75 2.00
8 Marcel Dionne Dave Taylor .50 1.25
9 Brian Bellows Dino Ciccarelli .60 1.50
10 Larry Robinson Guy Carbonneau .60 1.50
11 Mel Bridgman Chico Resch .30 .75
12 Mike Bossy Bryan Trottier 1.00 2.50
13 Reijo Ruotsalainen Barry Beck .30 .75
14 Tim Kerr Mark Howe .30 .75
15 Mario Lemieux Mike Bullard 8.00 20.00
16 Peter Stastny Michel Goulet 1.00 2.50
17 Rob Ramage Brian Sutter .30 .75
18 Rick Vaive Borje Salming .40 1.00
19 Patrik Sundstrom Stan Smyl .30 .75
20 Rod Langway Mike Gartner .50 1.25
21 Dale Hawerchuk Paul MacLean .40 1.00
22 Stanley Cup Winners .30 .75
23 Prince of Wales Trophy Winners .30 .75
24 Clarence S. Campbell Bowl Winners .30 .75
25 Title Card .08 .25

1991-92 Sharks Sports Action

This 22-card standard-size set was issued by Sports Action and features members of the 1991-92 San Jose Sharks. The cards are printed on thin card stock. The fronts feature full-bleed glossy color action photos. The backs carry brief biography, career summary, and the team logo. The cards are unnumbered and checklisted below in alphabetical order.

COMPLETE SET (22) 4.00 10.00
1 Perry Anderson .20 .50
2 Perry Berezan .20 .50
3 Steve Bozek .20 .50
4 Dean Evason .20 .50
5 Pat Falloon .30 .75
6 Paul Fenton .20 .50
7 Link Gaetz .20 .50
8 Jeff Hackett .40 1.00
9 Ken Hammond .20 .50
10 Brian Hayward .30 .75
11 Tony Hrkac .20 .50
12 Kelly Kisio .25 .60
13 Brian Lawton .20 .50
14 Pat MacLeod .20 .50

15 Bob McGill .20 .50
16 Brian Mullen .20 .50
17 Jarmo Myllys .25 .60
18 Wayne Presley .20 .50
19 Neil Wilkinson .25 .60
20 Doug Wilson .40 1.00
21 Rob Zettler .20 .50
22 San Jose Sharks .30 .75

1997 Sharks Fleer All-Star Sheet

This odd-sized sheet was handed out to attendees of the '97 NHL All-Star Game to promote the '96-97 line of Fleer hockey products. The sheet also was available at the All-Star Fanfest card show. It features eight members of the hometown San Jose Sharks on three different types of Fleer cards; the brand pictured is listed after each player's name.

9 Sharks Complete Sheet 1.50 4.00
Doug Bodger Fleer Picks
Kelly Hrudey Metal Universe
Al Iafrate Metal Universe
Bernie Nicholls Metal Universe
Owen Nolan Fleer
Marcus Ragnarsson Fleer
Chris Terreri Fleer
Alexei Yegorov Fleer Picks

2001-02 Sharks Postcards

This set was given away by the team during the 2001-02 season. The checklist below is not believed to be complete. Please forward any info to hockeymag@beckett.com. Special thanks to Sgt. Randy Garcia of the Humboldt County Sheriff's Dept. for the checklist and image.

1 Adam Graves .75 2.00
2 Vincent Damphousse .40 1.00
3 Matt Bradley .40 1.00
4 Brad Stuart .40 1.00
5 Owen Nolan .75 2.00
6 Patrick Marleau .75 2.00
7 Gary Suter .40 1.00
8 Niklas Sundstrom .40 1.00
9 Marco Sturm .40 1.00
10 Mike Ricci .40 1.00
11 Marcus Ragnarsson .40 1.00
12 Scott Thornton .40 1.00
13 Scott Hannan .40 1.00
14 Todd Harvey .40 1.00
15 Bryan Marchment .40 1.00
16 Teemu Selanne 1.25 3.00

2002-03 Sharks Team Issue

These 4X 7 blank backs were issued by the team at promotional events. It's likely more exist in the set. If you can confirm this, please contact us at hockeymag@beckett.com.

COMPLETE SET 4.00 10.00
1 Vincent Damphousse .40 1.00
2 Adam Graves .40 1.00
3 Patrick Marleau .40 1.00
4 Evgeni Nabokov .75 2.00
5 Mike Rathje .40 1.00
6 Mike Ricci .40 1.00
7 Teemu Selanne 1.25 3.00
8 Marco Sturm .40 1.00

2003-04 Sharks Postcards

The checklist is likely incomplete. Please send additional info to hockeymag@beckett.com.

COMPLETE SET 5.00 12.00
1 Jonathan Cheechoo 1.25 3.00
2 Vincent Damphousse .40 1.00
3 Rob Davidson .40 1.00
4 Nils Ekman .40 1.00
5 Jim Fahey .40 1.00
6 Scott Hannan .40 1.00
7 Todd Harvey .40 1.00
8 Alexander Korolyuk .40 1.00
9 Patrick Marleau .75 2.00
10 Alyn McCauley .40 1.00
11 Kyle McLaren .40 1.00
12 Evgeni Nabokov .75 2.00
13 Tom Preissing .40 1.00
14 Wayne Primeau .40 1.00
15 Mike Rathje .40 1.00
16 Mike Ricci .40 1.00
17 Brad Stuart .40 1.00
18 Marco Sturm .40 1.00
19 Scott Thornton .40 1.00

1960-61 Shirriff Coins

This set of 120 coins (each measuring approximately 1 3/8" in diameter) features players from all six NHL teams. These plastic coins are in color and numbered on the front. The coins are checklisted below according to teams as follows: Toronto Maple Leafs (1-20), Montreal Canadiens (21-40), Detroit Red Wings (41-60), Chicago Blackhawks (61-80), New York Rangers (81-100), and Boston Bruins (101-120). The set was also issued on a limited basis as a factory set in a black presentation box.

COMPLETE SET (120) 250.00 500.00
1 Johnny Bower 5.00 10.00
2 Dick Duff 2.50 5.00
3 Carl Brewer 2.50 5.00
4 Red Kelly 5.00 10.00
5 Tim Horton 7.50 15.00
6 Allan Stanley 2.50 5.00
7 Bob Baun 2.50 5.00
8 Billy Harris 1.50 3.00
9 George Armstrong 3.00 6.00
10 Ron Stewart 1.50 3.00
11 Bert Olmstead 2.50 5.00
12 Frank Mahovlich 7.50 15.00
13 Bob Pulford 2.50 5.00
14 Gary Edmundson 1.50 3.00
15 Johnny Wilson 1.50 3.00
16 Larry Regan 1.50 3.00
17 Gerry James 2.00 4.00
18 Rudy Migay 1.50 3.00
19 Gerry Ehman 1.50 3.00
20 Punch Imlach CO 2.00 4.00
21 Jacques Plante 12.50 25.00
22 Dickie Moore 3.00 6.00
23 Don Marshall 1.50 3.00
24 Albert Langlois 1.50 3.00
25 Tom Johnson 2.50 5.00
26 Doug Harvey 5.00 10.00
27 Phil Goyette 1.50 3.00
28 Boom Boom Geoffrion 6.00 12.00
29 Marcel Bonin 1.50 3.00
30 Jean Beliveau 10.00 20.00
31 Ralph Backstrom 2.00 4.00
32 Andre Pronovost 1.50 3.00
33 Claude Provost 2.00 4.00
34 Henri Richard 7.50 15.00
35 Jean-Guy Talbot 2.00 4.00
36 J.C. Tremblay 2.00 4.00
37 Bob Turner 1.50 3.00
38 Bill Hicke 1.50 3.00
39 Charlie Hodge 4.00 8.00
40 Toe Blake CO 2.50 5.00
41 Terry Sawchuk 10.00 20.00
42 Gordie Howe 25.00 50.00
43 John McKenzie 1.50 3.00
44 Alex Delvecchio 5.00 10.00
45 Norm Ullman 3.00 6.00
46 Jack McIntyre 1.50 3.00
47 Barry Cullen 2.00 4.00
48 Val Fonteyne 1.50 3.00
49 Warren Godfrey 1.50 3.00
50 Pete Goegan 1.50 3.00
51 Gerry Melnyk 1.50 3.00
52 Marc Reaume 1.50 3.00
53 Gary Aldcorn 1.50 3.00
54 Len Lunde 1.50 3.00
55 Murray Oliver 1.50 3.00
56 Marcel Pronovost 2.50 5.00
57 Howie Glover 1.50 3.00
58 Gerry Odrowski 1.50 3.00
59 Parker MacDonald 1.50 3.00
60 Sid Abel CO 2.50 5.00
61 Glenn Hall 6.00 12.00
62 Ed Litzenberger 2.00 4.00
63 Bobby Hull 20.00 40.00
64 Tod Sloan 1.50 3.00
65 Murray Balfour 1.50 3.00
66 Pierre Pilote 2.50 5.00
67 Al Arbour 2.50 5.00
68 Earl Balfour 1.50 3.00
69 Eric Nesterenko 2.00 4.00
70 Ken Wharram 2.50 5.00
71 Stan Mikita 12.50 25.00
72 Ab McDonald 1.50 3.00
73 Elmer Vasko 2.00 4.00
74 Dollard St.Laurent 2.00 4.00
75 Ron Murphy 1.50 3.00
76 Jack Evans 1.50 3.00
77 Bill Hay 1.50 3.00
78 Reg Fleming 2.00 4.00
79 Cecil Hoekstra 1.50 3.00
80 Tommy Ivan CO 2.00 4.00
81 Jack McCartan 4.00 8.00
82 Red Sullivan 1.50 3.00
83 Camille Henry 2.00 4.00
84 Larry Popein 1.50 3.00
85 John Hanna 1.50 3.00
86 Harry Howell 2.50 5.00
87 Eddie Shack 5.00 10.00
88 Irv Spencer 1.50 3.00
89 Andy Bathgate 3.00 6.00
90 Bill Gadsby 2.50 5.00
91 Andy Hebenton 1.50 3.00
92 Earl Ingarfield 1.50 3.00
93 Don Johns 1.50 3.00
94 Dave Balon 1.50 3.00
95 Jim Morrison 1.50 3.00
96 Ken Schinkel 1.50 3.00
97 Lou Fontinato 1.50 3.00
98 Ted Hampson 1.50 3.00
99 Brian Cullen 2.00 4.00
100 Alf Pike CO 1.50 3.00
101 Don Simmons 2.50 5.00
102 Fern Flaman 2.50 5.00
103 Vic Stasiuk 2.00 4.00
104 Johnny Bucyk 5.00 10.00
105 Bronco Horvath 2.00 4.00
106 Doug Mohns 4.00 8.00
107 Leo Boivin 2.50 5.00
108 Don McKenney 1.50 3.00
109 Jean-Guy Gendron 1.50 3.00
110 Jerry Toppazzini 1.50 3.00
111 Dick Meissner 1.50 3.00
112 Autry Erickson 1.50 3.00
113 Jim Bartlett 1.50 3.00
114 Orval Tessier 2.00 4.00
115 Billy Carter 1.50 3.00
116 Dallas Smith 2.00 4.00
117 Leo Labine 1.50 3.00
118 Bob Armstrong 1.50 3.00
119 Bruce Gamble 2.50 5.00
120 Milt Schmidt CO 2.50 5.00

1961-62 Shirriff/Salada Coins

This set of 120 coins (each measuring approximately 1 3/8" in diameter) features players of the NHL, all six teams. These plastic coins are in color and numbered on the front. The coins are numbered according to teams as follows: Boston Bruins (1-20), Chicago Blackhawks (21-40), Toronto Maple Leafs (41-60), Detroit Red Wings (61-80), New York Rangers (81-100), and Montreal Canadiens (101-120). The coins were also produced in identical fashion for Salada with a Salada imprint; the Salada version has the same values as listed below. This was the only year of Shirriff coins where collectors could obtain plastic shields for displaying their collection. These shields are not considered part of the complete set.

COMPLETE SET (120) 200.00 400.00
1 Cliff Pennington 1.25 2.50
2 Dallas Smith 2.00 4.00
3 Andre Pronovost 1.25 2.50
4 Charlie Burns 1.25 2.50
5 Leo Boivin 2.50 5.00
6 Don McKenney 1.25 2.50
7 Johnny Bucyk 4.00 8.00
8 Murray Oliver 1.25 2.50
9 Jerry Toppazzini 1.25 2.50
10 Doug Mohns 2.00 4.00
11 Don Head 2.00 4.00
12 Bob Armstrong 1.25 2.50
13 Pat Stapleton 2.00 4.00
14 Orland Kurtenbach 2.00 4.00
15 Dick Meissner 1.25 2.50
16 Ted Green 2.00 4.00
17 Tom Williams 1.25 2.50
18 Autry Erickson 1.25 2.50
19 Phil Watson CO 2.50 5.00
20 Ed Chadwick 2.50 5.00
21 Wayne Hillman 5.00 10.00
22 Stan Mikita 6.00 12.00
23 Eric Nesterenko 2.00 4.00
24 Reg Fleming 1.25 2.50
25 Bobby Hull 12.50 25.00
26 Elmer Vasko 1.25 2.50
27 Pierre Pilote 2.50 5.00
28 Chico Maki 2.00 4.00
29 Glenn Hall 5.00 10.00
30 Murray Balfour 1.25 2.50
31 Bronco Horvath 1.50 3.00
32 Ken Wharram 2.00 4.00
33 Ab McDonald 1.25 2.50
34 Bill Hay 1.25 2.50
35 Dollard St.Laurent 2.00 4.00
36 Ron Murphy 1.25 2.50
37 Bob Turner 1.25 2.50
38 Gerry Melnyk 1.25 2.50
39 Jack Evans 1.25 2.50
40 Rudy Pilous CO 2.50 5.00
41 Johnny Bower 5.00 10.00
42 Allan Stanley 3.00 6.00
43 Frank Mahovlich 5.00 10.00
44 Tim Horton 7.50 15.00
45 Carl Brewer 2.00 4.00
46 Bob Pulford 2.50 5.00
47 Bob Nevin 2.00 4.00
48 Eddie Shack 4.00 8.00
49 Red Kelly 4.00 8.00
50 Bob Baun 2.00 4.00
51 George Armstrong 3.00 6.00
52 Bert Olmstead 2.50 5.00
53 Dick Duff 2.00 4.00
54 Billy Harris 2.00 4.00
55 Larry Keenan 1.25 2.50
56 Johnny MacMillan 1.25 2.50
57 Punch Imlach CO 2.50 5.00
58 Dave Keon 7.50 15.00
59 Larry Hillman 1.25 2.50
60 Al Arbour 2.50 5.00
61 Sid Abel CO 2.50 5.00
62 Warren Godfrey 1.25 2.50
63 Vic Stasiuk 1.25 2.50
64 Leo Labine 1.25 2.50
65 Howie Glover 1.25 2.50
66 Gordie Howe 20.00 40.00
67 Val Fonteyne 1.25 2.50
68 Marcel Pronovost 2.50 5.00
69 Parker MacDonald 1.25 2.50
70 Alex Delvecchio 4.00 8.00
71 Ed Litzenberger 1.25 2.50
72 Al Johnson 1.25 2.50
73 Bruce MacGregor 1.25 2.50
74 Howie Young 1.25 2.50
75 Pete Goegan 1.25 2.50
76 Norm Ullman 3.00 6.00
77 Terry Sawchuk 12.50 25.00
78 Gerry Odrowski 1.25 2.50
79 Bill Gadsby 2.50 5.00
80 Hank Bassen 2.00 4.00
81 Doug Harvey 4.00 8.00
82 Earl Ingarfield 1.25 2.50
83 Pat Hannigan 1.25 2.50
84 Dean Prentice 2.00 4.00
85 Gump Worsley 5.00 10.00
86 Irv Spencer 1.25 2.50
87 Camille Henry 2.00 4.00
88 Andy Bathgate 3.00 6.00
89 Harry Howell 2.50 5.00
90 Andy Hebenton 1.25 2.50
91 Red Sullivan 1.25 2.50
92 Ted Hampson 1.25 2.50
93 Jean-Guy Gendron 1.25 2.50
94 Albert Langlois 1.25 2.50
95 Larry Cahan 1.25 2.50
96 Bob Cunningham 1.25 2.50
97 Vic Hadfield 2.00 4.00
98 Jean Ratelle 5.00 10.00
99 Ken Schinkel 1.25 2.50
100 Johnny Wilson 1.25 2.50
101 Toe Blake CO 2.50 5.00
102 Jean Beliveau 10.00 20.00
103 Don Marshall 1.25 2.50
104 Boom Boom Geoffrion 6.00 12.00
105 Claude Provost 2.00 4.00
106 Tom Johnson 2.50 5.00
107 Dickie Moore 4.00 8.00
108 Bill Hicke 1.25 2.50
109 Jean-Guy Talbot 2.00 4.00
110 Henri Richard 5.00 10.00
111 Lou Fontinato 1.50 3.00
112 Gilles Tremblay 1.25 2.50
113 Jacques Plante 10.00 20.00
114 Ralph Backstrom 2.00 4.00
115 Marcel Bonin 1.25 2.50
116 Phil Goyette 1.25 2.50
117 Bobby Rousseau 2.00 4.00
118 J.C. Tremblay 2.00 4.00
119 Al MacNeil 1.25 2.50
120 Jean Gauthier 1.25 2.50
S1 Boston Bruins Shield 30.00 60.00
S2 Chicago Blackhawks Shield 30.00 60.00
S3 Detroit Red Wings Shield 30.00 60.00
S4 Montreal Canadiens Shield 30.00 60.00
S5 New York Rangers Shield 30.00 60.00
S6 Toronto Maple Leafs Shield 30.00 60.00

1962-63 Shirriff Coins

This set of 60 coins (each measuring approximately 1 1/2" in diameter) features 12 All-Stars, six Trophy winners, and players from Montreal (20) and Toronto (22). The four American teams in the NHL were not included in this set except where they appeared as All-Stars or Trophy winners. These metal coins are in color and numbered on the front. The backs are written in French and English.

COMPLETE SET (60) 200.00 400.00
1 Johnny Bower 5.00 10.00
2 Allan Stanley 2.00 4.00
3 Frank Mahovlich 10.00 20.00
4 Tim Horton 10.00 20.00
5 Carl Brewer 2.50 5.00
6 Bob Pulford 4.00 8.00
7 Bob Nevin 2.00 4.00
8 Eddie Shack 4.00 8.00
9 Red Kelly 4.00 8.00
10 George Armstrong 4.00 8.00
11 Bert Olmstead 3.00 6.00
12 Dick Duff 2.50 5.00
13 Billy Harris 2.00 4.00
14 Johnny MacMillan 2.00 4.00
15 Punch Imlach CO 2.00 4.00
16 Dave Keon 7.50 15.00
17 Larry Hillman 2.00 4.00
18 Ed Litzenberger 2.00 4.00
19 Bob Baun 3.00 6.00
20 Al Arbour 4.00 8.00
21 Ron Stewart 2.00 4.00
22 Don Simmons 3.00 6.00
23 Lou Fontinato 2.00 4.00
24 Gilles Tremblay 2.00 4.00
25 Jacques Plante 12.50 25.00
26 Ralph Backstrom 2.50 5.00
27 Marcel Bonin 2.00 4.00
28 Phil Goyette 2.00 4.00
29 Bobby Rousseau 2.50 5.00
30 J.C. Tremblay 2.50 5.00
31 Toe Blake CO 4.00 8.00
32 Jean Beliveau 10.00 20.00
33 Don Marshall 2.00 4.00
34 Boom Boom Geoffrion 6.00 12.00
35 Claude Provost 2.50 5.00
36 Tom Johnson 3.00 6.00
37 Dickie Moore 5.00 10.00
38 Bill Hicke 2.00 4.00
39 Jean-Guy Talbot 2.50 5.00
40 Al MacNeil 2.50 5.00
41 Henri Richard 7.50 15.00
42 Red Berenson 5.00 10.00
43 Jacques Plante AS 12.50 25.00
44 Jean-Guy Talbot AS 2.50 5.00
45 Doug Harvey AS 5.00 10.00
46 Stan Mikita AS 5.00 10.00
47 Bobby Hull AS 12.50 25.00
48 Andy Bathgate AS 4.00 8.00
49 Glenn Hall AS 5.00 10.00
50 Pierre Pilote AS 4.00 8.00
51 Carl Brewer AS 2.50 5.00
52 Dave Keon AS 7.50 15.00
53 Frank Mahovlich AS 7.50 15.00
54 Gordie Howe AS 20.00 40.00
55 Dave Keon Byng 7.50 15.00
56 Bobby Rousseau Calder 2.50 5.00
57 Bobby Hull Ross 12.50 25.00
58 Jacques Plante Vezina 12.50 25.00
59 Jacques Plante Hart 12.50 25.00
60 Doug Harvey Norris 5.00 10.00

1968-69 Shirriff Coins

This set of 176 coins (each measuring approximately 1 3/8" in diameter) features players from all of the teams in the NHL. These plastic coins are in color and numbered on the front. However the coins are numbered by Shirriff within each team and not for the whole set. The correspondence between the actual coin numbers and the numbers assigned below should be apparent. For those few situations where two coins from the same team have the same number, that number is listed in the checklist below next to the name. The coins are checklisted below according to teams as follows: Boston Bruins (1-16), Chicago Blackhawks (17-33), Detroit Red Wings (34-49), Los Angeles Kings (50-61), Minnesota North Stars (62-74), Montreal Canadiens (75-92), New York Rangers (93-108), Oakland Seals (109-121), Philadelphia Flyers (122-134), Pittsburgh Penguins (135-146), St. Louis Blues (147-158), and Toronto Maple Leafs (159-176). Some of the coins are quite challenging to find. It seems the higher numbers within each team and the coins from the players on the expansion teams are more difficult to find; these are marked by SP in the list below.

1 Eddie Shack 8.00 20.00
2 Ed Westfall 8.00 20.00
3 Don Awrey 10.00 25.00
4 Gerry Cheevers 10.00 25.00
5 Bobby Orr 80.00 150.00
6 Johnny Bucyk 10.00 25.00
7 Derek Sanderson 10.00 25.00
8 Phil Esposito 15.00 40.00
9 Fred Stanfield 12.00 30.00
10 Ken Hodge 12.00 30.00
11 John McKenzie 10.00 25.00
12 Ted Green 12.00 30.00
13 Dallas Smith SP 60.00 150.00
14 Gary Doak SP 60.00 150.00
15 Glen Sather SP 60.00 150.00
16 Tom Williams SP 80.00 150.00
17 Bobby Hull 20.00 50.00
18 Pat Stapleton 12.00 30.00
19 Wayne Maki 10.00 25.00
20 Denis DeJordy 10.00 25.00
21 Ken Wharram 10.00 25.00
22 Pit Martin 10.00 25.00
23 Chico Maki 5.00 12.00
24 Doug Mohns 8.00 20.00
25 Stan Mikita 10.00 25.00
26 Doug Jarrett 15.00 40.00
27 Dennis Hull 11 SP 40.00 100.00
28 Dennis Hull 11 30.00 80.00
29 Matt Ravlich 10.00 25.00
30 Dave Dryden SP 40.00 100.00
31 Eric Nesterenko SP 60.00 150.00
32 Gilles Marotte SP 60.00 150.00
33 Jim Pappin SP 60.00 150.00
34 Gary Bergman 10.00 25.00
35 Roger Crozier 10.00 25.00
36 Peter Mahovlich 10.00 25.00
37 Alex Delvecchio 10.00 25.00
38 Dean Prentice 10.00 25.00
39 Kent Douglas 12.00 30.00
40 Roy Edwards 10.00 25.00
41 Bruce MacGregor 12.00 30.00
42 Garry Unger 10.00 25.00
43 Pete Stemkowski 8.00 20.00
44 Gordie Howe 30.00 80.00
45 Frank Mahovlich 8.00 20.00
46 Bob Baun SP 150.00 250.00
47 Brian Conacher SP 40.00 100.00
48 Jim Watson SP 200.00 300.00
49 Nick Libett SP 50.00 125.00
50 Real Lemieux 8.00 20.00
51 Ted Irvine 8.00 20.00
52 Bob Wall 5.00 12.00
53 Bill White 8.00 20.00
54 Gord Labossiere 8.00 20.00
55 Eddie Joyal 8.00 20.00
56 Lowell MacDonald 8.00 20.00
57 Bill Flett 8.00 20.00
58 Wayne Rutledge 8.00 20.00
59 Dave Amadio 10.00 25.00
60 Skip Krake SP 30.00 80.00
61 Doug Robinson SP 25.00 60.00
62 Wayne Connelly 8.00 20.00
63 Bob Woytowich 8.00 20.00
64 Andre Boudrias 8.00 20.00
65 Bill Goldsworthy 8.00 20.00
66 Cesare Maniago 8.00 20.00
67 Milan Marcetta 8.00 20.00
68 Bill Collins SP 7 40.00 100.00
69 Claude Larose SP 7 40.00 100.00
70 Parker MacDonald 6.00 15.00
71 Ray Cullen 6.00 15.00
72 Mike McMahon 8.00 20.00
73 Bob McCord SP 25.00 60.00
74 Larry Hillman SP 30.00 80.00
75 Gump Worsley 8.00 20.00
76 Rogatien Vachon 8.00 20.00
77 Ted Harris 10.00 25.00
78 Jacques Laperriere 8.00 20.00
79 J.C. Tremblay 10.00 25.00
80 Jean Beliveau 20.00 50.00
81 Gilles Tremblay 8.00 20.00
82 Ralph Backstrom 8.00 20.00
83 Bobby Rousseau 8.00 20.00
84 John Ferguson 8.00 20.00
85 Dick Duff 8.00 20.00
86 Terry Harper 8.00 20.00
87 Yvan Cournoyer 10.00 25.00
88 Jacques Lemaire 8.00 20.00
89 Henri Richard 8.00 20.00
90 Claude Provost SP 50.00 125.00
91 Serge Savard SP 80.00 150.00
92 Mickey Redmond SP 80.00 150.00
93 Rod Seiling 8.00 20.00
94 Jean Ratelle 8.00 20.00
95 Ed Giacomin 12.00 30.00
96 Reg Fleming 8.00 20.00
97 Phil Goyette 8.00 20.00
98 Arnie Brown 8.00 20.00
99 Don Marshall 5.00 12.00
100 Orland Kurtenbach 8.00 20.00
101 Bob Nevin 10.00 25.00
102 Rod Gilbert 8.00 20.00
103 Harry Howell 8.00 20.00
104 Jim Neilson 12.00 30.00
105 Vic Hadfield SP 150.00 400.00
106 Larry Jeffrey SP 200.00 350.00
107 Dave Balon SP 80.00 150.00
108 Ron Stewart SP 300.00 400.00
109 Gerry Ehman 12.00 30.00
110 John Brenneman 15.00 40.00
111 Ted Hampson 25.00 60.00
112 Billy Harris 20.00 50.00
113 George Swarbrick SP 5 50.00 100.00
114 Carol Vadnais SP 5 900.00 1500.00
115 Gary Smith 12.00 30.00
116 Charlie Hodge 12.00 30.00
117 Bert Marshall 6.00 15.00
118 Bill Hicke 12.00 30.00
119 Tracy Pratt 10.00 25.00
120 Gary Jarrett SP 800.00 1200.00
121 Howie Young SP 800.00 1200.00
122 Bernie Parent 15.00 40.00
123 John Miszuk 8.00 20.00
124 Ed Hoekstra SP 3 50.00 100.00
125 Allan Stanley SP 3 60.00 150.00
126 Gary Dornhoefer 8.00 20.00
127 Doug Favell 10.00 25.00
128 Andre Lacroix 10.00 25.00
129 Brit Selby 6.00 15.00
130 Don Blackburn 8.00 20.00
131 Leon Rochefort 15.00 40.00
132 Forbes Kennedy 15.00 40.00
133 Claude Laforge SP 150.00 250.00
134 Pat Hannigan SP 50.00 125.00
135 Ken Schinkel 8.00 20.00
136 Earl Ingarfield 8.00 20.00
137 Val Fonteyne 8.00 20.00
138 Noel Price 10.00 25.00
139 Andy Bathgate 10.00 25.00
140 Les Binkley 12.00 30.00
141 Leo Boivin 12.00 30.00
142 Paul Andrea 6.00 15.00
143 Dunc McCallum 12.00 30.00
144 Keith McCreary 8.00 20.00
145 Lou Angotti SP 100.00 250.00
146 Wally Boyer SP 150.00 250.00
147 Ron Schock 10.00 25.00
148 Bob Plager 10.00 25.00
149 Al Arbour 6.00 15.00
150 Red Berenson 10.00 25.00
151 Glenn Hall 10.00 25.00
152 Jim Roberts 6.00 15.00
153 Noel Picard 8.00 20.00
154 Barclay Plager 8.00 20.00
155 Larry Keenan 8.00 20.00
156 Terry Crisp 10.00 25.00
157 Gary Sabourin SP 60.00 150.00
158 Ab McDonald SP 60.00 150.00
159 George Armstrong 10.00 25.00
160 Wayne Carleton 10.00 25.00
161 Paul Henderson 30.00 80.00
162 Bob Pulford 8.00 20.00
163 Mike Walton 6.00 15.00
164 Johnny Bower 10.00 25.00
165 Ron Ellis 10.00 25.00
166 Mike Pelyk 10.00 25.00
167 Murray Oliver 8.00 20.00
168 Norm Ullman 8.00 20.00
169 Dave Keon 25.00 60.00
170 Floyd Smith 10.00 25.00
171 Marcel Pronovost 10.00 25.00
172 Tim Horton 30.00 80.00
173 Bruce Gamble 10.00 25.00
174 Jim McKenny SP 80.00 150.00
175 Mike Byers SP 60.00 150.00
176 Pierre Pilote SP 80.00 150.00

1995-96 SkyBox Impact Promo Panel

Measuring 7" by 7", this perforated promo panel was issued by SkyBox to celebrate the inaugural edition of the SkyBox Impact hockey series. The left strip consists of ad copy, with four standard-size player cards filling out the rest of the panel. As indicated in the listing below, Blaine Lacher is featured on two cards: a regular card as well as a Deflector insert card. The only difference from their regular issue counterparts is that these cards have the word "SAMPLE" on a black rectangle in place of card number.

PAN Uncut Panel .75 2.00
Theo Fleury IQ
Blaine Lacher
Blaine Lacher D
Jeremy Roenick PP
1 Theo Fleury IQ .30 .75
2 Blaine Lacher .20 .50
3 Blaine Lacher D .20 .50
4 Jeremy Roenick PP .30 .75

1995-96 SkyBox Impact

The 1996 Skybox Impact set was issued in one series totaling 250 cards. The 10-card packs retailed for $1.29. Each pack included an NHL on Fox Slapshot Instant Win Game Card, offering a chance at more than 20,000 prizes. The unused game cards sell for about ten cents. The Blaine Lacher SkyMotion exchange card was randomly inserted at a rate of 1:360 packs. The exchange deadline for the Lacher SkyMotion card was December 31st, 1996. Prices for the expired card and the redeemed card are listed below.

COMPLETE SET (250) 6.00 15.00
1 Bobby Dollas .01 .05
2 Guy Hebert .02 .10
3 Paul Kariya .07 .20
4 Todd Krygier .01 .05
5 Oleg Tverdovsky .01 .05
6 Shaun Van Allen .01 .05
7 Ray Bourque .10 .30
8 Al Iafrate .02 .10
9 Blaine Lacher .01 .05
10 Joe Mullen .02 .10
11 Cam Neely .07 .20
12 Adam Oates .02 .10
13 Kevin Stevens .01 .05
14 Donald Audette .01 .05
15 Garry Galley .01 .05
16 Dominik Hasek .15 .40
17 Pat LaFontaine .07 .20
18 Derek Plante .01 .05
19 Alexei Zhitnik .01 .05
20 Steve Chiasson .01 .05
21 Theo Fleury .01 .05
22 Phil Housley .02 .10
23 Trevor Kidd .02 .10
24 Joe Nieuwendyk .02 .10
25 German Titov .01 .05
26 Zarley Zalapski .01 .05
27 Ed Belfour .07 .20
28 Chris Chelios .07 .20
29 Sergei Krivokrasov .01 .05
30 Joe Murphy .01 .05
31 Bernie Nicholls .01 .05
32 Patrick Poulin .01 .05
33 Jeremy Roenick .08 .25
34 Gary Suter .01 .05
35 Peter Forsberg .20 .50
36 Valeri Kamensky .02 .10
37 Claude Lemieux .01 .05
38 Curtis Leschyshyn .01 .05
39 Sandis Ozolinsh .01 .05
40 Mike Ricci .02 .10
41 Joe Sakic .15 .40
42 Jocelyn Thibault .07 .20
43 Bob Bassen .01 .05
44 Dave Gagner .01 .05
45 Todd Harvey .02 .10
46 Derian Hatcher .01 .05
47 Kevin Hatcher .01 .05
48 Mike Modano .10 .30
49 Andy Moog .07 .20
50 Dino Ciccarelli .02 .10
51 Paul Coffey .07 .20
52 Sergei Fedorov .10 .30
53 Vladimir Konstantinov .02 .10
54 Slava Kozlov .02 .10
55 Nicklas Lidstrom .07 .20
56 Chris Osgood .02 .10
57 Keith Primeau .01 .05
58 Steve Yzerman .40 1.00
59 Jason Arnott .01 .05
60 Curtis Joseph .07 .20
61 Igor Kravchuk .01 .05
62 Todd Marchant .01 .05
63 David Oliver .01 .05
64 Bill Ranford .02 .10
65 Doug Weight .02 .10
66 Stu Barnes .01 .05
67 Jesse Belanger .01 .05
68 Gord Murphy .01 .05
69 Magnus Svensson .01 .05
70 John Vanbiesbrouck .02 .10
71 Sean Burke .02 .10
72 Andrew Cassels .01 .05
73 Nelson Emerson .01 .05
74 Andrei Nikolishin .01 .05
75 Geoff Sanderson .01 .05
76 Brendan Shanahan .07 .20
77 Glen Wesley .01 .05
78 Rob Blake .02 .10
79 Wayne Gretzky .60 1.50
80 Dimitri Khristich .01 .05
81 Jari Kurri .07 .20
82 Darryl Sydor .01 .05
83 Rick Tocchet .02 .10
84 Vincent Damphousse .02 .10
85 Vladimir Malakhov .01 .05
86 Mark Recchi .02 .10
87 Patrick Roy .40 1.00
88 Brian Savage .02 .10
89 Pierre Turgeon .02 .10
90 Martin Brodeur .20 .50
91 Neal Broten .02 .10
92 Shawn Chambers .01 .05
93 John MacLean .02 .10
94 Randy McKay .01 .05
95 Scott Niedermayer .01 .05
96 Stephane Richer .02 .10
97 Scott Stevens .02 .10
98 Steve Thomas .01 .05
99 Wendel Clark .02 .10
100 Patrick Flatley .01 .05
101 Scott Lachance .01 .05
102 Brett Lindros .01 .05
103 Kirk Muller .01 .05
104 Tommy Salo RC .30 .75
105 Mathieu Schneider .01 .05
106 Dennis Vaske .01 .05
107 Ray Ferraro .01 .05
108 Adam Graves .01 .05
109 Alexei Kovalev .02 .10
110 Brian Leetch .02 .10
111 Mark Messier .07 .20
112 Mike Richter .07 .20
113 Luc Robitaille .02 .10
114 Ulf Samuelsson .01 .05
115 Pat Verbeek .01 .05
116 Don Beaupre .02 .10
117 Radek Bonk .01 .05
118 Alexandre Daigle .01 .05
119 Steve Duchesne .01 .05
120 Dan Quinn .01 .05
121 Martin Straka .01 .05
122 Alexei Yashin .01 .05
123 Rod Brind'Amour .01 .05
124 Eric Desjardins .01 .05
125 Ron Hextall .02 .10
126 John LeClair .02 .10
127 Eric Lindros .07 .20
128 Mikael Renberg .02 .10
129 Chris Therien .01 .05
130 Ron Francis .02 .10
131 Jaromir Jagr .10 .30
132 Mario Lemieux .40 1.00
133 Petr Nedved .02 .10
134 Tomas Sandstrom .01 .05
135 Bryan Smolinski .01 .05
136 Ken Wregget .02 .10
137 Sergei Zubov .01 .05
138 Shayne Corson .01 .05
139 Geoff Courtnall .01 .05
140 Dale Hawerchuk .07 .20
141 Brett Hull .08 .25
142 Ian Laperriere .02 .10
143 Al MacInnis .02 .10
144 Chris Pronger .07 .20
145 Esa Tikkanen .01 .05
146 Ulf Dahlen .01 .05
147 Jeff Friesen .01 .05
148 Arturs Irbe .02 .10
149 Craig Janney .01 .05
150 Owen Nolan .02 .10
151 Mike Rathje .01 .05
152 Ray Sheppard .01
153 Brian Bradley .01
154 Chris Gratton .01
155 Roman Hamrlik .02
156 Petr Klima .01
157 Daren Puppa .02
158 Dave Andreychuk .02
159 Mike Gartner .02
160 Todd Gill .01
161 Doug Gilmour .02
162 Kenny Jonsson .01
163 Larry Murphy .02
164 Felix Potvin .07
165 Mats Sundin .07
166 Jeff Brown .01
167 Pavel Bure .07
168 Russ Courtnall .01
169 Trevor Linden .02
170 Kirk McLean .02
171 Alexander Mogilny .02
172 Roman Oksiuta .01
173 Mike Ridley .01
174 Peter Bondra .02
175 Jim Carey .02
176 Sergei Gonchar .02
177 Dale Hunter .02
178 Calle Johansson .01
179 Joe Juneau .02
180 Michal Pivonka .01
181 Nikolai Khabibulin .02
182 Dave Manson .01
183 Teppo Numminen .01
184 Teemu Selanne .07
185 Keith Tkachuk .07
186 Darren Turcotte .01
187 Alexei Zhamnov .02
188 Chad Kilger RC .01
189 Kyle McLaren RC .01
190 Brian Holzinger RC .07
191 Wayne Primeau RC .01
192 Marty Murray .01
193 Eric Daze .02
194 Jon Klemm RC .01
195 Jere Lehtinen .01
196 Jason Bonsignore .01
197 Miroslav Satan RC .30
198 Ryan Smyth .02
199 Tyler Wright .01
200 Radek Dvorak RC .15
201 Ed Jovanovski .07
202 Jeff O'Neill .01
203 Aki Berg RC .02
204 Jamie Storr .02
205 Vitali Yachmenev .01
206 Saku Koivu .07
207 Denis Pederson .01
208 Todd Bertuzzi RC .50 1
209 Bryan McCabe .01
210 Dan Plante .08
211 Peter Ferraro .01
212 Darren Langdon RC .01
213 Niklas Sundstrom .01
214 Daniel Alfredsson RC .30
215 Garth Snow .02
216 Ian Moran .01
217 Richard Park .01
218 Jamie Rivers .01
219 Roman Vopat RC .01
220 Marcus Ragnarsson RC .02
221 Aaron Gavey .01
222 Daymond Langkow RC .15
223 Darby Hendrickson .01
224 Martin Gendron .01
225 Brendan Witt .01
226 Shane Doan RC .25
227 Deron Quint .01
228 Jim Carey HH .01
229 Peter Forsberg HH .10
230 Paul Kariya HH .07
231 David Oliver HH .01
232 Blaine Lacher HH .01
233 Todd Harvey HH .01
234 Todd Marchant HH .01
235 Jeff Friesen HH .01
236 Oleg Tverdovsky HH .01
237 Jason Arnott HH .01
238 Cam Neely PP .02
239 Keith Tkachuk PP .07
240 Owen Nolan PP .02
241 Keith Primeau PP .01
242 Peter Bondra PP .02
243 Jeremy Roenick PP .08
244 John LeClair PP .02
245 Mikael Renberg PP .02
246 Dave Andreychuk PP .02
247 Rick Tocchet PP .02
248 Checklist Card .02
249 Checklist Card .02
250 Checklist Card .02
NNO Blaine Lacher SkyMotion 4.00 10
NNO Blaine Lacher EXCH .25

1995-96 SkyBox Impact Deflectors

Randomly inserted in packs at a rate of 1:10, this 12 card set features top NHL goalies.

COMPLETE SET (12) 6.00 15
1 Dominik Hasek 1.00 2
2 Jim Carey .25
3 Felix Potvin .75 2
4 Sean Burke .25
5 Blaine Lacher .25
6 John Vanbiesbrouck .40 1
7 Jocelyn Thibault .40 1
8 Patrick Roy 2.00 5
9 Ed Belfour .40 1
10 Trevor Kidd .25
11 Martin Brodeur 1.50 4
12 Kirk McLean .25

1995-96 SkyBox Impact Countdown to Impact

Randomly inserted in hobby packs only at a rate of 1:60, this set features nine explosive stars whose names can be found on the backs of many fans jersi at NHL arenas across North America. The card fron also point to statistical milestones that are within ra for that player.

COMPLETE SET (9) 12.00 30
1 Eric Lindros 1.50 4
2 Jaromir Jagr 2.50 6
3 Mario Lemieux 4.00 10
4 Wayne Gretzky 6.00 15
5 Mark Messier 1.50 4
6 Sergei Fedorov 1.50 4
7 Paul Kariya 1.50 4
8 Doug Gilmour 1.00 2
9 Pavel Bure 1.50 4

1995-96 SkyBox Impact Ice Quake

andomly inserted in packs at a rate of 1:20, this 15-
ard set delivers the rumble that goalies feel when the
HL's best forwards have the puck on their sticks and
art skating towards the net.

OMPLETE SET (15) 15.00 40.00
Jaromir Jagr 2.50 6.00
Brett Hull 1.50 4.00
Pavel Bure 1.00 2.50
Eric Lindros 1.00 2.50
Mark Messier 1.50 4.00
Wayne Gretzky 6.00 15.00
Mario Lemieux 5.00 12.00
Peter Forsberg 2.50 6.00
Sergei Fedorov 1.50 4.00
0 Cam Neely 1.00 2.50
1 Owen Nolan .40 1.00
2 Alexei Zhamnov .40 1.00
3 Theo Fleury .40 1.00
4 Luc Robitaille .40 1.00
5 Teemu Selanne 1.00 2.50

1995-96 SkyBox Impact NHL On Fox

andomly inserted in packs at a rate of 1:3, this 18-
ard set showcases both bright young stars and the
ompany's strong affiliation with the NHL broadcasts
the Fox television network in the States.

OMPLETE SET (18) 2.00 5.00
Mariusz Czerkawski .20 .50
Roman Oksiuta .20 .50
David Oliver .20 .50
Adam Deadmarsh .20 .50
Denis Chasse .20 .50
Sergei Krivokrasov .20 .50
lan Laperriere .20 .50
Chris Therien .20 .50
Brian Savage .20 .50
0 Todd Marchant .20 .50
1 Jeff O'Neill .20 .50
2 Brett Lindros .20 .50
3 Kenny Jonsson .20 .50
4 Manny Fernandez .40 1.00
5 Brian Holzinger .20 .50
6 Niklas Sundstrom .20 .50
7 Eric Daze .20 .50
8 Chad Kilger .20 .50

1996-97 SkyBox Impact

is 175-card set featured color action player photos
118 seasoned stars plus a 20-card Rookies subset
119-#138) and a 10-card Power Play subset (#139-
48). These ten Power Play cards had front designs
at actually looked like miniature magazine covers. A
ecial Stanley Cup logo appeared on all Colorado
alanche player cards. The backs carried player stats,
o information, and a statement about the player as
itten by hockey HOF and Fox broadcaster Denis
otvin. A "John LeClair SkyPin Exchange" card,
serted at the rate of one in every 180 packs, entitled
e collector to send for a John LeClair "preview card"
om the proposed -- but never materialized -- SkyPin
ading card line. One "SkyBox/Fox Game" card was
serted in every pack which enabled the holder to win
g prizes from SkyBox, Fox, and the NHL.

OMPLETE SET (175) 10.00 25.00
Guy Hebert .07 .20
Paul Kariya .12 .30
Roman Oksiuta .05 .15
Teemu Selanne .20 .50
Ray Bourque .15 .40
Kyle McLaren .05 .15
Adam Oates .10 .25
Bill Ranford .07 .20
Rick Tocchet .07 .20
Dominik Hasek .15 .40
Pat LaFontaine .10 .25
Mike Peca .05 .15
Theo Fleury .20 .50
Trevor Kidd .05 .15
German Titov .05 .15
Tony Amonte .07 .20
Ed Belfour .10 .25
Chris Chelios .10 .25
Eric Daze .07 .20
Gary Suter .05 .15
Alexei Zhamnov .07 .20
Peter Forsberg .15 .40
Valeri Kamensky .07 .20
Uwe Krupp .05 .15
Claude Lemieux .05 .15
Sandis Ozolinsh .05 .15
Patrick Roy .25 .60
Joe Sakic .15 .40
Derian Hatcher .05 .15
Mike Modano .15 .40
Joe Nieuwendyk .10 .25
Sergei Zubov .05 .15
Paul Coffey .10 .25
Sergei Fedorov .15 .40
Vladimir Konstantinov .07 .20
Slava Kozlov .05 .15
Nicklas Lidstrom .12 .30
Chris Osgood .10 .25
Keith Primeau .05 .15
Steve Yzerman .25 .60
Jason Arnott .07 .20
Curtis Joseph .10 .25
Doug Weight .10 .25
Radek Dvorak .07 .20
Ed Jovanovski .07 .20
Scott Mellanby .07 .20
Rob Niedermayer .07 .20
Ray Sheppard .07 .20
Robert Svehla .05 .15
John Vanbiesbrouck .10 .25
Jeff Brown .05 .15
Sean Burke .05 .15
Andrew Cassels .05 .15
Geoff Sanderson .07 .20
Brendan Shanahan .12 .30
Byron Dafoe .05 .15
Ray Ferraro .05 .15
Dimitri Khristich .05 .15
Vitali Yachmenev .05 .15
Valeri Bure .05 .15
Vincent Damphousse .07 .20
Saku Koivu .10 .25
Mark Recchi .12 .30
Martin Rucinsky .05 .15
Jocelyn Thibault .10 .25
Pierre Turgeon .10 .25
Dave Andreychuk .10 .25
Martin Brodeur .20 .50
Bill Guerin .10 .25
Scott Niedermayer .10 .25
71 Scott Stevens .10 .25
72 Petr Sykora .05 .15
73 Steve Thomas .05 .15
74 Todd Bertuzzi .10 .25
75 Travis Green .07 .20
76 Kenny Jonsson .05 .15
77 Zigmund Palffy .10 .25
78 Adam Graves .05 .15
79 Wayne Gretzky .50 1.25
80 Alexei Kovalev .05 .15
81 Brian Leetch .10 .25
82 Mark Messier .15 .40
83 Mike Richter .10 .25
84 Ulf Samuelsson .05 .15
85 Niklas Sundstrom .05 .15
86 Daniel Alfredsson .10 .25
87 Radek Bonk .05 .15
88 Alexandre Daigle .05 .15
89 Steve Duchesne .05 .15
90 Damian Rhodes .07 .20
91 Alexei Yashin .07 .20
92 Rod Brind'Amour .10 .25
93 Eric Desjardins .07 .20
94 Dale Hawerchuk .12 .30
95 Ron Hextall .07 .20
96 John LeClair .10 .25
97 Eric Lindros .15 .40
98 Mikael Renberg .07 .20
99 Tom Barrasso .07 .20
100 Ron Francis .12 .30
101 Jaromir Jagr .25 .60
102 Mario Lemieux .30 .75
103 Petr Nedved .07 .20
104 Bryan Smolinski .05 .15
105 Nikolai Khabibulin .07 .20
106 Teppo Numminen .05 .15
107 Keith Tkachuk .10 .25
108 Jeremy Roenick .15 .40
109 Oleg Tverdovsky .07 .20
110 Shayne Corson .05 .15
111 Geoff Courtnall .05 .15
112 Grant Fuhr .10 .25
113 Brett Hull .50 1.25
114 Al MacInnis .10 .25
115 Chris Pronger .07 .20
116 Jeff Friesen .05 .15
117 Owen Nolan .10 .25
118 Marcus Ragnarsson .05 .15
119 Chris Terreri .07 .20
120 Brian Bradley .05 .15
121 Chris Gratton .07 .20
122 Roman Hamrlik .07 .20
123 Daren Puppa .07 .20
124 Alexander Selivanov .05 .15
125 Wendel Clark .07 .20
126 Doug Gilmour .12 .30
127 Kirk Muller .05 .15
128 Larry Murphy .07 .20
129 Felix Potvin .10 .25
130 Mats Sundin .10 .25
131 Pavel Bure .12 .30
132 Russ Courtnall .05 .15
133 Trevor Linden .07 .20
134 Kirk McLean .07 .20
135 Alexander Mogilny .07 .20
136 Peter Bondra .07 .20
137 Jim Carey .10 .25
138 Sylvain Cote .05 .15
139 Sergei Gonchar .05 .15
140 Phil Housley .07 .20
141 Joe Juneau .05 .15
142 Michal Pivonka .05 .15
143 Brendan Witt .05 .15
144 Nolan Baumgartner .05 .15
145 Martin Biron RC .12 .30
146 Jason Bonsignore .05 .15
147 Andrew Brunette RC .12 .30
148 Jason Doig .05 .15
149 Peter Ferraro .05 .15
150 Eric Fichaud .07 .20
151 Ladislav Kohn .05 .15
152 Jamie Langenbrunner .05 .15
153 Daymond Langkow .07 .20
154 Jay McKee RC .05 .15
155 Marty Murray
156 Wayne Primeau .05 .15
157 Jamie Pushor .05 .15
158 Jamie Rivers .05 .15
159 Jamie Storr .05 .15
160 Steve Sullivan RC .07 .20
161 Jose Theodore .12 .30
162 Roman Vopat .05 .15
163 Alexei Yegorov RC .10 .25
164 Daniel Alfredsson PP .10 .25
165 Niklas Andersson PP .05 .15
166 Todd Bertuzzi PP .10 .25
167 Valeri Bure PP .05 .15
168 Eric Daze PP .07 .20
169 Saku Koivu PP .10 .25
170 Miroslav Satan PP .05 .15
171 Petr Sykora PP .05 .15
172 Cory Stillman PP .05 .15
173 Vitali Yachmenev PP .05 .15
174 Checklist 1 .02 .10
175 Checklist 2 UER .02 .10
S1 John LeClair PROMO .10 .30

1996-97 SkyBox Impact BladeRunners

Randomly inserted at the rate of 1:3 packs, this 25-card set featured some of the fastest hockey players on ice. The fronts carried a color action player photo while the backs displayed player information.

COMPLETE SET (25) 15.00 40.00
1 Brian Bradley .30 .75
2 Chris Chelios .75 2.00
3 Peter Forsberg 2.50 5.00
4 Ron Francis .50 1.25
5 Mike Gartner .50 1.25
6 Doug Gilmour .50 1.25
7 Phil Housley .50 1.25
8 Brett Hull 1.00 2.50
9 Valeri Kamensky .50 1.25
10 Pat LaFontaine .75 2.00
11 John LeClair .75 2.00
12 Claude Lemieux .30 .75
13 Nicklas Lidstrom .75 2.00
14 Mark Messier .75 2.00
15 Alexander Mogilny .50 1.25
16 Petr Nedved .50 1.25
17 Adam Oates .50 1.25
18 Zigmund Palffy .50 1.25
19 Jeremy Roenick 1.00 2.50
20 Teemu Selanne .75 2.00
21 Brendan Shanahan .75 2.00
22 Keith Tkachuk .75 2.00
23 Pierre Turgeon .50 1.25
24 Doug Weight .50 1.25
25 Steve Yzerman 5.00 10.00

1996-97 SkyBox Impact Countdown to Impact

Randomly inserted in hobby packs only at the rate of 1:30, this 10-card insert set focused on the superstars of the game. The fronts displayed color player photos while the backs carried player information.

COMPLETE SET (10) 20.00 50.00
1 Pavel Bure 1.25 3.00
2 Sergei Fedorov 1.25 3.00
3 Wayne Gretzky 8.00 20.00
4 Jaromir Jagr 2.00 5.00
5 Ed Jovanovski .75 2.00
6 Paul Kariya 1.25 3.00
7 Mario Lemieux 6.00 15.00
8 Eric Lindros 1.25 3.00
9 Patrick Roy 6.00 15.00
10 Joe Sakic 3.00 8.00

1996-97 SkyBox Impact NHL on Fox

Randomly inserted at the rate of 1:10 packs, this 20-card set was a joint venture with Fox TV.

COMPLETE SET (20) 5.00 12.00
1 Daniel Alfredsson .40 1.00
2 Todd Bertuzzi .40 1.00
3 Ray Bourque 1.25 3.00
4 Valeri Bure .20 .50
5 Chris Chelios .75 2.00
6 Paul Coffey .75 2.00
7 Eric Daze .20 .50
8 Eric Desjardins .20 .50
9 Sergei Gonchar .20 .50
10 Phil Housley .20 .50
11 Ed Jovanovski .20 .50
12 Vladimir Konstantinov .75 2.00
13 Saku Koivu .75 2.00
14 Brian Leetch .40 1.00
15 Larry Murphy .20 .50
16 Teppo Numminen .20 .50
17 Sandis Ozolinsh .20 .50
18 Marcus Ragnarsson .20 .50
19 Petr Sykora .20 .50
20 Vitali Yachmenev .20 .50

1996-97 SkyBox Impact VersaTeam

Randomly inserted at the rate of 1:120 packs, this 10-card set featured the NHL's best multi-skilled players. The fronts displayed color player photos while the backs carried player information.

COMPLETE SET (10) 40.00 100.00
1 Pavel Bure 2.50 6.00
2 Sergei Fedorov 2.50 6.00
3 Peter Forsberg 4.00 10.00
4 Wayne Gretzky 12.00 25.00
5 Jaromir Jagr 4.00 10.00
6 Paul Kariya 2.50 6.00
7 Mario Lemieux 12.00 30.00
8 Eric Lindros 2.50 6.00
9 Joe Sakic 6.00 15.00
10 Teemu Selanne 2.50 6.00

1996-97 SkyBox Impact Zero Heroes

Randomly inserted in retail packs only at the rate of 1:30, this 10-card set featured the stingiest goaltenders in the league. The fronts displayed color player photos while the backs carried player information.

COMPLETE SET (10) 20.00 50.00
1 Ed Belfour 2.50 6.00
2 Sean Burke 1.25 3.00
3 Jim Carey 1.25 3.00
4 Dominik Hasek 4.00 10.00
5 Ron Hextall 2.50 6.00
6 Chris Osgood 2.50 6.00
7 Felix Potvin 2.50 6.00
8 Daren Puppa 1.25 3.00
9 Patrick Roy 10.00 25.00
10 John Vanbiesbrouck 2.50 6.00

1994-95 Slapshot Promos

This eight-card set features a sampling of the 1994-95 Slapshot cards, which were issued in team set form. The designs are identical to the regular cards, although some cards carry the disclaimer "Promo". The Jamie Rivers card actually is his 1993-94 card. The cards are unnumbered and checklisted below in alphabetical order.

COMPLETE SET (8) .75 2.00
1 David Belitski .20 .50
2 Dan Graham .01
3 Bill McGuigan .08 .25
4 Todd Norman .08 .25
5 Steve Rice .08 .25
6 Jamie Rivers .20 .50
7 Sudbury's World Juniors# .40 1.00
8 Ad Card .01 .05

1995-96 Slapshot

The 1995-96 Slapshot set features the players of the OHL and was issued in foil packs in one series totaling 440 cards. Randomly inserted into packs were promo cards and an autographed card of Zac Bierk. The set is notable for the inclusion of several top prospects, including Alexandre Volchkov, Boyd Devereaux, Joe Thornton, Daniel Cleary and Rico Fata.

COMPLETE SET (440) 20.00 50.00
1 Checklist .01 .05
2 Checklist .01 .05
3 Checklist .01 .05
4 Checklist .01 .05
5 David E. Branch .01 .05
6 Bert Templeton .01 .05
7 Chris George .01 .05
8 Chris Thompson .08 .25
9 Quade Lightbody .01 .05
10 Shane Delaronde .01 .05
11 Justin Robinson .01 .05
12 Shawn Frappier .01 .05
13 Lucio Nasato .08 .25
14 Jason Payne .01 .05
15 Jason Cannon .01 .05
16 Alexandre Volchkov .08 .25
17 Daniel Tkaczuk .20 .50
18 Gerry Lanigan .01 .05
19 Darrell Woodley .01 .05
20 Brian Barker .01 .05
21 Mauricio Alvarez .01 .05
22 Brock Boucher .01 .05
23 Jeff Cowan .15 .40
24 Jan Bulis .20 .50
25 Jeff Tetzlaff .01 .05
26 Caleb Ward .05 .15
27 Mike White .01 .05
28 Jeremy Miculinic .01 .05
29 Andrew Morrison .01 .05
30 Robert Dubois .01 .05
31 Kory Cooper .08 .25
32 Jason Gaggi .08 .25
33 Mike Van Volsen .01 .05
34 Paul McInness .01 .05
35 Harkie Stingh .01 .05
36 Robin Lacour .01 .05
37 Jamie Sokolsky .01 .05
38 Marc Dupuis .01 .05
39 Daniel Cleary .20 .50
40 David Peca .01 .05
41 Adam Robbins .01 .05
42 Steve Tracze .01 .05
43 James Boyd .01 .05
44 Jake Irsag .01 .05
45 Ryan Ready .01 .05
46 Walker McDonald .01 .05
47 Rob Guinn .01 .05
48 Rob Fitzgerald .01 .05
49 Joe Coombs .01 .05
50 Daniel Reja .01 .05
51 Joe Van Volsen .02 .10
52 Craig Mills .08 .25
53 Murray Hogg .01 .05
54 Andrei Shurupov .08 .25
55 Andrew Williamson .01 .05
56 Mike Minard .08 .25
57 Robert Esche .75 2.00
58 Lee Jinman .08 .25
59 Corey Neilson .07 .20
60 Troy Smith .01 .05
61 Mike Rucinski .07 .20
62 Colin Beardsmore .01 .05
63 Dan Pawlaczyk .01 .05
64 Scott Blair .01 .05
65 Mike Morrone .01 .05
66 Matt Ball .01 .05
67 Steve Dumonski .01 .05
68 Murray Sheehan .01 .05
69 Sean Haggerty .08 .25
70 Andrew Taylor .01 .05
71 Steve Wasylko .02 .10
72 Jan Vodrazka .01 .05
73 Dan Preston .01 .05
74 Jesse Boulerice .20 .50
75 Bryan Berard .30 .75
76 Nicolas Beaudoin .08 .25
77 Tom Buckley .02 .10
78 Mark Cadotte .07 .20
79 Greg Stephan .01 .05
80 Peter DeBoer .02 .10
81 Regan Stocco .01 .05
82 Andy Adams .08 .25
83 Brett Thompson .08 .25
84 Darryl McArthur .01 .05
85 Ryan Risidore .07 .20
86 Joel Cort .02 .10
87 Chris Hajt .08 .25
88 Bryan McKinney .01 .05
89 Dwayne Hay .20 .50
90 Andrew Clark .01 .05
91 Ryan Robichaud .01 .05
92 Mike Vellinga .01 .05
93 Jamie Wright .01 .05
94 Herbert Vasilijevs .01 .05
95 Dan Cloutier .75 2.00
96 Brian Wesenberg .08 .25
97 Michael Pittman .01 .05
98 Jeff Williams .01 .05
99 Todd Norman .08 .25
100 Brian Willsie .01 .05
101 Jason Jackman .07 .20
102 Mike Lankshear .05 .15
103 Andrew Long .07 .20
104 Nick Bootland .02 .10
105 E.J. McGuire .01 .05
106 Bujar Amidovski .20 .50
107 John Hultberg .08 .25
108 Eric Olsen .01 .05
109 Chris Allen .20 .50
110 Michael Tilson .01 .05
111 Jeff DaCosta .01 .05
112 Gord Walsh .01 .05
113 Matt Bradley .01 .05
114 Robert Mailloux .01 .05
115 Justin Davis .01 .05
116 Marc Moro .15 .40
117 Cail MacLean .01 .05
118 Jason Sands .01 .05
119 Matt Price .01 .05
120 Zdenek Skorepa .02 .10
121 Jason Morgan .01 .05
122 Mike Oliveira .08 .25
123 Colin Chaulk .01 .05
124 Dylan Taylor .01 .05
125 Kurt Johnston .01 .05
126 Bill Minkhorst .01 .05
127 Wes Swinson .08 .25
128 Adam Fleming .01 .05
129 Chris MacDonald .01 .05
130 Gary Agnew .01 .05
131 David Belitski .08 .25
132 Jarrett Rose .01 .05
133 Ryan Mougenel .01 .05
134 Rob Stanfield .01 .05
135 Duncan Fader .01 .05
136 Rob Maric .01 .05
137 Mark McMahon .01 .05
138 Serge Payer .01 .05
139 Paul Traynor .01 .05
140 Bogdan Rudenko .01 .05
141 Robert DeCiantis .05 .15
142 Andrew Dale .08 .25
143 Jeff Ambrosio .02 .10
144 Paul Doyle .07 .20
145 Bryan Duce .01 .05
146 Jason Byrnes .01 .05
147 Ryan Pepperall .08 .25
148 Wes Vander Wal .01 .05
149 Boyd Devereaux .20 .50
150 Keith Walsh .01 .05
151 Joe Birch .01 .05
152 Craig Nelson .01 .05
153 Brian Hayden .01 .05
154 Matt O'Dette .01 .05
155 Geoff Ward .01 .05
156 Frank Ivankovic .08 .25
157 Eoin McInerney .20 .50
158 Joel Dezainde .01 .05
159 Duncan Dalmao .01 .05
160 Brandon Sugden .20 .50
161 Jamie Wentzell .01 .05
162 Ryan Burgoyne .01 .05
163 Todd Crane .01 .05
164 Chad Cavanagh .01 .05
165 Andrew Fagan .01 .05
166 Ryan Gardner .01 .05
167 Kevin Boyd .01 .05
168 Kevin Barry .01 .05
169 Richard Pitirri .01 .05
170 Adam Colagiacomo .20 .50
171 Jason Brooks .01 .05
172 Justin McPolin .01 .05
173 Travis Riggin .01 .05
174 Steve Lowe .01 .05
175 Todd St. Louis .01 .05
176 Kevin Slota .01 .05
177 Ryan McKie .01 .05
178 Corey Isen .01 .05
179 Sasha Cucuz .01 .05
180 Tom Barrett .01 .05
181 Ken Carroll .01 .05
182 Ryan Penney .08 .25
183 Jay McKee .30 .75
184 Ryan Taylor .01 .05
185 Jeff Paul .01 .05
186 Jason Ward .20 .50
187 Jesse Black .02 .10
188 Steve Nimigon .07 .20
189 Chris Haskett .01 .05
190 Geoff Peters .08 .25
191 Ryan Cirillo .01 .05
192 David Froh .01 .05
193 Jeff Johnstone .01 .05
194 Shane Nash .07 .20
195 Jason Robinson .01 .05
196 Rich Vrataric .01 .05
197 Colin Pepperall .01 .05
198 Craig Jalbert .01 .05
199 Andrew Williamson .01 .05
200 Greg Tymchuk .01 .05
201 Chester Gallant .01 .05
202 Mike Perna .01 .05
203 Adam Nitel .20 .50
204 Dave Burkholder .01 .05
205 Chris Johnstone .01 .05
206 Elliott Faust .08 .25
207 Scott Roche .08 .25
208 Kam White .01 .05
209 Scott Atkins .01 .05
210 Luc Belliveau .01 .05
211 Jamie Vossen .01 .05
212 Ryan MacDonald .01 .05
213 Jim Midgley .01 .05
214 Steven Carpenter .01 .05
215 Jake Martel .01 .05
216 Alex Matvichuk .01 .05
217 Trevor Gallant .08 .25
218 Ryan Gillis .01 .05
219 Kris Cantu .01 .05
220 Mark Provenzano .01 .05
221 Brian Whitley .01 .05
222 Dustin Virag .01 .05
223 Lee Jinman .08 .25
224 Peter McCague .01 .05
225 Herb Bonvie .01 .05
226 Philippe Poirier .01 .05
227 Greg Labanski .01 .05
228 Milan Kostolny .08 .25
229 Ryan Power .01 .05
230 Shane Parker .01 .05
231 Travis Scott .08 .25
232 Tyrone Garner .08 .25
233 Marty Wilford .08 .25
234 Ole Anderson .01 .05
235 Ryan Tocher .01 .05
236 Nathan Perrott .30 .75
237 Brandon Coalter .01 .05
238 John Tripp .08 .25
239 Jay Legault .20 .50
240 Wayne Primeau .20 .50
241 Trevor Edgar .01 .05
242 Peter Hogan .01 .05
243 Warren Holmes .01 .05
244 Jason Metcalfe .01 .05
245 Mike Zanutto .01 .05
246 Jeff Ware .08 .25
247 Ian MacNeil .01 .05
248 Jan Snopek .07 .20
249 Kurt Walsh .01 .05
250 Marc Savard .30 .75
251 Darcy O'Shea .01 .05
252 Jason Sweitzer .01 .05
253 Ryan Lindsay .01 .05
254 Scott Seiling .01 .05
255 Stan Butler .08 .25
256 Tim Keyes .08 .25
257 Craig Hillier .08 .25
258 Craig Whynot .01 .05
259 David Bell .01 .05
260 Rich Bronila .01 .05
261 Roy Gray .01 .05
262 Nick Boynton .40 1.00
263 Mike Sim .08 .25
264 B.J. Johnston .01 .05
265 Niall Maynard .01 .05
266 Dan Tudin .08 .25
267 Jure Kovacavic .01 .05
268 Ben Gustavson .01 .05
269 Steve Zaryk .01 .05
270 Darren Debrie .01 .05
271 Troy Stonier .01 .05
272 David Nemirovsky .08 .25
273 Joel Trottier .08 .25
274 Mike Lavell .01 .05
275 Brian Campbell .20 .50
276 Chris Despatis .01 .05
277 Sean Blanchard .08 .25
278 Alyn McCauley .30 .75
279 Chris Pittman .07 .20
280 Daryl Rivers .01 .05
281 Brent Johnson .75 2.00
282 Shaun Gallant .01 .05
283 Shane Kenny .01 .05
284 Chris Biagini .01 .05
285 Jim Ensom .02 .10
286 Marek Babic .01 .05
287 Oleg Tsyrkunov .01 .05
288 Mike Loach .01 .05
289 Peter MacKellar .01 .05
290 Ryan Davis .01 .05
291 John Argiropoulos .01 .05
292 Jason Campbell .01 .05
293 Ryan Christie .20 .50
294 Dan Snyder .40 1.00
295 Steve Gallace .01 .05
296 Scott Seiling .01 .05
297 Jeremy Rebek .01 .05
298 Adam Mair .20 .50
299 Matt Osborne .01 .05
300 Mike Gelati .01 .05
301 Wayne Primeau .20 .50
302 Chris Wismer .01 .05
303 Larry Paleczny .08 .25
304 Kurt Walsh .01 .05
305 John Lovell .01 .05
306 Allan Hitchen .08 .25
307 Zac Bierk .20 .50
308 Mike Martone .01 .05
309 Jonathan Murphy .01 .05
310 Adrian Murray .01 .05
311 Rob Gifin .01 .05
312 Corey Crocker .08 .25
313 Cameron Mann .20 .50
314 Ryan Pawluk .01 .05
315 Jason MacMillan .01 .05
316 Shawn Thornton .40 1.00
317 Wade Dawe .01 .05
318 Eric Landry .01 .05
319 Steve Hogg .01 .05
320 Kevin Bolibruck .01 .05
321 Dave Duerden .08 .25
322 Mike Williams .01 .05
323 Andy Johnson .01 .05
324 Jaret Nixon .01 .05
325 Evgeny Korolev .08 .25
326 Matthew Lahey .01 .05
327 Ryan Schmidt .01 .05
328 Scott Barney .08 .25
329 Steve Jones .01 .05
330 Dave McQueen .01 .05
331 Jeff Salajko .08 .25
332 Patrick DesRochers .20 .50
333 Gerald Moriarity .01 .05
334 Allan Carr .01 .05
335 Tom Brown .01 .05
336 Andy Delmore .20 .50
337 Darren Mortier .01 .05
338 Aaron Brand .08 .25
339 Eric Boulton .40 1.00
340 Jonathan Sim .20 .50
341 Trevor Letowski .20 .50
342 Michael Hanson .01 .05
343 Todd Miller .01 .05
344 Brendan Yarema .01 .05
345 Brad Simms .01 .05
346 David Nemirovsky .08 .25
347 Jeff Brown .08 .25
348 Andrew Proskurnicki .01 .05
349 Wes Mason .08 .25
350 Scott Corbett .01 .05
351 Dave Bourque .01 .05
352 Sean Brown .20 .50
353 Marcin Snita .01 .05
354 Rich Brown .01 .05
355 Mark Hunter .01 .05
356 Michal Podolka .08 .25
357 Dan Cloutier .75 2.00
358 Cory Murphy .01 .05
359 Kevin Murnaghan .01 .05
360 Andre Payette .01 .05
361 Richard Uniacke .07 .20
362 Joe Seroski .05 .15
363 Joe Thornton 4.00 10.00
364 Ben Schust .01 .05
365 Peter Cava .01 .05
366 Darryl Green .01 .05
367 Trevor Tokarczyk .01 .05
368 Jeff Gies .01 .05
369 Rico Fata .20 .50
370 Brian Secord .01 .05
371 Scott Cherrey .05 .15
372 Brian Stacey .01 .05
373 Lee Cole .01 .05
374 Richard Jackman .20 .50
375 Jason Doyle .08 .25
376 Brian Stewart .02 .10
377 Blaine Fitzpatrick .01 .05
378 Robert Mulick .01 .05
379 Andy Adams .08 .25
380 Joe Paterson .01 .05
381 Dave MacDonald .08 .25
382 Stephan Valiquette .40 1.00
383 Tim Swartz .01 .05
384 Gregg Lalonde .01 .05
385 Tyson Flinn .01 .05
386 Ryan Sly .01 .05
387 Neal Martin .01 .05
388 Kevin Hansen .01 .05
389 Joe Lombardo .01 .05
390 Darryl Moxam .01 .05
391 Jeremy Adduono .05 .15
392 Ryan Shanahan .01 .05
393 Sean Venedam .05 .15
394 Andrew Dale .08 .25
395 Rob Butler .01 .05
396 Brian Scott .01 .05
397 Liam MacEachern .01 .05
398 Luc Gagne .01 .05
399 Richard Rochefort .01 .05
400 Noel Burkitt .01 .05
401 Simon Sherry .01 .05
402 Brad Domonsky .08 .25
403 Ron Newhook .15 .40
404 Serge Dunphy .01 .05
405 Todd Lalonde .01 .05
406 Ryan Gelinas .08 .25
407 Terry Joss .07 .20
408 Mike Martin .07 .20
409 Chris Van Dyk .07 .20
410 D.J. Smith .20 .50
411 Glenn Crawford .07 .20
412 Robert Blain .01 .05
413 Matt Masterson .01 .05
414 Adam Young .01 .05
415 Matt Cooke .40 1.00
416 Jeff Zehr .20 .50
417 Wes Ward .07 .20
418 Matt Elich .15 .40
419 Rob Shearer .15 .40
420 Dean Mando .01 .05
421 Chris Kerr .01 .05
422 Vladimir Kretchine .01 .05
423 Jeff Martin .01 .05
424 Valeri Svoboda .01 .05
425 Dave Geris .07 .20
426 Ryan Pawluk .01 .05
427 Ryan Shaver .01 .05
428 Cameron Kincaid .01 .05
429 Tim Findlay .08 .25
430 Tim Bryan .01 .05
431 Alexandre Volchkov .20 .50
432 Boyd Devereaux .40 1.00
433 Chris Allen .08 .25
434 Paul Doyle .07 .20
435 Wes Mason .08 .25
436 Chris Hajt .08 .25
437 Kurt Walsh .01 .05
438 Glenn Crawford .07 .20
439 Jeff Brown .08 .25
440 Geoff Peters .08 .25
NNO Zac Bierk autograph 2.00 5.00
NNO Jay McKee promo .20 .50
NNO Zac Bierk promo .20 .50
NNO Cameron Mann promo .20 .50
NNO Mike Martin promo .20 .50
NNO Nick Boynton promo .40 1.00
NNO Ryan Pepperall promo .20 .50
NNO Scott Roche promo .20 .50
NNO Sean Haggerty promo .20 .50
NNO Adam Colagiacomo promo .20 .50

1994-95 SP

Wayne Gretzky's card number 54 was released as a promo. The only discernible difference between the two versions is that the foil on the promo is a brighter gold than the regular issue card. A special Wayne Gretzky 2500 point card was inserted one per case. This card is designed horizontally with die-cutting of the top corners. Wayne appears on a gold background with "2500" in block numbers on the front of the card.

1 Paul Kariya .30 .75
2 Oleg Tverdovsky .20 .50
3 Stephan Lebeau .15 .40
4 Bob Corkum .15 .40
5 Guy Hebert .20 .50
6 Ray Bourque .40 1.00
7 Blaine Lacher RC .20 .50
8 Adam Oates .25 .60
9 Cam Neely .25 .60
10 Mariusz Czerkawski RC .25 .60
11 Bryan Smolinski .15 .40
12 Pat LaFontaine .25 .60
13 Alexander Mogilny .20 .50
14 Dominik Hasek .50 1.25
15 Dale Hawerchuk .30 .75
16 Alexei Zhitnik .20 .50
17 Theo Fleury .25 .60
18 German Titov .15 .40
19 Phil Housley .20 .50
20 Joe Nieuwendyk .25 .60
21 Trevor Kidd .20 .50
22 Jeremy Roenick .50 1.25
23 Chris Chelios .25 .60
24 Ed Belfour .25 .60
25 Bernie Nicholls .20 .50
26 Tony Amonte .20 .50
27 Joe Murphy .15 .40
28 Mike Modano .40 1.00
29 Trent Klatt .15 .40
30 Dave Gagner .20 .50
31 Kevin Hatcher .15 .40
32 Andy Moog .25 .60
33 Sergei Fedorov .40 1.00
34 Steve Yzerman .60 1.50
35 Slava Kozlov .20 .50
36 Paul Coffey .25 .60
37 Keith Primeau .25 .60
38 Ray Sheppard .20 .50
39 Doug Weight .20 .50
40 Jason Arnott .20 .50
41 Bill Ranford .20 .50
42 Shayne Corson .15 .40
43 Stu Barnes .15 .40
44 John Vanbiesbrouck .20 .50
45 Johan Garpenlov .15 .40
46 Bob Kudelski .15 .40
47 Scott Mellanby .20 .50
48 Chris Pronger .25 .60
49 Darren Turcotte .15 .40
50 Andrew Cassels .15 .40
51 Sean Burke .20 .50
52 Geoff Sanderson .20 .50
53 Rob Blake .25 .60
54A Wayne Gretzky 1.25 3.00
54B Wayne Gretzky PROMO 1.25 3.00
55 Rick Tocchet .20 .50
56 Tony Granato .15 .40
57 Jari Kurri .20 .50
58 Vincent Damphousse .20 .50
59 Patrick Roy .60 1.50
60 Vladimir Malakhov .15 .40
61 Pierre Turgeon .20 .50
62 Mark Recchi .30 .75
63 Martin Brodeur .60 1.50
64 Stephane Richer .20 .50
65 John MacLean .20 .50
66 Scott Stevens .25 .60
67 Scott Niedermayer .25 .60
68 Kirk Muller .15 .40
69 Ray Ferraro .15 .40
70 Brett Lindros .15 .40
71 Steve Thomas .15 .40
72 Pat Verbeek .20 .50
73 Mark Messier .25 .60
74 Brian Leetch .25 .60
75 Mike Richter .25 .60
76 Alexei Kovalev .15 .40
77 Adam Graves .15 .40
78 Sergei Zubov .15 .40
79 Alexei Yashin .25 .60
80 Radek Bonk RC .15 .40
81 Alexandre Daigle .15 .40
82 Don Beaupre .20 .50
83 Mikael Renberg .20 .50
84 Eric Lindros .25 .60
85 John LeClair .25 .60
86 Rod Brind'Amour .20 .50
87 Ron Hextall .20 .50
88 Ken Wregget .20 .50
89 Jaromir Jagr .60 1.50
90 Tomas Sandstrom .15 .40
91 John Cullen .15 .40
92 Ron Francis .30 .75
93 Luc Robitaille .25 .60
94 Joe Sakic .50 1.25
95 Owen Nolan .25 .60
96 Peter Forsberg .60 1.50
97 Wendel Clark .20 .50
98 Mike Ricci .15 .40
99 Stephane Fiset .20 .50
100 Brett Hull .50 1.25
101 Brendan Shanahan .30 .75
102 Curtis Joseph .40 1.00
103 Esa Tikkanen .15 .40
104 Al MacInnis .20 .50
105 Arturs Irbe .20 .50
106 Ray Whitney .15 .40
107 Sergei Makarov .15 .40
108 Sandis Ozolinsh .15 .40
109 Craig Janney .20 .50
110 Petr Klima .15 .40
111 Chris Gratton .15 .40
112 Roman Hamrlik .20 .50
113 Alexander Selivanov RC .20 .50
114 Brian Bradley .15 .40
115 Doug Gilmour .30 .75
116 Mats Sundin .20 .50
117 Felix Potvin .25 .60

118 Mike Ridley .15 .40
119 Dave Andreychuk .25 .60
120 Dmitri Mironov .15 .40
121 Pavel Bure .25 .60
122 Trevor Linden .20 .50
123 Jeff Brown .15 .40
124 Kirk McLean .20 .50
125 Geoff Courtnall .15 .40
126 Joe Juneau .20 .50
127 Dale Hunter .15 .40
128 Jim Carey RC .25 .60
129 Peter Bondra .20 .50
130 Dimitri Khristich .15 .40
131 Teemu Selanne .50 1.25
132 Keith Tkachuk .25 .60
133 Alexei Zhamnov .20 .50
134 Dave Manson .15 .40
135 Nelson Emerson .15 .40
136 Alexandre Daigle .15 .40
137 Jamie Storr .20 .50
138 Todd Harvey .15 .40
139 Wade Redden RC .40 1.00
140 Ed Jovanovski RC .40 1.00
141 Jamie Rivers RC .25 .60
142 Ryan Smyth RC .75 2.00
143 Jason Botterill .20 .50
144 Denis Pederson RC .20 .50
145 Jeff Friesen .15 .40
146 Dan Cloutier RC .40 1.00
147 Lee Sorochan RC .25 .60
148 Marty Murray .20 .50
149 Shean Donovan RC .25 .60
150 Larry Courville RC .25 .60
151 Jason Allison .20 .50
152 Jeff O'Neill RC .20 .50
153 Bryan McCabe .15 .40
154 Miloslav Guren RC .25 .60
155 Petr Buzek RC .25 .60
156 Tomas Blazek .25 .60
157 Josef Marha .25 .60
158 Jan Hlavac RC .40 1.00
159 Veli-Pekka Nutikka RC .25 .60
160 Kimmo Timonen .20 .50
161 Antti Aalto RC .20 .50
162 Janne Niinimaa .25 .60
163 Nikolai Zavarukhin .25 .60
164 Vadim Epantchinsev RC .20 .50
165 Alexander Korolyuk RC .25 .60
166 Dmitri Klevakin RC .20 .50
167 Vitali Yachmenev RC .25 .60
168 Niklas Sundstrom .25 .60
169 Anders Soderberg RC .20 .50
170 Anders Eriksson .20 .50
171 Jesper Mattsson RC .20 .50
172 Mattias Ohlund RC .40 1.00
173 Jason Bonsignore .25 .60
174 Bryan Berard RC .40 1.00
175 Richard Park .15 .40
176 Mike McBain RC .25 .60
177 Jason Doig RC .25 .60
178 Xavier Delisle RC .25 .60
179 Christian Dube RC .25 .60
180 Louis-Phil.Sevigny RC .25 .60
181 Jarome Iginla RC .75 2.00
182 Marc Savard RC .25 .60
183 Alyn McCauley RC .25 .60
184 Brad Mehalko RC .25 .60
185 Todd Norman RC .25 .60
186 Brian Scott RC .25 .60
187 Brad Larsen RC .25 .60
188 Jeff Ware RC .25 .60
189 Sergei Samsonov RC .25 .60
190 Andrei Petrunin RC .25 .60
191 Sean Haggerty RC .25 .60
192 Rory Fitzpatrick RC .25 .60
193 Deron Quint .15 .40
194 Jamie Langenbrunner .20 .50
195 Jeff Mitchell RC .20 .50
SP1 Wayne Gretzky 2500 1.25 3.00

1994-95 SP Die Cuts

This 195-card set is a parallel version of the regular issue. These were inserted at a rate of one per pack. They are distinguished by the die-cutting of the top and bottom right corners of the card, and the use of a silver instead of gold hologram. The numbering of the cards is consistent with the regular issue.

1 Paul Kariya .75 2.00
2 Oleg Tverdovsky .50 1.25
3 Stephan Lebeau .40 1.00
4 Bob Corkum .40 1.00
5 Guy Hebert .50 1.25
6 Ray Bourque 1.00 2.50
7 Blaine Lacher .50 1.25
8 Adam Oates .60 1.50
9 Cam Neely .60 1.50
10 Mariusz Czerkawski .60 1.50
11 Bryan Smolinski .40 1.00
12 Pat LaFontaine .60 1.50
13 Alexander Mogilny .50 1.25
14 Dominik Hasek 1.25 3.00
15 Dale Hawerchuk .75 2.00
16 Alexei Zhitnik .50 1.25
17 Theo Fleury .60 1.50
18 German Titov .40 1.00
19 Phil Housley .50 1.25
20 Joe Nieuwendyk .60 1.50
21 Trevor Kidd .50 1.25
22 Jeremy Roenick 1.25 3.00
23 Chris Chelios .60 1.50
24 Ed Belfour .60 1.50
25 Bernie Nicholls .50 1.25
26 Tony Amonte .50 1.25
27 Joe Murphy .40 1.00
28 Mike Modano 1.00 2.50
29 Trent Klatt .40 1.00
30 Dave Gagner .50 1.25
31 Kevin Hatcher .40 1.00
32 Andy Moog .60 1.50
33 Sergei Fedorov 1.00 2.50
34 Steve Yzerman 1.50 4.00
35 Slava Kozlov .50 1.25
36 Paul Coffey .60 1.50
37 Keith Primeau .60 1.50
38 Ray Sheppard .50 1.25
39 Doug Weight .50 1.25
40 Jason Arnott .50 1.25
41 Bill Ranford .50 1.25
42 Shayne Corson .40 1.00
43 Stu Barnes .40 1.00
44 John Vanbiesbrouck .50 1.25
45 Johan Garpenlov .40 1.00
46 Bob Kudelski .40 1.00
47 Scott Mellanby .50 1.25
48 Chris Pronger .60 1.50
49 Darren Turcotte .40 1.00
50 Andrew Cassels .40 1.00
51 Sean Burke .50 1.25
52 Geoff Sanderson .50 1.25
53 Rob Blake .60 1.50
54 Wayne Gretzky 3.00 8.00
55 Rick Tocchet .50 1.25
56 Tony Granato .40 1.00
57 Jari Kurri .50 1.25
58 Vincent Damphousse .50 1.25
59 Patrick Roy 1.50 4.00
60 Vladimir Malakhov .40 1.00
61 Pierre Turgeon .50 1.25
62 Mark Recchi .75 2.00
63 Martin Brodeur 1.50 4.00
64 Stephane Richer .50 1.25
65 John MacLean .50 1.25
66 Scott Stevens .60 1.50
67 Scott Niedermayer .60 1.50
68 Kirk Muller .40 1.00
69 Ray Ferraro .40 1.00
70 Brett Lindros .40 1.00
71 Steve Thomas .40 1.00
72 Pat Verbeek .50 1.25
73 Mark Messier .60 1.50
74 Brian Leetch .60 1.50
75 Mike Richter .60 1.50
76 Alexei Kovalev .40 1.00
77 Adam Graves .40 1.00
78 Sergei Zubov .40 1.00
79 Alexei Yashin .60 1.50
80 Radek Bonk .40 1.00
81 Alexandre Daigle .40 1.00
82 Don Beaupre .50 1.25
83 Mikael Renberg .50 1.25
84 Eric Lindros .60 1.50
85 John LeClair .60 1.50
86 Rod Brind'Amour .50 1.25
87 Ron Hextall .50 1.25
88 Ken Wregget .50 1.25
89 Jaromir Jagr 1.50 4.00
90 Tomas Sandstrom .40 1.00
91 John Cullen .40 1.00
92 Ron Francis .75 2.00
93 Luc Robitaille .60 1.50
94 Joe Sakic 1.25 3.00
95 Owen Nolan .60 1.50
96 Peter Forsberg 1.50 4.00
97 Wendel Clark .50 1.25
98 Mike Ricci .40 1.00
99 Stephane Fiset .50 1.25
100 Brett Hull 1.25 3.00
101 Brendan Shanahan .75 2.00
102 Curtis Joseph 1.00 2.50
103 Esa Tikkanen .40 1.00
104 Al MacInnis .50 1.25
105 Arturs Irbe .50 1.25
106 Ray Whitney .40 1.00
107 Sergei Makarov .40 1.00
108 Sandis Ozolinsh .40 1.00
109 Craig Janney .50 1.25
110 Petr Klima .40 1.00
111 Chris Gratton .40 1.00
112 Roman Hamrlik .50 1.25
113 Alexander Selivanov .50 1.25
114 Brian Bradley .40 1.00
115 Doug Gilmour .75 2.00
116 Mats Sundin .50 1.25
117 Felix Potvin .60 1.50
118 Mike Ridley .40 1.00
119 Dave Andreychuk .60 1.50
120 Dmitri Mironov .40 1.00
121 Pavel Bure .60 1.50
122 Trevor Linden .50 1.25
123 Jeff Brown .40 1.00
124 Kirk McLean .50 1.25
125 Geoff Courtnall .40 1.00
126 Joe Juneau .50 1.25
127 Dale Hunter .40 1.00
128 Jim Carey .60 1.50
129 Peter Bondra .50 1.25
130 Dimitri Khristich .40 1.00
131 Teemu Selanne 1.25 3.00
132 Keith Tkachuk .60 1.50
133 Alexei Zhamnov .50 1.25
134 Dave Manson .40 1.00
135 Nelson Emerson .40 1.00
136 Alexandre Daigle .40 1.00
137 Jamie Storr .50 1.25
138 Todd Harvey .40 1.00
139 Wade Redden 1.00 2.50
140 Ed Jovanovski 1.00 2.50
141 Jamie Rivers .60 1.50
142 Ryan Smyth 2.50 6.00
143 Jason Botterill .50 1.25
144 Denis Pederson .50 1.25
145 Jeff Friesen .40 1.00
146 Dan Cloutier 1.00 2.50
147 Lee Sorochan .60 1.50
148 Marty Murray .50 1.25
149 Shean Donovan .60 1.50
150 Larry Courville .60 1.50
151 Jason Allison .50 1.25
152 Jeff O'Neill .50 1.25
153 Bryan McCabe .40 1.00
154 Miloslav Guren .60 1.50
155 Petr Buzek .60 1.50
156 Tomas Blazek .60 1.50
157 Josef Marha .60 1.50
158 Jan Hlavac 1.00 2.50
159 Veli-Pekka Nutikka .60 1.50
160 Kimmo Timonen .50 1.25
161 Antti Aalto .50 1.25
162 Janne Niinimaa .60 1.50
163 Nikolai Zavarukhin .60 1.50
164 Vadim Epantchinsev .50 1.25
165 Alexander Korolyuk .60 1.50
166 Dmitri Klevakin .50 1.25
167 Vitali Yachmenev .60 1.50
168 Niklas Sundstrom .60 1.50
169 Anders Soderberg .50 1.25
170 Anders Eriksson .50 1.25
171 Jesper Mattsson .50 1.25
172 Mattias Ohlund 1.00 2.50
173 Jason Bonsignore .60 1.50
174 Bryan Berard 1.00 2.50
175 Richard Park .40 1.00
176 Mike McBain .60 1.50
177 Jason Doig .60 1.50
178 Xavier Delisle .60 1.50
179 Christian Dube .60 1.50
180 Louis-Philippe .60 1.50
181 Jarome Iginla 2.50 6.00
182 Marc Savard .60 1.50
183 Alyn McCauley .60 1.50
184 Brad Mehalko .60 1.50
185 Todd Norman .60 1.50
186 Brian Scott .60 1.50
187 Brad Larsen .60 1.50
188 Jeffrey Ware .60 1.50
189 Sergei Samsonov .60 1.50
190 Andrei Petrunin .60 1.50
191 Sean Haggerty .60 1.50
192 Rory Fitzpatrick .60 1.50
193 Deron Quint .40 1.00
194 Jamie Langenbrunner .50 1.25
195 Jeff Mitchell .50 1.25

1994-95 SP Premier

The 30 cards in this set were randomly inserted in SP at the rate of 1:9 packs. The cards are printed on white paper stock and have a full white border. The action photo has a ghosted background, making the picture look slightly out of focus. The set name is embossed on the lower card front. Player name and position are printed above and below the set name. Player photo and limited text are the back. A gold rectangular hologram is used on this version.

COMPLETE SET (30) 20.00 40.00
*DIE CUT: 4X TO 8X BASIC INSERTS
1 Paul Kariya .60 1.50
2 Peter Forsberg 1.50 4.00
3 Viktor Kozlov .30 .75
4 Todd Marchant .30 .75
5 Oleg Tverdovsky .15 .40
6 Todd Harvey .15 .40
7 Kenny Jonsson .30 .75
8 Blaine Lacher .30 .75
9 Radek Bonk .40 1.00
10 Brett Lindros .15 .40
11 Valeri Bure .30 .75
12 Brian Rolston .15 .40
13 David Oliver .15 .40
14 Ian Laperriere .15 .40
15 Adam Deadmarsh .30 .75
16 Pavel Bure .60 1.50
17 Wayne Gretzky 3.00 8.00
18 Jeremy Roenick .75 2.00
19 Dominik Hasek 1.25 3.00
20 Ray Bourque .75 2.00
21 Doug Gilmour .30 .75
22 Teemu Selanne .60 1.50
23 Cam Neely .60 1.50
24 Sergei Fedorov 1.00 2.50
25 Bernie Nicholls .15 .40
26 Jaromir Jagr .75 2.00
27 Joe Sakic 1.50 4.00
28 Mark Messier .60 1.50
29 Brett Hull .75 2.00
30 Eric Lindros .60 1.50

1995-96 SP

The 1995-96 Upper Deck SP set was issued in one series totaling 188 cards. The 8-card packs had an SRP of $4.39 each. The Great Connections inserts (GC1and GC2), were randomly inserted at the rate of 1:381 packs. There are two versions of card number 66. The first features Wayne Gretzky in an All-Star sweater. This was used as a promotional card and was issued with the dealer solicitation. The second is the regular number 66 found in packs and features Craig Johnson, a player acquired by the Kings in the Gretzky trade.

COMPLETE SET (188) 20.00 40.00
1 Paul Kariya .25 .60
2 Teemu Selanne .25 .60
3 Guy Hebert .10 .30
4 Steve Rucchin .10 .30
5 Ray Bourque .40 1.00
6 Cam Neely .25 .60
7 Adam Oates .10 .30
8 Kyle McLaren RC .05 .15
9 Bill Ranford .10 .30
10 Shawn McEachern .05 .15
11 Don Sweeney .05 .15
12 Pat LaFontaine .25 .60
13 Dominik Hasek .50 1.25
14 Brian Holzinger RC .25 .60
15 Alexei Zhitnik .05 .15
16 Theo Fleury .05 .15
17 Cory Stillman .05 .15
18 German Titov .05 .15
19 Phil Housley .10 .30
20 Michael Nylander .05 .15
21 Trevor Kidd .10 .30
22 Eric Daze .10 .30
23 Chris Chelios .25 .60
24 Jeremy Roenick .30 .75
25 Gary Suter .05 .15
26 Bernie Nicholls .05 .15
27 Ed Belfour .25 .60
28 Tony Amonte .10 .30
29 Peter Forsberg .60 1.50
30 Patrick Roy 1.25 3.00
31 Joe Sakic .50 1.25
32 Sandis Ozolinsh .05 .15
33 Adam Deadmarsh .05 .15
34 Stephane Fiset .10 .30
35 Claude Lemieux .05 .15
36 Mike Modano .40 1.00
37 Kevin Hatcher .05 .15
38 Joe Nieuwendyk .10 .30
39 Todd Harvey .10 .30
40 Derian Hatcher .05 .15
41 Jere Lehtinen .10 .30
42 Nicklas Lidstrom .25 .60
43 Mathieu Dandenault .05 .15
44 Sergei Fedorov .40 1.00
45 Paul Coffey .25 .60
46 Steve Yzerman 1.25 3.00
47 Keith Primeau .05 .15
48 Chris Osgood .10 .30
49 Vyacheslav Kozlov .10 .30
50 Doug Weight .10 .30
51 Jason Arnott .05 .15
52 Miroslav Satan RC 1.00 2.50
53 Zdeno Ciger .05 .15
54 Curtis Joseph .25 .60
55 Scott Mellanby .05 .15
56 John Vanbiesbrouck .10 .30
57 Jody Hull .05 .15
58 Ed Jovanovski .25 .60
59 Radek Dvorak RC .40 1.00
60 Rob Niedermayer .10 .30
61 Andrew Cassels .05 .15
62 Brendan Shanahan .25 .60
63 Nelson Emerson .05 .15
64 Jeff O'Neill .05 .15
65 Sean Burke .10 .30
66A Wayne Gretzky promo 4.00 10.00
66B Craig Johnson .05 .15
67 Dimitri Khristich .05 .15
68 Vitali Yachmenev .05 .15
69 Aki Berg RC .10 .30
70 Byron Dafoe .10 .30
71 Pierre Turgeon .10 .30
72 Mark Recchi .10 .30
73 Saku Koivu .25 .60
74 Valeri Bure .05 .15
75 Vincent Damphousse .05 .15
76 Jocelyn Thibault .25 .60
77 Patrice Brisebois .05 .15
78 John MacLean .10 .30
79 Martin Brodeur .60 1.50
80 Steve Thomas .10 .30
81 Scott Stevens .10 .30
82 Bill Guerin .10 .30
83 Petr Sykora RC 1.00 2.50
84 Scott Niedermayer .05 .15
85 Stephane Richer .10 .30
86 Zigmund Palffy .10 .30
87 Travis Green .10 .30
88 Todd Bertuzzi RC 2.00 5.00
89 Mathieu Schneider .05 .15
90 Eric Fichaud .10 .30
91 Bryan McCabe .05 .15
92 Mark Messier .25 .60
93 Pat Verbeek .05 .15
94 Brian Leetch .10 .30
95 Mike Richter .25 .60
96 Niklas Sundstrom .10 .30
97 Luc Robitaille .10 .30
98 Adam Graves .05 .15
99 Alexei Kovalev .05 .15
100 Daniel Alfredsson RC 2.00 5.00
101 Alexei Yashin .05 .15
102 Radek Bonk .05 .15
103 Alexandre Daigle .05 .15
104 Damian Rhodes .10 .30
105 Antti Tormanen .05 .15
106 Eric Lindros .25 .60
107 Mikael Renberg .10 .30
108 John LeClair .25 .60
109 Ron Hextall .10 .30
110 Rod Brind'Amour .10 .30
111 Joel Otto .05 .15
112 Eric Desjardins .10 .30
113 Mario Lemieux 1.25 3.00
114 Jaromir Jagr .40 1.00
115 Ron Francis .10 .30
116 Markus Naslund .25 .60
117 Sergei Zubov .05 .15
118 Tomas Sandstrom .05 .15
119 Tom Barrasso .10 .30
120 Richard Park .05 .15
121 Brett Hull .30 .75
122 Shayne Corson .05 .15
123 Dale Hawerchuk .25 .60
124 Chris Pronger .25 .60
125 Al MacInnis .10 .30
126 Grant Fuhr .25 .60
127 Wayne Gretzky 1.50 4.00
128 Geoff Courtnall .05 .15
129 Owen Nolan .10 .30
130 Ray Sheppard .05 .15
131 Chris Terreri .10 .30
132 Marcus Ragnarsson RC .10 .30
133 Jeff Friesen .05 .15
134 Doug Bodger .05 .15
135 Roman Hamrlik .10 .30
136 Petr Klima .05 .15
137 Daren Puppa .10 .30
138 Aaron Gavey .05 .15
139 Daymond Langkow RC .40 1.00
140 Alexander Selivanov .05 .15
141 Mats Sundin .25 .60
142 Kirk Muller .05 .15
143 Larry Murphy .10 .30
144 Doug Gilmour .10 .30
145 Darby Hendrickson .05 .15
146 Felix Potvin .25 .60
147 Kenny Jonsson .05 .15
148 Alexander Mogilny .10 .30
149 Pavel Bure .25 .60
150 Trevor Linden .10 .30
151 Corey Hirsch .10 .30
152 Kirk McLean .10 .30
153 Esa Tikkanen .05 .15
154 Cliff Ronning .05 .15
155 Peter Bondra .10 .30
156 Jim Carey .10 .30
157 Michal Pivonka .05 .15
158 Joe Juneau .05 .15
159 Dale Hunter .10 .30
160 Steve Konowalchuk .05 .15
161 Stefan Ustorf .05 .15
162 Brendan Witt .05 .15
163 Chad Kilger RC .05 .15
164 Keith Tkachuk .25 .60
165 Deron Quint .05 .15
166 Oleg Tverdovsky .05 .15
167 Alexei Zhamnov .10 .30
168 Igor Korolev .05 .15
169 Wade Redden .05 .15
170 Jarome Iginla .30 .75
171 Christian Dube .05 .15
172 Jason Podollan .05 .15
173 Alyn McCauley .10 .30
174 Nolan Baumgartner .05 .15
175 Jason Botterill .05 .15
176 Chris Phillips RC .30 .75
177 Dmitri Nabokov .10 .30
178 Andrei Petrunin .05 .15
179 Alexander Korolyuk .10 .30
180 Sergei Samsonov .60 1.50
181 Ilja Gorokhov RC .10 .30
182 Alexei Kolkunov RC .10 .30
183 Samuel Pahlsson RC .05 .15
184 Mattias Ohlund .05 .15
185 Marcus Nilsson RC .25 .60
186 Daniel Tjarnqvist RC .05 .15
187 Per Anton Lundstrom RC .05 .15
188 Fredrik Loven RC .05 .15
GC1 Wayne Gretzky 15.00 40.00
GC2 Sergei Samsonov 8.00 20.00

1995-96 SP Holoviews

Randomly inserted in packs at a rate of 1:5, this 20-card set utilizes UD's Holoview technology to great effect. There also exists a die-cut parallel version of this set (known as Special FX), issued 1:75 packs. Special FX cards are enhanced by rainbow foil, as well as the die-cutting. Multipliers to determine the value of these cards are listed below.

COMPLETE SET (20) 20.00 50.00
*SPECIAL FX: 1.25X TO 3X BASIC INSERTS
FX1 Teemu Selanne .60 1.50
FX2 Paul Kariya .60 1.50
FX3 Chris Chelios .60 1.50
FX4 Peter Forsberg 1.50 4.00
FX5 Sergei Fedorov 1.00 2.50
FX6 Paul Coffey .60 1.50
FX7 Steve Yzerman 3.00 8.00
FX8 Jason Arnott .15 .40
FX9 Doug Weight .30 .75
FX10 Wayne Gretzky 5.00 12.00
FX11 Vitali Yachmenev .15 .40
FX12 Martin Brodeur 1.50 4.00
FX13 Scott Stevens .30 .75
FX14 Mark Messier .60 1.50
FX15 Daniel Alfredsson 3.00 8.00
FX16 Eric Lindros .60 1.50
FX17 Mario Lemieux 3.00 8.00
FX18 Jaromir Jagr 1.00 2.50
FX19 Shayne Corson .15 .40
FX20 Pavel Bure .75 2.00

1995-96 SP Stars Etoiles

Randomly inserted in packs at a rate of 1:3, this 30-card set uses a double die-cut design to highlight the top athletes in the NHL. This version uses silver foil as it's primary element. There also is a gold foil parallel version, which is significantly tougher to pull. These cards were randomly inserted 1:61 packs.

COMPLETE SET (30) 25.00 50.00
*GOLD: 3X TO 6X BASIC INSERTS
E1 Paul Kariya .50 1.25
E2 Teemu Selanne .50 1.25
E3 Ray Bourque .75 2.00
E4 Cam Neely .50 1.25
E5 Pat LaFontaine .50 1.25
E6 Theo Fleury .60 1.50
E7 Jeremy Roenick .60 1.50
E8 Joe Sakic 1.00 2.50
E9 Patrick Roy 2.50 6.00
E10 Peter Forsberg 1.25 3.00
E11 Mike Modano .75 2.00
E12 Sergei Fedorov .75 2.00
E13 Paul Coffey .50 1.25
E14 Steve Yzerman 2.50 6.00
E15 Pierre Turgeon .25 .60
E16 Brendan Shanahan .50 1.25
E17 Wayne Gretzky 2.50 6.00
E18 Martin Brodeur 1.25 3.00
E19 Mark Messier .50 1.25
E20 Brian Leetch .25 .60
E21 Eric Lindros .50 1.25
E22 Mario Lemieux 2.50 6.00
E23 Jaromir Jagr .75 2.00
E24 Brett Hull .60 1.50
E25 Roman Hamrlik .25 .60
E26 Mats Sundin .50 1.25
E27 Felix Potvin .50 1.25
E28 Alexander Mogilny .25 .60
E29 Pavel Bure .50 1.25
E30 Keith Tkachuk .50 1.25

1996-97 SP

The 1996-97 SP set was issued in one series totaling 188 cards. The eight-card packs had a suggested retail price of $3.49 each. Printed on 20 pt. card stock, this set featured color action photos of 168 regular players from all 26 NHL teams and included a subset of 20 premier prospects. The backs carried player information and statistics. The Gretzky promo was distributed to dealers; it mirrored the regular issue save for the word SAMPLE written across the back.

COMPLETE SET (188) 15.00 40.00
1 Paul Kariya .25 .60
2 Teemu Selanne .40 1.00
3 Jari Kurri .20 .50
4 Darren Van Impe .12 .30
5 Guy Hebert .15 .40
6 Steve Rucchin .12 .30
7 Ray Bourque .30 .75
8 Kyle McLaren .12 .30
9 Bill Ranford .15 .40
10 Don Sweeney .12 .30
11 Adam Oates .20 .50
12 Rick Tocchet .15 .40
13 Ted Donato .12 .30
14 Curtis Brown .12 .30
15 Pat LaFontaine .20 .50
16 Derek Plante .12 .30
17 Dominik Hasek .30 .75
18 Brian Holzinger .15 .40
19 Alexei Zhitnik .12 .30
20 Theo Fleury .40 1.00
21 Trevor Kidd .12 .30
22 Steve Chiasson .12 .30
23 Jarome Iginla .25 .60
24 German Titov .12 .30
25 Zarley Zalapski .12 .30
26 Eric Daze .15 .40
27 Chris Chelios .20 .50
28 Ed Belfour .20 .50
29 Gary Suter .12 .30
30 Alexei Zhamnov .15 .40
31 Ethan Moreau RC .20 .50
32 Tony Amonte .15 .40
33 Peter Forsberg .30 .75
34 Joe Sakic .30 .75
35 Patrick Roy .50 1.25
36 Adam Deadmarsh .12 .30
37 Mike Ricci .12 .30
38 Adam Foote .12 .30
39 Claude Lemieux .12 .30
40 Mike Modano .30 .75
41 Pat Verbeek .12 .30
42 Todd Harvey .12 .30
43 Sergei Zubov .12 .30
44 Andy Moog .20 .50
45 Derian Hatcher .12 .30
46 Jamie Langenbrunner .12 .30
47 Steve Yzerman .50 1.25
48 Sergei Fedorov .30 .75
49 Slava Kozlov .12 .30
50 Brendan Shanahan .25 .60
51 Chris Osgood .20 .50
52 Nicklas Lidstrom .25 .60
53 Vladimir Konstantinov .15 .40
54 Curtis Joseph .20 .50
55 Jason Arnott .15 .40
56 Ryan Smyth .15 .40
57 Doug Weight .20 .50
58 Andrei Kovalenko .12 .30
59 Mariusz Czerkawski .12 .30
60 Ed Jovanovski .15 .40
61 John Vanbiesbrouck .20 .50
62 Rob Niedermayer .15 .40
63 Robert Svehla .12 .30
64 Brian Skrudland .12 .30
65 Scott Mellanby .15 .40
66 Ray Sheppard .15 .40
67 Jeff O'Neill .12 .30
68 Keith Primeau .12 .30
69 Geoff Sanderson .15 .40
70 Sean Burke .12 .30
71 Kevin Dineen .12 .30
72 Andrew Cassels .12 .30
73 Kevin Stevens .12 .30
74 Rob Blake .20 .50
75 Ed Olczyk .12 .30
76 Mattias Norstrom .12 .30
77 Stephane Fiset .15 .40
78 Vitali Yachmenev .12 .30
79 Saku Koivu .20 .50
80 Valeri Bure .12 .30
81 Jocelyn Thibault .20 .50
82 David Wilkie .12 .30
83 Stephane Richer .15 .40
84 Shayne Corson .12 .30
85 Mark Recchi .25 .60
86 Martin Brodeur .40 1.00
87 Bobby Holik
88 Petr Sykora .12 .30
89 Scott Stevens .20 .50
90 Scott Niedermayer .20 .50
91 Bill Guerin .20 .50
92 Eric Fichaud .15 .40
93 Kenny Jonsson .12 .30
94 Travis Green .15 .40
95 Derek King .12 .30
96 Todd Bertuzzi .20 .50
97 Zigmund Palffy .20 .50
98 Mark Messier .30 .75
99 Wayne Gretzky 1.00 2.50
100 Mike Richter .20 .50
101 Brian Leetch .20 .50
102 Luc Robitaille .20 .50
103 Adam Graves .12 .30
104 Alexei Kovalev .12 .30
105 Radek Bonk .12 .30
106 Alexandre Daigle .12 .30
107 Daniel Alfredsson .20 .50
108 Alexei Yashin .15 .40
109 Andreas Dackell RC .20 .50
110 Damian Rhodes .15 .40
111 Petr Svoboda .12 .30
112 John LeClair .20 .50
113 Eric Desjardins .15 .40
114 Eric Lindros .30 .75
115 Mikael Renberg .15 .40
116 Ron Hextall .15 .40
117 Dainius Zubrus RC .25 .60
118 Keith Tkachuk .20 .50
119 Jeremy Roenick .30 .75
120 Nikolai Khabibulin .15 .40
121 Oleg Tverdovsky .15 .40
122 Teppo Numminen .12 .30
123 Mike Gartner .20 .50
124 Cliff Ronning .12 .30
125 Mario Lemieux .60 1.50
126 Jaromir Jagr .50 1.25
127 Ron Francis .25 .60
128 Petr Nedved .15 .40
129 Darius Kasparaitis .12 .30
130 Kevin Hatcher .12 .30
131 Joe Mullen .15 .40
132 Joe Murphy .12 .30
133 Grant Fuhr .20 .50
134 Harry York RC .20 .50
135 Chris Pronger .15 .40
136 Brett Hull 1.00 2.50
137 Pierre Turgeon .20 .50
138 Owen Nolan .20 .50
139 Bernie Nicholls .12 .30
140 Tony Granato .12 .30
141 Kelly Hrudey .15 .40
142 Darren Turcotte .12 .30
143 Jeff Friesen .12 .30
144 Roman Hamrlik .15 .40
145 Chris Gratton .15 .40
146 Daymond Langkow .15 .40
147 Dino Ciccarelli .20 .50
148 Alexander Selivanov .12 .30
149 Brian Bradley .12 .30
150 Wendel Clark .15 .40
151 Mats Sundin .20 .50
152 Doug Gilmour .25 .60
153 Felix Potvin .20 .50
154 Larry Murphy .15 .40
155 Mathieu Schneider .12 .30
156 Kirk Muller .12 .30
157 Pavel Bure .25 .60
158 Alexander Mogilny .15 .40
159 Corey Hirsch .15 .40
160 Jyrki Lumme .12 .30
161 Russ Courtnall .12 .30
162 Mike Fountain RC
163 Peter Bondra .15 .40
164 Jim Carey .20 .50
165 Sergei Gonchar .12 .30
166 Joe Juneau .12 .30
167 Phil Housley .15 .40
168 Jason Allison .15 .40
169 Ruslan Salei RC .20 .50
170 Mattias Timander RC .20 .50
171 Vaclav Varada RC .20 .50
172 Jonas Hoglund .12 .30
173 Jason Podollan .15 .40
174 Jose Theodore .25 .60
175 Roman Turek RC .20 .50
176 Anders Eriksson .12 .30
177 Mike Grier RC .25 .60
178 Rem Murray RC .20 .50
179 Per Gustafsson RC .20 .50
180 Jay Pandolfo UER .20 .50
181 Kai Nurminen RC .20 .50
182 Bryan Berard .20 .50
183 Christian Dube .12 .30
184 Daniel Goneau RC .20 .50
185 Wade Redden .12 .30
186 Janne Niinimaa .20 .50
187 Jim Campbell .12 .30
188 Sergei Berezin RC .30 .75
P99 Wayne Gretzky PROMO 1.00 2.50

1996-97 SP Clearcut Winner

Randomly inserted in packs at a rate of 1:91, this 20-card set featured color player images in a chiseled-out ice block, die-cut card displaying a full body transparent Hologram.

CW1 Wayne Gretzky 20.00 50.00
CW2 Saku Koivu 2.50 6.00
CW3 Mario Lemieux 10.00 25.00
CW4 Sergei Fedorov 3.00 8.00
CW5 Paul Kariya 2.50 6.00
CW6 Patrick Roy 10.00 25.00
CW7 Jeremy Roenick 3.00 8.00
CW8 Brendan Shanahan 2.50 6.00
CW9 John Vanbiesbrouck 2.00 5.00
CW10 Doug Weight 2.00 5.00
CW11 Mark Messier 2.50 6.00
CW12 Mats Sundin 2.50 6.00
CW13 Paul Coffey 2.00 5.00
CW14 Theo Fleury 4.00 10.00
CW15 Steve Yzerman 8.00 20.00
CW16 Pavel Bure 2.50 6.00
CW17 Adam Deadmarsh 1.00 2.50
CW18 Chris Chelios 2.00 5.00
CW19 Joe Sakic 8.00 20.00
CW20 Eric Daze 1.00 2.50

1996-97 SP Holoview Collection

Randomly inserted in packs at a rate of 1:9, this 30-card set featured color player photos of some of the NHL's most elite stars printed on an all new design Holoview die-cut card.

COMPLETE SET (30) 20.00 50.00
HC1 Wayne Gretzky 6.00 15.00
HC2 Eric Daze .40 1.00
HC3 Doug Gilmour .60 1.50
HC4 Jason Arnott .60 1.50
HC5 Sergei Fedorov 1.50 4.00
HC6 Chris Chelios 1.00 2.50
HC7 Alexei Kovalev .60 1.5
HC8 Pat LaFontaine .40 1.0
HC9 Daniel Alfredsson .60 1.5
HC10 Chris Pronger .60 1.5
HC11 Jocelyn Thibault .60 1.5
HC12 Chris Gratton .40 1.0
HC13 Alexei Yashin .40 1.0
HC14 Peter Bondra .60 1.5
HC15 Saku Koivu 1.00 2.5
HC16 Valeri Bure .40 1.0
HC17 Joe Juneau .40 1.0
HC18 Tony Amonte 1.00 2.5
HC19 Brian Holzinger .40 1.0
HC20 Mats Sundin 1.00 2.5
HC21 Chris Osgood .60 1.5
HC22 Roman Hamrlik .40 1.0
HC23 Ray Bourque 2.00 5.0
HC24 Doug Weight .60 1.5
HC25 Mike Modano 1.50 4.0
HC26 Niklas Sundstrom .40 1.0
HC27 Mike Richter 1.00 2.5
HC28 Zigmund Palffy .60 1.5
HC29 Adam Oates .60 1.5
HC30 Dominik Hasek 2.00 5.0

1996-97 SP Inside Info

Inserted at the rate of one per box, this eight-card set featured color action player photos with a special pul out panel that displayed another photo of the same player and statistics. Cards are not numbered. We ha numbered them alphabetically. A gold version was al available and was seeded one in every two cases. Values for these cards can be determined by using th multipliers listed below.

COMPLETE SET (8) 20.00 50.0
*GOLDS: 2X TO 5X BASIC INSERTS
IN1 Wayne Gretzky 10.00 25.0
IN2 Keith Tkachuk 2.00 5.0
IN3 Brendan Shanahan 2.50 6.0
IN4 Teemu Selanne 3.00 8.0
IN5 Ray Bourque 3.00 8.0
IN6 Joe Sakic 4.00 10.0
IN7 Felix Potvin 3.00 8.0
IN8 Steve Yzerman 6.00 15.0

1996-97 SP Game Film

Randomly inserted in packs at a rate of 1:30, this 20-card set carried actual game photography featuring fil footage of favorite NHL players.

COMPLETE SET (20) 40.00 100.0
GF1 Wayne Gretzky 15.00 40.0
GF2 Peter Forsberg 4.00 10.0
GF3 Patrick Roy 10.00 25.0
GF4 Brett Hull 3.00 8.0
GF5 Keith Tkachuk 1.00 2.5
GF6 Eric Lindros 3.00 8.0
GF7 Felix Potvin 3.00 8.0
GF8 John Vanbiesbrouck 1.50 4.0
GF9 Paul Kariya 3.00 8.0
GF10 Mark Messier 2.50 6.0
GF11 Ed Belfour 2.50 6.0
GF12 Alexander Mogilny 1.00 2.5
GF13 Jim Carey 1.50 4.0
GF14 Ed Jovanovski 1.00 2.5
GF15 Theo Fleury 1.50 4.0
GF16 Doug Gilmour 1.50 4.0
GF17 John LeClair 1.00 2.5
GF18 Pat LaFontaine 1.00 2.5
GF19 Paul Coffey 1.50 4.0
GF20 Daniel Alfredsson 1.50 4.0

1996-97 SP SPx Force

Randomly inserted in packs at a rate of 1:360, this fiv card set featured top NHL players on a multi-image Holoview card. Each of the first four cards displayed a center, winger, goalie and rookie. The last card carrie the top player from each of the previous cards.

COMPLETE SET (5) 60.00 150.0
1 Lind./Lemieux/Forsb./Gretz. 25.00 60.0
2 Brett Hull 15.00 30.0
Jaromir Jagr
Pavel Bure
Teemu Selanne
3 Osgo./Hasek/Brod./Richt. 12.00 30.0
4 Eriks./Berard/Iginla/Berezin 8.00 20.0
5 Iginla/Jagr/Gretzky/Brodeur 20.00 50.0

1996-97 SP SPx Force Autographs

These four different autograph cards were randomly inserted one in 2,500 packs of 1996-97 SP. Besides the player's signature, the cards are parallel to the more common, unsigned SPx Force Inserts. Only 10 cards were signed by each player.

1 Wayne Gretzky AU 150.00 300.0
2 Jaromir Jagr AU 50.00 125.0
3 Martin Brodeur AU 60.00 150.0
4 Jarome Iginla AU 30.00 80.0

1997-98 SP Authentic

The 1997-98 SP Authentic set was issued in one seri totaling 198 cards and was distributed in five-card packs with a suggested retail price of $4.99. The fron features color player photos printed on 24 pt. card stock. The backs carry player information. The set contains the topical subset: Future Watch (169-198).

COMPLETE SET (198) 30.00 60.0
1 Teemu Selanne .30 .7
2 Sean Pronger .08 .2
3 Joe Sacco .08 .2
4 Tomas Sandstrom .08 .2
5 Steve Rucchin .08 .2
6 Paul Kariya .30 .7
7 Ted Donato .08 .2
8 Ray Bourque .50 1.2
9 Tim Taylor .08 .2
10 Jason Allison .08 .2
11 Kyle McLaren .08 .2
12 Dimitri Khristich .08 .2
13 Jason Dawe .08 .2
14 Dominik Hasek .60 1.5
15 Miroslav Satan .08 .2
16 Brian Holzinger .08 .2
17 Alexei Zhitnik .08 .2
18 Theo Fleury .08 .2
19 Cory Stillman .08 .2
20 Jarome Iginla .40 1.0
21 Sandy McCarthy .08 .2
22 German Titov .08 .2
23 Glen Wesley .08 .2
24 Keith Primeau .08 .2
25 Geoff Sanderson .25 .6
26 Gary Roberts .08 .2
27 Sami Kapanen .08 .2
28 Jeff O'Neill .08 .2
29 Tony Amonte .25 .6
30 Chris Chelios .30 .7
31 Eric Daze .25 .6
32 Alexei Zhamnov .08 .2
33 Chris Terreri .25 .6
34 Sergei Krivokrasov .08 .2
35 Joe Sakic .60 1.5
36 Peter Forsberg .75 2.0

7 Patrick Roy 1.50 4.00
3 Claude Lemieux .08 .25
Valeri Kamensky .25 .60
Adam Deadmarsh .08 .25
Sandis Ozolinsh .08 .25
2 Jari Kurri .25 .60
3 Mike Modano .50 1.25
4 Ed Belfour .30 .75
5 Derian Hatcher .08 .25
6 Sergei Zubov .08 .25
7 Jamie Langenbrunner .08 .25
3 Jere Lehtinen .08 .25
Joe Nieuwendyk .25 .60
Vyacheslav Kozlov .08 .25
Chris Osgood .25 .60
2 Steve Yzerman 1.50 4.00
3 Nicklas Lidstrom .30 .75
4 Igor Larionov .08 .25
5 Brendan Shanahan .30 .75
6 Anders Eriksson .08 .25
7 Darren McCarty .08 .25
3 Doug Weight .25 .60
Jason Arnott .08 .25
Curtis Joseph .30 .75
Ryan Smyth .25 .60
2 Dean McAmmond .08 .25
Mike Grier .08 .25
Kelly Buchberger .08 .25
Ed Jovanovski .25 .60
6 Ray Whitney .08 .25
7 Rob Niedermayer .08 .25
Scott Mellanby .08 .25
John Vanbiesbrouck .25 .60
Viktor Kozlov .08 .25
Jozef Stumpel .25 .60
2 Rob Blake .25 .60
Garry Galley .08 .25
Vladimir Tsyplakov .08 .25
Yanic Perreault .08 .25
Stephane Fiset .25 .60
Luc Robitaille .25 .60
Valeri Bure .08 .25
Mark Recchi .25 .60
Saku Koivu .30 .75
Andy Moog .25 .60
Vincent Damphousse .08 .25
Vladimir Malakhov .08 .25
Shayne Corson .08 .25
Scott Stevens .25 .60
Bill Guerin .25 .60
Martin Brodeur .75 2.00
Doug Gilmour .25 .60
Bobby Holik .08 .25
Petr Sykora .08 .25
Zigmund Palffy .25 .60
Bryan Berard .25 .60
Tommy Salo .25 .60
Travis Green .08 .25
Kenny Jonsson .08 .25
Todd Bertuzzi .30 .75
Robert Reichel .08 .25
Pat LaFontaine .30 .75
Wayne Gretzky 2.00 5.00
0 Brian Leetch .30 .75
1 Mike Richter .30 .75
2 Alexei Kovalev .08 .25
3 Adam Graves .08 .25
4 Niklas Sundstrom .08 .25
5 Alexei Yashin .08 .25
6 Daniel Alfredsson .25 .60
7 Alexandre Daigle .08 .25
8 Wade Redden .08 .25
9 Andreas Dackell .08 .25
0 Shawn McEachern .08 .25
1 Eric Lindros .30 .75
2 Chris Gratton .25 .60
3 Paul Coffey .30 .75
4 John LeClair .30 .75
5 Rod Brind'Amour .25 .60
6 Ron Hextall .25 .60
7 Dainius Zubrus .30 .75
8 Jeremy Roenick .40 1.00
9 Keith Tkachuk .30 .75
0 Nikolai Khabibulin .25 .60
1 Rick Tocchet .25 .60
2 Teppo Numminen .08 .25
3 Craig Janney .08 .25
4 Mike Gartner .25 .60
5 Jaromir Jagr .50 1.25
6 Ron Francis .25 .60
7 Kevin Hatcher .08 .25
8 Robert Dome RC .08 .25
9 Martin Straka .08 .25
0 Peter Skudra RC .08 .25
1 Owen Nolan .25 .60
2 Bernie Nicholls .08 .25
3 Mike Vernon .25 .60
4 Jeff Friesen .08 .25
5 Tony Granato .08 .25
6 Mike Ricci .08 .25
7 Jim Campbell .08 .25
8 Brett Hull .40 1.00
9 Chris Pronger .25 .60
0 Al MacInnis .25 .60
1 Pierre Turgeon .25 .60
2 Pavol Demitra .25 .60
3 Grant Fuhr .25 .60
Steve Duchesne .08 .25
Daymond Langkow .25 .60
Alexander Selivanov .08 .25
Daren Puppa .25 .60
3 Dino Ciccarelli .08 .25
Roman Hamrlik .25 .60
Mats Sundin .30 .75
Felix Potvin .30 .75
2 Wendel Clark .25 .60
3 Sergei Berezin .08 .25
4 Steve Sullivan .08 .25
Alexander Mogilny .25 .60
Pavel Bure .30 .75
Mark Messier .30 .75
3 Bret Hedican .08 .25
Kirk McLean .25 .60
Trevor Linden .25 .60
Dave Scatchard RC .08 .25
2 Adam Oates .25 .60
3 Joe Juneau .25 .60
Peter Bondra .25 .60
Bill Ranford .25 .60
Sergei Gonchar .08 .25
Calle Johansson .08 .25
3 Phil Housley .08 .25
Espen Knutsen RC .75 2.00
Pavel Trnka RC .25 .60
Joe Thornton 1.00 2.50
Sergei Samsonov .40 1.00

173 Erik Rasmussen .25 .60
174 Tyler Moss RC .25 .60
175 Derek Morris RC .40 1.00
176 Craig Mills .25 .60
177 Daniel Cleary .25 .60
178 Eric Messier RC .30 .75
179 Kevin Hodson .25 .60
180 Mike Knuble RC .25 .60
181 Boyd Deveraux .25 .60
182 Craig Millar RC .08 .25
183 Kevin Weekes RC 2.00 5.00
184 Donald MacLean RC .25 .60
185 Patrik Elias RC 3.00 8.00
186 Zdeno Chara RC 12.00 30.00
187 Chris Phillips .25 .60
188 Vaclav Prospal RC .30 .75
189 Brad Isbister .25 .60
190 Alexei Morozov .25 .60
191 Patrick Marleau .60 1.50
192 Marco Sturm RC .50 1.25
193 Brendan Morrison RC 1.25 3.00
194 Mike Johnson RC .30 .75
195 Alyn McCauley .25 .60
196 Mattias Ohlund .25 .60
197 Richard Zednik .25 .60
198 Jan Bulis RC .25 .60
99 Wayne Gretzky PROMO 3.00 8.00

1997-98 SP Authentic Authentics

Randomly inserted in packs at the rate of 1:288, these special "trade" cards could be redeemed for an assortment of Wayne Gretzky's signed momorabilia from Upper Deck Authenticated such as autographed jerseys, pucks, sticks and other items. Only three "SP Authentics Collection" cards were produced that could be redeemed for Wayne Gretzky's entire collection of autographed memorabilia. We have listed and priced only the autographed trading card below.

10 W.Gretzky 802 Card/184 25.00 50.00

1997-98 SP Authentic Icons

Randomly inserted in packs at the rate of 1:5, this 40-card set features color action photos of the most respected players of the NHL. Embossed and die cut parallels were also created and inserted randomly.

COMPLETE SET (40) 40.00 80.00
*EMBOSSED: .8X TO 2X BASIC INSERTS
*DIE CUT: 4X TO 10X BASIC INSERTS
I1 Pat LaFontaine .75 2.00
I2 Brett Hull 1.00 2.50
I3 Chris Chelios .75 2.00
I4 Joe Sakic 1.50 4.00
I5 John Vanbiesbrouck .60 1.50
I6 Patrik Elias .75 2.00
I7 Eric Lindros 1.25 3.00
I8 Jaromir Jagr 1.25 3.00
I9 Joe Thornton 1.50 4.00
I10 Brendan Shanahan .75 2.00
I11 Paul Kariya .75 2.00
I12 Peter Forsberg 2.00 5.00
I13 Ed Belfour .75 2.00
I14 Martin Brodeur 2.00 5.00
I15 Alexei Morozov .60 1.50
I16 Mark Messier .75 2.00
I17 John LeClair .75 2.00
I18 Luc Robitaille .60 1.50
I19 Teemu Selanne .75 2.00
I20 Theo Fleury .25 .60
I21 Steve Yzerman 2.00 5.00
I22 Chris Phillips .25 .60
I23 Keith Tkachuk .75 2.00
I24 Patrick Roy 2.00 5.00
I25 Mark Recchi .60 1.50
I26 Wayne Gretzky 3.00 8.00
I27 Dino Ciccarelli .25 .60
I28 Ray Bourque 1.25 3.00
I29 Tony Amonte .60 1.50
I30 Daniel Alfredsson .60 1.50
I31 Saku Koivu .75 2.00
I32 Doug Weight .60 1.50
I33 Mats Sundin .75 2.00
I34 Dominik Hasek 1.50 4.00
I35 Scott Stevens .60 1.50
I36 Pavel Bure .75 2.00
I37 Mike Modano 1.25 3.00
I38 Zigmund Palffy .60 1.50
I39 Brian Leetch .75 2.00
I40 Marco Sturm .75 2.00

1997-98 SP Authentic Mark of a Legend

Randomly inserted in packs at the rate of 1:198, this six-card set features autographed color portraits of six of the NHL's greatest all-time players.

M1 Gordie Howe/112 125.00 250.00
M2 Billy Smith/560 10.00 25.00
M3 Cam Neely/560 15.00 40.00
M4 Bryan Trottier/560 12.00 30.00
M5 Bobby Hull/560 25.00 60.00
M6 Wayne Gretzky/560 100.00 200.00

1997-98 SP Authentic Sign of the Times

Randomly inserted in packs at the rate of 1:23, this 29-card set features autographed color action photos of top players in the NHL. Exchange card expired 3/16/99.

BB Bryan Berard 2.00 5.00
BH Brett Hull 15.00 40.00
BH Brian Holzinger 2.00 5.00
CC Chris Chelios 6.00 15.00
DM Darren McCarty 4.00 10.00
DW Doug Weight 4.00 10.00
DZ Dainius Zubrus 4.00 10.00
GF Grant Fuhr 8.00 20.00
GH Guy Hebert 4.00 10.00
JI Jarome Iginla 6.00 15.00
JS Jaroslav Svejkovsky 2.00 5.00
JLA Jamie Langenbrunner 4.00 10.00
JT Joe Thornton 10.00 25.00
JTH Jose Theodore 8.00 20.00
MB Martin Brodeur 30.00 80.00
MG Mike Grier 4.00 10.00
MS Mats Sundin 15.00 40.00
NK Nikolai Khabibulin 6.00 15.00
NL Nicklas Lidstrom 10.00 25.00
PB Peter Bondra 4.00 10.00
PR Patrick Roy 30.00 80.00
RB Ray Bourque 20.00 50.00
RN Rob Niedermayer 4.00 10.00
SB Sergei Berezin 2.00 5.00
SS Sergei Samsonov 4.00 10.00
SY Steve Yzerman 50.00 100.00
TA Tony Amonte 4.00 10.00
WG Wayne Gretzky 75.00 150.00
YP Yanic Perreault 4.00 10.00

1997-98 SP Authentic Tradition

Randomly inserted in packs at the rate of 1:340, this six card sot features color action dual photos and autographs of a current star and an NHL legend.

T1 W.Gretzky/G.Howe/158 250.00 400.00
T2 P.Roy/B.Smith/333 40.00 100.00
T3 J.Thornton/C.Neely/352 25.00 60.00
T4 B.Berard/B.Trottier/352 8.00 20.00
T5 B.Hull/B.Hull/352 30.00 80.00
T6 R.Bourque/C.Neely/140 50.00 120.00

1998-99 SP Authentic

The 1998-99 SP Authentic set was issued in one series totaling 135 cards and was distributed in five-card packs with a suggested retail price of $4.99. The set features action color photos of 90 superstars of the NHL (1-90) and 45 top prospects (91-135) which are numbered to just 2000.

COMPLETE SET (135) 125.00 300.00
COMP.SET w/o SP's (90) 10.00 25.00
1 Paul Kariya .30 .75
2 Teemu Selanne .30 .75
3 Guy Hebert .25 .60
4 Sergei Samsonov .25 .60
5 Joe Thornton .50 1.25
6 Jason Allison .08 .25
7 Ray Bourque .50 1.25
8 Dominik Hasek .60 1.50
9 Michael Peca .08 .25
10 Michal Grosek .08 .25
11 Derek Morris .08 .25
12 Theo Fleury .08 .25
13 Jarome Iginla .40 1.00
14 Ron Francis .25 .60
15 Keith Primeau .08 .25
16 Sami Kapanen .08 .25
17 Tony Amonte .25 .60
18 Doug Gilmour .25 .60
19 Chris Chelios .30 .75
20 Peter Forsberg .75 2.00
21 Patrick Roy 1.00 2.50
22 Joe Sakic .60 1.50
23 Adam Deadmarsh .08 .25
24 Brett Hull .40 1.00
25 Mike Modano .50 1.25
26 Ed Belfour .30 .75
27 Jere Lehtinen .08 .25
28 Sergei Fedorov .50 1.25
29 Brendan Shanahan .30 .75
30 Chris Osgood .25 .60
31 Steve Yzerman 1.50 4.00
32 Nicklas Lidstrom .30 .75
33 Doug Weight .25 .60
34 Bill Guerin .25 .60
35 Tom Poti .08 .25
36 Rob Niedermayer .08 .25
37 Ed Jovanovski .08 .25
38 Luc Robitaille .25 .60
39 Rob Blake .25 .60
40 Glen Murray .08 .25
41 Saku Koivu .30 .75
42 Mark Recchi .25 .60
43 Vincent Damphousse .08 .25
44 Mike Dunham .25 .60
45 Sergei Krivokrasov .08 .25
46 Andrew Brunette .25 .60
47 Brendan Morrison .25 .60
48 Martin Brodeur 1.00 2.50
49 Scott Stevens .25 .60
50 Patrik Elias .25 .60
51 Trevor Linden .25 .60
52 Zigmund Palffy .25 .60
53 Bryan Berard .08 .25
54 Robert Reichel .08 .25
55 Mike Richter .30 .75
56 Wayne Gretzky 2.00 4.00
57 Brian Leetch .25 .60
58 Wade Redden .08 .25
59 Alexei Yashin .08 .25
60 Daniel Alfredsson .25 .60
61 Eric Lindros .30 .75
62 John Vanbiesbrouck .25 .60
63 John LeClair .30 .75
64 Rod Brind'Amour .25 .60
65 Jeremy Roenick .40 1.00
66 Keith Tkachuk .30 .75
67 Nikolai Khabibulin .25 .60
68 German Titov .08 .25
69 Martin Straka .08 .25
70 Jaromir Jagr .50 1.25
71 Chris Pronger .25 .60
72 Al MacInnis .25 .60
73 Pierre Turgeon .25 .60
74 Pavol Demitra .25 .60
75 Patrick Marleau .10 .30
76 Jeff Friesen .08 .25
77 Owen Nolan .08 .25
78 Bill Ranford .08 .25
79 Wendel Clark .25 .60
80 Craig Janney .08 .25
81 Mike Johnson .08 .25
82 Curtis Joseph .30 .75
83 Mats Sundin .30 .75
84 Mattias Ohlund .25 .60
85 Mark Messier .30 .75
86 Pavel Bure .30 .75
87 Olaf Kolzig .25 .60
88 Peter Bondra .25 .60
89 Joe Juneau .25 .60
90 Adam Oates .25 .60
91 Johan Davidsson 1.50 4.00
92 Rico Fata 1.50 4.00
93 Mike Maneluk RC 2.00 5.00
94 J-P Dumont 1.50 4.00
95 Milan Hejduk RC 8.00 20.00
96 Chris Drury 1.50 4.00
97 Mark Parrish RC 4.00 10.00
98 Oleg Kvasha RC 2.00 5.00
99 Josh Green RC 2.00 5.00
100 Olli Jokinen 1.50 4.00
101 Manny Malhotra 1.50 4.00
102 Eric Brewer 1.50 4.00
103 Mike Watt 1.50 4.00
104 Daniel Briere 6.00 15.00
105 Jean-Sebastien Aubin RC 4.00 10.00
106 Jan Hrdina RC 2.00 5.00
107 Marty Reasoner 1.50 4.00
108 Michal Handzus RC 4.00 10.00
109 Vincent Lecavalier 4.00 10.00
110 Tomas Kaberle RC 4.00 10.00
111 Bill Muckalt RC 2.00 5.00
112 Josh Holden 1.50 4.00
113 Matt Herr RC 2.00 5.00
114 Brian Finley RC 3.00 8.00
115 Maxime Ouellet RC 2.00 5.00
116 Kurtis Foster RC 2.00 5.00
117 Barret Jackman RC 4.00 10.00
118 Ross Lupaschuk RC 2.00 5.00
119 Steven McCarthy RC 2.00 5.00
120 Peter Reynolds RC 2.00 5.00
121 Bart Rushmer RC 2.00 5.00
122 Jonathon Zion RC 2.00 5.00
123 Kris Beech RC 3.00 8.00
124 Brandin Cote RC 2.00 5.00
125 Scott Kelman RC 2.00 5.00
126 Jamie Lundmark RC 3.00 8.00
127 Derek MacKenzie RC 2.00 5.00
128 Rory McDade RC 2.00 5.00
129 David Morisset RC 2.00 5.00
130 Mirko Murovic RC 2.00 5.00
131 Taylor Pyatt RC 4.00 10.00
132 Charlie Stephens 2.00 5.00
133 Kyle Wanvig RC 2.00 5.00
134 Krzystof Wieckowski RC 2.00 5.00
135 Michael Zigomanis RC 2.00 5.00

1998-99 SP Authentic Power Shift

Randomly inserted into packs, this 135-card set is parallel to the base set. Only 500 sets were made.

*1-90 POWER SHIFT: 4X TO 10X BAIC CARDS
*91-135 POWER SHIFT: 1X TO 3X BASIC SP

1998-99 SP Authentic Authentics

Randomly inserted into packs at the rate of 1:697, this set features hand numbered redemption cards for autographed merchandise and game used memorabilia. We have listed and priced only the autographed trading cards. The number of each item available is indicated below. The cards expired on February 23, 2000.

6 R.Blake Puck/75 12.50 25.00
7 R.Blake Photo/100 12.50 25.00
8 C.Chelios Photo/75 30.00 60.00
9 C.Chelios Puck/75 30.00 60.00
10 W.Gretzky Puck/50 125.00 250.00
11 W.Gretzky Photo/50 125.00 250.00
12 B.Hull Puck/90 30.00 60.00
13 K.Tkachuk Photo/75 30.00 60.00
14 K.Tkachuk Puck/75 30.00 60.00
15 S.Yzerman Card/50 50.00 100.00
16 S.Yzerman 2-card 75.00 150.00
17 S.Yzerman '98 BD Card/50 75.00 150.00

1998-99 SP Authentic Sign of the Times

Randomly inserted into packs at the rate of 1:23, this 50-card set features autographed color photos of top players and future stars of the NHL. Some of the autographs were obtained through redemption cards.

AD Adam Deadmarsh 2.00 5.00
AM Alexander Mogilny 8.00 20.00
AS Alex Selivanov 3.00 8.00
BB Bates Battaglia 2.00 5.00
BD Byron Dafoe 4.00 10.00
BF Brian Finley 2.00 5.00
BH Brett Hull 12.50 30.00
BJ Barret Jackman 8.00 20.00
CJ Curtis Joseph 8.00 20.00
CS Charlie Stephens 2.00 5.00
DA Daniel Alfredsson 6.00 15.00
DM David Morisset 2.00 5.00
DMA Derek Mackenzie 2.00 5.00
DW Doug Weight 5.00 12.00
EJ Ed Jovanovski 4.00 10.00
JA Jason Allison 2.00 5.00
JJ Joe Juneau 4.00 10.00
JS Jozef Stumpel 2.00 5.00
JT Joe Thornton 10.00 25.00
KB Kris Beech 2.00 5.00
KF Kurtis Foster 3.00 8.00
KT Keith Tkachuk 8.00 20.00
MAO Maxime Ouellet 3.00 8.00
MB Matthew Barnaby 2.00 5.00
MH Marian Hossa 8.00 20.00
MIM Mirko Murovic 2.00 5.00
MM Manny Malhotra 4.00 10.00
MMC Marty McSorley 5.00 12.00
MO Mattias Ohlund 2.00 5.00
MS Mats Sundin 20.00 50.00
MZ Michael Zigomanis 2.00 5.00
NL Nicklas Lidstrom 12.50 30.00
ON Owen Nolan 4.00 10.00
PB Pavel Bure 10.00 25.00
PBO Peter Bondra 4.00 10.00
PR Patrick Roy 30.00 80.00
PRE Peter Reynolds 2.00 5.00
RB Rob Blake 4.00 10.00
RL Ross Lupaschuk 2.00 5.00
RM Rory McDade 2.00 5.00
RN Rumun Ndur 2.00 5.00
RS Ryan Smyth 4.00 10.00
SG Sergei Gonchar 2.00 5.00
SK Scott Kelman 3.00 8.00
SM Steven McCarthy 2.00 5.00
SY Steve Yzerman 40.00 80.00
TH Tomas Holmstrom 5.00 12.00
TP Taylor Pyatt 5.00 12.00
VL Vincent Lecavalier 8.00 20.00
WG Wayne Gretzky 100.00 200.00

1998-99 SP Authentic Sign of the Times Gold

Randomly inserted into packs, this set is a parallel version of the regular SP Authentic Sign of the Times insert set with each card hand-numbered to the pictured player's jersey number. These numbers follow the player's name in the checklist below. Cards with print runs less than 25 are not priced due to scarcitiy.

AM A.Mogilny/89 25.00 50.00
AS Alex Selivanov/29 12.50 30.00
BD Byron Dafoe/34 20.00 50.00
BF Brian Finley/100 10.00 25.00
BJ Barret Jackman/100 10.00 25.00
CJ Curtis Joseph/31 50.00 125.00
CS Charlie Stephens/100 6.00 15.00
DM David Morisset/100 6.00 15.00
DMA Derek Mackenzie/100 6.00 15.00
DW Doug Weight/39 25.00 50.00
EJ E.Jovanovski/55 25.00 50.00
JA Jason Allison/41 10.00 25.00
JJ Joe Juneau/49 10.00 25.00
KB Kris Beech/100 6.00 15.00
KF Kurtis Foster/100 6.00 15.00
MAO Maxime Ouellet/100 10.00 25.00
MB Matthew Barnaby/36 10.00 25.00
MIM Mirko Murovic/100 6.00 15.00
MMC Marty McSorley/33 10.00 25.00
MZ Michael Zigomanis/100 8.00 20.00
PR Patrick Roy/33 200.00 350.00
PRE Petor Roynolds/100 6.00 15.00
RL Ross Lupaschuk/100 6.00 15.00
RM Rory McDade/100 6.00 15.00
RN Rumun Ndur/40 10.00 25.00
RS Ryan Smyth/94 12.50 30.00
SG Sergei Gonchar/55 12.50 30.00
SK Scott Kelman/100 6.00 15.00
SM Steven McCarthy/100 6.00 15.00
TH Tomas Holmstrom/96 10.00 25.00
TP Taylor Pyatt/100 15.00 30.00
WG Wayne Gretzky/99 200.00 300.00

1998-99 SP Authentic Snapshots

Randomly inserted in packs at the rate of 1:11, this 30-card set features unique images of the NHL's most exciting players. The backs carry player information.

COMPLETE SET (30) 30.00 60.00
SS1 Wayne Gretzky 4.00 10.00
SS2 Patrick Roy 3.00 8.00
SS3 Steve Yzerman 3.00 8.00
SS4 Brett Hull .75 2.00
SS5 Jaromir Jagr 1.00 2.50
SS6 Peter Forsberg 1.50 4.00
SS7 Dominik Hasek 1.25 3.00
SS8 Paul Kariya .60 1.50
SS9 Eric Lindros .60 1.50
SS10 Teemu Selanne .60 1.50
SS11 John LeClair .60 1.50
SS12 Mike Modano 1.00 2.50
SS13 Martin Brodeur 1.50 4.00
SS14 Brendan Shanahan .60 1.50
SS15 Ray Bourque 1.00 2.50
SS16 John Vanbiesbrouck .50 1.25
SS17 Brian Leetch .50 1.25
SS18 Vincent Lecavalier 4.00 10.00
SS19 Joe Sakic 1.25 3.00
SS20 Chris Drury .75 2.00
SS21 Eric Brewer 1.00 2.50
SS22 Jeremy Roenick .75 2.00
SS23 Mats Sundin .60 1.50
SS24 Zigmund Palffy .50 1.25
SS25 Keith Tkachuk .60 1.50
SS26 Sergei Samsonov .50 1.25
SS27 Curtis Joseph .60 1.50
SS28 Peter Bondra .50 1.25
SS29 Sergei Fedorov 1.00 2.50
SS30 Doug Gilmour .50 1.25

1998-99 SP Authentic Stat Masters

Randomly inserted into packs, this 30-card set features color photos of the NHL's best players printed on sequentially numbered cards based on the achievements of the player featured. Each player's card is sequentially numbered to the player's key accomplishment. These numbers follow the player's name in the checklist below.

COMPLETE SET (30) 200.00 400.00
STATED PRINT RUN 92-2000
S1 Brendan Shanahan/400 2.50 6.00
S2 Brett Hull/1000 3.00 8.00
S3 Dominik Hasek/200 10.00 25.00
S4 Doug Gilmour/1200 2.50 6.00
S5 Doug Weight/500 2.50 6.00
S6 Eric Lindros/115 8.00 20.00
S7 Jaromir Jagr/301 6.00 15.00
S8 Joe Sakic/900 3.00 8.00
S9 John LeClair/500 3.00 8.00
S10 John Vanbiesbrouck/306 2.50 6.00
S11 Keith Tkachuk/250 2.50 6.00
S12 Mark Messier/600 2.50 6.00
S13 Martin Brodeur/200 12.50 30.00
S14 Mike Modano/650 3.00 8.00
S15 Patrick Roy/400 10.00 25.00
S16 Paul Kariya/108 30.00 80.00
S17 Pavel Bure/500 2.50 6.00
S18 Peter Bondra/300 2.50 6.00
S19 Peter Forsberg/400 5.00 12.00
S20 Ray Bourque/1500 3.00 8.00
S21 Ron Francis/1500 2.50 6.00
S22 Sergei Fedorov/600 3.00 8.00
S23 Steve Yzerman/1500 5.00 12.00
S24 Steve Yzerman/900 6.00 15.00
S25 Steve Yzerman/500 10.00 25.00
S26 Teemu Selanne/300 2.50 6.00
S27 Vincent Lecavalier/1998 2.50 6.00
S28 Wayne Gretzky/92 75.00 200.00
S29 Wayne Gretzky/900 5.00 12.00
S30 Wayne Gretzky/2000 3.00 8.00

1999-00 SP Authentic

Released as a 135-card set, the 1999-00 SP Authentic base set is composed of 90-regular issue cards and 45-short printed Future Watch cards which are serial numbered out of 2000. This subset features some of the NHL's most promising prospects. Base cards have a white border and are enhanced by an embossed SP Authentic logo towards the bottom, and embossed framing along the top and bottom. The Future Watch subset contains a foil SP Authentic logo in the lower left front corner, and players are set against a green grid-line background. SP Authentic was released as 24-pack boxes containing 5-card packs that carried a suggested retail price of $4.99.

COMPLETE SET (135) 150.00 300.00
COMP.SET w/o SP's (90) 15.00 40.00
1 Paul Kariya .30 .75
2 Teemu Selanne .30 .75
3 Guy Hebert .25 .60
4 Ray Ferraro .08 .25
5 Andrew Brunette .25 .60
6 Joe Thornton .50 1.25
7 Ray Bourque .50 1.25
8 Sergei Samsonov .25 .60
9 Michael Peca .08 .25
10 Dominik Hasek .60 1.50
11 Miroslav Satan .08 .25
12 Maxim Afinogenov .08 .25
13 Valeri Bure .08 .25
14 Marc Savard .25 .60
15 Fred Brathwaite .25 .60
16 Ron Francis .25 .60
17 Arturs Irbe .25 .60
18 Sami Kapanen .08 .25
19 Tony Amonte .25 .60
20 Steve Passmore RC .40 1.00
21 Doug Gilmour .25 .60
22 Milan Hejduk .30 .75
23 Joe Sakic .60 1.50
24 Patrick Roy 1.50 4.00
25 Chris Drury .25 .60
26 Peter Forsberg .75 2.00
27 Mike Modano .50 1.25
28 Brett Hull .40 1.00
29 Ed Belfour .30 .75
30 Steve Yzerman 1.50 4.00
31 Chris Osgood .25 .60
32 Brendan Shanahan .30 .75
33 Sergei Fedorov .50 1.25
34 Doug Weight .25 .60
35 Bill Guerin .08 .25
36 Alexander Selivanov .08 .25
37 Pavel Bure .30 .75
38 Trevor Kidd .25 .60
39 Viktor Kozlov .08 .25
40 Luc Robitaille .25 .60
41 Zigmund Palffy .25 .60
42 Rob Blake .25 .60
43 Saku Koivu .30 .75
44 Mike Ribeiro .25 .60
45 Jose Theodore .40 1.00
46 David Legwand .25 .60
47 Mike Dunham .25 .60
48 Rob Valicevic RC .08 .25
49 Martin Brodeur .75 2.00
50 Claude Lemieux .08 .25
51 Scott Gomez .08 .25
52 Tim Connolly .08 .25
53 Roberto Luongo .40 1.00
54 Kenny Jonsson .08 .25
55 Mike Richter .30 .75
56 Theo Fleury .08 .25
57 Mike York .08 .25
58 Brian Leetch .30 .75
59 Radek Bonk .08 .25
60 Marian Hossa .30 .75
61 Patrick Lalime .25 .60
62 Keith Primeau .08 .25
63 Eric Lindros .30 .75
64 John LeClair .30 .75
65 Trevor Letowski .08 .25
66 Keith Tkachuk .30 .75
67 Jeremy Roenick .40 1.00
68 Jaromir Jagr .50 1.25
69 Alexei Kovalev .08 .25
70 Martin Straka .08 .25
71 Brad Stuart .08 .25
72 Steve Shields .25 .60
73 Owen Nolan .25 .60
74 Jeff Friesen .08 .25
75 Pavol Demitra .25 .60
76 Roman Turek .25 .60
77 Pierre Turgeon .25 .60
78 Vincent Lecavalier .30 .75
79 Dan Cloutier .25 .60
80 Chris Gratton .25 .60
81 Mats Sundin .30 .75
82 Bryan Berard .25 .60
83 Curtis Joseph .30 .75
84 Jonas Hoglund .08 .25
85 Mark Messier .30 .75
86 Peter Schaefer .08 .25
87 Alexander Mogilny .25 .60
88 Olaf Kolzig .25 .60
89 Adam Oates .25 .60
90 Peter Bondra .25 .60
91 Patrik Stefan RC 3.00 8.00
92 Dean Sylvester RC 2.00 5.00
93 Scott Fankhouser RC 2.00 5.00
94 Brian Campbell RC 2.00 5.00
95 Byron Ritchie RC 2.00 5.00
96 John Grahame RC 3.00 8.00
97 Andre Savage RC 2.00 5.00
98 Oleg Saprykin RC 3.00 8.00
99 Kyle Calder RC 3.00 8.00
100 Dan Hinote RC 3.00 8.00
101 Jonathan Sim RC 2.00 5.00
102 Marc Rodgers RC 2.00 5.00
103 Paul Comrie RC 2.00 5.00
104 Ivan Novoseltsev RC 2.00 5.00
105 Jason Blake RC 2.00 5.00
106 Brian Rafalski RC 3.00 8.00
107 John Madden RC 3.00 8.00
108 Jason Krog RC 3.00 8.00
109 Jorgen Jonsson RC 2.00 5.00
110 Kim Johnsson RC 2.00 5.00
111 Mike Fisher RC 3.00 8.00
112 Michal Rozsival RC 2.00 5.00
113 Mika Alatalo RC 2.00 5.00
114 Tyson Nash RC 2.00 5.00
115 Ladislav Nagy RC 6.00 15.00
116 Jochen Hecht RC 3.00 8.00
117 Adam Mair RC 2.00 5.00
118 Nikolai Antropov RC 5.00 12.00
119 Steve Kariya RC 2.00 5.00
120 Jeff Halpern RC 2.00 5.00
121 Alexandre Volchkov RC 2.00 5.00
122 Pavel Brendl RC 2.50 6.00
123 Sheldon Keefe RC 2.00 5.00
124 Branislav Mezei RC 2.00 5.00
125 Milan Kraft RC 2.00 5.00
126 Kristian Kudroc RC 2.00 5.00
127 Jaroslav Kristek RC 2.00 5.00
128 Alexander Buturlin RC 2.00 5.00
129 Andrei Shefer RC 2.00 5.00
130 Brad Moran RC 2.00 5.00
131 Ryan Jardine RC 2.00 5.00
132 Brett Lysak RC 2.00 5.00
133 Michal Sivek RC 2.00 5.00
134 Luke Sellars RC 2.00 5.00
135 Brad Ralph RC 2.00 5.00

1999-00 SP Authentic Buyback Autographs

Randomly inserted in packs at 1:287, this 66-card set features some of the NHL's most sought after autographs on Upper Deck and Upper Deck SP (Authentic) dating back to 1993-94. Each card is serial numbered out of how many were signed. Lower print runs are unpriced due to scarcity.

SERIAL #'d UNDER 25 NOT PRICED
1 P.Bure 94SP/65 30.00 60.00
2 P.Bure 94SPDC/4
3 P.Bure 94UDSPI/60 30.00 60.00
4 P.Bure 94UDSPIDC/2
5 P.Bure 94SP/1
6 P.Bure 95SP/3
7 P.Bure 95SPHol/1
8 P.Bure 96SP/16
9 P.Bure 97SPAIcon/3
10 P.Bure 98SPA/30 30.00 80.00
11 W.Gretzky 94SP/56 125.00 250.00
12 W.Gretzky 94SPDC/1
13 W.Gretzky 94UDSPI/16 150.00 300.00
14 W.Gretzky 94UDSPIDC/5
15 W.Gretzky 95SP/1
16 W.Gretzky 95SPPromo/2
17 W.Gretzky 96SP/13
18 W.Gretzky 97SPAIcon/2
19 W.Gretzky 98SPA/101 100.00 200.00
21 B.Hull 94SP/92 25.00 60.00
22 B.Hull 94UDSPI/17
23 B.Hull 94UDSPIDC/3
24 B.Hull 95SP/2
25 B.Hull 95SPStars/4
26 B.Hull 97SPA/4
27 B.Hull 97SPAIcon/1
28 B.Hull 98SPA/100 25.00 60.00
30 M.Johnson 97SPA/25 8.00 20.00
31 M.Johnson 98SPA/300 5.00 12.00
32 C.Joseph 94SP/65 12.00 30.00
33 C.Joseph 94SPDC/9
34 C.Joseph 94UDSPI/34 12.00 30.00
35 C.Joseph 94UDSPIDC/4
36 C.Joseph 96SP/29 12.00 30.00
37 C.Joseph 98SPA/200 8.00 20.00
39 J.LeClair 94SP/150 12.00 30.00
40 J.LeClair 94SPDC/10
41 J.LeClair 96SP/130 15.00 40.00
42 J.LeClair 98SPA/100 20.00 50.00
43 Z.Palffy 94UDSPI/75 12.00 30.00
44 Z.Palffy 94UDSPI/10
45 Z.Palffy 96SP/33 12.00 30.00
46 Z.Palffy 97SPA/3
47 Z.Palffy 98SPA/100 8.00 20.00
48 L.Robitaille 93SPI/16 25.00 50.00
49 L.Robitaille 94SP/20 25.00 50.00
50 L.Robitaille 94SPDC/19 50.00 40.00
51 L.Robitaille 94UDSPI/60 15.00 40.00
52 L.Robitaille 94UDSPIDC/9
53 L.Robitaille 98SPA/65 15.00 40.00
54 J.Roenick 93SPI/11
55 J.Roenick 94SP/70 25.00 60.00
56 J.Roenick 94SPDC/14
57 J.Roenick 94UDSPI/40 40.00 60.00
58 J.Roenick 94UDSPIDC/13
59 J.Roenick 95SP/3
60 J.Roenick 96SP/32 40.00 80.00
61 J.Roenick 98SPA/97 25.00 60.00
62 S.Samsonov 94SP/65 12.00 30.00
63 S.Samsonov 94SPDC/15
64 S.Samsonov 95SP/10
65 S.Samsonov 98SPA/255 8.00 20.00
66 S.Yzerman 93SPI/3
67 S.Yzerman 94SP/65 50.00 100.00
68 S.Yzerman 96SP/21
69 S.Yzerman 98SPA/77 50.00 100.00

1999-00 SP Authentic Honor Roll

Randomly seeded in packs at 1:24, this 6-card set places some of hockey's most dominating on a grey card with a centered foil background. Card backs carry an "HR" prefix.

COMPLETE SET (6) 15.00 30.00
HR1 Paul Kariya 2.50 6.00
HR2 Patrick Roy 5.00 12.00
HR3 Steve Yzerman 5.00 12.00
HR4 Martin Brodeur 2.50 6.00
HR5 Eric Lindros 1.50 4.00
HR6 Jaromir Jagr 1.50 4.00

1999-00 SP Authentic Legendary Heroes

Randomly inserted in packs at 1:72, this 5-card set pays homage to the NHL's past superstars. Card backs carry an "LH" prefix.

COMPLETE SET (5) 20.00 40.00
LH1 Wayne Gretzky 5.00 12.00
LH2 Bobby Orr 5.00 12.00
LH3 Gordie Howe 4.00 10.00
LH4 Maurice Richard 4.00 10.00
LH5 Bobby Hull 3.00 8.00

1999-00 SP Authentic Sign of the Times

Randomly seeded in packs at 1:23, this 32-card set features autographs from past superstars, current veteran players, and top prospects. Each card is set with a white box in the middle containing the player's autograph.

SGO Scott Gomez 3.00 8.00
AT Alex Tanguay 5.00 12.00
BC Brian Campbell 3.00 8.00
BH Bobby Hull 15.00 40.00
BHU Brett Hull 8.00 20.00
BM Bill Muckalt 3.00 8.00
BO Bobby Orr 50.00 100.00
BS Brad Stuart 3.00 8.00
CJ Curtis Joseph 8.00 20.00
DL David Legwand 3.00 8.00
DT Dave Tanabe 3.00 8.00
HG Gordie Howe 40.00 80.00
JH Jochen Hecht 3.00 8.00
JL John LeClair 5.00 12.00
JR Jeremy Roenick 8.00 20.00
JST Jozef Stumpel 2.50 6.00
LR Luc Robitaille 5.00 12.00
MH Marian Hossa 6.00 15.00
MRC Maurice Richard 150.00 250.00
MRI Mike Ribeiro 3.00 8.00
OS Oleg Saprykin 3.00 8.00
PB Pavel Bure 8.00 20.00
PM Paul Mara 3.00 8.00
PS Patrik Stefan 3.00 8.00
SF Sergei Fedorov 12.50 30.00
SG Simon Gagne 5.00 12.00
SS Sergei Samsonov 5.00 12.00
SY Steve Yzerman 15.00 40.00
TC Tim Connolly 3.00 8.00
TF Theo Fleury 8.00 20.00
WG Wayne Gretzky 100.00 200.00
ZP Zigmund Palffy 5.00 12.00

1999-00 SP Authentic Sign of the Times Gold

Randomly inserted in packs, this 32-card set parallels the base Sign of the Times insert set. Each card is serial numbered out of 25. Cards # CJ, PM, and WG were inserted in packs as redemption cards.

*UNLISTED GOLD: 2.5X TO 6X BASIC AU
HG Gordie Howe 250.00 500.00
MRC Maurice Richard 150.00 300.00
WG Wayne Gretzky 350.00 600.00

1999-00 SP Authentic Special Forces

Randomly inserted in packs at 1:12, this 10-card set showcases top players set against an all foil true-life background. Card backs carry an "SF" prefix.

COMPLETE SET (10) 12.00 25.00
SF1 Paul Kariya .60 1.50
SF2 Joe Sakic 1.25 3.00
SF3 Patrick Roy 3.00 8.00
SF4 Steve Yzerman 3.00 8.00
SF5 Mike Modano 1.00 2.50
SF6 Pavel Bure .75 2.00
SF7 Jaromir Jagr 1.00 2.50
SF8 Eric Lindros 1.00 2.50
SF9 Curtis Joseph .60 1.50
SF10 Steve Kariya .60 1.50

1999-00 SP Authentic Supreme Skill

Randomly sooded in packs at 1:4, this 11-card sot places NHL's most dominating against an all-foil true to life background. Card backs carry an "SS" prefix.

COMPLETE SET (11) 6.00 12.00
SS1 Paul Kariya .40 1.00
SS2 Teemu Selanne .40 1.00
SS3 Peter Forsberg 1.00 2.50
SS4 Brett Hull .50 1.25
SS5 Sergei Fedorov .75 2.00
SS6 Pavel Bure .50 1.25
SS7 Martin Brodeur 1.00 2.50
SS8 Theo Fleury .40 1.00
SS9 John LeClair .50 1.25
SS10 Keith Tkachuk .40 1.00
SS11 Jaromir Jagr .75 2.00

1999-00 SP Authentic Tomorrow's Headliners

Randomly inserted in packs at 1:10, this 10-card set features top prospects and young stars on an all-foil background. Card backs carry a "TH" prefix and contain a brief blurb about each player's standout skills.

COMPLETE SET (10)	8.00	20.00
TH1 Patrik Stefan	1.00	2.50
TH2 Joe Thornton	1.50	4.00
TH3 Maxim Afinogenov	1.00	2.50
TH4 Milan Hejduk	1.00	2.50
TH5 David Legwand	1.00	2.50
TH6 Scott Gomez	1.00	2.50
TH7 Marian Hossa	1.00	2.50
TH8 Jochen Hecht	1.00	2.50
TH9 Vincent Lecavalier	1.50	4.00
TH10 Steve Kariya	1.00	2.50

2000-01 SP Authentic

SP Authentic released these cards as a 165-card set with 75 short-printed rookies. The bas set design had white with blue and grey borders. The card fronts were highlighted with silver-foil lettering and logo. The card backs had a short summary about the player along with his statistics and a small photo. The short-printed rookies were serial numbered to 900.

1 Paul Kariya	.40	1.00
2 Jean-Sebastien Giguere	.25	.60
3 Oleg Tverdovsky	.20	.50
4 Patrik Stefan	.25	.60
5 Donald Audette	.25	.60
6 Damian Rhodes	.20	.50
7 Joe Thornton	.50	1.25
8 Jason Allison	.25	.60
9 Bill Guerin	.30	.75
10 Dominik Hasek	.50	1.25
11 Maxim Afinogenov	.20	.50
12 Doug Gilmour	.40	1.00
13 Valeri Bure	.25	.60
14 Marc Savard	.25	.60
15 Jarome Iginla	.30	.75
16 Ron Francis	.40	1.00
17 Jeff O'Neill	.25	.60
18 Sandis Ozolinsh	.25	.60
19 Steve Sullivan	.20	.50
20 Tony Amonte	.25	.60
21 Rob Blake	.30	.75
22 Ray Bourque	.50	1.25
23 Patrick Roy	.75	2.00
24 Peter Forsberg	.40	1.00
25 Joe Sakic	.50	1.25
26 Ron Tugnutt	.25	.60
27 Geoff Sanderson	.25	.60
28 Ed Belfour	.30	.75
29 Mike Modano	.50	1.25
30 Brett Hull	.50	1.25
31 Steve Yzerman	1.00	2.50
32 Brendan Shanahan	.40	1.00
33 Nicklas Lidstrom	.30	.75
34 Sergei Fedorov	.50	1.25
35 Doug Weight	.30	.75
36 Ryan Smyth	.25	.60
37 Tommy Salo	.25	.60
38 Pavel Bure	.40	1.00
39 Ray Whitney	.25	.60
40 Ivan Novoseltsev	.20	.50
41 Adam Deadmarsh	.25	.60
42 Zigmund Palffy	.30	.75
43 Luc Robitaille	.30	.75
44 Darby Hendrickson	.20	.50
45 Manny Fernandez	.25	.60
46 Jose Theodore	.40	1.00
47 Andrei Markov	.40	1.00
48 Trevor Linden	.30	.75
49 David Legwand	.30	.75
50 Mike Dunham	.20	.50
51 Cliff Ronning	.20	.50
52 Scott Gomez	.25	.60
53 Martin Brodeur	.60	1.50
54 Jason Arnott	.25	.60
55 Mark Messier	.50	1.25
56 Theo Fleury	.40	1.00
57 Brian Leetch	.30	.75
58 Tim Connolly	.20	.50
59 Brad Isbister	.20	.50
60 Taylor Pyatt	.20	.50
61 Alexei Yashin	.25	.60
62 Marian Hossa	.25	.60
63 Patrick Lalime	.25	.60
64 John LeClair	.30	.75
65 Simon Gagne	.30	.75
66 Mark Recchi	.40	1.00
67 Jeremy Roenick	.30	.75
68 Keith Tkachuk	.30	.75
69 Shane Doan	.25	.60
70 Jaromir Jagr	.75	2.00
71 Alexei Kovalev	.25	.60
72 Mario Lemieux	1.00	2.50
73 Owen Nolan	.30	.75
74 Patrick Marleau	.30	.75
75 Evgeni Nabokov	.25	.60
76 Pierre Turgeon	.30	.75
77 Chris Pronger	.25	.60
78 Roman Turek	.25	.60
79 Brad Richards	.30	.75
80 Vincent Lecavalier	.25	.60
81 Fredrik Modin	.20	.50
82 Mats Sundin	.30	.75
83 Curtis Joseph	.40	1.00
84 Gary Roberts	.20	.50
85 Daniel Sedin	.60	1.50
86 Henrik Sedin	.50	1.25
87 Markus Naslund	.25	.60
88 Peter Bondra	.25	.60
89 Olaf Kolzig	.30	.75
90 Adam Oates	.30	.75
91 Petr Tenkrat RC	2.00	5.00
92 Andy McDonald RC	4.00	10.00
93 Brad Tapper RC	2.00	5.00
94 Andrew Raycroft RC	5.00	12.00
95 Lee Goren RC	2.00	5.00
96 Josef Vasicek RC	5.00	12.00
97 Reto Von Arx RC	2.50	6.00
98 David Aebischer RC	5.00	12.00
99 Ville Nieminen RC	2.00	5.00
100 Serge Aubin RC	2.50	6.00
101 Rostislav Klesla RC	4.00	10.00
102 Marty Turco RC	4.00	10.00
103 Tyler Bouck RC	2.00	5.00
104 Jason Williams RC	3.00	8.00
105 Shawn Horcoff RC	4.00	10.00
106 Mike Comrie RC	5.00	12.00
107 Eric Belanger RC	2.50	6.00
108 Steven Reinprecht RC	3.00	8.00
109 Lubomir Visnovsky RC	4.00	10.00
110 Marian Gaborik RC	15.00	40.00
111 Peter Bartos RC	2.50	6.00
112 Scott Hartnell RC	8.00	20.00
113 Chris Mason RC	4.00	10.00
114 Rick DiPietro RC	10.00	25.00
115 Martin Havlat RC	10.00	25.00
116 Jani Hurme RC	2.00	5.00
117 Petr Hubacek RC	2.00	5.00
118 Justin Williams RC	5.00	12.00
119 Roman Cechmanek RC	2.50	6.00
120 Ruslan Fedotenko RC	2.00	5.00
121 Roman Simicek RC	2.00	5.00
122 Mark Smith RC	2.00	5.00
123 Alexander Kharitonov RC	2.00	5.00
124 Alexei Ponikarovsky RC	3.00	8.00
125 Matt Pettinger RC	2.00	5.00
126 Zdenek Blatny RC	2.00	5.00
127 Damian Surma RC	2.00	5.00
128 Marc-Andre Thinel RC	2.00	5.00
129 Fedor Fedorov RC	2.50	6.00
130 Jason Jaspers RC	2.00	5.00
131 Jordan Krestanovich RC	2.00	5.00
132 Jeff Bateman RC	2.00	5.00
133 Marc Chouinard RC	2.00	5.00
134 Darcy Hordichuk RC	2.00	5.00
135 Bryan Adams RC	2.00	5.00
136 Jarno Kultanen RC	2.00	5.00
137 Eric Boulton RC	2.00	5.00
138 Ronald Petrovicky RC	2.00	5.00
139 Martin Brochu RC	2.00	5.00
140 Craig Adams RC	2.00	5.00
141 Chris Nielsen RC	2.00	5.00
142 Petteri Nummelin RC	2.00	5.00
143 Brian Swanson RC	2.00	5.00
144 Michel Riesen RC	2.50	6.00
145 Lance Ward RC	2.00	5.00
146 Travis Scott RC	2.50	6.00
147 Lubomir Sekeras RC	2.00	5.00
148 Eric Landry RC	2.00	5.00
149 Greg Classen RC	2.00	5.00
150 Sascha Goc RC	2.00	5.00
151 Mike Commodore RC	2.00	5.00
152 Johan Holmqvist RC	2.00	5.00
153 Vitali Yeremeyev RC	2.50	6.00
154 Tomas Kloucek RC	2.00	5.00
155 Dale Purinton RC	2.00	5.00
156 Shane Hnidy RC	2.00	5.00
157 Todd Fedoruk RC	2.00	5.00
158 Jean-Guy Trudel RC	2.00	5.00
159 Ossi Vaananen RC	2.50	6.00
160 Greg Andrusak RC	2.50	6.00
161 Alexander Khavanov RC	2.00	5.00
162 Bryce Salvador RC	2.50	6.00
163 Reed Low RC	2.00	5.00
164 Petr Svoboda RC	2.50	6.00
165 Brent Sopel RC	3.00	8.00

2000-01 SP Authentic Buyback Autographs

Randomly inserted in packs of 2000-01 SP Authentic at a rate of 1:144, this 114 card set featured original SP cards that were purchased from the secondary market and autographed. Cards with lower print runs are unpriced due to scarcity.

1 B.Orr 99SPALH/49	150.00	300.00
2 S.Samsonov 94SP/3		
3 S.Samsonov 95SP/2		
4 S.Samsonov 97SPA/3		
5 S.Samsonov 98SPA/20		
6 S.Samsonov 99SPA/184	8.00	20.00
7 B.Dafoe 95SP/7		
8 M.Satan 95SP/6		
9 M.Satan 97SPA/3		
10 M.Satan 99SPA/145	20.00	40.00
11 P.Brendl 99SPA/3		
12 Bo.Hull 99SPALH/98	25.00	60.00
13 M.Hejduk 99SPA/200	10.00	25.00
14 M.Hejduk 99SPATH/143	12.50	30.00
15 R.Bourque 98SPASS/1		
16 R.Bourque 98SPA/24	75.00	200.00
17 R.Bourque 99SPA/122	20.00	50.00
18 M.Modano 94SP/61	20.00	50.00
19 M.Modano 95SP/10		
20 M.Modano 96SP/5		
21 M.Modano 97SPA/2		
22 M.Modano 97SPASM/1		
23 M.Modano 98SPA/40	25.00	60.00
24 M.Modano 99SPA/168	12.50	30.00
25 M.Modano 99SPASF/155	12.50	30.00
30 N.Lidstrom 98SPA/19		
31 Br.Hull 94SPDC/1		
32 Br.Hull 94SP/7		
33 Br.Hull 97SPA/3		
34 Br.Hull 97SPAIC/2		
35 Br.Hull 98SPA/16	25.00	60.00
36 Br.Hull 99SPA/119	20.00	50.00
37 T.Salo 97SPA/12		
38 P.Bure 94SP/2		
39 P.Bure 96SP/16	90.00	150.00
40 P.Bure 97SPA/6		
41 P.Bure 97SPAIC/2		
42 P.Bure 98SPA/1		
43 P.Bure 99SPA/225	15.00	30.00
44 P.Bure 99SPASF/154	15.00	30.00
45 P.Bure 99SPASS/69	15.00	40.00
46 I.Novoseltsev 99SPA/1		
47 L.Robitaille 94SP/36	25.00	60.00
48 L.Robitaille 94SPPRE/8		
49 L.Robitaille 95SP/1		
50 L.Robitaille 97SPA/6		
51 L.Robitaille 97SPAIC/6		
52 L.Robitaille 99SPA/97	15.00	40.00
53 M.Ribeiro 99SPA/117	12.50	30.00
54 D.Legwand 99SPA/214	6.00	15.00
55 D.Legwand 99SPATH/130	12.50	25.00
56 S.Gomez 99SPA/243	10.00	25.00
57 S.Gomez 99SPATH/157	12.50	30.00
58 P.Elias 97SPA/1		
59 P.Elias 98SPA/43	15.00	40.00
60 M.Brodeur 94SPDC/3		
61 M.Brodeur 95SP/11		
62 M.Brodeur 96SP/21		
63 M.Brodeur 98SPA/5		
64 W.Gretzky 94SP/4		
65 W.Gretzky 94SPDC/1		
66 W.Gretzky 96SP/2		
67 W.Gretzky 98SPA/4		
68 W.Gretzky 99SPALH/9		
69 M.Messier 94SP/50	40.00	80.00
70 M.Messier 95SP/9		
71 M.Messier 96SP/3		
72 M.Messier 97SPA/10		
73 M.Messier 98SPA/26	50.00	100.00
74 M.Messier 99SPA/147	30.00	60.00
75 M.Richter 94SP/5		
76 M.Richter 94SPPRE/8		
77 M.Richter 95SP/21	25.00	50.00
78 M.Richter 96SP/21		
79 M.Richter 97SPA/8		
80 M.Richter 98SPA/48	15.00	30.00
81 M.Richter 99SPA/214	10.00	25.00
82 M.York 99SPA/212	8.00	20.00
83 J.LeClair 94SP/12		
84 J.LeClair 95SP/24		
85 J.LeClair 96SP/14		
86 J.LeClair 97SPA/10		
87 J.LeClair 97SPAIC/6		
88 J.LeClair 98SPA/100	8.00	20.00
89 J.LeClair 99SPA/207	8.00	20.00
90 J.LeClair 99SPASS/116	15.00	40.00
91 J.Roenick 99SPA/98	15.00	40.00
92 M.Lemieux 95SP/19		
93 M.Lemieux 96SP/1		
94 M.Kraft 99SPA/3		
95 S.Shields 99SPA/195	6.00	15.00
96 C.Joseph 98SPA/14		
97 C.Joseph 99SPA/187	20.00	40.00
98 C.Joseph 99SPASF/135	15.00	40.00
99 F.Potvin 95SP/10		
100 F.Potvin 96SP/2		
101 F.Potvin 97SPA/5		
102 S.Yzerman 93UDSP/3		
103 S.Yzerman 94SP/22		
104 S.Yzerman 94SPDC/2		
105 S.Yzerman 94SPPRE/34	50.00	125.00
106 S.Yzerman 94SPPREDC/4		
107 S.Yzerman 95SPHOL/1		
108 S.Yzerman 95SP/2		
109 S.Yzerman 96SP/9		
110 S.Yzerman 98SPASS/1		
111 S.Yzerman 98SPA/5		
112 S.Yzerman 99SPA/152	30.00	80.00
113 S.Yzerman 99SPASF/35	50.00	125.00

2000-01 SP Authentic Honor

These cards were inserted into packs of SP Authentic at a rate of 1:24. The 7-card set featured the hottest players from the NHL. The cards carried a 'SP' prefix for their numbering.

COMPLETE SET (7)	8.00	20.00
SP1 Paul Kariya	.75	2.00
SP2 Patrick Roy	1.50	4.00
SP3 Pavel Bure	.75	2.00
SP4 Martin Brodeur	1.25	3.00
SP5 Mark Messier	1.00	2.50
SP6 Mario Lemieux	2.00	5.00
SP7 Jaromir Jagr	1.50	4.00

2000-01 SP Authentic Parents' Scrapbook

These cards were inserted into packs of SP Authentic at a rate of 1:24. The 7-card set featured the hottest players from the NHL. The cards carried a 'PS' prefix for their numbering.

COMPLETE SET (7)	4.00	10.00
PS1 Paul Kariya	.60	1.50
PS2 Joe Thornton	.75	2.00
PS3 Mike Modano	.75	2.00
PS4 Scott Gomez	.40	1.00
PS5 Martin Brodeur	1.00	2.50
PS6 John LeClair	.50	1.25
PS7 Vincent Lecavalier	.40	1.00

2000-01 SP Authentic Power Skaters

These cards were inserted into packs of SP Authentic at a rate of 1:24. The 7-card set featured Hall of Famers from the NHL. The cards carried a 'P' prefix for their numbering.

COMPLETE SET (7)	20.00	40.00
P1 Bobby Orr	2.00	5.00
P2 Bobby Hull	1.25	3.00
P3 Gordie Howe	2.00	5.00
P4 Wayne Gretzky	3.00	8.00
P5 Wayne Gretzky	3.00	8.00
P6 Wayne Gretzky	3.00	8.00
P7 Wayne Gretzky	3.00	8.00

2000-01 SP Authentic Sign of the Times

These cards were inserted into packs of SP Authentic at a rate of 1:23 for the single player autographs, 1:287 for the double autographs, and the triple autographs are serial numbered to 25.. The 68-card set featured some of the hottest players from the NHL. The cards used the player's initials for their numbering. Please note that there were 5 cards that were issued as exchange/redemption cards at time of release. Upper Deck has reported that only 19 of the Ray Bourque cards were produced.

AC Anson Carter	3.00	8.00
AE Anders Eriksson	3.00	8.00
AU Serge Aubin	3.00	8.00
BD Byron Dafoe	3.00	8.00
BH Bobby Hull	20.00	50.00
BI Martin Biron	3.00	8.00
BO Bobby Orr SP	75.00	150.00
BR Pavel Brendl	3.00	8.00
CJ Curtis Joseph	8.00	20.00
DG David Gosselin	3.00	8.00
DL David Legwand	3.00	8.00
DS Daniel Sedin	8.00	20.00
FP Felix Potvin	10.00	25.00
GH Gordie Howe	50.00	100.00
HA Martin Havlat	6.00	15.00
HS Henrik Sedin	8.00	20.00
IN Ivan Novoseltsev	3.00	8.00
JA Jean-Sebastien Aubin	3.00	8.00
JH Jani Hurme	3.00	8.00
JL John LeClair	8.00	20.00
JT Jose Theodore	10.00	25.00
LB Lubos Bartecko	8.00	20.00
LR Luc Robitaille	6.00	15.00
MB Martin Brodeur	25.00	60.00
MD Marc Denis	3.00	8.00
MG Marian Gaborik	15.00	30.00
MH Milan Hejduk SP	50.00	100.00
MK Milan Kraft	3.00	8.00
ML Mario Lemieux SP	150.00	300.00
MM Mark Messier SP	40.00	100.00
MO Mike Modano	10.00	25.00
MR Mike Richter	10.00	25.00
MS Miroslav Satan	3.00	8.00
MT Marty Turco	8.00	20.00
MY Mike York	3.00	8.00
NL Nicklas Lidstrom	10.00	25.00
PB Pavel Bure	8.00	20.00
PE Patrik Elias	4.00	10.00
PS Petr Sykora	3.00	8.00
RB Ray Bourque/19*	200.00	400.00
RD Rick DiPietro	8.00	20.00
RI Michel Riesen	3.00	8.00
RK Rostislav Klesla	3.00	8.00
RO Mike Ribeiro	4.00	10.00
RT Ron Tugnutt	4.00	10.00
SA Sergei Samsonov	6.00	15.00
SG Scott Gomez	4.00	10.00
SH Scott Hartnell	6.00	15.00
SR Steven Reinprecht	3.00	8.00
SS Steve Shields	3.00	8.00
SY Steve Yzerman	30.00	80.00
TS Tommy Salo	4.00	10.00
WG Wayne Gretzky SP	250.00	500.00
DBS M.Brodeur/P.Sykora	40.00	80.00
DBN P.Bure/I.Novoseltsev	10.00	25.00
DBY P.Brendl/M.York	8.00	20.00
DEG P.Elias/S.Gomez	8.00	20.00
DHG G.Howe/W.Gretzky	900.00	1500.00
DHH B.Hull/B.Hull	30.00	80.00
DLK M.Lemieux/M.Kraft	75.00	200.00
DMG M.Messier/W.Gretzky	350.00	600.00
DOB B.Orr/R.Bourque	100.00	200.00
DSS D.Sedin/H.Sedin	12.50	30.00
DYL S.Yzerman/N.Lidstrom	100.00	200.00
TBGE Brodr/Gmez/Elias/25	100.00	200.00
TGMF Grtzky/Mesr/Fuhr/25	700.00	1200.00
THLY Hull/Lem/Yzerman/25	250.00	500.00
THOG Howe/Grtzky/Orr/25	800.00	1600.00
TLMB LeClr/Modno/Bre/25	50.00	100.00

2000-01 SP Authentic Significant Stars

These cards were inserted into packs of SP Authentic at a rate of 1:24. The 7-card set featured the hottest players from the NHL. The cards carried a 'ST' prefix for their numbering.

COMPLETE SET (7)	8.00	15.00
ST1 Peter Forsberg	1.25	3.00
ST2 Brett Hull	.60	1.50
ST3 Steve Yzerman	2.50	6.00
ST4 Pavel Bure	.60	1.50
ST5 Mark Messier	.60	1.50
ST6 Jaromir Jagr	.75	2.00
ST7 Mario Lemieux	3.00	8.00

2000-01 SP Authentic Special Forces

These cards were inserted into packs of SP Authentic at a rate of 1:24. The 7-card set featured the hottest players from the NHL. The cards carried a 'SF' prefix for their numbering.

COMPLETE SET (7)	4.00	8.00
SF1 Teemu Selanne	1.00	2.50
SF2 Mike Modano	.75	2.00
SF3 Brendan Shanahan	.60	1.50
SF4 Pavel Bure	.60	1.50
SF5 John LeClair	.50	1.25
SF6 Keith Tkachuk	.50	1.25
SF7 Jaromir Jagr	1.25	3.00

2000-01 SP Authentic Super Stoppers

These cards were inserted into packs of SP Authentic at a rate of 1:24. The 7-card set featured the to goalies from the NHL. The cards carried a 'SS' prefix for their numbering.

COMPLETE SET (7)	4.00	8.00
SS1 Dominik Hasek	.75	2.00
SS2 Patrick Roy	1.25	3.00
SS3 Ed Belfour	.50	1.25
SS4 Martin Brodeur	1.00	2.50
SS5 Roman Turek	.40	1.00
SS6 Curtis Joseph	.60	1.50
SS7 Olaf Kolzig	.50	1.25

2001-02 SP Authentic

This 180-card set was released in mid-February with an SRP of $4.99 for a 5-card pack. The set consisted of 90 base cards, 50 Future Watch subset rookie cards (6 of which were autographed), 20 Future Greats subset cards and 20 All-Time Greats subset cards. Future Greats and All-Time Greats were serial-numbered out of 3500 while the Future Watch cards were serial-numbered to 900.

COMP.SET w/o SP's (90)	20.00	40.00
1 Jeff Friesen	.12	.30
2 Paul Kariya	.25	.60
3 Dany Heatley	.20	.50
4 Milan Hnilicka	.15	.40
5 Bill Guerin	.20	.50
6 Joe Thornton	.25	.60
7 Sergei Samsonov	.15	.40
8 Miroslav Satan	.15	.40
9 Martin Biron	.15	.40
10 J-P Dumont	.12	.30
11 Jarome Iginla	.20	.50
12 Roman Turek	.15	.40
13 Craig Conroy	.12	.30
14 Tony Amonte	.15	.40
15 Steve Sullivan	.12	.30
16 Joe Sakic	.30	.75
17 Milan Hejduk	.15	.40
18 Patrick Roy	.50	1.25
19 Rob Blake	.20	.50
20 Chris Drury	.15	.40
21 Ron Tugnutt	.15	.40
22 Geoff Sanderson	.12	.30
23 Mike Modano	.30	.75
24 Ed Belfour	.20	.50
25 Pierre Turgeon	.20	.50
26 Brett Hull	.25	.60
27 Dominik Hasek	.30	.75
28 Steve Yzerman	.60	1.50
29 Sergei Fedorov	.30	.75
30 Luc Robitaille	.20	.50
31 Brendan Shanahan	.25	.60
32 Tommy Salo	.15	.40
33 Ryan Smyth	.15	.40
34 Mike Comrie	.15	.40
35 Pavel Bure	.25	.60
36 Valeri Bure	.12	.30
37 Roberto Luongo	.30	.75
38 Jason Allison	.15	.40
39 Zigmund Palffy	.20	.50
40 Felix Potvin	.30	.75
41 Manny Fernandez	.15	.40
42 Marian Gaborik	.30	.75
43 Jose Theodore	.20	.50
44 Brian Savage	.12	.30
45 David Legwand	.15	.40
46 Mike Dunham	.15	.40
47 Patrik Elias	.20	.50
48 Martin Brodeur	.40	1.00
49 Jason Arnott	.15	.40
50 Scott Stevens	.20	.50
51 Chris Osgood	.20	.50
52 Alexei Yashin	.15	.40
53 Mark Parrish	.12	.30
54 Mark Messier	.30	.75
55 Eric Lindros	.30	.75
56 Petr Nedved	.15	.40
57 Marian Hossa	.15	.40
58 Radek Bonk	.12	.30
59 Daniel Alfredsson	.20	.50
60 Jeremy Roenick	.20	.50
61 John LeClair	.20	.50
62 Keith Primeau	.15	.40
63 Mark Recchi	.25	.60
64 Roman Cechmanek	.15	.40
65 Sean Burke	.12	.30
66 Michal Handzus	.12	.30
67 Shane Doan	.15	.40
68 Mario Lemieux	.60	1.50
69 Alexei Kovalev	.15	.40
70 Johan Hedberg	.15	.40
71 Teemu Selanne	.40	1.00
72 Owen Nolan	.20	.50
73 Evgeni Nabokov	.15	.40
74 Vincent Damphousse	.15	.40
75 Pavol Demitra	.25	.60
76 Doug Weight	.20	.50
77 Keith Tkachuk	.20	.50
78 Chris Pronger	.15	.40
79 Brad Richards	.20	.50
80 Vincent Lecavalier	.15	.40
81 Nikolai Khabibulin	.20	.50
82 Curtis Joseph	.20	.50
83 Mats Sundin	.20	.50
84 Alexander Mogilny	.15	.40
85 Markus Naslund	.20	.50
86 Daniel Sedin	.20	.50
87 Henrik Sedin	.20	.50
88 Peter Bondra	.20	.50
89 Olaf Kolzig	.20	.50
90 Jaromir Jagr	.50	1.25
91 Paul Kariya ATG	1.50	4.00
92 Ray Bourque ATG	2.00	5.00
93 Patrick Roy ATG	3.00	8.00
94 Joe Sakic ATG	2.00	5.00
95 Mike Modano ATG	2.00	5.00
96 Ed Belfour ATG	1.25	3.00
97 Steve Yzerman ATG	4.00	10.00
98 Dominik Hasek ATG	2.00	5.00
99 Gordie Howe ATG	4.00	10.00
100 Brett Hull ATG	1.50	4.00
101 Wayne Gretzky ATG	6.00	15.00
102 Martin Brodeur ATG	2.50	6.00
103 Mark Messier ATG	2.00	5.00
104 John LeClair ATG	1.25	3.00
105 Jeremy Roenick ATG	1.25	3.00
106 Mario Lemieux ATG	4.00	10.00
107 Teemu Selanne ATG	2.50	6.00
108 Al MacInnis ATG	1.25	3.00
109 Curtis Joseph ATG	1.25	3.00
110 Jaromir Jagr ATG	3.00	8.00
111 Dany Heatley FG	1.25	3.00
112 Mike Comrie FG	1.00	2.50
113 David Legwand FG	1.00	2.50
114 Justin Williams FG	.75	2.00
115 Mike Van Ryn FG	.75	2.00
116 Alex Tanguay FG	1.00	2.50
117 Manny Fernandez FG	1.00	2.50
118 Martin Havlat FG	1.00	2.50
119 Kris Beech FG	.75	2.00
120 Nikolai Antropov FG	.75	2.00
121 Patrik Stefan FG	1.00	2.50
122 Steven Reinprecht FG	.75	2.00
123 Marian Gaborik FG	2.00	5.00
124 Pavel Brendl FG	.75	2.00
125 Brad Stuart FG	.75	2.00
126 Martin Biron FG	1.00	2.50
127 Eric Belanger FG	.75	2.00
128 Rick DiPietro FG	1.00	2.50
129 Ladislav Nagy FG	.75	2.00
130 Brad Richards FG	1.25	3.00
131 Ilja Bryzgalov RC	4.00	10.00
132 Timo Parssinen RC	2.00	5.00
133 Kevin Sawyer RC	1.50	4.00
134 Brian Pothier RC	1.50	4.00
135 Kamil Piros RC	1.50	4.00
136 Ivan Huml RC	1.50	4.00
137 Scott Nichol RC	1.50	4.00
138 Jukka Hentunen RC	1.50	4.00
139 Erik Cole RC	3.00	8.00
140 Casey Hankinson RC	1.50	4.00
141 Jaroslav Obsut RC	1.50	4.00
142 Jody Shelley RC	2.00	5.00
143 Matt Davidson RC	1.50	4.00
144 Niko Kapanen RC	2.50	6.00
145 Pavel Datsyuk RC	30.00	60.00
146 Ty Conklin RC	2.50	6.00
147 Sean Selmser RC	1.50	4.00
148 Jason Chimera RC	1.50	4.00
149 Andrej Podkonicky RC	1.50	4.00
150 Niklas Hagman RC	2.00	5.00
151 Jaroslav Bednar RC	1.50	4.00
152 Mike Matteucci RC	1.50	4.00
153 Pascal Dupuis RC	2.50	6.00
154 Francis Belanger RC	2.00	5.00
155 Martti Jarventie	1.50	4.00
156 Pavel Skrbek RC	1.50	4.00
157 Martin Erat RC	2.50	6.00
158 Andreas Salomonsson RC	1.50	4.00
159 Scott Clemmensen RC	1.50	4.00
160 Josef Boumedienne RC	1.50	4.00
161 Peter Smrek RC	1.50	4.00
162 Mikael Samuelsson RC	2.00	5.00
163 Radek Martinek RC	1.50	4.00
164 Joel Kwiatkowski RC	1.50	4.00
165 Ivan Ciernik RC	1.50	4.00
166 Chris Neil RC	2.00	5.00
167 Jiri Dopita RC	1.50	4.00
168 Vaclav Pletka RC	1.50	4.00
169 David Cullen RC	1.50	4.00
170 Jeff Jillson RC	1.50	4.00
171 Mark Rycroft RC	2.00	5.00
172 Nikita Alexeev RC	1.50	4.00
173 Ryan Tobler RC	2.00	5.00
174 Bob Wren RC	1.50	4.00
175 Ilya Kovalchuk AU RC	30.00	60.00
176 Vaclav Nedorost AU RC	4.00	10.00
177 Kristian Huselius AU RC	6.00	15.00
178 Dan Blackburn AU RC	5.00	12.00
179 Krys Kolanos AU RC	4.00	10.00
180 Raffi Torres AU RC	10.00	25.00
NNO Pavel Bure SAMPLE	1.00	2.50

2001-02 SP Authentic Limited

This 150-card set paralleled the base set but each cards was serial-numbered out of 150.
*1-90 VETS/150: 3X TO 8X BASIC CARDS
*91-130 ATG/FG/150: .8X TO 2X SP/3500
*131-174 ROOK/150: .4X TO 1X RK/900
*175-180 RK.AU/150: .6X TO 1.5X AU/900

145 Pavel Datsyuk	100.00	200.00
175 Ilya Kovalchuk	60.00	120.00

2001-02 SP Authentic Limited Gold

This 150-card set paralleled the base set but each card was serial-numbered out of 25.
*1-90 VETS/25: 10X TO 25X BASIC CARDS
*91-130 ATG/FG/150: 2.5X TO 6X SP/3500
*131-174 ROOK/25: 1.2X TO 3X RK/900
*175-180 RK.AU/25: 1X TO 2.5X AU/900

145 Pavel Datsyuk	150.00	250.00
175 Ilya Kovalchuk	200.00	400.00

2001-02 SP Authentic Buybacks

Randomly inserted into packs, this 41-card set featured original Upper Deck cards that were purchased from the secondary market and autographed. Print runs for each card are listed below.

6 C.Joseph 99UDMVPSC/31	40.00	100.00
7 D.Heatley 00UD/50	200.00	400.00
9 D.Weight 91UD/20	20.00	50.00
13 M.Biron 00BDGG/41	25.00	60.00
14 M.Brodeur 00UDLGJ/30	60.00	150.00
16 M.Comrie 00BD/37	30.00	80.00
17 M.Gaborik 00UD/32	50.00	125.00
18 M.Havlat 00UD/37	40.00	100.00
20 M.Modano 90UD/75	20.00	50.00
21 M.Turco 00UD/37	30.00	80.00
22 O.Kolzig 00BDGG/20	20.00	50.00
26 R.Bourque 99MVPSCGS/20	40.00	100.00
28 R.DiPietro 00UD/31	20.00	50.00
29 R.Brind'Amour 90UD/95	12.50	30.00
30 R.Klesla 00UD/46	15.00	40.00
31 S.Hartnell 00UD/84	12.50	30.00

2001-02 SP Authentic Jerseys

This 30-card set featured game-worn jersey swatches and were divided between two different subsets: Notable Numbers and Personal Prolifics. Each card was serial-numbered to an individual statistic for the featured player.

NNBP Bob Probert/1034	8.00	20.00
NNBS Brendan Shanahan/955	6.00	15.00
NNCC Chris Chelios/1181	5.00	12.00
NNEL Eric Lindros/659	6.00	15.00
NNJK Jari Kurri/601	10.00	25.00
NNJL John LeClair/627	5.00	12.00
NNJS Joe Sakic/1178	10.00	25.00
NNKP Keith Primeau/496	4.00	10.00
NNMC Sandy McCarthy/1252	4.00	10.00
NNMG Mike Gartner/102	12.50	30.00
NNML Mario Lemieux/648	10.00	25.00
NNMM Mark Messier/651	6.00	15.00
NNMO Mike Modano/900	5.00	12.00
NNMR Mark Recchi/1010	4.00	10.00
NNPK Paul Kariya/531	5.00	12.00
NNRB Ray Bourque/1169	6.00	15.00
NNRT Rick Tocchet/950	4.00	10.00
NNSS Scott Stevens/1434	4.00	10.00
NNSY Steve Yzerman/1614	10.00	25.00
NNTD Tie Domi/1620	4.00	10.00
PPBH Brett Hull/86	20.00	50.00
PPJJ Jaromir Jagr/87	20.00	50.00
PPJS Joe Sakic/54	25.00	60.00
PPLR Luc Robitaille/63	12.00	30.00
PPMB Martin Brodeur/43	25.00	60.00
PPML Mario Lemieux/38	75.00	150.00
PPPR Patrick Roy/52	15.00	40.00
PPRB Ray Bourque/77	25.00	60.00
PPTS Teemu Selanne/76	20.00	50.00
PPWG Wayne Gretzky/92	60.00	150.00

2001-02 SP Authentic Sign of the Times

Randomly inserted into packs at overall odds of 1:24, this 82-card set featured autographs of one, two or three NHL players. Two player cards were serial-numbered out of 150 and triple player cards were serial-numbered to 25.

AI Arturs Irbe	6.00	15.00
AK Alexei Kovalev	6.00	15.00
AM Al MacInnis	6.00	15.00
BG Bill Guerin	5.00	12.00
BO Bobby Orr	100.00	200.00
BR Martin Brodeur	40.00	100.00
BS Brent Sopel	4.00	10.00
CJ Curtis Joseph	10.00	25.00
DH Dany Heatley	12.00	30.00
DS Daniel Sedin	6.00	15.00
DW Doug Weight	6.00	15.00
EB Ed Belfour	10.00	25.00
FP Felix Potvin	12.00	30.00
GH Gordie Howe	75.00	150.00
HA Martin Havlat	5.00	12.00
HE Johan Hedberg	4.00	10.00
HO Marian Hossa	6.00	15.00
HS Henrik Sedin	8.00	20.00
IK Ilya Kovalchuk	15.00	40.00
JA Jason Allison	4.00	10.00
JH Jochen Hecht	4.00	10.00
JI Jarome Iginla	10.00	25.00
JL John LeClair	8.00	20.00
JN Jeff O'Neill	4.00	10.00
JT Joe Thornton	12.50	30.00
KP Keith Primeau	5.00	12.00
MB Martin Biron	4.00	10.00
MC Mike Comrie	4.00	10.00
MF Manny Fernandez	6.00	15.00
MG Marian Gaborik	10.00	25.00
MH Milan Hejduk	8.00	20.00
MK Milan Kraft	4.00	10.00
MM Mike Modano	10.00	25.00
MN Markus Naslund	8.00	20.00
MR Mike Ribeiro	5.00	12.00
OK Olaf Kolzig	6.00	15.00
PB Pavel Bure	10.00	25.00
PR Patrick Roy/33	125.00	250.00
PS Patrik Stefan	4.00	10.00
RB Rod Brind'Amour	5.00	12.00
RB Rob Blake	4.00	10.00
RD Rick DiPietro	6.00	15.00
RK Rostislav Klesla	4.00	10.00
RL Roberto Luongo	20.00	50.00
SG Simon Gagne	8.00	20.00
SH Scott Hartnell	6.00	15.00
SY Steve Yzerman	30.00	80.00
TA Tony Amonte	6.00	15.00
TS Tommy Salo	5.00	12.00
TS Teemu Selanne	10.00	25.00
VL Vincent Lecavalier	8.00	20.00
WG Wayne Gretzky	125.00	250.00
ZP Zigmund Palffy	6.00	15.00
TRL Trevor Letowski	4.00	10.00
BB M.Brodeur/E.Belfour/150	30.00	80.00
BL P.Bure/R.Luongo/150	12.50	30.00
CH M.Comrie/J.Hecht/150	10.00	25.00
DL R.DiPietro/R.Luongo/150	15.00	40.00
ET P.Esposito/Thornton/150	15.00	40.00
FG Fernandez/Gaborik/150	12.00	30.00
GO G.Howe/B.Orr/150	150.00	300.00
HH M.Havlat/M.Hossa/150	12.00	30.00
HS J.Hedberg/T.Salo/150	12.50	30.00
HT M.Hossa/J.Thornton/150	20.00	50.00
HY G.Howe/S.Yzerman/150	125.00	250.0
IH J.Iginla/M.Hejduk/150	15.00	40.0
LR J.LeClair/M.Recchi/150	10.00	25.0
PP Z.Palffy/F.Potvin/150	12.50	30.0
SS D.Sedin/H.Sedin/150	15.00	40.0
TL Thornton/Lecavalier/150	25.00	60.0
WM D.Weight/MacInnis/150	10.00	25.0
YA S.Yzerman/J.Allison/150	30.00	80.0
BKK Bure/Kvlchk/Kovalv/25	100.00	250.0
BOB Bourque/Orr/Blake/25	150.00	300.0
GWA Guerin/Weight/Amonte/25	30.00	80.0
HBB Hejduk/Bourque/Blake/25	100.00	250.0
HGY Howe/Gretzky/Yzer/25	500.00	1000.0
HHS Havlat/Hejduk/Sykora/25	40.00	100.0
JBB Joseph/Brodeur/Belfr/25	125.00	250.0
PHG Palffy/Hossa/Gaborik/25	60.00	150.0
SDP Salo/DiPietro/Potvin/25	40.00	100.0
SSN Sedin/Sedin/Naslund/25	40.00	100.0

2002-03 SP Authentic

Released in late February, this 219-card set consisted of 90 veteran base cards, 15 shortprinted "Hat Trick" subset cards (serial-numbered to 1499), 30 shortprinted "Future Great" subset cards (serial numbered to 2003), 60 shortprinted rookies (serial-numbered to 900) and 20 shortprinted rookie autographs (serial-numbered to 999). Cards 202-218 were available only in packs of UD Rookie Update.

COMP.SET w/o SP's (90)	15.00	40.0
1 Jean-Sebastien Giguere	.30	.7
2 Paul Kariya	.40	1.0
3 Adam Oates	.30	.7
4 Dany Heatley	.30	.7
5 Ilya Kovalchuk	.40	1.0
6 Joe Thornton	.40	1.0
7 Sergei Samsonov	.25	.6
8 Steve Shields	.25	.6
9 Martin Biron	.25	.6
10 Miroslav Satan	.30	.7
11 Tim Connolly	.20	.5
12 Jarome Iginla	.30	.7
13 Roman Turek	.30	.7
14 Arturs Irbe	.25	.6
15 Rod Brind'Amour	.30	.7
16 Ron Francis	.40	1.0
17 Alexei Zhamnov	.25	.6
18 Eric Daze	.20	.5
19 Jocelyn Thibault	.25	.6
20 Chris Drury	.30	.7
21 Joe Sakic	.50	1.2
22 Patrick Roy	.75	2.0
23 Peter Forsberg	.40	1.0
24 Rob Blake	.30	.7
25 Ray Whitney	.25	.6
26 Marc Denis	.25	.6
27 Rostislav Klesla	.20	.5
28 Bill Guerin	.30	.7
29 Marty Turco	.30	.7
30 Mike Modano	.50	1.2
31 Brendan Shanahan	.40	1.0
32 Brett Hull	.40	1.0
33 Curtis Joseph	.30	.7
34 Nicklas Lidstrom	.30	.7
35 Sergei Fedorov	.50	1.2
36 Steve Yzerman	.60	1.5
37 Mike Comrie	.30	.7
38 Tommy Salo	.25	.6
39 Anson Carter	.25	.6
40 Roberto Luongo	.50	1.2
41 Olli Jokinen	.30	.7
42 Felix Potvin	.50	1.2
43 Zigmund Palffy	.30	.7
44 Jason Allison	.25	.6
45 Manny Fernandez	.25	.6
46 Marian Gaborik	.50	1.2
47 Jose Theodore	.30	.7
48 Saku Koivu	.30	.7
49 Yanic Perreault	.20	.5
50 Tomas Vokoun	.25	.6
51 David Legwand	.25	.6
52 Scott Hartnell	.30	.7
53 Martin Brodeur	.60	1.5
54 Patrik Elias	.30	.7
55 Jeff Friesen	.20	.5
56 Alexei Yashin	.30	.7
57 Chris Osgood	.25	.6
58 Michael Peca	.25	.6
59 Eric Lindros	.50	1.2
60 Bobby Holik	.25	.6
61 Pavel Bure	.40	1.0
62 Daniel Alfredsson	.30	.7
63 Marian Hossa	.25	.6
64 Patrick Lalime	.25	.6
65 Jeremy Roenick	.30	.7
66 Roman Cechmanek	.25	.6
67 Simon Gagne	.30	.7
68 John LeClair	.30	.7
69 Sean Burke	.25	.6
70 Tony Amonte	.25	.6
71 Daniel Briere	.25	.6
72 Alexei Kovalev	.30	.7
73 Mario Lemieux	1.00	2.5
74 Evgeni Nabokov	.25	.6
75 Owen Nolan	.30	.7
76 Teemu Selanne	.60	1.5
77 Doug Weight	.30	.7
78 Pavol Demitra	.40	1.0
79 Keith Tkachuk	.30	.7
80 Nikolai Khabibulin	.30	.7
81 Vincent Lecavalier	.25	.6
82 Alexander Mogilny	.25	.6
83 Ed Belfour	.30	.7
84 Mats Sundin	.30	.7
85 Markus Naslund	.25	.6
86 Ed Jovanovski	.25	.6
87 Todd Bertuzzi	.30	.7
88 Jaromir Jagr	.75	2.0
89 Olaf Kolzig	.30	.7
90 Peter Bondra	.30	.7
91 Paul Kariya HT	1.50	4.0
92 Joe Thornton HT	1.50	4.0
93 Jarome Iginla HT	1.25	3.0
94 Joe Sakic HT	2.00	5.0
95 Peter Forsberg HT	1.50	4.0
96 Steve Yzerman HT	2.50	6.0
97 Brendan Shanahan HT	1.50	4.0
98 Brett Hull HT	1.50	4.0
99 Wayne Gretzky HT	6.00	15.0
100 Eric Lindros HT	2.00	5.0
101 Pavel Bure HT	1.50	4.0
102 Mario Lemieux HT	4.00	10.0
103 Keith Tkachuk HT	1.25	3.0
104 Todd Bertuzzi HT	1.25	3.0
105 Peter Bondra HT	1.25	3.0
106 Andy McDonald FG	1.50	4.0
107 Dany Heatley FG	1.50	4.0
108 Ilya Kovalchuk FG	2.00	5.0
109 Ivan Huml FG	1.00	2.5
110 Maxim Afinogenov FG	1.00	2.5
111 Jaroslav Svoboda FG	1.00	2.5
112 Kyle Calder FG	1.00	2.5

Radim Vrbata FG	1.25	3.00
Rostislav Klesla FG	1.00	2.50
Pavel Datsyuk FG	2.00	5.00
Mike Comrie FG	1.50	4.00
Marcus Nilsson FG	1.00	2.50
Kristian Huselius FG	1.00	2.50
Marian Gaborik FG	2.50	6.00
Mike Ribeiro FG	1.25	3.00
Scott Hartnell FG	1.50	4.00
Brian Gionta FG	1.25	3.00
Raffi Torres FG	1.00	2.50
Dan Blackburn FG	1.25	3.00
Tom Poti FG	1.00	2.50
Petr Schastlivy FG	1.00	2.50
Pavel Brendl FG	1.00	2.50
Brian Boucher FG	1.25	3.00
Ville Nieminen FG	1.00	2.50
Jeff Jillson FG	1.00	2.50
Justin Papineau FG	1.00	2.50
Brad Richards FG	1.50	4.00
Nikita Alexeev FG	1.00	2.50
Nikolai Antropov FG	1.25	3.00
Matt Pettinger FG	1.00	2.50
Martin Gerber RC	3.00	8.00
Tim Thomas RC	8.00	20.00
Micki Dupont RC	2.00	5.00
Shawn Thornton RC	2.50	6.00
Matt Henderson RC	2.00	5.00
Jeff Paul RC	2.00	5.00
Lasse Pirjeta RC	2.00	5.00
Dmitri Bykov RC	2.00	5.00
Alex Henry RC	2.50	6.00
Kari Haakana RC	2.00	5.00
Ivan Majesky RC	2.00	5.00
Sylvain Blouin RC	2.00	5.00
Stephane Veilleux RC	2.00	5.00
Greg Koehler RC	2.00	5.00
Ray Schultz RC	2.00	5.00
Tomi Pettinen RC	2.00	5.00
Eric Godard RC	2.00	5.00
Dennis Seidenberg RC	3.00	8.00
Radovan Somik RC	2.00	5.00
Patrick Sharp RC	6.00	15.00
Lynn Loyns RC	2.00	5.00
Tom Koivisto RC	2.00	5.00
Curtis Sanford RC	5.00	12.00
Cody Rudkowsky RC	2.00	5.00
Steve Eminger RC	2.00	5.00
Shaone Morrisonn RC	2.00	5.00
Anton Volchenkov RC	2.00	5.00
Carlo Colaiacovo RC	3.00	8.00
Rickard Wallin RC	2.00	5.00
Matt Walker RC	2.00	5.00
Ryan Miller RC	10.00	25.00
Levente Szuper RC	3.00	8.00
Tomas Malec RC	2.00	5.00
Jim Fahey RC	2.00	5.00
Jonathan Hedstrom RC	2.00	5.00
Michael Leighton RC	3.00	8.00
Dany Sabourin RC	2.00	5.00
Mike Cammalleri RC	8.00	20.00
Craig Andersson RC	6.00	15.00
Darren Haydar RC	2.00	5.00
Vernon Fiddler RC	2.50	6.00
Curtis Murphy RC	2.00	5.00
Jared Aulin RC	2.00	5.00
Ian MacNeil RC	2.00	5.00
Dick Tarnstrom RC	2.00	5.00
Alexei Smirnov AU RC	4.00	10.00
Stanislav Chistov AU RC	3.00	8.00
Chuck Kobasew AU RC	4.00	10.00
Rick Nash AU RC	20.00	50.00
Pascal LeClaire AU RC	4.00	10.00
Henrik Zetterberg AU RC	30.00	80.00
Jay Bouwmeester AU RC	10.00	25.00
Alexander Frolov AU RC	6.00	15.00
Ron Hainsey AU RC	3.00	8.00
Adam Hall AU RC	3.00	8.00
Jason Spezza AU RC	25.00	60.00
Jeff Taffe AU RC	3.00	8.00
Kurt Sauer AU RC	3.00	8.00
Alexander Svitov AU RC	3.00	8.00
Mikael Tellqvist AU RC	3.00	8.00
Jordan Leopold AU RC	5.00	12.00
Ales Hemsky AU RC	8.00	20.00
P-M Bouchard AU RC	5.00	12.00
Scottie Upshall AU RC	4.00	10.00
Brooks Orpik AU RC	5.00	12.00
Steve Ott AU RC	6.00	15.00
Igor Radulov RC	2.00	5.00
Alexei Semenov RC	2.00	5.00
Mike Komisarek RC	3.00	8.00
Tomas Surovy RC	2.00	5.00
Jason Bacashihua RC	2.50	6.00
Ray Emery RC	6.00	15.00
Fernando Pisani RC	2.00	5.00
Simon Gamache RC	2.00	5.00
Ari Ahonen RC	2.00	5.00
Brandon Reid RC	2.00	5.00
Ryan Bayda RC	2.00	5.00
Niko Dimitrakos RC	2.00	5.00
Rob Davison RC	2.00	5.00
Konstantin Koltsov RC	2.50	6.00
Jarret Stoll RC	8.00	20.00
Cristobal Huet RC	4.00	10.00
Jason King RC	3.00	8.00
Tomas Kurka RC	2.00	5.00

2002-03 SP Authentic UD Promos

rted into copies of the April 2003 issue of Beckett key Collector, this 90-card set parallels the base Authentic set but carried a silver foil "UD Promo" np across the card fronts.

PROMO: .8X TO 2X BASIC CARDS

2002-03 SP Authentic Sign of the Times

33-card set carried authentic player autographs of two or three NHL players. Single autographs were rted at 1:96 packs, Dual autographs were serial-bered to 99 sets and triple autographs were serial-bered to 25 sets.

L AUTO PRINT RUN 99 SER.#'d SETS

PLE AUTO PRINT RUN 25 SER.#'d SETS

rturs Irbe		
Alexander Frolov	8.00	20.00
Pavel Brendl	4.00	10.00
Bobby Orr SP	50.00	120.00
Curtis Joseph SP	15.00	40.00
Dany Heatley	15.00	40.00
Erik Cole	4.00	10.00
Evgeni Nabokov SP	10.00	25.00
Gordie Howe	50.00	100.00
Ales Hemsky	8.00	20.00
Henrik Zetterberg	30.00	80.00
ay Bouwmeester	12.00	30.00
rome Iginla	10.00	25.00
ohn LeClair	4.00	10.00
oe Thornton	12.00	30.00
Justin Williams	4.00	10.00

MA Maxim Afinogenov	4.00	10.00
MB Martin Brodeur SP	30.00	80.00
MC Mike Comrie	8.00	20.00
MF Manny Fernandez	4.00	10.00
MH Martin Havlat	4.00	10.00
MK Milan Kraft	4.00	10.00
MN Markus Naslund	5.00	12.00
NK Nikolai Khabibulin SP	20.00	50.00
PB Pavel Bure	25.00	60.00
PR Patrick Roy	60.00	120.00
RB Ray Bourque	15.00	40.00
RN Rick Nash SP	40.00	100.00
SG Simon Gagne	6.00	15.00
SP Jason Spezza	25.00	60.00
SS Sergei Samsonov	4.00	10.00
SY Steve Yzerman	30.00	80.00
TS Teemu Selanne	12.00	30.00
WG Wayne Gretzky	125.00	250.00
BB B.Orr/Bouwmeester/99	60.00	150.00
BR P.Roy/R.Bourque/99	70.00	150.00
CI M.Comrie/J.Iginla/99	15.00	40.00
GB S.Gagne/P.Brendl/99	12.00	30.00
GC W.Gretzky/M.Comrie/99	80.00	150.00
GL S.Gagne/J.LeClair/99	15.00	40.00
GW W.Gretzky/G.Howe/99	500.00	800.00
KA Kovalchuk/Afinogenov/99	10.00	25.00
KH Kovalchuk/D.Heatley/99	30.00	80.00
KN Nabokov/Khabibulin/99	12.00	30.00
LW J.Leclair/J.Williams/99	12.00	30.00
MM M.Brodeur/M.Ouellet/99	30.00	80.00
OB B.Orr/R.Bourque/99	80.00	200.00
SN Selanne/E.Nabokov/99	20.00	50.00
ST Thornton/Samsonov/99	12.00	30.00
SZ Spezza/H.Zetterberg/99	30.00	80.00
YH S.Yzerman/G.Howe/99	125.00	250.00
YZ Yzerman/Zetterberg/99	60.00	120.00
GHO Gretzky/Howe/Orr/25	800.00	1200.00
HCI Heatley/Comrie/Iginla/25	60.00	120.00
OBT Orr/Bourque/Thornton/25	150.00	300.00
SZB Spezza/Zetter/Bouwm/25	60.00	120.00
TSB Thorntn/Sams/Bourqe/25	75.00	150.00

2002-03 SP Authentic Signed Patches

Limited to just 100 copies each, this 15-card set featured swatches of game jersey patches and authentic polayer autographs from some of the hottest rookies of the year.

*SINGLE COLOR: .25X TO .75X HI

PAF Alexander Frolov	25.00	60.00
PAH Ales Hemsky	25.00	60.00
PAS Alexander Svitov	12.00	30.00
PCK Chuck Kobasew	12.00	30.00
PHA Adam Hall	8.00	20.00
PHZ Henrik Zetterberg	150.00	300.00
PJB Jay Bouwmeester	15.00	40.00
PJL Jordan Leopold	15.00	40.00
PJS Jason Spezza	80.00	200.00
PPB P-M Bouchard	15.00	40.00
PRH Ron Hainsey	12.00	30.00
PRN Rick Nash	60.00	150.00
PSC Stanislav Chistov	8.00	20.00
PSM Alexei Smirnov	8.00	20.00
PSU Scottie Upshall	15.00	40.00

2002-03 SP Authentic Super Premium Jerseys

Randomly inserted, this memorabilia card set featured single, double or triple swatches of game used jerseys. Singles cards were serial-numbered to 599, doubles were numbered to 299 and triples were numbered to just 15. Triples are not priced due to scarcity.

SPAM Alexei Morozov	3.00	8.00
SPBG Bill Guerin	4.00	10.00
SPBI Martin Biron	3.00	8.00
SPBL Brian Leetch	4.00	10.00
SPBS Brendan Shanahan	5.00	12.00
SPDB Daniel Briere	4.00	10.00
SPDH Dan Hinote	3.00	8.00
SPEJ Ed Jovanovski	4.00	10.00
SPJA Jason Allison	3.00	8.00
SPJI Jarome Iginla	6.00	15.00
SPJJ Jaromir Jagr	6.00	15.00
SPJR Jeremy Roenick	6.00	15.00
SPJS Joe Sakic	8.00	20.00
SPJT Joe Thornton	6.00	15.00
SPMB Martin Brodeur	10.00	25.00
SPMD Marc Denis	3.00	8.00
SPML Mario Lemieux	10.00	25.00
SPMM Mike Modano	6.00	15.00
SPMN Markus Naslund	5.00	12.00
SPMS Mats Sundin	5.00	12.00
SPOK Olaf Kolzig	4.00	10.00
SPPF Peter Forsberg	5.00	12.00
SPPK Paul Kariya	5.00	12.00
SPPR Patrick Roy	10.00	25.00
SPSF Sergei Fedorov	6.00	15.00
SPSG Simon Gagne	5.00	12.00
SPSS Sergei Samsonov	4.00	10.00
SPSY Steve Yzerman	8.00	20.00
SPTH Jose Theodore	5.00	12.00
SPZP Zigmund Palffy	4.00	10.00
DPDS C.Drury/J.Sakic	6.00	15.00
DPFR P.Forsberg/P.Roy	12.00	30.00
DPGL M.Lemieux/W.Gretzky	25.00	60.00
DPKJ O.Kolzig/J.Jagr	8.00	20.00
DPMG M.Modano/B.Guerin	6.00	15.00
DPRG J.Roenick/S.Gagne	8.00	20.00
DPST S.Samsonov/J.Thornton	8.00	20.00
DPTK J.Theodore/S.Koivu	10.00	25.00
DPYS S.Yzerman/B.Shanahan	8.00	20.00
TPGLY Lemieux/Gretzky/Yzerman	125.00	250.00
TPRBB Roy/Brodeur/Belfour	50.00	100.00
TPTBN Thornton/Bourque/Neely	40.00	80.00

2003-04 SP Authentic

This 166-card set consisted of 90 veteran cards, 53 short-printed rookie cards (91-135 and 159-166) and 23 rookie autograph cards (136-158). Rookie cards were serial-numbered out of 900 and cards 159-166 were available in packs of UD Rookie Update.

COMP.SET w/o SP's (90)	15.00	30.00
1 Jean-Sebastien Giguere	.30	.75
2 Sergei Fedorov	.50	1.25
3 Stanislav Chistov	.20	.50
4 Dany Heatley	.30	.75
5 Ilya Kovalchuk	.30	.75
6 Felix Potvin	.50	1.25
7 Joe Thornton	.40	1.00
8 Sergei Samsonov	.25	.60
9 Chris Drury	.25	.60
10 Daniel Briere	.30	.75
11 Martin Biron	.25	.60
12 Jarome Iginla	.30	.75
13 Roman Turek	.25	.60
14 Jamie Storr	.25	.60
15 Ron Francis	.40	1.00
16 Alexei Zhamnov	.25	.60
17 Jocelyn Thibault	.25	.60
18 Tyler Arnason	.20	.50
19 David Aebischer	.25	.60
20 Joe Sakic	.50	1.25
21 Paul Kariya	.40	1.00
22 Peter Forsberg	.40	1.00
23 Marc Denis	.25	.60
24 Rick Nash	.30	.75
25 Todd Marchant	.20	.50
26 Bill Guerin	.30	.75
27 Marty Turco	.30	.75
28 Mike Modano	.50	1.25
29 Dominik Hasek	.50	1.25
30 Henrik Zetterberg	.40	1.00
31 Steve Yzerman	.75	2.00
32 Ales Hemsky	.30	.75
33 Raffi Torres	.20	.50
34 Adam Oates	.30	.75
35 Tommy Salo	.25	.60
36 Jay Bouwmeester	.30	.75
37 Olli Jokinen	.30	.75
38 Roberto Luongo	.50	1.25
39 Luc Robitaille	.30	.75
40 Roman Cechmanek	.25	.60
41 Zigmund Palffy	.30	.75
42 Manny Fernandez	.25	.60
43 Marian Gaborik	.50	1.25
44 Pierre-Marc Bouchard	.30	.75
45 Jose Theodore	.30	.75
46 Marcel Hossa	.20	.50
47 Michael Ryder	.25	.60
48 Saku Koivu	.30	.75
49 David Legwand	.25	.60
50 Tomas Vokoun	.25	.60
51 Martin Brodeur	.60	1.50
52 Patrik Elias	.30	.75
53 Scott Gomez	.25	.60
54 Scott Stevens	.30	.75
55 Alexei Yashin	.25	.60
56 Michael Peca	.25	.60
57 Rick DiPietro	.25	.60
58 Eric Lindros	.50	1.25
59 Mark Messier	.50	1.25
60 Mike Dunham	.25	.60
61 Jason Spezza	.30	.75
62 Marian Hossa	.25	.60
63 Patrick Lalime	.25	.60
64 Jeff Hackett	.25	.60
65 Jeremy Roenick	.30	.75
66 Simon Gagne	.30	.75
67 Mike Johnson	.20	.50
68 Sean Burke	.20	.50
69 Mario Lemieux	1.00	2.50
70 Martin Straka	.20	.50
71 Evgeni Nabokov	.25	.60
72 Patrick Marleau	.30	.75
73 Vincent Damphousse	.25	.60
74 Chris Osgood	.30	.75
75 Doug Weight	.30	.75
76 Keith Tkachuk	.30	.75
77 Pavol Demitra	.40	1.00
78 Nikolai Khabibulin	.30	.75
79 Vincent Lecavalier	.25	.60
80 Alexander Mogilny	.25	.60
81 Ed Belfour	.30	.75
82 Mats Sundin	.30	.75
83 Owen Nolan	.25	.60
84 Ed Jovanovski	.25	.60
85 Jason King	.20	.50
86 Markus Naslund	.30	.75
87 Todd Bertuzzi	.30	.75
88 Jaromir Jagr	.75	2.00
89 Olaf Kolzig	.30	.75
90 Peter Bondra	.25	.60
91 Andrew Hutchinson RC	2.50	6.00
92 Phil Osaer RC	2.50	6.00
93 Boyd Kane RC	2.50	6.00
94 Brent Krahn RC	2.50	6.00
95 Cody McCormick RC	3.00	8.00
96 Christoph Brandner RC	3.00	8.00
97 Dan Fritsche RC	2.50	6.00
98 David Hale RC	2.50	6.00
99 Esa Pirnes RC	2.50	6.00
100 Libor Pivko RC	2.50	6.00
101 Greg Campbell RC	2.50	6.00
102 John-Michael Liles RC	3.00	8.00
103 Mikhail Yakubov RC	2.50	6.00
104 Marek Svatos RC	5.00	12.00
105 Marek Zidlicky RC	2.50	6.00
106 Nathan Robinson RC	2.50	6.00
107 Matthew Lombardi RC	3.00	8.00
108 Matthew Spiller RC	3.00	8.00
109 Matt Murley RC	3.00	8.00
110 Maxim Kondratiev RC	2.50	6.00
111 Ryan Kesler RC	10.00	25.00
112 Paul Martin RC	3.00	8.00
113 Ryan Malone RC	5.00	12.00
114 Tim Gleason RC	3.00	8.00
115 Tom Preissing RC	3.00	8.00
116 Fredrik Sjostrom RC	4.00	10.00
117 Tony Martensson RC	2.50	6.00
118 Aaron Johnson RC	2.50	6.00
119 Seamus Kotyk RC	2.50	6.00
120 Pat Rissmiller RC	3.00	8.00
121 Jeff Hamilton RC	2.50	6.00
122 Sergei Zinovjev RC	2.50	6.00
123 Julien Vauclair RC	2.50	6.00
124 Nikolai Zherdev RC	5.00	12.00
125 Brent Burns RC	6.00	15.00
126 John Pohl RC	2.50	6.00
127 Dominic Moore RC	2.50	6.00
128 Rastislav Stana RC	4.00	10.00
129 Gavin Morgan RC	3.00	8.00
130 Darryl Bootland RC	3.00	8.00
131 Trevor Daley RC	4.00	10.00
132 Peter Sarno RC	2.50	6.00
133 Jed Ortmeyer RC	2.50	6.00
134 Nathan Smith RC	2.50	6.00
135 Grant McNeill RC	2.50	6.00
136 Joffrey Lupul AU RC	15.00	30.00
137 Eric Staal AU RC	30.00	60.00
138 Pavel Vorobiev AU RC	5.00	12.00
139 Tuomo Ruutu AU RC	6.00	15.00
140 Antoine Vermette AU RC	8.00	20.00
141 Antti Miettinen AU RC	6.00	15.00
142 Boyd Gordon AU RC	5.00	12.00
143 Nathan Horton AU RC	10.00	25.00
144 Tony Salmelainen AU RC	4.00	10.00
145 Christian Ehrhoff AU RC	5.00	12.00
146 Patrice Bergeron AU RC	30.00	80.00
147 Dan Hamhuis AU RC	5.00	12.00
148 Jordin Tootoo AU RC	8.00	20.00
149 Joni Pitkanen AU RC	6.00	15.00
150 Dustin Brown AU RC	8.00	20.00
151 Chris Higgins AU RC	8.00	20.00
152 Sean Bergenheim AU RC	5.00	12.00
153 Marc-Andre Fleury AU RC	30.00	80.00
154 Jiri Hudler AU RC	10.00	25.00
155 Milan Michalek AU RC	8.00	20.00
156 Peter Sejna AU RC	5.00	12.00
157 Matt Stajan AU RC	6.00	15.00
158 Alexander Semin AU RC	12.00	30.00
159 Niklas Kronwall RC	5.00	12.00
160 Derek Roy RC	4.00	10.00
161 Kyle Wellwood RC	4.00	10.00
162 Brad Boyes RC	4.00	10.00
163 Timofei Shishkanov RC	2.50	6.00
164 Jason Pominville RC	6.00	15.00
165 Aleksander Suglobov RC	2.50	6.00
166 Carl Corazzini RC	3.00	8.00

2003-04 SP Authentic Limited

*1-90 VETS/99: 4X TO 10X BASIC CARDS

1-90 VETERAN PRINT RUN 99

*91-135 ROOKIE/50: .8X TO 2X

*136-158 ROOK.AU/50: .8X TO 2X

91-158 ROOKIE PRINT RUN 50

59 Mark Messier	5.00	12.00
137 Eric Staal AU	75.00	150.00
146 Patrice Bergeron AU	60.00	120.00
153 Marc-Andre Fleury AU	50.00	120.00

2003-04 SP Authentic 10th Anniversary

COMPLETE SET (20)	10.00	20.00
PRINT RUN 1994 SER.#'d SETS		
*LIMITED: 1X TO 2.5X		
LTD PRINT RUN 99 SER.#'d SETS		
SP1 Wayne Gretzky	3.00	8.00
SP2 Patrick Roy	1.50	4.00
SP3 Steve Yzerman	1.50	4.00
SP4 Mario Lemieux	2.00	5.00
SP5 Teemu Selanne	.50	1.25
SP6 Joe Sakic	1.00	2.50
SP7 Jaromir Jagr	.75	2.00
SP8 Sergei Fedorov	.60	1.50
SP9 Mike Modano	.75	2.00
SP10 Brett Hull	.60	1.50
SP11 Jason Spezza	.50	1.25
SP12 Joe Thornton	.75	2.00
SP13 Rick Nash	.60	1.50
SP14 Marian Gaborik	.75	2.00
SP15 Ales Hemsky	.40	1.00
SP16 Marian Hossa	.40	1.00
SP17 Jean-Sebastien Giguere	.40	1.00
SP18 Martin Brodeur	1.25	3.00
SP19 Todd Bertuzzi	.40	1.00
SP20 Markus Naslund	.40	1.00

2003-04 SP Authentic Breakout Seasons

PRINT RUN 500 SER.#'d SETS

*LIMITED: .75X TO 2X

LTD PRINT RUN 99 SER.#'d SETS

B1 Steve Yzerman	4.00	10.00
B2 Martin Brodeur	4.00	10.00
B3 Nicklas Lidstrom	1.00	2.50
B4 Joe Thornton	1.50	3.00
B5 Jeremy Roenick	1.00	2.50
B6 Todd Bertuzzi	1.00	2.50
B7 Markus Naslund	1.00	2.50
B8 Sergei Fedorov	1.00	2.50
B9 Chris Pronger	.75	2.00
B10 Zigmund Palffy	.75	2.00
B11 Marian Gaborik	2.00	5.00
B12 Jose Theodore	1.25	3.00
B13 Mike Modano	1.50	3.00
B14 Vincent Lecavalier	1.00	2.50
B15 Jean-Sebastien Giguere	.75	2.00
B16 Keith Tkachuk	1.00	2.50
B17 Mats Sundin	1.00	2.50
B18 Paul Kariya	1.00	2.50
B19 Jarome Iginla	1.25	3.00
B20 Jaromir Jagr	1.50	3.00
B21 Dominik Hasek	1.50	4.00
B22 Teemu Selanne	1.00	2.50
B23 Jocelyn Thibault	.75	2.00
B24 Alexei Yashin	.75	2.00
B25 Ilya Kovalchuk	1.25	3.00
B26 Marian Hossa	1.00	2.50
B27 Ed Belfour	1.00	2.50
B28 Peter Forsberg	2.50	6.00
B29 Mario Lemieux	5.00	12.00
B30 Saku Koivu	1.00	2.50

2003-04 SP Authentic Foundations

PRINT RUN 250 SER.#'d SETS

*LIMITED: .6X TO 1.5X

LTD PRINT RUN 99 SER.#'d SETS

F1 S.Fedorov/J.Giguere	2.00	8.00
F2 J.Thornton/S.Samsonov	2.00	5.00
F3 P.Kariya/T.Selanne	2.00	5.00
F4 P.Forsberg/J.Sakic	4.00	10.00
F5 S.Yzerman/D.Hasek	4.00	10.00
F6 T.Bertuzzi/M.Naslund	2.00	5.00
F7 M.Modano/M.Turco	2.00	5.00
F8 M.Brodeur/S.Stevens	4.00	10.00
F9 M.Sundin/E.Belfour	3.00	8.00
F10 S.Koivu/J.Theodore	2.00	5.00

2003-04 SP Authentic Honors

PRINT RUN 900 SER.#'d SETS

*LIMITED: 1X TO 2.5X

LTD PRINT RUN 99 SER.#'d SETS

H1 Wayne Gretzky	5.00	12.00
H2 Wayne Gretzky	5.00	12.00
H3 Wayne Gretzky	5.00	12.00
H4 Gordie Howe	2.50	6.00
H5 Gordie Howe	2.50	6.00
H6 Gordie Howe	2.50	6.00
H7 Scotty Bowman	1.00	2.50
H8 Scotty Bowman	1.00	2.50
H9 Scotty Bowman	1.00	2.50
H10 Don Cherry	1.00	2.50
H11 Don Cherry	1.00	2.50
H12 Patrick Roy	3.00	10.00
H13 Patrick Roy	4.00	8.00
H14 Bobby Clarke	.60	1.50
H15 Marcel Dionne	.60	1.50
H16 Guy Lafleur	.75	2.00
H17 Mario Lemieux	4.00	10.00
H18 Jason Spezza	.75	2.00
H19 Jean-Sebastien Giguere	.60	1.50
H20 Mike Modano	1.25	3.00
H21 Rick Nash	1.00	2.50
H22 Todd Bertuzzi	.75	2.00
H23 Marian Gaborik	1.25	3.00
H24 Martin Brodeur	2.50	5.00
H25 Joe Thornton	1.25	3.00
H26 Ed Belfour	.75	2.00
H27 Saku Koivu	.75	2.00
H28 Steve Yzerman	3.00	8.00
H29 Markus Naslund	.75	2.00
H30 Marian Hossa	.75	2.00

2003-04 SP Authentic Sign of the Times

This 77-card set featured certified autographs. Overall odds were stated at 1:24. Single player autos were inserted at 1:26, dual player autos were serial-numbered to 99 copies and triple player autos were serial-numbered to 25.

AF Alexander Frolov	4.00	10.00
AH Adam Hall	3.00	8.00
AS Alexei Smirnov	3.00	8.00
BC Bobby Clarke SP	15.00	40.00
BO Bobby Orr	60.00	150.00
CK Chuck Kobasew	3.00	8.00
DA David Aebischer	4.00	10.00
DC Don Cherry	20.00	50.00
EL Eric Lindros SP	30.00	80.00
GL Guy Lafleur SP	20.00	50.00
HZ Henrik Zetterberg	10.00	25.00
IK Ilya Kovalchuk	5.00	12.00
JI Jarome Iginla	5.00	12.00
JK Jari Kurri	8.00	20.00
JL Jordan Leopold	3.00	8.00
JN Joe Nieuwendyk	5.00	12.00
JP Joni Pitkanen	5.00	12.00
JR Jeremy Roenick	5.00	12.00
JS Jason Spezza	5.00	12.00
JT Jose Theodore	5.00	12.00
KL Eric Staal SP	15.00	40.00
LM Lanny McDonald	8.00	20.00
MB Martin Brodeur	25.00	60.00
MC Mike Comrie	4.00	10.00
MG Marian Gaborik	8.00	20.00
MH Gordie Howe	80.00	150.00
MT Mikael Tellqvist SP	4.00	10.00
MT Marty Turco	5.00	12.00
PE Phil Esposito SP	15.00	40.00
PL Pascal Leclaire	3.00	8.00
PR Patrick Roy SP	50.00	120.00
RN Rick Nash	5.00	12.00
SB Scotty Bowman SP	20.00	50.00
SC Stanislav Chistov	3.00	8.00
SF Sergei Fedorov	12.00	30.00
SG Curtis Joseph	8.00	20.00
SH Scott Hartnell	5.00	12.00
SK Saku Koivu SP	15.00	40.00
SM Stan Mikita	6.00	15.00
SS Sergei Samsonov	4.00	10.00
TB Todd Bertuzzi	5.00	12.00
TR Tuomo Ruutu	5.00	12.00
WG Wayne Gretzky	150.00	250.00
ZP Zigmund Palffy	5.00	12.00
AHY Ales Hemsky	5.00	12.00
JLC John LeClair	5.00	12.00
JSG Jean-Sebastien Giguere	5.00	12.00
JTH Joe Thornton	8.00	20.00
MAF Marc-Andre Fleury	20.00	50.00
MHA Marian Hossa	10.00	25.00
BL P.Bure/E.Lindros	30.00	80.00
CF S.Chistov/S.Fedorov	20.00	50.00
CH M.Comrie/A.Hemsky	12.00	30.00
CR B.Clarke/J.Roenick	12.00	30.00
ET P.Esposito/J.Thornton	20.00	50.00
FG S.Fedorov/J.Giguere	20.00	50.00
FS E.Staal/M.Fleury	50.00	125.00
GK W.Gretzky/J.Kurri	150.00	250.00
GR J.Giguere/P.Roy	30.00	80.00
HS M.Hossa/J.Spezza	12.00	30.00
IM J.Iginla/L.McDonald	20.00	50.00
NB M.Naslund/T.Bertuzzi	12.00	30.00
NL R.Nash/P.Leclaire	12.00	30.00
TK J.Theodore/S.Koivu	12.00	30.00
BCY S.Bowman/D.Cherry	40.00	100.00
BTG Bossy/Trott/Gillies	60.00	150.00
CRG Clarke/Roen/Gagne	30.00	80.00
GCF Gig/Chistov/Fedorov	30.00	80.00
GKF Gretzky/Kurri/Fuhr	300.00	500.00
GMM Howe/Howe/Howe	400.00	500.00
GTS Gretzky/Thorn/Spezza	250.00	400.00
LFR Staal/Fleury/Ruutu	50.00	120.00
NSZ Nash/Spezz/Zetter	50.00	120.00
PAF Palffy/Aulin/Frolov	15.00	40.00
RGB Roy/Giguere/Brodeur	250.00	400.00

2003-04 SP Authentic Signed Patches

This 18-card set featured autographs as well as jersey patches from some of the hottest rookies of the 2003-04 season. Each card was serial-numbered to 100.

*SINGLE COLOR: .25X TO .75X

AM Antti Miettinen	15.00	40.00
AS Alexander Semin	60.00	120.00
CH Chris Higgins	20.00	50.00
DB Dustin Brown	75.00	150.00
DH Dan Hamhuis	20.00	50.00
ES Eric Staal	100.00	200.00
JH Jiri Hudler	25.00	60.00
JL Joffrey Lupul	40.00	80.00
JP Joni Pitkanen	25.00	60.00
JT Jordin Tootoo	60.00	120.00
MF Marc-Andre Fleury	75.00	150.00
MS Matt Stajan	25.00	60.00
NH Nathan Horton	30.00	80.00
PB Patrice Bergeron	100.00	200.00
PS Peter Sejna	25.00	60.00
SB Sean Bergenheim	30.00	80.00
TR Tuomo Ruutu	25.00	60.00
TS Tony Salmelainen	25.00	60.00

2004-05 SP Authentic

This 150-card set was released in late May 2005, it consisted of 90 veteran player cards, 6 rookie cards and 54 All-World subset cards which were inserted at one per pack.

COMPLETE SET (150)	20.00	50.00
COMP.SET w/o SP's (90)	8.00	20.00
1 Jean-Sebastien Giguere	.30	.75
2 Joffrey Lupul	.25	.60
3 Sergei Fedorov	.50	1.25
4 Dany Heatley	.30	.75
5 Ilya Kovalchuk	.30	.75
6 Kari Lehtonen	.40	1.00
7 Andrew Raycroft	.25	.60
8 Joe Thornton	.40	1.00
9 Patrice Bergeron	.40	1.00
10 Glen Murray	.25	.60
11 Mika Noronen	.25	.60
12 Miroslav Satan	.25	.60
13 Maxim Afinogenov	.20	.50
14 Jarome Iginla	.30	.75
15 Matthew Lombardi	.20	.50
16 Miikka Kiprusoff	.25	.60
17 Eric Staal	.40	1.00
18 Erik Cole	.25	.60
19 Tyler Arnason	.20	.50
20 Tuomo Ruutu	.25	.60
21 David Aebischer	.25	.60
22 Joe Sakic	.50	1.25
23 Peter Forsberg	.40	1.00
24 Milan Hejduk	.25	.60
25 Alex Tanguay	.25	.60
26 Rick Nash	.30	.75
27 Nikolai Zherdev	.25	.60
28 Mike Modano	.50	1.25
29 Bill Guerin	.30	.75
30 Marty Turco	.30	.75
31 Manny Legace	.25	.60
32 Pavel Datsyuk	.40	1.00
33 Brendan Shanahan	.40	1.00
34 Steve Yzerman	1.00	2.50
35 Henrik Zetterberg	.40	1.00
36 Jason Smith	.20	.50
37 Ryan Smyth	.25	.60
38 Ty Conklin	.25	.60
39 Nathan Horton	.30	.75
40 Roberto Luongo	.50	1.25
41 Olli Jokinen	.25	.60
42 Alexander Frolov	.25	.60
43 Zigmund Palffy	.30	.75
44 Marian Gaborik	.50	1.25
45 Manny Fernandez	.25	.60
46 Michael Ryder	.25	.60
47 Jose Theodore	.30	.75
48 Saku Koivu	.30	.75
49 Steve Sullivan	.20	.50
50 Jordin Tootoo	.20	.50
51 Tomas Vokoun	.25	.60
52 Martin Brodeur	.60	1.50
53 Patrik Elias	.30	.75
54 Scott Stevens	.30	.75
55 Eric Lindros	.50	1.25
56 Mark Messier	.75	2.00
57 Jaromir Jagr	.75	2.00
58 Michael Peca	.25	.60
59 Rick DiPietro	.25	.60
60 Daniel Alfredsson	.30	.75
61 Marian Hossa	.25	.60
62 Jason Spezza	.30	.75
63 Martin Havlat	.30	.75
64 Dominik Hasek	.50	1.25
65 Jeremy Roenick	.30	.75
66 Robert Esche	.25	.60
67 Simon Gagne	.30	.75
68 Brett Hull	.40	1.00
69 Mike Comrie	.25	.60
70 Shane Doan	.25	.60
71 Marc-Andre Fleury	.75	2.00
72 Mario Lemieux	1.00	2.50
73 Mark Recchi	.40	1.00
74 Evgeni Nabokov	.25	.60
75 Patrick Marleau	.30	.75
76 Chris Pronger	.25	.60
77 Doug Weight	.30	.75
78 Keith Tkachuk	.30	.75
79 Brad Richards	.30	.75
80 Nikolai Khabibulin	.30	.75
81 Martin St. Louis	.30	.75
82 Vincent Lecavalier	.25	.60
83 Owen Nolan	.25	.60
84 Ed Belfour	.30	.75
85 Mats Sundin	.30	.75
86 Gary Roberts	.20	.50
87 Ed Jovanovski	.25	.60
88 Markus Naslund	.30	.75
89 Trevor Linden	.30	.75
90 Olaf Kolzig	.30	.75
91 Brad Fast RC	.75	2.00
92 Brennan Evans RC	.75	2.00
93 Layne Ulmer RC	.60	1.50
94 Mel Angelstad RC	.60	1.50
95 Garret Stroshein RC	.60	1.50
96 Marcel Goc RC	1.00	2.50
97 Sergei Fedorov AW	1.25	3.00
98 Dany Heatley AW	.75	2.00
99 Joe Thornton AW	1.00	2.50
100 Glen Murray AW	.60	1.50
101 Ilya Kovalchuk AW	.75	2.00
102 Miroslav Satan AW	.60	1.50
103 Jarome Iginla AW	.75	2.00
104 Eric Daze AW	.60	1.50
105 Paul Kariya AW	1.00	2.50
106 Peter Forsberg AW	1.00	2.50
107 Joe Sakic AW	1.25	3.00
108 Patrick Roy AW	2.00	5.00
109 Milan Hejduk AW	.60	1.50
110 Mike Modano AW	1.25	3.00
111 Bill Guerin AW	.75	2.00
112 Nicklas Lidstrom AW	.75	2.00
113 Steve Yzerman AW	2.50	6.00
114 Brendan Shanahan AW	1.00	2.50
115 Martin St. Louis AW	.75	2.00
116 Roberto Luongo AW	1.25	3.00
117 Zigmund Palffy AW	.75	2.00
118 Luc Robitaille AW	.75	2.00
119 Marian Gaborik AW	1.25	3.00
120 Saku Koivu AW	.75	2.00
121 Jose Theodore AW	.75	2.00
122 Martin Brodeur AW	1.50	4.00
123 Scott Niedermayer AW	.75	2.00
124 Scott Stevens AW	.75	2.00
125 Patrik Elias AW	.75	2.00
126 Alexei Yashin AW	.60	1.50
127 Pavel Bure AW	1.00	2.50
128 Jaromir Jagr AW	2.00	5.00
129 Wayne Gretzky AW	4.00	10.00
130 Dominik Hasek AW	1.25	3.00
131 Marian Hossa AW	.60	1.50
132 Daniel Alfredsson AW	.75	2.00
133 Jeremy Roenick AW	.75	2.00
134 Keith Primeau AW	.75	2.00
135 John LeClair AW	.75	2.00
136 Tony Amonte AW	.60	1.50
137 Brett Hull AW	1.00	2.50
138 Mario Lemieux AW	2.50	6.00
139 Vincent Damphousse AW	.60	1.50
140 Keith Tkachuk AW	.75	2.00
141 Doug Weight AW	.75	2.00
142 Chris Pronger AW	.60	1.50
143 Vincent Lecavalier AW	.60	1.50
144 Nikolai Khabibulin AW	.75	2.00
145 Mats Sundin AW	.75	2.00
146 Ed Belfour AW	.75	2.00
147 Joe Nieuwendyk AW	.75	2.00
148 Brian Leetch AW	.75	2.00
149 Markus Naslund AW	.75	2.00
150 Olaf Kolzig AW	.75	2.00

2004-05 SP Authentic Buyback Autographs

This 201-card set followed the historical notion of "Buybacks" as being previously issued cards that were bought back by Upper Deck, autographed by the player and then serial-numbered for inclusion into SP Authentic. For 2004-05 SP Authentic, Upper Deck also bought back rookie cards and previously signed cards for inclusion in packs. Since those cards were not altered from their previous form, they are not listed seperately.

STATED PRINT RUN 1-55

13 A.Raycroft 03Rookie Upd/51	12.00	30.00
15 Bo.Hull 04Leg Sig/38	25.00	60.00
26 C.Drury 03Rookie Upd/23	8.00	20.00
35 D.Briere 03RK Upd/48	15.00	40.00
36 D.Heatley 03Rookie Upd/15	20.00	40.00
41 D.Aebischer 03Rookie Upd/50	12.00	30.00
44 D.Weight 03Beehive Jsy/23	10.00	25.00
50 E.Jovanovski 02SPA Sup Prem/21	12.00	30.00
55 E.Jovanovski 03Rookie Upd/55	10.00	25.00
58 Cheevers 04Leg Sig/45	20.00	50.00
59 Perreault 04Leg Sig/22	15.00	40.00
64 Zetterberg 03RK Upd/40	15.00	40.00
75 J.Spezza 03Rookie Upd/39	8.00	20.00
80 J.Bouwmeester 03Rookie Upd/48	10.00	25.00
84 Beliveau 04Leg Sig/49	30.00	60.00
93 Roenick 03RK Upd/20	20.00	50.00
100 Theodore 03RK Upd/29	30.00	80.00
104 L.McDonald 04Leg Sig/48	15.00	40.00
114 Mari.Hossa 03Rookie Upd/18	20.00	40.00
139 M.Turco 03RK Upd/35	15.00	40.00
147 M.Noronen 03Rookie Upd/35	10.00	25.00
153 M.Bossy 04Legend Sig/47	12.00	30.00
156 M.Ribeiro 03Rookie Upd/53	10.00	25.00
161 Khabibulin 03RK Upd/26	25.00	60.00
164 R.Leach 04Leg Sig/24	15.00	40.00
165 R.Robert 04Leg Sig/24	8.00	20.00
169 R.Nash 03RK Upd/41	15.00	40.00
173 Luongo 03RK Upd/45	15.00	40.00
174 R.Smyth 03Beehive Jsy/20	12.00	30.00
187 S.Mikita 04Leg Sig/30	10.00	25.00
192 S.Sullivan 02UD Speed Demon/20	10.00	25.00
193 S.Sullivan 03Rookie Upd/26	10.00	25.00
194 T.Esposito 04Leg Sig/18	20.00	40.00
200 Z.Palffy 03Rookie Upd/32	10.00	25.00

2004-05 SP Authentic Rookie Redemptions

This 51-card set was issued in packs as redemption cards redeemable for rookies who first skated in the 2005-06 season. Cards RR1-RR30 are team specific and cards RR31-RR51 were "Wild" cards. Print run was limited to 399 copies each. Please note that due to a printing error, cards 41 and 42 have a "PP" prefix.

RR1 Corey Perry	12.00	30.00
RR2 Braydon Coburn	4.00	10.00
RR3 Hannu Toivonen	4.00	10.00
RR4 Thomas Vanek	8.00	20.00
RR5 Dion Phaneuf	12.00	30.00
RR6 Cam Ward	10.00	25.00
RR7 Brent Seabrook	6.00	15.00
RR8 Wojtek Wolski	8.00	20.00
RR9 Gilbert Brule	4.00	10.00
RR10 Jussi Jokinen	5.00	12.00
RR11 Jim Howard	10.00	25.00
RR12 Brad Winchester	4.00	10.00
RR13 Rostislav Olesz	3.00	8.00
RR14 George Parros	4.00	10.00
RR15 Matt Foy	4.00	10.00
RR16 Alexander Perezhogin	3.00	8.00
RR17 Ryan Suter	6.00	15.00
RR18 Zach Parise	10.00	25.00
RR19 Robert Nilsson	4.00	10.00
RR20 Henrik Lundqvist	15.00	40.00
RR21 Andrej Meszaros	3.00	8.00
RR22 Jeff Carter	8.00	20.00
RR23 David Leneveu	3.00	8.00
RR24 Sidney Crosby	125.00	250.00
RR25 Ryane Clowe	6.00	15.00
RR26 Jeff Woywitka	4.00	10.00
RR27 Evgeny Artyukhin	5.00	12.00
RR28 Alexander Steen	6.00	15.00
RR29 Rob McVicar	3.00	8.00
RR30 Alexander Ovechkin	60.00	120.00
RR31 Peter Budaj	5.00	12.00
RR32 Rene Bourque	4.00	10.00
RR33 Duncan Keith	8.00	20.00
RR34 Lee Stempniak	5.00	12.00
RR35 Andrew Alberts	3.00	8.00
RR36 Milan Jurcina	3.00	8.00
RR37 Yann Danis	4.00	10.00
RR38 Keith Ballard	4.00	10.00
RR39 Eric Nystrom	4.00	10.00
RR40 Mike Richards	12.00	30.00
PP41 Kevin Nastiuk	3.00	8.00
PP42 Petteri Nokelainen	3.00	8.00
RR43 Chris Campoli	3.00	8.00
RR44 Andrew Wozniewski	3.00	8.00
RR45 Ryan Getzlaf	12.00	30.00
RR46 Maxime Talbot	4.00	10.00
RR47 Petr Prucha	5.00	12.00
RR48 Johan Franzen	6.00	15.00
RR49 Brandon Bochenski	3.00	8.00
RR50 Patrick Eaves	5.00	12.00
RR51 Jim Slater	3.00	8.00

2004-05 SP Authentic Rookie Review Autographed Patches

This 42-card set featured certified player autographs along with jersey patch swatches. Each card was serial-numbered out of 100.

PRINT RUN 100 SER.#'d SETS

RRAB David Aebischer	20.00	50.00
RRAF Alexander Frolov	20.00	50.00
RRBR Martin Brodeur	60.00	120.00
RRCD Chris Drury	20.00	50.00
RRDA Daniel Briere	25.00	60.00
RRDB Dustin Brown	20.00	50.00
RRDL David Legwand	15.00	40.00
RRDW Doug Weight	15.00	40.00
RREJ Ed Jovanovski	12.00	30.00
RRHE Milan Hejduk	25.00	60.00
RRHV Martin Havlat	25.00	60.00
RRHZ Henrik Zetterberg	25.00	60.00
RRIG Jarome Iginla	50.00	125.00
RRIK Ilya Kovalchuk	25.00	60.00
RRJB Jay Bouwmeester	15.00	40.00
RRJK Jari Kurri	40.00	100.00
RRJL Joffrey Lupul	20.00	50.00
RRJR Jeremy Roenick	20.00	50.00
RRJT Joe Thornton	30.00	80.00
RRKL Kari Lehtonen	20.00	50.00
RRKP Keith Primeau	15.00	40.00
RRMA Maxim Afinogenov	15.00	40.00
RRMG Marian Gaborik	30.00	80.00
RRMH Marcel Hossa	15.00	40.00
RRMN Markus Naslund	20.00	50.00
RRMP Mark Parrish	20.00	50.00
RRMR Michael Ryder	20.00	50.00
RRMT Marty Turco	15.00	40.00
RRNS Nathan Smith	15.00	40.00
RRPB Patrice Bergeron/90	30.00	80.00
RRPS Philippe Sauve	15.00	40.00
RRRE Robert Esche	12.00	30.00
RRRL Roberto Luongo	30.00	80.00
RRRN Rick Nash	40.00	100.00
RRRS Ryan Smyth	15.00	40.00
RRSC Stanislav Chistov	15.00	40.00

RRSG Simon Gagne 15.00 40.00
RRSP Jason Spezza 30.00 80.00
RRSW Stephen Weiss 15.00 40.00
RRWG Wayne Gretzky/12
RRZC Zdeno Chara 20.00 50.00

2004-05 SP Authentic Sign of the Times

For 2004-05, the Sign of the Times set featured autograph cards carrying 1, 2, 3, 4, 5 and 6 player autographs. Single autographs were inserted at 1:20. Dual-player autos were serial-numbered to 100 (unless otherwise noted below). Triple-player autos were serial-numbered out of 25. Quad-player autos were serial-numbered out of 20. Five player-autos were serial numbered out of 15 and six player-autos were serial-numbered to just 10 copies each. Please note that card #SS-AWS contained two autographs of each of the three players depicted and was a 1/1.

STAB David Aebischer 5.00 12.00
STAF Maxim Afinogenov 15.00 40.00
STAH Ales Hemsky 6.00 15.00
STAR Andrew Raycroft 6.00 15.00
STAT Alex Tanguay 6.00 15.00
STBA Milan Bartovic 4.00 10.00
STBB Brad Boyes 5.00 12.00
STBI Martin Biron 6.00 15.00
STBL Brian Leetch SP 30.00 80.00
STBM Brenden Morrow 6.00 15.00
STBO Scotty Bowman SP 30.00 80.00
STBR Brad Richards 8.00 20.00
STCD Chris Drury 5.00 12.00
STCH Chris Higgins 6.00 15.00
STCP Chris Pronger 6.00 15.00
STDB Daniel Briere 6.00 15.00
STDC Don Cherry 15.00 40.00
STDH Dany Heatley SP 15.00 40.00
STDL David Legwand 5.00 12.00
STDR Dwayne Roloson 6.00 15.00
STDU Dustin Brown 6.00 15.00
STDW Doug Weight SP 10.00 25.00
STEC Erik Cole 5.00 12.00
STEJ Ed Jovanovski 5.00 12.00
STES Eric Staal 12.00 30.00
STFL Marc-Andre Fleury 12.00 30.00
STFM Frank Mahovlich SP 30.00 80.00
STFR Alexander Frolov 4.00 10.00
STFS Fredrik Sjostrom 4.00 10.00
STGA Marian Gaborik 12.00 30.00
STGE Georges Laraque 4.00 10.00
STGH Gordie Howe 50.00 100.00
STGI Gilbert Perreault SP 30.00 80.00
STGL Guy Lafleur SP 75.00 150.00
STHA Dominik Hasek SP 20.00 50.00
STHO Nathan Horton 5.00 12.00
STHZ Henrik Zetterberg 15.00 40.00
STIK Ilya Kovalchuk 15.00 40.00
STJB Jay Bouwmeester 5.00 12.00
STJG Jean-Sebastien Giguere 6.00 15.00
STJI Jarome Iginla 15.00 40.00
STJL Joffrey Lupul 6.00 15.00
STJO Jose Theodore SP 15.00 40.00
STJR Jeremy Roenick 10.00 25.00
STJT Joe Thornton 12.50 30.00
STKL Kari Lehtonen 8.00 20.00
STKU Jari Kurri 10.00 25.00
STLE Manny Legace 4.00 10.00
STLM Lanny McDonald 8.00 20.00
STLN Ladislav Nagy 4.00 10.00
STLO Matthew Lombardi 4.00 10.00
STMA Marcel Hossa 4.00 10.00
STMB Martin Brodeur SP 75.00 150.00
STMH Milan Hejduk 8.00 20.00
STMJ Matt Stajan 5.00 12.00
STML John-Michael Liles 4.00 10.00
STMN Markus Naslund 6.00 15.00
STMO Brendan Morrison 5.00 12.00
STMP Michael Peca 5.00 12.00
STMT Marty Turco 6.00 15.00
STNK Nikolai Khabibulin 10.00 25.00
STNS Nathan Smith 4.00 10.00
STNZ Nikolai Zherdev 6.00 15.00
STPA Mark Parrish 4.00 10.00
STPB Patrice Bergeron 12.00 30.00
STPR Patrick Roy SP 150.00 300.00
STPS Philippe Sauve 4.00 10.00
STPW Peter Worrell 4.00 10.00
STRE Robert Esche 4.00 10.00
STRL Roberto Luongo 8.00 20.00
STRN Rick Nash 12.50 30.00
STRR Robyn Regehr 4.00 10.00
STRS Ryan Smyth 6.00 15.00
STRY Michael Ryder 6.00 15.00
STSC Stanislav Chistov 4.00 10.00
STSD Shane Doan 5.00 12.00
STSG Simon Gagne 8.00 20.00
STSK Saku Koivu 10.00 25.00
STSP Jason Spezza SP 25.00 50.00
STST Martin St. Louis 6.00 15.00
STSU Steve Sullivan 4.00 10.00
STSW Stephen Weiss 5.00 12.00
STTA Tyler Arnason 4.00 10.00
STTH Trent Hunter 4.00 10.00
STTU Tuomo Ruutu 6.00 15.00
STVL Vincent Lecavalier SP 125.00 250.00
STWG Wayne Gretzky SP 125.00 250.00
STZC Zdeno Chara 10.00 25.00
DSPR Perreault/Robert/25 25.00 60.00
DSAH Alfredsson/Hossa/100 12.00 30.00
DSBC Bowman/Cherry/25 60.00 120.00
DSBD M.Biron/C.Drury/100 10.00 25.00
DSBR Brodeur/Roy/25 150.00 300.00
DSBT Bossy/Trottier/25 50.00 125.00
DSCR R.Esche/J.Roenick/100 12.50 30.00
DSDS S.Doan/F.Sjostrom/100 10.00 25.00
DSEE T.Espo/P.Espo/25 75.00 125.00
DSFH G.Fuhr/G.Hall/25 50.00 100.00
DSHG Howe/Gretzky/25 400.00 650.00
DSHH M.Hossa/M.Hossa/100 15.00 40.00
DSHS D.Hasek/J.Spezza/100 20.00 50.00
DSIR J.Iginla/R.Regehr/100 20.00 50.00
DSKL Khabibulin/R.Luongo/100 20.00 50.00
DSKN Kovalchuk/Lehtonen/100 20.00 50.00
DSLB B.Leetch/E.Belfour/100 25.00 60.00
DSLK St.Louis/Kovalchuk/100 30.00 80.00
DSLL St. Louis/Lecavalier/25 30.00 80.00
DSLW G.Laraque/P.Worrell/100 12.00 30.00
DSMJ M.Ryder/J.Theodore/100 12.00 30.00
DSMT B.Morrow/M.Turco/100 12.00 30.00
DSMZ Naslund/Zetterberg/100 15.00 40.00
DSNH C.Neely/G.Howe/25 75.00 150.00
DSNJ Naslund/Jovanvski/100 15.00 40.00
DSNK Nabokov/Khabablin/100 12.00 30.00
DSNZ R.Nash/N.Zherdev/100 20.00 50.00
DSPH M.Peca/T.Hunter/100 10.00 25.00
DSPM P.Bergeron/M.Ryder/100 15.00 40.00
DSPW C.Pronger/D.Weight/100 12.00 30.00
DSRA R.Smyth/A.Hemsky/100 15.00 40.00
DSRL Raycroft/Lehtonen/100 15.00 40.00
DSRP R.Bourque/C.Neely/100 30.00 80.00
DSRR M.Ryder/M.Ribeiro/100 12.00 30.00
DSRT Raycroft/J.Thornton/100 15.00 40.00
DSSH J.Spezza/M.Havlat/100 15.00 40.00
DSST E.Staal/J.Thornton/100 25.00 60.00
DSTN J.Thornton/C.Neely/100 20.00 50.00
DSWL S.Weiss/R.Luongo/100 15.00 40.00
TSBNT Bourq/Neely/Thorn 75.00 150.00
TSBTG Bossy/Trottier/Gillies 75.00 125.00
TSCLR Clarke/Leach/Roenick 75.00 150.00
TSGKF Gretzky/Kurri/Fuhr 400.00 700.00
TSGRE Gagne/Roenick/Esche 30.00 80.00
TSHLK Heatly/Lehtnen/Kovlchk 75.00 150.00
TSHTA Hejduk/Tang/Aebischer 40.00 80.00
TSIKN Iginla/Kovalchuk/Nash 100.00 250.00
TSILN Iginla/St. Louis/Nash 75.00 150.00
TSKLL Khabi/Luongo/Lehton 50.00 125.00
TSLPJ Leetch/Pronger/Jovo 40.00 100.00
TSLRZ Lupul/Ruutu/Zherdev 25.00 60.00
TSLWH Luongo/Weiss/Horton 60.00 150.00
TSNSS Nash/Spezza/Staal 125.00 250.00
TSPBF Palffy/Brown/Frolov 25.00 60.00
TSRBT Raycroft/Belfour/Turco 50.00 120.00
TSRKR Ribeiro/Koivu/Ryder 50.00 100.00
TSRLB Roy/Luongo/Brodeur 250.00 500.00
TSSHZ Staal/Horton/Zherdev 50.00 100.00
TSTRB Thorntn/Raycrft/Brgrn 40.00 100.00
QSHRBG Bo.Hull/Robit/Bcyk/Gill 60.00 120.00
QSBBLK Berg/Brown/Lupul/Kslr 60.00 120.00
QSBDPB Beliv/Dnne/Perr/Bossy 90.00 150.00
QSBPBP Brqe/Prngr/Bouw/Pitk 60.00 120.00
QSBTCR Bcyk/Thrn/Chvrs/Rycr 50.00 100.00
QSFBRE Fuhr/Brod/Roy/T.Espo 175.00 300.00
QSFSHZ M.Flry/Staal/Hrtn/Zhrdv 50.00 100.00
QSGPRE Ggne/Prim/Rnick/Esch 60.00 120.00
QSGTDC Grzky/Thrn/Dnne/Clrk 250.00 400.00
QSHINS Hejd/Ignla/Nash/St.Lou 75.00 150.00
QSIKHL Iginl/Kbas/Hejduk/Liles 60.00 120.00
QSLKSN St.L/Koval/Hossa/Nasl 60.00 120.00
QSLRLK St.L/Rich/Lecav/Khab 75.00 150.00
QSMHCL Mikta/Bo.Hll/Clrke/Lch 75.00 150.00
QSNHKS Nash/Heat/Koval/Berg 75.00 150.00
QSTAHS Tang/Aebs/Hjdk/Sve 60.00 120.00
QSTPLS Thrnt/Prim/Lecav/Staal 75.00 150.00
QSVANC Nslnd/Mrrsn/Jovan/Kslr 50.00 100.00

2004-05 SP Authentic UD Promos

*UD PROMO: .8X TO 2X BASIC CARDS
1 Jean-Sebastien Giguere .60 1.50
2 Joffrey Lupul .50 1.25
3 Sergei Fedorov 1.00 2.50
4 Dany Heatley .60 1.50
5 Ilya Kovalchuk .60 1.50
6 Kari Lehtonen .75 2.00
7 Andrew Raycroft .50 1.25
8 Joe Thornton .75 2.00
9 Patrice Bergeron .75 2.00
10 Glen Murray .50 1.25
11 Mika Noronen .50 1.25
12 Miroslav Satan .50 1.25
13 Maxim Afinogenov .40 1.00
14 Jarome Iginla .60 1.50
15 Matthew Lombardi .40 1.00
16 Miikka Kiprusoff .50 1.25
17 Eric Staal .75 2.00
18 Erik Cole .50 1.25
19 Tyler Arnason .40 1.00
20 Tuomo Ruutu .50 1.25
21 David Aebischer .50 1.25
22 Joe Sakic 1.00 2.50
23 Peter Forsberg .75 2.00
24 Milan Hejduk .50 1.25
25 Alex Tanguay .50 1.25
26 Rick Nash .60 1.50
27 Nikolai Zherdev .50 1.25
28 Mike Modano 1.00 2.50
29 Bill Guerin .60 1.50
30 Marty Turco .60 1.50
31 Manny Legace .50 1.25
32 Pavel Datsyuk .75 2.00
33 Brendan Shanahan .75 2.00
34 Steve Yzerman 2.00 5.00
35 Henrik Zetterberg .75 2.00
36 Jason Smith .40 1.00
37 Ryan Smyth .50 1.25
38 Ty Conklin .50 1.25
39 Nathan Horton .60 1.50
40 Roberto Luongo 1.00 2.50
41 Olli Jokinen .50 1.25
42 Alexander Frolov .50 1.25
43 Zigmund Palffy .60 1.50
44 Marian Gaborik 1.00 2.50
45 Manny Fernandez .50 1.25
46 Michael Ryder .50 1.25
47 Jose Theodore .60 1.50
48 Saku Koivu .60 1.50
49 Steve Sullivan .40 1.00
50 Jordin Tootoo .40 1.00
51 Tomas Vokoun .50 1.25
52 Martin Brodeur 1.25 3.00
53 Patrik Elias .60 1.50
54 Scott Stevens .60 1.50
55 Eric Lindros 1.00 2.50
56 Mark Messier 1.50 4.00
57 Jaromir Jagr 1.50 4.00
58 Michael Peca .50 1.25
59 Rick DiPietro .50 1.25
60 Daniel Alfredsson .60 1.50
61 Marian Hossa .50 1.25
62 Jason Spezza .60 1.50
63 Martin Havlat .60 1.50
64 Dominik Hasek 1.00 2.50
65 Jeremy Roenick .60 1.50
66 Robert Esche .50 1.25
67 Simon Gagne .60 1.50
68 Brett Hull .75 2.00
69 Mike Comrie .50 1.25
70 Shane Doan .50 1.25
71 Marc-Andre Fleury 1.50 4.00
72 Mario Lemieux 2.00 5.00
73 Mark Recchi .75 2.00
74 Evgeni Nabokov .50 1.25
75 Patrick Marleau .60 1.50
76 Chris Pronger .50 1.25
77 Doug Weight .60 1.50
78 Keith Tkachuk .60 1.50
79 Brad Richards .60 1.50
80 Nikolai Khabibulin .60 1.50
81 Martin St. Louis .60 1.50
82 Vincent Lecavalier .50 1.25
83 Owen Nolan .50 1.25
84 Ed Belfour .60 1.50
85 Mats Sundin .60 1.50
86 Gary Roberts .40 1.00
87 Ed Jovanovski .50 1.25
88 Markus Naslund .60 1.50
89 Trevor Linden .60 1.50
90 Olaf Kolzig .60 1.50

2005-06 SP Authentic

COMP.SET w/o SP's (100) 12.50 30.00
101-130 STATED PRINT RUN 999
131-220 PRINT RUN 999
221-287 STATED PRINT RUN 1999
288-290 ISSUED IN ROOKIE UPDATE
1 Jean-Sebastien Giguere .40 1.00
2 Joffrey Lupul .30 .75
3 Teemu Selanne .75 2.00
4 Scott Niedermayer .40 1.00
5 Ilya Kovalchuk .40 1.00
6 Kari Lehtonen .30 .75
7 Marian Hossa .30 .75
8 Sergei Samsonov .30 .75
9 Brian Leetch .40 1.00
10 Andrew Raycroft .30 .75
11 Patrice Bergeron .50 1.25
12 Glen Murray .30 .75
13 Chris Drury .30 .75
14 Martin Biron .30 .75
15 Daniel Briere .40 1.00
16 Jarome Iginla .40 1.00
17 Miikka Kiprusoff .30 .75
18 Doug Weight .40 1.00
19 Martin Gerber .30 .75
20 Eric Staal .50 1.25
21 Nikolai Khabibulin .40 1.00
22 Tuomo Ruutu .40 1.00
23 Eric Daze .30 .75
24 Joe Sakic .60 1.50
25 Alex Tanguay .40 1.00
26 Milan Hejduk .30 .75
27 David Aebischer .30 .75
28 Rob Blake .40 1.00
29 Rick Nash .40 1.00
30 Sergei Fedorov .60 1.50
31 Mike Modano .60 1.50
32 Marty Turco .40 1.00
33 Bill Guerin .40 1.00
34 Brendan Shanahan .50 1.25
35 Steve Yzerman 1.00 2.50
36 Henrik Zetterberg .50 1.25
37 Pavel Datsyuk .50 1.25
38 Gordie Howe 1.25 3.00
39 Chris Pronger .30 .75
40 Michael Peca .30 .75
41 Ryan Smyth .30 .75
42 Wayne Gretzky 2.00 5.00
43 Roberto Luongo .60 1.50
44 Olli Jokinen .40 1.00
45 Luc Robitaille .40 1.00
46 Jeremy Roenick .40 1.00
47 Alexander Frolov .25 .60
48 Pavol Demitra .50 1.25
49 Marian Gaborik .60 1.50
50 Dwayne Roloson .30 .75
51 Jose Theodore .40 1.00
52 Saku Koivu .40 1.00
53 Mike Ribeiro .30 .75
54 Michael Ryder .30 .75
55 Paul Kariya .50 1.25
56 Tomas Vokoun .30 .75
57 Martin Brodeur .75 2.00
58 Patrik Elias .40 1.00
59 Scott Gomez .30 .75
60 Brian Gionta .30 .75
61 Miroslav Satan .30 .75
62 Alexei Yashin .30 .75
63 Rick DiPietro .30 .75
64 Mark Parrish .25 .60
65 Jaromir Jagr 1.00 2.50
66 Martin Straka .25 .60
67 Dominik Hasek .60 1.50
68 Dany Heatley .40 1.00
69 Wade Redden .25 .60
70 Martin Havlat .40 1.00
71 Daniel Alfredsson .40 1.00
72 Jason Spezza .40 1.00
73 Peter Forsberg .50 1.25
74 Keith Primeau .40 1.00
75 Simon Gagne .40 1.00
76 Robert Esche .30 .75
77 Shane Doan .30 .75
78 Curtis Joseph .40 1.00
79 Mario Lemieux 1.25 3.00
80 Zigmund Palffy .40 1.00
81 Mark Recchi .50 1.25
82 Jonathan Cheechoo .40 1.00
83 Evgeni Nabokov .30 .75
84 Patrick Marleau .40 1.00
85 Joe Thornton .50 1.25
86 Barret Jackman .25 .60
87 Keith Tkachuk .40 1.00
88 Martin St. Louis .40 1.00
89 Vincent Lecavalier .30 .75
90 Brad Richards .40 1.00
91 Sean Burke .25 .60
92 Eric Lindros .60 1.50
93 Mats Sundin .40 1.00
94 Ed Belfour .40 1.00
95 Matt Stajan .30 .75
96 Jason Allison .30 .75
97 Todd Bertuzzi .40 1.00
98 Markus Naslund .40 1.00
99 Brendan Morrison .25 .60
100 Olaf Kolzig .40 1.00
101 Mario Lemieux/999 6.00 15.00
102 Joe Sakic/999 3.00 8.00
103 Jaromir Jagr/999 5.00 12.00
104 Mike Modano/999 3.00 8.00
105 Dominik Hasek/999 3.00 8.00
106 Ilya Kovalchuk/999 2.00 5.00
107 Steve Yzerman/999 5.00 12.00
108 Nikolai Khabibulin/999 2.00 5.00
109 Joe Thornton/999 2.50 6.00
110 Jarome Iginla/999 2.00 5.00
111 Martin St. Louis/999 2.00 5.00
112 Paul Kariya/999 2.50 6.00
113 Martin Brodeur/999 4.00 10.00
114 Mats Sundin/999 2.00 5.00
115 Peter Forsberg/999 2.50 6.00
116 Jean-Sebastien Giguere/999 2.00 5.00
117 Marian Hossa/999 1.50 4.00
118 Alex Tanguay/999 2.00 5.00
119 Rick Nash/999 2.00 5.00
120 Jeremy Roenick/999 2.00 5.00
121 Dany Heatley/999 2.00 5.00
122 Brendan Shanahan/999 2.50 6.00
123 Jose Theodore/999 2.00 5.00
124 Patrik Elias/999 2.00 5.00
125 Curtis Joseph/999 2.00 5.00
126 Evgeni Nabokov/999 1.50 4.00
127 Vincent Lecavalier/999 1.50 4.00
128 Markus Naslund/999 2.00 5.00
129 Olaf Kolzig/999 2.00 5.00
130 Doug Weight/999 2.00 5.00
131 Ryan Getzlaf AU RC 25.00 60.00
132 Corey Perry AU RC 25.00 60.00
133 Braydon Coburn AU RC 6.00 15.00
134 Jim Slater AU RC 5.00 12.00
135 Hannu Toivonen AU RC 6.00 15.00
136 Andrew Alberts AU RC 4.00 10.00
137 Milan Jurcina AU RC 5.00 12.00
138 Kevin Dallman AU RC 5.00 12.00
139 Thomas Vanek AU RC 12.00 30.00
140 Dion Phaneuf AU RC 8.00 20.00
141 Eric Nystrom AU RC 5.00 12.00
142 Cam Ward AU RC 12.00 30.00
143 Kevin Nastiuk AU RC 4.00 10.00
144 Niklas Nordgren AU RC 6.00 15.00
145 Brent Seabrook AU RC 20.00 50.00
146 Cam Barker AU RC 25.00 60.00
147 Duncan Keith AU RC 50.00 125.00
148 Rene Bourque AU RC 6.00 15.00
149 Wojtek Wolski AU RC 6.00 15.00
150 Peter Budaj AU RC 8.00 20.00
151 Gilbert Brule AU RC 6.00 15.00
152 Jaroslav Balastik AU RC 4.00 10.00
153 Jussi Jokinen AU RC 6.00 15.00
154 Johan Franzen AU RC 10.00 25.00
155 Jim Howard AU RC 12.00 30.00
156 Brett Lebda AU RC 4.00 10.00
157 Brad Winchester AU RC 6.00 15.00
158 Rostislav Olesz AU RC 5.00 12.00
159 Anthony Stewart AU RC 5.00 12.00
160 George Parros AU RC 5.00 12.00
161 Matt Foy AU RC 4.00 10.00
162 Derek Boogaard AU RC 8.00 20.00
163 Alexander Perezhogin AU RC 5.00 12.00
164 Yann Danis AU RC 5.00 12.00
165 Raitis Ivanans AU RC 4.00 10.00
166 Ryan Suter AU RC 8.00 20.00
167 Zach Parise AU RC 15.00 40.00
168 Robert Nilsson AU RC 6.00 15.00
169 Petteri Nokelainen AU RC 4.00 10.00
170 Al Montoya AU RC 6.00 15.00
171 Henrik Lundqvist AU RC 60.00 150.00
172 Petr Prucha AU RC 4.00 10.00
173 Ryan Hollweg AU RC 4.00 10.00
174 Patrick Eaves AU RC 6.00 15.00
175 Brandon Bochenski AU RC 6.00 15.00
176 Andrej Meszaros AU RC 5.00 12.00
177 Jeff Carter AU RC 12.00 30.00
178 Mike Richards AU RC 10.00 25.00
179 David Leneveu AU RC 4.00 10.00
180 Keith Ballard AU RC 4.00 10.00
181 Sidney Crosby AU RC 700.00 1000.00
182 Maxime Talbot AU RC 6.00 15.00
183 Josh Gorges AU RC 5.00 12.00
184 Ryane Clowe AU RC 8.00 20.00
185 Jay McClement AU RC 4.00 10.00
186 Jeff Hoggan AU RC 4.00 10.00
187 Jeff Woywitka AU RC 4.00 10.00
188 Alexander Steen AU RC 8.00 20.00
189 Andy Wozniewski AU RC 5.00 12.00
190 Alexander Ovechkin AU RC 250.00 500.00
191 Ryan Whitney AU RC 6.00 15.00
192 R.J. Umberger AU RC 6.00 15.00
193 Mikko Koivu AU RC 6.00 15.00
194 Steve Bernier AU RC 6.00 15.00
195 Timo Helbling AU RC 4.00 10.00
196 Ryan Craig AU RC 4.00 10.00
197 Valtteri Filppula AU RC 8.00 20.00
198 Daniel Paille AU RC 6.00 15.00
199 Danny Richmond AU RC 4.00 10.00
200 Maxim Lapierre AU RC 6.00 15.00
201 Barry Tallackson AU RC 5.00 12.00
202 Chris Campoli AU RC 4.00 10.00
203 Jeremy Colliton AU RC 4.00 10.00
204 Christoph Schubert AU RC 4.00 10.00
205 Kevin Bieksa AU RC 8.00 20.00
206 Jordan Sigalet AU RC 4.00 10.00
207 Adam Berkhoel AU RC 5.00 12.00
208 Erik Christensen AU RC 4.00 10.00
209 Ole-Kristian Tollefsen AU RC 5.00 12.00
210 Dimitri Patzold AU RC 4.00 10.00
211 Brad Richardson AU RC 6.00 15.00
212 Lee Stempniak AU RC 6.00 15.00
213 Andrei Kostitsyn AU RC 8.00 20.00
214 Evgeny Artyukhin AU RC 5.00 12.00
215 Ben Eager AU RC 5.00 12.00
216 Andrew Ladd AU RC 8.00 20.00
217 Jeff Tambellini AU RC 4.00 10.00
218 Kyle Quincey AU RC 5.00 12.00
219 Tomas Fleischmann AU RC 6.00 15.00
220 Jakub Klepis AU RC 4.00 10.00
221 Michael Wall RC 2.00 5.00
222 Zenon Konopka RC 1.50 4.00
223 Vojtech Polak RC 1.50 4.00
224 Martin St. Pierre RC 1.50 4.00
225 Steve Goertzen RC 1.50 4.00
226 Andrew Penner RC 2.00 5.00
227 Danny Syvret RC 1.50 4.00
228 Jeff Giuliano RC 2.00 5.00
229 Adam Hauser RC 2.00 5.00
230 Kyle Brodziak RC 1.50 4.00
231 Cam Janssen RC 2.00 5.00
232 Kevin Colley RC 2.00 5.00
233 Chris Holt RC 1.50 4.00
234 Greg Jacina RC 1.50 4.00
235 Yanick Lehoux RC 2.50 6.00
236 Brian McGrattan RC 1.50 4.00
237 Colin Hemingway RC 1.50 4.00
238 Paul Ranger RC 1.50 4.00
239 Gerald Coleman RC 1.50 4.00
240 Dennis Wideman RC 1.50 4.00
241 Junior Lessard RC 1.50 4.00
242 Matt Jones RC 1.50 4.00
243 Brian Eklund RC 2.00 5.00
244 Nick Tarnasky RC 1.50 4.00
245 Bruno Gervais RC 1.50 4.00
246 Staffan Kronwall RC 1.50 4.00
247 Dustin Penner RC 2.50 6.00
248 Kevin Klein RC 1.50 4.00
249 Rob McVicar RC 2.00 5.00
250 Eric Healey RC 2.00 5.00
251 Ben Guite RC 2.00 5.00
252 Nathan Paetsch RC 2.00 5.00
253 Jiri Novotny RC 2.00 5.00
254 Richie Regehr RC 1.50 4.00
255 Mark Giordano RC 2.50 6.00
256 Chad Larose RC 1.50 4.00
257 Corey Crawford RC 8.00 20.00
258 Vitaly Kolesnik RC 2.00 5.00
259 Geoff Platt RC 2.00 5.00
260 Matt Greene RC 1.50 4.00
261 Jean-Francois Jacques RC 1.50 4.00
262 Rob Globke RC 1.50 4.00
263 Petr Taticek RC 2.00 5.00
264 Petr Kanko RC 2.00 5.00
265 Matt Ryan RC 2.00 5.00
266 Connor James RC 2.00 5.00
267 Richard Petiot RC 2.00 5.00
268 Mark Streit RC 1.50 4.00
269 Jean-Philippe Cote RC 1.50 4.00
270 Jonathan Ferland RC 2.00 5.00
271 Pekka Rinne RC 10.00 25.00
272 Jason Ryznar RC 1.50 4.00
273 Josh Gratton RC 2.00 5.00
274 Alexandre Picard RC 1.50 4.00
275 Colby Armstrong RC 2.50 6.00
276 Grant Stevenson RC 1.50 4.00
277 Doug Murray RC 1.50 4.00
278 Chris Beckford-Tseu RC 2.00 5.00
279 Jon DiSalvatore RC 2.00 5.00
280 Mike Glumac RC 2.00 5.00
281 Darren Reid RC 1.50 4.00
282 Doug O'Brien RC 1.50 4.00
283 Jay Harrison RC 2.00 5.00
284 Rick Rypien RC 3.00 8.00
285 Alexandre Burrows RC 3.00 8.00
286 David Steckel RC 2.00 5.00
287 Mike Green RC 3.00 8.00
288 Ben Walter AU RC 4.00 10.00
289 Alexandre Picard AU RC 4.00 10.00
290 Chris Thorburn AU RC 5.00 12.00

2005-06 SP Authentic Limited

*1-100 VETS: 6X TO 15X BASIC CARDS
*101-130 VETS: 1.2X TO 3X BASIC CARDS
*131-220 ROOK.JSY AU: 1X TO 2.5X BASIC RC
*221-287 ROOKIES: 1.5X TO 4X BASIC RC
STATED PRINT RUN 100 SERIAL #'d SETS
147 D.Keith PATCH AU 100.00 200.00
181 S.Crosby PATCH AU 750.00 1200.00
190 A. Ovechkin PATCH AU 250.00 500.00

2005-06 SP Authentic Chirography

PRINT RUN 50 SER.#'d SETS
SPAR Andrew Raycroft 10.00 25.00
SPAT Alex Tanguay 10.00 25.00
SPAY Alexei Yashin 8.00 20.00
SPCP Chris Pronger 10.00 25.00
SPDH Dany Heatley 12.00 30.00
SPEB Ed Belfour 10.00 25.00
SPEN Evgeni Nabokov 10.00 25.00
SPHK Dominik Hasek 20.00 50.00
SPHV Martin Havlat 10.00 25.00
SPIK Ilya Kovalchuk 20.00 50.00
SPJG Jean-Sebastien Giguere 10.00 25.00
SPJI Jarome Iginla 15.00 40.00
SPJO Joe Thornton 25.00 50.00
SPJR Jeremy Roenick 20.00 50.00
SPJT Jose Theodore 12.00 30.00
SPMB Martin Brodeur 40.00 100.00
SPMG Marian Gaborik 20.00 50.00
SPMH Milan Hejduk 8.00 20.00
SPML Manny Legace 8.00 20.00
SPMM Mike Modano 15.00 40.00
SPMN Markus Naslund 10.00 25.00
SPOK Olaf Kolzig 12.00 30.00
SPPB Patrice Bergeron 10.00 25.00
SPRL Roberto Luongo 15.00 40.00
SPRN Rick Nash 15.00 40.00
SPSL Martin St. Louis 10.00 25.00
SPTV Tomas Vokoun 10.00 25.00
SPVL Vincent Lecavalier 25.00 60.00

2005-06 SP Authentic Marks of Distinction

STATED PRINT RUN 25 SERIAL #'d SETS
MDAO Alexander Ovechkin 200.00 300.00
MDAR Andrew Raycroft 15.00 40.00
MDAT Alex Tanguay 20.00 50.00
MDAY Alexei Yashin 8.00 20.00
MDBL Brian Leetch 20.00 50.00
MDBO Ray Bourque 60.00 120.00
MDBR Brad Richards 25.00 60.00
MDCP Chris Pronger 20.00 50.00
MDDH Dany Heatley 25.00 60.00
MDDW Doug Weight 15.00 40.00
MDEB Ed Belfour 50.00 100.00
MDGH Gordie Howe 100.00 200.00
MDGL Guy Lafleur 50.00 125.00
MDHV Martin Havlat 12.00 30.00
MDIK Ilya Kovalchuk 30.00 80.00
MDJC Jonathan Cheechoo 30.00 60.00
MDJG Jean-Sebastien Giguere 20.00 40.00
MDJI Jarome Iginla 40.00 80.00
MDJO Joe Thornton 40.00 80.00
MDJR Jeremy Roenick 25.00 60.00
MDJS Jason Spezza 20.00 50.00
MDJT Jose Theodore 30.00 60.00
MDKL Kari Lehtonen 25.00 60.00
MDKP Keith Primeau 12.00 30.00
MDMD Marcel Dionne 30.00 60.00
MDMH Milan Hejduk 15.00 40.00
MDMM Mike Modano 30.00 60.00
MDMN Markus Naslund 15.00 40.00
MDMS Mats Sundin
MDPB Patrice Bergeron 25.00 50.00
MDPE Phil Esposito 30.00 60.00
MDPR Patrick Roy 100.00 200.00
MDRB Rob Blake 12.00 30.00
MDRL Roberto Luongo 50.00 100.00
MDRN Rick Nash 50.00 100.00
MDSC Sidney Crosby 400.00 800.00
MDSG Simon Gagne 12.00 30.00
MDSK Saku Koivu 40.00 80.00
MDSL Martin St. Louis 20.00 50.00
MDSN Scott Niedermayer 15.00 40.00
MDVL Vincent Lecavalier 40.00 80.00

2005-06 SP Authentic Prestigious Pairings

PPBN Bourque/Neely/50 40.00 80.00
PPBP Blake/Pronger/100 15.00 40.00
PPBS Belfour/Sundin/50
PPCE Cheevers/P. Espo/50
PPCR Carter/Richards/100 30.00 80.00
PPDT Dionne/Taylor/100 25.00 60.00
PPEP Esche/Pitkanen/100 5.00 12.00
PPFK Fuhr/Kurri/50 25.00 60.00
PPGR Gaborik/Roloson/100 12.00 30.00
PPGS Lafleur/Koivu/50 25.00 60.00
PPHB Horton/Bouw./100
PPHE Bo.Hull/T.Espo/50 60.00 150.00
PPHG Howe/Gretzky/50 275.00 400.00
PPHV Hasek/Vokoun/100 15.00 40.00
PPIS Iginla/St. Louis/50 20.00 50.00
PPKN Khabi./Nabokov/100 8.00 20.00
PPLH Legace/Howard/100 15.00 40.00
PPLK Lehtonen/Koval./100 15.00 40.00
PPLM Lundqvist/Montoya/100 15.00 40.00
PPLR Lecav./Richards/100 20.00 50.00
PPMB Miller/Biron/100 20.00 50.00
PPNL Naslund/Linden/100 20.00 50.00
PPNZ Nash/Zherdev/100 15.00 40.00
PPOS Olesz/Stewart/100 5.00 12.00
PPPG Perry/Getzlaf/100 20.00 50.00
PPPH Parrish/Hunter/100 5.00 12.00
PPPN Phan./Nyst./100 30.00 80.00
PPPO Phanf/Ovech/50 EXCH 100.00 200.00
PPPV Perreault/Vanek/100 15.00 40.00
PPRA Ruutu/Arnason/100 5.00 12.00
PPRB Roy/Brodeur/50 125.00 250.00
PPRP Recchi/Palffy/100
PPRR Ryder/Ribeiro/100 8.00 20.00
PPTB Trottier/Bossy/50 15.00 40.00
PPTC Thornton/Cheech/100 25.00 60.00
PPTF Thibault/Fleury/100 12.00 30.00
PPTW Tkachuk/Weight/100
PPTZ Turco/Zubov/100 8.00 20.00

2005-06 SP Authentic Rookie Authentics

STATED PRINT RUN 250 SER.#'d SETS
RAAM Andrej Meszaros 8.00 20.00
RAAO Alexander Ovechkin 75.00 150.00
RAAP Alexander Perezhogin 8.00 20.00
RAAS Alexander Steen 10.00 25.00
RABC Braydon Coburn 8.00 20.00
RABS Brent Seabrook 8.00 20.00
RABW Brad Winchester 8.00 20.00
RACB Cam Barker
RACP Corey Perry 12.00 30.00
RACW Cam Ward 12.00 30.00
RADP Dion Phaneuf
RAEN Eric Nystrom 8.00 20.00
RAGB Gilbert Brule 10.00 25.00
RAHL Henrik Lundqvist 20.00 50.00
RAHT Hannu Toivonen 8.00 20.00
RAJC Jeff Carter 15.00 40.00
RAJH Jim Howard 15.00 40.00
RAJJ Jussi Jokinen 8.00 20.00
RAJW Jeff Woywitka 8.00 20.00
RAKB Keith Ballard 8.00 20.00
RAMR Mike Richards 12.00 30.00
RARG Ryan Getzlaf 12.00 30.00
RARN Robert Nilsson 8.00 20.00
RARO Rostislav Olesz 10.00 25.00
RARS Ryan Suter 10.00 25.00
RAST Anthony Stewart 8.00 20.00
RATV Thomas Vanek 15.00 40.00
RAWW Wojtek Wolski 10.00 25.00
RAYD Yann Danis 8.00 20.00
RAZP Zach Parise 20.00 50.00

2005-06 SP Authentic Scripts to Success

PRINT RUN 100 SER.#'d SETS
SSAF Alexander Frolov 6.00 15.00
SSAH Ales Hemsky 6.00 15.00
SSAR Andrew Raycroft 6.00 15.00
SSCB Christian Backman 4.00 10.00
SSCC Carlo Colaiacovo 4.00 10.00
SSDB Dustin Brown 6.00 15.00
SSDF Dan Fritsche 4.00 10.00
SSES Eric Staal 12.00 30.00
SSFT Fedor Tyutin 4.00 10.00
SSHZ Henrik Zetterberg 10.00 25.00
SSJB Jay Bouwmeester 6.00 15.00
SSJC Jonathan Cheechoo 8.00 20.00
SSJL Jamie Lundmark 4.00 10.00
SSJM John-Michael Liles 4.00 10.00
SSJP Joni Pitkanen 4.00 10.00
SSJR Jani Rita 4.00 10.00
SSKL Kari Lehtonen 10.00 25.00
SSLU Joffrey Lupul 4.00 10.00
SSMF Marc-Andre Fleury 12.00 30.00
SSMH Marcel Hossa 4.00 10.00
SSMR Mike Ribeiro 4.00 10.00
SSMS Matt Stajan 5.00 12.00
SSPB Patrice Bergeron 12.00 30.00
SSPL Pascal Leclaire 4.00 10.00
SSPS Philippe Sauve 6.00 15.00
SSRK Ryan Kesler 6.00 15.00
SSRM Ryan Miller 12.00 30.00
SSRY Michael Ryder 8.00 20.00
SSTA Tyler Arnason 4.00 10.00
SSTR Tuomo Ruutu 10.00 25.00

2005-06 SP Authentic Sign of the Times

STATED ODDS 1:24
AF Alexander Frolov 3.00 8.00
AR Andrew Raycroft 4.00 10.00
AT Jason Arnott 4.00 10.00
AY Alexei Yashin 4.00 10.00
BL Brett Lebda 3.00 8.00
BO Derek Boogaard 8.00 20.00
BR Brian Rafalski 4.00 10.00
BW Jay Bouwmeester 5.00 12.00
CB Christian Backman 3.00 8.00
CC Carlo Colaiacovo 3.00 8.00
CO Craig Conroy 3.00 8.00
CP Chris Pronger SP 8.00 20.00
CS Cory Stillman 3.00 8.00
DB Dustin Brown 5.00 12.00
DC Dan Cloutier 4.00 10.00
DF Dan Fritsche 3.00 8.00
DH Dany Heatley SP 15.00 40.00
DK Duncan Keith 15.00 40.00
DW Doug Weight 5.00 12.00
ED Eric Daze 4.00 10.00
ES Eric Staal 8.00 20.00
FT Fedor Tyutin 3.00 8.00
GL Georges Laraque 4.00 10.00
GM Glen Murray SP 15.00 40.00
GP George Parros 3.00 8.00
HE Timo Helbling 3.00 8.00
HG Jeff Hoggan 3.00 8.00
HO Marcel Hossa 3.00 8.00
HV Martin Havlat 5.00 12.00
HZ Henrik Zetterberg 6.00 15.00
IL Ian Laperriere 3.00 8.00
JA Jani Rita 3.00 8.00
JB Jaroslav Balastik 3.00 8.00
JC Jonathan Cheechoo 5.00 12.00
JH Jochen Hecht 3.00 8.00
JI Jarome Iginla SP 20.00 50.00
JL Jamie Lundmark 3.00 8.00
JM John-Michael Liles 3.00 8.00
JO Jeff O'Neill 3.00 8.00
JP Joni Pitkanen 3.00 8.00
JR Jeremy Roenick SP 15.00 40.00
JS Jim Slater 4.00 10.00
JT Jocelyn Thibault 4.00 10.00
KD Kris Draper 6.00 15.00
KE Kevin Dallman 4.00 10.00
KH Kristian Huselius 3.00 8.00
KL Kari Lehtonen 4.00 10.00
KP Keith Primeau 5.00 12.00
KW Kevin Weekes 4.00 10.00
LU Joffrey Lupul 4.00 10.00
MA Marc-Andre Fleury 10.00 25.00
MB Matthew Barnaby 3.00 8.00
MG Martin Gerber 4.00 10.00
MR Mike Ribeiro 4.00 10.00
MS Matt Stajan 4.00 10.00
MT Maxime Talbot 5.00 12.00
MW Brenden Morrow 4.00 10
NN Niklas Nordgren 5.00 12
NY Michael Nylander 3.00 8.
OS Chris Osgood 5.00 12
PB Patrice Bergeron 8.00 20.
PL Pascal Leclaire 4.00 10.
PM Pierre-Marc Bouchard 5.00 12.
PS Philippe Sauve 4.00 10.
RA Raitis Ivanans 3.00 8
RH Ryan Hollweg 3.00 8
RI Brad Richards 5.00 12
RK Ryan Kesler 6.00 15
RL Roberto Luongo SP 8.00 20
RM Ryan Miller 5.00 12.
RN Rob Niedermayer 4.00 10.
RO Dwayne Roloson 4.00 10.
RS Ryan Smith 4.00 10.
RY Michael Ryder 6.00 15.
RZ Richard Zednik 3.00 8.
SA Miroslav Satan 4.00 10.
SB Sean Burke 3.00 8.
SC Sidney Crosby 150.00 300.
SL Martin St. Louis SP 15.00 40.
SN Scott Niedermayer 6.00 15.
SP Jason Spezza 8.00 20.
SS Sheldon Souray 3.00 8.
ST Marco Sturm 3.00 8.
SZ Sergei Zubov 4.00 10
TA Tyler Arnason 3.00 8
TG Tim Gleason 3.00 8.
TH Trent Hunter 3.00 8.
TL Trevor Linden 5.00 12.
TP Tom Poti 3.00 8.
TU Tuomo Ruutu 5.00 12.
VL Vincent Lecavalier 6.00 15.
VP Vaclav Prospal 3.00 8.
WG Wayne Gretzky/15 SP 250.00 500.

2005-06 SP Authentic Sign of the Times Duals

STATED ODDS 1:288
DAS N.Antropov/M.Stajan 6.00 15.
DBM P.Bergeron/G.Murray 8.00 20.
DCS E.Cole/E.Staal 10.00 25.
DDV C.Drury/T.Vanek 10.00 25.
DGW M.Gerber/C.Ward 8.00 20.
DHK M.Hossa/I.Kovalchuk 12.00 30.
DKO O.Kolzig/A.Ovechkin 30.00 80.
DKP S.Koivu/A.Perezhogin 12.00 30.
DLO M.Legace/C.Osgood 10.00 25.
DLP J.Lupul/C.Perry 8.00 20.
DMA M.Modano/J.Arnott 10.00 25.
DMC B.Morrison/D.Cloutier 6.00 15.
DNB R.Nash/G.Brule 25.00 60.
DNC E.Nabokov/Cheechoo 10.00 25.
DNN Niedermayer Bros. 12.00 30.
DPH M.Peca/A.Hemsky 6.00 15.
DPR K.Primeau/M.Richards 10.00 25.
DPS C.Pronger/R.Smyth 10.00 25.
DRR J.Roenick/L.Robitaille 20.00 50.
DRT A.Raycroft/H.Toivonen 6.00 15.
DSH J.Spezza/D.Heatley 25.00 60.
DSS T.Steen/A.Steen 10.00 25.
DTD J.Theodore/Y.Danis 8.00 20.
DWL K.Weekes/H.Lundqvist 15.00 40.
DYS A.Yashin/M.Satan 6.00 15.
DZF Zetterberg/J.Franzen 12.50 30.

2006-07 SP Authentic

COMP.SET w/o SPs (100) 10.00 25.
101-160 NOTABLE PRINT RUN 999
161-250 ROOKIE PRINT RUN 999
1 Alexander Ovechkin 1.25 3.
2 Olaf Kolzig .30
3 Markus Naslund .25
4 Roberto Luongo .50 1.
5 Brendan Morrison .20
6 Mats Sundin .30
7 Michael Peca .25
8 Alexander Steen .30
9 Andrew Raycroft .25
10 Vincent Lecavalier .25
11 Martin St. Louis .30
12 Brad Richards .30
13 Doug Weight .30
14 Keith Tkachuk .30
15 Manny Legace .25
16 Joe Thornton .40 1.
17 Patrick Marleau .30
18 Jonathan Cheechoo .30
19 Vesa Toskala .25
20 Sidney Crosby 1.25 3.
21 Marc-Andre Fleury .50 1.
22 Mark Recchi .40 1.
23 Mario Lemieux 1.00 2.
24 Shane Doan .25
25 Jeremy Roenick .30
26 Owen Nolan .25
27 Curtis Joseph .30
28 Peter Forsberg .40 1.
29 Simon Gagne .30
30 Jeff Carter .30
31 Mike Richards .30
32 Jason Spezza .30
33 Daniel Alfredsson .30
34 Dany Heatley .30
35 Martin Gerber .25
36 Jaromir Jagr .75 2.
37 Brendan Shanahan .40 1.
38 Henrik Lundqvist .60 1.
39 Petr Prucha .25
40 Miroslav Satan .25
41 Rick DiPietro .25
42 Alexei Yashin .25
43 Martin Brodeur .60 1.
44 Patrik Elias .30
45 Brian Gionta .25
46 Paul Kariya .40 1.
47 Tomas Vokoun .25
48 Saku Koivu .30
49 Michael Ryder .20
50 Cristobal Huet .25
51 Chris Higgins .20
52 Pavol Demitra .40 1.
53 Marian Gaborik .40 1.
54 Manny Fernandez .25
55 Wayne Gretzky 1.50 4.
56 Rob Blake .30
57 Alexander Frolov .20
58 Ed Belfour .30
59 Olli Jokinen .30
60 Todd Bertuzzi .30
61 Ryan Smyth .25
62 Ales Hemsky .25
63 Joffrey Lupul .25
64 Gordie Howe 1.00 2.
65 Henrik Zetterberg .40 1.
66 Dominik Hasek .40 1.
67 Pavel Datsyuk .40 1.
68 Nicklas Lidstrom .30
69 Marty Turco .30

Mike Modano .50 1.25
Eric Lindros .50 1.25
Rick Nash .30 .75
Pascal LeClaire .25 .60
Sergei Fedorov .50 1.25
Joe Sakic .50 1.25
Jose Theodore .30 .75
Milan Hejduk .25 .60
Marek Svatos .20 .50
Martin Havlat .20 .50
Tuomo Ruutu .30 .75
Nikolai Khabibulin .30 .75
Eric Staal .40 1.00
Cam Ward .30 .75
Rod Brind`Amour .30 .75
Miikka Kiprusoff .25 .60
Alex Tanguay .20 .50
Jarome Iginla .30 .75
Dion Phaneuf .30 .75
Ryan Miller .30 .75
Chris Drury .25 .60
Daniel Briere .30 .75
Patrice Bergeron .40 1.00
Brad Boyes .20 .50
Zdeno Chara .30 .75
Bobby Orr 1.00 2.50
Marian Hossa .25 .60
Kari Lehtonen .25 .60
Ilya Kovalchuk .30 .75
Chris Pronger .25 .60
Teemu Selanne .60 1.50
Ales Hemsky N .75 2.00
Alexander Frolov N .60 1.50
Alexander Ovechkin N 4.00 10.00
Alexander Steen N 1.00 2.50
Bobby Orr N 3.00 8.00
Brendan Shanahan N 1.25 3.00
Cam Ward N 1.00 2.50
Dany Heatley N 1.00 2.50
Dion Phaneuf N 1.00 2.50
Dominik Hasek N 1.25 3.00
Doug Weight N 1.00 2.50
Ed Belfour N 1.00 2.50
Eric Staal N 1.25 3.00
Gordie Howe N 3.00 8.00
Henrik Lundqvist N 2.00 5.00
Henrik Zetterberg N 1.25 3.00
Ilya Kovalchuk N 1.00 2.50
Jarome Iginla N 1.00 2.50
Jaromir Jagr N 2.50 6.00
Larry Robinson N 1.00 2.50
Jason Spezza N 1.00 2.50
Jay Bouwmeester N 1.00 2.50
Jeremy Roenick N 1.00 2.50
Joe Sakic N 1.50 4.00
Joe Thornton N 1.25 3.00
Jonathan Cheechoo N 1.00 2.50
Jose Theodore N 1.00 2.50
Kari Lehtonen N .75 2.00
Marc-Andre Fleury N 1.50 4.00
Marian Gaborik N 1.25 3.00
Mario Lemieux N 3.00 8.00
Markus Naslund N .75 2.00
Martin Brodeur N 2.00 5.00
Scott Stevens N 1.00 2.50
Martin Havlat N .60 1.50
Martin St. Louis N 1.00 2.50
Mats Sundin N 1.00 2.50
Michael Ryder N .60 1.50
Miikka Kiprusoff N .75 2.00
Mike Modano N 1.50 4.00
Milan Hejduk N .75 2.00
Nicklas Lidstrom N 1.00 2.50
Patrice Bergeron N 1.25 3.00
Patrick Roy N 2.50 6.00
Paul Kariya N 1.25 3.00
Peter Forsberg N 1.25 3.00
Bobby Clarke N 1.00 2.50
Ray Bourque N 1.50 4.00
Rick Nash N 1.00 2.50
Rob Blake N 1.00 2.50
Roberto Luongo N 1.50 4.00
Ryan Miller N 1.00 2.50
Saku Koivu N 1.00 2.50
Shane Doan N .75 2.00
Sidney Crosby N 6.00 15.00
Simon Gagne N 1.00 2.50
Teemu Selanne N 2.00 5.00
Tomas Vokoun N .75 2.00
Vincent Lecavalier N .75 2.00
Wayne Gretzky N 5.00 12.00
Ryan Shannon AU RC 4.00 10.00
Shane O'Brien AU RC 4.00 10.00
Phil Kessel AU RC 25.00 50.00
Mark Stuart AU RC 4.00 10.00
Matt Lashoff AU RC 4.00 10.00
Yan Stastny AU RC 4.00 10.00
Nate Thompson AU RC 4.00 10.00
Drew Stafford AU RC 6.00 15.00
Dustin Boyd AU RC 4.00 10.00
Brandon Prust AU RC 4.00 10.00
Dave Bolland AU RC 6.00 15.00
Michael Blunden AU RC 4.00 10.00
Dustin Byfuglien AU RC 10.00 25.00
Paul Stastny AU RC 10.00 25.00
Karri Ramo AU RC 4.00 10.00
Loui Eriksson AU RC 10.00 25.00
Tomas Kopecky AU RC 5.00 12.00
Ladislav Smid AU RC 4.00 10.00
M-A Pouliot AU RC 4.00 10.00
Niklas Grossman AU RC 10.00 25.00
Patrick Thoresen AU RC 4.00 10.00
Janis Sprukts AU RC 4.00 10.00
P.O'Sullivan AU RC 6.00 15.00
Anze Kopitar AU RC 30.00 80.00
K.Pushkarev AU RC 5.00 12.00
G.Latendresse AU RC 6.00 15.00
Shea Weber AU RC 15.00 40.00
A.Radulov AU RC 20.00 50.00
Travis Zajac AU RC 8.00 20.00
Jarkko Immonen AU RC 4.00 10.00
Nigel Dawes AU RC 4.00 10.00
Kelly Guard AU RC 5.00 12.00
Ryan Potulny AU RC 4.00 10.00
Benoit Pouliot AU RC 5.00 12.00
Keith Yandle AU RC 8.00 20.00
Evgeni Malkin AU RC 125.00 200.00
Noah Welch AU RC 4.00 10.00
Jordan Staal AU RC 8.00 20.00
Michel Ouellet AU RC 5.00 12.00
K.Letang AU RC 25.00 60.00
Matt Carle AU RC 4.00 10.00
M-E Vlasic AU RC 4.00 10.00
Roman Polak AU RC 5.00 12.00
Jeremy Williams AU RC 4.00 10.00
Ian White AU RC 5.00 12.00
Jesse Schultz AU RC 4.00 10.00
Brendan Bell AU RC 4.00 10.00
Luc Bourdon AU RC 6.00 15.00
Alexander Edler AU RC 6.00 15.00
Eric Fehr AU RC 6.00 15.00

211 Daren Machesney RC 2.00 5.00
212 Nathan McIver RC 2.00 5.00
213 Patrick Coulombe RC 2.00 5.00
214 Alexei Mikhnov RC 2.00 5.00
215 Kris Newbury RC 2.00 5.00
216 Blair Jones RC 2.00 5.00
217 Marek Schwarz RC 3.00 8.00
218 David Backes RC 8.00 20.00
219 Joe Pavelski RC 10.00 25.00
220 Patrick Fischer RC 2.00 5.00
221 Bill Thomas RC 2.00 5.00
222 Triston Grant RC 2.00 5.00
223 Lars Jonsson RC 2.00 5.00
224 David Printz RC 2.00 5.00
225 Jussi Timonen RC 2.50 6.00
226 Martin Houle RC 2.50 6.00
227 Josh Hennessy RC 2.00 5.00
228 Blake Comeau RC 3.00 8.00
229 Masi Marjamaki RC 2.00 5.00
230 Ben Ondrus RC 2.00 5.00
231 Fredrik Norrena RC 2.00 5.00
232 Johnny Oduya RC 3.00 8.00
233 Enver Lisin RC 2.00 5.00
234 Mikhail Grabovski RC 6.00 15.00
235 Mikko Lehtonen RC 2.50 6.00
236 Niklas Backstrom RC 4.00 10.00
237 Miroslav Kopriva RC 2.00 5.00
238 Benoit Pouliot RC 2.50 6.00
239 Peter Harrold RC 2.00 5.00
240 David Booth RC 2.50 6.00
241 Drew Larman RC 2.00 5.00
242 Jan Hejda RC 2.00 5.00
243 Jeff Deslauriers RC 2.00 5.00
244 Stefan Liv RC 2.00 5.00
245 Adam Burish RC 3.00 8.00
246 Michael Funk RC 2.00 5.00
247 Mike Card RC 2.00 5.00
248 Adam Dennis RC 2.00 5.00
249 Clarke MacArthur RC 2.50 6.00
250 David McKee RC 2.00 5.00

2006-07 SP Authentic Chirography

STATED PRINT RUN 75 SER.#'d SETS
AF Alexander Frolov 8.00 20.00
AH Ales Hemsky 6.00 15.00
AK Anze Kopitar 25.00 60.00
BB Brad Boyes 4.00 10.00
CP Corey Perry 8.00 20.00
DH Dany Heatley 12.00 30.00
DR Dwayne Roloson 4.00 10.00
DT Darcy Tucker 8.00 20.00
EM Evgeni Malkin 30.00 80.00
ES Eric Staal 8.00 20.00
GE Martin Gerber 8.00 20.00
HA Dominik Hasek 15.00 40.00
HE Milan Hejduk 6.00 15.00
JC Jonathan Cheechoo 8.00 20.00
JI Jarome Iginla 20.00 50.00
JS Jordan Staal 15.00 40.00
KD Kris Draper 6.00 15.00
MC Mike Cammalleri 8.00 20.00
MF Marc-Andre Fleury 15.00 40.00
MG Marian Gaborik 12.00 30.00
MH Martin Havlat 6.00 15.00
MM Mike Modano 10.00 25.00
MP Michael Peca 8.00 20.00
MS Marek Svatos 6.00 15.00
MT Marty Turco 8.00 20.00
NL Nicklas Lidstrom 15.00 30.00
PE Patrik Elias 6.00 15.00
PM Patrick Marleau 8.00 20.00
PO Patrick O'Sullivan 12.00 30.00
PP Petr Prucha 4.00 10.00
RM Ryan Miller 15.00 40.00
RN Rick Nash 15.00 40.00
RS Matt Carle 6.00 15.00
SC Sidney Crosby EXCH 100.00 200.00
TV Tomas Vokoun 8.00 20.00

2006-07 SP Authentic Limited

*1-100 LIMITED: 4X TO 10X BASIC CARDS
*101-160 NOTABLES: 1.2X TO 3X
*161-210 ROOKIE PATCH AU: 1.2X TO 3X
*211-250 ROOKIES: 1.2X TO 3X
STATED PRINT RUN 100 SER.#'d SETS
184 Anze Kopitar JSY AU 125.00 250.00
196 Evgeni Malkin JSY AU 250.00 400.00
198 Jordan Staal JSY AU 50.00 100.00
209 Alexander Edler JSY AU 30.00 80.00

2006-07 SP Authentic Sign of the Times

The Phaneuf single was not part of the original checklist and may not have been issued in packs. However, a handful of copies were circulated, apparently by company employees, and thus it is included in this listing but without a price. The Bernier single was not included in packs, but was released later as a redemption replacement single.

STATED ODDS 1:24
STAF Alexander Frolov 4.00 10.00
STAH Ales Hemsky 5.00 12.00
STAR Andrew Raycroft 5.00 12.00
STBG Brian Gionta 5.00 12.00
STBH Bobby Hull SP 12.00 30.00
STBO Bobby Orr 50.00 125.00
STBU Johnny Bucyk 10.00 25.00
STCA Colby Armstrong SP 10.00 25.00
STCP Corey Perry 6.00 15.00
STCW Cam Ward 6.00 15.00
STDC Don Cherry 15.00 40.00
STDH Dominik Hasek 20.00 50.00
STDP Dion Phaneuf 12.00 30.00
STDR Dwayne Roloson 5.00 12.00
STDS Denis Savard 8.00 20.00
STEL Patrik Elias 6.00 15.00
STEM Evgeni Malkin 25.00 60.00
STES Eric Staal 8.00 20.00
STGB Gilbert Brule 5.00 12.00
STGE Martin Gerber SP 5.00 12.00
STGH Gordie Howe 50.00 125.00
STGO Scott Gomez 5.00 12.00
STHE Dany Heatley 6.00 15.00
STHJ Milan Hejduk 5.00 12.00
STIB Ray Bourque SP 25.00 60.00
STJB Jean Beliveau SP EXCH 150.00 250.00
STJC Jonathan Cheechoo 6.00 15.00
STJE Jeff Carter 6.00 15.00
STJG Jean-Sebastien Giguere 6.00 15.00
STJI Jarome Iginla 6.00 15.00
STJK Jari Kurri 6.00 15.00
STJM Joe Mullen 5.00 12.00
STJS Jarret Stoll 5.00 12.00
STJT Jose Theodore 6.00 15.00
STJW Justin Williams 5.00 12.00
STKD Kris Draper 4.00 10.00
STLR Luc Robitaille SP 25.00 60.00
STMA Matt Carle 4.00 10.00
STMB Martin Brodeur 30.00 80.00
STMF Marc-Andre Fleury 15.00 40.00
STMH Martin Havlat 4.00 10.00
STMI Ryan Miller 6.00 15.00
STML Mario Lemieux SP 80.00 150.00
STMM Mike Modano 10.00 25.00
STMO Brenden Morrow 5.00 12.00
STMT Marty Turco 6.00 15.00
STNL Nicklas Lidstrom 6.00 15.00
STPB Pierre-Marc Bouchard SP 6.00 15.00
STPE Michael Peca 5.00 12.00
STPK Phil Kessel 10.00 25.00
STPM Patrick Marleau SP 6.00 15.00
STPP Petr Prucha SP 5.00 12.00
STRN Rick Nash 6.00 15.00
STRS Ryan Smyth 5.00 12.00
STRY Michael Ryder 4.00 10.00
STSB Steve Bernier 4.00 10.00
STSC Sidney Crosby 80.00 200.00
STSK Saku Koivu SP 6.00 15.00
STSV Marek Svatos 4.00 10.00
STTE Tony Esposito 15.00 40.00
STTV Tomas Vokoun 5.00 12.00
STVT Vesa Toskala 5.00 12.00
STWC Wendel Clark 12.00 30.00
STWG Wayne Gretzky 150.00 300.00
STWO Willie O'Ree SP 20.00 50.00

2006-07 SP Authentic Sign of the Times Duals

STAS G.Anderson/R.Smyth 12.00 30.00
STBE R.Ellis/J.Bower 20.00 50.00
STBG M.Bossy/C.Gillies 15.00 40.00
STBM R.Blake/L.Murphy 12.00 30.00
STBW M.Brodeur/C.Ward 30.00 80.00
STCB J.Cheechoo/S.Bernier 12.00 30.00
STCC B.Clarke/J.Carter 12.00 30.00
STCG D. Ciccarelli/M. Gaborik 15.00 40.00
STCT G.Cheevers/H.Toivonen 12.00 30.00
STDS S.Koivu/D.Savard 15.00 40.00
STDV M.Dionne/R.Vachon 20.00 50.00
STDW D.Gilmour/W.Clark 20.00 50.00
STEG P.Elias/B.Gionta 12.00 30.00
STET T.Esposito/M.Turco 12.00 30.00
STFK A.Frolov/A.Kopitar 15.00 40.00
STFM B.Federko/J.Mullen 10.00 25.00
STGL M.Lemieux/W.Gretzky SP 300.00 400.00
STGR G.Fuhr/R.Miller 15.00 40.00
STHA D.Aebischer/C.Huet 10.00 25.00
STHE D.Heatley/P.Eaves 12.00 30.00
STHK M.Havlat/N.Khabibulin 12.00 30.00
STHO B.Orr/G.Howe 150.00 300.00
STHS M.Hejduk/M.Svatos 10.00 25.00
STIT Iginla/Tanguay 12.00 30.00
STKB P.Bergeron/P.Kessel 20.00 50.00
STKL I.Kovalchuk/K.Lehtonen 12.00 30.00
STLB R.Luongo/R.Brodeur 20.00 50.00
STLG S.Gagne/R.Leach 12.00 30.00
STLM M.Lemieux/E.Malkin SP 100.00 200.00
STLR G.Lafleur/M.Ryder 15.00 40.00
STLS N.Lidstrom/B.Salming 20.00 50.00
STLT V.Lecavalier/J.Thornton 15.00 40.00
STMC G.Lafleur/L.Robinson 15.00 40.00
STMM M.Modano/B.Morrow 20.00 50.00
STMR M.Modano/M.Ribeiro 20.00 50.00
STNB R.Nash/G.Brule 12.00 30.00
STNK C.Neely/P.Kessel 20.00 50.00
STOB B.Orr/R.Bourque 80.00 150.00
STPJ P.Marleau/J.Cheechoo 12.00 30.00
STPP Z.Parise/J.Parise 15.00 40.00
STQC P.Stastny/P.Stastny 20.00 50.00
STRB P.Roy/M.Brodeur SP 100.00 200.00
STRL M.Ryder/G.Latendresse 12.00 30.00
STRP D.Potvin/L.Robinson 12.00 30.00
STRR D.Roloson/B.Ranford 12.00 30.00
STRT L.Robitaille/D.Taylor 12.00 30.00
STSA C.Armstrong/J.Staal 20.00 50.00
STSS E.Staal/J.Staal 20.00 50.00
STSW E.Staal/C.Ward 15.00 40.00
STVA Vokoun/Arnott 10.00 25.00
STVH T.Vokoun/D.Hasek 15.00 40.00
STWR S.Weber/A.Radulov 20.00 50.00

2006-07 SP Authentic Sign of the Times Triples

ST3BBK Boyes/Berg/Kessel 25.00 60.00
ST3BEK Ellis/Bower/Kelly 30.00 80.00
ST3COS Cheev/O'Reilly/Sand 25.00 60.00
ST3DBM Drury/Briere/Miller 15.00 40.00
ST3HNS Heatley/Nash/Staal 20.00 50.00
ST3HTS Hejduk/Theo/Svatos 15.00 40.00
ST3ITK Iginla/Tang/Kipper 15.00 40.00
ST3LFM Mario/Fleury/Malkin 200.00 300.00
ST3LGH Lemieux/Gretz/Howe 600.00 800.00
ST3LHZ Lidstrom/Holm/Zetter 40.00 100.00
ST3LRS Lafleur/Shutt/Robin 20.00 50.00
ST3MTC Marleau/Thorn/Chee 20.00 50.00
ST3MTM Modano/Turco/Morr 30.00 80.00
ST3NLM Nasl/Luongo/Morris 25.00 60.00
ST3OBE Espo/Orr/Bourque 150.00 250.00
ST3PGB Parrish/Gabby/Bouch 20.00 50.00
ST3RBW Roy/Brodeur/Ward 100.00 250.00
ST3RHG Redden/Heats/Gerb 15.00 40.00
ST3RKH Higgins/Koivu/Ryder 15.00 40.00
ST3RPT Raycroft/Peca/Tuck 12.00 30.00
ST3SSH Smyth/Stoll/Hemsky 12.00 30.00
ST3SSS Stastnys 25.00 60.00
ST3WSW Williams/Staal/Ward 20.00 50.00
ST3SUT1 Sutter/Sutter/Sutter 20.00 50.00
ST3SUT2 Sutter/Sutter/Sutter 15.00 40.00

2007-08 SP Authentic

COMP.SET w/o SP's (100) 10.00 25.00
101-160 NOTABLES PRINT RUN 1999
161-190 ROOKIE PRINT RUN 999
191-250 ROOKIE AU PRINT RUN 999
1 Daniel Briere .30 .75
2 Simon Gagne .30 .75
3 Jeff Carter .30 .75
4 Alexander Ovechkin 1.25 3.00
5 Olaf Kolzig .30 .75
6 Alexander Semin .30 .75
7 Patrice Bergeron .40 1.00
8 Marc Savard .20 .50
9 Phil Kessel .40 1.00
10 Tomas Vokoun .25 .60
11 Nathan Horton .30 .75
12 Olli Jokinen .25 .60
13 Eric Staal .40 1.00
14 Cam Ward .30 .75
15 Rod Brind`Amour .30 .75
16 Saku Koivu .30 .75
17 Michael Ryder .20 .50
18 Guillaume Latendresse .25 .60
19 Cristobal Huet .25 .60
20 Mats Sundin .30 .75
21 Vesa Toskala .25 .60
22 Darcy Tucker .25 .60
23 Alexander Steen .30 .75
24 Rick DiPietro .25 .60
25 Bill Guerin .30 .75
26 Miroslav Satan .25 .60
27 Vincent Lecavalier .25 .60
28 Brad Richards .30 .75
29 Martin St. Louis .30 .75
30 Jaromir Jagr .75 2.00
31 Henrik Lundqvist .40 1.00
32 Brendan Shanahan .40 1.00
33 Chris Drury .25 .60
34 Sidney Crosby 1.25 3.00
35 Evgeni Malkin 1.00 2.50
36 Marc-Andre Fleury .50 1.25
37 Jordan Staal .30 .75
38 Dany Heatley .30 .75
39 Ray Emery .25 .60
40 Jason Spezza .30 .75
41 Daniel Alfredsson .30 .75
42 Ilya Kovalchuk .30 .75
43 Kari Lehtonen .25 .60
44 Marian Hossa .25 .60
45 Martin Brodeur .60 1.50
46 Patrik Elias .30 .75
47 Zach Parise .40 1.00
48 Ryan Miller .30 .75
49 Thomas Vanek .40 1.00
50 Jason Pominville .30 .75
51 Shane Doan .25 .60
52 Ilya Bryzgalov .30 .75
53 Ed Jovanovski .25 .60
54 Anze Kopitar .50 1.25
55 Rob Blake .30 .75
56 Alexander Frolov .20 .50
57 Martin Havlat .30 .75
58 Nikolai Khabibulin .30 .75
59 Tuomo Ruutu .30 .75
60 Ales Hemsky .25 .60
61 Joni Pitkanen .20 .50
62 Dwayne Roloson .25 .60
63 Rick Nash .30 .75
64 Sergei Fedorov .50 1.25
65 David Vyborny .20 .50
66 Paul Kariya .40 1.00
67 Manny Legace .25 .60
68 Keith Tkachuk .30 .75
69 Joe Sakic .50 1.25
70 Ryan Smyth .25 .60
71 Paul Stastny .30 .75
72 Milan Hejduk .25 .60
73 Jarome Iginla .30 .75
74 Miikka Kiprusoff .25 .60
75 Alex Tanguay .20 .50
76 Dion Phaneuf .30 .75
77 Marian Gaborik .40 1.00
78 Mikko Koivu .25 .60
79 Niklas Backstrom .30 .75
80 Mike Modano .50 1.25
81 Marty Turco .30 .75
82 Mike Ribeiro .25 .60
83 Joe Thornton .40 1.00
84 Jonathan Cheechoo .30 .75
85 Patrick Marleau .30 .75
86 Chris Mason .25 .60
87 Alexander Radulov .30 .75
88 Jason Arnott .25 .60
89 Roberto Luongo .40 1.00
90 Markus Naslund .30 .75
91 Henrik Sedin .30 .75
92 Daniel Sedin .30 .75
93 Ryan Getzlaf .50 1.25
94 Jean-Sebastien Giguere .30 .75
95 Doug Weight .30 .75
96 Chris Pronger .25 .60
97 Pavel Datsyuk .40 1.00
98 Nicklas Lidstrom .30 .75
99 Henrik Zetterberg .40 1.00
100 Dominik Hasek .40 1.00
101 Alexander Ovechkin NOT 5.00 12.00
102 Markus Naslund NOT 1.25 3.00
103 Roberto Luongo NOT 1.50 4.00
104 Frank Mahovlich NOT 1.50 4.00
105 Mats Sundin NOT 1.25 3.00
106 Martin St. Louis NOT 1.25 3.00
107 Vincent Lecavalier NOT 1.00 2.50
108 Paul Kariya NOT 1.50 4.00
109 Brad Boyes NOT .75 2.00
110 Patrick Marleau NOT 1.25 3.00
111 Joe Thornton NOT 1.50 4.00
112 Evgeni Malkin NOT 4.00 10.00
113 Marc-Andre Fleury NOT 2.00 5.00
114 Mario Lemieux NOT 4.00 10.00
115 Sidney Crosby NOT 5.00 12.00
116 Shane Doan NOT 1.00 2.50
117 Bernie Parent NOT 1.25 3.00
118 Bobby Clarke NOT 1.25 3.00
119 Daniel Briere NOT 1.25 3.00
120 Ron Hextall NOT 2.00 5.00
121 Simon Gagne NOT 1.25 3.00
122 Dany Heatley NOT 1.25 3.00
123 Ray Emery NOT 1.00 2.50
124 Brendan Shanahan NOT 1.50 4.00
125 Jaromir Jagr NOT 3.00 8.00
126 Mark Messier NOT 2.00 5.00
127 Rick DiPietro NOT 1.00 2.50
128 Zach Parise NOT 1.50 4.00
129 Martin Brodeur NOT 2.50 6.00
130 Guy Lafleur NOT 1.50 4.00
131 Larry Robinson NOT 1.25 3.00
132 Saku Koivu NOT 1.25 3.00
133 Marian Gaborik NOT 1.50 4.00
134 Luc Robitaille NOT 1.25 3.00
135 Tomas Vokoun NOT 1.00 2.50
136 Grant Fuhr NOT 1.25 3.00
137 Jari Kurri NOT 1.25 3.00
138 Wayne Gretzky NOT 6.00 15.00
139 Henrik Zetterberg NOT 1.50 4.00
140 Dominik Hasek NOT 1.50 4.00
141 Gordie Howe NOT 3.00 8.00
142 Nicklas Lidstrom NOT 1.25 3.00
143 Mike Modano NOT 2.00 5.00
144 Rick Nash NOT 1.25 3.00
145 Paul Stastny NOT 1.25 3.00
146 Joe Sakic NOT 2.00 5.00
147 Bobby Hull NOT 2.00 5.00
148 Stan Mikita NOT 1.50 4.00
149 Tony Esposito NOT 1.25 3.00
150 Jarome Iginla NOT 1.25 3.00
151 Miikka Kiprusoff NOT 1.00 2.50
152 Gilbert Perreault NOT 1.25 3.00
153 Thomas Vanek NOT 1.50 4.00
154 Bobby Orr NOT 4.00 10.00
155 Johnny Bucyk NOT 1.00 2.50
156 Patrice Bergeron NOT 1.50 4.00
157 Phil Esposito NOT 2.00 5.00
158 Ray Bourque NOT 2.00 5.00
159 J-S Giguere NOT 1.25 3.00
160 Ryan Getzlaf NOT 2.00 5.00
161 Petteri Wirtanen RC 2.50 6.00
162 Kent Huskins RC 2.50 6.00
163 Mike Weber RC 2.50 6.00
164 Mark Mancari RC 3.00 8.00
165 Kris Russell RC 3.00 8.00
166 Matt Keetley RC 3.00 8.00
167 David Moss RC 4.00 10.00
168 Magnus Johansson RC 2.50 6.00
169 David Koci RC 2.50 6.00
170 Jeff Finger RC 2.50 6.00
171 Tomas Popperle RC 3.00 8.00
172 Chris Conner RC 2.50 6.00
173 Joel Lundqvist RC 2.50 6.00
174 Matt Ellis RC 3.00 8.00
175 Bryan Young RC 2.50 6.00
176 Liam Reddox RC 2.50 6.00
177 Jonathan Quick RC 100.00 200.00
178 Cal Clutterbuck RC 4.00 10.00
179 Sergei Kostitsyn RC 3.00 8.00
180 Ryan O'Byrne RC 4.00 10.00
181 Mark Fraser RC 2.50 6.00
182 Cody Bass RC 3.00 8.00
183 Riley Cote RC 3.00 8.00
184 Craig Weller RC 2.50 6.00
185 Daniel Winnik RC 3.00 8.00
186 Tyler Kennedy RC 4.00 10.00
187 Lukas Kaspar RC 2.50 6.00
188 Tomas Plihal RC 3.00 8.00
189 Mike Lundin RC 2.50 6.00
190 Chris Bourque RC 3.00 8.00
191 Jonas Hiller AU RC 6.00 15.00
192 Drew Miller AU RC 4.00 10.00
193 Bobby Ryan AU RC 8.00 20.00
194 Ryan Carter AU RC 3.00 8.00
195 Bryan Little AU RC 5.00 12.00
196 Brett Sterling AU RC 3.00 8.00
197 Tobias Enstrom AU RC 6.00 15.00
198 Ondrej Pavelec AU RC 6.00 15.00
199 Milan Lucic AU RC 15.00 40.00
200 David Krejci AU RC 15.00 30.00
201 Tuukka Rask AU RC 40.00 80.00
202 Curtis McElhinney AU RC 5.00 12.00
203 Jonathan Toews AU RC 150.00 225.00
204 Patrick Kane AU RC 125.00 200.00
205 Jaroslav Hlinka AU RC 4.00 10.00
206 Tyler Weiman AU RC 4.00 10.00
207 Jonathan Sigalet AU RC 3.00 8.00
208 Jared Boll AU RC 4.00 10.00
209 Marc Methot AU RC 3.00 8.00
210 Matt Niskanen AU RC 5.00 12.00
211 Tobias Stephan AU RC 4.00 10.00
212 Andrew Cogliano AU RC 5.00 12.00
213 Sam Gagner AU RC 6.00 15.00
214 Tom Gilbert AU RC 4.00 10.00
215 Rob Schremp AU RC 4.00 10.00
216 Cory Murphy AU RC 3.00 8.00
217 Stefan Meyer AU RC 4.00 10.00
218 Jack Johnson AU RC 4.00 10.00
219 Jonathan Bernier AU RC 15.00 40.00
220 Lauri Tukonen AU RC 3.00 8.00
221 Petr Kalus AU RC 3.00 8.00
222 James Sheppard AU RC 3.00 8.00
223 Jaroslav Halak AU RC 10.00 25.00
224 Kyle Chipchura AU RC 5.00 12.00
225 Carey Price AU RC 150.00 250.00
226 Ville Koistinen AU RC 3.00 8.00
227 Nicklas Bergfors AU RC 3.00 8.00
228 Andy Greene AU RC 4.00 10.00
229 Frans Nielsen AU RC 5.00 12.00
230 Ryan Callahan AU RC 6.00 15.00
231 Marc Staal AU RC 5.00 12.00
232 Brandon Dubinsky AU RC 6.00 15.00
233 Daniel Girardi AU RC 4.00 10.00
234 Brian Elliott AU RC 6.00 15.00
235 Nick Foligno AU RC 6.00 15.00
236 Ryan Parent AU RC 3.00 8.00
237 Peter Mueller AU RC 4.00 10.00
238 Martin Hanzal AU RC 4.00 10.00
239 Daniel Carcillo AU RC 4.00 10.00
240 Torrey Mitchell AU RC 4.00 10.00
241 Devin Setoguchi AU RC 5.00 12.00
242 Erik Johnson AU RC 5.00 12.00
243 David Perron AU RC 5.00 12.00
244 Steve Wagner AU RC 3.00 8.00
245 Matt Smaby AU RC 3.00 8.00
246 Anton Stralman AU RC 3.00 8.00
247 Jiri Tlusty AU RC 5.00 12.00
248 Jannik Hansen AU RC 4.00 10.00
249 Mason Raymond AU RC 5.00 12.00
250 Nicklas Backstrom AU RC 15.00 30.00

2007-08 SP Authentic Limited

*1-100 VETS: 1.5X TO 4X BASIC CARDS
*101-160 NOTABLE: .6X TO 1.5X
*161-190 ROOKIES: .8X TO 2X
STATED PRINT RUN 100 SER.#'d SETS
177 Jonathan Quick 150.00 250.00
191 Jonas Hiller AU PATCH 20.00 50.00
192 Drew Miller AU PATCH 12.00 30.00
193 Bobby Ryan AU PATCH 25.00 60.00
194 Ryan Carter AU PATCH 10.00 25.00
195 Bryan Little AU PATCH 12.00 30.00
196 Brett Sterling AU PATCH 10.00 25.00
197 Tobias Enstrom AU PATCH 20.00 50.00
198 Ondrej Pavelec AU PATCH 25.00 60.00
199 Milan Lucic AU PATCH 75.00 150.00
200 David Krejci AU PATCH 50.00 100.00
201 Tuukka Rask AU PATCH
202 Curtis McElhinney AU PATCH 15.00 40.00
203 Jonathan Toews AU PATCH 300.00 500.00
204 Patrick Kane AU PATCH 250.00 400.00
205 Jaroslav Hlinka AU PATCH 12.00 30.00
206 Tyler Weiman AU PATCH 12.00 30.00
207 Jonathan Sigalet AU PATCH 10.00 25.00
208 Jared Boll AU PATCH 12.00 30.00
209 Marc Methot AU PATCH 10.00 25.00
210 Matt Niskanen AU PATCH 15.00 40.00
211 Tobias Stephan AU PATCH 12.00 30.00
212 Andrew Cogliano AU PATCH 15.00 40.00
213 Sam Gagner AU PATCH 20.00 50.00
214 Tom Gilbert AU PATCH 12.00 30.00
215 Rob Schremp AU PATCH 12.00 30.00
216 Cory Murphy AU PATCH
217 Stefan Meyer AU PATCH
218 Jack Johnson AU PATCH 12.00 30.00
219 Jonathan Bernier AU PATCH 40.00 100.00
220 Lauri Tukonen AU PATCH 10.00 25.00
221 Petr Kalus AU PATCH 10.00 25.00
222 James Sheppard AU PATCH 10.00 25.00
223 Jaroslav Halak AU PATCH 20.00 50.00
224 Kyle Chipchura AU PATCH 15.00 40.00
225 Carey Price AU PATCH 150.00 250.00
226 Ville Koistinen AU PATCH 10.00 25.00
227 Nicklas Bergfors AU PATCH 10.00 25.00
228 Andy Greene AU PATCH 12.00 30.00
229 Frans Nielsen AU PATCH 15.00 40.00
230 Ryan Callahan AU PATCH 20.00 50.00
231 Marc Staal AU PATCH 15.00 40.00
232 B.Dubinsky AU PATCH 20.00 50.00
233 Daniel Girardi AU PATCH 12.00 30.00
234 Brian Elliott AU PATCH 20.00 50.00
235 Nick Foligno AU PATCH 20.00 50.00
236 Ryan Parent AU PATCH 10.00 25.00
237 Peter Mueller AU PATCH 12.00 30.00
238 Martin Hanzal AU PATCH 12.00 30.00
239 Daniel Carcillo AU PATCH 12.00 30.00
240 Torrey Mitchell AU PATCH 12.00 30.00
241 Devin Setoguchi AU PATCH 15.00 40.00
242 Erik Johnson AU PATCH 15.00 40.00
243 David Perron AU PATCH 15.00 40.00
244 Steve Wagner AU PATCH 10.00 25.00
245 Matt Smaby AU PATCH 10.00 25.00
246 Anton Stralman AU PATCH 10.00 25.00
247 Jiri Tlusty AU PATCH 15.00 40.00
248 Jannik Hansen AU PATCH 12.00 30.00
249 Mason Raymond AU PATCH 15.00 40.00
250 N.Backstrom AU PATCH 50.00 100.00

2007-08 SP Authentic Chirography

STATED PRINT RUN 75 SERIAL #'d SETS
AO Alexander Ovechkin 40.00 100.00
AR Alexander Radulov 10.00 25.00
DH Dany Heatley 12.00 30.00
IK Ilya Kovalchuk 15.00 40.00
JG Jean-Sebastien Giguere 6.00 15.00
JI Jarome Iginla 12.00 30.00
JT Joe Thornton 12.50 30.00
MB Martin Brodeur 25.00 60.00
MG Marian Gaborik 8.00 20.00
MM Mike Modano 12.50 30.00
MN Markus Naslund 10.00 25.00
NL Nicklas Lidstrom 12.50 30.00
PB Patrice Bergeron 8.00 20.00
RM Ryan Miller 12.00 30.00
RN Rick Nash 12.00 30.00
SC Sidney Crosby 100.00 200.00
SD Shane Doan 10.00 25.00
SG Simon Gagne 10.00 25.00
SK Saku Koivu 10.00 25.00
VL Vincent Lecavalier 12.50 30.00

2007-08 SP Authentic Holoview FX

COMPLETE SET (42) 50.00 100.00
STATED ODDS 1:12
FX1 Alexander Ovechkin 5.00 12.00
FX2 Alexander Radulov 1.25 3.00
FX3 Patrick Kane 5.00 12.00
FX4 Brendan Shanahan 1.50 4.00
FX5 Dany Heatley 1.25 3.00
FX6 Dwayne Roloson 1.00 2.50
FX7 Eric Staal 1.50 4.00
FX8 Evgeni Malkin 4.00 10.00
FX9 Henrik Zetterberg 1.50 4.00
FX10 Ilya Kovalchuk 1.25 3.00
FX11 Jarome Iginla 1.25 3.00
FX12 Jaromir Jagr 3.00 8.00
FX13 Jason Spezza 1.25 3.00
FX14 Jean-Sebastien Giguere 1.25 3.00
FX15 Joe Sakic 2.00 5.00
FX16 Joe Thornton 1.50 4.00
FX17 Marian Gaborik 1.50 4.00
FX18 Markus Naslund 1.25 3.00
FX19 Martin Brodeur 2.50 6.00
FX20 Martin St. Louis 1.25 3.00
FX21 Marty Turco 1.25 3.00
FX22 Mats Sundin 1.25 3.00
FX23 Michael Ryder .75 2.00
FX24 Miikka Kiprusoff 1.00 2.50
FX25 Mike Modano 2.00 5.00
FX26 Nicklas Lidstrom 1.25 3.00
FX27 Patrice Bergeron 1.50 4.00
FX28 Patrick Marleau 1.25 3.00
FX29 Paul Kariya 1.50 4.00
FX30 Phil Kessel 1.50 4.00
FX31 Rick Nash 1.25 3.00
FX32 Roberto Luongo 1.50 4.00
FX33 Ryan Getzlaf 2.00 5.00
FX34 Ryan Smyth 1.00 2.50
FX35 Saku Koivu 1.25 3.00
FX36 Jonathan Toews 5.00 12.00
FX37 Sidney Crosby 5.00 12.00
FX38 Simon Gagne 1.25 3.00
FX39 Thomas Vanek 1.50 4.00
FX40 Carey Price 8.00 20.00
FX41 Vincent Lecavalier 1.00 2.50
FX42 Zach Parise 1.50 4.00

2007-08 SP Authentic Holoview FX Die Cuts

*DIE CUTS: .8X TO 2X BASIC
STATED ODDS 1:144

2007-08 SP Authentic Prestigious Pairings

STATED PRINT RUN 100 SER.#'d SETS
PPCR J.Cheechoo/M.Ryder 8.00 20.00
PPDH D.Heatley/S.Doan 12.00 30.00
PPGS M.St. Louis/S.Gagne 8.00 20.00
PPGT J.Giguere/M.Turco 12.00 30.00
PPHG M.Gaborik/M.Hossa EXCH 8.00 20.00
PPIN J.Iginla/R.Nash 12.00 30.00
PPJJ E.Johnson/J.Johnson 12.00 30.00
PPKR Kovalchuk/Radulov EXCH 15.00 40.00
PPKS P.Stastny/A.Kopitar EXCH 12.00 30.00
PPLS Lidstrom/Salming EXCH 12.00 30.00
PPLT Thornton/Lecavalier EXCH 15.00 40.00
PPMM M.Modano/J.Mullen 12.00 30.00
PPOM A.Ovechkin/E.Malkin 75.00 150.00
PPRP C.Perry/M.Richards EXCH 12.00 30.00
PPTB P.Bergeron/A.Tanguay 8.00 20.00
PPVH D.Hasek/T.Vokoun EXCH 12.00 30.00
PPVL T.Vanek/G.Latendresse 12.00 30.00

2007-08 SP Authentic Rookie Review Autographed Patches

STATED PRINT RUN 100 SERIAL #'d SETS
RRAK Anze Kopitar 30.00 80.00
RRAO Alexander Ovechkin 60.00 120.00
RRAR Andrew Raycroft 15.00 40.00
RRAT Alex Tanguay 12.00 30.00
RRBL Brian Leetch 15.00 40.00
RRCD Chris Drury 15.00 40.00
RRCW Cam Ward 20.00 50.00
RRDC Dino Ciccarelli 20.00 50.00
RRDH Dale Hawerchuk 25.00 60.00
RREM Evgeni Malkin 50.00 100.00
RREN Evgeni Nabokov 15.00 40.00
RRHE Dany Heatley 20.00 50.00
RRJC Jonathan Cheechoo 20.00 50.00
RRJI Jarome Iginla 15.00 40.00
RRJP Joni Pitkanen 12.00 30.00
RRJT Joe Thornton 20.00 50.00
RRJW Justin Williams 15.00 40.00
RRKB Kevin Bieksa 15.00 40.00
RRKD Kris Draper 10.00 25.00
RRMG Marian Gaborik 20.00 50.00
RRMH Marian Hossa 15.00 40.00
RRMM Mike Modano 30.00 80.00
RRMR Mike Ribeiro 15.00 40.00
RRMS Marc Savard 12.00 30.00
RRMT Marty Turco 20.00 50.00
RRNL Nicklas Lidstrom 20.00 50.00
RRPB Patrice Bergeron 25.00 50.00
RRPS Paul Stastny 15.00 40.00
RRRB Ray Bourque 25.00 60.00
RRRN Rick Nash 20.00 50.00
RRSC Sidney Crosby 100.00 200.00
RRSG Scott Gomez 15.00 40.00
RRST Peter Stastny 15.00 40.00
RRTH Jose Theodore 20.00 50.00

2007-08 SP Authentic Sign of the Times

STATED ODDS 1:14
STAC Andrew Cogliano 6.00 15.00
STAF Alexander Frolov 4.00 10.00
STAK Anze Kopitar 10.00 25.00
STAM Andy McDonald 5.00 12.00
STAO Adam Oates 6.00 15.00
STAT Alex Tanguay 4.00 10.00
STBA Nicklas Backstrom 10.00 25.00
STBB Brad Boyes 4.00 10.00
STBC Bobby Clarke 10.00 25.00
STBE Steve Bernier 8.00 20.00
STBF Bernie Federko 4.00 10.00
STBG Brian Gionta 5.00 12.00
STBI Kevin Bieksa 5.00 12.00
STBL Bryan Little 5.00 12.00
STBO Bobby Orr SP 175.00 300.00
STBP Bob Probert 20.00 50.00
STBR Dustin Brown 6.00 15.00
STCG Clark Gillies 6.00 15.00
STCK Chuck Kobasew 4.00 10.00
STCP Carey Price 25.00 50.00
STDB Dustin Boyd 4.00 10.00
STDG Doug Gilmour 8.00 20.00
STDH Dominik Hasek 12.00 30.00
STDT Darcy Tucker 5.00 12.00
STDW Doug Wilson 5.00 12.00
STEJ Erik Johnson 8.00 20.00
STEM Evgeni Malkin 25.00 60.00
STER Loui Eriksson 6.00 15.00
STES Eric Staal 8.00 20.00
STFP Fernando Pisani 4.00 10.00
STGB Gilbert Brule 5.00 12.00
STGF Grant Fuhr 12.00 30.00
STGH Gordie Howe SP 75.00 150.00
STHL Hakan Loob 4.00 10.00
STJA Jason Arnott 5.00 12.00
STJB Jonathan Bernier 6.00 15.00
STJC Jonathan Cheechoo 8.00 20.00
STJG Jean-Sebastien Giguere 6.00 15.00
STJI Jarome Iginla 10.00 25.00
STJJ Jack Johnson 5.00 12.00
STJK Jari Kurri SP 25.00 60.00
STJP Joni Pitkanen 4.00 10.00
STJS Jordan Staal 15.00 40.00
STJT Jonathan Toews 50.00 100.00
STJW Justin Williams 5.00 12.00
STKA Petr Kalus 4.00 10.00
STKB Keith Ballard 4.00 10.00
STKD Kris Draper 4.00 10.00
STKE Ryan Kesler 8.00 20.00
STKH Kelly Hrudey 5.00 12.00
STLE Brian Leetch 8.00 20.00
STLM Lanny McDonald 6.00 15.00
STMB Martin Brodeur SP 60.00 120.00
STMC Mike Cammalleri 5.00 12.00
STMD Marcel Dionne 30.00 60.00
STMF Marc-Andre Fleury 15.00 40.00
STMG Marian Gaborik 8.00 20.00
STMH Marian Hossa 5.00 12.00
STML Mario Lemieux SP 175.00 300.00
STMM Mark Messier 30.00 80.00
STMN Markus Naslund 6.00 15.00
STMO Mike Modano 15.00 40.00
STMP Marc-Antoine Pouliot 4.00 10.00
STMR Michael Ryder 4.00 10.00
STMS Marc Savard 4.00 10.00
STMT Marty Turco 8.00 20.00
STNB Nicklas Backstrom 20.00 50.00
STNF Nick Foligno 10.00 25.00
STNG Niklas Grossman 4.00 10.00
STNO Fredrik Norrena 4.00 10.00
STNZ Nikolai Zherdev 4.00 10.00
STOV Alexander Ovechkin 25.00 60.00
STPK Patrick Kane 50.00 100.00
STPM Peter Mueller 5.00 12.00
STPO Patrick O'Sullivan 5.00 12.00
STPP Petr Prucha 4.00 10.00
STPR Brandon Prust 4.00 10.00
STPS Paul Stastny 6.00 15.00
STRA Andrew Raycroft 5.00 12.00
STRI Mike Richards 6.00 15.00
STRK Red Kelly 8.00 20.00
STRP Ryan Parent 8.00 20.00
STRS Rob Schremp 5.00 12.00
STRY Ryan Potulny 4.00 10.00
STSA Miroslav Satan 5.00 12.00
STSB Scotty Bowman 10.00 25.00
STSC Sidney Crosby SP 125.00 250.00
STSD Shane Doan 5.00 12.00
STSS Steve Shutt 6.00 15.00
STST Martin St. Louis 6.00 15.00
STTK Tomas Kopecky 5.00 12.00
STTV Tomas Vokoun 5.00 12.00
STVF Valtteri Filppula 6.00 15.00
STVL Vincent Lecavalier 10.00 25.00
STWG Wayne Gretzky SP 300.00 400.00

2007-08 SP Authentic Sign of the Times Duals

STATED ODDS 1:288
ST2AN Ovechkin/Backstrom 75.00 150.00
ST2BC B.Clarke/J.Bucyk 15.00 40.00
ST2BG M.Bossy/C.Gillies 15.00 40.00
ST2BK P.Bergeron/P.Kessel 15.00 40.00
ST2CB Cheechoo/Bernier 8.00 20.00
ST2CG Cogliano/Gagner 15.00 40.00
ST2CH B.Clarke/R.Hextall 20.00 50.00
ST2DH D.Heatley/S.Doan 12.00 30.00
ST2FK A.Frolov/A.Kopitar 8.00 20.00
ST2FR G.Fuhr/B.Ranford 12.00 30.00
ST2FS M.Fleury/J.Staal 20.00 50.00
ST2GS M.Gaborik/J.Sheppard 15.00 40.00
ST2HM G.Howe/M.Messier 100.00 200.00
ST2IT J.Iginla/A.Tanguay 12.00 30.00
ST2KL I.Kovalchuk/B.Little 12.00 30.00
ST2LH Lidstrom/Holmstrom 15.00 40.00
ST2LS Lecavalier/M.St. Louis 15.00 40.00
ST2MM M.Modano/B.Morrow 20.00 50.00
ST2MP A.McDonald/C.Perry 10.00 25.00
ST2MR E.Malkin/A.Radulov 25.00 60.00
ST2NB R.Nash/G.Brule 12.00 30.00
ST2NK M.Naslund/R.Kesler 15.00 40.00
ST2OB B.Orr/R.Bourque 150.00 300.00
ST2RL Ryder/Latendresse 10.00 25.00
ST2SS E.Staal/J.Staal 10.00 25.00
ST2TK J.Toews/P.Kane 100.00 200.00
ST2VS T.Vanek/D.Stafford 15.00 40.00
ST2VT V.Filppula/T.Kopecky 12.00 30.00
ST2WS P.Stastny/W.Wolski 12.00 30.00

2007-08 SP Authentic Sign of the Times Triples

Six cards were released in packs as redemption cards: Malkin/Fleury/Staal, Hasek/Lidstrom/Draper, Nash/Brule/Zherdev, Price/Ryder/Latendresse, Staal/Staal/Staal and Stastny/Wolski/Svatos.
STATED PRIN RUN 25 SERIAL #'d SETS
ST3FMS Malkin/Fleury/Staal 100.00 200.00
ST3GPR Getzlaf/Perry/Ryan 60.00 120.00
ST3GRL Gagne/Richards/Lupul 40.00 80.00
ST3HLD Hasek/Lidstrom/Draper 60.00 120.00
ST3KJB Kopitar/Johnson/Bernier 175.00 300.00
ST3MRT Modano/Turco/Ribeiro 30.00 80.00
ST3MSS Sittler/Salming/Mahov 40.00 80.00
ST3MVS Miller/Vanek/Stafford 25.00 60.00
ST3NZB Nash/Brule/Zherdev 40.00 80.00
ST3OJK Ovech/Johnson/Kane 100.00 200.00
ST3PHP Roy/Brodeur/Price 125.00 250.00
ST3PRL Price/Ryder/Latend 75.00 150.00
ST3RGP Roloson/Gagner/Pitkanen 30.00 60.00
ST3SBK Bergeron/Kessel/Savard 40.00 80.00
ST3SSS Staal/Staal/Staal 125.00 250.00
ST3SWS Stastny/Wolski/Svatos 50.00 100.00

2008-09 SP Authentic

This set was released on April 1, 2009. The base set consists of 250 cards.
COMP.SET w/o SPs (100) 10.00 25.00
NOTABLE/999 STATED ODDS 1:18
ROOKIE/999 STATED ODDS 1:24
ROOKIE AU/999 STATED ODDS 1:48
1 Zach Parise .30 .75
2 Wayne Gretzky 1.50 4.00
3 Vincent Lecavalier .25 .60
4 Vesa Toskala .25 .60
5 Mike Cammalleri .25 .60
6 Tomas Vokoun .25 .60
7 Tomas Kaberle .20 .50
8 Thomas Vanek .30 .75
9 Simon Gagne .30 .75
10 Sidney Crosby 1.25 3.00
11 Sam Gagner .25 .60
12 Shane Doan .25 .60
13 Scott Niedermayer .30 .75
14 Saku Koivu .30 .75
15 Ryan Miller .30 .75
16 Ryan Getzlaf .50 1.25
17 Rod Brind`Amour .30 .75
18 Roberto Luongo .40 1.00
19 Rick Nash .30 .75
20 Rick DiPietro .25 .60
21 Phil Kessel .40 1.00
22 Peter Mueller .25 .60
23 Pavel Datsyuk .40 1.00
24 Paul Stastny .30 .75
25 Paul Kariya .40 1.00
26 Patrik Elias .30 .75
27 Patrick Sharp .30 .75
28 Mikko Koivu .25 .60
29 Patrick Kane .60 1.50
30 Pascal Leclaire .25 .60
31 Olli Jokinen .25 .60
32 Nikolai Zherdev .20 .50
33 Niklas Backstrom .30 .75
34 Nicklas Lidstrom .30 .75
35 Nicklas Backstrom .50 1.25
36 Nathan Horton .25 .60
37 Milan Hejduk .25 .60
38 Mike Richards .30 .75
39 Andrew Cogliano .25 .60
40 Mike Modano .50 1.25
41 Miikka Kiprusoff .25 .60
42 Mikhail Grabovski .30 .75
43 Marty Turco .30 .75
44 Martin St. Louis .30 .75
45 Martin Brodeur .60 1.50
46 Martin Biron .25 .60
47 Doug Weight .30 .75
48 Miroslav Satan .30 .75
49 Marian Hossa .25 .60
50 Marian Gaborik .40 1.00
51 Marc-Andre Fleury .50 1.25
52 Marc Savard .20 .50
53 Kari Lehtonen .25 .60
54 Jordan Staal .30 .75
55 Jonathan Toews .75 2.00
56 Jonathan Cheechoo .30 .75
57 Johan Franzen .30 .75
58 Joe Thornton .40 1.00
59 Joe Sakic .50 1.25
60 Jean-Sebastien Giguere .30 .75
61 Jason Spezza .30 .75
62 Jason Pominville .30 .75
63 Jason Arnott .25 .60
64 Jarome Iginla .30 .75
65 Dustin Brown .30 .75
66 Ilya Kovalchuk .30 .75
67 Henrik Zetterberg .40 1.00
68 Henrik Sedin .30 .75
69 Henrik Lundqvist .40 1.00
70 Tomas Plekanec .30 .75
71 Gordie Howe .75 2.00
72 Evgeni Nabokov .25 .60
73 Evgeni Malkin 1.00 2.50
74 Eric Staal .40 1.00
75 Dion Phaneuf .30 .75
76 Derek Roy .20 .50
77 Dany Heatley .30 .75
78 Daniel Sedin .30 .75
79 Daniel Briere .30 .75
80 Daniel Alfredsson .30 .75
81 Dan Ellis .20 .50
82 Cristobal Huet .25 .60
83 Alexander Semin .30 .75
84 Teemu Selanne .60 1.50
85 Chris Osgood .30 .75
86 Chris Drury .25 .60
87 Carey Price 1.25 3.00
88 Cam Ward .30 .75
89 Markus Naslund .25 .60
90 Brian Campbell .25 .60
91 Brad Richards .30 .75
92 Brad Boyes .20 .50
93 Patrice Bergeron .40 1.00
94 Mats Sundin .30 .75
95 Anze Kopitar .50 1.25
96 Alexander Ovechkin 1.25 3.00
97 Alexander Frolov .20 .50
98 Alex Tanguay .20 .50
99 Alex Kovalev .25 .60
100 Ales Hemsky .25 .60
101 Alexander Ovechkin N 5.00 12.00
102 Bernie Parent N 1.25 3.00
103 Bobby Clarke N 1.25 3.00
104 Bobby Hull N 2.00 5.00
105 Bobby Orr N 4.00 10.00
106 Mike Bossy N 1.25 3.00
107 Carey Price N 5.00 12.00
108 Chris Chelios N 1.25 3.00
109 Daniel Briere N 1.25 3.00
110 Dany Heatley N 1.25 3.00
111 Evgeni Malkin N 4.00 10.00
112 Guy Carbonneau N 1.25 3.00
113 Gordie Howe N 3.00 8.00
114 Grant Fuhr N 1.25 3.00
115 Guy Lafleur N 1.50 4.00
116 Henrik Lundqvist N 1.50 4.00
117 Henrik Zetterberg N 1.50 4.00
118 Jarome Iginla N 1.25 3.00
119 Jason Spezza N 1.25 3.00
120 Jean-Sebastien Giguere N 1.25 3.00
121 Joe Sakic N 2.00 5.00
122 Joe Thornton N 1.50 4.00
123 Johnny Bucyk N 1.25 3.00
124 Jonathan Toews N 3.00 8.00
125 Luc Robitaille N 1.25 3.00
126 Marc-Andre Fleury N 2.00 5.00
127 Marian Gaborik N 1.50 4.00
128 Mario Lemieux N 4.00 10.00
129 Mark Messier N 1.50 4.00
130 Markus Naslund N 1.00 2.50
131 Martin Brodeur N 2.50 6.00
132 Martin St. Louis N 1.25 3.00
133 Keith Tkachuk N 1.25 3.00
134 Mike Modano N 2.00 5.00
135 Nicklas Lidstrom N 1.25 3.00
136 Patrick Kane N 2.50 6.00
137 Paul Kariya N 1.50 4.00
138 Peter Forsberg N 1.50 4.00
139 Phil Esposito N 2.00 5.00
140 Ray Bourque N 2.00 5.00
141 Rick DiPietro N 1.00 2.50
142 Rick Nash N 1.25 3.00
143 Jeremy Roenick N 1.25 3.00
144 Roberto Luongo N 1.50 4.00
145 Mike Richards N 1.25 3.00
146 Miikka Kiprusoff N 1.00 2.50
147 Ryan Miller N 1.25 3.00
148 Saku Koivu N 1.25 3.00
149 Shane Doan N 1.00 2.50
150 Sidney Crosby N 5.00 12.00
151 Simon Gagne N 1.25 3.00
152 Stan Mikita N 1.50 4.00
153 Teemu Selanne N 2.50 6.00
154 Patrick Roy N 3.00 8.00
155 Thomas Vanek N 1.25 3.00
156 Tomas Vokoun N 1.00 2.50
157 Tony Esposito N 1.25 3.00
158 Vincent Lecavalier N 1.00 2.50
159 Wayne Gretzky N 6.00 15.00
160 Zach Parise N 1.25 3.00
161 Adam Pardy RC 2.50 6.00
162 Matthew Halischuk RC 2.00 5.00
163 Karl Alzner RC 2.00 5.00
164 Brendan Mikkelson RC 2.00 5.00
165 Trevor Lewis RC 3.00 8.00
166 Michal Repik RC 3.00 8.00
167 Chris Porter RC 3.00 8.00
168 Brad Staubitz RC 2.50 6.00
169 Cam Paddock RC 2.00 5.00
170 Jonas Frogren RC 2.00 5.00
171 Ben Bishop RC 5.00 12.00
172 Ben Maxwell RC 3.00 8.00
173 Nathan Gerbe RC 3.00 8.00
174 Tim Kennedy RC 3.00 8.00
175 Jesse Winchester RC 2.00 5.00
176 Simeon Varlamov RC 6.00 15.00
177 John Mitchell RC 2.50 6.00
178 Max Pacioretty RC 30.00 80.00
179 Chris Stewart RC 3.00 8.00
180 Brett Festerling RC 2.50 6.00
181 Mike Brown RC 4.00 10.00
182 Kenndal McArdle RC 2.50 6.00
183 Cory Schneider RC 8.00 20.00
184 Derek Dorsett RC 4.00 10.00
185 Ryan Jones RC 3.00 8.00
186 Ty Wishart RC 2.50 6.00
187 Theo Peckham RC 3.00 8.00
188 Tom Cavanagh RC 2.50 6.00
189 Wayne Simmonds RC 5.00 12.00
190 Janne Pesonen RC 2.50 6.00
191 Luke Schenn AU RC 6.00 15.00
192 Zach Bogosian AU RC 5.00 12.00
193 Justin Abdelkader AU RC 8.00 20.00
194 Ryan Jones AU RC 5.00 12.00
195 Brandon Sutter AU RC 25.00 60.00
196 Derick Brassard AU RC 4.00 10.00
197 Marc-Andre Gragnani RC 2.50 6.00
198 James Neal AU RC 10.00 25.00
199 Colton Gillies AU RC 4.00 10.00
200 Kyle Okposo AU RC 5.00 12.00
201 Brian Boyle AU RC 4.00 10.00
202 Petr Vrana AU RC 3.00 8.00
203 Zach Boychuk AU RC 5.00 12.00
204 Kevin Porter RC 2.50 6.00
205 Patric Hornqvist AU RC 5.00 12.00
206 Nikita Filatov AU RC 15.00 40.00
207 Mark Fistric AU RC 4.00 10.00
208 Dan LaCosta RC 3.00 8.00
209 Steve Mason AU RC 8.00 20.00
210 Erik Ersberg AU RC 4.00 10.00
211 Ryan Stone AU RC 3.00 8.00
212 Jon Filewich AU RC 4.00 10.00
213 Tyler Plante RC 2.50 6.00
214 Matt D'Agostini AU RC 4.00 10.00
215 Adam Pineault RC 2.50 6.00
216 Shawn Matthias AU RC 5.00 12.00
217 Viktor Tikhonov AU RC 4.00 10.00
218 Nikolai Kulemin AU RC 5.00 12.00
219 Blake Wheeler AU RC 15.00 40.00
220 Mattias Ritola AU RC 4.00 10.00
221 Tom Sestito RC 3.00 8.00
222 Darren Helm AU RC 5.00 12.00
223 Danny Taylor RC 2.50 6.00
224 Josh Bailey AU RC 30.00 80.00
225 Luca Sbisa AU RC 3.00 8.00
226 Jamie McGinn AU RC 5.00 12.00
227 Andrew Ebbett RC 2.00 5.00
228 Boris Valabik RC 3.00 8.00
229 Oscar Moller AU RC 4.00 10.00
230 Jonathan Ericsson AU RC 5.00 12.00
231 Alex Pietrangelo AU RC 12.00 30.00
232 Robbie Earl AU RC 3.00 8.00
233 Ilya Zubov AU RC 4.00 10.00
234 Teddy Purcell AU RC 6.00 15.00
235 Justin Pogge RC 3.00 8.00
236 Brian Lee AU RC 4.00 10.00
237 Claude Giroux AU RC 40.00 100.00
238 Vladimir Mihalik AU RC 3.00 8.00
239 Patrik Berglund AU RC 4.00 10.00
240 Lauri Korpikoski AU RC 3.00 8.00
241 Michael Frolik AU RC 5.00 12.00
242 Alex Goligoski AU RC 6.00 15.00
243 T.J. Oshie AU RC 20.00 50.00
244 Drew Doughty AU RC 35.00 60.00
245 Mikkel Boedker AU RC 6.00 15.00
246 Kyle Turris AU RC 10.00 25.00
247 Steven Stamkos AU RC 125.00 250.00
248 Jakub Voracek AU RC 12.00 30.00
249 Fabian Brunnstrom AU RC 4.00 10.00
250 Andreas Nodl AU RC 3.00 8.00

2008-09 SP Authentic Limited

*1-100 VETS: 2X TO 5X BASIC CARDS
*101-160 NOTABLE: .8X TO 2X
*161-250 ROOKIES: .6X TO 1.5X
STATED PRINT RUN 100 SER.#'d SETS
35 Nicklas Backstrom 2.50 6.00

2008-09 SP Authentic Holoview FX

COMPLETE SET (42) 60.00 120.00
STATED ODDS 1:12
FX43 Colton Gillies 1.00 2.50
FX44 Teemu Selanne 2.50 6.00
FX45 Ilya Kovalchuk 1.25 3.00
FX46 Marc Savard .75 2.00
FX47 Ryan Miller 1.25 3.00
FX48 Jarome Iginla 1.25 3.00
FX49 Dion Phaneuf 1.25 3.00
FX50 Eric Staal 1.50 4.00
FX51 Patrick Kane 2.50 6.00
FX52 Jonathan Toews 3.00 8.00
FX53 Paul Stastny 1.25 3.00
FX54 Rick Nash 1.25 3.00
FX55 Brenden Morrow 1.00 2.50
FX56 Brad Richards 1.25 3.00
FX57 Henrik Zetterberg 1.50 4.00
FX58 Marian Hossa 1.00 2.50
FX59 Nicklas Lidstrom 1.25 3.00
FX60 Shawn Horcoff .75 2.00
FX61 Sam Gagner 1.00 2.50
FX62 Fabian Brunnstrom 1.00 2.50
FX63 Anze Kopitar 2.00 5.00
FX64 Marian Gaborik 1.50 4.00
FX65 Saku Koivu 1.25 3.00
FX66 Carey Price 5.00 12.00
FX67 Steven Stamkos 8.00 20.00
FX68 Martin Brodeur 2.50 6.00
FX69 Rick DiPietro 1.00 2.50
FX70 Dany Heatley 1.25 3.00
FX71 Mike Richards 1.25 3.00
FX72 Peter Mueller 1.00 2.50
FX73 Evgeni Malkin 4.00 10.00
FX74 Marc-Andre Fleury 2.00 5.00
FX75 Sidney Crosby 5.00 12.00
FX76 Jonathan Cheechoo 1.25 3.00
FX77 Joe Thornton 1.50 4.00
FX78 Blake Wheeler 3.00 8.00
FX79 Vincent Lecavalier 1.00 2.50
FX80 Kyle Turris 2.00 5.00
FX81 Jakub Voracek 2.50 6.00
FX82 Roberto Luongo 1.50 4.00
FX83 Alexander Ovechkin 5.00 12.00
FX84 Nicklas Backstrom 2.00 5.00

2008-09 SP Authentic Holoview FX Die Cuts

*SINGLES: 1.2X TO 3X BASIC INSERTS
STATED ODDS 1:288
FX84 Nicklas Backstrom 6.00 15.00

2008-09 SP Authentic Limited Autographed Patches

STATED PRINT RUN 100 SER.#'d SETS
191 Luke Schenn 20.00 50.00
192 Zach Bogosian 15.00 40.00
193 Justin Abdelkader 25.00 60.00
194 Ryan Jones 15.00 40.00
195 Brandon Sutter 40.00 80.00
196 Derick Brassard 12.00 30.00
197 Marc-Andre Gragnani
198 James Neal 20.00 50.00
199 Colton Gillies 12.00 30.00
200 Kyle Okposo
201 Brian Boyle 12.00 30.00
202 Petr Vrana 10.00 25.00
203 Zach Boychuk 15.00 40.00
204 Kevin Porter
205 Patric Hornqvist 15.00 40.00
206 Nikita Filatov 40.00 100.00
207 Mark Fistric 12.00 30.00
208 Dan LaCosta
209 Steve Mason 25.00 60.00
210 Erik Ersberg 12.00 30.00
211 Ryan Stone 10.00 25.00
212 Jon Filewich 12.00 30.00
213 Tyler Plante
214 Matt D'Agostini 12.00 30.00
215 Adam Pineault
216 Shawn Matthias 15.00 40.00
217 Viktor Tikhonov 12.00 30.00
218 Nikolai Kulemin 15.00 40.00
219 Blake Wheeler 40.00 100.00
220 Mattias Ritola 12.00 30.00
221 Tom Sestito
222 Darren Helm 15.00 40.00
223 Danny Taylor
224 Josh Bailey 20.00 50.00
225 Luca Sbisa 10.00 25.00
226 Jamie McGinn 15.00 40.00
227 Andrew Ebbett
228 Boris Valabik
229 Oscar Moller 12.00 30.00
230 Jonathan Ericsson 15.00 40.00
231 Alex Pietrangelo 20.00 50.00
232 Robbie Earl 10.00 25.00
233 Ilya Zubov 12.00 30.00
234 Teddy Purcell 20.00 50.00
235 Nathan Oystrick
236 Brian Lee 12.00 30.00
237 Claude Giroux 125.00 250.00
238 Vladimir Mihalik 10.00 25.00
239 Patrik Berglund 12.00 30.00
240 Lauri Korpikoski 10.00 25.00
241 Michael Frolik 15.00 40.00
242 Alex Goligoski 20.00 50.00
243 T.J. Oshie 40.00 80.00
244 Drew Doughty 60.00 120.00
245 Mikkel Boedker 15.00 40.00
246 Kyle Turris 25.00 60.00
247 Steven Stamkos 300.00 600.00
248 Jakub Voracek 15.00 40.00
249 Fabian Brunnstrom 12.00 30.00
250 Andreas Nodl 10.00 25.00

2008-09 SP Authentic Marks of Distinction

STATED PRINT RUN 25 SER.#'d SETS
MDBH Bobby Hull 75.00 150.00
MDBO Bobby Orr 175.00 300.00
MDGH Gordie Howe 125.00 200.00
MDMB Martin Brodeur 100.00 200.00
MDMM Mark Messier 100.00 200.00
MDPR Patrick Roy 125.00 200.00
MDSC Sidney Crosby 100.00 200.00
MDWG Wayne Gretzky 200.00 350.00

2008-09 SP Authentic Penned Perfection

STATED PRINT RUN 50 SERIAL #'d SETS
PPCP Carey Price 40.00 100.00
PPDH Dany Heatley
PPES Eric Staal 12.00 30.00
PPHZ Henrik Zetterberg 12.00 30.00
PPJG Jean-Sebastien Giguere 10.00 25.00
PPJI Jarome Iginla 12.00 30.00
PPJT Joe Thornton 12.00 30.00
PPMG Nicklas Backstrom 15.00 40.00
PPMN Markus Naslund 8.00 20.00
PPMR Mike Richards 40.00 80.00
PPNL Nicklas Lidstrom 20.00 50.00
PPPB Patrice Bergeron 12.00 30.00
PPPK Patrick Kane 20.00 50.00
PPPM Peter Mueller 8.00 20.00
PPRM Ryan Miller 10.00 25.00
PPRN Rick Nash 20.00 40.00
PPSK Saku Koivu 10.00 25.00
PPTO Jonathan Toews 25.00 60.00

2008-09 SP Authentic Rookie Review Autographed Patches

STATED PRINT RUN 100 SERIAL #'d SETS
RRBM Brenden Morrow 10.00 25.00
RRCD Chris Drury 10.00 25.00
RRCP Carey Price 50.00 100.00
RRCW Cam Ward 12.00 30.00
RRDH Dany Heatley 12.00 30.00
RRDK Dominik Hasek 15.00 40.00
RREM Evgeni Malkin 25.00 60.00
RRES Eric Staal 15.00 40.00
RRHZ Henrik Zetterberg 15.00 40.00
RRJI Jarome Iginla 12.00 30.00
RRJS Jordan Staal 12.00 30.00
RRJT Jonathan Toews 40.00 80.00
RRMB Martin Brodeur 40.00 80.00
RRMF Marc-Andre Fleury 40.00 80.00
RRMH Marian Hossa 10.00 25.00
RRMM Mike Modano 15.00 40.00
RRMR Mike Richards 12.00 30.00
RRMT Marty Turco 12.00 30.00
RRNL Nicklas Lidstrom 25.00 50.00
RRPK Patrick Kane 30.00 80.00
RRPS Paul Stastny 10.00 25.00
RRRG Ryan Getzlaf 20.00 50.00
RRRM Ryan Miller 20.00 50.00
RRRN Rick Nash 12.00 30.00
RRSC Sidney Crosby 100.00 200.00
RRSG Scott Gomez 10.00 25.00
RRTH Joe Thornton 20.00 50.00
RRVL Vincent Lecavalier 20.00 50.00

2008-09 SP Authentic Sign of the Times

STATED ODDS 1:14
STAP Alex Pietrangelo 4.00 10.00
STBB Brian Boyle 2.50 6.00
STBD Mikkel Boedker 4.00 10.00
STBH Bobby Hull 25.00 60.00
STBO Ray Bourque 30.00 80.00
STBS Brandon Sutter 3.00 8.00
STCA Carey Price 30.00 60.00
STCW Cam Ward 5.00 12.00
STDC Daniel Carcillo 3.00 8.00
STDD Drew Doughty 8.00 20.00
STDH Darren Helm 3.00 8.00
STDS Drew Stafford 4.00 10.00
STEM Evgeni Malkin 20.00 50.00
STES Eric Staal 6.00 15.00
STFL Marc-Andre Fleury 15.00 40.00
STGH Gordie Howe 60.00 120.00
STHE T.J. Hensick 4.00 10.00
STHZ Henrik Zetterberg 20.00 50.00
STJF Jon Filewich 2.50 6.00
STJH Josh Harding 5.00 12.00
STJI Jarome Iginla 5.00 12.00
STJK Jari Kurri 8.00 20.00
STJM Joe Mullen 4.00 10.00
STJO Joe Thornton 15.00 40.00
STJT Jonathan Toews 25.00 50.00
STJV Jakub Voracek 12.50 25.00
STKA Patrick Kane 25.00 50.00
STKO Kyle Okposo 3.00 8.00
STKT Kyle Turris 5.00 12.00
STLS Luke Schenn 4.00 10.00
STMB Martin Brodeur 75.00 150.00
STME Mark Messier
STMI Mike Iggulden 4.00 10.00
STMK Mike Richards 5.00 12.00
STOR Bobby Orr 75.00 150.00
STPK Phil Kessel 6.00 15.00
STRE Robbie Earl 2.00 5.00
STRM Ryan Miller 8.00 20.00
STRN Rick Nash 15.00 40.00
STRS Ryan Stone 2.00 5.00
STSA Denis Savard 6.00 15.00
STSC Sidney Crosby 75.00 150.00
STSH James Sheppard 3.00 8.00
STSM Steve Mason 12.00 30.00
STSS Steven Stamkos 20.00 50.00
STST Paul Stastny 5.00 12.00
STTE Tobias Enstrom 3.00 8.00
STTJ T.J. Oshie 12.00 30.00
STTV Tomas Vokoun 4.00 10.00
STVA Thomas Vanek 5.00 12.00
STVL Vincent Lecavalier 15.00 40.00
STWG Wayne Gretzky 150.00 300.00
STZB Zach Bogosian 3.00 8.00
STZH Zach Boychuk 3.00 8.00

2008-09 SP Authentic Sign of the Times Duals

STATED ODDS 1:288
ST2BF M.Brodeur/M.Fleury 40.00 80.00
ST2BM S.Mason/D.Brassard 10.00 25.00
ST2EE T.Esposito/P.Esposito 20.00 50.00
ST2GM W.Gretzky/M.Messier 250.00 400.00
ST2HT B.Hull/J.Toews 50.00 100.00
ST2HZ D.Heatley/I.Zubov 10.00 25.00
ST2KP K.Okposo/P.Kessel 12.00 30.00
ST2KS P.Kane/J.Skille 15.00 40.00
ST2KT S.Koivu/A.Tanguay 15.00 40.00
ST2LM M.Lemieux/E.Malkin 75.00 150.00
ST2LT J.Thornton/V.Lecavalier 12.00 30.00
ST2MT M.Modano/M.Turco 15.00 40.00
ST2OB B.Orr/R.Bourque 100.00 200.00
ST2PK C.Price/P.Kane 40.00 100.00
ST2PP P.Stastny/P.Stastny 15.00 40.00
ST2PT P.Mueller/K.Turris 25.00 60.00
ST2RC M.Richards/J.Carter 20.00 50.00
ST2RK L.Robitaille/J.Kurri 20.00 50.00
ST2SS J.Staal/M.Staal 10.00 25.00
ST2SW E.Staal/C.Ward 12.00 30.00
ST2ZH G.Howe/H.Zetterberg 60.00 120.00

2008-09 SP Authentic Sign of the Times Triples

STATED PRINT RUN 25 SER.#'d SETS
ST3BHS Harding/Shpprd/Bchrd
ST3BTK Kane/Toews/Backstrm 100.00 175.00
ST3CHS Hextall/Clarke/Schultz 50.00 100.00
ST3GND Naslund/Gomez/Drury 50.00 100.00
ST3GNT Turco/Nabkv/Giguer 30.00 60.00
ST3IHN Heatley/Iginla/Nash 40.00 100.00
ST3KTH Koivu/Tanguy/Higgins 50.00 100.00
ST3LBC Bouchrd/Carbon/Lafler 40.00 100.00
ST3LBM Messier/Mario/Bourque 150.00 300.00
ST3MCT Mueller/Turris/Carcillo 20.00 40.00
ST3MRM Modano/Morrow/Rbero 25.00 60.00
ST3MSG Gilmour/Mahov/Salming 40.00 100.00
ST3OGH Gretzky/Howe/Orr 600.00 1000.00
ST3PMV Miller/Vanek/Pominvle 60.00 120.00
ST3RBP Roy/Brodeur/Price 100.00 200.00
ST3SSS Staal/Staal/Staal 40.00 80.00

2009-10 SP Authentic

COMP.SET w/o SPS (100) 10.00 25.00
101-160 ESS PRINT RUN 1999
161-200 ROOKIE PRINT RUN 999
201-260 ROOKIE AU PRINT RUN 999
1 Phil Kessel .40 1.00
2 Luke Schenn .25 .60
3 Doug Weight .30 .75
4 Drew Doughty .40 1.00
5 Carey Price 1.25 3.00
6 Vincent Lecavalier .25 .60
7 Joe Thornton .30 .75
8 Alexander Ovechkin 1.25 3.00
9 Steve Mason .25 .60
10 Dany Heatley .30 .75
11 Peter Mueller .25 .60
12 Henrik Zetterberg .40 1.00
13 Ryan Getzlaf .50 1.25
14 Claude Giroux .30 .75
15 Tomas Vokoun .25 .60
16 Roberto Luongo .40 1.00
17 Ilya Kovalchuk .30 .75
18 Mike Richards .30 .75
19 Jonathan Toews .60 1.50
20 Marian Gaborik .40 1.00
21 Mike Modano .50 1.25
22 Eric Staal .40 1.00
23 Pekka Rinne .40 1.00
24 Miikka Kiprusoff .25 .60
25 Jason Pominville .30 .75
26 Paul Stastny .30 .75
27 Paul Kariya .40 1.00
28 Mikko Koivu .30 .75
29 Marc-Andre Fleury .50 1.25
30 Martin Brodeur .60 1.50
31 Sam Gagner .25 .60
32 Nicklas Lidstrom .30 .75
33 Jakub Voracek .30 .75
34 Chris Pronger .25 .60
35 Marc Staal .30 .75
36 Kris Versteeg .30 .75
37 Martin St. Louis .30 .75
38 Olli Jokinen .25 .60
39 Martin Havlat .25 .60
40 Jason Spezza .30 .75
41 Chris Stewart .25 .60
42 Brad Richards .30 .75
43 Bryan Little .30 .75
44 Nikolai Khabibulin .30 .75
45 Derek Roy .25 .60
46 Bobby Ryan .30 .75
47 Scott Gomez .25 .60
48 Shea Weber .25 .60
49 Henrik Lundqvist .50 1.25
50 Johan Franzen .30 .75
51 Tim Thomas .30 .75
52 Patrick Marleau .30 .75
53 Evgeni Malkin 1.00 2.50
54 Anze Kopitar .50 1.25
55 Jeff Carter .30 .75
56 Mike Ribeiro .25 .60
57 Tomas Kaberle .20 .50
58 Shane Doan .25 .60
59 Zach Parise .30 .75
60 Alex Kovalev .30 .75
61 Rick Nash .25 .60
62 Mike Green .30 .75
63 Andrei Markov .30 .75
64 Marian Hossa .25 .60
65 Nathan Horton .30 .75
66 Daniel Sedin .30 .75
67 Kyle Okposo .30 .75
68 Dion Phaneuf .40 1.00
69 Cam Ward .30 .75
70 Milan Hejduk .25 .60
71 Blake Wheeler .30 .75
72 Patrik Berglund .20 .50
73 Ales Hemsky .25 .60
74 Kari Lehtonen .25 .60
75 Niklas Backstrom .30 .75
76 Thomas Vanek .30 .75
77 Scott Niedermayer .30 .75
78 Simon Gagne .30 .75
79 Steven Stamkos .60 1.50
80 Jason Arnott .25 .60
81 Chris Drury .25 .60
82 Pavel Datsyuk .40 1.00
83 Nikolai Kulemin .25 .60
84 Ryan Smyth .25 .60
85 Marty Turco .30 .75
86 Mike Cammalleri .25 .60
87 Sidney Crosby 1.25 3.00
88 Patrick Kane .60 1.50
89 Patrik Elias .30 .75
90 Devin Setoguchi .25 .60
91 Zdeno Chara .30 .75
92 Andrew Cogliano .25 .60
93 Josh Bailey .25 .60
94 Derick Brassard .30 .75
95 Daniel Alfredsson .30 .75
96 Jarome Iginla .30 .75
97 Rod Brind`Amour .30 .75
98 Semyon Varlamov .30 .75
99 Henrik Sedin .30 .75
100 Ryan Miller .30 .75
101 Alexander Ovechkin ESS 3.00 8.00
102 Bobby Hull ESS 1.00 2.50
103 Bobby Orr ESS 2.50 6.00
104 Bobby Ryan ESS .75 2.00
105 Bryan Little ESS .75 2.00
106 Cam Neely ESS .75 2.00
107 Cam Ward ESS .75 2.00
108 Carey Price ESS 3.00 8.00
109 Dany Heatley ESS .75 2.00
110 Drew Doughty ESS 1.00 2.50
111 Eric Staal ESS 1.00 2.50
112 Evgeni Malkin ESS 2.50 6.00
113 Gordie Howe ESS 2.00 5.00
114 Henrik Lundqvist ESS 1.25 3.00
115 Henrik Zetterberg ESS 1.00 2.50
116 Ilya Kovalchuk ESS .75 2.00
117 Jarome Iginla ESS .75 2.00
118 Jason Spezza ESS .75 2.00
119 Jean Beliveau ESS .75 2.00
120 Jeff Carter ESS .75 2.00
121 Joe Thornton ESS .75 2.00
122 Johan Franzen ESS .75 2.00
123 Jonathan Toews ESS 1.50 4.00
124 Luke Schenn ESS .60 1.50
125 Marc-Andre Fleury ESS 1.25 3.00
126 Marian Gaborik ESS 1.00 2.50
127 Marian Hossa ESS .60 1.50
128 Mario Lemieux ESS 2.50 6.00
129 Mark Messier ESS 1.00 2.50
130 Martin Brodeur ESS 1.50 4.00
131 Martin St. Louis ESS .75 2.00
132 Marty Turco ESS .75 2.00
133 Miikka Kiprusoff ESS .60 1.50
134 Mike Richards ESS .75 2.00
135 Mikko Koivu ESS .75 2.00
136 Nicklas Backstrom ESS 1.25 3.00
137 Niklas Backstrom ESS .75 2.00
138 Nikolai Khabibulin ESS .75 2.00
139 Patrick Kane ESS 1.50 4.00
140 Patrick Marleau ESS .75 2.00
141 Patrick Roy ESS 2.00 5.00
142 Paul Kariya ESS 1.00 2.50
143 Paul Stastny ESS .75 2.00
144 Pavel Datsyuk ESS 1.00 2.50
145 Rick Nash ESS .60 1.50
146 Roberto Luongo ESS 1.00 2.50
147 Ryan Getzlaf ESS 1.25 3.00
148 Ryan Miller ESS .75 2.00
149 Sam Gagner ESS .60 1.50
150 Shane Doan ESS .60 1.50
151 Shea Weber ESS .60 1.50
152 Sidney Crosby ESS 3.00 8.00
153 Steve Mason ESS .60 1.50
154 Steve Yzerman ESS 2.00 5.00
155 Thomas Vanek ESS .75 2.00
156 Tim Thomas ESS .75 2.00
157 Vincent Lecavalier ESS .60 1.50
158 Wayne Gretzky ESS 4.00 10.00
159 Zach Parise ESS .75 2.00
160 Zdeno Chara ESS .75 2.00
161 Lars Eller RC 3.00 8.00
162 Ryan Wilson RC 3.00 8.00
163 Aaron Gagnon RC 2.00 5.00
164 James Reimer RC 8.00 20.00
165 Anton Khudobin RC 3.00 8.00
166 Scott Parse RC 3.00 8.00
167 Mathieu Carle RC 3.00 8.00
168 Alexander Salak RC 2.50 6.00
169 Mario Bliznak RC 3.00 8.00
170 Steven Zalewski RC 2.50 6.00
171 Peter Olvecky RC 3.00 8.00
172 Tom Pyatt RC 3.00 8.00
173 Ryan O'Marra RC 2.00 5.00
174 Deryk Engelland RC 4.00 10.00
175 Mathieu Perreault RC 5.00 12.00
176 Francis Wathier RC 2.50 6.00
177 Philippe Dupuis RC 3.00 8.00
178 David Laliberte RC 2.50 6.00
179 Shaun Heshka RC 3.00 8.00
180 Teemu Laakso RC 2.00 5.00
181 Ryan White RC 4.00 10.00
182 Victor Oreskovich RC 2.50 6.00
183 Davis Drewiske RC 3.00 8.00
184 Ryan Vesce RC 2.50 6.00
185 Peter Regin RC 2.50 6.00
186 Bobby Sanguinetti RC 2.00 5.00
187 Tyson Strachan RC 2.00 5.00
188 Guillaume Desbiens RC 3.00 8.00
189 Mika Pyorala RC 2.50 6.00
190 Devan Dubnyk RC 6.00 15.00
191 Phil Oreskovic RC 3.00 8.00
192 Andreas Thuresson RC 2.50 6.00
193 Jakub Kindl RC 3.00 8.00
194 Drayson Bowman RC 3.00 8.00
195 Johan Backlund RC 3.00 8.00
196 Ryan Stoa RC 2.50 6.00
197 Braden Holtby RC 15.00 40.00
198 Keaton Ellerby RC 2.50 6.00
199 Matthew Corrente RC 2.50 6.00
200 Alexander Sulzer RC 2.00 5.00
201 John Tavares AU RC 150.00 250.00
202 Victor Hedman AU RC 25.00 60.00
203 Matt Duchene AU RC 15.00 40.00
204 Colin Wilson AU RC 5.00 12.00
205 Tyler Bozak AU RC 8.00 20.00
206 James van Riemsdyk AU RC 10.00 25.00
207 Evander Kane AU RC 12.00 30.00
208 Michael Grabner AU RC 5.00 12.00
209 Erik Karlsson AU RC 80.00 200.00
210 Matt Gilroy AU RC 5.00 12.00
211 Tyler Myers AU RC 8.00 20.00
212 Antti Niemi AU RC 8.00 20.00
213 Ville Leino AU RC 4.00 10.00
214 Yannick Weber AU RC 5.00 12.00
215 Jonas Gustavsson AU RC 6.00 15.00
216 Brian Salcido AU RC 4.00 10.00
217 Spencer Machacek AU RC 5.00 12.00
218 Chris Butler AU RC 5.00 12.00
219 Lars Eller AU 5.00 12.00
220 Benn Ferriero AU RC 6.00 15.00
221 Alec Martinez AU RC 8.00 20.00
222 Ryan O'Reilly AU RC 10.00 25.00
223 Jamie Benn AU RC 25.00 60.00
224 Byron Bitz AU RC 5.00 12.00
225 John Scott AU RC 6.00 15.00
226 Riku Helenius AU RC 6.00 15.00
227 Jesse Joensuu AU RC 5.00 12.00
228 Cody Franson AU RC 6.00 15.00
229 Matt Beleskey AU RC 5.00 12.00
230 Dmitry Kulikov AU RC 6.00 15.00
231 Michael Del Zotto AU RC 6.00 15.00
232 Ivan Vishnevskiy AU RC 5.00 12.00
233 Jhonas Enroth AU RC 8.00 20
234 Christian Hanson AU RC 6.00 15
235 Mikael Backlund AU RC 6.00 15
236 Michal Neuvirth AU RC 10.00 25
237 Ray Macias AU RC 5.00 12
238 Cal O'Reilly AU RC 5.00 12
239 Taylor Chorney AU RC 6.00 15
240 Oskars Bartulis AU RC 6.00 15
241 Mike Santorelli AU RC 6.00 15
242 Tom Wandell AU RC 25.00 60
243 Andrew MacDonald AU RC 4.00 10
244 Artem Anisimov AU RC 6.00 15
245 Matt Pelech AU RC 6.00 15
246 Peter Regin AU 5.00 12
247 Ryan O'Marra AU 4.00 10
248 Joel Rechlicz AU RC 4.00 10
249 Jason Demers AU RC 10.00 25
250 Sergei Shirokov AU RC 4.00 10
251 Jay Rosehill AU RC 6.00 15
252 Frazer McLaren AU RC 5.00 12
253 Michael Sauer AU RC 5.00 12
254 Kris Chucko AU RC 5.00 12
255 T.J. Galiardi AU RC 6.00 15
256 Luca Caputi AU RC 20.00 50
257 Viktor Stalberg AU RC 6.00 15
258 Perttu Lindgren AU RC 5.00 12
259 Logan Couture AU RC 15.00 40
260 Brad Marchand AU RC 30.00 80

2009-10 SP Authentic Limite Autographed Patches

STATED PRINT RUN 100 SER.#'d SETS
201 John Tavares 200.00 400
202 Victor Hedman 25.00 60
203 Matt Duchene 125.00 250
204 Colin Wilson 12.00 25
205 Tyler Bozak 25.00 60
206 James van Riemsdyk 25.00 60
207 Evander Kane 60.00 120
208 Michael Grabner 15.00 40
209 Erik Karlsson 100.00 200
210 Matt Gilroy 15.00 40
211 Tyler Myers 25.00 60
212 Antti Niemi 75.00 150
213 Ville Leino 12.00 30
214 Yannick Weber 15.00 40
215 Jonas Gustavsson 20.00 50
216 Brian Salcido 12.00 30
217 Spencer Machacek 15.00 40
218 Chris Butler 10.00 25
219 Lars Eller 25.00 50
220 Benn Ferriero 15.00 40
221 Alec Martinez 20.00 50
222 Ryan O'Reilly 30.00 80
223 Jamie Benn 100.00 200
224 Byron Bitz 12.00 30
225 John Scott 50.00 120
226 Riku Helenius 15.00 40
227 Jesse Joensuu 12.00 30
228 Cody Franson 12.00 30
229 Matt Beleskey 12.00 30
230 Dmitry Kulikov 15.00 40
231 Michael Del Zotto 15.00 40
232 Ivan Vishnevskiy 12.00 30
233 Jhonas Enroth 15.00 40
234 Christian Hanson 15.00 40
235 Mikael Backlund 15.00 40
236 Michal Neuvirth 20.00 50
237 Ray Macias 12.00 30
238 Cal O'Reilly 12.00 30
240 Oskars Bartulis 15.00 40
241 Mike Santorelli 15.00 40
243 Andrew MacDonald 10.00 25
244 Artem Anisimov 15.00 40
245 Matt Pelech 15.00 40
247 Ryan O'Marra 10.00 25
248 Joel Rechlicz 10.00 25
249 Jason Demers 25.00 60
250 Sergei Shirokov 10.00 25
251 Jay Rosehill 15.00 40
252 Frazer McLaren 12.00 30
253 Michael Sauer 12.00 30
254 Kris Chucko 12.00 30
255 T.J. Galiardi 15.00 40
257 Viktor Stalberg 15.00 40
258 Perttu Lindgren 12.00 30
259 Logan Couture 50.00 100
260 Brad Marchand 40.00 100

2009-10 SP Authentic Chirography

STATED PRINT RUN 50 SER.#'d SETS
AM Andrei Markov 10.00 25
AO Alexander Ovechkin 60.00 120
AZ Anze Kopitar 15.00 40
BR Bobby Ryan 10.00 25
CD Chris Drury 8.00 20
CG Claude Giroux 20.00 40
DE Derick Brassard 10.00 25
DS Devin Setoguchi 8.00 20
EN Evgeni Nabokov 8.00 20
ES Eric Staal 8.00 20
JS James Sheppard 6.00 15
JT Jonathan Toews 30.00 60
LS Luke Schenn
MF Marc-Andre Fleury 15.00 40
MM Mike Modano 15.00 40
MR Mike Ribeiro 8.00 20
PD Pavel Datsyuk 12.00 30
PK Phil Kessel 12.00 30
PM Peter Mueller 8.00 20
PS Paul Stastny 10.00 25
RI Mike Richards 15.00 40
RM Ryan Miller 10.00 25
SC Sidney Crosby 100.00 200
SM Steve Mason 8.00 20
SS Steven Stamkos 30.00 60
ST Jordan Staal 10.00 25
SW Shea Weber 8.00 20
TV Tomas Vokoun 8.00 20
VF Valtteri Filppula 10.00 25

2009-10 SP Authentic Holovie FX

COMPLETE SET (42) 75.00 150
STATED ODDS 1:12
FX1 Alexander Ovechkin 5.00 12
FX2 Anze Kopitar 2.00 5

3 Bobby Orr 4.00 10.00
4 Carey Price 5.00 12.00
5 Dany Heatley 1.25 3.00
6 Eric Staal 1.50 4.00
7 Evgeni Malkin 4.00 10.00
8 Gordie Howe 3.00 8.00
9 Henrik Zetterberg 1.50 4.00
10 Ilya Kovalchuk 1.25 3.00
11 Jarome Iginla 1.25 3.00
12 Jason Spezza 1.25 3.00
13 Jeff Carter 1.25 3.00
14 Joe Thornton 1.25 3.00
15 John Tavares 6.00 15.00
16 Jonathan Toews 2.50 6.00
17 Marc-Andre Fleury 2.00 5.00
18 Marian Gaborik 1.50 4.00
19 Mario Lemieux 4.00 10.00
20 Mark Messier 1.50 4.00
21 Martin Brodeur 2.50 6.00
22 Matt Duchene 2.50 6.00
23 Mike Modano 2.00 5.00
24 Mikko Koivu 1.25 3.00
25 Patrick Kane 2.50 6.00
26 Patrick Roy 3.00 8.00
27 Paul Kariya 1.50 4.00
28 Paul Stastny 1.25 3.00
29 Pavel Datsyuk 1.50 4.00
30 Phil Kessel 1.50 4.00
31 Rick Nash 1.00 2.50
32 Roberto Luongo 1.50 4.00
33 Ryan Getzlaf 2.00 5.00
34 Ryan Miller 1.25 3.00
35 Sam Gagner 1.00 2.50
36 Shane Doan 1.00 2.50
37 Sidney Crosby 5.00 12.00
38 Steve Yzerman 3.00 8.00
39 Tim Thomas 1.25 3.00
40 Victor Hedman 2.50 6.00
41 Vincent Lecavalier 1.00 2.50
42 Wayne Gretzky 6.00 15.00

2009-10 SP Authentic Holoview FX Die Cuts

INGLES: 1.5X TO 4X HOLOVIEW
TATED ODDS 1:288

2009-10 SP Authentic Marks of Distinction

TATED PRINT RUN 25 SER.#'d SETS
DAK Anze Kopitar 20.00 50.00
DAO Alexander Ovechkin 60.00 150.00
DBL Brian Lee 12.00 30.00
DBO Zach Boychuk 10.00 25.00
DBW Blake Wheeler
DCP Carey Price 50.00 125.00
DCW Cam Ward 12.00 30.00
DDH Dany Heatley 12.00 30.00
DES Eric Staal 15.00 40.00
DGA Simon Gagne 12.00 30.00
DHL Henrik Lundqvist
DIK Ilya Kovalchuk 8.00 20.00
DJA Jason Arnott 10.00 25.00
DJB Josh Bailey
DJC Jeff Carter 15.00 40.00
DJI Jarome Iginla 12.00 30.00
DJT Jonathan Toews 25.00 60.00
DKA Karl Alzner 8.00 20.00
DMB Martin Brodeur 60.00 120.00
DMG Marian Gaborik 15.00 40.00
DMS Martin St. Louis 12.00 30.00
DMT Marty Turco 12.00 30.00
DNL Nicklas Lidstrom 12.00 30.00
DPD Pavel Datsyuk 15.00 40.00
DSC Sidney Crosby 150.00 300.00
DSD Shane Doan 10.00 25.00
DSG Scott Gomez 10.00 25.00
DSS Steven Stamkos 40.00 80.00
DTH Joe Thornton 12.00 30.00
DVO Tomas Vokoun 15.00 40.00
DZB Zach Bogosian 8.00 20.00

2009-10 SP Authentic Prestigious Pairings

TATED PRINT RUN 100 SER.#'d SETS
PBC S.Bowman/D.Cherry 40.00 80.00
PBS Stamkos/Brassard 20.00 50.00
PCG J.Carter/Cl.Giroux 10.00 25.00
PEG Elias/Gaborik 12.00 30.00
PFS Staal/Fleury 20.00 50.00
PGP Price/Gomez 20.00 50.00
PHH Howe/Howe 50.00 100.00
PIS Iginla/Staal 12.00 30.00
PKK P.Kessel/P.Kane 20.00 50.00
PLD Delvecchio/Lindsay
PLS N.Lidstrom/B.Salming 10.00 25.00
PMJ Staal/M.Richards EXCH
PMR M.Modano/M.Ribeiro 15.00 40.00
PMT K.Turris/P.Mueller 10.00 25.00
PNB D.Brassard/R.Nash 15.00 40.00
POB Ovechkin/Backstrom 40.00 100.00
PPB Berglund/Perron 15.00 40.00
PPV T.Vanek/J.Pominville
PPW D.Phaneuf/S.Weber
PRS D.Setoguchi/B.Ryan 12.00 30.00
PTH Heatley/Thornton 15.00 40.00
PTT Thornton/Toews 20.00 50.00
PTW Ward/Turco 10.00 25.00
PVS Lecavalier/Stamkos 20.00 50.00
PYM Yzerman/Messier 60.00 120.00
PZB N.Backstrom/H.Zetterberg 15.00 40.00

2009-10 SP Authentic Rookie Review Autographed Patches

TATED PRINT RUN 100 SER.#'d SETS
P STATED PRINT RUN 25 SER.#'d SETS
RAK Anze Kopitar/100 25.00 60.00
RAM Al MacInnis/25 60.00 120.00
RAO Alexander Ovechkin/25 100.00 200.00
RBL Brian Leetch/25 20.00 50.00
RCD Chris Drury/100 10.00 25.00
RCN Cam Neely/25 30.00 80.00
RCW Cam Ward/100 20.00 50.00
RDG Doug Gilmour/100 20.00 40.00
RDH Dany Heatley/25 20.00 50.00
REM Evgeni Malkin/25
RES Eric Staal/100 12.00 30.00
RHL Henrik Lundqvist/100 25.00 60.00
RHS Henrik Sedin/100 15.00 40.00
RHZ Henrik Zetterberg/25 25.00 60.00
RIK Ilya Kovalchuk/25 20.00 50.00
RJA Jason Arnott/100 12.00 30.00
RJC Jeff Carter/100 12.00 30.00
RJD J.P. Dumont/100 10.00 25.00
RJG Jean-Sebastian Giguere/100 15.00 40.00
RJI Jarome Iginla/25 30.00 80.00
RJT Joe Thornton/25 20.00 50.00
RLM Lanny McDonald/100 15.00 40.00
RLR Luc Robitaille/100 15.00 40.00
RMG Marian Gaborik/25 40.00 100.00
RMH Milan Hejduk/100 12.00 30.00
RMM Mike Modano/100 25.00 60.00
RMS Martin St. Louis/100 15.00 40.00

RRMT Marty Turco/100 20.00 50.00
RRMV Andrei Markov/100 15.00 40.00
RRNB Nicklas Backstrom/25 50.00 100.00
RRPD Pavel Datsyuk/100 30.00 60.00
RRPL Pascal Leclaire/100 15.00 40.00
RRPR Patrick Roy/25 100.00 200.00
RRPS Peter Stastny/100 15.00 40.00
RRRI Mike Ribeiro/100 8.00 20.00
RRRO Larry Robinson/25 20.00 50.00
RRRS Ryan Smyth/100 12.00 30.00
RRSG Scott Gomez/100 12.00 30.00
RRSI Simon Gagne/100 15.00 40.00
RRSS Steve Shutt/100 15.00 40.00
RRSY Steve Yzerman/25 100.00 200.00
RRTV Thomas Vanek/100 15.00 40.00
RRVL Vincent Lecavalier/25 12.00 30.00
RRVO Tomas Vokoun/100 12.00 30.00

2009-10 SP Authentic Sign of the Times

OVERALL AU ODDS 1:8
STAA Artem Anisimov A 6.00 15.00
STAC Andrew Cogliano 5.00 12.00
STAE Andrew Ebbett 4.00 10.00
STAK Anze Kopitar 10.00 25.00
STAL Andrew Ladd 8.00 20.00
STAO Adam Oates 6.00 15.00
STAP Alex Pietrangelo 5.00 12.00
STBA Mikael Backlund 6.00 15.00
STBH Bobby Hull 15.00 40.00
STBL Brian Leetch 8.00 20.00
STBM Ben Maxwell 5.00 12.00
STBO Bobby Orr 75.00 150.00
STBR Bobby Ryan 6.00 15.00
STBS Brandon Sutter 5.00 12.00
STBW Blake Wheeler C 6.00 15.00
STCG Colton Gillies 6.00 15.00
STCH Christian Hanson 6.00 15.00
STCP Carey Price 20.00 40.00
STDB David Backes 6.00 15.00
STDC Daniel Carcillo 4.00 10.00
STDH Dale Hawerchuk C 8.00 20.00
STDP Dion Phaneuf A 8.00 20.00
STDS Darryl Sutter 5.00 12.00
STDU Matt Duchene 15.00 40.00
STEE Erik Ersberg 5.00 12.00
STEJ Jhonas Enroth 8.00 20.00
STEK Evander Kane 10.00 25.00
STEN Eric Nystrom 5.00 12.00
STES Eric Staal 6.00 15.00
STFB Fabian Brunnstrom 5.00 12.00
STFO Nick Foligno 5.00 12.00
STGA Simon Gagne 6.00 15.00
STGU Jonas Gustavsson 12.00 30.00
STHL Henrik Lundqvist 15.00 30.00
STIK Ilya Kovalchuk A 6.00 15.00
STIV Ivan Vishnevskiy 5.00 12.00
STJA Jason Arnott 5.00 12.00
STJB Josh Bailey 5.00 12.00
STJD J.P. Dumont 4.00 10.00
STJE Jonathan Ericsson 5.00 12.00
STJG Jean-Sebastian Giguere A 10.00 25.00
STJH Josh Harding 6.00 15.00
STJI Jarome Iginla SP 50.00 100.00
STJJ Jack Johnson 4.00 10.00
STJK Jari Kurri B 8.00 20.00
STJS James Sheppard 4.00 10.00
STJT Jonathan Toews 30.00 60.00
STKA Karl Alzner 4.00 10.00
STLS Luke Schenn C 6.00 15.00
STMA Andrei Markov 6.00 15.00
STMG Marian Gaborik 8.00 20.00
STMI Mikkel Boedker 4.00 10.00
STML Maxim Lapierre 4.00 10.00
STMP Max Pacioretty 8.00 20.00
STMS Mark Streit 4.00 10.00
STMT Maxime Talbot 6.00 15.00
STNB Nicklas Backstrom 10.00 25.00
STNG Nathan Gerbe 5.00 12.00
STOM Oscar Moller 4.00 10.00
STOV Alexander Ovechkin 25.00 60.00
STPD Pavel Datsyuk 15.00 40.00
STPK Phil Kessel 8.00 20.00
STPM Peter Mueller 5.00 12.00
STRI Mike Richards 6.00 15.00
STRM Ryan Miller 10.00 25.00
STSC Sidney Crosby SP 125.00 250.00
STSG Scott Gomez 5.00 12.00
STSM Martin St. Louis 6.00 15.00
STSS Steven Stamkos 20.00 50.00
STST Jordan Staal 6.00 15.00
STSW Stephen Weiss B 4.00 10.00
STSY Steve Yzerman SP 175.00 300.00
STTA John Tavares 25.00 50.00
STTK Tim Kennedy 5.00 12.00
STTV Thomas Vanek 6.00 15.00
STTW Ty Wishart 5.00 12.00
STVF Valtteri Filppula 6.00 15.00
STVH Victor Hedman 10.00 25.00
STVL Ville Leino 5.00 12.00
STVO Tomas Vokoun C 5.00 12.00
STVR James van Riemsdyk 12.00 30.00
STWE Shea Weber 5.00 12.00
STZB Zach Bogosian C 5.00 12.00

2009-10 SP Authentic Sign of the Times Duals

OVERALL AU ODDS 1:8
ST2AW J.Arnott/C.Wilson 10.00 25.00
ST2BH J.Harding/N.Backstrom
ST2BL L.Sbisa/B.Salcido
ST2BO D.Backes/T.Oshie
ST2BW P.Bergeron/B.Wheeler
ST2DC M.Duchene/P.Stastny 20.00 50.00
ST2DM P.Mueller/S.Doan 8.00 20.00
ST2DW S.Weber/J.Dumont 8.00 20.00
ST2EO P.Esposito/B.Orr 75.00 150.00
ST2EZ E.Staal/Z.Boychuk 12.00 30.00
ST2FF M.Foligno/N.Foligno 8.00 20.00
ST2FK J.Kurri/G.Fuhr 20.00 50.00
ST2FL V.Filppula/V.Leino 10.00 25.00
ST2FM N.Filatov/M.Mayorov
ST2FV I.Vishnevskiy/M.Fistric 8.00 20.00
ST2GA M.Green/K.Alzner 10.00 25.00
ST2GG C.Gillies/C.Gillies
ST2GL M.Gaborik/H.Lundqvist 20.00 50.00
ST2GS L.Schenn/J.Gustavsson 12.00 30.00
ST2HB T.Bozak/C.Hanson 20.00 50.00
ST2HD A.Delvecchio/G.Howe
ST2HT J.Toews/B.Hull 40.00 100.00
ST2IB J.Iginla/M.Backlund 10.00 25.00
ST2JD D.Doughty/J.Johnson 12.00 30.00
ST2KM A.Kopitar/O.Moller
ST2LE J.Ericsson/N.Lidstrom 10.00 25.00
ST2LF N.Foligno/P.Leclaire 10.00 25.00
ST2LG S.Gomez/M.Lapierre
ST2LM B.Leetch/M.Messier 20.00 50.00
ST2LP M.Pacioretty/M.Lapierre
ST2MA A.Anisimov/M.Gaborik 12.00 30.00
ST2MM T.Myers/R.Miller 15.00 40.00
ST2MP C.Price/A.Markov 40.00 100.00

ST2MW A.Markov/Y.Weber 10.00 25.00
ST2NC K.Chucko/E.Nystrom 8.00 20.00
ST2NV M.Neuvirth/S.Varlamov 15.00 40.00
ST2NW C.Neely/B.Wheeler
ST2OC P.O'Sullivan/A.Cogliano
ST2OM A.Ovechkin/E.Malkin 100.00 200.00
ST2PP D.Phaneuf/M.Pelech 12.00 30.00
ST2RB M.Beleskey/B.Ryan 10.00 25.00
ST2RC D.Carcillo/M.Richards
ST2SB M.Streit/J.Bailey 15.00 40.00
ST2SG J.Sheppard/C.Gillies 15.00 40.00
ST2SM M.Stajan/J.Mitchell 8.00 20.00
ST2SS P.Stastny/P.Stastny 10.00 25.00
ST2ST S.Stamkos/M.St. Louis 20.00 50.00
ST2SU B.Sutter/B.Sutter 8.00 20.00
ST2TC L.Caputi/M.Talbot 10.00 25.00
ST2TS M.Talbot/J.Staal 10.00 25.00
ST2VB Z.Bogosian/B.Valabik
ST2VK T.Kennedy/T.Vanek 15.00 40.00
ST2VW T.Vokoun/S.Weiss 8.00 20.00

2009-10 SP Authentic Sign of the Times Triples

STATED PRINT RUN 25 SER.#'d SETS
ST3ADO Arnott/Dumont/O'Reilly
ST3BBM Brnstrm/Moller/Backlnd 15.00 40.00
ST3BEM Brodeur/T.Espo/Mason 30.00 80.00
ST3BMM Leetch/M.Staal/Sauer
ST3CGR Richrds/Gagne/Clrk 60.00 120.00
ST3DOM Datsyk/Ovech/Malk 200.00 300.00
ST3FME Fuhr/Miller/Enroth 60.00 120.00
ST3GSP Paclorty/Gomz/Shutt 40.00 100.00
ST3LEE Lndqvst/Ersberg/Enroth 20.00 50.00
ST3LHD Lindsay/Howe/Delvec
ST3LPM Mason/Price/Leclar 50.00 100.00
ST3LSS Lecav/St.L/Stamkos 60.00 120.00
ST3LYG Gretz/Yzermn/Mario 350.00 500.00
ST3LYR Yzermn/Leetch/Robit 75.00 150.00
ST3MRW Weber/Robsn/Markv 40.00 100.00
ST3RCG Richards/Carter/Giroux
ST3SBS E.Staal/Sutter/Boychuk 10.00 25.00
ST3YZH Howe/Yzermn/Zetter 125.00 250.00

2010-11 SP Authentic

COMP.SET w/o SPs (150) 12.00 30.00
151-208 ESS PRINT RUN 1999
209-248 ROOKIE PRINT RUN 999
249-310 ROOKIE AU PRINT RUN 999
1 Sidney Crosby 1.25 3.00
2 Ryan Kesler .30 .75
3 Phil Kessel .40 1.00
4 Thomas Vanek .30 .75
5 James van Riemsdyk .50 1.25
6 Tomas Holmstrom .20 .50
7 Tyler Myers .30 .75
8 Milan Hejduk .25 .60
9 Tomas Vokoun .25 .60
10 Paul Stastny .30 .75
11 Martin St. Louis .30 .75
12 Jeff Carter .30 .75
13 Ryan Miller .30 .75
14 John Tavares .60 1.50
15 Blake Wheeler .30 .75
16 Victor Hedman .40 1.00
17 Nicklas Backstrom .50 1.25
18 Michael Frolik .20 .50
19 Derick Brassard .30 .75
20 Shea Weber .25 .60
21 Matt Duchene .30 .75
22 Mike Green .30 .75
23 Daniel Sedin .30 .75
24 Jason Arnott .25 .60
25 Jakub Voracek .30 .75
26 Evander Kane .30 .75
27 Joe Pavelski .30 .75
28 Patrice Bergeron .40 1.00
29 Claude Giroux .30 .75
30 Devin Setoguchi .25 .60
31 Alexander Ovechkin 1.25 3.00
32 Steven Stamkos .60 1.50
33 Jarome Iginla .30 .75
34 Joe Thornton .30 .75
35 Martin Brodeur .60 1.50
36 Rick Nash .30 .75
37 Jonathan Toews .60 1.50
38 Patrick Kane .60 1.50
39 Drew Doughty .30 .75
40 Evgeni Malkin 1.00 2.50
41 Pavel Datsyuk .40 1.00
42 Shane Doan .25 .60
43 Nicklas Lidstrom .30 .75
44 Mike Richards .30 .75
45 Marc-Andre Fleury .50 1.25
46 Carey Price 1.25 3.00
47 Johan Franzen .30 .75
48 Ryan Getzlaf .50 1.25
49 Jean-Sebastien Giguere .25 .60
50 Eric Lindros .50 1.25
51 Joe Sakic .50 1.25
52 Ray Bourque .50 1.25
53 Luc Robitaille .30 .75
54 Guy Lafleur .40 1.00
55 Cam Neely .30 .75
56 Chris Osgood .30 .75
57 Steve Yzerman .75 2.00
58 Mark Messier .50 1.25
59 Mario Lemieux 1.00 2.50
60 Wayne Gretzky 1.50 4.00
61 Vincent Lecavalier .25 .60
62 Jaroslav Halak .30 .75
63 Ilya Bryzgalov .25 .60
64 Mike Fisher .30 .75
65 Daniel Alfredsson .30 .75
66 Josh Bailey .25 .60
67 Patric Hornqvist .25 .60
68 Tomas Plekanec .30 .75
69 Andrew Brunette .20 .50
70 Alexander Semin .30 .75
71 Gilbert Brule .30 .75
72 Alexandre Burrows .30 .75
73 James Neal .30 .75
74 Craig Anderson .30 .75
75 Marty Turco .30 .75
76 Cam Ward .30 .75
77 Derek Roy .30 .75
78 Dustin Byfuglien .30 .75
79 Bobby Ryan .30 .75
80 Steve Mason .25 .60
81 Miikka Kiprusoff .25 .60
82 Tuukka Rask .30 .75
83A Semyon Varlamov .30 .75
83B Corey Perry .30 .75
85 Luke Schenn .25 .60
86 Ryan Smyth .25 .60
87 Andrei Markov .30 .75
88 Jamie Langenbrunner .20 .50
89 Henrik Lundqvist .50 1.25
90 Chris Pronger .25 .60
91 Dany Heatley .25 .60
92 Dan Boyle .25 .60
93 Mark Streit .20 .50
94 Teemu Selanne .60 1.50
95 Jussi Jokinen .20 .50
96 Zdeno Chara .25 .60
97 Jonas Hiller .25 .60
98 Patrick Sharp .30 .75
99 Roberto Luongo .30 .75
100 Kari Lehtonen .25 .60
101 David Backes .30 .75
102 Chris Drury .25 .60
103 David Clarkson .20 .50
104 Jim Howard .40 1.00
105 Henrik Sedin .30 .75
106 Dion Phaneuf .30 .75
107 Jonathan Quick .50 1.25
108 Scott Gomez .25 .60
109 Antoine Vermette .20 .50
110 Guillaume Latendresse .25 .60
111 Rene Bourque .20 .50
112 Eric Staal .40 1.00
113 Mike Smith .30 .75
114 Michael Leighton .25 .60
115 Marian Gaborik .40 1.00
116 Patrick Marleau .30 .75
117 Andy McDonald .25 .60
118 Jason Spezza .20 .50
119 Mike Ribeiro .25 .60
120 Ales Hemsky .25 .60
121 Anze Kopitar .50 1.25
122 Loui Eriksson .25 .60
123 Brandon Sutter .25 .60
124 Sam Gagner .25 .60
125 Niklas Backstrom .30 .75
126 Nik Antropov .25 .60
127 Henrik Zetterberg .40 1.00
128 Dustin Penner .20 .50
129 Mikko Koivu .30 .75
130 Mike Modano .50 1.25
131 Marian Hossa .25 .60
132 Marc Savard .20 .50
133 Steve Sullivan .20 .50
134 Zach Parise .30 .75
135 Wojtek Wolski .20 .50
136 Mikael Samuelsson .20 .50
137 Brian Elliott .25 .60
138 Jordan Staal .30 .75
139 Brian Gionta .25 .60
140 Rick DiPietro .25 .60
141 Stephen Weiss .25 .60
142 Alex Tanguay .20 .50
143 Dustin Brown .30 .75
144 Brandon Dubinsky .25 .60
145 Erik Johnson .20 .50
146 J.P. Dumont .20 .50
147 Ville Leino .25 .60
148 Brad Richards .30 .75
149 Ilya Kovalchuk .30 .75
150 Pekka Rinne .40 1.00
151 Milan Lucic ESS .75 2.00
152 Teemu Selanne ESS 1.50 4.00
153 Joe Sakic ESS 1.25 3.00
154 Jakub Voracek ESS .75 2.00
155 Lanny McDonald ESS .75 2.00
156 Dustin Penner ESS .50 1.25
157 Mike Modano ESS 1.25 3.00
158 Patrik Elias ESS .75 2.00
159 Guillaume Latendresse ESS .60 1.50
160 Guy Lafleur ESS 1.00 2.50
161 Daniel Alfredsson ESS .75 2.00
162 Phil Esposito ESS 1.25 3.00
163 Alexander Ovechkin ESS 3.00 8.00
164 Evgeni Malkin ESS 2.50 6.00
165 Pekka Rinne ESS 1.00 2.50
166 Mario Lemieux ESS 2.50 6.00
167 Tony Esposito ESS .75 2.00
168 Tyler Myers ESS .75 2.00
169 Nicklas Lidstrom ESS .75 2.00
170 Milan Hejduk ESS .60 1.50
171 Duncan Keith ESS .75 2.00
172 Mikko Koivu ESS .75 2.00
173 Brandon Dubinsky ESS .60 1.50
174 Martin Brodeur ESS 1.50 4.00
175 Bobby Clarke ESS .75 2.00
176 Jaroslav Halak ESS .75 2.00
177 Steven Stamkos ESS 1.50 4.00
178 Henrik Sedin ESS .75 2.00
179 Eric Staal ESS 1.00 2.50
180 Corey Perry ESS .75 2.00
181 Dan Boyle ESS .60 1.50
182 Chris Pronger ESS .60 1.50
183 Phil Kessel ESS 1.00 2.50
184 Mike Green ESS .75 2.00
185 Anze Kopitar ESS 1.25 3.00
186 Jonathan Toews ESS 1.50 4.00
187 Sidney Crosby ESS 3.00 8.00
188 Mike Cammalleri ESS .75 2.00
189 Ray Bourque ESS 1.25 3.00
190 Dustin Byfuglien ESS .75 2.00
191 Brad Richards ESS .75 2.00
192 Johan Franzen ESS .75 2.00
193 Patrice Bergeron ESS 1.00 2.50
194 Dustin Brown ESS .75 2.00
195 Matt Duchene ESS .75 2.00
196 Jean-Sebastien Giguere ESS .60 1.50
197 Alexandre Burrows ESS .75 2.00
198 Doug Gilmour ESS 1.00 2.50
199 Wayne Gretzky ESS 4.00 10.00
200 Steve Yzerman ESS 2.00 5.00
201 Ilya Bryzgalov ESS .60 1.50
202 Jussi Jokinen ESS .50 1.25
203 Gilbert Perreault ESS .75 2.00
204 Joe Thornton ESS .75 2.00
205 Mark Messier ESS 1.25 3.00
206 Rick Nash ESS .75 2.00
207 Patrick Roy ESS 2.00 5.00
208 Gordie Howe ESS 2.00 5.00
209 Matt Kassian RC 3.00 8.00
210 Linus Klasen RC 3.00 8.00
211 Jon Matsumoto RC 3.00 8.00
212 Mark Dekanich RC 3.00 8.00
213 Adam McQuaid RC 4.00 10.00
214 Tomas Tatar RC 12.50 25.00
215 Korbinian Holzer RC 3.00 8.00
216 Jonas Holos RC 3.00 8.00
217 Jeremy Morin RC 3.00 8.00
218 Ben Smith RC 3.00 8.00
219 Nick Holden RC 3.00 8.00
220 Brandon McMillan RC 3.00 8.00
221 Travis Hamonic RC 4.00 10.00
222 Mats Zuccarello-Aasen RC 5.00 12.00
223 Evgeny Dadonov RC 4.00 10.00
224 Linus Omark RC 8.00 20.00
225 Patrice Cormier RC 4.00 10.00
226 Nikita Nikitin RC 3.00 8.00
227 Mike Moore RC 3.00 8.00
228 Jake Muzzin RC 3.00 8.00
229 Marco Scandella RC 3.00 8.00
230 Brad Mills RC 3.00 8.00
231 Alexander Urbom RC 3.00 8.00
232 Matt Taormina RC 3.00 8.00
233 Matt Martin RC 5.00 12.00
234 Alexander Vasyunov RC 3.00 8.00
235 Mark Fayne RC 3.00 8.00
236 Olivier Magnan-Grenier RC 3.00 8.00
237 Stephen Gionta RC 4.00 10.00
238 Derek Smith RC 3.00 8.00
239 Robin Lehner RC 6.00 15.00
240 Justin Braun RC 3.00 8.00
241 Brett MacLean RC 4.00 10.00
242 Johan Harju RC 3.00 8.00
243 Ryan Reaves RC 4.00 10.00
244 Jim O'Brien RC 4.00 10.00
245 Keith Aulie RC 3.00 8.00
246 Nicholas Drazenovic RC 4.00 10.00
247 Ryan McDonagh RC 8.00 20.00
248 Brian Fahey RC 3.00 8.00
249 Marcus Johansson AU RC 8.00 20.00
250 Nazem Kadri AU RC 15.00 40.00
251 Dustin Tokarski AU RC 5.00 12.00
252 Dana Tyrell AU RC 5.00 12.00
253 Tommy Wingels AU RC 5.00 12.00
254 Eric Tangradi AU RC 5.00 12.00
255 Nick Johnson AU RC 4.00 10.00
256 A.Pechurski AU RC 6.00 15.00
257 Joe Fallon AU RC 5.00 12.00
258 O.Ekman-Larsson AU RC 8.00 20.00
259 Sergei Bobrovsky AU RC 12.00 30.00
260 Kaspars Daugavins AU RC 6.00 15.00
261 Jared Cowen AU RC 5.00 12.00
262 Derek Stepan AU RC 10.00 25.00
263 Evgeny Grachev AU RC 5.00 12.00
264 Nino Niederreiter AU RC 6.00 15.00
265 Dustin Kohn AU RC 5.00 12.00
266 Eric Wellwood AU RC 6.00 15.00
267 Nick Palmieri AU RC 5.00 12.00
268 Jacob Josefson AU RC 5.00 12.00
269 Anders Lindback AU RC 5.00 12.00
270 Nick Spaling AU RC 5.00 12.00
271 P.K. Subban AU RC 40.00 80.00
272 J.T. Wyman AU RC 5.00 12.00
273 Justin Falk AU RC 4.00 10.00
274 Cody Almond AU RC 5.00 12.00
275 Maxim Noreau AU RC 4.00 10.00
276 Casey Wellman AU RC 5.00 12.00
277 Brayden Schenn AU RC 10.00 25.00
278 Kyle Clifford AU RC 5.00 12.00
279 Magnus Paajarvi AU RC 6.00 15.00
280 Taylor Hall AU RC 40.00 100.00
281 Jordan Eberle AU RC 30.00 60.00
282 Alex Plante AU RC 5.00 12.00
283 Mattias Tedenby AU RC 4.00 10.00
284 Evan Brophey AU RC 5.00 12.00
285 Philip Larsen AU RC 5.00 12.00
286 Brandon Pirri AU RC 5.00 12.00
287 Luke Adam AU RC 5.00 12.00
288 K.Shattenkirk AU RC 10.00 25.00
289 Colby Cohen AU RC 5.00 12.00
290 Chad Kolarik AU RC 5.00 12.00
291 Mark Olver AU RC 5.00 12.00
292 Brandon Yip AU RC 5.00 12.00
293 Justin Mercier AU RC 5.00 12.00
294 Nick Leddy AU RC 8.00 20.00
295 Jeff Skinner AU RC 12.00 30.00
296 Jamie McBain AU RC 5.00 12.00
297 Zac Dalpe AU RC 5.00 12.00
298 Ian Cole AU RC 5.00 12.00
299 Henrik Karlsson AU RC 5.00 12.00
300 T.J. Brodie AU RC 5.00 12.00
301 Tyler Seguin AU RC 60.00 100.00
302 Zach Hamill AU RC 5.00 12.00
303 A.Bodnarchuk AU RC 5.00 12.00
304 Jordan Caron AU RC 8.00 20.00
305 A.Burmistrov AU RC 5.00 12.00
306 Arturs Kulda AU RC 5.00 12.00
307 Cam Fowler AU RC 6.00 15.00
308 Kyle Palmieri AU RC 10.00 25.00
309 T.McCollum AU RC 6.00 15.00
310 Jacob Markstrom AU RC 20.00 50.00

2010-11 SP Authentic Limited Autographed Patches

STATED PRINT RUN 25-100
1 Sidney Crosby/100 75.00 150.00
2 Ryan Kesler/100 20.00 50.00
3 Phil Kessel/100 20.00 50.00
4 Thomas Vanek/100 15.00 40.00
5 James van Riemsdyk/100 20.00 50.00
6 Tomas Holmstrom/100 10.00 25.00
8 Milan Hejduk/100 12.00 30.00
9 Tomas Vokoun/100 12.00 30.00
10 Paul Stastny/100 15.00 40.00
11 Martin St. Louis/100 15.00 40.00
12 Jeff Carter/100 15.00 40.00
13 Ryan Miller/100 15.00 40.00
14 John Tavares/100 30.00 60.00
15 Blake Wheeler/100 15.00 40.00
16 Victor Hedman/100 20.00 50.00
17 Nicklas Backstrom/100 25.00 50.00
20 Shea Weber/100 12.00 30.00
22 Mike Green/100 20.00 50.00
27 Joe Pavelski/100 15.00 40.00
28 Patrice Bergeron/100 30.00 80.00
30 Devin Setoguchi/100 12.00 30.00
31 Alexander Ovechkin/25 125.00 225.00
32 Steven Stamkos/25 60.00 120.00
33 Jarome Iginla/25 30.00 80.00
34 Joe Thornton/25 30.00 80.00
36 Rick Nash/25 30.00 80.00
37 Jonathan Toews/25 60.00 120.00
38 Patrick Kane/25 40.00 100.00
40 Evgeni Malkin/25 50.00 100.00
41 Pavel Datsyuk/25 40.00 80.00
43 Nicklas Lidstrom/25 60.00 120.00
45 Marc-Andre Fleury/25 25.00 60.00
46 Carey Price/25 100.00 200.00
47 Johan Franzen/25 30.00 80.00
48 Ryan Getzlaf/25 25.00 60.00
50 Eric Lindros/25 125.00 250.00
51 Joe Sakic/25 100.00 200.00
52 Ray Bourque/25 125.00 250.00
53 Luc Robitaille/25 40.00 100.00
54 Guy Lafleur/25 60.00 125.00
55 Cam Neely/25 60.00 120.00
56 Chris Osgood/25 50.00 100.00
57 Steve Yzerman/25 150.00 250.00
58 Mark Messier/25 100.00 200.00
59 Mario Lemieux/25 100.00 200.00
60 Wayne Gretzky/25 400.00 700.00
249 Marcus Johansson 50.00 100.00
250 Nazem Kadri 30.00 80.00
251 Dustin Tokarski 10.00 25.00
252 Dana Tyrell 12.00 30.00
253 Tommy Wingels 12.00 30.00
254 Eric Tangradi 12.00 30.00
255 Nick Johnson 12.00 30.00
256 Alexander Pechurski 15.00 40.00
257 Joe Fallon 12.00 30.00
258 Oliver Ekman-Larsson 20.00 50.00
259 Sergei Bobrovsky 30.00 80.00
260 Kaspars Daugavins 15.00 40.00
261 Jared Cowen 12.00 30.00
262 Derek Stepan 20.00 50.00
263 Evgeny Grachev 12.00 30.00
264 Nino Niederreiter 15.00 40.00
265 Dustin Kohn 12.00 30.00
266 Eric Wellwood 12.00 30.00
267 Nick Palmieri 12.00 30.00
268 Jacob Josefson 12.00 30.00
269 Anders Lindback 15.00 40.00
270 Nick Spaling 12.00 30.00
271 P.K. Subban 80.00 150.00
272 J.T. Wyman 12.00 30.00
273 Justin Falk 10.00 25.00
274 Cody Almond 10.00 25.00
275 Maxim Noreau 10.00 25.00
276 Casey Wellman 12.00 30.00
277 Brayden Schenn 40.00 100.00
278 Kyle Clifford 12.00 30.00
279 Magnus Paajarvi 15.00 40.00
280 Taylor Hall 100.00 200.00
281 Jordan Eberle 40.00 100.00
282 Alex Plante 12.00 30.00
283 Mattias Tedenby 10.00 25.00
284 Evan Brophey 12.00 30.00
285 Philip Larsen 12.00 30.00
286 Brandon Pirri 20.00 50.00
287 Luke Adam 25.00 60.00
288 Kevin Shattenkirk 20.00 50.00
289 Colby Cohen 12.00 30.00
290 Chad Kolarik 12.00 30.00
291 Mark Olver 12.00 30.00
292 Brandon Yip 12.00 30.00
293 Justin Mercier 12.00 30.00
294 Nick Leddy 20.00 50.00
295 Jeff Skinner 100.00 200.00
296 Jamie McBain 12.00 30.00
297 Zac Dalpe 12.00 30.00
298 Ian Cole 12.00 30.00
299 Henrik Karlsson 12.00 30.00
300 T.J. Brodie 12.00 30.00
301 Tyler Seguin 125.00 200.00
302 Zach Hamill 12.00 30.00
303 Andrew Bodnarchuk 12.00 30.00
304 Jordan Caron 20.00 50.00
305 Alexander Burmistrov 25.00 60.00
306 Arturs Kulda 30.00 80.00
307 Cam Fowler 20.00 50.00
308 Kyle Palmieri 25.00 60.00
309 Thomas McCollum 15.00 40.00
310 Jacob Markstrom 60.00 120.00

2010-11 SP Authentic Chirography

STATED PRINT RUN 50 SER.#'d SETS
CAK Anze Kopitar 15.00 40.00
CCP Carey Price 40.00 100.00
CHL Henrik Lundqvist 15.00 40.00
CJC Jeff Carter
CJG Jean-Sebastien Giguere
CJI Jarome Iginla 10.00 25.00
CJP Joe Pavelski 10.00 25.00
CJT John Tavares 20.00 50.00
CJV James van Riemsdyk 15.00 40.00
CMH Marian Hossa 15.00 40.00
CMM Mike Modano 15.00 40.00
COV Alexander Ovechkin 60.00 120.00
CPD Pavel Datsyuk 15.00 40.00
CPK Patrick Kane 20.00 50.00
CRM Ryan Miller 15.00 40.00
CRN Rick Nash 15.00 40.00
CSC Sidney Crosby 75.00 150.00
CSS Steven Stamkos 20.00 50.00
CTH Joe Thornton 10.00 25.00
CTO Jonathan Toews 20.00 50.00

2010-11 SP Authentic Holoview FX

COMPLETE SET (42) 75.00 150.00
STATED ODDS 1:12
*DIE CUTS: 1.5X TO 4X BASIC INSERTS
FX1 Wayne Gretzky 6.00 15.00
FX2 Mikko Koivu 1.25 3.00
FX3 Gilbert Perreault 1.25 3.00
FX4 Bobby Orr 4.00 10.00
FX5 Rick Nash 1.25 3.00
FX6 Martin Brodeur 2.50 6.00
FX7 Henrik Zetterberg 1.50 4.00
FX8 Alexander Ovechkin 5.00 12.00
FX9 Gordie Howe 3.00 8.00
FX10 Daniel Briere 1.25 3.00
FX11 Mark Messier 2.00 5.00
FX12 David Perron .75 2.00
FX13 Dion Phaneuf 1.25 3.00
FX14 Thomas Vanek 1.25 3.00
FX15 Dustin Penner .75 2.00
FX16 Drew Doughty 1.25 3.00
FX17 Guy Lafleur 1.50 4.00
FX18 Eric Staal 1.50 4.00
FX19 Steve Yzerman 3.00 8.00
FX20 Nicklas Lidstrom 1.25 3.00
FX21 Henrik Lundqvist 2.00 5.00
FX22 Henrik Sedin 1.25 3.00
FX23 Mario Lemieux 4.00 10.00
FX24 Patrick Marleau 1.25 3.00
FX25 John Tavares 2.50 6.00
FX26 Ilya Kovalchuk 1.25 3.00
FX27 Brian Gionta 1.00 2.50
FX28 Evgeni Malkin 4.00 10.00
FX29 Mike Richards 1.25 3.00
FX30 Matt Duchene 1.25 3.00
FX31 Jarome Iginla 1.25 3.00
FX32 Bobby Ryan 1.25 3.00
FX33 Patrick Roy 3.00 8.00
FX34 Mike Ribeiro 1.00 2.50
FX35 Daniel Alfredsson 1.25 3.00
FX36 Jonathan Toews 2.50 6.00
FX37 Shane Doan 1.00 2.50
FX38 Steven Stamkos 2.50 6.00
FX39 Duncan Keith 1.25 3.00
FX40 Joe Pavelski 1.25 3.00
FX41 Martin St. Louis 1.25 3.00
FX42 Sidney Crosby 5.00 12.00

2010-11 SP Authentic Marks of Distinction

STATED PRINT RUN 25 SER.#'d SETS
MDAO Alexander Ovechkin 60.00 120.00
MDBC Bobby Clarke 50.00 100.00
MDBO Bobby Orr 200.00 300.00
MDCN Cam Neely 15.00 40.00
MDCP Carey Price 50.00 100.00
MDEM Evgeni Malkin 50.00 100.00
MDGH Gordie Howe 125.00 250.00
MDGL Guy Lafleur 50.00 100.00
MDHL Henrik Lundqvist 25.00 60.00
MDJI Jarome Iginla 40.00 80.00
MDJT John Tavares 30.00 80.00
MDLR Luc Robitaille 30.00 80.00
MDMH Milan Hejduk 25.00 60.00
MDMI Mike Bossy 15.00 40.00
MDML Mario Lemieux 60.00 125.00
MDMM Mark Messier 40.00 80.00
MDPD Pavel Datsyuk 25.00 60.00
MDPE Phil Esposito 25.00 60.00
MDPK Patrick Kane 50.00 100.00
MDPR Patrick Roy 75.00 150.00
MDRH Ron Hextall 20.00 50.00
MDRM Ryan Miller 15.00 40.00
MDRN Rick Nash 25.00 60.00
MDSC Sidney Crosby 100.00 200.00
MDSS Steven Stamkos 30.00 80.00
MDTH Joe Thornton 15.00 40.00
MDTO Jonathan Toews 30.00 80.00
MDWG Wayne Gretzky 250.00 400.00

2010-11 SP Authentic Prestigious Pairings

STATED PRINT RUN 50 SER.#'d SETS
PPBO J.Bucyk/B.Orr 60.00 120.00
PPBP D.Potvin/M.Bossy 20.00 40.00
PPCR M.Richards/B.Clarke
PPEE P.Esposito/T.Esposito 30.00 60.00
PPEO P.Esposito/B.Orr 75.00 150.00
PPGB M.Green/N.Backstrom 30.00 80.00
PPGM M.Messier/W.Gretzky 200.00 300.00
PPHG W.Gretzky/G.Howe 250.00 400.00
PPHM B.Hull/S.Mikita 30.00 80.00
PPIN R.Nash/J.Iginla 25.00 60.00
PPLR G.Lafleur/L.Robinson 25.00 50.00
PPLY M.Lemieux/S.Yzerman 75.00 150.00
PPMS J.Staal/E.Malkin 15.00 40.00
PPOF C.Osgood/M.Fleury 20.00 50.00
PPOS A.Ovechkin/S.Stamkos 60.00 120.00
PPPV G.Perreault/T.Vanek 15.00 40.00
PPRB R.Bourque/P.Roy 60.00 120.00
PPRK L.Robitaille/J.Kurri 15.00 40.00
PPSD P.Stastny/M.Duchene 10.00 25.00
PPTK P.Kane/J.Toews 60.00 100.00
PPTP J.Thornton/J.Pavelski 10.00 25.00
PPTS J.Tavares/S.Stamkos 50.00 100.00
PPVP R.Vachon/C.Price 50.00 100.00

2010-11 SP Authentic Sign of the Times

OVERALL STATED AU ODDS 1:12
SOTAB Alexander Burmistrov 3.00 8.00
SOTAC Andrew Cogliano 3.00 8.00
SOTAN Antti Niemi
SOTAO Alexander Ovechkin 75.00 150.00
SOTAT Alex Tanguay 3.00 8.00
SOTBA Josh Bailey 10.00 25.00
SOTBC Bobby Clarke 15.00 40.00
SOTBM Barry Melrose 4.00 10.00
SOTBN Brayden Schenn 12.00 30.00
SOTBO Bobby Orr 60.00 120.00
SOTBR Bobby Ryan
SOTBS Bobby Sanguinetti 3.00 8.00
SOTCA Jeff Carter
SOTCO Chris Osgood 5.00 12.00
SOTCP Carey Price 25.00 60.00
SOTCR Sidney Crosby SP 75.00 150.00
SOTCS Chris Stewart
SOTCW Cam Ward 8.00 20.00
SOTDG Doug Gilmour
SOTDH Dany Heatley 10.00 25.00
SOTDS Devin Setoguchi 4.00 10.00
SOTEK Evander Kane
SOTEL Eric Lindros
SOTEM Evgeni Malkin 15.00 40.00
SOTES Eric Staal 8.00 20.00
SOTET Eric Tangradi 4.00 10.00
SOTGH Gordie Howe 60.00 120.00
SOTGR Wayne Gretzky SP 200.00 400.00
SOTHE Milan Hejduk 4.00 10.00
SOTHL Henrik Lundqvist 10.00 25.00
SOTJA Jay Bouwmeester 6.00 15.00
SOTJB Jamie Benn 12.50 30.00
SOTJC Jared Cowen 3.00 8.00
SOTJE Jordan Eberle 30.00 80.00
SOTJF Johan Franzen 8.00 20.00
SOTJG Jean-Sebastien Giguere 12.00 30.00
SOTJH Jaroslav Halak 12.00 30.00
SOTJI Jarome Iginla 8.00 20.00
SOTJK Jari Kurri 8.00 20.00
SOTJM Jamie McBain 4.00 10.00
SOTJP Joe Pavelski 5.00 12.00
SOTJS Jack Skille 4.00 10.00
SOTJT Joe Thornton 20.00 50.00
SOTJV James van Riemsdyk 8.00 20.00
SOTLC Logan Couture 6.00 15.00
SOTLE Lars Eller 4.00 10.00
SOTLR Luc Robitaille 20.00 50.00
SOTMA Mario Lemieux SP 125.00 250.00
SOTMB Martin Brodeur
SOTMC Matthew Corrente 4.00 10.00
SOTMD Matt Duchene
SOTMF Marc-Andre Fleury 12.00 30.00
SOTMH Marian Hossa 10.00 25.00
SOTMJ Marcus Johansson 6.00 15.00
SOTML Mario Lemieux 75.00 135.00
SOTMM Mark Messier 75.00 150.00
SOTMO Mike Modano 10.00 25.00
SOTMP Magnus Paajarvi 4.00 10.00
SOTMR Mike Richards
SOTMS Marc Staal
SOTMT Marty Turco
SOTNB Nicklas Bergfors 4.00 10.00
SOTNL Nicklas Lidstrom 12.00 30.00
SOTNZ Nazem Kadri 10.00 25.00
SOTPB Patrice Bergeron
SOTPD Pavel Datsyuk 20.00 50.00
SOTPE Phil Esposito 12.00 30.00
SOTPK Patrick Kane 15.00 40.00
SOTPL Perttu Lindgren 3.00 8.00
SOTPM Peter Mueller 4.00 10.00
SOTPR Patrick Roy 60.00 120.00
SOTPS P.K. Subban 40.00 80.00
SOTRB Ray Bourque 25.00 60.00
SOTRE Ray Emery 15.00 40.00
SOTRI Brad Richards 6.00 15.00
SOTRK Ryan Kesler 10.00 25.00
SOTRM Ryan Miller 10.00 25.00
SOTRN Rick Nash 8.00 20.00
SOTRV Rogie Vachon 12.00 30.00
SOTSC Cory Schneider 6.00 15.00
SOTSH James Sheppard 3.00 8.00
SOTSI Sidney Crosby 75.00 150.00
SOTSK Jeff Skinner 15.00 30.00
SOTSN Derek Stepan 6.00 15.00
SOTSS Steven Stamkos 20.00 50.00
SOTTA John Tavares 15.00 30.00
SOTTE Tony Esposito 25.00 50.00
SOTTH Taylor Hall 40.00 80.00
SOTTK Tim Kennedy 3.00 8.00
SOTTM Tyler Myers
SOTTO Jonathan Toews 30.00 60.00
SOTTS Tyler Seguin 25.00 50.00
SOTTV Thomas Vanek 5.00 12.00
SOTVH Victor Hedman 6.00 15.00
SOTWG Wayne Gretzky 175.00 350.00
SOTWI Colin Wilson 4.00 10.00
SOTWS Wayne Simmonds
SOTZH Zach Hamill 3.00 8.00

2010-11 SP Authentic Sign of the Times Duals

STATED ODDS 1:288
ST2BB N.Bergfors/D.Byfuglien 8.00 20.00
ST2BG J.Giguere/M.Brodeur 60.00 120.00
ST2BH J.Halak/D.Backes 8.00 20.00
ST2BL H.Lundqvist/M.Brodeur
ST2BP P.Kessel/B.Salming 15.00 30.00
ST2BT A.Tanguay/J.Bouwmeester 10.00 25.00
ST2CM J.Cowen/J.McBain 6.00 15.00
ST2CR B.Clarke/M.Richards
ST2DA A.Pietrangelo/D.Backes 10.00 25.00
ST2DG D.Stepan/E.Grachev 12.00 30.00
ST2DH D.Doughty/V.Hedman 10.00 25.00
ST2DY M.Duchene/B.Yip 8.00 20.00
ST2ET M.Turco/T.Esposito 20.00 40.00
ST2FH R.Hextall/G.Fuhr 20.00 50.00
ST2GF J.Giguere/M.Fleury 20.00 50.00
ST2HE J.Eberle/T.Hall 100.00 175.00
ST2HH M.Howe/G.Howe 50.00 100.00
ST2HK M.Hossa/P.Kane 20.00 50.00
ST2HP J.Halak/C.Price 30.00 80.00
ST2IK J.Iginla/R.Kesler 8.00 20.00
ST2IS W.Simmonds/J.Iginla
ST2IT J.Iginla/A.Tanguay
ST2KP J.Kurri/M.Paajarvi 8.00 20.00
ST2LD P.Datsyuk/N.Lidstrom 40.00 80.00
ST2LF N.Lidstrom/J.Franzen 20.00 50.00
ST2LM E.Malkin/M.Lemieux 30.00 80.00
ST2MD M.Modano/P.Datsyuk 25.00 60.00
ST2NB P.Bergeron/C.Neely
ST2NM R.Nash/S.Mason 15.00 40.00
ST2OB J.Bailey/K.Okposo
ST2OG B.Orr/W.Gretzky 300.00 400.00
ST2OM A.Ovechkin/E.Malkin
ST2OR B.Orr/B.Orr 150.00 250.00
ST2OV A.Ovechkin/S.Varlamov 60.00 120.00
ST2PK P.Kessel/D.Phaneuf 15.00 40.00
ST2PM C.Price/S.Mason 40.00 80.00
ST2PN P.Subban/N.Kadri 30.00 80.00
ST2PS P.Subban/C.Price 100.00 200.00
ST2PV G.Perreault/T.Vanek 10.00 25.00
ST2QN P.Stastny/G.Lafleur 25.00 60.00
ST2RL M.Richards/V.Leino
ST2RP P.Roy/C.Price 75.00 150.00
ST2RR B.Richards/M.Ribeiro
ST2SC T.Seguin/J.Caron 25.00 60.00
ST2SD S.Crosby/S.Crosby 150.00 250.00
ST2SH D.Setoguchi/D.Heatley
ST2SK J.Sakic/J.Sakic 125.00 250.00
ST2SS P.Stastny/P.Stastny 20.00 50.00
ST2SU D.Sutter/B.Sutter
ST2TB J.Bailey/J.Tavares 15.00 40.00
ST2TM E.Malkin/M.Talbot 25.00 60.00
ST2TP J.Thornton/J.Pavelski 8.00 20.00
ST2TS J.Tavares/S.Stamkos 30.00 80.00
ST2TT J.Toews/J.Toews 40.00 80.00
ST2VB J.Bernier/R.Vachon 12.00 30.00
ST2WG D.Wilson/D.Gilmour 15.00 40.00
ST2COL J.Sakic/R.Bourque 125.00 250.00
ST2TBL S.Stamkos/S.Gagne 15.00 40.00

2010-11 SP Authentic Sign of the Times Triples

STATED PRINT RUN 25 SER.#'d SETS
ST31ST Kane/Stamkos/Tavares 100.00 175.00
ST3CHI Toews/Kane/Turco 40.00 100.00
ST3EDM Hall/Eberle/Paajarvi 125.00 250.00
ST3GR8 Lemieux/Yzerman/Messier 100.00 175.00
ST3HOF Gretzky/Howe/Orr 650.00 1000.00
ST3MTL Price/Roy/Vachon 125.00 200.00
ST3TBL Lecav/Hedman/Stamkos 75.00 150.00
ST3TCF Getzlaf/Nash/Iginla 75.00 150.00
ST3IIHF Dionne/Clarke/Esposito 60.00 120.00
ST3ROOK Subban/Kadri/Cowen 125.00 250.00

2010-11 SP Authentic By The Letter Legend Last Name

This autograph set was randomly inserted into packs and features the Lettermen style. To obtain the complete print run, take the actual serial-numbering on the card and multiply that by the player's last name. The only exceptions appear to be for Jim Jackson and Robert Horry, which should spell out "Legend".
STATED PRINT RUN 30 TO 149 SER.#'d SETS
MOST PRINT RUNS BASED ON LAST NAME
TOTAL PRINT RUN LISTED WITH ASTERISK
LSC Sidney Crosby/180* 150.00 300.00

2011-12 SP Authentic

COMP.SET w/o RC's (150) 10.00 25.00
ESSENTIAL ODDS 1:12 HOB
181-220 ROOKIE/999 ODDS 1:36 HOB
221-280 ROOK.AU/999 ODDS 1:24 HOB
EXCH EXPIRATION: 6/20/2014
1 P.K. Subban .50 1.25
2 Jordan Eberle .25 .60
3 Sam Gagner .20 .50
4 David Clarkson .15 .40
5 Brandon Dubinsky .20 .50
6 Tyler Ennis .20 .50
7 Derek Roy .20 .50
8 Chris Osgood .25 .60
9 Lars Eller .20 .50
10 Bobby Ryan .25 .60
11 Nick Foligno .20 .50
12 Logan Couture .25 .60
13 Jaroslav Halak .25 .60
14 Matt Duchene .25 .60
15 Devin Setoguchi .20 .50
16 Nicklas Backstrom .40 1.00
17 Mike Modano .40 1.00
18 Alexander Ovechkin 1.00 2.50
19 Ryan Getzlaf .40 1.00
20 Tuukka Rask .25 .60
21 Derick Brassard .25 .60
22 Patrice Bergeron .30 .75
23 Carey Price .75 2.00
24 Ryan Kesler .25 .60
25 Jonathan Toews .50 1.25
26 Nikolai Kulemin .25 .60
27 Taylor Hall .50 1.25
28 Patrick Marleau .25 .60
29 Kari Lehtonen .20 .50
30 Sidney Crosby 1.00 2.50
31 Tyler Seguin .50 1.25
32 Keith Yandle .25 .60
33 Martin Brodeur .50 1.25
34 Jakub Voracek .25 .60
35 Shea Weber .20 .50
36 Jarome Iginla .25 .60
37 Jay Bouwmeester .25 .60
38 Ryan Smyth .20 .50
39 Steven Stamkos .50 1.25
40 Craig Anderson .25 .60
41 Brad Richards .25 .60
42 Patrick Kane .50 1.25
43 Jordan Staal .25 .60
44 Jonas Hiller .20 .50
45 Nathan Horton .25 .60
46 Thomas Vanek .25 .60
47 Eric Staal .30 .75
48 Ryan Miller .25 .60
49 Trevor Linden .25 .60
50 Larry Robinson .25 .60
51 Bill Barber .25 .60
52 Bill Ranford .25 .60
53 Brad Park .20 .50
54 Brett Hull .30 .75
55 Luc Robitaille .25 .60
56 Joe Sakic .40 1.00
57 Wayne Gretzky 1.25 3.00
58 Roberto Luongo .25 .60
59 Brendan Shanahan .30 .75
60 Zach Parise .25 .60
61 Tim Thomas .25 .60
62 Tyler Myers .25 .60
63 Miikka Kiprusoff .25 .60
64 Tomas Holmstrom .15 .40
65 Colin Wilson .20 .50
66 Jim Howard .25 .60
67 Daniel Sedin .25 .60
68 Patrik Berglund .20 .50
69 Brent Burns .30 .75
70 Evander Kane .25 .60
71 Kevin Shattenkirk .20 .50
72 Vincent Lecavalier .20 .50
73 Mike Green .25 .60
74 Tomas Vokoun .20 .50
75 Chris Stewart .20 .50
76 Loui Eriksson .20 .50
77 Chris Pronger .20 .50
78 Alexandre Burrows .25 .60
79 Marc-Andre Fleury .40 1.00
80 Rick Nash .25 .60
81 Marcus Johansson .20 .50
82 Ilya Kovalchuk .25 .60
83 T.J. Oshie .40 1.00
84 Dan Cleary .25 .60
85 Brenden Morrow .20 .50
86 Henrik Sedin .25 .60
87 Radim Vrbata .20 .50
88 Martin St. Louis .25 .60
89 John Tavares .50 1.25
90 Ilya Bryzgalov .25 .60
91 Ville Leino .20 .50
92 Dany Heatley .20 .50
93 Ondrej Pavelec .25 .60
94 Bobby Orr .75 2.00
95 Pekka Rinne .30 .75
96 Jeff Skinner .25 .60
97 Patrick Sharp .25 .60
98 Teemu Selanne .50 1.25
99 Antoine Vermette .15 .40
100 Dan Boyle .20 .50
101 David Jones .15 .40
102 James Neal .25 .60
103 Joe Thornton .25 .60
104 Jose Theodore .25 .60
105 Matt Moulson .20 .50
106 Mike Ribeiro .20 .50
107 Mikko Koivu .20 .50
108 Stephen Weiss .20 .50
109 Zdeno Chara .25 .60
110 Ryan Suter .15 .40
111 Ryane Clowe .15 .40
112 Scott Gomez .20 .50
113 Semyon Varlamov .25 .60
114 Shane Doan .20 .50
115 Phil Kessel .30 .75
116 Ryan Callahan .25 .60
117 Steve Mason UER .20 .50
(Allen York pictured on front)
118 Daniel Alfredsson .25 .60
119 Niklas Backstrom .25 .60
120 Pavel Datsyuk .30 .75
121 Josh Gorges .15 .40
122 Dion Phaneuf .25 .60
123 Henrik Zetterberg .30 .75
124 Magnus Paajarvi .20 .50
125 Luke Adam .20 .50
126 Cam Ward .25 .60
127 Corey Perry .25 .60
128 Mark Giordano .20 .50
129 Brian Campbell .15 .40
130 Claude Giroux .25 .60
131 Dwayne Roloson .20 .50
132 James Reimer .25 .60
133 Johan Franzen .25 .60
134 Erik Karlsson .50 1.25
135 Drew Doughty .25 .60
136 Jussi Jokinen .15 .40
137 Paul Stastny .25 .60
138 Marian Hossa .20 .50
139 Michael Grabner .20 .50
140 James van Riemsdyk .25 .60
141 Henrik Lundqvist .30 .75
142 Nicklas Lidstrom .25 .60
143 Daniel Briere .25 .60
144 Anze Kopitar .40 1.00
145 Corey Crawford .30 .75
146 Erik Johnson .15 .40
147 Mike Richards .25 .60
148 Dustin Byfuglien .25 .60
149 Evgeni Malkin .75 2.00
150 Dustin Brown .25 .60
151 Corey Perry ESS .75 2.00
152 Bobby Orr ESS 2.50 6.00
153 Tim Thomas ESS .75 2.00
154 Ryan Miller ESS .75 2.00
155 Jarome Iginla ESS .75 2.00
156 Jeff Skinner ESS .75 2.00
157 Jonathan Toews ESS 1.50 4.00
158 Matt Duchene ESS .75 2.00
159 Jamie Benn ESS 1.00 2.50
160 Jim Howard ESS .75 2.00
161 Taylor Hall ESS 1.50 4.00
162 Anze Kopitar ESS 1.25 3.00
163 Mike Richards ESS .75 2.00
164 Mikko Koivu ESS .60 1.50
165 Carey Price ESS 2.50 6.00
166 P.K. Subban ESS 1.50 4.00
167 Zach Parise ESS .75 2.00
168 Ilya Kovalchuk ESS .75 2.00
169 Martin Brodeur ESS 1.50 4.00
170 John Tavares ESS 1.50 4.00
171 Wayne Gretzky ESS 4.00 10.00
172 Mark Messier ESS 1.00 2.50
173 Henrik Lundqvist ESS 1.00 2.50
174 Eric Lindros ESS 1.25 3.00
175 Jaromir Jagr ESS 2.00 5.00
176 Sidney Crosby ESS 3.00 8.00
177 Steven Stamkos ESS 1.50 4.00
178 Phil Kessel ESS 1.00 2.50
179 Roberto Luongo ESS .75 2.00
180 Alexander Ovechkin ESS 3.00 8.00
181 Peter Holland RC 2.50 6.00
182 Pat Maroon RC 2.50 6.00
183 Iiro Tarkki RC 3.00 8.00
184 Brayden McNabb RC 2.50 6.00
185 Marcus Foligno RC 4.00 10.00
186 Leland Irving RC 2.50 6.00
187 Andrew Shaw RC 6.00 15.00
188 Jimmy Hayes RC 3.00 8.00
189 Brad Malone RC 2.50 6.00
190 Ryan Russell RC 3.00 8.00
191 Matt Fraser RC 3.00 8.00
192 Brendan Smith RC 2.50 6.00
193 Milan Kytnar RC 3.00 8.00
194 Greg Rallo RC 3.00 8.00
195 Brian Foster RC 3.00 8.00
196 Jarod Palmer RC 2.50 6.00
197 Kris Fredheim RC 2.50 6.00
198 David McIntyre RC 2.50 6.00
199 Frederic St. Denis RC 2.50 6.00
200 Mattias Ekholm RC 2.50 6.00
201 Ryan Ellis RC 2.50 6.00
202 Roman Josi RC 4.00 10.00
203 Keith Kinkaid RC 2.50 6.00
204 David Ullstrom RC 2.50 6.00
205 Calvin de Haan RC 2.50 6.00
206 Mikko Koskinen RC 3.00 8.00
207 Anders Nilsson RC 2.50 6.00
208 Stu Bickel RC 2.50 6.00
209 Carl Hagelin RC 4.00 10.00
210 Andre Petersson RC 3.00 8.00
211 Erik Condra RC 2.50 6.00
212 Mark Borowiecki RC 3.00 8.00
213 Zac Rinaldo RC 2.50 6.00
214 Harry Zolnierczyk RC 2.50 6.00
215 Kevin Marshall RC 2.50 6.00
216 Marc-Andre Bourdon RC 2.50 6.00
217 Robert Bortuzzo RC 2.50 6.00
218 Carl Sneep RC 2.50 6.00
219 Cade Fairchild RC 2.00 5.00
220 Dmitry Orlov RC 3.00 8.00
221 Gustav Nyquist AU RC 12.00 30.00
222 Andy Miele AU RC 4.00 10.00
223 Colten Teubert AU RC 4.00 10.00
224 Cody Hodgson AU RC 8.00 20.00
225 Jake Gardiner AU RC 10.00 25.00
226 Carl Klingberg AU RC 4.00 10.00
227 Mika Zibanejad AU RC 10.00 25.00
228 Mark Scheifele AU RC 25.00 60.00
229 Aaron Palushaj AU RC 4.00 10.00
230 Adam Larsson AU RC 8.00 20.00
231 Matt Read AU RC 8.00 20.00
232 Matt Frattin AU RC 4.00 10.00
233 Blake Geoffrion AU RC 4.00 10.00
234 Smith-Pelly AU RC EXCH 12.00 30.00
235 Erik Gudbranson AU RC 8.00 20.00
236 Jonathon Blum AU RC 4.00 10.00
237 Anton Lander AU RC 10.00 25.00
238 Brandon Saad AU RC 12.00 30.00
239 Adam Henrique AU RC 8.00 20.00
240 Brett Connolly AU RC 4.00 10.00
241 Harri Sateri AU RC 4.00 10.00
242 Joe Colborne AU RC 4.00 10.00
243 Marcus Kruger AU RC 6.00 15.00
244 Greg Nemisz AU RC 4.00 10.00
245 Ryan Johansen AU RC 12.00 30.00
246 Sean Couturier AU RC 12.00 30.00
247 G.Landeskog AU RC 15.00 40.00
248 Nugent-Hopkins AU RC 30.00 80.00
249 Roman Horak AU RC 4.00 10.00
250 John Moore AU RC 4.00 10.00
251 Colin Greening AU RC 4.00 10.00
252 Cam Atkinson AU RC 10.00 25.00
253 T.Vincour AU RC EXCH 4.00 10.00
254 Yann Sauve AU RC 4.00 10.00
255 Alexei Emelin AU RC 4.00 10.00
256 Cody Eakin AU RC 5.00 12.00
257 Justin Faulk AU RC 6.00 15.00
258 Cameron Gaunce AU RC 3.00 8.00
259 Joe Vitale AU RC 4.00 10.00
260 Brendon Nash AU RC 4.00 10.00
261 Erik Gustafsson AU RC 5.00 12.00
262 Raphael Diaz AU RC 4.00 10.00
263 David Savard AU RC 4.00 10.00
264 Tim Erixon AU RC 4.00 10.00
265 Teemu Hartikainen AU RC 4.00 10.00
266 Ben Scrivens AU RC 8.00 20.00
267 Paul Postma AU RC 4.00 10.00
268 Craig Smith AU RC 5.00 12.00
269 Patrick Wiercioch AU RC 4.00 10.00
270 Alex Stalock AU 4.00 10.00
271 Brett Bulmer AU RC 4.00 10.00
272 Stephane Da Costa AU RC 4.00 10.00
273 Viatcheslav Voynov AU RC 4.00 10.00
274 Simon Despres AU RC 4.00 10.00
275 Louis Leblanc AU RC 4.00 10.00
276 Lance Bouma AU RC 4.00 10.00
277 Brian Strait AU RC 5.00 12.00
278 Ben Holmstrom AU RC 4.00 10.00
279 Zack Kassian AU RC 8.00 20.00
280 Lennart Petrell AU RC 5.00 12.00

2011-12 SP Authentic Chirography

STATED PRINT RUN 50 SER.#'d SETS
EXCH EXPIRATION: 6/20/2014
CBM Brad Marchand 15.00 30.00
CBO Bobby Orr 60.00 120.00
CCG Claude Giroux 20.00 40.00
CCP Carey Price 30.00 80.00
CDP Dion Phaneuf 10.00 25.00
CDR Derek Roy 8.00 20.00
CEM Evgeni Malkin EXCH
CES Eric Staal 12.00 30.00
CHL Henrik Lundqvist 30.00 60.00
CJE Jordan Eberle 25.00 60.00
CJP Joe Pavelski 10.00 25.00
CJS Jeff Skinner 20.00 40.00
CLC Logan Couture 12.00 30.00
CMD Matt Duchene 10.00 25.00
CNB Nicklas Backstrom 15.00 40.00
CNH Nathan Horton 10.00 25.00
CPK Patrick Kane 30.00 60.00
CPS P.K. Subban 20.00 50.00
CRK Ryan Kesler 15.00 40.00
CRM Ryan Miller 10.00 25.00
CSC Sidney Crosby 60.00 120.00
CSS Steven Stamkos 30.00 80.00
CTV Thomas Vanek 10.00 25.00

2011-12 SP Authentic Holoview FX

STATED ODDS 1:12 HOBBY
*DIE CUTS: 1.2X TO 3X BASIC INSERTS
RFX1 Devante Smith-Pelly 1.50 4.00
RFX2 Greg Nemisz 1.00 2.50
RFX3 Marcus Kruger 1.50 4.00
RFX4 Brandon Saad 2.00 5.00
RFX5 Gabriel Landeskog 2.00 5.00
RFX6 Ryan Johansen 2.00 5.00
RFX7 Ryan Nugent-Hopkins 10.00 25.00
RFX8 Teemu Hartikainen 1.00 2.50
RFX9 Anton Lander 1.00 2.50
RFX10 Lennart Petrell 1.25 3.00
RFX11 Erik Gudbranson 1.25 3.00
RFX12 Aaron Palushaj 1.00 2.50
RFX13 Craig Smith 1.25 3.00
RFX14 Jonathon Blum 1.00 2.50
RFX15 Blake Geoffrion 1.00 2.50
RFX16 Adam Henrique 2.50 6.00
RFX17 Adam Larsson 1.25 3.00
RFX18 Tim Erixon 1.00 2.50
RFX19 Mika Zibanejad 2.50 6.00
RFX20 David Rundblad 1.00 2.50
RFX21 Sean Couturier 2.00 5.00
RFX22 Matt Read 2.00 5.00
RFX23 Harri Sateri 1.00 2.50
RFX24 Brett Connolly 1.00 2.50
RFX25 Jake Gardiner 1.50 4.00
RFX26 Joe Colborne 1.00 2.50
RFX27 Matt Frattin 1.00 2.50
RFX28 Cody Hodgson 2.00 5.00
RFX29 Carl Klingberg 1.00 2.50
RFX30 Mark Scheifele 2.50 6.00

2011-12 SP Authentic Limited Patches

1-15 STATED PRINT RUN 100
17-60 STATED PRINT RUN 10-25
*ROOKIE AU/100: 1.2X TO 3X BASIC AU RC
221-280 ROOKIE PRINT RUN 100
EXCH EXPIRATION: 6/20/2014
1 P.K. Subban AU/100 20.00 50.00
2 Jordan Eberle AU/100 20.00 50.00
3 Sam Gagner AU/100 12.00 30.00
4 David Clarkson AU/100 10.00 25.00
6 Tyler Ennis AU/100 10.00 25.00
7 Derek Roy AU/100 12.00 30.00
8 Chris Osgood AU/100 15.00 40.00
9 Lars Eller AU/100 12.00 30.00
12 Logan Couture AU/100 12.00 30.00
13 Jaroslav Halak AU/100 15.00 40.00
14 Matt Duchene AU/100 20.00 50.00
15 Devin Setoguchi AU/100 10.00 25.00
16 Nicklas Backstrom AU/25 50.00 125.00
17 Mike Modano AU/25 40.00 100.00
18 Alexander Ovechkin AU/25 40.00 80.00
19 Ryan Getzlaf AU/25 30.00 80.00
20 Tuukka Rask AU/25 30.00 80.00
21 Derick Brassard AU/25 20.00 50.00
22 Patrice Bergeron AU/25 50.00 100.00
23 Carey Price AU/25 60.00 120.00
24 Ryan Kesler AU/25 25.00 60.00
25 Jonathan Toews AU/25 60.00 120.00
26 Nikolai Kulemin AU/25 20.00 50.00
27 Taylor Hall AU/25 75.00 150.00
28 Patrick Marleau AU/25 25.00 60.00
29 Kari Lehtonen AU/25
30 Sidney Crosby AU/25 100.00 175.00
31 Tyler Seguin AU/25 40.00 100.00
33 Martin Brodeur AU/25 EXCH 60.00 120.00
35 Jarome Iginla AU/25 25.00 60.00
37 Jay Bouwmeester AU/25 25.00 60.00
39 Shea Weber AU/25
39 Steven Stamkos AU/25 75.00 150.00
41 Brad Richards AU/25 30.00 80.00
42 Patrick Kane AU/25 25.00 60.00
43 Jordan Staal AU/25 25.00 60.00
44 Jonas Hiller AU/25 25.00 60.00
45 Nathan Horton AU/25 25.00 60.00
46 Thomas Vanek AU/25 15.00 40.00
47 Eric Staal AU/25 20.00 50.00
48 Ryan Miller AU/25 30.00 80.00
49 Trevor Linden AU/25 50.00 100.00
50 Larry Robinson AU/25 30.00 80.00
51 Bill Barber AU/25 30.00 80.00
52 Bill Ranford AU/25 30.00 80.00
53 Brad Park AU/25 25.00 60.00
54 Brett Hull AU/25 40.00 100.00
56 Joe Sakic AU/25 50.00 100.00
58 Roberto Luongo/25 12.00 30.00
59 Brendan Shanahan/25 15.00 40.00
60 Zach Parise/25 12.00 30.00
240 Brett Connolly AU/100 12.00 30.00
247 Gabriel Landeskog AU/100 40.00 100.00
248 Ryan Nugent-Hopkins AU/100 100.00 200.00

2011-12 SP Authentic Marks of Distinction

STATED PRINT RUN 25 SER.#'d SETS
EXCH EXPIRATION: 6/20/2014
MDAO Alexander Ovechkin
MDBO Bobby Orr 125.00 250.00
MDBY Mike Bossy 25.00 50.00
MDCP Carey Price 50.00 120.00
MDDH Dale Hawerchuk 25.00 60.00
MDDR Derek Roy 12.00 30.00
MDEL Eric Lindros
MDEM Evgeni Malkin EXCH
MDGP Gilbert Perreault 15.00 40.00
MDHL Henrik Lundqvist 30.00 60.00
MDJI Jarome Iginla 20.00 50.00
MDJS Joe Sakic 40.00 80.00
MDJT Joe Thornton 25.00 50.00
MDMB Martin Brodeur EXCH
MDML Mario Lemieux 100.00 200.00
MDMM Mark Messier 40.00 100.00
MDMN Markus Naslund 12.00 30.00
MDPK Patrick Kane 30.00 80.00
MDPS P.K. Subban 25.00 50.00
MDRF Ron Francis 20.00 50.00
MDRM Ryan Miller 12.00 30.00
MDSC Sidney Crosby 100.00 175.00
MDSS Steven Stamkos 50.00 100.00
MDTH Taylor Hall 50.00 100.00
MDTO Jonathan Toews 30.00 80.00
MDWG Wayne Gretzky EXCH 150.00 250.00

2011-12 SP Authentic Prestigious Pairings

STATED PRINT RUN 35 SER.#'d SETS
EXCH EXPIRATION: 6/20/2014
PPBB D.Boyle/B.Burns 15.00 40.00
PPBL Lafleur/Beliveau EXCH
PPCA P.Coffey/G.Fuhr
PPEH T.Hall/J.Eberle 50.00 100.00
PPES P.Subban/L.Eller 25.00 60.00
PPGL H.Lundqvist/M.Gaborik 15.00 40.00
PPGV C.Giroux/Van Riemsdyk 12.00 30.00
PPHF M.Hossa/M.Frolik 10.00 25.00
PPHH B.Hull/B.Hull 75.00 150.00
PPHM D.Hasek/R.Miller 30.00 60.00
PPHO B.Hull/A.Oates 60.00 120.00
PPKH C.Hodgson/R.Kesler 30.00 60.00
PPLF M.Lemieux/R.Francis 60.00 120.00
PPMM J.Moore/S.Mason 8.00 20.00
PPOR B.Orr/L.Robinson 80.00 150.00
PPPC J.Pavelski/L.Couture 12.00 30.00
PPRK L.Robitaille/J.Kurri 25.00 50.00
PPSL S.Stamkos/Lecavalier 50.00 100.00
PPTK J.Toews/P.Kane 50.00 125.00
PPVR T.Vanek/D.Roy 12.00 30.00

2011-12 SP Authentic Rookie Extended

COMPLETE SET (100) 30.00 80.00
STATED ODDS 1:2 HOBBY
R1 Peter Holland .75 2.00
R2 Iiro Tarkki 1.00 2.50
R3 Devante Smith-Pelly 1.25 3.00
R4 Pat Maroon .75 2.00
R5 Corey Tropp .75 2.00
R6 T.J. Brennan .75 2.00
R7 Cody Hodgson 1.50 4.00
R8 Lance Bouma .75 2.00
R9 Roman Horak .75 2.00
R10 Leland Irving .75 2.00
R11 Greg Nemisz .75 2.00
R12 Mike Murphy .75 2.00
R13 Justin Faulk 1.25 3.00
R14 Brandon Saad 1.50 4.00
R15 Marcus Kruger 1.25 3.00
R16 Cameron Gaunce .60 1.50
R17 Gabriel Landeskog 1.50 4.00
R18 David Savard .75 2.00
R19 Cam Atkinson 2.00 5.00
R20 Tomas Kubalik .75 2.00
R21 John Moore .75 2.00
R22 Allen York 1.00 2.50
R23 Ryan Johansen 1.50 4.00
R24 Tomas Vincour .75 2.00
R25 Colton Sceviour .75 2.00
R26 Gustav Nyquist 2.00 5.00
R27 Brendan Smith .75 2.00
R28 Chris Vande Velde 1.25 3.00
R29 Teemu Hartikainen .75 2.00
R30 Lennart Petrell 1.00 2.50
R31 Anton Lander .75 2.00
R32 Colten Teubert .75 2.00
R33 Ryan Nugent-Hopkins 3.00 8.00
R34 Scott Timmins .75 2.00
R35 Hugh Jessiman .75 2.00
R36 Bracken Kearns .75 2.00
R37 Erik Gudbranson 1.00 2.50
R38 Viatcheslav Voynov .75 2.00
R39 Brett Bulmer .75 2.00
R40 Chad Rau .75 2.00
R41 Carson McMillan 1.00 2.50
R42 Kris Fredheim .75 2.00
R43 Raphael Diaz .75 2.00
R44 Brendon Nash .75 2.00
R45 Aaron Palushaj .75 2.00
R46 Alexei Emelin .75 2.00
R47 Frederic St. Denis .75 2.00
R48 Louis Leblanc .75 2.00
R49 Blake Geoffrion .75 2.00
R50 Jonathon Blum .75 2.00
R51 Craig Smith 1.00 2.50
R52 Ryan Ellis .75 2.00
R53 Jeremy Smith 1.00 2.50
R54 Keith Kinkaid .75 2.00
R55 Adam Henrique 2.00 5.00
R56 Adam Larsson 1.00 2.50
R57 Shane Sims .75 2.00
R58 Calvin de Haan .75 2.00
R59 Mikko Koskinen 1.00 2.50
R60 Matt Campanale .75 2.00
R61 Anders Nilsson .75 2.00
R62 David Ullstrom .75 2.00
R63 Carl Hagelin 1.25 3.00
R64 Tim Erixon .75 2.00
R65 Andre Petersson 1.00 2.50
R66 Patrick Wiercioch .75 2.00
R67 Colin Greening .75 2.00
R68 Roman Wick 1.00 2.50
R69 Andre Benoit 1.00 2.50
R70 Stephane Da Costa .75 2.00
R71 Erik Condra .75 2.00
R72 Mika Zibanejad 2.00 5.00
R73 Ben Holmstrom .75 2.00
R74 Erik Gustafsson 1.00 2.50
R75 Matt Read 1.50 4.00
R76 Harry Zolnierczyk .75 2.00
R77 Zac Rinaldo .75 2.00
R78 Kevin Marshall .75 2.00
R79 Sean Couturier 1.50 4.00
R80 David Rundblad .75 2.00
R81 Simon Despres .75 2.00
R82 Joe Vitale .75 2.00
R83 Brian Strait 1.00 2.50
R84 Robert Bortuzzo .75 2.00
R85 Harri Sateri .75 2.00
R86 Pierre-Cedric Labrie .75 2.00
R87 Brett Connolly .75 2.00
R88 Mike Angelidis 1.00 2.50
R89 Matt Frattin .75 2.00
R90 Jake Gardiner 1.25 3.00
R91 Joe Colborne .75 2.00
R92 Yann Sauve .75 2.00
R93 Eddie Lack .75 2.00
R94 Zack Kassian 1.00 2.50
R95 Tomas Kundratek 1.00 2.50
R96 Cody Eakin 1.00 2.50
R97 Dmitry Orlov 1.00 2.50
R98 Paul Postma .75 2.00
R99 Carl Klingberg .75 2.00
R100 Mark Scheifele 2.00 5.00

2011-12 SP Authentic Sign of the Times

GROUP A ODDS 1:1560 HOB
GROUP B ODDS 1:452 HOB
GROUP C ODDS 1:335 HOB
GROUP D ODDS 1:172 HOB
GROUP E ODDS 1:41 HOB
EXCH EXPIRATION: 6/25/2014
SOTAL Andrew Ladd E 4.00 10.00
SOTAM Andrei Markov C 6.00 15.00
SOTAN Antti Niemi C 5.00 12.00
SOTAO A.Ovechkin A EXCH 50.00 100.00
SOTAP Alex Pietrangelo B 6.00 15.00
SOTAS Alex Stalock B 5.00 12.00
SOTBB Bill Barber D 6.00 15.00
SOTBC Bobby Clarke A 25.00 60.00
SOTBL Jared Boll E 2.50 6.00
SOTBM Richard Bachman E 3.00 8.00
SOTBO Bobby Orr D 60.00 120.00
SOTBR Bill Ranford E 6.00 15.00
SOTBW Drayson Bowman E 3.00 8.00
SOTCE Cory Emmerton E 5.00 12.00
SOTCG Claude Giroux 20.00 40.00
SOTCH Cody Hodgson B 10.00 25.00
SOTCL Claude Lemieux D 6.00 15.00
SOTCN Brett Connolly D 3.00 8.00
SOTCO Cal O'Reilly E 2.50 6.00
SOTCS Cory Schneider E 6.00 15.00
SOTCU Sean Couturier E 10.00 25.00
SOTDB Dan Boyle C 5.00 12.00
SOTDG Daniel Girardi E 4.00 10.00
SOTDP Dion Phaneuf B 12.00 30.00
SOTDR Derek Roy C 5.00 12.00
SOTDS Dave Schultz C 8.00 20.00
SOTEB Jordan Eberle C 40.00 80.00
SOTEM Evgeni Malkin C 15.00 40.00
SOTES Eric Staal 5.00 12.00
SOTEW Eric Wellwood D 5.00 12.00
SOTHL Henrik Lundqvist B 30.00 60.00
SOTJB Josh Bailey D 3.00 8.00
SOTJD Jordan Staal A 10.00 25.00
SOTJE Jonathan Ericsson E 3.00 8.00
SOTJH Josh Harding E 4.00 10.00
SOTJK Jack Skille E 3.00 8.00
SOTJM John Moore B 5.00 12.00
SOTJO Jonathon Blum B 5.00 12.00
SOTJP J.P. Dumont E 2.50 6.00
SOTJS James Sheppard E 2.50 6.00
SOTJT Jonathan Toews A 40.00 80.00
SOTKA Keith Aulie E 3.00 8.00
SOTLC Luca Caputi E 2.50 6.00
SOTLE Brian Lee E 3.00 8.00
SOTLI Trevor Linden D 8.00 20.00
SOTLK Gabriel Landeskog B 20.00 50.00
SOTLO Logan Couture C 10.00 25.00
SOTMA Brett MacLean E 4.00 10.00
SOTMC Philip McRae E 3.00 8.00
SOTMD Michael Del Zotto D 5.00 12.00
SOTME Barry Melrose C 5.00 12.00
SOTMF Michael Frolik 2.50 6.00
SOTMH Matthew Halischuk E 2.50 6.00
SOTMK Jacob Markstrom C 12.50 25.00
SOTML Maxim Lapierre E 3.00 8.00
SOTMM Milan Michalek 2.50 6.00
SOTMS Matt Stajan D 4.00 10.00
SOTMU Peter Mueller D 4.00 10.00
SOTMX Ben Maxwell E 3.00 8.00
SOTNF Nick Foligno C 5.00 12.00
SOTNG Nicklas Grossman E 2.50 6.00
SOTNH Nathan Horton A 30.00 60.00
SOTPD Pavel Datsyuk A 30.00 60.00
SOTPK Patrick Kane B 20.00 50.00
SOTPL Pascal Leclaire D 3.00 8.00
SOTPM Patrick Marleau E 4.00 10.00
SOTPS P.K. Subban C 20.00 50.00
SOTRG Ryan Getzlaf D 5.00 12.00
SOTRJ Ryan Jones E 5.00 12.00
SOTRK Ryan Kesler C 8.00 20.00
SOTRM Ryan Miller B 8.00 20.00
SOTRNH Ryan Nugent-Hopkins D 20.00 50.00
SOTRO Mike Ribeiro 3.00 8.00
SOTRY Ryan O'Reilly E 4.00 10.00
SOTSB Sergei Bobrovsky E 5.00 12.00
SOTSC Sidney Crosby A 75.00 150.00
SOTSF Mark Scheifele D 8.00 20.00
SOTSG Sam Gagner B 10.00 25.00
SOTSK Sergei Kostitsyn 2.50 6.00
SOTSM Shawn Matthias A 15.00 30.00
SOTSS Steven Stamkos B 25.00 50.00
SOTSV Steve Mason B 10.00 25.00
SOTSW Shea Weber
(inserted in 2015-16 SP Authentic)
SOTTG Tim Gleason E 2.50 6.00
SOTTH Taylor Hall B 20.00 50.00
SOTTM Thomas McCollum C 5.00 12.00
SOTTS Tyler Seguin B 20.00 50.00
SOTTV John Tavares B 20.00 40.00
SOTWC Wendel Clark B 15.00 30.00
SOTWG Wayne Gretzky A 200.00 350.00

2011-12 SP Authentic Sign of the Times Duals

GROUP A ODDS 1:22,618 HOBBY
GROUP B ODDS 1:2770 HOBBY
GROUP C ODDS 1:3553 HOBBY
GROUP D ODDS 1:574 HOBBY
VAN RIEM/GIRX ODDS 1:10,175 '13-14 SPA
OVERALL STATED ODDS 1:288 HOBBY
EXCH EXPIRATION: 6/25/2014
SOT2BM B.Barber/R.MacLeish C 15.00 40.00
SOT2BP Pietrangelo/D.Backes D 12.00 30.00
SOT2BR B.Orr/R.Bourque A 125.00 200.00
SOT2CH Hodgson/J.Colborne B 40.00 80.00
SOT2CT Couture/J.Thornton B 30.00 60.00
SOT2DH S.Doan/M.Hanzal D 8.00 20.00
SOT2EA Ericsson/Abdelkader D 8.00 20.00
SOT2GE J.Eberle/S.Gagner 20.00 50.00
SOT2GG Wayne Gretzky dual 300.00 500.00
SOT2GR R.Getzlaf/B.Ryan B 20.00 50.00
SOT2HC Hedman/B.Connolly B 15.00 40.00
SOT2HK B.Hull/P.Kane
SOT2HM T.Myers/R.Miller B 12.00 30.00
SOT2HS Heatley/Setoguchi B 10.00 25.00
SOT2JJ J.Markstrom/J.Skille D 10.00 25.00
SOT2JM J.Boll/J.Moore D 8.00 20.00
SOT2KK P.Kane/R.Kesler B 40.00 80.00
SOT2LD Lidstrom/P.Datsyuk B 25.00 60.00
SOT2LF P.Leclaire/N.Foligno D 8.00 20.00
SOT2MB P.Marleau/D.Boyle B 10.00 25.00
SOT2ME MacLean/Ekman-Larsson 10.00 25.00
SOT2MS Santorelli/S.Matthias D 6.00 15.00
SOT2MT S.Mikita/J.Toews 60.00 120.00
SOT2PK P.K. Subban Dual D 40.00 80.00
SOT2PS C.Price/P.Subban B 40.00 80.00
SOT2RB Ribeiro/Bachman 8.00 20.00
SOT2RL P.Roy/C.Lemieux A 125.00 250.00
SOT2RV D.Roy/T.Vanek C 12.00 30.00
SOT2RY Nugent-Hopkins Dual D 30.00 80.00
SOT2SH H.Sateri/A.Stalock C 15.00 30.00
SOT2SK Scheifele/C.Klingberg C 20.00 50.00
SOT2SM M.Stajan/B.Mikkelson D 6.00 15.00
SOT2SS S.Stamkos Dual D 60.00 120.00
SOT2TS S.Stamkos/J.Tavares D 50.00 100.00
SOT2VG Van Riemsdyk/C.Giroux
SOTMYS Mystery Redemption 50.00 100.00

2011-12 SP Authentic Sign of the Times Triples

STATED PRINT RUN 25 SER.#'d SETS
SOT3#1 Ngnt-Hp/Hall/Tavrs 125.00 250.00
SOT3BOS Orr/P.Espo/Bucyk 175.00 300.00
SOT3BUF R.Millr/Vank/Myers 20.00 50.00
SOT3CHI Toews/Hossa/Kane 125.00 200.00
SOT3EDM Eberle/Pjarvi/Hall 30.00 60.00
SOT3GR8 Lemx/Sakic/Mssr 150.00 250.00
SOT3PHI Girx/vn Riems/Schn 40.00 100.00
SOT3QGF Roy/Brodr/Giguere 150.00 250.00
SOT3SJS Thrntn/Mrlu/Coutre 40.00 80.00
SOT3CANR Ngnt-Hp/Hdgs/Schf 100.00 175.00
SOT3CAPS Ovchkn/Bckstrm/Carlsn 40.00 80.00
SOT3JETS Hwrchk/Doan/Kne 50.00 100.00
SOT3KING Gretzky/Kurri/Robit 200.00 350.00
SOT3USAR Lndskog/Ctrier/Cnolly 30.00 60.00

2011-12 SP Authentic Signature Stoppers

STATED PRINT RUN 25 SER.#'d SETS
SSCP Carey Price 50.00 120.00
SSCW Cam Ward 15.00 40.00
SSHL Henrik Lundqvist 40.00 80.00
SSJH Jonas Hiller EXCH 20.00 50.00
SSMB Martin Brodeur 50.00 100.00
SSPR Pekka Rinne 20.00 50.00
SSRH Ron Hextall 25.00 60.00
SSRO Patrick Roy 75.00 150.00
SSSM Steve Mason 12.00 30.00
SSTV Tomas Vokoun 12.00 30.00

2012-13 SP Authentic

151-180 AM STATED ODDS 1:6
181-190 AM STATED ODDS 1:18
191-205 TC STATED ODDS 1:12
206-210 TC STATED ODDS 1:36
211-235 AU RC STATED PRINT RUN 999
EXCH EXPIRATION: 5/16/2015
1 Carey Price .75 2.0
2 Claude Giroux .25 .6
3 Bobby Ryan .25 .6
4 Jaroslav Halak .25 .6
5 Jamie Benn .30 .7
6 James Neal .25 .6
7 Jordan Eberle .25 .6
8 Braden Holtby .40 1.0
9 Adam Henrique .25 .6
10 Simon Gagne .25 .6
11 Brad Marchand .30 .7
12 Gabriel Landeskog .25 .6
13 Sean Couturier .25 .6
14 Ryan Kesler .25 .6
15 Taylor Hall .50 1.2
16 Pekka Rinne .30 .7
17 Milan Hejduk .20 .5
18 Ales Hemsky .20 .5
19 Derek Roy .20 .5
20 P.K. Subban .40 1.0
21 Ryan Nugent-Hopkins .25 .6
22 Anze Kopitar .40 1.0
23 Patrice Bergeron .30 .7
24 Ed Belfour .25 .6
25 Dino Ciccarelli .25 .6
26 Drew Doughty .25 .6
27 Brett Hull .25 .6
28 Alexander Ovechkin 1.00 2.5
29 Henrik Lundqvist .30 .7
30 Evgeni Malkin .75 2.0
31 Pavel Datsyuk .30 .7
32 Curtis Joseph .25 .6
33 Jordan Staal .25 .6
34 Ryan Getzlaf .40 1.0
35 Ray Bourque .40 1.0
36 Doug Gilmour .30 .7
37 Eric Lindros .40 1.0
38 Mark Messier .30 .7
39 Martin Brodeur .50 1.2
40 Jaromir Jagr .60 1.5
41 Joe Sakic .40 1.0
42 Mario Lemieux .75 2.0
43 Bryan Trottier .30 .7
44 Wayne Gretzky 1.25 3.0
45 Brendan Shanahan .30 .7
46 Henrik Zetterberg .30 .7
47 Zdeno Chara .25 .6
48 Jason Spezza .25 .6
49 Ilya Kovalchuk .25 .6
50 Zach Parise .25 .6
51 Bobby Orr .75 2.0
52 Andrew Shaw .25 .6
53 Devin Setoguchi .20 .5
54 Cam Ward .25 .6
55 Bobby Hull .25 .6
56 Lars Eller .20 .5
57 Mark Scheifele .30 .7
58 Jean Beliveau .25 .6
59 Carl Hagelin .25 .6
60 Bernie Parent .25 .6
61 Zack Kassian .20 .5
62 Saku Koivu .25 .6
63 Tony Esposito .25 .6
64 Ron Hextall .25 .6
65 Patrick Roy .60 1.5
66 Wendel Clark .25 .6
67 Tyler Seguin .40 1.0
68 Steve Mason .20 .5
69 Nicklas Backstrom .40 1.0
70 Matt Read .20 .5
71 Oliver Ekman-Larsson .25 .6
72 Guy Lafleur .30 .7
73 Erik Karlsson .50 1.2
74 Clark Gillies .25 .6
75 Brayden Schenn .25 .6
76 Dustin Byfuglien .25 .6
77 Gilbert Perreault .25 .6
78 Cam Fowler .20 .5
79 Alex Pietrangelo .20 .5
80 Bill Ranford .25 .6
81 Marc Staal .20 .5
82 Logan Couture .25 .6
83 Joe Thornton .25 .6
84 Jonas Hiller .20 .5
85 Evander Kane .25 .6
86 Brad Park .20 .5
87 Brandon Dubinsky .20 .5
88 Doug Gilmour .30 .7
89 David Backes .25 .6
90 Alexander Burmistrov .20 .5
91 Andrew Ladd .25 .6
92 Derek Stepan .25 .6
93 Dany Heatley .20 .5
94 Antti Niemi .20 .5
95 Marian Hossa .20 .5
96 Steven Stamkos .50 1.2
97 Shane Doan .20 .5
98 Patric Hornqvist .20 .5
99 Magnus Paajarvi .20 .5
100 Dion Phaneuf .25 .6
101 Stephen Weiss .20 .5
102 Luc Robitaille .25 .6
103 Trevor Linden .25 .6
104 Marc-Andre Fleury .40 1.0
105 Kris Versteeg .20 .5
106 Paul Stastny .25 .6
107 Josh Gorges .20 .5
108 Nick Foligno .20 .5
109 Nikolai Kulemin .20 .5
110 Jean-Sebastien Giguere .20 .5
111 Tuukka Rask .25 .6
112 Mike Ribeiro .20 .5
113 John Tavares .50 1.2
114 Marcel Dionne .30 .7
115 Mike Bossy .25 .6
116 Kevin Shattenkirk .25 .6
117 Marian Gaborik .25 .6
118 Patrick Marleau .25 .6
119 Dale Hawerchuk .30 .7
120 Scott Niedermayer .25 .6
121 Jonathan Toews .50 1.2
122 Dominik Hasek .30 .7
123 Nicklas Lidstrom .25 .6
124 Louis Leblanc .25 .6
125 Martin St. Louis .25 .6
126 Jeff Carter .25 .6
127 Cody Hodgson .25 .6
128 Peter Stastny .20 .5
129 Patrick Kane .50 1.2
130 Jonathan Quick .40 1.0
131 Rick Nash .25 .6
132 Eric Staal .30 .7
133 Ryan Miller .25 .6
134 Tomas Vokoun .20 .5
135 Mikkel Boedker .15 .4
136 Markus Naslund .20 .5
137 Matt Duchene .25 .6
138 Jarome Iginla .25 .6
139 Luke Adam .20 .5
140 Dustin Brown .25 .6
141 Mike Richards .25 .6

42 Ryan Callahan .25 .60
43 James van Riemsdyk .25 .60
44 Shea Weber .20 .50
45 Phil Esposito .40 1.00
46 Jeff Skinner .25 .60
47 Nathan Horton .25 .60
48 Vincent Lecavalier .20 .50
49 Phil Kessel .30 .75
50 Sidney Crosby 1.00 2.50
51 Zdeno Chara AM .75 2.00
52 Bobby Orr AM 2.50 6.00
53 Tyler Seguin AM 1.25 3.00
54 Jeff Skinner AM .75 2.00
55 Jonathan Toews AM 1.50 4.00
56 Gabriel Landeskog AM .75 2.00
57 Ryan Nugent-Hopkins AM .75 2.00
58 Jordan Eberle AM .75 2.00
59 Sam Gagner AM .60 1.50
60 Taylor Hall AM 1.50 4.00
61 Ron Francis AM 1.00 2.50
62 Wayne Gretzky AM 4.00 10.00
63 Jonathan Quick AM 1.25 3.00
64 Dustin Brown AM .75 2.00
65 Drew Doughty AM .75 2.00
66 Anze Kopitar AM 1.25 3.00
67 Patrick Roy AM 2.00 5.00
68 Pekka Rinne AM 1.00 2.50
69 Martin Brodeur AM 1.50 4.00
70 Chris Kreider AM 1.25 3.00
71 Mats Sundin AM .75 2.00
72 Pavel Bure AM 1.00 2.50
73 Erik Karlsson AM 1.50 4.00
74 Sidney Crosby AM 3.00 8.00
75 Evgeni Malkin AM 2.50 6.00
76 James Neal AM .75 2.00
77 Mario Lemieux AM 2.50 6.00
78 Brett Hull AM .75 2.00
79 Cory Schneider AM .60 1.50
80 Alexander Ovechkin AM 3.00 8.00
81 Skc/Sndn/Bre/Ots AM 1.25 3.00
82 W.Gretzky/P.Roy AM 4.00 10.00
83 T.Hall/J.Eberle AM 1.50 4.00
84 M.Sundin/J.Sakic AM 1.25 3.00
85 B.Orr/P.Esposito AM 2.50 6.00
86 M.Lemieux/J.Jagr AM 2.00 5.00
87 Kreider/M.Brodeur AM 1.50 4.00
88 B.Hull/B.Hull AM .75 2.00
89 T.Hall/T.Seguin AM 1.50 4.00
90 J.Halak/Pietrangelo AM .75 2.00
91 Theoren Fleury TC 1.00 2.50
92 Brayden Schenn TC .75 2.00
93 Carey Price TC 2.50 6.00
94 Sidney Crosby TC 3.00 8.00
95 Adam Henrique TC .75 2.00
96 Jordan Eberle TC .75 2.00
97 Jeff Skinner TC .75 2.00
98 John Tavares TC 1.50 4.00
99 Bobby Orr TC 2.50 6.00
100 Mario Lemieux TC 2.50 6.00
101 P.K. Subban TC 1.25 3.00
102 Martin Brodeur TC 1.50 4.00
103 Joe Sakic TC 1.25 3.00
104 Jonathan Toews TC 1.50 4.00
105 Wayne Gretzky TC 4.00 10.00
106 J.Tavares/J.Eberle TC 1.50 4.00
107 P.Subban/J.Eberle TC 1.25 3.00
108 Gretzky/Lemieux TC 4.00 10.00
109 M.Lemieux/J.Sakic TC 2.00 5.00
110 Hodgson/Duchene TC .75 2.00
111 Maxime Sauve AU RC 3.00 8.00
112 Sven Baertschi AU RC 4.00 10.00
113 Akim Aliu AU RC 3.00 8.00
114 Brandon Bollig AU RC 3.00 8.00
115 Tyson Barrie AU RC 6.00 15.00
116 Cody Goloubef AU RC 25.00 50.00
117 Reilly Smith AU RC EXCH 15.00 30.00
118 Brenden Dillon AU RC 20.00 40.00
119 Scott Glennie AU RC 3.00 8.00
120 Riley Sheahan AU RC 3.00 8.00
121 Jordan Nolan AU RC 3.00 8.00
122 Jason Zucker AU RC 4.00 10.00
123 Tyler Cuma AU RC 3.00 8.00
124 Gabriel Dumont AU RC 3.00 8.00
125 Chet Pickard AU RC 3.00 8.00
126 Casey Cizikas AU RC 20.00 40.00
127 Chris Kreider AU RC 15.00 40.00
128 Jakob Silfverberg AU RC 6.00 15.00
129 Mark Stone AU RC 15.00 40.00
130 Michael Stone AU RC 3.00 8.00
131 Jake Allen AU RC 10.00 25.00
132 Jaden Schwartz AU RC 12.50 25.00
133 J.T. Brown AU RC 10.00 25.00
134 Carter Ashton AU RC 2.50 6.00
135 Jussi Rynnas AU RC 3.00 8.00

2012-13 SP Authentic 1994-95 SP Retro

STATED ODDS 1:4
SP1 Tyson Barrie 1.50 4.00
SP2 Jussi Rynnas .75 2.00
SP3 Mats Sundin 1.50 4.00
SP4 Pavel Bure 2.00 5.00
SP5 Jakob Silfverberg 1.50 4.00
SP6 Sven Baertschi 1.00 2.50
SP7 Evander Kane 1.50 4.00
SP8 Dale Hawerchuk 2.00 5.00
SP9 Mark Scheifele 1.25 3.00
SP10 Andrew Ladd 1.50 4.00
SP11 Alexander Ovechkin 6.00 15.00
SP12 Nicklas Backstrom 2.50 6.00
SP13 Braden Holtby 2.50 6.00
SP14 Cody Hodgson 1.50 4.00
SP15 Ryan Kesler 1.50 4.00
SP16 Cory Schneider 1.25 3.00
SP17 Trevor Linden 1.50 4.00
SP18 Phil Kessel 2.00 5.00
SP19 Dion Phaneuf 1.50 4.00
SP20 Vincent Lecavalier 1.25 3.00
SP21 Steven Stamkos 3.00 8.00
SP22 Jaroslav Halak 1.50 4.00
SP23 Brett Hull 1.50 4.00
SP24 Jaden Schwartz 1.50 4.00
SP25 Jake Allen 2.50 6.00
SP26 Antti Niemi 1.25 3.00
SP27 Patrick Marleau 1.50 4.00
SP28 Joe Thornton 1.50 4.00
SP29 Logan Couture 1.50 4.00
SP30 Jordan Staal 1.50 4.00
SP31 Evgeni Malkin 5.00 12.00
SP32 Mario Lemieux 5.00 12.00
SP33 Marc-Andre Fleury 2.50 6.00
SP34 Sidney Crosby 6.00 15.00
SP35 Paul Coffey 1.50 4.00
SP36 Eric Lindros 2.50 6.00
SP37 Bobby Clarke 1.50 4.00
SP38 Jaromir Jagr 4.00 10.00
SP39 Claude Giroux 1.50 4.00
SP40 Brayden Schenn 1.50 4.00
SP41 Sean Couturier 1.50 4.00
SP42 Dominik Hasek 2.00 5.00
SP43 Erik Karlsson 3.00 8.00
SP44 Ryan Callahan 1.50 4.00
SP45 Marian Gaborik 1.50 4.00
SP46 Henrik Lundqvist 2.00 5.00
SP47 Mark Messier 2.00 5.00
SP48 Chris Kreider 1.50 4.00
SP49 Bryan Trottier 2.00 5.00
SP50 John Tavares 3.00 8.00
SP51 Mike Bossy 1.50 4.00
SP52 Martin Brodeur 3.00 8.00
SP53 Pekka Rinne 2.00 5.00
SP54 Jean Beliveau 2.00 5.00
SP55 Carey Price 5.00 12.00
SP56 Larry Robinson 1.50 4.00
SP57 P.K. Subban 2.50 6.00
SP58 Guy Lafleur 2.50 6.00
SP59 Josh Gorges 1.25 3.00
SP60 Jeff Carter 1.50 4.00
SP61 Anze Kopitar 2.50 6.00
SP62 Mike Richards 1.50 4.00
SP63 Luc Robitaille 1.50 4.00
SP64 Drew Doughty 1.50 4.00
SP65 Dustin Brown 1.50 4.00
SP66 Jonathan Quick 2.50 6.00
SP67 Ron Francis 2.00 5.00
SP68 Ryan Nugent-Hopkins 1.50 4.00
SP69 Taylor Hall 3.00 8.00
SP70 Grant Fuhr 1.50 4.00
SP71 Jari Kurri 1.50 4.00
SP72 Jordan Eberle 1.50 4.00
SP73 Wayne Gretzky 5.00 12.00
SP74 Bill Ranford 1.50 4.00
SP75 Pavel Datsyuk 2.00 5.00
SP76 Nicklas Lidstrom 1.50 4.00
SP77 Johan Franzen 1.50 4.00
SP78 Riley Sheahan 1.25 3.00
SP79 Rick Nash 1.50 4.00
SP80 Joe Sakic 2.50 6.00
SP81 Patrick Roy 4.00 10.00
SP82 Matt Duchene 1.50 4.00
SP83 Paul Stastny 1.50 4.00
SP84 Gabriel Landeskog 1.50 4.00
SP85 Patrick Kane 3.00 8.00
SP86 Bobby Hull 1.50 4.00
SP87 Jonathan Toews 3.00 8.00
SP88 Ed Belfour 1.50 4.00
SP89 Jeff Skinner 1.50 4.00
SP90 Jarome Iginla 1.50 4.00
SP91 Thomas Vanek 1.50 4.00
SP92 Ryan Miller 1.50 4.00
SP93 Ray Bourque 2.50 6.00
SP94 Bobby Orr 5.00 12.00
SP95 Phil Esposito 2.50 6.00
SP96 Cam Neely 1.50 4.00
SP97 Brad Marchand 2.00 5.00
SP98 Tyler Seguin 2.50 6.00
SP99 Ryan Getzlaf 2.50 6.00
SP100 Jonas Hiller 1.25 3.00

2012-13 SP Authentic 1994-95 SP Retro Die Cut Autographs

GROUP B ODDS 1:730
GROUP C ODDS 1:170
OVERALL ODDS 1:96
GROUP A2 ODDS 1:8480 '13-14 SPA
GROUP B2 ODDS 1:2260 '13-14 SPA
GROUP C2 ODDS 1:350 '13-14 SPA
EXCH EXPIRATION: 5/16/2015
SP1 Tyson Barrie C 8.00 20.00
SP2 Jussi Rynnas C 5.00 12.00
SP4 Pavel Bure B 25.00 60.00
SP5 Jakob Silfverberg C 15.00 30.00
SP6 Sven Baertschi C 5.00 12.00
SP8 Dale Hawerchuk
SP9 Mark Scheifele C2 6.00 15.00
SP10 Andrew Ladd C 5.00 12.00
SP13 Braden Holtby C2 8.00 20.00
SP14 Cody Hodgson C2 5.00 12.00
SP15 Ryan Kesler C 6.00 15.00
SP16 Cory Schneider C2 4.00 10.00
SP17 Trevor Linden B 15.00 30.00
SP18 Phil Kessel B2 10.00 25.00
SP19 Dion Phaneuf B2 5.00 12.00
SP22 Jaroslav Halak C2 5.00 12.00
SP24 Jaden Schwartz C 8.00 20.00
SP25 Jake Allen C 12.00 30.00
SP26 Antti Niemi C2 4.00 10.00
SP27 Patrick Marleau B2
SP28 Joe Thornton B 10.00 25.00
SP29 Logan Couture B 8.00 20.00
SP30 Jordan Staal C 5.00 12.00
SP32 Mario Lemieux A 75.00 135.00
SP33 Marc-Andre Fleury B2 12.00 30.00
SP37 Bobby Clarke B 20.00 40.00
SP38 Jaromir Jagr C 20.00 40.00
SP39 Claude Giroux B2 20.00 40.00
SP40 Brayden Schenn C 6.00 15.00
SP48 Chris Kreider C 15.00 40.00
SP49 Bryan Trottier A 30.00 60.00
SP50 John Tavares C 12.00 30.00
SP51 Mike Bossy B 10.00 25.00
SP53 Pekka Rinne C2 6.00 15.00
SP55 Carey Price B 15.00 30.00
SP56 Larry Robinson B 8.00 20.00
SP57 P.K. Subban 12.00 30.00
SP58 Guy Lafleur B
SP59 Josh Gorges C2 4.00 10.00
SP60 Jeff Carter B2 20.00 50.00
SP61 Anze Kopitar B 12.00 30.00
SP63 Luc Robitaille B 12.50 25.00
SP65 Dustin Brown B 10.00 25.00
SP66 Jonathan Quick B EXCH
SP67 Ron Francis A 25.00 50.00
SP69 Taylor Hall B EXCH 30.00 60.00
SP70 Grant Fuhr B2 8.00 20.00
SP71 Jari Kurri C2 5.00 12.00
SP72 Jordan Eberle B2 8.00 20.00
SP74 Bill Ranford C 15.00 30.00
SP75 Pavel Datsyuk B2 12.00 30.00
SP76 Nicklas Lidstrom B 15.00 30.00
SP77 Johan Franzen C2 5.00 12.00
SP78 Riley Sheahan C 6.00 15.00
SP79 Rick Nash 30.00 60.00
SP80 Joe Sakic A 30.00 60.00
SP82 Matt Duchene C2 5.00 12.00
SP83 Paul Stastny C2 5.00 12.00
SP84 Gabriel Landeskog C 12.00 30.00
SP85 Patrick Kane B EXCH 20.00 40.00
SP86 Bobby Hull B 40.00 80.00
SP96 Cam Neely B 15.00 40.00
SP97 Brad Marchand C2 6.00 15.00
SP99 Ryan Getzlaf
SP100 Jonas Hiller C 4.00 10.00

2012-13 SP Authentic All-Time Chirography

STATED PRINT RUN 15 SER.#'d SETS
ATCBH Bobby Hull 40.00 80.00
ATCBO Bobby Orr 125.00 200.00
ATCGP Gilbert Perreault
ATCJB Jean Beliveau 90.00 150.00
ATCWG Wayne Gretzky 250.00 400.00

2012-13 SP Authentic Buyback Autographs

79 S.Stamkos '09-10 SPA 30.00 60.00

2012-13 SP Authentic Chirography

STATED PRINT RUN 35 SER.#'d SETS
SPCBM Brad Marchand 15.00 40.00
SPCCG Claude Giroux 12.00 30.00
SPCCP Carey Price 25.00 50.00
SPCDP Dion Phaneuf 12.00 30.00
SPCEK Erik Karlsson 25.00 60.00
SPCIK Ilya Kovalchuk 12.00 30.00
SPCJT Jonathan Toews 25.00 50.00
SPCMB Martin Brodeur 40.00 80.00
SPCSC Sidney Crosby 90.00 150.00
SPCTV John Tavares 25.00 60.00

2012-13 SP Authentic Limited Autographs

51-150 GROUP A ODDS 1:1804
51-150 GROUP B ODDS 1:1300
51-150 GROUP C ODDS 1:479
51-150 GROUP D ODDS 1:325
51-150 OVERALL ODDS 1:100
152-180 GROUP A ODDS 1:1755
152-180 GROUP B ODDS 1:717
152-180 OVERALL ODDS 1:480
182-188 STATED ODDS 1:3360
191-205 TC GROUP A ODDS 1:6832
191-205 TC GROUP B ODDS 1:6832
191-205 TC GROUP C ODDS 1:1300
191-205 TC OVERALL ODDS 1:960
206-209 STATED ODDS 1:6816
EXCH EXPIRATION: 5/16/2015
51 Bobby Orr C 75.00 125.00
52 Andrew Shaw C 12.50 25.00
54 Cam Ward B 8.00 20.00
55 Bobby Hull A
56 Lars Eller D 6.00 15.00
57 Mark Scheifele C 8.00 20.00
58 Jean Beliveau A
59 Carl Hagelin D 5.00 12.00
61 Zack Kassian D 4.00 10.00
62 Saku Koivu A
63 Tony Esposito A
64 Ron Hextall B
65 Patrick Roy B 75.00 135.00
66 Wendel Clark A
67 Tyler Seguin A 12.00 30.00
68 Steve Mason C 4.00 10.00
70 Matt Read C 4.00 10.00
72 Guy Lafleur A 20.00 50.00
74 Clark Gillies C 6.00 15.00
75 Brayden Schenn C 8.00 20.00
77 Gilbert Perreault A 10.00 25.00
79 Alex Pietrangelo C 10.00 25.00
80 Bill Ranford C 12.00 30.00
81 Marc Staal C 10.00 25.00
82 Logan Couture A 8.00 20.00
83 Joe Thornton B 8.00 20.00
84 Jonas Hiller D 4.00 10.00
86 Brad Park C 6.00 15.00
87 Brandon Dubinsky C 4.00 10.00
88 Doug Gilmour A 30.00 60.00
89 David Backes B 8.00 20.00
91 Andrew Ladd D 5.00 12.00
93 Dany Heatley A
94 Antti Niemi C 4.00 10.00
97 Shane Doan C 4.00 10.00
99 Magnus Paajarvi C 4.00 10.00
100 Dion Phaneuf A 10.00 25.00
101 Stephen Weiss C 4.00 10.00
102 Luc Robitaille B 10.00 25.00
103 Trevor Linden A
104 Marc-Andre Fleury A 20.00 40.00
106 Paul Stastny B 8.00 20.00
107 Josh Gorges C 4.00 10.00
108 Nick Foligno D 4.00 10.00
109 Nikolai Kulemin D 4.00 10.00
110 Jean-Sebastien Giguere A
113 John Tavares B 30.00 60.00
114 Marcel Dionne A
115 Mike Bossy A 15.00 40.00
116 Kevin Shattenkirk C 5.00 12.00
117 Marian Gaborik A
118 Patrick Marleau A 10.00 25.00
119 Dale Hawerchuk A
121 Jonathan Toews B EXCH 40.00 80.00
122 Dominik Hasek A
123 Nicklas Lidstrom A 25.00 50.00
124 Louis Leblanc D 5.00 12.00
125 Martin St. Louis B 8.00 20.00
126 Jeff Carter B 12.00 30.00
127 Cody Hodgson C 5.00 12.00
128 Peter Stastny B 20.00 40.00
129 Patrick Kane A
131 Rick Nash A
132 Eric Staal B 10.00 25.00
133 Ryan Miller C 5.00 12.00
135 Mikkel Boedker D 3.00 8.00
136 Markus Naslund A 15.00 30.00
137 Matt Duchene B 8.00 20.00
138 Jarome Iginla A 30.00 60.00
139 Luke Adam D 4.00 10.00
140 Dustin Brown A 10.00 25.00
141 Mike Richards B
143 James van Riemsdyk C 5.00 12.00
144 Shea Weber C 5.00 12.00
145 Phil Esposito A
146 Jeff Skinner B 8.00 20.00
149 Phil Kessel A 12.00 30.00
150 Sidney Crosby A 50.00 100.00
152 Bobby Orr AM A 200.00 350.00
153 Tyler Seguin AM B 12.00 30.00
154 Jeff Skinner AM B 12.00 30.00
155 Jonathan Toews AM A 75.00 125.00
156 Gabriel Landeskog AM B 12.00 30.00
157 Ryan Nugent-Hopkins AM A 25.00 50.00
158 Jordan Eberle AM B 12.00 30.00
159 Sam Gagner AM B 10.00 25.00
160 Taylor Hall AM A 60.00 120.00
161 Ron Francis AM A 20.00 50.00
162 Wayne Gretzky AM A 200.00 350.00
164 Dustin Brown AM B 12.00 30.00
166 Anze Kopitar AM A
167 Patrick Roy AM A 100.00 175.00
168 Pekka Rinne AM B 15.00 40.00
169 Martin Brodeur AM A 100.00 175.00
170 Chris Kreider AM B 10.00 25.00
171 Mats Sundin AM A 60.00 120.00
172 Pavel Bure AM A 40.00 80.00
173 Erik Karlsson AM B 25.00 60.00
174 Sidney Crosby AM A 100.00 175.00
175 Evgeni Malkin AM A 60.00 120.00
176 James Neal AM B 12.00 30.00
177 Mario Lemieux AM A
178 Brett Hull AM A 50.00 100.00
179 Cory Schneider AM B 10.00 25.00
180 Alexander Ovechkin AM A 90.00 150.00
181 Sakc/Sndn/Bre/Otes AM A
182 W.Gretzky/P.Roy AM
183 T.Hall/J.Eberle AM B 50.00 100.00
184 J.Sakic/M.Sundin AM A 90.00 150.00
185 B.Orr/P.Esposito AM 125.00 250.00
186 M.Lemieux/J.Jagr AM 125.00 250.00
187 C.Kreider/M.Brodeur AM
188 B.Hull/B.Hull AM 150.00 250.00
190 J.Halak/Pietrangelo AM B 30.00 60.00
191 Theoren Fleury TC B 40.00 80.00
192 Brayden Schenn TC C 15.00 40.00
193 Carey Price TC B 50.00 100.00
194 Sidney Crosby TC A
195 Adam Henrique TC C 15.00 40.00
196 Jordan Eberle TC 15.00 40.00
197 Jeff Skinner TC C 15.00 40.00
198 John Tavares TC C 25.00 60.00
199 Bobby Orr TC C 100.00 200.00
200 Mario Lemieux TC A
201 P.K. Subban TC
202 Martin Brodeur TC A
203 Joe Sakic TC A
204 Jonathan Toews TC 40.00 80.00
205 Wayne Gretzky TC A 175.00 300.00
206 Tavares/J.Eberle TC EXCH 75.00 125.00
208 W.Gretzky/M.Lemieux TC
209 M.Lemieux/J.Sakic TC 100.00 200.00
210 C.Hodgson/Duchene TC 50.00 100.00

2012-13 SP Authentic Limited Autographed Patches

1-150 VETERAN PRINT RUN 10-100
EXCH EXPIRATION: 5/16/2015
1 Carey Price AU/100 30.00 60.00
2 Claude Giroux/100 20.00 40.00
3 Bobby Ryan AU/100 10.00 25.00
6 James Neal AU/25 25.00 60.00
7 Jordan Eberle/25
8 Braden Holtby/25 15.00 40.00
9 Adam Henrique AU/25 30.00 80.00
10 Simon Gagne/100 10.00 25.00
11 Brad Marchand/100 12.00 30.00
12 Gabriel Landeskog/100 10.00 25.00
14 Ryan Kesler AU/100 10.00 25.00
15 Taylor Hall/100 20.00 50.00
16 Pekka Rinne/100 12.00 30.00
17 Milan Hejduk 12.00 30.00
18 Ales Hemsky/100 12.00 30.00
19 Derek Roy/25 15.00 40.00
20 P.K. Subban AU/100 30.00 60.00
22 Anze Kopitar AU/25 60.00 120.00
23 Patrice Bergeron/25 25.00 50.00
24 Ed Belfour AU/25 25.00 60.00
27 Brett Hull AU/25 50.00 100.00
28 Alexander Ovechkin AU/25 75.00 135.00
32 Curtis Joseph/25 20.00 50.00
34 Ryan Getzlaf AU/25
(inserted in 2015-16 SP Authentic)
35 Ray Bourque AU/25 40.00 100.00
56 Lars Eller AU/25 15.00 40.00
59 Carl Hagelin AU/25 30.00 80.00
64 Ron Hextall/25 40.00 80.00
70 Matt Read AU/25 15.00 40.00
75 Brayden Schenn AU/25 20.00 50.00
80 Bill Ranford AU/25 20.00 50.00
81 Marc Staal/25 15.00 40.00
104 Marc-Andre Fleury/25 30.00 80.00
107 Josh Gorges/25 15.00 40.00
117 Marian Gaborik/25 20.00 50.00
118 Patrick Marleau/25 20.00 50.00
136 Markus Naslund AU/25 15.00 40.00
137 Matt Duchene/25 20.00 50.00
141 Mike Richards/25 20.00 50.00
144 Shea Weber/25 15.00 40.00
211 Maxime Sauve AU/100 8.00 20.00
212 Sven Baertschi AU/100 10.00 25.00
213 Akim Aliu AU/100 8.00 20.00
214 Brandon Bollig AU/100 8.00 20.00
215 Tyson Barrie AU/100 15.00 40.00
217 Reilly Smith AU/100
(inserted in 2015-16 SP Authentic)
218 Brenden Dillon AU/100 8.00 20.00
219 Scott Glennie AU/100 8.00 20.00
220 Riley Sheahan AU/100 8.00 20.00
221 Jordan Nolan AU/100 8.00 20.00
222 Jason Zucker AU/100 10.00 25.00
223 Tyler Cuma AU/100 8.00 20.00
224 Gabriel Dumont AU/100 8.00 20.00
225 Chet Pickard AU/100 8.00 20.00
226 Casey Cizikas AU/100 8.00 20.00
227 Chris Kreider AU/100 15.00 40.00
228 Jakob Silfverberg AU/100 12.00 30.00
229 Mark Stone AU/100 15.00 40.00
230 Michael Stone AU/100 8.00 20.00
231 Jake Allen AU/100 25.00 60.00
232 Jaden Schwartz AU/100 30.00 80.00
233 J.T. Brown/100 8.00 20.00
234 Carter Ashton AU/100 6.00 15.00
235 Jussi Rynnas AU/100 8.00 20.00

2012-13 SP Authentic Marks of Distinction

STATED PRINT RUN 25 SER.#'d SETS
MDBT Bryan Trottier 20.00 40.00
MDCP Carey Price 30.00 60.00
MDEL Eric Lindros
MDEM Evgeni Malkin 25.00 50.00
MDJE Jordan Eberle 15.00 40.00
MDJJ Jaromir Jagr 40.00 80.00
MDJS Joe Sakic 50.00 100.00
MDNL Nicklas Lidstrom 30.00 60.00
MDPK Patrick Kane 40.00 80.00
MDPV Pavel Bure 50.00 100.00
MDRN Ryan Nugent-Hopkins
(inserted in 2015-16 SP Authentic)
MDSC Sidney Crosby EXCH 100.00 175.00
MDSU Mats Sundin 40.00 80.00
MDTH Taylor Hall 20.00 50.00
MDWG Wayne Gretzky 175.00 300.00

2012-13 SP Authentic Premier Chirography

STATED PRINT RUN 65 SER.#'d SETS
PTCCK Chris Kreider 10.00 25.00
PTCJE Jordan Eberle 10.00 25.00
PTCJS Jeff Skinner 10.00 25.00
PTCRN Nugent-Hopkins
PTCSB Sven Baertschi 6.00 15.00
PTCSC Jaden Schwartz 10.00 25.00
PTCTH Taylor Hall 12.00 30.00
PTCTS Tyler Seguin 15.00 40.00

2012-13 SP Authentic Sign of the Times

GROUP A ODDS 1:1508
GROUP B ODDS 1:428
GROUP C ODDS 1:34
GROUP A2 ODDS 1:10,175 '13-14 SPA
GROUP B2 ODDS 1:1140 '13-14 SPA
OVERALL ODDS 1:31
SOTAA Akim Aliu C 3.00 8.00
SOTAH Adam Henrique B 6.00 15.00
SOTBM Brad Marchand D2 10.00 25.00
SOTBO Bobby Orr A 75.00 150.00
SOTBP Brad Park B 8.00 20.00
SOTBS Brayden Schenn TC B 6.00 15.00
SOTBT Bryan Trottier TC B 15.00 40.00
SOTBU Pavel Bure A 60.00 120.00
SOTBV Alexander Burmistrov C 3.00 8.00
SOTBW J.T. Brown C 3.00 8.00
SOTCA Carter Ashton TC C 3.00 8.00
SOTCC Casey Cizikas TC C 3.00 8.00
SOTCG Claude Giroux A2 75.00 150.00
SOTCH Cody Hodgson B2 6.00 15.00
SOTCK Chris Kreider B2 6.00 15.00
SOTCP Carey Price TC A 40.00 80.00
SOTCW Cam Ward TC B 8.00 20.00
SOTCY Carey Price A 60.00 120.00
SOTDB Dustin Brown B 6.00 15.00
SOTDD Devan Dubnyk C 4.00 10.00
SOTDH Calvin de Haan TC C 3.00 8.00
SOTEL Eric Lindros A
SOTFL Theoren Fleury A 125.00 200.00
SOTFY Theoren Fleury TC A 100.00 175.00
SOTGL Guy Lafleur A
SOTGO Michel Goulet B 8.00 20.00
SOTGR Wayne Gretzky TC A 250.00 400.00
SOTJA Jake Allen TC C 10.00 25.00
SOTJB Jean Beliveau A 100.00 175.00
SOTJE Jordan Eberle A2
SOTJJ Jaromir Jagr A
SOTJR Jussi Rynnas C 4.00 10.00
SOTJS Jakob Silfverberg C 5.00 12.00
SOTJZ Jason Zucker C 4.00 10.00
SOTLE Mario Lemieux TC A
SOTLI Eric Lindros TC A
SOTLR Luc Robitaille AS A 20.00 40.00
SOTMB Martin Brodeur A
SOTME Mark Messier TC A 60.00 100.00
SOTMF Marc-Andre Fleury A 40.00 80.00
SOTML Mario Lemieux A 60.00 120.00
SOTMM Mark Messier A 60.00 100.00
SOTMO Andy Moog B 15.00 30.00
SOTOR Bobby Orr TC A 200.00 350.00
SOTPC Paul Coffey A2 40.00 80.00
SOTPR Patrick Roy AS A 60.00 120.00
SOTPS P.K. Subban
SOTRA Bill Ranford B 8.00 20.00
SOTRE Ryan Ellis TC C 2.50 6.00
SOTRG Ryan Getzlaf A2
SOTRI Pekka Rinne B2 10.00 25.00
SOTRN Ryan Nugent-Hopkins
(inserted in 2015-16 SP Authentic)
SOTRS Riley Sheahan C 3.00 8.00
SOTSC Sidney Crosby A
SOTSG Scott Glennie C 3.00 8.00
SOTSJ Jaden Schwartz TC C 6.00 15.00
SOTSK Jeff Skinner TC B 8.00 20.00
SOTSU Mats Sundin A2
SOTSZ Dave Schultz B2 10.00 25.00
SOTTB Tyson Barrie TC C 5.00 12.00
SOTTH Taylor Hall B2 12.00 30.00
SOTWG Wayne Gretzky A 150.00 250.00

2012-13 SP Authentic Sign of the Times Duals

GROUP B ODDS 1:1259
GROUP C ODDS 1:628
OVERALL ODDS 1:384
EXCH EXPIRATION: 5/16/2015
ST2AS J.Allen/J.Schwartz C 20.00 50.00
ST2BG J.Benn/S.Glennie
ST2BK D.Brown/A.Kopitar B 25.00 60.00
ST2EH T.Hall/J.Eberle B 50.00 100.00
ST2FC R.Francis/P.Coffey B 20.00 50.00
ST2FS M.Fleury/J.Staal B 25.00 60.00
ST2GJ G.Lafleur/J.Beliveau B 60.00 120.00
ST2HH Br.Hull/Bo.Hull B 30.00 60.00
ST2IN J.Iginla/R.Nash TC B 15.00 40.00
ST2JK Johansen/Kassian TC C 10.00 25.00
ST2KS P.Kane/A.Shaw B EXCH 40.00 80.00
ST2LC L.Leblanc/C.Cizikas TC C 8.00 20.00
ST2ND J.Neal/S.Despres C 12.00 30.00
ST2OH A.Ovechkin/B.Holtby C 30.00 80.00
ST2PC L.Couture/J.Pavelski C 10.00 25.00
ST2PP Carey Price dual B 30.00 60.00
ST2PS P.Subban/C.Price B 20.00 50.00
ST2TT John Tavares dual C 40.00 80.00
SOT2EE J.Eberle/J.Eberle
SOT2SK D.Stepan/C.Kreider

2012-13 SP Authentic Sign of the Times Triples

STATED PRINT RUN 25 SER.#'d SETS
SOT3BOS Mrchnd/Brgrn/Sgn
SOT3EDM Gretzky/Messier/Kurri 200.00 350.00
SOT3OIL RNH/Hall/Eberle 100.00 200.00
SOT3STL Schwartz/Allen/Ptrnglo 30.00 60.00
SOT3VAN Kesler/Schnder/Burrws 40.00 80.00
SOT3WJC Tavares/Eberle/Subban
SOT3BEES Orr/Bourque/Park 150.00 250.00
SOT3PITT Lemieux/Jagr/Francis 150.00 250.00
SOT3ROOK Kreidr/Schwrtz/Brtschi 40.00 100.00

2012-13 SP Authentic Signature Stoppers

STATED PRINT RUN 25 SER.#'d SETS
SSAM Andy Moog 25.00 50.00
SSCP Carey Price 30.00 60.00
SSCS Cory Schneider 30.00 60.00
SSDH Dominik Hasek 50.00 100.00
SSEB Ed Belfour 30.00 60.00
SSJH Jaroslav Halak 25.00 50.00
SSJQ Jonathan Quick EXCH 60.00 120.00
SSMB Martin Brodeur 60.00 120.00
SSPR Pekka Rinne 15.00 40.00
SSRO Patrick Roy 75.00 150.00

2012-13 SP Authentic SPx Inserts

TWO PER SPx PACK
1 Teemu Selanne 2.50 6.00
2 Milan Lucic 1.25 3.00
3 Ryan Miller 1.25 3.00
4 Jarome Iginla 1.25 3.00
5 Jeff Skinner 1.25 3.00
6 Jonathan Toews 2.50 6.00
7 Jack Johnson .75 2.00
8 Johan Franzen 1.25 3.00
9 Ryan Nugent-Hopkins 1.25 3.00
10 Wayne Gretzky 6.00 15.00
11 Stephen Weiss 1.00 2.50
12 Mike Richards 1.25 3.00
13 Jonathan Quick 2.00 5.00
14 Carey Price 4.00 10.00
15 Pekka Rinne 1.50 4.00
16 Ilya Kovalchuk 1.25 3.00
17 John Tavares 2.50 6.00
18 Marian Gaborik 1.25 3.00
19 Henrik Lundqvist 1.50 4.00
20 Jason Spezza 1.25 3.00
21 Claude Giroux 1.25 3.00
22 Eric Lindros 2.00 5.00
23 Evgeni Malkin 4.00 10.00
24 Sidney Crosby 5.00 12.00
25 Mario Lemieux 3.00 8.00
26 Antti Niemi 1.00 2.50
27 David Backes 1.25 3.00
28 Steven Stamkos 2.50 6.00
29 Alexander Ovechkin 5.00 12.00
30 Ondrej Pavelec 1.25 3.00

2012-13 SP Authentic SPx Inserts Rookie Jersey Autographs

1-17 STATED PRINT RUN 275
18-25 STATED PRINT RUN 175
1 Maxime Sauve JSY AU/275 5.00 12.00
2 Akim Aliu JSY AU/275 5.00 12.00
3 Brandon Bollig JSY AU/275 5.00 12.00
4 Cody Goloubef JSY AU/275 5.00 12.00
7 Scott Glennie JSY AU/275 5.00 12.00
8 Riley Sheahan JSY AU/275 5.00 12.00
9 Jordan Nolan JSY AU/275 5.00 12.00
10 Jason Zucker JSY AU/275 6.00 15.00
11 Tyler Cuma JSY AU/275 5.00 12.00
12 Gabriel Dumont JSY AU/275 5.00 12.00
13 Chet Pickard JSY AU/275 5.00 12.00
14 Casey Cizikas JSY AU/275 5.00 12.00
15 Mark Stone JSY AU/275 10.00 25.00
16 Michael Stone JSY AU/275 5.00 12.00
17 J.T. Brown JSY AU/275 5.00 12.00
18 Sven Baertschi JSY AU/175 8.00 20.00
19 Tyson Barrie JSY AU/175 12.00 30.00
20 Chris Kreider JSY AU/175 12.00 30.00
21 Jakob Silfverberg JSY AU/175 12.00 30.00
22 Jake Allen JSY AU/175 20.00 50.00
23 Jaden Schwartz JSY AU/175 12.00 30.00
24 Carter Ashton JSY AU/175 5.00 12.00
25 Jussi Rynnas JSY AU/175 6.00 15.00

2012-13 SP Authentic SPx Inserts Rookie Patch Autographs

*1-17 PATCH AU/30: 1X TO 2.5X JSY AU/275
*18-25 PATCH AU/30: .8X TO 2X JSY AU/175
5 Reilly Smith 25.00 60.00
18 Sven Baertschi 50.00 100.00
20 Chris Kreider 75.00 120.00
21 Jakob Silfverberg 50.00 100.00

2013-14 SP Authentic

COMP.SET w/o RC's (200) 10.00 25.00
151-190 AM STATED ODDS 1:5
191-200 AM STATED ODDS 1:17
201-260 ROOKIE PRINT RUN 1299
261-320 ROOKIE AU PRINT RUN 999
EXCH EXPIRATION: 5/30/2016
1 Jonas Hiller .20 .50
2 Markus Naslund .20 .50
3 Kris Letang .25 .60
4 Jonathan Bernier .25 .60
5 Steve Mason .20 .50
6 Doug Wilson .20 .50
7 David Backes .25 .60
8 Chris Pronger .20 .50
9 Chris Osgood .25 .60
10 Alexandre Burrows .25 .60
11 Jason Spezza .25 .60
12 Shea Weber .20 .50
13 Shane Doan .20 .50
14 Tyler Seguin .40 1.00
15 Mikko Koivu .20 .50
16 John LeClair .25 .60
17 Gabriel Landeskog .20 .50
18 Dustin Brown .25 .60
19 Andrew Ladd .25 .60
20 Ales Hemsky .15 .40
21 Anze Kopitar .40 1.00
22 Claude Giroux .25 .60
23 Joe Sakic .40 1.00
24 Dominik Hasek .30 .75
25 Theoren Fleury .30 .75
26 Dion Phaneuf .25 .60
27 Eric Staal .30 .75
28 Corey Perry .25 .60
29 Joe Thornton .25 .60
30 Vincent Lecavalier .20 .50
31 Taylor Hall .50 1.25
32 Ryan Nugent-Hopkins .25 .60
33 Matt Duchene .25 .60
34 Al MacInnis .25 .60
35 Brett Hull .25 .60
36 Curtis Joseph .25 .60
37 Doug Gilmour .30 .75
38 Ed Belfour .25 .60
39 Jonathan Toews .50 1.25
40 Martin Brodeur .50 1.25
41 Eric Lindros .40 1.00
42 Luc Robitaille .25 .60
43 Mats Sundin .25 .60
44 Alexander Ovechkin 1.00 2.50
45 Patrick Roy .60 1.50
46 Steve Yzerman .50 1.25
47 Dominik Hasek .30 .75
48 Sidney Crosby 1.00 2.50
49 Mario Lemieux .75 2.00
50 Wayne Gretzky 1.25 3.00
51 Adam Henrique .25 .60
52 Alex Pietrangelo .20 .50
53 Alex Tanguay .15 .40
54 Alexander Burmistrov .20 .50
55 Andy Moog .25 .60
56 Arturs Irbe .20 .50
57 Bobby Clarke .25 .60
58 Bobby Hull .25 .60
59 Bobby Orr .75 2.00
60 Bobby Ryan .25 .60
61 Brent Seabrook .25 .60
62 Braden Holtby .40 1.00
63 Brayden Schenn .25 .60
64 Brian Campbell .15 .40
65 Carey Price .75 2.00
66 Carl Hagelin .25 .60
67 Chris Kunitz .25 .60
68 Cody Franson .15 .40
69 Cody Hodgson .25 .60
70 Cory Schneider .20 .50
71 Craig Anderson .25 .60
72 Dany Heatley .20 .50
73 David Clarkson .15 .40
74 Derek Roy .20 .50
75 Drew Doughty .25 .60
76 Erik Karlsson .50 1.25
77 Evander Kane .25 .60
78 Evgeni Malkin .75 2.00
79 Evgeni Nabokov .20 .50
80 Gilbert Perreault .25 .60
81 Grant Fuhr .25 .60
82 Guy Lafleur .30 .75
83 Henrik Lundqvist .30 .75
84 Ilya Kovalchuk .25 .60
85 Jacob Markstrom .20 .50
86 Jakub Voracek .25 .60
87 James Neal .25 .60
88 James Reimer .25 .60
89 Jarome Iginla .25 .60
90 Jaroslav Halak .25 .60
91 Jason Spezza .25 .60
92 Jean Beliveau .25 .60
93 Jeff Carter .25 .60
94 Jeff Skinner .20 .50
95 Jiri Tlusty .20 .50
96 Bill Barber .25 .60
97 Joe Pavelski .25 .60
98 John Tavares .50 1.25
99 Jonas Hiller .20 .50
100 Jordan Staal .25 .60
101 Josh Harding .25 .60
102 Kari Lehtonen .20 .50
103 Keith Yandle .25 .60
104 Kevin Shattenkirk .25 .60
105 Lanny McDonald .25 .60
106 Loui Eriksson .20 .50
107 Luc Robitaille .25 .60
108 Marian Gaborik .25 .60
109 Marian Hossa .20 .50
110 Mark Messier .30 .75
111 Martin St. Louis .25 .60
112 Matt Duchene .25 .60
113 Matt Moulson .20 .50
114 Mike Modano .40 1.00
115 Mike Ribeiro .20 .50
116 Mike Richards .25 .60
117 Mike Smith .25 .60
118 Nazem Kadri .25 .60
119 Bryan Bickell .15 .40
120 Nicklas Lidstrom .25 .60
121 Oliver Ekman-Larsson .20 .50
122 Ondrej Pavelec .25 .60
123 P.K. Subban .40 1.00
124 Patric Hornqvist .20 .50
125 Patrick Kane .50 1.25
126 Patrick Marleau .25 .60
127 Paul Coffey .25 .60
128 Paul Stastny .25 .60
129 Pavel Datsyuk .30 .75
130 Pekka Rinne .30 .75
131 Phil Kessel .30 .75
132 Ray Bourque .40 1.00
133 Rick Nash .25 .60
134 Ryan Ellis .15 .40
135 Ryan Johansen .30 .75
136 Ryan Kesler .25 .60
137 Ryan Suter .15 .40
138 Scott Hartnell .25 .60
139 Sergei Bobrovsky .25 .60
140 Stan Mikita .30 .75
141 Steven Stamkos .50 1.25
142 Ted Lindsay .25 .60
143 Teddy Purcell .25 .60
144 Teemu Selanne .50 1.25
145 Thomas Vanek .25 .60
146 Tomas Fleischmann .15 .40
147 Tuukka Rask .25 .60
148 Tyler Seguin .40 1.00
149 Zach Parise .25 .60
150 Zdeno Chara .25 .60
151 Viktor Fasth AM .75 2.00
152 Patrice Bergeron AM 1.00 2.50
153 Ray Bourque AM 1.25 3.00
154 Bobby Orr AM 2.50 6.00
155 Tyler Seguin AM 1.25 3.00
156 Cody Hodgson AM .75 2.00
157 Thomas Vanek AM .75 2.00
158 Eric Staal AM 1.00 2.50
159 Patrick Sharp AM .75 2.00
160 Jonathan Toews AM 1.50 4.00
161 Patrick Kane AM 1.50 4.00
162 Gabriel Landeskog AM .60 1.50
163 Patrick Roy AM 2.00 5.00
164 Brett Hull AM .75 2.00
165 Jordan Eberle AM .75 2.00
166 Nail Yakupov AM 2.50 6.00
167 Taylor Hall AM 1.50 4.00
168 Wayne Gretzky AM 4.00 10.00
169 Jonathan Huberdeau AM 2.00 5.00
170 Slava Voynov AM .60 1.50
171 Jonathan Quick AM 1.25 3.00
172 Luc Robitaille AM .75 2.00
173 Ryan Nugent-Hopkins AM .75 2.00
174 Anze Kopitar AM 1.25 3.00
175 Zach Parise AM .75 2.00
176 Marcel Dionne AM 1.00 2.50
177 Beau Bennett AM 1.00 2.50
178 Brendan Gallagher AM 2.50 6.00
179 Pekka Rinne AM 1.00 2.50
180 Jaromir Jagr AM 2.00 5.00
181 Cory Conacher AM .50 1.25
182 Aleksander Barkov AM 2.00 5.00
183 Sidney Crosby AM 3.00 8.00
184 Tomas Hertl AM 1.00 2.50
185 Mario Lemieux AM 2.50 6.00
186 Mats Sundin AM .75 2.00
187 Nazem Kadri AM .75 2.00
188 Pavel Bure AM 1.00 2.50
189 Nathan MacKinnon AM 3.00 8.00
190 Alexander Ovechkin AM 3.00 8.00
191 MacKinnon/S.Jones AM 3.00 8.00
192 MacKinnon/A.Barkov AM 3.00 8.00
193 E.Staal/A.Ladd AM 1.00 2.50
194 Perry/Getzlaf/Penner AM 1.25 3.00
195 J.Toews/P.Sharp AM 1.50 4.00
196 E.Malkin/M.Lemieux AM 2.50 6.00
197 J.Toews/C.Crawford AM 1.50 4.00
198 Bergeron/Marchand AM 1.00 2.50
199 J.Quick/D.Penner AM 1.25 3.00
200 P.Kane/J.Toews AM 1.50 4.00
201 Edward Pasquale RC 1.25 3.00
202 Ryan Stanton RC 2.00 5.00
203 Jarred Tinordi RC 2.00 5.00
204 Jayson Megna RC 2.00 5.00
205 Jared Staal RC 2.00 5.00
206 Josh Leivo RC 2.00 5.00
207 Ryan Spooner RC 2.00 5.00
208 Eric Gryba RC 1.50 4.00
209 Drew Shore RC 1.50 4.00
210 Nathan Beaulieu RC 1.50 4.00
211 Jeff Zatkoff RC 2.00 5.00
212 Luke Gazdic RC 1.50 4.00
213 Cameron Schilling RC 1.25 3.00
214 Carl Soderberg RC 2.00 5.00
215 Patrick Bordeleau RC 2.00 5.00
216 Brian Dumoulin RC 2.00 5.00
217 Thomas Hickey RC 1.50 4.00
218 Mark Barberio RC 1.25 3.00
219 Reid Boucher RC 2.00 5.00
220 Anthony Peluso RC 1.25 3.00
221 Frank Corrado RC 1.25 3.00
222 Jon Merrill RC 2.00 5.00
223 Tom Wilson RC 3.00 8.00
224 Ondrej Palat RC 2.50 6.00
225 Xavier Ouellet RC 2.00 5.00
226 Patrick Holland RC 3.00 8.00
227 Spencer Abbott RC 1.50 4.00
228 Sami Aittokallio RC 2.00 5.00
229 Linden Vey RC 1.25 3.00
230 Mark Pysyk RC 2.00 5.00
231 Frederik Andersen RC 3.00 8.00

232 Ryan Strome RC 2.50 6.00
233 Nikita Zadorov RC 2.00 5.00
234 Rickard Rakell RC 2.00 5.00
235 John Gibson RC 6.00 15.00
236 Eric Gelinas RC 2.00 5.00
237 Matthew Irwin RC 1.50 4.00
238 Martin Jones RC 5.00 12.00
239 J.T. Miller RC 2.00 5.00
240 Johan Larsson RC 1.50 4.00
241 Philipp Grubauer RC 2.00 5.00
242 Tomas Jurco RC 3.00 8.00
243 Andrej Sustr RC 1.25 3.00
244 Antti Raanta RC 2.50 6.00
245 Cody Ceci RC 1.50 4.00
246 Victor Bartley RC 1.50 4.00
247 Antoine Roussel RC 2.00 5.00
248 Richard Panik RC 2.00 5.00
249 Tyler Johnson RC 5.00 12.00
250 Freddie Hamilton RC 2.00 5.00
251 J.Audy-Marchessault RC 4.00 10.00
252 Nick Bjugstad RC 2.50 6.00
253 Jerry D'Amigo RC 2.00 5.00
254 Jonas Brodin RC 1.50 4.00
255 Viktor Fasth RC 2.00 5.00
256 Austin Watson RC 1.50 4.00
257 Reto Berra RC 2.00 5.00
258 Tyler Pitlick RC 2.00 5.00
259 Martin Marincin RC 1.50 4.00
260 Darcy Kuemper RC 2.00 5.00
261 Brian Lashoff AU RC 4.00 10.00
262 Ryan Murphy AU RC EXCH 15.00 40.00
263 Damien Brunner AU RC 4.00 10.00
264 Petr Mrazek AU RC 10.00 25.00
265 Nail Yakupov AU RC 15.00 40.00
266 Max Reinhart AU RC 5.00 12.00
267 Tanner Pearson AU RC 5.00 12.00
268 Morgan Rielly AU RC 12.00 30.00
269 Filip Forsberg AU RC 25.00 60.00
270 Seth Jones AU RC 5.00 12.00
271 Valeri Nichushkin AU RC 5.00 12.00
272 Sean Monahan AU RC 8.00 20.00
273 Cory Conacher AU RC 3.00 8.00
274 Tyler Toffoli AU RC 10.00 25.00
275 Radko Gudas AU RC 5.00 12.00
276 V.Tarasenko AU RC EXCH 100.00 250.00
277 Alex Galchenyuk AU RC 25.00 60.00
278 Jesper Fast AU RC 4.00 10.00
279 J.Huberdeau AU RC 12.00 30.00
280 Jordan Schroeder AU RC 5.00 12.00
281 Justin Fontaine AU RC 5.00 12.00
282 Elias Lindholm AU RC 8.00 20.00
283 Justin Schultz AU RC 5.00 12.00
284 Alex Killorn AU RC 8.00 20.00
285 Mark Arcobello AU RC 5.00 12.00
286 Nicklas Jensen AU RC 4.00 10.00
287 Hampus Lindholm AU RC 8.00 20.00
288 Beau Bennett AU RC 6.00 15.00
289 Calvin Pickard AU RC 5.00 12.00
290 Matt Nieto AU RC EXCH 40.00 100.00
291 Connor Carrick AU RC 25.00 60.00
292 Emerson Etem AU RC 5.00 12.00
293 Charlie Coyle AU RC 5.00 12.00
294 Brock Nelson AU RC 5.00 12.00
295 Michael Bournival AU RC 5.00 12.00
296 John Gibson AU 40.00 100.00
297 Ryan Murray AU RC 8.00 20.00
298 Alex Chiasson AU RC 5.00 12.00
299 Boone Jenner AU RC 5.00 12.00
300 R.Ristolainen AU RC 8.00 20.00
301 Lucas Lessio AU RC 3.00 8.00
302 Joakim Nordstrom AU RC 4.00 10.00
303 Jack Campbell AU RC 4.00 10.00
304 Dougie Hamilton AU RC 10.00 25.00
305 Olli Maatta AU RC 8.00 20.00
306 Michael Latta AU RC 4.00 10.00
307 Danny DeKeyser AU RC 6.00 15.00
308 Tomas Hertl AU RC 6.00 15.00
309 Z.Girgensons AU RC 15.00 40.00
310 Scott Laughton AU RC 5.00 12.00
311 Will Acton AU RC 4.00 10.00
312 N.MacKinnon AU RC 40.00 100.00
313 Jacob Trouba AU RC 8.00 20.00
314 Mathew Dumba AU RC 5.00 12.00
315 Mike Kostka AU RC 4.00 10.00
316 A.Barkov AU RC 20.00 50.00
317 Anton Belov AU RC 5.00 12.00
318 Brendan Gallagher AU RC 15.00 40.00
319 Mikael Granlund AU RC 8.00 20.00
320 Mikhail Grigorenko AU RC 15.00 40.00

2013-14 SP Authentic Limited

1-19 JSY AU PRINT RUN 100
23-40 JSY AU PRINT RUN 25
42-49 UNPRICED JSY AU PRINT RUN 10
51-149 UNPRICED AU GRP A ODDS 1:9560
51-149 AU GROUP B ODDS 1:2660
51-149 AU GROUP C ODDS 1:1125
51-149 AU GROUP D ODDS 1:1400
51-149 AU GROUP E ODDS 1:800
51-149 AU OVERALL ODDS 1:300 HOB
151-189 UNPRICED AM AU GRP A ODDS 1:13,440
151-189 UNPRICED AM AU GRP B ODDS 1:6880
151-189 UNPRICED AM AU GRP C ODDS 1:7800
151-189 AM AU GROUP D ODDS 1:4000
151-189 AM AU GROUP E ODDS 1:2600
151-189 AM AU GROUP F ODDS 1:900
151-189 AM AU OVERALL ODDS 1:480 HOB
191-200 UNPRICED AM AU GRP A ODDS 1:14,140
191-200 AM AU GROUP B ODDS 1:6600
191-200 AM AU OVERALL ODDS 1:4500 HOB
*201-260 ROOKIE/25: 1.2X TO 3X BASIC RC
EXCH EXPIRATION: 5/30/2016
1 Jonas Hiller JSY AU/100 8.00 20.00
2 Markus Naslund JSY AU/100 10.00 25.00
3 Kris Letang JSY AU/100
(inserted in 2015-16 SP Authentic)
5 Steve Mason JSY AU/100 20.00 50.00
6 Doug Wilson JSY AU/100 10.00 25.00
7 David Backes JSY AU/100 10.00 25.00
8 Chris Pronger JSY AU/100 8.00 20.00
9 Chris Osgood JSY AU/100 10.00 25.00
11 Jason Spezza JSY AU/100 10.00 25.00
12 Shea Weber JSY AU/100
(inserted in 2015-16 SP Authentic)
14 Tyler Seguin JSY AU/100 15.00 40.00
15 Mikko Koivu JSY AU/100 8.00 20.00
16 John LeClair JSY AU/100 10.00 25.00
17 Gabriel Landeskog JSY AU/100
(inserted in 2015-16 SP Authentic)
18 Dustin Brown JSY AU/100 8.00 20.00
19 Andrew Ladd JSY AU/100 10.00 25.00
21 Anze Kopitar JSY AU/25 40.00 80.00
22 Claude Giroux JSY AU/25
(inserted in 2015-16 SP Authentic)
23 Joe Sakic JSY AU/25 40.00 80.00
24 Dominik Hasek JSY AU/25 20.00 50.00
25 Theoren Fleury JSY AU/25 15.00 40.00
26 Dion Phaneuf JSY AU/25 12.00 30.00
27 Eric Staal JSY AU/25 20.00 40.00
28 Corey Perry JSY AU/25 25.00 50.00
29 Joe Thornton JSY AU/25 30.00 60.00
33 Matt Duchene JSY AU/25
(inserted in 2015-16 SP Authentic)
34 Al MacInnis JSY AU/25 30.00 60.00
35 Brett Hull JSY AU/25 30.00 60.00
36 Curtis Joseph JSY AU/25 10.00 25.00
37 Doug Gilmour JSY AU/25 30.00 60.00
38 Ed Belfour JSY AU/25 30.00 60.00
39 Jonathan Toews JSY AU/25 75.00 150.00
40 Martin Brodeur JSY AU/25 50.00 100.00
51 Adam Henrique AU D 8.00 20.00
52 Alex Pietrangelo AU C 6.00 15.00
53 Alex Tanguay AU C 5.00 12.00
55 Andy Moog AU E 8.00 20.00
56 Arturs Irbe AU C 10.00 25.00
57 Bobby Clarke AU C 25.00 50.00
58 Bobby Hull AU A
59 Bobby Orr AU E 50.00 100.00
60 Bobby Ryan AU B
61 Brent Seabrook AU C
62 Braden Holtby AU D 12.00 30.00
63 Brayden Schenn AU C
65 Carey Price AU A
66 Carl Hagelin AU E 8.00 20.00
67 Chris Kunitz AU D 8.00 20.00
68 Cody Franson AU C 10.00 25.00
69 Cody Hodgson AU B
(inserted in 2015-16 SP Authentic)
70 Cory Schneider AU E 6.00 15.00
72 Dany Heatley AU B
74 Derek Roy AU E 6.00 15.00
78 Evgeni Malkin AU B 12.00 30.00
80 Gilbert Perreault AU C 6.00 15.00
81 Grant Fuhr AU B 10.00 25.00
82 Guy Lafleur AU B 15.00 40.00
85 Jacob Markstrom AU E 5.00 12.00
87 James Neal AU D 8.00 20.00
89 Jarome Iginla AU B
90 Jaroslav Halak AU C 8.00 20.00
92 Jean Beliveau AU A
94 Jeff Skinner AU A
95 Jiri Tlusty AU E 5.00 12.00
96 Bill Barber AU E 8.00 20.00
97 Joe Pavelski AU D 8.00 20.00
98 John Tavares AU C 12.00 30.00
99 Jonas Hiller AU C 6.00 15.00
100 Jordan Staal AU C 8.00 20.00
101 Josh Harding AU E 8.00 20.00
104 Kevin Shattenkirk AU E 8.00 20.00
106 Loui Eriksson AU D 6.00 15.00
107 Luc Robitaille AU B 10.00 25.00
110 Mark Messier AU A
112 Matt Duchene AU C 8.00 20.00
114 Mike Modano AU B
117 Mike Smith AU D 8.00 20.00
119 Bryan Bickell AU E 5.00 12.00
120 Nicklas Lidstrom AU B
123 P.K. Subban AU A
(inserted in 2015-16 SP Authentic)
124 Patric Hornqvist AU D 6.00 15.00
125 Patrick Kane AU A 15.00 40.00
126 Patrick Marleau AU B 10.00 25.00
127 Paul Coffey AU A
128 Paul Stastny AU C 8.00 20.00
130 Pekka Rinne AU A
(inserted in 2015-16 SP Authentic)
131 Phil Kessel AU B 12.00 30.00
132 Ray Bourque AU A
133 Rick Nash AU B
134 Ryan Ellis AU E 5.00 12.00
136 Ryan Kesler AU C 8.00 20.00
137 Ryan Suter AU B
(inserted in 2015-16 SP Authentic)
138 Scott Hartnell AU C 8.00 20.00
139 Sergei Bobrovsky AU D 8.00 20.00
140 Stan Mikita AU A
143 Teddy Purcell AU D 5.00 12.00
148 Tyler Seguin AU C 12.00 30.00
149 Zach Parise AU B 8.00 20.00
151 Viktor Fasth AM AU F 8.00 20.00
152 Patrice Bergeron AM AU B
153 Ray Bourque AM AU B
154 Bobby Orr AM AU D 125.00 250.00
155 Tyler Seguin AM AU C
156 Cody Hodgson AM AU E 8.00 20.00
158 Eric Staal AM AU B 12.00 30.00
159 Patrick Sharp AM AU A 40.00 80.00
160 Jonathan Toews AM AU A 50.00 100.00
161 Patrick Kane AM AU A 50.00 100.00
162 G.Landeskog AM AU E 12.00 30.00
163 Patrick Roy AM AU B
164 Brett Hull AM AU A 50.00 100.00
165 Jordan Eberle AM AU D 12.00 30.00
166 Nail Yakupov AM AU D 25.00 60.00
168 Wayne Gretzky AM AU C
169 J.Huberdeau AM AU F 8.00 20.00
172 Luc Robitaille AM AU B
173 Ryan Nugent-Hopkins AM AU B 12.00 30.00
(inserted in 2015-16 SP Authentic)
174 Anze Kopitar AM AU C 12.00 30.00
175 Zach Parise AM AU C 12.00 30.00
176 Marcel Dionne AM AU B 40.00 80.00
177 Beau Bennett AM AU F 12.00 30.00
178 B.Gallagher AM AU F 12.00 30.00
179 Pekka Rinne AM AU B
(inserted in 2015-16 SP Authentic)
180 Jaromir Jagr AM AU B 75.00 120.00
181 Cory Conacher AM AU E 5.00 12.00
182 A.Barkov AM AU F 15.00 40.00
184 Tomas Hertl AM AU F 15.00 40.00
185 Mario Lemieux AM AU A
186 Mats Sundin AM AU C 40.00 100.00
188 Pavel Bure AM AU A
(inserted in 2015-16 SP Authentic)
189 MacKinnon AM AU D EXCH 50.00 100.00
190 A.Ovechkin AM AU A
191 MacKin/S.Jones AM AU 40.00 80.00
192 MacKin/A.Barkov AM AU 40.00 80.00
195 J.Toews/P.Sharp AM AU
196 E.Malkin/Lemieux AM AU 100.00 200.00
200 P.Kane/J.Toews AM AU 100.00 200.00
261 Brian Lashoff JSY AU 8.00 20.00
262 Ryan Murphy JSY AU 10.00 25.00
263 Damien Brunner JSY AU 8.00 20.00
264 Petr Mrazek JSY AU 15.00 40.00
265 Nail Yakupov JSY AU 50.00 100.00
266 Max Reinhart JSY AU 10.00 25.00
267 Tanner Pearson JSY AU 15.00 40.00
268 Morgan Rielly JSY AU 20.00 50.00
269 Filip Forsberg JSY AU 60.00 120.00
270 Seth Jones JSY AU 30.00 80.00
271 Valeri Nichushkin JSY AU EXCH 30.00 80.00
272 Sean Monahan JSY AU 40.00 100.00
273 Cory Conacher JSY AU 6.00 15.00
274 Tyler Toffoli JSY AU 40.00 100.00
275 Radko Gudas JSY AU 12.00 30.00
276 Vladimir Tarasenko JSY AU 125.00 250.00
277 Alex Galchenyuk JSY AU 75.00 150.00
278 Jesper Fast JSY AU 8.00 20.00
279 Jonathan Huberdeau JSY AU 40.00 100.00
280 Jordan Schroeder JSY AU 12.00 30.00
281 Justin Fontaine JSY AU 12.00 30.00
282 Elias Lindholm JSY AU 15.00 40.00
283 Justin Schultz JSY AU 10.00 25.00
284 Alex Killorn JSY AU 20.00 50.00
285 Mark Arcobello JSY AU 10.00 25.00
286 Nicklas Jensen JSY AU 8.00 20.00
287 Hampus Lindholm JSY AU 15.00 40.00
288 Beau Bennett JSY AU 20.00 50.00
289 Calvin Pickard JSY AU 10.00 25.00
290 Matt Nieto JSY AU 10.00 25.00
291 Connor Carrick JSY AU 8.00 20.00
292 Emerson Etem JSY AU 10.00 25.00
293 Charlie Coyle JSY AU 60.00 120.00
294 Brock Nelson JSY AU 10.00 25.00
295 Michael Bournival JSY AU 10.00 25.00
296 John Gibson JSY AU
(inserted in 2015-16 SP Authentic)
297 Ryan Murray JSY AU 15.00 40.00
298 Alex Chiasson JSY AU 10.00 25.00
299 Boone Jenner JSY AU 20.00 50.00
301 Lucas Lessio JSY AU 6.00 15.00
302 Joakim Nordstrom JSY AU 8.00 20.00
303 Jack Campbell JSY AU 12.00 30.00
304 Dougie Hamilton JSY AU 25.00 60.00
305 Olli Maatta JSY AU 40.00 80.00
306 Michael Latta JSY AU 10.00 25.00
307 Danny DeKeyser JSY AU 10.00 25.00
308 Tomas Hertl JSY AU 12.00 30.00
309 Z.Girgensons JSY AU 20.00 50.00
310 Scott Laughton JSY AU 10.00 25.00
311 Will Acton JSY AU 10.00 25.00
312 MacKinnon JSY AU EXCH 300.00 600.00
313 Jacob Trouba JSY AU 15.00 40.00
314 Mathew Dumba JSY AU 15.00 40.00
315 Mike Kostka JSY AU 8.00 20.00
316 Aleksander Barkov JSY AU 60.00 120.00
318 B.Gallagher JSY AU EXCH 60.00 120.00
319 Mikael Granlund JSY AU 15.00 40.00
320 M.Grigorenko JSY AU 12.00 30.00

2013-14 SP Authentic 1993-94 SP Retro

STATED ODDS 1:4 HOBBY
931 Bryan Bickell 1.00 2.50
932 Andy Moog 1.50 4.00
933 Bobby Orr 3.00 8.00
934 Brad Marchand 2.00 5.00
935 Tyler Seguin 2.50 6.00
936 Cody Hodgson 1.50 4.00
937 Jordan Staal 1.50 4.00
938 Jeff Skinner 1.25 3.00
939 Brent Seabrook 1.50 4.00
9310 Patrick Kane 3.00 8.00
9311 Jonathan Toews 3.00 8.00
9312 Joe Sakic 2.50 6.00
9313 Patrick Roy 2.50 6.00
9314 Peter Forsberg 1.50 4.00
9315 Gabriel Landeskog 1.25 3.00
9316 Steve Yzerman 3.00 8.00
9317 Ales Hemsky 1.00 2.50
9318 Ryan Nugent-Hopkins 1.50 4.00
9319 Taylor Hall 3.00 8.00
9320 Jordan Eberle 1.50 4.00
9321 Wayne Gretzky 4.00 10.00
9322 Devan Dubnyk 1.50 4.00
9323 Anze Kopitar 2.50 6.00
9324 Dustin Brown 1.50 4.00
9325 Jonathan Quick 2.50 6.00
9326 Ryan Suter 1.00 2.50
9327 Zach Parise 1.50 4.00
9328 Carey Price 5.00 12.00
9329 Rick Nash 1.50 4.00
9330 Pekka Rinne 2.00 5.00
9331 Martin Brodeur 3.00 8.00
9332 Adam Henrique 1.50 4.00
9333 John Tavares 3.00 8.00
9334 Erik Karlsson 3.00 8.00
9335 Scott Hartnell 1.50 4.00
9336 Claude Giroux 1.50 4.00
9337 Eric Lindros 2.50 6.00
9338 Paul Coffey 1.50 4.00
9339 Evgeni Malkin 5.00 12.00
9340 Mario Lemieux 5.00 12.00
9341 Kris Letang 1.50 4.00
9342 Sidney Crosby 3.00 8.00
9343 Arturs Irbe 1.25 3.00
9344 Patrick Marleau 1.50 4.00
9345 Jaroslav Halak 1.50 4.00
9346 Brett Hull 1.50 4.00
9347 Alex Pietrangelo 1.25 3.00
9348 Chris Pronger 1.25 3.00
9349 Steven Stamkos 3.00 8.00
9350 Mats Sundin 1.50 4.00
9351 Jonathan Bernier 1.50 4.00
9352 Phil Kessel 2.00 5.00
9353 Dion Phaneuf 1.50 4.00
9354 James van Riemsdyk 1.50 4.00
9355 Felix Potvin 2.50 6.00
9356 Pavel Bure 2.00 5.00
9357 Alexandre Burrows 1.50 4.00
9358 Cory Schneider 1.25 3.00
9359 Alexander Ovechkin 6.00 15.00
9360 Evander Kane 1.50 4.00

2013-14 SP Authentic 1993-94 SP Retro Autographs

GROUP A STATED ODDS 1:3,500
GROUP B STATED ODDS 1:1,540
GROUP C STATED ODDS 1:2,300
GROUP D STATED ODDS 1:475
931 Bryan Bickell D 3.00 8.00
932 Andy Moog D 5.00 12.00
933 Bobby Orr C 100.00 200.00
935 Tyler Seguin C
936 Cody Hodgson D 5.00 12.00
937 Jordan Staal C 5.00 12.00
938 Jeff Skinner D 8.00 20.00
939 Brent Seabrook D 8.00 20.00
9310 Patrick Kane A
9311 Jonathan Toews A 40.00 80.00
9312 Joe Sakic A 40.00 80.00
9313 Patrick Roy A 50.00 100.00
9314 Peter Forsberg A
9315 Gabriel Landeskog D 6.00 15.00
9316 Steve Yzerman A
9318 Ryan Nugent-Hopkins B
(inserted in 2015-16 SP Authentic)
9320 Jordan Eberle A
(inserted in 2015-16 SP Authentic)
9321 Wayne Gretzky A
9322 Devan Dubnyk D 5.00 12.00
9323 Anze Kopitar B
9324 Dustin Brown B 8.00 20.00
9326 Ryan Suter D 8.00 20.00
9327 Zach Parise B 10.00 25.00
9328 Carey Price A 40.00 100.00
9329 Rick Nash C 10.00 25.00
9330 Pekka Rinne B
9331 Martin Brodeur A 40.00 80.00
9332 Adam Henrique D 8.00 20.00
9333 John Tavares D 10.00 25.00
9335 Scott Hartnell B 10.00 25.00
9336 Claude Giroux C 8.00 20.00
9338 Paul Coffey C 10.00 25.00
9339 Evgeni Malkin B 20.00 50.00
9340 Mario Lemieux A 75.00 150.00
9341 Kris Letang B
9343 Arturs Irbe B 40.00 100.00
9344 Patrick Marleau B 8.00 20.00
9345 Jaroslav Halak D 5.00 12.00
9346 Brett Hull B 20.00 50.00
9347 Alex Pietrangelo D 4.00 10.00
9348 Chris Pronger B 4.00 10.00
9350 Mats Sundin A 40.00 80.00
9351 Jonathan Bernier B 10.00 25.00
9352 Phil Kessel B 8.00 20.00
9353 Dion Phaneuf C
9354 James van Riemsdyk D 5.00 12.00
9355 Felix Potvin B 12.00 30.00
9356 Pavel Bure A
(inserted in 2015-16 SP Authentic)
9358 Cory Schneider B 4.00 10.00
9359 Alexander Ovechkin A

2013-14 SP Authentic 1993-94 SP Retro Premier Prospects

STATED ODDS 1:15 HOBBY
PP1 Cory Conacher .50 1.25
PP2 Mikhail Grigorenko 1.00 2.50
PP3 Aleksander Barkov 2.00 5.00
PP4 Vladimir Tarasenko 3.00 8.00
PP5 Dougie Hamilton 1.50 4.00
PP6 Boone Jenner .75 2.00
PP7 Charlie Coyle .75 2.00
PP8 Seth Jones .75 2.00
PP9 Elias Lindholm 1.25 3.00
PP10 Valeri Nichushkin .75 2.00
PP11 Nail Yakupov 2.50 6.00
PP12 Jonathan Huberdeau 2.00 5.00
PP13 Zemgus Girgensons 1.50 4.00
PP14 Jordan Schroeder .75 2.00
PP15 Justin Schultz .75 2.00
PP16 Ryan Murray 1.25 3.00
PP17 Tyler Toffoli 1.50 4.00
PP18 Tom Wilson 1.25 3.00
PP19 Hampus Lindholm 1.25 3.00
PP20 Jacob Trouba 1.25 3.00
PP21 Nathan MacKinnon 3.00 8.00
PP22 Connor Carrick .60 1.50
PP23 Brendan Gallagher 2.50 6.00
PP24 Rasmus Ristolainen 1.25 3.00
PP25 Morgan Rielly 2.00 5.00
PP26 Sean Monahan 1.25 3.00
PP27 Ryan Murphy .75 2.00
PP28 Damien Brunner .60 1.50
PP29 Alex Galchenyuk 4.00 10.00
PP30 Tomas Hertl 1.00 2.50

2013-14 SP Authentic 1993-94 SP Retro Premier Prospects Gold Autographs

STATED PRINT RUN 99 SER.#'d SETS
PP1 Cory Conacher 4.00 10.00
PP2 Mikhail Grigorenko 8.00 20.00
PP3 Aleksander Barkov 12.00 30.00
PP4 Vladimir Tarasenko 12.00 30.00
PP5 Dougie Hamilton 12.00 30.00
PP6 Boone Jenner 8.00 20.00
PP7 Charlie Coyle 6.00 15.00
PP8 Seth Jones 6.00 15.00
PP9 Elias Lindholm 10.00 25.00
PP10 Valeri Nichushkin 6.00 15.00
PP11 Nail Yakupov 20.00 50.00
PP12 Jonathan Huberdeau 15.00 40.00
PP13 Zemgus Girgensons 12.00 30.00
PP14 Jordan Schroeder 4.00 10.00
PP15 Justin Schultz 6.00 15.00
PP16 Ryan Murray 8.00 20.00
PP17 Tyler Toffoli 12.00 30.00
PP18 Tom Wilson 8.00 20.00
PP19 Hampus Lindholm 10.00 25.00
PP20 Jacob Trouba 10.00 25.00
PP21 Nathan MacKinnon 30.00 80.00
PP22 Connor Carrick 5.00 12.00
PP23 Brendan Gallagher 15.00 40.00
PP25 Morgan Rielly 15.00 40.00
PP26 Sean Monahan 10.00 25.00
PP27 Ryan Murphy 6.00 15.00
PP28 Damien Brunner 4.00 10.00
PP29 Alex Galchenyuk 30.00 80.00
PP30 Tomas Hertl 15.00 40.00

2013-14 SP Authentic 1993-94 SP Retro Silver Skates

STATED ODDS 1:15 HOBBY
R1 Wayne Gretzky 5.00 12.00
R2 Mario Lemieux 3.00 8.00
R3 John Tavares 2.00 5.00
R4 Jordan Eberle 1.00 2.50
R5 Taylor Hall 2.00 5.00
R6 Rick Nash 1.00 2.50
R7 Ryan Nugent-Hopkins 1.00 2.50
R8 Gabriel Landeskog .75 2.00
R9 Bobby Orr 3.00 8.00
R10 Jonathan Bernier 1.00 2.50
R11 Sidney Crosby 4.00 10.00
R12 Jonathan Toews 2.00 5.00
R13 Joe Sakic 1.50 4.00
R14 Steve Yzerman 2.00 5.00
R15 Alexander Ovechkin 4.00 10.00
R16 Nail Yakupov 2.50 6.00
R17 Alex Galchenyuk 4.00 10.00
R18 Sean Monahan 1.25 3.00
R19 Jonathan Huberdeau 2.00 5.00
R20 Elias Lindholm 1.25 3.00
R21 Morgan Rielly 2.00 5.00
R22 Mikhail Grigorenko 1.00 2.50
R23 Nathan MacKinnon 3.00 8.00
R24 Tomas Hertl 1.00 2.50
R25 Justin Schultz .75 2.00
R26 Dougie Hamilton 1.50 4.00
R27 Aleksander Barkov 2.00 5.00
R28 Ryan Murray 1.25 3.00
R29 Valeri Nichushkin .75 2.00
R30 Seth Jones .75 2.00

2013-14 SP Authentic 1993-94 SP Retro Silver Skates Autographs

R1 Wayne Gretzky B
R2 Mario Lemieux A
R3 John Tavares B 15.00 40.00
R4 Jordan Eberle B 8.00 20.00
(inserted in 2015-16 SP Authentic)
R6 Rick Nash B 12.00 30.00
R7 Ryan Nugent-Hopkins A 12.00 30.00
(inserted in 2015-16 SP Authentic)
R8 Gabriel Landeskog B 8.00 20.00
R9 Bobby Orr B 100.00 200.00
R10 Jonathan Bernier B 15.00 40.00
R12 Jonathan Toews B 20.00 50.00
R13 Joe Sakic B 25.00 60.00
R14 Steve Yzerman B 80.00 150.00
R15 Alexander Ovechkin A
R16 Nail Yakupov 12.00 30.00
R17 Alex Galchenyuk 40.00 100.00
R18 Sean Monahan 25.00 60.00
R19 Jonathan Huberdeau 15.00 40.00
R20 Elias Lindholm 10.00 25.00
R21 Morgan Rielly 20.00 50.00
R22 Mikhail Grigorenko 25.00 60.00
R23 Nathan MacKinnon 30.00 80.00
R24 Tomas Hertl 25.00 60.00
R25 Justin Schultz 6.00 15.00
R26 Dougie Hamilton 15.00 40.00
R27 Aleksander Barkov 15.00 40.00
R28 Ryan Murray 10.00 25.00
R29 Valeri Nichushkin 15.00 40.00
R30 Seth Jones 6.00 15.00

2013-14 SP Authentic Chirography

STATED PRINT RUN 35 SER.#'d SETS
CAO Alexander Ovechkin
CCG Claude Giroux 12.00 30.00
CCP Carey Price 40.00 80.00
CCS Cory Schneider 10.00 25.00
CDP Dion Phaneuf
CEM Evgeni Malkin 25.00 50.00
CGL Gabriel Landeskog 8.00 20.00
CJB Jonathan Bernier 12.00 30.00
CJE Jordan Eberle
(inserted in 2015-16 SP Authentic)
CJN James Neal 12.00 30.00
CJT Jonathan Toews 30.00 60.00
CJV James van Riemsdyk 8.00 20.00
CMB Martin Brodeur 20.00 50.00
CMK Mikko Koivu 10.00 25.00
CNH Ryan Nugent-Hopkins
(inserted in 2015-16 SP Authentic)
CPD Pavel Datsyuk 15.00 40.00
CPK Patrick Kane 20.00 50.00
CPR Pekka Rinne 15.00 40.00
CRG Ryan Getzlaf 20.00 50.00
CRN Rick Nash 12.00 30.00
CRS Ryan Suter 10.00 25.00
CTA John Tavares 15.00 40.00
CTS Tyler Seguin 12.00 30.00
CZP Zach Parise 12.00 30.00

2013-14 SP Authentic Marks of Distinction

STATED PRINT RUN 25 SER.#'d SETS
MDAO Alexander Ovechkin
MDCP Carey Price
MDEM Evgeni Malkin 25.00 50.00
MDJB Jean Beliveau 60.00 100.00
MDJS Joe Sakic 40.00 80.00
MDJT Jonathan Toews 30.00 80.00
MDMK Mikko Koivu 12.00 30.00
MDML Mario Lemieux 50.00 100.00
MDMM Mark Messier 25.00 50.00
MDMS Mats Sundin 60.00 100.00
MDPB Pavel Bure
(inserted in 2015-16 SP Authentic)
MDPK Patrick Kane EXCH 30.00 60.00
MDPR Patrick Roy 40.00 100.00
MDRN Ryan Nugent-Hopkins
(inserted in 2015-16 SP Authentic)
MDSP Jason Spezza
MDTA John Tavares 30.00 60.00
MDWG Wayne Gretzky 200.00 400.00
MDZP Zach Parise 15.00 40.00

2013-14 SP Authentic Premier Chirography

STATED PRINT RUN 75 SER.#'d SETS
PCAG Alex Galchenyuk 20.00 50.00
PCBB Beau Bennett 5.00 12.00
PCBE Nathan Beaulieu 10.00 25.00
PCBG Brendan Gallagher 12.00 30.00
PCCC Charlie Coyle 4.00 10.00
PCCO Cory Conacher 2.50 6.00
PCDB Damien Brunner 3.00 8.00
PCDH Dougie Hamilton 8.00 20.00
PCEE Emerson Etem 4.00 10.00
PCGR Mikael Granlund 6.00 15.00
PCJC Jack Campbell 3.00 8.00
PCJH Jonathan Huberdeau 10.00 25.00
PCJO Jamie Oleksiak 3.00 8.00
PCJS Justin Schultz 4.00 10.00
PCMG Mikhail Grigorenko 10.00 25.00
PCNB Nick Bjugstad 5.00 12.00
PCNY Nail Yakupov 12.00 30.00
PCPM Petr Mrazek 8.00 20.00
PCQH Quinton Howden 4.00 10.00
PCRS Ryan Spooner 6.00 15.00
PCSC Jordan Schroeder 5.00 12.00
PCSL Scott Laughton 4.00 10.00
PCSM Stefan Matteau 3.00 8.00
PCTT Tyler Toffoli 10.00 25.00
PCTW Tom Wilson 6.00 15.00
PCVF Viktor Fasth 4.00 10.00

2013-14 SP Authentic Sign of the Times

GROUP A STATED ODDS 1:11,300
GROUP B STATED ODDS 1:5140
GROUP C STATED ODDS 1:1080
GROUP D STATED ODDS 1:385
GROUP E STATED ODDS 1:150
OVERALL STATED ODDS 1:100
SOTAG Alex Goligoski E 4.00 10.00
SOTAI Arturs Irbe D 8.00 20.00
SOTAL Alex Galchenyuk C 15.00 40.00
SOTBN Brock Nelson E 6.00 15.00
SOTBO Bobby Orr C 50.00 100.00
SOTBS Brent Seabrook B 6.00 15.00
SOTCF Cody Franson C 5.00 12.00
SOTCK Chris Kreider B 6.00 15.00
SOTCO Charlie Coyle D 6.00 15.00
SOTCT Christian Thomas D 5.00 12.00
SOTDD Devan Dubnyk B 8.00 20.00
SOTDS Dave Schultz B 6.00 15.00
SOTHI Thomas Hickey E 5.00 12.00
SOTJB Jean Beliveau A
SOTJE Jordan Eberle C 10.00 25.00
SOTJN James Neal B
(inserted in 2015-16 SP Authentic)
SOTJP Jean-Gabriel Pageau D 5.00 12.00
SOTJS Jaden Schwartz C 4.00 10.00
SOTJT Joe Thornton A 25.00
SOTMG Michel Goulet B 10.00 25.00
SOTMI Mikhail Grigorenko D 6.00 15.00
SOTMS Mats Sundin A 80.00 150.00
SOTNB Nick Bjugstad E 5.00 12.00
SOTNY Nail Yakupov D 12.00 30.00
SOTOS Chris Osgood A
SOTPB Pavel Bure A 150.00 250.00
(inserted in 2015-16 SP Authentic)
SOTPI Calvin Pickard E 5.00 12.00
SOTPS Mark Pysyk D 6.00 15.00
SOTRE Ryan Ellis C 4.00 10.00
SOTRI Pekka Rinne B 8.00 20.00
SOTRM Ryan Murphy E 5.00 12.00
SOTRN Ryan Nugent-Hopkins B
(inserted in 2015-16 SP Authentic)
SOTSL Scott Laughton D 5.00 12.00
SOTTF Theoren Fleury A 30.00 60.00
SOTWG Wayne Gretzky B 125.00 250.00

2013-14 SP Authentic Sign of the Times Duals

STATED PRINT RUN 25 SER.#'d SETS
SOT2AA A.Niemi/A.Irbe 40.00 100.00
SOT2GC M.Granlund/C.Coyle
SOT2GG Galchenyuk/Gallagher 60.00 120.00
SOT2GM W.Gretzky/M.Messier
SOT2JR S.Jones/M.Rielly 20.00 50.00
SOT2LM E.Lindholm/Monahan 40.00 80.00
SOT2LO B.Orr/N.Lidstrom 90.00 150.00
SOT2MF T.Fleury/A.MacInnis
SOT2MJ R.Murray/B.Jenner
SOT2MY MacKinnon/N.Yakupov 50.00 120.00
SOT2NH V.Nichushkin/T.Hertl 25.00 60.00
SOT2RS P.Roy/J.Sakic 50.00 100.00
SOT2SY N.Yakupov/J.Schultz 20.00 50.00
SOT2TB J.Trouba/A.Barkov 20.00 50.00

2014-15 SP Authentic

EXCH EXPIRATION: 6/9/2017
1 Dustin Brown .20 .50
2 Claude Giroux .25 .60
3 Mike Modano .40 1.00
4 Joe Sakic .40 1.00
5 Kyle Turris .25 .60
6 Logan Couture .25 .60
7 Olli Maatta .25 .60
8 Tyler Toffoli .25 .60
9 Adam Oates .25 .60
10 Joe Pavelski .25 .60
11 Mark Scheifele .30 .75
12 Wayne Gretzky 1.25 3.00
13 Ryan Nugent-Hopkins .25 .60
14 Patrick Kane .50 1.25
15 Tyler Johnson .25 .60
16 Sidney Crosby 1.00 2.50
17 Carey Price .75 2.00
18 Tyler Seguin .40 1.00
19 Shea Weber .20 .50
20 Patrick Roy .60 1.50
21 Vladimir Tarasenko .40 1.00
22 James van Riemsdyk .25 .60
23 Sean Couturier .25 .60
24 Nick Bjugstad .20 .50
25 Chris Chelios .25 .60
26 Damien Brunner .15 .40
27 Mike Gartner .25 .60
28 Mats Zuccarello .25 .60
29 Jeremy Roenick .25 .60
30 Ryan Miller .25 .60
31 Vincent Lecavalier .20 .50
32 Sergei Bobrovsky .25 .60
33 Antti Niemi .20 .50
34 Mario Lemieux .75 2.00
35 Dustin Byfuglien .25 .60
36 Torey Krug .25 .60
37 Marian Gaborik .25 .60
38 Mark Messier .25 .60
39 Jaromir Jagr .60 1.50
40 Teemu Selanne .50 1.25
41 John Tavares .50 1.25
42 Taylor Hall .50 1.25
43 Patrick Sharp .25 .60
44 Frederik Andersen .20 .50
45 Max Pacioretty .25 .60
46 Jim Howard .25 .60
47 Kari Lehtonen .20 .50
48 Zach Parise .25 .60
49 John Gibson .30 .75
50 Filip Forsberg .30 .75
51 Nathan MacKinnon .50 1.25
52 Evgeni Malkin .75 2.00
53 Cory Schneider .20 .50
54 Nicklas Lidstrom .25 .60
55 David Backes .25 .60
56 David Krejci .25 .60
57 Pavel Datsyuk .30 .75
58 Alexander Ovechkin 1.00 2.50
59 Anze Kopitar .40 1.00
60 Eric Staal .30 .75
61 Patrik Berglund .15 .40
62 Mikhail Grigorenko .25 .60
63 Rob Brown .20 .50
64 Ryan O'Reilly .25 .60
65 Paul Stastny .25 .60
66 Devan Dubnyk .25 .60
67 Brian Leetch .25 .60
68 Johan Franzen .25 .60
69 Morgan Rielly .25 .60
70 Pekka Rinne .30 .75
71 Martin St. Louis .25 .60
72 P.A. Parenteau .15 .40
73 Ryan Strome .20 .50
74 Brandon Saad .25 .60
75 Jari Kurri .25 .60
76 Ryan Suter .25 .60
77 Mats Sundin .25 .60
78 Adam Henrique .25 .60
79 Denis Savard .30 .75
80 Patrik Elias .25 .60
81 Pierre Turgeon .25 .60
82 James Neal .25 .60
83 Colton Orr .15 .40
84 Matt Duchene .25 .60
85 Antti Raanta .25 .60
86 Trevor Linden .25 .60
87 Kyle Quincey .15 .40
88 Martin Jones .25 .60
89 Alex Galchenyuk .40 1.00
90 Mike Liut .20 .50
91 Mike Richter .25 .60
92 Steven Stamkos .50 1.25
93 Henrik Lundqvist .30 .75
94 Henrik Zetterberg .30 .75
95 Nicklas Backstrom .40 1.00
96 Tomas Hertl .25 .60
97 Ryan Kesler .25 .60
98 Brad Marchand .30 .75
99 Alec Martinez .15 .40
100 Phil Kessel .30 .75
101 Patrick Marleau .25 .60
102 Jacob Trouba .20 .50
103 Martin Brodeur .50 1.25
104 Ryan Getzlaf .40 1.00
105 Craig Anderson .25 .60
106 Blake Wheeler .25 .60
107 Jakub Voracek .25 .60
108 Darryl Sittler .25 .60
109 P.K. Subban .40 1.00
110 Drew Doughty .25 .60
111 Bobby Ryan .25 .60
112 Derek Stepan .25 .60
113 Kyle Okposo .25 .60
114 Tomas Tatar .20 .50
115 Patrice Bergeron .30 .75
116 Niklas Kronwall .20 .50
117 Zdeno Chara .25 .60
118 Chris Kreider .25 .60
119 Theoren Fleury .30 .75
120 Valeri Nichushkin .20 .50
121 Aleksander Barkov .25 .60
122 Seth Jones .20 .50
123 Ben Scrivens .20 .50
124 Ondrej Palat .20 .50
125 Corey Perry .25 .60
126 Gustav Nyquist .20 .50
127 Alexander Steen .25 .60
128 Alex Pietrangelo .20 .50
129 Bobby Orr .75 2.00
130 Tomas Plekanec .25 .60
131 Darcy Kuemper .20 .50
132 Jonathan Quick .40 1.00
133 David Perron .15 .40
134 Chris Kunitz .25 .60
135 Ryan Johansen .30 .75
136 Brandon Dubinsky .20 .50
137 Ryan Murray .15 .40
138 T.J. Oshie .40 1.00
139 Andrew Cogliano .15 .40
140 Jarome Iginla .25 .60
141 Ryan McDonagh .25 .60
142 Rick Nash .25 .60
143 Ben Bishop .25 .60
144 Steve Mason .20 .50
145 Charlie Coyle .20 .50
146 Tom Barrasso .25 .60
147 David Desharnais .25 .60
148 Justin Williams .20 .50
149 Jonathan Bernier .25 .60
150 Elias Lindholm .25 .60
151 Tomas Hertl AM .75 2.00
152 Mike Smith AM .75 2.00
153 Teemu Selanne AM 1.50 4.00
154 Justin Williams AM .60 1.50
155 Corey Crawford AM 1.00 2.50
156 Nathan MacKinnon AM 1.50 4.00
157 Seth Jones AM .60 1.50
158 John Gibson AM 1.00 2.50
159 Carey Price AM 2.50 6.00
160 Martin St. Louis AM .75 2.00
161 Jonathan Bernier AM .75 2.00
162 Andre Burakovsky AM 1.25 3.00
163 Sidney Crosby AM 3.00 8.00
164 Aleksander Barkov AM .75 2.00
165 Jonathan Drouin AM 2.00 5.00
166 Semyon Varlamov AM .75 2.00
167 Alec Martinez AM .50 1.25
168 Jonathan Toews AM 1.50 4.00
169 Mats Zuccarello AM .75 2.00
170 Henrik Lundqvist AM 1.00 2.50
171 Ekbld/Rnhrt/Drstl AM 5.00 12.00
172 J.Pavelski/P.Marleau AM 1.00 2.50
173 J.Benn/T.Seguin AM 1.50 4.00
174 D.Nurse/L.Draisaitl AM 5.00 12.00
175 J.Quick/A.Kopitar AM 1.50 4.00
176 T.Toffoli/T.Pearson AM 1.00 2.50
177 J.Sekac/S.Andrighetto AM 1.25 3.00
178 M.Modano/R.Blake AM 1.50 4.00
179 D.Stepan/R.Nash AM 1.00 2.50
180 D.Hasek/P.Forsberg AM 1.25 3.00
181 Bobby Orr ATM 2.50 6.00
182 Brian Leetch ATM .75 2.00
183 Mike Modano ATM 1.25 3.00
184 Wayne Gretzky ATM 4.00 10.00
185 Jonathan Toews ATM 1.50 4.00
186 John Vanbiesbrouck ATM .75 2.00
187 Mike Krushelnyski ATM .60 1.50
188 Steve Yzerman ATM 1.50 4.00
189 Teemu Selanne ATM 1.50 4.00
190 Chris Chelios ATM .75 2.00
191 Jaromir Jagr ATM 2.00 5.00
192 Arturs Irbe ATM .60 1.50
193 Paul Coffey ATM .75 2.00
194 Mike Bossy ATM .75 2.00
195 Jean Beliveau ATM .75 2.00
196 M.Messier/M.Richter ATM 1.25 3.00
197 C.Chelios/D.Hasek ATM 1.50 4.00
198 W.Gretzky/W.Gretzky ATM 6.00 15.00
199 M.Bossy/W.Gretzky ATM 6.00 15.00
200 G.Lafleur/M.Dionne ATM 1.50 4.00
201 Iiro Pakarinen RC 1.50 4.00
202 Sam Carrick RC 2.00 5.00
203 Brandon Davidson RC 2.00 5.00
204 Miikka Salomaki RC 2.00 5.00
205 Kristers Gudlevskis RC 2.00 5.00
206 Oscar Klefbom RC 4.00 10.00
207 Tyler Gaudet RC 1.50 4.00
208 Jyrki Jokipakka RC 2.00 5.00
209 Brody Sutter RC 1.25 3.00
210 Barclay Goodrow RC 2.00 5.00
211 Klas Dahlbeck RC 1.50 4.00
212 Joe Whitney RC 1.25 3.00
213 Joel Armia RC 2.00 5.00
214 John Persson RC 1.50 4.00
215 Nikita Nesterov RC 2.00 5.00
216 Phoenix Copley RC 2.50 6.00
217 Scott Darling RC 5.00 12.00
218 Joe Morrow RC 2.50 6.00
219 Christopher Gibson RC 3.00 8.00
220 Petteri Lindbohm RC 1.50 4.00
221 Jordan Binnington RC 2.00 5.00
222 Seth Helgeson RC 1.50 4.00
223 Mike Halmo RC 1.25 3.00
224 Max Friberg RC 1.50 4.00
225 Rob Zepp RC 3.00 8.00
226 Brandon Gormley RC 2.00 5.00
227 Jonathan Racine RC 2.00 5.00
228 Joey Hishon RC 2.50 6.00
229 Bill Arnold RC 1.50 4.00
230 Brendan Shinnimin RC 1.50 4.00
231 Tyler Graovac RC 1.50 4.00
232 Jordan Martinook RC 1.50 4.00
233 Scott Mayfield RC 1.50 4.00
234 Josh Jooris RC 2.00 5.00
235 Bobby Farnham RC 2.00 5.00
236 Cedric Paquette RC 2.00 5.00
237 Troy Grosenick RC 2.00 5.00
238 Bryan Rust RC 15.00 40.00
239 Landon Ferraro RC 1.25 3.00
240 Colin Smith RC 2.00 5.00
241 Dominik Uher RC 1.50 4.00
242 Scott Harrington RC 2.00 5.00
243 Bogdan Yakimov RC 2.00 5.00
244 Tyler Wotherspoon RC 2.00 5.00
245 Pierre-Edouard Bellemare RC 2.00 5.00
246 Petter Granberg RC 1.50 4.00
247 Adam Clendening RC 2.00 5.00
248 Johan Sundstrom RC 2.00 5.00
249 Chris Wagner RC 2.00 5.00
250 Brandon DeFazio RC 1.50 4.00
251 John Klingberg RC 6.00 15.00
252 Nicolas Deschamps RC 2.00 5.00
253 Borna Rendulic RC 2.00 5.00
254 Tim Schaller RC 1.25 3.00
255 Andrey Makarov RC 2.00 5.00
256 Anton Forsberg RC 2.00 5.00

57 Scott Wilson RC 1.50 4.00
58 Andrew Agozzino RC 1.50 4.00
59 Cody Kunyk RC 1.25 3.00
60 Matt Lindblad RC 1.50 4.00
61 William Karlsson AU RC 20.00 50.00
62 Darnell Nurse AU RC 15.00 40.00
63 Jake McCabe AU RC 5.00 12.00
64 Patrick Brown AU RC 5.00 12.00
65 Joni Ortio AU RC 20.00 50.00
66 Mark Visentin AU RC 5.00 12.00
67 Corban Knight AU RC 5.00 12.00
68 Stuart Percy AU RC 5.00 12.00
69 Phillip Danault AU RC 5.00 12.00
70 Patrik Nemeth AU RC 5.00 12.00
71 Colton Sissons AU RC 5.00 12.00
72 Curtis McKenzie AU RC 4.00 10.00
73 Sam Reinhart AU RC 12.00 30.00
74 Melker Karlsson AU RC 5.00 12.00
75 Nicolas Deslauriers AU RC 5.00 12.00
76 Christian Folin AU RC 5.00 12.00
77 Leon Draisaitl AU RC 150.00 300.00
78 Sven Andrighetto AU RC 20.00 50.00
79 Chris Tierney AU RC 15.00 40.00
80 Trevor van Riemsdyk AU RC 8.00 20.00
81 A.Hammond AU RC EXCH 8.00 20.00
82 David Pastrnak AU RC 60.00 150.00
83 Vincent Trocheck AU RC 6.00 15.00
84 T.Teravainen AU RC EXCH 15.00 40.00
85 Bo Horvat AU RC 30.00 80.00
86 A.Duclair AU RC EXCH 25.00 60.00
87 Damon Severson AU RC 5.00 12.00
88 Evgeny Kuznetsov AU RC 25.00 60.00
89 Rocco Grimaldi AU RC 5.00 12.00
90 Dennis Everberg AU RC 5.00 12.00
91 Alexander Wennberg AU RC 10.00 25.00
92 Derrick Pouliot AU RC 6.00 15.00
93 Ryan Sproul AU RC 5.00 12.00
94 Kevin Hayes AU RC 15.00 40.00
95 Jiri Sekac AU RC 5.00 12.00
96 V.Namestnikov AU RC EXCH 40.00 100.00
97 Tobias Rieder AU RC EXCH 25.00 60.00
98 Brandon Kozun AU RC 4.00 10.00
99 Shayne Gostisbehere AU RC 25.00 60.00
100 Marko Dano AU RC 5.00 12.00
101 Calle Jarnkrok AU RC EXCH 25.00 60.00
102 Seth Griffith AU RC EXCH 40.00 100.00
103 Griffin Reinhart AU RC 6.00 15.00
104 Alexander Khokhlachev AU RC 5.00 12.00
105 Laurent Brossoit AU RC 5.00 12.00
106 J.Gaudreau AU RC EXCH 60.00 150.00
107 Brett Ritchie AU RC 5.00 12.00
108 Markus Granlund AU RC 8.00 20.00
109 Aaron Ekblad AU RC 20.00 50.00
110 Andrei Vasilevskiy AU RC 30.00 80.00
111 Adam Lowry AU RC 5.00 12.00
112 Andre Burakovsky AU RC 12.00 30.00
113 Jonathan Drouin AU RC 50.00 120.00
114 Curtis Lazar AU RC 6.00 15.00
115 Mirco Mueller AU RC 5.00 12.00
116 Teemu Pulkkinen AU RC 6.00 15.00
117 Ty Rattie AU RC EXCH 20.00 50.00
118 Victor Rask AU RC 30.00 80.00
119 Kerby Rychel AU RC 4.00 10.00
120 Jori Lehtera AU RC 25.00 60.00

2014-15 SP Authentic Limited

Dustin Brown JSY AU/100 10.00 25.00
Mike Modano JSY AU/25 30.00 80.00
Joe Sakic JSY AU/25 EXCH 30.00 80.00
Kyle Turris JSY AU/100 12.00 30.00
Logan Couture JSY AU/25 20.00 50.00
(inserted in 2015-16 SP Authentic)
Olli Maatta JSY AU/100 12.00 30.00
(inserted in 2015-16 SP Authentic)
Adam Oates JSY AU/25 30.00 80.00
(inserted in 2015-16 SP Authentic)
0 Joe Pavelski JSY AU/100 12.00 30.00
1 Mark Scheifele JSY AU/100 15.00 40.00
7 Carey Price JSY AU/25 60.00 150.00
8 Tyler Seguin JSY AU/25 30.00 80.00
(inserted in 2015-16 SP Authentic)
9 Shea Weber JSY AU/25 15.00 40.00
(inserted in 2015-16 SP Authentic)
2 James van Riemsdyk JSY AU/25 20.00 50.00
(inserted in 2015-16 SP Authentic)
3 Sean Couturier JSY AU/100 12.00 30.00
(inserted in 2015-16 SP Authentic)
5 Chris Chelios JSY AU/25 30.00 80.00
7 Mike Gartner JSY AU/25 20.00 50.00
8 Mats Zuccarello JSY AU/100 15.00 40.00
(inserted in 2015-16 SP Authentic)
9 Jeremy Roenick JSY AU/100 12.00 30.00
(inserted in 2015-16 SP Authentic)
2 Sergei Bobrovsky JSY AU/25 20.00 50.00
(inserted in 2015-16 SP Authentic)
6 Torey Krug JSY AU/100 12.00 30.00
7 Marian Gaborik JSY AU/100 12.00 30.00
(inserted in 2015-16 SP Authentic)
5 Max Pacioretty JSY AU/25 20.00 50.00
(inserted in 2015-16 SP Authentic)
6 Jim Howard JSY AU/100 12.00 30.00
7 Kari Lehtonen JSY AU/100 10.00 25.00
9 John Gibson JSY AU/100 15.00 40.00
1 MacKinnon JSY AU/25 EXCH 60.00 150.00
3 Cory Schneider JSY AU/25 15.00 40.00
5 David Backes JSY AU/100 12.00 30.00
7 Pavel Datsyuk JSY AU/25 40.00 100.00
8 Ovechkin JSY AU/25 EXCH 80.00 200.00
0 Eric Staal JSY AU/25 25.00 60.00
3 Rob Brown AU D 8.00 20.00
5 Paul Stastny AU B 10.00 25.00
(inserted in 2015-16 SP Authentic)
6 Devan Dubnyk AU C 10.00 25.00
7 Brian Leetch AU B 10.00 25.00
(inserted in 2015-16 SP Authentic)
8 Johan Franzen AU C 10.00 25.00
9 Morgan Rielly AU C 15.00 40.00
2 P.A. Parenteau AU D 6.00 15.00
(inserted in 2015-16 SP Authentic)
3 Ryan Strome AU C 8.00 20.00
(inserted in 2015-16 SP Authentic)
4 Brandon Saad AU C 10.00 25.00
(inserted in 2015-16 SP Authentic)
5 Jari Kurri AU C 10.00 25.00
6 Ryan Suter AU B 10.00 25.00
(inserted in 2015-16 SP Authentic)
7 Mats Sundin AU A 25.00 60.00
9 Denis Savard AU B 12.00 30.00
1 Pierre Turgeon AU B 10.00 25.00
6 Trevor Linden AU D 10.00 25.00
7 Kyle Quincey AU D 6.00 15.00
9 Alex Galchenyuk AU C 15.00 40.00
(inserted in 2015-16 SP Authentic)
0 Mike Liut AU B 8.00 20.00
6 Tomas Hertl AU D 10.00 25.00
(inserted in 2015-16 SP Authentic)
7 Ryan Kesler AU B 10.00 25.00
(inserted in 2015-16 SP Authentic)
01 Patrick Marleau AU B 10.00 25.00
(inserted in 2015-16 SP Authentic)
03 Martin Brodeur AU A 40.00 100.00
108 Darryl Sittler AU A 15.00 40.00
(inserted in 2015-16 SP Authentic)
119 Theoren Fleury AU B 15.00 40.00
120 Val Nichushkin AU C 8.00 20.00
(inserted in 2015-16 SP Authentic)
122 Seth Jones AU C 8.00 20.00
129 Bobby Orr AU B 80.00 150.00
136 Brandon Dubinsky AU C 8.00 20.00
(inserted in 2015-16 SP Authentic)
140 Jarome Iginla AU A 15.00 40.00
141 Ryan McDonagh AU C 10.00 25.00
142 Rick Nash AU B 10.00 25.00
145 Charlie Coyle AU D 8.00 20.00
(inserted in 2015-16 SP Authentic)
146 Tom Barrasso AU B 8.00 20.00
149 Jonathan Bernier AU B 8.00 20.00
151 Tomas Hertl AM AU B 12.00 30.00
153 Teemu Selanne AM AU B 40.00 100.00
156 Nathan MacKinnon AM AU 20.00 50.00
(inserted in 2015-16 SP Authentic)
157 Seth Jones AM AU B 10.00 25.00
158 John Gibson AM AU B 10.00 25.00
159 Carey Price AM AU B 40.00 100.00
161 J.Bernier AM AU B 12.00 30.00
162 A.Burakovsky AM AU B 15.00 40.00
163 Sidney Crosby AM AU A 250.00 350.00
164 A.Barkov AM AU B 10.00 25.00
165 J.Drouin AM AU B 25.00 60.00
168 J.Toews AM AU B 60.00 150.00
169 Mats Zuccarello AM AU 10.00 25.00
(inserted in 2015-16 SP Authentic)
171 Ekblad/S.Rein/Drais AM AU 50.00 120.00
172 J.Pavelski/P.Marteau AM AU 20.00 50.00
174 Nurse/L.Draisaitl AM AU 50.00 120.00
177 J.Sekac/S.Andrighetto AM AU 12.00 30.00
178 Modano/R.Blake AM AU 80.00 200.00
180 D.Hasek/P.Forsberg AM AU 40.00 100.00
181 Bobby Orr ATM AU 80.00 150.00
182 Brian Leetch ATM AU 10.00 25.00
(inserted in 2015-16 SP Authentic)
183 Mike Modano ATM AU 25.00 60.00
184 Wayne Gretzky ATM AU 200.00 500.00
185 Jonathan Toews ATM AU 60.00 150.00
186 J.Vanbiesbrouck ATM AU 10.00 25.00
187 Mike Krushelnyski ATM AU 8.00 20.00
188 Steve Yzerman ATM AU 50.00 120.00
189 Teemu Selanne ATM AU 60.00 150.00
190 Chris Chelios ATM AU 10.00 25.00
191 Jaromir Jagr ATM AU 50.00 120.00
192 Arturs Irbe ATM AU 8.00 20.00
193 Paul Coffey ATM AU 10.00 25.00
194 Mike Bossy ATM AU 10.00 25.00
197 Chelios/D.Hasek ATM AU 80.00 150.00
198 W.Gretzky dual ATM AU 350.00 450.00
199 Bossy/Gretzky ATM AU 200.00 300.00
200 Lafleur/Dionne ATM AU 40.00 100.00
201 Iiro Pakarinen 5.00 12.00
202 Sam Carrick 6.00 15.00
203 Brandon Davidson 6.00 15.00
204 Miikka Salomaki 6.00 15.00
205 Kristers Gudlevskis 6.00 15.00
206 Oscar Klefbom 25.00 60.00
207 Tyler Gaudet 5.00 12.00
208 Jyrki Jokipakka 6.00 15.00
209 Brody Sutter 4.00 10.00
210 Barclay Goodrow 6.00 15.00
211 Klas Dahlbeck 5.00 12.00
212 Joe Whitney 4.00 10.00
213 Joel Armia 6.00 15.00
214 John Persson 5.00 12.00
215 Nikita Nesterov 6.00 15.00
216 Phoenix Copley 8.00 20.00
217 Scott Darling 15.00 40.00
218 Joe Morrow 8.00 20.00
219 Christopher Gibson 10.00 25.00
220 Petteri Lindbohm 5.00 12.00
221 Jordan Binnington 6.00 15.00
222 Seth Helgeson 5.00 12.00
223 Mike Halmo 4.00 10.00
224 Max Friberg 5.00 12.00
225 Rob Zepp 10.00 25.00
226 Brandon Gormley 6.00 15.00
227 Jonathan Racine 6.00 15.00
228 Joey Hishon 8.00 20.00
229 Bill Arnold 5.00 12.00
230 Brendan Shinnimin 5.00 12.00
231 Tyler Graovac 5.00 12.00
232 Jordan Martinook 5.00 12.00
233 Scott Mayfield 5.00 12.00
234 Josh Jooris 6.00 15.00
235 Bobby Farnham 6.00 15.00
236 Cedric Paquette 6.00 15.00
237 Troy Grosenick 6.00 15.00
238 Bryan Rust 20.00 50.00
239 Landon Ferraro 4.00 10.00
240 Colin Smith 6.00 15.00
241 Dominik Uher 5.00 12.00
242 Scott Harrington 6.00 15.00
243 Bogdan Yakimov 6.00 15.00
244 Tyler Wotherspoon 6.00 15.00
245 Pierre-Edouard Bellemare 6.00 15.00
246 Petter Granberg 5.00 12.00
247 Adam Clendening 6.00 15.00
248 Johan Sundstrom 6.00 15.00
249 Chris Wagner 6.00 15.00
250 Brandon Defazio 5.00 12.00
251 John Klingberg 20.00 50.00
252 Nicolas Deschamps 6.00 15.00
253 Borna Rendulic 6.00 15.00
254 Tim Schaller 4.00 10.00
255 Andrey Makarov 6.00 15.00
256 Anton Forsberg 6.00 15.00
257 Scott Wilson 5.00 12.00
258 Andrew Agozzino 5.00 12.00
259 Cody Kunyk 4.00 10.00
260 Matt Lindblad 5.00 12.00
261 William Karlsson JSY AU/100 50.00 120.00
262 Darnell Nurse JSY AU/100 40.00 100.00
263 Jake McCabe JSY AU/100 12.00 30.00
264 Patrick Brown JSY AU/100 12.00 30.00
265 Joni Ortio JSY AU/100 15.00 40.00
(inserted in 2015-16 SP Authentic)
266 Mark Visentin JSY AU/100 12.00 30.00
267 Corban Knight JSY AU/100 12.00 30.00
268 Stuart Percy JSY AU/100 12.00 30.00
269 Phillip Danault JSY AU/100 12.00 30.00
(inserted in 2015-16 SP Authentic)
270 Patrik Nemeth JSY AU/100 12.00 30.00
271 Colton Sissons JSY AU/100 12.00 30.00
272 Curtis McKenzie JSY AU/100 10.00 25.00
273 Sam Reinhart JSY AU/100 40.00 100.00
275 N.Deslauriers JSY AU/100 12.00 30.00
277 L.Draisaitl JSY AU/100 EXCH 200.00 350.00
279 Chris Tierney JSY AU/100 12.00 30.00
(inserted in 2015-16 SP Authentic)
281 A.Hammond JSY AU/100 EXCH 20.00 50.00
282 D.Pastrnak JSY AU/100 EXCH 80.00 200.00
283 V.Trocheck JSY AU/100 15.00 40.00
284 T.Teravainen JSY AU/100 EXCH 20.00 50.00
285 Bo Horvat JSY AU/100 80.00 200.00
286 Anthony Duclair JSY AU/100 20.00 50.00
287 D.Severson JSY AU/100 12.00 30.00
288 E.Kuznetsov JSY AU/100 50.00 120.00
289 Rocco Grimaldi JSY AU/100 12.00 30.00
290 D.Everberg JSY AU/100 12.00 30.00
291 A.Wennberg JSY AU/100 25.00 60.00
293 Ryan Sproul JSY AU/100 12.00 30.00
294 Kevin Hayes JSY AU/100 40.00 100.00
(inserted in 2015-16 SP Authentic)
295 Jiri Sekac JSY AU/100 12.00 30.00
296 Vladislav Namestnikov JSY AU/100 20.00 50.00
297 Tobias Rieder JSY AU/100 12.00 30.00
(inserted in 2015-16 SP Authentic)
298 Brandon Kozun JSY AU/100 10.00 25.00
299 S.Gostisbehere JSY AU/100 50.00 125.00
300 Marko Dano JSY AU/100 12.00 30.00
302 Seth Griffith JSY AU/100 15.00 40.00
(inserted in 2015-16 SP Authentic)
303 G.Reinhart JSY AU/100 15.00 40.00
304 A.Khokhlachev JSY AU/100 12.00 30.00
305 Laurent Brossoit JSY AU/100 12.00 30.00
306 J.Gaudreau JSY AU/100 EXCH 100.00 250.00
309 Aaron Ekblad JSY AU/100 50.00 120.00
310 A.Vasilevskiy JSY AU/100 25.00 60.00
311 Adam Lowry JSY AU/100 12.00 30.00
312 A.Burakovsky JSY AU/100 20.00 50.00
313 J.Drouin JSY AU/100 80.00 200.00
314 Curtis Lazar JSY AU/100 25.00 60.00
315 Mirco Mueller JSY AU/100 12.00 30.00
316 T.Pulkkinen JSY AU/100 15.00 40.00
317 Ty Rattie JSY AU/100 15.00 40.00
(inserted in 2015-16 SP Authentic)
318 Victor Rask JSY AU/100 20.00 50.00
(inserted in 2015-16 SP Authentic)
319 Kerby Rychel JSY AU/100 10.00 25.00
320 Jori Lehtera JSY AU/100 15.00 40.00
(inserted in 2015-16 SP Authentic)

2014-15 SP Authentic '94-95 SP Retro

1-80 STATED ODDS 1:5 HOBBY
81-100 STATED ODDS 1:17 HOBBY
1 Marty McSorley 1.50 4.00
2 Ryan Miller 1.50 4.00
3 Ryan Kesler 1.50 4.00
4 Vincent Lecavalier 1.25 3.00
5 Scott Hartnell 1.50 4.00
6 Steve Larmer 1.25 3.00
7 Mark Messier 1.50 4.00
8 Bobby Clarke 1.50 4.00
9 David Krejci 1.50 4.00
10 Wayne Gretzky 8.00 20.00
11 Alec Martinez 1.00 2.50
12 Vincent Damphousse 1.25 3.00
13 Mike Gartner 1.50 4.00
14 Jeremy Roenick 1.50 4.00
15 Jamie Benn 2.00 5.00
16 Phil Esposito 2.50 6.00
17 Jari Kurri 1.50 4.00
18 Jarome Iginla 1.50 4.00
19 Olaf Kolzig 1.50 4.00
20 Patrick Sharp 1.50 4.00
21 Henrik Lundqvist 2.00 5.00
22 Roberto Luongo 1.50 4.00
23 Evgeni Malkin 5.00 12.00
24 Marian Hossa 1.25 3.00
25 Teemu Selanne 3.00 8.00
26 Joe Pavelski 1.50 4.00
27 Jaromir Jagr 4.00 10.00
28 Matt Duchene 1.50 4.00
29 John LeClair 1.50 4.00
30 Patrick Roy 4.00 10.00
31 Andy Moog 1.50 4.00
32 Bill Ranford 1.50 4.00
33 Sergei Bobrovsky 1.50 4.00
34 Jeff Skinner 1.50 4.00
35 Pete Peeters 1.25 3.00
36 Denis Savard 2.00 5.00
37 Richard Brodeur 1.50 4.00
38 Mario Lemieux 5.00 12.00
39 Felix Potvin 2.50 6.00
40 Pavel Datsyuk 2.00 5.00
41 Pierre Turgeon 1.50 4.00
42 Chris Chelios 1.50 4.00
43 Derek Stepan 1.50 4.00
44 Theoren Fleury 2.00 5.00
45 Carey Price 5.00 12.00
46 Gabriel Landeskog 1.25 3.00
47 Brian Bellows 1.25 3.00
48 John Tavares 3.00 8.00
49 Sean Monahan 1.50 4.00
50 Ryan Suter 1.50 4.00
51 Brendan Gallagher 1.50 4.00
52 Torey Krug 1.50 4.00
53 Mats Sundin 1.50 4.00
54 Johan Franzen 1.50 4.00
55 Guy Lafleur 2.00 5.00
56 Patrik Elias 1.50 4.00
57 Mike Liut 1.25 3.00
58 Ryan McDonagh 1.50 4.00
59 Joe Sakic 2.50 6.00
60 Henrik Zetterberg 2.00 5.00
61 Tom Barrasso 1.50 4.00
62 Dominik Hasek 2.00 5.00
63 Jakub Voracek 1.50 4.00
64 Bobby Orr 5.00 12.00
65 Jonathan Bernier 1.50 4.00
66 Jason Pominville 1.25 3.00
67 Logan Couture 1.50 4.00
68 Martin Brodeur 3.00 8.00
69 Brad Park 1.25 3.00
70 Jaroslav Halak 1.25 3.00
71 Brian Leetch 1.50 4.00
72 Jim Howard 1.50 4.00
73 Paul Stastny 1.50 4.00
74 Arturs Irbe 1.25 3.00
75 Sean Couturier 1.50 4.00
76 Rick Nash 1.50 4.00
77 Nicklas Lidstrom 1.50 4.00
78 Shea Weber 1.25 3.00
79 Tony Esposito 1.50 4.00
80 Brandon Dubinsky 1.25 3.00
81 Evgeny Kuznetsov 8.00 20.00
82 Sam Reinhart 4.00 10.00
83 Victor Rask 2.00 5.00
84 Teuvo Teravainen 4.00 10.00
85 Alexander Wennberg 4.00 10.00
86 David Pastrnak 5.00 12.00
87 Calle Jarnkrok 2.00 5.00
88 Aaron Ekblad 4.00 10.00
89 Curtis Lazar 2.50 6.00
90 Leon Draisaitl 10.00 25.00
91 Vincent Trocheck 2.50 6.00
92 Damon Severson 2.00 5.00
93 Griffin Reinhart 2.50 6.00
94 Anthony Duclair 3.00 8.00
95 Johnny Gaudreau 6.00 15.00
96 Vladislav Namestnikov 3.00 8.00
97 Andre Burakovsky 4.00 10.00
98 Jonathan Drouin 4.00 10.00
99 Jiri Sekac 2.00 5.00
100 Darnell Nurse 6.00 15.00

2014-15 SP Authentic '94-95 SP Retro Die Cut Autographs

GROUP A VETS STATED ODDS 1:3,855
GROUP B VETS STATED ODDS 1:890
GROUP C VETS STATED ODDS 1:360
GROUP A ROOK STATED ODDS 1:750
GROUP B ROOK STATED ODDS 1:355
OVERALL ODDS 1:240 HOBBY
1 Marty McSorley C 6.00 15.00
3 Ryan Kesler C 6.00 15.00
(inserted in 2015-16 SP Authentic)
6 Steve Larmer C 6.00 15.00
7 Mark Messier B 25.00 60.00
9 David Krejci C 8.00 20.00
10 Wayne Gretzky A 250.00 350.00
12 Vincent Damphousse C 5.00 12.00
13 Mike Gartner C 6.00 15.00
14 Jeremy Roenick B 6.00 15.00
(inserted in 2015-16 SP Authentic)
15 Jamie Benn C 8.00 20.00
(inserted in 2015-16 SP Authentic)
16 Phil Esposito A 25.00 60.00
(inserted in 2015-16 SP Authentic)
17 Jari Kurri B 15.00 40.00
18 Jarome Iginla A 15.00 40.00
23 Evgeni Malkin B 20.00 50.00
25 Teemu Selanne B 25.00 60.00
26 Joe Pavelski B 6.00 15.00
27 Jaromir Jagr A 60.00 150.00
30 Patrick Roy A 40.00 100.00
33 Sergei Bobrovsky C 6.00 15.00
(inserted in 2015-16 SP Authentic)
35 Pete Peeters C 5.00 12.00
(inserted in 2015-16 SP Authentic)
36 Denis Savard B 8.00 20.00
37 Richard Brodeur C 6.00 15.00
38 Mario Lemieux A 80.00 150.00
39 Felix Potvin C 10.00 25.00
41 Pierre Turgeon B 15.00 40.00
42 Chris Chelios B 12.00 30.00
44 Theoren Fleury B 15.00 40.00
45 Carey Price B 30.00 80.00
46 Gabriel Landeskog C 5.00 12.00
(inserted in 2015-16 SP Authentic)
48 John Tavares C 12.00 30.00
(inserted in 2015-16 SP Authentic)
49 Sean Monahan C 6.00 15.00
(inserted in 2015-16 SP Authentic)
50 Ryan Suter B 6.00 15.00
(inserted in 2015-16 SP Authentic)
52 Torey Krug C 6.00 15.00
53 Mats Sundin A 25.00 60.00
54 Johan Franzen C 6.00 15.00
57 Mike Liut C 5.00 12.00
58 Ryan McDonagh C 6.00 15.00
59 Joe Sakic A 30.00 80.00
61 Tom Barrasso C 6.00 15.00
62 Dominik Hasek A 25.00 60.00
64 Bobby Orr A 100.00 200.00
65 Jonathan Bernier C 6.00 15.00
67 Logan Couture C 6.00 15.00
(inserted in 2015-16 SP Authentic)
68 Martin Brodeur B 40.00 100.00
69 Brad Park B 5.00 12.00
71 Brian Leetch B 6.00 15.00
(inserted in 2015-16 SP Authentic)
72 Jim Howard C 6.00 15.00
73 Paul Stastny C 6.00 15.00
74 Arturs Irbe B 5.00 12.00
75 Sean Couturier C 6.00 15.00
(inserted in 2015-16 SP Authentic)
76 Rick Nash B 10.00 25.00
77 Nicklas Lidstrom B 12.00 30.00
78 Shea Weber B 5.00 12.00
(inserted in 2015-16 SP Authentic)
79 Tony Esposito A 25.00 60.00
(inserted in 2015-16 SP Authentic)
80 Brandon Dubinsky C 5.00 12.00
81 Evgeny Kuznetsov B 25.00 60.00
82 Sam Reinhart A 20.00 50.00
83 Victor Rask 6.00 15.00
(inserted in 2015-16 SP Authentic)
84 Teuvo Teravainen 10.00 25.00
(inserted in 2015-16 SP Authentic)
85 Alexander Wennberg B 12.00 30.00
86 David Pastrnak 25.00 60.00
(inserted in 2015-16 SP Authentic)
88 Aaron Ekblad B 15.00 40.00
89 Curtis Lazar B 8.00 20.00
90 Leon Draisaitl 30.00 80.00
(inserted in 2015-16 SP Authentic)
91 Vincent Trocheck B 8.00 20.00
92 Damon Severson B 6.00 15.00
93 Griffin Reinhart A 8.00 20.00
94 Anthony Duclair 10.00 25.00
(inserted in 2015-16 SP Authentic)
95 Johnny Gaudreau A 30.00 80.00
96 Vladislav Namestnikov 10.00 25.00
97 Andre Burakovsky A 10.00 25.00
98 Jonathan Drouin A 15.00 40.00
99 Jiri Sekac B 6.00 15.00
100 Darnell Nurse B 12.00 30.00

2014-15 SP Authentic Buyback Autographs

142 Nicklas Lidstrom '11-12 SPA/20 15.00 40.00

2014-15 SP Authentic Chirography

CAG Alex Galchenyuk
(inserted in 2015-16 SP Authentic)
CEM Evgeni Malkin 20.00 50.00
CES Eric Staal 8.00 20.00
CGL Gabriel Landeskog
(inserted in 2015-16 SP Authentic)
CJB Jonathan Bernier
CJJ Jaromir Jagr 40.00 80.00
CJT John Tavares 15.00 30.00
CJV James van Riemsdyk
(inserted in 2015-16 SP Authentic)
CLC Logan Couture
(inserted in 2015-16 SP Authentic)
CSW Shea Weber
(inserted in 2015-16 SP Authentic)

2014-15 SP Authentic Marks of Distinction

MDBO Bobby Orr 100.00 200.00
MDGL Guy Lafleur 30.00 80.00
MDJB Jonathan Bernier 20.00 50.00
MDJJ Jaromir Jagr 40.00 100.00
MDJT John Tavares 40.00 100.00
MDMG Mike Gartner 20.00 50.00
MDMP Max Pacioretty 20.00 50.00
(inserted in 2015-16 SP Authentic)
MDMS Mats Sundin 30.00 80.00
MDTE Tony Esposito 25.00 60.00
(inserted in 2015-16 SP Authentic)
MDTO Jonathan Toews 50.00 120.00
MDWG Wayne Gretzky

2014-15 SP Authentic Premier Chirography

PCAE Aaron Ekblad 30.00 60.00
PCEK Evgeny Kuznetsov 12.00 30.00
PCGI John Gibson
(inserted in 2015-16 SP Authentic)
PCJD Jonathan Drouin
PCJG Johnny Gaudreau 40.00 80.00
PCLD Leon Draisaitl
(inserted in 2015-16 SP Authentic)
PCMR Morgan Rielly 12.00 30.00
PCNM Nathan MacKinnon
(inserted in 2015-16 SP Authentic)
PCTR Ty Rattie
(inserted in 2015-16 SP Authentic)
PCTT Teuvo Teravainen
(inserted in 2015-16 SP Authentic)
PCVN Val Nichushkin
(inserted in 2015-16 SP Authentic)

2014-15 SP Authentic Sign of the Times

GROUP A STATED ODDS 1:3,225 HOBBY
GROUP B STATED ODDS 1:1,505 HOBBY
GROUP C STATED ODDS 1:1,004 HOBBY
GROUP D STATED ODDS 1:572 HOBBY
GROUP E STATED ODDS 1:292 HOBBY
OVERALL STATED ODDS 1:140 HOBBY
SOTTAI Arturs Irbe D 5.00 12.00
SOTTBL Brian Leetch A 6.00 15.00
(inserted in 2015-16 SP Authentic)
SOTTBO Bobby Orr A 100.00 200.00
SOTTBR Richard Brodeur C 6.00 15.00
SOTTCC Chris Chelios B 15.00 40.00
SOTTCF Cody Franson E 4.00 10.00
SOTTCN Cam Neely D 6.00 15.00
SOTTDD Devan Dubnyk E 6.00 15.00
SOTTDK David Krejci E 6.00 15.00
SOTTFP Felix Potvin D 10.00 25.00
SOTTJH Jim Howard E 6.00 15.00
SOTTJK Jari Kurri C 6.00 15.00
SOTTJS Joe Sakic A 15.00 40.00
(inserted in 2015-16 SP Authentic)
SOTTJV James van Riemsdyk A 6.00 15.00
(inserted in 2015-16 SP Authentic)
SOTTLC Logan Couture A 15.00 40.00
(inserted in 2015-16 SP Authentic)
SOTTMK Mike Krushelnyski D 5.00 12.00
SOTTMS Mark Scheifele E 8.00 20.00
SOTTMZ Mats Zuccarello A 8.00 20.00
(inserted in 2015-16 SP Authentic)
SOTTPG Philipp Grubauer B 6.00 15.00
(inserted in 2015-16 SP Authentic)
SOTTPS Paul Stastny A 6.00 15.00
(inserted in 2015-16 SP Authentic)
SOTTPT Pierre Turgeon B 15.00 40.00
SOTTRB Rob Brown C 8.00 20.00
SOTTRS Ryan Strome A 5.00 12.00
(inserted in 2015-16 SP Authentic)
SOTTSB Sergei Bobrovsky B 6.00 15.00
(inserted in 2015-16 SP Authentic)
SOTTTK Torey Krug B 6.00 15.00
(inserted in 2015-16 SP Authentic)
SOTTTL Trevor Linden B 6.00 15.00
SOTTWG Wayne Gretzky A 250.00 350.00

2014-15 SP Authentic Sign of the Times Duals

ST2DM M.Duchene/N.MacKinnon 30.00 80.00
ST2DN D.Nurse/L.Draisaitl 40.00 100.00
ST2ED J.Drouin/A.Ekblad 30.00 80.00
ST2FP M.Fleury/C.Price 40.00 100.00
ST2GA F.Andersen/J.Gibson 15.00 40.00
ST2KG W.Gretzky/J.Kurri 200.00 400.00
ST2LD P.Datsyuk/N.Lidstrom 25.00 60.00
ST2PC J.Pavelski/L.Couture 10.00 25.00
ST2PF F.Potvin/G.Fuhr 25.00 60.00
ST2PS R.Suter/Z.Parise 25.00 60.00
ST2RR S.Reinhart/G.Reinhart 25.00 60.00
ST2YL S.Yzerman/N.Lidstrom 80.00 150.00

2014-15 SP Authentic Sign of the Times Triples

STATED PRINT RUN 15 SER.#'d SETS
ST3RC Ekbld/Rnhrt/Drstl
ST3AVS Landeskog/Duchene/MacKinnon
ST3DEF Orr/Brqe/Prk 250.00 400.00
ST3GR8 Grtzky/Mssr/Lmx 500.00 600.00
ST3LOS Kptr/Brwn/Tffli 80.00 150.00
ST3MIN Coyle/Granlund/Parise 30.00 80.00
ST3NYI Tvrs/Okpso/Strme 60.00 100.00
ST3BEES Brqe/Krshlnski/Ptrs

2015-16 SP Authentic

1 Alexander Ovechkin 1.00 2.50
2 Ryan Strome .20 .50
3 P.K. Subban .40 1.00
4 Jim Howard .25 .60
5 Marian Gaborik .25 .60
6 Adam Henrique .25 .60
7 Gabriel Landeskog .25 .60
8 Chris Chelios .25 .60
9 Kari Lehtonen .20 .50
10 Nathan MacKinnon .50 1.25
11 Nazem Kadri .20 .50
12 Patrice Bergeron .30 .75
13 Bo Horvat .40 1.00
14 Zemgus Girgensons .20 .50
15 Marc-Andre Fleury .40 1.00
16 Joe Pavelski .25 .60
17 Matt Duchene .25 .60
18 James van Riemsdyk .25 .60
19 Corey Crawford .30 .75
20 Rick Nash .25 .60
21 Frederik Andersen .20 .50
22 Tyler Seguin .40 1.00
23 Roberto Luongo .25 .60
24 Alex Galchenyuk .30 .75
25 Steve Mason .20 .50
26 Zach Parise .25 .60
27 Pavel Datsyuk .30 .75
28 Logan Couture .25 .60
29 Anthony Duclair .20 .50
30 Taylor Hall .50 1.25
31 Tomas Plekanec .25 .60
32 Tyler Johnson .20 .50
33 Justin Faulk .25 .60
34 Tuukka Rask .25 .60
35 Ryan Getzlaf .40 1.00
36 Sergei Bobrovsky .25 .60
37 Jonathan Quick .40 1.00
38 Mike Hoffman .20 .50
39 Daniel Sedin .25 .60
40 Jakub Voracek .25 .60
41 Ondrej Pavelec .25 .60
42 Jordan Eberle .25 .60
43 Tyler Ennis .20 .50
44 Filip Forsberg .30 .75
45 Oliver Ekman-Larsson .20 .50
46 Carey Price .75 2.00
47 Corey Perry .25 .60
48 Claude Giroux .25 .60
49 Ben Bishop .25 .60
50 Dustin Byfuglien .25 .60
51 Loui Eriksson .20 .50
52 Jason Pominville .20 .50
53 David Krejci .20 .50
54 Chris Kreider .25 .60
55 Anze Kopitar .40 1.00
56 Jeff Skinner .20 .50
57 Jaden Schwartz .30 .75
58 John Carlson .30 .75
59 Max Pacioretty .25 .60
60 Jonathan Toews .50 1.25
61 Brent Burns .30 .75
62 Ryan Kesler .25 .60
63 John Tavares .50 1.25
64 Duncan Keith .25 .60
65 Jonathan Bernier .25 .60
66 Braden Holtby .40 1.00
67 Jamie Benn .30 .75
68 Jiri Hudler .20 .50
69 David Backes .25 .60
70 Jaromir Jagr .60 1.50
71 Drew Doughty .25 .60
72 Aaron Ekblad .25 .60
73 Jason Spezza .20 .50
74 Jonas Hiller .20 .50
75 Ryan Nugent-Hopkins .25 .60
76 Henrik Lundqvist .30 .75
77 Vladimir Tarasenko .40 1.00
78 Steven Stamkos .50 1.25
79 Brandon Saad .25 .60
80 Johnny Gaudreau .40 1.00
81 Jaroslav Halak .20 .50
82 Ryan Miller .25 .60
83 Eric Staal .30 .75
84 Mikael Granlund .20 .50
85 Patrick Roy .60 1.50
86 Jarome Iginla .25 .60
87 Sidney Crosby 1.00 2.50
88 Patrick Kane .50 1.25
89 Phil Kessel .40 1.00
90 Ryan O'Reilly .25 .60
91 Cory Schneider .20 .50
92 Tyler Toffoli .25 .60
93 Evgeni Malkin .75 2.00
94 Blake Wheeler .25 .60
95 Henrik Zetterberg .30 .75
96 Erik Karlsson .50 1.25
97 Roman Josi .25 .60
98 Kyle Turris .20 .50
99 Pekka Rinne .30 .75
100 Devan Dubnyk .25 .60
101 Theoren Fleury 1.00 2.50
102 Bob Nystrom .60 1.50
103 Glenn Hall .60 1.50
104 Gerry Cheevers .75 2.00
105 Pierre Turgeon .75 2.00
106 Al MacInnis .75 2.00
107 Willi Plett .75 2.00
108 Doug Weight .75 2.00
109 Brian Leetch .75 2.00
110 Bob Bourne .60 1.50
111 Joe Sakic 1.25 3.00
112 Mike Modano 1.25 3.00
113 Bobby Orr 2.50 6.00
114 Bill Guerin .75 2.00
115 Luc Robitaille 1.00 2.50
116 Curtis Joseph .75 2.00
117 Glenn Anderson .75 2.00
118 Steve Yzerman 1.25 3.00
119 Bobby Hull .75 2.00
120 Lanny McDonald .75 2.00
121 Doug Gilmour 1.00 2.50
122 Bobby Clarke .75 2.00
123 Denis Savard 1.00 2.50
124 Mario Lemieux 2.50 6.00
125 Teemu Selanne 1.50 4.00
126 Martin Brodeur 1.50 4.00
127 Felix Potvin 1.25 3.00
128 Borje Salming .75 2.00
129 Peter Forsberg .75 2.00
130 Wayne Gretzky 4.00 10.00
131 Bobby Orr ATM 3.00 8.00
132 Darryl Sittler ATM 1.00 2.50
133 Guy Lafleur ATM 1.25 3.00
134 Willi Plett ATM 1.00 2.50
135 Wayne Gretzky ATM 5.00 12.00
136 Marcel Dionne ATM 1.25 3.00
137 Doug Gilmour ATM 1.25 3.00
138 Steve Yzerman ATM 1.50 4.00
139 Theoren Fleury ATM 1.25 3.00
140 Mike Gartner ATM 1.00 2.50
141 Cam Neely ATM 1.00 2.50
142 Felix Potvin ATM 1.50 4.00
143 John Tavares AM 2.00 5.00
144 Nikolaj Ehlers AM 2.00 5.00
145 Jason Spezza AM .75 2.00
146 Carey Price AM 3.00 8.00
147 Alexander Ovechkin AM 4.00 10.00
148 Ondrej Pavelec AM 1.00 2.50
149 Jamie Benn AM 1.25 3.00
150 Aaron Ekblad AM 1.00 2.50
151 Jaromir Jagr AM 2.50 6.00
152 Zach Parise AM 1.00 2.50
153 Connor McDavid AM 8.00 20.00
154 Dylan Larkin AM 3.00 8.00
155 W.Gretzky/M.Messier ATM 6.00 15.00
156 J.Sakic/P.Roy ATM 3.00 8.00
157 Lidstrom/Yzerman/Chelios ATM 2.00 5.00
158 A.Ovechkin/J.Toews AM 5.00 12.00
159 J.Toews/P.Sharp AM 2.50 6.00
160 C.McDavid/T.Hall AM RC 10.00 25.00
161 T.Selanne/C.Perry FI 15.00 40.00
162 P.Roy/C.Price FI 25.00 60.00
163 O.Ekman-Larsson/S.Doan FI 6.00 15.00
164 B.Orr/P.Bergeron FI 25.00 60.00
165 G.Perreault/T.Ennis FI 8.00 20.00
166 T.Fleury/J.Gaudreau FI 12.00 30.00
167 M.Liut/E.Staal FI 10.00 25.00
168 B.Hull/J.Toews FI 15.00 40.00
169 J.Sakic/G.Landeskog FI 12.00 30.00
170 R.Nash/N.Foligno FI 8.00 20.00
171 M.Modano/J.Benn FI 12.00 30.00
172 S.Yzerman/H.Zetterberg FI 12.00 30.00
173 W.Gretzky/C.McDavid FI 100.00 250.00
174 R.Luongo/A.Ekblad FI 8.00 20.00
175 M.Dionne/A.Kopitar FI 12.00 30.00
176 M.Koivu/Z.Parise FI 8.00 20.00
177 S.Weber/F.Forsberg FI 10.00 25.00
178 M.Brodeur/C.Schneider FI 15.00 40.00
179 M.Bossy/J.Tavares FI 15.00 40.00
180 M.Messier/H.Lundqvist FI 12.00 30.00
181 M.Hossa/E.Karlsson FI 15.00 40.00
182 B.Clarke/C.Giroux FI 8.00 20.00
183 M.Lemieux/E.Malkin FI 25.00 60.00
184 A.Irbe/J.Pavelski FI 8.00 20.00
185 B.Hull/V.Tarasenko FI 12.00 30.00
186 M.St. Louis/S.Stamkos FI 15.00 40.00
187 D.Gilmour/N.Kadri FI 10.00 25.00
188 M.Naslund/H.Sedin FI 8.00 20.00
189 M.Gartner/A.Ovechkin FI 30.00 80.00
190 A.Ladd/M.Scheifele FI 10.00 25.00
191 Jack Eichel RC 25.00 60.00
192 Michael Mersch RC 6.00 15.00
193 Taylor Leier RC 6.00 15.00
194 Joseph Blandisi RC 6.00 15.00
195 Gustav Olofsson RC 6.00 15.00
196 Chris Wideman RC 6.00 15.00
197 Jujhar Khaira RC 5.00 12.00
198 Sergei Kalinin RC 5.00 12.00
199 Alexandre Grenier RC 5.00 12.00
200 Juuse Saros RC 8.00 20.00
201 Phil Di Giuseppe RC 6.00 15.00
202 Tomas Nosek RC 6.00 15.00
203 Jaccob Slavin RC 5.00 12.00
204 Ryan Dzingel RC 4.00 10.00
205 Laurent Dauphin RC 6.00 15.00
206 Ryan Carpenter RC 6.00 15.00
207 Brett Pesce RC 5.00 12.00
208 Frank Vatrano RC 12.00 30.00
209 Bud Holloway RC 6.00 15.00
210 Shea Theodore RC 6.00 15.00
211 Slater Koekkoek RC 5.00 12.00
212 Stanislav Galiev RC 6.00 15.00
213 Joonas Korpisalo RC 8.00 20.00
214 Yanni Gourde RC 12.00 30.00
215 Garret Sparks RC 8.00 20.00
216 Daniel Carr RC 5.00 12.00
217 Louis Domingue RC 6.00 15.00
218 Christoph Bertschy RC 5.00 12.00
219 Petr Straka RC 5.00 12.00
220 Matt Murray AU RC 40.00 100.00
221 Chris Driedger RC 5.00 12.00
222 Adam Pelech RC 5.00 12.00
223 Mark Alt RC 4.00 10.00
224 Nick Shore RC 6.00 15.00
225 Connor Hellebuyck RC 15.00 40.00
226 Connor McDavid AU RC 1000.00 1500.00
227 Zachary Fucale AU RC 8.00 20.00
228 Josh Anderson AU RC 8.00 20.00
229 Antoine Bibeau AU RC 8.00 20.00
230 Nick Cousins AU RC 8.00 20.00
231 Henrik Samuelsson AU RC 6.00 15.00
232 Ryan Hartman AU RC 10.00 25.00
233 Matt Puempel AU RC 6.00 15.00
234 Emile Poirier AU RC 8.00 20.00
235 Malcolm Subban AU RC 25.00 60.00
236 Jacob de la Rose AU RC 8.00 20.00
237 Kevin Fiala AU RC 8.00 20.00
238 Sam Bennett AU RC 10.00 25.00
239 Shane Prince AU RC 6.00 15.00
240 Chandler Stephenson AU RC 8.00 20.00
241 Devin Shore AU RC 8.00 20.00
242 Max Domi AU RC 100.00 250.00
243 Kyle Baun AU RC 8.00 20.00
244 Ronalds Kenins AU RC 8.00 20.00
245 Jared McCann AU RC 8.00 20.00
246 Nicolas Petan AU RC 8.00 20.00
247 Viktor Arvidsson AU RC 10.00 25.00
248 Dylan DeMelo AU RC 6.00 15.00
249 Sergei Plotnikov AU RC 20.00 50.00
250 Robby Fabbri AU RC 10.00 25.00
251 Charles Hudon AU RC 8.00 20.00
252 Derek Forbort AU RC 6.00 15.00
253 Ben Hutton AU RC 8.00 20.00
254 Mike Condon AU RC 8.00 20.00
255 Matt O'Connor AU RC 6.00 15.00
256 Joonas Donskoi AU RC 8.00 20.00
257 Connor Brickley AU RC 6.00 15.00
258 Artemi Panarin AU RC 50.00 120.00
259 Stefan Noesen AU RC 6.00 15.00
260 Dylan Larkin AU RC 25.00 60.00
261 Hunter Shinkaruk AU RC 8.00 20.00
262 Anthony Stolarz AU RC 8.00 20.00
263 Radek Faksa AU RC 8.00 20.00
264 Sam Brittain AU RC 8.00 20.00
265 Noah Hanifin AU RC 10.00 25.00
266 Nikolay Goldobin AU RC 8.00 20.00
267 Brock McGinn AU RC 8.00 20.00
268 Colton Parayko AU RC 10.00 25.00
269 Nick Ritchie AU RC 8.00 20.00
270 Brady Skjei AU RC 40.00 100.00
271 Anton Slepyshev AU RC 6.00 15.00
272 Mattias Janmark AU RC 8.00 20.00
273 Linus Ullmark AU RC 10.00 25.00
274 Colin Miller AU RC 6.00 15.00
275 Oscar Lindberg AU RC 8.00 20.00
276 Mikko Rantanen AU RC 15.00 40.00
277 Jake Virtanen AU RC 10.00 25.00
278 Andreas Athanasiou AU RC 20.00 50.00
279 Vincent Hinostroza AU RC 5.00 12.00
280 Daniel Sprong AU RC 25.00 60.00
281 Andrew Copp AU RC 8.00 20.00
282 Mike McCarron AU RC 20.00 50.00
283 Brendan Gaunce AU RC 10.00 25.00
284 Jordan Weal AU RC 8.00 20.00
285 Nikolaj Ehlers AU RC 15.00 40.00

2015-16 SP Authentic '95-96 SP Retro

R1 Corey Perry 1.50 4.00
R2 Oliver Ekman-Larsson 1.25 3.00
R3 Sean Monahan 1.50 4.00
R4 Jonathan Toews 3.00 8.00
R5 Nathan MacKinnon 3.00 8.00
R6 Jamie Benn 2.00 5.00
R7 Taylor Hall 3.00 8.00
R8 Anze Kopitar 2.50 6.00
R9 Zach Parise 1.50 4.00
R10 Roman Josi 1.50 4.00
R11 Joe Pavelski 1.50 4.00
R12 Jaden Schwartz 2.00 5.00
R13 Radim Vrbata 1.25 3.00
R14 Andrew Ladd 1.50 4.00
R15 David Pastrnak 2.50 6.00
R16 Zemgus Girgensons 1.25 3.00
R17 Jeff Skinner 1.25 3.00
R18 Brandon Saad 1.50 4.00
R19 Tomas Tatar 1.25 3.00
R20 Aaron Ekblad 1.50 4.00
R21 Alex Galchenyuk 2.00 5.00
R22 Cory Schneider 1.25 3.00
R23 John Tavares 3.00 8.00
R24 Rick Nash 1.50 4.00
R25 Erik Karlsson 3.00 8.00
R26 Jakub Voracek 1.50 4.00
R27 Sidney Crosby 6.00 15.00
R28 Tyler Johnson 1.25 3.00
R29 James van Riemsdyk 1.50 4.00
R30 Alexander Ovechkin 6.00 15.00
R31 Bobby Orr 12.00 30.00
R32 Dominik Hasek 5.00 12.00
R33 Guy Lafleur 5.00 12.00
R34 Joe Sakic 6.00 15.00
R35 Wayne Gretzky 20.00 50.00
R36 Connor McDavid 15.00 40.00
R37 Max Domi 4.00 10.00
R38 Sam Bennett 2.50 6.00
R39 Mike Condon 2.00 5.00
R40 Jared McCann 2.00 5.00
R41 Mikko Rantanen 4.00 10.00
R42 Artemi Panarin 6.00 15.00

R43 Jake Virtanen 2.50 6.00
R44 Daniel Sprong 4.00 10.00
R45 Zachary Fucale 2.00 5.00
R46 Noah Hanifin 2.50 6.00
R47 Malcolm Subban 5.00 12.00
R48 Sergei Plotnikov 1.50 4.00
R49 Emile Poirier 2.00 5.00
R50 Shane Prince 1.50 4.00
R51 Nick Ritchie 2.00 5.00
R52 Stanislav Galiev 2.00 5.00
R53 Oscar Lindberg 2.00 5.00
R54 Nikolay Goldobin 2.00 5.00
R55 Colton Parayko 2.50 6.00
R56 Kevin Fiala 2.00 5.00
R57 Robby Fabbri 2.50 6.00
R58 Nikolaj Ehlers 4.00 10.00
R59 Dylan Larkin 6.00 15.00
R60 Jack Eichel 8.00 20.00

2015-16 SP Authentic '95-96 SP Retro Gold Autographs

R3 Sean Monahan
R4 Jonathan Toews A
R6 Jamie Benn C 20.00 50.00
R7 Taylor Hall C 10.00 25.00
R8 Anze Kopitar B
R9 Zach Parise B
R11 Joe Pavelski C 20.00 50.00
R14 Andrew Ladd D
R16 Zemgus Girgensons D
R18 Brandon Saad D 10.00 25.00
R19 Tomas Tatar E 6.00 15.00
R20 Aaron Ekblad C 12.00 30.00
R21 Alex Galchenyuk D 25.00 60.00
R22 Cory Schneider E 6.00 15.00
R23 John Tavares B 25.00 60.00
R24 Rick Nash C 15.00 40.00
R26 Jakub Voracek C 15.00 40.00
R27 Sidney Crosby A
R28 Tyler Johnson E 6.00 15.00
R29 James Van Riemsdyk
R30 Alexander Ovechkin A
R31 Bobby Orr C
R32 Dominik Hasek B 40.00 100.00
R33 Guy Lafleur
R34 Joe Sakic B
R35 Wayne Gretzky A
R36 Connor McDavid A 400.00 600.00
R38 Sam Bennett A
R39 Mike Condon C 5.00 12.00
R40 Jared McCann C 5.00 12.00
R41 Mikko Rantanen
R43 Jake Virtanen A 30.00 80.00
R45 Zachary Fucale C 12.00 30.00
R46 Noah Hanifin
R49 Emile Poirier C 5.00 12.00
R50 Shane Prince B 5.00 12.00
R52 Stanislav Galiev C 5.00 12.00
R53 Oscar Lindberg C 6.00 15.00
R54 Nikolay Goldobin C 5.00 12.00
R55 Colton Parayko C 8.00 20.00
R56 Kevin Fiala B 6.00 15.00
R57 Robby Fabbri C 10.00 25.00
R58 Nikolaj Ehlers B 12.00 30.00
R59 Dylan Larkin B 40.00 80.00

2015-16 SP Authentic Authentic Moments Booklet Autographs

ABAH Andrew Hammond C 25.00 60.00
ABAO Alexander Ovechkin A
ABBB Ben Bishop C 25.00 6.00
ABBO Bobby Orr B 300.00 500.00
ABBS Borje Salming A
ABCM Connor McDavid A
ABCP Carey Price B
ABDG Doug Gilmour B 30.00 80.00
ABDL Dylan Larkin C 150.00 300.00
ABJB Jamie Benn B 100.00 200.00
ABJG Johnny Gaudreau B
ABJH Jiri Hudler C 40.00 100.00
ABJT John Tavares B 100.00 200.00
ABKT Kyle Turris C 25.00 60.00
ABMD Max Domi A
ABML Mario Lemieux A
ABRF Robby Fabbri C 40.00 100.00
ABRI Pekka Rinne B 25.00 60.00
ABSB Sam Bennett C 50.00 120.00
ABSC Sidney Crosby A
ABTJ Tyler Johnson C 30.00 80.00
ABWG Wayne Gretzky A

2015-16 SP Authentic Great White North Autographs

GWNAE Aaron Ekblad D 12.00 30.00
GWNBB Brent Burns D 15.00 40.00
GWNCM Connor McDavid A 400.00 800.00
GWNJT Jonathan Toews B 80.00 200.00
GWNKT Kyle Turris E 10.00 25.00
GWNMD Matt Duchene D 12.00 30.00
GWNNR Nick Ritchie 12.00 30.00
GWNRN Rick Nash C 15.00 40.00
GWNRS Ryan Strome E 10.00 25.00
GWNSR Sam Reinhart D 12.00 30.00
GWNTA John Tavares C 30.00 80.00
GWNTH Taylor Hall C 30.00 80.00
GWNTT Tyler Toffoli 12.00 30.00
GWNWG Wayne Gretzky A 250.00 500.00

2015-16 SP Authentic Limited Patch Autographs

226 Connor McDavid/100 800.00 1600.00
232 Ryan Hartman/100 20.00 50.00
238 Sam Bennett/100 75.00 200.00
250 Robby Fabbri/100 40.00 100.00
255 Matt O'Connor/100 20.00 50.00
258 Artemi Panarin/100 150.00 300.00
260 Dylan Larkin/100 250.00 400.00
263 Radek Faksa/100 30.00 80.00
276 Mikko Rantanen/100 40.00 100.00
277 Jake Virtanen/100 40.00 100.00
278 Andreas Athanasiou/100 60.00 120.00
282 Mike McCarron/100 40.00 100.00
285 Nikolaj Ehlers/100 40.00 100.00

2015-16 SP Authentic Marks of Distinction

MDAK Anze Kopitar 30.00 80.00
MDAO Alexander Ovechkin
MDBB Ben Bishop 15.00 40.00
MDCM Connor McDavid 350.00 500.00
MDCP Carey Price
MDDD Devan Dubnyk 20.00 50.00
MDDL Dylan Larkin 150.00 300.00
MDEM Evgeni Malkin
MDJB Jamie Benn 30.00 80.00
MDJI Jarome Iginla 12.00 30.00
MDJJ Jaromir Jagr 100.00 200.00
MDJP Joe Pavelski 20.00 50.00
MDJT John Tavares
MDPD Pavel Datsyuk 25.00 60.00
MDRN Rick Nash 20.00 50.00
MDSC Sidney Crosby 150.00 300.00
MDTH Taylor Hall 12.00 30.00
MDTJ Tyler Johnson 15.00 40.00
MDTO Jonathan Toews 50.00 120.00
MDZG Zemgus Girgensons 10.00 25.00
MDZP Zach Parise 8.00 20.00

2015-16 SP Authentic Scripted Stoppers

SSAH Andrew Hammond D 8.00 20.00
SSAI Arturs Irbe D 8.00 20.00
SSCP Carey Price B 75.00 150.00
SSCS Cory Schneider C 12.00 30.00
SSDD Devan Dubnyk C 10.00 25.00
SSDH Dominik Hasek B 75.00 150.00
SSFP Felix Potvin C 20.00 50.00
SSMB Martin Brodeur B 75.00 150.00
SSPR Patrick Roy A
SSSB Sergei Bobrovsky C 8.00 20.00
SSSM Steve Mason D 8.00 20.00

2015-16 SP Authentic Sign of the Times

SOTTAE Aaron Ekblad D 8.00 20.00
SOTTAG Alex Galchenyuk D 10.00 25.00
SOTTAH Andrew Hammond F 25.00 60.00
SOTTAK Anze Kopitar C 12.00 30.00
SOTTAL Andrew Ladd E 8.00 20.00
SOTTAO Alexander Ovechkin B 30.00 80.00
SOTTBB Brent Burns C 10.00 25.00
SOTTBO Bobby Orr A 80.00 150.00
SOTTBR Bobby Ryan D 6.00 15.00
SOTTBS Matt Beleskey F 5.00 12.00
SOTTCL Curtis Lazar F 6.00 15.00
SOTTCP Carey Price B 30.00 80.00
SOTTDH Dougie Hamilton E 8.00 20.00
SOTTDK David Krejci C 6.00 15.00
SOTTEM Evgeni Malkin B 25.00 60.00
SOTTGL Gabriel Landeskog D 8.00 20.00
SOTTJF Justin Faulk E 8.00 20.00
SOTTJH Jiri Hudler F 6.00 15.00
SOTTJJ Jaromir Jagr B 40.00 100.00
SOTTJL John LeClair D 8.00 20.00
SOTTJP Joe Pavelski D 8.00 20.00
SOTTJV Jakub Voracek D 8.00 20.00
SOTTKH Kevin Hayes F 8.00 20.00
SOTTKT Kyle Turris F 6.00 15.00
SOTTLA Guy Lafleur A 10.00 25.00
SOTTMB Martin Biron D 6.00 15.00
SOTTMH Mike Hoffman F 6.00 15.00
SOTTMM Matt Moulson F 6.00 15.00
SOTTMN Markus Naslund D 6.00 15.00
SOTTMS Mark Scheifele F 10.00 25.00
SOTTMT Marty Turco E 8.00 20.00
SOTTNK Nikita Kucherov E 12.00 30.00
SOTTNY Nail Yakupov E 6.00 15.00
SOTTPE Corey Perry C 8.00 20.00
SOTTPM Patrick Marleau C 8.00 20.00
SOTTRH Ron Hextall C 8.00 20.00
SOTTRM Ryan Miller C 8.00 20.00
SOTTRO Ryan O'Reilly B 8.00 20.00
SOTTSM Sean Monahan C 8.00 20.00
SOTTST Mark Stone F 6.00 15.00
SOTTTA Tomas Tatar F 6.00 15.00
SOTTTJ Tyler Johnson E 6.00 15.00
SOTTTK Torey Krug D 8.00 20.00
SOTTTT Tyler Toffoli C 8.00 20.00
SOTTWG Wayne Gretzky A 150.00 300.00
SOTTZG Zemgus Girgensons C 6.00 15.00

2015-16 SP Authentic Sign of the Times Duals

ST2GP A.Galchenyuk/C.Price 80.00 200.00
ST2HB S.Hartnell/S.Bobrovsky 10.00 25.00
ST2HM T.Hall/C.McDavid 250.00 600.00
ST2HS A.Henrique/C.Schneider 15.00 40.00
ST2JB B.Bishop/T.Johnson 12.00 30.00
ST2LA J.Lehtera/J.Allen 12.00 30.00
ST2LL A.Ladd/A.Lowry 15.00 40.00
ST2LT A.Lee/J.Tavares 15.00 40.00
ST2PC J.Pavelski/L.Couture 15.00 40.00
ST2TL D.Larkin/T.Tatar 30.00 80.00
ST2VB J.van Riemsdyk/J.Bernier 8.00 20.00
ST2VM J.Voracek/S.Mason 30.00 80.00

2015-16 SP Authentic Sign of the Times Rookies

SOTRAA Andreas Athanasiou/299 15.00 40.00
SOTRBG Brendan Gaunce/299 8.00 20.00
SOTRCH Charles Hudon/299 6.00 15.00
SOTRCM Connor McDavid/99 300.00 500.00
SOTRCP Colton Parayko/299 8.00 20.00
SOTRCS Chandler Stephenson/299 6.00 15.00
SOTRDL Dylan Larkin/99 100.00 200.00
SOTREP Emile Poirier/299 6.00 15.00
SOTRJD Joonas Donskoi/299 6.00 15.00
SOTRJM Jared McCann/299 6.00 15.00
SOTRJV Jake Virtanen/199 15.00 40.00
SOTRLU Linus Ullmark/299 8.00 20.00
SOTRMC Mike Condon/299 15.00 40.00
SOTRMI Colin Miller/299 5.00 12.00
SOTRMJ Mattias Janmark/299 6.00 15.00
SOTRMM Mike McCarron/299 12.00 30.00
SOTRMR Mikko Rantanen/199 12.00 30.00
SOTRNE Nikolaj Ehlers/99 20.00 50.00
SOTRNH Noah Hanifin/199 8.00 20.00
SOTROL Oscar Lindberg/199 6.00 15.00
SOTRRF Robby Fabbri/199 8.00 20.00
SOTRSB Sam Bennett/99 40.00 100.00
SOTRVA Viktor Arvidsson/299 8.00 20.00
SOTRVH Vincent Hinostroza/299 4.00 10.00
SOTRZF Zachary Fucale/299 15.00 40.00

2015-16 SP Authentic Sign of the Times Rookies Inscriptions

SOTRCH Charles Hudon Hudy/25 25.00 60.00
SOTRCS Chandler Stephenson Stevie/25 25.00 60.00
SOTRJD Joonas Donskoi Menn Sharks/25 30.00 80.00
SOTRJV Jake Virtanen Big Country/15 40.00 100.00
SOTRMC Mike Condon Condo/25 20.00 50.00
SOTRMI Colin Miller Millsie/25 15.00 40.00
SOTROL Oscar Lindberg Ogie/15 20.00 50.00
SOTRRF Robby Fabbri FABBS/15 25.00 60.00
SOTRVA Viktor Arvidsson Go Preds Go/25 25.00 60.00
SOTRVH Vincent Hinostroza Lets go Hawks/25 20.00 50.00
SOTRZF Zachary Fucale Fucs/25 20.00 50.00

2016-17 SP Authentic

1 Patrick Kane .50 1.25
2 Erik Karlsson .50 1.25
3 Nathan MacKinnon .50 1.25
4 Kyle Okposo .25 .60
5 Aaron Ekblad .25 .60
6 Mika Zibanejad .25 .60
7 Taylor Hall .50 1.25
8 Alexander Ovechkin 1.00 2.50
9 Matt Duchene .25 .60
10 Adam Henrique .25 .60
11 Anze Kopitar .40 1.00
12 Marian Gaborik .25 .60
13 Ryan Johansen .30 .75
14 Jamie Benn .30 .75
15 Nino Niederreiter .25 .60
16 Joe Pavelski .25 .60
17 Jaden Schwartz .30 .75
18 Derick Brassard .25 .60
19 Jonathan Toews .50 1.25
20 Brayden Schenn .25 .60
21 Derek Stepan .20 .50
22 Shayne Gostisbehere .30 .75
23 Sean Monahan .25 .60
24 Leon Draisaitl .30 .75
25 Daniel Sedin .25 .60
26 Mark Stone .25 .60
27 Alex Galchenyuk .30 .75
28 Jake Muzzin .20 .50
29 Marc-Andre Fleury .40 1.00
30 Henrik Lundqvist .25 .60
31 Carey Price .75 2.00
32 Joe Thornton .25 .60
33 Evgeny Kuznetsov .40 1.00
34 P.K. Subban .40 1.00
35 Cory Schneider .20 .50
36 Evgeni Malkin .75 2.00
37 Corey Perry .25 .60
38 Johnny Gaudreau .40 1.00
39 Steven Stamkos .50 1.25
40 Henrik Zetterberg .30 .75
41 Oliver Ekman-Larsson .20 .50
42 Nazem Kadri .20 .50
43 Jeff Skinner .25 .60
44 Artemi Panarin .30 .75
45 Gabriel Landeskog .20 .50
46 Tyler Seguin .40 1.00
47 Boone Jenner .25 .60
48 Max Domi .30 .75
49 Elias Lindholm .25 .60
50 Zach Parise .25 .60
51 Andrew Ladd .25 .60
52 David Krejci .25 .60
53 Blake Wheeler .25 .60
54 Ryan Getzlaf .40 1.00
55 Robby Fabbri .25 .60
56 Artem Anisimov .20 .50
57 Mats Zuccarello .25 .60
58 Braden Holtby .40 1.00
59 Roman Josi .25 .60
60 Jonathan Drouin .30 .75
61 Milan Lucic .20 .50
62 Ryan Spooner .20 .50
63 Victor Hedman .30 .75
64 Mike Hoffman .20 .50
65 Tom Wilson .25 .60
66 Filip Forsberg .30 .75
67 Max Pacioretty .25 .60
68 Jaromir Jagr .60 1.50
69 Nikolaj Ehlers .25 .60
70 Mikkel Boedker .20 .50
71 Dylan Larkin .40 1.00
72 Jiri Hudler .20 .50
73 Tyler Toffoli .25 .60
74 Tomas Tatar .20 .50
75 Matt Murray .40 1.00
76 Rickard Rakell .25 .60
77 Jonathan Quick .40 1.00
78 Jarome Iginla .25 .60
79 Patrice Bergeron .30 .75
80 Jack Eichel .50 1.25
81 Brendan Gallagher .30 .75
82 Mikko Koivu .20 .50
83 Anthony Duclair .25 .60
84 Claude Giroux .25 .60
85 David Backes .25 .60
86 Nikita Kucherov .40 1.00
87 Sidney Crosby 1.00 2.50
88 Brent Burns .30 .75
89 Morgan Rielly .20 .50
90 Ryan O'Reilly .25 .60
91 John Tavares .50 1.25
92 Mark Scheifele .30 .75
93 Sam Bennett .30 .75
94 Vladimir Tarasenko .40 1.00
95 Kris Letang .25 .60
96 Brandon Saad .25 .60
97 Connor McDavid 1.25 3.00
98 Loui Eriksson .25 .60
99 Shea Weber .20 .50
100 Corey Crawford .30 .75
101 Jaromir Jagr AM 3.00 8.00
102 Marian Hossa AM 1.00 2.50
103 Patrick Kane AM 2.50 6.00
104 Joe Thornton AM 1.25 3.00
105 Artemi Panarin AM 1.50 4.00
106 Connor McDavid AM 6.00 15.00
107 Henrik Lundqvist AM 1.25 3.00
108 Sidney Crosby AM 5.00 12.00
109 P.K. Subban AM 2.00 5.00
110 Carey Price AM 4.00 10.00
111 Auston Matthews AM 8.00 20.00
112 Jimmy Vesey AM 2.50 6.00
113 Mitch Marner AM 6.00 15.00
114 Patrik Laine AM 5.00 12.00
115 Wayne Gretzky AM 6.00 15.00
116 William Nylander FW AU RC 80.00 150.00
117 Charlie Lindgren FW AU RC 15.00 40.00
118 Oliver Bjorkstrand FW AU RC 6.00 15.00
119 Steven Santini FW AU RC 6.00 15.00
120 Connor Brown FW AU RC 12.00 30.00
121 Ryan Pulock FW AU RC 8.00 20.00
122 Dominik Simon FW AU RC 8.00 20.00
123 Esa Lindell FW AU RC 8.00 20.00
124 Anthony Mantha FW AU RC 30.00 80.00
125 Chris Bigras FW AU RC 6.00 15.00
126 Kasperi Kapanen FW RC 8.00 20.00
127 Oliver Kylington FW AU RC 6.00 15.00
128 Pontus Aberg FW AU RC 10.00 25.00
129 Hudson Fasching FW AU RC 8.00 20.00
130 Trevor Carrick FW AU RC 8.00 20.00
131 Sonny Milano FW AU RC 10.00 25.00
132 Mark McNeill FW AU RC 8.00 20.00
133 Tom Kuhnhackl FW AU RC 6.00 15.00
134 Pavel Zacha FW AU RC 10.00 25.00
135 Nikita Soshnikov FW AU RC 5.00 12.00
136 Sergey Tolchinsky FW AU RC 6.00 15.00
137 Mike Reilly FW AU RC 6.00 15.00
138 Jason Dickinson FW AU RC 6.00 15.00
139 Josh Morrissey FW AU RC 10.00 25.00
140 Justin Bailey FW AU RC 8.00 20.00
141 Brendan Leipsic FW AU RC 8.00 20.00
142 Oskar Sundqvist FW AU RC 8.00 20.00
143 Michael Matheson FW AU RC 15.00 40.00
144 Daniel Altshuller FW AU RC 6.00 15.00
145 Miles Wood FW AU RC 6.00 15.00
146 Auston Matthews FW AU RC 800.00 1200.00
147 Patrik Laine FW AU RC 150.00 300.00
148 Mitch Marner FW AU RC 80.00 200.00
149 Jesse Puljujarvi FW AU RC 20.00 50.00
150 Matthew Tkachuk FW AU RC 25.00 60.00
151 Dylan Strome FW AU RC 15.00 40.00
152 Jimmy Vesey FW AU RC 15.00 40.00
153 Ivan Provorov FW AU RC 15.00 40.00
154 Travis Konecny FW AU RC 15.00 40.00
155 Joel Eriksson Ek FW AU RC 8.00 20.00
156 Zach Werenski FW AU RC 15.00 40.00
157 Kyle Connor FW AU RC 25.00 60.00
158 Sebastian Aho FW AU RC 25.00 60.00
159 Anthony Beauvillier FW AU RC 8.00 20.00
160 Brayden Point FW AU RC 30.00 80.00
161 Christian Dvorak FW AU RC 8.00 20.00
162 Danton Heinen FW AU RC 12.00 30.00
163 Tyler Motte FW AU RC 8.00 20.00
164 Troy Stecher FW RC 8.00 20.00
165 Mikhail Sergachev FW AU RC 25.00 60.00
166 Timo Meier FW AU RC 8.00 20.00
167 Nick Baptiste FW AU RC 8.00 20.00
168 Gustav Forsling FW AU RC 8.00 20.00
169 Lawson Crouse FW AU RC 6.00 15.00
170 Mathew Barzal FW AU RC 100.00 200.00
171 Denis Malgin FW RC 8.00 20.00
172 Anthony DeAngelo FW AU RC 8.00 20.00
173 Thomas Chabot FW AU RC 15.00 40.00
174 Stephen Johns FW RC 6.00 15.00
175 Nick Schmaltz FW RC 8.00 20.00
176 Brandon Carlo FW AU RC 8.00 20.00
177 Artturi Lehkonen FW RC 8.00 20.00
178 Jakob Chychrun FW AU RC 8.00 20.00
179 Zach Sanford FW RC 8.00 20.00
180 Pavel Buchnevich FW AU RC 12.00 30.00
181 Kevin Labanc FW AU RC 8.00 20.00
182 Jake Guentzel FW AU RC 60.00 150.00
183 John Quenneville FW AU RC 8.00 20.00
184 Jakub Vrana FW AU RC 8.00 20.00
185 Thatcher Demko FW AU RC 15.00 40.00
186 Brendan Perlini FW AU RC 8.00 20.00
187 Tyler Bertuzzi FW AU RC 10.00 25.00
188 Brendan Guhle FW AU RC 8.00 20.00
189 A.J. Greer FW AU RC 8.00 20.00
190 Blake Speers FW AU RC 8.00 20.00
191 Troy Stecher FW AU RC 8.00 20.00
192 Nikita Tryamkin FW AU RC 6.00 15.00
193 Brandon Tanev FW AU RC 8.00 20.00
194 Brandon Montour FW AU RC 8.00 20.00
195 Nic Dowd FW AU RC 8.00 20.00
196 Zach Hyman FW AU RC 15.00 40.00
197 Tristan Jarry FW AU RC 15.00 40.00

2016-17 SP Authentic Gold

*GOLD/99: 1X TO 2.5X BASIC INSERTS
106 Connor McDavid AM 20.00 50.00
115 Wayne Gretzky AM 25.00 60.00

2016-17 SP Authentic Future Watch Inscribed Autographs

*ROOKIES: .6X TO 1.5X BASIC CARDS
116 William Nylander 2/29/16 80.00 200.00
147 Patrik Laine 10/13/16 150.00 300.00
148 Mitch Marner 10/12/16 200.00 400.00
149 Jesse Puljujarvi 10/12/16 60.00 150.00

2016-17 SP Authentic Global Chirography

CZEDK David Krejci D 6.00 15.00
FINPL Patrik Laine C 150.00 250.00
NIRON Owen Nolan C 6.00 15.00
SVKMA Marian Gaborik C 6.00 15.00
SVKPB Peter Bondra D 6.00 15.00
SWEHZ Henrik Zetterberg B 20.00 50.00
USAAM Auston Matthews A 350.00 600.00
USAPA Pat LaFontaine C 6.00 15.00

2016-17 SP Authentic Great White North Autographs

GWNAL Andrew Ladd D 5.00 12.00
GWNAM Anthony Mantha D 15.00 40.00
GWNDS Dylan Strome C 10.00 25.00
GWNJB Jamie Benn A 12.00 30.00
GWNJT Joe Thornton A 8.00 20.00
GWNLR Luc Robitaille B 50.00 120.00
GWNMB Mike Bossy A 8.00 20.00
GWNMM Mark Messier A 12.00 30.00
GWNRO Ryan O'Reilly D 6.00 15.00

2016-17 SP Authentic Limited Patch Autographs

*LIMITED/25: 40X TO 100X BASIC CARDS
*LIMTED/50: 30X TO 80X BASIC CARDS
FW/100: .75X TO 2X BASIC CARD
29 Marc-Andre Fleury/50 50.00 120.00
50 Zach Parise/25 40.00 100.00
68 Jaromir Jagr/25 150.00 250.00
116 William Nylander FW/100 150.00 300.00
117 Charlie Lindgren FW/100 50.00 120.00
124 Anthony Mantha FW/100 80.00 150.00
146 Auston Matthews FW/100 1000.00 1500.00
147 Patrik Laine FW/100 300.00 450.00
148 Mitch Marner FW/100 200.00 400.00
149 Jesse Puljujarvi FW/100 80.00 200.00
156 Zach Werenski FW/100 60.00 150.00
160 Brayden Point FW/100 80.00 200.00

2016-17 SP Authentic Marks of Distinction

MDCP Carey Price 60.00 150.00
MDHL Henrik Lundqvist 40.00 100.00
MDHZ Henrik Zetterberg 30.00 80.00
MDJT Jonathan Toews 40.00 100.00
MDMM Mitch Marner 150.00 250.00
MDPL Patrik Laine 250.00 350.00
MDTA John Tavares 25.00 60.00

2016-17 SP Authentic Sign of the Times

SOTTAH Adam Henrique D 5.00 12.00
SOTTBE Brian Elliott E 4.00 10.00
SOTTBO Peter Bondra D 5.00 12.00
SOTTCH Carl Hagelin D 5.00 12.00
SOTTCM Connor McDavid A 250.00 350.00
SOTTDB David Backes D 5.00 12.00
SOTTDS Darryl Sittler B 15.00 40.00
SOTTHL Henrik Lundqvist C 25.00 60.00
SOTTHZ Henrik Zetterberg B 15.00 40.00
SOTTJM Jake Muzzin E 4.00 10.00
SOTTJT Joe Thornton A 80.00 150.00
SOTTLD Leon Draisaitl D 15.00 40.00
SOTTLM Larry Murphy B 5.00 12.00
SOTTMM Matt Murray E 15.00 40.00
SOTTPL Pat LaFontaine C 5.00 12.00
SOTTRS Ryan Spooner E 4.00 10.00
SOTTTL Trevor Linden B 6.00 15.00
SOTTVR Victor Rask E 4.00 10.00
SOTTWG Wayne Gretzky A 250.00 400.00
SOTTZP Zach Parise B 5.00 12.00
SOTTTO Jonathan Toews 15.00 40.00

2016-17 SP Authentic Sign of the Times Rookies

SOTRAM Anthony Mantha/99 25.00 60.00
SOTRAM Auston Matthews/35 400.00 700.00
SOTRBL Brendan Leipsic/199 6.00 15.00
SOTRDS Dylan Strome/199 12.00 30.00
SOTRHF Hudson Fasching/199 6.00 15.00
SOTRJD Jason Dickinson/199 5.00 12.00
SOTRJP Jesse Puljujarvi/199 15.00 40.00
SOTRJV Jimmy Vesey/199 12.00 30.00
SOTRKC Kyle Connor/199 15.00 40.00
SOTRMM Michael Matheson/199 6.00 15.00
SOTRMM Mitch Marner/199 80.00 150.00
SOTRNS Nikita Soshnikov/199 4.00 10.00
SOTRPL Patrik Laine/99 100.00 200.00
SOTRPZ Pavel Zacha/99 8.00 20.00
SOTRSM Sonny Milano/199 8.00 20.00
SOTRWN William Nylander/99 80.00 200.00

2016-17 SP Authentic Silver Skates Gold

SSAM Auston Matthews 30.00 80.00

2016-17 SP Authentic Spectrum Autographs

COMMON CARD 4.00 10.00
SEMISTARS 5.00 12.00
UNLISTED STARS 6.00 15.00
5 Aaron Ekblad B 6.00 15.00
7 Taylor Hall B 12.00 30.00
10 Adam Henrique C 6.00 15.00
11 Anze Kopitar B 25.00 60.00
12 Marian Gaborik B 6.00 15.00
14 Jamie Benn B 8.00 20.00
15 Nino Niederreiter D 6.00 15.00
16 Joe Pavelski B 15.00 40.00
20 Brayden Schenn C 6.00 15.00
24 Leon Draisaitl C 25.00 60.00
26 Mark Stone C 6.00 15.00
28 Jake Muzzin D 5.00 12.00
29 Marc-Andre Fleury B 25.00 60.00
30 Henrik Lundqvist A 60.00 150.00
31 Carey Price A 80.00 150.00
32 Joe Thornton A 30.00 80.00
35 Cory Schneider C 5.00 12.00
36 Evgeni Malkin A 40.00 100.00
40 Henrik Zetterberg B 20.00 50.00
46 Tyler Seguin A 20.00 50.00
47 Boone Jenner D 6.00 15.00
50 Zach Parise B 6.00 15.00
51 Andrew Ladd C 6.00 15.00
52 David Krejci C 6.00 15.00
55 Robby Fabbri D 6.00 15.00
56 Artem Anisimov D 5.00 12.00
62 Ryan Spooner D 5.00 12.00
64 Mike Hoffman C 5.00 12.00
65 Tom Wilson D 6.00 15.00
68 Jaromir Jagr A 80.00 150.00
69 Nikolaj Ehlers D 6.00 15.00
72 Jiri Hudler D 5.00 12.00
73 Tyler Toffoli C 6.00 15.00
75 Matt Murray D 10.00 25.00
78 Jarome Iginla A 20.00 50.00
85 David Backes B 6.00 15.00
86 Nikita Kucherov C 10.00 25.00
88 Brent Burns D 8.00 20.00
90 Ryan O'Reilly C 6.00 15.00
91 John Tavares B 12.00 30.00
92 Mark Scheifele D 8.00 20.00
97 Connor McDavid A
98 Loui Eriksson C 6.00 15.00
101 Jaromir Jagr AM B 125.00 200.00
104 Joe Thornton AM C 8.00 20.00
106 Connor McDavid AM B
107 Henrik Lundqvist AM B 50.00 120.00
110 Carey Price AM B
111 Auston Matthews AM A
112 Jimmy Vesey AM D 12.00 30.00
113 Mitch Marner AM C 80.00 150.00
114 Patrik Laine AM D 100.00 200.00
115 Wayne Gretzky AM B

2016-17 SP Authentic Spectrum FX

S1 Patrick Kane 2.50 6.00
S2 Carey Price 4.00 10.00
S3 Johnny Gaudreau 2.00 5.00
S4 Steven Stamkos 2.50 6.00
S5 Connor McDavid 6.00 15.00
S6 Nathan MacKinnon 2.50 6.00
S7 Taylor Hall 2.50 6.00
S8 Jeff Skinner 1.25 3.00
S9 Mark Scheifele 1.50 4.00
S10 Alexander Ovechkin 5.00 12.00
S11 Erik Karlsson 2.50 6.00
S12 Jack Eichel 2.50 6.00
S13 Jonathan Quick 2.00 5.00
S14 Jamie Benn 1.50 4.00
S15 Sidney Crosby 5.00 12.00
S16 Shayne Gostisbehere 1.50 4.00
S17 David Pastrnak 2.00 5.00
S18 Brent Burns 1.50 4.00
S19 Jaromir Jagr 3.00 8.00
S20 John Tavares 2.50 6.00
S21 Max Domi 1.50 4.00
S22 Daniel Sedin 1.25 3.00
S23 P.K. Subban 2.00 5.00
S24 Brandon Saad 1.25 3.00
S25 Henrik Zetterberg 1.50 4.00
S26 Nazem Kadri 1.00 2.50
S27 Mikko Koivu 1.00 2.50
S28 Ryan Getzlaf 2.00 5.00
S29 Derek Stepan 1.00 2.50
S30 Vladimir Tarasenko 2.00 5.00
S31 Tyler Seguin 2.00 5.00
S32 Milan Lucic 1.00 2.50
S33 Tyler Toffoli 1.25 3.00
S34 Dylan Larkin 2.00 5.00
S35 Evgeni Malkin 4.00 10.00
S36 Nikita Kucherov 2.00 5.00
S37 Artemi Panarin 1.50 4.00
S38 Alex Galchenyuk 1.50 4.00
S39 Bobby Orr 4.00 10.00
S40 Wayne Gretzky 6.00 15.00
S41 Anthony DeAngelo FW 1.25 3.00
S42 Tyler Bertuzzi FW 3.00 8.00
S43 Jacob Larsson FW 4.00 10.00
S44 Artturi Lehkonen FW 2.50 6.00
S45 Brendan Guhle FW 2.50 6.00
S46 Kasperi Kapanen FW 5.00 12.00
S47 Oliver Bjorkstrand FW 2.00 5.00
S48 Tristan Jarry FW 5.00 12.00
S49 Michael Matheson FW 2.50 6.00
S50 Nick Schmaltz FW 2.50 6.00
S51 Julius Honka FW 2.50 6.00
S52 Zach Hyman FW 3.00 8.00
S53 Thatcher Demko FW 5.00 12.00
S54 Zach Sanford FW 2.50 6.00
S55 Jake Guentzel FW 10.00 25.00
S56 A.J. Greer FW 2.50 6.00
S57 Troy Stecher FW 2.50 6.00
S58 Josh Morrissey FW 3.00 8.00
S59 Thomas Chabot FW 5.00 12.00
S60 Ondrej Kase FW 2.50 6.00
S61 Denis Malgin FW 2.50 6.00
S62 Sonny Milano FW 3.00 8.00
S63 Nic Dowd FW 2.50 6.00
S64 Mark Jankowski FW 2.00 5.00
S65 Drake Caggiula FW 2.50 6.00
S66 John Quenneville FW 2.50 6.00
S67 Nikita Zaitsev FW 2.50 6.00
S68 Gustav Forsling FW 2.50 6.00
S69 Danton Heinen FW 4.00 10.00
S70 Brendan Leipsic FW 2.50 6.00
S71 Connor Brown FW 4.00 10.00
S72 Brandon Carlo FW 2.50 6.00
S73 Dylan Strome FW 5.00 12.00
S74 Anthony Beauvillier FW 2.50 6.00
S75 Lawson Crouse FW 2.00 5.00
S76 Kyle Connor FW 6.00 15.00
S77 Joel Eriksson Ek FW 2.50 6.00
S78 Sebastian Aho FW 5.00 12.00
S79 Pavel Buchnevich FW 4.00 10.00
S80 Mathew Barzal FW 8.00 20.00
S81 Christian Dvorak FW 2.50 6.00
S82 Brayden Point FW 6.00 15.00
S83 Tyler Motte FW 2.50 6.00
S84 Jakub Vrana FW 2.50 6.00
S85 Brendan Perlini FW 2.50 6.00
S86 Travis Konecny FW 5.00 12.00
S87 Pavel Zacha FW 3.00 8.00
S88 Kevin Labanc FW 2.50 6.00
S89 Jakob Chychrun FW 2.50 6.00
S90 Ivan Provorov FW 5.00 12.00
S91 Zach Werenski FW 5.00 12.00
S92 Anthony Mantha FW 6.00 15.00
S93 Mikhail Sergachev FW 5.00 12.00
S94 Matthew Tkachuk FW 8.00 20.00
S95 William Nylander FW 10.00 25.00
S96 Jimmy Vesey FW 5.00 12.00
S97 Jesse Puljujarvi FW 6.00 15.00
S98 Mitch Marner FW 25.00 60.00
S99 Patrik Laine FW 25.00 60.00
S100 Auston Matthews FWB 100.00 200.00

2016-17 SP Authentic Spectrum FX Gold

*FW/50: .75X TO 2X BASIC INSERTS
S80 Mathew Barzal FW 25.00 60.00
S98 Mitch Marner FW 60.00 150.00
S99 Patrik Laine FW 100.00 250.00
S100 Auston Matthews FW 150.00 300.00

2017-18 SP Authentic

1 Connor McDavid 1.00 2.50
2 Oliver Ekman-Larsson .25 .60
3 Cam Atkinson .25 .60
4 Jamie Benn .30 .75
5 Matt Murray .40 1.00
6 Mark Scheifele .30 .75
7 Victor Hedman .30 .75
8 Wayne Simmonds .30 .75
9 Duncan Keith .25 .60
10 Auston Matthews 1.00 2.50
11 Sebastian Aho .25 .60
12 Ryan Kesler .25 .60
13 Johnny Gaudreau .40 1.00
14 P.K. Subban .25 .60
15 Patrik Laine .40 1.00
16 Jason Pominville .20 .50
17 Jonathan Drouin .25 .60
18 David Pastrnak .40 1.00
19 Marcus Johansson .20 .50
20 John Tavares .50 1.25
21 Henrik Lundqvist .40 1.00
22 Joe Pavelski .25 .60
23 Brandon Saad .25 .60
24 Anthony Mantha .25 .60
25 Nathan MacKinnon .50 1.25
26 Jaden Schwartz .30 .75
27 Henrik Sedin .25 .60
28 Aleksander Barkov .25 .60
29 Mikael Granlund .25 .60
30 Alexander Ovechkin 1.00 2.50
31 Marc-Andre Fleury .40 1.00
32 Mike Hoffman .20 .50
33 Leon Draisaitl .40 1.00
34 Christian Dvorak .20 .50
35 Patrick Marleau .25 .60
36 Jordan Eberle .25 .60
37 Alexander Wennberg .20 .50
38 Andrew Ladd .25 .60
39 Ryan O'Reilly .25 .60
40 Tyler Seguin .40 1.00
41 Ivan Provorov .25 .60
42 Anze Kopitar .40 1.00
43 Logan Couture .25 .60
44 Matthew Tkachuk .25 .60
45 Sidney Crosby 1.00 2.50
46 Max Pacioretty .25 .60
47 Tomas Tatar .25 .60
48 Gabriel Landeskog .20 .50
49 Jimmy Vesey .25 .60
50 Jonathan Toews .50 1.25
51 Corey Perry .25 .60
52 Nick Bonino .20 .50
53 Reilly Smith .25 .60
54 Brad Marchand .30 .75
55 Steven Stamkos .50 1.25
56 Erik Karlsson .30 .75
57 T.J. Oshie .40 1.00
58 Noah Hanifin .25 .60
59 Bo Horvat .25 .60
60 Taylor Hall .50 1.25
61 Roberto Luongo .25 .60
62 Devan Dubnyk .25 .60
63 Jakub Voracek .25 .60
64 Jack Eichel .40 1.00
65 Jaromir Jagr .60 1.50
66 William Nylander .40 1.00
67 Colton Parayko .25 .60
68 Henrik Zetterberg .25 .60
69 Dustin Byfuglien .25 .60
70 Mikko Rantanen .25 .60
71 Artemi Panarin .25 .60
72 Kevin Shattenkirk .25 .60
73 Derek Stepan .20 .50
74 Mark Giordano .20 .50
75 Patrick Kane .50 1.25
76 Ryan Johansen .25 .60
77 Carey Price .75 2.00
78 Pavel Zacha .25 .60
79 Brent Burns .30 .75
80 Nino Niederreiter .20 .50
81 John Gibson .25 .60
82 Nikita Kucherov .40 1.00
83 Scott Darling .20 .50
84 Jeff Carter .25 .60
85 Jake Guentzel .30 [illegible]
86 Ben Bishop .25 [illegible]
87 Evgeny Kuznetsov .40 1.0
88 Vladimir Tarasenko .40 1.0
89 Ryan Strome .20 [illegible]
90 James Neal .20 [illegible]
91 Mitch Marner .40 1.0
92 Phil Kessel .30 [illegible]
93 Tuukka Rask .25 [illegible]
94 Vincent Trocheck .20 [illegible]
95 Conor Sheary .25 [illegible]
96 Pavel Bure .25 [illegible]
97 Mario Lemieux .75 2.0
98 Darryl Sittler .25 [illegible]
99 Wayne Gretzky 1.25 3.0
100 Patrick Roy .60 1.5
101 Alexander Ovechkin AM 1.00 2.5
102 Sidney Crosby AM 1.00 2.5
103 Henrik Sedin AM .25 [illegible]
104 Connor McDavid AM 1.00 2.5
105 Auston Matthews AM 1.00 2.5
106 Corey Perry AM .25 [illegible]
107 Colton Sissons AM .20 [illegible]
108 Patrick Marleau AM .25 [illegible]
109 Evgeni Malkin AM .75 2.0
110 Roberto Luongo AM .25 [illegible]
111 Leon Draisaitl AM .40 1.0
112 Joe Thornton AM .25 [illegible]
113 Detroit Red Wings AM .25 [illegible]
114 Los Angeles Kings/Vancouver Canucks AM .25 [illegible]
115 Nico Hischier AM .75 2.0
116 Charlie McAvoy FW AU RC 40.00 100.0
117 Jack Roslovic FW AU RC 10.00 25.0
118 Adrian Kempe FW AU RC 10.00 25.0
119 Alex Tuch FW AU RC 20.00 50.0
120 Clayton Keller FW AU RC 40.00 100.0
121 Jordan Schmaltz FW AU RC 10.00 25.0
122 J.T. Compher FW AU RC 10.00 25.0
123 Jon Gillies FW AU RC 8.00 20.0
124 Riley Barber FW AU RC 6.00 15.0
125 Brock Boeser FW AU RC 150.00 250.0
126 Lucas Wallmark FW AU RC 8.00 20.0
127 Jakob Forsbacka-Karlsson FW AU RC 8.00 20.0
128 Gabriel Carlsson FW AU RC 6.00 15.0
129 Evgeny Svechnikov FW AU RC 15.00 40.0
130 Josh Ho-Sang FW AU RC 10.00 25.0
131 Mike Vecchione FW AU RC 6.00 15.0
132 Colin White FW AU RC 8.00 20.0
133 Denis Gurianov FW AU RC 8.00 20.0
134 Vladislav Kamenev FW AU RC 12.00 30.0
135 Tyson Jost FW AU RC 15.00 40.0
136 Jonny Brodzinski FW AU RC 8.00 20.0
137 Ivan Barbashev FW AU RC 8.00 20.0
138 Nikita Scherbak FW AU RC 15.00 40.0
139 Valentin Zykov FW AU RC 8.00 20.0
140 Alexander Nylander FW AU RC 12.00 30.0
141 Samuel Morin FW AU RC 8.00 20.0
142 Christian Fischer FW AU RC 10.00 25.0
143 Peter Cehlarik FW AU RC 8.00 20.0
144 Nolan Patrick FW RC 15.00 40.0
145 Nico Hischier FW RC 25.00 60.0
146 Anders Bjork FW AU RC 10.00 25.0
147 Alex DeBrincat FW AU RC 30.00 80.0
148 Haydn Fleury FW AU RC 8.00 20.0
149 Alex Formenton FW AU RC 8.00 20.0
150 Pierre-Luc Dubois FW AU RC 30.00 80.0
151 Owen Tippett FW AU RC 15.00 40.0
152 Luke Kunin FW RC 8.00 20.0
153 Vince Dunn FW AU RC 8.00 20.0
154 Christian Djoos FW AU RC 8.00 20.0
155 Jake DeBrusk FW RC 12.00 30.0
156 Robert Hagg FW AU RC 8.00 20.0
157 Michael Amadio FW AU RC 8.00 20.0
158 Ville Husso FW AU RC 8.00 20.0
159 Janne Kuokkanen FW AU RC 8.00 20.0
160 Kailer Yamamoto FW AU RC 20.00 50.0
161 Logan Brown FW RC 8.00 20.0
162 Jesper Bratt FW RC 12.00 30.0
163 Martin Necas FW RC 8.00 20.0
164 Tucker Poolman FW AU RC 8.00 20.0
165 Victor Mete FW AU RC 8.00 20.0
166 Remi Elie FW AU RC 6.00 15.0
167 Madison Bowey FW RC 6.00 15.0
168 Calle Rosen FW RC 8.00 20.0
169 Tage Thompson FW AU RC 12.00 30.0
170 Will Butcher FW AU RC 10.00 25.0
171 Filip Chlapik FW AU RC 8.00 20.0
172 Ian McCoshen FW AU RC 8.00 20.0
173 Alex Kerfoot FW AU RC 8.00 20.0
174 Filip Chytil FW AU RC 12.00 30.0
175 Nick Merkley FW AU RC 8.00 20.0
176 Samuel Girard FW AU RC 8.00 20.0
177 Nicolas Kerdiles FW AU RC 8.00 20.0
178 Tim Heed FW AU RC 8.00 20.0
179 Nathan Walker FW AU RC 8.00 20.0
180 Brendan Lemieux FW AU RC 8.00 20.0
181 Alex Nedeljkovic FW AU RC 6.00 15.0
182 Andrew Mangiapane FW AU RC 8.00 20.0
183 Kalle Kossila FW AU RC 6.00 15.0
184 Adin Hill FW AU RC 8.00 20.0
185 Alexandre Carrier FW AU RC 6.00 15.0
186 Andrew Poturalski FW AU RC 8.00 20.0
187 Roland McKeown FW AU RC 8.00 20.0
188 Kyle Capobianco FW RC 8.00 20.0
189 Christian Jaros FW RC 8.00 20.0
190 Jan Rutta FW RC 8.00 20.0
191 Kevin Roy FW RC 8.00 20.0
192 Alex Iafallo FW AU RC 8.00 20.0

2017-18 SP Authentic '07-08 Retro Rookie Patch Autographs

RAB Anders Bjork 25.00 60.0
RAD Alex DeBrincat 50.00 125.0
RAT Alex Tuch 100.00 250.0
RBB Brock Boeser 400.00 500.0
RCF Christian Fischer 25.00 60.0
RCK Clayton Keller 50.00 125.0
RFC Filip Chlapik 20.00 50.0
RHF Haydn Fleury 20.00 50.0
RJH Josh Ho-Sang 100.00 200.0
ROT Owen Tippett 50.00 125.0
RRH Robert Hagg 20.00 50.0
RTJ Tyson Jost 100.00 200.0
RTT Tage Thompson 30.00 80.0
RVD Vince Dunn 20.00 50.0
RVM Victor Mete 40.00 100.0
RWB Will Butcher 25.00 60.0

2017-18 SP Authentic '90-91 Retro Draft Picks

RDPAM Auston Matthews 6.00 15.0
RDPAO Alexander Ovechkin 6.00 15.0
RDPBB Brock Boeser 8.00 20.0
RDPCK Clayton Keller 4.00 10.0
RDPCM Connor McDavid 6.00 15.0
RDPEK Erik Karlsson 2.00 5.0
RDPJD Jonathan Drouin 1.50 4.0
RDPPL Patrik Laine 2.50 6.0
RDPSS Steven Stamkos 3.00 8.0
RDPTH Taylor Hall 3.00 8.0

2017-18 SP Authentic '90-91 Retro Draft Picks Autographs

PAM Auston Matthews/25
PAO Alexander Ovechkin/25 100.00 200.00
PBB Brock Boeser/50
PCK Clayton Keller/50 30.00 80.00
PCM Connor McDavid/25 300.00 400.00
PEK Erik Karlsson/25
PPL Patrik Laine/50 100.00 200.00
PSS Steven Stamkos/25
PTH Taylor Hall/50

2017-18 SP Authentic Future Watch Inscribed Autographs

6 Charlie McAvoy 60.00 150.00
4/12/17
0 Clayton Keller 150.00 250.00
3/27/17
5 Brock Boeser 500.00 600.00
3/25/17
7 Alex DeBrincat 150.00 250.00
10/5/17

2017-18 SP Authentic Global Chirography

ERLD Leon Draisaitl A 25.00 60.00
DRAW Mats Zuccarello A 25.00 60.00
ORP Richard Panik B 4.00 10.00
WEVH Victor Hedman A 6.00 15.00
SACK Clayton Keller B 25.00 60.00
SAJV John Vanbiesbrouck A 25.00 60.00
SAPH Phil Housley B 4.00 10.00

2017-18 SP Authentic Great White North Signatures

WNBB Bill Barber D 8.00 20.00
WNJH Josh Ho-Sang E 6.00 15.00
WNMD Marcel Dionne B 30.00 80.00
WNMM Matt Murray C 25.00 60.00
WNSS Steven Stamkos A 100.00 200.00
WNTJ Tyson Jost D 8.00 20.00

2017-18 SP Authentic Marks of Distinction

DAK Anze Kopitar 25.00 60.00
DCK Clayton Keller 100.00 200.00
DCM Connor McDavid
DSS Steven Stamkos
DVT Vladimir Tarasenko 30.00 80.00

2017-18 SP Authentic Rookie Year Milestones

YMAE Aaron Ekblad .50 1.25
YMAM Auston Matthews 2.00 5.00
YMAO Alexander Ovechkin 2.00 5.00
YMBR Martin Brodeur 1.00 2.50
YMCM Connor McDavid 2.00 5.00
YMDH Dale Hawerchuk .60 1.50
YMDK Duncan Keith .50 1.25
YMEB Ed Belfour .60 1.50
YMEM Evgeni Malkin 1.50 4.00
YMGL Gabriel Landeskog .40 1.00
YMJG Jake Guentzel .60 1.50
YMLM Larry Murphy .40 1.00
YMMB Mike Bossy .75 2.00
YMMD Marcel Dionne .60 1.50
YMML Mario Lemieux 1.50 4.00
YMMM Mike Modano .75 2.00
YMNL Nicklas Lidstrom .40 1.00
YMNM Nathan MacKinnon 1.00 2.50
YMPB Pavel Bure .50 1.25
YMPF Peter Forsberg .75 2.00
YMPK Patrick Kane 1.00 2.50
YMRB Ray Bourque .75 2.00
YMSA Terry Sawchuk .40 1.00
YMSC Sidney Crosby 2.00 5.00
YMSM Steve Mason .40 1.00
YMSY Steve Yzerman .60 1.50
YMTB Tom Barrasso .40 1.00
YMTE Tony Esposito .50 1.25
YMTS Teemu Selanne .60 1.50
YMWG Wayne Gretzky 2.50 6.00

2017-18 SP Authentic Rookie Year Milestones Autographs

YMAE Aaron Ekblad/39 6.00 15.00
YMCM Connor McDavid/16
YMDK Duncan Keith/21 25.00 60.00
YMJG Jake Guentzel/21 40.00 100.00
YMMD Marcel Dionne/49
YMTB Tom Barrasso/26

2017-18 SP Authentic Sign of the Times

OTTAN Craig Anderson F 5.00 12.00
OTTCA Cam Atkinson G 5.00 12.00
OTTCN Cam Neely B 30.00 80.00
OTTCP Carey Price A
OTTCS Conor Sheary G 5.00 12.00
OTTDP Denis Potvin E 5.00 12.00
OTTFP Felix Potvin E 8.00 20.00
OTTGC Gerry Cheevers E 10.00 25.00
OTTJC Jeff Carter C 5.00 12.00
OTTJG Jake Guentzel D 12.00 30.00
OTTJK Jari Kurri D 5.00 12.00
OTTJP Jason Pominville C 4.00 10.00
OTTJT Jacob Trouba G 4.00 10.00
OTTKS Kevin Shattenkirk C 5.00 12.00
OTTLC Logan Couture C 5.00 12.00
OTTMF Marc-Andre Fleury B 100.00 200.00
OTTMH Mike Hoffman G 4.00 10.00
OTTML Mario Lemieux B 80.00 150.00
OTTMR Mikko Rantanen F 5.00 12.00
OTTMT Matthew Tkachuk G 5.00 12.00
OTTPA Colton Parayko F 5.00 12.00
OTTPH Phil Housley D 4.00 10.00
OTTPK Patrick Kane B 25.00 60.00
OTTPL Patrik Laine B 40.00 100.00
OTTPM Petr Mrazek G 5.00 12.00
OTTPT Pierre Turgeon E 5.00 12.00
OTTRH Ron Hextall E 5.00 12.00
OTTRL Rod Langway G 5.00 12.00
OTTRP Richard Panik G 4.00 10.00
OTTSB Sergei Bobrovsky D 5.00 12.00
OTTSI Charlie Simmer G 5.00 12.00
OTTSS Steven Stamkos A
OTTTA Tony Amonte F 5.00 12.00
OTTTB Tom Barrasso D 4.00 10.00
OTTTP Tanner Pearson G 4.00 10.00
OTTVT Vincent Trocheck C 4.00 10.00
OTTZH Zach Hyman G 4.00 10.00

2017-18 SP Authentic Spectrum FX

S1 Auston Matthews 5.00 12.00
S2 Marc-Andre Fleury 2.00 5.00
S3 Phil Kessel 1.50 4.00
S4 Brandon Saad 1.25 3.00
S5 Alexander Ovechkin 5.00 12.00
S6 Kevin Shattenkirk 1.25 3.00
S7 Brent Burns 1.50 4.00
S8 Artemi Panarin 1.25 3.00
S9 Sean Couturier 1.00 2.50
S10 Carey Price 4.00 10.00
S11 Teuvo Teravainen 1.00 2.50
S12 Oliver Ekman-Larsson 1.25 3.00
S13 Ben Bishop 1.25 3.00
S14 Jack Eichel 2.00 5.00
S15 Jaromir Jagr 3.00 8.00
S16 Tomas Tatar 1.25 3.00
S17 Henrik Sedin 1.25 3.00
S18 Anze Kopitar 2.00 5.00
S19 Roberto Luongo 1.25 3.00
S20 Connor McDavid 5.00 12.00
S21 Gabriel Landeskog 1.00 2.50
S22 Corey Perry 1.25 3.00
S23 Nikita Kucherov 2.00 5.00
S24 Eric Staal 1.50 4.00
S25 Erik Karlsson 1.50 4.00
S26 Marcus Johansson 1.00 2.50
S27 Mitch Marner 2.00 5.00
S28 Johnny Gaudreau 2.00 5.00
S29 Leon Draisaitl 2.00 5.00
S30 P.K. Subban 1.25 3.00
S31 Tuukka Rask 1.25 3.00
S32 John Tavares 2.50 6.00
S33 William Karlsson 2.50 6.00
S34 Evgeny Kuznetsov 2.00 5.00
S35 Vladimir Tarasenko 2.00 5.00
S36 Patrik Laine 2.00 5.00
S37 Sidney Crosby 5.00 12.00
S38 Patrick Roy 3.00 8.00
S39 Mario Lemieux 4.00 10.00
S40 Wayne Gretzky 6.00 15.00
S41 Janne Kuokkanen FW 2.00 5.00
S42 Evgeny Svechnikov FW 4.00 10.00
S43 Nikita Scherbak FW 4.00 10.00
S44 J.T. Compher FW 2.50 6.00
S45 Calle Rosen FW 2.00 5.00
S46 Henrik Haapala FW 2.00 5.00
S47 Michael Amadio FW 2.00 5.00
S48 Alex Formenton FW 2.00 5.00
S49 Ivan Barbashev FW 2.00 5.00
S50 Jakob Forsbacka-Karlsson FW 2.00 5.00
S51 Denis Gurianov FW 2.00 5.00
S52 Eric Comrie FW 1.50 4.00
S53 Haydn Fleury FW 2.00 5.00
S54 Kevin Roy FW 2.00 5.00
S55 Ville Husso FW 2.00 5.00
S56 Samuel Girard FW 2.00 5.00
S57 Jake Dotchin FW 1.50 4.00
S58 Vince Dunn FW 2.00 5.00
S59 Alexandre Carrier FW 1.50 4.00
S60 John Hayden FW 1.50 4.00
S61 Lucas Wallmark FW 2.00 5.00
S62 Joakim Ryan FW 2.00 5.00
S63 Jon Gillies FW 2.00 5.00
S64 Christian Djoos FW 2.00 5.00
S65 Madison Bowey FW 1.50 4.00
S66 Samuel Blais FW 2.00 5.00
S67 Christian Jaros FW 2.00 5.00
S68 Travis Sanheim FW 2.00 5.00
S69 Andreas Borgman FW 2.00 5.00
S70 Carter Rowney FW 1.50 4.00
S71 Will Butcher FW 4.00 10.00
S72 Jake DeBrusk FW 5.00 12.00
S73 Adrian Kempe FW 4.00 10.00
S74 Logan Brown FW 3.00 8.00
S75 Alex Kerfoot FW 3.00 8.00
S76 Victor Mete FW 3.00 8.00
S77 Robert Hagg FW 3.00 8.00
S78 Jack Roslovic FW 4.00 10.00
S79 Filip Chytil FW 3.00 8.00
S80 Anders Bjork FW 4.00 10.00
S81 Alex Tuch FW 8.00 20.00
S82 Martin Necas FW 3.00 8.00
S83 Luke Kunin FW 3.00 8.00
S84 Colin White FW 3.00 8.00
S85 Owen Tippett FW 6.00 15.00
S86 Nick Merkley FW 3.00 8.00
S87 Josh Ho-Sang FW 4.00 10.00
S88 Tage Thompson FW 5.00 12.00
S89 Christian Fischer FW 4.00 10.00
S90 Jesper Bratt FW 5.00 12.00
S91 Nico Hischier FW 25.00 60.00
S92 Clayton Keller FW 20.00 50.00
S93 Charlie McAvoy FW 25.00 60.00
S94 Kailer Yamamoto FW 20.00 50.00
S95 Pierre-Luc Dubois FW 15.00 40.00
S96 Alex DeBrincat FW 20.00 50.00
S97 Alexander Nylander FW 12.00 30.00
S98 Tyson Jost FW 15.00 40.00
S99 Nolan Patrick FW 15.00 40.00
S100 Brock Boeser FW 6.00 15.00

2000-01 SP Game Used

The SP Game-Used set was released as a 90-card set with 30 short-printed rookies, serial numbered to 900. The card fronts featured a full color photo of the featured player. The card design had grey and white boarders, along with silver-foil highlights. The card backs had a small color photo of the featured player along with his statistics and a brief summary of his 2000-01 season.

COMP.SET w/o SP's (60) 30.00 80.00
1 Paul Kariya 1.25 3.00
2 Teemu Selanne 2.00 5.00
3 Patrik Stefan .75 2.00
4 Byron Dafoe .75 2.00
5 Joe Thornton 1.50 4.00
6 Dominik Hasek 1.50 4.00
7 Maxim Afinogenov .60 1.50
8 Valeri Bure .75 2.00
9 Ron Francis 1.25 3.00
10 Arturs Irbe .75 2.00
11 Tony Amonte .75 2.00
12 Steve Sullivan .60 1.50
13 Patrick Roy 2.50 6.00
14 Joe Sakic 1.50 4.00
15 Peter Forsberg 1.25 3.00
16 Ray Bourque 1.50 4.00
17 Ron Tugnutt .75 2.00
18 Mike Modano 1.50 4.00
19 Brett Hull 1.50 4.00
20 Ed Belfour 1.00 2.50
21 Steve Yzerman 3.00 8.00
22 Brendan Shanahan 1.25 3.00
23 Sergei Fedorov 1.50 4.00
24 Nicklas Lidstrom 1.00 2.50
25 Doug Weight 1.00 2.50
26 Tommy Salo .75 2.00
27 Pavel Bure 1.25 3.00
28 Trevor Kidd .60 1.50
29 Luc Robitaille 1.00 2.50
30 Zigmund Palffy 1.00 2.50
31 Manny Fernandez .75 2.00
32 Jose Theodore 1.25 3.00
33 Trevor Linden 1.00 2.50
34 Mike Dunham .60 1.50
35 David Legwand 1.00 2.50
36 Martin Brodeur 2.00 5.00
37 Scott Gomez .75 2.00
38 Tim Connolly .60 1.50
39 John Vanbiesbrouck .75 2.00
40 Mike Richter 1.00 2.50
41 Mark Messier 1.50 4.00
42 Marian Hossa .75 2.00
43 Alexei Yashin .75 2.00
44 Brian Boucher .75 2.00
45 John LeClair 1.00 2.50
46 Jeremy Roenick 1.00 2.50
47 Keith Tkachuk 1.00 2.50
48 Jaromir Jagr 2.50 6.00
49 Mario Lemieux 3.00 8.00
50 Steve Shields .60 1.50
51 Owen Nolan 1.00 2.50
52 Roman Turek .75 2.00
53 Pavol Demitra 1.25 3.00
54 Vincent Lecavalier .75 2.00
55 Curtis Joseph 1.25 3.00
56 Mats Sundin 1.00 2.50
57 Daniel Sedin 2.00 5.00
58 Henrik Sedin 1.50 4.00
59 Olaf Kolzig 1.00 2.50
60 Chris Simon .60 1.50
61 Jonas Ronnqvist RC 2.00 5.00
62 Andy McDonald RC 4.00 10.00
63 Andrew Raycroft RC 5.00 12.00
64 Josef Vasicek RC 5.00 12.00
65 David Aebischer RC 4.00 10.00
66 Rostislav Klesla RC 4.00 10.00
67 Marty Turco RC 6.00 15.00
68 Tyler Bouck RC 2.00 5.00
69 Steven Reinprecht RC 3.00 8.00
70 Marian Gaborik RC 8.00 20.00
71 Scott Hartnell RC 5.00 12.00
72 Greg Classen RC 2.00 5.00
73 Rick DiPietro RC 10.00 25.00
74 Jason LaBarbera RC 2.50 6.00
75 Martin Havlat RC 6.00 15.00
76 Jani Hurme RC 2.00 5.00
77 Roman Cechmanek RC 2.50 6.00
78 Ruslan Fedotenko RC 2.00 5.00
79 Justin Williams RC 5.00 12.00
80 Roman Simicek RC 2.00 5.00
81 Mark Smith RC 2.00 5.00
82 Matt Elich RC 2.50 6.00
83 Alexander Kharitonov RC 2.00 5.00
84 Fedor Fedorov RC 2.50 6.00
85 Marc-Andre Thinel RC 2.00 5.00
86 Zdenek Blatny RC 2.00 5.00
87 Jeff Bateman RC 2.00 5.00
88 Jason Jaspers RC 2.00 5.00
89 Jordan Krestanovich RC 2.00 5.00
90 Damian Surma RC 2.00 5.00

2000-01 SP Game Used Patch Cards

Randomly inserted in SP Game-Used Edition packs, the 29-card set featured jersey patch swatches. The set had 5 combo player swatches. The card numbers carried a 'P' prefix and a 'D' prefix on the combo cards. The cards were serial numbered to 50.

DFR P.Forsberg/P.Roy 75.00 200.00
DJL J.Jagr/M.Lemieux 125.00 300.00
DKG P.Kariya/W.Gretzky 150.00 300.00
DMG M.Messier/W.Gretzky 200.00 400.00
DOB B.Orr/R.Bourque 200.00 400.00
PBB Brian Boucher 20.00 50.00
PBH Brett Hull 30.00 80.00
PBO Bobby Orr 150.00 300.00
PGH Gordie Howe 50.00 120.00
PJJ Jaromir Jagr 30.00 80.00
PJL John LeClair 25.00 60.00
PJR Jeremy Roenick 30.00 80.00
PJS Joe Sakic 50.00 125.00
PKT Keith Tkachuk 25.00 60.00
PMB Martin Brodeur 60.00 150.00
PML Mario Lemieux 125.00 300.00
PMM Mark Messier 60.00 150.00
PMO Mike Modano 30.00 80.00
PMS Mats Sundin 20.00 50.00
PPB Pavel Bure 25.00 60.00
PPF Peter Forsberg 50.00 125.00
PPK Paul Kariya 25.00 60.00
PPR Patrick Roy 75.00 200.00
PRB Ray Bourque 50.00 125.00
PSF Sergei Fedorov 25.00 60.00
PSY Steve Yzerman 75.00 200.00
PTA Tony Amonte 20.00 50.00
PTS Teemu Selanne 30.00 80.00
PWG Wayne Gretzky 150.00 300.00

2000-01 SP Game Used Tools of the Game

Randomly inserted in SP Game-Used Edition packs, the 38-card set featured game-used jersey swatches. The card numbers had the player's initials in place of the number.

*EXCLUSIVE/350: .6X TO 1.5X BASIC JSY
EXCL.STAT.PRINT RUN 350 SER #'d SETS
AM Al MacInnis 3.00 8.00
BB Brian Boucher 3.00 8.00
BD Byron Dafoe 3.00 8.00
BH Brett Hull 5.00 12.00
BL Brian Leetch 4.00 10.00
CO Chris Osgood 3.00 8.00
DL David Legwand 3.00 8.00
EL Eric Lindros 4.00 10.00
GH Gordie Howe 20.00 40.00
JJ Jaromir Jagr 6.00 15.00
JL John LeClair 4.00 10.00
JN Joe Nieuwendyk 3.00 8.00
JR Jeremy Roenick 5.00 12.00
JS Joe Sakic 8.00 20.00
KT Keith Tkachuk 4.00 10.00
MB Martin Brodeur 8.00 20.00
MH Michal Handzus 3.00 8.00
ML Mario Lemieux 8.00 20.00
MM Mark Messier 4.00 10.00
MO Mike Modano 5.00 12.00
MP Michael Peca 3.00 8.00
MR Mike Richter 6.00 15.00
MS Mats Sundin 4.00 10.00
NL Nicklas Lidstrom 4.00 10.00
PB Pavel Bure 4.00 10.00
PD Pavol Demitra 3.00 8.00
PF Peter Forsberg 6.00 15.00
PK Paul Kariya 4.00 10.00
PM Patrick Marleau 3.00 8.00
PR Patrick Roy 10.00 25.00
RB Ray Bourque 8.00 20.00
SF Sergei Fedorov 6.00 15.00
SO Sandis Ozolinsh 3.00 8.00
SS Sergei Samsonov 3.00 8.00
SY Steve Yzerman 10.00 25.00
TA Tony Amonte 3.00 8.00
TS Teemu Selanne 4.00 10.00
WG Wayne Gretzky 15.00 40.00

2000-01 SP Game Used Tools of the Game Combos

Randomly inserted in SP Game-Used Edition packs, the 21-card set featured combo game-used jersey swatches. The cards were serial numbered to 100.

CBF P.Bure/S.Fedorov 20.00 50.00
CBR M.Brodeur/M.Richter 25.00 60.00
CDM P.Demitra/A.MacInnis 15.00 40.00
CGS D.Gilmour/M.Sundin 20.00 50.00
CGY S.Gomez/M.York 15.00 40.00
CHB B.Hull/E.Belfour 15.00 40.00
CHG G.Howe/W.Gretzky 75.00 150.00
CHP D.Hasek/M.Peca 15.00 40.00
CKS P.Kariya/T.Selanne 15.00 40.00
CLB B.Boucher/J.LeClair 15.00 40.00
CLG M.Lemieux/W.Gretzky 75.00 150.00
CLJ M.Lemieux/J.Jagr 50.00 120.00
CMG M.Messier/W.Gretzky 75.00 150.00
CMN M.Modano/J.Nieuwendyk 15.00 40.00
COL C.Osgood/N.Lidstrom 15.00 40.00
CRF P.Roy/P.Forsberg 25.00 60.00
CRT J.Roenick/K.Tkachuk 15.00 40.00
CSD B.Dafoe/S.Samsonov 15.00 40.00
CSH B.Shanahan/G.Howe 40.00 100.00
CSS J.Sakic/J.Sakic 40.00 100.00
CYH S.Yzerman/G.Howe 40.00 100.00

2000-01 SP Game Used Tools of the Game Autographed Bronze

Randomly inserted in SP Game-Used Edition packs, the 8-card set featured game-used jersey swatches and the individual player's autograph. The cards were serial numbered to 300.

*SILVER/100: .6X TO 1.5X BRONZE
SILVER STATED PRINT RUN 100
*GOLD/25: .8X TO 2X BRONZE
GOLD STATED PRINT RUN 25
ABR Brett Hull 20.00 50.00
AJL John LeClair 12.50 30.00
APB Pavel Bure 12.50 30.00
ARB Ray Bourque 25.00 60.00
ARL Roberto Luongo 20.00 50.00
ASG Scott Gomez 8.00 20.00
ASY Steve Yzerman 50.00 125.00
AWG Wayne Gretzky 125.00 250.00

2001-02 SP Game Used

Released in mid January 2001, this 100-card set carried an SRP of $29.99 per pack. Each pack contained three cards with a game-used insert card in every pack. The base set consisted of 60 veteran player cards and Rookie Cards (#61-100) which were serial numbered to 499.

COMPLETE SET (100) 125.00 250.00
COMP.SET w/o SP's (60) 30.00 80.00
1 Paul Kariya 1.25 3.00
2 Dany Heatley 1.00 2.50
3 Joe Thornton 1.25 3.00
4 Bill Guerin 1.00 2.50
5 Miroslav Satan .75 2.00
6 Roman Turek .75 2.00
7 Jeff O'Neill .60 1.50
8 Tony Amonte .75 2.00
9 Rob Blake 1.00 2.50
10 Joe Sakic 1.50 4.00
11 Chris Drury .75 2.00
12 Patrick Roy 2.50 6.00
13 Ron Tugnutt .75 2.00
14 Mike Modano 1.50 4.00
15 Ed Belfour 1.00 2.50
16 Pierre Turgeon 1.00 2.50
17 Brendan Shanahan 1.25 3.00
18 Steve Yzerman 3.00 8.00
19 Brett Hull 1.25 3.00
20 Dominik Hasek 1.50 4.00
21 Luc Robitaille 1.00 2.50
22 Mike Comrie .75 2.00
23 Pavel Bure 1.25 3.00
24 Valeri Bure .60 1.50
25 Adam Deadmarsh .75 2.00
26 Zigmund Palffy 1.00 2.50
27 Marian Gaborik 1.50 4.00
28 Jose Theodore 1.00 2.50
29 Mike Dunham .75 2.00
30 Patrik Elias 1.00 2.50
31 Martin Brodeur 2.00 5.00
32 Rick DiPietro .75 2.00
33 Alexei Yashin .75 2.00
34 Eric Lindros 1.50 4.00
35 Mark Messier 1.50 4.00
36 Marian Hossa .75 2.00
37 Radek Bonk .60 1.50
38 John LeClair 1.00 2.50
39 Jeremy Roenick 1.00 2.50
40 Pavel Brendl .60 1.50
41 Roman Cechmanek .75 2.00
42 Sean Burke .60 1.50
43 Mario Lemieux 3.00 8.00
44 Johan Hedberg .75 2.00
45 Alexei Kovalev .75 2.00
46 Teemu Selanne 2.00 5.00
47 Evgeni Nabokov .75 2.00
48 Keith Tkachuk 1.00 2.50
49 Chris Pronger .75 2.00
50 Pavol Demitra 1.25 3.00
51 Doug Weight 1.00 2.50
52 Vincent Lecavalier .75 2.00
53 Curtis Joseph 1.00 2.50
54 Alexander Mogilny .75 2.00
55 Mats Sundin 1.00 2.50
56 Markus Naslund 1.00 2.50
57 Daniel Sedin 1.00 2.50
58 Jaromir Jagr 2.50 6.00
59 Olaf Kolzig 1.00 2.50
60 Peter Bondra 1.00 2.50
61 Ilja Bryzgalov RC 5.00 12.00
62 Timo Parssinen RC 2.50 6.00
63 Kevin Sawyer RC 2.00 5.00
64 Brian Pothier RC 2.00 5.00
65 Kamil Piros RC 2.00 5.00
66 Ilya Kovalchuk RC 15.00 40.00
67 Zdenek Kutlak RC 2.00 5.00
68 Scott Nichol RC 2.00 5.00
69 Erik Cole RC 4.00 10.00
70 Jaroslav Obsut RC 2.00 5.00
71 Vaclav Nedorost RC 2.00 5.00
72 Mathieu Darche RC 3.00 8.00
73 Matt Davidson RC 2.00 5.00
74 Niko Kapanen RC 3.00 8.00
75 Pavel Datsyuk RC 25.00 50.00
76 Ty Conklin RC 3.00 8.00
77 Jason Chimera RC 2.00 5.00
78 Niklas Hagman RC 2.50 6.00
79 Kristian Huselius RC 3.00 8.00
80 Jaroslav Bednar RC 2.00 5.00
81 Nick Schultz RC 2.00 5.00
82 Travis Roche RC 2.00 5.00
83 Martin Erat RC 3.00 8.00
84 Scott Clemmensen RC 2.00 5.00
85 Josef Boumedienne RC 2.00 5.00
86 Raffi Torres RC 3.00 8.00
87 Radek Martinek RC 2.00 5.00
88 Dan Blackburn RC 2.50 6.00
89 Peter Smrek RC 2.00 5.00
90 Ivan Ciernik RC 2.00 5.00
91 Chris Neil RC 2.50 6.00
92 Vaclav Pletka RC 2.00 5.00
93 Jiri Dopita RC 2.00 5.00
94 Krys Kolanos RC 2.00 5.00
95 Jeff Jillson RC 2.00 5.00
96 Mark Rycroft RC 2.50 6.00
97 Ryan Tobler RC 2.50 6.00
98 Nikita Alexeev RC 2.00 5.00
99 Chris Corrinet RC 2.00 5.00
100 Brian Sutherby RC 2.00 5.00

2001-02 SP Game Used Authentic Fabric

Inserted on per pack, this 77-card set featured game-worn jersey swatches from one, two, three or four players. Dual player cards were serial-numbered to 100 each, triple player cards were serial-numbered to 25, and quadruple player cards were serial-numbered to 10.

SINGLE JSY STATED ODDS 1:1
*GOLD/300: .5X TO 1.2X BASIC JSY
*GOLD/50: .6X TO 1.5X BASIC JSY
AFAK Alexei Kovalev 3.00 8.00
AFBB Brian Boucher 3.00 8.00
AFBG Bill Guerin 3.00 8.00
AFBJ Brent Johnson 3.00 8.00
AFBN Radek Bonk 3.00 8.00
AFBS Brendan Shanahan 4.00 10.00
AFBU Pavel Bure SP 10.00 25.00
AFCO Chris Osgood 3.00 8.00
AFDH Dominik Hasek 6.00 15.00
AFEB Ed Belfour 4.00 10.00
AFFP Felix Potvin 5.00 12.00
AFGE Wayne Gretzky SP 20.00 50.00
AFGH Gordie Howe 15.00 40.00
AFGR Wayne Gretzky SP 20.00 50.00
AFJB Jaroslav Bednar 3.00 8.00
AFJD J-P Dumont 3.00 8.00
AFJH Jan Hlavac 3.00 8.00
AFJI Jarome Iginla 6.00 15.00
AFJJ Jaromir Jagr SP 12.50 30.00
AFJL John LeClair 4.00 10.00
AFJN Joe Nieuwendyk 3.00 8.00
AFJO Jose Theodore 6.00 15.00
AFJS Joe Sakic 6.00 15.00
AFJT Joe Thornton 10.00 25.00
AFKA Paul Kariya SP 15.00 40.00
AFKP Keith Primeau 3.00 8.00
AFLR Luc Robitaille 3.00 8.00
AFMA Maxim Afinogenov 3.00 8.00
AFMB Martin Brodeur 10.00 25.00
AFML Mario Lemieux 10.00 25.00
AFMM Mike Modano 5.00 12.00
AFMN Mika Noronen 3.00 8.00
AFMN Markus Naslund 4.00 10.00
AFMO Mike Modano SP 10.00 25.00
AFMR Mark Recchi 3.00 8.00
AFMS Miroslav Satan 3.00 8.00
AFMY Mike York 3.00 8.00
AFON Owen Nolan 3.00 8.00
AFPB Peter Bondra 4.00 10.00
AFPD Pavol Demitra 3.00 8.00
AFPF Peter Forsberg 6.00 15.00
AFPK Paul Kariya 4.00 10.00
AFPM Patrick Marleau 3.00 8.00
AFPR Patrick Roy 12.50 30.00
AFRB Ray Bourque 6.00 15.00
AFRD Radek Dvorak 3.00 8.00
AFRF Ruslan Fedotenko 3.00 8.00
AFRF Rico Fata 3.00 8.00
AFRL Robert Lang 3.00 8.00
AFSA Joe Sakic SP 12.50 30.00
AFSF Sergei Fedorov 5.00 12.00
AFSK Saku Koivu 4.00 10.00
AFSS Scott Stevens SP 10.00 25.00
AFSV Marc Savard 3.00 8.00
AFSY Steve Yzerman 10.00 25.00
AFTF Theo Fleury 5.00 12.00
AFTS Teemu Selanne SP 4.00 10.00
AFWG Wayne Gretzky SP 20.00 50.00
AFZP Zigmund Palffy 3.00 8.00
DFAB M.Afinogenov/M.Biron 6.00 15.00
DFBR M.Brodeur/P.Roy 30.00 80.00
DFDS J-P Dumont/M.Satan 6.00 15.00
DFFD T.Fleury/R.Dvorak 12.00 30.00
DFFS S.Fedorov/B.Shanahan 10.00 25.00
DFFS P.Forsberg/J.Sakic 15.00 40.00
DFIS J.Iginla/M.Savard 10.00 25.00
DFLB J.LeClair/B.Boucher 8.00 20.00
DFLG M.Lemieux/W.Gretzky 60.00 150.00
DFLK M.Lemieux/A.Kovalev 12.00 30.00
DFMB M.Modano/E.Belfour 8.00 20.00
DFNB M.Naslund/P.Bondra 10.00 25.00
DFPK Paul Kariya Dual 6.00 12.00
DFPL K.Primeau/J.LeClair 8.00 20.00
DFPP Z.Palffy/F.Potvin 15.00 40.00
DFPT F.Potvin/J.Theodore 20.00 50.00
DFRF M.Recchi/R.Fedotenko 10.00 25.00
DFTG J.Thornton/B.Guerin 15.00 40.00
DFYO S.Yzerman/C.Osgood 15.00 40.00
TFFSR Forsberg/Sakic/Roy 125.00 250.00
TFLKL Lemieux/Kovalev/Lang 125.00 200.00
TFLRP LeClair/Recchi/Primeau 30.00 80.00
TFMNB Modano/Nieuwy/Belfour 25.00 60.00
TFYSF Yzerman/Shanny/Fedorov 125.00 250.00

2001-02 SP Game Used Inked Sweaters

Randomly inserted, this 40-card set featured swatches of game-worn jerseys and player autographs. Single player cards were serial-numbered to 100 unless otherwise noted below. Dual player cards were serial-numbered to just 10 and are not priced due to scarcity.

SCJ Curtis Joseph/50 20.00 50.00
SEB Ed Belfour/50 25.00 60.00
SGA Simon Gagne/50 20.00 50.00
SGH Gordie Howe/50 100.00 200.00
SJL John LeClair/50 15.00 40.00
SMB Martin Brodeur/50 75.00 150.00
SRB Ray Bourque/50 25.00 60.00
SSY Steve Yzerman/50 75.00 200.00
SWG Wayne Gretzky/50 200.00 400.00
ISAK Alexei Kovalev/100 10.00 25.00
ISCJ Curtis Joseph/100 15.00 40.00
ISHS Henrik Sedin/100 15.00 40.00
ISJI Jarome Iginla/100 25.00 60.00
ISJL John LeClair/100 15.00 40.00
ISJT Joe Thornton/100 40.00 80.00
ISMB Martin Brodeur/100 40.00 100.00
ISMB Martin Biron/100 5.00 12.00
ISMH Marian Hossa/100 12.00 30.00
ISMM Mike Modano/100 20.00 50.00
ISOK Olaf Kolzig/100 10.00 25.00
ISRB Ray Bourque/100 50.00 100.00
ISSG Simon Gagne/100 15.00 40.00
ISSY Steve Yzerman/100 75.00 150.00
ISVL Vincent Lecavalier/100 15.00 40.00
ISZP Zigmund Palffy/100 10.00 25.00

2001-02 SP Game Used Patches

Randomly inserted, this 55-card set featured patch swatches from one, two or three different players' jerseys. Single player cards were serial-numbered out of 50, dual player cards were serial-numbered out of 25, and triple player cards were serial numbered to just 10 copies each. Triple player cards are not priced due to scarcity.

PBI Martin Biron 10.00 25.00
PBO Peter Bondra 10.00 25.00
PBS Brendan Shanahan 15.00 40.00
PCJ Curtis Joseph 25.00 60.00
PEB Ed Belfour 20.00 50.00
PJH Jani Hurme 10.00 25.00
PJI Jarome Iginla 20.00 50.00
PJJ Jaromir Jagr 25.00 60.00
PJL John LeClair 10.00 25.00
PJS Joe Sakic 25.00 60.00
PJT Joe Thornton 15.00 40.00
PKP Keith Primeau 10.00 25.00
PMB Martin Brodeur 25.00 60.00
PMH Marian Hossa 15.00 40.00
PML Mario Lemieux 60.00 150.00
PMM Mike Modano 20.00 50.00
PMS Mats Sundin 15.00 40.00
POK Olaf Kolzig 15.00 40.00
PPB Pavel Bure 15.00 40.00
PPF Peter Forsberg 25.00 60.00
PPK Paul Kariya 15.00 40.00
PPR Patrick Roy 60.00 150.00
PPS Patrik Stefan 10.00 25.00
PSA Miroslav Satan 15.00 40.00
PSF Sergei Fedorov 20.00 50.00
PSG Simon Gagne 15.00 40.00
PSS Sergei Samsonov 15.00 40.00
PSY Steve Yzerman 40.00 100.00
PTA Tony Amonte 15.00 40.00
PWG Wayne Gretzky 75.00 150.00
CPAI T.Amonte/J.Iginla 30.00 80.00
CPBA P.Bondra/T.Amonte 20.00 50.00
CPBJ M.Brodeur/C.Joseph 75.00 200.00
CPGK S.Gagne/P.Kariya 20.00 50.00
CPHB J.Hurme/M.Brodeur 60.00 150.00
CPHH J.Hurme/M.Hossa 25.00 60.00
CPHL M.Hossa/J.LeClair 25.00 60.00
CPJB J.Jagr/P.Bondra 50.00 100.00
CPKB O.Kolzig/P.Bondra 30.00 80.00
CPKR O.Kolzig/P.Roy 75.00 200.00
CPKS P.Kariya/S.Samsonov 30.00 80.00
CPLJ M.Lemieux/J. Jagr 100.00 200.00
CPLP J.LeClair/K.Primeau 25.00 60.00
CPPG K.Primeau/S.Gagne 30.00 80.00
CPSB B.Shanahan/P.Bure 30.00 80.00
CPSJ M.Sundin/C.Joseph 20.00 50.00
CPSK M.Satan/P.Kariya 20.00 50.00
CPSR J.Sakic/P.Roy 150.00 350.00
CPSY B.Shanahan/S.Yzerman 75.00 150.00
CPYF S.Yzerman/S.Fedorov 75.00 200.00
TPJBB Joseph/Brodeur/Belfour
TPKYB Kariya/Yzerman/Bure
TPLGY Lemieux/Gretzky/Yzerman
TPSLS Samsonov/LeClair/Shanny
TPSSP Stefan/Sakic/Primeau

2001-02 SP Game Used Patches Autographs

This 20-card set partially paralleled the regular patch set, but included authentic autographs of the featured player(s). Single player cards were serial-numbered out of 50 and dual player cards were serial-numbered to just 10 copies each.

SPCJ Curtis Joseph 50.00 100.00
SPEB Ed Belfour 40.00 100.00
SPJI Jarome Iginla 30.00 80.00
SPJL John LeClair 25.00 60.00
SPJT Joe Thornton 25.00 60.00
SPKP Keith Primeau 25.00 60.00
SPMB Martin Brodeur 75.00 150.00
SPMB Martin Biron 30.00 80.00
SPMH Marian Hossa 30.00 80.00
SPOK Olaf Kolzig 30.00 80.00
SPPB Pavel Bure 30.00 80.00
SPPB Peter Bondra 30.00 80.00
SPPS Patrik Stefan 30.00 80.00
SPSG Simon Gagne 30.00 80.00
SPSS Sergei Samsonov 30.00 80.00
SPSY Steve Yzerman 75.00 200.00
SPTA Tony Amonte 30.00 80.00
SPTH Jose Theodore 40.00 100.00
SPTS Teemu Selanne 40.00 100.00
SPWG Wayne Gretzky 200.00 400.00

2001-02 SP Game Used Tools of the Game

Randomly inserted, this 52-card set featured one, two or three swatches of game-used gear from the player(s) featured. Single player cards were serial-numbered out of 100 (unless otherwise noted below), dual player cards were serial-numbered out of 50 and triple player cards were serial numbered out of 35.

TAC Anson Carter/100 12.50 30.00
TBB Brian Boucher/100 12.50 30.00
TBD Byron Dafoe/100 12.50 30.00
TCO Chris Osgood/100 12.50 30.00
TDA Byron Dafoe/100 12.50 30.00
TDF Byron Dafoe/100 12.50 30.00
TGF Grant Fuhr/100 15.00 40.00
TGP Gilbert Perreault/92 20.00 50.00
TJA Jaromir Jagr/100 15.00 40.00
TJF Jeff Friesen/100 8.00 20.00
TJH Johan Hedberg/100 10.00 25.00
TJJ Jaromir Jagr/100 15.00 40.00
TJT Joe Thornton/36 40.00 100.00
TLE John LeClair/100 10.00 25.00
TMM Mark Messier/100 12.50 30.00
TOK Olaf Kolzig/100 12.50 30.00
TPR Patrick Roy/100 30.00 80.00
TRA Bill Ranford/100 8.00 20.00
TRC Roman Cechmanek/100 12.50 30.00
TRD Rick DiPietro/100
TSA Sergei Samsonov/83 12.50 30.00
TSF Sergei Fedorov/100 12.50 30.00
TSS Sergei Samsonov/100 12.50 30.00
TSY Steve Yzerman/30 75.00 200.00
TTE Tony Esposito/100 15.00 40.00
TTH Jose Theodore/100 20.00 50.00
TWG Wayne Gretzky/71 100.00 250.00
CTCB R.Cechmanek/B.Boucher 20.00 50.00
CTCH R.Cechmanek/J.Hedberg 20.00 50.00
CTCS A.Carter/S.Samsonov 20.00 50.00
CTDB B.Dafoe/B.Boucher 20.00 50.00
CTDC B.Dafoe/G.Cheevers 20.00 50.00
CTEC T.Esposito/G.Cheevers 25.00 60.00
CTFC G.Fuhr/R.Cechmanek 20.00 50.00
CTFF S.Fedorov/J.Friesen 20.00 50.00
CTFR S.Fedorov/P.Roy 25.00 60.00
CTHD J.Hedberg/B.Dafoe 20.00 50.00
CTKB O.Kolzig/B.Boucher 20.00 50.00
CTKT O.Kolzig/J.Theodore 20.00 50.00
CTLJ J.LeClair/J.Jagr 25.00 60.00
CTRC P.Roy/R.Cechmanek 25.00 60.00
CTRF P.Roy/G.Fuhr 30.00 80.00
CTRF B.Ranford/G.Fuhr 20.00 50.00
CTSF S.Samsonov/S.Fedorov 20.00 50.00
CTTD J.Theodore/B.Dafoe 20.00 50.00
TTDER Dafoe/Esposito/Roy 60.00 120.00
TTFCF Friesen/Carter/Fedorov 30.00 80.00
TTFSL Fedorov/Samsonov/LeClair 40.00 100.00
TTHCR Hedberg/Cheevers/Roy 60.00 150.00
TTKCH Kolzig/Cech/Hedberg 40.00 100.00
TTRBK Roy/Boucher/Kolzig 75.00 150.00
TTRFE Ranford/Fuhr/Esposito 40.00 100.00

2001-02 SP Game Used Tools of the Game Autographs

This 22-card set featured swatches of game-worn gear as well as authentic player autographs of the player(s) featured. Single player cards were serial-numbered out of 100 while dual player cards were serial-numbered out of 35.

STBR Bill Ranford 20.00 50.00
STGF Grant Fuhr 20.00 50.00
STGP Gilbert Perrault 30.00 80.00
STJH Johan Hedberg 15.00 40.00
STJL John LeClair 12.00 30.00
STJT Jose Theodore 25.00 60.00
STJT Joe Thornton 25.00 60.00
STKP Keith Primeau 20.00 50.00
STLE John LeClair 15.00 40.00
STPB Peter Bondra 15.00 40.00
STRB Ray Bourque 40.00 100.00
STSA Sergei Samsonov 15.00 40.00
STSM Sergei Samsonov 15.00 40.00
STSY Steve Yzerman 60.00 120.00
STTS Teemu Selanne 20.00 50.00
SCBS R.Bourque/S.Samsonov 100.00 200.00
SCLT J.LeClair/J.Thornton 75.00 200.00
SCPS K.Primeau/S.Samsonov 25.00 60.00
SCPY K.Primeau/S.Yzerman 60.00 150.00
SCRF B.Ranford/G.Fuhr 40.00 100.00
SCRH B.Ranford/J.Hedberg 40.00 100.00
SCTY J.Thornton/S.Yzerman 125.00 250.00

2002-03 SP Game Used

Released in March of 2003, this 103-card set carried an SRP of $29.99. There were two subsets; All-Star Flashbacks (51-65) and New Grooves (66-103). The All-Star Flashbacks were serial-numbered out of 999 and the New Grooves rookie cards were serial-numbered out of 750.

COMP.SET w/o SP's (50) 60.00 125.00
1 Paul Kariya 1.25 3.00
2 Ilya Kovalchuk 1.25 3.00
3 Dany Heatley 1.00 2.50
4 Joe Thornton 1.25 3.00
5 Sergei Samsonov .75 2.00
6 Martin Biron .75 2.00
7 Jarome Iginla 1.00 2.50
8 Jeff O'Neill .60 1.50
9 Ron Francis 1.25 3.00
10 Eric Daze .60 1.50
11 Peter Forsberg 1.25 3.00
12 Joe Sakic 1.50 4.00
13 Patrick Roy 2.50 6.00
14 Marc Denis .75 2.00
15 Bill Guerin 1.00 2.50
16 Mike Modano 1.50 4.00
17 Steve Yzerman 2.00 5.00
18 Brendan Shanahan 1.25 3.00
19 Curtis Joseph 1.00 2.50
20 Mike Comrie 1.00 2.50
21 Roberto Luongo 1.50 4.00
22 Felix Potvin 1.50 4.00
23 Zigmund Palffy 1.00 2.50
24 Marian Gaborik 1.50 4.00
25 Jose Theodore 1.00 2.50
26 Saku Koivu 1.00 2.50
27 Mike Dunham .75 2.00
28 Martin Brodeur 2.00 5.00
29 Patrik Elias 1.00 2.50
30 Mike Peca .75 2.00
31 Alexei Yashin .75 2.00
32 Eric Lindros 1.50 4.00
33 Pavel Bure 1.25 3.00
34 Martin Havlat .75 2.00
35 Daniel Alfredsson 1.00 2.50
36 Simon Gagne 1.00 2.50
37 Jeremy Roenick 1.00 2.50
38 Sean Burke .60 1.50
39 Tony Amonte .75 2.00
40 Mario Lemieux 3.00 8.00
41 Owen Nolan 1.00 2.50
42 Evgeni Nabokov .75 2.00
43 Chris Pronger .75 2.00
44 Keith Tkachuk 1.00 2.50
45 Vincent Lecavalier .75 2.00
46 Mats Sundin 1.00 2.50
47 Ed Belfour 1.00 2.50
48 Markus Naslund .75 2.00
49 Olaf Kolzig 1.00 2.50
50 Jaromir Jagr 2.50 6.00
51 Gordie Howe AF 6.00 15.00
52 Mario Lemieux AF 6.00 15.00
53 Wayne Gretzky AF 10.00 25.00
54 Mario Lemieux AF 6.00 15.00
55 Wayne Gretzky AF 10.00 25.00
56 Vincent Damphousse AF 1.50 4.00
57 Brett Hull AF 2.50 6.00
58 Mike Richter AF 2.00 5.00
59 Ray Bourque AF 3.00 8.00
60 Mark Recchi AF 2.50 6.00
61 Teemu Selanne AF 4.00 10.00
62 Wayne Gretzky AF 10.00 25.00
63 Pavel Bure AF 2.50 6.00
64 Bill Guerin AF 2.00 5.00
65 Eric Daze AF 1.25 3.00
66 Alexei Smirnov RC 1.50 4.00
67 Stanislav Chistov RC 1.25 3.00

Card	Low	High
68 Martin Gerber RC	2.00	5.00
69 Kurt Sauer RC	1.25	3.00
70 Chuck Kobasew RC	1.50	4.00
71 Jordan Leopold RC	2.00	5.00
72 Jeff Paul RC	1.25	3.00
73 Rick Nash RC	12.50	30.00
74 Lasse Pirjeta RC	1.25	3.00
75 Henrik Zetterberg RC	10.00	25.00
76 Dmitri Bykov RC	1.25	3.00
77 Ales Hemsky RC	5.00	12.00
78 Jay Bouwmeester RC	4.00	10.00
79 Alexander Frolov RC	2.50	6.00
80 Sylvain Blouin RC	1.25	3.00
81 P-M Bouchard RC	2.00	5.00
82 Jason Spezza RC	10.00	25.00
83 Ron Hainsey RC	1.25	3.00
84 Adam Hall RC	1.25	3.00
85 Scottie Upshall RC	1.50	4.00
86 Anton Volchenkov RC	1.25	3.00
87 Dennis Seidenberg RC	2.00	5.00
88 Patrick Sharp RC	4.00	10.00
89 Jeff Taffe RC	1.25	3.00
90 Cody Rudkowsky RC	1.25	3.00
91 Tom Koivisto RC	1.25	3.00
92 Curtis Sanford RC	2.00	5.00
93 Alexander Svitov RC	1.25	3.00
94 Carlo Colaiacovo RC	2.00	5.00
95 Steve Eminger RC	1.25	3.00
96 Shaone Morrisonn RC	1.25	3.00
97 Ryan Miller RC	8.00	20.00
98 Levente Szuper RC	2.00	5.00
99 Mike Cammalleri RC	4.00	10.00
100 Stephane Veilleux RC	1.25	3.00
101 Darren Haydar RC	1.25	3.00
102 Lynn Loyns RC	1.25	3.00
103 Mikael Tellqvist RC	1.25	3.00

2002-03 SP Game Used Authentic Fabrics

Randomly inserted, this 102-card set featured single or dual swatches of game-worn jerseys on the card fronts. Each card was serial-numbered in silver foil out of 225.

Card	Low	High
AFAM Tony Amonte	3.00	8.00
AFAT Alex Tanguay	3.00	8.00
AFAY Alexei Yashin	3.00	8.00
AFBB Brian Boucher	3.00	8.00
AFBD Peter Bondra	3.00	8.00
AFBG Bill Guerin	3.00	8.00
AFBH Brett Hull	6.00	15.00
AFBI Martin Biron	3.00	8.00
AFBL Brian Leetch	3.00	8.00
AFBO Peter Bondra	3.00	8.00
AFBQ Ray Bourque	8.00	20.00
AFBS Brendan Shanahan	4.00	10.00
AFCD Chris Drury	3.00	8.00
AFCK Roman Cechmanek	3.00	8.00
AFDA Eric Daze	3.00	8.00
AFDB Donald Brashear	3.00	8.00
AFDR Chris Drury	3.00	8.00
AFED Eric Daze	3.00	8.00
AFFO Peter Forsberg	8.00	20.00
AFFP Felix Potvin	6.00	15.00
AFFV Sergei Fedorov	5.00	12.00
AFGI Jean-Sebastien Giguere	3.00	8.00
AFGM Glen Murray	3.00	8.00
AFGU Bill Guerin	3.00	8.00
AFGY Wayne Gretzky	25.00	60.00
AFHE Milan Hejduk	4.00	10.00
AFHO Marian Hossa	4.00	10.00
AFHU Brett Hull	5.00	12.00
AFIK Ilya Kovalchuk	8.00	20.00
AFJA Jason Allison	3.00	8.00
AFJF Jeff Friesen	3.00	8.00
AFJG Jean-Sebastien Giguere	3.00	8.00
AFJI Jarome Iginla	8.00	20.00
AFJJ Jaromir Jagr	6.00	15.00
AFJL John LeClair	4.00	10.00
AFJR Jeremy Roenick	6.00	15.00
AFJS Joe Sakic	8.00	20.00
AFJT Joe Thornton	6.00	15.00
AFJW Justin Williams	3.00	8.00
AFKA Paul Kariya	4.00	10.00
AFKK Ilya Kovalchuk	8.00	20.00
AFKO Alexei Kovalev	3.00	8.00
AFKP Keith Primeau	3.00	8.00
AFKV Alexei Kovalev	3.00	8.00
AFMB Martin Brodeur	15.00	40.00
AFMD Marc Denis	3.00	8.00
AFMH Marian Hossa	4.00	10.00
AFML Mario Lemieux	15.00	40.00
AFMM Mike Modano	5.00	12.00
AFMN Markus Naslund	4.00	10.00
AFMO Mike Modano	8.00	20.00
AFMR Mark Recchi	3.00	8.00
AFMS Mats Sundin	4.00	10.00
AFMT Mats Sundin	4.00	10.00
AFNA Markus Naslund	4.00	10.00
AFOK Olaf Kolzig	3.00	8.00
AFPB Pavel Bure	4.00	10.00
AFPD Pavol Demitra	3.00	8.00
AFPK Paul Kariya	4.00	10.00
AFPM Patrick Marleau	3.00	8.00
AFPR Patrick Roy	12.00	30.00
AFPU Keith Primeau	3.00	8.00
AFRB Ray Bourque	6.00	15.00
AFRC Roman Cechmanek	3.00	8.00
AFRO Jeremy Roenick	6.00	15.00
AFRW Ray Whitney	3.00	8.00
AFRY Patrick Roy	15.00	40.00
AFSA Miroslav Satan	3.00	8.00
AFSC Joe Sakic	10.00	25.00
AFSD Shane Doan	3.00	8.00
AFSF Sergei Fedorov	8.00	20.00
AFSH Steve Shields	3.00	8.00
AFSK Saku Koivu	4.00	10.00
AFSN Brendan Shanahan	4.00	10.00
AFSS Sergei Samsonov	3.00	8.00
AFSU Steve Sullivan	3.00	8.00
AFSV Sergei Samsonov	3.00	8.00
AFSY Steve Yzerman	15.00	40.00
AFTA Alex Tanguay	3.00	8.00
AFTH Jose Theodore	8.00	20.00
AFTT Jocelyn Thibault	3.00	8.00
AFWG Wayne Gretzky	25.00	60.00
AFZP Zigmund Palffy	4.00	10.00
CFCS T.Connolly/M.Satan	5.00	12.00
CFDT P.Demitra/K.Tkachuk	6.00	15.00
CFFO Peter Forsberg Dual	20.00	50.00
CFFP Felix Potvin Dual	8.00	20.00
CFGR Wayne Gretzky Dual	25.00	60.00
CFJB J.Jagr/P.Bondra	6.00	15.00
CFJJ Jaromir Jagr Dual	10.00	25.00
CFJS Joe Sakic Dual	12.50	30.00
CFLK M.Lemieux/P.Kariya	15.00	40.00
CFMO Mike Modano Dual	8.00	20.00
CFNB J.Nieuwendyk/M.Brodeur	10.00	25.00
CFSH B.Shanahan/B.Hull	6.00	15.00
CFTB J.Thibault/M.Brodeur	10.00	25.00
CFTK J.Theodore/S.Koivu	12.50	30.00
CFTL K.Tkachuk/J.LeClair	6.00	15.00
CFTS J.Thornton/S.Samsonov	6.00	15.00
CFWD D.Weight/P.Demitra	6.00	15.00
CFWG Wayne Gretzky Dual	30.00	80.00
CFYR S.Yzerman/L.Robitaille	10.00	25.00

2002-03 SP Game Used Authentic Fabrics Gold

This 83-card set paralleled the basic insert set but each card was serial-numbered in gold foil to just 99 copies.

*GOLD: .5X TO 1.25X BASIC JERSEYS
GOLD PRINT RUN 99 SER.#'d SETS

2002-03 SP Game Used First Rounder Patches

Randomly inserted, this 58-card set featured swatches of game-worn jersey patches from the featured player. Each card was serial-numbered out of 30 on the card front and carried a "PC" prefix on the card back.

Card	Low	High
AD Adam Deadmarsh	15.00	40.00
AK Alexei Kovalev	15.00	40.00
AL Jason Allison	15.00	40.00
AT Alex Tanguay	15.00	40.00
AY Alexei Yashin	20.00	50.00
BB Brian Boucher	15.00	40.00
BG Bill Guerin	15.00	40.00
BI Martin Biron	15.00	40.00
BS Brendan Shanahan	20.00	50.00
CP Chris Pronger	15.00	40.00
DB Daniel Briere	15.00	40.00
DL David Legwand	15.00	40.00
EL Eric Lindros	25.00	60.00
GO Sergei Gonchar	15.00	40.00
IK Ilya Kovalchuk	25.00	60.00
JA Jason Arnott	15.00	40.00
JD J-P Dumont	15.00	40.00
JG Jean-Sebastien Giguere	15.00	40.00
JI Jarome Iginla	25.00	60.00
JJ Jaromir Jagr	30.00	80.00
JR Jeremy Roenick	30.00	80.00
JS Joe Sakic	40.00	100.00
JT Joe Thornton	30.00	80.00
JW Justin Williams	15.00	40.00
KK Krys Kolanos	15.00	40.00
KP Keith Primeau	15.00	40.00
KT Keith Tkachuk	25.00	60.00
MA Manny Malhotra	15.00	40.00
MB Martin Brodeur	40.00	100.00
MD Marc Denis	15.00	40.00
ML Mario Lemieux	60.00	150.00
MM Mike Modano	30.00	80.00
MN Markus Naslund	20.00	50.00
MS Mats Sundin	25.00	60.00
NO Mika Noronen	15.00	40.00
OK Olaf Kolzig	20.00	50.00
ON Owen Nolan	15.00	40.00
PF Peter Forsberg	30.00	80.00
PK Paul Kariya	20.00	50.00
PM Patrick Marleau	15.00	40.00
PS Patrik Stefan	15.00	40.00
RB Ray Bourque	40.00	100.00
RK Rostislav Klesla	15.00	40.00
RL Roberto Luongo	25.00	60.00
RT Raffi Torres	15.00	40.00
SD Shane Doan	15.00	40.00
SG Simon Gagne	20.00	50.00
SH Scott Hartnell	20.00	50.00
SK Saku Koivu	20.00	50.00
SS Sergei Samsonov	20.00	50.00
SY Steve Yzerman	75.00	150.00
TC Tim Connolly	15.00	40.00
TL Trevor Linden	15.00	40.00
TP Taylor Pyatt	15.00	40.00
TS Teemu Selanne	20.00	50.00
VL Vincent Lecavalier	25.00	60.00
BLA Dan Blackburn	15.00	40.00
BLE Brian Leetch	25.00	60.00

2002-03 SP Game Used Future Fabrics

Randomly inserted, this 31-card set featured swatches of game-worn jerseys on the card fronts. Each card was serial-numbered in silver foil out of 225.

Card	Low	High
FFAE David Aebischer	3.00	8.00
FFAT Alex Tanguay	3.00	8.00
FFBJ Brent Johnson	3.00	8.00
FFBM Brenden Morrow	3.00	8.00
FFCA Kyle Calder	3.00	8.00
FFDA Denis Arkhipov	3.00	8.00
FFDB Daniel Briere	3.00	8.00
FFEB Eric Belanger	3.00	8.00
FFHA Jeff Halpern	3.00	8.00
FFIB Ilja Bryzgalov	4.00	10.00
FFIK Ilya Kovalchuk	6.00	15.00
FFJG Jean-Sebastien Giguere	3.00	8.00
FFJH Jeff Halpern	3.00	8.00
FFKC Kyle Calder	3.00	8.00
FFKO Ilya Kovalchuk	6.00	15.00
FFMA Maxim Afinogenov	3.00	8.00
FFMB Mark Bell	3.00	8.00
FFME Martin Erat	3.00	8.00
FFMM Manny Malhotra	3.00	8.00
FFMP Matt Pettinger	3.00	8.00
FFMR Mike Ribeiro	3.00	8.00
FFMT Marty Turco	3.00	8.00
FFPB Pavel Brendl	3.00	8.00
FFRI Mike Ribeiro	3.00	8.00
FFRK Rostislav Klesla	3.00	8.00
FFSG Simon Gagne	4.00	10.00
FFSH Scott Hartnell	4.00	10.00
FFSR Steven Reinprecht	3.00	8.00
FFTC Tim Connolly	3.00	8.00
FFTP Taylor Pyatt	3.00	8.00
FFVN Ville Nieminen	3.00	8.00

2002-03 SP Game Used Future Fabrics Gold

This 31-card set paralleled the basic insert set but each card was serial-numbered in gold foil to just 99 copies.

*GOLD: .5X TO 1.25X BASIC JERSEY

2002-03 SP Game Used Piece of History

Randomly inserted, this 87-card set featured swatches of game-worn jerseys on the card fronts. Each card was serial-numbered in silver foil out of 225.

*GOLD/99: .6X TO 1.5X BASIC JSY/225

Card	Low	High
PHAD Adam Deadmarsh	4.00	10.00
PHAL Jason Allison	4.00	10.00
PHAM Tony Amonte	4.00	10.00
PHAT Alex Tanguay	4.00	10.00
PHAY Alexei Yashin	4.00	10.00
PHAZ Alexei Zhamnov	4.00	10.00
PHBD Peter Bondra	5.00	12.00
PHBH Brett Hull	6.00	15.00
PHBI Martin Biron	4.00	10.00
PHBL Brian Leetch	5.00	12.00
PHBO Peter Bondra	5.00	12.00
PHBQ Ray Bourque	8.00	20.00
PHBS Brendan Shanahan	6.00	15.00
PHCC Chris Chelios	5.00	12.00
PHCD Chris Drury	5.00	12.00
PHCJ Curtis Joseph	5.00	12.00
PHCK Roman Cechmanek	4.00	10.00
PHCL Claude Lemieux	4.00	10.00
PHDL David Legwand	4.00	10.00
PHDR Chris Drury	5.00	12.00
PHDU Mike Dunham	4.00	10.00
PHED Eric Daze	3.00	8.00
PHEK Espen Knutsen	3.00	8.00
PHEL Eric Lindros	8.00	20.00
PHFO Peter Forsberg	6.00	15.00
PHFP Felix Potvin	8.00	20.00
PHFV Sergei Fedorov	8.00	20.00
PHGO Sergei Gonchar	4.00	10.00
PHGU Bill Guerin	5.00	12.00
PHGY Wayne Gretzky	25.00	60.00
PHJA Jason Allison	4.00	10.00
PHJD J.P. Dumont	3.00	8.00
PHJG Jaromir Jagr	12.00	30.00
PHJI Jarome Iginla	5.00	12.00
PHJJ Jaromir Jagr	12.00	30.00
PHJL John LeClair	5.00	12.00
PHJN Joe Nieuwendyk	5.00	12.00
PHJO Jocelyn Thibault	4.00	10.00
PHJR Jeremy Roenick	5.00	12.00
PHJS Joe Sakic	8.00	20.00
PHJT Joe Thornton	6.00	15.00
PHKA Paul Kariya	6.00	15.00
PHKK Ilya Kovalchuk	6.00	15.00
PHKO Steve Konowalchuk	3.00	8.00
PHKP Keith Primeau	5.00	12.00
PHKU Saku Koivu	5.00	12.00
PHLM Nicklas Lidstrom	5.00	12.00
PHMB Martin Brodeur	10.00	25.00
PHMD Marc Denis	4.00	10.00
PHMH Milan Hejduk	4.00	10.00
PHML Mario Lemieux	15.00	40.00
PHMM Mike Modano	8.00	20.00
PHMN Markus Naslund	4.00	10.00
PHMO Mike Modano	8.00	20.00
PHMR Mark Recchi	6.00	15.00
PHMS Mats Sundin	5.00	12.00
PHMY Mike York	3.00	8.00
PHNA Markus Naslund	4.00	10.00
PHNL Nicklas Lidstrom	5.00	12.00
PHPB Pavel Bure	6.00	15.00
PHPF Peter Forsberg	6.00	15.00
PHPK Paul Kariya	6.00	15.00
PHPM Patrick Marleau	5.00	12.00
PHPR Patrick Roy	12.00	30.00
PHRB Ray Bourque	8.00	20.00
PHRC Roman Cechmanek	4.00	10.00
PHRK Jeremy Roenick	5.00	12.00
PHRO Rob Blake	5.00	12.00
PHRT Roman Turek	5.00	12.00
PHRY Patrick Roy	12.00	30.00
PHSA Marc Savard	3.00	8.00
PHSB Sean Burke	3.00	8.00
PHSC Joe Sakic	8.00	20.00
PHSF Sergei Fedorov	8.00	20.00
PHSG Simon Gagne	5.00	12.00
PHSH Brendan Shanahan	6.00	15.00
PHSK Saku Koivu	5.00	12.00
PHSS Sergei Samsonov	4.00	10.00
PHSU Mats Sundin	5.00	12.00
PHSV Sergei Samsonov	4.00	10.00
PHSY Steve Yzerman	10.00	25.00
PHTA Alex Tanguay	4.00	10.00
PHTC Tim Connolly	3.00	8.00
PHTH Jose Theodore	5.00	12.00
PHTS Teemu Selanne	10.00	25.00
PHTT Jocelyn Thibault	4.00	10.00
PHZP Zigmund Palffy	5.00	12.00

2002-03 SP Game Used Signature Style

Inserted at 1:12, this 32-card set featured authentic player autographs. Each card carried a "SS" prefix on the card backs.

Card	Low	High
AF Alexander Frolov	8.00	20.00
BO Bobby Orr	125.00	250.00
BR Pavel Brendl	5.00	12.00
CJ Curtis Joseph	12.00	30.00
DH Dany Heatley	10.00	25.00
EB Ed Belfour	15.00	40.00
EC Erik Cole	5.00	12.00
GH Gordie Howe	50.00	125.00
IK Ilya Kovalchuk	12.00	30.00
JI Jarome Iginla	10.00	25.00
JL John LeClair	5.00	12.00
JT Joe Thornton	12.00	30.00
JW Justin Williams	5.00	12.00
KH Kristian Huselius	5.00	12.00
MA Maxim Afinogenov	5.00	12.00
MB Martin Brodeur	40.00	100.00
MC Mike Comrie	5.00	12.00
MFO Manny Fernandez	5.00	12.00
MH Martin Havlat	5.00	12.00
MK Milan Kraft	6.00	12.00
NK Nikolai Khabibulin	8.00	20.00
PB Pavel Bure	8.00	20.00
PR Patrick Roy	50.00	125.00
RB Ray Bourque	20.00	50.00
SC Stanislav Chistov	6.00	15.00
SG Simon Gagne	6.00	15.00
SH Scott Hartnell	6.00	15.00
SP Jason Spezza	20.00	50.00
SS Sergei Samsonov	6.00	15.00
SY Steve Yzerman	30.00	80.00
TS Teemu Selanne	6.00	15.00
WG Wayne Gretzky	150.00	300.00

2002-03 SP Game Used Tools of the Game

Randomly inserted, this 30-card set featured swatches of game-worn gloves or goalie leg pads on the card fronts. Each card was serial-numbered in silver foil out of 99. Cards carried a "TG" prefix on the card backs.

Card	Low	High
AK Alexei Kovalev G	8.00	20.00
AM Alexander Mogilny G	8.00	20.00
BB Brian Boucher P	8.00	20.00
BD Byron Dafoe P	8.00	20.00
BE Ed Belfour P	12.50	30.00
BH Brett Hull G	15.00	40.00
BS Brendan Shanahan G	12.50	30.00
DH Dominik Hasek P	15.00	40.00
EB Ed Belfour G	12.50	30.00
JF Jeff Friesen G	8.00	20.00
JJ Jaromir Jagr G	12.00	30.00
JL John LeClair G	12.50	30.00
JR Jeremy Roenick G	15.00	40.00
JT Joe Thornton G	15.00	40.00
KP Keith Primeau G	8.00	20.00
KT Keith Tkachuk G	10.00	25.00
MD Marc Denis P	8.00	20.00
MS Mats Sundin G	12.50	30.00
OK Olaf Kolzig P	8.00	20.00
PB Peter Bondra G	8.00	20.00
PR Patrick Roy P	20.00	50.00
RC Roman Cechmanek P	8.00	20.00
RD Rick DiPietro P	8.00	20.00
RF Ron Francis G	8.00	20.00
RL Roberto Luongo P	15.00	40.00
SF Sergei Fedorov G	12.50	30.00
SH Steve Shields P	8.00	20.00
SS Sergei Samsonov G	8.00	20.00
TH Jose Theodore P	12.00	30.00
TS Teemu Selanne G	12.50	30.00

2003-04 SP Game Used

This 130-card set consisted of 50 veteran cards; Tier 1 rookie cards (51-82 and 123-130) serial-numbered to 600; Tier 2 rookies (83-92) serial-numbered to 99 and veteran jersey cards (93-122). Cards 123-130 were only available in packs of UD Rookie Update and were serial-numbered out of 600.

Card	Low	High
COMP.SET w/o SP's (50)	25.00	60.00
1 Jean-Sebastien Giguere	1.00	2.50
2 Sergei Fedorov	1.50	4.00
3 Dany Heatley	1.00	2.50
4 Ilya Kovalchuk	1.00	2.50
5 Joe Thornton	1.25	3.00
6 Sergei Samsonov	.75	2.00
7 Chris Drury	.75	2.00
8 Jarome Iginla	1.00	2.50
9 Ron Francis	1.25	3.00
10 Jocelyn Thibault	.75	2.00
11 Joe Sakic	1.50	4.00
12 Peter Forsberg	1.25	3.00
13 Paul Kariya	1.25	3.00
14 Rick Nash	1.00	2.50
15 Marty Turco	1.00	2.50
16 Mike Modano	1.50	4.00
17 Steve Yzerman	2.50	6.00
18 Dominik Hasek	1.50	4.00
19 Ales Hemsky	1.00	2.50
20 Mike Comrie	.75	2.00
21 Roberto Luongo	1.50	4.00
22 Zigmund Palffy	1.00	2.50
23 Marian Gaborik	1.50	4.00
24 Jose Theodore	1.00	2.50
25 Saku Koivu	1.00	2.50
26 Tomas Vokoun	.75	2.00
27 Martin Brodeur	2.00	5.00
28 Alexei Yashin	.75	2.00
29 Eric Lindros	1.50	4.00
30 Pavel Bure	1.25	3.00
31 Patrick Lalime	.75	2.00
32 Marian Hossa	.75	2.00
33 Jason Spezza	1.00	2.50
34 Simon Gagne	1.00	2.50
35 Jeremy Roenick	1.00	2.50
36 Sean Burke	.60	1.50
37 Mario Lemieux	3.00	8.00
38 Niko Dimitrakos	.60	1.50
39 Evgeni Nabokov	.75	2.00
40 Al MacInnis	1.00	2.50
41 Keith Tkachuk	1.00	2.50
42 Chris Pronger	.75	2.00
43 Nikolai Khabibulin	1.00	2.50
44 Vincent Lecavalier	.75	2.00
45 Owen Nolan	.75	2.00
46 Ed Belfour	1.00	2.50
47 Mats Sundin	1.00	2.50
48 Markus Naslund	1.00	2.50
49 Todd Bertuzzi	1.00	2.50
50 Jaromir Jagr	2.50	6.00
51 Jiri Hudler RC	5.00	12.00
52 Patrice Bergeron RC	10.00	25.00
53 Milan Bartovic RC	2.50	6.00
54 Matthew Lombardi RC	2.50	6.00
55 Lasse Kukkonen RC	2.00	5.00
56 Travis Moen RC	2.50	6.00
57 Marek Svatos RC	4.00	10.00
58 John-Michael Liles RC	2.50	6.00
59 Cody McCormick RC	2.50	6.00
60 Dan Fritsche RC	2.00	5.00
61 Antti Miettinen RC	3.00	8.00
62 Esa Pirnes RC	2.00	5.00
63 Tim Gleason RC	2.50	6.00
64 Brent Burns RC	5.00	12.00
65 Christoph Brandner RC	2.50	6.00
66 Chris Higgins RC	4.00	10.00
67 Dan Hamhuis RC	2.50	6.00
68 Marek Zidlicky RC	2.00	5.00
69 Wade Brookbank RC	2.50	6.00
70 David Hale RC	2.00	5.00
71 Paul Martin RC	2.50	6.00
72 Sean Bergenheim RC	2.50	6.00
73 Antoine Vermette RC	4.00	10.00
74 Matthew Spiller RC	2.50	6.00
75 Matt Murley RC	2.50	6.00
76 Christian Ehrhoff RC	2.50	6.00
77 Alexander Semin RC	6.00	15.00
78 Tom Preissing RC	2.50	6.00
79 Peter Sejna RC	2.50	6.00
80 Maxim Kondratiev RC	2.00	5.00
81 Matt Stajan RC	3.00	8.00
82 Boyd Gordon RC	2.50	6.00
83 Joffrey Lupul RC	15.00	40.00
84 Eric Staal RC	30.00	80.00
85 Tuomo Ruutu RC	10.00	25.00
86 Pavel Vorobiev RC	8.00	20.00
87 Nathan Horton RC	15.00	40.00
88 Dustin Brown RC	12.00	30.00
89 Jordin Tootoo RC	12.00	30.00
90 Joni Pitkanen RC	10.00	25.00
91 Marc-Andre Fleury RC	50.00	100.00
92 Milan Michalek RC	12.00	30.00
93 Joe Thornton JSY	6.00	15.00
94 Jason Blake JSY	3.00	8.00
95 Pavol Demitra JSY	6.00	15.00
96 Martin St. Louis JSY	5.00	12.00
97 Zigmund Palffy JSY	5.00	12.00
98 Sean Burke JSY	3.00	8.00
99 Todd Marchant JSY	3.00	8.00
100 Jarome Iginla JSY	5.00	12.00
101 Doug Weight JSY	5.00	12.00
102 Henrik Zetterberg JSY	6.00	15.00
103 Ilya Kovalchuk JSY	5.00	12.00
104 Alexei Yashin JSY	4.00	10.00
105 Mario Lemieux JSY	10.00	25.00
106 Milan Hejduk JSY	4.00	10.00
107 Martin Biron JSY	4.00	10.00
108 Tomas Vokoun JSY	4.00	10.00
109 Tommy Salo JSY	4.00	10.00
110 Anson Carter JSY	4.00	10.00
111 Nikoali Khabibulin JSY	5.00	12.00
112 Keith Tkachuk JSY	5.00	12.00
113 Martin Brodeur JSY	10.00	25.00
114 Steve Yzerman JSY	6.00	15.00
115 Jeremy Roenick JSY	5.00	12.00
116 Mike Modano JSY	8.00	20.00
117 Marian Hossa JSY	4.00	10.00
118 Paul Kariya JSY	6.00	15.00
119 Marty Turco JSY	5.00	12.00
120 Peter Forsberg JSY	6.00	15.00
121 Todd Bertuzzi JSY	5.00	12.00
122 David Aebischer JSY	4.00	10.00
123 Fedor Tyutin RC	2.00	5.00
124 John Pohl RC	2.00	5.00
125 Ryan Kesler RC	10.00	25.00
126 Fredrik Sjostrom RC	3.00	8.00
127 Aaron Johnson RC	2.00	5.00
128 Brad Boyes RC	3.00	8.00
129 Nikolai Zherdev RC	4.00	10.00
130 Tomas Plekanec RC	6.00	15.00

2003-04 SP Game Used Gold

*1-50 VETS/40: 2.5X TO 6X BASIC CARDS
*51-82 ROOKIES/40: .8X TO 2X RC/600
*83-92 ROOKIES/25: .4X TO 1X RC/99
*93-122 JERSEYS/30: .8X TO 2X BASIC JSY

2003-04 SP Game Used Authentic Fabrics

This 72-card set featured single, dual or quad jersey swatches. Single and dual swatch cards were serial-numbered to 99 while quad swatch cards were serial-numbered out of 55.

Card	Low	High
AFAF Alexander Frolov	5.00	12.00
AFEL Eric Lindros	6.00	15.00
AFHA Marcel Hossa	3.00	8.00
AFJG J-S Giguere	5.00	12.00
AFJI Jarome Iginla	10.00	25.00
AFJJ Jaromir Jagr	10.00	25.00
AFJR Jeremy Roenick	10.00	25.00
AFJS Jason Spezza	8.00	20.00
AFJT Joe Thornton	10.00	25.00
AFMH Marian Hossa	6.00	15.00
AFML Mario Lemieux	15.00	40.00
AFON Owen Nolan	5.00	12.00
AFPR Patrick Roy	15.00	40.00
AFPS Peter Sejna	3.00	8.00
AFRL Roberto Luongo	8.00	20.00
AFRN Rick Nash	12.50	30.00
AFSF Sergei Fedorov	10.00	25.00
AFSG Simon Gagne	6.00	15.00
AFSK Saku Koivu	5.00	12.00
AFTB Todd Bertuzzi	5.00	12.00
AFWG Wayne Gretzky	30.00	80.00
AFZP Zigmund Palffy	4.00	10.00
DFBJ R.Blake/E.Jovanovski	8.00	20.00
DFBL J.Bouwmeester/R.Luongo	15.00	40.00
DFBP M.Brodeur/P.Leclaire	15.00	40.00
DFBR M.Brodeur/P.Roy	25.00	60.00
DFBT Z.Palffy/A.Frolov	8.00	20.00
DFCM C.Drury/M.Satan	6.00	15.00
DFDS T.Domi/J.Shelley	8.00	20.00
DFFS P.Forsberg/J.Sakic	15.00	40.00
DFGR J.Giguere/P.Roy	15.00	40.00
DFGS W.Gretzky/J.Spezza	40.00	100.00
DFHC A.Hemsky/M.Comrie	8.00	20.00
DFHG G.Howe/W.Gretzky	50.00	125.00
DFHH M.Hossa/M.Hossa	10.00	25.00
DFHK D.Heatley/I.Kovalchuk	12.00	30.00
DFHL D.Hasek/N.Lidstrom	10.00	25.00
DFHY B.Hull/S.Yzerman	15.00	40.00
DFJB J.Jagr/P.Bondra	8.00	20.00
DFKF P.Kariya/P.Forsberg	12.00	30.00
DFKH S.Koivu/M.Hossa	8.00	20.00
DFKS P.Kariya/T.Selanne	8.00	20.00
DFLG M.Lemieux/W.Gretzky	50.00	125.00
DFLK G.Lafleur/S.Koivu	8.00	20.00
DFLP B.Leetch/T.Poti	8.00	20.00
DFMT M.Modano/M.Turco	15.00	40.00
DFNB M.Naslund/T.Bertuzzi	12.00	30.00
DFND R.Nash/M.Denis	8.00	20.00
DFNM R.Nash/T.Marchant	8.00	20.00
DFPC Z.Palffy/R.Cechmanek	6.00	15.00
DFRG J.Roenick/S.Gagne	8.00	20.00
DFSG S.Bowman/G.Lafleur	15.00	40.00
DFSH J.Spezza/M.Hossa	15.00	40.00
DFTK J.Theodore/S.Koivu	12.50	30.00
DFTM J.Thornton/G.Murray	8.00	20.00
DFVN V.Lecavalier/N.Khabibulin	8.00	20.00
DFWT D.Weight/K.Tkachuk	6.00	15.00
DFYH S.Yzerman/G.Howe	30.00	80.00
DFYP A.Yashin/M.Peca	6.00	15.00
DFZH H.Zetterberg/B.Hull	15.00	40.00
DFZT A.Zhamnov/J.Thibault	6.00	15.00
QARGL Amnte/Roen/Gags/LeC	25.00	60.00
QFSKS Frsbrg/Seln/Krya/Sakic	40.00	100.00
QKTHK Kvu/Thdre/Hsa/Kmisrk	30.00	80.00
QLGHL Lem/Gretz/Howe/Lafleur	150.00	350.00
QMGTM Modn/Grin/Trco/Morr	25.00	60.00
QNBJM Naslund/Bert/Jov/Morr	25.00	60.00
QRGBT Roy/J-S G/Brodr/Turco	60.00	150.00
QSAHL Spza/Alfrd/Hssa/Lalime	25.00	60.00
QSNBM Sndin/Nolan/Blfr/Mogil	25.00	60.00
QSNZH Spza/Nsh/Zettr/Hmsky	60.00	150.00
QYBHH Yzrm/Bowm/Hull/Hask	60.00	120.00

2003-04 SP Game Used Double Threads

This 27-card set featured dual-patch swatches of the featured players. Each card was serial-numbered out of 60.

Card	Low	High
DTAR D.Aebischer/P.Roy	40.00	100.00
DTBL J.Bouwmeester/R.Luongo	20.00	50.00
DTBR M.Brodeur/P.Roy	60.00	150.00
DTDS C.Drury/M.Satan	20.00	50.00
DTFS P.Forsberg/J.Sakic	20.00	50.00
DTKH S.Koivu/M.Hossa	20.00	50.00
DTKS P.Kariya/T.Selanne	20.00	50.00
DTLG M.Lemieux/W.Gretzky	75.00	150.00
DTLK V.Lecavalier/N.Khabibulin	20.00	50.00
DTLS V.Lecavalier/M.St. Louis	20.00	50.00
DTMG M.Modano/B.Guerin	20.00	50.00
DTMT M.Modano/M.Turco	20.00	50.00
DTNB M.Naslund/T.Bertuzzi	20.00	50.00
DTND R.Nash/M.Denis	25.00	60.00
DTNN R.Niedermayer/S.Niedermayer	25.00	60.00
DTPF Z.Palffy/A.Frolov	20.00	50.00
DTPK P.Kariya/P.Kariya	20.00	50.00
DTRA J.Roenick/T.Amonte	20.00	50.00
DTSB M.Sundin/E.Belfour	25.00	60.00
DTSF S.Fedorov/S.Fedorov	40.00	100.00
DTSH J.Spezza/M.Hossa	25.00	60.00
DTSN M.Sundin/O.Nolan	25.00	60.00
DTTM J.Thornton/G.Murray	20.00	50.00
DTTS J.Thornton/S.Samsonov	20.00	50.00
DTWG W.Gretzky/W.Gretzky	150.00	400.00
DTYZ S.Yzerman/H.Zetterberg	25.00	60.00
DTZT A.Zhamnov/J.Thibault	20.00	50.00

2003-04 SP Game Used Game Gear

PRINT RUN 99 SERIAL #'d SETS

Card	Low	High
GGBB Brian Boucher	6.00	15.00
GGBD Byron Dafoe	6.00	15.00
GGCJ Curtis Joseph	8.00	20.00
GGCO Chris Osgood	6.00	15.00
GGDH Dominik Hasek	12.50	30.00
GGGF Grant Fuhr	15.00	40.00
GGJF Jeff Friesen	6.00	15.00
GGJGR Jaromir Jagr	12.50	30.00
GGJH Johan Hedberg/36	6.00	15.00
GGJJ Jaromir Jagr	12.50	30.00
GGJT Jose Theodore	12.50	30.00
GGMB Martin Brodeur	15.00	40.00
GGMD Marc Denis	6.00	15.00
GGMS Mats Sundin	8.00	20.00
GGMT Marty Turco	6.00	15.00
GGOK Olaf Kolzig	6.00	15.00
GGPL Patrick Lalime	6.00	15.00
GGPR Patrick Roy	15.00	40.00
GGRC Roman Cechmanek	6.00	15.00
GGRD Rick DiPietro	6.00	15.00
GGRL Roberto Luongo	12.50	30.00
GGSAM Sergei Samsonov	6.00	15.00
GGSS Steve Shields	6.00	15.00
GGTS Teemu Selanne	8.00	20.00
GGTSA Tommy Salo	6.00	15.00

2003-04 SP Game Used Game Gear Combo

*COMBO: .5X TO 1.5X BASIC GEAR
PRINT RUN 85 SERIAL #'d SETS

2003-04 SP Game Used Limited Threads

PRINT RUN 75 SERIAL #'d SETS
*GOLD/21: .6X TO 1.5X BASIC JSY/75

Card	Low	High
LTAH Ales Hemsky	6.00	15.00
LTAK Ales Kotalik	6.00	15.00
LTAY Alexei Yashin	6.00	15.00
LTBG Bill Guerin	6.00	15.00
LTBL Brian Leetch	6.00	15.00
LTCD Chris Drury	6.00	15.00
LTDH Dany Heatley	10.00	25.00
LTDHA Dominik Hasek	12.50	30.00
LTG1 Wayne Gretzky	30.00	80.00
LTGL Guy Lafleur	12.50	30.00
LTIK Ilya Kovalchuk	10.00	25.00
LTJB Jay Bouwmeester	6.00	15.00
LTJBU Johnny Bucyk	6.00	15.00
LTJJ Jaromir Jagr	10.00	25.00
LTJS Jason Spezza	12.50	30.00
LTJSG Jean-Sebastien Giguere	6.00	15.00
LTJT Joe Thornton	12.50	30.00
LTJTH Jocelyn Thibault	6.00	15.00
LTLM Lanny McDonald	6.00	15.00
LTMB Mike Bossy	6.00	15.00
LTMH Gordie Howe	25.00	60.00
LTMHO Marian Hossa	6.00	15.00
LTMM Mike Modano	10.00	25.00
LTMN Markus Naslund	6.00	15.00
LTMS Mats Sundin	8.00	20.00
LTMT Marty Turco	6.00	15.00
LTPD Pavel Datsyuk	15.00	40.00
LTPF Peter Forsberg	15.00	40.00
LTPK Paul Kariya	6.00	15.00
LTPR Patrick Roy	20.00	60.00
LTRL Roberto Luongo	10.00	25.00
LTRN Rick Nash	10.00	25.00
LTSB Scotty Bowman	15.00	40.00
LTSF Sergei Fedorov	10.00	25.00
LTSU Scottie Upshall	6.00	15.00
LTSY Steve Yzerman	12.50	30.00
LTTA Tony Amonte	6.00	15.00
LTTB Todd Bertuzzi	6.00	15.00
LTTS Teemu Selanne	8.00	20.00
LTVL Vincent Lecavalier	8.00	20.00
LTWG Wayne Gretzky	30.00	80.00
LTWGR Wayne Gretzky	30.00	80.00

2003-04 SP Game Used Rookie Exclusives Autographs

PRINT RUN 100 SERIAL #'d SETS

Card	Low	High
RE1 Patrice Bergeron	20.00	50.00
RE2 Dustin Brown	15.00	30.00
RE3 Marc-Andre Fleury	30.00	80.00
RE4 Nathan Horton	15.00	40.00
RE5 Jiri Hudler	10.00	25.00
RE6 Joffrey Lupul	10.00	25.00
RE7 Joni Pitkanen	10.00	25.00
RE8 Tuomo Ruutu	15.00	40.00
RE9 Eric Staal	25.00	60.00
RE10 Jordin Tootoo	15.00	40.00

2003-04 SP Game Used Signers

STATED ODDS 1:7

Card	Low	High
SPSBO Bobby Orr	60.00	150.00
SPSCJ Curtis Joseph	6.00	15.00
SPSDA David Aebischer	6.00	15.00
SPSEL Eric Lindros	12.50	30.00
SPSGH Gordie Howe	30.00	80.00
SPSHA Marian Hossa	6.00	15.00
SPSHV Martin Havlat	6.00	15.00
SPSHZ Henrik Zetterberg	10.00	25.00
SPSJB Jaromir Jagr SP	25.00	50.00
SPSJI Jarome Iginla	10.00	25.00
SPSJR Jeremy Roenick	8.00	20.00
SPSJS Jason Spezza	8.00	20.00
SPSJT Joe Thornton	10.00	25.00
SPSMG Marian Gaborik	10.00	25.00
SPSMH Marcel Hossa	6.00	15.00
SPSMT Marty Turco	6.00	15.00
SPSPB Pavel Bure	6.00	15.00
SPSPR Patrick Roy SP	60.00	120.00
SPSRB Ray Bourque	15.00	40.00
SPSRL Roberto Luongo	12.50	30.00
SPSRN Rick Nash	12.50	30.00
SPSSF Sergei Fedorov	12.50	30.00
SPSTB Todd Bertuzzi	6.00	15.00
SPSWG Wayne Gretzky SP	75.00	200.00
SSJSG Jean-Sebastien Giguere	6.00	15.00

2005-06 SP Game Used

This 240-card set was issued in both product-specific unopened and as inserts in Rookie Update. Cards numbered 1-190 were issued in three-card packs with an $29.99 SRP, which came six to a box and six boxes to a case. Cards numbered 1-100 are veterans while cards 101-240 are all Rookie Cards and all of those cards were issued to a stated print run of 999 serial numbered copies.

COMP.SET w/o SP's (100) 25.00 60.00
101-240 ROOKIE PRINT RUN 999
191-240 ISSUED IN ROOKIE UPDATE

Card	Low	High
1 Jean-Sebastien Giguere	1.00	2.50
2 Teemu Selanne	2.00	5.00
3 Scott Niedermayer	1.00	2.50
4 Ilya Kovalchuk	1.00	2.50
5 Kari Lehtonen	.75	2.00
6 Marian Hossa	.75	2.00
7 Peter Bondra	.75	2.00
8 Glen Murray	.75	2.00
9 Brian Leetch	1.00	2.50
10 Andrew Raycroft	.75	2.00
11 Patrice Bergeron	1.25	3.00
12 Chris Drury	.75	2.00
13 Martin Biron	.75	2.00
14 Maxim Afinogenov	.60	1.50
15 Jarome Iginla	1.00	2.50
16 Miikka Kiprusoff	.75	2.00
17 Tony Amonte	.75	2.00
18 Erik Cole	.75	2.00
19 Eric Staal	1.25	3.00
20 Nikolai Khabibulin	1.00	2.50
21 Tuomo Ruutu	1.00	2.50
22 Tyler Arnason	.60	1.50
23 Joe Sakic	1.50	4.00
24 Milan Hejduk	.75	2.00
25 Alex Tanguay	1.00	2.50
26 David Aebischer	.75	2.00
27 Rob Blake	1.00	2.50
28 Rick Nash	1.00	2.50
29 Nikolai Zherdev	.60	1.50
30 Sergei Fedorov	1.50	4.00
31 Mike Modano	1.50	4.00
32 Bill Guerin	1.00	2.50
33 Marty Turco	1.00	2.50
34 Brendan Shanahan	1.25	3.00
35 Steve Yzerman	2.50	6.00
36 Pavel Datsyuk	1.25	3.00
37 Henrik Zetterberg	1.25	3.00
38 Manny Legace	1.00	2.50
39 Ryan Smyth	.75	2.00
40 Chris Pronger	.75	2.00
41 Ty Conklin	.75	2.00
42 Stephen Weiss	.60	1.50
43 Joe Nieuwendyk	1.00	2.50
44 Roberto Luongo	1.50	4.00
45 Jeremy Roenick	1.00	2.50
46 Luc Robitaille	1.00	2.50
47 Pavol Demitra	1.25	3.00
48 Alexander Frolov	.60	1.50
49 Marian Gaborik	1.50	4.00
50 Dwayne Roloson	.75	2.00
51 Mike Ribeiro	.75	2.00
52 Jose Theodore	1.00	2.50
53 Michael Ryder	.75	2.00
54 Saku Koivu	1.00	2.50
55 Paul Kariya	1.25	3.00
56 Steve Sullivan	.60	1.50
57 Tomas Vokoun	.75	2.00
58 Martin Brodeur	2.00	5.00
59 Patrik Elias	1.00	2.50
60 Scott Gomez	.75	2.00
61 Alexander Mogilny	.75	2.00
62 Alexei Yashin	.75	2.00
63 Miroslav Satan	.75	2.00
64 Rick DiPietro	.75	2.00
65 Mark Parrish	.60	1.50
66 Kevin Weekes	.75	2.00
67 Jaromir Jagr	2.50	6.00
68 Dany Heatley	1.00	2.50
69 Dominik Hasek	1.50	4.00
70 Jason Spezza	1.00	2.50
71 Martin Havlat	1.00	2.50
72 Peter Forsberg	1.25	3.00
73 Keith Primeau	1.00	2.50
74 Simon Gagne	1.00	2.50
75 Robert Esche	.75	2.00
76 Shane Doan	.75	2.00
77 Curtis Joseph	1.00	2.50
78 John LeClair	1.00	2.50
79 Mario Lemieux	3.00	8.00
80 Zigmund Palffy	1.00	2.50
81 Joe Thornton	1.25	3.00
82 Jonathan Cheechoo	1.00	2.50
83 Evgeni Nabokov	.75	2.00
84 Patrick Marleau	1.00	2.50
85 Keith Tkachuk	1.00	2.50
86 Doug Weight	1.00	2.50
87 Martin St. Louis	1.00	2.50
88 Vincent Lecavalier	.75	2.00
89 Brad Richards	1.00	2.50
90 Sean Burke	.60	1.50
91 Mats Sundin	1.00	2.50
92 Ed Belfour	1.00	2.50
93 Eric Lindros	1.50	4.00
94 Jason Allison	.75	2.00
95 Nik Antropov	.75	2.00
96 Markus Naslund	1.00	2.50
97 Brendan Morrison	.60	1.50
98 Todd Bertuzzi	1.00	2.50
99 Olaf Kolzig	1.00	2.50
100 Brendan Witt	.60	1.50
101 Sidney Crosby RC	60.00	120.00
102 Brandon Bochenski RC	3.00	8.00
103 Rostislav Olesz RC	2.50	6.00
104 Jeff Hoggan RC	2.00	5.00
105 Brett Lebda RC	2.00	5.00
106 Brad Winchester RC	3.00	8.00
107 Wojtek Wolski RC	6.00	15.00
108 Patrick Eaves RC	3.00	8.00
109 Braydon Coburn RC	3.00	8.00
110 Yann Danis RC	2.50	6.00
111 Alexander Ovechkin RC	25.00	60.00
112 Peter Budaj RC	4.00	10.00
113 Jeff Carter RC	8.00	20.00
114 Duncan Keith RC	6.00	15.00
115 Mike Richards RC	8.00	20.00
116 Rene Bourque RC	3.00	8.00
117 Keith Ballard RC	2.50	6.00
118 Thomas Vanek RC	8.00	20.00
119 Robert Nilsson RC	3.00	8.00
120 Kevin Nastiuk RC	2.00	5.00
121 Jaroslav Balastik RC	2.00	5.00
122 Brent Seabrook RC	6.00	15.00
123 Maxime Talbot RC	3.00	8.00
124 Niklas Nordgren RC	3.00	8.00
125 David Leneveu RC	2.50	6.00
126 Eric Nystrom RC	2.50	6.00
127 Timo Helbling RC	2.00	5.00
128 George Parros RC	2.00	5.00
129 Lee Stempniak RC	3.00	8.00
130 Dion Phaneuf RC	10.00	25.00
131 Henrik Lundqvist RC	10.00	25.00
132 Cam Ward RC	5.00	12.00
133 Ryan Hollweg RC	2.00	5.00
134 Corey Perry RC	8.00	20.00
135 Matt Foy RC	2.00	5.00
136 Alexander Steen RC	6.00	15.00
137 Jim Slater RC	2.50	6.00
138 Ryan Suter RC	4.00	10.00
139 Gilbert Brule RC	3.00	8.00
140 Andrej Meszaros RC	2.50	6.00
141 Andrew Alberts RC	2.00	5.00
142 Zach Parise RC	8.00	20.00
143 Kevin Dallman RC	2.50	6.00
144 Chris Campoli RC	2.00	5.00
145 Johan Franzen RC	5.00	12.00
146 Jay McClement RC	2.00	5.00
147 Ryan Getzlaf RC	10.00	25.00
148 Alexander Perezhogin RC	2.50	6.00
149 Andrew Wozniewski RC	2.50	6.00
150 Jim Howard RC	8.00	20.00
151 Jeff Woywitka RC	2.00	5.00
152 Hannu Toivonen RC	3.00	8.00
153 Petteri Nokelainen RC	2.00	5.00

164 Jussi Jokinen RC 3.00 8.00
165 Ryane Clowe RC 4.00 10.00
166 Milan Jurcina RC 2.50 6.00
167 Mark Streit RC 2.00 5.00
168 Raitis Ivanans RC 2.00 5.00
169 Petr Prucha RC 3.00 8.00
170 Josh Gorges RC 2.50 6.00
171 Anthony Stewart RC 2.50 6.00
172 Alvaro Montoya RC 3.00 8.00
173 Paul Ranger RC 2.00 5.00
174 Chris Holt RC 2.00 5.00
175 Wade Skolney RC 2.00 5.00
176 Cam Barker RC 2.50 6.00
177 Adam Berkhoel RC 2.50 6.00
178 Kyle Brodziak RC 2.00 5.00
179 Brian McGrattan RC 2.00 5.00
170 Mikko Koivu RC 4.00 10.00
171 Derek Boogaard RC 4.00 10.00
172 Nick Tarnasky RC 2.00 5.00
173 Evgeny Artyukhin RC 2.50 6.00
174 Colin Hemingway RC 2.00 5.00
175 Michael Wall RC 2.50 6.00
176 Steve Goertzen RC 2.00 5.00
177 Junior Lessard RC 2.00 5.00
178 Vojtech Polak RC 2.00 5.00
179 Jakub Klepis RC 2.00 5.00
180 Jordan Sigalet RC 2.00 5.00
181 Steve Bernier RC 3.00 8.00
182 Dimitri Patzold RC 2.00 5.00
183 R.J. Umberger RC 3.00 8.00
184 Christoph Schubert RC 2.00 5.00
185 Staffan Kronwall RC 2.00 5.00
186 Ryan Whitney RC 3.00 8.00
187 Erik Christensen RC 2.00 5.00
188 Brian Eklund RC 2.50 6.00
189 Rob McVicar RC 2.50 6.00
190 Tomas Fleischmann RC 3.00 8.00
191 Zenon Konopka RC 2.00 5.00
192 Dustin Penner RC 3.00 8.00
193 Ben Walter RC 2.00 5.00
194 Daniel Paille RC 3.00 8.00
195 Chris Thorburn RC 2.50 6.00
196 Richie Regehr RC 2.00 5.00
197 Andrew Ladd RC 4.00 10.00
198 Chad Larose RC 2.00 5.00
199 Danny Richmond RC 2.00 5.00
200 Martin St. Pierre RC 2.00 5.00
201 Corey Crawford RC 10.00 25.00
202 Brad Richardson RC 3.00 8.00
203 Vitaly Kolesnik RC 2.50 6.00
204 Alexandre Picard RC 2.00 5.00
205 Ole-Kristian Tollefsen RC 2.50 6.00
206 Joakim Lindstrom RC 2.00 5.00
207 Kyle Quincey RC 2.50 6.00
208 Valtteri Filppula RC 4.00 10.00
209 Danny Syvret RC 2.00 5.00
210 Matt Greene RC 2.00 5.00
211 J-F Jacques RC 2.00 5.00
212 Greg Jacina RC 2.00 5.00
213 Rob Globke RC 2.00 5.00
214 Yanick Lehoux RC 3.00 8.00
215 Jeff Tambellini RC 2.00 5.00
216 Petr Kanko RC 2.50 6.00
217 Maxim Lapierre RC 3.00 8.00
218 J-P Cote RC 2.00 5.00
219 Andrei Kostitsyn RC 4.00 10.00
220 Kevin Klein RC 2.00 5.00
221 Pekka Rinne RC 8.00 20.00
222 Barry Tallackson RC 2.50 6.00
223 Jason Ryznar RC 2.00 5.00
224 Jeremy Colliton RC 2.00 5.00
225 Bruno Gervais RC 2.00 5.00
226 Stefan Ruzicka RC 2.00 5.00
227 Ben Eager RC 2.50 6.00
228 Alexandre Picard RC 2.00 5.00
229 Matt Jones RC 2.00 5.00
230 Colby Armstrong RC 3.00 8.00
231 Doug Murray RC 2.00 5.00
232 Grant Stevenson RC 2.00 5.00
233 Dennis Wideman RC 2.00 5.00
234 Doug O'Brien RC 2.00 5.00
235 Darren Reid RC 2.00 5.00
236 Ryan Craig RC 2.00 5.00
237 Jay Harrison RC 2.50 6.00
238 Tomas Mojzis RC 2.00 5.00
239 Kevin Bieksa RC 4.00 10.00
240 Mike Green RC 4.00 10.00

2005-06 SP Game Used Gold

*1-100 VETS/100: 1X TO 2.5X BASIC CARDS
1-100 PRINT RUN 100 SER.#'d SETS
*101-190 ROOK/25: 1.2X TO 3X BASIC RC
101-190 ROOKIE PRINT RUN 25
101 Sidney Crosby 200.00 350.00
111 Alexander Ovechkin 125.00 250.00

2005-06 SP Game Used Authentic Fabrics

OVERALL MEMORABILIA ODDS 1:1
AFAE David Aebischer 3.00 8.00
AFAF Alexander Frolov 2.50 6.00
AFAR Andrew Raycroft 3.00 8.00
AFAT Alex Tanguay 4.00 10.00
AFAY Alexei Yashin 3.00 8.00
AFBE Daniel Briere 4.00 10.00
AFBG Bill Guerin 4.00 10.00
AFBL Rob Blake 4.00 10.00
AFBM Brendan Morrison 2.50 6.00
AFBO Mike Bossy 4.00 10.00
AFBR Martin Brodeur 8.00 20.00
AFBS Brendan Shanahan 5.00 12.00
AFCD Chris Drury 3.00 8.00
AFCJ Curtis Joseph 4.00 10.00
AFCN Cam Neely 5.00 12.00
AFCP Chris Pronger 3.00 8.00
AFDA Daniel Alfredsson 4.00 10.00
AFDB Dustin Brown 4.00 10.00
AFDC Dan Cloutier 3.00 8.00
AFDE Pavol Demitra 5.00 12.00
AFDH Dany Heatley 4.00 10.00
AFDW Doug Weight 4.00 10.00
AFEB Ed Belfour 4.00 10.00
AFGM Glen Murray 3.00 8.00
AFGO Scott Gomez 3.00 8.00
AFHA Dominik Hasek 6.00 15.00
AFHJ Milan Hejduk 3.00 8.00
AFHO Marian Hossa 3.00 8.00
AFHU Trent Hunter 2.50 6.00
AFHV Martin Havlat 4.00 10.00
AFHZ Henrik Zetterberg 5.00 12.00
AFIK Ilya Kovalchuk 4.00 10.00
AFJB Jay Bouwmeester 4.00 10.00
AFJC Jonathan Cheechoo 4.00 10.00
AFJF Jeff Friesen 2.50 6.00
AFJG Jean-Sebastien Giguere 4.00 10.00
AFJI Jarome Iginla 4.00 10.00
AFJJ Jaromir Jagr 10.00 25.00
AFJH Jeremy Roenick 4.00 10.00
AFJS Joe Sakic 6.00 15.00
AFJT Joe Thornton 5.00 12.00
AFKD Kris Draper 5.00 12.00
AFKL Kari Lehtonen 3.00 8.00
AFKP Keith Primeau 4.00 10.00
AFKT Keith Tkachuk 4.00 10.00
AFLE Manny Legace 4.00 10.00
AFMB Martin Biron 3.00 8.00
AFMD Marcel Dionne SP 6.00 15.00
AFMG Marian Gaborik 6.00 15.00
AFMI Mike Ribeiro 3.00 8.00
AFML Mario Lemieux 10.00 25.00
AFMM Mike Modano 6.00 15.00
AFMN Markus Naslund 4.00 10.00
AFMP Mark Parrish 2.50 6.00
AFMR Mark Recchi 5.00 12.00
AFMT Marty Turco 4.00 10.00
AFMW Brenden Morrow 3.00 8.00
AFNH Nathan Horton 4.00 10.00
AFNK Nikolai Khabibulin 4.00 10.00
AFNL Nicklas Lidstrom 4.00 10.00
AFNZ Nikolai Zherdev 2.50 6.00
AFOK Olaf Kolzig 4.00 10.00
AFPB Patrice Bergeron 5.00 12.00
AFPD Pavel Datsyuk 5.00 12.00
AFPE Patrik Elias 4.00 10.00
AFPF Peter Forsberg 5.00 12.00
AFPK Paul Kariya 5.00 12.00
AFPM Patrick Marleau 4.00 10.00
AFPR Patrick Roy 10.00 25.00
AFRB Ray Bourque 6.00 15.00
AFRD Rick DiPietro 3.00 8.00
AFRE Robert Esche 3.00 8.00
AFRI Brad Richards 4.00 10.00
AFRL Roberto Luongo 6.00 15.00
AFRN Rick Nash 4.00 10.00
AFRS Ryan Smyth 3.00 8.00
AFRY Michael Ryder 3.00 8.00
AFSA Miroslav Satan 3.00 8.00
AFSD Shane Doan 3.00 8.00
AFSF Sergei Fedorov 6.00 15.00
AFSG Simon Gagne 4.00 10.00
AFSK Saku Koivu 4.00 10.00
AFSP Jason Spezza 6.00 15.00
AFST Matt Stajan 3.00 8.00
AFSU Mats Sundin 4.00 10.00
AFSW Stephen Weiss 2.50 6.00
AFSY Steve Yzerman 8.00 20.00
AFTB Todd Bertuzzi 4.00 10.00
AFTC Ty Conklin 3.00 8.00
AFTH Jose Theodore 4.00 10.00
AFTP Tom Poti 2.50 6.00
AFTR Tuomo Ruutu 4.00 10.00
AFTV Tomas Vokoun 3.00 8.00
AFVL Vincent Lecavalier 3.00 8.00
AFZC Zdeno Chara 4.00 10.00
AFZP Zigmund Palffy 4.00 10.00

2005-06 SP Game Used Authentic Fabrics Autographs

STATED PRINT RUN 75 SER.#'d SETS
AAFAE David Aebischer 10.00 25.00
AAFAF Alexander Frolov 8.00 20.00
AAFAR Andrew Raycroft 10.00 25.00
AAFAT Alex Tanguay 12.00 30.00
AAFAY Alexei Yashin 10.00 25.00
AAFBE Daniel Briere 12.00 30.00
AAFBL Rob Blake 12.00 30.00
AAFBM Brendan Morrison 8.00 20.00
AAFBO Mike Bossy 15.00 40.00
AAFCD Chris Drury 10.00 25.00
AAFCN Cam Neely 25.00 50.00
AAFCP Chris Pronger 12.00 30.00
AAFDA Daniel Alfredsson 15.00 40.00
AAFDB Dustin Brown 12.00 30.00
AAFDC Dan Cloutier 10.00 25.00
AAFDH Dany Heatley 12.00 30.00
AAFDW Doug Weight 12.00 30.00
AAFGM Glen Murray 10.00 25.00
AAFHA Dominik Hasek 20.00 50.00
AAFHJ Milan Hejduk 10.00 25.00
AAFHO Marian Hossa 10.00 25.00
AAFHU Trent Hunter 8.00 20.00
AAFHV Martin Havlat 12.00 30.00
AAFHZ Henrik Zetterberg 15.00 40.00
AAFIK Ilya Kovalchuk 12.00 30.00
AAFJB Jay Bouwmeester 12.00 30.00
AAFJC Jonathan Cheechoo 15.00 40.00
AAFJG Jean-Sebastien Giguere 12.00 30.00
AAFJI Jarome Iginla 12.00 30.00
AAFJR Jeremy Roenick 15.00 40.00
AAFJT Joe Thornton 15.00 40.00
AAFKD Kris Draper 15.00 40.00
AAFKL Kari Lehtonen 10.00 25.00
AAFKP Keith Primeau 10.00 25.00
AAFLE Manny Legace 12.00 30.00
AAFMB Martin Biron 10.00 25.00
AAFMD Marcel Dionne 12.00 30.00
AAFMI Mike Ribeiro 10.00 25.00
AAFMN Markus Naslund 12.00 30.00
AAFMP Mark Parrish 8.00 20.00
AAFMS Martin St. Louis 8.00 20.00
AAFMT Marty Turco 12.00 30.00
AAFMW Brenden Morrow 10.00 25.00
AAFNH Nathan Horton 12.00 30.00
AAFNZ Nikolai Zherdev 8.00 20.00
AAFOK Olaf Kolzig 12.00 30.00
AAFPB Patrice Bergeron 15.00 40.00
AAFRE Robert Esche 10.00 25.00
AAFRI Brad Richards 12.00 30.00
AAFRL Roberto Luongo 15.00 40.00
AAFRN Rick Nash 15.00 40.00
AAFRS Ryan Smyth 10.00 25.00
AAFRY Michael Ryder 10.00 25.00
AAFSA Miroslav Satan 10.00 25.00
AAFSD Shane Doan 10.00 25.00
AAFSG Simon Gagne 12.00 30.00
AAFSP Jason Spezza 15.00 40.00
AAFST Matt Stajan 10.00 25.00
AAFSW Stephen Weiss 8.00 20.00
AAFTB Todd Bertuzzi 12.00 30.00
AAFTC Ty Conklin 10.00 25.00
AAFTH Jose Theodore 12.00 30.00
AAFTP Tom Poti 8.00 20.00
AAFTR Tuomo Ruutu 12.00 30.00
AAFVL Vincent Lecavalier 15.00 40.00
AAFWG Wayne Gretzky 150.00 250.00
AAFZC Zdeno Chara 12.00 30.00

2005-06 SP Game Used Authentic Fabrics Dual

STATED PRINT RUN 100 SER.#'d SETS
AH D.Alfredsson/D.Heatley 6.00 15.00
BB M.Biron/D.Briere 6.00 15.00
BF D.Brown/A.Frolov 6.00 15.00
BM E.Belfour/B.McCabe 6.00 15.00
BN M.Biron/M.Noronen 5.00 12.00
CO P.Roy/R.Bourque 15.00 40.00
DH S.Doan/B.Hull 8.00 20.00
DJ D.Heatley/J.Spezza 6.00 15.00
EB P.Elias/M.Brodeur 12.00 30.00
ER R.Esche/P.Forsberg 8.00 20.00
GH W.Gretzky/G.Howe 25.00 60.00
GK W.Gretzky/J.Kurri 30.00 80.00
GS J.Giguere/T.Selanne 12.00 30.00
HH D.Hasek/M.Havlat 10.00 25.00
HK M.Hossa/I.Kovalchuk 6.00 15.00
HL A.Hall/D.Legwand 5.00 12.00
HS T.Hunter/M.Satan 5.00 12.00
IK J.Iginla/M.Kiprusoff 6.00 15.00
IS J.Iginla/M.St.Louis 6.00 15.00
KK N.Khabibulin/M.Kiprusoff 6.00 15.00
KT S.Koivu/J.Theodore 6.00 15.00
KV P.Kariya/T.Vokoun 8.00 20.00
LN K.Lehtonen/M.Noronen 5.00 12.00
LS V.Lecavalier/M.St. Louis 6.00 15.00
MC P.Marleau/J.Cheechoo 6.00 15.00
MO M.Sundin/O.Nolan 6.00 15.00
MT M.Naslund/T.Bertuzzi 6.00 15.00
NB C.Neely/R.Bourque 10.00 25.00
NT R.Nash/J.Thornton 10.00 25.00
NY B.Trottier/M.Bossy 8.00 20.00
PB J.Thornton/P.Bergeron 8.00 20.00
PC C.Pronger/T.Conklin 5.00 12.00
PE J.Pitkanen/R.Esche 5.00 12.00
PG K.Primeau/S.Gagne 6.00 15.00
RA R.Torres/A.Hemsky 5.00 12.00
RB M.Ribeiro/P.Bergeron 8.00 20.00
RF D.Roloson/M.Fernandez 5.00 12.00
RR M.Ryder/M.Ribeiro 5.00 12.00
SA J.Spezza/D.Alfredsson 6.00 15.00
SB J.Sakic/R.Blake 10.00 25.00
SC R.Smyth/T.Conklin 5.00 12.00
SP D.Sittler/G.Perreault 6.00 15.00
SR P.Sauve/A.Raycroft 5.00 12.00
SS M.Stajan/E.Staal 8.00 20.00
TH A.Tanguay/M.Hejduk 6.00 15.00
TM M.Turco/M.Modano 10.00 25.00
WB P.Worrell/D.Brashear 4.00 10.00
WH S.Weiss/N.Horton 6.00 15.00
WT D.Weight/K.Tkachuk 6.00 15.00
YS S.Yzerman/B.Shanahan 15.00 40.00
ZD H.Zetterberg/K.Draper 8.00 20.00

2005-06 SP Game Used Authentic Fabrics Dual Autographs

STATED PRINT RUN 25 SER.#'d SETS
AH D.Alfredsson/D.Heatley
BB M.Biron/D.Briere 20.00 50.00
CO P.Roy/R.Bourque 125.00 200.00
DJ D.Heatley/J.Spezza 40.00 100.00
DT M.Dionne/B.Trottier 20.00 50.00
GH W.Gretzky/G.Howe 300.00 500.00
HH D.Hasek/M.Havlat 30.00 80.00
HK M.Hossa/I.Kovalchuk 25.00 60.00
HS T.Hunter/M.Satan 15.00 40.00
IS J.Iginla/M.St.Louis 20.00 50.00
KT S.Koivu/J.Theodore 30.00 80.00
LD G.Lafleur/M.Dionne 60.00 125.00
LN K.Lehtonen/M.Noronen 20.00 50.00
LS V.Lecavalier/M.St. Louis 40.00 100.00
MO M.Sundin/O.Nolan 30.00 80.00
MT M.Naslund/T.Bertuzzi 20.00 50.00
NB C.Neely/R.Bourque 75.00 150.00
NT R.Nash/J.Thornton 50.00 125.00
PB J.Thornton/P.Bergeron 25.00 60.00
PC C.Pronger/T.Conklin 20.00 50.00
PE J.Pitkanen/R.Esche 15.00 40.00
PG K.Primeau/S.Gagne 15.00 40.00
RB M.Ribeiro/P.Bergeron 15.00 40.00
RR M.Ryder/M.Ribeiro 15.00 40.00
SA J.Spezza/D.Alfredsson
SR P.Sauve/A.Raycroft 15.00 40.00
SS M.Stajan/E.Staal 25.00 60.00
TH A.Tanguay/M.Hejduk 25.00 60.00
TM M.Turco/M.Modano 20.00 50.00
WH S.Weiss/N.Horton 15.00 40.00

2005-06 SP Game Used Authentic Fabrics Gold

*GOLD/100: .8X TO 2X BASIC JSY
GOLD STATED PRINT RUN 100
AFMD Marcel Dionne 8.00 20.00
AFWG Wayne Gretzky 40.00 100.00

2005-06 SP Game Used Authentic Fabrics Triple

STATED PRINT RUN 25 SER.#'d SETS
ARS Alfredsson/Richards/St.Louis 40.00 80.00
BBP Bourque/Blake/Pronger 20.00 50.00
BBT Broduer/Belfour/Turco 30.00 80.00
BIS Brodeur/Iginla/St.Louis 60.00 125.00
BTR Brodeur/Theodore/Roy 75.00 150.00
CEA Conklin/Esche/Aebischer 20.00 50.00
CNP Chara/Niedermeyar/Pronger 30.00 60.00
CRH Chara/Redden/Hasek 30.00 60.00
DBS Domi/Brashear/Simon 20.00 50.00
DKF Datsyuk/Kovalchuk/Fedorov 40.00 100.00
DLP Draper/Lehtinen/Peca 30.00 60.00
GLY Gretzky/Lemieux/Yzerman 175.00 300.00
GNP Gonchar/Niedermayer/Pronger 20.00 50.00
HJH Hasek/Jagr/Havlat 50.00 100.00
HND Hull/Nagy/Doan 20.00 50.00
INK Iginla/Nash/Kovalchuk 40.00 80.00
ISL Iginla/Shanahan/Linden 40.00 80.00
KNS Kovalchuk/Naslund/Stillman 20.00 50.00
KRT Kiprusoff/Roloson/Turco 40.00 80.00
KSK Kurri/Selanne/Koivu 60.00 125.00
MLR Modano/Linden/Roenick 30.00 80.00
NKL Noronen/Kiprusoff/Lehtonen 40.00 80.00
NPJ Nolan/Primeau/Jagr 30.00 60.00
NSL Nolan/Sundin/Lindros 25.00 60.00
PCS Pronger/Conklin/Smyth 20.00 50.00
RLA Raycroft/Lehtonen/Aebischer 30.00 80.00
SEL Sakic/Elias/Lang 25.00 60.00
SFI St.Louis/Forsberg/Iginla 30.00 60.00
SFN Sundin/Forsberg/Naslund 25.00 60.00
SHA St. Louis/Hossa/Alfredsson 20.00 50.00
SNI St.Louis/Naslund/Iginla 40.00 80.00
TBM Thornton/Bergeron/Murray 30.00 60.00
TSY Thornton/Sakic/Yzerman 50.00 100.00
VKL Vokoun/Kariya/Legwand 20.00 50.00
YSP Yashin/Satan/Parrish 30.00 60.00

2005-06 SP Game Used Authentic Fabrics Patches

*PATCH/75: 1.2X TO 3X BASIC JSY
STATED PRINT RUN 75 SER.#'d SETS
APMD Marcel Dionne 12.00 30.00
APWG Wayne Gretzky 50.00 120.00

2005-06 SP Game Used Authentic Fabrics Autographs Patch

*PATCH/50: .6X TO 1.5X FABRIC AU/75
STATED PRINT RUN 50 SER.#'d SETS
AAPWG Wayne Gretzky 150.00 300.00

2005-06 SP Game Used Authentic Fabrics Dual Patches

*DUAL PATCH/35: .8X TO 2X DUAL JSY
PRINT RUN 35 SER.#'d SETS
GH W.Gretzky/G.Howe 150.00 300.00
GK W.Gretzky/J.Kurri 100.00 250.00
GL W.Gretzky/M.Lemieux 150.00 300.00
LD Guy Lafleur/Marcel Dionne 20.00 50.00

2005-06 SP Game Used Auto Draft

STATED PRINT RUN 1-241
ADAF Alexander Frolov/20 12.00 30.00
ADAL Daniel Alfredsson/133 8.00 20.00
ADAM Alvaro Montoya/29 25.00 60.00
ADAP A. Perezhogin/25 15.00 40.00
ADAS Alexander Steen/24 30.00 60.00
ADBR Brad Richards/64 10.00 25.00
ADBU Peter Budaj/63 15.00 40.00
ADBW Brad Winchester/35 12.00 30.00
ADBY Matthew Barnaby/83 6.00 15.00
ADCA Michael Cammalleri/49 12.00 30.00
ADCC Craig Conroy/123 5.00 12.00
ADCD Chris Drury/72 8.00 20.00
ADCP Corey Perry/28 25.00 60.00
ADCW Cam Ward/25 30.00 75.00
ADDA David Aebischer/161 6.00 15.00
ADDB Daniel Briere/24 15.00 40.00
ADDC Dan Cloutier/26 12.00 30.00
ADDF Dan Fritsche/46 8.00 20.00
ADDK Duncan Keith/54 25.00 50.00
ADDL David Leneveu/46 10.00 25.00
ADDM Darren McCarty/46 8.00 20.00
ADEC Erik Cole/71 8.00 20.00
ADED Eric Daze/90 8.00 20.00
ADFT Fedor Tyutin/40 8.00 20.00
ADGL Georges Laraque/31 15.00 40.00
ADHE Jochen Hecht/49 8.00 20.00
ADHT Hannu Toivonen/29 20.00 50.00
ADHV Martin Havlat/26 25.00 60.00
ADJC Jonathan Cheechoo/29 25.00 60.00
ADJF Johan Franzen/97 15.00 40.00
ADJH Jim Howard/64 15.00 40.00
ADJJ Jussi Jokinen/192 8.00 20.00
ADJK Jari Kurri/69 15.00 40.00
ADJS Jim Slater/30 10.00 25.00
ADJT Jose Theodore/44 15.00 40.00
ADJV Josef Vasicek/91 6.00 15.00
ADJW Justin Williams/28 12.00 30.00
ADKD Kris Draper/62 12.00 30.00
ADKH Kristian Huselius/47 8.00 20.00
ADKW Kevin Weekes/41 10.00 25.00
ADLR Luc Robitaille/171 50.00 100.00
ADMA Maxim Afinogenov/69 6.00 15.00
ADMB Martin Brodeur/20 60.00 150.00
ADMC Jay McClement/57 6.00 15.00
ADMF Matt Foy/175 5.00 12.00
ADMH Milan Hejduk/87 8.00 20.00
ADMI Milan Bartovic/35 8.00 20.00
ADMJ Milan Jurcina/241 6.00 15.00
ADMN Markus Naslund/16 15.00 40.00
ADMR Mike Ribeiro/45 10.00 25.00
ADMS Matt Stajan/57 8.00 20.00
ADMW Brenden Morrow/25 12.00 30.00
ADNK Nikolai Khabibulin/204 8.00 20.00
ADNO Mika Noronen/21
ADNY Michael Nylander/59 6.00 15.00
ADPB Patrice Bergeron/45 30.00 60.00
ADPE Patrick Eaves/29 15.00 40.00
ADPR Patrick Roy/51 75.00 150.00
ADPS Philippe Sauve/38 10.00 25.00
ADRB Rob Blake/70 10.00 25.00
ADRC Mark Recchi/67
ADRE Robert Esche/139 6.00 15.00
ADRG Ryan Getzlaf/19 60.00 150.00
ADRI Mike Richards/24 50.00 100.00
ADRK Ryan Kesler/23 20.00 50.00
ADSB Sean Burke/24 10.00 25.00
ADSG Simon Gagne/22 30.00 60.00
ADSH Sheldon Souray/71 6.00 15.00
ADSK Saku Koivu/21 30.00 60.00
ADSS Steve Sullivan/233 5.00 12.00
ADSV Marc Savard/91 6.00 15.00
ADSZ Sergei Zubov/85 8.00 20.00
ADTA Tyler Arnason/183 5.00 12.00
ADTB Todd Bertuzzi/23 15.00 40.00
ADTG Tim Gleason/23 10.00 25.00
ADTH Trent Hunter/150 5.00 12.00
ADTP Tom Poti/59 6.00 15.00
ADTS Timofei Shishkanov/33 8.00 20.00
ADVP Vaclav Prospal/71 6.00 15.00
ADZC Zdeno Chara/56 10.00 25.00

2005-06 SP Game Used Awesome Authentics

STATED PRINT RUN 75-100
*GOLD/25: .6X TO 1.5X BASIC JSY/75-100
AAAF Alexander Frolov
AAAH Ales Hemsky 10.00 25.00
AAAR Andrew Raycroft 10.00 25.00
AAAT Alex Tanguay 12.00 30.00
AAAY Alexei Yashin 10.00 25.00
AABG Bill Guerin 12.00 30.00
AABI Martin Biron 10.00 25.00
AABM Bryan McCabe 8.00 20.00
AABR Brad Richards 12.00 30.00
AABS Brendan Shanahan 15.00 40.00
AACD Chris Drury 10.00 25.00
AACJ Curtis Joseph 12.00 30.00
AACP Chris Pronger 10.00 25.00
AADA Daniel Alfredsson 12.00 30.00
AADB Daniel Briere 12.00 30.00
AADC Dan Cloutier 10.00 25.00
AADH Dany Heatley 10.00 25.00
AADL David Legwand 10.00 25.00
AADU Dustin Brown 12.00 30.00
AADW Doug Weight 12.00 30.00
AAEB Ed Belfour 12.00 30.00
AAEL Eric Lindros 20.00 50.00
AAES Eric Staal 15.00 40.00
AAGM Glen Murray 10.00 25.00
AAHJ Milan Hejduk 10.00 25.00
AAHK Dominik Hasek/75 15.00 40.00
AAHV Martin Havlat 12.00 30.00
AAHZ Henrik Zetterberg 15.00 40.00
AAIK Ilya Kovalchuk 10.00 25.00
AAJB Jay Bouwmeester 12.00 30.00
AAJG Jean-Sebastien Giguere 12.00 30.00
AAJI Jarome Iginla 10.00 25.00
AAJJ Jaromir Jagr 15.00 40.00
AAJL John LeClair 12.00 30.00
AAJO Joe Thornton 12.00 30.00
AAJR Jeremy Roenick 10.00 25.00
AAJS Jason Spezza 10.00 25.00
AAJT Jocelyn Thibault 10.00 25.00
AAJW Justin Williams 10.00 25.00
AAKP Keith Primeau 12.00 30.00
AAKT Keith Tkachuk 12.00 30.00
AALN Ladislav Nagy 8.00 20.00
AALU Joffrey Lupul 10.00 25.00
AALX Mario Lemieux 25.00 60.00
AAMB Martin Brodeur 25.00 60.00
AAMF Manny Fernandez 10.00 25.00
AAMG Marian Gaborik 12.00 30.00
AAMK Miikka Kiprusoff 10.00 25.00
AAML Manny Legace 12.00 30.00
AAMM Mike Modano 10.00 25.00
AAMN Markus Naslund 12.00 30.00
AAMO Brendan Morrison 8.00 20.00
AAMP Mark Parrish 8.00 20.00
AAMS Matt Stajan 10.00 25.00
AAMT Marty Turco 12.00 30.00
AAMW Brenden Morrow 10.00 25.00
AANH Nathan Horton 12.00 30.00
AANK Nikolai Khabibulin 12.00 30.00
AANL Nicklas Lidstrom 12.00 30.00
AANZ Nikolai Zherdev 8.00 20.00
AAOK Olaf Kolzig 12.00 30.00
AAPB Patrice Bergeron 15.00 40.00
AAPE Patrik Elias 12.00 30.00
AAPF Peter Forsberg 12.00 30.00
AAPK Paul Kariya 15.00 40.00
AARA Brian Rafalski 10.00 25.00
AARB Rob Blake 12.00 30.00
AARD Rick DiPietro 10.00 25.00
AARE Mark Recchi 15.00 40.00
AARF Ruslan Fedotenko 8.00 20.00
AARL Roberto Luongo 12.00 30.00
AARN Rick Nash 10.00 25.00
AARO Robert Esche 10.00 25.00
AARS Ryan Smyth 10.00 25.00
AARY Michael Ryder 10.00 25.00
AARZ Richard Zednik 8.00 20.00
AASA Joe Sakic 12.00 30.00
AASD Shane Doan 10.00 25.00
AASF Sergei Fedorov/75 20.00 50.00
AASG Simon Gagne 12.00 30.00
AASK Saku Koivu 12.00 30.00
AASL Martin St. Louis 12.00 30.00
AASU Mats Sundin 12.00 30.00
AASY Steve Yzerman 25.00 60.00
AATC Ty Conklin 10.00 25.00
AATH Jose Theodore 10.00 25.00
AATR Tuomo Ruutu 12.00 30.00
AATS Teemu Selanne 25.00 60.00
AATV Tomas Vokoun 10.00 25.00
AAVL Vincent Lecavalier 10.00 25.00
AAWR Wade Redden 8.00 20.00
AAZP Zigmund Palffy 12.00 30.00

2005-06 SP Game Used Game Gear

STATED PRINT RUN 45-100
GGAF Maxim Afinogenov 5.00 12.00
GGAK Alexei Kovalev 6.00 15.00
GGAM Alexander Mogilny 6.00 15.00
GGAO Alexander Ovechkin 30.00 80.00
GGAP Alexander Perezhogin 6.00 15.00
GGAR Andrew Raycroft 6.00 15.00
GGAS Alexander Steen 15.00 40.00
GGAT Alex Tanguay/45 10.00 25.00
GGBA Rod Brind'Amour 8.00 20.00
GGBE Patrice Bergeron 10.00 25.00
GGBG Bill Guerin 8.00 20.00
GGBL Rob Blake 8.00 20.00
GGBO Ray Bourque 12.00 30.00
GGBR Martin Brodeur 12.00 30.00
GGBS Billy Smith 5.00 12.00
GGBT Bryan Trottier 5.00 12.00
GGCB Cam Barker 6.00 15.00
GGCD Chris Drury 6.00 15.00
GGCE Christian Ehrhoff 5.00 12.00
GGCH Jonathan Cheechoo 8.00 20.00
GGCN Cam Neely 8.00 20.00
GGCP Chris Pronger 6.00 15.00
GGDB Daniel Briere 8.00 20.00
GGDH Dany Heatley 8.00 20.00
GGDL David Legwand 6.00 15.00
GGDP Dion Phaneuf 12.00 30.00
GGEN Eric Nystrom 6.00 15.00
GGES Eric Staal 10.00 25.00
GGGB Gilbert Brule 8.00 20.00
GGGL Guy Lafleur 10.00 25.00
GGHA Dominik Hasek 12.00 30.00
GGHL Henrik Lundqvist 12.00 30.00
GGHT Hannu Toivonen 6.00 15.00
GGHZ Henrik Zetterberg 10.00 25.00
GGIK Ilya Kovalchuk 8.00 20.00
GGJB Jean Beliveau 10.00 25.00
GGJC Jeff Carter 8.00 20.00
GGJF Jeff Friesen 5.00 12.00
GGJG Jean-Sebastien Giguere 8.00 20.00
GGJH Jim Howard 8.00 20.00
GGJI Jarome Iginla 8.00 20.00
GGJJ Jaromir Jagr 20.00 50.00
GGJO Joe Thornton 10.00 25.00
GGJP Joni Pitkanen 5.00 12.00
GGJR Jeremy Roenick 8.00 20.00
GGJS Jason Spezza 8.00 20.00
GGKP Keith Primeau 8.00 20.00
GGKT Keith Tkachuk 8.00 20.00
GGMA Paul Martin 5.00 12.00
GGMB Mike Bossy 8.00 20.00
GGML Mario Lemieux 12.00 30.00
GGMM Mike Modano 12.00 30.00
GGMR Mike Ribeiro 6.00 15.00
GGMT Marty Turco 8.00 20.00
GGOK Olaf Kolzig 8.00 20.00
GGOR Brooks Orpik 6.00 15.00
GGPB Peter Bondra 6.00 15.00
GGPE Corey Perry 6.00 15.00
GGPF Peter Forsberg 10.00 25.00
GGPK Paul Kariya 10.00 25.00
GGPM Pierre-Marc Bouchard 8.00 20.00
GGPS Philippe Sauve 6.00 15.00
GGRB Ray Bourque 12.00 30.00
GGRF Ruslan Fedotenko 5.00 12.00
GGRG Ryan Getzlaf 10.00 25.00
GGRI Mike Richards 6.00 15.00
GGRK Rostislav Klesla 5.00 12.00
GGRM Ryan Malone 5.00 12.00
GGRN Rick Nash 8.00 20.00
GGRT Raffi Torres 5.00 12.00
GGRY Michael Ryder 6.00 15.00
GGSA Joe Sakic 12.00 30.00
GGSC Sidney Crosby 50.00 125.00
GGSG Simon Gagne 8.00 20.00
GGSH Brendan Shanahan 10.00 25.00
GGSK Saku Koivu 8.00 20.00
GGST Anthony Stewart 6.00 15.00
GGSU Mats Sundin 8.00 20.00
GGSY Steve Yzerman 15.00 40.00
GGTH Trent Hunter 5.00 12.00
GGTV Thomas Vanek 8.00 20.00
GGWW Wojtek Wolski 8.00 20.00
GGYD Yann Danis 6.00 15.00
GGZP Zach Parise 10.00 25.00
GGBH2 Bobby Hull 12.00 30.00
GGGH1 Gordie Howe 12.00 30.00
GGGH2 Gordie Howe 12.00 30.00
GGPR1 Patrick Roy 15.00 40.00
GGPR2 Patrick Roy 20.00 50.00

2005-06 SP Game Used Heritage Classic Jerseys

STATED PRINT RUN 100 SER.#'d SETS
*PATCH/25: .8X TO 2X BASIC JSY/100
HCBR Bill Ranford 8.00 20.00
HCBS Borje Salming 8.00 20.00
HCDG Doug Gilmour 10.00 25.00
HCDS Darryl Sittler 6.00 15.00
HCDW Tiger Williams 6.00 15.00
HCGF Grant Fuhr 8.00 20.00
HCKM Kirk Muller 5.00 12.00
HCLM Larry Murphy 6.00 15.00
HCMC Lanny McDonald 8.00 20.00
HCMK Mike Krushelnyski 5.00 12.00
HCPS Peter Stastny 8.00 20.00
HCRB Ray Bourque 10.00 20.00
HCRE Ron Ellis 5.00 12.00
HCRL Rod Langway 6.00 15.00
HCRV Rick Vaive 5.00 12.00
HCSS Steve Shutt 8.00 20.00
HCWC Wendel Clark 8.00 20.00

2005-06 SP Game Used Heritage Classic Jerseys Autographs

STATED PRINT RUN 100 SER.#'d SETS
HCABR Bill Ranford 12.00 30.00
HCABS Borje Salming 12.00 30.00
HCADG Doug Gilmour 20.00 50.00
HCADS Darryl Sittler 15.00 40.00
HCADW Tiger Williams 10.00 25.00
HCAGF Grant Fuhr 15.00 40.00
HCAKM Kirk Muller 8.00 20.00
HCALM Larry Murphy 10.00 25.00
HCAMC Lanny McDonald 15.00 40.00
HCAMK Mike Krushelnyski 8.00 20.00
HCAPS Peter Stastny 10.00 25.00
HCARB Ray Bourque 20.00 50.00
HCARE Ron Ellis 10.00 25.00
HCARL Rod Langway 10.00 25.00
HCARV Rick Vaive 10.00 25.00
HCASS Steve Shutt 10.00 25.00
HCAWC Wendel Clark 20.00 50.00

2005-06 SP Game Used Oldtimer's Challenge Jerseys

STATED PRINT RUN 100 SER.#'d SETS
*PATCH/25: .8X TO 2X BASIC JSY/100
OCBB Bob Bourne 4.00 10.00
OCBO Ray Bourque 10.00 25.00
OCBP Bob Probert 5.00 12.00
OCDB Doug Bodger 4.00 10.00
OCDG Doug Gilmour 10.00 25.00
OCDS Darryl Sittler 6.00 15.00
OCDW Tiger Williams 4.00 10.00
OCGA Glenn Anderson 4.00 10.00
OCGF Grant Fuhr 6.00 15.00
OCGL Guy Lafleur 5.00 12.00
OCGP Gilbert Perreault 4.00 10.00
OCKM Kirk Muller 4.00 10.00
OCMC Lanny McDonald 6.00 15.00
OCRB Richard Brodeur 4.00 10.00
OCSS Steve Shutt 4.00 10.00

2005-06 SP Game Used Oldtimer's Challenge Jerseys Autographs

STATED PRINT RUN 100 SER.#'d SETS
OCABB Bob Bourne 10.00 25.00
OCABO Ray Bourque 20.00 50.00
OCABP Bob Probert 12.00 30.00
OCADB Doug Bodger 10.00 25.00
OCADG Doug Gilmour 20.00 50.00
OCADS Darryl Sittler 15.00 40.00
OCADW Tiger Williams 10.00 25.00
OCAGA Glenn Anderson 10.00 25.00
OCAGF Grant Fuhr 15.00 40.00
OCAGL Guy Lafleur 20.00 50.00
OCAGP Gilbert Perreault 10.00 25.00
OCAKM Kirk Muller 10.00 25.00
OCAMC Lanny McDonald 15.00 40.00
OCARB Richard Brodeur 10.00 25.00
OCASS Steve Shutt 10.00 25.00

2005-06 SP Game Used Rookie Exclusive Autographs

STATED PRINT RUN 100 SER.#'d SETS
REAA Andrew Alberts 4.00 10.00
REAL Al Montoya 6.00 15.00
REAM Andrej Meszaros 5.00 12.00
REAO Alexander Ovechkin 75.00 150.00
REAP Alexander Perezhogin 5.00 12.00
REAS Alexander Steen 12.00 30.00
REAW Andrew Wozniewski 5.00 12.00
REBB Brandon Bochenski 6.00 15.00
REBC Braydon Coburn 6.00 15.00
REBL Brett Lebda 4.00 10.00
REBS Brent Seabrook 12.00 30.00
REBW Brad Winchester 6.00 15.00
RECB Cam Barker ERR 5.00 12.00
RECC Chris Campoli 4.00 10.00
RECP Corey Perry 15.00 40.00
RECW Cam Ward 20.00 50.00
REDK Duncan Keith 15.00 40.00
REDL David Leneveu 5.00 12.00
REDP Dion Phaneuf 12.50 30.00
REEN Eric Nystrom 5.00 12.00
REGB Gilbert Brule 6.00 15.00
REGP George Parros 4.00 10.00
REHL Henrik Lundqvist 25.00 60.00
REHT Hannu Toivonen 6.00 15.00
REJB Jaroslav Balastik 4.00 10.00
REJC Jeff Carter 12.00 30.00
REJF Johan Franzen 20.00 40.00
REJG Josh Gorges 5.00 12.00
REJH Jim Howard 15.00 40.00
REJJ Jussi Jokinen 6.00 15.00
REJM Jay McClement 4.00 10.00
REJS Jim Slater 5.00 12.00
REJW Jeff Woywitka 4.00 10.00
REKB Keith Ballard 5.00 12.00
REKD Kevin Dallman 5.00 12.00
REKN Kevin Nastiuk 4.00 10.00
RELS Lee Stempniak 6.00 15.00
REMF Matt Foy 4.00 10.00
REMJ Milan Jurcina 5.00 12.00
REMR Mike Richards 15.00 40.00
REMT Maxime Talbot 6.00 15.00
RENN Niklas Nordgren 6.00 15.00
REPB Peter Budaj 8.00 20.00
REPE Patrick Eaves 6.00 15.00
REPN Petteri Nokelainen 4.00 10.00
REPP Petr Prucha 6.00 15.00
RERB Rene Bourque 6.00 15.00
RERC Ryane Clowe 8.00 20.00
RERG Ryan Getzlaf 25.00 60.00
RERH Ryan Hollweg 4.00 10.00
RERI Raitis Ivanans 4.00 10.00
RERN Robert Nilsson 6.00 15.00
RERO Rostislav Olesz 5.00 12.00
RERS Ryan Suter 8.00 20.00
RESC Sidney Crosby 175.00 300.00
REST Anthony Stewart 5.00 12.00
RETV Thomas Vanek 20.00 50.00
REWW Wojtek Wolski 15.00 40.00
REYD Yann Danis 5.00 12.00
REZP Zach Parise 15.00 40.00

2005-06 SP Game Used SIGnificance

STATED PRINT RUN 100 SER.#'d SETS
SAF Alexander Frolov 5.00 12.00
SAL Daniel Alfredsson 8.00 20.00
SAY Alexei Yashin 6.00 15.00
SBM Brendan Morrison 5.00 12.00
SBR Brad Richards 8.00 20.00
SCD Chris Drury 6.00 15.00
SCO Chris Osgood 8.00 20.00
SCP Chris Pronger 6.00 15.00
SCS Cory Stillman 6.00 15.00
SDA David Aebischer 6.00 15.00
SDB Dustin Brown 8.00 20.00
SDC Dan Cloutier 6.00 15.00
SDH Dany Heatley 8.00 20.00
SDL David Legwand 6.00 15.00
SDM Darren McCarty 5.00 12.00
SDR Dwayne Roloson 6.00 15.00
SEC Erik Cole 6.00 15.00
SED Eric Daze 6.00 15.00
SEJ Ed Jovanovski 6.00 15.00
SEN Evgeni Nabokov 6.00 15.00
SES Eric Staal 10.00 25.00
GH Gordie Howe 40.00 80.00
SGM Glen Murray 6.00 15.00
SHO Marian Hossa 6.00 15.00
SHZ Henrik Zetterberg 10.00 25.00
SIK Ilya Kovalchuk 15.00 40.00
SJA Jason Arnott 6.00 15.00
SJB Jay Bouwmeester 8.00 20.00
SJC Jonathan Cheechoo 8.00 20.00
SJI Jarome Iginla 8.00 20.00
SJL Joffrey Lupul 6.00 15.00
SJN Jocelyn Thibault 6.00 15.00
SJO Jeff O'Neill 5.00 12.00
SJP Joni Pitkanen 5.00 12.00
SJR Jeremy Roenick 8.00 20.00
SJS Jason Spezza 12.00 30.00
SJT Joe Thornton 15.00 40.00
SKD Kris Draper 10.00 25.00
SKP Keith Primeau 8.00 20.00
SMB Martin Brodeur 30.00 80.00
SMC Mike Cammalleri 8.00 20.00
SMH Martin Havlat 8.00 20.00
SML Manny Legace 8.00 20.00
SMN Markus Naslund 8.00 20.00
SMP Mark Parrish 5.00 12.00
SMR Michael Ryder 6.00 15.00
SMS Miroslav Satan 6.00 15.00
SMT Marty Turco 8.00 20.00
SMW Brenden Morrow 6.00 15.00
SNY Michael Nylander 5.00 12.00
SNZ Nikolai Zherdev 5.00 12.00
SOK Olaf Kolzig 8.00 20.00
SPB Patrice Bergeron 10.00 25.00
SPM Pierre-Marc Bouchard 8.00 20.00
SPR Patrick Roy 50.00 100.00
SPS Philippe Sauve 6.00 15.00
SRA Brian Rafalski 6.00 15.00
SRB Rob Blake 8.00 20.00
SRE Robert Esche 6.00 15.00
SRF Ruslan Fedotenko 5.00 12.00
SRL Roberto Luongo 12.00 30.00
SRM Ryan Miller 8.00 20.00
SRN Rick Nash 8.00 20.00
SRO Rob Niedermayer 6.00 15.00
SRS Ryan Smyth 6.00 15.00
SSB Sean Burke 5.00 12.00
SSD Shane Doan 6.00 15.00
SSL Martin St. Louis 8.00 20.00
SSN Scott Niedermayer 8.00 20.00
SSS Sheldon Souray 5.00 12.00
SSU Mats Sundin 8.00 20.00
SSW Stephen Weiss 5.00 12.00
SSZ Sergei Zubov 6.00 15.00
STA Tyler Arnason 5.00 12.00
STH Trent Hunter 5.00 12.00
STL Trevor Linden 8.00 20.00
SVL Vincent Lecavalier 6.00 15.00
SVP Vaclav Prospal 5.00 12.00
SZC Zdeno Chara 8.00 20.00

2005-06 SP Game Used SIGnificance Gold

*GOLD/25: .6X TO 1.5X BASIC AUTO
SGH Gordie Howe 75.00 175.00
SMB Martin Brodeur 75.00 150.00
SPR Patrick Roy 75.00 150.00

2005-06 SP Game Used SIGnificance Extra

STATED PRINT RUN 25 SER.#'d SETS
BL M.Brodeur/R.Luongo 50.00 120.00
CR J.Cheechoo/M.Ryder 20.00 50.00
FB A.Frolov/D.Brown 12.50 30.00
GH G.Howe/W.Gretzky 300.00 500.00
HH D.Heatley/M.Havlat 25.00 60.00
HK M.Hossa/I.Kovalchuk 25.00 60.00
HP T.Hunter/M.Parrish
IH J.Iginla/M.Hejduk 20.00 50.00
MS R.Miller/P.Sauve 15.00 40.00
MT B.Morrow/M.Turco 12.50 30.00
NM M.Naslund/B.Morrison 15.00 40.00
PE K.Primeau/R.Esche 12.50 30.00
RR M.Ryder/M.Ribeiro 12.00 30.00
SA M.Sundin/N.Antropov 15.00 40.00
SC R.Smyth/T.Conklin 12.00 30.00
SF M.St. Louis/R.Fedotenko 12.00 30.00
TA M.Turco/D.Aebischer 12.00 30.00
TB J.Thornton/P.Bergeron 25.00 50.00
WH S.Weiss/N.Horton 20.00 50.00
ZN N.Zherdev/R.Nash 20.00 50.00

2005-06 SP Game Used Significant Numbers

SNAF Alexander Frolov/24 10.00 25.00
SNAM Alvaro Montoya/29 15.00 40.00
SNAP A. Perezhogin/42 8.00 20.00
SNAY Alexei Yashin/79 10.00 25.00
SNBR Brian Rafalski/28 15.00 40.00
SNBU Peter Budaj/31 30.00 60.00
SNBY Mike Bossy/22
SNCB Cam Barker/25 ERR 25.00 60.00
SNCO Corey Perry/61 20.00 50.00
SNCP Chris Pronger/44 10.00 25.00
SNCW Cam Ward/30 25.00 60.00
SNDB Dustin Brown/23
SNDC Dan Cloutier/39 12.00 30.00
SNDL David Leneveu/30 15.00 40.00
SNDW Doug Weight/39 10.00 25.00
SNEA Patrick Eaves/44 8.00 20.00
SNEB Ed Belfour/20 40.00 100.00
SNED Eric Daze/55 8.00 20.00
SNEJ Ed Jovanovski/55 8.00 20.00
SNEN Eric Nystrom/23 15.00 40.00

SNGM Glen Murray/27 20.00 50.00
SNGP George Parros/57 8.00 20.00
SNHK Dominik Hasek/39 25.00 60.00
SNHL Henrik Lundqvist/30 50.00 120.00
SNHT Hannu Toivonen/33 12.00 30.00
SNHZ Henrik Zetterberg/40 15.00 40.00
SNJF Johan Franzen/39 12.00 30.00
SNJH Jim Howard/35 25.00 60.00
SNJJ Jussi Jokinen/36 10.00 25.00
SNJP Joni Pitkanen/44 8.00 20.00
SNJR Jeremy Roenick/97 12.00 30.00
SNJT Jose Theodore/61 15.00 40.00
SNJW Jeff Woywitka/29 12.00 30.00
SNKD Kris Draper/33 10.00 25.00
SNKL Kari Lehtonen/32 15.00 40.00
SNKP Keith Primeau/25 10.00 25.00
SNLR Luc Robitaille/20 15.00 40.00
SNMB Martin Brodeur/30 75.00 150.00
SNMH Milan Hejduk/23 10.00 25.00
SNMJ Milan Jurcina/62 8.00 20.00
SNMP Michael Peca/37 10.00 25.00
SNMS Miroslav Satan/81 8.00 20.00
SNMT Marty Turco/35 15.00 40.00
SNNA Nik Antropov/80 8.00 20.00
SNNI Robert Nilsson/21 12.00 30.00
SNNK Nikolai Khabibulin/53 15.00 40.00
SNON Jeff O'Neill/92 8.00 20.00
SNPB Patrice Bergeron/37 20.00 50.00
SNPE Phil Esposito/77 25.00 60.00
SNPM P-M Bouchard/96 8.00 20.00
SNPR Patrick Roy/33 75.00 150.00
SNRB Ray Bourque/77 25.00 60.00
SNRG Ryan Getzlaf/51 15.00 40.00
SNRN Rick Nash/61 20.00 50.00
SNRO Rostislav Olesz/85 6.00 15.00
SNRS Ryan Smyth/94 8.00 20.00
SNRY Michael Ryder/73 10.00 25.00
SNSC Sidney Crosby/87 200.00 350.00
SNSL Martin St. Louis/26 15.00 40.00
SNSM Ryan Suter/20 15.00 40.00
SNSN Scott Niedermayer/27 12.00 30.00
SNST Anthony Stewart/57 8.00 20.00
SNTB Todd Bertuzzi/44 15.00 40.00
SNTV Thomas Vanek/26 30.00 80.00
SNYD Yann Danis/75 8.00 20.00
SNZP Zach Parise/9

2005-06 SP Game Used Statscriptions

STAF Alexander Frolov/79 10.00 25.00
STAH Ales Hemsky/64 10.00 25.00
STAR Andrew Raycroft/29 15.00 40.00
STAY Alexei Yashin/44 8.00 20.00
STBA Matthew Barnaby/43 8.00 20.00
STBG Bernie Geoffrion/50 30.00 80.00
STBH Bobby Hull/58 20.00 50.00
STBM Bryan McCabe/63 8.00 20.00
STBP Brad Park/57 6.00 15.00
STBR Brendan Morrison/71 6.00 15.00
STBT Bryan Trottier/50 8.00 20.00
STCB Christian Backman/18 10.00 25.00
STCC Craig Conroy/69 5.00 12.00
STCD Chris Drury/50 8.00 20.00
STCO Chris Osgood/45 8.00 20.00
STDA Daniel Alfredsson/37 15.00 40.00
STDB Dustin Brown/31 8.00 20.00
STDC Dan Cloutier/33 8.00 20.00
STDH Dany Heatley/41 15.00 40.00
STDL David Legwand/48 8.00 20.00
STDT Dave Taylor/47 6.00 15.00
STDW Doug Weight/79 10.00 25.00
STED Eric Daze/38 8.00 20.00
STES Eric Staal/81 12.00 30.00
STFT Fedor Tyutin/25 8.00 20.00
STGL Guy Lafleur/60 12.00 30.00
STGM Glen Murray/44 8.00 20.00
STHO Marcel Hossa/59 8.00 20.00
STHV Martin Havlat/31 15.00 40.00
STHZ Henrik Zetterberg/44 20.00 50.00
STIL Ian Laperriere/78 8.00 20.00
STJA Jason Arnott/68 6.00 15.00
STJB Jay Bouwmeester/82 6.00 15.00
STJC Jonathan Cheechoo/63 12.00 30.00
STJH Jochen Hecht/52 8.00 20.00
STJI Jarome Iginla/52 20.00 50.00
STJL Jamie Lundmark/29 8.00 20.00
STJM John-Michael Liles/79 5.00 12.00
STJO Jeff O'Neill/41 8.00 20.00
STJP Joni Pitkanen/71 6.00 15.00
STJS Jason Spezza/55 15.00 40.00
STJT Jocelyn Thibault/36 10.00 25.00
STJV Josef Vasicek/45 10.00 25.00
STKD Kris Draper/40 8.00 20.00
STKH Kristian Huselius/45 6.00 15.00
STKL Kari Lehtonen/30 20.00 50.00
STKP Keith Primeau/57 6.00 15.00
STKT Kimmo Timonen/55 6.00 15.00
STKW Kevin Weekes/66 6.00 15.00
STLM Larry Murphy/63 6.00 15.00
STLU Joffrey Lupul/34 10.00 25.00
STLU Roberto Luongo/25 20.00 50.00
STMA Marc-Andre Fleury/46 30.00 60.00
STMB Mike Bossy/69 10.00 25.00
STMD Marcel Dionne/59 12.00 30.00
STMG Martin Gerber/54 8.00 20.00
STMN Michael Nylander/64 8.00 20.00
STMR Mike Ribeiro/65 6.00 15.00
STMS Matt Stajan/27 12.00 30.00
STMT Marty Turco/37 12.00 30.00
STMW Brenden Morrow/48 6.00 15.00
STNA Nik Antropov/45 6.00 15.00
STNH Nathan Horton/55 6.00 15.00
STNZ Nikolai Zherdev/34 10.00 25.00
STOK Olaf Kolzig/41 20.00 50.00
STPB Patrice Bergeron/39 20.00 40.00
STPC Grant Fuhr/40 25.00 60.00
STPL Pascal Leclaire/62 8.00 20.00
STPM Pierre-Marc Bouchard/42 8.00 20.00
STPS Peter Stastny/47 10.00 25.00
STRA Brian Rafalski/52 8.00 20.00
STRB Rob Blake/68 8.00 20.00
STRF Ruslan Fedotenko/39 8.00 20.00
STRK Ryan Kesler/28 25.00 60.00
STRL Reggie Leach/61 8.00 20.00
STRM Ryan Miller/18 25.00 50.00
STRN Rob Niedermayer/61 8.00 20.00
STRS Ryan Smyth/39 12.00 30.00
STRV Rogie Vachon/33 12.00 30.00
STRY Michael Ryder/63 10.00 25.00
STRZ Richard Zednik/50 6.00 15.00
STSA Philippe Sauve/27 10.00 25.00
STSB Sean Burke/35 8.00 20.00
STSD Shane Doan/68 6.00 15.00
STSG Simon Gagne/66 10.00 25.00
STSL Martin St. Louis/38 12.00 30.00
STSN Scott Niedermayer/57 8.00 20.00
STST Marco Sturm/48 10.00 25.00
STSZ Sergei Zubov/79 6.00 15.00
STTA Tyler Arnason/55 8.00 20.00
STTE Tony Esposito/35 15.00 40.00
STTH Trent Hunter/51 6.00 15.00
STTL Trevor Linden/25 40.00 100.00
STTP Tom Poti/48 6.00 15.00
STTR Tuomo Ruutu/44 10.00 25.00
STVL Vincent Lecavalier/33 30.00 80.00
STVR Mike Van Ryn/37 10.00 25.00
STWC Wayne Cashman/30 8.00 20.00

2006-07 SP Game Used

COMPLETE SET w/o SPs (100) 50.00 100.00
101-160 ROOKIE PRINT RUN 999
1 Chris Pronger .60 1.50
2 Teemu Selanne 1.50 4.00
3 Jean-Sebastien Giguere .75 2.00
4 Ilya Kovalchuk .75 2.00
5 Kari Lehtonen .60 1.50
6 Marian Hossa .60 1.50
7 Patrice Bergeron 1.00 2.50
8 Brad Boyes .50 1.25
9 Hannu Toivonen .60 1.50
10 Bobby Orr 2.50 6.00
11 Ryan Miller .75 2.00
12 Chris Drury .60 1.50
13 Jarome Iginla .75 2.00
14 Miikka Kiprusoff .60 1.50
15 Alex Tanguay .50 1.25
16 Dion Phaneuf .75 2.00
17 Eric Staal 1.00 2.50
18 Cam Ward .75 2.00
19 Erik Cole .60 1.50
20 Rod Brind'Amour .75 2.00
21 Nikolai Khabibulin .75 2.00
22 Martin Havlat .50 1.25
23 Tuomo Ruutu .75 2.00
24 Joe Sakic 1.25 3.00
25 Jose Theodore .75 2.00
26 Milan Hejduk .60 1.50
27 Marek Svatos .50 1.25
28 Rick Nash .75 2.00
29 Sergei Fedorov 1.25 3.00
30 Pascal LeClaire .60 1.50
31 Mike Modano 1.25 3.00
32 Marty Turco .75 2.00
33 Eric Lindros 1.25 3.00
34 Gordie Howe 1.50 4.00
35 Henrik Zetterberg 1.00 2.50
36 Pavel Datsyuk 1.00 2.50
37 Dominik Hasek 1.00 2.50
38 Nicklas Lidstrom .75 2.00
39 Ales Hemsky .60 1.50
40 Ryan Smyth .60 1.50
41 Joffrey Lupul .60 1.50
42 Ed Belfour .75 2.00
43 Jay Bouwmeester .75 2.00
44 Todd Bertuzzi .75 2.00
45 Olli Jokinen .75 2.00
46 Wayne Gretzky 4.00 10.00
47 Alexander Frolov .50 1.25
48 Rob Blake .75 2.00
49 Marian Gaborik 1.00 2.50
50 Manny Fernandez .60 1.50
51 Pavol Demitra 1.00 2.50
52 Cristobal Huet .60 1.50
53 Patrick Roy 2.00 5.00
54 Michael Ryder .50 1.25
55 Saku Koivu .75 2.00
56 Alexei Kovalev .60 1.50
57 Paul Kariya 1.00 2.50
58 Tomas Vokoun .60 1.50
59 Jason Arnott .60 1.50
60 Martin Brodeur 1.50 4.00
61 Brian Gionta .60 1.50
62 Patrik Elias .75 2.00
63 Alexei Yashin .60 1.50
64 Miroslav Satan .60 1.50
65 Brendan Shanahan 1.00 2.50
66 Jaromir Jagr 2.00 5.00
67 Henrik Lundqvist 1.50 4.00
68 Dany Heatley .75 2.00
69 Martin Gerber .60 1.50
70 Daniel Alfredsson .75 2.00
71 Jason Spezza .75 2.00
72 Simon Gagne .75 2.00
73 Peter Forsberg 1.00 2.50
74 Jeff Carter .75 2.00
75 Joni Pitkanen .50 1.25
76 Shane Doan .60 1.50
77 Jeremy Roenick .75 2.00
78 Owen Nolan .60 1.50
79 Curtis Joseph .75 2.00
80 Sidney Crosby 3.00 8.00
81 Mario Lemieux 2.50 6.00
82 Marc-Andre Fleury 1.25 3.00
83 Mark Recchi 1.00 2.50
84 Joe Thornton 1.00 2.50
85 Patrick Marleau .75 2.00
86 Jonathan Cheechoo .75 2.00
87 Doug Weight .75 2.00
88 Keith Tkachuk .75 2.00
89 Vincent Lecavalier .60 1.50
90 Martin St. Louis .75 2.00
91 Brad Richards .75 2.00
92 Alexander Steen .75 2.00
93 Mats Sundin .75 2.00
94 Andrew Raycroft .60 1.50
95 Michael Peca .60 1.50
96 Markus Naslund .60 1.50
97 Roberto Luongo 1.25 3.00
98 Brendan Morrison .50 1.25
99 Alexander Ovechkin 3.00 8.00
100 Olaf Kolzig .75 2.00
101 Shane O'Brien RC 2.00 5.00
102 Ryan Shannon RC 2.00 5.00
103 Yan Stastny RC 2.00 5.00
104 Mark Stuart RC 2.00 5.00
105 Nate Thompson RC 2.00 5.00
106 Phil Kessel RC 5.00 12.00
107 Matt Lashoff RC 2.00 5.00
108 Dave Bolland RC 3.00 8.00
109 Michael Blunden RC 2.00 5.00
110 Dustin Byfuglien RC 5.00 12.00
111 Paul Stastny RC 5.00 12.00
112 Fredrik Norrena RC 2.00 5.00
113 Loui Eriksson RC 3.00 8.00
114 Tomas Kopecky RC 2.50 6.00
115 Alexei Mikhnov RC 2.00 5.00
116 Marc-Antoine Pouliot RC 2.00 5.00
117 Patrick Thoresen RC 2.00 5.00
118 Ladislav Smid RC 2.00 5.00
119 Janis Sprukts RC 2.00 5.00
120 Konstantin Pushkarev RC 2.50 6.00
121 Patrick O'Sullivan RC 3.00 8.00
122 Anze Kopitar RC 8.00 20.00
123 Benoit Pouliot RC 2.50 6.00
124 Miroslav Kopriva RC 2.00 5.00
125 Niklas Backstrom RC 4.00 10.00
126 Guillaume Latendresse RC 3.00 8.00
127 Alexander Radulov RC 4.00 10.00
128 Shea Weber RC 5.00 12.00
129 Mikko Lehtonen RC 2.50 6.00
130 Alex Brooks RC 2.00 5.00
131 John Oduya RC 3.00 8.00
132 Travis Zajac RC 4.00 10.00
133 Drew Stafford RC 3.00 8.00
134 Masi Marjamaki RC 2.00 5.00
135 Jarkko Immonen RC 2.00 5.00
136 Nigel Dawes RC 2.00 5.00
137 Alexei Kaigorodov RC 2.00 5.00
138 Lars Jonsson RC 2.00 5.00
139 Ryan Potulny RC 2.00 5.00
140 Triston Grant RC 2.00 5.00
141 Enver Lisin RC 2.00 5.00
142 Brandon Prust RC 2.00 5.00
143 Keith Yandle RC 4.00 10.00
144 Patrick Fischer RC 2.00 5.00
145 Noah Welch RC 2.00 5.00
146 Michel Ouellet RC 2.50 6.00
147 Jordan Staal RC 8.00 20.00
148 Kristopher Letang RC 8.00 20.00
149 Evgeni Malkin RC 15.00 40.00
150 Matt Carle RC 2.00 5.00
151 Marc-Edouard Vlasic RC 2.00 5.00
152 D.J. King RC 2.00 5.00
153 Roman Polak RC 2.50 6.00
154 Ben Ondrus RC 2.00 5.00
155 Brendan Bell RC 2.00 5.00
156 Ian White RC 2.50 6.00
157 Dustin Boyd RC 2.00 5.00
158 Luc Bourdon RC 3.00 8.00
159 Eric Fehr RC 3.00 8.00
160 Jonas Johansson RC 2.00 5.00

2006-07 SP Game Used Gold

*1-100 VETS: 2X TO 5X BASIC CARDS
*101-160 ROOKIES: 1X TO 2.5X BASIC RC
GOLD STATED PRINT RUN 100

2006-07 SP Game Used Rainbow

*1-100 VETS: 4X TO 10X BASIC CARDS
*101-160 ROOKIES: 2X TO 5X BASIC RC
STATED PRINT RUN 25 SER.#'d SETS
149 Evgeni Malkin 100.00 200.00

2006-07 SP Game Used Authentic Fabrics

OVERALL MEM. ODDS 1:1
AFAF Alexander Frolov 4.00 10.00
AFAH Ales Hemsky 5.00 12.00
AFAL Daniel Alfredsson 6.00 15.00
AFAO Alexander Ovechkin SP 15.00 40.00
AFAS Alexander Steen 6.00 15.00
AFAT Alex Tanguay 4.00 10.00
AFAY Alexei Yashin 5.00 12.00
AFBB Brad Boyes 4.00 10.00
AFBG Brian Gionta 5.00 12.00
AFBL Brian Leetch 6.00 15.00
AFBM Brenden Morrow 5.00 12.00
AFBO Pierre-Marc Bouchard 6.00 15.00
AFBR Brad Richards 6.00 15.00
AFBS Brendan Shanahan 8.00 20.00
AFCD Chris Drury 5.00 12.00
AFCJ Curtis Joseph 6.00 15.00
AFCS Curtis Sanford 5.00 12.00
AFCW Cam Ward 6.00 15.00
AFDA David Aebischer 5.00 12.00
AFDE Pavol Demitra 8.00 20.00
AFDH Dominik Hasek 6.00 15.00
AFDP Dion Phaneuf 5.00 12.00
AFDR Dwayne Roloson 5.00 12.00
AFDS Daniel Sedin 6.00 15.00
AFDW Doug Weight 6.00 15.00
AFEB Ed Belfour 6.00 15.00
AFEJ Ed Jovanovski 5.00 12.00
AFES Eric Staal 8.00 20.00
AFGA Simon Gagne 6.00 15.00
AFGR Gary Roberts 4.00 10.00
AFHE Dany Heatley 6.00 15.00
AFHL Henrik Lundqvist 12.00 30.00
AFHS Henrik Sedin 6.00 15.00
AFHT Hannu Toivonen 5.00 12.00
AFHZ Henrik Zetterberg 8.00 20.00
AFIK Ilya Kovalchuk SP 8.00 20.00
AFJB Jay Bouwmeester 6.00 15.00
AFJC Jeff Carter 6.00 15.00
AFJD J.P. Dumont 4.00 10.00
AFJI Jarome Iginla 6.00 15.00
AFJJ Jaromir Jagr SP 15.00 40.00
AFJL Jere Lehtinen 4.00 10.00
AFJN Joe Nieuwendyk 6.00 15.00
AFJP Joni Pitkanen 4.00 10.00
AFJS Joe Sakic 8.00 20.00
AFJT Joe Thornton 6.00 15.00
AFJW Jason Williams 4.00 10.00
AFLU Joffrey Lupul 5.00 12.00
AFMA Mark Recchi 8.00 20.00
AFMB Martin Brodeur SP 12.00 30.00
AFMC Mike Cammalleri 4.00 10.00
AFME Martin Erat 4.00 10.00
AFMF Manny Fernandez 5.00 12.00
AFMG Marian Gaborik 8.00 20.00
AFMH Milan Hejduk 5.00 12.00
AFMI Miroslav Satan 5.00 12.00
AFMM Mike Modano 8.00 20.00
AFMN Markus Naslund 5.00 12.00
AFMO Brendan Morrison 4.00 10.00
AFMP Michael Peca 5.00 12.00
AFMR Michael Ryder 4.00 10.00
AFMS Mats Sundin 6.00 15.00
AFNH Nathan Horton 6.00 15.00
AFNL Nicklas Lidstrom 6.00 15.00
AFOK Olaf Kolzig 6.00 15.00
AFPB Patrice Bergeron 8.00 20.00
AFPD Pavel Datsyuk 8.00 20.00
AFPE Patrik Elias 6.00 15.00
AFPF Peter Forsberg 6.00 15.00
AFPK Paul Kariya 5.00 12.00
AFPL Pascal LeClaire 5.00 12.00
AFPM Patrick Marleau 6.00 15.00
AFPS Patrik Stefan 4.00 10.00
AFPT Pierre Turgeon 6.00 15.00
AFRB Rob Blake 6.00 15.00
AFRD Rick DiPietro 5.00 12.00
AFRE Robert Esche 5.00 12.00
AFRF Ruslan Fedotenko 4.00 10.00
AFRG Ryan Getzlaf 10.00 25.00
AFRL Roberto Luongo 10.00 25.00
AFRM Ryan Malone 4.00 10.00
AFRN Rick Nash 6.00 15.00
AFRS Ryan Smyth 5.00 12.00
AFSC Sidney Crosby SP 40.00 80.00
AFSF Sergei Fedorov 10.00 25.00
AFSG Scott Gomez 5.00 12.00
AFSJ Matt Stajan 5.00 12.00
AFSK Saku Koivu 6.00 15.00
AFSM Martin St. Louis 6.00 15.00
AFSN Scott Niedermayer 6.00 15.00
AFSP Jason Spezza 6.00 15.00
AFSS Sergei Samsonov 5.00 12.00
AFST Jarret Stoll 5.00 12.00
AFSU Steve Sullivan 4.00 10.00
AFTA Tony Amonte 5.00 12.00
AFTH Tomas Holmstrom 5.00 12.00
AFTS Teemu Selanne 12.00 30.00
AFTT Tim Thomas 8.00 20.00
AFTV Tomas Vokoun 5.00 12.00
AFVL Vincent Lecavalier 5.00 12.00

2006-07 SP Game Used Authentic Fabrics Parallel

*PARALLEL 1X to 1.25X
STATED PRINT RUN 100 SER.#'d SETS

2006-07 SP Game Used Authentic Fabrics Patches

*PATCHES: 2X to 4X HI BASE JERSEYS
PRINT RUN 50 SER. #'d SETS

2006-07 SP Game Used Authentic Fabrics Dual

STATED PRINT RUN 100 SER.#'d SETS
AF2AB M.Afinogenov/D.Briere 6.00 15.00
AF2AH D.Aebischer/C.Huet 8.00 20.00
AF2AS J.Arnott/S.Sullivan 3.00 8.00
AF2BF R.Blake/A.Frolov 4.00 10.00
AF2BG M.Brodeur/B.Gionta 10.00 25.00
AF2BH J.Bouwmeester/N.Horton 3.00 8.00
AF2DG P.Demitra/M.Gaborik 6.00 15.00
AF2DM C.Drury/R.Miller 6.00 15.00
AF2FC P.Forsberg/J.Carter 6.00 15.00
AF2HK M.Havlat/N.Khabibulin 6.00 15.00
AF2HL A.Hemsky/J.Lupul 3.00 8.00
AF2HO D.Hasek/C.Osgood 10.00 25.00
AF2HS M.Hejduk/M.Svatos 3.00 8.00
AF2HZ T.Holmstrom/H.Zetterberg 8.00 20.00
AF2IK J.Iginla/M.Kiprusoff 10.00 25.00
AF2JL J.Jagr/H.Lundqvist 10.00 25.00
AF2KG S.Kapanen/S.Gagne 3.00 8.00
AF2KH M.Hossa/I.Kovalchuk 6.00 15.00
AF2KO O.Kolzig/A.Ovechkin 12.00 30.00
AF2KR S.Koivu/M.Ryder 4.00 10.00
AF2KV P.Kariya/T.Vokoun 6.00 15.00
AF2LC P.LeClaire/T.Conklin 3.00 8.00
AF2LJ J.Lehtinen/J.Jokinen 3.00 8.00
AF2LR V.Lecavalier/B.Richards 8.00 20.00
AF2ML M.Modano/E.Lindros 6.00 15.00
AF2MT P.Marleau/J.Thornton 8.00 20.00
AF2ND O.Nolan/S.Doan 4.00 10.00
AF2NF R.Nash/S.Fedorov 8.00 20.00
AF2NL M.Naslund/R.Luongo 6.00 15.00
AF2PB M.Parrish/P.Bouchard 3.00 8.00
AF2PT M.Peca/D.Tucker 4.00 10.00
AF2RC M.Recchi/S.Crosby 20.00 50.00
AF2RL G.Lapointe/L.Robinson 4.00 15.00
AF2SB M.Savard/P.Bergeron 6.00 15.00
AF2SC B.Stuart/Z.Chara 3.00 8.00
AF2SD M.Satan/R.DiPietro 4.00 10.00
AF2SH J.Spezza/D.Heatley 8.00 20.00
AF2SJ B.Shanahan/J.Jagr 10.00 25.00
AF2SP T.Selanne/C.Perry 6.00 15.00
AF2SS M.Sundin/A.Steen 6.00 15.00
AF2SW E.Staal/C.Ward 6.00 15.00
AF2TK A.Tanguay/C.Kobasew 4.00 10.00
AF2TM M.Turco/B.Morrow 4.00 10.00
AF2TP R.Torres/F.Pisani 3.00 8.00
AF2TS P.Turgeon/J.Sakic 8.00 20.00
AF2TT H.Toivonen/T.Thomas 4.00 10.00
AF2WB J.Williams/R.Brind'Amour 3.00 8.00
AF2WG D.Weight/B.Guerin 3.00 8.00

2006-07 SP Game Used Authentic Fabrics Dual Patches

*PATCHES: 2X to 4X DUAL JSY HI
PRINT RUN 25 #'d SETS

2006-07 SP Game Used Authentic Fabrics Triple

PRINT RUN 25 #'d SETS
AF3ANA Selan/Prong/Nied 20.00 50.00
AF3ATL Hossa/Kovy/Lehton 25.00 60.00
AF3BOS Boyes/Chara/Berg 20.00 50.00
AF3BUF Drury/Briere/Miller 25.00 60.00
AF3CAR Brind/Staal/Ward 20.00 50.00
AF3CGY Iggy/Tanguay/Kipper 30.00 80.00
AF3CHI Havlat/Ruutu/Khabi 15.00 40.00
AF3CLB LeClaire/Nash/Fedorov 25.00 60.00
AF3COL Sakic/Hejduk/Theo 40.00 100.00
AF3DAL Modano/Lind/Turco 25.00 60.00
AF3DET Hasek/Lidstrom/Zetty 40.00 100.00
AF3EDM Smyth/Rolo/Hemsky 15.00 40.00
AF3FLA Belfour/Bert/Bouw 20.00 50.00
AF3LAK Blake/Frolov/Cam 15.00 40.00
AF3MIN Demitra/Gabby/Bouch 20.00 50.00
AF3MTL Samson/Koivu/Ryder 30.00 80.00
AF3NAS Kariya/Vokoun/Arnott 20.00 50.00
AF3NJD Brodeur/Elias/Gionta 30.00 80.00
AF3NYI Satan/Yashin/DiPietro 20.00 50.00
AF3NYR Shanny/Jagr/Lundqvist 50.00 100.00
AF3OTT Alfred/Spezza/Heatley 25.00 60.00
AF3PHI Forsberg/Esche/Gagne 20.00 50.00
AF3PHX Joseph/Roenick/Doan 15.00 40.00
AF3PIT Recchi/Malone/Crosby 40.00 100.00
AF3SJS Marleau/Thorn/Chee 25.00 60.00
AF3STL Weight/Tkachuk/Leg 15.00 40.00
AF3TBL Lecav/Richards/St. Lou 30.00 80.00
AF3TOR Sundin/Raycroft/Steen 20.00 50.00
AF3VAN Naslund/Sedin/Sedin 25.00 60.00
AF3WAS Ovech/Kolzig/Zednik 30.00 80.00

2006-07 SP Game Used Inked Sweaters

PRINT RUN 100 #'d SETS
SP PRINT RUN 25 #'d SETS
ISAF Alexander Frolov 6.00 15.00
ISAH Ales Hemsky 8.00 20.00
ISAN Antero Niittymaki 10.00 25.00
ISAO Alexander Ovechkin SP 75.00 150.00
ISAR Andrew Raycroft 10.00 25.00
ISAY Alexei Yashin 6.00 15.00
ISBB Brad Boyes 6.00 15.00
ISBG Brian Gionta 6.00 15.00
ISBM Bryan McCabe 6.00 15.00
ISBS Borje Salming SP 15.00 30.00
ISCA Matt Carle 10.00 25.00
ISCH Chris Higgins 10.00 25.00
ISCN Cam Neely SP 25.00 60.00
ISCP Chris Pronger SP 15.00 40.00
ISCW Cam Ward 8.00 20.00
ISDA Dany Heatley 10.00 25.00
ISDB Daniel Briere 12.00 30.00
ISDH Dominik Hasek SP 40.00 80.00
ISDI Dion Phaneuf SP 25.00 60.00
ISDR Dwayne Roloson 10.00 25.00
ISDS Denis Savard SP 15.00 40.00
ISDT Darcy Tucker 10.00 25.00
ISEF Eric Fehr 6.00 15.00
ISEL Patrik Elias 8.00 20.00
ISES Eric Staal 12.00 30.00
ISFP Fernando Pisani 6.00 15.00
ISGE Martin Gerber 8.00 20.00
ISGH Gordie Howe SP
ISHA Martin Havlat 10.00 25.00
ISHE Milan Hejduk 8.00 20.00
ISHO Tomas Holmstrom 8.00 20.00
ISHT Hannu Toivonen 10.00 25.00
ISHU Cristobal Huet 10.00 25.00
ISIK Ilya Kovalchuk SP 25.00 60.00
ISIM Jarkko Immonen 8.00 20.00
ISJA Jason Arnott 6.00 15.00
ISJI Jarome Iginla SP 15.00 40.00
ISJL Joffrey Lupul 6.00 15.00
ISJP Joni Pitkanen 6.00 15.00
ISJS Jarret Stoll 6.00 15.00
ISJT Joe Thornton SP 25.00 60.00
ISJW Justin Williams 6.00 15.00
ISKD Kris Draper 6.00 15.00
ISKL Kari Lehtonen 10.00 25.00
ISKO Mikko Koivu 8.00 20.00
ISLN Ladislav Nagy 6.00 15.00
ISLR Luc Robitaille SP
ISMA Al MacInnis SP 20.00 50.00
ISMB Martin Brodeur SP 60.00 150.00
ISMC Mike Cammalleri 8.00 20.00
ISMG Marian Gaborik 15.00 40.00
ISMI Ryan Miller 12.00 30.00
ISML Mario Lemieux SP 100.00 200.00
ISMM Milan Michalek 6.00 15.00
ISMO Mike Modano SP 20.00 50.00
ISMP Mark Parrish 6.00 15.00
ISMR Mike Ribeiro 6.00 15.00
ISMT Marty Turco 10.00 25.00
ISNL Nicklas Lidstrom SP 25.00 60.00
ISNZ Nikolai Zherdev 6.00 15.00
ISPB Pierre-Marc Bouchard 6.00 15.00
ISPE Michael Peca 6.00 15.00
ISPM Patrick Marleau 8.00 20.00
ISPO Marc-Antoine Pouliot 8.00 20.00
ISPP Petr Prucha 8.00 20.00
ISPR Patrick Roy SP 125.00 250.00
ISRG Ryan Getzlaf 10.00 25.00
ISRH Ron Hextall SP 20.00 50.00
ISRI Mike Richards 8.00 20.00
ISRN Rick Nash SP 25.00 60.00
ISRS Ryan Smyth 10.00 25.00
ISSA Marc Savard 8.00 20.00
ISSB Steve Bernier 8.00 20.00
ISSC Sidney Crosby 75.00 150.00
ISSG Scott Gomez 8.00 20.00
ISSK Saku Koivu SP 20.00 50.00
ISSV Marek Svatos 8.00 20.00
ISSW Shea Weber 10.00 25.00
ISTV Tomas Vokoun 10.00 25.00
ISVL Vincent Lecavalier SP 25.00 60.00
ISVT Vesa Toskala 10.00 25.00
ISWG Wayne Gretzky SP EXCH 200.00 300.00
ISWR Wade Redden 6.00 15.00
ISZC Zdeno Chara 6.00 15.00

2006-07 SP Game Used Inked Sweaters Patches

*PATCHES: 1.25X to 2X JSY HI
PRINT RUN 25 #'d SETS
ISAF Alexander Frolov 12.00 30.00
ISAH Ales Hemsky 15.00 40.00
ISAN Antero Niittymaki 25.00 60.00
ISAO Alexander Ovechkin SP 200.00 350.00
ISAR Andrew Raycroft 30.00 80.00
ISAY Alexei Yashin 12.00 30.00
ISBB Brad Boyes 12.00 30.00
ISBG Brian Gionta 12.00 30.00
ISBM Bryan McCabe 12.00 30.00
ISBS Borje Salming SP
ISCA Matt Carle 20.00 50.00
ISCH Chris Higgins 20.00 50.00
ISCN Cam Neely SP
ISCP Chris Pronger SP
ISCW Cam Ward 20.00 50.00
ISDA Dany Heatley 20.00 50.00
ISDB Daniel Briere 25.00 60.00
ISDH Dominik Hasek SP
ISDI Dion Phaneuf SP
ISDR Dwayne Roloson 20.00 50.00
ISDS Denis Savard SP
ISDT Darcy Tucker 20.00 50.00
ISEF Eric Fehr 12.00 30.00
ISEL Patrik Elias 15.00 40.00
ISES Eric Staal 20.00 50.00
ISFP Fernando Pisani 12.00 30.00
ISGE Martin Gerber 15.00 40.00
ISHA Martin Havlat 20.00 50.00
ISHE Milan Hejduk 15.00 40.00
ISHO Tomas Holmstrom 15.00 40.00
ISHT Hannu Toivonen 20.00 50.00
ISHU Cristobal Huet 30.00 80.00
ISIK Ilya Kovalchuk SP 60.00 100.00
ISIM Jarkko Immonen 15.00 40.00
ISJA Jason Arnott 12.00 30.00
ISJI Jarome Iginla SP 60.00 120.00
ISJL Joffrey Lupul 12.00 30.00
ISJP Joni Pitkanen 12.00 30.00
ISJS Jarret Stoll 12.00 30.00
ISJT Joe Thornton SP 125.00 200.00
ISJW Justin Williams 12.00 30.00
ISKD Kris Draper 15.00 40.00
ISKL Kari Lehtonen 20.00 50.00
ISKO Mikko Koivu 20.00 50.00
ISLN Ladislav Nagy 12.00 30.00
ISLR Luc Robitaille SP
ISMA Al MacInnis SP
ISMB Martin Brodeur SP
ISMC Mike Cammalleri 15.00 40.00
ISMG Marian Gaborik 30.00 80.00
ISMI Ryan Miller 25.00 60.00
ISML Mario Lemieux SP
ISMM Milan Michalek 12.00 30.00
ISMO Mike Modano SP
ISMP Mark Parrish 12.00 30.00
ISMR Mike Ribeiro 12.00 30.00
ISMT Marty Turco 20.00 50.00
ISNZ Nikolai Zherdev 12.00 30.00
ISPB Pierre-Marc Bouchard 12.00 30.00
ISPE Michael Peca
ISPM Patrick Marleau 15.00 40.00
ISPO Marc-Antoine Pouliot 15.00 40.00
ISPP Petr Prucha 15.00 40.00
ISPR Patrick Roy SP
ISRG Ryan Getzlaf 30.00 50.00
ISRI Mike Richards 15.00 40.00
ISRN Rick Nash SP
ISRS Ryan Smyth 20.00 50.00
ISSA Marc Savard 15.00 40.00
ISSB Steve Bernier 15.00 40.00
ISSC Sidney Crosby 200.00 350.00
ISSG Scott Gomez 15.00 40.00
ISSK Saku Koivu SP
ISSV Marek Svatos 15.00 40.00
ISSW Shea Weber 20.00 50.00
ISTH Jose Theodore SP
ISTV Tomas Vokoun 15.00 40.00
ISVL Vincent Lecavalier SP 75.00 150.00
ISVT Vesa Toskala 25.00 60.00
ISWG Wayne Gretzky SP EXCH
ISWR Wade Redden 12.00 30.00
ISZC Zdeno Chara 12.00 30.00

2006-07 SP Game Used Inked Sweaters Dual

PRINT RUN 50 #'d SETS
SP PRINT RUN 10 #'d SETS
IS2AS J.Arnott/S.Sullivan 8.00 20.00
IS2BB B.Boyes/P.Bergeron 12.00 30.00
IS2BL M.Brodeur/R.Luongo SP
IS2BP D.Potvin/R.Bourque SP
IS2CL B.Clarke/G.Lafleur SP
IS2CP G.Cheevers/B.Park 15.00 40.00
IS2DM C.Drury/R.Miller 15.00 40.00
IS2EG P.Elias/B.Gionta 10.00 25.00
IS2EP R.Esche/J.Pitkanen 8.00 20.00
IS2FC A.Frolov/M.Cammelleri 10.00 25.00
IS2FR G.Fuhr/B.Ranford 20.00 50.00
IS2GB M.Gaborik/P.Bouchard 20.00 50.00
IS2GC S.Gagne/J.Carter
IS2GL M.Lemieux/W.Gretzky SP
IS2HA D.Aebischer/C.Huet 15.00 40.00
IS2HH M.Handzus/M.Havlat 8.00 20.00
IS2HO D.Hasek/C.Osgood 20.00 50.00
IS2HS J.Stoll/A.Hemsky 8.00 20.00
IS2HT M.Hejduk/J.Theodore 10.00 25.00
IS2HV T.Vokoun/D.Hasek SP
IS2IT J.Iginla/A.Tanguay 15.00 40.00
IS2KL I.Kovalchuk/K.Lehtonen 25.00 60.00
IS2KR S.Koivu/M.Ryder 12.00 30.00
IS2LP H.Lundqvist/P.Prucha 25.00 60.00
IS2LS N.Lidstrom/B.Salming 20.00 50.00
IS2MC P.Marleau/J.Cheechoo 15.00 40.00
IS2MM J.Mullen/A.MacInnis 12.00 30.00
IS2MS M.Savard/G.Murray 10.00 25.00
IS2MT M.Modano/M.Turco 12.00 30.00
IS2NH D.Heatley/R.Nash 20.00 50.00
IS2NM M.Naslund/B.Morrison 12.00 30.00
IS2OJ O.Jokinen/J.Bouwmeester 8.00 20.00
IS2OK Kovalchuk/Ovechkin SP
IS2PT M.Peca/D.Tucker 15.00 40.00
IS2RB P.Roy/R.Bourque SP
IS2RD J.Roenick/S.Doan 10.00 25.00
IS2RG W.Redden/M.Gerber 10.00 25.00
IS2RS A.Raycroft/A.Steen 15.00 40.00
IS2RT L.Robitaille/D.Taylor 25.00 60.00
IS2SD M.St. Louis/M.Denis 12.00 30.00
IS2SR R.Smyth/D.Roloson 12.00 30.00
IS2SS J.Spezza/E.Staal SP
IS2SW J.Williams/E.Staal 10.00 25.00
IS2SY M.Satan/A.Yashin 8.00 20.00
IS2VW T.Vokoun/S.Weber 12.00 30.00
IS2WP T.Williams/B.Probert 12.00 30.00
IS2WR D.Roloson/C.Ward 12.00 30.00
IS2ZH T.Holmstrom/H.Zetterberg 20.00 50.00
IS2HH2 B.Hull/G.Howe SP

2006-07 SP Game Used Legendary Fabrics

LFBC Bobby Clarke/100 6.00 15.00
LFGH Gordie Howe/25 20.00 50.00
LFGL Guy Lafleur/100 10.00 25.00
LFJB Jean Beliveau/100 12.00 30.00
LFMB Mike Bossy/100 6.00 15.00
LFML Mario Lemieux/25 30.00 80.00
LFPE Phil Esposito/25 12.00 30.00
LFPR Patrick Roy/25 30.00 80.00
LFRB Ray Bourque/25 20.00 50.00
LFWG Wayne Gretzky/25 75.00 150.00

2006-07 SP Game Used Legendary Fabrics Autographs

PRINT RUN 100 #'d SETS
LFBC Bobby Clarke 15.00 40.00
LFGH Gordie Howe 50.00 120.00
LFGL Guy Lafleur 20.00 50.00
LFJB Jean Beliveau 25.00 60.00
LFMB Mike Bossy 15.00 40.00
LFML Mario Lemieux SP 50.00 125.00
LFPE Phil Esposito SP 15.00 40.00
LFPR Patrick Roy SP
LFRB Ray Bourque SP 50.00 100.00
LFWG Wayne Gretzky SP EXCH 250.00 400.00

2006-07 SP Game Used Letter Marks

STATED PRINT RUN 50 #'d SETS
LMAF Alexander Frolov 20.00 50.00
LMAK Andrei Kostitsyn 20.00 50.00
LMAL Andrew Ladd 20.00 50.00
LMAN Antero Niittymaki 20.00 50.00
LMBB Brad Boyes 15.00 40.00
LMBG Brian Gionta 20.00 50.00
LMBM Brenden Morrow 20.00 50.00
LMBP Bernie Parent EXCH 20.00 50.00
LMBQ Ray Bourque 30.00 80.00
LMBR Bill Ranford EXCH 20.00 50.00
LMCG Clark Gillies 20.00 50.00
LMCH Cristobal Huet 15.00 40.00
LMCK Chuck Kobasew 12.00 30.00
LMCN Cam Neely 30.00 80.00
LMCW Cam Ward 30.00 80.00
LMDC Dino Ciccarelli EXCH 20.00 50.00
LMDP Denis Potvin 15.00 40.00
LMDR Dwayne Roloson 12.00 30.00
LMDS Denis Savard 50.00 100.00
LMDW Dave Williams 20.00 50.00
LMEC Erik Cole 20.00 50.00
LMEL Patrik Elias 30.00 80.00
LMEM Evgeni Malkin
LMES Eric Staal 30.00 80.00
LMFP Fernando Pisani 20.00 50.00
LMGC Gerry Cheevers 20.00 50.00
LMGL G.Latendresse EXCH 20.00 50.00
LMHA Dominik Hasek EXCH 60.00 100.00
LMHE Milan Hejduk 30.00 80.00
LMHO Gordie Howe 50.00 100.00
LMIK Ilya Kovalchuk EXCH 25.00 60.00
LMJA Jason Arnott 15.00 40.00
LMJC Jeff Carter 20.00 50.00
LMJI Jarome Iginla 30.00 80.00
LMJJ Jussi Jokinen 20.00 60.00
LMJL Joffrey Lupul 15.00 40.00
LMJP Joni Pitkanen 20.00 50.00
LMJT Jose Theodore 20.00 50.00
LMKD Kris Draper 20.00 50.00
LMLR Luc Robitaille 30.00 80.00
LMLU Roberto Luongo 100.00 200.00
LMMA Matt Carle 15.00 40.00
LMMB Martin Brodeur 150.00 300.00
LMMF Marc-Andre Fleury 60.00 120.00
LMMG Marian Gaborik 25.00 60.00
LMMI Mike Cammalleri 20.00 50.00
LMMM Mike Modano 50.00 100.00
LMMN Markus Naslund 20.00 50.00
LMMR Michael Ryder 20.00 50.00
LMMT Marty Turco 20.00 50.00
LMNL Nicklas Lidstrom 25.00 60.00
LMOJ Olli Jokinen 20.00 50.00
LMOR Bobby Orr 125.00 250.00
LMPE Michael Peca 20.00 50.00
LMPI P-M Bouchard 20.00 50.00
LMPK Phil Kessel 20.00 50.00
LMPM Patrick Marleau 20.00 50.00
LMPO Ryan Potulny 20.00 50.00
LMPP Petr Prucha 25.00 60.00
LMRH Ron Hextall 50.00 100.00
LMRI Mike Ribeiro 20.00 50.00
LMRL Reggie Leach EXCH 20.00 50.00
LMRM Mike Richards 25.00 60.00
LMRV Rogie Vachon 30.00 80.00
LMRY Ryan Miller 40.00 100.00
LMSB Steve Bernier 15.00 40.00
LMSC Sidney Crosby 200.00 400.00
LMSK Saku Koivu 30.00 80.00
LMSM Ryan Smyth 25.00 60.00
LMSV Marek Svatos 15.00 40.00
LMTH Tomas Holmstrom 20.00 50.00
LMTL Ted Lindsay 30.00 80.00
LMTO Terry O'Reilly 20.00 50.00
LMVA Thomas Vanek 50.00 100.00
LMWG Wayne Gretzky EXCH 200.00 400.00
LMZC Zdeno Chara 25.00 60.00

2006-07 SP Game Used Rookie Exclusives Autographs

STATED PRINT RUN 100
REAB Adam Burish 10.00 25.00
REAE Alexander Edler 10.00 25.00
REAK Anze Kopitar 25.00 60.00
REAL Alex Brooks 6.00 15.00
REAR Alexander Radulov 12.00 30.00
REBB Brendan Bell 6.00 15.00
REBO Ben Ondrus 6.00 15.00
REBR Mike Brown 6.00 15.00
RECA Mike Card 6.00 15.00
REDB Dustin Byfuglien 15.00 40.00
REDL Drew Larman 6.00 15.00
REDS Drew Stafford 10.00 25.00
REDU Dustin Boyd 6.00 15.00
REEF Eric Fehr 10.00 25.00
REEM Evgeni Malkin 40.00 80.00
REGL Guillaume Latendresse 10.00 25.00
REIW Ian White 8.00 20.00
REJF Jean-Francois Racine 8.00 20.00
REJI Jarkko Immonen 6.00 15.00
REJS Jordan Staal 15.00 40.00
REJW Jeremy Williams 6.00 15.00
REKP Konstantin Pushkarev 8.00 20.00
REKY Keith Yandle 12.00 30.00
RELE Loui Eriksson 10.00 25.00
RELS Ladislav Smid 6.00 15.00
REMB Michael Blunden 6.00 15.00
REMC Matt Carle 6.00 15.00
REMM Masi Marjamaki 6.00 15.00
REMO Michel Ouellet 8.00 20.00
REMP Marc-Antoine Pouliot 6.00 15.00
REMS Mark Stuart 6.00 15.00
REMV Marc-Edouard Vlasic 6.00 15.00
REND Nigel Dawes 6.00 15.00
RENM Nathan McIver 6.00 15.00
RENO Fredrik Norrena 6.00 15.00
RENW Noah Welch 6.00 15.00
REPO Patrick O'Sullivan 10.00 25.00
REPK Phil Kessel 15.00 40.00
REPO Ryan Potulny 6.00 15.00
REPS Paul Stastny 15.00 40.00
REPT Patrick Thoresen 6.00 15.00
RERS Ryan Shannon 6.00 15.00
RESO Shane O'Brien 6.00 15.00
RESP Janis Sprukts 6.00 15.00
RESW Shea Weber 15.00 40.00
RETK Tomas Kopecky 8.00 20.00
RETZ Travis Zajac 12.00 30.00
REYS Yan Stastny 6.00 15.00

2006-07 SP Game Used SIGnificance

STATED PRINT RUN 50 #'d SETS
SAF Alexander Frolov 8.00 20.00
SAH Ales Hemsky 8.00 20.00
SAK Andrei Kostitsyn 6.00 15.00
SAL Andrew Ladd 8.00 20.00
SAM Al Montoya 8.00 20.00
SAN Antero Niittymaki 8.00 20.00
SBG Brian Gionta 8.00 20.00
SBM Bryan McCabe 6.00 15.00
SBN Bob Nystrom 6.00 15.00
SBR Daniel Briere 8.00 20.00
SCB Cam Barker 6.00 15.00
SCH Cristobal Huet 10.00 25.00
SCK Chuck Kobasew 6.00 15.00
SCN Cam Neely 12.00 30.00
SCW Cam Ward 10.00 25.00
SDB Dustin Brown 8.00 20.00
SDC Don Cherry 20.00 40.00
SDE Denis Savard 8.00 20.00
SDK Duncan Keith 8.00 20.00
SDP Denis Potvin 6.00 15.00
SDR Dwayne Roloson 6.00 15.00
SDS Derek Sanderson 8.00 20.00
SDT Dave Taylor 6.00 15.00
SEC Erik Cole 6.00 15.00
SEM Evgeni Malkin 40.00 80.00
SEN Eric Nystrom 6.00 15.00
SES Eric Staal 8.00 20.00
SFP Fernando Pisani 6.00 15.00
SGA Marian Gaborik 12.00 30.00
SGH Gordie Howe 50.00 100.00
SGL Guillaume Latendresse 10.00 25.00
SHI Chris Higgins 6.00 15.00
SHO Marcel Hossa 5.00 12.00
SHT Hannu Toivonen 6.00 15.00
SHZ Henrik Zetterberg 12.00 30.00
SIK Ilya Kovalchuk 15.00 40.00
SJA Jason Arnott 8.00 20.00
SJB Jay Bouwmeester 8.00 20.00
SJC Jeff Carter 8.00 20.00
SJP Joni Pitkanen 6.00 15.00
SJS Jarret Stoll 8.00 20.00
SKB Keith Ballard 6.00 15.00
SKD Kris Draper 8.00 20.00
SKL Kari Lehtonen 10.00 25.00
SKO Mikko Koivu 8.00 20.00
SLE Reggie Leach 8.00 20.00
SLN Ladislav Nagy 5.00 12.00
SMA Ryan Malone 6.00 15.00
SMB Martin Brodeur 40.00 100.00
SMC Mike Cammalleri 8.00 20.00
SMD Andy McDonald 6.00 15.00
SMG Martin Gerber 8.00 20.00
SMH Michal Handzus 5.00 12.00
SMM Milan Michalek 6.00 15.00
SMP Michael Peca 6.00 15.00
SMR Mike Richards 8.00 20.00

MT Marty Turco 8.00 20.00
NH Nathan Horton 8.00 20.00
NZ Nikolai Zherdev 5.00 12.00
PA Mark Parrish 5.00 12.00
PB Pierre-Marc Bouchard 6.00 15.00
PH Chris Phillips 5.00 12.00
PP Petr Prucha 6.00 15.00
RB Richard Brodeur 8.00 20.00
RE Robert Esche 6.00 15.00
RF Ruslan Fedotenko 5.00 12.00
RH Ron Hextall 15.00 40.00
RI Mike Ribeiro 5.00 12.00
RK Rostislav Klesla 5.00 12.00
RM Ryan Miller 20.00 50.00
RN Rick Nash 10.00 25.00
RS Ryan Smyth 6.00 15.00
RV Rogie Vachon 15.00 40.00
RW Ryan Whitney 5.00 12.00
RY Michael Ryder 6.00 15.00
SA Marc Savard 8.00 20.00
SB Steve Bernier 6.00 15.00
SC Sidney Crosby 100.00 200.00
SV Marek Svatos 6.00 15.00
SW Stephen Weiss 6.00 15.00
TH Tomas Holmstrom 6.00 15.00
TL Ted Lindsay 8.00 20.00
TO Terry O'Reilly 8.00 20.00
TU Darcy Tucker 8.00 20.00
TV Tomas Vokoun 8.00 20.00
VA Thomas Vanek 10.00 25.00
VF Valtteri Filppula 8.00 20.00
VT Vesa Toskala 8.00 20.00
WR Wade Redden 5.00 12.00
ZC Zdeno Chara 8.00 20.00

2007-08 SP Game Used

This set was issued into the hobby in three-card packs, with a $29.99 SRP, which came six packs to a box and 12 boxes to a case. Cards numbered 1-100 are veterans while cards 101-200 are Rookie Cards. Within the Rookie Card subset: Cards numbered 101-190 were issued to a stated print run of 999 serial numbered sets and cards 191-200 were issued to a stated print run of 99 serial numbered sets.

COMP.SET w/o SPs (100) 25.00 60.00
(101-190) PRINT RUN 999 SER.#'d SETS
(191-200) PRINT RUN 99 SER.#'d SETS
Alexander Ovechkin 3.00 8.00
Olaf Kolzig .75 2.00
Alexander Semin .75 2.00
Roberto Luongo 1.00 2.50
Markus Naslund .75 2.00
Henrik Sedin .75 2.00
Daniel Sedin .75 2.00
Mats Sundin .75 2.00
Vesa Toskala .60 1.50
0 Darcy Tucker .60 1.50
1 Alexander Steen .75 2.00
2 Martin St. Louis .75 2.00
3 Vincent Lecavalier .60 1.50
4 Brad Richards .75 2.00
5 Doug Weight .75 2.00
6 Keith Tkachuk .75 2.00
7 Paul Kariya 1.00 2.50
8 Joe Thornton 1.00 2.50
9 Jonathan Cheechoo .75 2.00
20 Evgeni Nabokov .60 1.50
21 Patrick Marleau .75 2.00
22 Jordan Staal .75 2.00
23 Sidney Crosby 3.00 8.00
24 Marc-Andre Fleury 1.25 3.00
25 Evgeni Malkin 2.50 6.00
26 Shane Doan .60 1.50
27 Ed Jovanovski .60 1.50
28 Simon Gagne .75 2.00
29 Daniel Briere .75 2.00
30 Jeff Carter .75 2.00
31 Jason Spezza .75 2.00
32 Daniel Alfredsson .75 2.00
33 Ray Emery .60 1.50
34 Dany Heatley .75 2.00
35 Jaromir Jagr 2.00 5.00
36 Henrik Lundqvist 1.00 2.50
37 Chris Drury .60 1.50
38 Bill Guerin .75 2.00
39 Rick DiPietro .60 1.50
40 Miroslav Satan .60 1.50
41 Martin Brodeur 1.50 4.00
42 Patrik Elias .75 2.00
43 Zach Parise 1.00 2.50
44 Chris Mason .60 1.50
45 Alexander Radulov .75 2.00
46 Jason Arnott .60 1.50
47 Saku Koivu .75 2.00
48 Cristobal Huet .60 1.50
49 Michael Ryder .50 1.25
50 Guillaume Latendresse .60 1.50
51 Marian Gaborik 1.00 2.50
52 Pierre-Marc Bouchard .75 2.00
53 Mikko Koivu .60 1.50
54 Anze Kopitar 1.25 3.00
55 Rob Blake .75 2.00
56 Alexander Frolov .50 1.25
57 Tomas Vokoun .60 1.50
58 Nathan Horton .75 2.00
59 Olli Jokinen .60 1.50
60 Dwayne Roloson .60 1.50
61 Ales Hemsky .60 1.50
62 Jarret Stoll .60 1.50
63 Pavel Datsyuk 1.00 2.50
64 Henrik Zetterberg 1.00 2.50
65 Nicklas Lidstrom .75 2.00
66 Dominik Hasek 1.00 2.50
67 Mike Modano 1.25 3.00
68 Marty Turco .75 2.00
69 Mike Ribeiro .60 1.50
70 Rick Nash .75 2.00
71 Sergei Fedorov 1.25 3.00
72 David Vyborny .50 1.25
73 Joe Sakic 1.25 3.00
74 Ryan Smyth .60 1.50
75 Milan Hejduk .60 1.50
76 Paul Stastny .75 2.00
77 Nikolai Khabibulin .75 2.00
78 Martin Havlat .75 2.00
79 Tuomo Ruutu .75 2.00
80 Eric Staal 1.00 2.50
81 Cam Ward .75 2.00
82 Justin Williams .60 1.50
83 Jarome Iginla .75 2.00
84 Alex Tanguay .50 1.25
85 Miikka Kiprusoff .60 1.50
86 Dion Phaneuf .75 2.00
87 Thomas Vanek 1.00 2.50
88 Ryan Miller .75 2.00
89 Jason Pominville .75 2.00
90 Drew Stafford .60 1.50
91 Patrice Bergeron 1.00 2.50
92 Manny Fernandez .60 1.50
93 Phil Kessel 1.00 2.50
94 Ilya Kovalchuk .75 2.00
95 Marian Hossa .60 1.50
96 Kari Lehtonen .60 1.50
97 Chris Pronger .60 1.50
98 Ryan Getzlaf 1.25 3.00
99 Jean-Sebastien Giguere .75 2.00
100 Scott Niedermayer .75 2.00
101 Jeff Schultz RC 5.00 12.00
102 Jamie Hunt RC 4.00 10.00
103 Mason Raymond RC 6.00 15.00
104 Jannik Hansen RC 5.00 12.00
105 Matt Smaby RC 4.00 10.00
106 Mike Lundin RC 4.00 10.00
107 Erik Johnson RC 6.00 15.00
108 David Perron RC 6.00 15.00
109 Steve Wagner RC 4.00 10.00
110 Torrey Mitchell RC 5.00 12.00
111 Tomas Plihal RC 5.00 12.00
112 Martin Hanzal RC 5.00 12.00
113 Craig Weller RC 4.00 10.00
114 Daniel Winnik RC 5.00 12.00
115 Daniel Carcillo RC 5.00 12.00
116 Ryan Parent RC 4.00 10.00
117 Stefan Meyer RC 5.00 12.00
118 Denis Tolpeko RC 4.00 10.00
119 Nathan Guenin RC 5.00 12.00
120 Riley Cote RC 5.00 12.00
121 Danny Bois RC 4.00 10.00
122 Nick Foligno RC 8.00 20.00
123 Brian Elliott RC 8.00 20.00
124 Marc Staal RC 6.00 15.00
125 Brandon Dubinsky RC 8.00 20.00
126 Ryan Callahan RC 8.00 20.00
127 Daniel Girardi RC 5.00 12.00
128 Frans Nielsen RC 6.00 15.00
129 Drew Fata RC 4.00 10.00
130 Nicklas Bergfors RC 4.00 10.00
131 Andy Greene RC 5.00 12.00
132 Mark Fraser RC 4.00 10.00
133 David Clarkson RC 6.00 15.00
134 Rod Pelley RC 4.00 10.00
135 Ville Koistinen RC 4.00 10.00
136 Rich Peverley RC 6.00 15.00
137 Kyle Chipchura RC 6.00 15.00
138 Jaroslav Halak RC 10.00 25.00
139 Duncan Milroy RC 4.00 10.00
140 Petr Kalus RC 4.00 10.00
141 Lauri Tukonen RC 4.00 10.00
142 Jonathan Bernier RC 10.00 25.00
143 Jack Johnson RC 5.00 12.00
144 Brady Murray RC 4.00 10.00
145 John Zeiler RC 4.00 10.00
146 Shay Stephenson RC 4.00 10.00
147 Joe Piskula RC 4.00 10.00
148 Gabe Gauthier RC 4.00 10.00
149 Martin Lojek RC 4.00 10.00
150 Cory Murphy RC 4.00 10.00
151 Rob Schremp RC 5.00 12.00
152 Andrew Cogliano RC 6.00 15.00
153 Tom Gilbert RC 5.00 12.00
154 Bryan Young RC 4.00 10.00
155 Zach Stortini RC 4.00 10.00
156 Sebastien Bisaillon RC 4.00 10.00
157 Matt Ellis RC 5.00 12.00
158 Matt Niskanen RC 6.00 15.00
159 Tobias Stephan RC 5.00 12.00
160 Joel Lundqvist RC 4.00 10.00
161 Chris Conner RC 4.00 10.00
162 Kris Russell RC 5.00 12.00
163 Tomas Popperle RC 5.00 12.00
164 Marc Methot RC 4.00 10.00
165 Jared Boll RC 5.00 12.00
166 Curtis Glencross RC 6.00 15.00
167 Tyler Weiman RC 5.00 12.00
168 Jaroslav Hlinka RC 5.00 12.00
169 Jeff Finger RC 4.00 10.00
170 Colin Fraser RC 4.00 10.00
171 Bryan Bickell RC 8.00 20.00
172 Magnus Johansson RC 4.00 10.00
173 Jonas Nordqvist RC 4.00 10.00
174 David Koci RC 4.00 10.00
175 Curtis McElhinney RC 6.00 15.00
176 Matt Keetley RC 5.00 12.00
177 David Moss RC 6.00 15.00
178 Tomi Maki RC 4.00 10.00
179 Mark Mancari RC 5.00 12.00
180 Patrick Kaleta RC 4.00 10.00
181 David Krejci RC 12.00 30.00
182 Milan Lucic RC 10.00 25.00
183 Jonathan Sigalet RC 4.00 10.00
184 Brett Sterling RC 4.00 10.00
185 Tobias Enstrom RC 6.00 15.00
186 Ondrej Pavelec RC 8.00 20.00
187 Drew Miller RC 5.00 12.00
188 Ryan Carter RC 4.00 10.00
189 Jonas Hiller RC 8.00 20.00
190 Kent Huskins RC 4.00 10.00
191 Nick Backstrom/99 RC 40.00 80.00
192 Peter Mueller/99 RC 12.00 30.00
193 Jiri Tlusty/99 RC 15.00 40.00
194 Carey Price/99 RC 60.00 120.00
195 J. Sheppard/99 RC 10.00 25.00
196 D. Setoguchi/99 RC 15.00 40.00
197 Sam Gagner/99 RC 20.00 50.00
198 J. Toews/99 RC 75.00 150.00
199 Patrick Kane/99 RC 60.00 120.00
200 Bryan Little/99 RC 15.00 40.00

2007-08 SP Game Used Gold

*1-100 GOLD/100: 2.5X TO 6X BASIC CARDS
1-100 STATED PRINT RUN 100
*101-190 ROOK/50: .8X TO 2X BASIC RC
*1910-200 ROOKIE/50: .4X TO 1X BASIC RC
101-200 ROOKIE PRINT RUN 50
194 Carey Price 75.00 135.00
198 Jonathan Toews 60.00 120.00
199 Patrick Kane 50.00 100.00

2007-08 SP Game Used Spectrum

*SPEC (1-100): 3X TO 8X
*SPEC RCs (101-190): 1.2X TO 3X
*SPEC RCs (191-200): .6X TO1.5X
STATED PRINT RUN 25 SER.#'d SETS
194 Carey Price 60.00 120.00
198 Jonathan Toews 75.00 150.00
199 Patrick Kane 60.00 120.00

2007-08 SP Game Used Authentic Fabrics

*PATCH/50: 1.5X TO 4X BASIC JSY
*RAINBOW/100: .8X TO 2X JSY
AFAK Alex Kovalev 4.00 10.00
AFAO Adam Oates 5.00 12.00
AFAR Alexander Radulov 5.00 12.00
AFAS Anton Stastny 3.00 8.00
AFAY Alexei Yashin 4.00 10.00
AFBB Bob Bourne 3.00 8.00
AFBG Bill Guerin 5.00 12.00
AFBI Bill Ranford 5.00 12.00
AFBM Brendan Morrison 3.00 8.00
AFBO Brad Boyes 3.00 8.00
AFBP Bob Probert 4.00 10.00
AFBR Brandon Bochenski 3.00 8.00
AFBS Billy Smith 5.00 12.00
AFBW Brendan Witt 3.00 8.00
AFCA Colby Armstrong 3.00 8.00
AFCC Chris Chelios 5.00 12.00
AFCD Chris Drury 4.00 10.00
AFCH Chris Higgins 3.00 8.00
AFCN Cam Neely 5.00 12.00
AFCO Mike Commodore 3.00 8.00
AFCW Cam Ward 5.00 12.00
AFDA Daniel Alfredsson 5.00 12.00
AFDG Doug Gilmour 6.00 15.00
AFDH Dale Hawerchuk 6.00 15.00
AFDL David Legwand 4.00 10.00
AFDR Dwayne Roloson 4.00 10.00
AFDW Doug Weight 5.00 12.00
AFEB Ed Belfour 5.00 12.00
AFEN Evgeni Nabokov 4.00 10.00
AFES Eric Staal 6.00 15.00
AFEV Evgeni Malkin 15.00 40.00
AFFM Frank Mahovlich 6.00 15.00
AFGF Grant Fuhr 5.00 12.00
AFGI Brian Gionta 4.00 10.00
AFGM Glen Murray 4.00 10.00
AFGR Gary Roberts 3.00 8.00
AFHE Dany Heatley 5.00 12.00
AFHL Henrik Lundqvist 6.00 15.00
AFHT Hannu Toivonen 4.00 10.00
AFIK Ilya Kovalchuk 5.00 12.00
AFJB Jay Bouwmeester 5.00 12.00
AFJC Jonathan Cheechoo 5.00 12.00
AFJG Jean-Sebastien Giguere 5.00 12.00
AFJI Jarome Iginla 5.00 12.00
AFJJ Jaromir Jagr 12.00 30.00
AFJL Joffrey Lupul 4.00 10.00
AFJO Joe Sakic 8.00 20.00
AFJP Joni Pitkanen 3.00 8.00
AFJS Jarret Stoll 4.00 10.00
AFJT Joe Thornton 6.00 15.00
AFJU Jussi Jokinen 3.00 8.00
AFJW Justin Williams 4.00 10.00
AFKL Kari Lehtonen 4.00 10.00
AFKO Anze Kopitar 8.00 20.00
AFKT Keith Tkachuk 5.00 12.00
AFLN Ladislav Nagy 3.00 8.00
AFLR Larry Robinson 5.00 12.00
AFMA Marc Savard 3.00 8.00
AFMB Martin Brodeur 10.00 25.00
AFMC Bryan McCabe 3.00 8.00
AFMF Manny Fernandez 4.00 10.00
AFMG Marian Gaborik 6.00 15.00
AFMH Marian Hossa 4.00 10.00
AFMK Mikko Koivu 4.00 10.00
AFML Manny Legace 4.00 10.00
AFMM Mike Modano 8.00 20.00
AFMN Markus Naslund 5.00 12.00
AFMO Brenden Morrow 4.00 10.00
AFMR Mike Ribeiro 4.00 10.00
AFMS Miroslav Satan 4.00 10.00
AFMT Marty Turco 5.00 12.00
AFON Owen Nolan 4.00 10.00
AFOV Alexander Ovechkin 8.00 20.00
AFPB Patrice Bergeron 6.00 15.00
AFPD Pavel Datsyuk 6.00 15.00
AFPE Patrik Elias 5.00 12.00
AFPR Patrick Roy 10.00 25.00
AFRA Andrew Raycroft 4.00 10.00
AFRB Brian Rafalski 4.00 10.00
AFRE Mark Recchi 6.00 15.00
AFRI Brad Richards 5.00 12.00
AFRL Roberto Luongo 6.00 15.00
AFRN Rick Nash 5.00 12.00
AFRS Ryan Smyth 4.00 10.00
AFRY Michael Ryder 3.00 8.00
AFSA Borje Salming 5.00 12.00
AFSC Sidney Crosby 8.00 20.00
AFSG Simon Gagne 5.00 12.00
AFSH Brendan Shanahan 6.00 15.00
AFSK Saku Koivu 5.00 12.00
AFSM Martin St. Louis 5.00 12.00
AFSN Scott Niedermayer 5.00 12.00
AFSP Jason Spezza 5.00 12.00
AFST Brad Stuart 3.00 8.00
AFSU Mats Sundin 5.00 12.00
AFSV Marek Svatos 3.00 8.00
AFTH Jose Theodore 5.00 12.00
AFTW Tiger Williams 4.00 10.00
AFVL Vincent Lecavalier 4.00 10.00

2007-08 SP Game Used Authentic Fabrics Duals

STATED PRINT RUN 100 SER.#'d SETS
*PATCH/25: 1.2X TO 3X BASIC DUAL
AF2AD Tanguay/Phaneuf 4.00 10.00
AF2AH Alfredsson/Heatley 4.00 10.00
AF2AM Afinogenov/Miller 4.00 10.00
AF2BB E.Belfour/M.Brodeur 8.00 20.00
AF2BG M.Brodeur/B.Gionta 8.00 20.00
AF2BH Bouwmeester/Horton 4.00 10.00
AF2BK P.Bergeron/P.Kessel 5.00 12.00
AF2BL M.Brodeur/R.Luongo 8.00 20.00
AF2BW Brind'Amour/Ward 4.00 10.00
AF2CB J.Cheechoo/S.Bernier 4.00 10.00
AF2CM S.Crosby/E.Malkin 30.00 60.00
AF2CO S.Crosby/A.Ovechkin 30.00 60.00
AF2CR C.Chelios/B.Rafalski 4.00 10.00
AF2CS M.Commodore/E.Staal 5.00 12.00
AF2DD K.Draper/P.Datsyuk 5.00 12.00
AF2DG P.Demitra/M.Gaborik 5.00 12.00
AF2DS R.DiPietro/B.Smith 4.00 10.00
AF2EJ E.Staal/J.Staal 5.00 12.00
AF2FB Fernandez/Bergeron 5.00 12.00
AF2FR G.Fuhr/B.Ranford 4.00 10.00
AF2FS P.Forsberg/B.Salming 5.00 12.00
AF2FT Fernandez/Toivonen 3.00 8.00
AF2GB Gaborik/Bouchard 5.00 12.00
AF2GC S.Gagne/J.Carter 4.00 10.00
AF2GJ M.Green/M.Jurcina 4.00 10.00
AF2GK M.Gaborik/M.Koivu 5.00 12.00
AF2GL S.Gagne/J.Lupul 4.00 10.00
AF2GS B.Guerin/M.Satan 4.00 10.00
AF2HD D.Hasek/P.Datsyuk 5.00 12.00
AF2HK Hossa/Kovalchuk 4.00 10.00
AF2HL D.Hasek/N.Lidstrom 5.00 12.00
AF2IK J.Iginla/M.Kiprusoff 4.00 10.00
AF2JC J.Jagr/C.Drury 10.00 25.00
AF2JD J.Spezza/D.Heatley 4.00 10.00
AF2JH O.Jokinen/N.Horton 4.00 10.00
AF2JJ J.Sakic/J.Thornton 6.00 15.00
AF2JL J.Jagr/H.Lundqvist 10.00 25.00
AF2JP J.Jagr/P.Prucha 10.00 25.00
AF2JR J.Sakic/R.Smyth 6.00 15.00
AF2KB P.Kariya/B.Boyes 5.00 12.00
AF2KK S.Koivu/M.Koivu 4.00 10.00
AF2KT P.Kariya/K.Tkachuk 5.00 12.00
AF2LA D.Legwand/J.Arnott 3.00 8.00
AF2LB P.Leclaire/G.Brule 3.00 8.00
AF2LC Lemieux/Crosby 20.00 50.00
AF2LH M.Ryder/C.Huet 3.00 8.00
AF2LJ J.Lehtinen/J.Jokinen 2.50 6.00
AF2LM M.Lemieux/M.Messier 12.00 30.00
AF2LR D.Legwand/A.Radulov 4.00 10.00
AF2LZ Lidstrom/Zetterberg 5.00 12.00
AF2MA M.Sundin/A.Raycroft 4.00 10.00
AF2MB M.Sundin/B.Salming 4.00 10.00
AF2MC M.Ryder/C.Higgins 2.50 6.00
AF2MJ M.Modano/J.Mullen 3.00 8.00
AF2ML M.Sundin/A.Steen 4.00 10.00
AF2MM L.McDonald/J.Mullen 3.00 8.00
AF2MR M.Modano/M.Ribeiro 6.00 15.00
AF2MT Marleau/Thornton 5.00 12.00
AF2NB C.Neely/R.Bourque 6.00 15.00
AF2NG Niedermayer/Giguere 4.00 10.00
AF2NI O.Nolan/J.Iginla 4.00 10.00
AF2NK L.Nagy/A.Kopitar 6.00 15.00
AF2NL M.Naslund/R.Luongo 5.00 12.00
AF2NM Havlat/Khabibulin 4.00 10.00
AF2NO C.Neely/A.Oates 4.00 10.00
AF2OM A.Ovechkin/E.Malkin 15.00 40.00
AF2PB M.Parrish/P.Bouchard 4.00 10.00
AF2PM D.Phaneuf/A.MacInnis 4.00 10.00
AF2PV G.Perreault/T.Vanek 5.00 12.00
AF2RB P.Roy/M.Brodeur 12.00 30.00
AF2RH D.Roloson/A.Hemsky 3.00 8.00
AF2RR G.Roberts/M.Recchi 5.00 12.00
AF2SA S.Koivu/A.Kovalev 4.00 10.00
AF2SB B.Smith/B.Bourne 4.00 10.00
AF2SC M.Comrie/M.Satan 3.00 8.00
AF2SE H.Sedin/D.Sedin 4.00 10.00
AF2SF M.Sundin/P.Forsberg 5.00 12.00
AF2SH S.Samsonov/M.Havlat 4.00 10.00
AF2SL M.Legace/B.Boyes 3.00 8.00
AF2SM M.Savard/G.Murray 3.00 8.00
AF2SN Selanne/Niedermayer 8.00 20.00
AF2SP J.Stoll/F.Pisani 3.00 8.00
AF2SR S.Shutt/L.Robinson 4.00 10.00
AF2SS J.Sakic/P.Stastny 6.00 15.00
AF2ST J.Sakic/J.Theodore 6.00 15.00
AF2SW M.Svatos/W.Wolski 3.00 8.00
AF2TC Thornton/Cheechoo 5.00 12.00
AF2TM M.Turco/B.Morrow 4.00 10.00
AF2TO M.Stajan/A.Steen 4.00 10.00
AF2TP R.Torres/F.Pisani 2.50 6.00
AF2VB Lecavalier/B.Richards 4.00 10.00
AF2VC M.Naslund/M.Ohlund 4.00 10.00
AF2VJ T.Vokoun/O.Jokinen 3.00 8.00
AF2WK D.Wilson/D.Keith 4.00 10.00
AF2WS J.Williams/E.Staal 5.00 12.00
AF2WT D.Weight/K.Tkachuk 4.00 10.00
AF2ZF N.Zherdev/S.Fedorov 5.00 12.00

2007-08 SP Game Used Authentic Fabrics Triples

STATED PRINT RUN 25 SER.#'d SETS
AF3AMV Afino/Miller/Vanek 25.00 50.00
AF3ASH Alfred/Spezza/Heatley 25.00 50.00
AF3BCC Blake/Calder/Cammi 12.00 30.00
AF3BEG Brodeur/Elias/Gionta 30.00 60.00
AF3BLK Brodeur/Luongo/Kip 25.00 60.00
AF3BPG Bertuzzi/Perry/Getzlaf 15.00 40.00
AF3BSW Brind/Staal/Ward 15.00 40.00
AF3CCW Commo/Cole/Williams 12.00 30.00
AF3CVP Connolly/Vanek/Paille 12.00 30.00
AF3DGK Demitra/Gabor/Koivu 12.00 30.00
AF3FBK Fernan/Berger/Kessel 25.00 50.00
AF3FCM Fleury/Crosby/Malkin
AF3GBB Gagne/Briere/Biron 25.00 50.00
AF3GDH Gomez/Drury/Hollweg 25.00 50.00
AF3GSD Guerin/Satan/DiPietro 12.00 30.00
AF3HDD Hasek/Draper/Datsyuk 30.00 60.00
AF3HKL Hossa/Koval/Lehtonen
AF3HSB Hejduk/Svatos/Budaj 15.00 40.00
AF3ITK Iginla/Tanguay/Kipr 15.00 40.00
AF3JSP Jagr/Straka/Prucha 25.00 50.00
AF3KGO Kolzig/Green/Ovechkin 40.00 80.00
AF3KPK Kovalev/Perezh/Kostit 12.00 30.00
AF3KRK Koivu/Ryder/Kovalev 30.00 60.00
AF3KWT Kariya/Weight/Tkach 10.00 25.00
AF3LAR Legwand/Arnott/Radul 15.00 40.00
AF3LBS Legace/Boyes/Stemp 10.00 25.00
AF3LGM Lemieux/Gretz/Messier
AF3LHZ Lidstrom/Holmstrom/Zett 20.00 50.00
AF3LNF Fedor/Leclaire/Nash 12.00 30.00
AF3LRC Lupul/Richards/Carter 10.00 25.00
AF3LRS Lecav/Richard/St. Lou 15.00 40.00
AF3LSS Luongo/Sedin/Sedin
AF3MBC Michalek/Bernier/Carle 10.00 25.00
AF3MMM Lanny/Mullen/MacInnis 12.00 30.00
AF3MRT Modano/Ribeiro/Turco 12.00 30.00
AF3NFK Nagy/Frolov/Kopitar
AF3NMK Naslund/Morris/Kesler 15.00 40.00
AF3NRL Nolan/Regehr/Lombo 10.00 25.00
AF3PBM Parrish/Bouch/Moore 10.00 25.00
AF3REM Redden/Emery/Mesz 12.00 30.00
AF3RMA Recchi/Malone/Armstr 10.00 25.00
AF3SFA Sundin/Forsberg/Alfred 30.00 60.00
AF3SHR Sams/Havlat/Ruutu 12.00 30.00
AF3SKK Seabrook/Keith/Khabi 10.00 25.00
AF3SLT Sakic/Lecav/Thornton 25.00 50.00
AF3SMC Savard/Murray/Chara 15.00 40.00
AF3SMT Sundin/McCabe/Tosk 15.00 40.00
AF3SNG Selanne/Nied/Giggy 12.00 30.00
AF3SRH Stoll/Roloson/Hemsky 12.00 30.00
AF3SSJ Sakic/Shanahan/Jagr 15.00 40.00
AF3SSW Stajan/Steen/White 10.00 25.00
AF3STS Sakic/Theod/Smyth 15.00 40.00
AF3SWV Savard/Wilson/Vaive 10.00 25.00
AF3THP Torres/Horcoff/Pisani 10.00 25.00
AF3TNC Thorn/Nabokov/Cheech
AF3VJB Vokoun/Jokinen/Bouw 12.00 30.00
AF3VSB Vyborny/Shelley/Brule 10.00 25.00
AF3ZLM Zubov/Leht/Morrow 15.00 40.00

2007-00 SP Game Used Extra SIGnificance

STATED PRINT RUN 10-25
XSAM A.Stastny/M.Stastny 25.00 50.00
XSBB K.Bieksa/L.Bourdon 25.00 50.00
XSBO S.Samsonov/R.Bourque 10.00 25.00
XSCC K.Calder/M.Cammalleri 10.00 25.00
XSDB B.Sutter/D.Sutter 12.00 30.00
XSGD S.Gomez/N.Dawes 12.00 30.00
XSGH W.Gretzky/G.Howe 250.00 350.00
XSHP A.Hemsky/J.Pitkanen 15.00 40.00
XSJP J.Johnson/R.Parent 10.00 25.00
XSKS R.Kesler/R.Shannon 20.00 50.00
XSMA R.Malone/C.Armstrong 20.00 40.00
XSMD Afinogenov/Stafford 10.00 25.00
XSMT M.Modano/M.Turco 20.00 50.00
XSMW M.Svatos/W.Wolski 12.00 30.00
XSPD P.Prucha/N.Dawes 12.00 30.00
XSRC M.Richards/J.Carter 30.00 60.00
XSRH M.Ryder/C.Huet 12.00 30.00
XSSR S.Bernier/R.Clowe 12.00 30.00
XSSW E.Staal/C.Ward 15.00 40.00
XSTC M.Talbot/E.Christensen 15.00 30.00
XSVP M.Vlasic/J.Pavelski 20.00 50.00
XSWC S.Weber/M.Carle 10.00 25.00
XSWL R.Whitney/K.Letang 12.00 30.00
XSWR S.Weber/A.Radulov 10.00 25.00
XSZB N.Zherdev/G.Brule 15.00 40.00

2007-08 SP Game Used Inked Sweaters

STATED PRINT RUN 50 SER.#'d SETS
*PATCH/25: .5X TO 1.2X JSY AU/50
ISAF Alexander Frolov 8.00 20.00
ISAH Ales Hemsky 10.00 25.00
ISAK Andrei Kostitsyn 10.00 25.00
ISAR Alexander Radulov 12.00 30.00
ISAT Alex Tanguay 8.00 20.00
ISBB Brad Boyes 8.00 20.00
ISBF Bernie Federko 8.00 20.00
ISBG Brian Gionta 10.00 25.00
ISBM Brendan Morrison 8.00 20.00
ISBO Pierre-Marc Bouchard 12.00 30.00
ISBR Daniel Briere 12.00 30.00
ISCH Cristobal Huet 10.00 25.00
ISCK Chuck Kobasew 8.00 20.00
ISCP Corey Perry 12.00 30.00
ISCW Cam Ward 12.00 30.00
ISDB Dustin Brown 12.00 30.00
ISDH Dany Heatley 20.00 50.00
ISDP Dion Phaneuf 12.00 30.00
ISDR Dwayne Roloson 10.00 25.00
ISDW Doug Wilson 10.00 25.00
ISEM Evgeni Malkin 30.00 80.00
ISES Eric Staal 15.00 40.00
ISFP Fernando Pisani 8.00 20.00
ISGA Simon Gagne 12.00 30.00
ISGB Gilbert Brule 10.00 25.00
ISGE Martin Gerber 10.00 25.00
ISGL Guy Lafleur 30.00 80.00
ISGM Glen Murray 10.00 25.00
ISHE Milan Hejduk 10.00 25.00
ISHL Henrik Lundqvist 15.00 40.00
ISHT Hannu Toivonen 10.00 25.00
ISHU Trent Hunter 8.00 20.00
ISIW Ian White 8.00 20.00
ISJA Jason Arnott 10.00 25.00
ISJB Jay Bouwmeester 12.00 30.00
ISJC Jeff Carter 12.00 30.00
ISJG Jean-Sebastien Giguere 12.00 30.00
ISJI Jarome Iginla 12.00 30.00
ISJO Jonathan Cheechoo 12.00 30.00
ISJS Jarret Stoll 10.00 25.00
ISJT Jose Theodore 12.00 30.00
ISJW Justin Williams 10.00 25.00
ISKB Kevin Bieksa 10.00 25.00
ISKC Kyle Calder 8.00 20.00
ISKD Kris Draper 8.00 20.00
ISKL Kari Lehtonen 10.00 25.00
ISKO Anze Kopitar 20.00 50.00
ISLI John-Michael Liles 8.00 20.00
ISLN Ladislav Nagy 8.00 20.00
ISLS Ladislav Smid 8.00 20.00
ISMA Martin St. Louis 12.00 30.00
ISMB Martin Biron 10.00 25.00
ISMC Matt Carle 8.00 20.00
ISMF Marc-Andre Fleury 20.00 50.00
ISMG Marian Gaborik 15.00 40.00
ISMH Martin Havlat 12.00 30.00
ISMI Mike Richards 12.00 30.00
ISMJ Milan Jurcina 8.00 20.00
ISMM Mike Modano 20.00 50.00
ISMN Markus Naslund 12.00 30.00
ISMO Brenden Morrow 10.00 25.00
ISMP Marc-Antoine Pouliot 8.00 20.00
ISMR Michael Ryder 8.00 20.00
ISMS Marc Savard 8.00 20.00
ISMT Marty Turco 12.00 30.00
ISNH Nathan Horton 12.00 30.00
ISNL Nicklas Lidstrom 12.00 30.00
ISNZ Nikolai Zherdev 8.00 20.00
ISPB Patrice Bergeron 15.00 40.00
ISPE Patrik Elias 12.00 30.00
ISPK Phil Kessel 15.00 40.00
ISPL Pascal Leclaire 10.00 25.00
ISPP Petr Prucha 8.00 20.00
ISRA Andrew Raycroft 10.00 25.00
ISRE Robert Esche 10.00 25.00
ISRG Ryan Getzlaf 20.00 50.00
ISRI Mike Ribeiro 10.00 25.00
ISRK Ryan Kesler 15.00 40.00
ISRM Ryan Malone 8.00 20.00
ISRN Rick Nash 12.00 30.00
ISRY Ryan Miller 12.00 30.00
ISSA Miroslav Satan 10.00 25.00
ISSB Steve Bernier 8.00 20.00
ISSC Sidney Crosby 75.00 150.00
ISSD Shane Doan 10.00 25.00
ISSG Scott Gomez 10.00 25.00
ISSV Marek Svatos 8.00 20.00
ISSW Shea Weber 10.00 25.00
ISTF Tomas Fleischmann 8.00 20.00
ISTH Tomas Holmstrom 10.00 25.00
ISTV Tomas Vokoun 10.00 25.00
ISVL Vincent Lecavalier 10.00 25.00
ISWE Stephen Weiss 8.00 20.00
ISWW Wojtek Wolski 10.00 25.00
ISZP Zach Parise 15.00 40.00

2007-08 SP Game Used Inked Sweaters Dual

STATED PRINT RUN 25 #'d SETS
IS2CB Cheechoo/Bernier 15.00 30.00
IS2DA D.Roloson/A.Hemsky 10.00 25.00
IS2EG P.Elias/B.Gionta 10.00 25.00
IS2FK A.Frolov/A.Kopitar 20.00 40.00
IS2FM M.Fleury/E.Malkin 40.00 80.00
IS2GB M.Gaborik/P.Bouchard 10.00 25.00
IS2GC S.Gagne/J.Carter 20.00 40.00
IS2GH J.Giguere/D.Heatley 15.00 30.00
IS2GP S.Gomez/P.Prucha 20.00 50.00
IS2HL D.Hasek/N.Lidstrom 30.00 60.00
IS2HS M.Hejduk/M.Svatos
IS2IP J.Iginla/D.Phaneuf 40.00 80.00
IS2LT Lecavalier/Thornton 15.00 40.00
IS2MR M.Modano/M.Ribeiro 20.00 40.00
IS2MW R.Miller/C.Ward 20.00 40.00
IS2NM M.Naslund/B.Morrison 15.00 30.00
IS2OR A.Ovechkin/A.Radulov
IS2PG C.Perry/R.Getzlaf 20.00 50.00
IS2RB P.Roy/R.Bourque 75.00 150.00
IS2RH M.Ryder/C.Huet 20.00 40.00
IS2SB M.Savard/P.Bergeron 12.00 30.00
IS2SN M.St. Louis/R.Nash 15.00 40.00
IS2VH T.Vokoun/N.Horton 15.00 30.00
IS2WS J.Williams/E.Staal 12.00 30.00

2007-08 SP Game Used Legendary Fabrics

STATED PRINT RUN 100 SER.#'d SETS
LFAM Al MacInnis 10.00 25.00
LFAO Adam Oates 10.00 25.00
LFBB Bob Bourne 6.00 15.00
LFBC Bobby Clarke 10.00 25.00
LFBN Bernie Nicholls 6.00 15.00
LFBP Bob Probert 8.00 20.00
LFBR Bill Ranford 10.00 25.00
LFBS Billy Smith 10.00 25.00
LFBU Johnny Bucyk 8.00 20.00
LFCN Cam Neely 10.00 25.00
LFDC Dino Ciccarelli 10.00 25.00
LFDE Denis Savard 12.00 30.00
LFDG Doug Gilmour 12.00 30.00
LFDH Dale Hawerchuk 12.00 30.00
LFDW Doug Wilson 8.00 20.00
LFFM Frank Mahovlich 12.00 30.00
LFGA Glenn Anderson 10.00 25.00
LFGF Grant Fuhr 10.00 25.00
LFGL Guy Lafleur 10.00 25.00
LFGP Gilbert Perreault 10.00 25.00
LFJM Joe Mullen 8.00 20.00
LFLM Lanny McDonald 10.00 25.00
LFLR Larry Robinson 10.00 25.00
LFML Mario Lemieux 20.00 40.00
LFMM Mark Messier 12.00 30.00
LFMU Larry Murphy 8.00 20.00
LFNY Bob Nystrom 6.00 15.00
LFPR Patrick Roy 20.00 40.00
LFPS Peter Stastny 8.00 20.00
LFRB Ray Bourque 12.00 30.00
LFRH Ron Hextall 8.00 20.00
LFRI Richard Brodeur 8.00 20.00
LFRO Luc Robitaille 8.00 20.00
LFRV Rogie Vachon 10.00 25.00
LFSA Borje Salming 10.00 25.00
LFSH Steve Shutt 10.00 25.00
LFSS Scott Stevens 10.00 25.00
LFTW Tiger Williams 8.00 20.00
LFWG Wayne Gretzky 20.00 50.00
LFZP Zigmund Palffy 10.00 25.00

2007-08 SP Game Used Legendary Fabrics Autographs

STATED PRINT RUN 10-25
LAFAM Al MacInnis 15.00 40.00
LAFAO Adam Oates
LAFBB Bob Bourne 10.00 25.00
LAFBC Bobby Clarke
LAFBN Bernie Nicholls 10.00 25.00
LAFBP Bob Probert
LAFBR Bill Ranford
LAFBS Billy Smith 15.00 40.00
LAFBU Johnny Bucyk
LAFCN Cam Neely 20.00 50.00
LAFDC Dino Ciccarelli 15.00 40.00
LAFDE Denis Savard
LAFDG Doug Gilmour 20.00 50.00
LAFDH Dale Hawerchuk 20.00 50.00
LAFDW Doug Wilson 12.00 30.00
LAFFM Frank Mahovlich 25.00 60.00
LAFGA Glenn Anderson 15.00 40.00
LAFGF Grant Fuhr 15.00 40.00
LAFGL Guy Lafleur
LAFGP Gilbert Perreault 15.00 40.00
LAFJM Joe Mullen 12.00 30.00
LAFLM Lanny McDonald
LAFLR Larry Robinson 15.00 40.00
LAFML Mario Lemieux 75.00 150.00
LAFMU Larry Murphy
LAFNY Bob Nystrom 12.00 30.00
LAFPR Patrick Roy 60.00 120.00
LAFPS Peter Stastny 12.00 30.00
LAFRB Ray Bourque 40.00 80.00
LAFRH Ron Hextall 15.00 40.00
LAFRI Richard Brodeur 12.00 30.00
LAFRO Luc Robitaille 15.00 40.00
LAFSA Borje Salming 15.00 40.00
LAFSH Steve Shutt
LAFSS Scott Stevens
LAFTW Tiger Williams 15.00 40.00
LAFWG Wayne Gretzky 125.00 200.00
LAFZP Zigmund Palffy

2007-08 SP Game Used Legends Classic Jerseys

STATED PRINT RUN 100 SER.#'d SETS
*PATCH/50: .8X TO 2X JSY/100
HGJAS Anton Stastny 4.00 10.00
HGJBB Bob Bourne 4.00 10.00
HGJBG Butch Goring
HGJBN Bernie Nicholls 4.00 10.00
HGJBR Bill Ranford 6.00 15.00
HGJBS Billy Smith 6.00 15.00
HGJBT Bryan Trottier 8.00 20.00
HGJDG Doug Gilmour 8.00 20.00
HGJDH Dale Hawerchuk 8.00 20.00
HGJDS Darryl Sittler 5.00 12.00
HGJGA Glenn Anderson 6.00 15.00
HGJGF Grant Fuhr 6.00 15.00
HGJHA Dale Hawerchuk 8.00 20.00
HGJJM Joe Mullen 5.00 12.00
HGJLM Lanny McDonald 6.00 15.00
HGJLR Larry Robinson 6.00 15.00
HGJMU Larry Murphy 5.00 12.00
HGJPS Peter Stastny 5.00 12.00
HGJRB Richard Brodeur 5.00 12.00
HGJRE Ron Ellis 4.00 10.00
HGJRV Rick Vaive 5.00 12.00
HGJSA Borje Salming 6.00 15.00
HGJSS Steve Shutt 6.00 15.00
HGJTW Tiger Williams 5.00 12.00
HGJWC Wendel Clark 6.00 15.00

2007-08 SP Game Used Legends Classic Jerseys Autographs

STATED PRINT RUN 50 SER.#'d SETS
*PATCH AU/25: .8X TO 2X JSY AU/50
HGJAS Anton Stastny 8.00 20.00
HGJBB Bob Bourne 8.00 20.00
HGJBN Bernie Nicholls 8.00 20.00
HGJBR Bill Ranford 12.00 30.00
HGJBS Billy Smith 12.00 30.00
HGJBT Bryan Trottier 15.00 40.00
HGJDG Doug Gilmour 15.00 40.00
HGJDH Dale Hawerchuk 15.00 40.00
HGJDS Darryl Sittler 10.00 25.00
HGJGA Glenn Anderson 12.00 30.00
HGJGF Grant Fuhr 12.00 30.00
HGJHA Dale Hawerchuk 15.00 40.00
HGJJM Joe Mullen 10.00 25.00
HGJLM Lanny McDonald 12.00 30.00
HGJLR Larry Robinson 12.00 30.00
HGJMU Larry Murphy 10.00 25.00
HGJPS Peter Stastny 10.00 25.00
HGJRB Richard Brodeur 10.00 25.00
HGJRE Ron Ellis 8.00 20.00
HGJRV Rick Vaive 10.00 25.00
HGJSA Borje Salming 12.00 30.00
HGJSS Steve Shutt 12.00 30.00
HGJTW Tiger Williams 10.00 25.00
HGJWC Wendel Clark 8.00 20.00

2007-08 SP Game Used Letter Marks

STATED PRINT RUN 50 #'d SETS
LMAC A. Cogliano EXCH 15.00 40.00
LMAF Alexander Frolov 15.00 40.00
LMAH Ales Hemsky 25.00 60.00
LMAK Anze Kopitar 50.00 100.00
LMAM Al MacInnis 15.00 40.00
LMAT Alex Tanguay
LMBC Bobby Clarke 50.00 80.00
LMBF Bernie Federko 15.00 40.00
LMBG Brian Gionta
LMBN Bob Nystrom
LMBP Bernie Parent 50.00 100.00
LMBU Johnny Bucyk 25.00 60.00
LMCA M. Cammalleri EXCH 15.00 40.00
LMCG Clark Gillies 15.00 40.00
LMCN Cam Neely 40.00 80.00
LMCP Corey Perry
LMCW Cam Ward 25.00 60.00
LMDM Dickie Moore
LMDP Denis Potvin 15.00 40.00
LMDT Darcy Tucker
LMDW Doug Wilson 15.00 40.00
LMEM Evgeni Malkin 75.00 120.00
LMES Eric Staal 25.00 60.00
LMGC Gerry Cheevers
LMGH Gordie Howe 75.00 120.00
LMHE M. Hejduk EXCH 15.00 40.00
LMJB Jean Beliveau 40.00 80.00
LMJG Jean-Sebastien Giguere 15.00 40.00
LMJJ Jack Johnson 15.00 40.00
LMJK Jari Kurri 40.00 80.00
LMJS Jordan Staal 25.00 60.00
LMJT Jonathan Toews 100.00 200.00
LMKD Kris Draper 15.00 40.00
LMKE Phil Kessel 25.00 60.00
LMLA Guy Lafleur 50.00 100.00
LMMB Mike Bossy 60.00 80.00
LMMC Andy McDonald 15.00 40.00
LMMD Marcel Dionne 25.00 60.00
LMMF Marc-Andre Fleury 50.00 100.00
LMMR Mike Ribeiro
LMMS Milt Schmidt 15.00 40.00
LMMU Peter Mueller 20.00 50.00
LMPA Paul Henderson
LMPE Phil Esposito 40.00 80.00
LMPK Patrick Kane 75.00 150.00
LMPR Carey Price 125.00 250.00
LMPS Paul Stastny
LMRA Andrew Raycroft 15.00 40.00
LMRH Ron Hextall 50.00 100.00
LMRM Ryan Miller 25.00 60.00
LMRS Rob Schremp 25.00 60.00
LMSK Jack Skille
LMSM Stan Mikita 25.00 60.00
LMTE Tony Esposito 100.00 200.00
LMTL Ted Lindsay 20.00 50.00
LMTO Terry O'Reilly 25.00 60.00
LMTV Tomas Vokoun 50.00 80.00
LMVL V. Lecavalier/25 EXCH 60.00 100.00
LMWG Wayne Gretzky 200.00 400.00

2007-08 SP Game Used Number Marks

STATED PRINT RUN 25 SER.#'d SETS
NMAH Ales Hemsky 15.00 40.00
NMAK Anze Kopitar 25.00 60.00
NMAO Alexander Ovechkin 175.00 300.00
NMAR Andrew Raycroft 20.00 50.00
NMBC Bobby Clarke 75.00 150.00
NMBF Bernie Federko
NMBH Bobby Hull 40.00 100.00
NMBO Bobby Orr 200.00 400.00
NMBR Martin Brodeur 175.00 300.00
NMCA Jeff Carter 30.00 80.00
NMCP Corey Perry
NMCW Cam Ward 15.00 40.00
NMDH Dany Heatley
NMDP Dion Phaneuf
NMDR Dwayne Roloson 15.00 40.00
NMDT Darcy Tucker
NMEM Evgeni Malkin 100.00 200.00
NMES Eric Staal 25.00 60.00
NMGH Gordie Howe 125.00 250.00
NMGP Gilbert Perreault 30.00 80.00
NMHA Dominik Hasek 75.00 150.00
NMHL Henrik Lundqvist 75.00 150.00
NMIK Ilya Kovalchuk
NMJC Jonathan Cheechoo 30.00 80.00
NMJI Jarome Iginla 75.00 150.00
NMJJ J. Johnson EXCH 40.00 100.00
NMJK Jari Kurri 40.00 100.00
NMJS Jordan Staal 50.00 100.00
NMJT Jose Theodore 15.00 40.00
NMMB Mike Bossy 75.00 150.00
NMMC M. Cammalleri EXCH 20.00 50.00
NMMG Marian Gaborik
NMMN Markus Naslund 15.00 40.00
NMMO Mike Modano 75.00 150.00
NMMR Michael Ryder 15.00 40.00
NMMS Martin St. Louis 25.00 60.00
NMMT Marty Turco 20.00 50.00
NMNL Nicklas Lidstrom 75.00 125.00
NMPE Patrik Elias 20.00 50.00
NMPK Phil Kessel 25.00 60.00
NMPR Pat LaFontaine
NMPS Paul Stastny 40.00 100.00
NMRA Alexander Radulov 40.00 100.00
NMRB R. Bourque EXCH 75.00 150.00
NMRM Ryan Miller 40.00 100.00
NMRN Rick Nash 75.00 150.00
NMRS Rob Schremp
NMSA Miroslav Satan 15.00 40.00
NMSC Sidney Crosby 200.00 400.00
NMSD Shane Doan 75.00 150.00
NMSG Simon Gagne 15.00 40.00
NMSK Saku Koivu
NMSV Marek Svatos 25.00 60.00
NMTE Tony Esposito 40.00 100.00
NMTH Joe Thornton 30.00 80.00
NMTV Tomas Vokoun 25.00 60.00
NMVL Vincent Lecavalier 40.00 100.00
NMWG Wayne Gretzky 200.00 400.00
NMZP Zach Parise

2007-08 SP Game Used Rookie Exclusives Autographs

STATED PRINT RUN 100 SER.#'d SETS
REAC Andrew Cogliano 10.00 25.00
REAG Andy Greene 8.00 20.00
REAS Anton Stralman 6.00 15.00
REBA Nicklas Backstrom 30.00 60.00
REBD Brandon Dubinsky 15.00 40.00
REBE Jonathan Bernier 12.00 30.00

REBL Bryan Little 8.00 20.00
REBR Bobby Ryan 15.00 40.00
REBS Brett Sterling 6.00 15.00
RECA Ryan Callahan 12.00 30.00
RECM Curtis McElhinney 10.00 25.00
RECP Carey Price 75.00 150.00
REDC Daniel Carcillo 8.00 20.00
REDG Daniel Girardi 8.00 20.00
REDK David Krejci 20.00 40.00
REDM Drew Miller 8.00 20.00
REDP David Perron 10.00 25.00
REDS Devin Setoguchi 10.00 25.00
REEJ Erik Johnson 10.00 25.00
REEL Brian Elliott 12.00 30.00
REFN Frans Nielsen 10.00 25.00
REHA Jaroslav Halak 10.00 25.00
REHL Jaroslav Hlinka 8.00 20.00
REJA Jannik Hansen 8.00 20.00
REJB Jared Boll 8.00 20.00
REJH Jonas Hiller 12.00 30.00
REJJ Jack Johnson 8.00 20.00
REJS Jonathan Sigalet 6.00 15.00
REJT Jonathan Toews 60.00 120.00
REKR Kris Russell 8.00 20.00
RELT Lauri Tukonen 6.00 15.00
REMA Matt Smaby 6.00 15.00
REME Matt Ellis 8.00 20.00
REMH Martin Hanzal 8.00 20.00
REML Milan Lucic 25.00 50.00
REMM Marc Methot 6.00 15.00
REMN Matt Niskanen 10.00 25.00
REMR Mason Raymond 10.00 25.00
REMS Marc Staal 10.00 25.00
REMU Cory Murphy 6.00 15.00
RENB Nicklas Bergfors 6.00 15.00
RENF Nick Foligno 12.00 30.00
REOP Ondrej Pavelec 12.00 30.00
REPA Ryan Parent 6.00 15.00
REPK Patrick Kane 50.00 100.00
REPM Peter Mueller 12.00 30.00
RERC Ryan Carter 6.00 15.00
RERP Rod Pelley 6.00 15.00
RERS Rob Schremp 8.00 20.00
RESG S. Gagner EXCH 15.00 40.00
RESH James Sheppard 6.00 15.00
RESM Stefan Meyer 8.00 20.00
RETE Tobias Enstrom 10.00 25.00
RETG Tom Gilbert 8.00 20.00
RETL Jiri Tlusty 10.00 25.00
RETM Torrey Mitchell 8.00 20.00
RETP Tomas Plihal 8.00 20.00
RETS Tobias Stephan 8.00 20.00
RETW Tyler Weiman 8.00 20.00

2007-08 SP Game Used SIGnificance

STATED PRINT RUN 50 SER.#'d SETS
SAA Andrew Alberts 5.00 12.00
SAF Alexander Frolov 5.00 12.00
SAK Andrei Kostitsyn 6.00 15.00
SAM Al Montoya 6.00 15.00
SAO Adam Oates 8.00 20.00
SAR Alexander Radulov 12.00 30.00
SBB Brad Boyes 5.00 12.00
SBC Blake Comeau 5.00 12.00
SBG Brian Gionta 6.00 15.00
SBI Kevin Bieksa 6.00 15.00
SBM Barry Melrose 6.00 15.00
SBO David Booth 5.00 12.00
SBP Benoit Pouliot 5.00 12.00
SBW Ben Walter 5.00 12.00
SCA Colby Armstrong 5.00 12.00
SCB Christian Backman 5.00 12.00
SCH Chuck Kobasew 5.00 12.00
SCK Chris Kunitz 8.00 20.00
SCM Matt Carle 5.00 12.00
SCP Chris Phillips 5.00 12.00
SCR Craig MacTavish 5.00 12.00
SDA Daniel Briere 8.00 20.00
SDB Dustin Brown 8.00 20.00
SDK Duncan Keith 8.00 20.00
SDS Drew Stafford 6.00 15.00
SDW Doug Wilson 6.00 15.00
SEC Erik Christensen 5.00 12.00
SEF Eric Fehr 5.00 12.00
SFN Fredrik Norrena 5.00 12.00
SGH Gordie Howe 50.00 100.00
SHA Michal Handzus 6.00 15.00
SHL Hakan Loob 5.00 12.00
SIW Ian White 5.00 12.00
SJA Jason Arnott 6.00 15.00
SJG Josh Gorges 5.00 12.00
SJI Jarkko Immonen 5.00 12.00
SJM Jay McClement 5.00 12.00
SJP Joe Pavelski 8.00 20.00
SKB Keith Ballard 5.00 12.00
SKC Kyle Calder 5.00 12.00
SKD Kris Draper 5.00 12.00
SKH Kristian Huselius 5.00 12.00
SKL Rostislav Klesla 5.00 12.00
SKO Anze Kopitar 12.00 30.00
SKQ Kyle Quincey 5.00 12.00
SLA Pat LaFontaine 8.00 20.00
SLE Loui Eriksson 8.00 20.00
SLI John-Michael Liles 5.00 12.00
SLN Ladislav Nagy 5.00 12.00
SMA Maxim Afinogenov 5.00 12.00
SMB Martin Biron 6.00 15.00
SMC Andy McDonald 6.00 15.00
SMG Martin Gerber 6.00 15.00
SMH Marcel Hossa 5.00 12.00
SMI Mike Cammalleri 6.00 15.00
SMJ Milan Jurcina 5.00 12.00
SML Maxim Lapierre 5.00 12.00
SMN Markus Naslund 8.00 20.00
SMR Mike Richards 8.00 20.00
SMS Marek Svatos 5.00 12.00
SMT Maxime Talbot 8.00 20.00
SMV Marc-Edouard Vlasic 5.00 12.00
SNZ Nikolai Zherdev 5.00 12.00
SON Ben Ondrus 5.00 12.00
SPB Brandon Prust 5.00 12.00
SPE Corey Perry 8.00 20.00
SPI Pierre-Marc Bouchard 8.00 20.00
SPL Pascal Leclaire 6.00 15.00
SPO Patrick O'Sullivan 6.00 15.00
SPP Petr Prucha 5.00 12.00
SPR Bob Probert 6.00 15.00
SRB Rene Bourque 5.00 12.00
SRC Ryane Clowe 6.00 15.00
SRD Ron Duguay 15.00 40.00
SRG Ryan Getzlaf 12.00 30.00
SRK Red Kelly 6.00 15.00
SRL Rejean Lemelin 6.00 15.00
SRM Ryan Malone 5.00 12.00
SRP Ryan Potulny 5.00 12.00
SRW Ryan Whitney 6.00 15.00
SSB Steve Bernier 5.00 12.00
SSC Milt Schmidt 6.00 15.00
SSD Shane Doan 6.00 15.00
SSG Scott Gomez 6.00 15.00
SSI Sidney Crosby 100.00 200.00
SSS Sergei Samsonov 6.00 15.00
SST Mark Stuart 5.00 12.00
SSW Shea Weber 6.00 15.00
STH Tomas Holmstrom 6.00 15.00
STV Thomas Vanek 10.00 25.00
SVF Valtteri Filppula 8.00 20.00
SVO Tomas Vokoun 6.00 15.00
SWE Stephen Weiss 5.00 12.00
SWG Wayne Gretzky 100.00 200.00
SWW Wojtek Wolski 6.00 15.00
SYS Yan Stastny 5.00 12.00
SZP Zach Parise 12.00 30.00

2007-08 SP Game Used SIGnificant Numbers

SNAF Alexander Frolov/24 12.00 30.00
SNAR Alexander Radulov/47 10.00 25.00
SNAT Alex Tanguay/40 8.00 20.00
SNBB Brad Boyes/38 8.00 20.00
SNBC Bobby Clarke/16
SNBN Bob Nystrom/23
SNBR Bill Ranford/30 15.00 40.00
SNBS Borje Salming/21
SNCA Colby Armstrong/20
SNCW Cam Ward/30 8.00 20.00
SNDC Dino Ciccarelli/22 10.00 25.00
SNDG Doug Gilmour/93 6.00 15.00
SNDH Dany Heatley/15 8.00 20.00
SNDS Darryl Sittler/27 10.00 25.00
SNEM Evgeni Malkin/71 15.00 40.00
SNFM Frank Mahovlich/27 15.00 40.00
SNGB Gilbert Brule/17 8.00 20.00
SNGF Grant Fuhr/31 20.00 40.00
SNHA Dominik Hasek/39 12.00 30.00
SNHL Henrik Lundqvist/30 15.00 40.00
SNIK Ilya Kovalchuk/17
SNJA Jason Arnott/19 8.00 20.00
SNJE Jeff Carter/17
SNJG Jean-Sebastien Giguere/35 15.00 40.00
SNJK Jari Kurri/17
SNJS Jarret Stoll/16
SNJT Joe Thornton/19 20.00 50.00
SNKD Kris Draper/33
SNKL Kari Lehtonen/32 15.00 40.00
SNMB Martin Brodeur/30 20.00 50.00
SNMF Marc-Andre Fleury/29
SNMH Milan Hejduk/23 10.00 25.00
SNMN Markus Naslund/19 15.00 40.00
SNMR Michael Ryder/73 4.00 10.00
SNMS Marc Savard/71 8.00 20.00
SNMT Marty Turco/35
SNPB Patrice Bergeron/37 12.00 30.00
SNRG Ryan Getzlaf/15 8.00 20.00
SNRH Ron Hextall/27 15.00 40.00
SNRI Mike Ribeiro/71 4.00 10.00
SNRM Ryan Miller/30 15.00 40.00
SNRN Rick Nash/61 8.00 20.00
SNSC Sidney Crosby/87 30.00 80.00
SNSD Shane Doan/19 10.00 25.00
SNSS Steve Shutt/22
SNST Martin St. Louis/26 10.00 25.00
SNTH Tomas Holmstrom/96 10.00 25.00
SNTJ Jose Theodore/60 5.00 12.00
SNTV Tomas Vokoun/29 15.00 40.00

2008-09 SP Game Used

This set was released on January 28, 2009. The base set consists of 200 cards. Cards 1-100 feature veterans, and cards 101-200 are all rookies. Cards 101-190 are serial numbered of 999, and cards 191-200 are serial numbered of 99..

COMP.SET w/o SPs (100) 30.00 60.00
101-190 ROOKIE PRINT RUN 999
191-200 ROOKIE PRINT RUN 99
1 Scott Niedermayer .75 2.00
2 Corey Perry .75 2.00
3 Chris Pronger .60 1.50
4 Ryan Getzlaf 1.25 3.00
5 Jean-Sebastien Giguere .75 2.00
6 Ilya Kovalchuk .75 2.00
7 Kari Lehtonen .60 1.50
8 Marc Savard .50 1.25
9 Bobby Orr 2.50 6.00
10 Michael Ryder .50 1.25
11 Phil Kessel 1.00 2.50
12 Thomas Vanek .75 2.00
13 Ryan Miller .75 2.00
14 Jason Pominville .75 2.00
15 Derek Roy .50 1.25
16 Jarome Iginla .75 2.00
17 Miikka Kiprusoff .60 1.50
18 Dion Phaneuf .75 2.00
19 Eric Staal 1.00 2.50
20 Cam Ward .75 2.00
21 Brian Campbell .60 1.50
22 Patrick Sharp .75 2.00
23 Jonathan Toews 2.00 5.00
24 Patrick Kane 1.50 4.00
25 Cristobal Huet .60 1.50
26 Patrick Roy 2.00 5.00
27 Joe Sakic 1.25 3.00
28 Milan Hejduk .60 1.50
29 Paul Stastny .75 2.00
30 Rick Nash .75 2.00
31 Pascal Leclaire .60 1.50
32 Brad Richards .75 2.00
33 Mike Modano 1.25 3.00
34 Marty Turco .75 2.00
35 Mike Ribeiro .60 1.50
36 Chris Osgood .75 2.00
37 Johan Franzen .75 2.00
38 Pavel Datsyuk 1.00 2.50
39 Henrik Zetterberg 1.00 2.50
40 Nicklas Lidstrom .75 2.00
41 Marian Hossa .60 1.50
42 Shawn Horcoff .50 1.25
43 Ales Hemsky .60 1.50
44 Tomas Vokoun .60 1.50
45 Nathan Horton .60 1.50
46 Gordie Howe 2.00 5.00
47 Wayne Gretzky 4.00 10.00
48 Anze Kopitar 1.25 3.00
49 Alexander Frolov .50 1.25
50 Brent Burns 1.00 2.50
51 Marian Gaborik 1.00 2.50
52 Pierre-Marc Bouchard .75 2.00
53 Niklas Backstrom .75 2.00
54 Alex Tanguay .50 1.25
55 Carey Price 3.00 8.00
56 Saku Koivu .75 2.00
57 Alex Kovalev .60 1.50
58 J.P. Dumont .50 1.25
59 Dan Ellis .50 1.25
60 Jason Arnott .60 1.50
61 Martin Brodeur 1.50 4.00
62 Patrik Elias .75 2.00
63 Zach Parise .75 2.00
64 Rick DiPietro .60 1.50
65 Nikolai Zherdev .50 1.25
66 Mark Messier 1.00 2.50
67 Brian Leetch .75 2.00
68 Henrik Lundqvist 1.00 2.50
69 Chris Drury .60 1.50
70 Jason Spezza .75 2.00
71 Daniel Alfredsson .75 2.00
72 Dany Heatley .75 2.00
73 Mike Richards .75 2.00
74 Martin Biron .60 1.50
75 Simon Gagne .75 2.00
76 Daniel Briere .75 2.00
77 Olli Jokinen .60 1.50
78 Shane Doan .60 1.50
79 Peter Mueller .60 1.50
80 Miroslav Satan .75 2.00
81 Mario Lemieux 2.50 6.00
82 Jordan Staal .75 2.00
83 Sidney Crosby 3.00 8.00
84 Marc-Andre Fleury 1.25 3.00
85 Evgeni Malkin 2.50 6.00
86 Rob Blake .75 2.00
87 Joe Thornton 1.00 2.50
88 Jonathan Cheechoo .75 2.00
89 Evgeni Nabokov .60 1.50
90 Brad Boyes .50 1.25
91 Paul Kariya 1.00 2.50
92 Martin St. Louis .75 2.00
93 Vincent Lecavalier .60 1.50
94 Mats Sundin .75 2.00
95 Vesa Toskala .60 1.50
96 Roberto Luongo 1.00 2.50
97 Henrik Sedin .75 2.00
98 Daniel Sedin .75 2.00
99 Nicklas Backstrom 1.25 3.00
100 Alexander Ovechkin 3.00 8.00
101 Adam Pineault RC 3.00 8.00
102 Alex Foster RC 3.00 8.00
103 Alex Goligoski RC 5.00 12.00
104 Andrew Ebbett RC 2.50 6.00
105 Andrew Murray RC 3.00 8.00
106 B.J. Crombeen RC 2.50 6.00
107 Boris Valabik RC 4.00 10.00
108 Brandon Nolan RC 3.00 8.00
109 Brian Boyle RC 3.00 8.00
110 Brian Lee RC 3.00 8.00
111 Chris Minard RC 4.00 10.00
112 Claude Giroux RC 10.00 25.00
113 Nikita Filatov RC 4.00 10.00
114 Cody McLeod RC 3.00 8.00
115 Colin Stuart RC 3.00 8.00
116 Corey Locke RC 3.00 8.00
117 Dan LaCosta RC 4.00 10.00
118 Danny Taylor RC 3.00 8.00
119 Darren Helm RC 4.00 10.00
120 Darryl Boyce RC 3.00 8.00
121 David Brine RC 2.50 6.00
122 Derick Brassard RC 3.00 8.00
123 Erik Ersberg RC 3.00 8.00
124 Garrett Stafford RC 4.00 10.00
125 Ilya Zubov RC 3.00 8.00
126 Jack Hillen RC 3.00 8.00
127 Jesse Winchester RC 2.50 6.00
128 Joe Jensen RC 4.00 10.00
129 Joey Mormina RC 3.00 8.00
130 Jon Filewich RC 3.00 8.00
131 Jonathan Ericsson RC 4.00 10.00
132 Jordan Hendry RC 3.00 8.00
133 Jordan LaVallee RC 4.00 10.00
134 Justin Abdelkader RC 6.00 15.00
135 Brandon Sutter RC 4.00 10.00
136 Kyle Greentree RC 4.00 10.00
137 Kyle Okposo RC 4.00 10.00
138 James Neal RC 8.00 20.00
139 Lauri Korpikoski RC 2.50 6.00
140 Marc-Andre Gragnani RC 3.00 8.00
141 Mark Fistric RC 3.00 8.00
142 Matt D'Agostini RC 3.00 8.00
143 Mattias Ritola RC 3.00 8.00
144 Mike Brown RC 5.00 12.00
145 Mike Iggulden RC 3.00 8.00
146 Mike Mole RC 3.00 8.00
147 Niklas Hjalmarsson RC 6.00 15.00
148 Pascal Pelletier RC 2.50 6.00
149 Luca Sbisa RC 2.50 6.00
150 Robbie Earl RC 2.50 6.00
151 Ryan Stone RC 2.50 6.00
152 Sami Lepisto RC 3.00 8.00
153 Shawn Matthias RC 4.00 10.00
154 Steve Mason RC 6.00 15.00
155 Colton Gillies RC 3.00 8.00
156 Michael Frolik RC 4.00 10.00
157 Nikolai Kulemin RC 4.00 10.00
158 T.J. Oshie RC 8.00 20.00
159 Patrik Berglund RC 3.00 8.00
160 Patric Hornqvist RC 4.00 10.00
161 Ryan Jones RC 4.00 10.00
162 Chris Porter RC 4.00 10.00
163 Viktor Tikhonov RC 3.00 8.00
164 Kevin Porter RC 3.00 8.00
165 Jonas Frogren RC 2.50 6.00
166 John Mitchell RC 3.00 8.00
167 Paul Bissonnette RC 5.00 12.00
168 Derek Dorsett RC 5.00 12.00
169 Janne Niskala RC 4.00 10.00
170 Vladimir Mihalik RC 2.50 6.00
171 Jared Ross RC 4.00 10.00
172 Wayne Simmonds RC 6.00 15.00
173 Adam Pardy RC 3.00 8.00
174 Dane Byers RC 3.00 8.00
175 Mitch Fritz RC 3.00 8.00
176 Zach Fitzgerald RC 4.00 10.00
177 Ben Bishop RC 6.00 15.00
178 Anssi Salmela RC 4.00 10.00
179 Andreas Nodl RC 2.50 6.00
180 Petr Vrana RC 2.50 6.00
181 Zach Boychuk RC 4.00 10.00
182 Nathan Oystrick RC 4.00 10.00
183 Oscar Moller RC 3.00 8.00
184 Teddy Purcell RC 5.00 12.00
185 Theo Peckham RC 4.00 10.00
186 Tim Conboy RC 3.00 8.00
187 Tim Ramholt RC 3.00 8.00
188 Tom Cavanagh RC 3.00 8.00
189 Tom Sestito RC 4.00 10.00
190 Tyler Plante RC 3.00 8.00
191 Mikkel Boedker RC 15.00 40.00
192 Kyle Turris RC 20.00 50.00
193 Fabian Brunnstrom RC 10.00 25.00
194 Jakub Voracek RC 15.00 40.00
195 Blake Wheeler RC 30.00 80.00
196 Luke Schenn RC 15.00 40.00
197 Zach Bogosian RC 12.00 30.00
198 Alex Pietrangelo RC 15.00 40.00
199 Drew Doughty RC 40.00 80.00
200 Steven Stamkos RC 100.00 175.00

2008-09 SP Game Used Gold

*GOLD (1-100): .8X TO 2X BASE
*GOLD (101-190): .5X TO 1.2X BASE
1-190 STATED PRINT RUN 100
*GOLD (191-200): .2X TO .5X BASE
191-200 STATED PRINT RUN 50
99 Nicklas Backstrom 2.50 6.00
192 Kyle Turris 30.00 80.00
200 Steven Stamkos 75.00 150.00

2008-09 SP Game Used Platinum

Although this set is called SP Game Used Platinum, it is highlighted with red foil markings and it is serial numbered to 25.

*PLATINUM (1-100): 2X TO 5X BASE
*PLATINUM (101-190): 1.2X TO 3X BASE
*GOLD (191-200): .3X TO .8X BASE
99 Nicklas Backstrom 6.00 15.00
200 Steven Stamkos 60.00 150.00

2008-09 SP Game Used Authentic Fabrics Duos

STATED PRINT RUN 100 SERIAL #'d SETS
AF2AN V.Toskala/N.Antropov 4.00 10.00
AF2BG M.Brodeur/D.Gilmour 10.00 25.00
AF2BJ A.Kopitar/J.Johnson 8.00 20.00
AF2BL M.Brodeur/R.Luongo 10.00 25.00
AF2BM M.Brodeur/R.Miller 10.00 25.00
AF2BP M.Brodeur/C.Price 20.00 50.00
AF2BR M.Richards/D.Briere 5.00 12.00
AF2CM S.Crosby/E.Malkin 20.00 50.00
AF2CR C.Chelios/B.Rafalski 5.00 12.00
AF2CT E.Cole/T.Thomas 5.00 12.00
AF2CW E.Cole/G.Brule 4.00 10.00
AF2DB P.Demitra/S.Bernier 6.00 15.00
AF2DK S.Fedorov/I.Kovalchuk 8.00 20.00
AF2DM E.Malkin/R.Fedotenko 15.00 40.00
AF2DW J.Dumont/S.Weber 4.00 10.00
AF2ED J.Dumont/D.Legwand 4.00 10.00
AF2EE P.Esposito/T.Esposito 8.00 20.00
AF2EJ E.Staal/J.Staal 6.00 15.00
AF2EP Z.Parise/P.Elias 5.00 12.00
AF2FM E.Malkin/S.Fedorov 15.00 40.00
AF2FN M.Fleury/A.Niittymaki 6.00 15.00
AF2FO M.Fleury/C.Osgood 6.00 15.00
AF2FP T.Fleury/D.Phaneuf 6.00 15.00
AF2GB M.Gaborik/P.Bouchard 6.00 15.00
AF2GC S.Gagne/J.Carter 5.00 12.00
AF2GD S.Gomez/C.Drury 4.00 10.00
AF2GK M.Gaborik/M.Koivu 6.00 15.00
AF2GP Z.Parise/B.Gionta 5.00 12.00
AF2GW S.Gonchar/R.Whitney 5.00 12.00
AF2HF P.Forsberg/M.Hejduk 6.00 15.00
AF2HG S.Horcoff/S.Gagner 4.00 10.00
AF2HH M.Hossa/M.Hossa 4.00 10.00
AF2IK A.Kovalev/I.Kovalchuk 5.00 12.00
AF2JH S.Doan/O.Jokinen 4.00 10.00
AF2JJ J.Johnson/E.Johnson 4.00 10.00
AF2JM J.Staal/E.Johnson 8.00 20.00
AF2JP J.Sakic/P.Stastny 8.00 20.00
AF2JR J.Spezza/R.Nash 5.00 12.00
AF2KK S.Koivu/A.Kovalev 5.00 12.00
AF2KM I.Kovalchuk/E.Malkin 15.00 40.00
AF2KO A.Ovechkin/I.Kovalchuk 20.00 50.00
AF2KP P.Kariya/D.Perron 6.00 15.00
AF2KV S.Koivu/M.Koivu 5.00 12.00
AF2LA L.McDonald/A.MacInnis 5.00 12.00
AF2LB R.Luongo/S.Bernier 6.00 15.00
AF2LC M.Lemieux/S.Crosby 20.00 50.00
AF2LH N.Lidstrom/T.Holmstrom 5.00 12.00
AF2LI V.Lecavalier/M.Lundin 4.00 10.00
AF2LN H.Lundqvist/M.Naslund 6.00 15.00
AF2LS V.Lecavalier/M.St. Louis 5.00 12.00
AF2LT R.Luongo/M.Turco 6.00 15.00
AF2MG M.Modano/B.Guerin 8.00 20.00
AF2MJ J.Sakic/M.Svatos 8.00 20.00
AF2MM M.Gaborik/M.Hossa 6.00 15.00
AF2MP A.MacInnis/D.Phaneuf 5.00 12.00
AF2MS B.Salming/L.McDonald 5.00 12.00
AF2NH M.Naslund/T.Holmstrom 4.00 10.00
AF2NK E.Nabokov/M.Kiprusoff 4.00 10.00
AF2NL V.Lecavalier/R.Nash 5.00 12.00
AF2NS R.Nash/M.St. Louis 5.00 12.00
AF2OB A.Ovechkin/N.Backstrom 20.00 50.00
AF2OF A.Ovechkin/S.Fedorov 20.00 50.00
AF2PB P.Kessel/Bergeron
AF2PC D.Phaneuf/Z.Chara 5.00 12.00
AF2PG R.Getzlaf/Perry 8.00 20.00
AF2PS P.Sharp/B.Seabrook 5.00 12.00
AF2PZ M.Naslund/N.Zherdev 4.00 10.00
AF2RB P.Bouchard/M.Koivu 5.00 12.00
AF2RD L.Robitaille/M.Dionne 6.00 15.00
AF2RF P.Roy/P.Forsberg 12.00 30.00
AF2RJ R.Smyth/J.Spezza 5.00 12.00
AF2RN L.Robitaille/B.Nicholls 5.00 12.00
AF2SD M.Staal/C.Drury 5.00 12.00
AF2SF M.Sundin/P.Forsberg 6.00 15.00
AF2SG T.Selanne/R.Getzlaf 10.00 25.00
AF2SL M.Savard/M.Lucic 8.00 20.00
AF2SM S.Doan/P.Mueller 4.00 10.00
AF2SN M.Sundin/M.Naslund 5.00 12.00
AF2SS J.Sakic/R.Smyth 8.00 20.00
AF2TB M.Turco/P.Budaj 5.00 12.00
AF2TC J.Thornton/J.Cheechoo 6.00 15.00
AF2TL K.Lehtonen/V.Toskala 4.00 10.00
AF2TM V.Lecavalier/R.Malone 4.00 10.00
AF2TN J.Thornton/R.Nash 6.00 15.00
AF2TP J.Toews/C.Price 20.00 50.00
AF2TR T.Rask/V.Toskala 5.00 12.00
AF2TT T.Thomas/T.Rask 5.00 12.00
AF2VH D.Hasek/T.Vokoun 6.00 15.00
AF2WL W.Redden/H.Lundqvist 6.00 15.00
AF2ZC E.Malkin/H.Zetterberg 15.00 40.00
AF2ZD N.Zherdev/C.Drury 4.00 10.00
AF2ZF S.Fedorov/M.Afinogenov 8.00 20.00
AF2ZM Z.Parise/M.Modano 8.00 20.00

2008-09 SP Game Used Authentic Fabrics Duos Patches

STATED PRINT RUN 25 SERIAL #'d SETS
AF2AN V.Toskala/N.Antropov 8.00 20.00
AF2BB D.Briere/P.Bergeron 12.00 30.00
AF2BG M.Brodeur/D.Gilmour 20.00 50.00
AF2BJ J.Johnson/A.Kopitar 15.00 40.00
AF2BK N.Backstrom/P.Kane 15.00 40.00
AF2BL M.Brodeur/R.Luongo
AF2BM R.Miller/M.Brodeur 20.00 50.00
AF2BP M.Brodeur/C.Price 20.00 50.00
AF2BR D.Briere/M.Richards 15.00 40.00
AF2CM S.Crosby/E.Malkin 40.00 100.00
AF2CR C.Chelios/B.Rafalski 10.00 25.00
AF2CT E.Cole/T.Thomas 10.00 25.00
AF2CW E.Cole/G.Brule
AF2DB P.Demitra/S.Bernier
AF2DK I.Kovalchuk/S.Fedorov 15.00 40.00
AF2DM E.Malkin/R.Fedotenko
AF2DW J.Dumont/S.Weber
AF2ED J.Dumont/D.Legwand 8.00 20.00
AF2EE P.Esposito/T.Esposito 15.00 40.00
AF2EJ E.Staal/J.Staal
AF2EP P.Elias/Z.Parise 10.00 25.00
AF2FM S.Fedorov/E.Malkin 30.00 80.00
AF2FN A.Niittymaki/M.Fleury 15.00 40.00
AF2FO C.Osgood/M.Fleury 15.00 40.00
AF2FP D.Phaneuf/T.Fleury
AF2GB M.Gaborik/P.Bouchard 12.00 30.00
AF2GC S.Gagne/J.Carter 10.00 25.00
AF2GD S.Gomez/C.Drury 8.00 20.00
AF2GK M.Gaborik/M.Koivu 12.00 30.00
AF2GP B.Gionta/Z.Parise 10.00 25.00
AF2GW S.Gonchar/R.Whitney
AF2HF M.Hejduk/P.Forsberg
AF2HG S.Horcoff/S.Gagner
AF2HH M.Hossa/M.Hossa 10.00 25.00
AF2IK A.Kovalev/I.Kovalchuk 10.00 25.00
AF2JH O.Jokinen/S.Doan
AF2JJ J.Johnson/E.Johnson 8.00 20.00
AF2JM M.Fleury/J.Staal
AF2JP J.Sakic/P.Stastny
AF2JR J.Spezza/R.Nash 15.00 40.00
AF2KK S.Koivu/A.Kovalev
AF2KM I.Kovalchuk/E.Malkin 30.00 80.00
AF2KO I.Kovalchuk/A.Ovechkin
AF2KP P.Kariya/D.Perron 12.00 30.00
AF2KV S.Koivu/M.Koivu 10.00 25.00
AF2LA L.McDonald/A.MacInnis 10.00 25.00
AF2LB R.Luongo/S.Bernier 12.00 30.00
AF2LC M.Lemieux/S.Crosby 40.00 100.00
AF2LE K.Lehtonen/T.Enstrom 15.00 40.00
AF2LH N.Lidstrom/T.Holmstrom
AF2LI V.Lecavalier/M.Lundin
AF2LN H.Lundqvist/M.Naslund
AF2LR J.Lehtinen/M.Ribeiro 8.00 20.00
AF2LS V.Lecavalier/M.St. Louis 10.00 25.00
AF2LT M.Turco/R.Luongo 12.00 30.00
AF2MG M.Modano/B.Guerin
AF2MJ J.Sakic/M.Svatos 15.00 40.00
AF2MM M.Hossa/M.Gaborik 15.00 30.00
AF2MP D.Phaneuf/A.MacInnis 10.00 25.00
AF2MS L.McDonald/B.Salming 10.00 25.00
AF2NH T.Holmstrom/M.Naslund 8.00 20.00
AF2NK E.Nabokov/M.Kiprusoff
AF2NL V.Lecavalier/R.Nash 10.00 25.00
AF2NS M.St. Louis/R.Nash 10.00 25.00
AF2OB A.Ovechkin/N.Backstrom 40.00 100.00
AF2OF S.Fedorov/A.Ovechkin 40.00 100.00
AF2PA G.Perreault/M.Afinogenov 10.00 25.00
AF2PB P.Bergeron/P.Kessel 12.00 30.00
AF2PC Z.Chara/D.Phaneuf 10.00 25.00
AF2PG C.Perry/R.Getzlaf 15.00 40.00
AF2PS P.Sharp/B.Seabrook 8.00 20.00
AF2PZ M.Naslund/N.Zherdev 8.00 20.00
AF2RB P.Bouchard/M.Koivu 10.00 25.00
AF2RD L.Robitaille/M.Dionne
AF2RF P.Roy/P.Forsberg 25.00 60.00
AF2RJ J.Spezza/R.Smyth 10.00 25.00
AF2RN L.Robitaille/B.Nicholls
AF2SA D.Stafford/M.Afinogenov 8.00 20.00
AF2SD C.Drury/M.Staal
AF2SF M.Sundin/P.Forsberg 12.00 30.00
AF2SG T.Selanne/R.Getzlaf 20.00 50.00
AF2SL M.Savard/M.Lucic 15.00 40.00
AF2SM S.Doan/P.Mueller 8.00 20.00
AF2SN M.Sundin/M.Naslund 10.00 25.00
AF2SS J.Sakic/R.Smyth 15.00 40.00
AF2TB M.Turco/P.Budaj
AF2TC J.Thornton/J.Cheechoo 12.00 30.00
AF2TK J.Toews/P.Kane 25.00 60.00
AF2TL V.Toskala/K.Lehtonen 8.00 20.00
AF2TM V.Lecavalier/R.Malone 8.00 20.00
AF2TN J.Thornton/R.Nash 12.00 30.00
AF2TP J.Toews/C.Price 40.00 100.00
AF2TR V.Toskala/T.Rask 10.00 25.00
AF2TT T.Thomas/T.Rask
AF2VH T.Vokoun/D.Hasek 12.00 30.00
AF2WL W.Radden/H.Lundqvist 12.00 30.00
AF2ZC H.Zetterberg/E.Malkin
AF2ZD C.Drury/N.Zherdev
AF2ZF S.Fedorov/M.Afinogenov 12.00 30.00
AF2ZM M.Modano/Z.Parise 15.00 40.00

2008-09 SP Game Used Authentic Fabrics Trios

*PATCH/15: .6X TO 1.5X BASIC TRIO/25
AF3BEP Brodeur/Elias/Parise 15.00 40.00
AF3BKJ Kopitar/Johnson/Brown 12.00 30.00
AF3BLF Brodeur/Luongo/Fleury 15.00 40.00
AF3BLM Brodeur/Lundqvist/Miller 15.00 40.00
AF3BMG Backstrom/Gagner/Mueller 12.00 30.00
AF3BSS Brind/Staal/Samsnv 10.00 25.00
AF3CHO Hasek/Osgood/Chelios 10.00 25.00
AF3CTN Crosby/Toews/Nash 30.00 80.00
AF3DKO Ovech/Koval/Zherdev 30.00 80.00
AF3DWS Dumont/Weber/Sullivan 6.00 15.00
AF3GBR Richards/Briere/Gagne 8.00 20.00
AF3GGP Gaborik/Getzlaf/Parise 12.00 30.00
AF3GHC Gretzky/Howe/Crosby 40.00 100.00
AF3GND Gomez/Drury/Naslund 6.00 15.00
AF3HCG Horcoff/Cole/Gagner 6.00 15.00
AF3HEG Gaborik/Hossa/Elias 10.00 25.00
AF3HEW Hull/Esposito/Wilson 12.00 30.00
AF3HSW Smyth/Wolski/Hejduk 6.00 15.00
AF3JDM Doan/Mueller/Jokinen
AF3KBJ Kariya/Johnson/Perron 10.00 25.00
AF3KOM Ovech/Malkin/Koval 15.00 40.00
AF3LBD Luongo/Bernier/Demitra 10.00 25.00
AF3LCM Lemieux/Crosby/Malkin 30.00 80.00
AF3LNZ Lndqvst/Naslnd/Zherdv 10.00 25.00
AF3LPG Lids/Phanf/Gonchar 8.00 20.00
AF3LSM Lecav/St. Louis/Malone
AF3LTS Lecav/St.Louis/Thorntn
AF3MFM McDld/Fleury/Macln 10.00 25.00
AF3MGP Staal/Gagner/Perron
AF3MPG Getzlaf/Perry/Morrison
AF3MRL Modano/Ribeiro/Lehtinen
AF3MSS Modano/Sundin/Shanhn
AF3NGB Gaborik/Bouchard/Nolan 10.00 25.00
AF3OGB OvechBackstrm/Green 15.00 40.00
AF3RBP Roy/Brodeur/Price 30.00 80.00
AF3RSF Roy/Sakic/Forsberg
AF3RTL Turco/Lehtinen/Ribeiro 8.00 20.00
AF3SAA Koivu/Kostitsyn/Kovalev
AF3SAS Sundin/Antropov/Stajan
AF3SFW Fleury/Sykora/Whitney 12.00 30.00
AF3SHF Sakic/Forsberg/Hejduk 12.00 30.00
AF3SKF Selanne/Kariya/Fedorov 15.00 40.00
AF3SKJ Selanne/Koivu/Jokinen
AF3SKK Selanne/Koivu/Koivu 15.00 40.00
AF3SNF Sundin/Naslund/Frsbrg 10.00 25.00
AF3SNH Naslund/Sundin/Holstrm 8.00 20.00
AF3SPG Selanne/Getzlaf/Perry 15.00 40.00
AF3SSS Staal/Staal/Staal
AF3SSW Sakic/Smyth/Wolski 12.00 30.00
AF3TKL Kiprusoff/Lehtn/Tskala
AF3TLM Lndqvst/Miller/Tskala 10.00 25.00
AF3TNC Thorn/Checho/Nabkv 10.00 25.00
AF3VKL Kolzig/Lehton/Vokoun 8.00 20.00
AF3WSS Staal/Samsonov/Williams
AF3ZGF Fedorov/Zubov/Gonchar
AF3ZLC Zetter/Lidstrom/Chelios 10.00 25.00

2008-09 SP Game Used Dual Authentic Fabrics

AFAM Andrei Markov 6.00 15.00
AFAN Antero Niittymaki 5.00 12.00
AFAO Alexander Ovechkin 10.00 25.00
AFAS Anton Stastny 4.00 10.00
AFBB Bob Bourne 4.00 10.00
AFBG Patrice Bergeron 8.00 20.00
AFBL Rob Blake 6.00 15.00
AFBN Bernie Nicholls 5.00 12.00
AFBQ Ray Bourque 10.00 25.00
AFBR Steve Bernier 4.00 10.00
AFBS Billy Smith 6.00 15.00
AFBZ Todd Bertuzzi 6.00 15.00
AFCC Chris Chelios 6.00 15.00
AFCH Jonathan Cheechoo 6.00 15.00
AFDB Doug Gilmour 8.00 20.00
AFDC Dino Ciccarelli 6.00 15.00
AFDE Pavol Demitra 8.00 20.00
AFDH Dominik Hasek 8.00 20.00
AFDL Darryl Sittler 6.00 15.00
AFDP Dion Phaneuf 6.00 15.00
AFDS Denis Savard 8.00 20.00
AFDW Doug Weight 6.00 15.00
AFEL Patrik Elias 6.00 15.00
AFEM Evgeni Malkin 20.00 50.00
AFES Eric Staal 8.00 20.00
AFGA Glenn Anderson 6.00 15.00
AFGN Simon Gagne 6.00 15.00
AFGP Gilbert Perreault 6.00 15.00
AFHK Roman Hamrlik 5.00 12.00
AFHL Henrik Lundqvist 8.00 20.00
AFHM Marian Hossa 5.00 12.00
AFHO Tomas Holmstrom 5.00 12.00
AFHW Dale Hawerchuk 8.00 20.00
AFIK Ilya Kovalchuk 6.00 15.00
AFJL Jere Lehtinen 4.00 10.00
AFJM Joe Mullen 5.00 12.00
AFJS Jordan Staal 6.00 15.00
AFJW Justin Williams 5.00 12.00
AFKL Kari Lehtonen 5.00 12.00
AFKM Mike Komisarek 4.00 10.00
AFKO Mikko Koivu 5.00 12.00
AFKV Saku Koivu 6.00 15.00
AFLG Roberto Luongo 8.00 20.00
AFLM Lanny McDonald 6.00 15.00
AFLR Larry Robinson 6.00 15.00
AFMA Maxim Afinogenov
AFMB Martin Brodeur 12.00 30.00
AFME Ryan Malone 4.00 10.00
AFMF Marc-Andre Fleury 10.00 25.00
AFMG Marian Gaborik 8.00 20.00
AFMH Milan Hejduk 5.00 12.00
AFMK Miikka Kiprusoff 5.00 12.00
AFMM Mike Modano 10.00 25.00
AFMN Manny Fernandez 5.00 12.00
AFMP Michael Peca 5.00 12.00
AFMR Mike Ribeiro 5.00 12.00
AFMS Marek Svatos 4.00 10.00
AFMT Marty Turco 6.00 15.00
AFNL Nicklas Lidstrom 6.00 15.00
AFNS Markus Naslund 5.00 12.00
AFNZ Nikolai Zherdev 4.00 10.00
AFOJ Olli Jokinen 5.00 12.00
AFPA Paul Kariya 8.00 20.00
AFPB Pierre-Marc Bouchard 6.00 15.00
AFPF Peter Forsberg 8.00 20.00
AFPK Phil Kessel 8.00 20.00
AFRB Richard Brodeur 5.00 12.00
AFRD Rod Brind'Amour 6.00 15.00
AFRE Ron Ellis 4.00 10.00
AFRF Ruslan Fedotenko 4.00 10.00
AFRG Ryan Getzlaf 10.00 25.00
AFRH Ron Hextall 10.00 25.00
AFRK Ryan Kesler 8.00 20.00
AFRL Rod Langway 5.00 12.00
AFRM Ryan Miller 6.00 15.00
AFRN Rick Nash 6.00 15.00
AFRO Patrick Roy 15.00 40.00
AFRS Ryan Smyth 5.00 12.00
AFRY Michael Ryder 4.00 10.00
AFSC Sidney Crosby 12.00 30.00
AFSD Shane Doan 5.00 12.00
AFSF Sergei Fedorov 10.00 25.00
AFSH Shawn Horcoff 4.00 10.00
AFSK Joe Sakic 10.00 25.00
AFSP Jason Spezza 6.00 15.00
AFSS Steve Shutt 6.00 15.00
AFST Miroslav Satan 6.00 15.00
AFSU Mats Sundin 6.00 15.00
AFSV Marc Savard 4.00 10.00
AFSY Peter Stastny 6.00 15.00
AFSZ Sergei Zubov 5.00 12.00
AFTH Tim Thomas 6.00 15.00
AFTR Tuukka Rask 6.00 15.00
AFTS Teemu Selanne 12.00 30.00
AFTW Tiger Williams 5.00 12.00
AFVL Vincent Lecavalier 5.00 12.00
AFVO Tomas Vokoun 5.00 12.00
AFVT Vesa Toskala 5.00 12.00
AFWB Shea Weber 5.00 12.00
AFZP Zach Parise 6.00 15.00

2008-09 SP Game Used Dual Authentic Fabrics Gold

*GOLD:.5X TO 1.2X BASE
STATED PRINT RUN 50 SERIAL #'d SETS

2008-09 SP Game Used Dual Authentic Fabrics Platinum

*PLATINUM: .6X TO 1.5X BASE
STATED PRINT RUN 25 SERIAL #'d SETS

2008-09 SP Game Used Extra SIGnificance

STATED PRINT RUN 25 SERIAL #'d SETS
XSGBC Carcillo/Burish 10.00 25.00
XSGBE M.Brodeur/P.Elias 40.00 80.00
XSGBK P.Kane/N.Backstrom 25.00 60.00
XSGBM B.Dubinsky/M.Staal 15.00 40.00
XSGCG S.Gagner/A.Cogliano 10.00 25.00
XSGCH Hextall/Clarke 20.00 50.00
XSGCM P.Mueller/D.Carcillo 10.00 25.00
XSGDB Sittler/Salming 12.00 30.00
XSGDD B.Dubinsky/C.Drury 12.00 30.00
XSGDK Setoguchi/Letang 12.00 30.00
XSGDT Dionne/Taylor 15.00 40.00
XSGDV D.Cleary/V.Filppula 12.00 30.00
XSGEE T.Esposito/P.Esposito 20.00 50.00
XSGEJ E.Staal/J.Staal
XSGEM E.Lach/M.Schmidt 20.00 50.00
XSGES P.Esposito/D.Sanderson
XSGGB N.Backstrom/M.Green 15.00 40.00
XSGGS B.Smith/C.Gillies 12.00 30.00
XSGHD K.Draper/T.Holmstrom 12.00 30.00
XSGHG D.Heatley/M.Gerber 15.00 40.00
XSGHM H.Zetterberg/M.Hossa 15.00 40.00
XSGHP C.Price/J.Halak 25.00 60.00
XSGHS J.Harding/J.Sheppard
XSGIC J.Iginla/M.Cammalleri 15.00 40.00
XSGIK Kovalchuk/Lehtonen 15.00 40.00
XSGIP J.Iginla/D.Phaneuf 20.00 50.00
XSGJP J.Pominville/D.Paille 12.00 30.00
XSGKN K.Chipchura/N.Foligno 8.00 20.00
XSGKT K.Lehtonen/T.Enstrom
XSGLE Lidstrom/Enstrom 12.00 30.00
XSGLS Lecavalier/St. Louis 12.00 30.00
XSGMD Mancari/Paille 10.00 25.00
XSGMF T.Fleury/J.Mullen 15.00 40.00
XSGMG B.Gionta/M.Modano 15.00 40.00
XSGMH Miller/Harding 12.00 30.00
XSGMJ M.Staal/J.Staal 12.00 30.00
XSGMM Modano/Morrow 20.00 50.00
XSGMP Hejduk/Stastny 12.00 30.00
XSGMS Miller/Stafford 12.00 30.00
XSGNP E.Nabokov/D.Patzold 12.00 30.00
XSGNT N.Horton/T.Vokoun
XSGOB Ovechkin/Backstrom 50.00 125.00
XSGOM E.Malkin/A.Ovechkin 50.00 125.00
XSGPP P.Bergeron/P.Kessel 12.00 30.00
XSGPT Stastny/Hensick 12.00 30.00
XSGPV Vanek/Pominville 12.00 30.00
XSGRC M.Richards/J.Carter 12.00 30.00
XSGRK Raymond/Kesler 15.00 40.00
XSGRM B.Morrow/M.Ribeiro 15.00 40.00
XSGRT R.Clowe/T.Mitchell 15.00 40.00
XSGS2 Stastny/Stastny 12.00 30.00
XSGSH Smyth/Hejduk 10.00 25.00
XSGSS D.Sedin/H.Sedin
XSGST J.Tlusty/M.Stajan 12.00 30.00
XSGSW E.Staal/C.Ward 12.00 30.00
XSGTF Fleury/Talbot 20.00 50.00
XSGTH C.Higgins/A.Tanguay
XSGTK J.Toews/P.Kane 30.00 80.00
XSGTM Thornton/Michalek 15.00 40.00
XSGTP C.Price/J.Toews 50.00 120.00
XSGVP T.Vanek/D.Paille
XSGVW Ward/Vokoun 12.00 30.00
XSGZK S.Gagner/S.Kostitsyn 10.00 25.00

2008-09 SP Game Used Inked Sweaters Dual

STATED PRINT RUN 25 SERIAL #'d SETS
INKAL McDonald/MacInnis
INKBM M.Brodeur/R.Miller 30.00 80.00
INKBP M.Brodeur/C.Price 40.00 80.00
INKBV P.Budaj/T.Vokoun 12.00 30.00
INKFS M.Fleury/J.Staal 25.00 60.00
INKKM E.Malkin/I.Kovalchuk 50.00 100.00
INKLG W.Gretzky/M.Lemieux 300.00 450.00
INKLS Lecavalier/St. Louis 15.00 40.00
INKLZ N.Lidstrom/H.Zetterberg 20.00 50.00
INKMM Modano/Ribeiro 25.00 60.00
INKMT M.Modano/M.Turco 25.00 60.00
INKNZ Naslund/Zherdev 12.00 30.00
INKOB Ovechkin/Backstrom 60.00 150.00
INKSC Gomez/Drury 12.00 30.00
INKSH R.Smyth/M.Hejduk 12.00 30.00
INKSW C.Ward/E.Staal 20.00 50.00
INKTK P.Kane/J.Toews 40.00 100.00
INKZH H.Zetterberg/M.Hossa 20.00 50.00

2008-09 SP Game Used Letter Marks

STATED PRINT RUN 50 SERIAL #'d SETS
LMBP Bob Probert 40.00 80.00
LMCA Daniel Carcillo 12.00 30.00
LMDS Denis Savard 25.00 60.00
LMEJ Erik Johnson 15.00 40.00
LMEM Evgeni Malkin 50.00 100.00
LMGC Guy Carbonneau 20.00 50.00
LMHS Henrik Sedin 20.00 50.00
LMJI Jarome Iginla 20.00 50.00
LMKT Kyle Turris 60.00 120.00
LMLR Luc Robitaille 20.00 50.00
LMMH Marian Hossa 15.00 40.00
LMMK Mike Knuble 12.00 30.00
LMMM Mark Messier 50.00 100.00
LMNH Nathan Horton 15.00 40.00
LMPK Phil Kessel 20.00 50.00
LMPS Paul Stastny 20.00 50.00
LMRG Ryan Getzlaf 20.00 50.00
LMRK Red Kelly 20.00 50.00
LMSC Sidney Crosby 125.00 250.00
LMSE Daniel Sedin 20.00 50.00
LMTV Thomas Vanek 20.00 50.00

2008-09 SP Game Used Letter Marks Nickname Edition

STATED PRINT RUN 50 SERIAL #'d SETS
NEBH Bobby Hull 30.00 80.00
NEBN Bob Nystrom 12.00 30.00
NEDC Don Cherry 50.00 125.00
NEDG Doug Gilmour 25.00 60.00
NEDS Dave Schultz 20.00 50.00
NEEM Evgeni Malkin 30.00 80.00
NEEN Evgeni Nabokov 15.00 40.00
NEES Eddie Shack 15.00 40.00
NEGH Gordie Howe 100.00 175.00
NEJB Johnny Bucyk 20.00 50.00
NEJI Jarome Iginla 15.00 40.00
NELR Luc Robitaille 20.00 50.00
NEMF Marc-Andre Fleury 40.00 80.00
NEML Mario Lemieux 60.00 150.00
NEMM Mark Messier 75.00 150.00
NEMN Markus Naslund 15.00 40.00
NEMT Marty Turco 20.00 50.00
NERS Ryan Smyth
NETE Tony Esposito 50.00 100.00
NETO Terry O'Reilly 15.00 40.00

2008-09 SP Game Used Number Marks

STATED PRINT RUN 9-25
NMAD Alex Delvecchio 30.00 80.00
NMBB Bob Baun 25.00 60.00
NMBC Bobby Clarke 25.00 60.00
NMBD Brandon Dubinsky 20.00 50.00
NMBN Bernie Nicholls 20.00 50.00
NMBO Pierre-Marc Bouchard 25.00 60.00
NMBR Bobby Ryan 25.00 60.00
NMBS Borje Salming 25.00 60.00
NMCB Cam Barker 15.00 40.00
NMCG Clark Gillies 25.00 60.00
NMCP Carey Price 100.00 250.00
NMDB Dan Boyle 20.00 50.00
NMDP Dustin Penner 20.00 50.00
NMDS Drew Stafford 20.00 50.00
NMES Eric Staal 30.00 80.00
NMGF Grant Fuhr 25.00 60.00
NMGL Guillaume Latendresse 15.00 40.00
NMJB Jonathan Bernier 30.00 80.00
NMJM Joe Mullen 20.00 50.00
NMJT Jonathan Toews 60.00 150.00
NMLM Lanny McDonald 25.00 60.00
NMMC Marty McSorley 25.00 60.00
NMMH Martin Havlat 25.00 60.00
NMMM Milan Michalek 15.00 40.00
NMMR Mike Ribeiro 20.00 50.00
NMMS Marco Sturm
NMPB Peter Budaj 20.00 50.00
NMPE Patrik Elias 25.00 60.00
NMPK Patrick Kane 50.00 125.00
NMPS Peter Stastny 25.00 60.00
NMRA Bill Ranford 25.00 60.00
NMRV Rogie Vachon 15.00 40.00
NMSB Steve Bernier 15.00 40.00
NMSE Devin Setoguchi/30 20.00 50.00
NMSS Steve Shutt 25.00 60.00
NMST Martin St. Louis 25.00 60.00

NMTF Theoren Fleury 30.00 80.00
NMTH Tomas Holmstrom 20.00 50.00
NMWG Wayne Gretzky/9

2008-09 SP Game Used Rookie Exclusive Autographs

STATED PRINT RUN 100 SERIAL #'d SETS
REAE Andrew Ebbett 4.00 10.00
REAG Alex Goligoski 8.00 20.00
REAP Adam Pineault 5.00 12.00
REBB Brian Boyle 5.00 12.00
REBL Brian Lee 5.00 12.00
REBO Zach Boychuk 6.00 15.00
REBS Brandon Sutter 6.00 15.00
REBV Boris Valabik 6.00 15.00
REBW Blake Wheeler 15.00 40.00
RECG Claude Giroux 40.00 80.00
REDB Derick Brassard 5.00 12.00
REDD Drew Doughty 15.00 40.00
REDH Darren Helm 6.00 15.00
REDL Dan LaCosta 6.00 15.00
REEE Erik Ersberg 5.00 12.00
REFB Fabian Brunnstrom 5.00 12.00
REFR Jonas Frogren 4.00 10.00
REGI Colton Gillies 5.00 12.00
REIG Mike Iggulden 5.00 12.00
REIZ Ilya Zubov 5.00 12.00
REJA Justin Abdelkader 10.00 25.00
REJE Jonathan Ericsson 6.00 15.00
REJF Jon Filewich 5.00 12.00
REJM John Mitchell 5.00 12.00
REJN James Neal 8.00 20.00
REJV Jakub Voracek 12.00 30.00
REKO Kyle Okposo 6.00 15.00
REKP Kevin Porter 5.00 12.00
REKT Kyle Turris 10.00 25.00
RELK Lauri Korpikoski 4.00 10.00
RELS Luca Sbisa 4.00 10.00
REMA Steve Mason 8.00 20.00
REMB Mikkel Boedker 8.00 20.00
REMD Matt D'Agostini 5.00 12.00
REMF Mark Fistric 5.00 12.00
REMG Marc-Andre Gragnani 5.00 12.00
REMI Michael Frolik 6.00 15.00
REMR Mattias Ritola 5.00 12.00
RENF Nikita Filatov 6.00 15.00
RENK Nikolai Kulemin 6.00 15.00
RENO Nathan Oystrick
REOM Oscar Moller 5.00 12.00
REPB Patrik Berglund 5.00 12.00
REPH Patric Hornqvist 6.00 15.00
REPI Alex Pietrangelo 8.00 20.00
REPV Petr Vrana 4.00 10.00
RERE Robbie Earl 4.00 10.00
RERJ Ryan Jones 6.00 15.00
RERS Ryan Stone 4.00 10.00
RESC Luke Schenn 8.00 20.00
RESM Shawn Matthias 6.00 15.00
RESS Steven Stamkos 100.00 175.00
RETO T.J. Oshie 12.00 30.00
RETS Tom Sestito 6.00 15.00
REVM Vladimir Mihalik 4.00 10.00
REVT Viktor Tikhonov 5.00 12.00
REZB Zach Bogosian 6.00 15.00

2008-09 SP Game Used SIGnificance

STATED PRINT RUN 50 SERIAL #'d SETS
SIGAC Andrew Cogliano 6.00 15.00
SIGAE Alexander Edler 5.00 12.00
SIGAM Al MacInnis
SIGAO Alexander Ovechkin 30.00 80.00
SIGAT Alex Tanguay 5.00 12.00
SIGBB Bob Baun 8.00 20.00
SIGBD Brandon Dubinsky 6.00 15.00
SIGBE Jonathan Bernier 8.00 20.00
SIGBG Brian Gionta 6.00 15.00
SIGBM Brenden Morrow 6.00 15.00
SIGBO Brad Boyes 5.00 12.00
SIGCA Daniel Carcillo 5.00 12.00
SIGCB Cam Barker 5.00 12.00
SIGCD Chris Drury 6.00 15.00
SIGCI Dino Ciccarelli 6.00 15.00
SIGCK Chris Kunitz 8.00 20.00
SIGCP Carey Price 30.00 80.00
SIGCS Cory Stillman 5.00 12.00
SIGCW Cam Ward 8.00 20.00
SIGDA David Perron 6.00 15.00
SIGDB David Booth 8.00 20.00
SIGDC Dan Cleary 6.00 15.00
SIGDJ David Jones 5.00 12.00
SIGDP Daniel Paille 5.00 12.00
SIGDR Dwayne Roloson 6.00 15.00
SIGDS Daniel Sedin 8.00 20.00
SIGEJ Erik Johnson 6.00 15.00
SIGEL Patrik Elias
SIGEM Evgeni Malkin 25.00 60.00
SIGES Eric Staal 10.00 25.00
SIGFN Fredrik Norrena 5.00 12.00
SIGGZ Scott Gomez 6.00 15.00
SIGHA Michal Handzus 6.00 15.00
SIGHE Milan Hejduk 6.00 15.00
SIGHI Jonas Hiller 6.00 15.00
SIGHO Tomas Holmstrom 6.00 15.00
SIGJC Jeff Carter 8.00 20.00
SIGJH Jaroslav Halak 8.00 20.00
SIGJI Jarome Iginla 8.00 20.00
SIGJJ Jack Johnson 5.00 12.00
SIGJL Joffrey Lupul 6.00 15.00
SIGJP Jason Pominville 8.00 20.00
SIGJS Jordan Staal 8.00 20.00
SIGJT Jiri Tlusty 6.00 15.00
SIGKA Petr Kalus 8.00 20.00
SIGKC Kyle Chipchura
SIGKE Phil Kessel 10.00 25.00
SIGKL Kari Lehtonen 6.00 15.00
SIGKO Chuck Kobasew 5.00 12.00
SIGLE Kristopher Letang 15.00 40.00
SIGMA Matt Stajan
SIGMC Bryan McCabe 5.00 12.00
SIGMF Marc-Andre Fleury 10.00 25.00
SIGMH Martin Havlat 8.00 20.00
SIGMI Ryan Miller 10.00 25.00
SIGMK Mike Knuble 5.00 12.00
SIGMM Milan Michalek
SIGMR Mason Raymond 8.00 20.00
SIGMS Marco Sturm 8.00 20.00
SIGMT Maxime Talbot 8.00 20.00
SIGNB Nicklas Backstrom 12.00 30.00
SIGNI I Nathan Horton
SIGNZ Nikolai Zherdev 5.00 12.00
SIGPA Paul Stastny 8.00 20.00
SIGPB Pierre-Marc Bouchard 8.00 20.00
SIGPE Corey Perry
SIGPH Dion Phaneuf 8.00 20.00
SIGPK Patrick Kane 25.00 50.00
SIGPM Peter Mueller
SIGPS Peter Stastny 8.00 20.00
SIGRI Mike Ribeiro
SIGRM Ryan Malone 5.00 12.00
SIGRS Ryan Smyth 6.00 15.00
SIGSB Steve Bernier
SIGSE Devin Setoguchi 6.00 15.00
SIGSG Sam Gagner 6.00 15.00
SIGSK Sergei Kostitsyn 5.00 12.00
SIGST Martin St. Louis 8.00 20.00
SIGTE Tobias Enstrom 5.00 12.00
SIGTH T.J. Hensick 6.00 15.00
SIGTM Torrey Mitchell
SIGTO Jonathan Toews 20.00 50.00
SIGTR Tuukka Rask 8.00 20.00
SIGTV Thomas Vanek 8.00 20.00
SIGTY Tyler Kennedy
SIGTZ Travis Zajac 6.00 15.00
SIGVO Tomas Vokoun 6.00 15.00

2008-09 SP Game Used SIGnificant Numbers Dual Swatches

STATED PRINT RUN 2-96 SERIAL #'d SETS
SNBE Patrice Bergeron/37 20.00 50.00
SNBL Brian Lee/55
SNBS Borje Salming/21
SNBY Mike Bossy/22
SNCD Chris Drury/23
SNCP Carey Price/31 20.00 50.00
SNCW Cam Ward/30 10.00 25.00
SNDB Derick Brassard/16
SNDC Dino Ciccarelli/20
SNDP David Perron/57 10.00 25.00
SNDR Dwayne Roloson/35 12.00 30.00
SNEL Patrik Elias/26 20.00 40.00
SNFT Mark Fistric/28
SNGF Grant Fuhr/31 15.00 40.00
SNGX Claude Giroux/56 40.00 80.00
SNHE Milan Hejduk/23
SNHZ Henrik Zetterberg/40 15.00 40.00
SNIK Ilya Kovalchuk/17
SNJC Jeff Carter/17
SNJT Joe Thornton/19
SNKT Kyle Turris/91 25.00 50.00
SNKY Kyle Okposo/21
SNMB Martin Brodeur/30 50.00 100.00
SNMF Marc-Andre Fleury/29 30.00 60.00
SNMH Marian Hossa/81 12.00 30.00
SNMI Ryan Miller/30 15.00 40.00
SNML Milan Lucic/17
SNMN Markus Naslund/91
SNMR Michael Ryder/73 10.00 25.00
SNMS Steve Mason/30 15.00 40.00
SNMT Marty Turco/35 10.00 25.00
SNNB Nicklas Backstrom/19
SNNH Nathan Horton/16
SNPB Pierre-Marc Bouchard/96 8.00 20.00
SNPK Phil Kessel/81 15.00 40.00
SNPM Peter Mueller/88 10.00 25.00
SNPS Paul Stastny/26 15.00 40.00
SNRC Mike Richards/18
SNRG Ryan Getzlaf/15
SNRI Mike Ribeiro/63 8.00 20.00
SNRS Ryan Smyth/94 8.00 20.00
SNSB Steve Bernier/56
SNSC Sidney Crosby/87 60.00 120.00
SNSL Martin St. Louis/26 15.00 40.00
SNSS Steve Shutt/22 15.00 40.00
SNTH Tomas Holmstrom/96 10.00 25.00
SNTO Jonathan Toews/19
SNTR Tuukka Rask/40 15.00 40.00
SNVO Tomas Vokoun/29 15.00 40.00

2008-09 SP Game Used SIGnificant Swatches

STATED PRINT RUN 50 SERIAL #'d SETS
SSAG Alex Goligoski 15.00 40.00
SSAL Al MacInnis 12.00 30.00
SSAO Adam Oates 12.00 30.00
SSAP Adam Pineault 10.00 25.00
SSBB Bob Bourne 8.00 20.00
SSBL Brian Lee 10.00 25.00
SSBO Pierre-Marc Bouchard 12.00 30.00
SSBS Mike Bossy 12.00 30.00
SSBT Mark Fistric
SSBU Peter Budaj 10.00 25.00
SSBY Brian Boyle 10.00 25.00
SSCC Dino Ciccarelli 12.00 30.00
SSCD Chris Drury 10.00 25.00
SSCO Chris Osgood 20.00 40.00
SSCP Corey Perry 12.00 30.00
SSCS Cory Stillman 8.00 20.00
SSDA David Perron 10.00 25.00
SSDB Derick Brassard 10.00 25.00
SSDC Dino Ciccarelli 12.00 30.00
SSDG Doug Gilmour 15.00 40.00
SSDP Daniel Paille 8.00 20.00
SSDS Drew Stafford 10.00 25.00
SSDT Darcy Tucker 10.00 25.00
SSEJ Erik Johnson 10.00 25.00
SSEM Evgeni Malkin 50.00 100.00
SSES Eric Staal 15.00 40.00
SSGB Gilbert Brule 8.00 20.00
SSGC Guy Carbonneau 12.00 30.00
SSGH Gordie Howe 60.00 120.00
SSGP Gilbert Perreault 12.00 30.00
SSGX Claude Giroux 30.00 80.00
SSGZ Scott Gomez 10.00 25.00
SSIK Ilya Kovalchuk 12.00 30.00
SSIZ Ilya Zubov 10.00 25.00
SSJB Johnny Bucyk 12.00 30.00
SSJC Jeff Carter 12.00 30.00
SSJJ Jack Johnson 8.00 20.00
SSJK Jari Kurri 12.00 30.00
SSJO Joe Thornton
SSJS Jordan Staal 12.00 30.00
SSJT Jonathan Toews 30.00 80.00
SSKA Patrick Kane 25.00 60.00
SSKT Kyle Turris 20.00 50.00
SSLE Kristopher Letang 12.00 30.00
SSLM Lanny McDonald 12.00 30.00
SSLU Joffrey Lupul 10.00 25.00
SSMA Ryan Malone 8.00 20.00
SSMD Marcel Dionne 15.00 40.00
SSMG Marc-Andre Gragnani 10.00 25.00
SSMH Milan Hejduk 10.00 25.00
SSMI Mike Lundin 8.00 20.00
SSML Milan Lucic 20.00 50.00
SSMN Matt Niskanen 10.00 25.00
SSMO Brendan Morrison 8.00 20.00
SSMP Michael Peca 10.00 25.00
SSMR Mike Ribeiro 10.00 25.00
SSMT Marty Turco 12.00 30.00
SSNB Nicklas Backstrom 12.00 30.00
SSNH Nathan Horton 10.00 25.00
SSNZ Nikolai Zherdev 8.00 20.00
SSOK Kyle Okposo 12.00 30.00
SSOV Alexander Ovechkin 60.00 125.00
SSPB Patrice Bergeron 15.00 40.00
SSPE Patrik Elias 12.00 30.00
SSPH Chris Phillips 8.00 20.00
SSPK Phil Kessel 15.00 40.00
SSPM Peter Mueller 10.00 25.00
SSPO Denis Potvin 12.00 30.00
SSPR Carey Price 30.00 80.00
SSPS Paul Stastny 12.00 30.00
SSPT Peter Stastny 12.00 30.00
SSRB Richard Brodeur 10.00 25.00
SSRE Robbie Earl 8.00 20.00
SSRH Ron Hextall 20.00 50.00
SSRI Mike Richards 12.00 30.00
SSRK Ryan Kesler 15.00 40.00
SSRL Rod Langway 10.00 25.00
SSRM Ryan Miller 12.00 30.00
SSRN Ryan Stone 8.00 20.00
SSRV Rick Vaive 8.00 20.00
SSSB Steve Bernier 8.00 20.00
SSSG Sam Gagner 10.00 25.00
SSSH Shawn Matthias 12.00 30.00
SSST Matt Stajan 10.00 25.00
SSSV Steve Mason 15.00 40.00
SSSW Stephen Weiss 8.00 20.00
SSTF Theoren Fleury 15.00 40.00
SSTH Tomas Holmstrom 10.00 25.00
SSTR Tuukka Rask 12.00 30.00
SSVO Tomas Vokoun 10.00 25.00

2008-09 SP Game Used Team Marks

STATED PRINT RUN 25-50
TMAM Al MacInnis 12.00 30.00
TMAO Alexander Ovechkin/25 100.00 200.00
TMBC Bobby Clarke 12.00 30.00
TMBF Bernie Federko 10.00 25.00
TMBO Bobby Orr 75.00 150.00
TMCN Cam Neely 12.00 30.00
TMCP Carey Price 50.00 100.00
TMCW Cam Ward 12.00 30.00
TMEL Patrik Elias 12.00 30.00
TMEM Evgeni Malkin 25.00 60.00
TMEN Evgeni Nabokov 10.00 25.00
TMES Eric Staal 15.00 40.00
TMGA Sam Gagner 10.00 25.00
TMGF Grant Fuhr 12.00 30.00
TMGH Gordie Howe 75.00 150.00
TMGP Gilbert Perreault 12.00 30.00
TMHE Dany Heatley 20.00 50.00
TMHS Henrik Sedin 12.00 30.00
TMJC Jeff Carter 12.00 30.00
TMJI Jarome Iginla 12.00 30.00
TMJK Jari Kurri 12.00 30.00
TMJM Joe Mullen 10.00 25.00
TMJT Jonathan Toews 30.00 80.00
TMLR Luc Robitaille 12.00 30.00
TMMB Martin Brodeur/25 50.00 100.00
TMME Mark Messier 50.00 100.00
TMMF Marc-Andre Fleury 20.00 50.00
TMMI Mike Bossy 12.00 30.00
TMMM Mike Modano 20.00 50.00
TMMN Markus Naslund 10.00 25.00
TMMS Martin St. Louis 12.00 30.00
TMNL Nicklas Lidstrom 12.00 30.00
TMPK Patrick Kane 25.00 60.00
TMPS Paul Stastny 15.00 40.00
TMRB Ray Bourque/25 50.00 100.00
TMRG Ryan Getzlaf 20.00 50.00
TMRL Rod Langway 12.00 30.00
TMRM Ryan Miller 12.00 30.00
TMRO Larry Robinson 12.00 30.00
TMSC Sidney Crosby 75.00 150.00
TMST Peter Stastny 20.00 50.00
TMTE Tony Esposito 30.00 80.00
TMTV Thomas Vanek 12.00 30.00

2008-09 SP Game Used Triple Authentic Fabrics

*GOLD/25: .6X TO 1.5X BASIC INSERTS
3AFAM Andrei Markov 6.00 15.00
3AFAO Adam Oates 6.00 15.00
3AFAS Anton Stastny 4.00 10.00
3AFBB Bob Bourne 4.00 10.00
3AFBL Rob Blake 6.00 15.00
3AFBN Brendan Morrison 4.00 10.00
3AFBO Pierre-Marc Bouchard 6.00 15.00
3AFBQ Ray Bourque 10.00 25.00
3AFBU Peter Budaj 5.00 12.00
3AFBY Billy Smith 6.00 15.00
3AFCA Carey Price 25.00 60.00
3AFCC Dino Ciccarelli 6.00 15.00
3AFCH Jonathan Cheechoo 6.00 15.00
3AFCJ Curtis Joseph 6.00 15.00
3AFCL David Clarkson 5.00 12.00
3AFCM Mike Commodore 4.00 10.00
3AFDC Dino Ciccarelli 6.00 15.00
3AFDG Doug Gilmour 8.00 20.00
3AFDH Dominik Hasek 8.00 20.00
3AFDP Dion Phaneuf 6.00 15.00
3AFDT Darcy Tucker 5.00 12.00
3AFEM Evgeni Malkin 20.00 50.00
3AFES Eric Staal 8.00 20.00
3AFFM Frank Mahovlich 6.00 15.00
3AFGA Simon Gagne 6.00 15.00
3AFGN Glenn Anderson 6.00 15.00
3AFHA Dale Hawerchuk 8.00 20.00
3AFHL Henrik Lundqvist 8.00 20.00
3AFHO Marian Hossa 5.00 12.00
3AFHR Trent Hunter 4.00 10.00
3AFJM Joe Mullen 5.00 12.00
3AFJT Jonathan Toews 15.00 40.00
3AFJW Justin Williams 5.00 12.00
3AFKA Paul Kariya 8.00 20.00
3AFKK Mike Komisarek 4.00 10.00
3AFKL Kari Lehtonen 5.00 12.00
3AFKO Mikko Koivu 5.00 12.00
3AFLA Rod Langway 5.00 12.00
3AFLG Robert Lang 4.00 10.00
3AFLM Lanny McDonald 6.00 15.00
3AFLT Brian Leetch 6.00 15.00
3AFLW Rod Langway 5.00 12.00
3AFMB Martin Brodeur 12.00 30.00
3AFMC Bryan McCabe 4.00 10.00
3AFMD Lanny McDonald 6.00 15.00
3AFME Ryan Malone 4.00 10.00
3AFMF Marc-Andre Fleury 10.00 25.00
3AFMG Marian Gaborik 8.00 20.00
3AFMH Milan Hejduk 5.00 12.00
3AFMK Miikka Kiprusoff 5.00 12.00
3AFMM Mike Modano 10.00 25.00
3AFMN Markus Naslund 5.00 12.00
3AFMR Michael Ryder 4.00 10.00
3AFMT Matt Carle 4.00 10.00
3AFMY Marty Turco 6.00 15.00
3AFNC Bernie Nicholls 5.00 12.00
3AFNL Nicklas Lidstrom 6.00 15.00
3AFNY Cam Neely 6.00 15.00
3AFNZ Nikolai Zherdev 4.00 10.00
3AFOK Olaf Kolzig 6.00 15.00
3AFOV Alexander Ovechkin 25.00 60.00
3AFPB Patrice Bergeron 8.00 20.00
3AFPE Gilbert Perreault 6.00 15.00
3AFPF Peter Forsberg 8.00 20.00
3AFPK Patrick Roy 15.00 40.00
3AFPM Patrick Marleau 6.00 15.00
3AFPT Peter Stastny 6.00 15.00
3AFRB Rod Brind'Amour 6.00 15.00
3AFRD Richard Brodeur 5.00 12.00
3AFRL Roberto Luongo 8.00 20.00
3AFRM Ryan Miller 6.00 15.00
3AFRN Rick Nash 6.00 15.00
3AFRV Rick Vaive 4.00 10.00
3AFRW Ryan Whitney 6.00 15.00
3AFRY Ryan Smyth 5.00 12.00
3AFSA Borje Salming 6.00 15.00
3AFSB Steve Bernier 4.00 10.00
3AFSC Sidney Crosby 20.00 50.00
3AFSF Sergei Fedorov 10.00 25.00
3AFSI Darryl Sittler 6.00 15.00
3AFSK Saku Koivu 6.00 15.00
3AFSL Steve Sullivan 5.00 12.00
3AFSS Sergei Samsonov 5.00 12.00
3AFST Jordan Staal 6.00 15.00
3AFSU Mats Sundin 6.00 15.00
3AFSV Steve Shutt 6.00 15.00
3AFSW Shea Weber 5.00 12.00
3AFTH Tomas Holmstrom 5.00 12.00
3AFTL Trevor Linden 6.00 15.00
3AFTP Tomas Plekanec 6.00 15.00
3AFTS Teemu Selanne 12.00 30.00
3AFTT Tim Thomas 6.00 15.00
3AFTU Tuomo Ruutu 6.00 15.00
3AFTW Tiger Williams 5.00 12.00
3AFVL Vincent Lecavalier 5.00 12.00
3AFVT Vesa Toskala 5.00 12.00
3AFWR Wade Redden 4.00 10.00
3AFWW Wojtek Wolski 5.00 12.00
3AFZP Zach Parise 6.00 15.00
3AFZV Sergei Zubov 5.00 12.00

2009-10 SP Game Used

COMP.SET w/o SPs (100) 40.00 80.00
(101-190) PRINT RUN 999 SER.#'d SETS
(191-200) PRINT RUN 99 SER.#'d SETS
1 Ryan Getzlaf 1.00 2.50
2 Teemu Selanne 1.25 3.00
3 Saku Koivu .60 1.50
4 Ilya Kovalchuk .60 1.50
5 Nik Antropov .50 1.25
6 Bryan Little .60 1.50
7 Zdeno Chara .60 1.50
8 Tim Thomas .60 1.50
9 Marc Savard .40 1.00
10 Milan Lucic .50 1.25
11 Thomas Vanek .60 1.50
12 Ryan Miller .60 1.50
13 Derek Roy .50 1.25
14 Jason Pominville .60 1.50
15 Jarome Iginla .60 1.50
16 Olli Jokinen .50 1.25
17 Dion Phaneuf .75 2.00
18 Miikka Kiprusoff .50 1.25
19 Eric Staal .75 2.00
20 Cam Ward .60 1.50
21 Rod Brind`Amour .60 1.50
22 Jonathan Toews 1.25 3.00
23 Patrick Kane 1.25 3.00
24 Marian Hossa .50 1.25
25 Brian Campbell .50 1.25
26 Milan Hejduk .50 1.25
27 Paul Stastny .60 1.50
28 Craig Anderson .60 1.50
29 Rick Nash .50 1.25
30 Steve Mason .50 1.25
31 Derick Brassard .60 1.50
32 Mike Modano 1.00 2.50
33 Mike Ribeiro .50 1.25
34 Marty Turco .60 1.50
35 Henrik Zetterberg .75 2.00
36 Pavel Datsyuk .75 2.00
37 Johan Franzen .60 1.50
38 Nicklas Lidstrom .60 1.50
39 Ales Hemsky .50 1.25
40 Nikolai Khabibulin .60 1.50
41 Sam Gagner .50 1.25
42 Andrew Cogliano .50 1.25
43 Tomas Vokoun .50 1.25
44 David Booth .40 1.00
45 Michael Frolik .50 1.25
46 Drew Doughty .75 2.00
47 Ryan Smyth .50 1.25
48 Anze Kopitar 1.00 2.50
49 Mikko Koivu .60 1.50
50 Niklas Backstrom .60 1.50
51 Martin Havlat .50 1.25
52 Carey Price 2.50 6.00
53 Scott Gomez .50 1.25
54 Mike Cammalleri .50 1.25
55 Andrei Markov .60 1.50
56 Pekka Rinne .75 2.00
57 Jason Arnott .50 1.25
58 Shea Weber .50 1.25
59 Martin Brodeur 1.25 3.00
60 Patrik Elias .60 1.50
61 Zach Parise .60 1.50
62 Kyle Okposo .60 1.50
63 Doug Weight .60 1.50
64 Josh Bailey .50 1.25
65 Henrik Lundqvist 1.00 2.50
66 Marian Gaborik .75 2.00
67 Chris Drury .50 1.25
68 Jason Spezza .60 1.50
69 Daniel Alfredsson .60 1.50
70 Jonathan Cheechoo .60 1.50
71 Mike Richards .60 1.50
72 Jeff Carter .60 1.50
73 Simon Gagne .60 1.50
74 Shane Doan .50 1.25
75 Peter Mueller .50 1.25
76 Ilya Bryzgalov .50 1.25
77 Sidney Crosby 2.50 6.00
78 Evgeni Malkin 2.00 5.00
79 Marc-Andre Fleury 1.00 2.50
80 Jordan Staal .60 1.50
81 Joe Thornton .60 1.50
82 Dany Heatley .60 1.50
83 Patrick Marleau .60 1.50
84 Devin Setoguchi .50 1.25
85 David Perron .40 1.00
86 Paul Kariya .75 2.00
87 Patrik Berglund .40 1.00
88 Steven Stamkos 1.25 3.00
89 Vincent Lecavalier .50 1.25
90 Martin St. Louis .60 1.50
91 Phil Kessel .75 2.00
92 Luke Schenn .50 1.25
93 Tomas Kaberle .40 1.00
94 Roberto Luongo .75 2.00
95 Daniel Sedin .60 1.50
96 Henrik Sedin .60 1.50
97 Ryan Kesler .60 1.50
98 Alexander Ovechkin 2.50 6.00
99 Nicklas Backstrom 1.00 2.50
100 Mike Green .60 1.50
101 Yannick Weber RC 4.00 10.00
102 Wes O'Neill RC 4.00 10.00
103 Ville Leino RC 3.00 8.00
104 Viktor Stalberg RC 4.00 10.00
105 Tyson Strachan RC 2.50 6.00
106 Tyler Myers RC 6.00 15.00
107 Troy Bodie RC 3.00 8.00
108 Tom Wandell RC 4.00 10.00
109 Tim Wallace RC 2.50 6.00
110 Teemu Laakso RC 2.50 6.00
111 Taylor Chorney RC 4.00 10.00
112 T.J. Galiardi RC 4.00 10.00
113 Spencer Machacek RC 4.00 10.00
114 Sergei Shirokov RC 2.50 6.00
115 Sean Collins RC 3.00 8.00
116 Sean Bentivoglio RC 3.00 8.00
117 Tyler Ennis RC 5.00 12.00
118 Ryan Wilson RC 4.00 10.00
119 Ryan Vesce RC 3.00 8.00
120 Ryan O'Reilly RC 6.00 15.00
121 Riley Armstrong RC 3.00 8.00
122 Riku Helenius RC 4.00 10.00
123 Ray Macias RC 3.00 8.00
124 Peter Regin RC 3.00 8.00
125 Perttu Lindgren RC 3.00 8.00
126 Daniel Larsson RC 3.00 8.00
127 Mike Santorelli RC 4.00 10.00
128 Mike McKenna RC 3.00 8.00
129 Mikael Backlund RC 4.00 10.00
130 Mika Pyorala RC 3.00 8.00
131 Michal Neuvirth RC 6.00 15.00
132 John Carlson RC 6.00 15.00
133 Michael Sauer RC 3.00 8.00
134 Michael Del Zotto RC 4.00 10.00
135 Matt Pelech RC 4.00 10.00
136 Matt Hendricks RC 3.00 8.00
137 Matt Gilroy RC 4.00 10.00
138 Matt Climie RC 3.00 8.00
139 Matt Beleskey RC 3.00 8.00
140 Luca Caputi RC 4.00 10.00
141 Logan Couture RC 8.00 20.00
142 Lars Eller RC 4.00 10.00
143 Kris Chucko RC 3.00 8.00
144 Kevin Westgarth RC 3.00 8.00
145 Kevin Quick RC 2.50 6.00
146 John Scott RC 4.00 10.00
147 John Negrin RC 4.00 10.00
148 Johan Backlund RC 4.00 10.00
149 Joel Rechlicz RC 2.50 6.00
150 Jhonas Enroth RC 5.00 12.00
151 Jesse Joensuu RC 3.00 8.00
152 Jay Rosehill RC 4.00 10.00
153 Jay Beagle RC 5.00 12.00
154 Jason Demers RC 6.00 15.00
155 Matthew Corrente RC 3.00 8.00
156 Jamie Fraser RC 3.00 8.00
157 James Reimer RC 10.00 25.00
158 Devan Dubnyk RC 8.00 20.00
159 Jaime Sifers RC 3.00 8.00
160 Ivan Vishnevskiy RC 3.00 8.00
161 Ilkka Pikkarainen RC 4.00 10.00
162 Geoff Kinrade RC 4.00 10.00
163 Frazer McLaren RC 3.00 8.00
164 Bobby Sanguinetti RC 2.50 6.00
165 Erik Karlsson RC 12.50 25.00
166 Dmitry Kulikov RC 4.00 10.00
167 Derek Peltier RC 2.50 6.00
168 Davis Drewiske RC 4.00 10.00
169 David Van Der Gulik RC 3.00 8.00
170 David Sloane RC 4.00 10.00
171 David Schlemko RC 3.00 8.00
172 Jakub Kindl RC 4.00 10.00
173 Colin Wilson RC 4.00 10.00
174 Cody Franson RC 4.00 10.00
175 Christian Hanson RC 4.00 10.00
176 Chris Durno RC 3.00 8.00
177 Cal O'Reilly RC 3.00 8.00
178 Byron Bitz RC 3.00 8.00
179 Bryan Rodney RC 3.00 8.00
180 Brian Salcido RC 3.00 8.00
181 Brandon Segal RC 3.00 8.00
182 Brad Marchand RC 10.00 25.00
183 Benn Ferriero RC 4.00 10.00
184 Ben Lovejoy RC 4.00 10.00
185 Artem Anisimov RC 4.00 10.00
186 Andrew MacDonald RC 2.50 6.00
187 Alexander Sulzer RC 2.50 6.00
188 Alec Martinez RC 5.00 12.00
189 Aaron MacKenzie RC 4.00 10.00
190 Aaron Gagnon RC 2.50 6.00
191 Jamie Benn RC/99 30.00 60.00
192 Victor Hedman RC/99 20.00 50.00
193 Tyler Bozak RC/99 15.00 40.00
194 Antti Niemi RC/99 15.00 40.00
195 Michael Grabner RC/99 10.00 25.00
196 Evander Kane RC/99 15.00 40.00
197 Jonas Gustavsson RC/99 10.00 25.00
198 James van Riemsdyk RC/99 20.00 50.00
199 Matt Duchene RC/99 40.00 80.00
200 John Tavares RC/99 40.00 100.00

2009-10 SP Game Used Gold

*GOLD 1-100: 1.2X TO 3X BASE
1-100 PRINT RUN 100 SER.#'d SETS
*GOLD ROOKIES 101-190: .5X TO 1.2X BASE
*GOLD ROOKIES 191-200: .25X TO.6X BASE
101-200 PRINT RUN 50 SER.#'d SETS
61 Zach Parise 2.50 6.00
99 Nicklas Backstrom 4.00 10.00
101 Yannick Weber 6.00 15.00
140 Luca Caputi 6.00 15.00
199 Matt Duchene 25.00 60.00
200 John Tavares 30.00 80.00

2009-10 SP Game Used Authentic Fabrics

*GOLD/100: .5X TO 1.2X BASIC JSY
*PATCH/35: 1X TO 2.5X BASIC JSY
OVERALL G-U/AU ODDS 1 PER PACK
AFAC Andrew Cogliano 3.00 8.00
AFAF Alexander Frolov 3.00 8.00
AFAM Andrei Markov 4.00 10.00
AFAO Adam Oates 4.00 10.00
AFAS Alexander Semin 4.00 10.00
AFBC Brian Campbell 3.00 8.00
AFBL Brian Leetch 4.00 10.00
AFBO David Booth 2.50 6.00
AFBW Blake Wheeler 4.00 10.00
AFCN Cam Neely 4.00 10.00
AFCP Carey Price 15.00 40.00
AFDD Drew Doughty 5.00 12.00
AFDE Derick Brassard 4.00 10.00
AFDG Doug Gilmour 5.00 12.00
AFDP Dion Phaneuf 5.00 12.00
AFDR Derek Roy 3.00 8.00
AFDS Daniel Sedin 4.00 10.00
AFDY Darcy Tucker 3.00 8.00
AFEM Evgeni Malkin 12.00 30.00
AFGF Grant Fuhr 4.00 10.00
AFGH Gordie Howe 10.00 25.00
AFGI Claude Giroux 4.00 10.00
AFGR Mike Green 4.00 10.00
AFGW Gump Worsley 6.00 15.00
AFHL Henrik Lundqvist 6.00 15.00
AFHS Henrik Sedin 4.00 10.00
AFHZ Henrik Zetterberg 5.00 12.00
AFIK Ilya Kovalchuk 4.00 10.00
AFJA Jason Arnott 3.00 8.00
AFJB Jay Bouwmeester 4.00 10.00
AFJC Jeff Carter 4.00 10.00
AFJD J.P. Dumont 2.50 6.00
AFJF Johan Franzen 4.00 10.00
AFJP Jason Pominville 4.00 10.00
AFJS Jason Spezza 4.00 10.00
AFJT Joe Thornton 4.00 10.00
AFJV Jakub Voracek 4.00 10.00
AFKE Phil Kessel 5.00 12.00
AFKM Mike Komisarek 3.00 8.00
AFLS Luke Schenn 3.00 8.00
AFMB Martin Brodeur 8.00 20.00
AFMC Mike Cammalleri 3.00 8.00
AFME Ryan Malone 2.50 6.00
AFMF Marc-Andre Fleury 6.00 15.00
AFMG Marian Gaborik 5.00 12.00
AFMK Miikka Kiprusoff 3.00 8.00
AFML Milan Lucic 3.00 8.00
AFMM Mike Modano 6.00 15.00
AFMR Mike Richards 4.00 10.00
AFMS Martin St. Louis
AFMT Marty Turco 4.00 10.00
AFNB Nicklas Backstrom 6.00 15.00
AFNF Nick Foligno 3.00 8.00
AFNH Nathan Horton 4.00 10.00
AFNL Nicklas Lidstrom 4.00 10.00
AFOV Alexander Ovechkin 6.00 15.00
AFPA Paul Stastny 4.00 10.00
AFPB Patrik Berglund 2.50 6.00
AFPD Pavel Datsyuk 5.00 12.00
AFPK Patrick Kane 8.00 20.00
AFPO Patrick O'Sullivan 3.00 8.00
AFPR Patrick Roy 10.00 25.00
AFRH Roman Hamrlik 2.50 6.00
AFRK Ryan Kesler 4.00 10.00
AFRL Roberto Luongo 5.00 12.00
AFRM Ryan Miller 4.00 10.00
AFRN Rick Nash 3.00 8.00
AFRS Ryan Smyth 3.00 8.00
AFSC Sidney Crosby 10.00 25.00
AFSG Sam Gagner 3.00 8.00
AFSK Saku Koivu 4.00 10.00
AFSM Steve Mason 3.00 8.00
AFSS Steven Stamkos 8.00 20.00
AFST Jordan Staal 4.00 10.00
AFSW Shea Weber 3.00 8.00
AFSY Steve Yzerman 10.00 25.00
AFTK Tomas Kaberle 2.50 6.00
AFTT Tim Thomas 4.00 10.00
AFTU Tuukka Rask 4.00 10.00
AFTV Thomas Vanek 4.00 10.00
AFVL Vincent Lecavalier 3.00 8.00
AFVO Tomas Vokoun 3.00 8.00
AFWG Wayne Gretzky 15.00 40.00
AFZP Zach Parise 4.00 10.00

2009-10 SP Game Used Authentic Fabrics Dual

STATED PRINT RUN 100 SER.#'d SETS
AF2AA Frolov/Kopitar 8.00 20.00
AF2AD Arnott/Dumont 4.00 10.00
AF2AG Cogliano/Gagner 4.00 10.00
AF2AW Arnott/Weber 4.00 10.00
AF2BO Brown/O'Sullivan 4.00 10.00
AF2BP Brodeur/Parise 10.00 25.00
AF2BS Brind`Amour/Staal 6.00 15.00
AF2BV Brassard/Voracek 5.00 12.00
AF2CG Clark/Gilmour 8.00 20.00
AF2CM Crosby/Malkin 20.00 50.00
AF2CO Crosby/Ovechkin 20.00 50.00
AF2CT Campbell/Toews 10.00 25.00
AF2DB Doughty/Bogosian 6.00 15.00
AF2DH Sedin/Sedin 5.00 12.00
AF2DL Doan/Lombardi 4.00 10.00
AF2DR Smyth/Brown 4.00 10.00
AF2DW Dumont/Weber 4.00 10.00
AF2DZ Datsyuk/Zetterberg 6.00 15.00
AF2EC Staal/Ward 6.00 15.00
AF2EF Emery/Fleury 8.00 20.00
AF2FC Fleury/Crosby 20.00 50.00
AF2FK Fuhr/Kurri 5.00 12.00
AF2FS Fleury/Staal 8.00 20.00
AF2GC Gomez/Cammalleri 4.00 10.00
AF2GD Green/Doughty 6.00 15.00
AF2GK Gaborik/Kessel 6.00 15.00
AF2GM Gilmour/MacInnis 6.00 15.00
AF2HB Horton/Booth 5.00 12.00
AF2HD Holmstrom/Datsyuk 6.00 15.00
AF2HF Holmstrom/Franzen 5.00 12.00
AF2HH Hossa/Huet 5.00 12.00
AF2HM Hamrlik/Markov 5.00 12.00
AF2HW Redden/Lundqvist 8.00 20.00
AF2IK Iginla/Kiprusoff 5.00 12.00
AF2JC Carter/Giroux 5.00 12.00
AF2JD Bouwmeester/Phaneuf 6.00 15.00
AF2JI Jokinen/Iginla 5.00 12.00
AF2KL Kovalchuk/Lehtonen 5.00 12.00
AF2KP Kariya/Perron 6.00 15.00
AF2KR Luongo/Kiprusoff 6.00 15.00
AF2KS Kane/Stamkos 10.00 25.00
AF2LI Lecavalier/Iginla 5.00 12.00
AF2LN Neely/Lucic 5.00 12.00
AF2LR Luongo/Raymond 6.00 15.00
AF2LS Lidstrom/Salming 5.00 12.00
AF2LZ Lidstrom/Zetterberg 6.00 15.00
AF2MM Modano/Turco 8.00 20.00
AF2MR Modano/Richards 8.00 20.00
AF2MS McDonald/Sittler 6.00 15.00
AF2MW Svatos/Wolski 3.00 8.00
AF2NB Neely/Bourque 8.00 20.00
AF2NM Nash/Mason 4.00 10.00
AF2NV Nash/Voracek 5.00 12.00
AF2OB Ovechkin/Backstrom 12.00 30.00
AF2OM Ovechkin/Malkin 20.00 50.00
AF2PK Parise/Kane 10.00 25.00
AF2PM Price/Mason 20.00 50.00
AF2PP Stastny/Stastny 5.00 12.00
AF2PR Pominville/Roy 5.00 12.00
AF2RC Richards/Carter 5.00 12.00
AF2RD Sedin/Kesler 5.00 12.00
AF2RJ Pominville/Miller 5.00 12.00
AF2RL Roy/Luongo 12.00 30.00
AF2RR Luongo/Kesler 6.00 15.00
AF2RS Miller/Stafford 5.00 12.00
AF2RV Roy/Vanek 5.00 12.00
AF2SB Stoll/Brown 4.00 10.00
AF2SD Smyth/Doughty 6.00 15.00
AF2SR Shutt/Robinson 5.00 12.00
AF2SS Staal/Staal 6.00 15.00
AF2SW Svatos/Stastny 5.00 12.00
AF2TD Vanek/Stafford 5.00 12.00
AF2TL Kaberle/Schenn 4.00 10.00
AF2TM Thomas/Lucic 8.00 20.00
AF2TR Ryder/Thomas 5.00 12.00
AF2VH Vokoun/Horton 5.00 12.00
AF2VS Lecavalier/Stamkos 10.00 25.00
AF2WH Weiss/Horton 5.00 12.00
AF2YB Yzerman/Bowman 12.00 30.00
AF2YG Yzerman/Gretzky 25.00 60.00
AF2ZL Schenn/Bogosian 4.00 10.00

2009-10 SP Game Used Authentic Fabrics Dual Patches

*SINGLES: .8X TO 2X BASIC INSERTS
STATED PRINT RUN 25 SER.#'d SETS
AF2DZ Datsyuk/Zetterberg 25.00 60.00
AF2KP Kariya/Perron 12.00 30.00
AF2NV Nash/Voracek 12.00 30.00

2009-10 SP Game Used Authentic Fabrics Triples

STATED PRINT RUN 25 SER.#'d SETS
*PATCH/15: .6X TO 1.5X BASIC TRIPLE
AF3ADW Arntt/Dumnt/Webr 6.00 15.00
AF3ASF Alfred/Speza/Foligno 8.00 20.00
AF3BLM Brodeur/Lund/Miller 15.00 40.00
AF3BSO Brown/Stafford/Okposo 8.00 20.00
AF3BSW Brind`Amr/Staal/Ward
AF3BVM Brassard/Voracek/Mason 8.00 20.00
AF3CBP Brodeur/Prise/Clrksn 15.00 40.00
AF3CMS Crosby/Malkin/Staal 30.00 80.00
AF3COM Crosby/Ovech/Malkin 30.00 80.00
AF3DSB Doughty/Schenn/Bogosn 10.00 25.00
AF3DSS Demitra/Sedin/Sedin 15.00 40.00
AF3ERC Emery/Richards/Carter 8.00 20.00
AF3FBK Frolov/Brown/Kopitar 12.00 30.00
AF3FCM Fleury/Crosby/Malkin 30.00 80.00
AF3FGT Laraque/Brashear/Lucic 6.00 15.00
AF3GMP Gomez/Markov/Price 30.00 80.00
AF3HTK Hossa/Toews/Kane 15.00 40.00
AF3IKP Iginla/Kiprsff/Phneuf 10.00 25.00
AF3KKS Kabrle/Komis/Schenn 6.00 15.00
AF3KOG Khabib/O'Sullivan/Gagner
AF3KSM Kovlchk/Smin/Malkin 25.00 60.00
AF3LHN Lecav/Heatley/Nash 8.00 20.00
AF3LHZ Lidstrm/Homstrm/Ztter 10.00 25.00
AF3LKR Luongo/Keslr/Rymnd 10.00 25.00
AF3LMS Lecav/Malne/Stmkos 15.00 40.00
AF3LOD Lidstrm/Osgd/Datsyuk 10.00 25.00
AF3LSS Lecav/St.Louis/Stmkos 15.00 40.00
AF3MAH McDonld/Andersn/Hawerck 10.00 25.00
AF3MMM McDnld/Mulln/McInnis 15.00 40.00
AF3MRT Modano/Ribeiro/Turco 12.00 30.00
AF3MSH McDnld/Shutt/Hawer 10.00 25.00
AF3MVS Miller/Vanek/Stafford 8.00 20.00
AF3NBV Nash/Brassard/Voracek 8.00 20.00
AF3OCG O'Sullivan/Cogliano/Gagner 6.00 15.00
AF3OGB Ovech/Green/Backs 20.00 50.00
AF3PHM Hamrlik/Markv/Pleknc 15.00 40.00
AF3PMC Markov/Camml/Pleknc 15.00 40.00
AF3PMV Pominville/Miller/Vanek 8.00 20.00
AF3PVS Pominvle/Vanek/Staffrd 8.00 20.00
AF3RBM Roy/Brodeur/Mason 20.00 50.00
AF3RCG Richards/Carter/Giroux 8.00 20.00
AF3RGL Redden/Gaboik/Lund 12.00 30.00
AF3RHD Luongo/Sedin/Sedin 10.00 25.00
AF3SBS Samsonov/Brind/Staal 10.00 25.00
AF3SGB Semin/Green/Backstrom 12.00 30.00
AF3SNT Spezza/Nash/Toews 15.00 40.00
AF3SOB Semin/Ovech/Backs 30.00 80.00
AF3SSK Sedin/Sedin/Kesler 30.00 80.00
AF3SSS Staal/Staal/Staal 10.00 25.00
AF3VHB Vokoun/Horton/Booth 8.00 20.00
AF3YGM Yzermn/Grtzky/Messr 40.00 100.00
AF3DROP Laraque/Komisarek/Lucic 6.00 15.00

2009-10 SP Game Used Extra SIGnificance

STATED PRINT RUN 25 SER.#'d SETS
SIGTV Beliveau/Bouchard 30.00 60.00
XSGBO Oshie/Berglund 15.00 40.00
XSGBP Backes/Pietrangelo 15.00 40.00
XSGCG Cogliano/Gagner 8.00 20.00
XSGCS Price/Mason 30.00 80.00
XSGDZ Datsyuk/Zetterberg 30.00 60.00
XSGEE Esposito/Esposito 15.00 40.00
XSGEJ Staal/Staal 12.00 30.00
XSGFH Fuhr/Hawerchuk 12.00 30.00
XSGGB Green/Backstrom 15.00 40.00
XSGGK Kurri/Gretzky 125.00 200.00
XSGGL Gaborik/Lundqvist 15.00 40.00
XSGGS Schenn/Gustavsson 12.00 30.00
XSGGW Green/Weber 10.00 25.00
XSGHD Sedin/Sedin 25.00 50.00
XSGHR Ryan/Hiller 20.00 50.00
XSGIP Iginla/Phaneuf 12.00 30.00
XSGJB Johnson/Bernier 10.00 25.00
XSGJM Tavares/Duchene 40.00 100.00
XSGKJ Kessel/Gustavsson 12.00 30.00
XSGKO O'Reilly/Carcillo 8.00 20.00
XSGLD Lindsay/Delvecchio 20.00 40.00
XSGLM Lemieux/Malkin 75.00 150.00
XSGLS Lecavalier/Stamkos 20.00 50.00
XSGML Leetch/Messier 40.00 80.00
XSGMV Miller/Vanek 12.00 30.00
XSGOB Okposo/Bailey 10.00 25.00
XSGOE Ersberg/Moller 10.00 25.00
XSGOH Orr/Hull 125.00 200.00
XSGOK Kovalchuk/Ovechkin 60.00 120.00
XSGOM Ovechkin/Malkin 60.00 120.00
XSGRB Roy/Brodeur 75.00 150.00
XSGRM Markov/Robinson 10.00 25.00
XSGTK Toews/Kane 40.00 80.00
XSGYG Yzerman/Howe 100.00 200.00
XSGZM Zetterberg/Malkin 30.00 80.00

2009-10 SP Game Used Inked Sweaters

STATED PRINT RUN 15-50
ISAC Andrew Cogliano 6.00 15.00
ISBW Blake Wheeler 8.00 20.00
ISCW Cam Ward 8.00 20.00
ISDC Matt Duchene 40.00 80.00
ISDD Drew Doughty 10.00 25.00
ISDP Dion Phaneuf 10.00 25.00
ISDS Daniel Sedin 8.00 20.00
ISDZ Michael Del Zotto 8.00 20.00
ISEK Evander Kane 15.00 40.00
ISEM Evgeni Malkin/15 40.00 80.00
ISGB Michael Grabner 8.00 20.00
ISGH Gordie Howe/15 75.00 150.00
ISGO Scott Gomez 6.00 15.00
ISGR Mike Green 8.00 20.00
ISGV Jonas Gustavsson 20.00 50.00
ISGX Claude Giroux 8.00 20.00
ISHL Henrik Lundqvist 25.00 50.00
ISHS Henrik Sedin 8.00 20.00

ISJA Jason Arnott 6.00 15.00
ISJC Jeff Carter 8.00 20.00
ISJD J.P. Dumont 5.00 12.00
ISJI Jarome Iginla/15 40.00 80.00
ISJS Jordan Staal 8.00 20.00
ISJV Jakub Voracek 8.00 20.00
ISLS Luke Schenn 6.00 15.00
ISMB Martin Brodeur/15 50.00 100.00
ISMF Marc-Andre Fleury 20.00 50.00
ISMG Marian Gaborik 10.00 25.00
ISML Mario Lemieux/15 60.00 120.00
ISNF Nick Foligno 6.00 15.00
ISNH Nathan Horton 8.00 20.00
ISNK Nikolai Khabibulin 8.00 20.00
ISNL Nicklas Lidstrom 12.00 30.00
ISOV Alexander Ovechkin/15 40.00 100.00
ISPM Peter Mueller 6.00 15.00
ISPR Patrick Roy/15
ISPS Paul Stastny 8.00 20.00
ISSC Sidney Crosby/15 100.00 200.00
ISSD Shane Doan 6.00 15.00
ISSG Sam Gagner 6.00 15.00
ISSM Steve Mason 6.00 15.00
ISST Steven Stamkos 15.00 40.00
ISSW Shea Weber 6.00 15.00
ISSY Steve Yzerman/15 75.00 150.00
ISTA John Tavares 20.00 50.00
ISVO Tomas Vokoun 6.00 15.00
ISVR James van Riemsdyk 15.00 40.00
ISWG Wayne Gretzky/15 175.00 300.00

2009-10 SP Game Used Inked Sweaters Dual

STATED PRINT RUN 5-15
AF6LA Arnott/Dumont 12.00 30.00
DISBL Brodeur/Lundqvist
DISBW Bucyk/Wheeler
DISCG Cogliano/Gagner 12.00 30.00
DISDH Sedin/Sedin 15.00 40.00
DISFS Fleury/Staal 25.00 50.00
DISGM Gomez/Markov
DISGY Yzerman/Gretzky
DISHH Hull/Howe
DISHL Lidstrom/Holmstrom 30.00 60.00
DISIP Iginla/Phaneuf 20.00 50.00
DISIT Thornton/Iginla
DISLM Lemieux/Malkin
DISLZ Lidstrom/Zetterberg 20.00 50.00
DISML Leetch/Messier
DISNO Neely/Oates 15.00 40.00
DISOB Okposo/Bailey 15.00 40.00
DISOR Robitaille/Ovechkin
DISPM Price/Mason
DISPP Stastny/Stastny 20.00 50.00
DISRB Roy/Bourque
DISRK Kane/van Riemsdyk 30.00 80.00
DISSM Mason/Stamkos 30.00 80.00
DISST Tavares/Stamkos
DISTD Tavares/Duchene 100.00 200.00
DISVH Vokoun/Horton 15.00 40.00
DISYL Yzerman/Lidstrom 60.00 120.00
DISZH Holmstrom/Zetterberg

2009-10 SP Game Used Legends Classic

STATED PRINT RUN 100 SER.#'d SETS
LCBB Bob Bourne 4.00 10.00
LCBS Billy Smith 5.00 12.00
LCDH Dale Hawerchuk 6.00 15.00
LCGA Glenn Anderson 5.00 12.00
LCLM Lanny McDonald 5.00 12.00
LCPS Peter Stastny 5.00 12.00
LCRL Rod Langway 4.00 10.00
LCSA Borje Salming 5.00 12.00
LCSS Steve Shutt 5.00 12.00
LCTW Tiger Williams 4.00 10.00

2009-10 SP Game Used Legends Classic Patches

*SINGLES: .6X TO 1.5X BASIC INSERTS
STATED PRINT RUN 25 SER.#'d SETS

2009-10 SP Game Used Letter Marks

STATED PRINT RUN 50 SER.#'d SETS
LMAA Artem Anisimov 15.00 40.00
LMAL Andrew Ladd 15.00 40.00
LMBO Mikkel Boedker 10.00 25.00
LMBR Bobby Ryan 15.00 40.00
LMBW Blake Wheeler 15.00 40.00
LMCG Claude Giroux 15.00 40.00
LMCH Christian Hanson 15.00 40.00
LMDB David Backes 40.00 80.00
LMDC Daniel Carcillo 25.00 60.00
LMDP Dion Phaneuf 20.00 50.00
LMGH Gordie Howe 40.00 100.00
LMIV Ivan Vishnevskiy 12.00 30.00
LMJA Justin Abdelkader 12.00 30.00
LMJC Jeff Carter 15.00 40.00
LMJE Jhonas Enroth 20.00 50.00
LMJI Jarome Iginla 20.00 50.00
LMJK Jari Kurri 15.00 40.00
LMJT Jonathan Toews 30.00 80.00
LMJV Jakub Voracek 15.00 40.00
LMKE Phil Kessel 20.00 50.00
LMLS Luke Schenn 12.00 30.00
LMMB Mikael Backlund 15.00 40.00
LMMG Mike Green 15.00 40.00
LMMP Max Pacioretty 20.00 50.00
LMMR Mike Richards 15.00 40.00
LMNB Nicklas Backstrom 25.00 60.00
LMNG Nathan Gerbe 12.00 30.00
LMPD Pavel Datsyuk 30.00 80.00
LMPK Patrick Kane 75.00 125.00
LMRM Ryan Miller 15.00 40.00
LMSM Steve Mason 12.00 30.00
LMSS Steven Stamkos 30.00 80.00
LMSY Steve Yzerman 75.00 150.00
LMTK Tyler Kennedy 15.00 40.00
LMTV Thomas Vanek 15.00 40.00
LMVL Ville Leino 12.00 30.00

2009-10 SP Game Used Marks of a Nation

STATED PRINT RUN 50 SER.#'d SETS
MNAA Artem Anisimov 15.00 40.00
MNAF Marc-Andre Fleury 40.00 80.00
MNAK Anze Kopitar 25.00 60.00
MNBA Mikael Backlund 15.00 40.00
MNBH Bobby Hull 20.00 50.00
MNBL Brian Leetch 15.00 40.00
MNBO Bobby Orr 100.00 200.00
MNCP Carey Price 60.00 150.00
MNCW Cam Ward 15.00 40.00
MNDB David Backes 20.00 50.00
MNDP Dion Phaneuf 20.00 50.00
MNEM Evgeni Malkin 30.00 80.00
MNGH Gordie Howe 40.00 100.00
MNHZ Henrik Zetterberg 20.00 50.00
MNIV Ivan Vishnevskiy 12.00 30.00
MNJA Justin Abdelkader 12.00 30.00
MNJC Jeff Carter 15.00 40.00
MNJD J.P. Dumont 10.00 25.00
MNJI Jarome Iginla 15.00 40.00
MNJK Jari Kurri 15.00 40.00
MNJT Jonathan Toews 30.00 80.00
MNKE Phil Kessel 25.00 50.00
MNLC Luca Caputi 15.00 40.00
MNLS Luke Schenn 40.00 80.00
MNLV Vincent Lecavalier 12.00 30.00
MNMB Martin Brodeur 40.00 100.00
MNMG Mike Green 15.00 40.00
MNMH Marian Hossa 12.00 30.00
MNML Mario Lemieux 50.00 120.00
MNMM Mark Messier 40.00 100.00
MNMN Markus Naslund 12.00 30.00
MNMR Mike Richards 15.00 40.00
MNNB Nicklas Backstrom 25.00 60.00
MNNL Nicklas Lidstrom 40.00 80.00
MNPB Patrik Berglund 15.00 40.00
MNPD Pavel Datsyuk 40.00 80.00
MNPE Phil Esposito 25.00 60.00
MNPK Patrick Kane 30.00 80.00
MNPR Patrick Roy 60.00 120.00
MNRG Ryan Getzlaf 25.00 60.00
MNRH Riku Helenius 15.00 40.00
MNRM Ryan Miller 30.00 80.00
MNRN Rick Nash 25.00 60.00
MNSC Sidney Crosby 150.00 250.00
MNSD Shane Doan 12.00 30.00
MNSG Scott Gomez 12.00 30.00
MNSK Saku Koivu 40.00 80.00
MNSM Steve Mason 20.00 50.00
MNSS Steven Stamkos 30.00 80.00
MNSW Shea Weber 25.00 50.00
MNSY Steve Yzerman 125.00 200.00
MNTO T.J. Oshie 25.00 60.00
MNTV Thomas Vanek 20.00 50.00
MNVL Ville Leino 12.00 30.00
MNWG Wayne Gretzky 150.00 300.00
MNYW Yannick Weber 15.00 40.00

2009-10 SP Game Used Rookie Exclusives Autographs

REAA Artem Anisimov 6.00 15.00
REAM Alec Martinez 8.00 20.00
REAN Antti Niemi 10.00 25.00
REBA Mikael Backlund 6.00 15.00
REBB Byron Bitz 5.00 12.00
REBF Benn Ferriero 6.00 15.00
REBM Brad Marchand 15.00 40.00
REBS Brian Salcido 5.00 12.00
RECB Chris Butler 6.00 15.00
RECF Cody Franson 6.00 15.00
RECH Christian Hanson 6.00 15.00
RECO Cal O'Reilly 5.00 12.00
RECW Colin Wilson 6.00 15.00
REDE Michael Del Zotto 6.00 15.00
REDK Dmitry Kulikov 6.00 15.00
REEK Erik Karlsson 30.00 60.00
REFM Frazer McLaren 5.00 12.00
REGR Michael Grabner 6.00 15.00
REIV Ivan Vishnevskiy 5.00 12.00
REJB Jamie Benn 20.00 50.00
REJD Jason Demers 10.00 25.00
REJE Jhonas Enroth 8.00 20.00
REJG Jonas Gustavsson 40.00 80.00
REJJ Jesse Joensuu 5.00 12.00
REJR Jay Rosehill 6.00 15.00
REJS John Scott 6.00 15.00
REJT John Tavares 40.00 100.00
REJV James van Riemsdyk 12.00 30.00
REKA Evander Kane 12.00 30.00
REKC Kris Chucko 5.00 12.00
RELC Luca Caputi 6.00 15.00
RELG Logan Couture 12.00 30.00
REMA Andrew MacDonald 4.00 10.00
REMB Matt Beleskey 5.00 12.00
REMD Matt Duchene 15.00 40.00
REMG Matt Gilroy 6.00 15.00
REMH Matt Hendricks 5.00 12.00
REMN Michal Neuvirth 10.00 25.00
REMP Matt Pelech 6.00 15.00
REMS Michael Sauer 5.00 12.00
REPL Perttu Lindgren 5.00 12.00
REPR Peter Regin 5.00 12.00
RERE Joel Rechlicz 4.00 10.00
RERH Riku Helenius 6.00 15.00
RERM Ray Macias 5.00 12.00
RERO Ryan O'Reilly 10.00 25.00
RESA Mike Santorelli 6.00 15.00
RESM Spencer Machacek 6.00 15.00
RESS Sergei Shirokov 4.00 10.00
RETB Tyler Bozak 10.00 25.00
RETC Taylor Chorney 6.00 15.00
RETG T.J. Galiardi 6.00 15.00
RETM Tyler Myers 8.00 20.00
RETW Tom Wandell 6.00 15.00
REVH Victor Hedman 12.00 30.00
REVL Ville Leino 5.00 12.00
REVS Viktor Stalberg 6.00 15.00
REYW Yannick Weber 6.00 15.00

2009-10 SP Game Used SIGnificance

STATED PRINT RUN 50 SER.#'d SETS
FSCTG Artem Anisimov
SIGAC Andrew Cogliano 6.00 15.00
SIGAG Alex Goligoski
SIGAK Anze Kopitar 12.00 30.00
SIGAO Alexander Ovechkin/25 50.00 125.00
SIGAP Alex Pietrangelo 6.00 15.00
SIGBA Josh Bailey 6.00 15.00
SIGBK Mikael Backlund 8.00 20.00
SIGBL Brian Leetch 10.00 25.00
SIGBO Bobby Orr/25 100.00 200.00
SIGBR Mikkel Boedker 5.00 12.00
SIGBW Blake Wheeler 8.00 20.00
SIGBZ Todd Bertuzzi 10.00 25.00
SIGCN Cam Neely 8.00 20.00
SIGCO Colton Gillies 8.00 20.00
SIGCP Carey Price 30.00 80.00
SIGDA Darren Helm 6.00 15.00
SIGDC Daniel Carcillo 5.00 12.00
SIGDD Drew Doughty 10.00 25.00
SIGDH Dale Hawerchuk 10.00 25.00
SIGDP Daniel Paille
SIGDS Daniel Sedin 8.00 20.00
SIGDZ Michael Del Zotto 8.00 20.00
SIGEE Erik Ersberg 6.00 15.00
SIGEM Evgeni Malkin 20.00 50.00
SIGEN Evgeni Nabokov 6.00 15.00
SIGES Eric Staal 10.00 25.00
SIGGA Sam Gagner 6.00 15.00
SIGGB Gilbert Brule 10.00 25.00
SIGGH Gordie Howe/25 30.00 80.00
SIGGI Claude Giroux 8.00 20.00
SIGGP Gilbert Perreault 8.00 20.00
SIGGR Mike Green 8.00 20.00
SIGGV Jonas Gustavsson 10.00 25.00
SIGHK Jaroslav Halak 25.00 50.00
SIGHL Henrik Lundqvist 12.00 30.00
SIGHS Henrik Sedin 8.00 20.00
SIGHZ Henrik Zetterberg 10.00 25.00
SIGIV Ivan Vishnevskiy 6.00 15.00
SIGJA Justin Abdelkader 6.00 15.00
SIGJC Jeff Carter 8.00 20.00
SIGJD J.P. Dumont 5.00 12.00
SIGJE Jonathan Ericsson 6.00 15.00
SIGJM John-Michael Liles 5.00 12.00
SIGJN James Neal 8.00 20.00
SIGJS Jordan Staal 8.00 20.00
SIGJV Jakub Voracek 8.00 20.00
SIGKO Kyle Okposo 10.00 25.00
SIGKP Kevin Porter 5.00 12.00
SIGLC Luca Caputi 8.00 20.00
SIGLS Luke Schenn 6.00 15.00
SIGMA Steve Mason 6.00 15.00
SIGMB Martin Brodeur/25 25.00 60.00
SIGMD Matt Duchene 15.00 40.00
SIGMG Marian Gaborik 10.00 25.00
SIGMK Mike Knuble 20.00 50.00
SIGML Mario Lemieux/25 40.00 100.00
SIGMM Mark Messier/25 20.00 50.00
SIGNB Nicklas Backstrom 12.00 30.00
SIGNL Nicklas Lidstrom 8.00 20.00
SIGNV Michal Neuvirth 12.00 30.00
SIGOM Oscar Moller 5.00 12.00
SIGOR Terry O'Reilly 12.00 30.00
SIGPH Dion Phaneuf 10.00 25.00
SIGPN Dustin Penner 5.00 12.00
SIGPR Patrick Roy/25 30.00 80.00
SIGRA Mason Raymond 15.00 40.00
SIGRM Ryan Miller 15.00 40.00
SIGRN Rick Nash 6.00 15.00
SIGSC Sidney Crosby/25 75.00 150.00
SIGSE Devin Setoguchi 6.00 15.00
SIGSK Jack Skille 5.00 12.00
SIGST Steven Stamkos 15.00 40.00
SIGSW Shea Weber 6.00 15.00
SIGSY Steve Yzerman/25 75.00 150.00
SIGTA John Tavares 40.00 100.00
SIGTO Jonathan Toews 15.00 40.00
SIGTV Thomas Vanek 8.00 20.00
SIGTW Ty Wishart 6.00 15.00
SIGVR James van Riemsdyk 25.00 50.00
SIGWG Wayne Gretzky/25 100.00 200.00
SIGZB Zach Bogosian

2009-10 SP Game Used SIGnificant Numbers

STATED PRINT RUN 1-91
SNAA Artem Anisimov/42 10.00 25.00
SNBA Mikael Backlund/60 10.00 25.00
SNBW Blake Wheeler/26 12.00 30.00
SNCP Carey Price/31 40.00 100.00
SNCW Cam Ward/30 10.00 25.00
SNDS Daniel Sedin/22 12.00 30.00
SNEM Evgeni Malkin/71 30.00 80.00
SNGB Michael Grabner/20 25.00 50.00
SNGF Grant Fuhr/31 10.00 25.00
SNGR Mike Green/52 10.00 25.00
SNHL Henrik Lundqvist/30 15.00 40.00
SNHS Henrik Sedin/33 10.00 25.00
SNHZ Henrik Zetterberg/40 12.00 30.00
SNIK Ilya Kovalchuk/17
SNIV Ivan Vishnevskiy/59 8.00 20.00
SNJA Jason Arnott/19 10.00 25.00
SNJC Jeff Carter/17
SNJD J.P. Dumont/71 6.00 15.00
SNJK Jari Kurri/17
SNJO Jonathan Toews/19 30.00 60.00
SNJP Jason Pominville/29 12.00 30.00
SNJT Joe Thornton/19 12.00 30.00
SNKE Phil Kessel/81 12.00 30.00
SNKO Kyle Okposo/21 12.00 30.00
SNLR Larry Robinson/19 12.00 30.00
SNMB Martin Brodeur/30 40.00 80.00
SNMF Marc-Andre Fleury/29 30.00 60.00
SNMR Mason Raymond/21 10.00 25.00
SNMT Marty Turco/35 10.00 25.00
SNNB Nicklas Backstrom/19 30.00 60.00
SNNF Nick Foligno/71 8.00 20.00
SNPK Patrick Kane/88 20.00 50.00
SNPR Patrick Roy/33 60.00 120.00
SNPS Paul Stastny/26 12.00 30.00
SNPT Peter Stastny/26 12.00 30.00
SNRB Ray Bourque/77 15.00 40.00
SNRI Mike Richards/18 12.00 30.00
SNRM Ryan Miller/30 10.00 25.00
SNRN Rick Nash/61 8.00 20.00
SNSC Sidney Crosby/87 75.00 150.00
SNSD Shane Doan/19 10.00 25.00
SNSG Sam Gagner/89 8.00 20.00
SNSS Steve Shutt/22 20.00 40.00
SNST Steven Stamkos/91 30.00 60.00
SNSY Steve Yzerman/19 40.00 80.00
SNTV Thomas Vanek/26 12.00 30.00
SNVO Tomas Vokoun/29 10.00 25.00
SNVR James van Riemsdyk/51 25.00 60.00
SNYW Yannick Weber/68 10.00 25.00

2010-11 SP Game Used

COMP.SET w/o SPs (100) 50.00 100.00
101-190 PRINT RUN 699 SER.#'d SETS
191-200 PRINT RUN 99 SER.#'d SETS
1 Ryan Getzlaf 1.50 4.00
2 Bobby Ryan 1.00 2.50
3 Jonas Hiller .75 2.00
4 Dustin Byfuglien 1.00 2.50
5 Evander Kane 1.00 2.50
6 Zdeno Chara .75 2.00
7 Tuukka Rask 1.00 2.50
8 Patrice Bergeron 1.25 3.00
9 Thomas Vanek 1.00 2.50
10 Ryan Miller 1.00 2.50
11 Tyler Myers 1.00 2.50
12 Rene Bourque .60 1.50
13 Jarome Iginla 1.00 2.50
14 Alex Tanguay .60 1.50
15 Miikka Kiprusoff .75 2.00
16 Eric Staal 1.25 3.00
17 Cam Ward 1.00 2.50
18 Jussi Jokinen .60 1.50
19 Jonathan Toews 2.00 5.00
20 Patrick Kane 2.00 5.00
21 Marian Hossa .75 2.00
22 Duncan Keith 1.00 2.50
23 Marty Turco 1.00 2.50
24 Matt Duchene 1.00 2.50
25 Paul Stastny 1.00 2.50
26 Craig Anderson 1.00 2.50
27 Rick Nash 1.00 2.50
28 Steve Mason .75 2.00
29 Jakub Voracek 1.00 2.50
30 Kari Lehtonen .75 2.00
31 Mike Ribeiro .75 2.00
32 Brad Richards 1.00 2.50
33 Jim Howard 1.25 3.00
34 Henrik Zetterberg 1.25 3.00
35 Pavel Datsyuk 1.25 3.00
36 Nicklas Lidstrom 1.00 2.50
37 Ales Hemsky .75 2.00
38 Sam Gagner .75 2.00
39 Dustin Penner .60 1.50
40 Stephen Weiss .75 2.00
41 Tomas Vokoun .75 2.00
42 Drew Doughty 1.00 2.50
43 Ryan Smyth .75 2.00
44 Anze Kopitar 1.50 4.00
45 Mikko Koivu 1.00 2.50
46 Niklas Backstrom 1.00 2.50
47 Guillaume Latendresse .75 2.00
48 Andrew Brunette .60 1.50
49 Tomas Plekanec 1.00 2.50
50 Carey Price 4.00 10.00
51 Scott Gomez .75 2.00
52 Mike Cammalleri 1.00 2.50
53 Brian Gionta .75 2.00
54 Pekka Rinne 1.25 3.00
55 Patric Hornqvist .75 2.00
56 Shea Weber .75 2.00
57 Martin Brodeur 2.00 5.00
58 Patrik Elias 1.00 2.50
59 Zach Parise 1.00 2.50
60 Ilya Kovalchuk 1.00 2.50
61 Rick DiPietro .75 2.00
62 Kyle Okposo 1.00 2.50
63 John Tavares 2.00 5.00
64 Henrik Lundqvist 1.50 4.00
65 Marian Gaborik 1.25 3.00
66 Chris Drury .75 2.00
67 Jason Spezza .60 1.50
68 Daniel Alfredsson 1.00 2.50
69 Chris Pronger .75 2.00
70 Mike Richards 1.00 2.50
71 Jeff Carter 1.00 2.50
72 Claude Giroux 1.00 2.50
73 Michael Leighton .75 2.00
74 Shane Doan .75 2.00
75 Wojtek Wolski .60 1.50
76 Ilya Bryzgalov .75 2.00
77 Sidney Crosby 4.00 10.00
78 Evgeni Malkin 3.00 8.00
79 Marc-Andre Fleury 1.50 4.00
80 Joe Thornton 1.00 2.50
81 Dany Heatley .75 2.00
82 Patrick Marleau 1.00 2.50
83 Devin Setoguchi .75 2.00
84 Jaroslav Halak 1.00 2.50
85 Patrik Berglund .60 1.50
86 Steven Stamkos 2.00 5.00
87 Vincent Lecavalier .75 2.00
88 Martin St. Louis 1.00 2.50
89 Dion Phaneuf 1.00 2.50
90 Phil Kessel 1.25 3.00
91 Luke Schenn .75 2.00
92 Jean-Sebastien Giguere .75 2.00
93 Roberto Luongo 1.00 2.50
94 Daniel Sedin 1.00 2.50
95 Henrik Sedin 1.00 2.50
96 Alexandre Burrows 1.00 2.50
97 Semyon Varlamov 1.00 2.50
98 Alexander Ovechkin 4.00 10.00
99 Nicklas Backstrom 1.50 4.00
100 Mike Green 1.00 2.50
101 Mattias Tedenby RC 2.00 5.00
102 Luke Adam RC 2.50 6.00
103 Evgeny Grachev RC 2.50 6.00
104 Mark Dekanich RC 2.50 6.00
105 Adam McQuaid RC 3.00 8.00
106 Jeff Penner RC 4.00 10.00
107 Brandon Pirri RC 2.50 6.00
108 Jonas Holos RC 2.50 6.00
109 Nikita Nikitin RC 2.50 6.00
110 Kyle Wilson RC 3.00 8.00
111 Maxime Fortunus RC 2.00 5.00
112 Marco Scandella RC 2.50 6.00
113 Kevin Shattenkirk RC 5.00 12.00
114 Ian Cole RC 2.50 6.00
115 Kyle Palmieri RC 5.00 12.00
116 Robin Lehner RC 5.00 12.00
117 Marc-Andre Cliche RC 2.00 5.00
118 Richard Clune RC 3.00 8.00
119 Corey Elkins RC 2.00 5.00
120 Jake Muzzin RC 2.50 6.00
121 Clayton Stoner RC 2.50 6.00
122 Nate Prosser RC 2.50 6.00
123 Alexander Urbom RC 2.50 6.00
124 Matt Taormina RC 2.50 6.00
125 Matt Martin RC 4.00 10.00
126 Matt Kassian RC 2.50 6.00
127 Michael Haley RC 2.50 6.00
128 Mark Flood RC 2.00 5.00
129 Keith Aulie RC 2.50 6.00
130 Derek Smith RC 2.50 6.00
131 Bobby Butler RC 2.50 6.00
132 Jeremy Duchesne RC 3.00 8.00
133 Jeremy Morin RC 2.50 6.00
134 John McCarthy RC 2.50 6.00
135 Ryan Reaves RC 3.00 8.00
136 Colby Cohen RC 2.50 6.00
137 Brayden Irwin RC 2.50 6.00
138 Guillaume Desbiens 3.00 8.00
139 Evan Oberg RC 3.00 8.00
140 Brian Fahey RC 2.50 6.00
141 Marcus Johansson RC 4.00 10.00
142 Dustin Tokarski RC 2.50 6.00
143 Dana Tyrell RC 2.50 6.00
144 Tommy Wingels RC 2.50 6.00
145 Eric Tangradi RC 2.50 6.00
146 Nick Johnson RC 2.00 5.00
147 Alexander Pechurski RC 3.00 8.00
148 Evan Brophey RC 2.50 6.00
149 Oliver Ekman-Larsson RC 4.00 10.00
150 Sergei Bobrovsky RC 6.00 15.00
151 Kaspars Daugavins RC 3.00 8.00
152 Jared Cowen RC 2.50 6.00
153 Matt Zaba RC 3.00 8.00
154 Nino Niederreiter RC 3.00 8.00
155 Dustin Kohn RC 2.50 6.00
156 Dylan Reese RC 2.50 6.00
157 Nick Palmieri RC 2.50 6.00
158 Jacob Josefson RC 2.50 6.00
159 Anders Lindback RC 2.50 6.00
160 Nick Spaling RC 2.50 6.00
161 J.T. Wyman RC 2.50 6.00
162 Justin Falk RC 2.00 5.00
163 Cody Almond RC 2.50 6.00
164 Maxim Noreau RC 2.00 5.00
165 Casey Wellman RC 2.50 6.00
166 Kyle Clifford RC 2.50 6.00
167 Alex Plante RC 2.50 6.00
168 Dean Arsene RC 2.50 6.00
169 Johan Motin RC 2.00 5.00
170 Philip Larsen RC 2.50 6.00
171 Raymond Sawada RC 2.00 5.00
172 Eric Wellwood RC 3.00 8.00
173 Tomas Kana RC 2.50 6.00
174 Grant Clitsome RC 2.50 6.00
175 Chad Kolarik RC 2.50 6.00
176 Mark Olver RC 2.50 6.00
177 Brandon Yip RC 2.50 6.00
178 Justin Mercier RC 2.50 6.00
179 Nick Leddy RC 2.50 6.00
180 Jamie McBain RC 2.50 6.00
181 Zac Dalpe RC 2.50 6.00
182 Jerome Samson RC 2.50 6.00
183 Henrik Karlsson RC 2.50 6.00
184 T.J. Brodie RC 2.50 6.00
185 Zach Hamill RC 2.50 6.00
186 Andrew Bodnarchuk RC 2.50 6.00
187 Jordan Caron RC 4.00 10.00
188 Arturs Kulda RC 2.50 6.00
189 Cam Fowler RC 3.00 8.00
190 Nick Bonino RC 3.00 8.00
191 Derek Stepan/99 RC 15.00 40.00
192 Alexander Burmistrov/99 RC 8.00 20.00
193 Jeff Skinner/99 RC 15.00 40.00
194 Brayden Schenn/99 RC 12.00 30.00
195 Jordan Eberle/99 RC 40.00 100.00
196 Magnus Paajarvi/99 RC 10.00 25.00
197 Nazem Kadri/99 RC 30.00 60.00
198 P.K. Subban/99 RC 50.00 120.00
199 Tyler Seguin/99 RC 60.00 100.00
200 Taylor Hall/99 RC 40.00 100.00

2010-11 SP Game Used Gold

*1-100 GOLD: 1X TO 2.5X BASE
1-100 PRINT RUN 100 SER.#'d SETS
*101-190 GOLD: .6X TO 1.5X BASE
*191-200 GOLD: .3X TO .8X BASE
101-200 PRINT RUN 50 SER.#'d SETS
99 Nicklas Backstrom 4.00 10.00

2010-11 SP Game Used Authentic Fabrics

OVERALL STATED ODDS 1 PER PACK
*GOLD/60-100: .5X TO 1.2X BASIC JSY
AFAB Alexandre Burrows 4.00 10.00
AFAH Ales Hemsky 3.00 8.00
AFAK Anze Kopitar 6.00 15.00
AFAN Antti Niemi 3.00 8.00
AFAO Alexander Ovechkin 10.00 25.00
AFBA Nicklas Backstrom 6.00 15.00
AFBL Brian Leetch 4.00 10.00
AFBR Brad Richards 4.00 10.00
AFBS Borje Salming 4.00 10.00
AFCG Claude Giroux 4.00 10.00
AFCN Cam Neely 4.00 10.00
AFCP Carey Price 15.00 40.00
AFCW Cam Ward 4.00 10.00
AFDA Daniel Alfredsson 4.00 10.00
AFDB Dustin Byfuglien 4.00 10.00
AFDC Daniel Carcillo 2.50 6.00
AFDD Drew Doughty 4.00 10.00
AFDE Derick Brassard 4.00 10.00
AFDH Dany Heatley 3.00 8.00
AFDK Duncan Keith 4.00 10.00
AFDP Dion Phaneuf 4.00 10.00
AFDS Daniel Sedin 4.00 10.00
AFEK Evander Kane 4.00 10.00
AFEL Patrik Elias 4.00 10.00
AFEM Evgeni Malkin 12.00 30.00
AFFR Johan Franzen 4.00 10.00
AFGA Marian Gaborik 5.00 12.00
AFGF Grant Fuhr 4.00 10.00
AFHE Milan Hejduk 3.00 8.00
AFHL Henrik Lundqvist 6.00 15.00
AFHZ Henrik Zetterberg 5.00 12.00
AFIK Ilya Kovalchuk 4.00 10.00
AFJA Jason Arnott 3.00 8.00
AFJC Jeff Carter 4.00 10.00
AFJD J.P. Dumont 2.50 6.00
AFJG Jean-Sebastien Giguere 3.00 8.00
AFJI Jarome Iginla 4.00 10.00
AFJJ Jack Johnson 2.50 6.00
AFJL Jamie Langenbrunner 2.50 6.00
AFJO Joe Sakic 6.00 15.00
AFJP Joe Pavelski 4.00 10.00
AFJV James van Riemsdyk 6.00 15.00
AFKA Patrick Kane 8.00 20.00
AFKI Miikka Kiprusoff 3.00 8.00
AFLE Mario Lemieux 12.00 30.00
AFLS Luke Schenn 3.00 8.00
AFLU Loui Eriksson 3.00 8.00
AFMB Martin Brodeur 8.00 20.00
AFMC Mike Cammalleri 4.00 10.00
AFMD Matt Duchene 4.00 10.00
AFMG Mike Green 4.00 10.00
AFMH Marian Hossa 3.00 8.00
AFML Milan Lucic 4.00 10.00
AFMM Mark Messier 6.00 15.00
AFMR Mike Richards 4.00 10.00
AFMS Marc Savard 2.50 6.00
AFNB Niklas Backstrom 4.00 10.00
AFNK Nikolai Kulemin 3.00 8.00
AFNL Nicklas Lidstrom 4.00 10.00
AFOA Adam Oates 4.00 10.00
AFPB Patrice Bergeron 5.00 12.00
AFPD Pavel Datsyuk 5.00 12.00
AFPK Phil Kessel 5.00 12.00
AFPM Patrick Marleau 4.00 10.00
AFPR Patrick Roy 10.00 25.00
AFPS Paul Stastny 4.00 10.00
AFRB Rene Bourque 2.50 6.00
AFRG Ryan Getzlaf 6.00 15.00
AFRK Ryan Kesler 4.00 10.00
AFRL Roberto Luongo 4.00 10.00
AFRN Rick Nash 4.00 10.00
AFSC Sidney Crosby 8.00 20.00
AFSD Shane Doan 3.00 8.00
AFSH Patrick Sharp 4.00 10.00
AFSM Steve Mason 3.00 8.00
AFSP Jason Spezza 2.50 6.00
AFSS Steven Stamkos 8.00 20.00
AFST Martin St. Louis 4.00 10.00
AFTA John Tavares 8.00 20.00
AFVK Tomas Vokoun 3.00 8.00
AFVO Jakub Voracek 4.00 10.00
AFWG Wayne Gretzky 10.00 25.00
AFZP Zach Parise 4.00 10.00

2010-11 SP Game Used Authentic Fabrics Patches

*PATCH/35: 1X TO 2.5X BASIC JSY
STATED PRINT RUN 35 SER.#'d SETS
AFBA Nicklas Backstrom 15.00 40.00
AFBS Borje Salming/20 20.00 50.00

2010-11 SP Game Used Authentic Fabrics Dual

STATED PRINT RUN 100 SER.#'d SETS
*PATCH/25: .8X TO 2X DUAL
AF2AE J.Arnott/P.Elias 5.00 12.00
AF2AS D.Alfredsson/J.Spezza 5.00 12.00
AF2BK D.Brown/A.Kopitar 8.00 20.00
AF2BP Z.Parise/M.Brodeur 10.00 25.00
AF2CM S.Crosby/E.Malkin 15.00 40.00
AF2CO S.Crosby/A.Ovechkin 15.00 40.00
AF2CR Z.Chara/T.Rask 5.00 12.00
AF2CV J.van Riemsdyk/J.Carter 8.00 20.00
AF2DG M.Dionne/W.Gretzky 20.00 50.00
AF2DW J.Dumont/S.Weber 4.00 10.00
AF2GL M.Gaborik/H.Lundqvist 8.00 20.00
AF2GP J.Giguere/D.Phaneuf 5.00 12.00
AF2GV M.Green/S.Varlamov 5.00 12.00
AF2HD H.Sedin/D.Sedin 5.00 12.00
AF2HG M.Hossa/M.Gaborik 6.00 15.00
AF2HP A.Hemsky/D.Penner 4.00 10.00
AF2IB R.Bourque/J.Iginla 5.00 12.00
AF2JD J.Johnson/D.Doughty 5.00 12.00
AF2KB E.Kane/D.Byfuglien 5.00 12.00
AF2KK P.Kessel/N.Kulemin 6.00 15.00
AF2KM M.Messier/J.Kurri 8.00 20.00
AF2KR M.Kiprusoff/T.Rask 5.00 12.00
AF2LC S.Crosby/M.Lemieux 15.00 40.00
AF2LM R.Luongo/R.Miller 5.00 12.00
AF2LR M.Lucic/T.Rask 5.00 12.00
AF2LS S.Stamkos/V.Lecavalier 6.00 20.00
AF2MH P.Marleau/D.Heatley 5.00 12.00
AF2MN M.Koivu/N.Backstrom 5.00 12.00
AF2NB C.Neely/R.Bourque 8.00 20.00
AF2NV R.Nash/J.Voracek 5.00 12.00
AF2OB N.Backstrom/A.Ovechkin 8.00 20.00
AF2PD D.Keith/P.Kane 10.00 25.00
AF2PP C.Price/T.Plekanec 20.00 50.00
AF2PR R.Bourque/P.Roy 12.00 30.00
AF2RB P.Roy/M.Brodeur 12.00 30.00
AF2RG M.Richards/C.Giroux 5.00 12.00
AF2SD M.Duchene/P.Stastny 5.00 12.00
AF2SO A.Semin/A.Ovechkin 8.00 20.00
AF2SS M.St. Louis/S.Stamkos 8.00 20.00
AF2SW C.Ward/E.Staal 6.00 15.00
AF2SZ S.Crosby/Z.Parise 15.00 40.00
AF2TD J.Tavares/M.Duchene 10.00 25.00
AF2TK D.Keith/J.Toews 10.00 25.00
AF2TP J.Pavelski/J.Thornton 5.00 12.00
AF2WL L.Robitaille/W.Gretzky 20.00 50.00
AF2YD S.Yzerman/P.Datsyuk 10.00 25.00
AF2YL S.Yzerman/N.Lidstrom 10.00 25.00
AF2ZB H.Zetterberg/N.Backstrom 8.00 20.00

2010-11 SP Game Used Authentic Fabrics Triples

STATED PRINT RUN 25 SER.#'d SETS
*PATCH/15: .6X TO 1.5X BASIC TRIPLE/25
AF3ANA Ryan/Getzlaf/Hiller 12.00 30.00
AF3ATL Antrpv/Kane/Byfugl 8.00 20.00
AF3BOS Bergrn/Chara/Rask 12.00 30.00
AF3CAL Brque/Kiprusoff/Iginla 8.00 20.00
AF3CAR Ruutu/Staal/Ward 10.00 25.00
AF3CBS Nash/Voracek/Mason 8.00 20.00
AF3CHI Keith/Toews/Kane 15.00 40.00
AF3COL Stastny/Hejduk/Duchn 8.00 20.00
AF3DAL Rchrds/Eriksson/Lehton 8.00 20.00
AF3DET Howard/Datsyuk/Zetter 15.00 40.00
AF3FLA Frolik/Weiss/Vokoun 6.00 15.00
AF3LAK Kopitar/Brown/Doughty 12.00 30.00
AF3MIN Koivu/Latend/Backstrm 8.00 20.00
AF3MON Price/Plekanec/Cammal 30.00 80.00
AF3NJD Kvalchk/Brdeur/Parise 15.00 40.00
AF3NSH Dumont/Weber/Rinne 10.00 25.00
AF3NYI DiPietro/Tavres/Okpso 15.00 40.00
AF3NYR Lundqvist/Gaborik/Drury 12.00 30.00
AF3OTT Alfrdssn/Gnchar/Spezza 8.00 20.00
AF3PHI Carter/Richards/van R 12.00 30.00
AF3PIT Crosby/Fleury/Malkin 30.00 80.00
AF3SJS Thrntn/Mrleau/Setgchi 8.00 20.00
AF3STL Johnsn/Berglnd/Backes 8.00 20.00
AF3TBL Lecav/St. Lou/Stamks 12.00 30.00
AF3TOR Giguere/Kessel/Phaneuf 15.00 40.00
AF3VAN Luongo/Sedin/Sedin 8.00 20.00
AF3WAS Ovech/Bckstrm/Varl 30.00 80.00

2010-11 SP Game Used Career Legacy

STATED PRINT RUN 9-75
CL2BG Brian Gionta/40 5.00 12.00
CL2BL Brian Leetch/75 6.00 15.00
CL2JK Jari Kurri/75 6.00 15.00
CL2LM Lanny McDonald/75 6.00 15.00
CL2PE Phil Esposito/25 8.00 20.00
CL2PR Patrick Roy/75 15.00 40.00
CL2RB Ray Bourque/75 10.00 25.00
CL3DH Dany Heatley/35 10.00 25.00
CL3WG Wayne Gretzky/25 50.00 100.00

2010-11 SP Game Used Championship Marks

STATED PRINT RUN 50 SER.#'d SETS
CMAL Andrew Ladd 50.00 100.00
CMAN Antti Niemi 50.00 100.00
CMDB Dustin Byfuglien
CMJT Jonathan Toews 125.00 200.00
CMMH Marian Hossa 50.00 100.00
CMPK Patrick Kane 100.00 175.00
CMPS Patrick Sharp 30.00 60.00

2010-11 SP Game Used Extra SIGnificance

STATED PRINT RUN 25 SER.#'d SETS
XSGBF M.Fleury/M.Brodeur 25.00 60.00
XSGBG M.Bossy/C.Gillies 12.00 30.00
XSGBM R.Miller/M.Brodeur 25.00 60.00
XSGBO B.Orr/R.Bourque 125.00 250.00
XSGBR M.Brodeur/P.Roy 75.00 150.00
XSGCG J.Carter/C.Giroux 12.00 30.00
XSGDT T.Seguin/D.Stepan 40.00 80.00
XSGEB P.Esposito/J.Bucyk 20.00 50.00
XSGEE T.Esposito/P.Esposito 30.00 80.00
XSGFM M.Fleury/E.Malkin 40.00 100.00
XSGGG Gustavsson/Giguere 15.00 40.00
XSGGH W.Gretzky/G.Howe 200.00 300.00
XSGHE T.Hall/J.Eberle 75.00 150.00
XSGHG M.Gaborik/M.Hossa 15.00 40.00
XSGHM D.Hasek/R.Miller 20.00 50.00
XSGHS D.Heatley/D.Setoguchi 10.00 25.00
XSGIB M.Backlund/J.Iginla 12.00 30.00
XSGIT J.Iginla/A.Tanguay 12.00 30.00
XSGJD J.Tavares/D.Stepan 50.00 100.00
XSGKO A.Ovechkin/I.Kovalchuk 60.00 120.00
XSGKS P.Subban/N.Kadri 40.00 100.00
XSGMS D.Savard/S.Mikita 15.00 40.00
XSGNM R.Nash/S.Mason 12.00 30.00
XSGOB A.Ovechkin/N.Backstrom 60.00 120.00
XSGOR L.Robinson/B.Orr 100.00 200.00
XSGPG J.Giguere/D.Phaneuf 12.00 30.00
XSGRB P.Bergeron/M.Ryder 15.00 40.00
XSGRC M.Richards/J.Carter 20.00 50.00
XSGRN T.Rask/A.Niemi 12.00 30.00
XSGSK A.Kopitar/R.Smyth 12.00 30.00
XSGTB J.Bailey/J.Tavares 20.00 50.00
XSGTD J.Tavares/M.Duchene 25.00 60.00
XSGYL N.Lidstrom/S.Yzerman 100.00 200.00

2010-11 SP Game Used Inked Sweaters

STATED PRINT RUN 15-50
PRINT RUNS LESS THAN 25 NOT PRICED
ISAO Alexander Ovechkin/15 50.00 125.00
ISBY Brandon Yip 6.00 15.00
ISCA Jeff Carter 8.00 20.00
ISDC Daniel Carcillo 5.00 12.00
ISDS Devin Setoguchi 6.00 15.00
ISEM Evgeni Malkin 20.00 50.00
ISET Eric Tangradi 6.00 15.00
ISGF Grant Fuhr 12.00 30.00
ISGU Jonas Gustavsson 12.00 30.00
ISHL Henrik Lundqvist 15.00 40.00
ISIK Ilya Kovalchuk 15.00 40.00
ISJC Jared Cowen 6.00 15.00
ISJF Johan Franzen 10.00 25.00
ISJG Jean-Sebastien Giguere 10.00 25.00
ISJI Jarome Iginla 8.00 20.00
ISJM Jamie McBain 6.00 15.00
ISJT John Tavares 15.00 40.00
ISJV Jakub Voracek 8.00 20.00
ISMB Martin Brodeur/15 40.00 80.00
ISMF Marc-Andre Fleury 12.00 30.00
ISMG Marian Gaborik 10.00 25.00
ISML Mario Lemieux/15 40.00 100.00
ISMM Mark Messier/15 20.00 50.00
ISMR Mike Richards 20.00 50.00
ISMS Martin St. Louis 8.00 20.00
ISNB Nicklas Backstrom 12.00 30.00
ISNH Nathan Horton 6.00 15.00
ISNK Nazem Kadri 15.00 40.00
ISNL Nicklas Lidstrom 12.00 30.00
ISPE Phil Esposito 15.00 40.00
ISPR Patrick Roy/15 40.00 80.00
ISPS Paul Stastny 8.00 20.00
ISRB Ray Bourque 12.00 30.00
ISRM Ryan Miller 12.00 30.00
ISRN Rick Nash 10.00 25.00
ISSC Sidney Crosby/15 60.00 120.00
ISVA James van Riemsdyk 12.00 30.00
ISWG Wayne Gretzky/15 125.00 250.00
ISYZ Steve Yzerman/15 30.00 80.00
ISZH Zach Hamill 6.00 15.00

2010-11 SP Game Used Letter Marks

STATED PRINT RUN 50 SER.#'d SETS
LMAN Antti Niemi 12.00 30.00
LMAO Alexander Ovechkin 75.00 125.00
LMBS Brent Sutter 10.00 25.00
LMBY Brandon Yip 12.00 30.00
LMCS Chris Stewart 12.00 30.00
LMDS Devin Setoguchi 12.00 30.00
LMEK Evander Kane 15.00 40.00
LMET Eric Tangradi 12.00 30.00
LMIK Ilya Kovalchuk 20.00 50.00
LMJC Jared Cowen 12.00 30.00
LMJG Jonas Gustavsson 20.00 50.00
LMJI Jarome Iginla 15.00 40.00
LMJT John Tavares 30.00 80.00
LMJV James van Riemsdyk 25.00 60.00
LMLE Lars Eller 50.00 100.00
LMLR Luc Robitaille 15.00 40.00
LMMD Matt Duchene 15.00 40.00
LMML Mario Lemieux 60.00 120.00
LMNK Nazem Kadri 25.00 60.00
LMPK Patrick Kane 30.00 80.00
LMPS P.K. Subban 100.00 200.00
LMRK Ryan Kesler 30.00 80.00
LMSC Sidney Crosby 100.00 200.00
LMSG Sam Gagner 12.00 30.00
LMSS Steven Stamkos 60.00 120.00
LMSU Duane Sutter 10.00 25.00
LMTM Tyler Myers 15.00 40.00
LMTO Jonathan Toews 30.00 80.00
LMWC Wendel Clark 15.00 40.00

2010-11 SP Game Used Number Marks

STATED PRINT RUN 25 SER.#'d SETS
NMAO Alexander Ovechkin 75.00 150.00
NMBC Bobby Clarke 25.00 60.00
NMBO Bobby Orr 200.00 350.00
NMEM Evgeni Malkin 50.00 120.00
NMJS Joe Sakic 30.00 80.00
NMJT John Tavares 40.00 100.00
NMJV James van Riemsdyk 20.00 50.00
NMMB Martin Brodeur 40.00 100.00
NMMD Matt Duchene 40.00 100.00
NMMR Mike Richards 40.00 100.00
NMPK Patrick Kane 40.00 100.00
NMSA Joe Sakic 30.00 80.00
NMSC Sidney Crosby 150.00 300.00
NMSS Steven Stamkos 60.00 120.00
NMSY Steve Yzerman 50.00 125.00
NMTO Jonathan Toews 50.00 100.00
NMWG Wayne Gretzky 300.00 450.00

2010-11 SP Game Used Retro Marks

STATED PRINT RUN 50 SER.#'d SETS
RMBO Bobby Orr 100.00 200.00
RMGL Guy Lafleur 40.00 80.00
RMJS Joe Sakic 25.00 60.00
RMME Mark Messier 25.00 60.00
RMMM Mike Modano 25.00 60.00
RMPE Phil Esposito 15.00 40.00
RMSC Sidney Crosby 150.00 300.00

2010-11 SP Game Used Rookie Exclusives Autographs

STATED PRINT RUN 100 SER.#'d SETS
REAB Alexander Burmistrov 12.00 30.00
REAK Arturs Kulda 5.00 12.00
REAL Anders Lindback 5.00 12.00
REBO Andrew Bodnarchuk 5.00 12.00
REBS Brayden Schenn 10.00 25.00
REBY Brandon Yip 10.00 25.00
RECA Cody Almond 5.00 12.00
RECO Jared Cowen 5.00 12.00
REDA Dean Arsene 5.00 12.00
REDR Dylan Reese 5.00 12.00
REDS Derek Stepan 20.00 50.00
REDT Dustin Tokarski 5.00 12.00
REEG Evgeny Grachev 5.00 12.00
REET Eric Tangradi 5.00 12.00
REGC Grant Clitsome 5.00 12.00
REHK Henrik Karlsson 5.00 12.00
REJC Jordan Caron 8.00 20.00
REJE Jordan Eberle 40.00 80.00

REJM Jamie McBain 5.00 12.00
REJO Johan Motin 4.00 10.00
REJS Jeff Skinner 15.00 40.00
REKC Kyle Clifford 5.00 12.00
REKD Kaspars Daugavins 6.00 15.00
REKS Kevin Shattenkirk 10.00 25.00
REMJ Marcus Johansson 10.00 25.00
REMN Maxim Noreau 4.00 10.00
REMO Mark Olver 5.00 12.00
REMP Magnus Paajarvi 6.00 15.00
REMT Mattias Tedenby 4.00 10.00
RENB Nick Bonino 6.00 15.00
RENJ Nick Johnson 4.00 10.00
RENK Nazem Kadri 12.50 30.00
RENL Nick Leddy 5.00 12.00
RENN Nino Niederreiter 6.00 15.00
RENP Nate Prosser 5.00 12.00
RENS Nick Spaling 5.00 12.00
REPA Nick Palmieri 5.00 12.00
REPE Alexander Pechurski 6.00 15.00
REPS P.K. Subban 30.00 80.00
RESB Sergei Bobrovsky 12.00 30.00
RETB T.J. Brodie 5.00 12.00
RETH Taylor Hall 50.00 120.00
RETS Tyler Seguin 30.00 60.00
RETW Tommy Wingels 5.00 12.00
RETY Dana Tyrell 5.00 12.00
REZD Zac Dalpe 5.00 12.00
REZH Zach Hamill 5.00 12.00

2010-11 SP Game Used SIGnificance

STATED PRINT RUN 15-50
SIGAK Anze Kopitar 12.00 30.00
SIGAN Antti Niemi 6.00 15.00
SIGAO Alexander Ovechkin/15 40.00 100.00
SIGBA Mikael Backlund 5.00 12.00
SIGBL Brian Leetch 8.00 20.00
SIGBO Bobby Orr/15 100.00 200.00
SIGBR Bobby Ryan
SIGBS Brayden Schenn 10.00 25.00
SIGCA Jeff Carter 8.00 20.00
SIGCD Chris Drury 6.00 15.00
SIGCG Claude Giroux 8.00 20.00
SIGCN Cam Neely 15.00 40.00
SIGCP Carey Price 20.00 50.00
SIGCW Cam Ward 8.00 20.00
SIGDB Dan Boyle 6.00 15.00
SIGDD Drew Doughty 8.00 20.00
SIGDG Doug Gilmour 10.00 25.00
SIGDH Dany Heatley 6.00 15.00
SIGDP Dion Phaneuf 8.00 20.00
SIGDS Daniel Sedin
SIGEK Evander Kane 8.00 20.00
SIGEL Patrik Elias 8.00 20.00
SIGEM Evgeni Malkin 25.00 60.00
SIGEP Phil Esposito 12.00 30.00
SIGES Eric Staal
SIGET Eric Tangradi 6.00 15.00
SIGGF Grant Fuhr 8.00 20.00
SIGGH Gordie Howe/15 60.00 120.00
SIGGL Guillaume Latendresse 6.00 15.00
SIGGU Jonas Gustavsson 10.00 25.00
SIGHE Milan Hejduk 6.00 15.00
SIGHL Henrik Lundqvist 12.00 30.00
SIGHS Henrik Sedin
SIGIK Ilya Kovalchuk 12.00 30.00
SIGIL Igor Larionov 8.00 20.00
SIGJB Josh Bailey 6.00 15.00
SIGJC Jared Cowen 6.00 15.00
SIGJD J.P. Dumont 5.00 12.00
SIGJE Jordan Eberle 15.00 40.00
SIGJG Jean-Sebastien Giguere 12.00 30.00
SIGJH Jonas Hiller 6.00 15.00
SIGJI Jarome Iginla 8.00 20.00
SIGJK Jari Kurri/15 12.00 30.00
SIGJS Jordan Staal 8.00 20.00
SIGJT Jonathan Toews/15
SIGJV James van Riemsdyk 12.00 30.00
SIGKE Phil Kessel 10.00 25.00
SIGLC Logan Couture 12.00 30.00
SIGLM Lanny McDonald 8.00 20.00
SIGLR Luc Robitaille 8.00 20.00
SIGLS Luke Schenn 6.00 15.00
SIGMB Martin Brodeur/15 30.00 60.00
SIGMC Rick MacLeish
SIGMD Matt Duchene
SIGMF Marc-Andre Fleury 12.00 30.00
SIGMG Mike Green
SIGMH Marian Hossa 10.00 25.00
SIGMM Mark Messier/15 40.00 80.00
SIGMP Magnus Paajarvi 8.00 20.00
SIGMR Mike Ribeiro 6.00 15.00
SIGMS Martin St. Louis 8.00 20.00
SIGNB Nicklas Backstrom 12.00 30.00
SIGNK Nazem Kadri 15.00 40.00
SIGNL Nicklas Lidstrom 10.00 25.00
SIGPB Patrice Bergeron 10.00 25.00
SIGPD Pavel Datsyuk
SIGPE Corey Perry
SIGPH Patric Hornqvist
SIGPK Patrick Kane
SIGPM Patrick Marleau
SIGPR Patrick Roy/15 60.00 120.00
SIGPS P.K. Subban
SIGRG Ryan Getzlaf 12.00 30.00
SIGRI Mike Richards 8.00 20.00
SIGRM Ryan Miller 8.00 20.00
SIGRN Rick Nash 8.00 20.00
SIGRS Ryan Smyth 6.00 15.00
SIGSD Derek Stepan 12.00 30.00
SIGSE Devin Setoguchi 6.00 15.00
SIGSG Scott Gomez
SIGSJ Jeff Skinner 30.00 80.00
SIGSK Saku Koivu 12.00 30.00
SIGSM Stan Mikita 12.00 30.00
SIGSS Steven Stamkos
SIGST Paul Stastny 8.00 20.00
SIGSV Semyon Varlamov
SIGSW Shea Weber 6.00 15.00
SIGSY Steve Yzerman/15 60.00 120.00
SIGTA John Tavares 15.00 40.00
SIGTB Tyler Bozak
SIGTE Tony Esposito 15.00 40.00
SIGTH Taylor Hall 20.00 50.00
SIGTM Tyler Myers
SIGTR Tuukka Rask 8.00 20.00
SIGTS Tyler Seguin 25.00 60.00
SIGTV Tomas Vokoun 6.00 15.00
SIGVH Victor Hedman 10.00 25.00
SIGVL Vincent Lecavalier 6.00 15.00
SIGWG Wayne Gretzky/15 200.00 350.00
SIGWI Colin Wilson

2010-11 SP Game Used SIGnificant Numbers Autographs

STATED PRINT RUN 1-93
SNAN Antti Niemi/31 8.00 20.00
SNBP Brad Park/22 15.00 40.00
SNBY Brandon Yip/59 15.00 40.00
SNCG Claude Giroux/28 25.00 60.00
SNCN Cam Neely/21 25.00 50.00
SNCO Jared Cowen/48 15.00 40.00
SNCP Carey Price/31 25.00 60.00
SNCW Cam Ward/30 10.00 25.00
SNEM Evgeni Malkin/71 25.00 60.00
SNET Eric Tangradi/56 8.00 20.00
SNGF Grant Fuhr/31 25.00 50.00
SNGI Jean-Sebastien Giguere/35 12.00 30.00
SNHL Henrik Lundqvist/30 15.00 40.00
SNJF Johan Franzen/93 10.00 25.00
SNJV James van Riemsdyk/21 25.00 50.00
SNKU Nikolai Kulemin/41 8.00 20.00
SNLR Luc Robitaille/20 25.00 50.00
SNMB Martin Brodeur/30 20.00 50.00
SNMF Marc-Andre Fleury/29 20.00 50.00
SNMH Milan Hejduk/23 15.00 40.00
SNMP Magnus Paajarvi/91 10.00 25.00
SNMS Martin St. Louis/26 12.00 30.00
SNNK Nazem Kadri/43 25.00 60.00
SNPE Patrik Elias/26 15.00 40.00
SNPK Phil Kessel/81 10.00 25.00
SNPS P.K. Subban/76 40.00 100.00
SNRM Ryan Miller/30 15.00 40.00
SNRN Rick Nash/61 12.00 30.00
SNSC Sidney Crosby/87 100.00 200.00
SNSD Derek Stepan/21 25.00 50.00
SNSS Steven Stamkos/91 30.00 80.00
SNST Paul Stastny/26 12.00 30.00
SNTA John Tavares/91 20.00 50.00
SNTE Tony Esposito/35 15.00 40.00
SNTR Tuukka Rask/40 10.00 25.00
SNTS Tyler Seguin/19 40.00 100.00
SNTV Thomas Vanek/26 12.00 30.00
SNVH Victor Hedman/77 12.00 30.00
SNVO Jakub Voracek/93 10.00 25.00
SNZH Zach Hamill/52 8.00 20.00

2010-11 SP Game Used Team Marks

STATED PRINT RUN 50 SER.#'d SETS
TMAA Artem Anisimov 12.00 30.00
TMAO Adam Oates 25.00 60.00
TMBF Benn Ferriero 10.00 25.00
TMBO Bobby Orr 150.00 250.00
TMCD Chris Drury 12.00 30.00
TMCK Chris Kunitz 15.00 40.00
TMCN Cam Neely 40.00 100.00
TMCO Chris Osgood 15.00 40.00
TMDB Dan Boyle 12.00 30.00
TMDH Dany Heatley 12.00 30.00
TMDS Devin Setoguchi 12.00 30.00
TMEM Evgeni Malkin 50.00 125.00
TMET Eric Tangradi 12.00 30.00
TMGI Matt Gilroy 10.00 25.00
TMHL Henrik Lundqvist 25.00 60.00
TMJB Johnny Bucyk 25.00 60.00
TMJS Jordan Staal 15.00 40.00
TMJT Joe Thornton 20.00 50.00
TMLC Logan Couture 25.00 60.00
TMLR Luc Robitaille 15.00 40.00
TMMD Michael Del Zotto 10.00 25.00
TMMF Marc-Andre Fleury 30.00 80.00
TMMG Marian Gaborik 20.00 50.00
TMMS Michael Sauer 10.00 25.00
TMMT Maxime Talbot 25.00 60.00
TMNJ Nick Johnson 10.00 25.00
TMNL Nicklas Lidstrom 30.00 80.00
TMPD Pavel Datsyuk 20.00 50.00
TMPE Phil Esposito 25.00 60.00
TMRB Ray Bourque 25.00 60.00
TMSC Sidney Crosby 75.00 150.00
TMSY Steve Yzerman 50.00 100.00
TMTH Tomas Holmstrom 20.00 50.00
TMVF Valtteri Filppula 15.00 40.00

2011-12 SP Game Used

COMP.SET w/o RC's (100) 50.00 80.00
101-190 ROOKIE/699 ODDS 1:3 HOB
191-200 ROOKIE PRINT RUN 99
1 Ryan Getzlaf 1.50 4.00
2 Bobby Ryan 1.00 2.50
3 Jonas Hiller .75 2.00
4 Corey Perry 1.00 2.50
5 Zdeno Chara 1.00 2.50
6 Tim Thomas 1.00 2.50
7 David Krejci 1.00 2.50
8 Nathan Horton 1.00 2.50
9 Brad Marchand 1.25 3.00
10 Bobby Orr 3.00 8.00
11 Tyler Seguin 2.00 5.00
12 Thomas Vanek 1.00 2.50
13 Ryan Miller 1.00 2.50
14 Drew Stafford 1.00 2.50
15 Jarome Iginla 1.00 2.50
16 Miikka Kiprusoff 1.00 2.50
17 Eric Staal 1.25 3.00
18 Cam Ward 1.00 2.50
19 Jeff Skinner 1.00 2.50
20 Jonathan Toews 2.00 5.00
21 Patrick Kane 2.00 5.00
22 Marian Hossa .75 2.00
23 Matt Duchene 1.00 2.50
24 Paul Stastny 1.00 2.50
25 Rick Nash 1.00 2.50
26 Jeff Carter 1.00 2.50
27 Brenden Morrow .75 2.00
28 Jim Howard 1.00 2.50
29 Henrik Zetterberg 1.25 3.00
30 Pavel Datsyuk 1.25 3.00
31 Nicklas Lidstrom 1.00 2.50
32 Johan Franzen 1.00 2.50
33 Paul Coffey 1.00 2.50
34 Ales Hemsky .75 2.00
35 Jordan Eberle 1.00 2.50
36 Taylor Hall 2.00 5.00
37 Ryan Smyth .75 2.00
38 Wayne Gretzky 5.00 12.00
39 Tomas Fleischmann .60 1.50
40 Ron Francis 1.25 3.00
41 Drew Doughty 1.00 2.50
42 Anze Kopitar 1.50 4.00
43 Mike Richards 1.00 2.50
44 Mikko Koivu .75 2.00
45 Niklas Backstrom 1.00 2.50
46 Dany Heatley .75 2.00
47 Patrick Roy 2.50 6.00
48 Tomas Plekanec 1.00 2.50
49 Carey Price 3.00 8.00
50 P.K. Subban 2.00 5.00
51 Michael Cammalleri .75 2.00
52 Brian Gionta .75 2.00
53 Jean Beliveau 1.00 2.50
54 Pekka Rinne 1.25 3.00
55 Shea Weber .75 2.00
56 Martin Brodeur 2.00 5.00
57 Travis Zajac .75 2.00
58 Zach Parise 1.00 2.50
59 Ilya Kovalchuk 1.00 2.50
60 Michael Grabner .75 2.00
61 John Tavares 2.00 5.00
62 Mark Messier 1.25 3.00
63 Brad Richards 1.00 2.50
64 Henrik Lundqvist 1.25 3.00
65 Marian Gaborik 1.25 3.00
66 Craig Anderson 1.00 2.50
67 Jason Spezza 1.00 2.50
68 Daniel Alfredsson 1.00 2.50
69 Jaromir Jagr 2.50 6.00
70 Chris Pronger .75 2.00
71 Claude Giroux 1.00 2.50
72 Eric Lindros 1.50 4.00
73 Shane Doan .75 2.00
74 Mario Lemieux 3.00 8.00
75 Jordan Staal 1.00 2.50
76 Sidney Crosby 4.00 10.00
77 Evgeni Malkin 3.00 8.00
78 Marc-Andre Fleury 1.50 4.00
79 Joe Thornton 1.00 2.50
80 Patrick Marleau 1.00 2.50
81 Logan Couture 1.00 2.50
82 Jaroslav Halak 1.00 2.50
83 David Backes 1.00 2.50
84 Steven Stamkos 2.00 5.00
85 Vincent Lecavalier .75 2.00
86 Dwayne Roloson .75 2.00
87 James Reimer 1.00 2.50
88 Dion Phaneuf 1.00 2.50
89 Phil Kessel 1.25 3.00
90 Ryan Kesler 1.00 2.50
91 Roberto Luongo 1.00 2.50
92 Daniel Sedin 1.00 2.50
93 Henrik Sedin 1.00 2.50
94 Alexandre Burrows 1.00 2.50
95 Alexander Semin 1.00 2.50
96 Alexander Ovechkin 4.00 10.00
97 Nicklas Backstrom 1.50 4.00
98 Mike Green 1.00 2.50
99 Ondrej Pavelec 1.00 2.50
100 Evander Kane 1.00 2.50
101 Chris Vande Velde RC 4.00 10.00
102 Mark Katic RC 2.50 6.00
103 Cam Talbot RC 6.00 15.00
104 David Rundblad RC 2.50 6.00
105 Maxime Macenauer RC 2.50 6.00
106 Lance Bouma RC 2.50 6.00
107 Alex Stalock 2.50 6.00
108 Patrick Wiercioch RC 2.50 6.00
109 Craig Smith RC 3.00 8.00
110 Paul Postma RC 2.50 6.00
111 Ben Scrivens RC 4.00 10.00
112 Tim Erixon RC 2.50 6.00
113 David Savard RC 2.50 6.00
114 Raphael Diaz RC 2.50 6.00
115 Jean-Philippe Levasseur RC 2.50 6.00
116 Shane Sims RC 2.50 6.00
117 Simon Despres RC 2.50 6.00
118 Keith Kinkaid RC 2.50 6.00
119 Ben Holmstrom RC 2.50 6.00
120 Brett Bulmer RC 2.50 6.00
121 Teemu Hartikainen RC 2.50 6.00
122 Erik Gustafsson RC 3.00 8.00
123 Brendon Nash RC 2.50 6.00
124 Joe Vitale RC 2.50 6.00
125 Tomas Vincour RC 2.50 6.00
126 Cam Atkinson RC 6.00 15.00
127 Colin Greening RC 2.50 6.00
128 Roman Horak RC 2.50 6.00
129 Jonathon Blum RC 2.50 6.00
130 Blake Geoffrion RC 2.50 6.00
131 Matt Frattin RC 2.50 6.00
132 Matt Read RC 5.00 12.00
133 Aaron Palushaj RC 2.50 6.00
134 Carl Klingberg RC 2.50 6.00
135 Jake Gardiner RC 4.00 10.00
136 Scott Timmins RC 2.50 6.00
137 Justin DiBenedetto RC 2.00 5.00
138 Brandon Saad RC 5.00 12.00
139 Roman Wick RC 3.00 8.00
140 Mikko Koskinen RC 3.00 8.00
141 Tomas Kubalik RC 2.50 6.00
142 Drew Bagnall RC 2.50 6.00
143 John Moore RC 2.50 6.00
144 Devante Smith-Pelly RC 4.00 10.00
145 Colton Sceviour RC 2.50 6.00
146 Hugh Jessiman RC 2.50 6.00
147 Carson McMillan RC 3.00 8.00
148 Jamie Doornbosch RC 2.50 6.00
149 Matt Campanale RC 2.50 6.00
150 Andre Benoit RC 3.00 8.00
151 Brian Strait RC 3.00 8.00
152 Harry Zolnierczyk RC 2.50 6.00
153 Lennart Petrell RC 3.00 8.00
154 Zac Rinaldo RC 2.50 6.00
155 Todd Ford RC 3.00 8.00
156 Viatcheslav Voynov RC 2.50 6.00
157 Stephane Da Costa RC 2.50 6.00
158 Cameron Gaunce RC 2.00 5.00
159 Justin Faulk RC 4.00 10.00
160 Erik Condra RC 2.50 6.00
161 Alexei Emelin RC 2.50 6.00
162 Yann Sauve RC 2.50 6.00
163 Greg Nemisz RC 2.50 6.00
164 Marcus Kruger RC 4.00 10.00
165 Joe Colborne RC 2.50 6.00
166 Harri Sateri RC 2.50 6.00
167 Adam Henrique RC 5.00 12.00
168 Anton Lander RC 2.50 6.00
169 Bracken Kearns RC 2.50 6.00
170 Allen York RC 3.00 8.00
171 Andy Miele RC 2.50 6.00
172 Ryan Thang RC 2.00 5.00
173 Pat Maroon RC 2.50 6.00
174 Cody Eakin RC 3.00 8.00
175 Gustav Nyquist RC 6.00 15.00
176 Corey Tropp RC 2.50 6.00
177 Peter Holland RC 2.50 6.00
178 Robert Bortuzzo RC 2.50 6.00
179 Colten Teubert RC 2.50 6.00
180 Mattias Ekholm RC 2.50 6.00
181 Brendan Smith RC 2.50 6.00
182 Eddie Lack RC 2.50 6.00
183 Frederic St. Denis RC 2.50 6.00
184 Anders Nilsson RC 2.50 6.00
185 Kris Fredheim RC 2.50 6.00
186 Dmitry Orlov RC 3.00 8.00
187 Kevin Marshall RC 2.50 6.00
188 David Ullstrom RC 2.50 6.00
189 Louis Leblanc RC 2.50 6.00
190 Zack Kassian RC 3.00 8.00
191 Erik Gudbranson/99 RC 12.00 30.00
192 Adam Larsson/99 RC 25.00 50.00
193 Mika Zibanejad/99 RC 20.00 50.00
194 Mark Scheifele/99 RC 25.00 60.00
195 Brett Connolly/99 RC 20.00 40.00
196 Ryan Johansen/99 RC 30.00 60.00
197 Cody Hodgson/99 RC 20.00 50.00
198 Sean Couturier/99 RC 12.00 30.00
199 Gabriel Landeskog/99 RC 20.00 50.00
200 R.Nugent-Hopkins/99 RC 75.00 150.00

2011-12 SP Game Used Gold

*1-100 VETS/100: 1.2X TO 3X BASIC CARDS
1-100 VETERAN PRINT RUN 100
*101-190 ROOK/50: .6X TO 1.5X BASIC RC
101-200 ROOKIE PRINT RUN 50
97 Nicklas Backstrom 5.00 12.00
191 Erik Gudbranson AU 12.00 30.00
192 Adam Larsson AU 12.00 30.00
193 Mika Zibanejad AU 12.00 30.00
194 Mark Scheifele AU 15.00 40.00
195 Brett Connolly AU 10.00 25.00
196 Ryan Johansen AU 20.00 50.00
197 Cody Hodgson AU 40.00 100.00
198 Sean Couturier AU 15.00 40.00
199 Gabriel Landeskog AU 40.00 100.00
200 Ryan Nugent-Hopkins AU 125.00 250.00

2011-12 SP Game Used 500 Goal Club Marks

STATED PRINT RUN 25 SER.#'d SETS
EXCH EXPIRATION: 3/23/2014
500GCBH Brett Hull EXCH 60.00 120.00
500GCDH Dale Hawerchuk EXCH 50.00 100.00
500GCHU Bobby Hull 60.00 120.00
500GCJB Johnny Bucyk EXCH 30.00 60.00
500GCJK Jari Kurri EXCH 50.00 100.00
500GCMB Mike Bossy 40.00 80.00
500GCMG Mike Gartner 30.00 60.00
500GCML Mario Lemieux EXCH 100.00 200.00
500GCMM Mike Modano EXCH 30.00 60.00
500GCRF Ron Francis 15.00 40.00
500GCWG Wayne Gretzky EXCH 200.00 300.00

2011-12 SP Game Used Authentic Fabrics

STATED PRINT RUN 100 SER.#'d SETS
*PATCH/25-35: .8X TO 2X BASIC JSY/100
AFAB Alexandre Burrows 4.00 10.00
AFAH Ales Hemsky 3.00 8.00
AFAK Anze Kopitar 6.00 15.00
AFAN Antti Niemi 3.00 8.00
AFAO Alexander Ovechkin 15.00 40.00
AFAS Alexander Semin 4.00 10.00
AFAT Alex Tanguay 2.50 6.00
AFAV Antoine Vermette 2.50 6.00
AFBH Brett Hull 5.00 12.00
AFBK David Backes 4.00 10.00
AFBP Brad Park 3.00 8.00
AFBR Daniel Briere 4.00 10.00
AFBY Dustin Byfuglien 4.00 10.00
AFCG Claude Giroux 4.00 10.00
AFCH Cody Hodgson 8.00 20.00
AFCK Matt Carkner 3.00 8.00
AFCN Cam Neely 4.00 10.00
AFCP Carey Price 12.00 30.00
AFDA Daniel Alfredsson 4.00 10.00
AFDB Dan Boyle 3.00 8.00
AFDC Dan Cleary 4.00 10.00
AFDD Drew Doughty 4.00 10.00
AFDE Derick Brassard 4.00 10.00
AFDK Duncan Keith 4.00 10.00
AFDR Derek Roy 3.00 8.00
AFDS Daniel Sedin 4.00 10.00
AFDU Dustin Penner 3.00 8.00
AFDW Drew Stafford 4.00 10.00
AFEM Evgeni Malkin 12.00 30.00
AFES Eric Staal 5.00 12.00
AFGL Guillaume Latendresse 3.00 8.00
AFGR Mike Green 4.00 10.00
AFHE Milan Hejduk 3.00 8.00
AFHL Henrik Lundqvist 4.00 10.00
AFHS Henrik Sedin 4.00 10.00
AFHZ Henrik Zetterberg 6.00 15.00
AFIB Ilya Bryzgalov 4.00 10.00
AFIK Ilya Kovalchuk 4.00 10.00
AFJC Jeff Carter 4.00 10.00
AFJE Jordan Eberle 5.00 12.00
AFJF Johan Franzen 4.00 10.00
AFJH Jim Howard 8.00 20.00
AFJI Jarome Iginla 4.00 10.00
AFJS Jason Spezza 4.00 10.00
AFJT John Tavares 8.00 20.00
AFJV James van Riemsdyk 4.00 10.00
AFKE Phil Kessel 5.00 12.00
AFKO Mikko Koivu 3.00 8.00
AFLC Logan Couture 4.00 10.00
AFLE Loui Eriksson 3.00 8.00
AFLU Milan Lucic 4.00 10.00
AFMB Martin Brodeur 8.00 20.00
AFMC Michael Cammalleri 3.00 8.00
AFMD Matt Duchene 4.00 10.00
AFMG Marian Gaborik 5.00 12.00
AFMH Marian Hossa 3.00 8.00
AFMK Miikka Kiprusoff 4.00 10.00
AFML Mario Lemieux 12.00 30.00
AFMM Mark Messier 5.00 12.00
AFMP Magnus Paajarvi 3.00 8.00
AFMR Mike Richards 4.00 10.00
AFMS Martin St. Louis 4.00 10.00
AFNB Nicklas Backstrom 6.00 15.00
AFNH Nathan Horton 4.00 10.00
AFNK Nikolai Kulemin 4.00 10.00
AFPA Paul Stastny 4.00 10.00
AFPB Patrice Bergeron 5.00 12.00
AFPD Pavel Datsyuk 5.00 12.00
AFPE Corey Perry 4.00 10.00
AFPG Chris Pronger 3.00 8.00
AFPK Patrick Kane 8.00 20.00
AFPM Patrick Marleau 4.00 10.00
AFPR Patrick Roy 10.00 25.00
AFPS Patrick Sharp 4.00 10.00
AFRB Ray Bourque 8.00 20.00
AFRG Ryan Getzlaf 6.00 15.00
AFRI Brad Richards 4.00 10.00
AFRK Ryan Kesler 4.00 10.00
AFRL Roberto Luongo 4.00 10.00
AFRM Ryan Miller 4.00 10.00
AFRN Rick Nash 4.00 10.00
AFRS Ryan Smyth 3.00 8.00
AFRY Bobby Ryan 4.00 10.00
AFSB Sergei Bobrovsky 4.00 10.00
AFSC Sidney Crosby 15.00 40.00
AFSD Shane Doan 3.00 8.00
AFSH Scott Hartnell 4.00 10.00
AFSM Steve Mason 3.00 8.00
AFSN Scott Niedermayer 4.00 10.00
AFSS Steven Stamkos 8.00 20.00
AFST Jordan Staal 4.00 10.00
AFSW Shea Weber 3.00 8.00
AFTE Tyler Ennis 3.00 8.00
AFTH Taylor Hall 6.00 15.00
AFTO Jonathan Toews 8.00 20.00
AFTS Tyler Seguin 8.00 20.00
AFTV Thomas Vanek 4.00 10.00
AFWG Wayne Gretzky 20.00 50.00
AFZC Zdeno Chara 4.00 10.00
AFZP Zach Parise 4.00 10.00

2011-12 SP Game Used Authentic Fabrics Gold

GROUP A ODDS 1:715 HOB
COMMON GROUP B-D 2.00 5.00
GRP B-D SEMISTARS 2.50 6.00
GRP B-D UNL.STARS 3.00 8.00
GROUP B ODDS 1:223 HOB
GROUP C ODDS 1:2.5 HOB
GROUP D ODDS 1:6 HOB
OVERALL GOLD ODDS 1:2 HOB
SAME PLAYER: SAME GROUP: SAME PRICE
AFAO1 Alexander Ovechkin 8 C 12.00 30.00
AFBH1 Brett Hull 1 C 5.00 12.00
AFBY1 Dustin Byfuglien B C 4.00 10.00
AFCG1 Claude Giroux 2 C 6.00 10.00
AFCH1 Cody Hodgson D C 3.00 8.00
AFCK1 Matt Carkner E C 5.00 12.00
AFCN1 Cam Neely B C 3.00 8.00
AFCP1 Carey Price B C 10.00 25.00
AFDC1 Dan Cleary 1 C 4.00 10.00
AFDK1 Duncan Keith D C 4.00 10.00
AFEM1 Evgeni Malkin E C 10.00 25.00
AFHL1 Henrik Lundqvist G C 4.00 10.00
AFHZ1 Henrik Zetterberg E C 4.00 10.00
AFIK1 Ilya Kovalchuk K C 3.00 8.00
AFJE1 Jordan Eberle 1 C 6.00 15.00
AFJF1 Johan Franzen G C 3.00 8.00
AFJH1 Jim Howard H C 3.00 8.00
AFJI1 Jarome Iginla G C 4.00 10.00
AFJT1 John Tavares 1 C 6.00 15.00
AFMB1 Martin Brodeur 0 C 8.00 10.00
AFML1 Mario Lemieux 6 C 8.00 20.00
AFMM1 Mark Messier B C 4.00 10.00
AFMP1 Magnus Paajarvi 1 C 2.50 6.00
AFNB1 Nicklas Backstrom A D 5.00 12.00
AFNB2 Nicklas Backstrom H C 5.00 12.00
AFNB3 Nicklas Backstrom S C 5.00 12.00
AFNB4 Nicklas Backstrom W D 5.00 12.00
AFPB1 Patrice Bergeron C D 4.00 10.00
AFPD1 Pavel Datsyuk # C 4.00 10.00
AFPK1 Patrick Kane A C 6.00 15.00
AFPR1 Patrick Roy 0 C 8.00 20.00
AFRB1 Ray Bourque # D 5.00 12.00
AFRL1 Roberto Luongo 1 C 3.00 8.00
AFSB1 Sergei Bobrovsky # D 3.00 8.00
AFSC1 Sidney Crosby I C 12.00 30.00
AFSS1 Steven Stamkos # C 6.00 15.00
AFTH1 Taylor Hall A C 6.00 15.00
AFTO1 Jonathan Toews 1 C 6.00 15.00
AFTS1 Tyler Seguin C C 6.00 15.00
AFWG1 Wayne Gretzky 1 A 25.00 60.00

2011-12 SP Game Used Authentic Fabrics Dual

DUAL STATED PRINT RUN 25-100
*PATCH/25: .8X TO 2X BASIC DUAL/100
AF2BG J.Benn/E.Godard/100 6.00 15.00
AF2BH D.Backes/J.Halak/100 5.00 12.00
AF2BK D.Byfuglien/E.Kane/100 5.00 12.00
AF2BP Brodeur/Parise/100 8.00 20.00
AF2BQ J.Quick/J.Bernier/100 8.00 20.00
AF2CK N.Kronwall/D.Cleary/100 5.00 12.00
AF2CL S.Crosby/K.Letang/100 20.00 50.00
AF2CS S.Crosby/J.Staal/100 20.00 50.00
AF2CZ Zetterberg/Cleary/100 6.00 15.00
AF2DF Datsyuk/J.Franzen/100 6.00 15.00
AF2EH J.Eberle/T.Hall/100 15.00 40.00
AF2EK Ericsson/N.Kronwall/100 5.00 12.00
AF2FJ M.Fleury/B.Johnson/100 8.00 20.00
AF2FK R.Francis/A.Kovalev/100 6.00 15.00
AF2GB Backstrom/M.Green/100 8.00 20.00
AF2GH R.Getzlaf/J.Hiller/100 6.00 15.00
AF2GK M.Koivu/Latendresse/100 4.00 10.00
AF2GL Gaborik/Lundqvist/100 8.00 20.00
AF2HO Howard/Osgood/100 5.00 12.00
AF2HS A.Hemsky/R.Smyth/100 4.00 10.00
AF2IK Iginla/Kiprusoff/100 6.00 15.00
AF2JR Bouwmster/Bourque/100 5.00 12.00
AF2KD Doughty/Kopitar/100 6.00 15.00
AF2KZ I.Kovalchuk/T.Zajac/100 5.00 12.00
AF2LB Brodeur/Luongo/100 12.00 30.00
AF2LG Gretzky/Lemieux/25 30.00 60.00
AF2LH Howard/Lidstrom/100 5.00 12.00
AF2LK Luongo/Kesler/100 8.00 20.00
AF2MB M.Staal/B.Dubinsky/100 5.00 12.00
AF2ME T.Ennis/T.Myers/100 5.00 12.00
AF2MG M.Messier/M.Gartner/100 6.00 15.00
AF2MV R.Miller/T.Vanek/100 5.00 12.00
AF2ND N.Horton/D.Krejci/100 5.00 12.00
AF2NM R.Nash/S.Mason/100 5.00 12.00
AF2NV Vokoun/M.Neuvirth/100 4.00 10.00
AF2PE T.Plekanec/L.Eller/100 5.00 12.00
AF2PG Perry/Getzlaf/100 6.00 15.00
AF2PH Pronger/S.Hartnell/100 5.00 12.00
AF2PO M.Paajarvi/L.Omark/100 5.00 12.00
AF2RO M.Ribeiro/S.Ott/100 4.00 10.00
AF2RS Robinson/P.Subban/100 10.00 25.00
AF2SD Duchene/P.Stastny/100 5.00 12.00
AF2SO Semin/Ovechkin/100 20.00 50.00
AF2SS H.Sedin/D.Sedin/100 5.00 12.00
AF2SW R.Suter/S.Weber/100 4.00 10.00
AF2TK J.Toews/P.Kane/100 10.00 25.00
AF2TM Moulson/Tavares/100 10.00 25.00
AF2TR T.Thomas/T.Rask/100 6.00 15.00
AF2VG Giroux/vanRiemsdk/100 5.00 12.00
AF2WB S.Weiss/D.Booth/100 4.00 10.00

2011-12 SP Game Used Authentic Fabrics Triples

STATED PRINT RUN 25 SER.#'d SETS
*PATCH/15: .8X TO 2X BASIC TRIPLE/25
AF3ANA Getzlaf/Ryan/Hiller 12.00 30.00
AF3ATL Byfuglien/Pavelec/Kane 8.00 20.00
AF3AVS Duchene/Stastny/Johnson 8.00 20.00
AF3BOS Rask/Chara/Bergeron 10.00 25.00
AF3BUF Miller/Myers/Vanek 8.00 20.00
AF3CBJ Brassard/Mason/Nash 8.00 20.00
AF3CGY Kiprusoff/Iginla/Bouwm 8.00 20.00
AF3COL Bourque/Roy/Sakic 20.00 50.00
AF3DET Lidstrm/Zettr/Frnzen 10.00 25.00
AF3EDM Eberle/Hall/Paajarvi 15.00 40.00
AF3LAK Doughty/Kopitar/Quick 12.00 30.00
AF3NYI Moulsn/Tavrs/Okpso 15.00 40.00
AF3NYR Gaborik/Stepan/Staal 10.00 25.00
AF3OIL Gretzky/Messier/Kurri 50.00 100.00
AF3OTT Alfreds/Spezza/Andrsn 8.00 20.00
AF3PHI Giroux/Van Rms/Prngr 8.00 20.00
AF3SJS Marleau/Thrntn/Havlat 8.00 20.00
AF3STL Halak/Pietra/Backes 8.00 20.00
AF3TBL Stamkos/St. Ls/Lecav 10.00 25.00
AF3TGH Orr/Parros/Carkner 12.00 30.00
AF3VAN Sedin/Sedin/Kesler 8.00 20.00
AF3WAS Back/Ovechkin/Semin 30.00 80.00
AF3FLYR Hartnell/Briere/van Rm 10.00 25.00
AF3PENS Crosby/Staal/Malkin 15.00 40.00

2011-12 SP Game Used Career Legacy Dual

STATED PRINT RUN 75 SER.#'d SETS
*PATCH/15: .8X TO 2X DUAL JSY/75
CL2BB Jay Bouwmeester 5.00 12.00
CL2EE Jordan Eberle 15.00 40.00
CL2GG Jean-Sebastien Giguere 5.00 12.00
CL2HH Brett Hull 8.00 20.00
CL2KK Phil Kessel 8.00 20.00

2011-12 SP Game Used Career Legacy Triple

STATED PRINT RUN 25 SER.#'d SETS
CL3MH Marian Hossa 10.00 25.00

2011-12 SP Game Used Championship Marks

STATED PRINT RUN 50 SER.#'d SETS
EXCH EXPIRATION: 3/26/2014
CMBM Brad Marchand EXCH 40.00 80.00
CMMR Michael Ryder EXCH 30.00 60.00
CMNH Nathan Horton EXCH 25.00 50.00
CMPB Patrice Bergeron EXCH 40.00 80.00
CMTS Tyler Seguin 30.00 80.00

2011-12 SP Game Used Extra SIGnificance

STATED PRINT RUN 25 SER.#'d SETS
EXCH EXPIRATION: 3/25/2014
XSIGAA Larsson/Henrique 25.00 50.00
XSIGBK D.Byfuglien/A.Kulda 25.00 50.00
XSIGBM R.Miller/M.Brodeur 25.00 60.00
XSIGBR B.Orr/R.Bourque 150.00 300.00
XSIGBS D.Backes/C.Stewart 12.00 30.00
XSIGBT M.Bossy/J.Tavares 30.00 60.00
XSIGBV Carter/Brassard EXCH 12.00 30.00
XSIGCB D.Boyle/L.Couture 12.00 30.00
XSIGCR S.Couturier/M.Read 20.00 50.00
XSIGDB B.Barber/D.Schultz 15.00 40.00
XSIGDD Heatley/Setoguchi 10.00 25.00
XSIGDF P.Datsyuk/J.Franzen 25.00 50.00
XSIGEH J.Eberle/T.Hall 75.00 150.00
XSIGEP J.Eberle/M.Paajarvi 30.00 60.00
XSIGGC W.Gretzky/P.Coffey 150.00 250.00
XSIGHR Horton/Marchand EXCH 10.00 25.00
XSIGIB J.Iginla/J.Bouwmeester 12.00 30.00
XSIGJJ J.Skinner/J.McBain 12.00 30.00
XSIGKD A.Kopitar/D.Doughty 25.00 50.00
XSIGKH R.Kesler/C.Hodgson 20.00 50.00
XSIGLF N.Lidstrom/J.Franzen 15.00 40.00
XSIGLT Twist/Lafleur 15.00 40.00
XSIGMK Kulemin/MacArthur 12.00 30.00
XSIGMS Marleau/Thornton 25.00 50.00
XSIGNL RNH/Landeskog 75.00 200.00
XSIGNS A.Niemi/A.Stalock 10.00 25.00
XSIGOB Ovechkin/Backstrom 30.00 80.00
XSIGOC Coffey/Orr EXCH 75.00 150.00
XSIGOL Ovechkin/Larionov 50.00 100.00
XSIGPC J.Pavelski/L.Couture 20.00 40.00
XSIGRG S.Gagne/M.Richards 12.00 30.00
XSIGRM RNH/Scheifele 125.00 250.00
XSIGRS P.Roy/J.Sakic 60.00 120.00
XSIGSB P.Bergeron/T.Seguin 40.00 80.00
XSIGSD D.Doughty/B.Seabrook 25.00 50.00
XSIGSL Seabrook/Leddy EXCH 15.00 40.00
XSIGSM Marchand/Seguin EXCH 30.00 60.00
XSIGST J.Toews/B.Seabrook 40.00 80.00
XSIGTK J.Toews/P.Kane 40.00 80.00
XSIGTM T.Tatar/T.McCollum 10.00 25.00
XSIGTS S.Stamkos/J.Tavares 40.00 80.00
XSIGVE T.Vanek/T.Ennis 12.00 30.00
XSIGWB S.Weber/J.Blum 10.00 25.00
XSIGZM Zuccarello-Aasen/McDonagh 12.00 30.00
XSIGZS Zuccarello-Aasen/D.Stepan 12.00 30.00

2011-12 SP Game Used Inked Sweaters

STATED PRINT RUN 5-50
ISAO Alexander Ovechkin/15 50.00 100.00
ISAP Alex Pietrangelo/50 12.00 30.00
ISBR Brad Richards/50 10.00 25.00
ISBS Brayden Schenn/50 20.00 40.00
ISCH Cody Hodgson/50 20.00 50.00
ISCP Carey Price/50 30.00 60.00
ISCU Sean Couturier/50 20.00 50.00
ISDR Stefan Della Rovere/50 6.00 15.00
ISEK Evander Kane/50 12.00 30.00
ISEM Evgeni Malkin/50 25.00 50.00
ISGL Gabriel Landeskog/50 25.00 60.00
ISHL Henrik Lundqvist/50 15.00 40.00
ISJB Jamie Benn/50 12.00 30.00
ISJC Jared Cowen/50 10.00 25.00
ISJE Jordan Eberle/50 30.00 60.00
ISJF Jeff Carter/50 10.00 25.00
ISJH Jaroslav Halak/50 10.00 25.00
ISJT Jonathan Toews/15 40.00 80.00
ISKA Keith Aulie/50 8.00 20.00
ISKV Kris Versteeg/50 8.00 20.00
ISMB Martin Brodeur/15 40.00 80.00
ISMF Marc-Andre Fleury/50 12.00 30.00
ISMG Marian Gaborik/50 12.00 30.00
ISML Mario Lemieux/15 60.00 120.00
ISMM Mark Messier/15 40.00 80.00
ISNB Nicklas Backstrom/50 15.00 40.00
ISNL Nicklas Lidstrom/50 15.00 40.00
ISPC Patrice Cormier/50 6.00 15.00
ISPR Patrick Roy/15 50.00 100.00
ISPS P.K. Subban/50 20.00 50.00
ISRK Ryan Kesler/50 10.00 25.00
ISRM Ryan Miller/50 15.00 30.00
ISRY Ryan Nugent-Hopkins/50 30.00 80.00
ISSC Sidney Crosby/15 75.00 150.00
ISSS Steven Stamkos/50 20.00 50.00
ISTE Tyler Ennis/50 8.00 20.00
ISTH Taylor Hall/50 30.00 60.00
ISTV Thomas Vanek/50 10.00 25.00
ISWG Wayne Gretzky/15 150.00 250.00

2011-12 SP Game Used Inked Sweaters Dual

STATED PRINT RUN 5-15
DISBP J.Bucyk/B.Park/15 20.00 50.00
DISCN J.Carter/R.Nash/15 15.00 40.00
DISDK Doughty/Kopitr/15 30.00 60.00
DISFR Fuhr/Ranford/15 40.00 80.00
DISGR R.Getzlaf/B.Ryan/15 25.00 50.00
DISHE T.Hall/J.Eberle/15 60.00 120.00
DISIT Iginla/Thornton/15 40.00 80.00
DISLG Lundqvst/Gabork/15 30.00 60.00
DISMR R.Miller/D.Roy/15 12.00 30.00
DISRG Richards/Gagne/15 20.00 50.00
DISTK J.Toews/P.Kane/15 50.00 100.00

2011-12 SP Game Used Letter Marks

STATED PRINT RUN 50 SER.#'d SETS
LMAS Alex Stalock 12.00 30.00
LMBB Bill Barber 15.00 40.00
LMCH Cody Hodgson 20.00 50.00
LMDB Dustin Byfuglien 15.00 40.00
LMEM Evgeni Malkin 30.00 60.00
LMJF Johan Franzen 15.00 40.00
LMJM Jacob Markstrom EXCH
LMJP Joe Pavelski 15.00 40.00
LMJS Jeff Skinner 25.00 60.00
LMJT Jonathan Toews 40.00 80.00
LMLR Larry Robinson 15.00 40.00
LMMH Milan Hejduk 15.00 40.00
LMMO John Moore 8.00 20.00
LMMT Maxime Talbot 15.00 40.00
LMNB Nicklas Backstrom 25.00 60.00
LMPB Patrice Bergeron EXCH
LMRL Reggie Leach 15.00 40.00
LMRN Rick Nash
LMRV Rogie Vachon 20.00 50.00
LMSM Steve Mason 12.00 30.00
LMTL Ted Lindsay 15.00 40.00
LMTV Tomas Vokoun 20.00 50.00
LMVA Thomas Vanek 15.00 40.00
LMVL Ville Leino 15.00 40.00
LMWC Wendel Clark 30.00 60.00

2011-12 SP Game Used Number Marks

STATED PRINT RUN 25 SER.#'d SETS
EXCH EXPIRATION: 3/25/2014
NMAO Ovechkin EXCH 60.00 120.00
NMAS Alex Stalock 15.00 40.00
NMBC Bobby Clarke 40.00 80.00
NMBY Dustin Byfuglien 15.00 40.00
NMCH Cody Hodgson 30.00 60.00
NMJE Jordan Eberle EXCH 100.00 175.00
NMJM Markstrom EXCH 30.00 60.00
NMJS Jeff Skinner EXCH 25.00 50.00
NMJV Jakub Voracek EXCH 30.00 60.00
NMMZ Zuccarello-Aasen EXCH 20.00 50.00
NMPS P.K. Subban EXCH 40.00 80.00
NMSC Sidney Crosby EXCH 150.00 250.00
NMSS Steven Stamkos 60.00 120.00
NMTS Tyler Seguin 40.00 100.00

2011-12 SP Game Used Rookie Exclusives Autographs

STATED PRINT RUN 100 SER.#'d SETS
REAH Adam Henrique 12.00 30.00
REAL Anton Lander 5.00 12.00
REAM Andy Miele 6.00 15.00
REAP Aaron Palushaj 5.00 12.00
REAS Alex Stalock 5.00 12.00
REBC Brett Connolly 8.00 20.00
REBE Ben Scrivens 8.00 20.00
REBG Blake Geoffrion 5.00 12.00
REBH Ben Holmstrom 6.00 15.00
REBN Brendon Nash 5.00 12.00
REBS Brandon Saad 10.00 25.00
RECA Cam Atkinson 12.00 30.00
RECG Cameron Gaunce 4.00 10.00
RECH Cody Hodgson 10.00 25.00
RECK Carl Klingberg 5.00 12.00
RECS Craig Smith EXCH 10.00 25.00
RECT Colten Teubert 8.00 20.00
REDS Devante Smith-Pelly EXCH 8.00 20.00
REEG Erik Gudbranson 6.00 15.00
REGL Gabriel Landeskog 20.00 50.00
REGN Greg Nemisz 5.00 12.00
REGR Colin Greening 10.00 25.00
REGU Erik Gustafsson EXCH 6.00 15.00
REGV Gustav Nyquist EXCH 15.00 40.00
REHS Harri Sateri 10.00 25.00
REJB Jonathon Blum 5.00 12.00
REJC Joe Colborne 5.00 12.00
REJF Justin Faulk 8.00 20.00
REJG Jake Gardiner 12.00 30.00
REJM John Moore 5.00 12.00
REJV Joe Vitale 5.00 12.00
RELA Adam Larsson 10.00 25.00
RELL Louis Leblanc 15.00 40.00
RELP Lennart Petrell 6.00 15.00
REMF Matt Frattin 10.00 25.00
REMK Marcus Kruger 12.00 25.00
REMR Matt Read 15.00 40.00
REMS Mark Scheifele 15.00 40.00
REMZ Mika Zibanejad 12.00 30.00
REPP Paul Postma 5.00 12.00
REPW Patrick Wiercioch 5.00 12.00
RERD Raphael Diaz EXCH 5.00 12.00
RERH Roman Horak 5.00 12.00
RERJ Ryan Johansen 10.00 25.00
RERN Ryan Nugent-Hopkins 30.00 80.00
RESA David Savard 5.00 12.00
RESC Sean Couturier 15.00 40.00
REST Brian Strait 6.00 15.00
RETE Tim Erixon 5.00 12.00
RETH Teemu Hartikainen 5.00 12.00
RETV Tomas Vincour 6.00 15.00
REVV Viatcheslav Voynov 5.00 12.00
REYS Yann Sauve 5.00 12.00
REZK Zack Kassian 15.00 40.00

2011-12 SP Game Used SIGnificance

STATED PRINT RUN 15-50
EXCH EXPIRATION: 3/22/2014
SIGAB Alexander Burmistrov/50 8.00 20.00
SIGAK Anze Kopitar/50 15.00 40.00
SIGAL Adam Larsson/50 8.00 20.00
SIGAN Antti Niemi/50 10.00 25.00
SIGAS Alex Stalock/50 6.00 15.00
SIGBA David Backes/50 8.00 20.00
SIGBB Bill Barber/50 8.00 20.00
SIGBC Brett Connolly/50 6.00 15.00
SIGBH Brett Hull/15 40.00 80.00
SIGBM Brad Marchand/50 EXCH 10.00 25.00
SIGBO Bobby Orr/15 150.00 250.00
SIGBR Bobby Ryan/50 8.00 20.00
SIGBS Brayden Schenn/50 10.00 25.00
SIGBY Dan Boyle/50 15.00 30.00
SIGCA Jeff Carter/50 EXCH 10.00 25.00
SIGCF Cam Fowler/50 6.00 15.00
SIGCG Claude Giroux/50 20.00 40.00
SIGCH Cody Hodgson/50 15.00 40.00
SIGCM Clarke MacArthur/50 6.00 15.00
SIGCP Carey Price/50 20.00 40.00
SIGCS Chris Stewart/50 6.00 15.00
SIGCU Sean Couturier/50 12.00 30.00
SIGCW Cam Ward/50 8.00 20.00
SIGDB Dustin Byfuglien/15 60.00 120.00
SIGDD Drew Doughty/50 10.00 25.00
SIGDP Dion Phaneuf/50 10.00 25.00
SIGDS Derek Stepan/50 8.00 20.00
SIGEC Jonathan Ericsson/50 6.00 15.00
SIGEG Evgeny Grachev/50 EX 6.00 15.00
SIGEK Evander Kane/50 10.00 25.00
SIGEM Evgeni Malkin/50 20.00 40.00
SIGFR Matt Frattin/50 8.00 20.00
SIGHA Jaroslav Halak/50 8.00 20.00
SIGHO Cody Hodgson/50 15.00 40.00
SIGHP Nugent-Hopkins/15 250.00 400.00
SIGJB Jonathon Blum/50 6.00 15.00
SIGJC Joe Colborne/50 6.00 15.00
SIGJE Jordan Eberle/50 25.00 50.00
SIGJH Jonas Hiller/50 6.00 15.00
SIGJK Jari Kurri/50 10.00 25.00
SIGJM Jacob Markstrom/50 8.00 20.00
SIGJS Jeff Skinner/50 10.00 25.00
SIGJT John Tavares/50 15.00 40.00
SIGJV James van Riemsdyk/50 8.00 20.00
SIGKE Phil Kessel/50 10.00 25.00
SIGKG Marcus Kruger/50 10.00 25.00

SIGKS Kevin Shattenkirk/50 6.00 15.00
SIGKV Kris Versteeg/50 6.00 15.00
SIGLC Logan Couture/50 8.00 20.00
SIGLD Gabriel Landeskog/50 25.00 50.00
SIGMA Rick MacLeish/50 8.00 20.00
SIGMB Martin Brodeur/15 60.00 120.00
SIGMC Thomas McCollum/50 6.00 15.00
SIGMD Matt Duchene/50 10.00 25.00
SIGMF Marc-Andre Fleury/50 12.00 30.00
SIGML Mario Lemieux/15 100.00 200.00
SIGMM Mark Messier/15 40.00 80.00
SIGMP Magnus Paajarvi/50 8.00 20.00
SIGMR Mike Richards/50 EXCH 10.00 25.00
SIGMS Martin St. Louis/50 10.00 25.00
SIGMZ Zuccarello-Aasen/50 8.00 20.00
SIGNB Nicklas Backstrom/50 8.00 20.00
SIGNH Nathan Horton/50 8.00 20.00
SIGNK Nazem Kadri/50 12.00 30.00
SIGOR Bobby Orr/50 75.00 150.00
SIGOV Alexander Ovechkin/15 60.00 150.00
SIGPA Patrice Bergeron/50 20.00 40.00
SIGPB Patrik Berglund/50 6.00 15.00
SIGPC Patrice Cormier/50 EXCH 6.00 15.00
SIGPM Patrick Marleau/50 8.00 20.00
SIGPR Patrick Roy/15 60.00 120.00
SIGPS Paul Stastny/50 8.00 20.00
SIGRF Bill Ranford/50 8.00 20.00
SIGRJ Ryan Johansen/50 12.00 30.00
SIGRK Ryan Kesler/50 10.00 25.00
SIGRM Ryan Miller/50 10.00 25.00
SIGRN Pekka Rinne/50 8.00 20.00
SIGRS Ryan Smyth/50 10.00 25.00
SIGRY Nugent-Hopkins/50 50.00 120.00
SIGSB Brent Seabrook/50 8.00 20.00
SIGSC Sidney Crosby/15 75.00 150.00
SIGSE Devin Setoguchi/50 6.00 15.00
SIGSF Mark Scheifele/50 20.00 50.00
SIGSG Simon Gagne/50 15.00 30.00
SIGSID Sidney Crosby/50 60.00 120.00
SIGSS Steven Stamkos/50 25.00 40.00
SIGST Jordan Staal/50 8.00 20.00
SIGSU P.K. Subban/50 20.00 50.00
SIGTB Tyler Bozak/50 6.00 15.00
SIGTH Taylor Hall/50 25.00 50.00
SIGTM Tyler Myers/50 8.00 20.00
SIGTO T.J. Oshie/50 12.00 30.00
SIGTR Tuukka Rask/50 10.00 25.00
SIGTS Tyler Seguin/15 30.00 60.00
SIGTT Tomas Tatar/50 6.00 15.00
SIGTV Thomas Vanek/50 8.00 20.00
SIGVL Ville Leino/50 6.00 15.00
SIGVO Tomas Vokoun/50 6.00 15.00
SIGWG Wayne Gretzky/15 175.00 300.00

2011-12 SP Game Used SIGnificant Numbers Autographs

STATED PRINT RUN 1-93
SNAH Ales Hemsky/83 12.00 30.00
SNAN Antti Niemi/31 15.00 40.00
SNBH Brett Hull/16 125.00 200.00
SNBP Brad Park/22 15.00 40.00
SNBR Brad Richards/19 20.00 40.00
SNBY Dustin Byfuglien/33 20.00 40.00
SNCG Claude Giroux/28 30.00 60.00
SNCM Clarke MacArthur/16 25.00 50.00
SNCP Carey Price/31 30.00 60.00
SNDB David Backes/25 15.00 40.00
SNDE Derick Brassard/16 EXCH
SNEG Erik Gudbranson/44 12.00 30.00
SNEM Evgeni Malkin/71 30.00 60.00
SNGL Gabriel Landeskog/92 25.00 60.00
SNHE Milan Hejduk/23 12.00 30.00
SNHL Henrik Lundqvist/30 30.00 60.00
SNIK Ilya Kovalchuk/17 25.00 50.00
SNJH Jaroslav Halak/41 15.00 40.00
SNJK Jari Kurri/17 20.00 50.00
SNJO Jonathan Toews/19 40.00 80.00
SNJT Joe Thornton/19 30.00 60.00
SNJV James van Riemsdyk/21 15.00 40.00
SNKE Phil Kessel/81 12.00 30.00
SNLR Luc Robitaille/20 20.00 40.00
SNMB Martin Brodeur/30 40.00 80.00
SNMF Marc-Andre Fleury/29 25.00 60.00
SNMH Marian Hossa/81 15.00 40.00
SNMP Magnus Paajarvi/91 8.00 20.00
SNMR Mike Richards/18 30.00 60.00
SNMS Martin St. Louis/26 12.00 30.00
SNMZ Mika Zibanejad/93 20.00 50.00
SNNB Nicklas Backstrom/19 25.00 50.00
SNNH Nathan Horton/18 30.00 60.00
SNNK Nikolai Kulemin/41 10.00 25.00
SNPA Paul Stastny/26 15.00 40.00
SNPB Patrice Bergeron/37 20.00 40.00
SNPE Patrik Elias/26 10.00 25.00
SNPS P.K. Subban/76 25.00 60.00
SNRG Ryan Getzlaf/15 25.00 50.00
SNRJ Ryan Johansen/19
SNRK Ryan Kesler/17 20.00 50.00
SNRM Ryan Miller/30 20.00 40.00
SNRN Ryan Nugent-Hopkins/93 40.00 100.00
SNSC Sidney Crosby/87 75.00 150.00
SNSS Steven Stamkos/91 40.00 80.00
SNTA John Tavares/91 25.00 50.00
SNTE Tyler Ennis/63 12.00 30.00
SNTO Tony Esposito/35 20.00 40.00
SNTR Tuukka Rask/40 15.00 40.00
SNTS Tyler Seguin/19 60.00 120.00
SNTV Thomas Vanek/26 12.00 30.00
SNVH Victor Hedman/77 12.00 30.00

2011-12 SP Game Used Team Marks Flyers

STATED PRINT RUN 50 SER.#'d SETS
TMBS Brayden Schenn EXCH 20.00 50.00
TMCG Claude Giroux EXCH 30.00 60.00
TMEW Eric Wellwood EXCH 20.00 40.00
TMMT Maxime Talbot 10.00 25.00
TMVK Jakub Voracek EXCH 15.00 40.00

2011-12 SP Game Used Team Marks Oilers

STATED PRINT RUN 25-50
TMCF Paul Coffey/25 40.00 80.00
TMDD Devan Dubnyk/50 25.00 50.00
TMGA G.Anderson/25 EXCH 25.00 50.00
TMGF Grant Fuhr/25 30.00 60.00
TMJE Jordan Eberle/50 60.00 150.00
TMJK Jari Kurri/25 EXCH 40.00 80.00
TMMM Mark Messier/25 30.00 60.00
TMMP M.Paajarvi/50 EXCH 20.00 50.00
TMSG Sam Gagner/50 EXCH 20.00 50.00
TMTH Taylor Hall/50 EXCH 60.00 120.00
TMWG W.Gretzky/25 EXCH 175.00 300.00

2011-12 SP Game Used Team Marks Team Canada

STATED PRINT RUN 50 SER.#'d SETS
TMAP Alex Pietrangelo 30.00 60.00
TMCH Cody Hodgson 40.00 80.00
TMDT Dustin Tokarski 20.00 50.00
TMEB Jordan Eberle 50.00 120.00
TMEK Evander Kane 25.00 50.00
TMJT John Tavares 50.00 100.00
TMPC Patrice Cormier EXCH 12.00 30.00
TMPS P.K. Subban 40.00 80.00
TMTE Tyler Ennis 20.00 50.00
TMTM Tyler Myers 15.00 40.00

2011-12 SP Game Used Trophy Marks Calder

STATED PRINT RUN 50 SER.#'d SETS
CALDERAO Alex Ovechkin EXCH 50.00 100.00
CALDEREM Evgeni Malkin EXCH 40.00 80.00
CALDERJS Jeff Skinner EXCH 30.00 60.00
CALDERPK Patrick Kane EXCH 30.00 60.00
CALDERSM Steve Mason 20.00 40.00
CALDERTM Tyler Myers EXCH 20.00 40.00

2011-12 SP Game Used Trophy Marks Hart

STATED PRINT RUN 25 SER.#'d SETS
HARTBH Bobby Hull 60.00 120.00
HARTBO Bobby Orr 125.00 250.00
HARTJB Jean Beliveau 50.00 100.00

2012-13 SP Game Used

COMP.SET w/o RC's (100) 15.00 40.00
1 Dale Hawerchuk .75 2.00
2 Evander Kane .60 1.50
3 Alexander Ovechkin 2.50 6.00
4 Braden Holtby 1.00 2.50
5 Pavel Bure .75 2.00
6 Ryan Kesler .60 1.50
7 Alexandre Burrows .60 1.50
8 Richard Brodeur .60 1.50
9 Curtis Joseph .60 1.50
10 Dion Phaneuf .60 1.50
11 Phil Kessel .75 2.00
12 Steven Stamkos 1.25 3.00
13 Vincent Lecavalier .50 1.25
14 Alex Pietrangelo .50 1.25
15 Brett Hull .60 1.50
16 David Backes .60 1.50
17 Jaroslav Halak .60 1.50
18 Patrick Marleau .60 1.50
19 Joe Pavelski .60 1.50
20 Antti Niemi .50 1.25
21 Logan Couture .60 1.50
22 James Neal .60 1.50
23 Evgeni Malkin 2.00 5.00
24 Marc-Andre Fleury 1.00 2.50
25 Mario Lemieux 2.00 5.00
26 Sidney Crosby 2.50 6.00
27 Claude Giroux .60 1.50
28 Eric Lindros 1.00 2.50
29 Bernie Parent .60 1.50
30 Brayden Schenn .60 1.50
31 Dave Schultz .60 1.50
32 Ron Hextall .60 1.50
33 Erik Karlsson 1.25 3.00
34 Rick Nash .60 1.50
35 Brad Richards .60 1.50
36 Marian Gaborik .60 1.50
37 Mark Messier .75 2.00
38 Henrik Lundqvist .75 2.00
39 Mike Bossy .60 1.50
40 John Tavares 1.25 3.00
41 Bryan Trottier .75 2.00
42 Ilya Kovalchuk .60 1.50
43 Martin Brodeur 1.25 3.00
44 Adam Henrique .60 1.50
45 Pekka Rinne .75 2.00
46 Guy Lafleur .75 2.00
47 Jean Beliveau .60 1.50
48 Larry Robinson .60 1.50
49 P.K. Subban 1.00 2.50
50 Carey Price 2.00 5.00
51 Dany Heatley .50 1.25
52 Jari Kurri .60 1.50
53 Wayne Gretzky 2.50 6.00
54 Anze Kopitar 1.00 2.50
55 Drew Doughty .60 1.50
56 Simon Gagne .60 1.50
57 Luc Robitaille .60 1.50
58 Jonathan Quick 1.00 2.50
59 Ron Francis .75 2.00
60 Kris Versteeg .50 1.25
61 Stephen Weiss .50 1.25
62 Grant Fuhr .60 1.50
63 Bill Ranford .60 1.50
64 Jordan Eberle .60 1.50
65 Paul Coffey .60 1.50
66 Ryan Nugent-Hopkins .60 1.50
67 Taylor Hall 1.25 3.00
68 Johan Franzen .60 1.50
69 Nicklas Lidstrom .60 1.50
70 Pavel Datsyuk .75 2.00
71 Jamie Benn .75 2.00
72 Jaromir Jagr 1.50 4.00
73 Joe Sakic 1.00 2.50
74 Matt Duchene .60 1.50
75 Gabriel Landeskog .60 1.50
76 Denis Savard .75 2.00
77 Doug Wilson .50 1.25
78 Ed Belfour .60 1.50
79 Jonathan Toews 1.25 3.00
80 Patrick Kane 1.25 3.00
81 Jeff Skinner .60 1.50
82 Eric Staal .75 2.00
83 Jordan Staal .60 1.50
84 Doug Gilmour .75 2.00
85 Jarome Iginla .60 1.50
86 Thomas Vanek .60 1.50
87 Derek Roy .50 1.25
88 Ryan Miller .60 1.50
89 Dominik Hasek .75 2.00
90 Cody Hodgson .60 1.50
91 Bobby Orr 2.00 5.00
92 Cam Neely .60 1.50
93 Brad Marchand .75 2.00
94 Tuukka Rask .60 1.50
95 Patrice Bergeron .75 2.00
96 Ray Bourque 1.00 2.50
97 Terry O'Reilly .50 1.25
98 Tyler Seguin 1.00 2.50
99 Bobby Ryan .60 1.50
100 Jonas Hiller .50 1.25
101 Mat Clark/73 RC 8.00 20.00
102 Carter Camper/58 RC 6.00 15.00
103 Maxime Sauve/75 RC 8.00 20.00
104 L. MacDermid/64 RC 8.00 20.00
105 Torey Krug/47 RC 20.00 50.00
106 M. Hutchinson/70 RC 15.00 40.00
107 Travis Turnbull/65 RC 8.00 20.00
108 Sven Baertschi/47 RC 12.00 30.00
109 Akim Aliu/29 RC 12.00 30.00
110 Jeremy Welsh/23 RC 12.00 30.00
111 Brandon Bollig/52 RC 8.00 20.00
112 Tyson Barrie/41 RC 20.00 50.00
113 Mike Connolly/18 RC 15.00 40.00
114 Dalton Prout/47 RC 8.00 20.00
115 Cody Goloubef/48 RC 10.00 25.00
116 Shawn Hunwick/31 RC 10.00 25.00
117 Andrew Joudrey/23 RC 12.00 30.00
118 Ryan Garbutt/40 RC 10.00 25.00
119 Reilly Smith/18 RC 20.00 50.00
120 Brenden Dillon/4 RC
121 Scott Glennie/15 RC
122 Riley Sheahan/15 RC 25.00 50.00
123 Philippe Cornet/51 RC 8.00 20.00
124 Colby Robak/47 RC 10.00 25.00
125 Jordan Nolan/71 RC 8.00 20.00
126 Kris Foucault/72 RC 8.00 20.00
127 Jason Zucker/16 RC 30.00 60.00
128 Tyler Cuma/65 RC 8.00 20.00
129 Chay Genoway/47 RC 10.00 25.00
130 Gabriel Dumont/37 RC 15.00 40.00
131 Robert Mayer/65 RC 10.00 25.00
132 Chet Pickard/37 RC 10.00 25.00
133 Aaron Ness/55 RC 8.00 20.00
134 Casey Cizikas/53 RC 8.00 20.00
135 Matt Donovan/46 RC 10.00 25.00
136 Chris Kreider/20 RC 60.00 120.00
137 Jakob Silfverberg/33 RC 50.00 100.00
138 Mark Stone/60 RC 25.00 50.00
139 Brandon Manning/23 RC 12.00 30.00
140 Michael Stone/26 RC 12.00 30.00
141 Matt Watkins/50 RC 8.00 20.00
142 Tyson Sexsmith/37 RC 30.00 60.00
143 Jake Allen/34 RC 30.00 80.00
144 Jaden Schwartz/9 RC
145 J.T. Brown/19 RC 15.00 40.00
146 Carter Ashton/37 RC 15.00 40.00
147 Ryan Hamilton/48 RC 10.00 25.00
148 Jussi Rynnas/40 RC 10.00 25.00

2012-13 SP Game Used Authentic Fabrics

GROUP A ODDS 1:183
GROUP B ODDS 1:143
GROUP C ODDS 1:27
GROUP D ODDS 1:6
OVERALL MEM ODDS 1:3
AFAK Anze Kopitar D 5.00 12.00
AFAO Alexander Ovechkin A 25.00 60.00
AFBH Brett Hull A 8.00 20.00
AFBR Bobby Ryan D 3.00 8.00
AFBS Brendan Shanahan D 4.00 10.00
AFCG Claude Giroux D 3.00 8.00
AFCJ Curtis Joseph A 8.00 20.00
AFCK Chris Kreider D 5.00 12.00
AFCP Carey Price D 10.00 25.00
AFDA Daniel Alfredsson D 4.00 10.00
AFDU Dustin Brown D 3.00 8.00
AFEL Eric Lindros D 5.00 12.00
AFGR Mike Green C 4.00 10.00
AFHE Milan Hejduk C 3.00 8.00
AFJC Jeff Carter D 3.00 8.00
AFJI Jarome Iginla B 5.00 12.00
AFJJ Jaromir Jagr B 12.00 30.00
AFJK Jake Allen D 6.00 15.00
AFJS Jason Spezza D 3.00 8.00
AFKA Evander Kane C 4.00 10.00
AFMB Martin Brodeur A 8.00 20.00
AFMF Marc-Andre Fleury D 5.00 12.00
AFMG Michael Grabner C 3.00 8.00
AFMK Miikka Kiprusoff D 2.50 6.00
AFMO Mike Modano B 8.00 20.00
AFRB Ray Bourque D 5.00 12.00
AFRF Ron Francis C 5.00 12.00
AFRG Ryan Getzlaf C 6.00 15.00
AFRI Pekka Rinne D 4.00 10.00
AFSG Scott Glennie C 3.00 8.00
AFSH Scott Hartnell D 3.00 8.00
AFSV Sven Baertschi D 2.50 6.00
AFTS Tyler Seguin D 5.00 12.00
AFZC Zdeno Chara D 3.00 8.00

2012-13 SP Game Used Authentic Fabrics Fight Straps

STATED PRINT RUN 15
AFAK Anze Kopitar 15.00 40.00
AFAO Alexander Ovechkin 40.00 100.00
AFBH Brett Hull 12.00 30.00
AFBR Bobby Ryan 10.00 25.00
AFBS Brendan Shanahan 15.00 40.00
AFCG Claude Giroux 10.00 25.00
AFCJ Curtis Joseph 10.00 25.00
AFCK Chris Kreider 10.00 25.00
AFCP Carey Price 30.00 80.00
AFDA Daniel Alfredsson 10.00 25.00
AFDU Dustin Brown 10.00 25.00
AFEL Eric Lindros 20.00 50.00
AFGR Mike Green 10.00 25.00
AFHE Milan Hejduk 8.00 20.00
AFJC Jeff Carter 10.00 25.00
AFJI Jarome Iginla 10.00 25.00
AFJJ Jaromir Jagr 25.00 60.00
AFJK Jake Allen 12.00 30.00
AFJS Jason Spezza 10.00 25.00
AFKA Evander Kane 10.00 25.00
AFMB Martin Brodeur 20.00 50.00
AFMF Marc-Andre Fleury 15.00 40.00
AFMG Michael Grabner 8.00 20.00
AFMK Miikka Kiprusoff 8.00 20.00
AFMO Mike Modano 20.00 50.00
AFRB Ray Bourque 20.00 50.00
AFRF Ron Francis 15.00 40.00
AFRG Ryan Getzlaf 15.00 40.00
AFRI Pekka Rinne 12.00 30.00
AFSG Scott Glennie 8.00 20.00
AFSH Scott Hartnell 10.00 25.00
AFSV Sven Baertschi 6.00 15.00
AFTS Tyler Seguin 15.00 40.00
AFZC Zdeno Chara 10.00 25.00

2012-13 SP Game Used Authentic Fabrics Gold

AFBH Brett Hull/16
AFBS Brendan Shanahan/14
AFCG Claude Giroux/28 12.00 30.00
AFCJ Curtis Joseph/31 8.00 20.00
AFCK Chris Kreider/20 20.00 50.00
AFCP Carey Price/31 25.00 60.00
AFDA Daniel Alfredsson/11
AFDU Dustin Brown/23 10.00 25.00
AFEL Eric Lindros/88 12.00 30.00
AFGR Mike Green/52 8.00 20.00
AFHE Milan Hejduk/23 8.00 20.00
AFJI Jarome Iginla/12
AFJJ Jaromir Jagr/68 20.00 50.00
AFJK Jake Allen/34 20.00 50.00
AFJS Jason Spezza/19 10.00 25.00
AFMB Martin Brodeur/30 20.00 50.00
AFMF Marc-Andre Fleury/29 15.00 40.00
AFMG Michael Grabner/40 6.00 15.00
AFMK Miikka Kiprusoff/34 6.00 15.00
AFRB Ray Bourque/77 8.00 20.00
AFRF Ron Francis/10
AFRG Ryan Getzlaf/15
AFRI Pekka Rinne/35 10.00 25.00
AFSG Scott Glennie/15 6.00 15.00
AFSH Scott Hartnell/19 8.00 20.00
AFSV Sven Baertschi/47 8.00 20.00
AFTS Tyler Seguin/19 20.00 40.00
AFZC Zdeno Chara/33 8.00 20.00

2012-13 SP Game Used Authentic Fabrics Patches

AFAK Anze Kopitar 12.00 30.00
AFAO Alexander Ovechkin 12.00 30.00
AFBH Brett Hull 12.00 30.00
AFBR Bobby Ryan 8.00 20.00
AFBS Brendan Shanahan 10.00 25.00
AFCG Claude Giroux 8.00 20.00
AFCJ Curtis Joseph 10.00 25.00
AFCK Chris Kreider 10.00 25.00
AFCP Carey Price 15.00 40.00
AFDA Daniel Alfredsson 12.00 30.00
AFDU Dustin Brown 10.00 25.00
AFEL Eric Lindros 15.00 40.00
AFGR Mike Green 8.00 20.00
AFHE Milan Hejduk 6.00 15.00
AFJC Jeff Carter 8.00 20.00
AFJI Jarome Iginla 12.50 30.00
AFJJ Jaromir Jagr 12.00 30.00
AFJK Jake Allen 15.00 40.00
AFJS Jason Spezza 8.00 20.00
AFKA Evander Kane 8.00 20.00
AFMB Martin Brodeur 12.00 30.00
AFMF Marc-Andre Fleury 15.00 40.00
AFMG Michael Grabner 6.00 15.00
AFMK Miikka Kiprusoff 10.00 25.00
AFMO Mike Modano 10.00 25.00
AFRB Ray Bourque 12.00 30.00
AFRF Ron Francis 10.00 25.00
AFRG Ryan Getzlaf 10.00 25.00
AFRI Pekka Rinne 10.00 25.00
AFSG Scott Glennie 6.00 15.00
AFSH Scott Hartnell 8.00 20.00
AFSV Sven Baertschi 6.00 15.00
AFTS Tyler Seguin 12.00 30.00
AFZC Zdeno Chara 8.00 20.00

2012-13 SP Game Used Authentic Fabrics Dual

*PATCH/25: .8X TO 2X BASIC DUAL
AF2CR S.Couturier/M.Read D 4.00 10.00
AF2CZ H.Zetterberg/D.Cleary D 5.00 12.00
AF2DD D.Brown/D.Penner D 4.00 10.00
AF2DF P.Datsyuk/J.Franzen D 5.00 12.00
AF2EA J.Ericsson/J.Abdelkader D 3.00 8.00
AF2EH J.Eberle/T.Hall C 8.00 20.00
AF2GB M.Green/N.Backstrom C 8.00 20.00
AF2GR R.Getzlaf/B.Ryan D 6.00 15.00
AF2GS P.Subban/J.Gorges D 6.00 15.00
AF2GV S.Varlamov/J.Giguere D 4.00 10.00
AF2HB S.Hartnell/D.Briere D 4.00 10.00
AF2IK J.Iginla/M.Kiprusoff 4.00 10.00
AF2KD A.Kopitar/D.Doughty D 6.00 15.00
AF2KE N.Kronwall/J.Ericsson D 3.00 8.00
AF2KH C.Kreider/C.Hagelin D 8.00 20.00
AF2LK R.Kesler/R.Luongo D 4.00 10.00
AF2MI M.Brodeur/I.Kovalchuk D 8.00 20.00
AF2MK D.Krejci/B.Marchand D 5.00 12.00
AF2MM T.Myers/R.Miller D 4.00 10.00
AF2PK O.Pavelec/E.Kane A 12.00 30.00
AF2RC M.Richards/J.Carter D 4.00 10.00
AF2TR T.Thomas/T.Rask D 4.00 10.00
AF2WV S.Weiss/K.Versteeg D 5.00 12.00

2012-13 SP Game Used Authentic Fabrics Eights

AF8USA USA Stars 75.00 200.00
AF8ALLSTAR All-Stars 150.00 300.00
AF8GOALIE Goalie Stars
AF8SWEDEN Swedish Stars

2012-13 SP Game Used Authentic Fabrics Fives

AF5BOS Boston 5 20.00 50.00
AF5BUF Buffalo 5 15.00 40.00
AF5CGY Calgary 5 20.00 50.00
AF5COL Colorado 5 15.00 40.00
AF5DET Detroit 5 20.00 50.00
AF5GR8 8 All-Time Greats 80.00 200.00
AF5LAK L.A. Kings 5 25.00 60.00
AF5STL St. Louis 5 15.00 40.00
AF5VAN Vancouver 5 15.00 40.00
AF5BEES Boston 5 25.00 60.00
AF5BLUE N.Y. Rangers 5 20.00 50.00
AF5LBBR Montreal 5 50.00 125.00
AF5PENS Pittsburgh 5 50.00 125.00

2012-13 SP Game Used Authentic Fabrics Quads

AF4BUF Miller/Vanek/Stafford/Myers 8.00 20.00
AF4LAK Gagne/Brown/Carter/Penner 8.00 20.00
AF4ASAK Spezza/Alfredsson/Karlsson/Anderson 15.00 40.00
AF4RBJB Brod/Roy/Belfr/Josph 20.00 50.00
AF4KINGS Rich/Quick/Dghty/Kop 12.00 30.00

2012-13 SP Game Used Authentic Fabrics Sevens

AF7GR8 All-Time Greats 150.00 300.00
AF7NYR N.Y. Rangers Stars 20.00 50.00
AF7PHI Philadelphia Flyers Stars 20.00 50.00
AF7GOALIE Goalie Greats
AF7ROOKIE Rookie Stars 50.00 120.00

2012-13 SP Game Used Authentic Fabrics Sixes

NYNY New York Stars 12.50 30.00
ANALA Anaheim/L.A. Stars 15.00 40.00
CGYVAN Calgary/Vancvr Stars 60.00 120.00
CHIDET Chicago/Detroit Stars 12.00 30.00
MTLBOS Montreal/Boston Stars 25.00 60.00
NYBOS NY/Boston Stars 30.00 60.00
PITPHI Pittsburgh/Philly Stars 15.00 40.00
PITWAS Pttsbrgh/Wshng Stars 40.00 80.00
STLDET St.Louis/Detroit Stars 30.00 60.00
WASTBY Wash/Tampa Stars 20.00 50.00

2012-13 SP Game Used Authentic Fabrics Team Canada

*PATCH/35: .8X TO 2X BASIC TC JSY
*FIGHT STRAP/15: 1.2X TO 3X TC GRP B-D
*FIGHT STRAP/15: .8X TO 2X TC GRP A
TC1 Carter Ashton D 2.50 6.00
TC2 Brett Connolly D 3.00 8.00
TC3 Dan Boyle C 3.00 8.00
TC4 Jared Cowen C 4.00 10.00
TC5 Casey Cizikas D 3.00 8.00
TC6 Colten Teubert C 2.50 6.00
TC7 Simon Despres D 3.00 8.00
TC8 Dany Heatley D 3.00 8.00
TC9 Calvin de Haan C 3.00 8.00
TC10 Erik Gudbranson C 4.00 10.00
TC11 Eric Staal D 5.00 12.00
TC12 Jamie Benn B 5.00 12.00
TC13 Ryan Ellis C 2.50 6.00
TC14 Patrice Bergeron D 5.00 12.00
TC15 Patrice Cormier C 4.00 10.00
TC16 Corey Perry D 4.00 10.00
TC17 Chris Pronger D 3.00 8.00
TC18 Chet Pickard D 3.00 8.00
TC19 Mark Scheifele D 5.00 12.00
TC20 Scott Niedermayer C 4.00 10.00
TC21 Devante Smith-Pelly C 3.00 8.00
TC22 Jaden Schwartz D 6.00 15.00
TC23 Tyson Barrie C 6.00 15.00
TC24 Wayne Gretzky A 40.00 80.00
TC25 Zach Boychuk C 2.50 6.00

2012-13 SP Game Used Authentic Fabrics Team Canada Gold

TC8 Dany Heatley/15 8.00 20.00
TC14 Patrice Bergeron/39 8.00 20.00
TC19 Mark Scheifele/19 8.00 20.00
TC20 Scott Niedermayer/27
TC21 Devante Smith-Pelly/22
TC23 Tyson Barrie/22
TC24 Wayne Gretzky/99 40.00 80.00

2012-13 SP Game Used Authentic Fabrics Team Canada Dual

*PATCH/25: .8X TO 2X BASIC DUAL
TC26 R.Nash/M.Richards 5.00 12.00
TC27 B.Connolly/D.Smith-Pelly 4.00 10.00
TC28 C.Goloubef/C.Teubert 4.00 10.00
TC29 K.Aulie/R.Ellis 3.00 8.00
TC30 C.Ashton/C.Cizikas 4.00 10.00
TC31 J.Iginla/R.Getzlaf 8.00 20.00

2012-13 SP Game Used Authentic Fabrics Team Canada Fives

TC42 Eak/Sch/Leb/Fol/Ciz 10.00 25.00

2012-13 SP Game Used Authentic Fabrics Team Canada Quads

TC37 Schw/Schf/Cnlly/Smt-Ply 12.00 30.00
TC38 Igin/Thrntn/Htley/Getzlf 15.00 40.00
TC39 Ellis/Gudbn/Olsn/de Hn 10.00 25.00
TC40 Cowen/Dsprs/Brrie/Ellis 15.00 40.00
TC41 Dghty/Keith/Byle/Wber 12.00 30.00

2012-13 SP Game Used Authentic Fabrics Team Canada Triples

TC32 Schwrtz/Cnnlly/Smith-Ply 6.00 15.00
TC33 Despres/Olsen/Barrie 6.00 15.00
TC34 Leblanc/Johansen/Foligno 8.00 20.00
TC35 Schwartz/Cizikas/Ashton 6.00 15.00
TC36 Boyle/Thornton/Heatley 6.00 15.00

2012-13 SP Game Used Authentic Fabrics Triples

*PATCH/15: 1.2X TO 3X BASIC TRIPLE
AF3ASK Alfredsson/Spezza/Karlsson 6.00 15.00
AF3CBS Chara/Bergeron/Seguin 8.00 20.00
AF3DSS Staal/Stepan/Kreider 8.00 20.00
AF3DVE Doan/Vermette/Ekman-Larsson 6.00 15.00
AF3GBC Brown/Carter/Gagne 5.00 12.00
AF3GRH Getzlaf/Ryan/Hiller 8.00 20.00
AF3IKC Iginla/Kiprusoff/Cammalleri 6.00 15.00
AF3MVM Miller/Vanek/Myers 5.00 12.00
AF3PHG Giroux/Hartnell/Schenn 5.00 12.00
AF3RQD Richards/Quick/Dghty 8.00 20.00
AF3SDL Stastny/Duchene/Land 5.00 12.00
AF3SHB Sakic/Hejduk/Bourque 8.00 20.00
AF3SSB Sedin/Burrows/Sedin 6.00 15.00

2012-13 SP Game Used Draft Day Marks

EACH CARD SERIAL #'d TO 10-35
TOTAL PRINT RUNS MUCH HIGHER
EACH HAS MULTIPLE CARDS OF EQUAL VALUE
DDMCA1 Carter Ashton A/35 5.00 12.00
DDMCG1 Cody Goloubef B/35 6.00 15.00
DDMCI1 Casey Cizikas A/35 12.00 30.00
DDMCK1 Chris Kreider D/35 25.00 60.00
DDMCP1 Chet Pickard A/35 6.00 15.00
DDMEK1 Erik Karlsson A/10 60.00 120.00
DDMJA1 Jake Allen A/35 20.00 50.00
DDMJS1 Jeff Skinner E/10 40.00 80.00
DDMJT1 John Tavares A/20* 50.00 100.00
DDMJZ1 Jason Zucker C/35 8.00 20.00
DDMLC1 Logan Couture C/10 30.00 60.00
DDMRN1 Nugent-Hopkins E/10 100.00 200.00
DDMSB1 Sven Baertschi A/35 8.00 20.00
DDMSC1 Jaden Schwartz A/35 12.00 30.00
DDMSG1 Scott Glennie E/70* 12.00 30.00
DDMSH1 Riley Sheahan A/70* 15.00 40.00
DDMSI1 Jakob Silfverberg B/35 15.00 40.00
DDMTB1 Tyson Barrie A/35 12.00 30.00

2012-13 SP Game Used Gold Autographs

1 Dale Hawerchuk B 10.00 25.00
2 Evander Kane C 8.00 20.00
3 Alexander Ovechkin B 30.00 60.00
5 Pavel Bure B 30.00 60.00
6 Ryan Kesler C 8.00 20.00
8 Richard Brodeur B 8.00 20.00
9 Curtis Joseph B 15.00 30.00
10 Dion Phaneuf C 8.00 20.00
11 Phil Kessel B 10.00 25.00
12 Steven Stamkos A 30.00 60.00
13 Vincent Lecavalier B 10.00 25.00
14 Alex Pietrangelo B 12.00 30.00
15 Brett Hull B 25.00 50.00
16 David Backes C 8.00 20.00
17 Jaroslav Halak C 8.00 20.00
18 Patrick Marleau B 10.00 25.00
19 Joe Pavelski C 8.00 20.00
20 Antti Niemi B 6.00 15.00
21 Logan Couture B 8.00 20.00
22 James Neal C 12.00 30.00
23 Evgeni Malkin A 40.00 80.00
24 Marc-Andre Fleury B 15.00 30.00
25 Mario Lemieux A 40.00 80.00
26 Sidney Crosby A 60.00 120.00
27 Claude Giroux B 12.00 30.00
28 Eric Lindros A 40.00 80.00
30 Brayden Schenn C 10.00 25.00
31 Dave Schultz C 10.00 25.00
32 Ron Hextall B 15.00 40.00
34 Rick Nash B 8.00 20.00
35 Brad Richards C 10.00 25.00
36 Marian Gaborik B 15.00 40.00
37 Mark Messier A 25.00 50.00
38 Henrik Lundqvist B 20.00 40.00
39 Mike Bossy B 10.00 25.00
40 John Tavares C 15.00 30.00
41 Bryan Trottier B 12.00 30.00
43 Martin Brodeur B 30.00 60.00
44 Adam Henrique C 12.00 30.00
45 Pekka Rinne C 10.00 25.00
46 Guy Lafleur B 15.00 40.00
47 Jean Beliveau B 30.00 60.00
48 Larry Robinson B
49 P.K. Subban B 15.00 40.00
50 Carey Price B 25.00 60.00
51 Dany Heatley B 12.50 30.00
52 Jari Kurri C 8.00 20.00
53 Wayne Gretzky A
54 Anze Kopitar B 12.00 30.00
55 Drew Doughty B 20.00 50.00
56 Simon Gagne B 8.00 20.00
57 Luc Robitaille B 15.00 40.00
59 Ron Francis B 10.00 25.00
60 Kris Versteeg A 12.00 30.00
61 Stephen Weiss C 5.00 12.00
62 Grant Fuhr B 15.00 30.00
63 Bill Ranford C 6.00 15.00
64 Jordan Eberle C 15.00 40.00
65 Paul Coffey B 10.00 25.00
66 Ryan Nugent-Hopkins B 30.00 60.00
67 Taylor Hall B 15.00 40.00
68 Johan Franzen B 8.00 20.00
69 Nicklas Lidstrom B 15.00 40.00
70 Pavel Datsyuk B 15.00 40.00
71 Jamie Benn C 10.00 25.00
72 Jaromir Jagr A 30.00 60.00
73 Joe Sakic A 30.00 60.00
74 Matt Duchene B 12.00 30.00
75 Gabriel Landeskog B 10.00 25.00
76 Denis Savard B 10.00 25.00
77 Doug Wilson C 6.00 15.00
78 Ed Belfour B 30.00 60.00
79 Jonathan Toews A
80 Patrick Kane B 12.00 30.00
81 Jeff Skinner B 8.00 20.00
82 Eric Staal C 10.00 25.00
83 Jordan Staal C 8.00 20.00
84 Doug Gilmour B 12.00 30.00
85 Jarome Iginla B 15.00 30.00
86 Thomas Vanek C 6.00 15.00
87 Derek Roy B 6.00 15.00
88 Ryan Miller B 15.00 30.00
89 Dominik Hasek B 30.00 60.00
90 Cody Hodgson C 12.50 30.00
91 Bobby Orr A 100.00 175.00
92 Cam Neely B 12.00 30.00
93 Brad Marchand B 12.00 30.00
94 Tuukka Rask C 15.00 30.00
95 Patrice Bergeron B 15.00 30.00
96 Ray Bourque B 12.00 30.00
98 Tyler Seguin B 15.00 40.00
99 Bobby Ryan C 8.00 20.00
100 Jonas Hiller C 6.00 15.00
103 Maxime Sauve 6.00 15.00
108 Sven Baertschi 8.00 20.00
109 Akim Aliu 6.00 15.00
111 Brandon Bollig 10.00 25.00
112 Tyson Barrie 12.00 30.00
115 Cody Goloubef 6.00 15.00
119 Reilly Smith 10.00 25.00
120 Brenden Dillon 6.00 15.00
122 Riley Sheahan 6.00 15.00
125 Jordan Nolan 6.00 15.00
127 Jason Zucker 8.00 20.00
128 Tyler Cuma 6.00 15.00
130 Gabriel Dumont 6.00 15.00
132 Chet Pickard 6.00 15.00
136 Chris Kreider 15.00 40.00
137 Jakob Silfverberg 12.00 30.00
138 Mark Stone 12.00 30.00
140 Michael Stone 6.00 15.00
143 Jake Allen 20.00 50.00
144 Jaden Schwartz 12.00 30.00
145 J.T. Brown 6.00 15.00
146 Carter Ashton 6.00 15.00
148 Jussi Rynnas 10.00 25.00

2012-13 SP Game Used Inked Rookie Sweaters

IRSCA Carter Ashton 6.00 15.00
IRSCK Chris Kreider 15.00 40.00
IRSCP Chet Pickard 8.00 20.00
IRSJA Jake Allen 25.00 60.00
IRSRS Riley Sheahan 12.00 30.00
IRSSB Sven Baertschi 10.00 25.00
IRSSC Jaden Schwartz 15.00 40.00
IRSTB Tyson Barrie 15.00 40.00

2012-13 SP Game Used Inked Sweaters

ISAO Alexander Ovechkin/25 40.00 80.00
ISBP Brad Park/50 8.00 20.00
ISBS Brayden Schenn/99 8.00 20.00
ISCH Carl Hagelin/50 12.00 30.00
ISCP Carey Price/25 30.00 80.00
ISCS Cory Schneider/99 10.00 25.00
ISDB Dustin Brown/99 8.00 20.00
ISEK Evander Kane/99 8.00 20.00
ISEM Evgeni Malkin/25 25.00 60.00
ISGA Mike Gartner/50 10.00 25.00
ISGL Gabriel Landeskog/99 8.00 20.00
ISHL Henrik Lundqvist/25 15.00 40.00
ISHO Cody Hodgson/99 8.00 20.00
ISJE Jordan Eberle/50 20.00 50.00
ISJH Jaroslav Halak/50 10.00 25.00
ISKS Kevin Shattenkirk/99 8.00 20.00
ISKV Kris Versteeg/25 8.00 20.00
ISLA Luke Adam/99 6.00 15.00
ISMF Marc-Andre Fleury/50 15.00 30.00
ISMH Milan Hejduk/50 8.00 20.00
ISMR Matt Read/99 6.00 15.00
ISNB Nicklas Backstrom/50 15.00 40.00
ISNL Nicklas Lidstrom/25 20.00 40.00
ISPS P.K. Subban/50 15.00 40.00
ISRE Ryan Ellis/99 5.00 12.00
ISRK Ryan Kesler/50 10.00 25.00
ISRM Ryan Miller/50 10.00 25.00
ISSM Craig Smith/99 5.00 12.00
ISSS Steven Stamkos/25 20.00 50.00
ISTH Taylor Hall/50 25.00 50.00

2012-13 SP Game Used SIGnificant Numbers Autographs

COMMON CARD/20-92 8.00 20.00
SEMISTARS/20-92 10.00 25.00
UNL.STARS/20-92 12.00 30.00
STATED PRINT RUN 3-92
SNAO Alexander Ovechkin/8
SNBH Brett Hull/16 50.00 100.00
SNCG Claude Giroux/28 12.00 30.00
SNCK Chris Kreider/20 20.00 50.00
SNCN Cam Neely/8
SNCP Carey Price/31 40.00 100.00
SNCU Sean Couturier/14
SNDD Drew Doughty/8
SNDE Jaden Schwartz/9
SNDH Dale Hawerchuk/10
SNDP Dion Phaneuf/3
SNEK Evander Kane/9
SNEM Evgeni Malkin/71 30.00 60.00
SNES Eric Staal/12
SNGL Gabriel Landeskog/92 15.00 40.00
SNGZ Wayne Gretzky/9
SNHE Milan Hejduk/23 10.00 25.00
SNHG Carl Hagelin/62 12.00 30.00
SNHL Henrik Lundqvist/30 25.00 50.00
SNJA Jake Allen/34 30.00 80.00
SNJE Jordan Eberle/14
SNJG Josh Gorges/26 10.00 25.00
SNJI Jarome Iginla/12
SNJO Jarome Iginla/19
SNMB Martin Brodeur/30 35.00 75.00
SNMD Matt Duchene/9
SNMF Marc-Andre Fleury/29 20.00 50.00
SNML Mario Lemieux/6
SNMM Mark Messier/11
SNPR Patrick Roy/3
SNPS P.K. Subban/76 20.00 50.00
SNRG Ryan Getzlaf/15 15.00 30.00
SNRK Ryan Kesler/17 15.00 40.00
SNSC Sidney Crosby/7
SNTH Taylor Hall/4
SNTS Tyler Seguin/19 20.00 50.00
SNTT Bryan Trottier/19 15.00 30.00

2012-13 SP Game Used Stanley Cup Finals Materials Net Cord

G1AK Anze Kopitar 50.00 100.00
G1AV Anton Volchenkov 15.00 40.00
G1CF Colin Fraser 15.00 40.00
G1JQ Jonathan Quick 75.00 150.00
G2DD Drew Doughty 40.00 80.00
G2DP Dustin Penner 15.00 40.00
G2JC Jeff Carter 25.00 50.00
G2JQ Jonathan Quick 50.00 100.00
G3AK Anze Kopitar 50.00 100.00
G3AM Alec Martinez 25.00 50.00
G3DB Dustin Brown 30.00 60.00
G3JQ Jonathan Quick 75.00 150.00
G3JW Justin Williams 30.00 80.00
G3MG Matt Greene 25.00 50.00
G3SV Viatcheslav Voynov 15.00 40.00
G3WG Wayne Gretzky 100.00 200.00
G3WM Willie Mitchell 25.00 60.00
G4AH Adam Henrique 40.00 80.00
G4AP Alexei Ponikarovsky 25.00 50.00
G4BS Bryce Salvador
G4DC David Clarkson 15.00 40.00
G4DZ Dainius Zubrus 15.00 40.00
G4IK Ilya Kovalchuk 40.00 80.00
G4MB Martin Brodeur 50.00 100.00
G4MF Mark Fayne 15.00 40.00
G4PE Patrik Elias 20.00 50.00
G5BS Bryce Salvador 25.00 50.00
G5MB Martin Brodeur 50.00 100.00
G5TZ Travis Zajac 15.00 40.00
G5ZP Zach Parise 25.00 60.00
G6DB Dustin Brown 30.00 60.00
G6DD Drew Doughty 40.00 80.00
G6DK Dwight King 25.00 50.00
G6JC Jeff Carter 40.00 80.00
G6JQ Jonathan Quick 60.00 120.00
G6JS Jarret Stoll 30.00 60.00
G6LR Luc Robitaille 30.00 80.00
G6MR Mike Richards 30.00 60.00
G6RS Rob Scuderi 25.00 50.00
G6SG Simon Gagne 40.00 80.00
G6TL Trevor Lewis 30.00 60.00

2012-13 SP Game Used Stanley Cup Finals Materials Net Skirt Autographs

SCUPAH Adam Henrique C 15.00 40.00
SCUPAK Anze Kopitar B 40.00 100.00
SCUPDB Dustin Brown C 30.00 80.00
SCUPDD Drew Doughty B 75.00 150.00
SCUPLR Luc Robitaille B 40.00 100.00
SCUPMB Martin Brodeur A 175.00 350.00
SCUPWG Wayne Gretzky A 350.00 600.00

2012-13 SP Game Used Tandem Twigs

TTLA W.Gretzky/M.Dionne 25.00 50.00
TTNY W.Gretzky/M.Messier 20.00 50.00
TTBEES P.Esposito/J.Bucyk 10.00 25.00
TTBOS P.Esposito/R.Bourque 10.00 25.00
TTEDM W.Gretzky/M.Messier 40.00 80.00
TTMTL J.Beliveau/G.Lafleur 15.00 40.00
TTOTT D.Alfredsson/D.Hasek 15.00 40.00

2013-14 SP Game Used

COMP.SET w/o RC's (100) 15.00 40.00
101-200 ROOKIE PRINT RUN 5-75
1 Dale Hawerchuk .60 1.50
2 Evander Kane .50 1.25
3 Alexander Ovechkin 2.00 5.00
4 Braden Holtby .75 2.00
5 Nicklas Backstrom .75 2.00
6 Alexandre Burrows .50 1.25
7 Markus Naslund .40 1.00
8 Ryan Kesler .50 1.25
9 Trevor Linden .50 1.25
10 Doug Gilmour .60 1.50
11 Nazem Kadri .50 1.25
12 Dion Phaneuf .50 1.25
13 Phil Kessel .60 1.50
14 Steven Stamkos 1.00 2.50
15 Chris Stewart .40 1.00
16 Curtis Joseph .50 1.25
17 Brett Hull .50 1.25
18 David Backes .50 1.25
19 Jaroslav Halak .50 1.25
20 Patrick Marleau .50 1.25
21 Joe Pavelski .50 1.25
22 Antti Niemi .40 1.00
23 Chris Kunitz .50 1.25
24 Kris Letang .50 1.25
25 Paul Coffey .50 1.25
26 Evgeni Malkin 1.50 4.00
27 James Neal .50 1.25
28 Mario Lemieux 1.50 4.00
29 Sidney Crosby 2.00 5.00
30 Mike Smith .50 1.25
31 Shane Doan .40 1.00
32 Claude Giroux .50 1.25
33 Eric Lindros .75 2.00
34 Scott Hartnell .50 1.25
35 Dave Schultz .50 1.25
36 Erik Karlsson 1.00 2.50
37 Jason Spezza .50 1.25
38 Rick Nash .50 1.25
39 Theoren Fleury .60 1.50
40 Mark Messier .60 1.50
41 Henrik Lundqvist .60 1.50
42 Mike Bossy .50 1.25
43 John Tavares 1.00 2.50
44 Cory Schneider .40 1.00
45 Adam Henrique .50 1.25
46 Martin Brodeur 1.00 2.50
47 Pekka Rinne .60 1.50
48 Jean Beliveau .50 1.25
49 Larry Robinson .50 1.25
50 P.K. Subban .75 2.00
51 Carey Price 1.50 4.00
52 Zach Parise .50 1.25
53 Mikko Koivu .40 1.00
54 Niklas Backstrom .40 1.00
55 Jari Kurri .50 1.25
56 Wayne Gretzky 2.50 6.00
57 Anze Kopitar .75 2.00
58 Drew Doughty .50 1.25
59 Mike Richards .50 1.25

Jeff Carter .50 1.25
Jonathan Quick .75 2.00
Ron Francis .60 1.50
Pavel Bure .60 1.50
Grant Fuhr .50 1.25
Bill Ranford .50 1.25
Jordan Eberle .50 1.25
7 Ryan Nugent-Hopkins .50 1.25
Taylor Hall 1.00 2.50
Chris Osgood .50 1.25
Nicklas Lidstrom .50 1.25
Pavel Datsyuk .60 1.50
2 Jamie Benn .60 1.50
3 Marian Gaborik .50 1.25
4 Joe Sakic .75 2.00
5 Matt Duchene .50 1.25
6 Gabriel Landeskog .40 1.00
7 Corey Crawford .60 1.50
8 Tony Esposito .50 1.25
9 Jonathan Toews 1.00 2.50
0 Marian Hossa .40 1.00
1 Patrick Kane 1.00 2.50
2 Jeff Skinner .40 1.00
3 Eric Staal .60 1.50
4 Jordan Staal .50 1.25
5 Jiri Tlusty .40 1.00
6 Thomas Vanek .50 1.25
7 Gilbert Perreault .50 1.25
8 Cody Hodgson .50 1.25
9 Cam Neely .50 1.25
0 Brad Marchand .60 1.50
1 Tuukka Rask .50 1.25
2 Patrice Bergeron .60 1.50
3 Ray Bourque .75 2.00
4 Terry O'Reilly .40 1.00
5 Bobby Orr 1.50 4.00
6 Zdeno Chara .50 1.25
7 Jonas Hiller .40 1.00
8 Corey Perry .50 1.25
9 Ryan Getzlaf .75 2.00
00 Teemu Selanne 1.00 2.50
01 Alex Galchenyuk/27 RC 200.00 350.00
02 Zemgus Girgensons/28 RC 60.00 120.00
03 Richard Panik/71 RC 10.00 25.00
04 Ryan Murray/27 RC 40.00 80.00
05 Michael Latta/46 RC 15.00 40.00
06 Hampus Lindholm/47 RC 20.00 50.00
07 Mikael Granlund/64 RC 15.00 40.00
08 Boone Jenner/38 RC 15.00 40.00
09 Anton Belov/77 RC 10.00 25.00
10 Matt Tennyson/80 RC 6.00 15.00
12 Ondrej Palat/18 RC 30.00 60.00
13 Justin Schultz/19 RC 60.00 120.00
14 Drew Shore/15 RC 25.00 60.00
15 Ryan Spooner/51 RC 12.00 30.00
16 Austin Watson/52 RC 10.00 25.00
117 Tom Wilson/43 RC 20.00 50.00
121 Eric Gryba/62 RC 8.00 20.00
122 Stefan Matteau/15 RC 12.00 30.00
123 Tanner Pearson/70 RC 15.00 40.00
125 Cristopher Nilstorp/41 RC 10.00 25.00
126 Mark Arcobello/26 RC 15.00 40.00
127 Jordan Schroeder/45 RC 12.00 30.00
128 Joakim Nordstrom/42 RC 10.00 25.00
129 Sami Vatanen/45 RC 12.00 30.00
130 Matthew Irwin/52 RC 10.00 25.00
131 Quinton Howden/42 RC 10.00 25.00
132 Emerson Etem/65 RC 10.00 25.00
133 Rasmus Ristolainen/55 RC 40.00 80.00
134 Josh Leivo/32 RC 12.00 30.00
135 Tomas Hertl/48 RC 30.00 80.00
136 Dougie Hamilton/27 RC 50.00 100.00
138 Elias Lindholm/16 RC 30.00 60.00
139 Calvin Pickard/31 RC 15.00 40.00
140 Brian Flynn/65 RC 8.00 20.00
142 Jonas Brodin/25 RC 12.00 30.00
144 Cameron Schilling/45 RC 8.00 20.00
146 Michael Bournival/49 RC 12.00 30.00
147 Lucas Lessio/22 RC 15.00 40.00
148 Nick Petrecki/54 RC 8.00 20.00
149 Mathew Dumba/55 RC 12.00 30.00
151 Carl Soderberg/34 RC 12.00 30.00
152 Nathan MacKinnon/29 RC 700.00 1000.00
153 Cory Conacher/89 RC 6.00 15.00
155 Jarred Tinordi/24 RC 15.00 40.00
156 Nicklas Jensen/46 RC 10.00 25.00
158 Andrej Sustr/62 RC 6.00 15.00
159 Jamie Devane/59 RC 10.00 25.00
160 Aleksander Barkov/16 RC 125.00 200.00
161 Alex Killorn/17 RC
163 Eric Gelinas/32 RC 12.00 30.00
165 Viktor Fasth/30 RC 12.00 30.00
167 Connor Carrick/58 RC 10.00 25.00
168 Vladimir Tarasenko/91 RC 60.00 120.00
169 Spencer Abbott/56 RC 10.00 25.00
171 Petr Mrazek/34 RC 25.00 60.00
172 Scott Laughton/21 RC 15.00 40.00
173 Matt Nieto/83 RC 8.00 20.00
174 Frank Corrado/26 RC 12.00 30.00
175 Chris Brown/44 RC 8.00 20.00
177 Christian Thomas/60 RC 8.00 20.00
179 Jean-Gabriel Pageau/44 RC 10.00 25.00
180 Rickard Rakell/67 RC 10.00 25.00
182 Edward Pasquale/32 RC 15.00 40.00
183 Sean Monahan/23 RC 100.00 200.00
184 Mikhail Grigorenko/25 RC 40.00 80.00
185 Nail Yakupov/64 RC 60.00 120.00
187 Valeri Nichushkin/43 RC 60.00 120.00
188 Max Reinhart/59 RC 12.00 30.00
189 Morgan Rielly/44 RC 50.00 100.00
190 Will Acton/41 RC 10.00 25.00
191 Brock Nelson/29 RC 15.00 40.00
192 Brian Lashoff/23 RC 12.00 30.00
193 Tye McGinn/15 RC 30.00 60.00
194 Tyler Toffoli/73 RC 30.00 60.00
196 Beau Bennett/19 RC 40.00 80.00
198 Nick Bjugstad/27 RC 25.00 50.00
199 Nathan Beaulieu/40 RC 15.00 40.00
200 Danny DeKeyser/65 RC 12.00 30.00

2013-14 SP Game Used Authentic Fabrics

GROUP A ODDS 1:86
GROUP B ODDS 1:136
GROUP C ODDS 1:24
GROUP D ODDS 1:6
OVERALL ODDS 1:4
*GOLD/52-99: .6X TO 1.5X BASIC JSY C-D
*GOLD/52-99: .5X TO 1.2X BASIC JSY A-B
*GOLD/31-46: .8X TO 2X BASIC JSY C-D
*GOLD/31-46: .6X TO 1.5X BASIC JSY A-B
*GOLD/15-26: 1X TO 2.5X BASIC JSY C-D
*GOLD/15-26: .8X TO 2X BASIC JSY A-B
*FIGHT STRAP/15: 1X TO 2.5X BASIC JSY C-D
*FIGHT STRAP/15: .8X TO 2X BASIC JSY A-B
*PATCH/35: 1X TO 2.5X BASIC JSY C-D
*PATCH/35: .8X TO 2X BASIC JSY A-B
AFAL Andrew Ladd D 3.00 8.00
AFAO Alexander Ovechkin C 12.00 30.00
AFBC Brian Campbell C 2.00 5.00
AFBE Brian Elliott D 2.50 6.00
AFBR Dustin Brown D 3.00 8.00
AFCP Carey Price D 4.00 10.00
AFCS Chris Stewart C 2.50 6.00
AFDB David Backes D 3.00 8.00
AFDK David Krejci D 3.00 8.00
AFDP Dion Phaneuf D 3.00 8.00
AFEL Eric Lindros A 6.00 15.00
AFES Eric Staal A 5.00 12.00
AFGF Grant Fuhr C 5.00 12.00
AFGL Gabriel Landeskog D 2.50 6.00
AFGR Mike Green D 3.00 8.00
AFHZ Henrik Zetterberg C 4.00 10.00
AFJA Jake Allen B 5.00 12.00
AFJB Jamie Benn D 4.00 10.00
AFJC Jeff Carter D 3.00 8.00
AFJE Jordan Eberle D 6.00 15.00
AFJH Jonas Hiller D 2.50 6.00
AFJQ Jonathan Quick D 5.00 12.00
AFJS Joe Sakic B 5.00 12.00
AFKL Kari Lehtonen D 2.50 6.00
AFKY Keith Yandle D 3.00 8.00
AFLE Lars Eller A 3.00 8.00
AFLS Luke Schenn D 2.00 5.00
AFLU Milan Lucic D 3.00 8.00
AFMC Michael Cammalleri D 2.50 6.00
AFMG Michel Goulet D 2.50 6.00
AFMK Mikko Koivu D 3.00 8.00
AFML Mario Lemieux A 12.00 30.00
AFMR Mike Richards D 3.00 8.00
AFMS Mats Sundin D 3.00 8.00
AFMT Maxime Talbot D 3.00 8.00
AFNB Nicklas Backstrom D 5.00 12.00
AFPA P.A. Parenteau D 2.00 5.00
AFPE Corey Perry D 3.00 8.00
AFPR Pekka Rinne D 4.00 10.00
AFPS P.K. Subban D 5.00 12.00
AFRC Ryan Callahan C 3.00 8.00
AFRG Ryan Getzlaf D 5.00 12.00
AFRN Ryan Nugent-Hopkins D 3.00 8.00
AFSC Sidney Crosby B 15.00 40.00
AFSD Shane Doan D 2.50 6.00
AFSG Simon Gagne D 3.00 8.00
AFST Paul Stastny C 3.00 8.00
AFSW Shea Weber D 2.50 6.00
AFTE Tyler Ennis D 3.00 8.00
AFTH Taylor Hall C 6.00 15.00
AFTM Tyler Myers A 3.00 8.00
AFTP Tomas Plekanec C 3.00 8.00
AFTV Thomas Vanek D 3.00 8.00
AFVV Slava Voynov D 2.50 6.00
AFWG Wayne Gretzky A 15.00 40.00
AFWS Wayne Simmonds A 5.00 12.00
AFZB Zach Bogosian A 3.00 8.00
AFZC Zdeno Chara C 3.00 8.00

2013-14 SP Game Used Authentic Fabrics Dual

GROUP A ODDS 1:1544
GROUP B ODDS 1:796
GROUP C ODDS 1:141
GROUP D ODDS 1:11
OVERALL ODDS 1:10
*PATCH/25: .8X TO 2X BASIC DUAL
AF2BM E.Belfour/M.Modano C 6.00 15.00
AF2BS D.Backes/C.Stewart D 4.00 10.00
AF2CB Z.Chara/R.Bourque D 6.00 15.00
AF2CR T.Rask/Z.Chara D 4.00 10.00
AF2DV D.Doughty/S.Voynov D 6.00 15.00
AF2DY Datsyuk/S.Yzerman D 10.00 25.00
AF2EH J.Eberle/T.Hall D 8.00 20.00
AF2EK I.Kovalchuk/P.Elias B 5.00 12.00
AF2FH P.Forsberg/R.Hextall D 5.00 12.00
AF2FL M.Fleury/K.Letang C 6.00 15.00
AF2GB Backstrom/M.Green D 6.00 15.00
AF2GP R.Getzlaf/C.Perry D 6.00 15.00
AF2HG A.Hemsky/S.Gagner D 3.00 8.00
AF2HH J.Howard/D.Hasek D 5.00 12.00
AF2KC D.Keith/C.Crawford D 5.00 12.00
AF2LB K.Lehtonen/J.Benn D 5.00 12.00
AF2LM M.Lucic/B.Marchand D 5.00 12.00
AF2LS R.Luongo/H.Sedin D 4.00 10.00
AF2MT Marleau/J.Thornton D 4.00 10.00
AF2NH M.Neuvirth/B.Holtby D 6.00 15.00
AF2NQ A.Niemi/J.Quick D 6.00 15.00
AF2OH B.Holtby/A.Ovechkin D 5.00 12.00
AF2PD Parenteau/M.Duchene D 4.00 10.00
AF2PE T.Plekanec/L.Eller D 4.00 10.00
AF2PK O.Pavelec/E.Kane D 4.00 10.00
AF2PS Plekanec/P.Subban A 10.00 25.00
AF2RC M.Richards/J.Carter D 4.00 10.00
AF2RW S.Weber/P.Rinne D 5.00 12.00
AF2SA J.Spezza/C.Anderson C 4.00 10.00
AF2SG M.Sundin/D.Gilmour D 6.00 15.00
AF2SH J.Sakic/M.Hejduk D 6.00 15.00
AF2VS T.Vanek/D.Stafford D 4.00 10.00
AF2YJ K.Yandle/C.Joseph D 4.00 10.00

2013-14 SP Game Used Authentic Fabrics Dual Patches

STATED PRINT RUN 25 SER.#'d SETS
AF2BL P.Bergeron/M.Lucic 10.00 25.00
AF2BM E.Belfour/M.Modano 12.00 30.00
AF2BS D.Backes/C.Stewart 8.00 20.00
AF2CB Z.Chara/R.Bourque 12.00 30.00
AF2CR T.Rask/Z.Chara 8.00 20.00
AF2CS R.Callahan/D.Stepan 8.00 20.00
AF2DV D.Doughty/S.Voynov 12.00 30.00
AF2EH J.Eberle/T.Hall 15.00 40.00
AF2EK I.Kovalchuk/P.Elias 8.00 20.00
AF2FL M.Fleury/K.Letang 12.00 30.00
AF2GB N.Backstrom/M.Green 12.00 30.00
AF2GL C.Giroux/S.Laughton 8.00 20.00
AF2GP R.Getzlaf/C.Perry 12.00 30.00
AF2GS C.Giroux/W.Simmonds 10.00 25.00
AF2HG A.Hemsky/S.Gagner 6.00 15.00
AF2HH J.Howard/D.Hasek 10.00 25.00
AF2KC D.Keith/C.Crawford 10.00 25.00
AF2KE N.Kronwall/J.Ericsson 6.00 15.00
AF2KY I.Kovalchuk/N.Yakupov 10.00 25.00
AF2LB K.Lehtonen/J.Benn 10.00 25.00
AF2LM M.Lucic/B.Marchand 10.00 25.00
AF2NH M.Neuvirth/B.Holtby 12.00 30.00
AF2NQ A.Niemi/J.Quick 12.00 30.00
AF2OH B.Holtby/A.Ovechkin 15.00 40.00
AF2PD P.Parenteau/M.Duchene 8.00 20.00
AF2PE T.Plekanec/L.Eller 8.00 20.00
AF2PS T.Plekanec/P.Subban 12.00 30.00
AF2RC M.Richards/J.Carter 8.00 20.00
AF2RW S.Weber/P.Rinne 10.00 25.00
AF2SA J.Spezza/C.Anderson 8.00 20.00
AF2SD P.Stastny/M.Duchene 8.00 20.00
AF2SH J.Sakic/M.Hejduk 12.00 30.00
AF2VS T.Vanek/D.Stafford 8.00 20.00
AF2YJ K.Yandle/C.Joseph 8.00 20.00

2013-14 SP Game Used Authentic Fabrics Eights

OVERALL ODDS 1:1325 HOB
AF8CAN Canadian Stars
AF8NET Goalie Stars
AF8RUS Russian Stars 40.00 80.00
AF8SWE Swedish Stars
AF8STAR All-Stars

2013-14 SP Game Used Authentic Fabrics Fives

STATED ODDS 1:108
AF5CAP Ovc/Grn/Hlt/Bks/Nv 50.00 125.00
AF5COL Dch/Lnd/Sts/McK/Prn 25.00 50.00
AF5DAL Lht/Bn/Nls/Dly/Cmp 12.00 30.00
AF5DET Dts/Hwd/Lds/Mrz/DKy 15.00 40.00
AF5EDM Hll/Ebr/Sch/Hms/RNH
AF5GR8 Grt/Ry/Yzr/Hwrk/Hll 60.00 120.00
AF5LAK Qck/Kpt/Crtr/Vyn/Tfli 25.00 60.00
AF5NJD Els/Kvlk/Hnr/Brdr/Zjc 25.00 60.00
AF5NYR Cln/Stp/Nsh/Lnd/Rch 12.00 30.00
AF5SJS Hrt/Ctr/Mrl/Ptrcki/Nmi 25.00 60.00
AF5STL Stw/Ptn/Elt/Bck/Brgl 12.00 30.00
AF5TOR Blf/Glm/Jsp/Lnd/Snd 20.00 50.00

2013-14 SP Game Used Authentic Fabrics Quads

GROUP A ODDS 1:1,460
GROUP B ODDS 1:105
OVERALL ODDS 1:98
AF4COL Dch/Lnds/Hjdk/Stst B 8.00 20.00
AF4DAL Mdn/Lhtn/Bnn/Dley B 12.00 30.00
AF4DET Yzm/Dts/Mrzk/DKy B 12.00 30.00
AF4EDM RNH/Ykv/Hll/Ebr B 12.00 30.00
AF4HOF Hll/Lmx/Skc/Sndn B 25.00 60.00
AF4KINGS Kptr/Qck/Dgh/Vyn B 12.00 30.00
AF4LAK Kptr/Rchr/Crtr/Wlms B 12.00 30.00
AF4NYR Stp/Nsh/Clhn/Hgln A 8.00 20.00
AF4OTT Spz/Andr/Krls/Cnch B 8.00 20.00
AF4PIT Mlkn/Ltng/Flry/Nl B 25.00 60.00
AF4STL Stwt/Aln/Ellt/Bcks B 10.00 25.00

2013-14 SP Game Used Authentic Fabrics Sevens

STATED ODDS 1:720
AF7G Goalie Stars 30.00 60.00
AF7CHI Chicago Stars
AF7EDM Edmonton Stars 25.00 50.00
AF7LAK L.A. Kings Stars 30.00 60.00
AF7MON Montreal Stars 40.00 80.00

2013-14 SP Game Used Authentic Fabrics Sixes

STATED ODDS 1:300 HOB
AF6BOSNYR Boston/NY Stars
AF6CARNAS Carolina/Nashville 15.00 40.00
AF6CHISTL Chicago/St.Louis 15.00 40.00
AF6COLDET Colorado/Detroit 15.00 40.00
AF6LAKANA LA/Anaheim Stars 15.00 40.00
AF6LAKSJS LA/San Jose Stars 15.00 40.00

2013-14 SP Game Used Authentic Fabrics Triples

GROUP A ODDS 1:740
GROUP B ODDS 1:30
OVERALL ODDS 1:28
*PATCH/15: 1.2X TO 3X BASIC TRIPLE
AF3ANA Gtzlf/Prry/Hller B 8.00 20.00
AF3AVS Brque/Roy/Skic B 12.00 30.00
AF3BUF Myrs/Adam/Vnek B 5.00 12.00
AF3CAPS Ovchkn/Bkstrm/Hltby B 6.00 15.00
AF3CHI Toews/Kne/Kth B 10.00 25.00
AF3DAL Lhtnen/Benn/Dley B 6.00 15.00
AF3DRW Yzrmn/Dtsyk/DKysr B 8.00 20.00
AF3EDM Hpkns/Ebrle/Hall B 6.00 15.00
AF3GR8 Roy/Grtzky/Lmeux B 25.00 50.00
AF3HOF Skic/Sndin/Lmeux B 15.00 40.00
AF3JETS Byfgln/Pvlec/Kane B 5.00 12.00
AF3KINGS Rchrds/Crtr/Kptr B 8.00 20.00
AF3LAK Quick/Dghty/Kptar B 5.00 12.00
AF3LBBR Sbbn/Prce/Glchnyk B 12.00 30.00
AF3NJD Brdeur/Kvlchk/Hnrqe B 10.00 25.00
AF3OIL Ykpv/Hpkns/Hall B 8.00 20.00
AF3OTT Spzza/Krlssn/Lhnr B 10.00 25.00
AF3USA Brwn/Ststny/Quick A 8.00 20.00
AF3WIN Bgsian/Kne/Byfgln B 5.00 12.00

2013-14 SP Game Used Draft Day Marks

EACH CARD SERIAL #'d TO 10-35
TOTAL PRINT RUNS MUCH HIGHER
EACH HAS MULTIPLE CARDS OF EQUAL VALUE
EXCH EXPIRATION: 1/6/2016
YEAR 2012-13 PRINTED ON BACKS
DDMAB1 A.Barkov A/35 20.00 50.00
DDMAG1 Alex Galchenyuk A/35 40.00 100.00
DDMAO1 A.Ovechkin C/10 60.00 120.00
DDMBH1 Brett Hull H/10 40.00 80.00
DDMBJ1 Nick Bjugstad A/35 15.00 40.00
DDMBN1 Brock Nelson E/35 12.00 30.00
DDMCC1 Charlie Coyle C/35 8.00 20.00
DDMCT1 Christian Thomas A/35 6.00 15.00
DDMDH1 Dougie Hamilton A/35 20.00 50.00
DDMDM1 Dylan McIlrath A/35 8.00 20.00
DDMEE1 Emerson Etem E/70* 8.00 20.00
DDMEL1 Eric Lindros D/10 40.00 80.00
DDMGR1 Mikael Granlund A/35 12.00 30.00
DDMJB1 Jonas Brodin B/35 6.00 15.00
DDMJC1 Jack Campbell A/35 12.00 30.00
DDMJH1 J.Huberdeau A/35 20.00 50.00
DDMJO1 Jamie Oleksiak A/35 6.00 15.00
DDMJU1 Justin Schultz C/35 8.00 20.00
DDMMA1 Stefan Matteau A/70* 6.00 15.00
DDMMD1 Mathew Dumba A/35 8.00 20.00
DDMMG1 M.Grigorenko E/35 10.00 25.00
DDMMJ1 Jon Merrill E/35 8.00 20.00
DDMMR1 Morgan Rielly E/35 40.00 80.00
DDMNB1 Nathan Beaulieu A/35 6.00 15.00
DDMNJ1 Nicklas Jensen E/70* 10.00 25.00
DDMNM1 N.MacKinnon A/35 75.00 150.00
DDMNY1 Nail Yakupov A/35 25.00 60.00
DDMPF1 Peter Forsberg B/10 100.00 175.00
DDMPK1 P.Kane A/10 EXCH 40.00 80.00
DDMPM1 Petr Mrazek A/35 15.00 40.00
DDMPR1 Patrick Roy O/10 150.00 225.00
DDMQH1 Quinton Howden D/35 8.00 20.00
DDMRM1 Ryan Murray A/35 12.00 30.00
DDMSJ1 Seth Jones E/35 15.00 40.00
DDMSM1 Sean Monahan A/70* 30.00 60.00
DDMTI1 Jarred Tinordi D/35 8.00 20.00
DDMTJ1 Jacob Trouba A/35 25.00 50.00
DDMTT1 Tyler Toffoli F/70* 30.00 60.00
DDMTW1 Tom Wilson I/35 15.00 40.00
DDMVN1 Valeri Nichushkin C/35 20.00 50.00
DDMZG1 Z.Girgensons E/35 25.00 50.00

2013-14 SP Game Used Gold Autographs

GROUP A ODDS 1:3540
GROUP B ODDS 1:104
GROUP C ODDS 1:125
GROUP D ODDS 1:84
OVERALL ODDS 1:42
1 Dale Hawerchuk C 10.00 25.00
3 Alexander Ovechkin B 25.00 60.00
6 Alexandre Burrows D 6.00 15.00
7 Markus Naslund C 6.00 15.00
8 Ryan Kesler C 8.00 20.00
9 Trevor Linden D 8.00 20.00
12 Dion Phaneuf C 8.00 20.00
13 Phil Kessel C 10.00 25.00
14 Steven Stamkos B 20.00 50.00
15 Chris Stewart B 8.00 20.00
16 Curtis Joseph C 8.00 20.00
17 Brett Hull A 15.00 40.00
18 David Backes D 6.00 15.00
19 Jaroslav Halak D 6.00 15.00
21 Joe Pavelski B
22 Antti Niemi D 5.00 12.00
23 Chris Kunitz D 6.00 15.00
25 Paul Coffey C 8.00 20.00
26 Evgeni Malkin B 30.00 80.00
28 Mario Lemieux B 60.00 100.00
29 Sidney Crosby B 60.00 150.00
31 Shane Doan D 4.00 10.00
34 Scott Hartnell D 6.00 15.00
35 Dave Schultz C 8.00 20.00
37 Jason Spezza B 8.00 20.00
38 Rick Nash B 20.00
40 Mark Messier A 25.00
42 Mike Bossy B 10.00 25.00
43 John Tavares D 15.00 30.00
44 Cory Schneider D 5.00 12.00
45 Adam Henrique C 10.00 25.00
48 Jean Beliveau B 30.00 60.00
49 Larry Robinson C 8.00 20.00
52 Zach Parise C 8.00 20.00
55 Jari Kurri C 8.00 20.00
56 Wayne Gretzky C 75.00 150.00
57 Anze Kopitar C 12.00 30.00
59 Mike Richards C 8.00 20.00
60 Jeff Carter C 12.00 30.00
62 Ron Francis B 12.00 30.00
64 Grant Fuhr B 10.00 25.00
65 Bill Ranford D 6.00 15.00
67 Ryan Nugent-Hopkins C 10.00 25.00
68 Taylor Hall C 15.00 40.00
69 Chris Osgood D 6.00 15.00
70 Nicklas Lidstrom C 5.00 12.00
71 Pavel Datsyuk B 40.00 80.00
72 Jamie Benn D 8.00 20.00
73 Marian Gaborik B 10.00 25.00
78 Tony Esposito B 15.00 30.00
82 Jeff Skinner B
83 Eric Staal B
84 Jordan Staal D 6.00 15.00
85 Jiri Tlusty D 4.00 10.00
87 Gilbert Perreault C 8.00 20.00
89 Cam Neely C 8.00 20.00
90 Brad Marchand B
91 Tuukka Rask D 10.00 25.00
92 Patrice Bergeron B 20.00 50.00
93 Ray Bourque B 25.00 50.00
94 Terry O'Reilly C 6.00 15.00
95 Bobby Orr C 60.00 120.00
101 Alex Galchenyuk D 15.00 40.00
103 Richard Panik B 5.00 12.00
104 Ryan Murray A 12.00 30.00
107 Mikael Granlund A 10.00 25.00
108 Boone Jenner D 15.00
113 Justin Schultz A 6.00 15.00
114 Drew Shore B 4.00 10.00
115 Ryan Spooner C 8.00 20.00
116 Austin Watson D 3.00 8.00
117 Tom Wilson D 6.00 15.00
122 Stefan Matteau D 3.00 8.00
123 Tanner Pearson D 6.00 15.00
127 Jordan Schroeder B 5.00 12.00
131 Quinton Howden D 3.00 8.00
132 Emerson Etem B 5.00 12.00
133 Rasmus Ristolainen B 8.00 20.00
135 Tomas Hertl D 8.00 20.00
136 Dougie Hamilton B 10.00 25.00
137 Thomas Hickey D 3.00 8.00
138 Elias Lindholm A 10.00 25.00
145 Alex Chiasson D 4.00 10.00
148 Nick Petrecki D 2.50 6.00
150 Mark Pysyk D 4.00 10.00
152 Nathan MacKinnon A 30.00 80.00
153 Cory Conacher C 3.00 8.00
155 Jarred Tinordi D 5.00 12.00
156 Nicklas Jensen C 4.00 10.00
160 Aleksander Barkov C 8.00 20.00
162 Seth Jones B 5.00 12.00
164 Jack Campbell D 3.00 8.00
165 Viktor Fasth D 4.00 10.00
170 Jamie Oleksiak D 3.00 8.00
171 Petr Mrazek B 15.00 40.00
172 Scott Laughton C 5.00 12.00
175 Chris Brown D 2.50 6.00
176 Jonathan Huberdeau A 10.00 25.00
177 Christian Thomas C 4.00 10.00
179 Jean-Gabriel Pageau D 3.00 8.00
181 Brendan Gallagher A 20.00 50.00
183 Sean Monahan B 8.00 20.00
184 Mikhail Grigorenko D 5.00 12.00
185 Nail Yakupov A 12.00 30.00
187 Valeri Nichushkin A 10.00 25.00
188 Max Reinhart D 4.00 10.00
189 Morgan Rielly B 20.00 40.00
191 Brock Nelson C 5.00 12.00
192 Brian Lashoff D 3.00 8.00
193 Tye McGinn D 5.00 12.00
194 Tyler Toffoli C 8.00 20.00
195 Jesper Fast D 3.00 8.00
196 Beau Bennett D 6.00 15.00
197 Jacob Trouba A 20.00 50.00
198 Nick Bjugstad C 6.00 15.00
199 Nathan Beaulieu D 3.00 8.00
200 Danny DeKeyser C 6.00 15.00

2013-14 SP Game Used Inked Rookie Sweaters

*PATCH/25: .6X TO 1.5X BASIC JSY AU
IRSAG Alex Galchenyuk 25.00 60.00
IRSBB Beau Bennett 6.00 15.00
IRSBG Brendan Gallagher 15.00 40.00
IRSCC Cory Conacher 3.00 8.00
IRSDH Dougie Hamilton 12.00 30.00
IRSEE Emerson Etem 6.00 15.00
IRSGR Mikhail Grigorenko 8.00 20.00
IRSJC Jack Campbell 5.00 12.00
IRSJH Jonathan Huberdeau 10.00 25.00
IRSJS Justin Schultz 5.00 12.00
IRSJT Jarred Tinordi 5.00 12.00
IRSMG Mikael Granlund 8.00 20.00
IRSNB Nathan Beaulieu 4.00 10.00
IRSNY Nail Yakupov 15.00 40.00
IRSPM Petr Mrazek 8.00 20.00
IRSQH Quinton Howden 4.00 10.00
IRSRS Ryan Spooner 8.00 20.00
IRSSC Jordan Schroeder 5.00 12.00
IRSSL Scott Laughton 8.00 20.00
IRSSM Stefan Matteau 6.00 15.00
IRSTT Tyler Toffoli 10.00 25.00
IRSVF Viktor Fasth 5.00 12.00

2013-14 SP Game Used Inked Sweaters

ISAH Adam Henrique/99 6.00 15.00
ISAK Anze Kopitar/99 8.00 20.00
ISAN Antti Niemi/99 10.00 25.00
ISAO Alexander Ovechkin/25
ISCP Carey Price/25 30.00 80.00
ISDB David Backes/99 6.00 15.00
ISDH Dale Hawerchuk/50 10.00 25.00
ISDP Dion Phaneuf/50 8.00 20.00
ISEM Evgeni Malkin/50 20.00 40.00
ISJS Jeff Skinner/50 6.00 15.00
ISJT Jonathan Toews/50
ISMB Martin Brodeur/25
ISMK Mikko Koivu/99 6.00 15.00
ISMR Matt Read/99 4.00 10.00
ISMS Marc Staal/99 5.00 12.00
ISPB Patrice Bergeron/50 15.00 40.00
ISPK Patrick Kane/25 20.00 50.00
ISRI Pekka Rinne/99 8.00 20.00
ISRN Ryan Nugent-Hopkins/50 8.00 20.00
ISSC Sidney Crosby/25 40.00 100.00
ISSG Sam Gagner/99 5.00 12.00
ISSW Shea Weber/50 6.00 15.00
ISTE Tony Esposito/25 20.00 50.00
ISTH Taylor Hall/50 15.00 40.00
ISVD Vincent Damphousse/99 5.00 12.00
ISWG Wayne Gretzky/25 150.00 300.00

2013-14 SP Game Used Rookie Fabrics

GROUP A ODDS 1:34 HOB
GROUP B ODDS 1:9 HOB
OVERALL ODDS 1:7 HOB
*FIGHT STRAP/15: 1.2X TO 3X BASIC JSY
*GOLD/40-91: .6X TO 1.5X BASIC JSY
*GOLD/25-34: .8X TO 2X BASIC JSY
*GOLD/19-24: 1X TO 2.5X BASIC JSY
*PATCH/35: .8X TO 2X BASIC JSY
RFAG Alex Galchenyuk B 6.00 15.00
RFBB Beau Bennett A 4.00 10.00
RFBG Brendan Gallagher B 5.00 12.00
RFCC Charlie Coyle B 2.50 6.00
RFCO Cory Conacher B 1.50 4.00
RFDB Damien Brunner B 2.00 5.00
RFDH Dougie Hamilton A 5.00 12.00
RFEE Emerson Etem A 2.50 6.00
RFGR Mikael Granlund B 4.00 10.00
RFJB Jonas Brodin B 2.00 5.00
RFJC Jack Campbell A 2.00 5.00
RFJH Jonathan Huberdeau B 4.00 10.00
RFJS Justin Schultz A 2.50 6.00
RFJT Jarred Tinordi B 2.50 6.00
RFMG Mikhail Grigorenko B 3.00 8.00
RFMO Sean Monahan B 8.00 20.00
RFMR Morgan Rielly B 6.00 15.00
RFMU Ryan Murray B 4.00 10.00
RFNB Nathan Beaulieu B 4.00 10.00
RFNM Nathan MacKinnon B 8.00 20.00
RFNY Nail Yakupov B 5.00 12.00
RFPM Petr Mrazek B 4.00 10.00
RFQH Quinton Howden B 2.00 5.00
RFRM Ryan Murphy B 2.50 6.00
RFSC Jordan Schroeder B 2.50 6.00
RFSL Scott Laughton B 2.50 6.00
RFTT Tyler Toffoli A 4.00 10.00
RFVF Viktor Fasth A 2.50 6.00
RFVN Valeri Nichushkin B 5.00 12.00
RFVT Vladimir Tarasenko B 4.00 10.00

2013-14 SP Game Used Rookie Fabrics Dual

OVERALL ODDS 1:18 HOB
*PATCH/25: .8X TO 2X BASIC DUAL
RF2BL B.Bennett/S.Laughton 3.00 8.00
RF2CG C.Coyle/M.Granlund 4.00 10.00
RF2CO J.Campbell/J.Oleksiak 2.00 5.00
RF2CP C.Conacher/J.Pageau 2.00 5.00
RF2DM D.DeKeyser/P.Mrazek 5.00 12.00
RF2GB A.Galchenyuk/N.Beaulieu 6.00 15.00
RF2GG A.Galchenyuk/B.Gallagher 6.00 15.00
RF2HH J.Huberdeau/Q.Howden 4.00 10.00
RF2HS D.Hamilton/R.Spooner 4.00 10.00
RF2MJ R.Murray/B.Jenner 4.00 10.00
RF2SY J.Schultz/N.Yakupov 5.00 12.00
RF2TG J.Tinordi/B.Gallagher 6.00 15.00
RF2TH T.Toffoli/T.Hertl 5.00 12.00
RF2YM N.Yakupov/N.MacKinnon 12.00 30.00

2013-14 SP Game Used Rookie Fabrics Fives

OVERALL ODDS 1:216 HOB
RF5DEF Hmln/Sch/Mph/Beli/Bdin 8.00 20.00
RF5FWD Yv/Gch/Hbr/Glghr/Cnc 20.00 50.00
RF5USA Etm/Cmbl/Cyl/Bnt/Schr 10.00 25.00
RF5EAST Hmt/Cnch/Glch/Ggr/Hbr 20.00 50.00
RF5WEST Ykv/Sch/MKn/Trsn/My 15.00 40.00
RF5CANADA Hbrd/Hw/Bel/Olk/Tfl 12.00 30.00

2013-14 SP Game Used Rookie Fabrics Quads

OVERALL ODDS 1:101 HOB
RF4MON Glch/Glghr/Tnrdi/Blieu 10.00 25.00
RF4RUS Grgn/Ykpv/Trsnko/Nch 10.00 25.00
RF4USA Etm/Bntt/Glchn/Tnrdi 8.00 20.00
RF4CAND Schltz/Hmltn/Mrph/Beli 5.00 12.00

2013-14 SP Game Used Rookie Fabrics Sevens

OVERALL ODD 1:900 HOB
RF7DEF Hm/Olk/Sc/Br/Tn/Bl/Mp
RF7FWD Cn/Gr/MK/Yk/Hb/Gl/Ts 20.00 50.00
RF7USA Et/Cy/Gc/Tn/Mu/Bn/Sc
RF7CANADA Sp/Olk/Sc/Hw/Bl/Lg/Py

2013-14 SP Game Used Rookie Fabrics Triples

OVERALL ODDS 1:69 HOB
RF3G Mrzk/Pckrd/Cmpbll 6.00 15.00
RF3ANA Fasth/Etem/Rakell 3.00 8.00
RF3FWD Trsnko/Ykpv/Glchnyk 8.00 20.00
RF3MIN Grnlnd/Brdn/Cyle 5.00 12.00
RF3MON Blieu/Gllghr/Glchnyk 10.00 25.00

2013-14 SP Game Used SIGnificant Numbers Autographs

SNAG Alex Galchenyuk/27 100.00 175.00
SNCC Cory Conacher/89 5.00 12.00
SNCH Carl Hagelin/62 8.00 20.00
SNCO Charlie Coyle/63 8.00 20.00
SNJS Joe Sakic/19 20.00 40.00
SNJT Jonathan Toews/19 30.00 60.00
SNNY Nail Yakupov/64 30.00 60.00
SNRN Ryan Nugent-Hopkins/93 15.00 40.00

2013-14 SP Game Used Stanley Cup Finals Materials Game Used Puck

STATED ODDS 1:1100
SCGUPAS Andrew Shaw
SCGUPBB Bryan Bickell
SCGUPBS Brent Seabrook
SCGUPCC Corey Crawford 40.00 80.00
SCGUPDB Dave Bolland
SCGUPDP Daniel Paille
SCGUPKA Patrick Kane
SCGUPML Milan Lucic 20.00 50.00
SCGUPPB Patrice Bergeron 30.00 80.00
SCGUPPK Patrick Kane
SCGUPRA Tuukka Rask 20.00 50.00
SCGUPTR Tuukka Rask 20.00 50.00

2013-14 SP Game Used Stanley Cup Finals Materials Net Cord

STATED PRINT RUN 25 SER.#'d SETS
MOST HAVE TWO+ CARDS OF EQUAL VALUE
G1AF Andrew Ference 20.00 50.00
G1AS Andrew Shaw 30.00 80.00
G1CC Corey Crawford 30.00 80.00
G1DB Dave Bolland 30.00 80.00
G1DK Duncan Keith 50.00 100.00
G1ML Milan Lucic 30.00 80.00
G2CK Chris Kelly 20.00 50.00
G2DP Daniel Paille 20.00 50.00
G2MH Marian Hossa 75.00 125.00
G2PS Patrick Sharp 30.00 80.00
G2TR Tuukka Rask 30.00 80.00
G2TS Tyler Seguin 30.00 60.00
G3AS Andrew Shaw 30.00 80.00
G3JT Jonathan Toews 75.00 150.00
G3PB Patrice Bergeron
G3TR Tuukka Rask 25.00 60.00
G3TS Tyler Seguin 30.00 60.00
G3ZC Zdeno Chara 30.00 60.00
G4BS Brent Seabrook 30.00 80.00
G4CC Corey Crawford 30.00 80.00
G4DK Duncan Keith 50.00 100.00
G4JB Johnny Boychuk 30.00 80.00
G4JJ Jaromir Jagr 30.00 80.00
G4MH Michal Handzus 25.00 60.00
G4PB Patrice Bergeron
G4PK Patrick Kane
G4PS Patrick Sharp 30.00 80.00
G5BB Bryan Bickell 20.00 50.00
G5CC Corey Crawford 30.00 80.00
G5JO Johnny Oduya 30.00 80.00
G5JT Jonathan Toews 75.00 150.00
G5MH Michal Handzus 25.00 60.00
G5PK Patrick Kane
G5ZC Zdeno Chara 30.00 60.00
G6BB Bryan Bickell 20.00 50.00
G6CC Corey Crawford 30.00 80.00
G6DB Dave Bolland 40.00 100.00
G6JT Jonathan Toews 100.00 200.00
G6ML Milan Lucic 30.00 80.00
G6PK Patrick Kane 75.00 150.00
G6PS Patrick Sharp 30.00 80.00

2013-14 SP Game Used Stanley Cup Finals Materials Net Skirt Autographs

GROUP A ODDS 1:1440
GROUP B ODDS 1:1200
OVERALL ODDS 1:650
SCNSAAS Andrew Shaw B 75.00 135.00
SCNSABM Brad Marchand
SCNSABS Brandon Saad 60.00 120.00
SCNSAJT Jonathan Toews A
SCNSAPB Patrice Bergeron
SCNSAPK Patrick Kane A 90.00 150.00
SCNSASE Brent Seabrook 50.00 100.00

2013-14 SP Game Used Tandem Twigs

GROUP A ODDS 1:540 HOB
GROUP B ODDS 1:270 HOB
GROUP C ODDS 1:180 HOB
OVERALL ODDS 1:90 HOB
TTPP M.Lemieux/R.Francis A
TTANA T.Selanne/R.Getzlaf C 20.00 50.00
TTAVA P.Roy/J.Sakic A 15.00 40.00
TTBOS R.Bourque/C.Neely B 15.00 40.00
TTCOL P.Roy/P.Forsberg A 15.00 40.00
TTDET P.Datsyuk/H.Zetterberg B 15.00 40.00
TTDRW S.Yzerman/N.Lidstrom A
TTEDM P.Coffey/J.Kurri B 10.00 25.00
TTLAK D.Doughty/A.Kopitar C 12.00 30.00
TTLOS J.Quick/D.Doughty C 15.00 40.00
TTMNS D.Ciccarelli/M.Modano B 15.00 40.00
TTNYR R.Nash/H.Lundqvist B 12.00 30.00
TTOIL M.Messier/G.Anderson A 12.00 30.00
TTPEN M.Lemieux/E.Malkin A 15.00 40.00
TTPHI E.Lindros/C.Giroux B 15.00 40.00
TTRAN H.Lundqvist/M.Staal C 12.00 30.00
TTSAB T.Vanek/R.Miller C 8.00 20.00
TTTOR D.Gilmour/P.Kessel B 15.00 40.00
TTDUCKS T.Selanne/S.Koivu C 20.00 50.00
TTKINGS W.Gretzky/L.Robitaille A 40.00 80.00
TTSTAAL E.Staal/M.Staal C 12.00 30.00
TTGOALIE D.Hasek/R.Miller C 12.00 30.00
TTOILERS M.Messier/P.Coffey A 15.00 40.00
TTRWINGS S.Yzerman/H.Zetterberg B

2013-14 SP Game Used Team Canada Fabrics

GROUP A STATED ODDS 1:337
GROUP B STATED ODDS 1:255
GROUP C STATED ODDS 1:34
OVERALL STATED ODDS 1:27
*FIGHT STRAP/15: 1.2X TO 3X JSY B-C
*FIGHT STRAP/15: 1X TO 2.5X JSY A
*GOLD/97: .5X TO 1.2X JSY B
*GOLD/17-28: 1X TO 2.5X JSY C
*PATCH/35: 1X TO 2.5X JSY B-C
*PATCH/35: .8X TO 2X JSY A
TCBG Brendan Gallagher C 6.00 15.00
TCDH Dougie Hamilton C 4.00 10.00
TCJH Jonathan Huberdeau C 5.00 12.00
TCJO Jamie Oleksiak A 4.00 10.00
TCJT Joe Thornton B 4.00 10.00
TCMF Marcus Foligno C 2.50 6.00
TCMP Mark Pysyk A 5.00 12.00
TCNB Nathan Beaulieu C 2.00 5.00
TCQH Quinton Howden C 3.00 8.00

2013-14 SP Game Used Team Canada Fabrics Dual

OVERALL ODDS 1:125 HOB
*PATCH/25: 1X TO 2.5X BASIC INSERTS
TC2HG Huberdeau/Gallagher 4.00 10.00
TC2HP D.Hamilton/M.Pysyk 4.00 10.00

2013-14 SP Game Used Team Canada Fabrics Quads

OVERALL ODDS 1:263
TC4DEF Hmltn/Pyk/Olksk/Blieu 5.00 12.00
TC42012F Hbrd/Gllgr/Hwdn/Stne 8.00 20.00

2013-14 SP Game Used Team Canada Fabrics Triples

*PATCH/15: 1X TO 2.5X BASIC TRIPLE
TC3HBO Hmltn/Blieu/Olksk 5.00 12.00
TC3HHG Hbrdau/Hwdn/Gllghr 5.00 12.00

2013-14 SP Game Used Winter Classic Materials Net Cord

WCNCAM Andrej Meszaros 12.00 30.00
WCNCAS Anton Stralman 12.00 30.00
WCNCBB Bill Barber 15.00 40.00
WCNCBC Bobby Clarke 20.00 50.00
WCNCBD Brandon Dubinsky 15.00 40.00
WCNCBI Stu Bickel 15.00 40.00
WCNCBL Brian Leetch 20.00 50.00
WCNCBO Brian Boyle 12.00 30.00
WCNCBP Brandon Prust 12.00 30.00
WCNCBR Brad Richards 20.00 50.00
WCNCBS Brayden Schenn 20.00 50.00
WCNCCG Claude Giroux 20.00 50.00
WCNCCH Carl Hagelin 20.00 50.00
WCNCCO Braydon Coburn 12.00 30.00
WCNCDB Daniel Briere 20.00 50.00
WCNCDG Daniel Girardi 12.00 30.00
WCNCDS Derek Stepan 20.00 50.00
WCNCEL Eric Lindros 15.00 40.00
WCNCGA Glenn Anderson 20.00 50.00
WCNCHL Henrik Lundqvist
WCNCJJ Jaromir Jagr 50.00 125.00
WCNCJM John Mitchell 12.00 30.00
WCNCJV James van Riemsdyk 20.00 50.00
WCNCMB Martin Biron 15.00 40.00
WCNCMC Matt Carle 15.00 40.00
WCNCMD Michael Del Zotto 15.00 40.00
WCNCMG Marian Gaborik 20.00 50.00
WCNCMI Mike Gartner 20.00 50.00
WCNCMM Mark Messier 40.00 80.00
WCNCMR Matt Read 12.00 30.00
WCNCMS Marc Staal 15.00 40.00
WCNCMT Maxime Talbot 15.00 40.00
WCNCPA Bernie Parent 25.00 60.00
WCNCRC Ryan Callahan 20.00 50.00
WCNCRM Ryan McDonagh 20.00 50.00
WCNCRU Michael Rupp 12.00 30.00
WCNCSB Sergei Bobrovsky 40.00 80.00
WCNCSC Sean Couturier 20.00 50.00
WCNCSH Scott Hartnell 20.00 50.00
WCNCVO Jakub Voracek 20.00 50.00
WCNCWS Wayne Simmonds 20.00 50.00

2013-14 SP Game Used Winter Classic Materials Net Skirt Autographs

UNPRICED GROUP A ODDS 1:5040
GROUP B ODDS 1:3360
OVERALL ODDS 1:2000
WCNSABS Brayden Schenn B 30.00 80.00
WCNSAMM Mark Messier A 40.00 100.00

2014-15 SP Game Used

1 Wayne Gretzky/99 15.00 30.00
2 Jakub Voracek/93 5.00 12.00
3 Ryan Nugent-Hopkins/93 5.00 12.00
4 Gabriel Landeskog/92 4.00 10.00
5 John Tavares/91 10.00 25.00
6 Steven Stamkos/91 6.00 15.00
7 Tyler Seguin/91 8.00 20.00
8 Sidney Crosby/87 12.00 30.00
9 Phil Kessel/81 6.00 15.00
10 Jeff Carter/77 5.00 12.00
11 P.K. Subban/76 8.00 20.00
12 T.J. Oshie/74 8.00 20.00
13 Sergei Bobrovsky/72 5.00 12.00
14 Evgeni Malkin/71 15.00 40.00
15 Jaromir Jagr/68 10.00 25.00
16 Max Pacioretty/67 6.00 15.00
17 Mario Lemieux/66 10.00 25.00
18 Erik Karlsson/65 12.00 30.00
19 Mikael Granlund/64 5.00 12.00
20 Tyler Ennis/63 5.00 12.00
21 Rick Nash/61 8.00 20.00
22 Roberto Luongo/58 6.00 15.00
23 Jeff Skinner/53 6.00 15.00
24 Tyler Johnson/50 6.00 15.00
25 Tomas Hertl/48 6.00 15.00
26 Jonathan Bernier/45 6.00 15.00
27 David Backes/42 8.00 20.00
28 Tuukka Rask/40 8.00 20.00
29 Henrik Zetterberg/40 8.00 20.00
30 Dominik Hasek/39 10.00 25.00
31 Doug Gilmour/39 10.00 25.00
32 Logan Couture/39 8.00 20.00
33 Patrice Bergeron/37 10.00 25.00
34 Steve Mason/35 6.00 15.00
35 Cory Schneider/35 6.00 15.00
36 Jim Howard/35 8.00 20.00
37 Pekka Rinne/35 10.00 25.00
38 Mike Richter/35 8.00 20.00
39 Dustin Byfuglien/33 8.00 20.00
40 Kari Lehtonen/32 6.00 15.00
41 Jonathan Quick/32 12.00 30.00
42 Carey Price/31 25.00 60.00
43 Antti Niemi/31 6.00 15.00
44 Eddie Lack/31 6.00 15.00
45 Philipp Grubauer/31 8.00 20.00
46 Henrik Lundqvist/30 10.00 25.00
47 Martin Brodeur/30 15.00 40.00
48 Nathan MacKinnon/29 20.00 50.00
49 Jason Pominville/29 8.00 20.00
50 Claude Giroux/28 12.00 30.00
51 Martin St. Louis/26 10.00 25.00
52 Matt Moulson/26 8.00 20.00
53 Blake Wheeler/26 10.00 25.00
54 Jiri Hudler/24 10.00 25.00
55 Dustin Brown/23 8.00 20.00
56 Mike Bossy/22 10.00 25.00
57 Peter Forsberg/21 10.00 25.00
58 James van Riemsdyk/21 10.00 25.00
59 Brandon Saad/20 10.00 25.00
60 Ryan Suter/20 10.00 25.00
61 Alexander Steen/20 10.00 25.00
62 Chris Kreider/20 10.00 25.00
63 Jonathan Toews/19 40.00 80.00
64 Shane Doan/19 8.00 20.00
65 Jason Spezza/19 10.00 25.00
66 Nicklas Backstrom/19 15.00 40.00
67 Steve Yzerman/19 40.00 80.00
68 James Neal/18 10.00 25.00
69 Bryan Little/18 10.00 25.00
70 Radim Vrbata/17 8.00 20.00
71 Brandon Dubinsky/17 8.00 20.00
72 Ryan Kesler/17 10.00 25.00
73 Andrew Ladd/16 10.00 25.00
74 Ryan Getzlaf/15 15.00 40.00
75 Jordan Eberle/14
76 Jamie Benn/14
77 Theoren Fleury/14
78 Pavel Datsyuk/13
79 Mats Sundin/13
80 Eric Staal/12
81 Anze Kopitar/11
82 Brendan Gallagher/11
83 Zach Parise/11
84 Mark Messier/11
85 Corey Perry/10
86 Pavel Bure/10
87 Guy Lafleur/10

88 Patrick Sharp/10
89 Matt Duchene/9
90 Teemu Selanne/8
91 Drew Doughty/8
92 Alexander Ovechkin/8
93 Joe Pavelski/8
94 Kyle Turris/7
95 Phil Esposito/7
96 Brent Seabrook/7
97 Shea Weber/6
98 Taylor Hall/4
99 Bobby Orr/4
100 Ryan Johansen/19
101 Bo Horvat/53 RC 75.00 125.00
102 Laurent Brossoit/1 RC
103 Cody Kunyk/28 RC 12.00 30.00
104 Landon Ferraro/29 RC 12.00 30.00
105 Oscar Klefbom/84 RC 20.00 40.00
106 Joe Whitney/9 RC
107 Patrik Nemeth/37 RC 15.00 40.00
108 Joni Ortio/37 RC 20.00 50.00
109 Jiri Sekac/26 RC 25.00 60.00
110 Andrey Makarov/35 RC 15.00 40.00
111 A.Wennberg/41 RC 25.00 60.00
112 Johan Sundstrom/28 RC 20.00 50.00
113 Griffin Reinhart/8 RC
114 Sam Reinhart/23 RC 200.00 350.00
115 Mike Halmo/43 RC 8.00 20.00
116 Vincent Trocheck/67 RC 12.00 30.00
117 John Persson/56 RC 12.00 30.00
118 Barclay Goodrow/89 RC 10.00 25.00
119 Jake McCabe/29 RC 15.00 40.00
120 Kevin Hayes/13 RC
121 Paul Carey/28 RC 12.00 30.00
122 Simon Moser/21 RC 15.00 40.00
123 Ty Rattie/18 RC
124 Curtis McKenzie/11 RC
125 Colton Sissons/84 RC 10.00 25.00
126 Seth Griffith/53 RC 25.00 50.00
127 Christian Folin/5 RC
128 Josh Manson/42 RC 10.00 25.00
129 Chris Wagner/62 RC 10.00 25.00
130 Victor Rask/49 RC 25.00 50.00
131 Petteri Lindbohm/48 RC 10.00 25.00
132 A.Khokhlachev/76 RC 12.00 30.00
133 Marko Dano/56 RC 12.00 30.00
134 Patrick Brown/36 RC 15.00 40.00
135 Cedric Paquette/54 RC 12.00 30.00
136 Mirco Mueller/41 RC 12.00 30.00
137 V.Namestnikov/65 RC 15.00 40.00
138 Joe Morrow/45 RC 15.00 40.00
139 Jonathan Drouin/27 RC 200.00 350.00
140 Josh Jooris/86 RC 20.00 40.00
141 Adam Lowry/17 RC 40.00 80.00
142 Andrew Hammond/30 RC 90.00 150.00
143 Nicolas Deschamps/94 RC 20.00 40.00
144 Kristers Gudlevskis/37 RC 25.00 50.00
145 Tobias Rieder/8 RC
146 Ryan Sproul/48 RC 12.00 30.00
147 Leon Draisaitl/29 RC 200.00 350.00
148 Calle Jarnkrok/19 RC 30.00 60.00
149 Matt Carey/25 RC 15.00 40.00
150 Corban Knight/10 RC
151 Bogdan Yakimov/39 RC 15.00 40.00
152 Petter Granberg/8 RC
153 Aaron Ekblad/5 RC
154 Curtis Lazar/27 RC 12.00 30.00
155 Kevin Czuczman/24 RC 15.00 40.00
156 Teuvo Teravainen/86 RC 30.00 60.00
157 Rocco Grimaldi/23 RC 20.00 50.00
158 Joonas Nattinen/28 RC 20.00 50.00
159 Peter LeBlanc/64 RC 20.00 40.00
160 Stuart Percy/50 RC 12.00 30.00
161 Tyler Wotherspoon/56 RC 15.00 30.00
162 Teemu Pulkkinen/56 RC 40.00 80.00
163 William Karlsson/38 RC 60.00 150.00
164 Damon Severson/28 RC 30.00 60.00
165 Justin Hodgman/12 RC
166 Joey Hishon/38 RC 20.00 50.00
167 Greg McKegg/39 RC 12.00 30.00
168 Michael Zalewski/40 RC 15.00 30.00
169 Justin Johnson/49 RC 12.00 30.00
170 Matt Lindblad/52 RC 10.00 25.00
171 Johnny Gaudreau/53 RC 250.00 400.00
172 Jori Lehtera/12 RC
173 Evgeny Kuznetsov/92 RC 30.00 60.00
174 Nicolas Deslauriers/44 RC 12.00 30.00
175 Phil Varone/84 RC 8.00 20.00
176 Andrej Nestrasil/49 RC 12.00 30.00
177 Scott Mayfield/42 RC 10.00 25.00
178 Brett Gallant/59 RC 10.00 25.00
179 Brandon Kozun/67 RC 8.00 20.00
180 Mark Visentin/40 RC 12.00 30.00
181 Mark Van Guilder/29 RC 20.00 50.00
182 Garrett Wilson/28 RC 15.00 40.00
183 Dennis Everberg/45 RC 12.00 30.00
184 Chris Tierney/50 RC 12.00 30.00
185 Nathan Lieuwen/50 RC 10.00 25.00
186 Jonathan Racine/58 RC 12.00 30.00
187 Jyrki Jokipakka/2 RC
188 Andre Burakovsky/65 RC 40.00 80.00
189 Brandon Gormley/33 RC 15.00 40.00
190 Anthony Duclair/63 RC 30.00 60.00
191 S.Gostisbehere/53 RC 50.00 125.00
192 Markus Granlund/60 RC 15.00 30.00
193 Bryce Van Brabant/48 RC 25.00 50.00
194 Bill Arnold/46 RC 10.00 25.00
195 Andy Andreoff/15 RC 30.00 60.00
196 T.van Riemsdyk/57 RC 20.00 50.00
197 Bobby Robins/64 RC 8.00 20.00
198 Adam Payerl/45 RC 10.00 25.00
199 P-E Bellemare/78 RC 12.00 30.00
200 Darnell Nurse/25 RC 60.00 100.00

2014-15 SP Game Used Authentic Fabrics

GROUP A ODDS 1:1341
GROUP B ODDS 1:844
GROUP C ODDS 1:265
GROUP D ODDS 1:138
GROUP E ODDS 1:5
AFAN Antti Niemi E 3.00 8.00
AFBR Rod Brind'Amour E 5.00 12.00
AFBS Brandon Sutter B
AFCC Corey Crawford D 12.00 30.00
AFCE Cody Eakin E 2.50 6.00
AFEB Ed Belfour E 6.00 15.00
AFEK Evander Kane E 4.00 10.00
AFGR Michael Grabner A 6.00 15.00
AFJM Jake Muzzin C 5.00 12.00
AFJR Jeremy Roenick E 6.00 15.00
AFJZ Jeff Zatkoff A 6.00 15.00
AFMG Mike Gartner E 5.00 12.00
AFNH Nathan Horton E 4.00 10.00
AFPP Pete Peeters E 5.00 12.00
AFRB Ray Bourque E 10.00 25.00
AFRF Ron Francis C 10.00 25.00
AFVL Vincent Lecavalier E 5.00 12.00

2014-15 SP Game Used Authentic Fabrics Patches

STATED PRINT RUN 35 SER.#'d SETS
AFAL Andrew Ladd 5.00 12.00
AFAN Antti Niemi 4.00 10.00
AFAT Alex Tanguay 3.00 8.00
AFBR Rod Brind'Amour 8.00 20.00
AFBS Brandon Sutter 4.00 10.00
AFCC Corey Crawford 20.00 40.00
AFCE Cody Eakin 3.00 8.00
AFCO Colton Orr 3.00 8.00
AFEB Ed Belfour 10.00 25.00
AFEK Evander Kane 5.00 12.00
AFGR Michael Grabner 4.00 10.00
AFHL Hampus Lindholm 8.00 20.00
AFJM Jake Muzzin 10.00 25.00
AFJR Jeremy Roenick 10.00 25.00
AFJT Joe Thornton 8.00 20.00
AFJZ Jeff Zatkoff 4.00 10.00
AFMG Mike Gartner 6.00 15.00
AFNH Nathan Horton 5.00 12.00
AFNL Nick Leddy 8.00 20.00
AFPB Pavel Bure 12.00 30.00
AFPP Pete Peeters 8.00 20.00
AFRB Ray Bourque 15.00 40.00
AFVL Vincent Lecavalier 8.00 20.00

2014-15 SP Game Used Authentic Fabrics Dual

GROUP A ODDS 1:543
GROUP B ODDS 1:38
GROUP C ODDS 1:7
OVERALL STATED ODDS 1:6
AF2AL C.Anderson/Lehner C 4.00 10.00
AF2BS M.Sundin/E.Belfour B 6.00 15.00
AF2CH D.Hasek/C.Chelios C 5.00 12.00
AF2GK R.Getzlaf/A.Kopitar C 6.00 15.00
AF2HH M.Hackett/Hodgson A
AF2HT B.Hull/M.Turco C 4.00 10.00
AF2HY T.Hall/N.Yakupov C 8.00 20.00
AF2KB P.Kessel/J.Bernier A 12.00 30.00
AF2KD D.Keith/D.Doughty B 6.00 15.00
AF2LB Lehtonen/E.Belfour C 8.00 20.00
AF2PM P.Bure/M.Lemieux C 10.00 25.00
AF2PS C.Price/P.Subban C 8.00 20.00
AF2RR P.Rinne/T.Rask C 5.00 12.00
AF2ZH Zetterberg/J.Howard B 6.00 15.00

2014-15 SP Game Used Authentic Fabrics Dual Patches

STATED PRINT RUN 25 SER.#'d SETS
AF2BL P.Bure/Luongo 10.00 25.00
AF2BR P.Bure/M.Richter 10.00 25.00
AF2BS M.Sundin/E.Belfour 8.00 20.00
AF2CH D.Hasek/C.Chelios 10.00 25.00
AF2GK R.Getzlaf/A.Kopitar 12.00 30.00
AF2HH M.Hackett/Hodgson
AF2HT B.Hull/M.Turco 20.00 50.00
AF2KB P.Kessel/J.Bernier
AF2KD D.Keith/D.Doughty 12.00 30.00
AF2LB Lehtonen/E.Belfour 15.00 40.00
AF2PM P.Bure/M.Lemieux 20.00 50.00
AF2PS C.Price/P.Subban 20.00 50.00
AF2RL J.LeClair/J.Roenick 8.00 20.00
AF2RR P.Rinne/T.Rask 10.00 25.00
AF2ZH Zetterberg/J.Howard 8.00 20.00

2014-15 SP Game Used Authentic Fabrics Quads

GROUP A ODDS 1:1086
GROUP B ODDS 1:165
GROUP C ODDS 1:20
AF4CAN Keith/Doughty/Price/Luongo C 8.00 20.00
AF4CHI Kruger/Leddy/Saad/Bickell A
AF4FIN Maatta/Niemi/Lehtonen/Rask B 8.00 20.00
AF4SJLA Niemi/Thornton/Quick/Brown C 6.00 15.00
AF4WINS Varlamov/Niemi/Fleury/Bishop C 8.00 20.00

2014-15 SP Game Used Authentic Fabrics Sixes

AF6BOSMON Bg/Mry/Ot/Blw/Trg/Ry
AF6CENTRAL Cr/Vrl/Lh/Rn/Pv/Kmp 12.00 30.00
AF6CHINYR Sd/Kth/Ld/Zc/Stp/Mc 10.00 25.00
AF6NYRMON Hg/Mre/Zc/Pc/Elr/Mrk 40.00 80.00
AF6PACIFIC St/Qk/Nm/Lk/Sc/Rm 15.00 40.00
AF6PHINYR Ct/Gx/Ms/Stp/Ln/McD 20.00 50.00

2014-15 SP Game Used Authentic Fabrics Triples

GROUP A ODDS 1:1200
GROUP B ODDS 1:296
GROUP C ODDS 1:8
AF3G Ramo/Smith/Scrivens A
AF3GK Smith/Lack/Ramo C 5.00 12.00
AF3QN Goulet/Nolan/Tardif C 5.00 12.00
AF3CBJ Bbrvsky/Hortn/Schltz C 5.00 12.00
AF3FIN Rask/Niemi/Lehtonen C 5.00 12.00
AF3FLY Coutr/Coburn/Giroux A
AF3LAK Brown/Toffoli/Quick C 8.00 20.00
AF3NET Lehtn/Kmper/Pavelec C 5.00 12.00
AF3NYR Moore/Zuccrl/Hagelin B 6.00 15.00
AF3BEES Brque/Murray/Oates C 8.00 20.00
AF3CAPS Kuzn/Green/Carlson A 30.00 80.00
AF3JETS Ladd/Kane/Pavelec C 5.00 12.00

2014-15 SP Game Used Authentic Fabrics Triples Patches

STATED PRINT RUN 15 SER.#'d SETS
AF3G Ramo/Smith/Scrivns 15.00 40.00
AF3GK Smith/Lack/Ramo
AF3QN Goulet/Nolan/Tardif
AF3CBJ Bbrvsky/Hortn/Schltz 30.00 60.00
AF3FIN Rask/Niemi/Lehtn 15.00 40.00
AF3FLY Coutr/Coburn/Giroux
AF3LAK Brown/Toffoli/Quick 25.00 60.00
AF3MON Pacior/Eller/Markov
AF3NET Lehtn/Kmper/Pavelec
AF3NYR Moore/Zuccrl/Hagelin
AF3VAN Lack/Sedin/Sedin 15.00 40.00
AF3BEES Brque/Murray/Oates 25.00 60.00
AF3CAPS Kuzn/Green/Carlson 60.00 150.00
AF3JETS Ladd/Kane/Pavelec 15.00 40.00

2014-15 SP Game Used Autographs Blue

UNPRICED GROUP A ODDS 1:650
GROUP B ODDS 1:135
GROUP C ODDS 1:60
GROUP D ODDS 1:25
GROUP E ODDS 1:15
1 Wayne Gretzky C 150.00 250.00
3 Ryan Nugent-Hopkins D 6.00 15.00
4 Gabriel Landeskog D 5.00 12.00
5 John Tavares E 12.00 30.00
6 Steven Stamkos C 25.00 50.00
7 Tyler Seguin C 12.00 30.00
8 Sidney Crosby A 75.00 135.00
9 Phil Kessel D 8.00 20.00
13 Sergei Bobrovsky E 6.00 15.00
14 Evgeni Malkin D 20.00 50.00
15 Jaromir Jagr A 40.00 80.00
16 Max Pacioretty D 6.00 15.00
17 Mario Lemieux A 60.00 120.00
19 Mikael Granlund E 5.00 12.00
21 Rick Nash C 20.00 50.00
23 Jeff Skinner D
24 Tyler Johnson E 15.00 30.00
25 Tomas Hertl E 15.00 30.00
26 Jonathan Bernier E 6.00 15.00
27 David Backes E 6.00 15.00
28 Tuukka Rask E 8.00 20.00
30 Dominik Hasek B 20.00 40.00
31 Doug Gilmour C 25.00 50.00
32 Logan Couture C 8.00 20.00
33 Patrice Bergeron D 12.00 30.00
34 Steve Mason E 5.00 12.00
35 Cory Schneider D 5.00 12.00
36 Jim Howard E 6.00 15.00
37 Pekka Rinne E 8.00 20.00
38 Mike Richter D 8.00 20.00
43 Antti Niemi D 5.00 12.00
45 Philipp Grubauer E 6.00 15.00
47 Martin Brodeur B 30.00 60.00
48 Nathan MacKinnon D 25.00 50.00
49 Jason Pominville E 5.00 12.00
50 Claude Giroux C 8.00 20.00
51 Martin St. Louis C 8.00 20.00
55 Dustin Brown D 5.00 12.00
56 Mike Bossy C 8.00 20.00
57 Peter Forsberg B 25.00 50.00
58 James van Riemsdyk C
59 Brandon Saad E 6.00 15.00
62 Chris Kreider A
63 Jonathan Toews C 25.00 50.00
64 Shane Doan E 5.00 12.00
65 Jason Spezza D 6.00 15.00
67 Steve Yzerman B
68 James Neal E 6.00 15.00
72 Ryan Kesler D 6.00 15.00
77 Theoren Fleury C 10.00 25.00
78 Pavel Datsyuk C 20.00 40.00
79 Mats Sundin B 30.00 60.00
80 Eric Staal D 8.00 20.00
81 Anze Kopitar D 12.00 30.00
82 Brendan Gallagher B
83 Zach Parise C 10.00 25.00
84 Mark Messier B 20.00 40.00
87 Guy Lafleur C
89 Matt Duchene D 6.00 15.00
90 Teemu Selanne B 15.00 30.00
92 Alexander Ovechkin B 40.00 100.00
93 Joe Pavelski E 6.00 15.00
94 Kyle Turris E 6.00 15.00
95 Phil Esposito B 20.00 40.00
97 Shea Weber C 6.00 15.00
98 Taylor Hall B
99 Bobby Orr D 60.00 120.00
100 Ryan Johansen E 8.00 20.00
101 Bo Horvat D 15.00 40.00
102 Laurent Brossoit D 4.00 10.00
105 Oscar Klefbom D 8.00 20.00
108 Joni Ortio C 12.00 30.00
109 Jiri Sekac D 6.00 15.00
111 Alexander Wennberg D 8.00 20.00
113 Griffin Reinhart D 10.00 25.00
114 Sam Reinhart D 10.00 25.00
116 Vincent Trocheck D 5.00 12.00
119 Jake McCabe D 4.00 10.00
120 Kevin Hayes C EXCH 20.00 40.00
123 Ty Rattie D 5.00 12.00
125 Colton Sissons D 4.00 10.00
132 Alexander Khokhlachev D 4.00 10.00
133 Marko Dano D 4.00 10.00
134 Patrick Brown D 4.00 10.00
136 Mirco Mueller D 8.00 20.00
137 Vladislav Namestnikov D 6.00 15.00
138 Joe Morrow D 8.00 20.00
139 Jonathan Drouin D 15.00 40.00
141 Adam Lowry D 4.00 10.00
145 Tobias Rieder D 3.00 8.00
146 Ryan Sproul D 4.00 10.00
147 Leon Draisaitl D 20.00 50.00
150 Corban Knight D 4.00 10.00
153 Aaron Ekblad D 12.00 30.00
154 Curtis Lazar D 10.00 25.00
156 Teuvo Teravainen D 15.00 40.00
157 Rocco Grimaldi D 8.00 20.00
158 Joonas Nattinen D 4.00 10.00
160 Stuart Percy D 4.00 10.00
161 Tyler Wotherspoon D 6.00 15.00
162 Teemu Pulkkinen D 10.00 25.00
164 Damon Severson D 4.00 10.00
166 Joey Hishon D 5.00 12.00
167 Greg McKegg D 3.00 8.00
171 Johnny Gaudreau D 20.00 50.00
172 Jori Lehtera A 25.00 50.00
173 Evgeny Kuznetsov D 12.00 30.00
176 Andrej Nestrasil D 4.00 10.00
179 Brandon Kozun D 3.00 8.00
180 Mark Visentin D 4.00 10.00
183 Dennis Everberg D 4.00 10.00
184 Chris Tierney D 4.00 10.00
188 Andre Burakovsky D 10.00 25.00
189 Brandon Gormley D 4.00 10.00
190 Anthony Duclair C 12.00 30.00
192 Markus Granlund B 10.00 25.00
196 Trevor van Riemsdyk D 15.00 40.00
200 Darnell Nurse D 10.00 25.00

2014-15 SP Game Used Buyback Autographs

31 Nicklas Lidstrom/20 30.00 60.00

2014-15 SP Game Used Career Legacy Jerseys

UNPRICED GROUP A ODDS 1:84
GROUP B ODDS 1:114
GROUP C ODDS 1:62
GROUP D ODDS 1:5
OVERALL STATED ODDS 1:4
CLDK Dominik Hasek D 12.00 30.00
CLEK Evander Kane C 4.00 10.00
CLJB Jonathan Bernier D 3.00 8.00
CLJJ Jaromir Jagr A 15.00 40.00
CLML Mario Lemieux B 10.00 25.00
CLSM Steve Mason D 2.50 6.00
CLSV Semyon Varlamov D 3.00 8.00

2014-15 SP Game Used Career Legacy Patches

CLAL Andrew Ladd/99 4.00 10.00
CLAT Alex Tanguay/99 8.00 20.00
CLBG Bill Guerin/99 6.00 15.00
CLCA Craig Anderson/50 5.00 12.00
CLDB Daniel Briere/99 10.00 25.00
CLDK Dominik Hasek/25 20.00 40.00
CLDP David Perron/99 2.50 6.00
CLJB Jonathan Bernier/99 15.00 40.00
CLJC Jeff Carter/99 4.00 10.00
CLJJ Jaromir Jagr/25 30.00 60.00
CLML Mario Lemieux/25 25.00 50.00
CLMR Mike Richards/99 4.00 10.00
CLSM Steve Mason/99 10.00 25.00
CLSV Semyon Varlamov/25 6.00 15.00
CLZC Zdeno Chara/99 4.00 10.00

2014-15 SP Game Used Draft Day Marks

EACH CARD SERIAL #'d TO 10-35
TOTAL PRINT RUNS MUCH HIGHER
EACH HAS MULTIPLE CARDS OF EQUAL VALUE
EXCH EXPIRATION: 12/15/2016
DDMAC1 Adam Clendening C 12.00 30.00
DDMAE1 Aaron Ekblad E 40.00 80.00
DDMBH1 Bo Horvat EXCH 30.00 60.00
DDMBR1 Bobby Ryan R 20.00 50.00
DDMCJ1 Calle Jarnkrok EXCH 10.00 25.00
DDMCL1 Curtis Lazar L 25.00 50.00
DDMDN1 Darnell Nurse N 15.00 40.00
DDMEK1 Evander Kane K 25.00 60.00
DDMFF1 Filip Forsberg F 50.00 100.00
DDMGO1 Brandon Gormley G 12.00 30.00
DDMJB1 Jonathan Bernier B 12.00 30.00
DDMJD1 Jonathan Drouin D 30.00 60.00
DDMJE1 Jordan Eberle E/30* 30.00 80.00
DDMJG1 Johnny Gaudreau G 50.00 100.00
DDMJH1 Joey Hishon H/70* 15.00 40.00
DDMJM1 Joe Morrow M 15.00 40.00
DDMJT1 Jonathan Toews T 50.00 100.00
DDMKR1 Kerby Rychel R 10.00 25.00
DDMKZ1 Evgeny Kuznetsov K 20.00 50.00
DDMLD1 Leon Draisaitl D 20.00 50.00
DDMMD1 Matt Duchene D
DDMMF1 Marc-Andre Fleury F 30.00 60.00
DDMMV1 Mark Visentin V 12.00 30.00
DDMNA1 V.Namestnikov N/70* 15.00 40.00
DDMPK1 Phil Kessel K 25.00 60.00
DDMRG1 Griffin Reinhart R/70* 15.00 40.00
DDMRS1 Ryan Strome S 15.00 40.00
DDMSR1 Sam Reinhart R/70* 25.00 60.00
DDMTR1 Ty Rattie R 15.00 40.00
DDMTV1 Teuvo Teravainen T 30.00 60.00
DDMZP1 Zach Parise P 25.00 50.00

2014-15 SP Game Used Gold Jerseys

GROUP A VET ODDS 1:386
GROUP B VET ODDS 1:53
GROUP C VET ODDS 1:47
GROUP D VET ODDS 1:27
GROUP E VET ODDS 1:2
1 Wayne Gretzky B 20.00 50.00
5 John Tavares D 6.00 15.00
6 Steven Stamkos E 6.00 15.00
8 Sidney Crosby E 8.00 20.00
11 P.K. Subban E 5.00 12.00
13 Sergei Bobrovsky E 3.00 8.00
14 Evgeni Malkin E 10.00 25.00
16 Max Pacioretty E 3.00 8.00
17 Mario Lemieux E 10.00 25.00
21 Rick Nash E 3.00 8.00
22 Roberto Luongo B 4.00 10.00
27 David Backes E 3.00 8.00
28 Tuukka Rask E 3.00 8.00
29 Henrik Zetterberg E 4.00 10.00
30 Dominik Hasek A 8.00 20.00
31 Doug Gilmour E 6.00 15.00
32 Logan Couture E 3.00 8.00
33 Patrice Bergeron C 5.00 12.00
35 Cory Schneider C 3.00 8.00
36 Jim Howard E 3.00 8.00
37 Pekka Rinne E 4.00 10.00
38 Mike Richter B 4.00 10.00
40 Kari Lehtonen E 2.50 6.00
41 Jonathan Quick E 5.00 12.00
42 Carey Price E 8.00 20.00
43 Antti Niemi E 2.50 6.00
44 Eddie Lack E 2.50 6.00
46 Henrik Lundqvist E 4.00 10.00
47 Martin Brodeur E 6.00 15.00
52 Matt Moulson E 2.50 6.00
55 Dustin Brown C 3.00 8.00
62 Chris Kreider E 3.00 8.00
66 Nicklas Backstrom E 5.00 12.00
67 Steve Yzerman E 6.00 15.00
73 Andrew Ladd E 3.00 8.00
75 Jordan Eberle E 3.00 8.00
76 Jamie Benn E 4.00 10.00
77 Theoren Fleury E 4.00 10.00
81 Anze Kopitar E 5.00 12.00
84 Mark Messier E 4.00 10.00
85 Corey Perry D 3.00 8.00
88 Patrick Sharp E 3.00 8.00
91 Drew Doughty E 3.00 8.00
92 Alexander Ovechkin E 12.00 30.00
95 Phil Esposito B 8.00 20.00
96 Brent Seabrook D 3.00 8.00
98 Taylor Hall E 6.00 15.00
101 Bo Horvat 8.00 20.00
102 Laurent Brossoit 4.00 10.00
105 Oscar Klefbom 8.00 20.00
107 Patrik Nemeth 4.00 10.00
108 Joni Ortio 5.00 12.00
111 Alexander Wennberg 8.00 20.00
113 Griffin Reinhart 5.00 12.00
114 Sam Reinhart 6.00 15.00
116 Vincent Trocheck 5.00 12.00
119 Jake McCabe 4.00 10.00
123 Ty Rattie 5.00 12.00
125 Colton Sissons 4.00 10.00
130 Victor Rask 4.00 10.00
132 Alexander Khokhlachev 4.00 10.00
133 Marko Dano 4.00 10.00
136 Mirco Mueller 4.00 10.00
137 Vladislav Namestnikov 5.00 12.00
139 Jonathan Drouin 6.00 15.00
146 Ryan Sproul 4.00 10.00
147 Leon Draisaitl 6.00 15.00
150 Corban Knight 4.00 10.00
151 Bogdan Yakimov 4.00 10.00
153 Aaron Ekblad 6.00 15.00
154 Curtis Lazar 5.00 12.00
156 Teuvo Teravainen 6.00 15.00
157 Rocco Grimaldi 4.00 10.00
160 Stuart Percy 4.00 10.00
161 Tyler Wotherspoon 4.00 10.00
162 Teemu Pulkkinen 5.00 12.00
164 Damon Severson 4.00 10.00
166 Joey Hishon 5.00 12.00
167 Greg McKegg 3.00 8.00
171 Johnny Gaudreau 8.00 20.00
173 Evgeny Kuznetsov 6.00 15.00
177 Scott Mayfield 3.00 8.00
180 Mark Visentin 4.00 10.00
184 Chris Tierney 4.00 10.00
188 Andre Burakovsky 6.00 15.00
189 Brandon Gormley 4.00 10.00
192 Markus Granlund 6.00 15.00
200 Darnell Nurse 12.00 30.00

2014-15 SP Game Used Gold Spectrum Materials

*101-200 ROOKIE/99: .6X TO 1.5X JERSEY/499
1 Wayne Gretzky/25 40.00 80.00
2 Jakub Voracek/25 10.00 25.00
4 Gabriel Landeskog/99 5.00 12.00
5 John Tavares/50 15.00 40.00
8 Sidney Crosby/50 25.00 60.00
9 Phil Kessel/50 10.00 25.00
10 Jeff Carter/50 8.00 20.00
11 P.K. Subban/50 12.00 30.00
13 Sergei Bobrovsky/25 10.00 25.00
15 Jaromir Jagr/50 20.00 50.00
16 Max Pacioretty/50 8.00 20.00
17 Mario Lemieux/50 10.00 25.00
18 Erik Karlsson/50 15.00 40.00
20 Tyler Ennis/99 5.00 12.00
22 Roberto Luongo/25 10.00 25.00
26 Jonathan Bernier/25 10.00 25.00
27 David Backes/99 6.00 15.00
28 Tuukka Rask/50 8.00 20.00
29 Henrik Zetterberg/50 10.00 25.00
30 Dominik Hasek/15 15.00 40.00
31 Doug Gilmour/99 10.00 25.00
32 Logan Couture/50 8.00 20.00
33 Patrice Bergeron/45 10.00 25.00
34 Steve Mason/50 6.00 15.00
35 Cory Schneider/99 5.00 12.00
36 Jim Howard/99 6.00 15.00
37 Pekka Rinne/50 10.00 25.00
38 Mike Richter/25 10.00 25.00
40 Kari Lehtonen/25 8.00 20.00
41 Jonathan Quick/50 12.00 30.00
42 Carey Price/99 20.00 50.00
43 Antti Niemi/50 6.00 15.00
44 Eddie Lack/99 5.00 12.00
45 Philipp Grubauer/50 8.00 20.00
46 Henrik Lundqvist/99 8.00 20.00
47 Martin Brodeur/50 20.00 40.00
50 Claude Giroux/99 6.00 15.00
51 Martin St. Louis/99 6.00 15.00
52 Matt Moulson/50 6.00 15.00
53 Blake Wheeler/90 6.00 15.00
55 Dustin Brown/99 5.00 12.00
57 Peter Forsberg/75 6.00 15.00
58 James van Riemsdyk/99 6.00 15.00
59 Brandon Saad/50 8.00 20.00
60 Ryan Suter/99 6.00 15.00
61 Alexander Steen/50 8.00 20.00
62 Chris Kreider/25 10.00 25.00
63 Jonathan Toews/25 20.00 50.00
64 Shane Doan/99 5.00 12.00
65 Jason Spezza/50 8.00 20.00
66 Nicklas Backstrom/25 15.00 40.00
67 Steve Yzerman/50 25.00 50.00
68 James Neal/90 6.00 15.00
69 Bryan Little/99 6.00 15.00
71 Brandon Dubinsky/90 5.00 12.00
73 Andrew Ladd/99 6.00 15.00
74 Ryan Getzlaf/25 15.00 40.00
75 Jordan Eberle/25 10.00 25.00
76 Jamie Benn/50 10.00 25.00
77 Theoren Fleury/25 15.00 40.00
78 Pavel Datsyuk/25 12.00 30.00
79 Mats Sundin/75 6.00 15.00
80 Eric Staal/75 8.00 20.00
81 Anze Kopitar/75 10.00 25.00
82 Brendan Gallagher/50 8.00 20.00
83 Zach Parise/50 8.00 20.00
84 Mark Messier/25 12.00 30.00
86 Pavel Bure/50 10.00 25.00
87 Guy Lafleur/99 8.00 20.00
88 Patrick Sharp/99 6.00 15.00
89 Matt Duchene/50 8.00 20.00
90 Teemu Selanne/50 20.00 50.00
91 Drew Doughty/99 6.00 15.00
92 Alexander Ovechkin/50 30.00 80.00
95 Phil Esposito/15
96 Brent Seabrook/25 10.00 25.00
97 Shea Weber/50 6.00 15.00
98 Taylor Hall/50 15.00 40.00
100 Ryan Johansen/50 10.00 25.00
171 Johnny Gaudreau/99 20.00 50.00

2014-15 SP Game Used Heritage Classic Materials Net Cord

HCNCAB Alexandre Burrows 15.00 40.00
HCNCAE Alexander Edler 10.00 25.00
HCNCCC Cody Ceci 10.00 25.00
HCNCCG Colin Greening 10.00 25.00
HCNCCM Clarke MacArthur 10.00 25.00
HCNCCN Chris Neil 10.00 25.00
HCNCDH Dan Hamhuis 10.00 25.00
HCNCDS Daniel Sedin 15.00 40.00
HCNCEC Erik Condra 15.00 40.00
HCNCEG Eric Gryba 15.00 40.00
HCNCEK Erik Karlsson 30.00 80.00
HCNCEL Eddie Lack 12.00 30.00
HCNCHS Henrik Sedin 15.00 40.00
HCNCJG Jason Garrison 10.00 25.00
HCNCJH Jannik Hansen 12.00 30.00
HCNCJS Jason Spezza 15.00 40.00
HCNCMM Milan Michalek 10.00 25.00
HCNCRK Ryan Kesler 15.00 40.00
HCNCZK Zack Kassian 12.00 30.00
HCNCZS Zack Smith 10.00 25.00

2014-15 SP Game Used Inked Rookie Sweaters

IRSAB Andre Burakovsky- 12.00 30.00
IRSAE Aaron Ekblad 15.00 40.00
IRSAK Alexander Khokhlachev 6.00 15.00
IRSAW Alexander Wennberg 10.00 25.00
IRSBG Brandon Gormley 5.00 12.00
IRSCK Corban Knight 6.00 15.00
IRSCL Curtis Lazar 12.00 30.00
IRSCT Chris Tierney 6.00 15.00
IRSDS Damon Severson 10.00 25.00
IRSEK Evgeny Kuznetsov 12.00 30.00
IRSGM Greg McKegg 5.00 12.00
IRSGR Griffin Reinhart 10.00 25.00
IRSJD Jonathan Drouin 15.00 40.00
IRSJG Johnny Gaudreau 30.00 80.00
IRSJH Joey Hishon 6.00 15.00
IRSJM Jake McCabe 8.00 20.00
IRSLB Laurent Brossoit 6.00 15.00
IRSLD Leon Draisaitl 10.00 25.00
IRSMD Marko Dano 10.00 25.00
IRSMM Mirco Mueller 15.00 40.00
IRSMV Mark Visentin 5.00 12.00
IRSRS Ryan Sproul 6.00 15.00
IRSSP Stuart Percy 6.00 15.00
IRSSR Sam Reinhart 15.00 40.00
IRSTR Ty Rattie 6.00 15.00
IRSTT Teuvo Teravainen 40.00 80.00
IRSVN Vladislav Namestnikov 8.00 20.00
IRSVT Vincent Trocheck 6.00 15.00

2014-15 SP Game Used Inked Rookie Sweaters Patches

*PATCH/49: .6X TO 1.5X BASIC JERSEY/149
IRSJG Johnny Gaudreau 150.00 250.00

2014-15 SP Game Used Inked Sweaters

ISAK Anze Kopitar/50 12.00 30.00
ISAO Adam Oates/50 15.00 30.00
ISBA David Backes/99 8.00 20.00
ISBH Brett Hull/25 25.00 50.00
ISCG Claude Giroux/99 15.00 30.00
ISCK Chris Kreider/99 8.00 20.00
ISDB Dustin Brown/99 6.00 15.00
ISDG Doug Gilmour/99 20.00 40.00
ISJB Jamie Benn/50 10.00 25.00
ISKL Kari Lehtonen/99 6.00 15.00
ISPE Phil Esposito/25 20.00 40.00
ISPF Peter Forsberg/50 25.00 50.00
ISPR Patrick Roy/25 75.00 135.00
ISPS Patrick Sharp/99 25.00 50.00
ISRB Ray Bourque/50 15.00 30.00
ISSC Sidney Crosby/25
ISSM Steve Mason/99 6.00 15.00
ISSY Steve Yzerman/25 40.00 80.00

2014-15 SP Game Used Stadium Series Materials Game Used Pucks

SSGUPBN Brock Nelson 15.00 40.00
SSGUPCP Corey Perry
SSGUPDC Daniel Carcillo 12.00 30.00
SSGUPDS Derek Stepan 20.00 50.00
SSGUPHL Henrik Lundqvist 50.00 100.00
SSGUPJQ Jonathan Quick 40.00 80.00
SSGUPMZ Mats Zuccarello 20.00 50.00
SSGUPPE Patrik Elias 25.00 50.00
SSGUPRG Ryan Getzlaf 30.00 80.00

2014-15 SP Game Used Stadium Series Materials Jerseys

GROUP A ODDS 1:102
GROUP B ODDS 1:66
GROUP C ODDS 1:13
GROUP D ODDS 1:9
GROUP E ODDS 1:3
OVERALL STATED ODDS 1:2
SSAG Andy Greene E 2.50 6.00
SSAH Adam Henrique C 6.00 15.00
SSBB Bryan Bickell C 4.00 10.00
SSBG Brian Gibbons C 4.00 10.00
SSBL Ben Lovejoy E 2.50 6.00
SSBS Brent Seabrook B 8.00 20.00
SSCK Chris Kunitz D 4.00 10.00
SSCS Cory Schneider E 3.00 8.00
SSDB Damien Brunner A 5.00 12.00
SSDK Duncan Keith E 4.00 10.00
SSDM Dominic Moore E 2.50 6.00
SSDS Derek Stepan E 4.00 10.00
SSFN Frans Nielsen C 4.00 10.00
SSFO Cam Fowler C 5.00 12.00
SSFR Colin Fraser E 2.50 6.00
SSHL Hampus Lindholm C 5.00 12.00
SSJM Jake Muzzin E 2.50 6.00
SSJN Jordan Nolan D 4.00 10.00
SSJT John Tavares E 8.00 20.00
SSJZ Jeff Zatkoff E 3.00 8.00
SSKC Kyle Clifford D 2.50 6.00
SSKK Kevin Klein E 2.50 6.00
SSMD Matt Donovan E 2.50 6.00
SSMF Matt Frattin E 3.00 8.00
SSMG Michael Grabner A 6.00 15.00
SSMK Marcus Kruger D 4.00 10.00
SSMN Matt Niskanen D 3.00 8.00
SSMZ Mats Zuccarello D 4.00 10.00
SSNB Nick Bonino D 2.50 6.00
SSOM Olli Maatta C 6.00 15.00
SSSA Brandon Saad B 8.00 20.00
SSSG Stephen Gionta E 2.50 6.00
SSTH Thomas Hickey E 2.50 6.00

2014-15 SP Game Used Stadium Series Materials Net Cord Dodger Stadium

LANCAC Andrew Cogliano 12.00 30.00
LANCAK Anze Kopitar 30.00 80.00
LANCCF Cam Fowler 15.00 40.00
LANCCP Corey Perry 15.00 40.00
LANCDB Dustin Brown 15.00 40.00
LANCDD Drew Doughty 20.00 50.00
LANCFB Francois Beauchemin 12.00 30.00
LANCJC Jeff Carter 20.00 50.00
LANCJH Jonas Hiller 15.00 40.00
LANCJM Jake Muzzin 12.00 30.00
LANCJQ Jonathan Quick 25.00 60.00
LANCJS Jarret Stoll
LANCJW Justin Williams 15.00 40.00
LANCKP Kyle Palmieri 15.00 40.00
LANCMB Matt Beleskey
LANCMR Mike Richards 15.00 40.00
LANCNB Nick Bonino 12.00 30.00
LANCRG Ryan Getzlaf
LANCSK Saku Koivu 20.00 50.00
LANCSV Slava Voynov 15.00 40.00
LANCTS Teemu Selanne 40.00 100.00

2014-15 SP Game Used Stadium Series Materials Net Cord Soldier Field

SSCHBB Bryan Bickell 15.00 40.00
SSCHBO Brooks Orpik 20.00 50.00
SSCHBS Brandon Sutter 20.00 50.00
SSCHCC Corey Crawford 30.00 80.00
SSCHCK Chris Kunitz 25.00 60.00
SSCHDK Duncan Keith 40.00 80.00
SSCHEM Evgeni Malkin 30.00 60.00
SSCHJJ Jussi Jokinen 15.00 40.00
SSCHJN James Neal 20.00 50.00
SSCHJT Jonathan Toews 50.00 100.00
SSCHKV Kris Versteeg 20.00 50.00
SSCHMF Marc-Andre Fleury 40.00 100.00
SSCHMH Michal Handzus 15.00 40.00
SSCHMR Michal Rozsival 15.00 40.00
SSCHNL Nick Leddy 20.00 50.00
SSCHOM Olli Maatta 25.00 60.00
SSCHPK Patrick Kane
SSCHPS Patrick Sharp
SSCHSA Brandon Saad 20.00 40.00
SSCHSC Sidney Crosby 60.00 120.00
SSCHSD Simon Despres 12.00 30.00

2014-15 SP Game Used Stadium Series Materials Patches

*PATCH/99: 1.5X TO 4X JSY D-E
*PATCH/99: 1X TO 2.5X JSY C
*PATCH/99: .8X TO 2X JSY A-B
SSJT John Tavares/30
SSTO Jonathan Toews/99 25.00 60.00

2014-15 SP Game Used Stanley Cup Finals Materials Game Used Pucks

SCFGUPAK Anze Kopitar G3 100.00 200.00
SCFGUPAM Alec Martinez G5 100.00 200.00
SCFGUPBB Brian Boyle G5 40.00 80.00
SCFGUPCH Carl Hagelin G1
SCFGUPDD Drew Doughty G1 60.00 120.00
SCFGUPHL Henrik Lundqvist G4
SCFGUPJC Jeff Carter G3 40.00 80.00
SCFGUPJQ Jonathan Quick G1
SCFGUPJW Justin Williams G1
SCFGUPLU Henrik Lundqvist G5
SCFGUPMG Marian Gaborik G5 50.00 100.00
SCFGUPMS Martin St. Louis G4
SCFGUPQU Jonathan Quick G3
SCFGUPTT Tyler Toffoli G5 100.00 200.00
SCFGUPWI Justin Williams G5

2014-15 SP Game Used Stanley Cup Finals Materials Net Cord

SCNCAK Anze Kopitar 40.00 100.00
SCNCAM Alec Martinez 15.00 40.00
SCNCAS Anton Stralman 15.00 40.00
SCNCBB Brian Boyle 15.00 40.00
SCNCBP Benoit Pouliot
SCNCBR Brad Richards
SCNCCH Carl Hagelin 25.00 60.00
SCNCCK Chris Kreider 25.00 60.00
SCNCDB Dustin Brown 20.00 50.00
SCNCDD Drew Doughty 20.00 50.00
SCNCDE Derick Brassard 25.00 60.00
SCNCDG Daniel Girardi 20.00 50.00
SCNCDK Dwight King 15.00 40.00
SCNCDM Dominic Moore 20.00 50.00
SCNCDO Derek Dorsett 15.00 40.00
SCNCDS Derek Stepan 25.00 60.00
SCNCGA Marian Gaborik 25.00 60.00
SCNCHL Henrik Lundqvist
SCNCJC Jeff Carter 25.00 60.00
SCNCJM Jake Muzzin 15.00 40.00
SCNCJN Jordan Nolan 25.00 60.00
SCNCJQ Jonathan Quick
SCNCJS Jarret Stoll
SCNCJW Justin Williams 20.00 50.00
SCNCKC Kyle Clifford 15.00 40.00
SCNCKK Kevin Klein 15.00 40.00
SCNCMG Matt Greene 15.00 40.00
SCNCMO John Moore 15.00 40.00
SCNCMR Mike Richards 25.00 60.00
SCNCMS Martin St. Louis 30.00 80.00
SCNCMZ Mats Zuccarello 25.00 60.00
SCNCRD Raphael Diaz
SCNCRM Ryan McDonagh 40.00 80.00
SCNCRN Rick Nash 25.00 60.00
SCNCRR Robyn Regehr 15.00 40.00
SCNCST Marc Staal 20.00 50.00
SCNCSV Slava Voynov 25.00 60.00
SCNCTL Trevor Lewis
SCNCTP Tanner Pearson 25.00 60.00
SCNCTT Tyler Toffoli 25.00 60.00
SCNCWM Willie Mitchell 15.00 40.00

2014-15 SP Game Used Winter Classic Materials Game Used Pucks

PUCK ODDS 1:845
WCGUPDA Daniel Alfredsson
WCGUPJB Jonathan Bernier 50.00 100.00
WCGUPJR James van Riemsdyk

2014-15 SP Game Used Winter Classic Materials Jerseys

GROUP A ODDS 1:34
GROUP B ODDS 1:27
OVERALL ODDS 1:15
*PATCH/99: .6X TO 1.5X BASIC A JERSEY
*PATCH/99: .8X TO 2X BASIC B JERSEY
WCCF Cody Franson A 10.00 25.00
WCDC David Clarkson A 8.00 20.00
WCJB Jonathan Bernier B 10.00 25.00
WCNK Nazem Kadri B 8.00 20.00

2014-15 SP Game Used Winter Classic Materials Net Cord

NET CORD/35 ODDS 1:120
WCBS Brendan Smith 20.00 50.00
WCCF Cody Franson 12.00 30.00
WCDA Daniel Alfredsson 15.00 40.00
WCDC David Clarkson 12.00 30.00
WCDD Danny DeKeyser 12.00 30.00
WCDP Dion Phaneuf 15.00 40.00
WCGN Gustav Nyquist 12.00 30.00
WCHZ Henrik Zetterberg 25.00 60.00
WCJA Justin Abdelkader 20.00 50.00
WCJH Jim Howard 15.00 40.00
WCJL Joffrey Lupul 12.00 30.00
WCJV James van Riemsdyk 15.00 40.00
WCKR Niklas Kronwall 12.00 30.00
WCKU Nikolai Kulemin 12.00 30.00
WCMR Morgan Rielly
WCNK Nazem Kadri 15.00 40.00
WCPD Pavel Datsyuk 30.00 80.00
WCPK Phil Kessel 25.00 60.00
WCTB Tyler Bozak 12.00 30.00
WCTT Tomas Tatar 12.00 30.00

2015-16 SP Game Used

1 Wayne Gretzky/99 15.00 30.00
2 Keith Yandle/93 5.00 12.00
3 Jakub Voracek/93 5.00 12.00
4 Steven Stamkos/91 10.00 25.00
5 John Tavares/91 10.00 25.00
6 Vladimir Tarasenko/91 8.00 20.00
7 Tyler Seguin/91 8.00 20.00
8 Jason Spezza/90 4.00 10.00
9 Brent Burns/88 6.00 15.00
10 Patrick Kane/88 10.00 25.00
11 David Pastrnak/88 8.00 20.00
12 Sidney Crosby/87 15.00 30.00
13 Nikita Kucherov/86 8.00 20.00
14 Marian Hossa/81 4.00 10.00
15 Phil Kessel/81 8.00 20.00
16 Phil Esposito/77 8.00 20.00
17 Victor Hedman/77 6.00 15.00
18 P.K. Subban/76 8.00 20.00
19 John Carlson/74 6.00 15.00
20 Tyler Toffoli/73 5.00 12.00
21 Sergei Bobrovsky/72 5.00 12.00
22 Evgeni Malkin/71 6.00 15.00
23 Nick Foligno/71 4.00 10.00
24 Jaromir Jagr/68 12.00 30.00
25 Max Pacioretty/67 5.00 12.00
26 Erik Karlsson/65 10.00 25.00
27 Mikael Granlund/64 4.00 10.00
28 Mark Stone/61 4.00 10.00
29 Roman Josi/59 5.00 12.00
30 Mark Scheifele/55 6.00 15.00
31 Jeff Skinner/53 4.00 10.00
32 Bo Horvat/53 8.00 20.00
33 David Krejci/46 5.00 12.00
34 Jonathan Bernier/45 6.00 15.00
35 Morgan Rielly/44 5.00 12.00
36 Henrik Zetterberg/40 8.00 20.00
37 Tuukka Rask/40 6.00 15.00
38 Logan Couture/39 6.00 15.00
39 Steve Mason/35 5.00 12.00
40 Cory Schneider/35 5.00 12.00
41 Pekka Rinne/35 8.00 20.00

42 Patrick Roy/33 25.00 50.00
43 Henrik Sedin/33 8.00 20.00
44 Zdeno Chara/33 15.00 30.00
45 Jonathan Quick/32 12.00 30.00
46 Carey Price/31 20.00 40.00
47 Frederik Andersen/31 6.00 15.00
48 Ryan Miller/30 15.00 30.00
49 Ben Bishop/30 8.00 20.00
50 Andrew Hammond/30 25.00 60.00
51 Henrik Lundqvist/30 10.00 25.00
52 Marc-Andre Fleury/29 12.00 30.00
53 Nathan MacKinnon/29 15.00 40.00
54 Claude Giroux/28 8.00 20.00
55 Ryan McDonagh/27 6.00 15.00
56 Anders Lee/27 8.00 20.00
57 Alex Galchenyuk/27 12.00 30.00
58 Nick Bjugstad/27 6.00 15.00
59 Blake Wheeler/26 8.00 20.00
60 Jiri Hudler/24 6.00 15.00
61 Sam Reinhart/23 8.00 20.00
62 Sean Monahan/23 8.00 20.00
63 Oliver Ekman-Larsson/23 6.00 15.00
64 Daniel Sedin/22 8.00 20.00
65 Peter Forsberg/21 8.00 20.00
66 James van Riemsdyk/21 8.00 20.00
67 Tomas Tatar/21 6.00 15.00
68 Derek Stepan/21 8.00 20.00
69 Ryan Johansen/19 12.00 30.00
70 Nicklas Backstrom/19 12.00 30.00
71 Jonathan Toews/19 30.00 60.00
72 Ondrej Palat/18 8.00 20.00
73 Ryan Strome/18 8.00 20.00
74 Jaden Schwartz/17 12.00 30.00
75 Ryan Kesler/17 10.00 25.00
76 Jason Zucker/16 8.00 20.00
77 Elias Lindholm/16 6.00 15.00
78 Ryan Getzlaf/15
79 Jordan Eberle/14
80 Jamie Benn/14
81 Johnny Gaudreau/13
82 Pavel Datsyuk/13
83 Mark Messier/11
84 Zach Parise/11
85 Brendan Gallagher/11
86 Jonathan Huberdeau/11
87 Guy Lafleur/10
88 Corey Perry/10
89 Matt Duchene/9
90 Filip Forsberg/9
91 Bobby Hull/9
92 Tyler Johnson/9
93 Alexander Ovechkin/8
94 Drew Doughty/8
95 Teemu Selanne/8
96 Joe Pavelski/8
97 Nicklas Lidstrom/5
98 Aaron Ekblad/5
99 Taylor Hall/4
100 Glenn Hall/1
101 Rasmus Rissanen/62 RC 8.00 20.00
102 Anton Slepyshev/42 RC 10.00 25.00
103 Curtis Hamilton/70 RC 10.00 25.00
104 Antoine Bibeau/30 RC 15.00 40.00
105 Artemi Panarin/72 RC 150.00 300.00
106 Andreas Athanasiou/72 RC 20.00 40.00
107 Ben Hutton/27 RC 15.00 40.00
108 Keegan Lowe/45 RC 12.00 30.00
109 Stefan Noesen/64 RC 8.00 20.00
110 Brian O'Neill/18 RC 15.00 40.00
111 Stanislav Galiev/49 RC 12.00 30.00
112 Viktor Svedberg/27 RC 12.00 30.00
113 Colin Miller/48 RC 10.00 25.00
114 Oscar Dansk/35 RC 20.00 50.00
115 Colton Parayko/55 RC 25.00 50.00
116 Henrik Samuelsson/55 RC 10.00 25.00
117 Connor Brickley/86 RC 8.00 20.00
118 Josh Anderson/53 RC 12.00 30.00
119 Jordan Oesterle/82 RC 6.00 15.00
120 Oscar Lindberg/24 RC 20.00 50.00
121 Daniel Sprong/41 RC 75.00 125.00
122 Dylan DeMelo/74 RC 8.00 20.00
123 Viktor Arvidsson/38 RC 20.00 50.00
124 Dylan Larkin/71 RC 150.00 300.00
125 Malcolm Subban/70 RC 35.00 60.00
126 Evgeny Medvedev/82 RC 20.00 40.00
127 Jack Eichel/15 RC 1200.00 1800.00
128 Jared McCann/91 RC 10.00 25.00
129 Brendan Ranford/64 RC 8.00 20.00
130 Mike Lee/30 RC 10.00 25.00
131 Joel Edmundson/6 RC
132 Logan Shaw/48 RC 20.00 40.00
133 Joonas Donskoi/27 RC 40.00 80.00
134 Mackenzie Skapski/70 RC 12.00 30.00
135 Jordan Weal/19 RC 20.00 50.00
136 Jean-Francois Berube/30 RC 12.00 30.00
137 Casey Bailey/37 RC 15.00 40.00
138 Devin Shore/17 RC 40.00 80.00
139 Tyler Bunz/34 RC 15.00 40.00
140 Mattias Janmark/13 RC
141 Nick Shore/21 RC 20.00 50.00
142 David Musil/87 RC 8.00 20.00
143 Slater Koekkoek/29 RC 12.00 30.00
144 Max Domi/16 RC 500.00 800.00
145 Tanner Kero/36 RC 15.00 40.00
146 Matt Puempel/26 RC 12.00 30.00
147 Mike Condon/39 RC 75.00 125.00
148 Louis Domingue/35 RC 30.00 60.00
149 Mikko Rantanen/96 RC 40.00 80.00
150 Nicolas Petan/19 RC 60.00 150.00
151 Luke Witkowski/53 RC 10.00 25.00
152 Brett Kulak/61 RC 8.00 20.00
153 Ronalds Kenins/41 RC 12.00 30.00
154 Mark Alt/39 RC 10.00 25.00
155 Robby Fabbri/15 RC 75.00 150.00
156 Sergei Plotnikov/61 RC 8.00 20.00
157 Nikolaj Ehlers/27 RC 175.00 300.00
158 Erik Gustafsson/52 RC 40.00 80.00
159 Sergey Kalinin/51 RC 10.00 25.00
160 Petr Straka/51 RC 40.00 80.00
161 Tyler Randell/64 RC 10.00 25.00
162 Danny Biega/41 RC 8.00 20.00
163 Connor Hellebuyck/37 RC 50.00 100.00
164 Brian Ferlin/68 RC 6.00 15.00
165 Joonas Kemppainen/41 RC 10.00 25.00
166 Alex Biega/55 RC 8.00 20.00
167 Sam Brittain/31 RC 15.00 40.00
168 Jake Virtanen/18 RC 500.00 750.00
169 Andrew Copp/9 RC
170 Noah Hanifin/5 RC
171 Ryan Hartman/38 RC 20.00 50.00
172 Brock McGinn/23 RC 40.00 80.00
173 Anthony Bitetto/2 RC
174 Derek Forbort/7 RC
175 Sam Bennett/93 RC 100.00 175.00
176 Bryan Lerg/11 RC
177 David Wolf/45 RC 12.00 30.00
178 Tommy Cross/56 RC 10.00 25.00
179 Nick Cousins/52 RC 12.00 30.00
180 Jacob de la Rose/25 RC 15.00 40.00
181 Kyle Baun/39 RC 15.00 40.00
182 Daniil Tarasov/71 RC 12.00 30.00
183 Radek Faksa/12 RC
184 Vincent Hinostroza/48 RC 8.00 20.00
185 Emile Poirier/57 RC 12.00 30.00
186 Shane Prince/10 RC
187 Chris Wideman/45 RC 12.00 30.00
188 Chris Driedger/32 RC 12.00 30.00
189 Nikolay Goldobin/82 RC 10.00 25.00
190 Chandler Stephenson/18 RC 30.00 60.00
191 Andrew Miller/58 RC 10.00 25.00
192 Ryan Bourque/25 RC 12.00 30.00
193 Brett Pesce/54 RC 10.00 25.00
194 Raman Hrabarenka/34 RC 15.00 40.00
195 Brendan Gaunce/50 RC 15.00 40.00
196 Max McCormick/89 RC 8.00 20.00
197 Connor McDavid/97 RC 800.00 1200.00
198 Kevin Fiala/56 RC 12.00 30.00
199 Linus Ullmark/35 RC 20.00 50.00
200 Matt O'Connor/29 RC 25.00 60.00
201 Brett Kulak/61 RC 10.00 25.00
202 Michael Mersch/49 RC 20.00 50.00
203 Dennis Rasmussen/70 RC 25.00 60.00
204 Juuse Saros/1 RC
205 Taylor Leier/58 RC 20.00 50.00
206 Marek Langhamer/30 RC 25.00 60.00
207 Conor Sheary/43 RC 50.00 125.00
208 Phil Di Giuseppe/34 RC 20.00 50.00
209 Garret Sparks/31 RC 300.00 400.00
210 Adam Pelech/50 RC 15.00 40.00
211 Joseph Blandisi/64 RC 20.00 50.00
212 Anthony Stolarz/65 RC 20.00 50.00
213 Brady Skjei/76 RC 40.00 100.00
214 Charles Hudon/54 RC 20.00 50.00
215 Michael Keranen/36 RC 15.00 40.00
216 Shea Theodore/53 RC 60.00 150.00
217 Mike McCarron/34 RC 60.00 150.00
218 Gustav Olofsson/23 RC 40.00 100.00
219 Fredrik Claesson/49 RC 30.00 80.00
220 Frank Vatrano/72 RC 60.00 150.00
221 Markus Hannikainen/33 RC 60.00 150.00
222 Jujhar Khaira/54 RC 15.00 40.00
223 Ryan Carpenter/40 RC 80.00 150.00
224 Zachary Fucale/30 RC 80.00 150.00
225 Jaccob Slavin/74 RC 15.00 40.00
226 Alexandre Grenier/65 RC 30.00 80.00
227 Andreas Martinsen/27 RC 25.00 60.00
228 Andrey Pedan/29 RC 30.00 80.00
229 Nick Ritchie/37 RC 300.00 400.00
230 Christoph Bertschy/47 RC 80.00 150.00
231 Daniel Carr/43 RC 40.00 100.00
232 Byron Froese/56 RC 15.00 40.00
233 Laurent Dauphin/76 RC 20.00 50.00
234 Joonas Korpisalo/70 RC 50.00 120.00
235 Matt Murray/30 RC 500.00 700.00
236 Ryan Dzingel/43 RC 100.00 200.00

2015-16 SP Game Used '14 Stadium Series Materials Net Cord Soldier Field

STATED PRINT RUN 35 SER.#'d SETS
SSNCBB Bryan Bickell 8.00 20.00
SSNCEM Evgeni Malkin 40.00 100.00
SSNCJN James Neal 12.00 30.00
SSNCJT Jonathan Toews 30.00 60.00
SSNCKV Kris Versteeg 10.00 25.00
SSNCPK Patrick Kane 30.00 60.00
SSNCPS Patrick Sharp 15.00 40.00
SSNCSC Sidney Crosby 30.00 60.00

2015-16 SP Game Used '14 Stadium Series Materials Net Cord Yankee Stadium

STATED PRINT RUN 35 SER.#'d SETS
SSNCBN Brock Nelson Jan.29 10.00 25.00
SSNCBP Benoit Pouliot Jan.29 8.00 20.00
SSNCCH Carl Hagelin Jan.25 15.00 40.00
SSNCDC Daniel Carcillo Jan.29 8.00 20.00
SSNCDM Dominic Moore Jan.25 15.00 40.00
SSNCDS Derek Stepan Jan.25 25.00 50.00
SSNCEN Evgeni Nabokov Jan.29 12.00 30.00
SSNCJJ Jaromir Jagr Jan.25 40.00 80.00
SSNCMS Marc Staal Jan.25 10.00 25.00
SSNCMZ Mats Zuccarello Jan.25 25.00 50.00
SSNCPE Patrik Elias Jan.25 12.00 30.00
SSNCRN Rick Nash Jan.25 12.00 30.00
SSNCTZ Travis Zajac Jan.25 10.00 25.00
SSNCHL1 Henrik Lundqvist Jan.25 80.00 80.00
SSNCHL2 Henrik Lundqvist Jan.29 40.00 80.00

2015-16 SP Game Used '14 Winter Classic Materials Net Cord

STATED PRINT RUN 35 SER.#'d SETS
WCNCDA Daniel Alfredsson 12.00 30.00
WCNCJA Justin Abdelkader 15.00 40.00
WCNCJB Jonathan Bernier 12.00 30.00
WCNCJL Joffrey Lupul 10.00 25.00
WCNCJV James van Riemsdyk 12.00 30.00
WCNCPD Pavel Datsyuk 15.00 40.00
WCNCTB Tyler Bozak 10.00 25.00

2015-16 SP Game Used All-Star Skills Fabrics

GROUP A ODDS 1:1669
GROUP B ODDS 1:297
GROUP C ODDS 1:157
GROUP D ODDS 1:13
GROUP E ODDS 1:2
OVERALL ODDS 2:3
AS1 Bobby Ryan E 2.50 6.00
AS2 Jakub Voracek C 3.00 8.00
AS3 Zemgus Girgensons E 2.50 6.00
AS4 Roberto Luongo E 3.00 8.00
AS5 Justin Faulk E 3.00 8.00
AS6 Steven Stamkos B 5.00 12.00
AS7 Phil Kessel E 5.00 12.00
AS8 Filip Forsberg D 4.00 10.00
AS9 Jonathan Drouin D 4.00 10.00
AS10 Vladimir Tarasenko D 5.00 12.00
AS11 Drew Doughty E 3.00 8.00
AS12 Jaroslav Halak E 3.00 8.00
AS13 Anze Kopitar E 5.00 12.00
AS14 Patrice Bergeron E 4.00 10.00
AS15 Tyler Seguin E 5.00 12.00
AS16 Kevin Shattenkirk E 2.50 6.00
AS17 Radim Vrbata E 2.50 6.00
AS18 Dustin Byfuglien E 3.00 8.00
AS19 Carey Price E 6.00 15.00
AS20 Corey Crawford E 4.00 10.00
AS21 Patrik Elias E 3.00 8.00
AS22 Jiri Sekac E 2.50 6.00
AS23 Ryan Nugent-Hopkins E 3.00 8.00
AS24 Marc-Andre Fleury E 5.00 12.00
AS25 Shea Weber E 2.50 6.00
AS26 Brian Elliott E 2.50 6.00
AS27 Claude Giroux E 3.00 8.00
AS28 Rick Nash D 3.00 8.00
AS29 Alexander Ovechkin E 5.00 12.00
AS31 Mike Hoffman E 2.50 6.00
AS32 Duncan Keith E 3.00 8.00
AS33 Oliver Ekman-Larsson E 2.50 6.00
AS34 Mark Giordano E 3.00 8.00
AS36 Brent Seabrook E 3.00 8.00
AS37 Brent Burns E 4.00 10.00
AS38 Nick Foligno D 2.50 6.00
AS39 Aaron Ekblad E 3.00 8.00
AS41 Ryan Getzlaf A 8.00 20.00
AS43 Ryan Suter D 2.00 5.00
AS44 Ryan Johansen E 4.00 10.00

2015-16 SP Game Used All-Star Skills Fabrics Patch

*PATCH/35: 1X TO 2.5X BASIC JSY
AS9 Jonathan Drouin 8.00 20.00
AS20 Corey Crawford 8.00 20.00
AS30 John Tavares 12.00 30.00
AS35 Jonathan Toews 12.00 30.00
AS40 Patrick Kane 15.00 40.00
AS42 Johnny Gaudreau 10.00 25.00

2015-16 SP Game Used All-Star Skills Dual Fabrics

STATED ODDS 1:3
*PATCH/35: .6X TO 1.5X BASIC DUAL
AS21 N.Foligno/J.Toews 5.00 12.00
AS22 N.Foligno/R.Johansen 5.00 12.00
AS23 S.Stamkos/J.Drouin 8.00 20.00
AS24 J.Tavares/J.Halak 8.00 20.00
AS25 R.Luongo/A.Ekblad 4.00 10.00
AS26 Gaudreau/M.Giordano 6.00 15.00
AS27 Tarasenko/Shattenkirk 6.00 15.00
AS28 D.Keith/B.Seabrook 4.00 10.00
AS29 D.Doughty/A.Kopitar 6.00 15.00
AS210 S.Weber/F.Forsberg 5.00 12.00
AS211 J.Voracek/C.Giroux 4.00 10.00
AS212 B.Ryan/M.Hoffman 3.00 8.00
AS213 J.Toews/P.Kane 8.00 20.00
AS214 J.Tavares/J.Voracek 8.00 20.00
AS215 P.Bergeron/P.Elias 5.00 12.00
AS216 R.Getzlaf/A.Kopitar 6.00 15.00
AS217 J.Tavares/R.Nash 8.00 20.00
AS218 R.Suter/K.Shattenkirk 3.00 8.00
AS219 D.Byfuglien/J.Faulk 4.00 10.00
AS220 B.Elliott/C.Crawford 5.00 12.00
AS221 M.Fleury/R.Luongo 6.00 15.00

2015-16 SP Game Used All-Star Skills Quad Fabrics

STATED ODDS 1:8
*PATCH/15: 1.2X TO 3X BASIC QUAD
AS41 Toews/Gtzlf/Tvres/Nash 10.00 25.00
AS42 Kane/Stmkos/Ovch/Kptr 20.00 50.00
AS43 Webr/Sbrk/Ekblad/Suter 5.00 12.00
AS44 Dghty/Keith/Burns/Byfgln 6.00 15.00
AS45 Crwfrd/Halk/Prce/M.Flry 15.00 40.00
AS46 Tvres/Trsnk/Frsbrg/Gdru 10.00 25.00
AS47 Ovch/Stmks/Tws/Tvres 20.00 50.00
AS48 Gtzaf/Segn/Kane/Kpitr 10.00 25.00
AS49 Frsbrg/Gdru/Grgns/RNH 8.00 20.00
AS410 Trsnko/Tvrs/Grx/RNH 10.00 25.00

2015-16 SP Game Used All-Star Skills Relics

STATED PRINT RUN 125 SER.#'d SETS
*GOLD/49: .5X TO 1.2X BASIC JSY/125
ASAE Aaron Ekblad 4.00 10.00
ASAK Anze Kopitar 6.00 15.00
ASAO Alexander Ovechkin 6.00 15.00
ASBB Brent Burns 5.00 12.00
ASBE Brian Elliott 3.00 8.00
ASBR Bobby Ryan 3.00 8.00
ASBS Brent Seabrook 4.00 10.00
ASCC Corey Crawford 5.00 12.00
ASCG Claude Giroux 4.00 10.00
ASCP Carey Price 10.00 25.00
ASDB Dustin Byfuglien 4.00 10.00
ASDD Drew Doughty 4.00 10.00
ASDK Duncan Keith 4.00 10.00
ASFF Filip Forsberg 5.00 12.00
ASJD Jonathan Drouin 5.00 12.00
ASJF Justin Faulk 4.00 10.00
ASJG Johnny Gaudreau 6.00 15.00
ASJH Jaroslav Halak 3.00 8.00
ASJS Jiri Sekac 3.00 8.00
ASJV Jakub Voracek 4.00 10.00
ASKE Phil Kessel 6.00 15.00
ASKS Kevin Shattenkirk 3.00 8.00
ASMF Marc-Andre Fleury 6.00 15.00
ASMG Mark Giordano 4.00 10.00
ASMH Mike Hoffman 3.00 8.00
ASNA Rick Nash 4.00 10.00
ASNF Nick Foligno 3.00 8.00
ASOE Oliver Ekman-Larsson 3.00 8.00
ASPB Patrice Bergeron 5.00 12.00
ASPE Patrik Elias 4.00 10.00
ASRG Ryan Getzlaf 6.00 15.00
ASRJ Ryan Johansen 5.00 12.00
ASRL Roberto Luongo 4.00 10.00
ASRN Ryan Nugent-Hopkins 4.00 10.00
ASRS Ryan Suter 2.50 6.00
ASRV Radim Vrbata 3.00 8.00
ASSS Steven Stamkos 8.00 20.00
ASSW Shea Weber 3.00 8.00
ASTS Tyler Seguin 6.00 15.00
ASVT Vladimir Tarasenko 6.00 15.00
ASZG Zemgus Girgensons 3.00 8.00

2015-16 SP Game Used All-Star Skills Relics Platinum Blue Patch

*BLUE/25: .8X TO 2X BASIC JSY/125
ASCC Corey Crawford 10.00 25.00
ASJD Jonathan Drouin 10.00 25.00
ASJT Jonathan Toews 15.00 40.00
ASPK Patrick Kane 15.00 40.00
ASTA John Tavares 15.00 40.00

2015-16 SP Game Used All-Star Skills Six Fabrics

GROUP A ODDS 1:168
GROUP B ODDS 1:55
GROUP C ODDS 1:13
OVERALL STATED ODDS 1:10
AS61 Wbr/Sbk/Ekb/Str/Grd/Flk 6.00 15.00
AS62 Dty/Kth/Byf/Brn/Shk/E-L 8.00 20.00
AS63 Crw/Lng/Hlk/Prc/Flry/Ell 20.00 50.00
AS65 Flg/Ovc/Kpt/Stm/Grx/Kne 30.00 80.00
AS66 Tws/Vrk/Trsk/Els/Fsg/Gdr 12.00 30.00
AS67 Jhn/Ksl/Ryn/Vrb/Gns/RNH 12.00 30.00
AS69 Tvr/Vrk/Nsh/Sgn/Frg/Ekb 20.00 50.00

2015-16 SP Game Used All-Star Skills Triple Fabrics Patch

STATED PRINT RUN 25 SER.#'d SETS
*BASE TRIPLE: .15X TO .4X PATCH/25
AS31 Hoffman/Drouin/Sekac 12.00 30.00
AS32 Seguin/Tavares/Tarasenko 20.00 50.00
AS33 Kessel/Kane/Gaudreau 20.00 50.00
AS34 Faulk/Giordano/Ekman-Larsson 10.00 25.00
AS35 Shattenkirk/Burns/Suter 12.00 30.00
AS36 Nugent-Hopkins/Vrbata/Gaudreau 15.00 40.00
AS37 Girgensons/Elias/Ryan 10.00 25.00
AS38 Forsberg/Bergeron/Stamkos 20.00 50.00
AS39 Tarasenko/Ryan/Vrbata 15.00 40.00
AS310 Kessel/Voracek/Kane 20.00 50.00
AS311 Foligno/Nash/Ovechkin 40.00 100.00
AS312 Nugent-Hopkins/Getzlaf/Johansen 15.00 40.00
AS313 Kopitar/Seguin/Tavares 20.00 50.00
AS314 Price/Fleury/Halak 30.00 80.00
AS315 Drouin/Gaudreau/Hoffman 15.00 40.00

2015-16 SP Game Used Autographs Blue

UNPRICED VET GRP A ODDS 1:1438
VET GROUP B ODDS 1:27
VET GROUP C ODDS 1:39
VET GROUP D ODDS 1:24
VET GROUP E ODDS 1:11
1-100 OVERALL VET ODDS 1:5
UNPRICED RK.GROUP A ODDS 1:977
ROOK.GROUP B ODDS 1:121
ROOK.GROUP C ODDS 1:12
ROOK.GROUP D ODDS 1:7
ROOK.GROUP E ODDS 1:3
102-198 OVERALL ROOKIE ODDS 1:2
1 Wayne Gretzky B 125.00 200.00
5 John Tavares C 6.00 15.00
7 Tyler Seguin B 10.00 25.00
8 Jason Spezza C 6.00 15.00
9 Brent Burns C 8.00 20.00
10 Patrick Kane B 30.00 60.00
12 Sidney Crosby B 60.00 150.00
15 Phil Kessel A
16 Phil Esposito B 10.00 25.00
17 Victor Hedman A
18 P.K. Subban A 20.00 50.00
19 John Carlson E 3.00 8.00
20 Tyler Toffoli E 4.00 10.00
22 Evgeni Malkin B 12.00 30.00
24 Jaromir Jagr B 25.00 50.00
25 Max Pacioretty C 4.00 10.00
27 Mikael Granlund E 3.00 8.00
30 Mark Scheifele E 4.00 10.00
31 Jeff Skinner C 3.00 8.00
32 Bo Horvat E 6.00 15.00
34 Jonathan Bernier C 4.00 10.00
38 Logan Couture B 8.00 20.00
39 Steve Mason D 3.00 8.00
40 Cory Schneider B 6.00 15.00
42 Patrick Roy B 50.00 120.00
45 Jonathan Quick B 15.00 40.00
46 Carey Price B 20.00 50.00
47 Frederik Andersen B 6.00 15.00
48 Ryan Miller B 8.00 20.00
49 Ben Bishop D 4.00 10.00
50 Andrew Hammond E 12.00 30.00
53 Nathan MacKinnon C 8.00 20.00
55 Ryan McDonagh D 3.00 8.00
56 Anders Lee E 3.00 8.00
57 Alex Galchenyuk C 5.00 12.00
59 Blake Wheeler B 8.00 20.00
61 Sam Reinhart C 6.00 15.00
65 Peter Forsberg B 12.00 30.00
66 James van Riemsdyk C
67 Tomas Tatar E 3.00 8.00
71 Jonathan Toews B 25.00 50.00
72 Ondrej Palat E 4.00 10.00
73 Ryan Strome E 3.00 8.00
75 Ryan Kesler D 4.00 10.00
76 Jason Zucker E 3.00 8.00
80 Jamie Benn B 10.00 25.00
81 Johnny Gaudreau D 8.00 20.00
82 Pavel Datsyuk B 10.00 25.00
83 Mark Messier B 12.00 30.00
84 Zach Parise B 8.00 20.00
85 Brendan Gallagher D 5.00 12.00
86 Jonathan Huberdeau B 8.00 20.00
87 Guy Lafleur B 10.00 25.00
88 Corey Perry B 8.00 20.00
89 Matt Duchene C 5.00 12.00
91 Bobby Hull B 10.00 25.00
92 Tyler Johnson D 3.00 8.00
93 Alexander Ovechkin B 25.00 50.00
95 Teemu Selanne B 15.00 40.00
96 Joe Pavelski B 8.00 20.00
97 Nicklas Lidstrom B 8.00 20.00
99 Taylor Hall B 15.00 40.00
100 Glenn Hall B 8.00 20.00
102 Anton Slepyshev D 3.00 8.00
104 Antoine Bibeau E 3.00 8.00
105 Artemi Panarin D 40.00 80.00
106 Andreas Athanasiou C 15.00 30.00
107 Ben Hutton C 4.00 10.00
109 Stefan Noesen E 2.50 6.00
113 Colin Miller E 5.00 12.00
115 Colton Parayko E 8.00 20.00
116 Henrik Samuelsson E 2.50 6.00
118 Josh Anderson E 3.00 8.00
120 Oscar Lindberg E 6.00 15.00
121 Daniel Sprong C 8.00 20.00
122 Dylan DeMelo D 2.50 6.00
124 Dylan Larkin C 75.00 135.00
125 Malcolm Subban D 6.00 15.00
128 Jared McCann E 3.00 8.00
129 Brendan Ranford E 2.50 6.00
133 Joonas Donskoi C 15.00 30.00
134 Mackenzie Skapski C 4.00 10.00
135 Jordan Weal D 3.00 8.00
136 Jean-Francois Berube E 2.50 6.00
140 Mattias Janmark C 4.00 10.00
141 Nick Shore B 5.00 12.00
143 Slater Koekkoek D 2.50 6.00
144 Max Domi C 8.00 20.00
146 Matt Puempel D 2.50 6.00
147 Mike Condon E 3.00 8.00
149 Mikko Rantanen C 8.00 20.00
150 Nicolas Petan D 3.00 8.00
153 Ronalds Kenins C 6.00 12.00
155 Robby Fabbri C 8.00 20.00
156 Sergei Plotnikov C 3.00 8.00
157 Nikolaj Ehlers D 6.00 15.00
163 Connor Hellebuyck C 10.00 25.00
167 Sam Brittain E 3.00 8.00
168 Jake Virtanen D 4.00 10.00
169 Andrew Copp E 3.00 8.00
170 Noah Hanifin C 5.00 12.00
172 Brock McGinn C 4.00 10.00
174 Derek Forbort B 8.00 20.00
175 Sam Bennett C 5.00 12.00
179 Nick Cousins D 3.00 8.00
180 Jacob de la Rose B 5.00 12.00
181 Kyle Baun E 3.00 8.00
183 Radek Faksa E 3.00 8.00
184 Vincent Hinostroza D 2.00 5.00
185 Emile Poirier C 6.00 15.00
186 Shane Prince D 2.50 6.00
189 Nikolay Goldobin C 4.00 10.00
190 Chandler Stephenson C 5.00 12.00
197 Connor McDavid A 350.00 500.00
198 Kevin Fiala C 4.00 10.00
201 Brett Kulak C 6.00 15.00
(inserted in 2015-16 Upper Deck Portfolio)
205 Taylor Leier C 8.00 20.00
(inserted in 2015-16 Upper Deck Portfolio)
208 Phil Di Giuseppe B 8.00 20.00
(inserted in 2015-16 Upper Deck Portfolio)
209 Garret Sparks A 10.00 25.00
(inserted in 2015-16 Upper Deck Portfolio)
210 Adam Pelech C 6.00 15.00
(inserted in 2015-16 Upper Deck Portfolio)
212 Anthony Stolarz C 8.00 20.00
(inserted in 2015-16 Upper Deck Portfolio)
213 Brady Skjei C 6.00 15.00
(inserted in 2015-16 Upper Deck Portfolio)
214 Charles Hudon A 8.00 20.00
(inserted in 2015-16 Upper Deck Portfolio)
216 Shea Theodore C 8.00 20.00
(inserted in 2015-16 Upper Deck Portfolio)
217 Mike McCarron A 10.00 25.00
(inserted in 2015-16 Upper Deck Portfolio)
218 Gustav Olofsson B 8.00 20.00
(inserted in 2015-16 Upper Deck Portfolio)
220 Frank Vatrano B 15.00 40.00
(inserted in 2015-16 Upper Deck Portfolio)
221 Markus Hannikainen B 6.00 15.00
(inserted in 2015-16 Upper Deck Portfolio)
222 Jujhar Khaira B 6.00 15.00
(inserted in 2015-16 Upper Deck Portfolio)
223 Ryan Carpenter C 8.00 20.00
(inserted in 2015-16 Upper Deck Portfolio)
224 Zachary Fucale A 8.00 20.00
(inserted in 2015-16 Upper Deck Portfolio)
225 Jaccob Slavin B 6.00 15.00
(inserted in 2015-16 Upper Deck Portfolio)
226 Alexandre Grenier C 6.00 15.00
(inserted in 2015-16 Upper Deck Portfolio)
229 Nick Ritchie A 8.00 20.00
(inserted in 2015-16 Upper Deck Portfolio)
230 Christoph Bertschy B 6.00 15.00
(inserted in 2015-16 Upper Deck Portfolio)
231 Daniel Carr C 6.00 15.00
(inserted in 2015-16 Upper Deck Portfolio)
232 Byron Froese B 6.00 15.00
(inserted in 2015-16 Upper Deck Portfolio)
234 Joonas Korpisalo C 10.00 25.00
(inserted in 2015-16 Upper Deck Portfolio)
235 Matt Murray A 100.00 250.00
(inserted in 2015-16 Upper Deck Portfolio)
236 Ryan Dzingel C 5.00 12.00
(inserted in 2015-16 Upper Deck Portfolio)

2015-16 SP Game Used Career Legacy Jerseys

STATED PRINT RUN 125 SER.#'d SETS
*GOLD/49: .5X TO 1.2X BASIC JSY/125
*BLUE/25: .8X TO 2X BASIC JSY/125
CLDS Denis Savard 5.00 12.00
CLJS Jason Spezza 3.00 8.00
CLJT Joe Thornton 4.00 10.00
CLJV Jakub Voracek 4.00 10.00
CLKL Kari Lehtonen 3.00 8.00
CLMG Marian Gaborik 4.00 10.00
CLML Martin St. Louis 4.00 10.00
CLTS Tyler Seguin 6.00 15.00

2015-16 SP Game Used Copper Jerseys

VET GROUP A ODDS 1:213
VET GROUP B ODDS 1:76
VET GROUP C ODDS 1:16
VET GROUP D ODDS 1:8
VET GROUP E ODDS 1:3
OVERALL VET ODDS 1:2
ROOKIE STATED PRINT RUN 399
1 Wayne Gretzky A 20.00 50.00
3 Jakub Voracek E 3.00 8.00
4 Steven Stamkos C 6.00 15.00
5 John Tavares C 6.00 15.00
6 Vladimir Tarasenko D 5.00 12.00
7 Tyler Seguin D 5.00 12.00
8 Jason Spezza E 2.50 6.00
9 Brent Burns D 4.00 10.00
10 Patrick Kane C 6.00 15.00
12 Sidney Crosby A 8.00 20.00
13 Nikita Kucherov E 5.00 12.00
14 Marian Hossa D 2.50 6.00
15 Phil Kessel D 5.00 12.00
17 Victor Hedman E 4.00 10.00
18 P.K. Subban E 5.00 12.00
19 John Carlson E 4.00 10.00
20 Tyler Toffoli E 3.00 8.00
21 Sergei Bobrovsky E 3.00 8.00
22 Evgeni Malkin D 10.00 25.00
25 Max Pacioretty D 3.00 8.00
26 Erik Karlsson E 6.00 15.00
27 Mikael Granlund E 2.50 6.00
28 Mark Stone E 2.50 6.00
29 Roman Josi E 3.00 8.00
30 Mark Scheifele E 4.00 10.00
31 Jeff Skinner D 2.50 6.00
33 David Krejci E 2.50 6.00
34 Jonathan Bernier E 3.00 8.00
35 Morgan Rielly E 2.50 6.00
36 Henrik Zetterberg B 5.00 12.00
37 Tuukka Rask C 3.00 8.00
38 Logan Couture D 3.00 8.00
39 Steve Mason E 2.50 6.00
40 Cory Schneider E 2.50 6.00
41 Pekka Rinne D 4.00 10.00
42 Patrick Roy A 10.00 25.00
43 Henrik Sedin D 3.00 8.00
44 Zdeno Chara D 3.00 8.00
45 Jonathan Quick D 5.00 12.00
46 Carey Price D 8.00 20.00
47 Frederik Andersen E 2.50 6.00
48 Ryan Miller E 3.00 8.00
50 Andrew Hammond E 10.00 25.00
51 Henrik Lundqvist C 4.00 10.00
52 Marc-Andre Fleury D 5.00 12.00
53 Nathan MacKinnon D 6.00 15.00
55 Ryan McDonagh E 2.50 6.00
56 Anders Lee E 3.00 8.00
57 Alex Galchenyuk C 4.00 10.00
58 Nick Bjugstad E 2.50 6.00
59 Blake Wheeler E 3.00 8.00
60 Jiri Hudler C 2.50 6.00
62 Sean Monahan D 3.00 8.00
63 Oliver Ekman-Larsson D 2.50 6.00
64 Daniel Sedin D 3.00 8.00
66 James van Riemsdyk C 3.00 8.00
67 Tomas Tatar E 2.50 6.00
68 Derek Stepan E 3.00 8.00
69 Ryan Johansen E 4.00 10.00
70 Nicklas Backstrom C 5.00 12.00
71 Jonathan Toews B 6.00 15.00
72 Ondrej Palat E 2.50 6.00
73 Ryan Strome E 2.50 6.00
74 Jaden Schwartz E 4.00 10.00
75 Ryan Kesler E 3.00 8.00
77 Elias Lindholm E 2.00 5.00
78 Ryan Getzlaf C 5.00 12.00
79 Jordan Eberle E 3.00 8.00
80 Jamie Benn C 4.00 10.00
81 Johnny Gaudreau D 5.00 12.00
82 Pavel Datsyuk B 5.00 12.00
83 Mark Messier A 6.00 15.00
84 Zach Parise D 3.00 8.00
85 Brendan Gallagher E 4.00 10.00
86 Jonathan Huberdeau E 3.00 8.00
87 Guy Lafleur A 5.00 12.00
88 Corey Perry E 3.00 8.00
90 Filip Forsberg C 4.00 10.00
92 Tyler Johnson B 3.00 8.00
93 Alexander Ovechkin C 5.00 12.00
94 Drew Doughty E 3.00 8.00
96 Joe Pavelski E 3.00 8.00
97 Nicklas Lidstrom C 3.00 8.00
98 Aaron Ekblad E 3.00 8.00
99 Taylor Hall D 6.00 15.00
100 Glenn Hall A 5.00 12.00
104 Antoine Bibeau 5.00 12.00
105 Artemi Panarin 15.00 30.00
106 Andreas Athanasiou 5.00 12.00
109 Stefan Noesen 4.00 10.00
111 Stanislav Galiev 5.00 12.00
114 Oscar Dansk 6.00 15.00
116 Henrik Samuelsson 4.00 10.00
118 Josh Anderson 5.00 12.00
121 Daniel Sprong 10.00 25.00
124 Dylan Larkin 15.00 40.00
125 Malcolm Subban 4.00 10.00
127 Jack Eichel 12.00 30.00
129 Brendan Ranford 4.00 10.00
134 Mackenzie Skapski 5.00 12.00
135 Jordan Weal 5.00 12.00
138 Devin Shore 5.00 12.00
141 Nick Shore 5.00 12.00
143 Slater Koekkoek 4.00 10.00
144 Max Domi 10.00 25.00
146 Matt Puempel 4.00 10.00
149 Mikko Rantanen 10.00 25.00
150 Nicolas Petan 5.00 12.00
153 Ronalds Kenins 5.00 12.00
155 Robby Fabbri 6.00 15.00
157 Nikolaj Ehlers 10.00 25.00
163 Connor Hellebuyck 12.00 30.00
168 Jake Virtanen 6.00 15.00
170 Noah Hanifin 6.00 15.00
171 Ryan Hartman 6.00 15.00
172 Brock McGinn 5.00 12.00
175 Sam Bennett 6.00 15.00
179 Nick Cousins 5.00 12.00
180 Jacob de la Rose 5.00 12.00
181 Kyle Baun 5.00 12.00
185 Emile Poirier 5.00 12.00
186 Shane Prince 4.00 10.00
189 Nikolay Goldobin 5.00 12.00
197 Connor McDavid 30.00 60.00
198 Kevin Fiala 5.00 12.00

2015-16 SP Game Used Draft Day Marks

STATED PRINT RUN 10-35
DDMAB Antoine Bibeau/35 8.00 20.00
DDMBG Brendan Gaunce/35 10.00 25.00
DDMCH Connor Hellebuyck/35 25.00 50.00
DDMCM Connor McDavid/35 400.00 600.00
DDMDF Derek Forbort/35 6.00 15.00
DDMDL Dylan Larkin/35 60.00 150.00
DDMEP Emile Poirier/35 8.00 20.00
DDMHS Henrik Samuelsson/35 6.00 15.00
DDMHS Hunter Shinkaruk/35 8.00 20.00
DDMHU Charles Hudon/35 12.00 30.00
DDMJV Jake Virtanen/35 10.00 25.00
DDMKF Kevin Fiala/35 8.00 20.00
DDMMD Max Domi/35 50.00 100.00
DDMMP Matt Puempel/35 6.00 15.00
DDMMS Mackenzie Skapski/35 8.00 20.00
DDMNC Nick Cousins/35 12.00 30.00
DDMNE Nikolaj Ehlers/35 15.00 40.00
DDMNH Noah Hanifin/35 10.00 25.00
DDMNP Nicolas Petan/35 12.00 30.00
DDMNR Nick Ritchie/35 8.00 20.00
DDMOK Oscar Klefbom/35 12.00 30.00
DDMRF Robby Fabbri/35 20.00 40.00
DDMRF Radek Faksa/35 8.00 20.00
DDMRH Ryan Hartman/35 10.00 25.00
DDMSB Sam Bennett/35 10.00 25.00
DDMSI Duncan Siemens/35 10.00 25.00
DDMSK Slater Koekkoek/35 6.00 15.00
DDMSN Stefan Noesen/35 6.00 15.00
DDMSP Shane Prince/35 6.00 15.00
DDMST Shea Theodore/35 8.00 20.00
DDMSU Malcolm Subban/35 20.00 40.00
DDMZF Zachary Fucale/35 30.00 60.00

2015-16 SP Game Used Gold Spectrum Materials

*ROOKIE/99: 1X TO 2.5X COPPER/399
1 Wayne Gretzky/5
3 Jakub Voracek/49 6.00 15.00
4 Steven Stamkos/25 15.00 40.00
5 John Tavares/15 15.00 40.00
6 Vladimir Tarasenko/49 10.00 25.00
7 Tyler Seguin/25 12.00 30.00
8 Jason Spezza/25 6.00 15.00
10 Patrick Kane/25 15.00 40.00
12 Sidney Crosby/5
13 Nikita Kucherov/99 8.00 20.00
14 Marian Hossa/25 6.00 15.00
15 Phil Kessel/25 12.00 30.00
16 Phil Esposito/5
17 Victor Hedman/99 6.00 15.00
18 P.K. Subban/25 12.00 30.00
19 John Carlson/49 8.00 20.00
20 Tyler Toffoli/49 6.00 15.00
21 Sergei Bobrovsky/49 6.00 15.00
22 Evgeni Malkin/25 25.00 60.00
25 Max Pacioretty/25 8.00 20.00
26 Erik Karlsson/49 12.00 30.00
27 Mikael Granlund/49 5.00 12.00
28 Mark Stone/99 4.00 10.00
29 Roman Josi/49 6.00 15.00
30 Mark Scheifele/99 6.00 15.00
31 Jeff Skinner/49 5.00 12.00
33 David Krejci/49 5.00 12.00
34 Jonathan Bernier/49 6.00 15.00
35 Morgan Rielly/49 5.00 12.00
36 Henrik Zetterberg/25 10.00 25.00
37 Tuukka Rask/25 8.00 20.00
38 Logan Couture/49 6.00 15.00
39 Steve Mason/49 5.00 12.00
40 Cory Schneider/49 5.00 12.00
41 Pekka Rinne/49 8.00 20.00
42 Patrick Roy/5
43 Henrik Sedin/25 8.00 20.00
44 Zdeno Chara/25 8.00 20.00
45 Jonathan Quick/49 10.00 25.00
46 Carey Price/25 25.00 60.00
47 Frederik Andersen/99 4.00 10.00
48 Ryan Miller/49 6.00 15.00
49 Ben Bishop/49 6.00 15.00
50 Andrew Hammond/99 15.00 40.00
51 Henrik Lundqvist/15 12.00 30.00
52 Marc-Andre Fleury/49 10.00 25.00
53 Nathan MacKinnon/25 15.00 40.00
54 Claude Giroux/25 8.00 20.00
55 Ryan McDonagh/49 5.00 12.00
56 Anders Lee/99 5.00 12.00
57 Alex Galchenyuk/25 10.00 25.00
58 Nick Bjugstad/99 4.00 10.00
59 Blake Wheeler/99 5.00 12.00
60 Jiri Hudler/49 5.00 12.00
61 Sam Reinhart/49 6.00 15.00
62 Sean Monahan/25 8.00 20.00
63 Oliver Ekman-Larsson/49 5.00 12.00
64 Daniel Sedin/25 8.00 20.00
65 Peter Forsberg/5
66 James van Riemsdyk/49 6.00 15.00
67 Tomas Tatar/99 4.00 10.00
70 Nicklas Backstrom/25 12.00 30.00
71 Jonathan Toews/25 15.00 40.00
72 Ondrej Palat/49 5.00 12.00
73 Ryan Strome/49 5.00 12.00
74 Jaden Schwartz/99 6.00 15.00
77 Elias Lindholm/49 4.00 10.00
78 Ryan Getzlaf/25 12.00 30.00
79 Jordan Eberle/49 6.00 15.00
80 Jamie Benn/49 8.00 20.00
81 Johnny Gaudreau/49 10.00 25.00
82 Pavel Datsyuk/25 10.00 25.00
83 Mark Messier/5
84 Zach Parise/49 6.00 15.00
85 Brendan Gallagher/49 8.00 20.00
86 Jonathan Huberdeau/49 6.00 15.00
88 Corey Perry/49 6.00 15.00
89 Matt Duchene/49 6.00 15.00
90 Filip Forsberg/25 10.00 25.00
92 Tyler Johnson/25 6.00 15.00
93 Alexander Ovechkin/5
94 Drew Doughty/49 6.00 15.00
95 Teemu Selanne/25 15.00 40.00
96 Joe Pavelski/49 6.00 15.00
97 Nicklas Lidstrom/15 8.00 20.00
98 Aaron Ekblad/49 6.00 15.00
99 Taylor Hall/25 15.00 40.00
100 Glenn Hall/5
171 Ryan Hartman/99 6.00 15.00
197 Connor McDavid/99 150.00 300.00

2015-16 SP Game Used Inked Rookie Sweaters

*PATCH/49: .6X TO 1.5X BASIC AU/149
EXCH EXPIRATION: 1/13/2018
IRSAB Antoine Bibeau 5.00 12.00
IRSAP Artemi Panarin EXCH 60.00 120.00
IRSBM Brock McGinn 5.00 12.00
IRSCM Connor McDavid 200.00 350.00
IRSDF Derek Forbort 4.00 10.00
IRSDL Dylan Larkin 75.00 150.00
IRSDS Daniel Sprong EXCH 10.00 25.00
IRSEP Emile Poirier EXCH 5.00 12.00
IRSHS Henrik Samuelsson 4.00 10.00
IRSJA Josh Anderson 5.00 12.00
IRSJR Jacob de la Rose 5.00 12.00
IRSJV Jake Virtanen EXCH 6.00 15.00
IRSKB Kyle Baun 5.00 12.00
IRSKF Kevin Fiala 5.00 12.00
IRSMD Max Domi EXCH 10.00 25.00
IRSMP Matt Puempel 4.00 10.00
IRSMR Mikko Rantanen EXCH 10.00 25.00
IRSNC Nick Cousins 6.00 15.00
IRSNE Nikolaj Ehlers 10.00 25.00
IRSNG Nikolay Goldobin 5.00 12.00
IRSNH Noah Hanifin 6.00 15.00
IRSNP Nicolas Petan 5.00 12.00
IRSRF Robby Fabbri 12.00 30.00
IRSRH Ryan Hartman 6.00 15.00
IRSRK Ronalds Kenins 5.00 12.00
IRSSB Sam Bennett EXCH 6.00 15.00
IRSSK Slater Koekkoek 4.00 10.00
IRSSN Stefan Noesen 4.00 10.00
IRSSP Shane Prince 4.00 10.00
IRSSU Malcolm Subban 10.00 25.00

2015-16 SP Game Used Inked Sweaters

ISCP Carey Price/25 40.00 80.00
ISDK David Krejci/99 6.00 15.00
ISJB Jonathan Bernier/50 8.00 20.00
ISJS Jeff Skinner/99 6.00 15.00
ISJT Jonathan Toews/25 30.00 60.00
ISJV Jakub Voracek/99 8.00 20.00
ISLR Luc Robitaille/25 15.00 40.00
ISMF Marc-Andre Fleury/99 12.00 30.00
ISMG Mikael Granlund/99 6.00 15.00
ISMK Mike Keane/99 6.00 15.00
ISMS Martin St. Louis/50 8.00 20.00
ISNM Nathan MacKinnon/50 15.00 40.00
ISPM Patrick Marleau/50 8.00 20.00
ISPS Paul Stastny/50 8.00 20.00
ISRK Ryan Kesler/99 8.00 20.00
ISSH Scott Hartnell/99 8.00 20.00
ISTA John Tavares/25 25.00 60.00
ISTH Tomas Hertl/99 8.00 20.00
ISTS Tyler Seguin/25 20.00 50.00
ISTT Tyler Toffoli/99 8.00 20.00

2015-16 SP Game Used Media Guide Booklets

STATED PRINT RUN 65 SER.#'d SETS
*PATCH/15: .8X TO 2X BASIC INSERTS/65
MGBV D.Backes/V.Tarasenko 12.00 30.00
MGCB P.Bergeron/Z.Chara 10.00 25.00
MGDJ R.Johansen/B.Dubinsky 10.00 25.00
MGDO M.Domi/O.Ekman-Larsson 8.00 20.00
MGEN R.Nugent-Hopkins/J.Eberle 8.00 20.00
MGFK M.Fleury/C.Kunitz 12.00 30.00
MGGB W.Gretzky/R.Blake 40.00 100.00
MGGC C.Coyle/M.Granlund 6.00 15.00
MGHE A.Ekblad/J.Huberdeau 8.00 20.00
MGIL J.Iginla/G.Landeskog 8.00 20.00
MGJJ J.Spezza/J.Benn 10.00 25.00
MGME C.McDavid/T.Hall 40.00 80.00
MGMG S.Monahan/J.Gaudreau 12.00 30.00
MGNK R.Nash/C.Kreider 8.00 20.00
MGOH A.Ovechkin/B.Holtby 15.00 40.00
MGOS R.Strome/K.Okposo 8.00 20.00
MGPC L.Couture/J.Pavelski 8.00 20.00
MGPG R.Getzlaf/C.Perry 12.00 30.00
MGQD J.Quick/D.Doughty 12.00 30.00
MGRK M.Rielly/N.Kadri 12.00 30.00
MGSK M.Keane/D.Savard 10.00 25.00
MGSP S.Stamkos/O.Palat 15.00 40.00
MGSS H.Sedin/D.Sedin 8.00 20.00
MGST J.Trouba/M.Scheifele 10.00 25.00
MGTK J.Toews/P.Kane 20.00 40.00
MGTZ K.Turris/M.Zibanejad 8.00 20.00
MGVG J.Voracek/C.Giroux 8.00 20.00
MGWJ S.Weber/S.Jones 6.00 15.00

2015-16 SP Game Used Rookie Phenoms Relics

STATED PRINT RUN 125 SER.#'d SETS
*BLUE/25: .8X TO 2X BASIC INSERTS
*GOLD/49: .6X TO 1.5X BASIC INSERTS
RPAB Antoine Bibeau 2.00 5.00
RPAP Artemi Panarin 15.00 40.00

Card	Low	High
RPCH Connor Hellebuyck	5.00	12.00
RPCM Connor McDavid	60.00	120.00
RPDL Dylan Larkin	25.00	50.00
RPDS Daniel Sprong	4.00	10.00
RPEP Emile Poirier	2.00	5.00
RPHS Henrik Samuelsson	1.50	4.00
RPJA Josh Anderson	2.00	5.00
RPJD Jacob de la Rose	2.00	5.00
RPJE Jack Eichel	25.00	50.00
RPJV Jake Virtanen	2.50	6.00
RPKF Kevin Fiala	2.00	5.00
RPMD Max Domi	4.00	10.00
RPMP Matt Puempel	1.50	4.00
RPMR Mikko Rantanen	4.00	10.00
RPNE Nikolaj Ehlers	5.00	12.00
RPNH Noah Hanifin	2.50	6.00
RPNP Nicolas Petan	2.00	5.00
RPRF Robby Fabbri	4.00	10.00
RPRH Ryan Hartman	2.50	6.00
RPRK Ronalds Kenins	3.00	8.00
RPSB Sam Bennett	2.50	6.00
RPSM Mackenzie Skapski	2.00	5.00
RPSP Shane Prince	1.50	4.00

2015-16 SP Game Used Stadium Series Relics

STATED PRINT RUN 125 SER.#'d SETS
*BLUE/25: .8X TO 2X BASIC JSY/125
*GOLD/49: .5X TO 1.2X BASIC JSY/125

Card	Low	High
LADB Dustin Brown	3.00	8.00
LADD Drew Doughty	4.00	10.00
LADK Dwight King	2.50	6.00
LAGR Matt Greene	2.50	6.00
LAJM Jamie McBain	2.50	6.00
LAJN Jordan Nolan	2.50	6.00
LAJW Justin Williams	3.00	8.00
LAMG Marian Gaborik	4.00	10.00
LAMJ Martin Jones	4.00	10.00
LANS Nick Shore	4.00	10.00
LATT Tyler Toffoli	4.00	10.00
SJAS Alex Stalock	2.50	6.00
SJBD Brenden Dillon	2.50	6.00
SJJS James Sheppard	2.50	6.00
SJLC Logan Couture	4.00	10.00
SJMI Matt Irwin	2.50	6.00
SJMK Melker Karlsson	2.50	6.00
SJMN Matt Nieto	2.50	6.00
SJPM Patrick Marleau	4.00	10.00

2015-16 SP Game Used Stanley Cup Finals Materials Net Cord

STATED PRINT RUN 25 SER.#'d SETS

Card	Low	High
SCNCAK Alex Killorn	25.00	60.00
SCNCAN Andrew Shaw	30.00	80.00
SCNCAS Anton Stralman	20.00	50.00
SCNCAV Antoine Vermette	20.00	50.00
SCNCBB Ben Bishop	30.00	80.00
SCNCBR Brad Richards	30.00	80.00
SCNCBS Brent Seabrook	30.00	80.00
SCNCCC Corey Crawford	40.00	100.00
SCNCCP Cedric Paquette	20.00	50.00
SCNCDK Duncan Keith	30.00	80.00
SCNCJB J.T. Brown	20.00	50.00
SCNCJD Jonathan Drouin	40.00	100.00
SCNCJG Jason Garrison	20.00	50.00
SCNCJO Johnny Oduya	25.00	60.00
SCNCJT Jonathan Toews	75.00	125.00
SCNCKT Kimmo Timonen	20.00	50.00
SCNCMH Marian Hossa	25.00	60.00
SCNCNH Niklas Hjalmarsson	20.00	50.00
SCNCNK Nikita Kucherov	50.00	120.00
SCNCOP Ondrej Palat	25.00	60.00
SCNCPK Patrick Kane	90.00	150.00
SCNCPS Patrick Sharp	30.00	80.00
SCNCRC Ryan Callahan	30.00	80.00
SCNCSA Brandon Saad	30.00	80.00
SCNCSS Steven Stamkos	60.00	150.00
SCNCTJ Tyler Johnson	25.00	60.00
SCNCTT Teuvo Teravainen	30.00	80.00
SCNCVA Andrei Vasilevskiy	40.00	100.00
SCNCVF Valtteri Filppula	25.00	60.00
SCNCVH Victor Hedman	40.00	100.00

2015-16 SP Game Used Supreme Gloves

STATED PRINT RUN 15 SER.#'d SETS

Card	Low	High
PAAK Anze Kopitar	30.00	80.00
PADB Dustin Brown	15.00	40.00
PADD Drew Doughty	20.00	50.00
PAJC Jeff Carter	20.00	50.00
PAMB Martin Brodeur	40.00	100.00
PAML Mario Lemieux	60.00	150.00
PAPA Pascal Dupuis	15.00	40.00
PARL Roberto Luongo	20.00	50.00
PASH Scott Hartnell	20.00	50.00
PASV Semyon Varlamov	20.00	50.00
PATT Tyler Toffoli	20.00	50.00

2015-16 SP Game Used Supreme Pads

STATED PRINT RUN 15 SER.#'d SETS

Card	Low	High
PACO Chris Osgood	12.00	30.00
PACP Carey Price	40.00	100.00
PAGF Grant Fuhr	50.00	100.00
PAJQ Jonathan Quick	30.00	80.00
PAMA Marc-Andre Fleury	20.00	50.00
PAPD Pavel Datsyuk	30.00	80.00

2015-16 SP Game Used Supreme Patches

STATED PRINT RUN 15 SER.#'d SETS

Card	Low	High
PAAE Alexander Edler	12.00	30.00
PAAG Alex Galchenyuk	25.00	60.00
PAAK Anze Kopitar	30.00	80.00
PAAM Alec Martinez	12.00	30.00
PAAP Alex Pietrangelo	15.00	40.00
PAAT Alex Tanguay	12.00	30.00
PABB Bob Bourne	15.00	40.00
PABE Patrik Berglund	12.00	30.00
PABH Braden Holtby	30.00	80.00
PABR Bill Ranford	20.00	50.00
PABW Blake Wheeler	20.00	50.00
PACA Craig Anderson	20.00	50.00
PACC Corey Crawford	25.00	60.00
PACG Claude Giroux	20.00	50.00
PACO Chris Osgood	20.00	50.00
PADB Dustin Brown	15.00	40.00
PADD Drew Doughty	20.00	50.00
PADG Doug Gilmour	25.00	60.00
PADK David Krejci	15.00	40.00
PADS Derek Stepan	20.00	50.00
PAEK Erik Karlsson	40.00	100.00
PAEM Evgeni Malkin	60.00	150.00
PAES Eric Staal	25.00	60.00
PAGF Grant Fuhr	20.00	50.00
PAGM Glen Murray	15.00	40.00
PAHZ Henrik Zetterberg	25.00	60.00
PAJB Jonathan Bernier	20.00	50.00
PAJC Jeff Carter	20.00	50.00
PAJH Jiri Hudler	15.00	40.00
PAJI Jarome Iginla	20.00	50.00
PAJJ Jack Johnson	12.00	30.00
PAJQ Jonathan Quick	30.00	80.00
PAJR Jeremy Roenick	20.00	50.00
PAJS Jason Spezza	15.00	40.00
PAJT John Tavares	40.00	100.00
PAKR Niklas Kronwall	15.00	40.00
PALA Gabriel Landeskog	20.00	50.00
PAMA Marc-Andre Fleury	30.00	80.00
PAMB Martin Brodeur	40.00	100.00
PAMG Mike Gartner	20.00	50.00
PAMI Mikael Granlund	15.00	40.00
PAMT Marty Turco	20.00	50.00
PANB Nicklas Backstrom	30.00	80.00
PAOV Alexander Ovechkin	80.00	200.00
PAPB Patrice Bergeron	25.00	60.00
PAPD Pavel Datsyuk	25.00	60.00
PAPE Corey Perry	20.00	50.00
PAPF Peter Forsberg	20.00	50.00
PAPK Patrick Kane	40.00	100.00
PAPM Patrick Marleau	20.00	50.00
PAPR Patrick Roy	50.00	120.00
PARB Rod Brind'Amour	15.00	40.00
PARG Ryan Getzlaf	30.00	80.00
PARI Morgan Rielly	15.00	40.00
PARJ Ryan Johansen	25.00	60.00
PARL Roberto Luongo	20.00	50.00
PARM Ryan McDonagh	15.00	40.00
PARY Bobby Ryan	15.00	40.00
PASA Denis Savard	25.00	60.00
PASB Brayden Schenn	20.00	50.00
PASC Sidney Crosby	80.00	200.00
PASD Shane Doan	15.00	40.00
PASE Daniel Sedin	20.00	50.00
PASH Scott Hartnell	20.00	50.00
PASJ Seth Jones	15.00	40.00
PAST Jordan Staal	20.00	50.00
PASU P.K. Subban	30.00	80.00
PASV Semyon Varlamov	20.00	50.00
PATH Joe Thornton	20.00	50.00
PATP Tanner Pearson	12.00	30.00
PATR Tuukka Rask	20.00	50.00
PATS Tyler Seguin	30.00	80.00
PAVD Vincent Damphousse	15.00	40.00
PAVH Victor Hedman	25.00	60.00
PAVO Jakub Voracek	20.00	50.00
PAWS Wayne Simmonds	25.00	60.00
PAZC Zdeno Chara	20.00	50.00
PATT Tyler Toffoli	20.00	50.00

2015-16 SP Game Used Supreme Skates

STATED PRINT RUN 15 SER.#'d SETS

Card	Low	High
PAEM Evgeni Malkin	50.00	125.00
PALU Milan Lucic	12.00	30.00
PAMD Marcel Dionne	20.00	50.00
PASB Brayden Schenn	15.00	40.00

2015-16 SP Game Used Supreme Sticks

STATED PRINT RUN 15 SER.#'d SETS

Card	Low	High
PAAG Alex Galchenyuk	25.00	60.00
PAAM Alec Martinez	12.00	30.00
PAAT Alex Tanguay	12.00	30.00
PABB Bob Bourne	15.00	40.00
PABC Bobby Clarke	20.00	50.00
PABE Patrik Berglund	12.00	30.00
PABL Rob Blake	20.00	50.00
PABR Bill Ranford	20.00	50.00
PABS Borje Salming	20.00	50.00
PABW Blake Wheeler	20.00	50.00
PACG Claude Giroux	20.00	50.00
PADE Devan Dubnyk	20.00	50.00
PADG Doug Gilmour	25.00	60.00
PADK David Krejci	15.00	40.00
PADS Derek Stepan	20.00	50.00
PAGC Guy Carbonneau	15.00	40.00
PAHZ Henrik Zetterberg	25.00	60.00
PAJB Jonathan Bernier	20.00	50.00
PAJH Jiri Hudler	15.00	40.00
PAJI Jarome Iginla	20.00	50.00
PAJJ Jack Johnson	12.00	30.00
PAJK Jari Kurri	20.00	50.00
PAJR Jeremy Roenick	20.00	50.00
PAJS Jason Spezza	15.00	40.00
PAJT John Tavares	40.00	100.00
PAKR Niklas Kronwall	15.00	40.00
PALR Larry Robinson	20.00	50.00
PAMG Mike Gartner	20.00	50.00
PAMM Mark Messier	30.00	80.00
PAMR Mike Richter	20.00	50.00
PAMT Marty Turco	20.00	50.00
PANB Nicklas Backstrom	30.00	80.00
PAOV Alexander Ovechkin	80.00	200.00
PAPB Patrice Bergeron	25.00	60.00
PAPF Peter Forsberg	20.00	50.00
PAPK Patrick Kane	40.00	100.00
PAPR Patrick Roy	50.00	120.00
PARM Ryan McDonagh	15.00	40.00
PASA Denis Savard	25.00	60.00
PASC Sidney Crosby	80.00	200.00
PASD Shane Doan	15.00	40.00
PASE Daniel Sedin	20.00	50.00
PASG Sam Gagner	15.00	40.00
PAST Jordan Staal	20.00	50.00
PASU P.K. Subban	30.00	80.00
PATE Teemu Selanne	40.00	100.00
PATH Joe Thornton	20.00	50.00
PATP Tanner Pearson	12.00	30.00
PAVA John Vanbiesbrouck	20.00	50.00
PAVD Vincent Damphousse	15.00	40.00
PAWC Wendel Clark	20.00	50.00
PAZC Zdeno Chara	20.00	50.00

2015-16 SP Game Used Winter Classic Materials Net Cord

STATED PRINT RUN 35 SER.#'d SETS

Card	Low	High
WCNCAO Alexander Ovechkin	40.00	80.00
WCNCBO Brooks Orpik	20.00	50.00
WCNCBR Brad Richards	15.00	40.00
WCNCBS Brandon Saad	15.00	40.00
WCNCCC Corey Crawford	20.00	50.00
WCNCDK Duncan Keith	15.00	40.00
WCNCEF Eric Fehr	10.00	25.00
WCNCEK Evgeny Kuznetsov	25.00	60.00
WCNCJC John Carlson	15.00	40.00
WCNCJH Jack Hillen	10.00	25.00
WCNCJO Johnny Oduya	12.00	30.00
WCNCJT Jonathan Toews	30.00	60.00
WCNCKA Karl Alzner	15.00	40.00
WCNCMG Mike Green	15.00	40.00
WCNCMH Marian Hossa	30.00	60.00
WCNCMK Marcus Kruger	15.00	40.00
WCNCMN Matt Niskanen	12.00	30.00
WCNCNB Nicklas Backstrom	30.00	60.00
WCNCNH Niklas Hjalmarsson	10.00	25.00
WCNCPK Patrick Kane	30.00	60.00
WCNCPS Patrick Sharp	15.00	40.00
WCNCSE Brent Seabrook	15.00	40.00
WCNCTB Troy Brouwer	15.00	40.00
WCNCTW Tom Wilson	15.00	40.00

2016-17 SP Game Used

Card	Low	High
1 Sidney Crosby/87	20.00	50.00
2 Robby Fabbri/15	10.00	25.00
3 Joe Thornton/19	10.00	25.00
4 Brayden Schenn/10		
5 Mark Stone/61	5.00	12.00
6 Max Pacioretty/67	5.00	12.00
7 David Pastrnak/88	8.00	20.00
8 Anze Kopitar/11		
9 Jonathan Huberdeau/11		
10 Jason Spezza/90	5.00	12.00
11 Andrew Ladd/16	10.00	25.00
12 Nathan MacKinnon/29	15.00	40.00
13 Sam Bennett/93	6.00	15.00
14 Rasmus Ristolainen/55	4.00	10.00
15 Anthony Duclair/10		
16 Taylor Hall/9		
17 Jakob Silfverberg/33	8.00	20.00
18 Jonathan Toews/19	20.00	50.00
19 Petr Mrazek/34	8.00	20.00
20 David Backes/42	6.00	15.00
21 Filip Forsberg/9		
22 Nino Niederreiter/22	8.00	20.00
23 Nick Foligno/71	4.00	10.00
24 Rick Nash/61	5.00	12.00
25 Alexander Ovechkin/8		
26 Nikita Kucherov/86	8.00	20.00
27 Morgan Rielly/44	5.00	12.00
28 Henrik Sedin/33	8.00	20.00
29 Blake Wheeler/26	8.00	20.00
30 Victor Rask/49	5.00	12.00
31 Ryan Kesler/17	10.00	25.00
32 Ryan Spooner/51	4.00	10.00
33 Carey Price/31	25.00	60.00
34 Jarome Iginla/12		
35 Max Domi/16	12.00	30.00
36 John Tavares/91	10.00	25.00
37 Corey Crawford/50	8.00	20.00
38 Mikael Granlund/64	4.00	10.00
39 Chris Kreider/20	10.00	25.00
40 John Klingberg/3		
41 Jake Allen/34	10.00	25.00
42 Phil Kessel/81	6.00	15.00
43 Nikolaj Ehlers/27	8.00	20.00
44 Tyler Johnson /9		
45 Mike Hoffman/68	4.00	10.00
46 Duncan Keith/2		
47 Ryan Miller/30	8.00	20.00
48 Ryan Getzlaf/15	15.00	40.00
49 Nazem Kadri/43	5.00	12.00
50 Connor McDavid/97	25.00	60.00
51 T.J. Oshie/77	8.00	20.00
52 Jaden Schwartz/17	12.00	30.00
53 Patrick Marleau/12		
54 Jakub Voracek/93	5.00	12.00
55 Victor Hedman/77	6.00	15.00
56 Alex Galchenyuk/27	10.00	25.00
57 Jaroslav Halak/41	6.00	15.00
58 Jeff Carter/77	5.00	12.00
59 Aleksander Barkov/16	10.00	25.00
60 Henrik Lundqvist/30	8.00	20.00
61 Boone Jenner/38	6.00	15.00
62 Gabriel Landeskog/92	4.00	10.00
63 Ryan Johansen/92	6.00	15.00
64 Jack Eichel/15	20.00	50.00
65 David Krejci/46	6.00	15.00
66 Derek Stepan/21	8.00	20.00
67 Bo Horvat/53	8.00	20.00
68 Cam Ward/30	8.00	20.00
69 Kyle Palmieri/21	8.00	20.00
70 Henrik Zetterberg/40	8.00	20.00
71 Jordan Eberle/14		
72 Sean Monahan/23	8.00	20.00
73 Patrick Sharp/10		
74 Tyler Toffoli/73	5.00	12.00
75 Zach Parise/11		
76 Brendan Gallagher/11		
77 Bobby Ryan/9		
78 Frederik Andersen/31	6.00	15.00
79 Michael Cammalleri/13		
80 Oliver Ekman-Larsson/23	6.00	15.00
81 Tom Wilson /43	6.00	15.00
82 Sam Reinhart/23	6.00	15.00
83 Jake Muzzin/6		
84 Mark Scheifele/55	6.00	15.00
85 Wayne Simmonds/17	12.00	30.00
86 Patrick Kane/88	10.00	25.00
87 Tomas Tatar/21	8.00	20.00
88 Anders Lee/27	8.00	20.00
89 Roberto Luongo/1		
90 Teuvo Teravainen/86	5.00	12.00
91 Matt Murray/30	12.00	30.00
92 Carl Hagelin/62	5.00	12.00
93 Igor Larionov/8		
94 Patrick Roy/33	20.00	50.00
95 Larry Murphy/55	5.00	12.00
96 Pat LaFontaine/16	10.00	25.00
97 Mario Lemieux/66	15.00	40.00
98 Felix Potvin/29	12.00	30.00
99 Pavel Bure/10		
100 Wayne Gretzky/99	25.00	60.00
101 Auston Matthews/34 RC	1250.00	1500.00
102 Pavel Zacha/37 RC	25.00	60.00
103 Christian Dvorak/18 RC	25.00	60.00
104 Nick Schmaltz/8 RC		
105 Justin Bailey/56 RC	15.00	40.00
106 Ivan Provorov/9 RC		
107 Chris Bigras/3 RC		
108 Matthew Tkachuk/19 RC	80.00	200.00
109 Kyle Connor/81 RC	40.00	100.00
110 William Nylander/29 RC	100.00	250.00
111 Mikhail Sergachev/22 RC	50.00	125.00
112 Brandon Carlo/25 RC	25.00	60.00
113 Dylan Strome/20 RC	50.00	125.00
114 Jacob Larsson/51 RC	25.00	60.00
115 Miles Wood/44 RC	15.00	40.00
116 Lawson Crouse/67 RC	12.00	30.00
117 Zach Sanford/82 RC	30.00	80.00
118 Daniel Altshuller/40 RC	15.00	40.00
119 Anthony Beauvillier/72 RC	15.00	40.00
120 Anthony Mantha/39 RC	50.00	120.00
121 Casey Nelson/34 RC	20.00	50.00
122 Ondrej Kase/86 RC	15.00	40.00
123 Dominik Simon/49 RC	20.00	50.00
124 Nikita Zaitsev/22 RC	25.00	60.00
125 Nikita Soshnikov/26 RC	15.00	40.00
126 Gustav Forsling/42 RC	20.00	50.00
127 Brandon Tanev/13 RC		
128 Esa Lindell/23 RC	25.00	60.00
129 Josh Archibald/45 RC	20.00	50.00
130 Mitch Marner/16 RC	700.00	900.00
131 Hudson Fasching/52 RC	15.00	40.00
132 Shane Harper/38 RC	30.00	80.00
133 Markus Nutivaara/65 RC	15.00	40.00
134 Nick Baptiste/73 RC	15.00	40.00
135 Oliver Bjorkstrand/28 RC	20.00	50.00
136 Sebastian Aho/20 RC	50.00	125.00
137 Ross Johnston/52 RC	15.00	40.00
138 Jared Coreau/31 RC	25.00	60.00
139 Jesse Puljujarvi/98 RC	40.00	100.00
140 Kasperi Kapanen/37 RC	40.00	100.00
141 Nick Sorensen /59 RC	15.00	40.00
142 Aaron Dell/30 RC	30.00	80.00
143 J.C. Lipon/46 RC	20.00	50.00
144 Roman Lyubimov/13 RC		
145 Pontus Aberg/46 RC	25.00	60.00
146 Kevin Labanc/62 RC	15.00	40.00
147 Artturi Lehkonen/62 RC	15.00	40.00
148 Michael Matheson/19 RC	25.00	60.00
149 Troy Stecher/51 RC	30.00	80.00
150 Sonny Milano/22 RC	30.00	80.00
151 Jimmy Vesey/26 RC	50.00	125.00
152 Denis Malgin/62 RC	15.00	40.00
153 Mike Reilly/4 RC		
154 Noel Acciari/55 RC	40.00	100.00
155 Oliver Kylington/58 RC	12.00	30.00
156 Lukas Sedlak/45 RC	20.00	50.00
157 Travis Konecny/11 RC		
158 Michal Kempny/6 RC		
159 Blake Speers/74 RC	15.00	40.00
160 Brendan Leipsic/49 RC	20.00	50.00
161 Tyler Motte/64 RC	15.00	40.00
162 Frederik Gauthier/54 RC	12.00	30.00
163 Nick Paul/13 RC		
164 Alan Quine/10 RC		
165 Sergey Tolchinsky/61 RC	12.00	30.00
166 Rob O'Gara/44 RC	20.00	50.00
167 Mathew Barzal/13 RC		
168 Ben Harpur/67 RC	15.00	40.00
169 Thomas Chabot/72 RC	40.00	100.00
170 Charlie Lindgren/40 RC	40.00	100.00
171 Nikita Tryamkin/88 RC	12.00	30.00
172 Danton Heinen/43 RC	30.00	80.00
173 Oskar Sundqvist/40 RC	20.00	50.00
174 Joel Eriksson Ek/14 RC		
175 Steven Santini/34 RC	15.00	40.00
176 Brayden Point/21 RC	60.00	150.00
177 Nic Dowd/26 RC	25.00	60.00
179 Jakob Chychrun/6 RC		
180 Connor Brown/12 RC		
181 Scott Kosmachuk/72 RC	15.00	40.00
182 Tristan Jarry/35 RC	40.00	100.00
183 Tobias Lindberg/46 RC	30.00	80.00
184 Blake Pietila/56 RC	15.00	40.00
185 Patrik Laine/29 RC	700.00	1000.00
186 Zach Werenski/8 RC		
187 Pavel Buchnevich/89 RC	40.00	100.00
188 Rinat Valiev/29 RC	30.00	80.00
189 Anthony DeAngelo/77 RC	15.00	40.00
190 Jason Dickinson/16 RC	20.00	50.00
191 Brett Lernout/36 RC	20.00	50.00
192 Josh Morrissey/44 RC	25.00	60.00
193 Tom Kuhnhackl/34 RC	15.00	40.00
194 Zach Hyman/11 RC		
195 Chase De Leo/77 RC	15.00	40.00
196 Mark McNeill/41 RC	20.00	50.00
197 Austin Czarnik/27 RC	40.00	100.00
198 Trevor Carrick/46 RC	20.00	50.00
199 Joseph Cramarossa/74 RC	15.00	40.00

2016-17 SP Game Used Gold

Card	Low	High
1 Sidney Crosby JSY B	25.00	60.00
2 Robby Fabbri JSY D	4.00	10.00
3 Joe Thornton JSY C	5.00	12.00
4 Brayden Schenn JSY D	4.00	10.00
5 Mark Stone JSY C	5.00	12.00
6 Max Pacioretty JSY C	5.00	12.00
8 Anze Kopitar JSY C	8.00	20.00
9 Jonathan Huberdeau JSY B	6.00	15.00
10 Jason Spezza JSY C	5.00	12.00
13 Sam Bennett JSY D	5.00	12.00
14 Rasmus Ristolainen JSY D	3.00	8.00
17 Jakob Silfverberg JSY D	4.00	10.00
18 Jonathan Toews JSY B	12.00	30.00
19 Petr Mrazek JSY C	5.00	12.00
20 David Backes JSY D	4.00	10.00
21 Filip Forsberg JSY D	5.00	12.00
22 Nino Niederreiter JSY D	4.00	10.00
23 Nick Foligno JSY D	3.00	8.00
24 Rick Nash JSY C	5.00	12.00
25 Alexander Ovechkin JSY B	25.00	60.00
27 Morgan Rielly JSY D	3.00	8.00
28 Henrik Sedin JSY C	5.00	12.00
29 Blake Wheeler JSY D	4.00	10.00
31 Ryan Kesler JSY C	5.00	12.00
33 Carey Price JSY B	20.00	50.00
34 Jarome Iginla JSY C	5.00	12.00
35 Max Domi JSY D	5.00	12.00
36 John Tavares JSY B	12.00	30.00
38 Mikael Granlund JSY D	3.00	8.00
39 Chris Kreider JSY C	5.00	12.00
40 John Klingberg JSY C	5.00	12.00
41 Jake Allen JSY D	5.00	12.00
42 Phil Kessel JSY C	6.00	15.00
43 Nikolaj Ehlers JSY D	4.00	10.00
45 Mike Hoffman JSY D	3.00	8.00
46 Duncan Keith JSY D	4.00	10.00
47 Ryan Miller JSY D	4.00	10.00
48 Ryan Getzlaf JSY C	8.00	20.00
49 Nazem Kadri JSY D	3.00	8.00
50 Connor McDavid JSY B	30.00	80.00
51 T.J. Oshie JSY D	6.00	15.00
52 Jaden Schwartz JSY D	5.00	12.00
53 Patrick Marleau JSY C	5.00	12.00
54 Jakub Voracek JSY D	4.00	10.00
55 Victor Hedman JSY C	6.00	15.00
56 Alex Galchenyuk JSY C	6.00	15.00
58 Jeff Carter JSY D	4.00	10.00
59 Aleksander Barkov JSY C	5.00	12.00
60 Henrik Lundqvist JSY C	5.00	12.00
62 Gabriel Landeskog JSY C	4.00	10.00
64 Jack Eichel JSY D	8.00	20.00
66 Derek Stepan JSY C	4.00	10.00
67 Bo Horvat JSY D	6.00	15.00
68 Cam Ward JSY D	4.00	10.00
70 Henrik Zetterberg JSY C	6.00	15.00
71 Jordan Eberle JSY D	4.00	10.00
72 Sean Monahan JSY D	4.00	10.00
73 Patrick Sharp JSY D	3.00	8.00
74 Tyler Toffoli JSY D	4.00	10.00
75 Zach Parise JSY D	4.00	10.00
76 Brendan Gallagher JSY C	6.00	15.00
78 Frederik Andersen JSY D	3.00	8.00
79 Michael Cammalleri JSY D	3.00	8.00
80 Oliver Ekman-Larsson JSY C	4.00	10.00
82 Sam Reinhart JSY D	3.00	8.00
83 Jake Muzzin JSY D	3.00	8.00
84 Mark Scheifele JSY A	10.00	25.00
85 Wayne Simmonds JSY D	5.00	12.00
86 Patrick Kane JSY B	12.00	30.00
87 Tomas Tatar JSY D	3.00	8.00
88 Anders Lee JSY D	4.00	10.00
89 Roberto Luongo JSY C	5.00	12.00
91 Matt Murray JSY C	8.00	20.00
93 Igor Larionov JSY B	6.00	15.00
94 Patrick Roy JSY A	20.00	50.00
95 Larry Murphy JSY B	6.00	15.00
97 Mario Lemieux JSY A	25.00	60.00
98 Felix Potvin JSY B	10.00	25.00
99 Pavel Bure JSY B	6.00	15.00
100 Wayne Gretzky JSY A	40.00	100.00
101 Auston Matthews JSY	25.00	60.00
102 Pavel Zacha JSY	5.00	12.00
103 Christian Dvorak JSY	4.00	10.00
104 Nick Schmaltz JSY	4.00	10.00
105 Justin Bailey JSY	4.00	10.00
106 Ivan Provorov JSY	8.00	20.00
107 Chris Bigras JSY	3.00	8.00
108 Matthew Tkachuk JSY	12.00	30.00
109 Kyle Connor JSY	10.00	25.00
111 Mikhail Sergachev JSY	8.00	20.00
112 Brandon Carlo JSY	4.00	10.00
113 Dylan Strome JSY	8.00	20.00
114 Jacob Larsson JSY	6.00	15.00
115 Miles Wood JSY	3.00	8.00
116 Lawson Crouse JSY	3.00	8.00
118 Daniel Altshuller JSY	3.00	8.00
119 Anthony Beauvillier JSY	4.00	10.00
120 Anthony Mantha JSY	10.00	25.00
123 Dominik Simon JSY	4.00	10.00
125 Nikita Soshnikov JSY	2.50	6.00
128 Esa Lindell JSY	4.00	10.00
130 Mitch Marner JSY	20.00	50.00
131 Hudson Fasching JSY	4.00	10.00
135 Oliver Bjorkstrand JSY	3.00	8.00
136 Sebastian Aho JSY	8.00	20.00
139 Jesse Puljujarvi JSY	10.00	25.00
140 Kasperi Kapanen JSY	8.00	20.00
143 J.C. Lipon JSY	4.00	10.00
145 Pontus Aberg JSY	5.00	12.00
146 Kevin Labanc JSY	4.00	10.00
148 Michael Matheson JSY	4.00	10.00
150 Sonny Milano JSY	5.00	12.00
151 Jimmy Vesey JSY	8.00	20.00
153 Mike Reilly JSY	3.00	8.00
155 Oliver Kylington JSY	3.00	8.00
160 Brendan Leipsic JSY	4.00	10.00
162 Frederik Gauthier JSY	3.00	8.00
170 Charlie Lindgren JSY	8.00	20.00
173 Oskar Sundqvist JSY	4.00	10.00
175 Steven Santini JSY	3.00	8.00
176 Brayden Point JSY	10.00	25.00
178 Ryan Pulock JSY	4.00	10.00
179 Jakob Chychrun JSY	4.00	10.00
180 Connor Brown JSY	6.00	15.00
185 Patrik Laine JSY	15.00	40.00
186 Zach Werenski JSY	8.00	20.00
187 Pavel Buchnevich JSY	6.00	15.00
189 Anthony DeAngelo JSY	4.00	10.00
190 Jason Dickinson JSY	3.00	8.00
193 Tom Kuhnhackl JSY	3.00	8.00
196 Mark McNeill JSY	4.00	10.00
198 Trevor Carrick JSY	4.00	10.00

2016-17 SP Game Used Red

Card	Low	High
2 Robby Fabbri JSY AU C	6.00	15.00
3 Joe Thornton JSY AU B	8.00	20.00
4 Brayden Schenn JSY AU C	6.00	15.00
5 Mark Stone JSY AU C	6.00	15.00
6 Max Pacioretty JSY AU B	8.00	20.00
8 Anze Kopitar JSY AU B	12.00	30.00
9 Jonathan Huberdeau JSY AU C	6.00	15.00
10 Jason Spezza JSY AU B	8.00	20.00
13 Sam Bennett JSY AU C	8.00	20.00
20 David Backes JSY AU B	8.00	20.00
22 Nino Niederreiter JSY AU C	6.00	15.00
24 Rick Nash JSY AU C	6.00	15.00
27 Morgan Rielly JSY AU C	5.00	12.00
33 Carey Price JSY AU B		
34 Jarome Iginla JSY AU B	8.00	20.00
36 John Tavares JSY AU B	15.00	40.00
41 Jake Allen JSY AU C	8.00	20.00
43 Nikolaj Ehlers JSY AU C	6.00	15.00
45 Mike Hoffman JSY AU C	5.00	12.00
47 Ryan Miller JSY AU C	6.00	15.00
50 Connor McDavid JSY AU B	125.00	250.00
52 Jaden Schwartz JSY AU C	8.00	20.00
53 Patrick Marleau JSY AU C	6.00	15.00
54 Jakub Voracek JSY AU C	6.00	15.00
56 Alex Galchenyuk JSY AU B	10.00	25.00
59 Aleksander Barkov JSY AU C	6.00	15.00
60 Henrik Lundqvist JSY AU B	8.00	20.00
62 Gabriel Landeskog JSY AU B	6.00	15.00
66 Derek Stepan JSY AU C	5.00	12.00
67 Bo Horvat JSY AU C	10.00	25.00
68 Cam Ward JSY AU C	6.00	15.00
70 Henrik Zetterberg JSY AU B	10.00	25.00
72 Sean Monahan JSY AU C	6.00	15.00
74 Tyler Toffoli JSY AU C	6.00	15.00
75 Zach Parise JSY AU B	8.00	20.00
76 Brendan Gallagher JSY AU B	10.00	25.00
77 Bobby Ryan JSY AU B	6.00	15.00
83 Jake Muzzin JSY AU C	5.00	12.00
84 Mark Scheifele JSY AU C	8.00	20.00
87 Tomas Tatar JSY AU C	5.00	12.00
88 Anders Lee JSY AU C	6.00	15.00
89 Roberto Luongo JSY AU B	8.00	20.00
91 Matt Murray JSY AU C	25.00	60.00
93 Igor Larionov JSY AU B	8.00	20.00
94 Patrick Roy JSY AU B	20.00	50.00
95 Larry Murphy JSY AU B	8.00	20.00
97 Mario Lemieux JSY AU B	25.00	60.00
98 Felix Potvin JSY AU B	12.00	30.00
99 Pavel Bure JSY AU B	8.00	20.00
100 Wayne Gretzky JSY AU B		
102 Pavel Zacha JSY AU C	8.00	20.00
103 Christian Dvorak JSY AU C	6.00	15.00
104 Nick Schmaltz JSY AU D	5.00	12.00
105 Justin Bailey JSY AU D	5.00	12.00
106 Ivan Provorov JSY AU B	15.00	40.00
107 Chris Bigras JSY AU D	4.00	10.00
108 Matthew Tkachuk JSY AU B	25.00	60.00
109 Kyle Connor JSY AU B	20.00	50.00
110 William Nylander JSY AU B	30.00	80.00
111 Mikhail Sergachev JSY AU B	15.00	40.00
113 Dylan Strome JSY AU C	12.00	30.00
115 Miles Wood JSY AU E	4.00	10.00
116 Lawson Crouse JSY AU D	4.00	10.00
118 Daniel Altshuller JSY AU E	4.00	10.00
119 Anthony Beauvillier JSY AU D	5.00	12.00
120 Anthony Mantha JSY AU C	15.00	40.00
123 Dominik Simon JSY AU C	6.00	15.00
125 Nikita Soshnikov JSY AU B	5.00	12.00
128 Esa Lindell JSY AU E	5.00	12.00
131 Hudson Fasching JSY AU D	5.00	12.00
135 Oliver Bjorkstrand JSY AU D	4.00	10.00
139 Jesse Puljujarvi JSY AU B	20.00	50.00
140 Kasperi Kapanen JSY AU C	12.00	30.00
143 J.C. Lipon JSY AU C	6.00	15.00
145 Pontus Aberg JSY AU C	8.00	20.00
146 Kevin Labanc JSY AU E	5.00	12.00
148 Michael Matheson JSY AU D	5.00	12.00
150 Sonny Milano JSY AU C	8.00	20.00
153 Mike Reilly JSY AU E	4.00	10.00
157 Travis Konecny JSY AU C	12.00	30.00
160 Brendan Leipsic JSY AU C	6.00	15.00
161 Tyler Motte JSY AU E	5.00	12.00
167 Mathew Barzal JSY AU B	25.00	60.00
169 Thomas Chabot JSY AU D	10.00	25.00
170 Charlie Lindgren JSY AU C	12.00	30.00
173 Oskar Sundqvist JSY AU D	5.00	12.00
175 Steven Santini JSY AU E	4.00	10.00
176 Brayden Point JSY AU C	15.00	40.00
178 Ryan Pulock JSY AU C	6.00	15.00
179 Jakob Chychrun JSY AU C	6.00	15.00
180 Connor Brown JSY AU C	10.00	25.00
185 Patrik Laine JSY AU B	30.00	80.00
186 Zach Werenski JSY AU B	15.00	40.00
187 Pavel Buchnevich JSY AU C	10.00	25.00
189 Anthony DeAngelo JSY AU E	5.00	12.00
190 Jason Dickinson JSY AU D	4.00	10.00
192 Josh Morrissey JSY AU D	6.00	15.00
193 Tom Kuhnhackl JSY AU D	4.00	10.00
196 Mark McNeill JSY AU E	5.00	12.00
198 Trevor Carrick JSY AU C	6.00	15.00

2016-17 SP Game Used All Star Skills Dual Fabrics

Card	Low	High
AS2BS J.Benn/T.Seguin	6.00	15.00
AS2HT T.Hall/V.Tarasenko	8.00	20.00
AS2KT P.Kane/J.Tavares	8.00	20.00
AS2LG D.Larkin/J.Gaudreau	6.00	15.00
AS2ML E.Malkin/K.Letang	12.00	30.00
AS2PB J.Pavelski/B.Burns	5.00	12.00
AS2PG C.Perry/J.Gibson	4.00	10.00
AS2QD J.Quick/D.Doughty	6.00	15.00
AS2SB S.Stamkos/B.Bishop	8.00	20.00
AS2SC C.Schneider/D.Dubnyk	4.00	10.00
AS2SK P.Subban/E.Karlsson	8.00	20.00

2016-17 SP Game Used All Star Skills Fabrics

Card	Low	High
ASAE		
ASBB Ben Bishop C	3.00	8.00
ASBH Braden Holtby B	6.00	15.00
ASBS Brandon Saad C	3.00	8.00
ASBU Brent Burns B	5.00	12.00
ASCG Claude Giroux C	3.00	8.00
ASCP Corey Perry B	4.00	10.00
ASCS Cory Schneider C	2.50	6.00
ASDB Dustin Byfuglien C	3.00	8.00
ASDD Devan Dubnyk C	3.00	8.00
ASDL Dylan Larkin B	6.00	15.00
ASDO Drew Doughty C	3.00	8.00
ASDS Daniel Sedin B	4.00	10.00
ASEK Erik Karlsson B	8.00	20.00
ASEM Evgeni Malkin A	15.00	40.00
ASGI John Gibson C	3.00	8.00
ASJB Jamie Benn A	6.00	15.00
ASJF Justin Faulk C	2.50	6.00
ASJG Johnny Gaudreau B	6.00	15.00
ASJJ Jaromir Jagr A	12.00	30.00
ASJN James Neal C	2.50	6.00
ASJP Joe Pavelski B	4.00	10.00
ASJQ Jonathan Quick C	5.00	12.00
ASJS John Scott C	3.00	8.00
ASJT John Tavares A	10.00	25.00
ASKL Kris Letang B	4.00	10.00
ASKU Evgeny Kuznetsov B	6.00	15.00
ASLK Leo Komarov C	3.00	8.00
ASMD Matt Duchene C	3.00	8.00
ASMG Mark Giordano C	2.50	6.00
ASNB Nicklas Backstrom C	5.00	12.00
ASPB Patrice Bergeron C	4.00	10.00
ASPK Patrick Kane A	10.00	25.00
ASPR Pekka Rinne C	4.00	10.00
ASPS P.K. Subban A	8.00	20.00
ASRJ Roman Josi C	3.00	8.00
ASRL Roberto Luongo A	5.00	12.00
ASRM Ryan McDonagh C	2.50	6.00
ASRO Ryan O'Reilly C	3.00	8.00
ASSS Steven Stamkos A	10.00	25.00
ASSW Shea Weber C	2.50	6.00
ASTH Taylor Hall A	10.00	25.00
ASTS Tyler Seguin A	8.00	20.00
ASVT Vladimir Tarasenko A	8.00	20.00

2016-17 SP Game Used All Star Skills Quad Fabrics

Card	Low	High
AS4NSH Neal/Josi/Weber/Rinne B	6.00	15.00
AS4CAPT Kane/Tavares/Scott/Jagr A	12.00	30.00
AS4DMEN Faulk/McDonagh Giordano/Byfuglien B	5.00	12.00
AS4SCUP Malkin/Letang Pavelski/Burns A	15.00	40.00
AS4SOCAL Doughty/Quick Perry/Gibson B	8.00	20.00

2016-17 SP Game Used All Star Skills Relic Blends

Card	Low	High
ASBAE Aaron Ekblad	5.00	12.00
ASBBB Ben Bishop	5.00	12.00
ASBBH Braden Holtby	8.00	20.00
ASBBS Brandon Saad	5.00	12.00
ASBBU Brent Burns	6.00	15.00
ASBCG Claude Giroux	5.00	12.00
ASBCP Corey Perry	5.00	12.00
ASBCS Cory Schneider	4.00	10.00
ASBDB Dustin Byfuglien	5.00	12.00
ASBDD Devan Dubnyk	5.00	12.00
ASBDL Dylan Larkin	8.00	20.00
ASBDO Drew Doughty	5.00	12.00
ASBDS Daniel Sedin	5.00	12.00
ASBEK Erik Karlsson	10.00	25.00
ASBEM Evgeni Malkin	15.00	40.00
ASBGI John Gibson	5.00	12.00
ASBJB Jamie Benn	6.00	15.00
ASBJF Justin Faulk	4.00	10.00
ASBJG Johnny Gaudreau	8.00	20.00
ASBJJ Jaromir Jagr	12.00	30.00
ASBJN James Neal	4.00	10.00
ASBJP Joe Pavelski	5.00	12.00
ASBJQ Jonathan Quick	8.00	20.00
ASBJS John Scott	5.00	12.00
ASBJT John Tavares	10.00	25.00
ASBKL Kris Letang	5.00	12.00
ASBKU Evgeny Kuznetsov	8.00	20.00
ASBLK Leo Komarov	5.00	12.00
ASBMD Matt Duchene	5.00	12.00
ASBMG Mark Giordano	4.00	10.00
ASBNB Nicklas Backstrom	8.00	20.00
ASBPB Patrice Bergeron	6.00	15.00
ASBPK Patrick Kane	10.00	25.00
ASBPR Pekka Rinne	6.00	15.00
ASBPS P.K. Subban	8.00	20.00
ASBRJ Roman Josi	5.00	12.00
ASBRL Roberto Luongo	5.00	12.00
ASBRM Ryan McDonagh	4.00	10.00
ASBRO Ryan O'Reilly	5.00	12.00
ASBSS Steven Stamkos	10.00	25.00
ASBSW Shea Weber	4.00	10.00
ASBTH Taylor Hall	10.00	25.00
ASBTS Tyler Seguin	8.00	20.00
ASBVT Vladimir Tarasenko	8.00	20.00

2016-17 SP Game Used All Star Skills Six Fabrics

Card	Low	High
AS6-DEF Karlsson/Doughty/Letang Subban/Burns/Josi B	12.00	30.00
AS6AFWD Larkin/Bergeron/Jagr Komarov/O'Reilly/Stamkos B	15.00	40.00
AS6CFWD Kane/Benn/Tarasenko Duchene/Seguin/Neal A	15.00	40.00
AS6FPNP Neal/Weber/Rinne Jagr/Ekblad/Luongo B	15.00	40.00
AS6MFWD Kuznetsov/Malkin/Tavares Giroux/Saad/Backstrom A	25.00	60.00
AS6PFWD Gaudreau/Hall Perry/Pavelski/Scott/Sedin B	12.00	30.00
AS6ASTARS Kane/Benn/Gaudreau Malkin/Kuznetsov/Tavares A	25.00	60.00

2016-17 SP Game Used All Star Skills Triple Fabrics

Card	Low	High
AS3BHQ Bishop/Holtby/Quick	6.00	15.00
AS3BKH Backstrom/Kuznetsov/Holtby	6.00	15.00
AS3EJL Ekblad/Jagr/Luongo	10.00	25.00
AS3GBB Giordano/Burns/Byfuglien	5.00	12.00
AS3KSE Karlsson/Subban/Ekblad	8.00	20.00
AS3SBS Saad/Bergeron/Scott	5.00	12.00
AS3SGP Stamkos/Giroux/Pavelski	8.00	20.00
AS3SHD Seguin/Hall/Duchene	8.00	20.00
AS3-SOK Sedin/O'Reilly/Komarov	4.00	10.00

2016-17 SP Game Used Autographs Blue

Card	Low	High
2 Robby Fabbri D	3.00	8.00
3 Joe Thornton A		
4 Brayden Schenn D	3.00	8.00
6 Max Pacioretty C	5.00	12.00
8 Anze Kopitar C	8.00	20.00
9 Jonathan Huberdeau C	5.00	12.00
10 Jason Spezza C	5.00	12.00
11 Andrew Ladd C	5.00	12.00
13 Sam Bennett C	6.00	15.00
16 Taylor Hall C	10.00	25.00
22 Nino Niederreiter D	3.00	8.00
24 Rick Nash B	8.00	20.00
25 Alexander Ovechkin A		
26 Nikita Kucherov D	5.00	12.00
27 Morgan Rielly C	4.00	10.00
32 Ryan Spooner D	2.50	6.00
33 Carey Price B	50.00	120.00
34 Jarome Iginla B	8.00	20.00
36 John Tavares B	15.00	40.00
41 Jake Allen D	4.00	10.00
43 Nikolaj Ehlers D	3.00	8.00
44 Tyler Johnson D	2.50	6.00
47 Ryan Miller C	5.00	12.00
50 Connor McDavid C	90.00	150.00
52 Jaden Schwartz D	4.00	10.00
53 Patrick Marleau C	5.00	12.00
54 Jakub Voracek C	5.00	12.00
56 Alex Galchenyuk B	10.00	25.00
57 Jaroslav Halak C	5.00	12.00
59 Aleksander Barkov C	5.00	12.00
60 Henrik Lundqvist B	25.00	60.00
61 Boone Jenner D	3.00	8.00
62 Gabriel Landeskog C	4.00	10.00
65 David Krejci C	5.00	12.00
66 Derek Stepan D	2.50	6.00
67 Bo Horvat D	5.00	12.00
68 Cam Ward C	5.00	12.00
69 Kyle Palmieri D	2.50	6.00
70 Henrik Zetterberg B	10.00	25.00
72 Sean Monahan C	5.00	12.00
74 Tyler Toffoli D	3.00	8.00
75 Zach Parise B	8.00	20.00
76 Brendan Gallagher C	6.00	15.00
77 Bobby Ryan C	4.00	10.00
81 Tom Wilson D	3.00	8.00
83 Jake Muzzin C	4.00	10.00
84 Mark Scheifele D	4.00	10.00
87 Tomas Tatar D	2.50	6.00
88 Anders Lee D	3.00	8.00
89 Roberto Luongo C	5.00	12.00
91 Matt Murray C	20.00	50.00
92 Carl Hagelin D	3.00	8.00
93 Igor Larionov B	8.00	20.00
94 Patrick Roy B	40.00	100.00
95 Larry Murphy C	5.00	12.00
97 Mario Lemieux B	50.00	120.00
98 Felix Potvin C	8.00	20.00
99 Pavel Bure B		
100 Wayne Gretzky C	200.00	300.00
101 Auston Matthews A	200.00	400.00
102 Pavel Zacha F	4.00	10.00
103 Christian Dvorak B	6.00	15.00
104 Nick Schmaltz D	4.00	10.00
105 Justin Bailey F	3.00	8.00
106 Ivan Provorov B	12.00	30.00
107 Chris Bigras F	2.50	6.00
108 Matthew Tkachuk C	15.00	40.00
109 Kyle Connor C	12.00	30.00
110 William Nylander C	20.00	50.00
111 Mikhail Sergachev B	12.00	30.00
113 Dylan Strome B	30.00	80.00
115 Miles Wood D	3.00	8.00
116 Lawson Crouse D	3.00	8.00
118 Daniel Altshuller E	3.00	8.00
119 Anthony Beauvillier B	6.00	15.00
120 Anthony Mantha D	10.00	25.00
123 Dominik Simon F	3.00	8.00
125 Nikita Soshnikov D	2.50	6.00
128 Esa Lindell F	3.00	8.00
131 Hudson Fasching B	6.00	15.00
135 Oliver Bjorkstrand F	2.50	6.00
139 Jesse Puljujarvi B	15.00	40.00
140 Kasperi Kapanen D	8.00	20.00
143 J.C. Lipon B	6.00	15.00
145 Pontus Aberg E	5.00	12.00
146 Kevin Labanc E	4.00	10.00
148 Michael Matheson F	3.00	8.00
150 Sonny Milano B	8.00	20.00
153 Mike Reilly F	2.50	6.00
157 Travis Konecny B		
160 Brendan Leipsic E	4.00	10.00
161 Tyler Motte D	4.00	10.00
165 Sergey Tolchinsky F	2.50	6.00
167 Mathew Barzal C	15.00	40.00
169 Thomas Chabot D	8.00	20.00
170 Charlie Lindgren F	6.00	15.00
172 Danton Heinen D	6.00	15.00
173 Oskar Sundqvist E	4.00	10.00
175 Steven Santini E	3.00	8.00
176 Brayden Point B	15.00	40.00
178 Ryan Pulock F	3.00	8.00
179 Jakob Chychrun F	3.00	8.00
180 Connor Brown F	5.00	12.00
185 Patrik Laine C		
186 Zach Werenski C	10.00	25.00
187 Pavel Buchnevich F	5.00	12.00
189 Anthony DeAngelo E	4.00	10.00
190 Jason Dickinson F	2.50	6.00
192 Josh Morrissey E	5.00	12.00
193 Tom Kuhnhackl D	3.00	8.00
195 Chase De Leo F	3.00	8.00
196 Mark McNeill F	3.00	8.00
198 Trevor Carrick F	3.00	8.00

2016-17 SP Game Used Banner Year All Star '16

Card	Low	High
BASAE Aaron Ekblad	5.00	12.00
BASBB Ben Bishop	5.00	12.00
BASBH Braden Holtby	8.00	20.00

BASBS Brandon Saad 5.00 12.00
BASBU Brent Burns 6.00 15.00
BASCG Claude Giroux 5.00 12.00
BASCP Corey Perry 5.00 12.00
BASCS Cory Schneider 4.00 10.00
BASDB Dustin Byfuglien 5.00 12.00
BASDD Devan Dubnyk 5.00 12.00
BASDL Dylan Larkin 8.00 20.00
BASDO Drew Doughty 5.00 12.00
BASDS Daniel Sedin 5.00 12.00
BASEK Evgeny Kuznetsov 8.00 20.00
BASEM Evgeni Malkin 15.00 40.00
BASGI John Gibson 5.00 12.00
BASJB Jamie Benn 6.00 15.00
BASJF Justin Faulk 4.00 10.00
BASJG Johnny Gaudreau 8.00 20.00
BASJJ Jaromir Jagr 12.00 30.00
BASJN James Neal 4.00 10.00
BASJP Joe Pavelski 5.00 12.00
BASJQ Jonathan Quick 8.00 20.00
BASJS John Scott SP 20.00 50.00
BASJT John Tavares 10.00 25.00
BASKA Erik Karlsson 10.00 25.00
BASKL Kris Letang 5.00 12.00
BASLK Leo Komarov 5.00 12.00
BASMD Matt Duchene 5.00 12.00
BASMG Mark Giordano 4.00 10.00
BASNB Nicklas Backstrom 8.00 20.00
BASPB Patrice Bergeron 6.00 15.00
BASPK Patrick Kane 10.00 25.00
BASPR Pekka Rinne 6.00 15.00
BASPS P.K. Subban 8.00 20.00
BASRJ Roman Josi 5.00 12.00
BASRL Roberto Luongo 5.00 12.00
BASRM Ryan McDonagh 4.00 10.00
BASRO Ryan O'Reilly 5.00 12.00
BASSS Steven Stamkos 10.00 25.00
BASSW Shea Weber 4.00 10.00
BASTH Taylor Hall 10.00 25.00
BASTS Tyler Seguin 8.00 20.00
BASVT Vladimir Tarasenko 8.00 20.00

2016-17 SP Game Used Banner Year All Star '16 Autographs

BASBU Brent Burns B 30.00 80.00
BASCS Cory Schneider B 20.00 50.00
BASGI John Gibson B 25.00 60.00
BASJB Jamie Benn B 30.00 80.00
BASJP Joe Pavelski B 25.00 60.00
BASJT John Tavares A 80.00 200.00
BASRJ Roman Josi B 25.00 60.00
BASRL Roberto Luongo A 40.00 100.00

2016-17 SP Game Used Banner Year Draft '12

BD12AA Andreas Athanasiou 6.00 15.00
BD12AG Alex Galchenyuk SP 8.00 20.00
BD12AV Andrei Vasilevskiy 8.00 20.00
BD12CB Connor Brown 10.00 25.00
BD12FA Frederik Andersen 5.00 12.00
BD12FF Filip Forsberg 8.00 20.00
BD12MM Matt Murray 10.00 25.00
BD12MR Morgan Rielly 5.00 12.00
BD12NY Nail Yakupov 5.00 12.00
BD12RM Ryan Murray 4.00 10.00
BD12SG Shayne Gostisbehere 8.00 20.00
BD12TH Tomas Hertl 6.00 15.00
BD12TT Teuvo Teravainen 6.00 15.00
BD12ZG Zemgus Girgensons 5.00 12.00

2016-17 SP Game Used Banner Year Draft '12 Autographs

BD12AA Andreas Athanasiou C 20.00 50.00
BD12AG Alex Galchenyuk B 20.00 50.00
BD12-MM Matt Murray C 20.00 50.00

2016-17 SP Game Used Banner Year Draft '14

BD14AE Aaron Ekblad SP 6.00 15.00
BD14DL Dylan Larkin 10.00 25.00
BD14DP David Pastrnak 10.00 25.00
BD14JV Jake Virtanen 8.00 20.00
BD14LD Leon Draisaitl 8.00 20.00
BD14NE Nikolaj Ehlers 6.00 15.00
BD14RF Robby Fabbri 6.00 15.00
BD14SB Sam Bennett 8.00 20.00
BD14SR Sam Reinhart 5.00 12.00
BD14WN William Nylander 25.00 60.00

2016-17 SP Game Used Banner Year Draft '14 Autographs

BD14AE Aaron Ekblad C 8.00 20.00
BD14LD Leon Draisaitl C 20.00 50.00
BD14SB Sam Bennett C 15.00 40.00
BD14-WN William Nylander B 30.00 80.00

2016-17 SP Game Used Banner Year Draft '15

BD15CM Connor McDavid 30.00 80.00
BD15DS Daniel Sprong 8.00 20.00
BD15JE Jack Eichel SP 12.00 30.00
BD15MA Mitch Marner 30.00 80.00
BD15NH Noah Hanifin 6.00 15.00
BD15PZ Pavel Zacha 8.00 20.00
BD15ST Dylan Strome 12.00 30.00

2016-17 SP Game Used Banner Year Draft '15 Autographs

BD15CM Connor McDavid B
BD15MA Mitch Marner A
BD15PZ Pavel Zacha C 10.00 25.00
BD15-ST Dylan Strome C 15.00 40.00

2016-17 SP Game Used Banner Year Draft '16

BD16AM Auston Matthews 40.00 100.00
BD16JP Jesse Puljujarvi SP 15.00 40.00
BD16MT Matthew Tkachuk 20.00 50.00
BD16-PL Patrik Laine 25.00 60.00

2016-17 SP Game Used Banner Year Draft '16 Autographs

BD16AM Auston Matthews B 200.00 300.00
BD16JP Jesse Puljujarvi B 50.00 120.00
BD16PL Patrik Laine B 150.00 300.00

2016-17 SP Game Used Banner Year Stadium Series '16

BSSAP Artemi Panarin 8.00 20.00
BSSCC Corey Crawford 8.00 20.00
BSSDL Dylan Larkin 10.00 25.00
BSSGL Gabriel Landeskog 5.00 12.00
BSSHZ Henrik Zetterberg 8.00 20.00
BSSJI Jarome Iginla 6.00 15.00
BSSJT Jonathan Toews 12.00 30.00
BSSMD Matt Duchene 6.00 15.00
BSSMK Mikko Koivu 5.00 12.00
BSSNM Nathan MacKinnon 12.00 30.00
BSSNN Nino Niederreiter 6.00 15.00
BSSPK Patrick Kane SP 12.00 30.00
BSSPM Petr Mrazek SP 6.00 15.00
BSSTT Tomas Tatar 5.00 12.00
BSSZP Zach Parise 6.00 15.00

2016-17 SP Game Used Banner Year Stadium Series '16 Autographs

BSSGL Gabriel Landeskog B 15.00 40.00
BSSHZ Henrik Zetterberg A 25.00 60.00
BSSJI Jarome Iginla B 20.00 50.00
BSSMD Matt Duchene B 20.00 50.00
BSSNN Nino Niederreiter B 20.00 50.00
BSSTT Tomas Tatar B 15.00 40.00
BSSZP Zach Parise B 20.00 50.00
BSS-JT Jonathan Toews A 40.00 100.00

2016-17 SP Game Used Banner Year Stanley Cup Finals

BSCAK Anze Kopitar 8.00 20.00
BSCBB Brent Burns 6.00 15.00
BSCBS Brandon Saad 5.00 12.00
BSCCC Corey Crawford SP 6.00 15.00
BSCDB Derick Brassard 5.00 12.00
BSCDD Drew Doughty SP 5.00 12.00
BSCDK Duncan Keith 5.00 12.00
BSCDS Derek Stepan 4.00 10.00
BSCEM Evgeni Malkin 15.00 40.00
BSCHL Henrik Lundqvist 5.00 12.00
BSCJC Jeff Carter 5.00 12.00
BSCJP Joe Pavelski 5.00 12.00
BSCJT Jonathan Toews 10.00 25.00
BSCJW Justin Williams 4.00 10.00
BSCKE Phil Kessel 6.00 15.00
BSCKL Kris Letang 5.00 12.00
BSCKR David Krejci 5.00 12.00
BSCMH Marian Hossa 4.00 10.00
BSCMJ Martin Jones 5.00 12.00
BSCMM Matt Murray SP 8.00 20.00
BSCMR Mike Richards 3.00 8.00
BSCMZ Mats Zuccarello 5.00 12.00
BSCPB Patrice Bergeron 6.00 15.00
BSCPK Patrick Kane 10.00 25.00
BSCSC Sidney Crosby 20.00 50.00
BSCTH Joe Thornton 5.00 12.00
BSCTR Tuukka Rask 5.00 12.00
BSCTT Tyler Toffoli 5.00 12.00
BSCZC Zdeno Chara 5.00 12.00
BSC-BM Brad Marchand 6.00 15.00

2016-17 SP Game Used Banner Year Stanley Cup Finals Autographs

BSCAK Anze Kopitar B 50.00 125.00
BSCDK David Krejci B 30.00 80.00
BSCHL Henrik Lundqvist A 30.00 80.00
BSCJT Jonathan Toews A 60.00 150.00
BSCMM Matt Murray B 50.00 125.00
BSCTH Joe Thornton B 30.00 80.00
BSCTT Tyler Toffoli B 30.00 80.00

2016-17 SP Game Used Banner Year Winter Classic

BWCAG Alex Galchenyuk 6.00 15.00
BWCAM Andrei Markov 5.00 12.00
BWCBG Brendan Gallagher SP 6.00 15.00
BWCBH Braden Holtby 8.00 20.00
BWCBS Brent Seabrook 4.00 10.00
BWCCC Corey Crawford 6.00 15.00
BWCEK Evgeny Kuznetsov 8.00 20.00
BWCJC John Carlson 6.00 15.00
BWCJT Jonathan Toews 10.00 25.00
BWCKE Duncan Keith 5.00 12.00
BWCLE Loui Eriksson 5.00 12.00
BWCMC Mike Condon 5.00 12.00
BWCMH Marian Hossa 4.00 10.00
BWCMJ Marcus Johansson 5.00 12.00
BWCMP Max Pacioretty 5.00 12.00
BWCMQ Adam McQuaid 3.00 8.00
BWCNB Nicklas Backstrom 8.00 20.00
BWCNH Niklas Hjalmarsson 4.00 10.00
BWCPB Patrice Bergeron 6.00 15.00
BWCPK Patrick Kane 10.00 25.00
BWCPS P.K. Subban 8.00 20.00
BWCRS Ryan Spooner 4.00 10.00
BWCTP Tomas Plekanec 5.00 12.00
BWCTR Tuukka Rask 5.00 12.00
BWCZC Zdeno Chara 5.00 12.00
BWC-AO Alexander Ovechkin SP 20.00 50.00

2016-17 SP Game Used Banner Year Winter Classic Autographs

BWCAG Alex Galchenyuk B 40.00 100.00
BWCAO Alexander Ovechkin A 125.00 300.00
BWCBG Brendan Gallagher B 40.00 100.00
BWCJT Jonathan Toews A 60.00 150.00
BWC-RS Ryan Spooner B 25.00 60.00

2016-17 SP Game Used Draft Day Marks

DDMAD Anthony DeAngelo/35 12.00 30.00
DDMAM Auston Matthews/10
DDMAM Anthony Mantha/35 40.00 100.00
DDMBM Brandon Montour/35 12.00 30.00
DDMBP Brendan Perlini/35 12.00 30.00
DDMBP Brayden Point/35 30.00 80.00
DDMCB Chris Bigras/35 10.00 25.00
DDMCD Christian Dvorak/35 12.00 30.00
DDMCS Cory Schneider/10
DDMDS Dylan Strome/35 25.00 60.00
DDMFA Hudson Fasching/35 12.00 30.00
DDMIP Ivan Provorov/35 30.00 80.00
DDMJC Jakob Chychrun/35 12.00 30.00
DDMJD Jason Dickinson/35 10.00 25.00
DDMJH Julius Honka/35 12.00 30.00
DDMJP Jesse Puljujarvi/35 30.00 80.00
DDMJV Jakub Vrana/35 12.00 30.00
DDMKC Kyle Connor/35 15.00 40.00
DDMKK Kasperi Kapanen/35 25.00 60.00
DDMLC Lawson Crouse/35 10.00 25.00
DDMMB Mathew Barzal/35 30.00 80.00
DDMMM Michael Matheson/35 12.00 30.00
DDMMM Mitch Marner/35 100.00 200.00
DDMMT Matthew Tkachuk/35 40.00 100.00
DDMNS Nick Schmaltz/35 12.00 30.00
DDMOB Oliver Bjorkstrand/35 10.00 25.00
DDMON Owen Nolan/10
DDMPB Pavel Buchnevich/35 20.00 50.00
DDMPL Patrik Laine/35 125.00 250.00
DDMPZ Pavel Zacha/35 15.00 40.00
DDMRN Rick Nash/10
DDMRP Ryan Pulock/35 12.00 30.00
DDMSM Sonny Milano/35 15.00 40.00
DDMTD Thatcher Demko/35 30.00 80.00
DDMTH Taylor Hall/10
DDMTK Travis Konecny/35 25.00 60.00
DDMTL Trevor Linden/10
DDMTM Timo Meier/35 12.00 30.00
DDMWN William Nylander/35 80.00 150.00
DDMZW Zach Werenski/35 25.00 60.00

2016-17 SP Game Used Frameworks Materials

FWAE Aaron Ekblad D 6.00 15.00
FWAH Adam Henrique D 6.00 15.00
FWAK Anze Kopitar C 12.00 30.00
FWAO Alexander Ovechkin C 30.00 80.00
FWBH Brett Hull B 10.00 25.00
FWBS Brandon Saad D 6.00 15.00
FWBW Blake Wheeler D 6.00 15.00
FWCA Carey Price B 30.00 80.00
FWCM Connor McDavid B 50.00 125.00
FWDS Daniel Sedin C 8.00 20.00
FWEM Evgeni Malkin B 30.00 80.00
FWHB Braden Holtby C 12.00 30.00
FWHL Henrik Lundqvist B 10.00 25.00
FWHZ Henrik Zetterberg A 20.00 50.00
FWJB Jamie Benn C 10.00 25.00
FWJG Johnny Gaudreau C 12.00 30.00
FWJJ Jaromir Jagr C 20.00 50.00
FWJS Jordan Staal D 6.00 15.00
FWJT Jonathan Toews B 20.00 50.00
FWKM Kirk McLean B 10.00 25.00
FWLR Larry Robinson A 15.00 40.00
FWMD Max Domi D 8.00 20.00
FWMJ Martin Jones D 6.00 15.00
FWML Mario Lemieux B 30.00 80.00
FWNK Nazem Kadri D 5.00 12.00
FWPB Patrice Bergeron D 8.00 20.00
FWPK Patrick Kane A 30.00 80.00
FWPR Patrick Roy B 25.00 60.00
FWRI Pekka Rinne C 10.00 25.00
FWSC Sidney Crosby B 40.00 100.00
FWSS Steven Stamkos C 15.00 40.00
FWSZ Steve Yzerman B 12.00 30.00
FWTA John Tavares B 20.00 50.00
FWTS Tyler Seguin C 12.00 30.00
FWVT Vladimir Tarasenko C 12.00 30.00
FWZP Zach Parise C 8.00 20.00

2016-17 SP Game Used Inked Sweaters

ISAE Aaron Ekblad/99 12.00 30.00
ISAH Adam Henrique/99 12.00 30.00
ISBB Brent Burns/50 20.00 50.00
ISHL Henrik Lundqvist/50 15.00 40.00
ISHZ Henrik Zetterberg/50 20.00 50.00
ISKM Kirk McLean/50 15.00 40.00
ISLD Leon Draisaitl/99 15.00 40.00
ISMB Matt Beleskey/99 10.00 25.00
ISMH Mike Hoffman/99 10.00 25.00
ISMP Max Pacioretty/50 15.00 40.00
ISMZ Mats Zuccarello/99 12.00 30.00
ISRJ Roman Josi/99 12.00 30.00

2016-17 SP Game Used Orange Rainbow Draft Year

1 Sidney Crosby/105 15.00 40.00
2 Robby Fabbri/114 4.00 10.00
3 Joe Thornton/197 3.00 8.00
4 Brayden Schenn/109 4.00 10.00
5 Mark Stone/110 4.00 10.00
6 Max Pacioretty/107 4.00 10.00
7 David Pastrnak/114 6.00 15.00
8 Anze Kopitar/105 6.00 15.00
9 Jonathan Huberdeau/111 4.00 10.00
10 Jason Spezza/101 4.00 10.00
11 Andrew Ladd/104 4.00 10.00
12 Nathan MacKinnon/113 8.00 20.00
13 Sam Bennett/114 5.00 12.00
14 Rasmus Ristolainen/113 3.00 8.00
15 Anthony Duclair/113 4.00 10.00
16 Taylor Hall/110 8.00 20.00
17 Jakob Silfverberg/109 4.00 10.00
18 Jonathan Toews/106 8.00 20.00
19 Petr Mrazek/110 4.00 10.00
20 David Backes/103 4.00 10.00
21 Filip Forsberg/112 5.00 12.00
22 Nino Niederreiter/110 4.00 10.00
23 Nick Foligno/106 3.00 8.00
24 Rick Nash/102 4.00 10.00
25 Alexander Ovechkin/104 15.00 40.00
26 Nikita Kucherov/111 6.00 15.00
27 Morgan Rielly/112 3.00 8.00
28 Henrik Sedin/199 3.00 8.00
29 Blake Wheeler/104 4.00 10.00
30 Victor Rask/111 3.00 8.00
31 Ryan Kesler/103 4.00 10.00
32 Ryan Spooner/110 3.00 8.00
33 Carey Price/105 12.00 30.00
34 Jarome Iginla/195 3.00 8.00
35 Max Domi/113 5.00 12.00
36 John Tavares/109 8.00 20.00
37 Corey Crawford/103 5.00 12.00
38 Mikael Granlund/110 3.00 8.00
39 Chris Kreider/109 4.00 10.00
40 John Klingberg/110 4.00 10.00
41 Jake Allen/108 5.00 12.00
42 Phil Kessel/106 5.00 12.00
43 Nikolaj Ehlers/114 4.00 10.00
44 Tyler Johnson /100 3.00 8.00
45 Mike Hoffman/109 3.00 8.00
46 Duncan Keith/102 4.00 10.00
47 Ryan Miller/199 3.00 8.00
48 Ryan Getzlaf/103 6.00 15.00
49 Nazem Kadri/109 3.00 8.00
50 Connor McDavid/115 20.00 50.00
51 T.J. Oshie/105 6.00 15.00
52 Jaden Schwartz/110 5.00 12.00
53 Patrick Marleau/197 3.00 8.00
54 Jakub Voracek/107 4.00 10.00
55 Victor Hedman/109 5.00 12.00
56 Alex Galchenyuk/112 5.00 12.00
57 Jaroslav Halak/103 4.00 10.00
58 Jeff Carter/103 4.00 10.00
59 Aleksander Barkov/113 4.00 10.00
60 Henrik Lundqvist/100 4.00 10.00
61 Boone Jenner/111 4.00 10.00
62 Gabriel Landeskog/111 3.00 8.00
63 Ryan Johansen/110 5.00 12.00
64 Jack Eichel/115 8.00 20.00
65 David Krejci/104 4.00 10.00
66 Derek Stepan/108 3.00 8.00
67 Bo Horvat/113 6.00 15.00
68 Cam Ward/102 4.00 10.00
69 Kyle Palmieri/109 3.00 8.00
70 Henrik Zetterberg/199 4.00 10.00
71 Jordan Eberle/108 4.00 10.00
72 Sean Monahan/113 4.00 10.00
73 Patrick Sharp/101 3.00 8.00
74 Tyler Toffoli/110 4.00 10.00
75 Zach Parise/103 4.00 10.00
76 Brendan Gallagher/110 5.00 12.00
77 Bobby Ryan/105 3.00 8.00
78 Frederik Andersen/110 3.00 8.00
79 Michael Cammalleri/101 3.00 8.00
80 Oliver Ekman-Larsson/109 3.00 8.00
81 Tom Wilson /112 4.00 10.00
82 Sam Reinhart/114 3.00 8.00
83 Jake Muzzin/107 3.00 8.00
84 Mark Scheifele/111 5.00 12.00
85 Wayne Simmonds/107 5.00 12.00
86 Patrick Kane/107 8.00 20.00
87 Tomas Tatar/109 3.00 8.00
88 Anders Lee/109 4.00 10.00
89 Roberto Luongo/197 3.00 8.00
90 Teuvo Teravainen/112 4.00 10.00
91 Matt Murray/112 6.00 15.00
92 Carl Hagelin/107 4.00 10.00
93 Igor Larionov/185 3.00 8.00
94 Patrick Roy/184 8.00 20.00
95 Larry Murphy/180 3.00 8.00
96 Pat LaFontaine/183 3.00 8.00
97 Mario Lemieux/184 10.00 25.00
98 Felix Potvin/190 5.00 12.00
99 Pavel Bure/189 3.00 8.00
100 Wayne Gretzky/100 20.00 50.00
101 Auston Matthews/116 80.00 150.00
102 Pavel Zacha/115 5.00 12.00
103 Christian Dvorak/114 4.00 10.00
104 Nick Schmaltz/114 4.00 10.00
105 Justin Bailey/113 4.00 10.00
106 Ivan Provorov/115 8.00 20.00
107 Chris Bigras/113 3.00 8.00
108 Matthew Tkachuk/116 12.00 30.00
109 Kyle Connor/115 10.00 25.00
110 William Nylander/114 15.00 40.00
111 Mikhail Sergachev/116 8.00 20.00
112 Brandon Carlo/115 4.00 10.00
113 Dylan Strome/115 8.00 20.00
114 Jacob Larsson/115 6.00 15.00
115 Miles Wood/113 3.00 8.00
116 Lawson Crouse/115 3.00 8.00
117 Zach Sanford/113 4.00 10.00
118 Daniel Altshuller/112 3.00 8.00
119 Anthony Beauvillier/115 4.00 10.00
120 Anthony Mantha/113 10.00 25.00
121 Casey Nelson/100 4.00 10.00
122 Ondrej Kase/114 4.00 10.00
123 Dominik Simon/115 4.00 10.00
124 Nikita Zaitsev/100 4.00 10.00
125 Nikita Soshnikov/100 2.50 6.00
126 Gustav Forsling/114 4.00 10.00
127 Brandon Tanev/100 4.00 10.00
128 Esa Lindell/112 4.00 10.00
129 Josh Archibald/111 4.00 10.00
130 Mitch Marner/115 25.00 60.00
131 Hudson Fasching/113 4.00 10.00
132 Shane Harper/100 6.00 15.00
133 Markus Nutivaara/100 4.00 10.00
134 Nick Baptiste/113 4.00 10.00
135 Oliver Bjorkstrand/113 3.00 8.00
136 Sebastian Aho/115 8.00 20.00
137 Ross Johnston/100 4.00 10.00
138 Jared Coreau/100 5.00 12.00
139 Jesse Puljujarvi/116 10.00 25.00
140 Kasperi Kapanen/114 8.00 20.00
141 Nick Sorensen /113 4.00 10.00
142 Aaron Dell/100 5.00 12.00
143 J.C. Lipon/113 4.00 10.00
144 Roman Lyubimov/100 4.00 10.00
145 Pontus Aberg/112 5.00 12.00
146 Kevin Labanc/114 4.00 10.00
147 Artturi Lehkonen/113 4.00 10.00
148 Michael Matheson/112 4.00 10.00
149 Troy Stecher/100 4.00 10.00
150 Sonny Milano/114 5.00 12.00
151 Jimmy Vesey/112 8.00 20.00
152 Denis Malgin/115 4.00 10.00
153 Mike Reilly/111 3.00 8.00
154 Noel Acciari/100 5.00 12.00
155 Oliver Kylington/115 3.00 8.00
156 Lukas Sedlak/111 4.00 10.00
157 Travis Konecny/115 8.00 20.00
158 Michal Kempny/100 4.00 10.00
159 Blake Speers/115 4.00 10.00
160 Brendan Leipsic/112 4.00 10.00
161 Tyler Motte/113 4.00 10.00
162 Frederik Gauthier/113 3.00 8.00
163 Nick Paul/113 5.00 12.00
164 Alan Quine/113 4.00 10.00
165 Sergey Tolchinsky/100 3.00 8.00
166 Rob O'Gara/111 4.00 10.00
167 Mathew Barzal/115 12.00 30.00
168 Ben Harpur/113 4.00 10.00
169 Thomas Chabot/115 8.00 20.00
170 Charlie Lindgren/100 8.00 20.00
171 Nikita Tryamkin/114 3.00 8.00
172 Danton Heinen/114 6.00 15.00
173 Oskar Sundqvist/112 4.00 10.00
174 Joel Eriksson Ek/115 4.00 10.00
175 Steven Santini/113 3.00 8.00
176 Brayden Point/114 10.00 25.00
177 Nic Dowd/109 4.00 10.00
178 Ryan Pulock/113 4.00 10.00
179 Jakob Chychrun/116 4.00 10.00
180 Connor Brown/112 6.00 15.00
181 Scott Kosmachuk/112 4.00 10.00
182 Tristan Jarry/113 8.00 20.00
183 Tobias Lindberg/113 6.00 15.00
184 Blake Pietila/111 4.00 10.00
185 Patrik Laine/116 30.00 80.00
186 Zach Werenski/115 8.00 20.00
187 Pavel Buchnevich/113 6.00 15.00
188 Rinat Valiev/114 5.00 12.00
189 Anthony DeAngelo/114 4.00 10.00
190 Jason Dickinson/113 3.00 8.00
191 Brett Lernout/114 4.00 10.00
192 Josh Morrissey/113 5.00 12.00
193 Tom Kuhnhackl/110 3.00 8.00
194 Zach Hyman/110 5.00 12.00
195 Chase De Leo/114 4.00 10.00
196 Mark McNeill/111 4.00 10.00
197 Austin Czarnik/100 6.00 15.00
198 Trevor Carrick/112 4.00 10.00
199 Joseph Cramarossa/111 4.00 10.00

2016-17 SP Game Used Red Spectrum

101 Auston Matthews PATCH AU 400.00 700.00
185 Patrik Laine PATCH AU 150.00 300.00

2016-17 SP Game Used Rookie Relic Blends

RRBAB Anthony Beauvillier 4.00 10.00
RRBAM Anthony Mantha 10.00 25.00
RRBAU Auston Matthews 25.00 60.00
RRBBL Brendan Leipsic 4.00 10.00
RRBCB Connor Brown 6.00 15.00
RRBCD Christian Dvorak 4.00 10.00
RRBDS Dylan Strome 8.00 20.00
RRBHF Hudson Fasching 4.00 10.00
RRBIP Ivan Provorov 8.00 20.00
RRBJM Josh Morrissey 5.00 12.00
RRBJP Jesse Puljujarvi 10.00 25.00
RRBJV Jimmy Vesey 8.00 20.00
RRBKC Kyle Connor 10.00 25.00
RRBKK Kasperi Kapanen 8.00 20.00
RRBMM Mitch Marner 20.00 50.00
RRBMT Matthew Tkachuk 12.00 30.00
RRBNS Nick Schmaltz 4.00 10.00
RRBPB Pavel Buchnevich 6.00 15.00
RRBPL Patrik Laine 20.00 50.00
RRBPZ Pavel Zacha 5.00 12.00
RRBSA Sebastian Aho 8.00 20.00
RRBSM Sonny Milano 5.00 12.00
RRBTK Travis Konecny 8.00 20.00
RRBTM Tyler Motte 4.00 10.00
RRBWN William Nylander 15.00 40.00
RRBZW Zach Werenski 8.00 20.00

2016-17 SP Game Used Rookie Sweaters

RSAM Auston Matthews 12.00 30.00
RSCB Connor Brown 3.00 8.00
RSCD Christian Dvorak 2.00 5.00
RSCL Charlie Lindgren 4.00 10.00
RSDS Dylan Strome 4.00 10.00
RSEL Esa Lindell 2.00 5.00
RSHF Hudson Fasching 2.00 5.00
RSIP Ivan Provorov 4.00 10.00
RSJD Brayden Point 5.00 12.00
RSJM Travis Konecny 4.00 10.00
RSJP Jesse Puljujarvi 5.00 12.00
RSJV Jimmy Vesey 4.00 10.00
RSKC Kyle Connor 5.00 12.00
RSKK Kasperi Kapanen 4.00 10.00
RSMA Anthony Mantha 5.00 12.00
RSMB Mathew Barzal 6.00 15.00
RSMI Michael Matheson 2.00 5.00
RSMM Mitch Marner 10.00 25.00
RSMR Mike Reilly 1.50 4.00
RSMT Matthew Tkachuk 6.00 15.00
RSNS Nick Schmaltz 2.00 5.00
RSOB Oliver Bjorkstrand 1.50 4.00
RSPB Pavel Buchnevich 3.00 8.00
RSPL Patrik Laine 8.00 20.00
RSPZ Pavel Zacha 2.50 6.00
RSSA Sebastian Aho 4.00 10.00
RSSM Sonny Milano 2.50 6.00
RSWN William Nylander 8.00 20.00
RSZW Zach Werenski 4.00 10.00

2016-17 SP Game Used Rookie Sweaters Inked Patch

*SINGLES: 1.25X TO 3X BASIC INSERTS
RSAM Auston Matthews/35 300.00 500.00
RSIP Ivan Provorov/99 40.00 100.00
RSMI Mitch Marner/35 100.00 200.00
RSPL Patrik Laine/99 150.00 300.00
RSWN William Nylander/99 50.00 120.00

2016-17 SP Game Used Stadium Series Materials Puck

SSGUPAP Artemi Panarin 25.00 60.00
SSGUPDL Dylan Larkin 30.00 80.00
SSGUPGL Gabriel Landeskog 15.00 40.00
SSGUPHZ Henrik Zetterberg 25.00 60.00
SSGUPJP Jason Pominville 15.00 40.00
SSGUPJT Jonathan Toews 40.00 100.00
SSGUPMD Matt Dumba 15.00 40.00
SSGUPNM Nathan MacKinnon 40.00 100.00
SSGUPNN Nino Niederreiter 20.00 50.00
SSGUPPK Patrick Kane 40.00 100.00
SSGUPTB Tyson Barrie 20.00 50.00
SSGUPTT Tomas Tatar 15.00 40.00

2016-17 SP Game Used Stadium Series Quad Fabrics

SS4CHI Toews/Keith/Shaw/Hjalmarsson 10.00 25.00
SS4COL MacKinnon/Iginla/Beauchemin/Holden 10.00 25.00
SS4DET Larkin/Abdelkader/Green/Glendening 8.00 20.00
SS4-MIN Parise/Niederreiter/Vanek/Carter 5.00 12.00

2016-17 SP Game Used Stadium Series Relic Blends

SSBAS Andrew Shaw 6.00 15.00
SSBDK Duncan Keith 6.00 15.00
SSBDL Dylan Larkin 10.00 25.00
SSBEJ Erik Johnson 4.00 10.00
SSBFB Francois Beauchemin 5.00 12.00
SSBHJ Niklas Hjalmarsson 5.00 12.00
SSBJA Justin Abdelkader 5.00 12.00
SSBJI Jarome Iginla 6.00 15.00
SSBJS Jared Spurgeon 4.00 10.00
SSBJT Jonathan Toews 12.00 30.00
SSBLG Luke Glendening 5.00 12.00
SSBMG Mike Green 6.00 15.00
SSBNH Nick Holden 4.00 10.00
SSBNM Nathan MacKinnon 12.00 30.00
SSBNN Nino Niederreiter 6.00 15.00
SSBRC Ryan Carter 5.00 12.00
SSBRS Riley Sheahan 5.00 12.00
SSBTV Trevor van Riemsdyk 5.00 12.00
SSBVA Thomas Vanek 5.00 12.00
SSBZP Zach Parise 6.00 15.00

2016-17 SP Game Used Stanley Cup Finals Materials Net Cord

SCNCBB Brent Burns 30.00 80.00
SCNCBR Bryan Rust 25.00 60.00
SCNCCH Carl Hagelin 25.00 60.00
SCNCCK Chris Kunitz 25.00 60.00
SCNCCS Conor Sheary 30.00 80.00
SCNCCT Chris Tierney Game 3 15.00 40.00
SCNCEM Evgeni Malkin 80.00 200.00
SCNCEV Evgeni Malkin 80.00 200.00
SCNCJB Justin Braun 15.00 40.00
SCNCJD Joonas Donskoi 20.00 50.00
SCNCJP Joe Pavelski 25.00 60.00
SCNCJT Joe Thornton 25.00 60.00
SCNCJW Joel Ward 20.00 50.00
SCNCKL Kris Letang 25.00 60.00
SCNCLC Logan Couture 25.00 60.00
SCNCMA Matt Murray 40.00 100.00
SCNCMC Matt Cullen 25.00 60.00
SCNCMJ Martin Jones 25.00 60.00
SCNCMK Melker Karlsson Game 5 20.00 50.00
SCNCMM Matt Murray 40.00 100.00
SCNCMV Marc-Edouard Vlasic 15.00 40.00
SCNCNB Nick Bonino 15.00 40.00
SCNCOM Olli Maatta 20.00 50.00
SCNCPH Patric Hornqvist 25.00 60.00
SCNCPK Phil Kessel 30.00 80.00
SCNCPM Patrick Marleau 25.00 60.00
SCNCSC Sidney Crosby 125.00 200.00
SCNCSI Sidney Crosby 125.00 200.00
SCNCTH Tomas Hertl 25.00 60.00
SCNCTJ Joe Thornton 25.00 60.00

2016-17 SP Game Used Winter Classic Materials Net Cord

WCNCAD Adam McQuaid 15.00 40.00
WCNCAG Alex Galchenyuk 30.00 80.00
WCNCAM Andrei Markov 25.00 60.00
WCNCBC Brett Connolly 20.00 50.00
WCNCBE Patrice Bergeron 30.00 80.00
WCNCBG Brendan Gallagher 30.00 80.00
WCNCDD David Desharnais 20.00 50.00
WCNCER Loui Eriksson 25.00 60.00
WCNCJH Jimmy Hayes 15.00 40.00
WCNCJM Joe Morrow 20.00 50.00
WCNCLE Lars Eller 20.00 50.00
WCNCMB Matt Beleskey 20.00 50.00
WCNCMC Mike Condon 25.00 60.00
WCNCMP Max Pacioretty 25.00 60.00
WCNCNB Nathan Beaulieu 15.00 40.00
WCNCPB Paul Byron 20.00 50.00
WCNCPS P.K. Subban 40.00 100.00
WCNCRS Ryan Spooner 20.00 50.00
WCNCTK Torey Krug 25.00 60.00
WCNCTP Tomas Plekanec 25.00 60.00
WCNCTR Tuukka Rask 25.00 60.00
WCNCZC Zdeno Chara 25.00 60.00

2017-18 SP Game Used

1 Auston Matthews/34 25.00 60.00
2 Victor Hedman/77
3 Tyler Seguin/91
4 Jake Guentzel/59
5 Henrik Zetterberg/40
8 Oliver Ekman-Larsson/23 10.00 25.00
10 Carey Price/31 12.00 30.00
11 Ryan O'Reilly/90
14 Sean Monahan/23 6.00 15.00
15 Vladimir Tarasenko/91 4.00 10.00
17 Patrik Laine/29 12.00 30.00
18 Ryan Spooner/51 4.00 10.00
19 Milan Lucic/27 5.00 12.00
20 Jonathan Toews/19 10.00 25.00
21 Aleksander Barkov/16 15.00 40.00
22 Roman Josi/59
23 Marc-Andre Fleury/29
24 Pavel Zacha/37 5.00 12.00
25 Erik Karlsson/65
26 Brock Nelson/29
27 Mats Zuccarello/36
28 Shayne Gostisbehere/53
29 Evgeny Kuznetsov/92 5.00 12.00
30 Loui Eriksson/21 6.00 15.00
31 Jason Spezza/90
32 Dylan Larkin/71 25.00 60.00
34 Sebastian Aho/20 10.00 25.00
35 Matt Murray/30 10.00 25.00
36 Logan Couture/39
37 John Gibson/36 6.00 15.00
38 Nikolaj Ehlers/27 10.00 25.00
41 Evgeni Malkin/71 6.00 15.00
42 Max Pacioretty/67
43 Patrice Bergeron/37 8.00 20.00
45 Steven Stamkos/91
46 Jonathan Quick/32
50 Sidney Crosby/87 15.00 40.00
51 Colton Parayko/55 15.00 40.00
52 William Karlsson/71 10.00 25.00
53 Leon Draisaitl/29 15.00 40.00
54 Pekka Rinne/35 6.00 15.00
55 Patrick Kane/88 5.00 12.00
56 Claude Giroux/28 15.00 40.00
59 Jonathan Drouin/92 10.00 25.00
60 Henrik Lundqvist/30
61 David Pastrnak/88
64 Henrik Sedin/33 8.00 20.00
65 Brent Burns/88 40.00 100.00
66 Nathan MacKinnon/29 8.00 20.00
68 Nikita Kucherov/86 6.00 15.00
69 Mark Stone/61
70 John Tavares/91
72 Ryan Johansen/92
73 Mark Scheifele/55
74 Mitch Marner/16 50.00 120.00
75 Derek Stepan/21 5.00 12.00
76 Nino Niederreiter/22
77 Connor McDavid/97 20.00 50.00
80 Steve Yzerman/19 15.00 40.00
83 Brett Hull/16
84 Ed Belfour/30 12.00 40.00
85 Wayne Gretzky/99 20.00 50.00
87 Charlie McAvoy/73 RC 300.00 400.00
88 Victor Mete/53 RC 50.00 120.00
89 Gabriel Carlsson/53 RC
90 Kailer Yamamoto/56 RC 50.00 120.00
92 Janne Kuokkanen/59 RC 15.00 40.00
93 Jan Rutta/44 RC 20.00 50.00
94 Evgeny Svechnikov/37 RC 25.00 60.00
95 Vadim Shipachyov/87 RC 40.00 100.00
96 Nathan Walker/78 RC 12.00 30.00
97 Tage Thompson/32 RC 60.00 150.00
98 Vladislav Kamenev/91 RC 12.00 30.00
99 Filip Chytil/72 RC 150.00 200.00
101 Valentin Zykov/73 RC 30.00 80.00
102 Alex Iafallo/19 RC 40.00 100.00
103 Marcus Sorensen/20 RC 40.00 100.00
104 Ville Husso/35 RC 40.00 100.00
105 Owen Tippett/74 RC 40.00 100.00
106 Jean-Sebastien Dea/39 RC
107 Ivan Barbashev/49 RC 30.00 80.00
108 Alex Formenton/59 RC 30.00 80.00
109 Brendan Lemieux/48 RC
111 Mike Vecchione/74 RC 20.00 50.00
112 Nelson Nogier/62 RC 15.00 40.00
113 Kevin Rooney/58 RC 25.00 60.00
117 John Hayden/40 RC
118 Andreas Borgman/55 RC 30.00 80.00
119 Christian Djoos/29 RC 40.00 100.00
120 Colin White/36 RC 50.00 120.00
121 Paul LaDue/38 RC
122 Evan McEneny/61 RC
123 Michael Kapla/32 RC 12.00 30.00
124 Alexandre Carrier/73 RC 15.00 40.00
127 Vince Dunn/29 RC 80.00 150.00
129 Filip Chlapik/78 RC 15.00 40.00
131 Riley Barber/24 RC 25.00 60.00
132 MacKenzie Weegar/52 RC
133 Michael Amadio/52 RC 20.00 50.00
135 Nikita Scherbak/38 RC
136 Peter Cehlarik/22 RC 40.00 100.00
137 Kalle Kossila/83 RC 10.00 25.00
138 Sean Malone/37 RC 40.00 100.00
139 Andrei Mironov/94 RC 15.00 40.00
140 Josh Ho-Sang/66 RC 40.00 100.00
141 Blake Coleman/40 RC 60.00 150.00
142 Viktor Antipin/93 RC 15.00 40.00
143 Rasmus Andersson/54 RC
145 Calle Rosen/48 RC
147 T.J. Tynan/68 RC 15.00 40.00
148 Remi Elie/40 RC
149 Andrew Poturalski/29 RC 15.00 40.00
150 Pierre-Luc Dubois/18 RC 150.00 250.00
151 Martin Necas/88 RC 40.00 100.00
152 Jonny Brodzinski/17 RC 30.00 80.00
153 Madison Bowey/22 RC 30.00 80.00
154 Anton Lindholm/54 RC 15.00 40.00
155 Jack Roslovic/52 RC 30.00 80.00
156 Samuel Girard/49 RC 25.00 60.00
157 Lucas Wallmark/72 RC 12.00 30.00
159 Dan Ronouf/20 RC 80.00 150.00
160 Jakob Forsbacka-Karlsson/23 RC
161 Jordan Schmaltz/43 RC
162 Denis Gurianov/34 RC 15.00 40.00
163 Christian Jaros/83 RC 25.00 60.00
164 Luke Kunin/19 RC
165 Tyson Jost/17 RC
166 Matt Lorito/22 RC
167 Garrett Mitchell/76 RC 30.00 80.00
168 Jake Dotchin/59 RC 25.00 60.00
170 Jake DeBrusk/74 RC
171 Jon Gillies/32 RC 20.00 50.00
173 Tim Heed/72 RC 20.00 50.00
174 Carter Rowney/37 RC 15.00 40.00
175 Jesper Bratt/63 RC 30.00 80.00
176 Samuel Blais/64 RC
177 Alex Tuch/89 RC 30.00 80.00
178 Robbie Russo/18 RC
179 J.T. Compher/37 RC 30.00 80.00
180 Christian Fischer/36 RC 25.00 60.00
181 Logan Brown/21 RC 60.00 150.00
182 Alexander Nylander/92 RC 25.00 60.00
183 Jaycob Megna/75 RC 15.00 40.00
184 Kurtis MacDermid/56 RC
185 Nolan Patrick/19 RC 600.00 700.00

2017-18 SP Game Used Gold

COMMON CARD 2.00 5.00
SEMISTARS 2.50 6.00
UNLISTED STARS 3.00 8.00
GRP A STATED ODDS 1:120
GRP B STATED ODDS 1:23
GRP C STATED ODDS 1:19
GRP D STATED ODDS 1:9
GRP E STATED ODDS 1:6
COMMON CARD/399 2.00 5.00
SEMISTARS 2.50 6.00
UNLISTED STARS 3.00 8.00
50 Sidney Crosby JSY A 15.00 40.00

2017-18 SP Game Used Orange Rainbow

1 Auston Matthews/140 8.00 20.00
2 Victor Hedman/116 2.50 6.00
3 Tyler Seguin/137 3.00 8.00
4 Jake Guentzel/116 2.50 6.00
5 Henrik Zetterberg/143 2.00 5.00
6 Corey Perry/150 2.00 5.00
7 Anze Kopitar/134 3.00 8.00
8 Oliver Ekman-Larsson/123 2.00 5.00
9 Artemi Panarin/134 2.00 5.00
10 Carey Price/144 6.00 15.00
11 Ryan O'Reilly/128 2.00 5.00
12 Joe Pavelski/141 2.00 5.00
13 Brayden Schenn/126 2.00 5.00
14 Sean Monahan/131 2.00 5.00
15 Vladimir Tarasenko/140 3.00 8.00
16 Matt Duchene/130 2.00 5.00
17 Patrik Laine/136 3.00 8.00
18 Ryan Spooner/113 1.50 4.00
19 Milan Lucic/130 2.00 5.00
20 Jonathan Toews/134 4.00 10.00
21 Aleksander Barkov/128 2.00 5.00
22 Roman Josi/115 2.00 5.00
23 Marc-Andre Fleury/142 3.00 8.00
24 Pavel Zacha/108 2.00 5.00
25 Erik Karlsson/121 2.50 6.00
26 Brock Nelson/126 1.50 4.00
27 Mats Zuccarello/126 2.00 5.00
28 Shayne Gostisbehere/117 2.00 5.00
29 Evgeny Kuznetsov/120 3.00 8.00
30 Loui Eriksson/136 1.50 4.00
31 Jason Spezza/134 2.00 5.00
32 Dylan Larkin/123 2.00 5.00
33 Patrick Marleau/144 2.00 5.00
34 Sebastian Aho/124 2.00 5.00
35 Matt Murray/132 3.00 8.00
36 Logan Couture/132 2.00 5.00
37 John Gibson/125 2.00 5.00
38 Nikolaj Ehlers/125 2.00 5.00
39 Tyson Barrie/113 2.00 5.00
40 Alexander Ovechkin/165 8.00 20.00
41 Evgeni Malkin/150 6.00 15.00
42 Max Pacioretty/139 2.00 5.00
43 Patrice Bergeron/132 2.50 6.00
44 Eric Staal/145 2.50 6.00
45 Steven Stamkos/160 4.00 10.00
46 Jonathan Quick/140 3.00 8.00
47 Cam Atkinson/135 2.00 5.00
48 Johnny Gaudreau/130 3.00 8.00
49 Jack Eichel/124 3.00 8.00
50 Sidney Crosby/151 8.00 20.00
51 Colton Parayko/109 2.00 5.00
52 William Karlsson/109 4.00 10.00
53 Leon Draisaitl/129 3.00 8.00
54 Pekka Rinne/143 2.50 6.00
55 Patrick Kane/146 4.00 10.00
56 Claude Giroux/128 2.00 5.00
57 Noah Hanifin/104 2.00 5.00
58 Adam Henrique/130 1.50 4.00
59 Jonathan Drouin/121 2.00 5.00
60 Henrik Lundqvist/139 3.00 8.00
61 David Pastrnak/134 3.00 8.00
62 Justin Abdelkader/123 1.50 4.00
63 Mark Giordano/121 1.50 4.00
64 Henrik Sedin/129 2.00 5.00
65 Brent Burns/129 2.50 6.00
66 Nathan MacKinnon/124 4.00 10.00
67 Roberto Luongo/147 2.00 5.00
68 Nikita Kucherov/140 3.00 8.00
69 Mark Stone/126 2.00 5.00
70 John Tavares/138 4.00 10.00
71 Jamie Benn/141 2.50 6.00
72 Ryan Johansen/133 2.00 5.00
73 Mark Scheifele/132 2.50 6.00
74 Mitch Marner/119 3.00 8.00
75 Derek Stepan/122 1.50 4.00
76 Nino Niederreiter/125 1.50 4.00
77 Connor McDavid/130 8.00 20.00
78 Mark Messier/150 3.00 8.00
79 Rod Langway/111 2.00 5.00
80 Steve Yzerman/165 2.50 6.00
81 Mark Recchi/153 2.50 6.00
82 Teemu Selanne/176 2.50 6.00
83 Brett Hull/186 2.00 5.00
84 Ed Belfour/143 2.50 6.00
85 Wayne Gretzky/192 10.00 25.00
86 Nico Hischier/117 20.00 50.00
87 Charlie McAvoy/116 20.00 50.00
88 Victor Mete/116 6.00 15.00
89 Gabriel Carlsson/115 5.00 12.00
90 Kailer Yamamoto/117 15.00 40.00
91 Adrian Kempe/114 8.00 20.00
92 Janne Kuokkanen/116 6.00 15.00
93 Jan Rutta/100 6.00 15.00
94 Evgeny Svechnikov/115 12.00 30.00
95 Vadim Shipachyov/100 20.00 50.00
96 Nathan Walker/114 6.00 15.00
97 Tage Thompson/116 10.00 25.00
98 Vladislav Kamenev/114 10.00 25.00
99 Filip Chytil/117 6.00 15.00
100 Clayton Keller/116 15.00 40.00
101 Valentin Zykov/113 6.00 15.00
102 Alex Iafallo/100 6.00 15.00
103 Marcus Sorensen/110 5.00 12.00
104 Ville Husso/114 5.00 12.00
105 Owen Tippett/117 12.00 30.00
106 Jean-Sebastien Dea/100 6.00 15.00
107 Ivan Barbashev/114 6.00 15.00
108 Alex Formenton/117 6.00 15.00

109 Brendan Lemieux/114 6.00 15.00
110 Anders Bjork/114 8.00 20.00
111 Mike Vecchione/100 5.00 12.00
112 Nelson Nogier/114 6.00 15.00
113 Kevin Rooney/100 6.00 15.00
114 Alex Kerfoot/112 6.00 15.00
115 Brock Boeser/115 25.00 60.00
116 Travis Sanheim/114 6.00 15.00
117 John Hayden/113 5.00 12.00
118 Andreas Borgman/100 6.00 15.00
119 Christian Djoos/112 6.00 15.00
120 Colin White/115 6.00 15.00
121 Paul LaDue/112 5.00 12.00
122 Evan McEneny/100 6.00 15.00
123 Michael Kapla/100 6.00 15.00
124 Alexandre Carrier/115 5.00 12.00
125 Haydn Fleury/114 6.00 15.00
126 Robert Hagg/113 6.00 15.00
127 Vince Dunn/115 6.00 15.00
128 Eric Comrie/113 5.00 12.00
129 Filip Chlapik/115 6.00 15.00
130 Alex DeBrincat/116 15.00 40.00
131 Riley Barber/112 5.00 12.00
132 MacKenzie Weegar/113 6.00 15.00
133 Michael Amadio/114 6.00 15.00
134 Griffen Molino/100 5.00 12.00
135 Nikita Scherbak/114 12.00 30.00
136 Peter Cehlarik/113 6.00 15.00
137 Kalle Kossila/100 5.00 12.00
138 Sean Malone/113 6.00 15.00
139 Andrei Mironov/115 6.00 15.00
140 Josh Ho-Sang/114 8.00 20.00
141 Blake Coleman/111 5.00 12.00
142 Viktor Antipin/100 6.00 15.00
143 Rasmus Andersson/115 6.00 15.00
144 Oscar Fantenberg/100 6.00 15.00
145 Calle Rosen/100 6.00 15.00
146 Tucker Poolman/113 6.00 15.00
147 T.J. Tynan/111 5.00 12.00
148 Remi Elie/113 5.00 12.00
149 Andrew Poturalski/100 6.00 15.00
150 Pierre-Luc Dubois/116 12.00 30.00
151 Martin Necas/117 6.00 15.00
152 Jonny Brodzinski/113 6.00 15.00
153 Madison Bowey/113 5.00 12.00
154 Anton Lindholm/114 6.00 15.00
155 Jack Roslovic/115 8.00 20.00
156 Samuel Girard/116 6.00 15.00
157 Lucas Wallmark/114 6.00 15.00
158 Ian McCoshen/113 6.00 15.00
159 Dan Renouf/100 5.00 12.00
160 Jakob Forsbacka-Karlsson/115 6.00 15.00
161 Jordan Schmaltz/112 8.00 20.00
162 Denis Gurianov/115 6.00 15.00
163 Christian Jaros/115 6.00 15.00
164 Luke Kunin/116 6.00 15.00
165 Tyson Jost/116 12.00 30.00
166 Matt Lorito/100 6.00 15.00
167 Garrett Mitchell/109 6.00 15.00
168 Jake Dotchin/112 5.00 12.00
169 Samuel Morin/113 6.00 15.00
170 Jake DeBrusk/115 10.00 25.00
171 Jon Gillies/112 6.00 15.00
172 Will Butcher/113 8.00 20.00
173 Tim Heed/110 6.00 15.00
174 Carter Rowney/100 5.00 12.00
175 Jesper Bratt/116 10.00 25.00
176 Samuel Blais/114 6.00 15.00
177 Alex Tuch/114 15.00 40.00
178 Robbie Russo/111 6.00 15.00
179 J.T. Compher/113 8.00 20.00
180 Christian Fischer/115 8.00 20.00
181 Logan Brown/116 6.00 15.00
182 Alexander Nylander/116 10.00 25.00
183 Jaycob Megna/112 6.00 15.00
184 Kurtis MacDermid/100 6.00 15.00
185 Nolan Patrick/117 12.00 30.00

2017-18 SP Game Used Rainbow

86 Nico Hischier/218 8.00 20.00
87 Charlie McAvoy/219 8.00 20.00
88 Victor Mete/219 2.50 6.00
89 Gabriel Carlsson/220 2.00 5.00
90 Kailer Yamamoto/219 6.00 15.00
91 Adrian Kempe/221 3.00 8.00
92 Janne Kuokkanen/219 2.50 6.00
93 Jan Rutta/227 2.50 6.00
94 Evgeny Svechnikov/221 5.00 12.00
95 Vadim Shipachyov/230 8.00 20.00
96 Nathan Walker/223 2.50 6.00
97 Tage Thompson/220 4.00 10.00
98 Vladislav Kamenev/221 4.00 10.00
99 Filip Chytil/218 2.50 6.00
100 Clayton Keller/219 6.00 15.00
101 Valentin Zykov/222 2.50 6.00
102 Alex Iafallo/223 2.50 6.00
103 Marcus Sorensen/225 2.00 5.00
104 Ville Husso/222 2.50 6.00
105 Owen Tippett/218 5.00 12.00
106 Jean-Sebastien Dea/223 2.50 6.00
107 Ivan Barbashev/221 2.50 6.00
108 Alex Formenton/218 2.50 6.00
109 Brendan Lemieux/221 2.50 6.00
110 Anders Bjork/221 3.00 8.00
111 Mike Vecchione/224 2.00 5.00
112 Nelson Nogier/221 2.50 6.00
113 Kevin Rooney/224 2.50 6.00
114 Alex Kerfoot/223 2.50 6.00
115 Brock Boeser/220 15.00 40.00
116 Travis Sanheim/221 2.50 6.00
117 John Hayden/222 2.00 5.00
118 Andreas Borgman/222 2.50 6.00
119 Christian Djoos/223 2.50 6.00
120 Colin White/220 2.50 6.00
121 Paul LaDue/225 2.00 5.00
122 Evan McEneny/223 2.50 6.00
123 Michael Kapla/223 2.50 6.00
124 Alexandre Carrier/221 2.00 5.00
125 Haydn Fleury/221 2.50 6.00
126 Robert Hagg/222 2.50 6.00
127 Vince Dunn/221 2.50 6.00
128 Eric Comrie/222 2.00 5.00
129 Filip Chlapik/220 2.50 6.00
130 Alex DeBrincat/219 6.00 15.00
131 Riley Barber/223 2.00 5.00
132 MacKenzie Weegar/223 2.50 6.00
133 Michael Amadio/221 2.50 6.00
134 Griffen Molino/223 2.00 5.00
135 Nikita Scherbak/221 5.00 12.00
136 Peter Cehlarik/222 2.50 6.00
137 Kalle Kossila/224 2.00 5.00
138 Sean Malone/222 2.50 6.00
139 Andrei Mironov/223 2.50 6.00
140 Josh Ho-Sang/221 3.00 8.00
141 Blake Coleman/225 2.00 5.00
142 Viktor Antipin/224 2.50 6.00
143 Rasmus Andersson/221 2.50 6.00
144 Oscar Fantenberg/226 2.50 6.00
145 Calle Rosen/223 2.50 6.00
146 Tucker Poolman/224 2.50 6.00
147 T.J. Tynan/225 2.00 5.00
148 Remi Elie/222 2.00 5.00
149 Andrew Poturalski/223 2.50 6.00
150 Pierre-Luc Dubois/219 5.00 12.00
151 Martin Necas/218 2.50 6.00
152 Jonny Brodzinski/224 2.50 6.00
153 Madison Bowey/222 2.00 5.00
154 Anton Lindholm/222 2.50 6.00
155 Jack Roslovic/220 3.00 8.00
156 Samuel Girard/219 2.50 6.00
157 Lucas Wallmark/222 2.50 6.00
158 Ian McCoshen/222 2.50 6.00
159 Dan Renouf/223 2.00 5.00
160 Jakob Forsbacka-Karlsson/221 2.50 6.00
161 Jordan Schmaltz/224 3.00 8.00
162 Denis Gurianov/220 2.50 6.00
163 Christian Jaros/221 2.50 6.00
164 Luke Kunin/219 2.50 6.00
165 Tyson Jost/219 5.00 12.00
166 Matt Lorito/227 2.50 6.00
167 Garrett Mitchell/226 2.50 6.00
168 Jake Dotchin/223 2.00 5.00
169 Samuel Morin/222 2.50 6.00
170 Jake DeBrusk/221 4.00 10.00
171 Jon Gillies/223 2.50 6.00
172 Will Butcher/222 3.00 8.00
173 Tim Heed/226 2.50 6.00
174 Carter Rowney/228 2.00 5.00
175 Jesper Bratt/219 4.00 10.00
176 Samuel Blais/221 2.50 6.00
177 Alex Tuch/221 6.00 15.00
178 Robbie Russo/224 2.50 6.00
179 J.T. Compher/222 3.00 8.00
180 Christian Fischer/220 3.00 8.00
181 Logan Brown/219 2.50 6.00
182 Alexander Nylander/219 4.00 10.00
183 Jaycob Megna/224 2.50 6.00
184 Kurtis MacDermid/223 2.50 6.00
185 Nolan Patrick/219 5.00 12.00

2017-18 SP Game Used '16 Heritage Classic Game Used Pucks

HCGUPCM Connor McDavid
HCGUPCT Cam Talbot 50.00 125.00
HCGUPLD Leon Draisaitl
HCGUPMC Connor McDavid
HCGUPMS Mark Scheifele 30.00 80.00
HCGUPPL Patrik Laine 30.00 80.00

2017-18 SP Game Used '16 Heritage Classic Materials Net Cord

HCNCAL Adam Larsson 12.00 30.00
HCNCBW Blake Wheeler 25.00 60.00
HCNCCM Connor McDavid 50.00 125.00
HCNCCT Cam Talbot 25.00 60.00
HCNCDB Dustin Byfuglien 30.00 80.00
HCNCLD Leon Draisaitl 20.00 50.00
HCNCML Milan Lucic 20.00 50.00
HCNCMS Mark Scheifele 25.00 60.00
HCNCNE Nikolaj Ehlers 25.00 60.00
HCNCOK Oscar Klefbom 25.00 60.00
HCNCPL Patrik Laine 40.00 100.00
HCNCRN Ryan Nugent-Hopkins 25.00 60.00

2017-18 SP Game Used '17 All Star Game Materials Net Cord

ASNCAM Auston Matthews 80.00 150.00
ASNCAO Alexander Ovechkin 30.00 80.00
ASNCBB Brent Burns
ASNCCM Connor McDavid
ASNCCP Carey Price 30.00 80.00
ASNCEK Erik Karlsson 25.00 60.00
ASNCJG Johnny Gaudreau 25.00 60.00
ASNCJT John Tavares 20.00 50.00
ASNCNM Nathan MacKinnon
ASNCPK Patrick Kane 25.00 60.00
ASNCPL Patrik Laine 50.00 125.00
ASNCPS P.K. Subban 20.00 50.00
ASNCRK Ryan Kesler
ASNCSB Sergei Bobrovsky
ASNCSC Sidney Crosby 60.00 150.00
ASNCTH Taylor Hall 10.00 25.00
ASNCTO Jonathan Toews 25.00 60.00
ASNCTS Tyler Seguin 30.00 80.00
ASNCVT Vladimir Tarasenko 30.00 80.00
ASNCWS Wayne Simmonds

2017-18 SP Game Used '17 All Star Game Used Pucks

ASGUPAM Auston Matthews
ASGUPAO Alexander Ovechkin 50.00 125.00
ASGUPBB Brent Burns
ASGUPCP Carey Price
ASGUPJG Johnny Gaudreau
ASGUPJT John Tavares 25.00 60.00
ASGUPPL Patrik Laine

2017-18 SP Game Used '17 All Star Skills Dual Fabrics

AS2BP B.Burns/J.Pavelski 5.00 12.00
AS2CD J.Carter/D.Doughty 4.00 10.00
AS2KH N.Kucherov/V.Hedman 6.00 15.00
AS2MO C.McDavid/A.Ovechkin 15.00 40.00
AS2MR B.Marchand/T.Rask 5.00 12.00
AS2OH A.Ovechkin/B.Holtby 15.00 40.00
AS2TK J.Toews/P.Kane 8.00 20.00
AS2WP S.Weber/C.Price 12.00 30.00

2017-18 SP Game Used '17 All Star Skills Dual Fabrics Patch

*PATCH/25: 1X TO 2.5X BASIC INSERTS
AS2MO Connor McDavid 80.00 150.00
Alexander Ovechkin

2017-18 SP Game Used '17 All Star Skills Fabrics

ASAM Auston Matthews 12.00 30.00
ASAO Alexander Ovechkin 12.00 30.00
ASBB Brent Burns 4.00 10.00
ASBH Braden Holtby 5.00 12.00
ASBM Brad Marchand 4.00 10.00
ASCA Cam Atkinson 3.00 8.00
ASCC Corey Crawford 4.00 10.00
ASCM Connor McDavid 12.00 30.00
ASCP Carey Price 10.00 25.00
ASDK Duncan Keith 3.00 8.00
ASDO Drew Doughty 3.00 8.00
ASEK Erik Karlsson 4.00 10.00
ASJG Johnny Gaudreau 5.00 12.00
ASJP Joe Pavelski 3.00 8.00
ASJT John Tavares 6.00 15.00
ASNK Nikita Kucherov 5.00 12.00
ASNM Nathan MacKinnon 6.00 15.00
ASPK Patrick Kane 6.00 15.00
ASPL Patrik Laine 5.00 12.00
ASPS P.K. Subban 3.00 8.00
ASRK Ryan Kesler 3.00 8.00
ASSC Sidney Crosby 12.00 30.00
ASSW Shea Weber 2.50 6.00
ASTA Vladimir Tarasenko 5.00 12.00
ASTH Taylor Hall 6.00 15.00
ASTO Jonathan Toews 6.00 15.00
ASTR Tuukka Rask 3.00 8.00
ASTS Tyler Seguin 5.00 12.00
ASVH Victor Hedman 4.00 10.00
ASWS Wayne Simmonds 4.00 10.00

2017-18 SP Game Used '17 All Star Skills Fabrics Patch

*PATCH/35: .75X TO 2X BASIC INSERTS
ASAM Auston Matthews 40.00 100.00

2017-18 SP Game Used '17 All Star Skills Quad Fabrics

AS4NET Price/Rask/Bobrovsky/Holtby 12.00 30.00
AS4DMEN Karlsson/Subban 5.00 12.00
Doughty/Burns
AS4HAWKS Toews/Kane/Keith/Crawford 8.00 20.00
AS4STARS Toews/Ovechkin 15.00 40.00
McDavid/MacKinnon

2017-18 SP Game Used '17 Centennial Classic Fabrics

CCAA Andreas Athanasiou 3.00 8.00
CCAM Anthony Mantha 3.00 8.00
CCCB Connor Brown 3.00 8.00
CCDL Dylan Larkin 3.00 8.00
CCFA Frederik Andersen 2.50 6.00
CCFN Frans Nielsen 2.50 6.00
CCMM Mitch Marner 5.00 12.00
CCNK Nazem Kadri 2.50 6.00
CCNZ Nikita Zaitsev 2.50 6.00
CCWN William Nylander 5.00 12.00

2017-18 SP Game Used '17 Centennial Classic Materials Net Cord

CCNCAA Andreas Athanasiou 20.00 50.00
CCNCAM Anthony Mantha 20.00 50.00
CCNCDL Dylan Larkin 30.00 80.00
CCNCFA Frederik Andersen 15.00 40.00
CCNCFN Frans Nielsen 15.00 40.00
CCNCGN Gustav Nyquist 20.00 50.00
CCNCHZ Henrik Zetterberg 20.00 50.00
CCNCJV James van Riemsdyk 20.00 50.00
CCNCMA Auston Matthews 80.00 200.00
CCNCMM Mitch Marner 30.00 80.00
CCNCMR Morgan Rielly 20.00 50.00
CCNCNK Nazem Kadri 15.00 40.00
CCNCNZ Nikita Zaitsev 15.00 40.00
CCNCTT Tomas Tatar 20.00 50.00
CCNCWN William Nylander 30.00 80.00
CCNCZH Zach Hyman 15.00 40.00

2017-18 SP Game Used '17 Centennial Classic Quad Fabrics

CC4DRW Mantha/Athanasiou 8.00 20.00
Nielsen/Helm
CC4TML Marner/Nylander 12.00 30.00
Kadri/Andersen

2017-18 SP Game Used '17 Stadium Series Fabrics

PFBM Brandon Manning 2.50 6.00
PFIP Ivan Provorov 3.00 8.00
PFMR Matt Read 2.50 6.00
PFWS Wayne Simmonds 4.00 10.00
PPEM Evgeni Malkin 10.00 25.00
PPJG Jake Guentzel 4.00 10.00
PPJS Justin Schultz 3.00 8.00
PPMA Marc-Andre Fleury 5.00 12.00
PPPH Patric Hornqvist 2.50 6.00
PPSC Sidney Crosby 12.00 30.00

2017-18 SP Game Used '17 Stadium Series Materials Net Cord

SSNCCG Claude Giroux 20.00 50.00
SSNCCH Carl Hagelin 20.00 50.00
SSNCCO Sean Couturier 15.00 40.00
SSNCEM Evgeni Malkin 60.00 150.00
SSNCJG Jake Guentzel 25.00 60.00
SSNCJS Justin Schultz 20.00 50.00
SSNCJV Jakub Voracek 20.00 50.00
SSNCMM Matt Murray 30.00 80.00
SSNCPK Phil Kessel 25.00 60.00
SSNCSC Sidney Crosby 80.00 200.00
SSNCSG Shayne Gostisbehere 20.00 50.00
SSNCWS Wayne Simmonds 25.00 60.00

2017-18 SP Game Used '17 Stadium Series Quad Fabrics

SS4FLY Simmonds/Manning 10.00 25.00
Provorov/Read
SS4PEN Malkin/Guentzel 25.00 60.00
Hornqvist/Fleury

2017-18 SP Game Used '17 Stanley Cup Finals Materials Net Cord

SCNCBD Brian Dumoulin 15.00 40.00
SCNCBR Bryan Rust 20.00 50.00
SCNCCH Carl Hagelin 20.00 50.00
SCNCCJ Calle Jarnkrok 15.00 40.00
SCNCCS Conor Sheary 20.00 50.00
SCNCEM Evgeni Malkin 60.00 150.00
SCNCFF Filip Forsberg 25.00 60.00
SCNCFI Mike Fisher 15.00 40.00
SCNCJG Jake Guentzel 25.00 60.00
SCNCJN James Neal 15.00 40.00
SCNCJS Justin Schultz 20.00 50.00
SCNCMF Marc-Andre Fleury 30.00 80.00
SCNCMM Matt Murray 30.00 80.00
SCNCPH Patric Hornqvist 15.00 40.00
SCNCPK Phil Kessel 25.00 60.00
SCNCPR Pekka Rinne 25.00 60.00
SCNCPS P.K. Subban 20.00 50.00
SCNCRE Ryan Ellis 15.00 40.00
SCNCRJ Roman Josi 20.00 50.00
SCNCSC Sidney Crosby 80.00 200.00
SCNCSI Colton Sissons 15.00 40.00
SCNCVA Viktor Arvidsson 15.00 40.00

2017-18 SP Game Used '17 Winter Classic Materials Net Cord

WCNCAA Artem Anisimov 15.00 40.00
WCNCAP Artemi Panarin 20.00 50.00
WCNCAS Alexander Steen 20.00 50.00
WCNCBS Brent Seabrook 15.00 40.00
WCNCCC Corey Crawford 25.00 60.00
WCNCDK Duncan Keith 20.00 50.00
WCNCJA Jake Allen 25.00 60.00
WCNCJS Jaden Schwartz 25.00 60.00
WCNCJT Jonathan Toews 40.00 100.00
WCNCPI Alex Pietrangelo 15.00 40.00
WCNCPK Patrick Kane 40.00 100.00
WCNCVT Vladimir Tarasenko 30.00 80.00

2017-18 SP Game Used Autographs Blue

1 Auston Matthews A
2 Victor Hedman B 8.00 20.00
3 Tyler Seguin A 10.00 25.00
4 Jake Guentzel E 8.00 20.00
9 Artemi Panarin C 6.00 15.00
10 Carey Price A
12 Joe Pavelski B 6.00 15.00
13 Brayden Schenn E 10.00 25.00
14 Sean Monahan D 6.00 15.00
15 Vladimir Tarasenko A
16 Matt Duchene D 6.00 15.00
17 Patrik Laine B 25.00 60.00
18 Ryan Spooner E 5.00 12.00
20 Jonathan Toews A 25.00 60.00
21 Aleksander Barkov C 6.00 15.00
23 Marc-Andre Fleury E 30.00 80.00
24 Pavel Zacha E 6.00 15.00
27 Mats Zuccarello B 6.00 15.00
31 Jason Spezza B 6.00 15.00
34 Sebastian Aho E 6.00 15.00
35 Matt Murray D 10.00 25.00
36 Logan Couture B 6.00 15.00
37 John Gibson E 6.00 15.00
38 Nikolaj Ehlers D 6.00 15.00
40 Alexander Ovechkin A
42 Max Pacioretty B
45 Steven Stamkos A
47 Cam Atkinson D 6.00 15.00
50 Sidney Crosby A
51 Colton Parayko E 6.00 15.00
52 William Karlsson B 25.00 60.00
53 Leon Draisaitl D 10.00 25.00
55 Patrick Kane A
57 Noah Hanifin E 6.00 15.00
58 Adam Henrique E 5.00 12.00
60 Henrik Lundqvist A 40.00 100.00
63 Mark Giordano E 5.00 12.00
67 Roberto Luongo B 12.00 30.00
68 Nikita Kucherov E 10.00 25.00
69 Mark Stone E 6.00 15.00
70 John Tavares A 12.00 30.00
73 Mark Scheifele C 8.00 20.00
74 Mitch Marner C 25.00 60.00
76 Nino Niederreiter D 5.00 12.00
77 Connor McDavid A
78 Mark Messier A 20.00 50.00
79 Rod Langway B 6.00 15.00
80 Steve Yzerman A
82 Teemu Selanne A 20.00 50.00
83 Brett Hull A
84 Ed Belfour A
85 Wayne Gretzky A 150.00 250.00
87 Charlie McAvoy B 40.00 100.00
88 Victor Mete C 25.00 60.00
89 Gabriel Carlsson A 4.00 10.00
91 Adrian Kempe D 6.00 15.00
94 Evgeny Svechnikov C 10.00 25.00
95 Vadim Shipachyov E 15.00 40.00
97 Tage Thompson E 8.00 20.00
98 Vladislav Kamenev E 8.00 20.00
100 Clayton Keller B 12.00 30.00
101 Valentin Zykov E 5.00 12.00
105 Owen Tippett C 8.00 20.00
107 Ivan Barbashev A 5.00 12.00
110 Anders Bjork D 8.00 20.00
111 Mike Vecchione E 8.00 20.00
115 Brock Boeser A 100.00 200.00
116 Travis Sanheim E 5.00 12.00
119 Christian Djoos C 15.00 40.00
125 Haydn Fleury E 5.00 12.00
126 Robert Hagg A 5.00 12.00
127 Vince Dunn B 12.00 30.00
129 Filip Chlapik D 5.00 12.00
130 Alex DeBrincat D 12.00 30.00
131 Riley Barber E 4.00 10.00
133 Michael Amadio C 8.00 20.00
135 Nikita Scherbak B 10.00 25.00
136 Peter Cehlarik D 8.00 20.00
140 Josh Ho-Sang A 6.00 15.00
146 Tucker Poolman C 8.00 20.00
149 Andrew Poturalski C 5.00 12.00
150 Pierre-Luc Dubois C 10.00 25.00
153 Madison Bowey E 4.00 10.00
155 Jack Roslovic E 6.00 15.00
161 Jordan Schmaltz C 6.00 15.00
162 Denis Gurianov E 5.00 12.00
164 Luke Kunin D 8.00 20.00
165 Tyson Jost D 10.00 25.00
169 Samuel Morin C 5.00 12.00
171 Jon Gillies C 5.00 12.00
172 Will Butcher C 8.00 20.00
175 Jesper Bratt C 15.00 40.00
177 Alex Tuch D 15.00 40.00
179 J.T. Compher C 6.00 15.00
180 Christian Fischer A 8.00 20.00
182 Alexander Nylander E 8.00 20.00

2017-18 SP Game Used Banner Year All Star '17

BASAM Auston Matthews 15.00 40.00
BASAO Alexander Ovechkin 12.00 30.00
BASBB Brent Burns 4.00 10.00
BASCA Cam Atkinson 3.00 8.00
BASCM Connor McDavid 12.00 30.00
BASJG Johnny Gaudreau 5.00 12.00
BASJT John Tavares 6.00 15.00
BASNM Nathan MacKinnon 6.00 15.00
BASPK P.K. Subban 3.00 8.00
BASPL Patrik Laine 5.00 12.00
BASSC Sidney Crosby 12.00 30.00
BASTO Jonathan Toews 6.00 15.00
BASVH Victor Hedman 4.00 10.00
BASWS Wayne Simmonds 4.00 10.00

2017-18 SP Game Used Banner Year Centennial Classic '17

BCCAM Auston Matthews 15.00 40.00
BCCDL Dylan Larkin 5.00 12.00
BCCFA Frederik Andersen 4.00 10.00
BCCGN Gustav Nyquist 5.00 12.00
BCCHZ Henrik Zetterberg 5.00 12.00
BCCJV James van Riemsdyk 5.00 12.00
BCCMA Anthony Mantha 5.00 12.00
BCCMM Mitch Marner 12.00 30.00
BCCMR Morgan Rielly 5.00 12.00
BCCTT Tomas Tatar 5.00 12.00

2017-18 SP Game Used Banner Year Draft '03

BD03BB Brent Burns 10.00 25.00
BD03CC Corey Crawford 10.00 25.00
BD03MF Marc-Andre Fleury 12.00 30.00
BD03PB Patrice Bergeron 12.00 30.00
BD03RK Ryan Kesler 8.00 20.00

2017-18 SP Game Used Banner Year Draft '14

BD14IB Ivan Barbashev 2.50 6.00
BD14JH Josh Ho-Sang 3.00 8.00

2017-18 SP Game Used Banner Year Draft '15

BD15ES Evgeny Svechnikov 5.00 12.00
BD15JR Jack Roslovic 3.00 8.00

2017-18 SP Game Used Banner Year Draft '15 Autographs

BD15ES Evgeny Svechnikov
BD15JR Jack Roslovic 12.00 30.00

2017-18 SP Game Used Banner Year Draft '16

BD16CK Clayton Keller 4.00 10.00
BD16CM Charlie McAvoy 5.00 12.00
BD16PD Pierre-Luc Dubois 3.00 8.00
BD16TJ Tyson Jost 3.00 8.00

2017-18 SP Game Used Banner Year Draft '17

BD17NH Nico Hischier 12.00 30.00
BD17NP Nolan Patrick 12.00 30.00

2017-18 SP Game Used Banner Year Stadium Series '17

BSSCG Claude Giroux 6.00 15.00
BSSEM Evgeni Malkin 20.00 50.00
BSSJG Jake Guentzel 8.00 20.00
BSSJV Jakub Voracek 6.00 15.00
BSSPH Patric Hornqvist 5.00 12.00
BSSPK Phil Kessel 8.00 20.00
BSSSG Shayne Gostisbehere 6.00 15.00
BSSWS Wayne Simmonds 8.00 20.00

2017-18 SP Game Used Banner Year Winter Classic '17

BWCAA Artem Anisimov 4.00 10.00
BWCCC Corey Crawford 6.00 15.00
BWCDK Duncan Keith 5.00 12.00
BWCJA Jake Allen 6.00 15.00
BWCJS Jaden Schwartz 6.00 15.00
BWCPK Patrick Kane 10.00 25.00
BWCRF Robby Fabbri 5.00 12.00
BWCVT Vladimir Tarasenko 8.00 20.00

2017-18 SP Game Used Draft Day Marks

DDMAD Alex DeBrincat 50.00 125.00
DDMAK Adrian Kempe 25.00 60.00
DDMAT Alex Tuch 50.00 120.00
DDMBB Brock Boeser 150.00 300.00
DDMCF Christian Fischer 25.00 60.00
DDMCK Clayton Keller 50.00 120.00
DDMCM Charlie McAvoy 60.00 150.00
DDMDG Denis Gurianov 20.00 50.00
DDMES Evgeny Svechnikov 40.00 100.00
DDMGC Gabriel Carlsson 15.00 40.00
DDMHF Haydn Fleury 20.00 50.00
DDMIB Ivan Barbashev 20.00 50.00
DDMJE Joel Eriksson Ek 20.00 50.00
DDMJG Jake Guentzel 40.00 100.00
DDMJG Jon Gillies 20.00 50.00
DDMJR Jack Roslovic 25.00 60.00
DDMLK Luke Kunin 20.00 50.00
DDMOT Owen Tippett 40.00 100.00
DDMPD Pierre-Luc Dubois 30.00 80.00
DDMSM Samuel Morin 20.00 50.00
DDMTJ Tyson Jost 40.00 100.00
DDMTT Tage Thompson 40.00 100.00
DDMVK Vladislav Kamenev 20.00 50.00
DDMVT Vladimir Tarasenko 40.00 100.00
DDMVZ Valentin Zykov 20.00 50.00

2017-18 SP Game Used Frameworks Materials

FWAG Alex Galchenyuk C 10.00 25.00
FWAL Andrew Ladd C 8.00 20.00
FWAM Anthony Mantha B 15.00 40.00
FWAW Alexander Wennberg A 6.00 15.00
FWBB Brent Burns B 10.00 25.00
FWBM Brad Marchand B 10.00 25.00
FWCC Corey Crawford C 10.00 25.00
FWCM Connor McDavid A 30.00 80.00
FWDG Doug Gilmour A 10.00 25.00
FWEB Ed Belfour B 10.00 25.00
FWEK Evgeny Kuznetsov A 12.00 30.00
FWHS Henrik Sedin B 8.00 20.00
FWJA Justin Abdelkader C 6.00 15.00
FWJH Jonathan Huberdeau C 6.00 15.00
FWJK John Klingberg C 6.00 15.00
FWJQ Jonathan Quick C 12.00 30.00
FWJS Joe Sakic A 10.00 25.00
FWKE Phil Kessel B 10.00 25.00
FWLD Leon Draisaitl B 12.00 30.00
FWMA Auston Matthews A 30.00 80.00
FWMK Mikko Koivu C 6.00 15.00
FWMM Mitch Marner B 12.00 30.00
FWMU Matt Murray B 12.00 30.00
FWMZ Mats Zuccarello B 8.00 20.00
FWNK Nikita Kucherov B 12.00 30.00
FWNM Nathan MacKinnon A 15.00 40.00
FWOE Oliver Ekman-Larsson B 8.00 20.00
FWPC Paul Coffey A 8.00 20.00
FWPF Peter Forsberg A 12.00 30.00
FWPL Patrik Laine B 12.00 30.00
FWPS P.K. Subban B 8.00 20.00
FWRB Ray Bourque A 12.00 30.00
FWRG Ryan Getzlaf B 8.00 20.00
FWRO Ryan O'Reilly B 8.00 20.00
FWSC Jaden Schwartz B 10.00 25.00
FWSG Shayne Gostisbehere C 8.00 20.00
FWSM Sean Monahan C 8.00 20.00
FWSW Shea Weber C 6.00 15.00
FWTH Taylor Hall B 15.00 40.00
FWVR Victor Rask C 8.00 20.00

2017-18 SP Game Used Goal Pucks

GPCA Cam Atkinson 15.00 40.00
GPDS Daniel Sedin 15.00 40.00
GPJP Joe Pavelski 15.00 40.00
GPJT Jonathan Toews 30.00 80.00
GPMG Mikael Granlund 15.00 40.00
GPMS Mark Stone 15.00 40.00
GPOE Oliver Ekman-Larsson 15.00 40.00
GPOP Ondrej Palat 15.00 40.00
GPRJ Roman Josi 15.00 40.00

2017-18 SP Game Used Inked Sweaters

ISAG Alex Galchenyuk/50 8.00 20.00
ISCC Chris Chelios/25 12.00 30.00
ISJO Joe Thornton/25 15.00 40.00
ISJT Jonathan Toews/25 30.00 80.00
ISMM Matt Murray/50 20.00 50.00
ISPL Patrik Laine/50 25.00 60.00
ISTA John Tavares/25 15.00 40.00
ISTS Tyler Seguin/50 8.00 20.00

2017-18 SP Game Used Inked Sweaters Patch

COMMON CARD 12.00 30.00
SEMISTARS 15.00 40.00
UNLISTED STARS 20.00 50.00
IPMM Matt Murray/25 40.00 100.00
IPPL Patrik Laine/25 40.00 100.00

2017-18 SP Game Used Rookie Sweaters

RSAB Anders Bjork/199 3.00 8.00
RSAD Alex DeBrincat/199 6.00 15.00
RSAK Adrian Kempe/199 3.00 8.00
RSAN Alexander Nylander/199 4.00 10.00
RSAT Alex Tuch/199 6.00 15.00
RSBB Brock Boeser/199 15.00 40.00
RSCF Christian Fischer/199 3.00 8.00
RSCK Clayton Keller/199 6.00 15.00
RSCM Charlie McAvoy/199 8.00 20.00
RSCW Colin White/199 2.50 6.00
RSES Evgeny Svechnikov/199 5.00 12.00
RSHF Haydn Fleury/199 2.50 6.00
RSIB Ivan Barbashev/199 2.50 6.00
RSJD Jake DeBrusk/199 4.00 10.00
RSJG Jon Gillies/199 2.50 6.00
RSJH Josh Ho-Sang/199 3.00 8.00
RSJK Janne Kuokkanen/199 2.50 6.00
RSJR Jack Roslovic/199 3.00 8.00
RSKY Kailer Yamamoto/199 6.00 15.00
RSLB Logan Brown/199 2.50 6.00
RSNH Nico Hischier/99 8.00 20.00
RSNP Nolan Patrick/99 5.00 12.00
RSNS Nikita Scherbak/199 5.00 12.00
RSOT Owen Tippett/199 5.00 12.00
RSPD Pierre-Luc Dubois/199 5.00 12.00
RSRB Riley Barber/199 2.00 5.00
RSSM Samuel Morin/199 2.50 6.00
RSTJ Tyson Jost/199 5.00 12.00
RSTT Tage Thompson/199 4.00 10.00
RSVS Vadim Shipachyov/199 8.00 20.00

2017-18 SP Game Used Rookie Sweaters Inked Patch

RSAB Anders Bjork 20.00 50.00
RSAD Alex DeBrincat 40.00 100.00
RSAK Adrian Kempe 20.00 50.00
RSAN Alexander Nylander 25.00 60.00
RSAT Alex Tuch 40.00 100.00
RSBB Brock Boeser 150.00 300.00
RSCF Christian Fischer 20.00 50.00
RSCK Clayton Keller 40.00 100.00
RSCM Charlie McAvoy 50.00 125.00
RSES Evgeny Svechnikov 30.00 80.00
RSHF Haydn Fleury 15.00 40.00
RSIB Ivan Barbashev 15.00 40.00
RSJG Jon Gillies 15.00 40.00
RSJH Josh Ho-Sang 20.00 50.00
RSJR Jack Roslovic 20.00 50.00
RSNS Nikita Scherbak 30.00 80.00
RSOT Owen Tippett 30.00 80.00
RSPD Pierre-Luc Dubois 30.00 80.00
RSRB Riley Barber 12.00 30.00
RSSM Samuel Morin 15.00 40.00
RSTJ Tyson Jost 30.00 80.00
RSTT Tage Thompson 25.00 60.00
RSVS Vadim Shipachyov 50.00 125.00

2017-18 SP Game Used Signing Day Marks

SDMMV Mike Vecchione 15.00 40.00
SDMVS Vadim Shipachyov 15.00 40.00

1994 Sportflics Pride of Texas

These four Sportflics cards were given away at the Pinnacle Booth during the National Convention in Houston. Thus they feature athletes from Texas professional sport franchises: Dallas Cowboys (1), Houston Oilers (2), and Dallas Stars (3-4). On the fronts, the standard-size cards display a color player cutout on a background consisting of the Houston skyline. A Special "The Pride of Texas" logo appears on each front. The backs carry biography and a brief player profile. The tagline on the bottom of each back indicates that just 2,500 of each card were produced.

COMPLETE SET (4) 6.00 15.00
N3 Mike Modano 2.50 6.00
N4 Derian Hatcher 1.50 4.00

1935 Sporting Events and Stars

Cards measure approximately 2" x 3". Cards feature black and white fronts, along with informative backs. Set features 96 cards and was issued by various cigarette makers including Senior Service, Junior Member, and Illingworth's.

31 Ice Hockey 20.00 40.00

1933 Sport Kings

The cards in this 48-card set measure 2 3/8" by 2 7/8". The 1933 Sport Kings set, issued by the Goudey Gum Company, contains cards for the most famous athletic heroes of the times. No less than 18 different sports are represented in the set. The baseball cards of Cobb, Hubbell, and Ruth, and the football cards of Rockne, Grange and Thorpe command premium prices. The cards were issued in one-card penny packs which came 100 packs to a box along with a piece of gum. The catalog designation for this set is R338.

COMPLETE SET 10000.00 16000.00
19 Eddie Shore Hockey 400.00 800.00
24 Howie Morenz HK 600.00 1000.00
29 Ace Bailey HK 250.00 400.00
30 Ivan Ching Johnson HK 250.00 400.00

2007 Sportkings

5 Martin Brodeur 5.00 12.00
19 Mario Lemieux 6.00 15.00
26 Maurice Richard 5.00 12.00
29 Patrick Roy 6.00 15.00
32 Terry Sawchuk 5.00 12.00
33 Milt Schmidt 4.00 10.00

2007 Sportkings Mini

*MINIS: 1X TO 2X BASIC
ONE PER PACK
ANNOUNCED PRINT RUN 93 SETS

2007 Sportkings Autograph Silver

RANDOM INSERTS IN PACKS
ANNOUNCED PRINT RUN B/WN 95-99 PER
AMB Martin Brodeur 25.00 50.00
AML Mario Lemieux 50.00 80.00
AMS Milt Schmidt 15.00 30.00
APR Patrick Roy 50.00 80.00

2007 Sportkings Autograph Gold

*GOLD: 1.2X TO 2X BASIC
RANDOM INSERTS IN PACKS
ANNOUNCED PRINT RUN 10 SETS

2007 Sportkings Autograph Memorabilia Silver

RANDOM INSERTS IN PACKS
ANNOUNCED PRINT RUN 40 SETS
AMMB Martin Brodeur Jsy 40.00 70.00
AMML Mario Lemieux Jsy 70.00 120.00
AMMS Milt Schmidt Jsy 20.00 40.00
AMPR Patrick Roy Jsy 60.00 100.00

2007 Sportkings Autograph Memorabilia Gold

*GOLD/10: 1.2X TO 2X SILVER/40
ANNOUNCED PRINT RUN 10 SETS
AMML Mario Lemieux Jsy 125.00 200.00
AMPR Patrick Roy Jsy 125.00 200.00

2007 Sportkings Cityscapes Silver

ANNOUNCED PRINT RUN 20 SETS
*GOLD: .5X TO 1.2X BASIC
GOLD ANNOUNCED PRINT RUN 10 SETS
RANDOM INSERTS IN PACKS
CS02 P.Rose/P.Roy 100.00 175.00
CS03 R.Clemens/M.Schmidt 20.00 40.00
CS07 R.Clemente/M.Lemieux 40.00 80.00
CS08 M.Johnson/T.Sawchuk 20.00 40.00

2007 Sportkings Decades Silver

ANNOUNCED PRINT RUN 20 SETS
*GOLD: .5X TO 1.2X BASIC
GOLD ANNOUNCED PRINT RUN 10 SETS
RANDOM INSERTS IN PACKS
D01 Williams/Richard/Musial 40.00 80.00
D02 Sawchuk/Shoe/Schmidt 40.00 80.00
D06 Aikman/Roy/Clemens 40.00 80.00

2007 Sportkings Double Memorabilia Silver

RANDOM INSERTS IN PACKS
ANNOUNCED PRINT RUN 4-40 SETS
DM15, DM16 ANNOUNCED PRINT RUN 4 PER
NO DM15, DM16 PRICING DUE TO SCARCITY
DM4 Mario Lemieux 20.00 50.00
DM5 Martin Brodeur 12.50 30.00
DM7 Patrick Roy 20.00 50.00

2007 Sportkings Double Memorabilia Gold

*GOLD: .6X TO 1.5X BASIC
RANDOM INSERTS IN PACKS
ANNOUNCED PRINT RUN 10 SETS
DM15, DM16 ANNOUNCED PRINT RUN 1 PER
NO DM15, DM16 PRICING DUE TO SCARCITY

2007 Sportkings Lumber Silver

RANDOM INSERTS IN PACKS
ANNOUNCED PRINT RUN 30 SETS
WORDED SWATCHES COMMAND PREMIUMS
L1 Martin Brodeur Stick 20.00 40.00
L2 Mario Lemieux Stick 25.00 50.00
L3 Patrick Roy Stick 30.00 60.00
L4 Terry Sawchuk Stick 25.00 50.00
L5 Maurice Richard Stick 30.00 60.00

2007 Sportkings Lumber Gold

*GOLD: .75X TO 1.5 BASIC
RANDOM INSERTS IN PACKS
ANNOUNCED PRINT RUN 10 SETS
WORDED SWATCHES COMMAND PREMIUMS

2007 Sportkings Patch Silver

ANNOUNCED PRINT RUN 20 SETS
P28-P30 ANNOUNCED PRINT RUN 4 PER
NO P28-P30 PRICING DUE TO SCARCITY
*GOLD: .6X TO 1.2X BASIC
GOLD ANNOUNCED PRINT RUN 10 SETS
GOLD P28-P30 ANCD. PRINT RUN 1 PER
GOLD P28-P30 NO PRICING AVAILABLE
RANDOM INSERTS IN PACKS
P11 Mario Lemieux Jsy 20.00 50.00
P12 Martin Brodeur Jsy 15.00 40.00
P14 Milt Schmidt Jsy 12.50 30.00
P17 Patrick Roy Jsy 30.00 60.00

2007 Sportkings Single Memorabilia Silver

RANDOM INSERTS IN PACKS
ANNOUNCED PRINT RUN 90 SETS
SM3, SM13 ANNOUNCED PRINT RUN 4 PER
NO SM3, SM13 PRICING DUE TO SCARCITY
SM11 Mario Lemieux Jsy 10.00 25.00
SM12 Martin Brodeur Jsy 6.00 15.00
SM14 Milt Schmidt Jsy 8.00 20.00
SM42 Patrick Roy Jsy 10.00 25.00

2007 Sportkings Triple Memorabilia Silver

ANNOUNCED PRINT RUN 10 SETS
TM7, TM8 ANNOUNCED PRINT RUN 4 PER
NO TM7, TM8 PRICING DUE TO SCARCITY
GOLD ANNOUNCED PRINT RUN 1 SET
NO GOLD PRICING DUE TO SCARCITY
RANDOM INSERTS IN PACKS
TM04 Mario Lemieux 50.00 100.00
TM05 Martin Brodeur 30.00 60.00
TM12 Sawchuk/Roy/Brodeur 50.00 100.00

2008 Sportkings

FIVE CARDS PER BOX
78 Mark Messier 5.00 10.00
84 Jean Beliveau 6.00 12.00
87 Georges Vezina 6.00 12.00
88 Jacques Plante 7.50 15.00
97 Bobby Hull 6.00 12.00
103 Brett Hull 5.00 10.00

2008 Sportkings Mini

*MINI: 1X TO 2X BASIC
ONE PER BOX

2008 Sportkings Autograph Silver

ANNOUNCED PRINT RUN B/WN 20-90 PER
RANDOM INSERTS IN PACKS
MM Mark Messier/80 * 35.00 70.00
BH1 Brett Hull/40 * 20.00 40.00
BH2 Brett Hull/40 * 20.00 40.00
JB1 Jean Belveau/50 * 25.00 50.00
JB2 Jean Beliveau/50 * 25.00 50.00
BHU1 Bobby Hull/40 * 20.00 40.00
BHU2 Bobby Hull/40 * 20.00 40.00

2008 Sportkings Autograph Memorabilia Silver

ANNOUNCED PRINT RUN B/WN 15-50 PER
NO GOLD PRICING DUE TO SCARCITY
RANDOM INSERTS IN PACKS
BH1 Brett Hull/40 * 25.00 50.00
BH2 Brett Hull/40 * 25.00 50.00
BHU1 Bobby Hull/40 * 25.00 50.00
BHU2 Bobby Hull/40 * 25.00 50.00
JBE Jean Beliveau/50 * 30.00 60.00
JBE2 Jean Beliveau/50 * 30.00 60.00
MM Mark Messier/40 * 40.00 80.00

2008 Sportkings Cityscapes Double Silver

RANDOM INSERTS IN PACKS
1 P.Roy/J.Elway 30.00 60.00
3 G.Carter/J.Beliveau 15.00 40.00
4 B.Hull/M.Irvin 15.00 40.00
5 E.Banks/B.Hull 20.00 50.00
6 B.Gibson/B.Hull 15.00 40.00
8 Pele/M.Messier 75.00 125.00
10 B.Sanders/B.Hull 20.00 50.00

2008 Sportkings Cityscapes Triple Silver
RANDOM INSERTS IN PACKS
2 Irvin/Aikman/Hull 20.00 50.00
5 Carter/Rose/Beliveau 30.00 60.00
6 Messier/Mattingly/Pele 75.00 125.00
7 Brock/Smith/Hull 20.00 50.00

2008 Sportkings Decades Silver
RANDOM INSERTS IN PACKS
1 Banks/Beliveau/Hogan 40.00 80.00
2 Brown/Plante/Marichal 20.00 50.00
4 Marino/Messier/Parish 30.00 60.00
5 Hull/Irvin/Olajuwon 20.00 50.00

2008 Sportkings Double Memorabilia Silver
RANDOM INSERTS IN PACKS
3 J.Plante/P.Roy 30.00 60.00

2008 Sportkings National Convention VIP Promo
11 Patrick Roy 5.00 12.00
Ching Johnson
16 Mark Messier 3.00 8.00
Eddie Shore

2008 Sportkings Papercuts
RANDOM INSERTS IN PACKS
ANNOUNCED PRINT RUN B/WN 1-10 PER
NO PRICING DUE TO SCARCITY

2008 Sportkings Passing the Torch Silver
RANDOM INSERTS IN PACKS
5 J.Beliveau/M.Messier 20.00 50.00
6 J.Plante/P.Roy 40.00 80.00

2008 Sportkings Patch Silver
RANDOM INSERTS IN PACKS
17 Mark Messier Edmonton 20.00 50.00
18 Mark Messier NY 20.00 50.00
19 Mark Messier Vancouver 20.00 50.00

2008 Sportkings Single Memorabilia Silver
RANDOM INSERTS IN PACKS
17 Jacques Plante 10.00 25.00
19 Jean Beliveau 12.50 30.00
28 Mark Messier 8.00 20.00
45 Bobby Hull 10.00 25.00

2008 Sportkings Triple Memorabilia Silver
RANDOM INSERTS IN PACKS
6 Beliveau/Lemieux/Richard 30.00 60.00
8 Messier/Lemieux/Hull 30.00 60.00
9 Mark Messier NY-Van-Edm 30.00 60.00
15 Sawchuk/Roy/Brodeur 50.00 100.00

2009 Sportkings
COMPLETE SET (52) 250.00 450.00
COMMON CARD (109-160) 5.00 12.00
SEMISTARS 6.00 15.00
UNLISTED STARS 8.00 20.00
142 Hobey Baker 5.00 12.00
143 Vladislav Tretiak 10.00 25.00
144 Phil Esposito 6.00 15.00
149 Howie Morenz 6.00 15.00

2009 Sportkings Mini
*MINI: .6X TO 1.5X BASIC CARDS
STATED ODDS ONE PER BOX
UNPRICED SILVER PRINT RUN 7 SETS
UNPRICED GOLD PRINT RUN 3 SETS

2009 Sportkings Autograph Silver
ANNOUNCED PRINT RUN B/WN 15-70 PER
UNPRICED GOLD PRINT RUN 10
PE1 Phil Esposito/40* 20.00 40.00
PE2 Phil Esposito/40* 20.00 40.00
VT1 Vladislav Tretiak/40* 40.00 80.00
VT2 Vladislav Tretiak/40* 40.00 80.00

2009 Sportkings Autograph Memorabilia Silver
ANNOUNCED PRINT RUN B/WN 15-40 PER
UNPRICED GOLD PRINT RUN 10
RANDOM INSERTS IN PACKS
PE1 Phil Esposito Jsy/40* 15.00 30.00
PE2 Phil Esposito Jsy/40* 15.00 30.00
VT1 Vladislav Tretiak Jsy/40* 40.00 80.00
VT2 Vladislav Tretiak Jsy/40* 40.00 80.00

2009 Sportkings Cityscapes Double Silver
ANNOUNCED PRINT RUN 19 SETS
UNPRICED GOLD PRINT RUN 1
RANDOM INSERTS IN PACKS
4 M.Schmidt Jsy/B.Parent Jsy 25.00 50.00
5 P.Esposito Jsy/Pele Jsy 25.00 50.00
7 D.Flutie Jsy/B.Hull Jsy 20.00 40.00

2009 Sportkings Cityscapes Triple Silver
ANNOUNCED PRINT RUN 19 SETS
UNPRICED GOLD PRINT RUN 1
RANDOM INSERTS IN PACKS
3 Taylor/Reggie/P.Esposito 25.00 50.00
4 Flutie/Bo.Hull/T.Esposito 20.00 40.00

2009 Sportkings Decades Silver
ANNOUNCED PRINT RUN 19 SETS
UNPRICED GOLD PRINT RUN 1
RANDOM INSERTS IN PACKS
2 Tretiak/Reggie/Karolyi 50.00 100.00

2009 Sportkings Double Memorabilia Silver
ANNOUNCED PRINT RUN B/WN 1-19
UNPRICED GOLD PRINT RUN 1
RANDOM INSERTS IN PACKS
12 P.Esposito/V.Tretiak/19* 40.00 80.00
15 H.Morenz/M.Richard/1*

2009 Sportkings National Convention VIP Promo
COMPLETE SET (7)
1 Lendl/Esposito/Wallace 4.00 10.00
Shamrock/Barry/Tyson
2 Leslie/Namath/Flutie/Tretiak/Oliva/Taro 5.00 12.00
7 Morenz/Pollard/Johnson 5.00 12.00
Nagurski/S.Smith/Pele

2009 Sportkings Patch Silver
ANNOUNCED PRINT RUN B/WN 4-19
UNPRICED GOLD PRINT RUN 1 SET
RANDOM INSERTS IN PACKS
1 Phil Esposito/19* 20.00 40.00
2 Phil Esposito/19* 20.00 40.00
11 Vladislav Tretiak/19* 50.00 100.00

2009 Sportkings Single Memorabilia Silver
ANNOUNCED PRINT RUN B/WN 4-29
UNPRICED GOLD PRINT RUN B/WN 1-4
RANDOM INSERTS IN PACKS
12 Phil Esposito Jsy/29* 10.00 15.00
16 Vladislav Tretiak Jsy/29* 30.00 60.00
25 Howie Morenz Jsy/4*

2009 Sportkings Triple Memorabilia Silver
ANNOUNCED PRINT RUN B/WN 3-19
UNPRICED GOLD PRINT RUN 1 SET
RANDOM INSERTS IN PACKS

2010 Sportkings
COMPLETE SET (48) 150.00 300.00
COMP.SET w/o ALI SP (47) 100.00 200.00
167 Jim Craig 5.00 12.00
178 Joe Sakic 4.00 10.00
183 Bernie Parent 5.00 12.00

2010 Sportkings Mini
COMPLETE SET (48) 175.00 350.00
*MINI: .5X TO 1.2X BASIC CARDS
STATED ODDS 1:2

2010 Sportkings Autograph Silver
ANNOUNCED PRINT RUN 10-50
UNPRICED GOLD PRINT RUN 5-10
ABP1 Bernie Parent/40* 15.00 30.00
ABP2 Bernie Parent/40* 15.00 30.00
AJC1 Jim Craig/35* 20.00 40.00
AJC2 Jim Craig/35* 20.00 40.00
AJS1 Joe Sakic/40* 25.00 50.00
AJS2 Joe Sakic/40* 25.00 50.00

2010 Sportkings Autograph Memorabilia Silver
ANNOUNCED PRINT RUN 10-40
UNPRICED GOLD PRINT RUN 5-10
AMBP1 Bernie Parent Jsy/40* 20.00 40.00
AMBP2 Bernie Parent Jsy/40* 20.00 40.00
AMJC1 Jim Craig Stick/20* 25.00 50.00
AMJC2 Jim Craig Stick/20* 25.00 50.00
AMJS1 Joe Sakic Jsy/40* 25.00 50.00
AMJS2 Joe Sakic Jsy/40* 25.00 50.00

2010 Sportkings Double Memorabilia Silver
STATED PRINT RUN 20 UNLESS NOTED
DM10 J.Sakic/J.Sakic 15.00 40.00

2010 Sportkings Patch Silver
STATED PRINT RUN 20
UNPRICED GOLD PRINT RUN 10
P1 Bernie Parent 25.00 60.00
P2 Joe Sakic
P7 Joe Sakic

2010 Sportkings Single Memorabilia Silver
STATED PRINT RUN 26 UNLESS NOTED
SM2 Bernie Parent 6.00 12.00
SM13 Joe Sakic 10.00 20.00

2010 Sportkings Triple Memorabilia Silver
SILVER PRINT RUN 4-20
UNPRICED GOLD PRINT RUN 1-10
TM1 Craig/Sakic/Parent 30.00 60.00

2010 Sportkings National Convention VIP Promo
11 Joe Sakic 1.50 4.00
14 Bernie Parent 1.25 3.00

2012 Sportkings
237 Mark Wells 4.00 10.00
238 Guy Lafleur 5.00 12.00
239 Paul Henderson 4.00 10.00

2012 Sportkings Mini
*MINI: .5X TO 1.2X BASIC CARDS
RANDOM INSERT IN PACKS

2012 Sportkings Autographs Silver
ANNOUNCED PRINT RUN 15-130
AMW Mark Wells 10.00 20.00

2012 Sportkings Cityscapes Double Silver
ANNOUNCED PRINT RUN 30
CS5 G.Lafleur/J.Beliveau 20.00 40.00
CS8 I.Thomas/G.Howe 15.00 30.00
CS11 T.Raines/P.Roy 10.00 20.00

2012 Sportkings Double Memorabilia Silver
ANNOUNCED PRINT RUN 60
DM7 G.Lafleur/P.Roy 20.00 40.00
DM9 G.Lafleur/G.Lafleur 15.00 30.00

2012 Sportkings Greatest Moments Silver
ANNOUNCED PRINT RUN 40
GM2 Guy Lafleur 10.00 20.00

2012 Sportkings Premium Back
*SINGLES: .5X TO 1.2X BASIC CARDS
STATED ODDS ONE PER PACK

2012 Sportkings Quad Memorabilia Silver
ANNOUNCED PRINT RUN 30
QM6 Laflr/Beliv/Richrd/Plant 30.00 60.00

2012 Sportkings Single Memorabilia Silver
ANNOUNCED PRINT RUN 90
SM5 Guy Lafleur 7.50 15.00

2012 Sportkings Triple Memorabilia Silver
ANNOUNCED PRINT RUN 30
TM6 Lafleur/Borg/Navratilova 20.00 40.00

2013 Sportkings
COMPLETE SET (48) 60.00 120.00
280 Gordie Howe 5.00 12.00
302 Toe Blake 3.00 8.00

2013 Sportkings Mini
*MINI: .5X TO 1.2X BASIC CARDS
STATED ODDS 1:2

2013 Sportkings Premium Back
*PREM.BACK: .5X TO 1.2X BASIC CARDS
ONE PREMIUM BACK PER BOX
302 Toe Blake SP 30.00 60.00

2013 Sportkings Autographs Silver
PRINT RUN 15-60
AGH1 Gordie Howe/20* 50.00 100.00
AGH2 Gordie Howe/20* 50.00 100.00
AGH3 Gordie Howe/20* 50.00 100.00
AGH4 Gordie Howe/20* 50.00 100.00

2013 Sportkings Cityscapes Double Silver
ANNOUNCED PRINT RUN 40
CSD1 S.Pippen/B.Hull 10.00 25.00
CSD5 G.Howe/C.Drexler 8.00 20.00

2013 Sportkings Cityscapes Triple Silver
ANNOUNCED PRINT RUN 30
CST2 Thomas/Pippen/Hull 10.00 25.00
CST3 O'Neal/Valenzuela/Sawchuk

2013 Sportkings Decades Silver
ANNOUNCED PRINT RUN 40
D2 Thom/Pipp/Strg/Yzer 10.00 25.00
D4 Howe/Hays/Robi/Jack 12.00 30.00

2013 Sportkings Four Sport Silver
ANNOUNCED PRINT RUN 19
FSQM3 Rive/Drex/Howe/Strug 12.00 30.00

2013 Sportkings Papercuts
STATED PRINT RUN 1 SER. #'d SET
UNPRICED DUE TO SCARCITY
PCTB Toe Blake

2013 Sportkings Single Memorabilia Silver
ANNOUNCED PRINT RUN 90
SM9 Gordie Howe/30*

2013 Sportkings National Convention VIP
COMPLETE SET (9) 6.00 15.00
VIP01 Bill Mosienko .60 1.50
VIP02 Bobby Hull 1.25 3.00
VIP03 Charlie Gardiner .60 1.50
VIP04 Glenn Hall .75 2.00
VIP05 Max Bentley .60 1.50
VIP06 Pierre Pilote .60 1.50
VIP07 Roy Conacher .60 1.50
VIP08 Stan Mikita .75 2.00
VIP09 Tony Esposito 1.00 2.50

1977-79 Sportscaster Series 1
COMPLETE SET (24) 17.50 35.00
102 Bobby Orr 2.50 5.00

1977-79 Sportscaster Series 2
COMPLETE SET (24) 30.00 60.00
206 Gordie Howe 5.00 10.00
213 The Stanley Cup 1.00 2.00

1977-79 Sportscaster Series 3
COMPLETE SET (24) 15.00 30.00
319 Phil and Tony 1.00 2.00

1977-79 Sportscaster Series 5
COMPLETE SET (24) 12.50 25.00
509 The USA vs. Czechoslovakia .75 1.50
520 Bobby Hull 2.50 5.00

1977-79 Sportscaster Series 6
COMPLETE SET (24) 12.50 25.00
607 Gump Worsley 1.00 2.00

1977-79 Sportscaster Series 7
COMPLETE SET (24) 15.00 30.00
708 USSR 1.00 2.00
717 Brad Park 1.00 2.00

1977-79 Sportscaster Series 10
COMPLETE SET (24) 17.50 35.00
1014 Jean Beliveau 1.50 3.00

1977-79 Sportscaster Series 11
COMPLETE SET (25) 20.00 40.00
1119 Hat Trick .50 1.00

1977-79 Sportscaster Series 12
COMPLETE SET (24) 12.50 25.00
1215 World Championship .75 1.50
1222 Stan Mikita 1.25 2.50

1977-79 Sportscaster Series 14
COMPLETE SET (24) 17.50 35.00
1423 Ken Dryden 2.00 4.00

1977-79 Sportscaster Series 15
COMPLETE SET (24) 12.50 25.00
1513 Yvan Cournoyer 1.25 2.50

1977-79 Sportscaster Series 17
COMPLETE SET (24) 10.00 20.00
1709 Denis Potvin 2.00 4.00

1977-79 Sportscaster Series 18
COMPLETE SET (24) 12.50 25.00
1823 Garry Unger .50 1.00

1977-79 Sportscaster Series 19
COMPLETE SET (24) 25.00 50.00
1915 World Championship 1.00 2.00

1977-79 Sportscaster Series 21
COMPLETE SET (24) 15.00 30.00
2112 The Equipment .25 .50

1977-79 Sportscaster Series 27
COMPLETE SET (24) 12.50 25.00
2724 National Hockey 1.50 3.00

1977-79 Sportscaster Series 29
COMPLETE SET (24) 17.50 35.00
2908 The Power Play 1.00 2.00

1977-79 Sportscaster Series 31
COMPLETE SET (24) 12.50 25.00
3103 Penalty Killing 1.25 2.50

1977-79 Sportscaster Series 33
COMPLETE SET (24) 10.00 20.00
3303 Lines in the Ice .75 1.50

1977-79 Sportscaster Series 35
COMPLETE SET (24) 15.00 30.00
3503 The Spengler Cup .25 .50

1977-79 Sportscaster Series 38
COMPLETE SET (24) 20.00 40.00
3807 The Seven Professional Trophies 1.50 3.00

1977-79 Sportscaster Series 43
COMPLETE SET (24) 12.50 25.00
4304 Major and Minor .75 1.50
4306 Rogie Vachon 1.00 2.00

1977-79 Sportscaster Series 44
COMPLETE SET (24) 12.50 25.00
4403 Jaroslav Jirik .50 1.00
4420 Gerry Cheevers 1.00 2.00

1977-79 Sportscaster Series 45
Card number 11 is not in our checklist. Any information on this missing card is greatly appreciated.
COMPLETE SET (24) 20.00 40.00
4513 Steve Shutt 1.00 2.00

1977-79 Sportscaster Series 46
COMPLETE SET (24) 12.50 25.00
4614 In the Corners .75 1.50
4621 Bryan Trottler 1.50 3.00

1977-79 Sportscaster Series 47
COMPLETE SET (24) 17.50 35.00
4716 Trio Grande 4.00 8.00
4718 Darryl Sittler 1.50 3.00

1977-79 Sportscaster Series 50
COMPLETE SET (24) 15.00 30.00
5003 Sticks 2.00 4.00
5004 Facemasks 2.00 4.00

1977-79 Sportscaster Series 51
COMPLETE SET (24) 20.00 40.00
5101 Czechoslovakia 1977 .75 1.50
5118 Guy Lafleur 1.50 3.00

1977-79 Sportscaster Series 55
COMPLETE SET (24) 12.50 25.00
5514 Jiri and Jaroslav 1.00 2.00
5523 World Hockey Assoc. 4.00 8.00

1977-79 Sportscaster Series 56
COMPLETE SET (24) 37.50 75.00
5605 Montreal Forum 2.50 5.00

1977-79 Sportscaster Series 60
COMPLETE SET (24) 37.50 75.00
6012 Bobby Clarke 4.00 8.00

1977-79 Sportscaster Series 61
COMPLETE SET (24) 50.00 100.00
6103 Lingo 2.50 5.00

1977-79 Sportscaster Series 62
COMPLETE SET (24) 40.00 80.00
6217 Lester Patrick 2.50 5.00

1977-79 Sportscaster Series 63
COMPLETE SET (24) 30.00 60.00
6309 The Howe Family 6.00 12.00

1977-79 Sportscaster Series 64
COMPLETE SET (24) 25.00 50.00
6416 Sudden Death 2.50 5.00

1977-79 Sportscaster Series 67
COMPLETE SET (24) 40.00 80.00
6721 Bill Chadwick 2.50 5.00

1977-79 Sportscaster Series 70
COMPLETE SET (24) 30.00 60.00
7006 Hall of Fame 2.00 4.00

1977-79 Sportscaster Series 71
COMPLETE SET (24) 40.00 80.00
7104 The Abrahamsson 2.00 4.00
7112 Anders Hedberg 2.50 5.00

1977-79 Sportscaster Series 73
COMPLETE SET (24) 40.00 80.00
7301 USSR vs. NHL 4.00 8.00
7311 Czechoslavakia 1976 2.50 5.00

1977-79 Sportscaster Series 74
COMPLETE SET (24) 200.00 400.00
7417 The 1978 WCH 2.00 4.00
7424 Vaclav Nedomansky 2.50 5.00

1977-79 Sportscaster Series 76
COMPLETE SET (24) 30.00 60.00
7603 NCAA Hockey 2.50 5.00

1977-79 Sportscaster Series 77
COMPLETE SET (24) 150.00 300.00
7710 Wayne Gretzky 125.00 250.00
7724 Expansion 2.00 4.00

1977-79 Sportscaster Series 78
COMPLETE SET (24) 150.00 300.00
7804 Real Cloutier 1.50 3.00

1977-79 Sportscaster Series 80
COMPLETE SET (24) 62.50 125.00
8018 John Davidson 3.00 6.00

1977-79 Sportscaster Series 81
COMPLETE SET (24) 62.50 125.00
8119 Jacques Lemaire 5.00 10.00

1977-79 Sportscaster Series 82
COMPLETE SET (24) 50.00 100.00
8205 Scotty Bowman 7.50 15.00
8223 Dave Dryden 2.50 5.00

1977-79 Sportscaster Series 102
COMPLETE SET (24) 75.00 150.00
10214 Charlamov Petrov 4.00 8.00

1977-79 Sportscaster Series 103
COMPLETE SET (24) 87.50 175.00
10308 Alexander Yakushev 4.00 8.00

1987 Sports Cube Game
3 1/2" by 5 3/8" cards with nine black and white portrait shots on front and questions on the back
COMPLETE SET (3) 8.00 20.00
1 James Naismith 6.00 15.00
Babe Ruth
America's Cup
Knute

1989 Sports Illustrated for Kids I
Since its debut issue in January 1989, SI for Kids has included a perforated sheet of nine standard-size cards bound into each magazine. The cards were consecutively numbered 1-324 through December 1991. The athletes featured represent an extremely wide spectrum of sports. Each card features color photos with variously colored borders. The borders are as follows: aqua (1-108), green (109-207), woodgrain (208-216), red (217-315), marble (316-324). The player's name is printed in a white bar at the top, while his or her sport appears at the bottom. The backs carry biographical information, career highlights, and a trivia question with answer. The cards' magazine issue date appears on the back in very small type. Although originally distributed in sheet form, the cards are frequently traded as singles. Thus, they are priced individually. The value of an intact sheet is equal to the sum of the nine cards plus a premium of up to 20%.
1 Mario Lemieux HK 4.00 10.00
15 Joe Nieuwendyk HK .40 1.00
19 Wayne Gretzky HK 5.00 12.00
25 Steve Yzerman HK 2.00 5.00
30 Sean Burke HK .40 1.00
82 Al MacInnis .40 1.00
Hockey
96 Pat LaFontaine HK .75 2.00
100 Mark Messier HK 2.00 5.00

1990 Sports Illustrated for Kids I
116 Brian Leetch HK 1.00 2.50
118 Denis Savard HK .30 .75
126 Dale Hawerchuk HK .30 .75
134 Ray Bourque HK 1.00 2.50
143 Grant Fuhr HK .50 1.25
193 Brett Hull HK 1.25 3.00
214 Gordie Howe HK 1.25 3.00

1991 Sports Illustrated for Kids I
224 Ron Hextall HK .30 .75
228 Bernie Nicholls HK .20 .50
238 Chris Chelios HK .50 1.25
250 Mike Liut .10 .30
Hockey
252 Joe Mullen HK .20 .50
254 Steve Larmer HK .20 .50
300 Paul Coffey HK .50 1.25
317 Bobby Orr HK 4.00 10.00

1992 Sports Illustrated for Kids II
Since its debut issue in January 1989, SI for Kids has included a perforated sheet of nine standard-size cards bound into each magazine. In January 1992, the card numbers started over again at 1. This listing comprises the cards contained from that magazine through the last 2000 issue. The athletes featured represent an extremely wide spectrum of sports. Each card features color photos with borders of various designs and colors. The borders are as follows: navy (1-9, 19-99), clouds (10-18, 55-63, 226-234), marble (100-108, 208-216, 316-324), pink (109-207), purple (217-225), blue (235-315), gold/silver (325-486), clouds (487-495) and gold/silver (496-621). The athlete's name is printed at the top while his or her sport appears at the bottom. The backs carry biographical information, career highlights, and a trivia question with answer. The cards' magazine issue date appears on the back in very small type. Although originally distributed in sheet form, the cards are frequently traded as singles. Thus, they are priced individually. The value of an intact sheet is equal to the sum of the nine cards plus a premium of up to 20 percent. The cards labeled as "MC" were issued in SI for Kids as part of a milk promotion.
9 Tom Barrasso HK .20 .50
10 Mike Eruzione HK .40 1.00
20 Brian Bellows HK .20 .50
33 Ed Belfour HK .25 .60
42 Mark Messier HK .40 1.00
93 Patrick Roy 3.00 8.00
Hockey

1993 Sports Illustrated for Kids II
117 Jaromir Jagr HK .40 1.00
125 Mario Lemieux HK 3.00 8.00
135 Eric Lindros HK .40 1.00
153 Wayne Gretzky HK 3.00 8.00
154 Alexander Mogilny HK .20 .50
191 Manon Rheaume HK 1.25 3.00
200 Teemu Selanne HK .60 1.50
211 Bobby Hull HK .75 2.00

1994 Sports Illustrated for Kids II
241 Luc Robitaille HK .20 .50
246 Mike Gartner HK .20 .50
259 Sergei Fedorov HK .30 .75
265 Cam Neely HK .20 .50
284 Mike Richter .25 .60
Hockey
303 Pavel Bure HK .25 .60
309 Doug Gilmour HK .20 .50
317 Phil Esposito HK .60 1.50

1996 Sports Illustrated for Kids II
435 Peter Bondra HK .20 .50
442 Dominik Hasek HK .60 1.50
453 Mario Lemieux HK 1.50 4.00
kid photo
465 Brendan Shanahan HK .25 .60
474 Steve Yzerman HK 2.00 5.00
499 Joe Sakic HK .60 1.50
525 Jaromir Jagr HK .40 1.00
527 Cammi Granato HK .40 1.00
540 Ed Jovanovski HK .20 .50

1997 Sports Illustrated for Kids II
546 Daren Puppa .20 .50
Hockey
547 Wayne Gretzky 3.00 8.00
Hockey
551 Erin Whitten HK .20 .50
557 Sergei Fedorov HK .30 .75
559 Patrick Roy HK 3.00 8.00
585 Chris Chelios HK .25 .60
601 Mats Sundin HK .25 .60
618 Claude Lemieux HK .20 .50
623 Eric Lindros HK .30 .75
cartoon
638 Brett Hull HK .30 .75

1998 Sports Illustrated for Kids II
657 John LeClair HK .25 .60
666 Mark Johnson HK .20 .50
710 Temmu Selanne HK .60 1.50
715 Pavel Bure HK .25 .60
755 Peter Forsberg HK 1.50 4.00

1999 Sports Illustrated for Kids II
765 Jaromir Jagr#[Hockey .40 1.00
767 Martin Brodeur HK 1.50 4.00
792 Paul Kariya HK 1.25 3.00
794 Eric Lindros HK .30 .75
805 Mike Modano HK .50 1.25
864 Ed Belfour HK .25 .60

2000 Sports Illustrated for Kids II
872 Wayne Gretzky HK 3.00 8.00
880 Paul Kariya HK 1.25 3.00
885 Al MacInnis HK .20 .50
907 Scott Gomez HK .20 .50
913 Roman Turek HK .20 .50
921 Pavel Bure HK .25 .60
930 Mark Recchi HK .20 .50
939 Ray Bourque HK .60 1.50
946 Theo Fleury HK .20 .50
957 Scott Stevens HK .20 .50

2001 Sports Illustrated for Kids
Since its debut issue in January 1989, SI for Kids has included a perforated sheet of nine standard-size cards bound into each magazine. In December 2000, for the second time, the card numbers started over again at 1. The athletes featured represent an extremely wide spectrum of sports. The athlete's name is printed at the top while his or her sport appears at the bottom. The backs carry biographical information, career highlights, and a trivia question with answer. The cards' magazine issue date appears on the back in very small type. Although originally distributed in sheet form, the cards are frequently traded as singles. Thus, they are priced individually. The value of an intact sheet is equal to the sum of the nine cards plus a premium of up to 20 percent.
COMPLETE SET (108) 25.00 50.00
9 Chris Pronger HK .20 .50
11 Mark Messier HK .25 .60
20 Tony Amonte HK .20 .50
31 Nadine Muzerall HK .20 .50
36 Zigmund Palffy HK .20 .50
37 Brian Leetch HK .20 .50
49 Joe Sakic HK .60 1.50
60 Sean Burke HK .20 .50
66 Alexei Kovalev HK .20 .50
76 Adam Oates HK .20 .50
82 Patrik Elias HK .20 .50
96 Nicklas Lidstrom HK .25 .60
106 Patrick Roy HK 2.50 6.00
108 Keith Tkachuk HK .25 .60

2002 Sports Illustrated for Kids
109 Peter Bondra HK .20 .50
121 Curtis Joseph HK .30 .75
127 Maria Rooth HK .20 .50
135 Brendan Shanahan HK .20 .50
139 Jeremy Roenick HK .25 .60
150 Nikolai Khabibulin HK .20 .50
159 Jaromir Jagr HK .40 1.00
168 Martin Brodeur HK 1.50 4.00
178 Jarome Iginla HK .20 .50
198 Ron Francis HK .20 .50
204 Jose Theodore HK .25 .60
214 Mats Sundin HK .25 .60
217 Peter Forsberg HK 1.50 4.00
225 Evgeni Nabokov HK .20 .50

2003 Sports Illustrated for Kids
Since its debut issue in January 1989, SI for Kids has included a perforated sheet of nine standard-size cards bound into each magazine. In January 2001, for the second time, the card numbers started over at 1. Listed below are the cards issued in magazines that carry 2003 cover dates. The athletes featured represent an extremely wide spectrum of sports. Although originally distributed in sheet form, the cards are frequently traded as singles. Thus, they are priced individually. The value of an intact sheet is equal to the sum of the nine cards plus a premium of up to 20 percent.
232 Dany Heatley HK .10 .30
238 Owen Nolan HK .10 .30
251 Markus Naslund HK .10 .30
260 Joe Sakic HK .10 .30
265 Jaromir Jagr HK .40 1.00
277 Brett Hull HK .30 .75
280 Todd Bertuzzi HK .10 .30
296 Milan Hejduk HK .10 .30
300 Jean-Sebastien Giguere HK .30 .75
301 Hayley Wickenheiser Wom.HK .10 .30
307 Scott Stevens HK .10 .30
316 Joe Thornton HK .20 .50
321 Al MacInnis HK .10 .30
330 Marty Turco HK .20 .50

2004 Sports Illustrated for Kids
ONE NINE-CARD SHEET PER MAGAZINE
340 Wayne Gretzky HK .75 2.00
343 Marian Hossa HK .20 .50
358 Alex Tanguay HK .10 .30
367 Martin Brodeur HK .40 1.00
371 Robert Lang HK .10 .30
384 Ilya Kovalchuk HK .20 .50
395 Dwayne Roloson HK .10 .30
403 Martin St. Louis HK .20 .50
413 Evgeni Nabokov HK .20 .50

2005 Sports Illustrated for Kids
450 Natalie Darwitz Women's HK .07 .20
469 Marty Sertich College HK .07 .20
534 Rick Nash HK .10 .30

2006 Sports Illustrated for Kids
1 Sidney Crosby HK .60 1.50
11 Roberto Luongo HK .20 .50
24 Jaromar Jagr HK .30 .75
33 Alex Ovechkin HK .40 1.00
41 Dominik Hasek HK .20 .50
47 Simon Gagne HK .10 .30
62 Eric Staal HK .20 .50
67 Nickas Lidstrom HK .20 .50
81 Teemu Selanne HK .20 .50
90 Chris Pronger HK .20 .50
96 Joe Thornton HK .25 .60
106 Pavel Datsyuk HK .20 .50

2007 Sports Illustrated for Kids
ONE NINE-CARD SHEET PER MAGAZINE
133 Kari Lehtonen HK .08 .25
136 Evgeni Malkin HK .40 1.00
150 Daniel Briere HK .08 .25
159 Dany Heatley HK .20 .50
166 Vincent LeCavalier HK .08 .25
178 Jason Spezza HK .08 .25
189 Scott Niedermayer HK .08 .25
193 Ryan Miller HK .20 .50
200 Alexander Ovechkin HK .40 1.00
215 Henrik Zetterberg HK .20 .50

2008 Sports Illustrated for Kids
233 Patrick Kane HK .30 .75
241 Marian Gaborik HK .20 .50
244 Jarome Iginla HK .20 .50
254 Henrik Lundqvist HK .20 .50
267 Daniel Alfredsson HK .10 .30
274 Ilya Kovalchuk HK .10 .30
286 Evgeni Nabokov HK .10 .30
303 Johan Franzen HK .10 .30
323 Martin Brodeur HK .25 .60

2009 Sports Illustrated for Kids
339 Ed Belfour HK
340 Luc Robitaille HK
349 Sidney Crosby ART HK
355 Tim Thomas HK
361 Patrick Marleau HK
377 Zach Parise HK
380 Alexander Ovechkin HK
390 Evgeni Malkin HK
413 Jeff Carter HK
416 Nicklas Lidstrom HK
432 Miikka Kiprusoff HK

2010 Sports Illustrated for Kids
435 Marian Gaborik HK
447 Martin Brodeur HK
454 Henrik Sedin HK
479 Jaroslav Halak HK
495 Patrick Kane HK
503 Steven Stamkos HK
510 Tuukka Rask HK
521 Patrick Marleau HK
524 Ryan Miller HK

2011 Sports Illustrated for Kids
4 Brad Richards HK
10 Sidney Crosby HK
26 Tim Thomas HK
29 Patrick Sharp HK
45 Corey Perry HK
49 Dwayne Roloson HK
71 Nicklas Lidstrom HK
80 Daniel Sedin HK
82 Carey Price HK
92 Phil Kessel HK

2012 Sports Illustrated for Kids
106 Nikolai Khabibulin HK
111 Claude Giroux HK
115 Hilary Knight HK
125 Jimmy Howard HK
127 Evgeni Malkin HK
144 Steven Stamkos HK
153 Jonathan Quick HK
173 Erik Karlsson HK
182 Zdeno Chara HK

2013 Sports Illustrated for Kids
218 Martin St. Louis HK
231 Tuukka Rask HK
236 Amanda Kessel HK
240 John Tavares HK
256 Sergei Bobrovsky HK
263 Patrick Kane HK
278 Alex Ovechkin HK
282 Connor McDavid HK

2015 Sports Illustrated for Kids
393 David Jacobson HK
400 Jack Eichel HK
413 Jakub Voracek HK
416 Nicklas Backstrom HK
421 Hannah Brandt HK
429 Zane McIntyre HK

1996-97 SPx
The 1996-97 SPx set was issued in one series totaling 50 cards. The one-card packs retailed for $3.49 each. Each die-cut card features a full-motion hologram. Two special cards of Wayne Gretzky were randomly inserted, including a tribute (found 1:95), and an autographed tribute (found just one in 1297 packs). An additional special insert is the Great Futures card, which includes holoview images of four young stars (Eric Daze, Daniel Alfredsson, Vitali Yachmenev, and Saku Koivu) and was randomly inserted at a rate of 1:75 packs.
COMPLETE SET (50) 20.00 50.00
1 Paul Kariya .60 1.50
2 Teemu Selanne .60 1.50
3 Ray Bourque 1.00 2.50
4 Cam Neely .60 1.50
5 Theo Fleury .40 1.00
6 Chris Chelios .60 1.50
7 Jeremy Roenick .75 2.00
8 Peter Forsberg 1.00 2.50
9 Joe Sakic 1.25 3.00
10 Patrick Roy 2.50 6.00
11 Mike Modano .75 2.00
12 Joe Nieuwendyk .50 1.25
13 Sergei Fedorov .75 2.00
14 Steve Yzerman 2.50 6.00
15 Paul Coffey .60 1.50
16 Chris Osgood .50 1.25
17 Doug Weight .50 1.25
18 Pat LaFontaine .60 1.50
19 Brendan Shanahan .60 1.50
20 Vitali Yachmenev .40 1.00
21 Saku Koivu .60 1.50
22 Pierre Turgeon .50 1.25
23 Petr Sykora .40 1.00
24 Scott Stevens .50 1.25
25 Martin Brodeur 1.50 4.00
26 Brian Leetch .60 1.50
27 Mark Messier .60 1.50
28 Mike Richter .60 1.50
29 Zigmund Palffy .50 1.25
30 Todd Bertuzzi .60 1.50
31 Alexei Yashin .40 1.00
32 Daniel Alfredsson .50 1.25
33 Eric Lindros .60 1.50
34 John LeClair .60 1.50
35 Keith Tkachuk .60 1.50
36 Alexei Zhamnov .50 1.25
37 Mario Lemieux 2.50 6.00
38 Jaromir Jagr 1.00 2.50
39 Wayne Gretzky 3.00 8.00
40 Brett Hull .75 2.00
41 Owen Nolan .50 1.25
42 Roman Hamrlik .50 1.25
43 Mats Sundin .60 1.50
44 Felix Potvin .60 1.50
45 Doug Gilmour .50 1.25
46 Pavel Bure .60 1.50
47 Alexander Mogilny .50 1.25
48 Jim Carey .60 1.50
49 Peter Bondra .50 1.25
50 Eric Daze .50 1.25
P39 W.Gretzky PROMO .40 1.00
GF1 Great Futures 5.00 12.00
GS1 W.Gretzky Tribute AU 100.00 200.00
GT1 W.Gretzky Tribute 8.00 20.00

1996-97 SPx Gold
A parallel to SPx, these cards feature gold foil stock and were inserted 1:7 packs.
*GOLD: 1.2X TO 3X BASIC CARDS

1996-97 SPx Holoview Heroes
Randomly inserted in packs at a rate of 1:24, this 10-card set also was die-cut with a full-motion hologram.
COMPLETE SET (10) 40.00 100.00
HH1 Ray Bourque 3.00 8.00
HH2 Patrick Roy 8.00 20.00
HH3 Steve Yzerman 8.00 20.00
HH4 Paul Coffey 2.00 5.00
HH5 Mark Messier 2.50 6.00
HH6 Mario Lemieux 8.00 20.00
HH7 Wayne Gretzky 10.00 25.00
HH8 Brett Hull 2.50 6.00
HH9 Doug Gilmour 2.00 5.00
HH10 Grant Fuhr 2.00 5.00

1997-98 SPx
The 1997-98 SPx set was issued in one series totaling 50 cards and was distributed in three-card packs with a suggested retail price of $5.99. The fronts features color action player photos printed on 32-point card stock utilizing decorative foil on the exclusive Light F/X/Holoview cards.
COMPLETE SET (50) 15.00 40.00
1 Paul Kariya .60 1.50
2 Teemu Selanne 1.00 2.50
3 Ray Bourque .75 2.00
4 Dominik Hasek .75 2.00
5 Pat LaFontaine .50 1.25
6 Theo Fleury .60 1.50
7 Jarome Iginla .50 1.25
8 Tony Amonte .40 1.00
9 Chris Chelios .50 1.25
10 Patrick Roy 1.25 3.00
11 Peter Forsberg .60 1.50
12 Joe Sakic .75 2.00
13 Mike Modano .75 2.00
14 Steve Yzerman 1.00 2.50
15 Sergei Fedorov .75 2.00
16 Brendan Shanahan .60 1.50
17 Doug Weight .50 1.25
18 Jason Arnott .40 1.00

19 Curtis Joseph .50 1.25
20 John Vanbiesbrouck .50 1.25
21 Ed Jovanovski .30 .75
22 Geoff Sanderson .40 1.00
23 Rob Blake .50 1.25
24 Saku Koivu .50 1.25
25 Doug Gilmour .60 1.50
26 Scott Stevens .50 1.25
27 Martin Brodeur 1.00 2.50
28 Zigmund Palffy .50 1.25
29 Bryan Berard .30 .75
30 Wayne Gretzky 2.50 6.00
30S Wayne Gretzky SAMPLE 2.50 6.00
31 Mike Richter .50 1.25
32 Mark Messier .75 2.00
33 Brian Leetch .50 1.25
34 Daniel Alfredsson .50 1.25
35 Alexei Yashin .40 1.00
36 Eric Lindros .75 2.00
37 Janne Niinimaa .40 1.00
38 John LeClair .50 1.25
39 Jeremy Roenick .60 1.50
40 Keith Tkachuk .50 1.25
41 Ron Francis .60 1.50
42 Jaromir Jagr 1.25 3.00
43 Brett Hull .60 1.50
44 Owen Nolan .50 1.25
45 Chris Gratton .30 .75
46 Mats Sundin .50 1.25
47 Pavel Bure .60 1.50
48 Adam Oates .50 1.25
49 Joe Juneau .40 1.00
50 Peter Bondra .40 1.00

1997-98 SPx Bronze

Randomly inserted in packs at the rate of 1:3, this 50-card set is parallel to the base set and is similar in design. The difference is found in the bronze foil enhancements of the cards.
*BRONZE: 1X TO 2X BASIC CARDS

1997-98 SPx Gold

Randomly inserted in packs at the rate of 1:17, this 50-card set is parallel to the base set and is similar in design. The difference is found in the gold foil enhancements of the cards.
*GOLD: 4X TO 10X BASIC CARDS

1997-98 SPx Silver

omly inserted in packs at the rate of 1:6, this 50-card set is parallel to the base set and is similar in design. The difference is found in the silver foil enhancements of the cards.
*SILVER: 1.5X TO 4X BASIC CARDS

1997-98 SPx Steel

Inserted one in every pack, this 50-card set is parallel to the base set and is similar in design. The difference is found in the gray foil enhancements of the cards.
*STEEL: .8X TO 2X BASIC CARDS
STEEL ODDS 1:1 HOB/RET

1997-98 SPx Dimension

Randomly inserted in packs at the rate of 1:54, this 20-card set features color action player photos printed with a rainbow Light F/X and Litho combination.
SPX1 Wayne Gretzky 20.00 50.00
SPX2 Jeremy Roenick 3.00 8.00
SPX3 Mark Messier 2.50 6.00
SPX4 Eric Lindros 2.50 6.00
SPX5 Doug Gilmour 2.00 5.00
SPX6 Pavel Bure 2.00 5.00
SPX7 Brendan Shanahan 2.00 5.00
SPX8 Bryan Berard 1.00 2.50
SPX9 Curtis Joseph 1.50 4.00
SPX10 Chris Chelios 1.50 4.00
SPX11 Sergei Fedorov 2.50 6.00
SPX12 Adam Oates 1.50 4.00
SPX13 Zigmund Palffy 1.50 4.00
SPX14 Theo Fleury 2.00 5.00
SPX15 Keith Tkachuk 1.50 4.00
SPX16 Peter Forsberg 2.00 5.00
SPX17 Mats Sundin 1.50 4.00
SPX18 Teemu Selanne 3.00 8.00
SPX19 Paul Kariya 2.00 5.00
SPX20 Brett Hull 2.00 5.00

1997-98 SPx DuoView

Randomly inserted in packs at the rate of 1:252, this 10-card set features two different holoview images of the player depicted on the card front in a unique silver and gold combination printed on Light F/X holoview cards.
COMPLETE SET (10) 125.00 250.00
1 Wayne Gretzky 30.00 80.00
2 Jaromir Jagr 8.00 20.00
3 Martin Brodeur 20.00 50.00
4 Jarome Iginla 6.00 15.00
5 Steve Yzerman 25.00 60.00
6 Patrick Roy 25.00 60.00
7 Doug Weight 4.00 10.00
8 John Vanbiesbrouck 4.00 10.00
9 Dominik Hasek 10.00 25.00
10 Joe Sakic 10.00 25.00

1997-98 SPx DuoView Autographs

Randomly inserted in packs, this six-card set is a partial parallel version of the DuoView insert set featuring gold foil enhancements and the pictured player's autograph. Only 100 of each card was produced and are sequentially hand numbered.
1 Wayne Gretzky 100.00 250.00
2 Jaromir Jagr 25.00 60.00
3 Martin Brodeur 50.00 120.00
4 Jarome Iginla 20.00 50.00
5 Patrick Roy 40.00 100.00
6 Doug Weight 12.50 30.00

1997-98 SPx Grand Finale

Randomly inserted in packs, this 50-card set is parallel to the base set and is similar in design. The difference is found in the gold foil enhancements and gold Holoview/Hologram on the cards. Only 50 of each card of this set was produced.
*GRAND FINALE: 20X TO 50X BASIC CARDS

1999-00 SPx

The 1999-00 Upper Deck SPx set was released as a 180-card set consisting of both veteran cards and prospect cards. Card numbers 162-180 are short printed, and the majority of them are autographed. The base card is printed on a rainbow holofoil card stock and enhanced with gold foil. Packaged in 18-pack boxes with three card packs, SPx carried a suggested retail price of $5.99. Each box also contained a 4-card pack of Wayne Gretzky exclusive cards.
COMPLETE SET (180) 125.00 250.00
COMP.SET w/o SP's (162) 40.00 80.00
1 Damian Rhodes .25 .60
2 Nelson Emerson .10 .30
3 Ray Ferraro .10 .30
4 Paul Kariya .30 .75
5 Steve Rucchin .15 .40
6 Guy Hebert .25 .60
7 Oleg Tverdovsky .10 .30
8 Ted Donato .10 .30
9 Ray Bourque .50 1.25
10 Sergei Samsonov .25 .60
11 Joe Thornton .50 1.25
12 Jason Allison .10 .30
13 Byron Dafoe .25 .60
14 Jonathan Girard .10 .30
15 Dominik Hasek .60 1.50
16 Alexei Zhitnik .10 .30
17 Michael Peca .25 .60
18 Cory Sarich .25 .60
19 Martin Biron .25 .60
20 Miroslav Satan .25 .60
21 Valeri Bure .10 .30
22 Derek Morris .10 .30
23 Phil Housley .25 .60
24 Jarome Iginla .40 1.00
25 Rico Fata .10 .30
26 Jean-Sebastien Giguere .25 .60
27 Marc Savard .10 .30
28 Arturs Irbe .25 .60
29 Keith Primeau .10 .30
30 Sami Kapanen .10 .30
31 Ron Francis .10 .30
32 Wendel Clark .25 .60
33 J-P Dumont .25 .60
34 Ty Jones .10 .30
35 Tony Amonte .25 .60
36 Jocelyn Thibault .25 .60
37 Doug Gilmour .25 .60
38 Bryan McCabe .10 .30
39 Joe Sakic .60 1.50
40 Peter Forsberg .75 2.00
41 Alex Tanguay .25 .60
42 Chris Drury .25 .60
43 Patrick Roy 1.50 4.00
44 Sandis Ozolinsh .10 .30
45 Adam Deadmarsh .10 .30
46 Milan Hejduk .30 .75
47 Mike Modano .50 1.25
48 Brett Hull .40 1.00
49 Darryl Sydor .25 .60
50 Ed Belfour .30 .75
51 Jere Lehtinen .25 .60
52 Jamie Langenbrunner .10 .30
53 Joe Nieuwendyk .25 .60
54 Sergei Fedorov .50 1.25
55 Steve Yzerman 1.50 4.00
56 Brendan Shanahan .30 .75
57 Chris Osgood .25 .60
58 Nicklas Lidstrom .30 .75
59 Igor Larionov .10 .30
60 Chris Chelios .30 .75
61 Bill Guerin .25 .60
62 Doug Weight .15 .40
63 Mike Grier .10 .30
64 Tommy Salo .25 .60
65 Bill Ranford .25 .60
66 Tom Poti .10 .30
67 Daniel Cleary .10 .30
68 Mark Parrish .10 .30
69 Pavel Bure .30 .75
70 Oleg Kvasha .10 .30
71 Viktor Kozlov .25 .60
72 Trevor Kidd .25 .60
73 Rob Blake .25 .60
74 Pavel Rosa .25 .60
75 Luc Robitaille .25 .60
76 Zigmund Palffy .25 .60
77 Aki Berg .10 .30
78 Saku Koivu .30 .75
79 Jeff Hackett .25 .60
80 Trevor Linden .25 .60
81 Cliff Ronning .25 .60
82 David Legwand .25 .60
83 Mike Dunham .25 .60
84 Scott Stevens .25 .60
85 Martin Brodeur .75 2.00
86 Patrik Elias .25 .60
87 Brendan Morrison .25 .60
88 Scott Niedermayer .10 .30
89 Vadim Sharifijanov .10 .30
90 Mike Watt .10 .30
91 Felix Potvin .30 .75
92 Eric Brewer .10 .30
93 Jorgen Jonsson RC .10 .30
94 Kenny Jonsson .10 .30
95 Olli Jokinen .25 .60
96 Theo Fleury .25 .60
97 Brian Leetch .30 .75
98 Mike Richter .30 .75
99 Petr Nedved .25 .60
100 Adam Graves .10 .30
101 Manny Malhotra .25 .60
102 Alexei Yashin .25 .60
103 Daniel Alfredsson .15 .40
104 Ron Tugnutt .25 .60
105 Magnus Arvedson .10 .30
106 Sami Salo .10 .30
107 Marian Hossa .30 .75
108 Eric Lindros .30 .75
109 John Vanbiesbrouck .25 .60
110 John LeClair .30 .75
111 Rod Brind'Amour .25 .60
112 Mark Recchi .20 .50
113 Eric Desjardins .25 .60
114 Jeremy Roenick .40 1.00
115 Keith Tkachuk .30 .75
116 Rick Tocchet .25 .60
117 Robert Esche RC 1.00 2.50
118 Nikolai Khabibulin .25 .60
119 Teppo Numminen .10 .30
120 Jaromir Jagr .50 1.25
121 Martin Straka .10 .30
122 Jan Hrdina .10 .30
123 German Titov .10 .30
124 Alexei Kovalev .25 .60
125 Matthew Barnaby .25 .60
126 Vincent Damphousse .10 .30
127 Owen Nolan .25 .60
128 Jeff Friesen .25 .60
129 Patrick Marleau .25 .60
130 Marco Sturm .25 .60
131 Mike Vernon .25 .60
132 Pavol Demitra .25 .60
133 Al MacInnis .25 .60
134 Pierre Turgeon .25 .60
135 Chris Pronger .25 .60
136 Jochen Hecht RC 1.00 2.50
137 Vincent Lecavalier .30 .75
138 Paul Mara .25 .60
139 Dan Cloutier .25 .60
140 Andrei Zyuzin .10 .30
141 Pavel Kubina .10 .30
142 Kevin Hodson .25 .60
143 Mats Sundin .30 .75
144 Curtis Joseph .30 .75
145 Sergei Berezin .25 .60
146 Bryan Berard .10 .30
147 Tomas Kaberle .10 .30
148 Daniil Markov .10 .30
149 Mark Messier .30 .75
150 Bill Muckalt .25 .60
151 Markus Naslund .30 .75
152 Mattias Ohlund .25 .60
153 Ed Jovanovski .10 .30
154 Steve Kariya RC 1.00 2.50
155 Josh Holden .10 .30
156 Richard Zednik .10 .30
157 Jaroslav Svejkovsky .10 .30
158 Adam Oates .25 .60
159 Peter Bondra .25 .60
160 Sergei Gonchar .10 .30
161 Olaf Kolzig .25 .60
162 Jan Bulis .10 .30
163 Patrik Stefan AU RC 8.00 20.00
164 Daniel Sedin AU 6.00 15.00
165 Henrik Sedin AU 8.00 20.00
166 Pavel Brendl AU RC 8.00 20.00
167 Brian Finley AU 5.00 12.00
168 Taylor Pyatt AU 8.00 20.00
169 Jamie Lundmark AU 6.00 15.00
170 Denis Shvidki 2.50 6.00
171 Jani Rita 2.50 6.00
172 Oleg Saprykin AU RC 6.00 15.00
173 Nick Boynton 2.50 6.00
174 Tim Connolly AU 6.00 15.00
175 Kris Beech AU 5.00 12.00
176 Roberto Luongo 4.00 10.00
177 David Legwand 3.00 8.00
178 Dave Tanabe 2.50 6.00
179 Barret Jackman 2.50 6.00
180 Maxime Ouellet 4.00 10.00

1999-00 SPx Radiance

Randomly inserted in packs, this 135-card set parallels the base SPx set. Cards are enhanced with green foil, and each card is serial numbered out of 100.
*RADIANCE 1-162: 20X TO 40X BASIC CARDS
*RADIANCE 163-180: 1X TO 3X BASIC SP
*RADIANCE 163-180: .5X TO 1.2X BASIC SP AU
164 Daniel Sedin 20.00 50.00
165 Henrik Sedin 25.00 60.00
166 Pavel Brendl 12.50 30.00
168 Taylor Pyatt 10.00 25.00

1999-00 SPx 99 Cheers

Randomly inserted in packs at 1:17, this 15-card set pays tribute to Wayne Gretzky by capturing some of his most magical moments. Card backs carry a "CH" prefix.
COMPLETE SET (15) 30.00 60.00
COMMON GRETZKY (CH1-15) 2.50 6.00

1999-00 SPx Highlight Heroes

Randomly seeded in packs at 1:9, this 10-card set focuses on 10 of the NHL's top superstars. Action photos are set against a rainbow holo-foil checkered background. Card backs carry an "HH" prefix.
COMPLETE SET (10) 15.00 30.00
HH1 Wayne Gretzky 4.00 10.00
HH2 Sergei Samsonov .60 1.50
HH3 Dominik Hasek 1.25 3.00
HH4 Jaromir Jagr 1.00 2.50
HH5 Patrick Roy 3.00 8.00
HH6 Paul Kariya 1.00 2.50
HH7 Pavel Bure .75 2.00
HH8 Peter Forsberg 1.50 4.00
HH9 Eric Lindros 1.50 4.00
HH10 Teemu Selanne 1.00 2.50

1999-00 SPx Prolifics

Randomly seeded in packs at 1:17, this 15-card set highlights the 15 most collectible defensive players in the NHL. Card backs carry a "P" prefix.
COMPLETE SET (15) 25.00 50.00
P1 Paul Kariya 1.00 2.50
P2 Jaromir Jagr 1.50 4.00
P3 Brett Hull 1.25 3.00
P4 Joe Sakic 2.00 5.00
P5 Sergei Samsonov 1.00 2.50
P6 Keith Tkachuk 1.00 2.50
P7 Brendan Shanahan 1.50 4.00
P8 Vincent Lecavalier 1.00 2.50
P9 Steve Yzerman 5.00 12.00
P10 Jeremy Roenick 1.25 3.00
P11 Mike Modano 1.50 4.00
P12 John LeClair 1.25 3.00
P13 Peter Forsberg 2.50 6.00
P14 Ray Bourque 1.50 4.00
P15 David Legwand 1.00 2.50

1999-00 SPx SPXcitement

Randomly seeded in packs at 1:3, this 20-card set features the most exciting NHL players on a holographic Light F/X background. Card backs carry an "X" prefix.
COMPLETE SET (20) 20.00 40.00
X1 Wayne Gretzky 3.00 8.00
X2 Patrick Roy 2.50 6.00
X3 Pavel Bure .60 1.50
X4 Steve Yzerman 2.50 6.00
X5 David Legwand .50 1.25
X6 Dominik Hasek 1.00 2.50
X7 Sergei Samsonov .50 1.25
X8 Patrik Stefan 1.00 2.50
X9 Eric Lindros .75 2.00
X10 Brett Hull .60 1.50
X11 Steve Kariya .50 1.25
X12 Keith Tkachuk .50 1.25
X13 Alex Tanguay .50 1.25
X14 Peter Forsberg 1.25 3.00
X15 Jaromir Jagr .75 2.00
X16 Paul Kariya .50 1.25
X17 Brendan Shanahan .75 2.00
X18 Mike Modano .75 2.00
X19 John LeClair .60 1.50
X20 Teemu Selanne .50 1.25

1999-00 SPx SPXtreme

Randomly inserted in packs at 1:6, this 20-card set showcases some of the most popular players in the NHL. Action shots are set against a holographic Light F/X background. Card backs carry an "XT" prefix.
COMPLETE SET (20) 20.00 40.00
XT1 Al MacInnis .50 1.25
XT2 Keith Tkachuk .60 1.50
XT3 Peter Forsberg 1.50 4.00
XT4 Teemu Selanne .60 1.50
XT5 Patrick Roy 3.00 8.00
XT6 Sergei Samsonov .50 1.25
XT7 Brendan Shanahan 1.00 2.50
XT8 Mike Modano 1.00 2.50
XT9 Eric Lindros 1.00 2.50
XT10 Paul Kariya .60 1.50
XT11 Jaromir Jagr 1.00 2.50
XT12 Brett Hull .75 2.00
XT13 Mats Sundin .60 1.50
XT14 Dominik Hasek 1.25 3.00
XT15 Ray Bourque 1.00 2.50
XT16 Curtis Joseph .60 1.50
XT17 John LeClair .75 2.00
XT18 Ed Belfour .60 1.50
XT19 David Legwand .50 1.25
XT20 Wayne Gretzky 4.00 10.00

1999-00 SPx Starscape

Randomly inserted in packs at 1:9, this 10-card set places NHL's hottest in action over a holographic foil backdrop. Card backs carry an "S" prefix.
COMPLETE SET (10) 12.00 25.00
S1 Brett Hull .75 2.00
S2 Jaromir Jagr 1.00 2.50
S3 Pavel Bure .75 2.00
S4 Dominik Hasek 1.25 3.00
S5 Eric Lindros 1.00 2.50
S6 Paul Kariya .60 1.50
S7 Peter Forsberg 1.50 4.00
S8 Teemu Selanne .60 1.50
S9 Patrick Roy 3.00 8.00
S10 Keith Tkachuk .60 1.50

1999-00 SPx Winning Materials

Randomly inserted in packs at 1:252, this 12-card set features players with a swatch of a game-used jersey and puck. Also released with the set were autographed versions of Brett Hull and Wayne Gretzky.
WM1 Mike Modano 12.00 30.00
WM2 Martin Brodeur 15.00 40.00
WM3 Steve Yzerman 25.00 60.00
WM4 Jaromir Jagr 15.00 40.00
WM5 Dominik Hasek 15.00 40.00
WM6 Brett Hull 12.00 30.00
WM7 Patrick Roy 20.00 50.00
WM8 Ray Bourque 15.00 40.00
WM9 Eric Lindros 12.00 30.00
WM10 Wayne Gretzky 50.00 100.00
WMA1 W.Gretzky AU/25 500.00 800.00
WMA2 B.Hull AU/25 125.00 300.00

2000-01 SPx

SPx originally issued the set of 130 cards with 30 short-printed rookies, and 10 short-printed jersey cards. SPx later released an update set of 57 cards, which included 35 short-printed rookies. The card front design used silver-foil and added rainbow-holofoil for the SPx logo. The jersey cards were available in packs of 2000-01 SPx at a rate of 1:13.
COMPLETE SET (130) 250.00 500.00
COMP.SET w/o SP's (90) 20.00 40.00
1 Paul Kariya .40 1.00
2 Teemu Selanne .60 1.50
3 Patrik Stefan .25 .60
4 Jason Allison .25 .60
5 Sergei Samsonov .25 .60
6 Dominik Hasek .50 1.25
7 Miroslav Satan .20 .50
8 Fred Brathwaite .25 .60
9 Valeri Bure .25 .60
10 Ron Francis .40 1.00
11 Arturs Irbe .25 .60
12 Tony Amonte .25 .60
13 Joe Sakic .50 1.25
14 Milan Hejduk .25 .60
15 Patrick Roy .75 2.00
16 Peter Forsberg .40 1.00
17 Ray Bourque .50 1.25
18 Ron Tugnutt .25 .60
19 Brett Hull .50 1.25
20 Ed Belfour .30 .75
21 Mike Modano .50 1.25
22 Sergei Fedorov .50 1.25
23 Brendan Shanahan .40 1.00
24 Chris Osgood .30 .75
25 Steve Yzerman 1.00 2.50
26 Doug Weight .30 .75
27 Tommy Salo .25 .60
28 Pavel Bure .40 1.00
29 Trevor Kidd .20 .50
30 Viktor Kozlov .20 .50
31 Rob Blake .30 .75
32 Zigmund Palffy .30 .75
33 Luc Robitaille .30 .75
34 Manny Fernandez .25 .60
35 Saku Koivu .30 .75
36 David Legwand .25 .60
37 Martin Brodeur .60 1.50
38 Patrik Elias .30 .75
39 Scott Gomez .25 .60
40 Scott Stevens .25 .60
41 Mariusz Czerkawski .20 .50
42 Tim Connolly .20 .50
43 Mark Messier .50 1.25
44 Mike York .20 .50
45 Theo Fleury .40 1.00
46 Marian Hossa .25 .60
47 Radek Bonk .25 .60
48 Simon Gagne .30 .75
49 Brian Boucher .25 .60
50 Rick Tocchet .25 .60
51 John LeClair .30 .75
52 Jeremy Roenick .30 .75
53 Keith Tkachuk .30 .75
54 Jaromir Jagr .75 2.00
55 Jean-Sebastien Aubin .25 .60
56 Jeff Friesen .25 .60
57 Steve Shields .25 .60
58 Brad Stuart .25 .60
59 Chris Pronger .25 .60
60 Pavol Demitra .40 1.00
61 Roman Turek .25 .60
62 Dan Cloutier .25 .60
63 Vincent Lecavalier .25 .60
64 Nikolai Antropov .25 .60
65 Curtis Joseph .40 1.00
66 Mats Sundin .30 .75
67 Felix Potvin .50 1.25
68 Markus Naslund .30 .75
69 Adam Oates .30 .75
70 Olaf Kolzig .30 .75
71 Peter Forsberg XE .40 1.00
72 Brendan Shanahan XE .40 1.00
73 Scott Stevens XE .30 .75
74 Mark Messier XE .50 1.25
75 John LeClair XE .30 .75
76 Keith Primeau XE .25 .60
77 Keith Tkachuk XE .30 .75
78 Jeremy Roenick XE .30 .75
79 Owen Nolan XE .30 .75
80 Chris Pronger XE .25 .60
81 Paul Kariya PRO .40 1.00
82 Dominik Hasek PRO .50 1.25
83 Patrick Roy PRO .75 2.00
84 Ray Bourque PRO .50 1.25
85 Mike Modano PRO .50 1.25
86 Steve Yzerman PRO 1.00 2.50
87 Pavel Bure PRO .40 1.00
88 Martin Brodeur PRO .60 1.50
89 John LeClair PRO .30 .75
90 Jaromir Jagr PRO .75 2.00
91 Herbert Vasiljevs RC 1.50 4.00
92 Eric Nickulas RC 1.50 4.00
93 Brandon Smith RC 1.50 4.00
94 Jeff Cowan RC 1.50 4.00
95 Serge Aubin RC 2.00 5.00
96 Mike Minard RC 2.50 6.00
97 Steven Reinprecht RC 2.50 6.00
98 David Gosselin RC 2.00 5.00
99 Colin White RC 1.50 4.00
100 Willie Mitchell RC 2.50 6.00
101 Steve Brule RC 1.50 4.00
102 Steve Valiquette RC 2.00 5.00
103 Petr Mika RC 1.50 4.00
104 Chris Kenady RC 1.50 4.00
105 Johan Witehall RC 1.50 4.00
106 Jani Hurme RC 1.50 4.00
107 Jean-Guy Trudel RC 1.50 4.00
108 Dale Rominski RC 1.50 4.00
109 Greg Andrusak RC 2.00 5.00
110 Martin Havlat RC 6.00 15.00
111 Jeremy Stevenson RC 1.50 4.00
112 Sergei Vyshedkevich RC 1.50 4.00
113 Johnathan Aitken RC 1.50 4.00
114 Keith Aldridge RC 1.50 4.00
115 Rich Parent RC 2.00 5.00
116 Kaspars Astashenko RC 1.50 4.00
117 Matt Elich RC 2.00 5.00
118 Dieter Kochan RC 1.50 4.00
119 Kyle Freadrich RC 1.50 4.00
120 Justin Williams RC 4.00 10.00
121 Andrew Raycroft JSY RC 6.00 15.00
122 Zdenek Blatny JSY RC 2.50 6.00
123 Pavel Brendl JSY 2.50 6.00
124 Jason Jaspers JSY RC 2.50 6.00
125 Fedor Fedorov JSY RC 3.00 8.00
126 Jordan Krestanovich JSY RC 2.50 6.00
127 Marc-Andre Thinel JSY RC 2.50 6.00
128 Damian Surma JSY RC 2.50 6.00
129 Jeff Bateman JSY RC 2.50 6.00
130 Sheldon Keefe JSY 2.50 6.00
131 Ray Ferraro .20 .50
132 Bill Guerin .30 .75
133 Ronald Petrovicky RC 1.00 2.50
134 Shane Willis .20 .50
135 Chris Nielsen RC 1.00 2.50
136 Petteri Nummelin RC 1.00 2.50
137 Igor Larionov .30 .75
138 Shawn Horcoff RC 2.00 5.00
139 Lance Ward RC 1.00 2.50
140 Manny Fernandez .25 .60
141 Scott Niedermayer .30 .75
142 Alexei Yashin .25 .60
143 Claude Lemieux .25 .60
144 Mario Lemieux 1.00 2.50
145 Milan Kraft .20 .50
146 Evgeni Nabokov .25 .60
147 Keith Tkachuk .30 .75
148 Gary Roberts .20 .50
149 Daniel Sedin .60 1.50
150 Henrik Sedin .50 1.25
151 Kris Beech .20 .50
152 Lee Goren RC 1.50 4.00
153 Pavel Kolarik RC 1.50 4.00
154 Greg Kuznik RC 1.50 4.00
155 Josef Vasicek RC 4.00 10.00
156 Rick Berry RC 1.50 4.00
157 David Aebischer RC 3.00 8.00
158 Rostislav Klesla RC 4.00 10.00
159 Marty Turco RC 3.00 8.00
160 Tyler Bouck RC 1.50 4.00
161 Mike Comrie RC 4.00 10.00
162 Eric Belanger RC 2.00 5.00
163 Marian Gaborik RC 10.00 25.00
164 Scott Hartnell RC 4.00 10.00
165 Jason Labarbera RC 2.00 5.00
166 Rick DiPietro RC 6.00 15.00
167 Ruslan Fedotenko RC 1.50 4.00
168 Petr Hubacek RC 1.50 4.00
169 Roman Cechmanek RC 2.00 5.00
170 Roman Simicek RC 1.50 4.00
171 Mark Smith RC 1.50 4.00
172 Jakub Cutta RC 1.50 4.00
173 Marc Chouinard RC 1.50 4.00
174 Darcy Hordichuk RC 1.50 4.00
175 Bryan Adams RC 1.50 4.00
176 Jarno Kultanen RC 1.50 4.00
177 Eric Boulton RC 1.50 4.00
178 Brian Swanson RC 1.50 4.00
179 Lubomir Sekeras RC 1.50 4.00
180 Eric Landry RC 1.50 4.00
181 Mike Commodore RC 1.50 4.00
182 Johan Holmqvist RC 1.50 4.00
183 Jeff Ulmer RC 1.50 4.00
184 Ossi Vaananen RC 2.00 5.00
185 Alexander Khavanov RC 1.50 4.00
186 Bryce Salvador RC 2.00 5.00
187 Reed Low RC 1.50 4.00

2000-01 SPx Spectrum

Randomly inserted in packs, this 130-card set parallels the base SPx set enhanced and sequentially numbered to 50.
*1-90 VETS/50: 10X TO 25X BASIC CARDS
*91-120 ROOKIES/50: 1.2X TO 3X RC/1500
*121-130 JSY/50: .8X TO 2X BASIC JSY
43 Mark Messier 12.00 30.00
74 Mark Messier XE 12.00 30.00

2000-01 SPx Highlight Heroes

Randomly inserted in packs at the rate of 1:7, this 14-card set features full color action photography with the words highlight heroes appearing as part of the background. Along the bottom of the card, the player's name and the words Highlight Heroes appear in silver foil.
COMPLETE SET (14) 10.00 20.00
HH1 Paul Kariya .60 1.50
HH2 Patrik Stefan .60 1.50
HH3 Joe Thornton 1.00 2.50
HH4 Valeri Bure .50 1.25
HH5 Milan Hejduk .60 1.50
HH6 Brett Hull .75 2.00
HH7 Brendan Shanahan 1.00 2.50
HH8 Pavel Bure .75 2.00
HH9 Marian Hossa .60 1.50
HH10 Brian Boucher .60 1.50
HH11 Jeremy Roenick .75 2.00
HH12 Jaromir Jagr 1.00 2.50
HH13 Chris Pronger .50 1.25
HH14 Curtis Joseph .60 1.50

2000-01 SPx Prolifics

Randomly inserted in packs at the rate of 1:14, this seven card set features an action photograph on the left side of the card front and a portrait style photo on the right. These two photos are separated by a silver foil line and the word Prolifics.
COMPLETE SET (7) 8.00 15.00
P1 Dominik Hasek 1.25 3.00
P2 Ray Bourque 1.25 3.00
P3 Brett Hull .75 2.00
P4 Steve Yzerman 3.00 8.00
P5 Mark Messier .75 2.00
P6 John LeClair .75 2.00
P7 Jaromir Jagr 1.00 2.50

2000-01 SPx Rookie Redemption

Randomly inserted in packs, this 30-card set was issued as team specific redemption cards that were redeemable for rookies who made their NHL debut in the 2001-02 season. Exchange cards expired 5/2002.
RR1 Ilja Bryzgalov 4.00 10.00
RR2 Ilya Kovalchuk 10.00 25.00
RR3 Ivan Huml 2.00 5.00
RR4 Ales Kotalik 2.50 6.00
RR5 Scott Nichol 2.00 5.00
RR6 Erik Cole 3.00 8.00
RR7 Casey Hankinson 2.00 5.00
RR8 Vaclav Nedorost 2.00 5.00
RR9 Martin Spanhel 2.00 5.00
RR10 Niko Kapanen 2.00 5.00
RR11 Pavel Datsyuk 12.00 30.00
RR12 Ty Conklin 4.00 10.00
RR13 Kristian Huselius 3.00 8.00
RR14 Jaroslav Bednar 2.00 5.00
RR15 Nick Schultz 2.00 5.00
RR16 Martti Jarventie 2.00 5.00
RR17 Martin Erat 4.00 10.00
RR18 Andreas Salomonsson 2.00 5.00
RR19 Raffi Torres 3.00 8.00
RR20 Dan Blackburn 2.50 6.00
RR21 Ivan Ciernik 2.00 5.00
RR22 Jiri Dopita 2.00 5.00
RR23 Krys Kolanos 2.00 5.00
RR24 Billy Tibbetts 2.00 5.00
RR25 Jeff Jillson 2.00 5.00
RR26 Mark Rycroft 2.00 5.00
RR27 Nikita Alexeev 2.00 5.00
RR28 Bob Wren 2.00 5.00
RR29 Pat Kavanagh 2.00 5.00
RR30 Brian Sutherby 2.00 5.00

2000-01 SPx SPXcitement

COMPLETE SET (14) 10.00 20.00
STATED ODDS 1:7
X1 Teemu Selanne .60 1.50
X2 Sergei Samsonov .50 1.25
X3 Tony Amonte .50 1.25
X4 Joe Sakic 1.25 3.00
X5 Mike Modano 1.00 2.50
X6 Sergei Fedorov 1.25 3.00
X7 Pavel Bure .75 2.00
X8 Martin Brodeur 1.50 4.00
X9 Simon Gagne .50 1.25
X10 Jaromir Jagr 1.00 2.50
X11 Jeff Friesen .50 1.25
X12 Roman Turek .50 1.25
X13 Vincent Lecavalier .60 1.50
X14 Mats Sundin .60 1.50

2000-01 SPx SPXtreme

COMPLETE SET (7) 8.00 15.00
STATED ODDS 1:14
S1 Paul Kariya .75 2.00
S2 Peter Forsberg 1.50 4.00
S3 Mike Modano 1.00 2.50
S4 Martin Brodeur 1.50 4.00
S5 Mark Messier .75 2.00
S6 John LeClair .75 2.00
S7 Jaromir Jagr 1.00 2.50

2000-01 SPx Winning Materials

Randomly seeded in SPx packs at the rate of 1:14 and UD Update packs at 1:60, this 48-card set features a player action photo and a swatch of a game worn jersey as well as a game used stick. Update cards are marked below.
AC Anson Carter SP 4.00 10.00
BH Brett Hull SP 8.00 20.00
BS Brendan Shanahan 6.00 15.00
CJ Curtis Joseph 6.00 15.00
CO Chris Osgood 5.00 12.00
DH Dominik Hasek 8.00 20.00
FP Felix Potvin 8.00 20.00
JJ Jaromir Jagr 12.00 30.00
JL John LeClair 5.00 12.00
JR Jeremy Roenick 5.00 12.00
JS Joe Sakic 8.00 20.00
KJ Kenny Jonsson 3.00 8.00
KT Keith Tkachuk 5.00 12.00
MB Martin Brodeur SP 10.00 25.00
ML Mario Lemieux 15.00 40.00
MM Mike Modano SP 8.00 20.00
NL Nicklas Lidstrom 5.00 12.00
PD Pavol Demitra SP 6.00 15.00
PF Peter Forsberg 6.00 15.00
PK Paul Kariya SP 6.00 15.00
PR Patrick Roy 12.00 30.00
RB Ray Bourque 8.00 20.00
SF Sergei Fedorov 8.00 20.00
SY Steve Yzerman 15.00 40.00
TO Tony Amonte 4.00 10.00
TS Teemu Selanne 10.00 25.00
WG Wayne Gretzky 25.00 60.00
PBO Peter Bondra SP 4.00 10.00
WBC Brian Boucher Upd 4.00 10.00
WBE Ed Belfour Upd 5.00 12.00
WBI Martin Biron Upd 4.00 10.00
WBO Ray Bourque Upd 8.00 20.00
WBU Valeri Bure Upd 4.00 10.00
WFE Sergei Fedorov Upd 8.00 20.00
WGR Wayne Gretzky Upd 25.00 60.00
WJJ Jaromir Jagr Upd 12.00 30.00
WKA Paul Kariya Upd 6.00 15.00
WLE John LeClair Upd 5.00 12.00
WLU Roberto Luongo Upd 8.00 20.00
WRE Jeremy Roenick Upd 5.00 12.00
WRO Patrick Roy Upd 12.00 30.00
WSA Miroslav Satan Upd 3.00 8.00
WSE Teemu Selanne Upd 10.00 25.00
WSU Mats Sundin Upd 5.00 12.00
WTB Jocelyn Thibault Upd 4.00 10.00
WTH Joe Thornton Upd 8.00 20.00
WTK Keith Tkachuk Upd 5.00 12.00
WYZ Steve Yzerman Upd 15.00 40.00

2000-01 SPx Winning Materials Autographs

Randomly inserted in packs, this 10-card set parallels the SPx Winning Materials set but adds an authentic player autograph. These cards were limited to 25 serial-numbered sets.
PRINT RUN 25
SBH Brett Hull 75.00 150.00
SCJ Curtis Joseph 40.00 100.00
SFP Felix Potvin 60.00 120.00
SJL John LeClair 40.00 100.00
SKT Keith Tkachuk 60.00 120.00
SMB Martin Brodeur 60.00 125.00
SML Mario Lemieux 150.00 300.00
SRB Ray Bourque 75.00 150.00
SSY Steve Yzerman 125.00 225.00
SWG Wayne Gretzky 150.00 300.00

2001-02 SPx

Released in mid-December 2001, this set originally consisted of 170 cards including 70 base cards, 42 rookie cards (91-132) short printed to 999, and 38 rookie threads cards (133-151) short printed to either 800 or 1500. The rookie threads subset had two versions, home and away, for each player. Cards 197-216 were available in random packs of UD Rookie Update and were serial-numbered to 999.
COMP.SET w/o SP's (155) 40.00 80.00
1 Paul Kariya .40 1.00
2 Patrik Stefan .25 .60
3 Sergei Samsonov .25 .60
4 Joe Thornton .40 1.00
5 Bill Guerin .30 .75
6 Martin Biron .25 .60
7 Miroslav Satan .25 .60
8 Jarome Iginla .30 .75
9 Marc Savard .20 .50
10 Arturs Irbe .20 .50
11 Tony Amonte .25 .60
12 Steve Sullivan .20 .50
13 Joe Sakic .50 1.25
14 Peter Forsberg .40 1.00
15 Ray Bourque .50 1.25
16 Milan Hejduk .25 .60
17 Patrick Roy .75 2.00
18 Ron Tugnutt .25 .60
19 Mike Modano .50 1.25
20 Ed Belfour .30 .75
21 Pierre Turgeon .30 .75
22 Steve Yzerman 1.00 2.50
23 Brendan Shanahan .40 1.00
24 Sergei Fedorov .50 1.25
25 Luc Robitaille .30 .75
26 Dominik Hasek .50 1.25
27 Tommy Salo .25 .60
28 Mike Comrie .25 .60
29 Pavel Bure .40 1.00
30 Zigmund Palffy .30 .75
31 Felix Potvin .50 1.25
32 Adam Deadmarsh .25 .60
33 Marian Gaborik .50 1.25
34 Saku Koivu .30 .75
35 David Legwand .25 .60
36 Mike Dunham .25 .60
37 Martin Brodeur .60 1.50
38 Patrik Elias .30 .75
39 Jason Arnott .25 .60
40 Michael Peca .25 .60
41 Rick DiPietro .25 .60
42 Mark Messier .50 1.25
43 Theo Fleury .40 1.00
44 Marian Hossa .25 .60
45 Radek Bonk .20 .50
46 Jeremy Roenick .30 .75
47 Roman Cechmanek .25 .60
48 Keith Primeau .25 .60
49 John LeClair .30 .75
50 Sean Burke .20 .50
51 Alexei Kovalev .25 .60
52 Mario Lemieux 1.00 2.50
53 Johan Hedberg .25 .60
54 Robert Lang .20 .50
55 Evgeni Nabokov .25 .60
56 Teemu Selanne .60 1.50
57 Owen Nolan .30 .75
58 Chris Pronger .25 .60
59 Keith Tkachuk .30 .75
60 Doug Weight .30 .75
61 Pavol Demitra .40 1.00
62 Brad Richards .30 .75
63 Vincent Lecavalier .25 .60
64 Curtis Joseph .30 .75
65 Mats Sundin .30 .75
66 Markus Naslund .30 .75
67 Daniel Sedin .30 .75
68 Jaromir Jagr .75 2.00
69 Peter Bondra .30 .75
70 Olaf Kolzig .30 .75
71 Paul Kariya XCT .40 1.00
72 Peter Forsberg XCT .40 1.00
73 Mike Modano XCT .50 1.25
74 Sergei Fedorov XCT .50 1.25
75 Steve Yzerman XCT 1.00 2.50
76 Pavel Bure XCT .40 1.00
77 Zigmund Palffy XCT .30 .75
78 Mario Lemieux XCT 1.00 2.50
79 Vincent Lecavalier XCT .25 .60
80 Markus Naslund XCT .30 .75
81 Joe Sakic XT .50 1.25
82 Chris Drury XT .25 .60
83 Patrick Roy XT .75 2.00
84 Mike Modano XT .50 1.25
85 Steve Yzerman XT 1.00 2.50
86 Pavel Bure XT .40 1.00
87 Martin Brodeur XT .60 1.50
88 John LeClair XT .30 .75
89 Mario Lemieux XT 1.00 2.50
90 Chris Pronger XT .25 .60
91 Timo Parssinen RC 1.50 4.00
92 Ilja Bryzgalov RC 3.00 8.00
93 Kevin Sawyer RC 1.25 3.00
94 Dany Heatley SP 2.00 5.00
95 Zdenek Kutlak RC 1.25 3.00
96 Greg Crozier RC 1.25 3.00
97 Mika Noronen SP 1.25 3.00
98 Scott Nichol RC 1.25 3.00
99 Erik Cole RC 2.50 6.00
100 Casey Hankinson RC 1.25 3.00
101 Vaclav Nedorost RC 1.25 3.00
102 Jaroslav Obsut RC 1.25 3.00
103 Niko Kapanen RC 2.00 5.00
104 Pavel Datsyuk RC 15.00 40.00
105 Niklas Hagman RC 1.50 4.00
106 Kristian Huselius RC 2.00 5.00
107 Andrej Podkonicky RC 1.25 3.00
108 Francis Belanger RC 1.50 4.00
109 Martin Erat RC 2.00 5.00
110 Bill Bowler RC 1.25 3.00
111 Scott Clemmensen RC 1.25 3.00
112 Josef Boumedienne RC 1.25 3.00
113 Andreas Salomonsson RC 1.25 3.00
114 Mike Jefferson RC 1.25 3.00
115 Stanislav Gron RC 1.25 3.00
116 Radek Martinek RC 1.25 3.00
117 Dan Blackburn RC 1.50 4.00
118 Chris Neil RC 1.50 4.00
119 Ivan Ciernik RC 1.25 3.00
120 Pavel Brendl SP 1.25 3.00
121 David Cullen RC 1.25 3.00

2 Billy Tibbetts RC 1.25 3.00
3 Miikka Kiprusoff SP 2.00 5.00
4 Jeff Jillson RC 1.25 3.00
25 Michel Larocque RC 1.25 3.00
26 Mark Rycroft RC 1.50 4.00
27 Thomas Ziegler RC 1.50 4.00
28 Nikita Alexeev RC 1.25 3.00
9 Bob Wren RC 1.25 3.00
0 Mike Brown SP 1.50 4.00
1 Pat Kavanagh RC 1.50 4.00
2 Brian Sutherby RC 1.25 3.00
3A Brian Pothier AW/800 RC 1.25 3.00
3H Brian Pothier HM/800 RC 1.25 3.00
4A Dan Snyder AW/1500 RC 1.50 4.00
4H Dan Snyder HM/1500 RC 1.50 4.00
5A Jody Shelley AW/1500 RC 1.50 4.00
5H Jody Shelley HM/1500 RC 1.50 4.00
6A M.Spanhel AW/1500 RC 1.25 3.00
6H M.Spanhel HM/1500 RC 1.25 3.00
7A M.Darche AW/1500 RC 2.00 5.00
7H M.Darche HM/1500 RC 2.00 5.00
8A M.Davidson AW/1500 RC 1.25 3.00
8H M.Davidson HM/1500 RC 1.25 3.00
9A S.Selmser AW/1500 RC 1.25 3.00
9H S.Selmser HM/1500 RC 1.25 3.00
0A Jason Chimera AW/800 RC 1.25 3.00
0H Jason Chimera HM/800 RC 1.25 3.00
1A M.Matteucci AW/1500 RC 1.25 3.00
1H M.Matteucci HM/1500 RC 1.25 3.00
2A Pascal Dupuis AW/800 RC 2.00 5.00
2H Pascal Dupuis HM/800 RC 2.00 5.00
3A Peter Smrek AW/800 RC 1.25 3.00
3H Peter Smrek HM/800 RC 1.25 3.00
4A M.Samuelsson AW/1500 RC 1.50 4.00
4H M.Samuelsson HM/1500 RC 1.50 4.00
5A J.Kwiatkowski AW/1500 RC 1.25 3.00
5H J.Kwiatkowski HM/1500 RC 1.25 3.00
6A Kirby Law AW/1500 RC 1.25 3.00
6H Kirby Law HM/1500 RC 1.25 3.00
7A T.Divisek AW/1500 RC 1.50 4.00
7H T.Divisek HM/1500 RC 1.50 4.00
8A I.Kovalchuk AW/800 RC 10.00 25.00
8H I.Kovalchuk HM/800 RC 10.00 25.00
9A J.Bednar AW/800 RC 1.25 3.00
9H J.Bednar HM/800 RC 1.25 3.00
0A Jiri Dopita AW/800 RC 1.25 3.00
0H Jiri Dopita HM/800 RC 1.25 3.00
1A Krys Kolanos AW/800 RC 1.25 3.00
1H Krys Kolanos HM/800 RC 1.25 3.00
2 Jeff Friesen .20 .50
3 Jean-Sebastien Giguere .25 .60
4 Dany Heatley .30 .75
5 Pascal Rheaume .20 .50
6 Andy Hilbert .20 .50
7 Jozef Stumpel .20 .50
8 Glen Murray .25 .60
9 Maxim Afinogenov .20 .50
0 Roman Turek .25 .60
1 Craig Conroy .20 .50
2 Jeff O'Neill .20 .50
3 Sami Kapanen .20 .50
4 Jocelyn Thibault .25 .60
5 Mark Bell .20 .50
6 Kyle Calder .20 .50
7 Alex Tanguay .25 .60
8 Darius Kasparaitis .20 .50
9 Chris Drury .25 .60
0 Radim Vrbata .20 .50
1 Rostislav Klesla .20 .50
72 Brett Hull .40 1.00
73 Jani Rita .20 .50
74 Mike York .20 .50
75 Roberto Luongo .50 1.25
76 Jason Allison .25 .60
77 Andrew Brunette .20 .50
78 Sergei Berezin .20 .50
79 Donald Audette .20 .50
80 Brian Gionta .25 .60
81 Alexei Yashin .25 .60
82 Chris Osgood .30 .75
83 Pavel Bure .40 1.00
84 Tom Poti .20 .50
85 Eric Lindros .50 1.25
86 Patrick Lalime .25 .60
87 Martin Havlat .25 .60
88 Brian Boucher .25 .60
89 Simon Gagne .30 .75
90 Brian Savage .20 .50
91 Brent Johnson .25 .60
92 Gordie Dwyer .20 .50
93 Nikolai Khabibulin .30 .75
94 Alexander Mogilny .25 .60
95 Brendan Morrison .25 .60
96 Trevor Linden .30 .75
97 Pasi Nurminen RC 1.25 3.00
98 Ivan Huml RC 1.25 3.00
99 Ales Kotalik RC 2.50 6.00
00 Mike Peluso RC 1.25 3.00
01 Riku Hahl RC 1.25 3.00
02 Kelly Fairchild RC 1.25 3.00
03 Blake Bellefeuille RC 1.25 3.00
04 Sean Avery RC 1.25 3.00
05 Brad Norton RC 1.25 3.00
06 Marcel Hossa RC 2.00 5.00
07 Olivier Michaud RC 2.00 5.00
08 Robert Schnabel RC 1.25 3.00
09 Christian Berglund RC 1.50 4.00
10 Raffi Torres RC 2.00 5.00
11 Toni Dahlman RC 1.25 3.00
12 Branko Radivojevic RC 1.25 3.00
13 Shane Endicott RC 1.25 3.00
14 Tom Kostopoulos RC 1.25 3.00
15 Sebastien Centomo RC 1.25 3.00
16 Karel Pilar RC 1.25 3.00
9 Steve Yzerman SAMPLE 2.00 5.00

2001-02 SPx Hidden Treasures

vailable in random packs of UD Rookie Update, this 2-card set featured swatches of game-used jerseys rom two or three different NHL players. Dual jerseys were inserted at a rate of 1:45 while triple jerseys were nserted at 1:90.

TAD M.Afinogenov/J.Dumont 8.00 20.00
TBJ P.Bondra/J.Jagr 10.00 25.00
TBN R.Blake/V.Nieminen 8.00 20.00
TFC R.Fedotenko/T.Connolly 8.00 20.00
TGW S.Gagne/J.Williams 8.00 20.00
THB M.Hejduk/R.Blake 8.00 20.00
TJD J.Allison/A.Deadmarsh 8.00 20.00
TPS Z.Palffy/M.Satan 8.00 20.00
TSF M.Sundin/P.Forsberg 10.00 25.00
TSG S.Sullivan/S.Gagne 8.00 20.00
TTD T.Amonte/C.Drury 8.00 20.00
TTP J.Thibault/F.Potvin 10.00 25.00
TTT J.Thibault/J.Theodore 8.00 20.00
TYL M.York/B.Leetch 8.00 20.00
TBSS Bondra/Selanne/Sundin 12.50 30.00
TBTT Brodeur/Thibault/Theodore 15.00 40.00
TDBA Dumont/Biron/Afinogenov 12.50 30.00
TDSA Daze/Sullivan/Amonte 12.50 30.00
TFSD Forsbrg/Shan./Deadmrsh 15.00 40.00
TTKBL Klesla/Blake/Lidstrom 12.50 30.00
TTTHN Tanguay/Hinote/Nieminen 12.50 30.00
TTYLS Yzerman/Lemieux/Sakic 100.00 200.00

2001-02 SPx Hockey Treasures

Inserted at a rate of 1:19, this 19-card set featured swatches of game-used jerseys and sticks of the featured players. Cards were silver in color and the swatches were aligned parallel to one another with a color photo of the given player on the right side of the card front.

HTBH Brett Hull 6.00 15.00
HTCJ Curtis Joseph 5.00 12.00
HTDH Dominik Hasek 8.00 20.00
HTHU Brett Hull 6.00 15.00
HTJI Jarome Iginla 6.00 15.00
HTJL John LeClair 5.00 12.00
HTJN Joe Nieuwendyk 6.00 15.00
HTKP Keith Primeau 5.00 12.00
HTLE John LeClair 5.00 12.00
HTMB Martin Brodeur 10.00 25.00
HTML Mario Lemieux 15.00 40.00
HTMM Mike Modano 8.00 20.00
HTMO Mike Modano 6.00 15.00
HTPR Patrick Roy 12.50 30.00
HTRC Roman Cechmanek 5.00 12.00
HTSF Sergei Fedorov 6.00 15.00
HTSS Sergei Samsonov 5.00 12.00
HTSY Steve Yzerman 12.50 30.00
HTTS Teemu Selanne 5.00 12.00

2001-02 SPx Hockey Treasures Autographs

This set partially paralleled the base hockey treasures set but also carried authentic player autographs. Each card was serial-numbered out of 50.

STBO Ray Bourque 75.00 200.00
STCJ Curtis Joseph 25.00 60.00
STJI Jarome Iginla 30.00 80.00
STJL John LeClair 15.00 40.00
STKE Keith Primeau 25.00 60.00
STKP Keith Primeau 25.00 60.00
STLE John LeClair 15.00 40.00
STRB Ray Bourque 75.00 150.00
STSY Steve Yzerman 75.00 200.00
STTU Marty Turco 30.00 80.00

2001-02 SPx Rookie Redemption

Randomly inserted into packs of UD Rookie Update, this 30-card set of redemption cards represented each team in the NHL. Redemption cards were redeemable for rookies who make their debut in the 2002/03 season. Cards were serial-numbered out of 1250. Redemption cards expire 4/30/2005.

R1 Stanislav Chistov 2.00 5.00
R2 Mark Hartigan 2.00 5.00
R3 Tim Thomas 8.00 20.00
R4 Henrik Tallinder 2.00 5.00
R5 Chuck Kobasew 4.00 10.00
R6 Jaroslav Svoboda 2.00 5.00
R7 Shawn Thornton 4.00 10.00
R8 Jeff Paul 2.00 5.00
R9 Rick Nash 10.00 25.00
R10 John Erskine 2.00 5.00
R11 Henrik Zetterberg 12.50 30.00
R12 Ales Hemsky 6.00 15.00
R13 Jay Bouwmeester 4.00 10.00
R14 Alexander Frolov 5.00 12.00
R15 Pierre-Marc Bouchard 4.00 10.00
R16 Ron Hainsey 2.00 5.00
R17 Scottie Upshall 5.00 12.00
R18 Steve Ott 4.00 10.00
R19 Eric Godard 2.00 5.00
R20 Jamie Lundmark 2.00 5.00
R21 Jason Spezza 8.00 20.00
R22 Radovan Somik 2.00 5.00
R23 Jeff Taffe 2.00 5.00
R24 Shane Endicott 2.00 5.00
R25 Lynn Loyns 2.00 5.00
R26 Curtis Sanford 2.00 5.00
R27 Alexander Svitov 2.00 5.00
R28 Carlo Colaiacovo 2.00 5.00
R29 Fedor Fedorov 2.00 5.00
R30 Steve Eminger 2.00 5.00

2001-02 SPx Rookie Treasures

Available in random packs of UD Rookie Update at a rate of 1:20, this 20-card set resembled the hockey treasures design but focused on rookies and prospects. Each card carried a swatch of game-worn jersey as well as game-used stick.

RTBP Brian Pothier 3.00 8.00
RTDA Mathieu Darche 3.00 8.00
RTDS Dan Snyder 6.00 15.00
RTIK Ilya Kovalchuk 12.00 30.00
RTJB Jaroslav Bednar 3.00 8.00
RTJC Jason Chimera 3.00 8.00
RTJD Jiri Dopita 3.00 8.00
RTJK Joel Kwiatkowski 3.00 8.00
RTJS Jody Shelley 6.00 15.00
RTKK Krys Kolanos 3.00 8.00
RTKL Kirby Law 3.00 8.00
RTMD Matt Davidson 3.00 8.00
RTMM Mike Matteucci 3.00 8.00
RTMS Martin Spanhel 3.00 8.00
RTMS Mikael Samuelsson 3.00 8.00
RTPD Pascal Dupuis 4.00 10.00
RTPS Peter Smrek 3.00 8.00
RTRT Raffi Torres 4.00 10.00
RTSS Sean Selmser 3.00 8.00
RTTD Tomas Divisek 3.00 8.00

2001-02 SPx Signs of Xcellence

Inserted at 1:279, this 9-card set featured authentic player autographs. Card fronts were gold toned and displayed a large signing area with a smaller player photo off to the side of the card and a silhouette of the player in the background.

BO Bobby Orr 150.00 250.00
DW Doug Weight 10.00 25.00
GH Gordie Howe 100.00 200.00
JL John LeClair 10.00 25.00
MC Mike Comrie 5.00 12.00
MM Mark Messier 40.00 100.00
SG Simon Gagne 10.00 25.00
TL Trevor Letowski 5.00 12.00
WG Wayne Gretzky 150.00 250.00

2001-02 SPx Yzerman Tribute

This 26-card set paid homage to the long-time captain of the Detroit Red Wings. Steve Yzerman. Cards 1-19 carried authentic autographs and were serial-numbered out of 19 each. Autograph cards were gold toned on the card fronts and each card carried a different small photo of Yzerman. Cards 20-26 were inserted at 1:140 and carried either one or two large pieces of game-used jersey and/or equipment. Cards 20-26 were blue toned in color and each carried a different small photo of Yzerman.

COMMON AUTO/19 175.00 300.00
COMMON DBL.MEM. (20-24) 15.00 40.00
COMMON SINGLE MEM. (25-26) 10.00 25.00

2002-03 SPx

Released in December 2002, this 193-card set consisted of 60 base veteran cards (1-60), 40 "Spxitement" subset cards (#61-100), 25 "SPx Prospects" cards numbered to 999 (#101-125), 20 "Career Achievement" cards (#126-145), 15 rookie jersey/autograph cards (#146-159 and #175), 15 rookie jersey cards numbered to 999 (#160-174) and 17 shortprinted rookie cards numbered to 999 (#176-193). Cards 176-193 were available only in packs of UD Rookie Update. Individual print runs for cards 126-159 and card 175 are listed below.

COMP.SET w/o SP's (100) 20.00 50.00
1 Paul Kariya .40 1.00
2 Jean-Sebastien Giguere .30 .75
3 Ilya Kovalchuk .40 1.00
4 Dany Heatley .30 .75
5 Joe Thornton .40 1.00
6 Sergei Samsonov .25 .60
7 Miroslav Satan .30 .75
8 Martin Biron .25 .60
9 Roman Turek .30 .75
10 Jarome Iginla .30 .75
11 Jeff O'Neill .20 .50
12 Ron Francis .40 1.00
13 Arturs Irbe .25 .60
14 Eric Daze .20 .50
15 Jocelyn Thibault .25 .60
16 Patrick Roy .75 2.00
17 Chris Drury .30 .75
18 Joe Sakic .50 1.25
19 Peter Forsberg .40 1.00
20 Rob Blake .30 .75
21 Rostislav Klesla .20 .50
22 Marc Denis .25 .60
23 Mike Modano .50 1.25
24 Marty Turco .30 .75
25 Bill Guerin .30 .75
26 Steve Yzerman .60 1.50
27 Sergei Fedorov .50 1.25
28 Nicklas Lidstrom .30 .75
29 Brett Hull .40 1.00
30 Curtis Joseph .30 .75
31 Brendan Shanahan .40 1.00
32 Mike Comrie .30 .75
33 Tommy Salo .25 .60
34 Roberto Luongo .50 1.25
35 Kristian Huselius .20 .50
36 Felix Potvin .50 1.25
37 Zigmund Palffy .30 .75
38 Marian Gaborik .50 1.25
39 Manny Fernandez .25 .60
40 Jose Theodore .30 .75
41 Saku Koivu .30 .75
42 Patrik Elias .30 .75
43 Martin Brodeur .60 1.50
44 Scott Hartnell .30 .75
45 Mike Dunham .25 .60
46 Alexei Yashin .25 .60
47 Chris Osgood .30 .75
48 Michael Peca .25 .60
49 Eric Lindros .50 1.25
50 Mike Richter .30 .75
51 Pavel Bure .40 1.00
52 Patrick Lalime .25 .60
53 Marian Hossa .25 .60
54 Daniel Alfredsson .30 .75
55 Jeremy Roenick .30 .75
56 Simon Gagne .30 .75
57 Roman Cechmanek .25 .60
58 Sean Burke .20 .50
59 Tony Amonte .25 .60
60 Alexei Kovalev .30 .75
61 Mario Lemieux 1.00 2.50
62 Owen Nolan .30 .75
63 Evgeni Nabokov .25 .60
64 Keith Tkachuk .30 .75
65 Chris Pronger .25 .60
66 Brent Johnson .25 .60
67 Nikolai Khabibulin .30 .75
68 Vincent Lecavalier .25 .60
69 Alexander Mogilny .25 .60
70 Mats Sundin .30 .75
71 Ed Belfour .30 .75
72 Todd Bertuzzi .30 .75
73 Markus Naslund .25 .60
74 Olaf Kolzig .30 .75
75 Jaromir Jagr .75 2.00
76 Paul Kariya .40 1.00
77 Adam Oates .30 .75
78 Sergei Samsonov .25 .60
79 Bobby Orr 1.00 2.50
80 Joe Thornton .40 1.00
81 Jeff O'Neill .20 .50
82 Ron Francis .40 1.00
83 Joe Sakic .50 1.25
84 Patrick Roy .75 2.00
85 Peter Forsberg .40 1.00
86 Bill Guerin .30 .75
87 Mike Modano .50 1.25
88 Curtis Joseph .30 .75
89 Gordie Howe 1.00 2.50
90 Steve Yzerman .60 1.50
91 Mike Comrie .30 .75
92 Jose Theodore .30 .75
93 Martin Brodeur .60 1.50
94 Pavel Bure .40 1.00
95 Wayne Gretzky 1.50 4.00
96 John LeClair .30 .75
97 Mario Lemieux 1.00 2.50
98 Evgeni Nabokov .25 .60
99 Mats Sundin .30 .75
100 Jaromir Jagr .75 2.00
101 Pasi Nurminen SPR 1.50 4.00
102 Mark Hartigan SPR 1.50 4.00
103 Andy Hilbert SPR 1.50 4.00
104 Henrik Tallinder SPR 1.50 4.00
105 Jaroslav Svoboda SPR 1.50 4.00
106 Riku Hahl SPR 1.50 4.00
107 Jordan Krestanovich SPR 1.50 4.00
108 Andrej Nedorost SPR 1.50 4.00
109 Sean Avery SPR 2.00 5.00
110 Jani Rita SPR 1.50 4.00
111 Stephen Weiss SPR 2.50 6.00
112 Lukas Krajicek SPR 2.00 5.00
113 Tony Virta SPR 1.50 4.00
114 Marcel Hossa SPR 1.50 4.00
115 Jan Lasak SPR 2.00 5.00
116 Jonas Andersson SPR 2.00 5.00
117 Trent Hunter SPR 1.50 4.00
118 Martin Prusek SPR 1.50 4.00
119 Bruno St. Jacques SPR 1.50 4.00
120 Branko Radivojevic SPR 1.50 4.00
121 Shane Endicott SPR 1.50 4.00
122 Justin Papineau SPR 1.50 4.00
123 Sebastien Centomo SPR 1.50 4.00
124 Karel Pilar SPR 1.50 4.00
125 Sebastien Charpentier SPR 1.50 4.00
126 Mark Messier CA/1804 2.50 6.00
127 Ron Francis CA/1701 2.00 5.00
128 Steve Yzerman CA/1662 3.00 8.00
129 Mario Lemieux CA/1601 5.00 12.00
130 Luc Robitaille CA/1288 1.50 4.00
131 Joe Sakic CA/1257 2.50 6.00
132 Brett Hull CA/1246 2.00 5.00
133 Al MacInnis CA/1204 1.50 4.00
134 Pierre Turgeon CA/1192 1.50 4.00
135 Jaromir Jagr CA/1158 4.00 10.00
136 Mark Recchi CA/1074 2.00 5.00
137 Brendan Shanahan CA/1030 2.00 5.00
138 Jeremy Roenick CA/1014 1.50 4.00
139 Mike Modano CA/977 2.50 6.00
140 Mats Sundin CA/942 1.50 4.00
141 Sergei Fedorov CA/871 2.50 6.00
142 Teemu Selanne CA/855 3.00 8.00
143 Pavel Bure CA/749 2.00 5.00
144 Peter Bondra CA/734 1.50 4.00
145 Eric Lindros CA/732 2.50 6.00
146 A.Smirnov JSY AU/1250 RC 6.00 15.00
147 K.Sauer JSY AU/1250 RC 5.00 12.00
148 C.Kobasew JSY AU/1250 RC 6.00 15.00
149 R.Nash JSY AU/500 RC 20.00 50.00
150 J.Bouwmster JSY AU/500 RC 5.00 12.00
151 H.Zetterberg JSY AU/1250 RC 20.00 50.00
152 P.Bouchard JSY AU/1250 RC 8.00 20.00
153 R.Hainsey JSY AU/1250 RC 5.00 12.00
154 A.Hall JSY AU/1250 RC 5.00 12.00
155 S.Upshall JSY AU/1250 RC 6.00 15.00
156 S.Chistov JSY AU/500 RC 5.00 12.00
157 J.Taffe JSY AU/1250 RC 5.00 12.00
158 M.Tellqvist JSY AU/1250 RC 5.00 12.00
159 A.Svitov JSY AU/1250 RC 5.00 12.00
160 Ales Hemsky JSY RC 8.00 20.00
161 Alexander Frolov JSY RC 6.00 15.00
162 Steve Eminger JSY RC 3.00 8.00
163 Anton Volchenkov JSY RC 3.00 8.00
164 Sylvain Blouin JSY RC 3.00 8.00
165 Greg Koehler JSY RC 3.00 8.00
166 Martin Gerber JSY RC 5.00 12.00
167 Micki Dupont JSY RC 3.00 8.00
168 Jordan Leopold JSY RC 5.00 12.00
169 Tomi Pettinen JSY RC 3.00 8.00
170 Lynn Loyns JSY RC 3.00 8.00
171 Matt Henderson JSY RC 3.00 8.00
172 Radovan Somik JSY RC 3.00 8.00
173 Patrick Sharp JSY RC 10.00 25.00
174 Jeff Paul JSY RC 3.00 8.00
175 J.Spezza JSY AU/500 RC 25.00 60.00
176 Pascal LeClaire RC 1.50 4.00
177 Steve Ott RC 2.50 6.00
178 Brooks Orpik RC 2.00 5.00
179 Jared Aulin RC 1.25 3.00
180 Brandon Reid RC 1.25 3.00
181 Ray Emery RC 4.00 10.00
182 Ari Ahonen RC 1.25 3.00
183 Niko Dimitrakos RC 1.25 3.00
184 Jarret Stoll RC 5.00 12.00
185 Cristobal Huet RC 2.50 6.00
186 Mike Komisarek RC 2.00 5.00
187 Ryan Miller RC 8.00 20.00
188 Jason Bacashihua RC 1.50 4.00
189 Carlo Colaiacovo RC 2.00 5.00
190 Mike Cammalleri RC 4.00 10.00
191 Fernando Pisani RC 1.25 3.00
192 Alexei Semenov RC 1.25 3.00
193 Konstantin Koltsov RC 1.50 4.00

2002-03 SPx Spectrum Silver

*1-100 VETS/199: 2X TO 5X BASIC CARDS

2002-03 SPx Milestones

This 15-card set featured game jersey swatches. Cards were serial-numbered out of 99.

MBL Brian Leetch 5.00 12.00
MBO Peter Bondra 5.00 12.00
MBS Brendan Shanahan 5.00 12.00
MJR Jeremy Roenick 8.00 20.00
MJS Joe Sakic 10.00 25.00
MMB Martin Brodeur 12.50 30.00
MML Mario Lemieux 12.50 30.00
MMM Mike Modano 8.00 20.00
MMR Mark Recchi 5.00 12.00
MPB Pavel Bure 5.00 12.00
MPR Patrick Roy 12.50 30.00
MSF Sergei Fedorov 8.00 20.00
MSH Brendan Shanahan 5.00 12.00
MSY Steve Yzerman 12.50 30.00
MTS Teemu Selanne 6.00 15.00

2002-03 SPx Milestones Gold

This 15-card set paralleled the base insert set but each card was serial-numbered out of 15 in gold foil on the card front. All cards carried a "M" prefix on the card backs. This set is not priced due to scarcity.

2002-03 SPx Milestones Silver

This 15-card set paralleled the base insert set but each card was serial-numbered out of 50 in silver foil on the card front. All cards carried a "M" prefix on the card backs.

*STARS: .75X TO 2X BASIC CARDS

2002-03 SPx Rookie Redemption

These 30 redemption cards were randomly inserted into packs and were redeemable for players making their debut in 2003-04. Cards R194-R214 were serial-numbered to 1500 and cards R215-223 were serial-numbered to 500.

R194 Matthew Lombardi 3.00 8.00
R195 Pavel Vorobiev 3.00 8.00
R196 Marek Svatos 4.00 10.00
R197 Cody McCormick 3.00 8.00
R198 John-Michael Liles 3.00 8.00
R199 Antti Miettinen 3.00 8.00
R200 Brent Burns 3.00 8.00
R201 Christoph Brandner 3.00 8.00
R202 Chris Higgins 4.00 10.00
R203 Dan Hamhuis 3.00 8.00
R204 Marek Zidlicky 3.00 8.00
R205 Paul Martin 3.00 8.00
R206 Sean Bergenheim 3.00 8.00
R207 Antoine Vermette 4.00 10.00
R208 Matthew Spiller 3.00 8.00
R209 Christian Ehrhoff 3.00 8.00
R210 Peter Sejna 3.00 8.00
R211 Maxim Kondratiev 3.00 8.00
R212 Matt Stajan 4.00 10.00
R213 Boyd Gordon 3.00 8.00
R214 Joffrey Lupul 5.00 12.00
R215 Patrice Bergeron 10.00 25.00
R216 Eric Staal 12.00 30.00
R217 Tuomo Ruutu 5.00 12.00
R218 Nathan Horton 6.00 15.00
R219 Dustin Brown 10.00 20.00
R220 Jordin Tootoo 5.00 12.00
R221 Joni Pitkanen 4.00 10.00
R222 Marc-Andre Fleury 20.00 50.00
R223 Milan Michalek 6.00 15.00

2002-03 SPx Smooth Skaters

This 17-card set featured game jersey swatches. Cards were serial-numbered out of 99.
ALL CARDS CARRY SS PREFIX

ED Eric Daze 5.00 12.00
JI Jarome Iginla 8.00 20.00
JJ Jaromir Jagr 8.00 20.00
JS Joe Sakic 10.00 25.00
JT Joe Thornton 10.00 25.00
ML Mario Lemieux 15.00 40.00
MM Mike Modano 8.00 20.00
MN Markus Naslund 5.00 12.00
MS Mats Sundin 5.00 12.00
PB Peter Bondra 5.00 12.00
PK Paul Kariya 5.00 12.00
SA Miroslav Satan 5.00 12.00
SG Simon Gagne 6.00 15.00
SS Sergei Samsonov 5.00 12.00
SU Steve Sullivan 5.00 12.00
SY Steve Yzerman 12.50 30.00
WG Wayne Gretzky 20.00 50.00

2002-03 SPx Smooth Skaters Gold

This 17-card set paralleled the base insert set but each card was serial-numbered out of 15 in gold foil on the card front. All cards carried a "SS" prefix on the card backs. This set is not priced due to scarcity.

2002-03 SPx Smooth Skaters Silver

This 17-card set paralleled the base insert set but each card was serial-numbered out of 50 in silver foil on the card front. All cards carried a "SS" prefix on the card backs.

*STARS: .75X TO 2 X BASIC CARDS

2002-03 SPx Winning Materials

This 35-card memorabilia set had a stated print run of 99 serial-numbered copies each.

WMAY Alexei Yashin 5.00 12.00
WMBI Martin Biron 6.00 15.00
WMBL Brian Leetch 6.00 15.00
WMBO Ray Bourque COL 15.00 40.00
WMCJ Curtis Joseph 6.00 15.00
WMDH Dominik Hasek 20.00 50.00
WMDL David Legwand 6.00 15.00
WMDU J-P Dumont 5.00 12.00
WMEL Eric Lindros 6.00 15.00
WMFP Felix Potvin 8.00 20.00
WMIK Ilya Kovalchuk 15.00 40.00
WMJA Jaromir Jagr JSY/JSY 10.00 25.00
WMJG Jean-Sebastien Giguere 5.00 12.00
WMJJ Jaromir Jagr JSY/STK 10.00 25.00
WMJR Jeremy Roenick 12.50 30.00
WMJT Joe Thornton 10.00 25.00
WMKA Paul Kariya JSY/JSY 6.00 15.00
WMKO Olaf Kolzig 6.00 15.00
WMLE John LeClair 6.00 15.00
WMMB Martin Brodeur 20.00 50.00
WMML Mario Lemieux 25.00 60.00
WMMM Mike Modano 10.00 25.00
WMMN Markus Naslund 6.00 15.00
WMPA Zigmund Palffy 6.00 15.00
WMPB Pavel Bure 6.00 15.00
WMPF Peter Forsberg 15.00 40.00
WMPK Paul Kariya JSY/STK 6.00 15.00
WMPR Keith Primeau 5.00 12.00
WMRB Ray Bourque BOS 15.00 40.00
WMRO Patrick Roy 20.00 50.00
WMSG Simon Gagne 8.00 20.00
WMSS Sergei Samsonov 6.00 15.00
WMSY Steve Yzerman 20.00 50.00
WMTH Jose Theodore 8.00 20.00
WMZP Zigmund Palffy 6.00 15.00

2002-03 SPx Winning Materials Silver

This 35-card set paralleled the base insert set but each card was serial-numbered out of 50 in silver foil on the card front. All cards carried a "WM" prefix on the card backs.

*STARS: .75X TO 2X BASIC CARDS

2002-03 SPx Xtreme Talents

This 28-card set featured game jersey swatches. Cards were serial-numbered out of 99.
ALL CARDS CARRY X PREFIX

2002-03 SPx Xtreme Talents Silver

This 28-card set paralleled the base insert set but each card was serial-numbered out of 50 in silver foil on the card front. All cards carried an "x" prefix on the card backs.

*STARS: .75X TO 2X BASIC CARDS

2003-04 SPx

This 240-card set consisted of several different subsets. Cards 1-100 were base veteran cards; cards 101-130 made up the Lasting Impressions subset and each card was serial-numbered out of 750; cards 131-155 made up the Xcite subset and each was serial-numbered out of 750; cards 156-175 made up the Next Generation subset and each was serial-numbered out of 500; cards 176-190 made up the Profiles subset and each was serial-numbered out of 250. Cards 191-207 and 230-240 were rookie cards that carried jersey swatches and were serial-numbered out of 999. Cards 208-229 were also rookie jersey cards but they also carried certified "cut" autographs; print runs for these can be found below. Cards 231-240 were only available in packs of UD Rookie Update.

COMP.SET w/o SP's (100) 25.00 50.00
1 Jean-Sebastien Giguere .30 .75
2 Stanislav Chistov .20 .50
3 Sergei Fedorov .50 1.25
4 Dany Heatley .30 .75
5 Ilya Kovalchuk .30 .75
6 Joe Thornton .40 1.00
7 Sergei Samsonov .25 .60
8 Glen Murray .25 .60
9 Felix Potvin .50 1.25
10 Miroslav Satan .25 .60
11 Maxim Afinogenov .20 .50
12 Chris Drury .25 .60
13 Jarome Iginla .30 .75
14 Roman Turek .25 .60
15 Steve Reinprecht .20 .50
16 Ron Francis .40 1.00
17 Jeff O'Neill .20 .50
18 Alexei Zhamnov .25 .60
19 Jocelyn Thibault .25 .60
20 Kyle Calder .20 .50
21 Joe Sakic .50 1.25
22 Teemu Selanne .60 1.50
23 Peter Forsberg .40 1.00
24 David Aebischer .25 .60
25 Paul Kariya .40 1.00
26 Marc Denis .25 .60
27 Rick Nash .30 .75
28 Todd Marchant .20 .50
29 Bill Guerin .30 .75
30 Marty Turco .30 .75
31 Mike Modano .50 1.25
32 Henrik Zetterberg .40 1.00
33 Brendan Shanahan .40 1.00
34 Steve Yzerman .75 2.00
35 Dominik Hasek .50 1.25
36 Ryan Smyth .25 .60
37 Ales Hemsky .30 .75
38 Tommy Salo .25 .60
39 Mike Comrie .25 .60
40 Stephen Weiss .20 .50
41 Roberto Luongo .50 1.25
42 Jay Bouwmeester .30 .75
43 Olli Jokinen .30 .75
44 Zigmund Palffy .30 .75
45 Alexander Frolov .25 .60
46 Roman Cechmanek .25 .60
47 Marian Gaborik .50 1.25
48 Manny Fernandez .25 .60
49 Pierre-Marc Bouchard .30 .75
50 Jose Theodore .30 .75
51 Saku Koivu .30 .75
52 Mike Komisarek .20 .50
53 Marcel Hossa .20 .50
54 Tomas Vokoun .25 .60
55 David Legwand .25 .60
56 Scott Stevens .30 .75
57 Martin Brodeur .60 1.50
58 Patrik Elias .30 .75
59 Jamie Langenbrunner .25 .60
60 Alexei Yashin .25 .60
61 Rick DiPietro .25 .60
62 Michael Peca .25 .60
63 Mike Dunham .25 .60
64 Eric Lindros .50 1.25
65 Alex Kovalev .25 .60
66 Patrick Lalime .25 .60
67 Marian Hossa .25 .60
68 Daniel Alfredsson .30 .75
69 Jason Spezza .30 .75
70 John LeClair .30 .75
71 Tony Amonte .25 .60
72 Simon Gagne .30 .75
73 Jeremy Roenick .30 .75
74 Chris Gratton .20 .50
75 Sean Burke .20 .50
76 Mike Johnson .20 .50
77 Martin Straka .20 .50
78 Mario Lemieux 1.00 2.50
79 Sebastien Caron .25 .60
80 Niko Dimitrakos .20 .50
81 Evgeni Nabokov .25 .60
82 Mike Ricci .25 .60
83 Chris Osgood .30 .75
84 Al MacInnis .30 .75
85 Keith Tkachuk .30 .75
86 Chris Pronger .25 .60
87 Nikolai Khabibulin .30 .75
88 Martin St. Louis .30 .75
89 Vincent Lecavalier .25 .60
90 Owen Nolan .25 .60
91 Alexander Mogilny .25 .60
92 Ed Belfour .30 .75
93 Mats Sundin .30 .75
94 Markus Naslund .30 .75
95 Johan Hedberg .25 .60
96 Todd Bertuzzi .30 .75
97 Ed Jovanovski .25 .60
98 Jaromir Jagr .75 2.00
99 Olaf Kolzig .30 .75
100 Peter Bondra .25 .60
101 Wayne Gretzky LI 12.00 30.00
102 Gordie Howe LI 8.00 20.00
103 Bobby Orr LI 8.00 20.00
104 Bobby Clarke LI 2.50 6.00
105 Scotty Bowman LI 2.50 6.00
106 Lanny McDonald LI 2.00 5.00
107 Stan Mikita LI 3.00 8.00
108 Ted Lindsay LI 2.50 6.00
109 Marcel Dionne LI 3.00 8.00
110 Johnny Bucyk LI 2.50 6.00
111 Jean Beliveau LI 3.00 8.00
112 Mike Bossy LI 2.50 6.00
113 Guy Lafleur LI 3.00 8.00
114 Mario Lemieux LI 8.00 20.00
115 Mark Messier LI 4.00 10.00
116 Patrick Roy LI 6.00 15.00
117 Martin Brodeur LI 5.00 12.00
118 Jarome Iginla LI 2.50 6.00
119 Mike Modano LI 4.00 10.00
120 Steve Yzerman LI 6.00 15.00
121 Peter Forsberg LI 3.00 8.00
122 Marian Gaborik LI 4.00 10.00
123 Scott Stevens LI 2.50 6.00
124 Paul Kariya LI 3.00 8.00
125 Tie Domi LI 2.00 5.00
126 Joe Sakic LI 4.00 10.00
127 Brendan Shanahan LI 3.00 8.00
128 Jeremy Roenick LI 2.50 6.00
129 Joe Thornton LI 3.00 8.00
130 Mats Sundin LI 2.50 6.00
131 Jean-Sebastien Giguere Xcite 2.50 6.00
132 Marian Gaborik Xcite 4.00 10.00
133 Joe Thornton Xcite 3.00 8.00
134 Saku Koivu Xcite 2.50 6.00
135 Dany Heatley Xcite 2.50 6.00
136 Vincent Lecavalier Xcite 2.00 5.00
137 Todd Bertuzzi Xcite 2.50 6.00
138 Sergei Fedorov Xcite 4.00 10.00
139 Marty Turco Xcite 2.50 6.00
140 Paul Kariya Xcite 3.00 8.00
141 Marian Hossa Xcite 2.00 5.00
142 Alexei Yashin Xcite 2.00 5.00
143 Zigmund Palffy Xcite 2.50 6.00
144 Mario Lemieux Xcite 8.00 20.00
145 Ilya Kovalchuk Xcite 2.50 6.00
146 Henrik Zetterberg Xcite 3.00 8.00
147 Mike Modano Xcite 4.00 10.00
148 Tony Amonte Xcite 2.00 5.00
149 Jason Spezza Xcite 2.50 6.00
150 Owen Nolan Xcite 2.00 5.00
151 Ales Hemsky Xcite 2.50 6.00
152 Markus Naslund Xcite 2.50 6.00
153 Teemu Selanne Xcite 5.00 12.00
154 Sergei Samsonov Xcite 2.00 5.00
155 Martin Brodeur Xcite 5.00 12.00
156 Dany Heatley NG 3.00 8.00
157 Marian Hossa NG 2.50 6.00
158 Jean-Sebastien Giguere NG 3.00 8.00
159 Joe Thornton NG 4.00 10.00
160 Henrik Zetterberg NG 4.00 10.00
161 Rick Nash NG 3.00 8.00
162 Jay Bouwmeester NG 3.00 8.00
163 Jason Spezza NG 3.00 8.00
164 Pavel Datsyuk NG 4.00 10.00
165 Mike Komisarek NG 2.00 5.00
166 Ales Hemsky NG 3.00 8.00
167 Marian Gaborik NG 5.00 12.00
168 Alexander Frolov NG 2.50 6.00
169 Steve Ott NG 2.50 6.00
170 Justin Williams NG 2.50 6.00
171 Pierre-Marc Bouchard NG 3.00 8.00
172 Ryan Miller NG 3.00 8.00
173 Ilya Kovalchuk NG 3.00 8.00
174 Kyle Calder NG 2.00 5.00
175 David Aebischer NG 2.50 6.00
176 Mario Lemieux PRO 15.00 40.00
177 Joe Thornton PRO 6.00 15.00
178 Martin Brodeur PRO 10.00 25.00
179 Steve Yzerman PRO 12.00 30.00
180 Joe Sakic PRO 8.00 20.00
181 Mats Sundin PRO 5.00 12.00
182 Saku Koivu PRO 5.00 12.00
183 Sergei Fedorov PRO 8.00 20.00
184 Jeremy Roenick PRO 5.00 12.00
185 Roberto Luongo PRO 8.00 20.00
186 Mike Modano PRO 8.00 20.00
187 Todd Bertuzzi PRO 5.00 12.00
188 Zigmund Palffy PRO 5.00 12.00
189 Jean-Sebastien Giguere PRO 5.00 12.00
190 Markus Naslund PRO 5.00 12.00
191 Dan Fritsche JSY RC 3.00 8.00
192 Tim Gleason JSY RC 4.00 10.00
193 Lasse Kukkonen JSY RC 3.00 8.00
194 John-Michael Liles JSY RC 4.00 10.00
195 Paul Martin JSY RC 4.00 10.00
196 Esa Pirnes JSY RC 3.00 8.00
197 Tom Preissing JSY RC 4.00 10.00
198 David Hale JSY RC 3.00 8.00
199 Marek Svatos JSY RC 6.00 15.00
200 Boyd Kane JSY RC 3.00 8.00
201 Matthew Lombardi JSY RC 4.00 10.00
202 Marek Zidlicky JSY RC 3.00 8.00
203 Matthew Spiller JSY RC 4.00 10.00
204 Andrew Peters JSY RC 4.00 10.00
205 Greg Campbell JSY RC 3.00 8.00
206 Sean Bergenheim JSY RC 4.00 10.00
207 Boyd Gordon JSY RC 4.00 10.00
208 P.Sejna JSY AU/925 RC 5.00 12.00
209 M.Stajan JSY AU/925 RC 6.00 15.00
210 M.Michalek JSY AU/925 RC 8.00 20.00
211 P.Vorobiev JSY AU/925 RC 5.00 12.00
212 D.Hamhuis JSY AU/925 RC 5.00 12.00
213 C.Higgins JSY AU/925 RC 8.00 20.00
214 A.Miettinen JSY AU/925 RC 6.00 15.00
215 C.Ehrhoff JSY AU/925 RC 5.00 12.00
216 A.Semin JSY AU/925 RC 10.00 25.00
217 A.Vermette JSY AU/925 RC 8.00 20.00
218 T.Moen JSY AU/925 RC 5.00 12.00
219 J.Pitkanen JSY AU/925 RC 6.00 15.00
220 P.Bergeron JSY AU/925 RC 25.00 50.00
221 J.Hudler JSY AU/925 RC 10.00 25.00
222 M.Fleury JSY AU/500 RC 30.00 80.00
223 D.Brown JSY AU/500 RC 10.00 25.00
224 J.Lupul JSY AU/925 RC 10.00 25.00
225 T.Ruutu JSY AU/500 RC 8.00 20.00
226 J.Tootoo JSY AU/500 RC 10.00 25.00
227 E.Staal JSY AU/500 RC 15.00 40.00
228 N.Horton JSY AU/500 RC 12.00 30.00
229 T.Salmalainen JSY AU/925 RC 4.00 10.00
230 John Pohl JSY RC 3.00 8.00
231 Sergei Zinovjev JSY RC 3.00 8.00
232 Ryan Kesler JSY RC 8.00 20.00
233 Dominic Moore JSY RC 3.00 8.00
234 Peter Sarno JSY RC 3.00 8.00
235 Ryan Malone JSY RC 6.00 15.00
236 Nikolai Zherdev JSY RC 6.00 15.00
237 Fredrik Sjostrom JSY RC 5.00 12.00
238 Derek Roy JSY RC 5.00 12.00
239 Mikko Luoma JSY RC 3.00 8.00
240 Trevor Daley JSY RC 5.00 12.00

2003-04 SPx Radiance

*1-100 VETS/50: 8X TO 20X BASIC CARDS
*101-155 LI/XCI/50: 1X TO 2.5X LI/XCI/750
*156-175 NG/50:: .8X TO 2X NG/500
*176-190 PRO/50: .5X TO 1.2X PO/250
*191-207 ROOK.JSY/50: .5X TO 1.2X JSY/999
*ROOK.JSY/AU/50: .6X TO 1.5X JSY AU/925
*ROOK.JSY/AU/50: .5X TO 1.2X JSY AU/500

115 Mark Messier LI 10.00 25.00
220 Patrice Bergeron 75.00 135.00
222 Marc-Andre Fleury 75.00 150.00
227 Eric Staal 40.00 80.00
228 Nathan Horton 30.00 60.00

2003-04 SPx Big Futures

PRINT RUN 99 SER.#'d SETS
*LIMITED: .75X TO 2X
LIMITED PRINT RUN 25 SER.#'d SETS

BFAA Ari Ahonen 6.00 15.00
BFAF Alexander Frolov 6.00 15.00
BFAH Ales Hemsky 10.00 25.00
BFAK Ales Kotalik 6.00 15.00
BFAS Alexander Svitov 6.00 15.00
BFBJ Barret Jackman 6.00 15.00
BFBO Brooks Orpik 6.00 15.00
BFCN Sebastien Caron 6.00 15.00
BFDB Dan Blackburn 6.00 15.00
BFDH Dany Heatley 10.00 25.00
BFHZ Henrik Zetterberg 12.50 30.00
BFIK Ilya Kovalchuk 12.50 30.00
BFIR Igor Radulov 6.00 15.00
BFJB Jay Bouwmeester 6.00 15.00
BFJB Jason Bacashihua 6.00 15.00
BFJL Jordan Leopold 6.00 15.00
BFJS Jason Spezza 12.50 30.00
BFJT Joe Thornton 15.00 40.00
BFMC Mike Cammalleri 8.00 20.00
BFMD Marc Denis 6.00 15.00
BFMG Mathieu Garon 6.00 15.00
BFMH Marcel Hossa 6.00 15.00
BFMP Mark Parrish 6.00 15.00
BFMT Marty Turco 8.00 20.00
BFOJ Olli Jokinen 6.00 15.00
BFPD Pavel Datsyuk 10.00 25.00
BFPL Pascal Leclaire 6.00 15.00
BFPMB Pierre-Marc Bouchard 6.00 15.00
BFRE Robert Esche 8.00 20.00
BFRN Rick Nash 12.50 30.00
BFSC Stanislav Chistov 6.00 15.00
BFSG Simon Gagne 10.00 25.00
BFSO Steve Ott 8.00 20.00
BFSW Stephen Weiss 8.00 20.00

2003-04 SPx Fantasy Franchise

PRINT RUN 75 SER.#'d SETS
*LIMITED/25: .5X TO 1.2X BASIC INSERTS

FFBLK Bure/Lindrs/Kova 10.00 25.00
FFDSA Drury/Satan/Afing 12.00 30.00
FFEHJ Elias/Hossa/Jagr 12.00 30.00
FFGC Fedrv/Gigre/Chstv 10.00 25.00
FFGRB Giguere/Roy/Brodr 30.00 80.00
FFHSL Hossa/Spez/Lalime 12.00 30.00
FFHYS Hull/Yzerman/Shan 25.00 60.00
FFHYZ Howe/Yzerman/Zett 40.00 100.00
FFKFB Koval/Fedorov/Bure 20.00 50.00
FFKSF Kariya/Selanne/Fors 25.00 60.00
FFKTH Kariya/Thorn/Heatley 15.00 40.00
FFLGH Lemieux/Gretz/Howe 50.00 120.00
FFLRA LeClair/JR/Amonte 15.00 40.00
FFMGT Modn/Guerin/Turco 15.00 40.00
FFNBM Naslund/Bert/Mrrison 15.00 40.00
FFNSM Nolan/Sundin/Mogilny 10.00 25.00
FFNSZ Nash/Spezza/Zetter 25.00 60.00

FFSBJ Steve/Brodeur/Jovo 15.00 40.00
FFTMS Thornt/Murry/Samsnv 15.00 40.00
FFTWM Tkchk/Wght/McInn 10.00 25.00

2003-04 SPx Hall Pass

PRINT RUN 75 SER.#'d SETS
*LIMITED: .75X TO 2X
LIMITED PRINT RUN 25 SER.#'d SETS
HPBH Brett Hull 15.00 40.00
HPCC Chris Chelios 10.00 25.00
HPDG Doug Gilmour 10.00 25.00
HPDH Dominik Hasek 12.50 30.00
HPMB Martin Brodeur 25.00 60.00
HPML Mario Lemieux 20.00 50.00
HPMM Mark Messier 12.50 30.00
HPPR Patrick Roy 20.00 50.00
HPRB Ray Bourque 12.50 30.00
HPRF Ron Francis 8.00 20.00

2003-04 SPx Origins

PRINT RUN 75 SER.#'d SETS
OAY Alexei Yashin 8.00 20.00
OBL Brian Leetch 8.00 20.00
OBS Brendan Shanahan 8.00 20.00
ODH Dany Heatley 15.00 40.00
ODW Doug Weight 8.00 20.00
OEB Ed Belfour 12.50 30.00
OHZ Henrik Zetterberg 15.00 40.00
OJI Jarome Iginla 12.50 30.00
OJJ Jaromir Jagr 15.00 40.00
OJR Jeremy Roenick 15.00 40.00
OJS Jason Spezza 10.00 25.00
OJSG Jean-Sebastien Giguere 8.00 20.00
OJT Joe Thornton 12.50 30.00
OMB Martin Brodeur 20.00 50.00
OMH Marian Hossa 10.00 25.00
OML Mario Lemieux 25.00 60.00
OMN Markus Naslund 8.00 20.00
OMS Mats Sundin 10.00 25.00
OON Owen Nolan 8.00 20.00
OPB Pavel Bure 8.00 20.00
OPE Patrik Elias 8.00 20.00
OPF Peter Forsberg 15.00 40.00
OPR Patrick Roy 20.00 50.00
OSF Sergei Fedorov 15.00 40.00
OSS Sergei Samsonov 8.00 20.00
OTS Teemu Selanne 10.00 25.00
OZP Zigmund Palffy 8.00 20.00

2003-04 SPx Signature Threads

This 26-card set featured over-sized jersey swatches and certified autographs. Each card was limited to 50 serial-numbered copies.

STAF Alexander Frolov 20.00 50.00
STAH Ales Hemsky 15.00 40.00
STEL Eric Lindros 20.00 50.00
STHZ Henrik Zetterberg 25.00 60.00
STIK Ilya Kovalchuk 40.00 100.00
STJI Jarome Iginla 25.00 60.00
STJL John LeClair 15.00 40.00
STJR Jeremy Roenick 30.00 80.00
STJS Jason Spezza 40.00 80.00
STJT Joe Thornton 40.00 100.00
STJT Jose Theodore 25.00 60.00
STJSG Jean-Sebastien Giguere 15.00 40.00
STMC Mike Comrie 15.00 40.00
STMG Marian Gaborik
STMH Marian Hossa 20.00 50.00
STMN Markus Naslund 20.00 50.00
STMT Marty Turco 15.00 40.00
STPB Pavel Bure 15.00 40.00
STRN Rick Nash 40.00 100.00
STSF Sergei Fedorov 25.00 60.00
STSK Saku Koivu 20.00 50.00
STSS Sergei Samsonov 15.00 40.00
STSY Steve Yzerman 75.00 150.00
STTB Todd Bertuzzi 20.00 50.00
STWG Wayne Gretzky 150.00 350.00
STZP Zigmund Palffy 15.00 40.00

2003-04 SPx Style

This 12-card set featured triple jersey swatches from some of the league's elite players. Cards were serial-numbered out of 99. A Limited parallel was also created and serial-numbered out of 25

*LIMITED: .5X TO 1.25X
SPXBG Brodeur/Giguere/Luongo 15.00 40.00
SPXBS Bertuzzi/Shanahan/Tkachuk 12.50 30.00
SPXBT Belfour/Turco/Esche 12.50 30.00
SPXDS Domi/Stock/Shelley 12.50 30.00
SPXGS Gretzky/Spezza/Thornton 75.00 200.00
SPXHH Hejduk/Hossa/Jagr 20.00 50.00
SPXHN Howe/Nash/Bertuzzi 25.00 60.00
SPXHT Howe/Thornton/Bertuzzi 20.00 50.00
SPXJB Jovanovksi/Blake/Chara 12.50 30.00
SPXLH Lemieux/Heatley/Fedorov 20.00 50.00
SPXNZ Naslund/Zetterberg/Sundin 20.00 50.00
SPXRB Roy/Brodeur/Giguere 25.00 60.00

2003-04 SPx VIP

PRINT RUN 50 SER.#'d SETS
*LIMITED: .6X TO 1.5X
LTD PRINT RUN 25 SER.#'d SETS
VIPDA C.Drury/M.Afinogenov 12.50 30.00
VIPFG S.Fedorov/J.Giguere 15.00 40.00
VIPFS P.Forsberg/J.Sakic 20.00 50.00
VIPKH S.Koivu/Marcel Hossa 12.50 30.00
VIPLS V.Lecavalier/M.St. Louis 15.00 40.00
VIPMG M.Modano/B.Guerin 12.50 30.00
VIPNB M.Naslund 12.50 30.00
T.Bertuzzi
VIPPF Z.Palffy/A.Frolov 12.50 30.00
VIPSB S.Stevens/M.Brodeur 25.00 60.00
VIPSK T.Selanne/P.Kariya 12.50 30.00
VIPTM J.Thornton/G.Murray 12.50 30.00
VIPYS S.Yzerman/B.Shanahan 25.00 60.00

2003-04 SPx Winning Materials

PRINT RUN 99 SER.#'d SETS
*LIMITED: .6X TO 1.5X
LTD PRINT RUN 25 SER.#'d SETS
WMAD Adam Deadmarsh 6.00 15.00
WMBE Ed Belfour 8.00 20.00
WMBL Rob Blake 6.00 15.00
WMBO Peter Bondra 8.00 20.00
WMCD Chris Drury 6.00 15.00
WMDB Dan Blackburn 6.00 15.00
WMDH Dominik Hasek 12.50 30.00
WMEB Ed Belfour 8.00 20.00
WMFO Peter Forsberg 12.50 30.00
WMGR Wayne Gretzky 40.00 100.00
WMGY Wayne Gretzky 40.00 100.00
WMJB Jay Bouwmeester 6.00 15.00
WMJF Jeff Friesen 6.00 15.00
WMJG Jaromir Jagr 10.00 25.00
WMJI Jarome Iginla 10.00 25.00
WMJJ Jaromir Jagr 10.00 25.00
WMJR Jeremy Roenick 12.50 30.00
WMJS Joe Sakic 15.00 40.00
WMJZ Jason Spezza 12.50 30.00
WMMD Mike Dunham 6.00 15.00
WMMH Marian Hossa 8.00 20.00
WMMM Mark Messier 15.00 40.00
WMMN Markus Naslund 8.00 20.00
WMMO Mike Modano 12.50 30.00
WMMS Mats Sundin 8.00 20.00
WMMT Marty Turco 6.00 15.00
WMPB Pavel Bure 8.00 20.00
WMPF Peter Forsberg 12.50 30.00
WMPK Paul Kariya 8.00 20.00
WMPR Patrick Roy 20.00 50.00
WMRB Ray Bourque 10.00 25.00
WMRN Rick Nash 15.00 40.00
WMRY Patrick Roy 20.00 50.00
WMSA Jason Spezza 12.50 30.00
WMSB Sean Burke 6.00 15.00
WMSF Sergei Fedorov 10.00 25.00
WMSW Stephen Weiss 6.00 15.00
WMTA Tony Amonte 6.00 15.00
WMTB Todd Bertuzzi 8.00 20.00
WMTH Jose Theodore 12.50 30.00
WMTS Teemu Selanne 8.00 20.00
WMWG Wayne Gretzky 30.00 80.00

2005-06 SPx

COMP.SET w/o SP's (90) 12.50 25.00
133-153 ROOKIE JSY PRINT RUN 1999
ROOKIE JSY AU PRINT RUN 499-1999
192-221/244-293 PRINT RUN 999
*MULTICOLOR JSY: 1X TO 2.5X HI
1 Jean-Sebastien Giguere .40 1.00
2 Sergei Fedorov .60 1.50
3 Ilya Kovalchuk .40 1.00
4 Kari Lehtonen .30 .75
5 Marian Hossa .30 .75
6 Patrice Bergeron .50 1.25
7 Joe Thornton .50 1.25
8 Andrew Raycroft .30 .75
9 Glen Murray .30 .75
10 Maxim Afinogenov .25 .60
11 Chris Drury .30 .75
12 Jarome Iginla .40 1.00
13 Miikka Kiprusoff .30 .75
14 Tony Amonte .30 .75
15 Erik Cole .30 .75
16 Eric Staal .50 1.25
17 Tuomo Ruutu .40 1.00
18 Nikolai Khabibulin .40 1.00
19 Joe Sakic .60 1.50
20 David Aebischer .30 .75
21 Milan Hejduk .30 .75
22 Alex Tanguay .40 1.00
23 Rick Nash .40 1.00
24 Nikolai Zherdev .25 .60
25 Mike Modano .60 1.50
26 Bill Guerin .40 1.00
27 Marty Turco .40 1.00
28 Steve Yzerman 1.00 2.50
29 Brendan Shanahan .50 1.25
30 Henrik Zetterberg .50 1.25
31 Nicklas Lidstrom .40 1.00
32 Ty Conklin .30 .75
33 Chris Pronger .30 .75
34 Ryan Smyth .30 .75
35 Roberto Luongo .60 1.50
36 Stephen Weiss .25 .60
37 Joe Nieuwendyk .40 1.00
38 Jeremy Roenick .40 1.00
39 Luc Robitaille .40 1.00
40 Alexander Frolov .25 .60
41 Marian Gaborik .60 1.50
42 Manny Fernandez .30 .75
43 Saku Koivu .40 1.00
44 Jose Theodore .40 1.00
45 Michael Ryder .30 .75
46 Mike Ribeiro .30 .75
47 Paul Kariya .50 1.25
48 Tomas Vokoun .30 .75
49 David Legwand .30 .75
50 Martin Brodeur .75 2.00
51 Patrik Elias .40 1.00
52 Alexander Mogilny .30 .75
53 Scott Gomez .30 .75
54 Alexei Yashin .30 .75
55 Rick DiPietro .30 .75
56 Miroslav Satan .30 .75
57 Jaromir Jagr 1.00 2.50
58 Tom Poti .25 .60
59 Kevin Weekes .30 .75
60 Dany Heatley .40 1.00
61 Daniel Alfredsson .40 1.00
62 Martin Havlat .40 1.00
63 Dominik Hasek .60 1.50
64 Jason Spezza .40 1.00
65 Peter Forsberg .50 1.25
66 Keith Primeau .40 1.00
67 Simon Gagne .40 1.00
68 Robert Esche .30 .75
69 Shane Doan .30 .75
70 Brett Hull .50 1.25
71 Curtis Joseph .40 1.00
72 Mario Lemieux 1.25 3.00
73 Zigmund Palffy .40 1.00
74 Mark Recchi .50 1.25
75 Evgeni Nabokov .30 .75
76 Patrick Marleau .40 1.00
77 Jonathan Cheechoo .40 1.00
78 Keith Tkachuk .40 1.00
79 Doug Weight .40 1.00
80 Vincent Lecavalier .30 .75
81 Sean Burke .25 .60
82 Brad Richards .40 1.00
83 Martin St. Louis .40 1.00
84 Mats Sundin .40 1.00
85 Ed Belfour .40 1.00
86 Jason Allison .30 .75
87 Eric Lindros .60 1.50
88 Markus Naslund .40 1.00
89 Brendan Morrison .25 .60
90 Olaf Kolzig .40 1.00
91 Bernie Geoffrion JSY AU 50.00 100.00
92 Bobby Hull JSY AU 25.00 60.00
93 Bobby Clarke JSY AU 25.00 60.00
94 Borje Salming JSY AU 15.00 40.00
95 Brian Leetch JSY AU 100.00 200.00
96 Bryan Trottier JSY AU 250.00 500.00
97 Cam Neely JSY AU 60.00 120.00
98 Dominik Hasek JSY AU 100.00 200.00
99 Doug Weight JSY AU 60.00 150.00
100 Ed Jovanovski JSY AU 25.00 60.00
101 Gerry Cheevers JSY AU 60.00 120.00
102 Gilbert Perreault JSY AU 60.00 120.00
103 Gordie Howe JSY AU 400.00 600.00
104 Grant Fuhr JSY AU 50.00 100.00
105 Guy Lafleur JSY AU 30.00 80.00
106 Jari Kurri JSY AU 15.00 40.00
107 Jeremy Roenick JSY AU 80.00 200.00
108 Johnny Bucyk JSY AU 50.00 100.00
109 Luc Robitaille JSY AU 40.00 100.00
110 Marcel Dionne JSY AU 25.00 60.00
111 Martin Brodeur JSY AU SP 500.00 800.00
112 Mats Sundin JSY AU SP 500.00 800.00
113 Mike Bossy JSY AU 25.00 60.00
114 Mike Modano JSY AU SP 300.00 500.00
115 Michael Peca JSY AU 20.00 50.00
116 Miroslav Satan JSY AU SP 150.00 300.00
117 Owen Nolan JSY AU/10
118 Peter Stastny JSY AU 25.00 60.00
119 Phil Esposito JSY AU SP 175.00 300.00
120 Ray Bourque JSY AU SP 500.00 1000.00
121 Roberto Luongo JSY AU 50.00 100.00
122 Rogie Vachon JSY AU 20.00 50.00
123 Ron Hextall JSY AU 60.00 150.00
124 Scotty Bowman JSY AU/10
125 Wayne Gretzky JSY AU/25 800.00 1200.00
126 Clark Gillies JSY AU SP 200.00 400.00
127 Lanny McDonald JSY AU 15.00 40.00
128 Tiger Williams JSY AU 15.00 40.00
129 Jean Beliveau JSY AU/25 250.00 400.00
130 Wayne Gretzky JSY AU/9
131 Butch Goring JSY AU 12.00 30.00
132 Guy Lapointe JSY AU 60.00 120.00
133 Duncan Keith JSY RC 10.00 25.00
134 Jaroslav Balastik JSY RC 3.00 8.00
135 Jay McClement JSY RC 3.00 8.00
136 Jeff Hoggan JSY RC 3.00 8.00
137 Andrew Alberts JSY RC 3.00 8.00
138 Kevin Dallman JSY RC 4.00 10.00
139 Maxime Talbot JSY RC 5.00 12.00
140 Raitis Ivanans JSY RC 3.00 8.00
141 Niklas Nordgren JSY RC 5.00 12.00
142 Kevin Nastiuk JSY RC 3.00 8.00
143 Jim Slater JSY RC 4.00 10.00
144 George Parros JSY RC 3.00 8.00
145 David Leneveu JSY RC 4.00 10.00
146 Andrew Wozniewski JSY RC 4.00 10.00
147 Ryan Hollweg JSY RC 3.00 8.00
148 Brett Lebda JSY RC 3.00 8.00
149 Patrick Eaves JSY RC 5.00 12.00
150 Ryane Clowe JSY RC 6.00 15.00
151 Josh Gorges JSY RC 4.00 10.00
152 Brad Winchester JSY RC 5.00 12.00
153 Matt Foy JSY RC 3.00 8.00
154 Wojtek Wolski JSY AU RC 4.00 10.00
155 Rene Bourque JSY AU RC 5.00 12.00
156 Gilbert Brule JSY AU RC 5.00 12.00
157 Jeff Woywitka JSY AU RC 3.00 8.00
158 Hannu Toivonen JSY AU RC 5.00 12.00
159 Al Montoya JSY AU RC 5.00 12.00
160 Yann Danis JSY AU RC 4.00 10.00
161 Alexander Perezhogin JSY AU RC 4.00 10.00
162 Cam Barker JSY AU RC 4.00 10.00
163 Zach Parise JSY AU RC 12.00 30.00
164 Dion Phaneuf JSY AU RC 8.00 20.00
165 Mike Richards JSY AU RC 10.00 25.00
166 Cam Ward JSY AU RC 8.00 20.00
167 Robert Nilsson JSY AU RC 5.00 12.00
168 Petteri Nokelainen JSY AU RC 3.00 8.00
169 Alexander Steen JSY AU RC 10.00 25.00
170 Ryan Getzlaf JSY AU RC 15.00 40.00
171 Corey Perry JSY AU RC 15.00 40.00
172 Rostislav Olesz JSY AU RC 4.00 10.00
173 Henrik Lundqvist JSY AU RC 25.00 60.00
174 Petr Prucha JSY AU RC 5.00 12.00
175 Jim Howard JSY AU RC 12.00 30.00
176 Johan Franzen JSY AU RC 8.00 20.00
177 Thomas Vanek JSY AU RC 10.00 25.00
178 Andrej Meszaros JSY AU RC 4.00 10.00
179 Brandon Bochenski JSY AU RC 5.00 12.00
180 Jussi Jokinen JSY AU RC 5.00 12.00
181 Braydon Coburn JSY AU RC 5.00 12.00
182 Ryan Suter JSY AU RC 6.00 15.00
183 Peter Budaj JSY AU RC 6.00 15.00
184 Brent Seabrook JSY AU RC 10.00 25.00
185 Keith Ballard JSY AU RC 4.00 10.00
186 Milan Jurcina JSY AU RC 4.00 10.00
187 Anthony Stewart JSY AU RC 4.00 10.00
188 Eric Nystrom JSY AU RC 4.00 10.00
189 Jeff Carter JSY AU/499 RC 15.00 40.00
190 Alex Ovechkin JSY AU/499 RC 150.00 250.00
191 Sidney Crosby JSY AU/499 RC 400.00 800.00
192 Lee Stempniak RC 2.50 6.00
193 Andy Roach RC 1.50 4.00
194 Colin Hemingway RC 1.50 4.00
195 Mark Streit RC 1.50 4.00
196 Wade Skolney RC 1.50 4.00
197 Chris Campoli RC 1.50 4.00
198 Paul Ranger RC 1.50 4.00
199 Kyle Brodziak RC 1.50 4.00
200 Chris Holt RC 1.50 4.00
201 Brian McGrattan RC 1.50 4.00
202 Adam Berkhoel RC 2.00 5.00
203 Nick Tarnasky RC 1.50 4.00
204 Evgeny Artyukhin RC 2.00 5.00
205 Timo Helbling RC 1.50 4.00
206 Derek Boogaard RC 3.00 8.00
207 Michael Wall RC 2.00 5.00
208 Steve Goertzen RC 1.50 4.00
209 Junior Lessard RC 1.50 4.00
210 Vojtech Polak RC 1.50 4.00
211 Andrew Penner RC 2.00 5.00
212 Jordan Sigalet RC 1.50 4.00
213 Kevin Colley RC 2.00 5.00
214 Dimitri Patzold RC 1.50 4.00
215 Christoph Schubert RC 1.50 4.00
216 Zenon Konopka RC 1.50 4.00
217 Staffan Kronwall RC 1.50 4.00
218 Erik Christensen RC 1.50 4.00
219 Brian Eklund RC 2.00 5.00
220 Rob McVicar RC 2.00 5.00
221 Tomas Fleischmann RC 2.50 6.00
222 Chris Thorburn JSY AU RC 4.00 10.00
223 Daniel Paille JSY AU RC 5.00 12.00
224 Andrew Ladd JSY AU RC 6.00 15.00
225 Danny Richmond JSY AU RC 3.00 8.00
226 Brad Richardson JSY AU RC 5.00 12.00
227 Ole-Kristian Tollefsen JSY AU RC 4.00 10.00
228 Alexandre Picard JSY AU RC 3.00 8.00
229 Kyle Quincey JSY AU RC 4.00 10.00
230 Valtteri Filppula JSY AU RC 6.00 15.00
231 Jeff Tambellini JSY AU RC 3.00 8.00
232 Mikko Koivu JSY AU RC 12.00 30.00
233 Maxim Lapierre JSY AU RC 5.00 12.00
234 Andrei Kostitsyn JSY AU RC 6.00 15.00
235 Barry Tallackson JSY AU RC 4.00 10.00
236 Jeremy Colliton JSY AU RC 3.00 8.00
237 R.J. Umberger JSY AU RC 5.00 12.00
238 Ben Eager JSY AU RC 4.00 10.00
239 Ryan Whitney JSY AU RC 5.00 12.00
240 Steve Bernier JSY AU RC 5.00 12.00
241 Ryan Craig JSY AU RC 3.00 8.00
242 Kevin Bieksa JSY AU RC 6.00 15.00
243 Jakub Klepis JSY AU RC 3.00 8.00
244 Dustin Penner RC 2.50 6.00
245 Ben Walter RC 1.50 4.00
246 Eric Healey RC 2.00 5.00
247 Nathan Paetsch RC 2.00 5.00
248 Jiri Novotny RC 2.00 5.00
249 Richie Regehr RC 1.50 4.00
250 Chad Larose RC 1.50 4.00
251 Martin St. Pierre RC 1.50 4.00
252 Corey Crawford RC 12.00 25.00
253 James Wisniewski RC 2.00 5.00
254 Vitaly Kolesnik RC 2.00 5.00
255 Geoff Platt RC 2.00 5.00
256 Joakim Lindstrom RC 1.50 4.00
257 Danny Syvret RC 1.50 4.00
258 Kyle Brodziak RC 1.50 4.00
259 J-F Jacques RC 1.50 4.00
260 Matt Greene RC 1.50 4.00
261 Greg Jacina RC 1.50 4.00
262 Rob Globke RC 1.50 4.00
263 Yanick Lehoux RC 2.50 6.00
264 Connor James RC 2.00 5.00
265 Richard Petiot RC 2.00 5.00
266 Petr Kanko RC 2.00 5.00
267 Matt Ryan RC 2.00 5.00
268 J-P Cote RC 1.50 4.00
269 Jonathan Ferland RC 2.00 5.00
270 Greg Zanon RC 2.00 5.00
271 Kevin Klein RC 1.50 4.00
272 Pekka Rinne RC 4.00 10.00
273 Cam Janssen RC 2.00 5.00
274 Jason Ryznar RC 1.50 4.00
275 Bruno Gervais RC 1.50 4.00
276 Stefan Ruzicka RC 1.50 4.00
277 Alexandre Picard RC 1.50 4.00
278 Matt Jones RC 1.50 4.00
279 Colby Armstrong RC 2.50 6.00
280 Doug Murray RC 1.50 4.00
281 Grant Stevenson RC 1.50 4.00
282 Dennis Wideman RC 1.50 4.00
283 Chris Beckford-Tseu RC 2.00 5.00
284 Gerald Coleman RC 1.50 4.00
285 Darren Reid RC 1.50 4.00
286 Doug O'Brien RC 1.50 4.00
287 Jay Harrison RC 2.00 5.00
288 Rick Rypien RC 4.00 10.00
289 Alexandre Burrows RC 3.00 8.00
290 Tomas Mojzis RC 1.50 4.00
291 David Steckel RC 2.00 5.00
292 Mike Green RC 3.00 8.00
293 Joey Tenute RC 2.00 5.00

2005-06 SPx Spectrum

*STARS: 15X TO 40X BASE HI
1-90 PRINT RUN 25 SER.#'d SETS
91-132 UNPRICED PRINT RUN 1
*ROOKIE JSY: .75 X TO 2X
*ROOKIE JSY/AU: 1X TO 2.5X
*ROOKIE: .6X TO 1.5X
133-221 PRINT RUN 25 SER.#'d SETS
28 Steve Yzerman 25.00 60.00
50 Martin Brodeur 25.00 60.00
72 Mario Lemieux 25.00 60.00
156 Gilbert Brule JSY AU 30.00 80.00
164 Dion Phaneuf JSY AU 60.00 150.00
166 Cam Ward JSY AU 60.00 120.00
170 Ryan Getzlaf JSY AU 60.00 120.00
173 Henrik Lundqvist JSY AU 100.00 250.00
189 Jeff Carter JSY AU 100.00 200.00
190 A.Ovechkin JSY AU 300.00 600.00
191 Sidney Crosby JSY AU 800.00 1200.00
224 Andrew Ladd 10.00 25.00
238 Ben Eager 6.00 15.00
242 Kevin Bieksa 10.00 25.00

2005-06 SPx Winning Combos

STATED PRINT RUN 350 SER.#'d SETS
*GOLD/99: .6X TO 1.5X BASIC JSY/350
WCAB D.Aebischer 5.00 12.00
R.Blake
WCAN S.Fedorov/T.Selanne 10.00 25.00
WCBA M.Biron/M.Afinogenov 4.00 10.00
WCBB R.Bourque/R.Blake 8.00 20.00
WCBE M.Brodeur/P.Elias 10.00 25.00
WCBF D.Brown/A.Frolov 5.00 12.00
WCBH J.Bouwmeester/N.Horton 5.00 12.00
WCBK M.Bossy/J.Kurri 5.00 12.00
WCBL R.Bourque/B.Leetch 8.00 20.00
WCBM T.Bertuzzi/B.Morrison 5.00 12.00
WCBN M.Biron/M.Noronen 4.00 10.00
WCBO G.Murray/J.Thornton 6.00 15.00
WCBP R.Blake/C.Pronger 5.00 12.00
WCBT M.Brodeur/J.Theodore 10.00 25.00
WCCH Z.Chara/M.Havlat 5.00 12.00
WCCN D.Cloutier/M.Naslund 5.00 12.00
WCCP T.Conklin/C.Pronger 4.00 10.00
WCDA B.Guerin/M.Modano 8.00 20.00
WCDB C.Drury/D.Briere 5.00 12.00
WCDN M.Denis/R.Nash 5.00 12.00
WCDR M.Dionne/L.Robitaille 6.00 15.00
WCED R.Smyth/A.Hemsky 4.00 10.00
WCEJ E.Staal/J.Williams 6.00 15.00
WCEM E.Belfour/M.Turco 5.00 12.00
WCFG S.Fedorov/J.Giguere 8.00 20.00
WCFL J.Bouwmeester/R.Luongo 8.00 20.00
WCFP P.Forsberg/K.Primeau 6.00 15.00
WCFR S.Fedorov/J.Roenick 8.00 20.00
WCFS P.Forsberg/J.Sakic 8.00 20.00
WCGC W.Gretzky/S.Crosby 30.00 80.00
WCGF M.Gaborik/M.Fernandez 8.00 20.00
WCGM W.Gretzky/M.Messier 20.00 50.00
WCGR S.Gagne/B.Richards 5.00 12.00
WCHA D.Heatley/D.Alfredsson 5.00 12.00
WCHD B.Hull/S.Doan 6.00 15.00
WCHH M.Hossa/M.Hossa 4.00 10.00
WCHJ B.Hull/C.Joseph 6.00 15.00
WCHK M.Hossa/S.Koivu 5.00 12.00
WCJM J.Jagr/M.Messier 12.00 30.00
WCJP J.Thornton/P.Bergeron 6.00 15.00
WCJY J.Jagr/A.Yashin 12.00 30.00
WCKI M.Kiprusoff/J.Iginla 5.00 12.00
WCKN M.Kiprusoff/E.Nabokov 4.00 10.00
WCKR N.Khabibulin/T.Ruutu 5.00 12.00
WCLA L.Robitaille/J.Roenick 5.00 12.00
WCLF M.Lemieux/J.LeClair 10.00 25.00
WCLJ M.Lemieux/J.Jagr 12.00 30.00
WCLK G.Lafleur/S.Koivu 6.00 15.00
WCMI M.Hossa/I.Kovalchuk 5.00 12.00
WCMM M.Modano/B.Morrow 8.00 20.00
WCMN B.Morrison/M.Naslund 5.00 12.00
WCMP M.Ribeiro/P.Bergeron 6.00 15.00
WCMT M.Messier/B.Trottier 8.00 20.00
WCNA O.Nolan/N.Antropov 4.00 10.00
WCND L.Nagy/S.Doan 4.00 10.00
WCNY M.Bossy/B.Trottier 6.00 15.00
WCNZ R.Nash/N.Zherdev 5.00 12.00
WCOT D.Heatley/M.Havlat 5.00 12.00
WCPE K.Primeau/R.Esche 5.00 12.00
WCPG K.Primeau/S.Gagne 5.00 12.00
WCPH M.Peca/A.Hemsky 4.00 10.00
WCPR Z.Palffy/M.Recchi 6.00 15.00
WCPS M.Parrish/M.Satan 4.00 10.00
WCRB A.Raycroft/P.Bergeron 6.00 15.00
WCRC W.Redden/Z.Chara 5.00 12.00
WCRK M.Ryder/S.Koivu 5.00 12.00
WCRL A.Raycroft/K.Lehtonen 4.00 10.00
WCRR M.Ryder/M.Ribeiro 4.00 10.00
WCRT M.Ribeiro/J.Theodore 5.00 12.00
WCRW H.Zetterberg/N.Lidstrom 6.00 15.00
WCSA J.Spezza/D.Alfredsson 5.00 12.00
WCSB J.Spezza/P.Bergeron 6.00 15.00
WCSC R.Smyth/T.Conklin 4.00 10.00
WCSF M.St. Louis/R.Fedotenko 5.00 12.00
WCSH J.Sakic/M.Hejduk 8.00 20.00
WCSL M.St.Louis/V.Lecavalier 5.00 12.00
WCSN M.Sundin/O.Nolan 5.00 12.00
WCSR S.Stevens/B.Rafalski 5.00 12.00
WCST M.Turco/B.Morrow 5.00 12.00
WCSW M.Stajan/J.Williams 4.00 10.00
WCSY B.Shanahan/S.Yzerman 10.00 25.00
WCTB B.Richards/V.Lecavalier 5.00 12.00
WCTH A.Tanguay/M.Hejduk 5.00 12.00
WCTM M.Turco/M.Modano 8.00 20.00
WCTO M.Sundin/E.Belfour 5.00 12.00
WCVA E.Jovanovski/B.Morrison 4.00 10.00
WCVH T.Vokoun/D.Hasek 8.00 20.00
WCWH S.Weiss/N.Horton 5.00 12.00
WCWL P.Worrell/G.Laraque 4.00 10.00
WCWM D.Weight/A.MacInnis 5.00 12.00
WCWT D.Weight/K.Tkachuk 5.00 12.00
WCZD H.Zetterberg/K.Draper 6.00 15.00
WCZL H.Zetterberg/M.Legace 6.00 15.00

2005-06 SPx Winning Combos Autographs

PRINT RUN 25 SER.#'d SETS
AWCAB David Aebischer 20.00 50.00
Rob Blake
AWCAK A.Raycroft/K.Lehtonen 50.00 100.00
AWCBA Martin Biron 30.00 80.00
Maxim Afinogenov
AWCBB R.Bourque/R.Blake 30.00 80.00
AWCBF Dustin Brown 20.00 50.00
Alexander Frolov
AWCBL Jay Bouwmeester 25.00 60.00
Roberto Luongo
AWCBN Martin Biron 20.00 50.00
Mikka Noronen
AWCBO Andrew Raycroft 25.00 60.00
Patrice Bergeron
AWCBP R.Blake/C.Pronger 30.00 80.00
AWCBT M.Brodeur/J.Theodore 75.00 150.00
AWCCH Zdeno Chara 25.00 60.00
Martin Havlat
AWCCP Ty Conklin 20.00 50.00
Chris Pronger
AWCDB Chris Drury 20.00 50.00
Daniel Briere
AWCDR M.Dionne/Robitaille 30.00 80.00
AWCGC W.Gretzky/S.Crosby 2500.00 3500.00
AWCGR Simon Gagne 20.00 50.00
Brad Richards
AWCHA Dany Heatley 30.00 80.00
Daniel Alfredsson
AWCHH Dany Heatley 30.00 80.00
Martin Havlat
AWCHK M. Hossa/I. Kovalchuk 50.00 100.00
AWCJM Ed Jovanovski 30.00 80.00
Brendan Morrison
AWCLA Robitaille/Roenick 30.00 80.00
AWCLK Guy Lafleur 30.00 80.00
Saku Koivu
AWCMM Mike Modano 30.00 80.00
Brenden Morrow
AWCMN Brendan Morrison 20.00 50.00
Markus Naslund
AWCMS Marcel Hossa 20.00 50.00
Saku Koivu
AWCNA Owen Nolan 20.00 50.00
Nik Antropov
AWCND Ladislav Nagy 25.00 60.00
Shane Doan
AWCNY M.Bossy/B.Trottier 30.00 80.00
AWCNZ Rick Nash 25.00 60.00
Nikolai Zherdev
AWCOT J.Spezza/D.Alfredsson 25.00 60.00
AWCPE Keith Primeau 20.00 50.00
Robert Esche
AWCPH Michael Peca 20.00 50.00
Ales Hemsky
AWCPS Mark Parrish 30.00 80.00
Miroslav Satan
AWCRB Mike Ribeiro 20.00 50.00
Patrice Bergeron
AWCRL B.Richards/Lecavalier 30.00 60.00
AWCRR Michael Ryder 30.00 80.00
Mike Ribeiro
AWCSA Matt Stajan 30.00 80.00
Nik Antropov
AWCSC Ryan Smyth 30.00 80.00
Ty Conklin
AWCSF Martin St. Louis 30.00 80.00
Ruslan Fedotenko
AWCSH Ryan Smyth 30.00 80.00
Ales Hemsky
AWCSL Martin St. Louis 30.00 80.00
Vincent Lecavalier
AWCSW Eric Staal 20.00 50.00
Justin Williams
AWCTB Joe Thornton 30.00 80.00
Patrice Bergeron
AWCTH Alex Tanguay 20.00 50.00
Milan Hejduk
AWCTM Marty Turco 20.00 50.00
Brenden Morrow
AWCWH Stephen Weiss 30.00 80.00
Nathan Horton
AWCWL Peter Worrell 30.00 80.00
Georges Laraque
AWCZD Zetterberg/K.Draper 30.00 80.00
AWCZL Henrik Zetterberg 30.00 80.00
Manny Legace

2005-06 SPx Winning Materials

STATED PRINT RUN 350 SER.#'d SETS
WMAE David Aebischer 3.00 8.00
WMAF Alexander Frolov 2.50 6.00
WMAH Ales Hemsky 3.00 8.00
WMAR Andrew Raycroft 3.00 8.00
WMAT Alex Tanguay 4.00 10.00
WMBG Bill Guerin 4.00 10.00
WMBH Brett Hull 5.00 12.00
WMBL Brian Leetch 4.00 10.00
WMBM Brendan Morrison 2.50 6.00
WMBR Brad Richards 4.00 10.00
WMBS Brendan Shanahan 5.00 12.00
WMBT Bryan Trottier 5.00 12.00
WMBY Mike Bossy 4.00 10.00
WMCD Chris Drury 3.00 8.00
WMCJ Curtis Joseph 4.00 10.00
WMCP Chris Pronger 3.00 8.00
WMDA Daniel Alfredsson 4.00 10.00
WMDB Daniel Briere 4.00 10.00
WMDH Dany Heatley 6.00 15.00
WMDW Doug Weight 4.00 10.00
WMEB Ed Belfour 4.00 10.00
WMED Eric Daze 3.00 8.00
WMEJ Ed Jovanovski 3.00 8.00
WMGL Guy Lafleur 5.00 12.00
WMHA Dominik Hasek 10.00 25.00
WMHO Marian Hossa 3.00 8.00
WMHV Martin Havlat 4.00 10.00
WMHZ Henrik Zetterberg 5.00 12.00
WMIK Ilya Kovalchuk 6.00 15.00
WMJG Jean-Sebastien Giguere 4.00 10.00
WMJI Jarome Iginla 6.00 15.00
WMJJ Jaromir Jagr 6.00 15.00
WMJL John LeClair 4.00 10.00
WMJO Jose Theodore 4.00 10.00
WMJR Jeremy Roenick 4.00 10.00
WMJS Joe Sakic 10.00 25.00
WMJT Joe Thornton 8.00 20.00
WMJW Justin Williams 3.00 8.00
WMKD Kris Draper 5.00 12.00
WMKF Miikka Kiprusoff 3.00 8.00
WMKL Kari Lehtonen 3.00 8.00
WMKP Keith Primeau 4.00 10.00
WMKT Keith Tkachuk 4.00 10.00
WMLN Ladislav Nagy 2.50 6.00
WMLR Luc Robitaille 4.00 10.00
WMLX Mario Lemieux 15.00 40.00
WMMB Martin Brodeur 12.00 30.00
WMMC Bryan McCabe 2.50 6.00
WMMD Marcel Dionne 5.00 12.00
WMMG Marian Gaborik 8.00 20.00
WMMH Milan Hejduk 3.00 8.00
WMML Manny Legace 4.00 10.00
WMMM Mike Modano 6.00 15.00
WMMN Markus Naslund 4.00 10.00
WMMP Mark Parrish 2.50 6.00
WMMR Mike Ribeiro 3.00 8.00
WMMS Mark Messier 6.00 15.00
WMMW Brenden Morrow 3.00 8.00
WMNA Nik Antropov 3.00 8.00
WMNH Nathan Horton 4.00 10.00
WMNK Nikolai Khabibulin 4.00 10.00
WMNZ Nikolai Zherdev 2.50 6.00
WMOK Olaf Kolzig 4.00 10.00
WMON Owen Nolan 3.00 8.00
WMPB Patrice Bergeron 5.00 12.00
WMPE Michael Peca 3.00 8.00
WMPF Peter Forsberg 6.00 15.00
WMPM Patrick Marleau 4.00 10.00
WMRE Robert Esche 3.00 8.00
WMRF Ruslan Fedotenko 2.50 6.00
WMRL Roberto Luongo 6.00 15.00
WMRN Rick Nash 4.00 10.00
WMRS Ryan Smyth 3.00 8.00
WMRY Michael Ryder 3.00 8.00
WMRZ Richard Zednik 2.50 6.00
WMSA Miroslav Satan 3.00 8.00
WMSC Sidney Crosby 40.00 80.00
WMSD Shane Doan 3.00 8.00
WMSF Sergei Fedorov 6.00 15.00
WMSG Simon Gagne 4.00 10.00
WMSK Saku Koivu 4.00 10.00
WMSL Martin St. Louis 4.00 10.00
WMSP Jason Spezza 4.00 10.00
WMST Matt Stajan 3.00 8.00
WMSU Mats Sundin 4.00 10.00
WMSW Stephen Weiss 2.50 6.00
WMSY Steve Yzerman 12.00 30.00
WMTC Ty Conklin 3.00 8.00
WMTR Tuomo Ruutu 4.00 10.00
WMTS Teemu Selanne 6.00 15.00
WMTU Marty Turco 4.00 10.00
WMVL Vincent Lecavalier 3.00 8.00
WMWG Wayne Gretzky 25.00 50.00
WMZC Zdeno Chara 4.00 10.00
WMZP Zigmund Palffy 4.00 10.00

2005-06 SPx Winning Materials Autographs

PRINT RUN 50 SER.#'d SETS
AWMAF Alexander Frolov 15.00 40.00
AWMAR Andrew Raycroft 15.00 40.00
AWMAT Alex Tanguay 15.00 40.00
AWMBL Brian Leetch 15.00 40.00
AWMBM Brenden Morrow 15.00 40.00
AWMBR Brad Richards 15.00 40.00
AWMCD Chris Drury 15.00 40.00
AWMCP Chris Pronger 15.00 40.00
AWMDA David Aebischer 15.00 40.00
AWMDH Dany Heatley 15.00 40.00
AWMDW Doug Weight 15.00 40.00
AWMED Eric Daze 15.00 40.00
AWMHA Dominik Hasek 40.00 80.00
AWMHO Marian Hossa 15.00 40.00
AWMHV Martin Havlat 15.00 40.00
AWMHZ Henrik Zetterberg 20.00 50.00
AWMIK Ilya Kovalchuk 30.00 80.00
AWMJI Jarome Iginla 25.00 60.00
AWMJO Joe Thornton 25.00 60.00
AWMJR Jeremy Roenick 20.00 50.00
AWMJS Jason Spezza 25.00 60.00
AWMJT Jose Theodore 20.00 50.00
AWMJW Justin Williams 15.00 40.00
AWMKD Kris Draper 15.00 40.00
AWMKP Keith Primeau 15.00 40.00
AWMMB Martin Brodeur 40.00 100.00
AWMMC Bryan McCabe 15.00 40.00
AWMMH Milan Hejduk 15.00 40.00
AWMMN Markus Naslund 20.00 50.00
AWMMO Mike Modano 30.00 60.00
AWMMR Mike Ribeiro 15.00 40.00
AWMMT Marty Turco 12.50 30.00
AWMNH Nathan Horton 15.00 40.00
AWMNZ Nikolai Zherdev 15.00 40.00
AWMOK Olaf Kolzig 12.50 30.00
AWMPE Michael Peca 15.00 40.00
AWMPR Patrick Roy 60.00 120.00
AWMRE Robert Esche 15.00 40.00
AWMRL Roberto Luongo 20.00 50.00
AWMRN Rick Nash 20.00 50.00
AWMRS Ryan Smyth 15.00 40.00
AWMRY Michael Ryder 15.00 40.00
AWMRZ Richard Zednik 15.00 40.00
AWMSD Shane Doan 15.00 40.00
AWMSG Simon Gagne 20.00 50.00
AWMSL Martin St. Louis 15.00 40.00
AWMTC Ty Conklin 15.00 40.00
AWMVL Vincent Lecavalier 25.00 60.00
AWMWG Wayne Gretzky 150.00 300.00
AWMZC Zdeno Chara 15.00 40.00

2005-06 SPx Winning Materials Gold

*GOLD: .6X TO 1.5X BASIC WM
PRINT RUN 99 SER.#'d SETS
WMES Eric Staal 12.00 30.00
WMMB Martin Brodeur 12.00 30.00
WMPK Paul Kariya 8.00 20.00
WMSC Sidney Crosby 50.00 120.00

2005-06 SPx Xcitement Legends

STATED PRINT RUN 499 SER.#'d SETS
XLBB Bill Barber 2.00 5.0
XLBC Bobby Clarke 2.50 6.0
XLBG Bernie Geoffrion 2.00 5.0
XLBH Bobby Hull 4.00 10.0
XLBN Bob Nystrom 1.50 4.0
XLBO Johnny Bower 3.00 8.0
XLBP Brad Park 2.00 5.0
XLBT Bryan Trottier 3.00 8.0
XLBU Johnny Bucyk 2.00 5.0
XLCG Clark Gillies 2.50 6.0
XLCN Cam Neely 2.50 6.0
XLDC Don Cherry 2.50 6.0
XLDM Dickie Moore 1.50 4.0
XLDS Denis Savard 3.00 8.0
XLDT Dave Taylor 2.00 5.0
XLFM Frank Mahovlich 2.50 6.0
XLGA Glenn Anderson 2.50 6.0
XLGC Gerry Cheevers 5.00 12.0
XLGF Grant Fuhr 2.50 6.0
XLGH Gordie Howe 8.00 20.0
XLGL Guy Lafleur 3.00 8.0
XLGO Butch Goring 1.50 4.0
XLGP Gilbert Perreault 2.50 6.0
XLHL Hakan Loob 1.50 4.0
XLJB Jean Beliveau 2.50 6.0
XLJK Jari Kurri 2.50 6.0
XLKH Ken Hodge 2.00 5.0
XLKM Ken Morrow 1.50 4.0
XLLA Guy Lapointe 2.00 5.0
XLLM Lanny McDonald 2.50 6.0
XLMB Mike Bossy 2.50 6.0
XLMD Marcel Dionne 3.00 8.0
XLMN Mats Naslund 2.50 6.0
XLPE Phil Esposito 4.00 10.0
XLPR Patrick Roy 6.00 15.0
XLPS Peter Stastny 2.50 6.0
XLRH Ron Hextall 4.00 10.0
XLRK Red Kelly 2.50 6.0
XLRL Reggie Leach 1.50 4.0
XLRM Rick Martin 1.50 4.0
XLRR Rene Robert 1.50 4.0
XLRV Rogie Vachon 3.00 8.0
XLSA Derek Sanderson 1.50 4.0
XLSB Scotty Bowman 2.00 5.0
XLSM Stan Mikita 3.00 8.0
XLTE Tony Esposito 2.50 6.0
XLTO Terry O'Reilly 2.00 5.0
XLTW Tiger Williams 2.00 5.0
XLWC Wayne Cashman 1.50 4.0
XLWG Wayne Gretzky 12.00 30.0

2005-06 SPx Xcitement Legends Gold

*GOLD: .75X TO 2X
PRINT RUN 99 SER.#'d SETS

2005-06 SPx Xcitement Rookies

PRINT RUN 999 SER.#'d SETS
*GOLD/99: .8X TO 2X BASIC INSERTS
XRAA Andrew Alberts 1.25 3.00
XRAM Andrej Meszaros 1.50 4.00
XRAO Alexander Ovechkin 8.00 20.00
XRAP Alexander Perezhogin 1.50 4.00
XRAS Alexander Steen 4.00 10.00
XRAW Andrew Wozniewski 1.50 4.00
XRBB Brandon Bochenski 2.00 5.00
XRBC Braydon Coburn 2.00 5.00
XRBS Brent Seabrook 4.00 10.00
XRCB Cam Barker 1.50 4.00
XRCC Chris Campoli 1.25 3.00
XRCP Corey Perry 8.00 20.00
XRCW Cam Ward 3.00 8.00
XRDK Duncan Keith 4.00 10.00
XRDL David Leneveu 1.50 4.00
XRDP Dion Phaneuf 3.00 8.00
XREN Eric Nystrom 1.50 4.00
XRGB Gilbert Brule 2.00 5.00
XRHL Henrik Lundqvist 8.00 20.00
XRHT Hannu Toivonen 2.00 5.00
XRJC Jeff Carter 3.00 8.00
XRJF Johan Franzen 3.00 8.00
XRJH Jim Howard 4.00 10.00
XRJJ Jussi Jokinen 2.00 5.00
XRJM Jay McClement 1.25 3.00
XRJS Jim Slater 1.50 4.00
XRJW Jeff Woywitka 1.25 3.00
XRKB Keith Ballard 1.50 4.00
XRKD Kevin Dallman 1.50 4.00
XRKN Kevin Nastiuk 1.25 3.00
XRMF Matt Foy 1.25 3.00
XRMJ Milan Jurcina 1.50 4.00
XRMO Alvaro Montoya 2.00 5.00
XRMR Mike Richards 4.00 10.00
XRMT Maxime Talbot 2.00 5.00
XRPB Peter Budaj 2.50 6.00
XRPN Petteri Nokelainen 1.25 3.00
XRPP Petr Prucha 2.00 5.00
XRRB Rene Bourque 2.00 5.00
XRRC Ryane Clowe 2.50 6.00
XRRG Ryan Getzlaf 5.00 12.00
XRRN Robert Nilsson 2.00 5.00
XRRO Rostislav Olesz 1.50 4.00
XRRS Ryan Suter 2.50 6.00
XRSC Sidney Crosby 25.00 60.00
XRST Anthony Stewart 1.50 4.00
XRTV Thomas Vanek 4.00 10.00
XRWW Wojtek Wolski 1.50 4.00
XRYD Yann Danis 1.50 4.00
XRZP Zach Parise 5.00 12.00

2005-06 SPx Xcitement Superstars

STATED PRINT RUN 499 SER.#'d SETS
XSAT Alex Tanguay 2.00 5.00
XSBG Bill Guerin 2.00 5.00
XSBH Brett Hull 2.50 6.00
XSBL Brian Leetch 2.00 5.00
XSBR Brad Richards 2.00 5.00
XSBS Brendan Shanahan 2.50 6.00
XSCP Chris Pronger 1.50 4.00
XSDA Daniel Alfredsson 2.00 5.00
XSDH Dany Heatley 2.00 5.00
XSEB Ed Belfour 2.00 5.00
XSED Eric Daze 1.50 4.00
XSEJ Ed Jovanovski 1.50 4.00
XSEN Evgeni Nabokov 1.50 4.00

HA Dominik Hasek 3.00 8.00
HK Milan Hejduk 1.50 4.00
HV Martin Havlat 2.00 5.00
HZ Henrik Zetterberg 2.50 6.00
K Ilya Kovalchuk 2.00 5.00
JI Jarome Iginla 2.00 5.00
JJ Jaromir Jagr 5.00 12.00
JO Joe Thornton 2.50 6.00
JR Jeremy Roenick 2.00 5.00
JS Joe Sakic 3.00 8.00
JT Jose Theodore 2.00 5.00
KD Kris Draper 2.50 6.00
KP Keith Primeau 2.00 5.00
KT Keith Tkachuk 2.00 5.00
LR Luc Robitaille 2.00 5.00
MB Martin Brodeur 4.00 10.00
MG Marian Gaborik 3.00 8.00
MH Marian Hossa 1.50 4.00
ML Mario Lemieux 6.00 15.00
MM Mark Messier 3.00 8.00
MN Markus Naslund 2.00 5.00
MO Mike Modano 3.00 8.00
MP Mark Parrish 1.25 3.00
MS Mats Sundin 2.00 5.00
MT Marty Turco 2.00 5.00
OK Olaf Kolzig 2.00 5.00
ON Owen Nolan 1.50 4.00
RB Rob Blake 2.00 5.00
RL Roberto Luongo 3.00 8.00
RN Rick Nash 2.00 5.00
SD Shane Doan 1.50 4.00
SF Sergei Fedorov 3.00 8.00
SG Simon Gagne 2.00 5.00
SK Saku Koivu 2.00 5.00
SL Martin St. Louis 2.00 5.00
SY Steve Yzerman 5.00 12.00
VL Vincent Lecavalier 1.50 4.00

2005-06 SPx Xcitement Superstars Gold

OLD: .5X TO 1.25X
INT RUN 99 SER.#'d SETS
MM Mark Messier 4.00 10.00

2006-07 SPx

is 213-card set was issued in four-card packs, with a 99 SRP, which came 18 packs to a box and 14 xes to a case. Cards numbered 1-100 feature erans while cards 101-121 have a player-worn sey swatch and cards numbered 122-142 have both layer-worn swatch and and an autograph. Cards mbered 143-163 are Rookie Cards with a player rn swatch while cards numbered 164-195 are okie Cards with both a player-worn swatch and an tograph. The set concludes with Rookie Cards from 6-213 which were issued to a stated print run of 99 serial numbered sets.

Chris Pronger .30 .75
Teemu Selanne .75 2.00
Jean-Sebastien Giguere .40 1.00
Kari Lehtonen .30 .75
Marian Hossa .30 .75
Ilya Kovalchuk .40 1.00
Patrice Bergeron .50 1.25
Zdeno Chara .40 1.00
Brad Boyes .25 .60
Ryan Miller .40 1.00
Chris Drury .30 .75
Alex Tanguay .25 .60
Dion Phaneuf .40 1.00
Jarome Iginla .40 1.00
Miikka Kiprusoff .30 .75
Eric Staal .50 1.25
Cam Ward .40 1.00
Rod Brind'Amour .40 1.00
Nikolai Khabibulin .40 1.00
Martin Havlat .25 .60
Tuomo Ruutu .40 1.00
Joe Sakic .60 1.50
Marek Svatos .25 .60
Jose Theodore .40 1.00
Milan Hejduk .30 .75
Rick Nash .40 1.00
Sergei Fedorov .60 1.50
Fredrik Modin .25 .60
Eric Lindros .60 1.50
Mike Modano .60 1.50
Brenden Morrow .30 .75
Marty Turco .40 1.00
Pavel Datsyuk .50 1.25
Gordie Howe 1.25 3.00
Nicklas Lidstrom .40 1.00
Henrik Zetterberg .50 1.25
Dominik Hasek .50 1.25
Ryan Smyth .30 .75
Ales Hemsky .30 .75
Joffrey Lupul .30 .75
Wayne Gretzky 2.00 5.00
Olli Jokinen .40 1.00
Todd Bertuzzi .40 1.00
Ed Belfour .40 1.00
Jay Bouwmeester .40 1.00
Alexander Frolov .25 .60
Rob Blake .40 1.00
Marian Gaborik .50 1.25
Manny Fernandez .30 .75
Pavol Demitra .50 1.25
Alexei Kovalev .30 .75
Cristobal Huet .30 .75
Saku Koivu .40 1.00
Michael Ryder .25 .60
Mike Ribeiro .30 .75
Paul Kariya .50 1.25
Tomas Vokoun .30 .75
Jason Arnott .30 .75
Martin Brodeur .75 2.00
Brian Gionta .30 .75
Patrik Elias .40 1.00
Scott Gomez .30 .75
Rick DiPietro .30 .75
Miroslav Satan .30 .75
Alexei Yashin .30 .75
Brendan Shanahan .50 1.25
Henrik Lundqvist .75 2.00
Jaromir Jagr 1.00 2.50
Petr Prucha .30 .75
Daniel Alfredsson .40 1.00
Jason Spezza .40 1.00
Dany Heatley .40 1.00
Martin Gerber .30 .75
Jeff Carter .40 1.00
Peter Forsberg .50 1.25
Simon Gagne .40 1.00
Shane Doan .30 .75
Jeremy Roenick .40 1.00
Curtis Joseph .40 1.00
Mark Recchi .50 1.25
Sidney Crosby 1.50 4.00
Marc-Andre Fleury .60 1.50
Mario Lemieux 1.25 3.00
Patrick Marleau .40 1.00
85 Joe Thornton .50 1.25
86 Jonathan Cheechoo .40 1.00
87 Keith Tkachuk .40 1.00
88 Doug Weight .40 1.00
89 Brad Richards .40 1.00
90 Vincent Lecavalier .30 .75
91 Martin St. Louis .40 1.00
92 Mats Sundin .40 1.00
93 Andrew Raycroft .30 .75
94 Darcy Tucker .30 .75
95 Alexander Steen .40 1.00
96 Roberto Luongo .60 1.50
97 Markus Naslund .30 .75
98 Brendan Morrison .25 .60
99 Olaf Kolzig .40 1.00
100 Alexander Ovechkin 1.50 4.00
101 Teemu Selanne JSY 12.00 30.00
102 Ilya Kovalchuk JSY 6.00 15.00
103 Jarome Iginla JSY 6.00 15.00
104 Mark Recchi JSY 8.00 20.00
105 Eric Staal JSY 8.00 20.00
106 Joe Sakic JSY 10.00 25.00
107 Sergei Fedorov JSY 10.00 25.00
108 Mike Modano JSY 10.00 25.00
109 Brendan Shanahan JSY 8.00 20.00
110 Mats Sundin JSY 6.00 15.00
111 Bill Ranford JSY 6.00 15.00
112 Roberto Luongo JSY 10.00 25.00
113 Alexei Kovalev JSY 5.00 12.00
114 Paul Kariya JSY 8.00 20.00
115 Jaromir Jagr JSY 15.00 40.00
116 Peter Forsberg JSY 8.00 20.00
117 Richard Brodeur JSY 5.00 12.00
118 Peter Stastny JSY 6.00 15.00
119 Ron Hextall JSY 10.00 25.00
120 Eric Lindros JSY 10.00 25.00
121 Dave Williams JSY 5.00 12.00
122 Cam Neely JSY AU 12.00 30.00
123 Ray Bourque JSY AU 40.00 100.00
124 Gilbert Perreault JSY AU 12.00 30.00
125 Lanny McDonald JSY AU 12.00 30.00
126 Gordie Howe JSY AU 100.00 200.00
127 Grant Fuhr JSY AU 15.00 40.00
128 Wayne Gretzky JSY AU 150.00 300.00
129 Guy Lafleur JSY AU 40.00 100.00
130 Patrick Roy JSY AU 40.00 100.00
131 Martin Brodeur JSY AU 30.00 80.00
132 Mike Bossy JSY AU 12.00 30.00
133 D. Hasek JSY AU 20.00 50.00
134 Sidney Crosby JSY AU 75.00 150.00
135 Mario Lemieux SP JSY AU 125.00 250.00
136 Al MacInnis JSY AU 12.00 30.00
137 Borje Salming JSY AU 12.00 30.00
138 Darryl Sittler SP JSY AU 100.00 200.00
139 Steve Shutt JSY AU 12.00 30.00
140 Ed Belfour JSY AU 12.00 30.00
141 Bobby Clarke JSY AU 12.00 30.00
142 Billy Smith JSY AU 12.00 30.00
143 Dustin Byfuglien JSY RC 6.00 15.00
144 D. Stafford JSY AU RC EXCH 5.00 12.00
145 Frank Doyle JSY RC 3.00 8.00
146 Carsen Germyn JSY RC 2.50 6.00
147 David Printz JSY RC 2.50 6.00
148 Masi Marjamaki JSY RC 2.50 6.00
149 K.Pushkarev JSY RC 3.00 8.00
150 Michel Ouellet JSY RC 3.00 8.00
151 Billy Thompson JSY RC 2.50 6.00
152 Filip Novak JSY RC 2.50 6.00
153 M. Kopriva JSY RC 2.50 6.00
154 J. Johansson JSY RC 2.50 6.00
155 Shane O'Brien JSY RC 2.50 6.00
156 John Oduya JSY RC 4.00 10.00
157 Fredrik Norrena JSY RC 2.50 6.00
158 N. Backstrom JSY RC 5.00 12.00
159 D.J. King JSY RC 2.50 6.00
160 P. Thoresen JSY RC 2.50 6.00
161 D. Boyd JSY AU RC EXCH 3.00 8.00
162 Mikko Lehtonen JSY RC 3.00 8.00
163 Roman Polak JSY RC 3.00 8.00
164 Yan Stastny JSY AU RC 3.00 8.00
165 Mark Stuart JSY AU RC 3.00 8.00
166 Eric Fehr JSY AU RC 5.00 12.00
167 R. Potulny JSY AU RC 3.00 8.00
168 Ben Ondrus JSY AU RC 3.00 8.00
169 B. Bell JSY AU RC 3.00 8.00
170 Ian White JSY AU RC 4.00 10.00
171 J. Williams JSY AU RC 3.00 8.00
172 M-A Pouliot JSY AU RC 3.00 8.00
173 Noah Welch JSY AU RC 3.00 8.00
174 Shea Weber JSY AU RC 10.00 25.00
175 Jarkko Immonen JSY AU RC 3.00 8.00
176 Tomas Kopecky JSY AU RC 4.00 10.00
177 Matt Carle JSY AU RC 3.00 8.00
178 Ryan Shannon JSY AU RC 3.00 8.00
179 Anze Kopitar JSY AU RC 15.00 40.00
180 Travis Zajac JSY AU RC 6.00 15.00
181 Nigel Dawes JSY AU RC 3.00 8.00
182 K. Letang JSY AU RC 12.00 30.00
183 M-E Vlasic JSY AU RC 3.00 8.00
184 L. Smid JSY AU RC 3.00 8.00
185 L. Eriksson JSY AU RC 8.00 20.00
186 Paul Stastny JSY AU RC 8.00 20.00
187 A. Kaigorodov RC 1.25 3.00
188 P. O'Sullivan JSY AU RC 6.00 15.00
189 Phil Kessel JSY AU RC 12.00 30.00
190 G. Latendresse JSY AU RC 6.00 15.00
191 Jordan Staal JSY AU RC 8.00 20.00
192 L Bourdon JSY AU RC EXCH 8.00 20.00
193 Evgeni Malkin JSY AU RC 50.00 100.00
194 Keith Yandle JSY AU RC 6.00 15.00
195 A. Radulov JSY AU RC 6.00 15.00
196 Rob Collins RC 1.25 3.00
197 Steve Regier RC 1.25 3.00
198 Matt Koalska RC 1.25 3.00
199 Ryan Caldwell RC 1.25 3.00
200 David Liffiton RC 1.25 3.00
201 Erik Reitz RC 1.25 3.00
202 Adam Burish RC 2.00 5.00
203 Alex Brooks RC 1.25 3.00
204 Joel Perrault RC 1.25 3.00
205 Nate Thompson RC 1.25 3.00
206 Janis Sprukts RC 1.25 3.00
207 Alexei Mikhnov RC 1.25 3.00
208 Dave Bolland RC 2.00 5.00
209 Michael Blunden RC 1.25 3.00
210 Lars Jonsson RC 1.25 3.00
211 Triston Grant RC 1.25 3.00
212 Matt Lashoff RC 1.25 3.00
213 Bill Thomas RC 1.25 3.00

2006-07 SPx Spectrum

*VETS: 12X TO 30X BASIC CARDS
*FLASHBACK FABRIC: 1X TO 2.5X
*ROOKIES: 1.2X TO 3X
*ROOKIE JSY: .8X TO 2X
STATED PRINT RUN 25 SER.#'d SETS
81 Sidney Crosby 100.00 250.00
123 Ray Bourque JSY AU 25.00 60.00
125 Lanny McDonald JSY AU 20.00 50.00
126 Gordie Howe JSY AU 75.00 150.00
127 Grant Fuhr JSY AU 20.00 50.00
128 Wayne Gretzky JSY AU 250.00 500.00
130 Patrick Roy JSY AU 60.00 120.00
131 Martin Brodeur JSY AU 30.00 80.00
134 Sidney Crosby JSY AU 150.00 300.00
140 Ed Belfour JSY AU 30.00 80.00
193 Evgeni Malkin JSY AU 175.00 350.00

2006-07 SPx SPxcitement

STATED PRINT RUN 999 SETS
*SPECTRUM/99: .8X TO 2X BASIC INSERTS
X1 Chris Pronger 1.50 4.00
X2 Teemu Selanne 4.00 10.00
X3 Ilya Kovalchuk 2.00 5.00
X4 Kari Lehtonen 1.50 4.00
X5 Marian Hossa 1.50 4.00
X6 Ray Bourque 3.00 8.00
X7 Cam Neely 2.00 5.00
X8 Patrice Bergeron 2.50 6.00
X9 Brad Boyes 1.25 3.00
X10 Phil Esposito 3.00 8.00
X11 Gilbert Perreault 2.00 5.00
X12 Ryan Miller 2.00 5.00
X13 Chris Drury 1.50 4.00
X14 Lanny McDonald 2.00 5.00
X15 Jarome Iginla 2.00 5.00
X16 Miikka Kiprusoff 1.50 4.00
X17 Alex Tanguay 1.25 3.00
X18 Dion Phaneuf 2.00 5.00
X19 Nikolai Khabibulin 2.00 5.00
X20 Martin Havlat 1.25 3.00
X21 Tuomo Ruutu 2.00 5.00
X22 Joe Sakic 3.00 8.00
X23 Jose Theodore 2.00 5.00
X24 Milan Hejduk 1.50 4.00
X25 Marek Svatos 1.25 3.00
X26 Rick Nash 2.00 5.00
X27 Sergei Fedorov 3.00 8.00
X28 Gilbert Brule 1.50 4.00
X29 Mike Modano 3.00 8.00
X30 Marty Turco 2.00 5.00
X31 Eric Lindros 3.00 8.00
X32 Brenden Morrow 1.50 4.00
X33 Gordie Howe 6.00 15.00
X34 Henrik Zetterberg 2.50 6.00
X35 Pavel Datsyuk 2.50 6.00
X36 Nicklas Lidstrom 2.00 5.00
X37 Ted Lindsay 1.50 4.00
X38 Grant Fuhr 2.00 5.00
X39 Wayne Gretzky 10.00 25.00
X40 Ales Hemsky 1.50 4.00
X41 Ryan Smyth 1.50 4.00
X42 Jay Bouwmeester 2.00 5.00
X43 Nathan Horton 2.00 5.00
X44 Olli Jokinen 2.00 5.00
X45 Todd Bertuzzi 2.00 5.00
X46 Ed Belfour 2.00 5.00
X47 Alexander Frolov 1.25 3.00
X48 Rob Blake 2.00 5.00
X49 Rogie Vachon 2.50 6.00
X50 Marian Gaborik 2.50 6.00
X51 Manny Fernandez 1.50 4.00
X52 Pavol Demitra 2.50 6.00
X53 Patrick Roy 5.00 12.00
X54 Guy Lafleur 2.50 6.00
X55 Saku Koivu 2.00 5.00
X56 Cristobal Huet 1.50 4.00
X57 Michael Ryder 1.25 3.00
X58 Paul Kariya 2.50 6.00
X59 Tomas Vokoun 1.50 4.00
X60 Martin Brodeur 4.00 10.00
X61 Patrik Elias 2.00 5.00
X62 Brian Gionta 1.50 4.00
X63 Mike Bossy 2.00 5.00
X64 Miroslav Satan 1.50 4.00
X65 Alexei Yashin 1.50 4.00
X66 Jaromir Jagr 5.00 12.00
X67 Henrik Lundqvist 4.00 10.00
X68 Brendan Shanahan 2.50 6.00
X69 Dany Heatley 2.00 5.00
X70 Jason Spezza 2.00 5.00
X71 Daniel Alfredsson 2.00 5.00
X72 Martin Gerber 1.50 4.00
X73 Peter Forsberg 2.50 6.00
X74 Simon Gagne 2.00 5.00
X75 Jeff Carter 2.00 5.00
X76 Shane Doan 1.50 4.00
X77 Jeremy Roenick 2.00 5.00
X78 Owen Nolan 1.50 4.00
X79 Mario Lemieux 6.00 15.00
X80 Sidney Crosby 8.00 20.00
X81 Marc-Andre Fleury 3.00 8.00
X82 Joe Thornton 2.50 6.00
X83 Jonathan Cheechoo 2.00 5.00
X84 Patrick Marleau 2.00 5.00
X85 Doug Weight 2.00 5.00
X86 Keith Tkachuk 2.00 5.00
X87 Joe Mullen 1.50 4.00
X88 Vincent Lecavalier 1.50 4.00
X89 Martin St. Louis 2.00 5.00
X90 Brad Richards 2.00 5.00
X91 Borje Salming 2.00 5.00
X92 Darryl Sittler 2.00 5.00
X93 Mats Sundin 2.00 5.00
X94 Andrew Raycroft 1.50 4.00
X95 Alexander Steen 2.00 5.00
X96 Markus Naslund 1.50 4.00
X97 Roberto Luongo 3.00 8.00
X98 Richard Brodeur 1.50 4.00
X99 Alexander Ovechkin 8.00 20.00
X100 Olaf Kolzig 2.00 5.00

2006-07 SPx Winning Materials

*SPECTRUM/99: .6X TO 1.5X BASIC JSY
WMAF Alexander Frolov 1.50 4.00
WMAH Ales Hemsky 2.00 5.00
WMAM Al MacInnis 2.50 6.00
WMAN Glenn Anderson 2.50 6.00
WMAO Alexander Ovechkin 10.00 25.00
WMAS Alexander Steen 2.50 6.00
WMAT Alex Tanguay 1.50 4.00
WMAY Alexei Yashin 2.00 5.00
WMBB Brad Boyes 1.50 4.00
WMBC Bobby Clarke 2.50 6.00
WMBG Bill Guerin 2.50 6.00
WMBL Brian Leetch 2.50 6.00
WMBM Bryan McCabe 1.50 4.00
WMBO Pierre-Marc Bouchard 2.50 6.00
WMBR Brad Richards 2.50 6.00
WMBS Billy Smith 2.50 6.00
WMBT Bryan Trottier 3.00 8.00
WMCA Jeff Carter 2.50 6.00
WMCC Chris Chelios 2.50 6.00
WMCD Chris Drury 2.00 5.00
WMCH Cristobal Huet 2.00 5.00
WMCJ Curtis Joseph 2.50 6.00
WMCN Cam Neely 2.50 6.00
WMCP Chris Pronger 2.00 5.00
WMCW Cam Ward 2.50 6.00
WMDA Daniel Alfredsson 2.50 6.00
WMDH Dany Heatley 2.50 6.00
WMDP Dion Phaneuf 2.50 6.00
WMDW Doug Weight 2.50 6.00
WMEB Ed Belfour 2.50 6.00
WMES Eric Staal 3.00 8.00
WMGA Simon Gagne 2.50 6.00
WMGF Grant Fuhr 2.50 6.00
WMGI Brian Gionta 2.00 5.00
WMHA Martin Havlat 1.50 4.00
WMHE Milan Hejduk 2.00 5.00
WMHK Dominik Hasek 3.00 8.00
WMHL Henrik Lundqvist 5.00 12.00
WMHO Tomas Holmstrom 2.00 5.00
WMHZ Henrik Zetterberg 3.00 8.00
WMIK Ilya Kovalchuk 2.50 6.00
WMJB Jay Bouwmeester 2.50 6.00
WMJC Jonathan Cheechoo 2.50 6.00
WMJG Jean-Sebastien Giguere 2.50 6.00
WMJI Jarome Iginla 2.50 6.00
WMJJ Jaromir Jagr 6.00 15.00
WMJL Joffrey Lupul 2.00 5.00
WMJS Joe Sakic 4.00 10.00
WMJT Jose Theodore 2.50 6.00
WMJW Justin Williams 2.00 5.00
WMKC Kyle Calder 1.50 4.00
WMKD Kris Draper 1.50 4.00
WMKL Kari Lehtonen 2.00 5.00
WMKT Keith Tkachuk 2.50 6.00
WMLM Lanny McDonald 2.50 6.00
WMMA Maxim Afinogenov 1.50 4.00
WMMB Martin Brodeur 5.00 12.00
WMMC Mike Cammalleri 1.50 4.00
WMMF Manny Fernandez 2.00 5.00
WMMG Marian Gaborik 3.00 8.00
WMMH Marian Hossa 2.00 5.00
WMMM Mike Modano 4.00 10.00
WMMN Markus Naslund 2.00 5.00
WMMO Brendan Morrison 1.50 4.00
WMMR Michael Ryder 1.50 4.00
WMMS Miroslav Satan 2.00 5.00
WMMT Marty Turco 2.50 6.00
WMMW Brenden Morrow 2.00 5.00
WMNL Nicklas Lidstrom 2.50 6.00
WMOJ Olli Jokinen 2.50 6.00
WMOK Olaf Kolzig 2.50 6.00
WMPB Patrice Bergeron 3.00 8.00
WMPD Pavel Datsyuk 3.00 8.00
WMPE Patrik Elias 2.50 6.00
WMPF Peter Forsberg 3.00 8.00
WMPK Paul Kariya 3.00 8.00
WMPM Patrick Marleau 2.50 6.00
WMPP Petr Prucha 2.00 5.00
WMPT Pierre Turgeon 2.50 6.00
WMRD Rick DiPietro 2.00 5.00
WMRE Robert Esche 2.00 5.00
WMRE Mark Recchi 3.00 8.00
WMRL Roberto Luongo 4.00 10.00
WMRN Rick Nash 2.50 6.00
WMRO Rob Blake 2.50 6.00
WMRS Ryan Smyth 2.00 5.00
WMSA Borje Salming 2.50 6.00
WMSC Sidney Crosby 10.00 25.00
WMSD Shane Doan 2.00 5.00
WMSF Sergei Federov 4.00 10.00
WMSG Scott Gomez 2.00 5.00
WMSK Saku Koivu 2.50 6.00
WMSP Jason Spezza 2.50 6.00
WMSS Sergei Samsonov 2.00 5.00
WMST Martin St. Louis 2.50 6.00
WMTH Joe Thornton 3.00 8.00
WMTR Tuomo Ruutu 2.50 6.00
WMTS Teemu Selanne 5.00 12.00
WMTV Tomas Vokoun 2.00 5.00
WMVL Vincent Lecavalier 2.00 5.00

2007-08 SPx

This 235-card set was released in January, 2008. The set was issued into the hobby in four-card packs, with a $6.99 SRP, which came 18 packs to a box and 14 boxes to a case. Cards numbered 1-100 feature active veterans while cards 101-125 feature a mix of active and retired players with a game-worn jersey swatch. Cards numbered 126-150 feature both game-worn jersey swatches as well as an autograph. Rookie Cards are 151-236 with cards 182-200 having a game-worn jersey swatch and cards 201-236 having both a player-worn jersey swatch and an autograph. A few players did not return their signatures in time for pack out and those cards could be redeemed until December 17.2009.

COMP.SET w/o SPs (100) 12.00 30.00
(151-180) PRINT RUN 999 SER.#'d SETS
(181-200) PRINT RUN 1599 SER.#'d SETS
(201-230) PRINT RUN 999 SER.#'d SETS
(231-235) PRINT RUN 499 SER.#'d SETS
1 Jean-Sebastien Giguere .40 1.00
2 Ryan Getzlaf .60 1.50
3 Scott Niedermayer .40 1.00
4 Chris Pronger .30 .75
5 Mike Modano .60 1.50
6 Mike Ribeiro .30 .75
7 Marty Turco .40 1.00
8 Anze Kopitar .60 1.50
9 Alexander Frolov .25 .60
10 Rob Blake .40 1.00
11 Shane Doan .30 .75
12 Ed Jovanovski .30 .75
13 David Aebischer .30 .75
14 Joe Thornton .50 1.25
15 Evgeni Nabokov .30 .75
16 Jonathan Cheechoo .40 1.00
17 Patrick Marleau .40 1.00
18 Jarome Iginla .40 1.00
19 Miikka Kiprusoff .30 .75
20 Alex Tanguay .25 .60
21 Dion Phaneuf .40 1.00
22 Joe Sakic .60 1.50
23 Paul Stastny .40 1.00
24 Milan Hejduk .30 .75
25 Ales Hemsky .30 .75
26 Dwayne Roloson .30 .75
27 Wayne Gretzky 2.00 5.00
28 Shawn Horcoff .25 .60
29 Marian Gaborik .50 1.25
30 Niklas Backstrom .40 1.00
31 Pierre-Marc Bouchard .40 1.00
32 Markus Naslund .40 1.00
33 Roberto Luongo .50 1.25
34 Henrik Sedin .40 1.00
35 Daniel Sedin .40 1.00
36 Martin Havlat .40 1.00
37 Nikolai Khabibulin .40 1.00
38 Duncan Keith .40 1.00
39 Rick Nash .40 1.00
40 Fredrik Norrena .25 .60
41 Sergei Fedorov .60 1.50
42 Henrik Zetterberg .50 1.25
43 Gordie Howe 1.00 2.50
44 Pavel Datsyuk .50 1.25
45 Nicklas Lidstrom .40 1.00
46 Chris Mason .30 .75
47 Steve Sullivan .25 .60
48 Alexander Radulov .40 1.00
49 Doug Weight .40 1.00
50 Manny Legace .30 .75
51 Paul Kariya .50 1.25
52 Ilya Kovalchuk .40 1.00
53 Kari Lehtonen .30 .75
54 Marian Hossa .30 .75
55 Eric Staal .50 1.25
56 Cam Ward .40 1.00
57 Justin Williams .30 .75
58 Nathan Horton .40 1.00
59 Tomas Vokoun .30 .75
60 Olli Jokinen .30 .75
61 Martin St. Louis .40 1.00
62 Vincent Lecavalier .30 .75
63 Brad Richards .40 1.00
64 Alexander Ovechkin 1.50 4.00
65 Olaf Kolzig .40 1.00
66 Alexander Semin .40 1.00
67 Patrice Bergeron .50 1.25
68 Bobby Orr 1.25 3.00
69 Phil Kessel .50 1.25
70 Jason Pominville .40 1.00
71 Ryan Miller .40 1.00
72 Thomas Vanek .50 1.25
73 Saku Koivu .40 1.00
74 Cristobal Huet .30 .75
75 Michael Ryder .25 .60
76 Guillaume Latendresse .30 .75
77 Daniel Alfredsson .40 1.00
78 Jason Spezza .40 1.00
79 Ray Emery .30 .75
00 Dany Heatley .40 1.00
81 Mats Sundin .40 1.00
82 Vesa Toskala .30 .75
83 Alexander Steen .40 1.00
84 Darcy Tucker .30 .75
85 Martin Brodeur .75 2.00
86 Patrik Elias .40 1.00
87 Zach Parise .50 1.25
88 Rick DiPietro .30 .75
89 Miroslav Satan .30 .75
90 Bill Guerin .40 1.00
91 Henrik Lundqvist .50 1.25
92 Jaromir Jagr 1.00 2.50
93 Mark Messier .60 1.50
94 Simon Gagne .40 1.00
95 Daniel Briere .40 1.00
96 Jeff Carter .40 1.00
97 Marc-Andre Fleury .60 1.50
98 Evgeni Malkin 1.25 3.00
99 Sidney Crosby 1.50 4.00
100 Mario Lemieux 1.25 3.00
101 Billy Smith JSY 8.00 20.00
102 Bob Nystrom JSY 5.00 12.00
103 Bobby Clarke JSY 8.00 20.00
104 Brendan Shanahan JSY 10.00 25.00
105 Brian Leetch JSY 8.00 20.00
106 Denis Savard JSY 10.00 25.00
107 Dino Ciccarelli JSY 8.00 20.00
108 Doug Gilmour JSY 10.00 25.00
109 Ed Belfour JSY 8.00 20.00
110 Frank Mahovlich JSY 10.00 25.00
111 Guy Lafleur JSY 10.00 25.00
112 Joe Sakic JSY 12.00 30.00
113 Keith Tkachuk JSY 8.00 20.00
114 Lanny McDonald JSY 8.00 20.00
115 Mark Recchi JSY 10.00 25.00
116 Mats Sundin JSY 8.00 20.00
117 Mike Modano JSY 12.00 30.00
118 Nicklas Lidstrom JSY 8.00 20.00
119 Paul Kariya JSY 10.00 25.00
120 Peter Forsberg JSY 10.00 25.00
121 Roberto Luongo JSY 10.00 25.00
122 Saku Koivu JSY 8.00 20.00
123 Sergei Fedorov JSY 12.00 30.00
124 Steve Shutt JSY 8.00 20.00
125 Teemu Selanne JSY 15.00 40.00
126 Al MacInnis JSY AU 20.00 50.00
127 Alexander Ovechkin JSY AU 75.00 150.00
128 Borje Salming JSY AU 20.00 50.00
129 Cam Neely JSY AU 20.00 50.00
130 D.Hawerchuk SP JSY AU 40.00 100.00
131 Dany Heatley JSY AU 20.00 50.00
132 Darryl Sittler JSY AU 15.00 40.00
133 Dominik Hasek JSY AU 30.00 80.00
134 Doug Wilson JSY AU 10.00 25.00
135 Evgeni Malkin JSY AU 25.00 60.00
136 Gordie Howe SP JSY AU 250.00 400.00
137 Grant Fuhr JSY AU 40.00 80.00
138 Jarome Iginla JSY AU 15.00 40.00
139 J.Beliveau SP JSY AU 150.00 250.00
140 Joe Thornton JSY AU 20.00 50.00
141 Larry Robinson JSY AU 20.00 50.00
142 M.Lemieux SP JSY AU 125.00 250.00
143 M.Messier SP JSY AU 60.00 120.00
144 Martin Brodeur JSY AU 40.00 100.00
145 Ray Bourque JSY AU 30.00 80.00
146 P.Roy SP JSY AU 100.00 200.00
147 Peter Stastny JSY AU 15.00 40.00
149 Sidney Crosby JSY AU 100.00 200.00
150 W.Gretzky SP JSY AU 300.00 600.00
151 Ryan Carter RC 1.50 4.00
152 Mark Mancari RC 2.00 5.00
153 Patrick Kaleta RC 1.50 4.00
154 David Moss RC 2.50 6.00
155 Colin Fraser RC 1.50 4.00
156 Bryan Bickell RC 3.00 8.00
157 Magnus Johansson RC 1.50 4.00
158 Jonas Nordqvist RC 1.50 4.00
159 Jeff Finger RC 1.50 4.00
160 Tomas Popperle RC 2.00 5.00
161 Chris Conner RC 1.50 4.00
162 Bryan Young RC 1.50 4.00
163 Sebastien Bisaillon RC 1.50 4.00
164 Zach Stortini RC 1.50 4.00
165 Martin Lojek RC 1.50 4.00
166 Joe Piskula RC 1.50 4.00
167 John Zeiler RC 1.50 4.00
168 Brady Murray RC 1.50 4.00
169 Rich Peverley RC 2.50 6.00
170 Mark Fraser RC 1.50 4.00
171 David Clarkson RC 2.50 6.00
172 Denis Tolpeko RC 1.50 4.00
173 Daniel Carcillo RC 2.00 5.00
174 Craig Weller RC 1.50 4.00
175 Daniel Winnik RC 2.00 5.00
176 Thomas Plihal RC 2.00 5.00
177 Steve Wagner RC 1.50 4.00
178 Mike Lundin RC 1.50 4.00
179 Jannik Hansen RC 2.00 5.00
180 Mason Raymond RC 2.50 6.00
181 Jonas Hiller JSY RC 6.00 15.00
182 Tobias Enstrom JSY RC 5.00 12.00
183 Jonathan Sigalet JSY RC 3.00 8.00
184 Jaroslav Hlinka JSY RC 4.00 10.00
185 Tyler Weiman JSY RC 4.00 10.00
186 Jared Boll JSY RC 4.00 10.00
187 Marc Methot JSY RC 3.00 8.00
188 Tobias Stephan JSY RC 4.00 10.00
189 Matt Niskanen JSY RC 5.00 12.00
190 Devin Setoguchi JSY RC 5.00 12.00
191 Matt Ellis JSY RC 4.00 10.00
192 Tom Gilbert JSY RC 4.00 10.00
193 Tuukka Rask JSY AU RC 12.00 30.00
194 Ville Koistinen JSY RC 3.00 8.00
195 Rod Pelley JSY RC 3.00 8.00
196 Brandon Dubinsky JSY RC 6.00 15.00
197 Daniel Girardi JSY RC 4.00 10.00
198 Ryan Parent JSY RC 3.00 8.00
199 Torrey Mitchell JSY RC 4.00 10.00
200 Matt Smaby JSY RC 3.00 8.00
201 Bobby Ryan JSY AU RC 6.00 15.00
202 Drew Miller JSY AU RC 6.00 15.00
203 Bryan Little JSY AU RC 8.00 20.00
204 Brett Sterling JSY AU RC 5.00 12.00
205 David Krejci JSY AU RC 15.00 30.00
206 Milan Lucic JSY AU RC 20.00 40.00
207 Curtis McElhinney JSY AU RC 8.00 20.00
208 Kris Russell JSY AU RC 6.00 15.00
209 Sam Gagner JSY AU RC 10.00 25.00
210 Andrew Cogliano JSY AU RC 8.00 20.00
211 Rob Schremp JSY AU RC 6.00 15.00
212 Steve Downie JSY AU RC 6.00 15.00
213 Jack Johnson JSY AU RC 6.00 15.00
214 Jonathan Bernier JSY AU RC 12.00 30.00
215 Lauri Tukonen JSY AU RC 5.00 12.00
216 Petr Kalus JSY AU RC 5.00 12.00
217 James Sheppard JSY AU RC 5.00 12.00
218 Kyle Chipchura JSY AU RC 8.00 20.00
219 Jaroslav Halak JSY AU RC 10.00 25.00
220 Nicklas Bergfors JSY AU RC 5.00 12.00
221 Andy Greene JSY AU RC 6.00 15.00
222 Frans Nielsen JSY AU RC 8.00 20.00
223 Ryan Callahan JSY AU RC 12.50 30.00
224 Marc Staal JSY AU RC 8.00 20.00
225 Nick Foligno JSY AU RC 10.00 25.00
226 Brian Elliott JSY AU RC 10.00 25.00
227 Martin Hanzal JSY AU RC 6.00 15.00
228 David Perron JSY AU RC 8.00 20.00
229 Erik Johnson JSY AU RC 8.00 20.00
230 Anton Stralman JSY AU RC 5.00 12.00
231 Jonathan Toews JSY AU RC 75.00 135.00
232 Patrick Kane JSY AU RC 80.00 150.00
233 Carey Price JSY AU RC 125.00 200.00
234 Jiri Tlusty JSY AU RC 12.00 30.00
235 Peter Mueller JSY AU RC 10.00 25.00
236 Nicklas Backstrom JSY AU RC 25.00 50.00

2007-08 SPx Spectrum

*SPEC JSY (1-100): 6X TO 15X
*SPEC JSY (101-125): .5X TO 1.2X
*SPEC JSY AU (126-150): .4X TO 1X
*SPEC (151-180): .8X TO 2X
*SPEC JSY (181-200): .5X TO 1.2X
*SPEC JSY AU (201-230): .5X TO 1.2X
*SPEC JSY AU (231-236): .4X TO 1X
STATED PRINT RUN 25 SER.#'d SETS
143 Mark Messier JSY AU 100.00 200.00
146 Patrick Roy JSY AU 100.00 200.00
149 Sidney Crosby JSY AU 200.00 400.00
150 Wayne Gretzky JSY AU
231 Jonathan Toews JSY AU 300.00 600.00
232 Patrick Kane JSY AU 350.00 600.00
233 Carey Price JSY AU 600.00 900.00
236 Nicklas Backstrom JSY AU 50.00 100.00

2007-08 SPx Force Quad Holograms

STATED ODDS 1:126
F1 Lem/Sid/Gretz/Mess 15.00 40.00
F2 Roy/Brod/Luon/Gig 10.00 25.00
F3 Sakic/Lecav/Joe/Spez 6.00 15.00
F4 Iggy/St. L/Heat/Howe 10.00 25.00
F5 Lids/Nied/Orr/Dion 12.00 30.00

2007-08 SPx SPXtreme

COMPLETE SET (70) 75.00 150.00
STATED ODDS 1:18
STATED PRINT RUN 999 #'d SETS
X1 Wayne Gretzky 5.00 12.00
X2 Mario Lemieux 3.00 8.00
X3 Bobby Orr 3.00 8.00
X4 Mark Messier 1.50 4.00
X5 Gordie Howe 2.50 6.00
X6 Patrick Roy 2.50 6.00
X7 Phil Esposito 1.50 4.00
X8 Tony Esposito 1.00 2.50
X9 Stan Mikita 1.25 3.00
X10 Grant Fuhr 1.00 2.50
X11 Luc Robitaille 1.00 2.50
X12 Guy Lafleur 1.25 3.00
X13 Mike Bossy 1.00 2.50
X14 Denis Potvin 1.00 2.50
X15 Bobby Clarke 1.00 2.50
X16 Bernie Parent 1.00 2.50
X17 Darryl Sittler .75 2.00
X18 Lanny McDonald 1.00 2.50
X19 Peter Stastny .75 2.00
X20 Dale Hawerchuk 1.25 3.00
X21 Jean-Sebastien Giguere 1.00 2.50
X22 Ilya Kovalchuk 1.00 2.50
X23 Patrice Bergeron 1.25 3.00
X24 Ryan Miller 1.00 2.50
X25 Jarome Iginla 1.00 2.50
X26 Eric Staal 1.25 3.00
X27 Joe Sakic 1.50 4.00
X28 Rick Nash 1.00 2.50
X29 Mike Modano 1.50 4.00
X30 Henrik Zetterberg 1.25 3.00
X31 Marian Gaborik 1.25 3.00
X32 Saku Koivu 1.00 2.50
X33 Tomas Vokoun .75 2.00
X34 Martin Brodeur 2.00 5.00
X35 Jaromir Jagr 2.50 6.00
X36 Dany Heatley 1.00 2.50
X37 Simon Gagne 1.00 2.50
X38 Sidney Crosby 4.00 10.00
X39 Evgeni Malkin 3.00 8.00
X40 Joe Thornton 1.25 3.00
X41 Vincent Lecavalier .75 2.00
X42 Mats Sundin 1.00 2.50
X43 Roberto Luongo 1.25 3.00
X44 Alexander Ovechkin 4.00 10.00
X45 Miikka Kiprusoff .75 2.00
X46 Thomas Vanek 1.25 3.00
X47 Teemu Selanne 2.00 5.00
X48 Anze Kopitar 1.50 4.00
X49 Miroslav Satan .75 2.00
X50 Daniel Alfredsson 1.00 2.50
X51 Rob Schremp .75 2.00
X52 Jack Johnson .75 2.00
X53 Petr Kalus .60 1.50
X54 Carey Price 10.00 25.00
X55 Patrick Kane 12.00 30.00
X56 Nicklas Backstrom 2.00 5.00
X57 Marc Staal 1.00 2.50
X58 Peter Mueller .75 2.00
X59 Jonathan Toews 15.00 40.00
X60 Bobby Ryan 1.50 4.00
X61 Nicklas Bergfors .60 1.50
X62 Erik Johnson 1.00 2.50
X63 Sam Gagner 1.25 3.00
X64 Kyle Chipchura 1.00 2.50
X65 Bryan Little .75 2.00
X66 Jonathan Bernier 1.50 4.00
X67 Andrew Cogliano 1.00 2.50
X68 Nick Foligno 1.25 3.00
X69 Brett Sterling .60 1.50
X70 James Sheppard .60 1.50

2007-08 SPx SPXtreme Spectrum

*SPECTRUM/25: 2.5X TO 6X BASIC INSERTS
STATED PRINT RUN 25 SER.#'d SETS
X4 Mark Messier 10.00 25.00
X54 Carey Price 50.00 120.00
X55 Patrick Kane 50.00 100.00
X59 Jonathan Toews 60.00 120.00

2007-08 SPx Winning Combos

STATED ODDS 1:18
WCAR J.Arnott/A.Radulov 5.00 12.00
WCBE M.Brodeur/P.Elias 10.00 25.00
WCBH E.Belfour/D.Hasek 6.00 15.00
WCBK P.Bergeron/P.Kessel 6.00 15.00
WCBL M.Brodeur/R.Luongo 8.00 20.00
WCBM M.Sundin/B.Salming 5.00 12.00
WCCM S.Crosby/E.Malkin 20.00 50.00
WCCO S.Crosby/A.Ovechkin 12.00 30.00
WCDA D.Sittler/A.Steen 5.00 12.00
WCDB Datsyuk/Brind'Amour 6.00 15.00
WCDG P.Demitra/M.Gaborik 6.00 15.00
WCDM D.Ciccarelli/M.Gaborik 6.00 15.00
WCDS R.DiPietro/B.Smith 5.00 12.00
WCDZ Datsyuk/Zetterberg 6.00 15.00
WCFK A.Frolov/A.Kopitar 8.00 20.00
WCFR G.Fuhr/D.Roloson 5.00 12.00
WCGB S.Gagne/M.Biron 5.00 12.00
WCHE D.Heatley/R.Emery 5.00 12.00
WCHK Havlat/Khabibulin 5.00 12.00
WCIM M.Hossa/I.Kovalchuk 5.00 12.00
WCIT J.Iginla/A.Tanguay 5.00 12.00
WCJD E.Jovanovski/S.Doan 4.00 10.00
WCJL J.Jagr/H.Lundqvist 12.00 30.00
WCJM J.Sakic/M.Hejduk 8.00 20.00
WCJS J.Jagr/P.Stastny 6.00 15.00
WCKO O.Kolzig/A.Ovechkin 8.00 20.00
WCKR S.Koivu/M.Ryder 5.00 12.00
WCLB N.Lidstrom/R.Bourque 8.00 20.00
WCLC M.Lemieux/S.Crosby 20.00 50.00
WCLH G.Lafleur/C.Higgins 6.00 15.00
WCLS Lecavalier/St. Louis 5.00 12.00
WCMM M.Modano/M.Turco 8.00 20.00
WCMT McDonald/Tanguay 5.00 12.00
WCMV R.Miller/T.Vanek 6.00 15.00
WCNF R.Nash/S.Fedorov 8.00 20.00
WCNG Niedermayer/Giguere 5.00 12.00
WCNK C.Neely/P.Kessel 6.00 15.00
WCNL M.Naslund/R.Luongo 6.00 15.00
WCOM A.Ovechkin/E.Malkin 15.00 40.00
WCPM D.Phaneuf/A.MacInnis 5.00 12.00
WCRB P.Roy/M.Brodeur 12.00 30.00
WCRH D.Roloson/A.Hemsky 4.00 10.00
WCSD M.Satan/R.DiPietro 4.00 10.00
WCSH D.Savard/M.Havlat 6.00 15.00
WCSS J.Sakic/B.Shanahan 6.00 15.00
WCST M.Sundin/D.Tucker 5.00 12.00
WCSW E.Staal/C.Ward 6.00 15.00
WCTN Thornton/Nabokov 6.00 15.00
WCVJ T.Vokoun/O.Jokinen 4.00 10.00
WCWK P.Kariya/D.Weight 6.00 15.00

2007-08 SPx Winning Combos Spectrum

*SPEC: .5X TO 1.2X
STATED PRINT RUN 99 SER.#'d SETS

2007-08 SPx Winning Materials

STATED ODDS 1:18
*SPECTRUM/99: .5X TO 1.2X BASIC INSERTS
WMAH Ales Hemsky 3.00 8.00
WMAM Al MacInnis 4.00 10.00
WMAO Alexander Ovechkin 15.00 40.00
WMAT Alex Tanguay 2.50 6.00
WMBR Brad Richards 4.00 10.00
WMCN Cam Neely 4.00 10.00
WMCW Cam Ward 4.00 10.00
WMDA Daniel Alfredsson 4.00 10.00
WMDB Daniel Briere 4.00 10.00
WMDH Dany Heatley 4.00 10.00
WMDP Dion Phaneuf 4.00 10.00
WMDR Dwayne Roloson 3.00 8.00
WMES Eric Staal 5.00 12.00
WMHA Dominik Hasek 5.00 12.00
WMHL Henrik Lundqvist 5.00 12.00
WMHZ Henrik Zetterberg 5.00 12.00
WMIK Ilya Kovalchuk 4.00 10.00
WMJC Jonathan Cheechoo 4.00 10.00
WMJG Jean-Sebastien Giguere 4.00 10.00
WMJI Jarome Iginla 4.00 10.00
WMJJ Jaromir Jagr 10.00 25.00
WMJS Joe Sakic 6.00 15.00
WMJT Joe Thornton 5.00 12.00
WMKL Kari Lehtonen 3.00 8.00
WMMB Martin Brodeur 8.00 20.00
WMMG Marian Gaborik 5.00 12.00
WMMH Marian Hossa 3.00 8.00
WMMM Mike Modano 6.00 15.00
WMMN Markus Naslund 4.00 10.00
WMMR Michael Ryder 2.50 6.00
WMMS Mats Sundin 4.00 10.00
WMMT Marty Turco 4.00 10.00
WMNL Nicklas Lidstrom 4.00 10.00
WMPB Patrice Bergeron 5.00 12.00
WMPD Pavel Datsyuk 5.00 12.00
WMPF Peter Forsberg 5.00 12.00
WMPK Paul Kariya 5.00 12.00
WMPO Denis Potvin 4.00 10.00
WMRL Roberto Luongo 5.00 12.00
WMRN Rick Nash 4.00 10.00
WMSA Borje Salming 4.00 10.00
WMSC Sidney Crosby 15.00 40.00
WMSG Simon Gagne 4.00 10.00
WMSK Saku Koivu 4.00 10.00
WMTS Teemu Selanne 8.00 20.00
WMTV Tomas Vokoun 3.00 8.00
WMVA Thomas Vanek 5.00 12.00
WMVL Vincent Lecavalier 3.00 8.00
WMVT Vesa Toskala 3.00 8.00
WMZP Zach Parise 5.00 12.00

2007-08 SPx Winning Materials Radiance Autographs

STATED PRINT RUN 25 SER.#'d SETS
WMAO Alexander Ovechkin 150.00 250.00
WMCN Cam Neely 12.00 30.00
WMDP Dion Phaneuf 40.00 80.00
WMHA Dominik Hasek 40.00 80.00
WMMG Marian Gaborik 40.00 80.00
WMNL Nicklas Lidstrom 30.00 60.00
WMSC Sidney Crosby 150.00 300.00

2008-09 SPx

This set was released on January 14, 2009. The base set consists of 249 cards.
COMP.SET w/o SPs (100) 15.00 40.00
101-130 ROOKIE PRINT RUN 499
131-148,150-155 JSY PRINT RUN 1299

149/156-184 ROOK.JSY AU PRINT RUN 999
185-190 ROOK.JSY AU PRINT RUN 499
191-220 FF JSY ODDS 1:126
221-250 STATED ODDS 1:252
1 Nicklas Backstrom .75 2.00
2 Alexander Ovechkin 2.00 5.00
3 Pavol Demitra .60 1.50
4 Roberto Luongo .60 1.50
5 Steve Bernier .30 .75
6 Mats Sundin .50 1.25
7 Vesa Toskala .40 1.00
8 Ryan Malone .30 .75
9 Vincent Lecavalier .40 1.00
10 Olaf Kolzig .50 1.25
11 David Perron .40 1.00
12 Paul Kariya .60 1.50
13 Joe Thornton .60 1.50
14 Jonathan Cheechoo .50 1.25
15 Patrick Marleau .50 1.25
16 Rob Blake .50 1.25
17 Jordan Staal .50 1.25
18 Sidney Crosby 2.00 5.00
19 Marc-Andre Fleury .75 2.00
20 Evgeni Malkin 1.50 4.00
21 Miroslav Satan .50 1.25
22 Shane Doan .40 1.00
23 Peter Mueller .40 1.00
24 Olli Jokinen .40 1.00
25 Mike Richards .50 1.25
26 Martin Biron .40 1.00
27 Simon Gagne .50 1.25
28 Daniel Briere .50 1.25
29 Jason Spezza .50 1.25
30 Martin Gerber .40 1.00
31 Chris Phillips .30 .75
32 Markus Naslund .40 1.00
33 Scott Gomez .40 1.00
34 Wade Redden .30 .75
35 Henrik Lundqvist .60 1.50
36 Chris Drury .40 1.00
37 Nikolai Zherdev .30 .75
38 Doug Weight .50 1.25
39 Rick DiPietro .40 1.00
40 Martin Brodeur 1.00 2.50
41 Patrik Elias .50 1.25
42 Zach Parise .50 1.25
43 Brian Gionta .40 1.00
44 Shea Weber .40 1.00
45 Jason Arnott .40 1.00
46 Carey Price 2.00 5.00
47 Saku Koivu .50 1.25
48 Alex Kovalev .40 1.00
49 Alex Tanguay .30 .75
50 Marian Gaborik .60 1.50
51 Pierre-Marc Bouchard .50 1.25
52 Anze Kopitar .75 2.00
53 Tomas Vokoun .40 1.00
54 Stephen Weiss .30 .75
55 Shawn Horcoff .30 .75
56 Dwayne Roloson .40 1.00
57 Sam Gagner .40 1.00
58 Marian Hossa .40 1.00
59 Tomas Holmstrom .40 1.00
60 Brian Rafalski .40 1.00
61 Henrik Zetterberg .60 1.50
62 Nicklas Lidstrom .50 1.25
63 Brad Richards .50 1.25
64 Mike Modano .75 2.00
65 Marty Turco .50 1.25
66 Mike Ribeiro .40 1.00
67 Jere Lehtinen .30 .75
68 Pascal Leclaire .40 1.00
69 Rick Nash .50 1.25
70 Joe Sakic .75 2.00
71 Milan Hejduk .40 1.00
72 Paul Stastny .50 1.25
73 Peter Forsberg .60 1.50
74 Marek Svatos .30 .75
75 Darcy Tucker .40 1.00
76 Patrick Sharp .50 1.25
77 Jonathan Toews 1.25 3.00
78 Patrick Kane 1.00 2.50
79 Eric Staal .60 1.50
80 Cam Ward .50 1.25
81 Justin Williams .40 1.00
82 Mike Cammalleri .40 1.00
83 Jarome Iginla .50 1.25
84 Todd Bertuzzi .50 1.25
85 Dion Phaneuf .50 1.25
86 Tuukka Rask .50 1.25
87 Ryan Miller .50 1.25
88 Maxim Afinogenov .30 .75
89 Marc Savard .30 .75
90 Patrice Bergeron .60 1.50
91 Phil Kessel .60 1.50
92 Tim Thomas .50 1.25
93 Zdeno Chara .50 1.25
94 Michael Ryder .30 .75
95 Ilya Kovalchuk .50 1.25
96 Kari Lehtonen .40 1.00
97 Tobias Enstrom .30 .75
98 Corey Perry .50 1.25
99 Ryan Getzlaf .75 2.00
100 Teemu Selanne 1.00 2.50
101 Adam Pardy RC 2.50 6.00
102 Wayne Simmonds RC 5.00 12.00
103 Nathan Oystrick RC 3.00 8.00
104 Anssi Salmela RC 3.00 8.00
105 Jared Ross RC 3.00 8.00
106 Chris Porter RC 3.00 8.00
107 Janne Niskala RC 3.00 8.00
108 John Mitchell RC 2.50 6.00
109 Mike Brown RC 4.00 10.00
110 Kyle Greentree RC 3.00 8.00
111 Sami Lepisto RC 2.50 6.00
112 Zach Fitzgerald RC 3.00 8.00
113 Darryl Boyce RC 2.50 6.00
114 Jesse Winchester RC 2.00 5.00
115 Corey Locke RC 2.50 6.00
116 Brandon Nolan RC 2.50 6.00
117 Jordan Hendry RC 2.50 6.00
118 Pascal Pelletier RC 2.00 5.00
119 Tom Cavanagh RC 2.50 6.00
120 Theo Peckham RC 3.00 8.00
121 B.J. Crombeen RC 2.00 5.00
122 Joe Jensen RC 3.00 8.00
123 Josh Bailey RC 4.00 10.00
124 Garrett Stafford RC 3.00 8.00
125 Jonas Frogren RC 2.00 5.00
126 Alex Foster RC 2.50 6.00
127 David Brine RC 2.00 5.00
128 Colin Stuart RC 2.50 6.00
129 Andrew Murray RC 2.50 6.00
130 Niklas Hjalmarsson RC 5.00 12.00
131 Jonathan Ericsson JSY RC 4.00 10.00
132 Darren Helm JSY RC 4.00 10.00
133 Erik Ersberg JSY RC 3.00 8.00
134 Matthew Halischuk JSY RC 2.50 6.00
135 Mark Fistric JSY RC 3.00 8.00
136 Adam Pineault JSY RC 3.00 8.00
137 Oscar Moller JSY RC 3.00 8.00
138 Matt D'Agostini JSY RC 3.00 8.00
139 Mattias Ritola JSY RC 3.00 8.00
140 Ryan Stone JSY RC 2.50 6.00
141 Mike Iggulden JSY RC 3.00 8.00
142 Andrew Ebbett JSY RC 2.50 6.00
143 Dan LaCosta JSY RC 4.00 10.00
144 Teddy Purcell JSY RC 5.00 12.00
145 Jamie McGinn JSY RC 4.00 10.00
146 Tim Ramholt JSY RC 3.00 8.00
147 Jon Filewich JSY RC 3.00 8.00
148 Boris Valabik JSY RC 4.00 10.00
149 Cory Schneider JSY AU RC 10.00 25.00
150 Tyler Plante JSY RC 3.00 8.00
151 Petr Vrana JSY RC 2.50 6.00
152 Brian Boyle JSY RC 3.00 8.00
153 Tom Sestito JSY RC 4.00 10.00
154 Ryan Jones JSY RC 4.00 10.00
155 Andreas Nodl JSY RC 2.50 6.00
156 James Neal JSY AU RC 10.00 25.00
157 Jakub Voracek JSY AU RC 10.00 25.00
158 T.J. Oshie JSY AU RC 10.00 25.00
159 Nikita Filatov JSY AU RC 5.00 12.00
160 Brandon Sutter JSY AU RC 5.00 12.00
161 Steve Mason JSY AU RC 8.00 20.00
162 Derick Brassard JSY AU RC 4.00 10.00
163 Kevin Porter JSY AU RC 4.00 10.00
164 Viktor Tikhonov JSY AU RC 4.00 10.00
165 J.Abdelkader JSY AU RC 8.00 20.00
166 Michael Frolik JSY AU RC 5.00 12.00
167 Zach Boychuk JSY AU RC 5.00 12.00
168 Shawn Matthias JSY AU RC 5.00 12.00
169 F.Brunnstrom JSY AU RC 4.00 10.00
170 Patric Hornqvist JSY AU RC 5.00 12.00
171 Nikolai Kulemin JSY AU RC 5.00 12.00
172 Colton Gillies JSY AU RC 4.00 10.00
173 Kyle Okposo JSY AU RC 5.00 12.00
174 Patrik Berglund JSY AU RC 4.00 10.00
175 Lauri Korpikoski JSY AU RC 3.00 8.00
176 Brian Lee JSY AU RC 4.00 10.00
177 Ilya Zubov JSY AU RC 4.00 10.00
178 Robbie Earl JSY AU RC 3.00 8.00
179 Claude Giroux JSY AU RC 20.00 50.00
180 A.Pietrangelo JSY AU RC 6.00 15.00
181 Alex Goligoski JSY AU RC 6.00 15.00
182 Vladimir Mihalik JSY AU RC 3.00 8.00
183 Luca Sbisa JSY AU RC 3.00 8.00
184 Mikkel Boedker JSY AU RC 6.00 15.00
185 Kyle Turris JSY AU RC 10.00 25.00
186 Blake Wheeler JSY AU RC 15.00 40.00
187 Luke Schenn JSY AU RC 8.00 20.00
188 Zach Bogosian JSY AU RC 6.00 15.00
189 Drew Doughty JSY AU RC 15.00 40.00
190 S.Stamkos JSY AU RC 60.00 150.00
191 Theoren Fleury FF JSY 10.00 25.00
192 Adam Oates FF JSY 8.00 20.00
193 Grant Fuhr FF JSY 8.00 20.00
194 Zach Parise FF JSY 8.00 20.00
195 Lanny McDonald FF JSY 8.00 20.00
196 Nicklas Lidstrom FF JSY 8.00 20.00
197 Martin Brodeur FF JSY 15.00 40.00
198 Paul Kariya FF JSY 10.00 25.00
199 Teemu Selanne FF JSY 15.00 40.00
200 Peter Forsberg FF JSY 10.00 25.00
201 Mike Bossy FF JSY 8.00 20.00
202 Jeremy Roenick FF JSY 8.00 20.00
203 Joe Sakic FF JSY 12.00 30.00
204 Brendan Shanahan FF JSY 10.00 25.00
205 Chris Chelios FF JSY 8.00 20.00
206 Dominik Hasek FF JSY 10.00 25.00
207 Borje Salming FF JSY 8.00 20.00
208 Frank Mahovlich FF JSY 8.00 20.00
209 Gerry Cheevers FF JSY 8.00 20.00
210 Olli Jokinen FF JSY 6.00 15.00
211 Mats Sundin FF JSY 8.00 20.00
212 Marian Hossa FF JSY 6.00 15.00
213 Guy Carbonneau FF JSY 8.00 20.00
214 Marian Gaborik FF JSY 10.00 25.00
215 Marcel Dionne FF JSY 10.00 25.00
217 Al MacInnis FF JSY 8.00 20.00
218 Rod Langway FF JSY 6.00 15.00
219 Chris Drury FF JSY 6.00 15.00
220 Dale Hawerchuk FF JSY 10.00 25.00
221 Sidney Crosby FF JSY AU 80.00 200.00
222 Brian Leetch FF JSY AU 12.00 30.00
223 Bryan Trottier FF JSY AU 15.00 40.00
224 Borje Salming FF JSY AU 12.00 30.00
225 Ryan Smyth FF JSY AU 10.00 25.00
226 Mario Lemieux FF JSY AU 60.00 120.00
227 Bob Bourne FF JSY AU 8.00 20.00
228 Ron Hextall FF JSY AU 20.00 50.00
229 Steve Shutt FF JSY AU 12.00 30.00
230 Lanny McDonald FF JSY AU 12.00 30.00
231 Mike Modano FF JSY AU 20.00 50.00
232 Simon Gagne FF JSY AU 12.00 30.00
233 Bernie Nicholls FF JSY AU 10.00 25.00
234 Johnny Bucyk FF JSY AU 12.00 30.00
235 Joe Thornton FF JSY AU 15.00 40.00
236 Dominik Hasek FF JSY AU 15.00 40.00
237 Rick Vaive FF JSY AU 8.00 20.00
238 Bobby Hull FF JSY AU 20.00 50.00
239 Alex Ovechkin FF JSY AU 50.00 125.00
240 Mark Messier FF JSY AU 15.00 40.00
241 Rod Langway FF JSY AU 10.00 25.00
242 Dino Ciccarelli FF JSY AU 12.00 30.00
243 Jari Kurri FF JSY AU 12.00 30.00
244 Luc Robitaille FF JSY AU 12.00 30.00
245 Ray Bourque FF JSY AU 20.00 50.00
246 V.Lecavalier FF JSY AU 10.00 25.00
247 Tony Esposito FF JSY AU 12.00 30.00
248 H.Zetterberg FF JSY AU 15.00 40.00
249 Patrick Roy FF JSY AU 75.00 150.00
250 Wayne Gretzky FF JSY AU 100.00 200.00

2008-09 SPx Spectrum

*1-100 VET JSY: 4X TO 10X BASE JSY
*101-130 ROOKIE: .8X TO 2X BASE
*131-155 ROOK.JSY: .8X TO 2X BASE
*156-184 ROOK.JSY AU: 1.5X TO 4X JSY AU/999
*185-190 ROOK.JSY AU: 1.2X TO 3X JSY AU/499
*191-220 FF JSY: .6X TO 1.5X BASE
*221-250 FF JSY AU: .6X TO 1.5X BASE
STATED PRINT RUN 25 SER.#'d SETS
1 Nicklas Backstrom JSY 8.00 20.00
179 Claude Giroux JSY AU 125.00 250.00
190 Steven Stamkos JSY AU 200.00 400.00

2008-09 SPx Memorable Moments

STATED ODDS 1:126
MMAM Al MacInnis 8.00 20.00
MMBH Bobby Hull 12.00 30.00
MMBO Bobby Orr 25.00 60.00
MMBS Billy Smith 8.00 20.00
MMBT Bryan Trottier 10.00 25.00
MMCJ Curtis Joseph 8.00 20.00
MMCP Chris Pronger 6.00 15.00
MMDA Dave Andreychuk 8.00 20.00
MMDC Dino Ciccarelli 8.00 20.00
MMDS Dave Schultz 8.00 20.00
MMGF Grant Fuhr 8.00 20.00
MMGH Gordie Howe 15.00 40.00
MMGL Guy Lafleur 10.00 25.00
MMGR Wayne Gretzky 20.00 50.00
MMHO Gordie Howe 20.00 50.00
MMHZ Henrik Zetterberg 10.00 25.00
MMJK Jari Kurri 8.00 20.00
MMJS Joe Sakic 10.00 25.00
MMJT Joe Thornton 10.00 25.00
MMLE Mario Lemieux 25.00 60.00
MMLR Larry Robinson 8.00 20.00
MMMB Martin Brodeur 15.00 40.00
MMMD Marcel Dionne 10.00 25.00
MMMI Mike Bossy 8.00 20.00
MMML Mario Lemieux 15.00 40.00
MMMM Mark Messier 10.00 25.00
MMMS Martin St. Louis 8.00 20.00
MMPE Phil Esposito 12.00 30.00
MMPF Peter Forsberg 10.00 25.00
MMPR Patrick Roy 20.00 50.00
MMRH Ron Hextall 12.00 30.00
MMRO Luc Robitaille 10.00 25.00
MMRV Rogie Vachon 10.00 25.00
MMSB Scotty Bowman 8.00 20.00
MMSC Sidney Crosby 20.00 50.00
MMSF Sergei Fedorov 12.00 30.00
MMSM Stan Mikita 10.00 25.00
MMTH Jose Theodore 8.00 20.00
MMTS Teemu Selanne 15.00 40.00
MMTW Tiger Williams 6.00 15.00
MMWA Wayne Gretzky 20.00 50.00
MMWG Wayne Gretzky 20.00 50.00

2008-09 SPx SPxcitement

COMPLETE SET (70) 150.00 300.00
STATED PRINT RUN 999 SERIAL #'d SETS
X1 Alexander Ovechkin 6.00 15.00
X2 Andrew Cogliano 1.25 3.00
X3 Anze Kopitar 2.50 6.00
X4 Bobby Clarke 1.50 4.00
X5 Bobby Hull 2.50 6.00
X6 Bobby Orr 5.00 12.00
X7 Cam Neely 1.50 4.00
X8 Carey Price 6.00 15.00
X9 Dale Hawerchuk 2.00 5.00
X10 Daniel Alfredsson 1.50 4.00
X11 Dany Heatley 1.50 4.00
X12 Darryl Sittler 1.50 4.00
X13 Denis Potvin 1.50 4.00
X14 Dino Ciccarelli 1.50 4.00
X15 Eric Staal 2.00 5.00
X16 Evgeni Malkin 5.00 12.00
X17 Frank Mahovlich 1.50 4.00
X18 Guy Lafleur 2.00 5.00
X19 Gordie Howe 4.00 10.00
X20 Grant Fuhr 1.50 4.00
X21 Gilbert Perreault 1.50 4.00
X22 Henrik Lundqvist 2.00 5.00
X23 Henrik Zetterberg 2.00 5.00
X24 Ilya Kovalchuk 1.50 4.00
X25 Jari Kurri 1.50 4.00
X26 Jarome Iginla 1.50 4.00
X27 Dion Phaneuf 1.50 4.00
X28 Jean-Sebastien Giguere 1.50 4.00
X29 Joe Sakic 2.50 6.00
X30 Joe Thornton 2.00 5.00
X31 Jonathan Toews 4.00 10.00
X32 Jordan Staal 1.50 4.00
X33 Kyle Okposo 1.50 4.00
X34 Kyle Turris 2.50 6.00
X35 Lanny McDonald 1.50 4.00
X36 Luc Robitaille 1.50 4.00
X37 Marian Gaborik 2.00 5.00
X38 Mario Lemieux 5.00 12.00
X39 Mark Messier 2.00 5.00
X40 Martin Brodeur 3.00 8.00
X41 Martin St. Louis 1.50 4.00
X42 Mats Sundin 1.50 4.00
X43 Miikka Kiprusoff 1.25 3.00
X44 Mike Bossy 1.50 4.00
X45 Mike Modano 2.50 6.00
X46 Nicklas Backstrom 2.50 6.00
X47 Patrick Kane 3.00 8.00
X48 Patrick Roy 4.00 10.00
X49 Paul Stastny 1.50 4.00
X50 Peter Mueller 1.25 3.00
X51 Peter Stastny 1.50 4.00
X52 Phil Esposito 2.50 6.00
X53 Rick Nash 1.50 4.00
X54 Roberto Luongo 2.00 5.00
X55 Ron Hextall 2.50 6.00
X56 Ryan Getzlaf 2.50 6.00
X57 Ryan Miller 1.50 4.00
X58 Saku Koivu 1.50 4.00
X59 Sam Gagner 1.25 3.00
X60 Sidney Crosby 6.00 15.00
X61 Stan Mikita 2.00 5.00
X62 Steve Mason 2.50 6.00
X63 Teemu Selanne 3.00 8.00
X64 Nikita Filatov 1.50 4.00
X65 Tony Esposito 1.50 4.00
X66 Vincent Lecavalier 1.25 3.00
X67 Wayne Gretzky 8.00 20.00
X68 Blake Wheeler 4.00 10.00
X69 Fabian Brunnstrom 1.25 3.00
X70 Steven Stamkos 10.00 25.00

2008-09 SPx Spxcitement Spectrum

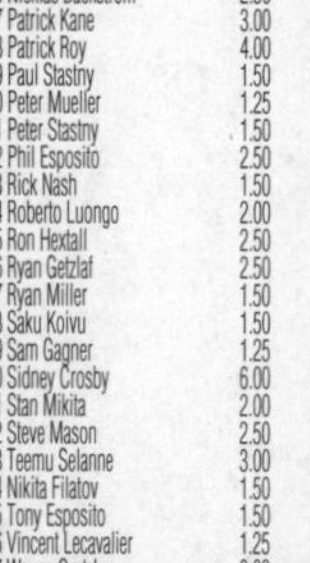

*SPECTRUM: 1X TO 2.5X BASE
STATED PRINT RUN 99 SERIAL #'d SETS
X46 Nicklas Backstrom 6.00 15.00

2008-09 SPx Winning Combos

STATED ODDS 1:18
*SPECTRUM: .5X TO 1.2X BASE
WCBG M.Gaborik/P.Bouchard 6.00 15.00
WCBM N.Backstrom/P.Mueller 8.00 20.00
WCBO R.Bourque/A.Oates 5.00 12.00
WCBP M.Brodeur/C.Price 20.00 50.00
WCCB E.Cole/G.Brule 4.00 10.00
WCCH R.Hextall/B.Clarke 8.00 20.00
WCCP J.Cheechoo/C.Perry 5.00 12.00
WCDL D.Sittler/L.McDonald 5.00 12.00
WCEE T.Esposito/P.Esposito 8.00 20.00
WCEI E.Malkin/I.Kovalchuk 15.00 40.00
WCEM E.Staal/M.Staal 6.00 15.00
WCFA G.Fuhr/G.Anderson 5.00 12.00
WCFB P.Forsberg/N.Backstrom 8.00 20.00
WCGB S.Gagner/N.Backstrom 8.00 20.00
WCGR S.Gagner/D.Roloson 4.00 10.00
WCGZ S.Gomez/N.Zherdev 4.00 10.00
WCHB M.Hejduk/P.Budaj 4.00 10.00
WCHE M.Hossa/P.Elias 5.00 12.00
WCHH B.Hull/D.Hawerchuk 8.00 20.00
WCHL D.Hasek/N.Lidstrom 6.00 15.00
WCHM D.Hasek/R.Miller 6.00 15.00
WCKC P.Kane/E.Cole 10.00 25.00
WCKH S.Koivu/C.Higgins 5.00 12.00
WCKK J.Kurri/S.Koivu 5.00 12.00
WCKS S.Koivu/S.Shutt 5.00 12.00
WCLC V.Lecavalier/J.Cheechoo 5.00 12.00
WCLH N.Lidstrom/T.Holmstrom 5.00 12.00
WCMG E.Malkin/S.Gagne 15.00 40.00
WCMK M.Modano/P.Kane 10.00 25.00
WCML M.Lemieux/M.Messier 10.00 25.00
WCMM L.McDonald/A.MacInnis 5.00 12.00
WCMV L.McDonald/R.Vaive 5.00 12.00
WCNE M.Naslund/P.Elias 5.00 12.00
WCNG M.Naslund/S.Gomez 4.00 10.00
WCNL R.Nash/V.Lecavalier 5.00 12.00
WCOK A.Ovechkin/I.Kovalchuk 10.00 25.00
WCOM A.Ovechkin/E.Malkin 20.00 50.00
WCPS R.Malone/S.Weiss 3.00 8.00
WCPZ R.Nash/M.Peca 5.00 12.00
WCRK M.Ryder/P.Kessel 6.00 15.00
WCRL L.Robinson/R.Langway 5.00 12.00
WCRM M.Ribeiro/M.Turco 5.00 12.00
WCSD S.Doan/R.Smyth 4.00 10.00
WCSH S.Shutt/C.Higgins 5.00 12.00
WCSM E.Staal/R.Malone 6.00 15.00
WCSS E.Staal/J.Staal 6.00 15.00
WCTK P.Kane/J.Toews 10.00 25.00
WCVH D.Hasek/T.Vokoun 12.00 30.00
WCZH H.Zetterberg/T.Holmstrom 6.00 15.00

2008-09 SPx Winning Combos Radiance Autographs

STATED PRINT RUN 25 SERIAL #'d SETS
WCBM N.Backstrom/P.Mueller 15.00 40.00
WCBO R.Bourque/A.Oates
WCBP M.Brodeur/C.Price 75.00 135.00
WCCH B.Clarke/R.Hextall 25.00 50.00
WCDL L.McDonald/D.Sittler 20.00 50.00
WCEE P.Esposito/T.Esposito 20.00 50.00
WCEI I.Kovalchuk/E.Malkin
WCEM E.Staal/M.Staal 15.00 40.00
WCFA G.Fuhr/G.Anderson 20.00 50.00
WCGB Gagner/Backstrom 20.00 50.00
WCGR D.Roloson/S.Gagner 15.00 40.00
WCGZ S.Gomez/N.Zherdev 15.00 40.00
WCHB M.Hejduk/P.Budaj
WCHE P.Elias/M.Hossa 20.00 50.00
WCHH B.Hull/D.Hawerchuk 30.00 60.00
WCHL N.Lidstrom/D.Hasek
WCHM R.Miller/D.Hasek 25.00 60.00
WCKC E.Cole/P.Kane 40.00 80.00
WCKK S.Koivu/J.Kurri 60.00 120.00
WCKS S.Koivu/S.Shutt 25.00 60.00
WCLC Lecavalier/Cheechoo
WCLH Holmstrom/Lidstrom 20.00 50.00
WCMG S.Gagne/E.Malkin 12.00 30.00
WCMK M.Modano/P.Kane 40.00 100.00
WCML M.Lemieux/M.Messier 150.00 250.00
WCMM McDonald/MacInnis 20.00 50.00
WCMV L.McDonald/R.Vaive 15.00 40.00
WCNE M.Naslund/P.Elias 20.00 50.00
WCNG S.Gomez/M.Naslund 20.00 50.00
WCNL R.Nash/V.Lecavalier 30.00 80.00
WCOK Kovalchuk/Ovechkin 50.00 100.00
WCOM A.Ovechkin/E.Malkin 75.00 150.00
WCPS S.Weiss/R.Malone 15.00 40.00
WCPZ M.Peca/R.Nash 20.00 50.00
WCRK P.Kessel/M.Ryder 75.00 125.00
WCRL Langway/Robinson 15.00 40.00
WCRM M.Ribeiro/M.Turco 12.00 30.00
WCSH S.Shutt/C.Higgins
WCSM R.Malone/E.Staal 20.00 50.00
WCSS J.Staal/E.Staal
WCTK J.Toews/P.Kane 50.00 100.00
WCVH T.Vokoun/D.Hasek 30.00 60.00
WCZH Zetterberg/Holmstrom 15.00 40.00

2008-09 SPx Winning Materials

STATED ODDS 1:18
*SPECTRUM/99: .5X TO 1.2X BASIC JSY
WMAM Andrei Markov 4.00 10.00
WMAO Adam Oates 4.00 10.00
WMBH Bobby Hull 6.00 15.00
WMCC Bobby Clarke 4.00 10.00
WMCH Jonathan Cheechoo 4.00 10.00
WMCN Cam Neely 4.00 10.00
WMCP Carey Price 15.00 40.00
WMDG Doug Gilmour 5.00 12.00
WMDH Dominik Hasek 5.00 12.00
WMES Eric Staal 5.00 12.00
WMGF Grant Fuhr 4.00 10.00
WMGG Sam Gagner 3.00 8.00
WMGZ Scott Gomez 3.00 8.00
WMHD Milan Hejduk 3.00 8.00
WMHG Chris Higgins 2.50 6.00
WMHZ Henrik Zetterberg 5.00 12.00
WMIK Ilya Kovalchuk 4.00 10.00
WMJM Joe Mullen 3.00 8.00
WMJS Jordan Staal 4.00 10.00
WMJT Jonathan Toews 10.00 25.00
WMKN Patrick Kane 8.00 20.00
WMLM Lanny McDonald 4.00 10.00
WMMB Martin Brodeur 8.00 20.00
WMMG Marian Gaborik 5.00 12.00
WMMH Marian Hossa 3.00 8.00
WMMM Mark Messier 5.00 12.00
WMMO Mike Modano 6.00 15.00
WMMP Michael Peca 3.00 8.00
WMMR Mike Ribeiro 3.00 8.00
WMNL Nicklas Lidstrom 4.00 10.00
WMOV Alexander Ovechkin 8.00 20.00
WMPE Patrik Elias 4.00 10.00
WMPK Phil Kessel 5.00 12.00
WMPM Peter Mueller 3.00 8.00
WMPS Peter Stastny 4.00 10.00
WMRL Rod Langway 3.00 8.00
WMRM Ryan Malone 2.50 6.00
WMRN Rick Nash 4.00 10.00
WMRV Rick Vaive 2.50 6.00
WMRY Michael Ryder 2.50 6.00
WMSB Steve Bernier 2.50 6.00
WMSC Sidney Crosby 10.00 25.00
WMSG Simon Gagne 4.00 10.00
WMSK Saku Koivu 4.00 10.00
WMSS Steve Shutt 4.00 10.00
WMST Matt Stajan 3.00 8.00
WMSW Shea Weber 3.00 8.00
WMTH Tomas Holmstrom 3.00 8.00
WMVL Vincent Lecavalier 3.00 8.00
WMWC Wendel Clark 4.00 10.00

2008-09 SPx Winning Materials Radiance Autographs

STATED PRINT RUN 25 SERIAL #'d SETS
WMAO Adam Oates
WMBH Bobby Hull 25.00 60.00
WMCC Bobby Clarke 15.00 40.00
WMCN Cam Neely 20.00 50.00
WMCP Carey Price 60.00 150.00
WMDG Doug Gilmour 15.00 40.00
WMDH Dominik Hasek 20.00 50.00
WMES Eric Staal 12.50 30.00
WMGF Grant Fuhr 15.00 40.00
WMGG Sam Gagner 10.00 25.00
WMGZ Scott Gomez
WMHD Milan Hejduk 12.00 30.00
WMHG Chris Higgins 40.00 100.00
WMHZ Henrik Zetterberg 40.00 80.00
WMIK Ilya Kovalchuk 15.00 40.00
WMJM Joe Mullen 12.00 30.00
WMJS Jordan Staal 15.00 40.00
WMJT Jonathan Toews 20.00 50.00
WMKN Patrick Kane 30.00 60.00
WMLM Lanny McDonald 15.00 40.00
WMMB Martin Brodeur 30.00 80.00
WMMH Marian Hossa 12.00 30.00
WMMM Mark Messier 50.00 100.00
WMMO Mike Modano
WMMP Michael Peca
WMMR Mike Ribeiro 12.00 30.00
WMNL Nicklas Lidstrom 25.00 50.00
WMOV Alexander Ovechkin 60.00 150.00
WMPE Patrik Elias 15.00 40.00
WMPK Phil Kessel 20.00 50.00
WMPM Peter Mueller 12.00 30.00
WMPS Peter Stastny 15.00 40.00
WMRL Rod Langway 10.00 25.00
WMRM Ryan Malone 10.00 25.00
WMRN Rick Nash 15.00 40.00
WMRV Rick Vaive 10.00 25.00
WMRY Michael Ryder 10.00 25.00
WMSB Steve Bernier
WMSC Sidney Crosby 100.00 200.00
WMSG Simon Gagne 15.00 40.00
WMSK Saku Koivu 15.00 40.00
WMSS Steve Shutt 15.00 40.00
WMST Matt Stajan 12.00 30.00
WMTH Tomas Holmstrom 15.00 40.00
WMVL Vincent Lecavalier 12.00 30.00
WMWC Wendel Clark 20.00 50.00

2008-09 SPx Winning Trios

All cards have a WT prefix.
STATED PRINT RUN 99 SERIAL #'d SETS
AKF Kovalv/Afinog/Fedor 12.00 30.00
AWL Arnott/Weber/Legwand 8.00 20.00
BMG Backstrm/Gagnr/Muell 15.00 40.00
BTK Backstrom/Toews/Kane 25.00 60.00
BTS Trottier/Bossy/Smith 12.00 30.00
CGY McDon/MacIns/Fleury 12.00 30.00
COM Crosby/Ovechkin/Malkin 25.00 60.00
DMJ Doan/Mueller/Jokinen 8.00 20.00
FCM Crosby/Malkin/Fleury 20.00 50.00
FSH Sakic/Forsberg/Hejduk 15.00 40.00
GBN Gaborik/Bouchrd/Nolan 12.00 30.00
GLM Gretz/Lemieux/Mess 40.00 100.00
GRC Richards/Carter/Gagne 10.00 25.00
HGA Howe/Gretzky/Beliveau 60.00 120.00
HLH Hasek/Lidstrm/Holmstrm 12.00 30.00
HPN Hextall/Parent/Niittymaki 15.00 40.00
HSF Forsberg/Smyth/Hejduk 12.00 30.00
KKS Kurri/Koivu/Selanne 20.00 50.00
KLS Kovalchk/Lecavalr/Staal 12.00 30.00
KTP Kariya/Tkachuk/Perron 12.00 30.00
LCN Lecavalr/Cheech/Nash 10.00 25.00
MLT Turco/Modano/Lehtinen 15.00 40.00
MSS Salming/McDonald/Sittler 10.00 25.00
NBO Neely/Bourque/Oates 15.00 40.00
NLP Nash/Leclaire/Peca 10.00 25.00
NLS Luongo/Demitra/Bernier 12.00 30.00
NPR Brodeur/Parise/Elias 15.00 40.00
OKK Ovech/Kovalck/Kovalev 20.00 50.00
OMK Ovech/Malkin/Kovalck 15.00 40.00
PKK Price/Kovalev/Koivu 30.00 80.00
PLG Phaneuf/Lidstrm/Gonchr 10.00 25.00
RBP Roy/Brodeur/Price 15.00 40.00
RDV Robitaille/Dionne/Vachon 12.00 30.00
RSB Roy/Sakic/Bourque 15.00 40.00
SBT Bergeron/Savard/Thomas 12.00 30.00
SFB Sund/Forsbrg/Backstrm 10.00 25.00
SKK Selanne/Koivu/Koivu 20.00 50.00
SNL Sund/Naslnd/Lndqvst 12.00 30.00
SSS Staal/Staal/Staal 12.00 30.00
STS Sundin/Toskala/Stajan 10.00 25.00
VHG Gaborik/Hossa/Vokoun 12.00 30.00

2009-10 SPx

COMP.SET w/o SPS (100) 12.00 30.00
(101-130) PRINT RUN 499 SER.#'d SETS
(131-152) PRINT RUN 799 SER.#'d SETS
(153-174) PRINT RUN 799 SER.#'d SETS
(175-180) PRINT RUN 499 SER.#'d SETS
(189-218) STATED ODDS 1:126
(219-248) STATED ODDS 1:252
1 Sidney Crosby 2.00 5.00
2 Phil Kessel .60 1.50
3 Mike Green .50 1.25
4 Henrik Lundqvist .75 2.00
5 Mark Messier .60 1.50
6 Devin Setoguchi .40 1.00
7 Jeff Carter .50 1.25
8 Henrik Zetterberg .60 1.50
9 Martin Brodeur 1.00 2.50
10 Jonathan Toews 1.00 2.50
11 Ryan Kesler .50 1.25
12 Bobby Orr 1.50 4.00
13 Eric Staal .60 1.50
14 David Perron .30 .75
15 Steven Stamkos 1.00 2.50
16 Steve Mason .40 1.00
17 Marc-Andre Fleury .75 2.00
18 Ilya Kovalchuk .50 1.25
19 Marian Gaborik .60 1.50
20 Miikka Kiprusoff .40 1.00
21 Ryan Getzlaf .75 2.00
22 Alexander Ovechkin 2.00 5.00
23 Tim Thomas .50 1.25
24 Dany Heatley .50 1.25
25 Andrew Cogliano .40 1.00
26 David Booth .30 .75
27 Pekka Rinne .60 1.50
28 Mike Ribeiro .40 1.00
29 Carey Price 2.00 5.00
30 Shane Doan .40 1.00
31 Brian Campbell .40 1.00
32 Ryan Miller .50 1.25
33 Mike Richards .50 1.25
34 Patrick Marleau .50 1.25
35 Nicklas Lidstrom .50 1.25
36 Luke Schenn .40 1.00
37 Anze Kopitar .75 2.00
38 Chris Drury .40 1.00
39 Tomas Vokoun .40 1.00
40 Rick DiPietro .40 1.00
41 Paul Stastny .50 1.25
42 Mario Lemieux 1.50 4.00
43 Sam Gagner .40 1.00
44 Jason Spezza .50 1.25
45 Martin St. Louis .50 1.25
46 Alexander Semin .50 1.25
47 Rick Nash .40 1.00
48 Cam Ward .50 1.25
49 Bobby Ryan .50 1.25
50 Tomas Kaberle .30 .75
51 Patrik Berglund .30 .75
52 Thomas Vanek .50 1.25
53 Andrei Markov .50 1.25
54 Pavel Datsyuk .60 1.50
55 Patrick Roy 1.25 3.00
56 Dion Phaneuf .60 1.50
57 Shea Weber .40 1.00
58 Patrik Elias .50 1.25
59 Bryan Little .50 1.25
60 Marty Turco .50 1.25
61 Jussi Jokinen .30 .75
62 Patrick Kane 1.00 2.50
63 Niklas Backstrom .50 1.25
64 Simon Gagne .50 1.25
65 Joe Thornton .50 1.25
66 Scottie Upshall .30 .75
67 Marian Hossa .40 1.00
68 Milan Hejduk .40 1.00
69 Marc Savard .30 .75
70 Kyle Okposo .50 1.25
71 Jason Blake .30 .75
72 Mike Modano .75 2.00
73 Jordan Staal .50 1.25
74 Ales Hemsky .40 1.00
75 Chris Osgood .50 1.25
76 Derek Roy .40 1.00
77 Daniel Alfredsson .50 1.25
78 Drew Doughty .60 1.50
79 Steve Yzerman 1.25 3.00
80 Roberto Luongo .60 1.50
81 Michael Frolik .40 1.00
82 Teemu Selanne 1.00 2.50
83 Ryan Smyth .40 1.00
84 Nicklas Backstrom .75 2.00
85 Mike Cammalleri .40 1.00
86 Peter Mueller .40 1.00
87 Kari Lehtonen .40 1.00
88 Gordie Howe 1.25 3.00
89 Scott Gomez .40 1.00
90 Jarome Iginla .50 1.25
91 David Backes .50 1.25
92 Zdeno Chara .50 1.25
93 Vincent Lecavalier .40 1.00
94 Mikko Koivu .50 1.25
95 Daniel Briere .50 1.25
96 Jason Arnott .40 1.00
97 Henrik Sedin .50 1.25
98 Derick Brassard .50 1.25
99 Wayne Gretzky 2.50 6.00
100 Zach Parise .50 1.25
101 Guillaume Desbiens RC 4.00 10.00
102 Davis Drewiske RC 4.00 10.00
103 Ryan Vesce RC 3.00 8.00
104 Alec Martinez RC 5.00 12.00
105 David Schlemko RC 3.00 8.00
106 Jay Beagle RC 5.00 12.00
107 Steven Zalewski RC 3.00 8.00
108 Tim Wallace RC 2.50 6.00
109 Geoff Kinrade RC 4.00 10.00
110 Teemu Laakso RC 2.50 6.00
111 Jakub Petruzalek RC 4.00 10.00
112 Matt Gilroy RC 4.00 10.00
113 Tyson Strachan RC 2.50 6.00
114 James Reimer RC 10.00 25.00
115 Sean Collins RC 3.00 8.00
116 Frazer McLaren RC 3.00 8.00
117 Johan Backlund RC 4.00 10.00
118 Mathieu Perreault RC 6.00 15.00
119 Kevin Quick RC 2.50 6.00
120 Mika Pyorala RC 3.00 8.00
121 Tim Stapleton RC 4.00 10.00
122 Chris Durno RC 3.00 8.00
123 Jaime Sifers RC 3.00 8.00
124 Troy Bodie RC 3.00 8.00
125 Braden Holtby RC 10.00 25.00
126 Sean Bentivoglio RC 3.00 8.00
127 Phil Oreskovic RC 4.00 10.00
128 James Wright RC 4.00 10.00
129 Bryan Rodney RC 3.00 8.00
130 Alexander Sulzer RC 2.50 6.00
131 Matt Beleskey JSY RC 4.00 10.00
132 Jason Demers JSY RC 8.00 20.00
133 Dmitry Kulikov JSY RC 5.00 12.00
134 Cal O'Reilly JSY RC 4.00 10.00
135 Jay Rosehill JSY RC 5.00 12.00
136 T.J. Galiardi JSY RC 5.00 12.00
137 Michael Sauer JSY RC 4.00 10.00
138 Ryan O'Marra JSY RC 3.00 8.00
139 Benn Ferriero JSY RC 5.00 12.00
140 Chris Butler JSY RC 5.00 12.00
141 Mike Santorelli JSY RC 5.00 12.00
142 Andrew MacDonald JSY RC 3.00 8.00
143 John Scott JSY RC 5.00 12.00
144 Matt Pelech JSY RC 5.00 12.00
145 Ray Macias JSY RC 4.00 10.00
146 Cody Franson JSY RC 5.00 12.00
147 Kris Chucko JSY RC 4.00 10.00
148 Joel Rechlicz JSY RC 3.00 8.00
149 Perttu Lindgren JSY RC 4.00 10.00
150 Sergei Shirokov JSY RC 3.00 8.00
151 Spencer Machacek JSY RC 5.00 12.00
152 Yannick Weber JSY RC 5.00 12.00
153 Artem Anisimov JSY AU RC 6.00 15.00
154 Brian Salcido JSY AU RC 5.00 12.00
155 C.Hanson JSY AU RC 6.00 15.00
156 I.Vishnevskiy JSY AU RC 5.00 12.00
157 Jhonas Enroth JSY AU RC 8.00 20.00
158 M.Grabner JSY AU RC 6.00 15.00
159 Luca Caputi JSY AU RC 6.00 15.00
160 Brad Marchand JSY AU RC 12.00 30.00
161 Mikael Backlund JSY AU RC 6.00 15.00
162 Riku Helenius JSY AU RC 6.00 15.00
163 Ville Leino JSY AU RC 5.00 12.00
164 Lars Eller JSY AU RC 6.00 15.00
165 Erik Karlsson JSY AU RC 15.00 40.00
166 Tyler Myers JSY AU RC 6.00 15.00
167 Ryan O'Reilly JSY AU RC 10.00 25.00
168 Jamie Benn JSY AU RC 25.00 50.00
169 Logan Couture JSY AU RC 12.00 30.00
170 Michael Del Zotto JSY AU RC 6.00 15.00
171 Viktor Stalberg JSY AU RC 6.00 15.00
172 Antti Niemi JSY AU RC 10.00 25.00
173 Tyler Bozak JSY AU RC 10.00 25.00
174 Colin Wilson JSY AU RC 6.00 15.00
175 M.Duchene JSY AU RC/499 15.00 40.00
176 Gustavsson JSY AU RC/499 8.00 20.00
177 V.Hedman JSY AU RC/499 15.00 40.00
178 E.Kane JSY AU RC/499 12.00 30.00
179 van Riems JSY AU RC/499 12.00 30.00
180 J.Tavares JSY AU RC/499 60.00 150.00
189 Doug Gilmour FF JSY 8.00 20.00
190 Alexander Ovechkin FF JSY 25.00 60.00
191 Tony Esposito FF JSY 10.00 25.00
192 Steve Shutt FF JSY 6.00 15.00
193 Jay Bouwmeester FF JSY 6.00 15.00
194 Adam Oates FF JSY 6.00 15.00
195 Joe Mullen FF JSY 5.00 12.00
196 Jari Kurri FF JSY 6.00 15.00
197 Patrick Kane FF JSY 12.00 30.00
198 Scott Gomez FF JSY 5.00 12.00
199 Paul Kariya FF JSY 8.00 20.00
200 Mike Modano FF JSY 10.00 25.00
201 Larry Murphy FF JSY 5.00 12.00
202 Luc Robitaille FF JSY 6.00 15.00
203 Nicklas Lidstrom FF JSY 6.00 15.00
204 Vincent Lecavalier FF JSY 5.00 12.00
205 Zach Parise FF JSY 6.00 15.00
206 Ray Bourque FF JSY 10.00 25.00
207 Bernie Federko FF JSY 5.00 12.00
208 Cam Neely FF JSY 6.00 15.00
209 Wade Redden FF JSY 4.00 10.00
210 Bob Bourne FF JSY 5.00 12.00
211 Larry Robinson FF JSY 6.00 15.00
212 Dale Hawerchuk FF JSY 8.00 20.00
213 Teemu Selanne FF JSY 12.00 30.00
214 Johnny Bucyk FF JSY 10.00 25.00
215 Brent Sutter FF JSY 4.00 10.00
216 Grant Fuhr FF JSY 6.00 15.00
217 Alex Tanguay FF JSY 4.00 10.00
218 Gilbert Perreault FF JSY 6.00 15.00
219 Steve Yzerman FF JSY AU 150.00 250.00
220 Martin Brodeur FF JSY AU 50.00 100.00
221 Evgeni Malkin FF JSY AU 30.00 60.00
222 Denis Savard FF JSY AU 20.00 50.00
223 Scotty Bowman FF JSY AU 30.00 60.00
224 Darryl Sittler FF JSY AU 12.00 30.00
225 Patrick Roy FF JSY AU 50.00 100.00
226 Wendel Clark FF JSY AU 15.00 40.00
227 Phil Esposito FF JSY AU 25.00 60.00
228 Patrick Marleau FF JSY AU 15.00 40.00
229 S.Niedermayer FF JSY AU 20.00 50.00
230 Marian Hossa FF JSY AU 12.00 30.00
231 Mark Messier FF JSY AU 40.00 100.00
232 Marcel Dionne FF JSY AU 20.00 50.00
233 Peter Stastny FF JSY AU 15.00 40.00
234 Mario Lemieux FF JSY AU 60.00 120.00
235 Carey Price FF JSY AU 30.00 80.00
236 Pavel Datsyuk FF JSY AU 20.00 50.00
237 Saku Koivu FF JSY AU 15.00 40.00
238 N.Khabibulin FF JSY AU 15.00 40.00
239 Gordie Howe FF JSY AU 75.00 150.00
240 Frank Mahovlich FF JSY AU 20.00 50.00
241 Guy Lafleur FF JSY AU 20.00 50.00
242 D.Ciccarelli FF JSY AU EXCH 15.00 40.00
243 G.Carbonneau FF JSY AU 25.00 60.00
244 Dany Heatley FF JSY AU 12.00 30.00
245 Sidney Crosby FF JSY AU 100.00 200.00
246 Glenn Anderson FF JSY AU 15.00 40.00
247 Dave Taylor FF JSY AU 15.00 40.00
248 Wayne Gretzky FF JSY AU 125.00 250.00

2009-10 SPx Spectrum

STATED PRINT RUN 25 SER.#'d SETS
1 Sidney Crosby JSY 25.00 60.00
2 Phil Kessel JSY 10.00 25.00
4 Henrik Lundqvist JSY 12.00 30.00
5 Mark Messier JSY 10.00 25.00
7 Jeff Carter JSY 8.00 20.00
8 Henrik Zetterberg JSY 10.00 25.00
9 Martin Brodeur JSY 15.00 40.00
10 Jonathan Toews JSY 15.00 40.00
11 Ryan Kesler JSY 8.00 20.00
13 Eric Staal JSY 10.00 25.00
17 Marc-Andre Fleury JSY 12.00 30.00
18 Ilya Kovalchuk JSY 8.00 20.00
19 Marian Gaborik JSY 10.00 25.00
20 Miikka Kiprusoff JSY 6.00 15.00
21 Ryan Getzlaf JSY 12.00 30.00
22 Alexander Ovechkin JSY 25.00 60.00
23 Tim Thomas JSY 8.00 20.00
24 Dany Heatley JSY
25 Andrew Cogliano JSY 6.00 15.00
26 David Booth JSY 8.00 20.00
27 Pekka Rinne JSY 10.00 25.00
28 Mike Ribeiro JSY 6.00 15.00
29 Carey Price JSY 30.00 80.00
30 Shane Doan JSY 6.00 15.00
31 Brian Campbell JSY
32 Ryan Miller JSY 8.00 20.00
33 Mike Richards JSY 8.00 20.00
34 Patrick Marleau JSY 8.00 20.00
35 Nicklas Lidstrom JSY 8.00 20.00
36 Luke Schenn JSY 6.00 15.00
37 Anze Kopitar JSY 12.00 30.00
38 Chris Drury JSY 6.00 15.00
39 Tomas Vokoun JSY 6.00 15.00
40 Rick DiPietro JSY 6.00 15.00
41 Paul Stastny JSY 8.00 20.00
42 Mario Lemieux JSY 25.00 60.00
43 Sam Gagner JSY 6.00 15.00
44 Jason Spezza JSY 8.00 20.00
45 Martin St. Louis JSY 8.00 20.00
46 Alexander Semin JSY 8.00 20.00
47 Rick Nash JSY 6.00 15.00
48 Cam Ward JSY 8.00 20.00
50 Tomas Kaberle JSY 5.00 12.00
51 Patrik Berglund JSY 5.00 12.00
52 Thomas Vanek JSY 8.00 20.00
53 Andrei Markov JSY 8.00 20.00
54 Pavel Datsyuk JSY 10.00 25.00
55 Patrick Roy JSY 20.00 50.00
56 Dion Phaneuf JSY 10.00 25.00
57 Shea Weber JSY 6.00 15.00
58 Patrik Elias JSY 8.00 20.00
60 Marty Turco JSY 8.00 20.00
61 Jussi Jokinen JSY 5.00 12.00
62 Patrick Kane JSY 15.00 40.00
64 Simon Gagne JSY 8.00 20.00
65 Joe Thornton JSY 8.00 20.00
67 Marian Hossa JSY 12.00 30.00
68 Milan Hejduk JSY 6.00 15.00
69 Marc Savard JSY 5.00 12.00
70 Kyle Okposo JSY 8.00 20.00
72 Mike Modano JSY 12.00 30.00
73 Jordan Staal JSY 8.00 20.00
74 Ales Hemsky JSY 6.00 15.00
75 Chris Osgood JSY 8.00 20.00
76 Derek Roy JSY 6.00 15.00
77 Daniel Alfredsson JSY 8.00 20.00
78 Drew Doughty JSY 10.00 25.00
79 Steve Yzerman JSY 20.00 50.00
80 Roberto Luongo JSY 10.00 25.00
81 Michael Frolik JSY
82 Teemu Selanne JSY 15.00 40.00
83 Ryan Smyth JSY 6.00 15.00
84 Nicklas Backstrom JSY 12.00 30.00
85 Mike Cammalleri JSY 15.00 40.00
86 Peter Mueller JSY 6.00 15.00
87 Kari Lehtonen JSY 6.00 15.00
88 Gordie Howe JSY 25.00 60.00
89 Scott Gomez JSY 6.00 15.00
90 Jarome Iginla JSY 8.00 20.00
93 Vincent Lecavalier JSY 6.00 15.00
94 Mikko Koivu JSY 8.00 20.00
96 Jason Arnott JSY 6.00 15.00
98 Derick Brassard JSY 10.00 25.00

9 Wayne Gretzky JSY	25.00	60.00
00 Zach Parise JSY	8.00	20.00
01 Guillaume Desbiens	5.00	12.00
02 Davis Drewiske	5.00	12.00
03 Ryan Vesce	4.00	10.00
04 Alec Martinez	6.00	15.00
05 David Schlemko	4.00	10.00
06 Jay Beagle	6.00	15.00
07 Steven Zalewski	4.00	10.00
08 Tim Wallace	3.00	8.00
09 Geoff Kinrade	5.00	12.00
10 Teemu Laakso	3.00	8.00
11 Jakub Petruzalek	5.00	12.00
12 Matt Gilroy	5.00	12.00
13 Tyson Strachan	3.00	8.00
14 James Reimer	15.00	40.00
15 Sean Collins	4.00	10.00
16 Frazer McLaren	4.00	10.00
17 Johan Backlund	5.00	12.00
18 Mathieu Perreault	8.00	20.00
19 Kevin Quick	3.00	8.00
20 Mika Pyorala	4.00	10.00
21 Tim Stapleton	5.00	12.00
22 Chris Durno	4.00	10.00
23 Jaime Sifers	4.00	10.00
24 Troy Bodie	4.00	10.00
25 Braden Holtby	12.00	30.00
26 Sean Bentivoglio	4.00	10.00
27 Phil Oreskovic	5.00	12.00
28 James Wright	5.00	12.00
29 Bryan Rodney		
30 Alexander Sulzer	3.00	8.00
31 Matt Beleskey PATCH	10.00	25.00
32 Jason Demers PATCH	20.00	50.00
33 Dmitry Kulikov PATCH	12.00	30.00
34 Cal O'Reilly PATCH	10.00	25.00
35 Jay Rosehill PATCH	12.00	30.00
36 T.J. Galiardi PATCH	12.00	30.00
37 Michael Sauer PATCH	10.00	25.00
38 Ryan O'Marra PATCH	8.00	20.00
39 Benn Ferriero PATCH	15.00	40.00
40 Chris Butler PATCH	12.00	30.00
41 Mike Santorelli PATCH	12.00	30.00
42 Andrew MacDonald PATCH	8.00	20.00
43 John Scott PATCH	12.50	30.00
44 Matt Pelech PATCH	12.00	30.00
45 Ray Macias PATCH	10.00	25.00
46 Cody Franson PATCH	12.00	30.00
47 Kris Chucko PATCH	10.00	25.00
48 Joel Rechlicz PATCH		
49 Perttu Lindgren PATCH	10.00	25.00
50 Sergei Shirokov PATCH	8.00	20.00
51 Spencer Machacek PATCH	12.00	30.00
52 Yannick Weber PATCH	12.00	30.00
53 Artem Anisimov PATCH AU	15.00	40.00
54 Brian Salcido PATCH AU	12.00	30.00
55 Christian Hanson PATCH AU	15.00	40.00
56 Vishnevskiy PATCH AU ERR	12.00	30.00
57 Jhonas Enroth PATCH AU	20.00	50.00
58 M.Grabner PATCH AU	15.00	40.00
59 Luca Caputi PATCH AU	15.00	40.00
60 Brad Marchand PATCH AU	15.00	40.00
61 M.Backlund PATCH AU	15.00	40.00
62 Riku Helenius PATCH AU	15.00	40.00
63 Ville Leino PATCH AU	12.00	30.00
64 Lars Eller PATCH AU	40.00	100.00
65 Erik Karlsson PATCH AU	75.00	150.00
66 Tyler Myers PATCH AU	250.00	400.00
68 Jamie Benn PATCH AU	50.00	125.00
69 Logan Couture PATCH AU	75.00	150.00
70 M.Del Zotto PATCH AU	15.00	40.00
71 Viktor Stalberg PATCH AU	15.00	40.00
72 Antti Niemi PATCH AU	25.00	60.00
73 Tyler Bozak PATCH AU	60.00	120.00
74 Colin Wilson PATCH AU	15.00	40.00
83 Matt Duchene PATCH AU	200.00	350.00
84 J.Gustavsson PATCH AU	100.00	200.00
85 Victor Hedman PATCH AU	60.00	120.00
86 Evander Kane PATCH AU	60.00	120.00
87 van Riemsdyk PATCH AU	100.00	200.00
88 John Tavares PATCH AU	250.00	500.00

2009-10 SPx Shadowbox

TATED ODDS 1:252

H1 Wayne Gretzky	125.00	200.00
H2 Evgeni Malkin	25.00	60.00
H3 Henrik Zetterberg	60.00	120.00
H4 Jeff Carter	30.00	60.00
H5 Rick Nash	12.00	30.00
H6 Zach Parise	15.00	40.00
H7 Joe Thornton	40.00	80.00
H8 Patrick Kane	60.00	120.00
H9 Bobby Orr	60.00	120.00
H10 Jarome Iginla	30.00	60.00
H11 Martin St. Louis	25.00	50.00
H12 Dany Heatley	15.00	40.00
H13 Ryan Getzlaf	15.00	40.00
H14 Jason Spezza	25.00	50.00
H15 Steve Yzerman	60.00	120.00
H16 Alexander Ovechkin	60.00	120.00
H17 Mario Lemieux	50.00	100.00
H18 Dion Phaneuf	12.00	30.00
H19 Cam Neely	15.00	40.00
H20 Ilya Kovalchuk	15.00	40.00
H21 Mike Richards		
H22 Jonathan Toews	60.00	120.00
H23 Nicklas Backstrom	15.00	40.00
H24 Mark Messier	40.00	80.00
H25 Pavel Datsyuk	30.00	60.00
H26 Eric Staal	25.00	50.00
H27 Mike Green	15.00	40.00
H28 Vincent Lecavalier	30.00	60.00
H29 Gordie Howe	40.00	100.00
H30 Sidney Crosby	40.00	100.00

2009-10 SPx Shadowbox Stoppers

TATED ODDS 1:252

T1 Martin Brodeur	15.00	40.00
T2 Patrick Roy	40.00	100.00
T3 Marc-Andre Fleury	30.00	60.00
T4 Roberto Luongo		
T5 Tony Esposito	20.00	50.00
T6 Miikka Kiprusoff	30.00	60.00
T7 Carey Price	40.00	80.00
T8 Henrik Lundqvist		
T9 Grant Fuhr	25.00	50.00
T10 Steve Mason	30.00	60.00
T11 Ron Hextall	25.00	50.00
T12 Ryan Miller	15.00	40.00

2009-10 SPx SPXcitement

OMPLETE SET (70)	200.00	400.00
TATED PRINT RUN 999 SER.#'d SETS		
1 Wayne Gretzky	8.00	20.00
2 Luke Schenn	1.25	3.00
3 Carey Price	6.00	15.00
4 Bobby Orr	5.00	12.00
5 Henrik Zetterberg	2.00	5.00
6 Marc-Andre Fleury	2.50	6.00
7 Thomas Vanek	1.50	4.00
8 Cam Neely	1.50	4.00
X9 Gordie Howe	4.00	10.00
X10 Patrick Marleau	1.50	4.00
X11 Mark Messier	2.00	5.00
X12 Miikka Kiprusoff	1.25	3.00
X13 John Tavares		
X14 Jonathan Toews	3.00	8.00
X15 Dany Heatley	1.50	4.00
X16 Bobby Clarke	1.50	4.00
X17 Steven Stamkos	3.00	8.00
X18 Alexander Ovechkin	6.00	15.00
X19 Steve Yzerman	4.00	10.00
X20 Phil Kessel	2.00	5.00
X21 Steve Mason	1.25	3.00
X22 Mike Bossy	1.50	4.00
X23 Sam Gagner	1.25	3.00
X24 Eric Staal	2.00	5.00
X25 Matt Duchene	3.00	8.00
X26 Ryan Getzlaf	2.50	6.00
X27 Evgeni Malkin	5.00	12.00
X28 Scott Gomez	1.25	3.00
X29 Joe Thornton	1.50	4.00
X30 Martin Brodeur	3.00	8.00
X31 Mike Ribeiro	1.25	3.00
X32 Pavel Datsyuk	2.00	5.00
X33 Patrick Roy	4.00	10.00
X34 Drew Doughty	2.00	5.00
X35 Vincent Lecavalier	1.25	3.00
X36 Mikko Koivu	1.50	4.00
X37 Zach Parise	1.50	4.00
X38 Marian Hossa	1.25	3.00
X39 Tomas Vokoun	1.25	3.00
X40 Jarome Iginla	1.50	4.00
X41 Ville Leino	1.25	3.00
X42 Henrik Lundqvist	2.50	6.00
X43 Jordan Staal	1.50	4.00
X44 Bobby Ryan	1.50	4.00
X45 Mike Green	1.50	4.00
X46 Ilya Kovalchuk	1.50	4.00
X47 Cam Ward	1.50	4.00
X48 Jonas Gustavsson	8.00	20.00
X49 Ryan Kesler	1.50	4.00
X50 Mikael Backlund	1.50	4.00
X51 Patrick Kane	3.00	8.00
X52 Jason Spezza	1.50	4.00
X53 Jeff Carter	1.50	4.00
X54 David Perron	1.00	2.50
X55 Shea Weber	1.25	3.00
X56 James van Riemsdyk	3.00	8.00
X57 Devin Setoguchi	1.25	3.00
X58 Tim Thomas	1.50	4.00
X59 Rick DiPietro	1.25	3.00
X60 Nicklas Lidstrom	1.50	4.00
X61 Rick Nash	1.25	3.00
X62 Artem Anisimov	1.50	4.00
X63 James Neal	1.50	4.00
X64 Ryan Miller	1.50	4.00
X65 Brian Campbell	1.25	3.00
X66 Mario Lemieux	5.00	12.00
X67 Paul Stastny	1.50	4.00
X68 Peter Mueller	1.25	3.00
X69 Roberto Luongo	2.00	5.00
X70 Sidney Crosby	6.00	15.00

2009-10 SPx SPXcitement Spectrum

*SINGLES: 1.5X TO 4X BASIC INSERTS
STATED PRINT RUN 25 SER.#'d SETS

X13 John Tavares	60.00	120.00
X37 Zach Parise	6.00	15.00
X48 Jonas Gustavsson	25.00	60.00

2009-10 SPx Winning Combos

STATED ODDS 1:18

WCBK Koivu/Bouchard	5.00	12.00
WCCB Chara/Bergeron	6.00	15.00
WCCG Gilmour/Clark	8.00	20.00
WCCM Crosby/Malkin	12.00	30.00
WCCO Crosby/Ovechkin	20.00	50.00
WCCT Campbell/Toews	10.00	25.00
WCCW Campbell/Wilson	4.00	10.00
WCDL Doan/Lombardi	4.00	10.00
WCEH Esposito/Huet	8.00	20.00
WCER Brind`Amour/Staal	6.00	15.00
WCFK Frolov/Kopitar	8.00	20.00
WCGD Gaborik/Drury	6.00	15.00
WCGF Fleury/Gilmour	8.00	20.00
WCGG Giguere/Getzlaf	8.00	20.00
WCGL Letang/Gonchar	5.00	12.00
WCHB Booth/Horton	5.00	12.00
WCHD Datsyuk/Holmstrom	6.00	15.00
WCHS Sharp/Hossa	5.00	12.00
WCHW Redden/Lundqvist	8.00	20.00
WCKF Kurri/Fuhr	5.00	12.00
WCKK Koivu/Koivu	5.00	12.00
WCKS Kurri/Selanne	10.00	25.00
WCLD Datsyuk/Lidstrom	6.00	15.00
WCLR Raymond/Luongo	6.00	15.00
WCLS Salming/Lidstrom	5.00	12.00
WCMC Ciccarelli/Modano	8.00	20.00
WCMR Richards/Modano	8.00	20.00
WCNB Bourque/Neely	8.00	20.00
WCNV Voracek/Nash	5.00	12.00
WCOB Ovechkin/Backstrom	15.00	40.00
WCOM Ovechkin/Malkin	15.00	40.00
WCPP Plekanec/Price	20.00	50.00
WCPR Pominville/Roy	5.00	12.00
WCRD Stafford/Miller	5.00	12.00
WCRL Roy/Luongo	12.00	30.00
WCRT Taylor/Robitaille	6.00	15.00
WCSB Stoll/Brown	4.00	10.00
WCSH Hawerchuk/Selanne	10.00	25.00
WCSK Sharp/Kane	10.00	25.00
WCSM Sittler/McDonald	6.00	15.00
WCSR Shutt/Robinson	5.00	12.00
WCSS Staal/Staal	6.00	15.00
WCSW Svatos/Wolski	3.00	8.00
WCYB Bowman/Yzerman	12.00	30.00

2009-10 SPx Winning Combos Spectrum

STATED PRINT RUN 25 SER.#'d SETS

WCBP Z.Parise/M.Brodeur	15.00	40.00
WCFC M.Fleury/S.Crosby	30.00	80.00
WCHS P.Sharp.M.Hossa	8.00	20.00
WCIK J.Iginla/M.Hossa	8.00	20.00
WCOB Ovechkin/Backstrom	20.00	50.00

2009-10 SPx Winning Materials

STATED ODDS 1:18
*PATCH/50: 1X TO 2.5X BASIC JSY

WMAC Andrew Cogliano	4.00	10.00
WMAF Alexander Frolov	4.00	10.00
WMBC Brian Campbell	4.00	10.00
WMBS Brent Seabrook	4.00	10.00
WMCH Cristobal Huet	5.00	12.00
WMCO Chris Osgood	5.00	12.00
WMCW Cam Ward	5.00	12.00
WMDB Dustin Brown	4.00	10.00
WMDC Dino Ciccarelli	5.00	12.00
WMDG Doug Gilmour	6.00	15.00
WMDH Dale Hawerchuk	6.00	15.00
WMDR Derek Roy	4.00	10.00
WMDS Darryl Sittler	6.00	15.00
WMDT Dave Taylor	6.00	15.00
WMFM Frank Mahovlich	6.00	15.00
WMGA Glenn Anderson	5.00	12.00
WMGP Gilbert Perreault	5.00	12.00
WMJB Josh Bailey	4.00	10.00
WMJC Jonathan Cheechoo	5.00	12.00
WMJG Jean-Sebastien Giguere	5.00	12.00
WMJI Jarome Iginla	5.00	12.00
WMJK Jari Kurri	5.00	12.00
WMJS Jason Spezza	5.00	12.00
WMJT Jonathan Toews	10.00	25.00
WMKL Kari Lehtonen	4.00	10.00
WMLM Lanny McDonald	5.00	12.00
WMLR Larry Robinson	5.00	12.00
WMLU Luc Robitaille	5.00	12.00
WMMD Marcel Dionne	6.00	15.00
WMMG Marian Gaborik	6.00	15.00
WMMI Milan Lucic	4.00	10.00
WMMK Mikko Koivu	5.00	12.00
WMMM Mark Messier	6.00	15.00
WMMT Marty Turco	5.00	12.00
WMNL Nicklas Lidstrom	5.00	12.00
WMPB Patrice Bergeron	6.00	15.00
WMPM Peter Mueller	4.00	10.00
WMPR Patrick Roy	12.00	30.00
WMPS Patrick Sharp	5.00	12.00
WMRD Rick DiPietro	4.00	10.00
WMRG Ryan Getzlaf	4.00	10.00
WMRL Roberto Luongo	6.00	15.00
WMSD Shane Doan	4.00	10.00
WMSG Simon Gagne	5.00	12.00
WMSK Saku Koivu	5.00	12.00
WMST Drew Stafford	5.00	12.00
WMWG Wayne Gretzky	25.00	60.00

2009-10 SPx Winning Materials Autographs

STATED PRINT RUN 50 SER.#'d SETS

AWMAK Anze Kopitar	20.00	50.00
AWMAO Adam Oates	12.00	30.00
AWMBC Bobby Clarke	15.00	40.00
AWMBH Bobby Hull	15.00	40.00
AWMBS Brent Sutter	8.00	20.00
AWMCN Cam Neely	12.00	30.00
AWMCP Carey Price	30.00	80.00
AWMDD Drew Doughty	15.00	40.00
AWMEM Evgeni Malkin	40.00	100.00
AWMES Eric Staal	15.00	40.00
AWMFR Michael Frolik	10.00	25.00
AWMHL Henrik Lundqvist	30.00	80.00
AWMIK Ilya Kovalchuk	12.00	30.00
AWMJK Jari Kurri	10.00	25.00
AWMJP Jason Pominville	12.00	30.00
AWMJT Joe Thornton	12.00	30.00
AWMJV Jakub Voracek	12.00	30.00
AWMLS Luke Schenn	10.00	25.00
AWMMB Martin Brodeur	40.00	100.00
AWMMF Marc-Andre Fleury	15.00	40.00
AWMMR Mason Raymond	20.00	50.00
AWMNB Nicklas Backstrom	20.00	50.00
AWMNH Nathan Horton	12.00	30.00
AWMPB Patrik Berglund	12.00	30.00
AWMPD Pavel Datsyuk	15.00	40.00
AWMPE Patrik Elias	12.00	30.00
AWMPH Dion Phaneuf	15.00	40.00
AWMPK Patrick Kane	25.00	60.00
AWMPL Pascal Leclaire	12.00	30.00
AWMPM Peter Mueller	10.00	25.00
AWMPR Pekka Rinne	15.00	40.00
AWMRH Ron Hextall	20.00	50.00
AWMRI Mike Richards	15.00	40.00
AWMRM Ryan Miller	20.00	50.00
AWMRN Rick Nash	10.00	25.00
AWMRY Michael Ryder	12.50	30.00
AWMSC Sidney Crosby	75.00	150.00
AWMSH Steve Shutt	12.00	30.00
AWMSW Shea Weber	10.00	25.00
AWMTE Tony Esposito	20.00	50.00
AWMTO Jonathan Toews	25.00	60.00
AWMTV Tomas Vokoun	10.00	25.00
AWMVA Thomas Vanek	12.00	30.00

2009-10 SPx Winning Trios

STATED PRINT RUN 50 SER.#'d SETS

WTALB Phaneuf/Iginla/Nieder		
WTAVS Hejduk/Wolski/Svatos	6.00	15.00
WTBBR Price/Gomez/Plekanc	30.00	80.00
WTBCO Price/Lucic/Kariya	30.00	80.00
WTBEL Clarkson/Cheech/Spez		
WTBOS Thomas/Bergern/Rydr	12.00	30.00
WTBRU Oates/Bourque/Neely	8.00	20.00
WTBUF Roy/Vanek/Stafford	8.00	20.00
WTBWK Hextall/Osgood/Redden	12.00	30.00
WTCAR Jokinen/Ruutu/Samsnv		
WTCBH Kane/Toews/Campbell	15.00	40.00
WTCBJ Voracek/Brassard/Nash	8.00	20.00
WTCGY McDonald/MacIns/Gilmr	10.00	25.00
WTCHF Mikita/Hull/Esposito	15.00	40.00
WTCHI Campbell/Sharp/Huet	10.00	25.00
WTCOL Stastny/Hejduk/Tucker	8.00	20.00
WTCON Zetter/Malkn/Nieder	15.00	40.00
WTCPT Mario/Messier/Gretzky	40.00	100.00
WTCZE Elias/Hejduk/Plekanec	8.00	20.00
WTDEF Bouwmstr/Phanf/Weber	10.00	25.00
WTDET Draper/Holmstrm/Lidstrm	8.00	20.00
WTDRW Osgood/Zetter/Datsyk	10.00	25.00
WTEDM Khabib/O'Sullvn/Cogli	8.00	20.00
WTEHF Messier/Fuhr/Kurri	10.00	25.00
WTFIN Selanne/Kurri/Koivu	12.00	30.00
WTFLD Lehtn/Rinne/Kiprusff	10.00	25.00
WTFLM Kiprusff/Iginla/Jokin	8.00	20.00
WTFND Kiprusff/Koivu/Selan	12.00	30.00
WTHAB Mahov/Shutt/Robnsn	10.00	25.00
WTHAR Ovechkin/Iginla/Crosby	15.00	40.00
WTHOF Mario/Yzermn/Messier	40.00	100.00
WTHRT Datsyk/Ovech/Malkn	20.00	50.00
WTHUR Staal/Brind`Amour/Ward	10.00	25.00
WTKAM Iginla/Doan/Nieder	8.00	20.00
WTKIN Dionne/Taylor/Murphy	15.00	40.00
WTKIT Roy/Richards/Robinsn	8.00	20.00
WTLAK Williams/Stoll/Brown	6.00	15.00
WTLAV Luongo/Bossy/Mario	25.00	60.00
WTLND Thorntn/Gagner/Carter	8.00	20.00
WTLON Ciccarelli/Gagner/Nash	8.00	20.00
WTLOS Kopitar/Doughty/Frolov	10.00	25.00
WTMHF Robinsn/Bellveau/Roy	30.00	60.00
WTMTL Shutt/Carbon/Robinsn	12.00	30.00
WTNYI Weight/Bailey/DiPietro	8.00	20.00
WTNYR Messi/Andersn/Leetch	10.00	25.00
WTOIL Messi/Kurri/Andersn		
WTOTT Spezza/Leclaire/Foligno	8.00	20.00
WTOTW Savard/Roy/Brind		
WTPEN Crosby/Staal/Malkin	25.00	60.00
WTPET Staal/Staal/Yzerman	20.00	50.00
WTPHI Carter/Richards/Gagne	15.00	40.00
WTPHX Mueller/Boedker/Doan	6.00	15.00
WTPIT Fleury/Letang/Gonchar	8.00	20.00
WTPOR Neely/Hossa/Messier	10.00	25.00
WTQMJ Luongo/Ribeiro/SLL	12.00	30.00
WTQUE Gagne/Lafleur/Ribeiro	12.00	30.00
WTRIM Lecav/Richrds/Crsby	15.00	40.00
WTRNG Staal/Gaborik/Drury	10.00	25.00
WTRRT Lecav/Ovech/Cheech	30.00	80.00
WTRUS Ovech/Koval/Malkn	20.00	50.00
WTSAB Vanek/Pominvill/Millr	12.00	30.00
WTSAS Ward/Schenn/Getzlf	12.00	30.00
WTSCC Getzlaf/Crsby/Datsyk	25.00	60.00
WTSEA Osgd/Andersn/Marleau	8.00	20.00
WTSHF Hawer/MacIns/Fedrk	12.00	30.00
WTSHO Brodr/Luongo/Kiprsff	15.00	40.00
WTSSM Espo/Gretz/Thorntn	50.00	100.00
WTSTR Richrds/Ribeo/Modno	12.00	30.00
WTSWE Lundqst/Lidstrm/Zetter	12.00	30.00
WTTHF Mahov/Sittler/McDnald	10.00	25.00
WTTML Clark/Andersn/Gilmour		
WTTOR Salmng/Mahov/McDnld	10.00	25.00
WTUDC Gretzky/Yzer/Crosby	100.00	200.00
WTUSA Modano/Parise/Miller	15.00	40.00
WTUSP Mullen/Parise/Modano	12.00	30.00
WTVAN Luongo/Raymnd/Bernier		
WTVIC Hextall/Fuhr/Roy	20.00	50.00
WTWNG Yzermn/Zettr/Howe	20.00	50.00

2010-11 SPx

COMP.SET w/o SPs (100)	10.00	25.00
LEGENDS PRINT RUN 999 SER.#'d SETS		
(116-155) PRINT RUN 499 SER.#'d SETS		
(156-165) PRINT RUN 799 SER.#'d SETS		
(166-191) PRINT RUN 799 SER.#'d SETS		
(192-197) PRINT RUN 499 SER.#'d SETS		
(198-228) STATED ODDS 1:126		
(229-257) STATED ODDS 1:252		
1 Corey Perry	.40	1.00
2 Ryan Getzlaf	.60	1.50
3 Bobby Ryan	.40	1.00
4 Dustin Byfuglien	.40	1.00
5 Evander Kane	.40	1.00
6 Nik Antropov	.30	.75
7 Blake Wheeler	.40	1.00
8 Tuukka Rask	.40	1.00
9 Patrice Bergeron	.50	1.25
10 Milan Lucic	.40	1.00
11 Tyler Myers	.40	1.00
12 Ryan Miller	.40	1.00
13 Thomas Vanek	.40	1.00
14 Jay Bouwmeester	.50	1.25
15 Jarome Iginla	.40	1.00
16 Miikka Kiprusoff	.30	.75
17 Tuomo Ruutu	.30	.75
18 Eric Staal	.50	1.25
19 Cam Ward	.40	1.00
20 Duncan Keith	.40	1.00
21 Patrick Kane	.75	2.00
22 Marian Hossa	.30	.75
23 Patrick Sharp	.40	1.00
24 Jonathan Toews	.75	2.00
25 Peter Mueller	.30	.75
26 Matt Duchene	.40	1.00
27 Paul Stastny	.40	1.00
28 Derick Brassard	.40	1.00
29 Rick Nash	.40	1.00
30 Steve Mason	.30	.75
31 Kari Lehtonen	.30	.75
32 Brad Richards	.40	1.00
33 Loui Eriksson	.30	.75
34 Johan Franzen	.40	1.00
35 Jim Howard	.50	1.25
36 Henrik Zetterberg	.50	1.25
37 Nicklas Lidstrom	.40	1.00
38 Pavel Datsyuk	.50	1.25
39 Ales Hemsky	.30	.75
40 Sam Gagner	.30	.75
41 Dustin Penner	.25	.60
42 Michael Frolik	.25	.60
43 Stephen Weiss	.30	.75
44 Tomas Vokoun	.30	.75
45 Anze Kopitar	.60	1.50
46 Drew Doughty	.40	1.00
47 Dustin Brown	.40	1.00
48 Guillaume Latendresse	.30	.75
49 Mikko Koivu	.40	1.00
50 Niklas Backstrom	.40	1.00
51 Tomas Plekanec	.40	1.00
52 Carey Price	1.50	4.00
53 Mike Cammalleri	.40	1.00
54 Pekka Rinne	.50	1.25
55 J.P. Dumont	.25	.60
56 Shea Weber	.30	.75
57 Ilya Kovalchuk	.40	1.00
58 Jamie Langenbrunner	.25	.60
59 Martin Brodeur	.75	2.00
60 Zach Parise	.40	1.00
61 Matt Moulson	.30	.75
62 Kyle Okposo	.40	1.00
63 John Tavares	.75	2.00
64 Marian Gaborik	.50	1.25
65 Henrik Lundqvist	.60	1.50
66 Chris Drury	.30	.75
67 Daniel Alfredsson	.40	1.00
68 Jason Spezza	.25	.60
69 Alex Kovalev	.40	1.00
70 Claude Giroux	.40	1.00
71 Jeff Carter	.40	1.00
72 James van Riemsdyk	.60	1.50
73 Chris Pronger	.30	.75
74 Mike Richards	.40	1.00
75 Ilya Bryzgalov	.30	.75
76 Shane Doan	.30	.75
77 Wojtek Wolski	.25	.60
78 Marc-Andre Fleury	.60	1.50
79 Evgeni Malkin	1.25	3.00
80 Jordan Staal	.40	1.00
81 Sidney Crosby	1.50	4.00
82 Dany Heatley	.30	.75
83 Joe Pavelski	.40	1.00
84 Joe Thornton	.40	1.00
85 Patrick Marleau	.40	1.00
86 T.J. Oshie	.60	1.50
87 David Backes	.40	1.00
88 Victor Hedman	.50	1.25
89 Steven Stamkos	.75	2.00
90 Martin St. Louis	.40	1.00
91 Phil Kessel	.50	1.25
92 Dion Phaneuf	.40	1.00
93 Jean-Sebastien Giguere	.30	.75
94 Henrik Sedin	.40	1.00
95 Ryan Kesler	.40	1.00
96 Roberto Luongo	.40	1.00
97 Daniel Sedin	.40	1.00
98 Alexander Ovechkin	1.50	4.00
99 Nicklas Backstrom	.60	1.50
100 Mike Green	.40	1.00
101 Bobby Orr	5.00	12.00
102 Lanny McDonald	1.50	4.00
103 Phil Esposito	2.50	6.00
104 Patrick Roy	4.00	10.00
105 Steve Yzerman	4.00	10.00
106 Jari Kurri	1.50	4.00
107 Gordie Howe	4.00	10.00
108 Wayne Gretzky	8.00	20.00
109 Guy Lafleur	2.00	5.00
110 Mike Bossy	1.50	4.00
111 Mark Messier	2.50	6.00
112 Bobby Clarke	1.50	4.00
113 Mario Lemieux	5.00	12.00
114 Peter Stastny	1.25	3.00
115 Red Kelly	1.50	4.00
116 Jonas Holos/499 RC	3.00	8.00
117 Brandon Pirri/499 RC	3.00	8.00
118 Alexander Urbom/499 RC	3.00	8.00
119 Matt Taormina/499 RC	3.00	8.00
120 Jake Muzzin/499 RC	3.00	8.00
121 Ryan Reaves/499 RC	4.00	10.00
122 Justin Mercier/499 RC	3.00	8.00
123 Robin Lehner/499 RC	6.00	15.00
124 Evan Brophey/499 RC	3.00	8.00
125 Nikita Nikitin/499 RC	3.00	8.00
126 Mattias Tedenby/499 RC	2.50	6.00
127 Kyle Wilson/499 RC	4.00	10.00
128 Adam McQuaid/499 RC	4.00	10.00
129 Mark Dekanich/499 RC	3.00	8.00
130 Guillaume Desbiens/499	4.00	10.00
131 Evan Oberg/499 RC	4.00	10.00
132 Jerome Samson/499 RC	3.00	8.00
133 Dustin Kohn/499 RC	3.00	8.00
134 Michael Haley/499 RC	3.00	8.00
135 Ian Cole/499 RC	3.00	8.00
136 Dylan Reese/499 RC	3.00	8.00
137 Corey Elkins/499 RC	2.50	6.00
138 Eric Wellwood/499 RC	4.00	10.00
139 Richard Clune/499 RC	4.00	10.00
140 Matt Kassian/499 RC	3.00	8.00
141 Colby Cohen/499 RC	3.00	8.00
142 Johan Motin/499 RC	2.50	6.00
143 Marco Scandella/499 RC	3.00	8.00
144 Jeremy Morin/499 RC	3.00	8.00
145 Brad Mills/499 RC	3.00	8.00
146 Mike Duco/499 RC	3.00	8.00
147 Alexander Pechurski/499 RC	4.00	10.00
148 Justin Falk/499 RC	2.50	6.00
149 Raymond Sawada/499 RC	2.50	6.00
150 Linus Klasen/499 RC	3.00	8.00
151 Clayton Stoner/499 RC	3.00	8.00
152 Dean Arsene/499 RC	3.00	8.00
153 Casey Wellman/499 RC	3.00	8.00
154 Maxime Fortunus/499 RC	2.50	6.00
155 Ben Smith/499 RC	3.00	8.00
156 Kaspars Daugavins JSY RC	5.00	12.00
157 Arturs Kulda JSY RC	4.00	10.00
158 Mark Olver JSY RC	4.00	10.00
159 Kyle Clifford JSY RC	4.00	10.00
160 Maxim Noreau JSY RC	3.00	8.00
161 Cody Almond JSY RC	4.00	10.00
162 Matt Martin JSY RC	6.00	15.00
163 Nick Palmieri JSY RC	4.00	10.00
164 Nick Johnson JSY RC	3.00	8.00
165 Justin Falk JSY RC	3.00	8.00
166 Luke Adam JSY AU RC	5.00	12.00
167 Dustin Tokarski JSY AU RC	5.00	12.00
168 Nick Leddy JSY AU RC	8.00	20.00
169 Jacob Josefson JSY AU RC	6.00	15.00
170 Alex Plante JSY AU RC	5.00	12.00
171 Evgeny Grachev JSY AU RC	5.00	12.00
172 Dana Tyrell JSY AU RC	5.00	12.00
173 K.Shattenkirk JSY AU RC	10.00	25.00
174 Anders Lindback JSY AU RC	5.00	12.00
175 Jordan Caron JSY AU RC	8.00	20.00
176 Brandon Yip JSY AU RC	5.00	12.00
177 Zach Hamill JSY AU RC	5.00	12.00
178 Jared Cowen JSY AU RC	5.00	12.00
179 Jamie McBain JSY AU RC	5.00	12.00
180 Cam Fowler JSY AU RC	8.00	20.00
181 Zac Dalpe JSY AU RC	5.00	12.00
182 Ekman-Larsson JSY AU RC	8.00	20.00
183 N.Niederreiter JSY AU RC	6.00	15.00
184 Eric Tangradi JSY AU RC	5.00	12.00
185 Henrik Karlsson JSY AU RC	5.00	12.00
186 S.Bobrovsky JSY AU RC	12.00	30.00
187 A.Burmistrov JSY AU RC	5.00	12.00
188 M.Johansson JSY AU RC	8.00	20.00
189 Jeff Skinner JSY AU RC	10.00	25.00
190 M.Paajarvi JSY AU RC	6.00	15.00
191 B.Schenn JSY AU RC	6.00	15.00
192 D.Stepan JSY AU/499 RC	12.00	30.00
193 N.Kadri JSY AU/499 RC	15.00	40.00
194 P.Subban JSY AU/499 RC	30.00	80.00
195 J.Eberle JSY AU/499 RC	15.00	40.00
196 T.Seguin JSY AU/499 RC	40.00	80.00
197 Taylor Hall JSY AU/499 RC	30.00	80.00
198 Adam Foote FF JSY	5.00	12.00
199 Alex Kovalev FF JSY	8.00	20.00
200 Alex Tanguay FF JSY	5.00	12.00
201 Alexander Frolov FF JSY	5.00	12.00
202 Bernie Nicholls FF JSY	8.00	20.00
203 Bob Probert FF JSY	6.00	15.00
204 Brendan Morrison FF JSY	6.00	15.00
206 Chris Pronger FF JSY	6.00	15.00
207 Darcy Tucker FF JSY	6.00	15.00
208 Dino Ciccarelli FF JSY	8.00	20.00
209 Donald Brashear FF JSY	12.00	30.00
210 Doug Weight FF JSY	8.00	20.00
211 Georges Laraque FF JSY		
212 Gump Worsley FF JSY	8.00	20.00
213 Ilya Kovalchuk FF JSY	8.00	20.00
214 Jarret Stoll FF JSY	6.00	15.00
215 Jason Arnott FF JSY	6.00	15.00
216 Jason Blake FF JSY	10.00	25.00
217 Joe Sakic FF JSY	12.00	30.00
218 Jose Theodore FF JSY	8.00	20.00
219 Kari Lehtonen FF JSY	6.00	15.00
220 Marc Savard FF JSY	8.00	20.00
221 Marian Hossa FF JSY	6.00	15.00
222 Olli Jokinen FF JSY	6.00	15.00
223 Paul Kariya FF JSY	10.00	25.00
224 Roberto Luongo FF JSY	8.00	20.00
225 Scott Gomez FF JSY	6.00	15.00
226 Teemu Selanne FF JSY	12.00	30.00
227 Wendel Clark FF JSY	12.00	30.00
228 Adam Oates FF JSY AU	15.00	40.00
229 Alex Ovechkin FF JSY AU	100.00	200.00
230 B.Bourne FF JSY AU EXCH	12.00	30.00
231 Borje Salming FF JSY AU	15.00	40.00
232 Brian Leetch FF JSY AU	15.00	40.00
233 Chris Drury FF JSY AU	20.00	50.00
234 Dale Hawerchuk FF JSY AU	12.00	30.00
235 Dany Heatley FF JSY AU	12.00	30.00
236 Darryl Sittler FF JSY AU	15.00	40.00
237 Doug Gilmour FF JSY AU	20.00	50.00
238 Gilbert Perreault FF JSY AU	20.00	50.00
239 Gordie Howe FF JSY AU		
240 Grant Fuhr FF JSY AU	15.00	40.00
241 J.P. Dumont FF JSY AU	10.00	25.00
242 Jari Kurri FF JSY AU EXCH	15.00	40.00
243 Jay Bouwmeester FF JSY AU	20.00	50.00
244 Larry Robinson FF JSY AU	15.00	40.00
245 Luc Robitaille FF JSY AU	15.00	40.00
246 Marcel Dionne FF JSY AU	20.00	50.00
247 M.Gaborik FF JSY AU EXCH	20.00	50.00
248 Mario Lemieux FF JSY AU	60.00	120.00
249 Mark Messier FF JSY AU	40.00	80.00
250 Markus Naslund FF JSY AU	20.00	50.00
251 Martin Brodeur FF JSY AU	50.00	100.00
252 Mike Modano FF JSY AU	25.00	60.00
253 Patrick Roy FF JSY AU	150.00	250.00
254 Sidney Crosby FF JSY AU	100.00	200.00
255 Simon Gagne FF JSY AU	15.00	40.00
256 Steve Yzerman FF JSY AU	100.00	200.00
257 Wayne Gretzky FF JSY AU	250.00	400.00

2010-11 SPx Spectrum

COMMON VET JSY (2-100)	4.00	10.00
VET JSY SEMISTARS	5.00	12.00
VET JSY UNL.STARS	6.00	15.00
*101-115: .5X TO 1.2X BASE		
*116-155: 1X TO 2.5X BASE		
*156-165: .8X TO 2X BASE		
*166-197: .6X TO 1.5X BASE		
STATED PRINT RUN 25 SER.#'d SETS		
2 Ryan Getzlaf JSY	10.00	25.00
5 Evander Kane JSY	6.00	15.00
11 Tyler Myers JSY	6.00	15.00
15 Jarome Iginla JSY	6.00	15.00
19 Cam Ward JSY	8.00	20.00
21 Patrick Kane JSY	12.00	30.00
26 Matt Duchene JSY	6.00	15.00
29 Rick Nash JSY	10.00	25.00
35 Jim Howard JSY	8.00	20.00
36 Henrik Zetterberg JSY	8.00	20.00
38 Pavel Datsyuk JSY	8.00	20.00
46 Drew Doughty JSY	6.00	15.00
52 Carey Price JSY	25.00	60.00
59 Martin Brodeur JSY	12.00	30.00
63 John Tavares JSY	12.00	30.00
64 Marian Gaborik JSY	8.00	20.00
65 Henrik Lundqvist JSY	10.00	25.00
67 Daniel Alfredsson JSY	8.00	20.00
70 Claude Giroux JSY	6.00	15.00
72 James van Riemsdyk JSY	10.00	25.00
79 Evgeni Malkin JSY	20.00	50.00
81 Sidney Crosby JSY	25.00	60.00
84 Joe Thornton JSY	6.00	15.00
89 Steven Stamkos JSY	12.00	30.00
93 Jean-Sebastien Giguere JSY	10.00	25.00
94 Henrik Sedin JSY	6.00	15.00
95 Ryan Kesler JSY	10.00	25.00
96 Roberto Luongo JSY	6.00	15.00
98 Alexander Ovechkin JSY	15.00	40.00
99 Nicklas Backstrom JSY	10.00	25.00
162 Matt Martin PATCH	15.00	40.00
175 Jordan Caron PATCH AU	40.00	80.00
176 Brandon Yip PATCH AU	25.00	60.00
180 Cam Fowler PATCH AU	75.00	150.00
181 Zac Dalpe PATCH AU	20.00	50.00
185 Henrik Karlsson PATCH AU	25.00	60.00
187 A.Burmistrov PATCH AU	50.00	100.00
188 M.Johansson PATCH AU	60.00	120.00
189 Jeff Skinner PATCH AU	30.00	80.00
191 Brayden Schenn PATCH AU	25.00	60.00
192 Derek Stepan PATCH AU	50.00	120.00
193 Nazem Kadri PATCH AU	30.00	80.00
194 P.K. Subban PATCH AU	150.00	300.00
195 Jordan Eberle PATCH AU	100.00	200.00
196 Tyler Seguin PATCH AU	100.00	200.00
197 Taylor Hall PATCH AU	100.00	200.00

2010-11 SPx Finite Rookies

COMP.SET w/o SPs (18)	100.00	175.00
F1-F18 PRINT RUN 499 SER.#'d SETS		
F19-F24 PRINT RUN 249 SER.#'d SETS		
F25-F30 PRINT RUN 99 SER.#'d SETS		
F1 Luke Adam	2.50	6.00
F2 Jacob Josefson	2.50	6.00
F3 Dustin Tokarski	2.50	6.00
F4 Evgeny Grachev	2.50	6.00
F5 Kevin Shattenkirk	6.00	15.00
F6 Dana Tyrell	2.50	6.00
F7 Anders Lindback	2.50	6.00
F8 Jordan Caron	4.00	10.00
F9 Brandon Yip	2.50	6.00
F10 Zach Hamill	2.50	6.00
F11 Jared Cowen	2.50	6.00
F12 Jamie McBain	2.50	6.00
F13 Cam Fowler	6.00	15.00
F14 Zac Dalpe	2.50	6.00
F15 Oliver Ekman-Larsson	4.00	10.00
F16 Nino Niederreiter	3.00	8.00
F17 Henrik Karlsson	2.50	6.00
F18 Sergei Bobrovsky	8.00	20.00
F19 Eric Tangradi/249	3.00	8.00
F20 Alexander Burmistrov/249	3.00	8.00
F21 Marcus Johansson/249	5.00	12.00
F22 Jeff Skinner/249	6.00	15.00
F23 Magnus Paajarvi/249	4.00	10.00
F24 Brayden Schenn/249	5.00	12.00
F25 Derek Stepan/99	10.00	25.00
F26 Nazem Kadri/99	10.00	25.00
F27 P.K. Subban/99	15.00	40.00
F28 Jordan Eberle/99	20.00	50.00
F29 Tyler Seguin/99	20.00	50.00
F30 Taylor Hall/99	40.00	80.00

2010-11 SPx Rookie Materials

STATED ODDS LEVEL 1 1:37
STATED ODDS LEVEL 2 1:252

RMAB Alexander Burmistrov L1	4.00	10.00
RMBS Brayden Schenn L1	3.00	8.00
RMDS Derek Stepan L2	5.00	12.00
RMJE Jordan Eberle L2	6.00	15.00
RMJJ Jacob Josefson L1	2.00	5.00
RMJS Jeff Skinner L1	4.00	10.00
RMMJ Marcus Johansson L1	3.00	8.00
RMMP Magnus Paajarvi L1	2.50	6.00
RMNK Nazem Kadri L2	8.00	20.00
RMNN Nino Niederreiter L1	2.50	6.00
RMOE Oliver Ekman-Larsson L1	4.00	10.00
RMPS P.K. Subban L2	8.00	20.00
RMSB Sergei Bobrovsky L1	5.00	12.00
RMTH Taylor Hall L2	10.00	25.00
RMTS Tyler Seguin L2	10.00	25.00
RMZD Zac Dalpe L1	4.00	10.00

2010-11 SPx Shadowbox

STATED ODDS 1:500

SB1 Wayne Gretzky	80.00	200.00
SB2 Mario Lemieux	50.00	120.00
SB3 Mark Messier	30.00	60.00
SB4 Brandon Yip	12.00	30.00
SB5 Evgeni Malkin	50.00	125.00
SB6 Jonathan Toews	30.00	80.00
SB7 John Tavares	30.00	80.00
SB8 Alexander Ovechkin	50.00	100.00
SB9 Matt Duchene	12.00	30.00
SB10 Tyler Myers	15.00	40.00
SB11 Steven Stamkos	20.00	50.00
SB12 Phil Esposito	25.00	60.00
SB13 Jari Kurri	15.00	40.00
SB14 Jarome Iginla	15.00	40.00
SB15 Bobby Hull	15.00	40.00
SB16 Henrik Zetterberg	20.00	50.00
SB17 Ray Bourque	25.00	60.00
SB18 Jamie McBain	12.00	30.00
SB19 Steve Yzerman	40.00	100.00
SB20 P.K. Subban	40.00	100.00
SB21 James van Riemsdyk	25.00	60.00
SB22 Nazem Kadri	40.00	100.00

2010-11 SPx Shadowbox Autographs

STATED ODDS LEVEL 1 1:1,663
STATED ODDS LEVEL 2 1:6,653

SBSBO Bobby Orr L1	300.00	600.00
SBSGH Gordie Howe L2	400.00	800.00
SBSSC Sidney Crosby L1 EXCH	250.00	500.00
SBSWG Wayne Gretzky L2	900.00	1500.00

2010-11 SPx Shadowbox Stoppers

STATED ODDS 1:805

ST1 Roberto Luongo	20.00	50.00
ST2 Henrik Lundqvist	30.00	80.00
ST3 Patrick Roy	60.00	120.00
ST4 Ilya Bryzgalov	15.00	40.00
ST5 Jim Howard	25.00	60.00
ST6 Ryan Miller	20.00	50.00
ST7 Martin Brodeur	40.00	100.00
ST8 Carey Price	80.00	200.00
ST9 Jean-Sebastien Giguere	20.00	50.00
ST10 Jonas Gustavsson	20.00	50.00
ST11 Jaroslav Halak	20.00	50.00
ST12 Miikka Kiprusoff	15.00	40.00

2010-11 SPx Winning Combos

STATED ODDS 1:18

WCAE P.Elias/J.Arnott	5.00	12.00
WCBB D.Backes/P.Berglund	5.00	12.00
WCBK D.Byfuglien/E.Kane	5.00	12.00
WCBL R.Luongo/M.Brodeur	10.00	25.00
WCBR P.Bergeron/T.Rask	6.00	15.00
WCCG D.Carcillo/C.Giroux	5.00	12.00
WCFM E.Malkin/M.Fleury	15.00	40.00
WCGF M.Fleury/J.Giguere	8.00	20.00
WCGM M.Messier/W.Gretzky	20.00	50.00
WCGS L.Schenn/J.Giguere	4.00	10.00
WCGV J.van Riemsdyk/C.Giroux	8.00	20.00
WCHG M.Gaborik/M.Hossa	6.00	15.00
WCHK M.Hossa/P.Kane	10.00	25.00
WCHS M.Hejduk/P.Stastny	5.00	12.00
WCJS S.Sullivan/J.Dumont	3.00	8.00
WCKB A.Burrows/R.Kesler	8.00	20.00
WCKD A.Kopitar/D.Doughty	8.00	20.00
WCKK P.Kessel/N.Kulemin	6.00	15.00
WCLB M.Brodeur/H.Lundqvist	10.00	25.00
WCLM R.Luongo/R.Miller	5.00	12.00
WCLS S.Stamkos/V.Lecavalier	10.00	25.00
WCMH P.Marleau/D.Heatley	5.00	12.00
WCMP P.Roy/M.Brodeur	12.00	30.00
WCNP C.Neely/B.Park	5.00	12.00
WCNV J.Voracek/R.Nash	5.00	12.00
WCOG M.Green/A.Ovechkin	12.00	30.00
WCOM A.Ovechkin/E.Malkin	12.00	30.00
WCPM C.Price/S.Mason	20.00	50.00
WCRB R.Bourque/P.Roy	10.00	25.00
WCRG W.Gretzky/L.Robitaille	15.00	40.00
WCSD M.Duchene/P.Stastny	5.00	12.00
WCSG S.Gagne/M.St. Louis	5.00	12.00
WCSH S.Stamkos/V.Hedman	10.00	25.00
WCSW C.Ward/E.Staal	6.00	15.00
WCTD J.Tavares/M.Duchene	10.00	25.00
WCVW T.Vokoun/S.Weiss	4.00	10.00
WCYL S.Yzerman/N.Lidstrom	12.00	30.00
WCZF J.Franzen/H.Zetterberg	6.00	15.00

2010-11 SPx Winning Combos Patches

STATED PRINT RUN 15 SER.#'d SETS

WCAE P.Elias/J.Arnott	12.00	30.00
WCAS J.Spezza/D.Alfredsson	12.00	30.00
WCBB D.Backes/P.Berglund	12.00	30.00
WCBK D.Byfuglien/E.Kane	12.00	30.00
WCBL R.Luongo/M.Brodeur	25.00	60.00
WCBR P.Bergeron/T.Rask	15.00	40.00
WCCG D.Carcillo/C.Giroux	12.00	30.00
WCFM E.Malkin/M.Fleury	40.00	100.00
WCGF M.Fleury/J.Giguere	20.00	50.00
WCGR M.Richards/C.Giroux	12.00	30.00
WCGS L.Schenn/J.Giguere	10.00	25.00
WCGV J.van Riemsdyk/C.Giroux	20.00	50.00
WCHG M.Gaborik/M.Hossa	15.00	40.00
WCHK M.Hossa/P.Kane	25.00	60.00
WCHS M.Hejduk/P.Stastny	12.00	30.00
WCIB R.Bourque/J.Iginla	12.00	30.00
WCJS S.Sullivan/J.Dumont	8.00	20.00
WCKB A.Burrows/R.Kesler	12.00	30.00
WCKD A.Kopitar/D.Doughty	20.00	50.00
WCKK P.Kessel/N.Kulemin	15.00	40.00
WCKR P.Kessel/B.Ryan	15.00	40.00
WCLB M.Brodeur/H.Lundqvist	25.00	60.00
WCLM R.Luongo/R.Miller	12.00	30.00
WCMH P.Marleau/D.Heatley	12.00	30.00
WCMS E.Malkin/J.Staal	40.00	100.00
WCNP C.Neely/B.Park	12.00	30.00
WCNT N.Backstrom/T.Rask	12.00	30.00
WCNV J.Voracek/R.Nash	12.00	30.00
WCOG M.Green/A.Ovechkin	25.00	60.00
WCOM A.Ovechkin/E.Malkin	50.00	125.00
WCPR M.Richards/C.Pronger	12.00	30.00
WCRK P.Kane/B.Ryan	20.00	50.00
WCRV D.Roy/T.Vanek	12.00	30.00
WCSD M.Duchene/P.Stastny	12.00	30.00
WCSG S.Gagne/M.St. Louis	12.00	30.00
WCSH S.Stamkos/V.Hedman	25.00	60.00
WCSS D.Sedin/H.Sedin	12.00	30.00
WCSW C.Ward/E.Staal	15.00	40.00
WCTD J.Tavares/M.Duchene	25.00	60.00
WCTP J.Thornton/J.Pavelski	12.00	30.00
WCVW T.Vokoun/S.Weiss	10.00	25.00
WCYL S.Yzerman/N.Lidstrom	30.00	80.00
WCZF J.Franzen/H.Zetterberg	15.00	40.00

2010-11 SPx Winning Materials

STATED ODDS 1:18

WMAK Anze Kopitar	6.00	15.00
WMAN Antti Niemi	3.00	8.00
WMAO Alexander Ovechkin	8.00	20.00
WMCG Claude Giroux	4.00	10.00
WMCN Cam Neely	4.00	10.00
WMCP Carey Price	15.00	40.00
WMCR Sidney Crosby	15.00	40.00
WMCW Cam Ward	4.00	10.00
WMDC Daniel Carcillo	2.50	6.00
WMDH Dany Heatley	3.00	8.00
WMDK Duncan Keith	6.00	15.00
WMDS Daniel Sedin	4.00	10.00
WMEK Evander Kane	4.00	10.00

WMEM Evgeni Malkin 12.00 30.00
WMES Eric Staal 5.00 12.00
WMGR Mike Green 4.00 10.00
WMHE Milan Hejduk 3.00 8.00
WMHZ Henrik Zetterberg 5.00 12.00
WMJC Jeff Carter 4.00 10.00
WMJG Jean-Sebastien Giguere 3.00 8.00
WMJS Jordan Staal 4.00 10.00
WMLR Luc Robitaille 4.00 10.00
WMMB Martin Brodeur 6.00 15.00
WMMD Matt Duchene 4.00 10.00
WMMG Marian Gaborik 5.00 12.00
WMMH Marian Hossa 3.00 8.00
WMMK Mikko Koivu 4.00 10.00
WMML Mario Lemieux 12.00 30.00
WMMM Mark Messier 6.00 15.00
WMPD Pavel Datsyuk 5.00 12.00
WMPE Patrik Elias 4.00 10.00
WMPK Patrick Kane 6.00 15.00
WMPS Patrick Sharp 4.00 10.00
WMRI Brad Richards 4.00 10.00
WMRK Ryan Kesler 6.00 15.00
WMSC Sidney Crosby 15.00 40.00
WMSD Shane Doan 3.00 8.00
WMSM Steve Mason 3.00 8.00
WMSY Steve Yzerman 10.00 25.00
WMTA John Tavares 8.00 20.00
WMVL Vincent Lecavalier 3.00 8.00
WMWG Wayne Gretzky 20.00 50.00

2010-11 SPx Winning Materials Autographs

AUTO PRINT RUN 15
WMAO Alexander Ovechkin 75.00 125.00
WMCP Carey Price 30.00 60.00
WMCR Sidney Crosby 90.00 150.00
WMCW Cam Ward 12.00 30.00
WMDH Dany Heatley 10.00 25.00
WMEK Evander Kane 12.00 30.00
WMEM Evgeni Malkin 30.00 60.00
WMES Eric Staal 12.00 30.00
WMHZ Henrik Zetterberg 30.00 60.00
WMJS Jordan Staal 20.00 50.00
WMMB Martin Brodeur 40.00 80.00
WMMD Matt Duchene 12.00 30.00
WMMH Marian Hossa 15.00 40.00
WMML Mario Lemieux 75.00 150.00
WMMM Mark Messier 30.00 60.00
WMRK Ryan Kesler 12.00 30.00
WMSC Sidney Crosby 90.00 150.00
WMSD Shane Doan 10.00 25.00
WMSS Steven Stamkos 40.00 80.00
WMSY Steve Yzerman 50.00 100.00
WMVL Vincent Lecavalier 20.00 50.00
WMWG Wayne Gretzky 175.00 300.00

2010-11 SPx Winning Materials Patches

*PATCH/35: 1X TO 2.5X BASIC WM
STATED PRINT RUN 35 SER.#'d SETS
WMAK Anze Kopitar 15.00 40.00
WMDC Daniel Carcillo 12.00 30.00
WMDS Daniel Sedin 15.00 40.00
WMHZ Henrik Zetterberg
WMJG Jean-Sebastien Giguere 10.00 25.00
WMML Mario Lemieux 40.00 100.00
WMRI Brad Richards 12.00 30.00
WMRK Ryan Kesler 15.00 40.00

2010-11 SPx Winning Trios

STATED PRINT RUN 50 SER.#'d SETS
WM31ST Stamkos/Kane/Tvares 15.00 40.00
WM3BOS Bergern/Lucic/Savard 10.00 25.00
WM3CGY McDnld/Mullen/Gilmour 10.00 25.00
WM3CPT Howe/Lidstrm/Yzermn 20.00 50.00
WM3DAL Ribeo/Eriksson/Richrds 8.00 20.00
WM3DEF Doughty/Myers/Weber 8.00 20.00
WM3DET Datsyuk/Zetter/Franzen 10.00 25.00
WM3FIN Rask/Kiprusff/Bckstrm
WM3GR8 Messier/Lemx/Gretzky 40.00 100.00
WM3HOF Yzermn/Lmieux/Mssier 25.00 60.00
WM3ISL Tavres/Okpso/Weight 12.00 30.00
WM3LAK Dghty/Brown/Kopitar 12.00 30.00
WM3MON Price/Gionta/Cammllri 30.00 80.00
WM3NYR Gabrik/Drury/Lndqvist 12.00 30.00
WM3RKP Tavares/Dchne/Myers 15.00 40.00
WM3RUS Datsyuk/Malkin/Ovech 15.00 40.00
WM3SLO Chara/Hossa/Gaborik 10.00 25.00
WM3TML Kulemin/Kess/Phaneuf 10.00 25.00
WM3VAN Burrows/Sedin/Kesler 15.00 40.00
WM3BEES Bourque/Chara/Park 12.00 30.00
WM3CAPS Ovech/Bckstrm/Grn 15.00 40.00
WM3ECAN Cammll/Kessel/Spezza 10.00 25.00
WM3NJD1 Langen/Elias/Brodr 12.00 30.00
WM3NJD2 Parise/Koval/Clarksn 8.00 20.00
WM3PITT Malkin/Crosby/Fleury 15.00 40.00
WM3SCF2 van R/Giroux/Carcillo 12.00 30.00
WM3SCW2 Keith/Hossa/Kane 15.00 40.00
WM3WCAN Penner/Sedin/Iginla 8.00 20.00
WM3WILD Bckstrm/Koivu/Bchrd 8.00 20.00
WM3FGHT2 Carkner/Carcillo/Orr 12.00 30.00
WM3GLDRS Ovech/Crsby/Stmkos 30.00 80.00

2011-12 SPx

COMP.SET w/o SP's (100) 12.00 30.00
101-121 LEGEND PRINT RUN 499
122-163 ROOKIE PRINT RUN 499
164-173 ROOKIE JSY PRINT RUN 799
174-199 ROOK.JSY AU PRINT RUN 799
200-205 ROOK.JSY AU PRINT RUN 499
VET JSY GROUP A ODDS 1:35,431
VET JSY GROUP B ODDS 1:16,872
VET JSY GROUP C ODDS 1:3615
VET JSY GROUP D ODDS 1:1070
VET JSY GROUP E ODDS 1:146
VET JSY AU GROUP A ODDS 1:32,210
VET JSY AU GROUP B ODDS 1:1817
VET JSY AU GROUP C ODDS 1:2834
VET JSY AU GROUP D ODDS 1:945
VET JSY AU GROUP E ODDS 1:472
1 Dustin Byfuglien .40 1.00
2 Ondrej Pavelec .40 1.00
3 Alexander Ovechkin 1.50 4.00
4 Nicklas Backstrom .60 1.50
5 Mike Green .40 1.00
6 Alexander Semin .40 1.00
7 Henrik Sedin .40 1.00
8 Ryan Kesler .40 1.00
9 Roberto Luongo .40 1.00
10 Daniel Sedin .40 1.00
11 Phil Kessel .50 1.25
12 Dion Phaneuf .40 1.00
13 Nikolai Kulemin .40 1.00
14 Steven Stamkos .75 2.00
15 Martin St. Louis .40 1.00
16 Vincent Lecavalier .30 .75
17 Patrik Berglund .30 .75
18 David Backes .40 1.00
19 Chris Stewart .30 .75
20 Jaroslav Halak .40 1.00
21 Joe Thornton .40 1.00
22 Patrick Marleau .40 1.00
23 Marc-Andre Fleury .60 1.50
24 Evgeni Malkin 1.25 3.00
25 Jordan Staal .40 1.00
26 Sidney Crosby 1.50 4.00
27 Oliver Ekman-Larsson .40 1.00
28 Ilya Bryzgalov .40 1.00
29 Claude Giroux .40 1.00
30 James van Riemsdyk .40 1.00
31 Chris Pronger .30 .75
32 Daniel Briere .40 1.00
33 Daniel Alfredsson .40 1.00
34 Jason Spezza .40 1.00
35 Marian Gaborik .50 1.25
36 Henrik Lundqvist .50 1.25
37 Derek Stepan .40 1.00
38 Brad Richards .40 1.00
39 Matt Moulson .30 .75
40 John Tavares .75 2.00
41 Ilya Kovalchuk .40 1.00
42 Martin Brodeur .75 2.00
43 Zach Parise .40 1.00
44 Pekka Rinne .50 1.25
45 Shea Weber .30 .75
46 Tomas Plekanec .40 1.00
47 Carey Price 1.25 3.00
48 Michael Cammalleri .30 .75
49 P.K. Subban .75 2.00
50 Dany Heatley .30 .75
51 Guillaume Latendresse .30 .75
52 Mikko Koivu .30 .75
53 Mike Richards .40 1.00
54 Anze Kopitar .60 1.50
55 Drew Doughty .40 1.00
56 Dustin Brown .40 1.00
57 Stephen Weiss .30 .75
58 David Booth .25 .60
59 Ales Hemsky .30 .75
60 Sam Gagner .30 .75
61 Magnus Paajarvi .30 .75
62 Jordan Eberle .40 1.00
63 Taylor Hall .75 2.00
64 Johan Franzen .40 1.00
65 Jim Howard .40 1.00
66 Henrik Zetterberg .50 1.25
67 Nicklas Lidstrom .40 1.00
68 Pavel Datsyuk .50 1.25
69 Kari Lehtonen .30 .75
70 Loui Eriksson .30 .75
71 Jeff Carter .40 1.00
72 Derick Brassard .40 1.00
73 Rick Nash .40 1.00
74 Steve Mason .30 .75
75 Peter Mueller .30 .75
76 Matt Duchene .40 1.00
77 Paul Stastny .40 1.00
78 Patrick Kane .75 2.00
79 Marian Hossa .30 .75
80 Patrick Sharp .40 1.00
81 Jonathan Toews .75 2.00
82 Tomas Kaberle .25 .60
83 Eric Staal .50 1.25
84 Jussi Jokinen .25 .60
85 Olli Jokinen .30 .75
86 Jay Bouwmeester .40 1.00
87 Jarome Iginla .40 1.00
88 Miikka Kiprusoff .40 1.00
89 Ryan Miller .40 1.00
90 Thomas Vanek .40 1.00
91 Drew Stafford .40 1.00
92 Derek Roy .30 .75
93 Patrice Bergeron .50 1.25
94 Milan Lucic .40 1.00
95 Tim Thomas .40 1.00
96 Zdeno Chara .40 1.00
97 Nathan Horton .40 1.00
98 Tyler Seguin .75 2.00
99 Bobby Ryan .40 1.00
100 Ryan Getzlaf .60 1.50
101 Bobby Orr LEG 6.00 15.00
102 Phil Esposito LEG 3.00 8.00
103 Cam Neely LEG 2.00 5.00
104 Bobby Hull LEG 2.00 5.00
105 Joe Sakic LEG 3.00 8.00
106 Alex Delvecchio LEG 1.50 4.00
107 Ted Lindsay LEG 2.00 5.00
108 Wayne Gretzky LEG 6.00 15.00
109 Paul Coffey LEG 2.00 5.00
110 Jari Kurri LEG 2.00 5.00
111 Ron Francis LEG 2.50 6.00
112 Guy Lafleur LEG 2.50 6.00
113 Jean Beliveau LEG 2.00 5.00
114 Patrick Roy LEG 6.00 15.00
115 Mike Bossy LEG 2.00 5.00
116 Mark Messier LEG 2.50 6.00
117 Pelle Lindbergh LEG 4.00 10.00
118 Bobby Clarke LEG 3.00 8.00
119 Mario Lemieux LEG 6.00 15.00
120 Richard Brodeur LEG 2.00 5.00
121 Dale Hawerchuk LEG 2.50 6.00
122 Allen York RC 3.00 8.00
123 David Ullstrom RC 2.50 6.00
124 Carl Klingberg RC 2.50 6.00
125 Andy Miele RC 2.50 6.00
126 Ben Holmstrom RC 2.50 6.00
127 Ben Scrivens RC 5.00 12.00
128 Bracken Kearns RC 2.50 6.00
129 Brendon Nash RC 2.50 6.00
130 Brian Strait RC 3.00 8.00
131 Cam Talbot RC 6.00 15.00
132 Cameron Gaunce RC 2.00 5.00
133 Carson McMillan RC 3.00 8.00
134 Chris Vande Velde RC 4.00 10.00
135 Cody Eakin RC 5.00 12.00
136 Stefan Elliott RC 2.50 6.00
137 Colton Sceviour RC 2.50 6.00
138 Corey Tropp RC 2.50 6.00
139 Drew Bagnall RC 2.50 6.00
140 Erik Gudbranson 3.00 8.00
141 Gustav Nyquist RC 10.00 25.00
142 Harry Zolnierczyk RC 2.50 6.00
143 Hugh Jessiman RC 2.50 6.00
144 Leland Irving RC 2.50 6.00
145 Joe Vitale RC 2.50 6.00
146 Keith Kinkaid RC 2.50 6.00
147 Lance Bouma RC 2.50 6.00
148 Mattias Ekholm RC 2.50 6.00
149 Maxime Macenauer RC 2.50 6.00
150 Pat Maroon RC 2.50 6.00
151 Patrick Wiercioch RC 2.50 6.00
152 Paul Postma RC 2.50 6.00
153 Peter Holland RC 2.50 6.00
154 Robert Bortuzzo RC 2.50 6.00
155 Roman Wick RC 3.00 8.00
156 Ryan Thang RC 2.00 5.00
157 Scott Timmins RC 2.50 6.00
158 Stephane Da Costa RC 2.50 6.00
159 Cade Fairchild RC 2.00 5.00
160 Tomas Kubalik RC 2.50 6.00
161 Viatcheslav Voynov RC 2.50 6.00
162 Brayden McNabb RC 2.50 6.00
163 Zac Rinaldo RC 2.50 6.00
164 David Rundblad JSY RC 3.00 8.00
165 Yann Sauve JSY RC 3.00 8.00
166 Teemu Hartikainen JSY RC 3.00 8.00
167 Cam Atkinson JSY RC 8.00 20.00
168 Brett Bulmer JSY RC 4.00 10.00
169 Alexei Emelin JSY RC 3.00 8.00
170 Raphael Diaz JSY RC 3.00 8.00
171 Colin Greening JSY RC 3.00 8.00
172 Colten Teubert JSY RC 3.00 8.00
173 Roman Horak JSY RC 3.00 8.00
174 Justin Faulk JSY AU RC 8.00 20.00
175 John Moore JSY AU RC 5.00 12.00
176 Tomas Vincour JSY AU RC 5.00 12.00
177 Zack Kassian JSY AU RC 8.00 20.00
178 Craig Smith JSY AU RC 6.00 15.00
179 Tim Erixon JSY AU RC 5.00 12.00
180 D.Smith-Pelly JSY AU RC 8.00 20.00
181 Greg Nemisz JSY AU RC 5.00 12.00
182 Marcus Kruger JSY AU RC 8.00 20.00
183 Brandon Saad JSY AU RC 15.00 30.00
184 Anton Lander JSY AU RC 5.00 12.00
185 E.Gudbranson JSY AU RC 6.00 15.00
186 Aaron Palushaj JSY AU RC 5.00 12.00
187 Jonathon Blum JSY AU RC 5.00 12.00
188 Blake Geoffrion JSY AU RC 5.00 12.00
189 Adam Henrique JSY AU RC 12.00 30.00
190 Adam Larsson JSY AU RC 6.00 15.00
191 M.Zibanejad JSY AU RC 6.00 15.00
192 Matt Read JSY AU RC 10.00 25.00
193 Louis Leblanc JSY AU RC 6.00 15.00
194 Jake Gardiner JSY AU RC 5.00 12.00
195 Joe Colborne JSY AU RC 5.00 12.00
196 Matt Frattin JSY AU RC 5.00 12.00
197 Brendan Smith JSY AU RC 6.00 15.00
198 R.Johansen JSY AU RC 10.00 25.00
199 Lennart Petrell JSY AU RC 6.00 15.00
200 Cody Hodgson JSY AU RC 12.00 30.00
201 Brett Connolly JSY AU RC 8.00 20.00
202 Mark Scheifele JSY AU RC 20.00 50.00
203 Sean Couturier JSY AU RC 8.00 20.00
204 G.Landeskog JSY AU RC 12.00 30.00
205 Nugent-Hopk JSY AU RC 30.00 80.00
206 Jaromir Jagr FF JSY E 12.00 30.00
207 Jaromir Jagr FF JSY D 20.00 50.00
208 Bernie Nicholls FF JSY E 5.00 12.00
209 Bill Ranford FF JSY D 8.00 20.00
210 Chris Higgins FF JSY C 8.00 20.00
211 Chris Pronger FF JSY B 6.00 15.00
212 Craig Anderson FF JSY E 5.00 12.00
213 Daniel Paille FF JSY E 3.00 8.00
214 Dave Taylor FF JSY E 4.00 10.00
215 Doug Weight FF JSY D 8.00 20.00
216 Dustin Penner FF JSY E 4.00 10.00
217 Ed Jovanovski FF JSY E 3.00 8.00
218 Erik Johnson FF JSY E 3.00 8.00
219 Jaromir Jagr FF JSY D 20.00 50.00
220 Ilya Kovalchuk FF JSY E 5.00 12.00
221 Langenbrunner FF JSY E 3.00 8.00
222 Jason Arnott FF JSY E 4.00 10.00
223 Joe Mullen FF JSY E 4.00 10.00
224 Jordan Leopold FF JSY E 3.00 8.00
225 Jose Theodore FF JSY E 5.00 12.00
226 Jussi Jokinen FF JSY A
227 Kari Lehtonen FF JSY E 4.00 10.00
228 Matt Stajan FF JSY E 4.00 10.00
229 Michael Frolik FF JSY E 3.00 8.00
230 Nik Antropov FF JSY D 6.00 15.00
231 Raffi Torres FF JSY E 3.00 8.00
232 Roberto Luongo FF JSY C 10.00 25.00
233 Saku Koivu FF JSY E 5.00 12.00
234 Scott Gomez FF JSY E 5.00 12.00
235 Sergei Gonchar FF JSY E 3.00 8.00
236 A.Ovechkin FF JSY AU B 50.00 100.00
237 Cam Neely FF JSY AU D 20.00 50.00
238 Chris Drury FF JSY AU C 10.00 25.00
239 Guy Lafleur FF JSY AU A 60.00 100.00
240 Jari Kurri FF JSY AU D 25.00 50.00
241 Jarome Iginla FF JSY AU C 12.00 30.00
242 Alex Tanguay FF JSY AU D 8.00 20.00
243 Kris Versteeg FF JSY AU E 10.00 25.00
244 L.Robinson FF JSY AU E 12.00 30.00
245 Luc Robitaille FF JSY AU E 12.00 30.00
246 Marcel Dionne FF JSY AU D 20.00 50.00
247 M.Lemieux FF JSY AU B 60.00 120.00
248 Mark Messier FF JSY AU B 30.00 60.00
249 M.Brodeur FF JSY AU B 40.00 80.00
250 Marty Turco FF JSY AU E 12.00 30.00
251 Mike Bossy FF JSY AU C 15.00 40.00
252 Mike Modano FF JSY AU B 20.00 50.00
253 Joe Thornton FF JSY AU B 20.00 40.00
254 Patrick Roy FF JSY AU B 40.00 80.00
255 Peter Mueller FF JSY AU E 10.00 25.00
256 Peter Stastny FF JSY AU D 12.00 30.00
257 Phil Esposito FF JSY AU B 20.00 40.00
258 Phil Kessel FF JSY AU C 15.00 40.00
259 Ray Bourque FF JSY AU B 30.00 60.00
260 Ray Emery FF JSY AU D 10.00 25.00
261 Ron Francis FF JSY AU B 15.00 30.00
262 Ron Hextall FF JSY AU B 25.00 50.00
263 Sidney Crosby FF JSY AU B 60.00 120.00
264 Tony Esposito FF JSY AU B 25.00 50.00
265 W.Gretzky FF JSY AU C 250.00 400.00

2011-12 SPx Spectrum

1-100 PATCH STATED PRINT RUN 15
*101-121 LEG/25: 1X TO 2.5X BASIC LEG/499
*122-163 ROOK/25: .6X TO 1.5X BASIC RC/499
*164-173 PATCH/35: 1X TO 2.5X JSY RC/799
*174-199 PTCH AU/25: 1X TO 2.5X JSY AU RC
*201-205 PTCH AU/25: 1X TO 2.5X JSY AU RC
EXCH EXPIRATION: 4/18/2014
1 Dustin Byfuglien PATCH 10.00 25.00
2 Ondrej Pavelec PATCH 10.00 25.00
3 Alexander Ovechkin PATCH 40.00 100.00
4 Nicklas Backstrom PATCH 15.00 40.00
5 Mike Green PATCH 10.00 25.00
6 Alexander Semin PATCH 10.00 25.00
7 Henrik Sedin PATCH 10.00 25.00
8 Ryan Kesler PATCH 10.00 25.00
9 Roberto Luongo PATCH 10.00 25.00
10 Daniel Sedin PATCH 10.00 25.00
11 Phil Kessel PATCH 12.00 30.00
12 Dion Phaneuf PATCH 10.00 25.00
13 Nikolai Kulemin PATCH 10.00 25.00
14 Steven Stamkos PATCH 20.00 50.00
15 Martin St. Louis PATCH 10.00 25.00
16 Vincent Lecavalier PATCH 8.00 20.00
17 Patrik Berglund PATCH 8.00 20.00
18 David Backes PATCH 10.00 25.00
19 Chris Stewart PATCH 8.00 20.00
20 Jaroslav Halak PATCH 10.00 25.00
21 Joe Thornton PATCH 10.00 25.00
22 Patrick Marleau PATCH 10.00 25.00
23 Marc-Andre Fleury PATCH 15.00 40.00
24 Evgeni Malkin PATCH 30.00 80.00
25 Jordan Staal PATCH 10.00 25.00
26 Sidney Crosby PATCH 30.00 80.00
27 Oliver Ekman-Larsson PATCH 10.00 25.00
28 Ilya Bryzgalov PATCH 10.00 25.00
29 Claude Giroux PATCH 10.00 25.00
30 James van Riemsdyk PATCH 10.00 25.00
31 Chris Pronger PATCH 8.00 20.00
32 Daniel Briere PATCH 10.00 25.00
33 Daniel Alfredsson PATCH 10.00 25.00
34 Jason Spezza PATCH 10.00 25.00
35 Marian Gaborik PATCH 12.00 30.00
36 Henrik Lundqvist PATCH 12.00 30.00
37 Derek Stepan PATCH 10.00 25.00
38 Brad Richards PATCH 10.00 25.00
39 Matt Moulson PATCH 8.00 20.00
40 John Tavares PATCH 20.00 50.00
41 Ilya Kovalchuk PATCH 10.00 25.00
42 Martin Brodeur PATCH 20.00 50.00
43 Zach Parise PATCH 10.00 25.00
44 Pekka Rinne PATCH 12.00 30.00
45 Shea Weber PATCH 8.00 20.00
46 Tomas Plekanec PATCH 10.00 25.00
47 Carey Price PATCH 30.00 80.00
48 Michael Cammalleri PATCH 8.00 20.00
49 P.K. Subban PATCH 20.00 50.00
50 Dany Heatley PATCH 8.00 20.00
51 Guillaume Latendresse PATCH 8.00 20.00
52 Mikko Koivu PATCH 8.00 20.00
53 Mike Richards PATCH 10.00 25.00
54 Anze Kopitar PATCH 15.00 40.00
55 Drew Doughty PATCH 10.00 25.00
56 Dustin Brown PATCH 10.00 25.00
57 Stephen Weiss PATCH 8.00 20.00
58 David Booth PATCH 6.00 15.00
59 Ales Hemsky PATCH 8.00 20.00
60 Sam Gagner PATCH 10.00 25.00
61 Magnus Paajarvi PATCH 8.00 20.00
62 Jordan Eberle PATCH 10.00 25.00
63 Taylor Hall PATCH 20.00 50.00
64 Johan Franzen PATCH 10.00 25.00
65 Jim Howard PATCH 10.00 25.00
66 Henrik Zetterberg PATCH 12.00 30.00
67 Nicklas Lidstrom PATCH 10.00 25.00
68 Pavel Datsyuk PATCH 12.00 30.00
69 Kari Lehtonen PATCH 12.00 30.00
70 Loui Eriksson PATCH 8.00 20.00
71 Jeff Carter PATCH 10.00 25.00
72 Derick Brassard PATCH 10.00 25.00
73 Rick Nash PATCH 10.00 25.00
74 Steve Mason PATCH 8.00 20.00
75 Peter Mueller PATCH 8.00 20.00
76 Matt Duchene PATCH 10.00 25.00
77 Paul Stastny PATCH 10.00 25.00
78 Patrick Kane PATCH 20.00 50.00
79 Marian Hossa PATCH 8.00 20.00
80 Patrick Sharp PATCH 10.00 25.00
81 Jonathan Toews PATCH 20.00 50.00
82 Tomas Kaberle PATCH 6.00 15.00
83 Eric Staal PATCH 12.00 30.00
84 Jussi Jokinen PATCH 6.00 15.00
85 Olli Jokinen PATCH 8.00 20.00
86 Jay Bouwmeester PATCH 10.00 25.00
87 Jarome Iginla PATCH 10.00 25.00
88 Miikka Kiprusoff PATCH 10.00 25.00
89 Ryan Miller PATCH 10.00 25.00
90 Thomas Vanek PATCH 10.00 25.00
91 Drew Stafford PATCH 10.00 25.00
92 Derek Roy PATCH 8.00 20.00
93 Patrice Bergeron PATCH 12.00 30.00
94 Milan Lucic PATCH 10.00 25.00
95 Tim Thomas PATCH 10.00 25.00
96 Zdeno Chara PATCH 10.00 25.00
97 Nathan Horton PATCH 10.00 25.00
98 Tyler Seguin PATCH 20.00 50.00
99 Bobby Ryan PATCH 10.00 25.00
100 Ryan Getzlaf PATCH 15.00 40.00
183 Brandon Saad PATCH AU 90.00 150.00
201 Brett Connolly PATCH AU 25.00 60.00
203 Sean Couturier PATCH AU 50.00 120.00
204 Gabriel Landeskog PATCH AU 75.00 150.00
205 Ryan Nugent-Hopkins PATCH AU 200.00 400.00

2011-12 SPx Finite Rookies

F1-F15 STATED PRINT RUN 499
F16-F27 STATED PRINT RUN 249
F28-F37 STATED PRINT RUN 99
F1 Alexei Emelin/499 2.00 5.00
F2 Andy Miele/499 2.00 5.00
F3 Anton Lander/499 2.00 5.00
F4 Blake Geoffrion/499 2.00 5.00
F5 Mika Zibanejad/499 5.00 12.00
F6 Carl Klingberg/499 2.00 5.00
F7 Colin Greening/499 2.00 5.00
F8 Colten Teubert/499 2.00 5.00
F9 Erik Gudbranson/499 2.50 6.00
F10 Joe Colborne/499 2.00 5.00
F11 Gustav Nyquist/499 6.00 15.00
F12 Jonathon Blum/499 2.00 5.00
F13 Peter Holland/499 2.00 5.00
F14 Raphael Diaz/499 2.00 5.00
F15 Tim Erixon/499 2.00 5.00
F16 Brandon Saad/249 5.00 12.00
F17 Teemu Hartikainen/249 2.50 6.00
F18 Marcus Kruger/249 4.00 10.00
F19 Devante Smith-Pelly/249 4.00 10.00
F20 Adam Henrique/249 6.00 15.00
F21 Craig Smith/249 3.00 8.00
F22 Matt Frattin/249 2.50 6.00
F23 Lennart Petrell/249 3.00 8.00
F24 Cody Eakin/249 3.00 8.00
F25 David Rundblad/249 2.50 6.00
F26 Jake Gardiner/249 4.00 10.00
F27 Matt Read/249 8.00 20.00
F28 Louis Leblanc/99 25.00 50.00
F29 Zack Kassian/99 8.00 20.00
F30 Ryan Johansen/99 8.00 20.00
F31 Adam Larsson/99 5.00 12.00
F32 Brett Connolly/99 4.00 10.00
F33 Cody Hodgson/99 12.00 30.00
F34 Sean Couturier/99 20.00 40.00
F35 Mark Scheifele/99 12.00 30.00
F36 Gabriel Landeskog/99 8.00 20.00
F37 Ryan Nugent-Hopkins/99 15.00 40.00

2011-12 SPx Rookie Materials

GROUP A STATED ODDS 1:37 HOB
GROUP B STATED ODDS 1:252 HOB
*PATCH/25: 1X TO 2.5X BASIC GRP A
*PATCH/15: 1X TO 2.5X BASIC GRP B
RMAL Adam Larsson 3.00 8.00
RMBC Brett Connolly 3.00 8.00
RMCE Cody Eakin 4.00 10.00
RMCH Cody Hodgson 8.00 20.00
RMCS Craig Smith 3.00 8.00
RMEG Erik Gudbranson 3.00 8.00
RMGL Gabriel Landeskog 8.00 20.00
RMJG Jake Gardiner 4.00 10.00
RMLL Louis Leblanc 12.00 30.00
RMMF Matt Frattin 2.50 6.00
RMMR Matt Read 5.00 12.00
RMMS Mark Scheifele 6.00 15.00
RMMZ Mika Zibanejad 6.00 15.00
RMRJ Ryan Johansen 6.00 15.00
RMRN Ryan Nugent-Hopkins 15.00 40.00
RMSC Sean Couturier 6.00 15.00
RMTH Teemu Hartikainen 2.50 6.00
RMZK Zack Kassian 3.00 8.00

2011-12 SPx Shadowbox

SB1-SB19 STATED ODDS 1:557 HOB
SB20 AU STATED ODDS 1:6800 HOB
SB1 Wayne Gretzky 60.00 120.00
SB2 Mario Lemieux 40.00 80.00
SB3 Mark Messier 20.00 50.00
SB4 Ron Francis 25.00 50.00
SB5 Joe Sakic 30.00 60.00
SB6 Mike Gartner 15.00 40.00
SB7 Guy Lafleur 20.00 50.00
SB8 Brett Hull 30.00 60.00
SB9 Jaromir Jagr 40.00 100.00
SB10 Evgeni Malkin 50.00 120.00
SB11 Alexander Ovechkin
SB12 Alexander Semin 10.00 25.00
SB13 Rick Nash 20.00 50.00
SB14 Ryan Getzlaf 25.00 60.00
SB15 Drew Doughty 15.00 40.00
SB16 Patrick Kane 20.00 50.00
SB17 Zach Parise 15.00 40.00
SB18 Ilya Kovalchuk 15.00 40.00
SB19 Nicklas Lidstrom 30.00 60.00
SB20 Steven Stamkos AU 60.00 150.00

2011-12 SPx Shadowbox Programme of Excellence

PE1-PE10 STATED ODDS 1:1058 HOB
PE11 AU STATED ODDS 1:6800 HOB
PE12 AU STATED ODDS 1:13,000 HOB
EXCH EXPIRATION 4/18/2014
PE1 John Tavares 30.00 80.00
PE2 P.K. Subban 25.00 60.00
PE3 Taylor Hall 30.00 80.00
PE4 Jordan Eberle 60.00 120.00
PE5 Tyler Ennis 12.00 30.00
PE6 Sidney Crosby 75.00 135.00
PE7 Jonathan Toews 40.00 80.00
PE8 Carey Price 40.00 80.00
PE9 Mike Richards 25.00 60.00
PE10 Roberto Luongo 50.00 100.00
PE11 Cody Hodgson AU 75.00 150.00
PE12 Wayne Gretzky AU EXCH

2011-12 SPx Shadowbox Stoppers

SBS1-SBS9 STATED ODDS 1:1130 HOB
SBS10 AU STATED ODDS 1:13,000 HOB
EXCH EXPIRATION: 4/18/2014
SBS1 Martin Brodeur 25.00 60.00
SBS2 Tim Thomas 30.00 60.00
SBS3 Bernie Parent 30.00 60.00
SBS4 Ryan Miller 15.00 40.00
SBS5 Corey Crawford 15.00 40.00
SBS6 Ondrej Pavelec 20.00 50.00
SBS7 Bill Ranford 15.00 40.00
SBS8 Terry Sawchuk 40.00 80.00
SBS9 Georges Vezina 50.00 100.00
SBS10 Patrick Roy AU EXCH 250.00 500.00

2011-12 SPx Winning Combos

GROUP A STATED ODDS 1:5624 HOB
GROUP B STATED ODDS 1:860 HOB
GROUP C STATED ODDS 1:289 HOB
GROUP D STATED ODDS 1:145 HOB
GROUP E STATED ODDS 1:22 HOB
*PATCH/15: .8X TO 2X BASIC GRP A
*PATCH/15: 1X TO 2.5X BASIC GRP B-C
WCAP A.Markov/P.Subban D 8.00 20.00
WCBH Bergeron/N.Horton E 6.00 15.00
WCBJ B.Schenn/J.Cowen E 5.00 12.00
WCBK D.Byfuglien/E.Kane E 5.00 12.00
WCBS P.Bergeron/E.Staal D 6.00 15.00
WCCF M.Fleury/S.Crosby C 10.00 25.00
WCCL M.Lemieux/S.Crosby C 20.00 50.00
WCDC Backes/C.Stewart E 5.00 12.00
WCDJ Cleary/Abdelkader E 5.00 12.00
WCEH T.Hall/J.Eberle E 8.00 20.00
WCFS M.Fleury/J.Staal E 8.00 20.00
WCGM Messier/W.Gretzky A 30.00 80.00
WCGR R.Getzlaf/B.Ryan E 8.00 20.00
WCGS M.Gaborik/D.Stepan E 6.00 15.00
WCGV Giroux/Van Riemsdyk E 6.00 15.00
WCHK V.Hedman/Karlsson E 10.00 25.00
WCHP Hemsky/M.Paajarvi E 5.00 12.00
WCHS H.Lundqvist/M.Staal E 6.00 15.00
WCIK J.Iginla/M.Kiprusoff E 5.00 12.00
WCKD Kopitar/D.Doughty D 8.00 20.00
WCKG J.Kurri/W.Gretzky B 12.00 30.00
WCKH R.Kesler/C.Hodgson C 4.00 10.00
WCKP Kovalchuk/Z.Parise E 6.00 15.00
WCLA Gagne/M.Richards E 5.00 12.00
WCLD Lidstrom/P.Datsyuk E 6.00 15.00
WCLK Luongo/M.Kiprusoff E 5.00 12.00
WCLM M.Lemieux/E.Malkin B 15.00 40.00
WCLS Lecavalier/St. Louis E 4.00 10.00
WCMK Kulemin/C.MacArthur E 5.00 12.00
WCMS R.Miller/D.Stafford E 5.00 12.00
WCNC M.Neuvirth/J.Carlson E 3.00 8.00
WCOB Ovechkin/Backstrom D 8.00 20.00
WCOG Ovechkin/M.Green C 5.00 12.00
WCPR P.Roy/R.Bourque D 8.00 20.00
WCRB P.Roy/M.Brodeur E 12.00 30.00
WCRG Robitaille/W.Gretzky A 25.00 50.00
WCRH Rinne/P.Hornqvist E 6.00 15.00
WCRL P.Roy/R.Luongo B 12.00 30.00
WCRV D.Roy/T.Vanek E 5.00 12.00
WCSD Duchene/P.Stastny E 4.00 10.00
WCSE D.Stafford/T.Ennis E 5.00 12.00
WCSS H.Sedin/D.Sedin E 5.00 12.00
WCTB Thornton/Bergeron D 5.00 12.00
WCTK J.Toews/P.Kane C 10.00 25.00
WCTM Moulson/J.Tavares E 5.00 12.00
WCTR T.Rask/T.Thomas E 5.00 12.00
WCTS J.Thornton/E.Staal D 5.00 12.00
WCVG J.Voracek/C.Giroux E 5.00 12.00
WCZF Zetterberg/Franzen E 5.00 12.00

2011-12 SPx Winning Materials

GROUP A STATED ODDS 1:3440 HOB
GROUP B STATED ODDS 1:350 HOB
GROUP C STATED ODDS 1:137 HOB
GROUP D STATED ODDS 1:90 HOB
GROUP E STATED ODDS 1:28 HOB
OVERALL ODDS 1:18 HOB
*PATCH/35: .6X TO 1.5X BASIC GRP B
*PATCH/35: .8X TO 2X BASIC GRP C-E
WMAH Ales Hemsky E 3.00 8.00
WMAK Anze Kopitar E 6.00 15.00
WMAO Alexander Ovechkin C 15.00 40.00
WMBA David Backes C 4.00 10.00
WMCN Cam Neely E 4.00 10.00
WMCS Chris Stewart E 3.00 8.00
WMDB Dustin Byfuglien C 4.00 10.00
WMDD Drew Doughty C 4.00 10.00
WMDR Derek Roy C 3.00 8.00
WMDS Daniel Sedin B 5.00 12.00
WMEL Eric Lindros E 6.00 15.00
WMEM Evgeni Malkin C 5.00 12.00
WMGL Guillaume Latendresse C 3.00 8.00
WMHL Henrik Lundqvist D 5.00 12.00
WMHW Jim Howard C 4.00 10.00
WMJC Jeff Carter E 4.00 10.00
WMJE Jordan Eberle D 5.00 12.00
WMJI Jarome Iginla E 4.00 10.00
WMJT Jonathan Toews D 8.00 20.00
WMKE Phil Kessel D 5.00 12.00
WMMB Martin Brodeur B 10.00 25.00
WMMD Matt Duchene E 4.00 10.00
WMMF Marc-Andre Fleury E 6.00 15.00
WMMG Marian Gaborik D 5.00 12.00
WMML Mario Lemieux B 8.00 20.00
WMMM Mark Messier B 6.00 15.00
WMMR Mike Richards E 4.00 10.00
WMMS Martin St. Louis D 4.00 10.00
WMNB Nicklas Backstrom E 6.00 15.00
WMNG Nathan Gerbe E 2.50 6.00
WMNL Nicklas Lidstrom C 5.00 12.00
WMPK Patrick Kane D 8.00 20.00
WMPM Patrick Marleau E 4.00 10.00
WMPR Pekka Rinne E 5.00 12.00
WMRB Ray Bourque E 6.00 15.00
WMRK Ryan Kesler C 4.00 10.00
WMRL Roberto Luongo E 4.00 10.00
WMRM Ryan Miller E 4.00 10.00
WMRN Rick Nash E 4.00 10.00
WMSC Sidney Crosby B 20.00 50.00
WMSF Drew Stafford E 4.00 10.00
WMSS Steven Stamkos B 10.00 25.00
WMST Jordan Staal D 4.00 10.00
WMTA John Tavares D 5.00 12.00
WMTH Taylor Hall B 10.00 25.00
WMTM Tyler Myers D 4.00 10.00
WMTS Tyler Seguin D 8.00 20.00
WMTV Thomas Vanek E 4.00 10.00
WMVL Vincent Lecavalier E 5.00 12.00
WMWG Wayne Gretzky A 50.00 100.00

2011-12 SPx Winning Materials Autographs

STATED PRINT RUN 15 SER.#'d SETS
EXCH EXPIRATION: 4/18/2014
WMAH Ales Hemsky 10.00 25.00
WMAK Anze Kopitar
WMAO Alexander Ovechkin 30.00 80.00
WMBA David Backes EXCH 12.00 30.00
WMCN Cam Neely 12.00 30.00
WMCS Chris Stewart 10.00 25.00
WMDB Dustin Byfuglien
WMDD Drew Doughty 12.00 30.00
WMDR Derek Roy 10.00 25.00
WMEL Eric Lindros 60.00 120.00
WMEM Evgeni Malkin 25.00 50.00
WMGL Guillaume Latendresse
WMHL Henrik Lundqvist 25.00 50.00
WMJC Jeff Carter EXCH 12.00 30.00
WMJE Jordan Eberle 50.00 100.00
WMJI Jarome Iginla 12.00 30.00
WMJT Jonathan Toews 25.00 50.00
WMKE Phil Kessel 15.00 40.00
WMMB Martin Brodeur 25.00 60.00
WMMD Matt Duchene 12.00 30.00
WMMF Marc-Andre Fleury 20.00 40.00
WMMG Marian Gaborik
WMML Mario Lemieux 50.00 100.00
WMMM Mark Messier
WMMR Mike Richards EXCH 20.00 40.00
WMMS Martin St. Louis 20.00 40.00
WMNB Nicklas Backstrom 20.00 50.00
WMNG Nathan Gerbe
WMNL Nicklas Lidstrom EXCH 12.00 30.00
WMPK Patrick Kane 15.00 40.00
WMPM Patrick Marleau 15.00 40.00
WMPR Pekka Rinne 15.00 40.00
WMRB Ray Bourque 20.00 50.00
WMRK Ryan Kesler 12.00 30.00
WMRM Ryan Miller
WMRN Rick Nash 12.00 30.00
WMSC Sidney Crosby 60.00 120.00
WMSS Steven Stamkos 30.00 60.00
WMST Jordan Staal 12.00 30.00
WMTA John Tavares 25.00 50.00
WMTH Taylor Hall
WMTM Tyler Myers 12.00 30.00
WMTS Tyler Seguin EXCH 30.00 60.00
WMTV Thomas Vanek 12.00 30.00
WMVL Vincent Lecavalier
WMWG Wayne Gretzky 175.00 300.00

2011-12 SPx Winning Trios

WIN TRIOS/50 ODDS 1:240 HOB
WTBCK Boychk/Cormier/Kane 6.00 15.00
WTBKD Kopitar/Doughty/Brown 10.00 25.00
WTBKP Brodeur/Kovlchk/Parse 12.00 30.00
WTCBP Bourque/Park/Chara 10.00 25.00
WTCOS Crosby/Ovech/Stamks 15.00 40.00
WTCPP Price/Pleknc/Cammall 20.00 50.00
WTCTL Lucic/Chara/Thomas 6.00 15.00
WTDRW Kronwll/Howrd/Ericssn 6.00 15.00
WTEHP Eberle/Hall/Paajarvi 8.00 20.00
WTFCM Crosby/Malkn/Fleury 15.00 40.00
WTGLS Lundqvst/Gabrk/Staal 8.00 20.00
WTGVP Giroux/vanRiems/Prngr 6.00 15.00
WTHTK Toews/Kane/Hossa 12.00 30.00
WTIBK Iginla/Bouwm/Kiprsff 8.00 20.00
WTIKB Iginla/Kiprsft/Bourque 6.00 15.00
WTKOM Ovech/Malkn/Koval 25.00 60.00
WTLDZ Lidstrm/Zetter/Datsyk 12.00 30.00
WTLGM Messier/Gretzky/Mario 30.00 60.00
WTLKB Keslr/Burrws/Luong 12.00 30.00
WTLSM Messier/Mario/Sakic 15.00 40.00
WTMPK Miller/Kessel/Parise 8.00 20.00
WTNHT RNH/Hall/Tavares 25.00 60.00
WTOCC Orr/Carcillo/Carkner 5.00 12.00
WTOPC Orr/Parros/Carkner 5.00 12.00
WTPGR Getzlaf/Ryan/Hiller 10.00 25.00
WTPMS Myers/Subbn/Pietrng 8.00 20.00
WTPRM Pominville/Roy/Miller 6.00 15.00
WTRFB Roy/Forsbrg/Bourq 15.00 40.00
WTRLE Ribiero/Lehtn/Erikssn 5.00 12.00
WTRMM Roy/Miller/Myers 6.00 15.00
WTSCK Spezza/Kessl/Camlri 8.00 20.00
WTSFA Spezza/Flgno/Alfrdssn 6.00 15.00
WTSIH Iginla/Hemsky/Sedin 6.00 15.00
WTSKK Kessel/Kulemin/Schenn 8.00 20.00
WTSOB Backstrm/Semn/Ovech 25.00 60.00
WTSTK Toews/Kane/Sharp 12.00 30.00
WTTAB Tokarski/Aulie/Benn 8.00 20.00
WTTBS Thorntn/Bergrn/Staal 8.00 20.00
WTTCG Luongo/Brodr/Fleury 12.00 30.00
WTTSH Stamkos/Hall/Tavares 12.00 30.00

2013-14 SPx

COMP.SET w/o RC's (100) 12.00 30.00
101-140 ROOKIE ODDS 1:2.5
141-160 ROOKIE ODDS 1:10
1 Bobby Ryan .40 1.00
2 Jonathan Toews .75 2.00
3 Shea Weber .30 .75
4 Ryan Suter .25 .60
5 Jamie Benn .50 1.25
6 Henrik Sedin .40 1.00
7 Eric Staal .50 1.25
8 Slava Voynov .40 1.00
9 Craig Anderson .40 1.00
10 Adam Henrique .40 1.00
11 Patrik Elias .40 1.00
12 Max Pacioretty .40 1.00
13 Ryan Johansen .50 1.25
14 Mike Ribeiro .30 .75
15 Cory Schneider .30 .75
16 Milan Lucic .40 1.00
17 James van Riemsdyk .40 1.00
18 Chris Stewart .30 .75
19 Tomas Fleischmann .25 .60
20 Jeff Skinner .30 .75
21 Ales Hemsky .25 .60
22 Derek Roy .30 .75
23 Oliver Ekman-Larsson .30 .75
24 Lee Stempniak .25 .60
25 David Krejci .40 1.00
26 Pascal Dupuis .25 .60
27 Claude Giroux .40 1.00
28 Matt Moulson .30 .75
29 Patrick Sharp .40 1.00
30 Kyle Okposo .40 1.00
31 Steven Stamkos .75 2.00
32 Tyler Ennis .30 .75
33 James Neal .40 1.00
34 Marian Gaborik .40 1.00
35 Carey Price 1.25 3.00
36 Ryan Callahan .40 1.00
37 Paul Stastny .40 1.00
38 Corey Perry .40 1.00
39 Jakub Voracek .40 1.00
40 Jordan Eberle .40 1.00
41 Sergei Bobrovsky .40 1.00
42 Tuukka Rask .40 1.00
43 Nicklas Backstrom .60 1.50
44 Jonathan Quick .60 1.50
45 Alex Pietrangelo .30 .75
46 Cam Ward .40 1.00
47 Joe Thornton .40 1.00
48 Henrik Lundqvist .50 1.25
49 Pavel Datsyuk .50 1.25
50 Anze Kopitar .60 1.50
51 Derek Stepan .40 1.00
52 Matt Duchene .40 1.00
53 Steve Mason .30 .75
54 Brent Seabrook .40 1.00
55 Erik Karlsson .75 2.00
56 Jim Howard .40 1.00
57 Evgeni Nabokov .30 .75
58 Phil Kessel .50 1.25
59 Evgeni Malkin 1.25 3.00
60 Jacob Markstrom .30 .75
61 David Legwand .30 .75
62 Chris Kunitz .40 1.00
63 Alexandre Burrows .40 1.00
64 Shane Doan .30 .75
65 Dan Boyle .30 .75
66 Zdeno Chara .40 1.00
67 David Clarkson .25 .60
68 Jakob Silfverberg .30 .75
69 Alexander Ovechkin 1.50 4.00
70 Andrew Ladd .40 1.00
71 Taylor Hall .75 2.00
72 P.A. Parenteau .25 .60
73 David Backes .40 1.00
74 Blake Wheeler .40 1.00
75 Mike Fisher .30 .75
76 Jonathan Bernier .40 1.00
77 Zach Parise .40 1.00
78 Jiri Tlusty .30 .75
79 Tyler Seguin .60 1.50
80 Nazem Kadri .40 1.00
81 Patrick Marleau .40 1.00
82 Martin Brodeur .75 2.00
83 Joe Pavelski .40 1.00
84 Niklas Kronwall .30 .75
85 Cody Hodgson .40 1.00
86 Mikael Backlund .30 .75
87 Logan Couture .40 1.00
88 Michael Cammalleri .30 .75
89 Evander Kane .40 1.00
90 Kari Lehtonen .30 .75
91 Ondrej Pavelec .40 1.00
92 Brian Elliott .30 .75
93 Sidney Crosby 1.50 4.00
94 Teddy Purcell .40 1.00
95 Patrick Kane .75 2.00
96 Henrik Zetterberg .50 1.25
97 Martin St. Louis .40 1.00
98 Gabriel Landeskog .30 .75
99 Ryan Getzlaf .60 1.50
100 Lars Eller .30 .75
101 Scott Laughton RC 1.25 3.00
102 Jack Campbell RC 1.00 2.50
103 Frank Corrado RC .75 2.00
104 Jacob Trouba RC 2.00 5.00
105 Tyler Toffoli RC 2.50 6.00
106 Marek Mazanec RC 1.25 3.00
107 Brett Bellemore RC 1.00 2.50
108 Eric Gryba RC 1.00 2.50
109 Calvin Pickard RC 1.25 3.00
110 Martin Jones RC 3.00 8.00
111 Jonas Brodin RC 1.00 2.50
112 Nathan Beaulieu RC 1.00 2.50
113 Jarred Tinordi RC 1.25 3.00
114 Max Reinhart RC 1.25 3.00
115 Nicklas Jensen RC 1.00 2.50
116 Tanner Pearson RC 1.25 3.00
117 Nikita Zadorov RC 1.25 3.00
118 Morgan Rielly RC 3.00 8.00
119 Michael Bournival RC 1.25 3.00
120 Cory Conacher RC .75 2.00
121 Frederik Andersen RC 2.00 5.00
122 Danny DeKeyser RC 1.50 4.00
123 Tomas Jurco RC 2.00 5.00
124 Radko Gudas RC 1.25 3.00
125 Alex Chiasson RC 1.25 3.00
126 Olli Maatta RC 2.00 5.00
127 Freddie Hamilton RC 1.25 3.00
128 Joakim Nordstrom RC 1.00 2.50
129 Justin Fontaine RC 1.25 3.00
130 Mark Arcobello RC 1.25 3.00
131 Jon Merrill RC 1.25 3.00
132 Zemgus Girgensons RC 2.50 6.00
133 Ryan Murphy RC 1.25 3.00
134 Damien Brunner RC 1.00 2.50
135 Ryan Strome RC 1.50 4.00
136 Sami Vatanen RC 1.25 3.00
137 Hampus Lindholm RC 2.00 5.00
138 Michael Latta RC 1.00 2.50
139 Mathew Dumba RC 1.25 3.00
140 Antti Raanta RC 1.50 4.00
141 Boone Jenner RC 1.25 3.00
142 Brendan Gallagher RC 4.00 10.00
143 Sean Monahan RC 2.00 5.00
144 Dougie Hamilton RC 2.50 6.00
145 Jonathan Huberdeau RC 3.00 8.00
146 Valeri Nichushkin RC 1.25 3.00
147 Alex Galchenyuk RC 8.00 20.00
148 Nail Yakupov RC 4.00 10.00
149 Seth Jones RC 1.25 3.00
150 Charlie Coyle RC 1.25 3.00

51 Nathan MacKinnon RC 5.00 12.00
52 Elias Lindholm RC 2.00 5.00
53 Vladimir Tarasenko RC 5.00 12.00
54 Mikhail Grigorenko RC 1.50 4.00
55 Aleksander Barkov RC 3.00 8.00
56 Ryan Murray RC 2.00 5.00
57 Justin Schultz RC 1.25 3.00
58 Rasmus Ristolainen RC 2.00 5.00
59 Tomas Hertl RC 1.50 4.00
60 Petr Mrazek RC 2.50 6.00
61 Tomas Jurco JSY AU/499 8.00 20.00
62 Ryan Murray JSY AU/499 8.00 20.00
63 Q.Howden AU/499 RC 4.00 10.00
64 A.Watson AU/499 RC 4.00 10.00
65 J.Schroeder AU/499 RC 5.00 12.00
66 A.Chiasson AU/499 5.00 12.00
67 F.Forsberg AU/499 RC 20.00 40.00
68 Nicklas Jensen JSY AU/499 6.00 15.00
69 D.Brunner AU/499 6.00 15.00
70 R.Spooner AU/499 RC 5.00 12.00
71 R.Ristolainen AU/499 8.00 20.00
72 B.Bennett AU/249 RC 8.00 20.00
73 C.Coyle AU/499 5.00 12.00
74 C.Conacher AU/499 3.00 8.00
75 Tarasenko JSY AU/249 EXCH 50.00 100.00
76 Mathew Dumba JSY AU/499 5.00 12.00
77 C.Thomas AU/499 RC 4.00 10.00
78 M.Granlund AU/499 RC 8.00 20.00
79 Morgan Rielly JSY AU/499 12.00 30.00
80 N.Bjugstad AU/499 RC 6.00 15.00
81 Jonas Brodin JSY AU/499 8.00 20.00
82 Jarred Tinordi JSY AU/499 5.00 12.00
83 Jack Campbell JSY AU/499 4.00 10.00
84 Petr Mrazek JSY AU/499 10.00 25.00
85 N.Beaulieu AU/499 4.00 10.00
86 M.Grigorenko AU/499 6.00 15.00
87 B.Nelson AU/499 RC 5.00 12.00
88 T.Pearson AU/499 8.00 20.00
89 E.Etem AU/499 RC 5.00 12.00
90 Elias Lindholm JSY AU/499 8.00 20.00
91 Ryan Murphy JSY AU/499 5.00 12.00
92 Jacob Trouba JSY AU/499 12.00 30.00
93 H.Lindholm AU/499 8.00 20.00
94 Tyler Toffoli JSY AU/499 12.50 25.00
95 S.Laughton AU/499 5.00 12.00
96 T.Wilson AU/499 RC 10.00 25.00
97 B.Jenner AU/499 5.00 12.00
98 V.Fasth AU/499 RC 5.00 12.00
99 V.Nichushkin AU/249 6.00 15.00
00 S.Monahan AU/249 10.00 25.00
01 A.Barkov AU/249 15.00 40.00
02 J.Huberdeau AU/249 12.00 30.00
03 Tomas Hertl JSY AU/249 15.00 40.00
04 Justin Schultz JSY AU/249 6.00 15.00
05 D.Hamilton AU/249 12.00 30.00
06 A.Galchenyuk AU/249 25.00 60.00
07 Seth Jones JSY AU/249 15.00 30.00
08 Nail Yakupov JSY AU/249 15.00 40.00
09 N.MacKinnon AU/249 40.00 100.00
10 B.Gallagher AU/249 25.00 50.00

2013-14 SPx Spectrum

01-160 AU STATED PRINT RUN 15
161-210 JSY AU/30: .8X TO 2X JSY AU/499
161-210 JSY AU/30: 1X TO 2.5X JSY AU/249
61-210 JSY AU STATED PRINT RUN 30
01 Scott Laughton AU 15.00 40.00
02 Jack Campbell AU 12.00 30.00
04 Jacob Trouba AU 40.00 100.00
05 Tyler Toffoli AU 20.00 50.00
12 Nathan Beaulieu AU 12.00 30.00
13 Jarred Tinordi AU 15.00 40.00
14 Max Reinhart AU 15.00 40.00
15 Nicklas Jensen AU 12.00 30.00
16 Tanner Pearson AU 15.00 40.00
18 Morgan Rielly AU 60.00 125.00
20 Cory Conacher AU 10.00 25.00
21 Frederik Andersen AU 40.00 80.00
22 Danny DeKeyser AU 20.00 50.00
23 Tomas Jurco AU
24 Radko Gudas AU 15.00 40.00
25 Alex Chiasson AU 15.00 40.00
28 Joakim Nordstrom AU 12.00 30.00
29 Justin Fontaine AU 15.00 40.00
30 Mark Arcobello AU 15.00 40.00
31 Jon Merrill AU 15.00 40.00
34 Damien Brunner AU 12.00 30.00
35 Ryan Strome AU 20.00 50.00
37 Hampus Lindholm AU 25.00 60.00
39 Mathew Dumba AU 15.00 40.00
41 Boone Jenner AU 15.00 40.00
43 Sean Monahan AU 50.00 100.00
44 Dougie Hamilton AU 50.00 100.00
45 Jonathan Huberdeau AU 40.00 80.00
46 Valeri Nichushkin AU 90.00 150.00
47 Alex Galchenyuk AU 75.00 150.00
48 Nail Yakupov AU 50.00 100.00
49 Seth Jones AU 40.00 80.00
50 Charlie Coyle AU 15.00 40.00
51 Nathan MacKinnon AU 100.00 200.00
52 Elias Lindholm AU 25.00 60.00
54 Mikhail Grigorenko AU 20.00 50.00
55 Aleksander Barkov AU 40.00 100.00
56 Ryan Murray AU 25.00 60.00
57 Justin Schultz AU 15.00 40.00
58 Rasmus Ristolainen AU 25.00 60.00
59 Tomas Hertl AU 20.00 50.00
60 Petr Mrazek AU 60.00 120.00
75 Vladimir Tarasenko PATCH AU 125.00 200.00
99 Valeri Nichushkin PATCH AU 15.00 40.00
03 Tomas Hertl PATCH AU 20.00 50.00
06 Alex Galchenyuk PATCH AU 125.00 250.00
08 Nail Yakupov PATCH AU 100.00 200.00
09 Nathan MacKinnon PATCH AU 400.00 600.00

2013-14 SPx 96-97 SPx Retro

-40 STATED ODDS 1:8
1-50 STATED ODDS 1:30
Taylor Hall 3.00 8.00
Chris Osgood 1.50 4.00
Ryan Getzlaf 2.50 6.00
Jarome Iginla 1.50 4.00
P.K. Subban 2.50 6.00
Bobby Clarke 2.00 5.00
Guy Lafleur 2.50 6.00
Jonathan Quick 2.50 6.00
Eric Lindros 3.00 8.00
0 Martin St. Louis 1.50 4.00
1 Grant Fuhr 2.00 5.00
2 Pavel Bure 2.00 5.00
3 Tony Esposito 2.00 5.00
4 Joe Thornton 1.50 4.00
5 Bobby Hull 2.00 5.00
6 Mats Sundin 2.00 5.00
7 Zdeno Chara 1.50 4.00
8 Mario Lemieux 6.00 15.00
9 Carey Price 5.00 12.00
0 Sidney Crosby 6.00 15.00
1 Bobby Orr 6.00 15.00
2 Henrik Zetterberg 2.00 5.00
3 Theoren Fleury 2.00 5.00
4 Steve Yzerman 4.00 10.00
25 Patrick Kane 3.00 8.00
26 Tyler Seguin 2.50 6.00
27 Patrick Roy 5.00 12.00
28 Mike Bossy 2.00 5.00
29 Scott Hartnell 1.50 4.00
30 Jonathan Toews 3.00 8.00
31 Luc Robitaille 1.50 4.00
32 Alexander Ovechkin 6.00 15.00
33 Claude Giroux 1.50 4.00
34 Brad Marchand 2.00 5.00
35 John Tavares 3.00 8.00
36 Wayne Gretzky 5.00 12.00
37 Martin Brodeur 3.00 8.00
38 Henrik Lundqvist 2.00 5.00
39 Zach Parise 1.50 4.00
40 Steven Stamkos 3.00 8.00
41 Nathan MacKinnon 6.00 15.00
42 Aleksander Barkov 4.00 10.00
43 Seth Jones 1.50 4.00
44 Elias Lindholm 2.50 6.00
45 Sean Monahan 2.50 6.00
46 Tomas Hertl 2.00 5.00
47 Ryan Murray 2.50 6.00
48 Jacob Trouba 2.50 6.00
49 Boone Jenner 1.50 4.00
50 Valeri Nichushkin 1.50 4.00

2013-14 SPx 96-97 SPx Retro Autographs

GROUP A ODDS 1:450
GROUP B ODDS 1:175
GROUP C ODDS 1:110
OVERALL ODDS 1:60
ARAG Alex Galchenyuk B 20.00 50.00
ARBB Beau Bennett A 25.00 50.00
ARBG Brendan Gallagher A 15.00 40.00
ARCC Charlie Coyle C 8.00 20.00
ARCO Cory Conacher C 6.00 15.00
ARDB Damien Brunner A 15.00 30.00
ARDH Dougie Hamilton B 20.00 40.00
ARFF Filip Forsberg B 15.00 40.00
ARGR Mikael Granlund B 10.00 25.00
ARJB Jonas Brodin C 6.00 15.00
ARJH Jonathan Huberdeau B 15.00 30.00
ARJS Justin Schultz B 6.00 15.00
ARMG Mikhail Grigorenko C 6.00 15.00
ARNB Nathan Beaulieu C 4.00 10.00
ARNY Nail Yakupov B 20.00 50.00
ARPM Petr Mrazek C 20.00 40.00
ARTT Tyler Toffoli C 10.00 25.00
ARVF Viktor Fasth C 5.00 12.00
ARVT Vladimir Tarasenko C 20.00 50.00

2013-14 SPx Buyback Autographs

39 W.Gretzky '96-97 SPx/24 150.00 250.00
63 J.Tavares '10-11 SPx/91 20.00 40.00
89 S.Stamkos '10-11 SPx/25

2013-14 SPx Rookie Materials

STATED ODDS 1:12
RMAG Alex Galchenyuk 6.00 15.00
RMBB Beau Bennett 3.00 8.00
RMBE Nathan Beaulieu 2.00 5.00
RMBG Brendan Gallagher 5.00 12.00
RMCC Cory Conacher 1.50 4.00
RMCO Charlie Coyle 2.50 6.00
RMDH Dougie Hamilton 5.00 12.00
RMEL Elias Lindholm 4.00 10.00
RMJB Jonas Brodin 2.00 5.00
RMJC Jack Campbell 2.00 5.00
RMJH Jonathan Huberdeau 5.00 12.00
RMJM J.T. Miller 2.50 6.00
RMJS Jordan Schroeder 2.50 6.00
RMJT Jarred Tinordi 2.50 6.00
RMMG Mikhail Grigorenko 3.00 8.00
RMMR Morgan Rielly 6.00 15.00
RMMU Ryan Murphy 2.50 6.00
RMNB Nick Bjugstad 3.00 8.00
RMNM Nathan MacKinnon 10.00 25.00
RMNY Nail Yakupov 5.00 12.00
RMPM Petr Mrazek 5.00 12.00
RMRM Ryan Murray 4.00 10.00
RMRR Rasmus Ristolainen 4.00 10.00
RMSC Justin Schultz 2.50 6.00
RMSJ Seth Jones 5.00 12.00
RMSM Sean Monahan 5.00 12.00
RMTH Tomas Hertl 6.00 15.00
RMTT Tyler Toffoli 5.00 12.00
RMVN Valeri Nichushkin 5.00 12.00
RMVT Vladimir Tarasenko 5.00 12.00

2013-14 SPx Rookie Materials Combos

GROUP A ODDS 1:467
GROUP A ODDS 1:234
GROUP A ODDS 1:146
OVERALL ODDS 1:72
*PATCH/25: 1.2X TO 3X BASIC COMBO
RM2D M.Dumba/R.Ristolainen C 5.00 12.00
RM21ST MacKinnon/Yakupov A 8.00 20.00
RM22ND R.Murray/A.Barkov A 5.00 12.00
RM2BUF Grigorenko/Girgensons C 6.00 15.00
RM2CAN Galchenyuk/Gallagher A 10.00 25.00
RM2CBJ B.Jenner/R.Murray B 5.00 12.00
RM2DAL Chiasson/Nichushkin B 6.00 15.00
RM2LAK T.Toffoli/T.Pearson C 5.00 12.00
RM2NET V.Fasth/P.Mrazek B 6.00 15.00
RM2NASH F.Forsberg/S.Jones B 8.00 20.00
RM2WILD C.Coyle/M.Dumba C 3.00 8.00
RM2SCORER S.Monahan/T.Hertl A 5.00 12.00

2013-14 SPx Rookie Materials Trios

GROUP A ODDS 1:1557
GROUP A ODDS 1:458
GROUP A ODDS 1:584
OVERALL STATED ODDS 1:216
RM3C Monhn/Galchn/Hubrd B 10.00 25.00
RM3D Jones/Rielly/Dumba A 10.00 25.00
RM3RW Taras/Bennett/Chiasn B 6.00 15.00
RM3CCE Conacher/Coyle/Etem C 4.00 10.00
RM3DEF Murray/Trouba/Ristol C 6.00 15.00
RM3NET Mrazek/Fasth/Cmpbl B 20.00 40.00
RM3FWDS MacKin/Taras/Yakpv A 20.00 40.00
RM3CENTER MacKin/Hertl/Jenner B 25.00 50.00

2013-14 SPx Shadowbox

STATED ODDS 1:144
SH1 Henrik Lundqvist 10.00 25.00
SH2 Dominik Hasek 10.00 25.00
SH3 Dany Heatley 6.00 15.00
SH4 Steven Stamkos 15.00 40.00
SH5 Sidney Crosby 25.00 60.00
SH6 Corey Crawford 10.00 25.00
SH7 Martin St. Louis 8.00 20.00
SH8 Bobby Orr 25.00 60.00
SH9 Alexander Ovechkin 30.00 80.00
SH10 Claude Giroux 8.00 20.00
SH11 Roberto Luongo 8.00 20.00
SH12 Nazem Kadri 8.00 20.00
SH13 Cory Conacher 6.00 15.00
SH14 Jakub Voracek 8.00 20.00
SH15 Eric Lindros 12.00 30.00
SH16 Brendan Gallagher 10.00 25.00
SH17 Evgeni Malkin 25.00 60.00
SH18 Shea Weber 6.00 15.00
SH19 Logan Couture 8.00 20.00
SH20 Marian Hossa 10.00 25.00
SH21 Milan Lucic 8.00 20.00
SH22 James van Riemsdyk 8.00 20.00
SH23 Henrik Zetterberg 10.00 25.00
SH24 Patrick Sharp 8.00 20.00
SH25 Chris Osgood 8.00 20.00
SH26 Drew Doughty 8.00 20.00
SH27 Grant Fuhr 8.00 20.00
SH28 Oliver Ekman-Larsson 6.00 15.00
SH29 Brent Seabrook 8.00 20.00
SH30 Claude Lemieux 6.00 15.00
SH31 P.K. Subban 12.00 30.00
SH32 Jonathan Quick 12.00 30.00
SH33 Thomas Vanek 8.00 20.00
SH34 Ryan Callahan 8.00 20.00
SH35 Corey Perry 8.00 20.00
SH36 Guy Lafleur 10.00 25.00

2013-14 SPx Winning Combos

GROUP A ODDS 1:2539
GROUP B ODDS 1:262
GROUP C ODDS 1:65
GROUP D ODDS 1:50
OVERALL STATED ODDS 1:24
*PATCH/15: .6X TO 1.5X COMBO GRP A
*PATCH/15: .8X TO 2X COMBO GRP B
*PATCH/15: 1X TO 2.5X COMBO GRP C-D
WCAQ A.Kopitar/J.Quick B 8.00 20.00
WCBB D.Backes/P.Berglund A 6.00 15.00
WCBG M.Grabner/J.Bailey D 3.00 8.00
WCBH E.Belfour/B.Hull A 6.00 15.00
WCBN P.Bure/M.Naslund B 6.00 15.00
WCBV D.Brown/S.Voynov D 4.00 10.00
WCCB R.Bourque/Z.Chara C 8.00 20.00
WCCS R.Callahan/D.Stepan B 4.00 10.00
WCEH J.Eberle/T.Hall C 5.00 12.00
WCGB M.Green/Backstrom D 6.00 15.00
WCGH R.Getzlaf/J.Hiller C 5.00 12.00
WCGP C.Price/J.Gorges C 5.00 12.00
WCHH D.Hasek/J.Howard B 8.00 20.00
WCHM R.Hextall/S.Mason D 6.00 15.00
WCHN T.Hall/Nugent-Hopkins C 5.00 12.00
WCKD A.Kopitar/D.Doughty D 6.00 15.00
WCLD N.Lidstrom/P.Datsyuk C 5.00 12.00
WCLF R.Francis/M.Lemieux B 8.00 20.00
WCLK R.Luongo/R.Kesler C 4.00 10.00
WCLS J.Spezza/R.Lehner C 4.00 10.00
WCMD D.Krejci/M.Lucic C 4.00 10.00
WCME R.Miller/T.Ennis D 4.00 10.00
WCMG M.Messier/M.Gartner A 15.00 40.00
WCML E.Lindros/M.Messier B 12.00 30.00
WCNF M.Naslund/R.Francis C 5.00 12.00
WCPF C.Perry/C.Fowler D 4.00 10.00
WCRC J.Carter/M.Richards D 4.00 10.00
WCRO Ovechkin/Robitaille B 20.00 50.00
WCRS L.Robinson/P.Subban B 8.00 20.00
WCRW P.Rinne/S.Weber D 5.00 12.00
WCSD Duchene/P.Stastny C 4.00 10.00
WCSK P.Sharp/D.Keith B 5.00 12.00
WCSW D.Savard/D.Wilson C 5.00 12.00

2013-14 SPx Winning Materials

GROUP A ODDS 1:1557
GROUP B ODDS 1:105
GROUP C ODDS 1:30
OVERALL STATED ODDS 1:24
*PATCH/15: 1.2X TO 3X BASIC GRP C
*PATCH/15: .8X TO 2X BASIC GRP A-B
WMAO Alexander Ovechkin C 12.00 30.00
WMCF Cam Fowler C 2.50 6.00
WMCP Carey Price B 15.00 40.00
WMDG Doug Gilmour B 6.00 15.00
WMDU Matt Duchene C 3.00 8.00
WMEK Erik Karlsson C 6.00 15.00
WMEL Eric Lindros B 8.00 20.00
WMGA Glenn Anderson B 5.00 12.00
WMHA Dominik Hasek B 6.00 15.00
WMJB Johnny Bucyk B 5.00 12.00
WMJC Jeff Carter C 3.00 8.00
WMJE Jordan Eberle C 3.00 8.00
WMJK Jari Kurri B 5.00 12.00
WMJS Jason Spezza C 3.00 8.00
WMLU Milan Lucic C 3.00 8.00
WMMD Marcel Dionne B 6.00 15.00
WMMF Marc-Andre Fleury C 5.00 12.00
WMMG Michel Goulet B 5.00 12.00
WMML Mario Lemieux B 15.00 40.00
WMMM Mark Messier A 6.00 15.00
WMMR Mike Richards C 3.00 8.00
WMPD Pavel Datsyuk C 4.00 10.00
WMPE Phil Esposito B 8.00 20.00
WMPR Patrick Roy A 12.00 30.00
WMPS P.K. Subban C 5.00 12.00
WMRB Ray Bourque B 8.00 20.00
WMRF Ron Francis B 6.00 15.00
WMRG Ryan Getzlaf C 5.00 12.00
WMRH Ron Hextall C 3.00 8.00
WMRL Roberto Luongo C 3.00 8.00
WMRM Ryan Miller B 4.00 10.00
WMRN Rick Nash C 3.00 8.00
WMSC Sidney Crosby C 15.00 40.00
WMSS Steven Stamkos C 6.00 15.00
WMTE Tony Esposito B 6.00 15.00
WMTH Taylor Hall C 6.00 15.00
WMTT Tony Twist C 3.00 8.00

2013-14 SPx Winning Trios

GROUP A ODDS 1:1442
GROUP B ODDS 1:125
OVERALL STATED ODDS 1:108
W3LA Richards/Cartr/Vynv B 6.00 15.00
W3AVS Ststny/Varlmv/Dchne B 6.00 15.00
W3BOS Lucic/Rask/Chara B 6.00 15.00
W3COL Roy/Sakic/Bourque B 15.00 40.00
W3DET Datsyuk/Zetter/Lidstrm B 8.00 20.00
W3DRW Howard/Mrazek/Hasek B 12.00 30.00
W3EDM Yakupov/RNH/Hall B 6.00 15.00
W3GR8 Gretzky/Lemx/Messier A 25.00 60.00
W3LAK Quick/Brown/Kopitar B 6.00 15.00
W3OIL Hall/Gagner/Eberle B 12.00 30.00
W3OTT Spezza/Karlsn/Lehner B 12.00 30.00
W3AMZG Lmux/Skic/Lndrs A 25.00 50.00
W3CAPS Ovech/Bckstrm/Holtby B 25.00 60.00
W3JETS Pavelec/Kane/Byfgln B 6.00 15.00
W3LBBR Gorges/Price/Subban B 20.00 50.00
W3PITT Fleury/Malkin/Letang A 12.00 30.00
W3KINGS Kopitr/Quick/Doughty B 10.00 25.00

2014-15 SPx

101-130 STATED ODDS 1:3 HOBBY
GROUP C FF ODDS 1:160 HOBBY
OVERALL FF ODDS 1:72
131-138 ROOKIE AU PRINT RUN 199
139-168 ROOKIE AU PRINT RUN 399
169-180 ROOKIE AU PRINT RUN 249
GROUP A FF ODDS 1:330 HOBBY
GROUP B FF ODDS 1:220 HOBBY
EXCH EXPIRATION: 1/20/2017
1 Andrew Cogliano .25 .60
2 Ryan Getzlaf .60 1.50
3 Corey Perry .40 1.00
4 Zdeno Chara .40 1.00
5 Tuukka Rask .40 1.00
6 Patrice Bergeron .50 1.25
7 Tyler Ennis .30 .75
8 Cody Hodgson .40 1.00
9 Jiri Hudler .30 .75
10 Sean Monahan .40 1.00
11 Eric Staal .50 1.25
12 Cam Ward .40 1.00
13 Jeff Skinner .40 1.00
14 Corey Crawford .50 1.25
15 Jonathan Toews .75 2.00
16 Patrick Kane .75 2.00
17 Duncan Keith .40 1.00
18 Matt Duchene .40 1.00
19 Nathan MacKinnon .75 2.00
20 Ryan O'Reilly .40 1.00
21 Ryan Johansen .50 1.25
22 Sergei Bobrovsky .40 1.00
23 Scott Hartnell .40 1.00
24 Tyler Seguin .60 1.50
25 Jamie Benn .50 1.25
26 Kari Lehtonen .30 .75
27 Henrik Zetterberg .50 1.25
28 Pavel Datsyuk .50 1.25
29 Gustav Nyquist .30 .75
30 Taylor Hall .75 2.00
31 Jordan Eberle .40 1.00
32 Ryan Nugent-Hopkins .40 1.00
33 Roberto Luongo .40 1.00
34 Scottie Upshall .25 .60
35 Anze Kopitar .60 1.50
36 Drew Doughty .40 1.00
37 Jonathan Quick .60 1.50
38 Marian Gaborik .40 1.00
39 Jason Pominville .30 .75
40 Zach Parise .40 1.00
41 Mikko Koivu .30 .75
42 P.K. Subban .60 1.50
43 Max Pacioretty .40 1.00
44 Carey Price 1.25 3.00
45 Pekka Rinne .50 1.25
46 Shea Weber .30 .75
47 James Neal .40 1.00
48 Jaromir Jagr 1.00 2.50
49 Adam Henrique .40 1.00
50 Cory Schneider .30 .75
51 Kyle Okposo .40 1.00
52 John Tavares .75 2.00
53 Jaroslav Halak .30 .75
54 Martin St. Louis .40 1.00
55 Henrik Lundqvist .50 1.25
56 Rick Nash .40 1.00
57 Erik Karlsson .75 2.00
58 Craig Anderson .40 1.00
59 Kyle Turris .40 1.00
60 Claude Giroux .40 1.00
61 Wayne Simmonds .50 1.25
62 Steve Mason .30 .75
63 Keith Yandle .40 1.00
64 Shane Doan .30 .75
65 Mike Smith .40 1.00
66 Sidney Crosby 1.50 4.00
67 Evgeni Malkin 1.25 3.00
68 Chris Kunitz .40 1.00
69 Marc-Andre Fleury .60 1.50
70 Joe Pavelski .40 1.00
71 Patrick Marleau .40 1.00
72 Logan Couture .40 1.00
73 Martin Brodeur .75 2.00
74 T.J. Oshie .60 1.50
75 David Backes .40 1.00
76 Steven Stamkos .75 2.00
77 Ben Bishop .40 1.00
78 Valtteri Filppula .40 1.00
79 Phil Kessel .50 1.25
80 James van Riemsdyk .40 1.00
81 James Reimer .40 1.00
82 Henrik Sedin .40 1.00
83 Daniel Sedin .40 1.00
84 Eddie Lack .30 .75
85 Alexander Ovechkin 1.50 4.00
86 Nicklas Backstrom .60 1.50
87 Joel Ward .25 .60
88 Blake Wheeler .40 1.00
89 Dustin Byfuglien .40 1.00
90 Evander Kane .40 1.00
91 Teemu Selanne .75 2.00
92 Mats Sundin .40 1.00
93 Bobby Clarke .40 1.00
94 Mark Messier .40 1.00
95 Joe Sakic .60 1.50
96 Guy Lafleur .50 1.25
97 Dominik Hasek .50 1.25
98 Steve Yzerman .75 2.00
99 Wayne Gretzky 2.00 5.00
100 Bobby Orr 1.25 3.00
101 Jordan Binnington RC 1.50 4.00
102 Landon Ferraro RC 1.00 2.50
103 Sven Andrighetto RC 2.00 5.00
104 Anton Forsberg RC 1.50 4.00
105 Shayne Gostisbehere RC 6.00 15.00
106 Troy Grosenick RC 1.50 4.00
107 William Karlsson RC 6.00 15.00
108 Petter Granberg RC 1.25 3.00
109 Markus Granlund RC 2.50 6.00
110 Josh Jooris RC 1.50 4.00
111 Sam Carrick RC 1.50 4.00
112 Mike Halmo RC 1.00 2.50
113 Scott Mayfield RC 1.25 3.00
114 Seth Helgeson RC 1.25 3.00
115 Kevin Czuczman RC 1.25 3.00
116 Borna Rendulic RC 1.50 4.00
117 Phillip Danault RC 1.50 4.00
118 Scott Darling RC 4.00 10.00
119 Colin Smith RC 1.50 4.00
120 Kevin Hayes RC 5.00 12.00
121 Johan Sundstrom RC 1.50 4.00
122 Mike Zalewski RC 1.25 3.00
123 Victor Rask RC 1.50 4.00
124 Andrew Agozzino RC 1.25 3.00
125 Andrey Makarov RC 1.50 4.00
126 Brody Sutter RC 1.00 2.50
127 Kristers Gudlevskis RC 1.50 4.00
128 Chris Wagner RC 1.50 4.00
129 Christian Folin RC 1.50 4.00
130 Oscar Klefbom RC 3.00 8.00
131 Curtis McKenzie AU RC EXCH 5.00 12.00
132 Joe Morrow AU RC 8.00 20.00
133 David Pastrnak AU RC 30.00 80.00
134 Brandon Kozun AU RC 5.00 12.00
135 Cedric Paquette AU RC 8.00 20.00
136 Joonas Nattinen AU RC 6.00 15.00
137 Tyler Wotherspoon AU RC 6.00 15.00
138 Stuart Percy AU RC 6.00 15.00
139 A.Clendening JSY AU RC 5.00 12.00
140 T.Pulkkinen JSY AU RC 12.50 25.00
141 Joni Ortio JSY AU RC 8.00 20.00
142 Patrik Nemeth JSY AU RC 5.00 12.00
143 Ryan Sproul JSY AU RC 5.00 12.00
144 A.Duclair JSY AU RC EXCH 8.00 20.00
145 Mark Visentin JSY AU RC 5.00 12.00
146 V.Namestnikov JSY AU RC 6.00 15.00
147 Calle Jarnkrok JSY AU RC 5.00 12.00
148 Kerby Rychel JSY AU RC 8.00 20.00
149 A.Wennberg JSY AU RC 10.00 25.00
150 A.Khokhlachev JSY AU RC 5.00 12.00
151 Joey Hishon JSY AU RC 6.00 15.00
152 Greg McKegg JSY AU RC 4.00 10.00
153 Ty Rattie JSY AU RC 6.00 15.00
154 Vincent Trocheck JSY AU RC 6.00 15.00
155 Chris Tierney JSY AU RC 6.00 15.00
156 Mirco Mueller JSY AU RC 5.00 12.00
157 Corban Knight JSY AU RC 5.00 12.00
158 Jake McCabe JSY AU RC 5.00 12.00
159 Tobias Rieder JSY AU RC 5.00 12.00
160 Griffin Reinhart JSY AU RC 6.00 15.00
161 Darnell Nurse JSY AU RC 15.00 30.00
162 Seth Griffith JSY AU RC 12.00 30.00
163 Marko Dano JSY AU RC 5.00 12.00
164 Colton Sissons JSY AU RC 5.00 12.00
165 Damon Severson JSY AU RC 5.00 12.00
166 Brandon Gormley JSY AU RC 5.00 12.00
167 Laurent Brossoit JSY AU RC 5.00 12.00
168 Adam Lowry JSY AU RC 5.00 12.00
169 J.Drouin JSY AU/249 RC 15.00 40.00
170 Jiri Sekac JSY AU/249 RC 6.00 15.00
171 T.Teravainen JSY AU/249 RC 25.00 50.00
172 Bo Horvat JSY AU/249 RC 20.00 40.00
173 E.Kuznetsov JSY AU/249 RC 25.00 60.00
174 Aaron Ekblad JSY AU/249 RC 20.00 50.00
175 Sam Reinhart JSY AU/249 RC 20.00 50.00
176 Leon Draisaitl JSY AU/249 RC 30.00 80.00
177 A.Burakovsky JSY AU/249 RC 10.00 25.00
178 Curtis Lazar JSY AU/249 RC 8.00 20.00
179 J.Gaudreau JSY AU/249 RC 25.00 60.00
180 Jori Lehtera JSY AU/249 RC EXCH 8.00 20.00
203 Marian Hossa FF JSY A 8.00 20.00
204 Marian Gaborik FF JSY C 3.00 8.00
205 Peter Forsberg FF JSY A 5.00 12.00
206 Nikolai Khabibulin FF JSY C 3.00 8.00
207 Zach Parise FF JSY A
208 Jonathan Bernier FF JSY C 3.00 8.00
209 Wayne Simmonds FF JSY C 4.00 10.00
210 Tyler Seguin FF JSY A 8.00 20.00
211 Rick Nash FF JSY C 3.00 8.00
212 Jeff Carter FF JSY C 3.00 8.00
213 Phil Kessel FF JSY C 4.00 10.00
214 Jaromir Jagr FF JSY B 8.00 20.00
215 Matt Moulson FF JSY C 2.50 6.00
216 Brad Richards FF JSY C 3.00 8.00
217 D.Alfredsson FF JSY 5.00 12.00
218 Joe Thornton FF JSY C 3.00 8.00
219 Brett Hull FF JSY A 5.00 12.00
220 Dale Hawerchuk FF JSY B 5.00 12.00
223 Doug Gilmour FF JSY B 5.00 12.00
224 Grant Fuhr FF JSY B 4.00 10.00
225 Dominik Hasek FF JSY B 5.00 12.00
226 Rob Blake FF JSY B 4.00 10.00
227 Ron Francis FF JSY B 5.00 12.00
228 Ed Belfour FF JSY B 4.00 10.00
229 Mario Lemieux FF JSY A 15.00 40.00
230 Patrick Roy FF JSY A 12.00 30.00
231 Mats Sundin FF JSY B 4.00 10.00
232 Steve Yzerman FF JSY A 10.00 25.00

2014-15 SPx Spectrum Blue

*132-138 AU/50: .6X TO 1.5X AU/199
*139-168 JSY AU/50: 1X TO 2.5X JSY AU/399
*169-180 JSY AU/50: .8X TO 2X JSY AU/249
174 Aaron Ekblad JSY AU 60.00 120.00
179 Johnny Gaudreau JSY AU 75.00 150.00
180 Jori Lehtera JSY AU EXCH 15.00 40.00

2014-15 SPx 97-98 SPx Retro

1-60 STATED ODDS 1:5
61-90 STATED ODDS 1:9
*ACTIVE/50: 1X TO 2.5X BASIC INSERTS
*RETIRED/50: .8X TO 2X BASIC INSERTS
1 Sidney Crosby 6.00 15.00
2 Ryan Getzlaf 2.50 6.00
3 Claude Giroux 1.50 4.00
4 Tyler Seguin 2.50 6.00
5 Corey Perry 1.50 4.00
6 Phil Kessel 2.00 5.00
7 Taylor Hall 3.00 8.00
8 Alexander Ovechkin 6.00 15.00
9 Joe Pavelski 1.50 4.00
10 Jamie Benn 2.00 5.00
11 Nicklas Backstrom 2.50 6.00
12 Evgeni Malkin 5.00 12.00
13 Anze Kopitar 2.50 6.00
14 Patrick Kane 3.00 8.00
15 Jonathan Toews 3.00 8.00
16 Matt Duchene 1.50 4.00
17 Martin St. Louis 1.50 4.00
18 Blake Wheeler 1.50 4.00
19 Kyle Okposo 1.50 4.00
20 Jaromir Jagr 4.00 10.00
21 John Tavares 3.00 8.00
22 Jordan Eberle 1.50 4.00
23 Erik Karlsson 3.00 8.00
24 Drew Doughty 1.50 4.00
25 Duncan Keith 1.50 4.00
26 P.K. Subban 2.50 6.00
27 Carey Price 5.00 12.00
28 Henrik Lundqvist 2.00 5.00
29 Jonathan Quick 2.50 6.00
30 Tuukka Rask 1.50 4.00
31 Roberto Luongo 1.50 4.00
32 Steven Stamkos 3.00 8.00
33 Patrice Bergeron 2.00 5.00
34 Zach Parise 1.50 4.00
35 Nathan MacKinnon 3.00 8.00
36 Shea Weber 1.25 3.00
37 Joe Thornton 1.50 4.00
38 Eric Staal 2.00 5.00
39 Martin Brodeur 6.00 15.00
40 Max Pacioretty 1.50 4.00
41 T.J. Oshie 2.50 6.00
42 Henrik Zetterberg 2.00 5.00
43 Pavel Datsyuk 2.50 6.00
44 Jonathan Bernier 1.50 4.00
45 Patrick Sharp 1.50 4.00
46 Mats Sundin 1.50 4.00
47 Jean Beliveau 3.00 8.00
48 Dominik Hasek 2.50 6.00
49 Teemu Selanne 3.00 8.00
50 Jeremy Roenick 2.00 5.00
51 Nicklas Lidstrom 2.00 5.00
52 Mike Bossy 2.00 5.00
53 Joe Sakic 3.00 8.00
54 Patrick Roy 5.00 12.00
55 Mario Lemieux 6.00 15.00
56 Guy Lafleur 2.50 6.00
57 Doug Harvey 2.00 5.00
58 Terry Sawchuk 2.00 5.00
59 Steve Yzerman 4.00 10.00
60 Wayne Gretzky 8.00 20.00
61 Teuvo Teravainen 2.50 6.00
62 Ty Rattie 2.00 5.00
63 Evgeny Kuznetsov 6.00 15.00
64 Brandon Gormley 1.50 4.00
65 Johnny Gaudreau 5.00 12.00
66 Marko Dano 1.50 4.00
67 Anthony Duclair 2.50 6.00
68 Chris Tierney 1.50 4.00
69 David Pastrnak 6.00 15.00
70 Stuart Percy 1.50 4.00
71 Alexander Khokhlachev 1.50 4.00
72 Sam Reinhart 5.00 12.00
73 Kerby Rychel 1.25 3.00
74 Adam Clendening 1.50 4.00
75 Jiri Sekac 1.50 4.00
76 Seth Griffith 2.00 5.00
77 Calle Jarnkrok 1.50 4.00
78 Damon Severson 1.50 4.00
79 Leon Draisaitl 8.00 20.00
80 Sven Andrighetto 2.00 5.00
81 Bo Horvat 5.00 12.00
82 Griffin Reinhart 2.00 5.00
83 Alexander Wennberg 3.00 8.00
84 Curtis Lazar 2.00 5.00
85 Kevin Hayes 5.00 12.00
86 Jori Lehtera 2.00 5.00
87 Andre Burakovsky 2.50 6.00
88 Darnell Nurse 5.00 12.00
89 Aaron Ekblad 6.00 15.00
90 Jonathan Drouin 4.00 10.00

2014-15 SPx Finite Rookies

1 Adam Clendening/299 2.00 5.00
2 Damon Severson/299 2.00 5.00
3 Alexander Khokhlachev/299 2.00 5.00
4 Brandon Kozun/299 1.50 4.00
5 Teuvo Teravainen/299 3.00 8.00
6 Evgeny Kuznetsov/299 8.00 20.00
7 Darnell Nurse/299 6.00 15.00
8 Vladislav Namestnikov/299 3.00 8.00
9 Seth Griffith/299 2.50 6.00
10 Jiri Sekac/299 2.00 5.00
11 Griffin Reinhart/299 2.50 6.00
12 Kevin Hayes/299 6.00 15.00
13 Brandon Gormley/299 2.00 5.00
14 Marko Dano/299 2.00 5.00
15 Ty Rattie/299 4.00 10.00
16 Alexander Wennberg/299 4.00 10.00
17 Stuart Percy/299 2.00 5.00
18 Victor Rask/299 2.00 5.00
19 Teemu Pulkkinen/299 2.50 6.00
20 Adam Lowry/299 2.00 5.00
21 Curtis Lazar/299 2.50 6.00
22 Andre Burakovsky/199 4.00 10.00
23 Johnny Gaudreau/199 12.00 30.00
24 Anthony Duclair/199 4.00 10.00
25 Sam Reinhart/199 8.00 20.00
26 Bo Horvat/199 8.00 20.00
27 Leon Draisaitl/199 12.00 30.00
28 Jonathan Drouin/149 6.00 15.00
29 Aaron Ekblad/149 12.00 30.00
30 Jori Lehtera/149 3.00 8.00

2014-15 SPx Finite Rookies Autographs

EXCH EXPIRATION: 1/17/2017
1 Adam Clendening/125 5.00 12.00
2 Damon Severson/125 5.00 12.00
3 Alexander Khokhlachev/125 5.00 12.00
4 Brandon Kozun/125 4.00 10.00
5 Teuvo Teravainen/125 20.00 40.00
6 Evgeny Kuznetsov/125 20.00 50.00
7 Darnell Nurse/125 15.00 30.00
8 Vladislav Namestnikov/125 8.00 20.00
9 Seth Griffith/125 6.00 15.00
10 Jiri Sekac/125 5.00 12.00
11 Griffin Reinhart/125 6.00 15.00
12 Kevin Hayes/125 EXCH 25.00 50.00
13 Brandon Gormley/125 5.00 12.00
14 Marko Dano/125 5.00 12.00
15 Ty Rattie/125 6.00 15.00
16 Alexander Wennberg/125 10.00 25.00
17 Stuart Percy/125 5.00 12.00
18 Victor Rask/125 5.00 12.00
19 Teemu Pulkkinen/125 8.00 20.00
20 Adam Lowry/125 5.00 12.00
21 Curtis Lazar/125 6.00 15.00
22 Andre Burakovsky/49 12.00 30.00
23 Johnny Gaudreau/49 75.00 125.00
24 Anthony Duclair/49 EXCH 25.00 50.00
25 Sam Reinhart/49 40.00 80.00
26 Bo Horvat/49 20.00 40.00
27 Leon Draisaitl/49 40.00 100.00
28 Jonathan Drouin/25 30.00 80.00
29 Aaron Ekblad/25 40.00 100.00
30 Jori Lehtera/25 12.00 30.00

2014-15 SPx Flashback Fabrics Patch

*203-232 PATCH/15: .8X TO 2X GRP A FF
*203-232 PATCH/15: 1X TO 2.5X GRP B FF
*203-232 PATCH/15: 1.2X TO 3X GRP C FF

2014-15 SPx Rookie Inaugural Jerseys

STATED ODDS 1:40 HOBBY
*PATCH/99: .6X TO 1.5X BASIC JSY
RPMAB Andre Burakovsky 4.00 10.00
RPMAE Aaron Ekblad 5.00 12.00
RPMAL Adam Lowry 2.50 6.00
RPMAW Alexander Wennberg 5.00 12.00
RPMBH Bo Horvat 8.00 20.00
RPMCJ Calle Jarnkrok 2.50 6.00
RPMCK Corban Knight 2.50 6.00
RPMCL Curtis Lazar 3.00 8.00
RPMCT Chris Tierney 2.50 6.00
RPMDN Darnell Nurse 8.00 20.00
RPMEK Evgeny Kuznetsov 10.00 25.00
RPMGR Griffin Reinhart 3.00 8.00
RPMJD Jonathan Drouin 6.00 15.00
RPMJG Johnny Gaudreau 10.00 25.00
RPMJH Joey Hishon 3.00 8.00
RPMLD Leon Draisaitl 12.00 30.00
RPMMD Marko Dano 2.50 6.00
RPMMV Alexander Khokhlachev 2.50 6.00
RPMSG Seth Griffith 3.00 8.00
RPMSR Sam Reinhart 8.00 20.00
RPMTR Ty Rattie 3.00 8.00
RPMTT Teuvo Teravainen 5.00 12.00
RPMWK Adam Clendening 2.50 6.00

2014-15 SPx Rookie Inaugural Jerseys Combos

*PATCH/49: .8X TO 2X BASIC JSY
RPM2EN A.Ekblad/D.Nurse 6.00 15.00
RPM2ER A.Ekblad/S.Reinhart 6.00 15.00
RPM2GK J.Gaudreau/C.Knight 6.00 15.00
RPM2GM B.Gormley/M.Visentin 3.00 8.00
RPM2KB Kuznetsov/Burakovsky 6.00 15.00
RPM2KG Khokhlachev/S.Griffith 4.00 10.00
RPM2ND D.Nurse/L.Draisaitl 5.00 12.00
RPM2RM S.Reinhart/J.McCabe 6.00 15.00
RPM2WD A.Wennberg/M.Dano 6.00 15.00

2014-15 SPx Rookie Inaugural Jerseys Trios

*PATCH/25: .8X TO 2X BASIC JSY
RPM3DNW Drouin/Nurse/Wenn 12.00 30.00
RPM3ENG Ekblad/Nurse/Gorm 15.00 40.00
RPM3ERD Ekblad/S.Rein/Drais 20.00 50.00
RPM3GOK Gaudr/Ortio/Knight 12.00 30.00
RPM3LRW Lazar/S.Rein/Wenn 6.00 15.00
RPM3NDB Nurse/Drais/Brossoit 20.00 50.00

2014-15 SPx Shadow Box

STATED ODDS 1:144 HOBBY
SH38-SH39 STATED ODDS 1:1,715 H
SH40-SH42 STATED ODDS 1:858 H
SH1 Sidney Crosby 30.00 80.00
SH2 Ryan Getzlaf 12.00 30.00
SH3 Claude Giroux 8.00 20.00
SH4 Tyler Seguin 12.00 30.00
SH5 Corey Perry 8.00 20.00
SH6 Taylor Hall 15.00 40.00
SH7 Alexander Ovechkin 30.00 80.00
SH8 Joe Pavelski 8.00 20.00
SH9 Jamie Benn 10.00 25.00
SH10 Anze Kopitar 12.00 30.00
SH11 Patrick Kane 15.00 40.00
SH12 Jonathan Toews 25.00 60.00
SH13 Martin St. Louis 8.00 20.00
SH14 Henrik Lundqvist 10.00 25.00
SH15 Jaromir Jagr 30.00 80.00
SH16 Nathan MacKinnon 15.00 40.00
SH17 P.K. Subban 12.00 30.00
SH18 Drew Doughty 8.00 20.00
SH19 Patrice Bergeron 10.00 25.00
SH20 Pavel Datsyuk 10.00 25.00
SH21 Zach Parise 8.00 20.00
SH22 Erik Karlsson 15.00 40.00
SH23 T.J. Oshie 12.00 30.00
SH24 Steven Stamkos 15.00 40.00
SH25 Jordan Eberle 8.00 20.00
SH26 Duncan Keith 8.00 20.00
SH27 Peter Forsberg 12.00 30.00
SH28 Joe Sakic 20.00 50.00
SH29 Doug Gilmour 15.00 40.00
SH30 Nicklas Lidstrom 8.00 20.00
SH31 Bobby Clarke 12.00 30.00
SH32 Bobby Orr 40.00 100.00
SH33 Dominik Hasek 15.00 40.00
SH34 Jean Beliveau 12.00 30.00
SH35 Doug Harvey 8.00 20.00
SH36 Mats Sundin 8.00 20.00
SH38 Teemu Selanne AU 40.00 80.00
SH39 Wayne Gretzky AU 150.00 250.00
SH40 Teuvo Teravainen AU 60.00 120.00
SH42 Evgeny Kuznetsov AU 50.00 100.00

2014-15 SPx Winning Combos

GROUP A STATED ODDS 1:1,950
GROUP B STATED ODDS 1:950
GROUP C STATED ODDS 1:205
GROUP D STATED ODDS 1:160
GROUP E STATED ODDS 1:65
OVERALL STATED ODDS 1:36
WCBF G.Fuhr/E.Belfour 5.00 12.00
WCBH M.Brodeur/A.Henrique 10.00 25.00
WCBK N.Kadri/J.Bernier 6.00 15.00
WCBV S.Bobrovsky/S.Varlamov 4.00 10.00
WCCN C.Crawford/A.Niemi 5.00 12.00
WCDK D.Doughty/D.Keith 4.00 10.00
WCDM E.Malkin/P.Datsyuk 6.00 15.00
WCDZ H.Zetterberg/P.Datsyuk 5.00 12.00
WCEH T.Hall/J.Eberle 8.00 20.00
WCEP E.Karlsson/P.Subban 8.00 20.00
WCGS C.Giroux/W.Simmonds 8.00 20.00
WCHB D.Harvey/J.Beliveau 10.00 25.00
WCHS T.Seguin/T.Hall 10.00 25.00
WCKD A.Kopitar/D.Doughty 6.00 15.00
WCKM E.Malkin/C.Kunitz 15.00 40.00
WCLF M.Lemieux/R.Francis 8.00 20.00
WCLH D.Harvey/G.Lafleur 15.00 30.00
WCLQ H.Lundqvist/J.Quick 10.00 25.00
WCLR K.Lehtonen/P.Rinne 6.00 15.00
WCLZ H.Zetterberg/N.Lidstrom
WCPP M.Pacioretty/C.Price 12.00 30.00
WCRB P.Roy/M.Brodeur 12.00 30.00
WCRL R.Nash/H.Lundqvist 10.00 25.00
WCRS J.Sakic/P.Roy 12.00 30.00
WCRW P.Rinne/S.Weber 6.00 15.00
WCSF P.Forsberg/J.Sakic 8.00 20.00
WCSK J.Kurri/T.Selanne 8.00 20.00
WCTK J.Toews/P.Kane 10.00 25.00
WCVB V.Hedman/B.Bishop 6.00 15.00
WCVD M.Duchene/S.Varlamov 4.00 10.00
WCYL S.Yzerman/N.Lidstrom

2014-15 SPx Winning Materials

GROUP A STATED ODDS 1:1,450
GROUP B STATED ODDS 1:970
GROUP C STATED ODDS 1:180
GROUP D STATED ODDS 1:165
GROUP E STATED ODDS 1:70
OVERALL STATED ODDS 1:36
WMAK Anze Kopitar B 8.00 20.00
WMBP Brad Park C 3.00 8.00
WMCG Claude Giroux C 4.00 10.00
WMCP Carey Price E 10.00 25.00
WMDB David Backes D 4.00 10.00
WMDD Drew Doughty E 3.00 8.00
WMDG Doug Gilmour C 5.00 12.00
WMDO Doug Harvey C 8.00 20.00
WMEM Evgeni Malkin C 12.00 30.00
WMES Eric Staal E 4.00 10.00
WMGF Grant Fuhr D 4.00 10.00
WMHA Dominik Hasek D 5.00 12.00
WMHL Henrik Lundqvist A 8.00 20.00
WMJB Jean Beliveau A 12.00 30.00
WMJQ Jonathan Quick C 6.00 15.00
WMLR Luc Robitaille E 3.00 8.00
WMMB Martin Brodeur E 6.00 15.00
WMMD Matt Duchene E 3.00 8.00
WMML Mario Lemieux C 10.00 25.00
WMOV Alexander Ovechkin D 15.00 40.00
WMSC Sidney Crosby B 12.00 30.00
WMTH Taylor Hall E 6.00 15.00
WMTO Jonathan Toews D 4.00 10.00
WMTR Tuukka Rask E 3.00 8.00
WMTS Tyler Seguin B 8.00 20.00

2015-16 SPx

101-130 STATED ODDS 1:3 HOBBY
131-138 ROOKIE AU PRINT RUN 299
139-165 ROOKIE AU PRINT RUN 499
166-172 RC AU PRINT RUN 199-399
1 Alexander Ovechkin 1.50 4.00
2 Carey Price 1.25 3.00
3 Cory Schneider .30 .75
4 David Backes .40 1.00
5 Erik Karlsson .75 2.00
6 Ryan Strome .30 .75
7 Sidney Crosby 1.50 4.00
8 Jarome Iginla .40 1.00
9 Corey Perry .40 1.00
10 James van Riemsdyk .40 1.00

11 Henrik Lundqvist .50 1.25
12 Oliver Ekman-Larsson .30 .75
13 Claude Giroux .40 1.00
14 Adam Henrique .40 1.00
15 Jamie Benn .50 1.25
16 Dustin Brown .30 .75
17 Brayden Schenn .40 1.00
18 Jonathan Toews .75 2.00
19 Jordan Eberle .40 1.00
20 Gabriel Landeskog .40 1.00
21 Zach Parise .40 1.00
22 Ryan O'Reilly .40 1.00
23 Steven Stamkos .75 2.00
24 Daniel Sedin .40 1.00
25 Logan Couture .40 1.00
26 Andrew Ladd .40 1.00
27 Johnny Gaudreau .60 1.50
28 Eric Staal .50 1.25
29 Brendan Gallagher .50 1.25
30 Aaron Ekblad .40 1.00
31 Filip Forsberg .50 1.25
32 P.K. Subban .60 1.50
33 Henrik Zetterberg .50 1.25
34 Evgeni Malkin 1.25 3.00
35 Tyler Johnson .30 .75
36 Anze Kopitar .60 1.50
37 Rick Nash .40 1.00
38 Nicklas Backstrom .60 1.50
39 Jiri Hudler .30 .75
40 Vladimir Tarasenko .60 1.50
41 Ben Bishop .40 1.00
42 Jonathan Bernier .40 1.00
43 Tyler Seguin .60 1.50
44 Radim Vrbata .30 .75
45 John Tavares .75 2.00
46 Joe Pavelski .40 1.00
47 Ryan Getzlaf .60 1.50
48 Max Pacioretty .40 1.00
49 Blake Wheeler .40 1.00
50 Brent Seabrook .40 1.00
51 Ryan Nugent-Hopkins .40 1.00
52 Jason Pominville .30 .75
53 Patrice Bergeron .50 1.25
54 Jordan Staal .40 1.00
55 Ryan Johansen .50 1.25
56 Bobby Hull .40 1.00
57 Martin St. Louis .40 1.00
58 Wayne Gretzky 2.00 5.00
59 Mark Messier .60 1.50
60 Grant Fuhr .40 1.00
61 Aaron Ekblad SC .40 1.00
62 Alex Galchenyuk SC .50 1.25
63 Viktor Arvidsson SC .50 1.25
64 Nathan MacKinnon SC .75 2.00
65 Max Domi SC .75 2.00
66 Tyler Johnson SC .30 .75
67 Sean Monahan SC .40 1.00
68 Aleksander Barkov SC .40 1.00
69 Mark Stone SC .30 .75
70 Nikolay Goldobin SC .40 1.00
71 Nikolaj Ehlers SC .75 2.00
72 Sam Bennett SC .50 1.25
73 Artemi Panarin SC 1.25 3.00
74 Dylan Larkin SC 1.25 3.00
75 Connor McDavid SC 5.00 12.00
76 Alexander Ovechkin SW 1.50 4.00
77 Bobby Ryan SW .30 .75
78 Ryan Johansen SW .50 1.25
79 Evgeni Malkin SW 1.25 3.00
80 Patrick Kane SW .75 2.00
81 Matt Duchene SW .40 1.00
82 Pavel Datsyuk SW .50 1.25
83 Johnny Gaudreau SW .60 1.50
84 Jason Spezza SW .30 .75
85 Jaromir Jagr SW 1.00 2.50
86 Aleksander Barkov SW .40 1.00
87 Sidney Crosby SW 1.50 4.00
88 Logan Couture SW .40 1.00
89 Connor McDavid SW 8.00 20.00
90 Matt Moulson SW .30 .75
91 Claude Giroux NOF .40 1.00
92 David Krejci NOF .30 .75
93 Alexander Ovechkin NOF 1.50 4.00
94 Joe Sakic NOF .60 1.50
95 Mario Lemieux NOF 1.25 3.00
96 Mike Bossy NOF .40 1.00
97 Jonathan Toews NOF .75 2.00
98 Nicklas Lidstrom NOF .40 1.00
99 Steve Yzerman NOF .60 1.50
100 Bobby Clarke NOF .40 1.00
101 Brian Ferlin RC 1.00 2.50
102 Luke Witkowski RC 1.25 3.00
103 Linus Ullmark RC 2.00 5.00
104 Byron Froese RC 1.25 3.00
105 Connor Brickley RC 1.25 3.00
106 Erik Gustafsson RC 2.50 6.00
107 Logan Shaw RC 1.50 4.00
108 Vincent Hinostroza RC 1.00 2.50
109 Chandler Stephenson RC 1.50 4.00
110 Zachary Fucale RC 1.50 4.00
111 Tommy Cross RC 1.25 3.00
112 Nick Shore RC 1.50 4.00
113 Chris Wideman RC 1.50 4.00
114 Joel Edmundson RC 1.25 3.00
115 Andrew Copp RC 1.50 4.00
116 Max McCormick RC 1.25 3.00
117 Brendan Ranford RC 1.25 3.00
118 Sergey Kalinin RC 1.25 3.00
119 Brett Pesce RC 1.25 3.00
120 Mike Condon RC 1.50 4.00
121 Chris Driedger RC 1.25 3.00
122 Tyler Randell RC 1.50 4.00
123 Tanner Kero RC 1.50 4.00
124 Viktor Svedberg RC 1.25 3.00
125 Brendan Gaunce RC 2.00 5.00
126 Dylan DeMelo RC 1.25 3.00
127 Joonas Kemppainen RC 1.25 3.00
128 Brian O'Neill RC 1.25 3.00
129 Anton Slepyshev RC 1.25 3.00
130 Evgeny Medvedev RC 1.25 3.00
131 Mike Condon AU 6.00 15.00
132 Sergei Plotnikov AU RC 5.00 12.00
133 Mattias Janmark AU RC 6.00 15.00
134 Ben Hutton AU RC 6.00 15.00
135 Andreas Athanasiou AU RC 20.00 50.00
136 Colton Parayko AU RC 8.00 20.00
137 Joonas Donskoi AU RC 6.00 15.00
138 Oscar Lindberg AU RC 6.00 15.00
139 Antoine Bibeau JSY AU/499 RC 5.00 12.00
140 Malcolm Subban JSY AU/499 RC 12.00 30.00
141 Matt Puempel JSY AU/499 RC 4.00 10.00
142 Nikolay Goldobin JSY AU/499 RC 5.00 12.00
143 Nick Cousins JSY AU/499 RC 5.00 12.00
144 Connor Hellebuyck JSY AU/499 RC 12.00 30.00
145 Shane Prince JSY AU/499 RC 4.00 10.00
146 Jordan Weal JSY AU/499 RC 5.00 12.00
147 Mikko Rantanen JSY AU/499 RC 10.00 25.00
148 Brendan Gaunce JSY AU/499 RC 6.00 15.00
149 Slater Koekkoek JSY AU/499 RC 4.00 10.00
150 Daniel Sprong JSY AU/499 RC 10.00 25.00
151 Ryan Hartman JSY AU/499 RC 6.00 15.00
152 Jared McCann JSY AU/499 RC 5.00 12.00
153 Jake Virtanen JSY AU/499 RC 6.00 15.00
154 Hunter Shinkaruk JSY AU/499 RC 5.00 12.00
155 Nick Ritchie JSY AU/499 RC 5.00 12.00
156 Derek Forbort JSY AU/499 RC 4.00 10.00
157 Zachary Fucale JSY AU/499 5.00 12.00
158 Kevin Fiala JSY AU/499 RC 5.00 12.00
159 Robby Fabbri JSY AU/499 RC 6.00 15.00
160 Henrik Samuelsson JSY AU/499 RC 4.00 10.00
161 Mackenzie Skapski JSY AU/499 RC 5.00 12.00
162 Noah Hanifin JSY AU/499 RC 6.00 15.00
163 Emile Poirier JSY AU/499 RC 5.00 12.00
164 Nicolas Petan JSY AU/499 RC 5.00 12.00
165 Brock McGinn JSY AU/499 RC 5.00 12.00
166 Sam Bennett JSY AU/399 RC 8.00 20.00
167 Nikolaj Ehlers JSY AU/399 RC 12.00 30.00
168 Dylan Larkin JSY AU/399 RC 60.00 120.00
169 Connor McDavid JSY AU/399 RC 250.00 400.00
170 Artemi Panarin JSY AU/399 RC 50.00 100.00
171 Max Domi JSY AU/199 RC 60.00 100.00
172 Jack Eichel JSY/399 RC 25.00 60.00

2015-16 SPx Red

*RED: .6X TO 1.5X AU/499 RC
*RED: .5X TO 1.2X AU/399 RC
*RED: .5X TO 1.2X AU/299 RC
STATED PRINT RUN 50 SER.#'d SETS
151 Ryan Hartman JSY AU 10.00 25.00
168 Dylan Larkin JSY AU 100.00 200.00
169 Connor McDavid JSY AU 650.00 800.00
170 Artemi Panarin JSY AU 100.00 200.00

2015-16 SPx '05-06 Retro Rookie Autograph Jerseys

STATED PRINT RUN 299-399
SPXRAB Antoine Bibeau/399 5.00 12.00
SPXRCH Connor Hellebuyck/399 12.00 30.00
SPXRCM Connor McDavid/299 250.00 450.00
SPXRDF Derek Forbort/399 4.00 10.00
SPXRDL Dylan Larkin/299 60.00 120.00
SPXRDS Daniel Sprong/399 10.00 25.00
SPXREP Emile Poirier/399 5.00 12.00
SPXRJA Josh Anderson/399 5.00 12.00
SPXRJM Jared McCann/399 5.00 12.00
SPXRJV Jake Virtanen/299 6.00 15.00
SPXRKB Kyle Baun/399 5.00 12.00
SPXRKF Kevin Fiala/399 5.00 12.00
SPXRMR Mikko Rantanen/399 10.00 25.00
SPXRNC Nick Cousins/399 5.00 12.00
SPXRNE Nikolaj Ehlers/299 10.00 25.00
SPXRNG Nikolay Goldobin/399 5.00 12.00
SPXRNH Noah Hanifin/399 6.00 15.00
SPXRNP Nicolas Petan/399 5.00 12.00
SPXRNR Nick Ritchie/399 5.00 12.00
SPXRRB Robby Fabbri/299 6.00 15.00
SPXRSH Hunter Shinkaruk/399 5.00 12.00
SPXRSP Shane Prince/399 4.00 10.00
SPXRZF Zachary Fucale/399 10.00 25.00

2015-16 SPx '05-06 Retro Rookie Jerseys

OVERALL STATED ODDS 1:16
GROUP A STATED ODDS 1:1,745
GROUP B STATED ODDS 1:50
GROUP C STATED ODDS 1:62
GROUP D STATED ODDS 1:39
SPXR-AB Antoine Bibeau D 2.50 6.00
SPXR-AP Artemi Panarin B 8.00 20.00
SPXR-BM Brock McGinn D 2.50 6.00
SPXR-CH Connor Hellebuyck D 6.00 15.00
SPXR-CM Connor McDavid B 40.00 80.00
SPXR-DF Derek Forbort D 2.00 5.00
SPXR-DL Dylan Larkin B 8.00 20.00
SPXR-DS Daniel Sprong C 5.00 12.00
SPXR-EP Emile Poirier A 6.00 15.00
SPXR-JA Josh Anderson D 2.50 6.00
SPXR-JE Jack Eichel B 10.00 25.00
SPXR-JM Jared McCann C 2.50 6.00
SPXR-JV Jake Virtanen B 3.00 8.00
SPXR-KB Kyle Baun D 2.50 6.00
SPXR-KF Kevin Fiala D 2.50 6.00
SPXR-MD Max Domi B 5.00 12.00
SPXR-MR Mikko Rantanen C 5.00 12.00
SPXR-NC Nick Cousins D 2.50 6.00
SPXR-NE Nikolaj Ehlers B 5.00 12.00
SPXR-NG Nikolay Goldobin B 2.50 6.00
SPXR-NH Noah Hanifin B 3.00 8.00
SPXR-NP Nicolas Petan C 2.50 6.00
SPXR-NR Nick Ritchie C 2.50 6.00
SPXR-RB Robby Fabbri B 3.00 8.00
SPXR-RH Ryan Hartman D 3.00 8.00
SPXR-SH Hunter Shinkaruk C 2.50 6.00
SPXR-SP Shane Prince C 2.00 5.00
SPXR-ZF Zachary Fucale D 2.50 6.00

2015-16 SPx Monochromatics

OVERALL STATED ODDS 1:20
GROUP A STATED ODDS 1:8,912
GROUP B STATED ODDS 1:275
GROUP C STATED ODDS 1:60
GROUP D STATED ODDS 1:34
MAE Aaron Ekblad C 4.00 10.00
MAH Adam Henrique D 4.00 10.00
MAO Alexander Ovechkin B 15.00 40.00
MBB Ben Bishop D 4.00 10.00
MBE Jamie Benn C 5.00 12.00
MBG Brendan Gallagher C 5.00 12.00
MBS Brayden Schenn D 4.00 10.00
MCG Claude Giroux C 4.00 10.00
MCP Carey Price B 12.00 30.00
MCS Cory Schneider D 3.00 8.00
MDB David Backes D 4.00 10.00
MDS Daniel Sedin D 4.00 10.00
MEM Evgeni Malkin B 12.00 30.00
MGF Grant Fuhr B 4.00 10.00
MGL Gabriel Landeskog D 4.00 10.00
MJE Jordan Eberle D 4.00 10.00
MJG Johnny Gaudreau C 6.00 15.00
MJH Jiri Hudler D 3.00 8.00
MJI Jarome Iginla C 4.00 10.00
MJS Jordan Staal D 4.00 10.00
MLC Logan Couture D 4.00 10.00
MMS Martin St. Louis B 4.00 10.00
MNB Nicklas Backstrom C 6.00 15.00
MNK Nazem Kadri A 3.00 8.00
MOE Oliver Ekman-Larsson C 3.00 8.00
MRJ Ryan Johansen C 5.00 12.00
MRN Ryan Nugent-Hopkins C 4.00 10.00
MRS Ryan Strome D 3.00 8.00
MSE Brent Seabrook D 4.00 10.00
MSS Steven Stamkos B 8.00 20.00
MTS Tyler Seguin B 6.00 15.00
MVT Vladimir Tarasenko B 6.00 15.00
MZP Zach Parise C 4.00 10.00

2015-16 SPx Sweet Shot Stick Signings

SSS-CM Connor McDavid 250.00 400.00
SSS-DL Dylan Larkin 25.00 60.00
SSS-DS Daniel Sprong 15.00 40.00
SSS-EP Emile Poirier 8.00 20.00
SSS-JD Jacob de la Rose 8.00 20.00
SSS-JM Jared McCann 8.00 20.00
SSS-KF Kevin Fiala 8.00 20.00
SSS-MR Mikko Rantanen 15.00 40.00
SSS-MS Malcolm Subban 20.00 50.00
SSS-NE Nikolaj Ehlers 15.00 40.00
SSS-NP Nicolas Petan 8.00 20.00
SSS-OL Oscar Lindberg 8.00 20.00
SSS-SP Shane Prince 6.00 15.00
SSS-WG Wayne Gretzky

2015-16 SPx X Jersey Dual

OVERALL STATED ODDS 1:70
GROUP A STATED ODDS 1:6,770
GROUP B STATED ODDS 1:395
GROUP C STATED ODDS 1:237
GROUP D STATED ODDS 1:135
XDBL S.Bennett/D.Larkin C 12.00 30.00
XDBS T.Seguin/J.Benn C 6.00 15.00
XDDL P.Datsyuk/N.Lidstrom A 5.00 12.00
XDDP M.Domi/A.Panarin B 12.00 30.00
XDHE N.Hanifin/J.Eichel B 15.00 40.00
XDKQ A.Kopitar/J.Quick C 6.00 15.00
XDKS R.Getzlaf/R.Kesler D 6.00 15.00
XDMG W.Gretzky/C.McDavid B 60.00 120.00
XDMP E.Malkin/C.Perry D 12.00 30.00
XDOB A.Ovechkin/N.Backstrom C 15.00 40.00
XDRB P.Roy/M.Brodeur B 10.00 25.00
XDSG P.Subban/A.Galchenyuk D 6.00 15.00
XDSL D.Stepan/H.Lundqvist D 5.00 12.00
XDTK J.Toews/P.Kane D 8.00 20.00

2015-16 SPx X Jersey Quad

OVERALL STATED ODDS 1:160
GROUP A STATED ODDS 1:1,160
GROUP B STATED ODDS 1:516
GROUP C STATED ODDS 1:290
XQBPPH Benn/Parise/Pavelski/Hall C 10.00 25.00
XQDPRE Domi/Panarin/Rantanen/Ehlers B 15.0040.00
XQFCRR Fleury/Coffey/Robitaille Robinson A 6.00 15.00
XQMHNE McDavid/Hall Nugent-Hopkins/Eberle A 40.00 100.00
XQOTSS Ovechkin/Tavares Seguin/Stamkos B 20.00 50.00
XQPKTV Perry/Kane/Tarasenko/Voracek C 10.0025.00
XQPRLR Price/Rinne/Lundqvist/Rask C 15.00 40.00
XQPSGP Pacioretty/Subban Galchenyuk/Price C 15.00 40.00
XQTKKC Toews/Kane/Keith/Crawford B 10.00 25.00

2016-17 SPx

1 John Gibson 3.00 8.00
2 Oliver Ekman-Larsson 2.50 6.00
3 David Krejci 3.00 8.00
4 Ray Bourque 5.00 12.00
5 Ryan O'Reilly 3.00 8.00
6 Dale Hawerchuk 4.00 10.00
7 Sean Monahan 3.00 8.00
8 Jonathan Toews 6.00 15.00
9 Patrick Kane 6.00 15.00
10 Nathan MacKinnon 6.00 15.00
11 Boone Jenner 3.00 8.00
12 Jamie Benn 4.00 10.00
13 Steve Yzerman 4.00 10.00
14 Dylan Larkin 5.00 12.00
15 Wayne Gretzky 15.00 40.00
16 Connor McDavid 15.00 40.00
17 Aleksander Barkov 3.00 8.00
18 Pavel Bure 3.00 8.00
19 Jaromir Jagr 8.00 20.00
20 Rob Blake 3.00 8.00
21 Drew Doughty 3.00 8.00
22 Zach Parise 3.00 8.00
23 Patrick Roy 8.00 20.00
24 Carey Price 10.00 25.00
25 Pekka Rinne 4.00 10.00
26 Cory Schneider 2.50 6.00
27 Jaroslav Halak 3.00 8.00
28 John Tavares 6.00 15.00
29 Derek Stepan 2.50 6.00
30 Rick Nash 3.00 8.00
31 Henrik Lundqvist 3.00 8.00
32 Mark Stone 3.00 8.00
33 Jakub Voracek 3.00 8.00
34 Sidney Crosby 12.00 30.00
35 Mario Lemieux 10.00 25.00
36 Joe Pavelski 3.00 8.00
37 Brent Burns 4.00 10.00
38 Jake Allen 4.00 10.00
39 Brett Hull 3.00 8.00
40 Steven Stamkos 6.00 15.00
41 Tyler Johnson 2.50 6.00
42 Nikita Kucherov 5.00 12.00
43 James van Riemsdyk 3.00 8.00
44 Morgan Rielly 2.50 6.00
45 Ryan Miller 3.00 8.00
46 Kirk McLean 3.00 8.00
47 Alexander Ovechkin 12.00 30.00
48 Braden Holtby 5.00 12.00
49 Mark Scheifele 4.00 10.00
50 Nikolaj Ehlers 3.00 8.00
51 William Nylander RC 12.00 30.00
52 Pavel Zacha RC 4.00 10.00
53 Anthony Mantha RC 8.00 20.00
54 Hudson Fasching RC 3.00 8.00
55 Kasperi Kapanen RC 6.00 15.00
56 Sonny Milano RC 4.00 10.00
57 Josh Morrissey RC 4.00 10.00
58 Justin Bailey RC 3.00 8.00
59 Connor Brown RC 5.00 12.00
60 Steven Santini RC 2.50 6.00
61 Oliver Bjorkstrand RC 2.50 6.00
62 Jason Dickinson RC 2.50 6.00
63 Nick Schmaltz RC 3.00 8.00
64 Dylan Strome RC 6.00 15.00
65 Kyle Connor RC 8.00 20.00
66 Mathew Barzal RC 10.00 25.00
67 Matthew Tkachuk RC 10.00 25.00
68 Mikhail Sergachev RC 6.00 15.00
69 Jimmy Vesey RC 6.00 15.00
70 Travis Konecny RC 6.00 15.00
71 Mitch Marner RC 20.00 50.00
72 Ivan Provorov RC 6.00 15.00
73 Jesse Puljujarvi RC 8.00 20.00
74 Patrik Laine RC 20.00 50.00
75 Auston Matthews RC 40.00 100.00

2016-17 SPx Blue

1 John Gibson AU/99 6.00 15.00
3 David Krejci AU/99 6.00 15.00
4 Ray Bourque AU/15
7 Sean Monahan AU/99 6.00 15.00
10 Nathan MacKinnon AU/49 20.00 50.00
11 Boone Jenner AU/99 6.00 15.00
12 Jamie Benn AU/49 12.00 30.00
13 Steve Yzerman AU/15
15 Wayne Gretzky AU/15
16 Connor McDavid AU/15
17 Aleksander Barkov AU/99 6.00 15.00
18 Pavel Bure AU/15
20 Rob Blake AU/15
22 Zach Parise AU/99 6.00 15.00
23 Patrick Roy AU/15
24 Carey Price AU/49 40.00 80.00
26 Cory Schneider AU/49 8.00 20.00
27 Jaroslav Halak AU/99 6.00 15.00
28 John Tavares AU/49 20.00 50.00
29 Derek Stepan AU/99 5.00 12.00
30 Rick Nash AU/99 6.00 15.00
31 Henrik Lundqvist AU/49 10.00 25.00
33 Jakub Voracek AU/99 6.00 15.00
35 Mario Lemieux AU/15
36 Joe Pavelski AU/99 6.00 15.00
37 Brent Burns AU/99 8.00 20.00
38 Jake Allen AU/99 8.00 20.00
39 Brett Hull AU/15
41 Tyler Johnson AU/99 5.00 12.00
42 Nikita Kucherov AU/99 10.00 25.00
43 James van Riemsdyk AU/99 6.00 15.00
44 Morgan Rielly AU/99 5.00 12.00
46 Kirk McLean AU/15
47 Alexander Ovechkin AU/15
49 Mark Scheifele AU/99 8.00 20.00
50 Nikolaj Ehlers AU/99 6.00 15.00
51 William Nylander AU/199 30.00 80.00
52 Pavel Zacha AU/199 8.00 20.00
54 Hudson Fasching AU/199 6.00 15.00
56 Sonny Milano AU/199 8.00 20.00
57 Josh Morrissey AU/199 8.00 20.00
58 Justin Bailey AU/199 6.00 15.00
59 Connor Brown AU/199 10.00 25.00
60 Steven Santini AU/199 5.00 12.00
61 Oliver Bjorkstrand AU/199 5.00 12.00
62 Jason Dickinson AU/199 5.00 12.00
63 Nick Schmaltz AU/199 6.00 15.00
64 Dylan Strome AU/199 12.00 30.00
66 Mathew Barzal AU/199 20.00 50.00
67 Matthew Tkachuk AU/199 20.00 50.00
68 Mikhail Sergachev AU/199 12.00 30.00
71 Mitch Marner AU/199 50.00 120.00
72 Ivan Provorov AU/199 12.00 30.00
73 Jesse Puljujarvi AU/199 20.00 50.00
74 Patrik Laine AU/199 75.00 150.00
75 Auston Matthews AU/25

2016-17 SPx Gold

7 Sean Monahan PATCH AU/49 15.00 40.00
10 Nathan MacKinnon PATCH AU/25 40.00 100.00
17 Aleksander Barkov PATCH AU/49 15.00 40.00
22 Zach Parise PATCH AU/49 15.00 40.00
24 Carey Price BLKR AU/25 50.00 120.00
26 Cory Schneider PATCH AU/25 15.00 40.00
27 Jaroslav Halak PATCH AU/49 15.00 40.00
28 John Tavares PATCH AU/25 40.00 100.00
29 Derek Stepan PATCH AU/49 12.00 30.00
31 Henrik Lundqvist PATCH AU/25 20.00 50.00
32 Mark Stone PATCH AU/49 15.00 40.00
33 Jakub Voracek PATCH AU/49 15.00 40.00
37 Brent Burns PATCH AU/49 20.00 50.00
38 Jake Allen PATCH AU/49 20.00 50.00
41 Tyler Johnson PATCH AU/49 12.00 30.00
42 Nikita Kucherov PATCH AU/49 25.00 60.00
43 James van Riemsdyk PATCH AU/49 15.00 40.00
44 Morgan Rielly PATCH AU/49 12.00 30.00
45 Ryan Miller STK AU/49 15.00 40.00
49 Mark Scheifele PATCH AU/49 20.00 50.00
50 Nikolaj Ehlers PATCH AU/49 15.00 40.00
51 William Nylander PATCH AU 40.00 80.00
52 Pavel Zacha PATCH AU 15.00 40.00
53 Anthony Mantha PATCH AU 30.00 80.00
54 Hudson Fasching PATCH AU 12.00 30.00
55 Kasperi Kapanen PATCH AU 25.00 60.00
56 Sonny Milano PATCH AU 15.00 40.00
57 Josh Morrissey PATCH AU 15.00 40.00
58 Justin Bailey PATCH AU 12.00 30.00
59 Connor Brown PATCH AU 20.00 50.00
60 Steven Santini PATCH AU 10.00 25.00
61 Oliver Bjorkstrand PATCH AU 10.00 25.00
62 Jason Dickinson PATCH AU 10.00 25.00
63 Nick Schmaltz PATCH AU 12.00 30.00
64 Dylan Strome PATCH AU 25.00 60.00
65 Kyle Connor PATCH AU 30.00 80.00
66 Mathew Barzal PATCH AU 30.00 80.00
67 Matthew Tkachuk PATCH AU 30.00 80.00
68 Mikhail Sergachev PATCH AU 25.00 60.00
70 Travis Konecny PATCH AU 15.00 40.00
71 Mitch Marner PATCH AU 175.00 300.00
72 Ivan Provorov PATCH AU 30.00 80.00
73 Jesse Puljujarvi PATCH AU 30.00 80.00
74 Patrik Laine PATCH AU 250.00 400.00
75 Auston Matthews PATCH AU 400.00 600.00

2016-17 SPx Red

1 John Gibson JSY C 4.00 10.00
2 Oliver Ekman-Larsson JSY B 3.00 8.00
5 Ryan O'Reilly JSY B 4.00 10.00
7 Sean Monahan JSY B 4.00 10.00
8 Jonathan Toews JSY B 8.00 20.00
10 Nathan MacKinnon JSY B 8.00 20.00
12 Jamie Benn JSY B 5.00 12.00
13 Steve Yzerman JSY 5.00 12.00
14 Dylan Larkin JSY C 6.00 15.00
15 Wayne Gretzky JSY 20.00 50.00
16 Connor McDavid JSY A 20.00 50.00
17 Aleksander Barkov JSY C 4.00 10.00
19 Jaromir Jagr JSY B 10.00 25.00
20 Rob Blake JSY 4.00 10.00
21 Drew Doughty JSY A 4.00 10.00
22 Zach Parise JSY C 4.00 10.00
23 Patrick Roy JSY 10.00 25.00
24 Carey Price JSY A 12.00 30.00
25 Pekka Rinne JSY C 5.00 12.00
26 Cory Schneider JSY C 3.00 8.00
28 John Tavares JSY B 8.00 20.00
29 Derek Stepan JSY C 3.00 8.00
31 Henrik Lundqvist JSY B 4.00 10.00
32 Mark Stone JSY C 4.00 10.00
33 Jakub Voracek JSY C 4.00 10.00
34 Sidney Crosby JSY A 15.00 40.00
35 Mario Lemieux JSY 12.00 30.00
37 Brent Burns JSY B 5.00 12.00
38 Jake Allen JSY C 5.00 12.00
39 Brett Hull JSY 4.00 10.00
40 Steven Stamkos JSY A 8.00 20.00
41 Tyler Johnson JSY B 3.00 8.00
42 Nikita Kucherov JSY B 6.00 15.00
43 James van Riemsdyk JSY C 4.00 10.00
44 Morgan Rielly JSY C 3.00 8.00
45 Ryan Miller JSY C 4.00 10.00
46 Kirk McLean JSY 4.00 10.00
47 Alexander Ovechkin JSY A 15.00 40.00
48 Braden Holtby JSY A 6.00 15.00
49 Mark Scheifele JSY B 5.00 12.00
51 William Nylander JSY 20.00 50.00
52 Pavel Zacha JSY 6.00 15.00
53 Anthony Mantha JSY 12.00 30.00
54 Hudson Fasching JSY 5.00 12.00
55 Kasperi Kapanen JSY 10.00 25.00
56 Sonny Milano JSY 6.00 15.00
57 Josh Morrissey JSY 6.00 15.00
58 Justin Bailey JSY 5.00 12.00
59 Connor Brown JSY 8.00 20.00
60 Steven Santini JSY 4.00 10.00
61 Oliver Bjorkstrand JSY 4.00 10.00
62 Jason Dickinson JSY 4.00 10.00
63 Nick Schmaltz JSY 5.00 12.00
64 Dylan Strome JSY 10.00 25.00
65 Kyle Connor JSY 12.00 30.00
66 Mathew Barzal JSY 15.00 40.00
67 Matthew Tkachuk JSY 15.00 40.00
68 Mikhail Sergachev JSY 10.00 25.00
69 Jimmy Vesey JSY 10.00 25.00
70 Travis Konecny JSY 10.00 25.00
71 Mitch Marner JSY 25.00 60.00
72 Ivan Provorov JSY 10.00 25.00
73 Jesse Puljujarvi JSY 12.00 30.00
74 Patrik Laine JSY 20.00 50.00
75 Auston Matthews JSY 30.00 80.00

2016-17 SPx Double XL Duos Materials

XDBM S.Bennett/S.Monahan/99 6.00 15.00
XDJL J.Jagr/R.Luongo/99 12.00 30.00
XDKH E.Kuznetsov/B.Holtby/99 8.00 20.00
XDLC P.Laine/K.Connor/99 20.00 50.00
XDLG M.Lemieux/W.Gretzky/49 30.00 80.00
XDMM A.Matthews/M.Marner/99 50.00 120.00
XDNB W.Nylander/C.Brown/99 20.00 50.00
XDRE S.Reinhart/J.Eichel/99 10.00 25.00
XDZS P.Zacha/S.Santini/99 6.00 15.00

2016-17 SPx Double XL Materials

XXLAH Adam Henrique/99 4.00 10.00
XXLAO Alexander Ovechkin/99 15.00 40.00
XXLBD Brandon Dubinsky/199 3.00 8.00
XXLBR Bill Ranford/99 4.00 10.00
XXLBS Brayden Schenn/199 3.00 8.00
XXLCG Claude Giroux/199 3.00 8.00
XXLDB Dustin Byfuglien/199 3.00 8.00
XXLEK Erik Karlsson/99 8.00 20.00
XXLFF Filip Forsberg/199 4.00 10.00
XXLGL Gabriel Landeskog/199 2.50 6.00
XXLHS Henrik Sedin/199 3.00 8.00
XXLJG Johnny Gaudreau/199 5.00 12.00
XXLJV Jimmy Vesey/199 6.00 15.00
XXLKC Kyle Connor/199 8.00 20.00
XXLMD Max Domi/199 4.00 10.00
XXLMM Mitch Marner/199 15.00 40.00
XXLNH Noah Hanifin/199 3.00 8.00
XXLNN Nino Niederreiter/199 3.00 8.00
XXLON Owen Nolan/99 4.00 10.00
XXLPZ Pavel Zacha/199 4.00 10.00
XXLSB Sam Bennett/199 4.00 10.00
XXLSC Sidney Crosby/199 12.00 30.00
XXLWN William Nylander/199 12.00 30.00

2016-17 SPx Extraordinary Material Autographs Black

EMAM Auston Matthews/25
EMBB Brent Burns/49
EMCM Connor McDavid/25
EMCS Cory Schneider/49
EMDT Dave Taylor/25
EMHL Henrik Lundqvist/25
EMHZ Henrik Zetterberg/25
EMIP Ivan Provorov/49
EMJS Jason Spezza/49
EMJT John Tavares/25
EMNK Nikita Kucherov/49
EMPL Patrik Laine/25
EMSB Sam Bennett/49
EMZP Zach Parise/49

2016-17 SPx Extraordinary Materials

EMAE Aaron Ekblad/25 10.00 25.00
EMAM Auston Matthews/25 60.00 150.00
EMBB Brent Burns/25 12.00 30.00
EMCS Cory Schneider/25 8.00 20.00
EMDT Dave Taylor/25 10.00 25.00
EMFF Filip Forsberg/25 12.00 30.00
EMGF Grant Fuhr/25 10.00 25.00
EMHL Henrik Lundqvist/25 10.00 25.00
EMIP Ivan Provorov/25 20.00 50.00
EMJS Jason Spezza/25 10.00 25.00
EMJT John Tavares/25 20.00 50.00
EMMM Mitch Marner/25 50.00 125.00
EMMS Mark Stone/25 10.00 25.00
EMNK Nikita Kucherov/25 15.00 40.00
EMPL Patrik Laine/25
EMSB Sam Bennett/25
EMZP Zach Parise/25

2016-17 SPx Extravagant Materials

EXAB Aleksander Barkov D 3.00 8.00
EXAM Anthony Mantha D 8.00 20.00
EXDD Drew Doughty C 3.00 8.00
EXDK Duncan Keith C 3.00 8.00
EXDS Dylan Strome D 6.00 15.00
EXEK Evgeny Kuznetsov D 5.00 12.00
EXEM Evgeni Malkin A 10.00 25.00
EXJC Jeff Carter A 3.00 8.00
EXJE Jack Eichel C 6.00 15.00
EXMJ Martin Jones D 3.00 8.00
EXML Mario Lemieux A 10.00 25.00
EXMR Morgan Rielly C 2.50 6.00
EXPB Patrice Bergeron C 4.00 10.00
EXPK Patrick Kane B 6.00 15.00
EXRG Ryan Getzlaf C 5.00 12.00
EXSS Steven Stamkos B 6.00 15.00
EXVH Victor Hedman D 4.00 10.00
EXVT Vladimir Tarasenko B 5.00 12.00

2016-17 SPx Extreme Black Holo Shield

EBAB Aleksander Barkov 5.00 12.00
EBAM Auston Matthews 50.00 120.00
EBAO Alexander Ovechkin 20.00 50.00
EBBB Brent Burns 6.00 15.00
EBBL Rob Blake 5.00 12.00
EBCD Christian Dvorak 5.00 12.00
EBCM Connor McDavid 25.00 60.00
EBCP Carey Price 15.00 40.00
EBDH Dale Hawerchuk 6.00 15.00
EBDK David Krejci 5.00 12.00
EBDL Dylan Larkin 8.00 20.00
EBDS Derek Stepan 4.00 10.00
EBHF Hudson Fasching 5.00 12.00
EBHL Henrik Lundqvist 5.00 12.00
EBIP Ivan Provorov 10.00 25.00
EBJA Jake Allen 6.00 15.00
EBJB Jamie Benn 6.00 15.00
EBJE Joel Eriksson Ek 5.00 12.00
EBJG John Gibson 5.00 12.00
EBJP Joe Pavelski 5.00 12.00
EBJT Jonathan Toews 10.00 25.00
EBJV Jakub Voracek 5.00 12.00
EBKC Kyle Connor 12.00 30.00
EBKM Kirk McLean 5.00 12.00
EBLA Patrik Laine 20.00 50.00
EBLE Loui Eriksson 5.00 12.00
EBMA Anthony Mantha 12.00 30.00
EBMB Mathew Barzal 15.00 40.00
EBMI Sonny Milano 6.00 15.00
EBMM Mitch Marner 25.00 60.00
EBMR Morgan Rielly 4.00 10.00
EBMS Mark Scheifele 6.00 15.00
EBMT Matthew Tkachuk 15.00 40.00
EBNK Nikita Kucherov 8.00 20.00
EBNM Nathan MacKinnon 10.00 25.00
EBPB Pavel Buchnevich 8.00 20.00
EBPK Patrick Kane 10.00 25.00
EBPU Jesse Puljujarvi 12.00 30.00
EBPZ Pavel Zacha 6.00 15.00
EBRB Ray Bourque 8.00 20.00
EBSA Sebastian Aho 10.00 25.00
EBSC Sidney Crosby 20.00 50.00
EBSE Mikhail Sergachev 10.00 25.00
EBSM Sean Monahan 5.00 12.00
EBTA John Tavares 10.00 25.00
EBTK Travis Konecny 10.00 25.00
EBVE Jimmy Vesey 10.00 25.00
EBWG Wayne Gretzky 25.00 60.00
EBWN William Nylander 20.00 50.00
EBZP Zach Parise 5.00 12.00

2016-17 SPx Ice Shredders Materials

ISAM Auston Matthews A 25.00 60.00
ISAO Alexander Ovechkin B 15.00 40.00
ISBW Blake Wheeler D 4.00 10.00
ISCM Connor McDavid B 20.00 50.00
ISDL Dylan Larkin C 6.00 15.00
ISEK Erik Karlsson C 8.00 20.00
ISGA Marian Gaborik D 4.00 10.00
ISGL Guy Lafleur A 5.00 12.00
ISJD Jonathan Drouin D 5.00 12.00
ISJT John Tavares B 8.00 20.00
ISJV Jimmy Vesey C 8.00 20.00
ISMG Mike Gartner B 4.00 10.00
ISNM Nathan MacKinnon C 8.00 20.00
ISPB Pavel Bure A 12.00 30.00
ISPK Phil Kessel D 5.00 12.00
ISPL Patrik Laine B 15.00 40.00
ISPZ Pavel Zacha C 5.00 12.00
ISSC Sidney Crosby A 15.00 40.00
ISWN William Nylander C 15.00 40.00

2016-17 SPx Ice Shredders Materials Premium Black

ISAM Auston Matthews/25 125.00 200.00
ISPL Patrik Laine/25 50.00 120.00

2016-17 SPx Impressions Autographs

IABB Brent Burns/199 12.00 30.00
IACC Chris Chelios/99 10.00 25.00
IADK David Krejci/199 10.00 25.00
IADT Dave Taylor/99 10.00 25.00
IAHL Henrik Lundqvist/25 20.00 50.00
IAHZ Henrik Zetterberg/25 25.00 60.00
IAIL Igor Larionov/25 20.00 50.00
IAJG John Gibson/199 10.00 25.00
IAJM Jake Muzzin/99 8.00 20.00
IALD Leon Draisaitl/199 12.00 30.00
IAMM Mike Modano/25 30.00 80.00
IAMS Mark Scheifele/199 12.00 30.00
IANB Nick Bjugstad/199 8.00 20.00
IANK Nikita Kucherov/99 15.00 40.00
IANN Nino Niederreiter/199 10.00 25.00
IARB Ray Bourque/25 30.00 80.00
IARJ Roman Josi/199 10.00 25.00
IAZP Zach Parise/99 10.00 25.00

2016-17 SPx Rookies

RAB Anthony Beauvillier 1.50 4.00
RAD Anthony DeAngelo 1.50 4.00
RAL Artturi Lehkonen 1.50 4.00
RAM Auston Matthews 25.00 60.00
RBI Chris Bigras 1.25 3.00
RBL Brendan Leipsic 1.50 4.00
RBP Brayden Point 4.00 10.00
RCB Connor Brown 2.50 6.00
RCD Christian Dvorak 1.50 4.00
RCL Charlie Lindgren 3.00 8.00
RDH Danton Heinen 2.50 6.00
RDL Chase De Leo 1.50 4.00
RDS Dylan Strome 3.00 8.00
REL Esa Lindell 1.50 4.00
RHF Hudson Fasching 1.50 4.00
RIP Ivan Provorov 3.00 8.00
RJB Justin Bailey 1.50 4.00
RJC Jakob Chychrun 1.50 4.00
RJE Joel Eriksson Ek 1.50 4.00
RJM Josh Morrissey 2.00 5.00
RJP Jesse Puljujarvi 4.00 10.00
RJV Jimmy Vesey 3.00 8.00
RKC Kyle Connor 4.00 10.00
RKK Kasperi Kapanen 3.00 8.00
RKL Kevin Labanc 1.50 4.00
RKU Tom Kuhnhackl 1.25 3.00
RLC Lawson Crouse 1.25 3.00
RMA Anthony Mantha 5.00 12.00
RMB Mathew Barzal 5.00 12.00
RMI Michael Matheson 1.50 4.00
RMM Mitch Marner 12.00 30.00
RMR Mike Reilly 1.25 3.00
RMS Mikhail Sergachev 3.00 8.00
RMT Matthew Tkachuk 5.00 12.00
RMW Miles Wood 1.25 3.00
RNS Nick Schmaltz 1.50 4.00
ROB Oliver Bjorkstrand 1.25 3.00
ROK Oliver Kylington 1.25 3.00
RPB Pavel Buchnevich 2.50 6.00
RPL Patrik Laine 10.00 25.00
RPZ Pavel Zacha 2.00 5.00
RRP Ryan Pulock 1.50 4.00
RSA Sebastian Aho 3.00 8.00
RSM Sonny Milano 2.00 5.00
RSO Nikita Soshnikov 1.00 2.50
RSS Steven Santini 1.25 3.00
RTK Travis Konecny 3.00 8.00
RTM Tyler Motte 1.50 4.00
RWN William Nylander 6.00 15.00
RZW Zach Werenski 3.00 8.00

2017-18 SPx

1 Sidney Crosby 6.00 15.00
2 Auston Matthews 6.00 15.00
3 Taylor Hall 3.00 8.00
4 Aleksander Barkov 1.50 4.00
5 Jonathan Toews 3.00 8.00
6 Marc-Andre Fleury 2.50 6.00
7 Carey Price 5.00 12.00
8 Erik Karlsson 2.00 5.00
9 Kevin Shattenkirk 1.50 4.00
10 Nikita Kucherov 2.50 6.00
11 Vladimir Tarasenko 2.50 6.00
12 Anze Kopitar 2.50 6.00
13 Patrik Laine 2.50 6.00
14 Alexander Wennberg 1.25 3.00
15 Henrik Zetterberg 1.50 4.00
16 John Tavares 3.00 8.00
17 Joe Pavelski 1.50 4.00
18 Devan Dubnyk 1.50 4.00
19 Alexander Ovechkin 6.00 15.00
20 Connor McDavid 6.00 15.00
21 Mario Lemieux 5.00 12.00
22 Patrick Roy 4.00 10.00
23 Pavel Bure 1.50 4.00
24 Steve Yzerman 2.00 5.00
25 Wayne Gretzky 8.00 20.00
26 Logan Brown RC 5.00 12.00
27 Will Butcher RC 6.00 15.00
28 Haydn Fleury RC 5.00 12.00
29 Adrian Kempe RC 6.00 15.00
30 Anders Bjork RC 6.00 15.00
31 Kailer Yamamoto RC 12.00 30.00
32 Jake DeBrusk RC 8.00 20.00
33 Luke Kunin RC 5.00 12.00
34 Owen Tippett RC 10.00 25.00
35 Alex Tuch RC 12.00 30.00
36 Jack Roslovic RC 6.00 15.00
37 Evgeny Svechnikov RC 10.00 25.00
38 Ivan Barbashev RC 5.00 12.00
39 Colin White RC 5.00 12.00
40 Josh Ho-Sang RC 6.00 15.00
41 Tyson Jost RC 10.00 25.00
42 Christian Fischer RC 6.00 15.00
43 Alexander Nylander RC 8.00 20.00
44 Charlie McAvoy RC 15.00 40.00
45 Brock Boeser RC 30.00 80.00
46 Clayton Keller RC 12.00 30.00
47 Pierre-Luc Dubois RC 10.00 25.00
48 Alex DeBrincat RC 12.00 30.00
49 Nolan Patrick RC 10.00 25.00
50 Nico Hischier RC 15.00 40.00

2017-18 SPx Double XL Duos Materials

XDBM A.Bjork/C.McAvoy/199 12.00 30.00
XDBT I.Barbashev/T.Thompson/199 6.00 15.00
XDFH J.Faulk/N.Hanifin/199 4.00 10.00
XDGB W.Gretzky/R.Blake/99 20.00 50.00
XDGN M.Granlund/N.Niederreiter/199 4.00 10.00
XDHB B.Hull/E.Belfour/99 12.00 30.00
XDMD C.McDavid/L.Draisaitl/199 15.00 40.00
XDML E.Malkin/K.Letang/199 12.00 30.00
XDSS H.Sedin/D.Sedin/199 4.00 10.00
XDTS J.Toews/B.Saad/199 8.00 20.00
XDWB C.White/L.Brown/199 4.00 10.00
XDYL S.Yzerman/I.Larionov/99 12.00 30.00

2017-18 SPx Extravagant Materials

EXBB Brent Burns C 3.00 8.00
EXBH Brett Hull B 2.50 6.00
EXBM Brad Marchand D 3.00 8.00
EXBW Blake Wheeler C 2.50 6.00
EXCC Corey Crawford E 3.00 8.00
EXCM Connor McDavid B 10.00 25.00
EXCP Corey Perry E 2.50 6.00
EXCT Cam Talbot E 2.50 6.00
EXDP David Pastrnak C 4.00 10.00
EXEK Erik Karlsson C 3.00 8.00
EXJB Jamie Benn D 3.00 8.00
EXJG Johnny Gaudreau D 4.00 10.00
EXJQ Jonathan Quick E 4.00 10.00
EXML Mario Lemieux A
EXMM Mitch Marner D 4.00 10.00
EXNM Nathan MacKinnon C 5.00 12.00
EXPA Colton Parayko E 2.50 6.00
EXSC Sidney Crosby B 10.00 25.00
EXWG Wayne Gretzky A
EXWN William Nylander D 4.00 10.00

2017-18 SPx Impressions Autographs

IAAB Aleksander Barkov/249 8.00 20.00
IABE Brian Elliott/249 8.00 20.00
IABH Brett Hull/25
IACA Cam Atkinson/249 8.00 20.00
IACS Conor Sheary/249 8.00 20.00
IAFM Frank Mahovlich/25
IAHL Henrik Lundqvist/25
IAJK Jari Kurri/249 8.00 20.00
IAJP Jason Pominville/249 6.00 15.00
IAJV John Vanbiesbrouck/249 8.00 20.00
IALC Logan Couture/125 8.00 20.00
IALD Leon Draisaitl/125 20.00 50.00
IALR Larry Robinson/125 10.00 25.00
IAMG Mark Giordano/249 6.00 15.00
IAMM Mark Messier/25
IANE Nikolaj Ehlers/249 8.00 20.00
IAPL Patrik Laine/125 20.00 50.00
IARB Rod Brind'Amour/249 8.00 20.00
IARL Roberto Luongo/125 8.00 20.00
IAWS Wayne Simmonds/125 10.00 25.00

2017-18 SPx Lasting Marks

LMBB Brock Boeser 100.00 200.00
LMBO Bobby Orr 100.00 200.00
LMCK Clayton Keller 30.00 80.00
LMDG Doug Gilmour 60.00 150.00
LMEM Evgeni Malkin
LMFK Jakob Forsbacka-Karlsson
LMGL Guy Lafleur
LMHS Josh Ho-Sang
LMJJ Joe Thornton
LMJT Jonathan Toews 25.00 60.00
LMMB Martin Brodeur
LMMP Max Pacioretty
LMPF Peter Forsberg 50.00 125.00
LMSS Steven Stamkos
LMVS Vadim Shipachyov

2017-18 SPx Materials

1 Sidney Crosby A 12.00 30.00
2 Auston Matthews A 12.00 30.00
3 Taylor Hall B 6.00 15.00
4 Aleksander Barkov C 3.00 8.00
5 Jonathan Toews A 6.00 15.00
6 Marc-Andre Fleury C 5.00 12.00
7 Carey Price B 10.00 25.00
8 Erik Karlsson A 4.00 10.00
9 Kevin Shattenkirk C 3.00 8.00
10 Nikita Kucherov B 5.00 12.00
11 Vladimir Tarasenko C 5.00 12.00
12 Anze Kopitar C 5.00 12.00
13 Patrik Laine C 5.00 12.00
14 Alexander Wennberg C 2.50 6.00
15 Henrik Zetterberg C 3.00 8.00
16 John Tavares A 6.00 15.00
17 Joe Pavelski C 3.00 8.00
18 Devan Dubnyk C 3.00 8.00
19 Alexander Ovechkin B 12.00 30.00
20 Connor McDavid A 12.00 30.00
21 Mario Lemieux B 25.00 60.00
22 Patrick Roy C 15.00 40.00
23 Pavel Bure C 20.00 50.00
24 Steve Yzerman B 15.00 40.00
25 Wayne Gretzky A 25.00 60.00

2017-18 SPx Rookies

RAD Alex DeBrincat 6.00 15.00
RAK Adrian Kempe 3.00 8.00
RAN Alexander Nylander 4.00 10.00
RBB Brock Boeser 20.00 50.00
RCF Christian Fischer 3.00 8.00
RCK Clayton Keller 6.00 15.00

CM Charlie McAvoy 8.00 20.00
CW Colin White 2.50 6.00
ES Evgeny Svechnikov 5.00 12.00
FC Filip Chytil 2.50 6.00
IB Ivan Barbashev 2.50 6.00
JH Josh Ho-Sang 3.00 8.00
JR Jack Roslovic 3.00 8.00
JT J.T. Compher 3.00 8.00
KY Kailer Yamamoto 6.00 15.00
LB Logan Brown 2.50 6.00
LK Luke Kunin 2.50 6.00
NH Nico Hischier 8.00 20.00
NP Nolan Patrick 5.00 12.00
NS Nikita Scherbak 5.00 12.00
OT Owen Tippett 5.00 12.00
PD Pierre-Luc Dubois 5.00 12.00
TJ Tyson Jost 5.00 12.00
VM Victor Mete 2.50 6.00
WB Will Butcher 3.00 8.00

2017-18 SPx Rookies Gold

PATCH/49: X TO X BASIC INSERTS
AK Adrian Kempe PATCH AU/49 25.00 60.00

2017-18 SPx Rookie Variations

5 Logan Brown AU/148 10.00 25.00
7 Will Butcher AU/148 12.00 30.00
8 Haydn Fleury AU/148 10.00 25.00
9 Adrian Kempe AU/148 12.00 30.00
0 Anders Bjork AU/148 12.00 30.00
Kailer Yamamoto AU/148 25.00 60.00
2 Jake DeBrusk AU/148 15.00 40.00
3 Luke Kunin AU/148 10.00 25.00
4 Owen Tippett AU/148 20.00 50.00
5 Alex Tuch AU/148 25.00 60.00
6 Jack Roslovic AU/148 12.00 30.00
7 Evgeny Svechnikov AU/148 20.00 50.00
8 Ivan Barbashev AU/148 10.00 25.00
9 Colin White AU/148 10.00 25.00
0 Josh Ho-Sang AU/148 12.00 30.00
Tyson Jost AU/148 20.00 50.00
Christian Fischer AU/148 12.00 30.00
Alexander Nylander AU/148 15.00 40.00
4 Charlie McAvoy AU/98 60.00 150.00
5 Brock Boeser AU/98 250.00 350.00
6 Clayton Keller AU/98 30.00 80.00
7 Pierre-Luc Dubois AU/98 20.00 50.00
8 Alex DeBrincat AU/98 25.00 60.00
9 Nolan Patrick/98 20.00 50.00
0 Nico Hischier/98 20.00 50.00

2017-18 SPx Rookies Autographs

AD Alex DeBrincat/199 20.00 50.00
AK Adrian Kempe/199 10.00 25.00
AN Alexander Nylander/199 12.00 30.00
BB Brock Boeser/99 100.00 200.00
CF Christian Fischer/199 10.00 25.00
CK Clayton Keller/99 15.00 40.00
CM Charlie McAvoy/99 60.00 150.00
CW Colin White/199 8.00 20.00
ES Evgeny Svechnikov/199 15.00 40.00
FC Filip Chytil/199 8.00 20.00
IB Ivan Barbashev/199 8.00 20.00
JH Josh Ho-Sang/199 10.00 25.00
JR Jack Roslovic/199 10.00 25.00
JT J.T. Compher/199 10.00 25.00
KY Kailer Yamamoto/199 20.00 50.00
LB Logan Brown/199 8.00 20.00
LK Luke Kunin/199 8.00 20.00
NS Nikita Scherbak/199 15.00 40.00
OT Owen Tippett/199 12.00 30.00
PD Pierre-Luc Dubois/199 15.00 40.00
TJ Tyson Jost/199 15.00 40.00
VM Victor Mete/199 8.00 20.00
WB Will Butcher/199 10.00 25.00

2017-18 SPx Rookies Materials

AD Alex DeBrincat 8.00 20.00
AK Adrian Kempe 4.00 10.00
AN Alexander Nylander 5.00 12.00
BB Brock Boeser 15.00 40.00
CF Christian Fischer 4.00 10.00
CK Clayton Keller 8.00 20.00
CM Charlie McAvoy 10.00 25.00
CW Colin White 3.00 8.00
ES Evgeny Svechnikov 6.00 15.00
FC Filip Chytil 3.00 8.00
IB Ivan Barbashev 3.00 8.00
JH Josh Ho-Sang 4.00 10.00
JR Jack Roslovic 4.00 10.00
JT J.T. Compher 4.00 10.00
KY Kailer Yamamoto 8.00 20.00
LB Logan Brown 3.00 8.00
LK Luke Kunin 3.00 8.00
NH Nico Hischier 10.00 25.00
NP Nolan Patrick 6.00 15.00
NS Nikita Scherbak 6.00 15.00
OT Owen Tippett 6.00 15.00
PD Pierre-Luc Dubois 6.00 15.00
TJ Tyson Jost 6.00 15.00

1998-99 SPx Finite

The 1998-99 SPx Finite hobby-only Series One was issued with a total of 180 cards. The three-card packs retail for $5.99 each. The 90 regular player cards (1-90) are sequentially numbered to 9,500 and feature color action player photos with a unique blue foil emblem embedded in the center of the cards. The set contains the subsets: Global Impact (91-120) sequentially numbered to 6,950, NHL Sure Shots, (121-150) numbered to 3,900, Marquee Performers (151-170) numbered to 2,625, and Living Legends (171-180) numbered to 1,620.

COMP.BASE SET (90) 30.00 80.00
Teemu Selanne .60 1.50
Guy Hebert .50 1.25
Josef Marha .20 .50
Travis Green .20 .50
Sergei Samsonov .50 1.25
Jason Allison .20 .50
Byron Dafoe .50 1.25
Dominik Hasek 1.25 3.00
Michael Peca .20 .50
0 Erik Rasmussen .20 .50
Matthew Barnaby .20 .50
2 Theo Fleury .20 .50
3 Derek Morris .20 .50
4 Valeri Bure .20 .50
5 Trevor Kidd .50 1.25
6 Sami Kapanen .20 .50
7 Bates Battaglia .20 .50
8 Tony Amonte .50 1.25
9 Dmitri Nabokov .20 .50
0 Daniel Cleary .20 .50
Jeff Hackett .50 1.25
2 Joe Sakic 1.25 3.00
3 Valeri Kamensky .50 1.25
4 Patrick Roy 2.00 5.00
5 Wade Belak .20 .50
6 Joe Nieuwendyk .50 1.25
7 Mike Keane .20 .50
8 Jere Lehtinen .20 .50
29 Ed Belfour .60 1.50
30 Steve Yzerman 3.00 8.00
31 Dmitri Mironov .20 .50
32 Brendan Shanahan .60 1.50
33 Nicklas Lidstrom .60 1.50
34 Doug Weight .50 1.25
35 Janne Niinimaa .20 .50
36 Bill Guerin .50 1.25
37 Ray Whitney .20 .50
38 Robert Svehla .20 .50
39 Ed Jovanovski .20 .50
40 Vladimir Tsyplakov .20 .50
41 Jozef Stumpel .50 1.25
42 Rob Blake .50 1.25
43 Mark Recchi .50 1.25
44 Andy Moog .50 1.25
45 Matt Higgins RC .20 .50
46 Martin Brodeur 1.50 4.00
47 Doug Gilmour .50 1.25
48 Brendan Morrison .50 1.25
49 Patrik Elias .50 1.25
50 Trevor Linden .50 1.25
51 Bryan Berard .20 .50
52 Zdeno Chara 3.00 8.00
53 Wayne Gretzky 3.00 8.00
54 Marc Savard .20 .50
55 Daniel Goneau .20 .50
56 Pat Lafontaine .60 1.50
57 Alexei Yashin .20 .50
58 Marian Hossa .60 1.50
59 Wade Redden .20 .50
60 John LeClair .60 1.50
61 Alexandre Daigle .20 .50
62 Rod Brind'Amour .50 1.25
63 Chris Therien .20 .50
64 Keith Tkachuk .60 1.50
65 Brad Isbister .20 .50
66 Nikolai Khabibulin .50 1.25
67 Robert Dome .20 .50
68 Alexei Morozov .20 .50
69 Stu Barnes .20 .50
70 Tom Barrasso .50 1.25
71 Owen Nolan .50 1.25
72 Marco Sturm .50 1.25
73 Patrick Marleau .20 .50
74 Pierre Turgeon .50 1.25
75 Chris Pronger .50 1.25
76 Pavol Demitra .50 1.25
77 Grant Fuhr .50 1.25
78 Stephane Richer .50 1.25
79 Zac Bierk RC .50 1.25
80 Alexander Selivanov .20 .50
81 Mike Johnson .50 1.25
82 Mats Sundin .60 1.50
83 Alyn McAuley .20 .50
84 Pavel Bure .60 1.50
85 Todd Bertuzzi .60 1.50
86 Garth Snow .50 1.25
87 Peter Bondra .50 1.25
88 Olaf Kolzig .50 1.25
89 Jan Bulis .20 .50
90 Sergei Gonchar .20 .50
91 Pavel Bure GI .75 2.00
92 Joe Sakic GI 2.00 5.00
93 Steve Yzerman GI 5.00 12.00
94 Jaromir Jagr GI 1.50 4.00
95 Peter Forsberg GI 2.50 6.00
96 Brendan Shanahan GI 1.00 2.50
97 Brett Hull GI 1.25 3.00
98 Alexei Yashin GI .75 2.00
99 Wayne Gretzky GI 6.00 15.00
100 Eric Lindros GI 1.00 2.50
101 Sergei Samsonov GI .75 2.00
102 John LeClair GI 1.00 2.50
103 Dominik Hasek GI 2.00 5.00
104 Teemu Selanne GI 1.00 2.50
105 Martin Brodeur GI 2.50 6.00
106 Tony Amonte GI .75 2.00
107 Theo Fleury GI .75 2.00
108 Rob Blake GI .75 2.00
109 Mike Modano GI 1.50 4.00
110 Peter Bondra GI .75 2.00
111 Brian Leetch GI 1.00 2.50
112 Nicklas Lidstrom GI 1.00 2.50
113 Doug Weight GI .75 2.00
114 Zigmund Palffy GI .60 1.50
115 Saku Koivu GI 1.00 2.50
116 Paul Kariya GI 1.00 2.50
117 Ray Bourque GI 1.50 4.00
118 Mats Sundin GI 1.00 2.50
119 Patrick Roy GI 1.50 4.00
120 Chris Chelios GI 1.00 2.50
121 Sergei Samsonov SS 1.50 4.00
122 Mike Johnson SS .60 1.50
123 Patrik Elias SS 1.50 4.00
124 Josef Marha SS .60 1.50
125 Dan Cloutier SS .60 1.50
126 Cameron Mann SS .60 1.50
127 Mattias Ohlund SS .60 1.50
128 Daniel Cleary SS .60 1.50
129 Anders Eriksson SS .60 1.50
130 Patrick Marleau SS .60 1.50
131 Jan Bulis SS .60 1.50
132 Alyn McAuley SS .60 1.50
133 Joe Thornton SS 3.00 8.00
134 Andrei Zyuzin SS .60 1.50
135 Richard Zednik SS .60 1.50
136 Derek Morris SS .60 1.50
137 Bates Battaglia SS .60 1.50
138 Mike Watt SS .60 1.50
139 Olli Jokinen SS 1.50 4.00
140 Marian Hossa SS 2.00 5.00
141 Daniel Goneau SS .60 1.50
142 Erik Rasmussen SS .60 1.50
143 Daniel Briere SS .60 1.50
144 Norm Maracle SS RC 2.50 6.00
145 Brendan Morrison SS 1.50 4.00
146 Brad Isbister SS .60 1.50
147 Robert Dome SS .60 1.50
148 Zac Bierk SS .60 1.50
149 Alexei Morozov SS .60 1.50
150 Marco Sturm SS .60 1.50
151 Wayne Gretzky MP 12.50 30.00
152 Eric Lindros MP 2.00 5.00
153 Paul Kariya MP 2.00 5.00
154 Patrick Roy MP 6.00 15.00
155 Sergei Samsonov MP 2.00 5.00
156 Steve Yzerman MP 8.00 20.00
157 Teemu Selanne MP 2.00 5.00
158 Brendan Shanahan MP 2.00 5.00
159 Dominik Hasek MP 4.00 10.00
160 Mark Messier MP 2.00 5.00
161 Martin Brodeur MP 6.00 15.00
162 Mats Sundin MP 2.00 5.00
163 Joe Sakic MP 4.00 10.00
164 John LeClair MP 2.00 5.00
165 Jaromir Jagr MP 4.00 10.00
166 Peter Forsberg MP 4.00 10.00
167 Theo Fleury MP 1.50 4.00
168 Peter Bondra MP 1.50 4.00
169 Mike Modano MP 3.00 8.00
170 Pavel Bure MP 2.00 5.00
171 Patrick Roy LL 12.50 30.00
172 Eric Lindros LL 6.00 15.00
173 Dominik Hasek LL 10.00 20.00
174 Jaromir Jagr LL 6.00 15.00
175 Steve Yzerman LL 12.50 30.00
176 Martin Brodeur LL 12.50 30.00
177 Ray Bourque LL 6.00 15.00
178 Peter Forsberg LL 10.00 25.00
179 Paul Kariya LL 6.00 15.00
180 Wayne Gretzky LL 8.00 20.00
S99 Wayne Gretzky SAMPLE .75 2.00

1998-99 SPx Finite Radiance

This 180-card gold foil parallel features the same players as in the SPx Finite base set, but with an extra added altered technology. Base radiance cards (#1-90) were serial numbered to 4750. Global impact radiance parallels (#91-120) were serial numbered to 3475, sure shots radiance parallels (#121-150) were numbered to 1300, and marquee performers radiance parallels (#151-170) were numbered to 875. Living legends radiance parallels (#171-180) were also serial numbered to 540.

*RADIANCE 1-90: .8X TO 2X BASIC CARDS
*RADIANCE GI 91-120 : .8X TO 2X BASIC CARDS
*RADIANCE SS 121-150: .8X TO 2X BASIC CARDS
*RADIANCE MP 151-170: 1X TO 2.5X BASIC CARDS
*RADIANCE LL 171-180: .8X TO 2X BASIC CARDS

1998-99 SPx Finite Spectrum

Sequentially numbered to 5500, this 180-card rainbow foil parallel again offers the same players as in the SPx Finite base set, but with an even further modified technology. Base spectrum parallels (#1-90) were serial numbered to 300. Global impact spectrum parallels (#91-120) were serial numbered to 225, sure shots spectrum parallels (#121-150) were numbered to 75, and marquee performers spectrum parallels (#151-170) were numbered to 25. Living legends spectrum parallels (#171-180) were also serial numbered to 1/1 and are not priced due to scarcity.

*SPECTRUM 1-90: 5X TO 15X BASIC CARDS
*SPECTRUM GI 91-120: 8X TO 18X BASIC CARDS
*SPECTRUM SS 121-150: 6X TO 15X BASIC CARDS
*SPECTRUM MP 151-170: 10X TO 20X BASIC CARDS

1998-99 SPx Top Prospects

The 1998-99 SPx Top Prospects set was issued in one series totaling 90 cards and features action color player photos with player information on the backs. Only 1,999 of cards 61-90 were printed. Cards 79 and 80 were only available signed.

COMPLETE SET (90) 60.00 150.00
COMP.SET w/o SP's (60) 15.00 40.00
1 Paul Kariya .60 1.50
2 Teemu Selanne .60 1.50
3 Ray Bourque 1.00 2.50
4 Sergei Samsonov .40 1.00
5 Joe Thornton 1.00 2.50
6 Dominik Hasek 1.25 3.00
7 Theo Fleury .40 1.00
8 Keith Primeau .20 .50
9 Tony Amonte .40 1.00
10 Doug Gilmour .40 1.00
11 J-P Dumont .20 .50
12 Chris Chelios .60 1.50
13 Peter Forsberg 1.50 4.00
14 Patrick Roy 3.00 8.00
15 Joe Sakic 1.25 3.00
16 Milan Hejduk RC 3.00 8.00
17 Chris Drury .40 1.00
18 Mike Modano 1.00 2.50
19 Brett Hull .75 2.00
20 Ed Belfour .60 1.50
21 Steve Yzerman 2.00 5.00
22 Brendan Shanahan .60 1.50
23 Sergei Fedorov 1.00 2.50
24 Chris Osgood .40 1.00
25 Nicklas Lidstrom .60 1.50
26 Bill Guerin .20 .50
27 Doug Weight .40 1.00
28 Tom Poti .20 .50
29 Mark Parrish RC 1.00 2.50
30 Rob Blake .40 1.00
31 Pavel Rosa RC .40 1.00
32 Vincent Damphousse .20 .50
33 Saku Koivu .60 1.50
34 Mike Dunham .20 .50
35 Martin Brodeur 1.50 4.00
36 Zigmund Palffy .40 1.00
37 Eric Brewer .20 .50
38 Wayne Gretzky 4.00 10.00
39 Brian Leetch .60 1.50
40 Manny Malhotra .20 .50
41 Petr Nedved .20 .50
42 Alexei Yashin .20 .50
43 Eric Lindros .60 1.50
44 John LeClair .40 1.00
45 John Vanbiesbrouck .40 1.00
46 Keith Tkachuk .40 1.00
47 Jeremy Roenick .75 2.00
48 Daniel Briere .20 .50
49 Jaromir Jagr 1.00 2.50
50 Patrick Marleau .40 1.00
51 Al MacInnis .20 .50
52 Chris Pronger .40 1.00
53 Vincent Lecavalier .60 1.50
54 Curtis Joseph .60 1.50
55 Mats Sundin .60 1.50
56 Tomas Kaberle RC 1.00 2.50
57 Mark Messier .60 1.50
58 Pavel Bure .60 1.50
59 Bill Muckalt RC .40 1.00
60 Peter Bondra .40 1.00
61 Brian Finley RC 1.50 4.00
62 Roberto Luongo 2.00 5.00
63 Mike Van Ryn 1.50 4.00
64 Harold Druken 1.50 4.00
65 Daniel Tkaczuk 1.50 4.00
66 Brenden Morrow RC 5.00 12.00
67 Jani Rita RC 1.50 4.00
68 Tommi Santala RC 1.50 4.00
69 Teemu Virkkunen RC 1.50 4.00
70 Arto Laaktikainen RC 1.50 4.00
71 Ilkka Mikkola RC 1.50 4.00
72 Miko Jokela RC 1.50 4.00
73 Kirill Safronov RC 1.50 4.00
74 Denis Shvidki 1.50 4.00
75 Denis Arkhipov RC 1.50 4.00
76 Maxim Afinogenov 2.00 5.00
77 Alexander Zevakhin RC 1.50 4.00
78 Alexei Volkov RC 1.50 4.00
79 Daniel Sedin AU 8.00 20.00
80 Henrik Sedin AU 8.00 20.00
81 Jimmie Olvestad RC 1.50 4.00
82 Mattias Weinhandl RC 1.50 4.00
83 Mathias Tjarnqvist RC 1.50 4.00
84 Jakob Johansson RC 1.50 4.00
85 Barrett Heisten RC 1.50 4.00
86 Tim Connolly RC 2.00 5.00
87 Andy Hilbert RC 1.50 4.00
88 David Legwand 1.50 4.00
89 Joe Blackburn RC 1.50 4.00
90 Dave Tanabe RC 1.50 4.00

1998-99 SPx Top Prospects Radiance

Randomly inserted in Finite Radiance hot packs only, this 90-card set is parallel to the base SPx Top Prospects set and is crash numbered to 100. A crash numbered 1 of 1 Spectrum parallel was also available and found only in Finite Spectrum hot packs. Spectrum parallels not priced due to scarcity.

*RADIANCE 1-60: 10X TO 25X BASIC CARDS
*RADIANCE 61-90: 1.2X TO 3X BASIC CARDS
*ROOKIES: 2X TO 5X BASIC CARDS

1998-99 SPx Top Prospects Highlight Heroes

Randomly inserted in packs at the rate of 1:8, this 30-card set features action color photos of top NHL players.

COMPLETE SET (30) 75.00 150.00
H1 Paul Kariya 1.50 4.00
H2 Teemu Selanne 1.50 4.00
H3 Ray Bourque 2.50 6.00
H4 Sergei Samsonov 1.25 3.00
H5 Dominik Hasek 3.00 8.00
H6 Theo Fleury 1.25 3.00
H7 Doug Gilmour 1.25 3.00
H8 Joe Sakic 3.00 8.00
H9 Patrick Roy 8.00 20.00
H10 Peter Forsberg 4.00 10.00
H11 Mike Modano 2.50 6.00
H12 Brett Hull 2.00 5.00
H13 Brendan Shanahan 1.50 4.00
H14 Steve Yzerman 8.00 20.00
H15 Sergei Fedorov 2.50 6.00
H16 Saku Koivu 1.50 4.00
H17 Martin Brodeur 4.00 10.00
H18 Wayne Gretzky 10.00 25.00
H19 Zigmund Palffy 1.25 3.00
H20 John Vanbiesbrouck 1.25 3.00
H21 Eric Lindros 1.50 4.00
H22 John LeClair 1.50 4.00
H23 Keith Tkachuk 1.50 4.00
H24 Jeremy Roenick 2.00 5.00
H25 Jaromir Jagr 2.50 6.00
H26 Vincent Lecavalier 1.50 4.00
H27 Mats Sundin 1.50 4.00
H28 Curtis Joseph 1.50 4.00
H29 Pavel Bure 1.50 4.00
H30 Peter Bondra 1.25 3.00

1998-99 SPx Top Prospects Lasting Impressions

COMPLETE SET (30) 40.00 80.00
STATED ODDS 1:3
L1 Vincent Lecavalier .75 2.00
L2 John Vanbiesbrouck .60 1.50
L3 Paul Kariya .75 2.00
L4 Keith Tkachuk .75 2.00
L5 Mike Modano 1.25 3.00
L6 Dominik Hasek 1.50 4.00
L7 Teemu Selanne .75 2.00
L8 Mats Sundin .75 2.00
L9 Brendan Shanahan .75 2.00
L10 Pavel Bure .75 2.00
L11 Theo Fleury .75 2.00
L12 Curtis Joseph .75 2.00
L13 Joe Sakic 1.50 4.00
L14 Eric Lindros .75 2.00
L15 Peter Bondra .60 1.50
L16 Brett Hull 1.00 2.50
L17 Ray Bourque 1.25 3.00
L18 Jaromir Jagr 1.25 3.00
L19 Steve Yzerman 4.00 10.00
L20 Jeremy Roenick 1.00 2.50
L21 Martin Brodeur 2.00 5.00
L22 Saku Koivu .75 2.00
L23 Patrick Roy 4.00 10.00
L24 John LeClair .75 2.00
L25 Doug Gilmour .60 1.50
L26 Sergei Fedorov 1.25 3.00
L27 Wayne Gretzky 5.00 12.00
L28 Peter Forsberg 2.00 5.00
L29 Zigmund Palffy .60 1.50
L30 Sergei Samsonov .60 1.50

1998-99 SPx Top Prospects Premier Stars

COMPLETE SET (30) 100.00 200.00
STATED ODDS 1:17
PS1 Wayne Gretzky 15.00 40.00
PS2 Sergei Samsonov 2.00 5.00
PS3 Ray Bourque 4.00 10.00
PS4 Dominik Hasek 5.00 12.00
PS5 Martin Brodeur 6.00 15.00
PS6 Brian Leetch 2.50 6.00
PS7 Mike Richter 2.50 6.00
PS8 Eric Lindros 3.00 8.00
PS9 John LeClair 2.50 6.00
PS10 John Vanbiesbrouck 2.00 5.00
PS11 Jaromir Jagr 4.00 10.00
PS12 Vincent Lecavalier 2.50 6.00
PS13 Mats Sundin 2.50 6.00
PS14 Curtis Joseph 2.50 6.00
PS15 Peter Bondra 2.00 5.00
PS16 Wayne Gretzky 15.00 40.00
PS17 Teemu Selanne 2.50 6.00
PS18 Paul Kariya 2.50 6.00
PS19 Theo Fleury 2.50 6.00
PS20 Tony Amonte 2.00 5.00
PS21 Patrick Roy 12.50 30.00
PS22 Joe Sakic 5.00 12.00
PS23 Peter Forsberg 6.00 15.00
PS24 Mike Modano 4.00 10.00
PS25 Brett Hull 3.00 8.00
PS26 Steve Yzerman 12.50 30.00
PS27 Brendan Shanahan 2.50 6.00
PS28 Doug Weight 2.00 5.00
PS29 Keith Tkachuk 2.50 6.00
PS30 Mark Messier 2.50 6.00

1998-99 SPx Top Prospects Winning Materials

Randomly inserted into packs at the rate of 1:251, this 12-card set features color player photos with pieces of the pictured player's game-used jersey and stick cut and affixed to the card.

CJ Curtis Joseph 8.00 20.00
CO Chris Osgood 8.00 20.00
EL Eric Lindros 10.00 25.00
FP Felix Potvin 10.00 25.00
JJ Jaromir Jagr 12.50 30.00
JL John LeClair 8.00 20.00
JS Joe Sakic 15.00 40.00
JV John Vanbiesbrouck 8.00 20.00
MR Mike Richter 8.00 20.00
MS Mats Sundin 8.00 20.00
PR Patrick Roy 30.00 80.00
RB Ray Bourque 15.00 40.00

1998-99 SPx Top Prospects Year of the Great One

Randomly inserted into packs at the rate of 1:17, this 30-card set features unique photos of Wayne Gretzky with notable quotes about his career from his father, various coaches, NHL greats and former teammates.

COMPLETE SET (30) 150.00 300.00
COMMON GRETZKY (WG1-WG30) 5.00 12.00

1992 Sport-Flash

This 15-card standard-size set was produced by Sport-Flash as the first series of "Hockey Stars since 1940". The accompanying certification of limited edition claims that the production run was 200,000 sets. Each set contained one autographed hockey card signed by the player. On a bright yellow card face, the fronts display close-up color photos enclosed by blue and black border stripes. The player's name appears in the bottom yellow border. The backs are bilingual and present biography, player profile, and career statistics. The cards are numbered on both sides.

COMPLETE SET (15) 4.00 10.00
1 Jacques Laperriere .25 .60
2 Larry Carriere .20 .50
3 Chuck Rayner .30 .75
4 Jean Beliveau .75 2.00
5 BoomBoom Geoffrion .60 1.50
6 Gilles Gilbert .30 .75
7 Marcel Bonin .20 .50
8 Leon Rochefort .20 .50
9 Maurice Richard 2.00 5.00
10 Rejean Houle .20 .50
11 Pierre Mondou .20 .50
12 Yvan Cournoyer .30 .75
13 Henri Richard .40 1.00
14 Checklist Card .02 .10
15 Certification of Limited Edition .02 .10

1992 Sport-Flash Autographs

Random inserts in the Sport-Flash sets. Each card is signed in blue Sharpie on the card front.

COMPLETE SET (15) 80.00 200.00
1 Jacques Laperriere 4.00 10.00
2 Larry Carriere 4.00 10.00
3 Chuck Rayner 4.00 10.00
4 Jean Beliveau 25.00 50.00
5 BoomBoom Geoffrion 12.00 30.00
6 Gilles Gilbert 4.00 10.00
7 Marcel Bonin 4.00 10.00
8 Leon Rochefort 4.00 10.00
9 Maurice Richard 20.00 50.00
10 Rejean Houle 4.00 10.00
11 Pierre Mondou 4.00 10.00
12 Yvan Cournoyer 8.00 20.00
13 Henri Richard 8.00 20.00

1991 Stadium Club Charter Member

This 50-card multi-sport standard-size set was sent to charter members in the Topps Stadium Club. The sports represented in the set are baseball (1-32), football (33-41), and hockey (42-50). The cards feature on the fronts full-bleed posed and action glossy color player photos. The player's name is shown in the light blue stripe that intersects the Stadium Club logo near the bottom of the picture. The words "Charter Member" are printed in gold foil lettering immediately below the stripe. The back design features a newspaper-like masthead (The Stadium Club Herald) complete with a headline announcing a major event in the player's season with copy below providing more information about the event. The cards are unnumbered and arranged below alphabetically within sports. Topps apparently made two printings of this set, which are most easily identifiable by the small asterisks on the bottom left of the card backs. The first printing cards have one asterisk, the second printing cards have two. The display box that contained the cards also included a Nolan Ryan bronze metallic card and a key chain. Very early members of the Stadium Club received a large size bronze metallic Nolan Ryan 1990 Topps card. It is valued below as well as the normal size Ryan metallic card. A third varation on the Ryan medallion has been found. This is another version of the 1991 Stadium Club charter member bronze medallion, except this one has a 24K logo on it. It is suspected that this might be a Home Shopping Newtork variety. No pricing is provided at this time for this piece due to lack of market information.

COMP.FACT SET (50) 6.00 15.00
42 Ed Belfour .20 .50
Belfour Cops
The Vezina
43 Ed Belfour .20 .50
Belfour Is Top Goalie
44 Ray Bourque .30 .75
45 Paul Coffey .30 .75
46 Wayne Gretzky 1.50 4.00
Gretzky Takes
No. 2000
47 Wayne Gretzky 1.50 4.00
The 700 Club
48 Brett Hull .30 .75
Brett's All Hart
49 Brett Hull .30 .75
Hull Joins 50-50
Club
50 Mario Lemieux 1.25 3.00

1991 Stadium Club Members Only

This 50-card multi-sport standard-size set was sent in three installments to members in the Topps Stadium Club. The first and second installments featured baseball players (card numbers 1-10 and 11-30), while the third spotlighted football (31-37) and hockey (38-50) players. The cards feature on the fronts full-bleed posed and action glossy color player photos. The player's name is shown in the light blue stripe that intersects the Stadium Club logo near the bottom of the picture. The words "Members Only" are printed in gold foil lettering immediately below the stripe. The back design features a newspaper-like masthead (The Stadium Club Herald) complete with a headline announcing a major event in the player's season with copy below providing more information about the event. The cards are unnumbered and arranged below alphabetically according to and within installments.

COMPLETE SET (50) 6.00 15.00
38 Pavel Bure .75 2.00
39 Guy Carbonneau .07 .20
40 Paul Coffey .30 .75
41 Mike Gartner .08 .25
Mike Makes It Two
42 Mike Gartner .08 .25
Mike Makes It 500
43 Michel Goulet .07 .20
44 Wayne Gretzky 2.00 5.00
45 Brett Hull .40 1.00
46 Brian Leetch .20 .50
47 Mario Lemieux 1.25 3.00
Mario Repeats As MVP
48 Mario Lemieux 1.25 3.00
Lemieux Takes 3rd
Ross Trophy
49 Mark Messier .30 .75
50 Patrick Roy 1.25 3.00

1991-92 Stadium Club

The 1991-92 Topps Stadium Club hockey set contains 400 standard-size cards. The fronts feature full-bleed glossy color player photos. At the bottom, the player's name appears in an aqua stripe that is bordered in gold. In the lower left or right corner the Stadium Club logo overlays the stripe. Against the background of a colorful drawing of a hockey rink, the horizontally oriented backs have a biography, The Sporting News Hockey Scouting Report (which consists of strengths and evaluative comments), statistics (last season and career totals), and a miniature photo of the player's first Topps card. There are many cards in the set that can be found with or without "The Sporting News" on the card back; these variations (no added premium) are 13, 16, 22, 46, 50, 60, 68, 149, 190, 204, 230, 249, 264, 276, 297, 298, 307, 320, 332, 339, 341, 342, 348, 351, and 362. There are no key Rookie Cards in this set.

1 Wayne Gretzky .75 2.00
2 Randy Moller .12 .30
3 Ray Ferraro .12 .30
4 Craig Wolanin .12 .30
5 Shayne Corson .12 .30
6 Chris Chelios .15 .40
7 Joe Mullen .12 .30
8 Ken Wregget .12 .30
9 Rob Cimetta .12 .30
10 Mike Liut .12 .30
11 Martin Gelinas .12 .30
12 Mario Marois .12 .30
13 Rick Vaive .10 .25
14 Brad McCrimmon .12 .30
15 Mark Hunter .12 .30
16 Jim Wiemer .12 .30
17 Sergio Momesso .12 .30
18 Claude Lemieux .12 .30
19 Brian Hayward .12 .30
20 Pat Flatley .12 .30
21 Mark Osborne .12 .30
22 Mike Hudson .12 .30
23 Rejean Lemelin .12 .30
24 Slava Fetisov .12 .30
25 Bobby Smith .12 .30
26 Kris King .12 .30
27 Randy Velischek .12 .30
28 Steve Bozek .12 .30
29 Mike Foligno .15 .40
30 Scott Arniel .12 .30
31 Sergei Makarov .12 .30
32 Rick Zombo .12 .30
33 Christian Ruuttu .12 .30
34 Gino Cavallini .12 .30
35 Rick Tocchet .12 .30
36 Jiri Hrdina .12 .30
37 Peter Bondra .12 .30
38 Craig Ludwig .12 .30
39 Mikael Andersson .12 .30
40 Bob Kudelski .10 .25
41 Guy Carbonneau .12 .30
42 Geoff Smith .12 .30
43 Russ Courtnall .12 .30
44 Michal Pivonka .12 .30
45 Todd Krygier .12 .30
46 Jeremy Roenick .40 1.00
47 Doug Brown .12 .30
48 Paul Cavallini .12 .30
49 Ron Sutter .12 .30
50 Paul Ranheim .15 .40
51 Mike Gartner .12 .30
52 Greg Adams .12 .30
53 Dave Capuano .12 .30
54 Mike Krushelnyski .12 .30
55 Ulf Dahlen .12 .30
56 Steven Finn .12 .30
57 Ed Olczyk .12 .30
58 Steve Duchesne .10 .25
59 Bob Probert .12 .30
60 Joe Nieuwendyk .12 .30
61 Petr Klima .12 .30
62 Uwe Krupp .12 .30
63 Jay Miller .12 .30
64 Cam Neely .15 .40
65 Phil Housley .12 .30
66 Michel Goulet .12 .30
67 Brett Hull .25 .60
68 Mike Ridley .12 .30
69 Esa Tikkanen .12 .30
70 Kjell Samuelsson .12 .30
71 Corey Millen RC .15 .40
72 Doug Lidster .12 .30
73 Ron Francis .20 .50
74 Scott Young .12 .30
75 Bob Sweeney .12 .30
76 Sean Burke .15 .40
77 Pierre Turgeon .12 .30
78 David Reid .10 .25
79 Al MacInnis .12 .30
80 Mike Hough .12 .30
81 Steve Yzerman .50 1.25
82 Derek King .10 .25
83 Brad Shaw .10 .25
84 Trevor Linden .12 .30
85 Rick Meagher .12 .30
86 Stephane Richer .12 .30
87 Brian Bellows .12 .30
88 Pete Peeters .10 .25
89 Adam Creighton .12 .30
90 Brent Ashton .12 .30
91 Bryan Trottier .20 .50
92 Mike Richter .15 .40
93 Dave Andreychuk .15 .40
94 Randy Carlyle .12 .30
95 Dave Christian .12 .30
96 Doug Gilmour .30 .75
97 Tony Granato .12 .30
98 Jeff Norton .12 .30
99 Neal Broten .12 .30
100 Jody Hull .10 .25
101 Shawn Burr .12 .30
102 Pat Verbeek .12 .30
103 Ken Daneyko .12 .30
104 Peter Zezel .10 .25
105 Kirk McLean .12 .30
106 Kelly Miller .12 .30
107 Patrick Roy .40 1.00
108 Adam Oates .15 .40
109 Steve Thomas .12 .30
110 Scott Mellanby .12 .30
111 Mark Messier .40 1.00
112 Larry Murphy .12 .30
113 Mark Janssens .12 .30
114 Doug Bodger .12 .30
115 Ron Tugnutt .12 .30
116 Glenn Anderson .15 .40
117 Dave Gagner .12 .30
118 Dino Ciccarelli .12 .30
119 Randy Burridge .12 .30
120 Kelly Hrudey .12 .30
121 Jimmy Carson .12 .30
122 Bruce Driver .12 .30
123 Pat LaFontaine .15 .40
124 Wendel Clark .15 .40
125 Peter Sidorkiewicz .12 .30
126 Gary Roberts .12 .30
127 Petr Svoboda .12 .30
128 Vincent Riendeau .12 .30
129 Brian Skrudland .12 .30
130 Tim Kerr .12 .30
131 Doug Wilson .12 .30
132 Pat Elynuik .12 .30
133 Craig MacTavish .12 .30
134 Troy Mallette .12 .30
135 Mike Ramsey .12 .30
136 Tony Hrkac .12 .30
137 Craig Simpson .10 .25
138 Jon Casey .12 .30
139 Steve Kasper .12 .30
140 Kevin Hatcher .12 .30
141 Dave Barr .12 .30
142 Brad Lauer .12 .30
143 Gary Suter .12 .30
144 John MacLean .12 .30
145 Dean Evason .12 .30
146 Vincent Damphousse .12 .30
147 Craig Janney .12 .30
148 Jeff Brown .12 .30
149 Geoff Courtnall .12 .30
150 Igor Larionov .12 .30
151 Jan Erixon .12 .30
152 Bob Essensa .12 .30
153 Gaetan Duchesne .10 .25
154 Jyrki Lumme .12 .30
155 Tom Barrasso .12 .30
156 Curtis Leschyshyn .12 .30
157 Benoit Hogue .12 .30
158 Gary Leeman .12 .30
159 Luc Robitaille .12 .30
160 Jamie Macoun .12 .30
161 Bob Carpenter .12 .30
162 Kevin Dineen .12 .30
163 Gary Nylund .12 .30
164 Dale Hunter .12 .30
165 Gerard Gallant .10 .25
166 Jacques Cloutier .12 .30
167 Troy Murray .12 .30
168 Phil Bourque .12 .30
169 Grant Ledyard .12 .30
170 Joel Otto .12 .30
171 Paul Ysebaert UER .12 .30
Photo actually Mike Sillinger
172 Luke Richardson .12 .30
173 Ron Hextall .15 .40
174 Mario Lemieux .60 1.50
175 Garry Galley .12 .30
176 Murray Craven .12 .30
177 Walt Poddubny .10 .25
178 Scott Pearson .12 .30
179 Kevin Lowe .12 .30
180 Brent Sutter .12 .30
181 Dirk Graham .12 .30
182 Pelle Eklund .12 .30
183 Sylvain Cote .12 .30
184 Rod Brind'Amour .12 .30
185 Fredrik Olausson .12 .30
186 Kelly Kisio .12 .30
187 Mike Modano .30 .75
188 Calle Johansson .12 .30
189 John Tonelli .12 .30
190 Glen Wesley .12 .30
191 Bob Errey .12 .30
192 Rich Sutter .12 .30
193 Kirk Muller .10 .25
194 Rob Zettler .12 .30
195 Alexander Mogilny .12 .30
196 Adrien Plavsic .12 .30
197 Daniel Marois .12 .30
198 Yves Racine .12 .30
199 Brendan Shanahan .20 .50
200 Rob Brown .12 .30
201 Brian Leetch .12 .30
202 Dave McLlwain .12 .30
203 Charlie Huddy .12 .30
204 David Volek .12 .30
205 Trent Yawney .12 .30
206 Brian MacLellan .12 .30
207 Thomas Steen .12 .30
208 Sylvain Lefebvre .12 .30
209 Tomas Sandstrom .12 .30
210 Mike McPhee .12 .30
211 Andy Moog .12 .30
212 Paul Coffey .12 .30
213 Denis Savard .20 .50
214 Eric Desjardins .15 .40
215 Wayne Presley .12 .30
216 Stephane Morin UER .12 .30
217 Ric Nattress .12 .30
218 Troy Gamble .10 .25
219 Terry Carkner .12 .30
220 Dave Hannan .12 .30
221 Randy Wood .12 .30
222 Brian Mullen .12 .30
223 Garth Butcher .12 .30
224 Tim Cheveldae .12 .30
225 Rod Langway .12 .30
226 Stephen Leach .12 .30
227 Perry Berezan .12 .30
228 Zarley Zalapski .12 .30
229 Patrik Sundstrom .12 .30
230 Steve Smith .15 .40
231 Daren Puppa .12 .30
232 Dave Taylor .12 .30
233 Ray Bourque .25 .60
234 Kevin Stevens .12 .30
235 Frank Musil .12 .30
236 Mike Keane .10 .25
237 Brian Propp .12 .30
238 Brent Fedyk .12 .30
239 Rob Ramage .12 .30
240 Robert Kron .12 .30

241 Mike McNeil .12 .30
242 Greg Gilbert .12 .30
243 Dan Quinn .12 .30
244 Chris Nilan .12 .30
245 Bernie Nicholls .12 .30
246 Don Beaupre .12 .30
247 Keith Acton .12 .30
248 Gord Murphy .12 .30
249 Bill Ranford .12 .30
250 Dave Chyzowski .10 .25
251 Clint Malarchuk .12 .30
252 Larry Robinson .10 .25
253 Dave Poulin .12 .30
254 Paul MacDermid .12 .30
255 Doug Smail .12 .30
256 Mark Recchi .20 .50
257 Brian Bradley .12 .30
258 Grant Fuhr .15 .40
259 Owen Nolan .15 .40
260 Hubie McDonough .12 .30
261 Mikko Makela .12 .30
262 Mathieu Schneider .12 .30
263 Peter Stastny .12 .30
264 Jim Hrivnak .12 .30
265 Scott Stevens .15 .40
266 Mike Tomlak .12 .30
267 Marty McSorley .12 .30
268 Johan Garpenlov .12 .30
269 Mike Vernon .12 .30
270 Steve Larmer .12 .30
271 Phil Sykes .12 .30
272 Jay Mazur .10 .25
273 John Ogrodnick .12 .30
274 Dave Ellett .12 .30
275 Randy Gilhen .12 .30
276 Tom Chorske .12 .30
277 James Patrick .12 .30
278 Darin Kimble .12 .30
279 Paul Cyr .12 .30
280 Petr Nedved .12 .30
281 Tony McKegney .12 .30
282 Alexei Kasatonov .10 .25
283 Stephen Lebeau .12 .30
284 Everett Sanipass .12 .30
285 Tony Tanti .12 .30
286 Kevin Miller .12 .30
287 Moe Mantha .12 .30
288 Alan May .12 .30
289 John Cullen .12 .30
290 Daniel Berthiaume .12 .30
291 Mark Pederson .12 .30
292 Laurie Boschman .12 .30
293 Neil Wilkinson .12 .30
294 Rick Wamsley .10 .25
295 Ken Linseman .12 .30
296 Jamie Leach .12 .30
297 Chris Terreri .12 .30
298 Cliff Ronning .12 .30
299 Bobby Holik .15 .40
300 Mats Sundin .15 .40
301 Carey Wilson .12 .30
302 Teppo Numminen .12 .30
303 Dave Lowry .12 .30
304 Joe Reekie .12 .30
305 Keith Primeau .12 .30
306 David Shaw .12 .30
307 Nick Kypreos .12 .30
308 Dave Manson .12 .30
309 Mick Vukota .12 .30
310 Todd Elik .12 .30
311 Michel Petit .12 .30
312 Dale Hawerchuk .20 .50
313 Joe Murphy .12 .30
314 Chris Dahlquist .12 .30
315 Petri Skriko .10 .25
316 Sergei Fedorov .25 .60
317 Lee Norwood .10 .25
318 Garry Valk .12 .30
319 Glen Featherstone .10 .25
320 Dave Snuggerud .10 .25
321 Doug Evans .10 .25
322 Marc Bureau .12 .30
323 John Vanbiesbrouck .12 .30
324 John McIntyre .12 .30
325 Wes Walz .12 .30
326 Daryl Reaugh .12 .30
327 Paul Fenton .12 .30
328 Ulf Samuelsson .12 .30
329 Andrew Cassels .12 .30
330 Alexei Gusarov RC .12 .30
331 John Druce .12 .30
332 Adam Graves .12 .30
333 Ed Belfour .40 1.00
334 Murray Baron .12 .30
335 John Tucker .10 .25
336 Todd Gill .12 .30
337 Martin Hostak .10 .25
338 Gino Odjick .12 .30
339 Eric Weinrich .15 .40
340 Todd Ewen .12 .30
341 Mike Hartman .12 .30
342 Danton Cole .05 .15
343 Jaromir Jagr .40 1.00
344 Mike Craig .12 .30
345 Mark Fitzpatrick .12 .30
346 Darren Turcotte .12 .30
347 Ron Wilson .12 .30
348 Rob Blake .15 .40
349 Dale Kushner .12 .30
350 Jeff Beukeboom .12 .30
351 Tim Bergland .12 .30
352 Peter Ing .12 .30
353 Wayne McBean .10 .25
354 Jim McKenzie RC .15 .40
355 Theo Fleury .12 .30
356 Jocelyn Lemieux .12 .30
357 Ken Hodge Jr. .15 .40
358 Shawn Anderson .12 .30
359 Dimitri Khristich .12 .30
360 Jon Morris .12 .30
361 Darrin Shannon .12 .30
362 Chris Joseph .12 .30
363 Normand Lacombe .12 .30
364 Frank Pietrangelo .12 .30
365 Joey Kocur .12 .30
366 Anatoli Semenov .12 .30
367 Bob Bassen .12 .30
368 Brad Jones .12 .30
369 Glenn Healy .15 .40
370 Don Sweeney .12 .30
371 Brad Dalgarno .10 .25
372 Al Iafrate .12 .30
373 Patrick Lebeau UER RC .12 .30
374 Terry Yake .12 .30
375 Roger Johansson .12 .30
376 Paul Broten .10 .25
377 Andre Racicot RC .12 .30
378 Scott Thornton .12 .30
379 Zdeno Ciger .12 .30
380 Paul Stanton .12 .30
381 Ray Sheppard .12 .30
382 Kevin Haller RC .15 .40
383 Vladimir Ruzicka .12 .30
384 Bryan Marchment RC .12 .30
385 Bill Berg .12 .30
386 Mike Ricci .15 .40
387 Pat Conacher .12 .30
388 Brian Glynn .12 .30
389 Joe Sakic .50 1.25
390 Mikhail Tatarinov .12 .30
391 Stephane Matteau .12 .30
392 Mark Tinordi .12 .30
393 Robert Reichel .30 .75
394 Tim Sweeney .12 .30
395 Rick Tabaracci .12 .30
396 Ken Sabourin .12 .30
397 Jeff Lazaro .12 .30
398 Checklist 1-133 .05 .15
399 Checklist 134-266 .05 .15
400 Checklist 267-400 .05 .15

1992 Stadium Club Members Only

This 50-card standard-size set was sent to 1992 Stadium Club members in four installments. In addition to the Stadium Club cards, the first installment included one "Top Draft Picks of the '90s" card (as a bonus) and a randomly chosen "Master Photo" printed on 5" by 7" white card stock. The third and fourth installments included hockey and football players in addition to baseball players. The cards feature full-bleed glossy color player photos. The fronts of the regular cards have the words "Members Only" printed in gold foil at the bottom along with the player's name and the Stadium Club logo. The backs feature a stadium scene with the scoreboard displaying, in yellow neon, a career highlight. The cards are unnumbered and checklisted below alphabetically, with the two-player cards listed at the end.

COMPLETE SET (50) 12.00 30.00
43 Neil Brady .07 .20
44 Mike Gartner .20 .50
45 Chris Kontos .20 .50
46 Jari Kurri .20 .50
47 Eric Lindros 1.50 4.00
48 Reggie Savage .20 .50
49 Teemu Selanne .30 .75
Selanne Rewrites
Record Books
50 Teemu Selanne .30 .75
Teemu Bests Bossy

1992-93 Stadium Club

This 501-card standard-size set features full-bleed color action player photos. The Stadium Club logo appears at the bottom and intersects a gold foil double stripe carrying the team name. The horizontal backs show an artist's rendering of a hockey rink as the background. A mini-reproduction of the player's first Topps card is shown as well as biography, statistics, and The Sporting News Skills Rating System. The Members Choice (241-250 and 251-260) subsets, showing full-bleed color photos, closes the first series and opens the second series. These backs have the same art work background with 1991-92 season statistics. The only notable Rookie Card is Guy Hebert.

1 Brett Hull .15 .40
2 Theo Fleury .15 .40
3 Joe Sakic .25 .60
4 Mike Modano .25 .60
5 Dmitri Mironov .05 .15
6 Yves Racine .05 .15
7 Igor Kravchuk .05 .15
8 Philippe Bozon .05 .15
9 Stephane Richer .07 .20
10 Dave Lowry .07 .20
11 Dean Evason .05 .15
12 Mark Fitzpatrick .07 .20
13 Dave Poulin .05 .15
14 Phil Housley .05 .15
15 Adrien Plavsic .05 .15
16 Claude Boivin .05 .15
17 Bill Guerin RC .20 .50
18 Wayne Gretzky .50 1.25
19 Steve Yzerman .25 .60
20 Joe Mullen .07 .20
21 Brad McCrimmon .05 .15
22 Dan Quinn .07 .20
23 Rob Blake .07 .20
24 Wayne Presley .05 .15
25 Zarley Zalapski .05 .15
26 Bryan Trottier .12 .30
27 Peter Sidorkiewicz .05 .15
28 John MacLean .07 .20
29 Brad Schlegel .05 .15
30 Marc Bureau .07 .20
31 Troy Murray .05 .15
32 Tony Amonte .07 .20
33 Rob DiMaio .05 .15
34 Joe Murphy .05 .15
35 Jim Waite .07 .20
36 Ron Sutter .05 .15
37 Joe Nieuwendyk .07 .20
38 Kevin Haller .05 .15
39 Andrew Cassels .05 .15
40 Dale Hunter .07 .20
41 Craig Janney .07 .20
42 Sergio Momesso .05 .15
43 Nicklas Lidstrom .07 .20
44 Luc Robitaille .07 .20
45 Adam Creighton .05 .15
46 Norm Maciver .05 .15
47 Mikhail Tatarinov .05 .15
48 Gary Roberts .05 .15
49 Gord Hynes .05 .15
50 Claude Lemieux .05 .15
51 Brad May .05 .15
52 Paul Stanton .05 .15
53 Rick Wamsley .05 .15
54 Steve Larmer .05 .15
55 Darrin Shannon .05 .15
56 Pat Falloon .05 .15
57 Chris Dahlquist .07 .20
58 John Vanbiesbrouck .07 .20
59 Sylvain Turgeon .05 .15
60 Jay More .05 .15
61 Randy Burridge .05 .15
62 Slava Kozlov .07 .20
63 Daniel Marois .05 .15
64 Curt Giles .05 .15
65 Brad Shaw .05 .15
66 Bill Ranford .07 .20
67 Frank Musil .07 .20
68 Steve Leach .05 .15
69 Michel Goulet .07 .20
70 Mathieu Schneider .05 .15
71 Steve Kasper .07 .20
72 Darryl Sydor .05 .15
73 Brian Leetch .07 .20
74 Chris Terreri .07 .20
75 Jim Johnson .07 .20
76 Rick Tocchet .07 .20
77 Teppo Numminen .05 .15
78 Owen Nolan .05 .15
79 Grant Ledyard .05 .15
80 Trevor Linden .07 .20
81 Luciano Borsato .05 .15
82 Derek King .05 .15
83 Robert Cimetta .07 .20
84 Geoff Smith .05 .15
85 Ray Sheppard .05 .15
86 Dimitri Khristich .05 .15
87 Chris Chelios .10 .25
88 Alexander Godynyuk .05 .15
89 Perry Anderson .05 .15
90 Neal Broten .07 .20
91 Brian Benning .05 .15
92 Brent Thompson .07 .20
93 Claude LaPointe .05 .15
94 Mario Lemieux .40 1.00
95 Pat LaFontaine .10 .25
96 Frank Pietrangelo .07 .20
97 Gerald Diduck .07 .20
98 Paul DiPietro .05 .15
99 Valeri Zelepukin .05 .15
100 Rick Zombo .05 .15
101 Daniel Berthiaume .07 .20
102 Tom Fitzgerald .05 .15
103 Ken Baumgartner .07 .20
104 Esa Tikkanen .05 .15
105 Steve Chiasson .05 .15
106 Bobby Holik .07 .20
107 Dominik Hasek .20 .50
108 Jeff Hackett .07 .20
109 Paul Broten .05 .15
110 Kevin Stevens .05 .15
111 Geoff Sanderson .07 .20
112 Donald Audette .07 .20
113 Jarmo Myllys .05 .15
114 Brian Skrudland .07 .20
115 Andrei Lomakin .05 .15
116 Keith Tkachuk .10 .25
117 John McIntyre .05 .15
118 Jacques Cloutier .07 .20
119 Michel Picard .07 .20
120 Dave Babych .07 .20
121 Dave Gagner .07 .20
122 Bob Carpenter .05 .15
123 Ray Ferraro .05 .15
124 Glenn Anderson .10 .25
125 Craig MacTavish .05 .15
126 Shawn Burr .05 .15
127 Tim Bergland .05 .15
128 Al MacInnis .07 .20
129 Jeff Beukeboom .05 .15
130 Ken Wregget .07 .20
131 Arturs Irbe .07 .20
132 Dave Andreychuk .10 .25
133 Patrick Roy .25 .60
134 Benoit Brunet .05 .15
135 Rick Tabaracci .05 .15
136 Jamie Baker .05 .15
137 Yanic Dupre .05 .15
138 Jari Kurri .10 .25
139 Adam Burt .05 .15
140 Peter Stastny .07 .20
141 Brad Jones .05 .15
142 Jeff Odgers .05 .15
143 Anatoli Semenov UER .05 .15
144 Paul Ranheim .05 .15
145 Sylvain Cote .07 .20
146 Brent Ashton .05 .15
147 Doug Bodger .05 .15
148 Bryan Marchment .07 .20
149 Bob Kudelski .07 .20
150 Adam Graves .05 .15
151 Scott Stevens .10 .25
152 Russ Courtnall .05 .15
153 Darcy Wakaluk .07 .20
154 Pelle Eklund .07 .20
155 Robert Kron .05 .15
156 Randy Ladouceur .05 .15
157 Ed Olczyk .05 .15
158 Jiri Hrdina .05 .15
159 John Tonelli .07 .20
160 John Cullen .05 .15
161 Jan Erixon .07 .20
162 David Shaw .07 .20
163 Brian Bradley .05 .15
164 Russ Romaniuk .05 .15
165 Eric Weinrich .05 .15
166 Steve Heinze .05 .15
167 Jeremy Roenick .15 .40
168 Mark Pederson .05 .15
169 Paul Coffey .10 .25
170 Bob Errey .07 .20
171 Brian Lawton .07 .20
172 Vincent Riendeau .07 .20
173 Marc Fortier .05 .15
174 Marc Bergevin .07 .20
175 Jim Sandlak .05 .15
176 Bob Bassen .05 .15
177 Uwe Krupp .05 .15
178 Paul MacDermid .07 .20
179 Bob Corkum .07 .20
180 Robert Reichel .05 .15
181 John LeClair .15 .40
182 Mike Hudson .05 .15
183 Mark Recchi .12 .30
184 Rollie Melanson .05 .15
185 Gordie Roberts .07 .20
186 Clint Malarchuk .05 .15
187 Kris King .05 .15
188 Adam Oates .10 .25
189 Jarrod Skalde .05 .15
190 Mike Lalor .07 .20
191 Vincent Damphousse .07 .20
192 Peter Ahola .05 .15
193 Kirk McLean .05 .15
194 Murray Baron .05 .15
195 Michel Petit .05 .15
196 Stephane Fiset .05 .15
197 Pat Verbeek .05 .15
198 Jon Casey .05 .15
199 Tim Cheveldae .05 .15
200 Mike Ridley .05 .15
201 Scott Lachance .05 .15
202 Rod Brind'Amour .05 .15
203 Bret Hedican RC .07 .20
204 Wendel Clark .07 .20
205 Shawn McEachern .05 .15
206 Randy Wood .05 .15
207 Ulf Dahlen .05 .15
208 Andy Brickley .07 .20
209 Scott Niedermayer .10 .25
210 Bob Essensa .07 .20
211 Patrick Poulin .05 .15
212 Johan Garpenlov .05 .15
213 Marty McInnis .05 .15
214 Josef Beranek .05 .15
215 Rod Langway .07 .20
216 Dave Christian .05 .15
217 Sergei Makarov .05 .15
218 Gerard Gallant .05 .15
219 Neil Wilkinson UER .05 .15
220 Tomas Sandstrom .07 .20
221 Shayne Corson .05 .15
222 John Ogrodnick .05 .15
223 Keith Acton .07 .20
224 Paul Fenton .07 .20
225 Rob Zettler .05 .15
226 Todd Elik .05 .15
227 Petr Svoboda .07 .20
228 Zdeno Ciger .05 .15
229 Kevin Miller .05 .15
230 Rich Pilon .05 .15
231 Pat Jablonski .07 .20
232 Greg Adams .05 .15
233 Martin Brodeur .25 .60
234 Dave Taylor .07 .20
235 Kelly Buchberger .05 .15
236 Steve Konroyd .07 .20
237 Guy Larose .05 .15
238 Patrice Brisebois .05 .15
239 Checklist 1-125 .05 .15
240 Checklist 126-250 .05 .15
241 Mark Messier MC .15 .40
242 Mike Richter MC .10 .25
243 Ed Belfour MC .10 .25
244 Sergei Fedorov MC .15 .40
245 Adam Oates MC .10 .25
246 Pavel Bure MC .20 .50
247 Luc Robitaille MC .07 .20
248 Brian Leetch MC .07 .20
249 Ray Bourque MC .15 .40
250 Tony Amonte MC .07 .20
251 Mario Lemieux MC .40 1.00
252 Patrick Roy MC .25 .60
253 Nicklas Lidstrom MC .07 .20
254 Steve Yzerman MC .25 .60
255 Jeremy Roenick MC .15 .40
256 Wayne Gretzky MC .50 1.25
257 Kevin Stevens MC .05 .15
258 Brett Hull MC .15 .40
259 Pat Falloon MC .05 .15
260 Guy Carbonneau MC .07 .20
261 Todd Gill .05 .15
262 Mike Sullivan .05 .15
263 Jeff Brown .07 .20
264 Joe Reekie .05 .15
265 Geoff Courtnall .05 .15
266 Mike Richter .10 .25
267 Ray Bourque .15 .40
268 Mike Craig .05 .15
269 Scott King .05 .15
270 Don Beaupre .07 .20
271 Ted Donato .05 .15
272 Gary Leeman .05 .15
273 Steve Weeks .05 .15
274 Keith Brown .07 .20
275 Greg Paslawski .05 .15
276 Pierre Turgeon .07 .20
277 Jimmy Carson .05 .15
278 Tom Fergus .07 .20
279 Glen Wesley .05 .15
280 Tomas Forslund .05 .15
281 Tony Granato .05 .15
282 Phil Bourque .05 .15
283 Dave Ellett .05 .15
284 David Bruce .05 .15
285 Stu Barnes .05 .15
286 Peter Bondra .07 .20
287 Garth Butcher .07 .20
288 Ron Hextall .07 .20
289 Guy Carbonneau .07 .20
290 Louie DeBrusk .05 .15
291 Dave Barr .05 .15
292 Ken Sutton .05 .15
293 Brian Bellows .07 .20
294 Mike McNeill .07 .20
295 Rob Brown .05 .15
296 Corey Millen .05 .15
297 Joe Juneau .05 .15
298 Jeff Chychrun UER .05 .15
299 Igor Larionov .05 .15
300 Sergei Fedorov .15 .40
301 Kevin Hatcher .05 .15
302 Al Iafrate .07 .20
303 James Black .05 .15
304 Steph Beauregard .07 .20
305 Joel Otto .05 .15
306 Nelson Emerson .05 .15
307 Gaetan Duchesne .05 .15
308 J.J. Daigneault .05 .15
309 Jamie Macoun .07 .20
310 Laurie Boschman .05 .15
311 Mike Gartner .07 .20
312 Tony Tanti .05 .15
313 Steve Duchesne .05 .15
314 Martin Gelinas .05 .15
315 Dominic Roussel .07 .20
316 Cam Neely .10 .25
317 Craig Wolanin .05 .15
318 Randy Gilhen .05 .15
319 David Volek .05 .15
320 Alexander Mogilny .07 .20
321 Jyrki Lumme .05 .15
322 Jeff Reese .05 .15
323 Greg Gilbert .07 .20
324 Jeff Norton .07 .20
325 Jim Hrivnak .07 .20
326 Eric Desjardins .07 .20
327 Curtis Joseph .10 .25
328 Ric Nattress .07 .20
329 Jamie Leach .05 .15
330 Christian Ruuttu .05 .15
331 Doug Brown .07 .20
332 Randy Carlyle .07 .20
333 Ed Belfour .10 .25
334 Doug Smail .05 .15
335 Hubie McDonough .05 .15
336 Pat MacLeod .05 .15
337 Don Sweeney .05 .15
338 Felix Potvin .20 .50
339 Kent Manderville .05 .15
340 Sergei Nemchinov .05 .15
341 Calle Johansson .05 .15
342 Dirk Graham .05 .15
343 Craig Billington .07 .20
344 Valeri Kamensky .05 .15
345 Mike Vernon .07 .20
346 Fredrik Olausson .05 .15
347 Peter Ing .05 .15
348 Mikael Andersson .05 .15
349 Mike Keane .05 .15
350 Stephane Quintal .05 .15
351 Tom Chorske .07 .20
352 Ron Francis .12 .30
353 Dana Murzyn .05 .15
354 Craig Ludwig .07 .20
355 Bob Probert .07 .20
356 Glenn Healy .07 .20
357 Troy Loney .05 .15
358 Vladimir Ruzicka .05 .15
359 Doug Gilmour .12 .30
360 Darren Turcotte .05 .15
361 Kelly Miller .05 .15
362 Dennis Vaske .05 .15
363 Stephane Matteau .05 .15
364 Brian Hayward .05 .15
365 Kevin Dineen .05 .15
366 Igor Ulanov .05 .15
367 Sylvain Lefebvre .05 .15
368 Petr Klima .05 .15
369 Steve Thomas .07 .20
370 Daren Puppa .07 .20
371 Brendan Shanahan .12 .30
372 Charlie Huddy .07 .20
373 Cliff Ronning .05 .15
374 Brian Propp .05 .15
375 Larry Murphy .07 .20
376 Bruce Driver .05 .15
377 Rob Pearson .05 .15
378 Paul Ysebaert .05 .15
379 Mark Osborne .05 .15
380 Doug Weight .20 .50
381 Kerry Huffman UER .05 .15
382 Michal Pivonka .05 .15
383 Steve Smith .05 .15
384 Steven Finn .05 .15
385 Kevin Lowe .07 .20
386 Mike Ramsey .05 .15
387 Kirk Muller .05 .15
388 John LeBlanc RC .07 .20
389 Rich Sutter .05 .15
390 Brent Fedyk .05 .15
391 Kelly Hrudey .07 .20
392 Slava Fetisov .05 .15
393 Glen Murray .05 .15
394 James Patrick .05 .15
395 Tom Draper .05 .15
396 Mark Hunter .07 .20
397 Wayne McBean .05 .15
398 Joe Sacco .05 .15
399 Dino Ciccarelli .07 .20
400 Brian Noonan .05 .15
401 Guy Hebert RC .15 .40
402 Peter Douris .05 .15
403 Gilbert Dionne .05 .15
404 Doug Lidster .07 .20
405 John Druce .05 .15
406 Alexei Kasatonov .05 .15
407 Chris Lindberg .05 .15
408 Mike Ricci .07 .20
409 Tom Kurvers .05 .15
410 Pat Elynuik .05 .15
411 Mike Donnelly .05 .15
412 Grant Fuhr .10 .25
413 Curtis Leschyshyn .07 .20
414 Derian Hatcher .05 .15
415 Michel Mongeau .07 .20
416 Tom Barrasso .07 .20
417 Joey Kocur .07 .20
418 Vladimir Konstantinov .10 .25
419 Dale Hawerchuk .12 .30
420 Brian Mullen .05 .15
421 Mark Greig .07 .20
422 Claude Vilgrain .07 .20
423 Gary Suter .05 .15
424 Garry Galley .05 .15
425 Benoit Hogue .05 .15
426 Jeff Finley RC .05 .15
427 Bobby Smith .07 .20
428 Brent Sutter .05 .15
429 Ron Wilson .07 .20
430 Andy Moog .07 .20
431 Stephan Lebeau .05 .15
432 Troy Mallette .05 .15
433 Peter Zezel .05 .15
434 Mike Hough .07 .20
435 Mark Tinordi .05 .15
436 Dave Manson .05 .15
437 Jim Paek .07 .20
438 Frantisek Kucera .07 .20
439 Rob Zamuner RC .07 .20
440 Ulf Samuelsson .05 .15
441 Perry Berezan .05 .15
442 Murray Craven .05 .15
443 Mark Messier .15 .40
444 Alexander Semak .05 .15
445 Gord Murphy .07 .20
446 Jocelyn Lemieux .05 .15
447 Paul Cavallini .05 .15
448 Bernie Nicholls .05 .15
449 Brent Gilchrist .05 .15
450 Randy McKay .07 .20
451 Alexei Gusarov .05 .15
452 Mike McPhee .05 .15
453 Kimbi Daniels .05 .15
454 Kelly Kisio .07 .20
455 Bob Sweeney .05 .15
456 Luke Richardson .07 .20
457 Petr Nedved .07 .20
458 Craig Berube .05 .15
459 Kay Whitmore .07 .20
460 Randy Velischek .05 .15
461 David Williams RC .05 .15
462 Scott Mellanby .05 .15
463 Terry Carkner .07 .20
464 Dale Craigwell .05 .15
465 Kevin Todd .05 .15
466 Kjell Samuelsson .07 .20
467 Denis Savard .12 .30
468 Adam Foote .07 .20
469 Stephane Morin .05 .15
470 Doug Wilson .07 .20
471 Shawn Cronin .05 .15
472 Brian Glynn UER .05 .15
473 Craig Simpson .05 .15
474 Todd Krygier .07 .20
475 Brad Miller .05 .15
476 Yvon Corriveau .05 .15
477 Patrick Flatley .07 .20
478 Mats Sundin .10 .25
479 Joe Cirella .07 .20
480 Gino Cavallini .05 .15
481 Marty McSorley .05 .15
482 Brad Marsh .07 .20
483 Bob McGill .05 .15
484 Randy Moller .05 .15
485 Keith Primeau .07 .20
486 Darin Kimble .05 .15
487 Mike Krushelnyski .05 .15
488 Sutter Brothers .05 .15
489 Pavel Bure .20 .50
490 Ray Whitney RC .15 .40
491 Dave McLlwain .05 .15
492 Per Djoos .07 .20
493 Garry Valk .05 .15
494 Mike Bullard .07 .20
495 Greg Hawgood .05 .15
496 Terry Yake .05 .15
497 Mike Hartman .05 .15
498 Jaromir Jagr .25 .60
499 Checklist 251-384 .05 .15
500 Checklist 385-500 .05 .15
501 Eric Lindros .30 .75

1993 Stadium Club Members Only

This 59-card standard-size set was mailed out to Stadium Club Members in four separate mailings. Each box contained several sports. The fronts have full-bleed color action player photos with the words "Members Only" printed in gold foil at the bottom along with the player's name and the Stadium Club logo. On a multi-colored background, the horizontal backs carry player information and a computer generated drawing of a baseball player. The cards are unnumbered and checklisted below alphabetically according to sport as follows: baseball (1-28), basketball (29-44), football (45-53), and hockey (54-59).

COMPLETE SET (59) 10.00 20.00
54 Peter Bondra .15 .40
55 Mike Gartner .08 .25
56 Mario Lemieux 1.00 2.50
57 Mike Richter .15 .40
58 Patrick Roy 1.25 3.00
59 Teemu Selanne .25 .60

1993-94 Stadium Club

This 500-card standard-size set features borderless color player action shots on the card fronts. The set was issued in two series of 250 cards each. Cards were printed for both the Canadian and U.S. markets. The O-Pee-Chee version has a U.S.A. copyright on back for series one cards only. The player's name appears in gold foil at the bottom, atop blue and gold foil stripes. Included is a ten-card Award Winners subset (141-150) that features the 1992-93 NHL Trophy winners. Rookie Cards include Jason Arnott, Chris Osgood, Jocelyn Thibault and German Titov.

1 Guy Carbonneau .05 .15
2 Joe Cirella .05 .15
3 Laurie Boschman .05 .15
4 Arturs Irbe .07 .20
5 Adam Creighton .05 .15
6 Mike McPhee .05 .15
7 Jeff Beukeboom .05 .15
8 Kevin Todd .05 .15
9 Yvon Corriveau .05 .15
10 Eric Lindros .30 .75
11 Martin Rucinsky .05 .15
12 Michel Goulet .05 .15
13 Scott Pellerin RC .10 .25
14 Mike Eagles .05 .15
15 Steve Heinze .05 .15
16 Gerard Gallant .05 .15
17 Kelly Miller .05 .15
18 Petr Nedved .05 .15
19 Joe Mullen .07 .20
20 Pat LaFontaine .10 .25
21 Garth Butcher .05 .15
22 Jeff Reese .05 .15
23 Dave Andreychuk .10 .25
24 Patrick Flatley .05 .15
25 Tomas Sandstrom .05 .15
26 Andre Racicot .05 .15
27 Patrice Brisebois .05 .15
28 Neal Broten .07 .20
29 Mark Freer .05 .15
30 Kelly Kisio .05 .15
31 Scott Mellanby .07 .20
32 Joe Sakic .25 .60
33 Kerry Huffman .05 .15
34 Evgeny Davydov .05 .15
35 Mark Messier .10 .25
36 Pat Verbeek .05 .15
37 Greg Gilbert .05 .15
38 John Tucker .05 .15
39 Claude Lemieux .05 .15
40 Shayne Corson .05 .15
41 Gordie Roberts .05 .15
42 Jiri Slegr .05 .15
43 Kevin Dineen .05 .15
44 Johan Garpenlov .05 .15
45 Sergei Fedorov .15 .40
46 Rich Sutter .05 .15
47 Dave Hannan .05 .15
48 Sylvain Lefebvre .05 .15
49 Pat Elynuik .05 .15
50 Ray Ferraro .05 .15
51 Brent Ashton .05 .15
52 Paul Stanton .05 .15
53 Kevin Haller .05 .15
54 Kelly Hrudey .07 .20
55 Russ Courtnall .05 .15
56 Alexei Zhamnov .07 .20
57 Andrei Lomakin .05 .15
58 Keith Brown .05 .15
59 Glen Murray .05 .15
60 Kay Whitmore .05 .15
61 Stephane Richer .07 .20
62 Todd Gill .05 .15
63 Bob Sweeney .05 .15
64 Mike Richter .10 .25
65 Brett Hull .15 .40
66 Sylvain Cote .05 .15
67 Kirk Muller .05 .15
68 Ronnie Stern .05 .15
69 Josef Beranek .05 .15
70 Steve Yzerman .25 .60
71 Don Beaupre .07 .20
72 Ed Courtenay .05 .15
73 Zdeno Ciger .05 .15
74 Andrew Cassels .05 .15
75 Roman Hamrlik .05 .15
76 Benoit Hogue .05 .15
77 Andrei Kovalenko .05 .15
78 Rod Brind'Amour .07 .20
79 Tom Barrasso .07 .20
80 Al Iafrate .05 .15
81 Brett Hedican .05 .15
82 Peter Bondra .07 .20
83 Ted Donato .05 .15
84 Chris Lindberg .05 .15
85 John Vanbiesbrouck .07 .20
86 Ron Sutter .05 .15
87 Luc Robitaille .07 .20
88 Brian Leetch .10 .25
89 Randy Wood .05 .15
90 Dirk Graham .05 .15
91 Alexander Mogilny .07 .20
92 Mike Keane .05 .15
93 Adam Oates .10 .25
94 Viacheslav Butsayev .05 .15
95 John LeClair .10 .25
96 Joe Nieuwendyk .07 .20
97 Mikael Andersson .05 .15
98 Jaromir Jagr .25 .60
99 Ed Belfour .10 .25
100 David Reid .05 .15
101 Darius Kasparaitis .05 .15
102 Zarley Zalapski .05 .15
103 Christian Ruuttu .05 .15
104 Phil Housley .07 .20
105 Al MacInnis .07 .20
106 Tommy Sjodin .05 .15
107 Richard Smehlik .05 .15
108 Jyrki Lumme .05 .15
109 Dominic Roussel .07 .20
110 Mike Gartner .07 .20
111 Bernie Nicholls .05 .15
112 Mark Howe .10 .25
113 Rich Pilon .05 .15
114 Jeff Odgers .05 .15
115 Gilbert Dionne .05 .15
116 Peter Zezel .05 .15
117 Don Sweeney .05 .15
118 Jimmy Carson .05 .15
119 Igor Korolev .05 .15
120 Bob Kudelski .05 .15
121 Dave Lowry .05 .15
122 Steve Kasper .05 .15
123 Mike Ridley .05 .15
124 Dave Tippett .05 .15
125 Cliff Ronning .05 .15
126 Bruce Driver .05 .15
127 Stephane Matteau .05 .15
128 Joel Otto .05 .15
129 Alexei Kovalev .07 .20
130 Mike Modano .15 .40
131 Bill Ranford .07 .20
132 Petr Svoboda .05 .15
133 Roger Johansson .05 .15
134 Marc Bureau .05 .15
135 Keith Tkachuk .10 .25
136 Mark Recchi .12 .30
137 Bob Probert .07 .20
138 Uwe Krupp .05 .15
139 Mike Sullivan .05 .15
140 Doug Gilmour .12 .30
141 Teemu Selanne TW .20 .50
142 Dave Poulin TW .05 .15
143 Mario Lemieux TW .40 1.00
144 Ed Belfour TW .10 .25
145 Pierre Turgeon TW .07 .20
146 Mario Lemieux TW .40 1.00
147 Chris Chelios TW .10 .25
148 Mario Lemieux TW .40 1.00
149 Doug Gilmour TW .12 .30
150 Ed Belfour TW .10 .25
151 Paul Ranheim .05 .15
152 Gino Cavallini .05 .15
153 Kevin Hatcher .05 .15
154 Marc Bergevin .05 .15
155 Marty McSorley .05 .15
156 Brian Bellows .07 .20
157 Patrick Poulin .05 .15
158 Kevin Stevens .05 .15
159 Bobby Holik .05 .15
160 Ray Bourque .15 .40
161 Bryan Marchment .05 .15
162 Curtis Joseph .10 .25
163 Kirk McLean .07 .20
164 Teppo Numminen .05 .15
165 Kevin Lowe .05 .15
166 Tim Cheveldae .07 .20
167 Brad Dalgarno .05 .15
168 Glenn Anderson .10 .25
169 Frank Musil .05 .15
170 Eric Desjardins .07 .20
171 Doug Zmolek .05 .15
172 Mark Lamb .05 .15
173 Craig Ludwig .05 .15
174 Rob Gaudreau RC .10 .25
175 Bob Carpenter .05 .15
176 Mike Ricci .05 .15
177 Brian Skrudland .05 .15
178 Dominik Hasek .20 .50
179 Pat Conacher .05 .15
180 Mark Janssens .05 .15
181 Brent Fedyk .05 .15
182 Rob DiMaio .05 .15
183 Dave Manson .05 .15
184 Janne Ojanen .05 .15
185 Ryan Walter .05 .15
186 Michael Nylander .05 .15
187 Steve Leach .05 .15
188 Jeff Brown .05 .15
189 Shawn McEachern .05 .15
190 Jeremy Roenick .15 .40
191 Darrin Shannon .05 .15
192 Wendel Clark .07 .20
193 Kevin Miller .05 .15
194 Paul DiPietro .05 .15
195 Steve Thomas .05 .15
196 Nicklas Lidstrom .10 .25
197 Ed Olczyk .05 .15
198 Robert Reichel .05 .15
199 Neil Brady .05 .15
200 Wayne Gretzky .50 1.25
201 Adrien Plavsic .05 .15
202 Joe Juneau .07 .20
203 Brad May .07 .20
204 Igor Kravchuk .05 .15
205 Keith Acton .05 .15
206 Ken Daneyko .05 .15
207 Sean Burke .05 .15
208 Jay More .05 .15
209 John Cullen .05 .15
210 Teemu Selanne .20 .50
211 Brent Sutter .05 .15
212 Brian Bradley .05 .15
213 Donald Audette .05 .15
214 Philippe Bozon .05 .15
215 Derek King .05 .15
216 Cam Neely .10 .25
217 Keith Primeau .05 .15
218 Steve Smith .05 .15
219 Ken Sutton .05 .15
220 Dale Hawerchuk .12 .30
221 Alexei Zhitnik .05 .15
222 Glen Wesley .05 .15
223 Nelson Emerson .05 .15
224 Pat Falloon .05 .15
225 Darryl Sydor .05 .15
226 Tony Amonte .07 .20
227 Brian Mullen .05 .15
228 Gary Suter .05 .15
229 David Shaw .05 .15
230 Troy Murray .05 .15
231 Patrick Roy .25 .60
232 Mitchel Petit .05 .15
233 Wayne Presley .05 .15
234 Keith Jones .05 .15
235 Gary Roberts .05 .15
236 Steve Larmer .07 .20
237 Valeri Kamensky .07 .20
238 Ulf Dahlen .05 .15
239 Danton Cole .05 .15
240 Vincent Damphousse .07 .20
241 Yuri Khmylev .05 .15
242 Stephane Quintal .05 .15
243 Peter Taglianetti .05 .15
244 Gary Leeman .05 .15

Card	Low	High
45 Sergei Nemchinov	.05	.15
46 Rob Blake	.07	.20
47 Steve Chiasson	.05	.15
48 Vladimir Malakhov	.05	.15
49 Checklist 1-125	.05	.15
50 Checklist 126-250	.05	.15
51 Kjell Samuelsson	.05	.15
52 Terry Carkner	.05	.15
53 Bill Lindsay	.05	.15
54 Bob Essensa	.07	.20
55 Jocelyn Lemieux	.05	.15
56 Joe Sacco	.05	.15
57 Marty McInnis	.05	.15
58 Warren Rychel	.05	.15
59 David Maley	.05	.15
60 Grant Fuhr	.10	.25
61 Scott Young	.05	.15
62 Ed Ronan	.05	.15
63 Micah Aivazoff RC	.10	.25
64 Murray Craven	.05	.15
65 Slava Fetisov	.05	.15
66 Chris Dahlquist	.05	.15
67 Norm Maciver	.05	.15
68 Alexander Godynyuk	.05	.15
69 Mikael Renberg	.10	.25
70 Adam Graves	.05	.15
71 Randy Ladouceur	.05	.15
72 Frank Pietrangelo	.07	.20
73 Basil McRae	.07	.20
74 Bryan Smolinski	.05	.15
75 Daren Puppa	.05	.15
76 Darcy Wakaluk	.05	.15
77 Dimitri Khristich	.05	.15
78 Vladimir Vujtek	.05	.15
79 Tom Kurvers	.05	.15
80 Felix Potvin	.20	.50
81 Keith Brown	.05	.15
82 Thomas Steen	.05	.15
83 Larry Murphy	.07	.20
84 Bob Corkum	.05	.15
85 Tony Granato	.05	.15
86 Cam Russell	.05	.15
87 John MacLean	.07	.20
88 Shawn Antoski	.05	.15
89 Pelle Eklund	.05	.15
90 Chris Pronger	.10	.25
91 Alexander Karpovtsev	.05	.15
92 Paul Laus RC	.05	.15
93 Jaroslav Otevrel	.05	.15
94 Dino Ciccarelli	.07	.20
95 Guy Hebert	.07	.20
96 Dave Karpa	.05	.15
97 Denis Savard	.12	.30
98 Jim Johnson	.05	.15
99 Kirk Maltby RC	.10	.25
00 Alexandre Daigle	.05	.15
01 Dave Poulin	.05	.15
02 James Patrick	.05	.15
03 Jon Casey	.07	.20
04 Yves Racine	.05	.15
05 Craig Simpson	.05	.15
06 Mike Krushelnyski	.05	.15
07 Mark Fitzpatrick	.05	.15
08 Charlie Huddy	.05	.15
09 Todd Ewen	.05	.15
10 Mario Lemieux	.40	1.00
11 Mark Astley RC	.10	.25
12 Sergei Zubov	.05	.15
13 Shawn Burr	.05	.15
14 Valeri Zelepukin	.05	.15
15 Stephane Fiset	.07	.20
16 C.J. Young	.05	.15
17 Luciano Borsato	.05	.15
18 Darcy Loewen	.05	.15
19 Mike Vernon	.07	.20
20 Chris Gratton	.07	.20
21 Matthew Barnaby	.07	.20
22 Mike Rathje	.05	.15
23 Sergio Momesso	.05	.15
24 David Volek	.05	.15
25 Ron Tugnutt	.07	.20
26 Jeff Hackett	.05	.15
27 Robb Stauber	.05	.15
28 Chris Terreri	.07	.20
29 Rick Tocchet	.07	.20
30 John Vanbiesbrouck	.07	.20
31 Drake Berehowsky	.05	.15
32 Alexei Kasatonov	.05	.15
33 Vladimir Konstantinov	.07	.20
34 John Blue	.07	.20
35 Craig Janney	.07	.20
36 Curtis Leschyshyn	.05	.15
37 Todd Krygier	.05	.15
38 Boris Mironov	.05	.15
39 Joby Messier RC	.10	.25
40 Tommy Soderstrom	.07	.20
41 Randy Cunneyworth	.05	.15
42 Mark Ferner RC	.05	.15
43 Stephan Lebeau	.05	.15
44 Jody Hull	.05	.15
45 Jason Arnott RC	.20	.50
46 Gerard Gallant	.05	.15
47 Stephane Richer	.07	.20
48 Jeff Shantz RC	.05	.15
49 Brian Skrudland	.05	.15
50 Chris Osgood RC	.60	1.50
51 Gary Shuchuk	.05	.15
52 Martin Brodeur	.25	.60
53 Bob Rouse	.05	.15
54 Doug Bodger	.05	.15
55 Mike Craig	.05	.15
56 Ulf Samuelsson	.05	.15
57 Trevor Linden	.07	.20
58 Dennis Vaske	.05	.15
59 Alexei Yashin	.07	.20
60 Paul Ysebaert	.05	.15
61 Shaun Van Allen	.05	.15
62 Sandis Ozolinsh	.05	.15
63 Todd Elik	.05	.15
64 German Titov RC	.10	.25
65 Alexander Semak	.05	.15
66 Allen Pedersen	.05	.15
67 Greg Johnson	.05	.15
68 Anatoli Semenov	.05	.15
69 Scott Mellanby	.07	.20
70 Mats Sundin	.07	.20
71 Mattias Norstrom RC	.10	.25
72 Glen Featherstone	.05	.15
73 Sergei Petrenko	.05	.15
74 Miko Donnolly	.05	.15
75 Nikolai Borschevsky	.05	.15
76 Rob Zamuner	.05	.15
77 Steven King	.05	.15
78 Rick Tabaracci	.05	.15
79 Dave Lowry	.05	.15
80 Pierre Turgeon	.07	.20
81 Garry Galley	.05	.15
82 Doug Weight	.07	.20
83 Scott Stevens	.10	.25
84 Mark Tinordi	.05	.15
85 Ron Francis	.12	.30
386 Mark Greig	.05	.15
387 Sean Hill	.05	.15
388 Slava Kozlov	.07	.20
389 Brendan Shanahan	.12	.30
390 Theo Fleury	.05	.15
391 Mathieu Schneider	.05	.15
392 Tom Fitzgerald	.05	.15
393 Markus Naslund	.10	.25
394 Travis Green	.07	.20
395 Troy Loney	.05	.15
396 Gord Donnelly	.05	.15
397 Owen Nolan	.07	.20
398 Steve Larmer	.07	.20
399 Dave Archibald	.05	.15
400 Jari Kurri	.10	.25
401 Jim Paek	.05	.15
402 Andrei Lomakin	.05	.15
403 Scott Niedermayer	.10	.25
404 Bob Errey	.05	.15
405 Michal Pivonka	.05	.15
406 Doug Lidster	.05	.15
407 Garry Valk	.05	.15
408 Geoff Sanderson	.07	.20
409 Stewart Malgunas RC	.10	.25
410 Craig MacTavish	.05	.15
411 Jaroslav Modry RC	.10	.25
412 Shawn Chambers	.05	.15
413 Geoff Courtnall	.05	.15
414 Mark Hardy	.05	.15
415 Martin Straka	.05	.15
416 Randy Burridge	.05	.15
417 Kent Manderville	.05	.15
418 Darren Rumble	.05	.15
419 Bill Houlder	.05	.15
420 Chris Chelios	.10	.25
421 Jim Hrivnak	.05	.15
422 Benoit Brunet	.05	.15
423 Aaron Ward RC	.10	.25
424 Alexei Gusarov	.05	.15
425 Mats Sundin SWE	.07	.20
426 Kjell Samuelsson	.05	.15
427 Mikael Andersson	.05	.15
428 Ulf Dahlen	.05	.15
429 Nicklas Lidstrom	.10	.25
430 Tommy Soderstrom SWE	.07	.20
431 Darrin Madeley RC	.10	.25
432 Kevin Dahl	.05	.15
433 Ron Hextall	.07	.20
434 Patrick Carnback RC	.10	.25
435 Randy Moller	.05	.15
436 Dave Gagner	.07	.20
437 Corey Millen	.05	.15
438 Olaf Kolzig	.07	.20
439 Gord Murphy	.05	.15
440 Cam Stewart RC	.10	.25
441 Darren McCarty RC	.15	.40
442 Frantisek Kucera	.05	.15
443 Ted Drury	.05	.15
444 Troy Mallette	.05	.15
445 Robin Bawa RC	.05	.15
446 Steven Rice	.05	.15
447 Pat Elynuik	.05	.15
448 Jim Cummins RC	.05	.15
449 Rob Niedermayer	.07	.20
450 Paul Coffey	.10	.25
451 Calle Johansson	.05	.15
452 Mike Needham	.05	.15
453 Glenn Healy	.07	.20
454 Dixon Ward	.05	.15
455 Al Iafrate	.05	.15
456 Jon Casey	.07	.20
457 Kevin Stevens USA	.05	.15
458 Tony Amonte	.07	.20
459 Chris Chelios	.10	.25
460 Pat LaFontaine USA	.10	.25
461 Jamie Baker	.05	.15
462 Andre Faust	.05	.15
463 Bobby Dollas	.05	.15
464 Steven Finn	.05	.15
465 Scott Lachance	.05	.15
466 Mike Hough	.05	.15
467 Bill Guerin	.05	.15
468 Dimitri Filimonov	.05	.15
469 Dave Ellett	.05	.15
470 Andy Moog	.10	.25
471 Scott Thomas RC	.10	.25
472 Trent Yawney	.05	.15
473 Tim Sweeney	.05	.15
474 Shjon Podein RC	.10	.25
475 J.J. Daigneault	.05	.15
476 Darren Turcotte	.05	.15
477 Esa Tikkanen	.05	.15
478 Vitali Karamnov	.05	.15
479 Jocelyn Thibault RC	.10	.25
480 Pavel Bure	.10	.25
481 Steve Konowalchuk	.05	.15
482 Sylvain Turgeon	.05	.15
483 Jeff Daniels	.05	.15
484 Dallas Drake RC	.10	.25
485 Iain Fraser RC	.10	.25
486 Joe Reekie	.05	.15
487 Evgeny Davydov	.05	.15
488 Jozef Stumpel	.05	.15
489 Brent Thompson	.05	.15
490 Terry Yake	.05	.15
491 Derek Plante RC	.10	.25
492 Dimitri Yushkevich	.05	.15
493 Wayne McBean	.05	.15
494 Derian Hatcher	.05	.15
495 Jeff Norton	.05	.15
496 Adam Foote	.05	.15
497 Mike Peluso	.05	.15
498 Rob Pearson	.05	.15
499 Checklist 251-375	.05	.15
500 Checklist 376-500	.05	.15

1993-94 Stadium Club Members Only Parallel

COMPLETE SET (500) 150.00 300.00
*MEMBERS ONLY: 3X TO 8X BASIC CARDS

1993-94 Stadium Club OPC

This O-Pee-Chee version has a "PTD in U.S.A." copyright line on back and was issued for series one cards only.

COMPLETE SET (250)	12.00	30.00
COMP.SERIES 1 (250)	6.00	15.00
COMP.SERIES 2 (250)	6.00	15.00

*O-PEE-CHEE: .4X TO 1X BASIC CARDS

1993-94 Stadium Club First Day Issue

Randomly inserted at a rate of 1:24 packs, the 500-cards parallel the basic Stadium Club set. The O-Pee-Chee version has a "PTD in U.S.A." copyright line on the back and was printed for series one cards only. The cards of Wayne Gretzky, Vincent Damphousse, Luc Robitaille and Wayne Presley can be found with the logo in either upper corner.
*VETS: 12X TO 30X BASIC CARDS
*ROOKIE STARS: 5X TO 12X BASIC RC
*SER.1 OPC: .5X TO 1.2X BASIC FIRST DAY

1993-94 Stadium Club All-Stars

Randomly inserted at the rate of 1:24 first-series packs, each of these 23 standard-size cards features two 1992-93 All-Stars, one from each conference. Both sides carry a posed color player photo superimposed over a stellar background. The cards are unnumbered.

Card	Low	High
COMPLETE SET (23)	30.00	60.00
*O-PEE-CHEE: .4X TO 1X BASIC INSERTS		
1 P.Roy/E.Belfour	6.00	15.00
2 R.Bourque/P.Coffey	2.00	5.00
3 A.Iafrate/C.Chelios	1.50	4.00
4 J.Jagr/B.Hull	2.00	5.00
5 P.LaFontaine/S.Yzerman	5.00	12.00
6 K.Stevens/P.Bure	2.00	5.00
7 C.Billington/J.Casey	.75	2.00
8 S.Duchesne/S.Chiasson	.75	2.00
9 S.Stevens/P.Housley	.75	2.00
10 P.Bondra/K.Kisio	1.50	4.00
11 A.Oates/B.Bradley	1.50	4.00
12 A.Mogilny/J.Kurri	1.50	4.00
13 P.Sidorkiewicz/M.Vernon	.75	2.00
14 Z.Zalapski/D.Manson	.75	2.00
15 B.Marsh/R.Carlyle	.75	2.00
16 K.Muller/G.Roberts	.75	2.00
17 J.Sakic/D.Gilmour	3.00	8.00
18 M.Recchi/L.Robitaille	1.50	4.00
19 K.Lowe/G.Butcher	.75	2.00
20 R.Tocchet/J.Roenick	2.00	5.00
21 P.Turgeon/M.Modano	2.00	5.00
22 M.Gartner/T.Selanne	2.00	5.00
23 M.Lemieux/W.Gretzky	10.00	25.00

1993-94 Stadium Club All-Stars Members Only Parallel

COMPLETE SET (23)
*MEMBERS ONLY: .6X TO 1.5X BASIC CARD

1993-94 Stadium Club Finest Inserts

Randomly inserted at the rate of 1:24 second-series packs, these 12 standard-size cards feature color player action cutouts on their multicolored metallic fronts. The player's name in gold lettering appears on a silver bar at the lower left. The horizontal back carries a color player photo on the left. The player's name and position appear at the top, with biography, career highlights, and statistics following below on a background that resembles blue ruffled silk. The cards are numbered on the back as "X of 12."

Card	Low	High
COMPLETE SET (12)	15.00	40.00
1 Wayne Gretzky	6.00	15.00
2 Jeff Brown	.20	.50
3 Brett Hull	1.25	3.00
4 Paul Coffey	.75	2.00
5 Felix Potvin	.75	2.00
6 Mike Gartner	.40	1.00
7 Luc Robitaille	.40	1.00
8 Marty McSorley	.20	.50
9 Gary Roberts	.20	.50
10 Mario Lemieux	5.00	12.00
11 Patrick Roy	5.00	12.00
12 Ray Bourque	1.50	4.00

1993-94 Stadium Club Finest Members Only Parallel

COMPLETE SET (12)
*MEMBERS ONLY: .6X TO 1.5X BASIC CARD

1993-94 Stadium Club Master Photos

Inserted one per U.S. box, and issued in two 12-card series, these 24 oversized cards measure 5" by 7". The fronts feature color player action shots framed by prismatic foil lines and set on a white card face. The cards are numbered on the back for both series as "X of 12," but are listed below as 1-24 to avoid confusion. Winner cards, which could be redeemed for one 5" X 7" card of each of the three players listed on the reverse, were inserted 1:24 packs of '93-94 Stadium Club

Card	Low	High
COMPLETE SET (24)	12.00	30.00
COMP.SERIES 1 (12)	8.00	20.00
COMP.SERIES 2 (12)	4.00	10.00
*WINNER EXCH: .5X TO 1.2X JUMBOS		
*WINNER MEM.ONLY: .6X TO 1.5X JUMBOS		
1 Pat LaFontaine	.30	.75
2 Doug Gilmour	.30	.75
3 Ray Bourque	.60	1.50
4 Teemu Selanne	.30	.75
5 Eric Lindros	.50	1.25
6 Ray Ferraro	.07	.20
7 Patrick Roy	2.50	6.00
8 Wayne Gretzky	4.00	10.00
9 Brett Hull	.50	1.25
10 John Vanbiesbrouck	.30	.75
11 Adam Oates	.15	.40
12 Tom Barrasso	.20	.50
13 Esa Tikkanen	.10	.25
14 Jari Kurri	.30	.75
15 Grant Fuhr	.40	1.00
16 Scott Lachance	.07	.20
17 Theo Fleury	.25	.75
18 Adam Graves	.07	.20
19 Rick Tabaracci	.15	.40
20 Pierre Turgeon	.15	.40
21 Steven Finn	.07	.20
22 Craig Janney	.15	.40
23 Mathieu Schneider	.07	.20
24 Felix Potvin	.75	2.00

1993-94 Stadium Club Team USA

Randomly inserted at the rate of 1:12 second-series packs, these 23 standard-size cards feature color player action shots on their borderless fronts. The player's name appears in gold-foil lettering over a blue stripe near the bottom. The gold foil USA Hockey logo appears in an upper corner. The cards are numbered on the back as "X of 23."

Card	Low	High
COMPLETE SET (23)	8.00	20.00
1 Mark Beaufait	.40	1.00
2 Jim Campbell	.60	1.50
3 Ted Crowley	.40	1.00
4 Mike Dunham	.60	1.50
5 Chris Ferraro	.40	1.00
6 Peter Ferraro	.40	1.00
7 Brett Hauer	.40	1.00
8 Darby Hendrickson	.40	1.00
9 Jon Hillebrandt	.40	1.00
10 Chris Imes	.40	1.00
11 Craig Johnson	.40	1.00
12 Peter Laviolette	.40	1.00
13 Jeff Lazaro	.40	1.00
14 John Lilley	.40	1.00
15 Todd Marchant	.60	1.50
16 Matt Martin	.40	1.00
17 Ian Moran	.40	1.00
18 Travis Richards	.40	1.00
19 Barry Richter	.40	1.00
20 David Roberts	.40	1.00
21 Brian Rolston	.60	1.50
22 David Sacco	.40	1.00
23 Jim Storm	.40	1.00

1993-94 Stadium Club Team USA Members Only Parallel

COMPLETE SET (23)
*MEMBERS ONLY: .8X TO 2X BASIC CARD

1994 Stadium Club Members Only 50

Issued to Stadium Club members, this 50-card standard-size set features 45 players who were involved with the 1994 All-Star game, Western Conference All-Stars (1-22), Eastern Conference All-Stars (23-45), and five Stadium Club Finest cards. The fronts have full-bleed color action player photos. The player's name is printed in the bottom left corner, the words "Topps Stadium Club Members Only" in gold foil appear in one of the top corners. On a black background, the horizontal backs carry a color player close-up shot, along with a player profile.

Card	Low	High
COMP.FACT SET (50)	8.00	20.00
1 Felix Potvin	.30	.75
2 Chris Chelios	.20	.50
3 Paul Coffey	.20	.50
4 Pavel Bure	.60	1.50
5 Wayne Gretzky	1.50	4.00
6 Brett Hull	.30	.75
7 Al MacInnis	.08	.25
8 Rob Blake	.08	.25
9 Alexei Kasatonov	.02	.10
10 Teemu Selanne	.50	1.25
11 Sandis Ozolinsh	.08	.25
12 Shayne Corson	.02	.10
13 Dave Andreychuk	.05	.15
14 Dave Taylor	.02	.10
15 Sergei Fedorov	.50	1.25
16 Brendan Shanahan	.40	1.00
17 Arturs Irbe	.20	.50
18 Joe Nieuwendyk	.08	.25
19 Russ Courtnall	.02	.10
20 Jeremy Roenick	.30	.75
21 Doug Gilmour	.20	.50
22 Curtis Joseph	.30	.75
23 Patrick Roy	1.25	3.00
24 Brian Leetch	.20	.50
25 Ray Bourque	.40	1.00
26 Alexander Mogilny	.20	.50
27 Mark Messier	.30	.75
28 Eric Lindros	.60	1.50
29 Garry Galley	.02	.10
30 Scott Stevens	.05	.15
31 Al Iafrate	.02	.10
32 Larry Murphy	.02	.10
33 Joe Mullen	.02	.10
34 Mark Recchi	.20	.50
35 Adam Graves	.05	.15
36 Geoff Sanderson	.02	.10
37 Adam Oates	.20	.50
38 Pierre Turgeon	.20	.50
39 Joe Sakic	.50	1.25
40 John Vanbiesbrouck	.20	.50
41 Brian Bradley	.02	.10
42 Alexei Yashin	.08	.25
43 Bob Kudelski	.02	.10
44 Jaromir Jagr	.75	2.00
45 Mike Richter	.30	.75
46 Martin Brodeur	.60	1.50
47 Mikael Renberg	.08	.25
48 Derek Plante	.02	.10
49 Jason Arnott	.08	.25
50 Alexandre Daigle	.02	.10

1994-95 Stadium Club

This 270-card standard-size set was issued in one series. Due to the NHL lock-out, series two was replaced on the production schedule by Finest; therefore, this set does not have a comprehensive player selection. There are 12 cards per pack and 24 packs per box. The card fronts feature a full-bleed photo with the player's name and set name printed in gold foil along the bottom. The backs feature two player photos and previous year stats. Subsets include Power Players (55-60), Great Expectations (110-119), Shutouts (178-190), Rink Report (201-204), and Trophy Winners (264-270). There are no key Rookie Cards in this set.

Card	Low	High
1 Mark Messier	.10	.25
2 Brad May	.05	.15
3 Mike Ricci	.05	.15
4 Scott Stevens	.10	.25
5 Keith Tkachuk	.10	.25
6 Guy Hebert	.07	.20
7 Jason Arnott	.07	.20
8 Cam Neely	.10	.25
9 Adam Graves	.05	.15
10 Pavel Bure	.10	.25
11 Jeff Odgers	.05	.15
12 Dimitri Khristich	.05	.15
13 Patrick Poulin	.05	.15
14 Mike Donnelly	.05	.15
15 Felix Potvin	.10	.25
16 Keith Primeau	.10	.25
17 Fred Knipscheer	.05	.15
18 Mike Keane	.05	.15
19 Vitali Prokhorov	.05	.15
20 Ray Ferraro	.05	.15
21 Shane Churla	.05	.15
22 Rob Niedermayer	.07	.20
23 Adam Creighton	.05	.15
24 Tommy Soderstrom	.07	.20
25 Theo Fleury	.10	.25
26 Jim Storm	.07	.20
27 Bret Hedican	.05	.15
28 Sean Hill	.05	.15
29 Bill Ranford	.07	.20
30 Derek Plante	.05	.15
31 Dave McLlwain	.05	.15
32 Iain Fraser	.05	.15
33 Patrick Roy	.25	.60
34 Martin Straka	.05	.15
35 Bruce Driver	.05	.15
36 Brian Skrudland	.05	.15
37 Bob Errey	.05	.15
38 Randy Cunneyworth	.05	.15
39 John Slaney	.05	.15
40 Ray Sheppard	.07	.20
41 Sergei Nemchinov	.05	.15
42 Dave Ellett	.05	.15
43 Vincent Riendeau	.05	.15
44 Trent Yawney	.05	.15
45 Dave Gagner	.07	.20
46 Igor Korolev	.05	.15
47 Gary Shuchuk	.07	.20
48 Rob Zamuner	.05	.15
49 Frantisek Kucera	.05	.15
50 Joe Mullen	.07	.20
51 Ron Hextall	.07	.20
52 J.J. Daigneault	.05	.15
53 Patrik Carnback	.05	.15
54 Steven Rice	.05	.15
55 Brian Leetch PP	.10	.25
56 Al MacInnis PP	.07	.20
57 Luc Robitaille PP	.10	.25
58 Dave Andreychuk PP	.10	.25
59 Jeremy Roenick PP	.20	.50
60 Mario Lemieux PP	.40	1.00
61 Dave Manson	.05	.15
62 Pat Falloon	.05	.15
63 Jesse Belanger	.05	.15
64 Philippe Boucher	.05	.15
65 Sergio Momesso	.10	.25
66 Evgeny Davydov	.05	.15
67 Alexei Gusarov	.07	.20
68 Jaromir Jagr	.25	.60
69 Randy Ladouceur	.07	.20
70 Chris Chelios	.10	.25
71 John Druce	.07	.20
72 Kris Draper	.05	.15
73 Joey Kocur	.05	.15
74 Rich Tabarraci	.07	.20
75 Mikael Andersson	.05	.15
76 Mark Osborne	.05	.15
77 Ray Bourque	.15	.40
78 Dimitri Yushkevich	.05	.15
79 Mike Vernon	.07	.20
80 Steve Thomas	.05	.15
81 Steve Duchesne	.05	.15
82 Dean Evason	.05	.15
83 Jason Smith	.07	.20
84 Bryan Marchment	.07	.20
85 Boris Mironov	.05	.15
86 Jeff Norton	.05	.15
87 Donald Audette	.05	.15
88 Eric Lindros	.10	.25
89 Garry Valk	.05	.15
90 Mats Sundin	.07	.20
91 Gerald Diduck	.05	.15
92 Jeff Shantz	.05	.15
93 Scott Niedermayer	.10	.25
94 Troy Mallette	.05	.15
95 John Vanbiesbrouck	.07	.20
96 Ron Francis	.12	.30
97 Slava Kozlov	.07	.20
98 Ken Baumgartner	.07	.20
99 Wayne Gretzky	.50	1.25
100 Brett Hull	.20	.50
101 Marc Bergevin	.05	.15
102 Owen Nolan	.10	.25
103 Bryan Smolinski	.05	.15
104 Lyle Odelein	.07	.20
105 Mike Ridley	.05	.15
106 Trevor Kidd	.07	.20
107 Derian Hatcher	.05	.15
108 Derek King	.05	.15
109 Rob Zettler	.05	.15
110 Alexandre Daigle GE	.05	.15
111 Chris Pronger GE	.10	.25
112 Chris Gratton GE	.05	.15
113 John Slaney GE	.05	.15
114 Jocelyn Thibault GE	.10	.25
115 Jason Arnott GE	.07	.20
116 Alexei Yashin GE	.10	.25
117 Rob Niedermayer GE	.07	.20
118 Jason Allison GE	.07	.20
119 Martin Brodeur GE	.25	.60
120 Pat Verbeek	.07	.20
121 Kelly Buchberger	.05	.15
122 Doug Lidster	.05	.15
123 Sergei Makarov	.05	.15
124 Kris King	.05	.15
125 Dominik Hasek	.20	.50
126 Martin Rucinsky	.05	.15
127 Kerry Huffman	.05	.15
128 Gord Murphy	.05	.15
129 Bobby Holik	.05	.15
130 Kirk Muller	.05	.15
131 Christian Ruuttu	.05	.15
132 Jyrki Lumme	.05	.15
133 Ken Wregget	.07	.20
134 Dale Hunter	.05	.15
135 Rob Blake	.10	.25
136 Petr Klima	.05	.15
137 Steve Heinze	.05	.15
138 Chris Osgood	.15	.40
139 John Lilley	.05	.15
140 Dave Andreychuk	.10	.25
141 Zarley Zalapski	.05	.15
142 Curtis Joseph	.15	.40
143 Brent Gilchrist	.05	.15
144 Vladimir Malakhov	.05	.15
145 Mikael Renberg	.07	.20
146 Robert Kron	.05	.15
147 Dean McAmmond	.05	.15
148 Doug Bodger	.05	.15
149 Ray Whitney	.05	.15
150 Brian Leetch	.10	.25
151 Martin Lapointe	.05	.15
152 Teppo Numminen	.05	.15
153 Scott Young	.05	.15
154 Nick Kypreos	.05	.15
155 Ed Belfour	.10	.25
156 Greg Adams	.05	.15
157 Brian Benning	.05	.15
158 Bob Carpenter	.05	.15
159 Vladimir Konstantinov	.07	.20
160 Rick Tocchet	.07	.20
161 Joe Sacco	.05	.15
162 Daren Puppa	.07	.20
163 Randy Burridge	.05	.15
164 Darryl Sydor	.05	.15
165 Jay More	.05	.15
166 Joe Nieuwendyk	.10	.25
167 Mike Eastwood	.05	.15
168 Murray Baron	.05	.15
169 Brent Fedyk	.05	.15
170 Russ Courtnall	.05	.15
171 Sean Burke	.07	.20
172 Uwe Krupp	.05	.15
173 Kevin Lowe	.05	.15
174 Guy Carbonneau	.05	.15
175 Alexei Yashin	.10	.25
176 Thomas Steen	.05	.15
177 Sandis Ozolinsh	.05	.15
178 Patrick Roy SO	.25	.60
179 Dominik Hasek SO	.20	.50
180 Ed Belfour SO	.10	.25
181 Mike Richter SO	.10	.25
182 Ron Hextall SO	.07	.20
183 Daren Puppa SO	.07	.20
184 Jon Casey SO	.07	.20
185 Felix Potvin SO	.10	.25
186 Martin Brodeur SO	.25	.60
187 Darcy Wakaluk SO	.07	.20
188 Kirk McLean SO	.07	.20
189 Mike Vernon SO	.07	.20
190 Arturs Irbe SO	.07	.20
191 Dino Ciccarelli	.07	.20
192 Steven Finn	.05	.15
193 Pierre Sevigny	.05	.15
194 Jim Dowd	.05	.15
195 Chris Gratton	.05	.15
196 Wayne Presley	.05	.15
197 Joel Otto	.05	.15
198 Fredrik Olausson	.05	.15
199 Jody Hull	.05	.15
200 Cliff Ronning	.05	.15
201 Darren Turcotte RR	.05	.15
202 Al Iafrate RR	.05	.15
203 Eric Lindros RR	.10	.25
204 Sandis Ozolinsh RR	.05	.15
205 Petr Nedved	.07	.20
206 Mark Lamb	.05	.15
207 Shaun Van Allen	.05	.15
208 Kelly Hrudey	.07	.20
209 Nikolai Borschevsky	.05	.15
210 Glen Wesley	.05	.15
211 Shawn McEachern	.05	.15
212 Mark Janssens	.05	.15
213 Brian Mullen	.05	.15
214 Craig Ludwig	.05	.15
215 Mike Rathje	.05	.15
216 Stephane Matteau	.05	.15
217 Tim Cheveldae	.07	.20
218 Brent Sutter	.07	.20
219 Gord Dineen UER Ottawa Senators (Listed as born	.05	.15
220 Kevin Hatcher	.05	.15
221 Todd Simon RC	.05	.15
222 Bill Lindsay	.05	.15
223 Kirk McLean	.07	.20
224 Chris Joseph	.05	.15
225 Valeri Zelepukin	.05	.15
226 Terry Yake	.05	.15
227 Benoit Brunet	.05	.15
228 Nicklas Lidstrom	.10	.25
229 Zdeno Ciger	.05	.15
230 Gary Roberts	.05	.15
231 Andy Moog	.10	.25
232 Ed Patterson	.05	.15
233 Philippe Bozon	.07	.20
234 Brent Hughes	.05	.15
235 Chris Pronger	.10	.25
236 Travis Green	.07	.20
237 Pat Conacher	.05	.15
238 Bob Rouse	.05	.15
239 Yves Racine	.05	.15
240 Nelson Emerson	.05	.15
241 Oleg Petrov	.05	.15
242 Steve Larmer	.07	.20
243 Dan Laperriere	.05	.15
244 John McIntyre	.05	.15
245 Alexander Semak	.05	.15
246 Stephane Fiset UER	.07	.20
247 Peter Bondra	.07	.20
248 Dale Hawerchuk	.12	.30
249 Jamie Baker	.05	.15
250 Sergei Fedorov	.15	.40
251 Derek Mayer	.05	.15
252 Ivan Droppa	.05	.15
253 Kent Manderville	.05	.15
254 Sergei Zholtok	.05	.15
255 Murray Craven	.05	.15
256 Todd Krygier	.05	.15
257 Brent Grieve RC	.05	.15
258 Esa Tikkanen	.05	.15
259 Brad Dalgarno	.05	.15
260 Russ Romaniuk	.05	.15
261 Stu Barnes	.05	.15
262 Dan Keczmer	.05	.15
263 Eric Desjardins	.07	.20
264 Martin Brodeur TW	.25	.60
265 Adam Graves TW	.05	.15
266 Cam Neely TW	.10	.25
267 Ray Bourque TW	.15	.40
268 Sergei Fedorov TW	.15	.40
269 Dominik Hasek TW	.20	.50
270 Wayne Gretzky TW	.50	1.25

1994-95 Stadium Club Members Only Parallel

Issued to Stadium Club members only, this set parallels the basic cards with the exception of the words "Topps Stadium Club Members Only" printed on the card front.
COMPLETE SET (270) 150.00 300.00
*MEMBERS ONLY: 3X TO 8X BASIC CARDS

1994-95 Stadium Club First Day Issue

This is a parallel to the 270 card basic set, inserted at a rate of 1:24 packs. The only difference is the silver foil "First Day Issue" logo on the card front.
*VETS: 15X TO 40X BASIC CARDS

1994-95 Stadium Club Dynasty and Destiny

According to published odds, the five cards in this set were randomly inserted at the rate of 1:24 packs. Collector and dealer reports suggest they are available at a much easier rate than listed. Each card features two players; one veteran and an up and coming player with the same type of skills. Photos and stats for each player are on the backs. Each card is numbered out of ten, signifying that five more cards were to be included in the never-produced second series.

Card	Low	High
COMPLETE SET (5)	5.00	12.00
1 T.Barrasso/A.Irbe	1.25	3.00
2 M.Messier/E.Lindros	1.50	4.00
3 B.Hull/P.Bure	2.00	5.00
4 Robitaille/Renberg	1.25	3.00
5 C.Chelios/C.Pronger	1.50	4.00

1994-95 Stadium Club Dynasty and Destiny Members Only Parallel

Issued to Stadium Club members only, this set parallels the basic cards with the exception of the words "Topps Stadium Club Members Only" printed on the card front.
*MEMBERS ONLY: .6X TO 1.5X BASIC CARD

1994-95 Stadium Club Finest Inserts

The nine cards in this set were inserted at the rate of 1:12 packs. The cards offer a completely different design from those of the basic Finest set which was released later in the season. These cards feature a cut-out player photo on a blue textured background. The player name is printed on a multi-color bar on the bottom of the card. Backs feature a small photo on the left with text information and limited stats. Cards are numbered out of nine.

Card	Low	High
COMPLETE SET (9)	15.00	40.00
1 Mario Lemieux	5.00	12.00
2 Brett Hull	1.25	3.00
3 Mark Messier	1.00	2.50
4 Wayne Gretzky	6.00	15.00
5 Pavel Bure	1.00	2.50
6 Sergei Fedorov	1.50	4.00
7 Brian Leetch	1.00	2.50
8 Ray Bourque	1.50	4.00
9 Patrick Roy	5.00	12.00

1994-95 Stadium Club Finest Inserts Members Only Parallel

Issued to Stadium Club members only, this set parallels the basic cards with the exception of the words "Topps Stadium Club Members Only" printed on the card front.
*MEMBERS ONLY: .6X TO 1.5X BASIC CARD

1994-95 Stadium Club Super Teams

The 26 cards in this set were inserted at the rate of 1:24 packs. The card fronts feature a photo of multiple players, or team action shot. The team name and set name are printed in speckled silver foil. Unlike most other inserts, these cards were part of an interactive game which allowed the holder to redeem the card for prizes if the pictured team won a division, conference or Stanley Cup championship. The backs have contest information and the teams record from the 1993-94 season. Holders of the New Jersey Devils card were able to redeem it for complete, specially stamped sets of Stadium Club and Finest. Winning division (Calgary, Detroit, Philadelphia, Quebec) and conference (Detroit, New Jersey) team cards were redeemable for packages of special stamped cards featuring members of that team.

Card	Low	High
COMPLETE SET (26)	25.00	60.00
1 Anaheim Mighty Ducks	1.00	2.50
2 Bruins/Oates/Bourque	1.00	2.50
3 Sabres/D.Hasek	1.00	2.50
4 Flames/Trefilov/Fleury	1.00	2.50
5 Blackhawks/E.Belfour	1.00	2.50
6 Stars/M.Modano	1.00	2.50
7 Detroit Red Wings	2.00	5.00
8 Edmonton Oilers	1.00	2.50
9 Florida Panthers	1.00	2.50
10 Hartford Whalers	1.00	2.50
11 Los Angeles Kings	1.00	2.50
12 Canadiens/P.Roy	2.50	6.00
13 Devils/M.Brodeur WIN	4.00	10.00
14 New York Islanders	1.00	2.50
15 Rangers/M.Messier	2.00	5.00
16 Ottawa Senators	1.00	2.50
17 Flyers/Lindros/Recchi/Bowen	1.00	2.50
18 Pittsburgh Penguins	2.00	5.00
19 Nordiques/J.Sakic	2.00	5.00
20 Blues/C.Joseph	1.00	2.50
21 San Jose Sharks	1.00	2.50
22 Tampa Bay Lightning	1.00	2.50
23 Toronto Maple Leafs	1.00	2.50
24 Canucks/P.Bure	2.00	5.00
25 Washington Capitals	1.00	2.50
26 Jets/Selanne/Zhamnov	2.00	5.00

1994-95 Stadium Club Super Teams Members Only Parallel

*MEMBERS ONLY: .6X TO 1.5X BASIC CARD

1994-95 Stadium Club Super Team Winner

These cards were the prizes of the interactive game which allowed the holder to redeem the card if the pictured team won a division, conference or Stanley Cup championship. Holders of the New Jersey Devils card were able to redeem it for complete, specially stamped sets of Stadium Club and Finest. Winning division (Calgary, Detroit, Philadelphia, Quebec) and conference (Detroit, New Jersey) team cards were redeemable for packages of special stamped cards featuring members of that team.
COMPLETE SET (270) 50.00 100.00
*ST WINNERS: 2X TO 5X BASIC CARDS

1995 Stadium Club Members Only 50

Topps produced a 50-card boxed set for each of the four major sports. With their club membership, members received one set of their choice and had the option of purchasing additional sets for $10.00 each. The five Finest cards (46-50) represent Topps' selection of the top 1994-95 rookies. The color action photos on the fronts have brightly-colored backgrounds and carry the distinctive Topps Stadium Club Members Only gold foil seal. The backs present a second color photo and player profile.

Card	Low	High
COMP. FACT SET (50)	10.00	25.00
1 Patrick Roy	1.00	2.50
2 Ray Bourque	.20	.50
3 Brian Leetch	.20	.50
4 Cam Neely	.15	.40
5 Jaromir Jagr	.60	1.50
6 Alexander Mogilny	.15	.40
7 John Vanbiesbrouck	.40	1.00
8 Geoff Sanderson	.05	.15
9 Mark Recchi	.08	.25
10 Scott Stevens	.02	.10
11 Roman Hamrlik	.05	.15
12 Dominik Hasek	.40	1.00
13 Joe Sakic	.40	1.00
14 Alexei Yashin	.20	.50
15 Eric Lindros	.60	1.50
16 Adam Oates	.08	.25
17 Ulf Samuelsson	.02	.10
18 Wendel Clark	.05	.15
19 Mark Messier	.30	.75
20 Pierre Turgeon	.08	.25
21 Mark Tinordi	.02	.10
22 Ron Francis	.08	.25
23 Jeff Brown	.02	.10
24 Tom Kurvers	.02	.10
25 Mike Modano	.30	.75
26 Mats Sundin	.20	.50
27 Jeremy Roenick	.20	.50
28 Kevin Hatcher	.02	.10
29 Curtis Joseph	.20	.50
30 Paul Coffey	.20	.50
31 Jason Arnott	.08	.25
32 Wayne Gretzky	1.25	3.00
33 Theo Fleury	.20	.50
34 Al MacInnis	.07	.20
35 Ed Belfour	.20	.50
36 Sergei Fedorov	.40	1.00
37 Brett Hull	.30	.75
38 Chris Chelios	.20	.50
39 Keith Tkachuk	.30	.75
40 Felix Potvin	.20	.50
41 Pavel Bure	.40	1.00
42 Ulf Dahlen	.02	.10
43 Teemu Selanne	.40	1.00
44 Doug Gilmour	.20	.50

45 Phil Housley .05 .15
46 Paul Kariya FIN 2.50 6.00
47 Peter Forsberg FIN 2.00 5.00
48 Jim Carey FIN .60 1.50
49 Todd Marchant FIN .20 .50
50 Blaine Lacher FIN .30 .75

1995-96 Stadium Club

The 1995-96 Stadium Club set was issued in one series totaling 225 cards. The 10-card packs retail for $2.50. The set features two subsets: Extreme Corps (163-189) and Extreme Rookies (190-207). One EC or ER subset card was included per hobby or retail pack (1:2 Canadian packs), making them somewhat more difficult to obtain than regular singles. Of note is the Stadium Club logo on the card fronts, which features the brand name translated into the primary language of the player featured. Rookie Cards in this set include Daniel Alfredsson. Two card number 2 were issued, no card #21.

1 Alexander Mogilny .07 .20
2A Ray Bourque .15 .40
2B Bill Ranford UER .07 .20
3 Garry Galley .05 .15
4 Glen Wesley .05 .15
5 Dave Andreychuk .10 .25
6 Daren Puppa .07 .20
7 Shayne Corson .05 .15
8 Kelly Hrudey .07 .20
9 Russ Courtnall .05 .15
10 Chris Chelios .10 .25
11 Ulf Samuelsson .05 .15
12 Mike Vernon .07 .20
13 Al MacInnis .10 .25
14 Joel Otto .05 .15
15 Patrick Roy .25 .60
16 Steve Thomas .07 .20
17 Pat Verbeek .07 .20
18 Joe Nieuwendyk .10 .25
19 Todd Krygier .05 .15
20 Steve Yzerman .12 .30
22 Ron Francis .12 .30
23 Sylvain Cote .05 .15
24 Grant Fuhr .10 .25
25 Brendan Shanahan .12 .30
26 John MacLean .07 .20
27 Darren Turcotte .05 .15
28 Bernie Nicholls .05 .15
29 Sean Burke .05 .15
30 Brian Leetch .10 .25
31 Dave Gagner .05 .15
32 Rick Tocchet .07 .20
33 Ron Hextall .10 .25
34 Paul Coffey .10 .25
35 John Vanbiesbrouck .07 .20
36 Rod Brind'Amour .10 .25
37 Brian Savage .05 .15
38 Nelson Emerson .05 .15
39 Brian Bradley .07 .20
40 Adam Oates .10 .25
41 Kirk McLean .07 .20
42 Kevin Hatcher .07 .20
43 Mike Keane .05 .15
44 Don Beaupre .07 .20
45 Scott Stevens .10 .25
46 Dale Hawerchuk .12 .30
47 Scott Young .05 .15
48 Mark Recchi .12 .30
49 Mike Richter .10 .25
50 Kevin Stevens .07 .20
51 Mike Ridley .05 .15
52 Joe Murphy .05 .15
53 Stephane Fiset .07 .20
54 Donald Audette .07 .20
55 Ed Belfour .07 .20
56 Rob Blake .07 .20
57 Adam Graves .07 .20
58 Arturs Irbe .07 .20
59 Mathieu Schneider .05 .15
60 Dominik Hasek .12 .30
61 Andrew Cassels .05 .15
62 Johan Garpenlov .05 .15
63 Kyle McLaren RC .05 .15
64 Petr Nedved .07 .20
65 Owen Nolan .10 .25
66 Keith Primeau .05 .15
67 Mark Tinordi .05 .15
68 Dimitri Khristich .05 .15
69 Chris Pronger .10 .25
70 Jaromir Jagr .25 .60
71 Mike Ricci .07 .20
72 Trevor Kidd .07 .20
73 Stu Barnes .05 .15
74 Doug Weight .10 .25
75 Mats Sundin .10 .25
76 Scott Niedermayer .10 .25
77 John LeClair .10 .25
78 Derian Hatcher .07 .20
79 Brad May .05 .15
80 Felix Potvin .10 .25
81 Derek King .07 .20
82 Guy Hebert .07 .20
83 Shawn McEachern .05 .15
84 Slava Kozlov .07 .20
85 Martin Brodeur .25 .60
86 Ray Whitney .07 .20
87 Martin Straka .05 .15
88 Keith Jones .07 .20
89 Roman Hamrlik .05 .15
90 Keith Tkachuk .10 .25
91 Jim Dowd .05 .15
92 Sergei Zubov .07 .20
93 Bryan McCabe .10 .25
94 Rob Niedermayer .07 .20
95 Alexei Zhamnov .10 .25
96 Zarley Zalapski .05 .15
97 Alexandre Daigle .05 .15
98 Jocelyn Thibault .07 .20
99 Zigmund Palffy .10 .25
100 Luc Robitaille .10 .25
101 Radek Bonk .05 .15
102 Todd Marchant .05 .15
103 Todd Harvey .05 .15
104 Blaine Lacher .07 .20
105 Peter Forsberg .25 .60
106 Jeff Friesen .05 .15
107 Kenny Jonsson .10 .25
108 Brett Lindros .05 .15
109 David Oliver .05 .15
110 Mikael Renberg .07 .20
111 Alexander Selivanov .07 .20
112 Stanislav Neckar .05 .15
113 Oleg Tverdovsky .10 .25
114 Shean Donovan .05 .15
115 Jim Carey .07 .20
116 Tony Granato .05 .15
117 Tony Amonte .07 .20
118 Tomas Sandstrom .07 .20
119 Rick Tabaracci .07 .20
120 Ray Ferraro .05 .15
121 Brian Noonan .05 .15
122 Miroslav Satan RC .12 .30
123 Sergio Momesso .05 .15
124 Gary Suter .07 .20
125 Eric Desjardins .07 .20
126 Steve Duchesne .05 .15
127 Zdeno Ciger .07 .20
128 Cliff Ronning .05 .15
129 Nicklas Lidstrom .10 .25
130 Bill Guerin .07 .20
131 Igor Korolev .05 .15
132 Roman Oksiuta .05 .15
133 Jesse Belanger .05 .15
134 Chris Gratton .05 .15
135 Chris Osgood .07 .20
136 Pat Peake .05 .15
137 Viktor Kozlov .07 .20
138 Aaron Gavey .05 .15
139 Zdenek Nedved .05 .15
140 Rhett Warrener .05 .15
141 Marko Kiprusoff .07 .20
142 Dan Quinn .07 .20
143 Alexei Zhitnik .05 .15
144 Larry Murphy .10 .25
145 Phil Housley .07 .20
146 Don Sweeney .05 .15
147 Jason Dawe .05 .15
148 Marcus Ragnarsson RC .12 .30
149 Andrei Nikolishin .05 .15
150 Dino Ciccarelli .07 .20
151 Jari Kurri .10 .25
152 Bob Probert .07 .20
153 Randy McKay .05 .15
154 Michael Nylander .05 .15
155 Wendel Clark .10 .25
156 Antti Tormanen RC .05 .15
157 Nikolai Khabibulin .07 .20
158 Tom Barrasso .07 .20
159 Vincent Damphousse .07 .20
160 Trevor Linden .10 .25
161 Valeri Kamensky .07 .20
162 Mike Gartner .10 .25
163 Cam Neely EC .25 .60
164 Pat LaFontaine EC .25 .60
165 Theo Fleury EC .30 .75
166 Jeremy Roenick EC .30 .75
167 Joe Sakic EC .40 1.00
168 Mike Modano EC .40 1.00
169 Sergei Fedorov EC .40 1.00
170 Scott Mellanby EC .20 .50
171 Jason Arnott EC .20 .50
172 Geoff Sanderson EC .15 .40
173 Wayne Gretzky EC 1.25 3.00
174 Paul Kariya EC .30 .75
175 Pierre Turgeon EC .25 .60
176 Stephane Richer EC .20 .50
177 Kirk Muller EC .20 .50
178 Mark Messier EC .40 1.00
179 Craig Janney EC .15 .40
180 Mario Lemieux EC .75 2.00
181 Eric Lindros EC .40 1.00
182 Alexei Yashin EC .20 .50
183 Brett Hull EC .30 .75
184 Doug Gilmour EC .30 .75
185 Petr Klima EC .15 .40
186 Pavel Bure EC .30 .75
187 Joe Juneau EC .20 .50
188 Teemu Selanne EC .50 1.25
189 Claude Lemieux EC .25 .60
190 Vitali Yachmenev ER .25 .60
191 Jason Bonsignore ER .15 .40
192 Jeff O'Neill ER .25 .60
193 Brendan Witt ER .25 .60
194 Brian Holzinger ER RC .50 1.25
195 Eric Daze ER .50 1.25
196 Ed Jovanovski ER .25 .60
197 Deron Quint ER .20 .50
198 Marty Murray ER .25 .60
199 Jere Lehtinen ER .20 .50
200 Radek Dvorak ER RC .30 .75
201 Aki Berg ER RC .25 .60
202 Chad Kilger ER RC .25 .60
203 Saku Koivu ER .25 .60
204 Todd Bertuzzi ER RC .30 .75
205 Niklas Sundstrom ER .25 .60
206 Daniel Alfredsson ER RC 1.25 3.00
207 Shane Doan ER RC .75 2.00
208 Richard Park .25 .60
209 Peter Bondra .25 .60
210 Bryan Smolinski .15 .40
211 Tommy Salo .40 1.00
212 Patrick Poulin .15 .40
213 Mathieu Dandenault RC .50 1.25
214 Steve Rucchin .20 .50
215 Ray Sheppard .20 .50
216 Robert Svehla RC .15 .40
217 Olaf Kolzig .20 .50
218 Alexei Kovalev .15 .40
219 Ian Moran .15 .40
220 Valeri Bure .15 .40
221 Dean Malkoc .15 .40
222 Jason Doig .25 .60
223 David Nemirovsky RC .20 .50
224 Jamie Pushor .20 .50
225 Ricard Persson .20 .50

1995-96 Stadium Club Members Only Parallel

Parallel to base set that was only available to members of Topps Stadium Club. Cards are distinguishable by an embossed Members only logo.

COMPLETE SET (225) 150.00 300.00
*MEMBERS ONLY: 3X TO 8X BASIC CARDS

1995-96 Stadium Club Extreme North

Randomly inserted in packs at a rate of 1:48, this 9-card set focuses on some of the best players on Canadian teams. The cards are printed on diffraction foil.

COMPLETE SET (9) 20.00 40.00
EN1 Pavel Bure 2.00 5.00
EN2 Teemu Selanne 2.00 5.00
EN3 Felix Potvin 2.00 5.00
EN4 Patrick Roy 8.00 20.00
EN5 Theo Fleury 1.25 3.00
EN6 Bill Ranford 1.25 3.00
EN7 Pierre Turgeon 1.25 3.00
EN8 Doug Gilmour 1.25 3.00
EN9 Alexander Mogilny 1.25 3.00

1995-96 Stadium Club Extreme North Members Only Parallel

Issued to Stadium Club members only, this set parallels the basic cards with the exception of the words "Topp's Stadium Club Members Only" printed on the card front.

*MEMBERS ONLY: .6X TO 1.5X BASIC INSERTS

1995-96 Stadium Club Fearless

Randomly inserted at a rate of 1:24 retail, and 1:48 hobby and Canadian packs, this 9-card set features hockey's toughest players on double diffraction foil-stamped cards.

COMPLETE SET (9) 8.00 15.00
F1 Brendan Shanahan 1.50 4.00
F2 Chris Chelios 1.50 4.00
F3 Keith Primeau .75 2.00
F4 Scott Stevens 1.25 3.00
F5 Rick Tocchet 1.25 3.00
F6 Kevin Stevens .75 2.00
F7 Ulf Samuelsson .75 2.00
F8 Wendel Clark 1.25 3.00
F9 Keith Tkachuk 1.50 4.00

1995-96 Stadium Club Fearless Members Only Parallel

Issued to Stadium Club members only, this set parallels the basic cards with the exception of the words "Topp's Stadium Club Members Only" printed on the card front.

*MEMBERS ONLY: .6X TO 1.5X BASIC INSERTS

1995-96 Stadium Club Generation TSC

COMPLETE SET (9) 15.00 30.00
GT1 Paul Kariya 1.50 4.00
GT2 Teemu Selanne 1.50 4.00
GT3 Jaromir Jagr 2.00 5.00
GT4 Peter Forsberg 3.00 8.00
GT5 Martin Brodeur 4.00 10.00
GT6 Jim Carey .75 2.00
GT7 Mikael Renberg .75 2.00
GT8 Scott Niedermayer .75 2.00
GT9 Ed Jovanovski .75 2.00

1995-96 Stadium Club Generation TSC Members Only Parallel

Issued to Stadium Club members only, this set parallels the basic cards with the exception of the words "Topp's Stadium Club Members Only" printed on the card front.

*MEMBERS ONLY: .6X TO 1.5X BASIC INSERTS

1995-96 Stadium Club Metalists

Randomly inserted at a rate of 1:48 hobby, 1:96 retail, and 1:192 Canadian packs, this 12-card set showcases players who have won two or more major awards during their career on the first ever laser-cut foil hockey cards.

COMPLETE SET (12) 25.00 60.00
M1 Wayne Gretzky 10.00 25.00
M2 Mario Lemieux 6.00 15.00
M3 Patrick Roy 6.00 15.00
M4 Ray Bourque 1.50 4.00
M5 Ed Belfour 1.50 4.00
M6 Tom Barrasso 1.00 2.50
M7 Joe Mullen 1.00 2.50
M8 Brian Leetch 1.00 2.50
M9 Mark Messier 1.50 4.00
M10 Dominik Hasek 3.00 8.00
M11 Paul Coffey 1.00 2.50
M12 Guy Carbonneau 1.00 2.50

1995-96 Stadium Club Metalists Members Only Parallel

Issued to Stadium Club members only, this set parallels the basic cards with the exception of the words "Topp's Stadium Club Members Only" printed on the card front.

*MEMBERS ONLY: .6X TO 1.5X BASIC INSERTS

1995-96 Stadium Club Nemeses

Randomly inserted at a rate of 1:24 hobby, 1:48 retail, and 1:96 Canadian packs, this 9-card set highlights two rival players together on one card. The cards use etched foil on each side.

COMPLETE SET (9) 25.00 60.00
N1 E.Lindros/S.Stevens 1.50 4.00
N2 W.Gretzky/M.Lemieux 10.00 25.00
N3 C.Lemieux/C.Neely 1.50 4.00
N4 P.Bure/M.Richter 1.50 4.00
N5 B.Leetch/R.Bourque 2.50 6.00
N6 M.Brodeur/D.Hasek 4.00 10.00
N7 D.Gilmour/S.Fedorov 2.50 6.00
N8 M.Messier/J.Otto 1.50 4.00
N9 P.Kariya/P.Forsberg 4.00 10.00

1995-96 Stadium Club Nemeses Members Only Parallel

Issued to Stadium Club members only, this set parallels the basic cards with the exception of the words "Topp's Stadium Club Members Only" printed on the card front.

*MEMBERS ONLY: .6X TO 1.5X BASIC INSERTS

1995-96 Stadium Club Power Streak

Randomly inserted at a rate of 1:12 retail, and 1:24 hobby and Canadian packs, this set features 10 players who have sustained prolonged goal scoring streaks. The cards are printed using Power Matrix technology.

COMPLETE SET (10) 5.00 12.00
PS1 Pierre Turgeon .40 1.00
PS2 Eric Lindros 1.25 3.00
PS3 Ron Francis .75 2.00
PS4 Paul Coffey .75 2.00
PS5 Mikael Renberg .40 1.00
PS6 John LeClair .40 1.00
PS7 Dino Ciccarelli .40 1.00
PS8 Wendel Clark .75 2.00
PS9 Brett Hull 1.25 3.00
PS10 Stephane Richer .40 1.00

1995-96 Stadium Club Power Streak Members Only Parallel

Issued to Stadium Club members only, this set parallels the basic cards with the exception of the words "Topp's Stadium Club Members Only" printed on the card front.

*MEMBERS ONLY: .6X TO 1.5X BASIC INSERTS

1995-96 Stadium Club Master Photo Test

This nine-card set measures approximately 3" by 5" and features color action player photos from the 1995-96 Stadium Club set inside a black border bearing the words Master Photo. The backs carry the TSC, NHL, and NHLPA logos. No further information on origin or distribution is available. The cards are unnumbered and checklisted below in alphabetical order. This may be an incomplete checklist; additional information would be appreciated.

COMPLETE SET (9) 25.00 60.00
1 Jason Arnott 2.00 5.00
2 Theo Fleury 4.00 10.00
3 Doug Gilmour 4.00 10.00
4 Trevor Linden 4.00 10.00
5 Kirk McLean 2.00 5.00
6 Alexander Mogilny 2.00 5.00
7 Felix Potvin 4.00 10.00
8 Mats Sundin 6.00 15.00
9 Alexei Yashin 2.00 5.00

1996 Stadium Club Members Only 50

This 50-card set was available through the direct marketing arm of the Topps Stadium Club. The first 45 cards feature the competitors in the 1996 NHL All-Star Game. The players are pictured in their AS sweaters over a stylized background. the back includes a portrait and player profile. The final five cards in the set picture some of the year's top rookies on Finest-style technology.

COMPLETE SET (50) 8.00 20.00
1 Wayne Gretzky 1.50 4.00
2 Paul Kariya 1.00 2.50
3 Brett Hull .30 .75
4 Chris Chelios .25 .60
5 Paul Coffey .25 .60
6 Ed Belfour .25 .60
7 Theo Fleury .25 .60
8 Owen Nolan .08 .25
9 Al MacInnis .08 .25
10 Alexander Mogilny .20 .50
11 Kevin Hatcher .02 .10
12 Doug Weight .15 .40
13 Felix Potvin .20 .50
14 Teemu Selanne .50 1.25
15 Sergei Fedorov .50 1.25
16 Larry Murphy .02 .10
17 Joe Sakic .50 1.25
18 Mats Sundin .25 .60
19 Nicklas Lidstrom .08 .25
20 Peter Forsberg .60 1.50
21 Chris Osgood .25 .60
22 Mike Gartner .05 .15
23 D.Savard .05 .15
C.MacTavish
24 Mario Lemieux 1.25 3.00
25 Jaromir Jagr .75 2.00
26 Brendan Shanahan .50 1.25
27 Scott Stevens .05 .15
28 Ray Bourque .30 .75
29 Martin Brodeur .60 1.50
30 Eric Lindros .75 2.00
31 Peter Bondra .25 .60
32 Scott Mellanby .02 .10
33 Brian Leetch .25 .60
34 John Vanbiesbrouck .25 .60
35 Pat Verbeek .07 .20
36 Cam Neely .20 .50
37 Roman Hamrlik .15 .40
38 Daniel Alfredsson .20 .50
39 Pierre Turgeon .20 .50
40 Mark Messier .30 .75
41 Eric Desjardins .02 .10
42 Dominik Hasek .50 1.25
43 John LeClair .40 1.00
44 Mathieu Schneider .02 .10
45 Ron Francis .20 .50
46 Saku Koivu 1.25 3.00
47 Ed Jovanovski .75 2.00
48 Vitali Yachmenev .40 1.00
49 Petr Sykora .75 2.00
50 Eric Daze .75 2.00

1999-00 Stadium Club Promos

Sent out to dealers with the press release for Stadium Club, this 6-card set debuts the new card design for the 1999-2000 brand.

COMPLETE SET (6) .75 2.00
PP1 Chris Osgood .20 .50
PP2 Steve Konowalchuk .08 .25
PP3 Jeremy Roenick .40 1.00
PP4 Rod Brind'Amour .20 .50
PP5 Mattias Norstrom .08 .25
PP6 Clarke Wilm .08 .25

1999-00 Stadium Club

Released as a 200-card set, Stadium Club featured flawless player action shots and blue foil highlights on every base card. Stadium Club was packaged in 24-pack boxes with packs containing six cards and one checklist. Packs carried a suggested retail price of $2.00.

COMPLETE SET (200) 30.00 60.00
1 Jaromir Jagr .30 .75
2 Mats Sundin .20 .50
3 Mark Messier .20 .50
4 Paul Kariya .20 .50
5 Ray Bourque .30 .75
6 Tony Amonte .15 .40
7 Dominik Hasek .40 1.00
8 Peter Forsberg .50 1.25
9 Pavel Bure .20 .50
10 Nicklas Lidstrom .20 .50
11 Kenny Jonsson .05 .15
12 Brian Leetch .20 .50
13 Eric Lindros .20 .50
14 Al MacInnis .15 .40
15 Keith Tkachuk .20 .50
16 Martin Brodeur .60 1.50
17 Saku Koivu .20 .50
18 Jeff Friesen .05 .15
19 Olaf Kolzig .15 .40
20 Mike Modano .30 .75
21 Jarome Iginla .25 .60
22 Alexei Kovalev .05 .15
23 Vincent Lecavalier .20 .50
24 Greg Johnson .05 .15
25 Ron Francis .15 .40
26 Steve Konowalchuk .05 .15
27 Luc Robitaille .15 .40
28 Alexei Yashin .05 .15
29 Mark Parrish .05 .15
30 Todd Warriner .05 .15
31 Brett Hull .25 .60
32 Steve Dubinsky .05 .15
33 Rod Brind'Amour .15 .40
34 Bill Muckalt .05 .15
35 Bryan Berard .05 .15
36 Manny Malhotra .15 .40
37 Jozef Stumpel .15 .40
38 Sergei Fedorov .30 .75
39 Roman Vopat .15 .40
40 Teemu Selanne .20 .50
41 Teppo Numminen .05 .15
42 Mats Lindgren .05 .15
43 Chris Gratton .05 .15
44 Owen Nolan .15 .40
45 Scott Niedermayer .05 .15
46 Sergei Krivokrasov .05 .15
47 Joe Sakic .40 1.00
48 Bill Guerin .05 .15
49 Shayne Corson .05 .15
50 Eric Daze .15 .40
51 Clarke Wilm .05 .15
52 Magnus Arvedson .05 .15
53 Sergei Berezin .05 .15
54 Derian Hatcher .05 .15
55 Jeremy Roenick .25 .60
56 Adam Oates .15 .40
57 Dixon Ward .05 .15
58 Petr Nedved .15 .40
59 Joe Reekie .05 .15
60 Milan Hejduk .20 .50
61 Mike Grier .05 .15
62 Martin Straka .05 .15
63 Petr Sykora .05 .15
64 Harry York .05 .15
65 John LeClair .20 .50
66 Patrick Roy .60 1.50
67 Arturs Irbe .15 .40
68 Murray Baron .05 .15
69 Felix Potvin .30 .75
70 Pavol Demitra .15 .40
71 Ray Whitney .15 .40
72 Patrick Marleau .20 .50
73 Tom Fitzgerald .05 .15
74 Jamal Mayers .05 .15
75 Joe Thornton .30 .75
76 Craig Rivet .05 .15
77 Ed Belfour .20 .50
78 Stephane Fiset .15 .40
79 Alexander Karpovtsev .05 .15
80 Miroslav Satan .05 .15
81 Doug Weight .15 .40
82 Marian Hossa .20 .50
83 Markus Naslund .20 .50
84 Derek Morris .05 .15
85 Mike Richter .20 .50
86 Scott Young .05 .15
87 Darcy Tucker .05 .15
88 Jason Allison .05 .15
89 Chris Osgood .15 .40
90 Doug Gilmour .15 .40
91 Ron Tugnutt .15 .40
92 Adam Deadmarsh .05 .15
93 Byron Dafoe .15 .40
94 Rick Tocchet .15 .40
95 Mike Johnson .05 .15
96 Guy Hebert .15 .40
97 Cory Stillman .15 .40
98 Daniel Alfredsson .15 .40
99 Tom Barrasso .15 .40
100 Peter Bondra .15 .40
101 Rob Blake .15 .40
102 Gary Roberts .05 .15
103 Cliff Ronning .15 .40
104 Jason Woolley .05 .15
105 Keith Primeau .05 .15
106 Brendan Shanahan .20 .50
107 Alexei Zhamnov .15 .40
108 Bobby Holik .05 .15
109 Mark Recchi .15 .40
110 Eric Brewer .05 .15
111 Mike Ricci .15 .40
112 Pierre Turgeon .15 .40
113 Martin Rucinsky .05 .15
114 Chris McAllister RC .05 .15
115 Patrik Elias .15 .40
116 Alexander Selivanov .05 .15
117 Fredrik Olausson .05 .15
118 Curtis Joseph .20 .50
119 Wade Redden .05 .15
120 Nikolai Khabibulin .15 .40
121 Chris Drury .15 .40
122 Chris Chelios .20 .50
123 Vincent Damphousse .05 .15
124 Mattias Ohlund .15 .40
125 Mike Dunham .15 .40
126 John Vanbiesbrouck .15 .40
127 John MacLean .15 .40
128 Jocelyn Thibault .15 .40
129 Jan Hrdina .05 .15
130 Mariusz Czerkawski .05 .15
131 Pavel Kubina .05 .15
132 Scott Stevens .15 .40
133 Mattias Norstrom .05 .15
134 Sami Kapanen .05 .15
135 Sergei Samsonov .15 .40
136 Tom Poti .05 .15
137 Steve Shields .15 .40
138 Anson Carter .15 .40
139 Chris McAlpine .05 .15
140 Rob Niedermayer .05 .15
141 Michael Peca .05 .15
142 Valeri Bure .05 .15
143 Joe Nieuwendyk .15 .40
144 Jose Theodore .25 .60
145 Steve Yzerman 1.00 2.50
146 Chris Pronger .15 .40
147 Marty McInnis .05 .15
148 Jere Lehtinen .15 .40
149 Adam Graves .05 .15
150 Deron Quint .05 .15
151 Ray Ferraro .05 .15
152 Niklas Sundstrom .05 .15
153 Damian Rhodes .15 .40
154 Zigmund Palffy .15 .40
155 Valeri Kamensky .15 .40
156 Oleg Tverdovsky .15 .40
157 Bill Ranford .15 .40
158 Kelly Buchberger .05 .15
159 Trevor Linden .05 .15
160 Bryan McCabe .05 .15
161 Dan Cloutier .05 .15
162 Olli Jokinen .15 .40
163 Theo Fleury .05 .15
164 Dave Andreychuk .15 .40
165 Gord Murphy .05 .15
166 Steve Duchesne .15 .40
167 Marc Savard .05 .15
168 Maxim Afinogenov .05 .15
169 Mark Eaton RC .15 .40
170 Pavel Patera RC .05 .15
171 Nikolai Antropov RC .60 1.50
172 Ivan Novoseltsev RC .40 1.00
173 Jochen Hecht RC 1.00 2.50
174 Mike Ribeiro .05 .15
175 Yuri Butsayev RC .05 .15
176 Jorgen Jonsson RC .05 .15
177 Dan Hinote RC .20 .50
178 Dave Tanabe .05 .15
179 John Grahame RC .50 1.25
180 Mika Alatalo RC .15 .40
181 Patrik Stefan RC .40 1.00
182 Mike Fisher RC .40 1.00
183 Niclas Havelid RC .15 .40
184 Paul Comrie RC .05 .15
185 Michal Rozsival RC .05 .15
186 Oleg Saprykin RC .40 1.00
187 Martin Skoula RC .20 .50
188 Simon Gagne .20 .50
189 Brian Rafalski RC .50 1.25
190 J-P Dumont .15 .40
191 Martin Biron .15 .40
192 Rico Fata .05 .15
193 Jan Hlavac .05 .15
194 Alex Tanguay .15 .40
195 Brad Stuart .15 .40
196 Brian Boucher .20 .50
197 Steve Kariya RC .20 .50
198 Scott Gomez .05 .15
199 Tim Connolly .25 .60
200 David Legwand .15 .40

1999-00 Stadium Club First Day Issue

Randomly inserted in Retail packs at the rate of one in 12, this 200-card set parallels the base Stadium Club set. Each card is enhanced with a foil "First Day Issue" stamp and is sequentially numbered to 150.

*VETS: 12.5X TO 30X BASIC CARDS
*ROOKIES: 3X TO 8X BASIC CARDS

1999-00 Stadium Club One of a Kind

Randomly inserted in Hobby packs, this 200-card set parallels the base Stadium Club set. Each card is sequentially numbered to 150.

*VETS: 12.5X TO 25X BASIC CARDS
*ROOKIES: 3X TO 8X BASIC CARDS

1999-00 Stadium Club Capture the Action

Randomly inserted in packs at the rate of 1:12, this 30-card set features blue borders on the top and bottom framing full color close up "in the game" action photographs. "Game View" parallels were also created and inserted at 1:118. The parallels were serial numbered to 100.

COMPLETE SET (30) 40.00 80.00
*GAME VIEW/100: 3X TO 8X BASIC INSERTS
CA1 Bill Muckalt .60 1.50
CA2 Chris Drury .75 2.00
CA3 Milan Hejduk 1.00 2.50
CA4 Mark Parrish .60 1.50
CA5 Marian Hossa 1.00 2.50
CA6 Manny Malhotra .75 2.00
CA7 J-P Dumont .75 2.00
CA8 Eric Brewer .60 1.50
CA9 Vincent Lecavalier 1.00 2.50
CA10 Jan Hrdina .60 1.50
CA11 Paul Kariya 1.00 2.50
CA12 Peter Forsberg 2.50 6.00
CA13 Eric Lindros 1.25 3.00
CA14 Martin Brodeur 2.50 6.00
CA15 Teemu Selanne 1.00 2.50
CA16 Keith Tkachuk 1.00 2.50
CA17 Mats Sundin 1.00 2.50
CA18 Pavel Bure 1.25 3.00
CA19 Mike Modano 1.50 4.00
CA20 Nicklas Lidstrom 1.25 3.00
CA21 Ray Bourque 1.50 4.00
CA22 Dominik Hasek 2.00 5.00
CA23 Patrick Roy 5.00 12.00
CA24 Mark Messier 1.00 2.50
CA25 Steve Yzerman 5.00 12.00
CA26 Jaromir Jagr 1.50 4.00
CA27 Paul Coffey 1.00 2.50
CA28 Brett Hull 1.25 3.00
CA29 Al MacInnis .75 2.00
CA30 Larry Murphy .75 2.00

1999-00 Stadium Club Chrome

Randomly inserted in packs at the rate of 1:4, this 50-card set utilizes the base card style, but issues this set on an all foil card stock. Chrome refractor parallels were also created and inserted at a rate of 1:8.

COMPLETE SET (50) 30.00 60.00
*REFRACTORS: .8X TO 2X BASIC INSERTS
1 Jaromir Jagr 1.00 2.50
2 Mats Sundin .60 1.50
3 Mark Messier .60 1.50
4 Paul Kariya .60 1.50
5 Ray Bourque 1.00 2.50
6 Tony Amonte .50 1.25
7 Dominik Hasek 1.25 3.00
8 Peter Forsberg 1.50 4.00
9 Pavel Bure .60 1.50
10 Nicklas Lidstrom .60 1.50
11 Brian Leetch .50 1.25
12 Eric Lindros .60 1.50
13 Al MacInnis .50 1.25
14 Keith Tkachuk .60 1.50
15 Martin Brodeur 1.50 4.00
16 Saku Koivu .60 1.50
17 Jeff Friesen .50 1.25
18 Mike Modano 1.00 2.50
19 Vincent Lecavalier .60 1.50
20 Luc Robitaille .50 1.25
21 Brett Hull .75 2.00
22 Teemu Selanne .60 1.50
23 Joe Sakic 1.25 3.00
24 Jeremy Roenick .75 2.00
25 John LeClair .60 1.50
26 Patrick Roy 3.00 8.00
27 Joe Thornton 1.00 2.50
28 Ed Belfour .60 1.50
29 Doug Weight .50 1.25
30 Marian Hossa .60 1.50
31 Chris Osgood .50 1.25
32 Daniel Alfredsson .50 1.25
33 Peter Bondra .50 1.25
34 Brendan Shanahan .60 1.50
35 Curtis Joseph .60 1.50
36 Chris Drury .50 1.25
37 Sergei Samsonov .50 1.25
38 Anson Carter .50 1.25
39 Joe Nieuwendyk .50 1.25
40 Steve Yzerman 3.00 8.00
41 Zigmund Palffy .50 1.25
42 Theo Fleury .50 1.25
43 Patrik Stefan 1.00 2.50
44 Simon Gagne .60 1.50
45 J-P Dumont .50 1.25
46 Alex Tanguay .50 1.25
47 Steve Kariya .50 1.25
48 Scott Gomez .50 1.25
49 Tim Connolly .75 2.00
50 David Legwand .50 1.25

1999-00 Stadium Club Chrome Oversized

Inserted one per hobby box, this 20-card set utilizes the same design as the base set on oversized cards. Refractor parallels were also created and inserted randomly.

COMPLETE SET (20) 50.00 100.00
*REFRACTORS: .8X TO 2X BASIC INSERTS
1 Jaromir Jagr 1.50 4.00
2 Mats Sundin 1.00 2.50
3 Paul Kariya 1.00 2.50
4 Ray Bourque 1.50 4.0
5 Dominik Hasek 2.00 5.0
6 Peter Forsberg 2.50 6.0
7 Pavel Bure 1.00 2.5
8 Eric Lindros 1.00 2.5
9 Martin Brodeur 2.50 6.0
10 Mike Modano 1.50 4.0
11 Teemu Selanne 1.00 2.5
12 Joe Sakic 2.00 5.0
13 Patrick Roy 5.00 12.0
14 Marian Hossa 1.00 2.5
15 Curtis Joseph 1.00 2.5
16 Steve Yzerman 5.00 12.0
17 Theo Fleury .75 2.0
18 Patrik Stefan 1.50 4.0
19 Steve Kariya .75 2.0
20 David Legwand .75 2.0

1999-00 Stadium Club Co-Signers

Randomly inserted in Hobby packs at the rate of 1:23 this 15-card set features two autographs on each card. Some cards were issued in exchange form.

CS1 C.Drury/B.Morrison 10.00 25.0
CS2 B.Morrison/M.Hossa 10.00 25.0
CS3 M.Hossa/C.Drury 10.00 25.0
CS4 J.Jagr/M.Sundin 30.00 80.0
CS5 J.Jagr/A.Yashin 25.00 60.0
CS6 J.LeClair/J.Jagr 40.00 100.0
CS7 A.Yashin/M.Sundin 12.00 30.0
CS8 M.Sundin/J.LeClair 12.00 30.0
CS9 A.Yashin/J.LeClair 10.00 25.0
CS10 C.Osgood/E.Belfour 30.00 80.0
CS11 C.Osgd/C.Joseph 25.00 60.0
CS12 E.Belfr/C.Joseph 30.00 80.0
CS13 R.Bourque/A.MacInnis 40.00 100.0
CS14 A.MacInnis/W.Redden 10.00 25.0
CS15 W.Redden/R.Bourque 25.00 60.0

1999-00 Stadium Club Eyes of the Game

Randomly seeded in packs at the rate of 1:15, this 10-card set features colored borders on the top and bottom and close up portrait photography of each respective player. Refractor parallels were also created and inserted at a rate of 1:75.

COMPLETE SET (10) 8.00 15.0
*REFRACTORS: 1.5X TO 4X BASIC INSERTS
EG1 Jaromir Jagr 1.00 2.5
EG2 Peter Forsberg 1.50 4.0
EG3 Paul Kariya .60 1.5
EG4 Teemu Selanne .60 1.5
EG5 Joe Sakic 1.25 3.0
EG6 Eric Lindros .60 1.5
EG7 Jason Allison .50 1.2
EG8 Mats Sundin .60 1.5
EG9 Pavol Demitra .50 1.2
EG10 Rod Brind'Amour .50 1.2

1999-00 Stadium Club Goalie Cam

Randomly seeded in packs at the rate of 1:24, this 7-card set puts collectors on the ice with photography taken from goalie cams.

COMPLETE SET (7) 8.00 15.0
GC1 Dominik Hasek 2.00 5.0
GC2 Martin Brodeur 2.50 6.0
GC3 Byron Dafoe .75 2.0
GC4 Olaf Kolzig .75 2.0
GC5 Mike Richter 1.00 2.5
GC6 Ron Tugnutt .75 2.0
GC7 Tom Barrasso .75 2.0

1999-00 Stadium Club Lone Sta Signatures

Released as a tier insert program, cards LS1-LS3 are seeded at 1:1675, cards LS4-LS9 are seeded at 1:558 card LS10 is seeded at 1:2233, and cards LS11-13 ar seeded at 1:419. Each card features an authentic playe autograph. Some players were released in exchange card form.

LS1 Jaromir Jagr 40.00 100.0
LS2 Alexei Yashin 5.00 12.0
LS3 Mats Sundin 25.00 60.0
LS4 Ray Bourque 25.00 60.0
LS5 Al MacInnis 6.00 15.0
LS6 Wade Redden 5.00 12.0
LS7 Chris Osgood 6.00 15.0
LS8 Ed Belfour 8.00 20.0
LS9 Curtis Joseph 20.00 50.0
LS10 John LeClair 8.00 20.0
LS11 Chris Drury 6.00 15.0
LS12 Brendan Morrison 6.00 15.0
LS13 Marian Hossa 8.00 20.0

1999-00 Stadium Club Onyx Extreme

Randomly inserted in packs at the rate of 1:15, this 10 card set features black textured borders around full color action player photos. Each card is enhanced wit silver foil highlights. A die-cut parallel was also created and inserted at a rate of 1:75.

COMPLETE SET (10) 8.00 15.0
*DIE-CUT: 1.5X TO 4X BASIC INSERTS
OE1 Jaromir Jagr 1.00 2.5
OE2 Peter Forsberg 1.50 4.0
OE3 Dominik Hasek 1.25 3.0
OE4 Eric Lindros .50 1.2
OE5 Paul Kariya .50 1.2
OE6 Joe Sakic 1.25 3.0
OE7 Nicklas Lidstrom .50 1.2
OE8 Teemu Selanne .50 1.2
OE9 John LeClair .50 1.2
OE10 Pavel Bure .50 1.2

1999-00 Stadium Club Souvenirs

Randomly inserted in Hobby packs at 1:118 for jersey and 1:197 for stick cards, this 6-card set features swatches of game used memorabilia. Stick cards were issued in redemption form. The MacInnis card appear to be short printed.

SAM Al MacInnis S 5.00 12.0
SCO Chris Osgood J 5.00 12.0
SEB Ed Belfour S 6.00 15.0
SJL John LeClair S 10.00 25.0
SMH Marian Hossa J 5.00 12.0
SMS Mats Sundin J 5.00 12.0

2000-01 Stadium Club

eased in mid December 2000, Stadium Club
nsists of a 260-card base set divided up into 227
ular player cards and 33 Draft Pick cards. Base set
ures a full bleed color photo on the top and a name
along the bottom enhanced with silver holofoil and
ured like ice. Stadium Club was packaged in 24-
k boxes with packs containing seven cards and
ried a suggested retail price of $2.45.

avel Bure .20 .50
rendan Shanahan .20 .50
hris Pronger .12 .30
oug Weight .15 .40
eter Forsberg .20 .50
aromir Jagr .40 1.00
d Belfour .15 .40
od Brind'Amour .15 .40
ike Richter .15 .40
Mike Ricci .12 .30
Dimitri Yushkevich .10 .25
Dominik Hasek .25 .60
Teemu Selanne .30 .75
Ed Jovanovski .12 .30
Damian Rhodes .10 .25
Martin Brodeur .30 .75
Keith Primeau .12 .30
Byron Dafoe .12 .30
Jeff Hackett .10 .25
Brad Isbister .10 .25
Jeremy Roenick .15 .40
Jocelyn Thibault .12 .30
Ray Bourque .25 .60
Steve Yzerman .50 1.25
Mike Dunham .10 .25
Bill Guerin .15 .40
Dan Cloutier .12 .30
Pavol Demitra .20 .50
Richard Smehlik .10 .25
Ron Francis .20 .50
Zigmund Palffy .15 .40
David Legwand .15 .40
Scott Stevens .15 .40
Daniel Alfredsson .15 .40
Michal Rozsival .10 .25
John LeClair .15 .40
Vincent Lecavalier .12 .30
Jason Allison .12 .30
Kenny Jonsson .10 .25
Patrick Roy .40 1.00
Derian Hatcher .12 .30
Chris Osgood .15 .40
Owen Nolan .15 .40
Mike York .10 .25
Ryan Smyth .12 .30
Alexei Kovalev .12 .30
Roman Turek .12 .30
Mark Recchi .20 .50
Ray Ferraro .10 .25
Sergei Samsonov .12 .30
Paul Kariya .20 .50
Jarome Iginla .15 .40
Martin Biron .12 .30
Tom Poti .10 .25
Trevor Linden .15 .40
Pierre Turgeon .15 .40
Scott Gomez .12 .30
Mattias Ohlund .10 .25
Tony Amonte .12 .30
Yannick Tremblay .10 .25
Cliff Ronning .10 .25
Marc Savard .12 .30
Viktor Kozlov .12 .30
Pavel Kubina .10 .25
Arturs Irbe .12 .30
Stephane Fiset .10 .25
John Madden .12 .30
Steve Shields .10 .25
Theo Fleury .20 .50
Chris Simon .10 .25
Andy Delmore .10 .25
Radek Bonk .12 .30
Michal Handzus .10 .25
Tommy Salo .12 .30
Felix Potvin .25 .60
Teppo Numminen .10 .25
Bobby Holik .10 .25
Phil Housley .12 .30
Sergei Gonchar .10 .25
Shawn McEachern .10 .25
Simon Gagne .15 .40
Mike Sillinger .10 .25
Tim Connolly .10 .25
Eric Daze .12 .30
Andrew Brunette .10 .25
Mike Modano .25 .60
Chris Drury .12 .30
Nicklas Lidstrom .15 .40
Joe Thornton .25 .60
Michael Peca .12 .30
Matt Cullen .10 .25
Robyn Regehr .10 .25
Todd Marchant .10 .25
Brett Hull .25 .60
Rob Blake .15 .40
Sergei Zholtok .10 .25
Eric Lindros .25 .60
Jean-Sebastien Aubin .12 .30
Jason Arnott .12 .30
Keith Tkachuk .15 .40
Wade Redden .10 .25
Sean Burke .10 .25
Marian Hossa .12 .30
Robert Lang .10 .25
Curtis Joseph .20 .50
Jeff Friesen .10 .25
Dennis Bonvie .10 .25
Alexander Korolyuk .10 .25
Eric Lacroix .10 .25
Todd Bertuzzi .12 .30
Bates Battaglia .10 .25
Jozef Stumpel .10 .25
Alexei Zhamnov .12 .30
Milan Hejduk .12 .30
Chris Chelios .15 .40
Adam Graves .12 .30
Patrik Stefan .12 .30
Guy Hebert .12 .30
Anson Carter .12 .30
Fred Brathwaite .12 .30
Maxim Afinogenov .10 .25
Eric Messier .10 .25
Ray Whitney .12 .30
Bob Bassen .10 .25
Patrick Lalime .12 .30
Jonas Hoglund .10 .25
Mike Johnson .10 .25
Peter Schaefer .10 .25
Olaf Kolzig .15 .40
Jamie Langenbrunner .12 .30
Scott Niedermayer .15 .40
Mariusz Czerkawski .10 .25
Petr Buzek .10 .25
134 Michal Grosek .10 .25
135 Valeri Bure .12 .30
136 Igor Korolev .10 .25
137 Oleg Tverdovsky .10 .25
138 Fredrik Modin .10 .25
139 Kyle McLaren .10 .25
140 Todd Gill .10 .25
141 Miroslav Satan .10 .25
142 Jeff O'Neill .12 .30
143 Steve Sullivan .10 .25
144 Jon Klemm .10 .25
145 Joe Nieuwendyk .15 .40
146 Luc Robitaille .15 .40
147 Patrice Brisebois .10 .25
148 Travis Green .10 .25
149 Patric Kjellberg .10 .25
150 Mats Sundin .15 .40
151 Brian Rolston .12 .30
152 Patrik Elias .15 .40
153 Markus Naslund .12 .30
154 Trevor Letowski .10 .25
155 Brad Stuart .12 .30
156 Doug Gilmour .20 .50
157 Alexander Mogilny .12 .30
158 Glen Wesley .10 .25
159 Petr Nedved .12 .30
160 Peter Bondra .12 .30
161 Alex Tanguay .12 .30
162 Steve Rucchin .10 .25
163 Nikolai Antropov .12 .30
164 Anders Eriksson .10 .25
165 Martin Rucinsky .10 .25
166 Trevor Kidd .10 .25
167 Zdeno Chara .15 .40
168 Adam Oates .15 .40
169 Eric Desjardins .12 .30
170 Petr Sykora .12 .30
171 Brenden Morrow .12 .30
172 AL MacInnis .15 .40
173 Ethan Moreau .10 .25
174 Chris Tamer .10 .25
175 Jaroslav Spacek .10 .25
176 Paul Mara .10 .25
177 Bryan Smolinski .12 .30
178 Yanic Perreault .10 .25
179 Vaclav Prospal .10 .25
180 Vitali Yachmenev .10 .25
181 Pavel Trnka .10 .25
182 Joe Sakic .25 .60
183 Vincent Damphousse .12 .30
184 Sergei Fedorov .25 .60
185 Brian Rafalski .10 .25
186 Jochen Hecht .10 .25
187 Shane Doan .12 .30
188 Saku Koivu .15 .40
189 Richard Zednik .10 .25
190 Brian Boucher .12 .30
191 Jeff Halpern .10 .25
192 Matt Cooke .10 .25
193 Darcy Tucker .10 .25
194 Brian Leetch .15 .40
195 Glen Murray .10 .25
196 Robert Svehla .10 .25
197 Kimmo Timonen .10 .25
198 Claude Lapointe .10 .25
199 Brian Savage .10 .25
200 Sami Kapanen .10 .25
201 Scott Pellerin .10 .25
202 Cam Stewart .10 .25
203 Sergei Krivokrasov .10 .25
204 Manny Fernandez .12 .30
205 Darby Hendrickson .10 .25
206 Jamie McLennan .10 .25
207 Kevyn Adams .10 .25
208 Lyle Odelein .10 .25
209 Marc Denis .12 .30
210 Ron Tugnutt .12 .30
211 Tyler Wright .10 .25
212 Geoff Sanderson .12 .30
213 Mark Messier .25 .60
214 Mike Vernon .12 .30
215 Dave Andreychuk .15 .40
216 Chris Murray .10 .25
217 Joe Juneau .12 .30
218 Vladimir Malakhov .10 .25
219 Paul Coffey .15 .40
220 Roberto Luongo .25 .60
221 Roman Hamrlik .12 .30
222 Sandis Ozolinsh .12 .30
223 Gary Roberts .10 .25
224 Boyd Devereaux .10 .25
225 Scott Thornton .12 .30
226 Igor Larionov .15 .40
227 John Vanbiesbrouck .12 .30
228 Milan Kraft SP .40 1.00
229 Steven McCarthy SP .40 1.00
230 Kris Beech SP .40 1.00
231 Henrik Sedin SP 1.00 2.50
232 Daniel Sedin SP 1.25 3.00
233 Oleg Saprykin SP .40 1.00
234 Maxime Ouellet SP .60 1.50
235 Taylor Pyatt SP .40 1.00
236 Brent Johnson SP .50 1.25
237 Shawn Heins SP .40 1.00
238 Mika Noronen SP .40 1.00
239 Samuel Pahlsson SP .40 1.00
240 Dimitri Kalinin SP .40 1.00
241 Marian Gaborik RC 3.00 8.00
242 Petr Svoboda RC .50 1.25
243 Niclas Wallin RC .50 1.25
244 Dale Purinton RC .40 1.00
245 Justin Williams RC 1.00 2.50
246 Roman Simicek RC .40 1.00
247 Brad Tapper RC .40 1.00
248 Rostislav Klesla RC 1.00 2.50
249 Martin Havlat RC 1.25 3.00
250 Scott Hartnell RC 1.00 2.50
251 Andrew Raycroft RC 1.00 2.50
252 Ossi Vaananen RC .50 1.25
253 Steven Reinprecht RC .60 1.50
254 Josef Vasicek RC 1.00 2.50
255 Petr Hubacek RC .40 1.00
256 Lubomir Sekeras RC .40 1.00
257 David Aebischer RC .75 2.00
258 Jani Hurme RC .40 1.00
259 Marty Turco RC 1.50 4.00
260 Jarno Kultanen RC .40 1.00

2000-01 Stadium Club Beam Team

Randomly inserted in packs at the rate of 1:53, this luminescent card features player photos on an ice rink background with laser cut accents and die cut borders. Each card is sequentially numbered to 500.

COMPLETE SET (30) 150.00 300.00
BT1 Paul Kariya 4.00 10.00
BT2 Peter Forsberg 10.00 25.00
BT3 Mike Modano 6.00 15.00
BT4 Steve Yzerman 12.00 30.00
BT5 Pavel Bure 5.00 12.00
BT6 Jaromir Jagr 6.00 15.00
BT7 Brett Hull 5.00 12.00
BT8 Joe Sakic 8.00 20.00
BT9 Scott Gomez 3.00 8.00
BT10 Teemu Selanne 8.00 20.00
BT11 Vincent Lecavalier 4.00 10.00
BT12 Patrick Roy 15.00 40.00
BT13 Martin Brodeur 10.00 25.00
BT14 Dominik Hasek 8.00 20.00
BT15 Joe Thornton 6.00 15.00
BT16 Valeri Bure 3.00 8.00
BT17 Ed Belfour 4.00 10.00
BT18 Ray Bourque 8.00 20.00
BT19 Mark Messier 5.00 12.00
BT20 Curtis Joseph 4.00 10.00
BT21 Jason Arnott 3.00 8.00
BT22 Brian Boucher 4.00 10.00
BT23 Tony Amonte 3.00 8.00
BT24 Milan Hejduk 4.00 10.00
BT25 Mark Recchi 3.00 8.00
BT26 Patrik Elias 3.00 8.00
BT27 Zigmund Palffy 3.00 8.00
BT28 Jeremy Roenick 5.00 12.00
BT29 Eric Lindros 6.00 15.00
BT30 Chris Pronger 3.00 8.00

2000-01 Stadium Club Capture the Action

Randomly inserted in packs at the rate of 1:12, this 15-card set features a base card design with borders along the top and bottom and places color action photography against a maroon and purple background. A game view parallel was also created, these cards had a stated print run of 100 sets.

COMPLETE SET (15) 10.00 20.00
*GAME VIEW/100: 4X TO 10X
CA1 Jaromir Jagr 1.00 2.50
CA2 Martin Brodeur 1.50 4.00
CA3 Scott Gomez .50 1.25
CA4 Ed Belfour .60 1.50
CA5 Dominik Hasek 1.25 3.00
CA6 Olaf Kolzig .50 1.25
CA7 Pavel Bure .60 1.50
CA8 John LeClair .60 1.50
CA9 Curtis Joseph .60 1.50
CA10 Chris Pronger .50 1.25
CA11 Peter Forsberg 1.50 4.00
CA12 Teemu Selanne .60 1.50
CA13 Patrik Stefan .50 1.25
CA14 Vincent Lecavalier .60 1.50
CA15 Tim Connolly .50 1.25

2000-01 Stadium Club Co-Signers

Randomly inserted in Hobby packs at the rate of 1:644, this four card set features a split card design with two players and their authentic autographs along the bottom in a whited out box.

CO1 P.Bure/P.Demitra 15.00 40.00
CO2 S.Gomez/M.Brodeur 60.00 150.00
CO3 N.Antropov/D.Alfredsson 12.00 30.00
CO4 A.Carter/M.York 15.00 40.00

2000-01 Stadium Club Glove Save

Randomly inserted in packs at the rate of 1:10, this 10-card set features an all die cut embossed card in the shape of a goalie glove.

COMPLETE SET (10) 20.00 40.00
GS1 Martin Brodeur 4.00 10.00
GS2 Ed Belfour 1.50 4.00
GS3 Patrick Roy 8.00 20.00
GS4 Curtis Joseph 1.50 4.00
GS5 Brian Boucher 1.25 3.00
GS6 Roman Turek 1.25 3.00
GS7 Olaf Kolzig 1.25 3.00
GS8 Dominik Hasek 3.00 8.00
GS9 Chris Osgood 1.25 3.00
GS10 Fred Brathwaite 1.25 3.00

2000-01 Stadium Club Lone Star Signatures

Randomly inserted in packs at the rate of 1:118 overall, this 10-card set features a base design with the player framed in the middle of an "ice rink" with a whited out portion centered along the bottom for an authentic player autograph.

LS1 Pavel Bure 10.00 25.00
LS2 Martin Brodeur 30.00 80.00
LS3 Scott Gomez 8.00 20.00
LS4 Daniel Alfredsson 8.00 20.00
LS5 Nikolai Antropov 8.00 20.00
LS6 Jose Theodore 10.00 25.00
LS7 Anson Carter 8.00 20.00
LS8 Pavol Demitra 8.00 20.00
LS9 Mike York 8.00 20.00
LS10 Brad Stuart 8.00 20.00

2000-01 Stadium Club Promos

COMPLETE SET (6) 2.00 4.00
PP1 Bill Guerin .30 .75
PP2 Alexei Kovalev .30 .75
PP3 Keith Primeau .30 .75
PP4 Jocelyn Thibault .30 .75
PP5 Brad Isbister .30 .75
PP6 Adam Graves .30 .75

2000-01 Stadium Club Souvenirs

Randomly inserted in packs at the rate of 1:88 overall, this eight card set features full color player photos coupled with a circular swatch of a game worn jersey.

SCS1 Wade Redden 6.00 15.00
SCS2 Joe Sakic 12.50 30.00
SCS3 Derian Hatcher 6.00 15.00
SCS4 Jeff Hackett 6.00 15.00
SCS5 Kenny Jonsson 6.00 15.00
SCS6 Sergei Samsonov 6.00 15.00
SCS7 Darren McCarty 10.00 25.00
SCS8 Tie Domi 6.00 15.00

2000-01 Stadium Club Special Forces

Randomly inserted in packs at the rate of 1:8, this 20-card set features a base design with purple borders along the top and bottom and full color player photography set against a holofoil background in the shape of an ice rink.

COMPLETE SET (20) 15.00 30.00
SF1 Scott Stevens .60 1.50
SF2 Chris Pronger .50 1.25
SF3 Paul Kariya .75 2.00
SF4 Peter Forsberg .75 2.00
SF5 Mike Modano 1.00 2.50
SF6 Steve Yzerman 2.00 5.00
SF7 Pavel Bure .75 2.00
SF8 Jaromir Jagr 1.50 4.00
SF9 John LeClair .60 1.50
SF10 Mats Sundin .60 1.50
SF11 Owen Nolan .60 1.50
SF12 Brendan Shanahan .75 2.00
SF13 Pavol Demitra .75 2.00
SF14 Nicklas Lidstrom .60 1.50
SF15 Ron Francis .75 2.00
SF16 Patrick Roy 1.50 4.00
SF17 Martin Brodeur 1.25 3.00
SF18 Dominik Hasek 1.00 2.50
SF19 Keith Tkachuk .60 1.50
SF20 Curtis Joseph .75 2.00

2001-02 Stadium Club

Released in November 2001, this 140-card set carried an SRP of $3.00 for a 6-card pack. The base set consisted of 100 veteran cards, 10 transactions cards (inserted 1:4), 10 Premium Prospects cards (inserted 1:4) and 20 rookies (inserted 1:8).

COMPLETE SET (140) 60.00 120.00
1 Martin Brodeur .40 1.00
2 Peter Forsberg .25 .60
3 Chris Pronger .15 .40
4 Paul Kariya .25 .60
5 Mike Modano .30 .75
6 Curtis Joseph .20 .50
7 Jason Allison .15 .40
8 Brendan Shanahan .25 .60
9 Peter Bondra .20 .50
10 Mark Messier .30 .75
11 Owen Nolan .20 .50
12 Saku Koivu .20 .50
13 Tony Amonte .15 .40
14 Vincent Lecavalier .15 .40
15 Marian Hossa .15 .40
16 Pavel Bure .25 .60
17 Daniel Sedin .20 .50
18 Mario Lemieux .60 1.50
19 Rick DiPietro .15 .40
20 Zigmund Palffy .20 .50
21 Ron Tugnutt .15 .40
22 Ron Francis .25 .60
23 Maxim Afinogenov .12 .30
24 Steve Yzerman .60 1.50
25 Ray Ferraro .12 .30
26 Tommy Salo .15 .40
27 Marian Gaborik .30 .75
28 Claude Lemieux .15 .40
29 David Legwand .15 .40
30 Roman Cechmanek .15 .40
31 Jarome Iginla .20 .50
32 Sergei Fedorov .30 .75
33 Bill Guerin .20 .50
34 Brian Leetch .20 .50
35 Alexei Kovalev .15 .40
36 Pavol Demitra .25 .60
37 Olaf Kolzig .20 .50
38 Jose Theodore .20 .50
39 Johan Hedberg .15 .40
40 Teemu Selanne .40 1.00
41 Adam Deadmarsh .15 .40
42 Miroslav Satan .15 .40
43 Henrik Sedin .20 .50
44 Ed Belfour .20 .50
45 Sean Burke .12 .30
46 Patrik Elias .20 .50
47 Daniel Alfredsson .20 .50
48 Evgeni Nabokov .15 .40
49 Markus Naslund .20 .50
50 Mats Sundin .20 .50
51 Milan Hejduk .15 .40
52 Eric Belanger .12 .30
53 Darren McCarty .12 .30
54 Keith Tkachuk .20 .50
55 Steve Sullivan .12 .30
56 Mark Recchi .25 .60
57 Rob Blake .20 .50
58 Manny Fernandez .15 .40
59 Patrick Lalime .15 .40
60 Adam Oates .20 .50
61 Joe Sakic .30 .75
62 Lubomir Visnovsky .12 .30
63 Jeff Halpern .12 .30
64 Shane Willis .12 .30
65 Todd Bertuzzi .20 .50
66 Jeff Friesen .12 .30
67 Mike Dunham .15 .40
68 Alex Tanguay .15 .40
69 J-P Dumont .12 .30
70 Patrick Marleau .20 .50
71 Martin Straka .12 .30
72 Petr Sykora .12 .30
73 Arturs Irbe .15 .40
74 Patrik Stefan .15 .40
75 Brad Richards .20 .50
76 Mike Comrie .15 .40
77 Jason Arnott .15 .40
78 Tie Domi .15 .40
79 Martin Havlat .15 .40
80 Roberto Luongo .30 .75
81 Nicklas Lidstrom .20 .50
82 Simon Gagne .20 .50
83 Marc Savard .12 .30
84 John LeClair .20 .50
85 Gary Roberts .12 .30
86 Ryan Smyth .15 .40
87 Patrick Roy .50 1.25
88 Petr Nedved .15 .40
89 Brent Johnson .15 .40
90 Scott Gomez .15 .40
91 Joe Thornton .25 .60
92 Felix Potvin .30 .75
93 Chris Drury .15 .40
94 Keith Primeau .15 .40
95 Rod Brind'Amour .20 .50
96 Joe Nieuwendyk .20 .50
97 Espen Knutsen .12 .30
98 Adam Foote .15 .40
99 Brad Isbister .12 .30
100 Marc Denis .15 .40
101 Eric Lindros TR .60 1.50
102 Alexei Yashin TR .30 .75
103 Dominik Hasek TR .60 1.50
104 Michael Peca TR .30 .75
105 Brett Hull TR .50 1.25
106 Pierre Turgeon TR .40 1.00
107 Doug Weight TR .40 1.00
108 Alexander Mogilny TR .30 .75
109 Jaromir Jagr TR 1.00 2.50
110 Jeremy Roenick TR .40 1.00
111 Dany Heatley PP 1.25 3.00
112 Rostislav Klesla PP .75 2.00
113 Pavel Brendl PP .75 2.00
114 Barrett Heisten PP .75 2.00
115 Miikka Kiprusoff PP 1.25 3.00
116 Kris Beech PP .75 2.00
117 Pierre Dagenais PP .75 2.00
118 Bryan Allen PP .75 2.00
119 Jason Williams PP .75 2.00
120 Milan Kraft PP .75 2.00
121 Ilya Kovalchuk RC 5.00 12.00
122 Peter Smrek RC 1.00 2.50
123 Jiri Dopita RC 1.00 2.50
124 Jeff Jillson RC 1.00 2.50
125 Jukka Hentunen RC 1.00 2.50
126 Vaclav Nedorost RC 1.00 2.50
127 Timo Parssinen RC 1.25 3.00
128 Niklas Hagman RC 1.25 3.00
129 Andreas Salomonsson RC 1.00 2.50
130 Scott Nichol RC 1.00 2.50
131 Dan Blackburn RC 1.25 3.00
132 Kristian Huselius RC 1.50 4.00
133 Ivan Ciernik RC 1.00 2.50
134 Scott Clemmensen RC 1.00 2.50
135 Pascal Dupuis RC 1.50 4.00
136 Jason Chimera RC 1.00 2.50
137 Erik Cole RC 2.00 5.00
138 Brian Sutherby RC 1.00 2.50
139 Pavel Datsyuk RC 6.00 15.00
140 Niko Kapanen RC 1.50 4.00

2001-02 Stadium Club Award Winners

This 140-card set paralleled the base set but each card was serial-numbered out of 100 and carried an "Award Winner" stamp. Collectors could redeem cards from this set for special NHL Award Winners sets if the card they held was of a player who won an NHL award during the 2001/02 season.

*VETS: 4X TO 10X BASIC CARDS
*ROOKIES: .5X TO 1.5X BASIC CARDS
31 Jarome Iginla 10.00 25.00
38 Jose Theodore 20.00 50.00
81 Nicklas Lidstrom 10.00 25.00
111 Dany Heatley 8.00 20.00

2001-02 Stadium Club Master Photos

This 140-card set paralleled the base set but each card was serial-numbered out of 100 and carried a silver "Master Photo" stamp. Stated odds for this set was 1:45.

*1-100 VETS/100: 8X TO 20X BASIC CARDS
*101-110 TR/100: 4X TO 10X BASIC TR
*111-120 PP/100: 1.2X TO 3X BASIC PP
*121-140 ROOKIE/100: 1X TO 2.5X BASIC RC

2001-02 Stadium Club Gallery

This 40-card set was inserted at 1:5 and featured color artist renditions of some of the top players in the league. Cards were printed on glossy stock and had white borders that resembled a picture frame.

COMPLETE SET (40) 30.00 60.00
*GOLD/50: 5X TO 12X BASIC INSERT
G1 Curtis Joseph .60 1.50
G2 Brendan Shanahan .60 1.50
G3 Mats Sundin .60 1.50
G4 Patrik Elias .50 1.25
G5 Martin Havlat .50 1.25
G6 Joe Sakic 1.25 3.00
G7 Mike Modano 1.00 2.50
G8 Chris Drury .50 1.25
G9 Scott Stevens .50 1.25
G10 Olaf Kolzig .50 1.25
G11 Roberto Luongo .75 2.00
G12 Roman Cechmanek .50 1.25
G13 Ed Belfour .60 1.50
G14 Teemu Selanne .60 1.50
G15 Henrik Sedin .60 1.50
G16 Jaromir Jagr 1.00 2.50
G17 Marian Gaborik 1.25 3.00
G18 John LeClair .60 1.50
G19 Keith Tkachuk .60 1.50
G20 Paul Kariya .60 1.50
G21 Mario Lemieux 4.00 10.00
G22 Sergei Fedorov 1.00 2.50
G23 Martin Brodeur 1.50 4.00
G24 Pavel Bure .60 1.50
G25 Mike Comrie .50 1.25
G26 Zigmund Palffy .50 1.25
G27 Milan Hejduk .60 1.50
G28 Nicklas Lidstrom .60 1.50
G29 Patrick Roy 3.00 8.00
G30 Bill Guerin .50 1.25
G31 Evgeni Nabokov .50 1.25
G32 Tony Amonte .50 1.25
G33 Peter Forsberg 1.50 4.00
G34 Rick DiPietro .50 1.25
G35 Saku Koivu .60 1.50
G36 Chris Pronger .50 1.25
G37 Steve Yzerman 3.00 8.00
G38 Daniel Sedin .60 1.50
G39 Vincent Lecavalier .60 1.50
G40 Mark Messier .60 1.50

2001-02 Stadium Club Heart and Soul

This 10-card set was inserted at a rate of 1:20 and featured full color action photos on white card fronts. The words "Heart and Soul" were printed in dark blue across the card top.

COMPLETE SET (10) 15.00 30.00
HS1 Mark Messier 1.00 2.50
HS2 Patrick Roy 4.00 10.00
HS3 Steve Yzerman 4.00 10.00
HS4 Mario Lemieux 5.00 12.00
HS5 Chris Pronger .60 1.50
HS6 Scott Stevens .60 1.50
HS7 Peter Forsberg 2.00 5.00
HS8 Curtis Joseph .60 1.50
HS9 Mike Modano 1.25 3.00
HS10 Brendan Shanahan 1.25 3.00

2001-02 Stadium Club Lone Star Signatures

Inserted at a rate of 1:120, this 7-card set featured authentic player autographs. Color player photos were printed on the top two-thirds of the card front, and a white autograph area was at the card bottom.

LS1 Milan Hejduk 8.00 20.00
LS2 Olaf Kolzig 8.00 20.00
LS3 Marian Gaborik 12.50 30.00
LS4 Martin Havlat 8.00 20.00
LS5 Patrik Elias 8.00 20.00
LS6 Adam Oates 8.00 20.00
LS7 Ilya Kovalchuk 12.50 30.00

2001-02 Stadium Club New Regime

Consisting of 11 regular insert cards and 9 autograph cards, this set featured goalie prospects from around the league. Regular cards were inserted at 1:9. Autographed cards carried a white autograph space at the bottom of each card and a Topps certified stamp on the card backs. The Turco, Hedberg and Aebiscer auto cards were inserted at 1:210, all other autos were inserted at 1:140.

NR1 Marty Turco 2.00 5.00
NR2 David Aebischer 2.00 5.00
NR3 Brent Johnson 2.00 5.00
NR4 Evgeni Nabokov 2.00 5.00
NR5 Marc Denis 2.00 5.00
NR6 Roberto Luongo 2.50 6.00
NR7 Manny Fernandez 2.00 5.00
NR8 Roman Cechmanek 2.00 5.00
NR9 Jani Hurme 2.00 5.00
NR10 Johan Hedberg 2.00 5.00
NR11 Rick DiPietro 2.00 5.00
NRABJ Brent Johnson AU 8.00 20.00
NRADA David Aebischer AU 10.00 25.00
NRAEN Evgeni Nabokov AU 8.00 20.00
NRAJHE Johan Hedberg AU 8.00 20.00
NRAMD Marc Denis AU 8.00 20.00
NRAMF Manny Fernandez AU 8.00 20.00
NRAMT Marty Turco AU 10.00 25.00
NRARC Roman Cechmanek AU 8.00 20.00
NRARL Roberto Luongo AU 10.00 25.00

2001-02 Stadium Club NHL Passport

This 20-card set was inserted at 1:10 and featured international stars who also represent their homelands during world competitions. Cards carried color player photos and a small replica of the player's homeland flag.

COMPLETE SET (20) 20.00 40.00
NHLP1 Peter Forsberg 1.50 4.00
NHLP2 Nicklas Lidstrom .60 1.50
NHLP3 Mats Sundin .60 1.50
NHLP4 Pavel Bure .75 2.00
NHLP5 Sergei Fedorov 1.25 3.00
NHLP6 Alexei Kovalev .50 1.25
NHLP7 Saku Koivu .60 1.50
NHLP8 Teemu Selanne .60 1.50
NHLP9 Roman Cechmanek .50 1.25
NHLP10 Patrik Elias .50 1.25
NHLP11 Milan Hejduk .60 1.50
NHLP12 Petr Sykora .50 1.25
NHLP13 Chris Drury .50 1.25
NHLP14 Bill Guerin .50 1.25
NHLP15 John LeClair .75 2.00
NHLP16 Mike Modano 1.00 2.50
NHLP17 Paul Kariya .60 1.50
NHLP18 Mario Lemieux 4.00 10.00
NHLP19 Joe Sakic 1.25 3.00
NHLP20 Steve Yzerman 3.00 8.00

2001-02 Stadium Club Perennials

This 15-card set was inserted at 1:7 and highlighted players who make the all-star team on a consistent basis.

COMPLETE SET (15) 20.00 40.00
P1 Pavel Bure .75 2.00
P2 Joe Sakic 1.25 3.00
P3 Martin Brodeur 1.50 4.00
P4 Peter Forsberg 1.50 4.00
P5 Patrick Roy 3.00 8.00
P6 John LeClair .75 2.00
P7 Paul Kariya .60 1.50
P8 Steve Yzerman 3.00 8.00
P9 Mario Lemieux 4.00 10.00
P10 Ed Belfour .60 1.50
P11 Keith Tkachuk .60 1.50
P12 Sergei Fedorov 1.25 3.00
P13 Curtis Joseph .60 1.50
P14 Zigmund Palffy .60 1.50
P15 Tony Amonte .60 1.50

2001-02 Stadium Club Souvenirs

This 35-card hobby only set featured one, two or three swatches of game-worn jerseys from the pictured player(s). Single player cards were inserted at 1:16, dual player cards were inserted at 1:986 and serial-numbered to 25 each. Triple player cards were inserted at 1:3616 and were serial-numbered to 25.

AZ Alexei Zhamnov 4.00 10.00
CO Chris Osgood 6.00 15.00
JI Jarome Iginla 15.00 40.00
JT Joe Thornton 8.00 20.00
MB Martin Brodeur 15.00 40.00
MP Matt Pettinger 4.00 10.00
MR Mark Recchi 6.00 15.00
MT Marty Turco 6.00 15.00
PB Pavel Bure 4.00 10.00
PF Peter Forsberg 15.00 40.00
PK Paul Kariya 8.00 20.00
PM Patrick Marleau 6.00 15.00
SB Sean Burke 6.00 15.00
SF Sergei Fedorov 10.00 25.00
SK Saku Koivu 4.00 10.00
TD Tie Domi 6.00 15.00
TK Tomas Kloucek 4.00 10.00
JHA Jeff Hackett 4.00 10.00
JHL Jan Hlavac 4.00 10.00
MAS Marc Savard 4.00 10.00
MIS Miroslav Satan 6.00 15.00
EBMB E.Belfour/M.Brodeur 60.00 120.00
JHSK J.Hackett/S.Koivu 20.00 50.00
JSCD J.Sakic/C.Drury 30.00 80.00
MTEB M.Turco/E.Belfour 20.00 50.00
PFCD P.Forsberg/C.Drury 30.00 80.00
PFJS P.Forsberg/J.Sakic 50.00 100.00
PRMB P.Roy/M.Brodeur 60.00 120.00
SFPB S.Fedorov/P.Bure 30.00 80.00
SSPB S.Samsonov/P.Bure 20.00 50.00
TDDM T.Domi/D.McCarty 20.00 50.00
TKMM T.Kloucek/M.Mottau 20.00 50.00
EBMBPR Belfour/Brodeur/Roy 100.00 250.00
JSCDPF Sakic/Drury/Forsberg 100.00 200.00
JTJASS Thorn/Allison/Samsonov 75.00 150.00

2001-02 Stadium Club Toronto Fall Expo

This 6-card set was available only by wrapper redemption from the Topps booth at the 2001 Toronto Fall expo. The cards paralleled the base set, but carry a expo logo on the card fronts and were numbered "# of 6" on the card backs.

COMPLETE SET (6) 1.50 4.00
1 Marian Hossa .40 1.00
2 Peter Forsberg .75 2.00
3 Daniel Alfredsson .20 .50
4 Nicklas Lidstrom .20 .50
5 Brendan Shanahan .30 .75
6 Pavel Bure .40 1.00

2002-03 Stadium Club

Released in mid-November, this 140-card set featured full-color action photos on the card fronts and player stats on the card backs. SP's were inserted at a rate of 1:8.

COMPLETE SET (140) 75.00 150.00
COMP.SET w/o SP's (120) 25.00 50.00
1 Jose Theodore .30 .75
2 Jarome Iginla .30 .75
3 Nicklas Lidstrom .30 .75
4 Ron Francis .40 1.00
5 Jaromir Jagr .75 2.00
6 Mario Lemieux 1.00 2.50
7 Owen Nolan .30 .75
8 Martin Brodeur .60 1.50
9 Joe Sakic .50 1.25
10 Ilya Kovalchuk .40 1.00
11 Mike Modano .50 1.25
12 Jason Allison .25 .60
13 Sean Burke .20 .50
14 Mats Sundin .30 .75
15 Markus Naslund .25 .60
16 Jeremy Roenick .30 .75
17 Eric Lindros .50 1.25
18 Brent Johnson .25 .60
19 Sergei Fedorov .50 1.25
20 Sergei Samsonov .25 .60
21 Chris Drury .30 .75
22 Ryan Smyth .25 .60
23 Scott Hartnell .30 .75
24 Simon Gagne .30 .75
25 Dan Cloutier .25 .60
26 Vincent Lecavalier .25 .60
27 Martin Havlat .25 .60
28 Patrik Elias .30 .75
29 Roberto Luongo .50 1.25
30 Rob Blake .30 .75
31 J-P Dumont .20 .50
32 Jeff O'Neill .20 .50
33 Pavel Datsyuk .40 1.00
34 Dan Blackburn .25 .60
35 Alexei Kovalev .30 .75
36 Olaf Kolzig .30 .75
37 Milan Hejduk .25 .60
38 Steve Yzerman .60 1.50
39 Marc Denis .25 .60
40 Michael Peca .25 .60
41 Saku Koivu .30 .75
42 Marian Gaborik .50 1.25
43 Brad Richards .30 .75
44 Alexander Mogilny .25 .60
45 Mike Comrie .30 .75
46 Peter Forsberg .40 1.00
47 Dany Heatley .30 .75
48 Steve Sullivan .20 .50
49 Keith Tkachuk .30 .75
50 Todd Bertuzzi .30 .75
51 Evgeni Nabokov .25 .60
52 David Legwand .25 .60
53 Scott Stevens .30 .75
54 Eric Daze .20 .50
55 Martin Biron .25 .60
56 Zigmund Palffy .30 .75
57 Paul Kariya .40 1.00
58 Krys Kolanos .20 .50
59 Pavel Bure .40 1.00
60 Darcy Tucker .20 .50
61 Marian Hossa .25 .60
62 Roman Cechmanek .25 .60
63 Mark Parrish .20 .50
64 Arturs Irbe .25 .60
65 Brian Rolston .25 .60
66 Marty Turco .30 .75
67 Peter Bondra .30 .75
68 Johan Hedberg .30 .75
69 Chris Pronger .25 .60
70 Patrick Lalime .25 .60
71 Mike Dunham .25 .60
72 Kristian Huselius .20 .50
73 Patrick Roy .75 2.00
74 Joe Thornton .40 1.00
75 Andrew Brunette .20 .50
76 Alexei Yashin .25 .60
77 John LeClair .30 .75
78 Miroslav Satan .30 .75
79 Doug Weight .30 .75
80 Gary Roberts .20 .50
81 Tommy Salo .25 .60
82 Daniel Alfredsson .30 .75
83 Marco Sturm .20 .50
84 Rostislav Klesla .20 .50
85 Richard Zednik .20 .50
86 Roman Turek .30 .75
87 Brian Leetch .30 .75
88 Chris Osgood .30 .75
89 Brendan Morrison .25 .60
90 Jocelyn Thibault .25 .60
91 Teemu Selanne .60 1.50
92 Jean-Sebastien Giguere .30 .75
93 Nikolai Khabibulin .30 .75
94 Pavol Demitra .40 1.00
95 Brendan Shanahan .40 1.00
96 Mark Recchi .40 1.00
97 Felix Potvin .50 1.25
98 Shane Doan .25 .60
99 Erik Cole .25 .60
100 Brett Hull .40 1.00
101 Curtis Joseph .30 .75
102 Bobby Holik .20 .50
103 Ed Belfour .30 .75
104 Bill Guerin .30 .75
105 Petr Sykora .25 .60
106 Scott Young .20 .50
107 Adam Oates .30 .75
108 Jeff Friesen .20 .50
109 Darius Kasparaitis .20 .50
110 Tony Amonte .25 .60
111 Marcel Hossa .20 .50
112 Jamie Lundmark .25 .60
113 Pavel Brendl .20 .50
114 Jaroslav Svoboda .20 .50
115 Stephen Weiss .30 .75
116 Martin Prusek .20 .50
117 Jani Rita .20 .50
118 Petr Cajanek .20 .50
119 Trent Hunter .20 .50
120 Jonathan Cheechoo .25 .60
121 Stanislav Chistov RC 1.00 2.50
122 Alexander Svitov RC 1.00 2.50
123 Alexander Frolov RC 2.00 5.00
124 Alexei Smirnov RC 1.25 3.00
125 Chuck Kobasew RC 1.25 3.00
126 Rick Nash RC 6.00 15.00
127 Henrik Zetterberg RC 8.00 20.00
128 Jay Bouwmeester RC 3.00 8.00
129 Ales Hemsky RC 4.00 10.00
130 Martin Gerber RC 1.50 4.00
131 Ron Hainsey RC 1.00 2.50
132 P-M Bouchard RC 1.50 4.00
133 Jason Spezza RC 5.00 12.00
134 Kurt Sauer RC 1.00 2.50
135 Lasse Pirjeta RC 1.00 2.50
136 Adam Hall RC 1.00 2.50
137 Dennis Seidenberg RC 1.50 4.00
138 Patrick Sharp RC 3.00 8.00
139 Steve Eminger RC 1.00 2.50
140 Dmitri Bykov RC 1.00 2.50

2002-03 Stadium Club Silver Decoy Cards

This 140-card set paralleled the base set but was printed on thicker card stock and carried a silver finish on the card fronts. They were inserted at one-per pack to discourage pack searching.
*DECOYS: .5X TO 1.2X BASIC CARDS

2002-03 Stadium Club Proofs

This 140-card proof set paralleled the base set but carried a "Proof" stamp and seria-numbering. Base cards were serial-numbered to 250 and rookies were serial-numbered to 100.
*1-120 VETS/250: 2X TO 5X BASIC CARDS
*121-140 ROOKIES/100: .8X TO 2X BASIC RC

2002-03 Stadium Club Beam Team

This 15-card set was inserted at a rate of 1:18.
COMPLETE SET (15) 20.00 40.00
BT1 Steve Yzerman 3.00 8.00
BT2 Mario Lemieux 4.00 10.00
BT3 Patrick Roy 3.00 8.00
BT4 Jarome Iginla 1.00 2.50
BT5 Jose Theodore .75 2.00
BT6 Brendan Shanahan 1.00 2.50
BT7 Chris Pronger .50 1.25
BT8 Dany Heatley .75 2.00
BT9 Joe Thornton 1.00 2.50
BT10 Peter Forsberg 1.50 4.00
BT11 Ron Francis .50 1.25
BT12 Owen Nolan .50 1.25
BT13 Todd Bertuzzi .60 1.50
BT14 Rob Blake .50 1.25
BT15 Paul Kariya .60 1.50

2002-03 Stadium Club Champions Fabric

Inserted at 1:68, this 10-card set featured swatches of game jerseys.
FC1 Rob Blake 4.00 10.00
FC2 Derian Hatcher 4.00 10.00
FC3 Alex Tanguay 4.00 10.00
FC4 Martin Brodeur 10.00 25.00
FC5 Milan Hejduk 4.00 10.00
FC6 Mike Modano 6.00 15.00
FC7 Scott Niedermayer 4.00 10.00
FC8 Brian Leetch 4.00 10.00
FC9 Sergei Zubov 4.00 10.00
FC10 Chris Drury 4.00 10.00

2002-03 Stadium Club Champions Patches

A parallel to the basic Champions Fabrics jerseys, this 9-card set featured swatches of game-worn jersey patches. Each card was serial-numberde to 25 copies each. Please note that Topps did not produce a patch variation of the Chris Drury card.
*PATCHES: 2X TO 5X BASIC JERSEY

2002-03 Stadium Club Lone Star Signatures Blue

Inserted at 1:56 packs, this 14-card set featured authentic player autographs in blue ink.
LSBG Brian Gionta 8.00 20.00
LSBR Brad Richards 8.00 20.00
LSCP Chris Pronger SP 12.50 30.00
LSDB Daniel Briere 8.00 20.00
LSEC Erik Cole 6.00 15.00
LSED Eric Daze 6.00 15.00
LSIL Ilya Kovalchuk 10.00 25.00
LSJI Jarome Iginla 12.50 30.00
LSJT Jose Theodore 12.50 30.00
LSPL Patrick Lalime 8.00 20.00
LSRK Rostislav Klesla 6.00 15.00
LSSG Simon Gagne 10.00 30.00
LSSW Stephen Weiss 8.00 20.00
LSTB Todd Bertuzzi 10.00 25.00

2002-03 Stadium Club Lone Star Signatures Red

Inserted at 1:144, this set paralleled the basic autograph set but player autographs were signed in red ink.
*RED SIGS: .5X TO 1.25X BLUE

2002-03 Stadium Club Passport Jerseys

Inserted at 1:40, this 14-card set featured swatches of game-worn jerseys affixed to a passport style card front. All cards carried a NHLP prefix.
1 Saku Koivu 5.00 12.00
2 Daniel Alfredsson 4.00 10.00
3 Eric Lindros 5.00 15.00
4 Mats Sundin 6.00 15.00
5 Todd Bertuzzi 5.00 12.00
6 Simon Gagne 6.00 15.00
7 Marian Hossa 5.00 12.00
8 Paul Kariya 5.00 12.00
9 Vincent Lecavalier 6.00 15.00
10 Miroslav Satan 4.00 10.00
11 Markus Naslund 6.00 15.00
12 Zigmund Palffy 4.00 10.00
13 Tony Amonte 4.00 10.00
14 Brian Rolston 4.00 10.00
15 Maxim Afinogenov 4.00 10.00
16 Sergei Samsonov 4.00 10.00
17 Marco Sturm 4.00 10.00

2002-03 Stadium Club Puck Stops Here

COMPLETE SET (15) 10.00 20.00
STATED ODDS 1:6
PSH1 Brent Johnson .50 1.25
PSH2 Roman Cechmanek .50 1.25
PSH3 Evgeni Nabokov .50 1.25
PSH4 Jose Theodore .75 2.00
PSH5 Martin Biron .50 1.25
PSH6 Chris Osgood .50 1.25
PSH7 Marty Turco .50 1.25
PSH8 Nikolai Khabibulin .60 1.50
PSH9 Roberto Luongo 1.00 2.50
PSH10 Martin Brodeur 1.25 3.00
PSH11 Sean Burke .50 1.25
PSH12 Tommy Salo .50 1.25
PSH13 Mike Richter .60 1.50
PSH14 Patrick Roy 1.50 4.00
PSH15 Jean-Sebastien Giguere .50 1.25

2002-03 Stadium Club St. Patrick Relics

This 16-card set honored the career of Patrick Roy. Single swatch jersey only odds were 1:237 and single swatch stick only cards were inserted at 1:3160. All other print runs are listed below. Print runs of 25 or less not priced due to scarcity.
ALL CARDS CARRY SP PREFIX
SAS P.Roy STK AU/50 100.00 250.00
CAJ P.Roy JSY 12.50 30.00
MCJ P.Roy JSY 12.50 30.00
CAJA P.Roy JSY AU/250 60.00 150.00
MCJA P.Roy JSY AU/250 60.00 150.00
SPS P.Roy STK 12.50 30.00
CAJP P.Roy PATCH/100 30.00 80.00
MCJP P.Roy PATCH/100 30.00 80.00
CAMCJ P.Roy 2 JSY/500 30.00 80.00
CAMCJA P.Roy 2 JSY AU/50 200.00 500.00
CAMCJS P.Roy JSY/STK/50 60.00 120.00
CAMCJSA P.Roy JSY/STK AU/25 200.00 500.00
CAJPA P.Roy PATCH AU/10
MCJPA P.Roy PATCH AU/10
CAMCJP P.Roy DUAL PATCH/25
CAMCJPA P.Roy DUAL PATCH AU/5

2002-03 Stadium Club World Stage

COMPLETE SET (20) 15.00 30.00
STATED ODDS 1:7
WS1 Sergei Fedorov 1.25 3.00
WS2 Chris Drury .50 1.25
WS3 Martin Brodeur 1.50 4.00
WS4 Joe Sakic 1.25 3.00
WS5 Mike Modano 1.00 2.50
WS6 Jeremy Roenick .75 2.00
WS7 Brett Hull .75 2.00
WS8 Ilya Kovalchuk 1.00 2.50
WS9 Nicklas Lidstrom .60 1.50
WS10 Jaromir Jagr 1.00 2.50
WS11 Alexei Yashin .50 1.25
WS12 Zigmund Palffy .50 1.25
WS13 Marian Gaborik .75 2.00
WS14 Teemu Selanne .60 1.50
WS15 Alexei Kovalev .50 1.25
WS16 Patrik Elias .50 1.25
WS17 Peter Bondra .50 1.25
WS18 Pavel Bure .75 2.00
WS19 Mats Sundin .60 1.50
WS20 Daniel Alfredsson .50 1.25

2002-03 Stadium Club YoungStars Relics

This 29-card set featured memorabilia worn during the NHL/Topps YoungStars game played in 2002. Single jersey swatch cards (S1-S23) were inserted at 1:28. Double swatch cards (DS1-DS6) were serial-numbered to 100. Odds for the MVP autographed puck were stated at 1:936 and there were only 200 copies available.
ALL CARDS CARRY YS PREFIX
YSS1 Ilya Kovalchuk 12.50 30.00
YSS2 Pavel Datsyuk 8.00 20.00
YSS3 Mike Comrie 4.00 10.00
YSS4 Dan Blackburn 4.00 10.00
YSS5 Dany Heatley 6.00 15.00
YSS6 Marian Gaborik 8.00 20.00
YSS7 Kristian Huselius 5.00 12.00
YSS8 David Legwand 5.00 12.00
YSS9 Roberto Luongo 8.00 20.00
YSS10 Brad Richards 5.00 12.00
YSS11 Justin Williams 5.00 12.00
YSS12 Kyle Calder 4.00 10.00
YSS13 Dave Tanabe 4.00 10.00
YSS14 Brenden Morrow 5.00 12.00
YSS15 Scott Hartnell 4.00 10.00
YSS16 Mike Fisher 5.00 12.00
YSS17 Tim Connolly 5.00 12.00
YSS18 Nick Boynton 4.00 10.00
YSS19 Paul Mara 4.00 10.00
YSS20 Mike Ribeiro 5.00 12.00
YSS21 Robyn Regehr 4.00 10.00
YSS22 Andrew Ference 4.00 10.00
YSS23 Karel Rachunek 4.00 10.00
YSDS1 D.Heatley/I.Kovalchuk 25.00 60.00
YSDS2 D.Legwand/S.Hartnell 10.00 25.00
YSDS3 K.Huselius/R.Luongo 20.00 50.00
YSDS4 M.Gaborik/P.Datsyuk 25.00 60.00
YSDS5 J.Williams/M.Comrie 8.00 20.00
YSDS6 B.Richards/D.Blackburn 10.00 25.00
APIK Kovalchuk Puck AU/200 20.00 50.00

1994-95 Stars HockeyKaps

Measuring approximately 1 3/4" in diameter, this set of 25 caps features the Dallas Stars. The caps were given away at Stars games on February 6, 9, 16 and 18. Additional caps could be obtained through a mail-in offer by sending a SASE along with proof-of-purchase from one 46 oz. or one six-pack of 10 oz. Tropicana Twister. A HockeyKap collector game board was also available through a mail-in offer for two proofs-of-purchase of the above-mentioned products. The fronts feature color head shots with a white border. The player's last name is printed in the white border. The backs are blank. The caps are unnumbered and checklisted below in alphabetical order.
COMPLETE SET (25) 3.00 8.00
1 Dave Barr .08 .25
2 Brad Berry .08 .25
3 Neal Broten .20 .50
4 Paul Broten .08 .25
5 Paul Cavallini .08 .25
6 Shane Churla .20 .50
7 Russ Courtnall .15 .40
8 Mike Craig .08 .25
9 Ulf Dahlen .15 .40
10 Dean Evason .08 .25
11 Dave Gagner .15 .40
12 Bob Gainey CO .15 .40
13 Brent Gilchrist .08 .25
14 Derian Hatcher .15 .40
15 Doug Jarvis ACO .02 .10
16 Jim Johnson .08 .25
17 Trent Klatt .08 .25
18 Grant Ledyard .08 .25
19 Craig Ludwig .08 .25
20 Mike McPhee .08 .25
21 Mike Modano .60 1.50
22 Andy Moog .40 1.00
23 Mark Tinordi .08 .25
24 Darcy Wakaluk .15 .40
25 Rick Wilson ACO .02 .10

1994-95 Stars Pinnacle Sheet

Produced by Pinnacle, this promo sheet was given out at Reunion Arena for the Dallas Stars game vs. the Red Wings on April 1, 1995. The sheet measures approximately 12 1/2" by 10 1/2". The left, perforated portion displays nine standard-size player cards, while the right portion consists of an advertisement to purchase 12-packs of Coke products at participating Texaco retailers. The design is the same as the 1994-95 Pinnacle hockey series, with the same numbering. The cards are listed below, beginning at the upper left of the sheet and moving toward the lower right corner.
COMPLETE SHEET (9) 2.00 5.00
3 Mike Modano .60 1.50
55 Derian Hatcher .20 .50
133 Russ Courtnall .20 .50
157 Darcy Wakaluk .20 .50
185 Brent Gilchrist .08 .25
262 Todd Harvey .20 .50
315 Andy Moog .40 1.00
334 Dave Gagner .20 .50
433 Paul Broten .08 .25

1994-95 Stars Postcards

This 23-postcard set of the Dallas Stars was produced by the club for promotional giveaways and autograph signings. The cards feature full-bleed action photos on the fronts, while the backs contain biographical and statistical information. As the cards are unnumbered, they are listed below in alphabetical order.
COMPLETE SET (23) 6.00 15.00
1 Paul Broten .20 .50
2 Paul Cavallini .20 .50
3 Shane Churla .30 .75
4 Gord Donnelly .20 .50
5 Mike Donnelly .20 .50
6 Dean Evason .20 .50
7 Dave Gagner .30 .75
8 Brent Gilchrist .20 .50
9 Todd Harvey .30 .75
10 Derian Hatcher .30 .75
11 Kevin Hatcher .20 .50
12 Mike Kennedy .20 .50
13 Trent Klatt .20 .50
14 Mike Lalor .20 .50
15 Grant Ledyard .20 .50
16 Craig Ludwig .20 .50
17 Richard Matvichuk .30 .75
18 Corey Millen .20 .50
19 Mike Modano 1.25 3.00
20 Andy Moog .75 2.00
21 Darcy Wakaluk .30 .75
22 Peter Zezel .20 .50
23 Doug Zmolek .20 .50

1994-95 Stars Score Sheet

This perforated sheet was given away February 2, 1995, at the Dallas Stars' home game against the San Jose Sharks. The sheet measures approximately 12 1/2" by 10 1/2"; the larger left portion consists of nine standard-size cards, while the smaller right portion presents an advertisement for 1994-95 Score hockey first series. The back of the ad portion mentions Tom Thumb grocery stores as a place to buy Score cards. The cards have the same design as the regular issue cards. Note, however, that Shane Churla does not have a card in the regular series; this is his only appearance on a 1994-95 Score card. The cards are listed below beginning in the upper left and moving across and down toward the lower right.
COMPLETE SHEET (9) 2.00 5.00
17 Mike McPhee .08 .25
43 Russ Courtnall .08 .25
68 Mark Tinordi .08 .25
94 Paul Cavallini .08 .25
113 Neal Broten .20 .50
148 Derian Hatcher .20 .50
173 Andy Moog .40 1.00
188 Mike Modano .60 1.50
NNO Shane Churla .40 1.00

1995-96 Stars Score Sheet

This perforated sheet was given away at a Dallas Stars game at Reunion Arena and measures approximately 12 1/2" by 10 1/2". The left portion displays nine cards with color action player photos while the right consists of sponsor logos and an advertisement to purchase six packs of Coke products at participating Texaco retailers. The cards are listed below beginning at the upper left of the sheet and moving toward the lower right corner.
COMPLETE SHEET (1) 2.00 5.00
12 Kevin Hatcher .08 .25
38 Todd Harvey .20 .50
64 Andy Moog .40 1.00
89 Greg Adams .20 .50
120 Mike Modano .75 2.00
197 Darcy Wakaluk .20 .50
225 Derian Hatcher .20 .50
229 Joe Nieuwendyk .40 1.00
261 Brent Gilchrist .08 .25

1996-97 Stars Postcards

This 27-postcard set was produced by the club for promotional giveaways and autograph signings. The cards feature full color action photos on the front; the backs have biographical information and complete career stats. As the cards are unnumbered, they are listed below alphabetically.
COMPLETE SET 6.00 15.00
1 Greg Adams .20 .50
2 Bob Bassen .20 .50
3 Neal Broten .30 .75
4 Guy Carbonneau .20 .50
5 Bob Gainey .20 .50
6 Brent Gilchrist .20 .50
7 Todd Harvey .30 .75
8 Derian Hatcher .30 .75
9 Ken Hitchcock CO .20 .50
10 Benoit Hogue .20 .50
11 Bill Huard .20 .50
12 Arturs Irbe .30 .75
13 Mike Kennedy .20 .50
14 Mike Lalor .20 .50
15 Jamie Langenbrunner .30 .75
16 Grant Ledyard .20 .50
17 Jere Lehtinen .30 .75
18 Craig Ludwig .20 .50
19 Grant Marshall .20 .50
20 Richard Matvichuk .20 .50
21 Mike Modano 1.00 2.50
22 Joe Nieuwendyk .30 .75
23 Andy Moog .60 1.50
24 Dave Reid .20 .50
25 Darryl Sydor .20 .50
26 Pat Verbeek .30 .75
27 Sergei Zubov .20 .50

1996-97 Stars Score Sheet

For the third straight season, Score and the Stars teamed up to distribute a special, perforated card sheet, this time at a match against the Edmonton Oilers on Sunday, February 23, as well as at a local card show the weekend following. The majority of the cards mirror those found in the 1996-97 Score set. Of note are the cards of Pat Verbeek and Sergei Zubov, which were updated to show them as members of the Stars; Jere Lehtinen, which features green ink on the back instead of red; and Derian Hatcher, who is not included in the regular Score set. Although it typically is sold in sheet form, it is listed below as singles because the unique cards have led to many dealers breaking it up.
COMPLETE SHEET 2.00 5.00
39 Greg Adams .20 .50
72 Mike Modano .75 2.00
86 Todd Harvey .20 .50
94 Pat Verbeek .20 .50
104 Andy Moog .40 1.00
152 Joe Nieuwendyk .30 .75
171 Sergei Zubov .20 .50
246 Jere Lehtinen .20 .50
NNO Derian Hatcher .20 .50

1997-98 Stars Postcards

COMPLETE SET (17) 4.00 10.00
1 Greg Adams .20 .50
2 Ed Belfour 1.00 2.50
3 Guy Carbonneau .20 .50
4 Bob Errey .20 .50
5 Derian Hatcher .20 .50
6 Benoit Hogue .20 .50
7 Jere Lehtinen .20 .50
8 Juha Lind .20 .50
9 Craig Ludwig .20 .50
10 Grant Marshall .20 .50
11 Mike Modano 1.00 2.50
12 Joe Nieuwendyk .60 1.50
13 Dave Reid .20 .50
14 Darryl Sydor .20 .50
15 Roman Turek .20 .50
16 Pat Verbeek .20 .50
17 Sergei Zubov .20 .50

1999-00 Stars Postcards

This 27-card set pictures the 1999-00 Dallas Stars and was sponsored by Southwest Airlines. Each card measures 4 1/4" by 6 1/4".
COMPLETE SET (27) 8.00 20.00
1 Keith Aldridge .20 .50
2 Ed Belfour .75 2.00
3 Guy Carbonneau .30 .75
4 Shawn Chambers .20 .50
5 Manny Fernandez .40 1.00
6 Aaron Gavey .20 .50
7 Derian Hatcher .30 .75
8 Brett Hull .75 2.00
9 Mike Keane .20 .50
10 Jamie Langenbrunner .30 .75
11 Jere Lehtinen .40 1.00
12 Alan Letang .20 .50
13 Juha Lind .20 .50
14 Warren Luhning .20 .50
15 Brad Lukowich .20 .50
16 Grant Marshall .20 .50
17 Richard Matvichuk .20 .50
18 Mike Modano 1.25 3.00
19 Chris Murray .20 .50
20 Joe Nieuwendyk .40 1.00
21 Pavel Patera .20 .50
22 Derek Plante .20 .50
23 Jamie Pushor .20 .50
24 Brian Skrudland .20 .50
25 Blake Sloan .20 .50
26 Darryl Sydor .20 .50
27 Sergei Zubov .20 .50

2000-01 Stars Postcards

This 26-card set was sponsored by Southwest Airlines. The front of each card features an on-ice photo of each player and is bordered on the left hand side in gold with the players name in green letters. The team logo is at the bottom left of each card front. The backs carry individual career stats as well as transactional history for each player.
COMPLETE SET (26) 8.00 20.00
1 Ed Belfour .80 2.00
2 Tyler Bouck .30 .75
3 Gerald Diduck .20 .50
4 Ted Donato .20 .50
5 Derian Hatcher .30 .75
6 Sami Helenius .20 .50
7 Ken Hitchcock HCO .20 .50
8 Brett Hull .80 2.00
9 Richard Jackman .20 .50
10 Mike Keane .20 .50
11 Jamie Langenbrunner .20 .50
12 Jere Lehtinen .60 1.50
13 Brad Lukowich .20 .50
14 Roman Lyashenko .30 .75
15 Grant Marshall .20 .50
16 Richard Matvichuk .20 .50
17 Mike Modano .80 2.00
18 Brenden Morrow .60 1.50
19 Kirk Muller .20 .50
20 Joe Nieuwendyk .30 .75
21 Jon Sim .20 .50
22 Blake Sloan .20 .50
23 Darryl Sydor .20 .50
24 Marty Turco .80 2.00
25 Shaun Van Allen .20 .50
26 Sergei Zubov .20 .50

2001-02 Stars Postcards

This set features the Dallas Stars. Singles were often handed out at player appearances. Sets could be obtained from the club with a donation to the Stars Foundation charity. The cards measures 4 X 6. The cards are listed in alphabetical order.
COMPLETE SET (26) 8.00 20.00
COMMON CARD (1-26)
1 Ed Belfour .75 2.00
2 Benoit Brunet .20 .50
3 Rob DiMaio .20 .50
4 John Erskine .20 .50
5 Derian Hatcher .30 .75
6 Sami Helenius .30 .75
7 Ken Hitchcock CO .20 .50
8 Benoit Hogue .20 .50
9 Valeri Kamensky .20 .50
10 Niko Kapanen .40 1.00
11 Jamie Langenbrunner .40 1.00
12 Jere Lehtinen .40 1.00
13 Brad Lukowich .20 .50
14 Roman Lyashenko .20 .50
15 Dave Manson .20 .50
16 Richard Matvichuk .20 .50
17 Mike Modano 1.25 3.00
18 Brenden Morrow .40 1.00
19 Kirk Muller .20 .50
20 Joe Nieuwendyk .40 1.00
21 Martin Rucinsky .20 .50
22 Darryl Sydor .20 .50
23 Marty Turco .60 1.50
24 Pierre Turgeon .30 .75
25 Pat Verbeek .20 .50
26 Sergei Zubov .20 .50

2001-02 Stars Team Issue

Little is known about this team issued set, but the cards below are known to exist. Please forward any additional info to hockeymag@beckett.com.
1 Brenden Morrow .75 2.00
2 Derian Hatcher .75 2.00
3 John Erskine .40 1.00
4 Niko Kapanen .40 1.00

2002-03 Stars Postcards

Issued by the team, this 24-card set measured 4" X 8". Card backs carried career stats for each player.
COMPLETE SET (24) 10.00 20.00
1 Scott Pellerin .20 .50
2 Sami Helenius .20 .50
3 John Erskine .40 1.00
4 Stephane Robidas .20 .50
5 Jere Lehtinen .60 1.50
6 Sergei Zubov .20 .50
7 Kirk Muller .20 .50
8 Brenden Morrow .40 1.00
9 Mike Modano 1.25 3.00
10 Richard Matvichuk .20 .50
11 Manny Malhotra .20 .50
12 Derian Hatcher .20 .50
13 Scott Young .20 .50
14 Niko Kapanen .40 1.00
15 Bill Guerin .60 1.50
16 Aaron Downey .75 2.00
17 Rob Dimaio .20 .50
18 Pierre Turgeon .30 .75
19 Marty Turco 1.25 3.00
20 Ron Tugnutt .40 1.00
21 Darryl Sydor .20 .50
22 Ulf Dahlen .20 .50
23 Philippe Boucher .20 .50
24 Jason Arnott .30 .75

2003-04 Stars Postcards

These cards were issued by the Stars for use at team events. Complete sets could also be purchased through the team. Although the majority of the cards are in colour, several late-season call-ups were issued in black and white.
COMPLETE SET (31) 10.00 20.00
1 Jason Arnott .20 .50
2 Stu Barnes .20 .50
3 Philippe Boucher .20 .50
4 Trevor Daley .20 .50
5 Rob DiMaio .20 .50
6 Aaron Downey .40 1.00
7 John Erskine .20 .50
8 Steve Gainey .20 .50
9 Bill Guerin .40 1.00
10 Niko Kapanen .30 .75
11 Jon Klemm .20 .50
12 Jere Lehtinen .40 1.00
13 Jeff MacMillan .20 .50
14 Richard Matvichuk .20 .50
15 Antti Miettinen .20 .50
16 Mike Modano .75 2.00
17 Gavin Morgan .20 .50
18 Brenden Morrow .60 1.50
19 Teppo Numminen .20 .50
20 David Oliver .20 .50
21 Steve Ott .75 2.00
22 Blake Sloan .20 .50
23 Mike Smith 1.25 3.00
24 Don Sweeney .20 .50
25 Mathias Tjarnqvist .20 .50
26 Ron Tugnutt .30 .75
27 Marty Turco .75 2.00
28 Pierre Turgeon .20 .50
29 Rob Valicevic .20 .50
30 Scott Young .20 .50
31 Sergei Zubov .20 .50

2006-07 Stars Team Postcards

Set includes a card of American Idol finalist Celena Rae, who sang the national anthems and was an intermission host for the Stars this season.
COMPLETE SET (28) 15.00 30.00
1 Krys Barch .75 2.00
2 Matthew Barnaby .75 2.00
3 Stu Barnes .40 1.00
4 Philippe Boucher .40 1.00
5 Trevor Daley .40 1.00
6 Loui Eriksson .75 2.00
7 Niklas Hagman .40 1.00
8 Jeff Halpern .40 1.00
9 Jussi Jokinen .40 1.00
10 Jon Klemm .40 1.00
11 Jere Lehtinen .75 2.00
12 Eric Lindros .75 2.00
13 Joel Lundqvist .75 2.00
14 Antti Miettinen .40 1.00
15 Mike Modano 1.25 3.00
16 Brenden Morrow .75 2.00
17 Steve Ott .75 2.00
18 Mike Ribeiro .40 1.00
19 Stephane Robidas .40 1.00
20 Mike Smith .75 2.00
21 Patrik Stefan .40 1.00
22 Darryl Sydor .40 1.00
23 Marty Turco .75 2.00
24 Sergei Zubov .40 1.00
25 Dave Tippett CO .10 .25
26 Celena Rae .40 1.00
27 Brett Hull 1.25 3.00
28 Craig Ludwig .40 1.00

2007-08 Stars Team Issue

COMPLETE SET (25) 15.00 30.00
1 Krys Barch .75 2.00
2 Stu Barnes .40 1.00
3 Philippe Boucher .40 1.00
4 Trevor Daley .40 1.00
5 Loui Eriksson .75 2.00
6 Todd Fedoruk .75 2.00
7 Niklas Grossman .40 1.00
8 Niklas Hagman .40 1.00
9 Jeff Halpern .40 1.00
10 Jussi Jokinen .40 1.00
11 Jere Lehtinen .75 2.00
12 Joel Lundqvist .40 1.00
13 Antti Miettinen .40 1.00
14 Mike Modano 1.25 3.00
15 Brenden Morrow 1.25 3.00
16 Matt Niskanen .75 2.00
17 Mattias Norstrom .40 1.00
18 Steve Ott .75 2.00
19 Mike Ribeiro .40 1.00
20 Stephane Robidas .40 1.00
21 Mike Smith .75 2.00
22 Marty Turco .75 2.00
23 Brad Winchester .40 1.00
24 Sergei Zubov .40 1.00
25 Dave Tippett HC .40 1.00

1975-76 Stingers Kahn's

This set of 14 photos was issued on wrappers of Kahn's Wieners and Beef Franks and features players of the Cincinnati Stingers of the WHA. The wrappers are approximately 2 11/16" wide and 11 5/8" long. The wiener wrappers are predominantly yellow and carry a 2" by 1 1/4" black-and-white posed photo of the player with a facsimile autograph inscribed across the picture. The beef frank wrappers are identical in design but predominantly red in color. The wrappers are unnumbered and checklisted below in alphabetical order.
COMPLETE SET (14) 62.50 125.00
1 Serge Aubry 5.00 10.00
2 Bryan Campbell 5.00 10.00
3 Rick Dudley 7.50 15.00
4 Pierre Guite 5.00 10.00
5 John Hughes 5.00 10.00
6 Claude Larose 6.00 12.00
7 Jacques Locas UER 5.00 10.00
8 Bernie MacNeil 5.00 10.00
9 Mike Pelyk 5.00 10.00
10 Ron Plumb 5.00 10.00
11 Dave Smedsmo 5.00 10.00
12 Dennis Sobchuk 5.00 10.00
13 Gene Sobchuk 5.00 10.00
14 Gary Veneruzzo 5.00 10.00

1976-77 Stingers Kahn's

This set of six photos was issued on wrappers of Kahn's Wieners and features players of the Cincinnati Stingers of the WHA. The wrappers are approximately 2 11/16" wide and 11 5/8" long. On a predominantly yellow wrapper with red lettering, a 2" by 1 1/4" black and white player action photo appears, with a facsimile autograph inscribed across the picture. The wrappers are unnumbered and checklisted below in alphabetical order. This set is distinguished from the previous year by the fact that these card photo poses (for the players in both sets) appear to be taken in an action sequence compared to the posed photographs taken the previous year.
COMPLETE SET (6) 62.50 125.00
1 Rick Dudley 15.00 30.00
2 Dave Inkpen 12.50 25.00
3 John Hughes 10.00 20.00
4 Claude Larose 12.50 25.00
5 Jacques Locas 10.00 20.00
6 Ron Plumb 10.00 20.00
7 Dennis Sobchuk 10.00 20.00

1997-98 Studio

The 1997-98 Studio set was issued in one series totaling 110 cards and was distributed in five-card packs with an 8x10 Studio Portrait enclosed. The fronts feature color player portraits, while the backs carry an action player photos and player information.
COMPLETE SET (110) 15.00 30.00
1 Wayne Gretzky 1.00 2.50
2 Dominik Hasek .30 .75
3 Eric Lindros .30 .75
4 Paul Kariya .25 .60
5 Jaromir Jagr .50 1.25
6 Brendan Shanahan .25 .60
7 Patrick Roy .50 1.25
8 Keith Tkachuk .20 .50
9 Mark Messier .30 .75
10 Steve Yzerman .40 1.00
11 Brett Hull .25 .60
12 Jarome Iginla .20 .50
13 Mike Modano .30 .75
14 Pavel Bure .25 .60
15 Peter Forsberg .25 .60
16 Ryan Smyth .15 .40
17 John Vanbiesbrouck .20 .50
18 Teemu Selanne .40 1.00
19 Saku Koivu .20 .50
20 Martin Brodeur .40 1.00
21 Sergei Fedorov .30 .75
22 John LeClair .20 .50
23 Joe Sakic .30 .75
24 Jose Theodore .20 .50
25 Marc Denis .20 .50
26 Dainius Zubrus .15 .40
27 Bryan Berard .12 .30
28 Ray Bourque .30 .75
29 Curtis Joseph .20 .50
30 Chris Chelios .20 .50
31 Alexei Yashin .15 .40
32 Adam Oates .20 .50
33 Anson Carter .12 .30
34 Jim Campbell .12 .30
35 Jason Arnott .15 .40
36 Derek Plante .15 .40
37 Guy Hebert .15 .40
38 Oleg Tverdovsky .15 .40
39 Ed Jovanovski .12 .30
40 Jeremy Roenick .25 .60
41 Scott Mellanby .15 .40
42 Keith Primeau .15 .40
43 Ron Hextall .20 .50
44 Daren Puppa .15 .40
45 Jim Carey .12 .30
46 Zigmund Palffy .20 .50
47 Jaroslav Svejkovsky .15 .40
48 Daymond Langkow .12 .30
49 Mikael Renberg .15 .40
50 Pat LaFontaine .20 .50
51 Mike Grier .15 .40
52 Stephane Fiset .15 .40
53 Luc Robitaille .20 .50
54 Joe Thornton .20 .50
55 Joe Nieuwendyk .20 .50
56 Mike Dunham .15 .40
57 Mark Recchi .25 .60
58 Ed Belfour .20 .50
59 Mike Richter .20 .50
60 Peter Bondra .15 .40
61 Trevor Kidd .12 .30
62 Sean Burke .12 .30
63 Nikolai Khabibulin .20 .50
64 Pierre Turgeon .20 .50
65 Dino Ciccarelli .20 .50
66 Felix Potvin .20 .50
67 Mats Sundin .20 .50
68 Joe Juneau .15 .40
69 Mike Vernon .15 .40
70 Adam Deadmarsh .12 .30
71 Damian Rhodes .15 .40
72 Mike Peca .15 .40
73 Jean-Sebastien Giguere .20 .50
74 Ron Francis .25 .60
75 Roman Hamrlik .15 .40
76 Vincent Damphousse .15 .40
77 Jocelyn Thibault .12 .30
78 Claude Lemieux .15 .40
79 Steve Shields RC .20 .50
80 Dimitri Khristich .15 .40
81 Theo Fleury .25 .60
82 Sandis Ozolinsh .15 .40
83 Ethan Moreau .12 .30
84 Geoff Sanderson .15 .40
85 Paul Coffey .20 .50
86 Brian Leetch .20 .50
87 Chris Osgood .20 .50
88 Kirk McLean .15 .40
89 Mike Gartner .20 .50
90 Chris Gratton .12 .30
91 Eric Fichaud .15 .40
92 Alexandre Daigle .12 .30
93 Doug Gilmour .25 .60
94 Daniel Alfredsson .20 .50
95 Doug Weight .20 .50
96 Derian Hatcher .15 .40
97 Wade Redden .12 .
98 Jeff Friesen .15 .
99 Tony Amonte .15 .
100 Janne Niinimaa .15 .
101 Trevor Linden .15 .
102 Grant Fuhr .20 .
103 Chris Phillips .15 .
104 Sergei Berezin .15 .
105 Brendan Shanahan CL .25 .
106 Steve Yzerman CL .40 1.
107 Teemu Selanne CL .40 1.
108 Eric Lindros CL .30 .
109 Wayne Gretzky CL 1.00 2.
110 Patrick Roy CL .50 1.
P3 Eric Lindros PROMO .30 .

1997-98 Studio Press Proofs Silver

Randomly inserted in packs, this 110-card set is parallel to the base set. The difference is found in th silver holographic foil and micro-etched borders. Ea card is numbered 1 of 1000.
*PP SILVER: 10X TO 25X BASIC CARDS

1997-98 Studio Press Proofs Gold

Randomly inserted in packs, this 110-card set is parallel to the regular Studio set. The difference is found in the special gold holographic foil and micro etched borders. Each card is numbered as 1 of 250.
*PP GOLD: 15X TO 40X BASIC CARDS

1997-98 Studio Hard Hats

Randomly inserted in packs, this 24-card set display color portraits of young and veteran stars printed on plastic card stock and featuring a die-cut helmet in t background. The cards are individually numbered to 3000.
COMPLETE SET (24) 75.00 150.
1 Wayne Gretzky 12.00 30.
2 Eric Lindros 3.00 8.
3 Paul Kariya 3.00 8.
4 Bryan Berard .75 2.
5 Dainius Zubrus .75 2.
6 Daymond Langkow .75 2.
7 Keith Tkachuk 1.50 4.
8 Ryan Smyth 1.50 4.
9 Brendan Shanahan 3.00 8.
10 Steve Yzerman 12.00 30.
11 Teemu Selanne 3.00 8.
12 Jarome Iginla 4.00 10.
13 Zigmund Palffy 1.50 4.
14 Sergei Berezin .75 2.
15 Saku Koivu 3.00 8.
16 Peter Forsberg 8.00 20.
17 Joe Sakic 6.00 15.
18 Pavel Bure 3.00 8.
19 Jaromir Jagr 5.00 12.
20 Brett Hull 4.00 10.
21 Sergei Fedorov 4.00 10.
22 Mike Grier .75 2.
23 Ethan Moreau .75 2.
24 Mats Sundin 3.00 8.

1997-98 Studio Portraits 8x10

Inserted one per pack, this 36-card set is a partial parallel 8" by 10" version of the base set and feature portraits of the top stars printed on large cards with signable UV coating.
COMPLETE SET (36) 30.00 60.
1 Wayne Gretzky 2.00 5.
2 Dominik Hasek .75 2.
3 Eric Lindros .50 1.
4 Paul Kariya .30 .
5 Jaromir Jagr .50 1.
6 Brendan Shanahan .30 .
7 Patrick Roy 1.50 4.
8 Keith Tkachuk .30 .
9 Mark Messier .40 1.
10 Steve Yzerman 1.25 3.
11 Brett Hull .50 1.
12 Jarome Iginla .50 1.
13 Mike Modano .50 1.
14 Pavel Bure .40 1.
15 Peter Forsberg .50 1.
16 Ryan Smyth .25 .
17 John Vanbiesbrouck .30 .
18 Teemu Selanne .40 1.
19 Saku Koivu .30 .
20 Martin Brodeur .50 1.
21 Sergei Fedorov .50 1.
22 Joe Thornton .75 2.
23 Joe Sakic .75 2.
24 Bryan Berard .30 .
25 John LeClair .40 1.
26 Marc Denis .25 .
27 Dainius Zubrus .30 .
28 Chris Chelios .40 1.
29 Jason Arnott .30 .
30 Jeremy Roenick .50 1.
31 Zigmund Palffy .25 .
32 Jaroslav Svejkovsky .25 .
33 Mike Richter .40 1.
34 Felix Potvin .50 1.
35 Brian Leetch .40 1.
36 Chris Osgood .40 1.
NNOA Martin Brodeur AU/700 40.00 100.
NNOB Jarome Iginla AU/1000 15.00 40.
NNOC Ryan Smyth AU/1000 6.00 15.

1997-98 Studio Silhouettes

Randomly inserted in packs, this 24-card set feature laser die-cutting of star players' facial features. The cards are sequentially numbered to 1,500. An 8"x10 parallel was also created and inserted into packs. These parallels were numbered to 3000.
COMPLETE SET (24) 100.00 200.
*8X10 JUMBO/3000: .3X TO .8X INSERT/1500
1 Wayne Gretzky 10.00 25.
2 Eric Lindros 3.00 8.
3 Patrick Roy 8.00 20.
4 Martin Brodeur 6.00 15.
5 Paul Kariya 2.50 6.
6 Mark Messier 3.00 8.
7 Dominik Hasek 5.00 12.
8 Brett Hull 4.00 10.
9 Pavel Bure 3.00 8.
10 Steve Yzerman 6.00 15.
11 Brendan Shanahan 3.00 8.
12 Joe Sakic 6.00 15.
13 Peter Forsberg 3.00 8.
14 Sergei Fedorov 4.00 10.
15 John LeClair 2.50 6.
16 John Vanbiesbrouck 2.50 6.
17 Teemu Selanne 3.00 8.
18 Keith Tkachuk 2.50 6.
19 Mike Modano 4.00 10.
20 Felix Potvin 5.00 12.
21 Ryan Smyth 2.00 5.
22 Jaromir Jagr 5.00 12.
23 Brian Leetch 2.50 6.
24 Jarome Iginla 5.00 12.

1995-96 Summit

e 1995-96 Summit set was issued in one series aling 200 cards. The 7-card packs had a suggested ail of $1.99 each. The set was highlighted by a uble thick 24-point card stock. The Cool Trade emption card was randomly inserted in 1:72 packs, d was redeemable for NHL Cool Trade Upgrade ds of Patrick Roy, Chris Chelios, Ray Bourque and m Neely. Rookie Cards include Daniel Alfredsson, dek Dvorak, Chad Kilger, and Kyle McLaren.

ark Messier .15 .40
aul Kariya .12 .30
lexei Zhamnov .10 .25
dam Oates .10 .25
ale Hunter .07 .20
aleri Kamensky .07 .20
avel Bure .12 .30
heo Fleury .12 .30
lats Sundin .10 .25
Joe Murphy .05 .15
Brian Bellows .07 .20
Owen Nolan .10 .25
Brett Hull .12 .30
Mike Modano .15 .40
Ulf Dahlen .05 .15
Paul Coffey .10 .25
Jaromir Jagr .25 .60
Jason Arnott .07 .20
Eric Lindros .15 .40
Jesse Belanger .05 .15
Alexandre Daigle .05 .15
Darren Turcotte .05 .15
Brian Leetch .10 .25
Wayne Gretzky .50 1.25
Mathieu Schneider .05 .15
Mark Recchi .12 .30
Martin Brodeur .25 .60
Igor Korolev .05 .15
Jocelyn Thibault .07 .20
Chris Pronger .10 .25
Sergei Fedorov .15 .40
Jari Kurri .10 .25
Ray Bourque .15 .40
Pat LaFontaine .10 .25
Don Beaupre .07 .20
Dave Andreychuk .10 .25
Oleg Tverdovsky .10 .25
Geoff Sanderson .05 .15
Chris Chelios .10 .25
Phil Housley .07 .20
Kevin Hatcher .07 .20
Ron Francis .12 .30
Pierre Turgeon .10 .25
Mikael Renberg .07 .20
Chris Gratton .05 .15
Tommy Soderstrom .07 .20
Stu Barnes .05 .15
Alexander Mogilny .07 .20
Craig Janney .05 .15
Scott Niedermayer .10 .25
Jim Carey .07 .20
Stephane Richer .07 .20
Dave Gagner .05 .15
Teemu Selanne .20 .50
Kelly Hrudey .07 .20
Roman Hamrlik .05 .15
Scott Mellanby .07 .20
Guy Hebert .07 .20
Gary Suter .07 .20
Travis Green .07 .20
Joe Sakic .15 .40
Doug Gilmour .12 .30
Peter Bondra .10 .25
Vincent Damphousse .07 .20
Dino Ciccarelli .07 .20
Adam Graves .07 .20
Kevin Stevens .07 .20
Jeff Friesen .05 .15
Kirk McLean .07 .20
Brad May .05 .15
Bill Ranford .07 .20
Derian Hatcher .07 .20
Glen Wesley .05 .15
Sergei Zubov .07 .20
John LeClair .10 .25
Igor Larionov .05 .15
Ray Sheppard .07 .20
Ulf Samuelsson .05 .15
Rod Brind'Amour .10 .25
Felix Potvin .10 .25
Cam Neely .10 .25
Jeremy Roenick .12 .30
Slava Kozlov .07 .20
Arturs Irbe .07 .20
Daren Puppa .07 .20
Rob Blake .07 .20
Steve Heinze .05 .15
Tom Barrasso .07 .20
Luc Robitaille .10 .25
Al MacInnis .10 .25
Petr Nedved .07 .20
Joe Mullen .07 .20
Mark Tinordi .05 .15
Tomas Sandstrom .07 .20
Dale Hawerchuk .12 .30
Andy Moog .10 .25
Alexei Kovalev .05 .15
David Oliver .05 .15
Patrick Poulin .05 .15
Tony Granato .05 .15
Alexei Yashin .07 .20
Trevor Linden .10 .25
Rick Tocchet .07 .20
Brett Lindros .05 .15
Rob Niedermayer .07 .20
John MacLean .07 .20
Pat Verbeek .07 .20
Ray Ferraro .05 .15
Mike Ricci .07 .20
Doug Weight .10 .25
Bill Guerin .07 .20
Ken Wregget .07 .20
Teppo Numminen .05 .15
Mike Vernon .07 .20
Mike Richter .10 .25
Dan Quinn .07 .20
Peter Forsberg .25 .60
Mario Lemieux .30 .75
Geoff Courtnall .05 .15
Ed Belfour .07 .20
Kirk Muller .07 .20
Chris Osgood .07 .20
Radek Bonk .05 .15
Brendan Shanahan .12 .30
Sean Burke .05 .15
Larry Murphy .10 .25
Blaine Lacher .07 .20
Russ Courtnall .05 .15
Claude Lemieux .10 .25
John Vanbiesbrouck .07 .20
131 Wendel Clark .10 .25
132 Nelson Emerson .05 .15
133 Ron Hextall .10 .25
134 Scott Stevens .10 .25
135 Bernie Nicholls .05 .15
136 Brian Skrudland .05 .15
137 Sandis Ozolinsh .07 .20
138 Trevor Kidd .07 .20
139 Joe Juneau .07 .20
140 Keith Primeau .05 .15
141 Petr Klima .05 .15
142 Viktor Kozlov .07 .20
143 Mike Gartner .10 .25
144 Zigmund Palffy .10 .25
145 Steve Duchesne .05 .15
146 Brian Bradley .07 .20
147 Michal Pivonka .05 .15
148 Todd Harvey .05 .15
149 Patrick Roy .25 .60
150 Gary Roberts .05 .15
151 Shayne Corson .05 .15
152 Keith Tkachuk .10 .25
153 Dimitri Khristich .05 .15
154 Steve Yzerman .12 .30
155 Shawn McEachern .05 .15
156 Bryan Smolinski .05 .15
157 Vladimir Malakhov .05 .15
158 Andrew Cassels .05 .15
159 Dominik Hasek .12 .30
160 Stephane Fiset .07 .20
161 Steve Thomas .07 .20
162 Joe Nieuwendyk .10 .25
163 Sergio Momesso .05 .15
164 Jyrki Lumme .05 .15
165 Tony Amonte .07 .20
166 Yanic Perreault .05 .15
167 Brian Savage .05 .15
168 Brian Holzinger RC .20 .50
169 Radek Dvorak RC .12 .30
170 Jamie Langenbrunner .05 .15
171 Ed Jovanovski .10 .25
172 Bryan McCabe .10 .25
173 Jere Lehtinen .07 .20
174 Antti Tormanen .05 .15
175 Aki Berg RC .10 .25
176 Ryan Smyth .07 .20
177 Shean Donovan .05 .15
178 Darby Hendrickson .05 .15
179 Chad Kilger RC .10 .25
180 Vitali Yachmenev .10 .25
181 Deron Quint .07 .20
182 Daniel Alfredsson RC .50 1.25
183 Jeff O'Neill .10 .25
184 Corey Hirsch .07 .20
185 Sandy Moger RC .05 .15
186 Saku Koivu .10 .25
187 Niklas Sundstrom .10 .25
188 Shane Doan RC .30 .75
189 Brendan Witt .10 .25
190 Eric Daze .20 .50
191 Marty Murray .10 .25
192 Byron Dafoe .07 .20
193 Todd Bertuzzi RC .12 .30
194 Kyle McLaren RC .05 .15
195 Marcus Ragnarsson RC .12 .30
196 Robert Svehla RC .05 .15
197 Valeri Bure .05 .15
198 Paul Coffey .10 .25
199 Checklist (1-198) .05 .15
200 Checklist (inserts) .05 .15

1995-96 Summit Artist's Proofs

This set is a parallel version of the regular Summit issue. The card fronts use a gold prismatic foil background, while the words "Artist's Proof" are stamped on the back. The cards were randomly inserted 1:36 packs.
*VETS: 20X TO 50X BASIC CARDS
*ROOKIES: 12X TO 30X

1995-96 Summit Ice

This lower end parallel set of the basic Summit issue features silver prismatic foil print technology on the front, and the words "Summit Ice" on the back. The cards were randomly inserted at a rate of 1:7 packs.
*VETS: 5X TO 12X BASIC CARDS
*ROOKIES: 3X TO 8X

1995-96 Summit GM's Choice

Randomly inserted at a rate of 1:37 packs, this 21-card set features Pinnacle consultant Mike McPhee selecting his top choices for an all-star "dream team". The appearance of the cards is boosted by the use of a holographic gold-foil background.

1 Patrick Roy 5.00 12.00
2 Martin Brodeur 5.00 12.00
3 Chris Chelios 2.00 5.00
4 Brian Leetch 2.00 5.00
5 Eric Lindros 3.00 8.00
6 Keith Tkachuk 2.00 5.00
7 Pavel Bure 2.50 6.00
8 Scott Stevens 2.00 5.00
9 Paul Coffey 2.00 5.00
10 Mario Lemieux 6.00 15.00
11 Jaromir Jagr 5.00 12.00
12 Cam Neely 2.00 5.00
13 Ray Bourque 3.00 8.00
14 Al MacInnis 2.00 5.00
15 Sergei Fedorov 3.00 8.00
16 Mark Messier 3.00 8.00
17 Brett Hull 2.50 6.00
18 Wayne Gretzky 10.00 25.00
19 Paul Kariya 2.50 6.00
20 Brendan Shanahan 2.50 6.00
21 Mike McPhee 2.00 5.00

1995-96 Summit In The Crease

Randomly inserted at a rate of 1:91 packs, this 15-card set showcases some of the hottest goaltenders in the league on cards utilizing Spectroetch technology.

COMPLETE SET (15) 25.00 60.00
1 Martin Brodeur 6.00 15.00
2 Dominik Hasek 4.00 10.00
3 Patrick Roy 10.00 25.00
4 Ed Belfour 2.00 5.00
5 Felix Potvin 2.00 5.00
6 Jim Carey 1.25 3.00
7 Jocelyn Thibault 1.25 3.00
8 Stephane Fiset 1.25 3.00
9 Chris Osgood 2.00 5.00
10 Ron Hextall 2.00 5.00
11 Mike Richter 2.00 5.00
12 Andy Moog 1.25 3.00
13 Sean Burke 1.25 3.00
14 Kirk McLean 1.25 3.00
15 John Vanbiesbrouck 2.00 5.00

1995-96 Summit Mad Hatters

Randomly inserted at a rate of 1:23 packs, this 15-card set pays tribute -- not surprisingly -- to some of the top hat trick artists of the 1994-95 season on Spectroetched cards.

COMPLETE SET (15) 15.00 30.00
1 Lindros 1.50 4.00
Nolan
Nicholls
2 Brett Hull 2.00 5.00
3 John LeClair .75 2.00
4 Cam Neely 1.50 4.00
5 Alexei Zhamnov .60 1.50
6 Jason Arnott .60 1.50
7 Pavel Bure 1.50 4.00
8 Wendel Clark .75 2.00
9 Sergei Fedorov 2.00 5.00
10 Jaromir Jagr 2.50 6.00
11 Peter Bondra .75 2.00
12 Alexei Yashin .60 1.50
13 Joe Nieuwendyk .75 2.00
14 Luc Robitaille .75 2.00
15 Todd Harvey .60 1.50

1996-97 Summit

This 200-card set was distributed in seven-card packs with a suggested retail price of $2.99. The fronts featured color action player photos while the backs carried player information. A 25-card "Rookies" subset and three checklists were included in this set. Key rookies include Kevin Hodson and Ethan Moreau.

COMPLETE SET (200) 15.00 30.00
1 Joe Sakic .30 .75
2 Dominik Hasek .30 .75
3 Paul Coffey .15 .40
4 Todd Gill .02 .10
5 Pat Verbeek .02 .10
6 John LeClair .15 .40
7 Joe Juneau .02 .10
8 Scott Mellanby .08 .25
9 Scott Stevens .08 .25
10 Ron Francis .08 .25
11 Larry Murphy .08 .25
12 Sandis Ozolinsh .02 .10
13 Luc Robitaille .08 .25
14 Grant Fuhr .08 .25
15 Adam Oates .08 .25
16 Keith Primeau .02 .10
17 Mark Recchi .08 .25
18 Brian Bradley .02 .10
19 Zdeno Ciger .02 .10
20 Zigmund Palffy .08 .25
21 Damian Rhodes .08 .25
22 Russ Courtnall .02 .10
23 Mike Modano .25 .60
24 Geoff Sanderson .08 .25
25 Michal Pivonka .02 .10
26 Randy Burridge .02 .10
27 Dimitri Khristich .02 .10
28 Mike Gartner .08 .25
29 Cam Neely .15 .40
30 Mathieu Schneider .02 .10
31 Steve Thomas .02 .10
32 Mario Lemieux .75 2.00
33 Darryl Sydor .02 .10
34 Alexei Yashin .02 .10
35 Brett Hull .20 .50
36 Trevor Kidd .08 .25
37 Alexei Zhamnov .08 .25
38 Uwe Krupp .02 .10
39 Brian Skrudland .02 .10
40 Igor Larionov .02 .10
41 Nikolai Khabibulin .08 .25
42 Pavel Bure .15 .40
43 Chris Chelios .15 .40
44 Andrew Cassels .02 .10
45 Owen Nolan .08 .25
46 Todd Harvey .02 .10
47 Jari Kurri .08 .25
48 Olaf Kolzig .08 .25
49 Greg Johnson .02 .10
50 Dominic Roussel .08 .25
51 Mats Sundin .15 .40
52 Robert Svehla .02 .10
53 Sandy Moger .02 .10
54 Darren Turcotte .02 .10
55 Teppo Numminen .02 .10
56 Benoit Hogue .02 .10
57 Scott Niedermayer .02 .10
58 Alexander Selivanov .02 .10
59 Valeri Kamensky .08 .25
60 Ken Wregget .08 .25
61 Travis Green .08 .25
62 Peter Bondra .08 .25
63 Vladimir Konstantinov .08 .25
64 Craig Janney .08 .25
65 Joe Nieuwendyk .08 .25
66 John Vanbiesbrouck .08 .25
67 Wayne Gretzky 1.00 2.50
68 Kirk McLean .08 .25
69 Alexei Zhitnik .02 .10
70 Mike Ricci .02 .10
71 Jeff Beukeboom .02 .10
72 Felix Potvin .15 .40
73 Mikael Renberg .08 .25
74 Jamie Baker .02 .10
75 Guy Hebert .08 .25
76 Steve Yzerman .75 2.00
77 Daren Puppa .08 .25
78 Scott Young .02 .10
79 Martin Gelinas .02 .10
80 Dave Gagner .08 .25
81 Tomas Sandstrom .02 .10
82 Alexei Kovalev .02 .10
83 Ray Whitney .02 .10
84 Vyacheslav Kozlov .02 .10
85 Jaromir Jagr .25 .60
86 Joe Murphy .02 .10
87 Patrick Roy .75 2.00
88 Ray Sheppard .08 .25
89 Chris Terreri .08 .25
90 Pierre Turgeon .08 .25
91 Theo Fleury .02 .10
92 Doug Weight .08 .25
93 Tom Barrasso .08 .25
94 Jim Carey .15 .40
95 Greg Adams .02 .10
96 Brian Leetch .15 .40
97 Ed Belfour .15 .40
98 Stephane Fiset .08 .25
99 Stephane Richer .08 .25
100 Ron Hextall .08 .25
101 Mike Vernon .00 .25
102 Jocelyn Thibault .15 .40
103 Jason Arnott .02 .10
104 Keith Tkachuk .15 .40
105 Sergei Fedorov .20 .50
106 Alexandre Daigle .02 .10
107 Alexander Mogilny .08 .25
108 German Titov .02 .10
109 Sean Burke .08 .25
110 Arturs Irbe .08 .25
111 Mark Messier .15 .40
112 Nicklas Lidstrom .15 .40
113 Claude Lemieux .02 .10
114 Martin Brodeur .40 1.00
115 Bernie Nicholls .02 .10
116 Paul Kariya .15 .40
117 Eric Lindros .15 .40
118 Doug Gilmour .08 .25
119 Sergei Zubov .02 .10
120 Adam Graves .02 .10
121 Phil Housley .08 .25
122 Bob Bassen .02 .10
123 Rod Brind'Amour .08 .25
124 Dave Andreychuk .08 .25
125 Corey Hirsch .08 .25
126 Kelly Hrudey .08 .25
127 Pat LaFontaine .15 .40
128 Slava Fetisov .02 .10
129 Oleg Tverdovsky .08 .25
130 Andy Moog .08 .25
131 Stu Barnes .02 .10
132 Roman Hamrlik .08 .25
133 Teemu Selanne .15 .40
134 Trevor Linden .08 .25
135 Chris Osgood .08 .25
136 Vincent Damphousse .02 .10
137 Shayne Corson .02 .10
138 Jeremy Roenick .20 .50
139 Brendan Shanahan .15 .40
140 Wendel Clark .08 .25
141 Ray Bourque .25 .60
142 Peter Forsberg .40 1.00
143 John MacLean .08 .25
144 Jeff Friesen .02 .10
145 Mike Richter .15 .40
146 Dave Reid .02 .10
147 Rob Niedermayer .08 .25
148 Petr Nedved .08 .25
149 Sylvain Lefebvre .02 .10
150 Curtis Joseph .15 .40
151 Eric Daze .08 .25
152 Saku Koivu .15 .40
153 Jere Lehtinen .02 .10
154 Todd Bertuzzi .15 .40
155 Chad Kilger .02 .10
156 Stephane Yelle .02 .10
157 Bryan McCabe .02 .10
158 Aaron Gavey .02 .10
159 Kyle McLaren .02 .10
160 Valeri Bure .02 .10
161 Antti Tormanen .02 .10
162 Brendan Witt .02 .10
163 Ed Jovanovski .08 .25
164 Aki Berg .02 .10
165 Marcus Ragnarsson .02 .10
166 Miroslav Satan .02 .10
167 Daniel Alfredsson .08 .25
168 Jeff O'Neill .02 .10
169 Radek Dvorak .02 .10
170 Petr Sykora .02 .10
171 Vitali Yachmenev .02 .10
172 Niklas Andersson .02 .10
173 Nolan Baumgartner .02 .10
174 Brandon Convery .02 .10
175 Ralph Intranuovo .02 .10
176 Niklas Sundblad .02 .10
177 Patrick Labrecque .08 .25
178 Eric Fichaud .08 .25
179 Martin Biron RC .75 2.00
180 Steve Sullivan RC .20 .50
181 Peter Ferraro .02 .10
182 Jose Theodore .20 .50
183 Kevin Hodson RC .15 .40
184 Ethan Moreau RC .15 .40
185 Curtis Brown .02 .10
186 Daymond Langkow .08 .25
187 Jan Caloun RC .02 .10
188 Landon Wilson .02 .10
189 Tommy Salo .08 .25
190 Anders Eriksson .02 .10
191 David Nemirovsky .02 .10
192 Jamie Langenbrunner .02 .10
193 Zdenek Nedved .02 .10
194 Todd Hlushko .02 .10
195 Alexei Yegorov RC .02 .10
196 Jamie Pushor .02 .10
197 Anders Myrvold .02 .10
198 Mark Messier CL .15 .40
199 Brett Hull CL .15 .40
200 Pavel Bure CL .15 .40

1996-97 Summit Artist's Proofs

Randomly inserted in packs at a rate of 1:35, this 200-card parallel set to the regular 1996-97 Summit set was distinguished in design by a holographic foil stamped Artist's Proof logo on the front.
*VETS: 20X TO 50X BASIC CARDS
*ROOKIES: 8X TO 20X

1996-97 Summit Ice

Randomly inserted in packs at the rate of 1:6, this 200-card parallel set featured prismatic foil printing which distinguished it from the regular Summit set. Values for all singles can be determined by using the multipliers below on the corresponding card from the base set.
*VETS: 6X TO 15X BASIC CARDS
*ROOKIES: 2.5X TO 6X

1996-97 Summit Metal

This 200 card set parallels the base set, and is printed on reflective foil board.

COMPLETE SET (200) 20.00 50.00
*METAL: 1.5X TO 4X BASIC CARDS

1996-97 Summit Premium Stock

A parallel to the standard Summit set, Premium Stock was distributed only to hobby outlets. Cards feature enhanced 24 pt. card stock with micro-etched foil backgrounds. Many of the Premium Stock cards came damaged out of the packs.

COMPLETE SET (200) 20.00 50.00
*VETS: 1.5X TO 4X BASIC CARDS
*ROOKIES: .6X TO 1.5X BASIC CARDS

1996-97 Summit High Voltage

This 16-card Spectroetch insert set spotlighted the high-energy play of the NHL's superstar elite. The fronts featured a color player image on a silver and black lightning displayed background. The backs carried another player photo with player information. Just 1,500 copies of each card in this set were produced and sequentially numbered. A parallel "Mirage" version of these cards was randomly inserted into packs and sequentially numbered to 600.

COMPLETE SET (16) 60.00 150.00
*MIRAGE: .8X TO 2X BASIC INSERTS
1 Mark Messier 4.00 10.00
2 Joe Sakic 8.00 20.00
3 Paul Kariya 4.00 10.00
4 Daniel Alfredsson 2.00 5.00
5 Wayne Gretzky 12.00 30.00
6 Peter Forsberg 6.00 15.00
7 Eric Daze 2.00 5.00
8 Mario Lemieux 8.00 20.00
9 Eric Lindros 4.00 10.00
10 Jeremy Roenick 4.00 10.00
11 Alexander Mogilny 2.00 5.00
12 Teemu Selanne 4.00 10.00
13 Sergei Fedorov 4.00 10.00
14 Saku Koivu 4.00 10.00
15 Jaromir Jagr 6.00 15.00
16 Brett Hull 4.00 10.00
P16 Eric Lindros PROMO 2.00 5.00

1996-97 Summit In The Crease

This 16-card insert set featured the NHL's top goalies. A gold-foil stamped print technology was utilized which gave the cards a distinctive feel and look, and created a sense of depth in the cards. 6,000 copies of each of the cards in this set were produced and sequentially numbered. A premium stock parallel was also created. The premium stock version had an enhanced foil background and was numbered with the prefix PSITC, and numbered to 600.

COMPLETE SET (16) 30.00 80.00
*PREM.STOCK: .8X TO 2X BASIC INSERTS
1 Patrick Roy 6.00 15.00
2 Mike Richter 2.50 6.00
3 Ed Belfour 2.50 6.00
4 Daren Puppa 1.50 4.00
5 Curtis Joseph 2.50 6.00
6 Jim Carey 1.50 4.00
7 Damian Rhodes 1.50 4.00
8 Martin Brodeur 6.00 15.00
9 Felix Potvin 3.00 8.00
10 John Vanbiesbrouck 2.00 5.00
11 Jocelyn Thibault 1.50 4.00
12 Nikolai Khabibulin 1.50 4.00
13 Chris Osgood 1.50 4.00
14 Dominik Hasek 4.00 10.00
15 Corey Hirsch 1.50 4.00
16 Ron Hextall 1.50 4.00

1996-97 Summit Untouchables

This 18-card insert set was an all-foil version of the regular series which honored 12 skaters who amassed 100 or more points and six goaltenders who notched 30 wins during the 1995-96 season. Although the cards were intended to mention this fact, all the goalie cards read 100 points along the bottom front, the same as the skaters. No corrected versions were produced. Just 1,000 copies of this set were produced and each card was sequentially numbered.

COMPLETE SET (18) 75.00 150.00
1 Mario Lemieux 10.00 25.00
2 Jaromir Jagr 4.00 10.00
3 Joe Sakic 8.00 20.00
4 Ron Francis 2.00 5.00
5 Peter Forsberg 4.00 10.00
6 Eric Lindros 5.00 12.00
7 Paul Kariya 3.00 8.00
8 Teemu Selanne 6.00 15.00
9 Alexander Mogilny 2.00 5.00
10 Sergei Fedorov 4.00 10.00
11 Doug Weight 2.00 5.00
12 Wayne Gretzky 25.00 60.00
13 Chris Osgood 2.00 5.00
14 Jim Carey 2.00 5.00
15 Patrick Roy 10.00 25.00
16 Martin Brodeur 8.00 20.00
17 Felix Potvin 6.00 15.00
18 Ron Hextall 3.00 8.00

1980 Superstar Matchbook

These collector issued matchbooks were issued in the New England area in 1980 and featured superstars from all sports but with an emphasis on players who made their fame in New England. Since these are unnumbered, we have sequenced them in alphabetical order.

COMPLETE SET 30.00 60.00
3 Ray Bourque 4.00 8.00
5 Gordie Howe 3.00 6.00
7 Guy LaFleur 2.00 4.00
9 Bobby Orr 5.00 10.00

1910-11 Sweet Caporal Postcards

These black-and-white photo postcards apparently were used by the artists working on the C55 cards of the next year, 1911-12. Printed by the British American Tobacco Co. in England, these cards were distributed by Imperial Tobacco of Canada. One card was reportedly packed in each 50-cigarette tin of Sweet Caporal cigarettes. The backs show the postcard design. The cards are checklisted below according to teams as follows: Quebec Bulldogs (1-8), Ottawa Senators (10-17), Renfrew Millionaires (18-26), Montreal Wanderers (27-36), and Montreal Canadiens (37-45).

COMPLETE SET (45) 9000.00 18000.00
1 Paddy Moran 250.00 500.00
2 Joe Hall 175.00 350.00
3 Barney Holden 100.00 200.00
4 Joe Malone 500.00 1000.00
5 Ed Oatman 100.00 200.00
6 Tom Dunderdale 175.00 350.00
7 Ken Mallen 100.00 200.00
8 Jack MacDonald 100.00 200.00
9 Fred Lake 100.00 200.00
10 Albert Kerr 100.00 200.00
11 Marty Walsh 175.00 350.00
12 Hamby Shore 100.00 200.00
13 Alex Currie 100.00 200.00
14 Bruce Ridpath 100.00 200.00
15 Bruce Stuart 175.00 350.00
16 Percy Lesueur 175.00 350.00
17 Jack Darragh 175.00 350.00
18 Steve Vair 100.00 200.00
19 Don Smith 100.00 200.00
20 Cyclone Taylor 600.00 1200.00
21 Bert Lindsay 125.00 250.00
22 H.L. Gilmour 175.00 350.00
23 Bobby Rowe 100.00 200.00
24 Sprague Cleghorn 300.00 600.00
25 Odie Cleghorn 125.00 250.00
26 Skein Ronan 100.00 200.00
27 Walter Smaill 125.00 250.00
28 Ernest Johnson 200.00 400.00
29 Jack Marshall 175.00 350.00
30 Harry Hyland 175.00 350.00
31 Art Ross 600.00 1200.00
32 Riley Hern 175.00 350.00
33 Gordon Roberts 175.00 350.00
34 Frank Glass 100.00 200.00
35 Ernest Russell 200.00 400.00
36 James Gardner 175.00 350.00
37 Art Bernier 100.00 200.00
38 Georges Vezina 2000.00 4000.00
39 Henri Dallaire 100.00 200.00
40 R.(Rocket) Power 100.00 200.00
41 Didier Pitre 175.00 350.00
42 Newsy Lalonde 600.00 1200.00
43 Eugene Payan 100.00 200.00
44 George Poulin 100.00 200.00
45 Jack Laviolette 200.00 400.00

1934-35 Sweet Caporal

This colorful set of 48 large (approximately 6 3/4" by 10 1/2") pictures were actually inserts in Montreal Forum programs during Canadiens and Maroons home games during the 1934-35 season. Apparently a different photo was inserted each game. Players in the checklist below are identified as part of the following teams, Montreal Canadiens (MC), Montreal Maroons (MM), Boston Bruins (BB), Chicago Blackhawks (CBH), Detroit Red Wings (DRW), New York Rangers (NYR), and Toronto Maple Leafs (TML). Card backs contain player biography and an ad for Sweet Caporal Cigarettes, both in French. The cards are unnumbered.

COMPLETE SET (48) 2500.00 5000.00
1 Gerald Carson MC 25.00 50.00
2 Nels Crutchfield MC 25.00 50.00
3 Wilfrid Cude MC 30.00 60.00
4 Roger Jenkins MC 25.00 50.00
5 Aurel Joliat MC 175.00 350.00
6 Joe Lamb MC 25.00 50.00
7 Wildor Larochelle MC 25.00 50.00
8 Pete Lepine MC 25.00 50.00
9 Georges Mantha MC 25.00 50.00
10 Sylvio Mantha MC 50.00 100.00
11 Jack McGill MC 25.00 50.00
12 Armand Mondou MC 25.00 50.00
13 Paul Marcel Raymond MC 25.00 50.00
14 Jack Riley MC 25.00 50.00
15 Russ Blinco MM 25.00 50.00
16 Herb Cain MM 40.00 80.00
17 Lionel Conacher MM 125.00 250.00
18 Alex Connell MM 62.50 125.00
19 Stewart Evans MM 25.00 50.00
20 Norman Gainor MM 25.00 50.00
21 Paul Haynes MM 25.00 50.00
22 Gus Marker MM 25.00 50.00
23 Baldy Northcott MM 30.00 60.00
24 Earl Robinson MM 25.00 50.00
25 Hooley Smith MM 50.00 100.00
26 Dave Trottier MM 25.00 50.00
27 Jimmy Ward MM 25.00 50.00
28 Cy Wentworth MM 30.00 60.00
29 Eddie Shore BB 250.00 500.00
30 Babe Siebert BB 62.50 125.00
31 Nels Stewart BB 75.00 150.00
32 Tiny Thompson BB 75.00 150.00
33 Lorne Chabot CBH 50.00 100.00
34 Mush March CBH 25.00 50.00
35 Howie Morenz CBH 400.00 800.00
36 Larry Aurie DRW 25.00 50.00
37 Ebbie Goodfellow DRW 50.00 100.00
38 Herbie Lewis DRW 25.00 50.00
39 Ralph Weiland DRW 50.00 100.00
40 Bill Cook NYR 50.00 100.00
41 Bun Cook NYR 50.00 100.00
42 Ivan(Ching) Johnson NYR 67.50 135.00
43 Dave Kerr NYR 40.00 80.00
44 King Clancy 200.00 400.00
45 Charlie Conacher TML 200.00 400.00
46 Red Horner TML 62.50 125.00
47 Busher Jackson TML 75.00 150.00
48 Joe Primeau TML 100.00 200.00

2006-07 Sweet Shot

This 160-card set was released in May, 2007. The set was issued into the hobby in four-card packs (tins) with an $85 SRP which came 20 packs (tins) to a case. Cards numbered 1-100 feature a mix of veterans and retired greats while cards 101-160 are all Rookie Cards which also have a player-worn jersey swatch. Those Rookie Cards were all issued to a stated print run of 499 serial numbered sets.

ROOKIE JSY STATED PRINT RUN 499
1 Teemu Selanne 2.00 5.00
2 Chris Pronger .75 2.00
3 Jean-Sebastien Giguere 1.00 2.50
4 Ilya Kovalchuk 1.00 2.50
5 Marian Hossa .75 2.00
6 Kari Lehtonen .75 2.00
7 Patrice Bergeron 1.25 3.00
8 Zdeno Chara 1.00 2.50
9 Cam Neely 1.00 2.50
10 Bobby Orr 8.00 20.00
11 Phil Esposito 1.50 4.00
12 Ray Bourque 1.50 4.00
13 Ryan Miller 1.00 2.50
14 Maxim Afinogenov .60 1.50
15 Chris Drury .75 2.00
16 Gilbert Perreault 1.00 2.50
17 Alex Tanguay .60 1.50
18 Dion Phaneuf 1.00 2.50
19 Jarome Iginla 1.00 2.50
20 Miikka Kiprusoff .75 2.00
21 Cam Ward 1.00 2.50
22 Eric Staal 1.25 3.00
23 Nikolai Khabibulin 1.00 2.50
24 Martin Havlat .60 1.50
25 Bobby Hull 1.50 4.00
26 Tony Esposito 1.00 2.50
27 Joe Sakic 1.50 4.00
28 Jose Theodore 1.00 2.50
29 Milan Hejduk .75 2.00
30 Patrick Roy 2.50 6.00
31 Rick Nash 1.00 2.50
32 Sergei Fedorov 1.50 4.00
33 Pascal LeClaire .75 2.00
34 Mike Modano 1.50 4.00
35 Eric Lindros 1.50 4.00
36 Marty Turco 1.00 2.50
37 Henrik Zetterberg 1.25 3.00
38 Nicklas Lidstrom 1.00 2.50
39 Pavel Datsyuk 1.25 3.00
40 Dominik Hasek 1.25 3.00
41 Gordie Howe 3.00 8.00
42 Ted Lindsay .75 2.00
43 Ales Hemsky .75 2.00
44 Dwayne Roloson .75 2.00
45 Wayne Gretzky 8.00 20.00
46 Jari Kurri 1.00 2.50
47 Grant Fuhr 1.00 2.50
48 Ed Belfour 1.00 2.50
49 Olli Jokinen 1.00 2.50
50 Rob Blake 1.00 2.50
51 Alexander Frolov .60 1.50
52 Manny Fernandez .75 2.00
53 Pavol Demitra 1.25 3.00
54 Marian Gaborik 1.25 3.00
55 Saku Koivu 1.00 2.50
56 Cristobal Huet .75 2.00
57 Michael Ryder .60 1.50
58 Guy Lafleur 1.25 3.00
59 Larry Robinson 1.00 2.50
60 Paul Kariya 1.25 3.00
61 Tomas Vokoun .75 2.00
62 Brian Gionta .75 2.00
63 Martin Brodeur 2.00 5.00
64 Patrik Elias 1.00 2.50
65 Rick DiPietro .75 2.00
66 Alexei Yashin .75 2.00
67 Mike Bossy 1.00 2.50
68 Billy Smith 1.00 2.50
69 Denis Potvin 1.00 2.50
70 Jaromir Jagr 2.50 6.00
71 Henrik Lundqvist 2.00 5.00
72 Brendan Shanahan 1.25 3.00
73 Dany Heatley 1.00 2.50
74 Jason Spezza 1.00 2.50
75 Daniel Alfredsson 1.00 2.50
76 Peter Forsberg 1.25 3.00
77 Simon Gagne 1.00 2.50
78 Bobby Clarke 1.00 2.50
79 Jeremy Roenick 1.00 2.50
80 Shane Doan .75 2.00
81 Curtis Joseph 1.00 2.50
82 Sidney Crosby 6.00 15.00
83 Marc-Andre Fleury 1.50 4.00
84 Mario Lemieux 3.00 8.00
85 Peter Stastny 1.00 2.50
86 Joe Thornton 1.25 3.00
87 Patrick Marleau 1.00 2.50
88 Jonathan Cheechoo 1.00 2.50
89 Doug Weight 1.00 2.50
90 Brad Richards 1.00 2.50
91 Vincent Lecavalier .75 2.00
92 Martin St. Louis 1.00 2.50
93 Mats Sundin 1.00 2.50
94 Andrew Raycroft .75 2.00
95 Darcy Tucker .75 2.00
96 Johnny Bower 1.50 4.00
97 Darryl Sittler 1.00 2.50
98 Roberto Luongo 1.50 4.00
99 Markus Naslund .75 2.00
100 Alexander Ovechkin 4.00 10.00
101 Shane O'Brien JSY RC 2.50 6.00
102 Ryan Shannon JSY RC 2.50 6.00
103 David McKee JSY RC 2.50 6.00
104 Phil Kessel JSY RC 6.00 15.00
105 Yan Stastny JSY RC 2.50 6.00
106 Mark Stuart JSY RC 2.50 6.00
107 Matt Lashoff JSY RC 2.50 6.00
108 Clarke MacArthur JSY RC 3.00 8.00
109 Drew Stafford JSY RC 4.00 10.00
110 Masi Marjamaki JSY RC 2.50 6.00
111 Michael Funk JSY RC 2.50 6.00
112 Brandon Prust JSY RC 2.50 6.00
113 Dustin Boyd JSY RC 2.50 6.00
114 Dustin Byfuglien JSY RC 6.00 15.00
115 Dave Bolland JSY RC 4.00 10.00
116 Michael Blunden JSY RC 2.50 6.00
117 Paul Stastny JSY RC 6.00 15.00
118 Fredrik Norrena JSY RC 2.50 6.00
119 Niklas Grossman JSY RC 4.00 10.00
120 Loui Eriksson JSY RC 4.00 10.00
121 Tomas Kopecky JSY RC 3.00 8.00
122 Stefan Liv JSY RC 2.50 6.00
123 Patrick Thoresen JSY RC 2.50 6.00
124 Marc-Antoine Pouliot JSY RC 2.50 6.00
125 Ladislav Smid JSY RC 2.50 6.00
126 Janis Sprukts JSY RC 2.50 6.00
127 Jeff Deslauriers JSY RC 2.50 6.00
128 David Booth JSY RC 3.00 8.00
129 Konstantin Pushkarev JSY RC 3.00 8.00
130 Anze Kopitar JSY RC 10.00 25.00
131 Patrick O'Sullivan JSY RC 4.00 10.00
132 Benoit Pouliot JSY RC 3.00 8.00
133 Niklas Backstrom JSY RC 5.00 12.00
134 Guillaume Latendresse JSY RC 4.00 10.00
135 Shea Weber JSY RC 6.00 15.00
136 Alexander Radulov JSY RC 5.00 12.00
137 Travis Zajac JSY RC 5.00 12.00
138 Nigel Dawes JSY RC 2.50 6.00
139 Jarkko Immonen JSY RC 2.50 6.00
140 Josh Hennessy JSY RC 2.50 6.00
141 Jussi Timonen JSY RC 3.00 8.00
142 Ryan Potulny JSY RC 2.50 6.00
143 Keith Yandle JSY RC 5.00 12.00
144 Michel Ouellet JSY RC 3.00 8.00
145 Jordan Staal JSY RC 6.00 15.00
146 Evgeni Malkin JSY RC 20.00 40.00
147 Noah Welch JSY RC 2.50 6.00
148 Kristopher Letang JSY RC 8.00 20.00
149 Matt Carle JSY RC 2.50 6.00
150 M-E Vlasic JSY RC 2.50 6.00
151 Joe Pavelski JSY RC 12.00 30.00
152 Marek Schwarz JSY RC 4.00 10.00
153 Karri Ramo JSY RC 2.50 6.00
154 Blair Jones JSY RC 2.50 6.00
155 Ian White JSY RC 3.00 8.00
156 Jeremy Williams JSY RC 2.50 6.00
157 Luc Bourdon JSY RC 4.00 10.00
158 Jesse Schultz JSY RC 2.50 6.00
159 Alexander Edler JSY RC 4.00 10.00
160 Eric Fehr JSY RC 4.00 10.00

2006-07 Sweet Shot Endorsed Equipment

STATED PRINT RUN 25 SER.#'d SETS
EEAR Andrew Raycroft 50.00 100.00
EEBR Bill Ranford 50.00 100.00
EEEB Ed Belfour 50.00 100.00
EEGC Gerry Cheevers 60.00 125.00
EEGF Grant Fuhr 50.00 100.00
EEJT Jose Theodore EXCH 30.00 80.00
EEMF Marc-Andre Fleury 100.00 150.00
EEMT Marty Turco 50.00 100.00
EEPR Patrick Roy 150.00 300.00
EETE Tony Esposito 60.00 125.00

2006-07 Sweet Shot Rookie Jerseys Autographs

STATED PRINT RUN 25 #'d SETS
101 Shane O'Brien 12.00 30.00
102 Ryan Shannon 12.00 30.00
103 David McKee 12.00 30.00
104 Phil Kessel 30.00 80.00
105 Yan Stastny 12.00 30.00
106 Mark Stuart 12.00 30.00
107 Matt Lashoff 12.00 30.00
108 Clarke MacArthur 15.00 40.00
109 Drew Stafford 40.00 100.00
110 Masi Marjamaki 12.00 30.00
111 Michael Funk 12.00 30.00
112 Brandon Prust 12.00 30.00
113 Dustin Boyd 12.00 30.00
114 Dustin Byfuglien 30.00 80.00
115 Dave Bolland 20.00 50.00
116 Michael Blunden 12.00 30.00
117 Paul Stastny 40.00 100.00
118 Fredrik Norrena 12.00 30.00
119 Niklas Grossman 20.00 50.00
120 Loui Eriksson 20.00 50.00

121 Tomas Kopecky 15.00 40.00
122 Stefan Liv 12.00 30.00
123 Patrick Thoresen 12.00 30.00
124 Marc-Antoine Pouliot 12.00 30.00
125 Ladislav Smid 12.00 30.00
126 Janis Sprukts 12.00 30.00
127 Jeff Deslauriers 12.00 30.00
128 David Booth 15.00 40.00
129 Konstantin Pushkarev 15.00 40.00
130 Anze Kopitar 50.00 120.00
131 Patrick O'Sullivan 20.00 50.00
132 Benoit Pouliot 15.00 40.00
133 Niklas Backstrom 25.00 60.00
134 Guillaume Latendresse 20.00 50.00
135 Shea Weber 30.00 80.00
136 Alexander Radulov 25.00 60.00
137 Travis Zajac 25.00 60.00
138 Nigel Dawes 12.00 30.00
139 Jarkko Immonen 12.00 30.00
140 Josh Hennessy 12.00 30.00
141 Jussi Timonen 15.00 40.00
142 Ryan Potulny 12.00 30.00
143 Keith Yandle 25.00 60.00
144 Michel Ouellet 15.00 40.00
145 Jordan Staal 40.00 100.00
146 Evgeni Malkin 75.00 200.00
147 Noah Welch 12.00 30.00
148 Kristopher Letang 40.00 100.00
149 Matt Carle 12.00 30.00
150 Marc-Edouard Vlasic 12.00 30.00
151 Joe Pavelski 60.00 150.00
152 Marek Schwarz 20.00 50.00
153 Karri Ramo 12.00 30.00
154 Blair Jones 12.00 30.00
155 Ian White 15.00 40.00
156 Jeremy Williams 12.00 30.00
157 Luc Bourdon 20.00 50.00
158 Jesse Schultz 12.00 30.00
159 Alexander Edler 20.00 50.00
160 Eric Fehr 20.00 50.00

2006-07 Sweet Shot Signature Shots/Saves

SSAF Alexander Frolov 5.00 12.00
SSAH Ales Hemsky 6.00 15.00
SSAK Anze Kopitar 20.00 50.00
SSAO Adam Oates 8.00 20.00
SSAR Andrew Raycroft 6.00 15.00
SSAT Alex Tanguay SP 5.00 12.00
SSBB Brad Boyes 5.00 12.00
SSBE Jean Beliveau SP 8.00 20.00
SSBF Bernie Federko 6.00 15.00
SSBG Brian Gionta 6.00 15.00
SSBH Bobby Hull SP 12.00 30.00
SSBI Martin Biron 6.00 15.00
SSBM Brenden Morrow 6.00 15.00
SSBO Pierre-Marc Bouchard 8.00 20.00
SSBR Martin Brodeur SP 15.00 40.00
SSCA Colby Armstrong 6.00 15.00
SSCH Jonathan Cheechoo 8.00 20.00
SSCI Dino Ciccarelli 8.00 20.00
SSCN Cam Neely SP 8.00 20.00
SSCP Corey Perry 8.00 20.00
SSCW Cam Ward 8.00 20.00
SSDC Don Cherry SP 12.00 30.00
SSDH Dominik Hasek 10.00 25.00
SSDI Dick Irvin 5.00 12.00
SSDP Denis Potvin SP 8.00 20.00
SSDR Dwayne Roloson 6.00 15.00
SSDS Drew Stafford 8.00 20.00
SSEM Evgeni Malkin 30.00 80.00
SSES Eric Staal 10.00 25.00
SSGB Gilbert Brule 6.00 15.00
SSGE Martin Gerber 6.00 15.00
SSGF Grant Fuhr SP 8.00 20.00
SSGH Gordie Howe 25.00 60.00
SSGL Guillaume Latendresse 8.00 20.00
SSGO Scott Gomez 6.00 15.00
SSHA Dale Hawerchuk 10.00 25.00
SSHE Dany Heatley SP 8.00 20.00
SSHI Chris Higgins 5.00 12.00
SSHU Cristobal Huet 6.00 15.00
SSHZ H. Zetterberg SP EXCH 10.00 25.00
SSIK Ilya Kovalchuk 8.00 20.00
SSJB Johnny Bucyk SP 8.00 20.00
SSJC Jeff Carter 8.00 20.00
SSJG Jean-Sebastien Giguere 8.00 20.00
SSJI Jarome Iginla 8.00 20.00
SSJP Joni Pitkanen 5.00 12.00
SSJS Jarret Stoll 6.00 15.00
SSJT Joe Thornton SP 10.00 25.00
SSKD Kris Draper 5.00 12.00
SSKL Kari Lehtonen 6.00 15.00
SSMA Matt Carle SP 5.00 12.00
SSMB Mike Bossy SP 8.00 20.00
SSMC Mike Cammalleri 5.00 12.00
SSME Barry Melrose 6.00 15.00
SSMF Marc-Andre Fleury 15.00 40.00
SSMG Marian Gaborik 10.00 25.00
SSMH Martin Havlat 5.00 12.00
SSMI Milan Hejduk 6.00 15.00
SSMK Miikka Kiprusoff 6.00 15.00
SSML Mario Lemieux SP 80.00 150.00
SSMM Marty McSorley 6.00 15.00
SSMO Mike Modano SP 15.00 40.00
SSMP Michael Peca 6.00 15.00
SSMR Michael Ryder 5.00 12.00
SSMS Marc Savard 5.00 12.00
SSMT Marty Turco 8.00 20.00
SSND Nigel Dawes 5.00 12.00
SSNL Nicklas Lidstrom SP 20.00 50.00
SSNZ Nikolai Zherdev 5.00 12.00
SSOR Bobby Orr 80.00 150.00
SSPB Patrice Bergeron 10.00 25.00
SSPE Patrik Elias 8.00 20.00
SSPK Phil Kessel 12.00 30.00
SSPM Patrick Marleau SP 8.00 20.00
SSPO Patrick O'Sullivan 8.00 20.00
SSPP Petr Prucha 6.00 15.00
SSPS Paul Stastny 12.00 30.00
SSRA Alexander Radulov 10.00 25.00
SSRB Ray Bourque SP 20.00 50.00
SSRH Ron Hextall 12.00 30.00
SSRM Ryan Miller 8.00 20.00
SSRN Rick Nash 8.00 20.00
SSRS Ryan Smyth 6.00 15.00
SSSC Sidney Crosby 60.00 150.00
SSSG Simon Gagne 8.00 20.00
SSST Jordan Staal 12.00 30.00
SSSV Marek Svatos 5.00 12.00
SSTH Jose Theodore SP 8.00 20.00
SSTO Terry O'Reilly 5.00 12.00
SSTV Tomas Vokoun 6.00 15.00
SSVL Vincent Lecavalier SP 12.00 30.00
SSVT Vesa Toskala 6.00 15.00
SSWG Wayne Gretzky SP 150.00 300.00
SSWO Willie O'Ree 12.00 30.00
SSZC Zdeno Chara 12.00 30.00

2006-07 Sweet Shot Signature Shots/Saves Ice Signings

STATED PRINT RUN 100 SER.#'d SETS
SSIAH Ales Hemsky 6.00 15.00
SSIAR Alex Radulov EXCH 15.00 40.00
SSIBB Brad Boyes 6.00 15.00
SSIBO Bobby Orr 100.00 200.00
SSICA Colby Armstrong 12.00 30.00
SSICW Cam Ward 10.00 25.00
SSIDH Dominik Hasek 25.00 60.00
SSIEM Evgeni Malkin 50.00 120.00
SSIES Eric Staal 10.00 25.00
SSIGH Gordie Howe 40.00 100.00
SSIHE Dany Heatley 15.00 40.00
SSIHZ Henrik Zetterberg 15.00 40.00
SSIIK Ilya Kovalchuk 12.00 30.00
SSIJG Jean-Sebastien Giguere 15.00 40.00
SSIJI Jarome Iginla 20.00 50.00
SSIJK Jari Kurri 20.00 50.00
SSIJS Jarret Stoll 6.00 15.00
SSIJT Joe Thornton 30.00 80.00
SSIKL Kari Lehtonen 12.00 30.00
SSILR Larry Robinson 10.00 25.00
SSIMB Martin Brodeur 25.00 60.00
SSIMD Marcel Dionne 10.00 25.00
SSIMG Marian Gaborik 20.00 50.00
SSIMH Martin Havlat 12.00 30.00
SSIMK Miikka Kiprusoff 15.00 40.00
SSIMM Mike Modano 12.00 30.00
SSIMR Michael Ryder 10.00 25.00
SSIMS Marek Svatos 6.00 15.00
SSIMT Marty Turco 12.00 30.00
SSINL Nicklas Lidstrom 20.00 50.00
SSIPE Patrik Elias 6.00 15.00
SSIPK Phil Kessel 20.00 50.00
SSIRB Ray Bourque 30.00 80.00
SSIRK Red Kelly 12.00 30.00
SSIRM Ryan Miller 20.00 50.00
SSIRN Rick Nash 15.00 40.00
SSISC Sidney Crosby 100.00 200.00
SSISG Simon Gagne 10.00 25.00
SSIST Jordan Staal 25.00 60.00
SSITV Tomas Vokoun 10.00 25.00
SSIWG Wayne Gretzky 150.00 300.00

2006-07 Sweet Shot Signature Shots/Saves Sticks

STATED PRINT RUN 25 SER.#'d SETS
SSSAB Andy Bathgate 15.00 40.00
SSSAF Alexander Frolov 15.00 40.00
SSSAH Ales Hemsky 25.00 60.00
SSSAK Anze Kopitar 75.00 150.00
SSSAR Andrew Raycroft 20.00 50.00
SSSBB Brad Boyes 40.00
SSSBC Bobby Clarke 25.00 60.00
SSSBG Brian Gionta 20.00 50.00
SSSBH Bobby Hull 40.00 100.00
SSSBM Brenden Morrow 25.00 60.00
SSSBO Mike Bossy 30.00 80.00
SSSBP Bernie Parent 50.00 125.00
SSSBR Brent Sutter 15.00 40.00
SSSBS Borje Salming 15.00 40.00
SSSBU Johnny Bucyk 20.00 50.00
SSSCA Colby Armstrong
SSSCD Chris Drury 25.00 60.00
SSSCH Cristobal Huet 20.00 50.00
SSSCN Cam Neely 30.00 80.00
SSSDC Don Cherry 75.00 150.00
SSSDE Denis Potvin 20.00 50.00
SSSDH Dominik Hasek 30.00 80.00
SSSDP Dion Phaneuf 30.00 60.00
SSSDR Dwayne Roloson 25.00 60.00
SSSDS Denis Savard 20.00 50.00
SSSDT Dave Taylor 20.00 50.00
SSSDW Doug Wilson 15.00 40.00
SSSEM Evgeni Malkin 50.00 120.00
SSSES Eric Staal 25.00 60.00
SSSGB Gilbert Brule 25.00 60.00
SSSGE Martin Gerber 15.00 30.00
SSSGF Grant Fuhr 30.00 80.00
SSSGH Gordie Howe 75.00 150.00
SSSGL Guillaume Latendresse 40.00 100.00
SSSGP Gilbert Perreault
SSSHE Dany Heatley 20.00 50.00
SSSHZ Henrik Zetterberg 40.00 100.00
SSSIK Ilya Kovalchuk 30.00 80.00
SSSJA Jason Arnott
SSSJB Jean Beliveau 50.00 125.00
SSSJC Jonathan Cheechoo 20.00 50.00
SSSJE Jeff Carter 20.00 50.00
SSSJI Jarome Iginla 30.00 80.00
SSSJK Jari Kurri 30.00 80.00
SSSJO Johnny Bower
SSSJR Jeremy Roenick 30.00 80.00
SSSJS Jordan Staal 100.00 200.00
SSSJT Jose Theodore
SSSKL Kari Lehtonen
SSSLA Guy Lafleur 40.00 100.00
SSSLR Luc Robitaille
SSSMA Matt Carle 15.00 40.00
SSSMB Martin Brodeur 100.00 200.00
SSSMC Mike Cammalleri 25.00 60.00
SSSMD Marcel Dionne 30.00 60.00
SSSMF Marc-Andre Fleury 25.00 60.00
SSSMG Marian Gaborik 20.00 50.00
SSSMH Martin Havlat 25.00 60.00
SSSMI Milan Hejduk
SSSMK Miikka Kiprusoff 25.00 60.00
SSSML Mario Lemieux 100.00 200.00
SSSMM Mike Modano 30.00 80.00
SSSMP Michael Peca
SSSMR Michael Ryder 25.00 60.00
SSSMS Marek Svatos 20.00 50.00
SSSMT Marty Turco 20.00 50.00
SSSNL Nicklas Lidstrom 25.00 60.00
SSSNZ Nikolai Zherdev 20.00 50.00
SSSOR Bobby Orr 200.00 400.00
SSSPA Patrice Bergeron 25.00 60.00
SSSPB Pierre-Marc Bouchard
SSSPE Patrik Elias 20.00 50.00
SSSPH Phil Esposito 50.00 125.00
SSSPK Phil Kessel 30.00 80.00
SSSPM Patrick Marleau 30.00 60.00
SSSPO Patrick O'Sullivan 15.00 40.00
SSSPS Paul Stastny 50.00 125.00
SSSRA Alexander Radulov 40.00 100.00
SSSRB Ray Bourque 40.00 100.00
SSSRH Ron Hextall 40.00 100.00
SSSRM Ryan Miller 25.00 60.00
SSSRN Rick Nash 25.00 60.00
SSSRO Larry Robinson 20.00 50.00
SSSRS Ryan Smyth 30.00 60.00
SSSRV Rick Vaive 25.00 60.00
SSSSC Sidney Crosby 150.00 300.00
SSSSG Scott Gomez 20.00 50.00
SSSSI Darryl Sittler 25.00 60.00
SSSSJ Jarret Stoll 15.00 40.00
SSSSK Saku Koivu 25.00 60.00
SSSST Peter Stastny 30.00 80.00
SSSSU Brian Sutter 15.00 40.00
SSSTE Tony Esposito 25.00 60.00
SSSTH Joe Thornton 40.00 100.00
SSSTL Ted Lindsay
SSSTV Tomas Vokoun 30.00 60.00
SSSVL Vincent Lecavalier 25.00 60.00
SSSWG Wayne Gretzky 300.00 500.00

2006-07 Sweet Shot Signature Sticks

STATED PRINT RUN 15 SER.#'d SETS
STAM Al MacInnis 30.00 80.00
STAO Adam Oates 20.00 50.00
STAR Andrew Raycroft 25.00 60.00
STBB Bob Bourne 25.00 60.00
STBC Bobby Clarke 60.00 125.00
STBH Bobby Hull 75.00 150.00
STBL Rob Blake 15.00 40.00
STBO Bobby Orr 400.00 600.00
STBP Bernie Parent 75.00 150.00
STBS Billy Smith 30.00 80.00
STCD Chris Drury 30.00 80.00
STCG Clark Gillies
STCH Cristobal Huet 30.00 80.00
STCW Cam Ward 30.00 80.00
STDA David Aebischer 30.00 80.00
STDB Daniel Briere 30.00 80.00
STDG Doug Gilmour 100.00 175.00
STDH Dominik Hasek 60.00 125.00
STDP Dion Phaneuf 30.00 80.00
STDR Dwayne Roloson 30.00 80.00
STEM Evgeni Malkin 100.00 200.00
STES Eric Staal 30.00 80.00
STFM Frank Mahovlich 60.00 150.00
STGH Gordie Howe 175.00 300.00
STGL Guy Lafleur 60.00 125.00
STGP Gilbert Perreault 40.00 100.00
STHA Dale Hawerchuk 30.00 80.00
STHE Dany Heatley 60.00 125.00
STHZ Henrik Zetterberg 75.00 150.00
STIK Ilya Kovalchuk 60.00 125.00
STJB Jean Beliveau 75.00 150.00
STJC Jonathan Cheechoo 60.00 125.00
STJG Jean-Sebastien Giguere 25.00 60.00
STJI Jarome Iginla 100.00 200.00
STJK Jari Kurri 60.00 125.00
STJL Joffrey Lupul 25.00 60.00
STJM Joe Mullen 25.00 60.00
STJP Joni Pitkanen 25.00 60.00
STJR Jeremy Roenick 75.00 150.00
STJT Joe Thornton 75.00 175.00
STKL Kari Lehtonen 30.00 80.00
STLE Manny Legace 25.00 60.00
STLM Larry Murphy 25.00 60.00
STLR Luc Robitaille 40.00 100.00
STMB Martin Brodeur 75.00 150.00
STMG Marian Gaborik 75.00 150.00
STMH Milan Hejduk 25.00 60.00
STMI Mike Bossy 75.00 125.00
STMK Miikka Kiprusoff 60.00 125.00
STML Mario Lemieux 175.00 300.00
STMM Mike Modano 60.00 125.00
STMN Markus Naslund 30.00 80.00
STMP Michael Peca 30.00 80.00
STMR Michael Ryder 30.00 80.00
STMS Martin St. Louis 40.00 100.00
STMT Marty Turco 30.00 80.00
STNL Nicklas Lidstrom 40.00 100.00
STNZ Nikolai Zherdev 30.00 80.00
STPB Patrice Bergeron 30.00 80.00
STPE Patrik Elias 25.00 60.00
STPI Pierre-Marc Bouchard 30.00 60.00
STPK Phil Kessel 60.00 125.00
STPM Patrick Marleau 30.00 80.00
STPO Denis Potvin 30.00 80.00
STPR Patrick Roy 150.00 300.00
STRB Ray Bourque 75.00 150.00
STRH Ron Hextall 30.00 80.00
STRM Ryan Malone 25.00 60.00
STRN Rick Nash 60.00 125.00
STRO Larry Robinson 25.00 60.00
STRY Ryan Miller 40.00 100.00
STSA Denis Savard 25.00 60.00
STSK Saku Koivu 40.00 100.00
STST Jordan Staal 100.00 200.00
STSV Marek Svatos 25.00 60.00
STTE Tony Esposito 30.00 80.00
STTR Tuomo Ruutu 25.00 60.00
STTV Tomas Vokoun 40.00 100.00
STWG Wayne Gretzky 500.00 800.00

2006-07 Sweet Shot Sweet Stitches

STATED PRINT RUN 200 SER.#'d SETS
*DUAL/50: .8X TO 2X SINGLE SWATCH
*TRIPLE/25: 1X TO 2.5X SINGLE SWATCH
SSAF Alexander Frolov 2.50 6.00
SSAH Ales Hemsky 3.00 8.00
SSAL Daniel Alfredsson 4.00 10.00
SSAN Antero Niittymaki 3.00 8.00
SSAO Alexander Ovechkin 15.00 40.00
SSAR Andrew Raycroft 3.00 8.00
SSAS Alexander Steen 4.00 10.00
SSAT Alex Tanguay 2.50 6.00
SSBG Brian Gionta 3.00 8.00
SSBL Rob Blake 4.00 10.00
SSBO Pierre-Marc Bouchard 4.00 10.00
SSBR Brendan Shanahan 5.00 12.00
SSBS Billy Smith 4.00 10.00
SSBT Bryan Trottier 5.00 12.00
SSCD Chris Drury 3.00 8.00
SSCH Cristobal Huet 3.00 8.00
SSCN Cam Neely 4.00 10.00
SSCP Chris Pronger 3.00 8.00
SSCW Cam Ward 4.00 10.00
SSDA Dany Heatley 4.00 10.00
SSDH Dominik Hasek 5.00 12.00
SSDP Dion Phaneuf 4.00 10.00
SSDS Darryl Sittler 4.00 10.00
SSDW Doug Weight 4.00 10.00
SSEL Eric Lindros 6.00 15.00
SSES Eric Staal 5.00 12.00
SSFM Frank Mahovlich 3.00 8.00
SSGF Grant Fuhr 4.00 10.00
SSGL Guy Lafleur 5.00 12.00
SSGP Gilbert Perreault 4.00 10.00
SSHA Dale Hawerchuk 5.00 12.00
SSHE Milan Hejduk 3.00 8.00
SSHL Henrik Lundqvist 8.00 20.00
SSHO Marian Hossa 3.00 8.00
SSHZ Henrik Zetterberg 5.00 12.00
SSIK Ilya Kovalchuk 4.00 10.00
SSJC Jonathan Cheechoo 4.00 10.00
SSJG Jean-Sebastien Giguere 4.00 10.00
SSJI Jarome Iginla 4.00 10.00
SSJJ Jaromir Jagr 10.00 25.00
SSJL Joffrey Lupul 3.00 8.00
SSJM Joe Mullen 3.00 8.00
SSJS Joe Sakic 6.00 15.00
SSJT Jose Theodore 4.00 10.00
SSKL Kari Lehtonen 3.00 8.00
SSLR Luc Robitaille 4.00 10.00
SSMA Maxim Afinogenov 2.50 6.00
SSMB Martin Brodeur 8.00 20.00
SSMF Manny Fernandez 3.00 8.00
SSMG Marian Gaborik 5.00 12.00
SSMH Martin Havlat 2.50 6.00
SSMI Mike Bossy 4.00 10.00
SSMK Miikka Kiprusoff 3.00 8.00
SSML Mario Lemieux 12.00 30.00
SSMM Mike Modano 6.00 15.00
SSMN Markus Naslund 3.00 8.00
SSMR Michael Ryder 2.50 6.00
SSMS Marek Svatos 2.50 6.00
SSMT Marty Turco 4.00 10.00
SSNL Nicklas Lidstrom 4.00 10.00
SSOJ Olli Jokinen 4.00 10.00
SSOK Olaf Kolzig 4.00 10.00
SSPB Patrice Bergeron 5.00 12.00
SSPD Pavel Datsyuk 5.00 12.00
SSPE Patrik Elias 4.00 10.00
SSPF Peter Forsberg 5.00 12.00
SSPK Paul Kariya 5.00 12.00
SSPL Pascal LeClaire 3.00 8.00
SSPM Patrick Marleau 4.00 10.00
SSPO Denis Potvin 4.00 10.00
SSPR Patrick Roy 10.00 25.00
SSPS Peter Stastny 4.00 10.00
SSRB Ray Bourque 6.00 15.00
SSRE Mark Recchi 5.00 12.00
SSRH Ron Hextall 6.00 15.00
SSRI Brad Richards 4.00 10.00
SSRL Roberto Luongo 6.00 15.00
SSRM Ryan Miller 4.00 10.00
SSRN Rick Nash 4.00 10.00
SSRO Larry Robinson 4.00 10.00
SSRS Ryan Smyth 3.00 8.00
SSRV Rogie Vachon 5.00 12.00
SSSA Miroslav Satan 3.00 8.00
SSSB Borje Salming 4.00 10.00
SSSC Sidney Crosby 12.00 30.00
SSSD Shane Doan 3.00 8.00
SSSF Sergei Fedorov 6.00 15.00
SSSH Steve Shutt 4.00 10.00
SSSK Saku Koivu 4.00 10.00
SSSP Jason Spezza 4.00 10.00
SSSS Sergei Samsonov 3.00 8.00
SSST Martin St. Louis 4.00 10.00
SSSU Mats Sundin 4.00 10.00
SSSZ Sergei Zubov 3.00 8.00
SSTH Joe Thornton 5.00 12.00
SSTS Teemu Selanne 8.00 20.00
SSTV Tomas Vokoun 3.00 8.00
SSVL Vincent Lecavalier 3.00 8.00
SSWG Wayne Gretzky 20.00 50.00
SSZC Zdeno Chara 4.00 10.00

2007-08 Sweet Shot

This set was released on May 14, 2008. The base set consists of 160 cards. Cards 1-100 feature veterans, and cards 101-160 are jersey rookie cards.

COMP.SET w/o SPs (100) 20.00 50.00
STATED PRINT RUN 599 SER.#'d SETS
1 Ales Hemsky .75 2.00
2 Al MacInnis 1.00 2.50
3 Alexander Ovechkin 4.00 10.00
4 Bobby Orr 3.00 8.00
5 Alexander Semin 1.00 2.50
6 Anze Kopitar 1.50 4.00
7 Bernie Federko .60 1.50
8 Cam Neely 1.00 2.50
9 Gordie Howe 2.50 6.00
10 Alexander Radulov 1.00 2.50
11 Mark Messier 1.50 4.00
12 Borje Salming 1.00 2.50
13 Brad Richards 1.00 2.50
14 Brendan Morrison .60 1.50
15 Brendan Shanahan 1.25 3.00
16 Brian Leetch 1.00 2.50
17 Billy Smith 1.00 2.50
18 Cam Ward 1.00 2.50
19 Daniel Alfredsson 1.00 2.50
20 Daniel Briere 1.00 2.50
21 Dany Heatley 1.00 2.50
22 Darryl Sittler .75 2.00
23 Denis Potvin 1.00 2.50
24 Dino Ciccarelli 1.00 2.50
25 Dion Phaneuf 1.00 2.50
26 Dominik Hasek 1.25 3.00
27 Manny Legace .75 2.00
28 Drew Stafford .75 2.00
29 Eric Staal 1.25 3.00
30 Patrice Bergeron 1.25 3.00
31 Frank Mahovlich 1.25 3.00
32 Gilbert Perreault 1.00 2.50
33 Patrick Roy 2.50 6.00
34 Grant Fuhr 1.00 2.50
35 Guy Lafleur 1.25 3.00
36 Henrik Lundqvist 1.25 3.00
37 Henrik Zetterberg 1.25 3.00
38 Ilya Kovalchuk 1.00 2.50
39 Jari Kurri 1.00 2.50
40 Jarome Iginla 1.00 2.50
41 Jaromir Jagr 2.50 6.00
42 Jason Spezza 1.00 2.50
43 Jean Beliveau 1.25 3.00
44 Jean-Sebastien Giguere 1.00 2.50
45 Joe Mullen .75 2.00
46 Joe Sakic 1.50 4.00
47 Joe Thornton 1.25 3.00
48 Johnny Bucyk .75 2.00
49 Jonathan Cheechoo 1.00 2.50
50 Jordan Staal 1.00 2.50
51 Kari Lehtonen .75 2.00
52 Larry Robinson 1.00 2.50
53 Luc Robitaille 1.00 2.50
54 Marc-Andre Fleury 1.50 4.00
55 Marian Gaborik 1.25 3.00
56 Marian Hossa .75 2.00
57 Miikka Kiprusoff .75 2.00
58 Bobby Hull 1.50 4.00
59 Mark Recchi 1.25 3.00
60 Markus Naslund 1.00 2.50
61 Martin Brodeur 2.00 5.00
62 Martin St. Louis 1.00 2.50
63 Marty Turco 1.00 2.50
64 Mats Sundin 1.00 2.50
65 Michael Ryder .60 1.50
66 Mario Lemieux 3.00 8.00
67 Mike Bossy 1.00 2.50
68 Mike Modano 1.50 4.00
69 Nathan Horton 1.00 2.50
70 Nicklas Lidstrom 1.00 2.50
71 Evgeni Malkin 3.00 8.00
72 Patrick Marleau 1.00 2.50
73 Bobby Clarke 1.00 2.50
74 Paul Kariya 1.25 3.00
75 Pavel Datsyuk 1.25 3.00
76 Peter Stastny .75 2.00
77 Ray Bourque 1.50 4.00
78 Phil Esposito 1.50 4.00
79 Phil Kessel 1.25 3.00
80 Paul Stastny 1.00 2.50
81 Rick DiPietro .75 2.00
82 Rick Nash 1.00 2.50
83 Roberto Luongo 1.25 3.00
84 Ron Hextall 1.50 4.00
85 Ryan Miller 1.00 2.50
86 Ryan Smyth .75 2.00
87 Sidney Crosby 4.00 10.00
88 Scott Niedermayer 1.00 2.50
89 Patrik Elias 1.00 2.50
90 Shane Doan .75 2.00
91 Saku Koivu 1.00 2.50
92 Simon Gagne 1.00 2.50
93 Stan Mikita 1.25 3.00
94 Teemu Selanne 2.00 5.00
95 Thomas Vanek 1.25 3.00
96 Tomas Vokoun .75 2.00
97 Tony Esposito 1.00 2.50
98 Vincent Lecavalier .75 2.00
99 Wayne Gretzky 5.00 12.00
100 Zach Parise 1.25 3.00
101 Bobby Ryan JSY RC 10.00 25.00
102 Jonathan Toews JSY RC 15.00 40.00
103 Sam Gagner JSY RC 8.00 20.00
104 Carey Price JSY RC 25.00 50.00
105 Nicklas Bergfors JSY RC 4.00 10.00
106 Erik Johnson JSY RC 6.00 15.00
107 Nicklas Backstrom JSY RC 12.00 30.00
108 Jack Johnson JSY RC 5.00 12.00
109 Jonathan Bernier JSY RC 10.00 25.00
110 Bryan Little JSY RC 6.00 15.00
111 Patrick Kane JSY RC 15.00 40.00
112 Kris Russell JSY RC 5.00 12.00
113 Matt Niskanen JSY RC 6.00 15.00
114 Andrew Cogliano JSY RC 6.00 15.00
115 Marc Staal JSY RC 6.00 15.00
116 Nick Foligno JSY RC 8.00 20.00
117 Peter Mueller JSY RC 5.00 12.00
118 Ondrej Pavelec JSY RC 8.00 20.00
119 Martin Hanzal JSY RC 5.00 12.00
120 Matt Smaby JSY RC 4.00 10.00
121 Petr Kalus JSY RC 4.00 10.00
122 Andy Greene JSY RC 5.00 12.00
123 Frans Nielsen JSY RC 6.00 15.00
124 Rob Schremp JSY RC 5.00 12.00
125 James Sheppard JSY RC 4.00 10.00
126 Kyle Chipchura JSY RC 6.00 15.00
127 Ryan Parent JSY RC 4.00 10.00
128 David Krejci JSY RC 12.50 25.00
129 Lauri Tukonen JSY RC 4.00 10.00
130 Tobias Enstrom JSY RC 6.00 15.00
131 Mason Raymond JSY RC 6.00 15.00
132 Brandon Dubinsky JSY RC 8.00 20.00
133 Curtis McElhinney JSY RC 6.00 15.00
134 Brian Elliott JSY RC 8.00 20.00
135 Drew Miller JSY RC 5.00 12.00
136 Ryan Callahan JSY RC 8.00 20.00
137 Ville Koistinen JSY RC 4.00 10.00
138 Torrey Mitchell JSY RC 5.00 12.00
139 David Perron JSY RC 6.00 15.00
140 Jannik Hansen JSY RC 5.00 12.00
141 Jaroslav Halak JSY RC 10.00 25.00
142 Sergei Kostitsyn JSY RC 5.00 12.00
143 Milan Lucic JSY RC 10.00 25.00
144 Tyler Weiman JSY RC 5.00 12.00
145 Jaroslav Hlinka JSY RC 5.00 12.00
146 Tobias Stephan JSY RC 5.00 12.00
147 Tuukka Rask JSY RC 8.00 20.00
148 Ryan Carter JSY RC 4.00 10.00
149 Jared Boll JSY RC 5.00 12.00
150 Casey Borer JSY RC 4.00 10.00
151 Steve Downie JSY RC 5.00 12.00
152 Lukas Kaspar JSY RC 4.00 10.00
153 Matt Ellis JSY RC 5.00 12.00
154 Jiri Tlusty JSY RC 6.00 15.00
155 Daniel Carcillo JSY RC 5.00 12.00
156 Devin Setoguchi JSY RC 6.00 15.00
157 T.J. Hensick JSY RC 5.00 12.00
158 Anton Stralman JSY RC 4.00 10.00
159 David Jones JSY RC 4.00 10.00
160 Jack Skille JSY RC 5.00 12.00

2007-08 Sweet Shot Rookie Jerseys Autographs

COMMON CARD/100 8.00 20.00
SEMISTARS/100 10.00 25.00
UNLISTED STARS/100 12.00 30.00
STATED PRINT RUN 100 SER.#'d SETS
101 Bobby Ryan 20.00 50.00
102 Jonathan Toews 60.00 120.00
103 Sam Gagner 12.00 30.00
104 Carey Price 60.00 120.00
106 Erik Johnson 12.00 30.00
107 Nicklas Backstrom 25.00 60.00
109 Jonathan Bernier 20.00 50.00
111 Patrick Kane 50.00 100.00
114 Andrew Cogliano 12.00 30.00
118 Ondrej Pavelec 15.00 40.00
128 David Krejci 25.00 50.00
136 Ryan Callahan 15.00 40.00
141 Jaroslav Halak 15.00 40.00
143 Milan Lucic 25.00 50.00
147 Tuukka Rask 40.00 80.00

2007-08 Sweet Shot Signature Saves Ice Signings

STATED PRINT RUN 100 SER.#'d SETS
SSRBP Bernie Parent 12.00 30.00
SSRBR Bill Ranford 12.00 30.00
SSRGF Grant Fuhr 12.00 30.00
SSRJG Jean-Sebastien Giguere 12.00 30.00
SSRMB Martin Brodeur 25.00 60.00
SSRMF Marc-Andre Fleury 20.00 50.00
SSRMT Marty Turco 12.00 30.00
SSRPR Patrick Roy/50 50.00 120.00
SSRRM Ryan Miller 12.00 30.00
SSRTE Tony Esposito 25.00 50.00

2007-08 Sweet Shot Signature Saves Puck Signings

STATED ODDS 1:2
SSPBI Bill Ranford 10.00 25.00
SSPBP Bernie Parent 10.00 25.00
SSPCP Carey Price 30.00 60.00
SSPGF Grant Fuhr 10.00 25.00
SSPHA Dominik Hasek 25.00 60.00
SSPJG Jean-Sebastien Giguere 10.00 25.00
SSPMT Marty Turco 10.00 25.00
SSPRA Andrew Raycroft 8.00 20.00
SSPRB Richard Brodeur 8.00 20.00
SSPRM Ryan Miller 10.00 25.00
SSPTE Tony Esposito 20.00 40.00

2007-08 Sweet Shot Signature Saves Stick Signings

STATED PRINT RUN 25 SERIAL #'d SETS
SSSBP Bernie Parent 25.00 60.00
SSSBR Bill Ranford 25.00 60.00
SSSCP Carey Price 100.00 200.00
SSSDH Dominik Hasek 30.00 80.00
SSSDR Dwayne Roloson 20.00 50.00
SSSGF Grant Fuhr 25.00 60.00
SSSJG Jean-Sebastien Giguere 20.00 50.00
SSSMB Martin Brodeur 50.00 125.00
SSSMT Marty Turco
SSSRH Ron Hextall 25.00 60.00
SSSRI Richard Brodeur 20.00 50.00
SSSRM Ryan Miller 25.00 60.00
SSSTE Tony Esposito 50.00 100.00
SSSVO Tomas Vokoun 20.00 50.00

2007-08 Sweet Shot Signature Shots Ice Signings

STATED PRINT RUN 100 SERIAL #'d SETS
SSRAK Anze Kopitar 20.00 50.00
SSRAT Alex Tanguay 8.00 20.00
SSRBO Mike Bossy 12.00 30.00
SSRDH Dany Heatley 12.00 30.00
SSRDP Denis Potvin 12.00 30.00
SSREM Evgeni Malkin 40.00 100.00
SSRGH Gordie Howe/50 50.00 100.00
SSRGL Guy Lafleur 30.00 60.00
SSRGP Gilbert Perreault 12.00 30.00
SSRHZ Henrik Zetterberg 15.00 40.00
SSRIK Ilya Kovalchuk 12.00 30.00
SSRJI Jarome Iginla 12.00 30.00
SSRJK Jari Kurri 12.00 30.00
SSRJT Joe Thornton 15.00 40.00
SSRLR Larry Robinson 12.00 30.00
SSRMG Marian Gaborik 15.00 40.00
SSRMM Mike Modano 20.00 50.00
SSRMN Markus Naslund 12.00 30.00
SSRMR Michael Ryder 8.00 20.00
SSRMS Martin St. Louis 12.00 30.00
SSRNL Nicklas Lidstrom 20.00 40.00
SSRPB Patrice Bergeron 15.00 40.00
SSRRB Ray Bourque 25.00 50.00
SSRRN Rick Nash 12.00 30.00
SSRSC Sidney Crosby 75.00 150.00
SSRSG Simon Gagne 12.00 30.00
SSRVL Vincent Lecavalier 10.00 25.00

2007-08 Sweet Shot Signature Shots Puck Signings

STATED ODDS 1:2
SSPAK Anze Kopitar 10.00 25.00
SSPAM Andy McDonald 5.00 12.00
SSPAR Alexander Radulov 6.00 15.00
SSPAT Alex Tanguay 4.00 10.00
SSPBB Brad Boyes 4.00 10.00
SSPBC Bobby Clarke 6.00 15.00
SSPBE1 Jean Beliveau
SSPBG Brian Gionta 5.00 12.00
SSPBH Bobby Hull
SSPBL Bryan Little 5.00 12.00
SSPBM Brendan Morrison 4.00 10.00
SSPBO Bobby Orr 75.00 150.00
SSPBR Bobby Ryan 10.00 25.00
SSPCA Mike Cammalleri 5.00 12.00
SSPDB Dan Boyle 5.00 12.00
SSPDM Dickie Moore
SSPDP David Perron 6.00 15.00
SSPDS Darryl Sutter 5.00 12.00
SSPDT Darcy Tucker 5.00 12.00
SSPDU Duane Sutter 4.00 10.00
SSPEJ Erik Johnson 6.00 15.00
SSPEM Evgeni Malkin 40.00 80.00
SSPGA Simon Gagne 6.00 15.00
SSPGH Gordie Howe 40.00 100.00
SSPGL Guy Lafleur 25.00 50.00
SSPGO Scott Gomez 5.00 12.00
SSPGP Gilbert Perreault 6.00 15.00
SSPIK Ilya Kovalchuk 15.00 30.00
SSPJC Jonathan Cheechoo 6.00 15.00
SSPJI Jarome Iginla 6.00 15.00
SSPJJ Jack Johnson 5.00 12.00
SSPJK Jari Kurri 6.00 15.00
SSPJP Joni Pitkanen 4.00 10.00
SSPJT Jonathan Toews 30.00 60.00
SSPKD Kris Draper 4.00 10.00
SSPKE Phil Kessel 8.00 20.00
SSPLR Larry Robinson 6.00 15.00
SSPMC Matt Carle 4.00 10.00
SSPMG Marian Gaborik 10.00 25.00
SSPMH Milan Hejduk 5.00 12.00
SSPMN Markus Naslund 6.00 15.00
SSPMO Brenden Morrow 5.00 12.00
SSPMP Michael Peca 5.00 12.00
SSPMR Michael Ryder 4.00 10.00
SSPMS Marc Staal 6.00 15.00
SSPMU Peter Mueller 5.00 12.00
SSPNB Nicklas Backstrom 12.00 30.00
SSPNF Nick Foligno 8.00 20.00
SSPNL Nicklas Lidstrom 10.00 25.00
SSPOS Patrick O'Sullivan 5.00 12.00
SSPPB Patrice Bergeron 8.00 20.00
SSPPE Corey Perry 6.00 15.00
SSPPK Patrick Kane 40.00 80.00
SSPPO Denis Potvin 6.00 15.00
SSPPS Paul Stastny 6.00 15.00
SSPRG Ryan Getzlaf 12.00 30.00
SSPRI Mike Richards 6.00 15.00
SSPRN Rick Nash 6.00 15.00
SSPRP Ryan Potulny 4.00 10.00
SSPRS Rob Schremp 5.00 12.00
SSPRV Rick Vaive 5.00 12.00
SSPSB Scotty Bowman 5.00 12.00
SSPSC Sidney Crosby 60.00 120.00
SSPSG Sam Gagner 8.00 20.00
SSPSH Steve Shutt 6.00 15.00
SSPSM Ryan Smyth 5.00 12.00
SSPST Martin St. Louis 6.00 15.00
SSPSU Brent Sutter 4.00 10.00
SSPSV Marek Svatos 4.00 10.00
SSPSW Stephen Weiss 4.00 10.00
SSPTH Tomas Holmstrom 6.00 15.00
SSPTS Tomas Steen 4.00 10.00
SSPTV Thomas Vanek 8.00 20.00
SSPVL Vincent Lecavalier 5.00 12.00
SSPWG Wayne Gretzky 150.00 300.00

2007-08 Sweet Shot Signature Shots Stick Signings

STATED PRINT RUN 25 SERIAL #'d SETS
SSSAK Anze Kopitar 25.00 60.00
SSSAM Al MacInnis 15.00 40.00
SSSAO Alexander Ovechkin 40.00 100.00
SSSAR Alexander Radulov
SSSAT Alex Tanguay 10.00 25.00
SSSBC Bobby Clarke 15.00 40.00
SSSBE Jean Beliveau 50.00 100.00
SSSBH Bobby Hull 50.00 100.00
SSSBL Brian Leetch 15.00 40.
SSSBM Brendan Morrison 10.00 25.
SSSBO Bobby Orr 175.00 300.
SSSCH Jonathan Cheechoo 15.00 40.
SSSCN Cam Neely 15.00 40.
SSSCR Sidney Crosby 150.00 250.
SSSDA Dany Heatley EXCH 15.00 40.
SSSDC Dino Ciccarelli 15.00 40.
SSSDS Darryl Sittler 15.00 40.
SSSDT Darcy Tucker 12.00 30.
SSSEM Evgeni Malkin 50.00 100.
SSSGH Gordie Howe 60.00 120.
SSSGL Guillaume Latendresse 12.00 30.
SSSGP Gilbert Perreault 25.00 50.
SSSHA Dale Hawerchuk 20.00 50.
SSSHE Milan Hejduk 12.00 30.
SSSHZ Henrik Zetterberg 20.00 50.
SSSIK Ilya Kovalchuk 15.00 40.
SSSJB Johnny Bucyk 12.00 30.
SSSJC Jeff Carter 15.00 40.
SSSJI Jarome Iginla 15.00 40.
SSSJJ Jack Johnson 12.00 30.
SSSJK Jari Kurri 15.00 40.
SSSJM Joe Mullen
SSSJS Jordan Staal 10.00 25.
SSSJT Jonathan Toews 150.00 300.
SSSKA Patrick Kane 150.00 300.
SSSLA Guy Lafleur 20.00 50.
SSSLM Lanny McDonald 15.00 40.
SSSLR Luc Robitaille 15.00 40.
SSSMD Marcel Dionne 20.00 50.
SSSME Mark Messier/10
SSSMG Marian Gaborik 20.00 50.
SSSMH Marian Hossa 12.00 30.
SSSMI Mike Bossy 12.00 30.
SSSML Mario Lemieux/10
SSSMM Mike Modano 25.00 60.
SSSMN Markus Naslund 15.00 40.
SSSMR Michael Ryder 10.00 25.
SSSMS Martin St. Louis 15.00 40.
SSSNH Nathan Horton 15.00 40.
SSSNL Nicklas Lidstrom 25.00 60.
SSSPB Patrice Bergeron 20.00 50.
SSSPK Phil Kessel 25.00 50.
SSSPM Peter Mueller 12.00 30.
SSSPO Denis Potvin
SSSPS Paul Stastny 15.00 40.
SSSRB Ray Bourque 40.00 80.
SSSRE Ron Ellis 12.00 30.
SSSRN Rick Nash 15.00 40.
SSSRO Larry Robinson
SSSRS Ryan Smyth 12.00 30.
SSSSA Borje Salming 15.00 40.
SSSSG Sam Gagner 20.00 50.
SSSSI Simon Gagne 15.00 40.
SSSSK Saku Koivu 15.00 40.
SSSSM Stan Mikita 20.00 50.
SSSSP Peter Stastny 12.00 30.
SSSSS Steve Shutt 15.00 40.
SSSSV Marek Svatos 10.00 25.
SSSTH Joe Thornton 20.00 50.
SSSTV Thomas Vanek 20.00 50.
SSSVL Vincent Lecavalier 25.00 50.
SSSWG Wayne Gretzky/10

2007-08 Sweet Shot Sweet Spo Signatures Baseball Skins

SBSBC Bobby Clarke 50.00 100.
SBSBH Bobby Hull 100.00 200.
SBSBO Bobby Orr 400.00 700.
SBSBP Bernie Parent 50.00 100.
SBSBU Johnny Bucyk 15.00 40.
SBSDH Dany Heatley 15.00 40.
SBSDP Denis Potvin 25.00 60.
SBSEM Evgeni Malkin 50.00 120.
SBSGH Gordie Howe 175.00 350.
SBSHA Dominik Hasek 30.00 80.
SBSHL Henrik Lundqvist 60.00 120.
SBSJI Jarome Iginla 40.00 100.
SBSJK Jari Kurri 20.00 50.
SBSJM Joe Mullen 25.00 60.
SBSJT Joe Thornton 50.00 100.
SBSLM Lanny McDonald 40.00 80.
SBSMB Martin Brodeur 100.00 200.
SBSMD Marcel Dionne 15.00 40.
SBSMF Marc-Andre Fleury 60.00 120.
SBSMH Milan Hejduk 15.00 40.
SBSML Mario Lemieux 200.00 400.
SBSMM Mark Messier 150.00 250.
SBSMN Markus Naslund 20.00 50.
SBSMR Michael Ryder 12.00 30.
SBSPB Patrice Bergeron 25.00 60.
SBSPR Patrick Roy 150.00 300.
SBSRH Ron Hextall 60.00 120.
SBSSC Sidney Crosby 200.00 350.
SBSTL Ted Lindsay 50.00 100.
SBSVL Vincent Lecavalier 40.00 80.

2007-08 Sweet Shot Sweet Stitches Triples

STATED PRINT RUN 299 SER.#'d SETS
SSTAH Ales Hemsky 4.00 10.
SSTAK Alex Kovalev 4.00 10.
SSTAM Al MacInnis 5.00 12.
SSTAO Alexander Ovechkin 20.00 50.
SSTAR Alexander Radulov 5.00 12.
SSTAS Alexander Steen 5.00 12.
SSTAT Alex Tanguay 3.00 8.
SSTBC Bobby Clarke 5.00 12.
SSTBL Brian Leetch 5.00 12.
SSTBN Bernie Nicholls 3.00 8.
SSTBO Mike Bossy 5.00 12.
SSTBS Brendan Shanahan 6.00 15.
SSTCN Cam Neely 5.00 12.
SSTCP Chris Pronger 4.00 10.
SSTDA Daniel Alfredsson 5.00 12.
SSTDE Denis Savard 6.00 15.
SSTDG Doug Gilmour 6.00 15.
SSTDH Dale Hawerchuk 6.00 15.
SSTDP Denis Potvin 5.00 12.
SSTDR Dwayne Roloson 4.00 10.
SSTDS Daniel Sedin 5.00 12.
SSTDW Doug Weight 5.00 12.
SSTEM Evgeni Malkin 12.00 30.
SSTEN Evgeni Nabokov 4.00 10.
SSTES Eric Staal 6.00 15.
SSTFM Frank Mahovlich 6.00 15.
SSTGF Grant Fuhr 5.00 12.
SSTGL Guy Lafleur 10.00 25.
SSTGP Gilbert Perreault 5.00 12.
SSTHA Dominik Hasek 6.00 15.
SSTHE Dany Heatley 5.00 12.
SSTHL Henrik Lundqvist 6.00 15.
SSTHM Milan Hejduk 4.00 10.
SSTHS Henrik Sedin 5.00 12.
SSTHZ Henrik Zetterberg 6.00 15.
SSTIK Ilya Kovalchuk 5.00 12.
SSTJI Jarome Iginla 5.00 12.
SSTJJ Jaromir Jagr 12.00 30.
SSTJO Joe Sakic 10.00 25.
SSTJS Jason Spezza 5.00 12.

SSTJT Joe Thornton 6.00 15.00
SSTKL Kari Lehtonen 4.00 10.00
SSTKO Anze Kopitar 8.00 20.00
SSTKP Miikka Kiprusoff 4.00 10.00
SSTLM Lanny McDonald 5.00 12.00
SSTLR Larry Robinson 5.00 12.00
SSTMA Martin Havlat 5.00 12.00
SSTMB Martin Brodeur 10.00 25.00
SSTMF Marc-Andre Fleury 8.00 20.00
SSTMG Marian Gaborik 6.00 15.00
SSTMH Marian Hossa 4.00 10.00
SSTMI Stan Mikita 6.00 15.00
SSTMK Mikko Koivu 4.00 10.00
SSTML Mario Lemieux 12.00 30.00
SSTMM Mark Messier 8.00 20.00
SSTMN Markus Naslund 5.00 12.00
SSTMO Mike Modano 8.00 20.00
SSTMR Mark Recchi 6.00 15.00
SSTMS Martin St. Louis 5.00 12.00
SSTMT Marty Turco 5.00 12.00
SSTMV Miroslav Satan 4.00 10.00
SSTNL Nicklas Lidstrom 5.00 12.00
SSTPB Patrice Bergeron 6.00 15.00
SSTPD Pavel Datsyuk 6.00 15.00
SSTPF Peter Forsberg 6.00 15.00
SSTPH Dion Phaneuf 5.00 12.00
SSTPK Paul Kariya 6.00 15.00
SSTPM Patrick Marleau 5.00 12.00
SSTPR Patrick Roy 12.00 30.00
SSTPS Peter Stastny 4.00 10.00
SSTRB Ray Bourque 8.00 20.00
SSTRE Ray Emery 4.00 10.00
SSTRG Ryan Getzlaf 8.00 20.00
SSTRH Ron Hextall 8.00 20.00
SSTRL Roberto Luongo 6.00 15.00
SSTRM Ryan Miller 5.00 12.00
SSTRN Rick Nash 5.00 12.00
SSTRO Luc Robitaille 5.00 12.00
SSTRS Ryan Smyth 4.00 10.00
SSTRV Rogie Vachon 6.00 15.00
SSTRY Michael Ryder 3.00 8.00
SSTSA Borje Salming 5.00 12.00
SSTSC Sidney Crosby 12.00 30.00
SSTSD Shane Doan 4.00 10.00
SSTSF Sergei Fedorov 8.00 20.00
SSTSG Simon Gagne 5.00 12.00
SSTSH Steve Shutt 5.00 12.00
SSTSI Darryl Sittler 4.00 10.00
SSTSK Saku Koivu 5.00 12.00
SSTSM Billy Smith 5.00 12.00
SSTSN Scott Niedermayer 5.00 12.00
SSTSS Scott Stevens 5.00 12.00
SSTST Jordan Staal 5.00 12.00
SSTSU Mats Sundin 5.00 12.00
SSTTS Teemu Selanne 10.00 25.00
SSTTV Tomas Vokoun 4.00 10.00
SSTTW Tiger Williams 4.00 10.00
SSTVL Vincent Lecavalier 4.00 10.00
SSTWG Wayne Gretzky 20.00 50.00
SSTZP Zach Parise 6.00 15.00

2017-18 Synergy Blue

VETS: .5X TO 1.25X RED
ROOKIES: .5X TO 1.25X RED
0 Auston Matthews 4.00 10.00

2017-18 Synergy Green

VETS: 1X TO 2.5X RED
ROOKIES: 1.25X TO 3X RED
0 Wayne Gretzky 12.00 30.00

2017-18 Synergy Purple

VETS: 1.5X TO 4X RED
ROOKIES: 2.5X TO 5X RED
9 Alex Tuch 40.00 100.00
2 Brock Boeser 80.00 150.00
3 Owen Tippett 15.00 40.00
4 Alex DeBrincat 20.00 50.00
5 Clayton Keller 25.00 60.00
6 Josh Ho-Sang 15.00 40.00
7 Pierre-Luc Dubois 25.00 60.00
8 Charlie McAvoy 25.00 60.00

2017-18 Synergy Red

OMMON CARD .40 1.00
EMISTARS .50 1.25
NLISTED STARS .60 1.50
OMMON RC 1.00 2.50
C.SEMISTARS 1.25 3.00
C.UNL.STAR 1.50 4.00
OUNTY: .6X TO 1.5X BASIC CARDS
Connor McDavid 2.50 6.00
Johnny Gaudreau 1.00 2.50
Henrik Zetterberg .60 1.50
Jamie Benn .75 2.00
P.K. Subban .60 1.50
Brad Marchand .75 2.00
John Tavares 1.25 3.00
Jack Eichel 1.00 2.50
Taylor Hall 1.25 3.00
Sidney Crosby 2.50 6.00
Claude Giroux .60 1.50
Vladimir Tarasenko 1.00 2.50
Aaron Ekblad .60 1.50
Leon Draisaitl 1.00 2.50
Carey Price 2.00 5.00
Ryan Getzlaf .60 1.50
Devan Dubnyk .60 1.50
Nathan MacKinnon 1.25 3.00
Max Domi .60 1.50
Alexander Ovechkin 2.50 6.00
Jonathan Toews 1.25 3.00
Drew Doughty .60 1.50
Nikita Kucherov 1.00 2.50
Mark Scheifele .75 2.00
Erik Karlsson .75 2.00
Daniel Sedin .60 1.50
Evgeni Malkin 2.00 5.00
Artemi Panarin .60 1.50
Nicklas Backstrom 1.00 2.50
Auston Matthews 3.00 8.00
Marc-Andre Fleury 1.00 2.50
David Pastrnak 1.00 2.50
Steven Stamkos 1.25 3.00
Brent Burns .75 2.00
Henrik Lundqvist 1.00 2.50
Jeff Skinner .50 1.25
Patrik Laine 1.00 2.50
Ryan Johansen .60 1.50
Jeff Carter .60 1.50
Patrick Kane 1.25 3.00
Mario Lemieux 2.00 5.00
Martin Brodeur 1.25 3.00
Pat LaFontaine .60 1.50
Pavel Bure .60 1.50
Patrick Roy 1.50 4.00
Joe Sakic .75 2.00
Mike Bossy 1.00 2.50
Ray Bourque 1.00 2.50
Mark Messier 1.00 2.50
Wayne Gretzky 3.00 8.00
Carter Rowney 1.25 3.00
Nicolas Kerdiles 1.50 4.00

53 Vince Dunn 1.50 4.00
54 Calle Rosen 1.50 4.00
55 Haydn Fleury 1.50 4.00
56 Tim Heed 1.50 4.00
57 Alex Kerfoot 1.50 4.00
58 Nikita Scherbak 3.00 8.00
59 J.T. Compher 2.00 5.00
60 Jack Roslovic 2.00 5.00
61 Denis Gurianov 1.50 4.00
62 Ivan Barbashev 1.50 4.00
63 Jakob Forsbacka-Karlsson 1.50 4.00
64 Samuel Girard 1.50 4.00
65 Madison Bowey 1.25 3.00
66 Lucas Wallmark 1.50 4.00
67 Janne Kuokkanen 1.50 4.00
68 Jon Gillies 1.50 4.00
69 Christian Fischer 2.00 5.00
70 Christian Djoos 1.50 4.00
71 Logan Brown 1.50 4.00
72 Alexander Nylander 2.50 6.00
73 Anders Bjork 2.00 5.00
74 Adrian Kempe 2.00 5.00
75 Colin White 1.50 4.00
76 Victor Mete 1.50 4.00
77 Luke Kunin 1.50 4.00
78 Tyson Jost 3.00 8.00
79 Jake DeBrusk 2.50 6.00
80 Kailer Yamamoto 4.00 10.00
81 Travis Sanheim 1.50 4.00
82 Jesper Bratt 2.50 6.00
83 Filip Chytil 1.50 4.00
84 Filip Chlapik 1.50 4.00
85 Evgeny Svechnikov 3.00 8.00
86 Tage Thompson 2.50 6.00
87 Samuel Blais 1.50 4.00
88 Martin Necas 1.50 4.00
89 Alex Tuch 4.00 10.00
90 Alex Formenton 1.50 4.00
91 Will Butcher 2.00 5.00
92 Brock Boeser 20.00 50.00
93 Owen Tippett 6.00 15.00
94 Alex DeBrincat 8.00 20.00
95 Clayton Keller 12.00 30.00
96 Josh Ho-Sang 8.00 20.00
97 Pierre-Luc Dubois 12.00 30.00
98 Charlie McAvoy 20.00 50.00
99 Nolan Patrick 3.00 8.00
100 Nico Hischier 8.00 20.00

2017-18 Synergy Autographs

AAA Artem Anisimov B 8.00 20.00
AAB Aleksander Barkov B 10.00 25.00
AAD Alex DeBrincat D 25.00 60.00
AAG Alex Galchenyuk B 12.00 30.00
AAL Anders Lee C 10.00 25.00
AAM Anthony Mantha C 10.00 25.00
AAN Alexander Nylander C 15.00 40.00
AAO Alexander Ovechkin A 40.00 100.00
AAT Alex Tuch D 25.00 60.00
AAV Andrei Vasilevskiy C 12.00 30.00
AAW Alexander Wennberg C 8.00 20.00
ABB Brock Boeser C 100.00 200.00
ABJ Anders Bjork C 12.00 30.00
ABO Bobby Orr C 80.00 150.00
ABS Brayden Schenn B 10.00 25.00
ACA Cam Atkinson C 10.00 25.00
ACF Christian Fischer D 12.00 30.00
ACK Clayton Keller C 25.00 60.00
ACM Connor McDavid A 40.00 100.00
ACP Carey Price A 30.00 80.00
ACS Conor Sheary C 10.00 25.00
ADG Denis Gurianov D 10.00 25.00
ADH Dominik Hasek A 10.00 25.00
ADS Darryl Sittler A 10.00 25.00
AEK Erik Karlsson A 12.00 30.00
AEM Evgeni Malkin A 30.00 80.00
AES Evgeny Svechnikov D 20.00 50.00
AFA Frederik Andersen C 8.00 20.00
AGI Jon Gillies D 10.00 25.00
AGL Guy Lafleur A 12.00 30.00
AGR Mikael Granlund C 10.00 25.00
AHL Henrik Lundqvist A 15.00 40.00
AJA Jake Allen B 12.00 30.00
AJB Jesper Bratt D 15.00 40.00
AJC John Carlson B 12.00 30.00
AJE Jeff Carter B 10.00 25.00
AJO Joe Sakic A 12.00 30.00
AJP Joe Pavelski B 10.00 25.00
AJR Jack Roslovic D 12.00 30.00
AJS Jason Spezza C 10.00 25.00
AJT Jonathan Toews A 20.00 50.00
AKA Evander Kane C 10.00 25.00
AKE Adrian Kempe D 12.00 30.00
AKP Kyle Palmieri C 8.00 20.00
ALD Leon Draisaitl B 15.00 40.00
ALK Luke Kunin C 10.00 25.00
AMA Auston Matthews A 40.00 100.00
AMB Madison Bowey D 8.00 20.00
AMC Charlie McAvoy B 30.00 80.00
AME Mark Messier A 15.00 40.00
AMF Marc-Andre Fleury B 15.00 40.00
AMG Mark Giordano C 8.00 20.00
AMI Mitch Marner B 15.00 40.00
AMM Matt Murray B 15.00 40.00
ANE Nikolaj Ehlers C 10.00 25.00
ANK Nikita Kucherov B 15.00 40.00
ANS Nikita Scherbak C 20.00 50.00
APB Pavel Buchnevich D 8.00 20.00
APD Pierre-Luc Dubois D 20.00 50.00
APK Patrick Kane B 20.00 50.00
APL Patrik Laine B 15.00 40.00
APO Jason Pominville C 8.00 20.00
APR Patrick Roy A 25.00 60.00
ARA Radek Faksa D 8.00 20.00
ARK Ryan Kesler B 10.00 25.00
ARL Roberto Luongo B 10.00 25.00
ARS Ryan Spooner C 8.00 20.00
ASA Sebastian Aho C 10.00 25.00
ASC Sidney Crosby A 40.00 100.00
ASK Brady Skjei C 8.00 20.00
ASM Samuel Morin D 10.00 25.00
ASS Steven Stamkos A 20.00 50.00
ASY Steve Yzerman A 12.00 30.00
ATA Tage Thompson D 15.00 40.00
ATJ Tylor Johnson B 8.00 20.00
ATS Tyler Seguin A 15.00 40.00
ATT Teuvo Teravainen C 8.00 20.00
ATV John Tavares A 20.00 50.00
ATY Tyson Jost D 20.00 50.00
AVH Victor Hedman B 12.00 30.00
AVK Vladislav Kamenev D 15.00 40.00
AVT Vladimir Tarasenko B 15.00 40.00
AVZ Valentin Zykov D 10.00 25.00
AWG Wayne Gretzky C 150.00 250.00
AWN William Nylander B 15.00 40.00
AWS Wayne Simmonds B 12.00 30.00

2017-18 Synergy Career Spanning

CS1 Wayne Gretzky 5.00 12.00
CS2 Steve Yzerman 1.25 3.00
CS3 Martin Brodeur 2.00 5.00
CS4 Ray Bourque 1.50 4.00
CS5 Lanny McDonald 1.00 2.50
CS6 Mark Messier 1.50 4.00
CS7 Mark Recchi 1.25 3.00
CS8 Dominik Hasek 1.00 2.50
CS9 Joe Sakic 1.25 3.00
CS10 Mario Lemieux 3.00 8.00

2017-18 Synergy Career Spanning Red

*RED/35: 1.5X TO 4X BASIC INSERTS
CS1 Wayne Gretzky 25.00 60.00

2017-18 Synergy Cast For Greatness

CG1 Sidney Crosby 40.00 100.00
CG2 Henrik Lundqvist 15.00 40.00
CG3 Mark Scheifele 12.00 30.00
CG4 Brad Marchand 12.00 30.00
CG5 Claude Giroux 10.00 25.00
CG6 Anze Kopitar 15.00 40.00
CG7 Henrik Zetterberg 10.00 25.00
CG8 Auston Matthews 40.00 100.00
CG9 Jamie Benn 12.00 30.00
CG10 Jonathan Toews 20.00 50.00
CG11 Marc-Andre Fleury 15.00 40.00
CG12 Ryan Getzlaf 10.00 25.00
CG13 Johnny Gaudreau 15.00 40.00
CG14 John Tavares 20.00 50.00
CG15 Patrik Laine 15.00 40.00
CG16 Mario Lemieux 30.00 80.00
CG17 Evgeni Malkin 30.00 80.00
CG18 Mark Messier 15.00 40.00
CG19 Nikita Kucherov 15.00 40.00
CG20 Erik Karlsson 12.00 30.00
CG21 Nolan Patrick 20.00 50.00
CG22 Brent Burns 12.00 30.00
CG23 Josh Ho-Sang 12.00 30.00
CG24 Steven Stamkos 20.00 50.00
CG25 Wayne Gretzky 50.00 120.00
CG26 Clayton Keller 25.00 60.00
CG27 Vladimir Tarasenko 15.00 40.00
CG28 Nicklas Backstrom 15.00 40.00
CG29 Bobby Orr 50.00 125.00
CG30 Patrick Kane 20.00 50.00
CG31 P.K. Subban 10.00 25.00
CG32 Pierre-Luc Dubois 20.00 50.00
CG33 Brock Boeser 50.00 125.00
CG34 Joe Sakic 12.00 30.00
CG35 Nico Hischier 30.00 80.00
CG36 Connor McDavid 40.00 100.00

2017-18 Synergy Color Shift

C1 Connor McDavid 30.00 80.00
C2 P.K. Subban 8.00 20.00
C3 John Tavares 15.00 40.00
C4 Nico Hischier 25.00 60.00
C5 Alex Ovechkin 30.00 80.00
C6 Jonathan Toews 15.00 40.00
C7 Patrik Laine 12.00 30.00
C8 Carey Price 25.00 60.00
C9 Johnny Gaudreau 12.00 30.00
C10 Sidney Crosby 30.00 80.00
C11 Mario Lemieux 25.00 60.00
C12 Steve Yzerman 10.00 25.00
C13 Ryan Getzlaf 8.00 20.00
C14 Brock Boeser 50.00 125.00
C15 Patrick Kane 15.00 40.00
C16 Brad Marchand 10.00 25.00
C17 Steven Stamkos 15.00 40.00
C18 Vladimir Tarasenko 12.00 30.00
C19 Nolan Patrick 15.00 40.00
C20 Auston Matthews 30.00 80.00
C21 Peter Forsberg 12.00 30.00
C22 Brent Burns 10.00 25.00
C23 Patrick Roy 20.00 50.00
C24 Henrik Lundqvist 12.00 30.00
C25 Erik Karlsson 10.00 25.00
C26 Pierre-Luc Dubois 15.00 40.00
C27 Evgeni Malkin 25.00 60.00
C28 Clayton Keller 20.00 50.00
C29 Nikita Kucherov 12.00 30.00
C30 Wayne Gretzky 50.00 125.00

2017-18 Synergy Exceptional Talent

ET1 Mark Scheifele 1.25 3.00
ET2 Henrik Lundqvist 1.50 4.00
ET3 Tyson Jost 2.00 5.00
ET4 Evgeny Svechnikov 2.00 5.00
ET5 Alexander Nylander 1.50 4.00
ET6 Owen Tippett 2.00 5.00
ET7 Filip Chytil 1.00 2.50
ET8 Brent Burns 1.25 3.00
ET9 Nikita Kucherov 1.50 4.00
ET10 Nicklas Backstrom 1.50 4.00
ET11 Jeff Carter 1.00 2.50
ET12 P.K. Subban 1.00 2.50
ET13 Artemi Panarin 1.00 2.50
ET14 Ryan Getzlaf 1.00 2.50
ET15 John Tavares 2.00 5.00
ET16 Steven Stamkos 2.00 5.00
ET17 Jack Eichel 1.50 4.00
ET18 Jamie Benn 1.25 3.00
ET19 Jonathan Toews 2.00 5.00
ET20 Patrik Laine 1.50 4.00
ET21 Johnny Gaudreau 1.50 4.00
ET22 Carey Price 3.00 8.00
ET23 Brad Marchand 1.25 3.00
ET24 Vladimir Tarasenko 1.50 4.00
ET25 Pierre-Luc Dubois 2.00 5.00
ET26 Will Butcher 1.25 3.00
ET27 Alex DeBrincat 2.50 6.00
ET28 Kailer Yamamoto 2.50 6.00
ET29 Alexander Ovechkin 4.00 10.00
ET30 Patrick Kane 2.00 5.00
ET31 Brock Boeser 5.00 12.00
ET32 Clayton Keller 2.50 6.00
ET33 Charlie McAvoy 3.00 8.00
ET34 Josh Ho-Sang 1.25 3.00
ET35 Erik Karlsson 1.25 3.00
ET36 Evgeni Malkin 3.00 8.00
ET37 Nico Hischier 3.00 8.00
ET38 Nolan Patrick 2.00 5.00
ET39 Auston Matthews 4.00 10.00
ET40 Connor McDavid 4.00 10.00
ET41 Sidney Crosby 4.00 10.00
ET42 Wayne Gretzky 5.00 12.00

2017-18 Synergy Impact Players

IP1 Wayne Gretzky 4.00 10.00
IP2 Henrik Zetterberg .75 2.00
IP3 Mitch Marner 1.25 3.00
IP4 Patrick Marleau .75 2.00
IP5 Nico Hischier 2.50 6.00
IP6 Corey Perry .75 2.00
IP7 Daniel Sedin .75 2.00
IP8 Drew Doughty .75 2.00
IP9 Brock Boeser 4.00 10.00
IP10 Steven Stamkos 1.50 4.00
IP11 Pavel Bure .75 2.00
IP12 Ryan McDonagh .60 1.50
IP13 Patrice Bergeron 1.00 2.50
IP14 Tyler Seguin 1.25 3.00
IP15 Patrik Laine 1.25 3.00
IP16 Filip Forsberg 1.00 2.50
IP17 Mike Bossy 1.25 3.00
IP18 Nolan Patrick 1.50 4.00
IP19 Ryan Johansen .75 2.00
IP20 Patrick Kane 1.50 4.00
IP21 Clayton Keller 2.00 5.00
IP22 Cam Atkinson .75 2.00
IP23 Evgeni Malkin 2.50 6.00
IP24 Marc-Andre Fleury 1.25 3.00
IP25 Connor McDavid 3.00 8.00
IP26 Nathan MacKinnon 1.50 4.00
IP27 Alex DeBrincat 2.00 5.00
IP28 Peter Forsberg 1.25 3.00
IP29 Taylor Hall 1.50 4.00
IP30 Erik Karlsson 1.00 2.50
IP31 Anders Bjork 1.00 2.50
IP32 Bobby Orr 2.50 6.00
IP33 Blake Wheeler .75 2.00
IP34 Duncan Keith .75 2.00
IP35 Dominik Hasek .75 2.00
IP36 Nikita Kucherov 1.25 3.00
IP37 Mario Lemieux 2.50 6.00
IP38 Nicklas Lidstrom .60 1.50
IP39 Claude Giroux .75 2.00
IP40 Auston Matthews 3.00 8.00
IP41 Pat LaFontaine .75 2.00
IP42 Will Butcher 1.00 2.50
IP43 Max Pacioretty .75 2.00
IP44 Kailer Yamamoto 2.00 5.00
IP45 Josh Ho-Sang 1.00 2.50
IP46 Shea Weber .60 1.50
IP47 Pierre-Luc Dubois 1.50 4.00
IP48 Jean Beliveau .75 2.00
IP49 Joe Pavelski .75 2.00
IP50 Sidney Crosby 3.00 8.00

2017-18 Synergy Impact Players Blue

*BLUE/26: 2X TO 5X BASIC INSERTS
IP15 Patrik Laine 15.00 40.00
IP32 Bobby Orr 25.00 60.00

2017-18 Synergy Noteworthy Newcomers

NN1 Nico Hischier 2.50 6.00
NN2 Evgeny Svechnikov 1.50 4.00
NN3 Haydn Fleury .75 2.00
NN4 Adrian Kempe 1.00 2.50
NN5 Pierre-Luc Dubois 1.50 4.00
NN6 Jack Roslovic 1.00 2.50
NN7 Owen Tippett 1.50 4.00
NN8 Tyson Jost 1.50 4.00
NN9 Anders Bjork 1.00 2.50
NN10 Clayton Keller 2.00 5.00
NN11 Colin White .75 2.00
NN12 Martin Necas .75 2.00
NN13 Jesper Bratt 1.25 3.00
NN14 Alex DeBrincat 2.00 5.00
NN15 Josh Ho-Sang 1.00 2.50
NN16 Filip Chytil .75 2.00
NN17 Alex Kerfoot .75 2.00
NN18 Logan Brown .75 2.00
NN19 Alexander Nylander 1.25 3.00
NN20 Charlie McAvoy 2.50 6.00
NN21 Ian McCoshen .75 2.00
NN22 Victor Mete .75 2.00
NN23 Christian Fischer 1.00 2.50
NN24 Will Butcher 1.00 2.50
NN25 Brock Boeser 4.00 10.00
NN26 Alex Tuch 2.00 5.00
NN27 Robert Hagg .75 2.00
NN28 Brendan Lemieux .75 2.00
NN29 Kailer Yamamoto 2.00 5.00
NN30 Nolan Patrick 1.50 4.00

2017-18 Synergy Noteworthy Newcomers Red

NN5 Pierre-Luc Dubois 12.00 30.00
NN12 Martin Necas 12.00 30.00

1981-82 TCMA

This 13-card set measures the standard size. The front features a color posed photo, with a thin black border on white card stock. The cards are numbered on the back and have biographical information as well as career highlights between two hockey sticks drawn on the sides of the card backs. Supposedly there were only 3000 sets produced. Eleven Hockey Hall of Famers are included in the set.

COMPLETE SET (13) 24.00 60.00
1 Norm Ullman 1.25 3.00
2 Gump Worsley 2.00 5.00
3 J.C. Tremblay .60 1.50
4 Lou Fontinato .60 1.50
5 Johnny Bucyk 1.25 3.00
6 Harry Howell .75 2.00
7 Henri Richard 2.00 5.00
8 Andy Bathgate 1.25 3.00
9 Bobby Orr 10.00 25.00
10 Frank Mahovlich 2.00 5.00
11 Jean Beliveau 4.00 10.00
12 Jacques Plante 4.00 10.00
13 Stan Mikita 3.00 8.00

1935 TCTA

This card measures approximately 3 1/2" x 5 1/2" and was printed in black and white.

NNO Maple Leaf Arena 25.00 50.00

1974 Team Canada L'Equipe WHA

This 24-photo set measures approximately 4 1/8" by 7 1/2" and features posed, glossy, black-and-white player photos on thin stock. The pictures are attached to red poster board. The player's name and two Team Canada L'Equipe logos appear in the white margin at the bottom. The backs are blank. The cards are unnumbered and checklisted below in alphabetical order.

COMPLETE SET (24) 25.00 50.00
1 Ralph Backstrom 1.00 2.00
2 Serge Bernier .75 1.50
3 Gerry Cheevers 5.00 10.00
4 Al Hamilton 1.00 2.00
5 Billy Harris CO .50 1.00
6 Jim Harrison .75 1.50
7 Ben Hatskin OWN .75 1.50
8 Paul Henderson 2.00 4.00
9 Rejean Houle 1.00 2.00
10 Mark Howe 4.00 8.00
11 Marty Howe 1.00 2.00
12 Bill Hunter .50 1.00
13 Gordon W. Juckes .50 1.00
14 Rick Ley 1.00 2.00
15 Frank Mahovlich 4.00 8.00
16 John McKenzie 1.00 2.00
17 Don McLeod .75 1.50
18 Rick Noonan .75 1.50
19 Brad Selwood .75 1.50
20 Rick Smith .75 1.50
21 Pat Stapleton 1.00 2.00
22 Marc Tardif 1.00 2.00
23 Mike Walton 1.00 2.00
24 Tom Webster 1.00 2.00

2002 Team Canada Coca Cola Coins

1 Mario Lemieux 4.00 10.00
2 Steve Yzerman 4.00 10.00
3 Joe Sakic 1.50 4.00
4 Chris Pronger 1.00 2.50
5 Owen Nolan 1.00 2.50
6 Scott Niedermayer 1.00 2.50
7 Rob Blake 1.00 2.50
8 Paul Kariya 1.50 4.00

1996-97 Team Out

The 1996-97 Team Out set was issued in one series totaling 89 cards. The cards were intended for use in a game, which is explained in the instructions included with the set. While the game itself never quite took off, the cards were quite popular with superstar and team collectors, which led to a fairly wide break of the product.

COMPLETE SET (89) 10.00 25.00
1 Paul Kariya .60 1.50
2 Luc Robitaille .08 .25
3 John LeClair .20 .50
4 Theo Fleury .20 .50
5 Scott Mellanby .08 .25
6 Adam Graves .08 .25
7 Esa Tikkanen .02 .10
8 Slava Kozlov .08 .25
9 Eric Daze .08 .25
10 Ryan Smyth .08 .25
11 Shayne Corson .08 .25
12 Kevin Stevens .08 .25
13 Murray Craven .02 .10
14 Keith Tkachuk .20 .50
15 Zigmund Palffy .20 .50
16 Eric Lindros .40 1.00
17 Mario Lemieux 1.00 2.50
18 Joe Sakic .40 1.00
19 Wayne Gretzky 1.25 3.00
20 Mark Messier .20 .50
21 Sergei Fedorov .40 1.00
22 Jason Arnott .08 .25
23 Chris Gratton .08 .25
24 Pierre Turgeon .08 .25
25 Mike Modano .20 .50
26 Saku Koivu .20 .50
27 Alexei Yashin .08 .25
28 Steve Yzerman .75 2.00
29 Peter Forsberg .40 1.00
30 Adam Oates .08 .25
31 Brett Hull .20 .50
32 Jaromir Jagr .40 1.00
33 Pavel Bure .40 1.00
34 Teemu Selanne .30 .75
35 Stephane Richer .02 .10
36 Mike Gartner .08 .25
37 Claude Lemieux .08 .25
38 Rick Tocchet .08 .25
39 Alexander Mogilny .08 .25
40 Peter Bondra .08 .25
41 Mats Sundin .08 .25
42 Daniel Alfredsson .08 .25
43 Owen Nolan .02 .10
44 Joe Juneau .08 .25
45 Mikael Renberg .08 .25
46 Chris Chelios .20 .50
47 Ray Bourque .30 .75
48 Scott Stevens .08 .25
49 Paul Coffey .20 .50
50 Glen Wesley .02 .10
51 Nicklas Lidstrom .20 .50
52 Scott Niedermayer .08 .25
53 Larry Murphy .02 .10
54 Sandis Ozolinsh .08 .25
55 Vladimir Malakhov .02 .10
56 Robert Svehla .02 .10
57 Steve Duchesne .02 .10
58 Sergei Gonchar .02 .10
59 Darius Kasparaitis .08 .25
60 Patrick Roy 1.00 2.50
61 Martin Brodeur .40 1.00
62 Mike Richter .20 .50
63 John Vanbiesbrouck .20 .50
64 Ron Hextall .08 .25
65 Nikolai Khabibulin .08 .25
66 Grant Fuhr .08 .25
67 Kirk McLean .08 .25
68 Jim Carey .20 .50
69 Dominik Hasek .30 .75
70 Ed Belfour .20 .50
71 Chris Osgood .20 .50
72 Guy Hebert .08 .25
73 Trevor Kidd .08 .25
74 Felix Potvin .20 .50
75 Roman Hamrlik .08 .25
76 Alexei Zhitnik .08 .25
77 Al MacInnis .02 .10
78 Brian Leetch .20 .50
79 Rob Blake .08 .25
80 Derian Hatcher .02 .10
81 Mathieu Schneider .02 .10
82 Gary Suter .02 .10
83 Jeff Brown .02 .10
84 Jyrki Lumme .02 .10
85 Ed Jovanovski .08 .25
86 Eric Desjardins .08 .25
87 Stephane Quintal .02 .10
88 Marcus Ragnarsson .02 .10
89 Zarley Zalapski .02 .10

2005-06 The Cup

1 Jean-Sebastien Giguere 6.00 15.00
2 Teemu Selanne 12.00 30.00
3 Ilya Kovalchuk 6.00 15.00
4 Marian Hossa 5.00 12.00
5 Kari Lehtonen 5.00 12.00
6 Cam Neely 6.00 15.00
7 Patrice Bergeron 8.00 20.00
8 Ray Bourque 10.00 25.00
9 Johnny Bucyk 5.00 12.00
10 Phil Esposito 10.00 25.00
11 Don Cherry 6.00 15.00
12 Brian Leetch 6.00 15.00
13 Gerry Cheevers 12.00 30.00
14 Gilbert Perreault 6.00 15.00
15 Chris Drury 5.00 12.00
16 Ryan Miller 6.00 15.00
17 Jarome Iginla 6.00 15.00
18 Lanny McDonald 6.00 15.00
19 Miikka Kiprusoff 5.00 12.00
20 Joe Mullen 5.00 12.00
21 Eric Staal 8.00 20.00
22 Doug Weight 6.00 15.00
23 Martin Gerber 5.00 12.00
24 Nikolai Khabibulin 6.00 15.00
25 Denis Savard 8.00 20.00
26 Bobby Hull 10.00 25.00
27 Tony Esposito 6.00 15.00
28 Joe Sakic 10.00 25.00
29 Alex Tanguay 6.00 15.00
30 Milan Hejduk 5.00 12.00
31 Jose Theodore 6.00 15.00
32 Marek Svatos 5.00 12.00
33 Rick Nash 6.00 15.00
34 Sergei Fedorov 10.00 25.00
35 Mike Modano 10.00 25.00
36 Marty Turco 6.00 15.00
37 Brenden Morrow 5.00 12.00
38 Steve Yzerman 15.00 40.00
39 Gordie Howe 20.00 50.00
40 Brendan Shanahan 8.00 20.00
41 Scotty Bowman 5.00 12.00
42 Pavel Datsyuk 8.00 20.00
43 Henrik Zetterberg 8.00 20.00
44 Chris Pronger 5.00 12.00
45 Wayne Gretzky 30.00 80.00
46 Grant Fuhr 6.00 15.00
47 Roberto Luongo 10.00 25.00
48 Olli Jokinen 6.00 15.00
49 Jeremy Roenick 6.00 15.00
50 Luc Robitaille 6.00 15.00
51 Rogie Vachon 8.00 20.00
52 Marian Gaborik 10.00 25.00
53 Saku Koivu 6.00 15.00
54 Jean Beliveau 6.00 15.00
55 Steve Shutt 6.00 15.00
56 Patrick Roy 15.00 40.00
57 Guy Lafleur 8.00 20.00
58 Guy Lapointe 5.00 12.00
59 Michael Ryder 5.00 12.00
60 Tomas Vokoun 5.00 12.00
61 Paul Kariya 8.00 20.00
62 Martin Brodeur 12.00 30.00
63 Patrik Elias 6.00 15.00
64 Alexei Yashin 5.00 12.00
65 Mike Bossy 6.00 15.00
66 Denis Potvin 6.00 15.00
67 Bryan Trottier 8.00 20.00
68 Clark Gillies 6.00 15.00
69 Jaromir Jagr 15.00 40.00
70 Dominik Hasek 10.00 25.00
71 Dany Heatley 6.00 15.00
72 Jason Spezza 6.00 15.00
73 Daniel Alfredsson 6.00 15.00
74 Peter Forsberg 8.00 20.00
75 Ron Hextall 10.00 25.00
76 Simon Gagne 6.00 15.00
77 Bobby Clarke 6.00 15.00
78 Keith Primeau 6.00 15.00
79 Bernie Parent 6.00 15.00
80 Shane Doan 5.00 12.00
81 Curtis Joseph 6.00 15.00
82 Mario Lemieux 20.00 50.00
83 Marc-Andre Fleury 10.00 25.00
84 Jonathan Cheechoo 6.00 15.00
85 Evgeni Nabokov 5.00 12.00
86 Joe Thornton 8.00 20.00
87 Patrick Marleau 6.00 15.00
88 Keith Tkachuk 6.00 15.00
89 Martin St. Louis 6.00 15.00
90 Vincent Lecavalier 5.00 12.00
91 Brad Richards 6.00 15.00
92 Ed Belfour 6.00 15.00
93 Darryl Sittler 5.00 12.00
94 Mats Sundin 6.00 15.00
95 Eric Lindros 10.00 25.00
96 Doug Gilmour 8.00 20.00
97 Markus Naslund 6.00 15.00
98 Todd Bertuzzi 6.00 15.00
99 Ed Jovanovski 5.00 12.00
100 Olaf Kolzig 6.00 15.00
101 R.Getzlaf JSY AU RC 150.00 300.00
102 R.Whitney JSY AU RC EX 20.00 50.00
103 R.J. Umberger JSY AU RC 40.00 100.00
104 Cam Ward JSY AU RC 40.00 100.00
105 B.Seabrook JSY AU RC 80.00 150.00
106 Eric Nystrom JSY AU RC 15.00 40.00
107 Gilbert Brule JSY AU RC 25.00 60.00
108 H.Toivonen JSY AU RC 20.00 50.00
109 R.Nilsson JSY AU RC 20.00 50.00
110 R.Olesz JSY AU RC 15.00 40.00
111 Ryan Suter JSY AU RC 40.00 100.00
112 J.Jokinen JSY AU RC EX 30.00 80.00
113 Zach Parise JSY AU RC 100.00 250.00
114 W.Wolski JSY AU RC 15.00 40.00
115 A.Meszaros JSY AU RC 15.00 40.00
116 J.Franzen JSY AU RC 30.00 80.00
117 P.Budaj JSY AU RC 25.00 60.00
118 D.Leneveu JSY AU RC 15.00 40.00
119 A.Alberts JSY AU RC 12.00 30.00
120 S.Bernier JSY AU RC 20.00 50.00
121 M.Koivu JSY AU RC 50.00 120.00
122 C.Campoli JSY AU RC 12.00 30.00
123 E.Artyukhin JSY AU RC 15.00 40.00
124 C.Schubert JSY AU RC 12.00 30.00
125 T.Fleischmann JSY AU RC 20.00 50.00
126 M.Talbot JSY AU RC 20.00 50.00
127 J.Sigalet JSY AU RC 12.00 30.00
128 D.Richmond JSY AU RC 12.00 30.00
129 M.Lapierre JSY AU RC 30.00 80.00
130 D.Patzold JSY AU RC 12.00 30.00
131 R.Bourque JSY AU RC 20.00 50.00
132 Y.Danis JSY AU RC 15.00 40.00
133 B.Winchester JSY AU RC 20.00 50.00
134 Jim Slater JSY AU RC 15.00 40.00
135 Petr Prucha JSY AU RC 20.00 50.00
136 Jim Howard JSY AU RC 80.00 200.00
137 P.Eaves JSY AU RC 20.00 50.00
138 R.Clowe JSY AU RC 25.00 60.00
139 B.Coburn JSY AU RC 20.00 50.00
140 B.Richardson JSY AU RC 20.00 50.00
141 M.Jurcina JSY AU RC 15.00 40.00
142 J.Woywitka JSY AU RC 12.00 30.00
143 A.Kostitsyn JSY AU RC 25.00 60.00
144 Derek Boogaard AU RC 20.00 50.00
145 B.Tallackson JSY AU RC 15.00 40.00
146 J.Klepis JSY AU RC EX 12.00 30.00
147 A.Montoya JSY AU RC 20.00 50.00
148 A.Ladd JSY AU RC 40.00 100.00
149 B.Bochenski JSY AU RC 20.00 50.00
150 J.Tambellini JSY AU RC 12.00 30.00
151 J.Balastik JSY AU RC 12.00 30.00
152 L.Stempniak JSY AU RC 20.00 50.00
153 K.Dallman JSY AU RC 15.00 40.00
154 N.Nordgren JSY AU RC 20.00 50.00
155 K.Nastiuk JSY AU RC 12.00 30.00
156 R.Craig JSY AU RC 12.00 30.00
157 E.Christensen JSY AU RC 12.00 30.00
158 C.Thorburn JSY AU RC 15.00 40.00
159 J.Gorges JSY AU RC 15.00 40.00
160 Matt Foy JSY AU RC 12.00 30.00
161 O.Tollefsen JSY AU RC 15.00 40.00
162 K.Bieksa JSY AU RC 25.00 60.00
163 K.Quincey JSY AU RC 15.00 40.00
164 A.Wozniewski JSY AU RC 15.00 40.00
165 Jeff Hoggan JSY AU RC 12.00 30.00
166 J.Colliton JSY AU RC 12.00 30.00
167 A.Picard JSY AU RC 12.00 30.00
168 Ben Eager JSY AU RC 15.00 40.00
169 D.Paille JSY AU RC 20.00 50.00
170 V.Filppula JSY AU RC 40.00 100.00
171 A. Perezhogin JSY AU RC 15.00 40.00
172 M.Richards JSY AU RC 60.00 120.00
173 Corey Perry JSY AU RC 150.00 300.00
174 A.Steen JSY AU RC 40.00 100.00
175 T.Vanek JSY AU RC 100.00 200.00
176 J.Carter JSY AU RC 125.00 250.00
177 H.Lundqvist JSY AU RC 350.00 600.00
178 D.Phaneuf JSY AU/99 RC 250.00 600.00
179 A.Ovechkin JSY AU/99 RC 2500.00 4000.00
180 S.Crosby JSY AU/99 RC 4500.00 8000.00
181 Brett Lebda AU RC 10.00 25.00
182 Jay McClement AU RC 10.00 25.00
183 Cam Barker JSY AU RC 15.00 40.00
184 P.Nokelainen AU RC 10.00 25.00
185 Keith Ballard AU RC 12.00 30.00
186 Duncan Keith AU RC 100.00 200.00
187 George Parros AU RC 10.00 25.00
188 Adam Berkhoel AU RC 12.00 30.00
189 Anthony Stewart AU RC 12.00 30.00
190 Ryan Hollweg AU RC 10.00 25.00
191 Ben Walter AU RC 10.00 25.00

2005-06 The Cup Gold

*1-100 GOLD: 1.2X TO 3X BASE HI
PRINT RUN 25 SER.#'d SETS
2 Teemu Selanne 30.00 80.00
3 Ilya Kovalchuk 25.00 60.00
8 Ray Bourque 25.00 60.00
11 Don Cherry 25.00 60.00
17 Jarome Iginla 25.00 60.00
21 Eric Staal 25.00 60.00
26 Bobby Hull 25.00 60.00
28 Joe Sakic 50.00 100.00
33 Rick Nash 40.00 80.00
35 Mike Modano 25.00 60.00
38 Steve Yzerman 60.00 125.00
39 Gordie Howe 30.00 80.00
42 Pavel Datsyuk 25.00 60.00
43 Henrik Zetterberg 25.00 60.00
45 Wayne Gretzky 250.00 400.00
47 Roberto Luongo 25.00 60.00
50 Luc Robitaille 25.00 60.00
52 Marian Gaborik 25.00 60.00
53 Saku Koivu 25.00 60.00
56 Patrick Roy 75.00 150.00
57 Guy Lafleur 25.00 60.00
62 Martin Brodeur 30.00 80.00
69 Jaromir Jagr 25.00 60.00
70 Dominik Hasek 25.00 60.00
71 Dany Heatley 25.00 60.00
72 Jason Spezza 25.00 60.00
74 Peter Forsberg 25.00 60.00
82 Mario Lemieux 60.00 150.00
83 Marc-Andre Fleury 25.00 60.00
86 Joe Thornton 25.00 60.00
90 Vincent Lecavalier 25.00 60.00

2005-06 The Cup Autographed Rookie Patches Gold Rainbow

STATED PRINT RUN 2-87
101 Ryan Getzlaf/51 250.00 500.00
102 Ryan Whitney/19
103 R.J. Umberger/20 75.00 150.00
104 Cam Ward/30 200.00 300.00
106 Eric Nystrom/23 75.00 150.00
107 Gilbert Brule/17 75.00 150.00
108 Hannu Toivonen/33 25.00 60.00
109 Robert Nilsson/21 100.00 200.00
110 Rostislav Olesz/85 20.00 50.00
111 Ryan Suter/20 75.00 150.00
112 Jussi Jokinen/36 80.00 150.00
116 Johan Franzen/39 100.00 200.00
117 Peter Budaj/31 125.00 250.00
118 David Leneveu/30 50.00 120.00
119 Andrew Alberts/41 30.00 60.00
120 Steve Bernier/26 75.00 150.00
121 Mikko Koivu/21 60.00 120.00
123 Evgeny Artyukhin/76 20.00 50.00
125 Tomas Fleischmann/43 60.00 120.00
126 Maxime Talbot/25 60.00 120.00
127 Jordan Sigalet/57 40.00 100.00
128 Danny Richmond/51 15.00 40.00
129 Maxim Lapierre/40 25.00 50.00
130 Dimitri Patzold/30 40.00 80.00
132 Yann Danis/75 15.00 40.00
133 Brad Winchester/26 30.00 60.00
134 Jim Slater/23 25.00 50.00
135 Petr Prucha/25 30.00 60.00
136 Jim Howard/35 125.00 200.00
137 Patrick Eaves/44 50.00 120.00
138 Ryane Clowe/29 75.00 150.00
141 Milan Jurcina/68 25.00 60.00
142 Jeff Woywitka/29 20.00 50.00
143 Andrei Kostitsyn/46 40.00 100.00
145 Barry Tallackson/27 25.00 50.00
146 Jakub Klepis/38 25.00 60.00
147 Alvaro Montoya/29 30.00 80.00
148 Andrew Ladd/16 40.00 80.00
151 Jaroslav Balastik/40 15.00 40.00
153 Kevin Dallman/38 25.00 50.00
154 Niklas Nordgren/44 15.00 40.00
155 Kevin Nastiuk/35 15.00 50.00
156 Ryan Craig/34 25.00 50.00
157 Erik Christensen/16 30.00 60.00
160 Matt Foy/83 15.00 50.00
161 Ole-Kristian Tollefsen/55 25.00 50.00
162 Kevin Bieksa/25 40.00 80.00
164 Andrew Wozniewski/56 15.00 40.00
165 Jeff Hoggan/22 30.00 60.00
166 Jeremy Colliton/27 40.00 80.00
167 Alexandre Picard/19 25.00 50.00
168 Ben Eager/55 25.00 50.00
169 Daniel Paille/20 60.00 120.00
171 Alexander Perezhogin/42 25.00 60.00
172 Mike Richards/18 125.00 250.00
173 Corey Perry/61 125.00 250.00
175 Thomas Vanek/26 125.00 250.00
176 Jeff Carter/17 175.00 350.00
177 Henrik Lundqvist/30 250.00 500.00
180 Sidney Crosby/87 3000.00 4500.00
183 Cam Barker/25 50.00 120.00
187 George Parros/57 30.00 60.00
189 Anthony Stewart/57

2005-06 The Cup Emblems of Endorsement

STATED PRINT RUN 10-15
EEAF Alexander Frolov
EEAO Alexander Ovechkin
EEAR Andrew Raycroft 75.00 150.00
EEAT Alex Tanguay 30.00 80.00
EEAY Alexei Yashin 25.00 60.00
EEBH Bobby Hull
EEBL Brian Leetch 30.00 80.00
EEBO Jay Bouwmeester 30.00 80.00
EEBQ Ray Bourque 60.00 120.00
EEBS Billy Smith
EEBY Mike Bossy
EECD Chris Drury
EECN Cam Neely 50.00 100.00
EECP Chris Pronger 25.00 60.00
EEDG Doug Gilmour 50.00 100.00
EEDH Dany Heatley 40.00 80.00
EEDS Darryl Sittler 25.00 60.00
EEDW Doug Weight
EEEB Ed Belfour
EEEN Evgeni Nabokov
EEES Eric Staal 40.00 100.00
EEFM Frank Mahovlich 30.00 80.00
EEGC Gerry Cheevers 50.00 100.00
EEGE Martin Gerber 25.00 60.00
EEGF Grant Fuhr/12
EEGL Guy Lafleur
EEGM Glen Murray 25.00 60.00
EEHK Dominik Hasek 60.00 120.00
EEHO Marian Hossa 25.00 60.00
EEHV Martin Havlat 50.00 100.00
EEHZ Henrik Zetterberg 75.00 150.00
EEIK Ilya Kovalchuk 50.00 100.00
EEJB Jean Beliveau 125.00 200.00
EEJC Jonathan Cheechoo 30.00 80.00
EEJG Jean-Sebastien Giguere 30.00 80.00
EEJI Jarome Iginla 60.00 120.00
EEJM Joe Mullen 25.00 60.00
EEJO Joe Thornton 40.00 100.00
EEJP Joni Pitkanen 20.00 50.00
EEJT Jose Theodore 30.00 80.00
EEKD Kris Draper 40.00 100.00
EEKL Kari Lehtonen 25.00 60.00
EEKP Keith Primeau 30.00 80.00
EELM Larry Murphy 25.00 60.00
EELR Luc Robitaille
EELU Joffrey Lupul 25.00 60.00
EEMB Martin Brodeur 100.00 200.00
EEMC Bryan McCabe 20.00 50.00
EEMG Marian Gaborik 50.00 125.00
EEMH Milan Hejduk 25.00 60.00
EEMK Miikka Kiprusoff 25.00 60.00
EEML Manny Legace 30.00 80.00
EEMM Mike Modano
EEMN Markus Naslund
EEMS Miroslav Satan
EEMT Marty Turco
EEMU Lanny McDonald
EEMW Brenden Morrow 25.00 60.00
EEOJ Olli Jokinen 30.00 80.00
EEOK Olaf Kolzig 30.00 80.00
EEPB Patrice Bergeron 100.00 175.00
EEPH Dion Phaneuf 60.00 120.00
EEPM Patrick Marleau 30.00 80.00
EEPR Patrick Roy 250.00 400.00
EERB Rob Blake
EERH Ron Hextall 100.00 175.00
EERL Roberto Luongo/10
EERM Ryan Miller 30.00 80.00
EERN Rick Nash 30.00 80.00
EERS Ryan Smyth
EERV Rogie Vachon
EERY Michael Ryder 25.00 60.00
EESC Sidney Crosby 500.00 800.00
EESG Simon Gagne
EESK Saku Koivu
EESL Martin St. Louis
EESN Scott Niedermayer
EESS Steve Shutt
EESV Marek Svatos 25.00 60.00
EETB Todd Bertuzzi 30.00 80.00
EETE Tony Esposito 50.00 100.00
EETI Tiger Williams 25.00 60.00
EETV Tomas Vokoun 50.00 100.00
EEVL Vincent Lecavalier 60.00 120.00
EEWR Wade Redden
EEZC Zdeno Chara

2005-06 The Cup Honorable Numbers

COMMON CARD/15-93 15.00 40.00
SEMISTARS/15-93 25.00 50.00
UNL.STARS/15-93 30.00 60.00
STATED PRINT RUN 1-93
HNAH Ales Hemsky/83 20.00 50.00
HNAO Alexander Ovechkin/8
HNAR Andrew Raycroft/1
HNAT Alex Tanguay/18 30.00 60.00
HNAY Alexei Yashin/79 25.00 60.00
HNBH Bobby Hull/9
HNBI Martin Biron/43 15.00 40.00
HNBK Rob Blake/4
HNBL Brian Leetch/22 75.00 150.00
HNBM Bryan McCabe/24 30.00 60.00
HNBT Bryan Trottier/19 50.00 100.00
HNBY Mike Bossy/22 30.00 80.00
HNCD Chris Drury/23 30.00 80.00
HNCH Jonathan Cheechoo/14
HNCN Cam Neely/8
HNCP Chris Pronger/44 30.00 60.00
HNDA David Aebischer/1
HNDG Doug Gilmour/93 40.00 80.00
HNDH Dany Heatley/15 50.00 100.00
HNDP Dion Phaneuf/3
HNDR Dwayne Roloson/30 25.00 50.00
HNDS Darryl Sittler/27 40.00 80.00
HNDW Doug Weight/39 25.00 50.00
HNED Eric Daze/55 15.00 40.00
HNER Eric Staal/12
HNGC Gerry Cheevers/30 50.00 100.00
HNGE Martin Gerber/29 30.00 60.00
HNGF Grant Fuhr/31 60.00 100.00
HNGL Guy Lafleur/10
HNGM Glen Murray/27 25.00 60.00
HNGP Gilbert Perreault/11
HNHK Dominik Hasek/39 50.00 100.00
HNHO Marian Hossa/18
HNHV Martin Havlat/9
HNIK Ilya Kovalchuk/17 75.00 150.00
HNJB Jean Beliveau/4
HNJC Jeff Carter/17
HNJI Jarome Iginla/12
HNJO Joe Thornton/19
HNJS Jean-Sebastien Giguere/35 20.00 50.00
HNJT Jose Theodore/60 40.00 80.00
HNKL Kari Lehtonen/32 50.00 120.00
HNKP Keith Primeau/25 12.00 30.00
HNLR Luc Robitaille/20 60.00 120.00
HNLU Joffrey Lupul/15
HNMB Martin Brodeur/30 150.00 250.00
HNMC Lanny McDonald/9
HNMG Marian Gaborik/10
HNMH Milan Hejduk/23 15.00 40.00
HNMK Miikka Kiprusoff/34 50.00 100.00
HNMN Markus Naslund/19
HNMO Brendan Morrison/7
HNMP Mark Parrish/37 20.00 50.00
HNMS Marek Svatos/40 40.00 80.00
HNMT Marty Turco/35 30.00 60.00
HNMW Brenden Morrow/10
HNOK Olaf Kolzig/37 50.00 100.00
HNPB Patrice Bergeron/37 40.00 80.00
HNPE Michael Peca/37 15.00 40.00
HNPM Patrick Marleau/12
HNPO Denis Potvin/5
HNPR Patrick Roy/33 150.00 300.00
HNRB Ray Bourque/77 40.00 80.00
HNRE Robert Esche/42 20.00 50.00
HNRH Ron Hextall/27 60.00 120.00
HNRL Roberto Luongo/1
HNRN Rick Nash/61 50.00 120.00
HNSA Miroslav Satan/81 25.00 60.00
HNSC Sidney Crosby/87 400.00 700.00
HNSG Simon Gagne/12
HNSK Saku Koivu/11
HNSL Martin St. Louis/26 30.00 60.00
HNST Matt Stajan/14
HNTB Todd Bertuzzi/44 15.00 40.00
HNTE Tony Esposito/35 40.00 80.00
HNTR Tuomo Ruutu/15 40.00 80.00
HNTV Tomas Vokoun/29 40.00 80.00
HNVL Vincent Lecavalier/4
HNWG Wayne Gretzky/9
HNZP Zigmund Palffy/33 30.00 60.00
HNDS2 Denis Savard/18 20.00 50.00

2005-06 The Cup Limited Logos Autographs

STATED PRINT RUN 4-50
LLAO Alexander Ovechkin 200.00 400.00
LLAT Alex Tanguay 25.00 60.00
LLAY Alexei Yashin 40.00 80.00
LLBH Bobby Hull/25
LLBI Martin Biron 30.00 80.00
LLBL Rob Blake 40.00 80.00
LLBS Billy Smith 50.00 100.00
LLBY Mike Bossy 60.00 125.00
LLCD Chris Drury 50.00 100.00
LLCN Cam Neely/4
LLCP Chris Pronger 60.00 125.00
LLDA David Aebischer 25.00 60.00
LLDG Doug Gilmour/15 150.00 250.00
LLDH Dany Heatley/14 100.00 200.00
LLDP Denis Potvin 60.00 125.00
LLDS Darryl Sittler/5
LLDW Doug Weight/35 30.00 60.00
LLED Eric Daze 40.00 80.00
LLEN Evgeni Nabokov/20 100.00 200.00
LLES Eric Staal 50.00 100.00
LLFM Frank Mahovlich/20 75.00 150.00
LLGE Martin Gerber 50.00 100.00
LLGF Grant Fuhr/45 50.00 100.00
LLGM Glen Murray 15.00 40.00
LLGP Gilbert Perreault 60.00 120.00
LLHA Dominik Hasek 60.00 100.00
LLHJ Milan Hejduk 40.00 80.00
LLHV Martin Havlat 20.00 50.00
LLIK Ilya Kovalchuk 25.00 60.00
LLJC Jonathan Cheechoo/25 50.00 100.00
LLJI Jarome Iginla 75.00 150.00
LLJO Joe Thornton 60.00 125.00
LLJS Jean-Sebastien Giguere 40.00 80.00
LLJT Jose Theodore 40.00 80.00
LLKD Kris Draper 25.00 60.00
LLKP Keith Primeau 12.00 30.00
LLLF Guy Lafleur/10
LLLM Lanny McDonald/25 50.00 100.00
LLLU Luc Robitaille 60.00 125.00
LLMB Martin Brodeur 100.00 200.00
LLMC Bryan McCabe 25.00 60.00
LLMG Marian Gaborik 30.00 80.00
LLMH Marian Hossa 40.00 80.00
LLMK Miikka Kiprusoff 75.00 150.00
LLML Manny Legace/10
LLMM Mike Modano 40.00 100.00
LLMN Markus Naslund 60.00 120.00
LLMO Brendan Morrison 25.00 60.00
LLMP Michael Peca/30 40.00 80.00
LLMT Marty Turco 40.00 80.00
LLMW Brenden Morrow 20.00 50.00
LLOJ Olli Jokinen 25.00 60.00
LLOK Olaf Kolzig 25.00 60.00
LLPB Patrice Bergeron/25 100.00 175.00
LLPM Patrick Marleau/30 50.00 100.00
LLPR Patrick Roy/21 250.00 400.00
LLRB Ray Bourque/45 50.00 100.00
LLRE Robert Esche 20.00 50.00
LLRL Roberto Luongo/40 40.00 100.00
LLRM Ryan Miller 25.00 60.00
LLRN Rick Nash/20 100.00 200.00
LLRS Ryan Smyth 60.00 125.00
LLRV Rogie Vachon/20
LLRY Michael Ryder 50.00 100.00
LLSA Miroslav Satan 25.00 60.00
LLSC Sidney Crosby 400.00 700.00
LLSD Shane Doan 50.00 100.00
LLSG Simon Gagne 20.00 50.00
LLSK Saku Koivu 25.00 60.00
LLSL Martin St. Louis/25 60.00 120.00
LLSN Scott Niedermayer 25.00 60.00
LLSS Steve Shutt 50.00 100.00
LLSW Stephen Weiss 25.00 60.00
LLTB Todd Bertuzzi 20.00 50.00
LLTC Ty Conklin 25.00 60.00
LLTE Tony Esposito/15 200.00 400.00
LLTV Tomas Vokoun 40.00 80.00
LLVL Vincent Lecavalier 60.00 125.00
LLZP Zigmund Palffy 30.00 75.00

2005-06 The Cup Noble Numbers

STATED PRINT RUN 1-68
NNBB Rob Blake
  Jay Bouwmeester/4
NNBC Brodeur/Cheevers/30 40.00 80.00
NNBE Ray Bourque
  Phil Esposito/7
NNBL Jean Beliveau
  Vincent Lecavalier/4
NNBS Bossy/Shutt/22 30.00 60.00
NNDZ Pavel Datsyuk
  Nikolai Zherdev/13
NNFJ Fuhr/Joseph/31 40.00 100.00
NNFS Forsberg/Salming/21 50.00 100.00
NNGM Simon Gagne
  Patrick Marleau/12
NNGT Giguere/Turco/35 25.00 60.00
NNGV Gerber/Vokoun/29 30.00 80.00
NNHD Hejduk/Drury/23 25.00 60.00
NNHM Bobby Hull
  Lanny McDonald/9
NNHR Dany Heatley
  Tuomo Ruutu/15
NNIG Jarome Iginla
  Simon Gagne/12
NNJJ Jagr/Jurcina/68 30.00 80.00
NNJS J.Spezza/Doan/19 25.00 50.00
NNKA Saku Koivu
  Daniel Alfredsson/11
NNKC Kovalchuk/Carter/17 60.00 125.00
NNKL Kiprusoff/Legace/34 30.00 60.00
NNLA Roberto Luongo
  David Aebischer/1
NNLM Lundqvist/Miller/30 60.00 120.00
NNLR Roberto Luongo
  Andrew Raycroft/1
NNMJ Murphy/Jovanovski/55 25.00 50.00
NNMK Mike Modano
  Paul Kariya/9
NNMM Lanny McDonald
  Joe Mullen/7
NNMS Mahovlich/Sittler/27 40.00 80.00
NNMT Joe Mullen
  Keith Tkachuk/7
NNNP Nash/Perry/61 30.00 80.00
NNPB Pronger/Bertuzzi/44 25.00 60.00
NNPK Gilbert Perreault
  Saku Koivu/11
NNPM Denis Potvin
  Larry Murphy/5
NNSC Brendan Shanahan
  Jonathan Cheechoo/14
NNSD Mats Sundin
  Pavel Datsyuk/13
NNSE Stastny/Elias/26 40.00 80.00
NNSI Eric Staal
  Jarome Iginla/12
NNSL Stastny/St. Louis/26 30.00 60.00
NNSM Eric Staal
  Patrick Marleau/12
NNSR Spezza/B.Richards/19 30.00 60.00
NNSS Mats Sundin
  Teemu Selanne/13
NNST D.Savard/Tanguay/18 25.00 50.00
NNTN Thornton/Naslund/19 30.00 60.00
NNTS Thornton/Spezza/19 30.00 60.00
NNYS Yzerman/Sakic/19 125.00 250.00
NNYT Yzerman/Thornton/19 60.00 120.00
NNZS Zetterberg/Svatos/40 25.00 100.00

2005-06 The Cup Platinum Rookies

PRINT RUN 25 SER.#'d SETS
101 Ryan Getzlaf 60.00 120.00
102 Ryan Whitney 50.00 100.00
103 R.J. Umberger 20.00 50.00
104 Cam Ward 25.00 60.00
105 Brent Seabrook 40.00 100.00
106 Eric Nystrom 15.00 40.00
107 Gilbert Brule 12.00 30.00
108 Hannu Toivonen 20.00 50.00
109 Robert Nilsson 20.00 50.00
110 Rostislav Olesz 15.00 40.00
111 Ryan Suter 25.00 60.00
112 Jussi Jokinen 20.00 50.00
113 Zach Parise 75.00 135.00
114 Wojtek Wolski 15.00 40.00
115 Andrej Meszaros 15.00 40.00
116 Johan Franzen 30.00 80.00
117 Peter Budaj 25.00 60.00
118 David Leneveu 15.00 40.00
119 Andrew Alberts 12.00 30.00
120 Steve Bernier 20.00 50.00
121 Mikko Koivu 25.00 60.00
122 Chris Campoli 12.00 30.00
123 Evgeny Artyukhin 15.00 40.00
124 Christoph Schubert 12.00 30.00
125 Tomas Fleischmann 20.00 50.00
126 Maxime Talbot 20.00 50.00
127 Jordan Sigalet 12.00 30.00
128 Danny Richmond 12.00 30.00
129 Maxim Lapierre 20.00 50.00
130 Dimitri Patzold 12.00 30.00
131 Rene Bourque 20.00 50.00
132 Yann Danis 15.00 40.00
133 Brad Winchester 20.00 50.00
134 Jim Slater 15.00 40.00
135 Petr Prucha 30.00 80.00
136 Jim Howard 40.00 100.00
137 Patrick Eaves 20.00 50.00
138 Ryane Clowe 25.00 60.00
139 Braydon Coburn 20.00 50.00
140 Brad Richardson 20.00 50.00
141 Milan Jurcina 15.00 40.00
142 Jeff Woywitka 12.00 30.00
143 Andrei Kostitsyn 20.00 50.00
144 Derek Boogaard 25.00 60.00
145 Barry Tallackson 15.00 40.00
146 Jakub Klepis 12.00 30.00
147 Alvaro Montoya 20.00 50.00
148 Andrew Ladd 25.00 60.00
149 Brandon Bochenski 20.00 50.00
150 Jeff Tambellini 12.00 30.00
151 Jaroslav Balastik 12.00 30.00
152 Lee Stempniak 20.00 50.00
153 Kevin Dallman 15.00 40.00
154 Niklas Nordgren 20.00 50.00
155 Kevin Nastiuk 12.00 30.00
156 Ryan Craig 12.00 30.00
157 Erik Christensen 12.00 30.00
158 Chris Thorburn 15.00 40.00
159 Josh Gorges 15.00 40.00
160 Matt Foy 12.00 30.00
161 Ole-Kristian Tollefsen 15.00 40.00
162 Kevin Bieksa 25.00 60.00
163 Kyle Quincey 15.00 40.00
164 Andrew Wozniewski 15.00 40.00
165 Jeff Hoggan 12.00 30.00
166 Jeremy Colliton 12.00 30.00
167 Alexandre Picard 12.00 30.00
168 Ben Eager 15.00 40.00
169 Daniel Paille 20.00 50.00
170 Valtteri Filppula 25.00 60.00
171 Alexander Perezhogin 15.00 40.00
172 Mike Richards 50.00 125.00
173 Corey Perry 75.00 150.00
174 Alexander Steen 50.00 100.00
175 Thomas Vanek 50.00 100.00
176 Jeff Carter 60.00 120.00
177 Henrik Lundqvist 100.00 200.00
178 Dion Phaneuf 50.00 120.00
179 Alexander Ovechkin 300.00 450.00
180 Sidney Crosby 800.00 1200.00
181 Brett Lebda 12.00 30.00
182 Jay McClement 12.00 30.00
183 Cam Barker 15.00 40.00
184 Petteri Nokelainen 12.00 30.00
185 Keith Ballard 15.00 40.00
186 Duncan Keith 40.00 100.00
187 George Parros 12.00 30.00
188 Adam Berkhoel 15.00 40.00
189 Anthony Stewart 15.00 40.00
190 Ryan Hollweg 12.00 30.00
191 Ben Walter 12.00 30.00

2005-06 The Cup Scripted Numbers

STATED PRINT RUN 1-61
SNBC Brodeur/Cheevers/30 50.00 100.00
SNBE Ray Bourque
  Phil Esposito/7
SNBL Mike Bossy 40.00 80.00
  Brian Leetch/22
SNBN Ed Belfour
  Evgeni Nabokov/20
SNBP Bergeron/Peca/37 30.00 60.00
SNBR Ed Belfour 30.00 60.00
  Luc Robitaille/20
SNBS Mike Bossy 40.00 80.00
  Steve Shutt/22
SNET Turco/Tony O/35 40.00 80.00
SNGM Simon Gagne
  Patrick Marleau/12
SNGT Giguere/Turco/35 30.00 60.00
SNGV Gerber/Vokoun/29 40.00 80.00
SNHD Hejduk/Drury/23 30.00 60.00
SNHH Bobby Hull
  Gordie Howe/9
SNHM Bobby Hull
  Lanny McDonald/9
SNJV Jean Beliveau
  Vincent Lecavalier/4
SNKC Ilya Kovalchuk
  Jeff Carter/17
SNKL Kiprusoff/Legace/34 40.00 100.00
SNLA Roberto Luongo
  David Aebischer/1
SNLB Vincent Lecavalier
  Rob Blake/4
SNLM Lundqvist/Miller/30 75.00 200.00
SNLR Roberto Luongo
  Andrew Raycroft/1
SNMH Mike Modano
  Martin Havlat/9
SNMM Lanny McDonald
  Joe Mullen/7
SNMN Murray/Nieder/27 25.00 60.00
SNMS Big M/Sittler/27 50.00 100.00
SNND Markus Naslund
  Shane Doan/19
SNNO Cam Neely
  Alexander Ovechkin/8
SNNP Nash/Perry/61 40.00 100.00
SNPB Pronger/Bertuzzi/44 25.00 60.00
SNPC Dion Phaneuf
  Zdeno Chara/3
SNSI Eric Staal
  Jarome Iginla/12
SNSM Eric Staal
  Patrick Marleau/12
SNST Denis Savard
  Alex Tanguay
  /18
SNTH Alex Tanguay
  Marian Hossa/18
SNTN Joe Thornton 40.00 80.00
  Markus Naslund/19
SNZS Zetterberg/Svatos/40 30.00 80.00

2005-06 The Cup Scripted Swatches

STATED PRINT RUN 4-25
SSAF Alexander Frolov/25 25.00 60.00
SSAH Ales Hemsky/25 50.00 125.00
SSAO Alexander Ovechkin/15
SSAR Andrew Raycroft/25 50.00 100.00
SSAS Alexander Steen/25 30.00 80.00
SSAT Alex Tanguay/25 30.00 80.00
SSAY Alexei Yashin/25 40.00 80.00
SSBH Bobby Hull/15 100.00 200.00
SSBL Rob Blake/25 50.00 100.00
SSBO Borje Salming/10
SSBY Mike Bossy/25 75.00 150.00
SSCD Chris Drury/25 25.00 60.00
SSCH Jonathan Cheechoo/10
SSCN Cam Neely/18
SSCP Chris Pronger/10
SSDG Doug Gilmour/25 40.00 100.00
SSDH Dany Heatley/25 40.00 100.00
SSDP Dion Phaneuf/25 50.00 100.00
SSDT Dave Taylor/25 40.00 100.00
SSDW Doug Weight/25 30.00 80.00
SSEN Evgeni Nabokov/25 75.00 125.00
SSER Eric Staal/25 30.00 80.00
SSGC Gerry Cheevers/25 60.00 120.00
SSGE Martin Gerber/25 60.00 100.00
SSGF Grant Fuhr/25 50.00 125.00
SSGL Guy Lafleur/20 100.00 200.00
SSGM Glen Murray/25 25.00 60.00
SSGP Gilbert Perreault/9
SSHK Dominik Hasek/25 75.00 150.00
SSHL Henrik Lundqvist/25 125.00 250.00
SSHO Marian Hossa/25 40.00 80.00
SSHV Martin Havlat/25 25.00 60.00
SSIK Ilya Kovalchuk/25 40.00 100.00
SSJB Jean Beliveau/25 125.00 250.00
SSJC Jeff Carter/25 60.00 125.00
SSJI Jarome Iginla/25 60.00 150.00
SSJO Joe Thornton/25 100.00 200.00
SSJS Jean-Sebastien Giguere/25 40.00 100.00
SSJT Jose Theodore/25 60.00 125.00
SSKL Kari Lehtonen/25 60.00 120.00
SSKP Keith Primeau/25 50.00 100.00
SSLR Luc Robitaille/25 75.00 150.00
SSLU Joffrey Lupul/25 40.00 80.00
SSMB Martin Brodeur/25 100.00 200.00
SSMC Lanny McDonald/10
SSMG Marian Gaborik/25 60.00 120.00
SSMH Milan Hejduk/25 30.00 80.00
SSMK Miikka Kiprusoff/25 75.00 150.00
SSMM Mike Modano/25 75.00 150.00
SSMN Markus Naslund/25 60.00 100.00
SSMO Brendan Morrison/25 25.00 60.00
SSMP Mark Parrish/25 25.00 50.00
SSMT Marty Turco/25 30.00 60.00
SSMW Brenden Morrow/25 25.00 60.00
SSOJ Olli Jokinen/25 40.00 80.00
SSOK Olaf Kolzig/25 50.00 125.00
SSPB Patrice Bergeron/10
SSPE Michael Peca/25 40.00 80.00
SSPM Patrick Marleau/15
SSPO Denis Potvin/15
SSRE Robert Esche/25 40.00 80.00
SSRL Roberto Luongo/5
SSRM Ryan Miller/25 60.00 100.00
SSRY Michael Ryder/25 50.00 100.00
SSSA Miroslav Satan/25 50.00 100.00
SSSC Sidney Crosby/10
SSSD Shane Doan/25 40.00 80.00
SSSG Simon Gagne/25 50.00 100.00
SSSK Saku Koivu/25 50.00 100.00
SSSL Martin St. Louis/15
SSSN Scott Niedermayer/15
SSST Matt Stajan/25 40.00 100.00
SSTB Todd Bertuzzi/25 40.00 100.00
SSTE Tony Esposito/25 60.00 120.00
SSTV Thomas Vanek/25 60.00 120.00
SSVL Vincent Lecavalier/25 60.00 120.00
SSZP Zigmund Palffy/25 40.00 80.00
SSPR1 Patrick Roy/25 125.00 250.00
SSPR2 Patrick Roy/25 125.00 250.00
SSRB1 Ray Bourque/25 75.00 150.00
SSRB2 Ray Bourque/25 60.00 125.00

2005-06 The Cup Signature Patches

STATED PRINT RUN 25-75
SPAF Alexander Frolov 12.00 30.00
SPAH Ales Hemsky 15.00 40.00
SPAO Alexander Ovechkin 250.00 500.00
SPAR Andrew Raycroft 15.00 40.00
SPAT Alex Tanguay 20.00 50.00
SPAY Alexei Yashin 15.00 40.00
SPBK Rob Blake 20.00 50.00
SPBL Brian Leetch 20.00 50.00
SPBS Billy Smith 30.00 80.00
SPBY Mike Bossy 30.00 80.00
SPCD Chris Drury 15.00 40.00
SPCN Cam Neely/25 60.00 100.00
SPCP Chris Pronger 40.00 80.00
SPDA David Aebischer 15.00 40.00
SPDG Doug Gilmour 25.00 60.00
SPDH Dany Heatley 20.00 50.00
SPDO Dominik Hasek 50.00 80.00
SPDP Dion Phaneuf 50.00 120.00
SPDW Doug Weight 20.00 50.00
SPES Eric Staal 30.00 80.00
SPFM Frank Mahovlich 20.00 50.00
SPGA Glenn Anderson 20.00 50.00
SPGC Gerry Cheevers/65 30.00 80.00
SPGE Martin Gerber 15.00 40.00
SPGL Guy Lafleur 25.00 60.00
SPGM Glen Murray 15.00 40.00
SPGO Scott Gomez 15.00 40.00
SPGP Gilbert Perreault/40 50.00 125.00
SPHJ Milan Hejduk 15.00 40.00
SPHL Henrik Lundqvist 60.00 120.00
SPHV Martin Havlat 20.00 50.00
SPIK Ilya Kovalchuk 30.00 80.00
SPJC Jeff Carter 50.00 120.00
SPJI Jarome Iginla 25.00 60.00
SPJM Joe Mullen 15.00 40.00
SPJO Joe Thornton 40.00 100.00
SPJP Joni Pitkanen 12.00 30.00
SPJS Jean-Sebastien Giguere 20.00 50.00
SPJT Jose Theodore 20.00 50.00
SPKD Kris Draper 25.00 60.00
SPKP Keith Primeau 20.00 50.00
SPLM Lanny McDonald 20.00 50.00
SPLR Luc Robitaille 25.00 60.00
SPLU Joffrey Lupul 15.00 40.00
SPMB Martin Brodeur 60.00 120.00
SPMG Marian Gaborik 25.00 60.00
SPMH Marian Hossa 15.00 40.00
SPMK Miikka Kiprusoff 40.00 100.00
SPMM Mike Modano 25.00 60.00
SPMN Markus Naslund 20.00 50.00
SPMP Mark Parrish 12.00 30.00
SPMR Mike Richards 25.00 60.00
SPMS Miroslav Satan 15.00 40.00
SPMT Marty Turco 20.00 50.00
SPOJ Olli Jokinen 20.00 50.00
SPOK Olaf Kolzig 20.00 50.00
SPPB Patrice Bergeron 25.00 60.00
SPPE Corey Perry/60 30.00 80.00
SPPO Denis Potvin 20.00 50.00
SPPR Patrick Roy 75.00 150.00
SPRB Ray Bourque 50.00 100.00
SPRE Robert Esche 15.00 40.00
SPRH Ron Hextall/40 50.00 100.00
SPRL Roberto Luongo 50.00 100.00
SPRM Ryan Miller 30.00 80.00
SPRN Rick Nash/40 40.00 100.00
SPRY Michael Ryder 15.00 40.00
SPSC Sidney Crosby 350.00 600.00
SPSD Shane Doan/25 50.00 100.00
SPSG Simon Gagne 20.00 50.00
SPSH Steve Shutt 20.00 50.00
SPSK Saku Koivu 20.00 50.00
SPSL Martin St. Louis/65 20.00 50.00
SPSN Scott Niedermayer 20.00 50.00
SPSV Marek Svatos 15.00 40.00
SPTB Todd Bertuzzi 20.00 50.00
SPTI Tiger Williams 15.00 40.00
SPTV Thomas Vanek 30.00 80.00
SPVL Vincent Lecavalier 25.00 60.00
SPVO Tomas Vokoun 15.00 40.00
SPWG Wayne Gretzky/25 400.00 750.00
SPWR Wade Redden 12.00 30.00
SPZC Zdeno Chara 20.00 50.00

2006-07 The Cup

This 174-card set was released in July, 2007. The set was issued into the hobby in four-card packs (boxes) that come six to a case. The set is broken down into a mix of Veterans/Retired Greats which are cards numbered 1-90 and are all issued to a stated print run of 249 serial numbered copies. Cards numbered 91-174 are Rookie Cards with cards 91-168 issued to a stated print run of 249 serial numbered sets and cards 169-174 issued to a stated print run of 99 serial numbered sets.

1 Teemu Selanne 10.00 25.00
2 Jean-Sebastien Giguere 5.00 12.00
3 Kari Lehtonen 4.00 10.00
4 Ilya Kovalchuk 5.00 12.00
5 Phil Esposito 8.00 20.00
6 Don Cherry 8.00 20.00
7 Ray Bourque 8.00 20.00
8 Bobby Orr 15.00 40.00
9 Cam Neely 5.00 12.00
10 Patrice Bergeron 6.00 15.00
11 Johnny Bucyk 5.00 12.00
12 Ryan Miller 5.00 12.00
13 Gilbert Perreault 5.00 12.00
14 Jarome Iginla 5.00 12.00
15 Miikka Kiprusoff 4.00 10.00
16 Al MacInnis 5.00 12.00
17 Eric Staal 6.00 15.00
18 Cam Ward 5.00 12.00
19 Bobby Hull 8.00 20.00
20 Tony Esposito 5.00 12.00
21 Stan Mikita 6.00 15.00
22 Joe Sakic 8.00 20.00
23 Patrick Roy 12.00 30.00
24 Rick Nash 5.00 12.00
25 Sergei Fedorov 8.00 20.00
26 Mike Modano 8.00 20.00
27 Dominik Hasek 6.00 15.00
28 Henrik Zetterberg 6.00 15.00
29 Gordie Howe 15.00 40.00
30 Scotty Bowman 4.00 10.00
31 Ted Lindsay 4.00 10.00
32 Red Kelly 4.00 10.00
33 Ales Hemsky 4.00 10.00
34 Grant Fuhr 5.00 12.00
35 Jari Kurri 5.00 12.00
36 Ed Belfour 5.00 12.00
37 Wayne Gretzky 25.00 60.00
38 Rob Blake 5.00 12.00
39 Marcel Dionne 6.00 15.00
40 Luc Robitaille 5.00 12.00
41 Rogie Vachon 6.00 15.00
42 Dino Ciccarelli 5.00 12.00
43 Marian Gaborik 6.00 15.00
44 Saku Koivu 5.00 12.00
45 Michael Ryder 3.00 8.00
46 Guy Lafleur 6.00 15.00
47 Larry Robinson 5.00 12.00
48 Jean Beliveau 5.00 12.00
49 Jacques Lemaire 4.00 10.00
50 Paul Kariya 6.00 15.00
51 Tomas Vokoun 4.00 10.00
52 Martin Brodeur 10.00 25.00
53 Scott Stevens 5.00 12.00
54 Alexei Yashin 4.00 10.00
55 Al Arbour 4.00 10.00
56 Mike Bossy 5.00 12.00
57 Billy Smith 5.00 12.00
58 Denis Potvin 5.00 12.00
59 Jaromir Jagr 12.00 30.00
60 Brendan Shanahan 6.00 15.00
61 Henrik Lundqvist 10.00 25.00
62 Gump Worsley 5.00 12.00
63 Andy Bathgate 4.00 10.00
64 Jason Spezza 5.00 12.00
65 Dany Heatley 5.00 12.00
66 Peter Forsberg 6.00 15.00
67 Simon Gagne 5.00 12.00
68 Bernie Parent 5.00 12.00
69 Bobby Clarke 5.00 12.00
70 Ron Hextall 8.00 20.00
71 Jeremy Roenick 5.00 12.00
72 Shane Doan 4.00 10.00
73 Sidney Crosby 20.00 50.00
74 Marc-Andre Fleury 8.00 20.00
75 Mario Lemieux 15.00 40.00
76 Peter Stastny 5.00 12.00
77 Joe Thornton 6.00 15.00
78 Jonathan Cheechoo 5.00 12.00
79 Patrick Marleau 5.00 12.00
80 Bernie Federko 4.00 10.00
81 Vincent Lecavalier 4.00 10.00
82 Mats Sundin 5.00 12.00
83 Frank Mahovlich 4.00 10.00
84 Darryl Sittler 5.00 12.00
85 Johnny Bower 8.00 20.00
86 Borje Salming 5.00 12.00
87 Roberto Luongo 8.00 20.00
88 Markus Naslund 4.00 10.00
89 Alexander Ovechkin 20.00 50.00
90 Dale Hawerchuk 6.00 15.00
91 Nate Thompson AU RC 6.00 15.00
92 Mike Brown AU RC 6.00 15.00
93 Mike Card AU RC 6.00 15.00
94 Adam Dennis AU RC 6.00 15.00
95 Carsen Germyn AU RC 6.00 15.00
96 Adam Burish AU RC 10.00 25.00
97 Drew Larman AU RC 6.00 15.00
98 Jonas Johansson AU RC 6.00 15.00
99 Joel Perrault AU RC 6.00 15.00
100 Mikko Lehtonen AU RC 8.00 20.00
101 Alex Brooks AU RC 6.00 15.00
102 Frank Doyle AU RC 8.00 20.00
103 Billy Thompson AU RC 6.00 15.00
104 Kelly Guard AU RC 8.00 20.00
105 David Printz AU RC 6.00 15.00
106 D.J. King AU RC 6.00 15.00
107 J-F. Racine AU RC 8.00 20.00
108 Nathan McIver AU RC 6.00 15.00
109 S.O'Brien JSY AU/50 60.00 120.00
110 R.Shannon JSY AU/125 RC 15.00 40.00
111 David McKee JSY AU RC 12.00 30.00
112 Mark Stuart JSY AU RC 12.00 30.00
113 Matt Lashoff JSY AU RC 12.00 30.00
114 D.Stafford JSY AU RC 20.00 50.00
115 C.MacArthur JSY AU RC EX 15.00 40.00
116 Michael Funk JSY AU RC 12.00 30.00
117 Brandon Prust JSY AU RC 12.00 30.00
118 Dustin Boyd JSY AU RC 12.00 30.00
119 D.Byfuglien JSY AU RC 30.00 80.00
120 Dave Bolland JSY AU RC 20.00 50.00
121 M. Blunden JSY AU RC 12.00 30.00
122 Filip Novak JSY AU RC 12.00 30.00
123 F.Norrena JSY AU RC 12.00 30.00
124 N.Grossman JSY AU RC 20.00 50.00
125 Loui Eriksson JSY AU RC 25.00 60.00
126 T.Kopecky JSY AU RC 15.00 40.00
127 Stefan Liv JSY AU RC 20.00 50.00
128 P. Thoresen JSY AU RC EX 12.00 30.00
129 M-A.Pouliot JSY AU RC 12.00 30.00
130 Ladislav Smid JSY AU RC 12.00 30.00
131 Janis Sprukts JSY AU RC 12.00 30.00
132 J.Deslauriers JSY AU RC 12.00 30.00
133 David Booth JSY AU RC 15.00 40.00
134 K.Pushkarev JSY AU RC 15.00 40.00
135 P. O'Sullivan JSY AU RC 20.00 50.00
136 B.Pouliot JSY AU RC 15.00 40.00
137 N.Backstrom JSY AU RC 25.00 60.00
138 G.Latendresse JSY AU RC 20.00 50.00
139 Shea Weber JSY AU RC 80.00 200.00
140 J.Oduya JSY AU RC 20.00 50.00
141 Travis Zajac JSY AU RC 25.00 60.00
142 M.Marjamaki JSY AU RC 12.00 30.00
143 Nigel Dawes JSY AU RC 12.00 30.00
144 J.Immonen JSY AU RC 12.00 30.00
145 J.Hennessy JSY AU RC 12.00 30.00
146 Ryan Potulny JSY AU RC 12.00 30.00
147 J.Timonen JSY AU RC 15.00 40.00
148 Keith Yandle JSY AU RC 25.00 60.00
149 Michel Ouellet JSY AU RC 15.00 40.00
150 Noah Welch JSY AU RC 12.00 30.00
151 K. Letang JSY AU RC 80.00 200.00
152 Joe Pavelski JSY AU RC 80.00 200.00
153 Matt Carle JSY AU RC 12.00 30.00
154 M-E Vlasic JSY AU RC 12.00 30.00
155 Yan Stastny JSY AU RC 12.00 30.00
156 M. Schwarz JSY AU RC 20.00 50.00
157 R. Polak JSY AU RC 15.00 40.00
158 Karri Ramo JSY AU RC 12.00 30.00
159 Blair Jones JSY AU RC 12.00 30.00
160 Brendan Bell JSY AU RC 12.00 30.00
161 Ian White JSY AU RC 15.00 40.00
162 Ben Ondrus JSY AU RC 12.00 30.00
163 J. Williams JSY AU RC 12.00 30.00
164 M.Kopriva JSY AU RC 12.00 30.00
165 L. Bourdon JSY AU RC 25.00 60.00
166 J. Schultz JSY AU RC 12.00 30.00
167 A. Edler JSY AU RC 20.00 50.00
168 Eric Fehr JSY AU RC 20.00 50.00
169 J.Staal JSY AU/99 RC 150.00 300.00
170 P.Kessel JSY AU/99 RC 150.00 300.00
171 E.Malkin JSY AU/99 RC 700.00 1500.00
172 P.Stastny JSY AU/99 RC 150.00 300.00
173 A.Kopitar JSY AU/99 RC 350.00 600.00
174 A.Radulov JSY AU/99 RC 80.00 200.00

2006-07 The Cup Foundations

STATED PRINT RUN 25 SER.#'d SETS
CQAH Ales Hemsky 12.00 30.00
CQAK Anze Kopitar 25.00 60.00
CQAM Al MacInnis 15.00 40.00
CQAO Adam Oates 15.00 40.00
CQAR Andrew Raycroft 12.00 30.00
CQAY Alexei Yashin 12.00 30.00
CQBB Brad Boyes 10.00 25.00
CQBL Rob Blake 15.00 40.00
CQBS Billy Smith 15.00 40.00
CQCJ Curtis Joseph 15.00 40.00
CQCN Cam Neely 15.00 40.00
CQCP Chris Pronger 12.00 30.00
CQCW Cam Ward 12.00 30.00
CQDA Daniel Alfredsson 15.00 40.00
CQDC Dino Ciccarelli 15.00 40.00
CQDG Doug Gilmour 20.00 50.00
CQDH Dale Hawerchuk 20.00 50.00
CQDS Denis Savard 20.00 50.00
CQEB Ed Belfour 15.00 40.00
CQEL Eric Lindros 25.00 60.00
CQEM Evgeni Malkin 40.00 100.00
CQEN Evgeni Nabokov 12.00 30.00
CQES Eric Staal 20.00 50.00
CQFM Frank Mahovlich 12.00 30.00
CQGC Gerry Cheevers 15.00 40.00
CQGF Grant Fuhr 15.00 40.00
CQGH Gordie Howe 30.00 80.00
CQGL Guy Lafleur 20.00 50.00
CQGP Gilbert Perreault 15.00 40.00
CQHA Dominik Hasek 20.00 50.00
CQHE Dany Heatley 15.00 40.00
CQHL Henrik Lundqvist 30.00 80.00
CQHM Milan Hejduk 12.00 30.00
CQHZ Henrik Zetterberg 20.00 50.00
CQIK Ilya Kovalchuk 15.00 40.00
CQJB Jean Beliveau 15.00 40.00
CQJC Jonathan Cheechoo 15.00 40.00
CQJI Jarome Iginla 15.00 40.00
CQJJ Jaromir Jagr 40.00 100.00
CQJK Jari Kurri 15.00 40.00
CQJO Joe Sakic 25.00 60.00
CQJR Jeremy Roenick 15.00 40.00
CQJS Jordan Staal 15.00 40.00
CQJT Joe Thornton 20.00 50.00
CQKE Phil Kessel 15.00 40.00
CQKL Kari Lehtonen 12.00 30.00
CQLM Lanny McDonald 15.00 40.00
CQLR Larry Robinson 15.00 40.00
CQMA Stan Mikita 20.00 50.00
CQMB Martin Brodeur 30.00 80.00
CQMD Marcel Dionne 20.00 50.00
CQMG Marian Gaborik 20.00 50.00
CQMH Marian Hossa 12.00 30.00
CQMI Mike Bossy 15.00 40.00
CQML Mario Lemieux 50.00 120.00
CQMM Mike Modano 25.00 60.00
CQMN Markus Naslund 12.00 30.00
CQMR Michael Ryder 10.00 25.00
CQMS Martin St. Louis 15.00 40.00
CQMT Marty Turco 15.00 40.00
CQNL Nicklas Lidstrom 15.00 40.00
CQOK Olaf Kolzig 15.00 40.00
CQOV Alexander Ovechkin 50.00 100.00
CQPB Patrice Bergeron 20.00 50.00
CQPD Pavel Datsyuk 20.00 50.00
CQPE Patrik Elias 15.00 40.00
CQPF Peter Forsberg 12.00 30.00
CQPH Dion Phaneuf 15.00 40.00
CQPK Paul Kariya 20.00 50.00
CQPM Patrick Marleau 15.00 40.00
CQPR Patrick Roy 60.00 150.00
CQPS Peter Stastny 15.00 40.00
CQRB Ray Bourque 25.00 60.00
CQRD Rick DiPietro 12.00 30.00
CQRE Ron Ellis 10.00 25.00
CQRH Ron Hextall 25.00 60.00
CQRL Roberto Luongo 25.00 60.00
CQRM Ryan Miller 15.00 40.00
CQRN Rick Nash 15.00 40.00
CQRO Luc Robitaille 15.00 40.00
CQRS Ryan Smyth 12.00 30.00
CQRV Rogie Vachon 20.00 50.00
CQSA Borje Salming 15.00 40.00
CQSC Sidney Crosby 75.00 200.00
CQSF Sergei Fedorov 25.00 60.00
CQSG Simon Gagne 15.00 40.00
CQSH Brendan Shanahan 20.00 50.00
CQSK Saku Koivu 15.00 40.00
CQSM Miroslav Satan 12.00 30.00
CQSP Jason Spezza 15.00 40.00
CQSS Scott Stevens 15.00 40.00
CQST Steve Shutt 15.00 40.00
CQSU Mats Sundin 15.00 40.00
CQTE Tony Esposito 15.00 40.00
CQTH Jose Theodore 15.00 40.00
CQTS Teemu Selanne 30.00 80.00
CQTV Tomas Vokoun 12.00 30.00
CQVL Vincent Lecavalier 12.00 30.00
CQWG Wayne Gretzky 75.00 150.00

2006-07 The Cup Enshrinements

STATED PRINT RUN 50 SER.#'d SETS
EAK Anze Kopitar 25.00 60.00
EAR Andrew Raycroft 10.00 25.00
EBO Bobby Orr 75.00 150.00
EBP Benoit Pouliot 10.00 25.00
ECD Chris Drury 10.00 25.00
ECN Cam Neely 20.00 50.00
ECW Cam Ward 15.00 40.00
EDB Dustin Boyd 10.00 25.00
EDH Dominik Hasek 25.00 60.00
EDP Dion Phaneuf 20.00 50.00
EDS Drew Stafford 15.00 40.00
EEM Evgeni Malkin 60.00 120.00
EES Eric Staal 15.00 40.00
EFM Frank Mahovlich 15.00 40.00
EGH Gordie Howe 40.00 100.00
EGL G. Latendresse 20.00 50.00

GR Wayne Gretzky 150.00 250.00
HE Dany Heatley 12.00 30.00
HZ Henrik Zetterberg 15.00 40.00
K Ilya Kovalchuk 15.00 40.00
IB Johnny Bucyk 10.00 25.00
IC Jonathan Cheechoo 15.00 40.00
IG J-S Giguere 15.00 40.00
II Jarome Iginla 15.00 40.00
IK Jari Kurri 15.00 40.00
IM Joe Mullen 10.00 25.00
IS Jordan Staal 15.00 40.00
IT Joe Thornton 15.00 40.00
KL Kari Lehtonen 15.00 40.00
LR Larry Robinson 10.00 25.00
MB Martin Brodeur 40.00 100.00
MD Marcel Dionne 15.00 40.00
MF Marc-Andre Fleury 20.00 50.00
MG Marian Gaborik 20.00 50.00
ML Mario Lemieux 75.00 150.00
MR Michael Ryder 10.00 25.00
MS Marek Svatos 10.00 25.00
MT Marty Turco 15.00 40.00
NL Nicklas Lidstrom 20.00 50.00
PK Phil Kessel 20.00 50.00
PL Pat LaFontaine 20.00 50.00
PR Patrick Roy 75.00 150.00
PS Paul Stastny 25.00 60.00
RA Alexander Radulov 15.00 40.00
RB Ray Bourque 25.00 60.00
RH Ron Hextall 15.00 40.00
RL Roberto Luongo
RM Ryan Miller 20.00 50.00
RN Rick Nash 20.00 50.00
RS Ryan Smyth 15.00 40.00
SC Sidney Crosby 100.00 200.00
SS Steve Shutt 10.00 25.00
ST Scott Stevens 15.00 40.00
TE Tony Esposito 20.00 50.00
TV Tomas Vokoun 15.00 40.00
TZ Travis Zajac 15.00 40.00
VA Thomas Vanek 15.00 40.00
VL Vincent Lecavalier 15.00 40.00
VT Vesa Toskala 15.00 40.00
WG Wayne Gretzky 150.00 250.00

2006-07 The Cup Gold

GOLD: 1X TO 2.5X HI COLUMN
STATED PRINT RUN 25 #'d SETS
Teemu Selanne 15.00 40.00
Jean-Sebastien Giguere 12.00 30.00
Kari Lehtonen 15.00 40.00
Ilya Kovalchuk 20.00 50.00
Phil Esposito 20.00 50.00
Don Cherry 15.00 40.00
Ray Bourque 25.00 60.00
Bobby Orr 50.00 100.00
Cam Neely 20.00 50.00
Patrice Bergeron 15.00 40.00
Johnny Bucyk 10.00 25.00
Ryan Miller 15.00 40.00
Gilbert Perreault 15.00 40.00
Jarome Iginla 20.00 50.00
Miikka Kiprusoff 15.00 40.00
Al MacInnis 8.00 20.00
Eric Staal 15.00 40.00
Cam Ward 15.00 40.00
Bobby Hull 25.00 60.00
Tony Esposito 15.00 40.00
Stan Mikita 15.00 40.00
Joe Sakic 30.00 80.00
Patrick Roy 40.00 100.00
Rick Nash 15.00 40.00
Sergei Fedorov 12.00 30.00
Mike Modano 15.00 40.00
Dominik Hasek 25.00 60.00
Henrik Zetterberg 20.00 50.00
Gordie Howe 30.00 80.00
Scotty Bowman 10.00 25.00
Ted Lindsay 8.00 20.00
Red Kelly 8.00 20.00
Ales Hemsky 8.00 20.00
Grant Fuhr 20.00 50.00
Jari Kurri 20.00 50.00
Ed Belfour 15.00 40.00
Wayne Gretzky 50.00 150.00
Rob Blake 12.00 30.00
Marcel Dionne 15.00 40.00
Luc Robitaille 12.00 30.00
Rogie Vachon 15.00 40.00
Dino Ciccarelli 8.00 20.00
Marian Gaborik 20.00 50.00
Saku Koivu 15.00 40.00
Michael Ryder 12.00 30.00
Guy Lafleur 25.00 60.00
Larry Robinson 12.00 30.00
Jean Beliveau 20.00 50.00
Jacques Lemaire 12.00 30.00
Paul Kariya 15.00 40.00
Tomas Vokoun 12.00 30.00
Martin Brodeur 40.00 100.00
Scott Stevens 12.00 30.00
Alexei Yashin 8.00 20.00
Al Arbour 8.00 20.00
Mike Bossy 12.00 30.00
Billy Smith 15.00 40.00
Denis Potvin 12.00 30.00
Jaromir Jagr 25.00 60.00
Brendan Shanahan 15.00 40.00
Henrik Lundqvist 20.00 50.00
Gump Worsley 12.00 30.00
Andy Bathgate 8.00 20.00
Jason Spezza 15.00 40.00
Dany Heatley 20.00 50.00
Peter Forsberg 25.00 60.00
Simon Gagne 15.00 40.00
Bernie Parent 12.00 30.00
Bobby Clarke 15.00 40.00
Ron Hextall 12.00 30.00
Jeremy Roenick 20.00 50.00
Shane Doan 8.00 20.00
Sidney Crosby 100.00 200.00
Marc-Andre Fleury 20.00 50.00
Mario Lemieux 40.00 100.00
Peter Stastny 10.00 25.00
Joe Thornton 25.00 60.00
Jonathan Cheechoo 15.00 40.00
Patrick Marleau 12.00 30.00
Bernie Federko 8.00 20.00
Vincent Lecavalier 15.00 40.00
Mats Sundin 15.00 40.00
Frank Mahovlich 15.00 40.00
Darryl Sittler 15.00 40.00
Johnny Bower 12.00 30.00
Borje Salming 12.00 30.00
Roberto Luongo 20.00 50.00
Markus Naslund 15.00 40.00
Alexander Ovechkin 40.00 100.00
Dale Hawerchuk 8.00 20.00

2006-07 The Cup Gold Rainbow Autographed Rookie Patches

STATED PRINT RUN 2-84
*WHITE SWATCHES: .5X to 1X LO
109 Shane O'Brien/37 30.00 80.00
110 Ryan Shannon/38 30.00 80.00
111 David McKee/41 30.00 80.00
112 Mark Stuart/45 25.00 60.00
113 Matt Lashoff/49 25.00 60.00
114 Drew Stafford/21 50.00 100.00
115 C. MacArthur/41 EXCH 50.00 100.00
117 Brandon Prust/37 20.00 50.00
118 Dustin Boyd/41 30.00 80.00
119 Dustin Byfuglien/52 40.00 100.00
120 Dave Bolland/36 50.00 100.00
121 Michael Blunden/28 20.00 50.00
122 Filip Novak/17 20.00 50.00
123 Fredrik Norrena/30 40.00 100.00
125 Loui Eriksson/21 60.00 120.00
126 Tomas Kopecky/32 20.00 50.00
127 Stefan Liv/32 25.00 60.00
128 Patrick Thoresen/28 20.00 50.00
129 M-A Pouliot/36 30.00 80.00
131 Janis Sprukts/38 25.00 60.00
132 Jeff Deslauriers/39 20.00 50.00
133 David Booth/46 25.00 60.00
136 Benoit Pouliot/67 25.00 60.00
137 Niklas Backstrom/32 60.00 150.00
138 G.Latendresse/84 50.00 100.00
140 Johnny Oduya/29 20.00 50.00
141 Travis Zajac/19 40.00 100.00
142 Masi Marjamaki/58 30.00 80.00
144 Jarkko Immonen/38 25.00 60.00
145 Josh Hennessy/36 30.00 80.00
147 J. Timonen/46 EXCH 25.00 60.00
151 Kris Letang/58 75.00 150.00
152 Joe Pavelski/53 75.00 150.00
153 Matt Carle/18
154 M-E Vlasic/44 30.00 80.00
155 Yan Stastny/43 25.00 60.00
156 M. Schwarz/40 EXCH
157 Roman Polak/46 15.00 40.00
158 Karri Ramo/31 25.00 60.00
159 Blair Jones/49 20.00 50.00
160 Brendan Bell/36 20.00 50.00
162 Ben Ondrus/46 20.00 50.00
163 Jeremy Williams/48 20.00 50.00
164 Miroslav Kopriva/31 25.00 60.00
166 Jesse Schultz/20 40.00 100.00
167 Alexander Edler/23 40.00 100.00
170 Phil Kessel/81 75.00 150.00
171 Evgeni Malkin/71 400.00 800.00
172 Paul Stastny/26 60.00 120.00
173 Anze Kopitar/11 500.00 700.00
174 A. Radulov/47 EXCH 150.00 300.00

2006-07 The Cup Gold Rainbow Autographed Rookies

91 Nate Thompson/52 10.00 25.00
92 Mike Brown/70 10.00 25.00
93 Mike Card/33 10.00 25.00
94 Adam Dennis/35
95 Carsen Germyn/39 10.00 25.00
96 Adam Burish/37 8.00 20.00
97 Drew Larman/50 10.00 25.00
98 Jonas Johansson/45 8.00 20.00
99 Joel Perrault/26 10.00 25.00
100 Mikko Lehtonen/42 8.00 20.00
101 Alex Brooks/8
102 Frank Doyle/1
103 Billy Thompson/31
104 Kelly Guard/32 12.00 30.00
105 David Printz/28 12.00 30.00
106 D.J. King/19 12.00 30.00
107 J-F Racine/35 12.00 30.00
108 Nathan McIver/45 10.00 25.00

2006-07 The Cup Honorable Numbers

STATED PRINT RUN 1-99
HNAH A. Hemsky/83 EXCH 25.00 60.00
HNAO Adam Oates/12
HNBC Bobby Clarke/16
HNBS Billy Smith/31 50.00 100.00
HNCH Jonathan Cheechoo/14
HNCW Cam Ward/30 40.00 80.00
HNDC D. Ciccarelli/20 EXCH 40.00 80.00
HNDE Denis Savard/18 60.00 125.00
HNDS Darryl Sittler/27 40.00 80.00
HNDW Doug Wilson/24 50.00 100.00
HNEM Evgeni Malkin/71 150.00 300.00
HNEN Evgeni Nabokov/20 50.00 100.00
HNES Eric Staal/12 20.00 50.00
HNGF Grant Fuhr/31 50.00 100.00
HNGL G. Latendresse/84 15.00 40.00
HNGO S. Gomez/23 EXCH 50.00 100.00
HNHA Dominik Hasek/39 40.00 80.00
HNHE Dany Heatley/15 20.00 50.00
HNHL Henrik Lundqvist/30 100.00 200.00
HNHM Milan Hejduk/23 30.00 80.00
HNHZ Henrik Zetterberg/40 75.00 150.00
HNIK Ilya Kovalchuk/17 40.00 100.00
HNJC Jeff Carter/17 60.00 125.00
HNJG Jean-Sebastien Giguere/35 40.00 80.00
HNJI Jarome Iginla/12 30.00 80.00
HNJK Jari Kurri/17 125.00 250.00
HNJS Jason Spezza/19 80.00 140.00
HNJT Joe Thornton/19 75.00 150.00
HNKL K.Lehtonen/32 EXCH 50.00 100.00
HNLE Loui Eriksson/21 30.00 80.00
HNLR Larry Robinson/19 40.00 80.00
HNMA Stan Mikita/21 60.00 125.00
HNMB Martin Brodeur/30 125.00 250.00
HNMC Matt Carle/18 40.00 100.00
HNMD Marcel Dionne/16 60.00 125.00
HNMH Martin Havlat/24 20.00 50.00
HNMI Mike Bossy/22 50.00 100.00
HNML Mario Lemieux/66 100.00 200.00
HNMN Markus Naslund/19 75.00 150.00
HNMR Michael Ryder/73 15.00 40.00
HNMS Martin St. Louis/26 50.00 100.00
HNMT Marty Turco/35 25.00 60.00
HNMU Larry Murphy/55 15.00 40.00
HNNZ Nikolai Zherdev/13 20.00 50.00
HNPA Paul Henderson/19 50.00 100.00
HNPD Patrice Bergeron/37 40.00 80.00
HNPE Patrik Elias/26 25.00 60.00
HNPK Phil Kessel/81 40.00 80.00
HNPL Pat LaFontaine/16
HNPM Patrick Marleau/12 50.00 100.00
HNPO Patrick O'Sullivan/12 30.00 80.00
HNPR Patrick Roy/33 125.00 250.00
HNPS Paul Stastny/26 50.00 120.00
HNRA A. Radulov/47 EXCH 60.00 125.00
HNRH Ron Hextall/27 40.00 100.00
HNRM Ryan Miller/30 50.00 120.00
HNRN Rick Nash/61 30.00 80.00
HNRO Luc Robitaille/20 25.00 60.00
HNRS Ryan Smyth/94 EXCH 25.00 60.00
HNSA Borje Salming/21 40.00 80.00
HNSC Sidney Crosby/87 150.00 300.00
HNSG Simon Gagne/12 30.00 80.00
HNSH Steve Shutt/22 25.00 60.00
HNSM Miroslav Satan/81 25.00 60.00
HNST Peter Stastny/26 40.00 80.00
HNSV Marek Svatos/40 25.00 60.00
HNTE Tony Esposito/35 60.00 125.00
HNTH Jose Theodore/60 12.00 30.00
HNTV Tomas Vokoun/29 40.00 80.00
HNTW Tiger Williams/22 25.00 60.00
HNWG Wayne Gretzky/99 250.00 500.00
HNZC Zdeno Chara/33 25.00 60.00

2006-07 The Cup Jerseys

STATED PRINT RUN 25 SER.#'d SETS
1 Teemu Selanne 15.00 40.00
2 Jean-Sebastien Giguere 8.00 20.00
3 Kari Lehtonen 6.00 15.00
4 Ilya Kovalchuk 8.00 20.00
7 Ray Bourque 12.00 30.00
9 Cam Neely 8.00 20.00
10 Patrice Bergeron 10.00 25.00
12 Ryan Miller 8.00 20.00
13 Gilbert Perreault
14 Jarome Iginla 8.00 20.00
15 Miikka Kiprusoff 6.00 15.00
16 Al MacInnis 8.00 20.00
17 Eric Staal 10.00 25.00
18 Cam Ward 8.00 20.00
19 Bobby Hull 15.00 40.00
20 Tony Esposito 8.00 20.00
21 Stan Mikita 10.00 25.00
22 Joe Sakic 25.00 60.00
23 Patrick Roy 40.00 100.00
24 Rick Nash 8.00 20.00
25 Sergei Fedorov 12.00 30.00
26 Mike Modano 12.00 30.00
27 Dominik Hasek 10.00 25.00
28 Henrik Zetterberg 10.00 25.00
29 Gordie Howe 30.00 60.00
33 Ales Hemsky 6.00 15.00
34 Grant Fuhr 8.00 20.00
35 Jari Kurri 8.00 20.00
36 Ed Belfour 8.00 20.00
37 Wayne Gretzky 100.00 225.00
38 Rob Blake 8.00 20.00
39 Marcel Dionne 10.00 25.00
40 Luc Robitaille 8.00 20.00
41 Rogie Vachon 10.00 25.00
42 Dino Ciccarelli 8.00 20.00
43 Marian Gaborik 20.00 50.00
44 Saku Koivu 8.00 20.00
45 Michael Ryder 5.00 12.00
46 Guy Lafleur 10.00 25.00
47 Larry Robinson 8.00 20.00
48 Jean Beliveau 25.00 60.00
50 Paul Kariya 10.00 25.00
51 Tomas Vokoun 6.00 15.00
52 Martin Brodeur 30.00 80.00
53 Scott Stevens 8.00 20.00
54 Alexei Yashin 5.00 20.00
56 Mike Bossy 12.00 30.00
57 Billy Smith 8.00 20.00
59 Jaromir Jagr 20.00 50.00
60 Brendan Shanahan 10.00 25.00
61 Henrik Lundqvist 15.00 40.00
62 Gump Worsley 8.00 20.00
64 Jason Spezza 8.00 20.00
65 Dany Heatley 8.00 20.00
66 Peter Forsberg 20.00 50.00
67 Simon Gagne 8.00 20.00
69 Bobby Clarke 8.00 20.00
70 Ron Hextall 12.00 30.00
71 Jeremy Roenick
72 Shane Doan 6.00 15.00
73 Sidney Crosby 75.00 150.00
74 Marc-Andre Fleury 12.00 30.00
75 Mario Lemieux 40.00 100.00
76 Peter Stastny 8.00 20.00
77 Joe Thornton 10.00 25.00
78 Jonathan Cheechoo 8.00 20.00
79 Patrick Marleau 8.00 20.00
80 Bernie Federko
81 Vincent Lecavalier 6.00 15.00
82 Mats Sundin 8.00 20.00
83 Frank Mahovlich 6.00 15.00
84 Darryl Sittler 8.00 20.00
86 Borje Salming 8.00 20.00
87 Roberto Luongo 12.00 30.00
88 Markus Naslund 6.00 15.00
89 Alexander Ovechkin 30.00 80.00
90 Dale Hawerchuk 8.00 20.00

2006-07 The Cup Limited Logos Autographs

STATED PRINT RUN 10-50
*SINGLE COLOR SWATCH: .5X TO 1X LO
LLAF Alexander Frolov/50 75.00 150.00
LLAH Ales Hemsky/50 30.00 80.00
LLAK Anze Kopitar/50 150.00 300.00
LLAM Al MacInnis/50 60.00 125.00
LLAO Adam Oates/50 30.00 80.00
LLAR Andrew Raycroft/50 30.00 80.00
LLAT Alex Tanguay/50 25.00 60.00
LLAY Alexei Yashin/50 30.00 80.00
LLBB Brad Boyes/50 20.00 50.00
LLBC Bobby Clarke/50 60.00 120.00
LLBF Bernie Federko/50 30.00 80.00
LLBG Brian Gionta/50 30.00 80.00
LLBL Bill Ranford/50 30.00 80.00
LLBO Mike Bossy/50 75.00 150.00
LLBS Billy Smith/50 30.00 80.00
LLCA Jeff Carter/50 50.00 120.00
LLCN Cam Neely/50 75.00 200.00
LLCW Cam Ward/50 30.00 80.00
LLDA David Aebischer/50 30.00 80.00
LLDB Daniel Briere/50 30.00 80.00
LLDC Dino Ciccarelli/50 30.00 80.00
LLDE Denis Savard/50 60.00 125.00
LLDG Doug Gilmour/50 75.00 150.00
LLDH Dale Hawerchuk/50 40.00 100.00
LLDO Dominik Hasek/50 60.00 125.00
LLDR Dwayne Roloson/50 30.00 80.00
LLDS Darryl Sittler/50 30.00 80.00
LLDW Doug Wilson/50 30.00 80.00
LLEM Evgeni Malkin/50 125.00 250.00
LLES Eric Staal/50 25.00 60.00
LLGA Glenn Anderson/50 25.00 60.00
LLGE Martin Gerber/50
LLGH Gordie Howe/10
LLGL Guy Lafleur/50 60.00 125.00
LLGP Gilbert Perreault/50 40.00 100.00
LLHE Dany Heatley/50 25.00 60.00
LLHL Henrik Lundqvist/50 100.00 200.00
LLHZ Henrik Zetterberg/50 75.00 150.00
LLIK Ilya Kovalchuk/50 40.00 100.00
LLJC Jonathan Cheechoo/50 30.00 80.00
LLJG Jean-Sebastien Giguere/50 50.00 100.00
LLJI Jarome Iginla/50 75.00 150.00
LLJK Jari Kurri/50 60.00 125.00
LLJM Joe Mullen/50 25.00 60.00
LLJR Jeremy Roenick/50 40.00 100.00
LLJS Jordan Staal/50 40.00 100.00
LLJT Joe Thornton/50 75.00 150.00
LLKL Kari Lehtonen/50 25.00 60.00
LLLM Lanny McDonald/50 20.00 50.00
LLLR Larry Robinson/50 30.00 80.00
LLMB Martin Brodeur/50 100.00 200.00
LLMG Marian Gaborik/50 30.00 80.00
LLMH Martin Havlat/50 25.00 60.00
LLMI Milan Hejduk/50 25.00 60.00
LLML Mario Lemieux/50 150.00 300.00
LLMM Mike Modano/50 40.00 100.00
LLMR Michael Ryder/50 25.00 60.00
LLMS Marek Svatos/50 20.00 50.00
LLMT Marty Turco/50 25.00 60.00
LLMU Larry Murphy/50
LLNK Nikolai Khabibulin/50 30.00 80.00
LLNL Nicklas Lidstrom/50 60.00 125.00
LLNZ Nikolai Zherdev/50 20.00 50.00
LLON Owen Nolan/50 25.00 60.00
LLOV Alexander Ovechkin/50 150.00 250.00
LLPA Paul Henderson/25 75.00 150.00
LLPB Patrice Bergeron/50 30.00 80.00
LLPE Patrik Elias/50 25.00 60.00
LLPH Dion Phaneuf/50 100.00 200.00
LLPK Phil Kessel/25 75.00 150.00
LLPL Pat LaFontaine/50 60.00 125.00
LLPM Patrick Marleau/50 30.00 80.00
LLPR Patrick Roy/50 150.00 300.00
LLPS Peter Stastny/50 30.00 80.00
LLRL Roberto Luongo/50 60.00 125.00
LLRM Ryan Miller/50 50.00 100.00
LLRN Rick Nash/50 60.00 150.00
LLRS Ryan Smyth/50 30.00 80.00
LLRV Rogie Vachon/50 30.00 80.00
LLSA Borje Salming/50 40.00 100.00
LLSC Sidney Crosby/50 300.00 600.00
LLSG Simon Gagne/50 30.00 80.00
LLSH Steve Shutt/50 30.00 80.00
LLSK Saku Koivu/50 30.00 80.00
LLSM Miroslav Satan/50 30.00 80.00
LLSS Scott Stevens/50 30.00 80.00
LLST Martin St. Louis/50 40.00 100.00
LLTB Todd Bertuzzi/50 30.00 80.00
LLTH Jose Theodore/50 25.00 60.00
LLTU Darcy Tucker/50 40.00 100.00
LLTV Tomas Vokoun/50 40.00 100.00
LLVL Vincent Lecavalier/50 100.00 200.00
LLVT Vesa Toskala/50 30.00 80.00
LLWC Wendel Clark/50 75.00 150.00
LLWG Wayne Gretzky/50 300.00 600.00
LLZC Zdeno Chara/50 30.00 80.00

2006-07 The Cup Rookies Platinum

STATED PRINT RUN 25 SER.#'d SETS
91 Nate Thompson 8.00 20.00
92 Mike Brown 8.00 20.00
93 Mike Card 8.00 20.00
94 Adam Dennis 8.00 20.00
95 Carsen Germyn 8.00 20.00
96 Adam Burish 12.00 30.00
97 Drew Larman 8.00 20.00
98 Jonas Johansson 8.00 20.00
99 Joel Perrault 8.00 20.00
100 Mikko Lehtonen 10.00 25.00
101 Alex Brooks 8.00 20.00
102 Frank Doyle 10.00 25.00
103 Billy Thompson 8.00 20.00
104 Kelly Guard 10.00 25.00
105 David Printz 8.00 20.00
106 D.J. King 8.00 20.00
107 Jean-Francois Racine 10.00 25.00
108 Nathan McIver 8.00 20.00
109 Shane O'Brien 8.00 20.00
110 Ryan Shannon 8.00 20.00
111 David McKee 8.00 20.00
112 Mark Stuart 8.00 20.00
113 Matt Lashoff 8.00 20.00
114 Drew Stafford 12.00 30.00
115 Clarke MacArthur 10.00 25.00
116 Michael Funk 8.00 20.00
117 Brandon Prust 8.00 20.00
118 Dustin Boyd 8.00 20.00
119 Dustin Byfuglien 20.00 50.00
120 Dave Bolland 12.00 30.00
121 Michael Blunden 8.00 20.00
122 Filip Novak 8.00 20.00
123 Fredrik Norrena 8.00 20.00
124 Niklas Grossman 12.00 30.00
125 Loui Eriksson 12.00 30.00
126 Tomas Kopecky 10.00 25.00
127 Stefan Liv 8.00 20.00
128 Patrick Thoresen 8.00 20.00
129 Marc-Antoine Pouliot 8.00 20.00
130 Ladislav Smid 8.00 20.00
131 Janis Sprukts 8.00 20.00
132 Jeff Drouin-Deslauriers 8.00 20.00
133 David Booth 10.00 25.00
134 Konstantin Pushkarev 10.00 25.00
135 Patrick O'Sullivan 12.00 30.00
136 Benoit Pouliot 10.00 25.00
137 Niklas Backstrom 15.00 40.00
138 Guillaume Latendresse 12.00 30.00
139 Shea Weber 20.00 50.00
140 Johnny Oduya 12.00 30.00
141 Travis Zajac 15.00 40.00
142 Masi Marjamaki 8.00 20.00
143 Nigel Dawes 8.00 20.00
144 Jarkko Immonen 8.00 20.00
145 Josh Hennessy 8.00 20.00
146 Ryan Potulny 8.00 20.00
147 Jussi Timonen 10.00 25.00
148 Keith Yandle 15.00 40.00
149 Michel Ouellet 10.00 25.00
150 Noah Welch 8.00 20.00
151 Kristopher Letang 50.00 125.00
152 Joe Pavelski 75.00 150.00
153 Matt Carle 8.00 20.00
154 Marc-Edouard Vlasic 8.00 20.00
155 Yan Stastny 8.00 20.00
156 Marek Schwarz 12.00 30.00
157 Roman Polak 10.00 25.00
158 Karri Ramo 8.00 20.00
159 Blair Jones 8.00 20.00
160 Brendan Bell 8.00 20.00
161 Ian White 10.00 25.00
162 Ben Ondrus 8.00 20.00
163 Jeremy Williams 8.00 20.00
164 Miroslav Kopriva 8.00 20.00
165 Luc Bourdon 12.00 30.00
166 Jesse Schultz 8.00 20.00
167 Alexander Edler 12.00 30.00
168 Eric Fehr 12.00 30.00
169 Jordan Staal 50.00 125.00
170 Phil Kessel 20.00 50.00
171 Evgeni Malkin 150.00 300.00
172 Paul Stastny 50.00 125.00
173 Anze Kopitar 60.00 125.00
174 Alexander Radulov 15.00 40.00

2006-07 The Cup Scripted Swatches

STATED PRINT RUN 25 SER.#'d SETS
SSAO Alexander Ovechkin 125.00 250.00
SSAR Andrew Raycroft 25.00 60.00
SSAT Alex Tanguay 25.00 60.00
SSBO Mike Bossy 50.00 100.00
SSBR Bill Ranford 30.00 80.00
SSBS Borje Salming 30.00 80.00
SSCD Chris Drury 25.00 60.00
SSCN Cam Neely 50.00 100.00
SSCW Cam Ward 25.00 60.00
SSDB Daniel Briere 30.00 80.00
SSDC D. Ciccarelli EXCH 30.00 80.00
SSDH Dale Hawerchuk 30.00 80.00
SSDS Denis Savard 30.00 80.00
SSDT Dave Taylor/10 125.00 250.00
SSDW Dave Williams 20.00 50.00
SSEM Evgeni Malkin 100.00 200.00
SSES Eric Staal 25.00 60.00
SSGA Glenn Anderson 25.00 60.00
SSGC Gerry Cheevers 30.00 80.00
SSGF Grant Fuhr 30.00 80.00
SSGL Guy Lafleur 50.00 100.00
SSGP Gilbert Perreault 30.00 80.00
SSHA Dominik Hasek 40.00 100.00
SSHE Dany Heatley 20.00 50.00
SSHL Henrik Lundqvist 100.00 200.00
SSHZ H. Zetterberg EXCH 75.00 150.00
SSIK Ilya Kovalchuk 30.00 80.00
SSJC Jonathan Cheechoo 25.00 60.00
SSJG Jean-Sebastien Giguere 25.00 60.00
SSJI Jarome Iginla 50.00 100.00
SSJK Jari Kurri 50.00 100.00
SSJM Joe Mullen 20.00 50.00
SSJS Jason Spezza
SSJT Joe Thornton 50.00 100.00
SSLR Larry Robinson 30.00 80.00
SSMB Martin Brodeur 150.00 250.00
SSMD Marcel Dionne 30.00 80.00
SSMG Marian Gaborik 30.00 80.00
SSMH Martin Havlat 20.00 50.00
SSMI Milan Hejduk 30.00 80.00
SSML Mario Lemieux 100.00 250.00
SSMM Mike Modano 30.00 80.00
SSMN Markus Naslund 30.00 80.00
SSMR Michael Ryder 25.00 60.00
SSMS Martin St. Louis 25.00 60.00
SSMT Marty Turco 25.00 60.00
SSNL Nicklas Lidstrom 30.00 80.00
SSPB Patrice Bergeron 30.00 80.00
SSPH Dion Phaneuf 30.00 80.00
SSPK Phil Kessel 30.00 80.00
SSPL P. LaFontaine EXCH 30.00 80.00
SSPM Patrick Marleau 25.00 60.00
SSPR Patrick Roy 75.00 150.00
SSRA A. Radulov EXCH 50.00 100.00
SSRB Ray Bourque 60.00 120.00
SSRE Ron Ellis 25.00 60.00
SSRH Ron Hextall 30.00 80.00
SSRL Roberto Luongo
SSRM Ryan Miller 50.00 100.00
SSRN Rick Nash 30.00 80.00
SSRO Luc Robitaille 30.00 80.00
SSRS Ryan Smyth 15.00 40.00
SSSC Sidney Crosby 150.00 300.00
SSSG Simon Gagne 25.00 60.00
SSSH Steve Shutt 20.00 50.00
SSSK Saku Koivu 25.00 60.00
SSSS Scott Stevens 60.00 125.00
SSST Jordan Staal 60.00 150.00
SSTE Tony Esposito 50.00 100.00
SSTH Jose Theodore 25.00 60.00
SSTV Tomas Vokoun 25.00 60.00
SSVL Vincent Lecavalier 50.00 100.00

2006-07 The Cup Signature Patches

STATED PRINT RUN 75 SER.#'d SETS
*WHITE SWATCHES: .5X TO 1X LO
SPAF Alexander Frolov 20.00 50.00
SPAH A. Hemsky EXCH 20.00 50.00
SPAK Anze Kopitar 40.00 100.00
SPAM Al MacInnis 25.00 60.00
SPAO Alexander Ovechkin 100.00 200.00
SPAR A. Radulov EXCH 25.00 60.00
SPAT Alex Tanguay 25.00 60.00
SPBC Bobby Clarke 40.00 80.00
SPBR Martin Brodeur 75.00 150.00
SPBS Billy Smith 25.00 60.00
SPCH Cristobal Huet 20.00 50.00
SPCN Cam Neely 25.00 60.00
SPCW Cam Ward 25.00 60.00
SPDA David Aebischer 15.00 40.00
SPDB Daniel Briere 15.00 40.00
SPDC D. Ciccarelli EXCH 25.00 60.00
SPDH Dale Hawerchuk 25.00 60.00
SPDI Dion Phaneuf 25.00 60.00
SPDS Denis Savard 25.00 60.00
SPDT Dave Taylor 25.00 60.00
SPDW Doug Wilson 15.00 40.00
SPEL Patrik Elias 15.00 40.00
SPEM Evgeni Malkin 75.00 150.00
SPES Eric Staal 20.00 50.00
SPGC Gerry Cheevers 30.00 60.00
SPGF Grant Fuhr 30.00 60.00
SPGH Gordie Howe/25 175.00 300.00
SPGL Guy Lafleur 25.00 60.00
SPGO Scott Gomez 20.00 50.00
SPGP Gilbert Perreault 25.00 60.00
SPHA Dominik Hasek 40.00 80.00
SPHE Dany Heatley 20.00 50.00
SPHZ H. Zetterberg EXCH 30.00 80.00
SPIK Ilya Kovalchuk 25.00 60.00
SPJC Jonathan Cheechoo 25.00 60.00
SPJG Jean-Sebastien Giguere 25.00 60.00
SPJI Jarome Iginla 30.00 80.00
SPJK Jari Kurri 20.00 50.00
SPJO Jordan Staal 30.00 60.00
SPJR Jeremy Roenick 25.00 60.00
SPJS J. Spezza EXCH 20.00 50.00
SPJT Joe Thornton 30.00 80.00
SPKL Kari Lehtonen 25.00 60.00
SPLA G. Latendresse 25.00 60.00
SPLB Luc Bourdon 30.00 60.00
SPLM Lanny McDonald 15.00 40.00
SPLR Larry Robinson 15.00 40.00
SPLX Mario Lemieux/25 250.00 400.00
SPMB Mike Bossy 40.00 80.00
SPMC Matt Carle 15.00 40.00
SPMD Marcel Dionne/25 50.00 120.00
SPMG Marian Gaborik 25.00 60.00
SPMI Milan Hejduk 25.00 60.00
SPMM Mike Modano 25.00 60.00
SPMR Michael Ryder 25.00 60.00
SPMS Martin St. Louis 20.00 50.00
SPMT Marty Turco 15.00 40.00
SPNL Nicklas Lidstrom 20.00 50.00
SPPA Brad Park 15.00 40.00
SPPB Patrice Bergeron 20.00 50.00
SPPH Paul Henderson 25.00 50.00
SPPK Phil Kessel 30.00 80.00
SPPM Patrick Marleau 20.00 50.00
SPPO Patrick O'Sullivan 20.00 50.00
SPPS Paul Stastny 40.00 100.00
SPRA Andrew Raycroft 12.00 30.00
SPRE Ron Ellis 15.00 40.00
SPRH Ron Hextall 25.00 60.00
SPRI Richard Brodeur 15.00 40.00
SPRL Roberto Luongo 30.00 60.00
SPRM Ryan Miller 25.00 60.00
SPRN Rick Nash 20.00 50.00
SPRO Luc Robitaille 40.00 80.00
SPRS Ryan Smyth 25.00 60.00
SPRV Rogie Vachon 25.00 60.00
SPSA Borje Salming 20.00 50.00
SPSC Sidney Crosby 175.00 350.00
SPSE Scott Stevens 50.00 100.00
SPSG Simon Gagne 12.00 30.00
SPSK Saku Koivu 20.00 50.00
SPSM Stan Mikita 30.00 80.00
SPSS Steve Shutt 20.00 50.00
SPST Peter Stastny 15.00 40.00
SPSU Brent Sutter 15.00 40.00
SPSV Marek Svatos 15.00 40.00
SPTB Todd Bertuzzi 20.00 50.00
SPTE Tony Esposito 25.00 60.00
SPTH Jose Theodore 15.00 40.00
SPTV Tomas Vokoun 15.00 40.00
SPVL Vincent Lecavalier 20.00 50.00
SPWG Wayne Gretzky/25 250.00 500.00
SPBO1 Ray Bourque 40.00 80.00
SPBO2 Ray Bourque 40.00 80.00
SPPR1 Patrick Roy 60.00 150.00
SPPR2 Patrick Roy 60.00 150.00

2006-07 The Cup Stanley Cup Signatures

STATED PRINT RUN 25 SER.#'d SETS
CSAA Al Arbour 30.00 60.00
CSAM Al MacInnis 40.00 80.00
CSAT Alex Tanguay 25.00 50.00
CSBA Bob Baun 30.00 60.00
CSBC Bobby Clarke 30.00 60.00
CSBD Butch Bouchard 40.00 80.00
CSBH Bobby Hull 50.00 100.00
CSBI Bill Ranford 40.00 100.00
CSBO Bobby Orr 150.00 300.00
CSBP Bernie Parent 40.00 80.00
CSBR Martin Brodeur 100.00 200.00
CSBS Billy Smith 40.00 80.00
CSBU Johnny Bucyk 40.00 80.00
CSCG Clark Gillies 25.00 50.00
CSCM Craig MacTavish 25.00 50.00
CSCS Clint Smith 60.00 125.00
CSCW Cam Ward 30.00 80.00
CSDG Doug Gilmour 30.00 60.00
CSDH Dominik Hasek 50.00 100.00
CSDP Denis Potvin 25.00 50.00
CSES Eric Staal 30.00 60.00
CSFM Frank Mahovlich 40.00 80.00
CSFR Frank Mahovlich 30.00 60.00
CSGA Glenn Anderson 40.00 80.00
CSGC Gerry Cheevers 30.00 60.00
CSGF Grant Fuhr 40.00 80.00
CSGH Gordie Howe 75.00 175.00
CSGL Guy Lafleur 60.00 125.00
CSHE Milan Hejduk 25.00 50.00
CSJB Jean Beliveau 50.00 100.00
CSJK Jari Kurri 40.00 100.00
CSJL Jacques Lemaire 30.00 60.00
CSJM Joe Mullen 30.00 60.00
CSJO Johnny Bower 25.00 60.00
CSKE Red Kelly 30.00 60.00
CSLA Larry Murphy
CSLE Elmer Lach 40.00 80.00
CSLR Larry Robinson 20.00 50.00
CSMB Mike Bossy 40.00 80.00
CSML Mario Lemieux 150.00 300.00
CSMM Mike Modano 50.00 100.00
CSMS Milt Schmidt 40.00 80.00
CSMU Joe Mullen 30.00 60.00
CSNL Nicklas Lidstrom 40.00 80.00
CSPE Phil Esposito 30.00 60.00
CSPR Patrick Roy 150.00 250.00
CSRB Ray Bourque 50.00 100.00
CSRK Red Kelly 20.00 50.00
CSRL Reggie Leach
CSRO Patrick Roy 75.00 150.00
CSRV Rogie Vachon 30.00 60.00
CSSB Scotty Bowman 40.00 80.00
CSSH Steve Shutt 25.00 50.00
CSSM Stan Mikita 30.00 60.00
CSSS Scott Stevens
CSST Martin St. Louis 25.00 50.00
CSTL Ted Lindsay 30.00 60.00
CSVL Vincent Lecavalier 30.00 60.00
CSWG W. Gretzky 350.00 550.00

2007-08 The Cup

1-100 STATED PRINT RUN 249
101-118 ROOKIE AU PRINT RUN 199
119-184 JSY AU PRINT RUN 249
185-190 ROOKIE JSY AU PRINT RUN 99
1 Dale Hawerchuk 6.00 15.00
2 Bobby Hull 8.00 20.00
3 Alexander Ovechkin 20.00 50.00
4 Dino Ciccarelli 5.00 12.00
5 Markus Naslund 5.00 12.00
6 Roberto Luongo 6.00 15.00
7 Richard Brodeur 4.00 10.00
8 Mats Sundin 5.00 12.00
9 Frank Mahovlich 6.00 15.00
10 Darryl Sittler 4.00 10.00
11 Borje Salming 5.00 12.00
12 Vincent Lecavalier 4.00 10.00
13 Martin St. Louis 5.00 12.00
14 Brad Richards 5.00 12.00
15 Paul Kariya 6.00 15.00
16 Bernie Federko 3.00 8.00
17 Joe Mullen 4.00 10.00
18 Joe Thornton 6.00 15.00
19 Jonathan Cheechoo 5.00 12.00
20 Patrick Marleau 5.00 12.00
21 Sidney Crosby 20.00 50.00
22 Evgeni Malkin 15.00 40.00
23 Mario Lemieux 15.00 40.00
24 Marc-Andre Fleury 8.00 20.00
25 Jordan Staal 5.00 12.00
26 Shane Doan 4.00 10.00
27 Simon Gagne 5.00 12.00
28 Bobby Clarke 5.00 12.00
29 Ron Hextall 8.00 20.00
30 Bernie Parent 5.00 12.00
31 Dany Heatley 5.00 12.00
32 Jason Spezza 5.00 12.00
33 Daniel Alfredsson 5.00 12.00
34 Mark Messier 8.00 20.00
35 Jaromir Jagr 12.00 30.00
36 Brendan Shanahan 6.00 15.00
37 Brian Leetch 5.00 12.00
38 Andy Bathgate 4.00 10.00
39 Mike Bossy 5.00 12.00
40 Clark Gillies 5.00 12.00
41 Denis Potvin 5.00 12.00
42 Billy Smith 5.00 12.00
43 Martin Brodeur 10.00 25.00
44 Zach Parise 6.00 15.00
45 Alexander Radulov 5.00 12.00
46 Peter Forsberg 6.00 15.00
47 Saku Koivu 5.00 12.00
48 Michael Ryder 3.00 8.00
49 Larry Robinson 5.00 12.00
50 Guy Lafleur 6.00 15.00
51 Patrick Roy 12.00 30.00
52 Jean Beliveau 6.00 15.00
53 Marian Gaborik 6.00 15.00
54 Mikko Koivu 4.00 10.00
55 Marcel Dionne 6.00 15.00
56 Anze Kopitar 8.00 20.00
57 Rob Blake 5.00 12.00
58 Gordie Howe 12.00 30.00
59 Tomas Vokoun 4.00 10.00
60 Jari Kurri 5.00 12.00
61 Grant Fuhr 5.00 12.00
62 Wayne Gretzky 25.00 60.00
63 Ales Hemsky 4.00 10.00
64 Dwayne Roloson 4.00 10.00
65 Dominik Hasek 6.00 15.00
66 Henrik Zetterberg 6.00 15.00
67 Nicklas Lidstrom 5.00 12.00
68 Pavel Datsyuk 6.00 15.00
69 Marty Turco 5.00 12.00
70 Mike Modano 8.00 20.00
71 Rick Nash 5.00 12.00
72 Sergei Fedorov 8.00 20.00
73 Joe Sakic 8.00 20.00
74 Paul Stastny 5.00 12.00
75 Milan Hejduk 4.00 10.00
76 Stan Mikita 6.00 15.00
77 Tony Esposito 5.00 12.00
78 Nikolai Khabibulin 5.00 12.00
79 Denis Savard 6.00 15.00
80 Eric Staal 6.00 15.00
81 Cam Ward 5.00 12.00
82 Jarome Iginla 5.00 12.00
83 Miikka Kiprusoff 4.00 10.00
84 Lanny McDonald 5.00 12.00
85 Al MacInnis 5.00 12.00
86 Ryan Miller 5.00 12.00
87 Gilbert Perreault 5.00 12.00
88 Thomas Vanek 6.00 15.00
89 Patrice Bergeron 6.00 15.00
90 Ray Bourque 8.00 20.00
91 Cam Neely 5.00 12.00
92 Bobby Orr 15.00 40.00
93 Johnny Bucyk 4.00 10.00
94 Phil Kessel 6.00 15.00
95 Ilya Kovalchuk 5.00 12.00
96 Marian Hossa 4.00 10.00
97 Kari Lehtonen 4.00 10.00
98 Jean-Sebastien Giguere 5.00 12.00
99 Ryan Getzlaf 8.00 20.00
100 Teemu Selanne 10.00 25.00
101 Matt Keetley AU RC 8.00 20.00
102 Tyler Kennedy AU RC 10.00 25.00
103 Petteri Wirtanen AU RC 6.00 15.00
104 Matt Hunwick AU RC 8.00 20.00
105 Tomas Popperle AU RC 8.00 20.00
106 Johnny Boychuk AU RC 10.00 25.00
107 Alexander Nikulin AU RC 8.00 20.00
108 Mark Mancari AU RC 8.00 20.00
109 Craig Weller AU RC 6.00 15.00
110 Jake Dowell AU RC 6.00 15.00
111 David Clarkson AU RC 10.00 25.00
112 Drew MacIntyre AU RC 8.00 20.00
113 Kris Versteeg AU RC 20.00 50.00
114 Greg Moore AU RC 8.00 20.00
115 Tomas Plihal AU RC 8.00 20.00
116 Mike Lundin AU RC 6.00 15.00
117 Rich Peverley AU RC 10.00 25.00
118 Cody Bass AU RC 8.00 20.00
119 Bobby Ryan JSY AU RC 25.00 60.00
120 Ondrej Pavelec JSY AU RC 20.00 50.00
121 Jack Johnson JSY AU RC 12.00 30.00
122 Nicklas Bergfors JSY AU RC 10.00 25.00
123 Erik Johnson JSY AU RC 15.00 40.00
124 Bryan Little JSY AU RC 15.00 40.00
125 Kris Russell JSY AU RC 12.00 30.00
126 Matt Niskanen JSY AU RC 15.00 40.00
127 A.Cogliano JSY AU RC 15.00 40.00
128 J.Bernier JSY AU RC 25.00 60.00
129 Marc Staal JSY AU RC 15.00 40.00
130 Nick Foligno JSY AU RC 20.00 50.00
131 Peter Mueller JSY AU RC 12.00 30.00
132 Brett Sterling JSY AU RC 10.00 25.00
133 Petr Kalus JSY AU RC 10.00 25.00
134 Rob Schremp JSY AU RC 12.00 30.00
135 Andy Greene JSY AU RC 12.00 30.00
136 Frans Nielsen JSY AU RC 15.00 40.00
137 Martin Hanzal JSY AU RC 12.00 30.00
138 Devin Setoguchi JSY AU RC 15.00 40.00
139 Matt Smaby JSY AU RC 10.00 25.00
140 James Sheppard JSY AU RC 10.00 25.00
141 Kyle Chipchura JSY AU RC 15.00 40.00
142 Ryan Parent JSY AU RC 10.00 25.00
143 David Krejci JSY AU RC 30.00 80.00
144 Lauri Tukonen JSY AU RC 10.00 25.00
145 Anton Stralman JSY AU RC 10.00 25.00
146 Tobias Enstrom JSY AU RC 15.00 40.00
147 B.Dubinsky JSY AU RC 20.00 50.00
148 M.Raymond JSY AU RC 15.00 40.00
149 Drew Miller JSY AU RC 12.00 30.00
150 Curtis McElhinney JSY AU RC 15.00 40.00
151 Ryan Callahan JSY AU RC 20.00 50.00
152 Brian Elliott JSY AU RC 20.00 50.00
153 J.Sigalet JSY AU RC 10.00 25.00
154 Ville Koistinen JSY AU RC 10.00 25.00
155 Torrey Mitchell JSY AU RC 12.00 30.00
156 David Perron JSY AU RC 15.00 40.00
157 Jannik Hansen JSY AU RC 12.00 30.00
158 Jaroslav Halak JSY AU RC 25.00 60.00
159 Milan Lucic JSY AU RC 50.00 125.00
160 Lukas Kaspar JSY AU RC 10.00 25.00
161 Marc Methot JSY AU RC 10.00 25.00
162 Tyler Weiman JSY AU RC 12.00 30.00
163 Ryan Carter JSY AU RC 10.00 25.00
164 Jared Boll JSY AU RC 12.00 30.00
165 Jonas Hiller JSY AU RC 20.00 50.00
166 J.Hlinka JSY AU RC 12.00 30.00

167 Matt Ellis JSY AU RC 12.00 30.00
168 Cory Murphy JSY AU RC 10.00 25.00
169 Steve Wagner JSY AU RC 10.00 25.00
170 Stefan Meyer JSY AU RC 12.00 30.00
171 Daniel Carcillo JSY AU RC 12.00 30.00
172 Tuukka Rask JSY AU RC 80.00 200.00
173 David Jones JSY AU RC 10.00 25.00
174 Tobias Stephan JSY AU RC 12.00 30.00
175 Tom Gilbert JSY AU RC 12.00 30.00
176 Cal Clutterbuck JSY AU RC 15.00 40.00
177 Rod Pelley JSY AU RC 10.00 25.00
178 Daniel Girardi JSY AU RC 12.00 30.00
179 Chris Bourque JSY AU RC 12.00 30.00
180 T.J. Hensick JSY AU RC 12.00 30.00
181 Steve Downie JSY AU RC 12.00 30.00
182 Jack Skille JSY AU RC 12.00 30.00
183 Casey Borer JSY AU RC 10.00 25.00
184 S.Kostitsyn JSY AU RC 12.00 30.00
185 P.Kane JSY AU/99 RC 1000.00 2000.00
186 S.Gagner JSY AU/99 RC 80.00 200.00
187 N.Backstrom JSY AU/99 RC 400.00 700.00
188 Jiri Tlusty JSY AU/99 RC 60.00 150.00
189 C.Price JSY AU/99 RC 1000.00 2000.00
190 J.Toews JSY AU/99 RC 1500.00 3000.00

2007-08 The Cup Gold

*1-100 GOLD/25: .8X TO 2X BASIC CARDS
STATED PRINT RUN 25 SER.#'d SETS

2007-08 The Cup Chirography

STATED PRINT RUN 50 SERIAL #'d SETS
CCAM Al MacInnis 12.00 30.00
CCAO Alexander Ovechkin 40.00 100.00
CCBC Bobby Clarke 12.00 30.00
CCBF Bernie Federko 8.00 20.00
CCBH Bobby Hull 20.00 50.00
CCBL Brian Leetch 12.00 30.00
CCBO Bobby Orr 75.00 150.00
CCBP Bernie Parent 12.00 30.00
CCBR Martin Brodeur 40.00 100.00
CCCG Clark Gillies 12.00 30.00
CCCN Cam Neely 12.00 30.00
CCDC Dino Ciccarelli 12.00 30.00
CCDH Dany Heatley 12.00 30.00
CCDP Denis Potvin 12.00 30.00
CCDS Darryl Sittler 12.00 30.00
CCEM Evgeni Malkin 30.00 80.00
CCES Eric Staal 15.00 40.00
CCFM Frank Mahovlich 15.00 40.00
CCGF Grant Fuhr 12.00 30.00
CCGH Gordie Howe 60.00 120.00
CCGL Guy Lafleur 25.00 60.00
CCGP Gilbert Perreault 12.00 30.00
CCHA Dale Hawerchuk 15.00 40.00
CCIK Ilya Kovalchuk 12.00 30.00
CCJB Jean Beliveau 25.00 50.00
CCJC Jonathan Cheechoo 12.00 30.00
CCJI Jarome Iginla 15.00 40.00
CCJK Jari Kurri 15.00 40.00
CCJM Joe Mullen 10.00 25.00
CCJT Joe Thornton 15.00 40.00
CCLM Lanny McDonald 15.00 40.00
CCLR Luc Robitaille 20.00 50.00
CCMB Mike Bossy 20.00 50.00
CCMD Marcel Dionne 15.00 40.00
CCMG Marian Gaborik 15.00 40.00
CCML Mario Lemieux 75.00 150.00
CCMM Mark Messier 50.00 100.00
CCMN Markus Naslund 12.00 30.00
CCMO Mike Modano 15.00 40.00
CCMS Martin St. Louis 15.00 40.00
CCMT Marty Turco 12.00 30.00
CCPE Phil Esposito 20.00 50.00
CCPR Patrick Roy 60.00 120.00
CCRB Ray Bourque 30.00 60.00
CCRH Ron Hextall 20.00 50.00
CCRO Larry Robinson 12.00 30.00
CCSA Borje Salming 12.00 30.00
CCSC Sidney Crosby 125.00 250.00
CCSD Shane Doan 10.00 25.00
CCSG Simon Gagne 20.00 50.00
CCSK Saku Koivu 20.00 50.00
CCSM Stan Mikita 20.00 50.00
CCTE Tony Esposito 25.00 50.00
CCVL Vincent Lecavalier 15.00 40.00
CCWG Wayne Gretzky 150.00 300.00

2007-08 The Cup Emblems of Endorsement

STATED PRINT RUN 4-15
EEAC Andrew Cogliano 25.00 60.00
EEAH Ales Hemsky
EEAK Anze Kopitar 40.00 100.00
EEAM Al MacInnis 25.00 60.00
EEAO Adam Oates 30.00 80.00
EEAR Alexander Radulov 25.00 60.00
EEAT Alex Tanguay 15.00 40.00
EEBC Bobby Clarke 30.00 80.00
EEBG Brian Gionta 20.00 50.00
EEBL Brian Leetch 30.00 80.00
EEBN Bernie Nicholls 25.00 50.00
EEBO Mike Bossy 40.00 100.00
EEBR Bill Ranford 25.00 60.00
EECD Chris Drury 20.00 50.00
EECH Jonathan Cheechoo 25.00 60.00
EECN Cam Neely 30.00 80.00
EECP Corey Perry
EECW Cam Ward
EECY Carey Price 175.00 300.00
EEDC Dino Ciccarelli 25.00 60.00
EEDG Doug Gilmour
EEDH Dale Hawerchuk 30.00 80.00
EEDR Dwayne Roloson 20.00 50.00
EEDS Darryl Sittler
EEEM Evgeni Malkin 125.00 200.00
EEEN Evgeni Nabokov
EEES Eric Staal 30.00 80.00
EEGA Sam Gagner 30.00 80.00
EEGF Grant Fuhr 75.00 125.00
EEGP Gilbert Perreault
EEHA Dominik Hasek 30.00 80.00
EEHE Dany Heatley
EEHZ Henrik Zetterberg 75.00 125.00
EEIK Ilya Kovalchuk
EEJA Jason Arnott 25.00 60.00
EEJB Jonathan Bernier
EEJC Jeff Carter 25.00 60.00
EEJG Jean-Sebastien Giguere 30.00 80.00
EEJI Jarome Iginla 175.00 300.00
EEJK Jari Kurri 50.00 100.00
EEJM Joe Mullen 20.00 50.00
EEJO Jonathan Toews 400.00 600.00
EEJS Jordan Staal 50.00 100.00
EEJT Joe Thornton 60.00 120.00
EEJW Justin Williams 20.00 50.00
EELM Lanny McDonald
EELR Larry Robinson 25.00 60.00
EEMB Martin Brodeur 75.00 125.00
EEMD Marcel Dionne 50.00 100.00
EEMF Marc-Andre Fleury 50.00 100.00
EEMG Marian Gaborik 30.00 80.00
EEMH Marian Hossa 20.00 50.00
EEMI Milan Hejduk 20.00 50.00
EEML Mario Lemieux 175.00 300.00
EEMM Mark Messier 90.00 150.00
EEMN Markus Naslund
EEMO Mike Modano 30.00 80.00
EEMS Marek Svatos 15.00 40.00
EEMT Marty Turco
EENB Nicklas Backstrom
EENL Nicklas Lidstrom 30.00 80.00
EEOV Alexander Ovechkin 250.00 400.00
EEPB Patrice Bergeron 30.00 80.00
EEPE Patrik Elias 25.00 60.00
EEPK Patrick Kane 300.00 500.00
EEPM Peter Mueller 20.00 50.00
EEPR Patrick Roy 125.00 250.00
EEPS Paul Stastny 25.00 60.00
EERB Ray Bourque 90.00 150.00
EERG Ryan Getzlaf 40.00 100.00
EERI Richard Brodeur 25.00 60.00
EERM Ryan Miller 30.00 80.00
EERN Rick Nash 30.00 80.00
EERO Luc Robitaille 40.00 100.00
EERS Ryan Smyth 20.00 50.00
EESA Borje Salming 25.00 60.00
EESC Sidney Crosby 450.00 700.00
EESD Shane Doan 20.00 50.00
EESG Simon Gagne 30.00 80.00
EESH Steve Shutt 30.00 80.00
EESK Saku Koivu 30.00 80.00
EESP Peter Stastny 25.00 60.00
EEST Martin St. Louis
EETE Tony Esposito 25.00 60.00
EETL Jiri Tlusty 25.00 60.00
EETR Tuomo Ruutu 25.00 60.00
EETV Thomas Vanek 30.00 80.00
EETW Tiger Williams
EEVL Vincent Lecavalier
EEVO Tomas Vokoun

2007-08 The Cup Enshrinements

STATED PRINT RUN 50 SERIAL #'d SETS
EAM Al MacInnis 15.00 40.00
EAO Alexander Ovechkin 60.00 150.00
EBC Bobby Clarke 15.00 40.00
EBF Bernie Federko 10.00 25.00
EBH Bobby Hull 25.00 60.00
EBL Brian Leetch 15.00 40.00
EBO Bobby Orr 100.00 200.00
EBP Bernie Parent 15.00 40.00
ECG Clark Gillies 15.00 40.00
ECN Cam Neely 15.00 40.00
EDC Dino Ciccarelli 15.00 40.00
EDH Dany Heatley 15.00 40.00
EDP Denis Potvin 15.00 40.00
EDS Darryl Sittler 12.00 30.00
EEM Evgeni Malkin 50.00 100.00
EES Eric Staal 12.00 30.00
EFM Frank Mahovlich 20.00 50.00
EGF Grant Fuhr 20.00 50.00
EGH Gordie Howe 50.00 100.00
EGL Guy Lafleur 20.00 50.00
EGP Gilbert Perreault 15.00 40.00
EHA Dale Hawerchuk 20.00 50.00
EIK Ilya Kovalchuk 15.00 40.00
EJB Jean Beliveau 20.00 50.00
EJC Jonathan Cheechoo 15.00 40.00
EJI Jarome Iginla 30.00 80.00
EJK Jari Kurri 15.00 40.00
EJM Joe Mullen 12.00 30.00
EJT Joe Thornton 20.00 50.00
ELM Lanny McDonald 15.00 40.00
ELR Luc Robitaille 15.00 40.00
EMB Martin Brodeur 30.00 80.00
EMD Marcel Dionne 20.00 50.00
EMG Marian Gaborik 20.00 50.00
EMI Mike Bossy 15.00 40.00
EML Mario Lemieux 75.00 150.00
EMM Mark Messier 60.00 120.00
EMN Markus Naslund 15.00 40.00
EMO Mike Modano 25.00 60.00
EMS Martin St. Louis 15.00 40.00
EMT Marty Turco 15.00 40.00
EPE Phil Esposito 25.00 60.00
EPR Patrick Roy 60.00 120.00
ERB Ray Bourque 25.00 60.00
ERH Ron Hextall 20.00 50.00
ERO Larry Robinson 15.00 40.00
ESA Borje Salming 15.00 40.00
ESC Sidney Crosby 100.00 200.00
ESD Shane Doan 12.00 30.00
ESG Simon Gagne 15.00 40.00
ESK Saku Koivu 12.00 30.00
ESM Stan Mikita 20.00 50.00
ETE Tony Esposito 30.00 60.00
EVL Vincent Lecavalier 12.00 30.00
EWG Wayne Gretzky 150.00 250.00

2007-08 The Cup Enshrinements Duals

COMPLETE SET (28)
STATED PRINT RUN 25 SERIAL #'d SETS
E2BG M.Bossy/C.Gillies 15.00 40.00
E2BR J.Beliveau/L.Robinson 30.00 80.00
E2CP B.Clarke/B.Parent 15.00 40.00
E2DH S.Doan/D.Heatley 15.00 40.00
E2EB P.Esposito/R.Bourque 25.00 60.00
E2EM T.Esposito/S.Mikita 25.00 60.00
E2EP T.Esposito/G.Perreault 25.00 60.00
E2FK G.Fuhr/J.Kurri 15.00 40.00
E2FM B.Federko/A.MacInnis 15.00 40.00
E2FS M.Fleury/J.Staal 25.00 60.00
E2GM W.Gretzky/M.Messier 175.00 250.00
E2GS S.Gagne/M.St. Louis 10.00 25.00
E2HM G.Howe/M.Messier 40.00 100.00
E2HP R.Hextall/B.Parent 25.00 60.00
E2IM J.Iginla/L.McDonald 15.00 40.00
E2KO Kovalchuk/Ovechkin 60.00 150.00
E2LC Lecavalier/Cheechoo 15.00 40.00
E2LM M.Lemieux/E.Malkin 50.00 125.00
E2LS Lidstrom/Salming 15.00 40.00
E2MM M.Modano/J.Mullen 12.00 30.00
E2MS F.Mahovlich/D.Sittler 20.00 50.00
E2OG B.Orr/W.Gretzky 80.00 200.00
E2OH B.Orr/G.Howe 50.00 125.00
E2PR D.Potvin/L.Robinson 15.00 40.00
E2RD L.Robitaille/M.Dionne 20.00 50.00
E2RH L.Robitaille/B.Hull 25.00 60.00
E2RL P.Roy/M.Lemieux 125.00 250.00
E2SH P.Stastny/D.Hawerchuk 15.00 40.00
E2TS J.Thornton/E.Staal 20.00 50.00

2007-08 The Cup Foundations

STATED PRINT RUN 25 SERIAL #'d SETS
CFAK Anze Kopitar 12.00 30.00
CFAM Al MacInnis 15.00 40.00
CFAO Adam Oates 8.00 20.00
CFAR Alexander Radulov 8.00 20.00
CFAS Alexander Steen 8.00 20.00
CFAT Alex Tanguay 5.00 12.00
CFBC Bobby Clarke 8.00 20.00
CFBH Bobby Hull 12.00 30.00
CFBL Brian Leetch 8.00 20.00
CFBO Mike Bossy 8.00 20.00
CFBR Bill Ranford 8.00 20.00
CFBS Billy Smith 8.00 20.00
CFBU Johnny Bucyk 6.00 15.00
CFCN Cam Neely 8.00 20.00
CFCP Chris Pronger 6.00 15.00
CFDA Daniel Alfredsson 8.00 20.00
CFDC Dino Ciccarelli 8.00 20.00
CFDE Denis Savard 10.00 25.00
CFDH Dale Hawerchuk 10.00 25.00
CFDP Denis Potvin 8.00 20.00
CFDR Dwayne Roloson 8.00 20.00
CFDS Darryl Sittler 6.00 15.00
CFEM Evgeni Malkin 15.00 40.00
CFEN Evgeni Nabokov 6.00 15.00
CFEP Phil Esposito 12.00 30.00
CFES Eric Staal 10.00 25.00
CFFM Frank Mahovlich 10.00 25.00
CFGF Grant Fuhr 8.00 20.00
CFGH Gordie Howe 40.00 80.00
CFGL Guy Lafleur
CFGP Gilbert Perreault
CFHA Dominik Hasek 10.00 25.00
CFHE Dany Heatley 8.00 20.00
CFHL Henrik Lundqvist 10.00 25.00
CFHO Marian Hossa 6.00 15.00
CFHZ Henrik Zetterberg 10.00 25.00
CFIK Ilya Kovalchuk 8.00 20.00
CFJB Jean Beliveau 10.00 25.00
CFJI Jarome Iginla 8.00 20.00
CFJJ Jaromir Jagr 20.00 50.00
CFJK Jari Kurri 8.00 20.00
CFJO Joe Sakic 12.00 30.00
CFJS Jason Spezza 8.00 20.00
CFJT Joe Thornton 10.00 25.00
CFKI Miikka Kiprusoff 6.00 15.00
CFKL Kari Lehtonen 6.00 15.00
CFLM Lanny McDonald 8.00 20.00
CFLR Larry Robinson
CFMB Martin Brodeur 15.00 40.00
CFMF Marc-Andre Fleury 12.00 30.00
CFMG Marian Gaborik 10.00 25.00
CFMH Milan Hejduk 6.00 15.00
CFMK Mikko Koivu
CFML Mario Lemieux 25.00 60.00
CFMM Mark Messier 20.00 50.00
CFMN Markus Naslund 8.00 20.00
CFMO Mike Modano 12.00 30.00
CFMR Mark Recchi 10.00 25.00
CFMS Martin St. Louis 8.00 20.00
CFNL Nicklas Lidstrom 8.00 20.00
CFOV Alexander Ovechkin 30.00 80.00
CFPB Patrice Bergeron 10.00 25.00
CFPD Pavel Datsyuk 10.00 25.00
CFPE Corey Perry 8.00 20.00
CFPF Peter Forsberg 10.00 25.00
CFPH Dion Phaneuf 8.00 20.00
CFPK Paul Kariya 10.00 25.00
CFPM Patrick Marleau 8.00 20.00
CFPR Patrick Roy 20.00 50.00
CFPS Peter Stastny 8.00 20.00
CFRB Ray Bourque 12.00 30.00
CFRE Ron Ellis 6.00 15.00
CFRH Ron Hextall 12.00 30.00
CFRI Brad Richards
CFRL Roberto Luongo 10.00 25.00
CFRN Rick Nash 8.00 20.00
CFRO Luc Robitaille 12.00 30.00
CFRS Ryan Smyth 6.00 15.00
CFRV Rogie Vachon 10.00 25.00
CFRY Michael Ryder 5.00 12.00
CFSA Borje Salming 8.00 20.00
CFSC Sidney Crosby 40.00 100.00
CFSD Shane Doan 6.00 15.00
CFSF Sergei Fedorov 12.00 30.00
CFSG Simon Gagne 8.00 20.00
CFSH Brendan Shanahan 10.00 25.00
CFSK Saku Koivu 8.00 20.00
CFSL Steve Sullivan 5.00 12.00
CFSM Stan Mikita 10.00 25.00
CFSN Scott Niedermayer
CFSS Steve Shutt 6.00 15.00
CFST Scott Stevens 8.00 20.00
CFSU Mats Sundin 8.00 20.00
CFTS Teemu Selanne 15.00 40.00
CFTV Tomas Vokoun 6.00 15.00
CFTW Tiger Williams 6.00 15.00
CFVL Vincent Lecavalier 6.00 15.00
CFVT Vesa Toskala 6.00 15.00
CFWG Wayne Gretzky 100.00 200.00
CFZP Zach Parise 10.00 25.00

2007-08 The Cup Gold Jerseys

*GOLD JSY: 1X TO 2.5X
STATED PRINT RUN 25 SERIAL #'d SETS
1 Dale Hawerchuk 15.00 40.00
2 Bobby Hull 20.00 50.00
3 Alexander Ovechkin 50.00 125.00
4 Dino Ciccarelli 12.00 30.00
5 Markus Naslund 12.00 30.00
6 Roberto Luongo 15.00 40.00
7 Richard Brodeur 10.00 25.00
8 Mats Sundin 12.00 30.00
9 Frank Mahovlich 15.00 40.00
10 Darryl Sittler 10.00 25.00
11 Borje Salming 12.00 30.00
12 Vincent Lecavalier 10.00 25.00
13 Martin St. Louis 12.00 30.00
14 Brad Richards 12.00 30.00
15 Paul Kariya 15.00 40.00
16 Bernie Federko 8.00 20.00
17 Joe Mullen 10.00 25.00
18 Joe Thornton 15.00 40.00
19 Jonathan Cheechoo 12.00 30.00
20 Patrick Marleau 12.00 30.00
21 Sidney Crosby 50.00 125.00
22 Evgeni Malkin 20.00 50.00
23 Mario Lemieux 40.00 100.00
24 Marc-Andre Fleury 20.00 50.00
25 Jordan Staal 12.00 30.00
26 Shane Doan 10.00 25.00
27 Simon Gagne 12.00 30.00
28 Bobby Clarke 12.00 30.00
29 Ron Hextall 20.00 50.00
30 Bernie Parent 12.00 30.00
31 Dany Heatley 12.00 30.00
32 Jason Spezza 15.00 40.00
33 Daniel Alfredsson 12.00 30.00
34 Mark Messier 20.00 50.00
35 Jaromir Jagr 30.00 80.00
36 Brendan Shanahan 15.00 40.00
37 Brian Leetch 12.00 30.00
39 Mike Bossy 12.00 30.00
40 Clark Gillies 12.00 30.00
41 Denis Potvin 12.00 30.00
42 Billy Smith 12.00 30.00
43 Martin Brodeur 25.00 60.00
44 Zach Parise 15.00 40.00
45 Alexander Radulov 12.00 30.00
46 Peter Forsberg 15.00 40.00
47 Saku Koivu 12.00 30.00
48 Michael Ryder 8.00 20.00
49 Larry Robinson 12.00 30.00
50 Guy Lafleur 15.00 40.00
51 Patrick Roy 30.00 80.00
52 Jean Beliveau 15.00 40.00
53 Marian Gaborik 15.00 40.00
54 Mikko Koivu 10.00 25.00
55 Marcel Dionne 15.00 40.00
56 Anze Kopitar 20.00 50.00
57 Rob Blake 12.00 30.00
58 Gordie Howe 30.00 80.00
59 Tomas Vokoun 10.00 25.00
60 Jari Kurri 12.00 30.00
61 Grant Fuhr 12.00 30.00
62 Wayne Gretzky 60.00 150.00
63 Ales Hemsky 10.00 25.00
64 Dwayne Roloson 10.00 25.00
65 Dominik Hasek 15.00 40.00
66 Henrik Zetterberg 15.00 40.00
67 Nicklas Lidstrom 12.00 30.00
68 Pavel Datsyuk 15.00 40.00
69 Marty Turco 12.00 30.00
70 Mike Modano 20.00 50.00
71 Rick Nash 12.00 30.00
72 Sergei Fedorov 12.00 30.00
73 Joe Sakic 20.00 50.00
74 Paul Stastny 12.00 30.00
75 Milan Hejduk 10.00 25.00
76 Stan Mikita 15.00 40.00
77 Tony Esposito 12.00 30.00
78 Nikolai Khabibulin 12.00 30.00
79 Denis Savard 15.00 40.00
80 Eric Staal 15.00 40.00
81 Cam Ward 12.00 30.00
82 Jarome Iginla 12.00 30.00
83 Miikka Kiprusoff 10.00 25.00
84 Lanny McDonald 12.00 30.00
85 Al MacInnis 12.00 30.00
86 Ryan Miller 12.00 30.00
87 Gilbert Perreault 12.00 30.00
88 Thomas Vanek 15.00 40.00
89 Patrice Bergeron 15.00 40.00
90 Ray Bourque 20.00 50.00
91 Cam Neely 12.00 30.00
93 Johnny Bucyk 10.00 25.00
94 Phil Kessel 15.00 40.00
95 Ilya Kovalchuk 12.00 30.00
96 Marian Hossa 10.00 25.00
97 Kari Lehtonen 10.00 25.00
98 Jean-Sebastien Giguere 12.00 30.00
99 Ryan Getzlaf 20.00 50.00
100 Teemu Selanne 25.00 60.00

2007-08 The Cup Gold Rainbow Autographed Rookies

STATED PRINT RUN 1-59
101 Matt Keetley/36 12.00 30.00
102 Tyler Kennedy/34 25.00 60.00
103 Petteri Wirtanen/56 6.00 15.00
104 Matt Hunwick/48 8.00 20.00
105 Tomas Popperle/1
106 Johnny Boychuk/28 15.00 40.00
107 Alexander Nikulin/6
108 Mark Mancari/25 50.00 100.00
109 Craig Weller/12
110 Jake Dowell/49 8.00 20.00
111 David Clarkson/27 25.00 60.00
112 Drew MacIntyre/34 15.00 40.00
113 Kris Versteeg/32 125.00 250.00
114 Greg Moore/47 15.00 40.00
115 Tomas Plihal/59 10.00 25.00
116 Mike Lundin/39 10.00 25.00
117 Rich Peverley/37 8.00 20.00
118 Cody Bass/21 15.00 40.00

2007-08 The Cup Gold Rainbow Autographed Rookie Patches

STATED PRINT RUN 1-89
119 Bobby Ryan/54 30.00 80.00
120 Ondrej Pavelec/33 30.00 60.00
121 Jack Johnson/33 40.00 100.00
128 Jonathan Bernier/45 60.00 120.00
129 Marc Staal/18
130 Nick Foligno/71 15.00 40.00
131 Peter Mueller/88 25.00 60.00
132 Brett Sterling/21 15.00 40.00
133 Petr Kalus/23 15.00 40.00
134 Rob Schremp/44 15.00 40.00
136 Frans Nielsen/51 20.00 50.00
138 Devin Setoguchi/16 30.00 80.00
139 Matt Smaby/32 25.00 60.00
140 James Sheppard/15 15.00 40.00
141 Kyle Chipchura/28 20.00 60.00
142 Ryan Parent/77 25.00 60.00
143 David Krejci/46 90.00 150.00
144 Lauri Tukonen/28 20.00 50.00
145 Anton Stralman/36 12.00 30.00
146 Tobias Enstrom/39 20.00 50.00
147 Brandon Dubinsky/54 40.00 100.00
148 Mason Raymond/21 30.00 80.00
149 Drew Miller/18 20.00 40.00
150 Curtis McElhinney/31 15.00 40.00
151 Ryan Callahan/43 25.00 60.00
152 Brian Elliott/30 25.00 60.00
153 Jonathan Sigalet/50 12.00 30.00
155 Torrey Mitchell/17 20.00 50.00
156 David Perron/57 20.00 50.00
157 Jannik Hansen/59 15.00 40.00
158 Jaroslav Halak/41 75.00 150.00
159 Milan Lucic/17 125.00 200.00
160 Lukas Kaspar/43 15.00 40.00
161 Marc Methot/48 12.00 30.00
162 Tyler Weiman/35 20.00 50.00
163 Ryan Carter/52 15.00 40.00
164 Jared Boll/40 20.00 50.00
166 Jaroslav Hlinka/17 20.00 50.00
168 Cory Murphy/21 25.00 60.00
169 Steve Wagner/49 12.00 30.00
170 Stefan Meyer/64 20.00 50.00
172 Tuukka Rask/40 125.00 250.00
173 David Jones/36 15.00 40.00
174 Tobias Stephan/31 15.00 40.00
175 Tom Gilbert/77 20.00 50.00
176 Cal Clutterbuck/22 25.00 60.00
177 Rod Pelley/22 15.00 40.00
178 Daniel Girardi/46 15.00 40.00
179 Chris Bourque/56 15.00 40.00
180 T.J. Hensick/34 15.00 40.00
181 Steve Downie/25 15.00 40.00
182 Jack Skille/48 25.00 60.00
183 Casey Borer/25 15.00 40.00
184 Sergei Kostitsyn/25 20.00 50.00
185 Patrick Kane/88 400.00 700.00
186 Sam Gagner/89 40.00 100.00
187 Nicklas Backstrom/19 250.00 400.00
188 Jiri Tlusty/41 60.00 120.00
189 Carey Price/31 600.00 1000.00
190 Jonathan Toews/19 1000.00 1500.00

2007-08 The Cup Honorable Numbers

STATED PRINT RUN 2-94
HNAC Andrew Cogliano/13
HNAM Al MacInnis/2
HNAO Alexander Ovechkin/8
HNBC Bobby Clarke/16 50.00 100.00
HNBL Brian Leetch/2
HNBN Bernie Nicholls/9
HNBR Martin Brodeur/30 150.00 300.00
HNBS Borje Salming/21
HNCN Cam Neely/8
HNCP Carey Price/31 300.00 600.00
HNDC Dino Ciccarelli/22 40.00 100.00
HNDH Dale Hawerchuk/10
HNDS Darryl Sittler/27 20.00 50.00
HNEM Evgeni Malkin/71 60.00 120.00
HNES Eric Staal/12
HNGA Sam Gagner/89 40.00 100.00
HNGF Grant Fuhr/31 40.00 80.00
HNGH Gordie Howe/9
HNGP Gilbert Perreault/11
HNHA Dominik Hasek/39 40.00 100.00
HNHE Dany Heatley/15 40.00 80.00
HNHZ Henrik Zetterberg/40 40.00 100.00
HNIK Ilya Kovalchuk/17 50.00 100.00
HNJB Jonathan Bernier/45 50.00 120.00
HNJC Jonathan Cheechoo/14
HNJG Jean-Sebastien Giguere/35 25.00 60.00
HNJI Jarome Iginla/12
HNJK Jari Kurri/17 50.00 100.00
HNJM Joe Mullen/7
HNJO Jonathan Toews/19 500.00 800.00
HNJS Jordan Staal/11
HNJT Joe Thornton/19 75.00 150.00
HNLM Lanny McDonald/9
HNLR Larry Robinson/19 40.00 80.00
HNMD Marcel Dionne/16 60.00 120.00
HNMF Marc-Andre Fleury/29 75.00 150.00
HNMG Marian Gaborik/10
HNML Mario Lemieux/66 175.00 350.00
HNMM Mark Messier/11
HNMN Markus Naslund/19 20.00 50.00
HNMO Mike Modano/9
HNMS Martin St. Louis/26 20.00 50.00
HNMT Marty Turco/35 20.00 50.00
HNNB Nicklas Backstrom/19 100.00 200.00
HNPE Phil Esposito/7
HNPK Patrick Kane/88 75.00 150.00
HNPM Peter Mueller/88 15.00 40.00
HNPR Patrick Roy/33 125.00 250.00
HNPS Paul Stastny/26 40.00 80.00
HNRB Ray Bourque/77 40.00 80.00
HNRG Ryan Getzlaf/15 50.00 100.00
HNRM Ryan Miller/30 40.00 100.00
HNRN Rick Nash/61 30.00 80.00
HNRO Luc Robitaille/20 25.00 60.00
HNRS Ryan Smyth/94 15.00 40.00
HNSC Sidney Crosby/87 150.00 300.00
HNSD Shane Doan/19 25.00 60.00
HNSG Simon Gagne/12
HNSH Steve Shutt/22 15.00 40.00
HNSK Saku Koivu/11
HNST Peter Stastny/26 50.00 100.00
HNTE Tony Esposito/35 40.00 80.00
HNTL Jiri Tlusty/41 25.00 60.00
HNTV Thomas Vanek/26 25.00 60.00
HNVL Vincent Lecavalier/4

2007-08 The Cup Honorable Numbers Dual

STATED PRINT RUN 2-81
HN2BS M.Bossy/S.Shutt/22 50.00 100.00
HN2DC M.Dionne/B.Clarke/16 40.00 100.00
HN2GT J.Giguere/M.Turco/35 40.00 100.00
HN2RC L.Robitaille/D.Ciccarelli/20 40.00 80.00
HN2SK M.Satan/P.Kessel/81 25.00 60.00
HN2SS P.Stastny/P.Stastny/26 60.00 150.00
HN2TD J.Thornton/S.Doan/19 40.00 100.00

2007-08 The Cup Limited Logos Autographs

STATED PRINT RUN 3-50
LLAC Andrew Cogliano/25 40.00 80.00
LLAH Ales Hemsky/50 20.00 50.00
LLAK Anze Kopitar/31 60.00 120.00
LLAM Al MacInnis/30 25.00 60.00
LLAO Adam Oates/50 25.00 60.00
LLAR Alexander Radulov/50 25.00 60.00
LLAT Alex Tanguay/50 15.00 40.00
LLBG Brian Gionta/50 20.00 50.00
LLBL Brian Leetch/50 25.00 60.00
LLBN Bernie Nicholls/50 25.00 60.00
LLBR Bill Ranford/50 25.00 60.00
LLCA Jeff Carter/50 40.00 80.00
LLCD Chris Drury/50 20.00 50.00
LLCN Cam Neely/25 60.00 120.00
LLCP Corey Perry/50
LLCW Cam Ward/50 25.00 60.00
LLCY Carey Price/50 200.00 400.00
LLDC Dino Ciccarelli/50 25.00 60.00
LLDG Doug Gilmour/50 30.00 80.00
LLDH Dale Hawerchuk/50 30.00 80.00
LLDR Dwayne Roloson/50 20.00 50.00
LLEL Patrik Elias/50 25.00 60.00
LLEM Evgeni Malkin/25 125.00 250.00
LLEN Evgeni Nabokov/50 20.00 50.00
LLES Eric Staal/50 30.00 80.00
LLGA Sam Gagner/25 60.00 120.00
LLGF Grant Fuhr/25 30.00 80.00
LLGL Guy Lafleur/3
LLGP Gilbert Perreault/25 30.00 80.00
LLHA Dominik Hasek/50 30.00 80.00
LLHE Dany Heatley/50 25.00 60.00
LLHZ Henrik Zetterberg/50 50.00 120.00
LLIK Ilya Kovalchuk/50 40.00 120.00
LLJA Jason Arnott/50 20.00 50.00
LLJB Jonathan Bernier/50 60.00 120.00
LLJC Jonathan Cheechoo/50 25.00 60.00
LLJG Jean-Sebastien Giguere/50 30.00 80.00
LLJI Jarome Iginla/50 30.00 80.00
LLJK Jari Kurri/25 30.00 80.00
LLJM Joe Mullen/50 20.00 50.00
LLJO Jonathan Toews/50 175.00 350.00
LLJS Jordan Staal/50 25.00 60.00
LLJT Joe Thornton/50 30.00 80.00
LLJW Justin Williams/50 20.00 50.00
LLLM Lanny McDonald/50 40.00 80.00
LLLR Larry Robinson/28 25.00 60.00
LLMA Martin Brodeur/50 75.00 150.00
LLMD Marcel Dionne/22 60.00 120.00
LLMF Marc-Andre Fleury/50 30.00 80.00
LLMG Marian Gaborik/50 40.00 100.00
LLMH Marian Hossa/50 30.00 80.00
LLMI Milan Hejduk/50 20.00 50.00
LLML Mario Lemieux/50 100.00 200.00
LLMM Mark Messier/50 50.00 100.00
LLMN Markus Naslund/50 25.00 60.00
LLMO Mike Modano/50 30.00 75.00
LLMS Martin St. Louis/50 25.00 60.00
LLMT Marty Turco/50 25.00 60.00
LLNB Nicklas Backstrom/50 90.00 150.00
LLNL Nicklas Lidstrom/50 60.00 120.00
LLOV Alexander Ovechkin/50 125.00 250.00
LLPB Patrice Bergeron/50 30.00 80.00
LLPK Patrick Kane/50 175.00 300.00
LLPM Peter Mueller/50 25.00 60.00
LLPR Patrick Roy/50 125.00 250.00
LLPS Paul Stastny/50 20.00 50.00
LLRB Ray Bourque/50 40.00 100.00
LLRG Ryan Getzlaf/50 40.00 100.00
LLRI Richard Brodeur/50 20.00 50.00
LLRM Ryan Miller/50 25.00 60.00
LLRN Rick Nash/50 25.00 60.00
LLRO Luc Robitaille/50 25.00 60.00
LLRS Ryan Smyth/50 20.00 50.00
LLSA Borje Salming/50 25.00 60.00
LLSC Sidney Crosby/50 300.00 500.00
LLSD Shane Doan/50 20.00 50.00
LLSG Simon Gagne/50 25.00 60.00
LLSH Steve Shutt/50 25.00 60.00
LLSK Saku Koivu/50 25.00 60.00
LLSM Stan Mikita/25 60.00 120.00
LLST Peter Stastny/32 60.00 120.00
LLSV Marek Svatos/50 15.00 40.00
LLTL Jiri Tlusty/50 25.00 60.00
LLTR Tuomo Ruutu/50 25.00 60.00
LLTV Thomas Vanek/50 25.00 60.00
LLVL Vincent Lecavalier/50 50.00 100.00
LLVO Tomas Vokoun/50 20.00 50.00
LLWG Wayne Gretzky/5

2007-08 The Cup Rookies Platinum

STATED PRINT RUN 25 SER.#'d SETS
101 Matt Keetley 8.00 20.00
102 Tyler Kennedy 10.00 25.00
103 Petteri Wirtanen 6.00 15.00
104 Matt Hunwick 8.00 20.00
105 Tomas Popperle 8.00 20.00
106 Johnny Boychuk 10.00 25.00
107 Alexander Nikulin 8.00 20.00
108 Mark Mancari 8.00 20.00
109 Craig Weller 6.00 15.00
110 Jake Dowell 6.00 15.00
111 David Clarkson 10.00 25.00
112 Drew MacIntyre 8.00 20.00
113 Kris Versteeg 50.00 120.00
114 Greg Moore 8.00 20.00
115 Tomas Plihal 8.00 20.00
116 Mike Lundin 6.00 15.00
117 Rich Peverley 10.00 25.00
118 Cody Bass 8.00 20.00
119 Bobby Ryan 15.00 40.00
120 Ondrej Pavelec 12.00 30.00
121 Jack Johnson 8.00 20.00
122 Nicklas Bergfors 6.00 15.00
123 Erik Johnson 10.00 25.00
124 Bryan Little 8.00 20.00
125 Kris Russell 8.00 20.00
126 Matt Niskanen 10.00 25.00
127 Andrew Cogliano 40.00 80.00
128 Jonathan Bernier 15.00 40.00
129 Marc Staal 10.00 25.00
130 Nick Foligno 12.00 30.00
131 Peter Mueller 8.00 20.00
132 Brett Sterling 6.00 15.00
133 Petr Kalus 6.00 15.00
134 Rob Schremp 8.00 20.00
135 Andy Greene 8.00 20.00
136 Frans Nielsen 10.00 25.00
137 Martin Hanzal 8.00 20.00
138 Devin Setoguchi 10.00 25.00
139 Matt Smaby 6.00 15.00
140 James Sheppard 6.00 15.00
141 Kyle Chipchura 10.00 25.00
142 Ryan Parent 6.00 15.00
143 David Krejci 30.00 60.00
144 Lauri Tukonen 6.00 15.00
145 Anton Stralman 6.00 15.00
146 Tobias Enstrom 10.00 25.00
147 Brandon Dubinsky 12.00 30.00
148 Mason Raymond 10.00 25.00
149 Drew Miller 8.00 20.00
150 Curtis McElhinney 10.00 25.00
151 Ryan Callahan 12.00 30.00
152 Brian Elliott 12.00 30.00
153 Jonathan Sigalet 6.00 15.00
154 Ville Koistinen 6.00 15.00
155 Torrey Mitchell 8.00 20.00
156 David Perron 10.00 25.00
157 Jannik Hansen 8.00 20.00
158 Jaroslav Halak 60.00 120.00
159 Milan Lucic 30.00 80.00
160 Lukas Kaspar 6.00 15.00
161 Marc Methot 6.00 15.00
162 Tyler Weiman 8.00 20.00
163 Ryan Carter 6.00 15.00
164 Jared Boll 8.00 20.00
165 Jonas Hiller 12.00 30.00
166 Jaroslav Hlinka 8.00 20.00
167 Matt Ellis 8.00 20.00
168 Cory Murphy 6.00 15.00
169 Steve Wagner 6.00 15.00
170 Stefan Meyer 8.00 20.00
171 Daniel Carcillo 8.00 20.00
172 Tuukka Rask 25.00 60.00
173 David Jones 6.00 15.00
174 Tobias Stephan 8.00 20.00
175 Tom Gilbert 8.00 20.00
176 Cal Clutterbuck 10.00 25.00
177 Rod Pelley 6.00 15.00
178 Daniel Girardi 8.00 20.00
179 Chris Bourque 8.00 20.00
180 T.J. Hensick 8.00 20.00
181 Steve Downie 8.00 20.00
182 Jack Skille 8.00 20.00
183 Casey Borer 6.00 15.00
184 Sergei Kostitsyn 25.00 60.00
185 Patrick Kane 100.00 200.00
186 Sam Gagner 40.00 80.00
187 Nicklas Backstrom 80.00 200.00
188 Jiri Tlusty 10.00 25.00
189 Carey Price 200.00 350.00
190 Jonathan Toews 75.00 150.00

2007-08 The Cup Scripted Swatches

STATED PRINT RUN 25 SERIAL #'d SETS
SSGH Gordie Howe/10
SSAC Andrew Cogliano 20.00 50.00
SSAO Alexander Ovechkin 75.00 150.00
SSAR Alexander Radulov 25.00 60.00
SSAT Alex Tanguay 20.00 50.00
SSBC Bobby Clarke 30.00 80.00
SSBL Brian Leetch 30.00 80.00
SSBR Martin Brodeur 100.00 200.00
SSCN Cam Neely/10
SSCP Carey Price 100.00 200.00
SSCW Cam Ward 30.00 80.00
SSDC Dino Ciccarelli 30.00 80.00
SSDG Doug Gilmour 40.00 100.00
SSDH Dale Hawerchuk 40.00 100.00
SSDS Darryl Sittler/10
SSEL Patrik Elias 30.00 80.00
SSEM Evgeni Malkin 75.00 150.00
SSES Eric Staal 40.00 100.00
SSGA Sam Gagner 25.00 60.00
SSGP Gilbert Perreault/10
SSHA Dominik Hasek 30.00 80.00
SSHE Dany Heatley 30.00 80.00
SSHZ Henrik Zetterberg 60.00 120.00
SSIK Ilya Kovalchuk 30.00 80.00
SSJB Jonathan Bernier 30.00 80.00
SSJG Jean-Sebastien Giguere 30.00 80.00
SSJI Jarome Iginla 30.00 80.00
SSJM Joe Mullen 25.00 60.00
SSJO Jonathan Toews 125.00 250.00
SSJS Jordan Staal 30.00 80.00
SSJT Joe Thornton 40.00 100.00
SSLM Lanny McDonald 30.00 80.00
SSLR Larry Robinson 30.00 80.00
SSMB Mike Bossy/10
SSMD Marcel Dionne 40.00 100.00
SSMF Marc-Andre Fleury 50.00 120.00
SSMG Marian Gaborik 40.00 100.00
SSMH Marian Hossa 25.00 60.00
SSMI Milan Hejduk 25.00 60.00
SSML Mario Lemieux 125.00 250.00
SSMM Mark Messier 125.00 250.00
SSMN Markus Naslund 30.00 80.00
SSMO Mike Modano 50.00 125.00
SSMS Martin St. Louis 25.00 60.00
SSMT Marty Turco 30.00 80.00
SSNB Nicklas Backstrom 100.00 200.00
SSNL Nicklas Lidstrom 30.00 80.00
SSPB Patrice Bergeron 40.00 100.00
SSPK Patrick Kane 75.00 150.00
SSPM Peter Mueller 25.00 60.00
SSPR Patrick Roy 100.00 200.00
SSPS Paul Stastny 30.00 80.00
SSRB Ray Bourque 60.00 120.00
SSRG Ryan Getzlaf 30.00 80.00
SSRM Ryan Miller 25.00 60.00
SSRN Rick Nash 30.00 80.00
SSRO Luc Robitaille 30.00 80.00
SSRS Ryan Smyth 25.00 60.00
SSSA Borje Salming 30.00 80.00
SSSC Sidney Crosby 200.00 300.00
SSSD Shane Doan 20.00 50.00
SSSG Simon Gagne 30.00 80.00
SSSH Steve Shutt 30.00 80.00
SSSK Saku Koivu 30.00 80.00
SSST Peter Stastny 25.00 60.00
SSTL Jiri Tlusty 20.00 50.00
SSVL Vincent Lecavalier 25.00 60.00
SSWG Wayne Gretzky 350.00 600.00

2007-08 The Cup Signature Patches

STATED PRINT RUN 10-75
SPAK Anze Kopitar/75 25.00 60.00
SPAO Alexander Ovechkin/75 75.00 150.00
SPAT Alex Tanguay/75 12.00 30.00
SPBL Brian Leetch/75 20.00 50.00
SPBR Martin Brodeur/25 75.00 150.00
SPBS Borje Salming/75 20.00 50.00
SPCD Chris Drury/75 15.00 40.00
SPCH Jonathan Cheechoo/75 20.00 50.00
SPCN Cam Neely/10
SPCP Carey Price/75 200.00 350.00
SPCW Cam Ward/75 20.00 50.00
SPDC Dino Ciccarelli/75 20.00 50.00
SPDH Dominik Hasek/25 75.00 150.00
SPEM Evgeni Malkin/75 15.00 40.00
SPES Eric Staal/75 25.00 60.00
SPGA Sam Gagner/75 25.00 60.00
SPGF Grant Fuhr/10
SPGP Gilbert Perreault/10
SPHA Dale Hawerchuk/75 25.00 60.00
SPHE Dany Heatley/75 20.00 50.00
SPIK Ilya Kovalchuk/75 20.00 50.00
SPJA Jason Arnott/75 15.00 40.00
SPJB Jonathan Bernier/75 20.00 50.00
SPJG Jean-Sebastien Giguere/75 20.00 50.00
SPJI Jarome Iginla/75 20.00 50.00
SPJM Joe Mullen/75 15.00 40.00
SPJS Jordan Staal/75 20.00 50.00
SPJT Joe Thornton/25 30.00 80.00
SPKE Patrick Kane/75 150.00 250.00
SPLM Lanny McDonald/75 20.00 50.00
SPLR Luc Robitaille/75 20.00 50.00
SPMB Mike Bossy/10
SPMG Marian Gaborik/75 30.00 80.00
SPMH Milan Hejduk/75 15.00 40.00
SPML Mario Lemieux/25 100.00 200.00
SPMM Mike Modano/75 25.00 60.00
SPMN Markus Naslund/75 20.00 50.00
SPMS Martin St. Louis/75 20.00 50.00
SPMT Marty Turco/75 20.00 50.00
SPNB Nicklas Backstrom/75 50.00 100.00
SPNL Nicklas Lidstrom/75 20.00 50.00
SPPB Patrice Bergeron/75 40.00 80.00
SPPE Patrik Elias/75 15.00 40.00
SPPK Phil Kessel/75 25.00 60.00
SPPM Peter Mueller/75 15.00 40.00
SPPR Patrick Roy/25 100.00 200.00
SPPS Peter Stastny/75 15.00 40.00
SPRB Ray Bourque/25 25.00 60.00
SPRM Ryan Miller/75 20.00 50.00
SPRN Rick Nash/75 20.00 50.00
SPSC Sidney Crosby/75 150.00 300.00
SPSD Shane Doan/75 15.00 40.00
SPSG Simon Gagne/75 15.00 40.00
SPSK Saku Koivu/75 25.00 60.00
SPST Paul Stastny/75 15.00 40.00
SPTL Jiri Tlusty/75 15.00 40.00
SPTO Jonathan Toews/75 150.00 250.00
SPTV Tomas Vokoun/75 15.00 40.00
SPVL Vincent Lecavalier/75 15.00 40.00

2007-08 The Cup Stanley Cup Signatures

STATED PRINT RUN 25 SERIAL #'d SETS
SCAM Andy McDonald 25.00 60.00
SCBC Bobby Clarke 30.00 80.00
SCBD Bill Dineen 25.00 60.00
SCBG Brian Gionta 25.00 60.00
SCBH Bobby Hull 40.00 100.00
SCBL Brian Leetch 30.00 80.00
SCBN Bob Nystrom 20.00 50.00
SCBO Mike Bossy 30.00 80.00

P Bernie Parent 40.00 100.00
S Brent Sutter 20.00 50.00
D Chris Drury 25.00 60.00
P Corey Perry
B Dan Boyle 25.00 60.00
P Denis Potvin 30.00 80.00
L Patrik Elias 20.00 50.00
M1 Frank Mahovlich 25.00 60.00
M2 Frank Mahovlich 25.00 60.00
F Grant Fuhr 25.00 60.00
H Gordie Howe 100.00 200.00
L Guy Lafleur 60.00 120.00
L Hakan Loob 25.00 60.00
A Jason Arnott 25.00 60.00
B Johnny Bucyk 30.00 80.00
G Jean-Sebastien Giguere 25.00 60.00
K Jari Kurri 30.00 80.00
W Justin Williams 15.00 40.00
D Kris Draper 20.00 50.00
M Lanny McDonald 30.00 80.00
R Larry Robinson 25.00 60.00
U Luc Robitaille 15.00 40.00
B Martin Brodeur 125.00 250.00
E Mark Messier 100.00 200.00
L Mario Lemieux 100.00 200.00
M Mark Messier 100.00 200.00
O Mike Modano 50.00 125.00
B Neal Broten 20.00 50.00
R Bobby Orr 200.00 400.00
E Phil Esposito 25.00 60.00
R1 Patrick Roy 125.00 250.00
R2 Patrick Roy 125.00 250.00
E Ron Ellis 20.00 50.00
G Ryan Getzlaf 25.00 60.00
A Denis Savard 20.00 50.00
B Scotty Bowman 25.00 60.00
C Scotty Bowman 25.00 60.00
G Scott Gomez
M Stan Mikita 40.00 100.00
U Duane Sutter 20.00 50.00
G Wayne Gretzky 300.00 500.00

2008-09 The Cup

0 STATED PRINT RUN 249
78 ROOKIE AU PRINT RUN 199
144 ROOK.JSY AU PRINT RUN 249
-150 ROOK.JSY AU PRINT RUN 99
ayne Gretzky 20.00 50.00
ncent Lecavalier 3.00 8.00
ny Esposito 4.00 10.00
omas Vanek 4.00 10.00
emu Selanne 8.00 20.00
ian Leetch 4.00 10.00
dney Crosby 15.00 40.00
aku Koivu 4.00 10.00
an Miller 4.00 10.00
Ryan Getzlaf 6.00 15.00
Ron Hextall 6.00 15.00
Roberto Luongo 5.00 12.00
Rick Nash 4.00 10.00
Ray Bourque 6.00 15.00
Phil Esposito 6.00 15.00
Brendan Shanahan 5.00 12.00
Pavel Datsyuk 5.00 12.00
Paul Stastny 4.00 10.00
Paul Kariya 5.00 12.00
Mats Sundin 4.00 10.00
Patrick Roy 10.00 25.00
Patrick Kane 8.00 20.00
Nicklas Lidstrom 4.00 10.00
Mike Richards 4.00 10.00
Marty Turco 4.00 10.00
Martin St. Louis 4.00 10.00
Martin Brodeur 8.00 20.00
Markus Naslund 3.00 8.00
Mark Messier 5.00 12.00
Mario Lemieux 12.00 30.00
Marian Gaborik 5.00 12.00
Marc-Andre Fleury 6.00 15.00
Luc Robitaille 4.00 10.00
Lanny McDonald 4.00 10.00
Jonathan Toews 10.00 25.00
Joe Thornton 5.00 12.00
Joe Sakic 6.00 15.00
Joe Mullen 3.00 8.00
Jean Beliveau 4.00 10.00
Jason Spezza 4.00 10.00
Jarome Iginla 4.00 10.00
Jari Kurri 4.00 10.00
Ilya Kovalchuk 4.00 10.00
Henrik Zetterberg 5.00 12.00
Guy Lafleur 5.00 12.00
Grant Fuhr 4.00 10.00
Gordie Howe 10.00 25.00
Frank Mahovlich 4.00 10.00
Evgeni Malkin 12.00 30.00
Eric Staal 5.00 12.00
Dominik Hasek 5.00 12.00
Dino Ciccarelli 4.00 10.00
Dany Heatley 4.00 10.00
Dale Hawerchuk 6.00 15.00
Carey Price 15.00 40.00
Cam Neely 4.00 10.00
Bobby Orr 12.00 30.00
Bobby Hull 6.00 15.00
Alexander Ovechkin 15.00 40.00
Al MacInnis 4.00 10.00
Nathan Oystrick AU RC 10.00 25.00
Marc-Andre Gragnani AU RC 8.00 20.00
Derek Dorsett AU RC 12.00 30.00
Maxsim Mayorov AU RC 10.00 25.00
Wayne Simmonds AU RC 30.00 80.00
Danny Taylor AU RC 8.00 20.00
Tim Ramholt AU RC 8.00 20.00
Mike Iggulden AU RC 8.00 20.00
Trevor Smith AU RC 8.00 20.00
Dane Byers AU RC 8.00 20.00
Dustin Jeffrey AU RC 10.00 25.00
Tom Cavanagh AU RC 8.00 20.00
Derek Joslin AU RC 8.00 20.00
Paul Szczechura AU RC 10.00 25.00
Jonas Frogren AU RC 6.00 15.00
John Mitchell AU RC 8.00 20.00
Simeon Varlamov AU RC 60.00 100.00
Oskar Osala AU RC 10.00 25.00
Andrew Ebbett JSY AU RC 10.00 25.00
B.Mikkelson JSY AU RC 10.00 25.00
81 Zach Bogosian JSY AU RC 15.00 40.00
82 Boris Valabik JSY AU RC 15.00 40.00
83 Nathan Gerbe JSY AU RC 15.00 40.00
84 Tim Kennedy JSY AU RC 15.00 40.00
85 Zach Boychuk JSY AU RC 15.00 40.00
86 Brandon Sutter JSY AU RC 15.00 40.00
87 Chris Stewart JSY AU RC 15.00 40.00
88 Dan LaCosta JSY AU RC 15.00 40.00
89 Steve Mason JSY AU RC 30.00 80.00
90 Tom Sestito JSY AU RC 15.00 40.00
91 Nikita Filatov JSY AU RC 15.00 40.00
92 Jakub Voracek JSY AU RC 60.00 100.00
93 Adam Pineault JSY AU RC 12.00 30.00
94 Derick Brassard JSY AU RC 12.00 30.00
95 Mark Fistric JSY AU RC 12.00 30.00
96 Fabian Brunnstrom JSY AU RC 12.00 30.00
97 James Neal JSY AU RC 30.00 80.00
98 J.Abdelkader JSY AU RC 30.00 60.00
99 J.Ericsson JSY AU RC 15.00 40.00
100 Mattias Ritola JSY AU RC 12.00 30.00
101 Darren Helm JSY AU RC 15.00 40.00
102 Michael Frolik JSY AU RC 15.00 40.00
103 Shawn Matthias JSY AU RC 15.00 40.00
104 Tyler Plante JSY AU RC 12.00 30.00
105 Michal Repik JSY AU RC 15.00 40.00
106 K.McArdle JSY AU RC 12.00 30.00
107 Brian Boyle JSY AU RC 12.00 30.00
108 Oscar Moller JSY AU RC 12.00 30.00
109 Erik Ersberg JSY AU RC 12.00 30.00
110 Teddy Purcell JSY AU RC 20.00 50.00
111 Colton Gillies JSY AU RC 12.00 30.00
112 Max Pacioretty JSY AU RC 150.00 250.00
113 Matt D'Agostini JSY AU RC 12.00 30.00
114 Ben Maxwell JSY AU RC 15.00 40.00
115 Patric Hornqvist JSY AU RC 40.00 80.00
116 Ryan Jones JSY AU RC 15.00 40.00
117 M.Halischuk JSY AU RC 10.00 25.00
118 Petr Vrana JSY AU RC 10.00 25.00
119 Josh Bailey JSY AU RC 20.00 50.00
120 Kyle Okposo JSY AU RC 40.00 80.00
121 Trevor Lewis JSY AU RC 15.00 40.00
122 Lauri Korpikoski JSY AU RC 10.00 25.00
123 Brian Lee JSY AU RC 12.00 30.00
124 Ilya Zubov JSY AU RC 12.00 30.00
125 Claude Giroux JSY AU RC 200.00 350.00
126 Luca Sbisa JSY AU RC 10.00 25.00
127 Andreas Nodl JSY AU RC 10.00 25.00
128 Viktor Tikhonov JSY AU RC 12.00 30.00
129 Kevin Porter JSY AU RC 12.00 30.00
130 Mikkel Boedker JSY AU RC 20.00 50.00
131 Alex Goligoski JSY AU RC 20.00 50.00
132 Jonathan Filewich JSY AU RC 12.00 30.00
133 Ryan Stone JSY AU RC 10.00 25.00
134 Jamie McGinn JSY AU RC 15.00 40.00
135 Alex Pietrangelo JSY AU RC 75.00 125.00
136 Patrik Berglund JSY AU RC 12.00 30.00
137 Ben Bishop JSY AU RC 30.00 80.00
138 T.J. Oshie JSY AU RC 40.00 80.00
139 Vladimir Mihalik JSY AU RC 10.00 25.00
140 Ty Wishart JSY AU RC 12.00 30.00
141 Robbie Earl JSY AU RC 10.00 25.00
142 Nikolai Kulemin JSY AU RC 15.00 40.00
143 Cory Schneider JSY AU RC 60.00 120.00
144 Karl Alzner JSY AU RC 10.00 25.00
145 J.Pogge JSY AU RC/99 25.00 60.00
146 D.Doughty JSY AU RC/99 300.00 500.00
147 B.Wheeler JSY AU RC/99 100.00 200.00
148 L.Schenn JSY AU RC/99 75.00 150.00
149 Kyle Turris JSY AU RC/99 125.00 200.00
150 S.Stamkos JSY AU RC/99 1500.00 2500.00

2008-09 The Cup Gold

*1-60 VETS/25: .8X TO 2X BASIC CARDS
COMMON ROOKIE (61-150) 8.00 20.00
ROOKIE SEMISTARS/25 10.00 25.00
ROOKIE UNL.STARS/25 12.00 30.00
STATED PRINT RUN 25 SER.#'d SETS
63 Derek Dorsett 12.00 30.00
64 Maxsim Mayorov 10.00 25.00
65 Wayne Simmonds 15.00 40.00
71 Dustin Jeffrey 10.00 25.00
77 Simeon Varlamov 150.00 250.00
78 Oskar Osala 10.00 25.00
83 Nathan Gerbe 12.00 30.00
87 Chris Stewart 12.00 30.00
89 Steve Mason 50.00 120.00
91 Nikita Filatov 25.00 60.00
92 Jakub Voracek 25.00 60.00
94 Derick Brassard 10.00 25.00
97 James Neal 20.00 50.00
98 Justin Abdelkader 25.00 50.00
99 Jonathan Ericsson 12.00 30.00
101 Darren Helm 8.00 20.00
102 Michael Frolik 12.00 30.00
110 Teddy Purcell 15.00 40.00
112 Max Pacioretty 50.00 125.00
113 Matt D'Agostini 10.00 25.00
114 Ben Maxwell 12.00 30.00
116 Ryan Jones 12.00 30.00
119 Josh Bailey 15.00 40.00
120 Kyle Okposo 12.00 30.00
121 Trevor Lewis 12.00 30.00
125 Claude Giroux 125.00 200.00
126 Luca Sbisa 8.00 20.00
130 Mikkel Boedker 15.00 40.00
131 Alex Goligoski 15.00 40.00
135 Alex Pietrangelo 15.00 40.00
136 Patrik Berglund 10.00 25.00
137 Ben Bishop 20.00 50.00
138 T.J. Oshie 25.00 60.00
143 Cory Schneider 30.00 80.00
144 Karl Alzner 8.00 20.00
145 Justin Pogge 12.00 30.00
146 Drew Doughty 40.00 80.00
147 Blake Wheeler 60.00 120.00
148 Luke Schenn 40.00 100.00
149 Kyle Turris 30.00 80.00
150 Steven Stamkos 250.00 400.00

2008-09 The Cup Gold Rainbow

61-78 AUTO PRINT RUN 15-77
79-150 PATCH AU PRINT RUN 2-96
61 Nathan Oystrick AU/47 12.00 30.00
62 Marc-Andre Gragnani AU/17 15.00 30.00
63 Derek Dorsett AU/15
64 Maxsim Mayorov AU/43 10.00 25.00
65 Wayne Simmonds AU/57 15.00 40.00
66 Danny Taylor AU/46 8.00 20.00
67 Tim Ramholt AU/47 12.00 30.00
68 Mike Iggulden AU/46 8.00 20.00
69 Trevor Smith AU/77 8.00 20.00
70 Dane Byers AU/54 8.00 20.00
71 Dustin Jeffrey AU/42 10.00 25.00
72 Tom Cavanagh AU/47 8.00 20.00
73 Derek Joslin AU/65 8.00 20.00
74 Paul Szczechura AU/38 10.00 25.00
75 Jonas Frogren AU/24 10.00 25.00
76 John Mitchell AU/39 10.00 25.00
77 Simeon Varlamov AU/40 40.00 100.00
78 Oskar Osala AU/48 10.00 25.00
79 Andrew Ebbett PATCH AU/48 6.00 15.00
80 Brendan Mikkelson PATCH AU/60 6.00 15.00
81 Zach Bogosian PATCH AU/4
82 Boris Valabik PATCH AU/48 30.00 80.00
83 Nathan Gerbe PATCH AU/42 25.00 60.00
84 Tim Kennedy PATCH AU/58 25.00 60.00
85 Zach Boychuk PATCH AU/23 30.00 80.00
86 Brandon Sutter PATCH AU/16 40.00 80.00
87 Chris Stewart PATCH AU/42 25.00 60.00
88 Dan LaCosta PATCH AU/29 20.00 50.00
89 Steve Mason PATCH AU/30 40.00 100.00
90 Tom Sestito PATCH AU/43 15.00 40.00
91 Nikita Filatov PATCH AU/28 25.00 60.00
92 J.Voracek PATCH AU/93 50.00 100.00
93 Adam Pineault PATCH AU/41 20.00 50.00
94 Derick Brassard PATCH AU/16
95 Mark Fistric PATCH AU/28 25.00 60.00
96 F.Brunnstrom PATCH AU/96 15.00 40.00
97 James Neal PATCH AU/18
99 J.Ericsson PATCH AU/52 20.00 50.00
100 M.Ritola PATCH AU/42 8.00 20.00
101 Darren Helm PATCH AU/43 30.00 80.00
102 M.Frolik PATCH AU/67 10.00 25.00
103 S.Matthias PATCH AU/41 15.00 40.00
104 Tyler Plante PATCH AU/35 25.00 60.00
105 Michal Repik PATCH AU/32 25.00 60.00
106 K.McArdle PATCH AU/71 10.00 25.00
107 Brian Boyle PATCH AU/22 20.00 50.00
108 Oscar Moller PATCH AU/51 20.00 50.00
109 Erik Ersberg PATCH AU/31 25.00 60.00
110 T.Purcell PATCH AU/54 25.00 60.00
111 Colton Gillies PATCH AU/18 20.00 40.00
112 M.Pacioretty PATCH AU/67 175.00 300.00
113 M.D'Agostini PATCH AU/36 25.00 60.00
114 Ben Maxwell PATCH AU/80 10.00 25.00
115 P.Hornqvist PATCH AU/27 25.00 60.00
116 Ryan Jones PATCH AU/28 20.00 50.00
117 M.Halischuk PATCH AU/63 20.00 50.00
118 Petr Vrana PATCH AU/22 20.00 50.00
119 Josh Bailey PATCH AU/12
120 Kyle Okposo PATCH AU/21 40.00 100.00
121 Trevor Lewis PATCH AU/61 10.00 25.00
122 L.Korpikoski PATCH AU/60 20.00 50.00
123 Brian Lee PATCH AU/55 15.00 40.00
124 Ilya Zubov PATCH AU/53 10.00 25.00
125 C.Giroux PATCH AU/28 300.00 450.00
126 Luca Sbisa PATCH AU/47 20.00 50.00
127 A.Nodl PATCH AU/41 12.00 30.00
128 V.Tikhonov PATCH AU/41 12.00 30.00
129 K.Porter PATCH AU/23 20.00 50.00
130 M.Boedker PATCH AU/89 15.00 40.00
131 A.Goligoski PATCH AU/67 12.00 30.00
132 J.Filewich PATCH AU/34 20.00 50.00
133 Ryan Stone PATCH AU/33 12.00 30.00
134 J.McGinn PATCH AU/64 20.00 50.00
135 A.Pietrangelo PATCH AU/52 30.00 80.00
136 P.Berglund PATCH AU/58 25.00 60.00
137 Ben Bishop PATCH AU/30 40.00 100.00
138 T.J. Oshie PATCH AU/74 30.00 80.00
139 V.Mihalik PATCH AU/56
140 Ty Wishart PATCH AU/3
141 Robbie Earl PATCH AU/52 6.00 15.00
142 N.Kulemin PATCH AU/41 20.00 50.00
143 C.Schneider PATCH AU/35 60.00 125.00
144 Karl Alzner PATCH AU/27
145 Justin Pogge PATCH AU/29 25.00 60.00
146 Drew Doughty PATCH AU/8
147 B.Wheeler PATCH AU/26 125.00 200.00
148 Luke Schenn PATCH AU/2
149 Kyle Turris PATCH AU/91 60.00 120.00
150 S.Stamkos PATCH AU/91 1000.00 1500.00

2008-09 The Cup Platinum Jerseys

STATED PRINT RUN 25 SER.#'d SETS
1 Wayne Gretzky 60.00 150.00
2 Vincent Lecavalier 10.00 25.00
3 Tony Esposito 12.00 30.00
4 Thomas Vanek 12.00 30.00
5 Teemu Selanne 25.00 60.00
6 Brian Leetch 12.00 30.00
7 Sidney Crosby 50.00 125.00
8 Saku Koivu 12.00 30.00
9 Ryan Miller 12.00 30.00
10 Ryan Getzlaf 20.00 50.00
11 Ron Hextall 20.00 50.00
12 Roberto Luongo 12.00 30.00
13 Rick Nash 12.00 30.00
14 Ray Bourque 20.00 50.00
15 Phil Esposito 20.00 50.00
16 Brendan Shanahan 15.00 40.00
17 Pavel Datsyuk 15.00 40.00
18 Paul Stastny 12.00 30.00
19 Paul Kariya 15.00 40.00
20 Mats Sundin 12.00 30.00
21 Patrick Roy 30.00 80.00
22 Patrick Kane 25.00 60.00
23 Nicklas Lidstrom 12.00 30.00
24 Mike Richards 12.00 30.00
25 Marty Turco 12.00 30.00
26 Martin St. Louis 12.00 30.00
27 Martin Brodeur 25.00 60.00
28 Markus Naslund 10.00 25.00
29 Mark Messier 15.00 40.00
30 Mario Lemieux 25.00 60.00
31 Marian Gaborik 15.00 40.00
32 Marc-Andre Fleury 20.00 50.00
33 Luc Robitaille 12.00 30.00
34 Lanny McDonald 12.00 30.00
35 Jonathan Toews 30.00 80.00
36 Joe Thornton 15.00 40.00
37 Joe Sakic 20.00 50.00
38 Joe Mullen 10.00 25.00
39 Jean Beliveau 12.00 30.00
40 Jason Spezza 12.00 30.00
41 Jarome Iginla 12.00 30.00
42 Jari Kurri 12.00 30.00
43 Ilya Kovalchuk 12.00 30.00
44 Henrik Zetterberg 15.00 40.00
45 Guy Lafleur 15.00 40.00
46 Grant Fuhr 12.00 30.00
47 Gordie Howe 30.00 80.00
48 Frank Mahovlich 12.00 30.00
49 Evgeni Malkin 40.00 100.00
50 Eric Staal 15.00 40.00
51 Dominik Hasek 15.00 40.00
52 Dino Ciccarelli 12.00 30.00
53 Dany Heatley 12.00 30.00
54 Dale Hawerchuk 15.00 40.00
55 Carey Price 50.00 120.00
56 Cam Neely 12.00 30.00
58 Bobby Hull 20.00 50.00
59 Alexander Ovechkin 25.00 60.00
60 Al MacInnis 12.00 30.00

2008-09 The Cup 20 Years of Greatness

COMMON GRETZKY 600.00 900.00

2008-09 The Cup Auto Draft Boards

STATED PRINT RUN 50 SER.#'d SETS
DBAC Andrew Cogliano 20.00 50.00
DBAK Anze Kopitar 40.00 100.00
DBAP Alex Pietrangelo 30.00 80.00
DBBE Jonathan Bernier 30.00 80.00
DBBO Zach Boychuk 25.00 60.00
DBBR Bobby Ryan 50.00 100.00
DBBS Brandon Sutter 30.00 80.00
DBCG Colton Gillies 20.00 50.00
DBCP Carey Price 175.00 300.00
DBCS Chris Stewart 30.00 80.00
DBDB Derick Brassard 50.00 120.00
DBDD Drew Doughty 125.00 250.00
DBDS Devin Setoguchi 40.00 100.00
DBFO Nick Foligno 40.00 80.00
DBGI Claude Giroux 175.00 300.00
DBJB Josh Bailey 30.00 80.00
DBJS Jordan Staal 40.00 100.00
DBJT Jonathan Toews 200.00 350.00
DBJV Jakub Voracek 40.00 100.00
DBKA Karl Alzner 15.00 40.00
DBKE Phil Kessel 60.00 120.00
DBKM Kenndal McArdle 20.00 50.00
DBKO Kyle Okposo 60.00 120.00
DBKT Kyle Turris 125.00 200.00
DBLE Brian Lee 20.00 50.00
DBLS Luke Schenn 75.00 150.00
DBLW Trevor Lewis 25.00 60.00
DBMB Mikkel Boedker 30.00 80.00
DBMF Michael Frolik
DBMH Martin Hanzal
DBMN Matt Niskanen
DBMP Max Pacioretty 100.00 175.00
DBMS Marc Staal 25.00 60.00
DBNB Nicklas Backstrom 100.00 200.00
DBNF Nikita Filatov 75.00 150.00
DBNI Nicklas Bergfors 40.00 100.00
DBPB Patrik Berglund 20.00 50.00
DBPK Patrick Kane 175.00 300.00
DBPM Peter Mueller 20.00 50.00
DBSB Luca Sbisa 15.00 40.00
DBSC Sidney Crosby 750.00 1000.00
DBSD Steve Downie 40.00 80.00
DBSG Sam Gagner 75.00 150.00
DBSH James Sheppard 15.00 40.00
DBSS Steven Stamkos 500.00 900.00
DBSV Simeon Varlamov 75.00 150.00
DBTO T.J. Oshie 75.00 150.00
DBTR Tuukka Rask 75.00 175.00
DBTW Ty Wishart 20.00 50.00
DBVT Viktor Tikhonov 20.00 50.00
DBZB Zach Bogosian 60.00 120.00

2008-09 The Cup Chirography

STATED PRINT RUN 50 SER.#'d SETS
CCAO Alexander Ovechkin 40.00 100.00
CCBH Bobby Hull 20.00 50.00
CCBO Bobby Orr 75.00 150.00
CCBR Martin Brodeur 50.00 100.00
CCEM Evgeni Malkin 40.00 100.00
CCFM Frank Mahovlich 15.00 40.00
CCGH Gordie Howe 50.00 100.00
CCGP Gilbert Perreault 12.00 30.00
CCIK Ilya Kovalchuk 12.00 30.00
CCJB Jean Beliveau 25.00 50.00
CCJI Jarome Iginla 12.00 30.00
CCJT Joe Thornton 15.00 40.00
CCMB Mike Bossy 12.00 30.00
CCML Mario Lemieux 50.00 100.00
CCMM Mark Messier 50.00 100.00
CCPE Phil Esposito 20.00 50.00
CCPR Patrick Roy 75.00 150.00
CCRB Ray Bourque 20.00 50.00
CCRH Ron Hextall 20.00 50.00
CCRO Larry Robinson 12.00 30.00
CCSC Sidney Crosby 75.00 150.00
CCVL Vincent Lecavalier 10.00 25.00
CCWG Wayne Gretzky 150.00 250.00

2008-09 The Cup Emblems of Endorsement

STATED PRINT RUN 15 SER.#'d SETS
EEJC Jeff Carter 60.00 120.00
EEJS Jordan Staal 30.00 60.00
EEPB Patrice Bergeron 30.00 60.00
EEAK Anze Kopitar 40.00 80.00
EEAO Adam Oates 30.00 60.00
EEAP Alex Pietrangelo 25.00 50.00
EEBE Patrik Berglund 30.00 60.00
EEBL Brian Leetch 25.00 50.00
EEBO Mikkel Boedker 25.00 50.00
EEBS Brandon Sutter 25.00 50.00
EECG Colton Gillies 30.00 60.00
EECN Cam Neely
EECP Carey Price 60.00 120.00
EECS Cory Schneider 20.00 40.00
EECW Cam Ward 20.00 50.00
EEDB Derick Brassard 30.00 80.00
EEDC Dino Ciccarelli 30.00 60.00
EEDD Drew Doughty 100.00 200.00
EEDG Doug Gilmour 50.00 100.00
EEDH Dale Hawerchuk 30.00 80.00
EEEM Evgeni Malkin 60.00 120.00
EEES Eric Staal 30.00 60.00
EEFB Fabian Brunnstrom 25.00 50.00
EEFR Michael Frolik 15.00 40.00
EEGA Simon Gagne 30.00 60.00
EEGH Gordie Howe 125.00 200.00
EEGK Marian Gaborik 30.00 60.00
EEHA Dominik Hasek 60.00 120.00
EEHE Dany Heatley 25.00 50.00
EEHL Henrik Lundqvist 50.00 100.00
EEHZ Henrik Zetterberg 75.00 150.00
EEIK Ilya Kovalchuk 30.00 80.00
EEJI Jarome Iginla 40.00 100.00
EEJN James Neal 30.00 60.00
EEJP Jean-Pierre Dumont 25.00 50.00
EEJT Joe Thornton 40.00 80.00
EEKO Kyle Okposo 40.00 80.00
EEKT Kyle Turris 50.00 100.00
EELE Mario Lemieux 125.00 250.00
EELM Lanny McDonald 30.00 60.00
EELS Luke Schenn 50.00 100.00
EEMB Martin Brodeur 90.00 150.00
EEMF Marc-Andre Fleury 50.00 100.00
EEMG Mike Green 40.00 80.00
EEMI Milan Hejduk 30.00 60.00
EEMM Mark Messier 90.00 150.00
EEMN Markus Naslund 25.00 50.00
EEMO Mike Modano 40.00 80.00
EEMS Martin St. Louis 30.00 60.00
EEMT Marty Turco 30.00 60.00
EENB Nicklas Backstrom 40.00 80.00
EENK Nikolai Kulemin 25.00 50.00
EENL Nicklas Lidstrom 50.00 100.00
EEOS T.J. Oshie 50.00 100.00
EEPE Corey Perry 40.00 80.00
EEPK Patrick Kane 50.00 100.00
EEPM Peter Mueller 30.00 60.00
EEPR Patrick Roy 125.00 200.00
EERB Ray Bourque 60.00 120.00
EERG Ryan Getzlaf
EERM Ryan Miller 30.00 80.00
EERN Rick Nash 20.00 50.00
EERO Luc Robitaille 40.00 80.00
EESC Sidney Crosby 300.00 500.00
EESG Sam Gagner 30.00 60.00
EESP Peter Stastny 40.00 80.00
EESS Steven Stamkos 350.00 600.00
EETO Jonathan Toews 40.00 80.00
EEVL Vincent Lecavalier 40.00 80.00
EEVO Tomas Vokoun 30.00 60.00
EEWG Wayne Gretzky 500.00 800.00
EEZA Zach Boychuk 20.00 40.00
EEZB Zach Bogosian 25.00 50.00

2008-09 The Cup Enshrinements

STATED PRINT RUN 50 SER.#'d SETS
CEAB Andy Bathgate 12.00 30.00
CEAO Alexander Ovechkin 60.00 120.00
CEBB Butch Bouchard 15.00 40.00
CEBC Bobby Clarke 12.00 30.00
CEBH Bobby Hull 20.00 50.00
CEBL Brian Leetch 12.00 30.00
CEBO Bobby Orr 75.00 150.00
CEBS Borje Salming 12.00 30.00
CEBU Johnny Bucyk 12.00 30.00
CECN Cam Neely 25.00 50.00
CEDH Dany Heatley 12.00 30.00
CEEM Evgeni Malkin 40.00 100.00
CEES Eric Staal 15.00 40.00
CEFM Frank Mahovlich 12.00 30.00
CEGF Grant Fuhr 12.00 30.00
CEGH Gordie Howe 60.00 120.00
CEGP Gilbert Perreault 12.00 30.00
CEHA Dominik Hasek 15.00 40.00
CEHZ Henrik Zetterberg 15.00 40.00
CEJB Jean Beliveau 25.00 50.00
CEJI Jarome Iginla 12.00 30.00
CEJK Jari Kurri 15.00 40.00
CEJO Johnny Bower 15.00 40.00
CEJT Joe Thornton 15.00 40.00
CELR Larry Robinson 12.00 30.00
CEMB Martin Brodeur 50.00 100.00
CEML Mario Lemieux 60.00 120.00
CEMM Mark Messier 50.00 100.00
CEMO Mike Modano 20.00 50.00
CENL Nicklas Lidstrom 12.00 30.00
CEPE Phil Esposito 20.00 50.00
CEPH Dion Phaneuf 12.00 30.00
CEPR Patrick Roy 50.00 100.00
CERB Ray Bourque 20.00 50.00
CERL Rod Langway 10.00 25.00
CERN Rick Nash 12.00 30.00
CESC Sidney Crosby 75.00 150.00
CETE Tony Esposito 12.00 30.00
CEWG Wayne Gretzky 150.00 250.00

2008-09 The Cup Enshrinements Dual

STATED PRINT RUN 25 SER.#'d SETS
CE2BH Beliveau/Howe 75.00 125.00
CE2BL Lindsay/Bouchard 25.00 60.00
CE2BM Bucyk/Mahovlich 20.00 50.00
CE2BT Turco/Brodeur 40.00 100.00
CE2HM Hull/Mikita 30.00 80.00
CE2HN Nash/Heatley 20.00 50.00
CE2IS Iginla/E.Staal 25.00 60.00
CE2KH Kurri/Hawerchuk 25.00 60.00
CE2KM Kovalchuk/Malkin 60.00 150.00
CE2LB B.Leetch/A.Bathgate 20.00 50.00
CE2LG Langway/Gillies 20.00 50.00
CE2NB Lidstrom/Salming 20.00 50.00
CE2PB Bowman/Potvin 20.00 50.00
CE2RD Roy/Duff 50.00 120.00
CE2SM Savard/Mullen 25.00 60.00

2008-09 The Cup Foundations Jerseys

STATED PRINT RUN 25 SER.#'d SETS
CFAK Anze Kopitar 12.00 30.00
CFAO Adam Oates 8.00 20.00
CFBC Bobby Clarke
CFBH Bobby Hull 12.00 30.00
CFBK Mikkel Boedker 10.00 25.00
CFBL Brian Leetch 8.00 20.00
CFBM Ben Maxwell
CFBS Brandon Sutter 8.00 20.00
CFBT Bryan Trottier 10.00 25.00
CFBU Johnny Bucyk 8.00 20.00
CFBW Blake Wheeler 20.00 50.00
CFCG Colton Gillies 6.00 15.00
CFCS Cory Schneider 15.00 40.00
CFDB Derick Brassard 6.00 15.00
CFDD Drew Doughty 20.00 50.00
CFDE Denis Savard 10.00 25.00
CFEM Evgeni Malkin 25.00 60.00
CFEP Phil Esposito 12.00 30.00
CFES Eric Staal 10.00 25.00
CFFB Fabian Brunnstrom 6.00 15.00
CFGF Grant Fuhr 8.00 20.00
CFGH Gordie Howe 20.00 50.00
CFHA Dominik Hasek 10.00 25.00
CFHE Dany Heatley 8.00 20.00
CFHL Henrik Lundqvist 10.00 25.00
CFHO Marian Hossa 6.00 15.00
CFHZ Henrik Zetterberg
CFIK Ilya Kovalchuk 8.00 20.00
CFJI Jarome Iginla 8.00 20.00
CFJK Carey Price 30.00 80.00
CFJN James Neal 15.00 40.00
CFJO Joe Sakic 12.00 30.00
CFJP Jean-Pierre Dumont 5.00 12.00
CFJS Jason Spezza 8.00 20.00
CFJT Joe Thornton 10.00 25.00
CFJV Jakub Voracek 15.00 40.00
CFKA Karl Alzner 5.00 12.00
CFKL Kari Lehtonen 6.00 15.00
CFKO Kyle Okposo 8.00 20.00
CFKT Kyle Turris 12.00 30.00
CFKV Alex Kovalev 6.00 15.00
CFLS Luke Schenn 10.00 25.00
CFMB Martin Brodeur 15.00 40.00
CFMF Marc-Andre Fleury 15.00 40.00
CFMG Sam Gagner 6.00 15.00
CFMH Milan Hejduk 6.00 15.00
CFMK Nicklas Backstrom 12.00 30.00
CFML Mario Lemieux 25.00 60.00
CFMM Mark Messier 10.00 25.00
CFMO Mike Modano 12.00 30.00
CFMR Mike Richards 8.00 20.00
CFMS Martin St. Louis 8.00 20.00
CFMT Marty Turco 8.00 20.00
CFNF Nikita Filatov 8.00 20.00
CFNL Nicklas Lidstrom 8.00 20.00
CFOV Alexander Ovechkin 30.00 80.00
CFPB Patrice Bergeron 10.00 25.00
CFPD Pavel Datsyuk 10.00 25.00
CFPH Dion Phaneuf 8.00 20.00
CFPK Paul Kariya 10.00 25.00
CFPR Patrick Roy 20.00 50.00
CFPS Paul Stastny 8.00 20.00
CFRB Ray Bourque 12.00 30.00
CFRL Roberto Luongo 10.00 25.00
CFRN Rick Nash 8.00 20.00
CFRS Ryan Smyth 6.00 15.00
CFRV Rogie Vachon 10.00 25.00
CFSC Sidney Crosby 60.00 120.00
CFSD Shane Doan 6.00 15.00
CFSF Sergei Fedorov 12.00 30.00
CFSG Simon Gagne 8.00 20.00
CFSK Saku Koivu 8.00 20.00
CFSL Jordan Staal 8.00 20.00
CFSS Steven Stamkos 30.00 80.00
CFST Chris Stewart 8.00 20.00
CFSU Mats Sundin 8.00 20.00
CFSV Simeon Varlamov
CFSY Peter Stastny 8.00 20.00
CFTH Tomas Holmstrom
CFTS Teemu Selanne 15.00 40.00
CFTV Thomas Vanek 8.00 20.00
CFTW Peter Mueller 6.00 15.00
CFVL Vincent Lecavalier 6.00 15.00
CFWG Wayne Gretzky 60.00 120.00
CFWR Wade Redden 5.00 12.00
CFZB Zach Bogosian 8.00 20.00
CFZP Zach Parise 8.00 20.00

2008-09 The Cup Honorable Numbers

STATED PRINT RUN 1-96
HNAP Alex Pietrangelo/27 15.00 40.00
HNBK Mikkel Boedker/89 20.00 50.00
HNBL Brian Leetch/2
HNBS Brandon Sutter/16
HNBW Blake Wheeler/26 60.00 120.00
HNCG Colton Gillies/18 25.00 50.00
HNCN Cam Neely/8
HNCP Carey Price/31 125.00 200.00
HNDB Derick Brassard/16
HNDC Dino Ciccarelli/22 20.00 50.00
HNDD Drew Doughty/8
HNEM Evgeni Malkin/71 60.00 120.00
HNES Eric Staal/12
HNFB Fabian Brunnstrom/96 25.00 60.00
HNGA Sam Gagner/89 30.00 80.00
HNGF Grant Fuhr/31 30.00 80.00
HNGL Guy Lafleur/10
HNHL Henrik Lundqvist/30 75.00 150.00
HNIK Ilya Kovalchuk/17 50.00 100.00
HNJI Jarome Iginla/12
HNJS Jordan Staal/11
HNJT Jonathan Toews/19 60.00 120.00
HNJV Jakub Voracek/93 30.00 60.00
HNKO Kyle Okposo/21 25.00 60.00
HNKT Kyle Turris/91 25.00 60.00
HNLS Luke Schenn/2
HNMB Martin Brodeur/30 100.00 200.00
HNMF Michael Frolik/67 20.00 50.00
HNML Mario Lemieux/66 100.00 200.00
HNMM Mark Messier/11
HNMT Marty Turco/35 30.00 80.00
HNNB Nicklas Backstrom/19 40.00 80.00
HNNF Nikita Filatov/28 25.00 60.00
HNPK Patrick Kane/88 100.00 175.00
HNPM Peter Mueller/88 25.00 60.00
HNPR Patrick Roy/33 125.00 250.00
HNRB Ray Bourque/77 50.00 100.00
HNRM Ryan Miller/30 25.00 60.00
HNRN Rick Nash/61 30.00 80.00
HNSC Sidney Crosby/87 200.00 350.00
HNSG Simon Gagne/12
HNSS Steven Stamkos/91 125.00 250.00
HNTH Joe Thornton/19
HNTV Thomas Vanek/26 25.00 60.00
HNVL Vincent Lecavalier/4
HNWG Wayne Gretzky/1
HNZB Zach Bogosian/4

2008-09 The Cup Honorable Numbers Dual

STATED PRINT RUN 5-91
HN2BM Brodeur/Miller/30 100.00 200.00
HN2BS Sutter/Brassard/16 25.00 60.00
HN2DB Doan/Backstrom/19
HN2FG Giroux/Filatov/28 75.00 150.00
HN2FP Price/Fuhr/31 40.00 100.00
HN2GS Stewart/Gerbe/42 20.00 50.00
HN2HG Getzlaf/Heatley/15 30.00 80.00
HN2KK Kurri/Kovalchuk/17 40.00 100.00
HN2KM Kane/Mueller/88 30.00 60.00
HN2NG GilliesNeal/18 30.00 80.00
HN2NR Richards/Neal/18
HN2SG Giguere/Schneider/35 40.00 100.00
HN2SS Stastny/Stastny/26 60.00 120.00
HN2SW Wheeler/Pa.Stastny/26 30.00 60.00
HN2TB Thornton/Backstrom/19 40.00 80.00
HN2TK Kulemin/Tikhonov/41 25.00 60.00
HN2TS Turris/Stamkos/91 100.00 200.00
HN2TT Toews/Thornton/19 50.00 100.00

2008-09 The Cup Limited Logos Autographs

STATED PRINT RUN 50 SER.#'d SETS
LLAP Alex Pietrangelo 15.00 40.00
LLBL Brian Leetch 20.00 50.00
LLBO Mikkel Boedker 15.00 40.00
LLBS Brandon Sutter 12.00 30.00
LLBW Blake Wheeler 50.00 120.00
LLCD Chris Drury 15.00 40.00
LLCG Colton Gillies 15.00 40.00
LLCP Carey Price 100.00 200.00
LLCS Cory Schneider 50.00 125.00
LLCW Cam Ward 25.00 60.00
LLDB Derick Brassard 20.00 50.00
LLDD Drew Doughty 75.00 150.00
LLDG Doug Gilmour 25.00 60.00
LLDH Dany Heatley 20.00 50.00
LLDS Daniel Sedin 20.00 50.00
LLEM Evgeni Malkin 100.00 200.00
LLES Eric Staal 25.00 60.00
LLFR Michael Frolik 12.00 30.00
LLGA Glenn Anderson 30.00 600.00
LLHA Dominik Hasek 25.00 60.00
LLHE Milan Hejduk 15.00 40.00
LLHL Henrik Lundqvist 75.00 150.00
LLHS Henrik Sedin 20.00 50.00
LLHZ Henrik Zetterberg 25.00 60.00
LLIK Ilya Kovalchuk 20.00 50.00
LLJC Jeff Carter 40.00 100.00
LLJI Jarome Iginla 20.00 50.00
LLJN James Neal 40.00 100.00
LLJS Jordan Staal 20.00 50.00
LLJT Joe Thornton 25.00 60.00
LLJV Jakub Voracek 50.00 100.00
LLKA Karl Alzner
LLKE Phil Kessel 25.00 60.00
LLKO Anze Kopitar 25.00 60.00
LLKT Kyle Turris 25.00 60.00
LLLK Lauri Korpikoski 12.00 30.00
LLLR Luc Robitaille 25.00 60.00
LLLS Luke Schenn 40.00 100.00
LLMB Martin Brodeur 100.00 200.00
LLMC Mike Cammalleri 15.00 40.00
LLMF Marc-Andre Fleury 50.00 100.00
LLMG Marian Gaborik 25.00 60.00
LLMH Marian Hossa
LLML Mario Lemieux 100.00 200.00
LLMM Mark Messier 60.00 120.00
LLMN Markus Naslund 15.00 40.00
LLMO Mike Modano 30.00 80.00
LLMS Martin St. Louis 20.00 50.00
LLMT Marty Turco 20.00 50.00
LLNB Nicklas Backstrom 30.00 80.00
LLNF Nikita Filatov 20.00 50.00
LLNK Nikolai Kulemin 20.00 50.00
LLNL Nicklas Lidstrom 40.00 80.00
LLOS T.J. Oshie 50.00 100.00
LLPB Patrice Bergeron 40.00 80.00
LLPD Pavel Datsyuk 40.00 100.00
LLPH Patric Hornqvist 20.00 50.00
LLPK Patrick Kane 50.00 100.00
LLPM Peter Mueller 15.00 40.00
LLPR Patrick Roy 100.00 200.00
LLPV Petr Vrana 12.00 30.00
LLRB Ray Bourque 30.00 80.00
LLRI Mike Richards 20.00 50.00
LLRM Ryan Miller 30.00 80.00
LLRN Rick Nash 30.00 80.00
LLSC Sidney Crosby 300.00 600.00
LLSG Sam Gagner 15.00 40.00
LLSH Steve Shutt 20.00 50.00
LLSI Simon Gagne 20.00 50.00
LLSK Saku Koivu 20.00 50.00
LLSP Peter Stastny 20.00 50.00
LLSS Steven Stamkos 250.00 500.00
LLTO Jonathan Toews 75.00 150.00
LLVL Vincent Lecavalier 30.00 80.00
LLVO Tomas Vokoun 15.00 40.00
LLZB Zach Bogosian 20.00 50.00

2008-09 The Cup Scripted Swatches

STATED PRINT RUN 25 SER.#'d SETS
SSBO Mikkel Boedker 20.00 50.00
SSBS Brandon Sutter 12.00 30.00
SSBW Blake Wheeler 40.00 100.00
SSCG Claude Giroux 75.00 150.00
SSCP Carey Price 60.00 120.00
SSCW Cam Ward 12.00 30.00
SSDB Derick Brassard 15.00 40.00
SSDC Dino Ciccarelli
SSDD Drew Doughty 40.00 100.00
SSDG Doug Gilmour 20.00 50.00
SSDH Dany Heatley 15.00 40.00
SSEM Evgeni Malkin 50.00 125.00
SSES Eric Staal 20.00 50.00
SSFB Fabian Brunnstrom 20.00 50.00
SSFR Michael Frolik 15.00 40.00
SSGA Simon Gagne 15.00 40.00
SSGI Colton Gillies 12.00 30.00
SSHA Dominik Hasek 20.00 50.00
SSHL Henrik Lundqvist 60.00 120.00
SSHZ Henrik Zetterberg 30.00 60.00
SSIK Ilya Kovalchuk 15.00 40.00
SSJI Jarome Iginla 15.00 40.00
SSJN James Neal 30.00 80.00
SSJT Joe Thornton 20.00 50.00
SSJV Jakub Voracek 25.00 60.00
SSKO Kyle Okposo 15.00 40.00
SSKT Kyle Turris 30.00 80.00
SSLS Luke Schenn 20.00 50.00
SSMB Martin Brodeur 60.00 120.00
SSMC Mike Cammalleri 12.00 30.00
SSMF Marc-Andre Fleury 25.00 60.00
SSML Mario Lemieux 75.00 150.00
SSMM Mark Messier 75.00 150.00
SSMN Markus Naslund 12.00 30.00
SSMS Martin St. Louis 15.00 40.00
SSMT Marty Turco 15.00 40.00
SSNB Nicklas Backstrom 25.00 60.00
SSNF Nikita Filatov 20.00 50.00
SSNL Nicklas Lidstrom 40.00 100.00
SSOS T.J. Oshie 40.00 80.00
SSPB Patrik Berglund 12.00 30.00
SSPH Patric Hornqvist 15.00 40.00
SSPK Patrick Kane 30.00 80.00
SSPM Peter Mueller 12.00 30.00
SSPR Patrick Roy 100.00 200.00
SSRN Rick Nash 25.00 60.00
SSSC Sidney Crosby 175.00 300.00
SSSD Shane Doan 12.00 30.00
SSSG Sam Gagner 12.00 30.00
SSSS Steven Stamkos 200.00 350.00
SSST Peter Stastny 15.00 40.00
SSTO Jonathan Toews 40.00 100.00
SSTV Thomas Vanek 15.00 40.00
SSVL Vincent Lecavalier 12.00 30.00
SSZB Zach Bogosian 15.00 40.00

2008-09 The Cup Signature Patches

STATED PRINT RUN 25-75
SPPS Paul Stastny 15.00 40.00
SPAK Anze Kopitar 25.00 60.00
SPBH Bobby Hull/25 40.00 100.00
SPBK Mikkel Boedker 20.00 50.00
SPBS Brandon Sutter 15.00 40.00
SPBW Blake Wheeler 40.00 100.00
SPCG Colton Gillies 12.00 30.00
SPCP Carey Price 60.00 150.00
SPDB Derick Brassard 15.00 40.00
SPDD Drew Doughty 40.00 100.00
SPDH Dany Heatley 15.00 40.00
SPEM Evgeni Malkin 50.00 125.00
SPES Eric Staal 20.00 50.00
SPFB Fabian Brunnstrom 12.00 30.00
SPFL Marc-Andre Fleury 20.00 50.00
SPGH Gordie Howe/25 100.00 200.00
SPHA Dale Hawerchuk 20.00 50.00
SPHK Dominik Hasek 20.00 50.00
SPIK Ilya Kovalchuk 15.00 40.00
SPJI Jarome Iginla 15.00 40.00
SPJN James Neal 20.00 50.00
SPJT Jonathan Toews 60.00 120.00
SPJV Jakub Voracek 30.00 60.00
SPKA Patrick Kane 50.00 100.00
SPKT Kyle Turris 25.00 50.00
SPLS Luke Schenn 20.00 50.00
SPMB Martin Brodeur/25 75.00 150.00
SPME Mark Messier/25 60.00 120.00
SPMF Michael Frolik 15.00 40.00
SPML Mario Lemieux/25 150.00 300.00
SPMM Mark Messier 60.00 120.00
SPMR Mike Richards 20.00 50.00
SPMS Martin St. Louis 15.00 40.00
SPMT Marty Turco 15.00 40.00
SPNB Nicklas Backstrom 25.00 60.00
SPNF Nikita Filatov 15.00 40.00
SPNL Nicklas Lidstrom 25.00 60.00
SPPK Phil Kessel 20.00 50.00
SPPM Peter Mueller 12.00 30.00
SPPR Patrick Roy/25 100.00 200.00
SPRB Ray Bourque 40.00 100.00
SPRN Rick Nash 15.00 40.00
SPSC Sidney Crosby/25 175.00 300.00
SPSG Simon Gagne 15.00 40.00
SPSS Steven Stamkos 200.00 400.00
SPTH Joe Thornton 20.00 50.00

SPVL Vincent Lecavalier 12.00 30.00
SPWG Wayne Gretzky/25 300.00 500.00
SPZB Zach Boychuk 15.00 40.00

2008-09 The Cup Stanley Cup Signatures

STATED PRINT RUN 50 SER.#'d SETS
SCSBH Bobby Hull 20.00 50.00
SCSBO Bobby Orr 100.00 200.00
SCSES Eric Staal 15.00 40.00
SCSFM Frank Mahovlich 12.00 30.00
SCSGF Grant Fuhr 25.00 50.00
SCSGH Gordie Howe 60.00 120.00
SCSHZ Henrik Zetterberg 25.00 60.00
SCSJB Jean Beliveau 25.00 50.00
SCSJM Joe Mullen 10.00 25.00
SCSLM Lanny McDonald 12.00 30.00
SCSMB Martin Brodeur 30.00 80.00
SCSMI Mike Bossy 25.00 60.00
SCSML Mario Lemieux 60.00 120.00
SCSMM Mark Messier 50.00 100.00
SCSMS Martin St. Louis 12.00 30.00
SCSNL Nicklas Lidstrom 20.00 50.00
SCSPD Pavel Datsyuk 25.00 60.00
SCSPR Patrick Roy 60.00 120.00
SCSRB Ray Bourque 20.00 50.00
SCSVL Vincent Lecavalier 15.00 40.00
SCSWG Wayne Gretzky 175.00 350.00

2008-09 The Cup Trios Jerseys

STATED PRINT RUN 15 SER.#'d SETS
CJ3BHH Hextall/Hasek/Brodeur 30.00 60.00
CJ3BMP MacIn/Phanf/Bourque 15.00 40.00
CJ3BNC Wheeler/Gillies/Frolik 25.00 60.00
CJ3BNO Bourque/Oates/Neely 30.00 60.00
CJ3CMF Fleury/Crosby/Malkin 50.00 100.00
CJ3COS Crosby/Ovech/Stamks 60.00 120.00
CJ3DMP Dionne/McDon/Perrlt 12.00 30.00
CJ3ELT Trottier/P.Espo/Lafleur 15.00 40.00
CJ3FSZ Sundin/Zetter/Forsbrg 12.00 30.00
CJ3GLC Crosby/Lemieux/Grtzky 60.00 120.00
CJ3GMH Howe/Gretzky/Messier 60.00 120.00
CJ3GMK Kopitar/Getzlaf/Mueller 15.00 40.00
CJ3GPC Cheech/Phanf/Getzlaf 12.00 30.00
CJ3HNT Heatley/Nash/Toews 15.00 40.00
CJ3HTK Hull/Kane/Toews 25.00 60.00
CJ3KKM Kovlev/S.Koivu/Markv 12.00 30.00
CJ3KMC Kane/Chelios/Modano 20.00 50.00
CJ3LRM Recchi/Lemieux/Mullen
CJ3LSS Spezza/Lecav/St. Lou 10.00 25.00
CJ3LTI Lecav/Iginla/Thornton 12.00 30.00
CJ3MAJ Anderson/Kurri/Messier 15.00 40.00
CJ3MLK Kovalv/Leetch/Messier 15.00 40.00
CJ3MMM McDon/MacInn/Mullen 10.00 25.00
CJ3OCI Iginla/Crosby/Ovechkin 50.00 100.00
CJ3OMK Ovech/Koval/Malkin 40.00 100.00
CJ3PMV Perreault/Vanek/Miller 25.00 60.00
CJ3PTK Toews/Price/Kane 40.00 100.00
CJ3QGF Roy/Luongo/Fleury 25.00 60.00
CJ3RBP Brodeur/Roy/Price 40.00 100.00
CJ3RSB Roy/Bourque/Sakic 25.00 60.00
CJ3SBK Savard/Bergrn/Kessel 15.00 40.00
CJ3SBP Bergrn/Parise/J.Staal 15.00 40.00
CJ3SEB Sakic/P.Espo/Bourque 15.00 40.00
CJ3SSF Sundin/Sakic/Forsberg 25.00 50.00
CJ3STB Turris/Stmks/Brunst 40.00 100.00
CJ3VFB Brassard/Vorck/Filatov 20.00 50.00

2009-10 The Cup

1-90 STATED PRINT RUN 249
91-111 ROOK.AU PRINT RUN 199
112-177 ROOK.JSY AU PRINT RUN 249
178-180 ROOK.JSY AU PRINT RUN 99
1 Sidney Crosby 12.00 30.00
2 Ray Bourque 5.00 12.00
3 Jarome Iginla 3.00 8.00
4 Marian Gaborik 4.00 10.00
5 Anze Kopitar 5.00 12.00
6 Shane Doan 2.50 6.00
7 Sam Gagner 2.50 6.00
8 Alexander Ovechkin 12.00 30.00
9 Jonathan Toews 6.00 15.00
10 David Perron 2.00 5.00
11 Mark Messier 4.00 10.00
12 Pavel Datsyuk 4.00 10.00
13 Phil Kessel 4.00 10.00
14 Brad Richards 3.00 8.00
15 Bobby Hull 4.00 10.00
16 Teemu Selanne 6.00 15.00
17 Vincent Lecavalier 2.50 6.00
18 Cam Ward 3.00 8.00
19 Steve Yzerman 8.00 20.00
20 Carey Price 12.00 30.00
21 Saku Koivu 3.00 8.00
22 Patrick Marleau 3.00 8.00
23 Bobby Orr 10.00 25.00
24 Paul Kariya 4.00 10.00
25 Steve Mason 2.50 6.00
26 Mike Richards 3.00 8.00
27 Denis Potvin 3.00 8.00
28 Borje Salming 3.00 8.00
29 Jean Beliveau 3.00 8.00
30 Marty Turco 3.00 8.00
31 Derick Brassard 3.00 8.00
32 Martin Brodeur 6.00 15.00
33 Henrik Sedin 3.00 8.00
34 Jason Spezza 3.00 8.00
35 Gilbert Perreault 3.00 8.00
36 Phil Esposito 5.00 12.00
37 Paul Stastny 3.00 8.00
38 Brian Leetch 3.00 8.00
39 Simon Gagne 3.00 8.00
40 Miikka Kiprusoff 2.50 6.00
41 Scott Niedermayer 3.00 8.00
42 Guy Lafleur 4.00 10.00
43 Marc-Andre Fleury 5.00 12.00
44 Chris Drury 2.50 6.00
45 Joe Thornton 3.00 8.00
46 Ron Hextall 5.00 12.00
47 Ryan Miller 3.00 8.00
48 Mario Lemieux 10.00 25.00
49 Luke Schenn 2.50 6.00
50 Rick DiPietro 2.50 6.00
51 Ilya Kovalchuk 3.00 8.00
52 Mike Bossy 3.00 8.00
53 Shea Weber 2.50 6.00
54 Jari Kurri 3.00 8.00
55 Drew Doughty 4.00 10.00
56 Henrik Zetterberg 4.00 10.00
57 Dino Ciccarelli 3.00 8.00
58 Steven Stamkos 6.00 15.00
59 Grant Fuhr 3.00 8.00
60 Patrick Roy 8.00 20.00
61 Rick Nash 2.50 6.00
62 Tomas Vokoun 2.50 6.00
63 Eric Staal 4.00 10.00
64 Luc Robitaille 3.00 8.00
65 Mikko Koivu 3.00 8.00
66 Cam Neely 3.00 8.00
67 Dale Hawerchuk 4.00 10.00
68 Patrick Kane 6.00 15.00
69 Ryan Getzlaf 5.00 12.00
70 Daniel Sedin 3.00 8.00
71 Evgeni Malkin 10.00 25.00
72 Gordie Howe 8.00 20.00
73 Andrew Cogliano 2.50 6.00
74 Henrik Lundqvist 5.00 12.00
75 Mike Modano 5.00 12.00
76 Peter Mueller 2.50 6.00
77 Roberto Luongo 4.00 10.00
78 Bobby Clarke 3.00 8.00
79 Thomas Vanek 3.00 8.00
80 Marian Hossa 2.50 6.00
81 Larry Robinson 3.00 8.00
82 Tim Thomas 3.00 8.00
83 Dany Heatley 3.00 8.00
84 Peter Stastny 3.00 8.00
85 Jeff Carter 3.00 8.00
86 Nicklas Lidstrom 3.00 8.00
87 Martin St. Louis 3.00 8.00
88 Clark Gillies 3.00 8.00
89 Zach Parise 3.00 8.00
90 Wayne Gretzky 15.00 40.00
91 Taylor Chorney AU RC 8.00 20.00
92 Anton Khudobin AU RC 12.00 30.00
93 Alexander Salak AU RC 6.00 15.00
94 John Negrin AU RC 8.00 20.00
95 James Reimer AU RC 20.00 50.00
96 Steven Zalewski AU RC 6.00 15.00
97 Teemu Laakso AU RC 5.00 12.00
98 Braden Holtby AU RC 80.00 200.00
99 Aaron Gagnon AU RC 5.00 12.00
100 Tom Pyatt AU RC 8.00 20.00
101 Mathieu Carle AU RC 8.00 20.00
102 Mark Letestu AU RC 8.00 20.00
103 Carl Gunnarsson AU RC 6.00 15.00
104 Mathieu Perreault AU RC 12.00 30.00
105 Ryan Vesce AU RC 6.00 15.00
106 Tom Wandell AU RC 8.00 20.00
107 Mike Brodeur AU RC 8.00 20.00
108 Phil Oreskovic AU RC 8.00 20.00
109 Peter Regin AU RC 6.00 15.00
110 Tyler Eckford AU RC 6.00 15.00
111 David Laliberte AU RC 6.00 15.00
112 Oskars Bartulis JSY AU RC 12.00 30.00
113 Ryan O'Marra JSY AU RC 8.00 20.00
114 Lars Eller JSY AU RC 12.00 30.00
115 Brad Marchand JSY AU RC 80.00 200.00
116 Logan Couture JSY AU RC 40.00 100.00
117 Perttu Lindgren JSY AU RC 10.00 25.00
118 M.Grabner JSY AU RC 15.00 40.00
119 Cody Franson JSY AU RC 15.00 40.00
120 Tyler Bozak JSY AU RC 20.00 50.00
121 Sergei Shirokov JSY AU RC 8.00 20.00
122 J.Gustavsson JSY AU RC 15.00 40.00
123 Viktor Stalberg JSY AU RC 12.00 30.00
124 Victor Hedman JSY AU RC 60.00 150.00
125 Erik Karlsson JSY AU RC 200.00 400.00
126 M.Del Zotto JSY AU RC 12.00 30.00
127 Matt Gilroy JSY AU RC 12.00 30.00
128 Colin Wilson JSY AU RC 12.00 30.00
129 Dmitry Kulikov JSY AU RC 12.00 30.00
130 Jamie Benn JSY AU RC 200.00 350.00
131 Ryan O'Reilly JSY AU RC 30.00 80.00
132 Tyler Myers JSY AU RC 25.00 60.00
133 Evander Kane JSY AU RC 40.00 100.00
134 Antti Niemi JSY AU RC 20.00 50.00
135 Ville Leino JSY AU RC 10.00 25.00
136 M.Neuvirth JSY AU RC 20.00 50.00
137 Matt Pelech JSY AU RC 12.00 30.00
138 Kris Chucko JSY AU RC 10.00 25.00
139 Riku Helenius JSY AU RC 12.00 30.00
140 I.Vishnevskiy JSY AU RC 10.00 25.00
141 Jhonas Enroth JSY AU RC 15.00 40.00
142 Artem Anisimov JSY AU RC 20.00 50.00
143 M.Backlund JSY AU RC 20.00 40.00
144 C.Hanson JSY AU RC 12.00 30.00
145 Yannick Weber JSY AU RC 12.00 30.00
146 T.J. Galiardi JSY AU RC 12.00 30.00
147 S.Machacek JSY AU RC 12.00 30.00
148 Luca Caputi JSY AU RC 12.00 30.00
149 Brian Salcido JSY AU RC 10.00 25.00
150 Matt Beleskey JSY AU RC 10.00 25.00
151 Michael Sauer JSY AU RC 10.00 25.00
152 Jesse Joensuu JSY AU RC 10.00 25.00
153 Cal O'Reilly JSY AU RC 10.00 25.00
154 Ray Macias JSY AU RC 10.00 25.00
155 Keaton Ellerby JSY AU RC 10.00 25.00
156 Jakub Kindl JSY AU RC 12.00 30.00
157 Mike Santorelli JSY AU RC 12.00 30.00
158 Drayson Bowman JSY AU RC 12.00 30.00
159 A.MacDonald JSY AU RC 8.00 20.00
160 Ryan Stoa JSY AU RC 10.00 25.00
161 John Scott JSY AU RC 25.00 60.00
162 Matt Hendricks JSY AU RC 10.00 25.00
163 Byron Bitz JSY AU RC 10.00 25.00
164 Joel Rechlicz JSY AU RC 8.00 20.00
165 Alec Martinez JSY AU RC 15.00 40.00
166 Jason Demers JSY AU RC 15.00 40.00
167 Benn Ferriero JSY AU RC 12.00 30.00
168 Frazer McLaren JSY AU RC 10.00 25.00
169 Matthew Corrente JSY AU RC 10.00 25.00
170 Jay Rosehill JSY AU RC 10.00 25.00
171 Chris Butler JSY AU RC 12.00 30.00
172 Tyler Ennis JSY AU RC 15.00 40.00
173 Daniel Larsson JSY AU RC 10.00 25.00
174 Bobby Sanguinetti JSY AU RC 8.00 20.00
175 Colin McDonald JSY AU RC 10.00 25.00
176 Devan Dubnyk JSY AU RC 30.00 80.00
177 Danny Irmen JSY AU RC 8.00 20.00
178 M.Duchene JSY AU RC/99 300.00 700.00
179 van Riems JSY AU RC/99 150.00 400.00
180 J.Tavares JSY AU RC/99 1500.00 2000.00

2009-10 The Cup Gold

*GOLD 1-90: .8X TO 2X BASE
COMMON ROOKIE (91-177) 8.00 20.00
ROOKIE SEMISTARS 10.00 25.00
ROOKIE UNL.STARS 12.00 30.00
STATED PRINT RUN 25 SER.#'d SETS
95 James Reimer 30.00 80.00
98 Braden Holtby 50.00 100.00
104 Mathieu Perreault 20.00 50.00
115 Brad Marchand 30.00 80.00
116 Logan Couture 25.00 60.00
120 Tyler Bozak 20.00 50.00
122 Jonas Gustavsson 15.00 40.00
123 Viktor Stalberg 12.00 30.00
124 Victor Hedman 25.00 60.00
125 Erik Karlsson 60.00 120.00
126 Michael Del Zotto 12.00 30.00
130 Jamie Benn 40.00 80.00
131 Ryan O'Reilly 20.00 50.00
132 Tyler Myers 20.00 50.00
134 Antti Niemi 25.00 60.00
136 Michal Neuvirth 15.00 40.00
141 Jhonas Enroth 15.00 40.00
148 Luca Caputi 12.00 30.00
150 Matt Beleskey 10.00 25.00
172 Tyler Ennis 15.00 40.00
176 Devan Dubnyk 15.00 40.00
178 Matt Duchene 40.00 100.00
179 James van Riemsdyk 60.00 120.00
180 John Tavares 125.00 250.00

2009-10 The Cup Gold Jerseys

STATED PRINT RUN 25 SER.#'d SETS
1 Sidney Crosby 40.00 100.00
2 Ray Bourque 15.00 40.00
3 Jarome Iginla 6.00 15.00
4 Marian Gaborik 8.00 20.00
5 Anze Kopitar 10.00 25.00
6 Shane Doan 5.00 12.00
7 Sam Gagner 5.00 12.00
8 Alexander Ovechkin 20.00 50.00
9 Jonathan Toews 12.00 30.00
11 Mark Messier 8.00 20.00
12 Pavel Datsyuk 12.00 30.00
13 Phil Kessel 8.00 20.00
14 Brad Richards 6.00 15.00
15 Bobby Hull 8.00 20.00
16 Teemu Selanne 12.00 30.00
17 Vincent Lecavalier 5.00 12.00
18 Cam Ward 6.00 15.00
19 Steve Yzerman 15.00 40.00
20 Carey Price 15.00 40.00
21 Saku Koivu 12.00 30.00
22 Patrick Marleau 8.00 20.00
24 Paul Kariya 12.00 30.00
25 Steve Mason 5.00 12.00
26 Mike Richards 6.00 15.00
27 Denis Potvin 6.00 15.00
28 Borje Salming 12.00 30.00
29 Jean Beliveau 15.00 40.00
30 Marty Turco 6.00 15.00
31 Derick Brassard 6.00 15.00
32 Martin Brodeur 12.00 30.00
33 Henrik Sedin 6.00 15.00
34 Jason Spezza 6.00 15.00
35 Gilbert Perreault 6.00 15.00
36 Phil Esposito 10.00 25.00
37 Paul Stastny 6.00 15.00
38 Brian Leetch 10.00 25.00
39 Simon Gagne 6.00 15.00
40 Miikka Kiprusoff 8.00 20.00
41 Scott Niedermayer 8.00 20.00
42 Guy Lafleur 8.00 20.00
43 Marc-Andre Fleury 20.00 50.00
44 Chris Drury 5.00 12.00
45 Joe Thornton 6.00 15.00
46 Ron Hextall 10.00 25.00
47 Ryan Miller 12.00 30.00
48 Mario Lemieux 20.00 50.00
49 Luke Schenn 5.00 12.00
50 Rick DiPietro 8.00 20.00
51 Ilya Kovalchuk 10.00 25.00
53 Shea Weber 10.00 25.00
54 Jari Kurri 12.00 30.00
55 Drew Doughty 8.00 20.00
56 Henrik Zetterberg 8.00 20.00
57 Dino Ciccarelli 6.00 15.00
58 Steven Stamkos 12.00 30.00
59 Grant Fuhr 20.00 50.00
60 Patrick Roy 25.00 60.00
61 Rick Nash 10.00 25.00
62 Tomas Vokoun 5.00 12.00
63 Eric Staal 8.00 20.00
64 Luc Robitaille 6.00 15.00
65 Mikko Koivu 12.00 30.00
66 Cam Neely 12.00 30.00
67 Dale Hawerchuk 15.00 40.00
68 Patrick Kane 12.00 30.00
69 Ryan Getzlaf 10.00 25.00
70 Daniel Sedin 6.00 15.00
71 Evgeni Malkin 20.00 50.00
72 Gordie Howe 15.00 40.00
73 Andrew Cogliano 5.00 12.00
74 Henrik Lundqvist 10.00 25.00
75 Mike Modano 10.00 25.00
76 Peter Mueller 5.00 12.00
77 Roberto Luongo 20.00 50.00
79 Thomas Vanek 8.00 20.00
80 Marian Hossa 5.00 12.00
81 Larry Robinson 6.00 15.00
82 Tim Thomas 6.00 15.00
83 Dany Heatley 6.00 15.00
84 Peter Stastny 8.00 20.00
85 Jeff Carter 8.00 20.00
86 Nicklas Lidstrom 10.00 25.00
87 Martin St. Louis 8.00 20.00
88 Clark Gillies 6.00 15.00
89 Zach Parise 8.00 20.00
90 Wayne Gretzky 40.00 100.00

2009-10 The Cup Auto Draft Boards

STATED PRINT RUN 25 SER.#'d SETS
DBBS Bobby Sanguinetti 15.00 40.00
DBCW Colin Wilson 25.00 60.00
DBDK Dmitry Kulikov 50.00 100.00
DBDU Matt Duchene 150.00 250.00
DBEK Erik Karlsson 175.00 300.00
DBIV Ivan Vishnevskiy 20.00 50.00
DBJK Jakub Kindl 50.00 100.00
DBJT John Tavares 250.00 500.00
DBJV James van Riemsdyk 60.00 120.00
DBKA Evander Kane 75.00 150.00
DBLC Logan Couture 100.00 200.00
DBLE Lars Eller 30.00 80.00
DBMB Mikael Backlund 60.00 120.00
DBMC Matthew Corrente 20.00 50.00
DBMD Michael Del Zotto 60.00 120.00
DBMG Michael Grabner 60.00 120.00
DBMP Matt Pelech 25.00 60.00
DBRH Riku Helenius 25.00 60.00
DBRO Ryan O'Marra 15.00 40.00
DBTE Tyler Ennis 40.00 100.00
DBTM Tyler Myers 100.00 200.00
DBVH Victor Hedman 40.00 100.00

2009-10 The Cup Emblems of Endorsement

STATED PRINT RUN 15 SER.#'d SETS
EEAO Alexander Ovechkin
EEBR Martin Brodeur 125.00 200.00
EEBS Bobby Sanguinetti 20.00 50.00
EECN Cam Neely 50.00 100.00
EECP Carey Price 175.00 300.00
EECW Colin Wilson 20.00 50.00
EEDB Drayson Bowman 20.00 50.00
EEDD Devan Dubnyk 40.00 100.00
EEDH Dany Heatley
EEDP Dion Phaneuf 25.00 60.00
EEEK Evander Kane 50.00 100.00
EEEM Evgeni Malkin 90.00 150.00
EEES Eric Staal 25.00 60.00
EEHZ Henrik Zetterberg 75.00 135.00
EEIK Ilya Kovalchuk 25.00 60.00
EEJC Jeff Carter 30.00 80.00
EEJG Jonas Gustavsson 25.00 60.00
EEJI Jarome Iginla 90.00 150.00
EEJK Jari Kurri 25.00 60.00
EEJT Joe Thornton 30.00 80.00
EEJV James van Riemsdyk 100.00 175.00
EEKA Patrick Kane 40.00 100.00
EELC Logan Couture 60.00 120.00
EEMD Matt Duchene 100.00 175.00
EEMF Marc-Andre Fleury 75.00 135.00
EEMG Marian Gaborik 25.00 60.00
EEML Mario Lemieux 150.00 250.00
EEMM Mark Messier 75.00 125.00
EEMO Mike Modano 30.00 80.00
EEMR Mike Richards 75.00 125.00
EEMS Martin St. Louis 20.00 50.00
EEMT Marty Turco 25.00 60.00
EENB Nicklas Backstrom 50.00 100.00
EENL Nicklas Lidstrom 60.00 120.00
EEPD Pavel Datsyuk 40.00 80.00
EEPK Phil Kessel 25.00 60.00
EEPR Patrick Roy
EERB Ray Bourque 50.00 100.00
EERH Ron Hextall
EERM Ryan Miller 30.00 80.00
EERN Rick Nash 75.00 125.00
EERO Luc Robitaille 25.00 60.00
EESC Sidney Crosby 300.00 500.00
EESD Shane Doan 25.00 60.00
EESM Steve Mason 25.00 60.00
EESS Sergei Shirokov 12.00 30.00
EEST Steven Stamkos 125.00 200.00
EESY Steve Yzerman 150.00 250.00
EETA John Tavares 150.00 250.00
EETM Tyler Myers 50.00 100.00
EETO Jonathan Toews 75.00 150.00
EETV Thomas Vanek 20.00 50.00
EEVH Victor Hedman 40.00 100.00
EEVL Vincent Lecavalier 25.00 60.00
EEVS Viktor Stalberg 20.00 50.00
EEWG Wayne Gretzky 500.00 800.00

2009-10 The Cup Enshrinements

STATED PRINT RUN 50 SER.#'d SETS
CEAO Alexander Ovechkin 30.00 80.00
CEBC Bobby Clarke 15.00 40.00
CEBH Bobby Hull 15.00 40.00
CEBO Bobby Orr 40.00 100.00
CECN Cam Neely 12.00 30.00
CECP Carey Price 50.00 125.00
CEDG Doug Gilmour 20.00 40.00
CEDH Dany Heatley
CEEK Evander Kane 15.00 40.00
CEEM Evgeni Malkin 40.00 100.00
CEES Eric Staal 15.00 40.00
CEGF Grant Fuhr 12.00 30.00
CEGH Gordie Howe 50.00 100.00
CEGP Gilbert Perreault 12.00 30.00
CEHL Henrik Lundqvist 20.00 50.00
CEHZ Henrik Zetterberg 15.00 40.00
CEIK Ilya Kovalchuk 12.00 30.00
CEJB Jean Beliveau 30.00 60.00
CEJC Jeff Carter 12.00 30.00
CEJI Jarome Iginla 12.00 30.00
CEJK Jari Kurri 12.00 30.00
CEJT Jonathan Toews 25.00 60.00
CEJV James van Riemsdyk 20.00 50.00
CEKA Patrick Kane 25.00 60.00
CELR Luc Robitaille 15.00 40.00
CEMB Martin Brodeur 25.00 60.00
CEMD Matt Duchene 20.00 50.00
CEME Mark Messier 30.00 80.00
CEMG Marian Gaborik 15.00 40.00
CEMI Mike Bossy 12.00 30.00
CEML Mario Lemieux 50.00 100.00
CEMM Mike Modano 15.00 40.00
CEMR Mike Richards 12.00 30.00
CEMS Martin St. Louis 12.00 30.00
CEMT Marty Turco 8.00 20.00
CENL Nicklas Lidstrom 12.00 30.00
CEPE Phil Esposito 20.00 50.00
CEPK Phil Kessel 15.00 40.00
CEPR Patrick Roy 75.00 150.00
CERB Ray Bourque 20.00 50.00
CERN Rick Nash 15.00 40.00
CERO Larry Robinson 12.00 30.00
CESC Sidney Crosby 75.00 150.00
CESY Steve Yzerman 60.00 120.00
CETA John Tavares 50.00 100.00
CETH Joe Thornton 12.00 30.00
CEVH Victor Hedman 25.00 60.00
CEVL Vincent Lecavalier 10.00 25.00
CEWG Wayne Gretzky 125.00 250.00

2009-10 The Cup Enshrinements Dual

STATED PRINT RUN 35 SER.#'d SETS
CE2BR Bourque/Orr 80.00 150.00
CE2BS Stalberg/Bozak 25.00 60.00
CE2CB Benn/Couture 30.00 80.00
CE2CR Richards/Clarke 15.00 40.00
CE2CV Carter/van Riemsdyk 15.00 40.00
CE2DM Datsyuk/Malkin 50.00 120.00
CE2DO O'Reilly/Duchene 30.00 80.00
CE2EN P.Esposito/Neely 25.00 60.00
CE2FW Wilson/Franson 15.00 40.00
CE2GB Bozak/Gustavsson 25.00 60.00
CE2GK Kessel/Gilmour 25.00 60.00
CE2GL Gaborik/Lundqvist 25.00 60.00
CE2GM Messier/Gretzky 150.00 300.00
CE2GS Shirokov/Grabner 15.00 40.00
CE2HT Toews/Hull 40.00 100.00
CE2IN Nash/Iginla 15.00 40.00
CE2KK Kovalchuk/Kane 30.00 80.00
CE2LD Leetch/Del Zotto 15.00 40.00
CE2LH Lidstrom/Hedman 30.00 80.00
CE2LY Yzerman/Lemieux 100.00 200.00
CE2ME Ennis/Myers 25.00 60.00
CE2MK Modano/Kane 30.00 80.00
CE2OB Ovech/Backstrm 60.00 150.00
CE2OM Ovechkin/Malkin 60.00 150.00
CE2PM Mason/Price 60.00 150.00
CE2RB Roy/Brodeur 80.00 150.00
CE2TD Tavares/Duchene 40.00 100.00
CE2TH Heatley/Thornton 15.00 40.00
CE2TS Tavares/Stamkos 50.00 120.00
CE2YH Yzerman/Howe 100.00 225.00

2009-10 The Cup Enshrinements Triples

STATED PRINT RUN 15 SER.#'d SETS
CE3BGH Hedman/Gstvsn/Bcklnd 40.00 80.00
CE3DOM Malkin/Ovech/Datsyuk 125.00 200.00
CE3EBO P.Espo/Bucyk/Orr 125.00 200.00
CE3FKM Messier/Kurri/Fuhr 90.00 150.00
CE3KVW E.Kane/Wilson/Rmsdyk 40.00 100.00
CE3LAM Leetch/G.Andrsn/Messier 60.00 120.00
CE3LYG Yzermn/Gretzky/Lemieux 400.00 600.00
CE3RBF M.Fleury/Brodeur/Roy 75.00 125.00
CE3RBL Roy/Beliveau/Lafleur 175.00 300.00
CE3TDH Hedmn/Tavares/Dchne 30.00 80.00

2009-10 The Cup Foundations Jerseys

STATED PRINT RUN 25 SER.#'d SETS
CFAK Anze Kopitar 12.00 30.00
CFAM Al MacInnis 10.00 25.00
CFAN Antti Niemi 8.00 20.00
CFAO Alexander Ovechkin 15.00 40.00
CFBA Mikael Backlund 5.00 12.00
CFBL Brian Leetch 6.00 15.00
CFBM Brad Marchand 12.00 30.00
CFBR Bobby Ryan 8.00 20.00
CFBS Borje Salming 12.00 30.00
CFCG Claude Giroux 12.00 30.00
CFCN Cam Neely 6.00 15.00
CFCP Carey Price 30.00 80.00
CFCW Colin Wilson 5.00 12.00
CFDB Derick Brassard 8.00 20.00
CFDD Drew Doughty 10.00 25.00
CFDE Michael Del Zotto 5.00 12.00
CFDH Dany Heatley 10.00 25.00
CFDS Devin Setoguchi 6.00 15.00
CFDU Matt Duchene 12.00 30.00
CFDW Doug Wilson 6.00 15.00
CFEK Evander Kane 8.00 20.00
CFEM Evgeni Malkin 15.00 40.00
CFES Phil Esposito 12.00 30.00
CFES Eric Staal 10.00 25.00
CFGA Glenn Anderson 5.00 12.00
CFGH Gordie Howe 15.00 40.00
CFGP Gilbert Perreault 6.00 15.00
CFGR Michael Grabner 5.00 12.00
CFHA Dale Hawerchuk 8.00 20.00
CFHL Henrik Lundqvist 12.00 30.00
CFHZ Henrik Zetterberg 10.00 25.00
CFIK Ilya Kovalchuk 8.00 20.00
CFJB Jamie Benn 15.00 40.00
CFJC Jeff Carter 8.00 20.00
CFJG Jonas Gustavsson 6.00 15.00
CFJI Jarome Iginla 8.00 20.00
CFJO Jordan Staal 8.00 20.00
CFJS Jason Spezza 8.00 20.00
CFJT Joe Thornton 8.00 25.00
CFJV James van Riemsdyk 25.00 60.00
CFKA Paul Kariya 10.00 25.00
CFKE Phil Kessel 10.00 25.00
CFKO Mikko Koivu 8.00 20.00
CFLC Logan Couture 10.00 25.00
CFLE Lars Eller 5.00 12.00
CFLM Lanny McDonald 6.00 15.00
CFLR Larry Robinson 6.00 15.00
CFMA Martin Brodeur 15.00 40.00
CFMD Marcel Dionne 8.00 20.00
CFME Mark Messier 8.00 20.00
CFMF Marc-Andre Fleury 12.00 30.00
CFMG Marian Gaborik 12.00 30.00
CFMH Marian Hossa 6.00 15.00
CFMK Miikka Kiprusoff 6.00 15.00
CFML Mario Lemieux 20.00 50.00
CFMM Mike Modano 12.00 30.00
CFMR Mike Richards 8.00 20.00
CFMS Martin St. Louis 8.00 20.00
CFMT Marty Turco 8.00 20.00
CFNB Nicklas Backstrom 12.00 30.00
CFNL Nicklas Lidstrom 8.00 20.00
CFPD Pavel Datsyuk 10.00 25.00
CFPE Peter Stastny 8.00 20.00
CFPK Patrick Kane 15.00 40.00
CFPM Patrick Marleau 8.00 20.00
CFPR Patrick Roy 15.00 40.00
CFPS Paul Stastny 8.00 20.00
CFRB Ray Bourque 10.00 25.00
CFRG Ryan Getzlaf 12.00 30.00
CFRH Ron Hextall 15.00 40.00
CFRL Roberto Luongo 12.00 30.00
CFRM Ryan Miller 8.00 20.00
CFRN Rick Nash 6.00 15.00
CFRO Ryan O'Reilly 8.00 20.00
CFSC Sidney Crosby 50.00 120.00
CFSD Shane Doan 6.00 15.00
CFSK Saku Koivu 8.00 20.00
CFSM Steve Mason 6.00 15.00
CFSS Steve Shutt 6.00 15.00
CFST Steven Stamkos 12.00 30.00
CFSY Steve Yzerman 15.00 40.00
CFTA John Tavares 25.00 60.00
CFTB Tyler Bozak 10.00 25.00
CFTE Tony Esposito 10.00 25.00
CFTM Tyler Myers 8.00 20.00
CFTO Jonathan Toews 15.00 40.00
CFTT Tim Thomas 8.00 20.00
CFTV Tomas Vokoun 10.00 25.00
CFVH Victor Hedman 10.00 25.00
CFVI Ville Leino 4.00 10.00
CFVL Vincent Lecavalier 8.00 20.00
CFWA Cam Ward 10.00 25.00
CFWG Wayne Gretzky 50.00 100.00
CFZC Zdeno Chara 10.00 25.00
CFZP Zach Parise 8.00 20.00

2009-10 The Cup Honorable Numbers

STATED PRINT RUN 1-97
HNCP Carey Price/31 50.00 120.00
HNCW Colin Wilson/33 20.00 50.00
HNEM Evgeni Malkin/71 40.00 100.00
HNGI Matt Gilroy/97 15.00 40.00
HNHL Henrik Lundqvist/30 40.00 100.00
HNHZ Henrik Zetterberg/40 75.00 150.00
HNIK Ilya Kovalchuk/17 30.00 80.00
HNJG Jonas Gustavsson/50 30.00 80.00
HNJK Jari Kurri/17 30.00 80.00
HNJT John Tavares/91 60.00 120.00
HNJV James van Riemsdyk/21 50.00 120.00
HNKA Erik Karlsson/65 75.00 150.00
HNKI Jakub Kindl/46 15.00 40.00
HNLC Logan Couture/39 30.00 80.00
HNLR Luc Robitaille/20 25.00 50.00
HNMA Martin Brodeur/30 60.00 120.00
HNMB Mikael Backlund/60 20.00 50.00
HNMF Marc-Andre Fleury/29 25.00 60.00
HNMG Mike Green/52 30.00 80.00
HNML Mario Lemieux/66 75.00 150.00
HNMR Mike Richards/18 25.00 60.00
HNMS Martin St. Louis/26 20.00 50.00
HNMT Marty Turco/35 20.00 50.00
HNNB Nicklas Backstrom/19 40.00 80.00
HNPA Patrick Kane/88 50.00 125.00
HNPE Patrik Elias/26 20.00 50.00
HNPK Phil Kessel/81 30.00 60.00
HNPS Paul Stastny/26 25.00 60.00
HNRB Ray Bourque/77 30.00 80.00
HNRM Ryan Miller/30 25.00 60.00
HNRN Rick Nash/61 30.00 60.00
HNRS Ryan Stoa/29 20.00 50.00
HNSD Shane Doan/19 30.00 60.00
HNSG Scott Gomez/91 15.00 40.00
HNSS Sergei Shirokov/25 15.00 40.00
HNSY Steve Yzerman/19 125.00 200.00
HNTH Joe Thornton/19 30.00 60.00
HNTM Tyler Myers/57 25.00 60.00
HNTO Jonathan Toews/19 50.00 100.00
HNVH Victor Hedman/77 25.00 60.00
HNVS Viktor Stalberg/45 15.00 40.00

2009-10 The Cup Honorable Numbers Dual

STATED PRINT RUN 2-91
HN2BH Hedman/Bourque/77 40.00 80.00
HN2BL Lundqvist/Brodeur/30 125.00 250.00
HN2EB P.Esposito/Bourque/77 50.00 120.00
HN2EN Eller/Nash/61 40.00 80.00
HN2ES Stastny/Elias/26 30.00 60.00
HN2GH Gaborik/Hawerchuk/10
HN2GT Gomez/Tavares/91 25.00 60.00
HN2HH Hull/Howe/9
HN2IS Iginla/Staal/12
HN2KC Kovalchuk/Carter/17 25.00 60.00
HN2KD Kane/Duchene/9
HN2KK Kovalchuk/Kurri/17 30.00 80.00
HN2KM Kane/Mueller/88 30.00 60.00
HN2LS Schenn/Leetch/2
HN2LV van Riemsdyk/Leino/21 25.00 60.00
HN2MD Modano/Duchene/9
HN2NO Ovechkin/Neely/8
HN2RC Ciccarelli/Robitaille/20
HN2SS Stastny/Stastny/26 20.00 50.00
HN2SW Sedin/Wilson/33
HN2TD Doan/Thornton/19
HN2TY Thornton/Yzerman/19 75.00 150.00
HN2YT Yzerman/Toews/19 125.00 200.00

2009-10 The Cup Limited Logos Autographs

STATED PRINT RUN 50 SER.#'d SETS
LLAO Alexander Ovechkin 75.00 150.00
LLBA Mikael Backlund 25.00 60.00
LLCN Cam Neely 30.00 80.00
LLCW Colin Wilson 30.00 80.00
LLDB Drayson Bowman 25.00 60.00
LLDK Dmitry Kulikov 25.00 60.00
LLDP Dion Phaneuf 20.00 50.00
LLDU Matt Duchene 40.00 100.00
LLEK Evander Kane 50.00 125.00
LLEM Evgeni Malkin 50.00 100.00
LLES Eric Staal 15.00 40.00
LLGI Matt Gilroy 15.00 40.00
LLGR Mike Green 30.00 80.00
LLHZ Henrik Zetterberg 40.00 100.00
LLIK Ilya Kovalchuk 25.00 60.00
LLJB Jamie Benn 75.00 135.00
LLJC Jeff Carter 25.00 60.00
LLJG Jonas Gustavsson 20.00 50.00
LLJI Jarome Iginla 25.00 60.00
LLJK Jakub Kindl 25.00 60.00
LLJT John Tavares 50.00 100.00
LLJV James van Riemsdyk 25.00 60.00
LLKA Erik Karlsson 60.00 150.00
LLKE Phil Kessel 30.00 80.00
LLLC Logan Couture 30.00 80.00
LLLE Ville Leino 25.00 60.00
LLMB Martin Brodeur 60.00 120.00
LLMD Michael Del Zotto 20.00 50.00
LLMG Marian Gaborik 30.00 80.00
LLML Mario Lemieux 75.00 150.00
LLMM Mike Modano 40.00 100.00
LLMR Mike Richards 25.00 60.00
LLMS Martin St. Louis 25.00 60.00
LLNB Nicklas Backstrom 30.00 80.00
LLOR Ryan O'Reilly 30.00 80.00
LLPD Pavel Datsyuk 20.00 50.00
LLPK Patrick Kane 60.00 120.00
LLPR Patrick Roy 100.00 200.00
LLRB Ray Bourque 40.00 100.00
LLRM Ryan Miller 25.00 60.00
LLRN Rick Nash 30.00 80.00
LLRO Luc Robitaille 40.00 100.00
LLSA Bobby Sanguinetti 15.00 40.00
LLSG Scott Gomez 20.00 50.00
LLSI Simon Gagne 15.00 40.00
LLSM Steve Mason 20.00 50.00
LLSS Sergei Shirokov 15.00 40.00
LLST Steven Stamkos 100.00 200.00
LLSY Steve Yzerman 75.00 150.00
LLTH Joe Thornton 25.00 60.00
LLTM Tyler Myers 30.00 80.00
LLTO Jonathan Toews 60.00 120.00
LLTV Thomas Vanek 20.00 50.00
LLVH Victor Hedman 40.00 80.00
LLVL Vincent Lecavalier 20.00 50.00
LLVS Viktor Stalberg 15.00 40.00

2009-10 The Cup Scripted Swatches

STATED PRINT RUN 25 SER.#'d SETS
SSAC Andrew Cogliano 12.00 30.00
SSAO Alexander Ovechkin 75.00 150.00
SSBL Brian Leetch 40.00 80.00
SSCP Carey Price 60.00 150.00
SSCW Colin Wilson 15.00 40.00
SSDP Dion Phaneuf 20.00 50.00
SSEK Evander Kane 30.00 80.00
SSEM Evgeni Malkin 75.00 150.00
SSHL Henrik Lundqvist 50.00 100.00
SSJB Jamie Benn 50.00 125.00
SSJC Jeff Carter 40.00 100.00
SSJG Jonas Gustavsson 20.00 50.00
SSJK Jari Kurri 40.00 100.00
SSJS Jordan Staal 15.00 40.00
SSJT Joe Thornton 15.00 40.00
SSJV James van Riemsdyk 30.00 80.00
SSKA Patrick Kane 30.00 80.00
SSLC Logan Couture 40.00 100.00
SSMA Martin Brodeur 60.00 120.00
SSMB Mikael Backlund 15.00 40.00
SSMD Matt Duchene 100.00 200.00
SSMF Marc-Andre Fleury 25.00 60.00
SSMG Marian Gaborik 25.00 60.00
SSMM Mike Modano 30.00 80.00
SSMR Mike Richards 30.00 80.00
SSMS Martin St. Louis 15.00 40.00
SSMT Marty Turco 15.00 40.00
SSPD Pavel Datsyuk 25.00 60.00
SSPK Phil Kessel 20.00 50.00
SSPS Paul Stastny 15.00 40.00
SSSC Sidney Crosby 100.00 200.00
SSSM Steve Mason 12.00 30.00
SSSS Steven Stamkos 75.00 150.00
SSSY Steve Yzerman 75.00 150.00
SSTA John Tavares 100.00 200.00
SSTM Tyler Myers 50.00 100.00
SSVH Victor Hedman 30.00 80.00
SSVL Vincent Lecavalier 12.00 30.00

2009-10 The Cup Signature Patches

STATED PRINT RUN 75 SER.#'d SETS
SPAA Artem Anisimov 12.00 30
SPAK Anze Kopitar 25.00 60
SPAO Alexander Ovechkin/25 100.00 200
SPBA Mikael Backlund 12.00 30
SPBE Jamie Benn 50.00 100
SPBH Bobby Hull/35 15.00 40
SPBL Brian Leetch 12.00 30
SPBO Tyler Bozak 20.00 50
SPBR Bobby Ryan/35 15.00 40
SPBS Brian Salcido 12.00 30
SPCD Chris Drury 12.00 30
SPCG Claude Giroux 30.00 80
SPCP Carey Price 75.00 150.
SPCU Logan Couture 25.00 60.
SPCW Colin Wilson 15.00 40.
SPDB Derick Brassard 15.00 40.
SPDG Doug Gilmour
SPDK Dmitry Kulikov 15.00 40.
SPDR Drayson Bowman 12.00 30.
SPDU Matt Duchene 40.00 100.
SPEK Evander Kane 25.00 60.
SPEM Evgeni Malkin 50.00 125.
SPES Eric Staal 20.00 50
SPGA Glenn Anderson 15.00 40
SPGI Matt Gilroy 12.00 30.
SPGO Scott Gomez 12.00 30.
SPHL Henrik Lundqvist 25.00 60.
SPHZ Henrik Zetterberg 20.00 50.
SPIK Ilya Kovalchuk 15.00 40.
SPJC Jeff Carter 15.00 40.
SPJG Jonas Gustavsson 15.00 40.
SPJI Jarome Iginla/25 40.00 100.
SPJK Jari Kurri 20.00 50.
SPJS Jordan Staal 20.00 50.
SPJT John Tavares 100.00 200.
SPJV James van Riemsdyk 25.00 60.
SPKA Erik Karlsson 50.00 100.
SPKE Phil Kessel 20.00 50.
SPKI Jakub Kindl 12.00 30.
SPLC Luca Caputi 15.00 40.
SPLE Ville Leino 10.00 25.
SPMA Martin Brodeur/25 60.00 120.
SPMD Michael Del Zotto 12.00 30.
SPMF Marc-Andre Fleury 25.00 60.
SPMG Marian Gaborik 20.00 50.
SPML Mario Lemieux/25 100.00 200.
SPMM Mark Messier/25 40.00 80.
SPMO Mike Modano 20.00 50.
SPMR Mike Richards 15.00 40.
SPMS Martin St. Louis 15.00 40.
SPMT Marty Turco 12.00 30.
SPNB Nicklas Backstrom 25.00 60.
SPNL Nicklas Lidstrom 15.00 40.
SPOR Ryan O'Reilly 20.00 50.
SPPD Pavel Datsyuk 40.00 100.
SPPE Phil Esposito/25 30.00 80.
SPPH Dion Phaneuf 12.00 30.
SPPK Patrick Kane 50.00 100.
SPPR Patrick Roy/25 75.00 150.
SPPS Paul Stastny 15.00 40.
SPRB Ray Bourque/25 30.00 80.
SPRH Ron Hextall/35 20.00 50.
SPRM Ryan Miller 20.00 50.
SPRN Rick Nash 15.00 40.
SPRO Luc Robitaille 20.00 50.
SPRS Ryan Stoa 10.00 25.
SPSC Sidney Crosby 175.00 300.
SPSD Shane Doan
SPSE Devin Setoguchi 12.00 30.
SPSH Sergei Shirokov 8.00 20.
SPSI Simon Gagne 15.00 40.
SPSM Steve Mason 12.00 30.
SPSS Steve Shutt 12.00 30.
SPST Steven Stamkos 40.00 100.
SPSW Shea Weber 20.00 50.
SPSY Steve Yzerman/25 60.00 120.
SPTH Joe Thornton 15.00 40.
SPTM Tyler Myers 20.00 50.
SPTO Jonathan Toews 40.00 80.
SPTV Thomas Vanek 15.00 40.
SPVH Victor Hedman 25.00 60.
SPVL Vincent Lecavalier 10.00 25.
SPVO Tomas Vokoun 12.00 30.
SPVS Viktor Stalberg 12.00 30.
SPWA Cam Ward 15.00 40.
SPWG Wayne Gretzky/25 200.00 400.

2009-10 The Cup Signature Patches Dual

STATED PRINT RUN 35 SER.#'d SETS
SP2BG Grabner/Backlund
SP2BN Bourque/Neely 60.00 120.
SP2CG Gagner/Cogliano
SP2CS Couture/Setoguchi 40.00 100.
SP2CT Carter/Toews 40.00 100.
SP2CV Carter/van Riemsdyk 40.00 100.
SP2DK Kane/Duchene
SP2DO Duchene/O'Reilly 40.00 100.
SP2FM Malkin/Fleury 50.00 100.
SP2FW Franson/Wilson 40.00 100.
SP2GA Gaborik/Anisimov
SP2GB Gustavsson/Bozak 20.00 50.
SP2GL Gaborik/Lundqvist 30.00 80.
SP2GM Messier/Gretzky 250.00 400.
SP2GP Gomez/Price 25.00 60.
SP2GS Grabner/Shirokov 20.00 50.
SP2HB Hanson/Bozak 25.00 60.
SP2HN Nash/Heatley
SP2HT Hossa/Toews 75.00 150.
SP2IB Backlund/Iginla 30.00 80.
SP2ID Iginla/Doan
SP2IS Iginla/St. Louis 25.00 60.
SP2JS Stalberg/Gustavsson 25.00 60.
SP2JV Hedman/Tavares 60.00 125.
SP2KB Bozak/Kessel
SP2KD Doughty/Kopitar 60.00 120.
SP2KK Kane/Kovalchuk 40.00 100.
SP2KM Kane/Modano
SP2KV Kane/van Riemsdyk 40.00 100.
SP2LD Leetch/Del Zotto
SP2LG Gretzky/Lemieux 400.00 700.
SP2LM Leetch/Messier 40.00 100.
SP2LN Niemi/Leino 50.00 100.
SP2LS Lecavalier/Stamkos 40.00 100.
SP2LY Yzerman/Lemieux 150.00 300.
SP2LZ Lidstrom/Zetterberg 50.00 100.
SP2MB Modano/Benn
SP2ME Miller/Enroth 30.00 80.
SP2MH Myers/Hedman 20.00 50.
SP2MJ Kurri/Messier 40.00 100.
SP2NB Nash/Brassard 30.00 80.
SP2OB Ovechkin/Backstrom
SP2OD Ovechkin/Datsyuk
SP2OG Ovechkin/Green
SP2OM Ovechkin/Malkin
SP2PM Mason/Price 25.00 60.
SP2PP Stastny/Stastny 20.00 50.
SP2SD Stastny/Duchene 40.00 100.

2SG Schenn/Gustavsson 40.00 80.00
2SS Sedin/Sedin
2SW Ward/Staal 25.00 60.00
2TC Thornton/Couture 40.00 100.00
2TD Duchene/Tavares 125.00 250.00
2TH Heatley/Thornton
2TK Kane/Toews 75.00 150.00
2TS Stamkos/Tavares 100.00 200.00
2TT Ennis/Myers 50.00 100.00
2VW Wilson/van Riemsdyk 30.00 80.00

2009-10 The Cup Stanley Cup Signatures

ATED PRINT RUN 50 SER.#'d SETS
AD Alex Delvecchio
AL Andrew Ladd 10.00 25.00
AM Al MacInnis 10.00 25.00
AN Glenn Anderson 10.00 25.00
AT Alex Tanguay 6.00 15.00
BB Bob Bourne
BC Bobby Clarke 10.00 25.00
BH Bobby Hull 20.00 50.00
BL Brian Leetch 12.00 30.00
BO Bobby Orr 60.00 120.00
CD Chris Drury 8.00 20.00
CG Clark Gillies 10.00 25.00
CO Chris Osgood
CW Cam Ward 10.00 25.00
DG Doug Gilmour 15.00 40.00
DP Denis Potvin 10.00 25.00
EM Evgeni Malkin 30.00 80.00
ES Eric Staal 12.00 30.00
GA Glenn Anderson 10.00 25.00
GF Grant Fuhr 10.00 25.00
GH Gordie Howe 25.00 60.00
HZ Henrik Zetterberg 25.00 60.00
JA Jason Arnott 8.00 20.00
JB Johnny Bucyk 12.00 30.00
JG Jean-Sebastien Giguere 12.00 30.00
JK Jari Kurri 15.00 40.00
JS Jordan Staal 20.00 50.00
LR Larry Robinson 10.00 25.00
MB Martin Brodeur 30.00 80.00
ME Mark Messier 30.00 80.00
MF Marc-Andre Fleury 20.00 50.00
MH Milan Hejduk 8.00 20.00
MI Mike Bossy 15.00 40.00
ML Mario Lemieux 40.00 100.00
MM Mark Messier 30.00 80.00
MO Mike Modano 15.00 40.00
MS Martin St. Louis 10.00 25.00
MT Maxime Talbot 15.00 40.00
NL Nicklas Lidstrom 15.00 40.00
PA Patrick Roy 50.00 100.00
PD Pavel Datsyuk 15.00 40.00
PE Patrik Elias 10.00 25.00
PH Phil Esposito 15.00 40.00
PR Patrick Roy 50.00 100.00
RB Ray Bourque 12.00 30.00
RO Luc Robitaille 12.00 30.00
SB Scotty Bowman 12.00 30.00
SC Sidney Crosby 100.00 200.00
SG Scott Gomez 8.00 20.00
SY Steve Yzerman 60.00 120.00
TH Tomas Holmstrom
TL Ted Lindsay 10.00 25.00
VF Valtteri Filppula 15.00 40.00
VL Vincent Lecavalier 15.00 40.00
WG Wayne Gretzky 150.00 250.00

2009-10 The Cup Stanley Cup Signatures Dual

ATED PRINT RUN 25 SER.#'d SETS
2AE Elias/Arnott 15.00 40.00
2BG Bossy/Gillies 25.00 60.00
2BO Bucyk/Orr 75.00 150.00
2BP Bossy/Potvin 25.00 60.00
2DT Drury/Tanguay 20.00 50.00
2DZ Zetterberg/Datsyuk 30.00 60.00
2EO Orr/Esposito 75.00 150.00
2FA Anderson/Fuhr 25.00 50.00
2FT Fleury/Talbot
2GA Delvecchio/Howe 30.00 80.00
2GB Gomez/Brodeur 25.00 60.00
2GM Gilmour/MacInnis 25.00 60.00
2HD Hejduk/Drury 10.00 25.00
2KG Kurri/Gretzky 150.00 300.00
2LD Delvecchio/Lindsay 20.00 50.00
2LM Leetch/Messier 40.00 100.00
2LS Lecavalier/St. Louis 15.00 40.00
2LZ Zetterberg/Lidstrom 30.00 80.00
2MC Modano/Carbonneau
2MS Malkin/Staal
2RB Roy/Bourque 40.00 80.00
2SB Boyle/St. Louis 12.00 30.00
2SL Staal/Ladd
2SW Ward/Staal 15.00 40.00
2WM Messier/Gretzky 150.00 250.00
2YB Yzerman/Bowman 60.00 120.00
2YR Yzerman/Robitaille 60.00 120.00

2009-10 The Cup Trios Jerseys

ATED PRINT RUN 25 SER.#'d SETS
ASK Alfredssn/Kovalv/Spez 8.00 20.00
BGB Gillies/Bossy/Bourne
BMR MacIns/Robinsn/Bourque 12.00 30.00
BPB Bourne/Bossy/Potvin
BSW Ward/Staal/Brind`Amour 15.00 40.00
CBP Backlund/Chucko/Pelech 8.00 20.00
CDF Demers/Ferriero/Couture 10.00 25.00
COM Malkin/Crosby/Ovechkin 30.00 80.00
CTS Stamkos/Crosby/Tavares 40.00 100.00
CWM Couture/Wilson/Mrchnd 15.00 40.00
DCP Clarke/Dionne/Perreault
DGL Drury/Lundqvist/Gaborik 12.00 30.00
DMO McDnld/O'Marra/Dubnyk 15.00 40.00
EHH Hull/Esposito/Howe 50.00 100.00
EME Ennis/Enroth/Myers 12.00 30.00
ENW Esposito/Wheeler/Neely
FCM Crosby/Fleury/Malkin 30.00 80.00
FKM Fuhr/Messier/Kurri
FOW Wilsn/Fransn/O'Reilly 8.00 20.00
GBS Stalberg/Bozak/Gustav 15.00 40.00
GDO Duchene/Galrdi/O'Rlly 20.00 50.00
GKH Karlsn/Gustav/Hedmn 25.00 60.00
HGV Hossa/Gaborik/Voracek 10.00 25.00
HTK Hossa/Kane/Toews 15.00 40.00
KBS Bozak/Kessel/Stalberg 12.00 30.00
KLK Kane/Lehtonen/Koval 12.00 30.00
KLN Lehton/Nieml/Klprusfl 12.00 30.00
KNG Koivu/Niedermyr/Getzlf 15.00 40.00
KOM Malkin/Koval/Ovech 30.00 80.00
KWM Marchand/Kane/Wilsn 20.00 50.00
LAM Messr/Andersn/Leetch 10.00 25.00
LCM Malkin/Mario/Crosby 30.00 80.00
LDZ Zetter/Lidstrm/Datsk 15.00 40.00
LEG Gustav/Lundqvst/Enroth 12.00 30.00
LIN Iginla/Nash/Lecavalier 8.00 20.00
LMM Modano/Leetch/Mullen
LPM Mason/Price/Luongo 30.00 80.00
LSD Leetch/Sanguntt/Del Z 8.00 20.00
LSH Salming/Lidstrm/Hedmn 15.00 40.00

CTLSS Lecav/St. Louis/Stamks 15.00 40.00
CTLVB Vishnevsk/Benn/Lindgrn 25.00 60.00
CTLYM Yzrmn/Mssr/Lemieux 25.00 60.00
CTLYT Lemx/Tavares/Yzermn 40.00 100.00
CTMGK McDnld/Gilmour/Kessel
CTMMG McDnld/Mullen/Gilmour
CTMRB Benn/Richards/Modano 25.00 60.00
CTMTC Couture/Thrntn/Mrleau 15.00 40.00
CTMVM Miller/Myers/Vanek 20.00 50.00
CTNBM Nash/Mason/Brassrd 8.00 20.00
CTPKW Wilson/Kane/Parise 15.00 40.00
CTRBF Brodeur/Roy/Fleury 20.00 50.00
CTRBL Roy/Brodeur/Luongo 20.00 50.00
CTRCR Roy/Robinson/Carbon 20.00 50.00
CTRCV Richards/Carter/van R 20.00 50.00
CTRST Richards/Toews/Stastny 15.00 40.00
CTRTG Robitaille/Taylor/Gretzky 40.00 100.00
CTSDG Del Zotto/Sangntti/Gilry 8.00 20.00
CTSDH Hawrchk/Selann/Doan
CTSDO Stastny/O'Reill/Duchen 12.00 30.00
CTSHN Heatly/Nash/St. Louis 8.00 20.00
CTSRL Lemaire/Robinson/Shutt 8.00 20.00
CTTDH Hedman/Tavars/Duchen 20.00 50.00
CTTKD Duchene/Tavares/Kane 30.00 80.00
CTVWG Wilson/vRmsdk/Gilry 20.00 50.00
CTYGM Messier/Yzermn/Gretz 40.00 100.00
CTYOD Yzermn/Osgood/Drapr 20.00 50.00
CTYZH Zetterbrg/Howe/Yzermn 40.00 100.00

2010-11 The Cup

1-90 STATED PRINT RUN 249
91-108 ROOKIE AU PRINT RUN 199
109-174 ROOKIE JSY AU PRINT RUN 249
175-180 ROOKIE JSY AU PRINT RUN 99
1 Mike Green 3.00 8.00
2 Alexander Ovechkin 12.00 30.00
3 Alexander Semin 3.00 8.00
4 Nicklas Backstrom 5.00 12.00
5 Roberto Luongo 3.00 8.00
6 Daniel Sedin 3.00 8.00
7 Henrik Sedin 3.00 8.00
8 Jean-Sebastien Giguere 2.50 6.00
9 Phil Kessel 4.00 10.00
10 Dion Phaneuf 3.00 8.00
11 Tyler Bozak 3.00 8.00
12 Vincent Lecavalier 2.50 6.00
13 Martin St. Louis 3.00 8.00
14 Steven Stamkos 6.00 15.00
15 Jaroslav Halak 3.00 8.00
16 Antti Niemi 2.50 6.00
17 Patrick Marleau 3.00 8.00
18 Dany Heatley 2.50 6.00
19 Joe Thornton 3.00 8.00
20 Jordan Staal 3.00 8.00
21 Evgeni Malkin 10.00 25.00
22 Mario Lemieux 8.00 20.00
23 Marc-Andre Fleury 5.00 12.00
24 Sidney Crosby 12.00 30.00
25 Shane Doan 2.50 6.00
26 Mike Richards 3.00 8.00
27 Jeff Carter 3.00 8.00
28 Bobby Clarke 2.50 6.00
29 Eric Lindros 4.00 10.00
30 Jason Spezza 2.00 5.00
31 Mark Messier 4.00 10.00
32 Marian Gaborik 4.00 10.00
33 Henrik Lundqvist 5.00 12.00
34 Brian Leetch 2.50 6.00
35 Clark Gillies 2.50 6.00
36 Mike Bossy 2.50 6.00
37 John Tavares 6.00 15.00
38 Denis Potvin 2.50 6.00
39 Zach Parise 3.00 8.00
40 Ilya Kovalchuk 3.00 8.00
41 Martin Brodeur 6.00 15.00
42 Shea Weber 2.50 6.00
43 Carey Price 12.00 30.00
44 Larry Robinson 2.50 6.00
45 Guy Lafleur 3.00 8.00
46 Lars Eller 2.50 6.00
47 Mikko Koivu 3.00 8.00
48 Marcel Dionne 3.00 8.00
49 Anze Kopitar 5.00 12.00
50 Wayne Gretzky 12.00 30.00
51 Luc Robitaille 2.50 6.00
52 Drew Doughty 3.00 8.00
53 Ron Francis 3.00 8.00
54 Gordie Howe 6.00 15.00
55 Tomas Vokoun 2.50 6.00
56 Grant Fuhr 2.50 6.00
57 Jari Kurri 2.50 6.00
58 Steve Yzerman 6.00 15.00
59 Pavel Datsyuk 4.00 10.00
60 Nicklas Lidstrom 3.00 8.00
61 Johan Franzen 3.00 8.00
62 Henrik Zetterberg 4.00 10.00
63 Brad Richards 3.00 8.00
64 Steve Mason 2.50 6.00
65 Rick Nash 3.00 8.00
66 Chris Stewart 2.50 6.00
67 Patrick Roy 6.00 15.00
68 Matt Duchene 3.00 8.00
69 Paul Stastny 3.00 8.00
70 Milan Hejduk 2.50 6.00
71 Ray Bourque 4.00 10.00
72 Bobby Hull 2.50 6.00
73 Jonathan Toews 6.00 15.00
74 Patrick Kane 6.00 15.00
75 Phil Esposito 4.00 10.00
76 Marty Turco 3.00 8.00
77 Cam Ward 3.00 8.00
78 Eric Staal 4.00 10.00
79 Jarome Iginla 3.00 8.00
80 Miikka Kiprusoff 2.50 6.00
81 Tyler Myers 3.00 8.00
82 Thomas Vanek 3.00 8.00
83 Ryan Miller 3.00 8.00
84 Gilbert Perreault 2.50 6.00
85 Bobby Orr 8.00 20.00
86 Tuukka Rask 3.00 8.00
87 Cam Neely 2.50 6.00
88 Evander Kane 3.00 8.00
89 Teemu Selanne 6.00 15.00
90 Ryan Getzlaf 5.00 12.00
91 Philip McRae AU RC 6.00 15.00
92 Nick Bonino AU RC 8.00 20.00
93 Derek Smith AU RC 6.00 15.00
94 Nikita Nikitin AU RC 6.00 15.00
95 Matt Hackott AU RC 8.00 20.00
96 Johan Motin AU RC 5.00 12.00
97 Adam McQuaid AU RC 10.00 25.00
98 Robin Lehner AU RC 12.00 30.00
99 Cory Emmerton AU RC 8.00 20.00
100 Jeff Penner AU RC 10.00 25.00
101 Brayden Irwin AU RC 6.00 15.00
102 Matt Kassian AU RC 6.00 15.00
103 Brandon McMillan AU RC 6.00 15.00
104 Grant Clitsome AU RC 6.00 15.00
105 Nate Prosser AU RC 6.00 15.00
106 Maxime Fortunus AU RC 5.00 12.00
107 Chad Kolarik AU RC 6.00 15.00
108 Richard Bachman AU RC 8.00 20.00
109 J.T. Wyman JSY AU RC 10.00 25.00
110 Tommy Wingels JSY AU RC 10.00 25.00
111 Dustin Kohn JSY AU RC 10.00 25.00
112 A.Bodnarchuk JSY AU RC 10.00 25.00
113 R.McDonagh JSY AU RC 40.00 100.00
114 K.Daugavins JSY AU RC 12.00 30.00
115 T.J. Brodie JSY AU RC 10.00 25.00
116 Jim O'Brien JSY AU RC 12.00 30.00
117 Brett MacLean JSY AU RC 12.00 30.00
118 Tomas Tatar JSY AU RC 30.00 80.00
119 Zuccarello-Aasen JSY AU RC 30.00 80.00
120 Patrice Cormier JSY AU RC 12.00 30.00
121 Casey Wellman JSY AU RC 10.00 25.00
122 Matt Martin JSY AU RC 25.00 60.00
123 S.Della Rovere JSY AU RC 10.00 25.00
124 Nick Spaling JSY AU RC 10.00 25.00
125 Justin Mercier JSY AU RC 10.00 25.00
126 Keith Aulie JSY AU RC 10.00 25.00
127 Nick Palmieri JSY AU RC 10.00 25.00
128 Philip Larsen JSY AU RC 10.00 25.00
129 Pechurski JSY AU RC EX 12.00 30.00
130 Justin Falk JSY AU RC 8.00 20.00
131 Maxim Noreau JSY AU RC 8.00 20.00
132 Arturs Kulda JSY AU RC 10.00 25.00
133 Mark Olver JSY AU RC 10.00 25.00
134 Cody Almond JSY AU RC 10.00 25.00
135 Nick Johnson JSY AU RC 8.00 20.00
136 Evan Brophey JSY AU RC 10.00 25.00
137 Jeremy Morin JSY AU RC 10.00 25.00
138 Jamie Arniel JSY AU RC 10.00 25.00
139 J.Markstrom JSY AU RC 25.00 60.00
140 Henrik Karlsson JSY AU RC 10.00 25.00
141 Kyle Clifford JSY AU RC 10.00 25.00
142 Alex Plante JSY AU RC 10.00 25.00
143 Ian Cole JSY AU RC 10.00 25.00
144 Jared Cowen JSY AU RC 10.00 25.00
145 Dana Tyrell JSY AU RC 10.00 25.00
146 M.Scandella JSY AU RC 10.00 25.00
147 D.Tokarski JSY AU RC 10.00 25.00
148 Zach Hamill JSY AU RC 10.00 25.00
149 Jamie McBain JSY AU RC 10.00 25.00
150 Colby Cohen JSY AU RC 10.00 25.00
151 Nick Leddy JSY AU RC 10.00 25.00
152 A.Lindback JSY AU RC 10.00 25.00
153 Brandon Pirri JSY AU RC 10.00 25.00
154 Brandon Yip JSY AU RC 10.00 25.00
155 Eric Wellwood JSY AU RC 12.00 30.00
156 T.McCollum JSY AU RC 12.00 30.00
157 C.Fowler JSY AU RC EXCH 12.00 30.00
158 Kyle Palmieri JSY AU RC 20.00 50.00
159 Eric Tangradi JSY AU RC 10.00 25.00
160 E.Grachev JSY AU RC 10.00 25.00
161 Zac Dalpe JSY AU RC 10.00 25.00
162 Luke Adam JSY AU RC 10.00 25.00
163 Ekman-Larsson JSY AU RC 30.00 80.00
164 K.Shattenkirk JSY AU RC 25.00 60.00
165 Johansson JSY AU RC EX 60.00 150.00
166 Jacob Josefson JSY AU RC 10.00 25.00
167 Jordan Caron JSY AU RC 15.00 40.00
168 B.Schenn JSY AU RC 30.00 80.00
169 N.Niederreiter JSY AU RC 20.00 50.00
170 Mattias Tedenby JSY AU RC 8.00 20.00
171 A.Burmistrov JSY AU RC 15.00 40.00
172 M.Paajarvi JSY AU RC 12.00 30.00
173 Derek Stepan JSY AU RC 20.00 50.00
174 Nazem Kadri JSY AU RC 50.00 120.00
175 S.Bobrovsky JSY AU RC 100.00 250.00
176 P.K. Subban JSY AU RC 400.00 750.00
177 Jeff Skinner JSY AU RC 100.00 250.00
178 Jordan Eberle JSY AU RC 400.00 1000.00
179 Tyler Seguin JSY AU RC 1000.00 2000.00
180 Taylor Hall JSY AU RC 600.00 1200.00

2010-11 The Cup Gold

*GOLD 1-90: .8X TO 2X BASE
COMMON ROOKIE (91-180) 8.00 20.00
ROOKIE SEMISTARS 10.00 25.00
ROOKIE UNL.STARS 12.00 30.00
STATED PRINT RUN 25 SER.#'d SETS
4 Nicklas Backstrom 10.00 25.00
22 Mario Lemieux 15.00 40.00
23 Marc-Andre Fleury 10.00 25.00
24 Sidney Crosby 25.00 60.00
27 Jeff Carter 12.00 30.00
29 Eric Lindros 12.00 30.00
50 Wayne Gretzky 50.00 100.00
98 Robin Lehner 20.00 50.00
99 Linus Omark 25.00 60.00
100 Jeff Penner 15.00 40.00
113 Ryan McDonagh 25.00 60.00
118 Tomas Tatar 30.00 60.00
119 Mats Zuccarello-Aasen 20.00 50.00
126 Keith Aulie 10.00 25.00
137 Jeremy Morin 10.00 25.00
139 Jacob Markstrom 15.00 40.00
156 Thomas McCollum 12.00 30.00
157 Cam Fowler 30.00 80.00
162 Luke Adam 10.00 25.00
163 Oliver Ekman-Larsson 15.00 40.00
164 Kevin Shattenkirk 20.00 50.00
165 Marcus Johansson 15.00 40.00
166 Jacob Josefson 10.00 25.00
167 Jordan Caron 15.00 40.00
168 Brayden Schenn 75.00 150.00
169 Nino Niederreiter 12.00 30.00
170 Mattias Tedenby 8.00 20.00
171 Alexander Burmistrov 10.00 25.00
172 Magnus Paajarvi 12.00 30.00
173 Derek Stepan 25.00 60.00
174 Nazem Kadri 30.00 80.00
175 Sergei Bobrovsky 25.00 60.00
176 P.K. Subban 100.00 200.00
177 Jeff Skinner 100.00 200.00
178 Jordan Eberle 100.00 200.00
179 Tyler Seguin 125.00 250.00
180 Taylor Hall 150.00 300.00

2010-11 The Cup Silver Jerseys

STATED PRINT RUN 25 SER.#'d SETS
1 Mike Green 6.00 15.00
2 Alexander Ovechkin 25.00 60.00
3 Alexander Semin 6.00 15.00
4 Nicklas Backstrom 10.00 25.00
5 Roberto Luongo 6.00 15.00
6 Daniel Sedin 8.00 20.00
7 Henrik Sedin 6.00 15.00
8 Jean-Sebastien Giguere
9 Phil Kessel 8.00 20.00
10 Dion Phaneuf 6.00 15.00
11 Tyler Bozak 6.00 15.00
12 Vincent Lecavalier 5.00 12.00
13 Martin St. Louis 8.00 20.00
14 Steven Stamkos 12.00 30.00
15 Jaroslav Halak 6.00 15.00
17 Patrick Marleau 6.00 15.00
19 Joe Thornton 6.00 15.00
20 Jordan Staal 6.00 15.00
21 Evgeni Malkin 20.00 50.00
22 Mario Lemieux 20.00 50.00
23 Marc-Andre Fleury 8.00 20.00
24 Sidney Crosby 25.00 60.00
25 Shane Doan 8.00 20.00
26 Mike Richards 6.00 15.00
27 Jeff Carter 6.00 15.00
29 Eric Lindros 6.00 15.00
30 Jason Spezza 4.00 10.00
31 Mark Messier 10.00 25.00
32 Marian Gaborik 12.00 30.00
33 Henrik Lundqvist 10.00 25.00
34 Brian Leetch 6.00 15.00
35 Clark Gillies 6.00 15.00
36 Mike Bossy 6.00 15.00
37 John Tavares 12.00 30.00
39 Zach Parise 6.00 15.00
40 Ilya Kovalchuk 6.00 15.00
41 Martin Brodeur 12.00 30.00
42 Shea Weber 5.00 12.00
43 Carey Price 25.00 60.00
44 Larry Robinson 6.00 15.00
46 Lars Eller 5.00 12.00
47 Mikko Koivu 6.00 15.00
48 Marcel Dionne 8.00 20.00
49 Anze Kopitar 10.00 25.00
50 Wayne Gretzky 30.00 80.00
51 Luc Robitaille 8.00 20.00
52 Drew Doughty 6.00 15.00
53 Ron Francis 8.00 20.00
54 Gordie Howe 15.00 40.00
55 Tomas Vokoun 5.00 12.00
57 Jari Kurri 6.00 15.00
58 Steve Yzerman 15.00 40.00
59 Pavel Datsyuk 8.00 20.00
60 Nicklas Lidstrom 6.00 15.00
61 Johan Franzen 8.00 20.00
62 Henrik Zetterberg 8.00 20.00
63 Brad Richards 6.00 15.00
64 Steve Mason 5.00 12.00
65 Rick Nash 6.00 15.00
66 Chris Stewart 5.00 12.00
67 Patrick Roy 15.00 40.00
68 Matt Duchene 6.00 15.00
69 Paul Stastny 6.00 15.00
70 Milan Hejduk 5.00 12.00
71 Ray Bourque 6.00 15.00
73 Jonathan Toews 12.00 30.00
74 Patrick Kane 12.00 30.00
75 Phil Esposito 10.00 25.00
76 Marty Turco 6.00 15.00
77 Cam Ward 6.00 15.00
78 Eric Staal 8.00 20.00
79 Jarome Iginla 6.00 15.00
80 Miikka Kiprusoff 5.00 12.00
81 Tyler Myers 6.00 15.00
82 Thomas Vanek 6.00 15.00
83 Ryan Miller 6.00 15.00
84 Gilbert Perreault 6.00 15.00
86 Tuukka Rask 6.00 15.00
87 Cam Neely 6.00 15.00
88 Evander Kane 6.00 15.00
90 Ryan Getzlaf 10.00 25.00

2010-11 The Cup Emblems of Endorsement

STATED PRINT RUN 15
EEAO Alexander Ovechkin 150.00 300.00
EEBR Martin Brodeur 100.00 200.00
EECP Carey Price 100.00 200.00
EEEL Eric Lindros 150.00 250.00
EEEM Evgeni Malkin 60.00 120.00
EEIL Igor Larionov 40.00 100.00
EEJE Jordan Eberle 200.00 400.00
EEJS Joe Sakic 150.00 250.00
EEJT John Tavares 40.00 100.00
EEMB Mike Bossy 60.00 120.00
EEMD Marcel Dionne 50.00 125.00
EEML Mario Lemieux 200.00 400.00
EEMM Mark Messier 60.00 150.00
EEMP Magnus Paajarvi 40.00 100.00
EENB Nicklas Backstrom 60.00 150.00
EEPD Pavel Datsyuk 50.00 125.00
EEPK Patrick Kane 80.00 200.00
EEPR Patrick Roy
EEPS P.K. Subban 200.00 400.00
EERF Ron Francis 40.00 100.00
EERM Ryan Miller 40.00 100.00
EESC Sidney Crosby EXCH 300.00 500.00
EESS Steven Stamkos 150.00 300.00
EESY Steve Yzerman 125.00 250.00
EETH Taylor Hall 200.00 400.00
EETO Jonathan Toews 100.00 200.00
EETS Tyler Seguin 125.00 300.00
EEWG Wayne Gretzky 600.00 1000.00

2010-11 The Cup Enshrinements

STATED PRINT RUN 50 SER.#'d SETS
CEAO Alexander Ovechkin 50.00 125.00
CEBC Bobby Clarke 12.00 30.00
CEBH Bobby Hull 15.00 40.00
CEBO Bobby Orr 75.00 150.00
CECN Cam Neely 12.00 30.00
CECP Carey Price 25.00 50.00
CECW Cam Ward 12.00 30.00
CEDI Marcel Dionne 15.00 40.00
CEDS Derek Stepan 12.00 30.00
CEEL Eric Lindros 30.00 60.00
CEEM Evgeni Malkin 40.00 100.00
CEES Eric Staal 15.00 40.00
CEGH Gordie Howe 60.00 120.00
CEGP Gilbert Perreault 12.00 30.00
CEHL Henrik Lundqvist 25.00 50.00
CEIL Igor Larionov 15.00 40.00
CEJB Johnny Bucyk 12.00 30.00
CEJE Jordan Eberle 50.00 100.00
CEJF Jeff Skinner 25.00 60.00
CEJG Jean-Sebastien Giguere 10.00 25.00
CEJH Jaroslav Halak 12.00 30.00
CEJI Jarome Iginla 12.00 30.00
CEJK Jari Kurri 12.00 30.00
CEJO Joe Thornton 12.00 30.00
CEJS Joe Sakic 20.00 50.00
CEJT Jonathan Toews 25.00 60.00
CEKE Phil Kessel 15.00 40.00
CELR Luc Robitaille 12.00 30.00
CEMB Martin Brodeur 25.00 60.00
CEMD Matt Duchene 12.00 30.00
CEME Mark Messier 25.00 60.00
CEMG Marian Gaborik 15.00 40.00
CEMH Milan Hejduk 10.00 25.00
CEMI Mike Bossy 12.00 30.00
CEML Mario Lemieux 50.00 100.00
CEMZ Mats Zuccarello-Aasen 12.00 30.00
CENB Nicklas Backstrom 15.00 40.00
CENK Nazem Kadri 20.00 50.00
CENL Nicklas Lidstrom 20.00 40.00
CEPE Phil Esposito 20.00 50.00
CEPK Patrick Kane 30.00 60.00
CEPR Patrick Roy 30.00 80.00
CEPS P.K. Subban 20.00 50.00
CERB Ray Bourque 20.00 50.00
CERF Ron Francis 20.00 50.00
CERG Ryan Getzlaf 20.00 50.00
CERK Red Kelly 10.00 25.00
CERM Ryan Miller 12.00 30.00
CERN Rick Nash 15.00 40.00
CESB Sergei Bobrovsky 15.00 40.00
CESC Sidney Crosby 75.00 150.00
CESY Steve Yzerman
CETA John Tavares 25.00 60.00
CETH Taylor Hall 25.00 60.00
CETS Tyler Seguin 25.00 60.00
CETV Thomas Vanek 12.00 30.00
CEWG Wayne Gretzky 100.00 200.00

2010-11 The Cup Enshrinements Dual

STATED PRINT RUN 35 SER.#'d SETS
CE2CR B.Clarke/M.Richards EX 20.00 50.00
CE2FH G.Howe/R.Francis 50.00 120.00
CE2GB G.Howe/B.Orr 100.00 200.00
CE2GH W.Gretzky/T.Hall 300.00 500.00
CE2GM W.Gretzky/M.Messier EX 175.00 300.00
CE2HC B.Hull/B.Clarke 40.00 100.00
CE2HD M.Duchene/M.Hejduk 20.00 50.00
CE2HE T.Hall/J.Eberle 75.00 150.00
CE2KK P.Kessel/N.Kadri 50.00 100.00
CE2KS J.Kurri/M.Paajarvi 30.00 80.00
CE2LB S.Bowman/I.Larionov 20.00 50.00
CE2ME M.Messier/J.Eberle 75.00 150.00
CE2MV R.Miller/T.Vanek 15.00 40.00
CE2NB C.Neely/R.Bourque 30.00 80.00
CE2OB Ovechkin/N.Bckstm EX 60.00 120.00
CE2OH B.Orr/B.Hull 100.00 200.00
CE2OM A.Ovechkin/E.Malkin EX 40.00 100.00
CE2PS C.Price/P.Subban 75.00 150.00
CE2RB P Roy/M.Brodeur 100.00 200.00
CE2RS J.Sakic/P.Roy EX 75.00 150.00
CE2SC S.Crosby/S.Crosby EX 200.00 350.00
CE2SD J.Sakic/M.Duchene EX 50.00 100.00
CE2SZ Zuccarello-Asn/Stepan 25.00 60.00
CE2TD J.Tavares/M.Duchene 30.00 60.00
CE2TK P.Kane/J.Toews 40.00 100.00
CE2TS S.Stamkos/J.Tavares EX 60.00 120.00
CE2TT T.Seguin/T.Rask 30.00 80.00
CE2YH S.Yzerman/G.Howe 100.00 200.00

2010-11 The Cup Enshrinements Triple

STATED PRINT RUN 15 SER.#'d SETS
CE3AVS Sakic/Roy/Bourque 125.00 250.00
CE3BOS Orr/Bucyk/Esposito 125.00 200.00
CE3CPT Gretzky/Mario/Yzerman 350.00 550.00
CE3EDM Gretzky/Messier/Kurri
CE3NYR Z-Aasen/Grachv/Stepn 40.00 80.00
CE3OG6 Howe/Orr/Hull 175.00 300.00
CE3OIL Hall/Eberle/Paajarvi 175.00 300.00
CE3RUS Ovechkn/Malkn/Dtsyk 100.00 200.00

2010-11 The Cup Foundations Jerseys

STATED PRINT RUN 25 SER.#'d SETS
CFAK Anze Kopitar 12.00 30.00
CFAO Alexander Ovechkin 30.00 80.00
CFBO Mike Bossy 12.00 30.00
CFCP Carey Price 30.00 80.00
CFDP Dion Phaneuf 8.00 20.00
CFDU Matt Duchene 8.00 20.00
CFEK Evander Kane 8.00 20.00
CFEM Evgeni Malkin
CFES Eric Staal 10.00 25.00
CFHL Henrik Lundqvist 12.00 30.00
CFIK Ilya Kovalchuk 8.00 20.00
CFIL Igor Larionov 12.00 30.00
CFJC Jeff Carter 8.00 20.00
CFJE Jordan Eberle 25.00 60.00
CFJF Johan Franzen 8.00 20.00
CFJG Jean-Sebastien Giguere 10.00 25.00
CFJH Jaroslav Halak 8.00 20.00
CFJI Jarome Iginla 8.00 20.00
CFJS Joe Sakic 15.00 40.00
CFJT Joe Thornton 8.00 20.00
CFKE Phil Kessel 10.00 25.00
CFLR Luc Robitaille 10.00 25.00
CFMB Martin Brodeur 15.00 40.00
CFMD Marcel Dionne 8.00 20.00
CFMG Marian Gaborik 10.00 25.00
CFML Mario Lemieux 20.00 50.00
CFMM Mark Messier 20.00 50.00
CFMP Magnus Paajarvi 5.00 12.00
CFMR Mike Richards 8.00 20.00
CFNB Nicklas Backstrom 12.00 30.00
CFNL Nicklas Lidstrom 8.00 20.00
CFPD Pavel Datsyuk 10.00 25.00
CFPK Patrick Kane 15.00 40.00
CFPS P.K. Subban 25.00 60.00
CFRF Ron Francis 15.00 40.00
CFRH Ron Hextall 8.00 20.00
CFRL Roberto Luongo 8.00 20.00
CFRM Ryan Miller 8.00 20.00
CFRN Rick Nash 8.00 20.00
CFSC Sidney Crosby 30.00 80.00
CFSS Steven Stamkos 15.00 40.00
CFSY Steve Yzerman 15.00 40.00
CFTA John Tavares 15.00 40.00
CFTH Taylor Hall 15.00 40.00
CFTO Jonathan Toews 15.00 40.00
CFTS Tyler Seguin 15.00 40.00
CFWG Wayne Gretzky 50.00 100.00
CFZP Zach Parise 8.00 20.00

2010-11 The Cup Foundations Jerseys Autographs

JSY AU PRINT RUN 15
CFAK Anze Kopitar 25.00 50.00
CFAO Alexander Ovechkin 60.00 120.00
CFBO Mike Bossy 25.00 50.00
CFCP Carey Price 50.00 100.00
CFDP Dion Phaneuf 15.00 40.00
CFDU Matt Duchene 15.00 40.00
CFEK Evander Kane 15.00 40.00
CFEM Evgeni Malkin 40.00 80.00
CFES Eric Staal 20.00 50.00
CFHL Henrik Lundqvist EXCH
CFIL Igor Larionov 25.00 50.00
CFJC Jeff Carter 15.00 40.00
CFJE Jordan Eberle 60.00 120.00
CFJF Johan Franzen 15.00 40.00
CFJG Jean-Sebastien Giguere 12.00 30.00
CFJH Jaroslav Halak 15.00 40.00
CFJI Jarome Iginla 15.00 40.00
CFJS Joe Sakic 40.00 80.00
CFJT Joe Thornton 15.00 40.00
CFKE Phil Kessel 20.00 50.00
CFLR Luc Robitaille 15.00 40.00
CFMB Martin Brodeur 40.00 80.00
CFMD Marcel Dionne 20.00 50.00
CFMG Marian Gaborik 15.00 40.00
CFML Mario Lemieux 60.00 120.00
CFMM Mark Messier 40.00 80.00
CFMP Magnus Paajarvi 25.00 50.00
CFNB Nicklas Backstrom 25.00 50.00
CFNL Nicklas Lidstrom 25.00 50.00
CFPD Pavel Datsyuk 30.00 60.00
CFPK Patrick Kane 40.00 80.00
CFPS P.K. Subban 40.00 100.00
CFRF Ron Francis 25.00 50.00
CFRH Ron Hextall 20.00 50.00
CFRM Ryan Miller 15.00 40.00
CFRN Rick Nash 15.00 40.00
CFSC Sidney Crosby 100.00 175.00
CFSS Steven Stamkos 50.00 100.00
CFSY Steve Yzerman 50.00 100.00
CFTA John Tavares 40.00 80.00
CFTH Taylor Hall 75.00 150.00
CFTO Jonathan Toews 75.00 150.00
CFWG Wayne Gretzky 200.00 350.00

2010-11 The Cup Honorable Numbers

STATED PRINT RUN 1-93
HNAK Anze Kopitar/11
HNAO Alex Ovechkin/8
HNBB Sergei Bobrovsky/35 40.00 80.00
HNBL Brian Leetch/2
HNBR Bobby Ryan/9
HNCN Cam Neely/8
HNCP Carey Price/31 50.00 100.00
HNCS Chris Stewart/25 20.00 50.00
HNCW Cam Ward/30 20.00 50.00
HNDP Dion Phaneuf/3
HNEK Evander Kane/9
HNEM Evgeni Malkin/71 50.00 100.00
HNES Eric Staal/12
HNHL Henrik Lundqvist/30 60.00 120.00
HNIL Igor Larionov/8
HNJC Jeff Carter/17 25.00 50.00
HNJE Jordan Eberle/14
HNJF Johan Franzen/93 20.00 50.00
HNJG J-S Giguere/35 20.00 50.00
HNJI Jarome Iginla/12
HNJO Joe Thornton/19 40.00 80.00
HNJS Joe Sakic/19 100.00 200.00
HNJT Jonathan Toews/19 60.00 120.00
HNJV James van Riemsdyk/21 25.00 60.00
HNKE Phil Kessel/81 15.00 40.00
HNKS Kevin Shattenkirk/8
HNLR Luc Robitaille/20 50.00 100.00
HNMA Martin Brodeur/30 50.00 100.00
HNMD Matt Duchene/9
HNME Mark Messier/11
HNMF Marc-Andre Fleury/29 50.00 120.00
HNMG Marian Gaborik/10
HNMH Marian Hossa/81 30.00 60.00
HNML Mario Lemieux/6
HNMP Magnus Paajarvi/91 15.00 40.00
HNMS Martin St. Louis/26 25.00 60.00
HNMZ Mats Zuccarello-Aasen/36 25.00 60.00
HNNB Nicklas Backstrom/19 40.00 80.00
HNNK Nazem Kadri/43 30.00 80.00
HNPE Derek Stepan/21 30.00 60.00
HNPK Patrick Kane/88 50.00 100.00
HNPR Patrick Roy/33 125.00 225.00
HNPS P.K. Subban/76 75.00 150.00
HNRB Ray Bourque/77 100.00 175.00
HNRF Ron Francis/10
HNRG Ryan Getzlaf/15 30.00 60.00
HNRI Brad Richards/91 15.00 40.00
HNRK Ryan Kesler/17 50.00 100.00
HNRM Ryan Miller/30 20.00 50.00
HNRN Rick Nash/61 30.00 80.00
HNSC Sidney Crosby/87 15.00 300.00
HNSD Shane Doan/19 25.00 50.00
HNSK Jeff Skinner/53 30.00 80.00
HNSM Steve Mason/1
HNSS Steven Stamkos/91 75.00 150.00
HNST Paul Stastny/26 20.00 50.00
HNSY Steve Yzerman/19 125.00 200.00
HNTA John Tavares/91 40.00 100.00
HNTH Taylor Hall/4
HNTM Tyler Myers/57 25.00 60.00
HNTR Tuukka Rask/40 40.00 80.00
HNTS Tyler Seguin/19 150.00 300.00
HNTT Tomas Tatar/12
HNTV Thomas Vanek/26 25.00 60.00
HNVL Vincent Lecavalier/4
HNWG Wayne Gretzky/9 EXCH

2010-11 The Cup Honorable Numbers Dual

STATED PRINT RUN 4-91
CARDS HAVE DHN PREFIX
BM Brodeur/Miller/30 EXCH 100.00 200.00
CC S.Crosby Dual/87 200.00 400.00
DJ D.Stepan/VanRmsdyk/21 30.00 60.00
ES T.Espo/S.Bobrvsky/35 40.00 80.00
HK M.Hossa/P.Kessel/81 25.00 60.00
KC R.Kesler/J.Carter/17 30.00 60.00
NB Naslund/Backstrom/19 50.00 100.00
SY J.Sakic/S.Yzerman/19 225.00 400.00
TS S.Stamkos/J.Tavares/91 60.00 120.00
TT Thornton/Toews/19
YS Yzerman/Seguin/19 EXCH 175.00 300.00

2010-11 The Cup Limited Logos Autographs

STATED PRINT RUN 10-50
LLAK Anze Kopitar 60.00 120.00
LLAO Alexander Ovechkin 75.00 150.00
LLBB Sergei Bobrovsky 30.00 80.00
LLBD Brandon Dubinsky 20.00 50.00
LLBO Mike Bossy/25 75.00 150.00
LLBS Brayden Schenn 30.00 80.00
LLCF Cam Fowler 25.00 60.00
LLCG Claude Giroux 30.00 80.00
LLCN Cam Neely 25.00 60.00
LLCP Carey Price 75.00 150.00
LLCW Cam Ward 25.00 60.00
LLDD Drew Doughty 60.00 150.00
LLDS Derek Stepan 20.00 50.00
LLDU Matt Duchene 25.00 60.00
LLEL Eric Lindros 60.00 120.00
LLEM Evgeni Malkin 75.00 125.00
LLHL Henrik Lundqvist 50.00 100.00
LLIL Igor Larionov/25 60.00 120.00
LLJE Jordan Eberle 100.00 200.00
LLJF Johan Franzen 15.00 40.00
LLJG Jean-Sebastien Giguere 25.00 60.00
LLJH Jaroslav Halak 40.00 80.00
LLJI Jarome Iginla 25.00 60.00
LLJS Joe Sakic 50.00 120.00
LLKE Phil Kessel 30.00 80.00
LLKN Patrick Kane 60.00 120.00
LLKS Kevin Shattenkirk 20.00 50.00
LLLR Luc Robitaille 40.00 80.00
LLMB Martin Brodeur 75.00 150.00
LLMD Marcel Dionne/25 100.00 200.00
LLMF Marc-Andre Fleury 25.00 60.00
LLMG Marian Gaborik 25.00 60.00
LLML Mario Lemieux 100.00 175.00
LLMM Mark Messier 50.00 120.00
LLMP Magnus Paajarvi 25.00 60.00
LLMZ Mats Zuccarello-Aasen 30.00 80.00
LLNB Nicklas Backstrom 25.00 60.00
LLNK Nazem Kadri 25.00 60.00
LLNL Nicklas Lidstrom 75.00 150.00
LLNN Nino Niederreiter 30.00 80.00
LLPA Paul Stastny 25.00 60.00
LLPD Pavel Datsyuk 50.00 100.00
LLPK P.K. Subban 75.00 150.00
LLPR Patrick Roy 100.00 200.00
LLRF Ron Francis 20.00 50.00
LLRG Ryan Getzlaf 40.00 100.00
LLRK Ryan Kesler 30.00 80.00
LLRM Ryan Miller 30.00 80.00
LLRN Rick Nash 30.00 80.00
LLSC Sidney Crosby 150.00 300.00
LLSK Jeff Skinner 75.00 150.00
LLSM Steve Mason 30.00 80.00
LLSS Steven Stamkos 75.00 150.00
LLST Jordan Staal 25.00 60.00
LLSY Steve Yzerman 60.00 120.00
LLTA John Tavares 40.00 100.00
LLTH Taylor Hall 75.00 150.00
LLTM Tyler Myers 25.00 60.00
LLTO Jonathan Toews 75.00 150.00
LLTR Tuukka Rask 40.00 100.00
LLTS Tyler Seguin 100.00 200.00
LLTT Tomas Tatar 50.00 100.00
LLTV Thomas Vanek 25.00 60.00
LLWG Wayne Gretzky/10 EXCH

2010-11 The Cup Auto Draft Boards

STATED PRINT RUN 25 SER.#'d SETS
DBAB Alexander Burmistrov 60.00 150.00
DBAP Alex Plante 30.00 80.00
DBBS Brayden Schenn 125.00 250.00
DBCA Jordan Caron 75.00 150.00
DBCF Cam Fowler EXCH 75.00 150.00
DBIC Ian Cole 20.00 50.00
DBJC Jared Cowen 20.00 50.00
DBJE Jordan Eberle 400.00 800.00
DBJJ Jacob Josefson 20.00 50.00
DBJN John Carlson 60.00 120.00
DBJS Jeff Skinner 225.00 400.00
DBKP Kyle Palmieri 40.00 100.00
DBKS Kevin Shattenkirk 40.00 80.00
DBMJ Marcus Johansson EXCH 100.00 200.00
DBMP Magnus Paajarvi 75.00 150.00
DBMT Mattias Tedenby 15.00 40.00
DBNK Nazem Kadri 100.00 200.00
DBNL Nick Leddy 40.00 80.00
DBNN Nino Niederreiter 60.00 120.00
DBOB Jim O'Brien 25.00 60.00
DBOE Oliver Ekman-Larsson 60.00 120.00
DBRM Ryan McDonagh 50.00 100.00
DBTH Taylor Hall 600.00 900.00
DBTS Tyler Seguin 250.00 500.00
DBZH Zach Hamill 30.00 80.00

2010-11 The Cup Rookie Bookmarks Dual Autographs

STATED PRINT RUN 25 SER.#'d SETS
RBKANA C.Fowler/K.Palmieri 30.00 80.00
RBKATL Burmistrov/P.Cormier 40.00 100.00
RBKCAR J.Skinner/Z.Dalpe 125.00 250.00
RBKCHI N.Leddy/J.Morin 125.00 200.00
RBKEDM J.Eberle/M.Paajarvi 100.00 200.00
RBKLAK B.Schenn/K.Clifford 100.00 200.00
RBKNJD M.Tedenby/J.Josefson 75.00 150.00
RBKNYR Stepan/Zuccarello-Asn 125.00 250.00
RBKPHI Bobrovsky/E.Wellwood 75.00 150.00
RBKPHX Ekman-Larsson/MacLn 40.00 100.00
RBK12 T.Hall/T.Seguin 300.00 600.00
RBKPKNK P.Subban/N.Kadri 200.00 400.00
RBKTBAY D.Tyrell/D.Tokarski 30.00 80.00

2010-11 The Cup Rookie Gear Autographs

STATED PRINT RUN 25 SER.#'d SETS
ARGAB Alexander Burmistrov 75.00 200.00
ARGBS Brayden Schenn 100.00 200.00
ARGDS Derek Stepan 100.00 200.00
ARGJC Jordan Caron 25.00 60.00
ARGJE Jordan Eberle 350.00 600.00
ARGJS Jeff Skinner 175.00 300.00
ARGKS Kevin Shattenkirk 60.00 120.00
ARGMJ Marcus Johansson EXCH 175.00 350.00
ARGMP Magnus Paajarvi 125.00 250.00
ARGMT Mattias Tedenby 25.00 60.00
ARGMZ Mats Zuccarello-Aasen 60.00 120.00
ARGNK Nazem Kadri 150.00 300.00
ARGNN Nino Niederreiter 40.00 100.00
ARGPS P.K. Subban 350.00 600.00
ARGSB Sergei Bobrovsky 125.00 250.00
ARGTH Taylor Hall 350.00 600.00
ARGTS Tyler Seguin 350.00 600.00
ARGTT Tomas Tatar 75.00 150.00

2010-11 The Cup Scripted Sticks

STATED PRINT RUN 35 SER.#'d SETS
SAO Alexander Ovechkin 200.00 350.00
SGH Gordie Howe 175.00 300.00
SPR Patrick Roy 150.00 300.00
SSC Sidney Crosby 250.00 500.00
SWG Wayne Gretzky 400.00 600.00

2010-11 The Cup Scripted Swatches

STATED PRINT RUN 35 SER.#'d SETS
SSAO Alexander Ovechkin 50.00 100.00
SSEL Eric Lindros 50.00 120.00
SSEM Evgeni Malkin 50.00 125.00
SSJE Jordan Eberle 75.00 150.00
SSJT Jonathan Toews 50.00 100.00
SSMB Martin Brodeur 50.00 120.00
SSML Mario Lemieux 100.00 175.00
SSMM Mark Messier 50.00 100.00
SSNB Nicklas Backstrom 40.00 80.00
SSPD Pavel Datsyuk 30.00 80.00
SSPK Patrick Kane 40.00 100.00
SSPS P.K. Subban 75.00 150.00
SSRF Ron Francis 25.00 60.00
SSRG Ryan Getzlaf 25.00 60.00
SSRM Ryan Miller 25.00 60.00
SSSC Sidney Crosby 200.00 300.00
SSSS Steven Stamkos 75.00 150.00
SSSY Steve Yzerman 60.00 120.00
SSTH Taylor Hall 150.00 300.00
SSTS Tyler Seguin 75.00 150.00
SSWG Wayne Gretzky EXCH 300.00 500.00

2010-11 The Cup Scripted Swatches Dual

STATED PRINT RUN 15 SER.#'d SETS
SS2BM M.Brodeur/R.Miller 75.00 150.00
SS2DK D.Doughty/A.Kopitar
SS2EP J.Eberle/M.Paajarvi 60.00 150.00
SS2GR W.Gretzky/L.Robitaille 300.00 600.00
SS2LC M.Lemieux/S.Crosby
SS2LF M.Lemieux/R.Francis 125.00 200.00
SS2NJ N.Lidstrom/J.Franzen 50.00 120.00
SS2OB A.Ovechkin/N.Backstrom
SS2OG E.Lindros/J.Tavares 75.00 150.00
SS2OM A.Ovechkin/E.Malkin 250.00 400.00
SS2RS P.Roy/J.Sakic 100.00 200.00
SS2TK J.Toews/P.Kane
SS2TT T.Hall/T.Seguin
SS2YL S.Yzerman/I.Larionov 100.00 175.00

2010-11 The Cup Signature Patches

STATED PRINT RUN 35-75
SPAB Alexander Burmistrov 10.00 25.00
SPAK Anze Kopitar 25.00 60.00
SPAN Antti Niemi 12.00 30.00
SPAO Alex Ovechkin/35 75.00 150.00
SPBB Sergei Bobrovsky 25.00 60.00
SPBD Brad Richards 15.00 40.00
SPBL Brian Leetch 12.00 30.00
SPBN Jonathan Bernier 12.00 30.00
SPBO Mike Bossy/35 20.00 50.00
SPBR Bobby Ryan 15.00 40.00
SPBS Brayden Schenn 15.00 40.00
SPBW Jay Bouwmeester 20.00 50.00
SPCD Chris Drury 12.00 30.00
SPCG Claude Giroux 15.00 40.00
SPCN Cam Neely 20.00 50.00
SPCW Cam Ward 15.00 40.00
SPDD Drew Doughty 15.00 40.00
SPDI Marcel Dionne/35 50.00 100.00
SPDK Derek Stepan 15.00 40.00
SPEG Evgeny Grachev 12.00 30.00
SPEK Evander Kane 15.00 40.00
SPEL Eric Lindros 25.00 60.00
SPEM Evgeni Malkin 50.00 125.00
SPES Eric Staal 12.50 30.00
SPET Eric Tangradi 12.00 30.00
SPHL Henrik Lundqvist 40.00 100.00
SPIL Igor Larionov/35 20.00 50.00
SPJC Jeff Carter 15.00 40.00
SPJE Jordan Eberle 40.00 100.00
SPJF Johan Franzen 15.00 40.00
(inserted in 2011-12 Cup packs)
SPJH Jaroslav Halak 15.00 40.00
SPJI Jarome Iginla 20.00 50.00
SPJO Jordan Caron 15.00 40.00
SPJS Joe Sakic/35 50.00 100.00
SPJT John Tavares 30.00 80.00
SPJV James van Riemsdyk 25.00 60.00
SPKA Patrick Kane 30.00 80.00
SPKS Phil Kessel 15.00 40.00
SPKV Kevin Shattenkirk 15.00 40.00
SPLR Larry Robinson 12.00 30.00
SPMA Marian Gaborik 20.00 50.00
SPMC Ryan McDonagh 20.00 50.00
SPMD Matt Duchene 20.00 50.00
SPMF Marc-Andre Fleury 20.00 50.00
SPMH Marian Hossa 30.00 60.00
SPML Mario Lemieux/35 100.00 200.00
SPMM Mark Messier/35 40.00 100.00
SPMS Martin St. Louis 15.00 30.00
SPMT Marty Turco 12.00 30.00
SPMZ Mats Zuccarello-Aasen 15.00 40.00
SPNB Nicklas Backstrom 25.00 60.00
SPNH Nathan Horton EXCH 12.00 30.00
SPNK Nazem Kadri 50.00 100.00
SPNL Nicklas Lidstrom 15.00 40.00
SPNN Nino Niederreiter 12.00 30.00
SPOE Oliver Ekman-Larsson 15.00 40.00
SPPC Patrice Cormier 15.00 40.00
SPPH Dion Phaneuf 15.00 40.00
SPPJ Magnus Paajarvi 12.00 30.00
SPPK P.K. Subban 60.00 120.00
SPPM Patrick Marleau 15.00 40.00
SPPS Paul Stastny 15.00 40.00
SPRF Ron Francis/35 25.00 60.00
SPRG Ryan Getzlaf 25.00 60.00
SPRH Ron Hextall 15.00 40.00
SPRK Ryan Kesler 12.00 30.00
SPRM Ryan Miller 25.00 60.00
SPRN Rick Nash 15.00 40.00
SPRO Luc Robitaille 15.00 40.00
SPRS Ryan Smyth 15.00 40.00
SPSC Sidney Crosby 100.00 200.00
SPSD Shane Doan 12.00 30.00
SPSE Devin Setoguchi 12.00 30.00
SPSK Jeff Skinner 20.00 50.00
SPSM Steve Mason 12.00 30.00
SPSS Steven Stamkos 50.00 100.00
SPST Jordan Staal 15.00 40.00
SPSV Semyon Varlamov 15.00 40.00
SPTH Taylor Hall 60.00 120.00
SPTM Tyler Myers 12.00 30.00
SPTO Jonathan Toews 30.00 80.00
SPTS Tyler Seguin 50.00 120.00
SPTT Tomas Tatar 40.00 80.00
SPVO Tomas Vokoun 12.00 30.00

2010-11 The Cup Signature Patches Dual

STATED PRINT RUN 35 SER.#'d SETS
SP2AT A.Pechurski/E.Tangradi 20.00 50.00
SP2BM M.Messier/B.Leetch 50.00 100.00
SP2CP C.Price/M.Cammalleri 75.00 150.00
SP2CS P.Subban/J.Cowen 50.00 120.00
SP2DS Dubinsky/Stepan 15.00 40.00
SP2EJ E.Staal/J.Staal 25.00 60.00
SP2GM W.Gretzky/M.Messier 250.00 400.00
SP2GR R.Getzlaf/B.Ryan 20.00 50.00
SP2HB J.Halak/D.Backes 15.00 40.00
SP2HE T.Hall/J.Eberle 200.00 400.00
SP2HT J.Toews/M.Hossa 75.00 100.00
SP2IB J.Iginla/J.Bouwmeester 20.00 50.00
SP2IK J.Iginla/E.Kane 20.00 50.00
SP2JM J.Staal/M.Staal 20.00 50.00
SP2KD A.Kopitar/D.Doughty 50.00 100.00
SP2LC M.Lemieux/S.Crosby 400.00 800.00
SP2LF N.Lidstrom/J.Franzen 30.00 80.00
SP2LG W.Gretzky/M.Lemieux 300.00 600.00
SP2LS V.Lecavalier/M.St. Louis 20.00 50.00
SP2LY M.Lemieux/S.Yzerman 100.00 200.00
SP2ME T.Myers/T.Ennis 25.00 60.00
SP2MJ J.Sakic/M.Duchene 50.00 120.00
SP2ML M.Modano/N.Lidstrom 40.00 80.00
SP2MV T.Vanek/R.Miller 15.00 40.00
SP2NB R.Bourque/C.Neely 30.00 80.00
SP2NM R.Nash/S.Mason 20.00 50.00
SP2OB Ovechkin/Backstrom 100.00 200.00
SP2PP P.Stastny/P.Stastny 20.00 50.00
SP2RB M.Brodeur/P.Roy 100.00 200.00
SP2SD P.Stastny/M.Duchene 20.00 50.00
SP2SK P.Subban/N.Kadri 40.00 100.00
SP2SS M.St. Louis/S.Stamkos 40.00 100.00
SP2SW E.Staal/C.Ward 25.00 60.00
SP2TD J.Tavares/M.Duchene 50.00 100.00
SP2TJ T.Hall/J.Tavares 75.00 150.00
SP2TK J.Toews/P.Kane 100.00 200.00
SP2TN J.Thornton/A.Niemi 20.00 50.00
SP2YL S.Yzerman/I.Larionov 75.00 150.00
SP2ZS Zuccarello-Asn/Stepan 20.00 50.00

2010-11 The Cup Stanley Cup Signatures

STATED PRINT RUN 50 SER.#'d SETS
SCAD Alex Delvecchio 8.00 20.00
SCAN Antti Niemi 8.00 20.00
SCAT Alex Tanguay 6.00 15.00
SCBC Bobby Clarke 15.00 40.00
SCBH Bobby Hull 12.00 30.00
SCBL Brian Leetch 15.00 40.00
SCBO Bobby Orr 60.00 120.00
SCBR Brad Richards 10.00 25.00
SCBS Brent Seabrook 15.00 40.00
SCCD Chris Drury 8.00 20.00
SCCG Clark Gillies 10.00 25.00
SCCW Cam Ward 10.00 25.00
SCDB Dustin Byfuglien 10.00 25.00
SCDG Doug Gilmour 12.00 30.00
SCDP Denis Potvin 10.00 25.00
SCEM Evgeni Malkin 30.00 80.00
SCES Eric Staal 12.00 30.00
SCFR Ron Francis 12.00 30.00
SCGA Glenn Anderson 10.00 25.00
SCGH Gordie Howe 60.00 120.00
SCHE Milan Hejduk 8.00 20.00
SCIL Igor Larionov 10.00 25.00
SCJB Johnny Bucyk 10.00 25.00
SCJF Johan Franzen 12.00 30.00
SCJG Jean-Sebastien Giguere 12.00 30.00
SCJK Jari Kurri 10.00 25.00
SCJS Joe Sakic 40.00 80.00
SCJT Jonathan Toews 40.00 80.00
SCKV Kris Versteeg 12.00 30.00
SCLF Guy Lafleur 25.00 60.00
SCLR Luc Robitaille 12.00 30.00
SCMA Mark Messier 20.00 50.00
SCMB Martin Brodeur 40.00 80.00
SCME Mark Messier 40.00 80.00
SCMF Marc-Andre Fleury 15.00 40.00
SCMH Marian Hossa 20.00 50.00
SCMI Mike Bossy 12.00 30.00
SCML Mario Lemieux 40.00 100.00
SCNL Nicklas Lidstrom 25.00 50.00
SCOS Chris Osgood 10.00 25.00
SCPA Patrick Roy 50.00 100.00
SCPE Phil Esposito 15.00 40.00
SCPK Patrick Kane 40.00 80.00
SCPR Patrick Roy 50.00 100.00
SCRB Ray Bourque 15.00 40.00
SCRK Red Kelly 10.00 25.00
SCRO Larry Robinson 10.00 25.00
SCSB Scotty Bowman 15.00 30.00
SCSC Sidney Crosby 100.00 175.00
SCST Jordan Staal 10.00 25.00
SCTL Ted Lindsay 10.00 25.00
SCVL Vincent Lecavalier 8.00 20.00
SCWG Wayne Gretzky 150.00 250.00

2010-11 The Cup Stanley Cup Signatures Dual

STATED PRINT RUN 25 SER.#'d SETS
SC2AE J.Arnott/P.Elias 12.00 30.00
SC2BG M.Bossy/C.Gillies 20.00 50.00
SC2BK D.Byfuglien/P.Kane 25.00 60.00
SC2BO B.Orr/J.Bucyk 60.00 120.00
SC2BP M.Bossy/D.Potvin 20.00 50.00
SC2DT M.Hejduk/C.Drury 10.00 25.00
SC2EA E.Staal/A.Ladd 15.00 40.00
SC2EO B.Orr/P.Esposito 60.00 120.00
SC2FM M.Fleury/E.Malkin 40.00 80.00
SC2GM W.Gretzky/M.Messier 125.00 250.00
SC2HD G.Howe/Delvecchio 60.00 120.00
SC2HN M.Hossa/A.Niemi 40.00 80.00
SC2JP J.Sakic/P.Roy 100.00 200.00
SC2KG W.Gretzky/J.Kurri 150.00 300.00
SC2LD T.Lindsay/Delvecchio 15.00 40.00
SC2LF M.Lemieux/R.Francis 60.00 120.00
SC2LM M.Messier/B.Leetch 40.00 80.00
SC2LR Lecavalier/B.Richards 20.00 50.00
SC2NJ N.Lidstrom/J.Franzen 30.00 80.00
SC2RB P.Roy/R.Bourque 50.00 100.00
SC2RS B.Richards/St. Louis 12.00 30.00
SC2SB J.Sakic/R.Bourque 75.00 150.00
SC2SW E.Staal/C.Ward 20.00 50.00
SC2TK J.Toews/P.Kane 50.00 100.00
SC2YL S.Yzerman/I.Larionov 60.00 120.00
SC2YR S.Yzerman/Robitaille 50.00 120.00

2010-11 The Cup Trios Jerseys

STATED PRINT RUN 25 SER.#'d SETS
C3BU Drury/DiPietro/Shatten 12.00 30.00
C3NY Stepan/Niederter/Adam 30.00 60.00
C3ANA Getzlaf/Perry/Fowler 12.00 30.00
C3ATL Cormier/Burmis/Kulda 8.00 20.00
C3AVS Duchn/Stastny/Muellr 8.00 20.00
C3BML Brodr/Miller/Lundqvist 15.00 40.00
C3BOS Rask/Bergeron/Horton 12.00 30.00
C3BUF Vanek/Myers/Miller 8.00 20.00
C3CAR Skinner/McBain/Dalpe 20.00 50.00
C3CHI Pirri/Leddy/Brophey 20.00 40.00
C3COL Sakic/Roy/Tanguay 20.00 50.00
C3CPT Sakic/Yzerman/Lemieux 15.00 40.00
C3DET Lidst/Zetter/Holmstrom 10.00 25.00
C3DRW Yzrmn/Larionv/Lidstrm 20.00 50.00
C3FLY Richrds/Cartr/Bobrvsky 15.00 40.00
C3GR8 Gretzky/Lemieux/Sakic 40.00 100.00
C3HSE Hall/Seguin/Eberle 30.00 80.00
C3LAK Doughty/Kopitar/Brown 15.00 40.00
C3MIN Scandella/Noreau/Almnd 6.00 15.00
C3NJD Tedenby/Josefsn/Palmri 6.00 15.00
C3NYI Tavrs/Niederrtr/Martn 15.00 40.00
C3NYR Lundqvst/Gabrik/Dbnsky 12.00 30.00
C3OIL Hall/Eberle/Paajarvi 40.00 100.00
C3OTT Spezza/Alfred/Kovalev 8.00 20.00
C3PEN Mario/Francs/Kovlv 15.00 40.00
C3PHI Clarke/Lindrs/Richrds 20.00 50.00
C3PHX Doan/Ekmn-Lars/MacLn 10.00 25.00
C3PIT Crosby/Malkin/Staal 20.00 50.00
C3SES Seguin/Eberle/Skinner 25.00 60.00
C3SJS Marleau/Htley/Thornton 8.00 20.00
C3STL Shatten/Cole/Dila Rvere 12.00 30.00
C3SWE Pjarvi/Johnsn/Tedenby 10.00 25.00
C3TBL Stamkos/St.Lou/Lecav 15.00 40.00
C3TCG Luongo/Brodeur/Fleury 25.00 60.00
C3TOR Giguer/Phaneuf/Kessl 20.00 50.00
C3VAN Luongo/Sedin/Sedin 20.00 50.00
C3WJC Kadri/Subban/Cowen 20.00 50.00
C3BEES Seguin/Caron/Hamill 25.00 60.00
C3BLUE Zucc-A/Stpan/Grchv 12.00 30.00
C3CAPS Ovech/Backstr/Green 15.00 40.00
C3GMGG Crosby/Toews/Perry 20.00 50.00
C3HABD Subbn/Markv/Hamrlk 20.00 50.00
C3HAWK Espo/Wilsn/Probrt 15.00 40.00
C3LBBR Price/Cammallr/Markv 20.00 50.00
C3PITT Tangradi/Pchski/Jhnsn 12.00 30.00
C3SCUP Toews/Kane/Hossa 20.00 50.00
C3WASH Ovech/Backstrm/Semn 30.00 80.00
C3WILD Koivu/Latend/Bouchrd 8.00 20.00
C3WISC Stepn/McBan/McDngh 20.00 50.00
C3CANES Staal/Skinner/Ward 12.00 30.00
C3CWALL Gilmour/Brodr/Hawr 25.00 60.00
C3GOALS Sid/Ovie/Stamks 25.00 60.00
C3KMLPS Igin/Doan/Niedermyr 8.00 20.00
C3LAGR8 Gretz/Dionn/Robitlle 40.00 100.00
C3RMSKI Sid/Richrds/Lecav 20.00 50.00
C3ROOKD Subbn/Ekmn-Lrs/Shattn 25.00 60.00
C3WNDSR Hall/Fowler/Wellwd 30.00 80.00
C3PHILLY Richrds/Cartr/Giroux 8.00 20.00

2011-12 The Cup

1-90 VETERAN PRINT RUN 249
91-108 ROOKIE AU PRINT RUN 199
109-174 ROOK.JSY AU PRINT RUN 249
175-180 ROOK.JSY AU PRINT RUN 99
EXCH EXPIRATION: 8/17/2014
1 Bobby Ryan 3.00 8.00
2 Ryan Getzlaf 5.00 12.00
3 Jonas Hiller 2.50 6.00
4 Ray Bourque 5.00 12.00
5 Bobby Orr 10.00 25.00
6 Phil Esposito 5.00 12.00
7 Cam Neely 3.00 8.00
8 Tim Thomas 4.00 10.00
9 Zdeno Chara 3.00 8.00
10 Nathan Horton 3.00 8.00
11 Tyler Seguin 6.00 15.00
12 Thomas Vanek 3.00 8.00
13 Ryan Miller 3.00 8.00
14 Derek Roy 2.50 6.00
15 Dominik Hasek 4.00 10.00
16 Miikka Kiprusoff 3.00 8.00
17 Jarome Iginla 3.00 8.00
18 Jeff Skinner 3.00 8.00
19 Patrick Kane 6.00 15.00
20 Tony Esposito 5.00 12.00
21 Bobby Hull 3.00 8.00
22 Jonathan Toews 6.00 15.00
23 Joe Sakic 5.00 12.00
24 Patrick Roy 8.00 20.00
25 Matt Duchene 3.00 8.00
26 Paul Stastny 3.00 8.00
27 Rick Nash 3.00 8.00
28 Jeff Carter 3.00 8.00
29 Steve Mason 2.50 6.00
30 Ed Belfour 3.00 8.00
31 Jim Howard 3.00 8.00
32 Pavel Datsyuk 4.00 10.00
33 Nicklas Lidstrom 3.00 8.00
34 Johan Franzen 3.00 8.00
35 Henrik Zetterberg 4.00 10.00
36 Ryan Smyth 2.50 6.00
37 Taylor Hall 6.00 15.00
38 Grant Fuhr 3.00 8.00
39 Jari Kurri 3.00 8.00
40 Jordan Eberle 3.00 8.00
41 Anze Kopitar 5.00 12.00
42 Mike Richards 3.00 8.00
43 Luc Robitaille 3.00 8.00
44 Drew Doughty 3.00 8.00
45 Mike Modano 5.00 12.00
46 Dino Ciccarelli 3.00 8.00
47 Carey Price 10.00 25.00
48 Larry Robinson 3.00 8.00
49 P.K. Subban 6.00 15.00
50 Pekka Rinne 4.00 10.00
51 Ilya Kovalchuk 3.00 8.00
52 Martin Brodeur 6.00 15.00
53 Zach Parise 3.00 8.00
54 John Tavares 6.00 15.00
55 Mike Bossy 3.00 8.00
56 Wayne Gretzky 15.00 40.00
57 Marian Gaborik 4.00 10.00
58 Henrik Lundqvist 4.00 10.00
59 Mark Messier 4.00 10.00
60 Jason Spezza 3.00 8.00
61 Eric Lindros 5.00 12.00
62 James van Riemsdyk 3.00 8.00
63 Jaromir Jagr 8.00 20.00
64 Claude Giroux 3.00 8.00
65 Jordan Staal 3.00 8.00
66 Evgeni Malkin 10.00 25.00
67 Mario Lemieux 10.00 25.00
68 Marc-Andre Fleury 5.00 12.00
69 Sidney Crosby 12.00 30.00
70 Ron Francis 4.00 10.00
71 Paul Coffey 3.00 8.00
72 Antti Niemi 2.50 6.00
73 Patrick Marleau 3.00 8.00
74 Joe Thornton 3.00 8.00
75 Logan Couture 3.00 8.00
76 Jaroslav Halak 3.00 8.00
77 Brett Hull 4.00 10.00
78 Vincent Lecavalier 2.50 6.00
79 Steven Stamkos 6.00 15.00
80 Phil Kessel 4.00 10.00
81 Dion Phaneuf 3.00 8.00
82 Roberto Luongo 3.00 8.00
83 Daniel Sedin 3.00 8.00
84 Henrik Sedin 3.00 8.00
85 Ryan Kesler 3.00 8.00
86 Trevor Linden 3.00 8.00
87 Alexander Ovechkin 12.00 30.00
88 Nicklas Backstrom 5.00 12.00
89 Dale Hawerchuk 4.00 10.00
90 Ondrej Pavelec 3.00 8.00
91 Zac Rinaldo RC 4.00 10.00
92 David Rundblad RC 4.00 10.00
93 Erik Condra RC 4.00 10.00
94 Robert Bortuzzo AU RC 6.00 15.00
95 Kevin Marshall AU RC 6.00 15.00
96 Ryan Thang AU RC 5.00 12.00
97 Pat Maroon AU RC 6.00 15.00
98 Eddie Lack AU RC 6.00 15.00
99 Jimmy Hayes AU RC 8.00 20.00
100 D.Ullstrom AU RC 6.00 15.00
101 Dylan Olsen AU RC 8.00 20.00
102 Frederic St. Denis AU RC 6.00 15.00
103 Brian Strait AU RC 8.00 20.00
104 Allen York AU RC 8.00 20.00
105 Stu Bickel AU RC 6.00 15.00
106 Paul Postma AU RC 6.00 15.00
107 Anders Nilsson AU RC 6.00 15.00
108 Mikko Koskinen AU RC 8.00 20.00
109 Ryan Ellis JSY AU RC 20.00 50.00
110 Marcus Foligno JSY AU RC 12.00 30.00
111 Zack Kassian JSY AU RC 10.00 25.00
112 B.McNabb JSY AU RC 8.00 20.00
113 Leland Irving JSY AU RC 8.00 20.00
114 Brendan Smith JSY AU RC 8.00 20.00
115 Peter Holland JSY AU RC 8.00 20.00
116 Gustav Nyquist JSY AU RC 30.00 80.00
117 Colten Teubert JSY AU RC 8.00 20.00
118 Andy Miele JSY AU RC 8.00 20.00
119 Jake Gardiner JSY AU RC 12.00 30.00
120 Carl Klingberg JSY AU RC 8.00 20.00
121 Mika Zibanejad JSY AU RC 20.00 50.00
122 Dmitry Orlov JSY AU RC EX 10.00 25.00
123 Aaron Palushaj JSY AU RC 8.00 20.00
124 Adam Larsson JSY AU RC 10.00 25.00
125 Matt Read JSY AU RC 15.00 40.00
126 Matt Frattin JSY AU RC 8.00 20.00
127 Blake Geoffrion JSY AU RC 8.00 20.00
128 D.Smith-Pelly JSY AU RC 12.00 30.00
129 E.Gudbranson JSY AU RC 10.00 25.00
130 Jonathon Blum JSY AU RC 8.00 20.00
131 Anton Lander JSY AU RC 8.00 20.00
132 Brandon Saad JSY AU RC 40.00 100.00
133 Adam Henrique JSY AU RC 15.00 40.00
134 Brett Connolly JSY AU RC 8.00 20.00
135 Harri Sateri JSY AU RC 8.00 20.00
136 Joe Colborne JSY AU RC 8.00 20.00
137 Marcus Kruger JSY AU RC 15.00 40.00
138 Greg Nemisz JSY AU RC 8.00 20.00
139 Ryan Johansen JSY AU RC 80.00 200.00
140 Simon Despres JSY AU RC 8.00 20.00
141 Keith Kinkaid JSY AU RC 8.00 20.00
142 Stefan Elliott JSY AU RC 8.00 20.00
143 Roman Horak JSY AU RC 8.00 20.00
144 John Moore JSY AU RC 8.00 20.00
145 Colin Greening JSY AU RC 8.00 20.00
146 Cam Atkinson JSY AU RC 20.00 50.00
147 Tomas Vincour JSY AU RC 8.00 20.00
148 Yann Sauve JSY AU RC 8.00 20.00
149 Alexei Emelin JSY AU RC 8.00 20.00
150 Cody Eakin JSY AU RC 10.00 25.00
151 Justin Faulk JSY AU RC 12.00 30.00
152 C.Gaunce JSY AU RC 6.00 15.00
153 Joe Vitale JSY AU RC 8.00 20.00
154 Brendon Nash JSY AU RC 8.00 20.00
155 Erik Gustafsson JSY AU RC 10.00 25.00
156 Raphael Diaz JSY AU RC 8.00 20.00
157 David Savard JSY AU RC 8.00 20.00
158 Tim Erixon JSY AU RC 8.00 20.00
159 T.Hartikainen JSY AU RC 8.00 20.00
160 Ben Scrivens JSY AU RC 12.00 30.00
161 Carl Hagelin JSY AU RC 12.00 30.00
162 Craig Smith JSY AU RC 10.00 25.00
163 P.Wiercioch JSY AU RC 8.00 20.00
164 Calvin de Haan JSY AU RC 8.00 20.00
165 Brett Bulmer JSY AU RC 8.00 20.00
166 Da Costa JSY AU RC 8.00 20.00
167 Voynov JSY AU RC EX 8.00 20.00
168 Roman Wick JSY AU RC 10.00 25.00
169 Mike Murphy JSY AU RC 8.00 20.00
170 Lance Bouma JSY AU RC 8.00 20.00
171 Andrew Shaw JSY AU RC 20.00 50.00
172 Ben Holmstrom JSY AU RC 8.00 20.00
173 Corey Tropp JSY AU RC 8.00 20.00
174 Lennart Petrell JSY AU RC 10.00 25.00
175 L.Leblanc JSY AU/99 RC 30.00 80.00
176 Scheifele JSY AU/99 RC 400.00 800.00
177 Hodgsn JSY AU/99 RC EX 60.00 150.00
178 S.Couturier JSY AU/99 RC 150.00 300.00
179 Landeskg JSY AU/99 RC 150.00 300.00
180 RNH JSY AU/99 RC 400.00 1000.00

2011-12 The Cup Gold

*1-90 VETS/25: 1X TO 2.5X BASIC CARDS
STATED PRINT RUN 25 SER.#'d SETS
88 Nicklas Backstrom 12.00 30.00
91 Zac Rinaldo 10.00 25.00
92 David Rundblad 10.00 25.00
93 Erik Condra 15.00 40.00
94 Robert Bortuzzo 10.00 25.00
95 Kevin Marshall 10.00 25.00
96 Ryan Thang 8.00 20.00
97 Pat Maroon 10.00 25.00
98 Eddie Lack 10.00 25.00
99 Jimmy Hayes 12.00 30.00
100 David Ullstrom 10.00 25.00
101 Dylan Olsen 12.00 30.00
102 Frederic St. Denis 10.00 25.00
103 Brian Strait 12.00 30.00
104 Allen York 12.00 30.00
105 Stu Bickel 10.00 25.00
106 Paul Postma 10.00 25.00
107 Anders Nilsson 10.00 25.00
108 Mikko Koskinen 12.00 30.00
109 Ryan Ellis 10.00 25.00
110 Marcus Foligno 30.00 75.00
111 Zack Kassian 12.00 30.00
112 Brayden McNabb 10.00 25.00
113 Leland Irving 10.00 25.00
114 Brendan Smith 10.00 25.00
115 Peter Holland 10.00 25.00
116 Gustav Nyquist 25.00 60.00
117 Colten Teubert 10.00 25.00
118 Andy Miele 10.00 25.00
119 Jake Gardiner 15.00 40.00
120 Carl Klingberg 10.00 25.00
121 Mika Zibanejad 25.00 60.00
122 Dmitry Orlov 12.00 30.00
123 Aaron Palushaj 10.00 25.00
124 Adam Larsson 12.00 30.00
125 Matt Read 20.00 50.00
126 Matt Frattin 10.00 25.00
127 Blake Geoffrion 10.00 25.00
128 Devante Smith-Pelly 15.00 40.00
129 Erik Gudbranson 12.00 30.00
130 Jonathon Blum 10.00 25.00
131 Anton Lander 15.00 40.00
132 Brandon Saad 20.00 50.00
133 Adam Henrique 25.00 60.00
134 Brett Connolly 10.00 25.00
135 Harri Sateri 10.00 25.00
136 Joe Colborne 15.00 40.00
137 Marcus Kruger 15.00 40.00
138 Greg Nemisz 10.00 25.00
139 Ryan Johansen 20.00 50.00
140 Simon Despres 10.00 25.00
141 Keith Kinkaid 10.00 25.00
142 Stefan Elliott 10.00 25.00
143 Roman Horak 10.00 25.00
144 John Moore 10.00 25.00
145 Colin Greening 10.00 25.00
146 Cam Atkinson 25.00 60.00
147 Tomas Vincour 10.00 25.00
148 Yann Sauve 10.00 25.00
149 Alexei Emelin 10.00 25.00
150 Cody Eakin 12.00 30.00
151 Justin Faulk 15.00 40.00
152 Cameron Gaunce 8.00 20.00
153 Joe Vitale 10.00 25.00
154 Brendon Nash 10.00 25.00
155 Erik Gustafsson 12.00 30.00
156 Raphael Diaz 10.00 25.00
157 David Savard 10.00 25.00
158 Tim Erixon 10.00 25.00
159 Teemu Hartikainen 15.00 40.00
160 Ben Scrivens 15.00 40.00
161 Carl Hagelin 30.00 80.00
162 Craig Smith 12.00 30.00
163 Patrick Wiercioch 10.00 25.00
164 Calvin de Haan 10.00 25.00
165 Brett Bulmer 10.00 25.00
166 Stephane Da Costa 15.00 40.00
167 Viatcheslav Voynov 10.00 25.00
168 Roman Wick 12.00 30.00
169 Mike Murphy 10.00 25.00
170 Lance Bouma 10.00 25.00
171 Andrew Shaw 25.00 60.00
172 Ben Holmstrom 12.00 30.00
173 Corey Tropp 10.00 25.00
174 Lennart Petrell 12.00 30.00
175 Louis Leblanc 10.00 25.00
176 Mark Scheifele 60.00 150.00
177 Cody Hodgson 20.00 50.00
178 Sean Couturier 20.00 50.00
179 Gabriel Landeskog 20.00 50.00
180 Ryan Nugent-Hopkins 100.00 200.00

2011-12 The Cup Gold Rainbow

1-90 UNPRICED JSY PRINT RUN 10
*ROOKIE/22-36: 1X TO 2.5X BASIC RC
*ROOKIE AU/41-81: .6X TO 1.5X BASIC AU RC
*ROOKIE AU/31-39: .8X TO 2X BASIC AU RC
94-108 ROOKIE AU PRINT RUN 1-81
*JSY AU/50-93: .5X TO 1.2X BASIC JSY AU RC
*JSY AU/30-49: .6X TO 1.5X BASIC JSY AU RC
*JSY AU/15-28: .8X TO 2X BASIC JSY AU RC
109-180 ROOKIE JSY AU PRINT RUN 2-93
EXCH EXPIRATION: 8/17/2014
137 Marcus Kruger JSY AU/16 40.00 100.00
171 Andrew Shaw JSY AU/65 60.00 120.00
175 Louis Leblanc JSY AU/71 50.00 120.00
176 Mark Scheifele JSY AU/55 100.00 250.00
179 Landeskog JSY AU/92 175.00 300.00
180 Nugent-Hopkins JSY AU/93 200.00 400.00

2011-12 The Cup Auto Draft Boards

STATED PRINT RUN 25 SER.#'d SETS
EXCH EXPIRATION: 8/26/2014
DBAL Adam Larsson 30.00 80.00
DBBC Brett Connolly 25.00 60.00
DBBS Brendan Smith 20.00 50.00
DBCH Cody Hodgson 40.00 100.00
DBCS Chris Summers 15.00 40.00
DBCT Colten Teubert 20.00 50.00
DBDH Calvin de Haan 30.00 80.00
DBDO Dylan Olsen 25.00 60.00
DBEG Erik Gudbranson 20.00 50.00
DBGL Gabriel Landeskog 75.00 150.00
DBGN Greg Nemisz 15.00 40.00
DBJB Jonathon Blum 20.00 50.00
DBJC Joe Colborne 15.00 40.00
DBJF Joe Finley 20.00 50.00
DBJG Jake Gardiner 30.00 80.00
DBJM John Moore 20.00 50.00
DBLI Leland Irving 20.00 50.00
DBLL Louis Leblanc 50.00 120.00
DBMS Mark Scheifele 50.00 125.00
DBMZ Mika Zibanejad 50.00 125.00
DBNH Riley Nash 20.00 50.00
DBPH Peter Holland 20.00 50.00
DBRE Ryan Ellis 20.00 50.00
DBRJ Ryan Johansen 40.00 100.00
DBRN Ryan Nugent-Hopkins 400.00 800.00
DBSC Sean Couturier 100.00 200.00
DBSD Simon Despres 25.00 60.00
DBTE Tim Erixon 20.00 50.00
DBTM Thomas McCollum 20.00 50.00
DBZK Zack Kassian 30.00 80.00

2011-12 The Cup Emblems of Endorsement

STATED PRINT RUN 10-15
EEBR Martin Brodeur/15
EECH Cody Hodgson/15 75.00 150.00
EEDS Denis Savard/15
EEEB Ed Belfour/15 50.00 100.00
EEEL Eric Lindros/15 125.00 200.00
EEEM Evgeni Malkin/15 150.00 250.00
EEES Eric Staal/15 30.00 80.00
EEGL Gabriel Landeskog/15
EEJI Jarome Iginla/15 40.00 80.00
EEJS Joe Sakic/15 75.00 150.00
EEJT Joe Thornton/15 40.00 80.00
EELL Louis Leblanc/15 50.00 100.00
EEMB Martin Brodeur/15 90.00 150.00
EEMF Marc-Andre Fleury/15 60.00 120.00
EEML Mario Lemieux/15 150.00 250.00
EEMO Mike Modano/15
EEPE Phil Esposito/15 90.00 150.00
EEPK Patrick Kane/15 75.00 135.00
EEPR Patrick Roy/15 75.00 150.00
EEPS P.K. Subban/15 75.00 150.00
EERF Ron Francis/15 60.00 100.00
EERN Rick Nash/15 20.00 50.00
EERY Ryan Nugent-Hopkins/15 300.00 600.00
EESC Sidney Crosby/15 200.00 400.00
EETH Taylor Hall/15 150.00 250.00
EETO Jonathan Toews/15 100.00 200.00
EETS Tyler Seguin/15 125.00 250.00
EEWG Wayne Gretzky/10

2011-12 The Cup Enshrinements

STATED PRINT RUN 50 SER.#'d SETS
CEAH Adam Henrique 15.00 40.00
CEAL Adam Larsson 12.00 30.00
CEAO Alexander Ovechkin 30.00 80.00
CEBB Bill Barber 8.00 20.00
CEBC Bobby Clarke 20.00 40.00
CEBH Brett Hull 25.00 50.00
CEBO Bobby Orr 60.00 120.00
CEBR Martin Brodeur 40.00 80.00
CEBU Johnny Bucyk 12.00 30.00
CECH Cody Hodgson 12.00 30.00
CECN Cam Neely 12.00 30.00
CECO Brett Connolly 10.00 25.00
CECP Carey Price 40.00 100.00
CECU Sean Couturier 12.00 30.00
CEDH Dominik Hasek 25.00 50.00
CEDS Dave Schultz 12.00 30.00
CEEB Ed Belfour 20.00 50.00
CEEL Eric Lindros 30.00 60.00
CEEM Evgeni Malkin 40.00 100.00
CEGF Grant Fuhr 12.00 30.00
CEGL Gabriel Landeskog 20.00 50.00
CEHA Dale Hawerchuk 15.00 40.00
CEHL Henrik Lundqvist 20.00 50.00
CEHU Bobby Hull 25.00 50.00
CEJE Jordan Eberle 15.00 40.00
CEJK Jari Kurri 15.00 30.00
CEJS Joe Sakic 30.00 60.00
CEJT Jonathan Toews 25.00 60.00
CELL Louis Leblanc 6.00 15.00
CELR Luc Robitaille 12.00 30.00
CEMB Mike Bossy 15.00 40.00
CEMD Matt Duchene 15.00 40.00
CEMG Mike Gartner 12.00 30.00
CEML Mario Lemieux 50.00 100.00
CEMM Mark Messier 25.00 50.00
CEMN Markus Naslund 10.00 25.00
CEMS Mark Scheifele 15.00 40.00
CENB Nicklas Backstrom 20.00 50.00
CENL Nicklas Lidstrom 20.00 50.00
CEPC Paul Coffey 12.00 30.00
CEPK Patrick Kane 25.00 60.00
CEPS P.K. Subban 25.00 60.00
CERB Ray Bourque 15.00 40.00
CERF Ron Francis 15.00 40.00
CERJ Ryan Johansen 15.00 40.00
CERM Ryan Miller 12.00 30.00
CERN Rick Nash 12.00 30.00
CERNH Ryan Nugent-Hopkins 40.00 100.00
CESC Sidney Crosby 75.00 150.00
CESK Jeff Skinner 12.00 30.00
CETA John Tavares 25.00 60.00
CETH Taylor Hall 25.00 60.00
CETK Tim Kerr 10.00 25.00
CETL Trevor Linden 15.00 40.00
CETS Tyler Seguin 20.00 50.00
CEWG Wayne Gretzky 125.00 200.00

2011-12 The Cup Enshrinements Dual

STATED PRINT RUN 25 SER.#'d SETS
CE2CM P.Coffey/M.Messier 30.00 60.00
CE2CR S.Couturier/M.Read 20.00 50.00
CE2EH T.Hall/J.Eberle 50.00 100.00
CE2EO P.Esposito/B.Orr 50.00 100.00
CE2FC R.Francis/P.Coffey 15.00 40.00
CE2FM E.Malkin/M.Fleury 40.00 100.00
CE2GM W.Gretzky/M.Messier 150.00 300.00
CE2GN Gretzky/Nugent-Hopkins 250.00 500.00
CE2HS T.Seguin/T.Hall 40.00 80.00
CE2HT B.Hull/J.Toews 50.00 100.00
CE2KH J.Kurri/T.Hartikainen 15.00 40.00
CE2KS Klingberg/M.Scheifele 15.00 40.00
CE2LC S.Crosby/Lemieux 200.00 400.00
CE2MK S.Mikita/P.Kane 30.00 60.00
CE2NB R.Bourque/C.Neely 30.00 60.00
CE2NL Nugent-Hopkins/Landes 40.00 100.00
CE2OB Ovechkin/Backstrom 40.00 100.00
CE2OH B.Orr/B.Hull 75.00 135.00
CE2PS C.Price/P.Subban 75.00 150.00
CE2RB P.Roy/M.Brodeur 100.00 200.00
CE2RG G.Fuhr/R.Miller 20.00 40.00
CE2RK M.Richards/Kopitar 15.00 40.00
CE2RL Lundqvist/B.Richards
CE2RS P.Roy/J.Sakic 60.00 120.00
CE2SB J.Sakic/R.Bourque 40.00 80.00
CE2SL P.Subban/L.Leblanc
CE2TD J.Tavares/M.Duchene 25.00 60.00
CE2TK P.Kane/J.Toews 50.00 100.00
CE2WM W.Gretzky/M.Messier 125.00 200.00

2011-12 The Cup Foundations Jerseys

STATED PRINT RUN 25 SER.#'d SETS
CFAH Adam Henrique 12.00 30.00
CFAO Alexander Ovechkin 30.00 80.00
CFCG Claude Giroux 8.00 20.00
CFCH Cody Hodgson 10.00 25.00
CFCP Carey Price 25.00 60.00
CFCS Chris Stewart 6.00 15.00
CFCU Sean Couturier 10.00 25.00
CFDB David Backes 8.00 20.00
CFDD Drew Doughty 8.00 20.00
CFDH Dale Hawerchuk 10.00 25.00
CFDR Derek Roy 6.00 15.00
CFDS Denis Savard 10.00 25.00
CFEL Eric Lindros 15.00 40.00
CFEM Evgeni Malkin 15.00 40.00
CFGL Gabriel Landeskog 10.00 25.00
CFHL Henrik Lundqvist 10.00 25.00
CFJC Jeff Carter 8.00 20.00
CFJE Jordan Eberle 8.00 20.00
CFJH Jaroslav Halak 8.00 20.00
CFJI Jarome Iginla 8.00 20.00
CFJS Joe Sakic 10.00 25.00
CFJT John Tavares 15.00 40.00
CFLL Louis Leblanc 5.00 12.00
CFLR Larry Robinson 8.00 20.00
CFMB Martin Brodeur 15.00 40.00
CFMD Matt Duchene 8.00 20.00
CFMF Marc-Andre Fleury 10.00 25.00
CFML Mario Lemieux 25.00 60.00
CFMM Mark Messier 10.00 25.00
CFMR Mike Richards 8.00 20.00
CFNB Nicklas Backstrom 12.00 30.00
CFNH Ryan Nugent-Hopkins 15.00 40.00
CFNL Nicklas Lidstrom 8.00 20.00
CFPK Patrick Kane 15.00 40.00
CFPR Patrick Roy 20.00 50.00
CFPS P.K. Subban 15.00 40.00
CFRF Ron Francis 10.00 25.00
CFRK Ryan Kesler 8.00 20.00
CFRL Roberto Luongo 8.00 20.00
CFRM Ryan Miller 8.00 20.00
CFRN Rick Nash 8.00 20.00
CFSC Sidney Crosby 30.00 80.00
CFSS Steven Stamkos 15.00 40.00
CFST Jordan Staal 8.00 20.00
CFTH Taylor Hall 15.00 40.00
CFTL Trevor Linden 12.00 30.00
CFTO Jonathan Toews 15.00 40.00
CFTT Tim Thomas 8.00 20.00
CFWG Wayne Gretzky 50.00 100.00
CFZP Zach Parise 8.00 20.00

2011-12 The Cup Foundations Jerseys Autographs

CFAH Adam Henrique
CFAO Alexander Ovechkin 50.00 100.00
CFCG Claude Giroux 20.00 50.00
CFCH Cody Hodgson 30.00 80.00
CFCP Carey Price 60.00 150.00
CFCU Sean Couturier 20.00 50.00
CFDB David Backes 20.00 50.00
CFDD Drew Doughty
CFDH Dale Hawerchuk 25.00 60.00
CFDR Derek Roy 15.00 40.00
CFDS Denis Savard 20.00 40.00
CFEL Eric Lindros 30.00 60.00
CFEM Evgeni Malkin 60.00 150.00
CFGL Gabriel Landeskog 40.00 80.00
CFHL Henrik Lundqvist 25.00 60.00
CFJC Jeff Carter 12.00 30.00
CFJE Jordan Eberle 20.00 50.00
CFJH Jaroslav Halak
CFJI Jarome Iginla 40.00 80.00
CFJT John Tavares 40.00 80.00
CFLL Louis Leblanc 15.00 40.00
CFLR Larry Robinson 20.00 50.00
CFMB Martin Brodeur 50.00 100.00
CFMD Matt Duchene 20.00 50.00
CFMF Marc-Andre Fleury 25.00 50.00
CFML Mario Lemieux 60.00 120.00
CFMM Mark Messier 40.00 80.00
CFNB Nicklas Backstrom 15.00 40.00
CFNH Ryan Nugent-Hopkins 40.00 100.00
CFNL Nicklas Lidstrom 30.00 80.00
CFPK Patrick Kane 40.00 100.00
CFPR Patrick Roy 60.00 120.00
CFPS P.K. Subban
CFRF Ron Francis 25.00 60.00
CFRK Ryan Kesler
CFRM Ryan Miller 20.00 50.00
CFRN Rick Nash
CFSC Sidney Crosby 150.00 250.00
CFST Jordan Staal 20.00 50.00
CFTH Taylor Hall 40.00 100.00
CFTL Trevor Linden 20.00 50.00
CFTO Jonathan Toews 40.00 100.00
CFWG Wayne Gretzky 250.00 400.00

2011-12 The Cup Honorable Numbers

STATED PRINT RUN 1-93
HNBM Brad Marchand/63 25.00 60.00
HNCG Claude Giroux/28 40.00 100.00
HNCO Chris Osgood/30 20.00 50.00
HNCP Carey Price/31 60.00 120.00
HNEM Evgeni Malkin/71 50.00 100.00
HNGL Gabriel Landeskog/92 30.00 80.
HNHG Cody Hodgson/18 40.00 100.
HNJF Johan Franzen/93 15.00 40.
HNJG J-S Giguere/35 15.00 40.
HNKE Evander Kane/29 20.00 50.
HNLR Luc Robitaille/20 30.00 60.
HNMB Martin Brodeur/30 40.00 100.
HNMH Marian Hossa/81 30.00 60.
HNNB Nicklas Backstrom/19 30.00 60.
HNPA Paul Stastny/26 20.00 50.
HNRG Ryan Getzlaf/15 30.00 60.
HNRH Nugent-Hopkins/93 50.00 120.
HNRK Ryan Kesler/17 40.00 80.
HNRM Ryan Miller/30 20.00 50.
HNRN Rick Nash/61 20.00 50.
HNSA Joe Sakic/19 40.00 100.
HNSC Sidney Crosby/87 150.00 300.
HNSF Mark Scheifele/55 40.00 100.
HNSN Scott Niedermayer/27 30.00 60.
HNTE Tony Esposito/35 30.00 60.
HNTO Jonathan Toews/19 125.00 225.
HNTS Tyler Seguin/19 40.00 100.
HNTV John Tavares/19 50.00 100.
HNVO Tomas Vokoun/29 40.00 80.

2011-12 The Cup Honorable Numbers Dual

STATED PRINT RUN 1-93
DHNBB M.Brodeur/E.Belfour/30 90.00 150.
DHNHL B.Hull/T.Linden/16 60.00 120.
DHNMI P.Marleau/J.Iginla/12 75.00 150.
DHNNB Backstrom/Naslnd/19 60.00 120.
DHNNZ RNH/M.Zibanejad/93 40.00 100.
DHNST J.Sakic/J.Toews/19 125.00 250.

2011-12 The Cup Silver Jersey

STATED PRINT RUN 25 SER.#'d SETS
1 Bobby Ryan 8.00 20.
2 Ryan Getzlaf 12.00 30.
3 Jonas Hiller 6.00 15.
4 Ray Bourque 12.00 30.
6 Phil Esposito 12.00 30.
7 Cam Neely 8.00 20.
8 Tim Thomas 8.00 20.
9 Zdeno Chara 8.00 20.
10 Nathan Horton 8.00 20.
11 Tyler Seguin 15.00 40.
12 Thomas Vanek 8.00 20.
13 Ryan Miller 8.00 20.
14 Derek Roy 6.00 15.
15 Dominik Hasek 10.00 25.
16 Miikka Kiprusoff 8.00 20.
17 Jarome Iginla 8.00 20.
18 Jeff Skinner 8.00 20.
19 Patrick Kane 15.00 40.
20 Tony Esposito 8.00 20.
22 Jonathan Toews 15.00 40.
23 Joe Sakic 12.00 30.
24 Patrick Roy 20.00 50.
25 Matt Duchene 8.00 20.
26 Paul Stastny 8.00 20.
27 Rick Nash 8.00 20.
28 Jeff Carter 8.00 20.
29 Steve Mason 6.00 15.
30 Ed Belfour 8.00 20.
31 Jim Howard 8.00 20.
32 Pavel Datsyuk 10.00 25.
33 Nicklas Lidstrom 8.00 20.
34 Johan Franzen 8.00 20.
35 Henrik Zetterberg 10.00 25.
36 Ryan Smyth 6.00 15.
37 Taylor Hall 15.00 40.
38 Grant Fuhr 8.00 20.
39 Jari Kurri 8.00 20.
40 Jordan Eberle 8.00 20.
41 Anze Kopitar 12.00 30.
42 Mike Richards 8.00 20.
43 Luc Robitaille 8.00 20.
44 Drew Doughty 8.00 20.
45 Mike Modano 12.00 30.
46 Dino Ciccarelli 8.00 20.
47 Carey Price 25.00 60.
48 Larry Robinson 8.00 20.
49 P.K. Subban 15.00 40.
50 Pekka Rinne 10.00 25.
51 Ilya Kovalchuk 8.00 20.
52 Martin Brodeur 15.00 40.
53 Zach Parise 8.00 20.
54 John Tavares 15.00 40.
56 Wayne Gretzky 40.00 100.
57 Marian Gaborik 10.00 25.
58 Henrik Lundqvist 10.00 25.
59 Mark Messier 10.00 25.
60 Jason Spezza 8.00 20.
61 Eric Lindros 12.00 30.
62 James van Riemsdyk 8.00 20.
63 Jaromir Jagr 20.00 50.
64 Claude Giroux 8.00 20.
65 Jordan Staal 8.00 20.
66 Evgeni Malkin 25.00 60.
67 Mario Lemieux 25.00 60.
68 Marc-Andre Fleury 12.00 30.
69 Sidney Crosby 30.00 80.
70 Ron Francis 10.00 25.
71 Paul Coffey 8.00 20.
72 Antti Niemi 6.00 15.
73 Patrick Marleau 10.00 25.
74 Joe Thornton 8.00 20.
75 Logan Couture 8.00 20.
76 Jaroslav Halak 8.00 20.
77 Brett Hull 10.00 25.
78 Vincent Lecavalier 6.00 15.
79 Steven Stamkos 15.00 40.
80 Phil Kessel 10.00 25.
81 Dion Phaneuf 8.00 20.
82 Roberto Luongo 8.00 20.
83 Daniel Sedin 8.00 20.
84 Henrik Sedin 8.00 20.
85 Ryan Kesler 8.00 20.
86 Trevor Linden 8.00 20.
87 Alexander Ovechkin 30.00 80.
88 Nicklas Backstrom 12.00 30.
89 Dale Hawerchuk 10.00 25.
90 Ondrej Pavelec 8.00 20.

2011-12 The Cup Limited Logos Autographs

STATED PRINT RUN 10-50
LLAH Adam Henrique/50 40.00 100.
LLAL Adam Larsson/50 20.00 50.
LLBC Brett Connolly/50 15.00 40.
LLBH Brett Hull/50 50.00 120.
LLBM Brad Marchand/50 25.00 60.
LLBR Bobby Ryan/50 20.00 50.
LLBS Brayden Schenn/50 20.00 50.
LLCG Claude Giroux/50 20.00 50.
LLCH Cody Hodgson/50 30.00 80.
LLCJ Curtis Joseph/50 20.00 50.
LLCP Carey Price/50 60.00 150.
LLCU Sean Couturier/50 8.00 20.
LLDD Drew Doughty/50 20.00 50.
LLDH Dany Heatley/50 15.00 40.

LDR Derek Roy/50 15.00 40.00
LEB Ed Belfour/50 20.00 50.00
LEK Evander Kane/50 20.00 50.00
LEL Eric Lindros/50 30.00 80.00
LEM Evgeni Malkin/50 50.00 120.00
LES Eric Staal/50 25.00 60.00
LGA Marian Gaborik/25 40.00 100.00
LGC Guy Carbonneau/50 20.00 50.00
LGL Gabriel Landeskog/50 30.00 80.00
LHO Cody Hodgson/50 30.00 80.00
LJE Jordan Eberle/50 20.00 50.00
LJF Johan Franzen/50 20.00 50.00
LJI Jarome Iginla/50 20.00 50.00
LJS Jordan Staal/50 20.00 50.00
LJT John Tavares/50 40.00 100.00
LLL Louis Leblanc/50 15.00 40.00
LMB Martin Brodeur/50 50.00 120.00
LMD Matt Duchene/50 20.00 50.00
LMF Marc-Andre Fleury/50 30.00 80.00
LMG Mike Gartner/50 20.00 50.00
LML Mario Lemieux/50 100.00 200.00
LNB Nicklas Backstrom/50 30.00 80.00
LNH Ryan Nugent-Hopkins/50 60.00 150.00
LPD Pavel Datsyuk/50 25.00 60.00
LPM Patrick Marleau/50 20.00 50.00
LPS P.K. Subban/50 40.00 100.00
LRB Ray Bourque/50 30.00 80.00
LRE Pekka Rinne/50 25.00 60.00
LRG Ryan Getzlaf/50 30.00 80.00
LRJ Ryan Johansen/50 30.00 80.00
LRK Ryan Kesler/50 20.00 50.00
LRM Ryan Miller/50 20.00 50.00
LRN Rick Nash/50 20.00 50.00
LSA Joe Sakic/50 50.00 120.00
LSC Sidney Crosby/50 150.00 300.00
LSF Mark Scheifele/50 40.00 100.00
LSU P.K. Subban/50 40.00 100.00
LTH Taylor Hall/50 40.00 100.00
LTL Trevor Linden/50 20.00 50.00
LTO Jonathan Toews/50 60.00 150.00
LTS Tyler Seguin/50 90.00 150.00
LTT Tony Twist/50 12.00 30.00
LZK Zack Kassian/50 20.00 50.00

2011-12 The Cup Rookie Bookmarks Dual Autographs

STATED PRINT RUN 25 SER.#'d SETS
RBCR S.Couturier/M.Read 75.00 150.00
RBHS Hodgson/M.Scheifele 75.00 150.00
RBLD L.Leblanc/R.Diaz 60.00 120.00
RBLH A.Larsson/A.Henrique 50.00 100.00
RBNL Nugent-Hpkins/Landskg 150.00 300.00
RBSG J.Gardiner/B.Scrivens 75.00 150.00
RBSN B.Smith/G.Nyquist 60.00 120.00
RBZG Zibanejad/C.Greening 50.00 100.00

2011-12 The Cup Rookie Evolution Video Cards

EACH RANDOMLY INSERTED IN PACKS
EAH Adam Henrique 125.00 200.00
EBC Brett Connolly 25.00 60.00
EBG Blake Geoffrion 25.00 60.00
EBS Brendan Smith 30.00 80.00
ECE Cody Eakin 30.00 80.00
EGL Gabriel Landeskog 30.00 80.00
EJG Jake Gardiner 50.00 100.00
EMZ Mika Zibanejad 30.00 80.00
ERE Ryan Ellis 40.00 100.00
ERN Ryan Nugent-Hopkins 100.00 200.00
ESD Simon Despres 30.00 80.00
EZK Zack Kassian 30.00 80.00
NO EXCH CARD 30.00 80.00

2011-12 The Cup Rookie Gear Autographs

STATED PRINT RUN 25 SER.#'d SETS
RGAH Adam Henrique 100.00 250.00
RGAL Adam Larsson 50.00 120.00
RGBC Brett Connolly 40.00 100.00
RGCE Cody Eakin 50.00 125.00
RGCH Cody Hodgson 80.00 200.00
RGCS Craig Smith 50.00 125.00
RGGL G.Landeskog 80.00 200.00
RGLL Louis Leblanc 40.00 100.00
RGMR Matt Read 80.00 200.00
RGMS Mark Scheifele 100.00 250.00
RGMZ Mika Zibanejad 100.00 250.00
RGRE Ryan Ellis 40.00 100.00
RGRJ Ryan Johansen 80.00 200.00
RGRN Ryan Nugent-Hopkins 200.00 400.00
RGSC Sean Couturier 80.00 200.00
RGZK Zack Kassian 50.00 125.00

2011-12 The Cup Scripted Sticks

STATED PRINT RUN 35 SER.#'d SETS
AO Alexander Ovechkin 100.00 175.00
BH Bobby Hull 30.00 60.00
CP Carey Price 75.00 150.00
DH Dale Hawerchuk 40.00 80.00
EL Eric Lindros 60.00 120.00
JS Joe Sakic 60.00 120.00
LR Larry Robinson 25.00 50.00
MB Martin Brodeur 100.00 200.00
MM Mark Messier 50.00 120.00
NL Nicklas Lidstrom 75.00 150.00
PR Patrick Roy 75.00 150.00
SC Sidney Crosby 200.00 350.00
WG Wayne Gretzky 300.00 500.00

2011-12 The Cup Scripted Sticks Dual

STATED PRINT RUN 15 SER.#'d SETS
SBL J.Beliveau/G.Lafleur 100.00 200.00
SBP M.Bossy/D.Potvin 60.00 120.00
SEB P.Esposito/J.Bucyk 60.00 120.00
SGM W.Gretzky/M.Messier
SKG W.Gretzky/J.Kurri
SLC S.Crosby/Lemieux
SMC D.Ciccarelli/M.Modano
SOM A.Ovechkin/E.Malkin
SRP P.Roy/C.Price 150.00 250.00
SRS P.Roy/J.Sakic 175.00 300.00

2011-12 The Cup Scripted Swatches

SAO Alexander Ovechkin/15 175.00 300.00
SBC Brett Connolly/35 25.00 50.00
SCU Sean Couturier/35 20.00 50.00
SGL G.Landeskog/35 EXCH 50.00 120.00
SJS Joe Sakic/35 75.00 150.00
SMB Martin Brodeur/35
SMF Marc-Andre Fleury/35 30.00 80.00
SML Mario Lemieux/35 100.00 175.00
SNH Nugent-Hopkins/35 75.00 150.00
SRF Ron Francis/35 25.00 60.00
SSC Sidney Crosby/35 150.00 250.00
SWG Wayne Gretzky/35 250.00 400.00

2011-12 The Cup Scripted Swatches Dual

STATED PRINT RUN 5-15
SSCF Coffey/Francis/15 50.00 100.00
SSCL S.Crosby/Lemieux/15

DSSCR Couturier/Read/15 40.00 100.00
DSSPS Price/Subban/15 100.00 200.00
DSSRG RNH/Landeskg/15 100.00 200.00
DSSRS Roy/Sakic/15 125.00 200.00

2011-12 The Cup Signature Patches

STATED PRINT RUN 35-75
SPAH Adam Henrique 20.00 50.00
SPAK Anze Kopitar 25.00 60.00
SPAO Alexander Ovechkin/35 50.00 100.00
SPBC Brett Connolly 15.00 40.00
SPBH Brett Hull/35 50.00 120.00
SPBJ Jonathon Blum 10.00 25.00
SPBR Bill Ranford 15.00 40.00
SPBY Dustin Byfuglien 15.00 40.00
SPCF Cam Fowler 12.00 30.00
SPCG Claude Giroux 15.00 40.00
SPCH Cody Hodgson 15.00 40.00
SPCO Chris Osgood 12.00 30.00
SPCP Carey Price/35 60.00 120.00
SPCU Sean Couturier 15.00 40.00
SPDB Dan Boyle 12.00 30.00
SPDD Drew Doughty 30.00 60.00
SPDE Devin Setoguchi 10.00 25.00
SPDH Dany Heatley 15.00 40.00
SPDP Dion Phaneuf 15.00 40.00
SPDR Derek Roy 12.00 30.00
SPDS Derek Stepan 15.00 40.00
SPDW Doug Wilson 12.00 30.00
SPEK Evander Kane 25.00 50.00
SPEL Eric Lindros/35 30.00 80.00
SPES Eric Staal 12.00 30.00
SPGL Gabriel Landeskog 25.00 60.00
SPGT Mike Gartner 20.00 50.00
SPJB Jay Bouwmeester 15.00 40.00
SPJC Jeff Carter 8.00 20.00
SPJE Jordan Eberle 20.00 50.00
SPJF Johan Franzen 12.00 30.00
SPJI Jarome Iginla 25.00 50.00
SPJM John Moore 12.00 30.00
SPJS Joe Sakic/35 30.00 80.00
SPJT Joe Thornton/35 15.00 40.00
SPLL Louis Leblanc 15.00 40.00
SPLR Larry Robinson 15.00 40.00
SPLU Luc Robitaille 25.00 50.00
SPMB Martin Brodeur/35 60.00 125.00
SPMD Matt Duchene 15.00 40.00
SPMF Marc-Andre Fleury 12.00 30.00
SPMH Marian Hossa 12.00 30.00
SPMK Mike Modano/35 25.00 60.00
SPML Mario Lemieux/35 50.00 100.00
SPNB Nicklas Backstrom 20.00 40.00
SPPA Paul Stastny 15.00 40.00
SPPD Pavel Datsyuk 20.00 50.00
SPPR Patrick Roy/35 75.00 150.00
SPPS P.K. Subban 30.00 80.00
SPRF Ron Francis/35 25.00 60.00
SPRG Ryan Getzlaf 12.00 30.00
SPRH Ron Hextall 15.00 40.00
SPRJ Ryan Johansen 20.00 50.00
SPRK Ryan Kesler 10.00 25.00
SPRM Ryan Miller 15.00 40.00
SPRN Rick Nash 25.00 50.00
SPRNH Ryan Nugent-Hopkins 50.00 100.00
SPRY Bobby Ryan 15.00 40.00
SPSC Sidney Crosby/35 100.00 200.00
SPSE Brent Seabrook 15.00 40.00
SPST Jordan Staal 15.00 40.00
SPSV Denis Savard 12.00 30.00
SPSW Shea Weber
SPTE Tony Esposito/35 30.00 60.00
SPTH Taylor Hall 25.00 50.00
SPTM Tyler Myers
SPTS Tyler Seguin 25.00 60.00
SPTW Jonathan Toews 30.00 60.00
SPVA James van Riemsdyk 15.00 40.00
SPVO Tomas Vokoun 12.00 30.00
SPWG Wayne Gretzky/35 250.00 400.00
SPZK Zack Kassian 12.00 30.00

2011-12 The Cup Signature Patches Dual

SP2AA Henriq/Lrssn/35 20.00 50.00
SP2BM Richrds/Gabrk/35
SP2BS Boyle/Seabrook/35 15.00 40.00
SP2CL Crosby/Lemieux/25 300.00 600.00
SP2DD Heatley/Setogch/35 15.00 40.00
SP2DS Dubinsky/Stepan/35 20.00 50.00
SP2EP Eberle/Paajarvi/35 30.00 80.00
SP2FC Francis/Coffey/35 20.00 50.00
SP2FS Fleury/Staal/35 30.00 80.00
SP2GR Getzlaf/Ryan/35 30.00 80.00
SP2GV Giroux/vanRmsdk/35 25.00 60.00
SP2HC Hodgson/Benn/25 30.00 80.00
SP2HS Heatley/Staal/35 30.00 60.00
SP2IB Iginla/Bouwmstr/35 20.00 50.00
SP2LS Lecav/St.Louis/35 30.00 60.00
SP2MT Marleau/Thorntn/35 30.00 60.00
SP2MV Miller/Vanek/35
SP2NB Neely/Bourque/35 40.00 80.00
SP2NL RNH/Landeskog/35 EX 60.00 120.00
SP2NM Mason/Nash/35 12.00 30.00
SP2OB Ovechkn/Backstrm/35 40.00 80.00
SP2PS Price/Subban/35 75.00 135.00
SP2RA RNH/Lander/35 EX 75.00 150.00
SP2RG M.Richards/Gagne/35 20.00 50.00
SP2RM Roy/Miller/35 25.00 50.00
SP2RS Roy/Sakic/35 75.00 150.00
SP2RV Roy/Vanek/35
SP2SD Stastny/Duchene/35 20.00 50.00
SP2SG Sakic/Gretzky/35 300.00 450.00
SP2SK Scheifel/Klingbrg/35 30.00 80.00
SP2SL Lafleur/Stastny/35 25.00 60.00
SP2SM Couturier/Read/35 25.00 60.00
SP2TH Tavares/Hall/35 EXCH 50.00 100.00
SP2TT Hall/Seguin/35 40.00 80.00
SP2WB S.Weber/D.Boyle/35 15.00 40.00

2011-12 The Cup Stanley Cup Signatures

STATED PRINT RUN 50 SER.#'d SETS
SCSAD Alex Delvecchio 12.00 30.00
SCSAT Alex Tanguay 8.00 20.00
SCSBB Bill Barber 10.00 25.00
SCSBC Bobby Clarke 12.00 30.00
SCSBH Bobby Hull 25.00 60.00
SCSBL Brian Leetch 12.00 30.00
SCSBM Brad Marchand 25.00 60.00
SCSBO Bobby Orr 60.00 120.00
SCSBW Johnny Bower 20.00 50.00
SCSCL Claude Lemieux 10.00 25.00
SCSCO Paul Coffey
SCSCR Sidney Crosby 90.00 150.00
SCSDP Denis Potvin 12.00 30.00
SCSDS Denis Savard 20.00 40.00
SCSEB Ed Belfour 20.00 40.00
SCSEM Evgeni Malkin 30.00 60.00
SCSGA Glenn Anderson 12.00 30.00
SCSGF Grant Fuhr 12.00 30.00
SCSGL Guy Lafleur 12.00 30.00
SCSHE Milan Hejduk 10.00 25.00
SCSHU Brett Hull 25.00 50.00
SCSIL Igor Larionov 12.00 30.00
SCSJB Johnny Bucyk 12.00 30.00
SCSJF Johan Franzen 12.00 30.00
SCSJG Jean-Sebastien Giguere 20.00 40.00
SCSJK Jari Kurri 15.00 40.00
SCSJS Joe Sakic 25.00 50.00
SCSJT Jonathan Toews 30.00 60.00
SCSLR Larry Robinson 12.00 30.00
SCSMA Mark Messier 30.00 60.00
SCSMB Martin Brodeur 30.00 60.00
SCSME Mark Messier 30.00 60.00
SCSMF Marc-Andre Fleury 20.00 40.00
SCSMH Marian Hossa 20.00 50.00
SCSMI Mike Bossy 15.00 40.00
SCSML Mario Lemieux 50.00 100.00
SCSMM Mike Modano 20.00 40.00
SCSMS Milt Schmidt 15.00 40.00
SCSNL Nicklas Lidstrom 25.00 50.00
SCSPC Paul Coffey 20.00 40.00
SCSPD Pavel Datsyuk 25.00 50.00
SCSPE Phil Esposito 20.00 50.00
SCSPK Patrick Kane 40.00 80.00
SCSRB Ray Bourque 25.00 50.00
SCSRF Ron Francis 25.00 50.00
SCSRG Ryan Getzlaf 12.00 30.00
SCSRK Red Kelly 12.00 30.00
SCSRM Rick MacLeish 12.00 30.00
SCSRO Patrick Roy 60.00 120.00
SCSSC Dave Schultz 12.00 30.00
SCSSN Scott Niedermayer 12.00 30.00
SCSST Jordan Staal 12.00 30.00
SCSTL Ted Lindsay 12.00 30.00
SCSTS Tyler Seguin 40.00 80.00
SCSWG Wayne Gretzky 150.00 300.00

2011-12 The Cup Stanley Cup Signatures Dual

STATED PRINT RUN 25 SER.#'d SETS
SC2BG C.Gillies/M.Bossy EX 15.00 40.00
SC2BM P.Bergeron/Marchand 30.00 80.00
SC2BN M.Brodeur/S.Niedermayer
SC2BP D.Potvin/M.Bossy 25.00 50.00
SC2BT B.Marchand/T.Seguin 25.00 60.00
SC2CL M.Lemieux/P.Coffey 60.00 125.00
SC2CM M.Messier/P.Coffey 30.00 60.00
SC2DF J.Franzen/P.Datsyuk 25.00 50.00
SC2DL N.Lidstrom/P.Datsyuk 30.00 60.00
SC2EO B.Orr/P.Esposito 75.00 150.00
SC2FC P.Coffey/R.Francis EX 30.00 60.00
SC2FK G.Fuhr/J.Kurri EX 20.00 50.00
SC2GM W.Gretzky/M.Messier EX 175.00 350.00
SC2HM B.Hull/S.Mikita 50.00 100.00
SC2HT J.Toews/M.Hossa 40.00 100.00
SC2KG W.Gretzky/J.Kurri 175.00 300.00
SC2LC S.Crosby/Lemieux 150.00 300.00
SC2LD A.Delvecchio/T.Lindsay 25.00 60.00
SC2LF M.Lemieux/R.Francis 60.00 125.00
SC2LL I.Larionov/N.Lidstrom 25.00 60.00
SC2LM M.Messier/B.Leetch
SC2MS E.Malkin/J.Staal 30.00 80.00
SC2OS B.Orr/M.Schmidt 75.00 150.00
SC2PG P.Coffey/G.Fuhr 25.00 60.00
SC2RB P.Roy/R.Bourque 50.00 125.00
SC2RR Patrick Roy 125.00 250.00
SC2RS J.Sakic/P.Roy 75.00 125.00
SC2SB J.Sakic/R.Bourque 40.00 80.00
SC2TK J.Toews/P.Kane 75.00 150.00

2011-12 The Cup Trios Jerseys

STATED PRINT RUN 25 SER.#'d SETS
C3ANA Perry/Getzlaf/Ryan 12.00 30.00
C3AVS Duchene/Ststny/Lndskg 15.00 30.00
C3BOS Bergeron/Horton/Seguin 12.00 30.00
C3BUF Miller/Vanek/Myers 8.00 20.00
C3CHI Crawford/Keith/Sharp 10.00 25.00
C3DRW Shanhn/Hasek/Lidstrm 10.00 25.00
C3LAK Kopitar/Richards/Brown 12.00 30.00
C3NJD Parise/Brodeur/Kovalchk 15.00 40.00
C3NYI Tavares/Moulson/Grabnr 10.00 25.00
C3NYR Callahan/Dubinsky/Stepn 8.00 20.00
C3OIL Hall/RNH/Eberle 20.00 50.00
C3PHI Giroux/Briere/vanRiems 8.00 20.00
C3QGF Brodeur/Luongo/Fleury 15.00 40.00
C3STL Halak/Pietrangelo/Stwrt 10.00 25.00
C3VAN Luongo/Sedin/Sedin 10.00 25.00
C3BEES Thomas/Krejci/Chara 8.00 20.00
C3BLUE Lundqvist/Staal/Gaborik 10.00 25.00
C3CAPS Ovech/Backstrom/Semin 30.00 80.00
C3JAGR Jagr/Jagr/Jagr 20.00 50.00
C3PENS Malkin/Staal/Fleury 25.00 60.00
C3PITT Fleury/Malkin/Letang 25.00 60.00
C3RAVS Landskg/Elliott/Gaunce 12.00 30.00
C3RCBJ Johnsn/Moore/Savard 12.00 30.00
C3RNJD Larsson/Henrq/Kinkaid 15.00 40.00
C3RPHI Coutier/Read/Gustafsn 12.00 30.00
C3WASH Green/Ovech/Vokoun 30.00 80.00
C3WJC1 Schenn/Coutier/Kassian 8.00 20.00
C3WJC2 Connolly/Leblanc/Johnsn 10.00 25.00
C3WJC3 Despres/Ellis/Gudbrnsn 8.00 20.00
C3BEESD Thomas/Rask/Chara 8.00 20.00
C3BLUES Hull/Joseph/Twist 15.00 40.00
C3DUCKS Hiller/Getzlaf/Fowler 12.00 30.00
C3GOLD1 Toews/Iginla/Staal 15.00 40.00
C3GOLD2 Perry/Bergrn/Morrow 12.00 30.00
C3GOLD3 Luongo/Brodr/Fleury 15.00 40.00
C3GOLD4 Seabrk/Dghty/Wbr 12.00 30.00
C3GOLD5 Thorntn/Marlu/Heatly 10.00 25.00
C3GOLD6 Nash/Richrds/Getzlf 12.00 30.00
C3GOLD7 Keith/Prongr/Niedrmyr 8.00 20.00
C3HAWKS Toews/Kane/Hossa 25.00 50.00
C3KINGS Quick/Dghty/Johnsn 20.00 50.00
C3NUCKS Hodgsn/Keslr/Burrws 12.00 30.00
C3RJETS Scheifl/Klingbrg/Pstm 15.00 40.00
C3RMTL1 Leblanc/Emelin/Diaz 6.00 15.00
C3RMTL2 Leblanc/Palshj/Nash 6.00 15.00
C3RNASH Ellis/Smith/Blum 8.00 20.00
C3ROIL1 RNH/Teubrt/Hartkn 20.00 50.00
C3ROIL2 RNH/Petrell/Lander 30.00 80.00
C3RPENS Despres/Vitale/Strait 15.00 40.00
C3RSENS Zibanjd/Grng/Wrcch 15.00 40.00
C3SABRE Roy/Staffrd/Pomnvll 8.00 20.00
C3WINGS Howrd/Frnzn/Krnwll 8.00 20.00
C390PENS Mario/Jagr/Murphy 25.00 50.00
C3ALLSTARG Brodeur/Belfr/Jsph 15.00 40.00
C3BHAWKS Savard/Wilsn/Espo 10.00 25.00
C3FLAMES Iginla/Cammllr/Kiprsff 8.00 20.00
C3RFLAMES Irving/Nemisz/Hork 6.00 15.00
C3RLEAFS Gardinr/Colbrn/Frttn 10.00 25.00
C3RSABRE Kassn/Flgno/McNb 40.00 100.00
C3STAR90S Mario/Sakic/Jagr 30.00 60.00

2012-13 The Cup

EXCH EXPIRATION: 9/27/2015
1 Ryan Getzlaf 6.00 15.00
2 Teemu Selanne 8.00 20.00
3 Ray Bourque 6.00 15.00
4 Bobby Orr 12.00 30.00
5 Tuukka Rask 4.00 10.00
6 Cam Neely 4.00 10.00
7 Zdeno Chara 4.00 10.00
8 Tyler Seguin 6.00 15.00
9 Brad Marchand 5.00 12.00
10 Thomas Vanek 4.00 10.00
11 Theoren Fleury 5.00 12.00
12 Miikka Kiprusoff 3.00 8.00
13 Jarome Iginla 4.00 10.00
14 Jeff Skinner 4.00 10.00
15 Phil Esposito 6.00 15.00
16 Patrick Kane 8.00 20.00
17 Tony Esposito 4.00 10.00
18 Bobby Hull 4.00 10.00
19 Jonathan Toews 8.00 20.00
20 Joe Sakic 6.00 15.00
21 Patrick Roy 10.00 25.00
22 Matt Duchene 4.00 10.00
23 Gabriel Landeskog 4.00 10.00
24 Jaromir Jagr 10.00 25.00
25 Dominik Hasek 5.00 12.00
26 Jim Howard 4.00 10.00
27 Pavel Datsyuk 5.00 12.00
28 Nicklas Lidstrom 4.00 10.00
29 Johan Franzen 4.00 10.00
30 Henrik Zetterberg 5.00 12.00
31 Ryan Smyth 3.00 8.00
32 Taylor Hall 8.00 20.00
33 Grant Fuhr 4.00 10.00
34 Jari Kurri 4.00 10.00
35 Jordan Eberle 4.00 10.00
36 Paul Coffey 4.00 10.00
37 Andy Moog 4.00 10.00
38 Ryan Nugent-Hopkins 4.00 10.00
39 Ed Belfour 4.00 10.00
40 Jeff Carter 4.00 10.00
41 Anze Kopitar 6.00 15.00
42 Mike Richards 4.00 10.00
43 Luc Robitaille 4.00 10.00
44 Drew Doughty 4.00 10.00
45 Wayne Gretzky 20.00 50.00
46 Jonathan Quick 6.00 15.00
47 Mike Modano 6.00 15.00
48 Zach Parise 4.00 10.00
49 Carey Price 12.00 30.00
50 Larry Robinson 4.00 10.00
51 P.K. Subban 6.00 15.00
52 Pekka Rinne 5.00 12.00
53 Ilya Kovalchuk 4.00 10.00
54 Martin Brodeur 8.00 20.00
55 Adam Henrique 4.00 10.00
56 John Tavares 8.00 20.00
57 Mike Bossy 4.00 10.00
58 Rick Nash 4.00 10.00
59 Marian Gaborik 4.00 10.00
60 Henrik Lundqvist 5.00 12.00
61 Mark Messier 5.00 12.00
62 Jason Spezza 4.00 10.00
63 Eric Lindros 6.00 15.00
64 Claude Giroux 4.00 10.00
65 Evgeni Malkin 12.00 30.00
66 Mario Lemieux 12.00 30.00
67 Marc-Andre Fleury 6.00 15.00
68 Sidney Crosby 15.00 40.00
69 Ron Francis 5.00 12.00
70 Kris Letang 4.00 10.00
71 Scott Hartnell 4.00 10.00
72 Antti Niemi 3.00 8.00
73 Patrick Marleau 4.00 10.00
74 Logan Couture 4.00 10.00
75 Jaroslav Halak 4.00 10.00
76 Brett Hull 4.00 10.00
77 Steven Stamkos 8.00 20.00
78 Phil Kessel 5.00 12.00
79 Dion Phaneuf 4.00 10.00
80 Mats Sundin 4.00 10.00
81 Alexandre Burrows 4.00 10.00
82 Daniel Sedin 4.00 10.00
83 Henrik Sedin 4.00 10.00
84 Ryan Kesler 4.00 10.00
85 Trevor Linden 4.00 10.00
86 Pavel Bure 5.00 12.00
87 Alexander Ovechkin 15.00 40.00
88 Nicklas Backstrom 6.00 15.00
89 Dale Hawerchuk 5.00 12.00
90 Ondrej Pavelec 4.00 10.00
91 M.Sauve JSY AU/249 RC 8.00 20.00
92 L.MacDermid JSY AU/249 RC 8.00 20.00
93 Torey Krug JSY AU/249 RC 30.00 80.00
94 M.Hutchinson JSY AU/249 RC 15.00 40.00
95 Akim Aliu JSY AU/249 RC 8.00 20.00
96 J.Welsh JSY AU/249 RC 8.00 20.00
97 Brandon Bollig JSY AU/249 RC 8.00 20.00
98 T.Barrie JSY AU/249 RC 20.00 50.00
99 M.Connolly JSY AU/249 RC 8.00 20.00
100 D.Prout JSY AU/249 RC 8.00 20.00
101 C.Goloubef JSY AU/249 RC 8.00 20.00
102 S.Hunwick JSY AU/249 RC 8.00 20.00
103 R.Garbutt JSY AU/249 RC 8.00 20.00
104 Reilly Smith JSY AU/249 RC 15.00 40.00
105 B.Dillon JSY AU/249 RC 8.00 20.00
106 S.Glennie JSY AU/249 RC 8.00 20.00
107 R.Sheahan JSY AU/249 RC 15.00 40.00
108 Philippe Cornet/199 RC 4.00 10.00
109 J.Nolan JSY AU/249 RC 8.00 20.00
110 J.Zucker JSY AU/249 RC 25.00 60.00
111 Tyler Cuma JSY AU/249 RC 8.00 20.00
112 C.Genoway JSY AU/249 RC 8.00 20.00
113 G.Dumont JSY AU/249 RC 8.00 20.00
114 Robert Mayer/199 RC 5.00 12.00
115 C.Pickard JSY AU/249 RC 12.00 30.00
116 Aaron Ness JSY AU/249 RC 8.00 20.00
117 C.Cizikas JSY AU/249 RC 12.00 30.00
118 M.Donovan JSY AU/249 RC 8.00 20.00
119 J.Silfverberg JSY AU/249 RC 25.00 60.00
120 Mark Stone JSY AU/249 RC 25.00 60.00
121 B.Manning JSY AU/249 RC 8.00 20.00
122 M.Stone JSY AU/249 RC 8.00 20.00
123 M.Watkins JSY AU/249 RC 8.00 20.00
124 Tyson Sexsmith/199 RC 4.00 10.00
125 Jake Allen JSY AU/249 RC 40.00 100.00
126 J.T. Brown JSY AU/249 RC 8.00 20.00
127 C.Ashton JSY AU/249 RC 6.00 15.00
128 R.Hamilton JSY AU/249 RC 8.00 20.00
129 J.Rynnas JSY AU/249 RC 8.00 20.00
130 S.Baertschi JSY AU/99 RC 80.00 200.00
131 Chris Kreider JSY AU/99 RC 100.00 300.00
132 J.Schwartz JSY AU/99 RC 100.00 300.00

2012-13 The Cup Gold

*1-90 VETS/25: 1X TO 2.5X BASIC CARDS
88 Nicklas Backstrom 12.00 30.00
91 Maxime Sauve 6.00 15.00
92 Lane MacDermid 6.00 15.00
93 Torey Krug 25.00 60.00
94 Michael Hutchinson 12.00 30.00
95 Akim Aliu 6.00 15.00
96 Jeremy Welsh 6.00 15.00
97 Brandon Bollig 6.00 15.00
98 Tyson Barrie 12.00 30.00
99 Mike Connolly 6.00 15.00
100 Dalton Prout 6.00 15.00
101 Cody Goloubef 6.00 15.00
102 Shawn Hunwick 6.00 15.00
103 Ryan Garbutt 8.00 20.00
104 Reilly Smith 12.00 30.00
105 Brenden Dillon 6.00 15.00
106 Scott Glennie 6.00 15.00
107 Riley Sheahan 10.00 25.00
108 Philippe Cornet 6.00 15.00
109 Jordan Nolan 6.00 15.00
110 Jason Zucker 8.00 20.00
111 Tyler Cuma 6.00 15.00
112 Chay Genoway 6.00 15.00
113 Gabriel Dumont 6.00 15.00
114 Robert Mayer 8.00 20.00
115 Chet Pickard 6.00 15.00
116 Aaron Ness 6.00 15.00
117 Casey Cizikas 6.00 15.00
118 Matt Donovan 6.00 15.00
119 Jakob Silfverberg 25.00 50.00
120 Mark Stone 12.00 30.00
121 Brandon Manning 6.00 15.00
122 Michael Stone 6.00 15.00
123 Matt Watkins 6.00 15.00
124 Tyson Sexsmith 6.00 15.00
125 Jake Allen 20.00 50.00
126 J.T. Brown 6.00 15.00
127 Carter Ashton 5.00 12.00
128 Ryan Hamilton 6.00 15.00
129 Jussi Rynnas 6.00 15.00
130 Sven Baertschi 8.00 20.00
131 Chris Kreider 20.00 50.00
132 Jaden Schwartz 20.00 50.00

2012-13 The Cup Gold Rainbow

*ROOKIE/55-74: .5X TO 1.2X JSY AU RC/249
*ROOKIE/31-49: .6X TO 1.5X JSY AU RC/249
*ROOKIE/20-29: .8X TO 2X JSY AU RC/249
*ROOKIE/15-18: 1X TO 2.5X JSY AU RC/249
93 Torey Krug JSY AU/47 60.00 120.00
119 Jakob Silfverberg JSY AU/33 30.00 80.00
130 Sven Baertschi JSY AU/47 30.00 80.00
131 Chris Kreider JSY AU/20 150.00 300.00

2012-13 The Cup Auto Draft Boards

DBCA Carter Ashton 25.00 50.00
DBCK Chris Kreider 60.00 120.00
DBCP Chet Pickard 25.00 50.00
DBJS Jaden Schwartz 75.00 135.00
DBRS Riley Sheahan 25.00 50.00
DBSB Sven Baertschi 20.00 50.00
DBTC Tyler Cuma 15.00 40.00

2012-13 The Cup Brilliance Autographs

GROUP A ODDS 1:19
GROUP B ODDS 1:14
GROUP C ODDS 1:10
OVERALL ODDS 1:5
BAM Andy Moog C 20.00 50.00
BAO Alexander Ovechkin A 30.00 80.00
BBH Brett Hull A 25.00 60.00
BBO Bobby Orr C 60.00 100.00
BCK Chris Kreider C 15.00 40.00
BCP Carey Price C 30.00 80.00
BEL Eric Lindros A 30.00 80.00
BEM Evgeni Malkin 25.00 50.00
BGL Gabriel Landeskog 12.00 30.00
BJA Jaden Schwartz C 12.00 30.00
BJE Jordan Eberle 20.00 40.00
BJI Jarome Iginla A 20.00 50.00
BJJ Jaromir Jagr A 50.00 100.00
BJQ Jonathan Quick 20.00 40.00
BJS Jeff Skinner C 12.00 30.00
BJT Jonathan Toews B 30.00 60.00
BMB Martin Brodeur 40.00 80.00
BMF Marc-Andre Fleury B 15.00 40.00
BML Mario Lemieux A 60.00 120.00
BMM Mark Messier A 30.00 60.00
BMS Mats Sundin A 40.00 80.00
BPB Pavel Bure A 50.00 100.00
BPF Peter Forsberg B 50.00 100.00
BPK Patrick Kane B 40.00 100.00
BPR Patrick Roy A 50.00 100.00
BPS P.K. Subban 20.00 50.00
BRI Pekka Rinne 12.00 30.00
BRN R.Nugent-Hopkins B EXCH 20.00 50.00
BSA Joe Sakic A 30.00 60.00
BSB Sven Baertschi C 8.00 20.00
BSC Sidney Crosby A 90.00 150.00
BSE Teemu Selanne 25.00 50.00
BTA John Tavares C 20.00 50.00
BTF Theoren Fleury B 15.00 40.00
BTH Taylor Hall B 40.00 100.00
BTL Trevor Linden B 12.00 30.00
BTS Tyler Seguin 20.00 40.00
BWG Wayne Gretzky A 350.00 500.00
BZP Zach Parise B 20.00 50.00

2012-13 The Cup Emblems of Endorsement

EEBU Pavel Bure 250.00 400.00
EECK Chris Kreider 100.00 200.00
EEDH Dale Hawerchuk 50.00 100.00
EEEB Ed Belfour 60.00 120.00
EEEL Eric Lindros 40.00 100.00
EEJE Jordan Eberle 60.00 120.00
EEJS Joe Sakic TC 100.00 175.00
EEMB Martin Brodeur 100.00 200.00
EEMF Marc-Andre Fleury TC 75.00 125.00
EEML Mario Lemieux 200.00 350.00
EEPB Patrice Bergeron 60.00 120.00
EEPF Peter Forsberg 175.00 300.00
EEPR Patrick Roy 175.00 300.00
EEPS P.K. Subban 40.00 80.00
(inserted in 14-15 The Cup)
EESA Joe Sakic Avs 100.00 175.00
EESN Mats Sundin 125.00 200.00
EESV Sven Baertschi 60.00 120.00
EESW Jaden Schwartz 125.00 200.00
EEWG Wayne Gretzky 500.00 750.00

2012-13 The Cup Enshrinements

CEAM Andy Moog 10.00 25.00
CEAO Alexander Ovechkin 30.00 80.00
CEBC Bobby Clarke 12.00 30.00
CEBE Jean Beliveau 30.00 60.00
CEBH Brett Hull 25.00 60.00
CEBM Brad Marchand 10.00 25.00
CEBO Bobby Orr 60.00 120.00
CEDR Martin Brodeur 25.00 60.00
CECJ Curtis Joseph 15.00 40.00
CECK Chris Kreider 12.00 30.00
CECN Cam Neely 12.00 30.00
CECP Carey Price 25.00 50.00
CEDH Dominik Hasek 25.00 50.00
CEDS Dave Schultz 10.00 25.00
CEEB Ed Belfour 20.00 50.00
CEEL Eric Lindros 20.00 50.00
CEEM Evgeni Malkin 40.00 100.00
CEGF Grant Fuhr 15.00 40.00
CEGL Guy Lafleur 20.00 50.00
CEGP Gilbert Perreault 12.00 30.00
CEHA Dale Hawerchuk 15.00 40.00
CEHU Bobby Hull 20.00 50.00
CEJA Jaden Schwartz 10.00 25.00
CEJB Johnny Bucyk 10.00 25.00
CEJE Jordan Eberle 12.00 30.00
CEJK Jari Kurri 12.00 30.00
CEJR Jussi Rynnas 5.00 12.00
CEJS Jakob Silfverberg 12.00 30.00
CEJT Jonathan Toews 25.00 60.00
CEKV Mikko Koivu 10.00 25.00
CELA Gabriel Landeskog 8.00 20.00
CEMB Mike Bossy 15.00 40.00
CEML Mario Lemieux 50.00 100.00
CEMM Mark Messier 25.00 50.00
CEMS Mats Sundin 15.00 40.00
CEPB Pavel Bure 30.00 80.00
CEPC Paul Coffey 12.00 30.00
CEPE Phil Esposito 20.00 50.00
CEPF Peter Forsberg 30.00 80.00
CEPK Patrick Kane 25.00 60.00
CEPR Patrick Roy 40.00 100.00
CEPS P.K. Subban 15.00 40.00
CERB Ray Bourque 20.00 50.00
CERF Ron Francis 10.00 25.00
CESA Joe Sakic 20.00 50.00
CESB Sven Baertschi 6.00 15.00
CESC Sidney Crosby EXCH 75.00 135.00
CESE Teemu Selanne 20.00 50.00
CESK Jeff Skinner 10.00 25.00
CETA John Tavares 25.00 60.00
CETF Theoren Fleury 15.00 40.00
CETH Taylor Hall 25.00 60.00
CETS Tyler Seguin 20.00 50.00
CEVD Vincent Damphousse 15.00 40.00
CEWG Wayne Gretzky 150.00 250.00
CEZP Zach Parise 20.00 50.00

2012-13 The Cup Foundations Jerseys

CFAB Alexandre Burrows 6.00 15.00
CFAL Jake Allen 6.00 15.00
CFAO Alexander Ovechkin 12.00 30.00
CFBH Braden Holtby 10.00 25.00
CFBM Brad Marchand 8.00 20.00
CFBU Pavel Bure 15.00 40.00
CFCG Claude Giroux 6.00 15.00
CFCK Chris Kreider 8.00 20.00
CFCP Carey Price 20.00 50.00
CFDD Drew Doughty 6.00 15.00
CFDH Dale Hawerchuk 8.00 20.00
CFEL Eric Lindros 15.00 30.00
CFEM Evgeni Malkin 8.00 20.00
CFGL Gabriel Landeskog 6.00 15.00
CFJA Jaden Schwartz 5.00 12.00
CFJE Jordan Eberle 6.00 15.00
CFJI Jarome Iginla 8.00 20.00
CFJN James Neal 8.00 20.00
CFJQ Jonathan Quick 10.00 25.00
CFJS Jeff Skinner 6.00 15.00
CFJT Jonathan Toews 12.00 30.00
CFLX Claude Lemieux 5.00 12.00
CFMB Martin Brodeur 12.00 30.00
CFMD Matt Duchene 6.00 15.00
CFMF Marc-Andre Fleury 8.00 20.00
CFML Mario Lemieux 15.00 40.00
CFMR Mike Richards 6.00 15.00
CFPB Patrice Bergeron 8.00 20.00
CFPC Paul Coffey 6.00 15.00
CFPF Peter Forsberg 8.00 20.00
CFPM Patrick Marleau 6.00 15.00
CFPR Patrick Roy 15.00 40.00
CFPS P.K. Subban 10.00 25.00
CFRF Ron Francis 8.00 20.00
CFRK Ryan Kesler 8.00 20.00
CFRN Ryan Nugent-Hopkins 6.00 15.00
CFSA Joe Sakic 10.00 25.00
CFSB Sven Baertschi 3.00 8.00
CFSC Sidney Crosby 25.00 60.00
CFSS Steven Stamkos 12.00 30.00
CFSV Jakob Silfverberg 8.00 20.00
CFTF Theoren Fleury 8.00 20.00
CFTH Taylor Hall 12.00 30.00
CFTR Tuukka Rask 8.00 20.00
CFTS Tyler Seguin 10.00 25.00
CFWG Wayne Gretzky 30.00 80.00

2012-13 The Cup Foundations Jerseys Autographs

CFAL Jake Allen 30.00 60.00
CFAO Alexander Ovechkin 75.00 125.00
CFBH Braden Holtby 20.00 50.00
CFBM Brad Marchand 25.00 60.00
CFBU Pavel Bure 75.00 125.00
CFCK Chris Kreider 20.00 50.00
CFCP Carey Price EXCH 50.00 100.00
CFDH Dale Hawerchuk 30.00 80.00
CFEL Eric Lindros 60.00 120.00
CFGL Gabriel Landeskog 15.00 40.00
CFJA Jaden Schwartz 20.00 50.00
CFJE Jordan Eberle 20.00 40.00
CFJI Jarome Iginla 25.00 60.00
CFJQ Jonathan Quick 30.00 60.00
CFJS Jeff Skinner 15.00 40.00
CFLX Claude Lemieux 15.00 40.00
CFMB Martin Brodeur 40.00 80.00
CFMD Matt Duchene 20.00 50.00
CFMF Marc-Andre Fleury 20.00 50.00
CFML Mario Lemieux 60.00 120.00
CFMR Mike Richards 25.00 60.00
CFMS Mats Sundin 30.00 80.00
CFPB Patrice Bergeron 25.00 60.00
CFPC Paul Coffey 40.00 80.00
CFPF Peter Forsberg 40.00 80.00
CFPM Patrick Marleau
CFPR Patrick Roy 75.00 135.00
CFPS P.K. Subban
CFRF Ron Francis 30.00 80.00
CFRK Ryan Kesler 25.00 60.00
CFSA Joe Sakic 25.00 60.00
CFSB Sven Baertschi 20.00 50.00
CFSV Jakob Silfverberg 30.00 60.00
CFTF Theoren Fleury 40.00 80.00
CFTH Taylor Hall 30.00 80.00
CFTS Tyler Seguin 15.00 40.00
CFWG Wayne Gretzky 250.00 400.00

2012-13 The Cup Honorable Numbers

HNCP Carey Price/31 50.00 120.00
HNJE Jordan Eberle/14
HNMB Martin Brodeur/30 60.00 120.00
HNSA Joe Sakic/19 60.00 120.00
HNSB Sven Baertschi/47 40.00 100.00

2012-13 The Cup Honorable Numbers Dual

DHNJP C.Joseph/C.Price/31 90.00 150.00
DHNMI J.Iginla/P.Marleau/12 50.00 100.00
DHNSD M.Sundin/Datsyuk/13 100.00 200.00

2012-13 The Cup Limited Logos Autographs

LLAH Adam Henrique/50 20.00 50.00
LLAJ Jake Allen/50 30.00 60.00
LLBM Brad Marchand/25 25.00 60.00
LLCA Carter Ashton/50 15.00 40.00
LLCJ Curtis Joseph/25 30.00 80.00
LLCK Chris Kreider/50 25.00 60.00
LLCP Carey Price/50 60.00 120.00
LLCS Cory Schneider/50 20.00 50.00
LLDG Doug Gilmour/50 40.00 100.00
LLDO Dominik Hasek/50 25.00 60.00
LLEB Ed Belfour/50 25.00 60.00
LLEL Eric Lindros/50 30.00 80.00
LLGG Sam Gagner/50 20.00 50.00
LLGL Gabriel Landeskog/50 25.00 60.00
LLGO Michel Goulet/25 20.00 50.00
LLHT Scott Hartnell/50 20.00 50.00
LLJE Jordan Eberle/50 20.00 50.00
LLJI Jarome Iginla/50 30.00 80.00
LLJJ Jaromir Jagr/50 60.00 150.00
LLJS Joe Sakic/50 50.00 120.00
LLJZ Jason Zucker/25 15.00 40.00
LLLX Claude Lemieux/50 20.00 50.00
LLMA Mark Stone/50 25.00 60.00
LLMB Martin Brodeur/50 50.00 125.00
LLMD Matt Duchene/25 40.00 80.00
LLMF Marc-Andre Fleury/30 40.00 80.00
LLML Mario Lemieux/25 75.00 135.00
LLMR Mike Richards/50 20.00 50.00
LLNL Nicklas Lidstrom/50 30.00 80.00
LLPB Patrice Bergeron/50 30.00 80.00
LLPC Paul Coffey/50 25.00 60.00
LLPF Peter Forsberg/50 EXCH 60.00 120.00
LLPI Chet Pickard/40 12.00 30.00
LLPM Patrick Marleau/50 25.00 60.00
LLRF Ron Francis/25 40.00 100.00
LLRG Ryan Getzlaf/50 40.00 100.00
LLRI Pekka Rinne/50 25.00 60.00
LLRK Ryan Kesler/40 20.00 50.00
LLRY Reilly Smith/50 25.00 50.00
LLSB Sven Baertschi/50 20.00 50.00
LLSU Mats Sundin/50 30.00 80.00
LLSV Jakob Silfverberg/40 25.00 60.00
LLSY Paul Stastny/50 15.00 40.00
LLTL Theoren Fleury/40 40.00 80.00
LLTY Tyson Barrie/50 15.00 40.00

2012-13 The Cup Rookie Bookmarks Dual Autographs

DABAS J.Allen/J.Schwartz 75.00 135.00
DABBS S.Baertschi/J.Silfverberg 60.00 120.00
DABSK C.Kreider/J.Schwartz 75.00 150.00

2012-13 The Cup Rookie Evolution Video Cards

EVO Redemption Card 20.00 50.00

2012-13 The Cup Rookie Gear Autographs

ARGCA Carter Ashton 15.00 40.00
ARGCK Chris Kreider 40.00 100.00
ARGCP Chet Pickard 20.00 50.00
ARGJA Jake Allen 50.00 100.00
ARGJR Jussi Rynnas 30.00 80.00
ARGJS Jaden Schwartz 40.00 100.00
ARGJZ Jason Zucker 25.00 60.00
ARGRS Riley Sheahan 40.00 80.00
ARGSB Sven Baertschi 60.00 120.00
ARGSI Jakob Silfverberg 50.00 100.00
ARGTB Tyson Barrie 40.00 100.00

2012-13 The Cup Scripted Sticks

SSAO Alexander Ovechkin 75.00 150.00
SSEL Eric Lindros 50.00 100.00
SSJB Jean Beliveau 100.00 175.00
SSJS Joe Sakic 50.00 120.00
SSMB Martin Brodeur 50.00 120.00
SSML Mario Lemieux 125.00 250.00
SSMM Mark Messier 90.00 150.00
SSPB Pavel Bure 100.00 200.00
SSPC Paul Coffey
SSPR Patrick Roy 75.00 150.00
SSTS Teemu Selanne 40.00 100.00
SSWG Wayne Gretzky 300.00 600.00

2012-13 The Cup Scripted Sticks Dual

DSSBL J.Beliveau/G.Lafleur 90.00 150.00
DSSBO P.Bure/A.Ovechkin 200.00 350.00
DSSBS P.Bergeron/T.Seguin
DSSEE P.Esposito/T.Esposito 60.00 120.00
DSSGH W.Gretzky/B.Hull 350.00 500.00
DSSRG P.Roy/W.Gretzky 400.00 600.00
DSSSB J.Sakic/R.Bourque 100.00 175.00
DSSSH Hawrchk/Selanne 100.00 200.00

2012-13 The Cup Scripted Swatches

SWAO Alexander Ovechkin/35 60.00 120.00
SWBH Brett Hull/35 75.00 150.00
SWCK Chris Kreider/35 30.00 80.00
SWEL Eric Lindros/35 40.00 100.00
SWJJ Jaromir Jagr/35 50.00 100.00
SWJS Jaden Schwartz/35 40.00 100.00
SWMB Martin Brodeur 50.00 100.00
SWML Mario Lemieux/15 100.00 175.00
SWPB Pavel Bure/35 75.00 150.00
SWSA Joe Sakic/35 50.00 100.00
SWSN Mats Sundin/35 50.00 100.00
SWSV Sven Baertschi/35 25.00 60.00
SWTF Theoren Fleury/35 40.00 100.00

2012-13 The Cup Scripted Swatches Dual

DSWJL M.Lemieux/J.Jagr 150.00 250.00
DSWLG C.Giroux/E.Lindros 175.00 300.00
DSWOB P.Bure/A.Ovechkin 200.00 350.00
DSWSH D.Hawerchuk/T.Selanne 90.00 150.00

2012-13 The Cup Signature Patches

SPAB Alexandre Burrows/99 15.00 40.00
SPAO Alexander Ovechkin/35 60.00 120.00
SPBH Braden Holtby/99 15.00 40.00
SPBM Brad Marchand/99 20.00 50.00
SPBR Bobby Ryan/99 10.00 25.00
SPBS Brayden Schenn/99 10.00 25.00
SPCJ Curtis Joseph/75 15.00 40.00
SPCK Chris Kreider/99 30.00 60.00
SPCO Chris Osgood/99 15.00 40.00
SPCP Carey Price/35 40.00 80.00
SPCS Cory Schneider/99 12.00 30.00
SPDB Dustin Brown/99 15.00 40.00
SPDH Dominik Hasek/75 30.00 80.00
SPEB Ed Belfour/75 12.00 30.00
SPEL Eric Lindros/35 20.00 50.00
SPFZ Johan Franzen/75 12.00 30.00
SPGL Gabriel Landeskog/75 15.00 40.00
SPGU Michel Goulet/75 12.00 30.00
SPHE Adam Henrique/99 12.00 30.00
SPHU Brett Hull/35 30.00 60.00
SPJA Jake Allen/75 25.00 60.00
SPJE Jordan Eberle/75 15.00 40.00
SPJF Jeff Skinner/75 15.00 40.00
SPJI Jarome Iginla/75 15.00 40.00
SPJJ Jaromir Jagr/35 50.00 125.00

Card	Low	High
SPJN James Neal/75	10.00	25.00
SPJS Joe Sakic/35	30.00	80.00
SPLR Luc Robitaille/75	15.00	40.00
SPLX Mario Lemieux/15	75.00	150.00
SPMA Patrick Marleau/75	15.00	40.00
SPMB Martin Brodeur/35	60.00	120.00
SPMD Matt Duchene/99	10.00	25.00
SPMF Marc-Andre Fleury/75	25.00	60.00
SPMP Magnus Paajarvi/75	10.00	25.00
SPMS Marc Staal/99	12.00	30.00
SPNF Nick Foligno/75	12.00	30.00
SPPB Patrice Bergeron/75	20.00	50.00
SPPC Paul Coffey/35	15.00	40.00
SPPD Pavel Datsyuk/75	20.00	50.00
SPPR Patrick Roy/15	75.00	135.00
SPPS P.K. Subban/75	30.00	60.00
SPPV Pavel Bure/35	100.00	175.00
SPRB Ray Bourque/75	30.00	60.00
SPRE Pekka Rinne/75	20.00	50.00
SPRG Ryan Getzlaf/75	25.00	60.00
SPRH Ron Hextall/25	20.00	50.00
SPRK Ryan Kesler/35	12.00	30.00
SPRS Ryan Smyth/75	12.00	30.00
SPSB Sven Baertschi/99	12.00	30.00
SPSC Jaden Schwartz/99	15.00	40.00
SPSD Shane Doan/75	12.00	30.00
SPSI Jakob Silfverberg/99	15.00	40.00
SPSN Mats Sundin/35	40.00	80.00
SPSU Mats Sundin/75	20.00	50.00
SPSW Stephen Weiss/99	12.00	30.00
SPTF Theoren Fleury/35	25.00	60.00
SPTS Teemu Selanne/75	40.00	80.00
SPWG Wayne Gretzky/15	350.00	500.00

2012-13 The Cup Signature Patches Dual

Card	Low	High
DSPCB B.Schenn/C.Giroux		
DSPEH J.Eberle/T.Hall	25.00	60.00
DSPGB S.Gagne/D.Brown	15.00	40.00
DSPGR B.Ryan/R.Getzlaf	25.00	50.00
DSPGS R.Smith/S.Glennie	15.00	40.00
DSPIB J.Iginla/S.Baertschi	25.00	60.00
DSPLJ J.Jagr/M.Lemieux	150.00	250.00
DSPRP C.Pickard/P.Rinne	25.00	60.00
DSPSJ Baertschi/Silfverberg	30.00	80.00
DSPSK J.Schwartz/C.Kreider	40.00	80.00

2012-13 The Cup Silver Jerseys

Card	Low	High
1 Ryan Getzlaf	8.00	20.00
3 Ray Bourque	10.00	25.00
5 Tuukka Rask	6.00	15.00
6 Cam Neely	6.00	15.00
7 Zdeno Chara	6.00	15.00
8 Tyler Seguin	10.00	25.00
9 Brad Marchand	8.00	20.00
10 Thomas Vanek	6.00	15.00
12 Miikka Kiprusoff	5.00	12.00
14 Jeff Skinner	6.00	15.00
15 Phil Esposito	8.00	20.00
16 Patrick Kane	12.00	30.00
17 Tony Esposito	6.00	15.00
20 Joe Sakic	10.00	25.00
21 Patrick Roy	15.00	40.00
22 Matt Duchene	6.00	15.00
23 Gabriel Landeskog	6.00	15.00
24 Jaromir Jagr	12.00	30.00
26 Jim Howard	6.00	15.00
27 Pavel Datsyuk	8.00	20.00
30 Henrik Zetterberg	8.00	20.00
32 Taylor Hall	12.00	30.00
34 Jari Kurri	6.00	15.00
35 Jordan Eberle	6.00	15.00
36 Paul Coffey	6.00	15.00
38 Ryan Nugent-Hopkins	6.00	15.00
39 Ed Belfour	8.00	20.00
40 Jeff Carter	6.00	15.00
41 Anze Kopitar	10.00	25.00
42 Mike Richards	6.00	15.00
43 Luc Robitaille	6.00	15.00
44 Drew Doughty	8.00	20.00
45 Wayne Gretzky	30.00	80.00
46 Jonathan Quick	10.00	25.00
49 Carey Price	20.00	50.00
50 Larry Robinson	8.00	20.00
51 P.K. Subban	10.00	25.00
52 Pekka Rinne	8.00	20.00
53 Ilya Kovalchuk	6.00	15.00
54 Martin Brodeur	12.00	30.00
55 Adam Henrique	6.00	15.00
56 John Tavares	12.00	30.00
59 Marian Gaborik	6.00	15.00
62 Jason Spezza	6.00	15.00
63 Eric Lindros	10.00	25.00
64 Claude Giroux	6.00	15.00
65 Evgeni Malkin	20.00	50.00
66 Mario Lemieux	20.00	50.00
67 Marc-Andre Fleury	8.00	20.00
68 Sidney Crosby	25.00	60.00
69 Ron Francis	8.00	20.00
71 Scott Hartnell	6.00	15.00
73 Patrick Marleau	6.00	15.00
74 Logan Couture	8.00	20.00
75 Jaroslav Halak	6.00	15.00
76 Brett Hull	10.00	25.00
77 Steven Stamkos	12.00	30.00
78 Phil Kessel	8.00	20.00
79 Dion Phaneuf	6.00	15.00
80 Mats Sundin	6.00	15.00
81 Alexandre Burrows	6.00	15.00
83 Henrik Sedin	8.00	20.00
84 Ryan Kesler	10.00	25.00
86 Pavel Bure	15.00	40.00
87 Alexander Ovechkin	15.00	40.00
88 Nicklas Backstrom	10.00	25.00
89 Dale Hawerchuk	8.00	20.00
90 Ondrej Pavelec	10.00	25.00

2012-13 The Cup Trios Jerseys

Card	Low	High
C3TC Pickard/Benn/Kane	10.00	25.00
C3AVS Ststny/Dchne/Landskg	8.00	20.00
C3CGY Kiprusoff/Aliu/Baertschi	5.00	12.00
C3CHI Keith/Crawford/Bolland	10.00	25.00
C3DET Krnwall/Filppula/Ericsson	8.00	20.00
C3DRW Datsyuk/Zettrbrg/Franzn	10.00	25.00
C3LAK Brown/Kopitar/Doughty	12.00	30.00
C3LAK Kopitar/Quick/Doughty	12.00	30.00
C3MTL Markov/Subban/Diaz	8.00	20.00
C3NJD Brodr/Clrksn/Kovalchk	10.00	25.00
C3OIL Eberle/Hall/Nugent-Hop	10.00	25.00
C3PHX Doan/Bdkr/Ekman-Lars	8.00	20.00
C3TML Phaneuf/Kessel/Kulmn	10.00	25.00
C3BEES Chara/Horton/Rask	8.00	20.00
C3DALL Glennie/Garbutt/Smith	12.00	30.00
C3GOON Domi/Twist/Probert	20.00	50.00
C3HABS Gionta/Plekanec/Eller	8.00	20.00
C3LBBR Price/Subban/Eller	12.00	30.00
C3PITT Fleury/Letang/Malkin	25.00	60.00
C3SENS Alfreds/Spzza/Andersn	8.00	20.00
C3WASH Ovechkin/Green/Holtby	10.00	25.00
C3ASTAR Brodeur/Belfour/Joseph	12.00	30.00
C3BLUES Perron/Schwartz/Allen	12.00	30.00
C3DUCKS Perry/Getzlaf/Ryan	12.00	30.00
C3KINGS Penner/Richards/Carter	8.00	20.00
C3PFBRG Forsberg triple	10.00	25.00
C3ROOK2 Ashton/Glennie/Cizikas	6.00	15.00
C3ROOK4 Pickard/Allen/Rynnas	12.00	30.00
C3BOS Chara/Bergeron/Lucic	10.00	25.00
C3DEVILS Kovlchk/Henrq/Larsn	8.00	20.00
C3DSTARS Hull/Lindros/Modano	12.00	30.00
C3FLYERS Schenn/Couturier/Read	12.00	30.00

2013-14 The Cup

EXCH EXPIRATION: 9/24/2016

Card	Low	High
1 Corey Perry	3.00	8.00
2 Ryan Getzlaf	5.00	12.00
3 Jonas Hiller	2.50	6.00
4 Teemu Selanne	6.00	15.00
5 Bobby Orr	10.00	25.00
6 Milan Lucic	3.00	8.00
7 Brad Marchand	4.00	10.00
8 Ray Bourque	5.00	12.00
9 Tuukka Rask	3.00	8.00
10 Dominik Hasek	4.00	10.00
11 Theoren Fleury	4.00	10.00
12 Al MacInnis	3.00	8.00
13 Eric Staal	4.00	10.00
14 Corey Crawford	4.00	10.00
15 Tony Esposito	3.00	8.00
16 Patrick Kane	6.00	15.00
17 Jonathan Toews	6.00	15.00
18 Brent Seabrook	3.00	8.00
19 Matt Duchene	3.00	8.00
20 Joe Sakic	5.00	12.00
21 Peter Forsberg	3.00	8.00
22 Marian Gaborik	3.00	8.00
23 Sergei Bobrovsky	3.00	8.00
24 Ed Belfour	3.00	8.00
25 Pavel Datsyuk	4.00	10.00
26 Jim Howard	3.00	8.00
27 Steve Yzerman	6.00	15.00
28 Nicklas Lidstrom	3.00	8.00
29 Johan Franzen	3.00	8.00
30 Henrik Zetterberg	4.00	10.00
31 Chris Osgood	3.00	8.00
32 Glenn Anderson	3.00	8.00
33 Grant Fuhr	3.00	8.00
34 Wayne Gretzky	15.00	40.00
35 Jordan Eberle	3.00	8.00
36 Taylor Hall	6.00	15.00
37 Drew Doughty	3.00	8.00
38 Luc Robitaille	3.00	8.00
39 Jonathan Quick	5.00	12.00
40 Jari Kurri	3.00	8.00
41 Anze Kopitar	5.00	12.00
42 Zach Parise	3.00	8.00
43 Ryan Suter	2.00	5.00
44 Dany Heatley	2.50	6.00
45 Larry Robinson	3.00	8.00
46 P.K. Subban	5.00	12.00
47 Patrick Roy	8.00	20.00
48 Carey Price	10.00	25.00
49 Pekka Rinne	4.00	10.00
50 Shea Weber	2.50	6.00
51 Martin Brodeur	6.00	15.00
52 Jaromir Jagr	8.00	20.00
53 Thomas Vanek	3.00	8.00
54 John Tavares	6.00	15.00
55 Mike Bossy	3.00	8.00
56 Mark Messier	4.00	10.00
57 Eric Lindros	5.00	12.00
58 Rick Nash	3.00	8.00
59 Phil Esposito	5.00	12.00
60 Henrik Lundqvist	4.00	10.00
61 Craig Anderson	3.00	8.00
62 Jason Spezza	3.00	8.00
63 Bobby Clarke	3.00	8.00
64 Claude Giroux	3.00	8.00
65 Shane Doan	2.50	6.00
66 Mario Lemieux	10.00	25.00
67 Evgeni Malkin	10.00	25.00
68 Marc-Andre Fleury	5.00	12.00
69 Sidney Crosby	12.00	30.00
70 Paul Coffey	3.00	8.00
71 Kris Letang	3.00	8.00
72 Logan Couture	3.00	8.00
73 Antti Niemi	2.50	6.00
74 Curtis Joseph	3.00	8.00
75 Jaroslav Halak	3.00	8.00
76 Martin St. Louis	3.00	8.00
77 Steven Stamkos	6.00	15.00
78 Phil Kessel	4.00	10.00
79 Nazem Kadri	3.00	8.00
80 Mats Sundin	3.00	8.00
81 Pavel Bure	4.00	10.00
82 Roberto Luongo	3.00	8.00
83 Alexandre Burrows	3.00	8.00
84 Ryan Kesler	3.00	8.00
85 Nicklas Backstrom	5.00	12.00
86 Braden Holtby	5.00	12.00
87 Alexander Ovechkin	12.00	30.00
88 Bobby Hull	3.00	8.00
89 Dale Hawerchuk	4.00	10.00
90 Vincent Damphousse	2.50	6.00
91 Sami Vatanen RC	5.00	12.00
92 J.T. Miller RC	5.00	12.00
93 Connor Carrick AU RC	6.00	15.00
94 Reid Boucher AU RC	8.00	20.00
95 Eric Gelinas AU RC	8.00	20.00
96 Martin Marincin AU RC	6.00	15.00
97 Ondrej Palat AU RC	20.00	50.00
98 Jeff Zatkoff AU RC	8.00	20.00
99 Marek Mazanec AU RC	8.00	20.00
100 Darcy Kuemper AU RC	8.00	20.00
101 Antti Raanta JSY AU/249 RC	20.00	50.00
102 Chris Brown JSY AU/249 RC	10.00	25.00
103 Jesper Fast JSY AU/249 RC	12.00	30.00
104 A.Ciasson JSY AU/249 RC	15.00	40.00
105 Petr Mrazek JSY AU/249 RC	60.00	150.00
106 Laughton JSY AU/249 RC	15.00	40.00
107 T.Hickey JSY AU/249 RC	12.00	30.00
108 D.Brunner JSY AU/249 RC	12.00	30.00
109 John Gibson JSY AU/249 RC	60.00	150.00
110 M.Bournival JSY AU/249 RC	15.00	40.00
111 J.Fontaine JSY AU/249 RC	15.00	40.00
112 Ristolainen JSY AU/249 RC	30.00	80.00
113 S.Matteau JSY AU/249 RC	12.00	30.00
114 M.Granlund JSY AU/249 RC	30.00	80.00
115 Jonas Brodin JSY AU/249 RC	12.00	30.00
116 Viktor Fasth JSY AU/249 RC	15.00	40.00
117 Will Acton JSY AU/249 RC	12.00	30.00
118 D.DeKeyser JSY AU/249 RC	20.00	50.00
119 Seth Jones JSY AU/249 RC	15.00	40.00
120 Q.Howden JSY AU/249 RC	12.00	30.00
121 Morgan Rielly JSY AU/249 RC	60.00	150.00
122 R.Rakell JSY AU/249 RC	40.00	100.00
123 J.Nordstrom JSY AU/249 RC	12.00	30.00
124 P.Grubauer JSY AU/249 RC	15.00	40.00
125 Justin Schultz JSY AU/249 RC	25.00	60.00
126 M.Dumba JSY AU/249 RC	20.00	50.00
127 Dylan McIlrath JSY AU/249 RC	10.00	25.00
128 Brock Nelson JSY AU/249 RC	15.00	40.00
129 Dmitrij Jaskin JSY AU/249 RC	15.00	40.00
130 Tomas Jurco JSY AU/249 RC	25.00	60.00
131 E.Pasquale JSY AU/249 RC	10.00	25.00
132 Ryan Strome JSY AU/249 RC	40.00	100.00
133 Martin Jones JSY AU/249 RC	40.00	100.00
134 A.Watson JSY AU/249 RC	12.00	30.00
135 Filip Forsberg JSY AU/249 RC	80.00	200.00
136 Drew Shore JSY AU/249 RC	12.00	30.00
137 J.Schroeder JSY AU/249 RC	15.00	40.00
138 B.Gallagher JSY AU/249 RC	80.00	200.00
139 Charlie Coyle JSY AU/249 RC	30.00	80.00
140 N.Bjugstad JSY AU/249 RC	20.00	50.00
141 Max Reinhart JSY AU/249 RC	15.00	40.00
142 R.Sooner JSY AU/249 RC	15.00	40.00
143 Matt Irwin JSY AU/249 RC	12.00	30.00
144 N.Jensen JSY AU/249 RC	12.00	30.00
145 Gustafsson JSY AU/249 RC	20.00	50.00
146 N.Beaulieu JSY AU/249 RC	12.00	30.00
147 Brian Flynn JSY AU/249 RC	12.00	30.00
148 Carl Soderberg JSY AU/249 RC	15.00	40.00
149 C.Thomas JSY AU/249 RC	12.00	30.00
150 Ryan Murphy JSY AU/249 RC	15.00	40.00
151 Grigorenko JSY AU/249 RC	20.00	50.00
152 Tyler Toffoli JSY AU/249 RC	30.00	80.00
153 Ryan Murray JSY AU/249 RC	25.00	60.00
154 Cory Conacher JSY AU/249 RC	10.00	25.00
155 Tom Wilson JSY AU/249 RC	25.00	60.00
156 T.Pearson JSY AU/249 RC	25.00	60.00
157 Josh Leivo JSY AU/249 RC	15.00	40.00
158 Lucas Lessio JSY AU/249 RC	10.00	25.00
159 Linden Vey JSY AU/249 RC	10.00	25.00
160 Tarasenko JSY AU/249 RC EX	300.00	800.00
161 Xavier Ouellet JSY AU/249 RC	15.00	40.00
162 J.Campbell JSY AU/249 RC	12.00	30.00
163 D.Hamilton JSY AU/249 RC	30.00	80.00
164 F.Andersen JSY AU/249 RC	60.00	150.00
165 H.Lindholm JSY AU/249 RC	25.00	60.00
166 Mark Arcobello JSY AU/249 RC	15.00	40.00
167 Tyler Johnson JSY AU/249 RC	50.00	125.00
168 Alex Killorn JSY AU/249 RC	15.00	40.00
169 F.Hamilton JSY AU/249 RC	15.00	40.00
170 A.Barkov JSY AU/249 RC	60.00	150.00
171 Olli Maatta JSY AU/249 RC	25.00	60.00
172 Beau Bennett JSY AU/249 RC	20.00	50.00
173 N.Zadorov JSY AU/249 RC	15.00	40.00
174 Emerson Etem JSY AU/249 RC	15.00	40.00
175 Jon Merrill JSY AU/249 RC	15.00	40.00
176 Boone Jenner JSY AU/249 RC	25.00	60.00
177 Matt Nieto JSY AU/249 RC	12.00	30.00
178 Elias Lindholm JSY AU/249 RC	25.00	60.00
179 Jarred Tinordi JSY AU/249 RC	15.00	40.00
180 Michael Latta JSY AU/249 RC	12.00	30.00
181 Jacob Trouba JSY AU/249 RC	25.00	60.00
182 Girgensons JSY AU/249 RC	30.00	80.00
183 Cody Ceci JSY AU/249 RC	12.00	30.00
184 Huberdeau JSY AU/249 RC	40.00	100.00
185 Nichushkin JSY AU/99 RC EX	60.00	150.00
186 Yakupov JSY AU/99 RC EX	100.00	250.00
187 N.MacKinnon JSY AU/99 RC	600.00	1000.00
188 Galchenyuk JSY AU/99 RC	400.00	1000.00
189 Tomas Hertl JSY AU/99 RC	100.00	250.00
190 S.Monahan JSY AU/99 RC	400.00	1000.00

2013-14 The Cup Gold

*1-90 VETS/25: 1X TO 2.5X BASIC CARDS
*91-92 ROOK/25: .6X TO 1.5X BASIC ROOK
*93-99 ROOK AU/25: .6X TO 1.5X BASIC AU/99

Card	Low	High
14 Corey Crawford	10.00	25.00
85 Nicklas Backstrom	12.00	30.00
101 Antti Raanta AU	15.00	40.00
102 Chris Brown AU	8.00	20.00
103 Jesper Fast AU	10.00	25.00
104 Alex Chiasson AU	12.00	30.00
105 Petr Mrazek AU	25.00	60.00
106 Scott Laughton AU	12.00	30.00
107 Thomas Hickey AU	10.00	25.00
108 Damien Brunner AU	10.00	25.00
109 John Gibson AU	40.00	100.00
110 Michael Bournival AU	12.00	30.00
111 Justin Fontaine AU	12.00	30.00
112 Rasmus Ristolainen AU	20.00	50.00
113 Stefan Matteau AU	10.00	25.00
114 Mikael Granlund AU		
115 Jonas Brodin AU	10.00	25.00
116 Viktor Fasth AU	12.00	30.00
117 Will Acton AU	10.00	25.00
118 Danny DeKeyser AU	15.00	40.00
119 Seth Jones AU	12.00	30.00
120 Quinton Howden AU	10.00	25.00
121 Morgan Rielly AU	30.00	80.00
122 Rickard Rakell AU	12.00	30.00
123 Joakim Nordstrom AU	10.00	25.00
124 Philipp Grubauer AU	12.00	30.00
125 Justin Schultz AU	10.00	25.00
126 Mathew Dumba AU	12.00	30.00
127 Dylan McIlrath AU	8.00	20.00
128 Brock Nelson AU	12.00	30.00
129 Dmitrij Jaskin AU	12.00	30.00
130 Tomas Jurco AU	20.00	50.00
131 Edward Pasquale AU	8.00	20.00
132 Ryan Strome AU	15.00	40.00
133 Martin Jones AU	20.00	50.00
134 Austin Watson AU	10.00	25.00
135 Filip Forsberg AU	50.00	100.00
136 Drew Shore AU	10.00	25.00
137 Jordan Schroeder AU	12.00	30.00
138 Brendan Gallagher AU	40.00	100.00
139 Charlie Coyle AU	12.00	30.00
140 Nick Bjugstad AU	15.00	40.00
141 Max Reinhart AU	10.00	25.00
142 Ryan Spooner AU	12.00	30.00
143 Matt Irwin AU	10.00	25.00
144 Nicklas Jensen AU	10.00	25.00
145 Johan Gustafsson AU	12.00	30.00
146 Nathan Beaulieu AU	10.00	25.00
147 Brian Flynn AU	10.00	25.00
148 Carl Soderberg AU	12.00	30.00
149 Christian Thomas AU	10.00	25.00
150 Ryan Murphy AU	12.00	30.00
151 Mikhail Grigorenko AU	15.00	40.00
152 Tyler Toffoli AU	40.00	80.00
154 Cory Conacher AU	8.00	20.00
155 Tom Wilson AU	15.00	40.00
156 Tanner Pearson AU	30.00	60.00
157 Josh Leivo AU	12.00	30.00
158 Lucas Lessio AU	8.00	20.00
159 Linden Vey AU	8.00	20.00
161 Xavier Ouellet AU	12.00	30.00
163 Dougie Hamilton AU	25.00	60.00
164 Frederik Andersen AU	20.00	50.00
165 Hampus Lindholm AU	20.00	50.00
166 Mark Arcobello AU	12.00	30.00
167 Tyler Johnson AU	125.00	200.00
168 Alex Killorn AU	12.00	30.00
169 Freddie Hamilton AU	10.00	25.00
170 Aleksander Barkov AU	30.00	80.00
171 Olli Maatta AU	20.00	50.00
172 Beau Bennett AU	20.00	50.00
173 Nikita Zadorov AU	12.00	30.00
174 Emerson Etem AU	12.00	30.00
175 Jon Merrill AU	12.00	30.00
176 Boone Jenner AU	12.00	30.00
177 Matt Nieto AU	10.00	25.00
178 Elias Lindholm AU	20.00	50.00
179 Jarred Tinordi AU	12.00	30.00
180 Michael Latta AU	10.00	25.00
181 Jacob Trouba AU	20.00	50.00
182 Zemgus Girgensons AU	25.00	60.00
183 Cody Ceci AU	10.00	25.00
184 Jonathan Huberdeau AU	30.00	80.00
185 Valeri Nichushkin AU	30.00	60.00
186 Nail Yakupov AU	40.00	100.00
187 Nathan MacKinnon AU	150.00	300.00
188 Alex Galchenyuk AU	100.00	200.00
189 Tomas Hertl AU	15.00	40.00
190 Sean Monahan AU	20.00	50.00

2013-14 The Cup Gold Rainbow

*ROOKIE/51-89: .5X TO 1.2X RC/249
*ROOKIE/30-49: .6X TO 1.5X RC/249
*ROOKIE/20-29: .8X TO 2X RC/249
*ROOKIE/15-19: 1X TO 2.5X RC/249

Card	Low	High
185 V.Nichushkin JSY AU/43	100.00	200.00
186 Nail Yakupov JSY AU/64	100.00	200.00
187 N.MacKinnon JSY AU/29	350.00	700.00
188 A.Galchenyuk JSY AU/27	200.00	400.00
189 Tomas Hertl JSY AU/48	100.00	200.00
190 S.Monahan JSY AU/23	150.00	250.00

2013-14 The Cup Auto Draft Boards

Card	Low	High
DBBN Brock Nelson	40.00	80.00
DBBR Jonas Brodin	12.00	30.00
DBCC Charlie Coyle	15.00	40.00
DBEE Emerson Etem	15.00	40.00
DBHA Dougie Hamilton	30.00	80.00
DBJH Jonathan Huberdeau	75.00	150.00
DBMG Mikael Granlund	25.00	60.00
DBNB Nathan Beaulieu	25.00	60.00
DBNJ Nicklas Jensen	12.00	30.00
DBPY Mark Pysyk	15.00	40.00
DBQH Quinton Howden	12.00	30.00
DBRR Rickard Rakell	15.00	40.00
DBRS Ryan Strome	40.00	80.00
DBSJ Jordan Schroeder	15.00	40.00
DBVT Vladimir Tarasenko		

2013-14 The Cup Brilliance Autographs

Card	Low	High
BAK Anze Kopitar	20.00	50.00
BAN Antti Niemi	10.00	25.00
BAO Alexander Ovechkin	40.00	80.00
BBB Bill Barber	12.00	30.00
BBC Bobby Clarke	15.00	40.00
BBH Bobby Hull	12.00	30.00
BBO Bobby Orr	75.00	150.00
BBR Bill Ranford	12.00	30.00
BCL Claude Lemieux	12.00	30.00
BCN Cam Neely	12.00	30.00
BCP Corey Perry	12.00	30.00
BCS Cory Schneider	10.00	25.00
BDH Dominik Hasek	40.00	100.00
BDP Dion Phaneuf	12.00	30.00
BDS Darryl Sittler	12.00	30.00
BEB Ed Belfour	12.00	30.00
BEK Evander Kane	12.00	30.00
BEM Evgeni Malkin	40.00	100.00
BES Eric Staal	15.00	40.00
BFP Felix Potvin	12.00	30.00
BGA Glenn Anderson	12.00	30.00
BGF Grant Fuhr	12.00	30.00
BGI Clark Gillies	12.00	30.00
BGL Guy Lafleur	25.00	50.00
BGO Michel Goulet	10.00	25.00
BGP Gilbert Perreault	12.00	30.00
BHU Brett Hull	20.00	40.00
BJB Johnny Bucyk	10.00	25.00
BJI Jarome Iginla	12.00	30.00
BJJ Jaromir Jagr	50.00	100.00
BJK Jari Kurri	12.00	30.00
BJT Jonathan Toews	30.00	60.00
BKA Patrick Kane	30.00	60.00
BLR Larry Robinson	12.00	30.00
BMA Marian Gaborik	15.00	40.00
BMB Mike Bossy	12.00	30.00
BMD Marcel Dionne	15.00	40.00
BMF Marc-Andre Fleury	20.00	40.00
BMG Mike Gartner	12.00	30.00
BML Mario Lemieux	50.00	100.00
BMN Markus Naslund	10.00	25.00
BMS Mats Sundin	25.00	50.00
BMT Marty Turco	12.00	30.00
BPE Phil Esposito	20.00	50.00
BPF Peter Forsberg	25.00	50.00
BPK Phil Kessel	15.00	40.00
BPR Patrick Roy	60.00	120.00
BRB Ray Bourque	20.00	50.00
BRF Ron Francis	15.00	40.00
BRH Ron Hextall	15.00	40.00
BRI Mike Richter	12.00	30.00
BRV Rogie Vachon	15.00	40.00
BRY Bobby Ryan	12.00	30.00
BSC Sidney Crosby	100.00	200.00
BSM Stan Mikita	20.00	40.00
BSS Steve Shutt	10.00	25.00
BSW Shea Weber	10.00	25.00
BSY Steve Yzerman		
BTA Taylor Hall	25.00	60.00
BTE Tony Esposito	20.00	40.00
BTF Theoren Fleury	15.00	40.00
BTS Tyler Seguin	20.00	50.00
BWG Wayne Gretzky	250.00	400.00
BZP Zach Parise	12.00	30.00

2013-14 The Cup Emblems of Endorsement

Card	Low	High
EEAG Alex Galchenyuk/15	150.00	300.00
EEAK Anze Kopitar		
EEAO Alexander Ovechkin/15	125.00	250.00
EEBB Brian Bellows/15	30.00	80.00
EEBG Brendan Gallagher/15	75.00	150.00
EEBH Brett Hull/15	60.00	120.00
EECC Cory Conacher/15	25.00	60.00
EECJ Curtis Joseph/15	40.00	100.00
EEDH Dominik Hasek/15	60.00	125.00
EEEB Ed Belfour/15	75.00	150.00
EEGC Guy Carbonneau/15	40.00	100.00
EEGF Grant Fuhr/15	40.00	100.00
EEHA Dougie Hamilton/15	75.00	150.00
EEJH Jonathan Huberdeau/15	100.00	200.00
EEJQ Jonathan Quick	60.00	100.00
EEJR Jeremy Roenick/15	40.00	100.00
EEJS Justin Schultz/15	100.00	200.00
EELI Elias Lindholm/15	40.00	100.00
EEMG Mikhail Grigorenko/15	60.00	120.00
EEML Mario Lemieux/15	100.00	200.00
EEMM Mike Modano/15	70.00	150.00
EEMS Mats Sundin/15	75.00	150.00
EENY Nail Yakupov/15		
EEPC Paul Coffey/15	40.00	100.00
EEPE Corey Perry/15	40.00	100.00
EEPF Peter Forsberg/15 EXCH	60.00	120.00
EEPR Patrick Roy/15	125.00	250.00
EERB Ray Bourque/15	75.00	150.00
EERN Rick Nash/15	40.00	100.00
EESA Joe Sakic/15	75.00	150.00
EESC Sidney Crosby/15		
EESJ Seth Jones/15	40.00	80.00
EESM Sean Monahan/15	60.00	120.00
EESP Jason Spezza/15	40.00	100.00
EETH Tomas Hertl/15	75.00	150.00
EETL Trevor Linden/15	75.00	150.00
EEVN Valeri Nichushkin/15	90.00	150.00

2013-14 The Cup Enshrinements

Card	Low	High
CEAB Aleksander Barkov	12.00	30.00
CEAG Alex Galchenyuk	25.00	60.00
CEAK Anze Kopitar	25.00	50.00
CEAM Al MacInnis	10.00	25.00
CEAN Antti Niemi	8.00	20.00
CEAO Adam Oates	10.00	25.00
CEBB Bill Barber	10.00	25.00
CEBC Bobby Clarke	12.00	30.00
CEBH Bobby Hull	15.00	40.00
CEBJ Boone Jenner	8.00	20.00
CEBO Bobby Orr	50.00	100.00
CEBR Bill Ranford	10.00	25.00
CECG Clark Gillies	10.00	25.00
CECL Claude Lemieux	10.00	25.00
CEDS Darryl Sittler	10.00	25.00
CEES Eric Staal	12.00	30.00
CEFF Filip Forsberg	15.00	40.00
CEFP Felix Potvin	20.00	50.00
CEGA Glenn Anderson	10.00	25.00
CEGF Grant Fuhr	10.00	25.00
CEGL Guy Lafleur	12.00	30.00
CEGM Glen Murray	8.00	20.00
CEGP Gilbert Perreault	10.00	25.00
CEGR Mikhail Grigorenko	6.00	15.00
CEJA Jacob Trouba	8.00	20.00
CEJB Johnny Bucyk	8.00	20.00
CEJH Jonathan Huberdeau	12.00	30.00
CEJI Jarome Iginla	10.00	25.00
CEJK Jari Kurri	10.00	25.00
CEJQ Jonathan Quick	15.00	40.00
CEJS Justin Schultz	10.00	25.00
CEJT Jonathan Toews	20.00	50.00
CELI Elias Lindholm	8.00	20.00
CELR Larry Robinson	10.00	25.00
CEMB Mike Bossy	10.00	25.00
CEMD Marcel Dionne	12.00	30.00
CEMG Mikael Granlund	8.00	20.00
CEMI Mike Gartner	10.00	25.00
CENL Nicklas Lidstrom	15.00	40.00
CENM Nathan MacKinnon	40.00	100.00
CENY Nail Yakupov	15.00	40.00
CEPB Pavel Bure	20.00	50.00
CEPC Paul Coffey	10.00	25.00
CEPE Phil Esposito	15.00	40.00
CEPK Phil Kessel	12.00	30.00
CERB Ray Bourque	15.00	40.00
CERH Ron Hextall	10.00	25.00
CERI Richard Brodeur	10.00	25.00
CERM Ryan Murray	8.00	20.00
CERR Rasmus Ristolainen	8.00	20.00
CERV Rogie Vachon	12.00	30.00
CERY Bobby Ryan	10.00	25.00
CESE Sean Monahan	8.00	20.00
CESJ Seth Jones	5.00	12.00
CESK Saku Koivu	10.00	25.00
CESM Stan Mikita	12.00	30.00
CESS Steve Shutt	8.00	20.00
CETE Tony Esposito	10.00	25.00
CETH Tomas Hertl	15.00	40.00
CEVN Valeri Nichushkin	5.00	12.00
CEVT Vladimir Tarasenko		
CEWG Wayne Gretzky	125.00	250.00
CEZP Zach Parise	10.00	25.00

2013-14 The Cup Enshrinements Dual

Card	Low	High
CE2BG M.Bossy/C.Gillies	20.00	50.00
CE2CB B.Barber/B.Clarke	25.00	60.00
CE2DV M.Dionne/R.Vachon	30.00	80.00
CE2FE V.Fasth/E.Etem	20.00	50.00
CE2GG Galchenyuk/Gallagher	60.00	120.00
CE2HB A.Barkov/Huberdeau	25.00	60.00
CE2HM D.Hasek/R.Miller	30.00	80.00
CE2JF S.Jones/F.Forsberg	30.00	80.00
CE2JM B.Jenner/R.Murray	15.00	40.00
CE2KP P.Kessel/D.Phaneuf		
CE2LS G.Lafleur/S.Shutt	25.00	60.00
CE2MC J.Campbell/P.Mrazek	20.00	50.00
CE2MY MacKinnon/Yakupov	100.00	200.00
CE2OB B.Orr/J.Bucyk	60.00	120.00
CE2WJ S.Weber/S.Jones	12.00	30.00
CE2YS Yakupov/J.Schultz	25.00	60.00
CE21983 B.Hull/S.Mikita		
CE21988 G.Lafleur/T.Esposito	25.00	60.00
CE21989 D.Sittler/B.Park	20.00	50.00
CE21990 G.Perreault/B.Barber	20.00	50.00
CE22011 D.Gilmour/E.Belfour		
CE22012A M.Sundin/J.Sakic	30.00	80.00

2013-14 The Cup Foundations Jerseys

Card	Low	High
CFAB Aleksander Barkov	8.00	20.00
CFAN Antti Niemi	5.00	12.00
CFAO Alexander Ovechkin	25.00	60.00
CFBB Bryan Bickell	4.00	10.00
CFCP Corey Perry	6.00	15.00
CFDH Dominik Hasek	8.00	20.00
CFEB Ed Belfour	6.00	15.00
CFEL Elias Lindholm	10.00	25.00
CFES Eric Lindros	10.00	25.00
CFJH Jim Howard	6.00	15.00
CFJQ Jonathan Quick	10.00	25.00
CFJR Jeremy Roenick	6.00	15.00
CFKL Phil Kessel	8.00	20.00
CFLR Luc Robitaille	6.00	15.00
CFMA Patrick Marleau	6.00	15.00
CFME Mark Messier	8.00	20.00
CFMG Mike Gartner	6.00	15.00
CFML Mario Lemieux	20.00	50.00
CFMS Mats Sundin	6.00	15.00
CFNM Nathan MacKinnon	20.00	40.00
CFPB Pavel Bure	15.00	40.00
CFPR Pekka Rinne	8.00	20.00
CFPS P.K. Subban	12.00	30.00
CFRB Ray Bourque	10.00	25.00
CFRF Ron Francis	8.00	20.00
CFRL Roberto Luongo	6.00	15.00
CFRO Patrick Roy	15.00	40.00
CFRS Ryan Strome	4.00	10.00
CFSC Sidney Crosby	20.00	50.00
CFSD Shane Doan	5.00	12.00
CFSJ Seth Jones	3.00	8.00
CFSM Sean Monahan	5.00	12.00
CFSW Shea Weber	5.00	12.00
CFTE Tony Esposito	10.00	25.00
CFTH Taylor Hall	10.00	25.00
CFTS Tyler Seguin	10.00	25.00
CFVT Vladimir Tarasenko	12.00	30.00
CFWG Wayne Gretzky	25.00	60.00

2013-14 The Cup Foundations Jerseys Autographs

Card	Low	High
CFAB Aleksander Barkov		
CFAN Antti Niemi	25.00	60.00
CFAO Alexander Ovechkin	125.00	300.00
CFBB Bryan Bickell	20.00	50.00
CFCJ Curtis Joseph		
CFCP Corey Perry		
CFDH Dominik Hasek	40.00	100.00
CFEB Ed Belfour		
CFEL Elias Lindholm	25.00	60.00
CFGF Grant Fuhr	30.00	80.00
CFHA Dale Hawerchuk	40.00	100.00
CFJH Jim Howard	25.00	60.00
CFJQ Jonathan Quick		
CFKL Phil Kessel	20.00	50.00
CFLR Luc Robitaille	30.00	80.00
CFMA Patrick Marleau	30.00	80.00
CFME Mark Messier	40.00	100.00
CFMG Mike Gartner	30.00	80.00
CFML Mario Lemieux	75.00	150.00
CFMS Mats Sundin	30.00	80.00
CFNM Nathan MacKinnon	60.00	150.00
CFPB Pavel Bure	60.00	120.00
CFPF Peter Forsberg		
CFPR Pekka Rinne		
CFRB Ray Bourque	50.00	125.00
CFRF Ron Francis		
CFRO Patrick Roy	60.00	120.00
CFRS Ryan Strome		
CFSC Sidney Crosby EXCH	100.00	200.00
CFSJ Seth Jones	15.00	40.00
CFSM Sean Monahan	40.00	80.00
CFSW Shea Weber	25.00	60.00
CFTF Theoren Fleury		
CFTH Taylor Hall	60.00	150.00
CFTS Tyler Seguin	50.00	120.00
CFVT Vladimir Tarasenko		
CFWG Wayne Gretzky	300.00	400.00

2013-14 The Cup Honorable Numbers

Card	Low	High
HNAB Aleksander Barkov/16	40.00	80.00
HNAG Alex Galchenyuk/27	200.00	400.00
HNAK Anze Kopitar		
HNBB Beau Bennett/19	25.00	60.00
HNBH Brett Hull/16	100.00	175.00
HNBI Bryan Bickell/29	20.00	50.00
HNBJ Boone Jenner/38	20.00	50.00
HNCC Cory Conacher/89	12.00	30.00
HNCH Cody Hodgson/19	20.00	50.00
HNCJ Curtis Joseph/31	100.00	200.00
HNCP Carey Price/31	75.00	150.00
HNDO Dominik Hasek/39	60.00	120.00
HNDW Doug Weight		
HNEB Ed Belfour		
HNEE Emerson Etem/65	15.00	40.00
HNEL Elias Lindholm/16	30.00	80.00
HNGC Guy Carbonneau/21	50.00	100.00
HNGF Grant Fuhr/31	75.00	150.00
HNGR Mikhail Grigorenko/25	60.00	120.00
HNHA Dougie Hamilton/27	40.00	100.00
HNHE Tomas Hertl/48	60.00	120.00
HNJQ Jonathan Quick		
HNJS Justin Schultz/19	20.00	50.00
HNJT Jonathan Toews/19	150.00	300.00
HNLC Logan Couture/39	60.00	120.00
HNLO Martin St. Louis/26	30.00	60.00
HNLR Luc Robitaille/20	40.00	100.00
HNMB Martin Brodeur/30	75.00	150.00
HNMG Mike Gartner/22	50.00	100.00
HNMI Mikael Granlund/64	25.00	60.00
HNMJ Martin Jones/31	30.00	80.00
HNMO Sean Monahan/23	100.00	200.00
HNMR Morgan Rielly/44	40.00	100.00
HNNM Nathan MacKinnon/29	150.00	300.00
HNNY Nail Yakupov/64	30.00	60.00
HNPF Peter Forsberg/21	60.00	120.00
HNPM Petr Mrazek/34	40.00	100.00
HNPR Pekka Rinne		
HNRH Ryan Nugent-Hopkins		
HNRM Ryan Murray		
HNRS Ryan Spooner/51	15.00	40.00
HNSA Joe Sakic/19	30.00	80.00
HNSL Scott Laughton/21	20.00	50.00
HNSM Stan Mikita/21	60.00	120.00
HNSY Steve Yzerman/19	40.00	100.00
HNTT Tyler Toffoli/73	60.00	120.00
HNTW Tom Wilson/43	30.00	80.00
HNVF Viktor Fasth/30	20.00	50.00
HNVT Vladimir Tarasenko/91		

2013-14 The Cup Honorable Numbers Dual

Card	Low	High
HNBL A.Barkov/Lindholm/16	20.00	50.00
HNBR Belfour/L.Robitaille/20	30.00	80.00
HNGM Galchenyuk/Murray/27	75.00	150.00
HNGY Yakupov/Granlund/64	50.00	120.00
HNSN J.Sakic/M.Naslund/19	50.00	120.00
HNST J.Toews/J.Spezza/19	100.00	200.00
HNWN Nichushkin/T.Wilson/43	40.00	100.00
HNYT S.Yzerman/J.Toews/19	125.00	250.00

2013-14 The Cup Limited Logos Autographs

Card	Low	High
LLAB Aleksander Barkov/50	30.00	80.00
LLAG Alex Galchenyuk/50	75.00	150.00
LLAH Adam Henrique/50	20.00	50.00
LLAK Anze Kopitar		
LLAL Alex Chiasson/50	12.00	30.00
LLAN Antti Niemi/50	20.00	50.00
LLAO Alexander Ovechkin/25	100.00	200.00
LLAT Alex Tanguay/50	15.00	40.00
LLBA David Backes/50	25.00	60.00
LLBG Brendan Gallagher/50	40.00	100.00
LLBJ Boone Jenner/50	15.00	40.00
LLCC Charlie Coyle/50	15.00	40.00
LLCF Cody Franson/50	15.00	40.00
LLCK Chris Kreider/50	15.00	40.00
LLCO Cory Conacher/50	8.00	20.00
LLCP Carey Price/25	100.00	125.00
LLCT Christian Thomas/50	15.00	40.00
LLDB Damien Brunner/50	15.00	40.00
LLDH Dominik Hasek/25	50.00	125.00
LLDL David Legwand/50	15.00	40.00
LLDM Dylan McIlrath/50	8.00	20.00
LLDW Doug Weight		
LLEM Evgeni Malkin/25	75.00	150.00
LLFO Peter Forsberg/25	50.00	100.00
LLGF Grant Fuhr/50	25.00	60.00
LLGR Mikhail Grigorenko/50	15.00	40.00
LLGU Bill Guerin/50	25.00	60.00
LLHA Dale Hawerchuk/50	20.00	50.00
LLJA Jason Spezza/50	20.00	50.00
LLJF Justin Fontaine/50	12.00	30.00
LLJH Jonathan Huberdeau/50	30.00	80.00
LLJK Jari Kurri/50	25.00	60.00
LLJL John LeClair/50	15.00	40.00
LLJM Jon Merrill/50	15.00	40.00
LLJO John Tavares/25	60.00	120.00
LLJS Justin Schultz/50	12.00	30.00
LLJT Joe Thornton/50	30.00	80.0
LLKL Kari Lehtonen/50	20.00	50.0
LLKT Kyle Turris/50	15.00	40.0
LLLI Elias Lindholm/50	25.00	60.0
LLMC Ryan McDonagh/50	40.00	80.0
LLMD Matt Duchene/50	25.00	60.0
LLMG Mikael Granlund/50	20.00	50.0
LLMN Markus Naslund/50	20.00	50.0
LLMO Mike Modano/50	30.00	80.0
LLMP Max Pacioretty/50	30.00	80.0
LLMR Morgan Rielly/50	25.00	60.0
LLMS Mats Sundin/25	25.00	60.0
LLMU Ryan Murphy/50	12.00	30.0
LLNA Markus Naslund/25	25.00	60.0
LLNM Nathan MacKinnon/50	60.00	150.0
LLNY Nail Yakupov/50	30.00	80.0
LLPE Patrik Elias/50	25.00	60.0
LLPM Petr Mrazek/50	25.00	60.0
LLPP P.A. Parenteau/25	25.00	60.0
LLRB Richard Brodeur/25	30.00	80.0
LLRI Mike Richter/25		
LLRM Ryan Murray		
LLRN Rick Nash/50	25.00	60.0
LLRO Jeremy Roenick/50	20.00	50.0
LLRR Rasmus Ristolainen/50	20.00	50.0
LLRS Ryan Smyth/50	25.00	60.0
LLRY Ryan Strome/50	15.00	40.0
LLSB Sergei Bobrovsky/50	25.00	60.0
LLSG Simon Gagne/50	15.00	40.0
LLSH Scott Hartnell/50	20.00	50.0
LLSJ Seth Jones/50	15.00	40.0
LLSK Saku Koivu/50	25.00	60.0
LLSM Sean Monahan/50	20.00	50.0
LLST Steve Mason/50	20.00	50.0
LLSW Shea Weber/50	15.00	40.0
LLTH Tomas Hertl/50	30.00	80.0
LLTJ Tomas Jurco/50	20.00	50.0
LLTP Tomas Plekanec/50	25.00	60.0
LLTR Jacob Trouba/50	20.00	50.0
LLVN Valeri Nichushkin/50	20.00	50.0
LLVT Vladimir Tarasenko/50		
LLZG Zemgus Girgensons/50	30.00	80.0

2013-14 The Cup Rookie Bookmarks Dual Autographs

Card	Low	High
DABBT N.Beaulieu/J.Tinordi	60.00	120.0
DABFJ S.Jones/F.Forsberg	60.00	120.0
DABFM P.Mrazek/V.Fasth	40.00	100.0
DABGC M.Granlund/C.Coyle	60.00	120.0
DABGG A.Galchenyuk/B.Gallagher	150.00	250.0
DABHB J.Huberdeau/A.Barkov	100.00	200.0
DABMY N.MacKinnon/N.Yakupov	150.00	300.0
DABSH D.Hamilton/R.Spooner	40.00	80.0
DABSY N.Yakupov/J.Schultz	30.00	80.0
DABTP T.Toffoli/T.Pearson	90.00	150.0

2013-14 The Cup Rookie Brilliance Autographs

Card	Low	High
BAB Aleksander Barkov	15.00	40.0
BBJ Boone Jenner	8.00	20.0
BCC Cory Conacher	5.00	12.0
BFF Filip Forsberg	20.00	50.0
BGR Mikael Granlund	12.00	30.0
BHA Dougie Hamilton	15.00	40.0
BJH Jonathan Huberdeau	15.00	40.0
BJS Justin Schultz	8.00	20.0
BMR Morgan Rielly	20.00	50.0
BNM Nathan MacKinnon	60.00	125.0
BNY Nail Yakupov	15.00	40.0
BSJ Seth Jones	8.00	20.0
BTH Tomas Hertl	15.00	40.0
BVF Viktor Fasth	8.00	20.0
BVN Valeri Nichushkin	12.00	30.0
BVT Vladimir Tarasenko		

2013-14 The Cup Rookie Evolution Video Cards

Card	Low	High
EVOAG Alex Galchenyuk	40.00	100.0
EVOCC Charlie Coyle	10.00	25.0
EVOJH Jonathan Huberdeau	25.00	60.0
EVONY Nail Yakupov	30.00	80.0
EVOSZ Justin Schultz	20.00	50.0
EVOTT Tyler Toffoli	40.00	80.0

2013-14 The Cup Rookie Gear Autographs

Card	Low	High
ARGAG Alex Galchenyuk	150.00	300.0
ARGBB Beau Bennett	40.00	100.0
ARGBG Brendan Gallagher	150.00	250.0
ARGCC Cory Conacher	15.00	40.0
ARGDB Damien Brunner	25.00	60.0
ARGDH Dougie Hamilton	75.00	150.0
ARGEE Emerson Etem	25.00	60.0
ARGEL Elias Lindholm	40.00	100.0
ARGFF Filip Forsberg	60.00	120.0
ARGGR Mikael Granlund	50.00	100.0
ARGJH Jonathan Huberdeau	75.00	150.0
ARGJS Justin Schultz	25.00	60.0
ARGMG Mikhail Grigorenko	30.00	80.0
ARGNM Nathan MacKinnon	300.00	600.0
ARGNY Nail Yakupov	60.00	120.0
ARGPM Petr Mrazek	75.00	150.0
ARGSJ Seth Jones	30.00	80.0
ARGSM Sean Monahan	60.00	120.0
ARGVF Viktor Fasth	25.00	60.0
ARGVT Vladimir Tarasenko		

2013-14 The Cup Scripted Sticks

Card	Low	High
SSAK Anze Kopitar		
SSAM Al MacInnis	25.00	60.0
SSBH Bobby Hull	25.00	60.0
SSCN Cam Neely	25.00	60.0
SSCP Carey Price	60.00	120.0
SSDG Doug Gilmour	40.00	80.0
SSDH Dale Hawerchuk	30.00	80.0
SSDP Dion Phaneuf	25.00	60.0
SSEM Evgeni Malkin	80.00	200.0
SSGA Marian Gaborik	25.00	60.0
SSGC Guy Carbonneau	25.00	60.0
SSGF Grant Fuhr	50.00	100.0
SSGL Guy Lafleur	50.00	100.0
SSHE Dany Heatley	20.00	50.0
SSHU Brett Hull	60.00	120.0
SSJK Jari Kurri	30.00	80.0
SSJL John LeClair	40.00	80.0
SSJS Joe Sakic	60.00	120.0
SSKE Phil Kessel	40.00	80.0
SSLC Logan Couture	25.00	60.0
SSLR Larry Robinson	25.00	60.0
SSMB Mike Bossy	25.00	60.0
SSMG Mike Gartner	25.00	60.0
SSMM Mark Messier	50.00	100.0
SSPC Paul Coffey	25.00	60.0
SSPE Phil Esposito	40.00	80.0
SSPF Peter Forsberg	75.00	150.0
SSPK Patrick Kane	50.00	125.0
SSPS P.K. Subban		
SSRB Ray Bourque	40.00	100.0
SSRF Ron Francis	30.00	80.0
SSSC Sidney Crosby	150.00	250.0

SSTE Tony Esposito 50.00 100.00
SSTH Taylor Hall 50.00 125.00
SSWG Wayne Gretzky 300.00 500.00

2013-14 The Cup Scripted Sticks Dual

DSSCL G.Carbonneau/J.LeClair 75.00 150.00
DSSCR G.Carbonneau/L.Robinson 30.00 80.00
DSSFM G.Fuhr/R.Miller 40.00 100.00
DSSGG D.Gilmour/M.Gartner 50.00 120.00
DSSGK W.Gretzky/J.Kurri 250.00 350.00
DSSKG W.Gretzky/J.Kurri 250.00 350.00
DSSMG M.Messier/M.Gartner
DSSNB R.Bourque/C.Neely 60.00 125.00
DSSRG W.Gretzky/L.Robitaille 250.00 350.00
DSSRK L.Robitaille/J.Kurri 40.00 100.00
DSSRP C.Price/P.Roy 250.00 350.00
DSSSD M.Duchene/P.Stastny
DSSSF P.Forsberg/J.Sakic 150.00 250.00
DSSYH S.Yzerman/D.Hasek 100.00 200.00

2013-14 The Cup Scripted Swatches

SWAB Aleksander Barkov/35 25.00 60.00
SWAH Adam Henrique/35 15.00 40.00
SWAN Antti Niemi/35 12.00 30.00
SWAO Alexander Ovechkin/15 100.00 250.00
SWBB Brian Bellows/35 15.00 40.00
SWCC Charlie Coyle/35 10.00 25.00
SWCP Carey Price/35 50.00 100.00
SWDW Doug Weight/35 15.00 40.00
SWGF Grant Fuhr/35 50.00 100.00
SWGL Gabriel Landeskog/35 12.00 30.00
SWJF Justin Fontaine/35 15.00 40.00
SWJH Jonas Hiller/15 15.00 40.00
SWJJ Jaromir Jagr/35 60.00 120.00
SWJS Jason Spezza/35 15.00 40.00
SWMD Matt Duchene/15 40.00 80.00
SWMF Marc-Andre Fleury/35 25.00 50.00
SWMG Mikael Granlund/35 20.00 50.00
SWMR Morgan Rielly/35 25.00 60.00
SWMS Mats Sundin/35 30.00 60.00
SWNM Nathan MacKinnon/35 100.00 200.00
SWNY Nail Yakupov/35 30.00 80.00
SWPA Patrik Elias/35 15.00 40.00
SWPE Corey Perry/35 15.00 40.00
SWPF Peter Forsberg/35 40.00 100.00
SWPM Petr Mrazek/35 30.00 80.00
SWRB Richard Brodeur/35 20.00 50.00
SWRM Ryan Miller/35 15.00 40.00
SWRS Ryan Strome/35 20.00 50.00
SWSA Joe Sakic/35 60.00 120.00
SWSC Sidney Crosby/35 EXCH 100.00 200.00
SWSJ Seth Jones/35 10.00 25.00
SWST Martin St. Louis/35 15.00 40.00
SWSW Shea Weber/15 25.00 60.00
SWSY Steve Yzerman/35 50.00 100.00
SWTH Taylor Hall/35 40.00 80.00
SWTT Tyler Toffoli/35 25.00 60.00
SWVT Vladimir Tarasenko/35

2013-14 The Cup Scripted Swatches Dual

DSSBM E.Belfour/M.Modano 50.00 100.00
DSSBS E.Belfour/M.Sundin 50.00 100.00
DSSHN T.Hall/R.Nugent-Hopkins
DSSHY T.Hall/N.Yakupov 100.00 200.00
DSSJH C.Joseph/B.Hull 100.00 200.00
DSSKH D.Krejci/D.Hamilton 40.00 100.00
DSSKP C.Perry/S.Koivu
DSSRW P.Rinne/S.Weber
DSSSF P.Forsberg/J.Sakic 75.00 150.00
DSSST P.Sharp/J.Toews 75.00 150.00

2013-14 The Cup Signature Patches

SPAA Marc Staal/99 6.00 15.00
SPAG Alex Galchenyuk/99 40.00 100.00
SPAH Adam Henrique/99 12.00 30.00
SPAK Anze Kopitar/99
SPAO Alexander Ovechkin/25 50.00 100.00
SPBB Bill Barber/99 8.00 20.00
SPBG Brendan Gallagher/99 25.00 60.00
SPBJ Boone Jenner/99 10.00 25.00
SPCA Carey Price/99 30.00 80.00
SPCC Cory Conacher/99 5.00 12.00
SPCH Cody Hodgson/99 8.00 20.00
SPCP Corey Perry/99 12.00 30.00
SPCS Cory Schneider/25 15.00 40.00
SPDK David Krejci/99
SPDM Dylan McIlrath/99 5.00 12.00
SPDU Mathew Dumba/99 8.00 20.00
SPDW Doug Weight/99
SPES Eric Staal/25 15.00 40.00
SPGL Guy Lafleur/99 30.00 80.00
SPGM Glen Murray/99 8.00 20.00
SPHU Jonathan Huberdeau/99 20.00 50.00
SPJB Jonathan Bernier/25 20.00 50.00
SPJH Jonas Hiller/99 12.00 30.00
SPJO Jordan Schroeder/99 8.00 20.00
SPJS Jason Spezza/99 8.00 20.00
SPJT John Tavares/25 40.00 100.00
SPKL Kari Lehtonen/99 8.00 20.00
SPLC Logan Couture/25 20.00 50.00
SPLR Luc Robitaille/25 20.00 50.00
SPMB Martin Brodeur/25 60.00 120.00
SPMG Mikhail Grigorenko/99 10.00 25.00
SPMM Mike Modano/99 25.00 60.00
SPMN Markus Naslund/99 8.00 20.00
SPMS Mats Sundin/25 50.00 100.00
SPNM Nathan MacKinnon/99 100.00 200.00
SPNY Nail Yakupov/99 20.00 50.00
SPPB Pavel Bure/25 60.00 120.00
SPPE Patrik Elias/99 8.00 20.00
SPPP P.A. Parenteau/99 5.00 12.00
SPPR Pekka Rinne/99 15.00 40.00
SPRI Morgan Rielly/99 20.00 50.00
SPRK Ryan Kesler/99 8.00 20.00
SPRM Ryan Miller/25 20.00 50.00
SPRR Tyler Toffoli/99 15.00 40.00
SPRS Ryan Strome/99 15.00 40.00
SPSC Sidney Crosby/25 150.00 250.00
SPSE Tyler Seguin/99 15.00 40.00
SPSM Sean Monahan/99 12.00 30.00
SPSW Shea Weber/25 15.00 40.00
SPTH Tomas Hertl/99 10.00 25.00
SPVN Valeri Nichushkin/99 12.00 30.00
SPZG Zemgus Girgensons/99 12.00 30.00

2013-14 The Cup Signature Patches Dual

DSPBH M.Brodeur/Henrique/35 30.00 60.00
DSPBP D.Phaneuf/J.Bernier/35
DSPGG Gallagher/Galchnyk/35 60.00 120.00
DSPHM J.Howard/P.Mrazek/35 25.00 60.00
DSPJH C.Joseph/D.Hasek/15 60.00 120.00
DSPJS M.Sundin/C.Joseph/15 50.00 100.00
DSPKP D.Phaneuf/P.Kessel/35
DSPLG Gretzky/M.Lemieux/15
DSPMB G.Murray/R.Bourque/35
DSPML Landeskog/MacKinn/35 100.00 200.00
DSPNM MacKinnon/Duchne/35 100.00 200.00
DSPNS M.Staal/R.Nash/35
DSPPE C.Perry/E.Etem/35 12.00 30.00
DSPPJ J.Bernier/P.Kessel/35
DSPRG J.Roenick/C.Giroux/35 20.00 40.00
DSPRR Robitaille/J.Roenick/35 25.00 50.00
DSPSF P.Forsberg/J.Sakic/15 100.00 200.00
DSPSS J.Sakic/M.Sundin/15 75.00 150.00
DSPTC C.Conacher/K.Turris/35 8.00 20.00
DSPTD Tavares/M.Duchene/35 40.00 80.00
DSPTV Seguin/V.Nichushkin/35 20.00 50.00
DSPWJ S.Jones/S.Weber/35 12.00 30.00
DSPYO S.Yzerman/C.Osgood/15 75.00 150.00

2013-14 The Cup Signature Renditions

SRAB Aleksander Barkov 15.00 40.00
SRAG Alex Galchenyuk 40.00 100.00
SRBB Bill Barber 15.00 40.00
SRBC Bobby Clarke
SRBH Bobby Hull 30.00 60.00
SRBO Bobby Orr 50.00 100.00
SRCL Claude Lemieux
SRCN Cam Neely 15.00 40.00
SRDH Dominik Hasek 30.00 60.00
SREB Ed Belfour
SREM Evgeni Malkin 50.00 125.00
SRES Eric Staal 20.00 50.00
SRGF Grant Fuhr 15.00 40.00
SRGL Guy Lafleur 20.00 50.00
SRGP Gilbert Perreault 15.00 40.00
SRGR Mikhail Grigorenko 12.00 30.00
SRGW Wayne Gretzky 200.00 300.00
SRHE Tomas Hertl 30.00 80.00
SRHU Brett Hull 30.00 60.00
SRJH Jonathan Huberdeau 15.00 40.00
SRJJ Jaromir Jagr 50.00 100.00
SRJK Jari Kurri 15.00 40.00
SRJP Jean-Gabriel Pageau 12.00 30.00
SRJQ Jonathan Quick
SRJT John Tavares 30.00 80.00
SRKE Phil Kessel 20.00 50.00
SRLI Elias Lindholm 20.00 50.00
SRLR Larry Robinson 15.00 40.00
SRMB Martin Brodeur 40.00 80.00
SRMD Marcel Dionne 25.00 50.00
SRMG Mike Gartner 15.00 40.00
SRMI Mike Bossy 15.00 40.00
SRMM Mark Messier 30.00 60.00
SRMO Sean Monahan 20.00 50.00
SRMS Mats Sundin 30.00 60.00
SRMT Marty Turco 15.00 40.00
SRNL Nicklas Lidstrom 15.00 40.00
SRNM Nathan MacKinnon 75.00 150.00
SRNY Nail Yakupov 20.00 50.00
SROR Bobby Orr 50.00 100.00
SRPC Paul Coffey 15.00 40.00
SRPE Phil Esposito 25.00 60.00
SRPK Patrick Kane 30.00 60.00
SRRB Ray Bourque 25.00 60.00
SRRF Ron Francis 20.00 50.00
SRRH Ron Hextall 15.00 40.00
SRRM Ryan Murray
SRRV Rogie Vachon 20.00 50.00
SRSB Sergei Bobrovsky 15.00 40.00
SRSJ Seth Jones 10.00 25.00
SRSM Stan Mikita 20.00 50.00
SRSW Shea Weber 15.00 40.00
SRTE Tony Esposito 15.00 40.00
SRTF Theoren Fleury 20.00 50.00
SRTH Taylor Hall 30.00 80.00
SRTO Jonathan Toews 30.00 80.00
SRTS Tyler Seguin 25.00 60.00
SRVL Valeri Nichushkin 20.00 50.00
SRVT Vladimir Tarasenko
SRWA Wayne Gretzky 200.00 300.00
SRWG Wayne Gretzky 200.00 300.00

2013-14 The Cup Signature Renditions Combos

SRCAP A.Oates/P.Bure 50.00 120.00
SRCCB B.Barber/B.Clarke
SRCED M.Dionne/P.Esposito
SRCGM Gretzky/M.Messier 250.00 500.00
SRCHL D.Hasek/N.Lidstrom 60.00 120.00
SRCHM B.Hull/S.Mikita 50.00 125.00
SRCHO B.Hull/A.Oates 40.00 100.00
SRCHY N.Yakupov/T.Hall
SRCLG Gretzky/M.Lemieux 500.00 700.00
SRCLJ J.Jagr/M.Lemieux 100.00 200.00
SRCLS S.Shutt/G.Lafleur 60.00 120.00
SRCMB Barkov/MacKinnon 75.00 150.00
SRCOH C.Osgood/D.Hasek
SRCPG R.Getzlaf/C.Perry
SRCPK D.Phaneuf/P.Kessel
SRCRS J.Sakic/P.Roy
SRCRV P.Roy/R.Vachon 100.00 250.00
SRCSN M.Naslund/M.Sundin 40.00 100.00
SRCSR B.Ryan/J.Spezza
SRCSS M.Sundin/J.Sakic
SRCTK J.Toews/P.Kane 100.00 200.00
SRCWM W.Gretzky/M.Messier 300.00 500.00
SRCYB S.Bowman/S.Yzerman 80.00 200.00
SRCYO S.Yzerman/A.Oates 80.00 200.00
SRCGRM Ranfrd/Mssr/Gretzky
SRCRSM MacKinn/Sakic/Roy 250.00 500.00
SRCSLF Sundn/Ldstrm/Forsbrg 60.00 120.00

2013-14 The Cup Silver Jerseys

1 Corey Perry 6.00 15.00
2 Ryan Getzlaf 10.00 25.00
3 Jonas Hiller 5.00 12.00
4 Teemu Selanne 12.00 30.00
6 Milan Lucic 6.00 15.00
7 Brad Marchand 8.00 20.00
8 Ray Bourque 12.00 30.00
9 Tuukka Rask 6.00 15.00
13 Eric Staal 8.00 20.00
14 Corey Crawford 8.00 20.00
15 Tony Esposito 6.00 15.00
16 Patrick Kane 12.00 30.00
17 Jonathan Toews 12.00 30.00
18 Brent Seabrook 6.00 15.00
19 Matt Duchene 6.00 15.00
20 Joe Sakic 10.00 25.00
21 Peter Forsberg 6.00 15.00
23 Sergei Bobrovsky 6.00 15.00
25 Pavel Datsyuk 8.00 20.00
26 Jim Howard 6.00 15.00
27 Steve Yzerman 12.00 30.00
28 Nicklas Lidstrom 6.00 15.00
29 Johan Franzen 6.00 15.00
30 Henrik Zetterberg 8.00 20.00
31 Chris Osgood 6.00 15.00
33 Grant Fuhr 8.00 20.00
34 Wayne Gretzky 40.00 100.00
35 Jordan Eberle 6.00 15.00
36 Taylor Hall 12.00 30.00
37 Drew Doughty 8.00 20.00
38 Luc Robitaille 8.00 20.00
39 Jonathan Quick 10.00 25.00
41 Anze Kopitar 10.00 25.00
46 P.K. Subban 10.00 25.00
47 Patrick Roy 15.00 40.00
48 Carey Price 20.00 50.00
49 Pekka Rinne 8.00 20.00
50 Shea Weber 5.00 12.00
51 Martin Brodeur 12.00 30.00
53 Thomas Vanek 6.00 15.00
54 John Tavares 12.00 30.00
55 Mike Bossy 8.00 20.00
56 Mark Messier 8.00 20.00
57 Eric Lindros 10.00 25.00
60 Henrik Lundqvist 8.00 20.00
61 Craig Anderson 6.00 15.00
62 Jason Spezza 6.00 15.00
64 Claude Giroux 6.00 15.00
65 Shane Doan 5.00 12.00
66 Mario Lemieux 20.00 50.00
67 Evgeni Malkin 20.00 50.00
68 Marc-Andre Fleury 10.00 25.00
69 Sidney Crosby 25.00 60.00
71 Kris Letang 6.00 15.00
72 Logan Couture 6.00 15.00
73 Antti Niemi 5.00 12.00
75 Jaroslav Halak 6.00 15.00
76 Martin St. Louis 8.00 20.00
77 Steven Stamkos 12.00 30.00
78 Phil Kessel 8.00 20.00
80 Mats Sundin 6.00 15.00
82 Roberto Luongo 6.00 15.00
84 Ryan Kesler 6.00 15.00
85 Nicklas Backstrom 10.00 25.00
86 Braden Holtby 10.00 25.00
87 Alexander Ovechkin 25.00 60.00
89 Dale Hawerchuk 8.00 20.00

2013-14 The Cup Trios Jerseys

C3AD Slnne/Kvu/Gtzlf 10.00 25.00
C3BB Mrchnd/Lcc/Krjci 10.00 25.00
C3EO NgntHpkns/Ykpv/Hll 12.00 30.00
C3VC Kslr/Schrdr/Edlr 8.00 20.00
C3WC Crlsn/Grn/Bckstrm 12.00 30.00
C3ANA Fsth/Gbsn/Andrsn 15.00 40.00
C3AVS Ry/Skc/McKnn 25.00 50.00
C3BEES Prk/Mrry/Brque 12.00 30.00
C3BLUES Elltt/Trsnko/Brglnd 20.00 50.00
C3BOS Spner/Sdrbrg/Hmltn 15.00 40.00
C3BUF Grgnko/Rstln/Grgsns 10.00 25.00
C3CAN Blieu/Tnrdi/Brnvl 8.00 20.00
C3CAPS Ovchkn/Crrck/Hltby 30.00 80.00
C3CAR Wrd/Stl/Lndhlm 12.00 30.00
C3CHI Shrp/Sbrk/Bckll 8.00 20.00
C3COL Dchne/Ststny/Lndskg 8.00 20.00
C3DAL Nchshkn/Sgn/Chssn 8.00 20.00
C3DET Hsk/Hwrd/Mrzk 10.00 25.00
C3DEV Hnrque/Schder/Mrrll 8.00 20.00
C3DRW Hwrd/Dtsyk/Frnzn 10.00 25.00
C3DUCKS Gtzlf/Prry/Etm 12.00 30.00
C3EDM Ykpv/Schltz/Hll 15.00 40.00
C3FLO Hbrdeau/Brkv/Hwdn 12.00 30.00
C3FLY Lghtn/Grx/Hrtnll 8.00 20.00
C3GOAL Fhr/Jsph/Hxtll 12.00 30.00
C3GR8 Hll/Chls/Frsbrg 8.00 20.00
C3HABS Bnvl/Gllghr/Glchnyk 15.00 40.00
C3HAWKS Shrp/Kne/Tws 15.00 40.00
C3KINGS Prsn/Vy/Jnes 12.00 30.00
C3LAK Kptr/Tffli/Rchrds 15.00 40.00
C3LBBR Glchnyk/Pcrtty/Mrkv 15.00 40.00
C3LEAFS Blfr/Fhr/Brnr 8.00 20.00
C3LOS Kptr/Tffli/Qck 15.00 40.00
C3MINW Grnlnd/Cyle/Brdn 8.00 20.00
C3MON Prce/Ry/Thdre 25.00 50.00
C3MTL Prce/Gllghr/Glchnyk 15.00 40.00
C3NASH Jnes/Rnne/Wbr 6.00 15.00
C3NET Hsk/Espsto/Blfr 12.00 30.00
C3NJD Brdr/Zjc/Mrrll 15.00 40.00
C3NYI Tvrs/Nlsn/Hcky 15.00 40.00
C3NYR Grtnr/Lndrs/Flry 12.00 30.00
C3OIL Hll/Ebrle/NgntHpkns 15.00 40.00
C3OILRS Hmsky/Schltz/Hll 15.00 40.00
C3OTT Hsk/Spzza/Krlssn 20.00 40.00
C3PEN Lmx/Mlkn/Bnntt 15.00 40.00
C3PHI Rnck/Hxtll/LeClr 8.00 20.00
C3PIT Mlkn/Flry/Ltng 25.00 60.00
C3PREDS Frsbrg/Wtsn/Jnes 12.00 30.00
C3RWINGS Lshft/DKysr/Jrco 8.00 20.00
C3STAR Nsh/Kth/Sknnr 12.00 30.00
C3STARS Lhtnn/Bnn/Cmpbll 10.00 25.00
C3TBL Pnk/Kllrn/Gds 8.00 20.00
C3TOR Blfr/Sndn/Lndrs 12.00 30.00
C3VAN Kslr/Edlr/Jnsn 8.00 20.00
C3WAS Bckstrm/Grn/Wlsn 12.00 30.00
C3WINGS Hwrd/Mrzk/Jrco 10.00 25.00

2014-15 The Cup

1-174 STATED PRINT RUN 249
175-180 STATED PRINT RUN 99
EXCH EXPIRATION: 9/1/2017
1 Teemu Selanne 6.00 15.00
2 Ryan Getzlaf 5.00 12.00
3 Shane Doan 2.50 6.00
4 Bobby Orr 6.00 15.00
5 Patrice Bergeron 4.00 10.00
6 Phil Esposito 5.00 12.00
7 Ray Bourque 5.00 12.00
8 Tuukka Rask 3.00 8.00
9 Cam Neely 3.00 8.00
10 Zemgus Girgensons 3.00 8.00
11 Dominik Hasek 4.00 10.00
12 Sean Monahan 3.00 8.00
13 Theoren Fleury 4.00 10.00
14 Eric Staal 4.00 10.00
15 Jonathan Toews 6.00 15.00
16 Patrick Kane 6.00 15.00
17 Patrick Sharp 3.00 8.00
18 Steve Larmer 2.50 6.00
19 Nathan MacKinnon 6.00 15.00
20 Matt Duchene 3.00 8.00
21 Semyon Varlamov 3.00 8.00
22 Joe Sakic 5.00 12.00
23 Gabriel Landeskog 2.50 6.00
24 Rob Blake 3.00 8.00
25 Sergei Bobrovsky 3.00 8.00
26 Brandon Dubinsky 2.50 6.00
27 Tyler Seguin 5.00 12.00
28 Jason Spezza 3.00 8.00
29 Jamie Benn 4.00 10.00
30 Pavel Datsyuk 4.00 10.00
31 Chris Chelios 3.00 8.00
32 Steve Yzerman 6.00 15.00
33 Henrik Zetterberg 4.00 10.00
34 Wayne Gretzky 15.00 40.00
35 Taylor Hall 6.00 15.00
36 Ryan Nugent-Hopkins 3.00 8.00
37 Glenn Anderson 3.00 8.00
38 Roberto Luongo 3.00 8.00
39 Aleksander Barkov 3.00 8.00
40 Jonathan Quick 5.00 12.00
41 Marian Gaborik 3.00 8.00
42 Anze Kopitar 5.00 12.00
43 Zach Parise 3.00 8.00
44 Thomas Vanek 3.00 8.00
45 P.K. Subban 5.00 12.00
46 Max Pacioretty 3.00 8.00
47 Patrick Roy 8.00 20.00
48 Vincent Damphousse 2.50 6.00
49 Carey Price 10.00 25.00
50 Alex Galchenyuk 5.00 12.00
51 Filip Forsberg 4.00 10.00
52 Pekka Rinne 4.00 10.00
53 Shea Weber 2.50 6.00
54 Jaromir Jagr 8.00 20.00
55 Cory Schneider 2.50 6.00
56 Kyle Okposo 3.00 8.00
57 John Tavares 6.00 15.00
58 Mike Bossy 3.00 8.00
59 Henrik Lundqvist 4.00 10.00
60 Rick Nash 3.00 8.00
61 Martin St. Louis 3.00 8.00
62 John Vanbiesbrouck 3.00 8.00
63 Mark Messier 3.00 8.00
64 Erik Karlsson 6.00 15.00
65 Bobby Ryan 3.00 8.00
66 Claude Giroux 3.00 8.00
67 Sidney Crosby 10.00 25.00
68 Evgeni Malkin 10.00 25.00
69 Marc-Andre Fleury 5.00 12.00
70 Mario Lemieux 10.00 25.00
71 Mats Sundin 3.00 8.00
72 Logan Couture 3.00 8.00
73 Joe Pavelski 3.00 8.00
74 Arturs Irbe 3.00 8.00
75 Tomas Hertl 3.00 8.00
76 David Backes 3.00 8.00
77 Vladimir Tarasenko 5.00 12.00
78 Brett Hull 3.00 8.00
79 Steven Stamkos 6.00 15.00
80 Ben Bishop 3.00 8.00
81 Darryl Sittler 3.00 8.00
82 Phil Kessel 4.00 10.00
83 Jonathan Bernier 3.00 8.00
84 James van Riemsdyk 3.00 8.00
85 Ryan Miller 3.00 8.00
86 Trevor Linden 3.00 8.00
87 Nicklas Backstrom 5.00 12.00
88 Alexander Ovechkin 12.00 30.00
89 Mike Gartner 3.00 8.00
90 Evander Kane 3.00 8.00
91 Joel Armia RC 5.00 12.00
92 Klas Dahlbeck AU RC 6.00 15.00
93 Andrej Nestrasil AU RC 8.00 20.00
94 Scott Mayfield AU RC 6.00 15.00
95 Patrick Brown AU RC 8.00 20.00
96 Patrik Nemeth AU RC 8.00 20.00
97 Corban Knight AU RC 8.00 20.00
98 Joey Hishon AU RC 10.00 25.00
99 Mike Halmo AU RC 5.00 12.00
100 Laurent Brossoit AU RC EXCH 25.00 50.00
101 Joonas Nattinen JSY AU RC 10.00 25.00
102 Liam O'Brien JSY AU RC EXCH 10.00 25.00
103 Curtis McKenzie JSY AU RC 8.00 20.00
104 C.Paquette JSY AU RC EX 25.00 50.00
105 Tyler Graovac JSY AU RC 8.00 20.00
106 Jake McCabe JSY AU RC 10.00 25.00
107 N.Deslauriers JSY AU RC 10.00 25.00
108 Seth Helgeson JSY AU RC 8.00 20.00
109 Dennis Everberg JSY AU RC 10.00 25.00
110 Colin Smith JSY AU RC EXCH 20.00 40.00
111 Rocco Grimaldi JSY AU RC 10.00 25.00
112 Greg McKegg JSY AU RC 8.00 20.00
113 Bryan Rust JSY AU RC 80.00 150.00
114 J.Klingberg JSY AU RC EXCH 30.00 80.00
115 P-E Bellemare JSY AU RC 12.00 30.00
116 Rob Zepp JSY AU RC 15.00 40.00
117 Mark Visentin JSY AU RC 10.00 25.00
118 M.Karlsson JSY AU RC 10.00 25.00
119 Christian Folin JSY AU RC 10.00 25.00
120 Brandon Kozun JSY AU RC 8.00 20.00
121 Wotherspoon JSY AU/249 RC 10.00 25.00
122 Derrick Pouliot JSY AU RC 12.00 30.00
123 Barclay Goodrow JSY AU RC 10.00 25.00
124 A.Vasilevskiy JSY AU RC 100.00 250.00
125 B.Gormley JSY AU RC 10.00 25.00
126 Ryan Sproul JSY AU RC 10.00 25.00
127 Joni Ortio JSY AU RC 12.00 30.00
128 Calle Jarnkrok JSY AU RC 10.00 25.00
129 Scott Harrington JSY AU RC 10.00 25.00
130 Griffin Reinhart JSY AU RC 12.00 30.00
131 Andy Andreoff JSY AU RC 10.00 25.00
132 Justin Hodgman JSY AU RC 8.00 20.00
133 Khokhlachev JSY AU RC EX 10.00 25.00
134 Josh Jooris JSY AU RC 10.00 25.00
135 P.Lindbohm JSY AU RC EX 15.00 40.00
136 Hammond JSY AU RC EXCH 15.00 40.00
137 M.Granlund JSY AU RC EX 20.00 40.00
138 Jordan Binnington JSY AU RC 10.00 25.00
139 Scott Darling JSY AU RC 60.00 120.00
140 Vincent Trocheck JSY AU RC 20.00 40.00
141 Colton Sissons JSY AU RC 10.00 25.00
142 Joe Morrow JSY AU RC 12.00 30.00
143 Teemu Pulkkinen JSY AU RC 15.00 40.00
144 Namestnikov JSY AU/249 RC EX 40.00 100.00
145 Brett Ritchie JSY AU RC 10.00 25.00
146 Mirco Mueller JSY AU RC 10.00 25.00
147 Marko Dano JSY AU RC 30.00 60.00
148 Ty Rattie JSY AU RC 15.00 40.00
149 A.Clendening JSY AU/249 RC 10.00 25.00
150 Tobias Rieder JSY AU RC 10.00 25.00
151 Victor Rask JSY AU RC 12.00 30.00
152 Karlsson JSY AU RC EXCH 80.00 150.00
153 B.Yakimov JSY AU/249 RC 12.00 30.00
154 K.Hayes JSY AU RC EXCH 30.00 80.00
155 T.van Riemsdyk JSY AU/249 RC 25.00 50.00
156 Pastrnak JSY AU/249 RC EXCH 250.00 400.00
157 S.Andrighetto JSY AU/249 RC 12.00 30.00
158 Adam Lowry JSY AU RC 10.00 25.00
159 C.Tierney JSY AU RC EXCH 25.00 50.00
160 L.Draisaitl JSY AU RC EXCH 200.00 500.00
161 Kerby Rychel JSY AU RC 8.00 20.00
162 Darnell Nurse JSY AU RC 40.00 100.00
163 S.Gostisbehere JSY AU/249 RC 100.00 200.00
164 D.Severson JSY AU/249 RC 10.00 25.00
165 Phillip Danault JSY AU RC 10.00 25.00
166 Stuart Percy JSY AU RC 10.00 25.00
167 Jiri Sekac JSY AU RC 10.00 25.00
168 S.Griffith JSY AU RC EXCH 25.00 50.00
169 A.Wennberg JSY AU/249 RC 20.00 50.00
170 Curtis Lazar JSY AU RC 20.00 50.00
171 Duclair JSY AU/249 RC EXCH 60.00 100.00
172 Jori Lehtera JSY AU RC 12.00 30.00
173 E.Kuznetsov JSY AU/249 RC 150.00 250.00
174 A.Burakovsky JSY AU/249 RC 30.00 80.00
175 J.Gaudreau JSY AU/99 RC 750.00 1500.00
176 Bo Horvat JSY AU/99 RC 200.00 500.00
177 T.Teravainen JSY AU/99 RC 125.00 300.00
178 Sam Reinhart JSY AU/99 RC 200.00 400.00
179 Aaron Ekblad JSY AU/99 RC 200.00 500.00
180 Drouin JSY AU/99 RC EXCH 300.00 600.00

2014-15 The Cup Gold Spectrum

*ROOKIES/25: .6X TO 1.5X BASIC RC/249
1-88 UNPRICED STATED PRINT RUN 5
91-180 STATED PRINT RUN 25
EXCH EXPIRATION: 8/31/2017
91 Joel Armia 8.00 20.00
92 Klas Dahlbeck AU 10.00 25.00
93 Andrej Nestrasil AU 12.00 30.00
94 Scott Mayfield AU 10.00 25.00
95 Patrick Brown AU 12.00 30.00
96 Patrik Nemeth AU 12.00 30.00
97 Corban Knight AU 12.00 30.00
99 Mike Halmo AU 8.00 20.00
101 Joonas Nattinen AU 12.00 30.00
102 Liam O'Brien AU 12.00 30.00
103 Curtis McKenzie AU 10.00 25.00
104 Cedric Paquette AU 12.00 30.00
105 Tyler Graovac AU 10.00 25.00
106 Jake McCabe AU 12.00 30.00
107 Nicolas Deslauriers AU 12.00 30.00
108 Seth Helgeson AU 10.00 25.00
109 Dennis Everberg AU 12.00 30.00
110 Colin Smith AU 12.00 30.00
111 Rocco Grimaldi AU 12.00 30.00
112 Greg McKegg AU 10.00 25.00
113 Bryan Rust AU 60.00 120.00
114 John Klingberg AU 125.00 200.00
115 Pierre-Edouard Bellemare AU 15.00 40.00
116 Rob Zepp AU 20.00 50.00
117 Mark Visentin AU 12.00 30.00
118 Melker Karlsson AU 12.00 30.00
119 Christian Folin AU 12.00 30.00
120 Brandon Kozun AU 10.00 25.00
121 Tyler Wotherspoon AU 12.00 30.00
122 Derrick Pouliot AU 15.00 40.00
123 Barclay Goodrow AU 12.00 30.00
124 Andrei Vasilevskiy AU 125.00 250.00
125 Brandon Gormley AU 12.00 30.00
126 Ryan Sproul AU 12.00 30.00
127 Joni Ortio AU 15.00 40.00
129 Scott Harrington AU 12.00 30.00
130 Griffin Reinhart AU 12.00 30.00
131 Andy Andreoff AU 12.00 30.00
135 Petteri Lindbohm AU 10.00 25.00
137 Markus Granlund AU 20.00 50.00
138 Jordan Binnington AU 12.00 30.00
139 Scott Darling AU 50.00 100.00
140 Vincent Trocheck AU 25.00 50.00
141 Colton Sissons AU 12.00 30.00
142 Joe Morrow AU 15.00 40.00
143 Teemu Pulkkinen AU 60.00 100.00
147 Marko Dano AU 12.00 30.00
148 Ty Rattie AU 15.00 40.00
149 Adam Clendening AU 12.00 30.00
150 Tobias Rieder AU 12.00 30.00
151 Victor Rask AU 12.00 30.00
152 William Karlsson AU 100.00 200.00
153 Bogdan Yakimov AU 12.00 30.00
154 Kevin Hayes AU 50.00 120.00
155 Trevor van Riemsdyk AU 20.00 50.00
156 David Pastrnak AU 75.00 135.00
157 Sven Andrighetto AU 15.00 40.00
158 Adam Lowry AU 12.00 30.00
160 Leon Draisaitl AU 40.00 80.00
161 Kerby Rychel AU 10.00 25.00
162 Darnell Nurse AU 40.00 80.00
163 Shayne Gostisbehere AU 60.00 100.00
164 Damon Severson AU 12.00 30.00
165 Phillip Danault AU 12.00 30.00
166 Stuart Percy AU 12.00 30.00
167 Jiri Sekac AU 12.00 30.00
169 Alexander Wennberg AU 25.00 60.00
170 Curtis Lazar AU 15.00 40.00
172 Jori Lehtera AU 15.00 40.00
173 Evgeny Kuznetsov AU 60.00 100.00
174 Andre Burakovsky AU 40.00 80.00
175 Johnny Gaudreau AU 125.00 250.00
176 Bo Horvat AU 60.00 120.00
177 Teuvo Teravainen AU 75.00 150.00
178 Sam Reinhart AU 60.00 120.00
179 Aaron Ekblad AU 60.00 120.00
180 Jonathan Drouin AU 100.00 200.00

2014-15 The Cup Auto Draft Boards

STATED PRINT RUN 25 SER.#'d SETS
ARDBBG Brandon Gormley 15.00 40.00
ARDBEK Evgeny Kuznetsov 90.00 150.00
ARDBJM Joe Morrow 20.00 50.00
ARDBKH Kevin Hayes 60.00 120.00
ARDBMV Mark Visentin 15.00 40.00
ARDBOK Oscar Klefbom 40.00 80.00
ARDBPD Phillip Danault 15.00 40.00
ARDBSP Stuart Percy 15.00 40.00

2014-15 The Cup Brilliance Autographs

GROUP A ODDS 1:90
GROUP B ODDS 1:35
GROUP C ODDS 1:34
GROUP D ODDS 1:13
GROUP E ODDS 1:12
OVERALL GROUP ODDS 1:4
BAO Adam Oates E 15.00 30.00
BBO Bobby Orr B 90.00 150.00
BCC Chris Chelios B 15.00 30.00
BCN Cam Neely C 10.00 25.00
BDA Dave Schultz E 10.00 25.00
BDH Dominik Hasek C 40.00 80.00
BDS Denis Savard D 12.00 30.00
BES Eric Staal D 12.00 30.00
BFP Felix Potvin D 25.00 50.00
BHU Brett Hull D 15.00 40.00
BJI Jarome Iginla D 20.00 40.00
BJL John LeClair E 15.00 30.00
BJP Joe Pavelski E 12.00 30.00
BJR Jeremy Roenick B 12.00 30.00
BJT John Tavares D 25.00 50.00
BMB Mike Bossy C 12.00 30.00
BMC Marty McSorley E 10.00 25.00
BML Mario Lemieux A 60.00 100.00
BMM Mark Messier A 30.00 60.00
BMN Markus Naslund D 8.00 20.00
BMP Max Pacioretty B 12.00 30.00
BNL Nicklas Lidstrom B 20.00 40.00
BPR Patrick Roy A 50.00 100.00
BPT Pierre Turgeon E 10.00 25.00
BSC Sidney Crosby A 100.00 175.00
BSW Shea Weber E 8.00 20.00
BSY Steve Yzerman B 60.00 100.00
BTB Tom Barrasso D 10.00 25.00
BTF Theoren Fleury D 12.00 30.00
BTH Taylor Hall C 20.00 40.00
BTS Teemu Selanne D 25.00 50.00
BWG Wayne Gretzky A 150.00 250.00

2014-15 The Cup Emblems of Endorsement

STATED PRINT RUN 15 SER.#'d SETS
EEAE Aaron Ekblad 175.00 300.00
EEAV Andrei Vasilevskiy
EEBR Brett Ritchie 25.00 60.00
EECC Charlie Coyle 25.00 60.00
EECJ Curtis Joseph 40.00 80.00
EEDB Dustin Brown 20.00 50.00
EEDP Derrick Pouliot 25.00 60.00
EEDW Doug Weight 30.00 60.00
EEES Eric Staal 30.00 60.00
EEJB Jonathan Bernier
EEJD Jonathan Drouin 40.00 100.00
EEJI Jarome Iginla 50.00 100.00
EEJR Jeremy Roenick 25.00 60.00
EEJS Joe Sakic 75.00 125.00
EEJT John Tavares 125.00 200.00
EEMB Martin Brodeur 125.00 200.00
EEMF Marc-Andre Fleury 50.00 100.00
EEMG Marian Gaborik 90.00 150.00
EEMS Mats Sundin 40.00 80.00
EERB Rob Blake 25.00 60.00
EESP Jason Spezza 25.00 60.00
EEST Martin St. Louis 25.00 60.00
EEWG Wayne Gretzky

2014-15 The Cup Enshrinements

EAE Aaron Ekblad/99 25.00 50.00
EAI Arturs Irbe/99 6.00 15.00
(inserted in 2015-16 The Cup)
EAO Alexander Ovechkin/25 40.00 80.00
EBE Jamie Benn/99 12.00 30.00
EBO Bobby Orr/25 100.00 200.00
ECL Curtis Lazar/99 6.00 15.00
ECN Cam Neely/50 25.00 50.00
ECP Carey Price/50 40.00 80.00
EDA Dave Schultz/50 10.00 25.00
EDH Dominik Hasek/50 30.00 60.00
EDP David Pastrnak/99 30.00 60.00
EDS Damon Severson/99 6.00 15.00
EEK Evgeny Kuznetsov/99 20.00 40.00
EEM Evgeni Malkin/50 40.00 100.00
(inserted in 2015-16 The Cup)
EES Eric Staal/99 12.00 30.00
EGF Grant Fuhr/50 20.00 40.00
EGM Glen Murray/99 8.00 20.00
EHU Brett Hull/25 30.00 60.00
EJB Jordan Binnington/99 5.00 12.00
EJG Johnny Gaudreau/99 40.00 80.00
EJI Jarome Iginla/99 15.00 30.00
EJJ Jaromir Jagr/50 40.00 80.00
EJL Jori Lehtera/99 12.00 30.00
EJP Joe Pavelski/99 12.00 30.00
EJR Jeremy Roenick/50 20.00 40.00
EJT John Tavares/50 25.00 50.00
EKR Kerby Rychel/99 6.00 15.00
ELS Leon Draisaitl/99 25.00 50.00
EMA Marty McSorley/99 10.00 25.00
EMB Martin Brodeur/25
EMI Mike Bossy/50 20.00 40.00
EML Mario Lemieux/25 60.00 120.00
EMM Mark Messier/25 30.00 60.00
EMP Max Pacioretty/99 12.00 30.00
EMS Mats Sundin/50 40.00 100.00
(inserted in 2015-16 The Cup)
EPR Patrick Roy/25 50.00 100.00
ESA Sven Andrighetto/99 8.00 20.00
ESC Sidney Crosby/50 75.00 135.00
ESE Jiri Sekac/99 5.00 12.00
ESL Steve Larmer/99 10.00 25.00
ESM Sean Monahan/99 20.00 40.00
ESP Stuart Percy/99 5.00 12.00
ESR Sam Reinhart/99 25.00 50.00
ESW Shea Weber/50 8.00 20.00
ESY Steve Yzerman/25
ETB Tom Barrasso/99 10.00 25.00
ETH Taylor Hall/50 15.00 40.00
ETO Jonathan Toews/50 40.00 100.00
(inserted in 2015-16 The Cup)
ETS Teemu Selanne/99 40.00 80.00
ETT Teuvo Teravainen/99 30.00 60.00
EWG Wayne Gretzky/25

2014-15 The Cup Enshrinements Dual

STATED PRINT RUN 25 SER.#'d SETS
E2BG W.Gretzky/R.Blake 175.00 300.00
E2BS J.Benn/J.Spezza
E2DE A.Ekblad/J.Drouin
E2DO A.Ovechkin/P.Datsyuk 75.00 135.00
E2EA Kuznetsov/Burakovsky 30.00 60.00
E2MK M.Messier/J.Kurri 40.00 80.00
E2PP C.Price/M.Pacioretty 100.00 175.00
E2RR S.Reinhart/G.Reinhart 25.00 60.00
E2VB Vasilevskiy/J.Binnington 25.00 60.00
E2YL S.Yzerman/N.Lidstrom 60.00 100.00

2014-15 The Cup Exquisite Collection Inserts

1 Wayne Gretzky AU/25 175.00 300.00
2 Mike Bossy AU/25 15.00 40.00
3 Grant Fuhr AU/25 15.00 40.00
4 Alexander Ovechkin AU/25 60.00 100.00
5 Bobby Orr AU/25 100.00 200.00
6 Mario Lemieux AU/25 100.00 175.00
7 Guy Lafleur AU/25 20.00 50.00
8 Carey Price AU/25 40.00 80.00
9 Jaromir Jagr AU/25 40.00 80.00
10 Ray Bourque AU/25 30.00 60.00
11 Mark Messier AU/25 40.00 80.00
12 Patrick Roy AU/25 75.00 135.00
13 Marcel Dionne AU/25 20.00 50.00
14 Jonathan Toews AU/25 90.00 150.00
15 Sidney Crosby AU/25 125.00 200.00
17 Kerby Rychel JSY AU/52 15.00 40.00
19 A.Duclair JSY AU/63 EX 40.00 80.00
21 N.Deslauriers JSY AU/44 20.00 50.00
22 A.Hammond JSY AU/30 EXCH 100.00 200.00
23 A.Burakovsky JSY AU/65 50.00 100.00
24 A.Vasilevskiy JSY AU/88 40.00 80.00
25 Colton Sissons JSY AU/84 20.00 50.00
26 William Karlsson JSY AU/38 80.00 200.00
27 T.Teravainen JSY AU/86 125.00 250.00
28 Jake McCabe JSY AU/29 30.00 60.00
29 Curtis Lazar JSY AU/27 60.00 120.00
30 Josh Jooris JSY AU/86 30.00 60.00
31 B.Yakimov JSY AU/39 40.00 80.00
32 T.van Riemsdyk JSY AU/57 30.00 80.00
33 Adam Lowry JSY AU/17
34 Seth Helgeson JSY AU/25 40.00 80.00
35 Andy Andreoff JSY AU/15 50.00 100.00
36 V.Namestnikov JSY AU/65 EX 50.00 100.00
37 Darnell Nurse JSY AU/25 50.00 100.00
38 E.Kuznetsov JSY AU/92 175.00 300.00
39 Joni Ortio JSY AU/37 25.00 60.00
40 V.Trocheck JSY AU/67 25.00 60.00
41 Brandon Gormley JSY AU/33 30.00 60.00
42 Jiri Sekac JSY AU/26 30.00 60.00
46 Mark Visentin JSY AU/29 25.00 60.00
47 C.Tierney JSY AU/50 EXCH 20.00 50.00
48 Teemu Pulkkinen JSY AU/56 60.00 100.00
49 Brandon Kozun JSY AU/67 15.00 40.00
50 Leon Draisaitl JSY AU/29 90.00 150.00
51 David Pastrnak JSY AU/88 175.00 300.00
52 P-E Bellemare JSY AU/78 20.00 50.00
53 Barclay Goodrow JSY AU/89 20.00 50.00
54 Joe Morrow JSY AU/45 30.00 60.00
56 Joey Hishon JSY AU/38 25.00 60.00
57 A.Wennberg JSY AU/41 40.00 100.00
58 Phillip Danault JSY AU/24 25.00 60.00
60 S.Andrighetto JSY AU/58 25.00 60.00
61 Ty Rattie JSY AU/18 75.00 135.00
62 Brett Ritchie JSY AU/25 30.00 80.00
63 Mirco Mueller JSY AU/41 20.00 50.00
64 Dennis Everberg JSY AU/45 20.00 50.00
65 J.Drouin JSY AU/27 EX 175.00 300.00
66 Victor Rask JSY AU/49 20.00 50.00
67 Liam O'Brien JSY AU/87 20.00 50.00
68 Sam Reinhart JSY AU/23 175.00 300.00
69 Joonas Nattinen JSY AU/28 25.00 60.00
70 Patrik Nemeth JSY AU/37 20.00 50.00
71 Jordan Binnington JSY AU/30
72 T.Wotherspoon JSY AU/56 20.00 50.00
73 Damon Severson JSY AU/28 40.00 80.00
75 Derrick Pouliot JSY AU/25 40.00 80.00
78 Stuart Percy JSY AU/50 20.00 50.00
79 Ryan Sproul JSY AU/48 20.00 50.00
80 Calle Jarnkrok JSY AU/19
81 Rocco Grimaldi JSY AU/23 40.00 80.00
82 Bo Horvat JSY AU/53 125.00 200.00
83 Patrick Brown JSY AU/36 20.00 50.00
85 J.Gaudreau JSY AU/53 200.00 350.00
86 Seth Griffith JSY AU/53 25.00 60.00
87 Greg McKegg JSY AU/39 15.00 40.00
88 Marko Dano JSY AU/56 50.00 100.00
89 M.Granlund JSY AU/60 EX 30.00 80.00

2014-15 The Cup Foundations Jerseys

STATED PRINT RUN 25 SER.#'d SETS
CFAE Aaron Ekblad
CFAF Marc-Andre Fleury 10.00 25.00
CFAO Alexander Ovechkin 25.00 60.00
CFRH Brett Hull 8.00 20.00
CFCH Cody Hodgson 6.00 15.00
CFCK Chris Kunitz 6.00 15.00
CFDB David Backes 6.00 15.00
CFDE Derek Stepan 6.00 15.00
CFDK David Krejci 6.00 15.00
CFDO Dominik Hasek 8.00 20.00
CFDS Denis Savard 8.00 20.00
CFDU Dustin Brown 5.00 12.00
CFEB Ed Belfour 6.00 15.00
CFES Eric Staal 8.00 20.00
CFFA Frederik Andersen 5.00 12.00
CFGF Grant Fuhr 6.00 15.00
CFHA Dale Hawerchuk 8.00 20.00
CFHE Tomas Hertl 6.00 15.00
CFJJ Jaromir Jagr 12.00 30.00
CFJP Jason Pominville 5.00 12.00
CFJT John Tavares 12.00 30.00
CFKO Kyle Okposo 6.00 15.00
CFLC Logan Couture 6.00 15.00
CFMA Steve Mason 5.00 12.00
CFMG Marian Gaborik 6.00 15.00
CFML Mario Lemieux 20.00 50.00
CFMM Matt Moulson 5.00 12.00
CFNK Niklas Kronwall 5.00 12.00
CFNM Nathan MacKinnon 12.00 30.00
CFNU Ryan Nugent-Hopkins 6.00 15.00
CFPA Joe Pavelski 6.00 15.00
CFPF Peter Forsberg 6.00 15.00
CFPK Phil Kessel 8.00 20.00
CFPR Patrick Roy 15.00 40.00
CFPS Paul Stastny 6.00 15.00
CFRG Ryan Getzlaf 10.00 25.00
CFRM Ryan Miller 6.00 15.00
CFRN Rick Nash 6.00 15.00
CFSB Sergei Bobrovsky 6.00 15.00
CFSC Sidney Crosby 25.00 50.00
CFSH Patrick Sharp 6.00 15.00
CFSJ Seth Jones 5.00 12.00
CFSS Steven Stamkos 12.00 30.00
CFSW Shea Weber 5.00 12.00

2014-15 The Cup Foundations Jerseys Autographs

STATED PRINT RUN 15 SER.#'d SETS
CFAE Aaron Ekblad 60.00 100.00
CFAF Marc-Andre Fleury 20.00 50.00
CFAO Alexander Ovechkin 40.00 80.00
CFBH Brett Hull 20.00 50.00
CFBI Martin Biron 15.00 40.00
CFCH Cody Hodgson 20.00 50.00
CFCK Chris Kunitz 20.00 50.00
CFDB David Backes 20.00 50.00
CFDE Derek Stepan
CFDK David Krejci 20.00 50.00
CFDO Dominik Hasek 40.00 80.00
CFDS Denis Savard
CFDU Dustin Brown 15.00 40.00
CFES Eric Staal
CFFA Frederik Andersen
CFGF Grant Fuhr
CFHE Tomas Hertl 20.00 50.00
CFJJ Jaromir Jagr 60.00 100.00
CFJP Jason Pominville
CFJT John Tavares
CFKO Kyle Okposo 20.00 50.00
CFMA Steve Mason 15.00 40.00
CFMG Marian Gaborik 40.00 80.00
CFML Mario Lemieux 75.00 135.00
CFMM Matt Moulson 15.00 40.00
CFNU Ryan Nugent-Hopkins 30.00 60.00
CFPA Joe Pavelski 20.00 50.00
CFPR Patrick Roy
CFRM Ryan Miller 20.00 50.00
CFSC Sidney Crosby 125.00 200.00
CFSJ Seth Jones
CFSW Shea Weber 15.00 40.00

2014-15 The Cup Honorable Numbers

HNAB Aleksander Barkov/16 20.00 50.00
HNCP Carey Price/31 90.00 150.00
HNDB Dustin Brown/23 15.00 40.00
HNDS Denis Savard/18 25.00 50.00
HNDW Doug Weight/39 25.00 50.00
HNJG John Gibson/36 25.00 50.00
HNJP Jason Pominville/29 12.00 30.00
HNJQ Jonathan Quick/32 40.00 80.00
HNKO Kyle Okposo/21 25.00 60.00
HNMB Martin Biron/43 15.00 40.00
HNNB Nick Bjugstad/27
HNPE Patrik Elias/26 25.00 50.00
HNPK Patrick Kane/8
HNRJ Ryan Johansen/19 15.00 40.00
HNRK Ryan Kesler/17 25.00 60.00
HNRM Ryan Miller/30 25.00 50.00
HNRS Ryan Strome/18 20.00 50.00
HNSH Scott Hartnell/43 15.00 40.00
HNSM Sean Monahan/23 60.00 100.00

2014-15 The Cup Honorable Numbers Dual

DHNNM M.Messier/O.Nolan/11 40.00 80.00
DHNSY S.Yzerman/J.Sakic/19 125.00 200.00

2014-15 The Cup Limited Logos Autographs

LLAB Aleksander Barkov/50 15.00 40.00
LLAE Aaron Ekblad/50 75.00 150.00
LLAG Alex Galchenyuk/50 40.00 80.00
LLAN Antti Niemi/50 12.00 30.00
LLBG Bill Guerin/50 15.00 40.00

LLBH Brett Hull/25 60.00 120.00
LLBR Bobby Ryan/50 20.00 50.00
LLCC Charlie Coyle/50 12.00 30.00
LLCH Cody Hodgson/50 15.00 40.00
LLCK Chris Kunitz/50 15.00 40.00
LLCP Carey Price/25 75.00 125.00
LLDB David Backes/50 15.00 40.00
LLDU Dustin Brown/50 12.00 30.00
LLDW Doug Weight/50 15.00 40.00
LLGA Marian Gaborik/50 20.00 50.00
LLGF Grant Fuhr/25 60.00 120.00
LLGI John Gibson/50 20.00 50.00
LLGM Glen Murray/50 12.00 30.00
LLGN Gustav Nyquist/50 12.00 30.00
LLJB Jamie Benn/25 30.00 80.00
LLJD Jonathan Drouin/50 75.00 135.00
LLJG Johnny Gaudreau/50 125.00 200.00
LLJH Jonathan Huberdeau/50 15.00 40.00
LLJI Jarome Iginla/50 20.00 50.00
LLJJ Jaromir Jagr/25 60.00 120.00
LLJL John LeClair/50 20.00 50.00
LLJP Jason Pominville/50 12.00 30.00
LLJR James van Riemsdyk/50 15.00 40.00
LLJS Joe Sakic/25 EXCH 60.00 120.00
LLJT John Tavares/25 50.00 125.00
LLJU Tomas Jurco/50 15.00 40.00
LLKL Kari Lehtonen/50 12.00 30.00
LLKO Kyle Okposo/50 15.00 40.00
LLKU Evgeny Kuznetsov/50 60.00 100.00
LLLD Leon Draisaitl/50
LLMB Martin Biron/50 12.00 30.00
LLMG Mikael Granlund/50 12.00 30.00
LLMO Matt Moulson/50 12.00 30.00
LLMP Max Pacioretty/50 30.00 60.00
LLMR Morgan Rielly/50 15.00 40.00
LLMS Mats Sundin/25 40.00 80.00
LLMZ Mats Zuccarello/50 15.00 40.00
LLOK Olaf Kolzig/50 20.00 50.00
LLON Owen Nolan/50 12.00 30.00
LLPD Pavel Datsyuk/50 40.00 80.00
LLPK Patrick Kane/50
LLPM Patrick Marleau/50 15.00 40.00
LLRA Ray Bourque/25 50.00 100.00
LLRB Rod Brind'Amour/50 15.00 40.00
LLRI Rick Nash/50 15.00 40.00
LLRJ Ryan Johansen/50 20.00 50.00
LLRK Ryan Kesler/50 20.00 50.00
LLRM Ryan McDonagh/50 15.00 40.00
LLRY Ryan Miller/50 15.00 40.00
LLSJ Seth Jones/50 12.00 30.00
LLSK Jeff Skinner/50 15.00 40.00
LLSM Sean Monahan/50 15.00 40.00
LLSP Jason Spezza/50 15.00 40.00
LLSR Sam Reinhart/50 75.00 135.00
LLST Steve Mason/50 12.00 30.00
LLSV Semyon Varlamov/50 15.00 40.00
LLSW Shea Weber/50 15.00 40.00
LLTH Tomas Hertl/50 15.00 40.00
LLTJ Jonathan Toews/25
LLTR Jacob Trouba/50 12.00 30.00
LLTS Teemu Selanne/25 50.00 100.00
LLZP Zach Parise/50 25.00 50.00

2014-15 The Cup Rookie Bookmarks Dual Autographs

STATED PRINT RUN 25 SER.#'d SETS
DARBBK Burakovsky/Kuznetsov 75.00 150.00
DARBPK S.Percy/B.Kozun 25.00 60.00
DARBWR A.Wennberg/K.Rychel 50.00 125.00

2014-15 The Cup Rookie Gear Autographs

STATED PRINT RUN 25 SER.#'d SETS
ARGAE Aaron Ekblad 100.00 175.00
ARGAW Alexander Wennberg 40.00 100.00
ARGBH Bo Horvat 75.00 135.00
ARGCL Curtis Lazar 40.00 80.00
ARGDS Damon Severson 20.00 50.00
ARGGR Griffin Reinhart 40.00 80.00
ARGJD Jonathan Drouin EXCH 75.00 125.00
ARGLD Leon Draisaitl
ARGSA Sven Andrighetto 25.00 60.00
ARGSR Sam Reinhart 60.00 150.00

2014-15 The Cup Scripted Sticks

STATED PRINT RUN 35 SER.#'d SETS
SSAM Andy Moog 25.00 60.00
SSAO Alexander Ovechkin 50.00 100.00
SSBH Brett Hull
SSBL Rob Blake 25.00 60.00
SSBP Brad Park 15.00 40.00
SSCC Chris Chelios 25.00 60.00
SSES Eric Staal
SSGL Glenn Anderson 25.00 60.00
SSJI Jarome Iginla 25.00 60.00
SSLA Guy Lafleur 30.00 80.00
SSMB Martin Brodeur 60.00 120.00
SSMD Marcel Dionne 30.00 80.00
SSMG Marian Gaborik 40.00 80.00
SSML Mario Lemieux 100.00 200.00
SSMM Marty McSorley
SSMR Mike Richter
SSPR Patrick Roy 125.00 200.00
SSRB Ray Bourque 40.00 80.00
SSRF Ron Francis 20.00 50.00
SSSC Sidney Crosby 125.00 200.00
SSSL Steve Larmer 15.00 40.00
SSSP Jason Spezza 20.00 50.00
SSSY Steve Yzerman 50.00 100.00
SSTS Teemu Selanne 40.00 80.00
SSWC Wendel Clark 25.00 60.00
SSWG Wayne Gretzky 175.00 300.00

2014-15 The Cup Scripted Sticks Dual

STATED PRINT RUN 15 SER.#'d SETS
DSPBD M.Dionne/R.Blake 60.00 120.00
DSPBG W.Gretzky/R.Blake 150.00 250.00
DSPBP R.Bourque/B.Park 60.00 120.00
DSPCD V.Damphousse/W.Clark 50.00 100.00
DSPGA W.Gretzky/G.Anderson
DSPGL W.Gretzky/M.Lemieux
DSPKB J.Kurri/R.Blake
DSPPS R.Suter/Z.Parise 60.00 120.00
DSPSK J.Kurri/T.Selanne 60.00 120.00
DSPVM M.Messier/J.Vanbiesbrouck
DSPYH B.Hull/S.Yzerman 75.00 150.00

2014-15 The Cup Scripted Swatches

STATED PRINT RUN 35 SER.#'d SETS
SWAO Alexander Ovechkin 50.00 100.00
SWBH Brett Hull 30.00 60.00
SWBR Dustin Brown 12.00 30.00
SWCC Chris Chelios 15.00 40.00
SWCO Chris Osgood 15.00 40.00
SWCP Carey Price 30.00 60.00
SWCW Cam Ward 15.00 40.00
SWDB David Backes 15.00 40.00
SWDS Denis Savard 12.00 30.00
SWDW Doug Weight 15.00 40.00
SWGN Gustav Nyquist 15.00 40.00
SWJL John LeClair 15.00 40.00
SWJP Jason Pominville 12.00 30.00
SWJS Jeff Skinner 15.00 40.00
SWJT John Tavares 40.00 80.00
SWKO Kyle Okposo 15.00 40.00
SWKT Kyle Turris 15.00 40.00
SWMB Martin Biron 12.00 30.00
SWMG Marian Gaborik 25.00 50.00
SWMP Max Pacioretty 25.00 50.00
SWMZ Mats Zuccarello 25.00 50.00
SWPD Pavel Datsyuk 25.00 50.00
SWPM Patrick Marleau 15.00 40.00
SWRK Ryan Kesler 15.00 40.00
SWRN Rick Nash 15.00 40.00
SWSA Joe Sakic EXCH 40.00 80.00
SWSM Sean Monahan 15.00 40.00
SWSW Shea Weber 15.00 40.00
SWTH Taylor Hall 30.00 60.00

2014-15 The Cup Scripted Swatches Dual

STATED PRINT RUN 15 SER.#'d SETS
DSSMH M.Moulson/C.Hodgson 30.00 60.00
DSSSF P.Forsberg/J.Sakic 60.00 120.00

2014-15 The Cup Signature Patches

SPAB Aleksander Barkov/99 10.00 25.00
SPAE Aaron Ekblad/99 40.00 80.00
SPAV Andrei Vasilevskiy/99 25.00 60.00
SPBH Bo Horvat/99 40.00 80.00
SPBI Ben Bishop/99 12.00 30.00
SPBR Brett Ritchie/99 10.00 25.00
SPCK Chris Kunitz/99 12.00 30.00
SPCW Cam Ward/99 15.00 40.00
SPDB Dustin Brown/99 10.00 25.00
SPDK David Krejci/99 12.00 30.00
SPDP Derrick Pouliot/99 10.00 25.00
SPDW Doug Weight/99 12.00 30.00
SPGN Gustav Nyquist/99 30.00 60.00
SPGR Mikael Granlund/99 10.00 25.00
SPJA Jake Allen/99 15.00 40.00
SPJB Jonathan Bernier/25 15.00 40.00
SPJG John Gibson/99 12.00 30.00
SPJH Jonathan Huberdeau/99 12.00 30.00
SPJI Jarome Iginla/25
SPJL John LeClair/99 12.00 30.00
SPJP Jason Pominville/99 10.00 25.00
SPJS Joe Sakic/25
SPJV James van Riemsdyk/99 12.00 30.00
SPKA Patrick Kane/25
SPLD Leon Draisaitl/99 75.00 150.00
SPMB Martin Biron/99 12.00 30.00
SPMN Markus Naslund/99 10.00 25.00
SPOK Olaf Kolzig/99 15.00 40.00
SPOV Alexander Ovechkin/25 60.00 120.00
SPRB Ray Bourque/25 40.00 80.00
SPRJ Ryan Johansen/99 15.00 40.00
SPRK Ryan Kesler/99 12.00 30.00
SPRM Rod Brind'Amour/99 12.00 30.00
SPSG Shayne Gostisbehere/99 100.00 200.00
SPSH Scott Hartnell/99 12.00 30.00
SPSK Jeff Skinner/99 12.00 30.00
SPSM Sean Monahan/99 15.00 40.00
SPSP Jason Spezza/99 12.00 30.00
SPSR Sam Reinhart/99 30.00 60.00
SPSV Semyon Varlamov/99 10.00 25.00
SPTJ Tomas Jurco/99 12.00 30.00
SPVD Vincent Damphousse/99 10.00 25.00
SPZP Zach Parise/99 15.00 40.00

2014-15 The Cup Signature Patches Dual

DSPDN L.Draisaitl/D.Nurse/35 20.00 50.00
DSPHB Huberdeau/A.Barkov/35 20.00 50.00
DSPJL J.Jagr/M.Lemieux/15 125.00 200.00
DSPJT J.Pavelski/T.Hertl/15 30.00 60.00
DSPKB Kuznetsov/Burakovsky/35 40.00 80.00
DSPPH J.Pavelski/T.Hertl/35 40.00 80.00
DSPRL J.LeClair/J.Roenick/35 30.00 60.00
DSPRR S.Reinhart/G.Reinhart/35 30.00 60.00
DSPWW Doug Weight/35
DSPYL S.Yzerman/N.Lidstrom/15

2014-15 The Cup Signature Renditions

GROUP A ODDS 1:107
GROUP B ODDS 1:46
GROUP C ODDS 1:22
GROUP D ODDS 1:17
GROUP E ODDS 1:16
OVERALL STATED ODDS 1:4
SRBC Bobby Clarke D 15.00 40.00
SRBE Jamie Benn D 12.00 30.00
SRBO Bobby Orr D 50.00 120.00
SRCR Sidney Crosby A 150.00 250.00
SRDS Darryl Sittler C 10.00 25.00
SRES Eric Staal E 12.00 30.00
SRGA Marian Gaborik D 15.00 30.00
SRGL Guy Lafleur C 20.00 40.00
SRGR Wayne Gretzky B 200.00 300.00
SRHU Brett Hull C 25.00 60.00
SRJI Jarome Iginla C 10.00 25.00
SRJJ Jaromir Jagr B 40.00 100.00
SRJP Joe Pavelski E 10.00 25.00
SRJV James van Riemsdyk E 10.00 25.00
SRLE Mario Lemieux A 80.00 150.00
SRMB Mike Bossy C 15.00 40.00
SRMD Marcel Dionne D 12.00 30.00
SRML Mario Lemieux A 80.00 150.00
SRMM Mark Messier A 30.00 80.00
SRPD Pavel Datsyuk C 20.00 40.00
SRPE Phil Esposito A 25.00 50.00
SRPR Carey Price D 40.00 100.00
SRRB Ray Bourque B 25.00 60.00
SRSC Sidney Crosby B 150.00 250.00
SRSE Teemu Selanne B 25.00 60.00
SRSY Steve Yzerman A 40.00 100.00
SRTA John Tavares E 20.00 50.00
SRTH Taylor Hall D 15.00 30.00
SRTS Teemu Selanne C 25.00 60.00
SRWA Wayne Gretzky B 200.00 300.00
SRWC Wendel Clark E 15.00 40.00
SRWG Wayne Gretzky A 250.00 400.00
SRYZ Steve Yzerman B 30.00 80.00
SRZP Zach Parise C 12.00 30.00

2014-15 The Cup Signature Renditions Combos

GROUP A ODDS 1:380
GROUP B ODDS 1:245
GROUP C ODDS 1:225
OVERALL STATED ODDS 1:90
SRCGM W.Gretzky/M.Messier 175.00 300.00
SRCHD P.Datsyuk/B.Hull 75.00 125.00
SRCJB M.Brodeur/J.Jagr 100.00 175.00
SRCOT J.Tavares/K.Okposo 40.00 80.00
SRCYH D.Hasek/S.Yzerman 60.00 120.00
SRCDRAFT Ekb/Rnht/Drstl EX 50.00 100.00

2014-15 The Cup Trios Jerseys

STATED PRINT RUN 25 SER.#'d SETS
*PATCH/10: 1X TO 2.5X BASIC JSY/25
C3ANA Gtzlf/Kslr/Prry 12.00 30.00
C3AVS Skc/Ry/Blke
C3BEES Ots/Brqe/Mrry 12.00 30.00
C3BOLTS Drn/Vslvsky/Nmstnkv 20.00 50.00
C3BRUINS Brgrn/Chra/Rsk 12.00 30.00
C3BUF Mlsn/Grgnsns/Hdgsn 8.00 20.00
C3CAN Mllr/Sdn/Sdn 8.00 20.00
C3CAPS Ovchkn/Bckstrm/Kzntsv 30.00 80.00
C3CAR Stl/Sknnr/Lndhlm 10.00 25.00
C3CB Sd/Hssa/Shrp 10.00 25.00
C3CBJ Wnnbrg/Dno/Rychl 10.00 25.00
C3CGY Mnhn/Gdru/Hllr 15.00 40.00
C3CHI Trvnn/Clndnng/Dnlt 8.00 20.00
C3CHIC Crwfrd/Kth/Sbrk 10.00 25.00
C3COL Ignla/Dchne/Lndskg 8.00 20.00
C3D Ekbld/Nrse/Plt 12.00 30.00
C3DAL Sgn/Spzza/Bnn 12.00 30.00
C3DEF Wbr/Dghty/Sbbn 12.00 30.00
C3DET Zttrbrg/Krnwll/Dtsyk 10.00 25.00
C3EDM Hll/NgntHpkns/Ebrle 15.00 40.00
C3FIN Rsk/Rnne/Nmi 10.00 25.00
C3FLA Brkv/Hbrdu/Bjgstd 8.00 20.00
C3GOALS Sgn/Nsh/Pvlski 12.00 30.00
C3GR8 Stmks/Ovchkn/Prry 30.00 80.00
C3HAWKS Shrp/Tws/Kne 15.00 40.00
C3JAC Jhnsn/Hrtnll/Bbrvsky 10.00 25.00
C3JETS Whlr/Trba/Schfle 10.00 25.00
C3KINGS Qck/Kptr/Dghty 12.00 30.00
C3LAK Crtr/Tffli/Prsn 8.00 20.00
C3MET Nsh/Tvrs/Jgr 15.00 40.00
C3MTL Prce/Pcrtty/Sbbn 25.00 60.00
C3NET Vslvsky/Bnngtn/Ortio 15.00 40.00
C3NJD Jgr/Hnrqe/Schndr 20.00 50.00
C3NYI Tvrs/Okpso/Strme 15.00 40.00
C3NYR Nsh/St.Ls/Zccrllo 8.00 20.00
C3OTT Ryn/Zbnjd/Trrs 8.00 20.00
C3PHI Schnn/Vrck/Grx 8.00 20.00
C3PIT Kntz/Flry/Mlkn 25.00 60.00
C3PRED Rnne/Wbr/Jns 10.00 25.00
C3ROOK1 Drn/Gdru/Rnhrt 15.00 40.00
C3ROOK2 Drn/Ekbld/Drstl 20.00 50.00
C3SHARKS Pvlski/Mrlu/Hrtl 8.00 20.00
C3SJS Thrntn/Ctre/Nmi 8.00 20.00
C3ST Bcks/Trsnko/Oshe 12.00 30.00
C3STARS Gtzlf/Tws/Grx 15.00 40.00
C3TBL Hdmn/Bshp/Stmks 15.00 40.00
C3TML Brnr/Kssl/vn Rmsdk 10.00 25.00
C3TOR Kssl/Kdri/vn Rmsdk 10.00 25.00
C3VAN Sdn/Kssn/Brrws 8.00 20.00
C3WAS Bckstrm/Crlsn/Hltby 12.00 30.00
C3WILD Prse/Pmnvlle/Grnlnd 8.00 20.00
C3WIN Pvlc/Kne/Schfle 10.00 25.00
C3ZONA Ggnr/Dn/EkmnLrssn 6.00 15.00

2015-16 The Cup

1 Wayne Gretzky 15.00 40.00
2 Corey Perry 3.00 8.00
3 Ryan Getzlaf 5.00 12.00
4 Teemu Selanne 6.00 15.00
5 Oliver Ekman-Larsson 2.50 6.00
6 Anthony Duclair 2.50 6.00
7 Tuukka Rask 3.00 8.00
8 David Krejci 2.50 6.00
9 Bobby Orr 10.00 25.00
10 Patrice Bergeron 4.00 10.00
11 Rasmus Ristolainen 2.50 6.00
12 Ryan O'Reilly 3.00 8.00
13 Jiri Hudler 2.50 6.00
14 Johnny Gaudreau 5.00 12.00
15 Sean Monahan 3.00 8.00
16 Cam Ward 3.00 8.00
17 Justin Faulk 3.00 8.00
18 Duncan Keith 3.00 8.00
19 Jonathan Toews 6.00 15.00
20 Patrick Kane 6.00 15.00
21 Jarome Iginla 3.00 8.00
22 Matt Duchene 3.00 8.00
23 Nathan MacKinnon 6.00 15.00
24 Joe Sakic 5.00 12.00
25 Patrick Roy 8.00 20.00
26 Sergei Bobrovsky 3.00 8.00
27 Scott Hartnell 3.00 8.00
28 Jason Spezza 2.50 6.00
29 Tyler Seguin 5.00 12.00
30 Jamie Benn 4.00 10.00
31 Tomas Tatar 2.50 6.00
32 Pavel Datsyuk 4.00 10.00
33 Henrik Zetterberg 4.00 10.00
34 Steve Yzerman 5.00 12.00
35 Dominik Hasek 4.00 10.00
36 Paul Coffey 3.00 8.00
37 Taylor Hall 6.00 15.00
38 Ryan Nugent-Hopkins 3.00 8.00
39 Roberto Luongo 3.00 8.00
40 Aaron Ekblad 3.00 8.00
41 Jaromir Jagr 8.00 20.00
42 Jonathan Quick 5.00 12.00
43 Tyler Toffoli 3.00 8.00
44 Anze Kopitar 5.00 12.00
45 Zach Parise 3.00 8.00
46 Jason Zucker 2.50 6.00
47 Alex Galchenyuk 4.00 10.00
48 Guy Lafleur 4.00 10.00
49 Carey Price 10.00 25.00
50 Max Pacioretty 3.00 8.00
51 Filip Forsberg 4.00 10.00
52 Shea Weber 2.50 6.00
53 Pekka Rinne 4.00 10.00
54 Martin Brodeur 6.00 15.00
55 Cory Schneider 2.50 6.00
56 Adam Henrique 3.00 8.00
57 Anders Lee 3.00 8.00
58 John Tavares 6.00 15.00
59 Jaroslav Halak 2.50 6.00
60 Ryan Strome 2.50 6.00
61 Henrik Lundqvist 4.00 10.00
62 Rick Nash 3.00 8.00
63 Mats Zuccarello 2.50 6.00
64 Mark Messier 5.00 12.00
65 Kyle Turris 2.50 6.00
66 Erik Karlsson 6.00 15.00
67 Mark Stone 2.50 6.00
68 Mike Hoffman 2.50 6.00
69 Claude Giroux 3.00 8.00
70 Jakub Voracek 3.00 8.00
71 Steve Mason 2.50 6.00
72 Sidney Crosby 12.00 30.00
73 Evgeni Malkin 10.00 25.00
74 Mario Lemieux 10.00 25.00
75 Marc-Andre Fleury 5.00 12.00
76 Peter Forsberg 3.00 8.00
77 Brent Burns 4.00 10.00
78 Joe Pavelski 3.00 8.00
79 Patrick Marleau 3.00 8.00
80 Jori Lehtera 2.50 6.00
81 Vladimir Tarasenko 5.00 12.00
82 Jake Allen 4.00 10.00
83 Victor Hedman 4.00 10.00
84 Steven Stamkos 6.00 15.00
85 Nikita Kucherov 5.00 12.00
86 Morgan Rielly 2.50 6.00
87 James van Riemsdyk 3.00 8.00
88 Doug Gilmour 4.00 10.00
89 Nazem Kadri 2.50 6.00
90 Ryan Miller 3.00 8.00
91 Henrik Sedin 3.00 8.00
92 Daniel Sedin 3.00 8.00
93 Pavel Bure 5.00 12.00
94 Evgeny Kuznetsov 5.00 12.00
95 Alexander Ovechkin 12.00 30.00
96 Nicklas Backstrom 5.00 12.00
97 Braden Holtby 5.00 12.00
98 Blake Wheeler 3.00 8.00
99 Mark Scheifele 4.00 10.00
100 Andrew Ladd 3.00 8.00
101 Joonas Kemppainen AU RC 8.00 20.00
102 Byron Froese AU RC 8.00 20.00
103 Frank Vatrano AU RC 20.00 50.00
104 Adam Pelech AU RC 8.00 20.00
105 Brett Kulak AU RC 8.00 20.00
106 Christoph Bertschy AU RC 8.00 20.00
107 Tanner Kero AU RC 12.00 30.00
108 Michael Keranen AU RC 8.00 20.00
109 Daniel Carr AU RC 8.00 20.00
110 Max McCormick AU RC 8.00 20.00
111 Petr Straka AU RC 8.00 20.00
112 Sergei Kalinin AU RC 15.00 40.00
113 Tyler Randell AU RC 10.00 25.00
114 Viktor Svedberg JSY AU RC 12.00 30.00
115 Matt Murray JSY AU RC 150.00 300.00
116 Jaccob Slavin JSY AU RC 12.00 30.00
117 Linus Ullmark JSY AU RC 20.00 50.00
118 Juuse Saros JSY AU RC 30.00 80.00
119 Andrew Copp JSY AU RC 15.00 40.00
120 Chris Wideman JSY AU RC 15.00 40.00
121 Sergei Plotnikov JSY AU RC 12.00 30.00
122 Phil Di Giuseppe JSY AU RC 15.00 40.00
123 Joseph Blandisi JSY AU RC 15.00 40.00
124 Louis Domingue JSY AU RC 15.00 40.00
125 Keegan Lowe JSY AU RC 15.00 40.00
126 Mike Condon JSY AU RC 15.00 40.00
127 Chris Driedger JSY AU RC 12.00 30.00
128 Mike McCarron JSY AU RC 20.00 50.00
129 Joonas Korpisalo JSY AU RC 30.00 80.00
130 Robby Fabbri JSY AU RC 20.00 50.00
131 Anton Slepyshev JSY AU RC 12.00 30.00
132 Mark Alt JSY AU RC 10.00 25.00
133 Jean-Francois Berube JSY AU RC 12.00 30.00
134 Joonas Donskoi JSY AU RC 15.00 40.00
135 Charles Hudon JSY AU RC 15.00 40.00
136 Mattias Janmark JSY AU RC 15.00 40.00
137 Matt O'Connor JSY AU RC 12.00 30.00
138 Taylor Leier JSY AU RC 15.00 40.00
139 Viktor Arvidsson JSY AU RC 30.00 80.00
140 Garret Sparks JSY AU RC 20.00 50.00
141 Dylan DeMelo JSY AU RC 12.00 30.00
142 Colin Miller JSY AU RC 12.00 30.00
143 Sam Brittain JSY AU RC 15.00 40.00
144 Ben Hutton JSY AU RC 15.00 40.00
145 Antoine Bibeau JSY AU RC 15.00 40.00
146 Stefan Noesen JSY AU RC 12.00 30.00
147 David Musil JSY AU RC 12.00 30.00
148 Ronalds Kenins JSY AU RC 15.00 40.00
149 Radek Faksa JSY AU RC 15.00 40.00
150 Joel Edmundson JSY AU RC 12.00 30.00
151 Mackenzie Skapski JSY AU RC 15.00 40.00
152 Devin Shore JSY AU RC 15.00 40.00
153 Jujhar Khaira JSY AU RC 12.00 30.00
154 Andreas Athanasiou JSY AU RC 40.00 100.00
155 Jordan Weal JSY AU RC 15.00 40.00
156 Nick Cousins JSY AU RC 15.00 40.00
157 Jacob de la Rose JSY AU RC 15.00 40.00
158 Henrik Samuelsson JSY AU RC 12.00 30.00
159 Duncan Siemens JSY AU RC 20.00 50.00
160 Kyle Baun JSY AU RC 15.00 40.00
161 Derek Forbort JSY AU RC 12.00 30.00
162 Slater Koekkoek JSY AU RC 12.00 30.00
163 Laurent Dauphin JSY AU RC 15.00 40.00
164 Vincent Hinostroza JSY AU RC 10.00 25.00
165 Colton Parayko JSY AU RC 20.00 50.00
166 Mikko Rantanen JSY AU RC 80.00 200.00
167 Nicolas Petan JSY AU RC 15.00 40.00
168 Daniel Sprong JSY AU RC 30.00 80.00
169 Jared McCann JSY AU RC 15.00 40.00
170 Gustav Olofsson JSY AU RC 15.00 40.00
171 Josh Anderson JSY AU RC 15.00 40.00
172 Malcolm Subban JSY AU RC 40.00 100.00
173 Brendan Ranford JSY AU RC 12.00 30.00
174 Shea Theodore JSY AU RC 15.00 40.00
175 Zachary Fucale JSY AU RC 15.00 40.00
176 Emile Poirier JSY AU RC 15.00 40.00
177 Matt Puempel JSY AU RC 12.00 30.00
178 Nikolay Goldobin JSY AU RC 15.00 40.00
179 Kevin Fiala JSY AU RC 15.00 40.00
180 Brock McGinn JSY AU RC 15.00 40.00
181 Nick Ritchie JSY AU RC 15.00 40.00
182 Shane Prince JSY AU RC 12.00 30.00
183 Jake Virtanen JSY AU RC 20.00 50.00
184 Anthony Stolarz JSY AU RC 15.00 40.00
185 Brady Skjei JSY AU RC 12.00 30.00
186 Ryan Hartman JSY AU RC 20.00 50.00
187 Connor Hellebuyck JSY AU RC 100.00 250.00
188 Hunter Shinkaruk JSY AU RC 15.00 40.00
189 Brendan Gaunce JSY AU RC 20.00 50.00
190 Brett Pesce JSY AU RC 12.00 30.00
191 Chandler Stephenson JSY AU RC 15.00 40.00
192 Noah Hanifin JSY AU RC 20.00 50.00
193 Oscar Lindberg JSY AU RC 15.00 40.00
194 Sam Bennett JSY AU/99 RC 250.00 500.00
195 Artemi Panarin JSY AU/99 RC 350.00 600.00
196 Nikolaj Ehlers JSY AU/99 RC 350.00 600.00
197 Connor McDavid JSY AU/99 RC 12000.00 15000.00
198 Max Domi JSY AU/99 RC 250.00 600.00
199 Dylan Larkin JSY AU/99 RC 350.00 700.00
200 Jack Eichel JSY/99 RC 600.00 1000.00

2015-16 The Cup Gold

*ROOKIES: .6X TO 1.50X BASIC CARDS
115 Matt Murray JSY AU 200.00 500.00
126 Mike Condon JSY AU 15.00 40.00
128 Mike McCarron JSY AU 15.00 40.00
130 Robby Fabbri JSY AU 40.00 100.00
135 Charles Hudon JSY AU 40.00 100.00
139 Viktor Arvidsson JSY AU 50.00 125.00
168 Daniel Sprong JSY AU 30.00 80.00
183 Jake Virtanen JSY AU 50.00 125.00
186 Ryan Hartman JSY AU 25.00 60.00
187 Connor Hellebuyck JSY AU 80.00 200.00

2015-16 The Cup Gold Spectrum

*ROOKIES: .5X TO 1.25X BASIC CARDS
115 Matt Murray AU 60.00 150.00
130 Robby Fabbri AU 20.00 50.00
135 Charles Hudon AU 15.00 40.00
139 Viktor Arvidsson AU 25.00 60.00
168 Daniel Sprong AU 20.00 50.00
183 Jake Virtanen AU 20.00 50.00
187 Connor Hellebuyck AU 60.00 150.00

2015-16 The Cup 12-Way Relics

12WRC1 ROOKIES 250.00 400.00
12WCOLO AVS 30.00 80.00
12WVET1 VETS 80.00 150.00
12WFLYERS FLYERS
12WKINGS KINGS

2015-16 The Cup 6-Way Relics

6WCAN CANADA
6WNET NETMINDERS 40.00 100.00
6WRC1 ROOKIES 1 100.00 250.00
6WRC2 ROOKIES 2 20.00 50.00
6WVAN CANUCKS 25.00 60.00
6WVET VETS 40.00 100.00
6WARIZ COYOTES 20.00 50.00
6WHAWKS BLACK HAWKS 60.00 150.00
6WWINGS RED WINGS 40.00 100.00
6WFLAMES FLAMES 20.00 50.00
6WOILERS OILERS
6WSABRES SABRES 30.00 80.00

2015-16 The Cup Enshrinements

EAE Aaron Ekblad/99 10.00 25.00
EAG Alex Galchenyuk/99 12.00 30.00
EAI Arturs Irbe 8.00 20.00
EAM Al MacInnis/99 10.00 25.00
EAO Alexander Ovechkin/25 40.00 100.00
EBO Bobby Orr/25 100.00 200.00
ECM Connor McDavid/99 500.00 700.00
EDH Dominik Hasek/99 25.00 60.00
EDL Dylan Larkin/99 30.00 80.00
EGA Glenn Anderson/99 10.00 25.00
EGC Guy Carbonneau/99 8.00 20.00
EJD Jonathan Drouin/99 12.00 30.00
EJG Johnny Gaudreau/99 15.00 40.00
EJK Jari Kurri/99 10.00 25.00
EJP Joe Pavelski/99 10.00 25.00
EJT Jonathan Toews/99 25.00 60.00
EML Mario Lemieux/25 80.00 200.00
ENE Nikolaj Ehlers/99 20.00 50.00
EPB Pavel Bure/99 25.00 60.00
EPR Patrick Roy/25 60.00 150.00
ERM Ryan Miller/99 10.00 25.00
ESB Sam Bennett/99 12.00 30.00
ESC Sidney Crosby/25
ESE Tyler Seguin/99 15.00 40.00
ETF Theoren Fleury/99 12.00 30.00
ETS Teemu Selanne/99 25.00 60.00
EWG Wayne Gretzky/25 300.00 400.00
EZF Zachary Fucale/99 10.00 25.00

2015-16 The Cup Enshrinements Dual

E2BS J.Benn/T.Seguin/25 30.00 80.00
E2JE J.Jagr/A.Ekblad/25 50.00 120.00
E2MB M.Messier/P.Bure/25 60.00 150.00
E2RH L.Robitaille/B.Hull/25 40.00 100.00

2015-16 The Cup Foundations Jerseys

CFAB Aleksander Barkov 5.00 12.00
CFAE Aaron Ekblad 5.00 12.00
CFAG Alex Galchenyuk 6.00 15.00
CFAL Andrew Ladd 5.00 12.00
CFAO Alexander Ovechkin 20.00 50.00
CFAP Artemi Panarin 15.00 40.00
CFCM Connor McDavid 60.00 150.00
CFCP Carey Price 15.00 40.00
CFCW Cam Ward 5.00 12.00
CFDL Dylan Larkin 15.00 40.00
CFEM Evgeni Malkin 15.00 40.00
CFGF Grant Fuhr 5.00 12.00
CFGH Glenn Hall 4.00 10.00
CFJC John Carlson 6.00 15.00
CFJE Jack Eichel 20.00 50.00
CFJF Justin Faulk 5.00 12.00
CFJG Johnny Gaudreau 8.00 20.00
CFJH Jiri Hudler 4.00 10.00
CFJJ Jaromir Jagr 12.00 30.00
CFJS Joe Sakic 8.00 20.00
CFJT John Tavares 10.00 25.00
CFLE Anders Lee 5.00 12.00
CFMA Mark Scheifele 6.00 15.00
CFMD Max Domi 10.00 25.00
CFMH Mike Hoffman 4.00 10.00
CFML Mario Lemieux 15.00 40.00
CFMS Martin St. Louis 5.00 12.00
CFNE Nikolaj Ehlers 10.00 25.00
CFNR Nick Ritchie 5.00 12.00
CFPB Pavel Bure 8.00 20.00
CFPD Pavel Datsyuk 6.00 15.00
CFPR Patrick Roy 12.00 30.00
CFRF Robby Fabbri 6.00 15.00
CFRM Ryan Miller 5.00 12.00
CFRN Rick Nash 5.00 12.00
CFSB Sam Bennett 6.00 15.00
CFSC Sidney Crosby 20.00 50.00
CFSY Steve Yzerman 8.00 20.00
CFTH Taylor Hall 10.00 25.00
CFTO Jonathan Toews 10.00 25.00
CFTT Tyler Toffoli 5.00 12.00
CFWG Wayne Gretzky 25.00 60.00
CFZF Zachary Fucale 5.00 12.00

2015-16 The Cup Honorable Numbers

HNAG Alex Galchenyuk/27 40.00 100.00
HNAL Anders Lee/27 25.00 60.00
HNCW Cam Ward/30 15.00 40.00
HNDE Derek Stepan/21 30.00 80.00
HNJB Jamie Benn/14 30.00 80.00
HNJH Jiri Hudler/24 20.00 50.00
HNJI Jarome Iginla/12 25.00 60.00
HNJJ Jaromir Jagr/68 80.00 200.00
HNJT Jonathan Toews/19 125.00 200.00
HNMF Marc-Andre Fleury/29 40.00 100.00
HNMH Mike Hoffman/68 15.00 40.00
HNMK Mike Keane/12 25.00 60.00
HNMP Max Pacioretty/67 25.00 60.00
HNMR Morgan Rielly/44 80.00 150.00
HNMS Mark Stone/61 15.00 40.00
HNNM Nathan MacKinnon/29 30.00 80.00
HNON Owen Nolan/11 40.00 100.00
HNPF Peter Forsberg/21 60.00 150.00
HNPT Pierre Turgeon/87 40.00 100.00
HNRB Rod Brind'Amour/17 30.00 80.00
HNRO Ryan O'Reilly/90 40.00 100.00
HNSC Mark Scheifele/55 25.00 60.00
HNST Martin St. Louis/26 25.00 60.00
HNTF Theoren Fleury/14 50.00 125.00
HNTT Tyler Toffoli/73 20.00 50.00
HNVT Vladimir Tarasenko/91 40.00 100.00
HNWP Willi Plett/25 30.00 80.00

2015-16 The Cup Honorable Numbers Dual

DHNFB J.Benn/T.Fleury/14
DHNGL A.Galchenyuk/A.Lee/27
DHNIK J.Iginla/M.Keane/12
DHNMW R.Miller/C.Ward/30 80.00 150.00
DHNVS D.Stepan/J.van Reimsdyk/21

2015-16 The Cup Honorable Numbers Rookies

HNRCM Connor McDavid/97 600.00 1500.00
HNRDL Dylan Larkin/71 175.00 300.00
HNRJM Jared McCann/91 20.00 50.00
HNRMD Max Domi/16
HNRNE Nikolaj Ehlers/27 60.00 150.00
HNRNR Nick Ritchie/37 15.00 40.00
HNRRF Robby Fabbri/15 60.00 150.00
HNRSB Sam Bennett/93 25.00 60.00
HNRZF Zachary Fucale/30 30.00 80.00

2015-16 The Cup Limited Logos Autographs

LLAG Alex Galchenyuk/50 30.00 80.00
LLAK Anze Kopitar/50 40.00 100.00
LLBB Ben Bishop/50 25.00 60.00
LLBH Brett Hull/25 30.00 80.00
LLBL Rob Blake/50 25.00 60.00
LLCM Connor McDavid/50 700.00 1500.00
LLCP Carey Price/25 100.00 200.00
LLDK David Krejci/50
LLDO Max Domi/50 50.00 125.00
LLDU Matt Duchene/50 25.00 60.00
LLEM Evgeni Malkin/25 100.00 250.00
LLJB Jamie Benn/50 30.00 80.00
LLJC John Carlson/50 25.00 60.00
LLJE Jack Eichel/50 (No Auto) 100.00 250.00
LLJF Justin Faulk/50 25.00 60.00
LLJG Johnny Gaudreau/50 40.00 100.00
LLJJ Jaromir Jagr/50 60.00 150.00
LLJP Joe Pavelski/50 25.00 60.00
LLJR Jeremy Roenick/50 80.00 150.00
LLJS Joe Sakic/25 100.00 200.00
LLJT Jonathan Toews/25
LLMA Nathan MacKinnon/50 50.00 125.00
LLMD Marcel Dionne/50 60.00 150.00
LLMF Marc-Andre Fleury/50 40.00 100.00
LLMH Mike Hoffman/50 20.00 50.00
LLMM Mike Modano/50 40.00 100.00
LLMP Max Pacioretty/50 25.00 60.00
LLMS Martin St. Louis/50 25.00 60.00
LLNE Nikolaj Ehlers/50 50.00 125.00
LLNH Noah Hanifin/50 30.00 80.00
LLON Owen Nolan/50 20.00 50.00
LLOV Alexander Ovechkin/25 60.00 150.00
LLPC Paul Coffey/25 60.00 150.00
LLPT Pierre Turgeon/50 25.00 60.00
LLRB Ray Bourque/25 50.00 125.00
LLRM Ryan Miller/50 25.00 60.00
LLSB Sam Bennett/50 30.00 80.00
LLSE Tyler Seguin/50 40.00 100.00
LLTA John Tavares/50 50.00 125.00
LLTH Taylor Hall/50 50.00 125.00
LLTJ Tyler Johnson/50 20.00 50.00
LLTS Teemu Selanne/25 60.00 150.00

2015-16 The Cup Monumental Sticks

MSDD Drew Doughty/20 20.00 50.00
MSDH Doug Harvey/15 50.00 125.00
MSDS Daniel Sedin/20 20.00 50.00
MSHZ Henrik Zetterberg/20 25.00 60.00
MSJB Jean Beliveau/20 100.00 200.00
MSJQ Jonathan Quick/20 30.00 80.00
MSLR Luc Robitaille/20 25.00 60.00
MSMB Martin Brodeur/20 60.00 150.00
MSML Mario Lemieux/20 60.00 150.00
MSPB Patrice Bergeron/20 50.00 125.00
MSPF Peter Forsberg/20 40.00 100.00
MSPK Phil Kessel/20 30.00 80.00
MSPS P.K. Subban/20 30.00 80.00
MSRG Ryan Getzlaf/20 30.00 80.00

2015-16 The Cup Monumental Sticks Autographs

AMSBO Ray Bourque/15 80.00 150.00
AMSFP Felix Potvin/20 80.00 200.00
AMSLR Larry Robinson/15 40.00 100.00
AMSRB Rob Blake/20 50.00 125.00
AMSRM Ryan Miller/20 30.00 80.00

2015-16 The Cup Monumental Sticks Dual Autographs

DMSBB M.Bossy/B.Bourne/15
DMSLG B.Guerin/J.LeClair/20 50.00 125.00
DMSPP C.Price/M.Pacioretty/15 80.00 200.00
DMSRS J.Roenick/D.Savard/15 60.00 150.00

2015-16 The Cup Quads Jerseys

C4CAN Bure/Sedin/Sedin/Virtanen 8.00 20.00
C4CAP Ovechkin/Carlson Backstrom/Holtby
C4EDM Gretzky/Hall/Eberle McDavid 40.00 100.00
C4FLO Bure/Jagr/Huberdeau/Luongo 12.00 30.00
C4NYR Fleury/St. Louis/Nash/Lundqvist 6.00 15.00
C4TBL Kucherov/Hedman/Johnson Stamkos 10.00 25.00
C4ARIZ Roenick/Hanzal Ekman-Larsson/Domi 10.00 25.00
C4HABS Pacioretty/Galchenyuk Price/Condon 15.00 40.00
C4JETS Wheeler/Scheifele Ehlers/Hellebuyck 12.00 30.00
C4RET1 Messier/Yzerman/Lemieux/Sakic 15.00 40.00
C4RET2 Robinson/Bourque/Coffey/Blake 8.00 20.00
C4RET4 Forsberg/LeClair/Hextall/Roenick 5.00 12.00
C4RET5 Brodeur/Roy/Hall/Fuhr 12.00 30.00
C4RIV1 Zuccarello/Tavares/Nash/Lee 10.00 25.00
C4RIV2 Bergeron/Subban Eriksson/Pacioretty 8.00 20.00
C4RIV3 Hall/Gaudreau/Eberle/Monahan 10.00 25.00
C4BLUES Tarasenko/Steen Shattenkirk/Backes 8.00 20.00
C4DUCKS Perry/Getzlaf/Ritchie/Theodore 8.00 20.00
C4HAWKS Savard/Toews/Kane/Panarin 15.00 40.00
C4KINGS Toffoli/Kopitar/Carter/Brown 8.00 20.00
C4SABRE Hawerchuk/Ristolainen O'Reilly/Eichel 20.00 50.00
C4STARS Spezza/Benn/Seguin/Lehtonen 8.00 20.00
C4BRUINS Bourque/Bergeron/Krejci/Rask 8.00 20.00
C4FLAMES Fleury/Monahan Gaudreau/Bennett 8.00 20.00
C4FLYERS Simmonds/Giroux Voracek/Schenn 6.00 15.00
C4POINT1 Jagr/Thornton/Iginla/Hossa 12.00 30.00
C4POINT2 Marleau/Elias/Sedin/Datsyuk 6.00 15.00
C4VEZINA Price/Rask Bobrovsky/Lundqvist 15.00 40.00

2015-16 The Cup Rookie Bookmarks Dual Autographs

DARBFP R.Fabbri/C.Parayko
DARBFR K.Fiala/M.Rantanen
DARBHF Z.Fucale/C.Hudon
DARBLS O.Lindberg/D.Sprong 30.00 80.00
DARBME N.Ehlers/J.McCann
DARBML C.McDavid/D.Larkin
DARBPP S.Prince/M.Puempel
DARBSC M.Subban/M.Condon 50.00 120.00
DARBVS J.Virtanen/H.Shinkaruk

2015-16 The Cup Rookie Gear Relic Autographs

ARGAP Artemi Panarin 100.00 200.00
ARGCH Charles Hudon 20.00 50.00
ARGCM Connor McDavid 500.00 800.00
ARGDL Dylan Larkin 150.00 300.00
ARGHS Hunter Shinkaruk 20.00 50.00
ARGJM Jared McCann 20.00 50.00
ARGJV Jake Virtanen 30.00 80.00
ARGKF Kevin Fiala 40.00 100.00
ARGMC Mike Condon 20.00 50.00
ARGMR Mikko Rantanen 30.00 80.00
ARGMS Malcolm Subban 30.00 80.00
ARGNE Nikolaj Ehlers 25.00 60.00
ARGNG Nikolay Goldobin 50.00 120.00
ARGNH Noah Hanifin 20.00 50.00
ARGNR Nick Ritchie 15.00 40.00
ARGOL Oscar Lindberg 20.00 50.00
ARGSB Sam Bennett 60.00 150.00
ARGZF Zachary Fucale 30.00 80.00

2015-16 The Cup Scripted Sticks

SSAK Anze Kopitar 40.00 100.00
SSAO Alexander Ovechkin 100.00 250.00
SSBC Bobby Clarke 25.00 60.00
SSBG Brendan Gallagher 30.00 80.00
SSBS Borje Salming 25.00 60.00
SSCJ Curtis Joseph 25.00 60.00
SSCP Carey Price 80.00 200.00
SSDG Doug Gilmour 30.00 80.00
SSDH Dominik Hasek 30.00 80.00
SSDS Denis Savard 30.00 80.00
SSFP Felix Potvin 40.00 100.00
SSJI Jarome Iginla 25.00 60.00
SSJJ Jaromir Jagr 60.00 150.00
SSJK Jari Kurri 25.00 60.00
SSJS Joe Sakic 40.00 100.00
SSLR Larry Robinson 25.00 60.00
SSMB Martin Brodeur 50.00 125.00
SSML Mario Lemieux 80.00 200.00
SSMM Mark Messier 40.00 100.00
SSMP Max Pacioretty 25.00 60.00
SSPR Patrick Roy 60.00 150.00
SSRB Rob Blake 25.00 60.00
SSRO Luc Robitaille 30.00 80.00
SSSC Sidney Crosby 100.00 250.00
SSSY Steve Yzerman 40.00 100.00
SSTS Teemu Selanne 50.00 125.00

2015-16 The Cup Scripted Swatches

SWAK Anze Kopitar 40.00 100.00
SWAO Alexander Ovechkin 100.00 250.00
SWCM Connor McDavid 500.00 800.00
SWDL Dylan Larkin 80.00 200.00
SWEM Evgeni Malkin 80.00 200.00
SWJB Jamie Benn 30.00 80.00
SWJF Justin Faulk 25.00 60.00
SWJG Johnny Gaudreau 40.00 100.00
SWJI Jarome Iginla 25.00 60.00
SWJJ Jaromir Jagr 60.00 150.00
SWJT Jonathan Toews 50.00 125.00
SWJV Jake Virtanen 30.00 80.00
SWMD Max Domi 50.00 125.00
SWML Mario Lemieux 80.00 200.00
SWNM Nathan MacKinnon 50.00 125.00
SWON Owen Nolan 20.00 50.00
SWPC Paul Coffey 25.00 60.00
SWPR Carey Price 80.00 200.00
SWRF Robby Fabbri 30.00 80.00
SWRO Patrick Roy 60.00 150.00
SWSB Sam Bennett 30.00 80.00
SWSC Sidney Crosby 100.00 250.00
SWTH Taylor Hall 50.00 125.00
SWTS Teemu Selanne 50.00 125.00
SWWG Wayne Gretzky
SWZF Zachary Fucale 25.00 60.00

2015-16 The Cup Signature Patches

SPAE Aaron Ekblad/99 25.00 60.00
SPAK Anze Kopitar/99 40.00 100.00
SPAO Alexander Ovechkin/25 125.00 300.00
SPBG Brendan Gallagher/99 30.00 80.00
SPCC Chris Chelios/99 25.00 60.00
SPCM Connor McDavid/99 500.00 1200.00
SPDL Dylan Larkin/99 80.00 200.00
SPDS Daniel Sprong/99 50.00 125.00
SPHS Hunter Shinkaruk/99 25.00 60.00
SPJB Jamie Benn/99 30.00 80.00
SPJG Johnny Gaudreau/99 40.00 100.00
SPJH Jiri Hudler/99 20.00 50.00
SPJI Jarome Iginla/99 25.00 60.00
SPJJ Jaromir Jagr/25 80.00 200.00
SPJM Jared McCann/99 25.00 60.00
SPJP Joe Pavelski/99 25.00 60.00
SPJR Jeremy Roenick/25 30.00 80.00
SPJT John Tavares/99 50.00 125.00
SPKF Kevin Fiala/99 25.00 60.00
SPLR Luc Robitaille/99 30.00 80.00
SPMC Mike Condon/99 25.00 60.00
SPMF Marc-Andre Fleury/99 40.00 100.00
SPMG Marian Gaborik/25
SPMP Max Pacioretty/99 25.00 60.00
SPMR Mikko Rantanen/99 50.00 125.00
SPMS Mark Stone/99
SPNE Nikolaj Ehlers/99 50.00 125.00
SPNH Noah Hanifin/99 30.00 80.00
SPNR Nick Ritchie/99 25.00 60.00
SPOL Oscar Lindberg/99 25.00 60.00
SPPA Colton Parayko/99 30.00 80.00
SPPB Pavel Bure/99 40.00 100.00
SPPC Paul Coffey/25 30.00 80.00
SPPD Pavel Datsyuk/99 30.00 80.00
SPPR Carey Price/25 100.00 250.00
SPRF Robby Fabbri/99 30.00 80.00
SPRM Ryan Miller/99 40.00 100.00
SPRN Rick Nash/99 25.00 60.00
SPRO Ryan O'Reilly/99 25.00 60.00
SPSB Sam Bennett/99 30.00 80.00
SPSC Sidney Crosby/25
SPSE Teemu Selanne/25 60.00 150.00
SPSH Shea Theodore/99 25.00 60.00
SPST Martin St. Louis/25 30.00 80.00
SPSU Malcolm Subban/99 60.00 150.00
SPTH Taylor Hall/99 50.00 125.00
SPTO Jonathan Toews/25 60.00 150.00
SPTS Tyler Seguin/99
SPVI Jake Virtanen/99 30.00 80.00
SPZF Zachary Fucale/99 25.00 60.00

2015-16 The Cup Signature Renditions

SRAO Alexander Ovechkin 40.00 100.00
SRBC Bobby Clarke 10.00 25.00
SRBO Bobby Orr 30.00 80.00
SRCM Connor McDavid 300.00 500.00
SRCP Carey Price 40.00 100.00
SRDG Doug Gilmour 30.00 80.00
SRDL Dylan Larkin 30.00 80.00
SREM Evgeni Malkin 25.00 60.00
SRFP Felix Potvin 15.00 40.00
SRGC Guy Carbonneau 8.00 20.00
SRJJ Jaromir Jagr
SRJT Jonathan Toews 40.00 100.00
SRNM Nathan MacKinnon

Card	Low	High
OL Oscar Lindberg	10.00	25.00
PB Pavel Bure	15.00	40.00
RB Rod Brind'Amour	8.00	20.00
RM Ryan Miller	15.00	40.00
RO Ryan O'Reilly	10.00	25.00
SM Sean Monahan	10.00	25.00
TF Theoren Fleury	12.00	30.00
TH Taylor Hall	20.00	50.00
WG Wayne Gretzky	200.00	400.00

2015-16 The Cup Trios Jerseys

Card	Low	High
LW Ovechkin/Benn/Hall	40.00	100.00
RW Kane/Tarasenko/Toffoli	20.00	50.00
CAL Gaudreau/Monahan/Hamilton	15.00	40.00
CAP Ovechkin/Holtby/Kuznetsov	40.00	100.00
CBJ Foligno/Saad/Hartnell	10.00	25.00
CEN Seguin/Toews/Malkin	30.00	80.00
FLO Barkov/Luongo/Jagr	25.00	60.00
NET Holtby/Price/Rask	30.00	80.00
NYI Tavares/Halak/Lee	20.00	50.00
NYR Zuccarello/Lundqvist/Nash	12.00	30.00
TBL Kucherov/Bishop/Stamkos	20.00	50.00
VAN Sedin/Miller/Sedin	10.00	25.00
COLO Landeskog/MacKinnon/Duchene	20.00	50.00
COYO Smith/Ekman-Larsson/Duclair	10.00	25.00
HABS Gallagher/Price/Pacioretty	30.00	80.00
JETS Scheifele/Wheeler/Byfuglien	12.00	30.00
NASH Josi/Rinne/Weber	12.00	30.00
RET1 Sakic/Yzerman/Lemieux	30.00	80.00
RET2 Coffey/Savard/Hawerchuk	12.00	30.00
RET5 Sakic/Bourque/Roy	25.00	60.00
ROTY Ekblad/MacKinnon/Panarin	30.00	80.00
WILD Koivu/Dubnyk/Parise	10.00	25.00
BLUES Tarasenko/Allen/Steen	15.00	40.00
CANES Lindholm/Faulk/Skinner	10.00	25.00
DUCKS Perry/Andersen/Getzlaf	15.00	40.00
LEAFS Rielly/van Riemsdyk/Kadri	8.00	20.00
PENGU Malkin/Fleury/Kessel	30.00	80.00
ROOK1 McDavid/Eichel/Larkin	80.00	200.00
ROOK2 McDavid/Panarin/Domi	80.00	200.00
ROOK3 Eichel/Bennett/Virtanen	40.00	100.00
ROOK4 Panarin/Hinostroza/Hartman	30.00	80.00
ROOK5 Theodore/Ritchie/Noesen	10.00	25.00
ROOK6 McCarron/Condon/Fucale	10.00	25.00
ROOK7 Lindberg/Skjei/Skapski	10.00	25.00
ROOK8 Hanifin/Pesce/McGinn	12.00	30.00
ROOK9 Virtanen/McCann/Hutton	12.00	30.00
STARS Seguin/Benn/Sharp	15.00	40.00
BRUINS Bergeron/Rask/Eriksson	12.00	30.00
DEVILS Henrique/Schneider/Cammalleri	10.00	25.00
GOALIE Crawford/Quick/Lundqvist	15.00	40.00
OILERS Nugent-Hopkins/Hall/Eberle	20.00	50.00
ROOK10 Ehlers/Hellebuyck/Petan	25.00	60.00
SABRES O'Reilly/Reinhart/Ristolainen	10.00	25.00
SHARKS Pavelski/Jones/Marleau	10.00	25.00

2016-17 The Cup

Card	Low	High
Steve Yzerman	6.00	15.00
Ray Bourque	8.00	20.00
Corey Perry	5.00	12.00
John Gibson	5.00	12.00
Teemu Selanne	10.00	25.00
Oliver Ekman-Larsson	4.00	10.00
Max Domi	6.00	15.00
David Backes	5.00	12.00
Patrice Bergeron	6.00	15.00
Bobby Orr	15.00	40.00
Cam Neely	5.00	12.00
Ryan O'Reilly	5.00	12.00
Jack Eichel	10.00	25.00
Dale Hawerchuk	6.00	15.00
Mark Giordano	4.00	10.00
Sam Bennett	6.00	15.00
Sean Monahan	5.00	12.00
Jordan Staal	5.00	12.00
Teuvo Teravainen	5.00	12.00
Cam Ward	5.00	12.00
Artemi Panarin	6.00	15.00
Jonathan Toews	10.00	25.00
Chris Chelios	5.00	12.00
Patrick Kane	10.00	25.00
Nathan MacKinnon	10.00	25.00
Matt Duchene	5.00	12.00
Joe Sakic	8.00	20.00
Brandon Saad	5.00	12.00
Boone Jenner	5.00	12.00
Sergei Bobrovsky	5.00	12.00
Jamie Benn	6.00	15.00
Tyler Seguin	8.00	20.00
Mike Modano	8.00	20.00
Andreas Athanasiou	5.00	12.00
Dylan Larkin	8.00	20.00
Henrik Zetterberg	6.00	15.00
Igor Larionov	5.00	12.00
Leon Draisaitl	6.00	15.00
Connor McDavid	25.00	60.00
Wayne Gretzky	25.00	60.00
Jaromir Jagr	12.00	30.00
Aaron Ekblad	5.00	12.00
Roberto Luongo	5.00	12.00
Tyler Toffoli	5.00	12.00
Anze Kopitar	8.00	20.00
Drew Doughty	5.00	12.00
Jake Muzzin	4.00	10.00
Devan Dubnyk	5.00	12.00
Nino Niederreiter	5.00	12.00
Ryan Suter	4.00	10.00
Alex Galchenyuk	6.00	15.00
Patrick Roy	12.00	30.00
Shea Weber	4.00	10.00
Carey Price	15.00	40.00
P.K. Subban	8.00	20.00
Ryan Johansen	6.00	15.00
Roman Josi	5.00	12.00
Taylor Hall	10.00	25.00
Cory Schneider	4.00	10.00
Martin Brodeur	10.00	25.00
Adam Henrique	5.00	12.00
Pat LaFontaine	5.00	12.00
John Tavares	10.00	25.00
Andrew Ladd	5.00	12.00
Erik Karlsson	10.00	25.00
Mike Hoffman	4.00	10.00
Bobby Ryan	4.00	10.00
Craig Anderson	5.00	12.00
Claude Giroux	5.00	12.00
Bobby Clarke	5.00	12.00
Jakub Voracek	5.00	12.00
Jeremy Roenick	5.00	12.00
Matt Murray	8.00	20.00
Sidney Crosby	20.00	50.00
Mario Lemieux	15.00	40.00
Evgeni Malkin	15.00	40.00
Joe Pavelski	5.00	12.00
Brent Burns	6.00	15.00
Martin Jones	5.00	12.00
Joe Thornton	5.00	12.00
Alex Pietrangelo	4.00	10.00
Brett Hull	5.00	12.00
Vladimir Tarasenko	8.00	20.00
Jake Allen	6.00	15.00
85 Steven Stamkos	10.00	25.00
86 Dave Andreychuk	5.00	12.00
87 Nikita Kucherov	8.00	20.00
88 Nazem Kadri	4.00	10.00
89 Morgan Rielly	4.00	10.00
90 Felix Potvin	8.00	20.00
91 Frederik Andersen	4.00	10.00
92 Daniel Sedin	5.00	12.00
93 Loui Eriksson	5.00	12.00
94 Bo Horvat	8.00	20.00
95 Alexander Ovechkin	20.00	50.00
96 Braden Holtby	8.00	20.00
97 Nicklas Backstrom	8.00	20.00
98 Blake Wheeler	5.00	12.00
99 Nikolaj Ehlers	5.00	12.00
100 Mark Scheifele	6.00	15.00
101 Ivan Provorov JSY AU/249 RC	40.00	100.00
102 Matthew Tkachuk JSY AU/249 RC	80.00	200.00
103 Pavel Zacha JSY AU/249 RC	25.00	60.00
104 Anthony Mantha JSY AU/249 RC	250.00	400.00
105 Travis Konecny JSY AU/249 RC	40.00	100.00
106 Sebastian Aho JSY AU/249 RC	40.00	100.00
107 Mathew Barzal JSY AU/249 RC	350.00	700.00
108 Dylan Strome JSY AU/249 RC	40.00	100.00
109 Zach Werenski JSY AU/249 RC	80.00	200.00
110 Pavel Buchnevich JSY AU/249 RC	50.00	125.00
111 Tyler Motte JSY AU/249 RC	20.00	50.00
112 Kyle Connor JSY AU/249 RC	60.00	150.00
113 Stephen Johns JSY AU/249 RC	15.00	40.00
114 Troy Stecher AU/249 RC	20.00	50.00
115 Tyler Bertuzzi JSY AU/249 RC	25.00	60.00
116 Zach Hyman JSY AU/249 RC	30.00	80.00
117 Nic Dowd JSY AU/249 RC	20.00	50.00
118 Nick Baptiste JSY AU/249 RC	20.00	50.00
119 Gustav Forsling JSY AU/249 RC	20.00	50.00
120 Brendan Guhle JSY AU/249 RC	20.00	50.00
121 Brandon Tanev JSY AU/249 RC	20.00	50.00
122 Mark Jankowski JSY AU/249 RC	15.00	40.00
123 Nikita Tryamkin JSY AU/249 RC	15.00	40.00
124 Tristan Jarry JSY AU/249 RC	40.00	100.00
125 A.J. Greer JSY AU/249 RC	20.00	50.00
126 Artturi Lehkonen JSY AU/249 RC	25.00	60.00
127 Austin Czarnik JSY AU/249 RC	30.00	80.00
128 Danton Heinen JSY AU/249 RC	30.00	80.00
129 Sergey Tolchinsky JSY AU/249 RC	15.00	40.00
130 Brandon Montour JSY AU/249 RC	20.00	50.00
131 Jakub Vrana JSY AU/249 RC	20.00	50.00
132 Timo Meier JSY AU/249 RC	20.00	50.00
133 Thatcher Demko JSY AU/249 RC	50.00	125.00
134 Jake Guentzel JSY AU/249 RC	150.00	350.00
135 Julius Honka JSY AU/249 RC	20.00	50.00
136 Michael Matheson JSY AU/249 RC	20.00	50.00
137 Jakob Chychrun JSY AU/249 RC	20.00	50.00
138 Nikita Soshnikov JSY AU/249 RC	12.00	30.00
139 Brendan Perlini JSY AU/249 RC	20.00	50.00
140 Mikhail Sergachev JSY AU/249 RC	80.00	200.00
141 Anthony Beauvillier JSY AU/249 RC	25.00	60.00
142 Brayden Point JSY AU/249 RC	200.00	300.00
143 Christian Dvorak JSY AU/249 RC	20.00	50.00
144 Joel Eriksson Ek JSY AU/249 RC	20.00	50.00
145 Kasperi Kapanen JSY AU/249 RC	40.00	100.00
146 Anthony DeAngelo JSY AU/249 RC	20.00	50.00
147 Tom Kuhnhackl JSY AU/249 RC	15.00	40.00
148 Dominik Simon JSY AU/249 RC	20.00	50.00
149 Trevor Carrick JSY AU/249 RC	20.00	50.00
150 Brendan Leipsic JSY AU/249 RC	20.00	50.00
151 Nick Schmaltz JSY AU/249 RC	20.00	50.00
152 Esa Lindell JSY AU/249 RC	20.00	50.00
153 Hudson Fasching JSY AU/249 RC	20.00	50.00
154 Justin Bailey JSY AU/249 RC	20.00	50.00
155 Connor Brown JSY AU/249 RC	30.00	80.00
156 Mike Reilly JSY AU/249 RC	15.00	40.00
157 Steven Santini JSY AU/249 RC	15.00	40.00
158 Chase De Leo JSY AU/249 RC	20.00	50.00
159 Oliver Bjorkstrand JSY AU/249 RC	15.00	40.00
160 Daniel Altshuller JSY AU/249 RC	15.00	40.00
161 Lawson Crouse JSY AU/249 RC	15.00	40.00
162 Chris Bigras JSY AU/249 RC	15.00	40.00
163 Blake Speers JSY AU/249 RC	20.00	50.00
164 John Quenneville JSY AU/249 RC	20.00	50.00
165 Pontus Aberg JSY AU/249 RC	25.00	60.00
166 JC Lipon JSY AU/249 RC	20.00	50.00
167 Josh Morrissey JSY AU/249 RC	25.00	60.00
168 Jason Dickinson JSY AU/249 RC	15.00	40.00
169 Oskar Sundqvist JSY AU/249 RC	20.00	50.00
170 Mark McNeill JSY AU/249 RC	20.00	50.00
171 Kevin Labanc JSY AU/249 RC	20.00	50.00
172 Sonny Milano JSY AU/249 RC	25.00	60.00
173 Thomas Chabot JSY AU/249 RC	40.00	100.00
174 Ryan Pulock JSY AU/249 RC	20.00	50.00
175 Patrik Laine JSY AU/99 RC	1500.00	2000.00
176 Mitch Marner JSY AU/99 RC	900.00	1500.00
177 Jesse Puljujarvi JSY AU/99 RC	350.00	600.00
178 William Nylander JSY AU/99 RC	500.00	800.00
179 Jimmy Vesey JSY AU/99 RC	450.00	700.00
180 Auston Matthews JSY AU/99 RC	7000.00	12000.00
181 Miles Wood JSY AU/249 RC	15.00	40.00
182 Oliver Kylington JSY AU/249 RC	15.00	40.00
183 Charlie Lindgren JSY AU/249 RC	30.00	80.00
184 Brandon Carlo JSY AU/249 RC	20.00	50.00
185 Jared Coreau RC	6.00	15.00
186 Markus Nutivaara RC	5.00	12.00
187 Adam Erne RC	8.00	20.00
188 Alan Quine RC	5.00	12.00
189 Joseph Cramarossa RC	5.00	12.00
190 Lukas Sedlak RC	5.00	12.00
191 Wade Megan RC	5.00	12.00
192 Matthew Benning RC	6.00	15.00
193 Nikita Zaitsev RC	5.00	12.00
194 Aaron Dell RC	6.00	15.00
195 Drake Caggiula RC	5.00	12.00
196 Denis Malgin RC	5.00	12.00
197 William Carrier RC	5.00	12.00
198 Jacob Larsson RC	8.00	20.00
199 Ondrej Kase RC	5.00	12.00
200 Kevin Gravel RC	6.00	15.00

2016-17 The Cup Brilliance Autographs

Card	Low	High
BAG Alex Galchenyuk B	12.00	30.00
BAM Auston Matthews A		
BAV Andrei Vasilevskiy D	12.00	30.00
BDS Darryl Sittler A	25.00	60.00
BFA Frederik Andersen D	8.00	20.00
BJG John Gibson D	10.00	25.00
BJH Julius Honka D	10.00	25.00
BJP Jesse Puljujarvi C	25.00	60.00
BLA Patrik Laine A		
BLD Leon Draisaitl C	50.00	125.00
BMH Mike Hoffman C	8.00	20.00
BMM Matt Murray C	30.00	80.00
BMT Matthew Tkachuk C	30.00	80.00
BNE Nikolaj Ehlers D	10.00	25.00
BNK Nikita Kucherov C	20.00	50.00
BNN Nino Niederreiter D	10.00	25.00
BPB Peter Bondra C	20.00	50.00
BPL Pat LaFontaine C	10.00	25.00
BRJ Roman Josi B	25.00	60.00
BRK Ryan Kesler B	10.00	25.00
BRV Rogie Vachon B	20.00	50.00
BSA Derek Sanderson C	25.00	60.00
BTB Tyson Barrie C	10.00	25.00
BTD Thatcher Demko D	30.00	80.00
BTF Theoren Fleury B	25.00	60.00
BTK Travis Konecny D	30.00	80.00
BVD Vincent Damphousse B	20.00	50.00
BWC Wendel Clark A	25.00	60.00
BWG Wayne Gretzky A		

2016-17 The Cup Enshrinements

Card	Low	High
EAB Anthony Beauvillier/99	10.00	25.00
EAG Alex Galchenyuk/99	12.00	30.00
EAO Alexander Ovechkin/25	80.00	150.00
EBC Bobby Clarke/99	15.00	40.00
ECN Cam Neely/99	10.00	25.00
EDP Denis Potvin/99	10.00	25.00
EDS Derek Sanderson/99	25.00	60.00
EEM Evgeni Malkin/99	30.00	80.00
EGL Guy Lafleur/25	80.00	150.00
EIP Ivan Provorov/99	30.00	80.00
EJE Joel Eriksson Ek/99	10.00	25.00
EJM Jake Muzzin/99	8.00	20.00
EJT Joe Thornton/99	20.00	50.00
EJV Jimmy Vesey/99	20.00	50.00
EKM Kirk Muller/99	10.00	25.00
ELD Leon Draisaitl/99	50.00	125.00
ELE Loui Eriksson/99	10.00	25.00
EMB Martin Brodeur/25	80.00	200.00
EMG Mark Giordano/99	8.00	20.00
EMH Mike Hoffman/99	8.00	20.00
EMR Morgan Rielly/99	8.00	20.00
EMS Mark Scheifele/99	12.00	30.00
EPH Phil Housley/99	40.00	100.00
EPK Patrick Kane/99	40.00	100.00
ERL Roberto Luongo/99	15.00	40.00
ESC Sidney Crosby/25	200.00	400.00
EWG Wayne Gretzky/25	250.00	400.00
EZW Zach Werenski/99	25.00	60.00

2016-17 The Cup Enshrinements Dual

Card	Low	High
E2LC P.Laine/K.Connor/25	300.00	400.00
E2SL J.Sakic/G.Lafleur/25	80.00	150.00
E2SM D.Sittler/L.McDonald/25	60.00	150.00

2016-17 The Cup Foundations Jerseys

Card	Low	High
FAE Aaron Ekblad/25	8.00	20.00
FAG Alex Galchenyuk/25	10.00	25.00
FAK Anze Kopitar/25	12.00	30.00
FAM Auston Matthews/49	100.00	250.00
FAO Alexander Ovechkin/25	30.00	80.00
FAP Alex Pietrangelo/25	6.00	15.00
FAV Andrei Vasilevskiy/25	10.00	25.00
FAW Alexander Wennberg/25	6.00	15.00
FBB Brent Burns/25	10.00	25.00
FBE Brian Elliott/25	6.00	15.00
FCM Connor McDavid/25	40.00	100.00
FCP Carey Price/25	25.00	60.00
FDB David Backes/25	8.00	20.00
FDD Devan Dubnyk/25	8.00	20.00
FEK Erik Karlsson/25	15.00	40.00
FEM Evgeni Malkin/25	25.00	60.00
FES Eric Staal/25	10.00	25.00
FHL Henrik Lundqvist/25	8.00	20.00
FHZ Henrik Zetterberg/25	10.00	25.00
FJA Jake Allen/25	10.00	25.00
FJG John Gibson/25	8.00	20.00
FJJ Joe Thornton/25	8.00	20.00
FJM Jake Muzzin/25	6.00	15.00
FJP Jesse Puljujarvi/49	20.00	50.00
FJT Jonathan Toews/25	15.00	40.00
FJV Jimmy Vesey/49	15.00	40.00
FLE Loui Eriksson/25	8.00	20.00
FMA Anthony Mantha/49	20.00	50.00
FMG Mark Giordano/25	6.00	15.00
FMH Mike Hoffman/25	6.00	15.00
FMM Mitch Marner/49	40.00	100.00
FMR Morgan Rielly/25	6.00	15.00
FMS Mark Scheifele/25	10.00	25.00
FMT Matthew Tkachuk/49	25.00	60.00
FMZ Mats Zuccarello/25	8.00	20.00
FPB Pavel Buchnevich/49	12.00	30.00
FPK Patrick Kane/25	15.00	40.00
FPL Patrik Laine/49	30.00	80.00
FPS P.K. Subban/25	12.00	30.00
FRK Ryan Kesler/25	8.00	20.00
FRL Roberto Luongo/25	8.00	20.00
FSB Sergei Bobrovsky/25	8.00	20.00
FSC Sidney Crosby/25	30.00	80.00
FSS Steven Stamkos/25	15.00	40.00
FTA John Tavares/25	15.00	40.00
FTH Taylor Hall/25	15.00	40.00
FTK Travis Konecny/49	15.00	40.00
FTS Tyler Seguin/25	12.00	30.00
FWS Wayne Simmonds/25	10.00	25.00
FZW Zach Werenski/49	15.00	40.00

2016-17 The Cup Honorable Numbers

Card	Low	High
HNAM Auston Matthews/34	1000.00	3000.00
HNAV Andrei Vasilevskiy/88	30.00	80.00
HNCC Chris Chelios/24	20.00	50.00
HNCP Carey Price/31		
HNDB David Backes/42	20.00	50.00
HNHL Henrik Lundqvist/30		
HNJE Joel Eriksson Ek/14		
HNJG Jake Guentzel/59	200.00	300.00
HNJP Jesse Puljujarvi/98	40.00	100.00
HNJS Joe Sakic/19	50.00	125.00
HNJT Joe Thornton/19	30.00	80.00
HNLD Leon Draisaitl/29	150.00	250.00
HNMA Michael Matheson/19	15.00	40.00
HNMM Matt Murray/30		
HNMR Morgan Rielly/44	20.00	50.00
HNMS Mark Scheifele/55	20.00	50.00
HNNE Nikolaj Ehlers/27		
HNNN Nino Niederreiter/22	25.00	60.00
HNPB Pavel Buchnevich/89	25.00	60.00
HNPL Patrik Laine/29	150.00	250.00
HNPR Patrick Roy/33		
HNRK Ryan Kesler/17	15.00	40.00
HNTS Tyler Seguin/91	50.00	125.00
HNVE Jimmy Vesey/26		
HNWS Wayne Simmonds/17		

2016-17 The Cup Honorable Numbers Dual

Card	Low	High
HN2ST T.Seguin/J.Tavares/91	40.00	100.00
HN2TT J.Thornton/J.Toews/19		
HN2YS S.Yzerman/J.Sakic/19		

2016-17 The Cup Rookie Bookmarks Dual Autographs

Card	Low	High
DARBKP T.Konecny/I.Provorov	60.00	150.00
DARBLC P.Laine/K.Connor		
DARBMB M.Marner/C.Brown		
DARBSL M.Sergachev/A.Lehkonen	50.00	125.00
DARBVB J.Vesey/P.Buchnevich		
DARBWB Z.Werenski/O.Bjorkstrand		

2016-17 The Cup Scripted Materials

Card	Low	High
SMAB Aleksander Barkov	15.00	40.00
SMAE Aaron Ekblad	15.00	40.00
SMAG Alex Galchenyuk	20.00	50.00
SMAM Auston Matthews	400.00	500.00
SMAO Alexander Ovechkin	60.00	150.00
SMAV Andrei Vasilevskiy	20.00	50.00
SMAW Alexander Wennberg	12.00	30.00
SMBE Brian Elliott	12.00	30.00
SMBH Brett Hull	15.00	40.00
SMBS Brayden Schenn	15.00	40.00
SMCM Connor McDavid	200.00	300.00
SMCP Carey Price	50.00	125.00
SMCS Cory Schneider	12.00	30.00
SMDB David Backes	15.00	40.00
SMEM Evgeni Malkin	50.00	125.00
SMFA Frederik Andersen	12.00	30.00
SMGL Guy Lafleur	80.00	150.00
SMHL Henrik Lundqvist	15.00	40.00
SMHZ Henrik Zetterberg	20.00	50.00
SMIL Igor Larionov	25.00	60.00
SMJE Joel Eriksson Ek	15.00	40.00
SMJG John Gibson	15.00	40.00
SMJI Jarome Iginla	15.00	40.00
SMJJ Joe Thornton	15.00	40.00
SMJM Jake Muzzin	12.00	30.00
SMJO Roman Josi	15.00	40.00
SMJP Jesse Puljujarvi	40.00	100.00
SMJT Jonathan Toews	30.00	80.00
SMJV Jimmy Vesey	100.00	200.00
SMLD Leon Draisaitl	80.00	150.00
SMLE Loui Eriksson	15.00	40.00
SMMG Mark Giordano	12.00	30.00
SMMH Mike Hoffman	12.00	30.00
SMMM Matt Murray	25.00	60.00
SMMR Morgan Rielly	12.00	30.00
SMMS Mark Scheifele	20.00	50.00
SMMT Mark Stone	15.00	40.00
SMNK Nikita Kucherov	25.00	60.00
SMNN Nino Niederreiter	15.00	40.00
SMPC Paul Coffey	15.00	40.00
SMPE Corey Perry	15.00	40.00
SMPK Patrick Kane	30.00	80.00
SMPL Patrik Laine	100.00	250.00
SMRK Ryan Kesler	15.00	40.00
SMSC Sidney Crosby	200.00	300.00
SMTA John Tavares	30.00	80.00
SMTH Taylor Hall	30.00	80.00
SMTK Travis Konecny	30.00	80.00
SMTS Tyler Seguin	25.00	60.00
SMWS Wayne Simmonds	20.00	50.00
SMZW Zach Werenski	30.00	80.00

2016-17 The Cup Signature Materials

Card	Low	High
SIAB Anthony Beauvillier/99	15.00	40.00
SIAG Alex Galchenyuk/99	20.00	50.00
SIAM Auston Matthews/99	550.00	700.00
SIAO Alexander Ovechkin/25	80.00	150.00
SIAV Andrei Vasilevskiy/99	20.00	50.00
SIBE Brian Elliott/99	12.00	30.00
SIBH Bo Horvat/99	25.00	60.00
SIBM Brandon Montour/99	15.00	40.00
SICD Christian Dvorak/99	15.00	40.00
SICM Connor McDavid/25	250.00	450.00
SICP Carey Price/25	80.00	150.00
SIEM Evgeni Malkin/25	80.00	150.00
SIHL Henrik Lundqvist/25	60.00	150.00
SIHZ Henrik Zetterberg/99	20.00	50.00
SIJE Joel Eriksson Ek/99	15.00	40.00
SIJH Julius Honka/99	15.00	40.00
SIJJ Jaromir Jagr/25	150.00	250.00
SIJM Jake Muzzin/99	12.00	30.00
SIJP Jesse Puljujarvi/99	40.00	100.00
SIJS Jaden Schwartz/99	20.00	50.00
SIJV Jimmy Vesey/99	30.00	80.00
SIKC Kyle Connor/99	40.00	100.00
SIMA Anthony Mantha/99	80.00	150.00
SIMB Mathew Barzal/99	50.00	125.00
SIMG Mark Giordano/99	12.00	30.00
SIMH Mike Hoffman/99	12.00	30.00
SIMM Michael Matheson/99	15.00	40.00
SIMR Morgan Rielly/99	12.00	30.00
SIMS Mark Scheifele/99	20.00	50.00
SIMT Matthew Tkachuk/99	80.00	200.00
SINE Nikolaj Ehlers/99	15.00	40.00
SINN Nino Niederreiter/99	15.00	40.00
SINS Nick Schmaltz/99	15.00	40.00
SIPB Pavel Buchnevich/99	25.00	60.00
SIPE Corey Perry/99	15.00	40.00
SIPK Patrick Kane/25	80.00	150.00
SIPL Patrik Laine/99	150.00	300.00
SIRK Ryan Kesler/99	15.00	40.00
SIRL Roberto Luongo/99	15.00	40.00
SIRN Rick Nash/99	15.00	40.00
SIRS Ryan Spooner/99	12.00	30.00
SISC Sidney Crosby/25	300.00	400.00
SITA John Tavares/99	30.00	80.00
SITB Tyson Barrie/99	15.00	40.00
SITH Joe Thornton/99	15.00	40.00
SITM Timo Meier/99	15.00	40.00
SIWS Wayne Simmonds/99	20.00	50.00
SIZW Zach Werenski/99	30.00	80.00

2016-17 The Cup Signature Materials Dual

Card	Low	High
SI2AD A.Matthews/D.Gilmour/15		
SI2BE A.Barkov/A.Ekblad/35	25.00	60.00
SI2BS J.Benn/T.Seguin/35	25.00	60.00
SI2CL P.Coffey/N.Lidstrom/15		
SI2HE B.Horvat/L.Eriksson/35	40.00	100.00
SI2KT P.Kane/J.Toews/15		
SI2LM N.Lidstrom/L.Murphy/15		
SI2PG C.Price/A.Galchenyuk/35	100.00	200.00
SI2SM S.Monahan/M.Giordano/35	40.00	100.00
SI2SS W.Simmonds/B.Schenn/35	25.00	60.00

2016-17 The Cup Signature Renditions

Card	Low	High
SRAM Auston Matthews C	450.00	600.00
SRAO Alexander Ovechkin C	60.00	150.00
SRBO Bobby Orr A	150.00	250.00
SRCM Connor McDavid B	300.00	400.00
SRCN Cam Neely E	15.00	40.00
SRCP Carey Price C	50.00	125.00
SRDA Dave Andreychuk E	15.00	40.00
SREM Evgeni Malkin D	50.00	125.00
SRHL Henrik Lundqvist C	30.00	80.00
SRJE Joel Eriksson Ek E	15.00	40.00
SRJJ Jaromir Jagr B	100.00	200.00
SRJT Joe Thornton D	25.00	60.00
SRJV Jimmy Vesey E	30.00	80.00
SRLM Lanny McDonald D	15.00	40.00
SRMD Marcel Dionne E	20.00	50.00
SRML Mario Lemieux A	150.00	250.00
SRMO Mike Modano D	25.00	60.00
SRPH Phil Housley E	15.00	40.00
SRPL Patrik Laine D	60.00	150.00
SRPR Patrick Roy B	80.00	150.00
SRRB Ray Bourque C	25.00	60.00
SRRL Roberto Luongo E	15.00	40.00
SRSC Sidney Crosby B	400.00	500.00
SRWG Wayne Gretzky A	300.00	400.00
SRZW Zach Werenski E	30.00	80.00

2016-17 The Cup Signature Renditions Combos

Card	Low	High
SR2CB P.Coffey/R.Bourque	80.00	150.00
SR2CL C.Chelios/N.Lidstrom	80.00	150.00
SR2KG J.Kurri/W.Gretzky		

2016-17 The Cup Ticket Inscriptions

Card	Low	High
TBAK Anze Kopitar/17	150.00	250.00
TBAO Alexander Ovechkin/16		
TBBS Brayden Schenn/14	40.00	100.00
TBGN Gustav Nyquist/12	50.00	125.00
TBPE Corey Perry/13		
TBPK Patrick Kane/12		
TBRN Rick Nash/15		
TBTA John Tavares/27	150.00	250.00
TBTS Tyler Seguin/16		
TBWS Wayne Simmonds/23		

2016-17 The Cup Trios Jerseys

Card	Low	High
C3ACR Chychrun/Strome/Dvorak	15.00	40.00
C3ANA Gibson/Getzlaf/Perry	10.00	25.00
C3ARI Domi/Ekman-Larsson/Smith	8.00	20.00
C3ASL Thornton/Jagr/Iginla	15.00	40.00
C3AVS Sakic/Roy/Blake	15.00	40.00
C3BB1 Marchand/Bergeron/Pastrnak	10.00	25.00
C3BB2 Spooner/Rask/Backes	6.00	15.00
C3BJR Bjorkstrand/Werenski/Milano	12.00	30.00
C3BUF O'Reilly/Eichel/Reinhart	12.00	30.00
C3CAL Monahan/Gaudreau/Bennett	10.00	25.00
C3CAR Hanifin/Teravainen/Lindholm	6.00	15.00
C3CBH Kane/Toews/Crawford	12.00	30.00
C3CBJ Wennberg/Bobrovsky/Jones	6.00	15.00
C3COL MacKinnon/Barrie/Duchene	12.00	30.00
C3DAL Seguin/Benn/Klingberg	10.00	25.00
C3DEF Hedman/Burns/Weber	8.00	20.00
C3DET Yzerman/Lidstrom/Larionov	8.00	20.00
C3DRW Larkin/Zetterberg/Athanasiou	10.00	25.00
C3EDM Lucic/McDavid/Draisaitl	40.00	100.00
C3FLO Trocheck/Ekblad/Barkov	6.00	15.00
C3GOA Dubnyk/Holtby/Bobrovsky	10.00	25.00
C3LA1 Toffoli/Kopitar/Carter	10.00	25.00
C3LA2 Doughty/Quick/Muzzin	10.00	25.00
C3MCR Lehkonen/Sergachev/Lindgren	12.00	30.00
C3MLR Nylander/Matthews/Marner	80.00	200.00
C3MON Pacioretty/Price/Weber	20.00	50.00
C3MW1 Suter/Dubnyk/Staal	8.00	20.00
C3MW2 Parise/Koivu/Niederreiter	6.00	15.00
C3NAS Forsberg/Subban/Johansen	10.00	25.00
C3NJD Henrique/Schneider/Hall	12.00	30.00
C3NOR Keith/Karlsson/Doughty	12.00	30.00
C3NYI Nelson/Tavares/Leddy	12.00	30.00
C3NYR Nash/McDonagh/Zibanejad	6.00	15.00
C3OIL Kurri/Gretzky/Messier	30.00	80.00
C3OTT Hoffman/Karlsson/Stone	12.00	30.00
C3PHI Schenn/Giroux/Simmonds	8.00	20.00
C3PIT Kessel/Malkin/Letang	20.00	50.00
C3RRT Perry/Stamkos/Ovechkin	25.00	60.00
C3SAS Marleau/Thornton/Couture	6.00	15.00
C3SCW Martinez/Letang/Keith	6.00	15.00
C3SEL Toews/Bergeron/Kopitar	12.00	30.00
C3SJS Burns/Pavelski/Jones	8.00	20.00
C3STL Pietrangelo/Tarasenko/Fabbri	10.00	25.00
C3TBL Hedman/Stamkos/Kucherov	12.00	30.00
C3TML Rielly/Andersen/Kadri	5.00	12.00
C3VAN Eriksson/Sedin/Sedin	6.00	15.00
C3WC1 Backstrom/Ovechkin/Holtby	25.00	60.00
C3WC2 Oshie/Kuznetsov/Burakovsky	10.00	25.00
C3WIN Scheifele/Wheeler/Byfuglien	8.00	20.00
C3WJR Connor/Laine/Morrissey	25.00	60.00

2002-03 Thrashers Postcards

This 20-card set was issued by the team.

Card	Low	High
COMPLETE SET (20)	10.00	25.00
1 Lubos Bartecko	.40	1.00
2 Yuri Butsayev	.40	1.00
3 Jeff Cowan	.40	1.00
4 Dany Heatley	2.00	5.00
5 Milan Hnilicka	.40	1.00
6 Tony Hrkac	.40	1.00
7 Frantisek Kaberle	.40	1.00
8 Ilya Kovalchuk	2.00	5.00
9 Slava Kozlov	.40	1.00
10 Francis Lessard	.40	1.00
11 Pasi Nurminen	.60	1.50
12 Jeff Odgers	.60	1.50
13 Kamil Piros	.40	1.00
14 Dan Snyder	.75	2.00
15 Patrik Stefan	.40	1.00
16 Per Svartvadet	.40	1.00
16 Andy Sutton	.40	1.00
17 Chris Tamer	.40	1.00
18 Brad Tapper	.40	1.00
20 J.P. Vigier	.40	1.00

2003-04 Thrashers Postcards

Issued by the team at public events or in response to fan requests, these are standard postcard size. The checklist may not be complete.

Card	Low	High
COMPLETE SET (23)	10.00	25.00
1 Serge Aubin	.40	1.00
2 Jeff Cowan	.40	1.00
3 Byron Dafoe	.60	1.50
4 Garnet Exelby	.60	1.50
5 Bob Hartley CO	.20	.50
6 Frank Kaberle	.40	1.00
7 Tomas Kloucek	.40	1.00
8 Slava Kozlov	.40	1.00
9 Ilya Kovalchuk	2.00	5.00
10 Brad Larsen	.40	1.00
11 Francis Lessard	.40	1.00
12 Ivan Majesky	.40	1.00
13 Shawn McEachern	.40	1.00
14 Pasi Nurminen	.40	1.00
15 Ronald Petrovicky	.40	1.00
16 Randy Robitaille	.40	1.00
17 Marc Savard	.60	1.50
18 Ben Simon	.40	1.00
19 Patrik Stefan	.40	1.00
20 Andy Sutton	.40	1.00
21 Chris Tamer	.40	1.00
22 Daniel Tjarnqvist	.40	1.00
23 J.P. Vigier	.40	1.00

2000-01 Titanium

Released in April 2001, this 150-card set had a hobby SRP of $14.99 for a 5-card pack and a retail SRP of $3.99 for a 3-card pack. The product is also known as Prive Stock Titanium. Hobby packs featured a memorabilia card in every pack. The set also boasted 50 randomly inserted Short Prints of rookies and prospects, serial numbered to just 99 in hobby packs and 199 in retail. The base cards were printed on a premium holographic foil base containing a color action player photo on a team logo background.

Card	Low	High
COMPLETE SET w/o SP's (100)	25.00	50.00
1 Paul Kariya	.40	1.00
2 Teemu Selanne	.60	1.50
3 Donald Audette	.25	.60
4 Jason Allison	.25	.60
5 Byron Dafoe	.25	.60
6 Bill Guerin	.30	.75
7 Joe Thornton	.50	1.25
8 J-P Dumont	.20	.50
9 Doug Gilmour	.40	1.00
10 Dominik Hasek	.50	1.25
11 Jarome Iginla	.30	.75
12 Marc Savard	.25	.60
13 Mike Vernon	.25	.60
14 Ron Francis	.40	1.00
15 Arturs Irbe	.25	.60
16 Tony Amonte	.25	.60
17 Steve Sullivan	.20	.50
18 Jocelyn Thibault	.25	.60
19 Ray Bourque	.50	1.25
20 Peter Forsberg	.40	1.00
21 Milan Hejduk	.25	.60
22 Patrick Roy	.75	2.00
23 Joe Sakic	.50	1.25
24 Alex Tanguay	.25	.60
25 Geoff Sanderson	.25	.60
26 Ron Tugnutt	.25	.60
27 Ed Belfour	.30	.75
28 Brett Hull	.50	1.25
29 Mike Modano	.50	1.25
30 Joe Nieuwendyk	.30	.75
31 Sergei Fedorov	.50	1.25
32 Manny Legace	.20	.50
33 Nicklas Lidstrom	.30	.75
34 Brendan Shanahan	.40	1.00
35 Steve Yzerman	1.00	2.50
36 Tommy Salo	.25	.60
37 Ryan Smyth	.25	.60
38 Doug Weight	.30	.75
39 Pavel Bure	.40	1.00
40 Trevor Kidd	.20	.50
41 Rob Blake	.30	.75
42 Ziggy Palffy	.30	.75
43 Luc Robitaille	.30	.75
44 Jamie Storr	.25	.60
45 Manny Fernandez	.25	.60
46 Scott Pellerin	.20	.50
47 Saku Koivu	.30	.75
48 Trevor Linden	.30	.75
49 Martin Rucinsky	.20	.50
50 Jose Theodore	.40	1.00
51 David Legwand	.30	.75
52 Cliff Ronning	.20	.50
53 Jason Arnott	.25	.60
54 Martin Brodeur	.60	1.50
55 Patrik Elias	.30	.75
56 Alexander Mogilny	.25	.60
57 Tim Connolly	.20	.50
58 Mariusz Czerkawski	.20	.50
59 John Vanbiesbrouck	.25	.60
60 Theo Fleury	.40	1.00
61 Brian Leetch	.30	.75
62 Mark Messier	.50	1.25
63 Mike Richter	.30	.75
64 Radek Bonk	.25	.60
65 Marian Hossa	.25	.60
66 Patrick Lalime	.25	.60
67 Alexei Yashin	.25	.60
68 Brian Boucher	.25	.60
69 Simon Gagne	.30	.75
70 John LeClair	.30	.75
71 Eric Lindros	.50	1.25
72 Sean Burke	.20	.50
73 Jeremy Roenick	.30	.75
74 Keith Tkachuk	.30	.75
75 Jaromir Jagr	.75	2.00
76 Alexei Kovalev	.25	.60
77 Mario Lemieux	1.00	2.50
78 Garth Snow	.25	.60
79 Martin Straka	.25	.60
80 Pavol Demitra	.40	1.00
81 Chris Pronger	.25	.60
82 Roman Turek	.25	.60
83 Pierre Turgeon	.30	.75
84 Vincent Damphousse	.25	.60
85 Patrick Marleau	.30	.75
86 Owen Nolan	.30	.75
87 Steve Shields	.20	.50
88 Mike Johnson	.20	.50
89 Vincent Lecavalier	.25	.60
90 Sergei Berezin	.20	.50
91 Curtis Joseph	.40	1.00
92 Gary Roberts	.20	.50
93 Mats Sundin	.30	.75
94 Andrew Cassels	.20	.50
95 Brendan Morrison	.30	.75
96 Markus Naslund	.25	.60
97 Felix Potvin	.50	1.25
98 Peter Bondra	.25	.60
99 Olaf Kolzig	.30	.75
100 Adam Oates	.30	.75
101 Samuel Pahlsson SP	6.00	15.00
102 Scott Fankhouser SP	6.00	15.00
103 Tomi Kallio SP	6.00	15.00
104 Brad Tapper SP RC	6.00	15.00
105 Andrew Raycroft SP RC	10.00	25.00
106 Denis Hamel SP	6.00	15.00
107 Jeff Cowan SP RC	6.00	15.00
108 Oleg Saprykin SP	6.00	15.00
109 Josef Vasicek SP RC	15.00	40.00
110 Shane Willis SP	6.00	15.00
111 David Aebischer SP RC	12.00	30.00
112 Serge Aubin SP RC	8.00	20.00
113 Marc Denis SP	8.00	20.00
114 Chris Nielsen SP RC	6.00	15.00
115 David Vyborny SP	6.00	15.00
116 Marty Turco SP RC	15.00	40.00
117 Mike Comrie SP RC	15.00	40.00
118 Shawn Horcoff SP RC	12.00	30.00
119 Dominic Pittis SP	6.00	15.00
120 Roberto Luongo SP	15.00	40.00
121 Ivan Novoseltsev SP	6.00	15.00
122 Serge Payer SP	6.00	15.00
123 Denis Shvidki SP	6.00	15.00
124 Steven Reinprecht SP RC	10.00	25.00
125 Lubomir Visnovsky SP RC	12.00	30.00
126 Marian Gaborik SP RC	40.00	100.00
127 Filip Kuba SP	6.00	15.00
128 Mathieu Garon SP	6.00	15.00
129 Eric Landry SP RC	6.00	15.00
130 Andrei Markov SP	12.00	30.00
131 Marian Cisar SP	6.00	15.00
132 Scott Hartnell SP RC	15.00	40.00
133 Rick DiPietro SP RC	25.00	60.00
134 Martin Havlat SP RC	20.00	50.00
135 Jani Hurme SP RC	6.00	15.00
136 Petr Schastlivy SP	6.00	15.00
137 Ruslan Fedotenko SP RC	6.00	15.00
138 Justin Williams SP RC	15.00	40.00
139 Robert Esche SP	6.00	15.00
140 Milan Kraft SP	6.00	15.00
141 Brent Johnson SP	8.00	20.00
142 Reed Low SP RC	6.00	15.00
143 Evgeni Nabokov SP	8.00	20.00
144 Alexander Kharitonov SP RC	6.00	15.00
145 Dieter Kochan SP RC	6.00	15.00
146 Brad Richards SP	10.00	25.00
147 Adam Mair SP	6.00	15.00
148 Daniel Sedin SP	20.00	50.00
149 Henrik Sedin SP	15.00	40.00
150 Trent Whitfield SP	6.00	15.00

2000-01 Titanium Blue

This 100-card set paralleled the Pacific Private Stock Titanium base set. The cards had a blue tone and were serial numbered to the depicted player's jersey number.

*VETS/60-97: 5X TO 12X BASIC CARDS
*VETS/30-45: 8X TO 20X BASIC CARDS
*VETS/15-29: 10X TO 25X BASIC CARDS

2000-01 Titanium Gold

This 100-card set paralleled the Pacific Private Stock Titanium base set. The cards had a gold tone and were serial numbered to 99. They were available in random hobby packs only.

*GOLD/99: 5X TO 12X BASIC CARDS

Card	Low	High
62 Mark Messier	8.00	20.00

2000-01 Titanium Premiere Date

Inserted at a rate of 1 per hobby box, this 100-card set paralleled the Pacific Private Stock Titanium base set. The cards were serial numbered to 185.

*PREM.DATE/185: 4X TO 10X BASIC CARDS

2000-01 Titanium Red

This 100-card set paralleled the Pacific Private Stock Titanium base set. The cards had a red tone and were serial numbered to 299. They were available in random retail packs only.

*RED/299: 3X TO 8X BASIC CARDS

Card	Low	High
62 Mark Messier	5.00	12.00

2000-01 Titanium Retail

Released through retail channels, this 150-card set is the same as the hobby set in most ways. The base cards were printed on a premium holographic foil base containing a color action player photo on a team logo background. SP's were serial numbered out of 199.

*1-100 VETS: .4X TO 1X HOBBY
*101-150 ROOK/SP/199: .25X TO .6X SP/99

Card	Low	High
62 Mark Messier	.60	1.50

2000-01 Titanium All-Stars

Randomly inserted and serial-numbered to 1000, this die-cut set actually represents two different sets of all-star players. All-stars from the North American team and from the World team are featured. Card numbers do not carry a NA or W prefix, but it is added below for checklisting purposes.

Card	Low	High
COMPLETE SET (20)	50.00	100.00
1W Dominik Hasek	2.50	6.00
1NA Paul Kariya	1.25	3.00
2W Peter Forsberg	3.00	8.00
2NA Bill Guerin	1.00	2.50
3W Sergei Fedorov	2.50	6.00
3NA Ray Bourque	2.50	6.00
4W Nicklas Lidstrom	1.25	3.00
4NA Patrick Roy	6.00	15.00
5W Pavel Bure	1.50	4.00
5NA Joe Sakic	2.50	6.00
6W Ziggy Palffy	1.00	2.50
6NA Brett Hull	1.50	4.00
7W Marian Hossa	1.25	3.00
7NA Martin Brodeur	4.00	10.00
8W Evgeni Nabokov	2.50	6.00
8NA Theo Fleury	1.00	2.50
9W Mats Sundin	1.25	3.00
9NA Mario Lemieux	6.00	15.00
10A North-American Team/100	8.00	20.00
10W World Team/100	8.00	20.00

2000-01 Titanium Game Gear

Inserted at a rate of 1:1 hobby and 1:49 retail, these cards feature game-used swatches of jerseys or sticks. Cards 1-50 were stick cards and 51-150 were jersey cards. Each stick card is serial numbered and the total is listed beside the player's name below. Cards 152-155 are dual player cards and carry two swatches of jersey. Dual player cards are serial numbered out of 100.

1-50 STICK PRINT RUN 193-255
*PATCH/250-450: .8X TO 2X BASIC JSY
*PATCH/50-200: 1X TO 2.5X BASIC JSY

Card	Low	High
1 Phil Housley/212	6.00	15.00
2 Martin Gelinas/255	6.00	12.00
3 Sami Kapanen/246	6.00	15.00
4 Sandis Ozolinsh/244	6.00	15.00
5 Tony Amonte/251	6.00	15.00
6 Alexei Zhamnov/206	6.00	15.00
7 Peter Forsberg/235	8.00	20.00
8 Patrick Roy/255	15.00	40.00
9 Joe Sakic/224	12.00	30.00
10 Stephane Yelle/253	6.00	12.00
11 Marc Denis/253	6.00	12.00
12 Kevin Dineen/248	5.00	12.00
13 Ron Tugnutt/253	6.00	15.00
14 Ted Donato/247	6.00	12.00
15 Brett Hull/224	10.00	25.00
16 Chris Chelios/252	8.00	20.00
17 Steve Yzerman/212	20.00	50.00
18 Olli Jokinen/249	6.00	15.00
19 Rob Blake/253	6.00	15.00
20 Rob Blake/251	6.00	15.00
21 Nelson Emerson/193	6.00	12.00
22 Ziggy Palffy/252	6.00	15.00
23 Zigmund Palffy	6.00	15.00
24 Bryan Smolinski/213	5.00	12.00
25 Jozef Stumpel/252	6.00	12.00
26 Jeff Hackett/245	6.00	12.00
27 Trevor Linden/246	8.00	20.00
28 Trevor Linden/247	6.00	20.00
29 Eric Weinrich/252	5.00	12.00
30 Alexander Mogilny/251	6.00	15.00
31 Mariusz Czerkawski/251	6.00	12.00
32 Radek Dvorak/205	6.00	15.00
33 Theo Fleury/203	6.00	20.00
34 Adam Graves/242	6.00	15.00
35 Valeri Kamensky/237	6.00	15.00
36 Brian Leetch/206	6.00	15.00
37 Sandy McCarthy/214	6.00	15.00
38 Kirk McLean/254	8.00	20.00
39 Kirk McLean/251	8.00	20.00

40 Petr Nedved/253 6.00 15.00
41 Daniel Alfredsson/251 6.00 15.00
42 John LeClair/248 8.00 20.00
43 Teppo Numminen/254 6.00 12.00
44 Mario Lemieux/254 15.00 40.00
45 Roman Turek/255 6.00 15.00
46 Yanic Perreault/245 6.00 12.00
47 Gary Roberts/211 6.00 15.00
48 Andrew Cassels/254 6.00 12.00
49 Felix Potvin/254 10.00 25.00
50 Steve Konowalchuk/243 6.00 12.00
51 Guy Hebert 3.00 8.00
52 Guy Hebert 3.00 8.00
53 Mike Leclerc 2.50 6.00
54 Teemu Selanne 6.00 15.00
55 Per Johan Axelsson 2.50 6.00
56 Byron Dafoe 2.50 6.00
57 Andre Savage 2.50 6.00
58 Stu Barnes 2.50 6.00
59 Dominik Hasek 8.00 20.00
60 Erik Rasmussen 2.50 6.00
61 Rob Ray 2.50 6.00
62 Richard Smehlik 2.50 6.00
63 Alexei Zhitnik 3.00 8.00
64 Fred Brathwaite 2.50 6.00
65 Valeri Bure 2.50 6.00
66 Rico Fata 2.50 6.00
67 Phil Housley 3.00 8.00
68 Jarome Iginla 5.00 12.00
69 Marc Savard 3.00 8.00
70 Jeff Shantz 2.50 6.00
71 Cory Stillman 2.50 6.00
72 Boris Mironov 2.50 6.00
73 Alexei Zhamnov 3.00 8.00
74 Peter Forsberg 4.00 10.00
75 Jon Klemm 2.50 6.00
76 Aaron Miller 2.50 6.00
77 Dave Reid 2.50 6.00
78 Patrick Roy 12.00 30.00
79 Joe Sakic 8.00 20.00
80 Lyle Odelein 2.50 6.00
81 Ed Belfour 4.00 10.00
82 Derian Hatcher 2.50 6.00
83 Benoit Hogue 2.50 6.00
84 Brett Hull 5.00 12.00
85 Mike Keane 2.50 6.00
86 Jamie Langenbrunner 2.50 6.00
87 Jere Lehtinen 2.50 6.00
88 Grant Marshall 2.50 6.00
89 Mike Modano 5.00 12.00
90 Joe Nieuwendyk 3.00 8.00
91 Blake Sloan 2.50 6.00
92 Darryl Sydor 2.50 6.00
93 Sergei Zubov 2.50 6.00
94 Chris Chelios 4.00 10.00
95 Mathieu Dandenault 4.00 10.00
96 Chris Osgood 4.00 10.00
97 Brendan Shanahan 4.00 10.00
98 Steve Yzerman 10.00 25.00
99 Robert Svehla 2.50 6.00
100 Benoit Brunet 2.50 6.00
101 Eric Weinrich 2.50 6.00
102 Sergei Zholtok 4.00 10.00
103 Patric Kjellberg 2.50 6.00
104 David Legwand 3.00 8.00
105 Martin Brodeur 12.50 30.00
106 Scott Niedermayer 3.00 8.00
107 Chris Terreri 2.50 6.00
108 Mariusz Czerkawski 2.50 6.00
109 Wade Flaherty 2.50 6.00
110 Kenny Jonsson 2.50 6.00
111 Theo Fleury 4.00 10.00
112 Theo Fleury 4.00 10.00
113 Adam Graves 3.00 8.00
114 Brian Leetch 3.00 8.00
115 Sylvain Lefebvre 2.50 6.00
116 Manny Malhotra 2.50 6.00
117 Petr Nedved 2.50 6.00
118 Mike Richter 4.00 10.00
119 Daniel Alfredsson 3.00 8.00
120 Alexei Yashin 3.00 8.00
121 Eric Desjardins 2.50 6.00
122 John LeClair 4.00 10.00
123 Mika Alatalo 2.50 6.00
124 Sean Burke 2.50 6.00
125 Shane Doan 2.50 6.00
126 Nikolai Khabibulin 4.00 10.00
127 Jyrki Lumme 2.50 6.00
128 Teppo Numminen 2.50 6.00
129 Jeremy Roenick 5.00 12.00
130 Jean-Sebastien Aubin 4.00 10.00
131 Rene Corbet 2.50 6.00
132 Jan Hrdina 2.50 6.00
133 Jaromir Jagr 6.00 15.00
134 Darius Kasparaitis 2.50 6.00
135 Alexei Kovalev 3.00 8.00
136 Robert Lang 2.50 6.00
137 Alexei Morozov 2.50 6.00
138 Rich Parent 2.50 6.00
139 Wayne Primeau 2.50 6.00
140 Michal Rozsival 2.50 6.00
141 Kevin Stevens 2.50 6.00
142 Martin Straka 2.50 6.00
143 Matthew Barnaby 2.50 6.00
144 Tie Domi 2.50 6.00
145 Glenn Healy 2.50 6.00
146 Curtis Joseph 4.00 10.00
147 Dimitri Yushkevich 2.50 6.00
148 Dan Cloutier 2.50 6.00
149 Felix Potvin 5.00 12.00
150 Olaf Kolzig 3.00 8.00
151 Mario Lemieux/100 30.00 80.00
152 M.Lemieux/J.Jagr/100 100.00 200.00
153 P.Forsberg/J.Sakic/100 20.00 50.00
154 B.Hull/M.Modano/100 25.00 60.00
155 Kovalev/Straka/100 15.00 40.00

2000-01 Titanium Three-Star Selections

Randomly inserted in packs, these cards highlight some of the top rookies, stars and goalies in the league. Cards 1-10 feature goalies and were numbered out of 1400. Cards 11-20 feature veteran stars and were numbered out of 1100. Cards 21-30 feature star rookies and are numbered to just 750.

COMPLETE SET (30) 40.00 80.00
1 Dominik Hasek 1.25 3.00
2 Patrick Roy 3.00 8.00
3 Ed Belfour .75 2.00
4 Martin Brodeur 1.50 4.00
5 Mike Richter .75 2.00
6 Brian Boucher .60 1.50
7 Roman Turek .60 1.50
8 Curtis Joseph .75 2.00
9 Felix Potvin 1.50 4.00
10 Olaf Kolzig .60 1.50
11 Paul Kariya .75 2.00
12 Joe Sakic 1.50 4.00
13 Mike Modano 1.25 3.00
14 Sergei Fedorov 1.25 3.00
15 Ziggy Palffy .60 1.50
16 Theo Fleury .60 1.50
17 Jaromir Jagr 1.25 3.00
18 Mario Lemieux 5.00 12.00
19 Vincent Lecavalier .75 2.00
20 Mats Sundin .75 2.00
21 Shane Willis 1.50 4.00
22 Steven Reinprecht 2.00 5.00
23 Marian Gaborik 6.00 15.00
24 Rick DiPietro 5.00 12.00
25 Martin Havlat 6.00 15.00
26 Brent Johnson 1.25 3.00
27 Evgeni Nabokov 4.00 10.00
28 Brad Richards 2.00 5.00
29 Daniel Sedin 2.00 5.00
30 Henrik Sedin 2.00 5.00

2001-02 Titanium

Released in early April 2002, this set consisted of 144 base cards and 40 rookies short printed to the particular player's jersey number. Each card featured a full color action photo on a mirrored card front with a hologram image of the player in the background. Card backs carry individual stats and a short bio.

COMP.SET w/o SP's (144) 15.00 40.00
1 Jeff Friesen .20 .50
2 Jean-Sebastien Giguere .25 .60
3 Paul Kariya .40 1.00
4 Dany Heatley .30 .75
5 Milan Hnilicka .25 .60
6 Patrik Stefan .25 .60
7 Byron Dafoe .25 .60
8 Bill Guerin .30 .75
9 Brian Rolston .25 .60
10 Sergei Samsonov .25 .60
11 Joe Thornton .40 1.00
12 Stu Barnes .25 .60
13 Martin Biron .25 .60
14 Tim Connolly .20 .50
15 J-P Dumont .20 .50
16 Miroslav Satan .25 .60
17 Craig Conroy .20 .50
18 Jarome Iginla .30 .75
19 Dean McAmmond .20 .50
20 Derek Morris .20 .50
21 Marc Savard .20 .50
22 Roman Turek .25 .60
23 Tom Barrasso .25 .60
24 Ron Francis .40 1.00
25 Arturs Irbe .25 .60
26 Sami Kapanen .20 .50
27 Jeff O'Neill .20 .50
28 Tony Amonte .25 .60
29 Mark Bell .20 .50
30 Kyle Calder .20 .50
31 Eric Daze .25 .60
32 Jocelyn Thibault .25 .60
33 Alexei Zhamnov .25 .60
34 Rob Blake .30 .75
35 Milan Hejduk .25 .60
36 Patrick Roy .75 2.00
37 Joe Sakic .50 1.25
38 Radim Vrbata .20 .50
39 Marc Denis .25 .60
40 Rostislav Klesla .20 .50
41 Ron Tugnutt .25 .60
42 Ray Whitney .20 .50
43 Ed Belfour .30 .75
44 Jere Lehtinen .25 .60
45 Mike Modano .50 1.25
46 Joe Nieuwendyk .30 .75
47 Pierre Turgeon .30 .75
48 Sergei Fedorov .50 1.25
49 Dominik Hasek .50 1.25
50 Brett Hull .40 1.00
51 Nicklas Lidstrom .30 .75
52 Luc Robitaille .30 .75
53 Brendan Shanahan .40 1.00
54 Steve Yzerman 1.00 2.50
55 Anson Carter .25 .60
56 Mike Comrie .25 .60
57 Tommy Salo .25 .60
58 Ryan Smyth .25 .60
59 Pavel Bure .40 1.00
60 Viktor Kozlov .20 .50
61 Roberto Luongo .50 1.25
62 Marcus Nilsson .20 .50
63 Jason Allison .25 .60
64 Adam Deadmarsh .25 .60
65 Steve Heinze .20 .50
66 Zigmund Palffy .30 .75
67 Felix Potvin .50 1.25
68 Andrew Brunette .20 .50
69 Jim Dowd .20 .50
70 Marian Gaborik .50 1.25
71 Dwayne Roloson .25 .60
72 Doug Gilmour .40 1.00
73 Yanic Perreault .20 .50
74 Mike Ribeiro .25 .60
75 Brian Savage .20 .50
76 Jose Theodore .30 .75
77 Mike Dunham .25 .60
78 Scott Hartnell .30 .75
79 David Legwand .25 .60
80 Cliff Ronning .20 .50
81 Jason Arnott .25 .60
82 Martin Brodeur .60 1.50
83 J-F Damphousse .20 .50
84 Patrik Elias .30 .75
85 Scott Stevens .30 .75
86 Mariusz Czerkawski .20 .50
87 Rick DiPietro .25 .60
88 Chris Osgood .30 .75
89 Mark Parrish .20 .50
90 Michael Peca .25 .60
91 Alexei Yashin .25 .60
92 Theo Fleury .40 1.00
93 Brian Leetch .30 .75
94 Eric Lindros .50 1.25
95 Mark Messier .50 1.25
96 Mike Richter .30 .75
97 Mike York .20 .50
98 Daniel Alfredsson .30 .75
99 Martin Havlat .25 .60
100 Marian Hossa .25 .60
101 Patrick Lalime .25 .60
102 Todd White .20 .50
103 Roman Cechmanek .25 .60
104 Simon Gagne .30 .75
105 John LeClair .30 .75
106 Mark Recchi .40 1.00
107 Jeremy Roenick .30 .75
108 Sean Burke .20 .50
109 Daymond Langkow .25 .60
110 Claude Lemieux .25 .60
111 Johan Hedberg .25 .60
112 Alexei Kovalev .25 .60
113 Robert Lang .20 .50
114 Mario Lemieux 1.00 2.50
115 Pavol Demitra .40 1.00
116 Brent Johnson .25 .60
117 Al MacInnis .30 .75
118 Chris Pronger .25 .60
119 Keith Tkachuk .30 .75
120 Doug Weight .30 .75
121 Vincent Damphousse .25 .60
122 Evgeni Nabokov .25 .60
123 Owen Nolan .30 .75
124 Teemu Selanne .60 1.50
125 Nikolai Khabibulin .30 .75
126 Vincent Lecavalier .25 .60
127 Brad Richards .30 .75
128 Martin St. Louis .30 .75
129 Curtis Joseph .30 .75
130 Alexander Mogilny .25 .60
131 Gary Roberts .20 .50
132 Mats Sundin .30 .75
133 Darcy Tucker .20 .50
134 Todd Bertuzzi .30 .75
135 Dan Cloutier .25 .60
136 Brendan Morrison .25 .60
137 Markus Naslund .30 .75
138 Daniel Sedin .30 .75
139 Henrik Sedin .30 .75
140 Peter Bondra .30 .75
141 Sergei Gonchar .20 .50
142 Jaromir Jagr .75 2.00
143 Olaf Kolzig .30 .75
144 Adam Oates .30 .75
145 Ilja Bryzgalov/30 RC 30.00 80.00
146 Timo Parssinen/29 RC 20.00 50.00
147 Ilya Kovalchuk/17 RC 150.00 250.00
148 Kamil Piros/25 RC 15.00 40.00
149 Brian Pothier/3 RC
150 Andy Hilbert/29 RC 15.00 40.00
151 Jukka Hentunen/24 RC 15.00 40.00
152 Erik Cole/26 RC 30.00 80.00
153 Vaclav Nedorost/22 RC 15.00 40.00
154 John Erskine/3 RC
155 Niko Kapanen/39 RC 20.00 50.00
156 Pavel Datsyuk/13 RC
157 Jason Chimera/28 RC 15.00 40.00
158 Ty Conklin/1 RC
159 Jussi Markkanen/30 RC 12.00 30.00
160 Niklas Hagman/14 RC
161 Kristian Huselius/22 RC 25.00 60.00
162 Jaroslav Bednar/7 RC
163 David Cullen/24 RC 15.00 40.00
164 Pascal Dupuis/11 RC
165 Nick Schultz/55 RC 10.00 25.00
166 Martin Erat/19 RC 25.00 60.00
167 Brian Gionta/14 RC
168 Andreas Salomonsson/15 RC 15.00 40.00
169 Radek Martinek/24 RC 15.00 40.00
170 Raffi Torres/16 RC 25.00 60.00
171 Dan Blackburn/31 RC 15.00 40.00
172 Mikael Samuelsson/37 RC 15.00 40.00
173 Chris Neil/25 RC 20.00 50.00
174 Jiri Dopita/20 RC 15.00 40.00
175 Bruno St. Jacques/42 RC 12.00 30.00
176 Krystofer Kolanos/36 RC 12.00 30.00
177 Josef Melichar/2 RC
178 Billy Tibbetts/12 RC
179 Mark Rycroft/42 RC 15.00 40.00
180 Jeff Jillson/5 RC
181 Nikita Alexeev/15 RC 15.00 40.00
182 Brad Leeb/38 RC 15.00 40.00
183 Chris Corrinet/48 RC 10.00 25.00
184 Brian Sutherby/41 RC 12.00 30.00

2001-02 Titanium Hobby Red

This 144-card set directly paralleled the base hobby set with red foil highlights. Each card was also serial numbered out of 94 on the card front.
*RED/94: 5X TO 12X BASIC HOBBY

2001-02 Titanium Premiere Date

This 144-card set was a parallel to the base set but carried a Premiere Date stamp on the card fronts. Each card was serial numbered out of 94, and these cards were available in hobby packs only at a rate of 1:7.
*VETS/94: 5X TO 12X BASIC HOBBY

2001-02 Titanium Retail

This 184-card set resembles the hobby version, but the card stock was slightly thicker and the mirrored effect on the hobby card fronts was removed for this version. Rookies in the retail version were serial-numbered out of 534.
*1-144 VETS: .4X TO 1X HOBBY
145 Ilja Bryzgalov RC 6.00 15.00
146 Timo Parssinen RC 3.00 8.00
147 Ilya Kovalchuk RC 15.00 40.00
148 Kamil Piros RC 2.50 6.00
149 Brian Pothier RC 2.50 6.00
150 Andy Hilbert SP 2.50 6.00
151 Jukka Hentunen RC 2.50 6.00
152 Erik Cole RC 5.00 12.00
153 Vaclav Nedorost RC 2.50 6.00
154 John Erskine RC 2.50 6.00
155 Niko Kapanen RC 4.00 10.00
156 Pavel Datsyuk RC 15.00 40.00
157 Jason Chimera RC 2.50 6.00
158 Ty Conklin RC 4.00 10.00
159 Jussi Markkanen SP 2.50 6.00
160 Niklas Hagman RC 3.00 8.00
161 Kristian Huselius RC 4.00 10.00
162 Jaroslav Bednar RC 2.50 6.00
163 David Cullen RC 2.50 6.00
164 Pascal Dupuis RC 4.00 10.00
165 Nick Schultz RC 2.50 6.00
166 Martin Erat RC 4.00 10.00
167 Brian Gionta SP 3.00 8.00
168 Andreas Salomonsson RC 2.50 6.00
169 Radek Martinek RC 2.50 6.00
170 Raffi Torres RC 4.00 10.00
171 Dan Blackburn RC 3.00 8.00
172 Mikael Samuelsson RC 3.00 8.00
173 Chris Neil RC 3.00 8.00
174 Jiri Dopita RC 2.50 6.00
175 Bruno St. Jacques RC 2.50 6.00
176 Krystofer Kolanos RC 2.50 6.00
177 Josef Melichar SP 2.50 6.00
178 Billy Tibbetts RC 2.50 6.00
179 Mark Rycroft RC 3.00 8.00
180 Jeff Jillson RC 2.50 6.00
181 Nikita Alexeev RC 2.50 6.00
182 Brad Leeb SP 3.00 8.00
183 Chris Corrinet RC 2.50 6.00
184 Brian Sutherby RC 2.50 6.00

2001-02 Titanium Retail Red

This 144-card set directly paralleled the base retail set with red foil highlights. Each card was also serial numbered out of 131 on the card front.
*RED/131: 4X TO 10X BASIC HOBBY

2001-02 Titanium All-Stars

Inserted at a rate of 1:7 hobby and 1:25 retail packs, this 20 card set featured players chosen for the 2002 NHL All-Star Game. The cards carried a photo of the given player on the front alongside a bronze foil logo from the game.

COMPLETE SET (20) 12.00 30.00
1 Joe Thornton 1.00 2.50
2 Jarome Iginla .75 2.00
3 Sami Kapanen .50 1.25
4 Eric Daze .50 1.25
5 Rob Blake .50 1.25
6 Patrick Roy 3.00 8.00
7 Dominik Hasek 1.25 3.00
8 Sergei Fedorov 1.25 3.00
9 Nicklas Lidstrom .60 1.50
10 Brendan Shanahan 1.00 2.50
11 Zigmund Palffy .50 1.25
12 Jose Theodore .75 2.00
13 Patrik Elias .50 1.25
14 Alexei Yashin .50 1.25
15 Chris Pronger .50 1.25
16 Owen Nolan .50 1.25
17 Teemu Selanne .60 1.50
18 Nikolai Khabibulin .60 1.50
19 Mats Sundin .60 1.50
20 Jaromir Jagr 1.00 2.50

2001-02 Titanium Double-Sided Jerseys

Inserted at one per hobby pack and 1:25 retail, this 75-card set featured game-worn jersey swatches of two players; one on front and one on back alongside color photos of the given player.

1 S.Rucchin/P.Kariya 4.00 10.00
2 J.Friesen/O.Tverdovsky 2.50 6.00
3 S.Samsonov/B.Guerin 4.00 10.00
4 J.Dumont/A.Zhitnik 2.50 6.00
5 M.Savard/R.Turek 2.50 6.00
6 R.Turek/B.Boughner 2.50 6.00
7 J.Iginla/M.Savard 4.00 10.00
8 T.Amonte/B.Mironov 2.50 6.00
9 K.Calder/M.Nylander 2.50 6.00
10 A.Zhamnov/S.Sullivan 2.50 6.00
11 M.Hejduk/C.Drury 3.00 8.00
12 J.Sakic/A.Tanguay 5.00 12.00
13 P.Roy/R.Blake 15.00 40.00
14 A.Tanguay/V.Nedorost 3.00 8.00
15 L.Odelein/J.McLennan 2.50 6.00
16 M.Modano/J.Langenbrunner 4.00 10.00
17 F.Potvin/Z.Palffy 4.00 10.00
18 A.Deadmarsh/B.Smolinski 2.50 6.00
19 R.Blake/A.Miller 2.50 6.00
20 J.Theodore/F.Potvin 3.00 8.00
21 J.Dumont/S.Stevens 2.50 6.00
22 C.Ronning/T.Fitzgerald 2.50 6.00
23 I.Kovalchuk/D.Heatley 10.00 25.00
24 E.Daze/M.Bell 2.50 6.00
25 E.Lindros/T.Fleury 4.00 10.00
26 B.Leetch/R.Fata 2.50 6.00
27 E.Lindros/M.Messier 6.00 15.00
28 M.York/T.Fleury 2.50 6.00
29 M.Richter/B.Leetch 4.00 10.00
30 D.Alfredsson/M.Sundin 6.00 15.00
31 P.Brendl/J.Hrdina 2.50 6.00
32 M.Lemieux/A.Morozov 15.00 40.00
33 P.Brendl/J.Beranek 2.50 6.00
34 M.Straka/M.Rozsival 2.50 6.00
35 J.Hrdina/I.Moran 2.50 6.00
36 A.Kovalev/R.Parent 2.50 6.00
37 M.Eastwood/F.Brathwaite 2.50 6.00
38 S.Young/J.Hecht 2.50 6.00
39 T.Selanne/I.Kovalchuk STK 15.00 40.00
40 V.Lecavalier/P.Svoboda 4.00 10.00
41 C.Joseph/G.Healy 4.00 10.00
42 M.Sundin/J.Sakic 8.00 20.00
43 J.Jagr/D.Zubrus 6.00 15.00
44 T.Barrasso/A.Irbe 4.00 10.00
45 R.Francis/J.O'Neill 2.50 6.00
46 R.Brind'mour/E.Cole 4.00 10.00
47 M.Havlat/M.Hossa 4.00 10.00
48 D.Alfredsson/P.Lalime 4.00 10.00
49 J.Dopita/R.Cechmanek 2.50 6.00
50 J.Roenick/J.LeClair 4.00 10.00
51 S.Gagne/J.LeClair 4.00 10.00
52 M.Modano/P.Turgeon 5.00 12.00
53 M.Turco/E.Belfour 4.00 10.00
54 H.Sedin/D.Sedin 4.00 10.00
55 T.Bertuzzi/B.Morrison 3.00 8.00
56 M.Naslund/D.Cloutier 4.00 10.00
57 B.Morrison/M.Turco 3.00 8.00
58 M.Naslund/D.Alfredsson 4.00 10.00
59 J.Roenick/T.Barrasso 4.00 10.00
60 M.Havlat/R.Cechmanek 2.50 6.00
61 R.Francis/A.Irbe 4.00 10.00
62 J.O'Neill/E.Cole 2.50 6.00
63 M.Hossa/J.Dopita 2.50 6.00
64 P.Lalime/S.Gagne 4.00 10.00
65 E.Belfour/P.Turgeon 5.00 12.00
66 M.Biron/M.Satan 3.00 8.00
67 M.Gaborik/M.Fernandez 6.00 15.00
68 M.Brodeur/J.Arnott 8.00 20.00
69 P.Elias/S.Gomez 3.00 8.00
70 J.McLennan/F.Kuba 2.50 6.00
71 K.Kolanos/D.Langkow 2.50 6.00
72 M.Handzus/S.Berezin 2.50 6.00
73 S.Sullivan/M.Bell 2.50 6.00
74 J.Thornton/B.Guerin 6.00 15.00
75 J.Allison/Z.Palffy 2.50 6.00

2001-02 Titanium Double-Sided Patches

This 55-card set partially paralleled the jersey set but featured game-worn jersey patch swatches. Individual print runs are listed below.

1 S.Rucchin/P.Kariya/56 10.00 25.00
2 J.Friesen/O.Tverdovsky/213 10.00 25.00
3 S.Samsonov/B.Guerin/215 10.00 25.00
4 J.Dumont/A. Zhitnik/181 10.00 25.00
9 K.Calder/M.Nylander/46 10.00 25.00
11 M.Hejduk/C.Drury/219 8.00 20.00
12 J.Sakic/A.Tanguay/259 12.00 30.00
13 P.Roy/R.Blake/39 30.00 80.00
14 A.Tanguay/V.Nedorost/117 10.00 25.00
16 M.Modano/J.Langenbrunner/19 12.00 30.00
17 F.Potvin/Z.Palffy/174 20.00 50.00
18 A.Deadmarsh/B.Smolinski/163 10.00 25.00
20 J.Theodore/F.Potvin/94 12.00 30.00
21 J.Dumont/S.Stevens/255 10.00 25.00
24 E.Daze/M.Bell/116 10.00 25.00
25 E.Lindros/T.Fleury/288 12.00 30.00
26 B.Leetch/R.Fata/198 10.00 25.00
27 E.Lindros/M.Messier/166 20.00 50.00
29 M.Richter/B.Leetch/104 12.50 30.00
30 D.Alfredsson/M.Sundin/63 10.00 25.00
33 P.Brendl/J.Beranek/39 10.00 25.00
34 M.Straka/M.Rozsival/302 10.00 25.00
35 J.Hrdina/I.Moran/88 10.00 25.00
38 S.Young/J.Hecht/62 10.00 25.00
40 V.Lecavalier/P.Svoboda/45 10.00 25.00
41 C.Joseph/G.Healy/140 10.00 25.00
42 M.Sundin/J.Sakic/53 25.00 60.00
43 J.Jagr/D.Zubrus/56 15.00 40.00
44 T.Barrasso/A.Irbe/199 10.00 25.00
45 R.Francis/J.O'Neill/194 10.00 25.00
46 R.Brind'mour/E.Cole/215 12.00 30.00
47 M.Havlat/M.Hossa/118 12.00 30.00
48 D.Alfredsson/P.Lalime/114 12.00 30.00
49 J.Dopita/R.Cechmanek/202 10.00 25.00
50 J.Roenick/J.LeClair/216 10.00 25.00
51 S.Gagne/J.LeClair/169 10.00 25.00
52 M.Modano/P.Turgeon/216 12.00 30.00
53 M.Turco/E.Belfour/212 10.00 25.00
54 H.Sedin/D.Sedin/218 10.00 25.00
55 T.Bertuzzi/B.Morrison/215 10.00 25.00
56 M.Naslund/D.Cloutier/164 10.00 25.00
57 B.Morrison/M.Turco/119 10.00 25.00
58 M.Naslund
D.Alfredsson/164 10.00 25.00
59 J.Roenick/T.Barrasso/113 10.00 25.00
60 M.Havlat/R.Cechmanek/109 10.00 25.00
61 R.Francis/A.Irbe/154 12.00 30.00
62 J.O'Neill/E.Cole/163 12.00 30.00
63 M.Hossa/J.Dopita/166 10.00 25.00
64 P.Lalime/S.Gagne/163 10.00 25.00
65 E.Belfour/P.Turgeon/165 10.00 25.00
66 M.Biron/M.Satan/256 8.00 20.00
67 M.Gaborik/M.Fernandez/104 15.00 40.00
69 P.Elias/S.Gomez/260 8.00 20.00
70 J.McLennan/F.Kuba/569 10.00 25.00
71 K.Kolanos/D.Langkow/116 10.00 25.00
72 M.Handzus/S.Berezin/260 10.00 25.00
73 S.Sullivan/M.Bell/264 10.00 25.00
75 J.Allison/Z.Palffy/106 10.00 25.00

2001-02 Titanium Rookie Team

This ten card set was inserted in hobby packs at 1:121 and each card was serial-numbered out of 70. Each card featured a player from the year's rookie class with both an action photo and a head shot.

1 Dany Heatley 10.00 25.00
2 Ilya Kovalchuk 10.00 25.00
3 Erik Cole 8.00 20.00
4 Mark Bell 4.00 10.00
5 Radim Vrbata 2.00 5.00
6 Kristian Huselius 2.00 5.00
7 Mike Ribeiro 2.00 5.00
8 Rick DiPietro 6.00 15.00
9 Raffi Torres 4.00 10.00
10 Krystofer Kolanos 2.00 5.00

2001-02 Titanium Saturday Knights

COMPLETE SET (20) 40.00 80.00
STATED ODDS 1:25 HOBBY/1:97 RETAIL
1 Paul Kariya 1.00 2.50
2 Joe Thornton 1.50 4.00
3 Jarome Iginla 1.25 3.00
4 Ed Belfour 1.00 2.50
5 Dominik Hasek 2.00 5.00
6 Brendan Shanahan 1.50 4.00
7 Steve Yzerman 5.00 12.00
8 Mike Comrie .75 2.00
9 Pavel Bure 1.25 3.00
10 Marian Gaborik 2.00 5.00
11 Jose Theodore 1.25 3.00
12 Martin Brodeur 2.50 6.00
13 Mike Peca .75 2.00
14 Eric Lindros 1.50 4.00
15 Daniel Alfredsson .75 2.00
16 Martin Havlat .75 2.00
17 Jeremy Roenick 1.25 3.00
18 Mario Lemieux 6.00 15.00
19 Curtis Joseph 1.00 2.50
20 Mats Sundin 1.00 2.50

2001-02 Titanium Three-Star Selections

This 30-card set featured top goalies, veterans and rookies with full color action photos on the card front surrounded by gold foil highlights. Cards 1-10 were seeded at 1:7 hobby packs/1:25 retail, cards 11-20 were seeded at 1:13 hobby/1:49 retail, and cards 21-30 were seeded at 1:25 hobby/1:97 retail.

COMPLETE SET (30) 15.00 40.00
1 Roman Turek .50 1.25
2 Tom Barrasso .50 1.25
3 Patrick Roy 3.00 8.00
4 Dominik Hasek 1.25 3.00
5 Martin Brodeur 1.50 4.00
6 Chris Osgood .50 1.25
7 Mike Richter .60 1.50
8 Evgeni Nabokov .50 1.25
9 Nikolai Khabibulin .60 1.50
10 Curtis Joseph .60 1.50
11 Paul Kariya .60 1.50
12 Jarome Iginla 1.00 2.50
13 Joe Sakic 1.50 4.00
14 Brendan Shanahan .60 1.50
15 Steve Yzerman 4.00 10.00
16 Eric Lindros .60 1.50
17 Mike York .50 1.25
18 Mario Lemieux 5.00 12.00
19 Mats Sundin .75 2.00
20 Jaromir Jagr 1.00 2.50
21 Dany Heatley 4.00 10.00
22 Ilya Kovalchuk 6.00 15.00
23 Erik Cole 2.00 5.00
24 Mark Bell 1.50 4.00
25 Radim Vrbata 1.50 4.00
26 Kristian Huselius 1.50 4.00
27 Mike Ribeiro 1.50 4.00
28 Rick DiPietro 1.50 4.00
29 Raffi Torres 1.50 4.00
30 Krystofer Kolanos 1.50 4.00

2002-03 Titanium

This 140-card set consisted of 100 base veteran cards and 40 rookie cards shortprinted to 99 copies each. Cards were highlighted by gold foil.

COMP.SET w/o SP's (100) 20.00 50.00
1 Jean-Sebastien Giguere .40 1.00
2 Paul Kariya .50 1.25
3 Petr Sykora .30 .75
4 Dany Heatley .40 1.00
5 Ilya Kovalchuk .50 1.25
6 Pasi Nurminen .25 .60
7 Glen Murray .30 .75
8 Brian Rolston .30 .75
9 Steve Shields .30 .75
10 Joe Thornton .50 1.25
11 Martin Biron .30 .75
12 Chris Gratton .25 .60
13 Miroslav Satan .40 1.00
14 Chris Drury .40 1.00
15 Jarome Iginla .40 1.00
16 Roman Turek .40 1.00
17 Rod Brind'Amour .40 1.00
18 Ron Francis .50 1.25
19 Jeff O'Neill .25 .60
20 Kevin Weekes .30 .75
21 Tyler Arnason .40 1.00
22 Theo Fleury .50 1.25
23 Jocelyn Thibault .30 .75
24 Peter Forsberg .50 1.25
25 Milan Hejduk .30 .75
26 Patrick Roy 1.00 2.50
27 Joe Sakic .60 1.50
28 Andrew Cassels .25 .60
29 Marc Denis .30 .75
30 Geoff Sanderson .30 .75
31 Bill Guerin .40 1.00
32 Mike Modano .60 1.50
33 Marty Turco .40 1.00
34 Pierre Turgeon .40 1.00
35 Sergei Fedorov .60 1.50
36 Brett Hull .50 1.25
37 Curtis Joseph .40 1.00
38 Nicklas Lidstrom .40 1.00
39 Brendan Shanahan .50 1.25
40 Steve Yzerman .75 2.00
41 Anson Carter .30 .75
42 Mike Comrie .40 1.00
43 Tommy Salo .30 .75
44 Ryan Smyth .30 .75
45 Kristian Huselius .25 .60
46 Olli Jokinen .40 1.00
47 Roberto Luongo .60 1.50
48 Jason Allison .30 .75
49 Eric Belanger .25 .60
50 Ziggy Palffy .40 1.00
51 Felix Potvin .60 1.50
52 Manny Fernandez .30 .75
53 Marian Gaborik .60 1.50
54 Cliff Ronning .25 .60
55 Saku Koivu .40 1.00
56 Yanic Perreault .25 .60
57 Jose Theodore .40 1.00
58 Richard Zednik .25 .60
59 Andreas Johansson .25 .60
60 David Legwand .30 .75
61 Tomas Vokoun .30 .75
62 Martin Brodeur .75 2.00
63 Scott Gomez .30 .75
64 John Madden .25 .60
65 Rick DiPietro .30 .75
66 Michael Peca .30 .75
67 Alexei Yashin .30 .75
68 Pavel Bure .50 1.25
69 Eric Lindros .60 1.50
70 Tom Poti .25 .60
71 Daniel Alfredsson .40 1.00
72 Marian Hossa .30 .75
73 Patrick Lalime .30 .75
74 Roman Cechmanek .30 .75
75 Simon Gagne .40 1.00
76 Jeremy Roenick .40 1.00
77 Tony Amonte .30 .75
78 Brian Boucher .30 .75
79 Shane Doan .30 .75
80 Johan Hedberg .40 1.00
81 Alex Kovalev .40 1.00
82 Mario Lemieux 1.25 3.00
83 Brent Johnson .30 .75
84 Cory Stillman .25 .60
85 Doug Weight .40 1.00
86 Patrick Marleau .40 1.00
87 Evgeni Nabokov .30 .75
88 Teemu Selanne .75 2.00
89 Nikolai Khabibulin .40 1.00
90 Vincent Lecavalier .30 .75
91 Martin St. Louis .40 1.00
92 Ed Belfour .40 1.00
93 Alexander Mogilny .30 .75
94 Mats Sundin .40 1.00
95 Todd Bertuzzi .40 1.00
96 Dan Cloutier .30 .75
97 Brendan Morrison .30 .75
98 Markus Naslund .30 .75
99 Jaromir Jagr 1.00 2.50
100 Michael Nylander .25 .60
101 Stanislav Chistov RC 6.00 15.00
102 Martin Gerber RC 10.00 25.00
103 Kurt Sauer RC 6.00 15.00
104 Alexei Smirnov RC 8.00 20.00
105 Shaone Morrisonn RC 6.00 15.00
106 Tim Thomas RC 20.00 50.00
107 Ryan Miller RC 30.00 80.00
108 Chuck Kobasew RC 8.00 20.00
109 Jordan Leopold RC 10.00 25.00
110 Pascal Leclaire RC 8.00 20.00
111 Rick Nash RC 75.00 150.00
112 Steve Ott RC 12.00 30.00
113 Dmitri Bykov RC 6.00 15.00
114 Henrik Zetterberg RC 40.00 100.00
115 Ales Hemsky RC 25.00 60.00
116 Jay Bouwmeester RC 20.00 50.00
117 Michael Cammalleri RC 20.00 50.00
118 Alexander Frolov RC 12.00 30.00
119 P-M Bouchard RC 10.00 25.00
120 Stephane Veilleux RC 6.00 15.00
121 Kyle Wanvig 6.00 15.00
122 Ron Hainsey RC 6.00 15.00
123 Vernon Fiddler RC 8.00 20.00
124 Adam Hall RC 6.00 15.00
125 Scottie Upshall RC 8.00 20.00
126 Jason Spezza RC 100.00 175.00
127 Anton Volchenkov RC 6.00 15.00
128 Dennis Seidenberg RC 10.00 25.00
129 Radovan Somik RC 6.00 15.00
130 Jeff Taffe RC 6.00 15.00
131 Sebastien Caron 8.00 20.00
132 Brooks Orpik RC 10.00 25.00
133 Dick Tarnstrom RC 6.00 15.00
134 Tom Koivisto RC 6.00 15.00
135 Curtis Sanford RC 10.00 25.00
136 Lynn Loyns RC 6.00 15.00
137 Alexander Svitov RC 6.00 15.00
138 Carlo Colaiacovo RC 10.00 25.00
139 Mikael Tellqvist RC 6.00 15.00
140 Steve Eminger RC 6.00 15.00

2002-03 Titanium Blue

*1-100 VETS/450: 1X TO 2.5X BASIC CARDS
*101-140 SP/450: .1X TO .25X BASIC SP
STATED PRINT RUN 450 SER.#'d SETS

2002-03 Titanium Red

*1-100 VETS/299: 1.2X TO 3X BASIC CARDS
*101-140 SP/299: .12X TO .3X BASIC SP
STATED PRINT RUN 299 SER.#'d SETS

2002-03 Titanium Retail

These cards mirrored the hobby set but carried silver foil highlights.

COMP.SET w/o SP's (100) 20.00 50.00
*1-100 VETS: .4X TO 1X HOBBY
*101-40 SP/1475: .06X TO .15X HOB
SP PRINT RUN 1475 SER.#'d SETS

2002-03 Titanium Jerseys

Inserted one per hobby pack, this 75-card set featu swatches of game worn jerseys. Each card was individually serial-numbered. A retail variation was also created that carried silver foil in place of the go foil on the hobby version.

JERSEY PRINT RUN 150-1403
*PATCH/100-250: 1X TO 2.5X JSY/503-1403
*PATCH/100-250: .8X TO 2X JSY/253-439
*PATCH/110-225: .6X TO 1.5X JSY/253-439
*PATCH/40-85: 1.2X TO 3X JSY/561-1099
*PATCH/60-65: 1X TO 2.5X JSY/228-316
*PATCH/20-35: 1.5X TO 4X JSY/606-1307
*PATCH/15: 2X TO 5X JSY/1249
*PATCH/15: 1.5X TO 4X JSY/439
*RETAIL/99-160: .6X TO 1.5X HOB/503-1403
*RETAIL/99-160: .5X TO 1.2X HOB/253-439
1 Mike Leclerc/376 2.50 6
2 Dany Heatley/715 3.00 8
3 Ilya Kovalchuk/606 4.00 10.
4 Patrik Stefan/1183 2.50 6.
5 Joe Thornton/160 6.00 15.
6 Martin Biron/1019 2.50 6.
7 J-P Dumont/948 2.00 5.
8 Rod Brind'Amour/1231 3.00 8.
9 Arturs Irbe/829 2.50 6.
10 Jeff O'Neill/283 2.50 6.
11 Chris Drury/514 3.00 8.
12 Roman Turek/1160 3.00 8.
13 Mark Bell/957 2.00 5.
14 Sergei Berezin/304 2.50 6.
15 Steve Sullivan/641 2.00 5.
16 Rob Blake/1020 3.00 8.
17 Milan Hejduk/1160 2.50 6.
18 Patrick Roy/150 15.00 40.
19 Rostislav Klesla/1099 2.00 5.
20 Geoff Sanderson/1307 2.50 6.
21 Ron Tugnutt/1338 2.50 6.
22 Marty Turco/552 3.00 8.
23 Sergei Fedorov/561 5.00 12.
24 Dominik Hasek/253 6.00 15.
25 Brett Hull/899 4.00 10.
26 Luc Robitaille/717 3.00 8.
27 Jason Williams/1270 2.00 5.
28 Mike Comrie/503 3.00 8.
29 Tommy Salo/801 2.50 6.
30 Ryan Smyth/1052 2.50 6.
31 Valeri Bure/1352 2.50 6.
32 Kristian Huselius/1305 2.00 5.
33 Roberto Luongo/1403 5.00 12.0
34 Marian Gaborik/342 6.00 15.0
35 Yanic Perreault/1285 2.00 5.0
36 Jose Theodore/316 4.00 10.0
37 David Legwand/857 2.50 6.0
38 Scott Walker/1307 2.00 5.0
39 Scott Gomez/872 2.50 6.0
40 Scott Stevens/1273 3.00 8.0
41 Michael Peca/553 2.50 6.0
42 Alexei Yashin/743 2.50 6.0
43 Pavel Bure/908 4.00 10.0
44 Eric Lindros/583 5.00 12.0
45 Mark Messier/809 5.00 12.0
46 Daniel Alfredsson/532 3.00 8.0
47 Martin Havlat/545 2.50 6.0
48 Patrick Lalime/826 2.50 6.0
49 Simon Gagne/1028 3.00 8.0
50 Michal Handzus/636 2.50 6.0
51 Tomi Kallio/1301 2.00 5.0
52 John LeClair/942 3.00 8.0
53 Johan Hedberg/1004 3.00 8.0
54 Mario Lemieux/288 12.00 30.0
55 Toby Petersen/1320 2.00 5.0
56 Pavol Demitra/1256 4.00 10.0
57 Ray Ferraro/1288 2.50 6.0
58 Chris Pronger/1249 2.50 6.0
59 Keith Tkachuk/914 3.00 8.0
60 Sergei Varlamov/1152 2.50 6.0
61 Miikka Kiprusoff/1203 2.50 6.0
62 Patrick Marleau/730 3.00 8.0
63 Owen Nolan/439 4.00 10.0
64 Nikolai Khabibulin/1002 3.00 8.0
65 Fredrik Modin/1260 2.00 5.0
66 Alexander Mogilny/710 2.50 6.0
67 Gary Roberts/1260 2.00 5.0
68 Darcy Tucker/1260 2.00 5.0
69 Dan Cloutier/867 2.50 6.0
70 Brendan Morrison/638 2.50 6.0
71 Daniel Sedin/1105 3.00 8.0
72 Henrik Sedin/1100 3.00 8.0
73 Peter Bondra/1289 3.00 8.0
74 Jaromir Jagr/171 12.00 30.0
75 Olaf Kolzig/1303 3.00 8.0

2002-03 Titanium Saturday Knights

COMPLETE SET (10) 10.00 25.0
STATED ODDS 1:17
1 Jarome Iginla 1.00 2.5
2 Patrick Roy 3.00 8.0
3 Joe Sakic 1.50 4.0
4 Steve Yzerman 3.00 8.0
5 Jose Theodore 1.00 2.5
6 Marian Hossa .75 2.0
7 Mario Lemieux 4.00 10.0
8 Ed Belfour .75 2.0
9 Mats Sundin .75 2.0
10 Todd Bertuzzi .75 2.0

2002-03 Titanium Masked Marauders

COMPLETE SET (8) 10.00 25.0
STATED ODDS 1:25
1 Patrick Roy 3.00 8.0
2 Marty Turco 1.25 3.0
3 Curtis Joseph 1.25 3.0
4 Jose Theodore 1.50 4.0
5 Martin Brodeur 2.50 6.0
6 Nikolai Khabibulin 1.25 3.0
7 Ed Belfour 1.25 3.0
8 Dan Cloutier 1.25 3.0

2002-03 Titanium Right on Target

COMPLETE SET (20) 20.00 50.0
STATED ODDS 1:9
1 Stanislav Chistov 1.25 3.0
2 Ivan Huml .75 2.0
3 Chuck Kobasew 1.25 3.0
4 Jordan Leopold .75 2.0
5 Tyler Arnason .75 2.0
6 Rick Nash 2.50 6.0
7 Henrik Zetterberg 2.00 5.0
8 Ales Hemsky 1.50 4.0
9 Jay Bouwmeester 1.25 3.0
10 Stephen Weiss 1.25 3.0
11 Michael Cammalleri 1.25 3.0
12 Alexander Frolov 1.25 3.0
13 P-M Bouchard 1.25 3.0
14 Scottie Upshall 1.25 3.0
15 Rick DiPietro 1.50 4.0
16 Jamie Lundmark .75 2.0

7 Jason Spezza 2.00 5.00
8 Barret Jackman .75 2.00
9 Jonathan Cheechoo 1.25 3.00
0 Fedor Fedorov .75 2.00

2002-03 Titanium Shadows

COMPLETE SET (6) 30.00 60.00
STATED ODDS 1:49
Ilya Kovalchuk 1.50 4.00
Joe Thornton 1.50 4.00
Patrick Roy 6.00 15.00
Joe Sakic 2.50 6.00
Steve Yzerman 6.00 15.00
Marian Gaborik 2.00 6.00

2003-04 Titanium

This 215-card set consisted of 100 veteran cards (1-100); 40 short-printed rookie cards (101-140) serial-numbered to 99; 50 veteran jersey cards (141-190) serial-numbered out of 875 (unless noted otherwise); 15 short-printed veteran jersey cards (191-205) serial-numbered to 99 (unless otherwise noted) and 10 short-printed rookie jersey cards (individual numbers are listed below). Titanium Hobby carried gold foil highlights which distinguished it from the Retail brand.

COMP.SET w/o SP's (100) 15.00 30.00
Martin Gerber .15 .40
Steve Rucchin .15 .40
Petr Sykora .20 .50
Frantisek Kaberle .15 .40
Slava Kozlov .20 .50
Pasi Nurminen .20 .50
Marc Savard .20 .50
Mike Knuble .15 .40
Glen Murray .20 .50
10 Felix Potvin .40 1.00
11 Andrew Raycroft .20 .50
12 Martin Biron .20 .50
13 Daniel Briere .25 .60
14 J-P Dumont .15 .40
15 Miroslav Satan .20 .50
16 Shean Donovan .15 .40
17 Miikka Kiprusoff .20 .50
18 Jordan Leopold .15 .40
19 Erik Cole .20 .50
20 Ron Francis .30 .75
21 Jeff O'Neill .15 .40
22 Josef Vasicek .15 .40
23 Kevin Weekes .20 .50
24 Mark Bell .15 .40
25 Kyle Calder .15 .40
26 Jocelyn Thibault .20 .50
27 Alexei Zhamnov .20 .50
28 Rob Blake .25 .60
29 Alex Tanguay .20 .50
30 Marc Denis .20 .50
31 Rick Nash .25 .60
32 David Vyborny .15 .40
33 Jason Arnott .20 .50
34 Jere Lehtinen .20 .50
35 Pavel Datsyuk .30 .75
36 Dominik Hasek .40 1.00
37 Curtis Joseph .25 .60
38 Henrik Zetterberg .30 .75
39 Tommy Salo .20 .50
40 Raffi Torres .15 .40
41 Mike York .15 .40
42 Valeri Bure .15 .40
43 Viktor Kozlov .15 .40
44 Stephen Weiss .15 .40
45 Roman Cechmanek .20 .50
46 Alexander Frolov .20 .50
47 Cristobal Huet .20 .50
48 Luc Robitaille .25 .60
49 Andrew Brunette .15 .40
50 Alexandre Daigle .20 .50
51 Manny Fernandez .20 .50
52 Marian Gaborik .40 1.00
53 Dwayne Roloson .20 .50
54 Marcel Hossa .15 .40
55 Mike Ribeiro .20 .50
56 Michael Ryder .20 .50
57 Sheldon Souray .15 .40
58 David Legwand .20 .50
59 Tomas Vokoun .20 .50
60 Jeff Friesen .15 .40
61 Scott Gomez .20 .50
62 Scott Niedermayer .25 .60
63 Jason Blake .15 .40
64 Mariusz Czerkawski .15 .40
65 Trent Hunter .15 .40
66 Garth Snow .20 .50
67 Mike Dunham .20 .50
68 Brian Leetch .25 .60
69 Mark Messier .40 1.00
70 Radek Bonk .20 .50
71 Zdeno Chara .25 .60
72 Peter Schaefer .15 .40
73 Tony Amonte .20 .50
74 Robert Esche .15 .40
75 Michal Handzus .20 .50
76 Mark Recchi .30 .75
77 Sean Burke .15 .40
78 Shane Doan .20 .50
79 Ladislav Nagy .15 .40
80 Sebastien Caron .20 .50
81 Rico Fata .15 .40
82 Dick Tarnstrom .15 .40
83 Pavol Demitra .30 .75
84 Chris Pronger .20 .50
85 Keith Tkachuk .25 .60
86 Jonathan Cheechoo .20 .50
87 Vincent Damphousse .20 .50
88 Patrick Marleau .25 .60
89 Evgeni Nabokov .20 .50
90 Marco Sturm .15 .40
91 John Grahame .15 .40
92 Cory Stillman .15 .40
93 Joe Nieuwendyk .25 .60
94 Darcy Tucker .20 .50
95 Jason King .15 .40
96 Daniel Sedin .25 .60
97 Henrik Sedin .25 .60
98 Peter Bondra .20 .50
99 Sergei Gonchar .15 .40
100 Robert Lang .15 .40
101 Garrett Burnett RC 3.00 8.00
102 Tony Martensson RC 3.00 8.00
103 Sergei Zinovjev RC 3.00 8.00
104 Andrew Peters RC 4.00 10.00
105 Brent Krahn RC 3.00 8.00
106 Eric Staal RC 20.00 50.00
107 Travis Moen RC 4.00 10.00
108 Tuomo Ruutu RC 5.00 12.00
109 Pavel Vorobiev RC 4.00 10.00
110 Mikhail Yakubov RC 3.00 8.00
111 Cody McCormick RC 4.00 10.00
112 Dan Fritsche RC 3.00 8.00
113 Kent McDonell RC 4.00 10.00
114 Nikolai Zherdev RC 6.00 15.00
115 Trevor Daley RC 5.00 12.00
116 Antti Miettinen RC 5.00 12.00
117 Jiri Hudler RC 8.00 20.00
118 Niklas Kronwall RC 6.00 15.00
119 Nathan Robinson RC 3.00 8.00
120 Peter Sarno RC 3.00 8.00
121 Tim Gleason RC 4.00 10.00
122 Esa Pirnes RC 3.00 8.00
123 Brent Burns RC 8.00 20.00
124 Dan Hamhuis RC 4.00 10.00
125 Marek Zidlicky RC 3.00 8.00
126 David Hale RC 3.00 8.00
127 Paul Martin RC 4.00 10.00
128 Sean Bergenheim RC 4.00 10.00
129 Dominic Moore RC 3.00 8.00
130 Joni Pitkanen RC 5.00 12.00
131 Fredrik Sjostrom RC 5.00 12.00
132 Marc-Andre Fleury RC 40.00 100.00
133 Matt Murley RC 4.00 10.00
134 John Pohl RC 3.00 8.00
135 Peter Sejna RC 4.00 10.00
136 Milan Michalek RC 6.00 15.00
137 Maxim Kondratiev RC 3.00 8.00
138 Ryan Kesler RC 15.00 40.00
139 Alexander Semin RC 10.00 25.00
140 Rastislav Stana RC 5.00 12.00
141 Stanislav Chistov JSY 2.00 5.00
142 Sergei Fedorov JSY 5.00 12.00
143 J-S Giguere JSY 3.00 8.00
144 Sergei Samsonov JSY 2.50 6.00
145 Ryan Miller JSY/785 3.00 8.00
146 Jarome Iginla JSY 3.00 8.00
147 David Aebischer JSY 2.50 6.00
148 Milan Hejduk JSY 2.50 6.00
149 Joe Sakic JSY 5.00 12.00
150 Teemu Selanne JSY 6.00 15.00
151 Mike Modano JSY 5.00 12.00
152 Marty Turco JSY 3.00 8.00
153 Brendan Shanahan JSY 4.00 10.00
154 Ales Hemsky JSY 3.00 8.00
155 Ryan Smyth JSY 2.50 6.00
156 Jay Bouwmeester JSY 3.00 8.00
157 Olli Jokinen JSY 3.00 8.00
158 Roberto Luongo JSY 5.00 12.00
159 Jason Allison JSY 2.50 6.00
160 Ziggy Palffy JSY 3.00 8.00
161 Saku Koivu JSY 3.00 8.00
162 Jose Theodore JSY 3.00 8.00
163 Richard Zednik JSY 2.00 5.00
164 Martin Erat JSY 2.00 5.00
165 Scott Walker JSY 2.00 5.00
166 Patrik Elias JSY 3.00 8.00
167 Rick DiPietro JSY 2.50 6.00
168 Michael Peca JSY 2.50 6.00
169 Alexei Yashin JSY 2.50 6.00
170 Jaromir Jagr JSY 8.00 20.00
171 Eric Lindros JSY 5.00 12.00
172 Daniel Alfredsson JSY 3.00 8.00
173 Marian Hossa JSY 2.50 6.00
174 Patrick Lalime JSY 2.50 6.00
175 Jason Spezza JSY 3.00 8.00
176 Jeff Hackett JSY 2.50 6.00
177 Jeremy Roenick JSY 3.00 8.00
178 Barret Jackman JSY 2.00 5.00
179 Chris Osgood JSY 3.00 8.00
180 Doug Weight JSY 3.00 8.00
181 Nikolai Khabibulin JSY 3.00 8.00
182 Vincent Lecavalier JSY 2.50 6.00
183 Martin St. Louis JSY/640 3.00 8.00
184 Owen Nolan JSY 2.50 6.00
185 Gary Roberts JSY/835 2.00 5.00
186 Mats Sundin JSY 3.00 8.00
187 Dan Cloutier JSY 2.50 6.00
188 Brendan Morrison JSY 2.50 6.00
189 Markus Naslund JSY 3.00 8.00
190 Olaf Kolzig JSY 3.00 8.00
191 Ilya Kovalchuk JSY 4.00 10.00
192 Dany Heatley JSY/39 4.00 10.00
193 Joe Thornton JSY 5.00 12.00
194 Peter Forsberg JSY 5.00 12.00
195 Paul Kariya JSY 5.00 12.00
196 Bill Guerin JSY 4.00 10.00
197 Brett Hull JSY 5.00 12.00
198 Nicklas Lidstrom JSY 4.00 10.00
199 Steve Yzerman JSY 10.00 25.00
200 Martin Brodeur JSY 10.00 25.00
201 Pavel Bure JSY 5.00 12.00
202 John LeClair JSY 4.00 10.00
203 Mario Lemieux JSY 12.00 30.00
204 Ed Belfour JSY 4.00 10.00
205 Todd Bertuzzi JSY 4.00 10.00
206 Joffrey Lupul/15 30.00 60.00
207 Patrice Bergeron/37 60.00 150.00
208 Matthew Lombardi/18 15.00 30.00
209 Nathan Horton/16 60.00 120.00
210 Dustin Brown/23 40.00 80.00
211 Christopher Higgins/88 5.00 12.00
212 Jordin Tootoo/55 20.00 50.00
213 Antoine Vermette/20
214 Matt Stajan/14
215 Boyd Gordon/15 12.00 30.00

2003-04 Titanium Hobby Jersey Number Parallels

This 190-card partial parallel set differed from the base set in that the player's jersey number was on the card front in place of the team logo. Cards 1-100 were serial-numbered to 150 sets; cards 101-140 were serial-numbered to 199 sets and cards 141-190 were serial-numbered to 50 sets.

*1-100 VETS/150: 3X TO 8X BASIC CARDS
*101-140 ROOKIES/199: .15X TO .4X RC/99
*JERSEY/50: .8X TO 2X JSY/640-875
69 Mark Messier 4.00 10.00

2003-04 Titanium Patches

*PATCH/25-165: .8X TO 2X BASIC JSY
STATED PRINT RUN 5-165

2003-04 Titanium Retail

The Retail set carried silver foil highlights that distinguished it from the Hobby set.

*1-100 VETS: .4X TO 1X HOBBY
*101-140 ROOK/750: .1X TO .3X HOB/99
*141-190 JSY/170: .5X TO 1.2X JSY/640-875
69 Mark Messier .50 1.25

2003-04 Titanium Retail Jersey Number Parallels

This 140-card partial parallel set differed from the base set in that the player's jersey number was on the card front in place of the team logo. Cards 1-100 were serial-numbered to 250 sets and cards 101-140 were serial-numbered to 225 sets.

*1-100 VETS/250: 2.5X TO 6X BASIC CARDS
*101-140 ROOKIES/225: .15X TO .4X RC/99
69 Mark Messier 3.00 8.00

2003-04 Titanium Highlight Reels

COMPLETE SET (8) 10.00 25.00
STATED ODDS 1:17 HOBBY
1 Ilya Kovalchuk 1.25 3.00
2 Joe Thornton 1.25 3.00
3 Peter Forsberg 1.50 4.00
4 Joe Sakic 1.50 4.00
5 Dominik Hasek 1.50 4.00
6 Steve Yzerman 3.00 8.00
7 Martin Brodeur 2.00 5.00
8 Mario Lemieux 3.00 8.00

2003-04 Titanium Masked Marauders

COMPLETE SET (10) 10.00 20.00
STATED ODDS 1:9
1 Jean-Sebastien Giguere .60 1.50
2 David Aebischer .60 1.50
3 Marty Turco .60 1.50
4 Dominik Hasek 1.50 4.00
5 Jose Theodore 1.00 2.50
6 Martin Brodeur 2.00 5.00
7 Rick DiPietro .60 1.50
8 Patrick Lalime .60 1.50
9 Nikolai Khabibulin .75 2.00
10 Ed Belfour .75 2.00

2003-04 Titanium Right on Target

COMPLETE SET (16) 10.00 20.00
STATED ODDS 1:5
1 Joffrey Lupul .30 .75
2 Patrice Bergeron 1.50 4.00
3 Eric Staal .75 2.00
4 Rick Nash .50 1.25
5 Henrik Zetterberg .60 1.50
6 Ales Hemsky .30 .75
7 Jay Bouwmeester .30 .75
8 Nathan Horton .75 2.00
9 Michael Ryder .30 .75
10 Jordin Tootoo .60 1.50
11 Jason Spezza .60 1.50
12 Joni Pitkanen .30 .75
13 Marc-Andre Fleury 2.00 5.00
14 Barret Jackman .30 .75
15 Matt Stajan .30 .75
16 Jason King .30 .75

2003-04 Titanium Stat Masters

COMPLETE SET (10) 8.00 15.00
STATED ODDS 1:9
1 Sergei Fedorov .75 2.00
2 Ilya Kovalchuk .75 2.00
3 Peter Forsberg 1.00 2.50
4 Rick Nash .75 2.00
5 Pavel Datsyuk .60 1.50
6 Brett Hull .75 2.00
7 Marian Hossa .60 1.50
8 Mario Lemieux 1.50 4.00
9 Todd Bertuzzi .60 1.50
10 Markus Naslund .60 1.50

2000-01 Titanium Draft Day Edition

This 176-card set was released at the 2001 NHL Draft in 2-card packs containing one jersey card and one short-printed first year player per pack. Cards 1-100 were jersey cards while cards 101-176 were shortprinted prospect cards serial numbered to 1000. The set introduced 25 new players not included in Titanium.

COMP.SET w/o JSYs (76) 150.00 350.00
1 Jean-Sebastien Giguere/1010 3.00 8.00
2 Mike Leclerc/520 3.00 8.00
3 P.J. Axelsson/520 3.00 8.00
4 Byron Dafoe/520 3.00 8.00
5 Kyle McLaren/520 3.00 8.00
6 Sergei Samsonov/520 6.00 15.00
7 Don Sweeney/535 3.00 8.00
8 Joe Thornton/535 8.00 20.00
9 Eric Weinrich/1020 3.00 8.00
10 Stu Barnes/535 3.00 8.00
11 Dominik Hasek/535 8.00 20.00
12 Erik Rasmussen/1020 3.00 8.00
13 Fred Brathwaite/1010 3.00 8.00
14 Valeri Bure/1020 3.00 8.00
15 Marc Savard/1020 3.00 8.00
16 Tony Amonte/1020 3.00 8.00
17 Eric Daze/1020 3.00 8.00
18 Boris Mironov/1020 3.00 8.00
19 Michael Nylander/1020 3.00 8.00
20 Steve Sullivan/1020 3.00 8.00
21 Jocelyn Thibault/1020 3.00 8.00
22 Alexei Zhamnov/1020 3.00 8.00
23 Chris Dingman/520 3.00 8.00
24 Peter Forsberg/520 10.00 25.00
25 Patrick Roy/68 75.00 200.00
26 Joe Sakic/535 8.00 20.00
27 Lyle Odelein/535 3.00 8.00
28 Ed Belfour/110 10.00 25.00
29 Derian Hatcher/990 3.00 8.00
30 Brett Hull/115 12.00 30.00
31 Jamie Langenbrunner/985 3.00 8.00
32 Jere Lehtinen/520 3.00 8.00
33 Mike Modano/1015 6.00 15.00
34 Joe Nieuwendyk/1015 3.00 8.00
35 Darryl Sydor/835 3.00 8.00
36 Chris Chelios/520 4.00 10.00
37 Matthieu Dandenault/520 3.00 8.00
38 Nicklas Lidstrom/110 6.00 15.00
39 Darren McCarty/520 3.00 8.00
40 Chris Osgood/1020 3.00 8.00
41 Brendan Shanahan/520 6.00 15.00
42 Steve Yzerman/105 25.00 60.00
43 Anson Carter/55 12.50 30.00
44 Ryan Smyth/1015 3.00 8.00
45 Doug Weight/520 3.00 8.00
46 Pavel Bure/55 15.00 40.00
47 Robert Svehla/1015 3.00 8.00
48 Felix Potvin/100 10.00 25.00
49 Benoit Brunet/1015 3.00 8.00
50 Jeff Hackett/520 3.00 8.00
51 Sergei Zholtok/1010 3.00 8.00
52 Mike Dunham/1020 3.00 8.00
53 Tom Fitzgerald/520 3.00 8.00
54 Patric Kjellberg/520 3.00 8.00
55 David Legwand/520 3.00 8.00
56 Cliff Ronning/520 3.00 8.00
57 Kimmo Timonen/520 3.00 8.00
58 Scott Walker/520 3.00 8.00
59 Bobby Holik/520 3.00 8.00
60 Scott Niedermayer/995 3.00 8.00
61 Mariusz Czerkawski/1020 3.00 8.00
62 Kenny Jonsson/520 3.00 8.00
63 Claude Lapointe/1015 3.00 8.00
64 Chris Terreri/1020 3.00 8.00
65 Theo Fleury/870 3.00 8.00
66 Brian Leetch/520 3.00 8.00
67 Petr Nedved/1015 3.00 8.00
68 Mike Richter/1010 4.00 10.00
69 Mike York/1015 3.00 8.00
70 Daniel Alfredsson/520 3.00 8.00
71 Alexei Yashin/285 3.00 8.00
72 Eric Desjardins/520 3.00 8.00
73 John LeClair/520 4.00 10.00
74 Mika Alatalo/535 3.00 8.00
75 Sean Burke/1010 3.00 8.00
76 Shane Doan/535 3.00 8.00
77 Jyrki Lumme/520 3.00 8.00
78 Jeremy Roenick/520 6.00 15.00
79 Radoslav Suchy/1015 2.50 6.00
80 Jean-Sebastien Aubin/1015 3.00 8.00
81 Jan Hrdina/1020 3.00 8.00
82 Jaromir Jagr/520 8.00 20.00
83 Darius Kasparaitis/1010 3.00 8.00
84 Alexei Kovalev/1015 3.00 8.00
85 Milan Kraft/1015 3.00 8.00
86 Mario Lemieux/115 25.00 60.00
87 Kevin Stevens/1020 3.00 8.00
88 Martin Straka/1010 3.00 8.00
89 Dallas Drake/535 3.00 8.00
90 Cory Stillman/1010 3.00 8.00
91 Vincent Damphousse/1015 3.00 8.00
92 Teemu Selanne/1020 4.00 10.00
93 Vincent Lecavalier/535 6.00 15.00
94 Shayne Corson/1010 3.00 8.00
95 Tie Domi/535 3.00 8.00
96 Curtis Joseph/535 6.00 15.00
97 Mats Sundin/535 6.00 15.00
98 Peter Bondra/15 30.00 60.00
99 Ulf Dahlen/535 3.00 8.00
100 Dainius Zubrus/520 3.00 8.00
101 Samuel Pahlsson 1.50 4.00
102 Scott Fankhouser 1.50 4.00
103 Tomi Kallio 1.50 4.00
104 Brad Tapper RC 2.00 5.00
105 Andrew Raycroft RC 6.00 15.00
106 Denis Hamel 1.50 4.00
107 Jeff Cowan RC 2.00 5.00
108 Oleg Saprykin 1.50 4.00
109 Josef Vasicek RC 2.00 5.00
110 Shane Willis 1.50 4.00
111 David Aebischer RC 6.00 15.00
112 Serge Aubin RC 2.00 5.00
113 Marc Denis 1.50 4.00
114 Chris Nielsen RC 2.00 5.00
115 David Vyborny 1.50 4.00
116 Marty Turco RC 8.00 20.00
117 Mike Comrie RC 3.00 8.00
118 Shawn Horcoff RC 3.00 8.00
119 Dominic Pittis 1.50 4.00
120 Roberto Luongo 2.50 6.00
121 Ivan Novoseltsev 1.50 4.00
122 Serge Payer 1.50 4.00
123 Denis Shvidki 1.50 4.00
124 Steven Reinprecht RC 3.00 8.00
125 Lubomir Visnovsky RC 2.00 5.00
126 Marian Gaborik RC 8.00 20.00
127 Filip Kuba 1.50 4.00
128 Mathieu Garon 1.50 4.00
129 Eric Landry RC 2.00 5.00
130 Andrei Markov 4.00 10.00
131 Marian Cisar 1.50 4.00
132 Scott Hartnell RC 4.00 10.00
133 Rick DiPietro RC 6.00 15.00
134 Martin Havlat RC 6.00 15.00
135 Jani Hurme RC 3.00 8.00
136 Petr Schastlivy 1.50 4.00
137 Ruslan Fedotenko RC 2.00 5.00
138 Justin Williams RC 4.00 10.00
139 Robert Esche 1.50 4.00
140 Milan Kraft 1.50 4.00
141 Brent Johnson 1.50 4.00
142 Reed Low RC 2.00 5.00
143 Evgeni Nabokov 6.00 15.00
144 Alexander Kharitonov RC 2.00 5.00
145 Dieter Kochan RC 2.00 5.00
146 Brad Richards 1.50 4.00
147 Adam Mair 1.50 4.00
148 Daniel Sedin 2.00 5.00
149 Henrik Sedin 2.00 5.00
150 Trent Whitfield 1.50 4.00
151 Marc Chouinard RC 2.00 5.00
152 Jonas Ronnqvist RC 2.00 5.00
153 Petr Tenkrat RC 2.00 5.00
154 Ronald Petrovicky RC 2.00 5.00
155 Craig Adams RC 2.00 5.00
156 Niclas Wallin RC 2.00 5.00
157 Rostislav Klesla RC 3.00 8.00
158 Petteri Nummelin RC 2.00 5.00
159 Tyler Bouck RC 2.00 5.00
160 Michel Riesen RC 2.00 5.00
161 Eric Belanger RC 2.00 5.00
162 Roman Simicek RC 2.00 5.00
163 Xavier Delisle 1.50 4.00
164 Greg Classen RC 2.00 5.00
165 Mike Commodore RC 2.00 5.00
166 Sascha Goc RC 2.00 5.00
167 Jeff Ulmer RC 2.00 5.00
168 Shane Hnidy RC 2.00 5.00
169 Roman Cechmanek RC 2.00 5.00
170 Todd Fedoruk RC 2.00 5.00
171 Ossi Vaananen RC 2.00 5.00
172 Bryce Salvador RC 2.00 5.00
173 Mark Smith RC 2.00 5.00
174 Mike Brown RC 2.00 5.00
175 Jakub Cutta RC 2.00 5.00
176 Johan Hedberg RC 3.00 8.00

2000-01 Titanium Draft Day Edition Patches

This 74-card set is a partial parallel to the jersey cards in the base set (#1-100). Please note that the cards have unique print runs which are player specific and each features a patch swatch.

*PATCHES: 1.2X TO 3X BASIC JSY
STATED PRINT RUN 24-120
8 Joe Thornton/24 30.00 80.00
44 Ryan Smyth/24 15.00 40.00
46 Pavel Bure/116 15.00 40.00

2000-01 Titanium Draft Day Edition Promos

Produced as promotional give-aways, this 76-card set resembles the base set in every way except that they are numbered XXXX/1000 and have the word "sample" printed across the back. According to reports, approximately 150 sets were produced.

COMPLETE SET (76) 200.00 400.00
101 Samuel Pahlsson 2.00 5.00
102 Scott Fankhouser 2.00 5.00
103 Tomi Kallio 2.00 5.00
104 Brad Tapper 2.00 5.00
105 Andrew Raycroft 3.00 8.00
106 Denis Hamel 2.00 5.00
107 Jeff Cowan 2.00 5.00
108 Oleg Saprykin 2.00 5.00
109 Josef Vasicek 2.00 5.00
110 Shane Willis 2.00 5.00
111 David Aebischer 2.00 5.00
112 Serge Aubin 2.00 5.00
113 Marc Denis 3.00 8.00
114 Chris Nielsen 2.00 5.00
115 David Vyborny 2.00 5.00
116 Marty Turco 3.00 8.00
117 Mike Comrie 2.00 5.00
118 Shawn Horcoff 2.00 5.00
119 Dominic Pittis 2.00 5.00
120 Roberto Luongo 5.00 12.00
121 Ivan Novoseltsev 2.00 5.00
122 Serge Payer 2.00 5.00
123 Denis Shvidki 2.00 5.00
124 Steven Reinprecht 2.00 5.00
125 Lubomir Visnovsky 2.00 5.00
126 Marian Gaborik 8.00 20.00
127 Filip Kuba 2.00 5.00
128 Mathieu Garon 2.00 5.00
129 Eric Landry 2.00 5.00
130 Andrei Markov 5.00 12.00
131 Marian Cisar 2.00 5.00
132 Scott Hartnell 3.00 8.00
133 Rick DiPietro 3.00 8.00
134 Martin Havlat 3.00 8.00
135 Jani Hurme 2.00 5.00
136 Petr Schastlivy 2.00 5.00
137 Ruslan Fedotenko 2.00 5.00
138 Justin Williams 2.00 5.00
139 Robert Esche 2.00 5.00
140 Milan Kraft 2.00 5.00
141 Brent Johnson 2.00 5.00
142 Reed Low 2.00 5.00
143 Evgeni Nabokov 2.00 5.00
144 Alexander Kharitonov 3.00 8.00
145 Dieter Kochan 2.00 5.00
146 Brad Richards 3.00 8.00
147 Adam Mair 2.00 5.00
148 Daniel Sedin 8.00 20.00
149 Henrik Sedin 8.00 20.00
150 Trent Whitfield 2.00 5.00
151 Marc Chouinard 2.00 5.00
152 Jonas Ronnqvist 2.00 5.00
153 Petr Tenkrat 2.00 5.00
154 Ronald Petrovicky 2.00 5.00
155 Craig Adams 2.00 5.00
156 Niclas Wallin 2.00 5.00
157 Rostislav Klesla 2.00 5.00
158 Petteri Nummelin 2.00 5.00
159 Tyler Bouck 2.00 5.00
160 Michel Riesen 2.00 5.00
161 Eric Belanger 2.00 5.00
162 Roman Simicek 2.00 5.00
163 Xavier Delisle 2.00 5.00
164 Greg Classen 2.00 5.00
165 Mike Commodore 2.00 5.00
166 Sascha Goc 2.00 5.00
167 Jeff Ulmer 2.00 5.00
168 Shane Hnidy 2.00 5.00
169 Roman Cechmanek 2.00 5.00
170 Todd Fedoruk 2.00 5.00
171 Ossi Vaananen 2.00 5.00
172 Bryce Salvador 2.00 5.00
173 Mark Smith 2.00 5.00
174 Mike Brown 2.00 5.00
175 Jakub Cutta 2.00 5.00
176 Johan Hedberg 2.00 5.00

2001-02 Titanium Draft Day Edition

Released in conjunction with the 2002 NHL Entry Draft as a stand alone product, this 172-card set featured 100 veteran jersey cards and 72 short printed (serial numberd to 780) non-memorabilia rookies and prospects. An autographed version of the Ilya Kovalchuk card was also randomly seeded in packs and numbered to just 500 copies.

1 Jeff Friesen 3.00 8.00
1AU Ilya Kovalchuk AU/500* 15.00 40.00
2 Paul Kariya 5.00 12.00
3 Oleg Tverdovsky 3.00 8.00
4 Dany Heatley 5.00 12.00
5 Milan Hnilicka 5.00 12.00
6 Tomi Kallio 3.00 8.00
7 Ilya Kovalchuk 6.00 15.00
8 Patrik Stefan 3.00 8.00
9 Bill Guerin 5.00 12.00
10 Kyle McLaren 3.00 8.00
11 Joe Thornton 6.00 15.00
12 Martin Biron 5.00 12.00
13 J-P Dumont 3.00 8.00
14 Erik Rasmussen 3.00 8.00
15 Jarome Iginla 6.00 15.00
16 Marc Savard 3.00 8.00
17 Roman Turek 5.00 12.00
18 Erik Cole 4.00 10.00
19 Jeff O'Neill 3.00 8.00
20 Tony Amonte 5.00 12.00
21 Kyle Calder 3.00 8.00
22 Tom Fitzgerald 3.00 8.00
23 Phil Housley 3.00 8.00
24 Steve Sullivan 3.00 8.00
25 Rob Blake 5.00 12.00
26 Vaclav Nedorost 2.50 6.00
27 Joe Sakic 8.00 20.00
28 Alex Tanguay 5.00 12.00
29 Marc Denis 5.00 12.00
30 Rostislav Klesla 3.00 8.00
31 Ron Tugnutt 5.00 12.00
32 Jason Arnott 3.00 8.00
33 Derian Hatcher 3.00 8.00
34 Mike Modano 6.00 15.00
35 Pierre Turgeon 5.00 12.00
36 Sergei Zubov 3.00 8.00
37 Dominik Hasek 8.00 20.00
38 Brett Hull 5.00 12.00
39 Mike Comrie 5.00 12.00
40 Jochen Hecht 2.50 6.00
41 Jason Allison 2.50 6.00
42 Adam Deadmarsh 2.50 6.00
43 Felix Potvin 6.00 15.00
44 Manny Fernandez 5.00 12.00
45 Marian Gaborik 6.00 15.00
46 Filip Kuba 2.50 6.00
47 Jamie McLennan 2.50 6.00
48 Sergei Berezin 2.50 6.00
49 Jeff Hackett 5.00 12.00
50 Jukka Hentunen 2.50 6.00
51 Martin Brodeur 6.00 15.00
52 Scott Gomez 2.50 6.00
53 Bobby Holik 2.50 6.00
54 Jamie Langenbrunner 2.50 6.00
55 Scott Stevens 5.00 12.00
56 Mats Lindgren 2.50 6.00
57 Kip Miller 2.50 6.00
58 Chris Osgood 5.00 12.00
59 Theo Fleury 3.00 8.00
60 Brian Leetch 5.00 12.00
61 Eric Lindros 5.00 12.00
62 Mark Messier 5.00 12.00
63 Mike Richter 5.00 12.00
64 Daniel Alfredsson 5.00 12.00
65 Martin Havlat 5.00 12.00
66 Marian Hossa 5.00 12.00
67 Patrick Lalime 5.00 12.00
68 Roman Cechmanek 3.00 8.00
69 Jiri Dopita 2.50 6.00
70 Simon Gagne 5.00 12.00
71 John LeClair 5.00 12.00
72 Jeremy Roenick 6.00 15.00
73 Michal Handzus 2.50 6.00
74 Krystofer Kolanos 2.50 6.00
75 Daymond Langkow 2.50 6.00
76 Teppo Numminen 2.50 6.00
77 Kris Beech 2.50 6.00
78 Johan Hedberg 3.00 8.00
79 Robert Lang 2.50 6.00
80 Mario Lemieux 15.00 40.00
81 Rich Parent 2.50 6.00
82 Toby Petersen 2.50 6.00
83 Mike Eastwood 2.50 6.00
84 Ray Ferraro 2.50 6.00
85 Patrick Marleau 5.00 12.00
86 Evgeni Nabokov 5.00 12.00
87 Owen Nolan 5.00 12.00
88 Vincent Lecavalier 5.00 12.00
89 Tom Barrasso 5.00 12.00
90 Mats Sundin 5.00 12.00
91 Dimitri Yushkevich 2.50 6.00
92 Todd Bertuzzi 5.00 12.00
93 Andrew Cassels 2.50 6.00
94 Dan Cloutier 5.00 12.00
95 Brendan Morrison 4.00 12.00
96 Markus Naslund 5.00 12.00
97 Daniel Sedin 5.00 12.00
98 Henrik Sedin 5.00 12.00
99 Peter Bondra 5.00 12.00
100 Jaromir Jagr 8.00 20.00
101 Ilja Bryzgalov RC 3.00 8.00
102 Andy McDonald 2.00 5.00
103 Timo Parssinen RC 2.00 5.00
104 Dany Heatley 4.00 10.00
105 Ilya Kovalchuk RC 12.00 30.00
106 Pasi Nurminen RC 2.50 6.00
107 Kamil Piros RC 2.00 5.00
108 Brian Pothier RC 2.00 5.00
109 Daniel Tjarnqvist 2.00 5.00
110 Andy Hilbert 2.00 5.00
111 Ales Kotalik RC 2.50 6.00
112 Mika Noronen 2.00 5.00
113 Erik Cole RC 4.00 10.00
114 Tyler Arnason RC 2.50 6.00
115 Mark Bell 2.00 5.00
116 Vaclav Nedorost RC 2.00 5.00
117 Radim Vrbata 2.00 5.00
118 Brian Willsie 2.00 5.00
119 Mathieu Darche RC 2.00 5.00
120 Rostislav Klesla 4.00 10.00
121 Jody Shelley RC 2.50 6.00
122 Martin Spanhel RC 2.00 5.00
123 John Erskine RC 2.00 5.00
124 Niko Kapanen RC 2.50 6.00
125 Sean Avery RC 2.00 5.00
126 Pavel Datsyuk RC 8.00 20.00
127 Maxim Kuznetsov 2.00 5.00
128 Jason Chimera RC 2.00 5.00
129 Ty Conklin RC 2.00 5.00
130 Jussi Markkanen 2.00 5.00
131 Niklas Hagman RC 2.00 5.00
132 Kristian Huselius RC 2.50 6.00
133 Stephen Weiss RC 4.00 10.00
134 Jaroslav Bednar RC 2.00 5.00
135 David Cullen RC 2.00 5.00
136 Pascal Dupuis RC 2.50 6.00
137 Nick Schultz RC 2.00 5.00
138 Mathieu Garon 2.00 5.00
139 Marcel Hossa RC 2.00 5.00
140 Mike Ribeiro 2.00 5.00
141 Bubba Berenzweig 2.00 5.00
142 Martin Erat RC 2.00 5.00
143 Jukka Hentunen RC 2.00 5.00
144 Nathan Perrott RC 2.00 5.00
145 Christian Berglund RC 2.00 5.00
146 Scott Clemmensen RC 2.00 5.00
147 J-F Damphousse 2.00 5.00
148 Brian Gionta 2.00 5.00
149 Andreas Salomonsson RC 2.00 5.00
150 Radek Martinek RC 2.00 5.00
151 Raffi Torres RC 2.50 6.00
152 Dan Blackburn RC 3.00 8.00
153 Mikael Samuelsson RC 2.00 5.00
154 Chris Neil RC 2.00 5.00
155 Pavel Brendl 2.00 5.00
156 Jiri Dopita RC 2.00 5.00
157 Bruno St. Jacques RC 2.00 5.00
158 Billy Tibbetts RC 2.00 5.00
159 Darcy Hordichuk 2.00 5.00
160 Krystofer Kolanos RC 2.00 5.00
161 Josef Melichar 2.00 5.00
162 Mark Rycroft RC 2.00 5.00
163 Sergei Varlamov 2.00 5.00
164 Matt Bradley 2.00 5.00
165 Jeff Jillson RC 2.00 5.00
166 Vesa Toskala 2.00 5.00
167 Nikita Alexeev RC 2.00 5.00
168 Alexei Ponikarovsky 2.00 5.00
169 Chris Corrinet RC 2.00 5.00
170 Stephen Peat 2.00 5.00
171 Matt Pettinger 2.00 5.00
172 Brian Sutherby RC 2.00 5.00

1993 Titrex Guy Lafleur Insert

This standard-size card was inserted in Canadian packages of Power Bar, made by Titrex International, a firm specializing in dietary products. Also included in the package was an order form in French for ordering the 24-card Guy Lafleur Collection set. The card features on its front and back a horizontal borderless shot of Guy Lafleur on ice wearing a Titrex jersey, with the Guy Lafleur Collection logo appearing at the bottom. The front has a glossy finish, and Lafleur's name is highlighted in gold foil. The unglossy back carries the Titrex logo at the upper left, and also has the years Lafleur played for each hockey team within a gray stripe down the left edge. The card is unnumbered.

1 Guy Lafleur 1.25 3.00
(Wearing Titrex jersey)

1994 Titrex Guy Lafleur

This 24-card standard size set presents the progression of Guy Lafleur's career. The cards were printed on heavier card stock and came with a card storage album measuring approximately 6 1/4" by 8" and a certificate of authenticity. The borderless fronts feature both horizontal and vertical black-and-white photos. The Guy Lafleur Collection emblem appears inside a red rectangle at the bottom. On a white background with a fading red stripe to the left, the backs carry horizontal and vertical black-and-white photos with the date and a brief photo description (in French and English) below. The cards are unnumbered and checklisted below in chronological order. The set could be obtained by mailing in the order form (plus 24.95 Canadian) that accompanied the 1993 Titrex Guy Lafleur Power Bar Insert in packages of Titrex's Power Bar.

COMPLETE SET (24) 12.00 30.00
COMMON LAFLEUR (1-24) .75 2.00

1954-55 Topps

Topps introduced its first hockey set in 1954-55. The issue includes 60 cards of players on the four American (Boston, Chicago, Detroit and New York) teams. Cards measure approximately 2 5/8" by 3 3/4". Color fronts feature the player on a white background with facsimile autograph and team logo. The player's name, team name and position appear in bottom borders that are in team colors. The backs, printed in red and blue, contain player biographies, 1953-54 statistics and a hockey fact section. The cards were printed in the USA. Rookie Cards include Camille Henry and Doug Mohns. An early and very popular card of Gordie Howe is the main attraction in this set.

COMPLETE SET (60) 3000.00 4500.00
1 Dick Gamble 75.00 150.00
2 Bob Chrystal RC 20.00 40.00
3 Harry Howell 50.00 100.00
4 Johnny Wilson 20.00 40.00
5 Red Kelly 75.00 150.00
6 Real Chevrefils 20.00 40.00
7 Bob Armstrong 20.00 40.00
8 Gordie Howe 1200.00 1800.00
9 Benny Woit 20.00 40.00
10 Gump Worsley 125.00 200.00
11 Andy Bathgate 50.00 100.00
12 Bucky Hollingworth RC 20.00 40.00
13 Ray Timgren 20.00 40.00
14 Jack Evans 20.00 40.00
15 Paul Ronty 20.00 40.00
16 Glen Skov 20.00 40.00
17 Gus Mortson 20.00 40.00
18 Doug Mohns RC 75.00 125.00
19 Leo Labine 25.00 60.00
20 Bill Gadsby 40.00 80.00
21 Jerry Toppazzini 25.00 60.00
22 Wally Hergesheimer 20.00 40.00
23 Danny Lewicki 20.00 40.00
24 Metro Prystai 20.00 40.00
25 Fern Flaman 25.00 60.00
26 Al Rollins 40.00 80.00
27 Marcel Pronovost 40.00 80.00
28 Lou Jankowski 20.00 40.00
29 Nick Mickoski 20.00 40.00
30 Frank Martin 20.00 40.00
31 Lorne Ferguson 20.00 40.00
32 Camille Henry RC 40.00 80.00
33 Pete Conacher 25.00 60.00
34 Marty Pavelich 20.00 40.00
35 Don McKenney RC 40.00 80.00
36 Fleming Mackell 25.00 60.00
37 Jim Henry 40.00 80.00
38 Hal Laycoe 20.00 40.00
39 Alex Delvecchio 75.00 150.00
40 Larry Wilson 20.00 40.00
41 Allan Stanley 50.00 100.00
42 George Sullivan 20.00 40.00
43 Jack McIntyre 20.00 40.00
44 Ivan Irwin RC 20.00 40.00
45 Tony Leswick 20.00 40.00
46 Bob Goldham 20.00 40.00
47 Cal Gardner 25.00 60.00
48 Ed Sandford 20.00 40.00
49 Bill Quackenbush 40.00 80.00
50 Warren Godfrey 20.00 40.00
51 Ted Lindsay 75.00 150.00
52 Earl Reibel 25.00 60.00
53 Don Raleigh 20.00 40.00
54 Bill Mosienko 40.00 80.00
55 Larry Popein RC 25.00 60.00
56 Edgar Laprade 25.00 60.00
57 Bill Dineen 25.00 60.00
58 Terry Sawchuk 400.00 700.00
59 Marcel Bonin RC 25.00 50.00
60 Milt Schmidt 150.00 250.00

1957-58 Topps

After a two year hiatus, Topps returned to producing hockey cards for 1957-58. Reportedly, Topps spent the interim evaluating the hockey card market. Cards in this 66-card set were reduced to measure the standard 2 1/2" by 3 1/2". The players in this set are from the four U.S. based teams. The cards are in team order: Boston 1-18, Chicago 19-33, Detroit 34-50 and New York 51-66. Bilingual backs feature 1956-57 statistics, a short player biography and a cartoon question and answer section. Rookie Cards in this include Johnny Bucyk, Glenn Hall, Pierre Pilote, and Norm Ullman.

COMPLETE SET (66) 1500.00 3000.00
1 Real Chevrefils 30.00 50.00
2 Jack Bionda RC 15.00 25.00
3 Bob Armstrong 12.00 20.00
4 Fern Flaman 15.00 25.00
5 Jerry Toppazzini 12.00 20.00
6 Larry Regan RC 12.00 20.00
7 Bronco Horvath RC 18.00 30.00
8 Jack Caffery 12.00 20.00
9 Leo Labine 15.00 25.00
10 Johnny Bucyk RC 175.00 300.00
11 Vic Stasiuk 12.00 20.00
12 Doug Mohns 15.00 25.00
13 Don McKenney 12.00 20.00
14 Don Simmons RC 15.00 25.00
15 Allan Stanley 18.00 30.00
16 Fleming Mackell 15.00 25.00
17 Larry Hillman RC 15.00 25.00
18 Leo Boivin 15.00 25.00
19 Bob Bailey 12.00 20.00
20 Glenn Hall RC 250.00 400.00
21 Ted Lindsay 40.00 80.00
22 Pierre Pilote RC 60.00 100.00
23 Jim Thomson 12.00 20.00
24 Eric Nesterenko 15.00 25.00
25 Gus Mortson 12.00 20.00
26 Ed Litzenberger RC 18.00 30.00
27 Elmer Vasko RC 18.00 30.00
28 Jack McIntyre 12.00 20.00
29 Ron Murphy 12.00 20.00
30 Glen Skov 12.00 20.00
31 Hec Lalande RC 12.00 20.00
32 Nick Mickoski 12.00 20.00
33 Wally Hergesheimer 12.00 20.00
34 Alex Delvecchio 30.00 50.00
35 Terry Sawchuk UER 150.00 250.00
36 Guyle Fielder RC 15.00 25.00
37 Tom McCarthy 12.00 20.00
38 Al Arbour 25.00 40.00
39 Billy Dea RC 12.00 20.00
40 Lorne Ferguson 12.00 20.00
41 Warren Godfrey 12.00 20.00
42 Gordie Howe 300.00 500.00

43 Marcel Pronovost 15.00 25.00
44 Bill McNeil RC 12.00 20.00
45 Earl Reibel 12.00 20.00
46 Norm Ullman RC 150.00 250.00
47 Johnny Wilson 12.00 20.00
48 Red Kelly 30.00 50.00
49 Bill Dineen 15.00 25.00
50 Forbes Kennedy RC 15.00 25.00
51 Harry Howell 25.00 40.00
52 Jean-Guy Gendron RC 15.00 25.00
53 Gump Worsley 60.00 100.00
54 Larry Popein 12.00 20.00
55 Jack Evans 12.00 20.00
56 George Sullivan 12.00 20.00
57 Gerry Foley RC 12.00 20.00
58 Andy Hebenton RC 15.00 25.00
59 Larry Cahan 12.00 20.00
60 Andy Bathgate 25.00 40.00
61 Danny Lewicki 12.00 20.00
62 Dean Prentice 15.00 25.00
63 Camille Henry 15.00 25.00
64 Lou Fontinato RC 25.00 40.00
65 Bill Gadsby 18.00 30.00
66 Dave Creighton 30.00 50.00

1958-59 Topps

The 1958-59 Topps set contains 66 color standard-size cards of players from the four U.S. based teams. Bilingual backs feature 1957-58 statistics, player biographies and a cartoon information section on the player. The set features the Rookie Card of Bobby Hull. Due to being the last card and subject to wear, as well as being chronically off-center, the Hull card is quite scarce in top grades. Other Rookie Cards include Eddie Shack and Ken Wharram.

COMPLETE SET (66) 3000.00 4500.00
1 Bob Armstrong 25.00 40.00
2 Terry Sawchuk 100.00 175.00
3 Glen Skov 10.00 20.00
4 Leo Labine 12.50 25.00
5 Dollard St.Laurent 10.00 20.00
6 Danny Lewicki 10.00 20.00
7 John Hanna RC 10.00 20.00
8 Gordie Howe UER 250.00 400.00
9 Vic Stasiuk 10.00 20.00
10 Larry Regan 10.00 20.00
11 Forbes Kennedy 10.00 20.00
12 Elmer Vasko 12.50 25.00
13 Glenn Hall 90.00 150.00
14 Ken Wharram RC 12.50 25.00
15 Len Lunde RC 10.00 20.00
16 Ed Litzenberger 12.50 25.00
17 Norm Johnson RC 10.00 20.00
18 Earl Ingarfield RC 10.00 20.00
19 Les Colwill RC 10.00 20.00
20 Leo Boivin 12.50 25.00
21 Andy Bathgate 25.00 40.00
22 Johnny Wilson 10.00 20.00
23 Larry Cahan 10.00 20.00
24 Marcel Pronovost 12.50 25.00
25 Larry Hillman 12.50 25.00
26 Jim Bartlett RC 10.00 20.00
27 Nick Mickoski 10.00 20.00
28 Larry Popein 10.00 20.00
29 Fleming Mackell 12.50 25.00
30 Eddie Shack RC 150.00 250.00
31 Jack Evans 10.00 20.00
32 Dean Prentice 12.50 25.00
33 Claude Laforge RC 10.00 20.00
34 Bill Gadsby 18.00 30.00
35 Bronco Horvath 12.50 25.00
36 Pierre Pilote 30.00 50.00
37 Earl Balfour 10.00 20.00
38 Gus Mortson 10.00 20.00
39 Gump Worsley 50.00 80.00
40 Johnny Bucyk 75.00 125.00
41 Lou Fontinato 12.50 25.00
42 Tod Sloan 10.00 20.00
43 Charlie Burns RC 10.00 20.00
44 Don Simmons 12.50 25.00
45 Jerry Toppazzini 10.00 20.00
46 Andy Hebenton 10.00 20.00
47 Pete Goegan RC 10.00 20.00
48 George Sullivan 10.00 20.00
49 Hank Ciesla RC 10.00 20.00
50 Doug Mohns 10.00 20.00
51 Jean-Guy Gendron 10.00 20.00
52 Alex Delvecchio 25.00 40.00
53 Eric Nesterenko 12.50 25.00
54 Camille Henry 12.50 25.00
55 Lorne Ferguson 10.00 20.00
56 Fern Flaman 12.50 25.00
57 Earl Reibel 10.00 20.00
58 Warren Godfrey 10.00 20.00
59 Ron Murphy 10.00 20.00
60 Harry Howell 18.00 30.00
61 Red Kelly 25.00 40.00
62 Don McKenney 10.00 20.00
63 Ted Lindsay 25.00 40.00
64 Al Arbour 12.50 25.00
65 Norm Ullman 60.00 100.00
66 Bobby Hull RC 2200.00 3000.00

1959-60 Topps

The 1959-60 Topps set contains 66 color standard-size cards of players from the four U.S. based teams. The fronts have the player's name and position at the bottom with team name and logo at the top. Bilingual backs feature 1958-59 statistics, a short biography and a cartoon question section.

COMPLETE SET (66) 1200.00 2000.00
1 Eric Nesterenko 30.00 50.00
2 Pierre Pilote 25.00 40.00
3 Elmer Vasko 15.00 25.00
4 Peter Goegan 10.00 20.00
5 Lou Fontinato 15.00 25.00
6 Ted Lindsay 25.00 40.00
7 Leo Labine 15.00 25.00
8 Alex Delvecchio 25.00 40.00
9 Don McKenney UER 10.00 20.00
10 Earl Ingarfield 10.00 20.00
11 Don Simmons 15.00 25.00
12 Glen Skov 10.00 20.00
13 Tod Sloan 10.00 20.00
14 Vic Stasiuk 10.00 20.00
15 Gump Worsley 35.00 60.00
16 Andy Hebenton 15.00 25.00
17 Dean Prentice 15.00 25.00
18 Pronovost/Bartlett IA 15.00 25.00
19 Fleming Mackell 15.00 25.00
20 Harry Howell 15.00 25.00
21 Larry Popein 10.00 20.00
22 Len Lunde 10.00 20.00
23 Johnny Bucyk 35.00 60.00
24 Jean-Guy Gendron 10.00 20.00
25 Barry Cullen 10.00 20.00
26 Leo Boivin 15.00 25.00
27 Warren Godfrey 10.00 20.00
28 G.Hall/C.Henry IA 25.00 40.00
29 Fern Flaman 15.00 25.00
30 Jack Evans 10.00 20.00
31 John Hanna 10.00 20.00
32 Glenn Hall 60.00 100.00
33 Murray Balfour RC 15.00 25.00
34 Andy Bathgate 25.00 40.00
35 Al Arbour 15.00 25.00
36 Jim Morrison 10.00 20.00
37 Nick Mickoski 10.00 20.00
38 Jerry Toppazzini 10.00 20.00
39 Bob Armstrong 10.00 20.00
40 Charlie Burns UER 10.00 20.00
41 Bill McNeil 10.00 20.00
42 Terry Sawchuk 90.00 150.00
43 Dollard St.Laurent 10.00 20.00
44 Marcel Pronovost 15.00 25.00
45 Norm Ullman 35.00 60.00
46 Camille Henry 15.00 25.00
47 Bobby Hull 400.00 600.00
48 G.Howe/J.Evans IA 50.00 80.00
49 Lou Marcon RC 10.00 20.00
50 Earl Balfour 10.00 20.00
51 Jim Bartlett 10.00 20.00
52 Forbes Kennedy 10.00 20.00
53 N.Mickoski/J.Hanna IA 10.00 20.00
54 G.Worsley/H.Howell IA 25.00 40.00
55 Brian Cullen 10.00 20.00
56 Bronco Horvath 15.00 25.00
57 Eddie Shack 60.00 100.00
58 Doug Mohns 15.00 25.00
59 George Sullivan 10.00 20.00
60 P.Pilote/F.Mackell IA 10.00 20.00
61 Ed Litzenberger 10.00 20.00
62 Bill Gadsby 18.00 30.00
63 Gordie Howe 250.00 400.00
64 Claude Laforge 10.00 20.00
65 Red Kelly 25.00 40.00
66 Ron Murphy 30.00 50.00

1960-61 Topps

The 1960-61 Topps set contains 66 color standard-size cards featuring players from Boston (1-20), Chicago (23-42) and New York (45-63). In addition to player and team names, the typical card front features color patterns according to the player's team. The backs are bilingual and have 1959-60 statistics and a cartoon trivia quiz. Cards titled "All-Time Greats" are an attractive feature to this set and include the likes of Georges Vezina and Eddie Shore. The All-Time Great players are indicated by ATG in the checklist below. Stan Mikita's Rookie Card is part of this set. The existence of an album issued by Topps to store this set has recently been confirmed. It is valued at approximately $150.

COMPLETE SET (66) 1100.00 1800.00
1 Lester Patrick ATG 40.00 80.00
2 Paddy Moran ATG 10.00 20.00
3 Joe Malone ATG 15.00 30.00
4 Ernest Johnson 7.50 15.00
5 Nels Stewart ATG 15.00 30.00
6 Bill Hay RC 10.00 20.00
7 Eddie Shack 40.00 80.00
8 Cy Denneny ATG 7.50 15.00
9 Jim Morrison 6.00 12.00
10 Bill Cook ATG 7.50 15.00
11 Johnny Bucyk 25.00 50.00
12 Murray Balfour 6.00 12.00
13 Leo Labine 6.00 12.00
14 Stan Mikita RC 250.00 400.00
15 George Hay ATG RC 7.50 15.00
16 Red Dutton ATG 7.50 15.00
17 Dickie Boon ATG RC 6.00 12.00
18 George Sullivan 6.00 12.00
19 Georges Vezina ATG 30.00 60.00
20 Eddie Shore ATG 30.00 60.00
21 Ed Litzenberger 6.00 12.00
22 Bill Gadsby 10.00 20.00
23 Elmer Vasko 6.00 12.00
24 Charlie Burns 6.00 12.00
25 Glenn Hall 40.00 80.00
26 Dit Clapper ATG 15.00 30.00
27 Art Ross ATG 25.00 50.00
28 Jerry Toppazzini 6.00 12.00
29 Frank Boucher ATG 7.50 15.00
30 Jack Evans 6.00 12.00
31 Jean-Guy Gendron 6.00 12.00
32 Chuck Gardiner ATG 12.50 25.00
33 Ab McDonald 6.00 20.00
34 Frank Fredrickson ATG RC 7.50 15.00
35 Frank Nighbor ATG 12.50 25.00
36 Gump Worsley 30.00 60.00
37 Dean Prentice 7.50 15.00
38 Hugh Lehman ATG RC 7.50 15.00
39 Jack McCartan RC 15.00 30.00
40 Don McKenney UER 6.00 12.00
(Misspelled McKenny
on card front
41 Ron Murphy 6.00 12.00
42 Andy Hebenton 6.00 12.00
43 Don Simmons 7.50 15.00
44 Herb Gardiner ATG 7.50 15.00
45 Andy Bathgate 12.50 25.00
46 Cyclone Taylor ATG 15.00 40.00
47 King Clancy ATG 25.00 50.00
48 Newsy Lalonde ATG 15.00 30.00
49 Harry Howell 7.50 15.00
50 Ken Schinkel RC 6.00 12.00
51 Tod Sloan 6.00 12.00
52 Doug Mohns 7.50 15.00
53 Camille Henry 7.50 15.00
54 Bronco Horvath 6.00 12.00
55 Tiny Thompson ATG 20.00 40.00
56 Bob Armstrong 6.00 12.00
57 Fern Flaman 7.50 15.00
58 Bobby Hull 250.00 400.00
59 Howie Morenz ATG 30.00 60.00
60 Dick Irvin ATG RC 15.00 30.00
61 Lou Fontinato 6.00 12.00
62 Leo Boivin 7.50 15.00
63 Moose Goheen ATG RC 7.50 15.00
64 Al Arbour 7.50 15.00
65 Pierre Pilote 15.00 30.00
66 Vic Stasiuk 15.00 30.00

1961-62 Topps Stamps

There are 52 stamps in this scarce set. They were issued as pairs as an insert in 1961-62 Topps Hockey regular issue card packs. The players in the set are either members of the Boston Bruins (BB), Chicago Blackhawks (CBH), New York Rangers (NYR), or All-Time Greats (ATG). The stamps are unnumbered, so they are listed below alphabetically.

COMPLETE SET (52) 900.00 1500.00
*PANELS: .6X TO 1.5X SUM OF SINGLE STAMPS
1 Murray Balfour 15.00 30.00
2 Andy Bathgate 15.00 30.00
3 Leo Boivin 12.50 25.00
4 Dickie Boon 15.00 30.00
5 Frank Boucher 20.00 40.00
6 Johnny Bucyk 20.00 40.00
7 Charlie Burns 10.00 20.00
8 King Clancy 20.00 50.00
9 Dit Clapper 15.00 30.00
10 Sprague Cleghorn 20.00 40.00
11 Alex Connell 15.00 30.00
12 Bill Cook 15.00 30.00
13 Cy Denneny 15.00 30.00
14 Jack Evans 10.00 20.00
15 Frank Frederickson 15.00 30.00
16 Chuck Gardiner 15.00 30.00
17 Herb Gardiner 15.00 30.00
18 Eddie Gerard 15.00 30.00
19 Moose Goheen 15.00 30.00
20 Glenn Hall 25.00 50.00
21 Doug Harvey 20.00 40.00
22 Bill Hay 15.00 30.00
23 George Hay 15.00 30.00
24 Andy Hebenton 10.00 20.00
25 Camille Henry 12.50 25.00
26 Bronco Horvath 10.00 20.00
27 Harry Howell 12.50 25.00
28 Bobby Hull 75.00 150.00
29 Dick Irvin 15.00 30.00
30 Ernest Johnson 15.00 30.00
31 Newsy Lalonde 20.00 40.00
32 Albert Langlois 15.00 30.00
33 Hugh Lehman 15.00 30.00
34 Joe Malone 20.00 40.00
35 Don McKenney 10.00 20.00
36 Stan Mikita 50.00 100.00
37 Doug Mohns 10.00 20.00
38 Paddy Moran 15.00 30.00
39 Howie Morenz 30.00 60.00
40 Ron Murphy 15.00 30.00
41 Frank Nighbor 25.00 50.00
42 Murray Oliver 10.00 20.00
43 Pierre Pilote 15.00 30.00
44 Dean Prentice 10.00 20.00
45 Andre Pronovost 10.00 20.00
46 Art Ross 25.00 50.00
47 Dallas Smith 10.00 20.00
48 Nels Stewart 15.00 30.00
49 Cyclone Taylor 15.00 30.00
50 Elmer Vasko 10.00 20.00
51 Georges Vezina 40.00 80.00
52 Gump Worsley 20.00 40.00

1961-62 Topps

The 1961-62 Topps set contains 66 color standard-size cards featuring players from Boston, Chicago and New York. The card numbering in this set is basically by team order, e.g., Boston Bruins (1-22), Chicago Blackhawks (23-44), and New York Rangers (45-65). Bilingual backs contain 1960-61 statistics and brief career highlights. For the first time, Topps cards were printed in Canada. Rookie Cards include New York Ranger stars Rod Gilbert and Jean Ratelle. The set marks the debut of team and checklist cards within Topps hockey card sets.

COMPLETE SET (66) 750.00 1500.00
1 Phil Watson CO 15.00 25.00
2 Ted Green RC 25.00 40.00
3 Earl Balfour 7.00 12.00
4 Dallas Smith RC 15.00 25.00
5 Andre Pronovost UER 7.00 12.00
(Misspelled Provonost
on card back
6 Dick Meissner RC 7.00 12.00
7 Leo Boivin 9.00 15.00
8 Johnny Bucyk 25.00 40.00
9 Jerry Toppazzini 7.00 12.00
10 Doug Mohns 9.00 15.00
11 Charlie Burns 7.00 12.00
12 Don McKenney 7.00 12.00
13 Bob Armstrong 7.00 12.00
14 Murray Oliver 7.00 12.00
15 Orland Kurtenbach RC 15.00 25.00
16 Terry Gray RC 7.00 12.00
17 Don Head RC 9.00 15.00
18 Pat Stapleton RC 15.00 25.00
19 Cliff Pennington RC 7.00 12.00
20 Bruins Team Picture 25.00 40.00
21 E.Balfour/F.Flaman IA 8.00 14.00
22 A.Bathgate/G.Hall IA 15.00 25.00
23 Rudy Pilous CO RC 9.00 15.00
24 Pierre Pilote 15.00 25.00
25 Elmer Vasko 7.00 12.00
26 Reg Fleming RC 9.00 15.00
27 Ab McDonald 7.00 12.00
28 Eric Nesterenko 9.00 15.00
29 Bobby Hull 150.00 300.00
30 Ken Wharram 9.00 15.00
31 Dollard St.Laurent 7.00 12.00
32 Glenn Hall 40.00 60.00
33 Murray Balfour 7.00 12.00
34 Ron Murphy 7.00 12.00
35 Bill Hay 9.00 15.00
36 Stan Mikita 100.00 150.00
37 Denis DeJordy RC 25.00 40.00
38 Wayne Hillman RC 9.00 15.00
39 Rino Robazzo RC 7.00 12.00
40 Bronco Horvath 7.00 12.00
41 Bob Turner 7.00 12.00
42 Blackhawks Team Picture 25.00 40.00
43 Ken Wharram IA 9.00 15.00
44 St.Laurent/G.Hall IA 15.00 25.00
45 Doug Harvey CO 25.00 40.00
46 Junior Langlois 7.00 12.00
47 Irv Spencer RC 7.00 12.00
48 George Sullivan 7.00 12.00
49 Earl Ingarfield 7.00 12.00
50 Gump Worsley 25.00 40.00
51 Harry Howell 9.00 15.00
52 Larry Cahan 7.00 12.00
53 Andy Bathgate 12.00 20.00
54 Dean Prentice 9.00 15.00
55 Andy Hebenton 7.00 12.00
56 Camille Henry 9.00 15.00
57 Jean-Guy Gendron 7.00 12.00
58 Pat Hannigan RC 7.00 12.00
59 Ted Hampson 7.00 12.00
60 Jean Ratelle RC 75.00 150.00
61 Al Lebrun RC 7.00 12.00
62 Rod Gilbert RC 75.00 150.00
63 Rangers Team Picture 25.00 40.00
64 D.Meissner/G.Worsley IA 12.00 20.00
65 Gump Worsley IA 12.00 20.00
66 Checklist Card 175.00 300.00

1962-63 Topps

The 1962-63 Topps set contains 66 color standard-size cards featuring players from Boston, Chicago, and New York. The card numbering in this set is by team order, e.g., Boston Bruins (1-22), Chicago Blackhawks (23-44), and New York Rangers (45-65). Included within the numbering sequence are team cards. Bilingual backs feature 1961-62 statistics and career highlights. The cards were printed in Canada. Rookie Cards include Vic Hadfield, Chico Maki, and Jim "The Chief" Neilson.

COMPLETE SET (66) 800.00 1300.00
1 Phil Watson CO 15.00 25.00
2 Bob Perreault RC 10.00 20.00
3 Bruce Gamble RC 20.00 40.00
4 Warren Godfrey 7.00 12.00
5 Leo Boivin 9.00 15.00
6 Doug Mohns 9.00 15.00
7 Ted Green 9.00 15.00
8 Pat Stapleton 9.00 15.00
9 Dallas Smith 9.00 15.00
10 Don McKenney 7.00 12.00
11 Johnny Bucyk 18.00 30.00
12 Murray Oliver 7.00 12.00
13 Jerry Toppazzini 7.00 12.00
14 Cliff Pennington 7.00 12.00
15 Charlie Burns 7.00 12.00
16 Jean-Guy Gendron 7.00 12.00
17 Irv Spencer 7.00 12.00
18 Wayne Connelly 7.00 12.00
19 Andre Pronovost 7.00 12.00
20 Terry Gray 7.00 12.00
21 Tom Williams RC 9.00 15.00
22 Bruins Team 25.00 40.00
23 Rudy Pilous CO 7.00 12.00
24 Glenn Hall 35.00 50.00
25 Denis DeJordy 9.00 15.00
26 Jack Evans 7.00 12.00
27 Elmer Vasko 7.00 12.00
28 Pierre Pilote 12.00 20.00
29 Bob Turner 7.00 12.00
30 Dollard St.Laurent 7.00 12.00
31 Wayne Hillman 9.00 15.00
32 Al McNeil 7.00 12.00
33 Bobby Hull 175.00 300.00
34 Stan Mikita 60.00 125.00
35 Bill Hay 9.00 15.00
36 Murray Balfour 7.00 12.00
37 Chico Maki RC 12.00 20.00
38 Ab McDonald 7.00 12.00
39 Ken Wharram 9.00 15.00
40 Ron Murphy 6.00 12.00
41 Eric Nesterenko 8.00 12.00
42 Reg Fleming 9.00 15.00
43 Murray Hall RC 7.00 12.00
44 Blackhawks Team 25.00 40.00
45 Gump Worsley 25.00 40.00
46 Harry Howell 7.00 12.00
47 Albert Langlois 7.00 12.00
48 Larry Cahan 7.00 12.00
49 Jim Neilson RC 12.00 20.00
50 Al Lebrun 7.00 12.00
51 Earl Ingarfield 7.00 12.00
52 Andy Bathgate 12.00 20.00
53 Dean Prentice 9.00 15.00
54 Andy Hebenton 7.00 12.00
55 Ted Hampson 7.00 12.00
56 Dave Balon RC 7.00 12.00
57 Bert Olmstead 9.00 15.00
58 Jean Ratelle 30.00 50.00
59 Rod Gilbert 30.00 50.00
60 Vic Hadfield RC 30.00 50.00
61 Frank Paice TR RC 7.00 12.00
62 Camille Henry 9.00 15.00
63 Bronco Horvath 7.00 12.00
64 Pat Hannigan 7.00 12.00
65 Rangers Team 25.00 40.00
66 Checklist Card 150.00 250.00

1962-63 Topps Hockey Bucks

These "bucks" are actually inserts printed to look like Canadian currency on thin paper stock. They were distributed as an inserted folded in one buck per wax pack. Since these bucks are unnumbered, they are ordered below in alphabetical order by player's name. The bucks are approximately 4 1/16" by 1 11/16"; there is no information on the backs, just a green-patterned design.

COMPLETE SET (24) 600.00 1000.00
1 Dave Balon 20.00 40.00
2 Andy Bathgate 20.00 40.00
3 Leo Boivin 20.00 40.00
4 Johnny Bucyk 25.00 50.00
5 Reg Fleming 20.00 40.00
6 Warren Godfrey 20.00 40.00
7 Ted Green 20.00 40.00
8 Glenn Hall 40.00 80.00
9 Bill Hay 25.00 50.00
10 Andy Hebenton 20.00 40.00
11 Harry Howell 20.00 40.00
12 Bobby Hull 100.00 200.00
13 Earl Ingarfield 20.00 40.00
14 Albert Langlois 20.00 40.00
15 Ab McDonald 20.00 40.00
16 Don McKenney 20.00 40.00
17 Stan Mikita 50.00 100.00
18 Doug Mohns 20.00 40.00
19 Murray Oliver 20.00 40.00
20 Pierre Pilote 25.00 50.00
21 Dean Prentice 20.00 40.00
22 Jerry Toppazzini 20.00 40.00
23 Elmer Vasko 20.00 40.00
24 Gump Worsley 40.00 80.00

1963-64 Topps

The 1963-64 Topps standard-size set contains 66 color cards featuring players and team cards from Boston (1-21), Chicago (22-43) and New York (44-65). Bilingual backs contain 1962-63 statistics and a short player biography. A question section, the answer for which could be obtained by rubbing the edge of a coin over a blank space under the question, also appears on the card backs. The cards were printed in Canada. The notable Rookie Cards in this set are Ed Johnston, Gilles Villemure, and Ed Westfall. Jacques Plante makes his first appearance in a Topps set.

COMPLETE SET (66) 700.00 1000.00
1 Milt Schmidt CO 15.00 25.00
2 Ed Johnston RC 25.00 50.00
3 Doug Mohns 8.00 12.00
4 Tom Johnson 8.00 12.00
5 Leo Boivin 8.00 12.00
6 Bob McCord RC 6.00 10.00
7 Ted Green 8.00 12.00
8 Ed Westfall RC 18.00 30.00
9 Charlie Burns 6.00 10.00
10 Murray Oliver 8.00 12.00
11 Johnny Bucyk 15.00 25.00
12 Tom Williams 8.00 12.00
13 Dean Prentice 8.00 12.00
14 Bob Leiter RC 6.00 10.00
15 Andy Hebenton 6.00 10.00
16 Jean-Guy Gendron 6.00 10.00
17 Wayne Rivers RC 6.00 10.00
18 Jerry Toppazzini 6.00 10.00
19 Forbes Kennedy 6.00 10.00
20 Orland Kurtenbach 8.00 12.00
21 Bruins Team 25.00 40.00
22 Billy Reay CO 8.00 12.00
23 Glenn Hall 25.00 40.00
24 Denis DeJordy 8.00 12.00
25 Pierre Pilote 10.00 15.00
26 Elmer Vasko 6.00 10.00
27 Wayne Hillman 8.00 12.00
28 Al McNeil 6.00 10.00
29 Howie Young RC 6.00 10.00
30 Ed Van Impe RC 10.00 15.00
31 R.Fleming/G.Howe 10.00 15.00
32 Bob Turner 6.00 10.00
33 Bobby Hull 150.00 250.00
34 Bill Hay 8.00 12.00
35 Murray Balfour 6.00 10.00
36 Stan Mikita 60.00 100.00
37 Ab McDonald 6.00 10.00
38 Ken Wharram 8.00 12.00
39 Eric Nesterenko 8.00 12.00
40 Ron Murphy 6.00 10.00
41 Chico Maki 6.00 10.00
42 John McKenzie 10.00 15.00
43 Blackhawks Team 25.00 40.00
44 George Sullivan 6.00 10.00
45 Jacques Plante 75.00 125.00
46 Gilles Villemure RC 18.00 30.00
47 Doug Harvey 18.00 30.00
48 Harry Howell 8.00 12.00
49 Albert Langlois 6.00 10.00
50 Jim Neilson 8.00 12.00
51 Larry Cahan 6.00 10.00
52 Andy Bathgate 10.00 15.00
53 Don McKenney 6.00 10.00
54 Vic Hadfield 10.00 15.00
55 Earl Ingarfield 6.00 10.00
56 Camille Henry 6.00 10.00
57 Rod Gilbert 18.00 30.00
58 P.Goyette/G.Howe 10.00 15.00
59 Don Marshall 8.00 12.00
60 Dick Meissner 6.00 10.00
61 Val Fonteyne 6.00 10.00
62 Ken Schinkel 6.00 10.00
63 Jean Ratelle 18.00 30.00
64 Don Johns RC 6.00 10.00
65 Rangers Team 25.00 40.00
66 Checklist Card 125.00 200.00

1964-65 Topps

The 1964-65 Topps hockey set features 110 color cards of players from all six NHL teams. The size of the card is larger than in previous years at 2 1/2" by 4 11/16". Colorful fronts contain a solid player background with team name at the top and player name and position at the bottom. Bilingual backs have 1963-64 statistics, a brief player bio and a cartoon section featuring a fact about the player. The cards were printed in Canada. Eleven of the card numbers in each series appear to have been short printed based upon configurations found on uncut sheets. They are designated SP below. Rookie Cards include single prints of Gary Dornhoefer and Marcel Paille found in the last series. Other Rookie Cards include Roger Crozier, Jim Pappin, Pit Martin, Rod Seiling and Lou Angotti.

COMPLETE SET (110) 4000.00 6000.00
1 Pit Martin RC 60.00 125.00
2 Gilles Tremblay 12.00 20.00
3 Terry Harper 15.00 25.00
4 John Ferguson 30.00 50.00
5 Elmer Vasko 12.00 20.00
6 Terry Sawchuk UER 65.00 100.00
7 Bill Hay 15.00 25.00
8 Gary Bergman SP RC 18.00 30.00
9 Doug Barkley 12.00 20.00
10 Bob McCord 12.00 20.00
11 Parker MacDonald 12.00 20.00
12 Glenn Hall 35.00 60.00
13 Albert Langlois 12.00 20.00
14 Camille Henry SP 18.00 30.00
15 Norm Ullman 18.00 30.00
16 Ab McDonald 12.00 20.00
17 Charlie Hodge 12.00 20.00
18 Orland Kurtenbach 12.00 20.00
19 Dean Prentice 12.00 20.00
20 Bobby Hull SP 200.00 350.00
21 Ed Johnston 15.00 25.00
22 Denis DeJordy 12.00 20.00
23 Claude Provost 12.00 20.00
24 Rod Gilbert 30.00 50.00
25 Doug Mohns 12.00 20.00
26 Al McNeil 12.00 20.00
27 Billy Harris SP 15.00 25.00
28 Ken Wharram SP 15.00 25.00
29 George Sullivan 12.00 20.00
30 John McKenzie 12.00 20.00
31 Stan Mikita 65.00 100.00
32 Ted Green SP 15.00 25.00
33 Jean Beliveau SP 75.00 150.00
34 Arnie Brown RC 12.00 20.00
35 Reg Fleming 12.00 20.00
36 Jim Mikol RC 12.00 20.00
37 Dave Balon 12.00 20.00
38 Billy Reay CO 12.00 20.00
39 Marcel Pronovost SP 18.00 30.00
40 Johnny Bower 35.00 60.00
41 Wayne Hillman 12.00 20.00
42 Floyd Smith 12.00 20.00
43 Toe Blake CO 18.00 30.00
44 Red Kelly 18.00 30.00
45 Punch Imlach CO 15.00 25.00
46 Dick Duff 15.00 25.00
47 Roger Crozier RC 35.00 60.00
48 Henri Richard SP 75.00 125.00
49 Larry Jeffrey 12.00 20.00
50 Leo Boivin 12.00 20.00
51 Ed Westfall SP 15.00 25.00
52 Jean-Guy Talbot 12.00 20.00
53 Jacques Laperriere 15.00 25.00
54 1st Checklist 175.00 300.00
55 2nd Checklist SP 300.00 500.00
56 Ron Murphy 35.00 60.00
57 Bob Baun 35.00 60.00
58 Tom Williams SP 75.00 150.00
59 Pierre Pilote SP 150.00 250.00
60 Bob Pulford 35.00 60.00
61 Red Berenson 25.00 50.00
62 Vic Hadfield 35.00 60.00
63 Bob Leiter 25.00 50.00
64 Jim Pappin RC 35.00 60.00
65 Earl Ingarfield 35.00 60.00
66 Lou Angotti RC 35.00 60.00
67 Rod Seiling RC 25.00 50.00
68 Jacques Plante 100.00 175.00
69 George Armstrong UER 40.00 100.00
70 Milt Schmidt CO 25.00 50.00
71 Eddie Shack 60.00 100.00
72 Gary Dornhoefer SP RC 100.00 200.00
73 Chico Maki SP 100.00 200.00
74 Gilles Villemure SP 100.00 200.00
75 Carl Brewer 35.00 60.00
76 Bruce MacGregor 35.00 60.00
77 Bob Nevin 35.00 60.00
78 Ralph Backstrom 35.00 60.00
79 Murray Oliver 35.00 60.00
80 Bobby Rousseau SP 75.00 150.00
81 Don McKenney 35.00 60.00
82 Ted Lindsay 50.00 80.00
83 Harry Howell 35.00 60.00
84 Doug Robinson RC 35.00 60.00
85 Frank Mahovlich 75.00 125.00
86 Andy Bathgate 50.00 80.00
87 Phil Goyette 35.00 60.00
88 J.C. Tremblay 35.00 60.00
89 Gordie Howe 250.00 400.00
90 Murray Balfour 35.00 60.00
91 Eric Nesterenko SP 75.00 150.00
92 Marcel Paille SP RC 150.00 250.00
93 Sid Abel CO 35.00 60.00
94 Dave Keon 60.00 100.00
95 Alex Delvecchio 50.00 80.00
96 Bill Gadsby 35.00 60.00
97 Don Marshall 25.00 50.00
98 Bill Hicke SP 75.00 150.00
99 Ron Stewart 35.00 60.00
100 Johnny Bucyk 50.00 80.00
101 Tom Johnson 35.00 60.00
102 Tim Horton 80.00 150.00
103 Jim Neilson 25.00 50.00
104 Allan Stanley 35.00 60.00
105 Tim Horton AS SP 200.00 350.00
106 Stan Mikita AS SP 175.00 300.00
107 Bobby Hull AS 125.00 200.00
108 Ken Wharram AS 35.00 60.00
109 Pierre Pilote AS 40.00 80.00
110 Glenn Hall AS 90.00 150.00

1965-66 Topps

The 1965-66 Topps set contains 128 standard-size cards. Bilingual backs contain 1964-65 statistics, a short biography and a scratch-off question section. The cards were printed in Canada. The cards are grouped by team: Montreal (1-10, 67-76), Toronto (11-20, 77-86), New York (21-30, 87-95), Boston (31-40, 96-105), Detroit (41-53, 106-112) and Chicago (54-65, 113-120). Cards 122-128 are quite scarce and considered single prints. The seven cards were not included on checklist card 121. Rookie Cards include Gerry Cheevers, Yvan Cournoyer, Phil Esposito, Ed Giacomin, Paul Henderson, Ken Hodge and Dennis Hull. Eleven cards in the set were double printed including Cournoyer's Rookie Card.

COMPLETE SET (128) 1700.00 2700.00
1 Toe Blake CO 35.00 60.00
2 Gump Worsley 18.00 40.00
3 Jacques Laperriere 6.00 10.00
4 Jean-Guy Talbot 5.00 8.00
5 Ted Harris RC 5.00 8.00
6 Jean Beliveau 35.00 60.00
7 Dick Duff 6.00 10.00
8 Claude Provost DP 4.00 6.00
9 Red Berenson 6.00 10.00
10 John Ferguson 6.00 10.00
11 Punch Imlach CO 6.00 10.00
12 Terry Sawchuk 45.00 75.00
13 Bob Baun 6.00 10.00
14 Kent Douglas 5.00 8.00
15 Red Kelly 12.00 20.00
16 Jim Pappin 6.00 10.00
17 Dave Keon 30.00 50.00
18 Bob Pulford 6.00 10.00
19 George Armstrong 9.00 15.00
20 Orland Kurtenbach 5.00 8.00
21 Ed Giacomin RC 90.00 150.00
22 Harry Howell 6.00 10.00
23 Rod Seiling 5.00 8.00
24 Mike McMahon RC 5.00 8.00
25 Jean Ratelle 15.00 25.00
26 Doug Robinson 5.00 8.00
27 Vic Hadfield 6.00 10.00
28 Garry Peters UER RC 5.00 8.00
29 Don Marshall 6.00 10.00
30 Bill Hicke 5.00 8.00
31 Gerry Cheevers RC 125.00 200.00
32 Leo Boivin 6.00 10.00
33 Albert Langlois 5.00 8.00
34 Murray Oliver DP 4.00 6.00
35 Tom Williams 5.00 8.00
36 Ron Schock RC 5.00 8.00
37 Ed Westfall 6.00 10.00
38 Gary Dornhoefer 6.00 10.00
39 Bob Dillabough 5.00 8.00
40 Paul Popiel RC 5.00 8.00
41 Sid Abel CO 6.00 10.00
42 Roger Crozier 6.00 10.00
43 Doug Barkley 5.00 8.00
44 Bill Gadsby 5.00 8.00
45 Bryan Watson RC 9.00 15.00
46 Bob McCord 5.00 8.00
47 Alex Delvecchio 9.00 15.00
48 Andy Bathgate 9.00 15.00
49 Norm Ullman 9.00 15.00
50 Ab McDonald 5.00 8.00
51 Paul Henderson RC 30.00 50.00
52 Pit Martin 6.00 10.00
53 Billy Harris DP 4.00 6.00
54 Billy Reay CO 6.00 10.00
55 Glenn Hall 18.00 40.00
56 Pierre Pilote 9.00 15.00
57 Al McNeil 5.00 8.00
58 Camille Henry 5.00 8.00
59 Bobby Hull 125.00 200.00
60 Stan Mikita 40.00 60.00
61 Ken Wharram 6.00 10.00
62 Bill Hay 6.00 10.00
63 Fred Stanfield RC 6.00 10.00
64 Dennis Hull DP RC 18.00 30.00
65 Ken Hodge RC 20.00 40.00
66 Checklist Card 125.00 200.00
67 Charlie Hodge 6.00 10.00
68 Terry Harper 5.00 8.00
69 J.C. Tremblay 6.00 10.00
70 Bobby Rousseau DP 4.00 6.00
71 Henri Richard 30.00 50.00
72 Dave Balon 5.00 8.00
73 Ralph Backstrom 6.00 10.00
74 Jim Roberts RC 6.00 10.00
75 Claude Larose RC 6.00 10.00
76 Yvan Cournoyer DP RC 70.00 100.00
77 Johnny Bower DP 15.00 25.00
78 Carl Brewer 6.00 10.00
79 Tim Horton 30.00 50.00
80 Marcel Pronovost 6.00 10.00
81 Frank Mahovlich 25.00 40.00
82 Ron Ellis RC 18.00 30.00
83 Larry Jeffrey 5.00 8.00
84 Peter Stemkowski RC 6.00 10.00
85 Eddie Joyal RC 5.00 8.00
86 Mike Walton RC 6.00 10.00
87 George Sullivan 5.00 8.00
88 Don Simmons 6.00 10.00
89 Jim Neilson 6.00 10.00
90 Arnie Brown 5.00 8.00
91 Rod Gilbert 15.00 25.00
92 Phil Goyette 5.00 8.00
93 Bob Nevin 6.00 10.00
94 John McKenzie 6.00 10.00
95 Ted Taylor RC 5.00 8.00
96 Milt Schmidt CO DP 6.00 10.00
97 Ed Johnston 6.00 10.00
98 Ted Green 6.00 10.00
99 Don Awrey RC 6.00 10.00
100 Bob Woytowich DP RC 4.00 6.00
101 Johnny Bucyk 12.00 20.00
102 Dean Prentice 6.00 10.00
103 Ron Stewart 5.00 8.00
104 Reg Fleming 5.00 8.00
105 Parker MacDonald 5.00 8.00
106 Hank Bassen 6.00 10.00
107 Gary Bergman 5.00 8.00
108 Gordie Howe DP 90.00 150.00
109 Floyd Smith 5.00 8.00
110 Bruce MacGregor 5.00 8.00
111 Ron Murphy 5.00 8.00
112 Don McKenney 5.00 8.00
113 Denis DeJordy DP 4.00 6.00
114 Elmer Vasko 5.00 8.00
115 Matt Ravlich RC 5.00 8.00
116 Phil Esposito RC 250.00 450.00
117 Chico Maki 5.00 8.00
118 Doug Mohns 6.00 10.00
119 Eric Nesterenko 6.00 10.00
120 Pat Stapleton 6.00 10.00
121 Checklist Card 125.00 200.00
122 Gordie Howe 600 SP 250.00 400.00
123 Toronto Maple Leafs SP 50.00 80.00
124 Chicago Blackhawks SP 50.00 80.00
125 Detroit Red Wings SP 50.00 80.00
126 Montreal Canadiens SP 50.00 80.00
127 New York Rangers SP 50.00 80.00
128 Boston Bruins SP 125.00 200.00

1966-67 Topps

At 132 standard-size cards, the 1966-67 issue was the largest Topps set to date. The front features a distinctive wood grain border with a television screen look. Bilingual backs feature a short biography, 1965-66 and career statistics. The cards are grouped by team: Montreal (1-10/67-75), Toronto (11-20/76-84), New York (21-30/85-93), Boston (31-41/94-101), Detroit (42-52/102-109) and Chicago (53-64/110-117). The cards were printed in Canada. The key card in the set is Bobby Orr's Rookie Card. Other Rookie Cards include Emile Francis, Harry Sinden and Peter Mahovlich. The backs of card numbers 127-132 form a puzzle of Bobby Orr.

COMPLETE SET (132) 2800.00 4500.00
1 Toe Blake CO 30.00 80.00
2 Gump Worsley 12.00 20.00
3 Jean-Guy Talbot 6.00 10.00
4 Gilles Tremblay 6.00 10.00
5 J.C. Tremblay 7.00 12.00
6 Jim Roberts 7.00 12.00
7 Bobby Rousseau 6.00 10.00
8 Henri Richard 20.00 35.00
9 Claude Provost 6.00 10.00
10 Claude Larose 7.00 12.00
11 Punch Imlach CO 7.00 12.00
12 Johnny Bower 15.00 25.00
13 Terry Sawchuk 35.00 60.00
14 Mike Walton 7.00 12.00
15 Pete Stemkowski 6.00 10.00
16 Allan Stanley 7.00 12.00
17 Eddie Shack 18.00 30.00
18 Brit Selby RC 7.00 12.00
19 Bob Pulford 7.00 12.00
20 Marcel Pronovost 7.00 12.00
21 Emile Francis CO RC 12.00 20.00
22 Rod Seiling 6.00 10.00
23 Ed Giacomin 30.00 50.00
24 Don Marshall 7.00 12.00
25 Orland Kurtenbach 6.00 10.00
26 Rod Gilbert 12.00 20.00
27 Bob Nevin 7.00 12.00
28 Phil Goyette 6.00 10.00
29 Jean Ratelle 12.00 20.00
30 Earl Ingarfield 6.00 10.00
31 Harry Sinden CO RC 25.00 40.00
32 Ed Westfall 7.00 12.00
33 Joe Watson RC 7.00 12.00
34 Bob Woytowich 6.00 10.00
35 Bobby Orr RC 2000.00 3500.00
36 Gilles Marotte RC 7.00 12.00
37 Ted Green 7.00 12.00
38 Tom Williams 6.00 10.00
39 Johnny Bucyk 12.00 20.00
40 Wayne Connelly 6.00 10.00
41 Pit Martin 7.00 12.00
42 Sid Abel CO 6.00 10.00
43 Roger Crozier 7.00 12.00
44 Andy Bathgate 7.00 12.00
45 Dean Prentice 6.00 10.00
46 Paul Henderson 9.00 15.00
47 Gary Bergman 6.00 10.00
48 Bryan Watson 7.00 12.00
49 Bob Wall RC 6.00 10.00
50 Leo Boivin 7.00 12.00
51 Bert Marshall RC 6.00 10.00
52 Norm Ullman 9.00 15.00
53 Billy Reay CO 7.00 12.00
54 Glenn Hall 15.00 25.00
55 Wally Boyer RC 6.00 10.00
56 Fred Stanfield 6.00 10.00
57 Pat Stapleton 7.00 12.00
58 Matt Ravlich 6.00 10.00
59 Pierre Pilote 7.00 12.00
60 Eric Nesterenko 7.00 12.00
61 Doug Mohns 7.00 12.00
62 Stan Mikita 30.00 50.00
63 Phil Esposito 75.00 125.00
64 Bobby Hull LL 50.00 75.00
65 C.Hodge/G.Worsley 15.00 25.00
66 Checklist Card 200.00 400.00
67 Jacques Laperriere 7.00 12.00
68 Terry Harper 6.00 10.00
69 Ted Harris 6.00 10.00
70 John Ferguson 7.00 12.00
71 Dick Duff 7.00 12.00
72 Yvan Cournoyer 30.00 50.00
73 Jean Beliveau 30.00 50.00
74 Dave Balon 6.00 10.00
75 Ralph Backstrom 7.00 12.00
76 Jim Pappin 6.00 10.00
77 Frank Mahovlich 25.00 40.00
78 Dave Keon 18.00 30.00
79 Red Kelly 12.00 20.00
80 Tim Horton 25.00 40.00
81 Ron Ellis 7.00 12.00
82 Kent Douglas 6.00 10.00
83 Bob Baun 7.00 12.00
84 George Armstrong 9.00 15.00
85 Bernie Geoffrion 15.00 25.00
86 Vic Hadfield 7.00 12.00

1958-59 Topps

7 Wayne Hillman 6.00 10.00
8 Jim Neilson 6.00 10.00
9 Al McNeil 6.00 10.00
0 Arnie Brown 6.00 10.00
1 Harry Howell 7.00 12.00
2 Red Berenson 7.00 12.00
3 Reg Fleming 6.00 10.00
4 Ron Stewart 6.00 10.00
5 Murray Oliver 6.00 10.00
6 Ron Murphy 6.00 10.00
7 John McKenzie 7.00 12.00
8 Bob Dillabough 6.00 10.00
9 Ed Johnston 7.00 12.00
00 Ron Schock 6.00 10.00
01 Dallas Smith 6.00 10.00
02 Alex Delvecchio 12.00 20.00
03 Peter Mahovlich RC 18.00 30.00
04 Bruce MacGregor 6.00 10.00
05 Murray Hall 6.00 10.00
06 Floyd Smith 6.00 10.00
07 Hank Bassen 7.00 12.00
08 Val Fonteyne 6.00 10.00
09 Gordie Howe 125.00 200.00
10 Chico Maki 6.00 10.00
11 Doug Jarrett RC 6.00 10.00
12 Bobby Hull 90.00 150.00
13 Dennis Hull 7.00 12.00
14 Ken Hodge 9.00 15.00
15 Denis DeJordy 7.00 12.00
16 Lou Angotti 6.00 10.00
17 Ken Wharram 6.00 10.00
18 Montreal Canadiens 15.00 25.00
19 Detroit Red Wings 15.00 25.00
20 Checklist Card 200.00 400.00
21 Gordie Howe AS 60.00 100.00
22 Jacques Laperriere AS 7.00 12.00
23 Pierre Pilote AS 7.00 12.00
24 Stan Mikita AS 20.00 40.00
125 Bobby Hull AS 50.00 80.00
126 Glenn Hall AS 15.00 30.00
127 Jean Beliveau AS 15.00 30.00
128 Allan Stanley AS 7.00 12.00
129 Pat Stapleton AS 7.00 12.00
130 Gump Worsley AS 15.00 30.00
131 Frank Mahovlich AS 15.00 30.00
132 Bobby Rousseau AS 15.00 30.00

1966-67 Topps USA Test

This 66-card standard-size set was apparently a test issue with limited distribution solely in America as it is quite scarce. The cards feature the same format as the 1966-67 Topps regular hockey cards. The primary difference is that the card backs in this scarce issue are only printed in English, i.e., no French. The card numbering has some similarities to the regular issue, e.g., Bobby Orr is number 35 in both sets, however there are also many differences from the regular Topps Canadian version which was mass produced. The wood grain border on the front of the cards is slightly lighter than that of the regular issue.

COMPLETE SET (66) 8000.00 12000.00
1 Dennis Hull 50.00 80.00
2 Gump Worsley 70.00 120.00
3 Dallas Smith 25.00 50.00
4 Gilles Tremblay 25.00 50.00
5 J.C. Tremblay 25.00 50.00
6 Ralph Backstrom 25.00 50.00
7 Bobby Rousseau 25.00 50.00
8 Henri Richard 125.00 200.00
9 Claude Provost 25.00 50.00
10 Red Berenson 25.00 50.00
11 Punch Imlach CO 25.00 50.00
12 Johnny Bower 70.00 120.00
13 Yvan Cournoyer 90.00 150.00
14 Mike Walton 25.00 50.00
15 Pete Stemkowski 25.00 50.00
16 Allan Stanley 40.00 70.00
17 George Armstrong 40.00 70.00
18 Harry Howell 35.00 60.00
19 Vic Hadfield 25.00 50.00
20 Marcel Pronovost 35.00 60.00
21 Pete Mahovlich 35.00 60.00
22 Rod Seiling 25.00 50.00
23 Gordie Howe 500.00 800.00
24 Don Marshall 25.00 50.00
25 Orland Kurtenbach 25.00 50.00
26 Rod Gilbert 50.00 80.00
27 Bob Nevin 25.00 50.00
28 Phil Goyette 25.00 50.00
29 Jean Ratelle 60.00 100.00
30 Dave Keon 90.00 150.00
31 Jean Beliveau 175.00 300.00
32 Ed Westfall 25.00 50.00
33 Ron Murphy 25.00 50.00
34 Wayne Hillman 25.00 50.00
35 Bobby Orr 5000.00 8000.00
36 Boom Boom Geoffrion 90.00 150.00
37 Ted Green 25.00 50.00
38 Tom Williams 25.00 50.00
39 Johnny Bucyk 50.00 80.00
40 Bobby Hull 350.00 600.00
41 Ted Harris 25.00 50.00
42 Red Kelly 50.00 80.00
43 Roger Crozier 35.00 60.00
44 Ken Wharram 25.00 50.00
45 Dean Prentice 25.00 50.00
46 Paul Henderson 50.00 80.00
47 Gary Bergman 25.00 50.00
48 Arnie Brown 25.00 50.00
49 Jim Pappin 25.00 50.00
50 Denis DeJordy 35.00 60.00
51 Frank Mahovlich 75.00 125.00
52 Norm Ullman 50.00 80.00
53 Chico Maki 25.00 50.00
54 Reg Fleming 25.00 50.00
55 Jim Neilson 25.00 50.00
56 Bruce MacGregor 25.00 50.00
57 Pat Stapleton 25.00 50.00
58 Matt Ravlich 25.00 50.00
59 Pierre Pilote 40.00 70.00
60 Eric Nesterenko 25.00 50.00
61 Doug Mohns 25.00 50.00
62 Stan Mikita 175.00 300.00
63 Alex Delvecchio 60.00 100.00
64 Ed Johnston 35.00 60.00
65 John Ferguson 35.00 60.00
66 John McKenzie 50.00 80.00

1967-68 Topps

The 1967-68 Topps set features 132 standard-size cards. Players on the six expansion teams (Los Angeles, Minnesota, Oakland, Philadelphia, Pittsburgh, and St. Louis) were not included until 1968-69. Bilingual backs feature a short biography, 1966-67 and career records. The backs are identical in format to the 1966-67 cards. The cards are grouped by team: Montreal (1-10/67-75), Toronto (11-20/76-83), New York (21-31/84-91), Boston (32-42/92-100), Detroit (43-52/101-108) and Chicago (53-63/109-117). The cards were printed in Canada. Rookie Cards include Jacques Lemaire, Derek Sanderson, Glen Sather, and Rogatien Vachon.

COMPLETE SET (132) 2000.00 3000.00
1 Gump Worsley 25.00 40.00
2 Dick Duff 6.00 10.00
3 Jacques Lemaire RC 40.00 80.00
4 Claude Larose 6.00 10.00
5 Gilles Tremblay 5.00 8.00
6 Terry Harper 5.00 8.00
7 Jacques Laperriere 6.00 10.00
8 Garry Monahan RC 5.00 8.00
9 Carol Vadnais RC 6.00 10.00
10 Ted Harris 5.00 8.00
11 Dave Keon 12.00 20.00
12 Pete Stemkowski 5.00 8.00
13 Allan Stanley 6.00 10.00
14 Ron Ellis 6.00 10.00
15 Mike Walton 6.00 10.00
16 Tim Horton 20.00 35.00
17 Brian Conacher RC 5.00 8.00
18 Bruce Gamble 6.00 10.00
19 Bob Pulford 6.00 10.00
20 Duane Rupp RC 5.00 8.00
21 Larry Jeffrey 5.00 8.00
22 Wayne Hillman 5.00 8.00
23 Don Marshall 6.00 10.00
24 Red Berenson 6.00 10.00
25 Phil Goyette 5.00 8.00
26 Camille Henry 5.00 8.00
27 Rod Seiling 5.00 8.00
28 Bob Nevin 6.00 10.00
29 Bernie Geoffrion 15.00 30.00
30 Reg Fleming 5.00 8.00
31 Jean Ratelle 9.00 15.00
32 Phil Esposito 40.00 75.00
33 Derek Sanderson RC 75.00 125.00
34 Eddie Shack 15.00 25.00
35 Ross Lonsberry RC 6.00 10.00
36 Fred Stanfield 5.00 8.00
37 Don Awrey UER 5.00 8.00
38 Glen Sather RC 18.00 30.00
39 John McKenzie 6.00 10.00
40 Tom Williams 5.00 8.00
41 Dallas Smith 5.00 8.00
42 Johnny Bucyk 12.00 20.00
43 Gordie Howe 90.00 150.00
44 Gary Jarrett RC 5.00 8.00
45 Dean Prentice 5.00 8.00
46 Bert Marshall 5.00 8.00
47 Gary Bergman 5.00 8.00
48 Roger Crozier 6.00 10.00
49 Howie Young 5.00 8.00
50 Doug Roberts RC 5.00 8.00
51 Alex Delvecchio 12.00 20.00
52 Floyd Smith 5.00 8.00
53 Doug Shelton RC 5.00 8.00
54 Gerry Goyer RC 5.00 8.00
55 Wayne Maki RC 5.00 8.00
56 Dennis Hull 6.00 10.00
57 Dave Dryden RC 9.00 15.00
58 Paul Terbenche RC 5.00 8.00
59 Gilles Marotte 5.00 8.00
60 Eric Nesterenko 6.00 10.00
61 Pat Stapleton 6.00 10.00
62 Pierre Pilote 6.00 10.00
63 Doug Mohns 5.00 8.00
64 Stan Mikita Triple 18.00 30.00
65 G.Hall/D.DeJordy 12.00 20.00
66 Checklist Card 150.00 250.00
67 Ralph Backstrom 6.00 10.00
68 Bobby Rousseau 5.00 8.00
69 John Ferguson 6.00 10.00
70 Yvan Cournoyer 18.00 30.00
71 Claude Provost 5.00 8.00
72 Henri Richard 15.00 25.00
73 J.C. Tremblay 6.00 10.00
74 Jean Beliveau 25.00 40.00
75 Rogatien Vachon RC 30.00 80.00
76 Johnny Bower 12.00 20.00
77 Wayne Carleton RC 5.00 8.00
78 Jim Pappin 5.00 8.00
79 Frank Mahovlich 15.00 25.00
80 Larry Hillman 5.00 8.00
81 Marcel Pronovost 6.00 10.00
82 Murray Oliver 5.00 8.00
83 George Armstrong 9.00 15.00
84 Harry Howell 6.00 10.00
85 Ed Giacomin 18.00 30.00
86 Gilles Villemure 6.00 10.00
87 Orland Kurtenbach 5.00 8.00
88 Vic Hadfield 6.00 10.00
89 Arnie Brown 5.00 8.00
90 Rod Gilbert 9.00 15.00
91 Jim Neilson 5.00 8.00
92 Bobby Orr 400.00 600.00
93 Skip Krake UER RC 5.00 8.00
94 Ted Green 6.00 10.00
95 Ed Westfall 6.00 10.00
96 Ed Johnston 6.00 10.00
97 Gary Doak RC 6.00 10.00
98 Ken Hodge 6.00 10.00
99 Gerry Cheevers 30.00 50.00
100 Ron Murphy 5.00 8.00
101 Norm Ullman 9.00 15.00
102 Bruce MacGregor 5.00 8.00
103 Paul Henderson 6.00 10.00
104 Jean-Guy Talbot 5.00 8.00
105 Bart Crashley RC 5.00 8.00
106 Roy Edwards RC 6.00 10.00
107 Jim Watson RC 5.00 8.00
108 Ted Hampson 5.00 8.00
109 Bill Orban RC 5.00 8.00
110 Geoffrey Powis RC 5.00 8.00
111 Chico Maki 5.00 8.00
112 Doug Jarrett 5.00 8.00
113 Bobby Hull 75.00 125.00
114 Stan Mikita 25.00 40.00
115 Denis DeJordy 6.00 10.00
116 Pit Martin 6.00 10.00
117 Ken Wharram 5.00 8.00
118 Bobby Orr Calder 150.00 300.00
119 Harry Howell Norris 5.00 8.00
120 Checklist Card 150.00 250.00
121 Harry Howell AS 5.00 8.00
122 Pierre Pilote AS 5.00 8.00
123 Ed Giacomin AS 9.00 15.00
124 Bobby Hull AS 50.00 80.00
125 Ken Wharram AS 5.00 8.00
126 Stan Mikita AS 15.00 25.00
127 Tim Horton AS 12.00 20.00
128 Bobby Orr AS 200.00 400.00
129 Glenn Hall AS 12.00 20.00
130 Don Marshall AS 5.00 8.00
131 Gordie Howe AS 60.00 100.00
132 Norm Ullman AS 12.00 20.00

1968-69 Topps

The 1968-69 Topps set consists of 132 standard-size cards featuring all 12 teams including the first cards of players from the six expansion teams. The fronts feature a horizontal format with the player in the foreground and an artistically rendered hockey scene in the background. The backs include a short biography, 1967-68 and career statistics as well as a cartoon-illustrated fact about the player. The cards are grouped by team: Boston (1-11), Chicago (12-22), Detroit (23-33), Los Angeles (34-44), Minnesota (45-55), Montreal (56-66), New York (67-77), Oakland (78-88), Philadelphia (89-99), Pittsburgh (100-110), St. Louis (111-120) and Toronto (122-132). With O-Pee-Chee printing cards for the Canadian market, text on back is English only. For the first time since 1960-61, Topps cards were printed in the U.S. The only Rookie Card of consequence is Bernie Parent.

COMPLETE SET (132) 450.00 750.00
1 Gerry Cheevers 12.00 20.00
2 Bobby Orr 150.00 250.00
3 Don Awrey UER 2.00 4.00
4 Ted Green 2.50 5.00
5 Johnny Bucyk 3.50 7.00
6 Derek Sanderson 15.00 25.00
7 Phil Esposito 18.00 30.00
8 Ken Hodge 2.50 5.00
9 John McKenzie 2.50 5.00
10 Fred Stanfield 2.00 4.00
11 Tom Williams 2.00 4.00
12 Denis DeJordy 2.50 5.00
13 Doug Jarrett 2.00 4.00
14 Gilles Marotte 2.00 4.00
15 Pat Stapleton 2.50 5.00
16 Bobby Hull 35.00 50.00
17 Chico Maki 2.00 4.00
18 Pit Martin 2.50 5.00
19 Doug Mohns 2.00 4.00
20 Stan Mikita 12.00 20.00
21 Jim Pappin 2.00 4.00
22 Ken Wharram 2.00 4.00
23 Roger Crozier 2.50 5.00
24 Bob Baun 2.50 5.00
25 Gary Bergman 2.00 4.00
26 Kent Douglas 2.00 4.00
27 Ron Harris 2.00 4.00
28 Alex Delvecchio 3.50 7.00
29 Gordie Howe 45.00 75.00
30 Bruce MacGregor 2.00 4.00
31 Frank Mahovlich 7.00 12.00
32 Dean Prentice 2.00 4.00
33 Pete Stemkowski 2.00 4.00
34 Terry Sawchuk 25.00 40.00
35 Larry Cahan 2.00 4.00
36 Real Lemieux RC 2.00 4.00
37 Bill White RC 3.00 6.00
38 Gord Labossiere 2.00 4.00
39 Ted Irvine 2.00 4.00
40 Eddie Joyal 2.00 4.00
41 Dale Rolfe RC 2.00 4.00
42 Lowell MacDonald RC 3.00 6.00
43 Skip Krake UER 2.00 4.00
44 Terry Gray 2.00 4.00
45 Cesare Maniago 2.50 5.00
46 Mike McMahon 2.00 4.00
47 Wayne Hillman 2.00 4.00
48 Larry Hillman 2.00 4.00
49 Bob Woytowich 2.00 4.00
50 Wayne Connelly 2.00 4.00
51 Claude Larose 2.00 4.00
52 Danny Grant UER 5.00 10.00
John Vanderburg pictured
53 Andre Boudrias 2.00 4.00
54 Ray Cullen RC 2.00 4.00
55 Parker MacDonald 2.00 4.00
56 Gump Worsley 6.00 10.00
57 Terry Harper 2.00 4.00
58 Jacques Laperriere 2.50 5.00
59 J.C. Tremblay 2.50 5.00
60 Ralph Backstrom 2.50 5.00
61 Jean Beliveau 9.00 15.00
62 Yvan Cournoyer 7.00 12.00
63 Jacques Lemaire 9.00 15.00
64 Henri Richard 7.00 12.00
65 Bobby Rousseau 2.00 4.00
66 Gilles Tremblay 2.00 4.00
67 Ed Giacomin 7.00 12.00
68 Arnie Brown 2.00 4.00
69 Harry Howell 2.50 5.00
70 Jim Neilson 2.00 4.00
71 Rod Seiling 2.00 4.00
72 Rod Gilbert 3.50 7.00
73 Phil Goyette 2.00 4.00
74 Vic Hadfield 2.50 5.00
75 Don Marshall 2.50 5.00
76 Bob Nevin 2.50 5.00
77 Jean Ratelle 3.50 7.00
78 Charlie Hodge 2.50 5.00
79 Bert Marshall 2.00 4.00
80 Billy Harris 2.00 4.00
81 Carol Vadnais 2.50 5.00
82 Howie Young 2.00 4.00
83 John Brenneman RC 2.00 4.00
84 Gerry Ehman 2.00 4.00
85 Ted Hampson 2.00 4.00
86 Bill Hicke 2.00 4.00
87 Gary Jarrett 2.00 4.00
88 Doug Roberts 2.00 4.00
89 Bernie Parent RC 40.00 60.00
90 Joe Watson 2.00 4.00
91 Ed Van Impe 2.00 4.00
92 Larry Zeidel 2.00 4.00
93 John Miszuk RC 2.00 4.00
94 Gary Dornhoefer 2.00 4.00
95 Leon Rochefort RC 2.00 4.00
96 Brit Selby 2.00 4.00
97 Forbes Kennedy 2.00 4.00
98 Ed Hoekstra 2.00 4.00
99 Garry Peters 2.00 4.00
100 Les Binkley RC 5.00 10.00
101 Leo Boivin 2.50 5.00
102 Earl Ingarfield 2.00 4.00
103 Lou Angotti 2.00 4.00
104 Andy Bathgate 3.00 6.00
105 Wally Boyer 2.00 4.00
106 Ken Schinkel 2.00 4.00
107 Ab McDonald 2.00 4.00
108 Charlie Burns 2.00 4.00
109 Val Fonteyne 2.00 4.00
110 Noel Price 2.00 4.00
111 Glenn Hall 6.00 10.00
112 Bob Plager RC 6.00 12.00
113 Jim Roberts 2.50 5.00
114 Red Berenson 2.00 4.00
115 Larry Keenan 2.00 4.00
116 Camille Henry 2.00 4.00
117 Gary Sabourin RC 2.00 4.00
118 Ron Schock 2.00 4.00
119 Gary Veneruzzo RC 2.00 4.00
120 Gerry Melnyk 2.00 4.00
121 Checklist Card 60.00 100.00
122 Johnny Bower 6.00 10.00
123 Tim Horton 8.00 15.00
124 Pierre Pilote 3.00 6.00
125 Marcel Pronovost 2.50 5.00
126 Ron Ellis 2.50 5.00
127 Paul Henderson 2.50 5.00
128 Dave Keon 4.00 7.00
129 Bob Pulford 2.50 5.00
130 Floyd Smith 2.00 4.00
131 Norm Ullman 3.00 6.00
132 Mike Walton 3.00 6.00

1969-70 Topps

The 1969-70 Topps set consists of 132 standard-size cards. The backs contain 1968-69 and career statistics, a short biography and a cartoon-illustrated fact about the player. Those players in this set who were also included in the insert set of stamps have a place on the card back for placing that player's stamp. This is not recommended as it would be considered a means of defacing the card and lowering its grade. The cards are grouped by team: Montreal (1-11), St. Louis (12-21), Boston (22-32), New York (33-43), Toronto (44-54), Detroit (55-65), Chicago (66-76), Oakland (77-87), Philadelphia (88-98), Los Angeles (99-109), Pittsburgh (110-120) and Minnesota (121-131). The only notable Rookie Card in the set is Serge Savard.

COMPLETE SET (132) 400.00 600.00
1 Gump Worsley 8.00 15.00
2 Ted Harris 1.50 3.00
3 Jacques Laperriere 2.00 4.00
4 Serge Savard RC 12.50 25.00
5 80 2.00 4.00
6 Yvan Cournoyer 2.50 5.00
7 John Ferguson 2.00 4.00
8 Jacques Lemaire 2.50 5.00
9 Bobby Rousseau 1.50 3.00
10 Jean Beliveau 7.00 12.00
11 Henri Richard 5.00 8.00
12 Glenn Hall 5.00 8.00
13 Bob Plager 1.50 3.00
14 Jim Roberts 1.50 3.00
15 Jean-Guy Talbot 2.00 4.00
16 Andre Boudrias 1.50 3.00
17 Camille Henry 1.50 3.00
18 Ab McDonald 1.50 3.00
19 Gary Sabourin 1.50 3.00
20 Red Berenson 1.50 3.00
21 Phil Goyette 1.50 3.00
22 Gerry Cheevers 6.00 10.00
23 Ted Green 1.50 3.00
24 Bobby Orr 75.00 125.00
25 Dallas Smith 1.50 3.00
26 Johnny Bucyk 3.00 6.00
27 Ken Hodge 2.00 4.00
28 John McKenzie 2.00 4.00
29 Ed Westfall 2.00 4.00
30 Phil Esposito 12.00 20.00
31 Derek Sanderson 9.00 15.00
32 Fred Stanfield 1.50 3.00
33 Ed Giacomin 6.00 10.00
34 Arnie Brown 1.50 3.00
35 Jim Neilson 1.50 3.00
36 Rod Seiling 1.50 3.00
37 Rod Gilbert 2.50 5.00
38 Vic Hadfield 2.00 4.00
39 Don Marshall 1.50 3.00
40 Bob Nevin 1.50 3.00
41 Ron Stewart 1.50 3.00
42 Jean Ratelle 2.50 5.00
43 Walt Tkaczuk RC 2.50 5.00
44 Bruce Gamble 2.00 4.00
45 Tim Horton 7.00 12.00
46 Ron Ellis 2.00 4.00
47 Paul Henderson 2.00 4.00
48 Brit Selby 1.50 3.00
49 Floyd Smith 1.50 3.00
50 Mike Walton 2.00 4.00
51 Dave Keon 2.50 5.00
52 Murray Oliver 1.50 3.00
53 Bob Pulford 2.00 4.00
54 Norm Ullman 2.50 5.00
55 Roger Crozier 2.00 4.00
56 Roy Edwards 2.00 4.00
57 Bob Baun 2.00 4.00
58 Gary Bergman 1.50 3.00
59 Carl Brewer 2.00 4.00
60 Wayne Connelly 1.50 3.00
61 Gordie Howe 30.00 50.00
62 Frank Mahovlich 5.00 8.00
63 Bruce MacGregor 1.50 3.00
64 Alex Delvecchio 3.00 6.00
65 Pete Stemkowski 1.50 3.00
66 Denis DeJordy 2.00 4.00
67 Doug Jarrett 1.50 3.00
68 Gilles Marotte 1.50 3.00
69 Pat Stapleton 2.00 4.00
70 Bobby Hull 25.00 40.00
71 Dennis Hull 2.00 4.00
72 Doug Mohns 1.50 3.00
73 Jim Pappin 1.50 3.00
74 Ken Wharram 1.50 3.00
75 Pit Martin 2.00 4.00
76 Stan Mikita 7.00 12.00
77 Charlie Hodge 2.00 4.00
78 Gary Smith 2.00 4.00
79 Harry Howell 2.00 4.00
80 Bert Marshall 1.50 3.00
81 Doug Roberts 1.50 3.00
82 Carol Vadnais 2.00 4.00
83 Gerry Ehman 1.50 3.00
84 Bill Hicke 1.50 3.00
85 Gary Jarrett 1.50 3.00
86 Ted Hampson 1.50 3.00
87 Earl Ingarfield 1.50 3.00
88 Doug Favell RC 5.00 10.00
89 Bernie Parent 10.00 20.00
90 Larry Hillman 1.50 3.00
91 Wayne Hillman 1.50 3.00
92 Ed Van Impe 1.50 3.00
93 Joe Watson 1.50 3.00
94 Gary Dornhoefer 2.00 4.00
95 Reg Fleming 1.50 3.00
96 Jean-Guy Gendron 1.50 3.00
97 Jim Johnson 1.50 3.00
98 Andre Lacroix 2.00 4.00
99 Gerry Desjardins RC 5.00 8.00
100 Dale Rolfe 1.50 3.00
101 Bill White 1.50 3.00
102 Bill Flett 1.50 3.00
103 Ted Irvine 1.50 3.00
104 Ross Lonsberry 1.50 3.00
105 Leon Rochefort 1.50 3.00
106 Eddie Shack 2.50 5.00
107 Dennis Hextall RC 2.50 5.00
108 Eddie Joyal 1.50 3.00
109 Gord Labossiere 1.50 3.00
110 Les Binkley 2.00 4.00
111 Tracy Pratt 1.50 3.00
112 Bryan Watson 1.50 3.00
113 Bob Woytowich 1.50 3.00
114 Keith McCreary 1.50 3.00
115 Dean Prentice 1.50 3.00
116 Glen Sather 2.00 4.00
117 Ken Schinkel 1.50 3.00
118 Wally Boyer 1.50 3.00
119 Val Fonteyne 1.50 3.00
120 Ron Schock 1.50 3.00
121 Cesare Maniago 2.00 4.00
122 Leo Boivin 2.00 4.00
123 Bob McCord 1.50 3.00
124 John Miszuk 1.50 3.00
125 Danny Grant UER 2.00 4.00
John Vanderburg pictured
126 Claude Larose 1.50 3.00
127 Jean-Paul Parise 2.00 4.00
128 Tom Williams 1.50 3.00
129 Charlie Burns 1.50 3.00
130 Ray Cullen 1.50 3.00
131 Danny O'Shea RC 1.50 3.00
132 Checklist Card 35.00 60.00

1970-71 Topps

The 1970-71 Topps set consists of 132 standard-size cards. Card fronts have solid player backgrounds that differ in color according to team. The player's name, team and position are at the bottom. The backs feature the player's 1969-70 and career statistics as well as a short biography. Players from the expansion Buffalo Sabres and Vancouver Canucks are included. For the most part, cards are grouped by team. However, team names on front are updated on some cards to reflect transactions that occurred late in the off-season. Rookie Cards include Wayne Cashman, Brad Park and Gilbert Perreault.

COMPLETE SET (132) 300.00 400.00
1 Gerry Cheevers 6.00 15.00
2 Johnny Bucyk 2.00 5.00
3 Bobby Orr 30.00 75.00
4 Don Awrey .75 1.50
5 Fred Stanfield .75 1.50
6 John McKenzie 1.00 2.50
7 Wayne Cashman RC 4.00 8.00
8 Ken Hodge 1.00 2.50
9 Wayne Carleton .75 1.50
10 Garnet Bailey RC 1.00 2.00
11 Phil Esposito 10.00 20.00
12 Lou Angotti .75 1.50
13 Jim Pappin .75 1.50
14 Dennis Hull 1.00 2.50
15 Bobby Hull 20.00 40.00
16 Doug Mohns .75 1.50
17 Pat Stapleton 1.00 2.50
18 Pit Martin 1.00 2.50
19 Eric Nesterenko 1.00 2.50
20 Stan Mikita 6.00 12.00
21 Roy Edwards 1.00 2.50
22 Frank Mahovlich 2.50 6.00
23 Ron Harris .75 1.50
24 Bob Baun 1.00 2.50
25 Pete Stemkowski .75 1.50
26 Garry Unger 1.00 2.50
27 Bruce MacGregor .75 1.50
28 Larry Jeffrey .75 1.50
29 Gordie Howe 25.00 50.00
30 Billy Dea .75 1.50
31 Denis DeJordy 1.00 2.50
32 Matt Ravlich .75 1.50
33 Dave Amadio .75 1.50
34 Gilles Marotte .75 1.50
35 Eddie Shack 1.50 4.00
36 Bob Pulford 1.00 2.50
37 Ross Lonsberry 1.00 2.50
38 Gord Labossiere .75 1.50
39 Eddie Joyal .75 1.50
40 Gump Worsley 1.50 4.00
41 Bob McCord .75 1.50
42 Leo Boivin 1.00 2.50
43 Tom Reid RC .75 1.50
44 Charlie Burns .75 1.50
45 Bob Barlow .75 1.50
46 Bill Goldsworthy 1.00 2.50
47 Danny Grant 1.00 2.50
48 Norm Beaudin RC .75 1.50
49 Rogatien Vachon 3.00 8.00
50 Yvan Cournoyer 1.50 4.00
51 Serge Savard 1.50 4.00
52 Jacques Laperriere 1.00 2.50
53 Terry Harper .75 1.50
54 Ralph Backstrom 1.00 2.50
55 Jean Beliveau 5.00 10.00
56 Claude Larose UER .75 1.50
57 Jacques Lemaire 1.50 4.00
58 Peter Mahovlich 1.00 2.50
59 Tim Horton 6.00 10.00
60 Bob Nevin .75 1.50
61 Dave Balon .75 1.50
62 Vic Hadfield 1.00 2.50
63 Rod Gilbert 1.50 4.00
64 Ron Stewart .75 1.50
65 Ted Irvine .75 1.50
66 Arnie Brown .75 1.50
67 Brad Park RC 12.50 25.00
68 Ed Giacomin 1.50 4.00
69 Gary Smith 1.00 2.50
70 Carol Vadnais 1.00 2.50
71 Doug Roberts .75 1.50
72 Harry Howell 1.00 2.50
73 Joe Szura .75 1.50
74 Mike Laughton .75 1.50
75 Gary Jarrett .75 1.50
76 Bill Hicke .75 1.50
77 Paul Andrea RC .75 1.50
78 Bernie Parent 9.00 15.00
79 Joe Watson .75 1.50
80 Ed Van Impe .75 1.50
81 Larry Hillman .75 1.50
82 George Swarbrick .75 1.50
83 Bill Sutherland .75 1.50
84 Andre Lacroix 1.00 2.50
85 Gary Dornhoefer 1.00 2.50
86 Jean-Guy Gendron .75 1.50
87 Al Smith RC 1.00 2.50
88 Bob Woytowich .75 1.50
89 Duane Rupp .75 1.50
90 Jim Morrison .75 1.50
91 Ron Schock .75 1.50
92 Ken Schinkel .75 1.50
93 Keith McCreary .75 1.50
94 Bryan Hextall 1.00 2.50
95 Wayne Hicks RC .75 1.50
96 Gary Sabourin .75 1.50
97 Ernie Wakely RC 1.00 2.50
98 Bob Wall .75 1.50
99 Barclay Plager 1.00 2.50
100 Jean-Guy Talbot .75 1.50
101 Gary Veneruzzo .75 1.50
102 Tim Ecclestone .75 1.50
103 Red Berenson 1.00 2.50
104 Larry Keenan .75 1.50
105 Bruce Gamble 1.00 2.50
106 Jim Dorey .75 1.50
107 Mike Pelyk RC .75 1.50
108 Rick Ley .75 1.50
109 Mike Walton .75 1.50
110 Norm Ullman 1.50 4.00
111 Brit Selby .75 1.50
112 Garry Monahan .75 1.50
113 George Armstrong 1.50 4.00
114 Gary Doak .75 1.50
115 Darryl Sly RC .75 1.50
116 Wayne Maki .75 1.50
117 Orland Kurtenbach .75 1.50
118 Murray Hall .75 1.50
119 Marc Reaume .75 1.50
120 Pat Quinn 3.00 5.00
121 Andre Boudrias .75 1.50
122 Paul Popiel .75 1.50
123 Paul Terbenche .75 1.50
124 Howie Menard .75 1.50
125 Gerry Meehan RC 1.50 4.00
126 Skip Krake .75 1.50
127 Phil Goyette .75 1.50
128 Reg Fleming .75 1.50
129 Don Marshall 1.00 2.50
130 Bill Inglis RC .75 1.50
131 Gilbert Perreault RC 20.00 40.00
132 Checklist Card 30.00 60.00

1970-71 Topps/OPC Sticker Stamps

This set consists of 33 unnumbered, full-color sticker stamps measuring 2 1/2" by 3 1/2". The backs are blank. The checklist below is ordered alphabetically for convenience. The sticker cards were issued as an insert in the regular issue wax packs of the 1970-71 Topps hockey as well as in first series wax packs of 1970-71 O-Pee-Chee.

COMPLETE SET (33) 300.00 450.00
1 Jean Beliveau 15.00 30.00
2 Red Berenson 6.00 12.00
3 Wayne Carleton 6.00 12.00
4 Tim Ecclestone 6.00 12.00
5 Ron Ellis 6.00 12.00
6 Phil Esposito 15.00 30.00
7 Tony Esposito 15.00 40.00
8 Bill Flett 6.00 12.00
9 Ed Giacomin 10.00 20.00
10 Rod Gilbert 10.00 20.00
11 Danny Grant 6.00 12.00
12 Bill Hicke 6.00 12.00
13 Gordie Howe 20.00 50.00
14 Bobby Hull 15.00 40.00
15 Earl Ingarfield 6.00 12.00
16 Eddie Joyal 6.00 12.00
17 Dave Keon 15.00 30.00
18 Andre Lacroix 6.00 12.00
19 Jacques Laperriere 6.00 12.00
20 Jacques Lemaire 10.00 20.00
21 Frank Mahovlich 10.00 20.00
22 Keith McCreary 6.00 12.00
23 Stan Mikita 10.00 20.00
24 Bobby Orr 40.00 100.00
25 Jean-Paul Parise 6.00 12.00
26 Jean Ratelle 7.50 20.00
27 Derek Sanderson 12.50 25.00
28 Frank St.Marseille 6.00 12.00
29 Ron Schock 6.00 12.00
30 Garry Unger 6.00 12.00
31 Carol Vadnais 6.00 12.00
32 Ed Van Impe 6.00 12.00
33 Bob Woytowich 6.00 12.00

1971-72 Topps

The 1971-72 Topps set consists of 132 standard-size cards. For the first time, Topps included the player's NHL year-by-year career record on back. A short player biography and a cartoon-illustrated fact about the player also appear on back. A League Leaders (1-6) subset is exclusive to the Topps set of this year. The only noteworthy Rookie Card is of Ken Dryden. An additional key card in the set is Gordie Howe (70). Howe does not have a basic card in the 1971-72 O-Pee-Chee set.

COMPLETE SET (132) 200.00 350.00
1 Espo/Bucyk/B.Hull LL 12.00 30.00
2 Orr/Espo/Bucyk LL 12.00 30.00
3 Espo/Orr/Bucyk LL 6.00 15.00
4 Espo/EJ/Cheev/Giaco LL 4.00 10.00
5 Giaco/Espo/Maniago LL 2.50 6.00
6 Plante/Giaco/T.Espo LL 5.00 12.00
7 Fred Stanfield .60 1.50
8 Mike Robitaille RC .60 1.50
9 Vic Hadfield .75 2.00
10 Jacques Plante 6.00 15.00
11 Bill White .60 1.50
12 Andre Boudrias .60 1.50
13 Jim Lorentz .60 1.50
14 Arnie Brown .60 1.50
15 Yvan Cournoyer 1.25 3.00
16 Bryan Hextall .75 2.00
17 Gary Croteau .60 1.50
18 Gilles Villemure .75 2.00
19 Serge Bernier RC .75 2.00
20 Phil Esposito 5.00 12.00
21 Charlie Burns .60 1.50
22 Doug Barrie RC .60 1.50
23 Eddie Joyal .60 1.50
24 Rosaire Paiement .60 1.50
25 Pat Stapleton .75 2.00
26 Garry Unger .75 2.00
27 Al Smith .75 2.00
28 Bob Woytowich .60 1.50
29 Marc Tardif .75 2.00
30 Norm Ullman 1.25 3.00
31 Tom Williams .60 1.50
32 Ted Harris .60 1.50
33 Andre Lacroix .75 2.00
34 Mike Byers .60 1.50
35 Johnny Bucyk 1.50 4.00
36 Roger Crozier .75 2.00
37 Alex Delvecchio 1.25 3.00
38 Frank St.Marseille .60 1.50
39 Pit Martin .75 2.00
40 Brad Park 4.00 10.00
41 Greg Polis RC .60 1.50
42 Orland Kurtenbach .60 1.50
43 Jim McKenny RC .60 1.50
44 Bob Nevin .60 1.50
45 Ken Dryden RC 75.00 125.00
46 Carol Vadnais .75 2.00
47 Bill Flett .60 1.50
48 Jim Johnson .60 1.50
49 Al Hamilton .60 1.50
50 Bobby Hull 25.00 40.00
51 Chris Bordeleau RC .60 1.50
52 Tim Ecclestone .60 1.50
53 Rod Seiling .60 1.50
54 Gerry Cheevers 2.50 6.00
55 Bill Goldsworthy .75 2.00
56 Ron Schock .60 1.50
57 Jim Dorey .60 1.50
58 Wayne Maki .60 1.50
59 Terry Harper .60 1.50
60 Gilbert Perreault 6.00 15.00
61 Ernie Hicke RC .60 1.50
62 Wayne Hillman .60 1.50
63 Denis DeJordy .75 2.00
64 Ken Schinkel .60 1.50
65 Derek Sanderson 2.50 6.00
66 Barclay Plager .75 2.00
67 Paul Henderson .75 2.00
68 Jude Drouin .60 1.50
69 Keith Magnuson .75 2.00
70 Gordie Howe 30.00 60.00
71 Jacques Lemaire 1.25 3.00
72 Doug Favell .75 2.00
73 Bert Marshall .60 1.50
74 Gerry Meehan .75 2.00
75 Walt Tkaczuk .75 2.00
76 Bob Berry RC 1.25 3.00
77 Syl Apps RC 1.25 3.00
78 Tom Webster .75 2.00
79 Danny Grant .75 2.00
80 Dave Keon 1.25 3.00
81 Ernie Wakely .75 2.00
82 John McKenzie .75 2.00
83 Doug Roberts .60 1.50
84 Peter Mahovlich .75 2.00
85 Dennis Hull .75 2.00
86 Juha Widing RC .60 1.50
87 Gary Doak .60 1.50
88 Phil Goyette .60 1.50
89 Gary Dornhoefer .75 2.00
90 Ed Giacomin 1.25 3.00
91 Red Berenson .75 2.00
92 Mike Pelyk .60 1.50
93 Gary Jarrett .60 1.50
94 Bob Pulford .75 2.00
95 Dale Tallon .75 2.00
96 Eddie Shack 1.25 3.00
97 Jean Ratelle 1.25 3.00
98 Jim Pappin .60 1.50
99 Roy Edwards .75 2.00
100 Bobby Orr 25.00 50.00
101 Ted Hampson .60 1.50
102 Mickey Redmond 1.25 3.00
103 Bob Plager .75 2.00
104 Bruce Gamble .75 2.00
105 Frank Mahovlich 1.50 4.00
106 Tony Featherstone RC .60 1.50
107 Tracy Pratt .60 1.50
108 Ralph Backstrom .75 2.00
109 Murray Hall .60 1.50
110 Tony Esposito 8.00 20.00
111 Checklist Card 30.00 60.00
112 Jim Neilson .60 1.50
113 Ron Ellis .75 2.00
114 Bobby Clarke 12.00 30.00
115 Ken Hodge .75 2.00
116 Jim Roberts .75 2.00
117 Cesare Maniago .75 2.00
118 Jean Pronovost .75 2.00
119 Gary Bergman .60 1.50
120 Henri Richard 1.50 4.00
121 Ross Lonsberry .60 1.50
122 Pat Quinn .75 2.00
123 Rod Gilbert 1.25 3.00
124 Gary Smith .75 2.00
125 Stan Mikita 4.00 10.00
126 Ed Van Impe .60 1.50
127 Wayne Connelly .60 1.50
128 Dennis Hextall .75 2.00
129 Wayne Cashman 1.25 3.00
130 J.C. Tremblay .75 2.00
131 Bernie Parent 1.50 4.00
132 Dunc McCallum RC 2.50 6.00

1972-73 Topps

The 1972-73 production marked Topps' largest set to date at 176 standard-size cards. Expansion plays a part in the increase as the Atlanta Flames and New York Islanders join the league. Tan borders include team name down the left side. A tan colored bar that crosses the bottom portion of the player photo includes the player's name and team logo. The back contains the year-by-year NHL career record of the player, a short biography and a cartoon illustrated fact about the player. The key cards in the set are the first Topps cards of Marcel Dionne and Guy Lafleur. The set was printed on two sheets of 132 cards creating 88 double-printed cards. The double prints are noted in the checklist below by DP. Topps gives collectors a look at the various NHL hardware in the Trophy subset (170-176).

COMPLETE SET (176) 200.00 400.00
1 Bruins Team DP 3.00 6.00
2 Playoff Game 1 .40 1.00
3 Playoff Game 2 .40 1.00
4 Playoff Game 3 .40 1.00
5 Playoff Game 4 DP .25 .50
6 Playoff Game 5 DP .40 1.00
7 Playoff Game 6 DP .25 .50
8 Stanley Cup Trophy 2.50 5.00
9 Ed Van Impe DP .25 .50
10 Yvan Cournoyer DP .60 1.50
11 Syl Apps DP .60 1.50
12 Bill Plager RC .60 1.50
13 Ed Johnston DP .25 .50
14 Walt Tkaczuk .50 1.25
15 Dale Tallon DP .25 .50
16 Gerry Meehan .50 1.25
17 Reggie Leach 1.50 3.00
18 Marcel Dionne DP 5.00 10.00
19 Andre Dupont RC .60 1.50
20 Tony Esposito 6.00 12.00
21 Bob Berry DP .25 .50
22 Craig Cameron .40 1.00
23 Ted Harris .40 1.00
24 Jacques Plante 6.00 12.00
25 Jacques Lemaire DP .60 1.50
26 Simon Nolet DP .25 .50
27 Keith McCreary DP .25 .50
28 Duane Rupp .40 1.00
29 Wayne Cashman .60 1.50
30 Brad Park 3.00 6.00
31 Roger Crozier .50 1.25
32 Wayne Maki .40 1.00
33 Tim Ecclestone .40 1.00
34 Rick Smith .40 1.00
35 Garry Unger DP .25 .50
36 Serge Bernier DP .25 .50
37 Brian Glennie .40 1.00
38 Gerry Desjardins DP .25 .50
39 Danny Grant .50 1.25
40 Bill White DP .25 .50
41 Gary Dornhoefer DP .25 .50

42 Peter Mahovlich .50 1.25
43 Greg Polis DP .25 .50
44 Larry Hale DP RC .25 .50
45 Dallas Smith .40 1.00
46 Orland Kurtenbach DP .25 .50
47 Steve Atkinson .40 1.00
48 Joey Johnston DP .25 .50
49 Gary Bergman .40 1.00
50 Jean Ratelle .60 1.50
51 Rogatien Vachon DP .60 1.50
52 Phil Roberto DP .25 .50
53 Brian Spencer DP .25 .50
54 Jim McKenny DP .25 .50
55 Gump Worsley .60 1.50
56 Stan Mikita DP 2.50 5.00
57 Guy Lapointe .50 1.25
58 Lew Morrison DP .25 .50
59 Ron Schock DP .25 .50
60 Johnny Bucyk 1.25 2.50
61 Espo/Hadf/B.Hull LL 6.00 10.00
62 Orr/Espo/Ratelle LL DP 6.00 12.00
63 Espo/Orr/Ratelle LL DP 6.00 12.00
64 Espo/Villem/Worsley LL 3.00 6.00
65 Wtsn/Magn/Dorn LL .40 1.00
66 Jim Neilson .40 1.00
67 Nick Libett DP .25 .50
68 Jim Lorentz .40 1.00
69 Gilles Meloche RC 3.00 6.00
70 Pat Stapleton .50 1.25
71 Frank St.Marseille DP .25 .50
72 Butch Goring .50 1.25
73 Paul Henderson DP .25 .50
74 Doug Favell .50 1.25
75 Jocelyn Guevremont DP .25 .50
76 Tom Miller RC .40 1.00
77 Bill MacMillan RC .40 1.00
78 Doug Mohns .40 1.00
79 Guy Lafleur DP 10.00 20.00
80 Rod Gilbert DP .60 1.50
81 Gary Doak .40 1.00
82 Dave Burrows DP RC .25 .50
83 Gary Croteau .40 1.00
84 Tracy Pratt DP .25 .50
85 Carol Vadnais DP .25 .50
86 Jacques Caron DP RC .40 1.00
87 Keith Magnuson .75 2.00
88 Dave Keon .60 1.50
89 Mike Corrigan .40 1.00
90 Bobby Clarke 8.00 15.00
91 Dunc Wilson DP .25 .50
92 Gerry Hart RC .40 1.00
93 Lou Nanne .50 1.25
94 Checklist 1-176 DP 15.00 25.00
95 Red Berenson DP .25 .50
96 Bob Plager .50 1.25
97 Jim Rutherford RC 3.00 6.00
98 Rick Foley DP RC .25 .50
99 Pit Martin DP .25 .50
100 Bobby Orr DP 20.00 50.00
101 Stan Gilbertson .40 1.00
102 Barry Wilkins .40 1.00
103 Terry Crisp DP .25 .50
104 Cesare Maniago DP .25 .50
105 Marc Tardif .40 1.00
106 Don Luce DP .25 .50
107 Mike Pelyk .40 1.00
108 Juha Widing DP .25 .50
109 Phil Myre DP RC 1.50 3.00
110 Vic Hadfield .50 1.25
111 Arnie Brown DP .25 .50
112 Ross Lonsberry DP .25 .50
113 Dick Redmond .40 1.00
114 Gary Smith .50 1.25
115 Bill Goldsworthy .50 1.25
116 Bryan Watson .40 1.00
117 Dave Balon DP .25 .50
118 Bill Mikkelson DP RC .25 .50
119 Terry Harper DP .25 .50
120 Gilbert Perreault DP 3.00 6.00
121 Tony Esposito AS1 3.00 6.00
122 Bobby Orr AS1 12.00 20.00
123 Brad Park AS1 1.50 3.00
124 Phil Esposito AS1 2.50 5.00
125 Rod Gilbert AS1 .40 1.00
126 Bobby Hull AS1 9.00 15.00
127 Ken Dryden AS2 DP 8.00 20.00
128 Bill White AS2 DP .25 .50
129 Pat Stapleton AS2 DP .25 .50
130 Jean Ratelle AS2 DP .60 1.50
131 Yvan Cournoyer AS2 DP .60 1.50
132 Vic Hadfield AS2 DP .25 .50
133 Ralph Backstrom DP .25 .50
134 Bob Baun DP .25 .50
135 Fred Stanfield DP .25 .50
136 Barclay Plager DP .25 .50
137 Gilles Villemure .50 1.25
138 Ron Harris DP .25 .50
139 Bill Flett DP .25 .50
140 Frank Mahovlich 2.00 4.00
141 Alex Delvecchio DP .60 1.50
142 Paul Popiel .40 1.00
143 Jean Pronovost DP .25 .50
144 Denis DeJordy DP .25 .50
145 Richard Martin DP 1.50 3.00
146 Ivan Boldirev RC .60 1.50
147 Jack Egers RC .40 1.00
148 Jim Pappin .40 1.00
149 Rod Seiling .40 1.00
150 Phil Esposito 5.00 10.00
151 Gary Edwards .50 1.25
152 Ron Ellis DP .25 .50
153 Jude Drouin .40 1.00
154 Ernie Hicke DP .25 .50
155 Mickey Redmond .60 1.50
156 Joe Watson DP .25 .50
157 Bryan Hextall .40 1.00
158 Andre Boudrias .40 1.00
159 Ed Westfall .50 1.25
160 Ken Dryden 18.00 30.00
161 Rene Robert DP RC 1.00 2.50
162 Bert Marshall DP .25 .50
163 Gary Sabourin .40 1.00
164 Dennis Hull .50 1.25
165 Ed Giacomin DP .60 1.50
166 Ken Hodge .50 1.25
167 Gilles Marotte DP .25 .50
168 Norm Ullman DP .60 1.50
169 Barry Gibbs RC .40 1.00
170 Art Ross Trophy .60 1.50
171 Hart Memorial Trophy .60 1.50
172 James Norris Trophy .60 1.50
173 Vezina Trophy DP .60 1.50
174 Calder Trophy DP .60 1.50
175 Lady Byng Trophy DP .60 1.50
176 Conn Smythe Trophy DP .60 1.50

1973-74 Topps

Once again increasing in size, the 1973-74 Topps set consists of 198 standard-size cards. The fronts of the cards have distinct colored borders including blue and green. This differs from O-Pee-Chee which used red borders for cards 1-198. The backs contain the player's 1972-73 season record, career numbers, a short biography and a cartoon-illustrated fact about the player. Team cards (92-107) give team and player records on the back. Since the set was printed on two 132-card sheets, there are 66 double-printed cards. These double prints are noted in the checklist below by DP. Rookie Cards include Bill Barber, Billy Smith and Dave Schultz. Ken Dryden (10) is only in the Topps set.

COMPLETE SET (198) 125.00 200.00
1 P.Espo/MacLeish LL 1.25 3.00
2 P.Espo/B.Clarke LL 1.25 3.00
3 P.Espo/B.Clarke LL 1.25 3.00
4 K.Dryden/T.Espo LL 2.50 6.00
5 D.Schultz/Schoenfeld LL 1.25 3.00
6 P.Espo/MacLeish LL 1.25 3.00
7 Paul Henderson DP .20 .50
8 Gregg Sheppard DP UER .20 .50
9 Rod Seiling DP .20 .50
10 Ken Dryden 25.00 40.00
11 Jean Pronovost DP .20 .50
12 Dick Redmond .30 .75
13 Keith McCreary DP .20 .50
14 Ted Harris DP .20 .50
15 Garry Unger .40 1.00
16 Neil Komadoski RC .30 .75
17 Marcel Dionne 6.00 10.00
18 Ernie Hicke DP .20 .50
19 Andre Boudrias .30 .75
20 Bill Flett .30 .75
21 Marshall Johnston .30 .75
22 Gerry Meehan .30 .75
23 Ed Johnston DP .20 .50
24 Serge Savard .50 1.25
25 Walt Tkaczuk .40 1.00
26 Johnny Bucyk .75 2.00
27 Dave Burrows .30 .75
28 Cliff Koroll .30 .75
29 Rey Comeau DP .20 .50
30 Barry Gibbs .30 .75
31 Wayne Stephenson .40 1.00
32 Dan Maloney DP .20 .50
33 Henry Boucha DP .30 .75
34 Gerry Hart .30 .75
35 Bobby Schmautz .30 .75
36 Ross Lonsberry DP .20 .50
37 Ted McAneeley .30 .75
38 Don Luce DP .20 .50
39 Jim McKenny DP .20 .50
40 Frank Mahovlich .50 1.25
41 Bill Fairbairn .30 .75
42 Dallas Smith .30 .75
43 Bryan Hextall .30 .75
44 Keith Magnuson .40 1.00
45 Dan Bouchard .40 1.00
46 Jean-Paul Parise DP .20 .50
47 Barclay Plager .40 1.00
48 Mike Corrigan .30 .75
49 Nick Libett DP .20 .50
50 Bobby Clarke 7.00 12.00
51 Bert Marshall DP .20 .50
52 Craig Patrick .40 1.00
53 Richard Lemieux .30 .75
54 Tracy Pratt DP .20 .50
55 Ron Ellis DP .20 .50
56 Jacques Lemaire .50 1.25
57 Steve Vickers DP .20 .50
58 Carol Vadnais .30 .75
59 Jim Rutherford DP .20 .50
60 Dennis Hull .40 1.00
61 Pat Quinn DP .20 .50
62 Bill Goldsworthy DP .30 .75
63 Fran Huck RC .30 .75
64 Rogatien Vachon DP .40 1.00
65 Gary Bergman DP .20 .50
66 Bernie Parent .50 1.25
67 Ed Westfall .40 1.00
68 Ivan Boldirev .40 1.00
69 Don Tannahill DP .20 .50
70 Gilbert Perreault DP 3.00 6.00
71 Mike Pelyk DP .20 .50
72 Guy Lafleur DP 7.50 15.00
73 Jean Ratelle .50 1.25
74 Gilles Gilbert DP RC 2.00 4.00
75 Greg Polis .30 .75
76 Doug Jarrett DP .20 .50
77 Phil Myre DP .20 .50
78 Fred Harvey DP .20 .50
79 Jack Egers .30 .75
80 Terry Harper .30 .75
81 Bill Barber RC 6.00 10.00
82 Roy Edwards DP .20 .50
83 Brian Spencer .40 1.00
84 Reggie Leach DP .30 .75
85 Dave Keon .50 1.25
86 Jim Schoenfeld .75 2.00
87 Henri Richard DP .40 1.00
88 Rod Gilbert DP .40 1.00
89 Don Marcotte DP .20 .50
90 Tony Esposito 3.00 6.00
91 Joe Watson .30 .75
92 Flames Team .75 1.50
93 Bruins Team .75 1.50
94 Sabres Team DP .75 1.50
95 Golden Seals Team DP .75 1.50
96 Blackhawks Team .75 1.50
97 Red Wings Team DP .75 1.50
98 Kings Team DP .75 1.50
99 North Stars Team .75 1.50
100 Canadiens Team .75 1.50
101 Islanders Teams .75 1.50
102 Rangers Team DP .75 1.50
103 Flyers Team DP .75 1.50
104 Penguins Team .75 1.50
105 Blues Team .75 1.50
106 Maple Leafs Team .75 1.50
107 Canucks Team .75 1.50
108 Roger Crozier DP .20 .50
109 Tom Reid .30 .75
110 Hilliard Graves RC .30 .75
111 Don Lever .40 1.00
112 Jim Pappin .30 .75
113 Ron Schock DP .20 .50
114 Gerry Desjardins .40 1.00
115 Yvan Cournoyer DP .30 .75
116 Checklist Card 12.00 20.00
117 Bob Leiter .30 .75
118 Ab DeMarco .30 .75
119 Doug Favell .40 1.00
120 Phil Esposito 3.00 6.00
121 Mike Robitaille .30 .75
122 Real Lemieux .30 .75
123 Jim Neilson .30 .75
124 Tim Ecclestone DP .20 .50
125 Jude Drouin .30 .75
126 Gary Smith DP .20 .50
127 Walt McKechnie .30 .75
128 Lowell MacDonald .30 .75
129 Dale Tallon DP .20 .50
130 Billy Harris RC .40 1.00
131 Randy Manery DP .20 .50
132 Darryl Sittler DP 3.00 6.00
133 Ken Hodge .40 1.00
134 Bob Plager .40 1.00
135 Rick MacLeish .75 2.00
136 Dennis Hextall .30 .75
137 Jacques Laperriere DP .30 .75
138 Butch Goring .40 1.00
139 Rene Robert .40 1.00
140 Ed Giacomin .50 1.25
141 Alex Delvecchio DP .30 .75
142 Jocelyn Guevremont .30 .75
143 Joey Johnston .30 .75
144 Bryan Watson DP .20 .50
145 Stan Mikita 3.00 5.00
146 Cesare Maniago .40 1.00
147 Craig Cameron .30 .75
148 Norm Ullman DP .30 .75
149 Dave Schultz RC 6.00 12.00
150 Bobby Orr 18.00 30.00
151 Phil Roberto .30 .75
152 Curt Bennett RC .30 .75
153 Gilles Villemure DP .20 .50
154 Chuck Lefley RC .30 .75
155 Richard Martin 1.00 2.50
156 Juha Widing .30 .75
157 Orland Kurtenbach .30 .75
158 Bill Collins DP .20 .50
159 Bob Stewart RC .30 .75
160 Syl Apps .40 1.00
161 Danny Grant .40 1.00
162 Billy Smith RC 15.00 25.00
163 Brian Glennie .30 .75
164 Pit Martin DP .20 .50
165 Brad Park 2.00 4.00
166 Wayne Cashman DP .30 .75
167 Gary Dornhoefer .30 .75
168 Steve Durbano RC .30 .75
169 Jacques Richard .30 .75
170 Guy Lapointe .40 1.00
171 Jim Lorentz .30 .75
172 Bob Berry DP .20 .50
173 Dennis Kearns .30 .75
174 Red Berenson .40 1.00
175 Gilles Meloche DP .20 .50
176 Al McDonough .30 .75
177 Dennis O'Brien RC .30 .75
178 Germaine Gagnon UER DP .20 .50
179 Rick Kehoe DP .20 .50
180 Bill White .30 .75
181 Vic Hadfield DP .20 .50
182 Derek Sanderson 1.50 3.00
183 Andre Dupont DP .20 .50
184 Gary Sabourin .30 .75
185 Larry Romanchych RC .30 .75
186 Peter Mahovlich .40 1.00
187 Dave Dryden .40 1.00
188 Gilles Marotte .30 .75
189 Bobby Lalonde .30 .75
190 Mickey Redmond .40 1.00
191 Series A .30 .75
192 Series B .30 .75
193 Series C .30 .75
194 Series D .30 .75
195 Series E .30 .75
196 Series F .30 .75
197 Series G .30 .75
198 Canadiens Champs 1.00 2.50

1973-74 Topps Team Stickers

COMPLETE SET (22) 50.00 100.00
1 Atlanta Flames/Sabres 2.00 5.00
2 Boston Bruins/Penguins 2.00 5.00
3 Boston Bruins/Rangers 2.00 5.00
4 Buffalo Sabres/Islanders 2.00 5.00
5 California Golden Seals/Blues 2.00 5.00
6 Chicago Blackhawks/Flames 2.00 5.00
7 Detroit Red Wings/Golden Seals 2.00 5.00
8 Detroit Red Wings/North Stars 2.00 5.00
9 Los Angeles Kings/Maple Leafs 2.00 5.00
10 Minnesota North Stars/Canadiens 2.00 5.00
11 Montreal Canadiens/Maple Leafs 2.00 5.00
12 Montreal Canadiens/Red Wings 2.00 5.00
13 New York Islanders/Bruins 2.00 5.00
14 New York Rangers/Black Hawks 2.00 5.00
15 New York Rangers/Canucks 2.00 5.00
16 Philadelphia Flyers/Red Wings 2.00 5.00
17 Pittsburgh Penguins/Black Hawks 2.00 5.00
18 St. Louis Blues/Canadiens 2.00 5.00
19 Toronto Maple Leafs/Bruins 2.00 5.00
20 Toronto Maple Leafs/Flyers 2.00 5.00
21 Vancouver Canucks/Rangers 2.00 5.00
22 NHL Logo/Kings 2.00 5.00

1974-75 Topps

Topps produced a set of 264 standard-size cards for 1974-75. Design of card fronts offers a hockey stick down the left side. The team name, player name and team logo appear at the bottom in a border that features one of the team colors. The backs feature the player's 1973-74 and career statistics, a short biography and a cartoon-illustrated fact about the player. Players from the 1974-75 expansion Washington Capitals and Kansas City Scouts (presently New Jersey Devils) appear in this set. The set marks the return of coach cards, including Don Cherry and Scotty Bowman.

COMPLETE SET (264) 125.00 200.00
1 P.Espo/Goldsworthy LL 1.50 3.00
2 B.Orr/D.Hextall LL 3.00 5.00
3 P.Espo/B.Clarke LL 2.00 4.00
4 D.Favell/B.Parent LL .60 1.50
5 B.Watson/D.Schultz LL .25 .60
6 M.Redmond/R.Mac LL .25 .60
7 Gary Bromley RC .30 .75
8 Bill Barber 2.00 4.00
9 Emile Francis CO .25 .60
10 Gilles Gilbert .60 1.50
11 John Davidson RC 4.00 8.00
12 Ron Ellis .40 1.00
13 Syl Apps .25 .60
14 Richard/Lysiak/McCreary TL .25 .60
15 Dan Bouchard .30 .75
16 Ivan Boldirev .30 .75
17 Gary Coalter RC .25 .60
18 Bob Berry .25 .60
19 Red Berenson .30 .75
20 Stan Mikita 2.00 4.00
21 Fred Shero CO RC 1.25 2.50
22 Gary Smith .30 .75
23 Bill Mikkelson .25 .60
24 Jacques Lemaire UER .60 1.50
25 Gilbert Perreault 2.00 4.00
26 Cesare Maniago .30 .75
27 Bobby Schmautz .25 .60
28 Espo/Orr/Bucyk TL 4.00 8.00
29 Steve Vickers .30 .75
30 Lowell MacDonald .25 .60
31 Fred Stanfield .25 .60
32 Ed Westfall .30 .75
33 Curt Bennett .25 .60
34 Bep Guidolin CO .25 .60
35 Cliff Koroll .25 .60
36 Gary Croteau .25 .60
37 Mike Corrigan .25 .60
38 Henry Boucha .25 .60
39 Ron Low .30 .75
40 Darryl Sittler 2.50 5.00
41 Tracy Pratt .25 .60
42 R.Martin/R.Robert TL .25 .60
43 Larry Carriere .25 .60
44 Gary Dornhoefer .30 .75
45 Denis Herron RC 1.25 2.50
46 Doug Favell .30 .75
47 Dave Gardner RC .25 .60
48 Morris Mott RC .25 .60
49 Marc Boileau CO .25 .60
50 Brad Park 1.50 3.00
51 Bob Leiter .25 .60
52 Tom Reid .25 .60
53 Serge Savard .60 1.50
54 Checklist 1-132 UER 7.00 12.00
55 Terry Harper .25 .60
56 Johnston/McKechnie TL .25 .60
57 Guy Charron .25 .60
58 Pit Martin .25 .60
59 Chris Evans .25 .60
60 Bernie Parent .60 1.50
61 Jim Lorentz .25 .60
62 Dave Kryskow RC .25 .60
63 Lou Angotti CO .25 .60
64 Bill Flett .25 .60
65 Vic Hadfield .30 .75
66 Wayne Merrick RC .25 .60
67 Andre Dupont .25 .60
68 Tom Lysiak RC .60 1.50
69 Pappin/Mikita/Bord TL .25 .60
70 Guy Lapointe .30 .75
71 Gerry O'Flaherty .25 .60
72 Marcel Dionne 3.00 6.00
73 Butch Deadmarsh RC .50 1.25
74 Butch Goring .30 .75
75 Keith Magnuson .25 .60
76 Red Kelly CO .25 .60
77 Pete Stemkowski .25 .60
78 Jim Roberts .25 .60
79 Don Luce .25 .60
80 Don Awrey .25 .60
81 Rick Kehoe .30 .75
82 Billy Smith 3.00 6.00
83 Jean-Paul Parise .25 .60
84 Redmond/Dionne/Hog TL .25 .60
85 Ed Van Impe .25 .60
86 Randy Manery .25 .60
87 Barclay Plager .30 .75
88 Inge Hammarstrom RC .25 .60
89 Ab DeMarco .25 .60
90 Bill White .25 .60
91 Al Arbour CO .60 1.50
92 Bob Stewart .25 .60
93 Jack Egers .25 .60
94 Don Lever .25 .60
95 Reggie Leach .30 .75
96 Dennis O'Brien .25 .60
97 Peter Mahovlich .30 .75
98 Goring/St.Marseille/Kozak TL .25 .60
99 Gerry Meehan .25 .60
100 Bobby Orr 15.00 30.00
101 Jean Potvin RC .25 .60
102 Rod Seiling .25 .60
103 Keith McCreary .25 .60
104 Phil Maloney CO RC .25 .60
105 Denis Dupere .25 .60
106 Steve Durbano .25 .60
107 Bob Plager UER .30 .75
108 Chris Oddleifson RC .25 .60
109 Jim Neilson .25 .60
110 Jean Pronovost .30 .75
111 Don Kozak RC .25 .60
112 Goldsworthy/Grant/Hex .30 .75
113 Jim Pappin .25 .60
114 Richard Lemieux .25 .60
115 Dennis Hextall .25 .60
116 Bill Hogaboam .25 .60
117 Canucks Leaders .25 .60
118 Jimmy Anderson CO .25 .60
119 Walt Tkaczuk .30 .75
120 Mickey Redmond .30 .75
121 Jim Schoenfeld .60 1.50
122 Jocelyn Guevremont .25 .60
123 Bob Nystrom .60 1.50
124 Cour/F.Mahov/Larose TL 1.00 2.00
125 Lew Morrison .25 .60
126 Terry Murray .30 .75
127 Richard Martin AS .30 .75
128 Ken Hodge AS .25 .60
129 Phil Esposito AS 1.25 2.50
130 Bobby Orr AS 7.00 12.00
131 Brad Park AS .75 2.00
132 Gilles Gilbert AS .25 .60
133 Lowell MacDonald AS .25 .60
134 Bill Goldsworthy AS .25 .60
135 Bobby Clarke AS 2.00 4.00
136 Bill White AS .25 .60
137 Dave Burrows AS .25 .60
138 Bernie Parent AS .60 1.50
139 Jacques Richard .25 .60
140 Yvan Cournoyer .60 1.50
141 R.Gilbert/B.Park TL .60 1.50
142 Rene Robert .30 .75
143 J. Bob Kelly RC .25 .60
144 Ross Lonsberry .25 .60
145 Jean Ratelle .60 1.50
146 Dallas Smith .25 .60
147 Bernie Geoffrion CO 1.25 2.50
148 Ted McAneeley .25 .60
149 Pierre Plante .25 .60
150 Dennis Hull .30 .75
151 Dave Keon .60 1.50
152 Dave Dunn RC .25 .60
153 Michel Belhumeur .30 .75
154 B.Clarke/D.Schultz TL 1.00 2.00
155 Ken Dryden 7.50 15.00
156 John Wright RC .25 .60
157 Larry Romanchych .25 .60
158 Ralph Stewart .25 .60
159 Mike Robitaille .25 .60
160 Ed Giacomin 1.00 2.00
161 Don Cherry CO RC 15.00 25.00
162 Checklist 133-264 7.00 12.00
163 Rick MacLeish .60 1.50
164 Greg Polis .25 .60
165 Carol Vadnais .25 .60
166 Pete Laframboise .25 .60
167 Ron Schock .25 .60
168 Lanny McDonald RC 6.00 12.00
169 Scouts Emblem .40 1.00
170 Tony Esposito 2.50 5.00
171 Pierre Jarry .25 .60
172 Dan Maloney .30 .75
173 Peter McDuffe .30 .75
174 Danny Grant .30 .75
175 John Stewart .25 .60
176 Floyd Smith CO .25 .60
177 Bert Marshall .25 .60
178 Chuck Lefley UER .25 .60
179 Gilles Villemure .30 .75
180 Borje Salming RC 6.00 12.00
181 Doug Mohns .25 .60
182 Barry Wilkins .25 .60
183 L.MacDonald/S.Apps TL .30 .75
184 Gregg Sheppard .25 .60
185 Joey Johnston .25 .60
186 Dick Redmond .25 .60
187 Simon Nolet .25 .60
188 Ron Stackhouse .25 .60
189 Marshall Johnston .25 .60
190 Richard Martin .60 1.50
191 Andre Boudrias .25 .60
192 Steve Atkinson .25 .60
193 Nick Libett .25 .60
194 Bob Murdoch RC .30 .75
195 Denis Potvin RC 15.00 25.00
196 Dave Schultz 1.00 2.00
197 G.Unger/P.Plante TL .25 .60
198 Jim McKenny .25 .60
199 Gerry Hart .25 .60
200 Phil Esposito 2.00 4.00
201 Rod Gilbert .60 1.50
202 Jacques Laperriere .30 .75
203 Barry Gibbs .25 .60
204 Billy Reay CO .30 .75
205 Gilles Meloche .30 .75
206 Wayne Cashman .30 .75
207 Dennis Ververgaert RC .25 .60
208 Phil Roberto .25 .60
209 Quarter Finals .35 .75
210 Quarter Finals .35 .75
211 Quarter Finals .35 .75
212 Quarter Finals .35 .75
213 Stanley Cup Semifinals .35 .75
214 Stanley Cup Semifinals .35 .75
215 Stanley Cup Finals .35 .75
216 Flyers Champions .60 1.50
217 Joe Watson .25 .60
218 Wayne Stephenson .30 .75
219 Sittler/Ullman/Hend TL .60 1.50
220 Bill Goldsworthy .30 .75
221 Don Marcotte .25 .60
222 Alex Delvecchio CO .25 .60
223 Stan Gilbertson .25 .60
224 Mike Murphy .25 .60
225 Jim Rutherford .30 .75
226 Phil Russell .25 .60
227 Lynn Powis .25 .60
228 Billy Harris .25 .60
229 Bob Pulford CO .30 .75
230 Ken Hodge .30 .75
231 Bill Fairbairn .25 .60
232 Guy Lafleur 7.00 12.00
233 Harris/Stew/Potvin TL 1.25 2.50
234 Fred Barrett .25 .60
235 Rogatien Vachon .75 2.00
236 Norm Ullman .60 1.50
237 Garry Unger .30 .75
238 Jack Gordon CO RC .25 .60
239 Johnny Bucyk .60 1.50
240 Bob Dailey RC .25 .60
241 Dave Burrows .25 .60
242 Len Frig RC .25 .60
243 Henri Richard Masterson .60 1.50
244 Phil Esposito Hart 1.25 2.50
245 Johnny Bucyk Byng .40 1.00
246 Phil Esposito Ross 1.25 2.50
247 Prince of Wales Trophy .30 .75
248 Bobby Orr Norris 7.00 12.00
249 Bernie Parent Vezina .60 1.50
250 Stanley Cup .40 1.00
251 Bernie Parent Smythe .60 1.50
252 Denis Potvin Calder 3.00 6.00
253 Flyers Campbell Trophy .30 .75
254 Pierre Bouchard .25 .60
255 Jude Drouin .25 .60
256 Capitals Emblem .40 1.00
257 Michel Plasse .30 .75
258 Juha Widing .25 .60
259 Bryan Watson .25 .60
260 Bobby Clarke 4.00 8.00
261 Scotty Bowman CO RC 15.00 25.00
262 Craig Patrick .30 .75
263 Craig Cameron .25 .60
264 Ted Irvine .60 1.50

1974-75 Topps Team Cloth Stickers

COMPLETE SET (24) 40.00 80.00
1 Atlanta Flames/Canadiens 1.50 4.00
2 Atlanta Flames/Penguins 1.50 4.00
3 Boston Bruins/Flames 1.50 4.00
4 Boston Bruins/Maple Leafs 1.50 4.00
5 Buffalo Sabres/Canucks 1.50 4.00
6 California Golden Seals Canadiens 1.50 4.00
7 Chicago Blackhawks/Bruins 1.50 4.00
8 Detroit Red Wings/Blues 1.50 4.00
9 Kansas City Scouts/Bruins 1.50 4.00
10 Los Angeles Kings/Black Hawks 1.50 4.00
11 Minnesota North Stars/Black Hawks 1.50 4.00
12 Montreal Canadiens/Flyers 1.50 4.00
13 Montreal Canadiens/Rangers 1.50 4.00
14 New York Islanders/North Stars 1.50 4.00
15 New York Rangers/Capitals 1.50 4.00
16 New York Rangers/Golden Seals 1.50 4.00
17 Philadelphia Flyers/Kings 1.50 4.00
18 Pittsburgh Penguins/Flames 1.50 4.00
19 St. Louis Blues/Islanders 1.50 4.00
20 Toronto Maple Leafs/Rangers 1.50 4.00
21 Toronto Maple Leafs/Red Wings 1.50 4.00
22 Vancouver Canucks/Sabres 1.50 4.00
23 Washington Capitals/Scouts 1.50 4.00
24 NHL Logo/Flyers 1.50 4.00
PUZ1 NHL Crest UL .40 1.00
PUZ2 NHL Crest UCL .40 1.00
PUZ3 NHL Crest UCR .40 1.00
PUZ4 NHL Crest UR .40 1.00
PUZ5 NHL Crest ML .40 1.00
PUZ6 NHL Crest MCL .40 1.00
PUZ7 NHL Crest MCR .40 1.00
PUZ8 NHL Crest MR .40 1.00
PUZ9 NHL Crest LL .40 1.00
PUZ10 NHL Crest LCL .40 1.00
PUZ11 NHL Crest LCR .40 1.00
PUZ12 NHL Crest LR .40 1.00

1975-76 Topps

At 330 standard-size cards, the 1975-76 Topps set stands as the company's largest until 1990-91. Fronts feature team name at top and player name at the bottom. The player's position appears in a puck at the bottom. The backs contain year-by-year and NHL career records, a short biography and a cartoon-illustrated hockey fact or referee's signal with interpretation. For the first time, team cards (81-98) with team checklist on back appear in a Topps set.

COMPLETE SET (330) 75.00 150.00
1 Stanley Cup Finals .60 1.50
2 Semi-Finals .20 .50
3 Semi-Finals .20 .50
4 Quarter Finals .20 .50
5 Quarter Finals .20 .50
6 Quarter Finals .20 .50
7 Quarter Finals .20 .50
8 Curt Bennett .20 .50
9 Johnny Bucyk .50 1.25
10 Gilbert Perreault 1.25 3.00
11 Darryl Edestrand .20 .50
12 Ivan Boldirev .20 .50
13 Nick Libett .20 .50
14 Jim McElmury RC .20 .50
15 Frank St.Marseille .20 .50
16 Blake Dunlop .20 .50
17 Yvon Lambert .30 .75
18 Gerry Hart .20 .50
19 Steve Vickers .20 .50
20 Rick MacLeish .30 .75
21 Bob Paradise .20 .50
22 Red Berenson .30 .75
23 Lanny McDonald 1.50 4.00
24 Mike Robitaille .20 .50
25 Ron Low .30 .75
26 Bryan Hextall .20 .50
27 Carol Vadnais .20 .50
28 Jim Lorentz .20 .50
29 Gary Simmons .30 .75
30 Stan Mikita 1.25 3.00
31 Bryan Watson .20 .50
32 Guy Charron .20 .50
33 Bob Murdoch .20 .50
34 Norm Gratton .20 .50
35 Ken Dryden 9.00 15.00
36 Jean Potvin .20 .50
37 Rick Middleton 1.50 3.00
38 Ed Van Impe .20 .50
39 Rick Kehoe .30 .75
40 Garry Unger .30 .75
41 Ian Turnbull .30 .75
42 Dennis Ververgaert .20 .50
43 Mike Marson RC .20 .50
44 Randy Manery .20 .50
45 Gilles Gilbert .30 .75
46 Rene Robert .30 .75
47 Bob Stewart .20 .50
48 Pit Martin .20 .50
49 Danny Grant .30 .75
50 Peter Mahovlich .30 .75
51 Dennis Patterson RC .20 .50
52 Mike Murphy .20 .50
53 Dennis O'Brien .20 .50
54 Garry Howatt .20 .50
55 Ed Giacomin .60 1.50
56 Andre Dupont .20 .50
57 Chuck Arnason .20 .50
58 Bob Gassoff RC .20 .50
59 Ron Ellis .30 .75
60 Andre Boudrias .20 .50
61 Yvon Labre .20 .50
62 Hilliard Graves .20 .50
63 Wayne Cashman .30 .75
64 Danny Gare RC 1.00 2.00
65 Rick Hampton .20 .50
66 Darcy Rota .20 .50
67 Bill Hogaboam .20 .50
68 Denis Herron .30 .75
69 Sheldon Kannegiesser .20 .50
70 Yvan Cournoyer UER .50 1.25
71 Ernie Hicke .20 .50
72 Bert Marshall .20 .50
73 Derek Sanderson .75 2.00
74 Tom Bladon .30 .75
75 Ron Schock .20 .50
76 Larry Sacharuk RC .20 .50
77 George Ferguson .20 .50
78 Ab DeMarco .20 .50
79 Tom Williams .20 .50
80 Phil Roberto .20 .50
81 Bruins Team CL 1.00 2.50
82 Seals Team CL 1.00 2.50
83 Sabres Team CL UER 1.00 2.50
84 Blackhawks CL UER 1.00 2.50
85 Flames Team CL 1.00 2.50
86 Kings Team CL 1.00 2.50
87 Red Wings Team CL 1.00 2.50
88 Scouts Team CL UER 1.00 2.50
89 North Stars Team CL 1.00 2.50
90 Canadiens Team CL 1.00 2.50
91 Maple Leafs Team CL 1.00 2.50
92 Islanders Team CL 1.00 2.50
93 Penguins Team CL 1.00 2.50
94 Rangers Team CL 1.00 2.50
95 Flyers Team CL UER 1.00 2.50
96 Blues Team CL 1.00 2.50
97 Canucks Team CL 1.00 2.50
98 Capitals Team CL 1.00 2.50
99 Checklist 1-110 6.00 10.00
100 Bobby Orr 12.00 20.00
101 Germaine Gagnon UER .20 .50
102 Phil Russell .20 .50
103 Billy Lochead .20 .50
104 Robin Burns .20 .50
105 Gary Edwards .30 .75
106 Dwight Bialowas .20 .50
107 D. Risebrough UER RC 1.25 2.50
108 Dave Lewis .20 .50
109 Bill Fairbairn .20 .50
110 Ross Lonsberry .20 .50
111 Ron Stackhouse .20 .50
112 Claude Larose .20 .50
113 Don Luce .20 .50
114 Errol Thompson RC .30 .75
115 Gary Smith .30 .75
116 Jack Lynch .20 .50
117 Jacques Richard .20 .50
118 Dallas Smith .20 .50
119 Dave Gardner .20 .50
120 Mickey Redmond .30 .75
121 John Marks .20 .50
122 Dave Hudson .20 .50
123 Bob Nevin .20 .50
124 Fred Barrett .20 .50
125 Gerry Desjardins .30 .75
126 Guy Lafleur UER 4.00 10.00
127 Jean-Paul Parise .20 .50
128 Walt Tkaczuk .30 .75
129 Gary Dornhoefer .30 .75
130 Syl Apps .20 .50
131 Bob Plager .30 .75
132 Stan Weir .20 .50
133 Tracy Pratt .20 .50
134 Jack Egers .20 .50
135 Eric Vail .20 .50
136 Al Sims .20 .50
137 Larry Patey .20 .50
138 Jim Schoenfeld .30 .75
139 Cliff Koroll .20 .50
140 Marcel Dionne 1.50 4.00
141 Jean-Guy Lagace .20 .50
142 Juha Widing .20 .50
143 Lou Nanne .30 .75
144 Serge Savard .50 1.25
145 Glenn Resch 1.25 3.00
146 Ron Greschner RC 1.00 2.00
147 Dave Schultz .30 .75
148 Barry Wilkins .20 .50
149 Floyd Thomson .20 .50
150 Darryl Sittler .50 1.25
151 Paulin Bordeleau .20 .50
152 Ron Lalonde RC .20 .50
153 Larry Romanchych .20 .50
154 Larry Carriere .20 .50
155 Andre Savard .20 .50
156 Dave Hrechkosy RC .20 .50
157 Bill White .20 .50
158 Dave Kryskow .20 .50
159 Denis Dupere .20 .50
160 Rogatien Vachon .60 1.50
161 Doug Rombough .20 .50
162 Murray Wilson .20 .50
163 Bob Bourne RC 1.00 2.00
164 Gilles Marotte .20 .50
165 Vic Hadfield .30 .75
166 Reggie Leach .30 .75
167 Jerry Butler .20 .50
168 Inge Hammarstrom .20 .50
169 Chris Oddleifson .20 .50
170 Greg Joly .20 .50
171 Checklist 111-220 6.00 10.00
172 Pat Quinn .30 .75
173 Dave Forbes .20 .50
174 Len Frig .20 .50
175 Richard Martin .30 .75
176 Keith Magnuson .20 .50
177 Dan Maloney .20 .50
178 Craig Patrick .30 .75
179 Tom Williams .20 .50
180 Bill Goldsworthy .30 .75
181 Steve Shutt .50 1.25
182 Ralph Stewart .20 .50
183 John Davidson 1.25 3.00
184 Bob Kelly .20 .50
185 Ed Johnston .30 .75
186 Dave Burrows .20 .50
187 Dave Dunn .20 .50
188 Dennis Kearns .20 .50
189 Bill Clement 1.25 3.00
190 Gilles Meloche .30 .75
191 Bob Leiter .20 .50
192 Jerry Korab .20 .50
193 Joey Johnston .20 .50
194 Walt McKechnie .20 .50
195 Wilf Paiement .20 .50
196 Bob Berry .20 .50
197 Dean Talafous RC .20 .50
198 Guy Lapointe .30 .75
199 Clark Gillies RC 2.00 4.00
200 Phil Esposito 1.25 3.00
201 Greg Polis .20 .50
202 Jimmy Watson .30 .75
203 Gord McRae RC .30 .75
204 Lowell MacDonald .20 .50
205 Barclay Plager .30 .75
206 Don Lever .20 .50
207 Bill Mikkelson .20 .50
208 Espo/Lafleur/Martin LL 1.25 3.00
209 Clarke/Orr/P.Mahov LL 1.50 4.00
210 Orr/Espo/Dionne LL 2.00 5.00
211 Schultz/Dupont/Rusl LL .20 .50
212 Espo/Martin/Grant LL .60 1.50
213 Parent/Vach/Dryden LL 2.00 5.00
214 Barry Gibbs .20 .50
215 Ken Hodge .30 .75
216 Jocelyn Guevremont .20 .50
217 Warren Williams RC .20 .50
218 Dick Redmond .20 .50
219 Jim Rutherford .30 .75
220 Simon Nolet .20 .50
221 Butch Goring .30 .75
222 Glen Sather .30 .75
223 Mario Tremblay RC 1.50 3.00
224 Jude Drouin .20 .50
225 Rod Gilbert .50 1.25
226 Bill Barber .50 1.25
227 Gary Inness RC .30 .75
228 Wayne Merrick .20 .50
229 Rod Seiling .20 .50
230 Tom Lysiak .30 .75
231 Bob Dailey .20 .50
232 Michel Belhumeur .30 .75
233 Bill Hajt RC .20 .50
234 Jim Pappin .20 .50
235 Gregg Sheppard .20 .50
236 Gary Bergman .20 .50
237 Randy Rota .20 .50
238 Neil Komadoski .20 .50
239 Craig Cameron .20 .50
240 Tony Esposito 1.25 3.00
241 Larry Robinson 2.50 6.00
242 Billy Harris .20 .50
243 Jean Ratelle .50 1.25
244 Ted Irvine UER .20 .50
245 Bob Neely .20 .50
246 Bobby Lalonde .20 .50
247 Ron Jones RC .20 .50
248 Rey Comeau .20 .50
249 Michel Plasse .30 .75
250 Bobby Clarke 2.50 6.00
251 Bobby Schmautz .20 .50
252 Peter McNab RC 1.25 2.50
253 Al MacAdam .20 .50
254 Dennis Hull .30 .75
255 Terry Harper .20 .50
256 Peter McDuffe .30 .75
257 Jean Hamel .20 .50
258 Jacques Lemaire .50 1.25
259 Bob Nystrom .30 .75
260 Brad Park .75 2.00
261 Cesare Maniago .30 .75
262 Don Saleski .20 .50
263 J. Bob Kelly .20 .50
264 Bob Hess RC .20 .50
265 Blaine Stoughton .30 .75
266 John Gould .20 .50
267 Checklist 221-330 6.00 10.00
268 Dan Bouchard .30 .75
269 Don Marcotte .20 .50
270 Jim Neilson .20 .50
271 Craig Ramsay .20 .50
272 Grant Mulvey RC .30 .75
273 Larry Giroux RC .20 .50
274 Real Lemieux .20 .50
275 Denis Potvin 2.50 6.00
276 Don Kozak .20 .50
277 Tom Reid .20 .50
278 Bob Gainey 1.50 4.00
279 Nick Beverley .20 .50
280 Jean Pronovost .30 .75
281 Joe Watson .20 .50
282 Chuck Lefley .20 .50
283 Borje Salming 2.00 5.00

4 Garnet Bailey .20 .50
5 Gregg Boddy .20 .50
6 Bobby Clarke AS1 1.25 3.00
7 Denis Potvin AS1 1.25 3.00
8 Bobby Orr AS1 6.00 10.00
9 Richard Martin AS1 .20 .50
0 Guy Lafleur AS1 1.50 4.00
1 Bernie Parent AS1 .50 1.25
2 Phil Esposito AS2 .75 2.00
3 Guy Lapointe AS2 .20 .50
4 Borje Salming AS2 1.00 2.50
5 Steve Vickers AS2 .20 .50
6 Rene Robert AS2 .20 .50
7 Rogatien Vachon AS2 .60 1.50
8 Buster Harvey RC .20 .50
9 Gary Sabourin .20 .50
0 Bernie Parent .50 1.25
1 Terry O'Reilly .30 .75
2 Ed Westfall .30 .75
3 Pete Stemkowski .20 .50
4 Pierre Bouchard .20 .50
5 Pierre Larouche RC 2.00 4.00
6 Lee Fogolin RC .30 .75
7 Gerry O'Flaherty .20 .50
8 Phil Myre .30 .75
9 Pierre Plante .20 .50
0 Dennis Hextall .20 .50
1 Jim McKenny .20 .50
2 Vic Venasky .20 .50
3 Flames Leaders .20 .50
4 Espo/Orr/Bucyk TL 2.00 5.00
5 Sabres Leaders .20 .50
6 Seals Leaders .20 .50
7 S.Mikita/J.Pappin TL .20 .50
8 D.Grant/M.Dionne TL .20 .50
9 Scouts Leaders .20 .50
0 Kings Leaders .20 .50
1 North Stars Leaders .20 .50
2 Lafleur/P.Mahov TL .60 1.50
3 Nystrom/Potvin/Gill TL .60 1.50
4 Vick/Gilbert/Ratelle TL .20 .50
5 R.Leach/B.Clarke TL .20 .50
6 Penguins Leaders .20 .50
7 Blues Leaders .20 .50
8 Darryl Sittler TL .60 1.50
9 Canucks Leaders .20 .50
0 Capitals Leaders .20 .50

1976-77 Topps

e 1976-77 Topps set contains 264 color standard-ze cards. The fronts contain team name and logo at e top with player name and position at the bottom. e backs feature 1975-76 and career statistics, career ghlights and a cartoon-illustrated fact. The first cards Colorado Rockies (formerly Kansas City) players pear this year. Rookie Cards in this set include Bryan ottier and Dennis Maruk.

OMPLETE SET (264) 100.00 200.00
Leach/Lafleur/Larou LL .75 2.00
Clarke/Lafleur/Perr/ LL .75 2.00
Lafleur/Clarke/Perr LL .75 2.00
Durbno/Watsn/Schultz LL .20 .50
Espo/Lafleur/Potvin LL .75 2.00
Dryden/Resch/Laroc LL 1.25 3.00
Gary Doak .20 .50
Jacques Richard .20 .50
Wayne Dillon .20 .50
0 Bernie Parent .75 2.00
1 Ed Westfall .25 .60
2 Dick Redmond .20 .50
3 Bryan Hextall .20 .50
4 Jean Pronovost .25 .60
5 Peter Mahovlich .25 .60
6 Danny Grant .25 .60
7 Phil Myre .25 .60
8 Wayne Merrick .20 .50
9 Steve Durbano .20 .50
0 Derek Sanderson .60 1.50
1 Mike Murphy .20 .50
2 Borje Salming 1.00 2.50
3 Mike Walton .20 .50
4 Randy Manery .20 .50
5 Ken Hodge .25 .60
6 Mel Bridgman RC .40 1.00
7 Jerry Korab .20 .50
8 Gilles Gratton .25 .60
9 Andre St.Laurent .20 .50
0 Yvan Cournoyer .40 1.00
1 Phil Russell .20 .50
2 Dennis Hextall .20 .50
3 Lowell MacDonald .20 .50
4 Dennis O'Brien .20 .50
5 Gerry Meehan .20 .50
6 Gilles Meloche .25 .60
7 Wilf Paiement .25 .60
8 Bob MacMillan RC .40 1.00
9 Ian Turnbull .25 .60
0 Rogatien Vachon .50 1.25
1 Nick Beverley .20 .50
2 Rene Robert .25 .60
3 Andre Savard .20 .50
4 Bob Gainey 1.00 2.50
5 Joe Watson .20 .50
6 Billy Smith 1.00 2.50
7 Darcy Rota .20 .50
8 Rick Lapointe RC .20 .50
9 Pierre Jarry .20 .50
0 Syl Apps .20 .50
1 Eric Vail .20 .50
2 Greg Joly .20 .50
3 Don Lever .20 .50
4 Bob Murdoch Seals .20 .50
5 Denis Herron .25 .60
6 Mike Bloom .20 .50
7 Bill Fairbairn .20 .50
8 Fred Stanfield .20 .50
9 Steve Shutt .75 2.00
60 Brad Park .60 1.50
61 Gilles Villemure .25 .60
62 Bert Marshall .20 .50
63 Chuck Lefley .20 .50
64 Simon Nolet .20 .50
65 Reggie Leach RB .25 .60
66 Darryl Sittler RB .40 1.00
67 Bryan Trottier RB 3.00 8.00
68 Garry Unger RB .25 .60
69 Ron Low .25 .60
70 Bobby Clarke 1.50 4.00
71 Michel Bergeron RC .20 .50
72 Ron Stackhouse .20 .50
73 Bill Hogaboam .20 .50
74 Bob Murdoch Kings .20 .50
75 Steve Vickers .20 .50
76 Pit Martin .20 .50
77 Gerry Hart .20 .50
78 Craig Ramsay .20 .50
79 Michel Larocque .25 .60
80 Jean Ratelle .40 1.00
81 Don Saleski .20 .50
82 Bill Clement .40 1.00
83 Dave Burrows .20 .50
84 Wayne Thomas .25 .60
85 John Gould .20 .50
86 Dennis Maruk RC 1.00 2.00
87 Ernie Hicke .20 .50
88 Jim Rutherford .25 .60
89 Dale Tallon .20 .50
90 Rod Gilbert .40 1.00
91 Marcel Dionne 1.25 3.00
92 Chuck Arnason .20 .50
93 Jean Potvin .20 .50
94 Don Luce .20 .50
95 Johnny Bucyk .40 1.00
96 Larry Goodenough .20 .50
97 Mario Tremblay .25 .60
98 Nelson Pyatt RC .20 .50
99 Brian Glennie .20 .50
100 Tony Esposito .75 2.00
101 Dan Maloney .20 .50
102 Barry Wilkins .20 .50
103 Dean Talafous .20 .50
104 Ed Staniowski RC .20 .50
105 Dallas Smith .20 .50
106 Jude Drouin .20 .50
107 Pat Hickey .20 .50
108 Jocelyn Guevremont .20 .50
109 Doug Risebrough .40 1.00
110 Reggie Leach .25 .60
111 Dan Bouchard .25 .60
112 Chris Oddleifson .20 .50
113 Rick Hampton .20 .50
114 John Marks .20 .50
115 Bryan Trottier RC 20.00 35.00
116 Checklist 1-132 3.00 6.00
117 Greg Polis .20 .50
118 Peter McNab .40 1.00
119 Jim Roberts .20 .50
120 Gerry Cheevers .75 2.00
121 Rick MacLeish .25 .60
122 Billy Lochead .20 .50
123 Tom Reid .20 .50
124 Rick Kehoe .25 .60
125 Keith Magnuson .20 .50
126 Clark Gillies .40 1.00
127 Rick Middleton .75 2.00
128 Bill Hajt .20 .50
129 Jacques Lemaire .40 1.00
130 Terry O'Reilly .40 1.00
131 Andre Dupont .20 .50
132 Flames Team CL .75 2.00
133 Bruins Team CL .75 2.00
134 Sabres Team CL .75 2.00
135 Seals Team CL .75 2.00
136 Blackhawks Team CL .75 2.00
137 Red Wings Team CL .75 2.00
138 Scouts Team CL .75 2.00
139 Kings Team CL .75 2.00
140 North Stars Team CL .75 2.00
141 Canadiens Team CL .75 2.00
142 Islanders Team CL .75 2.00
143 Rangers Team CL .75 2.00
144 Flyers Team CL .75 2.00
145 Penguins Team CL .75 2.00
146 Blues Team CL .75 2.00
147 Maple Leafs Team CL .75 2.00
148 Canucks Team CL .75 2.00
149 Capitals Team CL .75 2.00
150 Dave Schultz .60 1.50
151 Larry Robinson 1.50 4.00
152 Al Smith .25 .60
153 Bob Nystrom .25 .60
154 Ron Greschner UER .20 .50
155 Gregg Sheppard .20 .50
156 Alain Daigle .20 .50
157 Ed Van Impe .20 .50
158 Tim Young RC .25 .60
159 Gary Bergman .20 .50
160 Ed Giacomin .60 1.50
161 Yvon Labre .20 .50
162 Jim Lorentz .20 .50
163 Guy Lafleur 2.50 6.00
164 Tom Bladon .25 .60
165 Wayne Cashman .25 .60
166 Pete Stemkowski .20 .50
167 Grant Mulvey .20 .50
168 Yves Belanger RC .25 .60
169 Bill Goldsworthy .25 .60
170 Denis Potvin 1.50 4.00
171 Nick Libett .20 .50
172 Michel Plasse .25 .60
173 Lou Nanne .20 .50
174 Tom Lysiak .25 .60
175 Dennis Ververgaert .20 .50
176 Gary Simmons .25 .60
177 Pierre Bouchard .20 .50
178 Bill Barber .60 1.50
179 Darryl Edestrand .20 .50
180 Gilbert Perreault .75 2.00
181 Dave Maloney RC .40 1.00
182 Jean-Paul Parise .20 .50
183 Bobby Sheehan .20 .50
184 Pete Lopresti RC .25 .60
185 Don Kozak .20 .50
186 Guy Charron .20 .50
187 Stan Gilbertson .20 .50
188 Bill Nyrop RC .20 .50
189 Bobby Schmautz .20 .50
190 Wayne Stephenson .25 .60
191 Brian Spencer .20 .50
192 Gilles Marotte .20 .50
193 Lorne Henning .20 .50
194 Bob Neely .20 .50
195 Dennis Hull .25 .60
196 Walt McKechnie .20 .50
197 Curt Ridley RC .20 .50
198 Dwight Bialowas .20 .50
199 Pierre Larouche .40 1.00
200 Ken Dryden 6.00 12.00
201 Ross Lonsberry .20 .50
202 Curt Bennett .20 .50
203 Hartland Monahan RC .20 .50
204 John Davidson .75 2.00
205 Serge Savard .40 1.00
206 Garry Howatt .20 .50
207 Darryl Sittler 1.25 3.00
208 J.P. Bordeleau .20 .50
209 Henry Boucha .20 .50
210 Richard Martin .25 .60
211 Vic Venasky .20 .50
212 Buster Harvey .20 .50
213 Bobby Orr 10.00 20.00
214 Martin/Perrlt/Robert .75 2.00
215 Barber/Clarke/Leach 1.00 2.50
216 Gillies/Trottier/Harris 1.50 4.00
217 Gainey/Jarvis/Roberts .20 .50
218 MacDon/Apps/Pronvst .20 .50
219 Bob Kelly .20 .50
220 Walt Tkaczuk .20 .50
221 Dave Lewis .40 1.00
222 Danny Gare .40 1.00
223 Guy Lapointe .25 .60
224 Hank Nowak RC .20 .50
225 Stan Mikita 1.00 2.50
226 Vic Hadfield .25 .60
227 Bernie Wolfe RC .25 .60
228 Bryan Watson .20 .50
229 Ralph Stewart .20 .50
230 Gerry Desjardins .25 .60
231 John Bednarski RC .20 .50
232 Yvon Lambert .20 .50
233 Orest Kindrachuk .20 .50
234 Don Marcotte .20 .50
235 Bill White .20 .50
236 Red Berenson .25 .60
237 Al MacAdam .20 .50
238 Rick Blight RC .20 .50
239 Butch Goring .25 .60
240 Cesare Maniago .25 .60
241 Jim Schoenfeld .25 .60
242 Cliff Koroll .20 .50
243 Mickey Redmond .25 .60
244 Rick Chartraw .20 .50
245 Phil Esposito 1.00 2.50
246 Dave Forbes .20 .50
247 Jimmy Watson .20 .50
248 Ron Schock .20 .50
249 Fred Barrett .20 .50
250 Glenn Resch .75 2.00
251 Ivan Boldirev .20 .50
252 Billy Harris .20 .50
253 Lee Fogolin .20 .50
254 Murray Wilson .20 .50
255 Gilles Gilbert .25 .60
256 Gary Dornhoefer .25 .60
257 Carol Vadnais .20 .50
258 Checklist 133-264 3.00 6.00
259 Errol Thompson .20 .50
260 Garry Unger .25 .60
261 J. Bob Kelly .20 .50
262 Terry Harper .20 .50
263 Blake Dunlop .20 .50
264 Canadiens Champs .60 1.50

1976-77 Topps Glossy Inserts

This 22-card insert set was issued with the 1976-77 Topps hockey card set but not with the O-Pee-Chee hockey cards unlike the glossy insert produced "jointly" by Topps and O-Pee-Chee the next year. This set is very similar to (but much more difficult to find than) the glossy insert set of the following year. The cards were printed in the United States. These rounded-corner cards are approximately 2 1/4" by 3 1/4".

COMPLETE SET (22) 40.00 80.00
1 Bobby Clarke 2.00 4.00
2 Brad Park 1.25 2.50
3 Tony Esposito 1.50 3.00
4 Marcel Dionne 2.00 4.00
5 Ken Dryden 7.50 15.00
6 Glenn Resch 1.00 2.00
7 Phil Esposito 2.50 5.00
8 Darryl Sittler 1.50 3.00
9 Gilbert Perreault 1.00 2.00
10 Denis Potvin 2.00 4.00
11 Guy Lafleur 4.00 8.00
12 Bill Barber 1.00 2.00
13 Syl Apps .50 1.00
14 Johnny Bucyk 1.00 2.00
15 Bryan Trottier 7.50 15.00
16 Dennis Hull .50 1.00
17 Guy Lapointe .75 1.50
18 Rod Gilbert 1.25 2.50
19 Richard Martin .75 1.50
20 Bobby Orr 12.50 25.00
21 Reggie Leach .75 1.50
22 Jean Ratelle 1.25 2.50

1977-78 Topps

BOBBY ORR • DEFENSE
BLACK HAWKS

The 1977-78 Topps set consists of 264 standard-size cards. Cards 203 (Stan Gilbertson) and 255 (Bill Fairbairn) differ from those of O-Pee-Chee. Card fronts have team name and logo, player name and position at the bottom. Yearly statistics including minor league numbers are featured on the back along with a short biography and a cartoon-illustrated fact about the player. After the initial print run, Topps changed the photos on card numbers 131, 138, 149 and 152. Two of the changes (138 and 149) were necessary corrections. Rookie Cards include Mike Milbury and Mike Palmateer.

COMPLETE SET (264) 45.00 90.00
1 Shutt/Lafleur/Dionne LL 1.00 2.50
2 Lafleur/Dionne/Sal LL .60 1.50
3 Lafleur/Dionne/Shutt LL .75 2.00
4 Williams/Polnch/Gasff LL .15 .40
5 McDonald/Espo/Will LL .30 .75
6 Laroc/Dryden/Resch LL 1.00 2.50
7 Perr/Shutt/Lafleur LL .60 1.50
8 Dryden/Vach/Parent LL 1.25 3.00
9 Brian Spencer .10 .25
10 Denis Potvin AS2 .30 .75
11 Nick Fotiu .30 .75
12 Bob Murray .10 .25
13 Pete Lopresti .15 .40
14 J. Bob Kelly .10 .25
15 Rick MacLeish .30 .75
16 Terry Harper .10 .25
17 Willi Plett RC .30 .75
18 Peter McNab .15 .40
19 Wayne Thomas .15 .40
20 Pierre Bouchard .10 .25
21 Dennis Maruk .30 .75
22 Mike Murphy .10 .25
23 Cesare Maniago .15 .40
24 Paul Gardner RC .30 .75
25 Rod Gilbert .30 .75
26 Orest Kindrachuk .10 .25
27 Bill Hajt .10 .25
28 John Davidson .30 .75
29 Jean-Paul Parise .10 .25
30 Larry Robinson AS1 1.25 3.00
31 Yvon Labre .10 .25
32 Walt McKechnie .10 .25
33 Rick Kehoe .15 .40
34 Randy Holt RC .15 .40
35 Garry Unger .15 .40
36 Lou Nanne .10 .25
37 Dan Bouchard .15 .40
38 Darryl Sittler .75 2.00
39 Bob Murdoch .10 .25
40 Jean Ratelle .30 .75
41 Dave Maloney .10 .25
42 Danny Gare .30 .75
43 Jimmy Watson .10 .25
44 Tom Williams .10 .25
45 Serge Savard .30 .75
46 Derek Sanderson .30 .75
47 John Marks .10 .25
48 Al Cameron RC .10 .25
49 Dean Talafous .10 .25
50 Glenn Resch .30 .75
51 Ron Schock .10 .25
52 Gary Croteau .10 .25
53 Gerry Meehan .10 .25
54 Ed Staniowski .10 .25
55 Phil Esposito .75 2.00
56 Dennis Ververgaert .10 .25
57 Rick Wilson .10 .25
58 Jim Lorentz .10 .25
59 Bobby Schmautz .10 .25
60 Guy Lapointe AS2 .15 .40
61 Ivan Boldirev .10 .25
62 Bob Nystrom .10 .25
63 Rick Hampton .10 .25
64 Jack Valiquette .10 .25
65 Bernie Parent .60 1.50
66 Dave Burrows .10 .25
67 Butch Goring .15 .40
68 Checklist 1-132 2.00 4.00
69 Murray Wilson .10 .25
70 Ed Giacomin .30 .75
71 Flames Team CL .50 1.25
72 Bruins Team CL .50 1.25
73 Sabres Team CL .50 1.25
74 Blackhawks Team CL .50 1.25
75 Barons Team CL .50 1.25
76 Rockies Team CL .50 1.25
77 Red Wings Team CL .50 1.25
78 Kings Team CL .50 1.25
79 North Stars Team CL .50 1.25
80 Canadiens Team CL .50 1.25
81 Islanders Team CL .50 1.25
82 Rangers Team CL .50 1.25
83 Flyers Team CL .50 1.25
84 Penguins Team CL .50 1.25
85 Blues Team CL .50 1.25
86 Maple Leafs Team CL .50 1.25
87 Canucks Team CL .50 1.25
88 Capitals Team CL .50 1.25
89 Keith Magnuson .10 .25
90 Walt Tkaczuk .15 .40
91 Bill Nyrop .10 .25
92 Michel Plasse .15 .40
93 Bob Bourne .15 .40
94 Lee Fogolin .10 .25
95 Gregg Sheppard .10 .25
96 Hartland Monahan .10 .25
97 Curt Bennett .10 .25
98 Bob Dailey .10 .25
99 Bill Goldsworthy .15 .40
100 Ken Dryden AS1 3.00 8.00
101 Grant Mulvey .10 .25
102 Pierre Larouche .30 .75
103 Nick Libett .10 .25
104 Rick Smith .10 .25
105 Bryan Trottier 4.00 10.00
106 Pierre Jarry .10 .25
107 Red Berenson .15 .40
108 Jim Schoenfeld .15 .40
109 Gilles Meloche .15 .40
110 Lanny McDonald AS2 .60 1.50
111 Don Lever .10 .25
112 Greg Polis .10 .25
113 Gary Sargent RC .10 .25
114 Earl Anderson RC .10 .25
115 Bobby Clarke 1.25 3.00
116 Dave Lewis .10 .25
117 Darcy Rota .10 .25
118 Andre Savard .10 .25
119 Denis Herron .15 .40
120 Steve Shutt AS1 .30 .75
121 Mel Bridgman .10 .25
122 Buster Harvey .10 .25
123 Roland Eriksson RC .10 .25
124 Dale Tallon .10 .25
125 Gilles Gilbert .15 .40
126 Billy Harris .10 .25
127 Tom Lysiak .15 .40
128 Jerry Korab .10 .25
129 Bob Gainey .60 1.50
130 Wilf Paiement .15 .40
131A Tom Bladon Standing 1.00 2.00
131B Tom Bladon Skating .10 .25
132 Ernie Hicke .10 .25
133 J.P. LeBlanc .10 .25
134 Mike Milbury RC 2.50 5.00
135 Pit Martin .10 .25
136 Steve Vickers .10 .25
137 Don Awrey .10 .25
138A Bernie Wolfe MacAdam 1.00 2.00
138B Bernie Wolfe COR .10 .25
139 Doug Jarvis .30 .75
140 Borje Salming AS1 .60 1.50
141 Bob MacMillan .10 .25
142 Wayne Stephenson .15 .40
143 Dave Forbes .10 .25
144 Jean Potvin .10 .25
145 Guy Charron .10 .25
146 Cliff Koroll .10 .25
147 Danny Grant .15 .40
148 Bill Hogaboam UER .10 .25
149A Al MacAdam ERR Wolfe 1.00 2.00
149B Al MacAdam COR .10 .25
150 Gerry Desjardins .15 .40
151 Yvon Lambert .10 .25
152A Rick Lapointe ERR 2.00 5.00
152B Rick Lapointe COR .10 .25
153 Ed Westfall .15 .40
154 Carol Vadnais .10 .25
155 Johnny Bucyk .30 .75
156 J.P. Bordeleau .10 .25
157 Ron Stackhouse .10 .25
158 Glen Sharpley RC .10 .25
159 Michel Bergeron .10 .25
160 Rogatien Vachon AS2 .30 .75
161 Fred Stanfield .10 .25
162 Gerry Hart .10 .25
163 Mario Tremblay .15 .40
164 Andre Dupont .10 .25
165 Don Marcotte .10 .25
166 Wayne Dillon .10 .25
167 Claude Larose .10 .25
168 Eric Vail .10 .25
169 Tom Edur .10 .25
170 Tony Esposito .60 1.50
171 Andre St.Laurent .10 .25
172 Dan Maloney .10 .25
173 Dennis O'Brien .10 .25
174 Blair Chapman RC .10 .25
175 Dennis Kearns .10 .25
176 Wayne Merrick .10 .25
177 Michel Larocque .15 .40
178 Bob Kelly .10 .25
179 Dave Farrish RC .10 .25
180 Richard Martin AS2 .30 .75
181 Gary Doak .10 .25
182 Jude Drouin .10 .25
183 Barry Dean RC .10 .25
184 Gary Smith .15 .40
185 Reggie Leach .30 .75
186 Ian Turnbull .15 .40
187 Vic Venasky .10 .25
188 Wayne Bianchin RC .10 .25
189 Doug Risebrough .15 .40
190 Brad Park .30 .75
191 Craig Ramsay .10 .25
192 Ken Hodge .15 .40
193 Phil Myre .15 .40
194 Garry Howatt .10 .25
195 Stan Mikita .75 2.00
196 Garnet Bailey .10 .25
197 Dennis Hextall .10 .25
198 Nick Beverley .10 .25
199 Larry Patey .10 .25
200 Guy Lafleur AS1 2.00 5.00
201 Don Edwards RC 1.00 2.50
202 Gary Dornhoefer .15 .40
203 Stan Gilbertson .10 .25
204 Alex Pirus RC .10 .25
205 Peter Mahovlich .15 .40
206 Bert Marshall .10 .25
207 Gilles Gratton .15 .40
208 Alain Daigle .10 .25
209 Chris Oddleifson .10 .25
210 Gilbert Perreault AS2 .60 1.50
211 Mike Palmateer RC 2.50 5.00
212 Billy Lochead .10 .25
213 Dick Redmond .10 .25
214 Guy Lafleur RB .60 1.50
215 Ian Turnbull RB .10 .25
216 Guy Lafleur RB .60 1.50
217 Steve Shutt RB .30 .75
218 Guy Lafleur RB .60 1.50
219 Lorne Henning .10 .25
220 Terry O'Reilly .30 .75
221 Pat Hickey .10 .25
222 Rene Robert .15 .40
223 Tim Young .10 .25
224 Dunc Wilson .15 .40
225 Dennis Hull .15 .40
226 Rod Seiling .10 .25
227 Bill Barber .30 .75
228 Dennis Polonich RC .10 .25
229 Billy Smith .60 1.50
230 Yvan Cournoyer .30 .75
231 Don Luce .10 .25
232 Mike McEwen RC .10 .25
233 Don Saleski .10 .25
234 Wayne Cashman .30 .75
235 Phil Russell .10 .25
236 Mike Corrigan .10 .25
237 Guy Chouinard .15 .40
238 Steve Jensen RC .10 .25
239 Jim Rutherford .15 .40
240 Marcel Dionne AS1 1.25 2.50
241 Rejean Houle .10 .25
242 Jocelyn Guevremont .10 .25
243 Jim Harrison .10 .25
244 Don Murdoch RC .30 .75
245 Rick Green RC .30 .75
246 Rick Middleton .30 .75
247 Joe Watson .10 .25
248 Syl Apps .10 .25
249 Checklist 133-264 2.00 4.00
250 Clark Gillies .30 .75
251 Bobby Orr 9.00 15.00
252 Nelson Pyatt .10 .25
253 Gary McAdam RC .10 .25
254 Jacques Lemaire .30 .75
255 Bill Fairbairn .10 .25
256 Ron Greschner .15 .40
257 Ross Lonsberry .10 .25
258 Dave Gardner .10 .25
259 Rick Blight .10 .25
260 Gerry Cheevers .30 .75
261 Jean Pronovost .15 .40
262 Mon/NYI Semi-Finals .15 .40
263 Bruins Semi-Finals .15 .40
264 Canadiens Champs .30 .75

1977-78 Topps/O-Pee-Chee Glossy

This set of 22 numbered cards was issued with either square or round corners as an insert with both the Topps and O-Pee-Chee hockey cards of 1977-78. Cards were numbered on the back and measure 2 1/4" by 3 1/4". They are essentially the same as the O-Pee-Chee insert issue of the same year. The O-Pee-Chee inserts have the same card numbers and pictures, same values, but different copyright lines on the reverses. The cards are priced below for the round cornered version; the square cornered cards are worth approximately 10 percent more than the prices below.

COMPLETE SET (22) 7.50 15.00
1 Wayne Cashman .20 .40
2 Gerry Cheevers .75 1.50
3 Bobby Clarke .75 1.50
4 Marcel Dionne .75 1.50
5 Ken Dryden 2.00 4.00
6 Clark Gillies .20 .40
7 Guy Lafleur 1.25 2.50
8 Reggie Leach .18 .35
9 Rick MacLeish .25 .50
10 Dave Maloney .13 .25
11 Richard Martin .20 .40
12 Don Murdoch .13 .25
13 Brad Park .38 .75
14 Gilbert Perreault .50 1.00
15 Denis Potvin .75 1.50
16 Jean Ratelle .38 .75
17 Glenn Resch .38 .75
18 Larry Robinson .75 1.50
19 Steve Shutt .38 .75
20 Darryl Sittler .63 1.25
21 Rogatien Vachon .38 .75
22 Tim Young .13 .25

1978-79 Topps

The 1978-79 Topps set consists of 264 standard-size cards. Card fronts have team name, logo and player position in the top left corner. The player's name is within the top border. A short biography, yearly statistics including minor leagues and a facsimile autograph are included on the back.

COMPLETE SET (264) 40.00 80.00
1 Mike Bossy HL 4.00 8.00
2 Phil Esposito HL .40 1.00
3 Guy Lafleur HL .40 1.00
4 Darryl Sittler HL .25 .60
5 Garry Unger HL .15 .40
6 Gary Edwards .15 .40
7 Rick Blight .08 .25
8 Larry Patey .08 .25
9 Craig Ramsay .08 .25
10 Bryan Trottier AS1 2.00 5.00
11 Don Murdoch .08 .25
12 Phil Russell .08 .25
13 Doug Jarvis .15 .40
14 Gene Carr .08 .25
15 Bernie Parent .40 1.00
16 Perry Miller .08 .25
17 Kent-Erik Andersson RC .15 .40
18 Gregg Sheppard .08 .25
19 Dennis Owchar .08 .25
20 Rogatien Vachon .25 .60
21 Dan Maloney .08 .25
22 Guy Charron .08 .25
23 Dick Redmond .08 .25
24 Checklist 1-132 1.00 2.50
25 Anders Hedberg .15 .40
26 Mel Bridgman .15 .40
27 Lee Fogolin .08 .25
28 Gilles Meloche .15 .40
29 Garry Howatt .08 .25
30 Darryl Sittler AS2 .60 1.50
31 Curt Bennett .08 .25
32 Andre St.Laurent .08 .25
33 Blair Chapman .08 .25
34 Keith Magnuson .08 .25
35 Pierre Larouche .25 .60
36 Michel Plasse .15 .40
37 Gary Sargent .08 .25
38 Mike Walton .08 .25
39 Robert Picard RC .15 .40
40 Terry O'Reilly AS2 .15 .40
41 Dave Farrish .08 .25
42 Gary McAdam .08 .25
43 Joe Watson .08 .25
44 Yves Belanger .15 .40
45 Steve Jensen .08 .25
46 Bob Stewart .08 .25
47 Darcy Rota .08 .25
48 Dennis Hextall .08 .25
49 Bert Marshall .08 .25
50 Ken Dryden AS1 2.50 6.00
51 Peter Mahovlich .15 .40
52 Dennis Ververgaert .08 .25
53 Inge Hammarstrom .08 .25
54 Doug Favell .15 .40
55 Steve Vickers .08 .25
56 Syl Apps .08 .25
57 Errol Thompson .08 .25
58 Don Luce .08 .25
59 Mike Milbury .25 .60
60 Yvan Cournoyer .25 .60
61 Kirk Bowman .08 .25
62 Billy Smith .25 .60
63 Lafleur/Bossy/Shutt LL 1.50 4.00
64 Trott/Lafleur/Sitt LL .60 1.50
65 Lafleur/Trott/Sitt LL .60 1.50
66 Schitz/Wil/Polnich LL .10 .30
67 Bossy/Espo/Shutt LL 1.00 2.50
68 Dryden/Parent/Gilb LL 1.00 2.50
69 Lafleur/Barber/Sitt LL .50 1.25
70 Parent/Dryden/Espo LL 1.00 2.50
71 Bob Kelly .08 .25
72 Ron Stackhouse .08 .25
73 Wayne Dillon .08 .25
74 Jim Rutherford .15 .40
75 Stan Mikita .60 1.50
76 Bob Gainey .40 1.00
77 Gerry Hart .08 .25
78 Lanny McDonald .40 1.00
79 Brad Park .40 1.00
80 Richard Martin .25 .60
81 Bernie Wolfe .15 .40
82 Bob MacMillan .08 .25
83 Brad Maxwell RC .08 .25
84 Mike Fidler .08 .25
85 Carol Vadnais .08 .25
86 Don Lever .08 .25
87 Phil Myre .15 .40
88 Paul Gardner .08 .25
89 Bob Murray .08 .25
90 Guy Lafleur AS1 1.50 4.00
91 Bob Murdoch .08 .25
92 Ron Ellis .15 .40
93 Jude Drouin .08 .25
94 Jocelyn Guevremont .08 .25
95 Gilles Gilbert .15 .40
96 Bob Sirois .08 .25
97 Tom Lysiak .15 .40
98 Andre Dupont .08 .25
99 Per-Olov Brasar RC .08 .25
100 Phil Esposito .75 2.00
101 J.P. Bordeleau .08 .25
102 Pierre Mondou RC .40 1.00
103 Wayne Bianchin .08 .25
104 Dennis O'Brien .08 .25
105 Glenn Resch .25 .60
106 Dennis Polonich .08 .25
107 Kris Manery RC .08 .25
108 Bill Hajt .08 .25
109 Jere Gillis RC .08 .25
110 Garry Unger .15 .40
111 Nick Beverley .08 .25
112 Pat Hickey .08 .25
113 Rick Middleton .25 .60
114 Orest Kindrachuk .08 .25
115 Mike Bossy RC 20.00 40.00
116 Pierre Bouchard .08 .25
117 Alain Daigle .08 .25
118 Terry Martin .08 .25
119 Tom Edur .08 .25
120 Marcel Dionne .75 2.00
121 Barry Beck RC .50 1.25
122 Billy Lochead .08 .25
123 Paul Harrison .15 .40
124 Wayne Cashman .25 .60
125 Rick MacLeish .25 .60
126 Bob Bourne .15 .40
127 Ian Turnbull .08 .25
128 Gerry Meehan .08 .25
129 Eric Vail .08 .25
130 Gilbert Perreault .25 .60
131 Bob Dailey .08 .25
132 Dale McCourt RC .40 1.00
133 John Wensink RC .50 1.25
134 Bill Nyrop .08 .25
135 Ivan Boldirev .08 .25
136 Lucien DeBlois RC .08 .25
137 Brian Spencer .08 .25
138 Tim Young .08 .25
139 Ron Sedlbauer .08 .25
140 Gerry Cheevers .40 1.00
141 Dennis Maruk .15 .40
142 Barry Dean .08 .25
143 Bernie Federko RC 3.00 6.00
144 Stefan Persson RC .15 .40
145 Wilf Paiement .15 .40
146 Dale Tallon .08 .25
147 Yvon Lambert .08 .25
148 Greg Joly .08 .25
149 Dean Talafous .08 .25
150 Don Edwards AS2 .08 .25
151 Butch Goring .15 .40
152 Tom Bladon .08 .25
153 Bob Nystrom .08 .25
154 Ron Greschner .15 .40
155 Jean Ratelle .25 .60
156 Russ Anderson RC .08 .25
157 John Marks .08 .25
158 Michel Larocque .15 .40
159 Paul Woods RC .15 .40
160 Mike Palmateer .15 .40
161 Jim Lorentz .08 .25
162 Dave Lewis .08 .25
163 Harvey Bennett .08 .25
164 Rick Smith .08 .25
165 Reggie Leach .25 .60
166 Wayne Thomas .15 .40
167 Dave Forbes .08 .25
168 Doug Wilson RC 4.00 8.00
169 Dan Bouchard .15 .40
170 Steve Shutt AS2 .25 .60
171 Mike Kaszycki RC .08 .25
172 Denis Herron .15 .40
173 Rick Bowness .15 .40
174 Rick Hampton .08 .25
175 Glen Sharpley .08 .25
176 Bill Barber .25 .60
177 Ron Duguay RC 1.25 3.00
178 Jim Schoenfeld .15 .40
179 Pierre Plante .08 .25
180 Jacques Lemaire .25 .60
181 Stan Jonathan .08 .25
182 Billy Harris .08 .25
183 Chris Oddleifson .08 .25
184 Jean Pronovost .15 .40
185 Fred Barrett .08 .25
186 Ross Lonsberry .08 .25
187 Mike McEwen .08 .25
188 Rene Robert .15 .40
189 J. Bob Kelly .08 .25
190 Serge Savard AS2 .15 .40
191 Dennis Kearns .08 .25
192 Flames Team CL .20 .50
193 Bruins Team CL .20 .50
194 Sabres Team CL .20 .50
195 Blackhawks Team CL .20 .50
196 Rockies Team CL .20 .50
197 Red Wings Team CL .20 .50
198 Kings Team CL .20 .50
199 North Stars Team CL .20 .50
200 Canadiens Team CL .20 .50
201 Islanders Team CL .20 .50
202 Rangers Team CL .20 .50
203 Flyers Team CL .20 .50
204 Penguins Team CL .20 .50
205 Blues Team CL .20 .50
206 Maple Leafs Team CL .20 .50
207 Canucks Team CL .20 .50
208 Capitals Team CL .20 .50
209 Danny Gare .15 .40
210 Larry Robinson AS1 .60 1.50
211 John Davidson .25 .60
212 Peter McNab .15 .40
213 Rick Kehoe .15 .40
214 Terry Harper .08 .25
215 Bobby Clarke .75 2.00
216 Bryan Maxwell UER .08 .25
217 Ted Bulley .08 .25
218 Red Berenson .15 .40
219 Ron Grahame .15 .40
220 Clark Gillies AS1 .15 .40
221 Dave Maloney .08 .25
222 Derek Smith RC .08 .25
223 Wayne Stephenson .15 .40
224 John Van Boxmeer .08 .25
225 Dave Schultz .15 .40
226 Reed Larson RC .40 1.00
227 Rejean Houle .08 .25
228 Doug Hicks .08 .25
229 Mike Murphy .08 .25
230 Pete Lopresti .15 .40
231 Jerry Korab .08 .25
232 Ed Westfall .15 .40
233 Greg Malone RC .15 .40
234 Paul Holmgren .25 .60
235 Walt Tkaczuk .15 .40
236 Don Marcotte .08 .25
237 Ron Low .15 .40
238 Rick Chartraw .08 .25
239 Cliff Koroll .08 .25
240 Borje Salming AS1 .40 1.00
241 Roland Eriksson .08 .25
242 Ric Seiling RC .08 .25
243 Jim Bedard RC .20 .50
244 Peter Lee RC .15 .40
245 Denis Potvin AS2 .60 1.50
246 Greg Polis .08 .25
247 Jimmy Watson .08 .25
248 Bobby Schmautz .08 .25
249 Doug Risebrough .15 .40
250 Tony Esposito .50 1.25
251 Nick Libett .08 .25
252 Ron Zanussi RC .08 .25
253 Andre Savard .08 .25
254 Dave Burrows .08 .25
255 Ulf Nilsson .25 .60
256 Richard Mulhern .08 .25
257 Don Saleski .08 .25
258 Wayne Merrick .08 .25
259 Checklist 133-264 1.00 2.50
260 Guy Lapointe .15 .40
261 Grant Mulvey .08 .25
262 Stanley Cup: Semis .10 .30
263 Stanley Cup: Semis .10 .30
264 Stanley Cup Finals .40 1.00

1978-79 Topps Team Stickers

This set of 22 team inserts measures the standard size. Each insert consists of two stickers: a team logo and a second sticker consisting of three mini-stickers. The mini-stickers picture hockey equipment (mask, stick(s), or puck), a hockey word (center, defense, goal!, goalie, score! or wing), and a number between zero and nine. The backs are blank and the fronts carry a 1978 copyright date.

COMPLETE SET (17) 7.50 15.00
1 Atlanta Flames .75 1.50
2A Boston Bruins/Puck .75 1.50
2B Boston Bruins/Stick .75 2.00
3 Buffalo Sabres .50 1.00
4 Chicago Blackhawks .75 1.50
5 Colorado Rockies .75 1.50
6 Detroit Red Wings .75 1.50
7 Los Angeles Kings .50 1.00
8 Minnesota North Stars .50 1.00
9A Montreal Canadiens/Goalie .75 1.50
9B Montreal Canadiens/Puck .75 2.00
10A New York Islanders/Center .50 1.00
10B New York Islanders/Goal! .50 1.00
11A New York Rangers/Goalie .50 1.00

11B New York Rangers/Sticks .75 1.50
12A Philadelphia Flyers/Goalie .50 1.00
12B Philadelphia Flyers/Sticks .50 1.00
13 Pittsburgh Penguins .50 1.00
14 St. Louis Blues .50 1.00
15 Toronto Maple Leafs .75 1.50
16 Vancouver Canucks .50 1.00
17 Washington Capitals .50 1.00

1979-80 Topps

The 1979-80 Topps set consists of 264 standard-size cards. Card numbers 81 and 82 (Stanley Cup Playoffs), 163 (Ulf Nilsson RB) and 261 (NHL Entries) differ from those of O-Pee-Chee. Unopened packs consist of ten cards plus a piece of bubble gum. The fronts contain a blue border that is prone to chipping. The player's name, team and position are at the top with team logo at the bottom. Career and 1978-79 statistics, short biography and a cartoon-illustrated fact about the player appear on the back. Included in this set are players from the four remaining WHA franchises that were absorbed by the NHL. The franchises are the Edmonton Oilers, Hartford Whalers, Quebec Nordiques and Winnipeg Jets. The set features the Rookie Card of Wayne Gretzky and the last cards of a Hall of Fame crop including Gordie Howe, Bobby Hull, Ken Dryden and Stan Mikita.

COMPLETE SET (264) 400.00 600.00
1 Bossy/Dionne/Lafleur LL 1.50 4.00
2 Trott/Lafleur/Dionne LL .75 2.00
3 Trott/Dionne/Lafleur LL 1.00 2.50
4 Williams/Holt/Schultz LL .25 .60
5 Bossy/Dionne/Gardner LL 1.00 2.50
6 Dryden/Resch/Parent LL 1.25 3.00
7 Lafleur/Bossy/Trott/ LL 1.00 2.50
8A Dryden/Espo/Par LL ERR 3.00 8.00
8B Dryden/Espo/Par LL COR 1.50 4.00
9 Greg Malone .15 .40
10 Rick Middleton .25 .60
11 Greg Smith .15 .40
12 Rene Robert .25 .60
13 Doug Risebrough .25 .60
14 Bob Kelly .15 .40
15 Walt Tkaczuk .25 .60
16 John Marks .15 .40
17 Willie Huber RC .15 .40
18 Wayne Gretzky RC 350.00 550.00
19 Ron Sedlbauer .15 .40
20 Glenn Resch AS2 .25 .60
21 Blair Chapman .15 .40
22 Ron Zanussi .15 .40
23 Brad Park .40 1.00
24 Yvon Lambert .15 .40
25 Andre Savard .15 .40
26 Jimmy Watson .15 .40
27 Hal Philipoff RC .15 .40
28 Dan Bouchard .25 .60
29 Bob Sirois .15 .40
30 Ulf Nilsson .25 .60
31 Mike Murphy .15 .40
32 Stefan Persson .15 .40
33 Garry Unger .25 .60
34 Rejean Houle .15 .40
35 Barry Beck .25 .60
36 Tim Young .15 .40
37 Rick Dudley .15 .40
38 Wayne Stephenson .25 .60
39 Peter McNab .25 .60
40 Borje Salming AS2 .25 .60
41 Tom Lysiak .15 .40
42 Don Maloney RC .50 1.25
43 Mike Rogers .25 .60
44 Dave Lewis .15 .40
45 Peter Lee .15 .40
46 Marty Howe .40 1.00
47 Serge Bernier .15 .40
48 Paul Woods .15 .40
49 Bob Sauve .25 .60
50 Larry Robinson AS1 .60 1.50
51 Tom Gorence RC .25 .60
52 Gary Sargent .15 .40
53 Thomas Gradin RC .50 1.25
54 Dean Talafous .15 .40
55 Bob Murray .15 .40
56 Bob Bourne .25 .60
57 Larry Patey .15 .40
58 Ross Lonsberry .15 .40
59 Rick Smith .15 .40
60 Guy Chouinard .25 .60
61 Danny Gare .25 .60
62 Jim Bedard .25 .60
63 Dale McCourt .15 .40
64 Steve Payne RC .40 1.00
65 Pat Hughes RC .15 .40
66 Mike McEwen .15 .40
67 Reg Kerr RC .25 .60
68 Walt McKechnie .15 .40
69 Michel Plasse .25 .60
70 Denis Potvin AS1 .40 1.00
71 Dave Dryden .25 .60
72 Gary McAdam .15 .40
73 Andre St.Laurent .15 .40
74 Jerry Korab .15 .40
75 Rick MacLeish .40 1.00
76 Dennis Kearns .15 .40
77 Jean Pronovost .25 .60
78 Ron Greschner .25 .60
79 Wayne Cashman .40 1.00
80 Tony Esposito .40 1.00
81 Cup Semi-Finals .25 .60
82 Cup Semi-Finals .25 .60
83 Stanley Cup Finals .60 1.50
84 Brian Sutter .75 2.00
85 Gerry Cheevers .40 1.00
86 Pat Hickey .15 .40
87 Mike Kaszycki .15 .40
88 Grant Mulvey .15 .40
89 Derek Smith .15 .40
90 Steve Shutt .40 1.00
91 Robert Picard .15 .40
92 Dan Labraaten .15 .40
93 Glen Sharpley .15 .40
94 Denis Herron .25 .60
95 Reggie Leach .40 1.00
96 John Van Boxmeer .15 .40
97 Tiger Williams .40 1.00
98 Butch Goring .25 .60
99 Don Marcotte .15 .40
100 Bryan Trottier AS1 1.00 2.50
101 Serge Savard AS2 .40 1.00
102 Cliff Koroll .15 .40
103 Gary Smith .25 .60
104 Al MacAdam .15 .40
105 Don Edwards .25 .60
106 Errol Thompson .15 .40
107 Andre Lacroix .25 .60
108 Marc Tardif .25 .60
109 Rick Kehoe .25 .60
110 John Davidson .25 .60
111 Behn Wilson RC .25 .60
112 Doug Jarvis .25 .60
113 Tom Rowe RC .15 .40
114 Mike Milbury .25 .60
115 Billy Harris .15 .40
116 Greg Fox RC .15 .40
117 Curt Fraser RC .25 .60
118 Jean-Paul Parise .15 .40
119 Ric Seiling .15 .40
120 Darryl Sittler .40 1.00
121 Rick Lapointe .15 .40
122 Jim Rutherford .25 .60
123 Mario Tremblay .25 .60
124 Randy Carlyle .40 1.00
125 Bobby Clarke .60 1.50
126 Wayne Thomas .25 .60
127 Ivan Boldirev .15 .40
128 Ted Bulley .15 .40
129 Dick Redmond .15 .40
130 Clark Gillies AS1 .25 .60
131 Checklist 1-132 5.00 12.00
132 Vaclav Nedomansky .15 .40
133 Richard Mulhern .15 .40
134 Dave Schultz .40 1.00
135 Guy Lapointe .25 .60
136 Gilles Meloche .25 .60
137 Randy Pierce RC .15 .40
138 Cam Connor .15 .40
139 George Ferguson .15 .40
140 Bill Barber .40 1.00
141 Mike Walton .25 .60
142 Wayne Babych RC .40 1.00
143 Phil Russell .15 .40
144 Bobby Schmautz .15 .40
145 Carol Vadnais .15 .40
146 John Tonelli RC 2.00 5.00
147 Peter Marsh RC .25 .60
148 Thommie Bergman .15 .40
149 Richard Martin .40 1.00
150 Ken Dryden AS1 2.50 6.00
151 Kris Manery .15 .40
152 Guy Charron .15 .40
153 Lanny McDonald .40 1.00
154 Ron Stackhouse .15 .40
155 Stan Mikita .60 1.50
156 Paul Holmgren .25 .60
157 Perry Miller .15 .40
158 Gary Croteau .15 .40
159 Dave Maloney .15 .40
160 Marcel Dionne AS2 .75 2.00
161 Mike Bossy RB 1.00 2.50
162 Don Maloney RB .15 .40
163 Ulf Nilsson RB .25 .60
164 Brad Park RB .15 .40
165 Bryan Trottier RB .40 1.00
166 Al Hill RC .15 .40
167 Gary Bromley .25 .60
168 Don Murdoch .15 .40
169 Wayne Merrick .15 .40
170 Bob Gainey .40 1.00
171 Jim Schoenfeld .25 .60
172 Gregg Sheppard .15 .40
173 Dan Bolduc RC .15 .40
174 Blake Dunlop .15 .40
175 Gordie Howe 14.00 20.00
176 Richard Brodeur .40 1.00
177 Tom Younghans .15 .40
178 Andre Dupont .15 .40
179 Ed Johnstone RC .25 .60
180 Gilbert Perreault .40 1.00
181 Bob Lorimer RC .15 .40
182 John Wensink .15 .40
183 Lee Fogolin .15 .40
184 Greg Carroll RC .15 .40
185 Bobby Hull 10.00 15.00
186 Harold Snepsts .15 .40
187 Peter Mahovlich .25 .60
188 Eric Vail .15 .40
189 Phil Myre .25 .60
190 Wilf Paiement .25 .60
191 Charlie Simmer RC 2.00 5.00
192 Per-Olov Brasar .15 .40
193 Lorne Henning .15 .40
194 Don Luce .15 .40
195 Steve Vickers .15 .40
196 Bob Miller RC .15 .40
197 Mike Palmateer .40 1.00
198 Nick Libett .15 .40
199 Pat Ribble RC .15 .40
200 Guy Lafleur AS1 1.50 4.00
201 Mel Bridgman .25 .60
202 Morris Lukowich RC .25 .60
203 Don Lever .15 .40
204 Tom Bladon .15 .40
205 Garry Howatt .15 .40
206 Bobby Smith RC 2.00 4.00
207 Craig Ramsay .25 .60
208 Ron Duguay .25 .60
209 Gilles Gilbert .40 1.00
210 Bob MacMillan .15 .40
211 Pierre Mondou .15 .40
212 J.P. Bordeleau .15 .40
213 Reed Larson .25 .60
214 Dennis Ververgaert .15 .40
215 Bernie Federko .75 2.00
216 Mark Howe .75 2.00
217 Bob Nystrom .15 .40
218 Orest Kindrachuk .15 .40
219 Mike Fidler .15 .40
220 Phil Esposito .50 1.25
221 Bill Hajt .15 .40
222 Mark Napier .25 .60
223 Dennis Maruk .25 .60
224 Dennis Polonich .15 .40
225 Jean Ratelle .25 .60
226 Bob Dailey .15 .40
227 Alain Daigle .15 .40
228 Ian Turnbull .15 .40
229 Jack Valiquette .15 .40
230 Mike Bossy AS2 5.00 10.00
231 Brad Maxwell .15 .40
232 Dave Taylor 1.50 4.00
233 Pierre Larouche .40 1.00
234 Rod Schutt RC .15 .40
235 Rogatien Vachon .40 1.00
236 Ryan Walter RC .40 1.00
237 Checklist 133-264 5.00 12.00
238 Terry O'Reilly .40 1.00
239 Real Cloutier .25 .60
240 Anders Hedberg .25 .60
241 Ken Linseman RC 1.00 2.50
242 Billy Smith .40 1.00
243 Rick Chartraw .15 .40
244 Flames Team .60 1.50
245 Bruins Team .60 1.50
246 Sabres Team .60 1.50
247 Blackhawks Team .60 1.50
248 Rockies Team .60 1.50
249 Red Wings Team .60 1.50
250 Kings Team .60 1.50
251 North Stars Team .60 1.50
252 Canadiens Team 1.25 3.00
253 Islanders Team .75 2.00
254 Rangers Team .60 1.50
255 Flyers Team .60 1.50
256 Penguins Team .60 1.50
257 Blues Team .60 1.50
258 Maple Leafs Team .75 2.00
259 Canucks Team .75 2.00
260 Capitals Team .60 1.50
261 New NHL Entries CL 7.00 15.00
262 Jean Hamel .15 .40
263 Stan Jonathan .15 .40
264 Russ Anderson .60 1.50

1979-80 Topps Team Stickers

This set of team sticker inserts measures the standard size, 2 1/2" by 3 1/2". They were issued one per wax pack and carry a 1979 copyright date. Each team insert consists of two stickers on one card: a team logo and a second sticker that is subdivided into three mini-stickers. The three mini-stickers picture a hockey icon (stick, goalie, puck, etc.), a hockey word (goal, wing, score, defense), and a one-digit number. Many were essentially a re-issue of a 1978-79 sticker with a different copyright date. The horizontally oriented back has an offer for personalized trading cards which expired 12/31/80.

COMPLETE SET (22) 10.00 20.00
1 Atlanta Flames .60 1.50
2 Boston Bruins .60 1.50
3 Buffalo Sabres .50 1.25
4 Chicago Blackhawks .60 1.50
5 Colorado Rockies .60 1.50
6 Detroit Red Wings .60 1.50
7 Edmonton Oilers .60 1.50
8 Hartford Whalers .50 1.25
9 Los Angeles Kings .50 1.25
10 Minnesota North Stars .50 1.25
11A Montreal Canadiens goalie .60 1.50
11B Montreal Canadiens score .60 1.50
12 New York Islanders .50 1.25
13 New York Rangers .60 1.50
14 Philadelphia Flyers .50 1.25
15 Pittsburgh Penguins UER .60 1.50
16 Quebec Nordiques .60 1.50
17 St. Louis Blues .50 1.25
18 Toronto Maple Leafs .60 1.50
19 Vancouver Canucks .50 1.25
20 Washington Capitals .50 1.25
21 Winnipeg Jets .50 1.25

1980-81 Topps

The 1980-81 Topps set features 264 standard-size cards. The fronts contain a puck (black ink) at the bottom right which can be scratched-off to reveal the player's name. Yearly statistics including minor leagues, a short biography and a cartoon-illustrated hockey fact are included on the back. Members of the U.S. Olympic team are designated by USA.

COMPLETE SET (264) 100.00 200.00
*SCRATCHED: .20X to .40X
1 Flyers RB .30 .75
2 Ray Bourque RB 4.00 10.00
3 Wayne Gretzky RB 6.00 15.00
4 Charlie Simmer RB .30 .75
5 Billy Smith RB .20 .50
6 Jean Ratelle .20 .50
7 Dave Maloney .15 .40
8 Phil Myre .20 .50
9 Ken Morrow OLY RC .60 1.50
10 Guy Lafleur .60 1.50
11 Bill Derlago RC .15 .40
12 Doug Wilson .30 .75
13 Craig Ramsay .12 .30
14 Pat Boutette .12 .30
15 Eric Vail .12 .30
16 Mike Foligno TL .40 1.00
17 Bobby Smith .40 1.00
18 Rick Kehoe .15 .40
19 Joel Quenneville .12 .30
20 Marcel Dionne .40 1.00
21 Kevin McCarthy .12 .30
22 Jim Craig OLY RC 4.00 10.00
23 Steve Vickers .12 .30
24 Ken Linseman .20 .50
25 Mike Bossy 1.25 3.00
26 Serge Savard .25 .60
27 Grant Mulvey TL .15 .40
28 Pat Hickey .12 .30
29 Peter Sullivan .12 .30
30 Blaine Stoughton .15 .40
31 Mike Liut RC 2.00 5.00
32 Blair MacDonald .12 .30
33 Rick Green .12 .30
34 Al MacAdam .15 .40
35 Robbie Ftorek .12 .30
36 Dick Redmond .12 .30
37 Ron Duguay .15 .40
38 Danny Gare TL .15 .40
39 Brian Propp RC 2.00 5.00
40 Bryan Trottier .50 1.25
41 Rich Preston .12 .30
42 Pierre Mondou .12 .30
43 Reed Larson .12 .30
44 George Ferguson .12 .30
45 Guy Chouinard .20 .50
46 Billy Harris .12 .30
47 Gilles Meloche .20 .50
48 Blair Chapman .12 .30
49 Mike Gartner TL 1.50 4.00
50 Darryl Sittler .25 .60
51 Richard Martin .20 .50
52 Ivan Boldirev .12 .30
53 Craig Norwich RC .12 .30
54 Dennis Polonich .12 .30
55 Bobby Clarke .60 1.50
56 Terry O'Reilly .20 .50
57 Carol Vadnais .12 .30
58 Bob Gainey .25 .60
59 Blaine Stoughton TL .15 .40
60 Billy Smith .20 .50
61 Mike O'Connell RC .30 .75
62 Lanny McDonald .25 .60
63 Lee Fogolin .12 .30
64 Rocky Saganiuk RC .12 .30
65 Rolf Edberg RC .12 .30
66 Paul Shmyr .12 .30
67 Michel Goulet RC 4.00 10.00
68 Dan Bouchard .20 .50
69 Mark Johnson OLY RC .60 1.50
70 Reggie Leach .15 .40
71 Bernie Federko TL .40 1.00
72 Peter Mahovlich .20 .50
73 Anders Hedberg .20 .50
74 Brad Park .15 .40
75 Clark Gillies .20 .50
76 Doug Jarvis .12 .30
77 John Garrett .20 .50
78 Dave Hutchinson .12 .30
79 John Anderson RC .25 .60
80 Gilbert Perreault .20 .50
81 Marcel Dionne AS1 .40 1.00
82 Guy Lafleur AS1 .60 1.50
83 Charlie Simmer AS1 .30 .75
84 Larry Robinson AS1 .25 .60
85 Borje Salming AS1 .15 .40
86 Tony Esposito AS1 .30 .75
87 Wayne Gretzky AS2 8.00 20.00
88 Danny Gare AS2 .15 .40
89 Steve Shutt AS2 .15 .40
90 Barry Beck AS2 .15 .40
91 Mark Howe AS2 .30 .75
92 Don Edwards AS2 .15 .40
93 Tom McCarthy RC .12 .30
94 P.McNab/R.Middleton TL .20 .50
95 Mike Palmateer .20 .50
96 Jim Schoenfeld .20 .50
97 Jordy Douglas .12 .30
98 Keith Brown RC .15 .40
99 Dennis Ververgaert .12 .30
100 Phil Esposito .30 .75
101 Jack Brownschidle .12 .30
102 Bob Nystrom .12 .30
103 Steve Christoff OLY RC .20 .50
104 Rob Palmer .12 .30
105 Tiger Williams .15 .40
106 Kent Nilsson TL .15 .40
107 Morris Lukowich .20 .50
108 Jack Valiquette .12 .30
109 Richie Dunn RC .12 .30
110 Rogatien Vachon .25 .60
111 Mark Napier .12 .30
112 Gordie Roberts .12 .30
113 Stan Jonathan .12 .30
114 Brett Callighen .12 .30
115 Rick MacLeish .20 .50
116 Ulf Nilsson .20 .50
117 Rick Kehoe TL .15 .40
118 Dan Maloney .12 .30
119 Terry Ruskowski .12 .30
120 Denis Potvin .50 1.25
121 Wayne Stephenson .20 .50
122 Rich Leduc .12 .30
123 Checklist 1-132 1.50 4.00
124 Don Lever .12 .30
125 Jim Rutherford .20 .50
126 Ray Allison RC .12 .30
127 Mike Ramsey OLY RC 1.00 2.50
128 Stan Smyl TL .30 .75
129 Al Secord RC 1.00 2.50
130 Denis Herron .20 .50
131 Bob Dailey .12 .30
132 Dean Talafous .12 .30
133 Ian Turnbull .12 .30
134 Ron Sedlbauer .12 .30
135 Tom Bladon .12 .30
136 Bernie Federko .60 1.50
137 Dave Taylor .75 2.00
138 Bob Lorimer .12 .30
139 MacAdam/Payne TL .15 .40
140 Ray Bourque RC 15.00 40.00
141 Glen Hanlon .20 .50
142 Willy Lindstrom .12 .30
143 Mike Rogers .12 .30
144 Tony McKegney RC .15 .40
145 Behn Wilson .12 .30
146 Lucien DeBlois .12 .30
147 Dave Burrows .12 .30
148 Paul Woods .12 .30
149 Phil Esposito TL .30 .75
150 Tony Esposito .60 1.50
151 Pierre Larouche .20 .50
152 Brad Maxwell .12 .30
153 Stan Weir .12 .30
154 Ryan Walter .12 .30
155 Dale Hoganson .12 .30
156 Anders Kallur RC .12 .30
157 Paul Reinhart RC .40 1.00
158 Greg Millen .20 .50
159 Ric Seiling .12 .30
160 Mark Howe .60 1.50
161 Goals Leaders .30 .75
Danny Gare (1)
Charlie Simmer (1)
Blaine Stoughton (1)
162 Gretz/Dio/Laf LL 5.00 12.00
163 Gretz/Dio/Laf LL 4.00 10.00
164 Penalty Minutes Leaders .20 .50
Jimmy Mann (1)
Dave (Tiger) Williams (2)
Paul Holmgren (3)
165 Power Play Goals Leaders .40 1.00
Charlie Simmer (1)
Marcel Dionne (2)
Danny Gare (2)
Steve Shutt (2)
Darryl Sittler (2)
166 Goals Against Average Leaders .20 .50
Bob Sauve (1)
Denis Herron (2)
Don Edwards (3)
167 Game-Winning Goals Leaders .15 .40
Danny Gare (1)
Peter McNab (2)
Blaine Stoughton (2)
168 Espo/Chee/Gar/McN .30 .75
169 Perry Turnbull RC .12 .30
170 Barry Beck .15 .40
171 Charlie Simmer TL .30 .75
172 Paul Holmgren .20 .50
173 Willie Huber .12 .30
174 Tim Young .12 .30
175 Gilles Gilbert .20 .50
176 Dave Christian OLY RC .75 2.00
177 Lars Lindgren RC .12 .30
178 Real Cloutier .15 .40
179 Laurie Boschman RC .15 .40
180 Steve Shutt .15 .40
181 Bob Murray .12 .30
182 Wayne Gretzky TL 6.00 12.00
183 John Van Boxmeer .12 .30
184 Nick Fotiu .20 .50
185 Mike McEwen .12 .30
186 Greg Malone .12 .30
187 Mike Foligno RC 1.25 3.00
188 Dave Langevin RC .12 .30
189 Mel Bridgman .12 .30
190 John Davidson .20 .50
191 Mike Milbury .20 .50
192 Ron Zanussi .12 .30
193 Darryl Sittler TL .25 .60
194 John Marks .12 .30
195 Mike Gartner RC 8.00 20.00
196 Dave Lewis .12 .30
197 Kent Nilsson RC 1.00 2.50
198 Rick Ley .12 .30
199 Derek Smith .12 .30
200 Bill Barber .20 .50
201 Guy Lapointe .20 .50
202 Vaclav Nedomansky .12 .30
203 Don Murdoch .12 .30
204 Mike Bossy TL .60 1.50
205 Pierre Hamel RC .20 .50
206 Mike Eaves RC .12 .30
207 Doug Halward .12 .30
208 Stan Smyl RC .50 1.25
209 Mike Zuke RC .12 .30
210 Borje Salming .15 .40
211 Walt Tkaczuk .20 .50
212 Grant Mulvey .15 .40
213 Rob Ramage RC .40 1.00
214 Tom Rowe .12 .30
215 Don Edwards .15 .40
216 G.Lafleur/P.Larouche TL .60 1.50
217 Dan Labraaten .12 .30
218 Glen Sharpley .12 .30
219 Stefan Persson .12 .30
220 Peter McNab .15 .40
221 Doug Hicks .12 .30
222 Bengt Gustafsson RC .12 .30
223 Michel Dion .20 .50
224 Jimmy Watson .12 .30
225 Wilf Paiement .12 .30
226 Phil Russell .12 .30
227 Morris Lukowich TL .20 .50
228 Ron Stackhouse .12 .30
229 Ted Bulley .12 .30
230 Larry Robinson .25 .60
231 Don Maloney .12 .30
232 Rob McClanahan OLY RC .15 .40
233 Al Sims .12 .30
234 Errol Thompson .12 .30
235 Glenn Resch .20 .50
236 Bob Miller .12 .30
237 Gary Sargent .12 .30
238 Real Cloutier TL .15 .40
239 Rene Robert .25 .60
240 Charlie Simmer .60 1.50
241 Thomas Gradin .12 .30
242 Rick Vaive RC 1.25 3.00
243 Ron Wilson RC .12 .30
244 Brian Sutter .40 1.00
245 Dale McCourt .12 .30
246 Yvon Lambert .12 .30
247 Tom Lysiak .12 .30
248 Ron Greschner .12 .30
249 Reggie Leach TL .15 .40
250 Wayne Gretzky 20.00 50.00
251 Rick Middleton .20 .50
252 Al Smith .20 .50
253 Fred Barrett .12 .30
254 Butch Goring .20 .50
255 Robert Picard .12 .30
256 Marc Tardif .12 .30
257 Checklist 133-264 1.50 4.00
258 Barry Long .12 .30
259 Rene Robert TL .25 .60
260 Danny Gare .15 .40
261 Rejean Houle .12 .30
262 Stanley Cup Semifinals .15 .40
263 Stanley Cup Semifinals .15 .40
264 Stanley Cup Finals .50 1.25

1980-81 Topps Team Posters

The 1980-81 Topps pin-up posters were issued as folded inserts (approximately 5" by 7" horizontal) to the 1980-81 Topps regular hockey issue. These 16 numbered posters are in full color with a white border on very thin stock. The posters feature posed shots (on ice) of the entire 1979-80 hockey team. The name of the team is indicated in large letters to the left of the hockey puck, which contains the designation 1979-80 Season. Fold lines or creases are natural and do not detract from the condition of the poster. For some reason the Edmonton Oilers, Quebec Nordiques, and Winnipeg Jets were not included in this set.

COMPLETE SET (16) 12.50 25.00
1 New York Islanders .60 1.50
2 New York Rangers .75 2.00
3 Philadelphia Flyers .60 1.50
4 Boston Bruins 1.00 2.50
5 Whalers w/Howe 1.50 4.00
6 Buffalo Sabres .60 1.50
7 Chicago Blackhawks 1.00 2.50
8 Detroit Red Wings 1.00 2.50
9 Minn. North Stars .75 2.00
10 Toronto Maple Leafs 1.00 2.50
11 Montreal Canadiens 1.00 2.50
12 Colorado Rockies 1.00 2.50
13 Los Angeles Kings 1.25 3.00
14 Vancouver Canucks .60 1.50
15 St. Louis Blues .60 1.50
16 Washington Capitals .60 1.50

1981 Topps Thirst Break

This is a 56-card set of individual wax paper gum wrappers, similar to a Bazooka Comic. These wrappers were issued in Thirst Break Orange Gum, which was reportedly distributed in Pennsylvania and Ohio. Each of these small gum wrappers has a comic-style image of a particular great moment in sports. As the checklist below shows, many different sports are represented in this set. The wrappers each measure approximately 2 9/16" by 1 5/8". The wrappers are numbered in small print at the top. The backs of the wrappers are blank. The "1981 Topps" copyright is at the bottom of each card. There was an orange and green outer wrapper that did not have player images.

COMPLETE SET (56) 60.00 150.00
43 Gerry Cheevers .75 2.00
44 Dave Schultz .60 1.50
50 Bobby Hull 1.60 4.00
51 Bobby Hull 1.60 4.00
52 Bobby Hull 1.60 4.00

1981-82 Topps

Topps regionalized distribution of its 198-card standard-size set for 1981-82, and issued two types of wax boxes, commonly referred to as either "East" boxes or "West" boxes. There is no way to differentiate which type of box you have without opening the packs. While the first 66 cards of the set were distributed nationally in both pack types, cards numbered 67 East through 132 East and 67 West through 132 West were distributed regionally. The card fronts contain the Topps logo at the top, with team logo, player name and position at the bottom. The team name appears in large letters placed over the bottom portion of the photo. The backs feature player biographies and yearly statistics including minor leagues. As for the regionally distributed portions of the set, the card numbering is in order by team starting with Boston.

COMPLETE SET (198) 20.00 50.00
1 Dave Babych RC .25 .60
2 Bill Barber .12 .30
3 Barry Beck .20 .50
4 Mike Bossy .60 1.50
5 Ray Bourque 4.00 10.00
6 Guy Chouinard .15 .40
7 Dave Christian .12 .30
8 Bill Derlago .12 .30
9 Marcel Dionne .25 .60
10 Brian Engblom .12 .30
11 Tony Esposito .15 .40
12 Bernie Federko .12 .30
13 Bob Gainey .15 .40
14 Danny Gare .12 .30
15 Thomas Gradin .12 .30
16 Wayne Gretzky 8.00 20.00
17 Rick Kehoe .12 .30
18 Jari Kurri RC 4.00 10.00
19 Guy Lafleur .60 1.50
20 Mike Liut .20 .50
21 Dale McCourt .12 .30
22 Rick Middleton .12 .30
23 Mark Napier .12 .30
24 Kent Nilsson .12 .30
25 Wilf Paiement .12 .30
26 Willi Plett .12 .30
27 Denis Potvin .25 .60
28 Paul Reinhart .12 .30
29 Jacques Richard .12 .30
30 Pat Riggin RC .25 .60
31 Larry Robinson .20 .50
32 Mike Rogers .12 .30
33 Borje Salming .20 .50
34 Steve Shutt .12 .30
35 Charlie Simmer .15 .40
36 Darryl Sittler .20 .50
37 Bobby Smith .12 .30
38 Stan Smyl .20 .50
39 Peter Stastny RC 3.00 8.00
40 Dave Taylor .15 .40
41 Bryan Trottier .25 .60
42 Ian Turnbull .12 .30
43 Eric Vail .12 .30
44 Rick Vaive .20 .50
45 Behn Wilson .12 .30
46 Rick Middleton TL .12 .30
47 Danny Gare TL .12 .30
48 Kent Nilsson TL .12 .30
49 Tom Lysiak TL .12 .30
50 Lanny McDonald TL .12 .30
51 Dale McCourt TL .12 .30
52 Wayne Gretzky TL 2.50 6.00
53 Mike Rogers TL .12 .30
54 Marcel Dionne TL .25 .60
55 Bobby Smith TL .12 .30
56 Steve Shutt TL .12 .30
57 Mike Bossy TL .60 1.50
58 Anders Hedberg TL .12 .30
59 Bill Barber TL .12 .30
60 Rick Kehoe TL .12 .30
61 Peter Stastny TL .15 .40
62 Bernie Federko TL .12 .30
63 Wilf Paiement TL .12 .30
64 Thomas Gradin TL .12 .30
65 Dennis Maruk TL .12 .30
66 Dave Christian TL .12 .30
E67 Dwight Foster .12 .30
E68 Steve Kasper RC .40 1.00
E69 Peter McNab .12 .30
E70 Mike O'Connell .15 .40
E71 Terry O'Reilly .15 .40
E72 Brad Park .15 .40
E73 Dick Redmond .12 .30
E74 Rogatien Vachon .20 .50
E75 Don Edwards .12 .30
E76 Tony McKegney .12 .30
E77 Bob Sauve .15 .40
E78 Andre Savard .12 .30
E79 Derek Smith .12 .30
E80 John Van Boxmeer .12 .30
E81 Pat Boutette .12 .30
E82 Mark Howe .20 .50
E83 Dave Keon .20 .50
E84 Warren Miller RC .12 .30
E85 Al Sims .12 .30
E86 Blaine Stoughton .15 .40
E87 Bob Bourne .12 .30
E88 Clark Gillies .20 .50
E89 Butch Goring .15 .40
E90 Anders Kallur .12 .30
E91 Ken Morrow .15 .40
E92 Stefan Persson .12 .30
E93 Billy Smith .20 .50
E94 Mike Allison RC .12 .30
E95 John Davidson .20 .50
E96 Ron Duguay .15 .40
E97 Ron Greschner .12 .30
E98 Anders Hedberg .12 .30
E99 Ed Johnstone .12 .30
E100 Dave Maloney .12 .30
E101 Don Maloney .12 .30
E102 Ulf Nilsson .20 .50
E103 Bobby Clarke .20 .50
E104 Bob Dailey .12 .30
E105 Paul Holmgren .20 .50
E106 Reggie Leach .20 .50
E107 Ken Linseman .20 .50
E108 Rick MacLeish .15 .40
E109 Pete Peeters .20 .50
E110 Brian Propp .20 .50
E111 Checklist 1-132 .40 1.00
E112 Randy Carlyle .20 .50
E113 Paul Gardner .12 .30
E114 Peter Lee .12 .30
E115 Greg Millen .15 .40
E116 Rod Schutt .12 .30
E117 Mike Gartner 2.00 5.00
E118 Rick Green .12 .30
E119 Bob Kelly .12 .30
E120 Dennis Maruk .12 .30
E121 Mike Palmateer .12 .30
E122 Ryan Walter .12 .30
E123 Bill Barber SA .12 .30
E124 Barry Beck SA .20 .50
E125 Mike Bossy SA .60 1.50
E126 Ray Bourque SA 2.00 5.00
E127 Danny Gare SA .12 .30
E128 Rick Kehoe SA .12 .30
E129 Rick Middleton SA .12 .30
E130 Denis Potvin SA .25 .60
E131 Mike Rogers SA .12 .30
E132 Bryan Trottier SA .25 .60
W67 Keith Brown .12 .30
W68 Ted Bulley .12 .30
W69 Tim Higgins RC .12 .30
W70 Reg Kerr .12 .30
W71 Tom Lysiak .12 .30
W72 Grant Mulvey .12 .30
W73 Bob Murray .12 .30
W74 Terry Ruskowski .12 .30
W75 Denis Savard RC 5.00 12.00
W76 Glen Sharpley .12 .30
W77 Darryl Sutter RC .40 1.00
W78 Doug Wilson .15 .40
W79 Lucien DeBlois .12 .30
W80 Paul Gagne RC .12 .30
W81 Merlin Malinowski RC .12 .30
W82 Lanny McDonald .12 .30
W83 Joel Quenneville .12 .30
W84 Rob Ramage .15 .40
W85 Glenn Resch .15 .40
W86 Steve Tambellini .12 .30
W87 Mike Foligno .15 .40
W88 Gilles Gilbert .15 .40
W89 Willie Huber .12 .30
W90 Mark Kirton RC .12 .30
W91 Jim Korn RC .12 .30
W92 Reed Larson .12 .30
W93 Gary McAdam .12 .30
W94 Vaclav Nedomansky .12 .30
W95 John Ogrodnick .12 .30
W96 Billy Harris .12 .30
W97 Jerry Korab .12 .30
W98 Mario Lessard .15 .40
W99 Don Luce .12 .30
W100 Larry Murphy RC 4.00 10.00
W101 Mike Murphy .12 .30
W102 Kent-Erik Andersson .12 .30
W103 Don Beaupre RC 1.50 4.00
W104 Steve Christoff .12 .30
W105 Dino Ciccarelli RC 6.00 15.00
W106 Craig Hartsburg .12 .30
W107 Al MacAdam .12 .30
W108 Tom McCarthy .12 .30
W109 Gilles Meloche .15 .40
W110 Steve Payne .12 .30
W111 Gordie Roberts .12 .30
W112 Greg Smith .12 .30
W113 Tim Young .12 .30
W114 Wayne Babych .12 .30
W115 Blair Chapman .12 .30
W116 Tony Currie .12 .30
W117 Blake Dunlop .12 .30
W118 Ed Kea .12 .30
W119 Rick Lapointe .12 .30
W120 Checklist 1-132 .60 1.50
W121 Jorgen Pettersson RC .12 .30
W122 Brian Sutter .20 .50
W123 Perry Turnbull .12 .30
W124 Mike Zuke .12 .30
W125 Marcel Dionne SA .25 .60
W126 Tony Esposito SA .15 .40
W127 Bernie Federko SA .12 .30
W128 Mike Liut SA .20 .50
W129 Dale McCourt SA .12 .30
W130 Charlie Simmer SA .15 .40
W131 Bobby Smith SA .12 .30
W132 Dave Taylor SA .15 .40

1983 Topps History's Greatest Olympians

This 99-card boxed set was manufactured under license from the Los Angeles Olympic Organizing Committee. (Sporting a slightly different card design, the 1984 M and M's Olympic Heroes is a subset of this set.) Though widely known to have been produced by Topps, this company name appears nowhere on the cards. On a white card face, the fronts feature either color or black-and-white photos framed by a white inner border and a yellow outer border. The player's name appears in red print across the bottom of the front. On a red panel, the backs carry a headline and news brief. The cards are numbered on the upper left corner.

COMPLETE SET (99) 8.00 20.00
33 Jim Craig .20 .50
36 Mike Eruzione .30 .75

1984-85 Topps

After a two year hiatus, Topps returned to hockey with a set of 165 standard size cards. The set contains 66 single print cards which are noted in the checklist by SP. Teams from the United States have a greater player representation than the Canadian teams. Card fronts (much like 1983 Topps baseball) are color coordinated by team and feature two photos. A small photo at bottom right has player name, position and team name to the left. Card backs contain complete career statistics. Cards are in team order starting with Boston.

COMPLETE SET (165) 20.00 50.00
1 Ray Bourque .75 2.00
2 Keith Crowder SP .15 .40
3 Tom Fergus .15 .40
4 Doug Keans RC .20 .50
5 Gord Kluzak SP .15 .40
6 Mike Krushelnyski SP .15 .40
7 Nevin Markwart RC .15 .40
8 Rick Middleton .20 .50
9 Mike O'Connell .15 .40
10 Terry O'Reilly SP .20 .50
11 Barry Pederson .15 .40
12 Pete Peeters .20 .50
13 Dave Andreychuk SP RC .75 2.00
14 Tom Barrasso RC 1.25 3.00
15 Real Cloutier SP .15 .40
16 Mike Foligno .20 .50
17 Bill Hajt SP .15 .40
18 Phil Housley SP .25 .60
19 Gilbert Perreault .25 .60
20 Larry Playfair SP .15 .40
21 Craig Ramsay SP .15 .40
22 Mike Ramsey .15 .40
23 Lindy Ruff SP .15 .40
24 Ed Beers .15 .40
25 Rejean Lemelin SP .20 .50
26 Lanny McDonald .20 .50
27 Murray Bannerman .20 .50
28 Keith Brown SP .15 .40
29 Curt Fraser .15 .40
30 Steve Larmer .40 1.00
31 Tom Lysiak .15 .40
32 Bob Murray .15 .40
33 Jack O'Callahan SP RC .20 .50
34 Rich Preston .15 .40
35 Denis Savard .30 .75
36 Darryl Sutter .15 .40
37 Doug Wilson .20 .50
38 Ivan Boldirev .15 .40
39 Colin Campbell SP .15 .40
40 Ron Duguay SP .20 .50
41 Dwight Foster SP .15 .40
42 Danny Gare SP .15 .40
43 Ed Johnstone .15 .40
44 Reed Larson SP .15 .40
45 Eddie Mio SP .20 .50

46 John Ogrodnick	.15	.40
47 Brad Park	.20	.50
48 Greg Stefan SP RC	.20	.50
49 Steve Yzerman RC	12.00	30.00
50 Paul Coffey	.40	1.00
51 Wayne Gretzky	1.25	3.00
52 Jari Kurri	.50	1.25
53 Bob Crawford RC	.15	.40
54 Ron Francis	.50	1.25
55 Marty Howe	.15	.40
56 Mark Johnson SP	.15	.40
57 Greg Malone SP	.15	.40
58 Greg Millen SP	.20	.50
59 Ray Neufeld	.15	.40
60 Joel Quenneville SP	.15	.40
61 Risto Siltanen	.15	.40
62 Sylvain Turgeon RC	.20	.50
63 Mike Zuke SP	.15	.40
64 Marcel Dionne	.30	.75
65 Brian Engblom SP	.15	.40
66 Jim Fox SP	.15	.40
67 Bernie Nicholls	.50	1.25
68 Terry Ruskowski SP	.15	.40
69 Charlie Simmer	.20	.50
70 Don Beaupre	.20	.50
71 Brian Bellows	.20	.50
72 Neal Broten SP	.25	.60
73 Dino Ciccarelli	.25	.60
74 Paul Holmgren SP	.20	.50
75 Al MacAdam SP	.15	.40
76 Dennis Maruk	.20	.50
77 Brad Maxwell SP	.15	.40
78 Tom McCarthy SP	.15	.40
79 Gilles Meloche SP	.20	.50
80 Steve Payne	.15	.40
81 Guy Lafleur	.30	.75
82 Larry Robinson	.25	.60
83 Bobby Smith	.20	.50
84 Mel Bridgman	.15	.40
85 Joe Cirella	.15	.40
86 Don Lever	.15	.40
87 Dave Lewis	.15	.40
88 Jan Ludvig RC	.15	.40
89 Glenn Resch	.20	.50
90 Pat Verbeek RC	2.50	6.00
91 Mike Bossy	.50	1.25
92 Bob Bourne	.15	.40
93 Greg Gilbert RC	.20	.50
94 Clark Gillies SP	.25	.60
95 Butch Goring SP	.20	.50
96 Pat LaFontaine SP RC	2.50	6.00
97 Ken Morrow	.15	.40
98 Bob Nystrom SP	.15	.40
99 Stefan Persson SP	.15	.40
100 Denis Potvin	.25	.60
101 Billy Smith SP	.25	.60
102 Brent Sutter SP	.15	.40
103 John Tonelli	.20	.50
104 Bryan Trottier	.30	.75
105 Barry Beck	.15	.40
106 Glen Hanlon SP	.20	.50
107 Anders Hedberg SP	.20	.50
108 Pierre Larouche SP	.20	.50
109 Don Maloney SP	.15	.40
110 Mark Osborne SP	.15	.40
111 Larry Patey	.15	.40
112 James Patrick RC	.25	.60
113 Mark Pavelich SP	.15	.40
114 Mike Rogers SP	.15	.40
115 Reijo Ruotsalainen SP	.15	.40
116 Peter Sundstrom SP RC	.20	.50
117 Bob Froese	.20	.50
118 Mark Howe	.25	.60
119 Tim Kerr SP	.20	.50
120 Dave Poulin RC	.40	1.00
121 Darryl Sittler SP	.25	.60
122 Ron Sutter RC	.25	.60
123 Mike Bullard SP	.15	.40
124 Ron Flockhart SP	.15	.40
125 Rick Kehoe	.20	.50
126 Kevin McCarthy SP	.15	.40
127 Mark Taylor	.15	.40
128 Dan Bouchard SP	.20	.50
129 Michel Goulet	.20	.50
130 Peter Stastny SP	.25	.60
131 Bernie Federko	.20	.50
132 Mike Liut	.20	.50
133 Joe Mullen SP	.40	1.00
134 Rob Ramage	.15	.40
135 Brian Sutter	.20	.50
136 John Anderson SP	.15	.40
137 Dan Daoust	.15	.40
138 Rick Vaive	.15	.40
139 Darcy Rota SP	.15	.40
140 Stan Smyl SP	.15	.40
141 Tony Tanti	.15	.40
142 Dave Christian SP	.15	.40
143 Mike Gartner SP	.75	2.00
144 Bengt Gustafsson SP	.15	.40
145 Doug Jarvis	.15	.40
146 Al Jensen	.20	.50
147 Rod Langway	.20	.50
148 Pat Riggin	.20	.50
149 Scott Stevens SP	.75	2.00
150 Dave Babych	.15	.40
151 Laurie Boschman	.15	.40
152 Dale Hawerchuk	.75	2.00
153 Michel Goulet AS	.20	.50
154 Wayne Gretzky AS	1.25	3.00
155 Mike Bossy AS	.50	1.25
156 Rod Langway AS	.20	.50
157 Ray Bourque AS	.75	2.00
158 Tom Barrasso AS	1.25	3.00
159 Mark Messier AS	.40	1.00
160 Bryan Trottier AS	.30	.75
161 Jari Kurri AS	.50	1.25
162 Denis Potvin AS	.25	.60
163 Paul Coffey AS	.40	1.00
164 Pat Riggin AS	.20	.50
165 Checklist 1-165 SP	.60	1.50

1985-86 Topps

This set of 165 standard-size cards is very similar to Topps' hockey set of the previous season in that there are 66 single prints. The single prints are noted in the checklist by SP. Unopened packs consist of 12 cards plus one sticker and a piece of bubble gum. The fronts have player name and position at the bottom with the team logo at the top right or left. Backs contain complete career statistics and personal notes. The key Rookie Card is Mario Lemieux.

COMPLETE SET (165)	125.00	225.00
1 Lanny McDonald	.40	1.00
2 Mike O'Connell SP	.25	.60
3 Curt Fraser SP	.25	.60
4 Steve Penney	.25	.60
5 Brian Engblom	.25	.60
6 Ron Sutter	.25	.60
7 Joe Mullen	.25	.60
8 Rod Langway	.25	.60
9 Mario Lemieux RC	50.00	120.00
10 Dave Babych	.25	.60
11 Bob Nystrom	.25	.60
12 Andy Moog SP	.75	2.00
13 Dino Ciccarelli	.25	.60
14 Dwight Foster SP	.25	.60
15 James Patrick SP	.25	.60
16 Thomas Gradin SP	.25	.60
17 Mike Foligno	.25	.60
18 Mario Gosselin RC	.25	.60
19 Mike Zuke SP	.25	.60
20 John Anderson SP	.25	.60
21 Dave Pichette	.25	.60
22 Nick Fotiu SP	.25	.60
23 Tom Lysiak	.20	.50
24 Peter Zezel RC	.50	1.25
25 Denis Potvin	.20	.50
26 Bob Carpenter	.20	.50
27 Murray Bannerman SP	.20	.50
28 Gordie Roberts SP	.20	.50
29 Steve Yzerman	6.00	15.00
30 Phil Russell	.20	.50
31 Peter Stastny	.20	.50
32 Craig Ramsay SP	.20	.50
33 Terry Ruskowski SP	.20	.50
34 Kevin Dineen SP RC	1.00	2.50
35 Mark Howe	.25	.60
36 Glenn Resch	.20	.50
37 Danny Gare SP	.20	.50
38 Doug Bodger RC	.20	.50
39 Mike Rogers	.25	.60
40 Ray Bourque	1.25	3.00
41 John Tonelli	.20	.50
42 Mel Bridgman	.25	.60
43 Sylvain Turgeon SP	.20	.50
44 Mark Johnson	.25	.60
45 Doug Wilson	.20	.50
46 Mike Gartner	.40	1.00
47 Brent Peterson	.25	.60
48 Paul Reinhart SP	.20	.50
49 Mike Krushelnyski	.25	.60
50 Brian Bellows	.20	.50
51 Chris Chelios	1.50	4.00
52 Barry Pederson SP	.25	.60
53 Murray Craven SP	.20	.50
54 Pierre Larouche SP	.20	.50
55 Reed Larson	.20	.50
56 Pat Verbeek SP	.20	.50
57 Randy Carlyle	.20	.50
58 Ray Neufeld SP	.20	.50
59 Keith Brown SP	.25	.60
60 Bryan Trottier	.30	.75
61 Jim Fox SP	.25	.60
62 Scott Stevens	.40	1.00
63 Phil Housley	.20	.50
64 Rick Middleton	.20	.50
65 Steve Payne	.20	.50
66 Dave Lewis	.20	.50
67 Mike Bullard	.20	.50
68 Stan Smyl SP	.20	.50
69 Mark Pavelich SP	.20	.50
70 John Ogrodnick	.20	.50
71 Bill Derlago SP	.20	.50
72 Brad Marsh SP	.20	.50
73 Denis Savard	.30	.75
74 Mark Fusco RC	.20	.50
75 Pete Peeters	.20	.50
76 Doug Gilmour	2.50	6.00
77 Mike Ramsey	.20	.50
78 Anton Stastny SP	.20	.50
79 Steve Kasper SP	.20	.50
80 Bryan Erickson SP RC	.20	.50
81 Clark Gillies	.25	.60
82 Keith Acton	.20	.50
83 Pat Flatley	.20	.50
84 Kirk Muller RC	1.00	2.50
85 Paul Coffey	1.25	3.00
86 Ed Olczyk RC	.25	.60
87 Charlie Simmer SP	.25	.60
88 Mike Liut	.25	.60
89 Dave Maloney	.25	.60
90 Marcel Dionne	.30	.75
91 Tim Kerr	.25	.60
92 Ivan Boldirev SP	.25	.60
93 Ken Morrow SP	.25	.60
94 Don Maloney SP	.25	.60
95 Rejean Lemelin	.25	.60
96 Curt Giles	.25	.60
97 Bob Bourne	.25	.60
98 Joe Cirella	.25	.60
99 Dave Christian SP	.25	.60
100 Darryl Sutter	.25	.60
101 Kelly Kisio	.25	.60
102 Mats Naslund	.25	.60
103 Joel Quenneville SP	.25	.60
104 Bernie Federko	.25	.60
105 Tom Barrasso	.25	.60
106 Rick Vaive	.25	.60
107 Brent Sutter	.25	.60
108 Wayne Babych	.20	.50
109 Dale Hawerchuk	.40	1.00
110 Pelle Lindbergh SP	4.00	10.00
111 Dennis Maruk SP	.15	.40
112 Reijo Ruotsalainen SP	.15	.40
113 Tom Fergus SP	.15	.40
114 Bob Murray SP	.15	.40
115 Patrik Sundstrom	.20	.50
116 Ron Duguay SP	.20	.50
117 Alan Haworth SP	.15	.40
118 Greg Malone	.15	.40
119 Bill Hajt	.15	.40
120 Wayne Gretzky	8.00	20.00
121 Craig Redmond	.15	.40
122 Kelly Hrudey RC	1.25	3.00
123 Tomas Sandstrom RC	1.25	3.00
124 Neal Broten	.20	.50
125 Moe Mantha SP	.20	.50
126 Greg Gilbert SP	.20	.50
127 Bruce Driver SP RC	.25	.60
128 Dave Poulin	.20	.50
129 Morris Lukowich SP	.20	.50
130 Mike Bossy	.60	1.50
131 Larry Playfair SP	.20	.50
132 Steve Larmer	.20	.50
133 Doug Keans SP	.20	.50
134 Bob Manno	.25	.60
135 Brian Sutter	.25	.60
136 Pat Riggin	.25	.60
137 Pat LaFontaine	.75	2.00
138 Barry Beck SP	.25	.60
139 Rich Preston SP	.25	.60
140 Ron Francis	1.00	2.50
141 Brian Propp SP	.25	.60
142 Don Beaupre	.25	.60
143 Dave Andreychuk SP	.25	.60
144 Ed Beers	.20	.50
145 Paul MacLean	.20	.50
146 Troy Murray SP	.25	.60
147 Larry Robinson	.25	.60
148 Bernie Nicholls	.25	.60
149 Glen Hanlon SP	.25	.60
150 Michel Goulet	.25	.80
151 Doug Jarvis SP	.25	.60
152 Warren Young	.20	.50
153 Tony Tanti	.20	.50
154 Tomas Jonsson SP	.20	.50
155 Jari Kurri	1.00	2.50
156 Tony McKegney	.20	.50
157 Greg Stefan SP	.20	.50
158 Brad McCrimmon SP	.20	.50
159 Keith Crowder SP	.20	.50
160 Gilbert Perreault	.25	.60
161 Tim Bothwell SP	.20	.50
162 Bob Crawford SP	.20	.50
163 Paul Gagne SP	.20	.50
164 Dan Daoust SP	.20	.50
165 Checklist 1-165 SP	1.00	2.50

1985-86 Topps Box Bottoms

This 16-card standard-size set was issued in sets of four on the bottom of the 1985-86 Topps wax pack boxes. Complete box bottom panels are valued at a 25 percent premium above the prices listed below. The back, written in English, includes statistical information. The cards are lettered rather than numbered. The key card in the set is Mario Lemieux, pictured in his Rookie Card year.

COMPLETE SET (16)	26.00	65.00
A Brian Bellows	.25	.60
B Ray Bourque	1.00	2.50
C Bob Carpenter	.15	.40
D Chris Chelios	1.50	4.00
E Marcel Dionne	.50	1.25
F Ron Francis	1.00	2.50
G Wayne Gretzky	10.00	25.00
H Tim Kerr	.15	.40
I Mario Lemieux	20.00	50.00
J John Ogrodnick	.15	.40
K Gilbert Perreault	.30	.75
L Glenn Resch	.25	.60
M Reijo Ruotsalainen	.15	.40
N Brian Sutter	.25	.60
O John Tonelli	.15	.40
P Doug Wilson	.25	.60

1985-86 Topps Sticker Inserts

This set of 33 "Hockey Helmet Stickers" features stickers of 12 All-Star players (1-12) and 21 stickers of team logos, pucks, and numbers. The stickers were inserted in with the 1985-86 Topps hockey regular issue wax packs and as such are also 2 1/2" by 3 1/2". The card backs are printed in blue and red on white card stock. These inserts were also included in some O-Pee-Chee packs that year, which may explain why this particular year of stickers is relatively plentiful. The last seven team stickers can be found with the team logos on the top or bottom.

COMPLETE SET (33)	8.00	20.00
1 John Ogrodnick	.10	.25
2 Wayne Gretzky	4.00	10.00
3 Jari Kurri	.40	1.00
4 Paul Coffey	.60	1.50
5 Ray Bourque	.60	1.50
6 Pelle Lindbergh	1.50	4.00
7 John Tonelli	.10	.25
8 Dale Hawerchuk	.30	.75
9 Mike Bossy	.40	1.00
10 Rod Langway	.10	.25
11 Doug Wilson	.10	.25
12 Tom Barrasso	.30	.75
13 Toronto Maple Leafs	.15	.40
14 Buffalo Sabres	.10	.25
15 Detroit Red Wings	.10	.25
16 Pittsburgh Penguins	.10	.25
17 New York Rangers	.10	.25
18 Calgary Flames	.10	.25
19 Winnipeg Jets	.10	.25
20 Quebec Nordiques	.10	.25
21 Chicago Blackhawks	.10	.25
22 Los Angeles Kings	.10	.25
23 Montreal Canadiens	.15	.40
24 Vancouver Canucks	.10	.25
25 Hartford Whalers	.15	.40
26 Philadelphia Flyers	.10	.25
27 New Jersey Devils	.10	.25
28 St. Louis Blues	.10	.25
29 Minnesota North Stars	.10	.25
30 Washington Capitals	.10	.25
31 Boston Bruins	.10	.25
32 New York Islanders	.10	.25
33 Edmonton Oilers	.10	.25

1986-87 Topps

This set of 198 cards measures the standard size. There are 66 double prints that are noted in the checklist by DP. Card fronts feature player name, team, team logo and position at the bottom with a team colored stripe up the right border. Card backs contain complete career statistics and career highlights. The key Rookie Card in this set is Patrick Roy.

COMPLETE SET (198)	75.00	150.00
1 Ray Bourque	1.00	2.50
2 Pat LaFontaine DP	.60	1.50
3 Wayne Gretzky	10.00	25.00
4 Lindy Ruff	.05	.15
5 Brad McCrimmon	.05	.15
6 Tiger Williams	.15	.40
7 Denis Savard DP	.15	.40
8 Lanny McDonald	.05	.15
9 John Vanbiesbrouck DP RC	5.00	10.00
10 Greg Adams RC	.30	.75
11 Steve Yzerman	7.50	15.00
12 Craig Hartsburg	.05	.15
13 John Anderson DP	.05	.15
14 Bob Bourne DP	.05	.15
15 Kjell Dahlin RC	.05	.15
16 Dave Andreychuk	.30	.75
17 Rob Ramage DP	.05	.15
18 Ron Greschner DP	.05	.15
19 Bruce Driver	.05	.15
20 Peter Stastny	.15	.40
21 Dave Christian	.05	.15
22 Doug Keans	.05	.15
23 Scott Bjugstad RC	.05	.15
24 Doug Bodger DP	.05	.15
25 Troy Murray DP	.05	.15
26 Al Iafrate	.30	.75
27 Kelly Hrudey	.30	.75
28 Doug Jarvis	.05	.15
29 Rich Sutter	.05	.15
30 Marcel Dionne	.15	.40
31 Curt Fraser	.05	.15
32 Doug Lidster	.05	.15
33 Brian MacLellan	.05	.15
34 Barry Pederson	.05	.15
35 Craig Laughlin	.05	.15
36 Ilkka Sinisalo DP	.05	.15
37 John MacLean RC	1.00	2.50
38 Brian Mullen	.05	.15
39 Duane Sutter DP	.05	.15
40 Brian Engblom	.05	.15
41 Chris Cichocki	.05	.15
42 Gordie Roberts	.05	.15
43 Ron Francis	.60	1.50
44 Joe Mullen	.30	.75
45 Moe Mantha DP	.05	.15
46 Pat Verbeek	.05	.15
47 Clint Malarchuk RC	.30	.75
48 Bob Brooke DP	.05	.15
49 Darryl Sutter DP	.05	.15
50 Stan Smyl DP	.05	.15
51 Greg Stefan	.15	.40
52 Bill Hajt DP	.05	.15
53 Patrick Roy RC	30.00	80.00
54 Gord Kluzak	.05	.15
55 Bob Froese DP	.05	.15
56 Grant Fuhr	1.00	2.50
57 Mark Hunter DP	.05	.15
58 Dana Murzyn RC	.15	.40
59 Mike Gartner	.30	.75
60 Dennis Maruk	.05	.15
61 Rich Preston	.05	.15
62 Larry Robinson DP	.05	.15
63 Dave Taylor DP	.05	.15
64 Bob Murray DP	.05	.15
65 Ken Morrow	.15	.40
66 Mike Ridley RC	.30	.75
67 John Tucker RC	.05	.15
68 Miroslav Frycer	.05	.15
69 Danny Gare	.15	.40
70 Randy Burridge RC	.30	.75
71 Dave Poulin	.05	.15
72 Brian Sutter	.15	.40
73 Dave Babych	.05	.15
74 Dale Hawerchuk DP	.30	.75
75 Brian Bellows	.05	.15
76 Dave Pasin DP RC	.05	.15
77 Pete Peeters DP	.05	.15
78 Tomas Jonsson DP	.05	.15
79 Gilbert Perreault DP	.05	.15
80 Glenn Anderson DP	.30	.75
81 Don Maloney	.05	.15
82 Ed Olczyk DP	.05	.15
83 Mike Bullard DP	.05	.15
84 Tom Fergus	.05	.15
85 Dave Lewis	.05	.15
86 Brian Propp	.15	.40
87 John Ogrodnick	.05	.15
88 Kevin Dineen DP	.30	.75
89 Don Beaupre	.15	.40
90 Mike Bossy DP	.50	1.25
91 Tom Barrasso DP	.30	.75
92 Michel Goulet DP	.05	.15
93 Doug Gilmour	1.25	3.00
94 Kirk Muller	.30	.75
95 Larry Melnyk DP RC	.05	.15
96 Bob Gainey DP	.30	.75
97 Steve Kasper	.05	.15
98 Petr Klima RC	.15	.40
99 Neal Broten DP	.05	.15
100 Al Secord DP	.05	.15
101 Bryan Erickson DP	.05	.15
102 Rejean Lemelin	.15	.40
103 Sylvain Turgeon	.05	.15
104 Bob Nystrom	.05	.15
105 Bernie Federko	.15	.40
106 Doug Wilson DP	.05	.15
107 Alan Haworth	.05	.15
108 Jari Kurri	.60	1.50
109 Ron Sutter	.05	.15
110 Reed Larson DP	.05	.15
111 Terry Ruskowski DP	.05	.15
112 Mark Johnson DP	.05	.15
113 James Patrick	.05	.15
114 Paul MacLean	.05	.15
115 Mike Ramsey DP	.05	.15
116 Kelly Kisio DP	.05	.15
117 Brent Sutter	.05	.15
118 Joel Quenneville	.05	.15
119 Curt Giles DP	.05	.15
120 Tony Tanti DP	.05	.15
121 Doug Sulliman DP	.05	.15
122 Mario Lemieux	10.00	25.00
123 Mark Howe DP	.05	.15
124 Bob Sauve	.15	.40
125 Anton Stastny	.05	.15
126 Scott Stevens DP	.30	.75
127 Mike Foligno	.05	.15
128 Reijo Ruotsalainen DP	.05	.15
129 Denis Potvin	.15	.40
130 Keith Crowder	.05	.15
131 Bob Janecyk DP	.05	.15
132 John Tonelli	.05	.15
133 Mike Liut DP	.05	.15
134 Tim Kerr DP	.05	.15
135 Al Jensen	.15	.40
136 Mel Bridgman	.05	.15
137 Paul Coffey DP	.60	1.50
138 Dino Ciccarelli DP	.15	.40
139 Steve Larmer	.30	.75
140 Mike O'Connell	.05	.15
141 Clark Gillies	.15	.40
142 Phil Russell DP	.05	.15
143 Dirk Graham DP RC	.30	.75
144 Randy Carlyle	.05	.15
145 Charlie Simmer	.05	.15
146 Ron Flockhart DP	.05	.15
147 Tom Laidlaw	.05	.15
148 Dave Tippett RC	.15	.40
149 Wendel Clark DP RC	3.00	8.00
150 Bob Carpenter DP	.05	.15
151 Bill Watson RC	.05	.15
152 Roberto Romano DP RC	.05	.15
153 Doug Shedden	.05	.15
154 Phil Housley	.40	.75
155 Bryan Trottier	.30	.75
156 Patrik Sundstrom DP	.05	.15
157 Rick Middleton DP	.05	.15
158 Glenn Resch	.15	.40
159 Bernie Nicholls DP	.30	.75
160 Ray Ferraro RC	1.00	2.50
161 Mats Naslund DP	.05	.15
162 Pat Flatley DP	.05	.15
163 Joe Cirella	.05	.15
164 Rod Langway DP	.05	.15
165 Checklist 1-99	.30	.75
166 Carey Wilson	.05	.15
167 Murray Craven	.05	.15
168 Paul Gillis RC	.05	.15
169 Borje Salming	.05	.15
170 Perry Turnbull	.05	.15
171 Chris Chelios	1.25	3.00
172 Keith Acton	.05	.15
173 Al MacInnis	2.00	5.00
174 Russ Courtnall RC	1.00	2.50
175 Brad Marsh	.05	.15
176 Guy Carbonneau	.15	.40
177 Ray Neufeld	.05	.15
178 Craig MacTavish RC	.30	.75
179 Rick Lanz	.05	.15
180 Murray Bannerman	.15	.40
181 Brent Ashton	.05	.15
182 Jim Peplinski	.05	.15
183 Mark Napier	.05	.15
184 Laurie Boschman	.05	.15
185 Larry Murphy	.15	.40
186 Mark Messier	.30	.75
187 Risto Siltanen	.05	.15
188 Bobby Smith	.15	.40
189 Gary Suter RC	.75	2.00
190 Peter Zezel	.05	.15
191 Rick Vaive	.05	.15
192 Dale Hunter	.15	.40
193 Mike Krushelnyski	.05	.15
194 Scott Arniel	.05	.15
195 Larry Playfair	.05	.15
196 Doug Risebrough	.05	.15
197 Kevin Lowe	.05	.15
198 Checklist 100-198	.30	.75

1986-87 Topps Box Bottoms

This sixteen-card standard-size set was issued in sets of four on the bottom of the 1986-87 Topps wax pack boxes. Complete box bottom panels are valued at a 25 percent premium above the prices listed below. The front presents a color action photo with various color borders, with the team's logo in the lower right hand corner. The back includes statistical information, is written in English, and is printed on blue with black ink. The cards are lettered rather than numbered.

COMPLETE SET (16)	14.00	35.00
A Greg Adams	.20	.50
B Mike Bossy	.40	1.00
C Dave Christian	.08	.25
D Mike Foligno	.08	.25
E Michel Goulet	.20	.50
F Wayne Gretzky	6.00	15.00
G Tim Kerr	.08	.25
H Jari Kurri	.60	1.50
I Mario Lemieux	8.00	20.00
J Lanny McDonald	.20	.50
K Bernie Nicholls	.20	.50
L Mike Ridley	.20	.50
M Larry Robinson	.20	.50
N Denis Savard	.20	.50
O Brian Sutter	.08	.25
P Bryan Trottier	.30	.75

1986-87 Topps Sticker Inserts

This set of 33 "Hockey Helmet Stickers" features stickers of 12 All-Star players (1-12) and 21 stickers of team logos, pucks, and numbers. The stickers were inserted in with the 1986-87 Topps hockey regular issue wax packs and as such are also 2 1/2" by 3 1/2". The card backs are printed in blue and red on white card stock. The last seven team stickers can be found with the team logos on the top or bottom.

COMPLETE SET (33)	12.00	30.00
1 John Vanbiesbrouck	3.00	8.00
2 Michel Goulet	.20	.50
3 Wayne Gretzky	4.00	10.00
4 Mike Bossy	.40	1.00
5 Paul Coffey	.60	1.50
6 Mark Howe	.15	.40
7 Bob Froese	.15	.40
8 Mats Naslund	.15	.40
9 Mario Lemieux	4.00	10.00
10 Jari Kurri	.60	1.50
11 Ray Bourque	.75	2.00
12 Larry Robinson	.20	.50
13 Toronto Maple Leafs	.08	.25
14 Buffalo Sabres	.05	.15
15 Detroit Red Wings	.08	.25
16 Pittsburgh Penguins	.05	.15
17 New York Rangers	.08	.25
18 Calgary Flames	.05	.15
19 Winnipeg Jets	.05	.15
20 Quebec Nordiques	.05	.15
21 Chicago Blackhawks	.08	.25
22 Los Angeles Kings	.05	.15
23 Montreal Canadiens	.08	.25
24 Vancouver Canucks	.05	.15
25 Hartford Whalers	.05	.15
26 Philadelphia Flyers	.05	.15
27 New Jersey Devils	.05	.15
28 St. Louis Blues	.05	.15
29 Minnesota North Stars	.05	.15
30 Washington Capitals	.05	.15
31 Boston Bruins	.08	.25
32 New York Islanders	.05	.15
33 Edmonton Oilers	.05	.15

1987-88 Topps

The 1987-88 Topps hockey set contains 198 standard size cards. There are 66 double printed cards which are indicated by DP below. Again, unopened packs had 12 cards plus one sticker and a piece of gum. The fronts feature a design that includes a hockey stick at the bottom with which the player's name is located. At bottom right, the team name appears in a large puck. The card backs contain career statistics, game winning goals from 1986-87 and highlights.

COMPLETE SET (198)	30.00	80.00
1 Denis Potvin DP	.20	.50
2 Rick Tocchet RC	3.00	8.00
3 Dave Andreychuk	.25	.60
4 Stan Smyl	.20	.50
5 Dave Babych DP	.20	.50
6 Pat Verbeek	.20	.50
7 Esa Tikkanen RC	2.00	5.00
8 Mike Ridley	.20	.50
9 Randy Carlyle	.20	.50
10 Greg Paslawski RC	.20	.50
11 Neal Broten	.20	.50
12 Wendel Clark DP	1.00	2.50
13 Bill Ranford DP RC	2.00	5.00
14 Doug Wilson	.20	.50
15 Mario Lemieux	8.00	20.00
16 Mats Naslund	.20	.50
17 Mel Bridgman	.20	.50
18 James Patrick DP	.20	.50
19 Rollie Melanson	.20	.50
20 Lanny McDonald	.20	.50
21 Peter Stastny	.20	.50
22 Murray Craven	.20	.50
23 Ulf Samuelsson DP RC	.75	2.00
24 Michael Thelven DP UER (Misspelled Thelvin	.20	.50
25 Scott Stevens	.25	.60
26 Petr Klima	.20	.50
27 Brent Sutter DP	.20	.50
28 Tomas Sandstrom	.20	.50
29 Tim Bothwell	.20	.50
30 Bob Carpenter DP	.20	.50
31 Brian MacLellan DP	.20	.50
32 John Chabot	.20	.50
33 Phil Housley DP	.20	.50
34 Patrik Sundstrom DP	.20	.50
35 Dave Ellett	.20	.50
36 John Vanbiesbrouck	2.50	6.00
37 Dave Lewis	.20	.50
38 Tom McCarthy DP	.20	.50
39 Dave Poulin	.20	.50
40 Mike Foligno	.20	.50
41 Gordie Roberts	.20	.50
42 Luc Robitaille RC	8.00	20.00
43 Duane Sutter	.20	.50
44 Pete Peeters	.20	.50
45 John Anderson	.20	.50
46 Aaron Broten	.20	.50
47 Keith Brown	.20	.50
48 Bobby Smith	.20	.50
49 Don Maloney	.20	.50
50 Mark Hunter	.20	.50
51 Moe Mantha	.20	.50
52 Charlie Simmer	.20	.50
53 Wayne Gretzky	6.00	15.00
54 Mark Howe	.25	.60
55 Bob Gould	.20	.50
56 Steve Yzerman DP	2.50	6.00
57 Larry Playfair	.20	.50
58 Alain Chevrier	.20	.50
59 Steve Larmer	.20	.50
60 Bryan Trottier	.30	.75
61 Stewart Gavin DP	.25	.60
62 Russ Courtnall DP	.25	.60
63 Mike Ramsey DP	.25	.60
64 Bob Brooke	.25	.60
65 Rick Wamsley DP	.25	.60
66 Ken Morrow DP	.25	.60
67 Gerard Gallant UER RC	.25	.60
68 Kevin Hatcher RC	.60	1.50
69 Cam Neely	.75	2.00
70 Sylvain Turgeon DP	.25	.60
71 Peter Zezel	.25	.60
72 Al MacInnis	1.00	2.50
73 Terry Ruskowski DP	.25	.60
74 Troy Murray	.25	.60
75 Jim Fox DP	.25	.60
76 Kelly Kisio	.25	.60
77 Michel Goulet DP	.25	.60
78 Tom Barrasso DP	.25	.60
79 Bruce Driver DP	.25	.60
80 Craig Simpson DP RC	.40	1.00
81 Dino Ciccarelli	.25	.60
82 Gary Nylund DP	.25	.60
83 Bernie Federko	.25	.60
84 John Tonelli DP	.25	.60
85 Brad McCrimmon DP	.25	.60
86 Dave Tippett DP	.25	.60
87 Ray Bourque DP	.75	2.00
88 Dave Christian	.25	.60
89 Glen Hanlon	.25	.60
90 Brian Curran	.25	.60
91 Paul MacLean	.25	.60
92 Jimmy Carson RC	.25	.60
93 Willie Huber	.25	.60
94 Brian Bellows	.20	.50
95 Doug Jarvis DP	.25	.60
96 Clark Gillies	.25	.60
97 Tony Tanti	.25	.60
98 Pelle Eklund DP RC	.25	.60
99 Paul Coffey	1.00	2.50
100 Brent Ashton DP	.25	.60
101 Mark Johnson	.25	.60
102 Greg Johnston RC	.25	.60
103 Ron Flockhart	.25	.60
104 Ed Olczyk	.25	.60
105 Mike Bossy	.40	1.00
106 Chris Chelios	1.00	2.50
107 Gilles Meloche	.25	.60
108 Rod Langway	.25	.60
109 Ray Ferraro DP	.25	.60
110 Ron Duguay DP	.20	.50
111 Al Secord DP	.25	.60
112 Mark Messier	.25	.60
113 Ron Sutter	.25	.60
114 Darren Veitch RC	.25	.60
115 Rick Middleton DP	.25	.60
116 Doug Sulliman	.25	.60
117 Dennis Maruk DP	.25	.60
118 Dave Taylor	.25	.60
119 Kelly Hrudey	.25	.60
120 Tom Fergus	.25	.60
121 Christian Ruuttu RC	.25	.60
122 Brian Benning RC	.25	.60
123 Adam Oates RC	5.00	12.00
124 Kevin Dineen	.25	.60
125 Doug Bodger DP	.25	.60
126 Joe Mullen	.25	.60
127 Denis Savard	.30	.75
128 Brad Marsh	.25	.60
129 Marcel Dionne DP	.30	.75
130 Bryan Erickson	.25	.60
131 Reed Larson DP	.25	.60
132 Don Beaupre	.25	.60
133 Larry Murphy DP	.25	.60
134 John Ogrodnick DP	.25	.60
135 Greg Adams DP	.25	.60
136 Pat Flatley	.25	.60
137 Scott Arniel DP	.25	.60
138 Dana Murzyn	.25	.60
139 Greg C. Adams	.15	.40
140 Bob Sauve	.15	.40
141 Mike O'Connell	.15	.40
142 Walt Poddubny DP	.15	.40
143 Paul Reinhart	.15	.40
144 Tim Kerr DP	.15	.40
145 Brian Lawton RC	.15	.40
146 Gino Cavallini RC	.15	.40
147 Doug Keans DP	.15	.40
148 Jari Kurri	.15	.40
149 Dale Hawerchuk	.30	.75
150 Randy Cunneyworth RC	.20	.50
151 Jay Wells	.15	.40
152 Mike Liut DP	.15	.40
153 Steve Konroyd	.15	.40
154 John Tucker	.15	.40
155 Rick Vaive DP	.15	.40
156 Bob Murray	.15	.40
157 Kirk Muller DP	.15	.40
158 Brian Propp	.15	.40
159 Ron Greschner	.15	.40
160 Rob Ramage	.15	.40
161 Craig Laughlin	.15	.40
162 Steve Kasper DP	.20	.50
163 Patrick Roy	8.00	20.00
164 Shawn Burr DP RC	.20	.50
165 Craig Hartsburg DP	.20	.50
166 Dean Evason RC	.20	.50
167 Bob Bourne	.20	.50
168 Mike Gartner	.20	.50
169 Ron Hextall RC	4.00	10.00
170 Joe Cirella	.20	.50
171 Dan Quinn DP	.20	.50
172 Tony McKegney	.20	.50
173 Pat LaFontaine DP	.25	.60
174 Allen Pedersen DP RC	.20	.50
175 Doug Gilmour	.30	.75
176 Gary Suter DP	.20	.50
177 Barry Pederson DP	.20	.50
178 Grant Fuhr DP	.50	1.25
179 Wayne Presley RC	.20	.50
180 Wilf Paiement	.20	.50
181 Doug Smail	.25	.60
182 Doug Crossman DP	.25	.60
183 Bernie Nicholls UER (Misspelled Nichols on card front)	.25	.60
184 Dirk Graham UER (Misspelled Dick on card front)	.25	.60
185 Anton Stastny	.25	.60
186 Greg Stefan	.25	.60
187 Ron Francis	.30	.75
188 Steve Thomas DP	.25	.60
189 Kelly Miller RC	.25	.60
190 Tomas Jonsson	.25	.60
191 John MacLean	.25	.60
192 Larry Robinson DP	.20	.50
193 Doug Wickenheiser DP	.20	.50
194 Keith Crowder DP	.20	.50
195 Bob Froese	.20	.50
196 Jim Johnson	.20	.50
197 Checklist 1-99	.30	.75
198 Checklist 100-198	.30	.75

1987-88 Topps Box Bottoms

This sixteen-card standard-size set was issued in sets of four on the bottom of the 1987-88 Topps wax pack boxes. The cards feature team scoring leaders. Complete box bottom panels are valued at a 25 percent premium above the prices listed below. The cards are in the same design as the 1987-88 Topps regular issues except they are bordered in yellow. The backs are printed in red and black ink and give statistical information. The cards are lettered rather than numbered.

COMPLETE SET (16)	10.00	25.00
A Wayne Gretzky	4.00	10.00
B Tim Kerr	.08	.25
C Steve Yzerman	2.00	5.00
D Luc Robitaille	1.50	4.00
E Doug Gilmour	.40	1.00
F Ray Bourque	.75	2.00
G Joe Mullen	.20	.50
H Larry Murphy	.20	.50
I Dale Hawerchuk	.25	.60
J Ron Francis	.40	1.00
K Walt Poddubny	.05	.15
L Mats Naslund	.15	.40
M Michel Goulet	.20	.50
N Denis Savard	.20	.50
O Bryan Trottier	.25	.60
P Russ Courtnall	.20	.50

1987-88 Topps Sticker Inserts

This set of 33 "Hockey Helmet Stickers" features stickers of 12 All-Star players (1-12) and 21 stickers of team logos, pucks, and numbers. The stickers were inserted in with the 1987-88 Topps hockey regular issue wax packs and as such are also 2 1/2" by 3 1/2". The card backs are printed in blue and red on white card stock. The last seven team stickers can be found with the team logos on the top or bottom.

COMPLETE SET (33)	8.00	20.00
1 Ray Bourque	.75	2.00
2 Ron Hextall	1.00	2.50
3 Mark Howe	.15	.40
4 Jari Kurri	.30	.75
5 Wayne Gretzky	3.00	8.00
6 Michel Goulet	.15	.40
7 Larry Murphy	.15	.40
8 Mike Liut	.15	.40
9 Al MacInnis	.20	.50
10 Tim Kerr	.08	.25
11 Mario Lemieux	4.00	10.00
12 Luc Robitaille	1.50	4.00
13 Toronto Maple Leafs	.08	.25
14 Buffalo Sabres	.05	.15
15 Detroit Red Wings	.08	.25
16 Pittsburgh Penguins	.05	.15
17 New York Rangers	.08	.25
18 Calgary Flames	.05	.15
19 Winnipeg Jets	.05	.15
20 Quebec Nordiques	.05	.15
21 Chicago Blackhawks	.05	.15
22 Los Angeles Kings	.05	.15
23 Montreal Canadiens	.08	.25
24 Vancouver Canucks	.05	.15
25 Hartford Whalers	.05	.15
26 Philadelphia Flyers	.05	.15
27 New Jersey Devils	.05	.15
28 St. Louis Blues	.05	.15
29 Minnesota North Stars	.05	.15
30 Washington Capitals	.05	.15
31 Boston Bruins	.08	.25
32 New York Islanders	.05	.15
33 Edmonton Oilers	.05	.15

1988-89 Topps

The 1988-89 Topps hockey set contains 198 standard size cards. There are 66 double printed cards that are indicated by DP in the checklist below. The fronts feature colored borders and each player's team logo. The backs contain yearly statistics, playoff statistics, game winning goals from 1987-88 and highlights. Wayne Gretzky (120) appears as a King for the first time. The press conference photo has Gretzky holding his new Kings jersey. Be careful of counterfeit Brett Hull RCs.

COMPLETE SET (198)	15.00	40.00
1 Mario Lemieux DP	2.50	6.00
2 Bob Joyce DP RC	.25	.60
3 Joel Quenneville DP	.20	.50
4 Tony McKegney	.20	.50
5 Stephane Richer DP	.20	.50
6 Mark Howe DP	.25	.60
7 Brent Sutter DP	.20	.50
8 Gilles Meloche DP	.20	.50
9 Jimmy Carson DP	.20	.50
10 John MacLean	.20	.50
11 Gary Leeman	.20	.50
12 Gerard Gallant DP	.20	.50
13 Marcel Dionne	.30	.75
14 Dave Christian DP	.20	.50
15 Gary Nylund	.20	.50
16 Joe Nieuwendyk RC	2.00	6.00
17 Billy Smith DP	.25	.60
18 Christian Ruuttu	.20	.50
19 Randy Cunneyworth	.20	.50
20 Brian Lawton	.20	.50
21 Scott Mellanby DP RC	.75	2.00
22 Peter Stastny DP	.20	.50
23 Gord Kluzak	.20	.50
24 Sylvain Turgeon	.20	.50

25 Clint Malarchuk .20 .50
26 Denis Savard .30 .75
27 Craig Simpson .20 .50
28 Petr Klima .20 .50
29 Pat Verbeek .20 .50
30 Moe Mantha .20 .50
31 Chris Nilan .20 .50
32 Barry Pederson .20 .50
33 Randy Burridge .20 .50
34 Ron Hextall .50 1.25
35 Gaston Gingras .20 .50
36 Kevin Dineen DP .20 .50
37 Tom Laidlaw .20 .50
38 Paul MacLean DP .20 .50
39 John Chabot DP .20 .50
40 Lindy Ruff .20 .50
41 Dan Quinn DP .20 .50
42 Don Beaupre .20 .50
43 Gary Suter .20 .50
44 Mikko Makela DP RC .20 .50
45 Mark Johnson DP .20 .50
46 Dave Taylor .20 .50
47 Ulf Dahlen DP RC .20 .50
48 Jeff Sharples RC .20 .50
49 Chris Chelios .60 1.50
50 Mike Gartner DP .20 .50
51 Darren Pang DP RC .75 2.00
52 Ron Francis .30 .75
53 Ken Morrow .20 .50
54 Michel Goulet .20 .50
55 Ray Sheppard RC .75 2.00
56 Doug Gilmour .30 .75
57 David Shaw DP .20 .50
58 Cam Neely DP .60 1.50
59 Grant Fuhr DP .50 1.25
60 Scott Stevens .25 .60
61 Bob Brooke .25 .60
62 Dave Hunter .25 .60
63 Alan Kerr RC .25 .60
64 Brad Marsh .25 .60
65 Dale Hawerchuk DP .30 .75
66 Brett Hull DP RC 8.00 20.00
67 Patrik Sundstrom DP .25 .60
68 Greg Stefan .25 .60
69 James Patrick .25 .60
70 Dale Hunter DP .25 .60
71 Al Iafrate .25 .60
72 Bob Carpenter .25 .60
73 Ray Bourque DP .75 2.00
74 John Tucker DP .25 .60
75 Carey Wilson .25 .60
76 Joe Mullen .25 .60
77 Rick Vaive .25 .60
78 Shawn Burr DP .25 .60
79 Murray Craven DP .25 .60
80 Clark Gillies .25 .60
81 Bernie Federko .25 .60
82 Tony Tanti .25 .60
83 Greg Gilbert .25 .60
84 Kirk Muller .25 .60
85 Dave Tippett .25 .60
86 Kevin Hatcher DP .25 .60
87 Rick Middleton DP .25 .60
88 Bobby Smith .25 .60
89 Doug Wilson DP .25 .60
90 Scott Arniel .25 .60
91 Brian Mullen .25 .60
92 Mike O'Connell DP .15 .40
93 Mark Messier DP .50 1.25
94 Sean Burke RC 1.00 2.50
95 Brian Bellows DP .20 .50
96 Doug Bodger .15 .40
97 Bryan Trottier .30 .75
98 Anton Stastny .15 .40
99 Checklist 1-99 .20 .60
100 Dave Poulin DP .15 .40
101 Bob Bourne DP .15 .40
102 John Vanbiesbrouck .15 .40
103 Allen Pedersen .15 .40
104 Mike Ridley .15 .40
105 Andrew McBain .15 .40
106 Troy Murray DP .15 .40
107 Tom Barrasso .15 .40
108 Tomas Jonsson .15 .40
109 Rob Brown RC .15 .40
110 Hakan Loob DP .15 .40
111 Ilkka Sinisalo DP .15 .40
112 Dave Archibald RC .15 .40
113 Doug Halward .15 .40
114 Ray Ferraro .15 .40
115 Doug Brown RC .15 .40
116 Patrick Roy DP 1.50 4.00
117 Greg Millen .15 .40
118 Ken Linseman .15 .40
119 Phil Housley DP .15 .40
120 Wayne Gretzky Sweater 8.00 20.00
121 Tomas Sandstrom .15 .40
122 Brendan Shanahan RC 6.00 15.00
123 Pat LaFontaine .25 .60
124 Luc Robitaille DP 1.00 2.50
125 Ed Olczyk DP .15 .40
126 Ron Sutter .15 .40
127 Mike Liut .15 .40
128 Brent Ashton DP .15 .40
129 Tony Hrkac RC .15 .40
130 Kelly Miller .15 .40
131 Alan Haworth .15 .40
132 Dave McLlwain RC .15 .40
133 Mike Ramsey .15 .40
134 Bob Sweeney RC .20 .50
135 Dirk Graham DP .20 .50
136 Ulf Samuelsson .20 .50
137 Petri Skriko .20 .50
138 Aaron Broten DP .20 .50
139 Jim Fox .20 .50
140 Randy Wood DP RC .20 .50
141 Larry Murphy .20 .50
142 Daniel Berthiaume DP .20 .50
143 Kelly Kisio .20 .50
144 Neal Broten .20 .50
145 Reed Larson .20 .50
146 Peter Zezel DP .20 .50
147 Jari Kurri .20 .50
148 Jim Johnson .20 .50
149 Gino Cavallini DP .20 .50
150 Glen Hanlon DP .20 .50
151 Bengt Gustafsson .20 .50
152 Mike Bullard DP .20 .50
153 John Ogrodnick .20 .50
154 Steve Larmer .20 .50
155 Kelly Hrudey .20 .50
156 Mats Naslund .20 .50
157 Bruce Driver .20 .50
158 Randy Hillier .20 .50
159 Craig Hartsburg .20 .50
160 Rollie Melanson .20 .50
161 Adam Oates DP .50 1.25
162 Greg Adams DP .15 .40
163 Dave Andreychuk DP .25 .60
164 Dave Babych .20 .50
165 Brian Noonan RC .20 .50
166 Glen Wesley RC .20 .50
167 Dave Ellett .20 .50
168 Brian Propp .20 .50
169 Bernie Nicholls .20 .50
170 Walt Poddubny .20 .50
171 Steve Konroyd .20 .50
172 Doug Sulliman DP .20 .50
173 Mario Gosselin .20 .50
174 Brian Benning .20 .50
175 Dino Ciccarelli .20 .50
176 Steve Kasper .20 .50
177 Rick Tocchet .60 1.50
178 Brad McCrimmon .20 .50
179 Paul Coffey .50 1.25
180 Pete Peeters .20 .50
181 Bob Probert DP RC 1.50 4.00
182 Steve Duchesne DP RC .60 1.50
183 Russ Courtnall .20 .50
184 Mike Foligno DP .20 .50
185 Wayne Presley DP .20 .50
186 Rejean Lemelin .20 .50
187 Mark Hunter .20 .50
188 Joe Cirella .20 .50
189 Glenn Anderson DP .25 .60
190 John Anderson .15 .40
191 Pat Flatley .15 .40
192 Rod Langway .15 .40
193 Brian MacLellan .20 .50
194 Pierre Turgeon RC 3.00 8.00
195 Brian Hayward .20 .50
196 Steve Yzerman DP .75 2.00
197 Doug Crossman .20 .50
198 Checklist 100-198 .25 .60

1988-89 Topps Box Bottoms

This sixteen-card standard-size set was issued in sets of four on the bottom of the 1988-89 Topps wax pack boxes. The cards feature team scoring leaders. Complete box bottom panels are valued at a 25 percent premium above the prices listed below. The cards are in the same design as the 1988-89 Topps regular issues except they are bordered only in gray. The backs are printed in purple on orange background and give statistical information. The cards are lettered rather than numbered.

COMPLETE SET (16) 5.60 14.00
A Ron Francis .30 .75
B Wayne Gretzky 2.50 6.00
C Pat LaFontaine .30 .75
D Bobby Smith .08 .25
E Bernie Federko .08 .25
F Kirk Muller .20 .50
G Ed Olczyk .05 .15
H Denis Savard .20 .50
I Ray Bourque .60 1.50
J Murray Craven .05 .15
Brian Propp
K Dale Hawerchuk .20 .50
L Steve Yzerman 1.25 3.00
M Dave Andreychuk .15 .40
N Mike Gartner .20 .50
O Hakan Loob .08 .25
P Luc Robitaille .40 1.00

1988-89 Topps Sticker Inserts

This set of 33 "Hockey Helmet Stickers" features stickers of 12 All-Star players (1-12) and 21 stickers of team logos, pucks, and numbers. The stickers were inserted in with the 1988-89 Topps hockey regular issue wax packs and as such are also 2 1/2" by 3 1/2". The card backs are printed in blue and red on white card stock. The last seven team stickers can be found with the team logos on the top or bottom.

COMPLETE SET (33) 6.00 15.00
1 Luc Robitaille .60 1.50
2 Mario Lemieux 1.50 4.00
3 Hakan Loob .08 .25
4 Scott Stevens .15 .40
5 Ray Bourque .30 .75
6 Grant Fuhr .20 .50
7 Michel Goulet .15 .40
8 Wayne Gretzky 2.00 5.00
9 Cam Neely .30 .75
10 Brad McCrimmon .08 .25
11 Gary Suter .08 .25
12 Patrick Roy 2.00 5.00
13 Toronto Maple Leafs .08 .25
14 Buffalo Sabres .05 .15
15 Detroit Red Wings .08 .25
16 Pittsburgh Penguins .05 .15
17 New York Rangers .08 .25
18 Calgary Flames .05 .15
19 Winnipeg Jets .05 .15
20 Quebec Nordiques .05 .15
21 Chicago Blackhawks .08 .25
22 Los Angeles Kings .05 .15
23 Montreal Canadiens .08 .25
24 Vancouver Canucks .05 .15
25 Hartford Whalers .05 .15
26 Philadelphia Flyers .05 .15
27 New Jersey Devils .05 .15
28 St. Louis Blues .05 .15
29 Minnesota North Stars .05 .15
30 Washington Capitals .05 .15
31 Boston Bruins .08 .25
32 New York Islanders .05 .15
33 Edmonton Oilers .05 .15

1989-90 Topps

The 1989-90 Topps set contains 198 standard-size cards. There are 66 double-printed cards which are marked as DP in the checklist below. The fronts feature blue borders on top and bottom that are prone to chipping. An ice blue border is on either side. A team logo and the player's name are at the bottom. The backs contain yearly statistics, playoff statistics, game-winning goals from 1988-89 and highlights. The key Rookie Card in this set is Joe Sakic.

COMPLETE SET (198) 15.00 30.00
1 Mario Lemieux 1.50 4.00
2 Ulf Dahlen DP .25 .60
3 Terry Carkner RC .25 .60
4 Tony McKegney .25 .60
5 Denis Savard .30 .75
6 Derek King DP RC .25 .60
7 Lanny McDonald .25 .60
8 John Tonelli .25 .60
9 Tom Kurvers DP .25 .60
10 Dave Archibald .25 .60
11 Peter Sidorkiewicz RC .25 .60
12 Esa Tikkanen .25 .60
13 Dave Barr .25 .60
14 Brent Sutter .25 .60
15 Cam Neely .25 .60
16 Calle Johansson RC .20 .50
17 Patrick Roy DP 1.00 2.50
18 Dale DeGray DP RC .20 .50
19 Phil Bourque RC .20 .50
20 Kevin Dineen .20 .50
21 Mike Bullard DP .20 .50
22 Gary Leeman .20 .50
23 Greg Stefan DP .20 .50
24 Brian Mullen .20 .50
25 Pierre Turgeon DP .50 1.25
26 Bob Rouse DP .20 .50
27 Peter Zezel .20 .50
28 Jeff Brown DP .20 .50
29 Andy Brickley DP RC .20 .50
30 Mike Gartner .20 .50
31 Darren Pang .20 .50
32 Pat Verbeek .20 .50
33 Petri Skriko DP .20 .50
34 Tom Laidlaw .20 .50
35 Randy Wood .20 .50
36 Tom Barrasso DP .20 .50
37 John Tucker DP .20 .50
38 Andrew McBain .20 .50
39 David Shaw DP .20 .50
40 Rejean Lemelin .20 .50
41 Dino Ciccarelli DP .20 .50
42 Jeff Sharples .20 .50
43 Jari Kurri .20 .50
44 Murray Craven DP .20 .50
45 Cliff Ronning DP RC .75 2.00
46 Dave Babych .20 .50
47 Bernie Nicholls DP .20 .50
48 Jon Casey RC .20 .50
49 Al MacInnis .20 .50
50 Bob Errey DP RC .20 .50
51 Glen Wesley .20 .50
52 Dirk Graham .20 .50
53 Guy Carbonneau DP .20 .50
54 Tomas Sandstrom .20 .50
55 Rod Langway DP .20 .50
56 Patrik Sundstrom .20 .50
57 Michel Goulet .20 .50
58 Dave Taylor .20 .50
59 Phil Housley .20 .50
60 Pat LaFontaine DP .25 .60
61 Kirk McLean DP RC .30 .75
62 Ken Linseman .20 .50
63A Randy Cunneyworth PIT .20 .50
63B Randy Cunneyworth WIN .20 .50
64 Tony Hrkac DP .20 .50
65 Mark Messier DP .20 .50
66 Carey Wilson DP .20 .50
67 Stephen Leach RC .20 .50
68 Christian Ruuttu .20 .50
69 Dave Ellett .20 .50
70 Ray Ferraro .20 .50
71 Colin Patterson RC .20 .50
72 Tim Kerr .20 .50
73 Bob Joyce .20 .50
74 Doug Gilmour DP .30 .75
75 Lee Norwood DP .20 .50
76 Dale Hunter .20 .50
77 Jim Johnson DP .20 .50
78 Mike Foligno DP .25 .60
79 Al Iafrate DP .25 .60
80 Rick Tocchet DP .25 .60
81 Greg Hawgood DP RC .25 .60
82 Steve Thomas .25 .60
83 Steve Yzerman DP .60 1.50
84 Mike McPhee .25 .60
85 David Volek DP RC .25 .60
86 Brian Benning .25 .60
87 Neal Broten .25 .60
88 Luc Robitaille .25 .60
89 Trevor Linden RC .75 2.00
90 James Patrick DP .25 .60
91 Brian Lawton .25 .60
92 Sean Burke DP .25 .60
93 Scott Stevens .25 .60
94 Pat Elynuik DP RC .25 .60
95 Paul Coffey .25 .60
96 Jan Erixon DP .25 .60
97 Mike Liut .25 .60
98 Wayne Presley .25 .60
99 Craig Simpson .25 .60
100 Kjell Samuelsson RC .25 .60
101 Shawn Burr DP .25 .60
102 John MacLean .25 .60
103 Tom Fergus .25 .60
104 Mike Krushelnyski .25 .60
105 Gary Nylund .25 .60
106 Dave Andreychuk .25 .60
107 Bernie Federko .25 .60
108 Gary Suter .25 .60
109 Dave Gagner DP .25 .60
110 Ray Bourque .40 1.00
111 Geoff Courtnall RC .50 1.25
112 Doug Wilson .25 .60
113 Joe Sakic RC 6.00 15.00
114 John Vanbiesbrouck .25 .60
115 Dave Poulin .25 .60
116 Rick Meagher .15 .40
117 Kirk Muller DP .15 .40
118 Mats Naslund .15 .40
119 Ray Sheppard .15 .40
120 Jeff Norton RC .20 .50
121 Randy Burridge DP .15 .40
122 Dale Hawerchuk DP .30 .75
123 Steve Duchesne .15 .40
124 John Anderson .15 .40
125 Rick Vaive DP .15 .40
126 Randy Hillier .15 .40
127 Jimmy Carson .15 .40
128 Larry Murphy .15 .40
129 Paul MacLean DP .15 .40
130 Joe Cirella .15 .40
131 Kelly Miller DP .15 .40
132 Alain Chevrier DP .15 .40
133 Ed Olczyk .15 .40
134 Dave Tippett .15 .40
135 Bob Sweeney .15 .40
136 Brian Leetch RC 2.50 6.00
137 Greg Millen .15 .40
138 Joe Nieuwendyk .15 .40
139 Brian Propp .15 .40
140 Mike Ramsey .15 .40
141 Mike Allison .15 .40
142 Shawn Chambers RC .15 .40
143 Peter Stastny DP .15 .40
144 Glen Hanlon .15 .40
145 John Cullen RC .20 .50
146 Kevin Hatcher .20 .50
147 Brendan Shanahan .30 .75
148 Paul Reinhart .20 .50
149 Bryan Trottier .30 .75
150 Dave Manson RC .20 .50
151 Marc Habscheid DP RC .20 .50
152 Dan Quinn .20 .50
153 Stephane Richer DP .20 .50
154 Doug Bodger DP .20 .50
155 Ron Hextall .20 .50
156 Wayne Gretzky 1.25 3.00
157 Steve Tuttle DP RC .25 .60
158 Charlie Huddy DP .25 .60
159 Dave Christian DP .25 .60
160 Andy Moog .25 .60
161 Tony Granato RC .25 .60
162 Sylvain Cote RC .25 .60
163 Mike Vernon .30 .75
164 Steve Chiasson RC .20 .50
165 Mike Ridley .20 .50
166 Kelly Hrudey .20 .50
167 Bob Carpenter DP .20 .50
168 Zarley Zalapski RC .20 .50
169 Derek Laxdal RC .25 .60
170 Clint Malarchuk DP .25 .60
171 Kelly Kisio .25 .60
172 Gerard Gallant .25 .60
173 Ron Sutter .25 .60
174 Chris Chelios .25 .60
175 Ron Francis .30 .75
176 Gino Cavallini .20 .50
177 Brian Bellows DP .20 .50
178 Greg C. Adams DP .20 .50
179 Steve Larmer .20 .50
180 Aaron Broten .20 .50
181 Brent Ashton DP .20 .50
182 Gerald Diduck DP RC .20 .50
183 Paul MacDermid RC .20 .50
184 Walt Poddubny DP .20 .50
185 Adam Oates .25 .60
186 Brett Hull 2.00 5.00
187 Scott Arniel .20 .50
188 Bobby Smith .20 .50
189 Guy Lafleur .30 .75
190 Craig Janney RC .30 .75
191 Mark Howe .25 .60
192 Grant Fuhr DP .50 1.25
193 Rob Brown .15 .40
194 Steve Kasper DP .15 .40
195 Pete Peeters .15 .40
196 Joe Mullen .15 .40
197 Checklist 1-99 .30 .75
198 Checklist 100-198 DP .30 .75

1989-90 Topps Box Bottoms

This sixteen-card standard-size set was issued in sets of four on the bottom of the 1989-90 Topps wax pack boxes. The cards feature sixteen NHL star players who were scoring leaders on their teams. Complete box bottom panels are valued at a 25 percent premium above the prices listed below. A color action photo appears on the front and the player's name, team, and team logo at the bottom of the picture. The back is printed in red and black ink and gives the player's position and statistical information. The cards are lettered rather than numbered. The set features such NHL stars as Wayne Gretzky, Brett Hull, and Mario Lemieux.

COMPLETE SET (16) 4.00 10.00
A Mario Lemieux 1.50 4.00
B Mike Ridley .08 .25
C Tomas Sandstrom .08 .25
D Petri Skriko .08 .25
E Wayne Gretzky 1.50 4.00
F Brett Hull .75 2.00
G Tim Kerr .08 .25
H Mats Naslund .08 .25
I Jari Kurri .20 .50
J Steve Larmer .20 .50
K Cam Neely .30 .75
L Steve Yzerman .75 2.00
M Kevin Dineen .08 .25
N Dave Gagner .15 .40
O Joe Mullen .15 .40
P Pierre Turgeon .30 .75

1989-90 Topps Sticker Inserts

This 33-card standard-size set was issued as a one per pack insert in the 1989-90 Topps Hockey packs. This set is divided into the first 12 cards being the 1989-90 NHL all-stars and the next 21 cards being the various team logos along with some number stickers and stickers of hockey pucks. For some reason Topps apparently printed these sticker cards on sheets in such a way that there were three complete sets of 33 and then three more rows of 11 double-printed cards instead of merely printing four complete sets on the printing sheet.

COMPLETE SET (33) 4.00 10.00
1 Chris Chelios .30 .75
2 Gerard Gallant DP .05 .15
3 Mario Lemieux 2.00 5.00
4 Al MacInnis .20 .50
5 Joe Mullen DP .08 .25
6 Patrick Roy 1.50 4.00
7 Ray Bourque .30 .75
8 Rob Brown .08 .25
9 Geoff Courtnall DP .08 .25
10 Steve Duchesne DP .05 .15
11 Wayne Gretzky 2.00 5.00
12 Mike Vernon .15 .40
13 Toronto Maple Leafs .05 .15
14 Buffalo Sabres .05 .15
15 Detroit Red Wings .05 .15
16 Pittsburgh Penguins .05 .15
17 New York Rangers .05 .15
18 Calgary Flames .05 .15
19 Winnipeg Jets .05 .15
20 Quebec Nordiques .05 .15
21 Chicago Blackhawks .05 .15
22 Los Angeles Kings .05 .15
23 Montreal Canadiens .05 .15
24 Vancouver Canucks .05 .15
25 Hartford Whalers .05 .15
26 Philadelphia Flyers .05 .15
27 New Jersey Devils DP .02 .10
28 St. Louis Blues DP .02 .10
29 Minn. North Stars DP .02 .10
30 Washington Capitals DP .02 .10
31 Boston Bruins DP .02 .10
32 New York Islanders DP .02 .10
33 Edmonton Oilers DP .02 .10

1990-91 Topps

The 1990-91 Topps hockey set contains 396 standard-size cards. The fronts feature color action photos with color borders (according to team) on all four sides. A hockey stick is superimposed over the picture at the top border. The backs have yearly statistics, playoff statistics, and game winning goals from 1989-90. Included in the set is a three-card Tribute to Wayne Gretzky (1-3). Team cards have action scenes with the team's previous season standings and power play stats on back.

*TIFFANY: 3X TO 8X BASIC CARDS
ANNOUNCED PRINT RUN 3000 SETS
1 Wayne Gretzky Indy .50 1.25
2 Wayne Gretzky Oilers .50 1.25
3 Wayne Gretzky LA .50 1.25
4 Brett Hull HL .20 .50
5 Jari Kurri HL UER .12 .30
misspelled Jarri
6 Bryan Trottier HL .12 .30
7 Jeremy Roenick RC .75 2.00
8 Brian Propp .10 .25
9 Jim Hrivnak RC .10 .25
10 Mick Vukota RC .10 .25
11 Tom Kurvers .10 .25
12 Ulf Dahlen .10 .25
13 Bernie Nicholls .10 .25
14 Peter Sidorkiewicz .10 .25
15 Peter Zezel .10 .25
16 Mike Hartman RC .10 .25
17 Kings Team .10 .25
18 Jim Sandlak .10 .25
19 Rob Brown .20 .50
20 Paul Ranheim RC .10 .25
21 Rick Zombo RC .10 .25
22 Paul Gillis .07 .20
23 Brian Hayward .10 .25
24 Brent Ashton .10 .25
25 Mark Lamb .10 .25
26 Rick Tocchet .10 .25
27 Slava Fetisov RC .20 .50
28 Denis Savard .12 .30
29 Chris Chelios .10 .25
30 Janne Ojanen RC .10 .25
31 Don Maloney .10 .25
32 Allan Bester .10 .25
33 Geoff Smith RC .10 .25
34 Daniel Shank RC .10 .25
35 Mikael Andersson RC .10 .25
36 Gino Cavallini .10 .25
37 Rob Murphy RC .10 .25
38 Flames Team .10 .25
39 Laurie Boschman .07 .20
40 Craig Wolanin RC .07 .20
41 Phil Bourque .07 .20
42 Alexander Mogilny RC .50 1.25
43 Ray Bourque .15 .40
44 Mike Liut .07 .20
45 Ron Sutter .07 .20
46 Bob Kudelski RC .07 .20
47 Larry Murphy .07 .20
48 Darren Turcotte RC .07 .20
49 Paul Ysebaert RC .07 .20
50 Alan Kerr .07 .20
51 Randy Carlyle .07 .20
52 Iiro Jarvi .07 .20
53 Don Barber RC .07 .20
54 Carey Wilson .07 .20
55 Joey Kocur RC .20 .50
56 Steve Larmer .07 .20
57 Paul Cavallini .07 .20
58 Shayne Corson .07 .20
59 Canucks Team .07 .20
60 Sergei Makarov RC .20 .50
61 Kjell Samuelsson .07 .20
62 Tony Granato .07 .20
63 Tom Fergus .07 .20
64 Martin Gelinas RC .20 .50
65 Tom Barrasso .07 .20
66 Pierre Turgeon .07 .20
67 Randy Cunneyworth .07 .20
68 Michal Pivonka RC .07 .20
69 Cam Neely .10 .25
70 Brian Bellows .07 .20
71 Pat Elynuik .07 .20
72 Doug Crossman .07 .20
73 Sylvain Turgeon .07 .20
74 Shawn Burr .07 .20
75 John Vanbiesbrouck .07 .20
76 Steve Bozek .07 .20
77 Brett Hull .20 .50
78 Zarley Zalapski .07 .20
79 Wendel Clark .10 .25
80 Flyers Team .10 .25
Kjell Samuelsson
Wendell Young
81 Kelly Miller .05 .15
82 Mark Pederson RC .10 .25
83 Adam Creighton .05 .15
84 Scott Young .05 .15
85 Petr Klima .05 .15
86 Steve Duchesne .05 .15
87 Joe Nieuwendyk .05 .15
88 Andy Brickley .05 .15
89 Phil Housley .07 .20
90 Neal Broten .05 .15
91 Al Iafrate .05 .15
92 Steve Thomas .05 .15
93 Guy Carbonneau .05 .15
94 Steve Chiasson .05 .15
95 Mike Tomlak RC .10 .25
96 Roger Johansson RC .10 .25
97 Randy Wood .05 .15
98 Jim Johnson .05 .15
99 Bob Sweeney .05 .15
100 Dino Ciccarelli .10 .25
101 Rangers Team .10 .25
James Patrick
102 Mike Ramsey .05 .15
103 Kelly Hrudey .05 .15
104 Dave Ellett .05 .15
105 Bob Brooke .05 .15
106 Greg Adams .05 .15
107 Joe Cirella .05 .15
108 Jari Kurri .12 .30
109 Pete Peeters .05 .15
110 Paul MacLean .07 .20
111 Doug Wilson .10 .25
112 Pat Verbeek .07 .20
113 Bob Beers RC .07 .20
114 Mike O'Connell .07 .20
115 Brian Bradley .07 .20
116 Paul Coffey .10 .25
117 Doug Brown .07 .20
118 Aaron Broten .07 .20
119 Bob Essensa RC .15 .40
120 Wayne Gretzky UER .50 1.25
121 Vincent Damphousse .07 .20
122 Nordiques Team .07 .20
Paul Gillis
123 Mike Foligno .07 .20
124 Russ Courtnall .10 .25
125 Rick Meagher .07 .20
126 Craig Fisher RC .10 .25
127 Al MacInnis .07 .20
128 Derek King .10 .25
129 Dale Hunter .10 .25
130 Mark Messier UER .20 .50
131 James Patrick UER .10 .25
(Orange border rather than blue)
132 Checklist 1-132 .05 .15
133 Red Wings Team .30 .75
Steve Yzerman
134 Barry Pederson .07 .20
135 Gary Leeman .07 .20
136 Doug Gilmour .12 .30
137 Mike McPhee .07 .20
138 Bob Murray .07 .20
139 Bob Carpenter .07 .20
140 Sean Burke .07 .20
141 Dale Hawerchuk .12 .30
142 Guy Lafleur .12 .30
143 Lindy Ruff .07 .20
144 Whalers Team .07 .20
Brad Shaw
145 Glenn Anderson .10 .25
146 Dave Chyzowski RC .07 .20
147 Kevin Hatcher .07 .20
148 Rick Vaive .07 .20
149 Adam Oates .10 .25
150 Garth Butcher .07 .20
151 Basil McRae .07 .20
152 Ilkka Sinisalo .07 .20
153 Steve Kasper .07 .20
154 Greg Paslawski .07 .20
155 Brad Marsh .07 .20
156 Esa Tikkanen .07 .20
157 Tony Tanti .07 .20
158 Mario Marois .07 .20
159 Sylvain Lefebvre RC .07 .20
160 Troy Murray .07 .20
161 Gary Roberts .10 .25
162 Randy Ladouceur .10 .25
163 John Chabot .10 .25
164 Calle Johansson .10 .25
165 Bruins Team .15 .40
Ray Bourque
166 Jeff Norton .10 .25
167 Mike Krushelnyski .10 .25
168 Dave Gagner .10 .25
169 Dave Andreychuk .10 .25
170 Dave Capuano RC .10 .25
171 Curtis Joseph RC .50 1.25
172 Bruce Driver .10 .25
173 Scott Mellanby .10 .25
174 John Ogrodnick .10 .25
175 Mario Lemieux .40 1.00
176 Marc Fortier .07 .20
177 Vincent Riendeau RC .10 .25
178 Mark Johnson .07 .20
179 Dirk Graham .07 .20
180 Jets Team .10 .25
181 Robb Stauber RC .10 .25
182 Christian Ruuttu .07 .20
183 Dave Tippett .07 .20
184 Pat LaFontaine .10 .25
185 Mark Howe .10 .25
186 Stephane Richer .10 .25
187 Jan Erixon .10 .25
188 Neil Sheehy .10 .25
189 Craig MacTavish .07 .20
190 Randy Burridge .07 .20
191 Bernie Federko .07 .20
192 Shawn Chambers .07 .20
193 Mark Messier AS1 .20 .50
194 Luc Robitaille AS1 .10 .25
195 Brett Hull AS1 .20 .50
196 Ray Bourque AS1 .15 .40
197 Al Macinnis AS1 .07 .20
198 Patrick Roy AS1 .25 .60
199 Wayne Gretzky AS2 .50 1.25
200 Brian Bellows AS2 .07 .20
201 Cam Neely AS2 .10 .25
202 Paul Coffey AS2 .10 .25
203 Doug Wilson AS2 .10 .25
204 Daren Puppa AS2 UER .07 .20
205 Gary Suter .10 .25
206 Ed Olczyk .10 .25
207 Doug Lidster .10 .25
208 John Cullen .10 .25
209 Luc Robitaille .10 .25
210 Tim Kerr .10 .25
211 Scott Stevens .10 .25
212 Craig Janney .10 .25
213 Kevin Dineen .10 .25
214 Jim Waite RC .10 .25
215 Benoit Hogue .10 .25
216 Curtis Leschyshyn RC .07 .20
217 Brad Lauer .07 .20
218 Joe Mullen .07 .20
219 Patrick Roy .25 .60
220 Blues Team .10 .25
Jeff Brown
221 Brian Leetch .12 .30
222 Steve Yzerman .30 .75
223 Steph Beauregard RC .07 .20
224 John MacLean .07 .20
225 Trevor Linden .07 .20
226 Bill Ranford .07 .20
227 Mark Osborne .07 .20
228 Curt Giles .07 .20
229 Mikko Makela .07 .20
230 Bob Errey .07 .20
231 Jimmy Carson .07 .20
232 Kay Whitmore RC .07 .20
233 Gary Nylund .07 .20
234 Jiri Hrdina RC .07 .20
235 Stephen Leach .07 .20
236 Greg Hawgood .07 .20
237 Jocelyn Lemieux RC .07 .20
238 Daren Puppa .07 .20
239 Kelly Kisio .07 .20
240 Craig Simpson .07 .20
241 Maple Leafs Team .07 .20
Vincent Damphousse
242 Fredrik Olausson .07 .20
243 Ron Hextall .07 .20
244 Sergio Momesso RC .07 .20
245 Kirk Muller .07 .20
246 Petr Svoboda .07 .20
247 Daniel Berthiaume .07 .20
248 Andrew McBain .07 .20
249 Jeff Jackson UER .07 .20
250 Randy Gilhen RC .05 .15
251 Oilers Team .20 .50
Adam Graves
252 Rick Bennett RC .05 .15
253 Don Beaupre .05 .15
254 Pelle Eklund .05 .15
255 Greg Gilbert .05 .15
256 Gordie Roberts .05 .15
257 Kirk McLean .05 .15
258 Brent Sutter .07 .20
259 Brendan Shanahan .12 .30
260 Todd Krygier RC .07 .20
261 Larry Robinson UER .07 .20
262 Sabres Team .07 .20
Phil Housley
263 Dave Christian .07 .20
264 Checklist 133-264 .05 .15
265 Jamie Macoun .07 .20
266 Glen Hanlon .07 .20
267 Daniel Marois .07 .20
268 Doug Smail .07 .20
269 Jon Casey .10 .25
270 Brian Skrudland .07 .20
271 Michel Petit .07 .20
272 Dan Quinn .07 .20
273 Geoff Courtnall .07 .20
274 Mike Bullard .07 .20
275 Randy Gregg .07 .20
276 Keith Brown .07 .20
277 Troy Mallette RC .07 .20
278 Steve Tuttle .07 .20
279 Brad Shaw RC .07 .20
280 Mark Recchi RC .30 .75
281 John Tonelli .07 .20
282 Doug Bodger .07 .20
283 Thomas Steen .07 .20
284 Devils Team .20 .50
Chris Terreri
285 Lee Norwood .07 .20
286 Brian MacLellan .07 .20
287 Bobby Smith .07 .20
288 Rob Cimetta RC .07 .20
289 Rob Zettler RC .07 .20
290 David Reid RC .10 .25
291 Bryan Trottier .12 .30
292 Brian Mullen .10 .25
293 Paul Reinhart .10 .25
294 Andy Moog .10 .25
295 Jeff Brown .10 .25
296 Ryan Walter .10 .25
297 Trent Yawney .10 .25
298 John Druce RC .10 .25
299 Dave McLlwain UER .10 .25
(Card says shoots right, should be left)
300 David Volek .10 .25
301 Tomas Sandstrom .10 .25
302 Gord Murphy RC .10 .25
303 Lou Franceschetti RC .10 .25
304 Dana Murzyn .10 .25
305 North Stars Team .10 .25
Jon Casey
306 Patrik Sundstrom .10 .25
307 Kevin Lowe .10 .25
308 Dave Barr .10 .25
309 Wendell Young RC .10 .25
310 Darrin Shannon RC .10 .25
311 Ron Francis .12 .30
312 Stephane Fiset RC .20 .50
313 Paul Fenton .10 .25
314 Dave Taylor .10 .25
315 Islanders Team .10 .25
Pat LaFontaine
316 Petri Skriko .10 .25
317 Rob Ramage .10 .25
318 Murray Craven .10 .25
319 Gaetan Duchesne .10 .25
320 Brad McCrimmon .10 .25
321 Grant Fuhr .10 .25
322 Gerard Gallant .05 .15
323 Tommy Albelin .05 .15
324 Scott Arniel .05 .15
325 Mike Keane RC .05 .15
326 Penguins Team .05 .15
Randy Gilhen
327 Mike Ridley .05 .15
328 Dave Babych .05 .15
329 Michel Goulet .05 .15
330 Mike Richter RC .30 .75
331 Garry Galley RC .05 .15
332 Rod Brind'Amour RC .20 .50
333 Tony McKegney .05 .15
334 Peter Stastny .07 .20
335 Greg Millen .07 .20
336 Ray Ferraro .07 .20
337 Miloslav Horava RC .07 .20
338 Paul MacDermid .07 .20
339 Craig Coxe RC .07 .20
340 Dave Snuggerud RC .07 .20
341 Mike Lalor RC .07 .20
342 Marc Habscheid .07 .20
343 Rejean Lemelin .07 .20
344 Charlie Huddy .07 .20
345 Ken Linseman .07 .20
346 Canadiens Team .07 .20
Sylvain Lefebvre
347 Troy Loney RC .10 .25
348 Mike Modano RC .60 1.50
349 Jeff Reese RC .10 .25
350 Pat Flatley .10 .25
351 Mike Vernon .10 .25
352 Todd Elik RC .10 .25
353 Rod Langway .10 .25
354 Moe Mantha .10 .25
355 Keith Acton .10 .25
356 Scott Pearson RC .10 .25
357 Perry Berezan RC .10 .25
358 Alexei Kasatonov RC .10 .25
359 Igor Larionov RC .20 .50
360 Kevin Stevens RC .20 .50
361 Yves Racine RC .10 .25
362 Dave Poulin .10 .25
363 Blackhawks Team .10 .25
Dave Manson
Doug Wilson
364 Yvon Corriveau RC .07 .20
365 Brian Benning .07 .20
366 Hubie McDonough RC .07 .20
367 Ron Tugnutt .07 .20
368 Steve Smith .07 .20
369 Joel Otto .07 .20
370 Dave Lowry RC .07 .20
371 Clint Malarchuk .07 .20
372 Mathieu Schneider RC .07 .20
373 Mike Gartner .10 .25
374 John Tucker .07 .20
375 Chris Terreri RC .20 .50
376 Dean Evason .07 .20
377 Jamie Leach RC .07 .20
378 Jacques Cloutier RC .07 .20
379 Glen Wesley .07 .20
380 Vladimir Krutov RC .20 .50
381 Terry Carkner .07 .20
382 John McIntyre RC .07 .20
383 Ville Siren RC .07 .20
384 Joe Sakic .30 .75
385 Teppo Numminen RC .20 .50
386 Theo Fleury .12 .30
387 Glen Featherstone RC .07 .20
388 Stephan Lebeau RC .07 .20
389 Kevin McClelland .07 .20
390 Uwe Krupp .10 .25
391 Mark Janssens RC .10 .25
392 Marty McSorley .10 .25
393 Vladimir Ruzicka RC .10 .25
394 Capitals Team .10 .25
Kirk Muller
Scott Stevens
395 Mark Fitzpatrick RC .07 .20
396 Checklist 265-396 .05 .15

1990-91 Topps Tiffany

This is a parallel to the base set, and Topps announced that only 3000 sets were produced. The cards can be distinguished by a glossy coating not found on regular issued cards.

1990-91 Topps Box Bottoms

This 16-card standard-size set was issued in sets of four on the bottom of the 1990-91 Topps wax pack boxes. The cards are lettered rather than numbered. Complete box bottom panels are valued at a 25 percent premium above the prices listed below. The front design of these cards is essentially the same as the regular issue cards. The horizontally oriented backs have special statistics in blue lettering on a pale green background. The checklist does not agree with the actual grouping of the players in the four sets.

COMPLETE SET (16) 3.00 8.00
A Alexander Mogilny .50 1.25
B Jon Casey .15 .40
C Paul Coffey .25 .60
D Wayne Gretzky 1.00 2.50
E Patrick Roy .60 1.50
F Mike Modano .30 .75
G Mario Lemieux .60 1.50
H Al MacInnis .15 .40
I Ray Bourque .25 .60
J Steve Yzerman .40 1.00
K Darren Turcotte .08 .25
L Mike Vernon .15 .40
M Pierre Turgeon .20 .50
N Doug Wilson .08 .25
O Don Beaupre .15 .40
P Sergei Makarov .08 .25

1990-91 Topps Team Scoring Leaders

The 21-cards in this standard size set was included as a one per pack insert in the 1990-91 Topps hockey packs. This set has a glossy front with a full color action shot of the team's leading scorer while the back of the card has a list of the ten leading scorers for each team.

COMPLETE SET (21) 3.00 7.50
*TIFFANY: 3X TO 8X BASIC INSERTS
1 Steve Larmer .15 .40
2 Brett Hull .40 1.00
3 Cam Neely .20 .50
4 Stephane Richer .20 .50
5 Paul Reinhart .20 .50
6 Dino Ciccarelli .20 .50
7 Kirk Muller .15 .40
8 Joe Nieuwendyk .12 .30
9 Rick Tocchet .20 .50
10 Pat LaFontaine .20 .50
11 Dale Hawerchuk .25 .60
12 Wayne Gretzky 1.00 2.50
13 Gary Leeman .15 .40
14 Joe Sakic .60 1.50
15 Brian Bellows .15 .40
16 Mark Messier .40 1.00
17 Mario Lemieux .75 2.00
18 John Ogrodnick .20 .50
19 Steve Yzerman .60 1.50
20 Pierre Turgeon .15 .40
21 Ron Francis .25 .60

1991-92 Topps

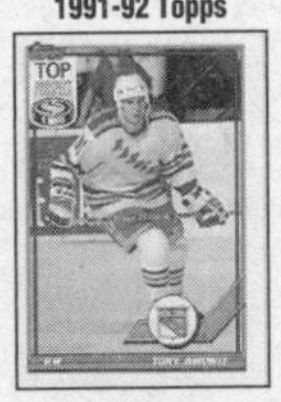

The 1991-92 O-Pee-Chee and Topps hockey sets contain 528 standard-size cards. Both sets feature a Guy Lafleur Tribute (1-3) and a Super Rookie (4-13) subset. Topps hockey cards were sold in 15-card packs that included a bonus team scoring leader card, whereas the O-Pee-Chee cards were sold in nine-card wax packs that included a stick of gum plus one insert card from a special 66-card insert set. The fronts have glossy color action player photos, with two different color border stripes and a white card face. In the lower right corner, the team logo appears as a hockey puck superimposed on a hockey stick. They present full player information, including biography, statistics, 1990-91 game-winning goals, and NHL playoff record (the OPC cards present player information in French as well as English). The card number appears next to a hockey skate in the upper right corner of the back. Rookie Cards in this set include Tony Amonte, Valeri Kamensky and John LeClair.

COMPLETE SET (528) 6.00 15.00
COMP.FACT.SET (528) 8.00 20.00
*O-PEE-CHEE: .5X TO 1.25X TOPPS
1 Guy Lafleur Tribute .12 .30
2 Guy Lafleur Tribute .12 .30
3 Guy Lafleur Tribute .12 .30
4 Ed Belfour SR .25 .60
5 Ken Hodge Jr. SR .10 .25
6 Rob Blake SR UER .10 .25
7 Bobby Holik SR .10 .25
8 Sergei Fedorov SR UER .15 .40
9 Jaromir Jagr SR .25 .60
10 Eric Weinrich SR .10 .25
11 Mike Richter SR .10 .25
12 Mats Sundin SR .10 .25
13 Mike Ricci SR .10 .25
14 Eric Desjardins .10 .25
15 Paul Ranheim .10 .25
16 Joe Sakic .30 .75
17 Curt Giles .10 .25
18 Mike Foligno .10 .25
19 Brad Marsh .10 .25
20 Ed Belfour .25 .60
21 Steve Smith .10 .25
22 Kirk Muller .05 .15
23 Kelly Chase .07 .20
24 Jim McKenzie RC .10 .25
25 Mick Vukota .07 .20
26 Tony Amonte RC .25 .60
27 Danton Cole .05 .15
28 Jay Mazur RC .05 .15
29 Pete Peeters .05 .15
30 Petri Skriko .05 .15
31 Steve Duchesne .05 .15
32 Sabres Team .05 .15
33 Phil Bourque UER .07 .20
34 Tim Bergland .07 .20
35 Tim Cheveldae .07 .20
36 Bill Armstrong RC .07 .20
37 John McIntyre .07 .20
38 Dave Andreychuk .10 .25
39 Curtis Leschyshyn .07 .20
40 Jaromir Jagr .25 .60
41 Craig Janney .07 .20
42 Doug Brown .07 .20
43 Ken Sabourin .07 .20
44 North Stars Team .05 .15
45 Fredrik Olausson UER .07 .20
46 Mike Gartner UER .07 .20
47 Mark Fitzpatrick .07 .20
48 Joe Murphy .07 .20
49 Doug Wilson .07 .20
50 Brian MacLellan .07 .20
51 Bob Bassen .07 .20
52 Robert Kron .07 .20
53 Roger Johansson .07 .20
54 Guy Carbonneau UER .07 .20
55 Rob Ramage .07 .20
56 Bobby Holik .10 .25
57 Alan May .07 .20
58 Rick Meagher .07 .20
59 Cliff Ronning .07 .20
60 Red Wings Team .05 .15
61 Bob Kudelski .05 .15
62 Wayne McBean .05 .15
63 Craig MacTavish .07 .20
64 Owen Nolan .10 .25
65 Dale Hawerchuk .12 .30
66 Ray Bourque .15 .40
67 Sean Burke .10 .25
68 Frank Musil .07 .20
69 Joe Mullen .07 .20
70 Drake Berehowsky .07 .20
71 Darren Turcotte .07 .20
72 Randy Carlyle .07 .20
73 Paul Cyr .07 .20
74 Dave Gagner .07 .20
75 Steve Larmer .07 .20
76 Petr Svoboda .07 .20
77 Keith Acton .07 .20
78 Dimitri Khristich .07 .20
79 Brad McCrimmon .07 .20
80 Pat LaFontaine UER .10 .25
81 Jeff Reese .07 .20
82 Mario Marois .07 .20
83 Rob Brown .07 .20
84 Grant Fuhr .10 .25
85 Carey Wilson .07 .20
86 Garry Galley .07 .20
87 Troy Murray .07 .20
88 Tony Granato .07 .20
89 Cord Murphy UER .07 .20
90 Brent Gilchrist .07 .20
91 Mike Richter .10 .25
92 Eric Weinrich .10 .25
93 Marc Bureau .07 .20
94 Bob Errey .07 .20
95 Dave McLlwain .07 .20
96 Nordiques Team .05 .15
97 Clint Malarchuk UER .07 .20
98 Shawn Antoski UER .07 .20
99 Bob Sweeney .07 .20
100 Stephen Leach .07 .20
101 Gary Nylund .07 .20
102 Lucien DeBlois .07 .20
103 Oilers Team .05 .15
104 Jimmy Carson .07 .20
105 Rod Langway .07 .20
106 Jeremy Roenick .25 .60
107 Mike Vernon .07 .20
108 Brian Leetch .07 .20
109 Mark Hunter .07 .20
110 Brian Bellows .07 .20
111 Pelle Eklund .07 .20
112 Rob Blake .10 .25
113 Mike Hough .07 .20
114 Frank Pietrangelo .07 .20
115 Christian Ruuttu .07 .20
116 Bryan Marchment RC .07 .20
117 Garry Valk .07 .20
118 Ken Daneyko UER .07 .20
119 Russ Courtnall .07 .20
120 Ron Wilson .07 .20
121 Shayne Stevenson .07 .20
122 Bill Berg .07 .20
123 Maple Leafs Team .05 .15
124 Glenn Anderson .10 .25
125 Kevin Miller .07 .20
126 Calle Johansson .07 .20
127 Jimmy Waite .07 .20
128 Allen Pedersen .07 .20
129 Brian Mullen .07 .20
130 Ron Francis .12 .30
131 Jergus Baca .07 .20
132 Checklist 1-132 .05 .15
133 Tony Tanti .07 .20
134 Wes Walz .07 .20
135 Stephan Lebeau .07 .20
136 Ken Wregget .07 .20
137 Scott Arniel UER .07 .20
138 Dave Taylor .07 .20
139 Steven Finn .07 .20
140 Brendan Shanahan .12 .30
141 Petr Nedved .07 .20
142 Chris Dahlquist .07 .20
143 Rich Sutter .07 .20
144 Joe Reekie .07 .20
145 Peter Ing .07 .20
146 Ken Linseman .07 .20
147 Dave Barr .07 .20
148 Al Iafrate .07 .20
149 Greg Gilbert .07 .20
150 Craig Ludwig .07 .20
151 Gary Suter .07 .20
152 Jan Erixon .07 .20
153 Mario Lemieux .40 1.00
154 Mike Liut UER .07 .20
155 Uwe Krupp .07 .20
156 Darin Kimble .07 .20
157 Shayne Corson .07 .20
158 Jets Team .05 .15
159 Stephane Morin UER .07 .20
160 Rick Tocchet .07 .20
161 John Tonelli UER .07 .20
162 Adrien Plavsic .07 .20
163 Jason Miller .07 .20
164 Tim Kerr .07 .20
165 Brent Sutter .07 .20
166 Michel Petit .07 .20
167 Adam Graves .07 .20
168 Jamie Macoun .07 .20
169 Terry Yake .07 .20
170 Bruins Team .05 .15
171 Alexander Mogilny .07 .20
172 Karl Dykhuis TP .07 .20
173 Tomas Sandstrom .07 .20
174 Bernie Nicholls .07 .20
175 Slava Fetisov .07 .20
176 Andrew Cassels .07 .20
177 Ulf Dahlen .07 .20
178 Brian Hayward .07 .20
179 Doug Lidster .07 .20
180 Dave Lowry .07 .20
181 Ron Tugnutt UER .07 .20
182 Ed Olczyk .07 .20
183 Paul Coffey .07 .20
184 Shawn Burr UER .07 .20
185 Whalers Team .05 .15
186 Mark Janssens .07 .20
187 Mike Craig .07 .20
188 Gary Leeman .07 .20
189 Phil Sykes .07 .20
190 Brett Hull LL .15 .40
191 Devils Team .05 .15
192 Cam Neely .10 .25
193 Petr Klima .07 .20
194 Mike Ricci .10 .25
195 Kelly Hrudey .07 .20
196 Mark Recchi .12 .30
197 Mikael Andersson .07 .20
198 Bob Probert .07 .20
199 Craig Wolanin .07 .20
200 Scott Mellanby .07 .20
201 Wayne Gretzky HL UER .50 1.25
202 Laurie Boschman .07 .20
203 Gino Odjick .07 .20
204 Garth Butcher .07 .20
205 Randy Wood .07 .20
206 John Druce .07 .20
207 Doug Bodger .07 .20
208 Doug Gilmour .20 .50
209 John LeClair RC .25 .60
210 Steve Thomas .07 .20
211 Kjell Samuelsson .07 .20
212 Daniel Marois .07 .20
213 Jiri Hrdina .07 .20
214 Darrin Shannon .07 .20
215 Rangers Team .05 .15
216 Bob McGill .07 .20
217 Dirk Graham UER .07 .20
218 Thomas Steen .07 .20
219 Mats Sundin .10 .25
220 Kevin Lowe UER .07 .20
221 Kirk McLean .07 .20
222 Jeff Brown .07 .20
223 Joe Nieuwendyk .07 .20
224 Wayne Gretzky LL .50 1.25
225 Marty McSorley .07 .20
226 John Cullen .07 .20
227 Brian Propp UER .07 .20
228 Yves Racine .07 .20
229 Dale Hunter .07 .20
230 Dennis Vaske .07 .20
231 Sylvain Turgeon .07 .20
232 Ron Sutter .07 .20
233 Chris Chelios .10 .25
234 Brian Bradley .07 .20
235 Scott Young .07 .20
236 Mike Ramsey UER .07 .20
237 Jon Casey .07 .20
238 Nevin Markwart .07 .20
239 John MacLean .07 .20
240 Brent Ashton .07 .20
241 Tony Hrkac .07 .20
242 Canucks Team .05 .15
243 Jeff Norton .07 .20
244 Martin Gelinas .07 .20
245 Mike Ridley .07 .20
246 Pat Jablonski RC .07 .20
247 Flames Team .05 .15
248 Paul Ysebaert .07 .20
249 Sylvain Cote .07 .20
250 Marc Habscheid .07 .20
251 Todd Elik .07 .20
252 Mike McPhee .07 .20
253 James Patrick .07 .20
254 Murray Craven .07 .20
255 Trent Yawney .07 .20
256 Rob Cimetta .07 .20
257 Wayne Gretzky LL .50 1.25
258 Wayne Gretzky AS .50 1.25
259 Brett Hull AS .15 .40
260 Luc Robitaille AS .07 .20
261 Ray Bourque AS .15 .40
262 Al MacInnis AS .07 .20
263 Ed Belfour AS .25 .60
264 Checklist 133-264 .05 .15
265 Adam Oates AS .10 .25
266 Cam Neely AS .10 .25
267 Kevin Stevens AS .07 .20
268 Chris Chelios AS .10 .25
269 Brian Leetch AS .07 .20
270 Patrick Roy AS .25 .60
271 Ed Belfour LL .25 .60
272 Rob Zettler .07 .20
273 Donald Audette .07 .20
274 Teppo Numminen .07 .20
275 Peter Stastny UER .07 .20
276 Dave Christian .07 .20
277 Larry Murphy .07 .20
278 Johan Garpenlov .07 .20
279 Tom Fitzgerald .07 .20
280 Gerald Diduck .07 .20
281 Gino Cavallini .07 .20
282 Theo Fleury .07 .20
283 Kings Team .05 .15
284 Jeff Beukeboom .07 .20
285 Kevin Dineen .07 .20
286 Jacques Cloutier .07 .20
287 Tom Chorske .07 .20
288 Ed Belfour LL .25 .60
289 Ray Sheppard .07 .20
290 Olaf Kolzig .07 .20
291 Terry Carkner .07 .20
292 Benoit Hogue .07 .20
293 Mike Peluso .07 .20
294 Bruce Driver .07 .20
295 Jari Kurri .07 .20
296 Peter Sidorkiewicz .07 .20
297 Scott Pearson .07 .20
298 Canadiens Team .05 .15
299 Vincent Damphousse .07 .20
300 John Carter .07 .20
301 Geoff Smith .07 .20
302 Steve Kasper UER .07 .20
303 Brett Hull .15 .40
304 Ray Ferraro .07 .20
305 Geoff Courtnall .07 .20
306 David Shaw .07 .20
307 Bob Essensa .07 .20
308 Mark Tinordi .07 .20
309 Keith Primeau .07 .20
310 Kevin Hatcher .07 .20
311 Chris Nilan .07 .20
312 Trevor Kidd TP .07 .20
313 Daniel Berthiaume .07 .20
314 Adam Creighton .07 .20
315 Everett Sanipass .07 .20
316 Ken Baumgartner .07 .20
317 Sheldon Kennedy .07 .20
318 Dave Capuano .07 .20
319 Don Sweeney .07 .20
320 Gary Roberts .07 .20
321 Wayne Gretzky .50 1.25
322 T.Fleury/M.McSorley UER .07 .20
323 Ulf Samuelsson .07 .20
324 Mike Krushelnyski .07 .20
325 Dean Evason .07 .20
326 Pat Elynuik .07 .20
327 Michal Pivonka .07 .20
328 Paul Cavallini .07 .20
329 Flyers Team .05 .15
330 Denis Savard .12 .30
331 Paul Fenton .07 .20
332 Jon Morris .07 .20
333 Daren Puppa .07 .20
334 Doug Smail .07 .20
335 Kelly Kisio .07 .20
336 Michel Goulet UER .07 .20
337 Mike Sillinger .07 .20
338 Andy Moog .07 .20
339 Paul Stanton .07 .20
340 Greg Adams .07 .20
341 Doug Crossman UER .07 .20
342 Kelly Miller .07 .20
343 Pat Flatley .07 .20
344 Zarley Zalapski .07 .20
345 Mark Osborne UER .07 .20
346 Mark Messier .25 .60
347 Blues Team .05 .15
348 Neil Wilkinson .07 .20
349 Brian Skrudland .07 .20
350 Lyle Odelein .07 .20
351 Luke Richardson .07 .20
352 Zdeno Ciger .07 .20
353 John Vanbiesbrouck .07 .20
354 Lou Franceschetti .07 .20
355 Alexei Gusarov RC .07 .20
356 Bill Ranford .07 .20
357 Normand Lacombe .07 .20
358 Randy Burridge .07 .20
359 Brian Benning .07 .20
360 Dave Hannan .07 .20
361 Todd Gill .07 .20
362 Peter Bondra .07 .20
363 Mike Hartman .07 .20
364 Trevor Linden .07 .20
365 John Ogrodnick .07 .20
366 Steve Konroyd .07 .20
367 Mike Modano .20 .50
368 Glenn Healy .10 .25
369 Stephane Richer .07 .20
370 Vincent Riendeau .07 .20
371 Randy Moller .07 .20
372 Penguins Team .05 .15
373 Murray Baron .07 .20
374 Troy Crowder .07 .20
375 Rick Tabaracci .07 .20
376 Brent Fedyk .07 .20
377 Randy Velischek .07 .20
378 Esa Tikkanen .07 .20
379 Rich Pilon .07 .20
380 Jeff Lazaro RC .07 .20
381 Dave Ellett .07 .20
382 Jeff Hackett .07 .20
383 Stephane Matteau .07 .20
384 Capitals Team .05 .15
385 Wayne Presley .07 .20
386 Grant Ledyard .07 .20
387 Kip Miller .07 .20
388 Dean Kennedy .07 .20
389 Hubie McDonough .07 .20
390 Anatoli Semenov .07 .20
391 Daryl Reaugh .07 .20
392 Mathieu Schneider .07 .20
393 Dan Quinn .07 .20
394 Claude Lemieux .07 .20
395 Phil Housley .07 .20
396 Checklist 265-396 .05 .15
397 Steve Bozek .07 .20
398 Bobby Smith .07 .20
399 Mark Pederson .07 .20
400 Kevin Todd RC .10 .25
401 Sergei Fedorov .15 .40
402 Tom Barrasso .07 .20
403 Brett Hull HL .15 .40
404 Bob Carpenter UER .07 .20
405 Luc Robitaille .07 .20
406 Mark Hardy .07 .20
407 Neil Sheehy .07 .20
408 Mike McNeil .07 .20
409 Dave Manson .07 .20
410 Mike Tomlak .07 .20
411 Robert Reichel .20 .50
412 Islanders Team .05 .15
413 Patrick Roy .25 .60
414 Shaun Van Allen RC .07 .20
415 Dale Kushner .07 .20
416 Pierre Turgeon .07 .20
417 Curtis Joseph .07 .20
418 Randy Gilhen .07 .20
419 Jyrki Lumme .07 .20
420 Neal Broten .07 .20
421 Kevin Stevens .07 .20
422 Chris Terreri .07 .20
423 David Reid .05 .15
424 Steve Yzerman .30 .75
425 Ed Belfour LL .25 .60
426 Jim Johnson .07 .20
427 Joey Kocur .07 .20
428 Joel Otto .07 .20
429 Dino Ciccarelli .07 .20
430 Blackhawks Team .05 .15
431 Claude Lapointe RC .07 .20
432 Chris Joseph .07 .20
433 Gaetan Duchesne .05 .15
434 Mike Keane .05 .15
435 Dave Chyzowski .05 .15
436 Glen Featherstone .05 .15
437 Jim Paek RC .10 .25
438 Doug Evans .05 .15
439 Alexei Kasatonov UER .05 .15
440 Ken Hodge Jr. .10 .25
441 Dave Snuggerud .05 .15
442 Brad Shaw .05 .15
443 Gerard Gallant .05 .15
444 Jiri Latal .05 .15
445 Peter Zezel .05 .15
446 Troy Gamble .05 .15
447 Craig Coxe .05 .15
448 Adam Oates .10 .25
449 Todd Krygier .07 .20
450 Andre Racicot RC .07 .20
451 Patrik Sundstrom .07 .20
452 Glen Wesley UER .07 .20
453 Jocelyn Lemieux .07 .20
454 Rick Zombo .07 .20
455 Derek King .05 .15
456 J.J. Daigneault .05 .15
457 Rick Vaive .05 .15
458 Larry Robinson .05 .15
459 Rick Wamsley .05 .15
460 Craig Simpson .05 .15
461 Corey Millen RC .10 .25
462 Sergio Momesso .07 .20
463 Paul MacDermid .07 .20
464 Wendel Clark .10 .25
465 Mikhail Tatarinov .07 .20
466 Mark Howe .10 .25
467 Jay Miller .07 .20
468 Grant Jennings .07 .20
469 Paul Gillis .07 .20
470 Ron Hextall .10 .25
471 Alexander Godynyuk RC .10 .25
472 Bryan Trottier .12 .30
473 Kevin Haller RC .10 .25
474 Troy Mallette .07 .20
475 Jim Wiemer .07 .20
476 David Maley .07 .20
477 Moe Mantha UER .07 .20
478 Brad Jones .07 .20
479 Craig Muni .07 .20
480 Igor Larionov .07 .20
481 Scott Stevens .10 .25
482 Sergei Makarov .07 .20
483 Mike Lalor .07 .20
484 Tony McKegney .07 .20
485 Perry Berezan .07 .20
486 Derrick Smith .07 .20
487 Jim Hrivnak .07 .20
488 David Volek .07 .20
489 Sylvain Lefebvre .07 .20
490 Rod Brind'Amour .07 .20
491 Al MacInnis .07 .20
492 Jamie Leach .07 .20
493 Robert Dirk .07 .20
494 Gordie Roberts .07 .20
495 Mike Hudson .07 .20
496 Frank Breault .07 .20
497 Rejean Lemelin .07 .20
498 Kris King .07 .20
499 Pat Verbeek .07 .20
500 Bryan Fogarty .07 .20
501 Perry Anderson .07 .20
502 Joe Cirella .07 .20
503 Mikko Makela .07 .20
504 Paul Coffey HL UER .07 .20
505 Don Beaupre .07 .20
506 Brian Glynn .07 .20
507 Dave Poulin .07 .20
508 Steve Chiasson .07 .20
509 Myles O'Connor RC .07 .20
510 Ilkka Sinisalo .07 .20
511 Nick Kypreos .07 .20
512 Doug Houda UER .07 .20
513 Valeri Kamensky RC .25 .60
514 Sergei Nemchinov .07 .20
515 Dmitri Mironov .07 .20
516 Brett Hull Hart .15 .40
517 Ray Bourque Norris .15 .40
518 Ed Belfour Calder .25 .60
519 Ed Belfour Vezina UER .25 .60
520 Wayne Gretzky Byng .50 1.25
521 Dirk Graham Selke .07 .20
522 Wayne Gretzky Ross .50 1.25
523 Mario Lemieux Smythe .40 1.00
524 Wayne Gretzky HL .50 1.25
525 San Jose Sharks Logo .05 .15
526 T.B.Lightning Logo .05 .15
527 Ottawa Senators Logo .05 .15
528 Checklist 397-528 .05 .15

1991-92 Topps/Bowman Preview Sheet

This nine-card unperforated sheet of Topps and Bowman hockey cards was sent to dealers to show them the graphic design of the coming year's hockey cards. It is common to find these cards being sold as single neatly cut from the sheet. The fronts of these preview cards are identical to the regular issue. In blue lettering, the backs have the player's name, the words "Pre-Production Sample", "1991 Topps (or as the case may be, Bowman) Card", and a tagline. The cards are unnumbered on the back and hence are listed below beginning with the upper left corner, counting across, and ending with the lower right corner. The cards are arranged so that Topps and Bowman cards alternate with one another.

COMPLETE SET (9) 3.00 8.00
1 Mario Lemieux (Topps) .75 2.00
2 Wayne Gretzky (Bowman) 1.25 3.00
3 Joe Sakic (Topps) .50 1.25
4 Ray Bourque (Bowman) .30 .75
5 Ed Belfour (Topps) .30 .75
6 Mark Messier (Bowman) .40 1.00
7 Pat LaFontaine (Topps) .20 .50
8 Steve Yzerman (Bowman) .50 1.25
9 Brett Hull (Topps) .40 1.00
NNO Uncut Panel 3.00 8.00

1991-92 Topps Team Scoring Leaders

This 21-card standard-size set was inserted at a rate of one per '91-92 Topps pack and features the top scorer from every team on the front, while the back ranks the top 10 point leaders for that team.

COMPLETE SET (21) 2.50 6.00
1 Pat Verbeek .15 .40
2 Dale Hawerchuk .15 .40
3 Steve Yzerman .60 1.50
4 Brian Leetch .20 .50
5 Mark Recchi .15 .40
6 Esa Tikkanen .02 .10
7 Dave Gagner .02 .10
8 Joe Sakic .40 1.00
9 Vincent Damphousse .15 .40
10 Wayne Gretzky 1.25 3.00
11 Phil Housley .02 .10
12 Pat LaFontaine .15 .40
13 Rick Tocchet .15 .40
14 Theo Fleury UER .15 .40
15 John MacLean .02 .10
16 Kevin Hatcher .02 .10
17 Trevor Linden .15 .40
18 Russ Courtnall .02 .10
19 Ray Bourque .20 .50
20 Brett Hull .25 .60
21 Steve Larmer .02 .10

1992-93 Topps

The 1992-93 Topps set contains 529 standard-size cards. Topps switched to white card stock this year allowing for a better looking product. Card fronts have team and player name at the bottom. Colorful backs include yearly statistics, playoff statistics and game-winning goals from 1991-92. The early print-run cards of Randy Moller (407) suffer from a print flaw which appears to be large finger impression on the card face. The only Rookie Card of note is Guy Hebert.

1 Wayne Gretzky .50 1.25
2 Brett Hull .15 .40
3 Felix Potvin .20 .50
4 Mark Tinordi .05 .15
5 Paul Coffey HL .10 .25
6 Tony Amonte SR .07 .20
7 Pat Falloon SR .05 .15
8 Pavel Bure SR .20 .50
9 Nicklas Lidstrom SR .07 .20
10 Dominic Roussel SR .07 .20
11 Nelson Emerson SR .05 .15
12 Donald Audette .07 .20
13 Gilbert Dionne SR .05 .15
14 Vladimir Konstantinov .10 .25
15 Kevin Todd .05 .15
16 Steve Leach .05 .15
17 Ed Olczyk .05 .15
18 Jim Hrivnak .07 .20
19 Gilbert Dionne .05 .15
20 Mike Vernon .07 .20
21 Dave Christian .05 .15
22 Ed Belfour .10 .25
23 Andrew Cassels .05 .15
24 Jaromir Jagr .25 .60
25 Arturs Irbe .07 .20
26 Petr Klima .05 .15
27 Randy Gilhen .05 .15
28 Ulf Dahlen .05 .15
29 Kelly Hrudey .07 .20
30 Dave Ellett .05 .15
31 Tom Fitzgerald .05 .15
32 Cam Neely .10 .25
33 Greg Paslawski .05 .15
34 Brad May .05 .15
35 Slava Kozlov .07 .20
36 Mark Hunter .07 .20
37 Steve Chiasson .05 .15
38 Joe Murphy .05 .15
39 Darryl Sydor .05 .15
40 Ron Hextall .07 .20
41 Jim Sandlak .05 .15
42 Dave Lowry .07 .20
43 Claude Lemieux .05 .15
44 Gerald Diduck .07 .20
45 Mike McPhee .05 .15
46 Rod Langway .07 .20
47 Guy Larose .05 .15
48 Craig Billington .07 .20
49 Daniel Marois .05 .15
50 Todd Nelson RC .07 .20
51 Jari Kurri .10 .25
52 Keith Brown .07 .20
53 Valeri Kamensky .05 .15
54 Jim Johnson .07 .20
55 Vincent Damphousse .07 .20
56 Pat Elynuik .05 .15
57 Jeff Beukeboom .05 .15
58 Paul Ysebaert .05 .15
59 Ken Sutton .05 .15
60 Dale Craigwell .05 .15
61 Marc Bergevin .07 .20
62 Stephane Beauregard .07 .20
63 Bob Probert .07 .20
64 Jergus Baca .07 .20
65 Brian Propp .05 .15
66 Jacques Cloutier .07 .20
67 Jim Thomson RC .07 .20
68 Anatoli Semenov .05 .15
69 Stephan Lebeau .05 .15
70 Rick Tocchet .07 .20
71 James Patrick .05 .15
72 Rob Brown .05 .15
73 Peter Ahola .05 .15
74 Bob Corkum .07 .20
75 Brent Sutter .05 .15
76 Neil Wilkinson .05 .15
77 Mark Osborne .05 .15
78 Ron Wilson .07 .20
79 Todd Richards .07 .20
80 Robert Kron .05 .15
81 Cliff Ronning .05 .15
82 Zarley Zalapski .05 .15
83 Randy Burridge .05 .15
84 Jarrod Skalde .05 .15
85 Gary Leeman .05 .15
86 Mike Ricci .07 .20
87 Dennis Vaske .05 .15
88 John LeBlanc RC .07 .20
89 Brad Shaw .05 .15
90 Rod Brind'Amour .05 .15
91 Colin Patterson .07 .20
92 Gerard Gallant .05 .15
93 Per Djoos .07 .20
94 Claude Lapointe .05 .15
95 Bob Errey .07 .20
96 Norm Maciver .05 .15
97 Todd Elik .05 .15
98 Chris Chelios .10 .25
99 Keith Primeau .07 .20
100 Jim Waite .07 .20
101 Luc Robitaille .07 .20
102 Keith Tkachuk .10 .25
103 Benoit Hogue .05 .15
104 Brian Mullen .05 .15
105 Joe Nieuwendyk .07 .20
106 Randy McKay .07 .20
107 Michal Pivonka .05 .15
108 Darcy Wakaluk .07 .20
109 Andy Brickley .07 .20
110 Patrick Roy LL .25 .60
111 Bob Sweeney .05 .15
112 Guy Hebert RC .15 .40
113 Joe Mullen .07 .20
114 Gord Murphy .07 .20
115 Evgeny Davydov .05 .15
116 Gary Roberts .05 .15
117 Pelle Eklund .07 .20
118 Tom Kurvers .05 .15
119 John Tonelli .07 .20
120 Fredrik Olausson .05 .15
121 Mike Donnelly .05 .15
122 Doug Gilmour .12 .30
123 Wayne Gretzky LL .50 1.25
124 Curtis Leschyshyn .07 .20
125 Guy Carbonneau .07 .20
126 Bill Ranford .07 .20
127 Ulf Samuelsson .05 .15
128 Joey Kocur .07 .20
129 Kevin Miller .05 .15
130 Kirk McLean .05 .15
131 Kevin Dineen .05 .15
132 John Cullen .05 .15
133 Al Iafrate .07 .20
134 Craig Janney .07 .20
135 Patrick Flatley .07 .20
136 Dominik Hasek .20 .50
137 Benoit Brunet .05 .15
138 Dave Babych .07 .20
139 Doug Brown .07 .20
140 Mike Lalor .07 .20
141 Thomas Steen .05 .15
142 Frank Musil .07 .20
143 Dan Quinn .07 .20
144 Dmitri Mironov .05 .15
145 Bob Kudelski .07 .20
146 Mike Bullard .07 .20
147 Randy Carlyle .07 .20
148 Kent Manderville .05 .15
149 Kevin Hatcher .05 .15
150 Steve Kasper .07 .20
151 Mikael Andersson .05 .15
152 Alexei Kasatonov .05 .15
153 Jan Erixon .07 .20
154 Craig Ludwig .07 .20
155 Dave Poulin .05 .15
156 Scott Stevens .10 .25
157 Robert Reichel .05 .15
158 Uwe Krupp .05 .15
159 Brian Noonan .05 .15
160 Stephane Richer .07 .20
161 Brent Thompson .07 .20
162 Glenn Anderson .10 .25
163 Joe Cirella .07 .20
164 Dave Andreychuk .10 .25
165 Vladimir Konstantinov .10 .25
166 Mike McNeill .07 .20
167 Darrin Shannon .05 .15
168 Rob Pearson .05 .15
169 John Vanbiesbrouck .07 .20
170 Randy Wood .05 .15
171 Marty McSorley .05 .15
172 Mike Hudson .05 .15
173 Paul Fenton .07 .20
174 Jeff Brown .07 .20
175 Mark Greig .07 .20
176 Gordie Roberts .07 .20
177 Josef Beranek .05 .15
178 Shawn Burr .05 .15
179 Marc Bureau .07 .20
180 Mikhail Tatarinov .05 .15
181 Robert Cimetta .07 .20
182 Paul Coffey UER .10 .25
183 Bob Essensa .07 .20
184 Joe Reekie .05 .15
185 Jeff Hackett .07 .20
186 Tomas Forslund .05 .15
187 Claude Vilgrain .07 .20
188 John Druce .05 .15
189 Patrice Brisebois .05 .15
190 Peter Douris .05 .15
191 Brent Ashton .05 .15
192 Eric Desjardins .07 .20
193 Nick Kypreos .05 .15
194 Dana Murzyn .05 .15
195 Don Beaupre .07 .20
196 Jeff Chychrun .05 .15
197 Dave Barr .05 .15
198 Brian Glynn .05 .15
199 Keith Acton .07 .20
200 Igor Kravchuk .05 .15
201 Shayne Corson .05 .15
202 Curt Giles .05 .15
203 Darren Turcotte .05 .15
204 David Volek .05 .15
205 Ray Whitney RC .15 .40
206 Donald Audette .07 .20
207 Steve Yzerman .25 .60
208 Craig Berube .05 .15
209 Bob McGill .05 .15
210 Stu Barnes .05 .15
211 Rob Blake .07 .20
212 Mario Lemieux .40 1.00
213 Dominic Roussel .07 .20
214 Sergio Momesso .05 .15
215 Brad Marsh .07 .20
216 Mark Fitzpatrick .07 .20
217 Ken Baumgartner .07 .20
218 Greg Gilbert .07 .20
219 Ric Nattress .07 .20
220 Theo Fleury .15 .40
221 Ray Bourque .15 .40
222 Steve Thomas .07 .20
223 Scott Niedermayer .10 .25
224 Jeff Lazaro .05 .15
225 Cheveldae/K.McLean LL .05 .15
226 Marc Fortier .05 .15
227 Rob Zettler .05 .15
228 Kevin Todd .05 .15
229 Tony Amonte .07 .20
230 Mark Lamb .05 .15
231 Chris Dahlquist .07 .20
232 James Black .05 .15
233 Paul Cavallini .05 .15
234 Gino Cavallini .05 .15
235 Tony Tanti .05 .15
236 Mike Ridley .05 .15
237 Curtis Joseph .10 .25
238 Mike Craig .05 .15
239 Luciano Borsato .05 .15
240 Brian Bellows .07 .20
241 Barry Pederson .05 .15
242 Tony Granato .05 .15
243 Jim Paek .07 .20
244 Tim Bergland .05 .15
245 Jay More .05 .15
246 Laurie Boschman .05 .15
247 Doug Bodger .05 .15
248 Murray Craven .05 .15
249 Kris Draper .05 .15
250 Brian Benning .05 .15
251 Jarmo Myllys .05 .15
252 Sergei Fedorov .15 .40
253 Mathieu Schneider .05 .15
254 Dave Gagner .07 .20
255 Michel Goulet .07 .20
256 Alexander Godynyuk .05 .15
257 Ray Sheppard .05 .15
258 Mark Messier AS .15 .40
259 Kevin Stevens AS .05 .15
260 Brett Hull AS .15 .40
261 Brian Leetch AS .07 .20
262 Ray Bourque AS .15 .40
263 Patrick Roy AS .25 .60
264 Mike Gartner HL .07 .20
265 Mario Lemieux AS .40 1.00
266 Luc Robitaille AS .07 .20
267 Mark Recchi AS .12 .30
268 Phil Housley AS .05 .15
269 Scott Stevens AS .10 .25
270 Kirk McLean AS .05 .15
271 Steve Duchesne .05 .15
272 Jiri Hrdina .05 .15
273 John MacLean .07 .20
274 Mark Messier .15 .40
275 Geoff Smith .05 .15
276 Russ Courtnall .05 .15
277 Yves Racine .05 .15
278 Tom Draper .05 .15
279 Charlie Huddy .07 .20
280 Trevor Kidd .07 .20
281 Garth Butcher .07 .20
282 Mike Sullivan .05 .15
283 Adam Burt .05 .15

284 Troy Murray .05 .15
285 Stephane Fiset .05 .15
286 Perry Anderson .05 .15
287 Sergei Nemchinov .05 .15
288 Rick Zombo .05 .15
289 Pierre Turgeon .07 .20
290 Kevin Lowe .07 .20
291 Brian Bradley .05 .15
292 Martin Gelinas UER .05 .15
293 Brian Leetch .07 .20
294 Peter Bondra .07 .20
295 Brendan Shanahan .12 .30
296 Dale Hawerchuk .12 .30
297 Mike Hough .07 .20
298 Rollie Melanson .05 .15
299 Brad Jones .05 .15
300 Jocelyn Lemieux .05 .15
301 Brad McCrimmon .05 .15
302 Marty McInnis .05 .15
303 Chris Terreri .07 .20
304 Dean Evason .05 .15
305 Glenn Healy .07 .20
306 Ken Hodge Jr. .05 .15
307 Mike Liut .05 .15
308 Gary Suter .05 .15
309 Neal Broten .07 .20
310 Tim Cheveldae .05 .15
311 Tom Fergus .07 .20
312 Petr Svoboda .07 .20
313 Tom Chorske .07 .20
314 Paul Ysebaert LL .05 .15
315 Steve Smith .05 .15
316 Stephane Morin .05 .15
317 Pat MacLeod .05 .15
318 Dino Ciccarelli .07 .20
319 Peter Zezel .05 .15
320 Chris Lindberg .05 .15
321 Grant Ledyard .05 .15
322 Ron Francis .12 .30
323 Adrien Plavsic .05 .15
324 Ray Ferraro .05 .15
325 Wendel Clark .07 .20
326 Corey Millen .05 .15
327 Mark Pederson .05 .15
328 Patrick Poulin .05 .15
329 Adam Graves .05 .15
330 Bobby Holik .07 .20
331 Kelly Kisio .07 .20
332 Peter Sidorkiewicz .05 .15
333 Vladimir Ruzicka .05 .15
334 J.J. Daigneault .05 .15
335 Troy Mallette .05 .15
336 Craig MacTavish .05 .15
337 Michel Petit .05 .15
338 Claude Loiselle .05 .15
339 Teppo Numminen .05 .15
340 Brett Hull LL .15 .40
341 Sylvain Lefebvre .05 .15
342 Perry Berezan .05 .15
343 Kevin Stevens .05 .15
344 Randy Ladouceur .05 .15
345 Pat LaFontaine .10 .25
346 Glen Wesley .05 .15
347 Michel Goulet HL .07 .20
348 Jamie Macoun .07 .20
349 Owen Nolan .05 .15
350 Grant Fuhr .10 .25
351 Tim Kerr .05 .15
352 Kjell Samuelsson .07 .20
353 Pavel Bure .20 .50
354 Murray Baron .05 .15
355 Paul Broten .05 .15
356 Craig Simpson .05 .15
357 Ken Daneyko .05 .15
358 Greg Hawgood .05 .15
359 Johan Garpenlov .05 .15
360 Garry Galley .05 .15
361 Paul DiPietro .05 .15
362 Jamie Leach .05 .15
363 Clint Malarchuk .05 .15
364 Dan Lambert .05 .15
365 Joe Juneau .05 .15
366 Scott Lachance .05 .15
367 Mike Richter .10 .25
368 Sheldon Kennedy .05 .15
369 John McIntyre .05 .15
370 Glen Murray .05 .15
371 Ron Sutter .05 .15
372 David Williams RC .05 .15
373 Bill Lindsay RC .05 .15
374 Todd Gill .05 .15
375 Sylvain Turgeon .05 .15
376 Dirk Graham .05 .15
377 Brad Schlegel .05 .15
378 Bob Carpenter .05 .15
379 Jon Casey .05 .15
380 Andrei Lomakin .05 .15
381 Kay Whitmore .07 .20
382 Alexander Mogilny .07 .20
383 Garry Valk .05 .15
384 Bruce Driver .05 .15
385 Jeff Reese .05 .15
386 Brent Gilchrist .05 .15
387 Kerry Huffman .05 .15
388 Bobby Smith .07 .20
389 Dave Manson .05 .15
390 Russ Romaniuk .05 .15
391 Paul MacDermid .07 .20
392 Louie DeBrusk .05 .15
393 Dave McLlwain .05 .15
394 Andy Moog .07 .20
395 Tie Domi .10 .25
396 Pat Jablonski .07 .20
397 Troy Loney .05 .15
398 Jimmy Carson .05 .15
399 Eric Weinrich .05 .15
400 Jeremy Roenick .15 .40
401 Brent Fedyk .05 .15
402 Geoff Sanderson .07 .20
403 Doug Lidster .07 .20
404 Mike Gartner .07 .20
405 Derian Hatcher .05 .15
406 Gaetan Duchesne .05 .15
407 Randy Moller .05 .15
408 Brian Skrudland .07 .20
409 Luke Richardson .07 .20
410 Mark Recchi .12 .30
411 Steve Konroyd .07 .20
412 Troy Gamble .05 .15
413 Greg Johnston .05 .15
414 Denis Savard .12 .30
415 Mats Sundin .10 .25
416 Bryan Trottier .12 .30
417 Don Sweeney .05 .15
418 Pat Falloon .05 .15
419 Alexander Semak .05 .15
420 David Shaw .07 .20
421 Tomas Sandstrom .07 .20
422 Petr Nedved .07 .20
423 Peter Ing .05 .15
424 Wayne Presley .05 .15
425 Rick Wamsley .05 .15
426 Rob Zamuner RC .07 .20
427 Claude Boivin .05 .15
428 Sylvain Cote .07 .20
429 Kevin Stevens HL .05 .15
430 Randy Velischek .05 .15
431 Derek King .05 .15
432 Terry Yake .05 .15
433 Philippe Bozon .05 .15
434 Rich Sutter .05 .15
435 Brian Lawton .07 .20
436 Brian Hayward .05 .15
437 Robert Dirk .07 .20
438 Bernie Nicholls .05 .15
439 Michel Picard .07 .20
440 Nicklas Lidstrom .07 .20
441 Mike Modano .25 .60
442 Phil Bourque .05 .15
443 Wayne McBean .05 .15
444 Scott Mellanby .05 .15
445 Kevin Haller .05 .15
446 Dave Taylor UER .07 .20
447 Larry Murphy .07 .20
448 David Bruce .05 .15
449 Steven Finn .05 .15
450 Mike Krushelnyski .05 .15
451 Adam Creighton .05 .15
452 Al MacInnis .07 .20
453 Rick Tabaracci .05 .15
454 Bob Bassen .05 .15
455 Kelly Buchberger .05 .15
456 Phil Housley .05 .15
457 Daren Puppa .07 .20
458 Slava Fetisov .05 .15
459 Doug Smail .05 .15
460 Paul Stanton .05 .15
461 Steve Weeks .05 .15
462 Valeri Zelepukin .05 .15
463 Stephane Matteau .05 .15
464 Dale Hunter .07 .20
465 Terry Carkner .07 .20
466 Vincent Riendeau .07 .20
467 Sergei Makarov .05 .15
468 Igor Ulanov .05 .15
469 Peter Stastny .07 .20
470 Dimitri Khristich .05 .15
471 Joel Otto .05 .15
472 Geoff Courtnall .05 .15
473 Mike Ramsey .05 .15
474 Yvon Corriveau .05 .15
475 Adam Oates .10 .25
476 Esa Tikkanen .05 .15
477 Doug Weight .20 .50
478 Mike Keane .05 .15
479 Kelly Miller .05 .15
480 Nelson Emerson .05 .15
481 Shawn McEachern .05 .15
482 Doug Wilson .07 .20
483 Jeff Odgers .05 .15
484 Stephane Quintal .05 .15
485 Christian Ruuttu .05 .15
486 Paul Ranheim .05 .15
487 Craig Wolanin .05 .15
488 Rob DiMaio .05 .15
489 Shawn Cronin .05 .15
490 Kirk Muller .05 .15
491 Patrick Roy LL .25 .60
492 Rich Pilon .05 .15
493 Pat Verbeek .05 .15
494 Ken Wregget .07 .20
495 Joe Sakic .25 .60
496 Zdeno Ciger .05 .15
497 Steve Larmer .05 .15
498 Calle Johansson .05 .15
499 Trevor Linden .07 .20
500 John LeClair .15 .40
501 Bryan Marchment .07 .20
502 Todd Krygier .07 .20
503 Tom Barrasso .07 .20
504 Mario Lemieux LL .40 1.00
505 Daniel Berthiaume UER .07 .20
506 Jamie Baker .05 .15
507 Greg Adams .05 .15
508 Patrick Roy .25 .60
509 Kris King .05 .15
510 Jyrki Lumme .05 .15
511 Darin Kimble .05 .15
512 Igor Larionov .05 .15
513 Martin Brodeur .25 .60
514 Denny Felsner RC .07 .20
515 Yanic Dupre .05 .15
516 Bill Guerin RC .20 .50
517 Bret Hedican RC UER .07 .20
518 Mike Hartman .05 .15
519 Steve Heinze UER .05 .15
520 Frantisek Kucera .07 .20
521 David Reid .05 .15
522 Frank Pietrangelo .07 .20
523 Martin Rucinsky .05 .15
524 Tony Hrkac .05 .15
525 Checklist 1-132 .05 .15
526 Checklist 133-264 .05 .15
527 Checklist 265-396 .05 .15
528 Checklist 397-528 UER .05 .15
529 Eric Lindros UER .30 .75

1992-93 Topps Gold

Gold foil versions of all 529 cards in the 1992-93 Topps Hockey set were produced: one was inserted in each foil pack, three in each jumbo pack, and 20 were included in factory sets as a bonus. Deciding against producing Gold checklists, Topps made cards 525-528 of players not featured in the basic set. On a white card face, the fronts display color action player photos inside a two-color picture frame. The player's name and team name appear in two short colored bars toward the bottom of the picture. The backs carry biography, statistics, and player profile. The following cards were printed in a horizontal format: 90, 164, 195, 225, 272, 307, 324, 337, 350, 366, 413 and 420.

*GOLD: 1.5X TO 4X BASIC INSERTS
1 Wayne Gretzky 8.00 20.00

1993-94 Topps Premier Promo Sheet

This nine-card promo sheet measures approximately 7 3/4" by 10 3/4" and features white-bordered color player photos on the front. The player's name and position appear at the bottom of each card within a team color-coded stripe, and the Premier logo is displayed in the lower left. The horizontal backs carry color player action shots on their left sides. At the top, the player's name, uniform number, team, and position appear within a team color-coded stripe. Below this, and to the right of the player photo, appear the player's biography and stats on a background that resembles white ruffled silk. The team, NHL, and NHLPA logos in the lower left round out the back.

COMPLETE SET (9) 1.50 4.00
1 Patrick Roy .60 1.50
15 Mike Vernon .15 .40
22 Jamie Baker .08 .25
100 Theo Fleury .15 .40
156 Geoff Sanderson .15 .40
244 Dave Lowry .08 .25
257 Scott Lachance .08 .25
601 Mark Messier .20 .50
602 Ray Bourque .20 .50

1993-94 Topps Premier

Both series of the 1993-94 Topps (and O-Pee-Chee) Premier hockey set consisted of 264 standard-size cards. The fronts feature white-bordered color player photos. The player's name and position appear at the bottom of each card within a team color-coded stripe, and the Premier logo is displayed in the lower left. The horizontal backs carry color player action shots on their left sides. Topical subsets featured are Super Rookies (121-130), and 1st Team All-Stars, 2nd Team All-Stars, and League Leaders scattered throughout the set. Except for some information in French on the backs, the O-Pee-Chee Premier set is identical to the Topps Premier set.

*GOLD VETS: 1.5X TO 4X BASIC CARDS
1 Patrick Roy .25 .60
2 Alexei Zhitnik .05 .15
3 Uwe Krupp .05 .15
4 Todd Gill .05 .15
5 Paul Stanton .05 .15
6 Petr Nedved .05 .15
7 Dale Hawerchuk .12 .30
8 Kevin Miller .05 .15
9 Nicklas Lidstrom .10 .25
10 Joe Sakic .25 .60
11 Thomas Steen .05 .15
12 Peter Bondra .07 .20
13 Brian Noonan .05 .15
14 Glen Featherstone .05 .15
15 Mike Vernon .07 .20
16 Janne Ojanen .05 .15
17 Neil Brady .05 .15
18 Dimitri Yushkevich .05 .15
19 Rob Zamuner .05 .15
20 Zarley Zalapski .05 .15
21 Mike Sullivan .05 .15
22 Jamie Baker .05 .15
23 Craig MacTavish .05 .15
24 Mark Tinordi .05 .15
25 Brian Leetch .10 .25
26 Brian Skrudland .05 .15
27 Keith Tkachuk .10 .25
28 Patrick Flatley .05 .15
29 Doug Bodger .05 .15
30 Felix Potvin .20 .50
31 Shawn Antoski .05 .15
32 Eric Desjardins .07 .20
33 Mike Donnelly .05 .15
34 Kjell Samuelsson .05 .15
35 Nelson Emerson .05 .15
36 Phil Housley .07 .20
37 Mario Lemieux LL .40 1.00
38 Shayne Corson .05 .15
39 Steve Smith .05 .15
40 Bob Kudelski .05 .15
41 Joe Cirella .05 .15
42 Sergei Nemchinov .05 .15
43 Kerry Huffman .05 .15
44 Bob Beers .05 .15
45 Al Iafrate .05 .15
46 Mike Modano .15 .40
47 Pat Verbeek .05 .15
48 Joel Otto .05 .15
49 Dino Ciccarelli .07 .20
50 Adam Oates .10 .25
51 Pat Elynuik .05 .15
52 Bobby Holik .05 .15
53 Johan Garpenlov .05 .15
54 Jeff Beukeboom .05 .15
55 Tommy Soderstrom .07 .20
56 Rob Blake .07 .20
57 Marty McInnis .05 .15
58 Dixon Ward .05 .15
59 Patrice Brisebois .05 .15
60 Ed Belfour .10 .25
61 Donald Audette .05 .15
62 Mike Ricci .05 .15
63 Fredrik Olausson .05 .15
64 Norm Maciver .05 .15
65 Andrew Cassels .05 .15
66 Tim Cheveldae .07 .20
67 David Reid .05 .15
68 Philippe Bozon .05 .15
69 Drake Berehowsky .05 .15
70 Tony Amonte .07 .20
71 Dave Manson .05 .15
72 Rick Tocchet .07 .20
73 Steve Kasper .05 .15
74 Assist Leader .10 .25
75 Ulf Dahlen .05 .15
76 Chris Lindberg .05 .15
77 Doug Wilson .05 .15
78 Mike Ridley .05 .15
79 Viacheslav Butsayev .05 .15
80 Scott Stevens .10 .25
81 Cliff Ronning .05 .15
82 Andrei Lomakin .05 .15
83 Shawn Burr .05 .15
84 Benoit Brunet .05 .15
85 Valeri Kamensky .07 .20
86 Randy Carlyle .05 .15
87 Chris Joseph .05 .15
88 Dirk Graham .05 .15
89 Ken Sutton .05 .15
90 Luc Robitaille AS .07 .20
91 Mario Lemieux AS .40 1.00
92 Teemu Selanne AS .20 .50
93 Ray Bourque AS .15 .40
94 Chris Chelios AS .10 .25
95 Ed Belfour AS .10 .25
96 Keith Jones .05 .15
97 Sylvain Turgeon .05 .15
98 Jim Johnson .05 .15
99 Michael Nylander .05 .15
100 Theo Fleury .05 .15
101 Shawn Chambers .05 .15
102 Alexander Semak .05 .15
103 Ron Sutter .05 .15
104 Glenn Anderson .10 .25
105 Jaromir Jagr .25 .60
106 Adam Graves .05 .15
107 Nikolai Borschevsky .05 .15
108 Vladimir Konstantinov .07 .20
109 Robb Stauber .05 .15
110 Arturs Irbe .07 .20
111 Felix Potvin LL .20 .50
112 Darius Kasparaitis .05 .15
113 Kirk McLean .07 .20
114 Glen Wesley .05 .15
115 Rod Brind'Amour .07 .20
116 Mike Eagles .05 .15
117 Brian Bradley .05 .15
118 Dave Christian .05 .15
119 Randy Wood .05 .15
120 Craig Janney .07 .20
121 Eric Lindros SR .30 .75
122 Tommy Soderstrom SR .07 .20
123 Shawn McEachern SR .05 .15
124 Andrei Kovalenko SR .05 .15
125 Joe Juneau SR .07 .20
126 Felix Potvin SR .20 .50
127 Dixon Ward SR .05 .15
128 Alexei Zhamnov SR .07 .20
129 Vladimir Malakhov SR .05 .15
130 Teemu Selanne SR .20 .50
131 Neal Broten .07 .20
132 Ulf Samuelsson .05 .15
133 Mark Janssens .05 .15
134 Claude Lemieux .05 .15
135 Mike Richter .10 .25
136 Doug Weight .07 .20
137 Rob Pearson .05 .15
138 Sylvain Cote .05 .15
139 Mike Keane .05 .15
140 Benoit Hogue .05 .15
141 Michel Petit .05 .15
142 Mark Freer .05 .15
143 Doug Zmolek .05 .15
144 Tony Granato .05 .15
145 Paul Coffey .10 .25
146 Ted Donato .05 .15
147 Brent Sutter .05 .15
148 A.Mogilny/T.Selanne LL .20 .50
149 James Patrick .05 .15
150 Mikael Andersson .05 .15
151 Steve Duchesne .05 .15
152 Terry Carkner .05 .15
153 Russ Courtnall .05 .15
154 Brian Mullen .05 .15
155 Martin Straka .05 .15
156 Geoff Sanderson .07 .20
157 Mark Howe .10 .25
158 Stephane Richer .07 .20
159 Doug Crossman .05 .15
160 John Vanbiesbrouck .07 .20
161 Bob Essensa .07 .20
162 Wayne Presley .05 .15
163 Mathieu Schneider .05 .15
164 Jiri Slegr .05 .15
165 Stephane Fiset .07 .20
166 Wendell Young .05 .15
167 Kevin Dineen .05 .15
168 Sandis Ozolinsh .05 .15
169 Mike Krushelnyski .05 .15
170 Kevin Stevens AS .05 .15
171 Pat LaFontaine AS .10 .25
172 Alexander Mogilny AS .07 .20
173 Larry Murphy AS .07 .20
174 Al Iafrate AS .05 .15
175 Tom Barrasso AS .07 .20
176 Derek King .05 .15
177 Bob Probert .07 .20
178 Gary Suter .05 .15
179 David Shaw .05 .15
180 Luc Robitaille .07 .20
181 John LeClair .10 .25
182 Troy Murray .05 .15
183 Dave Gagner .07 .20
184 Darcy Loewen .05 .15
185 Mario Lemieux LL .40 1.00
186 Pat Jablonski .05 .15
187 Alexei Kovalev .07 .20
188 Todd Krygier .05 .15
189 Larry Murphy .07 .20
190 Pierre Turgeon .07 .20
191 Craig Ludwig .05 .15
192 Brad May .07 .20
193 John MacLean .07 .20
194 Ron Wilson .05 .15
195 Eric Weinrich .05 .15
196 Steve Chiasson .05 .15
197 Dmitri Kvartalnov .05 .15
198 Andrei Kovalenko .05 .15
199 Rob Gaudreau RC .10 .25
200 Evgeny Davydov .05 .15
201 Adrien Plavsic .05 .15
202 Brian Bellows .07 .20
203 Doug Evans .05 .15
204 Tom Barrasso .07 .20
205 Joe Nieuwendyk .07 .20
206 Jari Kurri .10 .25
207 Bob Rouse .05 .15
208 Yvon Corriveau .05 .15
209 John Blue .07 .20
210 Dimitri Khristich .05 .15
211 Brent Fedyk .05 .15
212 Jody Hull .05 .15
213 Chris Terreri .07 .20
214 Mike McPhee .05 .15
215 Chris Kontos .05 .15
216 Greg Gilbert .05 .15
217 Sergei Zubov .05 .15
218 Grant Fuhr .10 .25
219 Charlie Huddy .05 .15
220 Mario Lemieux .40 1.00
221 Sheldon Kennedy .05 .15
222 Curtis Joseph .10 .25
223 Brad Dalgarno .05 .15
224 Bret Hedican .05 .15
225 Trevor Linden .07 .20
226 Darryl Sydor .05 .15
227 Jay More .05 .15
228 Dave Poulin .05 .15
229 Frank Musil .05 .15
230 Mark Recchi .12 .30
231 Craig Simpson .05 .15
232 Gino Cavallini .05 .15
233 Vincent Damphousse .07 .20
234 Luciano Borsato .05 .15
235 Dave Andreychuk .10 .25
236 Ken Daneyko .05 .15
237 Chris Chelios .10 .25
238 Andrew McBain .05 .15
239 Rick Tabaracci .05 .15
240 Steve Larmer .07 .20
241 Sean Burke .05 .15
242 Rob DiMaio .05 .15
243 Jim Paek .05 .15
244 Dave Lowry .05 .15
245 Alexander Mogilny .07 .20
246 Darren Turcotte .05 .15
247 Brendan Shanahan .12 .30
248 Peter Taglianetti .05 .15
249 Scott Mellanby .07 .20
250 Guy Carbonneau .05 .15
251 Claude LaPointe .05 .15
252 Pat Conacher .05 .15
253 Roger Johansson .05 .15
254 Cam Neely .10 .25
255 Garry Galley .05 .15
256 Keith Primeau .05 .15
257 Scott Lachance .05 .15
258 Bill Ranford .07 .20
259 Pat Falloon .05 .15
260 Pavel Bure .10 .25
261 Darrin Shannon .05 .15
262 Mike Foligno .05 .15
263 Checklist 1-132 .05 .15
264 Checklist 133-264 .05 .15
265 Peter Douris .05 .15
266 Warren Rychel .05 .15
267 Owen Nolan .07 .20
268 Mark Osborne .05 .15
269 Teppo Numminen .05 .15
270 Rob Niedermayer .07 .20
271 Mark Lamb .05 .15
272 Curtis Joseph .10 .25
273 Joe Murphy .05 .15
274 Bernie Nicholls .05 .15
275 Gord Roberts .05 .15
276 Al MacInnis .07 .20
277 Ken Wregget .05 .15
278 Calle Johansson .05 .15
279 Tom Kurvers .05 .15
280 Steve Yzerman .25 .60
281 Roman Hamrlik .05 .15
282 Esa Tikkanen .05 .15
283 Darrin Madeley RC .10 .25
284 Robert Dirk .05 .15
285 Derek Plante RC .10 .25
286 Ron Tugnutt .07 .20
287 Frank Pietrangelo .07 .20
288 Paul DiPietro .05 .15
289 Alexander Godynyuk .05 .15
290 Kirk Maltby RC .10 .25
291 Olaf Kolzig .07 .20
292 Vitali Karamnov .05 .15
293 Alexei Gusarov .05 .15
294 Bryan Erickson .05 .15
295 Jocelyn Lemieux .05 .15
296 Bryan Trottier .12 .30
297 Dave Ellett .05 .15
298 Tim Watters .05 .15
299 Joe Juneau .07 .20
300 Steve Thomas .05 .15
301 Mark Greig .05 .15
302 Jeff Reese .05 .15
303 Steven King .05 .15
304 Don Beaupre .07 .20
305 Denis Savard .12 .30
306 Greg Smyth .05 .15
307 Jaroslav Modry RC .10 .25
308 Petr Svoboda .05 .15
309 Mike Craig .05 .15
310 Eric Lindros .30 .75
311 Dana Murzyn .05 .15
312 Sean Hill .05 .15
313 Andre Racicot .05 .15
314 John Vanbiesbrouck .07 .20
315 Doug Lidster .05 .15
316 Garth Butcher .05 .15
317 Alexei Yashin .07 .20
318 Sergei Fedorov .15 .40
319 Louie DeBrusk .05 .15
320 Dominik Hasek CZE .20 .50
321 Michal Pivonka .05 .15
322 Bobby Holik .05 .15
323 Roman Hamrlik CZE .05 .15
324 Petr Svoboda .05 .15
325 Jaromir Jagr CZE .25 .60
326 Steven Finn .05 .15
327 Stephane Richer .07 .20
328 Claude Loiselle .05 .15
329 Joe Sacco .05 .15
330 Wayne Gretzky .50 1.25
331 Sylvain Lefebvre .05 .15
332 Sergei Bautin .05 .15
333 Craig Simpson .05 .15
334 Don Sweeney .05 .15
335 Dominic Roussel .07 .20
336 Scott Thomas RC .10 .25
337 Geoff Courtnall .05 .15
338 Tom Fitzgerald .05 .15
339 Kevin Haller .05 .15
340 Troy Loney .05 .15
341 Ronnie Stern .05 .15
342 Mark Astley RC .10 .25
343 Jeff Daniels .05 .15
344 Marc Bureau .05 .15
345 Micah Aivazoff RC .10 .25
346 Matthew Barnaby .07 .20
347 C.J. Young .05 .15
348 Dale Craigwell .05 .15
349 Ray Ferraro .05 .15
350 Ray Bourque .15 .40
351 Stu Barnes .05 .15
352 Alan Conroy RC .05 .15
353 Shawn McEachern .05 .15
354 Garry Valk .05 .15
355 Christian Ruuttu .05 .15
356 Darren Rumble .05 .15
357 Stu Grimson .05 .15
358 Alexander Karpovtsev .05 .15
359 Wendel Clark .07 .20
360 Michal Pivonka .05 .15
361 Peter Popovic RC .10 .25
362 Kevin Dahl .05 .15
363 Jeff Brown .05 .15
364 Daren Puppa .05 .15
365 Dallas Drake RC .10 .25
366 Dean McAmmond .05 .15
367 Martin Rucinsky .05 .15
368 Shane Churla .05 .15
369 Todd Ewen .05 .15
370 Kevin Stevens .05 .15
371 David Volek .05 .15
372 J.J. Daigneault .05 .15
373 Marc Bergevin .05 .15
374 Craig Billington .07 .20
375 Mike Gartner .07 .20
376 Jimmy Carson .05 .15
377 Bruce Driver .05 .15
378 Steve Heinze .05 .15
379 Patrick Carnback RC .10 .25
380 Wayne Gretzky CAN .50 1.25
381 Jeff Brown CAN .05 .15
382 Gary Roberts CAN .05 .15
383 Ray Bourque CAN .15 .40
384 Mike Gartner CAN .07 .20
385 Felix Potvin CAN .20 .50
386 Michel Goulet .05 .15
387 Dave Tippett .05 .15
388 Jim Waite .07 .20
389 Yuri Khmylev .05 .15
390 Doug Gilmour .12 .30
391 Brad McCrimmon .05 .15
392 Brent Severyn RC .10 .25
393 Jocelyn Thibault RC .10 .25
394 Boris Mironov .05 .15
395 Marty McSorley .05 .15
396 Shaun Van Allen .05 .15
397 Gary Leeman .05 .15
398 Ed Olczyk .05 .15
399 Darcy Wakaluk .05 .15
400 Murray Craven .05 .15
401 Martin Brodeur .25 .60
402 Paul Laus RC .05 .15
403 Bill Houlder .05 .15
404 Robert Reichel .05 .15
405 Alexandre Daigle .05 .15
406 Brent Thompson .05 .15
407 Keith Acton .05 .15
408 Dave Karpa .05 .15
409 Igor Korolev .05 .15
410 Chris Gratton .07 .20
411 Vincent Riendeau .05 .15
412 Darren McCarty RC .15 .40
413 Bob Carpenter .05 .15
414 Joe Cirella .05 .15
415 Stephane Matteau .05 .15
416 Jozef Stumpel .05 .15
417 Rich Pilon .05 .15
418 Mattias Norstrom RC .10 .25
419 Dmitri Moronov .05 .15
420 Alexei Zhamnov .07 .20
421 Bill Guerin .05 .15
422 Greg Hawgood .05 .15
423 Randy Cunneyworth .05 .15
424 Ron Francis .12 .30
425 Brett Hull .15 .40
426 Tim Sweeney .05 .15
427 Mike Rathje .05 .15
428 Dave Babych .05 .15
429 Chris Tancill .05 .15
430 Mark Messier .10 .25
431 Bob Sweeney .05 .15
432 Terry Yake .05 .15
433 Joe Reekie .05 .15
434 Tomas Sandstrom .05 .15
435 Kevin Hatcher .05 .15
436 Bill Lindsay .05 .15
437 Jon Casey .07 .20
438 Dennis Vaske .05 .15
439 Allen Pedersen .05 .15
440 Pavel Bure RUS .10 .25
441 Sergei Fedorov RUS .15 .40
442 Arturs Irbe LAT .07 .20
443 Darius Kasparaitis .05 .15
444 Evgeny Davydov .05 .15
445 Vladimir Malakhov .05 .15
446 Tom Barrasso .07 .20
447 Jeff Norton .05 .15
448 David Emma .05 .15
449 Pelle Eklund .05 .15
450 Jeremy Roenick .15 .40
451 Jesse Belanger .05 .15
452 Vitali Prokhorov .05 .15
453 Arto Blomsten .05 .15
454 Peter Zezel .05 .15
455 Kelly Kisio .05 .15
456 Zdeno Ciger .05 .15
457 Greg Johnson .05 .15
458 Dave Archibald .05 .15
459 Vladimir Vujtek .05 .15
460 Mats Sundin .07 .20
461 Dan Keczmer .05 .15
462 Stephan Lebeau .05 .15
463 Dominik Hasek .20 .50
464 Kevin Lowe .05 .15
465 Gord Murphy .05 .15
466 Bryan Smolinski .05 .15
467 Josef Beranek .05 .15
468 Ron Hextall .07 .20
469 Randy Ladouceur .05 .15
470 Scott Niedermayer .10 .25
471 Kelly Hrudey .07 .20
472 Mike Needham .05 .15
473 John Tucker .05 .15
474 Kelly Miller .05 .15
475 Jyrki Lumme .05 .15
476 Andy Moog .10 .25
477 Glen Murray .05 .15
478 Mark Ferner RC .05 .15
479 John Cullen .05 .15
480 Gilbert Dionne .05 .15
481 Paul Ranheim .05 .15
482 Mike Hough .05 .15
483 Teemu Selanne .20 .50
484 Aaron Ward RC .10 .25
485 Chris Pronger .10 .25
486 Glenn Healy .07 .20
487 Curtis Leschyshyn .05 .15
488 Jim Montgomery RC .10 .25
489 Travis Green .07 .20
490 Pat LaFontaine .10 .25
491 Bobby Dollas RC .05 .15
492 Alexei Kasatonov .05 .15
493 Corey Millen .05 .15
494 Slava Kozlov .07 .20
495 Igor Kravchuk .05 .15
496 Dimitri Filimonov .05 .15
497 Jeff Odgers .05 .15
498 Joe Mullen .07 .20
499 Gary Shuchuk .05 .15
500 Jeremy Roenick USA .15 .40
501 Tom Barrasso USA .07 .20
502 Keith Tkachuk USA .10 .25
503 Phil Housley USA .07 .20
504 Tony Granato USA .05 .15
505 Brian Leetch USA .10 .25
506 Anatoli Semenov .05 .15
507 Steve Leach .05 .15
508 Brian Skrudland .05 .15
509 Kirk Muller .05 .15
510 Gary Roberts .05 .15
511 Gerard Gallant .05 .15
512 Joey Kocur .05 .15
513 Tie Domi .05 .15
514 Kay Whitmore .05 .15
515 Vladimir Malakhov .05 .15
516 Stewart Malgunas RC .10 .25
517 Jamie Macoun .05 .15
518 Alan May .05 .15
519 Guy Hebert .07 .20
520 Derian Hatcher .05 .15
521 Richard Smehlik .05 .15
522 Joby Messier RC .10 .25
523 Trent Klatt .05 .15
524 Tom Chorske .05 .15
525 Iain Fraser RC .10 .25
526 Dan Laperriere .05 .15
527 Checklist .05 .15
528 Checklist .05 .15

1993-94 Topps Premier Black Gold

Randomly inserted in Topps packs, these 24 standard-size cards feature on their white-bordered fronts color player action shots set on ghosted and darkened backgrounds. Gold foil inner borders at the top and bottom carry multiple Premier Black Gold logos. The cards are numbered on the back. Collectors could also find in packs exchange (EXCH) Winner A EXCH, redeemable for the entire 12-card first-series set; Winner B EXCH, redeemable for the 12-card second series; and Winner AB EXCH, redeemable for the entire 24 card set. Each winner card pictured a small thumbnail image of all cards for that series and these winner cards were replaced once the set were mailed out. The replacement winner cards featured a checklist syle back instead of contest rules. The Winner cards expired May 31, 1994.

COMPLETE SET (24) 12.00 30.00
COMP.SERIES 1 (12) 6.00 15.00
COMP.SERIES 2 (12) 6.00 15.00
1 Teemu Selanne .50 1.25
2 Steve Duchesne .20 .50
3 Felix Potvin .50 1.25
4 Shawn McEachern .20 .50
5 Adam Oates .30 .75
6 Paul Coffey .40 1.00
7 Wayne Gretzky 3.00 8.00
8 Alexei Zhamnov .25 .60
9 Mario Lemieux 2.00 5.00
10 Gary Suter .20 .50
11 Tom Barrasso .30 .75
12 Joe Juneau .25 .60
13 Eric Lindros .50 1.25
14 Ed Belfour .40 1.00
15 Ray Bourque .60 1.50
16 Steve Yzerman 2.00 5.00
17 Andrei Kovalenko .20 .50
18 Curtis Joseph .30 .75
19 Phil Housley .25 .60
20 Pierre Turgeon .30 .75
21 Brett Hull .50 1.25
22 Patrick Roy 2.00 5.00
23 Larry Murphy .25 .60
24 Pat LaFontaine .40 1.00
A1 Winner A 1-12 EXCH 1.50 4.00
A2 Winner A 1-12 Prize .20 .50
B1 Winner B 13-24 EXCH 1.50 4.00
B2 Winner B 13-24 Prize .20 .50
AB1 Winner A/B 1-24 EXCH 2.50 6.00
AB2 Winner A/B 1-24 Prize .50 1.25

1993-94 Topps Premier Finest

Randomly inserted in both Topps and OPC second-series packs, these 12 standard-size cards feature on their metallic fronts color player action shots framed by a gold line and bordered in blue. The player's name and position appear in gold lettering in the lower blue margin. The cards are numbered on the back as "X of 12."

COMPLETE SET (12) 8.00 20.00
1 Alexandre Daigle .20 .50
2 Roman Hamrlik .40 1.00
3 Eric Lindros .75 2.00
4 Owen Nolan .40 1.00
5 Mats Sundin .75 2.00
6 Mike Modano 1.25 3.00
7 Pierre Turgeon .40 1.00
8 Joe Murphy .20 .50
9 Wendel Clark .40 1.00
10 Mario Lemieux 4.00 10.00
11 Dale Hawerchuk .40 1.00
12 Rob Ramage .20 .50

1993-94 Topps Premier Team USA

Randomly inserted at a rate of 1:12 second-series Topps Premier packs, these 23 standard-size cards feature borderless color player photos on their fronts. The player's name and the USA Hockey logo appear at the bottom in gold foil. The red, white, and blue back carries the player's name and position at the top, followed below by biography, player photo, career highlights, and statistics. The cards are numbered on the back as "X of 23."

COMPLETE SET (23) 10.00 20.00
1 Mike Dunham .75 2.00
2 Ian Moran .40 1.00
3 Peter Laviolette .40 1.00
4 Darby Hendrickson .40 1.00
5 Brian Rolston .75 2.00
6 Mark Beaufait .40 1.00
7 Travis Richards .40 1.00
8 John Lilley .40 1.00
9 Chris Ferraro .75 2.00
10 Jon Hillebrandt .40 1.00
11 Chris Imes .40 1.00
12 Ted Crowley .40 1.00
13 David Sacco .40 1.00
14 Todd Marchant .75 2.00
15 Peter Ferraro .40 1.00
16 David Roberts .40 1.00
17 Jim Campbell .75 2.00
18 Barry Richter .40 1.00
19 Craig Johnson .40 1.00
20 Brett Hauer .40 1.00
21 Jeff Lazaro .40 1.00
22 Jim Storm .40 1.00
23 Matt Martin .40 1.00

1994-95 Topps Premier

This 550-card set was issued in two series of 275 cards each. OPC packs contained 14 cards and Topps packs contained 12 cards. Both boxes contained 36 packs. It was announced in press material that no more than 2,000 cases of each series of the OPC version were printed. Because of this shorter quantity, OPC versions earn a slight premium. Card fronts feature a full white border with a color bar enclosing the player's name near the bottom. Position runs vertically down the right side of the name, team name directly below it. All text is printed in silver foil. Backs have a black border with a cutout player photo, full stats including playoffs, and personal information. The OPC back text is in French and English. The Topps version is in English only. Since some of the cards have no written text, such as the All-Star cards, they are impossible to positively identify as being from one set or the other. Both versions have "The Topps Company, Inc." printed on the back. Several subsets appear scattered throughout the set, including All-Stars, Goaltending Duos, League Leaders, Rookie Sensations, Team of the Future, Tools of the Game, The Trade and Power.

1 Mark Messier .10 .25
2 Darren Turcotte .05 .15
3 Mikhail Shtalenkov RC .05 .15
4 Rob Gaudreau .05 .15

5 Tony Amonte .07 .20
6 Stephane Quintal .05 .15
7 Iain Fraser .05 .15
8 Doug Weight .07 .20
9 German Titov .05 .15
10 Larry Murphy .07 .20
11 Danton Cole .05 .15
12 Pat Peake .05 .15
13 Chris Terreri .07 .20
14 Yuri Khmylev .05 .15
15 Paul Coffey .10 .25
16 Brian Savage .05 .15
17 Rod Brind'Amour .07 .20
18 Nathan Lafayette .05 .15
19 Gord Murphy .05 .15
20 Al Iafrate .05 .15
21 Kevin Miller .05 .15
22 Peter Zezel .05 .15
23 Sylvain Turgeon .05 .15
24 Mark Tinordi .05 .15
25 Jari Kurri .07 .20
26 Benoit Hogue .05 .15
27 Jeff Reese .05 .15
28 Brian Noonan .05 .15
29 Denis Tsygurov RC .10 .25
30 James Patrick .05 .15
31 Bob Corkum .05 .15
32 Valeri Kamensky .07 .20
33 Ray Whitney .05 .15
34 Joe Murphy .05 .15
35 Dominik Hasek AS .20 .50
36 Ray Bourque AS .15 .40
37 Brian Leetch AS .10 .25
38 Dave Andreychuk AS .10 .25
39 Pavel Bure AS .10 .25
40 Sergei Fedorov AS .15 .40
41 Bob Beers .07 .20
42 Byron Dafoe RC .30 .75
43 Lyle Odelein .07 .20
44 Markus Naslund .10 .25
45 Dean Chynoweth RC .05 .15
46 Trent Klatt .05 .15
47 Murray Craven .05 .15
48 Dave Mackey .05 .15
49 Norm Maciver .05 .15
50 Alexander Mogilny .07 .20
51 David Reid .05 .15
52 Nicklas Lidstrom .10 .25
53 Tom Fitzgerald .05 .15
54 Roman Hamrlik .07 .20
55 Wendel Clark .07 .20
56 Dominic Roussel .07 .20
57 Alexei Zhitnik .07 .20
58 Valeri Zelepukin .05 .15
59 Calle Johansson .05 .15
60 Craig Janney .07 .20
61 Randy Wood .05 .15
62 Curtis Leschyshyn .05 .15
63 Stephan Lebeau .05 .15
64 Dallas Drake .05 .15
65 Vincent Damphousse .07 .20
66 Scott Lachance .05 .15
67 Dirk Graham .05 .15
68 Kevin Smyth .05 .15
69 Denis Savard .12 .30
70 Mike Richter .10 .25
71 Ronnie Stern .05 .15
72 Kirk Maltby .05 .15
73 Kjell Samuelsson .05 .15
74 Neal Broten .07 .20
75 Trevor Linden .07 .20
76 Todd Elik .05 .15
77 Andrew McBain .05 .15
78 Alexei Kudashov .05 .15
79 Ken Daneyko .05 .15
80 D.Hasek/G.Fuhr GD .20 .50
81 A.Moog/D.Wakaluk GD .10 .25
82 Vanbiesbrouck/M.Fitz. GD .07 .20
83 M.Brodeur/C.Terreri GD .25 .60
84 T.Barrasso/K.Wregget GD .07 .20
85 K.McLean/K.Whitmore .07 .20
86 Darryl Sydor .05 .15
87 Chris Osgood .15 .40
88 Ted Donato .05 .15
89 Dave Lowry .05 .15
90 Mark Recchi .12 .30
91 Jim Montgomery .05 .15
92 Bill Houlder .05 .15
93 Richard Smehlik .05 .15
94 Benoit Brunet .05 .15
95 Teemu Selanne .20 .50
96 Paul Ranheim .05 .15
97 Andrei Kovalenko .05 .15
98 Grant Ledyard .05 .15
99 Brent Grieve RC .05 .15
100 Joe Juneau .07 .20
101 Martin Gelinas .05 .15
102 Jamie Macoun .05 .15
103 Craig MacTavish .05 .15
104 Micah Aivazoff .05 .15
105 Stephane Richer .07 .20
106 Eric Weinrich .05 .15
107 Pat Elynuik .05 .15
108 Tomas Sandstrom .05 .15
109 Darrin Madeley .05 .15
110 Al MacInnis .07 .20
111 Cam Stewart .05 .15
112 Dixon Ward .05 .15
113 Vlastimil Kroupa .05 .15
114 Rob DiMaio .05 .15
115 Pierre Turgeon .07 .20
116 Mike Hough .05 .15
117 John LeClair .10 .25
118 Dave Hannan .05 .15
119 Todd Ewen .05 .15
120 NY Rangers Champs .10 .25
121 Dave Manson .05 .15
122 Jocelyn Lemieux .05 .15
123 Jocelyn Thibault .10 .25
124 Scott Pearson .05 .15
125 Patrick Roy AS .25 .60
126 Scott Stevens AS .10 .25
127 Al MacInnis AS .07 .20
128 Adam Graves AS .05 .15
129 Cam Neely AS .10 .25
130 Wayne Gretzky AS .50 1.25
131 Tom Chorske .05 .15
132 John Tucker .05 .15
133 Steve Smith .05 .15
134 Kay Whitmore .05 .15
135 Adam Oates .10 .25
136 Bill Berg .05 .15
137 Wes Walz .05 .15
138 Jeff Beukeboom .05 .15
139 Ron Francis .12 .30
140 Alexandre Daigle .05 .15
141 Josef Beranek .05 .15
142 Tom Pederson .05 .15
143 Jamie McLennan .07 .20
144 Scott Mellanby .07 .20
145 Slava Kozlov .07 .20
146 Marty McSorley .05 .15
147 Tim Sweeney .05 .15
148 Luciano Borsato .05 .15
149 Jason Dawe .05 .15
150 Wayne Gretzky LL .50 1.25
151 Pavel Bure LL .10 .25
152 Dominik Hasek LL .20 .50
153 Scott Stevens LL .10 .25
154 Wayne Gretzky LL .50 1.25
155 Mike Richter LL .10 .25
156 Dominik Hasek LL .20 .50
157 Ted Drury .05 .15
158 Peter Popovic .05 .15
159 Alexei Kasatonov .05 .15
160 Mats Sundin .07 .20
161 Brad Shaw .05 .15
162 Bret Hedican .05 .15
163 Mike McPhee .05 .15
164 Martin Straka .05 .15
165 Dmitri Mironov .05 .15
166 Andrei Trefilov .05 .15
167 Joe Reekie .05 .15
168 Gary Suter .05 .15
169 Greg Gilbert .05 .15
170 Igor Larionov .05 .15
171 Mike Sillinger .05 .15
172 Igor Kravchuk .05 .15
173 Glen Murray .05 .15
174 Shawn Chambers .05 .15
175 John MacLean .07 .20
176 Yves Racine .05 .15
177 Andrei Lomakin .05 .15
178 Patrick Flatley .05 .15
179 Igor Ulanov .05 .15
180 Pat LaFontaine .10 .25
181 Mathieu Schneider .05 .15
182 Peter Stastny .07 .20
183 Tony Granato .05 .15
184 Peter Douris .05 .15
185 Alexei Kovalev .05 .15
186 Geoff Courtnall .05 .15
187 Richard Matvichuk .05 .15
188 Troy Murray .05 .15
189 Todd Gill .05 .15
190 Martin Brodeur RS .25 .60
191 Mikael Renberg RS .07 .20
192 Alexei Yashin RS .10 .25
193 Jason Arnott RS .07 .20
194 Derek Plante RS .05 .15
195 Alexandre Daigle RS .05 .15
196 Bryan Smolinski RS .05 .15
197 Jesse Belanger RS .05 .15
198 Chris Pronger RS .10 .25
199 Chris Osgood RS .15 .40
200 Jeremy Roenick .20 .50
201 Johan Garpenlov .05 .15
202 Dave Karpa .05 .15
203 Darren McCarty .05 .15
204 Claude Lemieux .10 .25
205 Geoff Sanderson .07 .20
206 Tom Barrasso .07 .20
207 Kevin Dineen .05 .15
208 Sylvain Cote .05 .15
209 Brent Gretzky .05 .15
210 Shayne Corson .05 .15
211 Darius Kasparaitis .05 .15
212 Peter Andersson .05 .15
213 Robert Reichel .05 .15
214 Jozef Stumpel .05 .15
215 Brendan Shanahan .12 .30
216 Craig Muni .05 .15
217 Alexei Zhamnov .07 .20
218 Robert Lang .05 .15
219 Brian Bellows .07 .20
220 Steven King .05 .15
221 Sergei Zubov .05 .15
222 Kelly Miller .05 .15
223 Ilya Byakin .05 .15
224 Chris Tamer RC .05 .15
225 Doug Gilmour .12 .30
226 Shawn Antoski .05 .15
227 Andrew Cassels .05 .15
228 Craig Wolanin .05 .15
229 Jon Casey .07 .20
230 Mike Modano .15 .40
231 Bill Guerin .07 .20
232 Gaetan Duchesne .05 .15
233 Steve Dubinsky .05 .15
234 Jason Bowen .05 .15
235 Steve Yzerman .25 .60
236 Dave Poulin .05 .15
237 Michael Nylander .07 .20
238 Felix Potvin FUT .10 .25
239 Sandis Ozolinsh FUT .05 .15
240 Scott Niedermayer FUT .10 .25
241 Eric Lindros FUT .10 .25
242 Keith Tkachuk FUT .10 .25
243 Teemu Selanne FUT .20 .50
244 Marty McInnis .05 .15
245 Bob Kudelski .05 .15
246 Paul Cavallini .05 .15
247 Brian Bradley .05 .15
248 Robb Stauber .05 .15
249 Jay Wells .05 .15
250 Mario Lemieux .40 1.00
251 Tommy Albelin .05 .15
252 Paul DiPietro .05 .15
253 Mike Gartner .10 .25
254 Darrin Shannon .05 .15
255 Alexander Karpovtsev .05 .15
256 Dave Babych .05 .15
257 Greg Johnson .05 .15
258 Frank Musil .05 .15
259 Michal Pivonka .07 .20
260 Arturs Irbe .07 .20
261 Paul Broten .05 .15
262 Don Sweeney .05 .15
263 Doug Brown .05 .15
264 Bobby Dollas .05 .15
265 Brian Skrudland .05 .15
266 Dan Plante RC .05 .15
267 Chad Penney .05 .15
268 Steve Leach .05 .15
269 Damian Rhodes .07 .20
270 Glenn Anderson .10 .25
271 Randy McKay .05 .15
272 Jeff Brown .05 .15
273 Steve Konowalchuk .05 .15
274 Checklist 1-136 .05 .15
275 Checklist 137-275 .05 .15
276 Sergei Fedorov TOTG .15 .40
277 Adam Oates TOTG .10 .25
278 Mark Messier TOTG .10 .25
279 Doug Gilmour TOTG .12 .30
280 Wayne Gretzky TOTG .50 1.25
281 Rick Tocchet .07 .20
282 Guy Carbonneau .05 .15
283 Peter Bondra .07 .20
284 Valeri Karpov RC .05 .15
285 Ed Belfour .10 .25
286 Petr Nedved .07 .20
287 Mikael Andersson .05 .15
288 Boris Mironov .05 .15
289 Donald Audette .05 .15
290 Kevin Stevens .05 .15
291 Cliff Ronning .05 .15
292 Bruce Driver .05 .15
293 Mariusz Czerkawski RC .10 .25
294 Mikael Renberg .07 .20
295 Theo Fleury .10 .25
296 Robert Kron .05 .15
297 Wendel Clark .07 .20
298 Dave Gagner .07 .20
299 Ulf Dahlen .05 .15
300 Keith Tkachuk .10 .25
301 Mike Ridley .05 .15
302 Mike Vernon .07 .20
303 Troy Mallette .05 .15
304 Derek King .05 .15
305 Kirk Muller .05 .15
306 Rob Niedermayer .07 .20
307 Ian Laperriere RC .10 .25
308 Mike Donnelly .05 .15
309 Joe Sacco .05 .15
310 Patrick Roy TOTG .25 .60
311 Tom Barrasso .07 .20
312 Dominik Hasek TOTG .20 .50
313 Felix Potvin TOTG .10 .25
314 Mike Richter .10 .25
315 Bobby Holik .05 .15
316 Patrick Poulin .05 .15
317 Stephane Matteau .05 .15
318 Petr Klima .05 .15
319 Fredrik Olausson .05 .15
320 Dale Hawerchuk .12 .30
321 Jim Dowd .05 .15
322 Chris Therien .05 .15
323 Ravil Gusmanov RC .05 .15
324 Vincent Riendeau .05 .15
325 Pavel Bure .10 .25
326 Jimmy Carson .05 .15
327 Steve Chiasson .05 .15
328 Ken Wregget .07 .20
329 Kenny Jonsson .05 .15
330 Keith Primeau .10 .25
331 Bob Errey .05 .15
332 Derian Hatcher .05 .15
333 Stephane Fiset .07 .20
334 Brent Severyn .05 .15
335 Ray Ferraro .05 .15
336 Pavol Demitra .12 .30
337 Valeri Bure .05 .15
338 Guy Hebert .07 .20
339 Matt Johnson RC .05 .15
340 Curtis Joseph .15 .40
341 Rob Pearson .05 .15
342 Jeff Shantz .05 .15
343 Eric Charron RC .10 .25
344 Jason Smith .07 .20
345 M.Sundin/W.Clark .07 .20
346 R.Tocchet/L.Robitaille .10 .25
347 A.MacInnis/P.Housley .07 .20
348 M.Vernon/S.Chiasson .07 .20
349 Craig Simpson .05 .15
350 Adam Graves .05 .15
351 Kevin Haller .05 .15
352 Nelson Emerson .05 .15
353 Phil Housley .07 .20
354 Shawn McEachern .05 .15
355 Felix Potvin .10 .25
356 Sergio Momesso .10 .25
357 Glen Wesley .05 .15
358 David Shaw .05 .15
359 Terry Carkner .05 .15
360 John Vanbiesbrouck .07 .20
361 Dean Evason .05 .15
362 Michal Sykora .05 .15
363 Troy Loney .05 .15
364 Sylvain Lefebvre .05 .15
365 Alexei Yashin .10 .25
366 Gilbert Dionne .05 .15
367 Rick Tabaracci .07 .20
368 Paul Ysebaert .05 .15
369 Craig Johnson .05 .15
370 Scott Stevens .10 .25
371 Philippe Boucher .05 .15
372 Garry Valk .05 .15
373 Jason Muzzatti .07 .20
374 Chris Joseph .05 .15
375 Wayne Gretzky .50 1.25
376 Teppo Numminen .05 .15
377 Oleg Petrov .05 .15
378 Patrik Juhlin RC .05 .15
379 Zarley Zalapski .05 .15
380 Martin Brodeur TOTF .25 .60
381 Chris Pronger TOTF .10 .25
382 Sergei Zubov TOTF .05 .15
383 Mikael Renberg TOTF .07 .20
384 Brett Lindros TOTF .05 .15
385 Peter Forsberg TOTF .25 .60
386 Brandon Convery .05 .15
387 Steve Heinze .05 .15
388 Glenn Healy .07 .20
389 Brian Benning .05 .15
390 Pat Verbeek .07 .20
391 Ulf Samuelsson .05 .15
392 Turner Stevenson .05 .15
393 Bob Rouse .05 .15
394 Steve Konroyd .05 .15
395 Russ Courtnall .05 .15
396 Sergei Makarov .05 .15
397 Kirk McLean .07 .20
398 Steven Finn .05 .15
399 Yan Kaminsky .05 .15
400 Eric Lindros .10 .25
401 Steve Duchesne .05 .15
402 John Slaney .05 .15
403 Bernie Nicholls .07 .20
404 Kelly Buchberger .05 .15
405 Paul Kariya .12 .30
406 Michel Petit .05 .15
407 Cale Hulse RC .07 .20
408 Sheldon Kennedy .05 .15
409 Brad May .05 .15
410 Daren Puppa .07 .20
411 Janne Laukkanen .07 .20
412 Mats Sundin .07 .20
413 Trevor Kidd .07 .20
414 Greg Adams .05 .15
415 Pavel Bure TOTG .10 .25
416 Teemu Selanne TOTG .20 .50
417 Brett Hull TOTG .20 .50
418 Steve Larmer .07 .20
419 Cam Neely TOTG .10 .25
420 Ray Bourque .15 .40
421 Andrei Nikolishin .05 .15
422 Jim Paek .05 .15
423 John Cullen .05 .15
424 Darcy Wakaluk .07 .20
425 Peter Forsberg .25 .60
426 Yves Racine .05 .15
427 Jody Hull .05 .15
428 Ron Sutter .05 .15
429 Ray Sheppard .07 .20
430 Sandis Ozolinsh .05 .15
431 Brent Grieve .05 .15
432 Shaun Van Allen .05 .15
433 Craig Berube .05 .15
434 Vladislav Boulin RC .10 .25
435 Bill Ranford .07 .20
436 Denny Felsner .05 .15
437 Jamie Storr .07 .20
438 Brian Rolston .05 .15
439 Chris Gratton .05 .15
440 Dominik Hasek .20 .50
441 Garth Butcher .07 .20
442 Jyrki Lumme .05 .15
443 Sergei Nemchinov .05 .15
444 Tie Domi .07 .20
445 Gary Roberts .05 .15
446 Dave McLlwain .05 .15
447 John Gruden RC .05 .15
448 Vladimir Konstantinov .07 .20
449 Adam Deadmarsh .05 .15
450 Brian Leetch TOTG .10 .25
451 Scott Stevens .10 .25
452 Mark Tinordi .05 .15
453 Al Iafrate .05 .15
454 Ray Bourque TOTG .15 .40
455 Patrick Roy .25 .60
456 Viktor Gordiouk .07 .20
457 Owen Nolan .10 .25
458 Stu Barnes .05 .15
459 Zigmund Palffy .07 .20
460 Jaromir Jagr .25 .60
461 Andrei Nazarov .05 .15
462 Kelly Hrudey .07 .20
463 Jason Wiemer RC .05 .15
464 Oleg Tverdovsky .07 .20
465 Brett Hull .20 .50
466 Luke Richardson .05 .15
467 Jason Allison .07 .20
468 Dimitri Yushkevich .05 .15
469 Todd Simon RC .05 .15
470 Martin Brodeur .25 .60
471 Thomas Steen .05 .15
472 Vesa Viitakoski .07 .20
473 Todd Harvey .05 .15
474 Kent Manderville .05 .15
475 Chris Chelios .10 .25
476 Joby Messier .05 .15
477 Jassen Cullimore .05 .15
478 Jamie Pushor .07 .20
479 Bryan Smolinski .05 .15
480 Joe Sakic .20 .50
481 David Wilkie .07 .20
482 Craig Billington .07 .20
483 Pat Neaton .07 .20
484 Chris Pronger .10 .25
485 Brian Leetch POW .10 .25
486 Chris Chelios .10 .25
487 Jeff Brown .05 .15
488 Al MacInnis .07 .20
489 Paul Coffey .10 .25
490 Ray Bourque POW .15 .40
491 Phil Housley .07 .20
492 Larry Murphy .07 .20
493 Sergei Zubov POW .05 .15
494 Scott Stevens .10 .25
495 Steve Thomas .05 .15
496 Jim Waite .05 .15
497 Mike Keane .05 .15
498 Rob Blake .10 .25
499 John Lilley .05 .15
500 Brian Leetch .10 .25
501 Derek Plante .05 .15
502 Tim Cheveldae .07 .20
503 Vladimir Vujtek .05 .15
504 Esa Tikkanen .05 .15
505 Cam Neely .10 .25
506 Dale Hunter .05 .15
507 Marc Bergevin .05 .15
508 Joel Otto .05 .15
509 Brent Fedyk .05 .15
510 Dave Andreychuk .10 .25
511 Andy Moog .10 .25
512 Jaroslav Modry .05 .15
513 Sergei Krivokrasov .05 .15
514 Brett Lindros .05 .15
515 Cory Stillman RC .05 .15
516 Jon Rohloff RC .10 .25
517 Joe Mullen .07 .20
518 Evgeny Davydov .05 .15
519 Scott Young .05 .15
520 Sergei Fedorov .15 .40
521 Pat Falloon .05 .15
522 Bill Lindsay .05 .15
523 Ron Tugnutt .07 .20
524 Anatoli Semenov .05 .15
525 Geoff Courtnall .05 .15
526 Luc Robitaille .10 .25
527 Geoff Sanderson .07 .20
528 Esa Tikkanen .05 .15
529 Brendan Shanahan TOTG .12 .30
530 Jason Arnott .07 .20
531 Michal Grosek RC .05 .15
532 Steve Larmer .07 .20
533 Eric Fichaud RC .10 .25
534 Dimitri Khristich .05 .15
535 Garry Galley .05 .15
536 Aaron Gavey .05 .15
537 Joe Nieuwendyk .10 .25
538 Mike Craig .05 .15
539 Scott Niedermayer .10 .25
540 Luc Robitaille .10 .25
541 Dino Ciccarelli .07 .20
542 Sean Burke .07 .20
543 Jiri Slegr .05 .15
544 Jesse Belanger .05 .15
545 Sean Hill .05 .15
546 Vladimir Malakhov .05 .15
547 Jeff Friesen .05 .15
548 Mike Ricci .05 .15
549 Checklist 276-414 .05 .15
550 Checklist 415-550 .05 .15

1994-95 Topps Premier Special Effects

One card from this parallel set was issued in every other pack of OPC and Topps Premier. The cards can be differentiated from the basic set by the reflective rainbow foil which appears in the card background when held at an angle to a light source. Card backs are the same. The OPC versions are slightly more desirable because they were printed in smaller quantities than the Topps cards. Cards 274, 275, 549 and 550 replaced the checklists with players not featured in the basic set.

*SER.1 SE VETS: 4X TO 10X BASIC CARDS
*SER.1 SE ROOKIES: 1.5X TO 4X
*SER.2 SE VETS: 6X TO 15X BASIC CARDS
*SER.2 SE ROOKIES: 3X TO 8X
CL REPLACE (274/275/540/55) .40 1.00

1994-95 Topps Premier Finest Inserts

The 23 cards in this set were randomly inserted at a rate of 1:36 Topps Premier series one packs. The set includes all players who scored at least 40 goals in 1993-94. Cards feature an isolated player photo over a textured rainbow background. A reflective rainbow border is broken up by the player name and his goal scoring mark. Premier Finest is written across the top of the card. Backs have a small player photo with brief personal information, and scoring breakdown by division. Cards are numbered "X" of 23.

COMPLETE SET (23) 15.00 40.00
1 Pavel Bure 1.50 4.00
2 Brett Hull 2.00 5.00
3 Sergei Fedorov 1.50 4.00
4 Dave Andreychuk .75 2.00
5 Brendan Shanahan 1.50 4.00
6 Ray Sheppard .40 1.00
7 Adam Graves .40 1.00
8 Cam Neely 1.50 4.00
9 Mike Modano 2.00 5.00
10 Wendel Clark .75 2.00
11 Jeremy Roenick 2.00 5.00
12 Eric Lindros 1.50 4.00
13 Luc Robitaille .75 2.00
14 Steve Thomas .40 1.00
15 Geoff Sanderson .40 1.00
16 Gary Roberts .40 1.00
17 Kevin Stevens .40 1.00
18 Keith Tkachuk .75 2.00
19 Theo Fleury .40 1.00
20 Robert Reichel .40 1.00
21 Mark Recchi .75 2.00
22 Vincent Damphousse .40 1.00
23 Bob Kudelski .40 1.00

1994-95 Topps Premier The Go To Guy

This 15-card set was issued in both Topps and OPC Premier series two product at the rate of 1:36 packs. There is no difference between the cards inserted in each product.

COMPLETE SET (15) 12.00 30.00
1 Wayne Gretzky 5.00 12.00
2 Joe Sakic 1.50 4.00
3 Brett Hull 1.00 2.50
4 Mike Modano 1.25 3.00
5 Pavel Bure .75 2.00
6 Pat LaFontaine .75 2.00
7 Theo Fleury .15 .40
8 Jeremy Roenick 1.00 2.50
9 Sergei Fedorov 1.00 2.50
10 Eric Lindros .75 2.00
11 Kirk Muller .15 .40
12 Steve Yzerman 4.00 10.00
13 Alexander Mogilny .30 .75
14 Doug Gilmour .30 .75
15 Mark Messier .75 2.00

1994-95 Topps Finest Bronze

This trio of sets were made available to collectors exclusively through Topps Stadium Club program. The sets cost approximately $95 each, including shipping, from the club. Each bronze card features embossed color action player images on a metallic background of the team logo in a marbleized black border and thin gold frame. The gold backs carry player information and career statistics. Cards 1-6 were issued as a first series in 1994.

1 Jaromir Jagr 12.00 30.00
2 Eric Lindros 12.00 30.00
3 Patrick Roy 20.00 50.00
4 Pavel Bure 10.00 25.00
5 Teemu Selanne 10.00 25.00
6 Doug Gilmour 8.00 20.00
7 Sergei Fedorov 10.00 25.00
8 Brett Hull 10.00 25.00
9 Paul Kariya 15.00 40.00
10 Cam Neely 8.00 20.00
11 Mats Sundin 8.00 20.00
12 Martin Brodeur 10.00 25.00
13 Jeremy Roenick 8.00 20.00
14 Brian Leetch 6.00 15.00
15 Mark Messier 8.00 20.00
16 Mario Lemieux 20.00 50.00
17 Peter Forsberg 12.00 30.00
18 Felix Potvin 8.00 20.00
19 Alexander Mogilny 4.00 10.00
20 Ray Bourque 12.00 30.00
21 Ed Jovanovski 6.00 15.00
22 Mikael Renberg 4.00 10.00

1995-96 Topps

The 385-card set was issued in two series of 220 and 165 cards, respectively. The 13-card packs had an SRP of $1.29.

COMPLETE SET (385) 15.00 40.00
COMP.SERIES 1 (220) 10.00 25.00
COMP.SERIES 2 (165) 6.00 15.00
1 Eric Lindros MM .10 .25
2 Dominik Hasek MM .07 .20
3 Jeremy Roenick MM .08 .25
4 Paul Coffey MM .07 .20
5 Mark Messier MM .07 .20
6 Peter Bondra MM .02 .10
7 Paul Kariya MM .07 .20
8 Chris Chelios .07 .20
9 Martin Brodeur MM .12 .30
10 Brett Hull MM .07 .20
11 Mike Vernon MM .02 .10
12 Trevor Linden MM .60 .15
13 Pat LaFontaine MM .02 .10
14 Geoff Sanderson MM .02 .10
15 Cam Neely MM .02 .10
16 Brendan Shanahan MM .07 .20
17 Jason Arnott MM .01 .05
18 Mikael Renberg MM .02 .10
19 Mats Sundin MM .07 .20
20 Pavel Bure MM .07 .20
21 Pierre Turgeon MM .02 .10
22 Alexei Zhamnov MM .01 .05
23 Blaine Lacher .02 .10
24 Brian Holzinger RC .07 .20
25 Theo Fleury .02 .10
26 Eric Daze .02 .10
27 Mike Kennedy .01 .05
28 Darren McCarty .01 .05
29 Todd Marchant .01 .05
30 Andrew Cassels .01 .05
31 Rob Niedermayer .02 .10
32 Eric Lacroix .01 .05
33 Steve Rucchin .01 .05
34 Turner Stevenson .01 .05
35 Sergei Brylin .01 .05
36 Mathieu Schneider .01 .05
37 Pat Verbeek .01 .05
38 Steve Larouche RC .01 .05
39 Rod Brind'Amour .02 .10
40 Luc Robitaille .02 .10
41 Brett Lindros .01 .05
42 Shean Donovan .01 .05
43 David Roberts .01 .05
44 Cory Cross .01 .05
45 Todd Warriner .01 .05
46 Yevgeny Namestnikov .01 .05
47 Sergei Gonchar .01 .05
48 Nikolai Khabibulin .02 .10
49 Alexei Zhitnik .01 .05
50 Ray Bourque .10 .30
51 Paul Kruse .01 .05
52 Murray Craven .01 .05
53 Andy Moog .07 .20
54 Keith Primeau .01 .05
55 Shayne Corson .01 .05
56 Johan Garpenlov .01 .05
57 Marek Malik .01 .05
58 Tony Granato .01 .05
59 Bob Corkum .01 .05
60 Patrick Roy .40 1.00
61 Chris McAlpine RC .01 .05
62 Chris Marinucci RC .01 .05
63 Jeff Beukeboom .01 .05
64 Radek Bonk .01 .05
65 John LeClair .07 .20
66 Len Barrie .01 .05
67 Teppo Numminen .01 .05
68 Ray Whitney .02 .10
69 Jeff Norton .01 .05
70 Chris Gratton .01 .05
71 Benoit Hogue .01 .05
72 Bret Hedican .01 .05
73 Keith Jones .02 .10
74 John Cullen .01 .05
75 Brian Leetch .02 .10
76 Dave Reid .01 .05
77 Dino Ciccarelli .02 .10
78 Gary Roberts .01 .05
79 Tony Amonte .02 .10
80 Mike Modano .10 .30
81 Doug Brown .01 .05
82 Scott Thornton .01 .05
83 Bill Lindsay .01 .05
84 Frantisek Kucera .01 .05
85 Wayne Gretzky .50 1.25
86 Joe Sacco .01 .05
87 Benoit Brunet .01 .05
88 Bill Guerin .02 .10
89 Travis Green .02 .10
90 Alexei Kovalev .01 .05
91 Stanislav Neckar .01 .05
92 Rob Dimaio .01 .05
93 Chris Joseph .01 .05
94 Craig Martin RC .01 .05
95 Craig Janney .01 .05
96 Greg Gilbert .01 .05
97 Alexander Semak .01 .05
98 Mike Gartner .02 .10
99 Cliff Ronning .01 .05
100 Mario Lemieux .40 1.00
101 Jassen Cullimore .01 .05
102 Steve Duchesne .01 .05
103 Derek Plante .01 .05
104 John Gruden .01 .05
105 Michal Sykora .01 .05
106 Trent Klatt .01 .05
107 Nicklas Lidstrom .07 .20
108 Luke Richardson .01 .05
109 Steven Rice .01 .05
110 Stu Barnes .01 .05
111 John Druce .01 .05
112 Guy Hebert .02 .10
113 Vladimir Malakhov .01 .05
114 Claude Lemieux .01 .05
115 Kirk Muller .01 .05
116 Darren Langdon RC .01 .05
117 Rob Gaudreau .01 .05
118 Karl Dykhuis .01 .05
119 Richard Park .01 .05
120 Dave Manson .01 .05
121 Andrei Nazarov .01 .05
122 Bernie Nicholls .01 .05
123 Mikael Andersson .01 .05
124 Todd Gill .01 .05
125 Trevor Linden .02 .10
126 Kelly Miller .01 .05
127 Don Sweeney .01 .05
128 Jason Dawe .01 .05
129 Steve Chiasson .01 .05
130 Ed Belfour .07 .20
131 Kerry Huffman .01 .05
132 Tim Taylor .01 .05
133 Kirk Maltby .02 .10
134 Jody Hull .01 .05
135 Sean Burke .02 .10
136 Philippe Boucher .01 .05
137 Valeri Karpov .01 .05
138 Yves Racine .01 .05
139 Patrick Flatley .01 .05
140 John MacLean .02 .10
141 Sergei Nemchinov .01 .05
142 Don Beaupre .02 .10
143 Kevin Dineen .01 .05
144 Ulf Samuelsson .01 .05
145 Al MacInnis .02 .10
146 Igor Korolev .01 .05
147 Pat Falloon .01 .05
148 Brian Bradley .01 .05
149 Josef Beranek .01 .05
150 Mats Sundin .07 .20
151 Sylvain Cote .01 .05
152 Keith Tkachuk .07 .20
153 Mariusz Czerkawski .01 .05
154 Trevor Kidd .02 .10
155 Garry Galley .01 .05
156 Gary Suter .01 .05
157 Grant Ledyard .01 .05
158 Doug Weight .02 .10
159 Jesse Belanger .01 .05
160 Mike Vernon .02 .10
161 Robert Kron .01 .05
162 Marty McSorley .01 .05
163 Todd Krygier .01 .05
164 Scott Niedermayer .01 .05
165 Mark Recchi .02 .10
166 Phil Housley .02 .10
167 Ron Hextall .02 .10
168 Richard Smehlik .01 .05
169 Chris Tamer .01 .05
170 Alexei Yashin .01 .05
171 Sergei Makarov .01 .05
172 Patrice Tardif .01 .05
173 Milos Holan .01 .05
174 J.C. Bergeron .01 .05
175 Dave Andreychuk .02 .10
176 Martin Gelinas .01 .05
177 Dale Hunter .02 .10
178 Kevin Haller .01 .05
179 Jeff Shantz .01 .05
180 Adam Oates .02 .10
181 Ronnie Stern .01 .05
182 Jamie Langenbrunner .02 .10
183 Mark Fitzpatrick .02 .10
184 Adam Burt .01 .05
185 Sergei Fedorov .10 .30
186 Robert Lang .01 .05
187 Craig Conroy RC .01 .05
188 Ken Daneyko .01 .05
189 Marko Tuomainen .01 .05
190 Ken Wregget .02 .10
191 Mike Rathje .01 .05
192 Dimitri Yushkevich .01 .05
193 Roman Hamrlik .02 .10
194 Russ Courtnall .01 .05
195 Teemu Selanne .07 .20
196 Jon Rohloff .01 .05
197 Derian Hatcher .01 .05
198 Mark Tinordi .01 .05
199 Patrice Brisebois .01 .05
200 Jaromir Jagr .10 .30
201 Randy McKay .01 .05
202 Derek King .01 .05
203 Tony Twist .02 .10
204 Jyrki Lumme .01 .05
205 Steve Smith .01 .05
206 Bob Rouse .01 .05
207 Dave Ellett .01 .05
208 Kevin Dean .01 .05
209 Rusty Fitzgerald RC .01 .05
210 Jim Carey .02 .10
211 Kenny Jonsson .01 .05
212 Mike Richter .07 .20
213 Glen Wesley .01 .05
214 Donald Audette .01 .05
215 Curtis Joseph .07 .20
216 Joe Juneau .01 .05
217 Paul Kariya .07 .20
218 1995 Stanley Cup Champions .02 .10
219 Checklist 1-110 .01 .05
220 Checklist 111-220 .01 .05
221 Cam Neely .07 .20
222 Wayne Primeau RC .01 .05
223 Yanic Perreault .01 .05
224 Pierre Turgeon .02 .10
225 Alexander Mogilny .02 .10
226 Daren Puppa .02 .10
227 Ulf Dahlen .01 .05
228 Tomas Sandstrom .01 .05
229 Shayne Corson .01 .05
230 Chris Chelios .07 .20
231 Stephane Richer .02 .10
232 Paul Ranheim .01 .05
233 Joe Nieuwendyk .02 .10
234 Doug Gilmour .02 .10
235 Jeremy Roenick .08 .25
236 Joel Otto .01 .05
237 Steve Yzerman .40 1.00
238 Petr Klima .01 .05
239 Jari Kurri .07 .20
240 Mark Messier .07 .20
241 Bill Ranford .02 .10
242 Grant Fuhr .07 .20
243 Brent Severyn .01 .05
244 Ron Francis .02 .10
245 Ray Ferraro .01 .05
246 Martin Straka .01 .05
247 Gerald Diduck .01 .05
248 Dimitri Khristich .01 .05
249 Wade Flaherty RC .02 .10
250 Pat LaFontaine .07 .20
251 Darren Turcotte .01 .05
252 John Vanbiesbrouck .02 .10
253 Brian Bellows .01 .05
254 Dave Gagner .01 .05
255 Larry Murphy .02 .10
256 Steve Thomas .02 .10
257 Robert Svehla RC .01 .05
258 Deron Quint .01 .05
259 Kjell Samuelsson .01 .05
260 Scott Mellanby .01 .05
261 Dan Quinn .01 .05
262 Tom Barrasso .02 .10
263 Zarley Zalapski .01 .05
264 Rick Tocchet .02 .10
265 Paul Coffey .07 .20
266 Joe Sakic .15 .40
267 Aki Berg RC .02 .10
268 Jeff Brown .01 .05
269 Wendel Clark .02 .10
270 Vincent Damphousse .01 .05
271 Dale Hawerchuk .07 .20
272 Rhett Warrener RC .01 .05
273 Kevin Hatcher .01 .05
274 Calle Johansson .01 .05
275 Scott Stevens .02 .10
276 Geoff Courtnall .01 .05
277 Kirk McLean .02 .10
278 Steve Heinze .01 .05
279 Sylvain Lefebvre .01 .05
280 Joe Murphy .01 .05
281 Mike Keane .01 .05
282 Kevin Stevens .01 .05
283 Miroslav Satan RC .25 .60
284 Stephane Fiset .02 .10
285 Jeff O'Neill .01 .05
286 Denny Lambert RC .01 .05
287 Marcus Ragnarsson RC .02 .10
288 Adam Deadmarsh .01 .05
289 Eric Weinrich .01 .05
290 Eric Desjardins .02 .10
291 Tim Cheveldae .02 .10
292 Glenn Healy .02 .10
293 Byron Dafoe .02 .10
294 Tom Fitzgerald .01 .05
295 Adam Graves .01 .05
296 Arturs Irbe UER front Aturs .02 .10
297 Shaun Van Allen .01 .05
298 Kelly Buchberger .01 .05
299 Bob Probert .05 .15
300 Pavel Bure .07 .20
301 Chad Kilger RC .01 .05
302 Dominik Hasek .15 .40
303 Bobby Holik .01 .05
304 Petr Nedved .02 .10
305 Owen Nolan .02 .10
306 Saku Koivu .07 .20
307 Rob Blake .02 .10
308 Chris Pronger .07 .20
309 Kyle McLaren RC .01 .05
310 Peter Bondra .02 .10
311 Nelson Emerson .01 .05
312 Bryan McCabe .01 .05
313 Darcy Wakaluk .02 .10
314 Shane Doan RC .25 .60
315 Felix Potvin .07 .20
316 Jim Dowd .01 .05
317 Roman Oksiuta .01 .05
318 Geoff Sanderson .01 .05
319 Radek Dvorak RC .15 .40
320 Paul Ysebaert .01 .05
321 Shawn McEachern .01 .05
322 Vyacheslav Kozlov .02 .10
323 Marty McInnis .01 .05

324 Ted Donato .01 .05
325 Martin Brodeur .20 .50
326 Patrick Poulin .01 .05
327 Eric Lindros .20 .50
328 Dallas Drake .01 .05
329 Sean Hill .01 .05
330 Michal Pivonka .01 .05
331 Alexei Zhamnov .02 .10
332 Cory Stillman .01 .05
333 Sergei Zubov .01 .05
334 Tommy Soderstrom .02 .10
335 Patrik Carnback .01 .05
336 Joe Dziedzic .01 .05
337 Steve Duchesne .01 .05
338 Marty Murray .01 .05
339 Todd Bertuzzi RC .50 1.25
340 Jason Arnott .01 .05
341 Niklas Sundstrom .02 .10
342 Alexandre Daigle .01 .05
343 Jocelyn Thibault .07 .20
344 Mikhail Shtalenkov .01 .05
345 Chris Osgood .02 .10
346 Brendan Witt .01 .05
347 Ian Laperriere .01 .05
348 Zigmund Palffy .02 .10
349 Brian Savage .01 .05
350 Mike Peca .02 .10
351 Vitali Yachmenev .01 .05
352 Luc Robitaille .02 .10
353 Mikael Renberg .02 .10
354 Ed Jovanovski .07 .20
355 Jason Doig .01 .05
356 Todd Harvey .02 .10
357 Viktor Kozlov .02 .10
358 Valeri Bure .01 .05
359 Peter Forsberg .20 .50
360 Jeff Friesen .01 .05
361 Andrei Nikolishin .01 .05
362 Brian Rolston .01 .05
363 Jamie Storr .02 .10
364 Chris Therien .01 .05
365 Oleg Tverdovsky .01 .05
366 David Oliver .01 .05
367 Alexander Selivanov .01 .05
368 Alex Stojanov .01 .05
369 Daniel Alfredsson RC .25 .60
370 Brendan Shanahan .07 .20
371 Yuri Khmylev .01 .05
372 Brett Hull .08 .25
373 Sergei Fedorov MM .07 .20
374 Jaromir Jagr MM .07 .20
375 Wayne Gretzky MM .40 1.00
376 Alexander Mogilny MM .02 .10
377 Patrick Roy MM .30 .75
378 Ed Belfour MM .07 .20
379 Luc Robitaille MM .02 .10
380 Peter Forsberg MM .07 .20
381 Adam Oates MM .02 .10
382 Theo Fleury MM .01 .05
383 Jim Carey MM .01 .05
384 Checklist 221-304 .01 .05
385 Checklist 305-385 .01 .05

1995-96 Topps O-Pee-Chee Parallel

The 1995-96 OPC Insert set is a parallel to the 1995-96 Topps set. The set is identical save for the silver foil OPC logo in place of the gold foil Topps. The cards were inserted one per second series Canadian foil pack; cards from both series were included in this manner and were not available in separate packs as in the past. Several of the cards on the D printing sheet were short printed according to Topps Canada.
COMPLETE SET (385)
*VETS: 6X TO 15X BASIC TOPPS
*ROOKIES: 2.5X TO 6X TOPPS
*SP's: 10X TO 25X TOPPS

1995-96 Topps Canadian Gold

These ten cards featured some of the top players to don their whites in Canadian rinks; they were randomly inserted at a rate of 1:36 series 1 Canadian retail packs. These packs, unlike the American ones, contained just five cards each.
COMPLETE SET (10) 30.00 60.00
1CG Patrick Roy 12.50 30.00
2CG Alexei Yashin 2.00 5.00
3CG Jason Arnott 2.00 5.00
4CG Trevor Kidd 2.00 5.00
5CG Pavel Bure 2.50 6.00
6CG Theo Fleury 2.00 5.00
7CG Pierre Turgeon 2.00 5.00
8CG Felix Potvin 2.50 6.00
9CG Teemu Selanne 2.50 6.00
10CG Mats Sundin 2.50 6.00

1995-96 Topps Canadian World Juniors

The cards in this set, featuring the member of the World Champion Canadian junior team, could be found randomly inserted at a rate of 1:18 series one Canadian Topps packs.
COMPLETE SET (22) 10.00 20.00
1CJ Wade Redden .60 1.50
2CJ Jamie Storr .60 1.50
3CJ Larry Courville .40 1.00
4CJ Jason Allison .60 1.50
5CJ Alexandre Daigle .40 1.00
6CJ Marty Murray .40 1.00
7CJ Bryan McCabe .60 1.50
8CJ Ryan Smyth .75 2.00
9CJ Lee Sorochan .40 1.00
10CJ Todd Harvey .40 1.00
11CJ Nolan Baumgartner .40 1.00
12CJ Denis Pederson .40 1.00
13CJ Shean Donovan .40 1.00
14CJ Jason Botterill .40 1.00
15CJ Jeff Friesen .40 1.00
16CJ Darcy Tucker .60 1.50
17CJ Chad Allan .40 1.00
18CJ Dan Cloutier .60 1.50
19CJ Eric Daze .40 1.00
20CJ Jeff O'Neill .40 1.00
21CJ Jamie Rivers .40 1.00
22CJ Ed Jovanovski .60 1.50

1995-96 Topps Hidden Gems

The cards in this chase set focus on star players who were mined in the sixth round or later of the NHL entry draft. The cards were randomly inserted in series 1 packs at a rate of 1:24.
COMPLETE SET (15) 8.00 20.00
1HG Theo Fleury .75 2.00
2HG Luc Robitaille .75 2.00
3HG Doug Gilmour .75 2.00
4HG Dominik Hasek 2.00 5.00
5HG Pavel Bure 1.25 3.00
6HG Peter Bondra .75 2.00
7HG Steve Larmer .40 1.00
8HG David Oliver .40 1.00
9HG Gary Suter .40 1.00
10HG Brett Hull 1.25 3.00
11HG Kevin Stevens .40 1.00
12HG Ron Hextall .75 2.00
13HG Kirk McLean .40 1.00
14HG Andy Moog .75 2.00
15HG Rick Tocchet .40 1.00

1995-96 Topps Home Grown Canada

These cards, randomly inserted in Canadian series two retail packs only (HGC1-HGC15) at a rate of 1:36 and randomly inserted in Canadian series 2 hobby packs only (HGC16-HGC30) at a rate of 1:36, feature players born in the Great White North. The hobby-only cards are somewhat harder to find, as Topps announced that an indeterminate number of the 1-15 cards were inserted in their place, resulting in fewer of the 16-30 cards being released.
COMPLETE SET (30) 40.00 80.00
HGC1 Patrick Roy 6.00 15.00
HGC2 Wendel Clark .60 1.50
HGC3 Pierre Turgeon .60 1.50
HGC4 Doug Gilmour .60 1.50
HGC5 Theo Fleury .30 .75
HGC6 Eric Lindros 1.25 3.00
HGC7 Paul Kariya 1.25 3.00
HGC8 Bill Ranford .60 1.50
HGC9 Ray Bourque 2.00 5.00
HGC10 Brendan Shanahan 1.25 3.00
HGC11 Paul Coffey 1.25 3.00
HGC12 Trevor Linden .60 1.50
HGC13 Trevor Kidd .60 1.50
HGC14 Alexandre Daigle .30 .75
HGC15 Chris Pronger 1.25 3.00
HGC16 Steve Yzerman 6.00 15.00
HGC17 Todd Harvey .60 1.50
HGC18 Felix Potvin 1.25 3.00
HGC19 Luc Robitaille .60 1.50
HGC20 Wayne Gretzky 8.00 20.00
HGC21 Keith Primeau .30 .75
HGC22 Al MacInnis .60 1.50
HGC23 Cam Neely 1.25 3.00
HGC24 Ed Belfour 1.25 3.00
HGC25 Joe Juneau .30 .75
HGC26 Adam Graves .30 .75
HGC27 Mark Recchi .60 1.50
HGC28 Stephane Richer .60 1.50
HGC29 Mark Messier 1.25 3.00
HGC30 Mario Lemieux 6.00 15.00

1995-96 Topps Home Grown USA

This 10-card set features some of the top US-born players in the NHL. The cards were randomly inserted at a rate of 1:36 series two US packs.
COMPLETE SET (10) 10.00 20.00
HGA1 Brian Leetch .60 1.50
HGA2 Jeremy Roenick 1.50 4.00
HGA3 Mike Modano 2.00 5.00
HGA4 Pat LaFontaine 1.25 3.00
HGA5 Keith Tkachuk 1.25 3.00
HGA6 Chris Chelios 1.25 3.00
HGA7 Darren Turcotte .30 .75
HGA8 John Vanbiesbrouck .60 1.50
HGA9 John LeClair 1.25 3.00
HGA10 Mike Richter 1.25 3.00

1995-96 Topps Marquee Men Power Boosters

This 33-card set is a parallel to the Marquee Men cards found in the base Topps issue, with numbering on the back matching those cards as well. Cards 1-22 were randomly inserted in series 1 packs at a rate of 1:36; cards 373-383 used the same odds in series 2 packs. Because there were more cards distributed throughout the series 1 production run (22 to 11) the series one cards are somewhat more difficult to acquire. These cards can be differentiated from the base issues by the use of much thicker 28-point card stock and the prismatic foil front.
1 Eric Lindros 2.00 5.00
2 Dominik Hasek 1.50 4.00
3 Jeremy Roenick 2.00 5.00
4 Paul Coffey 1.50 4.00
5 Mark Messier 1.50 4.00
6 Peter Bondra .75 2.00
7 Paul Kariya 1.50 4.00
8 Chris Chelios 1.50 4.00
9 Martin Brodeur 2.50 6.00
10 Brett Hull 1.50 4.00
11 Mike Vernon .75 2.00
12 Trevor Linden 1.25 3.00
13 Pat LaFontaine .75 2.00
14 Geoff Sanderson .75 2.00
15 Cam Neely .75 2.00
16 Brendan Shanahan 1.50 4.00
17 Jason Arnott .40 1.00
18 Mikael Renberg .75 2.00
19 Mats Sundin 1.50 4.00
20 Pavel Bure 1.50 4.00
21 Pierre Turgeon .75 2.00
22 Alexei Zhamnov .40 1.00
373 Sergei Fedorov 1.50 4.00
374 Jaromir Jagr 1.50 4.00
375 Wayne Gretzky 8.00 20.00
376 Alexander Mogilny .75 2.00
377 Patrick Roy 6.00 15.00
378 Ed Belfour 1.50 4.00
379 Luc Robitaille .75 2.00
380 Peter Forsberg 1.50 4.00
381 Adam Oates .75 2.00
382 Theo Fleury .40 1.00
383 Jim Carey .40 1.00

1995-96 Topps Mystery Finest

These unique chase cards featured three top positional stars on the back and an opaque protective foil covering on the front. When removed, it would reveal a full frontal shot of one of the three players on the back, hence the mystery. The cards, which utilized the Finest technology, were randomly inserted 1:36 series 2 packs. A parallel refractor version of the set also existed. These cards were much more difficult to pull, coming out of 1:216 packs. Multipliers for these cards are included in the headers below.
COMPLETE SET (22) 50.00 100.00
*REFRACTORS: 1.5X TO 4X BASIC INSERTS
M1 Wayne Gretzky 8.00 20.00
M2 Mario Lemieux 8.00 20.00
M3 Mark Messier 1.50 4.00
M4 Eric Lindros 2.00 5.00
M5 Sergei Fedorov 2.50 6.00
M6 Joe Sakic 3.00 8.00
M7 Brett Hull 2.00 5.00
M8 Jaromir Jagr 2.50 6.00
M9 Teemu Selanne 1.50 4.00
M10 Brendan Shanahan 1.50 4.00
M11 Cam Neely 1.50 4.00
M12 Mikael Renberg .75 2.00
M13 Paul Kariya 1.50 4.00
M14 Keith Tkachuk 1.50 4.00
M15 Pavel Bure 1.50 4.00
M16 Brian Leetch .75 2.00
M17 Scott Stevens .75 2.00
M18 Chris Chelios 1.50 4.00
M19 Dominik Hasek 3.00 8.00
M20 Patrick Roy 8.00 20.00
M21 Martin Brodeur 4.00 10.00
M22 Felix Potvin 2.00 5.00

1995-96 Topps New To The Game

This 22-card set featured some of the top players just beginning to make their marks in the NHL. The cards were inserted one per US series 1 retail packs.
COMPLETE SET (22) 3.00 8.00
1NG Jim Carey .20 .50
2NG Sergei Brylin .08 .25
3NG Todd Marchant .08 .25
4NG Oleg Tverdovsky .08 .25
5NG Paul Kariya .40 1.00
6NG Adam Deadmarsh .08 .25
7NG Mike Kennedy .08 .25
8NG Roman Oksiuta .08 .25
9NG Kenny Jonsson .08 .25
10NG Peter Forsberg 1.00 2.50
11NG Alexander Selivanov .08 .25
12NG Chris Therien .08 .25
13NG Brian Rolston .08 .25
14NG David Oliver .08 .25
15NG Blaine Lacher .20 .50
16NG Sergei Krivokrasov .08 .25
17NG Todd Harvey .20 .50
18NG Jeff Friesen .08 .25
19NG Mariusz Czerkawski .08 .25
20NG Ian Laperriere .08 .25
21NG Brian Savage .08 .25
22NG Andrei Nikolishin .08 .25

1995-96 Topps Power Lines

These ten three player-cards feature the top lines of the 1994-95 NHL season. The cards were randomly inserted in 1:12 series 1 packs.
COMPLETE SET (10) 4.00 10.00
1PL Lindros/LeClair/Renberg .40 1.00
2PL Tkachuk/Selanne/Zhamnov .40 1.00
3PL Graves/Messier/Verbeek .40 1.00
4PL Poulin/Roenick/Amonte .40 1.00
5PL Stevens/Jagr/Francis .75 2.00
6PL Dawe/LaFon./Mogilny .40 1.00
7PL Oates/Neely/Czerkawski .40 1.00
8PL Kozlov/Fedorov/Brown 1.00 2.50
9PL Damp./Turgeon/Recchi .40 1.00
10PL Peluso/Holik/McKay .40 1.00

1995-96 Topps Profiles

Mark Messier knows a bit about hockey, as he demonstrates here with his choices of and commentary on some of the game's finest. The cards were inserted in both series 1 (1-10) and series 2 (11-20) packs at a rate of 1:12.
COMPLETE SET (20) 12.00 30.00
PF1 Wayne Gretzky 4.00 10.00
PF2 Brian Leetch .30 .75
PF3 Patrick Roy 2.50 6.00
PF4 Jaromir Jagr 1.00 2.50
PF5 Sergei Fedorov 1.00 2.50
PF6 Martin Brodeur 1.50 4.00
PF7 Eric Lindros .60 1.50
PF8 Jeremy Roenick .75 2.00
PF9 John Vanbiesbrouck .30 .75
PF10 Cam Neely .60 1.50
PF11 Pavel Bure .60 1.50
PF12 Paul Coffey .60 1.50
PF13 Scott Stevens .30 .75
PF14 Dominik Hasek 1.25 3.00
PF15 Mario Lemieux 2.50 6.00
PF16 Ed Belfour .60 1.50
PF17 Doug Gilmour .30 .75
PF18 Teemu Selanne .60 1.50
PF19 Brett Hull .75 2.00
PF20 Joe Sakic 1.25 3.00

1995-96 Topps Rink Leaders

Topps selected players who are top guys both on the ice and in the dressing room for this ten-card tribute. The cards were randomly inserted in series 1 hobby packs at a rate of 1:36.
COMPLETE SET (10) 30.00 60.00
1RL Mark Messier 2.00 5.00
2RL Mario Lemieux 8.00 20.00
3RL Ray Bourque 3.00 8.00
4RL Brett Hull 2.50 6.00
5RL Pat LaFontaine 2.00 5.00
6RL Scott Stevens 1.00 2.50
7RL Keith Tkachuk 2.00 5.00
8RL Doug Gilmour 1.00 2.50
9RL Chris Chelios 2.00 5.00
10RL Wayne Gretzky 12.50 30.00

1995-96 Topps Young Stars

Topps honors fifteen of the brightest young stars in the game with this set which utilizes the Power Matrix printing technology. The cards were randomly inserted at 1:24 series 2 packs.
COMPLETE SET (15) 12.00 25.00
YS1 Paul Kariya 1.00 2.50
YS2 Martin Brodeur 2.50 6.00
YS3 Mikael Renberg .50 1.25
YS4 Peter Forsberg 2.50 6.00
YS5 Alexei Yashin UER .25 .60
YS6 Jeff Friesen .25 .60
YS7 Oleg Tverdovsky .25 .60
YS8 Jim Carey .50 1.25
YS9 Alexei Kovalev .25 .60
YS10 Jason Arnott .25 .60
YS11 Teemu Selanne 1.00 2.50
YS12 Chris Osgood .50 1.25
YS13 Roman Hamrlik .50 1.25
YS14 Scott Niedermayer .25 .60
YS15 Jaromir Jagr 1.50 4.00

1998-99 Topps

The 1998-99 Topps set was issued in one series totaling 242 cards. The 11-card packs retail for $1.29 each. The fronts featured color action photos and the backs carried player information and statistics.
1 Peter Forsberg .25 .60
2 Petr Sykora .10 .25
3 Byron Dafoe .12 .30
4 Ron Francis .20 .50
5 Alexei Yashin .12 .30
6 Dave Ellett .12 .30
7 Jamie Langenbrunner .10 .25
8 Doug Weight .15 .40
9 Jason Woolley .10 .25
10 Paul Coffey .15 .40
11 Uwe Krupp .10 .25
12 Tomas Sandstrom .10 .25
13 Scott Mellanby .10 .25
14 Vladimir Tsyplakov .10 .25
15 Martin Rucinsky .10 .25
16 Mikael Renberg .12 .30
17 Marco Sturm .10 .25
18 Eric Lindros .25 .60
19 Sean Burke .10 .25
20 Martin Brodeur .30 .75
21 Boyd Devereaux .10 .25
22 Kelly Buchberger .10 .25
23 Scott Stevens .15 .40
24 Jamie Storr .12 .30
25 Anders Eriksson .10 .25
26 Gary Suter .10 .25
27 Theo Fleury .20 .50
28 Steve Leach .10 .25
29 Felix Potvin .15 .40
30 Brett Hull .25 .60
31 Mike Grier .10 .25
32 Cale Hulse .10 .25
33 Larry Murphy .12 .30
34 Rick Tocchet .12 .30
35 Eric Desjardins .12 .30
36 Igor Kravchuk .10 .25
37 Rob Niedermayer .10 .25
38 Bryan Smolinski .10 .25
39 Valeri Kamensky .10 .25
40 Ryan Smyth .12 .30
41 Bruce Driver .10 .25
42 Mike Johnson .10 .25
43 Rob Zamuner .10 .25
44 Steve Duchesne .12 .30
45 Martin Straka .10 .25
46 Bill Houlder .10 .25
47 Craig Conroy .10 .25
48 Guy Hebert .12 .30
49 Colin Forbes .10 .25
50 Mike Modano .25 .60
51 Jamie Pushor .10 .25
52 Jarome Iginla .30 .75
53 Paul Kariya .20 .50
54 Mattias Ohlund .10 .25
55 Sergei Berezin .12 .30
56 Peter Zezel .10 .25
57 Teppo Numminen .10 .25
58 Dale Hunter .12 .30
59 Sandy Moger .10 .25
60 John LeClair .15 .40
61 Wade Redden .10 .25
62 Patrik Elias .15 .40
63 Rob Blake .15 .40
64 Todd Marchant .10 .25
65 Claude Lemieux .12 .30
66 Trevor Kidd .10 .25
67 Sergei Fedorov .25 .60
68 Joe Sakic .25 .60
69 Derek Morris .10 .25
70 Alexei Morozov .10 .25
71 Mats Sundin .15 .40
72 Daymond Langkow .10 .25
73 Kevin Hatcher .10 .25
74 Damian Rhodes .15 .40
75 Brian Leetch .15 .40
76 Saku Koivu .15 .40
77 Rick Tabaracci .10 .25
78 Bernie Nicholls .10 .25
79 Alyn McCauley .10 .25
80 Patrice Brisebois .10 .25
81 Bret Hedican .10 .25
82 Sandy McCarthy .10 .25
83 Viktor Kozlov .12 .30
84 Derek King .10 .25
85 Alexander Selivanov .10 .25
86 Mike Vernon .12 .30
87 Jeff Beukeboom .10 .25
88 Tommy Salo .12 .30
89 Adam Graves .10 .25
90 Randy McKay .12 .30
91 Rich Pilon .10 .25
92 Richard Zednik .10 .25
93 Jeff Hackett .10 .25
94 Michael Peca .10 .25
95 Brent Gilchrist .10 .25
96 Stu Grimson .10 .25
97 Bob Probert .10 .25
98 Stu Barnes .10 .25
99 Ruslan Salei .10 .25
100 Al MacInnis .15 .40
101 Ken Daneyko .10 .25
102 Paul Ranheim .10 .25
103 Marty McInnis .10 .25
104 Marian Hossa .12 .30
105 Darren McCarty .10 .25
106 Guy Carbonneau .10 .25
107 Dallas Drake .10 .25
108 Sergei Samsonov .12 .30
109 Teemu Selanne .30 .75
110 Checklist .02 .10
111 Jaromir Jagr .40 1.00
112 Joe Thornton .30 .75
113 Jon Klemm .10 .25
114 Grant Fuhr .15 .40
115 Nikolai Khabibulin .15 .40
116 Rod Brind'Amour .15 .40
117 Trevor Linden .12 .30
118 Vincent Damphousse .12 .30
119 Dino Ciccarelli .15 .40
120 Pat Verbeek .10 .25
121 Sandis Ozolinsh .10 .25
122 Garth Snow .12 .30
123 Ed Belfour .15 .40
124 Keith Primeau .10 .25
125 Jason Allison .12 .30
126 Peter Bondra .12 .30
127 Ulf Samuelsson .12 .30
128 Jeff Friesen .10 .25
129 Jason Bonsignore .10 .25
130 Daniel Alfredsson .15 .40
131 Bobby Holik .10 .25
132 Jozef Stumpel .12 .30
133 Brian Bellows .12 .30
134 Chris Osgood .15 .40
135 Alexei Zhamnov .10 .25
136 Mattias Norstrom .10 .25
137 Drake Berehowsky .10 .25
138 Mark Messier .25 .60
139 Geoff Courtnall .12 .30
140 Marc Bureau .10 .25
141 Don Sweeney .10 .25
142 Wendel Clark .12 .30
143 Scott Niedermayer .15 .40
144 Chris Therien .10 .25
145 Kirk Muller .10 .25
146 Wayne Primeau .10 .25
147 Tony Granato .10 .25
148 Derian Hatcher .10 .25
149 Daniel Briere .12 .30
150 Fredrik Olausson .10 .25
151 Joe Juneau .12 .30
152 Michal Grosek .10 .25
153 Janne Laukkanen .10 .25
154 Keith Tkachuk .15 .40
155 Marty McSorley .10 .25
156 Owen Nolan .15 .40
157 Mark Tinordi .10 .25
158 Steve Washburn .10 .25
159 Luke Richardson .10 .25
160 Kris King .10 .25
161 Joe Nieuwendyk .15 .40
162 Travis Green .10 .25
163 Dominik Hasek .30 .75
164 Dimitri Khristich .10 .25
165 Dave Manson .10 .25
166 Chris Chelios .15 .40
167 Claude LaPointe .10 .25
168 Kris Draper .10 .25
169 Brad Isbister .10 .25
170 Patrick Marleau .15 .40
171 Jeremy Roenick .25 .60
172 Darren Langdon .10 .25
173 Kevin Dineen .10 .25
174 Luc Robitaille .15 .40
175 Steve Yzerman .50 1.25
176 Sergei Zubov .10 .25
177 Ed Jovanovski .12 .30
178 Sami Kapanen .10 .25
179 Adam Oates .15 .40
180 Pavel Bure .20 .50
181 Chris Pronger .12 .30
182 Pat Falloon .10 .25
183 Darcy Tucker .10 .25
184 Zigmund Palffy .15 .40
185 Curtis Brown .10 .25
186 Curtis Joseph .15 .40
187 Valeri Zelepukin .10 .25
188 Russ Courtnall .10 .25
189 Adam Foote .10 .25
190 Patrick Roy .40 1.00
191 Cory Stillman .10 .25
192 Alexei Zhitnik .10 .25
193 Olaf Kolzig .15 .40
194 Mark Fitzpatrick .10 .25
195 Eric Daze .12 .30
196 Zarley Zalapski .10 .25
197 Niklas Sundstrom .10 .25
198 Bryan Berard .12 .30
199 Jason Arnott .12 .30
200 Mike Richter .15 .40
201 Ken Baumgartner .10 .25
202 Jason Dawe .10 .25
203 Nicklas Lidstrom .20 .50
204 Tony Amonte .12 .30
205 Kjell Samuelsson .10 .25
206 Ray Bourque .25 .60
207 Alexander Mogilny .12 .30
208 Pierre Turgeon .15 .40
209 Tom Barrasso .12 .30
210 Richard Matvichuk .10 .25
211 Sergei Krivokrasov .10 .25
212 Ted Drury .10 .25
213 Matthew Barnaby .10 .25
214 Denis Pederson .10 .25
215 John Vanbiesbrouck .12 .30
216 Brendan Shanahan .20 .50
217 Jocelyn Thibault .12 .30
218 Nelson Emerson .10 .25
219 Wayne Gretzky .75 2.00
220 Checklist .02 .10
221 Ramzi Abid RC .10 .25
222 Mark Bell RC .10 .25
223 Michael Henrich RC .10 .25
224 Vincent Lecavalier .30 .75
225 Rico Fata .12 .30
226 Bryan Allen .10 .25
227 Daniel Tkaczuk .10 .25
228 Brad Stuart RC .10 .25
229 Derrick Walser RC .10 .25
230 Jonathan Cheechoo RC 3.00 8.00
231 Sergei Varlamov .10 .25
232 Scott Gomez RC 2.00 5.00
233 Jeff Heerema RC .10 .25
234 David Legwand .10 .25
235 Manny Malhotra .15 .40
236 Michael Rupp RC .12 .30
237 Alex Tanguay .12 .30
238 Mathieu Biron RC .12 .30
239 Bujar Amidovski RC .12 .30
240 Brian Finley RC .12 .30
241 Philippe Sauve RC .75 2.00
242 Jiri Fischer RC .12 .30

1998-99 Topps O-Pee-Chee Parallel

This 242-card parallel set, offered only in Canadian hobby packs, offers the same players as the Topps base set, but was emblazoned with the O-Pee-Chee foil stamp logo.
*1-220 VETS: 5X TO 12X BASIC CARDS
*221-242 ROOKIES: 1.5X TO 4X

1998-99 Topps Autographs

Randomly inserted into packs at the rate of 1:209, this nine-card set features autographed color action player photos with player information on the backs.
A1 Jason Allison 4.00 10.00
A2 Sergei Samsonov 6.00 15.00
A3 John LeClair 8.00 20.00
A4 Mattias Ohlund 4.00 10.00
A5 Jaromir Jagr 25.00 60.00
A6 Keith Tkachuk 6.00 15.00
A7 Patrik Elias 4.00 10.00
A8 Dominik Hasek 25.00 60.00
A9 Brian Leetch 8.00 20.00

1998-99 Topps Blast From The Past

Randomly inserted in packs at a rate of 1:23, this 10-card insert set features early reprint cards of true heroes of the game including Gordie Howe, Phil Esposito and Stan Mikita. These cards resemble the originals in every way except a small note on the back that states "Reprint X of 10".
COMPLETE SET (10) 25.00 50.00
1 Wayne Gretzky 12.50 30.00
2 Mark Messier 4.00 10.00
3 Ray Bourque 5.00 12.00
4 Patrick Roy 6.00 15.00
5 Grant Fuhr 2.50 6.00
6 Brett Hull 3.00 8.00
7 Gordie Howe 5.00 12.00
8 Stan Mikita 2.50 6.00
9 Bobby Hull 3.00 8.00
10 Phil Esposito 2.50 6.00

1998-99 Topps Blast From The Past Autographs

Randomly inserted into packs at the rate of 1:1878, this 4-card set mirrored the basic inserts but included autographs of the retired players. The Mikita card had insertion odds of 1:3756.
7 Gordie Howe 60.00 150.00
8 Stan Mikita 30.00 80.00
9 Bobby Hull 40.00 100.00
10 Phil Esposito 30.00 80.00

1998-99 Topps Board Members

Randomly inserted in packs at a rate of 1:36, this 15-card insert features color action photography of superstar defensemen on vibrant foilboard.
COMPLETE SET (15) 10.00 25.00
B1 Chris Pronger 1.25 3.00
B2 Chris Chelios 1.50 4.00
B3 Brian Leetch 1.50 4.00
B4 Ray Bourque 2.00 5.00
B5 Mattias Ohlund .75 2.00
B6 Nicklas Lidstrom 1.50 4.00
B7 Sergei Zubov .75 2.00
B8 Scott Niedermayer .75 2.00
B9 Larry Murphy .75 2.00
B10 Sandis Ozolinsh .75 2.00
B11 Rob Blake 1.25 3.00
B12 Scott Stevens .75 2.00
B13 Derian Hatcher .75 2.00
B14 Kevin Hatcher .75 2.00
B15 Wade Redden .75 2.00

1998-99 Topps Ice Age 2000

Randomly inserted in packs at a rate of 1:12, this 15-card insert was printed with dot-matrix technology.
COMPLETE SET (15) 8.00 15.00
I1 Paul Kariya .60 1.50
I2 Marco Sturm .20 .50
I3 Jarome Iginla .75 2.00
I4 Denis Pederson .20 .50
I5 Wade Redden .20 .50
I6 Jason Allison .20 .50
I7 Chris Pronger .50 1.25
I8 Peter Forsberg 1.50 4.00
I9 Saku Koivu .60 1.50
I10 Eric Lindros .60 1.50
I11 Sergei Samsonov .50 1.25
I12 Mattias Ohlund .50 1.25
I13 Joe Thornton 1.00 2.50
I14 Mike Johnson .20 .50
I15 Nikolai Khabibulin .50 1.25

1998-99 Topps Local Legends

Randomly inserted in packs at a rate of 1:18, this worldly 15-card insert honors players on foilboard cards that actually depict that player's country of origin.
COMPLETE SET (15) 30.00 60.00
L1 Peter Forsberg 2.50 6.00
L2 Mats Sundin 1.00 2.50
L3 Zigmund Palffy .75 2.00
L4 Jaromir Jagr 1.50 4.00
L5 Dominik Hasek 2.00 5.00
L6 Martin Brodeur 2.50 6.00
L7 Wayne Gretzky 8.00 20.00
L8 Patrick Roy 5.00 12.00
L9 Eric Lindros 1.00 2.50
L10 Joe Sakic 2.00 5.00
L11 Mark Messier 1.00 2.50
L12 Mike Modano 1.50 4.00
L13 Sergei Fedorov 1.50 4.00
L14 Pavel Bure 1.00 2.50
L15 Teemu Selanne 1.00 2.50

1998-99 Topps Mystery Finest Bronze

Sequentially numbered and arranged by jersey (home, away and All-Star), this 20-card insert honors the 20 best players in the NHL today. The set was also grouped and randomly inserted in Bronze 1:36; Silver 1:72; and Gold 1:108 variations. Refractor parallels for each color were also created and inserted at the following rates: bronze at 1:108, silver at 1:216, and gold at 1:324.
COMPLETE SET (20) 40.00 80.00
*BRONZE REF.: .7X TO 1.5X BASIC INSERTS
*GOLD: .8X TO 2X BASIC INSERTS
*GOLD REF.: 4X TO 8X BASIC INSERTS
*SILVER: .6X TO 1.5X BASIC INSERTS
*SILVER REF.: 1X TO 2.5X BASIC INSERTS
M1 Teemu Selanne 1.50 4.00
M2 Olaf Kolzig 1.25 3.00
M3 Pavel Bure 1.50 4.00
M4 Wayne Gretzky 8.00 20.00
M5 Mike Modano 2.50 6.00
M6 Jaromir Jagr 2.50 6.00
M7 Dominik Hasek 3.00 8.00
M8 Peter Forsberg 4.00 10.00
M9 Eric Lindros 1.50 4.00
M10 John LeClair 1.50 4.00
M11 Zigmund Palffy 1.25 3.00
M12 Martin Brodeur 4.00 10.00
M13 Keith Tkachuk 1.50 4.00
M14 Peter Bondra 1.25 3.00
M15 Nicklas Lidstrom 1.50 4.00
M16 Patrick Roy 6.00 15.00
M17 Chris Chelios 1.25 3.00
M18 Saku Koivu 1.50 4.00
M19 Mark Messier 1.50 4.00
M20 Joe Sakic 3.00 8.00

1998-99 Topps Mystery Finest Gold

Sequentially numbered and arranged by jersey (home, away and All-Star), this 20-card insert honors the 20 best players in the NHL today. The set was also grouped and randomly inserted in Bronze 1:36; Silver 1:72; and Gold 1:108 variations.
M1 Teemu Selanne 2.50 6.00
M2 Olaf Kolzig 2.00 5.00
M3 Pavel Bure 2.50 6.00
M4 Wayne Gretzky 15.00 30.00
M5 Mike Modano 4.00 10.00
M6 Jaromir Jagr 4.00 10.00
M7 Dominik Hasek 5.00 12.00
M8 Peter Forsberg 5.00 12.00
M9 Eric Lindros 2.50 6.00
M10 John LeClair 2.50 6.00
M11 Zigmund Palffy 2.00 5.00
M12 Martin Brodeur 8.00 20.00
M13 Keith Tkachuk 2.50 6.00
M14 Peter Bondra 2.00 5.00
M15 Nicklas Lidstrom 3.00 8.00
M16 Patrick Roy 10.00 25.00
M17 Chris Chelios 2.00 5.00
M18 Saku Koivu 2.50 6.00
M19 Mark Messier 3.00 8.00
M20 Joe Sakic 6.00 15.00

1998-99 Topps Mystery Finest Silver

M1 Teemu Selanne 2.50 6.00
M2 Olaf Kolzig 2.00 5.00
M3 Pavel Bure 2.50 6.00
M4 Wayne Gretzky 15.00 40.00
M5 Mike Modano 3.00 8.00
M6 Jaromir Jagr 3.00 8.00
M7 Dominik Hasek 4.00 10.00
M8 Peter Forsberg 6.00 15.00
M9 Eric Lindros 2.50 6.00
M10 John LeClair 2.50 6.00
M11 Zigmund Palffy 2.00 5.00
M12 Martin Brodeur 8.00 20.00
M13 Keith Tkachuk 2.50 6.00
M14 Peter Bondra 2.00 5.00
M15 Nicklas Lidstrom 2.50 6.00
M16 Patrick Roy 10.00 25.00
M17 Chris Chelios 2.00 5.00
M18 Saku Koivu 2.00 5.00
M19 Mark Messier 2.50 6.00
M20 Joe Sakic 5.00 12.00

1998-99 Topps Season's Best

andomly inserted in packs at a rate of 1:8, this 30-card insert features color action photography in five distinct categories: NetMinders salutes the league's top goalies, Sharpshooters features the top scoring leaders, Puck Providers showcases assist leaders, Performers Plus features those that lead ice time by plus/minus ratio, and Ice Hot introduces the powerful rookies.
COMPLETE SET (30) 15.00 40.00
SB1 Dominik Hasek 1.50 4.00
SB2 Martin Brodeur 2.00 5.00
SB3 Ed Belfour .75 2.00
SB4 Curtis Joseph .75 2.00
SB5 Jeff Hackett .60 1.50
SB6 Tom Barrasso .60 1.50
SB7 Mike Johnson .30 .75
SB8 Sergei Samsonov .60 1.50
SB9 Patrik Elias .60 1.50
SB10 Patrick Marleau .60 1.50
SB11 Mattias Ohlund .60 1.50
SB12 Marco Sturm .30 .75
SB13 Teemu Selanne .75 2.00
SB14 Peter Bondra .60 1.50
SB15 Pavel Bure .75 2.00
SB16 John LeClair 1.00 2.50
SB17 Zigmund Palffy .60 1.50
SB18 Keith Tkachuk .75 2.00
SB19 Jaromir Jagr 1.25 3.00
SB20 Wayne Gretzky 4.00 10.00
SB21 Peter Forsberg 1.25 3.00
SB22 Ron Francis .60 1.50
SB23 Adam Oates .60 1.50
SB24 Jozef Stumpel .60 1.50
SB25 Chris Pronger .60 1.50
SB26 Larry Murphy .60 1.50
SB27 Jason Allison .30 .75
SB28 John LeClair .75 2.00
SB29 Randy McKay .30 .75
SB30 Dainius Zubrus .30 .75

1999-00 Topps Arena Giveaways

These promo cards were issued in various NHL cities as part of a stadium giveaway program that included six cards per team. Manufacturers Topps, Upper Deck, and Pacific were all represented with two cards per team set.
COMPLETE SET (30) 15.00 30.00
ANALK Ladislav Kohn .20 .50
ANAOT Oleg Tverdovsky .20 .50
ATLMJ Matt Johnson .20 .50
ATLPS Patrik Stefan .40 1.00
BOSJG Jonathan Girard .20 .50
BOSJT Joe Thornton 1.50 4.00
BUFMA Maxim Afinogenov .40 1.00
BUFMB Martin Biron .40 1.00
CALDG Denis Gauthier .20 .50
CALRR Robyn Regehr .20 .50
CARBB Bates Battaglia .20 .50
CARDT David Tanabe .20 .50
CHIED Eric Daze .20 .50
CHIJD J-P Dumont .20 .50
COLAT Alex Tanguay .40 1.00
COLMD Marc Denis .40 1.00
DALBM Brenden Morrow .75 2.00
DALJS Jon Sim .20 .50
DETJF Jiri Fischer .20 .50
DETMD Mathieu Dandenault .20 .50
EDMGL Georges Laraque .40 1.00
EDMPC Paul Comrie .20 .50
FLOIN Ivan Novoseltsev .20 .50
FLOOK Oleg Kvasha .20 .50
LAFK Frantisek Kaberle .20 .50
LAJS Jamie Storr .40 1.00
NASDL David Legwand .20 .50
NASTV Tomas Vokoun .40 1.00
NJPE Patrik Elias .20 .50
NJSG Scott Gomez .20 .50
NYIOJ Olli Jokinen .20 .50
NYIRL Roberto Luongo 2.00 5.00
NYRKJ Kim Johnsson .20 .50
NYRMY Mike York .20 .50
OTTMF Mike Fisher .20 .50
OTTMH Marian Hossa .40 1.00
PHORS Radoslav Suchy .20 .50
PHOTL Trevor Letowski .20 .50
PITAF Andrew Ference .20 .50
PITJH Jan Hrdina .20 .50
SJBS Brad Stuart .20 .50
SJMS Marco Sturm .20 .50
STLJH Jochen Hecht .20 .50
STLTN Tyson Nash .20 .50
TBPM Paul Mara .20 .50
TBVL Vincent Lecavalier 1.25 3.00
TORNA Nikolai Antropov .40 1.00
TORTK Tomas Kaberle .20 .50
VANEJ Ed Jovanovski .20 .50
VANSK Steve Kariya .40 1.00
WASJH Jeff Halpern .20 .50
WASRZ Richard Zednik .20 .50

1999-00 Topps

Released as a 286-card set, there are actually a total of 330-cards in this release. Five versions of cards 276-286 were released. The complete set prices below reflect sets with one version of cards 276-286. Base cards feature full color action shots with blue borders and gold foil highlights. The O-Pee-Chee version of this set exactly parallels the base set but with the O-Pee-Chee logo.
COMPLETE SET (275) 25.00 50.00
COMP.SET w/MMs (330) 60.00 120.00
1 Joe Sakic .25 .60
2 Alexei Yashin .12 .30
3 Paul Kariya .20 .50
4 Keith Tkachuk .15 .40
5 Jaromir Jagr .40 1.00
6 Mike Modano .25 .60
7 Eric Lindros .25 .60

Zigmund Palffy .15 .40
Dominik Hasek .25 .60
0 Pavel Bure .20 .50
1 Ray Bourque .25 .60
2 Peter Forsberg .15 .40
3 Al MacInnis .15 .40
4 Steve Yzerman .50 1.25
5 Mats Sundin .15 .40
6 Patrick Roy .60 1.50
7 Teemu Selanne .30 .75
8 Keith Primeau .10 .25
9 John LeClair .15 .40
20 Martin Brodeur .30 .75
21 Joe Thornton .25 .60
22 Rob Blake .15 .40
23 Ron Francis .20 .50
24 Grant Fuhr .15 .40
25 Nicklas Lidstrom .15 .40
26 Vladimir Orszagh RC .10 .25
27 Glen Wesley .10 .25
28 Adam Deadmarsh .10 .25
29 Zdeno Chara .15 .40
30 Brian Leetch .15 .40
31 Valeri Bure .10 .25
32 Ryan Smyth .12 .30
33 Jean-Sebastien Aubin .12 .30
34 Dave Reid .10 .25
35 Ed Jovanovski .12 .30
36 Anders Eriksson .10 .25
37 Mike Ricci .12 .30
38 Todd Bertuzzi .12 .30
39 Shawn Bates .10 .25
40 Kip Miller .10 .25
41 Jozef Stumpel .10 .25
42 Jeremy Roenick .15 .40
43 Todd Marchant .10 .25
44 Josh Holden .10 .25
45 Rob Niedermayer .10 .25
46 Cory Sarich .10 .25
47 Nikolai Khabibulin .12 .30
48 Marty McInnis .10 .25
49 Marty Reasoner .10 .25
50 Gary Roberts .10 .25
51 Manny Malhotra .12 .30
52 Adam Foote .12 .30
53 Luc Robitaille .15 .40
54 Bryan Marchment .12 .30
55 Mark Janssens .10 .25
56 Steve Heinze .10 .25
57 Cory Stillman .10 .25
58 Guy Hebert .15 .40
59 Mike Richter .15 .40
60 Jamie Langenbrunner .10 .25
61 Wade Redden .10 .25
62 Steve Smith .10 .25
63 Daniil Markov .10 .25
64 Erik Rasmussen .10 .25
65 Glen Murray .12 .30
66 Alexei Kovalev .12 .30
67 Peter Bondra .12 .30
68 Dimitri Khristich .10 .25
69 Sami Kapanen .10 .25
70 Tom Poti .10 .25
71 Trevor Linden .15 .40
72 Tomas Vokoun .15 .40
73 Steve Webb .10 .25
74 Jarome Iginla .15 .40
75 Scott Mellanby .10 .25
76 Mattias Ohlund .12 .30
77 Steve Konowalchuk .10 .25
78 Bryan Berard .10 .25
79 Chris Pronger .12 .30
80 Teppo Numminen .10 .25
81 John MacLean .12 .30
82 Jeff Hackett .10 .25
83 Ray Whitney .12 .30
84 Chris Osgood .15 .40
85 Doug Zmolek .10 .25
86 Curtis Brown .10 .25
87 Reid Simpson .10 .25
88 Milan Hejduk .12 .30
89 Donald Audette .10 .25
90 Saku Koivu .15 .40
91 Martin Straka .10 .25
92 Mark Messier .25 .60
93 Richard Zednik .10 .25
94 Curtis Joseph .15 .40
95 Colin Forbes .10 .25
96 Jeff Friesen .12 .30
97 Eric Brewer .10 .25
98 Darius Kasparaitis .12 .30
99 Marian Hossa .12 .30
100 Petr Sykora .12 .30
101 Vladimir Malakhov .10 .25
102 Jamie Storr .10 .25
103 Doug Gilmour .20 .50
104 Doug Weight .15 .40
105 Derian Hatcher .12 .30
106 Chris Drury .12 .30
107 Arturs Irbe .12 .30
108 Fred Brathwaite .10 .25
109 Jason Allison .12 .30
110 Roman Hamrlik .12 .30
111 Rico Fata .10 .25
112 Janne Niinimaa .10 .25
113 Kenny Jonsson .10 .25
114 Marco Sturm .12 .30
115 Steve Thomas .10 .25
116 Garth Snow .12 .30
117 Rick Tocchet .12 .30
118 Jean-Marc Pelletier .10 .25
119 Bobby Holik .10 .25
120 Sergei Fedorov .25 .60
121 J-P Dumont .12 .30
122 Jason Woolley .10 .25
123 James Patrick .10 .25
124 Blake Sloan .12 .30
125 Marcus Nilsson .10 .25
126 Shayne Corson .10 .25
127 Tom Fitzgerald .10 .25
128 Brian Rolston .12 .30
129 Ron Tugnutt .12 .30
130 Mark Recchi .20 .50
131 Matthew Barnaby .12 .30
132 Olaf Kolzig .15 .40
133 Paul Mara .10 .25
134 Patrick Marleau .15 .40
135 Magnus Arvedson .10 .25
136 Felix Potvin .25 .60
137 Bill Guerin .15 .40
138 Brett Hull .25 .60
139 Vitali Yachmenev .10 .25
140 Ruslan Salei .10 .25
141 Mark Parrish .10 .25
142 Randy Cunneyworth .10 .25
143 Damian Rhodes .10 .25
144 Daniel Briere .12 .30
145 Craig Conroy .10 .25
146 Sergei Gonchar .10 .25
147 Vincent Lecavalier .12 .30
148 Adam Graves .12 .30
149 Doug Bodger .10 .25
150 Jeff O'Neill .10 .25
151 Darby Hendrickson .10 .25
152 Sergei Samsonov .12 .30
153 Ed Belfour .15 .40
154 Robert Svehla .10 .25
155 Cliff Ronning .10 .25
156 Brendan Morrison .12 .30
157 Daniel Alfredsson .15 .40
158 Eric Desjardins .12 .30
159 Mike Vernon .12 .30
160 Vadim Sharifijanov .10 .25
161 Jaroslav Svejkovsky .10 .25
162 Michael Peca .12 .30
163 Shane Willis .10 .25
164 Sandis Ozolinsh .10 .25
165 Mathieu Dandenault .10 .25
166 Martin Rucinsky .10 .25
167 Scott Stevens .15 .40
168 Sami Salo .12 .30
169 Tom Barrasso .15 .40
170 Chris Gratton .10 .25
171 Markus Naslund .15 .40
172 Mike Johnson .12 .30
173 Bob Boughner .10 .25
174 Todd Simpson .10 .25
175 Fredrik Olausson .10 .25
176 Jocelyn Thibault .12 .30
177 Juha Ylonen .10 .25
178 Brad Bombardir .10 .25
179 Jan Hrdina .10 .25
180 Adrian Aucoin .10 .25
181 Mike Eagles .10 .25
182 Petr Nedved .10 .25
183 Rem Murray .10 .25
184 Mikael Renberg .10 .25
185 Mike Eastwood .10 .25
186 Byron Dafoe .10 .25
187 Tony Amonte .12 .30
188 Darren McCarty .10 .25
189 Sergei Krivokrasov .10 .25
190 Dave Lowry .10 .25
191 Michal Handzus .12 .30
192 Tie Domi .12 .30
193 Brian Holzinger .10 .25
194 Jason Arnott .12 .30
195 Jose Theodore .15 .40
196 Brendan Shanahan .20 .50
197 Derek Morris .10 .25
198 Steve Rucchin .10 .25
199 Kevin Hodson .10 .25
200 Oleg Kvasha .10 .25
201 John Vanbiesbrouck .12 .30
202 Adam Oates .15 .40
203 Anson Carter .12 .30
204 Sebastien Bordeleau .10 .25
205 Pavol Demitra .20 .50
206 Owen Nolan .15 .40
207 Pavel Rosa .10 .25
208 Petr Svoboda .12 .30
209 Tomas Kaberle .10 .25
210 Claude Lapointe .12 .30
211 Todd Harvey .10 .25
212 Trent McCleary .10 .25
213 Vyacheslav Kozlov .10 .25
214 Marc Denis .12 .30
215 Joe Nieuwendyk .15 .40
216 Kelly Buchberger .10 .25
217 Tommy Albelin .10 .25
218 Kyle McLaren .10 .25
219 Chris Chelios .15 .40
220 Joel Bouchard .10 .25
221 Mats Lindgren .10 .25
222 Jyrki Lumme .10 .25
223 Pierre Turgeon .15 .40
224 Bill Muckalt .10 .25
225 Antti Aalto .10 .25
226 Jere Lehtinen .12 .30
227 Theo Fleury .20 .50
228 Dmitri Mironov .10 .25
229 Scott Niedermayer .15 .40
230 Sean Burke .10 .25
231 Eric Daze .12 .30
232 Alexei Zhitnik .10 .25
233 Christian Matte .10 .25
234 Patrik Elias .15 .40
235 Alexandre Korolyuk .10 .25
236 Sergei Berezin .10 .25
237 Ray Ferraro .10 .25
238 Rod Brind'Amour .15 .40
239 Darcy Tucker .10 .25
240 Darryl Sydor .12 .30
241 Mike Dunham .10 .25
242 Marc Bergevin .10 .25
243 Ray Sheppard .10 .25
244 Miroslav Satan .12 .30
245 Andreas Dackell .10 .25
246 Mike Grier .10 .25
247 Alexei Zhamnov .10 .25
248 David Legwand .10 .25
249 Daniel Tkaczuk .10 .25
250 Roberto Luongo .20 .50
251 Simon Gagne .15 .40
252 Jamie Lundmark .12 .30
253 Alexandre Giroux RC .10 .25
254 Dusty Jamieson RC .12 .30
255 Jamie Chamberlain RC .12 .30
256 Radim Vrbata RC 1.50 4.00
257 Scott Cameron RC .12 .30
258 Simon LaJeunesse RC .30 .75
259 Tim Connolly .10 .25
260 Kris Beech .10 .25
261 Brian Finley .15 .40
262 Alex Auld RC .30 .75
263 Martin Grenier RC .12 .30
264 Sheldon Keefe RC .30 .75
265 Justin Mapletoft RC .12 .30
266 Edward Hill RC .12 .30
267 Nolan Yonkman RC .15 .40
268 Oleg Saprykin RC .15 .40
269 Branislav Mezei RC .10 .25
270 Chris Kelly RC .12 .30
271 Pavel Brendl RC .75 2.00
272 Brett Lysak RC .12 .30
273 Matt Carkner RC .12 .30
274 Luke Sellars RC .15 .40
275 Brad Ralph RC .12 .30
276A Ray Bourque MM .50 1.25
276B Ray Bourque MM .50 1.25
1996 All-Star MVP
276C Ray Bourque MM .50 1.25
5-time Norris Winner
276D Ray Bourque MM .50 1.25
1000 NHL Points
276E Ray Bourque MM .50 1.25
1980 Calder Trophy
277A Peter Forsberg MM .30 .75
277B Peter Forsberg MM .30 .75
3 All-Star Games
277C Peter Forsberg MM .30 .75
1994 Gold Medal
277D Peter Forsberg MM .30 .75
1994 Gold Medal Goal
277E Peter Forsberg MM .30 .75
1996 Stanley Cup
278A Joe Nieuwendyk MM .30 .75
278B Joe Nieuwendyk MM .30 .75
4 All-Star Games
278C Joe Nieuwendyk MM .30 .75
1999 Stanley Cup
278D Joe Nieuwendyk MM .30 .75
1999 Conn Smythe Trophy
278E Joe Nieuwendyk MM .30 .75
1988 Calder Trophy
279A Dominik Hasek MM .50 1.25
279B Dominik Hasek MM .50 1.25
5-time Vezina Winner
279C Dominik Hasek MM .50 1.25
2-time Pearson Winner
279D Dominik Hasek MM .50 1.25
4 All-Star Games
279E Dominik Hasek MM .50 1.25
1998 Gold Medal
280A Jaromir Jagr MM .75 2.00
280B Jaromir Jagr MM .75 2.00
1999 Hart Trophy
280C Jaromir Jagr MM .75 2.00
8 All-Star Games
280D Jaromir Jagr MM .75 2.00
3-time Scoring Leader
280E Jaromir Jagr MM .75 2.00
2-time Stanley Cup Winner
281A Paul Kariya MM .40 1.00
281B Paul Kariya MM .40 1.00
3 All-Star Games
281C Paul Kariya MM .40 1.00
50 goals 1995-96
281D Paul Kariya MM .40 1.00
1994 Silver Medal
281E Paul Kariya MM .40 1.00
1993 NCAA Champ
282A Eric Lindros MM .50 1.25
282B Eric Lindros MM .50 1.25
1992 Silver Medal
282C Eric Lindros MM .50 1.25
1995 Hart Trophy
282D Eric Lindros MM .50 1.25
1995 Pearson Award
282E Eric Lindros MM .50 1.25
5 All-Star Games
283A Mark Messier MM .50 1.25
283B Mark Messier MM .50 1.25
6-time Stanley Cup Winner
283C Mark Messier MM .50 1.25
13 All-Star Games
283D Mark Messier MM .50 1.25
2-time Hart Winner
283E Mark Messier MM .50 1.25
2-time Pearson Winner
284A Patrick Roy MM 1.25 3.00
284B Patrick Roy MM 1.25 3.00
8 All-Star Games
284C Patrick Roy MM 1.25 3.00
3-time Vezina Winner
284D Patrick Roy MM 1.25 3.00
2-time Conn Smythe Winner
284E Patrick Roy MM 1.25 3.00
Playoff Wins Leader
285A Joe Sakic MM .50 1.25
285B Joe Sakic MM .50 1.25
7 All-Star Games
285C Joe Sakic MM .50 1.25
1996 Stanley Cup
285D Joe Sakic MM .50 1.25
50 goals 1995-96
285E Joe Sakic MM .50 1.25
1996 Conn Smythe Trophy
286A Steve Yzerman MM 1.00 2.50
286B Steve Yzerman MM 1.00 2.50
8 All-Star Games
286C Steve Yzerman MM 1.00 2.50
1989 Pearson Award
286D Steve Yzerman MM 1.00 2.50
1998 Conn Smythe Trophy
286E Steve Yzerman MM 1.00 2.50
2-time Stanley Cup Winner

1999-00 Topps All-Topps

Randomly inserted in Topps and OPC packs at the rate of 1:18, this 15-card set features top players on a card with full color action shots and holographic foil highlights. Card backs carry an "AT" prefix.
COMPLETE SET (15) 20.00 40.00
AT1 Dominik Hasek 1.50 4.00
AT2 Martin Brodeur 2.00 5.00
AT3 Ray Bourque 1.25 3.00
AT4 Al MacInnis .75 2.00
AT5 Nicklas Lidstrom .75 2.00
AT6 Brian Leetch .75 2.00
AT7 John LeClair 1.00 2.50
AT8 Paul Kariya .75 2.00
AT9 Keith Tkachuk .75 2.00
AT10 Eric Lindros 1.25 3.00
AT11 Peter Forsberg 2.00 5.00
AT12 Steve Yzerman 4.00 10.00
AT13 Jaromir Jagr 1.25 3.00
AT14 Teemu Selanne .75 2.00
AT15 Pavel Bure 1.00 2.50

1999-00 Topps Autographs

Randomly inserted in Topps packs at the rate of 1:517, this 10-card set features authentic player autographs.
TA1 Joe Sakic 12.00 30.00
TA2 Dominik Hasek 15.00 40.00
TA3 Curtis Joseph 10.00 25.00
TA4 Alexei Yashin 8.00 20.00
TA5 Mats Sundin 15.00 40.00
TA6 Chris Drury 8.00 20.00
TA7 Milan Hejduk 10.00 25.00
TA8 Marian Hossa 10.00 25.00
TA9 Vincent Lecavalier 10.00 25.00
TA10 Joe Thornton 12.00 30.00

1999-00 Topps A-Men

COMPLETE SET (6) 6.00 12.00
STATED ODDS 1:10 TOPPS
AM1 Jaromir Jagr .75 2.00
AM2 Peter Forsberg 1.25 3.00
AM3 Paul Kariya 1.25 3.00
AM4 Teemu Selanne 1.25 3.00
AM5 Joe Sakic 1.00 2.50
AM6 Eric Lindros .75 2.00

1999-00 Topps Fantastic Finishers

COMPLETE SET (6) 3.00 8.00
STATED ODDS 1:10 TOPPS
FF1 Teemu Selanne .50 1.25
FF2 Jaromir Jagr .75 2.00
FF3 Tony Amonte .40 1.00
FF4 Alexei Yashin .40 1.00
FF5 John LeClair .60 1.50
FF6 Joe Sakic 1.00 2.50

1999-00 Topps Ice Futures

COMPLETE SET (6) 1.25 3.00
STATED ODDS 1:10 TOPPS
IF1 Mark Parrish .25 .60
IF2 Chris Drury .50 1.25
IF3 Bill Muckalt .25 .60
IF4 Marian Hossa .25 .60
IF5 Milan Hejduk .50 1.25
IF6 Brendan Morrison .50 1.25

1999-00 Topps Ice Masters

COMPLETE SET (20) 40.00 80.00
STATED ODDS 1:30 TOPPS
IM1 Joe Sakic 2.00 5.00
IM2 Dominik Hasek 2.00 5.00
IM3 Eric Lindros 1.50 4.00
IM4 Jaromir Jagr 1.50 4.00
IM5 John LeClair 1.25 3.00
IM6 Mats Sundin 1.25 3.00
IM7 Ray Bourque 1.50 4.00
IM8 Mike Modano 1.50 4.00
IM9 Peter Forsberg 2.50 6.00
IM10 Brian Leetch 1.25 3.00
IM11 Martin Brodeur 2.50 6.00
IM12 Al MacInnis 1.00 2.50
IM13 Paul Kariya 1.25 3.00
IM14 Alexei Yashin 1.00 2.50
IM15 Steve Yzerman 5.00 12.00
IM16 Ed Belfour 1.25 3.00
IM17 Keith Tkachuk 1.25 3.00
IM18 Patrick Roy 5.00 12.00
IM19 Nicklas Lidstrom 1.25 3.00
IM20 Teemu Selanne 1.25 3.00

1999-00 Topps Now Starring

COMPLETE SET (15) 10.00 20.00
STATED ODDS 1:18
NS1 Anson Carter .75 2.00
NS2 Marian Hossa .75 2.00
NS3 Michael Peca .75 2.00
NS4 Kenny Jonsson .60 1.50
NS5 Petr Sykora .60 1.50
NS6 Chris Drury .75 2.00
NS7 Byron Dafoe .75 2.00
NS8 Wade Redden .60 1.50
NS9 Jeff Friesen .60 1.50
NS10 Jamie Langenbrunner .60 1.50
NS11 Mike Johnson .60 1.50
NS12 Keith Primeau .60 1.50
NS13 Vincent Lecavalier .75 2.00
NS14 Mattias Ohlund .75 2.00
NS15 Pavol Demitra .75 2.00

1999-00 Topps Positive Performers

COMPLETE SET (6) 2.00 5.00
STATED ODDS 1:10 TOPPS
PP1 Alexander Karpovtsev .15 .40
PP2 John LeClair .60 1.50
PP3 Eric Lindros .75 2.00
PP4 Magnus Arvedson .15 .40
PP5 Al MacInnis .40 1.00
PP6 Jere Lehtinen .40 1.00

1999-00 Topps Postmasters

COMPLETE SET (6) 5.00 12.00
STATED ODDS 1:10 TOPPS
PM1 Dominik Hasek 1.00 2.50
PM2 Byron Dafoe .40 1.00
PM3 Nikolai Khabibulin .40 1.00
PM4 Ed Belfour .50 1.25
PM5 Patrick Roy 2.50 6.00
PM6 Martin Brodeur 1.25 3.00

1999-00 Topps Stanley Cup Heroes

Randomly inserted in Topps and OPC packs at the rate of 1:23, this 20-card die cut set features full color player shots in the foreground and the Stanley cup in the background. A refractor parallel was also created and inserted at a rate of 1:120.
COMPLETE SET (20) 50.00 120.00
*REFRACTORS: 1.5X TO 4X BASIC INSERTS
SC1 Mario Lemieux 6.00 15.00
SC2 Mike Bossy 4.00 10.00
SC3 Guy Lafleur 4.00 10.00
SC4 Rocket Richard 6.00 15.00
SC5 Lanny McDonald 2.00 5.00
SC6 Frank Mahovlich 2.00 5.00
SC7 Steve Yzerman 6.00 15.00
SC8 Mark Messier 4.00 10.00
SC9 Patrick Roy 6.00 15.00
SC10 Joe Sakic 4.00 10.00
SC11 Jaromir Jagr 4.00 10.00
SC12 Peter Forsberg 3.00 8.00
SC13 Claude Lemieux 1.50 4.00
SC14 Martin Brodeur 5.00 12.00
SC15 Brian Leetch 2.00 5.00
SC16 Mike Richter 3.00 8.00
SC17 Theo Fleury 2.00 5.00
SC18 Chris Osgood 4.00 10.00
SC19 Ed Belfour 4.00 10.00
SC20 Joe Nieuwendyk 2.00 5.00

1999-00 Topps Stanley Cup Heroes Autographs

Randomly inserted in Topps and OPC packs at the rate of 1:697, this 6-card set features a die cut card and authentic player autographs.
COMPLETE SET (6)
SCA1 Mario Lemieux 100.00 200.00
SCA2 Mike Bossy 40.00 80.00
SCA3 Guy Lafleur 40.00 100.00
SCA4 Maurice Richard 150.00 300.00
SCA5 Lanny McDonald 30.00 60.00
SCA6 Frank Mahovlich 30.00 60.00

1999-00 Topps Top of the World

COMPLETE SET (20) 30.00 80.00
STATED ODDS 1:30
TW1 Teemu Selanne 2.50 6.00
TW2 Saku Koivu 1.25 3.00
TW3 Jere Lehtinen 1.25 3.00
TW4 Peter Forsberg 2.50 6.00
TW5 Mats Sundin 1.50 4.00
TW6 Nicklas Lidstrom 2.00 5.00
TW7 Alexei Yashin 1.25 3.00
TW8 Nikolai Khabibulin 1.25 3.00
TW9 Pavel Bure 2.50 6.00
TW10 John LeClair 1.25 3.00
TW11 Keith Tkachuk 1.25 3.00
TW12 Mike Modano 4.00 10.00
TW13 Paul Kariya 1.50 4.00
TW14 Joe Sakic 4.00 10.00
TW15 Martin Brodeur 6.00 15.00
TW16 Dominik Hasek 2.50 6.00
TW17 Jaromir Jagr 4.00 10.00
TW18 Peter Bondra 1.25 3.00
TW19 Olaf Kolzig 1.25 3.00
TW20 Marco Sturm 1.25 3.00

2000 Topps AS Sittler

This single was issued as a wrapper redemption at the 2000 NHL All-Star Game by Topps.
1 Darryl Sittler 1.20 3.00

2000-01 Topps Promos

COMPLETE SET (6) .60 1.50
PP1 Mariusz Czerkawski .08 .20
PP2 Sami Kapanen .08 .20
PP3 Tommy Salo .20 .50
PP4 Radek Bonk .08 .20
PP5 Pat Verbeek .08 .20
PP6 Luc Robitaille .20 .50

2000-01 Topps

Released as a 330-card set, Topps features action player photography on each card with silver borders and gold foil highlights. Topps was packaged in 36-pack boxes with packs containing 10 cards and carried a suggested retail price of $1.29. The O-Pee-Chee release was essentially a parallel to Topps except for the company logo on the fronts and that card numbers 251-270 were exclusive to either Topps or O-Pee-Chee.
COMPLETE SET (330) 15.00 30.00
1 Jaromir Jagr .40 1.00
2 Patrick Roy .40 1.00
3 Paul Kariya .20 .50
4 Mats Sundin .15 .40
5 Ron Francis .20 .50
6 Pavel Bure .20 .50
7 John LeClair .15 .40
8 Olaf Kolzig .15 .40
9 Chris Pronger .12 .30
10 Jeremy Roenick .15 .40
11 Owen Nolan .15 .40
12 Theo Fleury .20 .50
13 Zigmund Palffy .15 .40
14 Patrik Stefan .12 .30
15 Jarome Iginla .15 .40
16 Joe Thornton .25 .60
17 Tony Amonte .12 .30
18 Mike Modano .25 .60
19 Alexander Mogilny .12 .30
20 Mark Messier .25 .60
21 Dominik Hasek .25 .60
22 Steve Yzerman .50 1.25
23 Marian Hossa .12 .30
24 David Legwand .15 .40
25 Jose Theodore .20 .50
26 Vincent Lecavalier .12 .30
27 Mike Ricci .12 .30
28 Scott Stevens .15 .40
29 Kevin Weekes .10 .25
30 Sean Burke .10 .25
31 Alexei Kovalev .12 .30
32 Trevor Linden .15 .40
33 Joe Juneau .12 .30
34 Niklas Sundstrom .10 .25
35 Dan Cloutier .12 .30
36 Drake Berehowsky .10 .25
37 Jonas Hoglund .10 .25
38 Sami Kapanen .10 .25
39 Matthew Barnaby .12 .30
40 Anson Carter .12 .30
41 Miroslav Satan .10 .25
42 Mark Recchi .20 .50
43 Pavol Demitra .20 .50
44 Peter Bondra .12 .30
45 Mike Richter .15 .40
46 Guy Hebert .12 .30
47 Robert Svehla .10 .25
48 Martin Skoula .12 .30
49 Ed Belfour .15 .40
50 Alexei Zhamnov .12 .30
51 Fred Brathwaite .12 .30
52 Andrew Brunette .10 .25
53 Byron Dafoe .12 .30
54 Claude Lemieux .12 .30
55 Sergei Berezin .10 .25
56 Felix Potvin .25 .60
57 Rod Brind'Amour .15 .40
58 Doug Gilmour .20 .50
59 Brett Hull .25 .60
60 Nicklas Lidstrom .15 .40
61 Mike York .10 .25
62 Al MacInnis .15 .40
63 Brian Boucher .12 .30
64 Teemu Selanne .30 .75
65 Mike Vernon .12 .30
66 Bill Guerin .15 .40
67 Ray Bourque .25 .60
68 Bryan McCabe .10 .25
69 Ray Ferraro .10 .25
70 Stephane Fiset .10 .25
71 Sergei Gonchar .10 .25
72 Mattias Ohlund .10 .25
73 Todd Marchant .10 .25
74 Derek Morris .10 .25
75 Brian Rolston .12 .30
76 Damian Rhodes .10 .25
77 Chris Drury .12 .30
78 Curtis Joseph .20 .50
79 Teppo Numminen .10 .25
80 Petr Nedved .12 .30
81 Doug Weight .15 .40
82 Arturs Irbe .12 .30
83 Chris Osgood .15 .40
84 Chris Gratton .10 .25
85 Jocelyn Thibault .12 .30
86 Oleg Tverdovsky .10 .25
87 Derian Hatcher .12 .30
88 Ray Whitney .12 .30
89 Saku Koivu .15 .40
90 Cliff Ronning .10 .25
91 Claude Lapointe .10 .25
92 Fredrik Modin .10 .25
93 Chris Simon .10 .25
94 Todd Harvey .12 .30
95 Martin Rucinsky .10 .25
96 Valeri Bure .12 .30
97 Brad Isbister .10 .25
98 Daymond Langkow .10 .25
99 Todd Bertuzzi .12 .30
100 Roman Turek .12 .30
101 Kenny Jonsson .10 .25
102 Mike Dunham .10 .25
103 Rob Blake .15 .40
104 Darius Kasparaitis .12 .30
105 Daniel Alfredsson .15 .40
106 Bobby Holik .10 .25
107 Tommy Salo .12 .30
108 Sergei Samsonov .12 .30
109 Joe Sakic .25 .60
110 Bryan Smolinski .12 .30
111 Luc Robitaille .15 .40
112 Ryan Smyth .12 .30
113 Eric Daze .12 .30
114 Mariusz Czerkawski .10 .25
115 Brendan Shanahan .20 .50
116 Brian Rafalski .10 .25
117 Mark Parrish .10 .25
118 Jamie Langenbrunner .12 .30
119 Peter Forsberg .20 .50
120 Phil Housley .12 .30
121 Jeff O'Neill .12 .30
122 Stu Barnes .12 .30
123 Glen Murray .10 .25
124 Jeff Hackett .10 .25
125 Sergei Fedorov .25 .60
126 Kyle McLaren .10 .25
127 Michael Nylander .10 .25
128 Sergei Zubov .10 .25
129 Steve Rucchin .12 .30
130 Nelson Emerson .10 .25
131 Martin Brodeur .30 .75
132 Mike Grier .10 .25
133 Paul Coffey .15 .40
134 Radek Bonk .12 .30
135 Marc Savard .12 .30
136 Milan Hejduk .12 .30
137 Curtis Brown .10 .25
138 Viktor Kozlov .12 .30
139 Jason Woolley .10 .25
140 Adam Foote .12 .30
141 Radek Dvorak .12 .30
142 Jason Arnott .12 .30
143 German Titov .10 .25
144 Scott Thornton .10 .25
145 Brendan Morrison .12 .30
146 Keith Tkachuk .15 .40
147 Patrik Elias .15 .40
148 Donald Audette .10 .25
149 Jochen Hecht .10 .25
150 Dave Scatchard .10 .25
151 Tom Barrasso .12 .30
152 Adam Deadmarsh .12 .30
153 Brian Leetch .15 .40
154 Sergei Krivokrasov .10 .25
155 Randy Robitaille .10 .25
156 Petr Sykora .12 .30
157 Dave Andreychuk .15 .40
158 Mathieu Biron .10 .25
159 Sergei Zholtok .10 .25
160 Shawn McEachern .10 .25
161 Steve Shields .12 .30
162 Petr Svoboda .10 .25
163 Nikolai Antropov .12 .30
164 Michal Handzus .10 .25
165 Martin Straka .12 .30
166 Shane Doan .12 .30
167 Eric Desjardins .12 .30
168 Peter Schaefer .10 .25
169 Adam Oates .15 .40
170 Scott Niedermayer .15 .40
171 Dallas Drake .10 .25
172 Josh Green .10 .25
173 Mike Sillinger .10 .25
174 Adam Graves .12 .30
175 Lubos Bartecko .10 .25
176 Steve Konowalchuk .10 .25
177 Jozef Stumpel .10 .25
178 Vincent Damphousse .12 .30
179 Tomas Kaberle .10 .25
180 Maxim Afinogenov .10 .25
181 Marty McInnis .12 .30
182 Chris Chelios .15 .40
183 Joe Nieuwendyk .15 .40
184 Petr Buzek .12 .30
185 Calle Johansson .10 .25
186 Jeff Friesen .10 .25
187 Paul Mara .10 .25
188 Markus Naslund .12 .30
189 Scott Young .10 .25
190 Trevor Letowski .10 .25
191 Steve Thomas .10 .25
192 Martin Biron .12 .30
193 Jason Allison .12 .30
194 Bob Probert .12 .30
195 Jere Lehtinen .10 .25
196 Tom Poti .10 .25
197 Eric Lindros .25 .60
198 Rob Niedermayer .12 .30
199 Gary Roberts .10 .25
200 Richard Zednik .10 .25
201 Dainius Zubrus .10 .25
202 Tom Fitzgerald .10 .25
203 Scott Gomez .12 .30
204 Travis Green .10 .25
205 Pierre Turgeon .15 .40
206 Ed Jovanovski .12 .30
207 Trevor Kidd .10 .25
208 Jan Hrdina .10 .25
209 Valeri Zelepukin .10 .25
210 Vaclav Prospal .10 .25
211 Matt Cullen .10 .25
212 Karlis Skrastins .10 .25
213 Robyn Regehr .10 .25
214 Darren McCarty .10 .25
215 John Madden .12 .30
216 Scott Mellanby .10 .25
217 Tim Connolly .10 .25
218 Pat Verbeek .12 .30
219 Richard Matvichuk .10 .25
220 Rick Tocchet .12 .30
221 Jan Hlavac .10 .25
222 Jeff Halpern .10 .25
223 Patrick Marleau .15 .40
224 Robert Lang .10 .25
225 Wade Redden .10 .25
226 Stephane Richer .10 .25
227 Kim Johnsson .10 .25
228 Greg Adams .10 .25
229 Alex Tanguay .12 .30
230 Andre Savage .10 .25
231 Slava Kozlov .12 .30
232 Steve Sullivan .10 .25
233 Alexander Selivanov .10 .25
234 Tommy Westlund .10 .25
235 Darcy Tucker .10 .25
236 Simon Gagne .15 .40
237 Brad Stuart .12 .30
238 Jean-Sebastien Aubin .12 .30
239 Mike Johnson .10 .25
240 Shayne Corson .10 .25
241 Michael Peca .12 .30
242 Keith Primeau .10 .25
243 Martin Lapointe .12 .30
244 Tie Domi .25 .60
245 Janne Niinimaa .10 .25
246 Brenden Morrow .12 .30
247 Sandis Ozolinsh .12 .30
248 Ron Tugnutt .12 .30
249 Andrei Nazarov .10 .25
250 Bates Battaglia .10 .25
251A Dean Sylvester .10 .25
252A Hal Gill .10 .25
253A Vladimir Tsyplakov .10 .25
254A Sean Hill .10 .25
255A Michal Grosek .10 .25
256A Darryl Sydor .10 .25
257A Igor Larionov .15 .40
258A Jaroslav Spacek .10 .25
259A Mattias Norstrom .10 .25
260A Ladislav Kohn .10 .25
261A Patric Kjellberg .10 .25
262A Marty Reasoner .10 .25
263A Zdeno Chara .15 .40
264A Mathieu Schneider .10 .25
265A John Vanbiesbrouck .12 .30
266A Jyrki Lumme .10 .25
267A Janne Laukkanen .10 .25
268A Alexander Korolyuk .10 .25
269A Pavel Kubina .10 .25
270A Ulf Dahlen .10 .25
271 Roberto Luongo .25 .60
272 Harold Druken .10 .25
273 Marc Denis .12 .30
274 Oleg Saprykin .10 .25
275 Glen Metropolit .10 .25
276 Mark Eaton .10 .25
277 Dmitri Yakushin .10 .25
278 Scott Hannan .10 .25
279 Dave Tanabe .10 .25
280 Jiri Fischer .10 .25
281 Dmitri Nabokov .10 .25
282 Ivan Novoseltsev .10 .25
283 Manny Fernandez .12 .30
284 Maxim Balmochnyk .10 .25
285 Brian Campbell .10 .25
286 Sergei Varlamov .10 .25
287 Ville Nieminen RC .10 .25
288 Colin White RC .10 .25
289 Mike Fisher .12 .30
290 Matt Elich RC .12 .30
291 Zenith Komarniski .10 .25
292 Eric Nickulas RC .10 .25
293 Steven McCarthy .10 .25
294 Jason Krog .10 .25
295 Robert Esche .10 .25
296 Adam Mair .10 .25
297 Ladislav Nagy .10 .25
298 S.Vyshedkevich RC .10 .25
299 Steve Begin .10 .25
300 Brad Ference .10 .25
301 Andy Delmore .10 .25
302 Brent Sopel RC .15 .40
303 Evgeni Nabokov .12 .30
304 David Gosselin RC .12 .30
305 Tavis Hansen .10 .25
306 Ray Giroux .10 .25
307 Serge Aubin RC .12 .30
308 Shane Willis .10 .25
309 Vitali Vishnevski .10 .25
310 Richard Jackman .10 .25
311 Petr Schastlivy .10 .25
312 Ryan Bonni .10 .25
313 Alexei Tezikov .10 .25
314 Zac Bierk .10 .25
315 Mike Ribeiro .12 .30
316 Darryl Laplante .10 .25
317 Kyle Calder .10 .25
318 Dimitri Kalinin .10 .25
319 Jean-Sebastien Giguere .12 .30
320 Willie Mitchell RC .15 .40
321 Stephen Valiquette RC .12 .30
322 Brian Willsie .10 .25
323 Jarkko Ruutu .10 .25
324 Jon Sim .10 .25
325 Jonathan Girard .10 .25
326 Martin Brodeur HL .30 .75
327 Ray Bourque HL .25 .60
328 The Bure Brothers HL .20 .50
329 Steve Yzerman HL .50 1.25
330 Brett Hull HL .25 .60
CL1 Checklist 1 .12 .30
CL2 Checklist 2 .12 .30
CL3 Checklist 3 .12 .30

2000-01 Topps Foil Parallel

Randomly inserted in Topps packs at the rate of 1:39 and OPC packs at the rate of 1:31, this 330-card set parallels the base Topps/OPC set on cards enhanced with an all foil card stock. Each card is sequentially numbered to 100. Topps Parallels are found in O-Pee-Chee packs and O-Pee-Chee Parallels are found in Topps packs. Card numbers 251-270 were exclusive to either Topps or OPC.
*FOIL/100: 15X TO 40X BASIC CARDS
20 Mark Messier 12.00 30.00

2000-01 Topps Autographs

Randomly inserted in packs at the rate of 1:502, this 11-card set features authentic player autographs on a card front that has action photography set against a whiteout background.
ACP Chris Pronger 6.00 15.00
AFB Fred Brathwaite 6.00 15.00
AJL John LeClair 10.00 25.00
AJT Jose Theodore 12.50 30.00
AMM Mike Modano 15.00 40.00
AMR Mark Recchi 6.00 15.00
ARB Ray Bourque 30.00 80.00
ART Roman Turek 6.00 15.00
ASG Scott Gomez 6.00 15.00

2000-01 Topps Combos

Randomly inserted in Topps packs at the rate of 1:12 and OPC packs at the rate of 1:24, this 10-card set features original artist rendered pictures that pair up some of the NHL's finest.
COMPLETE SET (10) 15.00 40.00
*JUMBOS: .5X TO 1.2X BASIC INSERTS
JUMBOS: ONE PER BOX
TC1 P.Bure/V.Bure 1.50 4.00
TC2 T.Selanne/P.Kariya 1.25 3.00
TC3 J.LeClair/T.Amonte 1.00 2.50
TC4 C.Joseph/D.Hasek 2.00 5.00
TC5 M.Modano/P.Forsberg 2.00 5.00
TC6 R.Bourque/C.Pronger 2.00 5.00
TC7 V.Lecavalier/J.Thornton 2.00 5.00
TC8 P.Roy/M.Brodeur 4.00 10.00
TC9 S.Yzerman/B.Hull 3.00 8.00
TC10 J.Jagr/M.Lemieux 3.00 8.00

2000-01 Topps Combos Jumbos

Randomly inserted in boxes, this 10-card set parallels the base Combos set on jumbo cards.
*JUMBOS: .5X TO 1.2X BASIC INSERTS
ONE PER BOX

2000-01 Topps Game Worn Sweaters

Randomly inserted in packs at the rate of 1:460, this six card set features swatches of authentic game worn jerseys.
GWAG Adam Graves 8.00 20.00
GWBH Bobby Holik 8.00 20.00
GWDL David Legwand 8.00 20.00
GWDM Darren McCarty 8.00 20.00
GWJJ Jaromir Jagr 10.00 25.00
GWTD Tie Domi 8.00 20.00

2000-01 Topps Hobby Masters
This 10-card set was inserted in Topps Hobby packs at the rate of 1:18 and OPC packs at the rate of 1:20.
COMPLETE SET (10) 12.00 30.00
HM1 Martin Brodeur 2.50 6.00
HM2 Pavel Bure 1.50 4.00
HM3 Peter Forsberg 1.50 4.00
HM4 Dominik Hasek 2.00 5.00
HM5 Jaromir Jagr 3.00 8.00
HM6 Curtis Joseph 1.50 4.00
HM7 Paul Kariya 1.50 4.00
HM8 Mike Modano 2.00 5.00
HM9 Patrick Roy 3.00 8.00
HM10 Steve Yzerman 4.00 10.00

2000-01 Topps Lemieux Reprints
Randomly inserted in packs at the rate of 1:12, this 23-card set pays tribute to Mario Lemieux by reprinting both his base Topps and O-Pee-Chee cards.
COMPLETE SET (23) 50.00 100.00
COMMON CARD (1-23) 3.00 8.00

2000-01 Topps Lemieux Reprints Autographs
Randomly seeded in packs at the rate of 1:5456, this 23-card set parallels the base Lemieux Reprints set on cards enhanced with a Mario Lemieux autograph.
COMMON CARD (1-23) 100.00 200.00

2000-01 Topps NHL Draft
Randomly inserted in packs at the rate of 1:31, this 14-card set features seven number one draft selections and seven of the NHL's standout players.
COMPLETE SET (14) 20.00 40.00
D1 Vincent Lecavalier 1.25 3.00
D2 Eric Lindros 2.00 5.00
D3 Mike Modano 2.00 5.00
D4 Owen Nolan 1.00 2.50
D5 Patrik Stefan 1.00 2.50
D6 Mats Sundin 1.25 3.00
D7 Joe Thornton 2.00 5.00
D8 Pavel Bure 1.50 4.00
D9 Anson Carter 1.00 2.50
D10 Pavol Demitra 1.00 2.50
D11 Doug Gilmour 1.25 3.00
D12 Dominik Hasek 2.50 6.00
D13 Brett Hull 1.50 4.00
D14 Luc Robitaille 1.00 2.50

2000-01 Topps Own the Game
Randomly inserted in packs at the rate of 1:7, this 30-card set spotlights NHL leaders in each of these three categories: Points (OTG1-OTG10), Wins (OTG11-OTG20), and Rookie Points (OTG21-OTG30).
COMPLETE SET (30) 20.00 50.00
OTG1 Jaromir Jagr 1.50 4.00
OTG2 Pavel Bure 1.00 2.50
OTG3 Mark Recchi .75 2.00
OTG4 Paul Kariya 1.00 2.50
OTG5 Teemu Selanne 1.00 2.50
OTG6 Owen Nolan .75 2.00
OTG7 Tony Amonte .75 2.00
OTG8 Mike Modano 1.25 3.00
OTG9 Joe Sakic 2.00 5.00
OTG10 Steve Yzerman 3.00 8.00
OTG11 Martin Brodeur 2.00 5.00
OTG12 Roman Turek .40 1.00
OTG13 Olaf Kolzig .75 2.00
OTG14 Curtis Joseph 1.00 2.50
OTG15 Arturs Irbe .75 2.00
OTG16 Patrick Roy 4.00 10.00
OTG17 Ed Belfour 1.00 2.50
OTG18 Chris Osgood .75 2.00
OTG19 Guy Hebert .75 2.00
OTG20 Steve Shields .75 2.00
OTG21 Scott Gomez .75 2.00
OTG22 Alex Tanguay .75 2.00
OTG23 Mike York .40 1.00
OTG24 Simon Gagne .75 2.00
OTG25 Jan Hlavac .40 1.00
OTG26 Trevor Letowski .40 1.00
OTG27 Brad Stuart .40 1.00
OTG28 Maxim Afinogenov .40 1.00
OTG29 Tim Connolly .40 1.00
OTG30 Jochen Hecht .40 1.00

2000-01 Topps Stanley Cup Heroes

Randomly inserted in packs at the rate of 1:55, this five card set features top NHL stars of the past on an all foil die cut card in the shape of the Stanley Cup.
COMPLETE SET (5) 20.00 40.00
SHBG Bob Gainey 4.00 10.00
SHBP Bernie Parent 5.00 12.00
SHBT Bryan Trottier 5.00 12.00
SHLR Larry Robinson 5.00 12.00
SHTL Ted Lindsay 4.00 10.00

2000-01 Topps Stanley Cup Heroes Autographs
Randomly inserted in packs at the rate of 1:1104, this five card set parallels the base Stanley Cup Heroes insert set but is enhanced with authentic player autographs.
SHBG Bob Gainey 25.00 60.00
SHBP Bernie Parent 30.00 60.00
SHBT Bryan Trottier 15.00 40.00
SHLR Larry Robinson 15.00 40.00
SHTL Ted Lindsay 25.00 60.00

2000-01 Topps 1000 Point Club
Randomly inserted in packs at the rate of 1:27, this 16-card set spotlights players that have accumulated more than 1000 points on an all foil insert card.
COMPLETE SET (16) 25.00 50.00
PC1 Mark Messier 1.50 4.00
PC2 Steve Yzerman 6.00 15.00
PC3 Ron Francis 1.00 2.50
PC4 Paul Coffey 1.25 3.00
PC5 Ray Bourque 2.50 6.00
PC6 Doug Gilmour 1.25 3.00
PC7 Adam Oates 1.00 2.50
PC8 Larry Murphy 1.00 2.50
PC9 Dave Andreychuk 1.00 2.50
PC10 Luc Robitaille 1.00 2.50
PC11 Phil Housley 1.00 2.50
PC12 Brett Hull 1.50 4.00
PC13 Al MacInnis 1.00 2.50
PC14 Pierre Turgeon 1.00 2.50
PC15 Joe Sakic 2.50 6.00
PC16 Pat Verbeek 1.00 2.50

2000-01 Topps Premier Plus Promos
COMPLETE SET (6)
PP1 Scott Gomez .75 2.00
PP2 Joe Sakic 1.25 3.00
PP3 Zigmund Palffy .75 2.00
PP4 Tony Amonte .75 2.00
PP5 David Legwand .75 2.00
PP6 Jeff Farkas .75 2.00

2001-02 Topps
2001-02 Topps was released in August as a 360-card set with cards #330-360 in packs as redemption cards for "to-be-determined" rookies. The list of rookies redeemable for these cards was not made public until November. Pack SRP was $1.49 for a 10-card pack and there were 36 packs per box. Cards carrying a "U" prefix were available in packs of Topps Chrome at 1:4. These cards were inserted as updates for players who had changed teams since the release of the base set. The "U" was added for checklisting purposes only, it was not printed on the cards.
COMPLETE SET (360) 60.00 150.00
COMP SET w/o RCs (330) 25.00 50.00
*UPDATE: .5X TO 1.2X BASIC CARDS
1 Mario Lemieux .60 1.50
2 Steve Yzerman .60 1.50
3 Martin Brodeur .40 1.00
4 Brian Leetch .20 .50
5 Tony Amonte .15 .40
6 Bill Guerin .20 .50
7 Olaf Kolzig .20 .50
8 Pavel Bure .25 .60
9 Patrick Marleau .20 .50
10 Mariusz Czerkawski .12 .30
11 Teemu Selanne .40 1.00
12 Alex Tanguay .15 .40
13 Keith Primeau .15 .40
14 Alexei Yashin Senator .15 .40
14U Alexei Yashin Islander .20 .50
15 Markus Naslund .20 .50
16 Chris Pronger .15 .40
17 Sergei Zubov .15 .40
18 Marian Gaborik .30 .75
19 Mats Sundin .20 .50
20 Kevin Weekes .15 .40
21 J.P. Dumont .12 .30
22 Nicklas Lidstrom .20 .50
23 Ron Francis .25 .60
24 Doug Weight Oilers .20 .50
24U Doug Weight Blues .25 .60
25 Zigmund Palffy .20 .50
26 Jason Allison .15 .40
27 Joe Sakic .30 .75
28 Paul Kariya .25 .60
29 Marian Hossa .15 .40
30 Owen Nolan .20 .50
31 Jason Arnott .15 .40
32 Jaromir Jagr Pens .50 1.25
32U Jaromir Jagr Caps .60 1.50
33 Justin Williams .12 .30
34 Peter Bondra .20 .50
35 Chris Drury .15 .40
36 Radek Bonk .12 .30
37 Theo Fleury .25 .60
38 Keith Tkachuk .20 .50
39 Rick DiPietro .15 .40
40 Ed Jovanovski .15 .40
41 Scott Stevens .20 .50
42 John LeClair .20 .50
43 Jochen Hecht .12 .30
44 Vincent Lecavalier .15 .40
45 Henrik Sedin .20 .50
46 David Aebischer .15 .40
47 Patrick Roy .50 1.25
48 Valeri Bure .12 .30
49 Dominik Hasek Sabres .30 .75
49U Dominik Hasek Red Wings .40 1.00
50 Ray Ferraro .12 .30
51 Milan Hejduk .15 .40
52 Mike Modano .30 .75
53 Sergei Fedorov .30 .75
54 Luc Robitaille .20 .50
55 Mark Messier .30 .75
56 Sean Burke .12 .30
57 Jeff Friesen .12 .30
58 Alexander Mogilny Devils .15 .40
58U Alexander Mogilny Leafs .20 .50
59 Roman Cechmanek .15 .40
60 Martin Straka .12 .30
61 Pavol Demitra .25 .60
62 Curtis Joseph .20 .50
63 Daniel Sedin .20 .50
64 Brad Richards .20 .50
65 Simon Gagne .20 .50
66 Saku Koivu .20 .50
67 Jamie McLennan .12 .30
68 Roberto Luongo .30 .75
69 Brendan Shanahan .25 .60
70 Espen Knutsen .12 .30
71 Rob Blake .20 .50
72 Steve Sullivan .12 .30
73 Arturs Irbe .15 .40
74 Maxim Afinogenov .12 .30
75 Patrik Stefan .15 .40
76 Scott Gomez .15 .40
77 Brad Isbister .12 .30
78 Robert Lang .12 .30
79 Pierre Turgeon Blues .20 .50
79U Pierre Turgeon Stars .25 .60
80 Gary Roberts .12 .30
81 Adam Oates .20 .50
82 Evgeni Nabokov .15 .40
83 Petr Nedved .15 .40
84 Mike Dunham .15 .40
85 Chris Osgood Red Wings .20 .50
85U Chris Osgood Islanders .25 .60
86 Brett Hull Stars .25 .60
86U Brett Hull Red Wings .30 .75
87 Peter Forsberg .25 .60
88 Joe Thornton .25 .60
89 Ray Bourque .30 .75
90 Ed Belfour .20 .50
91 Patrik Elias .20 .50
92 Michael York .12 .30
93 Martin Havlat .15 .40
94 Jeremy Roenick Coyotes .20 .50
94U Jeremy Roenick Flyers .25 .60
95 Alexei Kovalev .15 .40
96 Al MacInnis .15 .40
97 Marco Sturm .12 .30
98 Jose Theodore .20 .50
99 Joe Nieuwendyk .20 .50
100 Darren McCarty .12 .30
101 Mark Recchi .25 .60
102 Daniel Alfredsson .20 .50
103 Miroslav Satan .15 .40
104 Sergei Samsonov .15 .40
105 Roman Turek Blues .15 .40
105U Roman Turek Flames .20 .50
106 Jarome Iginla .20 .50
107 Jeff O'Neill .12 .30
108 Tommy Salo .15 .40
109 Petr Sykora .12 .30
110 Adam Deadmarsh .15 .40
111 Oleg Tverdovsky .12 .30
112 Damian Rhodes .15 .40
113 Bob Probert .15 .40
114 Jere Lehtinen .15 .40
115 Cale Hulse .12 .30
116 Andy Sutton .12 .30
117 Wade Redden .12 .30
118 Brad Stuart .12 .30
119 Tomas Kaberle .12 .30
120 Sergei Gonchar .12 .30
121 Jean-Sebastien Aubin .15 .40
122 Adam Graves .15 .40
123 Teppo Numminen .12 .30
124 Martin Rucinsky .12 .30
125 Scott Young .12 .30
126 Pat Verbeek .15 .40
127 Michael Nylander .12 .30
128 Marc Savard .12 .30
129 Brian Rolston .15 .40
130 Sandis Ozolinsh .12 .30
131 Mike Grier .12 .30
132 Eric Belanger .12 .30
133 Patrick Lalime .15 .40
134 Steve Thomas .12 .30
135 Viktor Kozlov .12 .30
136 Manny Legace .15 .40
137 Oleg Saprykin .12 .30
138 Sami Kapanen .12 .30
139 Janne Niinimaa .12 .30
140 Scott Hartnell .20 .50
141 Tim Connolly .12 .30
142 Travis Green .12 .30
143 Matthew Barnaby .12 .30
144 Brendan Morrison .15 .40
145 Darcy Tucker .12 .30
146 Gary Suter .15 .40
147 Mattias Ohlund .12 .30
148 Patric Kjellberg .12 .30
149 Lubomir Visnovsky .12 .30
150 Claude Lapointe .12 .30
151 Martin Skoula .15 .40
152 Mike Vernon .15 .40
153 Stu Barnes .15 .40
154 Brenden Morrow .15 .40
155 Jim Dowd .12 .30
156 Shane Doan .15 .40
157 Peter Schaefer .12 .30
158 Jeff Halpern .12 .30
159 Sergei Berezin .12 .30
160 Mike Ricci .15 .40
161 Radek Dvorak .15 .40
162 Brian Savage .12 .30
163 Bryan Smolinski .12 .30
164 Derian Hatcher .12 .30
165 Shane Willis .12 .30
166 Ron Tugnutt .15 .40
167 Peter Worrell .12 .30
168 Richard Zednik .15 .40
169 Todd Marchant .12 .30
170 Andrew Brunette .12 .30
171 Derek Morris .12 .30
172 Kyle Calder .12 .30
173 Felix Potvin .30 .75
174 Bobby Holik .12 .30
175 Manny Fernandez .15 .40
176 Rick Tocchet .12 .30
177 Jonas Hoglund .12 .30
178 Todd Bertuzzi .20 .50
179 Garth Snow .15 .40
180 Cliff Ronning .12 .30
181 Martin Lapointe .12 .30
182 Jason Smith .12 .30
183 Byron Dafoe .15 .40
184 Rob Niedermayer .15 .40
185 Steve Rucchin .12 .30
186 Alexei Zhamnov .15 .40
187 Mike Richter .20 .50
188 Michal Handzus .12 .30
189 Pavel Kubina .12 .30
190 Donald Brashear .12 .30
191 Trevor Letowski .12 .30
192 Randy McKay .12 .30
193 Trevor Linden .20 .50
194 Mike Sillinger .12 .30
195 David Vyborny .12 .30
196 Dave Tanabe .12 .30
197 Scott Niedermayer .20 .50
198 Anson Carter .15 .40
199 Mike Leclerc .12 .30
200 Dave Scatchard .12 .30
201 Jan Hrdina .12 .30
202 Brian Holzinger .12 .30
203 Steve Konowalchuk .12 .30
204 Tie Domi .15 .40
205 Brent Johnson .15 .40
206 Shawn McEachern .12 .30
207 Jozef Stumpel .12 .30
208 Jamie Langenbrunner .12 .30
209 Jocelyn Thibault .15 .40
210 Donald Audette .12 .30
211 Serge Aubin .12 .30
212 Andrew Cassels .12 .30
213 Tyson Nash .12 .30
214 Colin White .12 .30
215 Tom Poti .12 .30
216 Rod Brind'Amour .20 .50
217 Fred Brathwaite .15 .40
218 Marc Denis .15 .40
219 Roman Simicek .12 .30
220 Jan Hlavac .12 .30
221 Darius Kasparaitis .12 .30
222 Vincent Damphousse .15 .40
223 Bob Boughner .12 .30
224 Yanic Perreault .12 .30
225 Chris Simon .12 .30
226 Chris Gratton .12 .30
227 Josef Vasicek .12 .30
228 Slava Kozlov .15 .40
229 Kelly Buchberger .15 .40
230 Jeff Hackett .15 .40
231 Taylor Pyatt .12 .30
232 Niklas Sundstrom .15 .40
233 Dan Cloutier .15 .40
234 Eric Daze .15 .40
235 Ryan Smyth .15 .40
236 Marty McInnis .15 .40
237 John Madden .15 .40
238 Claude Lemieux .15 .40
239 Steve Heinze .12 .30
240 Nikolai Antropov .12 .30
241 Cory Stillman .12 .30
242 Geoff Sanderson .12 .30
243 Trevor Kidd .12 .30
244 David Legwand .15 .40
245 Eric Desjardins .15 .40
246 Fredrik Modin .12 .30
247 Brett Clark .12 .30
248 Bryan Muir .12 .30
249 Ron Sutter .15 .40
250 Ken Klee .12 .30
251 Steve Halko .12 .30
252 Steve McKenna .12 .30
253 Marc Bergevin .12 .30
254 Scott Lachance .12 .30
255 Jamie Rivers .12 .30
256 Dixon Ward .12 .30
257 Gord Murphy .12 .30
258 Bret Hedican .12 .30
259 Bob Corkum .12 .30
260 Brent Sopel .12 .30
261 Todd Simpson .12 .30
262 Reid Simpson .12 .30
263 Chris McAlpine .12 .30
264 Deron Quint .12 .30
265 Josh Holden .12 .30
266 Mike Mottau .12 .30
267 Jakub Cutta .12 .30
268 Maxime Ouellet .20 .50
269 Peter Smrek RC .12 .30
270 Daniel Corso .12 .30
271 Rostislav Klesla .12 .30
272 Mika Noronen .12 .30
273 Kris Beech .12 .30
274 Sheldon Keefe .12 .30
275 Miikka Kiprusoff .20 .50
276 Mathieu Garon .15 .40
277 Jason Chimera RC .12 .30
278 Mark Bell .12 .30
279 Chris Nielsen .12 .30
280 Eric Chouinard .12 .30
281 Pierre Dagenais .12 .30
282 Branislav Mezei .12 .30
283 Milan Kraft .12 .30
284 Tomas Kloucek .12 .30
285 Petr Schastlivy .12 .30
286 Lee Goren .12 .30
287 Daniel Tkaczuk .12 .30
288 Andreas Lilja .12 .30
289 Tomas Divisek RC .15 .40
290 Alexei Ponikarovsky .12 .30
291 Mikael Samuelsson RC .15 .40
292 Petr Svoboda .15 .40
293 Mike Comrie .15 .40
294 Johan Hedberg .15 .40
295 Tyler Moss .12 .30
296 Martin Spanhel RC .12 .30
297 Mike Brown .15 .40
298 Derek Gustafson .12 .30
299 Matt Pettinger .12 .30
300 Mike Commodore .12 .30
301 Antti-Jussi Niemi .12 .30
302 Brad Tapper .12 .30
303 Rick Berry .12 .30
304 Andrew Raycroft .15 .40
305 Bryan Allen .12 .30
306 Ivan Novoseltsev .12 .30
307 Jason Williams .12 .30
308 Gregg Naumenko .12 .30
309 Jiri Bicek .12 .30
310 Mathieu Darche RC .20 .50
311 Brian Campbell .12 .30
312 Jeff Farkas .12 .30
313 Rico Fata .12 .30
314 Kristian Kudroc .12 .30
315 Roman Cechmanek AS .12 .30
316 Nicklas Lidstrom AS .15 .40
317 Ray Bourque AS .25 .60
318 Joe Sakic AS .25 .60
319 Patrik Elias AS .15 .40
320 Jaromir Jagr AS .40 1.00
321 J. Madden/R. McKay .12 .30
322 Mark Recchi .20 .50
323 Vincent Damphousse .12 .30
324 Patrick Roy .40 1.00
325 Jaromir Jagr .40 1.00
326 Mario Lemieux 1.50 4.00
327 Mario Lemieux 1.50 4.00
328 Mario Lemieux 1.50 4.00
329 Mario Lemieux 1.50 4.00
330 Mario Lemieux 1.50 4.00
331 Ilya Kovalchuk RC 5.00 12.00
332 Dan Blackburn RC 1.25 3.00
333 Vaclav Nedorost RC 1.00 2.50
334 Krys Kolanos RC 1.00 2.50
335 Kristian Huselius RC 1.50 4.00
336 Martin Erat RC 1.50 4.00
337 Timo Parssinen RC 1.25 3.00
338 Scott Nichol RC 1.00 2.50
339 Nick Schultz RC 1.00 2.50
340 Jukka Hentunen RC 1.00 2.50
341 Pascal Dupuis RC 1.50 4.00
342 Radek Martinek RC 1.00 2.50
343 Scott Clemmensen RC 1.00 2.50
344 Jeff Jillson RC 1.00 2.50
345 Brian Sutherby RC 1.00 2.50
346 Nikita Alexeev RC 1.00 2.50
347 Niklas Hagman RC 1.25 3.00
348 Erik Cole RC 2.00 5.00
349 Pavel Datsyuk RC 5.00 12.00
350 Ilja Bryzgalov RC 2.50 6.00
351 Chris Neil RC 1.25 3.00
352 Mark Rycroft RC 1.25 3.00
353 Kamil Piros RC 1.00 2.50
354 Niko Kapanen RC 1.50 4.00
355 Jiri Dopita RC 1.00 2.50
356 Andreas Salomonsson RC 1.00 2.50
357 Ivan Ciernik RC 1.00 2.50
358 Jaroslav Bednar RC 1.00 2.50
359 Ty Conklin RC 1.50 4.00
360 Raffi Torres RC 1.50 4.00

2001-02 Topps 71-72 Heritage Parallel
Inserted at a rate of 1:1, this 110-card set parallels the first 110 cards of the Topps base set. The card fronts carry the same photo as the base cards, but use the 1971-72 Topps design. Card backs are the same as the base set.
*SINGLES: 1X TO 2.5X BASIC TOPPS

2001-02 Topps 71-72 Heritage Parallel Limited
*SINGLES/50: 12X TO 30X BASIC TOPPS
STATED ODDS 1:222 HOB, 1:171 RET
STATED PRINT RUN 50 SER.#'d SETS

2001-02 Topps OPC Parallel
Inserted at a rate of 1:4, this 330-card set parallel the base set except that card fronts carried the O-Pee-Chee stamp in silver. Card backs were the same as the base cards.
*OPC PARALLEL: 1.5X TO 4X BASIC CARDS
55 Mark Messier 1.25 3.00

2001-02 Topps Autographs
This 10-card set was inserted into hobby packs at a rate of 1:507 and retail packs at 1:390. Card fronts were a blue and white ice design with the white portion being where the players signed. Card backs carried a Topps certified sticker.
ACD Chris Drury 10.00 25.00
AEN Evgeni Nabokov 10.00 25.00
AGR Gary Roberts 8.00 20.00
AJA Jason Arnott 8.00 20.00
AMY Mike York 8.00 20.00
ARF Ron Francis 8.00 20.00
ASG Simon Gagne 12.00 30.00
AVL Vincent Lecavalier 20.00 50.00
AMHA Martin Havlat 8.00 20.00
AMHE Milan Hejduk 12.00 30.00

2001-02 Topps Captain's Cloth
Available only in hobby packs, this 3-card set featured four swatches of game-used jerseys from four different players who were the captains of their respective teams. Each swatch was affixed in the shape of a "C" on the card front. Card backs carried photos and bios of each player along with the Topps certified sticker.
CC1 Jagr/Sakic/Kariya/Lec. 150.00 300.00
CC2 Pronger/Koivu/Amon/Jagr 100.00 200.00
CC3 Franc/Allis/Kariya/Lecav 100.00 200.00

2001-02 Topps Game-Worn Jersey
Inserted at 1:253 hobby and 1:195 retail, this 10-card set featured game-worn jersey swatches of the featured players. Card backs carried a Topps certified sticker.
JBB Brian Boucher 6.00 15.00
JBH Brett Hull 10.00 25.00
JCD Chris Drury 8.00 20.00
JEB Ed Belfour 8.00 20.00
JJA Jason Arnott 6.00 15.00
JMY Mike York 6.00 15.00
JPK Paul Kariya 8.00 20.00
JRF Ron Francis 6.00 15.00
JSG Simon Gagne 8.00 20.00
JVL Vincent Lecavalier 6.00 15.00

2001-02 Topps Jumbo Jersey Autographs
Inserted at stated odds of 1:16,895 hobby and 1:12,996 retail, this 6-card set featured larger than normal swatches of game-worn jerseys. The jersey swatches were also signed by the featured player.
JJACD Chris Drury 25.00 60.00
JJAJA Jason Arnott 25.00 60.00
JJAMY Mike York 25.00 60.00
JJARF Ron Francis 25.00 60.00
JJASG Simon Gagne 25.00 60.00
JJAVL Vincent Lecavalier 40.00 100.00

2001-02 Topps Mario Lemieux Reprints
Inserted at 1:12 hobby and 1:10 retail, this 10-card set featured reprints of past Topps cards of Mario Lemieux.
COMPLETE SET (10) 15.00 40.00
COMMON CARD (1-10) 2.50 6.00

2001-02 Topps Mario Returns Autographs
Numbered to just 66 sets, this 5-card set parallels the Mario Returns base cards, but also feature a certified autograph on the card front. These cards were inserted at 1:7679 hobby and 1:5907 retail.
COMMON AUTO (1-5) 75.00 150.00

2001-02 Topps Own The Game
This 30-card set was inserted at 1:6 hobby and 1:5 retail. Cards were produced on foil stock and featured league leaders in points, wins and rookie points.
COMPLETE SET (30) 15.00 30.00
OTG1 Jaromir Jagr .60 1.50
OTG2 Joe Sakic .75 2.00
OTG3 Patrik Elias .30 .75
OTG4 Jason Allison .12 .30
OTG5 Alexei Kovalev .30 .75
OTG6 Martin Straka .12 .30
OTG7 Pavel Bure .50 1.25
OTG8 Doug Weight .30 .75
OTG9 Peter Forsberg .75 2.00
OTG10 Zigmund Palffy .30 .75
OTG11 Brad Richards .30 .75
OTG12 Shane Willis .12 .30
OTG13 Martin Havlat .30 .75
OTG14 Lubomir Visnovsky .12 .30
OTG15 Marian Gaborik .75 2.00
OTG16 Ruslan Fedotenko .30 .75
OTG17 Steven Reinprecht .12 .30
OTG18 Daniel Sedin .12 .30
OTG19 Karel Rachunek .12 .30
OTG20 David Vyborny .12 .30
OTG21 Martin Brodeur 1.00 2.50
OTG22 Patrick Roy 2.00 5.00
OTG23 Dominik Hasek .75 2.00
OTG24 Olaf Kolzig .30 .75
OTG25 Arturs Irbe .30 .75
OTG26 Patrick Lalime .30 .75
OTG27 Tommy Salo .30 .75
OTG28 Roman Cechmanek .30 .75
OTG29 Ed Belfour .40 1.00
OTG30 Curtis Joseph .40 1.00

2001-02 Topps Promos
COMPLETE SET (6) 1.50 4.00
PP1 Zigmund Palffy .40 1.00
PP2 Randy McKay .20 .50
PP3 Gary Roberts .20 .50
PP4 Manny Fernandez .40 1.00
PP5 Steve Sullivan .20 .50
PP6 Adam Oates .40 1.00

2001-02 Topps Rookie Reprints
This 4-card set was inserted in 1:22 hobby and 1:17 retail packs and featured reprints of rookie cards of four NHL Hall-of-Famers.
COMPLETE SET (4) 10.00 20.00
1 Denis Potvin 2.00 5.00
2 Yvan Cournoyer 2.00 5.00
3 Phil Esposito 2.00 5.00
4 Gerry Cheevers 2.00 5.00

2001-02 Topps Rookie Reprint Autographs
This 4-card set paralleled the regular rookie reprint set but included authentic autographs from the featured players. A Topps certified sticker was placed on the card backs of this set.
1 Denis Potvin 15.00 40.00
2 Yvan Cournoyer 15.00 40.00
3 Phil Esposito 15.00 40.00
4 Gerry Cheevers 15.00 40.00

2001-02 Topps Shot Masters

COMPLETE SET (18) 15.00 30.00
STATED ODDS 1:13 HOB, 1:10 RET
SM1 Mario Lemieux 2.50 6.00
SM2 Pavel Bure .50 1.25
SM3 Brett Hull .50 1.25
SM4 Joe Sakic .75 2.00
SM5 Jaromir Jagr .60 1.50
SM6 Steve Yzerman 2.00 5.00
SM7 Milan Hejduk .40 1.00
SM8 Tony Amonte .30 .75
SM9 Zigmund Palffy .30 .75
SM10 Paul Kariya .40 1.00
SM11 Bill Guerin .30 .75
SM12 Peter Bondra .40 1.00
SM13 Patrik Elias .30 .75
SM14 Alexei Kovalev .30 .75
SM15 John LeClair .50 1.25
SM16 Alexei Yashin 1.00 2.50
SM17 Teemu Selanne .40 1.00
SM18 Alexander Mogilny .30 .75

2001-02 Topps Stanley Cup Heroes
Inserted at 1:66 hobby and 1:51 retail, this 4-card set features vintage players on a chrome die-cut design.
COMPLETE SET (4) 15.00 30.00
SCHDP Denis Potvin 4.00 10.00
SCHGC Gerry Cheevers 5.00 12.00
SCHPE Phil Esposito 4.00 10.00
SCHYC Yvan Cournoyer 5.00 12.00

2001-02 Topps Stanley Cup Heroes Autographs
This set paralleled the base heroes set but included player autographs and a Topps certified sticker on the card backs. Odds for this set were 1:1584 hobby and 1:1218 retail.
SCHADP Denis Potvin 15.00 40.00
SCHAGC Gerry Cheevers 15.00 40.00
SCHAPE Phil Esposito 20.00 50.00
SCHAYC Yvan Cournoyer 15.00 40.00

2001-02 Topps Stars of the Game
Inserted at 1:12 hobby and 1:10 retail, this 10-card set highlighted players who were recognized most often as one of the "Three Stars of the Game" media voting during the 2000/01 season.
COMPLETE SET (10) 8.00 15.00
SG1 Mario Lemieux 2.50 6.00
SG2 Sean Burke .30 .75
SG3 Pavel Bure .50 1.25
SG4 Joe Sakic .75 2.00
SG5 Patrik Elias .30 .75
SG6 Mike Modano .60 1.50
SG7 Curtis Joseph .40 1.00
SG8 Alexei Kovalev .30 .75
SG9 Sergei Fedorov .75 2.00
SG10 Tommy Salo .30 .75

2002-03 Topps
This 340-card set was released as a 330 card set and an available 10-card rookie update set. The rookie update set was available by mail by sending in special redemption cards found in packs. Cards with a "U" prefix were update cards found in packs of Topps Chrome. The "U" prefix is for checklisting purposes only.
COMPLETE SET (340) 20.00 50.00
COMP.SET w/o ROOK.RED. (330) 15.00 40.00
1 Patrick Roy .50 1.25
2 Mario Lemieux .60 1.50
3 Martin Brodeur .40 1.00
4 Steve Yzerman .40 1.00
5 Jaromir Jagr .50 1.25
6 Chris Pronger .15 .40
7 John LeClair .20 .50
8 Paul Kariya .25 .60
9 Tony Amonte .15 .40
9U Tony Amonte update .15 .40
10 Joe Thornton .25 .60
11 Ilya Kovalchuk .25 .60
12 Jarome Iginla .20 .50
13 Mike Modano .30 .75
14 Vincent Lecavalier .15 .40
15 Michael Peca .15 .40
16 Pavel Bure .25 .60
17 Eric Lindros .30 .75
18 Felix Potvin .30 .75
19 Ron Francis .25 .60
20 Miroslav Satan .20 .50
21 Rostislav Klesla .12 .30
22 Mike Comrie .20 .50
23 Daniel Alfredsson .20 .50
24 Sean Burke .12 .30
25 David Legwand .15 .40
26 Marian Gaborik .30 .75
27 Saku Koivu .20 .50
28 Owen Nolan .20 .50
29 Mats Sundin .20 .50
30 J-P Dumont .12 .30
31 Chris Drury .20 .50
31U Chris Drury update .20 .50
32 Markus Naslund .15 .40
33 Anson Carter .15 .40
34 Dwayne Roloson .12 .30
35 Brad Isbister .12 .30
36 Daniel Briere .15 .40
37 Martin St. Louis .20 .50
38 Shayne Corson .12 .30
39 Keith Tkachuk .20 .50
40 Mark Recchi .25 .60
41 Patrice Brisebois .12 .30
42 Niklas Hagman .12 .30
43 Marc Denis .15 .40
44 Robyn Regehr .12 .30
45 Byron Dafoe .15 .40
46 Sergei Fedorov .30 .75
47 Andrew Brunette .12 .30
48 Denis Arkhipov .12 .30
49 Martin Havlat .15 .40
50 Mike Rathje .12 .30
51 Mattias Ohlund .12 .30
52 Ulf Dahlen .12 .30
53 Tim Connolly .12 .30
54 Valeri Bure .15 .40
55 Brian Boucher .15 .40
56 Pascal Dupuis .12 .30
57 Brian Leetch .20 .50
58 Daniel Sedin .20 .50
59 Kenny Jonsson .12 .30
60 Erik Cole .15 .40
61 Patrick Lalime .15 .40
62 Mike Leclerc .12 .30
63 Patrick Marleau .20 .50
64 Tom Poti .12 .30
65 Lubos Bartecko .12 .30
66 Tom Barrasso .15 .40
67 Ryan Smyth .15 .40
68 Sami Kapanen .12 .30
69 Michal Handzus .15 .40
70 Martin Straka .15 .40
71 Peter Forsberg .25 .60
72 Marc Savard .12 .30
73 Jeff Friesen .12 .30
73U Jeff Friesen update .12 .30
74 Manny Fernandez .15 .40
75 Jason Smith .12 .30
76 Mike Ribeiro .15 .40
77 Steve Heinze .12 .30
78 Adam Foote .12 .30
79 Sandy McCarthy .12 .30
80 Toni Lydman .12 .30
81 Tie Domi .15 .40
82 Scott Stevens .20 .50
83 Radim Vrbata .15 .40
84 Oleg Petrov .12 .30
85 Marty Turco .20 .50
86 Kristian Huselius .12 .30
87 Jeremy Roenick .20 .50
88 Gary Roberts .12 .30
89 Dean McAmmond .12 .30
90 Chris Chelios .20 .50
91 Andy McDonald .20 .50
92 Brett Hull .25 .60
93 Danny Markov .12 .30
94 Eric Daze .12 .30
95 Alex Tanguay .15 .40
96 Petr Nedved .12 .30
97 Simon Gagne .20 .50
98 Roman Turek .20 .50
99 Milan Hejduk .15 .40
100 Mariusz Czerkawski .12 .30
100U Mariusz Czerkawski update .12 .30
101 Jaroslav Modry .12 .30
102 Dan Cloutier .15 .40
103 Mark Bell .12 .30
104 Brendan Witt .12 .30
105 Teemu Selanne .40 1.00
106 Johan Hedberg .20 .50
107 Mike Ricci .15 .40
108 Roberto Luongo .30 .75
109 Vaclav Prospal .12 .30
110 Zigmund Palffy .20 .50
111 Ed Jovanovski .15 .40
112 Scott Gomez .15 .40
113 Pierre Turgeon .20 .50
114 Niklas Sundstrom .12 .30
115 Martin Biron .15 .40
116 Keith Primeau .20 .50
117 Jean-Sebastien Giguere .20 .50
118 Filip Kuba .12 .30
119 Dave Tanabe .12 .30
120 Brian Savage .12 .30
121 Alexei Zhamnov .15 .40
122 Brent Johnson .15 .40
123 Dan Blackburn .15 .40
124 Eric Belanger .12 .30
125 Janne Niinimaa .12 .30
126 Jonas Hoglund .12 .30
127 Marian Hossa .15 .40
128 Mike Richter .20 .50
129 Peter Bondra .20 .50
130 Rod Brind'Amour .20 .50
131 Shane Doan .15 .40
132 Viktor Kozlov .12 .30
133 Yanic Perreault .12 .30
134 Sergei Samsonov .15 .40
135 Nikolai Khabibulin .20 .50
136 Rob Ray .12 .30
137 Roman Cechmanek .15 .40
138 Patrik Stefan .15 .40
139 Matt Cullen .12 .30
140 Kim Johnsson .12 .30
141 Jim Dowd .12 .30
142 Glen Murray .15 .40
143 Dominik Hasek .30 .75
144 Brad Richards .20 .50
145 Cory Stillman .12 .30
146 Josef Vasicek .12 .30
147 Alexei Kovalev .20 .50
148 Adam Deadmarsh .15 .40
149 Brendan Morrison .15 .40
150 Eric Brewer .12 .30
151 Jason Arnott .15 .40
152 Brenden Morrow .15 .40
153 Manny Legace .20 .50
154 Michael Nylander .12 .30
155 Pavol Demitra .25 .60
156 Olaf Kolzig .20 .50
157 Sergei Berezin .12 .30
158 Teppo Numminen .15 .40
159 Vladimir Orszagh .12 .30
160 Brian Rafalski .12 .30
161 Doug Gilmour .25 .60
162 Jere Lehtinen .20 .50
163 Mark Parrish .12 .30
164 Petr Sykora .15 .40
164U Petr Sykora update .15 .40
165 Sergei Zholtok .12 .30
166 Wade Redden .12 .30
167 Scott Niedermayer .20 .50
168 Olli Jokinen .20 .50
169 Kyle Calder .12 .30
170 Jamie Langenbrunner .15 .40
171 Darcy Tucker .12 .30
172 Alexei Morozov .12 .30
173 Adam Oates .20 .50
173U Adam Oates update .20 .50
174 Chris Osgood .20 .50
175 Espen Knutsen .12 .30
176 Jochen Hecht .12 .30
177 Maxim Afinogenov .12 .30
178 Radek Dvorak .15 .40
179 Steve Sullivan .12 .30
180 Trevor Linden .20 .50
181 Tomi Kallio .12 .30
182 Robert Lang .12 .30
182U Robert Lang update .12 .30
183 Milan Hnilicka .15 .40
184 Justin Williams .15 .40
185 Greg Johnson .12 .30
186 Craig Conroy .12 .30
187 Alexander Mogilny .15 .40
188 Adrian Aucoin .12 .30
189 Fredrik Modin .12 .30

190 Jose Theodore .20 .50
191 Ray Whitney .15 .40
192 Mikael Renberg .12 .30
193 Mike Sillinger .12 .30
194 Richard Zednik .12 .30
195 Mike Dunham .15 .40
196 Joe Sakic .30 .75
197 Fred Brathwaite .15 .40
198 Chris Simon .12 .30
199 Al MacInnis .20 .50
200 Georges Laraque .15 .40
201 Jozef Stumpel .12 .30
202 Theo Fleury .25 .60
203 Rob Blake .20 .50
204 Todd White .12 .30
205 Dany Heatley .20 .50
206 Scott Hartnell .20 .50
207 Oleg Tverdovsky .12 .30
208 Krys Kolanos .12 .30
209 Ian Laperriere .15 .40
210 Vincent Damphousse .15 .40
211 Nick Boynton .12 .30
212 Curtis Joseph .20 .50
212U Curtis Joseph update .20 .50
213 Henrik Sedin .20 .50
214 Kris Beech .12 .30
215 Sandis Ozolinsh .15 .40
216 Ron Tugnutt .15 .40
217 Todd Bertuzzi .20 .50
218 Tommy Salo .15 .40
219 Martin Lapointe .15 .40
220 Derian Hatcher .15 .40
221 David Vyborny .12 .30
222 Jocelyn Thibault .15 .40
223 Nicklas Lidstrom .20 .50
224 Marcus Nilsson .12 .30
225 Sergei Zubov .15 .40
226 Bryan McCabe .12 .30
227 Claude Lemieux .15 .40
228 Jean-Luc Grand-Pierre .12 .30
229 Bill Guerin .20 .50
229U Bill Guerin update .20 .50
230 Sergei Brylin .12 .30
231 Bryan Smolinski .15 .40
232 Luc Robitaille .20 .50
233 Alexei Yashin .15 .40
234 Evgeni Nabokov .15 .40
235 Pavel Datsyuk .25 .60
236 Martin Erat .12 .30
237 Stu Barnes .12 .30
238 Derek Morris .12 .30
239 Bates Battaglia .12 .30
240 Jason Allison .15 .40
241 Peter Worrell .12 .30
242 Mark Messier .30 .75
243 Shawn Bates .12 .30
244 Daymond Langkow .15 .40
245 Ed Belfour .20 .50
245U Ed Belfour update .20 .50
246 Jan Hrdina .12 .30
247 Pavel Kubina .12 .30
248 Scott Young .12 .30
249 Curtis Brown .12 .30
250 Brian Rolston .15 .40
251 Jiri Dopita .12 .30
252 Kimmo Timonen .12 .30
253 Marco Sturm .12 .30
254 Arturs Irbe .15 .40
255 Joe Nieuwendyk .20 .50
256 Sergei Gonchar .15 .40
257 Doug Weight .20 .50
258 Jeff O'Neill .12 .30
259 Mike York .12 .30
260 Radek Bonk .15 .40
261 Patrik Elias .20 .50
262 Phil Housley .15 .40
263 Brendan Shanahan .25 .60
264 Sheldon Keefe .12 .30
265 Rick DiPietro .15 .40
266 J-F Fortin .12 .30
267 Jason Chimera .12 .30
268 Andy Hilbert .12 .30
269 Brian Gionta .15 .40
270 Sergei Varlamov .15 .40
271 Alex Auld .12 .30
272 Pavel Brendl .12 .30
273 Branko Radivojevic .12 .30
274 Kamil Piros .12 .30
275 Steve Gainey .12 .30
276 Mike Mottau .12 .30
277 Jimmie Olvestad .12 .30
278 Jeff Jillson .12 .30
279 Ilja Bryzgalov .15 .40
280 Taylor Pyatt .12 .30
281 Andrew Raycroft .15 .40
282 Christian Berglund .12 .30
283 Patrick DesRochers .12 .30
284 Lukas Krajicek .15 .40
285 Riku Hahl .12 .30
286 Ivan Huml .12 .30
287 Jani Rita .12 .30
288 Kristian Kudroc .12 .30
289 Juraj Kolnik .12 .30
290 John Erskine .12 .30
291 Brian Sutherby .12 .30
292 Bruno St-Jacques .12 .30
293 Nick Schultz .12 .30
294 Pasi Nurminen .12 .30
295 Norm Milley .12 .30
296 Marcel Hossa .12 .30
297 Ales Kotalik .12 .30
298 Bryan Allen .12 .30
299 Mika Noronen .15 .40
300 Tyler Arnason .20 .50
301 Petr Schastlivy .12 .30
302 Mike Van Ryn .12 .30
303 Steve Montador .12 .30
304 Denis Shvidki .12 .30
305 Stephen Weiss .20 .50
306 Nikita Alexeev .12 .30
307 Vaclav Nedorost .12 .30
308 Raffi Torres .12 .30
309 Guillaume Lefebvre .12 .30
310 Sean Avery .15 .40
311 Shane Endicott .12 .30
312 Ty Conklin .15 .40
313 J-F Damphousse .15 .40
314 Jeremy Roenick .20 .50
315 Ron Francis .25 .60
316 Brendan Shanahan .25 .60
317 Patrick Roy .50 1.25
318 Luc Robitaille .20 .50
319 Jose Theodore .20 .50
320 Patrick Roy .50 1.25
321 Sergei Gonchar .15 .40
322 Bryan McCabe .12 .30
323 Chris Chelios .20 .50
324 Nicklas Lidstrom .20 .50
325 Simon Gagne .20 .50
326 Brendan Shanahan .25 .60
327 Jaromir Jagr .50 1.25
328 Jarome Iginla .20 .50
329 Mats Sundin .20 .50
330 Joe Sakic .30 .75
331 Henrik Zetterberg RC 2.50 6.00
332 P-M Bouchard RC .40 1.00
333 Alexander Frolov RC .50 1.25
334 Alexander Svitov RC .25 .60
335 Jason Spezza RC 1.50 4.00
336 Jay Bouwmeester RC .75 2.00
337 Ales Hemsky RC 1.00 2.50
338 Rick Nash RC 2.00 5.00
339 Chuck Kobasew RC .30 .75
340 Stanislav Chistov RC .25 .60
NNO Rookie Redemption expired .20 .50

2002-03 Topps Factory Set Gold

Available only in gift box factory sets, this 340-card set paralleled the regular Topps and OPC sets but featured gold foil highlights instead of the silver highlights found on cards distributed in packs. Each gift box contained 330 veteran cards, a redemption card for a 10-card rookie subset, a 20-card Hometown Heroes set, and a Patrick Roy Reprint card.

COMP.BASE SET (330) 15.00 40.00
COMP.FACTORY SET (340) 25.00 50.00
*GOLD VETS: .5X TO 1.2X BASIC TOPPS
*GOLD ROOKIES: .6X TO 1.5X BASE RC
242 Mark Messier .40 1.00

2002-03 Topps O-Pee-Chee Blue

Inserted at 1:6 for the regular cards and 1:1813 for the rookie redemption card, this 331-card set paralleled the base Topps set but carried blue borders and blue foil highlights. The O-Pee-Chee logo was printed on the card fronts in place of the Topps logo and each card was serial-numbered out of 500.

*VETS/500: 3X TO 8X BASIC TOPPS
*ROOKIES/500: 1.5X TO 4X TOPPS RC
242 Mark Messier 2.50 6.00

2002-03 Topps O-Pee-Chee Red

Inserted at 1:25 for the regular cards and 1:9869 for the rookie redemption card, this 331-card set paralleled the base Topps set but carried red borders and red foil highlights. The O-Pee-Chee logo was printed on the card fronts in place of the Topps logo and each card was serial-numbered out of 100.

*VETS/100: 8X TO 20X BASIC TOPPS
*ROOKIES/100: 4X TO 10X TOPPS RC
242 Mark Messier 6.00 15.00

2002-03 Topps Captain's Cloth

This 17-card set fetured swatches of game jersey from team captains around the league. Single swatch cards were serial-numbered to 100 and inserted at 1:939. Multi-swatch cards were serial-numbered to 50 and inserted at 1:2691.

CC1 Lemieux/Sakic/Francis 75.00 200.00
CC2 Primeau/LeClair/Recchi 60.00 150.00
CC3 Hatcher/Zubov/Modano 75.00 150.00
CC4 Pronger/Kariya/Francis 60.00 125.00
CC5 Koivu/Naslund/Sundin 40.00 100.00
CC6 Lemieux 60.00 120.00
Sundin
Primeau
CC7 Kariya/Koivu/Sakic 60.00 150.00
CC8 Mario Lemieux 20.00 50.00
CC9 Keith Primeau 12.50 30.00
CC10 Markus Naslund 10.00 25.00
CC11 Mats Sundin 12.00 30.00
CC12 Paul Kariya 10.00 25.00
CC13 Joe Sakic 15.00 40.00
CC14 Saku Koivu 12.50 30.00
CC15 Ron Francis 15.00 40.00
CC16 Derian Hatcher 12.50 30.00
CC17 Chris Pronger 15.00 40.00

2002-03 Topps Coast to Coast

COMPLETE SET (10) 10.00 20.00
STATED ODDS 1:12
CC1 Mario Lemieux 4.00 10.00
CC2 Pavel Bure .75 2.00
CC3 Jarome Iginla .75 2.00
CC4 Mats Sundin .60 1.50
CC5 Peter Bondra .60 1.50
CC6 Ilya Kovalchuk .75 2.00
CC7 Joe Thornton 1.00 2.50
CC8 Paul Kariya .60 1.50
CC9 Joe Sakic 1.25 3.00
CC10 Patrik Elias .75 2.00

2002-03 Topps First Round Fabric

STATED ODDS 1:216
ALL CARDS CARRY FRF PREFIX
DB Dan Blackburn 6.00 15.00
EL Eric Lindros 8.00 20.00
KP Keith Primeau 6.00 15.00
MB Martin Biron 6.00 15.00
MM Mike Modano 10.00 25.00
MN Markus Naslund 10.00 25.00
MS Mats Sundin 10.00 25.00
PM Patrick Marleau 6.00 15.00
RD Radek Dvorak 6.00 15.00
SN Scott Niedermayer 6.00 15.00
JPD J-P Dumont 6.00 15.00

2002-03 Topps First Round Fabric Autographs

This autographed parallel was inserted at 1:1191 packs.

ALL CARDS CARRY FRF PREFIX
KP Keith Primeau 12.50 30.00
MB Martin Biron 12.50 30.00
MM Mike Modano 20.00 50.00
MS Mats Sundin 20.00 50.00
RD Radek Dvorak 12.50 30.00
SN Scott Niedermayer .15.00 40.00

2002-03 Topps Hometown Heroes

This 40-card set was split into two subsets: Canadian and USA heroes. Cards HHC1-HHC20 were available only in OPC packs and cards HHU1-HHU20 were inserted into Topps packs. Odds were 1:12.

COMP.USA SET (20) 15.00 30.00
*FACT.SET: .4X TO 1X BASIC INSERTS
HHU1 Martin Brodeur 1.25 3.00
HHU2 Joe Sakic .75 2.50
HHU3 Mario Lemieux 3.00 8.00
HHU4 Steve Yzerman 2.50 6.00
HHU5 Paul Kariya .50 1.25
HHU6 Mike Modano .75 2.00
HHU7 Brett Hull .60 1.50
HHU8 Bill Guerin .40 1.00
HHU9 Tony Amonte .40 1.00
HHU10 Jeremy Roenick .60 1.50
HHU11 John LeClair .50 1.25
HHU12 Brendan Shanahan .75 2.00
HHU13 Owen Nolan .40 1.00
HHU14 Al MacInnis .40 1.00
HHU15 Chris Pronger .40 1.00
HHU16 Doug Weight .40 1.00
HHU17 Ilya Kovalchuk .60 1.50
HHU18 Joe Thornton .75 2.00
HHU19 Patrick Roy 2.50 6.00
HHU20 Ron Francis .40 1.00

2002-03 Topps Own The Game

COMPLETE SET (20) 5.00 10.00
STATED ODDS 1:6
OTG1 Jarome Iginla .30 .75
OTG2 Markus Naslund .20 .50
OTG3 Todd Bertuzzi .20 .50
OTG4 Mats Sundin .20 .50
OTG5 Jaromir Jagr .30 .75
OTG6 Jarome Iginla .30 .75
OTG7 Mats Sundin .20 .50
OTG8 Bill Guerin .15 .40
OTG9 Glen Murray .15 .40
OTG10 Markus Naslund .20 .50
OTG11 Dany Heatley .25 .60
OTG12 Ilya Kovalchuk .30 .75
OTG13 Kristian Huselius .15 .40
OTG14 Erik Cole .15 .40
OTG15 Pavel Datsyuk .30 .75
OTG16 Dominik Hasek .40 1.00
OTG17 Martin Brodeur .60 1.50
OTG18 Evgeni Nabokov .15 .40
OTG19 Byron Dafoe .15 .40
OTG20 Brent Johnson .15 .40

2002-03 Topps Patrick Roy Reprints

Inserted at odds of 1:18, this 14-card set featured reprints of goalie great Patrick Roy. Each card carried a gold foil Topps logo on the card front.

COMMON CARD (1-14) 2.00 5.00
*FACT.SET: .5X TO 1.2X BASIC INSERTS
1 Patrick Roy '86-87 3.00 8.00
2 Patrick Roy 2.00 5.00
3 Patrick Roy 2.00 5.00
4 Patrick Roy 2.00 5.00
5 Patrick Roy 2.00 5.00
6 Patrick Roy 2.00 5.00
7 Patrick Roy 2.00 5.00
8 Patrick Roy 2.00 5.00
9 Patrick Roy 2.00 5.00
10 Patrick Roy 2.00 5.00
11 Patrick Roy 2.00 5.00
12 Patrick Roy 2.00 5.00
13 Patrick Roy 2.00 5.00
14 Patrick Roy 2.00 5.00

2002-03 Topps Patrick Roy Reprints Autographs

This 14-card set paralleled the regular reprint set but included a certified autograph on each card. This set was serial-numbered to just 33.

COMMON CARD (1-14) 60.00 150.00

2002-03 Topps Rookie Reprints

STATED ODDS 1:18
1 Pat LaFontaine 2.00 5.00
2 Mike Gartner 2.00 5.00
3 Pete Mahovlich 3.00 8.00
4 Andy Bathgate 3.00 8.00
5 Gump Worsley 3.00 8.00
6 Danny Gare 2.00 5.00
7 Harry Howell 2.00 5.00
8 Andy Moog 2.00 5.00
9 Keith Magnuson 2.00 5.00
10 Milt Schmidt 3.00 8.00
11 Glen Sather 2.00 5.00
12 Dick Duff 2.00 5.00
13 Garry Unger 2.00 5.00
14 Darren Pang 2.00 5.00
15 Chico Resch 3.00 8.00

2002-03 Topps Rookie Reprint Autographs

This autographed parallel was inserted at 1:1191 packs.

1 Pat LaFontaine 15.00 40.00
2 Mike Gartner 15.00 40.00
3 Pete Mahovlich 30.00 60.00
4 Andy Bathgate 25.00 60.00
5 Gump Worsley 25.00 60.00
6 Danny Gare 15.00 40.00
7 Harry Howell 15.00 40.00
8 Andy Moog 20.00 50.00
9 Keith Magnuson 40.00 100.00
10 Milt Schmidt 30.00 80.00
11 Glen Sather 30.00 80.00
12 Dick Duff 20.00 50.00
13 Garry Unger 30.00 80.00
14 Darren Pang 15.00 40.00
15 Chico Resch 12.00 30.00

2002-03 Topps Signs of the Future

Inserted at 1:1191, this 6-card set featured certified player autographs. All cards carried a "SF" prefix on the card back.

DL David Legwand 10.00 25.00
IK Ilya Kovalchuk 15.00 40.00
KK Krys Kolanos 10.00 25.00
MC Mike Comrie 10.00 25.00
MH Martin Havlat 12.50 30.00
RV Radim Vrbata 10.00 25.00

2002-03 Topps Stanley Cup Heroes

COMPLETE SET (5) 25.00 40.00
STATED ODDS 1:36
ALL CARDS CARRY SCH PREFIX
SCHDS Derek Sanderson 4.00 10.00
SCHJF John Ferguson 4.00 10.00
SCHRL Reggie Leach 4.00 10.00
SCHRM Rick MacLeish 4.00 10.00
SCHSS Steve Shutt 4.00 10.00

2002-03 Topps Stanley Cup Heroes Autographs

This autogrpahed parallel was inserted at 1:375 hobby packs.

ALL CARDS CARRY SCHA PREFIX
SCHDS Derek Sanderson 15.00 40.00
SCHJF John Ferguson 15.00 40.00
SCHRL Reggie Leach 12.50 30.00
SCHRM Rick MacLeish 20.00 50.00
SCHSS Steve Shutt 12.50 30.00

2002-03 Topps Promos

This set was released in late-Spring of 2002 to generate early buzz around the release of the 2002-03 Topps set.

COMPLETE SET (6) 1.50 4.00
PP1 Simon Gagne .40 1.00
PP2 Jason Allison .40 1.00
PP3 Sergei Gonchar .20 .50
PP4 Wade Redden .20 .50
PP5 Byron Dafoe .40 1.00
PP6 Patrik Elias .40 1.00

2003-04 Topps

Released in late-August, this 330-card set featured full-color action photos with blue-green borders on the card fronts. A rookie redemption card redeemable for cards 331-340 was also randomly inserted at 1:36.

COMPLETE SET (340) 30.00 60.00
*GOLD/50: 6X TO 15X BASIC CARDS
STATED PRINT RUN 50 SER.#'d SETS
1 Joe Thornton .25 .60
2 Chris Osgood .20 .50
3 Brian Rafalski .15 .40
4 Chris Chelios .20 .50
5 Marian Gaborik .30 .75
6 Pavel Bure .25 .60
7 Ladislav Nagy .12 .30
8 Stephen Weiss .12 .30
9 Mike Modano .30 .75
10 Paul Kariya .25 .60
11 Daymond Langkow .12 .30
12 Patrick Lalime .15 .40
13 Alyn McCauley .12 .30
14 Steve Rucchin .12 .30
15 Mike Johnson .12 .30
16 Georges Laraque .15 .40
17 Brian Sutherby .12 .30
18 Petr Sykora .15 .40
19 Joe Sakic .30 .75
20 Henrik Sedin .20 .50
21 Nikolai Khabibulin .20 .50
22 Kevin Weekes .15 .40
23 Jan Bulis .12 .30
24 Ales Kotalik .12 .30
25 Niko Kapanen .12 .30
26 Jaroslav Modry .12 .30
27 Dan Cloutier .15 .40
28 Olli Jokinen .20 .50
29 Todd Marchant .12 .30
30 Jaromir Jagr .50 1.25
31 Rick Nash .20 .50
32 Sami Kapanen .12 .30
33 Brian Boucher .15 .40
34 P.J. Stock .12 .30
35 Teemu Selanne .40 1.00
36 Ossi Vaananen .12 .30
37 Jan Hlavac .12 .30
38 Ville Nieminen .12 .30
39 Jere Lehtinen .15 .40
40 Markus Naslund .20 .50
41 Anson Carter .15 .40
42 Steve Sullivan .12 .30
43 Dwayne Roloson .15 .40
44 Frantisek Kaberle .12 .30
45 Cory Stillman .12 .30
46 Shawn Horcoff .12 .30
47 Robert Lang .12 .30
48 Barret Jackman .12 .30
49 Joe Nieuwendyk .20 .50
50 Alexei Kovalev .15 .40
51 Niclas Wallin .12 .30
52 Cory Sarich .12 .30
53 Brendan Witt .12 .30
54 Mike Fisher .12 .30
55 Ed Belfour .20 .50
56 Sergei Zubov .15 .40
57 Ryan Miller .20 .50
58 Tyler Arnason .12 .30
59 Matt Cooke .12 .30
60 Brian Leetch .20 .50
61 Pavel Datsyuk .25 .60
62 Miikka Kiprusoff .15 .40
63 Michal Handzus .15 .40
64 Steve Shields .15 .40
65 Jason Arnott .15 .40
66 Miroslav Satan .15 .40
67 Nick Schultz .12 .30
68 Daniel Briere .20 .50
69 Alexei Yashin .15 .40
70 Martin Straka .12 .30
71 Martin Biron .15 .40
72 Michael Peca .15 .40
73 Simon Gagne .20 .50
74 Alexei Morozov .12 .30
75 Owen Nolan .15 .40
76 Niklas Hagman .12 .30
77 Kim Johnsson .12 .30
78 David Legwand .15 .40
79 Mark Parrish .12 .30
80 Marcel Hossa .12 .30
81 Mike Rathje .12 .30
82 Ruslan Fedotenko .12 .30
83 Bryan Berard .15 .40
84 Richard Zednik .12 .30
85 Viktor Kozlov .12 .30
86 John Madden .12 .30
87 Roman Hamrlik .15 .40
88 Eric Lindros .30 .75
89 Patrik Elias .20 .50
90 Sergei Fedorov .30 .75
91 Pavel Kubina .12 .30
92 Chris Phillips .12 .30
93 Marc Savard .15 .40
94 Janne Niinimaa .12 .30
95 Michael Nylander .12 .30
96 Radek Bonk .15 .40
97 Dmitri Bykov .12 .30
98 Dave Scatchard .12 .30
99 Marian Hossa .15 .40
100 Mario Lemieux .60 1.50
101 Mark Messier .30 .75
102 Tim Connolly .12 .30
103 Henrik Zetterberg .25 .60
104 Brendan Morrison .15 .40
105 Craig Conroy .12 .30
106 Darcy Tucker .15 .40
107 Steve Konowalchuk .12 .30
108 Valeri Bure .12 .30
109 Rod Brind'Amour .20 .50
110 Jeremy Roenick .20 .50
111 Zdeno Chara .20 .50
112 Mathieu Schneider .12 .30
113 Scott Hartnell .20 .50
114 Vincent Damphousse .15 .40
115 Brian Gionta .15 .40
116 Jeff O'Neill .12 .30
117 Pascal Dupuis .12 .30
118 Patrik Stefan .12 .30
119 Eric Daze .15 .40
120 Jose Theodore .20 .50
121 Yanic Perreault .12 .30
122 Shawn McEachern .12 .30
123 Daniel Alfredsson .20 .50
124 Peter Bondra .15 .40
125 Doug Weight .20 .50
126 Chris Drury .15 .40
127 Ed Jovanovski .15 .40
128 Scott Stevens .20 .50
129 Adam Foote .12 .30
130 Curtis Joseph .20 .50
131 Phil Housley .12 .30
132 Philippe Boucher .12 .30
133 Patrice Brisebois .12 .30
134 Josef Vasicek .12 .30
135 Peter Worrell .12 .30
136 Mike Knuble .12 .30
137 Jocelyn Thibault .15 .40
138 Keith Primeau .20 .50
139 Marc Chouinard .12 .30
140 Mats Sundin .20 .50
141 Martin Skoula .12 .30
142 Sergei Gonchar .12 .30
143 Pavol Demitra .25 .60
144 Tie Domi .15 .40
145 Denis Arkhipov .12 .30
146 Oleg Saprykin .12 .30
147 Tommy Salo .15 .40
148 Andrei Markov .20 .50
149 Brent Johnson .15 .40
150 Jarome Iginla .20 .50
151 Darryl Sydor .12 .30
152 Bryan Smolinski .12 .30
153 Roberto Luongo .30 .75
154 Sandis Ozolinsh .12 .30
155 Alexander Svitov .12 .30
156 J.P. Dumont .12 .30
157 Mike York .12 .30
158 Martin Brodeur .40 1.00
159 Scott Gomez .15 .40
160 Peter Forsberg .25 .60
161 Kimmo Timonen .12 .30
162 Derek Morris .12 .30
163 Justin Williams .15 .40
164 Mike Comrie .15 .40
165 Mattias Weinhandl .12 .30
166 Dimitri Kalinin .12 .30
167 John LeClair .20 .50
168 Evgeni Nabokov .15 .40
169 Alexander Mogilny .15 .40
170 Derian Hatcher .12 .30
171 Adam Deadmarsh .15 .40
172 Alexei Smirnov .12 .30
173 Nikolai Antropov .15 .40
174 Radoslav Suchy .12 .30
175 Nick Boynton .12 .30
176 Marc Denis .15 .40
177 Ivan Huml .12 .30
178 Dan Blackburn .15 .40
179 Roman Cechmanek .15 .40
180 Tony Amonte .15 .40
181 Jason Blake .12 .30
182 Erik Cole .15 .40
183 P-M Bouchard .20 .50
184 Reed Low .12 .30
185 Geoff Sanderson .12 .30
186 Andrei Zyuzin .12 .30
187 Jean-Sebastien Giguere .20 .50
188 Patrick Marleau .20 .50
189 Nicklas Lidstrom .20 .50
190 Ilya Kovalchuk .20 .50
191 Petr Nedved .12 .30
192 Vincent Lecavalier .15 .40
193 Andreas Johansson .12 .30
194 Dennis Seidenberg .20 .50
195 Alex Tanguay .15 .40
196 Slava Kozlov .15 .40
197 Eric Brewer .12 .30
198 Adam Hall .12 .30
199 Steve Reinprecht .12 .30
200 Todd Bertuzzi .20 .50
201 Rob Blake .20 .50
202 Olaf Kolzig .20 .50
203 Roman Turek .15 .40
204 Brian Rolston .15 .40
205 Bill Guerin .20 .50
206 Johan Hedberg .15 .40
207 Vladimir Orszagh .12 .30
208 Jordan Leopold .12 .30
209 Donald Brashear .12 .30
210 Saku Koivu .20 .50
211 Dave Andreychuk .20 .50
212 Luc Robitaille .20 .50
213 Shaun Van Allen .12 .30
214 Trevor Linden .20 .50
215 Jason Allison .15 .40
216 Marty Turco .20 .50
217 Kyle McLaren .12 .30
218 Daniel Sedin .20 .50
219 Eric Belanger .12 .30
220 Mattias Ohlund .12 .30
221 Brad Richards .20 .50
222 Kyle Calder .12 .30
223 Alexander Frolov .15 .40
224 Tomas Kaberle .12 .30
225 Martin Havlat .20 .50
226 Patrick Roy .50 1.25
227 Jamie Lundmark .12 .30
228 Wade Redden .12 .30
229 Mark Recchi .25 .60
230 Tomas Vokoun .15 .40
231 Scott Niedermayer .20 .50
232 Bob Boughner .12 .30
233 Rick DiPietro .15 .40
234 Chris Gratton .12 .30
235 Keith Tkachuk .20 .50
236 Rostislav Klesla .12 .30
237 Ruslan Salei .12 .30
238 Jeff Friesen .12 .30
239 Felix Potvin .30 .75
240 Dany Heatley .20 .50
241 Brad Stuart .12 .30
242 Andrew Cassels .12 .30
243 Ray Whitney .15 .40
244 Chris Pronger .15 .40
245 Garth Snow .15 .40
246 Sean Hill .12 .30
247 Kristian Huselius .12 .30
248 Jamie Langenbrunner .15 .40
249 Martin St. Louis .20 .50
250 Ron Francis .25 .60
251 Tyler Wright .12 .30
252 Doug Gilmour .25 .60
253 Mike Dunham .15 .40
254 Jozef Stumpel .12 .30
255 Andrew Brunette .12 .30
256 Bobby Holik .12 .30
257 Brendan Shanahan .25 .60
258 Martin Gelinas .12 .30
259 Sergei Berezin .12 .30
260 Zigmund Palffy .20 .50
261 Yannick Tremblay .12 .30
262 Pasi Nurminen .15 .40
263 Robyn Regehr .12 .30
264 Espen Knutsen .12 .30
265 Al MacInnis .20 .50
266 Adam Oates .20 .50
267 Ryan Smyth .15 .40
268 Marco Sturm .12 .30
269 Tom Poti .12 .30
270 Brett Hull .25 .60
271 David Aebischer .15 .40
272 Milan Hejduk .15 .40
273 Steve McKenna .12 .30
274 Dick Tarnstrom .12 .30
275 Kenny Jonsson .12 .30
276 Glen Murray .15 .40
277 Stu Barnes .12 .30
278 Jay Bouwmeester .20 .50
279 Darius Kasparaitis BM .10 .25
280 Scott Stevens BM .15 .40
281 Zdeno Chara BM .15 .40
282 Donald Brashear BM .10 .25
283 Reed Low BM .10 .25
284 Jody Shelley BM .10 .25
285 Eric Cairns BM .10 .25
286 Brendan Witt BM .10 .25
287 Rob Ray BM .10 .25
288 Georges Laraque BM .12 .30
289 Brett Hull SH .20 .50
290 Martin Brodeur SH .30 .75
291 Jean-Sebastien Giguere SH .15 .40
292 Paul Kariya SH .20 .50
293 New Jersey Devils .15 .40
294 Marty Turco AS .15 .40
295 Patrick Lalime AS .12 .30
296 Paul Kariya AS .20 .50
297 Nicklas Lidstrom AS .15 .40
298 Al MacInnis AS .15 .40
299 Scott Stevens AS .15 .40
300 Marian Gaborik AS .25 .60
301 Dany Heatley AS .15 .40
302 Jaromir Jagr AS .40 1.00
303 Olli Jokinen AS .15 .40
304 Bill Guerin AS .15 .40
305 Todd Bertuzzi AS .15 .40
306 Bruno St. Jacques .12 .30
307 Mathieu Darche .12 .30
308 Mathias Johansson .12 .30
309 Joe DiPenta RC .30 .75
310 Milan Bartovic RC .30 .75
311 Rick Mrozik RC .25 .60
312 Kent McDonell RC .30 .75
313 Fernando Pisani .12 .30
314 Kip Brennan .12 .30
315 Miroslav Zalesak .12 .30
316 Peter Sejna RC .30 .75
317 Matt Stajan RC .40 1.00
318 Ivan Ciernik .12 .30
319 Shaone Morrisonn .12 .30
320 Garnet Exelby .12 .30
321 Ari Ahonen .12 .30
322 Mike Rupp .12 .30
323 Kris Vernarsky .12 .30
324 Tomas Kurka .12 .30
325 Brandon Reid .12 .30
326 Jim Vandermeer .12 .30
327 Jared Aulin .12 .30
328 Cristobal Huet .15 .40
329 Alexei Ponikarovsky .12 .30
330 Alexei Semenov .12 .30
331 Patrice Bergeron RC 2.50 6.00
332 Jiri Hudler RC 1.25 3.00
333 Antti Miettinen RC .75 2.00
334 Eric Staal RC 2.50 6.00
335 Nathan Horton RC 1.25 3.00
336 Joffrey Lupul RC 1.25 3.00
337 Tuomo Ruutu RC .75 2.00
338 Jordin Tootoo RC 1.00 2.50
339 Dustin Brown RC 1.00 2.50
340 Marc-Andre Fleury RC 3.00 8.00
NNO Rookie EXCH expired .20 .50

2003-04 Topps Blue

This 330-card set paralleled the base set but carried blue borders. These parallels were inserted at 1:4 and each card was serial numbered out of 500. The Rookie Redemption parallel card was inserted at 1:1298.

*1-330 VETS/500: 3X TO 8X BASIC CARDS
*309-317 ROOKIES/500: 1.5X TO 4X BASIC RC
*331-340 ROOKIES/500: .8X TO 2X BASIC RC
101 Mark Messier 2.50 6.00

2003-04 Topps Red

This 330-card set paralleled the base set but carried red borders. These parallels were inserted at 1:21and each card was serial numbered out of 100. The Rookie Redemption parallel card was inserted at 1:5468.

*1-330 VETS/100: 6X TO 15X BASIC CARDS
*309-317 ROOKIES/100: 3X TO 8X BASIC RC
*331-340 ROOKIES/100: 1.5X TO 4X BASIC RC

2003-04 Topps First Overall Fabrics

SINGLE JSY.ODDS 1:4734
SINGLE PRINT RUN 50 SER.#'D SETS
DUAL JSY.ODDS 1:3769
DUAL PRINT RUN 25 SER.#'d SETS
ALL CARDS CARRY FO PREFIX
EL Eric Lindros 20.00 50.00
IL Ilya Kovalchuk 25.00 60.00
JT Joe Thornton 30.00 80.00
ML Mario Lemieux 50.00 125.00
MM Mike Modano 20.00 50.00
MS Mats Sundin 15.00 40.00
RN Rick Nash 20.00 50.00
VL Vincent Lecavalier 20.00 50.00
JTIK J.Thornton/I.Kovalchuk 50.00 125.00
JTVL J.Thornton/V.Lecavalier 60.00 150.00
MLMM M.Lemieux/M.Modano 75.00 200.00
MLRN M.Lemieux/R.Nash 75.00 200.00
MMMS M.Modano/M.Sundin 75.00 200.00
MSEL M.Sundin/E.Lindros 50.00 125.00
RNIK R.Nash/I.Kovalchuk 60.00 150.00
VLEL V.Lecavalier/E.Lindros 50.00 125.00

2003-04 Topps First Round Fabrics

SINGLE JSY.ODDS 1:238
DUAL JSY.ODDS 1:9706
ALL CARDS CARRY FR PREFIX
AY Alexei Yashin 6.00 15.00
BG Bill Guerin 6.00 15.00
JB Jay Bouwmeester 6.00 15.00
JI Jarome Iginla 12.50 30.00
JJ Jaromir Jagr 10.00 25.00
JL Jamie Lundmark 6.00 15.00
JP Jason Spezza 10.00 25.00
TB Todd Bertuzzi 6.00 15.00
BGJI B.Guerin/J.Iginla 30.00 80.00
JJJL J.Jagr/J.Lundmark
JSJB J.Spezza/J.Bouwmeester 30.00 80.00
TBAY T.Bertuzzi/A.Yashin 50.00 125.00

2003-04 Topps Idols

Inserted at 1:12, this 60-card insert set consisted of 3 subsets: Canadian Idols; USA Idols and International Idols. USA and International Idols were found in Topps packs while Canadian Idols were found in Canadian packs.

CI1 Dany Heatley .60 1.50
CI2 Martin Brodeur 1.25 3.00
CI3 Todd Bertuzzi .60 1.50
CI4 Mario Lemieux 2.00 5.00
CI5 Joe Thornton .75 2.00
CI6 Ed Belfour .60 1.50
CI7 Michael Peca .50 1.25
CI8 Jarome Iginla .60 1.50
CI9 Marty Turco .60 1.50
CI10 Steve Yzerman 1.50 4.00
CI11 Patrick Lalime .50 1.25
CI12 Jose Theodore .60 1.50
CI13 Rick Nash .60 1.50
CI14 Joe Sakic 1.00 2.50
CI15 Vincent Lecavalier .50 1.25
CI16 Mark Messier 1.00 2.50
CI17 Brendan Shanahan .75 2.00
CI18 Patrick Roy 1.50 4.00
CI19 Paul Kariya .75 2.00
CI20 Jocelyn Thibault .50 1.25
II1 Marian Gaborik 1.00 2.50
II2 Alex Kovalev .50 1.25
II3 Patrik Elias .60 1.50
II4 Daniel Alfredsson .60 1.50
II5 Alexei Yashin .50 1.25
II6 Peter Bondra .50 1.25
II7 Milan Hejduk .50 1.25
II8 Sergei Fedorov 1.00 2.50
II9 Alexander Mogilny .50 1.25
II10 Olli Jokinen .60 1.50
II11 Pavel Bure .75 2.00
II12 Jaromir Jagr 1.50 4.00
II13 Nicklas Lidstrom .60 1.50
II14 Ilya Kovalchuk .60 1.50
II15 Teemu Selanne 1.25 3.00
II16 Marian Hossa .50 1.25
II17 Markus Naslund .60 1.50
II18 Peter Forsberg .75 2.00
II19 Saku Koivu .60 1.50
II20 Mats Sundin .60 1.50
UI1 Bill Guerin .60 1.50
UI2 Jeremy Roenick .60 1.50
UI3 Doug Weight .60 1.50
UI4 Chris Drury .50 1.25
UI5 Mike Modano 1.00 2.50
UI6 Chris Chelios .60 1.50
UI7 Scott Gomez .50 1.25
UI8 Brian Rolston .50 1.25
UI9 Keith Tkachuk .60 1.50
UI10 Mark Parrish .40 1.00
UI11 John LeClair .60 1.50
UI12 Mike Dunham .50 1.25
UI13 Tyler Arnason .40 1.00
UI14 Tony Amonte .50 1.25
UI15 Mike York .40 1.00
UI16 David Legwand .50 1.25
UI17 Brian Leetch .60 1.50
UI18 Brent Johnson .50 1.25
UI19 Erik Cole .50 1.25
UI20 Jamie Langenbrunner .50 1.25

2003-04 Topps Lost Rookies

This 11-card set features "rookie" cards of superstars who didn't have a card issued during their rookie season. Cards from this set were inserted at 1:12.

BH Brett Hull .60 1.50
BS Brendan Shanahan .50 1.25
CJ Curtis Joseph .50 1.25
EB Ed Belfour .50 1.25
JR Jeremy Roenick .60 1.50
JS Joe Sakic 1.00 2.50
ML Mario Lemieux 3.00 8.00
MM Mike Modano .75 2.00
PR Patrick Roy 2.50 6.00
RF Ron Francis .50 1.25
SY Steve Yzerman 2.50 6.00

2003-04 Topps Own the Game

COMPLETE SET (20) 6.00 12.00
STATED ODDS 1:6
OTG1 Peter Forsberg .60 1.50
OTG2 Markus Naslund .20 .50
OTG3 Joe Thornton .30 .75
OTG4 Milan Hejduk .20 .50
OTG5 Todd Bertuzzi .20 .50
OTG6 Henrik Zetterberg .30 .75
OTG7 Tyler Arnason .15 .40
OTG8 Rick Nash .30 .75
OTG9 Ales Kotalik .15 .40
OTG10 Niko Kapanen .15 .40
OTG11 Martin Brodeur .75 2.00
OTG12 Patrick Lalime .15 .40
OTG13 Ed Belfour .20 .50
OTG14 Patrick Roy 1.00 2.50
OTG15 Jean-Sebastien Giguere .15 .40
OTG16 Jody Shelley .15 .40
OTG17 Reed Low .15 .40
OTG18 Matt Johnson .15 .40
OTG19 Wade Belak .15 .40
OTG20 Peter Worrell .15 .40

2003-04 Topps Signs of Toughness

STATED ODDS 1:1277
GL Georges Laraque 12.50 30.00
KS Kevin Sawyer 12.50 30.00
PW Peter Worrell 12.50 30.00
RR Rob Ray 20.00 50.00
SM Sandy McCarthy 12.50 30.00
SP Scott Parker 12.50 30.00
PJS P.J. Stock 12.50 30.00

2003-04 Topps Signs of Youth

STATED ODDS 1:635
BG Brian Gionta 5.00 12.00
BR Brad Richards 12.50 30.00
IK Ilya Kovalchuk 12.00 30.00
KH Kristian Huselius 10.00 25.00
RN Rick Nash 20.00 50.00
SW Stephen Weiss 10.00 25.00

2003-04 Topps Stanley Cup Heroes

STATED ODDS 1:36
BC Bobby Clarke 4.00 10.00
BN Bobby Nystrom 4.00 10.00
BS Billy Smith 4.00 10.00
DS Dave Schultz 4.00 10.00
GF Grant Fuhr 5.00 12.00
JL Jacques Lemaire 4.00 10.00
SS Serge Savard 4.00 10.00

2003-04 Topps Stanley Cup Heroes Autographs
STATED ODDS 1:250
BC Bobby Clarke 15.00 40.00
BN Bobby Nystrom 12.50 30.00
BS Billy Smith 12.50 30.00
DS Dave Schultz 12.50 30.00
GF Grant Fuhr 15.00 40.00
JL Jacques Lemaire 12.50 30.00
SS Serge Savard

2003-04 Topps Tough Materials
SINGLE JSY.ODDS 1:191
DUAL JSY.ODDS 1:1505
DL Darren Langdon 6.00 15.00
EC Eric Cairns 6.00 15.00
GL Georges Laraque 8.00 20.00
KS Kevin Sawyer 6.00 15.00
PW Peter Worrell 8.00 20.00
RL Reed Low 6.00 15.00
RR Rob Ray 8.00 20.00
SM Sandy McCarthy 6.00 15.00
SP Scott Parker 6.00 15.00
PJS P.J. Stock 10.00 25.00
GLSP G.Laraque/S.Parker 20.00 50.00
KSRL K.Sawyer/R.Low 12.50 30.00
PSRR P.Stock/R.Ray 20.00 50.00
PWDL P.Worrell/D.Langdon 20.00 50.00
SMEC S.McCarthy/E.Cairns 15.00 40.00

2003-04 Topps Tough Materials Autographs
STATED ODDS 1:1277
GL Georges Laraque 15.00 40.00
KS Kevin Sawyer 12.00 30.00
PW Peter Worrell 12.00 30.00
RR Rob Ray 15.00 40.00
SM Sandy McCarthy 12.00 30.00
SP Scott Parker 15.00 40.00
PJS P.J. Stock 12.00 30.00

2003-04 Topps Promos
COMPLETE SET (6) 1.50 4.00
PP1 Marian Hossa .30 .75
PP2 Jaromir Jagr .40 1.00
PP3 Curtis Joseph .30 .75
PP4 Mike Modano .40 1.00
PP5 Markus Naslund .30 .75
PP6 Alexei Yashin .25 .60

2011 Topps Allen and Ginter Autographs
STATED ODDS 1:68 HOBBY
DUAL AUTO ODDS 1:56,000 HOBBY
EXCHANGE DEADLINE 6/30/2014
RTU Ron Turcotte 20.00 50.00

2011 Topps Allen and Ginter Relics
STATED ODDS 1:10 HOBBY
EXCHANGE DEADLINE 6/30/2014
RTU Ron Turcotte 8.00 20.00

2013 Topps Allen and Ginter
COMPLETE SET (350) 20.00 50.00
COMP.SET w/o SP's (300) 12.00 30.00
SP ODDS 1:2 HOBBY
104 Mike Richter .40 1.00
212 Barry Melrose .40 1.00

2013 Topps Allen and Ginter Framed Mini Relics
VERSION A ODDS 1:29 HOBBY
VERSION B ODDS 1:27 HOBBY
BM Barry Melrose 6.00 15.00

2013 Topps Allen and Ginter Autographs
STATED ODDS 1:49 HOBBY
EXCHANGE DEADLINE 07/31/2016
BM Barry Melrose 8.00 20.00
MH Mike Richter 6.00 15.00

2013 Topps Allen and Ginter Autographs Red Ink
STATED ODDS 1:931 HOBBY
PRINT RUNS B/WN 10-409 SER.#'d SETS
NO PRICING ON MOST DUE TO SCARCITY
EXCHANGE DEADLINE 07/31/2013

2013 Topps Allen and Ginter Mini
*MINI 1-300: .75X TO 2X BASIC
*MINI 1-300 RC: .5X TO 1.2X BASIC RC's
*MINI SP 301-350: .5X TO 1.2X BASIC SP
MINI SP ODDS 1:13 HOBBY
351-400 RANDOM WITHIN RIP CARDS
STATED PLATE ODDS 1:594 HOBBY
PLATE PRINT RUN 1 SET PER COLOR
BLACK-CYAN-MAGENTA-YELLOW ISSUED
NO PLATE PRICING DUE TO SCARCITY

2013 Topps Allen and Ginter Mini A and G Back
*A & G BACK: 1X TO 2.5X BASIC
*A & G BACK RCs: .6X TO 1.5X BASIC RCs
A & G BACK ODDS 1:5 HOBBY
*A & G BACK SP: .6X TO 1.5X BASIC SP
A & G BACK SP ODDS 1:65 HOBBY

2013 Topps Allen and Ginter Mini Black
*BLACK: 1.5X TO 4X BASIC
*BLACK RCs: 1X TO 2.5X BASIC RCs
BLACK ODDS 1:10 HOBBY
*BLACK SP: 1X TO 2.5X BASIC SP
BLACK SP ODDS 1:130 HOBBY

2013 Topps Allen and Ginter Mini No Card Number
*NO NBR: 4X TO 10X BASIC
*NO NBR RCs: 2.5X TO 6X BASIC RCs
*NO NBR SP: 1.2X TO 3X BASIC SP
STATED ODDS 1:102 HOBBY
ANNC'D PRINT RUN OF 50 SETS

2015 Topps Allen and Ginter
COMPLETE SET (350) 30.00 80.00
ORIGINAL BUYBACK ODDS 1:7958 HOBBY
ORIG.BUYBACK PRINT RUN 1 SER.#'d SET
269 Jeremy Roenick .25 .60

2015 Topps Allen and Ginter Mini
*MINI 1-300: 1X TO 2.5X BASIC
*MINI 1-300 RC: .5X TO 1.2X BASIC RCs
*MINI SP 301-350: .6X TO 1.5X BASIC
MINI SP ODDS 1:13 HOBBY
351-400 RANDOM WITHIN RIP CARDS
STATED PLATE ODDS 1:495 HOBBY
PLATE PRINT RUN 1 SET PER COLOR
BLACK-CYAN-MAGENTA-YELLOW ISSUED
NO PLATE PRICING DUE TO SCARCITY

2015 Topps Allen and Ginter Mini A and G Back
*MINI AG 1-300: 1.2X TO 3X BASIC
*MINI AG 1-300 RC: .6X TO 1.5X BASIC RCs
*MINI AG SP 301-350: .75X TO 2X BASIC
MINI AG ODDS 1:5 HOBBY
MINI AG SP ODDS 1:65 HOBBY

2015 Topps Allen and Ginter Mini Black
*MINI BLK 1-300: 2X TO 5X BASIC
*MINI BLK 1-300 RC: 1X TO 2.5X BASIC RCs
*MINI BLK SP 301-350: 1.2X TO 3X BASIC
MINI BLK ODDS 1:10 HOBBY
MINI BLK SP ODDS 1:130 HOBBY

2015 Topps Allen and Ginter Mini Flag Back
*MINI FLAG: 5X TO 12X BASIC
*MINI FLAG RC: 2.5X TO 6X BASIC RCs
MINI FLAG ODDS 1:157 HOBBY
STATED PRINT RUN 25 SER.#'d SETS

2015 Topps Allen and Ginter Mini No Card Number
*MINI NNO: 6X TO 15X BASIC
*MINI NNO RC: 3X TO 8X BASIC RCs
MINI NNO ODDS 1:79 HOBBY
ANNCD PRINT RUN OF 50 COPIES EACH

2015 Topps Allen and Ginter Mini Red
*MINI RED: 5X TO 12X BASIC
*MINI RED RC: 2.5X TO 6X BASIC RCs
MINI RED ODDS 1:12 HOBBY BOXES
STATED PRINT RUN 40 SER.#'d SETS

2015 Topps Allen and Ginter Framed Mini Autographs
STATED ODDS 1:54 HOBBY
EXCHANGE DEADLINE 6/30/2018
AGAJR Jeremy Roenick 12.00 30.00

2015 Topps Allen and Ginter Relics
GROUP A ODDS 1:24 HOBBY
GROUP B ODDS 1:24 HOBBY
FSRAJR Jeremy Roenick A 2.50 6.00

2003 Topps All-Star Block Party
Given away exclusively at the Topps booth during the 2003 NHL All-Star block party, this 6-card set resembles the base Topps set but carried different numbering and an All-Star log on the card fronts. Each card was numbered "X of 6".
COMPLETE SET (6) 12.00
1 Patrick Roy 2.00 5.00
2 Jaromir Jagr .80 2.00
3 Jarome Iginla .40 1.00
4 Henrik Zetterberg 1.60 3.00
5 Rick Nash 1.60 4.00
6 Jay Bouwmeester 1.20 2.00

2004 Topps NHL All-Star FANtasy
This 6-card set was given away via a wrapper redemption at the Topps booth during the 2004 NHL All-Star weekend. Cards are numbered "X of 6" on the card backs.
COMPLETE SET (6) 6.00 15.00
1 Marian Gaborik .60 1.50
2 Dwayne Roloson .60 1.50
3 Patrice Bergeron 1.50 5.00
4 Marc-Andre Fleury 2.00 5.00
5 Eric Staal 1.00 2.00
6 Tuomo Ruutu 1.25 3.00

2001-02 Topps Archives
Released in mid-February 2002, this 81-card set had an SRP of $4.00 for a 8-card pack and featured reprints of past Topps/OPC rookie cards. Each card was embossed with a gold Topps Archives stamp in the top right corner and printed on 24-point white card stock.
COMPLETE SET (81) 30.00 60.00
1 Andy Bathgate .50 1.25
2 Bill Gadsby .50 1.25
3 Tony Esposito .75 2.00
4 Harry Howell .40 1.00
5 Larry Robinson .40 1.00
6 Jacques Plante .75 2.00
7 Pierre Pilote .50 1.25
8 Glenn Hall .50 1.25
9 Dale Hunter .25 .60
10 Guy Lapointe .25 .60
11 Norm Ullman .40 1.00
12 Bryan Trottier .60 1.50
13 Alex Delvecchio .50 1.25
14 Stan Mikita .60 1.50
15 Neal Broten .25 .60
16 Bernie Parent .50 1.25
17 Johnny Bucyk .50 1.25
18 Rick Middleton .40 1.00
19 Bobby Clarke .50 1.25
20 Billy Smith .50 1.25
21 Peter Stastny .40 1.00
22 Tim Kerr .25 .60
23 Gerry Cheevers .60 1.50
24 Andy Moog .40 1.00
25 Dennis Hull .40 1.00
26 Nick Fotiu .25 .60
27 Marcel Dionne .40 1.00
28 Guy Lafleur .60 1.50
29 Yvan Cournoyer .50 1.25
30 Brian Mullen .25 .60
31 Wayne Cashman .25 .60
32 Steve Shutt .40 1.00
33 Grant Fuhr .40 1.00
34 Ed Johnston .40 1.00
35 Clark Gillies .25 .60
36 Rick MacLeish .25 .60
37 Denis Potvin .40 1.00
38 Bill Clement .25 .60
39 Darryl Sittler .50 1.25
40 Pierre Larouche .25 .60
41 Vic Hadfield .25 .60
42 Derek Sanderson .40 1.00
43 Reggie Leach .25 .60
44 Brian Propp .25 .60
45 Barry Melrose .40 1.00
46 Danny Gare .25 .60
47 Darren Pang .40 1.00
48 Dick Duff .25 .60
49 Joel Quenneville .25 .60
50 John Ferguson .40 1.00
51 Ed Westfall .25 .60
52 Johnny Bower .50 1.25
53 Serge Savard .50 1.25
54 Keith Magnuson .25 .60
55 Ken Hodge .25 .60
56 Garry Unger .25 .60
57 Lindy Ruff .25 .60
58 Glenn Resch .40 1.00
59 Gump Worsley .50 1.25
60 Bernie Federko .25 .60
61 Mike Foligno .25 .60
62 Milt Schmidt .40 1.00
63 Mike Bossy .40 1.00
64 Ron Low .40 1.00
65 Jacques Lemaire .50 1.25
66 Dave Schultz .40 1.00
67 Glen Sather .40 1.00
68 Doug Wilson .25 .60
69 Terry Sawchuk 1.00 2.50
70 Mike Milbury .25 .60
71 Terry O'Reilly .40 1.00
72 Red Kelly .50 1.25
73 Peter McNab .25 .60
74 Paul Holmgren .25 .60
75 Ken Linseman .25 .60
76 Tim Horton .50 1.25
77 Bobby Smith .25 .60
78 Bobby Hull .75 2.00
79 Pat LaFontaine .40 1.00
80 Pete Mahovlich .25 .60
81 Mike Gartner .40 1.00

2001-02 Topps Archives Arena Seats
This 28-card set was inserted at a rate of 1:10 and featured a piece of an arena seat from either Boston Gardens, Maple Leaf Gardens or the Montreal Forum. Each card carried a reprinted card photo alongside the seat piece.
ASAD Alex Delvecchio 6.00 15.00
ASBF Bernie Federko 12.00 30.00
ASBS Bobby Smith 5.00 12.00
ASBT Bryan Trottier 8.00 20.00
ASDH Dennis Hull 5.00 12.00
ASDS Derek Sanderson 6.00 15.00
ASDSI Darryl Sittler 5.00 12.00
ASDWI Doug Wilson 5.00 12.00
ASGC Gerry Cheevers 6.00 15.00
ASGHA Glenn Hall 6.00 15.00
ASGL Guy Lapointe 5.00 12.00
ASGLA Guy Lafleur 8.00 20.00
ASJB John Bucyk 5.00 12.00
ASJL Jacques Lemaire 6.00 15.00
ASKH Ken Hodge 5.00 12.00
ASLR Larry Robinson 5.00 12.00
ASMD Marcel Dionne 6.00 15.00
ASNB Neal Broten 12.00 30.00
ASNU Norm Ullman 5.00 12.00
ASPL Pierre Larouche 5.00 12.00
ASPP Pierre Pilote 5.00 12.00
ASSM Stan Mikita 8.00 20.00
ASSSA Serge Savard 6.00 15.00
ASSSH Steve Shutt 6.00 15.00
ASTE Tony Esposito 6.00 15.00
ASTO Terry O'Reilly 6.00 15.00
ASWC Wayne Cashman 5.00 12.00
ASYC Yvan Cournoyer 6.00 15.00

2001-02 Topps Archives Autographs
Inserted at an overall rate of 1:17 hobby or retail packs, these cards were reprints of rookie cards of past players adorned with authentic autographs. Card #20, originally checklisted as Billy Smith, was never released.
1 Gerry Cheevers 10.00 25.00
2 Yvan Cournoyer 10.00 25.00
3 Denis Potvin 10.00 25.00
4 John Bucyk 10.00 25.00
5 Glenn Hall 12.00 30.00
6 Pierre Pilote 10.00 25.00
7 Norm Ullman 10.00 25.00
8 Jacques Lemaire 10.00 25.00
9 Grant Fuhr 12.00 30.00
10 Stan Mikita 25.00 50.00
11 Guy Lafleur 20.00 50.00
12 Tony Esposito SP 25.00 60.00
13 Alex Delvecchio 10.00 25.00
14 Dennis Hull 10.00 25.00
15 Marcel Dionne 10.00 25.00
16 Bobby Clarke 12.00 30.00
17 Darryl Sittler 12.50 30.00
18 Dave Schultz SP 50.00 100.00
19 Bryan Trottier 10.00 25.00
21 Terry O'Reilly SP 25.00 60.00
22 Serge Savard SP 40.00 80.00
23 Vic Hadfield SP 60.00 150.00
24 Rick Middleton SP 100.00 200.00
25 Peter McNab SP 100.00 200.00
26 Peter Stastny SP 75.00 150.00
27 Ken Linseman SP 25.00 60.00
28 Ed Westfall SP 50.00 120.00
29 Clark Gillies SP 25.00 60.00
30 Bobby Hull SP 75.00 150.00

2001-02 Topps Archives Buyback Autoproofs
Inserted at a rate of 1:1696 hobby or retail packs, these cards were actual vintage cards that were bought back by Topps, autographed by the player and then randomly inserted into packs. Each card was serial-numbered out of 50.
1 Marcel Dionne '88-89 Top 10.00 25.00
2 Bobby Clarke 8.00 20.00
3 Denis Potvin 50.00 100.00
4 Guy Lafleur 15.00 40.00

2001-02 Topps Archives Relics
This 15-card set featured smaller rookie reprint photos alongside swatches of game-used jerseys and sticks. Jersey cards were inserted at 1:8 and stick cards were inserted at 1:264. Jersey swatches were affixed using a rubber seal around the swatch.
JAD Alex Delvecchio J 6.00 15.00
JAM Andy Moog J 5.00 12.00
JBC Bobby Clarke J 12.50 30.00
JBM Brian Mullen J 6.00 15.00
JEW Ed Westfall J 5.00 12.00
JGF Grant Fuhr J 8.00 20.00
JLR Larry Robinson J 6.00 15.00
JMG Mike Gartner J 5.00 12.00
JPM Pete Mahovlich J 5.00 12.00
JSM Stan Mikita J 8.00 20.00
JBIS Billy Smith J 6.00 15.00
JBOS Bobby Smith J 5.00 12.00
SBC Bobby Clarke S 12.50 30.00
SDH Dale Hawerchuk S 8.00 20.00
STE Tony Esposito S 12.50 30.00

2003-04 Topps C55
This 165-card set was released in late December and pays homage to the original 1911-12 C55 set. Ten different players have two different cards each depicting them in either a cropped head and shoulders shot or a full length body shot, the cards are noted below with a "B" suffix (for checklisting purposes only). The set is considered incomplete without these 10 variation cards. A complete original C55 set was also inserted into packs at a rate of 1:6390. Since the buyback cards were not altered, prices can be found under the original set listing.
COMPLETE SET (165) 20.00 50.00
1 Peter Forsberg .30 .75
1B Peter Forsberg Full Length .30 .75
2 Brian Leetch .25 .60
3 Jarome Iginla .25 .60
4 Scott Stevens .25 .60
5 Nicklas Lidstrom .25 .60
6 Patrick Lalime .20 .50
7 Henrik Zetterberg .30 .75
7B Henrik Zetterberg Full Length .30 .75
8 Patrick Marleau .25 .60
9 Mike Modano .40 1.00
10 Marian Hossa .20 .50
11 Owen Nolan .20 .50
12 John Madden .15 .40
13 Mats Sundin .25 .60
14 Adam Hall .15 .40
15 Ron Francis .30 .75
16 Peter Bondra .20 .50
17 Ilya Kovalchuk .25 .60
17B Ilya Kovalchuk Full Length .25 .60
18 Miroslav Satan .20 .50
19 Joe Sakic .40 1.00
20 Vincent Lecavalier .20 .50
21 Rick Nash .25 .60
21B Rick Nash Full Length .25 .60
22 Anson Carter .20 .50
23 Doug Weight .25 .60
24 Rick DiPietro .20 .50
25 Tyler Arnason .15 .40
26 Mike Johnson .15 .40
27 Jeremy Roenick .25 .60
28 Teemu Selanne .50 1.25
29 Roberto Luongo .40 1.00
30 Martin Brodeur .50 1.25
30B Martin Brodeur Full Length .50 1.25
31 Bill Guerin .25 .60
32 Tim Connolly .15 .40
33 Roman Turek .20 .50
34 Olli Jokinen .25 .60
35 Radek Bonk .20 .50
36 Steve Rucchin .15 .40
37 Barret Jackman .15 .40
38 Dominik Hasek .40 1.00
39 Petr Nedved .15 .40
40 Marian Gaborik .40 1.00
40B Marian Gaborik Full Length .40 1.00
41 Josef Vasicek .15 .40
42 Ladislav Nagy .15 .40
43 Felix Potvin .40 1.00
44 Jay Bouwmeester .25 .60
45 Sergei Gonchar .15 .40
46 Niklas Hagman .15 .40
47 Glen Murray .20 .50
48 Kyle Calder .15 .40
49 Ed Belfour .25 .60
50 Milan Hejduk .20 .50
51 Alex Kovalev .20 .50
52 Petr Sykora .20 .50
53 Scott Hartnell .25 .60
54 Tony Amonte .20 .50
55 Ed Jovanovski .20 .50
56 Sergei Zubov .20 .50
57 Mark Recchi .30 .75
58 Markus Naslund .25 .60
59 Zigmund Palffy .25 .60
60 Marty Turco .25 .60
61 Jocelyn Thibault .20 .50
62 Martin Biron .20 .50
63 Roman Hamrlik .20 .50
64 Stanislav Chistov .15 .40
65 Tomas Kaberle .15 .40
66 Mario Lemieux .75 2.00
66B Mario Lemieux Full Length .75 2.00
67 Rob Blake .25 .60
68 Jaromir Jagr .60 1.50
69 Nikolai Khabibulin .25 .60
70 Brett Hull .30 .75
71 Slava Kozlov .20 .50
72 Michael Peca .20 .50
73 Jeff O'Neill .15 .40
74 Joe Nieuwendyk .25 .60
75 Yanic Perreault .15 .40
76 Derian Hatcher .15 .40
77 Chris Gratton .15 .40
78 Olaf Kolzig .25 .60
79 Alexei Yashin .20 .50
80 Martin St. Louis .25 .60
81 Chris Pronger .20 .50
82 Dick Tarnstrom .15 .40
83 Nick Schultz .15 .40
84 Ossi Vaananen .15 .40
85 Tie Domi .20 .50
86 Patrik Elias .25 .60
87 Jim Vandermeer .15 .40
88 Alexei Morozov .15 .40
89 Alexander Mogilny .20 .50
90 Dany Heatley .25 .60
91 Marcel Hossa .15 .40
92 Mike Comrie .20 .50
92B Mike Comrie Full Length .20 .50
93 Niko Kapanen .15 .40
94 David Legwand .20 .50
95 Alex Tanguay .20 .50
96 Alyn McCauley .15 .40
97 Brendan Morrison .20 .50
98 Chris Drury .20 .50
99 Paul Kariya .30 .75
100 Joe Thornton .30 .75
100B Joe Thornton Full Length .30 .75
101 Tomas Vokoun .20 .50
102 Tommy Salo .20 .50
103 Brad Richards .25 .60
104 Geoff Sanderson .15 .40
105 Daniel Briere .25 .60
106 Mike Dunham .20 .50
107 Kyle McLaren .15 .40
108 Zdeno Chara .25 .60
109 Curtis Joseph .25 .60
110 Todd Bertuzzi .25 .60
111 Saku Koivu .25 .60
112 Martin Havlat .25 .60
113 Dave Andreychuk .25 .60
114 Dan Cloutier .20 .50
115 Pavol Demitra .30 .75
116 Dave Scatchard .15 .40
117 Ryan Smyth .20 .50
118 Craig Conroy .15 .40
119 Eric Brewer .15 .40
120 Jean-Sebastien Giguere .25 .60
120B J.Giguere Full Length .25 .60
121 Alexander Frolov .20 .50
122 Al MacInnis .25 .60
123 Martin Straka .15 .40
124 Brian Rolston .20 .50
125 Jamie Langenbrunner .20 .50
126 Pierre-Marc Bouchard .25 .60
127 Jan Bulis .15 .40
128 Rostislav Klesla .15 .40
129 Pasi Nurminen .20 .50
130 Jose Theodore .25 .60
131 Tuomo Ruutu RC 1.00 2.50
132 Andrew Peters RC .75 2.00
133 Jordin Tootoo RC 1.25 3.00
134 Joe DiPenta RC .75 2.00
135 Milan Bartovic RC .75 2.00
136 Rick Mrozik RC .60 1.50
137 Kent McDonell RC .75 2.00
138 Antti Miettinen RC 1.00 2.50
139 Alexander Semin RC 2.00 5.00
140 Dustin Brown RC 1.25 3.00
141 Peter Sejna RC .75 2.00
142 Matt Stajan RC 1.00 2.50
143 Brent Burns RC 1.50 4.00
144 Paul Martin RC .75 2.00
145 Antoine Vermette RC 1.25 3.00
146 Sean Bergenheim RC .75 2.00
147 Joni Pitkanen RC 1.00 2.50
148 Patrice Bergeron RC 3.00 8.00
149 Eric Staal RC 3.00 8.00
150 Dan Hamhuis RC .75 2.00
151 Marc-Andre Fleury RC 4.00 10.00
152 Jiri Hudler RC 1.50 4.00
153 David Hale RC .60 1.50
154 Milan Michalek RC 1.25 3.00
155 John-Michael Liles RC .75 2.00

2003-04 Topps C55 Minis
These mini-cards were inserted one per pack and parallel the base set. There were several different parallels of the mini set that carried differing card backs.
*1-30 VETS: .5X TO 1.2X BASIC CARDS
*131-155 ROOKIES: .5X TO 1.2X BASIC RC

2003-04 Topps C55 Minis American Back
*1-130 VETS: .8X TO 2X BASIC CARDS
*131-155 ROOKIES: .6X TO 1.5X BASIC RC
BLACK BACK STATED ODDS 1:9

2003-04 Topps C55 Minis American Back Red
*1-130 VETS: 2X TO 5X BASIC CARDS
*131-155 ROOKIES: 1X TO 2.5X BASIC RC
STATED ODDS 1:33

2003-04 Topps C55 Minis Brooklyn Back
*1-130 VETS: .8X TO 2X BASIC CARDS
*131-155 ROOKIES: .6X TO 1.5X BASIC RC
STATED ODDS 1:9

2003-04 Topps C55 Minis Hat Trick Back
*1-130 VETS: 2X TO 5X BASIC CARDS
*131-155 ROOKIES: 1X TO 2.5X BASIC RC
STATED ODDS 1:38

2003-04 Topps C55 Minis O Canada Back
*1-130 VETS: .8X TO 2X BASIC CARDS
*131-155 ROOKIES: .6X TO 1.5X BASIC RC
BLACK BACK STATED ODDS 1:9

2003-04 Topps C55 Minis O Canada Back Red
*1-130 VETS: 2X TO 5X BASIC CARDS
*131-155 ROOKIES: 1X TO 2.5X BASIC RC
STATED ODDS 1:33

2003-04 Topps C55 Minis Stanley Cup Back
*1-300 VETS: .6X TO 1.5X BASIC CARDS
*131-155 ROOKIES: .6X TO 1.5X BASIC RC
STATED ODDS 1:4

2003-04 Topps C55 Autographs
This 12-card set featured certified autographs on mini-cards. Each card was held in a grey "C55" holder and shrink wrapped in clear plastic.
GROUP A ODDS 1:81
GROUP B ODDS 1:417
GROUP C ODDS 1:71
TACD Chris Drury C 6.00 15.00
TAEC Erik Cole A 6.00 15.00
TAHZ Henrik Zetterberg A 10.00 25.00
TAIK Ilya Kovalchuk B 10.00 25.00
TAJG Jean-Sebastien Giguere A 8.00 20.00
TAKH Kristian Huselius A 6.00 15.00
TAMH Marian Hossa A 8.00 20.00
TAPE Patrik Elias C 6.00 15.00
TARN Rick Nash A 6.00 15.00
TARV Radim Vrbata C 6.00 15.00
TASW Stephen Weiss A 6.00 15.00
TATB Todd Bertuzzi C 8.00 20.00

2003-04 Topps C55 Award Winners
These decoy cards represented trophy winners from the previous campaign. Cards from this set and the Stanley Cup Winners set were inserted one per non-memorabilia pack.
1 Mighty Ducks of Anaheim .20 .50
2 New Jersey Devils .20 .50
3 Ottawa Senators .20 .50
4 Barret Jackman .20 .50
5 Brendan Shanahan .25 .60
6 Peter Forsberg .40 1.00
7 Martin Brodeur .50 1.25
8 Alexander Mogilny .20 .50
9 Steve Yzerman .75 2.00
10 Nicklas Lidstrom .25 .60
11 Markus Naslund .25 .60
12 Milan Hejduk .20 .50
13 Peter Forsberg .40 1.00
14 Jere Lehtinen .20 .50
15 Jean-Sebastien Giguere .20 .50
16 Martin Brodeur .50 1.25

2003-04 Topps C55 Relics
This 45-card set featured jersey swatches on mini-cards. Each card was held in a grey "C55" holder and shrink wrapped in clear plastic.
GROUP A ODDS 1:15788
GROUP B ODDS 1:948
GROUP C ODDS 1:268
GROUP D ODDS 1:56
GROUP E ODDS 1:15
TRAH Adam Hall E 3.00 8.00
TRAS Alexander Svitov E 3.00 8.00
TRAY Alexei Yashin E 3.00 8.00
TRBG Bill Guerin E 3.00 8.00
TRBH Brett Hull D 8.00 20.00
TRBM Brendan Morrison D 3.00 8.00
TRBRA Branko Radivojevic E 3.00 8.00
TRBR Brad Richards D 4.00 10.00
TRDA Daniel Alfredsson D 4.00 10.00
TRDH Dany Heatley C 6.00 15.00
TRDL David Legwand C 4.00 10.00
TREB Ed Belfour D 6.00 15.00
TRGL Georges Laraque E 3.00 8.00
TRIK Ilya Kovalchuk D 8.00 20.00
TRJB Jay Bouwmeester E 3.00 8.00
TRJI Jarome Iginla E 6.00 15.00
TRJJ Jaromir Jagr E 8.00 20.00
TRJL Jordan Leopold E 3.00 8.00
TRJS Jason Spezza E 6.00 15.00
TRJT Jose Theodore E 6.00 15.00
TRJTH Joe Thornton E 8.00 20.00
TRMC Mike Comrie B 8.00 20.00
TRMG Marian Gaborik E 8.00 20.00
TRMHE Milan Hejduk D 5.00 12.00
TRMH Marian Hossa E 5.00 12.00
TRML Mario Lemieux A 250.00 400.00
TRMM Mike Modano B 50.00 125.00
TRMN Markus Naslund D 5.00 12.00
TRMS Mats Sundin D 5.00 12.00
TRMT Marty Turco E 4.00 10.00
TRNK Nikolai Khabibulin E 5.00 12.00
TRNS Nick Schultz E 3.00 8.00
TRPB Pavel Bure E 8.00 20.00
TRPK Paul Kariya B 20.00 50.00
TRPL Patrick Lalime D 4.00 10.00
TRRB Rob Blake E 4.00 10.00
TRRL Roberto Luongo C 6.00 15.00
TRRM Ryan Miller E 6.00 15.00
TRRN Rick Nash E 6.00 15.00
TRSK Saku Koivu E 5.00 12.00
TRSN Scott Niedermayer B 20.00 50.00
TRSP Scott Parker E 3.00 8.00
TRTB Todd Bertuzzi E 5.00 12.00
TRTC Tim Connolly B 20.00 50.00
TRVL Vincent Lecavalier B 40.00 100.00

2003-04 Topps C55 Stanley Cup Winners
These decoy cards represented Cup winners from previous years. Cards from this set and the Award Winners set were inserted one per non-memorabilia pack.
1 Ottawa Senators .30 .75
2 New York Rangers .30 .75
3 Boston Bruins .30 .75
4 Montreal Canadiens .30 .75
5 Montreal Canadiens .30 .75
6 Toronto Maple Leafs .30 .75
7 New York Rangers .30 .75
8 Chicago Blackhawks .30 .75
9 Montreal Maroons .30 .75
10 Detroit Red Wings .30 .75
11 Detroit Red Wings .30 .75
12 Chicago Blackhawks .30 .75
13 Boston Bruins .30 .75
14 New York Rangers .30 .75
15 Boston Bruins .30 .75
16 Toronto Maple Leafs .30 .75
17 Detroit Red Wings .30 .75
18 Montreal Canadiens .30 .75
19 Toronto Maple Leafs .30 .75
20 Montreal Canadiens .30 .75
21 Toronto Maple Leafs .30 .75
22 Toronto Maple Leafs .30 .75
23 Toronto Maple Leafs .30 .75
24 Detroit Red Wings .30 .75
25 Toronto Maple Leafs .30 .75
26 Detroit Red Wings .30 .75
27 Montreal Canadiens .30 .75
28 Detroit Red Wings .30 .75
29 Detroit Red Wings .30 .75
30 Montreal Canadiens .30 .75
31 Montreal Canadiens .30 .75
32 Montreal Canadiens .30 .75
33 Montreal Canadiens .30 .75
34 Montreal Canadiens .30 .75
35 Chicago Blackhawks .30 .75
36 Toronto Maple Leafs .30 .75
37 Toronto Maple Leafs .30 .75
38 Toronto Maple Leafs .30 .75
39 Montreal Canadiens .30 .75
40 Montreal Canadiens .30 .75
41 Toronto Maple Leafs .30 .75
42 Montreal Canadiens .30 .75
43 Montreal Canadiens .30 .75
44 Boston Bruins .30 .75
45 Montreal Canadiens .30 .75
46 Boston Bruins .30 .75
47 Montreal Canadiens .30 .75
48 Philadelphia Flyers .30 .75
49 Philadelphia Flyers .30 .75
50 Montreal Canadiens .30 .75
51 Montreal Canadiens .30 .75
52 Montreal Canadiens .30 .75
53 Montreal Canadiens .30 .75
54 New York Islanders .30 .75
55 New York Islanders .30 .75
56 New York Islanders .30 .75
57 New York Islanders .30 .75
58 Edmonton Oilers .30 .75
59 Edmonton Oilers .30 .75
60 Montreal Canadiens .30 .75
61 Edmonton Oilers .30 .75
62 Edmonton Oilers .30 .75
63 Calgary Flames .30 .75
64 Edmonton Oilers .30 .75
65 Pittsburgh Penguins .30 .75
66 Pittsburgh Penguins .30 .75
67 Montreal Canadiens .30 .75
68 New York Rangers .30 .75
69 New Jersey Devils .30 .75
70 Colorado Avalanche .30 .75
71 Detroit Red Wings .30 .75
72 Detroit Red Wings .30 .75
73 Dallas Stars .30 .75
74 New Jersey Devils .30 .75
75 Colorado Avalanche .30 .75
76 Detroit Red Wings .30 .75
77 New Jersey Devils .30 .75

1999-00 Topps Chrome
The 1999-00 Topps/OPC Chrome set released as a 297-card set printed on 16-point foil stock and consisted of 247 regular player cards and 39 subset cards, (24) 1999 NHL Draft Picks, 4-CHL Stars, and 11-Magic Moments which is comprised of five different versions of each card highlighting five significant moments in each player's career. Packaged in 24-pack boxes and 4-card packs, Topps/OPC Chrome packs carried a suggested retail price of $3.00.
COMPLETE SET (297) 150.00 300.00
COMP.SET w/MMs (341) 200.00 400.00
FIVE VERSIONS OF MM 276-286 EXIST
ALL VERSIONS SAME VALUE
1 Joe Sakic .75 2.00
2 Alexei Yashin .40 1.00
3 Paul Kariya .60 1.50
4 Keith Tkachuk .50 1.25
5 Jaromir Jagr 1.25 3.00
6 Mike Modano .75 2.00
7 Eric Lindros .75 2.00
8 Zigmund Palffy .50 1.25
9 Dominik Hasek .75 2.00
10 Pavel Bure .60 1.50
11 Ray Bourque .75 2.00
12 Peter Forsberg .50 1.25
13 Al MacInnis .50 1.25
14 Steve Yzerman 1.50 4.00
15 Mats Sundin .50 1.25
16 Patrick Roy 2.00 5.00
17 Teemu Selanne 1.00 2.50
18 Keith Primeau .30 .75
19 John LeClair .50 1.25
20 Martin Brodeur 1.00 2.50
21 Joe Thornton .75 2.00
22 Rob Blake .50 1.25
23 Ron Francis .60 1.50
24 Grant Fuhr .50 1.25
25 Nicklas Lidstrom .50 1.25
26 Vladimir Orszagh RC .30 .75
27 Glen Wesley .30 .75
28 Adam Deadmarsh .30 .75
29 Zdeno Chara .50 1.25
30 Brian Leetch .50 1.25
31 Valeri Bure .30 .75
32 Ryan Smyth .40 1.00
33 Jean-Sebastien Aubin .40 1.00
34 Dave Reid .30 .75
35 Ed Jovanovski .40 1.00
36 Anders Eriksson .30 .75
37 Mike Ricci .40 1.00
38 Todd Bertuzzi .40 1.00
39 Shawn Bates .30 .75
40 Kip Miller .30 .75
41 Jozef Stumpel .30 .75
42 Jeremy Roenick .50 1.25
43 Todd Marchant .30 .75
44 Josh Holden .30 .75
45 Rob Niedermayer .30 .75
46 Cory Sarich .30 .75
47 Nikolai Khabibulin .40 1.00
48 Marty McInnis .30 .75
49 Marty Reasoner .30 .75
50 Gary Roberts .30 .75
51 Manny Malhotra .40 1.00
52 Adam Foote .40 1.00
53 Luc Robitaille .50 1.25
54 Bryan Marchment .40 1.00
55 Mark Janssens .30 .75
56 Steve Heinze .30 .75
57 Cory Stillman .30 .75
58 Guy Hebert .50 1.25
59 Mike Richter .50 1.25
60 Jamie Langenbrunner .30 .75
61 Wade Redden .30 .75
62 Steve Smith .30 .75
63 Daniil Markov .30 .75
64 Erik Rasmussen .30 .75
65 Glen Murray .40 1.00
66 Alexei Kovalev .40 1.00
67 Peter Bondra .40 1.00
68 Dimitri Khristich .30 .75
69 Sami Kapanen .30 .75
70 Tom Poti .30 .75
71 Trevor Linden .50 1.25
72 Tomas Vokoun .50 1.25
73 Steve Webb .30 .75
74 Jarome Iginla .50 1.25
75 Scott Mellanby .30 .75
76 Mattias Ohlund .40 1.00
77 Steve Konowalchuk .30 .75
78 Bryan Berard .30 .75
79 Chris Pronger .40 1.00
80 Teppo Numminen .30 .75
81 John MacLean .40 1.00
82 Jeff Hackett .30 .75
83 Ray Whitney .40 1.00
84 Chris Osgood .50 1.25
85 Doug Zmolek .30 .75
86 Curtis Brown .30 .75
87 Reid Simpson .30 .75
88 Milan Hejduk .40 1.00
89 Donald Audette .30 .75
90 Saku Koivu .50 1.25
91 Martin Straka .30 .75
92 Mark Messier .75 2.00
93 Richard Zednik .30 .75
94 Curtis Joseph .50 1.25
95 Colin Forbes .30 .75
96 Jeff Friesen .40 1.00
97 Eric Brewer .30 .75
98 Darius Kasparaitis .40 1.00
99 Marian Hossa .40 1.00
100 Petr Sykora .40 1.00
101 Vladimir Malakhov .30 .75
102 Jamie Storr .30 .75
103 Doug Gilmour .60 1.50
104 Doug Weight .50 1.25
105 Derian Hatcher .40 1.00
106 Chris Drury .40 1.00
107 Arturs Irbe .40 1.00
108 Fred Brathwaite .30 .75
109 Jason Allison .40 1.00
110 Roman Hamrlik .40 1.00
111 Rico Fata .30 .75
112 Janne Niinimaa .30 .75
113 Kenny Jonsson .30 .75
114 Marco Sturm .40 1.00
115 Steve Thomas .30 .75
116 Garth Snow .40 1.00
117 Rick Tocchet .40 1.00
118 Jean-Marc Pelletier .30 .75
119 Bobby Holik .30 .75
120 Sergei Fedorov .75 2.00
121 J-P Dumont .40 1.00
122 Jason Woolley .30 .75
123 James Patrick .30 .75
124 Blake Sloan .40 1.00
125 Marcus Nilsson .30 .75
126 Shayne Corson .30 .75
127 Tom Fitzgerald .30 .75
128 Brian Rolston .40 1.00
129 Ron Tugnutt .40 1.00
130 Mark Recchi .60 1.50
131 Matthew Barnaby .40 1.00
132 Olaf Kolzig .50 1.25
133 Paul Mara .30 .75
134 Patrick Marleau .50 1.25
135 Magnus Arvedson .30 .75
136 Felix Potvin .75 2.00
137 Bill Guerin .50 1.25
138 Brett Hull .75 2.00
139 Vitali Yachmenev .30 .75
140 Ruslan Salei .30 .75
141 Mark Parrish .30 .75

42 Randy Cunneyworth .30 .75
43 Damian Rhodes .30 .75
44 Daniel Briere .40 1.00
45 Craig Conroy .30 .75
46 Sergei Gonchar .30 .75
47 Vincent Lecavalier .40 1.00
48 Adam Graves .40 1.00
49 Doug Bodger .30 .75
50 Jeff O'Neill .30 .75
51 Darby Hendrickson .30 .75
52 Sergei Samsonov .40 1.00
53 Ed Belfour .50 1.25
54 Robert Svehla .30 .75
55 Cliff Ronning .30 .75
56 Brendan Morrison .40 1.00
57 Daniel Alfredsson .50 1.25
58 Eric Desjardins .40 1.00
59 Mike Vernon .40 1.00
60 Vadim Sharifijanov .30 .75
61 Jaroslav Svejkovsky .30 .75
62 Michael Peca .40 1.00
63 Shane Willis .30 .75
64 Sandis Ozolinsh .30 .75
65 Mathieu Dandenault .30 .75
66 Martin Rucinsky .30 .75
67 Scott Stevens .50 1.25
68 Sami Salo .40 1.00
69 Tom Barrasso .50 1.25
70 Chris Gratton .30 .75
71 Markus Naslund .50 1.25
72 Mike Johnson .40 1.00
73 Bob Boughner .30 .75
74 Todd Simpson .30 .75
75 Fredrik Olausson .30 .75
76 Jocelyn Thibault .40 1.00
77 Juha Ylonen .30 .75
78 Brad Bombardir .30 .75
79 Jan Hrdina .30 .75
80 Adrian Aucoin .30 .75
81 Mike Eagles .30 .75
82 Petr Nedved .30 .75
83 Rem Murray .30 .75
84 Mikael Renberg .30 .75
85 Mike Eastwood .30 .75
86 Byron Dafoe .30 .75
87 Tony Amonte .40 1.00
88 Darren McCarty .30 .75
89 Sergei Krivokrasov .30 .75
90 Dave Lowry .30 .75
91 Michal Handzus .40 1.00
92 Tie Domi .40 1.00
93 Brian Holzinger .30 .75
94 Jason Arnott .40 1.00
95 Jose Theodore .50 1.25
96 Brendan Shanahan .60 1.50
97 Derek Morris .30 .75
98 Steve Rucchin .30 .75
99 Kevin Hodson .30 .75
100 Oleg Kvasha .30 .75
101 John Vanbiesbrouck .40 1.00
102 Adam Oates .50 1.25
103 Anson Carter .40 1.00
104 Sebastien Bordeleau .30 .75
105 Pavol Demitra .60 1.50
106 Owen Nolan .50 1.25
107 Pavel Rosa .30 .75
108 Petr Svoboda .40 1.00
109 Tomas Kaberle .30 .75
110 Claude Lapointe .40 1.00
111 Todd Harvey .30 .75
112 Trent McCleary .30 .75
113 Vyacheslav Kozlov .30 .75
114 Marc Denis .40 1.00
115 Joe Nieuwendyk .50 1.25
116 Kelly Buchberger .30 .75
117 Tommy Albelin .30 .75
118 Kyle McLaren .30 .75
119 Chris Chelios .50 1.25
120 Joel Bouchard .30 .75
121 Mats Lindgren .30 .75
122 Jyrki Lumme .30 .75
123 Pierre Turgeon .50 1.25
124 Bill Muckalt .30 .75
125 Antti Aalto .30 .75
126 Jere Lehtinen .40 1.00
127 Theo Fleury .60 1.50
128 Dmitri Mironov .30 .75
129 Scott Niedermayer .50 1.25
130 Sean Burke .30 .75
131 Eric Daze .40 1.00
132 Alexei Zhitnik .30 .75
133 Christian Matte .30 .75
134 Patrik Elias .50 1.25
135 Alexandre Korolyuk .30 .75
136 Sergei Berezin .30 .75
137 Ray Ferraro .30 .75
138 Rod Brind'Amour .50 1.25
139 Darcy Tucker .30 .75
140 Darryl Sydor .40 1.00
141 Mike Dunham .30 .75
142 Marc Bergevin .30 .75
143 Ray Sheppard .30 .75
144 Miroslav Satan .40 1.00
145 Andreas Dackell .30 .75
146 Mike Grier .30 .75
147 Alexei Zhamnov .30 .75
148 David Legwand .30 .75
149 Daniel Tkaczuk .30 .75
250 Roberto Luongo .60 1.50
251 Simon Gagne .50 1.25
252 Jamie Lundmark .40 1.00
253 Alexandre Giroux RC .40 1.00
254 Dusty Jamieson RC .50 1.25
255 Jamie Chamberlain RC .50 1.25
256 Radim Vrbata RC 2.00 5.00
257 Scott Cameron RC .50 1.25
258 Simon Lajeunesse RC .60 1.50
259 Tim Connolly .30 .75
260 Kris Beech .30 .75
261 Brian Finley .50 1.25
262 Alex Auld RC .60 1.50
263 Martin Grenier RC .50 1.25
264 Sheldon Keefe RC .60 1.50
265 Justin Mapletoft RC .50 1.25
266 Edward Hill RC .50 1.25
267 Nolan Yonkman RC .60 1.50
268 Oleg Saprykin RC .60 1.50
269 Branislav Mezei RC .40 1.00
270 Chris Kelly RC .50 1.25
271 Pavel Brendl RC 1.00 2.50
272 Brett Lysak RC .50 1.25
273 Matt Carkner RC .50 1.25
274 Luke Sellars RC .60 1.50
275 Brad Ralph RC .50 1.25
276A Ray Bourque MM 1.50 4.00
276B Ray Bourque MM 1.50 4.00
1996 All-Star MVP
276C Ray Bourque MM 1.50 4.00
5-time Norris Winner
276D Ray Bourque MM 1.50 4.00
1000 NHL Points
276E Ray Bourque MM 1.50 4.00
1980 Calder Trophy
277A Peter Forsberg MM 1.00 2.50
277B Peter Forsberg MM 1.00 2.50
3 All-Star Games
277C Peter Forsberg MM 1.00 2.50
1994 Gold Medal
277D Peter Forsberg MM 1.00 2.50
1994 Gold Medal Goal
277E Peter Forsberg MM 1.00 2.50
1996 Stanley Cup
278A Joe Nieuwendyk MM 1.00 2.50
278B Joe Nieuwendyk MM 1.00 2.50
4 All-Star Games
278C Joe Nieuwendyk MM 1.00 2.50
1999 Stanley Cup
278D Joe Nieuwendyk MM 1.00 2.50
1999 Conn Smythe Trophy
278E Joe Nieuwendyk MM 1.00 2.50
1988 Calder Trophy
279A Dominik Hasek MM 1.50 4.00
279B Dominik Hasek MM 1.50 4.00
5-time Vezina Winner
279C Dominik Hasek MM 1.50 4.00
2-time Pearson Winner
279D Dominik Hasek MM 1.50 4.00
4 All-Star Games
279E Dominik Hasek MM 1.50 4.00
1998 Gold Medal
280A Jaromir Jagr MM 2.50 6.00
280B Jaromir Jagr MM 2.50 6.00
1999 Hart Trophy
280C Jaromir Jagr MM 2.50 6.00
8 All-Star Games
280D Jaromir Jagr MM 2.50 6.00
3-time Scoring Leader
280E Jaromir Jagr MM 2.50 6.00
2-time Stanley Cup Winner
281A Paul Kariya MM 1.25 3.00
281B Paul Kariya MM 1.25 3.00
3 All-Star Games
281C Paul Kariya MM 1.25 3.00
50 goals 1995-96
281D Paul Kariya MM 1.25 3.00
1994 Silver Medal
281E Paul Kariya MM 1.25 3.00
1993 NCAA Champ
282A Eric Lindros MM 1.50 4.00
282B Eric Lindros MM 1.50 4.00
1992 Silver Medal
282C Eric Lindros MM 1.50 4.00
1995 Hart Trophy
282D Eric Lindros MM 1.50 4.00
1995 Pearson Award
282E Eric Lindros MM 1.50 4.00
5 All-Star Games
283A Mark Messier MM 1.50 4.00
283B Mark Messier MM 1.50 4.00
6-time Stanley Cup Winner
283C Mark Messier MM 1.50 4.00
13 All-Star Games
283D Mark Messier MM 1.50 4.00
2-time Hart Winner
283E Mark Messier MM 1.50 4.00
2-time Pearson Winner
284A Patrick Roy MM 4.00 10.00
284B Patrick Roy MM 4.00 10.00
8 All-Star Games
284C Patrick Roy MM 4.00 10.00
3-time Vezina Winner
284D Patrick Roy MM 4.00 10.00
2-time Conn Smythe Winner
284E Patrick Roy MM 4.00 10.00
Playoff Wins Leader
285A Joe Sakic MM 1.50 4.00
285B Joe Sakic MM 1.50 4.00
7 All-Star Games
285C Joe Sakic MM 1.50 4.00
1996 Stanley Cup
285D Joe Sakic MM 1.50 4.00
50 goals 1995-96
285E Joe Sakic MM 1.50 4.00
1996 Conn Smythe Trophy
286A Steve Yzerman MM 3.00 8.00
286B Steve Yzerman MM 3.00 8.00
8 All-Star Games
286C Steve Yzerman MM 3.00 8.00
1989 Pearson Award
286D Steve Yzerman MM 3.00 8.00
1998 Conn Smythe Trophy
286E Steve Yzerman MM 3.00 8.00
2-time Stanley Cup Winner
287 Alex Tanguay .40 1.00
288 Brad Stuart .40 1.00
289 Brian Boucher .50 1.25
290 Steve Kariya RC .60 1.50
291 Scott Gomez .40 1.00
292 Mikko Eloranta RC .50 1.25
293 Patrik Stefan RC .60 1.50
294 John Madden RC .60 1.50
295 Per Svartvadet RC .40 1.00
296 Jiri Fischer .30 .75
297 Nikolai Antropov RC 1.50 4.00

1999-00 Topps Chrome Refractors

Randomly inserted in Topps packs at 1:12, this 297-card set parallels the base set and is enhanced by the rainbow holo-foil refractor effect. The card number on the back appears above, the word "REFRACTOR".
*VETERANS: 3X TO 8X BASIC CARDS
*253-297 ROOK: 2.5X TO 6X BASIC RC
*276-286 MM: 1.5X TO 4X BASIC MM
92 Mark Messier 6.00 15.00
283A Mark Messier MM 6.00 15.00
1984 Conn Smythe Trophy
283B Mark Messier MM 6.00 15.00
6-time Stanley Cup Winner
283C Mark Messier MM 6.00 15.00
13 All-Star Games
283D Mark Messier MM 6.00 15.00
2-time Hart Winner
283E Mark Messier MM 6.00 15.00
2-time Pearson Winner

1999-00 Topps Chrome All-Topps

Randomly seeded in Topps and OPC packs at 1:24, this 15-card set features brilliant action photography of the best active players at a particular position, while the card backs contain comparisons with all-time greats at that same position. Refractor parallels of this set were also randomly inserted at 1:120.
COMPLETE SET (15) 15.00 40.00
*REFRACTORS: 1.2X TO 3X BASIC INSERTS
AT1 Dominik Hasek 2.00 5.00
AT2 Martin Brodeur 2.50 6.00
AT3 Ray Bourque 1.50 4.00
AT4 Al MacInnis .75 2.00
AT5 Nicklas Lidstrom 1.00 2.50
AT6 Brian Leetch .75 2.00
AT7 John LeClair .75 2.00
AT8 Paul Kariya 1.00 2.50
AT9 Keith Tkachuk .75 2.00
AT10 Eric Lindros 1.00 2.50
AT11 Peter Forsberg 1.50 4.00
AT12 Steve Yzerman 4.00 10.00
AT13 Jaromir Jagr 1.50 4.00
AT14 Teemu Selanne 1.00 2.50
AT15 Pavel Bure 1.00 2.50

1999-00 Topps Chrome A-Men

Randomly inserted in Topps and OPC packs at 1:24, this 6-card set focuses on the NHL's leading assist men. Action photos are set against a silver foil background. Refractor parallels of this set were also randomly inserted at 1:120.
COMPLETE SET (6) 10.00 20.00
*REFRACTORS: 1.2X TO 3X BASIC INSERTS
AM1 Jaromir Jagr 1.50 4.00
AM2 Peter Forsberg 2.50 6.00
AM3 Paul Kariya 1.50 4.00
AM4 Teemu Selanne 1.50 4.00
AM5 Joe Sakic 2.00 5.00
AM6 Eric Lindros 1.50 4.00

1999-00 Topps Chrome Fantastic Finishers

Randomly inserted in Topps and OPC packs at 1:24, this 6-card set features the NHL's top goal scorers. Action player photos are set against a foil true-life background. Refractor parallels of this set were also randomly inserted at 1:120.
COMPLETE SET (6) 6.00 12.00
*REFRACTORS: 1.2X TO 3X BASIC INSERTS
FF1 Teemu Selanne 1.00 2.50
FF2 Jaromir Jagr 1.50 4.00
FF3 Tony Amonte .75 2.00
FF4 Alexei Yashin .75 2.00
FF5 John LeClair 1.00 2.50
FF6 Joe Sakic 2.00 5.00

1999-00 Topps Chrome Ice Futures

Randomly inserted in Topps and OPC packs at 1:24, this 6-card set focuses on the NHL's hottest prospects. Action photos are set against a blue foil checkerboard background. Refractor parallels of this set were also randomly inserted at 1:120.
COMPLETE SET (6) 4.00 10.00
*REFRACTORS: 1.2X TO 3X BASIC INSERTS
IF1 Mark Parrish .75 2.00
IF2 Chris Drury 1.00 2.50
IF3 Bill Muckalt .75 2.00
IF4 Marian Hossa 1.25 3.00
IF5 Milan Hejduk 1.00 2.50
IF6 Brendan Morrison .75 2.00

1999-00 Topps Chrome Ice Masters

Randomly inserted in Topps and OPC packs at 1:18, this 20-card set showcases some of hockey's elite players on a blue and silver foil card that is textured like ice. Refractor parallels of this set were also randomly inserted at 1:90.
COMPLETE SET (20) 25.00 50.00
*REFRACTORS: 1.2X TO 3X BASIC INSERTS
IM1 Joe Sakic 1.50 4.00
IM2 Dominik Hasek 1.50 4.00
IM3 Eric Lindros .75 2.00
IM4 Jaromir Jagr 1.25 3.00
IM5 John LeClair .75 2.00
IM6 Mats Sundin .75 2.00
IM7 Ray Bourque 1.25 3.00
IM8 Mike Modano 1.25 3.00
IM9 Peter Forsberg 2.00 5.00
IM10 Brian Leetch .75 2.00
IM11 Martin Brodeur 2.00 5.00
IM12 Al MacInnis .60 1.50
IM13 Paul Kariya .75 2.00
IM14 Alexei Yashin .60 1.50
IM15 Steve Yzerman 4.00 10.00
IM16 Ed Belfour .75 2.00
IM17 Keith Tkachuk .75 2.00
IM18 Patrick Roy 4.00 10.00
IM19 Nicklas Lidstrom .75 2.00
IM20 Teemu Selanne .75 2.00

1999-00 Topps Chrome Positive Performers

Randomly Inserted in Topps and OPC packs at 1:24, this 6-card set features players with the best plus/minus rating in the game.Refractor parallels of this set were also randomly inserted at 1:120.
COMPLETE SET (6) 3.00 8.00
*REFRACTORS: 1.2X TO 3X BASIC INSERTS
PP1 Alexander Karpovtsev .60 1.50
PP2 John LeClair 1.00 2.50
PP3 Eric Lindros 1.00 2.50
PP4 Magnus Arvedson .60 1.50
PP5 Al MacInnis .75 2.00
PP6 Jere Lehtinen .75 2.00

1999-00 Topps Chrome Postmasters

Randomly inserted in Topps and OPC packs at 1:24, this 6-card set focuses on the NHL's toughest goaltenders. Refractor parallels of this set were also randomly inserted at 1:120.
COMPLETE SET (6) 10.00 20.00
*REFRACTORS: 1.2X TO 3X BASIC INSERTS
PM1 Dominik Hasek 2.00 5.00
PM2 Byron Dafoe .75 2.00
PM3 Nikolai Khabibulin .75 2.00
PM4 Ed Belfour 1.00 2.50
PM5 Patrick Roy 5.00 12.00
PM6 Martin Brodeur 2.50 6.00

2000-01 Topps Chrome

Released in late January 2001, this 251-card set is comprised of 160 veteran cards, 5 Season Highlight cards, 55 NHL Prospects, and 30 Chrome Expansion cards. Cards #241-251 were sequentially numbered to 1250. Base cards have silver borders and are printed on an all chrome card stock. Two parallel versions were issued for the Expansion cards, numbers 241-251, and these cards are also sequentially numbered to 1250. Topps Chrome was packaged in 24-pack boxes with packs containing four cards and carried a suggested retail price of $3.00.
1 Jaromir Jagr .75 2.00
2 Patrick Roy .75 2.00
3 Paul Kariya .40 1.00
4 Mats Sundin .30 .75
5 Ron Francis .40 1.00
6 Pavel Bure .40 1.00
7 John LeClair .30 .75
8 Olaf Kolzig .30 .75
9 Chris Pronger .25 .60
10 Jeremy Roenick .30 .75
11 Owen Nolan .30 .75
12 Theo Fleury .40 1.00
13 Zigmund Palffy .30 .75
14 Patrik Stefan .25 .60
15 Jarome Iginla .30 .75
16 Joe Thornton .50 1.25
17 Tony Amonte .25 .60
18 Mike Modano .50 1.25
19 Mark Messier .50 1.25
20 Dominik Hasek .50 1.25
21 Steve Yzerman 1.00 2.50
22 Marian Hossa .25 .60
23 David Legwand .30 .75
24 Jose Theodore .40 1.00
25 Vincent Lecavalier .25 .60
26 Scott Stevens .30 .75
27 Mark Parrish .20 .50
28 Sean Burke .20 .50
29 Alexei Kovalev .25 .60
30 Dan Cloutier .25 .60
31 Sami Kapanen .20 .50
32 Anson Carter .25 .60
33 Miroslav Satan .20 .50
34 Mark Recchi .40 1.00
35 Pavol Demitra .40 1.00
36 Peter Bondra .25 .60
37 Mike Richter .30 .75
38 Guy Hebert .25 .60
39 Martin Skoula .25 .60
40 Ed Belfour .30 .75
41 Fred Brathwaite .25 .60
42 Andrew Brunette .20 .50
43 Byron Dafoe .25 .60
44 Felix Potvin .50 1.25
45 Rod Brind'Amour .30 .75
46 Doug Gilmour .40 1.00
47 Brett Hull .50 1.25
48 Nicklas Lidstrom .30 .75
49 Mike York .20 .50
50 Al MacInnis .30 .75
51 Brian Boucher .25 .60
52 Teemu Selanne .60 1.50
53 Bill Guerin .30 .75
54 Ray Bourque .50 1.25
55 Ray Ferraro .20 .50
56 Sergei Gonchar .20 .50
57 Mattias Ohlund .20 .50
58 Todd Marchant .20 .50
59 Damian Rhodes .20 .50
60 Chris Drury .25 .60
61 Curtis Joseph .40 1.00
62 Teppo Numminen .20 .50
63 Petr Nedved .25 .60
64 Doug Weight .30 .75
65 Arturs Irbe .25 .60
66 Chris Osgood .30 .75
67 Jocelyn Thibault .25 .60
68 Oleg Tverdovsky .20 .50
69 Derian Hatcher .25 .60
70 Ray Whitney .25 .60
71 Saku Koivu .30 .75
72 Cliff Ronning .20 .50
73 Claude Lapointe .20 .50
74 Chris Simon .20 .50
75 Martin Rucinsky .20 .50
76 Valeri Bure .25 .60
77 Brad Isbister .20 .50
78 Roman Turek .25 .60
79 Kenny Jonsson .20 .50
80 Mike Dunham .20 .50
81 Rob Blake .30 .75
82 Daniel Alfredsson .30 .75
83 Tommy Salo .25 .60
84 Sergei Samsonov .25 .60
85 Joe Sakic .50 1.25
86 Bryan Smolinski .25 .60
87 Luc Robitaille .30 .75
88 Mariusz Czerkawski .20 .50
89 Brendan Shanahan .40 1.00
90 Brian Rafalski .20 .50
91 Jamie Langenbrunner .25 .60
92 Peter Forsberg .40 1.00
93 Phil Housley .25 .60
94 Glen Murray .20 .50
95 Jeff Hackett .20 .50
96 Sergei Fedorov .50 1.25
97 Sergei Zubov .25 .60
98 Martin Brodeur .60 1.50
99 Mike Grier .20 .50
100 Paul Coffey .30 .75
101 Radek Bonk .25 .60
102 Milan Hejduk .25 .60
103 Viktor Kozlov .25 .60
104 Jason Arnott .25 .60
105 Brendan Morrison .30 .75
106 Keith Tkachuk .30 .75
107 Patrik Elias .30 .75
108 Jochen Hecht .20 .50
109 Brian Leetch .30 .75
110 Petr Sykora .25 .60
111 Dave Andreychuk .30 .75
112 Steve Shields .20 .50
113 Nikolai Antropov .25 .60
114 Martin Straka .25 .60
115 Eric Desjardins .25 .60
116 Adam Oates .30 .75
117 Adam Graves .25 .60
118 Jozef Stumpel .20 .50
119 Vincent Damphousse .25 .60
120 Maxim Afinogenov .20 .50
121 Chris Chelios .30 .75
122 Joe Nieuwendyk .30 .75
123 Petr Buzek .20 .50
124 Jeff Friesen .20 .50
125 Markus Naslund .25 .60
126 Trevor Letowski .20 .50
127 Steve Thomas .20 .50
128 Jason Allison .25 .60
129 Jere Lehtinen .25 .60
130 Tom Poti .20 .50
131 Eric Lindros .50 1.25
132 Rob Niedermayer .25 .60
133 Gary Roberts .20 .50
134 Scott Gomez .25 .60
135 Pierre Turgeon .30 .75
136 Trevor Kidd .20 .50
137 Jan Hrdina .20 .50
138 John Madden .25 .60
139 Tim Connolly .20 .50
140 Pat Verbeek .25 .60
141 Jeff Halpern .20 .50
142 Patrick Marleau .30 .75
143 Wade Redden .20 .50
144 Alex Tanguay .25 .60
145 Darcy Tucker .20 .50
146 Simon Gagne .30 .75
147 Brad Stuart .25 .60
148 Jean-Sebastien Aubin .25 .60
149 Mike Johnson .20 .50
150 Shayne Corson .20 .50
151 Michael Peca .25 .60
152 Keith Primeau .25 .60
153 Tie Domi .50 1.25
154 Brenden Morrow .25 .60
155 Sandis Ozolinsh .25 .60
156 Mike Keane .25 .60
157 Patric Kjellberg .20 .50
158 Patrick Lalime .25 .60
159 John Vanbiesbrouck .25 .60
160 Andrew Cassels .20 .50
161 Scott Stephens HL .25 .60
162 Ed Belfour HL .30 .75
163 Martin Brodeur HL .60 1.50
164 Mike Modano HL .50 1.25
165 Jason Arnott HL .25 .60
166 Roberto Luongo .50 1.25
167 Harold Druken .20 .50
168 Marc Denis .25 .60
169 Oleg Saprykin .20 .50
170 Glen Metropolit .20 .50
171 Daniel Sedin .60 1.50
172 Dmitri Yakushin .20 .50
173 Scott Hannan .20 .50
174 Dave Tanabe .20 .50
175 Jiri Fischer .20 .50
176 Dmitri Nabokov .20 .50
177 Ivan Novoseltsev .20 .50
178 Manny Fernandez .25 .60
179 Maxim Balmochnyk .20 .50
180 Brian Campbell .20 .50
181 Sergei Varlamov .20 .50
182 Ville Nieminen RC .20 .50
183 Colin White RC .20 .50
184 Mike Fisher .25 .60
185 Matt Elich RC .25 .60
186 Zenith Komarniski .20 .50
187 Eric Nickulas RC .20 .50
188 Steven McCarthy .20 .50
189 Jason Krog .20 .50
190 Robert Esche .20 .50
191 Adam Mair .20 .50
192 Ladislav Nagy .20 .50
193 Sergei Vyshedkevich RC .20 .50
194 Steve Begin .20 .50
195 Brad Ference .20 .50
196 Andy Delmore .20 .50
197 Brent Sopel RC .30 .75
198 Evgeni Nabokov .25 .60
199 David Gosselin RC .25 .60
200 Tavis Hansen .20 .50
201 Ray Giroux .20 .50
202 Serge Aubin RC .25 .60
203 Shane Willis .20 .50
204 Vitali Vishnevsky .20 .50
205 Richard Jackman .20 .50
206 Petr Schastlivy .20 .50
207 Ryan Bonni .20 .50
208 Alexei Tezikov .20 .50
209 Henrik Sedin .50 1.25
210 Mike Ribeiro .25 .60
211 Darryl Laplante .20 .50
212 Kyle Calder .20 .50
213 Dimitri Kalinin .20 .50
214 Jean-Sebastien Giguere .25 .60
215 Willie Mitchell RC .30 .75
216 Steve Valiquette RC .25 .60
217 Brian Willsie .20 .50
218 Jarkko Ruutu .20 .50
219 Jon Sim .20 .50
220 Jonathan Girard .20 .50
221 Ron Tugnutt .25 .60
222 Lyle Odelein .20 .50
223 Jean-Luc Grand-Pierre .20 .50
224 Geoff Sanderson .25 .60
225 Robert Kron .20 .50
226 Kevin Dineen .20 .50
227 Kevyn Adams .20 .50
228 Tyler Wright .20 .50
229 Jamie Pushor .20 .50
230 David Vyborny .20 .50
231 Jamie McLennan .20 .50
232 Jeff Nielsen .20 .50
233 Scott Pellerin .20 .50
234 Darby Hendrickson .20 .50
235 Jim Dowd .20 .50
236 Filip Kuba .20 .50
237 Stacy Roest .20 .50
238 Sean O'Donnell .20 .50
239 Aaron Gavey .20 .50
240 Sergei Krivokrasov .20 .50
241 Justin Williams RC 2.50 6.00
242 Marian Gaborik RC 3.00 8.00
243 Marty Turco RC 2.00 5.00
244 David Aebischer RC 2.00 5.00
245 Rostislav Klesla RC 2.50 6.00
246 Petr Hubacek RC 1.00 2.50
247 Scott Hartnell RC 2.50 6.00
248 Martin Havlat RC 3.00 8.00
249 Steven Reinprecht RC 1.50 4.00
250 Andrew Raycroft RC 2.50 6.00
251 Rick DiPietro RC 4.00 10.00

2000-01 Topps Chrome Blue

Randomly inserted in packs, this 11-card set parallels the base rookie cards from the Topps Chrome set, card numbers 241-251. Each card is enhanced with a blue border and is sequentially numbered to 1250.
*BLUE/1250: .4X TO 1X BASE SP/1250

2000-01 Topps Chrome Red

Randomly inserted in packs, this 11-card set parallels the base rookie cards from the Topps Chrome set, card numbers 241-251. Each card is enhanced with a red border and is sequentially numbered to 1250.
*RED/1250: .4X TO 1X BASE SP/1250

2000-01 Topps Chrome OPC Refractors

Randomly inserted in packs at the rate of 1:9 for card numbers 1-220, and 1:383 for card numbers 241-251, this 251-card set parallels the base Topps Chrome set enhanced with the O-Pee-Chee logo in the lower right hand corner and the rainbow holofoil refractor effect. Card numbers 241-251 are all sequentially numbered to 35.
*1-240 VETS: 1.5X TO 4X BASIC CARDS
*161-240 ROOKIE: 1X TO 2.5X RC
*241-250 ROOK/35: 1.5X TO 4X RC/1250
19 Mark Messier 3.00 8.00

2000-01 Topps Chrome OPC Refractors Blue

Randomly inserted in packs at the rate of 1:383, this 11-card set parallels the last 11 cards in the base Topps Chrome set, card numbers 241-251. Each card is enhanced with a blue border, the rainbow holofoil refractor effect, and is sequentially numbered to 35.
*SP ROOKIE/35: 1.5X TO 4X BASIC SP
BLUE OPC REF/35 ODDS 1:383

2000-01 Topps Chrome OPC Refractors Red

Randomly inserted in packs at the rate of 1:383, this 11-card set parallels the last 11 cards in the base Topps Chrome set, card numbers 241-251. Each card is enhanced with a red border, the rainbow holofoil refractor effect, and is sequentially numbered to 35.
*SP ROOKIE/35: 1.5X TO 4X BASIC SP

2000-01 Topps Chrome Refractors

Randomly inserted in packs at the rate of 1:9 for card numbers 1-220, and randomly inserted for card numbers 241-250, this 250-card set parallels the base Topps Chrome set enhanced with the Topps Chrome logo in one of the front lower corners and the rainbow holofoil refractor effect. Card numbers 241-251 are all sequentially numbered to 25.
*1-240 VETS: 2X TO 5X BASIC CARDS
*161-240 ROOKIES: 1.2X TO 3X RC
*241-251 ROOK/25: 2X TO 5X RC/1250
19 Mark Messier 4.00 10.00

2000-01 Topps Chrome Refractors Blue

Randomly inserted in packs, this 11-card set parallels the last 11 cards in the base Topps Chrome set, card numbers 241-251. Each card is enhanced with a blue border, the rainbow holofoil refractor effect, and is sequentially numbered to 25.
*SP ROOKIE/25: 2X TO 5X BASIC SP

2000-01 Topps Chrome Refractors Red

Randomly inserted in packs, this 11-card set parallels the last 11 cards in the base Topps Chrome set, card numbers 241-251. Each card is enhanced with a red border, the rainbow holofoil refractor effect, and is sequentially numbered to 25.
*SP ROOKIE/25: 2X TO 5X BASIC SP

2000-01 Topps Chrome Combos

Randomly inserted in packs at the rate of one in 20, this 10-card set features original artwork of two top NHL players. The bottom of the card has their names and a brief explanation why they are paired in a green box. Cards are printed on all chrome card stock. Refractor parallels of this set were also randomly inserted at 1:200.
COMPLETE SET (10) 15.00 40.00
TC1 P.Bure/V.Bure 1.00 2.50
TC2 T.Selanne/P.Kariya 1.00 2.50
TC3 J.LeClair/T.Amonte 1.00 2.50
TC4 C.Joseph/D.Hasek 2.00 5.00
TC5 M.Modano/P.Forsberg 3.00 8.00
TC6 R.Bourque/C.Pronger 2.00 5.00
TC7 V.Lecavalier/J.Thornton 1.00 2.50
TC8 P.Roy/M.Brodeur 5.00 12.00
TC9 S.Yzerman/B.Hull 4.00 10.00
TC10 J.Jagr/M.Lemieux 4.00 10.00

2000-01 Topps Chrome Hobby Masters Refractors

Randomly inserted in Hobby packs at the rate of 1:400, this 10-card set features a player photo with a diagonal line above the lower right hand corner with the player's name and the words "Hobby Master" in yellow. Backgrounds are enhanced with the rainbow holofoil refractor effect.
COMPLETE SET (10) 75.00 150.00
HM1 Martin Brodeur 10.00 25.00
HM2 Pavel Bure 6.00 15.00
HM3 Peter Forsberg 10.00 25.00
HM4 Dominik Hasek 8.00 20.00
HM5 Jaromir Jagr 6.00 15.00
HM6 Curtis Joseph 5.00 12.00
HM7 Paul Kariya 5.00 12.00
HM8 Mike Modano 5.00 12.00
HM9 Patrick Roy 20.00 50.00
HM10 Steve Yzerman 20.00 50.00

2000-01 Topps Chrome Mario Lemieux Reprints

Randomly inserted in packs at the rate of 1:18, this 23-card set features reprinted versions of Mario Lemieux's cards dating back to 85-86 Topps and OPC. Cards are printed on an all chrome card stock. Refractor parallels of this set were also randomly inserted at 1:180.
COMPLETE SET (23) 75.00 150.00
COMMON LEMIEUX (1-23) 5.00 12.00
*REFRACTOR: 1.2X TO 3X BASIC INSERT

2000-01 Topps Chrome Rocket's Flare

Randomly inserted in packs at the rate of 1:14, this 10-card set features top players on a die cut card stock. The bottom of the card is red and the player's name appears in a black name box. A silver die cut "diamond shape" appears behind a full color player action photo. Refractor parallels of this set were also randomly inserted at 1:140.
COMPLETE SET (10) 10.00 20.00
*REFRACTOR: .8X TO 2X BASIC INSERT
RF1 Pavel Bure 1.00 2.50
RF2 Paul Kariya 1.00 2.50
RF3 John LeClair 1.00 2.50
RF4 Jaromir Jagr 1.50 4.00
RF5 Luc Robitaille .75 2.00
RF6 Milan Hejduk 1.00 2.50
RF7 Tony Amonte .75 2.00
RF8 Patrik Elias .75 2.00
RF9 Miroslav Satan .75 2.00
RF10 Teemu Selanne 1.00 2.50

2000-01 Topps Chrome 1000 Point Club Refractors

Randomly inserted in Retail packs at the rate of 1:250, this 16-card set features 1000 point club members on an all holofoil refractor card. Player photos are in full color, and the words, "1000 Point Club" appear on the top of the card. Card numbers carry a "1000PC" prefix.
1 Mark Messier 5.00 12.00
2 Steve Yzerman 20.00 50.00
3 Ron Francis 3.00 8.00
4 Paul Coffey 4.00 10.00
5 Ray Bourque 8.00 20.00
6 Doug Gilmour 3.00 8.00
7 Adam Oates 3.00 8.00
8 Larry Murphy 3.00 8.00
9 Dave Andreychuk 3.00 8.00
10 Luc Robitaille 3.00 8.00
11 Phil Housley 3.00 8.00
12 Brett Hull 5.00 12.00
13 Al MacInnis 3.00 8.00
14 Pierre Turgeon 3.00 8.00
15 Joe Sakic 10.00 25.00
16 Pat Verbeek 3.00 8.00

2001-02 Topps Chrome

Released in late February 2002, this 182-card set carried an SRP of $3.00 for a 4-card pack. Cards were printed on a chromium card stock. Short printed rookie cards were inserted at 1:3. Update cards for the 2001-02 Topps base set were also randomly seeded in packs at 1:4.
COMPLETE SET (182) 50.00 120.00
1 Mario Lemieux 1.50 4.00
2 Steve Yzerman 1.50 4.00
3 Martin Brodeur 1.00 2.50
4 Brian Leetch .50 1.25
5 Tony Amonte .40 1.00
6 Bill Guerin .50 1.25
7 Olaf Kolzig .50 1.25
8 Pavel Bure .60 1.50
9 Patrick Marleau .50 1.25
10 Mariusz Czerkawski .30 .75
11 Teemu Selanne 1.00 2.50
12 Alex Tanguay .40 1.00
13 Keith Primeau .40 1.00
14 Alexei Yashin .40 1.00
15 Markus Naslund .50 1.25
16 Chris Pronger .40 1.00
17 Sergei Zubov .40 1.00
18 Marian Gaborik .75 2.00
19 Mats Sundin .50 1.25
20 David Legwand .40 1.00
21 J-P Dumont .30 .75
22 Nicklas Lidstrom .50 1.25
23 Ron Francis .60 1.50
24 Doug Weight .50 1.25
25 Zigmund Palffy .50 1.25
26 Jason Allison .40 1.00
27 Joe Sakic .75 2.00
28 Paul Kariya .60 1.50
29 Marian Hossa .40 1.00
30 Owen Nolan .50 1.25
31 Jason Arnott .40 1.00
32 Jaromir Jagr 1.25 3.00
33 Claude Lemieux .40 1.00
34 Peter Bondra .50 1.25
35 Chris Drury .40 1.00
36 Radek Bonk .30 .75
37 Theo Fleury .60 1.50
38 Keith Tkachuk .50 1.25
39 Rick DiPietro .40 1.00
40 Ed Jovanovski .40 1.00
41 Scott Stevens .50 1.25
42 John LeClair .50 1.25
43 Ryan Smyth .40 1.00
44 Vincent Lecavalier .40 1.00
45 Henrik Sedin .50 1.25
46 David Aebischer .40 1.00
47 Patrick Roy 1.25 3.00
48 Valeri Bure .30 .75
49 Dominik Hasek .75 2.00
50 Ray Ferraro .30 .75
51 Milan Hejduk .40 1.00
52 Mike Modano .75 2.00
53 Sergei Fedorov .75 2.00
54 Luc Robitaille .50 1.25
55 Mark Messier .75 2.00
56 Sean Burke .30 .75
57 Jeff Friesen .30 .75
58 Alexander Mogilny .40 1.00
59 Roman Cechmanek .40 1.00
60 Martin Straka .30 .75
61 Pavol Demitra .60 1.50
62 Curtis Joseph .50 1.25
63 Daniel Sedin .50 1.25
64 Brad Richards .50 1.25
65 Simon Gagne .50 1.25
66 Saku Koivu .50 1.25
67 Eric Daze .40 1.00
68 Roberto Luongo .75 2.00
69 Brendan Shanahan .60 1.50
70 Espen Knutsen .30 .75
71 Rob Blake .50 1.25
72 Steve Sullivan .30 .75
73 Arturs Irbe .40 1.00
74 Maxim Afinogenov .30 .75
75 Dan Cloutier .40 1.00
76 Josef Vasicek .30 .75
77 Vincent Damphousse .40 1.00
78 Robert Lang .30 .75
79 Pierre Turgeon .50 1.25
80 Gary Roberts .30 .75
81 Adam Oates .50 1.25
82 Evgeni Nabokov .40 1.00
83 Petr Nedved .40 1.00
84 Mike Dunham .40 1.00
85 Chris Osgood .50 1.25
86 Brett Hull .60 1.50
87 Peter Forsberg .60 1.50
88 Joe Thornton .60 1.50
89 Marc Denis .40 1.00
90 Ed Belfour .50 1.25
91 Patrik Elias .50 1.25
92 Michael York .30 .75
93 Martin Havlat .40 1.00
94 Jeremy Roenick .50 1.25
95 Alexei Kovalev .40 1.00
96 Al MacInnis .50 1.25
97 Marco Sturm .30 .75
98 Jose Theodore .50 1.25
99 Joe Nieuwendyk .50 1.25
100 Darren McCarty .30 .75
101 Mark Recchi .60 1.50
102 Daniel Alfredsson .50 1.25
103 Miroslav Satan .40 1.00
104 Sergei Samsonov .40 1.00
105 Roman Turek .40 1.00
106 Jarome Iginla .50 1.25
107 Jeff O'Neill .30 .75
108 Tommy Salo .40 1.00
109 Petr Sykora .30 .75
110 Adam Deadmarsh .40 1.00
111 Oleg Tverdovsky .30 .75
112 Sami Kapanen .30 .75
113 Scott Hartnell .50 1.25
114 Jere Lehtinen .40 1.00
115 Darcy Tucker .30 .75
116 Stu Barnes .40 1.00
117 Jim Dowd .30 .75
118 Derek Morris .30 .75
119 Felix Potvin .75 2.00
120 Manny Fernandez .40 1.00
121 Jason Smith .30 .75
122 Byron Dafoe .40 1.00
123 Teppo Numminen .30 .75

124 Mike Richter .50 1.25
125 Anson Carter .40 1.00
126 Jocelyn Thibault .40 1.00
127 Dany Heatley .50 1.25
128 Marc Savard .30 .75
129 Brian Rolston .40 1.00
130 Martin Biron .40 1.00
131 Mark Parrish .30 .75
132 Mike Peca .40 1.00
133 Patrick Lalime .40 1.00
134 Eric Lindros .75 2.00
135 Brian Boucher .40 1.00
136 Nikolai Khabibulin .50 1.25
137 John Madden .40 1.00
138 Rostislav Klesla .30 .75
139 Mika Noronen .30 .75
140 Kris Beech .30 .75
141 Miikka Kiprusoff .50 1.25
142 Mathieu Garon .40 1.00
143 Mark Bell .30 .75
144 Jussi Markkanen .30 .75
145 Mike Comrie .40 1.00
146 Johan Hedberg .40 1.00
147 Andrew Raycroft .40 1.00
148 Daniel Corso .30 .75
149 Ilya Kovalchuk RC 5.00 12.00
150 Dan Blackburn RC 1.25 3.00
151 Vaclav Nedorost RC 1.00 2.50
152 Krys Kolanos RC 1.00 2.50
153 Kristian Huselius RC 1.50 4.00
154 Martin Erat RC 1.50 4.00
155 Timo Parssinen RC 1.25 3.00
156 Scott Nichol RC 1.00 2.50
157 Nick Schultz RC 1.00 2.50
158 Jukka Hentunen RC 1.00 2.50
159 Pascal Dupuis RC 1.50 4.00
160 Radek Martinek RC 1.00 2.50
161 Scott Clemmensen RC 1.00 2.50
162 Jeff Jillson RC 1.00 2.50
163 Brian Sutherby RC 1.00 2.50
164 Nikita Alexeev RC 1.00 2.50
165 Niklas Hagman RC 1.25 3.00
166 Erik Cole RC 2.00 5.00
167 Pavel Datsyuk RC 5.00 12.00
168 Ilja Bryzgalov RC 2.50 6.00
169 Chris Neil RC 1.25 3.00
170 Mark Rycroft RC 1.25 3.00
171 Kamil Piros RC 1.00 2.50
172 Niko Kapanen RC 1.50 4.00
173 Jiri Dopita RC 1.00 2.50
174 Andreas Salomonsson RC 1.00 2.50
175 Ivan Ciernik RC 1.00 2.50
176 Jaroslav Bednar RC 1.00 2.50
177 Ty Conklin RC 1.50 4.00
178 Richard Scott RC 1.00 2.50
179 Raffi Torres RC 1.50 4.00
180 Vaclav Pletka RC 1.00 2.50
181 Mikael Samuelsson RC 1.25 3.00
182 Mike Farrell RC 1.00 2.50

2001-02 Topps Chrome Refractors

This 182-cards set paralleled the base set with the rainbow holofoil refractor effect. Refractors were inserted at a rate of 1:6 packs.
*1-148 VETS: 1.5X TO 4X BASIC CARDS
*149-182 ROOKIES: .8X TO 2X BASIC RC
55 Mark Messier 3.00 8.00

2001-02 Topps Chrome Black Border Refractors

Serial-numbered to just 50 copies each, this 182-card set paralleled the base set with a rainbow holofoil refractor effect and black borders.
*1-148 VETS/50: 5X TO 12X BASIC CARDS
*149-182 ROOKIE/50: 1.5X TO 4X BASIC RC
55 Mark Messier 10.00 25.00

2001-02 Topps Chrome Mario Lemieux Reprints

Inserted at 1:12, 10-card set featured reprints of past Topps cards of Mario Lemieux on chrome stock. Refractor parallels of this set were also created and inserted at 1:120.
COMPLETE SET (10) 30.00 60.00
COMMON LEMIEUX 3.00 8.00
*REFRACTOR: 1.2X TO 3X BASIC INSERT

2001-02 Topps Chrome Mario Returns

This 5-card set highlighted the return of Mario Lemieux to the NHL. Cards from this set were inserted at odds of 1:24. Refractor parallels of this set were also created and inserted at 1:240.
COMPLETE SET (5) 25.00 50.00
COMMON LEMIEUX (MR1-MR5) 4.00 10.00
*REFRACTOR: 1.2X TO 3X BASIC INSERT

2001-02 Topps Chrome Reprints

This 10-card set featured rookie card reprints of past greats on chrome stock. Cards from this set were inserted at 1:12 packs. A refractor parallel was also created and inserted at 1:120
COMPLETE SET (10) 15.00 40.00
*REFRACTOR: 1.2X TO 3X BASIC INSERTS
1 Billy Smith 2.00 5.00
2 Wayne Cashman 2.00 5.00
3 Barry Melrose 2.00 5.00
4 Bernie Federko 2.00 5.00
5 Neal Broten 2.00 5.00
6 Bill Clement 2.00 5.00
7 Guy Lapointe 2.00 5.00
8 Bernie Parent 2.00 5.00
9 Larry Robinson 2.00 5.00
10 Ken Hodge 2.00 5.00

2001-02 Topps Chrome Reprint Autographs

Inserted at 1:247, this 10-card set paralleled the reprints set but was enhanced with authentic autographs of the featured players. Card backs carried a Topps authentic sticker.
1 Billy Smith/200 12.50 30.00
2 Wayne Cashman/200 12.50 30.00
3 Barry Melrose/200 15.00 40.00
4 Bernie Federko 12.50 30.00
5 Neal Broten/200 12.50 30.00
6 Bill Clement/200 12.50 30.00
7 Guy Lapointe/200 12.50 30.00
8 Bernie Parent 20.00 50.00
9 Larry Robinson/200 15.00 40.00
10 Ken Hodge 12.50 30.00

2002 Topps Chrome All-Star Fantasy

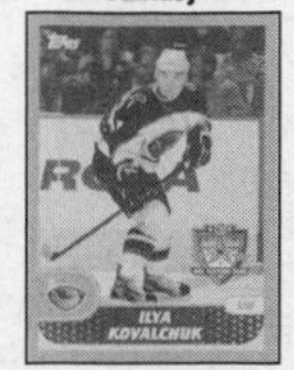

Available as wrapper redemptions from the Topps booth at the NHL All-Star Fantasy in Los Angeles, this 6-card set featured players involved in All-Star events. Each card was numbered "x of 6" on the card back. The card front carried the All-Star logo.
COMPLETE SET (6) 6.00 15.00
1 Paul Kariya 1.20 3.00
2 Zigmund Palffy .40 1.00
3 Joe Sakic 1.20 3.00
4 Jaromir Jagr 1.20 3.00
5 Dominik Hasek .80 2.00
6 Ilya Kovalchuk 2.00 5.00

2002-03 Topps Chrome

Released in February, this 181-card set consisted of 148 base veteran cards and 33 shortprinted rookie cards. Rookies were inserted at 1:3.
COMPLETE SET (182) 50.00 125.00
COMP.SET w/o SP's (148) 10.00 25.00
1 Patrick Roy 1.25 3.00
2 Mario Lemieux 1.50 4.00
3 Martin Brodeur 1.00 2.50
4 Steve Yzerman 1.00 2.50
5 Jaromir Jagr 1.25 3.00
6 Chris Pronger .40 1.00
7 John LeClair .50 1.25
8 Paul Kariya .60 1.50
9 Tony Amonte .40 1.00
10 Joe Thornton .60 1.50
11 Ilya Kovalchuk .60 1.50
12 Jarome Iginla .50 1.25
13 Mike Modano .75 2.00
14 Vincent Lecavalier .40 1.00
15 Michael Peca .40 1.00
16 Pavel Bure .60 1.50
17 Eric Lindros .75 2.00
18 Felix Potvin .75 2.00
19 Ron Francis .60 1.50
20 Miroslav Satan .50 1.25
21 Rostislav Klesla .30 .75
22 Mike Comrie .50 1.25
23 Daniel Alfredsson .50 1.25
24 Sean Burke .30 .75
25 David Legwand .40 1.00
26 Marian Gaborik .75 2.00
27 Saku Koivu .50 1.25
28 Owen Nolan .50 1.25
29 Mats Sundin .50 1.25
30 J-P Dumont .30 .75
31 Chris Drury .50 1.25
32 Markus Naslund .40 1.00
33 Anson Carter .40 1.00
34 Daniel Briere .40 1.00
35 Keith Tkachuk .50 1.25
36 Mark Recchi .60 1.50
37 Marc Denis .40 1.00
38 Sergei Fedorov .75 2.00
39 Andrew Brunette .30 .75
40 Martin Havlat .40 1.00
41 Brian Leetch .50 1.25
42 Erik Cole .40 1.00
43 Patrick Lalime .40 1.00
44 Patrick Marleau .50 1.25
45 Ryan Smyth .40 1.00
46 Sami Kapanen .30 .75
47 Martin Straka .40 1.00
48 Peter Forsberg .60 1.50
49 Jeff Friesen .30 .75
50 Manny Fernandez .40 1.00
51 Scott Stevens .50 1.25
52 Radim Vrbata .40 1.00
53 Marty Turco .50 1.25
54 Kristian Huselius .30 .75
55 Jeremy Roenick .50 1.25
56 Gary Roberts .30 .75
57 Chris Chelios .50 1.25
58 Brett Hull .60 1.50
59 Eric Daze .30 .75
60 Alex Tanguay .40 1.00
61 Simon Gagne .50 1.25
62 Roman Turek .50 1.25
63 Milan Hejduk .40 1.00
64 Mariusz Czerkawski .30 .75
65 Dan Cloutier .40 1.00
66 Teemu Selanne 1.00 2.50
67 Johan Hedberg .50 1.25
68 Mike Ricci .40 1.00
69 Roberto Luongo .75 2.00
70 Zigmund Palffy .50 1.25
71 Ed Jovanovski .40 1.00
72 Scott Gomez .40 1.00
73 Pierre Turgeon .50 1.25
74 Martin Biron .40 1.00
75 Keith Primeau .50 1.25
76 Jean-Sebastien Giguere .50 1.25
77 Alexei Zhamnov .40 1.00
78 Brent Johnson .40 1.00
79 Dan Blackburn .40 1.00
80 Mike Richter .50 1.25
81 Peter Bondra .50 1.25
82 Rod Brind'Amour .50 1.25
83 Shane Doan .40 1.00
84 Sergei Samsonov .40 1.00
85 Nikolai Khabibulin .50 1.25
86 Roman Cechmanek .40 1.00
87 Glen Murray .40 1.00
88 Brad Richards .50 1.25
89 Alexei Kovalev .50 1.25
90 Adam Deadmarsh .40 1.00
91 Brendan Morrison .40 1.00
92 Jason Arnott .40 1.00
93 Brenden Morrow .40 1.00
94 Pavol Demitra .60 1.50
95 Olaf Kolzig .50 1.25
96 Doug Gilmour .60 1.50
97 Jere Lehtinen .50 1.25
98 Petr Sykora .40 1.00
99 Wade Redden .30 .75
100 Adam Oates .50 1.25
101 Chris Osgood .50 1.25
102 Espen Knutsen .30 .75
103 Maxim Afinogenov .30 .75
104 Steve Sullivan .30 .75
105 Robert Lang .30 .75
106 Milan Hnilicka .40 1.00
107 Craig Conroy .30 .75
108 Alexander Mogilny .40 1.00
109 Jose Theodore .50 1.25
110 Mike Dunham .40 1.00
111 Joe Sakic .75 2.00
112 Al MacInnis .50 1.25
113 Marian Hossa .40 1.00
114 Rob Blake .50 1.25
115 Dany Heatley .50 1.25
116 Scott Hartnell .50 1.25
117 Krys Kolanos .30 .75
118 Vincent Damphousse .40 1.00
119 Curtis Joseph .50 1.25
120 Todd Bertuzzi .50 1.25
121 Tommy Salo .40 1.00
122 Jocelyn Thibault .40 1.00
123 Nicklas Lidstrom .50 1.25
124 Bryan McCabe .30 .75
125 Bill Guerin .50 1.25
126 Luc Robitaille .50 1.25
127 Alexei Yashin .40 1.00
128 Evgeni Nabokov .40 1.00
129 Pavel Datsyuk .60 1.50
130 Stu Barnes .30 .75
131 Derek Morris .30 .75
132 Jason Allison .40 1.00
133 Mark Messier .75 2.00
134 Ed Belfour .50 1.25
135 Scott Young .30 .75
136 Marco Sturm .30 .75
137 Arturs Irbe .40 1.00
138 Joe Nieuwendyk .50 1.25
139 Sergei Gonchar .40 1.00
140 Doug Weight .50 1.25
141 Jeff O'Neill .30 .75
142 Mike York .30 .75
143 Patrik Elias .50 1.25
144 Brendan Shanahan .60 1.50
145 Rick DiPietro .40 1.00
146 Jani Rita .30 .75
147 Stephen Weiss .50 1.25
148 Nikita Alexeev .30 .75
149 Micki DuPont RC .75 2.00
150 Ivan Majesky RC .75 2.00
151 Jason Spezza RC 5.00 12.00
152 Eric Godard RC .75 2.00
153 Shawn Thornton RC 1.00 2.50
154 Jeff Paul RC .75 2.00
155 Lasse Pirjeta RC .75 2.00
156 Adam Hall RC .75 2.00
157 Mikael Tellqvist RC .75 2.00
158 Tomi Pettinen RC .75 2.00
159 Radovan Somik RC .75 2.00
160 Jordan Leopold RC 1.25 3.00
161 Dmitri Bykov RC .75 2.00
162 Tim Thomas RC 3.00 8.00
163 Martin Gerber RC 1.25 3.00
164 Tom Koivisto RC .75 2.00
165 Patrick Sharp RC 2.50 6.00
166 Steve Eminger RC .75 2.00
167 Anton Volchenkov RC .75 2.00
168 Scottie Upshall RC 1.00 2.50
169 Ron Hainsey RC .75 2.00
170 Kurt Sauer RC .75 2.00
171 Jeff Taffe RC .75 2.00
172 Dennis Seidenberg RC 1.25 3.00
173 Stanislav Chistov RC .75 2.00
174 Chuck Kobasew RC 1.00 2.50
175 Rick Nash RC 6.00 15.00
176 Ales Hemsky RC 3.00 8.00
177 Jay Bouwmeester RC 2.50 6.00
178 Alexei Smirnov RC 1.00 2.50
179 Alexander Svitov RC .75 2.00
180 P-M Bouchard RC 1.25 3.00
181 Alexander Frolov RC 1.50 4.00
182 Henrik Zetterberg RC 6.00 15.00

2002-03 Topps Chrome Black Border Refractors

Inserted at 1:20, these refractor parallels mirrored the base set but carried black borders. Cards were serial-numbered to 100 copies each.
*1-148 VETS/100: 4X TO 10X BASIC CARDS
*149-182 ROOK/100: 1.5X TO 4X BASIC RC
133 Mark Messier 8.00 20.00

2002-03 Topps Chrome Refractors

*1-148 VETS: 2X TO 5X BASIC CARDS
*149-182 ROOKIES: 1X TO 2.5X BASIC RC
133 Mark Messier 4.00 10.00

2002-03 Topps Chrome e-Topps Decoy Cards

This 6-card set was inserted into packs of Topps Chrome as decoy cards to discourage pack searching. The cards advertised the upcoming release of 2003 e-Topps and pictured different player's e-Topps cards.
1 Jarome Iginla .30 .75
2 Pavel Bure .30 .75
3 Patrick Roy .30 .75
4 Mats Sundin .30 .75
5 Jaromir Jagr .30 .75
6 Martin Brodeur .30 .75

2002-03 Topps Chrome Chromographs

Inserted at 1:134, this 6-card set carried authentic player autographs.
CGBG Brian Gionta 6.00 15.00
CGBR Brad Richards 8.00 20.00
CGCJ Curtis Joseph 12.50 30.00
CGEC Erik Cole 5.00 12.00
CGRV Radim Vrbata 6.00 15.00
CGSW Stephen Weiss 5.00 12.00

2002-03 Topps Chrome First Round Fabric Patches

This 9-card set featured swatches of game jersey patches. Cards were serial-numbered to 50 copies each.
ALL CARDS CARRY FRFP PREFIX
DB Dan Blackburn 12.50 30.00
EL Eric Lindros 15.00 40.00
JP J-P Dumont 12.50 30.00
KP Keith Primeau 12.50 30.00
MB Martin Biron 12.50 30.00
MM Mike Modano 15.00 40.00
MN Markus Naslund 15.00 40.00
MS Mats Sundin 15.00 40.00
PM Patrick Marleau 12.50 30.00
RD Radek Dvorak 12.50 30.00
SN Scott Niedermayer 12.50 30.00

2002-03 Topps Chrome Patrick Roy Reprints

COMPLETE SET (25) 15.00 40.00
STATED ODDS 1:6
1 1986-87 Topps 1.00 2.50
2 1987-88 Topps 1.00 2.50
3 1988-89 Topps 1.00 2.50
4 1989-90 Topps 1.00 2.50
5 1990-91 Topps 1.00 2.50
6 1991-92 Topps 1.00 2.50
7 1992-93 Topps 1.00 2.50
8 1993-94 Premier 1.00 2.50
9 1994-95 Premier 1.00 2.50
10 1995-96 Topps 1.00 2.50
11 1998-99 Topps 1.00 2.50
12 1999-00 Topps 1.00 2.50
13 2000-01 Topps 1.00 2.50
14 2001-02 Topps 1.00 2.50
15 1986-87 OPC 1.00 2.50
16 1987-88 OPC 1.00 2.50
17 1988-89 OPC 1.00 2.50
18 1989-90 OPC 1.00 2.50
19 1990-91 OPC 1.00 2.50
20 1991-92 OPC 1.00 2.50
21 1992-93 OPC 1.00 2.50
22 1998-99 OPC 1.00 2.50
23 1999-00 OPC 1.00 2.50
24 2000-01 OPC 1.00 2.50
25 2001-02 OPC 1.00 2.50

2002-03 Topps Chrome Patrick Roy Reprints Refractors

*REFRACTOR: 2X TO 5X BASIC CARD

2002-03 Topps Chrome Patrick Roy Reprint Autographs

Inserted at 1:904 and serial-numbered to 400 copies each, this 2-card set carried certified autographs of Patrick Roy on reprints of his rookie cards.
COMMON CARD 40.00 80.00
COA Patrick Roy OPC 50.00 100.00
CTA Patrick Roy TOPPS 40.00 80.00

2002-03 Topps Chrome Patrick Roy Reprint Autograph Refractors

Inserted at 1:11,452, this 2-card set paralleled the basic autograph set on refractor card fronts. Each card was serial-numbered out of 33.
*REFRACTOR: 1.5X TO 4X BASIC AUTOGRAPH
COA Patrick Roy OPC 125.00 300.00
CTA Patrick Roy Topps 125.00 300.00

2002-03 Topps Chrome Patrick Roy Reprint Relics

This 4-card set featured jersey or patch swatches affixed to reprints of Roy's rookie cards. Jersey swatches were inserted at 1:1446 and patch swatches were inserted at 1:19,376. Jersey cards were serial-numbered to 250 and patches to 10. Patch cards are not priced due to scarcity.
PRJO1 P.Roy JSY OPC 20.00 50.00
PRJT1 P.Roy JSY TOPPS 25.00 60.00
PRP1 P.Roy PATCH OPC
PRPT1 P.Roy PATCH TOPPS

2002-03 Topps Chrome Patrick Roy Reprint Relics Refractors

Inserted at a rate of 1:5812, this 2-card set paralleled the base jersey cards on a refractor card front. Cards were serial-numbered to just 33 copies each.
PRJO1 Patrick Roy OPC Jersey 60.00 150.00
PRJT1 Patrick Roy Topps Jersey 60.00 150.00

2006 Upper Deck Employee Quad Jerseys

LJDJSCRB James/Jeter/Crosby/Bush 20.00 40.00

1998-99 Topps Gold Label Class 1

This 100-card set features color player photos printed on 35-point spectral-reflective rainbow polycarbonate stock with gold stamping. Each card showcases an NHL player on three different versions of his base card. Displayed in the foreground of the Class 1 set is a photo of the player with an action shot appearing in the background featuring players skating and goalies standing upright. Three parallel versions of the Class 1 set were also produced: The Black Label Parallel with the Black Topps Gold Label logo inserted at 1:18, the Red Label Parallel identified by the Red Topps Gold Label logo and sequentially numbered to 100 (inserted 1:73), and the One of One Parallel printed on special silver foil backs and numbered 1 of 1.
COMPLETE SET (100) 30.00 80.00
*CLASS I BLACK VETS: 2X TO 5X BASIC CARDS
*CLASS 1 BLACK ROOKIES: 1.2X TO 3X
*CLASS I RED VETS: 10X TO 25X BASIC CARDS
*CLASS 1 RED ROOKIES: 8X TO 20X
1 Brendan Shanahan .50 1.25
2 Mike Modano .75 2.00
3 Chris Chelios .50 1.25
4 Wayne Gretzky 3.00 8.00
5 Jaromir Jagr .75 2.00
6 Mark Messier .50 1.25
7 Teemu Selanne .50 1.25
8 Theo Fleury .10 .30
9 Ray Bourque .75 2.00
10 Martin Brodeur 1.25 3.00
11 Alexei Yashin .10 .30
12 Keith Tkachuk .50 1.25
13 Eric Lindros .50 1.25
14 Owen Nolan .40 1.00
15 Al MacInnis .40 1.00
16 Peter Bondra .40 1.00
17 Saku Koivu .50 1.25
18 Doug Weight .40 1.00
19 Robert Reichel .10 .30
20 Sergei Fedorov .75 2.00
21 Peter Forsberg 1.25 3.00
22 Ron Francis .40 1.00
23 Dimitri Khristich .10 .30
24 Ed Belfour .50 1.25
25 Oleg Kvasha RC .50 1.25
26 Ray Whitney .10 .30
27 Kenny Jonsson .10 .30
28 Randy McKay .10 .30
29 Pavol Demitra .40 1.00
30 Pierre Turgeon .40 1.00
31 Steve Yzerman 2.50 6.00
32 Ryan Smyth .40 1.00
33 Tony Amonte .40 1.00
34 Dominik Hasek 1.00 2.50
35 Jarome Iginla .60 1.50
36 Sami Kapanen .10 .30
37 Patrik Elias .40 1.00
38 Daniel Cleary .10 .30
39 Curtis Joseph .50 1.25
40 Joe Juneau .10 .30
41 Adam Graves .10 .30
42 Trevor Linden .40 1.00
43 Olli Jokinen .40 1.00
44 Joe Nieuwendyk .40 1.00
45 Sergei Samsonov .40 1.00
46 Rico Fata .10 .30
47 Mark Recchi .40 1.00
48 Rick Tocchet .40 1.00
49 Chris Pronger .40 1.00
50 Jason Allison .10 .30
51 Paul Kariya .50 1.25
52 Stu Barnes .10 .30
53 Mats Sundin .50 1.25
54 Mike Richter .50 1.25
55 Cliff Ronning .10 .30
56 Keith Primeau .10 .30
57 Guy Hebert .40 1.00
58 Nicklas Lidstrom .50 1.25
59 John Vanbiesbrouck .40 1.00
60 Jeff Friesen .10 .30
61 Vincent Lecavalier 1.00 2.50
62 Alexander Mogilny .40 1.00
63 Olaf Kolzig .40 1.00
64 Doug Gilmour .40 1.00
65 Joe Sakic 1.00 2.50
66 Mike Johnson .10 .30
67 Vincent Damphousse .10 .30
68 Eric Brewer .10 .30
69 Daniel Alfredsson .40 1.00
70 Nikolai Khabibulin .40 1.00
71 Marco Sturm .10 .30
72 Marty Reasoner .40 1.00
73 Bill Muckalt RC .10 .30
74 Pavel Bure .50 1.25
75 Bill Guerin .10 .30
76 Chris Osgood .40 1.00
77 Patrick Roy 2.50 6.00
78 Tom Barrasso .40 1.00
79 Alyn McCauley .10 .30
80 Adam Oates .40 1.00
81 Joe Thornton .75 2.00
82 Brendan Morrison .40 1.00
83 Mike Dunham .40 1.00
84 Jeremy Roenick .60 1.50
85 Brian Leetch .50 1.25
86 John LeClair .50 1.25
87 Mattias Ohlund .40 1.00
88 Wade Redden .10 .30
89 Mark Parrish RC 1.25 3.00
90 Milan Hejduk RC 1.25 3.00
91 Michael Peca .40 1.00
92 Brett Hull .60 1.50
93 Manny Malhotra .10 .30
94 Patrick Marleau .40 1.00
95 Grant Fuhr .40 1.00
96 Rob Blake .40 1.00
97 Damian Rhodes .40 1.00
98 Eric Daze .15 .60
99 Rod Brind'Amour .40 1.00
100 Scott Stevens .40 1.00

1998-99 Topps Gold Label Class 2

Randomly inserted into packs at the rate of one in six, this 100-card set features color player photos printed on 35-point spectral-reflective rainbow polycarbonate stock with gold stamping. Each card showcases an NHL player on three different version of his base card. Displayed in the foreground of the Class 2 set is a photo of the player with an action shot appearing in the background featuring players shooting and goalies sprawling. Three parallel versions of this set were also produced: The Black Label Parallel with the Black Topps Gold Label logo inserted at a rate 1:36, the Red Label Parallel identified by the Red Topps Gold Label logo and sequentially numbered to 50 (inserted at 1:146), and the One to One Parallel printed on special silver foil backs and numbered 1 of 1.
COMPLETE SET (100) 100.00 200.00
*CLASS 2: 1X TO 2.5X BASIC CLASS 1
*CLASS 2 BLACK: 1.5X TO 4X BASIC CLASS 1
*CLASS 2 RED: 8X TO 20X CLASS 1
*CLASS 2 RED ROOKIES: 6X TO 15X CLASS 1

1998-99 Topps Gold Label Class 3

Randomly inserted into packs at the rate of 1:12, this 100-card set features color player photos printed on 35-point spectral-reflective rainbow polycarbonate stock with gold stamping. Each card showcases an NHL player on three different version of his base card. Displayed in the foreground of the Class 3 set is a photo of the player with an action shot appearing in the background featuring players celebrating and goalies with their masks off. Three parallel versions of this set were also produced: The Black Label Parallel with the Black Topps Gold Label logo, the Red Label Parallel identified by the Red Topps Gold Label logo and sequentially numbered to 25 (inserted at 1:293) and the One to One Parallel printed on special silver foil backs and numbered 1 of 1.
COMPLETE SET (100) 150.00 300.00
*CLASS 3: 1.5X TO 4X BASIC CLASS 1
*CLASS 3 BLACK: 5X TO 12X BASIC CLASS 1
*CLASS 3 RED: 25X TO 60X BASIC CLASS 1
*CLASS 3 RED ROOKIES: 20X TO 50X CLASS 1

1998-99 Topps Gold Label Goal Race '99

Randomly inserted in packs at the rate of 1:18, this 10-card set features color action photos of the top players who strike fear in the hearts of goalies night after night. Three parallel versions of this set were also produced: Black Label Parallel with the Black Topps Gold Label logo and insertion rate of 1:54; Red Label Parallel with the Red Topps Gold Label logo, insertion rate of 1:795, and sequentially numbered to 92; and One of One parallel version printed on special silver foil backs and sequentially numbered 1 of 1.
*BLACK: .8X TO 2X BASIC INSERTS
*RED/92: 2.5X TO 6X BASIC INSERTS
GR1 Eric Lindros 2.50 6.00
GR2 John LeClair 2.00 5.00
GR3 Teemu Selanne 2.00 5.00
GR4 Paul Kariya 2.00 5.00
GR5 Jaromir Jagr 4.00 10.00
GR6 Keith Tkachuk 2.00 5.00
GR7 Theo Fleury 2.50 6.00
GR8 Brendan Shanahan 2.00 5.00
GR9 Tony Amonte 2.00 5.00
GR10 Joe Sakic 3.00 8.00

1999-00 Topps Gold Label Class 1

This 100-card set features color player photos printed on 35-point spectral-reflective rainbow polycarbonate stock with gold stamping. Each card showcases an NHL player on three different versions of his base card. Displayed in the foreground of the Class 1 set is a photo of the player with an action shot appearing in the background featuring players skating and goalies standing upright. Three parallel versions of this set were also produced: The Black Label Parallel with the Black Topps Gold Label logo (inserted 1:18), the Red Label Parallel identified by the Red Topps Gold Label logo and sequentially numbered to 100 (inserted 1:32), and the One to One Parallel numbered 1 of 1.
COMPLETE SET (100) 30.00 60.00
*CLASS 1 BLACK: 2X TO 5X BASIC CARDS
CLASS 1 BLACK ODDS 1:18
*CLASS 1 RED/100: 6X TO 15X BASIC CARDS
CLASS 1 RED/100 ODDS 1:32
*CLASS 2: .8X TO 2X CLASS 1
*CLASS 2 BLACK: 3X TO 8X CLASS 1
*CLASS 2 RED/50: 10X TO 25X CLASS 1
*CLASS 3: 1.5X TO 4X CLASS 1
*CLASS 3 BLACK: 10X TO 25X CLASS 1
*CLASS 3 RED/25: 20X TO 50X CLASS 1
1 Dominik Hasek .60 1.50
2 Al MacInnis .40 1.00
3 Luc Robitaille .40 1.00
4 Steve Yzerman 1.25 3.00
5 Michael Peca .30 .75
6 Keith Tkachuk .40 1.00
7 Saku Koivu .40 1.00
8 Tony Amonte .30 .75
9 Peter Bondra .30 .75
10 Pavel Bure .50 1.25
11 Ron Francis .50 1.25
12 Eric Lindros .60 1.50
13 Paul Kariya .50 1.25
14 Theo Fleury .50 1.25
15 Jaromir Jagr 1.00 2.50
16 Patrick Roy 1.50 4.00
17 Zigmund Palffy .40 1.00
18 Ed Belfour .40 1.00
19 Sergei Samsonov .30 .75
20 Nicklas Lidstrom .40 1.00
21 Pavol Demitra .50 1.25
22 Sergei Fedorov .60 1.50
23 Teemu Selanne .75 2.00
24 Martin Brodeur .75 2.00
25 John LeClair .40 1.00
26 Ray Bourque .60 1.50
27 Peter Forsberg .40 1.00
28 Doug Weight .40 1.00
29 Brian Leetch .40 1.00
30 Mark Recchi .50 1.25
31 Jason Allison .30 .75
32 Rob Blake .40 1.00
33 Scott Niedermayer .40 1.00
34 Chris Pronger .30 .75
35 Joe Sakic .60 1.50
36 Mark Messier .60 1.50
37 Daniel Alfredsson .40 1.00
38 Guy Hebert .40 1.00
39 Bobby Holik .25 .60
40 Joe Thornton .60 1.50
41 Ron Tugnutt .30 .75
42 Jeff Friesen .30 .75
43 Jeremy Roenick .40 1.00
44 Wade Redden .25 .60
45 Chris Osgood .40 1.00
46 Arturs Irbe .30 .75
47 Valeri Bure .25 .60
48 Chris Drury .30 .75
49 Owen Nolan .40 1.00
50 Kenny Jonsson .25 .60
51 Petr Sykora .30 .75
52 Byron Dafoe .25 .60
53 Brett Hull .60 1.50
54 Mike Richter .40 1.00
55 Brendan Shanahan .50 1.25
56 Mats Sundin .40 1.00
57 Miroslav Satan .30 .75
58 Markus Naslund .40 1.00
59 Rod Brind'Amour .40 1.00
60 Joe Nieuwendyk .40 1.00
61 Petr Nedved .25 .60
62 Sergei Berezin .25 .60
63 Trevor Linden .40 1.00
64 Marian Hossa .30 .75
65 Pierre Turgeon .40 1.00
66 Vincent Lecavalier .30 .75
67 Sami Kapanen .25 .60
68 Andrew Brunette .25 .60
69 Brian Savage .25 .60
70 Derian Hatcher .30 .75
71 Curtis Joseph .40 1.00
72 Scott Stevens .40 1.00
73 Radek Bonk .25 .60
74 Jarome Iginla .40 1.00
75 Adam Graves .30 .75
76 Alexander Selivanov .25 .60
77 Alexander Mogilny .30 .75
78 Cliff Ronning .25 .60
79 Vincent Damphousse .30 .75
80 Alexei Kovalev .30 .75
81 Yanic Perreault .25 .60
82 Alexander Korolyuk .25 .60
83 Jozef Stumpel .25 .60
84 Viktor Kozlov .25 .60
85 Mike Modano .60 1.50
86 David Legwand .25 .60
87 Scott Gomez .30 .75
88 Tim Connolly .25 .60
89 Brad Stuart .30 .75
90 Peter Schaefer .25 .60
91 Alex Tanguay .30 .75
92 Simon Gagne .40 1.00
93 Dave Tanabe .25 .60
94 Roberto Luongo .50 1.25
95 Martin Biron .30 .75
96 Mike Fisher RC .40 1.00
97 Patrik Stefan RC .40 1.00
98 Nikolai Antropov RC 1.00 2.50
99 Jochen Hecht RC .60 1.50
100 Steve Kariya RC .40 1.00

1999-00 Topps Gold Label Class 3

Randomly inserted into packs this 100-card set features color player photos printed on 35-point spectral-reflective rainbow polycarbonate stock with gold stamping. Each card showcases an NHL player on three different version of his base card. Displayed in the foreground of the Class 3 set is a photo of the player with an action shot appearing in the background featuring players celebrating and goalies with their masks off. Three parallel versions of this set were also produced: The Black Label Parallel with the Black Topps Gold Label logo (inserted 1:72), the Red Label Parallel identified by the Red Topps Gold Label logo and sequentially numbered to 25 (inserted 1:129) and the One to One Parallel numbered 1 of 1.
36 Mark Messier 2.50 6.00

1999-00 Topps Gold Label Fresh Gold

Randomly inserted in packs at one in 30, this 20-card set focuses on young stars looking to make their mark on the game. Each card features an action foreground shot and a silhouette background shot. Black and Red Label parallels of this set were also randomly inserted in packs. Black parallels were inserted at 1:150 and were red parallels were inserted at 1:644 and serial numbered to 25. Card backs carry an "FG" prefix.
COMPLETE SET (20) 15.00 30.00
*BLACK: 1.5X TO 4X BASIC INSERTS
*RED: 10X TO 25X BASIC INSERTS
FG1 Sergei Samsonov .75 2.00
FG2 Joe Thornton 2.00 5.00
FG3 Wade Redden .75 2.00
FG4 Chris Drury .75 2.00
FG5 Petr Sykora .75 2.00
FG6 Patrik Stefan 2.00 5.00
FG7 Anson Carter .75 2.00
FG8 Martin Biron .75 2.00
FG9 Alex Tanguay .75 2.00
FG10 Milan Hejduk 1.25 3.00
FG11 Mark Parrish .75 2.00
FG12 David Legwand .75 2.00
FG13 Brendan Morrison .75 2.00
FG14 Scott Gomez .75 2.00
FG15 Tim Connolly 1.25 3.00
FG16 Marian Hossa 1.25 3.00
FG17 Jan Hrdina .75 2.00
FG18 Steve Kariya .75 2.00
FG19 Jochen Hecht 1.50 4.00
FG20 Vincent Lecavalier 1.25 3.00

1999-00 Topps Gold Label Prime Gold

Randomly inserted in packs at one in 20, this 15-card set showcases 15 veterans who have set their own standards, and have influenced how future players will be evaluated. The foreground features a full color action shot that is set against a silhouette background shot. Black and Red label parallels were also released of this set. Black parallels were inserted at 1:100 and were red parallels were inserted at 1:859 and serial numbered to 25. Card backs carry a "PG" prefix.
COMPLETE SET (15) 30.00 60.00
*BLACK: 1.5X TO 4X BASIC CARDS
*RED/25: 10X TO 25X BASIC CARDS
PG1 Dominik Hasek 3.00 8.00
PG2 Paul Kariya 1.50 4.00
PG3 Theo Fleury 1.25 3.00
PG4 Jaromir Jagr 2.50 6.00
PG5 Zigmund Palffy 1.25 3.00
PG6 Nicklas Lidstrom 1.50 4.00
PG7 Teemu Selanne 1.50 4.00
PG8 John LeClair 1.50 4.00
PG9 Ray Bourque 2.50 6.00
PG10 Peter Forsberg 4.00 10.00
PG11 Joe Sakic 3.00 8.00
PG12 Jeremy Roenick 2.00 5.00
PG13 Mike Modano 2.50 6.00
PG14 Pavel Bure 1.50 4.00
PG15 Curtis Joseph 1.50 4.00

1999-00 Topps Gold Label Quest for the Cup

Randomly seeded in packs at 1:12, this 10-card set celebrates the 10 teams most likely to contend for the 2000 Stanley Cup. Card fronts feature the player that best represents his respective team set against the teams full color logo and the Stanley cup itself. Card backs carry a "QC" prefix. Black, red and gold parallels were also created and seeded randomly. Black parallels were inserted at 1:60. Red parallels were inserted at 1:1289 and were serial numbered to 25. Gold, black and red 1/1's also exist, but are not priced due to scarcity.
COMPLETE SET (10) 15.00 30.00
*BLACK: 1.5X TO 4X BASIC INSERTS
*RED/25: 20X TO 50X BASIC INSERTS
QC1 Steve Yzerman 4.00 10.00
QC2 Keith Tkachuk .75 2.00
QC3 Eric Lindros .75 2.00
QC4 Patrick Roy 3.00 8.00
QC5 Martin Brodeur 2.00 5.00
QC6 Chris Pronger .60 1.50
QC7 Daniel Alfredsson .60 1.50
QC8 Owen Nolan .60 1.50
QC9 Brett Hull 1.00 2.50
QC10 Mats Sundin .75 2.00

2000-01 Topps Gold Label Class 1

This 115-card set features color player photos printed on 35-point spectral-reflective rainbow styrene stock with gold stamping. Each card showcases an NHL player on three different versions of his base card. Displayed in the foreground of the Class 1 set is a photo of the player with an action shot appearing in the background featuring players skating and goalies standing upright. The last 15 cards in the set were sequentially numbered to 999. A gold parallel version of this set was also available in random packs where the same photos were used on gold tinted stock. In that version, cards 1-100 were sequentially numbered to 399 and cards 101-115 were numbered to 99. Topps Gold Label was packaged in 24-pack boxes with packs containing five cards and carried a suggested retail price of $5.00.
COMPLETE SET (115) 75.00 150.00
*CLS 1 GOLD VETS/399: 1.5X TO 4X CLS 1
*CLS 1 GOLD ROOK/99: .6X TO 1.5X CLS 1
*CLS 2 VETS: 1.2X TO 3X CLS 1
*CLS 2 ROOK/666: .5X TO 1.2X CLS 1
*CLS 2 GLD VETS/299: 2X TO 5X CLS 1
*CLS 2 GLD ROOK/66: .8X TO 2X CLS 1
*CLS 3 VETS: 2X TO 5X CLS 1
*CLS 3 ROOK/333: .6X TO 1.5X CLS 1
*CLS 3 GLD VETS/199: 2.5X TO 6X CLS 1
*CLS 3 GLD ROOK/33: 1.2X TO 3X CLS 1
1 Ray Bourque .60 1.50
2 Brendan Shanahan .50 1.25
3 Mark Recchi .50 1.25
4 Olaf Kolzig .40 1.00
5 Brett Hull .60 1.50
6 Valeri Bure .30 .75
7 Joe Thornton .60 1.50
8 Pavel Bure .50 1.25
9 Jeff Hackett .25 .60
10 Patrik Elias .40 1.00
11 Marian Hossa .30 .75
12 Patrick Marleau .40 1.00
13 Markus Naslund .30 .75
14 Jaromir Jagr 1.00 2.50
15 Tim Connolly .25 .60
16 Zigmund Palffy .40 1.00
17 Peter Forsberg .50 1.25
18 Byron Dafoe .30 .75
19 Patrik Stefan .30 .75
20 Arturs Irbe .30 .75
21 Jocelyn Thibault .30 .75
22 Bill Guerin .40 1.00
23 Keith Primeau .30 .75
24 Mats Sundin .40 1.00
25 Adam Oates .40 1.00
26 Owen Nolan .40 1.00
27 Mike Richter .40 1.00
28 Luc Robitaille .40 1.00
29 Chris Drury .30 .75
30 Maxim Afinogenov .25 .60
31 Jarome Iginla .40 1.00
32 Joe Nieuwendyk .40 1.00
33 Maxim Sushinski .25 .60
34 Daniel Alfredsson .40 1.00
35 Pierre Turgeon .40 1.00
36 Jason Allison .30 .75
37 Mario Lemieux 1.25 3.00

Sergei Fedorov .60 1.50
Paul Kariya .50 1.25
Scott Stevens .40 1.00
Keith Tkachuk .40 1.00
Curtis Joseph .50 1.25
Peter Bondra .30 .75
Roman Turek .30 .75
Alexei Kovalev .30 .75
Brian Boucher .30 .75
Mark Messier .60 1.50
Saku Koivu .40 1.00
Tommy Salo .30 .75
Ron Tugnutt .30 .75
Patrick Roy 1.00 2.50
Fred Brathwaite .30 .75
Donald Audette .30 .75
Doug Gilmour .50 1.25
Alexander Mogilny .30 .75
John LeClair .40 1.00
Scott Young .25 .60
Jeff Friesen .25 .60
Simon Gagne .40 1.00
Theo Fleury .50 1.25
Scott Gomez .30 .75
Guy Hebert .30 .75
Roberto Luongo .60 1.50
Mike Modano .60 1.50
Joe Sakic .60 1.50
Dominik Hasek .60 1.50
Pavol Demitra .50 1.25
Daniel Sedin .75 2.00
Vincent Lecavalier .30 .75
Jeremy Roenick .40 1.00
Martin Brodeur .75 2.00
Rob Blake .40 1.00
Ed Belfour .40 1.00
Tony Amonte .30 .75
Miroslav Satan .25 .60
Alexei Yashin .30 .75
Henrik Sedin .60 1.50
David Legwand .40 1.00
Steve Yzerman 1.25 3.00
Ron Francis .50 1.25
Milan Hejduk .30 .75
Teemu Selanne .75 2.00
Brad Isbister .25 .60
Jean-Sebastien Aubin .30 .75
Chris Pronger .30 .75
Nicklas Lidstrom .40 1.00
Brad Richards .40 1.00
Brent Johnson .30 .75
Oleg Saprykin .25 .60
Anson Carter .30 .75
Brian Leetch .40 1.00
Evgeni Nabokov .30 .75
Ian Laperriere .25 .60
Peter White .25 .60
Wes Walz .25 .60
Jason Arnott .30 .75
Tommy Albelin .25 .60
Jeff Toms .25 .60
Brad Brown .30 .75
0 Garry Valk .25 .60
1 Andrew Raycroft RC 3.00 8.00
2 Marian Gaborik RC 12.50 30.00
3 David Aebischer RC 2.50 6.00
4 Scott Hartnell RC 3.00 8.00
5 Marty Turco RC 2.50 6.00
6 Justin Williams RC 3.00 8.00
7 Steven Reinprecht RC 2.00 5.00
8 Josef Vasicek RC 3.00 8.00
9 Martin Havlat RC 8.00 20.00
0 Rostislav Klesla RC 3.00 8.00
1 Jani Hurme RC 1.25 3.00
2 Rick DiPietro RC 5.00 12.00
3 Alexander Kharitonov RC 1.25 3.00
4 Matt Pettinger RC 1.25 3.00
5 Roman Cechmanek RC 1.50 4.00

2000-01 Topps Gold Label Autographs

is 10-card set features authentic autographs of each ayer accompanied by an action photo and a large am logo on a reflective silver background. Each card so carries the Topps Certified Autograph stamp on ont and a Topps Genuine Issue sticker on card back. ese cards were available in random packs at stated lds of 1:57. The Gomez card was originally issued as exchange card.

ABB Brian Boucher 4.00 10.00
ABR Brad Richards 6.00 15.00
AJW Justin Williams 6.00 15.00
AMG Marian Gaborik 12.50 30.00
AMK Milan Kraft 4.00 10.00
AMT Marty Turco 8.00 20.00
AMY Mike York 4.00 10.00
ARB Ray Bourque 20.00 50.00
ASG Scott Gomez 4.00 10.00
ASH Scott Hartnell 8.00 20.00

2000-01 Topps Gold Label Behind the Mask

is 10-card set was available in random packs at a ated odd of 1:7. The card fronts featured a color tion shot of the player in the foreground over a larger ayer photo in the background. The players name is amped in gold on the front along with a color team go. A sparkle-texture treated parallel numbered 1 of 1 as also randomly available.

OMPLETE SET (10) 10.00 20.00
M1 Curtis Joseph .75 2.00
M2 Ed Belfour .75 2.00
M3 Dominik Hasek 1.50 4.00
M4 Martin Brodeur 2.00 5.00
M5 Brian Boucher .75 2.00
M6 Roman Turek .75 2.00
M7 Olaf Kolzig .75 2.00
M8 Patrick Roy 4.00 10.00
M9 Arturs Irbe .75 2.00
M10 Mike Richter .75 2.00

2000-01 Topps Gold Label Bullion

is 10-card set features photos of three teammates on gold team logo background. These cards were ailable in random packs at stated odds of 1:21. A arkle-texture treated parallel numbered 1 of 1 was so randomly available.

OMPLETE SET (10) 30.00 60.00
M.Brodeur/S.Gomez/J.Arnott 4.00 10.00
2 E.Belfour/M.Modano/B.Hull 3.00 8.00
3 Yzerman/Shanahan/Fedorov 6.00 12.00
4 P.Roy/Bourque/Forsberg 6.00 15.00
5 R.Turek/Pronger/Demitra 2.00 5.00
6 M.Sundin/C.Joseph/T.Domi 4.00 10.00
7 Roenick/Tkachuk/Numminen 3.00 8.00
8 J.Friesen/P.Marleau/O.Nolan 3.00 8.00
9 M.Messier/Leetch/M.Richter 2.00 5.00
10 D.Sedin/M.Naslund/H.Sedin 2.00 5.00

2000-01 Topps Gold Label Game-Worn Jerseys

This 6-card set was randomly available in packs at stated odds of 1:37. The card fronts featured a swatch of game-used jersey from the player featured along with an action photo of the player on a sparkle-texture treated foil. The card backs also contained a Topps Genuine Issue sticker.

GLJJL John LeClair 5.00 12.00
GLJKT Keith Tkachuk 5.00 12.00
GLJMB Martin Brodeur 10.00 25.00
GLJPF Peter Forsberg 10.00 25.00
GLJPM Patrick Marleau 5.00 12.00
GLJSF Sergei Fedorov 6.00 15.00

2000-01 Topps Gold Label Golden Greats

This 15-card set highlights players who scored 50-plus goals in a single season. The card fronts carry a gold-bordered action photo of the player. These cards were available in random packs at stated odds of 1:5. A sparkle-texture treated parallel numbered 1 of 1 was also randomly available.

GG1 Pavel Bure 1.25 3.00
GG2 Paul Kariya 1.00 2.50
GG3 Jaromir Jagr 1.50 4.00
GG4 John LeClair 1.00 2.50
GG5 Steve Yzerman 4.00 10.00
GG6 Brett Hull 1.25 3.00
GG7 Alexander Mogilny .75 2.00
GG8 Joe Sakic 2.00 5.00
GG9 Keith Tkachuk 1.00 2.50
GG10 Teemu Selanne 1.00 2.50
GG11 Sergei Fedorov 2.00 5.00
GG12 Luc Robitaille .75 2.00
GG13 Mike Modano 1.50 4.00
GG14 Brendan Shanahan 1.50 4.00
GG15 Jeremy Roenick 1.25 3.00

2000-01 Topps Gold Label New Generation

This 15-card set featured a color action photo of each player in the foreground and a larger photo of the players face in the background all set on a blue-bordered card front which also displayed the players name, position, and team logo. These cards were available in random packs at stated odds of 1:14. A sparkle-texture treated parallel numbered 1 of 1 was also randomly available.

NG1 Scott Gomez .75 2.00
NG2 Vincent Lecavalier 1.50 4.00
NG3 Joe Thornton 2.00 5.00
NG4 Alex Tanguay 1.25 3.00
NG5 Marian Hossa 1.50 4.00
NG6 Brad Stuart .75 2.00
NG7 Henrik Sedin .75 2.00
NG8 Marian Gaborik 3.00 8.00
NG9 Roberto Luongo 2.00 5.00
NG10 David Legwand .75 2.00
NG11 Daniel Sedin .75 2.00
NG12 Patrik Stefan .75 2.00
NG13 Brian Boucher 1.25 3.00
NG14 Chris Drury 1.25 3.00
NG15 Tim Connolly .75 2.00

2000-01 Topps Heritage

Topps Heritage was released in 2000-01 as a 247-card set. The cards had the same design as that of the 1954-55 Topps set. The rookies from the set were short-printed and serial numbered to 1955. They were available in packs at a rate of 1:12.

COMPLETE SET (247) 125.00 250.00
COMP.SET w/o SP's (219) 25.00 50.00
1 Ray Bourque .60 1.50
2 Martin Brodeur .75 2.00
3 Jaromir Jagr 1.00 2.50
4 Vincent Lecavalier .30 .75
5 Olaf Kolzig .40 1.00
6 Alexei Yashin .30 .75
7 Mark Messier .60 1.50
8 Paul Kariya .50 1.25
9 Pavel Bure .50 1.25
10 Steve Yzerman 1.25 3.00
11 Patrik Stefan .30 .75
12 Joe Thornton .60 1.50
13 Mats Sundin .40 1.00
14 Brett Hull .60 1.50
15 Zigmund Palffy .40 1.00
16 Peter Bondra .30 .75
17 Owen Nolan .40 1.00
18 Tony Amonte .30 .75
19 Henrik Sedin .60 1.50
20 Keith Tkachuk .40 1.00
21 Tim Connolly .25 .60
22 Doug Weight .40 1.00
23 Ed Belfour .40 1.00
24 Patrick Roy 1.00 2.50
25 Brad Richards .40 1.00
26 Dominik Hasek .60 1.50
27 Brendan Shanahan .50 1.25
28 Teemu Selanne .75 2.00
29 Scott Gomez .30 .75
30 John LeClair .40 1.00
31 Chris Pronger .30 .75
32 Ron Francis .50 1.25
33 Daniel Sedin .75 2.00
34 Curtis Joseph .50 1.25
35 Roman Turek .30 .75
36 Jeremy Roenick .40 1.00
37 Mark Recchi .50 1.25
38 Patrik Elias .40 1.00
39 Saku Koivu .40 1.00
40 Luc Robitaille .40 1.00
41 Sergei Fedorov .60 1.50
42 Peter Forsberg .50 1.25
43 Milan Kraft .25 .60
44 Jason Allison .30 .75
45 Mike Modano .60 1.50
46 Roberto Luongo .60 1.50
47 David Legwand .40 1.00
48 Pierre Turgeon .40 1.00
49 Maxime Ouellet .40 1.00
50 Oleg Saprykin .25 .60
51 Pavol Demitra .50 1.25
52 Adam Oates .40 1.00
53 Doug Gilmour .50 1.25
54 Joe Sakic .60 1.50
55 Daniel Alfredsson .40 1.00
56 Brian Leetch .40 1.00
57 Bill Guerin .40 1.00
58 Brent Johnson .30 .75
59 Scott Stevens .40 1.00
60 Rob Blake .40 1.00
61 Nicklas Lidstrom .40 1.00
62 Milan Hejduk .30 .75
63 Arturs Irbe .30 .75
64 Maxim Afinogenov .25 .60
65 Taylor Pyatt .25 .60
66 Tommy Salo .30 .75
67 Theo Fleury .50 1.25
68 Marian Hossa .30 .75
69 Simon Gagne .40 1.00
70 Jarome Iginla .40 1.00
71 Alexander Mogilny .30 .75
72 Chris Drury .30 .75
73 Mario Lemieux 1.25 3.00
74 Petr Hubacek RC 2.00 5.00
75 Marty Turco RC 4.00 10.00
76 Rostislav Klesla RC 5.00 12.00
77 Martin Havlat RC 6.00 15.00
78 David Aebischer RC 4.00 10.00
79 Reto Von Arx RC 2.50 6.00
80 Mike Comrie RC 5.00 12.00
81 Tomas Kloucek RC 2.00 5.00
82 Steven Reinprecht RC 3.00 8.00
83 Brad Tapper RC 2.00 5.00
84 Petr Svoboda RC 2.50 6.00
85 Marian Gaborik RC 10.00 25.00
86 Josef Vasicek RC 5.00 12.00
87 Lubomir Visnovsky RC 4.00 10.00
88 Roman Cechmanek RC 2.50 6.00
89 Reed Low RC 2.00 5.00
90 Jani Hurme RC 2.00 5.00
91 Petteri Nummelin RC 2.00 5.00
92 Colin White RC 2.00 5.00
93 Andrew Raycroft RC 5.00 12.00
94 Greg Classen RC 2.00 5.00
95 Alexander Kharitonov RC 2.50 6.00
96 Rick DiPietro RC 8.00 20.00
97 Justin Williams RC 5.00 12.00
98 Eric Belanger RC 2.50 6.00
99 Scott Hartnell RC 5.00 12.00
100 Michel Riesen RC 2.50 6.00
101 Brian Boucher .30 .75
102 Mike Richter .40 1.00
103 John Vanbiesbrouck .30 .75
104 Jamie McLennan .25 .60
105 Andrei Markov .50 1.25
106 Ron Tugnutt .30 .75
107 Jean-Sebastien Aubin .30 .75
108 Brad Stuart .30 .75
109 Gary Roberts .25 .60
110 Rod Brind'Amour .40 1.00
111 Keith Primeau .30 .75
112 Jeff Halpern .25 .60
113 Jochen Hecht .25 .60
114 Valeri Bure .30 .75
115 Donald Audette .30 .75
116 Brenden Morrow .30 .75
117 Mike Mottau .25 .60
118 Kevin Weekes .25 .60
119 Jamie Storr .30 .75
120 Shane Willis .25 .60
121 Matt Cooke .25 .60
122 Martin Lapointe .30 .75
123 Alexei Kovalev .30 .75
124 Felix Potvin .60 1.50
125 Sean Burke .25 .60
126 Jeff Hackett .25 .60
127 Brad Isbister .25 .60
128 Derian Hatcher .30 .75
129 Marc Savard .30 .75
130 Sergei Samsonov .30 .75
131 Maxim Sushinski .25 .60
132 Radek Bonk .30 .75
133 Mika Noronen .25 .60
134 Adam Graves .30 .75
135 Sheldon Keefe .25 .60
136 Markus Naslund .30 .75
137 Trevor Letowski .25 .60
138 Jeff Friesen .25 .60
139 Alex Tanguay .30 .75
140 Byron Dafoe .30 .75
141 Chris Osgood .40 1.00
142 Mike York .25 .60
143 Scott Young .25 .60
144 Sami Kapanen .25 .60
145 Evgeni Nabokov .30 .75
146 Brendan Morrison .40 1.00
147 Joe Nieuwendyk .40 1.00
148 Tomi Kallio .25 .60
149 Guy Hebert .30 .75
150 Randy McKay .25 .60
151 Mike Johnson .25 .60
152 Miroslav Satan .25 .60
153 Patrick Marleau .40 1.00
154 Jocelyn Thibault .30 .75
155 Martin Straka .30 .75
156 Fred Brathwaite .30 .75
157 Cliff Ronning .25 .60
158 Denis Shvidki .25 .60
159 Espen Knutsen .25 .60
160 Alexei Zhamnov .30 .75
161 Georges Laraque .30 .75
162 Jose Theodore .50 1.25
163 Rick Tocchet .30 .75
164 Donald Brashear .25 .60
165 Darren Langdon .25 .60
166 Rob Ray .25 .60
167 Matthew Barnaby .30 .75
168 Chris Simon .25 .60
169 Ken Belanger .25 .60
170 Tie Domi .60 1.50
171 Roman Hamrlik .30 .75
172 Olli Jokinen .30 .75
173 Steve Rucchin .25 .60
174 Jim Cummins .25 .60
175 Tyson Nash .25 .60
176 Scott Parker .25 .60
177 Matt Johnson .25 .60
178 Sandy McCarthy .25 .60
179 Daniel Cleary .30 .75
180 Michal Handzus .25 .60
181 Nikolai Antropov .30 .75
182 Scott Thornton .30 .75
183 Shane Doan .30 .75
184 Wade Redden .25 .60
185 Ray Whitney .30 .75
186 Teppo Numminen .25 .60
187 Pat Verbeek .30 .75
188 Bobby Holik .25 .60
189 Mike Dunham .25 .60
190 Rob Niedermayer .30 .75
191 Ray Ferraro .25 .60
192 Steve Sullivan .25 .60
193 Sergei Zubov .30 .75
194 Scott Walker .25 .60
195 Geoff Sanderson .30 .75
196 Bob Probert .30 .75
197 Andrew Brunette .25 .60
198 Marty Murray .25 .60
199 Steve Staios .25 .60
200 Kay Whitmore .25 .60
201 Jonas Hoglund .25 .60
202 Niklas Andersson .25 .60
203 Joaquin Gage .25 .60
204 Mike Ricci .30 .75
205 Bryan Helmer .25 .60
206 Patrick Traverse .25 .60
207 Mike Rucinski .25 .60
208 Brantt Myhres .25 .60
209 Claude Lapointe .25 .60
210 Frank Musil .25 .60
211 Sandis Ozolinsh .30 .75
212 Tomas Vokoun .30 .75
213 Jarrod Skalde .25 .60
214 Sergei Gonchar .25 .60
215 Anson Carter .30 .75
216 Steve Yzerman AS 1.00 2.50
217 Mike Modano AS .50 1.25
218 Paul Kariya AS .40 1.00
219 Brendan Shanahan AS .40 1.00
220 Pavel Bure AS .40 1.00
221 Jaromir Jagr AS .75 2.00
222 Chris Pronger AS .25 .60
223 Nicklas Lidstrom AS .30 .75
224 Rob Blake AS .30 .75
225 Eric Desjardins AS .25 .60
226 Olaf Kolzig AS .30 .75
227 Roman Turek AS .25 .60
228 S.Stevens C.Pronger LL .30 .75
229 S.Gomez A.Tanguay LL .25 .60
230 P.Bure O.Nolan LL .40 1.00
231 M.Brodeur R.Turek LL .60 1.50
232 M.Czerkawski O.Nolan LL .30 .75
233 J.Theodore E.Belfour LL .40 1.00
234 J.Madden T.Amonte LL .25 .60
235 J.Jagr P.Kariya LL .75 2.00
236 E.Desjardins N.Lidstrom LL .30 .75
237 B.Boucher R.Turek LL .25 .60
238 Steve Yzerman AW 1.00 2.50
239 Scott Stevens AW .30 .75
240 Scott Gomez AW .25 .60
241 Roman Turek AW .25 .60
242 Pavol Demitra AW .40 1.00
243 Pavel Bure AW .40 1.00
245 Jaromir Jagr AW .75 2.00
246 Chris Pronger AW .25 .60
247 New Jersey Devils SC .20 .50
244 Olaf Kolzig AW .30 .75

2000-01 Topps Heritage Chrome Parallel

Randomly inserted in packs of Topps Heritage, the 100-card parallel set featured the chrome version of the base set. The cards were serial numbered to 555.

*1-73 VETS/555: 2X TO 5X BASIC CARDS
*74-100 ROOK/555: .3X TO .8X BASE RC
7 Mark Messier 3.00 8.00

2000-01 Topps Heritage Arena Relics

Randomly inserted in packs of 2000-01 Topps Heritage at a rate of 1:128, this 15-card set featured original pieces from the old arenas. The 2 autographed cards were available in packs at a rate of 1:12345. The multi-piece arena relic was available in packs at a rate of 1:11536.

OSAJT Joe Thornton 10.00 25.00
OSAMM Mark Messier 12.50 30.00
OSAMS Mats Sundin 10.00 25.00
OSASK Saku Koivu 10.00 25.00
OSASY Steve Yzerman 12.50 30.00
OSATA Tony Amonte 10.00 25.00
OSABG Bill Gadsby 10.00 25.00
OSAGH Gordie Howe 12.00 30.00
OSALW Gump Worsley 10.00 25.00
OSAMR Maurice Richard 15.00 40.00
OSAMS Milt Schmidt 10.00 25.00
OSATK Ted Kennedy 10.00 25.00
OSA Multi Arena Relic/55 175.00 350.00
HAAGH Gordie Howe AU/25 250.00 400.00
HAALW Gump Worsley AU/25 150.00 250.00

2000-01 Topps Heritage Autographs

This 12-card set was randomly inserted in packs at a rate of 1:184 for the current players and 1:97 for the reprints of former NHL players. Please note that at the time of its release Topps included Joe Thornton and Tony Amonte as exchange/redemption cards. Tony Amonte did not sign his cards, the exchange card was redeemable for a similar card from other Topps issues.

HAAG Adam Graves 12.50 30.00
HACJ Curtis Joseph 12.50 30.00
HAJH Jeff Hackett 6.00 15.00
HAJT Joe Thornton 20.00 50.00
HASF Sergei Fedorov 20.00 50.00
HAAB Andy Bathgate 10.00 25.00
HAAD Alex Delvecchio 10.00 25.00
HAGH Gordie Howe 75.00 150.00
HALW Gump Worsley 15.00 40.00
HARK Red Kelly 12.50 30.00
HATL Ted Lindsay 12.50 30.00

2000-01 Topps Heritage Heroes

COMPLETE SET (20) 25.00 50.00
STATED ODDS: 1:14
HH1 Ray Bourque 1.50 4.00
HH2 Jaromir Jagr 1.25 3.00
HH3 Steve Yzerman 4.00 10.00
HH4 Mike Modano 1.25 3.00
HH5 Patrick Roy 4.00 10.00
HH6 Martin Brodeur 2.00 5.00
HH7 Mark Messier 1.00 2.50
HH8 Peter Forsberg 2.00 5.00
HH9 Scott Stevens .60 1.50
HH10 Teemu Selanne .75 2.00
HH11 Pavel Bure 1.00 2.50
HH12 Curtis Joseph .75 2.00
HH13 John LeClair 1.00 2.50
HH14 Brett Hull 1.00 2.50
HH15 Keith Tkachuk .75 2.00
HH16 Tony Amonte .60 1.50
HH17 Ed Belfour .75 2.00
HH18 Brendan Shanahan 1.25 3.00
HH19 Dominik Hasek 1.50 4.00
HH20 Paul Kariya .75 2.00

2000-01 Topps Heritage New Tradition

COMPLETE SET (10) 6.00 12.00
STATED ODDS: 1:8
NT1 Marian Hossa .50 1.25
NT2 Daniel Sedin .40 1.00
NT3 Milan Hejduk .50 1.25
NT4 Vincent Lecavalier .50 1.25
NT5 Joe Thornton .75 2.00
NT6 Scott Gomez .40 1.00
NT7 Chris Drury .40 1.00
NT8 Brian Boucher .40 1.00
NT9 Henrik Sedin .40 1.00
NT10 Marian Gaborik 2.00 5.00

2000-01 Topps Heritage Original Six Relics

Randomly inserted in packs at a rate of 1:409, this 16-card set featured original pieces from game-used hockey sticks or jerseys. The 2 autographed jersey cards that were available in packs at a rate of 1:8240. The multi-piece relics were available in packs at a rate of 1:11,536. The jersey cards were available in packs at a rate of 1:51. Tony Amonte did not sign his autograph cards, the exchange card was redeemed for similar cards from other Topps issues.

OSJAZ Alexei Zhamnov J 5.00 12.00
OSJCO Chris Osgood J 5.00 12.00
OSJJT Joe Thornton J 8.00 20.00
OSJSK Saku Koivu J 5.00 12.00
OSJTD Tie Domi J 5.00 12.00
OSJTF Theo Fleury J 5.00 12.00
OSSBP Bob Probert S 10.00 25.00
OSSJA Jason Allison S 10.00 25.00
OSSJH Jeff Hackett S 10.00 25.00
OSSMM Mark Messier S 10.00 25.00
OSSMS Mats Sundin S 10.00 25.00
OSSSY Steve Yzerman S 15.00 40.00
OSJ Alexei Zhamnov Theo Fleury Chris Osgood Joe Thornton Saku Koivu Tie Domi/55 125.00 250.00
OSJAJH Jeff Hackett JSY AU/25 40.00 80.00
OSJAJT Joe Thornton JSY AU/25 75.00 200.00

2001-02 Topps Heritage

Released in early December 2001, this 187-card set borrowed from the 1957-58 Topps design but included current day players. This set carried an SRP of $3.00 for an 8-card pack, and each pack included a stick of gum. Rookies and SPs (#138-187) were seeded at 1:3.

COMPLETE SET (187) 40.00 100.00
1 Mario Lemieux 1.00 2.50
2 Evgeni Nabokov .25 .60
3 Nicklas Lidstrom .30 .75
4 Patrik Elias .30 .75
5 Olaf Kolzig .30 .75
6 Mats Sundin .30 .75
7 Jason Allison .25 .60
8 Mike Modano .50 1.25
9 Keith Tkachuk .30 .75
10 John LeClair .30 .75
11 Pavel Bure .40 1.00
12 Tony Amonte .25 .60
13 Zigmund Palffy .30 .75
14 Mark Messier .50 1.25
15 Sean Burke .20 .50
16 Markus Naslund .30 .75
17 Milan Hejduk .25 .60
18 Teemu Selanne .60 1.50
19 Espen Knutsen .20 .50
20 David Legwand .25 .60
21 Saku Koivu .30 .75
22 Ron Francis .40 1.00
23 Ray Ferraro .20 .50
24 Brendan Shanahan .40 1.00
25 Rick DiPietro .25 .60
26 Brad Richards .30 .75
27 Henrik Sedin .30 .75
28 Marian Hossa .25 .60
29 Marian Gaborik .50 1.25
30 Ed Belfour .30 .75
31 Miroslav Satan .25 .60
32 Roberto Luongo .50 1.25
33 Brian Leetch .30 .75
34 Chris Pronger .25 .60
35 Peter Bondra .30 .75
36 Keith Primeau .25 .60
37 Johan Hedberg .25 .60
38 Steve Yzerman 1.00 2.50
39 Peter Forsberg .40 1.00
40 Jarome Iginla .30 .75
41 Jose Theodore .30 .75
42 Curtis Joseph .30 .75
43 Martin Havlat .25 .60
44 Sergei Fedorov .50 1.25
45 Arturs Irbe .25 .60
46 Martin Brodeur .60 1.50
47 Owen Nolan .30 .75
48 Daniel Sedin .30 .75
49 Mark Recchi .40 1.00
50 Adam Deadmarsh .25 .60
51 Tommy Salo .25 .60
52 Alexei Kovalev .25 .60
53 Steve Sullivan .20 .50
54 Paul Kariya .40 1.00
55 Vincent Lecavalier .25 .60
56 Alex Tanguay .25 .60
57 Joe Thornton .40 1.00
58 Brent Johnson .25 .60
59 Roman Cechmanek .25 .60
60 Petr Sykora .20 .50
61 J-P Dumont .20 .50
62 Mike Comrie .25 .60
63 Daniel Alfredsson .30 .75
64 Eric Daze .25 .60
65 Felix Potvin .50 1.25
66 Chris Drury .25 .60
67 Manny Fernandez .25 .60
68 Claude Lemieux .25 .60
69 Rob Blake .30 .75
70 Bill Guerin .30 .75
71 Mike Dunham .25 .60
72 Simon Gagne .30 .75
73 Jeff Friesen .20 .50
74 Joe Sakic .50 1.25
75 Jason Arnott .25 .60
76 Patrick Roy .75 2.00
77 Josef Vasicek .20 .50
78 Marty Turco .30 .75
79 Al MacInnis .30 .75
80 Anson Carter .25 .60
81 Tomi Kallio .20 .50
82 Eric Belanger .20 .50
83 Patrick Lalime .25 .60
84 Scott Young .20 .50
85 Scott Gomez .25 .60
86 Marc Denis .25 .60
87 Jeff O'Neill .20 .50
88 Sergei Samsonov .25 .60
89 Robert Lang .20 .50
90 Byron Dafoe .25 .60
91 Scott Stevens .30 .75
92 Adam Oates .30 .75
93 Patrick Marleau .30 .75
94 Petr Nedved .25 .60
95 Ryan Smyth .25 .60
96 Adam Foote .25 .60
97 Marc Savard .20 .50
98 Brad Isbister .20 .50
99 Martin Straka .20 .50
100 Joe Nieuwendyk .30 .75
101 Shane Willis .20 .50
102 Pavol Demitra .40 1.00
103 Jeff Halpern .20 .50
104 Sergei Zubov .25 .60
105 David Vyborny .20 .50
106 Gary Roberts .20 .50
107 Martin Biron .25 .60
109 Lubomir Visnovsky .20 .50
109 Fredrik Modin .20 .50
110 Brenden Morrow .25 .60
111 Stanley Cup Champs .40 1.00
112 Nicklas Lidstrom AS .25 .60
113 Jaromir Jagr AS .60 1.50
114 Patrik Elias AS .25 .60
115 Joe Sakic AS .40 1.00
116 Dominik Hasek AS .40 1.00
117 Rob Blake AS .25 .60
118 Scott Stevens AS .25 .60
119 Roman Cechmanek AS .20 .50
120 Mario Lemieux AS .75 2.00
121 Pavel Bure AS .30 .75
122 Luc Robitaille AS .25 .60
123 J.Jagr/J.Sakic LL .60 1.50
124 P.Bure/J.Sakic LL .40 1.00
125 P.Elias/J.Sakic LL .40 1.00
126 B.Leetch/N.Lidstrom LL .25 .60
127 A.Irbe/T.Salo LL .20 .50
128 M.Brodeur/P.Roy LL .60 1.50
129 M.Turco/R.Cechmanek LL .25 .60
130 Joe Sakic AW .40 1.00
131 Patrick Roy AW .60 1.50
132 Pavel Bure AW .30 .75
133 Evgeni Nabokov AW .20 .50
134 Nicklas Lidstrom AW .25 .60
135 Dominik Hasek AW .40 1.00
136 John Madden AW .20 .50
137 Jaromir Jagr AW .60 1.50
138 Ilya Kovalchuk RC 6.00 15.00
139 Niko Kapanen RC 2.50 6.00
140 Brian Sutherby RC 1.50 4.00
141 Jeff Jillson RC 1.50 4.00
142 Jiri Dopita RC 1.50 4.00
143 Andreas Salomonsson RC 1.50 4.00
144 Timo Parssinen RC 2.00 5.00
145 Vaclav Nedorost RC 1.50 4.00
146 Kristian Huselius RC 2.50 6.00
147 Dan Blackburn RC 2.00 5.00
148 Nikita Alexeev RC 1.50 4.00
149 Peter Smrek RC 1.50 4.00
150 Krys Kolanos RC 1.50 4.00
151 Pavel Datsyuk RC 6.00 15.00
152 Jaroslav Bednar RC 1.50 4.00
153 Chris Neil RC 2.00 5.00
154 Erik Cole RC 3.00 8.00
155 Niklas Hagman RC 2.00 5.00
156 Jason Chimera RC 1.50 4.00
157 Scott Clemmensen RC 1.50 4.00
158 Andrew Brunette .75 2.00
159 Dominik Hasek 2.00 5.00
160 Jaromir Jagr 3.00 8.00
161 Doug Weight 1.25 3.00
162 Brett Hull 1.50 4.00
163 Pierre Turgeon 1.25 3.00
164 Jeremy Roenick 1.25 3.00
165 Alexander Mogilny 1.00 2.50
166 Luc Robitaille 1.25 3.00
167 Michael Peca 1.00 2.50
168 Roman Turek 1.00 2.50
169 Martin Lapointe .75 2.00
170 Alexei Yashin 1.00 2.50
171 Adam Graves 1.00 2.50
172 Valeri Bure .75 2.00
173 Tim Connolly .75 2.00
174 Kris Beech .75 2.00
175 Donald Audette .75 2.00
176 Jochen Hecht .75 2.00
177 Fred Brathwaite 1.00 2.50
178 Rob Niedermayer 1.00 2.50
179 Eric Lindros 2.00 5.00
180 Bill Muckalt .75 2.00
181 Eric Weinrich .75 2.00
182 Taylor Pyatt .75 2.00
183 Pavel Brendl .75 2.00
184 Craig Berube .75 2.00
185 Dany Heatley 1.25 3.00
186 Ken Sutton .75 2.00
187 Slava Kozlov 1.00 2.50

2001-02 Topps Heritage Refractors

Printed on chrome reflective stock, this 110-card set paralleled the base set and was serial numbered to just 558 sets.

*REFRACTOR/558: 2.5X TO 6X BASIC CARDS
14 Mark Messier 3.00 8.00

2001-02 Topps Heritage Arena Relics

This 13-card hobby only set featured pieces of arena seats from the Montreal Forum and Boston Gardens. Cards featuring single players were inserted at 1:149. Dual player cards were serial-numbered to 100 and inserted at 1:994 Dual payer cards included two pieces of arena seats. Autographed versions of this set were inserted at 1:1491 for single player and 1:3976 for dual player. Autographed cards with dual players were serial-numbered out of 25.

RBG Bernie Geoffrion 6.00 15.00
RHR Henri Richard 6.00 15.00
RJBE Jean Beliveau 10.00 25.00
RJBU John Bucyk 8.00 20.00
RJBBG J.Bucyk/B.Geoffrion 30.00 80.00
RJBHR J.Bucyk/H.Richard 25.00 60.00
RJBJB J.Bucyk/J.Beliveau 30.00 80.00
ARBG Bernie Geoffrion AU 50.00 125.00
ARHR Henri Richard AU 40.00 100.00
ARJBE Jean Beliveau AU 50.00 120.00
ARJBU John Bucyk AU 40.00 100.00
ARJBBG Bucyk AU/Geoffrion AU 150.00 300.00
ARJBHR Bucyk AU/Richard AU 100.00 250.00
ARJBJB Bucyk AU/Beliveau AU 100.00 250.00

2001-02 Topps Heritage Autographs

This 16-card set featured authentic autographs of current and former players on the classic 1957-58 design. Current player cards were inserted at 1:156, reprints were inserted at 1:91 and cards #ABG, AHR and AJBE were inserted at 1:182. Overall odds of autograph cards were 1:44.

AAA Al Arbour 10.00 25.00
ABG Bernie Geoffrion 20.00 50.00
AGH Glenn Hall 12.00 30.00
AHH Harry Howell 10.00 25.00
AHR Henri Richard 12.00 30.00
AIK Ilya Kovalchuk 12.00 30.00
AJBE Jean Beliveau 30.00 60.00
AJBU John Bucyk 15.00 40.00
AJH Johan Hedberg 10.00 25.00
AJW Justin Williams 10.00 25.00
AMG Marian Gaborik 10.00 25.00
AMS Miroslav Satan 10.00 25.00
ANU Norm Ullman 12.00 30.00
AOK Olaf Kolzig 10.00 25.00
APP Pierre Pilote 10.00 25.00
AVL Vincent Lecavalier 10.00 25.00

2001-02 Topps Heritage Captain's Cloth

This 6-card set featured game-worn jersey swatches from team captains from around the league. Cards from this set were randomly inserted at 1:76 hobby packs.

CCAO Adam Oates 6.00 15.00
CCDH Derian Hatcher 6.00 15.00
CCED Eric Desjardins 8.00 20.00
CCPK Paul Kariya 8.00 20.00
CCSK Saku Koivu 8.00 20.00
CCVL Vincent Lecavalier 6.00 15.00

2001-02 Topps Heritage Jerseys

This 10-card hobby only set was inserted at overall odds of 1:17 packs. Cards from this set featured swatches of game-worn jerseys from the featured players.

JBL Brian Leetch 6.00 15.00
JJI Jarome Iginla 8.00 20.00
JJL John LeClair 6.00 15.00
JJT Joe Thornton 8.00 20.00
JMB Martin Brodeur 12.50 30.00
JMS Martin Straka 6.00 15.00
JPF Peter Forsberg 10.00 25.00
JPM Patrick Marleau 6.00 15.00
JRL Robert Lang 6.00 15.00
JSF Sergei Fedorov 8.00 20.00

2001-02 Topps Heritage Salute

This 9-card set featured 6 reprints from the 1957-58 Topps set and 3 "cards that never were" (S7-S9). Cards from this set were inserted at 1:16.

COMPLETE SET (9) 1.00 30.00
S1 John Bucyk 2.50 6.00
S2 Al Arbour 2.00 5.00
S3 Glenn Hall 2.50 6.00
S4 Harry Howell 2.00 5.00
S5 Pierre Pilote 2.00 5.00
S6 Norm Ullman 2.00 5.00
S7 Jean Beliveau 2.50 6.00
S8 Henri Richard 2.00 5.00
S9 Bernie Geoffrion 2.50 6.00

2001 Topps Heritage Avalanche NHL All-Star Game

This six card set was produced by Topps as a wrapper redemption for the 2001 All-Star Fan Fest. Base cards feature full color player action photos set against a white background with the Avalanche logo in the upper left hand corner and a blue and red border along the card bottom. Overlaying the pictures is a facsimile of the featured player's autograph.

COMPLETE SET (6) 12.00 30.00
1 Ray Bourque 3.20 8.00
2 Patrick Roy 4.00 10.00
3 Peter Forsberg 3.20 8.00
4 Joe Sakic 2.40 6.00
5 Milan Hejduk 1.60 4.00
6 Chris Drury 1.60 4.00

2002-03 Topps Heritage

Released in December 2002, this 180-card set borrowed from the classic "woodgrain" design of 1966-67 Topps. Cards 131-180 were inserted at a rate of 1:4. Original 1966-67 cards were also repurchased and randomly inserted into packs at 1:1687.

COMPLETE SET (180) 60.00 150.00
COMP.SET w/o SP's (130) 20.00 50.00
1 Nicklas Lidstrom .30 .75
2 Jarome Iginla .30 .75
3 Jose Theodore .30 .75
4 Ron Francis .40 1.00
5 Joe Thornton .40 1.00
6 Jaromir Jagr .75 2.00
7 Mario Lemieux 1.00 2.50
8 Roberto Luongo .50 1.25
9 Dany Heatley .30 .75
10 Pavel Bure .40 1.00
11 Brett Hull .40 1.00
12 Keith Tkachuk .30 .75
13 Mats Sundin .30 .75
14 Pavel Datsyuk .40 1.00
15 Daniel Alfredsson .30 .75
16 Marian Gaborik .50 1.25
17 Peter Forsberg .40 1.00
18 Miroslav Satan .30 .75
19 Martin Brodeur .60 1.50
20 Jeremy Roenick .30 .75
21 Teemu Selanne .60 1.50
22 Todd Bertuzzi .30 .75
23 Erik Cole .25 .60
24 Jason Allison .25 .60
25 Sean Burke .20 .50
26 Eric Daze .20 .50
27 Patrick Roy .75 2.00
28 Simon Gagne .30 .75
29 Nikolai Khabibulin .30 .75
30 Alexei Yashin .25 .60
31 Denis Arkhipov .20 .50
32 Steve Yzerman .60 1.50
33 Mike Modano .50 1.25
34 Joe Sakic .50 1.25
35 Sergei Samsonov .25 .60
36 Saku Koivu .30 .75
37 Paul Kariya .40 1.00
38 Doug Weight .30 .75
39 Tie Domi .25 .60
40 Kevin Weekes .25 .60
41 Rostislav Klesla .20 .50
42 Zigmund Palffy .30 .75

43 Chris Osgood .30 .75
44 Owen Nolan .30 .75
45 Markus Naslund .25 .60
46 Martin Biron .25 .60
47 Ryan Smyth .25 .60
48 Mike Dunham .25 .60
49 Martin Havlat .25 .60
50 Patrik Elias .30 .75
51 Peter Bondra .30 .75
52 Craig Conroy .20 .50
53 Rob Blake .30 .75
54 Mike Richter .30 .75
55 Stephen Weiss .30 .75
56 Johan Hedberg .30 .75
57 Brendan Morrison .25 .60
58 Chris Pronger .25 .60
59 Patrick Lalime .25 .60
60 David Legwand .25 .60
61 Jocelyn Thibault .25 .60
62 Mike Comrie .30 .75
63 Sergei Fedorov .50 1.25
64 Michael Peca .25 .60
65 Tommy Salo .25 .60
66 Scott Stevens .30 .75
67 Mark Recchi .40 1.00
68 Vincent Damphousse .25 .60
69 Vincent Lecavalier .25 .60
70 Olaf Kolzig .30 .75
71 Shane Doan .25 .60
72 Marty Turco .30 .75
73 Marian Hossa .25 .60
74 Eric Lindros .50 1.25
75 Brent Johnson .25 .60
76 John LeClair .30 .75
77 Dan Cloutier .25 .60
78 Radim Vrbata .25 .60
79 Ilya Kovalchuk .40 1.00
80 Brendan Shanahan .40 1.00
81 Stu Barnes .20 .50
82 Alexander Mogilny .25 .60
83 Felix Potvin .50 1.25
84 Jeff O'Neill .20 .50
85 Glen Murray .25 .60
86 Marc Denis .25 .60
87 Brad Richards .30 .75
88 Roman Cechmanek .25 .60
89 Brian Leetch .30 .75
90 Roman Turek .30 .75
91 Andrew Brunette .20 .50
92 Krys Kolanos .20 .50
93 Alyn McCauley .20 .50
94 Jean-Sebastien Giguere .30 .75
95 Alexei Kovalev .30 .75
96 Peter Worrell .20 .50
97 Alexei Zhamnov .25 .60
98 Evgeni Nabokov .25 .60
99 Pavol Demitra .40 1.00
100 Chris Drury .30 .75
101 Jarome Iginla .30 .75
102 Patrick Roy .75 2.00
103 Dany Heatley .30 .75
104 Nicklas Lidstrom .30 .75
105 Jose Theodore .30 .75
106 Michael Peca .25 .60
107 Ron Francis .40 1.00
108 J.Iginla/M.Sundin .30 .75
109 J.Iginla/M.Sundin .30 .75
110 J.Allison/A.Oates .30 .75
111 P.Datsyuk/D.Heatley .40 1.00
112 C.Chelios/J.Roenick .30 .75
113 N.Lidstrom/S.Gonchar .30 .75
114 K.Sawyer/P.Worrell .20 .50
115 R.Turek/M.Brodeur .60 1.50
116 P.Roy/J.Theodore .75 2.00
117 P.Roy/R.Cechmanek .75 2.00
118 Joe Sakic .50 1.25
119 Jarome Iginla .30 .75
120 Markus Naslund .25 .60
121 Nicklas Lidstrom .30 .75
122 Chris Chelios .30 .75
123 Patrick Roy .75 2.00
124 Mats Sundin .30 .75
125 Bill Guerin .30 .75
126 Brendan Shanahan .40 1.00
127 Rob Blake .30 .75
128 Sergei Gonchar .25 .60
129 Jose Theodore .30 .75
130 Stanley Cup Champions UER .30 .75
131 Henrik Zetterberg RC 6.00 15.00
132 Martin Gerber RC 1.25 3.00
133 Alexander Frolov RC 1.50 4.00
134 Alexei Smirnov RC 1.00 2.50
135 Stanislav Chistov RC .75 2.00
136 Alexander Svitov RC .75 2.00
137 Adam Hall RC .75 2.00
138 Jay Bouwmeester RC 2.50 6.00
139 Ales Hemsky RC 3.00 8.00
140 Rick Nash RC 6.00 15.00
141 Chuck Kobasew RC 1.00 2.50
142 Shawn Thornton RC 1.00 2.50
143 Dennis Seidenberg RC 1.25 3.00
144 Ron Hainsey RC .75 2.00
145 Kurt Sauer RC .75 2.00
146 Lasse Pirjeta RC .75 2.00
147 Jason Spezza RC 5.00 12.00
148 Tom Koivisto RC .75 2.00
149 P-M Bouchard RC 1.25 3.00
150 Patrick Sharp RC 2.50 6.00
151 Scottie Upshall RC 1.00 2.50
152 Steve Eminger RC .75 2.00
153 Radovan Somik RC .75 2.00
154 Anton Volchenkov RC .75 2.00
155 Dmitri Bykov RC .75 2.00
156 Bobby Holik SP .40 1.00
157 Curtis Joseph SP .60 1.50
158 Jeff Friesen SP .40 1.00
159 Petr Sykora SP .50 1.25
160 Ed Belfour SP .60 1.50
161 Darius Kasparaitis SP .40 1.00
162 Scott Young SP .40 1.00
163 Bill Guerin SP .60 1.50
164 Adam Oates SP .60 1.50
165 Tony Amonte SP .50 1.25
166 Jochen Hecht SP .40 1.00
167 Randy McKay SP .40 1.00
168 Jamie Lundmark SP .50 1.25
169 Mariusz Czerkawski SP .40 1.00
170 Bryan Berard SP .40 1.00
171 Shawn McEachern SP .40 1.00
172 Brian Boucher SP .50 1.25
173 Jiri Dopita SP .40 1.00
174 Erik Rasmussen SP .40 1.00
175 Robert Lang SP .40 1.00
176 Steve Shields SP .50 1.25
177 Kelly Buchberger SP .50 1.25
178 Andrew Cassels SP .40 1.00
179 Oleg Tverdovsky SP .40 1.00
180 Ron Tugnutt SP .50 1.25
CL1 Checklist 1 .10 .30
CL2 Checklist 2 .10 .30
CL3 Checklist 3 .10 .30
CL4 Checklist 4 .10 .30
CL5 Checklist 5 .10 .30
CL6 Checklist 6 .10 .30

2002-03 Topps Heritage Chrome Parallel

This 100-card set paralleled the base set on chrome card stock. Each card was serial-numbered out of 667 on the cardbacks.
*CHROME/667: 2X TO 5X BASIC CARDS

2002-03 Topps Heritage Autographs

Inserted at 1:55, this 9-card set featured certified player autographs in blue ink.
AM Al MacInnis 6.00 15.00
BM Bryan McCabe 5.00 12.00
CD Chris Drury 5.00 12.00
EC Erik Cole 5.00 12.00
KK Krys Kolanos 5.00 12.00
MP Mike Peca 5.00 12.00
PE Patrik Elias 5.00 12.00
SW Stephen Weiss 5.00 12.00
TB Todd Bertuzzi 5.00 12.00

2002-03 Topps Heritage Autographs Black

Inserted at 1:155, this parallel set carried player autographs in black ink.
*BLACK: .75X TO 2X BASIC AUTO

2002-03 Topps Heritage Autographs Red

Inserted at 1:495, this parallel set carried player autographs in red ink.
*RED: 1.5X TO 4X BASIC AUTO

2002-03 Topps Heritage Calder Cloth

This 8-card set featured swatches of game jerseys from past Calder trophy winners. Cards in group "A" were inserted at 1:1160 and cards in group "B" were inserted at 1:217.
ALL CARD CARRY CC PREFIX
BL Brian Leetch B 6.00 15.00
CD Chris Drury A 12.50 30.00
DA Daniel Alfredsson B 6.00 15.00
DH Dany Heatley B 15.00 40.00
MB Martin Brodeur A 12.00 30.00
PF Peter Forsberg A 15.00 40.00
SG Scott Gomez B 6.00 15.00
SS Sergei Samsonov A 8.00 20.00

2002-03 Topps Heritage Calder Cloth Patches

*PATCH: 1.25X TO 3X BASIC JERSEY
PATCH ODDS 1:2774

2002-03 Topps Heritage Crease Piece

Inserted at 1:39, this 9-card set carried swatches of goalie game jerseys.
ALL CARDS CARRY CP PREFIX
BB Brian Boucher 4.00 10.00
BD Byron Dafoe 4.00 10.00
DB Dan Blackburn 4.00 10.00
DC Dan Cloutier 4.00 10.00
FP Felix Potvin 5.00 12.00
ML Manny Legace 4.00 10.00
MT Marty Turco 5.00 12.00
PL Patrick Lalime 4.00 10.00
SB Sean Burke 4.00 10.00

2002-03 Topps Heritage Crease Piece Patches

*PATCH: 1X TO 2.5X BASE HI
STATED ODDS 1:775

2002-03 Topps Heritage Great Skates

This 10-card memorabilia set was inserted at 1:50.
ALL CARDS CARRY GS PREFIX
AK Alexei Kovalev 5.00 12.00
AT Alex Tanguay 5.00 12.00
BL Brian Leetch 5.00 12.00
BM Brendan Morrison 5.00 12.00
MH Milan Hejduk 6.00 15.00
MR Mark Recchi 5.00 12.00
MS Marco Sturm 5.00 12.00
SG Simon Gagne 6.00 15.00
TA Tony Amonte 5.00 12.00
MHO Marian Hossa 6.00 15.00

2002-03 Topps Heritage Great Skates Patches

*PATCH: 1.25X TO 3X BASE HI
STATED ODDS 1:1550

2002-03 Topps Heritage Reprint Autographs

Inserted at 1:139, this 5-card set partially paralleled the base reprint set but included certified autographs on the cardfronts. Cards carried a TMLA prefix on the cardbacks.
ES Eddie Shack 15.00 40.00
JB Johnny Bower 15.00 40.00
JP Jim Pappin 8.00 20.00
RK Red Kelly 10.00 25.00
RP Bob Pulford 15.00 40.00

2002-03 Topps Heritage Reprint Relics

Inserted at 1:127, this 7-card set paralleled the base reprint set but also featured a piece of stadium seat from Maple Leaf Gardens. Cards carried a TMLS prefix on the cardbacks.
ES Eddie Shack 10.00 25.00
JB Johnny Bower 10.00 25.00
JP Jim Pappin 8.00 20.00
RK Red Kelly 8.00 20.00
RP Robert Pulford 8.00 20.00
TH Tim Horton 15.00 40.00
TS Terry Sawchuk 20.00 50.00

2002-03 Topps Heritage Reprints

Inserted at 1:8, this 7-card set featured reprinted versions of original 1966-67 cards of members of the Toronto Maple Leafs. Cards carried a TML prefix on the cardbacks.
ES Eddie Shack 1.00 2.50
JB Johnny Bower 1.25 3.00
JP Jim Pappin 1.00 2.50
RK Red Kelly 1.25 3.00
RP Robert Pulford 1.00 2.50
TH Tim Horton 1.25 3.00
TS Terry Sawchuk 1.50 4.00

2002-03 Topps Heritage USA Test Parallel

In keeping with the tradition of the 1966-67 Topps set, this 10-card parallel set featured a sampling of players with much lighter woodgrain borders. This set was inserted at 1:20 packs.
2 Jarome Iginla 1.50 4.00
3 Jose Theodore 1.50 4.00
6 Jaromir Jagr 2.00 5.00
7 Mario Lemieux 8.00 20.00
10 Pavel Bure 1.25 3.00
13 Mats Sundin 1.25 3.00
17 Peter Forsberg 3.00 8.00
27 Patrick Roy 6.00 15.00
32 Steve Yzerman 6.00 15.00
79 Ilya Kovalchuk 1.50 4.00

1956 Topps Hocus Focus

The 1956 Topps Hocus Focus set is very similar in size and design to the 1948 Topps Magic Photos set. It contains at least 96 small (approximately 7/8" by 1 5/8") individual cards featuring a variety of sports and non-sport subjects. They were printed with both a series card number (by subject matter) on the back as well as a card number reflecting the entire set. The fronts were developed, much like a photograph, from a blank appearance by using moisture and sunlight. Due to varying degrees of photographic sensitivity, the clarity of these cards ranges from fully developed to poorly developed. A premium album holding 126-cards was also issued leading to the theory that there are actually 126 different cards. A few High Series (#97-126) cards have been discovered and cataloged below although a full 126-card checklist is yet unknown. The cards do reference the set name "Hocus Focus" on the backs unlike the 1948 Magic Photos. Finally, a slightly smaller version (roughly 7/8" by 1 7/16") of some of the cards has also been found, but a full checklist is not known.
61 Hockey 15.00 30.00

1948 Topps Magic Photos

The 1948 Topps Magic Photos set contains 252 small (approximately 7/8" by 1 7/16") individual cards featuring sport and non-sport subjects. They were issued in 19 lettered series with cards numbered within each series. The fronts were developed, much like a photograph, from a "blank" appearance by using moisture and sunlight. Due to varying degrees of photographic sensitivity, the clarity of these cards ranges from fully developed to poorly developed. This set contains Topps' first baseball cards. A premium album holding 126-cards was also issued. The set is sometimes confused with Topps' 1956 Hocus-Focus set, although the cards in this set are slightly smaller than those in the Hocus-Focus set. The checklist below is presented by series. Poorly developed cards are considered in lesser condition and hence have lesser value. The catalog designation for this set is R714-27. Each type of card subject has a letter prefix as follows: Boxing Champions (A), All-American Basketball (B), All-American Football (C), Wrestling Champions (D), Track and Field Champions (E), Stars of Stage and Screen (F), American Dogs (G), General Sports (H), Movie Stars (J), Baseball Hall of Fame (K), Aviation Pioneers (L), Famous Landmarks (M), American Inventors (N), American Military Leaders (O), American Explorers (P), Basketball Thrills (Q), Football Thrills (R), Figures of the Wild West (S), and General Sports (T).
COMPLETE SET (252) 3000.00 5000.00
T3 Ice Hockey 15.00 30.00

1983-84 Topps M&M's Olympic Heroes

This 44-card boxed standard-sized set is an abridgment of the 99-card 1983 Topps History's Greatest Olympians set. Though widely known to have been produced by Topps, this company name is found nowhere on the cards. On a white card face, the fronts display either color or black-and-white photos framed by a white inner border and a red outer border. The top of the red outer border carries the olympiad number, year, and city, while the player's name is printed across the bottom of the front. Inside a light blue border, the back carry a headline and news brief in brown ink. The M&M's logo adorns both sides of the cards. The cards are numbered on the back; note that numbering differs completely from that of the larger set.
COMPLETE SET (44) 8.00 20.00
13 Mike Eruzione .30 .75

1999 Topps Pearson Award

This card was available only by mail for those who voted online for Jaromir Jagr for the 1999 Lester B.Pearson award.
1 Jaromir Jagr 6.00 15.00

1996-97 Topps Picks

This limited production 90-card set was distributed in seven-card packs (five-cards in Canadian packs) with a suggested retail price of $.99. Topps and Fleer card companies joined together to each select a team of 90 hockey players. The cards in Topps set all have odd numbers because Topps had the first pick of players. Each card features color player photos with player career statistics, biographical information, and a "Topps Prediction" section which gave the upcoming season's goals, assists, wins and shutouts totals for each player as predicted by the Topps Sports Department. Each pack contained an official NHL/NHLPA Draft Game registration form which allowed the collectors the chance to draft their own players and create teams in order to win prizes in a fantasy league.
COMPLETE SET (90) 5.00 15.00
1 Jaromir Jagr .20 .50
3 Mario Lemieux .60 1.50
5 Peter Forsberg .30 .75
7 Teemu Selanne .10 .30
9 Alexander Mogilny .05 .15
11 Patrick Roy .60 1.50
13 Jim Carey .10 .30
15 Pavel Bure .10 .30
17 Sergei Fedorov .15 .40
19 Chris Chelios .10 .30
21 Sandis Ozolinsh .01 .05
23 Doug Weight .05 .15
25 Mark Messier .10 .30
27 Martin Brodeur .30 .75
29 Brett Hull .15 .40
31 Steve Yzerman .60 1.50
33 Kevin Hatcher .01 .05
35 Roman Hamrlik .05 .15
37 Petr Nedved .05 .15
39 Valeri Kamensky .05 .15
41 Gary Suter .01 .05
43 Mats Sundin .10 .30
45 Trevor Linden .05 .15
47 Jeremy Roenick .15 .40
49 Al MacInnis .05 .15
51 Mike Modano .20 .50
53 Mathieu Schneider .01 .05
55 Michal Pivonka .01 .05
57 Owen Nolan .05 .15
59 Martin Rucinsky .01 .05
61 Joe Nieuwendyk .05 .15
63 Mark Recchi .05 .15
65 Geoff Sanderson .05 .15
67 Vyacheslav Kozlov .01 .05
69 Pat Verbeek .01 .05
71 Brian Bradley .01 .05
73 Steve Duchesne .01 .05
75 Steve Thomas .01 .05
77 Eric Daze .05 .15
79 Alexei Kovalev .01 .05
81 Kevin Stevens .01 .05
83 Curtis Joseph .10 .30
85 Bill Ranford .05 .15
87 Luc Robitaille .05 .15
89 Claude Lemieux .01 .05
91 Sergei Gonchar .01 .05
93 Eric Desjardins .05 .15
95 Garry Galley .01 .05
97 Oleg Tverdovsky .05 .15
99 Rob Niedermayer .05 .15
101 Scott Mellanby .05 .15
103 Adam Deadmarsh .01 .05
105 Cliff Ronning .01 .05
107 Russ Courtnall .01 .05
109 Keith Primeau .01 .05
111 Rick Tocchet .05 .15
113 Scott Young .01 .05
115 Scott Stevens .05 .15
117 Al Iafrate .01 .05
119 Ray Ferraro .01 .05
121 Todd Bertuzzi .10 .30
123 Alexander Selivanov .01 .05
125 Steve Chiasson .01 .05
127 Dave Andreychuk .05 .15
129 Ray Sheppard .05 .15
131 Bernie Nicholls .01 .05
133 Tony Amonte .05 .15
135 Nelson Emerson .01 .05
137 Cam Neely .10 .30
139 Shayne Corson .01 .05
141 Bill Guerin .01 .05
143 Joe Murphy .01 .05
145 Cory Stillman .01 .05
147 Radek Bonk .01 .05
149 Geoff Courtnall .01 .05
151 Chad Kilger .01 .05
153 Sylvain Cote .01 .05
155 Glen Wesley .01 .05
157 Jeff Norton .01 .05
159 Rob Blake .05 .15
161 Calle Johansson .01 .05
163 Uwe Krupp .01 .05
165 James Patrick .01 .05
167 Dmitri Mironov .01 .05
169 Vladimir Konstantinov .05 .15
171 Mattias Norstrom .01 .05
173 David Wilkie .01 .05
175 Bryan McCabe .01 .05
177 Barry Richter .01 .05
179 Ed Belfour .10 .30
NNO CHECKLIST .02 .10

1996-97 Topps Picks 500 Club

Randomly inserted at the rate of 1:36 packs, this eight-card insert set featured the eight active players who had scored their 500th career goal by the end of the 1995-96 season. The set featured color player photos and player information printed on rainbow diffraction foilboard.
COMPLETE SET (8) 12.00 30.00
FC1 Wayne Gretzky 6.00 15.00
FC2 Mike Gartner .75 2.00
FC3 Jari Kurri .75 2.00
FC4 Dino Ciccarelli .75 2.00
FC5 Mario Lemieux 4.00 10.00
FC6 Mark Messier 1.25 3.00
FC7 Steve Yzerman 3.00 8.00
FC8 Dale Hawerchuk .75 2.00

1996-97 Topps Picks Fantasy Team

Randomly inserted at the rate of 1:24 packs, this 22 card set featured a dream team made up of the elite hockey stars which any NHL general manager would want playing for him. Printed with Power Matrix technology, the fronts displayed color player photos while the backs carried player information.
COMPLETE SET (22) 20.00 50.00
FT1 Patrick Roy 3.00 8.00
FT2 Chris Osgood .40 1.00
FT3 Martin Brodeur 2.00 5.00
FT4 Ray Bourque 1.25 3.00
FT5 Brian Leetch .75 2.00
FT6 Chris Chelios .75 2.00
FT7 Paul Coffey .75 2.00
FT8 Ed Jovanovski .40 1.00
FT9 Roman Hamrlik .40 1.00
FT10 Wayne Gretzky 4.00 10.00
FT11 Paul Kariya 1.25 3.00
FT12 Brett Hull 1.25 3.00
FT13 Pavel Bure 1.25 3.00
FT14 Jaromir Jagr 1.50 4.00
FT15 Mario Lemieux 3.00 8.00
FT16 Peter Forsberg 1.50 4.00
FT17 Sergei Fedorov 1.25 3.00
FT18 Jeremy Roenick 1.25 3.00
FT19 Alexander Mogilny .75 2.00
FT20 Joe Sakic 2.00 5.00
FT21 Teemu Selanne 1.25 3.00
FT22 Eric Lindros 1.25 3.00

1996-97 Topps Picks Ice D

Randomly inserted at the rate of 1:24 packs, this 15-card set featured five of the best defensemen and ten top goalies. Color player photos were printed on rainbow prismatic foil with player information on the backs.
COMPLETE SET (15) 20.00 40.00
ID1 Brian Leetch 1.25 3.00
ID2 Ray Bourque 2.00 5.00
ID3 Chris Chelios 1.25 3.00
ID4 Scott Stevens 1.00 2.50
ID5 Ed Jovanovski 1.00 2.50
ID6 Martin Brodeur 3.00 8.00
ID7 Patrick Roy 4.00 10.00
ID8 Chris Osgood 1.00 2.50
ID9 Jim Carey 1.25 3.00
ID10 Dominik Hasek 2.50 6.00
ID11 Ron Hextall 1.00 2.50
ID12 John Vanbiesbrouck 1.00 2.50
ID13 Mike Richter 1.25 3.00
ID14 Felix Potvin 1.25 3.00
ID15 Grant Fuhr 1.00 2.50

1996-97 Topps Picks OPC Inserts

Randomly inserted in Canadian packs only at the rate of 1:4, this 90-card set was parallel to the regular 1996-97 Topps NHL Picks set. These inserts are differentiated in that OPC cards have foil backgrounds and feature the OPC logo on the front. Values for the cards can be determined by using the multipliers below on the base cards.
*OPC: 4X TO 10X BASIC CARDS

1996-97 Topps Picks Rookie Stars

Inserted at the rate of one per pack, this 18-card set showcased hockey's best and brightest young stars. The fronts displayed color player photos while the back carried player information. OPC parallels were also created and inserted in random Canadian packs.
COMPLETE SET (18) 5.00 10.00
*OPC: 4X TO 10X BASIC INSERTS
RS1 Daniel Alfredsson .20 .50
RS2 Jere Lehtinen .60 1.50
RS3 Vitali Yachmenev .20 .50
RS4 Eric Daze .20 .50
RS5 Saku Koivu .60 1.50
RS6 Petr Sykora .20 .50
RS7 Marcus Ragnarsson .20 .50
RS8 Valeri Bure .20 .50
RS9 Cory Stillman .20 .50
RS10 Todd Bertuzzi .60 1.50
RS11 Ed Jovanovski .40 1.00
RS12 Miroslav Satan .40 1.00
RS13 Kyle McLaren .20 .50
RS14 Byron Dafoe .40 1.00
RS15 Eric Fichaud .20 .50
RS16 Corey Hirsch .20 .50
RS17 Jeff O'Neill .20 .50
RS18 Niklas Sundstrom .20 .50

1996-97 Topps Picks Top Shelf

Randomly inserted at the rate of 1:12 packs, this 15-card set featured red foil-stamped cards of the league's top scorers and award winners of the 1995-96 season. The fronts displayed color player photos while the backs carried player information.
COMPLETE SET (15) 15.00 40.00
TS1 John LeClair .60 1.50
TS2 Wayne Gretzky 4.00 10.00
TS3 Eric Lindros 1.00 2.50
TS4 Paul Kariya 1.00 2.50
TS5 Mark Messier 1.00 2.50
TS6 Jaromir Jagr 1.50 4.00
TS7 Peter Forsberg 1.50 4.00
TS8 Teemu Selanne 1.00 2.50
TS9 Alexander Mogilny .60 1.50
TS10 Brett Hull 1.25 3.00
TS11 Sergei Fedorov 1.25 3.00
TS12 Joe Sakic 2.00 5.00
TS13 Mats Sundin 1.00 2.50
TS14 Theo Fleury .60 1.50
TS15 Steve Yzerman 2.50 6.00

2009-10 Topps Puck Attax

COMPLETE SET (192) 25.00 60.00
1 Ryan Getzlaf .50 1.25
2 Corey Perry .30 .75
3 Teemu Selanne .60 1.50
4 Scott Niedermayer .30 .75
5 Ryan Whitney .20 .50
6 Jonas Hiller .25 .60
7 Bryan Little .30 .75
8 Ilya Kovalchuk .30 .75
9 Chris Thorburn .20 .50
10 Tobias Enstrom .30 .75
11 Ron Hainsey .20 .50
12 Kari Lehtonen .25 .60
13 Marc Savard .20 .50
14 David Krejci .30 .75
15 Milan Lucic .25 .60
16 Chuck Kobasew .20 .50
17 Zdeno Chara .30 .75
18 Dennis Wideman .20 .50
19 Tim Thomas .30 .75
20 Derek Roy .25 .60
21 Paul Gaustad .25 .60
22 Thomas Vanek .30 .75
23 Craig Rivet .20 .50
24 Toni Lydman .20 .50
25 Ryan Miller .30 .75
26 Olli Jokinen .25 .60
27 Jarome Iginla .30 .75
28 Curtis Glencross .20 .50
29 Dion Phaneuf .40 1.00
30 Jay Bouwmeester .30 .75
31 Miikka Kiprusoff .25 .60
32 Eric Staal .40 1.00
33 Chad LaRose .20 .50
34 Ray Whitney .25 .60
35 Joe Corvo .20 .50
36 Joni Pitkanen .25 .60
37 Cam Ward .30 .75
38 Jonathan Toews .60 1.50
39 Patrick Kane .60 1.50
40 Patrick Sharp .30 .75
41 Brian Campbell .25 .60
42 Duncan Keith .30 .75
43 Cristobal Huet .30 .75
44 Milan Hejduk .25 .60
45 Paul Stastny .30 .75
46 Cody McLeod .20 .50
47 John-Michael Liles .20 .50
48 Ruslan Salei .20 .50
49 Peter Budaj .25 .60
50 Rick Nash .25 .60
51 Kristian Huselius .20 .50
52 R.J. Umberger .25 .60
53 Fedor Tyutin .20 .50
54 Mike Commodore .20 .50
55 Steve Mason .25 .60
56 Mike Ribeiro .25 .60
57 Brad Richards .30 .75
58 Mike Modano .50 1.25
59 Matt Niskanen .25 .60
60 Stephane Robidas .20 .50
61 Marty Turco .30 .75
62 Dan Cleary .30 .75
63 Johan Franzen .30 .75
64 Pavel Datsyuk .40 1.00
65 Henrik Zetterberg .40 1.00
66 Brian Rafalski .20 .50
67 Nicklas Lidstrom .30 .75
68 Niklas Kronwall .25 .60
69 Chris Osgood .30 .75
70 Sam Gagner .25 .60
71 Ethan Moreau .20 .50
72 Ales Hemsky .25 .60
73 Sheldon Souray .20 .50
74 Tom Gilbert .20 .50
75 Denis Grebeshkov .20 .50
76 Nikolai Khabibulin .30 .75
77 Stephen Weiss .20 .50
78 David Booth .20 .50
79 Nathan Horton .30 .75
80 Keith Ballard .20 .50
81 Bryan McCabe .25 .60
82 Tomas Vokoun .25 .60
83 Ryan Smyth .25 .60
84 Anze Kopitar .50 1.25
85 Wayne Simmonds .40 1.00
86 Drew Doughty .40 1.00
87 Matt Greene .20 .50
88 Jonathan Quick .60 1.50
89 Martin Havlat .25 .60
90 Mikko Koivu .30 .75
91 Cal Clutterbuck .20 .50
92 Marek Zidlicky .20 .50
93 Brent Burns .40 1.00
94 Niklas Backstrom .30 .75
95 Mike Cammalleri .25 .60
96 Maxim Lapierre .20 .50
97 Andrei Kostitsyn .25 .60
98 Brian Gionta .25 .60
99 Scott Gomez .25 .60
100 Jaroslav Spacek .20 .50
101 Andrei Markov .30 .75
102 Carey Price 1.25 3.00
103 David Legwand .25 .60
104 Joel Ward .20 .50
105 Jason Arnott .25 .60
106 Shea Weber .25 .60
107 Ryan Suter .30 .75
108 Pekka Rinne .40 1.00
109 Zach Parise .30 .75
110 Patrik Elias .30 .75
111 Jamie Langenbrunner .20 .50
112 Paul Martin .20 .50
113 John Oduya .25 .60
114 Martin Brodeur .60 1.50
115 Doug Weight .30 .75
116 Frans Nielsen .20 .50
117 Kyle Okposo .30 .75
118 Mark Streit .20 .50
119 Bruno Gervais .20 .50
120 Dwayne Roloson .25 .60
121 Rick DiPietro .25 .60
122 Marian Gaborik .40 1.00
123 Brandon Dubinsky .25 .60
124 Chris Drury .25 .60
125 Sean Avery .25 .60
126 Dan Girardi .20 .50
127 Marc Staal .30 .75
128 Henrik Lundqvist .50 1.25
129 Jason Spezza .30 .75
130 Chris Kelly .25 .60
131 Daniel Alfredsson .30 .75
132 Filip Kuba .20 .50
133 Chris Campoli .20 .50
134 Pascal Leclaire .30 .75
135 Jeff Carter .30 .75
136 Mike Richards .30 .75
137 Arron Asham .25 .60
138 Chris Pronger .25 .60
139 Kimmo Timonen .25 .60
140 Braydon Coburn .20 .50
141 Ray Emery .25 .60
142 Matthew Lombardi .20 .50
143 Peter Mueller .25 .60
144 Shane Doan .25 .60
145 Zbynek Michalek .20 .50
146 Ed Jovanovski .20 .50
147 Ilya Bryzgalov .25 .60
148 Jason LaBarbera .25 .60
149 Maxime Talbot .30 .75
150 Evgeni Malkin 1.00 2.50
151 Sidney Crosby 1.25 3.00
152 Jordan Staal .30 .75
153 Kris Letang .30 .75
154 Sergei Gonchar .20 .50
155 Marc-Andre Fleury .50 1.25
156 Joe Thornton .30 .75
157 Ryane Clowe .25 .60
158 Devin Setoguchi .25 .60
159 Dan Boyle .25 .60
160 Rob Blake .30 .75
161 Evgeni Nabokov .25 .60
162 Brad Boyes .20 .50
163 Keith Tkachuk .30 .75
164 Jay McClement .20 .50
165 Barret Jackman .20 .50
166 Carlo Colaiacovo .20 .50
167 Chris Mason .25 .60
168 Vincent Lecavalier .25 .60
169 Steven Stamkos .60 1.50
170 Martin St. Louis .30 .75
171 Mattias Ohlund .20 .50
172 Andrej Meszaros .20 .50
173 Mike Smith .30 .75
174 Matt Stajan .25 .60
175 Jason Blake .20 .50
176 Alexei Ponikarovsky .20 .50
177 Luke Schenn .25 .60
178 Mike Komisarek .25 .60
179 Tomas Kaberle .20 .50
180 Vesa Toskala .30 .75
181 Henrik Sedin .30 .75
182 Alexandre Burrows .30 .75
183 Daniel Sedin .30 .75
184 Sami Salo .30 .75
185 Kevin Bieksa .25 .60
186 Roberto Luongo .40 1.00
187 Nicklas Backstrom .50 1.25
188 Alexamder Ovechkin 1.25 3.00
189 David Steckel .20 .50
190 Mike Green .30 .75
191 Shaone Morrisonn .20 .50
192 Simeon Varlamov .30 .75

2009-10 Topps Puck Attax Black Foil

*SINGLES: .8X TO 2X BASIC CARDS
STATED ODDS 1 PER PACK

2009-10 Topps Puck Attax Gold Foil

*SINGLES: 2X TO 5X BASIC CARDS

2009-10 Topps Puck Attax Platinum Blister

COMPLETE SET (6) 6.00 15.00
STATED ODDS 1 PER BLISTER
1 Mike Modano 1.50 4.00
2 Jarome Iginla 1.00 2.50
3 Ilya Kovalchuk 1.00 2.50
4 Rick Nash .75 2.00
5 Vincent Lecavalier .75 2.00
6 Henrik Sedin 1.00 2.50

2009-10 Topps Puck Attax Platinum Starter

COMPLETE SET (6) 10.00 25.00
STATED ODDS 1 PER STARTER PACK
1 Sidney Crosby 4.00 10.00
2 Alexamder Ovechkin 4.00 10.00
3 Eric Staal 1.25 3.00
4 Nicklas Lidstrom 1.00 2.50
5 Andrei Markov 1.00 2.50
6 Henrik Lundqvist 1.50 4.00

1999-00 Topps Premier Plus

Topps Premier Plus was released as a 140-card set comprised of 81 veteran cards and 59 prospect cards. Printed on a canvas card-stock, this set features crystal clear player action shots with a blue name box across the bottom for veterans and a red name box across the bottom for the prospects. Packaged at 24-packs per box and eight cards per pack, packs carried a suggested retail price of $2.50.
COMPLETE SET (140) 30.00 75.00
1 Curtis Joseph .20 .50
2 Peter Bondra .15 .40
3 Theo Fleury .05 .15
4 Steve Yzerman 1.00 2.50
5 Peter Forsberg .50 1.25
6 Ray Bourque .30 .75
7 Dominik Hasek .40 1.00
8 Chris Drury .15 .40
9 Brett Hull .25 .60
10 Chris Osgood .15 .40
11 Luc Robitaille .15 .40
12 Bobby Holik .15 .40
13 John LeClair .20 .50
14 Jeremy Roenick .25 .60
15 Owen Nolan .15 .40
16 Wade Redden .05 .15
17 Teemu Selanne .20 .50
18 Doug Weight .15 .40
19 Vincent Lecavalier .20 .50
20 Pierre Turgeon .15 .40
21 Ron Francis .15 .40
22 Sergei Samsonov .15 .40
23 Patrick Roy 1.00 2.50
24 Mark Messier .20 .50
25 Al MacInnis .15 .40
26 Mark Parrish .05 .15
27 Ron Tugnutt .15 .40
28 Joe Nieuwendyk .15 .40
29 Valeri Bure .05 .15
30 Jason Allison .05 .15
31 Tony Amonte .15 .40
32 Scott Niedermayer .05 .15
33 Kenny Jonsson .05 .15
34 Jaromir Jagr .30 .75
35 Sergei Berezin .15 .40
36 Olaf Kolzig .15 .40
37 Byron Dafoe .15 .40
38 Adam Deadmarsh .05 .15
39 Alexei Zhitnik .05 .15
40 Paul Kariya .20 .50
41 Chris Pronger .15 .40
42 Markus Naslund .20 .50
43 Damian Rhodes .15 .40
44 Marian Hossa .20 .50
45 Adam Graves .05 .15
46 Scott Stevens .15 .40
47 Nicklas Lidstrom .20 .50
48 Ed Belfour .20 .50
49 Miroslav Satan .15 .40
50 Rob Blake .15 .40
51 Petr Nedved .15 .40
52 Mark Recchi .15 .40
53 Jeff Friesen .05 .15
54 Mats Sundin .20 .50
55 Arturs Irbe .15 .40
56 Derian Hatcher .05 .15
57 Mike Modano .30 .75
58 Brendan Shanahan .20 .50
59 Zigmund Palffy .15 .40
60 Saku Koivu .20 .50
61 Brian Leetch .20 .50
62 Rod Brind'Amour .15 .40
63 Keith Tkachuk .20 .50
64 Pavol Demitra .15 .40
65 Magnus Arvedson .05 .15
66 Martin Brodeur .50 1.25
67 Chris Chelios .20 .50
68 Joe Sakic .40 1.00
69 Anson Carter .15 .40
70 Sergei Fedorov .30 .75
71 Pavel Bure .20 .50
72 Petr Sykora .05 .15
73 Daniel Alfredsson .15 .40
74 Guy Hebert .15 .40
75 Jere Lehtinen .15 .40
76 Mike Richter .20 .50
77 Michael Peca .15 .40
78 Sandis Ozolinsh .05 .15
79 Joe Thornton .30 .75
80 Eric Lindros .20 .50
81 Milan Hejduk .20 .50
82 Ladislav Nagy RC 1.00 2.50
83 Francis Bouillon RC .15 .40
84 Mark Eaton RC .30 .75
85 Robert Valicevic RC .15. .40
86 Sami Helenius RC .15 .40
87 Travis Brigley RC .15 .40
88 Glen Metropolit RC .60 1.50
89 Alan Letang RC .15 .40
90 Brad Chartrand RC .15 .40
91 Marc Rodgers RC .15 .40
92 Hans Jonsson RC .15 .40
93 Kim Johnsson RC .15 .40
94 Richard Lintner RC .15 .40
95 Andrew Ference .15 .40
96 Jeff Halpern RC .75 2.00
97 Brad Lukowich RC .15 .40
98 Tyson Nash RC .20 .50
99 Oleg Saprykin RC .75 2.00
100 John Grahame RC .75 2.00
101 Patrik Stefan RC .75 2.00
102 Jason Blake RC .15 .40
103 Kyle Calder RC .20 .50
104 John Madden RC .75 2.00
105 Dan Hinote RC .60 1.25
106 Pavel Patera RC .15 .40
107 Yuri Butsayev RC .15 .40
108 Paul Comrie RC .15 .40
109 Ivan Novoseltsev RC .60 1.50
110 Niclas Havelid RC .20 .50
111 Brian Rafalski RC .60 1.50
112 Jorgen Jonsson RC .15 .40
113 Mike Fisher RC .50 1.25
114 Mika Alatalo RC .15 .40
115 Michal Rozsival RC .15 .40
116 Jochen Hecht RC 1.00 2.50
117 Nikolai Antropov RC 1.00 2.50
118 Steve Kariya RC .60 1.50
119 Brian Campbell RC .15 .40
120 Maxim Afinogenov .05 .15
121 Roberto Luongo .25 .60
122 Petr Buzek .05 .15
123 Per Svartvadet RC .15 .40
124 Dave Tanabe .05 .15
125 Brad Stuart .15 .40
126 Michael York .05 .15
127 Jiri Fischer .05 .15
128 Peter Schaefer .15 .40
129 Martin Biron .15 .40
130 Rico Fata .05 .15

J-P Dumont .15 .40
2 Martin Skoula RC .60 1.50
3 Alex Tanguay .15 .40
4 Mike Ribeiro .15 .40
5 David Legwand .15 .40
6 Scott Gomez .05 .15
7 Tim Connolly .05 .15
8 Jan Hlavac .05 .15
9 Simon Gagne .20 .50
0 Brian Boucher .20 .50
W1 Chris Drury AU 10.00 20.00
0 Chris Drury JUMBO CHECKLIST
0 Curtis Joseph JUMBO CHECKLIST

999-00 Topps Premier Plus Foil Parallel

ndomly inserted in packs at 1:16, this die-cut foil allel is labeled on the back "Limited Edition of 250." rds are randomly inserted into packs.
ETS: 12X TO 30X BASIC CARDS
OKIES: 8X TO 20X BASIC CARDS

1999-00 Topps Premier Plus Calling All Calders

ndomly inserted in packs at 1:16, this 10-card set ures Calder Trophy winners spanning from the late 30's to 1999. This foil insert places player action its against a background that shows The Calder phy.
MPLETE SET (10) 12.00 25.00
C1 Chris Drury .75 2.00
C2 Sergei Samsonov 1.00 2.50
C3 Daniel Alfredsson .75 2.00
C4 Peter Forsberg 2.50 6.00
C5 Martin Brodeur 2.50 6.00
C6 Teemu Selanne .75 2.00
C7 Pavel Bure 1.25 3.00
C8 Ed Belfour 1.00 2.50
C9 Joe Nieuwendyk .75 2.00
C10 Brian Leetch 1.00 2.50

1999-00 Topps Premier Plus Club Signings

ndomly inserted in packs, this 9-card set featured hentic player autographs. Single autographs were erted at 1:476 and dual autos were inserted at 905.
1 Ray Bourque 30.00 60.00
2 Cam Neely 20.00 40.00
3 Curtis Joseph 12.50 30.00
4 Johnny Bower 12.50 30.00
5 Jaromir Jagr 25.00 60.00
6 Mario Lemieux 40.00 100.00
C1 R.Bourque/C.Neely 40.00 100.00
C2 C.Joseph/J.Bower 30.00 80.00
C3 J.Jagr/M.Lemieux 100.00 250.00

1999-00 Topps Premier Plus Code Red

MPLETE SET (8) 20.00 40.00
ATED ODDS 1:40
1 Keith Tkachuk 1.50 4.00
2 Teemu Selanne 1.50 4.00
3 Zigmund Palffy 1.50 4.00
4 Steve Yzerman 8.00 20.00
5 Theo Fleury 1.50 4.00
6 Jaromir Jagr 2.50 6.00
7 Peter Bondra 1.25 3.00
8 Pavel Bure 2.00 5.00

1999-00 Topps Premier Plus Feature Presentations

MPLETE SET (8) 8.00 15.00
ATED ODDS 1:10
1 Joe Sakic 1.25 3.00
2 Mark Messier .75 2.00
3 Steve Yzerman 3.00 8.00
4 Mike Modano 1.00 2.50
5 Paul Kariya .75 2.00
6 Pavel Bure .75 2.00
7 Jaromir Jagr 1.00 2.50
8 Ray Bourque 1.00 2.50

1999-00 Topps Premier Plus Game Pieces

ndomly inserted in packs, this 5-card set consists of ard front displaying a piece of game-used stick serted at 1:960) or game-used sweater (inserted at 90) from the league's top veterans and prospects.
CD Chris Drury S 40.00 100.00
DL David Legwand S 7.50 15.00
DW Doug Weight J 7.50 15.00
MR Mike Richter S 15.00 40.00
NL Nicklas Lidstrom J 7.50 15.00
SG Scott Gomez J 7.50 15.00

1999-00 Topps Premier Plus Imperial Guard

MPLETE SET(8) 20.00 40.00
ATED ODDS 1:40
Ed Belfour 1.50 4.00
Patrick Roy 8.00 20.00
Martin Brodeur 4.00 10.00
Dominik Hasek 3.00 8.00
Curtis Joseph 1.50 4.00
John Vanbiesbrouck 1.25 3.00
Mike Richter 1.50 4.00
Byron Dafoe 1.25 3.00

1999-00 Topps Premier Plus Premier Rookies

ndomly inserted in packs at 1:12, this 10-card set ures some of the NHL's eligible Calder Trophy ners. A parallel variation numbered to just 250 was o created and inserted at 1:229.
MPLETE SET (10) 10.00 20.00
IL/250: 1.5X TO 4X BASIC INSERTS
1 Alex Tanguay 1.50 4.00
2 Brad Stuart 1.25 3.00
3 Peter Schaefer .75 2.00
4 Scott Gomez .75 2.00
5 Patrik Stefan .75 2.00
6 Jochen Hecht 1.25 3.00
7 David Legwand 1.50 4.00
8 Steve Kariya 1.50 4.00
9 J-P Dumont 1.00 2.50
10 Simon Gagne 1.50 4.00

1999-00 Topps Premier Plus Premier Team

eded in packs at 1:12, this 10-card set pictures NHL erstars who have separated themselves from the t of the league. Card backs carry a "PT" prefix. A allel variation numbered to just 250 was also ated and inserted at 1:299.
MPLETE SET (10) 15.00 30.00
IL/250: 4X TO 10X BASIC INSERTS
1 Paul Kariya .75 2.00
2 Jaromir Jagr 1.25 3.00
3 Eric Lindros .75 2.00
4 Mike Modano 1.25 3.00
5 Mats Sundin .75 2.00
6 Peter Forsberg 2.00 5.00
PT7 Steve Yzerman 4.00 10.00
PT8 Patrick Roy 4.00 10.00
PT9 Martin Brodeur 2.00 5.00
PT10 Dominik Hasek 1.50 4.00

1999-00 Topps Premier Plus Signing Bonus

Randomly inserted in packs at 1:229, this 5-card set features five of the NHL's top prospects. Each card is autographed and contains the "Topps Certified Autograph" stamp and 3M authentication sticker. Card backs carry an "SB" prefix.
SB1 David Legwand 5.00 12.00
SB2 Scott Gomez 5.00 12.00
SB3 Peter Schaefer 5.00 12.00
SB4 Patrik Stefan 5.00 12.00
SB5 Alex Tanguay 10.00 25.00

1999-00 Topps Premier Plus The Next Ones

COMPLETE SET (8) 6.00 12.00
STATED ODDS 1:10
TNO1 Vincent Lecavalier 1.00 2.50
TNO2 Marian Hossa 1.00 2.50
TNO3 Chris Drury .75 2.00
TNO4 Joe Thornton 1.50 4.00
TNO5 Steve Kariya .30 .75
TNO6 David Legwand .75 2.00
TNO7 Patrik Stefan .30 .75
TNO8 Milan Hejduk 1.00 2.50

1999-00 Topps Premier Plus Promos

This set of six promo cards was widely distributed prior to the release of the Premier Plus set. The cards feature the same photos as the base cards, but different numbers, including a PP-prefix.
COMPLETE SET (6) 2.00 5.00
PP1 Curtis Joseph .60 1.50
PP2 J.P. Dumont .20 .50
PP3 Marian Hossa .60 1.50
PP4 Saku Koivu .30 .75
PP5 Chris Drury .40 1.00
PP6 Ron Francis .20 .50

2000-01 Topps Premier Plus

Topps Premier Plus was issued as a 140-card set with an additional NNO card of Scott Gomez with the checklist on the back. The card design had an embossed front and looked like the base Topps 2000-01. The card backs had a small photo of the featured player and some of his statistics from his NHL career.
COMPLETE SET (140) 30.00 60.00
1 Scott Gomez .15 .40
2 Brian Boucher .15 .40
3 Patrik Stefan .15 .40
4 David Legwand .20 .50
5 Tim Connolly .12 .30
6 Jaromir Jagr .50 1.25
7 Owen Nolan .20 .50
8 Patrick Roy .50 1.25
9 Joe Thornton .30 .75
10 Paul Kariya .25 .60
11 Mark Messier .30 .75
12 Jeremy Roenick .20 .50
13 Jeff Friesen .12 .30
14 Al MacInnis .20 .50
15 Curtis Joseph .25 .60
16 Olaf Kolzig .20 .50
17 Dominik Hasek .30 .75
18 Arturs Irbe .15 .40
19 Joe Sakic .30 .75
20 Sergei Fedorov .30 .75
21 Zigmund Palffy .20 .50
22 Jason Arnott .15 .40
23 Marian Hossa .15 .40
24 Pierre Turgeon .20 .50
25 Ron Tugnutt .15 .40
26 Valeri Bure .15 .40
27 Tony Amonte .15 .40
28 Jeff Hackett .12 .30
29 Mariusz Czerkawski .12 .30
30 Wade Redden .12 .30
31 Mark Recchi .25 .60
32 Jean-Sebastien Aubin .15 .40
33 Jason Allison .15 .40
34 Michael Peca .15 .40
35 Teemu Selanne .40 1.00
36 Martin Brodeur .40 1.00
37 Simon Gagne .20 .50
38 Chris Simon .12 .30
39 Doug Weight .20 .50
40 Jocelyn Thibault .15 .40
41 Ed Belfour .20 .50
42 Ray Bourque .30 .75
43 Mike Richter .20 .50
44 Curtis Leschyshyn .12 .30
45 Pavol Demitra .25 .60
46 Alexei Kovalev .15 .40
47 Brad Stuart .15 .40
48 Jarome Iginla .20 .50
49 Ron Francis .25 .60
50 Brendan Shanahan .25 .60
51 Rob Blake .20 .50
52 Miroslav Satan .12 .30
53 Theo Fleury .25 .60
54 John LeClair .20 .50
55 Roman Turek .15 .40
56 Brett Hull .30 .75
57 Peter Forsberg .25 .60
58 Steve Yzerman .60 1.50
59 Derian Hatcher .15 .40
60 Pavel Bure .25 .60
61 Patrik Elias .20 .50
62 Daniel Alfredsson .20 .50
63 Adam Oates .20 .50
64 Andrew Brunette .12 .30
65 Chris Pronger .15 .40
66 Mario Lemieux .60 1.50
67 Keith Tkachuk .20 .50
68 Markus Naslund .15 .40
69 Mike Modano .30 .75
70 Nicklas Lidstrom .20 .50
71 Scott Stevens .20 .50
72 Vincent Lecavalier .15 .40
73 Luc Robitaille .20 .50
74 Mats Sundin .20 .50
75 Milan Hejduk .15 .40
76 Rod Brind'amour .20 .50
77 Tommy Salo .15 .40
78 Byron Dafoe .15 .40
79 Doug Gilmour .25 .60
80 Guy Hebert .15 .40
81 Keith Primeau .15 .40
82 Chris Drury .15 .40
83 Saku Koivu .20 .50
84 Alexei Yashin .15 .40
85 Martin St. Louis .20 .50
86 Steve McCarthy .12 .30
87 Henrik Sedin .30 .75
88 Kris Beech .12 .30
89 Dimitri Kalinin .12 .30
90 Maxime Ouellet .20 .50
91 Shawn Heins .12 .30
92 Mika Noronen .12 .30
93 Taylor Pyatt .12 .30
94 Brent Johnson .15 .40
95 Oleg Saprykin .12 .30
96 Daniel Tkaczuk .15 .40
97 Daniel Sedin .40 1.00
98 Milan Kraft .12 .30
99 Jeff Farkas .12 .30
100 Denis Shvidki .12 .30
101 Mathieu Garon .12 .30
102 Mike Mottau .12 .30
103 Andrei Markov .25 .60
104 Brad Richards .20 .50
105 Brian Swanson RC .25 .60
106 Josef Vasicek RC .60 1.50
107 Reto Von Arx RC .30 .75
108 Lubomir Sekeras RC .25 .60
109 Ruslan Fedotenko RC .25 .60
110 Roman Simicek RC .25 .60
111 Michel Riesen RC .30 .75
112 Petteri Nummelin RC .25 .60
113 Brad Tapper RC .25 .60
114 Alexander Kharitonov RC .25 .60
115 Andrew Raycroft RC .60 1.50
116 Ossi Vaananen RC .30 .75
117 Tyler Bouck RC .25 .60
118 Steven Reinprecht RC .40 1.00
119 Rostislav Klesla RC .60 1.50
120 Martin Havlat RC 1.00 2.50
121 Scott Hartnell RC .60 1.50
122 David Aebischer RC .75 2.00
123 Bryce Salvador RC .30 .75
124 Jani Hurme RC .25 .60
125 Eric Belanger RC .30 .75
126 Marty Turco RC 1.25 3.00
127 Rick DiPietro RC 1.00 2.50
128 Justin Williams RC .60 1.50
129 Dale Purinton RC .25 .60
130 Marian Gaborik RC 2.00 5.00
131 Petr Svoboda RC .30 .75
132 Niclas Wallin RC .30 .75
133 Petr Hubacek RC .25 .60
134 Colin White RC .25 .60
135 Greg Classen RC .25 .60
136 Roman Cechmanek RC .30 .75
137 Eric Boulton RC .25 .60
138 Sascha Goc RC .25 .60
139 Lubomir Visnovsky RC .50 1.25
140 Ronald Petrovicky RC .25 .60
NNO Scott Gomez CL .12 .30

2000-01 Topps Premier Plus Blue Ice

Randomly inserted in packs of 2000-01 Topps Premier Plus at a rate of 1:15, this 140-card set is parallel to the base set. The cards were serial numbered to 250.The card design was the same as the base set with the exceptions of a red border instead of blue and the Ice in the photo was blue, the cards were die-cut on all 4 sides and the card front used an embossed foilboard design.
*1-104 VETS/250: 4X TO 10X BASIC CARDS
*105-140 ROOK/250: 2X TO 5X BASIC RC
BLUE/250 STATED ODDS 1:15
11 Mark Messier 3.00 8.00

2000-01 Topps Premier Plus Aspirations

COMPLETE SET (10) 10.00 20.00
STATED ODDS 1:16
PA1 Scott Gomez .75 2.00
PA2 Vincent Lecavalier 1.25 3.00
PA3 Maxim Afinogenov .75 2.00
PA4 Milan Hejduk 1.25 3.00
PA5 Joe Thornton 2.00 5.00
PA6 Marian Hossa 1.25 3.00
PA7 Oleg Saprykin .75 2.00
PA8 Shane Willis .75 2.00
PA9 David Legwand 1.00 2.50
PA10 Tim Connolly .75 2.00

2000-01 Topps Premier Plus Club Signings

The Signings were randomly inserted in packs of 2000-01 Topps Premier Plus at a rate of 1:219 for the single signed cards and a rate of 1:1751 for the dual signed cards.
CS1 Billy Smith 8.00 20.00
CS2 John Vanbiesbrouck 10.00 25.00
CS3 John LeClair 8.00 20.00
CS4 Bobby Clarke 12.50 30.00
CS5 Luc Robitaille 8.00 20.00
CS6 Marcel Dionne 8.00 20.00
CSC1 J.V'brouck/B.Smith 30.00 80.00
CSC2 J.LeClair/B.Clarke 30.00 80.00
CSC3 L.Robitaille/M.Dionne 30.00 60.00

2000-01 Topps Premier Plus Game-Used Memorabilia

Randomly inserted in packs of 2000-01 Topps Premier Plus at a rate of 1:66 for the jersey cards, 1:658 for the stick cards, and 1:1752 for the combo relic cards. The 18-card set featured pieces of game-used memorabilia from the NHL.
GPAO Adam Oates S 8.00 20.00
GPEB Ed Belfour S 20.00 50.00
GPJI Jarome Iginla J 12.00 30.00
GPJV John Vanbiesbrouck S 15.00 40.00
GPKB Kris Beech J 4.00 10.00
GPMB Max Balmochnyk J 4.00 10.00
GPMT Marty Turco J 8.00 20.00
GPOS Oleg Saprykin J 4.00 10.00
GPRF Rico Fata J 4.00 10.00
GPTP Taylor Pyatt J 4.00 10.00
GPTS Teemu Selanne S 12.00 30.00
GPVB Valeri Bure J 4.00 10.00
GPAOKB K.Beech/A.Oates 8.00 20.00
GPEBMT M.Turco/E.Belfour 30.00 80.00
GPJIRF R.Fata/J.Iginla 20.00 50.00
GPJVTP T.Pyatt/J.V'brouck 20.00 50.00
GPTSMB Balmoc'/Selanne 12.00 30.00
GPVBOS O.Saprykin/V.Bure 8.00 20.00

2000-01 Topps Premier Plus Masters of the Break

COMPLETE SET (20) 30.00 60.00
STATED ODDS 1:24
MB1 Jaromir Jagr 1.50 4.00
MB2 Teemu Selanne 1.00 2.50
MB3 Pavel Bure 1.25 3.00
MB4 Tony Amonte .75 2.00
MB5 Milan Hejduk 1.00 2.50
MB6 Patrik Elias .75 2.00
MB7 Paul Kariya 1.00 2.50
MB8 Peter Forsberg 2.50 6.00
MB9 Sergei Fedorov 2.00 5.00
MB10 Mike Modano 1.50 4.00
MB11 Martin Brodeur 2.50 6.00
MB12 Patrick Roy 5.00 12.00
MB13 Ed Belfour 1.00 2.50
MB14 Curtis Joseph 1.00 2.50
MB15 Dominik Hasek 2.00 5.00
MB16 Olaf Kolzig .60 1.50
MB17 Roman Turek .60 1.50
MB18 Brian Boucher 1.00 2.50
MB19 Mike Richter 1.00 2.50
MB20 Tommy Salo .60 1.50

2000-01 Topps Premier Plus Private Signings

Randomly inserted in packs of Topps Premier Plus at a rate of 1:175 for the rookies and 1:350 for the veterans and 1:526 for the Gomez. This 13-card set featured autographs from some of the top players in the NHL. The cards carried a 'PS' prefix except for the Gomez which carried a 'CT' prefix for the card number. Exchange expiration was 03/01/02.
CTW1 Scott Gomez Calder 10.00 25.00
PSBR Brad Richards 8.00 20.00
PSBS Brad Stuart 4.00 10.00
PSCP Chris Pronger 8.00 20.00
PSDS Daniel Sedin 8.00 20.00
PSEN Evgeni Nabokov 8.00 20.00
PSHS Henrik Sedin 8.00 20.00
PSJW Justin Williams 6.00 15.00
PSMB Martin Brodeur 25.00 60.00
PSMG Marian Gaborik 15.00 40.00
PSMK Milan Kraft 4.00 10.00
PSMT Marty Turco 10.00 25.00
PSSH Scott Hartnell 8.00 20.00

2000-01 Topps Premier Plus Rookies

Randomly inserted in packs of 2000-01 Topps Premier Plus at a rate of 1:12, the 10-card set highlighted the top newcomers to the NHL. A blue ice parallel variation numbered to just 250 was also created and inserted at 1:213.
COMPLETE SET (10) 10.00 20.00
*BLUE ICE/250: 1.2X TO 3X BASIC INSERT
PR1 Marian Gaborik 1.50 4.00
PR2 Henrik Sedin 1.50 4.00
PR3 Rostislav Klesla 1.25 3.00
PR4 Brad Richards 1.00 2.50
PR5 Justin Williams 1.25 3.00
PR6 Josef Vasicek 1.25 3.00
PR7 Daniel Sedin 2.00 5.00
PR8 Maxime Ouellet .75 2.00
PR9 Andrei Markov 1.00 2.50
PR10 Oleg Saprykin .60 1.50

2000-01 Topps Premier Plus Team

Randomly inserted in packs of 2000-01 Topps Premier Plus at a rate of 1:12, the 10-card set highlighted the top players from the NHL. A blue ice parallel variation numbered to just 250 was also created and inserted at 1:213.
COMPLETE SET (10) 8.00 15.00
*BLUE ICE/250: .6X TO 1.5X BASIC INSERT
PT1 Paul Kariya .50 1.25
PT2 Peter Forsberg 1.50 4.00
PT3 John LeClair .50 1.25
PT4 Mike Modano 1.00 2.50
PT5 Martin Brodeur 1.50 4.00
PT6 Pavel Bure .50 1.25
PT7 Curtis Joseph .50 1.25
PT8 Jaromir Jagr 1.00 2.50
PT9 Chris Pronger .50 1.25
PT10 Teemu Selanne .50 1.25

2000-01 Topps Premier Plus Trophy Tribute

COMPLETE SET (15) 15.00 30.00
STATED ODDS 1:16
TT1 Dominik Hasek 1.25 3.00
TT2 Jaromir Jagr 1.00 2.50
TT3 Patrick Roy 3.00 8.00
TT4 Chris Pronger .50 1.25
TT5 Paul Kariya .60 1.50
TT6 Ed Belfour .60 1.50
TT7 Mark Messier .75 2.00
TT8 Ray Bourque 1.25 3.00
TT9 Steve Yzerman 3.00 8.00
TT10 Sergei Fedorov 1.25 3.00
TT11 Brett Hull .75 2.00
TT12 Ron Francis .50 1.25
TT13 Pavel Bure .75 2.00
TT14 Teemu Selanne .60 1.50
TT15 Brian Leetch .50 1.25

2000-01 Topps Premier Plus World Premier

COMPLETE SET (20) 30.00 60.00
STATED ODDS 1:24
WP1 Patrick Roy 5.00 12.00
WP2 Martin Brodeur 2.50 6.00
WP3 Chris Pronger .75 2.00
WP4 Sergei Zubov .60 1.50
WP5 Scott Stevens .75 2.00
WP6 Ray Bourque 2.00 5.00
WP7 Nicklas Lidstrom 1.00 2.50
WP8 Rob Blake .75 2.00
WP9 Paul Kariya 1.00 2.50
WP10 John LeClair 1.25 3.00
WP11 Keith Tkackuk 1.00 2.50
WP12 Brendan Shanahan 1.50 4.00
WP13 Vincent Locavalicr 1.00 2.50
WP14 Steve Yzerman 5.00 12.00
WP15 Mike Modano 1.50 4.00
WP16 Peter Forsberg 2.50 6.00
WP17 Pavel Bure 1.25 3.00
WP18 Teemu Selanne 1.00 2.50
WP19 Brett Hull 1.25 3.00
WP20 Jaromir Jagr 1.50 4.00

2003-04 Topps Pristine

This 190-card set was released in January and was packaged 5 packs per box with 8 cards per pack. Each pack contained two additional packs with a memorabilia card and a "uncirculated " card in each pack. Uncircualted cards were incased in clear plastic slabs. Rookies in the set each had three different variations; common, uncommon and rare. Unpriced 1/1 Press Plates in 4 different colors also exist for each card below.
1 Jean-Sebastien Giguere .75 2.00
2 Slava Kozlov .60 1.50
3 Steve Shields .60 1.50
4 Martin Biron .60 1.50
5 Roman Turek .60 1.50
6 Kevin Weekes .60 1.50
7 Kyle Calder .50 1.25
8 Patrik Elias .75 2.00
9 Rob Blake .75 2.00
10 Marty Turco .75 2.00
11 Bill Guerin .75 2.00
12 Nicklas Lidstrom .75 2.00
13 Mike Comrie .60 1.50
14 Roberto Luongo 1.25 3.00
15 Ziggy Palffy .75 2.00
16 Paul Kariya 1.00 2.50
17 Stanislav Chistov .50 1.25
18 Andrew Brunette .50 1.25
19 Richard Zednik .50 1.25
20 Martin Brodeur 1.50 4.00
21 Alexei Yashin .60 1.50
22 Brian Leetch .75 2.00
23 Patrick Lalime .60 1.50
24 Simon Gagne .75 2.00
25 Mike Johnson .50 1.25
26 Mario Lemieux 2.50 6.00
27 Alyn McCauley .50 1.25
28 Kyle McLaren .50 1.25
29 Brent Johnson .60 1.50
30 Vincent Lecavalier .60 1.50
31 Ed Belfour .75 2.00
32 Todd Bertuzzi .75 2.00
33 Brendan Morrison .60 1.50
34 Olaf Kolzig .75 2.00
35 Ilya Kovalchuk .75 2.00
36 Johan Hedberg .60 1.50
37 Mike Knuble .50 1.25
38 Ales Kotalik .50 1.25
39 Chris Drury .60 1.50
40 Joe Thornton 1.00 2.50
41 Dominik Hasek 1.25 3.00
42 Daniel Alfredsson .75 2.00
43 Marc Denis .60 1.50
44 Mike Modano 1.25 3.00
45 Sergei Fedorov 1.25 3.00
46 Henrik Zetterberg 1.00 2.50
47 Tommy Salo .60 1.50
48 Olli Jokinen .75 2.00
49 Felix Potvin 1.25 3.00
50 Dany Heatley .75 2.00
51 Marian Gaborik 1.25 3.00
52 Saku Koivu .75 2.00
53 Tomas Vokoun .60 1.50
54 Eric Brewer .50 1.25
55 Rick DiPietro .60 1.50
56 Mike Dunham .60 1.50
57 Marian Hossa .60 1.50
58 Jeremy Roenick .75 2.00
59 Brian Boucher .60 1.50
60 Milan Hejduk .60 1.50
61 Patrick Marleau .75 2.00
62 Pavol Demitra 1.00 2.50
63 Al MacInnis .75 2.00
64 Nikolai Khabibulin .75 2.00
65 Mats Sundin .75 2.00
66 Miroslav Satan .60 1.50
67 Sergei Gonchar .50 1.25
68 Pasi Nurminen .60 1.50
69 Glen Murray .60 1.50
70 Brett Hull 1.00 2.50
71 Jarome Iginla .75 2.00
72 Ron Francis 1.00 2.50
73 Tyler Arnason .50 1.25
74 Joe Sakic 1.25 3.00
75 David Aebischer .60 1.50
76 Geoff Sanderson .50 1.25
77 Derian Hatcher .50 1.25
78 Jocelyn Thibault .60 1.50
79 Curtis Joseph .75 2.00
80 Markus Naslund .75 2.00
81 Kristian Huselius .50 1.25
82 Alexander Frolov .60 1.50
83 Petr Sykora .60 1.50
84 Dwayne Roloson .60 1.50
85 Jose Theodore .75 2.00
86 David Legwand .60 1.50
87 Scott Stevens .75 2.00
88 Michael Peca .60 1.50
89 Alex Kovalev .60 1.50
90 Jaromir Jagr 2.00 5.00
91 Tony Amonte .60 1.50
92 Daymond Langkow .50 1.25
93 Martin Straka .50 1.25
94 Evgeni Nabokov .60 1.50
95 Chris Pronger .60 1.50
96 Martin St. Louis .75 2.00
97 Alexander Mogilny .60 1.50
98 Owen Nolan .60 1.50
99 Dan Cloutier .60 1.50
100 Peter Forsberg 1.00 2.50
101 Tuomo Ruutu C RC 2.00 5.00
102 Tuomo Ruutu U 2.50 6.00
103 Tuomo Ruutu R 4.00 10.00
104 Marc-Andre Fleury C RC 8.00 20.00
105 Marc-Andre Fleury U 10.00 25.00
106 Marc-Andre Fleury R 15.00 40.00
107 Patrice Bergeron C RC 6.00 15.00
108 Patrice Bergeron U 8.00 20.00
109 Patrice Bergeron R 12.00 30.00
110 Milan Michalek C RC 2.50 6.00
111 Milan Michalek U 3.00 8.00
112 Milan Michalek R 5.00 12.00
113 Dominic Moore C RC 1.25 3.00
114 Dominic Moore U 1.50 4.00
115 Dominic Moore R 2.50 6.00
116 Dustin Brown C RC 2.50 6.00
117 Dustin Brown U 3.00 8.00
118 Dustin Brown R 5.00 12.00
119 Nathan Horton C RC 3.00 8.00
120 Nathan Horton U 4.00 10.00
121 Nathan Horton R 6.00 15.00
122 Chris Higgins C RC 2.50 6.00
123 Chris Higgins U 3.00 8.00
124 Chris Higgins R 5.00 12.00
125 Antti Miettinen C RC 2.00 5.00
126 Antti Miettinen U 2.50 6.00
127 Antti Miettinen R 4.00 10.00
128 Tom Preissing C RC 1.50 4.00
129 Tom Preissing U 2.00 5.00
130 Tom Preissing R 3.00 8.00
131 Marek Svatos C RC 2.50 6.00
132 Marek Svatos U 3.00 8.00
133 Marek Svatos R 5.00 12.00
134 Peter Sejna C RC 1.50 4.00
135 Peter Sejna U 2.00 5.00
136 Peter Sejna R 3.00 8.00
137 Matt Stajan C RC 2.00 5.00
138 Matt Stajan U 2.50 6.00
139 Matt Stajan R 4.00 10.00
140 Jiri Hudler C RC 3.00 8.00
141 Jiri Hudler U 4.00 10.00
142 Jiri Hudler R 6.00 15.00
143 Joni Pitkanen C RC 2.00 5.00
144 Joni Pitkanen U 2.50 6.00
145 Joni Pitkanen R 4.00 10.00
146 Garnet Exelby C 1.25 3.00
147 Garnet Exelby U 1.50 4.00
148 Garnet Exelby R 2.50 6.00
149 Eric Staal C RC 6.00 15.00
150 Eric Staal U 8.00 20.00
151 Eric Staal R 12.00 30.00
152 Sean Bergenheim C RC 1.50 4.00
153 Sean Bergenheim U 2.00 5.00
154 Sean Bergenheim R 3.00 8.00
155 Gregory Campbell C RC 1.25 3.00
156 Gregory Campbell U 1.50 4.00
157 Gregory Campbell R 2.50 6.00
158 Dan Hamhuis C RC 1.50 4.00
159 Dan Hamhuis U 2.00 5.00
160 Dan Hamhuis R 3.00 8.00
161 Maxim Kondratiev C RC 1.25 3.00
162 Maxim Kondratiev U 1.50 4.00
163 Maxim Kondratiev R 2.50 6.00
164 Matthew Lombardi C RC 1.50 4.00
165 Matthew Lombardi U 2.00 5.00
166 Matthew Lombardi R 3.00 8.00
167 Alexander Semin C RC 6.00 15.00
168 Alexander Semin U 8.00 20.00
169 Alexander Semin R 12.00 30.00
170 John-Michael Liles C RC 1.50 4.00
171 John-Michael Liles U 2.00 5.00
172 John-Michael Liles R 3.00 8.00
173 Andrew Peters C RC 1.50 4.00
174 Andrew Peters U 2.00 5.00
175 Andrew Peters R 3.00 8.00
176 Dan Fritsche C RC 1.25 3.00
177 Dan Fritsche U 1.50 4.00
178 Dan Fritsche R 2.50 6.00
179 Antoine Vermette C RC 2.50 6.00
180 Antoine Vermette U 3.00 8.00
181 Antoine Vermette R 5.00 12.00
182 David Hale C RC 1.25 3.00
183 David Hale U 1.50 4.00
184 David Hale R 2.50 6.00
185 Joffrey Lupul C RC 3.00 8.00
186 Joffrey Lupul U 4.00 10.00
187 Joffrey Lupul R 6.00 15.00
188 Jordin Tootoo C RC 2.50 6.00
189 Jordin Tootoo U 3.00 8.00
190 Jordin Tootoo R 5.00 12.00

2003-04 Topps Pristine Gold Refractor Die Cuts

One per box in boxtopper packs.
*1-100 VETS/33: 4X TO 10X BASIC CARDS
*COMMON ROOK/33: 1.5X TO 4X BASIC C
*UNCOMM.ROOK/33: 1.2X TO 3X BASIC U
*RARE ROOKIE/33: .8X TO 2X BASIC R

2003-04 Topps Pristine Refractors

*1-100 VET/59: 2.5X TO 6X BASIC CARDS
*COMMON ROOK/499: .5X TO 1.2X BASIC C
*UNCOMM.ROOK/199: .6X TO 1.5X BASIC U
*RARE ROOKIE/59: .5X TO 1.2X BASIC R

2003-04 Topps Pristine Autographs

This 7-card set featured certified autographs on silver metallic cards. A Gold metallic parallel was also created.
GROUP A ODDS 1:11
GROUP B ODDS 1:26
GROUP C ODDS 1:8
*GOLD: 1.5X TO 4X BASIC GRP B-C
*GOLD: 1X TO 2.5X BASIC GRP A
PERN Rick Nash A 12.00 30.00
PEMT Marty Turco C 6.00 15.00
PEMN Markus Naslund B 6.00 15.00
PEJG Jean-Sebastien Giguere A 6.00 15.00
PEMH Milan Hejduk A 6.00 15.00
PEMS Martin St. Louis C 8.00 20.00
PESC Stanislav Chistov C 3.00 8.00

2003-04 Topps Pristine Jersey Portions

GROUP A ODDS 4:5
GROUP B ODDS: 1:27
*REFRACTOR/25: 2X TO 5X BASIC JSY
PPJBMN Brendan Morrison A 3.00 8.00
PPJBMW Brenden Morrow A 3.00 8.00
PPJBRI Brad Richards A 6.00 15.00
PPJBRO Brian Rolston A 4.00 10.00
PPJDA Daniel Alfredsson A 3.00 8.00
PPJDBL Dan Blackburn A 4.00 10.00
PPJDC Dan Cloutier A 3.00 8.00
PPJDH Dany Heatley A 8.00 20.00
PPJDL David Legwand B 3.00 8.00
PPJED Eric Desjardins A 4.00 10.00
PPJEL Eric Lindros A 6.00 15.00
PPJFP Felix Potvin A 6.00 15.00
PPJIK Ilya Kovalchuk A 5.00 12.00
PPJJD J-P Dumont A 3.00 8.00
PPJJW Justin Williams A 3.00 8.00
PPJKP Keith Primeau A 4.00 10.00
PPJMA Maxim Afinogenov A 3.00 8.00
PPJMB Martin Biron A 4.00 10.00
PPJMG Marian Gaborik B 10.00 25.00
PPJMHE Milan Hejduk A 5.00 12.00
PPJMHO Marian Hossa A 4.00 10.00
PPJML Manny Legace A 6.00 15.00
PPJMSA Miroslav Satan A 4.00 10.00
PPJMSU Mats Sundin A 5.00 12.00
PPJMT Marty Turco B 5.00 12.00
PPJPL Patrick Lalime B 5.00 12.00
PPJPM Patrick Marleau A 3.00 8.00
PPJPR Patrick Roy B 12.00 30.00
PPJRB Rob Blake A 5.00 12.00
PPJRF Ron Francis A 4.00 10.00
PPJRL Roberto Luongo A 5.00 12.00
PPJSK Saku Koivu A 6.00 15.00
PPJTB Todd Bertuzzi B 4.00 10.00
PPJTV Tomas Vokoun A 4.00 10.00
PPJZP Zigmund Palffy A 3.00 8.00

2003-04 Topps Pristine Mini

Inserted at just one per box on average, these smaller cards were inserted into a fourth pack.
MINI AUTO ODDS 1:318
PMMSO Matt Stajan 2.00 5.00
PMNH Nathan Horton 3.00 8.00
PMMB Martin Brodeur 5.00 12.00
PMDH Dominik Hasek 3.00 8.00
PMES Eric Staal 6.00 15.00
PMJL Joffrey Lupul 3.00 8.00
PMMAF Marc-Andre Fleury 8.00 20.00
PMJTO Jordin Tootoo 2.50 6.00
PMJHU Jiri Hudler 3.00 8.00
PMPS Peter Sejna 1.50 4.00
PMAM Antti Miettinen 2.00 5.00
PMDB Dustin Brown 2.50 6.00
PMKW Kevin Weekes 1.50 4.00
PMSC Sebastien Caron 1.50 4.00
PMDR Dwayne Roloson 1.50 4.00
PMTS Tommy Salo 1.50 4.00
PMMDE Marc Denis 1.50 4.00
PMRE Robert Esche 1.25 3.00
PMTV Tomas Vokoun 1.50 4.00
PMSB Sean Burke 1.25 3.00
PMEN Evgeni Nabokov 1.50 4.00
PMCO Chris Osgood 2.00 5.00
PMPL Patrick Lalime 1.50 4.00
PMJT Jocelyn Thibault 1.50 4.00
PMRD Rick DiPietro 1.50 4.00
PMRC Roman Cechmanek 1.50 4.00
PMMBI Martin Biron 1.50 4.00
PMOK Olaf Kolzig 2.00 5.00
PMMT Marty Turco 2.00 5.00
PMDC Dan Cloutier 1.50 4.00
PMDA David Aebischer 1.50 4.00
PMPN Pasi Nurminen 1.50 4.00
PMRT Roman Turek 1.50 4.00
PMJSG Jean-Sebastien Giguere 2.00 5.00
PMMD Mike Dunham 1.50 4.00
PMRL Roberto Luongo 3.00 8.00
PMJTH Jose Theodore 3.00 8.00
PMFP Felix Potvin 3.00 8.00
PMNK Nikolai Khabibulin 2.00 5.00
PMEB Ed Belfour 2.00 5.00
PMAJG J-S Giguere AU 12.50 30.00

2003-04 Topps Pristine Patches

STATED ODDS 1:16
STATED PRINT RUN 50 SER.#'d SETS
PPDH Dany Heatley 15.00 40.00
PPPF Peter Forsberg 15.00 40.00
PPPD Pavel Datsyuk 12.00 30.00
PPIK Ilya Kovalchuk 12.00 30.00
PPPR Patrick Roy 30.00 80.00
PPJS Joe Sakic 15.00 40.00
PPMG Marian Gaborik 20.00 50.00
PPMM Mike Modano 15.00 40.00
PPVL Vincent Lecavalier 15.00 40.00
PPRB Rob Blake 8.00 20.00
PPMT Marty Turco 8.00 20.00
PPKH Kristian Huselius 8.00 20.00
PPZP Zigmund Palffy 8.00 20.00
PPPL Patrick Lalime 8.00 20.00
PPDA Daniel Alfredsson 10.00 25.00
PPMA Maxim Afinogenov 8.00 20.00
PPMB Martin Biron 8.00 20.00
PPMSA Miroslav Satan 8.00 20.00
PPMST Marco Sturm 8.00 20.00
PPJD J-P Dumont 8.00 20.00
PPJW Justin Williams 8.00 20.00
PPBRO Brian Rolston 8.00 20.00
PPKP Keith Primeau 8.00 20.00
PPBM Brendan Morrison 8.00 20.00
PPDL David Legwand 8.00 20.00
PPAT Alex Tanguay 8.00 20.00
PPML Manny Legace 8.00 20.00
PPDB Dan Blackburn 8.00 20.00
PPMC Mike Comrie 10.00 25.00
PPRL Roberto Luongo 12.00 30.00
PPJI Jarome Iginla 15.00 40.00
PPEL Eric Lindros 15.00 40.00
PPTB Todd Bertuzzi 8.00 20.00
PPSG Simon Gagne 12.00 30.00
PPMHO Marian Hossa 12.00 30.00
PPSK Saku Koivu 12.00 30.00
PPMHE Milan Hejduk 10.00 25.00
PPMSU Mats Sundin 12.00 30.00
PPMN Markus Naslund 10.00 25.00
PPJL John LeClair 8.00 20.00
PPFP Felix Potvin 15.00 40.00

2003-04 Topps Pristine Popular Demand Relics

GROUP A ODDS 1:127
GROUP B ODDS 1:12
GROUP C ODDS 1:5
*REFRACTOR/25: 1.5X TO 4X BASIC JSY
PDJT Joe Thornton C 8.00 20.00
PDPD Pavel Datsyuk C 6.00 15.00
PDPK Paul Kariya A 8.00 20.00
PDML Mario Lemieux A 20.00 50.00
PDSG Simon Gagne A 12.50 30.00
PDMN Markus Naslund A 6.00 15.00
PDJL John LeClair B 5.00 12.00
PDMM Mike Modano B 6.00 15.00
PDJSP Jason Spezza B 6.00 15.00
PDJJ Jaromir Jagr C 8.00 20.00
PDJI Jarome Iginla B 5.00 12.00
PDAZ Alexei Zhamnov B 4.00 10.00
PDMST Marco Sturm B 3.00 8.00
PDBG Bill Guerin C 4.00 10.00
PDMSK Martin Straka C 4.00 10.00
PDAY Alexei Yashin C 4.00 10.00
PDNK Nikolai Khabibulin C 4.00 10.00
PDTD Tie Domi B 4.00 10.00
PDKH Kristian Huselius C 3.00 8.00
PDTC Tim Connolly A 4.00 10.00
PDSN Scott Niedermayer B 4.00 10.00
PDJB Jay Bouwmeester C 4.00 10.00
PDMR Mark Recchi B 4.00 10.00
PDJTH Jose Theodore C 6.00 15.00
PDPB Pavel Bure C 5.00 12.00

2003-04 Topps Pristine Stick Portions

STATED ODDS: 1:27
PPSMM Mark Messier 8.00 20.00
PPSSY Steve Yzerman 20.00 50.00
PPSVB Valeri Bure 3.00 8.00
PPSED Eric Desjardins 4.00 10.00
PPSPS Patrik Stefan 4.00 10.00
PPSAO Adam Oates 5.00 12.00
PPSDA Daniel Alfredsson 5.00 12.00
PPSDW Doug Weight 5.00 12.00
PPSJI Jarome Iginla 6.00 15.00
PPSCJ Curtis Joseph 5.00 12.00
PPSJL John LeClair 5.00 12.00
PPSMS Mats Sundin 5.00 12.00

2001-02 Topps Reserve

Released in late January 2002, this 121-card hobby only set featured color player photos on gold sparkle card stock. Each 10-pack box contained an autographed team logo puck, a PSA graded serial-numbered rookie card, a non-graded serial-numbered rookie cards and two jersey cards. Rookie cards were serial-numbered to 1599, 1099, or 699. Approximately half of each rookie print run was graded.
COMP.SET w/o SP's (100) 40.00 80.00
1 Joe Sakic .60 1.50
2 Patrik Elias .40 1.00
3 Mario Lemieux 1.25 3.00
4 Chris Pronger .30 .75
5 Simon Gagne .40 1.00
6 Steve Yzerman 1.25 3.00
7 Bill Guerin .40 1.00
8 Pavel Bure .50 1.25

9 Mark Messier .60 1.50
10 Evgeni Nabokov .30 .75
11 Peter Bondra .40 1.00
12 Martin Havlat .30 .75
13 Mike Dunham .30 .75
14 Mike Comrie .30 .75
15 Ed Belfour .40 1.00
16 Tony Amonte .30 .75
17 Patrik Stefan .30 .75
18 Paul Kariya .50 1.25
19 Patrick Roy 1.00 2.50
20 Sean Burke .25 .60
21 Vincent Lecavalier .30 .75
22 Henrik Sedin .40 1.00
23 Petr Sykora .25 .60
24 Marian Gaborik .60 1.50
25 Rod Brind'Amour .40 1.00
26 Miroslav Satan .30 .75
27 Zigmund Palffy .40 1.00
28 Sergei Fedorov .60 1.50
29 Ron Tugnutt .30 .75
30 Jason Allison .30 .75
31 Marian Hossa .30 .75
32 John LeClair .40 1.00
33 Keith Tkachuk .40 1.00
34 Adam Oates .40 1.00
35 Johan Hedberg .30 .75
36 Saku Koivu .40 1.00
37 Peter Forsberg .50 1.25
38 Jarome Iginla .40 1.00
39 Nicklas Lidstrom .40 1.00
40 Martin Brodeur .75 2.00
41 Daniel Alfredsson .40 1.00
42 Alexei Kovalev .30 .75
43 Mats Sundin .40 1.00
44 Brian Leetch .40 1.00
45 Owen Nolan .40 1.00
46 Cliff Ronning .25 .60
47 Mike Modano .60 1.50
48 Milan Hejduk .30 .75
49 Joe Thornton .50 1.25
50 Ray Ferraro .25 .60
51 Geoff Sanderson .25 .60
52 Roberto Luongo .60 1.50
53 Manny Fernandez .30 .75
54 Mark Recchi .50 1.25
55 Curtis Joseph .40 1.00
56 Philippe Boucher .25 .60
57 Patrick Lalime .30 .75
58 Rick DiPietro .30 .75
59 Adam Deadmarsh .30 .75
60 Pierre Turgeon .40 1.00
61 Roman Turek .30 .75
62 Jeff Friesen .25 .60
63 Eric Lindros .60 1.50
64 Martin Straka .25 .60
65 Markus Naslund .40 1.00
66 J-P Dumont .25 .60
67 Daniel Sedin .40 1.00
68 Alexei Yashin .30 .75
69 Felix Potvin .60 1.50
70 Chris Drury .30 .75
71 Martin Biron .30 .75
72 Tommy Salo .30 .75
73 Stanislav Neckar .25 .60
74 Jaromir Jagr 1.00 2.50
75 Brendan Shanahan .50 1.25
76 Jose Theodore .40 1.00
77 Teemu Selanne .75 2.00
78 Alexander Mogilny .30 .75
79 Niclas Havelid .25 .60
80 Colin Forbes .25 .60
81 Michael Peca .30 .75
82 Jason Arnott .30 .75
83 Arturs Irbe .30 .75
84 Garry Valk .25 .60
85 Roman Cechmanek .30 .75
86 Scott Gomez .30 .75
87 Chris McAllister .25 .60
88 Shane Doan .30 .75
89 David Harlock .25 .60
90 Jeff O'Neill .25 .60
91 Rob Blake .40 1.00
92 Dominik Hasek .60 1.50
93 Olaf Kolzig .40 1.00
94 Brent Johnson .30 .75
95 Jeremy Roenick .40 1.00
96 Brad Richards .40 1.00
97 Steve Sullivan .25 .60
98 Alex Tanguay .30 .75
99 Brett Hull .50 1.25
100 Doug Weight .40 1.00
101 Niklas Hagman/1099 RC 2.00 5.00
102 Scott Clemmensen/1099 RC 1.50 4.00
103 Brian Sutherby/1099 RC 1.50 4.00
104 Erik Cole/1599 RC 3.00 8.00
105 Vaclav Nedorost/1599 RC 1.50 4.00
106 Jaroslav Bednar/1099 RC 1.50 4.00
107 Nick Schultz/699 RC 2.00 5.00
108 Jiri Dopita/699 RC 2.00 5.00
109 Krys Kolanos/1599 RC 1.50 4.00
110 Jukka Hentunen/1099 RC 1.50 4.00
111 Niko Kapanen/699 RC 3.00 8.00
112 Timo Parssinen/1099 RC 2.00 5.00
113 Kristian Huselius/1599 RC 2.50 6.00
114 A.Salomonsson RC/699 2.00 5.00
115 Ilya Kovalchuk/1599 RC 8.00 20.00
116 Dan Blackburn/1599 RC 2.00 5.00
117 Pavel Datsyuk/699 RC 12.50 30.00
118 Peter Smrek/699 RC 2.00 5.00
119 Jeff Jillson/1099 RC 1.50 4.00
120 Nikita Alexeev/1599 RC 1.50 4.00
121 Scott Nichol/699 RC 2.00 5.00

2001-02 Topps Reserve Jerseys

Inserted at 1:4 packs, this 56-card set featured swatches of game-worn jerseys alongside color player photos on team colored card fronts. All cards carried a "TR" prefix.
*EMBLEMS: 1X TO 2.5X JERSEYS
*NAME PLATES: 1X TO 2.5X JERSEYS
*PATCHES: 1.2X TO 3X JERSEYS
AK Alexei Kovalev 3.00 8.00
AO Adam Oates 3.00 8.00
AZ Alexei Zhamnov 3.00 8.00
BB Brian Boucher 3.00 8.00
BL Brian Leetch 5.00 12.00
CD Chris Drury 4.00 10.00
DH Derian Hatcher 3.00 8.00
DM Darren McCarty 5.00 12.00
DY Dimitri Yushkevich 3.00 8.00
EB Ed Belfour 5.00 12.00
ED Eric Desjardins 3.00 8.00
JH Jeff Hackett 3.00 8.00
JI Jarome Iginla 6.00 15.00
JL John LeClair 4.00 10.00
JS Joe Sakic 6.00 15.00
JT Joe Thornton 8.00 20.00
KJ Kenny Jonsson 3.00 8.00
KO Krzysztof Oliwa 3.00 8.00
MB Martin Brodeur 8.00 20.00
MC Mariusz Czerkawski 3.00 8.00
ML Mario Lemieux 10.00 25.00
MM Mike Mottau 3.00 8.00
MP Matt Pettinger 3.00 8.00
MR Mark Recchi 4.00 10.00
MT Marty Turco 5.00 12.00
MY Mike York 3.00 8.00
OS Oleg Saprykin 3.00 8.00
PB Pavel Bure 8.00 20.00
PF Peter Forsberg 6.00 15.00
PK Paul Kariya 5.00 12.00
PM Patrick Marleau 4.00 10.00
PR Patrick Roy 12.00 30.00
RL Robert Lang 3.00 8.00
SB Sean Burke 3.00 8.00
SF Sergei Fedorov 6.00 15.00
SG Simon Gagne 5.00 12.00
SK Saku Koivu 5.00 12.00
SM Shawn McEachern 3.00 8.00
SS Sergei Samsonov 5.00 12.00
SZ Sergei Zubov 3.00 8.00
TA Tony Amonte 4.00 10.00
TD Tie Domi 5.00 12.00
TF Theo Fleury 4.00 10.00
TK Tomas Kloucek 3.00 8.00
TL Trevor Letowski 3.00 8.00
TV Tomas Vokoun 5.00 12.00
VL Vincent Lecavalier 5.00 12.00
WR Wade Redden 3.00 8.00
DAB Daniel Briere 4.00 10.00
DOB Donald Brashear 4.00 10.00
JAI Jason Allison 4.00 10.00
JAR Jason Arnott 4.00 10.00
MIS Miroslav Satan 4.00 10.00
MSA Marc Savard 4.00 10.00
MST Martin Straka 4.00 10.00
ROF Ron Francis 4.00 10.00

2001-02 Topps Reserve Numbers

This 56-card set paralleled the base jersey set but each card carried a piece of the jersey number from the player's jersey. These cards were inserted at 1:29 packs. Each card carried a "TR#" prefix. Please note that card #JAH did not have a parent card in the base jersey set, thus it is priced seperately below.
*NUMBERS: 1X TO 2.5X JERSEYS
JAH Jan Hlavac 12.50 30.00

2000-01 Topps Stars

Released in late January 2001 as a 150-card set, Topps Stars features 97 veteran players, 3 retired stars on a gold background, 25 prospects on a silver background (#101-125) and 25 veteran and rookie Spotlight cards 126-150. Base card stock has a blue background with silver glitter and silver foil highlights around full color player action photography. Topps Stars was packaged in 24 pack boxes with packs containing six cards and carried a suggested retail price of $3.00.
COMPLETE SET (150) 15.00 40.00
1 Vincent Lecavalier .20 .50
2 Patrick Roy .60 1.50
3 Scott Gomez .20 .50
4 Steve Yzerman .75 2.00
5 Paul Kariya .30 .75
6 Dominik Hasek .40 1.00
7 Mike Modano .40 1.00
8 Zigmund Palffy .25 .60
9 John LeClair .25 .60
10 Mats Sundin .25 .60
11 Owen Nolan .25 .60
12 Tony Amonte .20 .50
13 Patrik Stefan .20 .50
14 Brett Hull .40 1.00
15 Chris Pronger .20 .50
16 Jeremy Roenick .25 .60
17 Martin Brodeur .50 1.25
18 Doug Weight .25 .60
19 Ray Bourque .40 1.00
20 Olaf Kolzig .25 .60
21 Jaromir Jagr .60 1.50
22 Daniel Alfredsson .25 .60
23 Jeff Hackett .15 .40
24 Jason Allison .20 .50
25 Joe Sakic .40 1.00
26 Brendan Shanahan .30 .75
27 David Legwand .25 .60
28 Tim Connolly .15 .40
29 Mark Recchi .30 .75
30 Brad Stuart .20 .50
31 Pierre Turgeon .25 .60
32 Ed Belfour .25 .60
33 Valeri Bure .20 .50
34 Pavel Bure .30 .75
35 Teemu Selanne .50 1.25
36 Patrik Elias .25 .60
37 Mattias Ohlund .15 .40
38 Rod Brind'Amour .25 .60
39 Derian Hatcher .20 .50
40 Peter Forsberg .30 .75
41 Eric Lindros .40 1.00
42 Curtis Joseph .30 .75
43 Keith Tkachuk .25 .60
44 Mike Ricci .20 .50
45 Al MacInnis .25 .60
46 Nicklas Lidstrom .25 .60
47 Rob Blake .25 .60
48 Scott Stevens .25 .60
49 Milan Hejduk .20 .50
50 Theo Fleury .30 .75
51 Joe Thornton .40 1.00
52 Tommy Salo .20 .50
53 Eric Desjardins .20 .50
54 Pavol Demitra .30 .75
55 Adam Oates .25 .60
56 Jeff Friesen .15 .40
57 Mariusz Czerkawski .15 .40
58 Luc Robitaille .25 .60
59 Jeff O'Neill .20 .50
60 Andrew Brunette .15 .40
61 Fred Brathwaite .20 .50
62 Robert Svehla .15 .40
63 Kimmo Timonen .15 .40
64 Teppo Numminen .15 .40
65 Nikolai Antropov .20 .50
66 Marian Hossa .20 .50
67 Joe Nieuwendyk .25 .60
68 Michael Peca .20 .50
69 Saku Koivu .25 .60
70 Alexei Kovalev .20 .50
71 Sergei Gonchar .15 .40
72 Brian Leetch .25 .60
73 Ryan Smyth .20 .50
74 Jarome Iginla .25 .60
75 Byron Dafoe .20 .50
76 Ray Whitney .20 .50
77 Wade Redden .15 .40
78 Pavel Kubina .15 .40
79 Markus Naslund .20 .50
80 Brian Boucher .20 .50
81 Martin Rucinsky .15 .40
82 Roman Turek .20 .50
83 Jocelyn Thibault .20 .50
84 Miroslav Satan .15 .40
85 Cliff Ronning .15 .40
86 Mike Richter .25 .60
87 Chris Chelios .25 .60
88 Arturs Irbe .20 .50
89 Steve Thomas .15 .40
90 Felix Potvin .40 1.00
91 Jason Arnott .20 .50
92 Mark Messier .40 1.00
93 Scott Pellerin .15 .40
94 John Vanbiesbrouck .20 .50
95 Dave Andreychuk .25 .60
96 Paul Coffey .25 .60
97 Ron Tugnutt .20 .50
98 Larry Robinson .25 .60
99 Billy Smith .25 .60
100 Mario Lemieux 1.50 4.00
101 Martin Havlat RC 1.00 2.50
102 Petr Hubacek RC .30 .75
103 Niclas Wallin RC .40 1.00
104 Alexander Khavanov RC .30 .75
105 Roman Cechmanek RC .40 1.00
106 Bryce Salvador RC .40 1.00
107 Jonas Ronnqvist RC .30 .75
108 Rostislav Klesla RC .75 2.00
109 Justin Williams RC .75 2.00
110 Sascha Goc RC .30 .75
111 Andrew Raycroft RC .75 2.00
112 Marty Turco RC .60 1.50
113 Marian Gaborik RC 1.00 2.50
114 Josef Vasicek RC .75 2.00
115 Steven Reinprecht RC .50 1.25
116 Jani Hurme RC .30 .75
117 David Aebischer RC .60 1.50
118 Dale Purinton RC .30 .75
119 Jarno Kultanen RC .30 .75
120 Petr Svoboda RC .40 1.00
121 Eric Belanger RC .40 1.00
122 Petteri Nummelin RC .30 .75
123 Michel Riesen RC .40 1.00
124 Jason Labarbera RC .40 1.00
125 Tyler Bouck RC .30 .75
126 Martin Brodeur SL .50 1.25
127 Pavel Bure SL .30 .75
128 Peter Forsberg SL .30 .75
129 Scott Gomez SL .20 .50
130 Dominik Hasek SL .40 1.00
131 Brett Hull SL .40 1.00
132 Jaromir Jagr SL .60 1.50
133 Curtis Joseph SL .30 .75
134 Paul Kariya SL .30 .75
135 Chris Pronger SL .20 .50
136 Patrick Roy SL .60 1.50
137 Joe Sakic SL .40 1.00
138 Teemu Selanne SL .50 1.25
139 Steve Yzerman SL .75 2.00
140 Vincent Lecavalier SL .20 .50
141 Samuel Pahlsson SL .15 .40
142 Maxime Ouellet SL .25 .60
143 Kris Beech SL .15 .40
144 Henrik Sedin SL .40 1.00
145 Daniel Sedin SL .50 1.25
146 Milan Kraft SL .15 .40
147 Marty Turco SL .20 .50
148 Oleg Saprykin SL .15 .40
149 Brent Johnson SL .20 .50
150 Marian Gaborik SL .30 .75

2000-01 Topps Stars Blue

Randomly inserted in packs at the rate of 1:8, this 150-card set parallels the base set enhanced with blue foil. Card numbers 126-150 are sequentially numbered to 99, and the rest are sequentially numbered to 299.
*1-100 VETS/299: 4X TO 10X BASIC CARDS
*101-125 ROOK/299: 2X TO 5X BASIC RC
*126-150 SL/99: 6X TO 15X BASIC SL
92 Mark Messier 4.00 10.00

2000-01 Topps Stars All-Star Authority

COMPLETE SET (11) 8.00 15.00
STATED ODDS 1:9
ASA1 Ray Bourque .60 1.50
ASA2 Brett Hull .40 1.00
ASA3 Mark Messier .40 1.00
ASA4 Patrick Roy 2.00 5.00
ASA5 Jaromir Jagr .60 1.50
ASA6 Dominik Hasek .60 1.50
ASA7 Teemu Selanne .40 1.00
ASA8 Steve Yzerman 2.00 5.00
ASA9 Joe Sakic .60 1.50
ASA10 Pavel Bure .50 1.25
ASA11 John LeClair .40 1.00

2000-01 Topps Stars Autographs

Randomly inserted in packs at the rate of 1:15 (combined odds between Game Gear and Autographs), this 10-card set features a framed player photo on the left side of the card front with a whiteout area extending from the left card border down along the bottom border of the card where the player autograph appears. Each card is enhanced with gold foil highlights.
ABB Brian Boucher 6.00 15.00
ACP Chris Pronger 10.00 25.00
ALR Larry Robinson 10.00 25.00
AML Mario Lemieux 75.00 150.00
AMM Mike Modano 15.00 40.00
AMY Mike York 6.00 15.00
AVL Vincent Lecavalier 10.00 25.00
ABSM Billy Smith 12.00 30.00
ABST Brad Stuart 6.00 15.00

2000-01 Topps Stars Game Gear

Randomly inserted in packs at the rate of 1:15 (combined odds between Game Gear and Autographs), this 18-card set featured either a swatch of game worn jersey or game used stick. Two different game gear autograph cards were also available, and randomly inserted in packs at the rate of 1:5568 for the jersey cards and 1:12528 for the stick cards. The Don Cherry suit cards were randomly inserted at 1:49 Canadian packs or 1:392 Canadian packs for the autographed version.
GGAG Adam Graves J 3.00 8.00
GGCP Chris Pronger J 4.00 10.00
GGDC Don Cherry Suit 10.00 25.00
GGDCA D.Cherry Suit/AU 40.00 100.00
GGDL David Legwand J 3.00 8.00
GGDM Darren McCarty J 3.00 8.00
GGJA Jason Allison J 3.00 8.00
GGKT Keith Tkachuk S 10.00 25.00
GGMC Mariusz Czerkawski J 3.00 8.00
GGML Martin Lapointe J 3.00 8.00
GGMM Mike Modano S 8.00 20.00
GGMR Mike Richter J 4.00 10.00
GGPH Phil Housley J 3.00 8.00
GGPR Patrick Roy J 15.00 40.00
GGRT Ron Tugnutt S 8.00 20.00
GGSZ Sergei Zubov J 3.00 8.00
GGTA Tony Amonte J 3.00 8.00
GGTS Teemu Selanne J 4.00 10.00
GGZP Zigmund Palffy S 10.00 25.00
GGMR Mark Recchi S 10.00 25.00
GGCP Chris Pronger J/AU 100.00 200.00
GGMM Mike Modano S/AU 150.00 300.00

2000-01 Topps Stars Progression

Randomly inserted in packs at the rate of 1:11, this nine-card set features three players of the same position on an all foil card stock. Three portrait style photos are set against a blue background with yellow foil highlights. From left to right, the photos feature an established veteran star, an established star, and a young star.
COMPLETE SET (9) 15.00 40.00
P1 M.Lemieux / Modano / Lecav 3.00 8.00
P2 M.Lemieux / Forsberg / Stefan 3.00 8.00
P3 M.Lemieux / Yzerman / Gomez 3.00 8.00
P4 B.Smith / Roy / Loungo 3.00 8.00
P5 B.Smith / Brodeur / Turco 2.00 5.00
P6 B.Smith / Belfour / Boucher 1.25 3.00
P7 Robinson / S.Stevens / Klesla .75 2.00
P8 Robinson / Bourque / Stuart 2.00 5.00
P9 Robinson / Pronger / Skoula .75 2.00

2000-01 Topps Stars Walk of Fame

COMPLETE SET (10) 10.00 20.00
STATED ODDS 1:10
WF1 Pavel Bure .60 1.50
WF2 Paul Kariya .60 1.50
WF3 Jaromir Jagr .75 2.00
WF4 Peter Forsberg 1.25 3.00
WF5 Mike Modano .60 1.50
WF6 Patrick Roy 2.50 6.00
WF7 Steve Yzerman 2.50 6.00
WF8 Dominik Hasek 1.00 2.50
WF9 John LeClair .60 1.50
WF10 Martin Brodeur 1.25 3.00

1995-96 Topps SuperSkills

The 1995-96 Topps SuperSkills set was issued in one series totaling 90 cards. The 11-card packs originally retailed for $3.99. The set was a special one-off project designed to capitalize on Topps sponsorship of the SuperSkills program held in conjunction with the 1996 All-Star Game in Boston. The set features the players who were expected to compete in the following categories: Puck Control (1-18), Fastest Skater (19-36), Hardest Shot (37-54), Accuracy Shooting (55-72) and Rapid Fire/Breakaway Relay (73-90). The packs clearly identified which conference and event the cards inside would picture. A one-card-per-pack parallel set, "Platinum", parallels the basic set save for a platinum gilded-edge, player name, and Topps logo. Base set is Gold. Multipliers can be found in the header below to determine values for these.
COMPLETE SET (90) 8.00 20.00
1 Mario Lemieux .75 2.00
2 Adam Oates .15 .40
3 Donald Audette .07 .20
4 Andrew Cassels .07 .20
5 Pat LaFontaine .15 .40
6 Mathieu Schneider .07 .20
7 Scott Stevens .07 .20
8 Mikael Renberg .15 .40
9 Pierre Turgeon .15 .40
10 Steve Yzerman .75 2.00
11 Russ Courtnall .07 .20
12 Oleg Tverdovsky .15 .40
13 Craig Janney .07 .20
14 Doug Gilmour .20 .50
15 Wayne Gretzky 1.25 3.00
16 Paul Kariya .60 1.50
17 Joe Sakic .40 1.00
18 Peter Forsberg .40 1.00
19 Brian Leetch .20 .50
20 Jaromir Jagr .40 1.00
21 Geoff Sanderson .07 .20
22 Rob Niedermayer .15 .40
23 Ray Ferraro .07 .20
24 Alexandre Daigle .07 .20
25 Joe Juneau .15 .40
26 Don Sweeney .07 .20
27 Scott Niedermayer .07 .20
28 Mike Gartner .07 .20
29 Paul Coffey .15 .40
30 Pavel Bure .40 1.00
31 Teemu Selanne .30 .75
32 Mats Sundin .20 .50
33 Trevor Linden .15 .40
34 Sergei Fedorov .30 .75
35 Theo Fleury .20 .50
36 Alexander Mogilny .15 .40
37 Garry Galley .07 .20
38 Stu Barnes .07 .20
39 Glen Wesley .07 .20
40 Eric Lindros .40 1.00
41 Stephane Richer .07 .20
42 John LeClair .20 .50
43 Pat Verbeek .15 .40
44 Bill Guerin .07 .20
45 Wendel Clark .15 .40
46 Mike Modano .20 .50
47 Keith Primeau .15 .40
48 Brett Hull .25 .60
49 Al MacInnis .15 .40
50 Chris Chelios .20 .50
51 Keith Tkachuk .20 .50
52 Dave Andreychuk .07 .20
53 Kevin Hatcher .07 .20
54 Chris Pronger .07 .20
55 Brendan Shanahan .20 .50
56 Luc Robitaille .15 .40
57 Ray Bourque .30 .75
58 Mark Recchi .15 .40
59 Brian Bradley .07 .20
60 Mark Messier .25 .60
61 Kevin Stevens .07 .20
62 John MacLean .07 .20
63 Cam Neely .20 .50
64 Rick Tocchet .07 .20
65 Jeremy Roenick .20 .50
66 Phil Housley .07 .20
67 Jason Arnott .15 .40
68 Todd Harvey .07 .20
69 Jeff Friesen .15 .40
70 Alexei Zhamnov .15 .40
71 David Oliver .07 .20
72 Bernie Nicholls .07 .20
73 Jim Carey .15 .40
74 Mike Richter .15 .40
75 Dominik Hasek .30 .75
76 Sean Burke .07 .20
77 Ron Hextall .15 .40
78 John Vanbiesbrouck .20 .50
79 Tom Barrasso .15 .40
80 Martin Brodeur .40 1.00
81 Patrick Roy .75 2.00
82 Trevor Kidd .15 .40
83 Andy Moog .15 .40
84 Mike Vernon .07 .20
85 Felix Potvin .20 .50
86 Bill Ranford .15 .40
87 Kelly Hrudey .15 .40
88 Grant Fuhr .15 .40
89 Kirk McLean .15 .40
90 Ed Belfour .20 .50

1995-96 Topps SuperSkills Platinum

COMPLETE SET (90) 15.00 40.00
*PLATINUM: .6X TO 1.5X BASIC CARDS
ONE PER PACK

1995-96 Topps SuperSkills Super Rookies

Inserted one per Topps SuperSkills pack, this 15-card set features the cream of the 1995-96 rookie crop on 20 point all-foil board stock with gild-edge technology.
COMPLETE SET (15) 4.80 12.00
SR1 Ed Jovanovski .20 .50
SR2 Jason Bonsignore .08 .25
SR3 Jeff O'Neill .40 1.00
SR4 Cory Stillman .08 .25
SR5 Chad Kilger .20 .50
SR6 Aki Berg .20 .50
SR7 Todd Bertuzzi 1.25 3.00
SR8 Shane Doan .40 1.00
SR9 Kyle McLaren .20 .50
SR10 Radek Dvorak .20 .50
SR11 Saku Koivu 1.25 3.00
SR12 Daniel Alfredsson .40 1.00
SR13 Antti Tormanen .08 .25
SR14 Niklas Sundstrom .20 .50
SR15 Vitali Yachmenev .08 .25

2002-03 Topps Total

Released in late February, this 440-card set was one of the largest base sets of the year.
COMPLETE SET (440) 15.00 40.00
1 Nicklas Lidstrom .15 .40
2 Mikko Eloranta .10 .25
3 Richard Park .10 .25
4 Eric Lindros .25 .60
5 Vincent Lecavalier .12 .30
6 Dany Heatley .15 .40
7 Roman Turek .15 .40
8 Rostislav Klesla .10 .25
9 Paul Kariya .20 .50
10 Marian Hossa .12 .30
11 Patrick Roy .40 1.00
12 Henrik Sedin .15 .40
13 Adam Graves .12 .30
14 Ian Laperriere .12 .30
15 Jiri Fischer .10 .25
16 Nick Schultz .10 .25
17 Steve Sullivan .10 .25
18 Sandis Ozolinsh .12 .30
19 Evgeni Nabokov .12 .30
20 Dimitri Khristich .10 .25
21 Danny Markov .10 .25
22 Adam Foote .10 .25
23 David Vyborny .10 .25
24 Jocelyn Thibault .12 .30
25 Mike Leclerc .10 .25
26 Pavol Demitra .20 .50
27 Scott Mellanby .10 .25
28 Brent Sopel .10 .25
29 Brad Isbister .10 .25
30 Sami Salo .10 .25
31 Jose Theodore .15 .40
32 Simon Gagne .15 .40
33 Rem Murray .10 .25
34 Mike Ricci .12 .30
35 Kim Johnsson .10 .25
36 Adam Oates .15 .40
37 Taylor Pyatt .10 .25
38 Rod Brind'Amour .15 .40
39 Mike Modano .25 .60
40 Jason Woolley .10 .25
41 Dimitri Yushkevich .10 .25
42 Craig Johnson .10 .25
43 Tony Hrkac .10 .25
44 Scott Young .10 .25
45 Marian Gaborik .25 .60
46 Patrik Stefan .12 .30
47 Jon Klemm .10 .25
48 Andy McDonald .15 .40
49 Chris Pronger .12 .30
50 Frantisek Kaberle .10 .25
51 Jean-Sebastien Giguere .15 .40
52 Luc Robitaille .15 .40
53 Scott Stevens .15 .40
54 Roberto Luongo .25 .60
55 Teppo Numminen .12 .30
56 Alyn McCauley .10 .25
57 John Grahame .10 .25
58 David Legwand .12 .30
59 Hal Gill .10 .25
60 Mattias Ohlund .10 .25
61 Radim Vrbata .12 .30
62 Doug Gilmour .20 .50
63 Vaclav Prospal .10 .25
64 Brian Leetch .15 .40
65 Sheldon Keefe .10 .25
66 Randy McKay .10 .25
67 Mikael Samuelsson .10 .25
68 Pavel Bure .20 .50
69 Zdeno Chara .15 .40
70 P.J. Stock .10 .25
71 Shawn McEachern .10 .25
72 Radek Martinek .10 .25
73 Mike Rathje .10 .25
74 Kenny Jonsson .10 .25
75 Jamie Langenbrunner .12 .30
76 Chris Phillips .10 .25
77 Zigmund Palffy .15 .40
78 Stu Barnes .10 .25
79 Robert Reichel .10 .25
80 Jason Allison .12 .30
81 Dimitri Kalinin .10 .25
82 Chris Simon .10 .25
83 Arturs Irbe .12 .30
84 Tony Amonte .12 .30
85 Ruslan Salei .10 .25
86 Pascal Rheaume .10 .25
87 Marc Denis .12 .30
88 Marc Chouinard .10 .25
89 Jim Dowd .10 .25
90 Claude Lemieux .12 .30
91 Alexei Zhamnov .12 .30
92 Al MacInnis .15 .40
93 Cory Stillman .10 .25
94 Bob Boughner .10 .25
95 Kris Draper .10 .25
96 Mario Lemieux .50 1.25
97 Sean Burke .10 .25
98 Wes Walz .10 .25
99 Brenden Morrow .12 .30
100 Dave Andreychuk .15 .40
101 Jaromir Jagr .40 1.00
102 Markus Naslund .12 .30
103 Nick Boynton .10 .25
104 Sean Hill .10 .25
105 Trevor Linden .15 .40
106 Bryan Berard .10 .25
107 Chris Neilson .10 .25
108 Marco Sturm .10 .25
109 Oleg Petrov .10 .25
110 Scott Gomez .12 .30
111 Luke Richardson .10 .25
112 Manny Malhotra .10 .25
113 Valeri Bure .12 .30
114 Marcel Hossa .10 .25
115 Todd Marchant .10 .25
116 Radek Bonk .12 .30
117 Matt Bradley .10 .25
118 Jochen Hecht .10 .25
119 Dan McGillis .10 .25
120 Adrian Aucoin .10 .25
121 Eric Belanger .10 .25
122 Peter Forsberg .20 .50
123 Alexei Morozov .10 .25
124 Jimmie Olvestad .10 .25
125 Ed Jovanovski .12 .30
126 Chris Drury .15 .40
127 Alexander Mogilny .12 .30
128 Stephen Weiss .15 .40
129 Manny Legace .15 .40
130 Jarome Iginla .15 .40
131 Doug Weight .15 .40
132 Martin St. Louis .15 .40
133 Alexander Khavanov .10 .25
134 Chris Chelios .15 .40
135 Viktor Kozlov .10 .25
136 Bret Hedican .10 .25
137 Denis Arkhipov .10 .25
138 Jere Lehtinen .15 .40
139 Mathieu Schneider .10 .25
140 Tomas Kaberle .10 .25
141 Brian Gionta .12 .30
142 Janne Niinimaa .10 .25
143 Mark Parrish .10 .25
144 Todd White .10 .25
145 Geoff Sanderson .12 .30
146 Yanic Perreault .10 .25
147 Roman Hamrlik .10 .25
148 Mike Fisher .10 .25
149 Jiri Dopita .10 .25
150 Claude Lapointe .10 .25
151 Vaclav Nedorost .10 .25
152 Mikael Renberg .10 .25
153 Jozef Stumpel .10 .25
154 Felix Potvin .25 .60
155 Chris Gratton .10 .25
156 Adam Deadmarsh .12 .30
157 Sergei Fedorov .25 .60
158 Mike Sillinger .10 .25
159 Kris Beech .10 .25
160 Grant Marshall .10 .25
161 Brent Johnson .12 .30
162 Alexei Kovalev .15 .40
163 Darren McCarty .12 .30
164 Marc Savard .10 .25
165 Janne Laukkanen .10 .25
166 Phil Housley .12 .30
167 Tomas Holmstrom .10 .25
168 Bill Guerin .15 .40
169 Darius Kasparaitis .10 .25
170 Jaroslav Modry .10 .25
171 Martin Gelinas .10 .25
172 Peter Bondra .15 .40
173 Steven Reinprecht .10 .25
174 Anson Carter .12 .30
175 Eric Brewer .10 .25
176 Magnus Arvedson .10 .25
177 Patrice Brisebois .10 .25
178 Sergei Brylin .10 .25
179 Vitali Vishnevski .10 .25
180 Marcus Nilsson .10 .25
181 Niklas Sundstrom .10 .25
182 Daymond Langkow .12 .30
183 Craig Conroy .10 .25
184 Gary Roberts .10 .25
185 Justin Williams .12 .30
186 Matt Cooke .10 .25
187 Pierre Turgeon .15. .40
188 Steve Konowalchuk .10 .25
189 Yannick Tremblay .10 .25
190 Tom Poti .10 .25
191 Sergei Zholtok .10 .25
192 Robyn Regehr .10 .25
193 Mike Richter .15 .40
194 Shawn Bates .10 .25
195 Pavel Trnka .10 .25
196 Martin Straka .12 .30
197 Jonas Hoglund .10 .25
198 Filip Kuba .10 .25
199 Chris Osgood .15 .40
200 Brad May .10 .25
201 David Aebischer .12 .30
202 Fred Brathwaite .12 .30
203 Lubos Bartecko .10 .25
204 Marty Turco .15 .40
205 Petr Nedved .10 .25
206 Shayne Corson .10 .25
207 Sergei Samsonov .12 .30
208 Patrik Elias .15 .40
209 Martin Erat .10 .25
210 Krystofer Kolanos .10 .25
211 Joe Thornton .20 .50
212 Ivan Novoseltsev .10 .25
213 Eric Messier .10
214 Daniel Cleary .12
215 Alex Tanguay .12
216 Robert Lang .10
217 Wade Redden .10
218 Scott Walker .10
219 Milan Hejduk .12
220 Ken Daneyko .10
221 J-P Dumont .10
222 Ian Moran .10
223 Christian Berglund .10
224 Alexei Yashin .12
225 Brad Stuart .10
226 Donald Brashear .10
227 Curtis Brown .10
228 John LeClair .15
229 Manny Fernandez .12
230 Maxim Afinogenov .10
231 Roman Cechmanek .12
232 Tyler Wright .10
233 Slava Kozlov .10
234 Tyler Arnason .15
235 Sandy McCarthy .10
236 Pascal Dupuis .10
237 Olaf Kolzig .15
238 Kyle Calder .10
239 Jeremy Roenick .15
240 Mathieu Dandenault .10
241 Jeff O'Neill .10
242 Dave Tanabe .10
243 Calle Johansson .10
244 Greg deVries .10
245 Andrew Brunette .10
246 Dan Hinote .10
247 Jason Smith .10
248 Mark Bell .10
249 Pavel Kubina .10
250 Teemu Selanne .30
251 Vladimir Orszagh .10
252 Brad Ference .10
253 Darryl Sydor .10
254 Vitali Yachmenev .10
255 Scott Hartnell .15
256 Fredrik Modin .10
257 Alexei Zhitnik .12
258 Brett Hull .20
259 Glen Murray .12
260 Michael Peca .12
261 Owen Nolan .15
262 Tie Domi .12
263 Ville Nieminen .10
264 Rob Blake .15
265 Greg Johnson .10
266 Andrei Markov .15
267 Josef Vasicek .10
268 Ryan Smyth .12
269 Vincent Damphousse .12
270 Mark Recchi .20
271 Rob Niedermayer .12
272 Mariusz Czerkawski .10
273 Glen Wesley .10
274 Brian Boucher .12
275 Bryan McCabe .10
276 Ron Tugnutt .12
277 Daniel Briere .12
278 Igor Larionov .15
279 Keith Tkachuk .15
280 Mats Sundin .15
281 Dwayne Roloson .10
282 Andrew Cassels .10
283 Brendan Morrison .12
284 Bryan Smolinski .12
285 Jan Hlavac .10
286 Jamal Mayers .10
287 Kevin Weekes .12
288 Tim Connolly .10
289 Steve Yzerman .30
290 Derek Morris .10
291 Derian Hatcher .12
292 Steve Shields .12
293 Martin Brodeur .30
294 Marcus Ragnarsson .10
295 Scott Thornton .10
296 Oleg Kvasha .10
297 Mike York .10
298 Tomi Kallio .10
299 Martin Skoula .10
300 Jeff Halpern .10
301 Ed Belfour .15
302 Andrew Ference .10
303 Nikolai Khabibulin .15
304 Bryce Salvador .10
305 Lubomir Visnovsky .10
306 Dan Cloutier .12
307 Andy Delmore .10
308 Martin Lapointe .12
309 Daniel Sedin .15
310 Kelly Buchberger .12
311 Darcy Tucker .10
312 Sergei Berezin .10
313 Ruslan Fedotenko .10
314 Mark Messier .25
315 Mike Comrie .15
316 Bobby Holik .10
317 Shane Doan .12
318 Michal Handzus .12
319 Joe Sakic .25
320 Kristian Huselius .10
321 Ben Clymer .10
322 Mattias Norstrom .10
323 Pavel Datsyuk .20
324 Richard Matvichuk .10
325 Dainius Zubrus .10
326 Craig Rivet .10
327 Eric Desjardins .10
328 Patrick Marleau .15
329 Mike Grier .10
330 Steve Rucchin .10
331 Kimmo Timonen .10
332 Brendan Witt .10
333 Sami Kapanen .10
334 Todd Bertuzzi .15
335 Ilya Kovalchuk .20
336 Donald Audette .10
337 Georges Laraque .12
338 Jason Arnott .12
339 John Madden .10
340 Petr Sykora .12
341 Tommy Salo .12
342 Daniel Alfredsson .15
343 Eric Weinrich .10
344 Radek Dvorak .12
345 Stephane Yelle .10
346 Sergei Zubov .12
347 Milan Hnilicka .12
348 Lubomir Sekeras .10
349 Espen Knutsen .10
350 Travis Green .10
351 Jan Hrdina .10
352 Paul Laus .10
353 Bates Battaglia .10

354 Miroslav Satan .15 .40
355 Craig Berube .10 .25
356 Sean O'Donnell .10 .25
357 Joe Nieuwendyk .15 .40
358 Patrick Lalime .12 .30
359 Brian Rafalski .10 .25
360 Michael Nylander .10 .25
361 Jean-Luc Grand Pierre .10 .25
362 Ron Francis .20 .50
363 Andrei Nikolishin .10 .25
364 Dallas Drake .12 .30
365 Eric Daze .10 .25
366 Andreas Dackell .10 .25
367 Scott Niedermayer .15 .40
368 Chris Clark .10 .25
369 Brendan Shanahan .20 .50
370 Tomas Vokoun .12 .30
371 Johan Hedberg .15 .40
372 Nikita Alexeev .10 .25
373 Dave Scatchard .10 .25
374 Matt Cullen .10 .25
375 Steve Thomas .10 .25
376 Brian Rolston .12 .30
377 Richard Zednik .10 .25
378 Sergei Gonchar .12 .30
379 Keith Primeau .15 .40
380 Jeff Friesen .10 .25
381 Keith Carney .10 .25
382 Kirk Maltby .10 .25
383 Erik Cole .12 .30
384 Martin Biron .12 .30
385 Jody Shelley .10 .25
386 Brad Richards .15 .40
387 Michal Rozsival .12 .30
388 Martin Havlat .12 .30
389 Igor Korolev .10 .25
390 Ladislav Nagy .10 .25
391 Curtis Joseph .15 .40
392 Toni Lydman .10 .25
393 Antti Laaksonen .10 .25
394 Jeff Jillson .10 .25
395 Saku Koivu .15 .40
396 Trevor Letowski .10 .25
397 Ray Whitney .12 .30
398 Olli Jokinen .15 .40
399 Colin White .10 .25
400 Mike Dunham .12 .30
401 Dan Blackburn .12 .30
402 Ron Hainsey RC .40 1.00
403 Scottie Upshall RC .50 1.25
404 Anton Volchenkov RC .40 1.00
405 Dmitri Bykov RC .40 1.00
406 Steve Eminger RC .40 1.00
407 Lasse Pirjeta RC .40 1.00
408 Tomi Pettinen RC .40 1.00
409 Ales Hemsky RC 1.50 4.00
410 Chuck Kobasew RC .50 1.25
411 Jason Spezza RC 2.50 6.00
412 Jeff Paul RC .40 1.00
413 Adam Hall RC .40 1.00
414 Rick Nash RC 3.00 8.00
415 Kurt Sauer RC .40 1.00
416 Alexander Frolov RC .75 2.00
417 Patrick Sharp RC 1.25 3.00
418 Alexei Smirnov RC .50 1.25
419 Tom Koivisto RC .40 1.00
420 Jay Bouwmeester RC 1.25 3.00
421 Mikael Tellqvist RC .40 1.00
422 P-M Bouchard RC .60 1.50
423 Radovan Somik RC .40 1.00
424 Ivan Majesky RC .40 1.00
425 Jamie Lundmark .12 .30
426 Henrik Zetterberg RC 4.00 10.00
427 Dennis Seidenberg RC .60 1.50
428 Jeff Taffe RC .40 1.00
429 Martin Gerber RC .60 1.50
430 Lynn Loyns RC .40 1.00
431 Micki DuPont RC .40 1.00
432 Jonathan Cheechoo .12 .30
433 Eric Godard RC .40 1.00
434 Stanislav Chistov RC .40 1.00
435 Alexander Svitov RC .40 1.00
436 Fedor Fedorov .10 .25
437 Stephane Veilleux RC .40 1.00
438 Curtis Sanford RC .60 1.50
439 Jordan Leopold RC .60 1.50
440 Carlo Colaiacovo RC .60 1.50

2002-03 Topps Total Award Winners

COMPLETE SET (10) 8.00 15.00
STATED ODDS 1:36
AW1 Jarome Iginla .75 2.00
AW2 Patrick Roy 2.50 6.00
AW3 Nicklas Lidstrom .60 1.50
AW4 Jose Theodore .75 2.00
AW5 Dany Heatley .75 2.00
AW6 Ron Francis .50 1.25
AW7 Eric Daze .50 1.25
AW8 Chris Chelios .60 1.50
AW9 Saku Koivu .60 1.50
AW10 Michael Peca .50 1.25

2002-03 Topps Total Production

COMPLETE SET (15) 6.00 12.00
STATED ODDS 1:12
TP1 Jarome Iginla .40 1.00
TP2 Joe Sakic .60 1.50
TP3 Mats Sundin .30 .75
TP4 Peter Forsberg .75 2.00
TP5 Bill Guerin .25 .60
TP6 Brendan Shanahan .50 1.25
TP7 Sergei Fedorov .60 1.50
TP8 Pavel Bure .40 1.00
TP9 Jeremy Roenick .40 1.00
TP10 Tony Amonte .25 .60
TP11 Teemu Selanne .30 .75
TP12 Alexander Mogilny .25 .60
TP13 Markus Naslund .30 .75
TP14 Todd Bertuzzi .30 .75
TP15 Jaromir Jagr .50 1.25

2002-03 Topps Total Signatures

Inserted at a rate of 1:926, this 6-card set looked like the base set but carried the "certified autograph" notation on the card fronts.
SBG Brian Gionta 8.00 20.00
SEC Erik Cole 10.00 25.00
SKK Krystofer Kolanos 10.00 25.00
SRK Rostislav Klesla 12.00 30.00
SRV Radim Vrbata 12.00 30.00
SSW Stephen Weiss 12.00 30.00

2002-03 Topps Total Team Checklists

COMPLETE SET (30) 6.00 15.00
TC1 Ilya Kovalchuk .40 1.00
TC2 Joe Thornton .40 1.00
TC3 Miroslav Satan .10 .25
TC4 Jarome Iginla .40 1.00
TC5 Ron Francis .10 .25
TC6 Jocelyn Thibault .10 .25
TTC7 Patrick Roy 1.25 3.00
TTC8 Rick Nash .40 1.00
TTC9 Mike Modano .40 1.00
TTC10 Steve Yzerman .75 2.00
TTC11 Tommy Salo .10 .25
TTC12 Roberto Luongo .40 1.00
TTC13 Jason Allison .10 .25
TTC14 Paul Kariya .30 .75
TTC15 Marian Gaborik .40 1.00
TTC16 Jose Theodore .40 1.00
TTC17 Mike Dunham .20 .50
TTC18 Martin Brodeur .75 2.00
TTC19 Michael Peca .10 .25
TTC20 Pavel Bure .30 .75
TTC21 Daniel Alfredsson .20 .50
TTC22 John LeClair .10 .25
TTC23 Tony Amonte .10 .25
TTC24 Mario Lemieux 1.25 3.00
TTC25 Owen Nolan .20 .50
TTC26 Keith Tkachuk .20 .50
TTC27 Nikolai Khabibulin .30 .75
TTC28 Mats Sundin .30 .75
TTC29 Todd Bertuzzi .10 .25
TTC30 Jaromir Jagr .60 1.50

2002-03 Topps Total Topps

COMPLETE SET (20) 8.00 15.00
STATED ODDS 1:6
TT1 Jarome Iginla .25 .60
TT2 Patrick Roy 1.00 2.50
TT3 Nicklas Lidstrom .20 .50
TT4 Jose Theodore .25 .60
TT5 Joe Sakic .40 1.00
TT6 Mats Sundin .20 .50
TT7 Ilya Kovalchuk .25 .60
TT8 Joe Thornton .30 .75
TT9 Mike Modano .30 .75
TT10 Brett Hull .25 .60
TT11 Steve Yzerman 1.00 2.50
TT12 Curtis Joseph .20 .50
TT13 Paul Kariya .20 .50
TT14 Patrik Elias .12 .30
TT15 Martin Brodeur .50 1.25
TT16 Eric Lindros .20 .50
TT17 Daniel Alfredsson .12 .30
TT18 Mario Lemieux 1.25 3.00
TT19 Owen Nolan .12 .30
TT20 Jaromir Jagr .30 .75

2003-04 Topps Traded

Released in late-April, this 165-card set consisted of 84 veterans who were traded earlier in the season and rookies who made their debut late in the season.
COMPLETE SET (165) 25.00 50.00
TT1 Felix Potvin .25 .60
TT2 Chris Drury .12 .30
TT3 Karel Rachunek .10 .25
TT4 Miikka Kiprusoff .12 .30
TT5 Justin Williams .12 .30
TT6 Bryan Berard .12 .30
TT7 Jim Vandermeer .10 .25
TT8 Shayne Corson .10 .25
TT9 Teemu Selanne .30 .75
TT10 Peter Worrell .10 .25
TT11 Darryl Sydor .10 .25
TT12 Todd Marchant .10 .25
TT13 Ray Whitney .12 .30
TT14 Robert Lang .10 .25
TT15 Adam Oates .15 .40
TT16 Jozef Stumpel .10 .25
TT17 Luc Robitaille .15 .40
TT18 Roman Cechmanek .12 .30
TT19 Martin Straka .10 .25
TT20 Sergei Fedorov .25 .60
TT21 Michael Nylander .10 .25
TT22 Steve Sullivan .10 .25
TT23 Steve Konowalchuk .10 .25
TT24 Valeri Bure .10 .25
TT25 Jaromir Jagr .40 1.00
TT26 Peter Bondra .12 .30
TT27 Mike Grier .10 .25
TT28 Cory Stillman .10 .25
TT29 Joe Nieuwendyk .15 .40
TT30 Brian Leetch .15 .40
TT31 Johan Hedberg .12 .30
TT32 Andrew Raycroft .12 .30
TT33 Chuck Kobasew .10 .25
TT34 Brett McLean .10 .25
TT35 Craig Andersson .15 .40
TT36 Michael Leighton .10 .25
TT37 Matthew Barnaby .12 .30
TT38 Philippe Sauve .12 .30
TT39 Chris Gratton .10 .25
TT40 Radek Dvorak .12 .30
TT41 Raffi Torres .10 .25
TT42 Ossi Vaananen .10 .25
TT43 Trent Klatt .10 .25
TT44 Alexander Daigle .12 .30
TT45 Sergei Gonchar .10 .25
TT46 Niklas Sundstrom .10 .25
TT47 Michael Ryder .12 .30
TT48 Igor Larionov .15 .40
TT49 Jan Hrdina .10 .25
TT50 Cliff Ronning .10 .25
TT51 Trent Hunter .10 .25
TT52 Alexei Zhamnov .12 .30
TT53 Tommy Salo .12 .30
TT54 Danny Markov .10 .25
TT55 Sean Burke .10 .25
TT56 Shane Doan .12 .30
TT57 Konstantin Koltsov .10 .25
TT58 Mike Danton .10 .25
TT59 John Grahame .10 .25
TT60 Dimitry Afanasenkov .12 .30
TT61 Bryan Marchment .10 .25
TT62 Mikael Tellqvist .12 .30
TT63 Jason King .10 .25
TT64 Anson Carter .12 .30
TT65 Steve Shields .12 .30
TT66 Ron Francis .20 .50
TT67 Petr Nedved .10 .25
TT68 Alexander Svitov .10 .25
TT69 Ville Nieminen .10 .25
TT70 Martin Skoula .10 .25
TT71 Steve Yzerman .40 1.00
TT72 Jason Spezza .15 .40
TT73 Stanislav Chistov .10 .25
TT74 Pascal Leclaire .10 .25
TT75 Mike Comrie .12 .30
TT76 Brent Johnson .12 .30
TT77 Mike Rupp .10 .25
TT78 Derek Morris .10 .25
TT79 Geoff Sanderson .10 .25
TT80 Martin Rucinsky .10 .25
TT81 Shaone Morrisonn .10 .25
TT82 Paul Kariya .20 .50
TT83 Alex Kovalev .12 .30
TT84 Jeff Jillson .10 .25
TT85 Kari Lehtonen RC 1.25 3.00
TT86 Karl Stewart RC .25 .60
TT87 Sergei Zinovjev RC .25 .60
TT88 Carl Corazzini RC .25 .60
TT89 Andrew Peters RC .30 .75
TT90 Derek Roy RC .40 1.00
TT91 Matthew Lombardi RC .30 .75
TT92 Alan Rourke RC .25 .60
TT93 Pavel Vorobiev RC .30 .75
TT94 Lasse Kukkonen RC .25 .60
TT95 Travis Moen RC .30 .75
TT96 Matt Keith RC .25 .60
TT97 Marek Svatos RC .50 1.25
TT98 Cody McCormick RC .30 .75
TT99 Mike Green RC .30 .75
TT100 Mikhail Kuleshov RC .25 .60
TT101 Dan Fritsche RC .25 .60
TT102 Nikolai Zherdev RC .50 1.25
TT103 Aaron Johnson RC .25 .60
TT104 Tim Jackman RC .30 .75
TT105 Trevor Daley RC .40 1.00
TT106 Nathan Robinson RC .25 .60
TT107 Niklas Kronwall RC .50 1.25
TT108 Darryl Bootland RC .30 .75
TT109 Tony Salmelainen RC .25 .60
TT110 Mike Bishai RC .25 .60
TT111 Gregory Campbell RC .25 .60
TT112 Tim Gleason RC .30 .75
TT113 Dustin Brown RC .50 1.25
TT114 Noah Clarke RC .25 .60
TT115 Chris Kunitz RC .50 1.25
TT116 Tony Martensson RC .25 .60
TT117 Brent Burns RC .60 1.50
TT118 Chris Higgins RC .50 1.25
TT119 Dan Hamhuis RC .30 .75
TT120 Marek Zidlicky RC .25 .60
TT121 Andrew Hutchinson RC .25 .60
TT122 Paul Martin RC .30 .75
TT123 Aleksandar Suglobov RC .25 .60
TT124 David Hale RC .25 .60
TT125 Sean Bergenheim RC .30 .75
TT126 Jed Ortmeyer RC .25 .60
TT127 Lawrence Nycholat RC .30 .75
TT128 Dominic Moore RC .25 .60
TT129 Fedor Tyutin RC .25 .60
TT130 Garth Murray RC .30 .75
TT131 Antoine Vermette RC .50 1.25
TT132 Joni Pitkanen RC .40 1.00
TT133 Antero Niittymaki RC .60 1.50
TT134 Matthew Spiller RC .30 .75
TT135 Fredrik Sjostrom RC .40 1.00
TT136 Ryan Malone RC .50 1.25
TT137 Matt Murley RC .30 .75
TT138 Andy Chiodo RC .25 .60
TT139 Tom Preissing RC .30 .75
TT140 Wade Brookbank RC .30 .75
TT141 Ryan Kesler RC 1.25 3.00
TT142 Nathan Smith RC .25 .60
TT143 Boyd Gordon RC .30 .75
TT144 Alexander Semin RC .75 2.00
TT145 Rastislav Stana RC .40 1.00
TT146 Cory Larose RC .25 .60
TT147 Rob Scuderi RC .30 .75
TT148 Ryan Barnes RC .25 .60
TT149 Matt Ellison RC .25 .60
TT150 Milan Michalek RC .50 1.25
TT151 Kyle Wellwood RC .40 1.00
TT152 Jame Pollock RC .25 .60
TT153 Dwayne Zinger RC .25 .60
TT154 Dan Ellis RC .30 .75
TT155 Patrick Leahy RC .30 .75
TT156 Jozef Balej RC .25 .60
TT157 Colton Orr RC .30 .75
TT158 Julien Vauclair RC .25 .60
TT159 Darcy Verot RC .25 .60
TT160 Christian Ehrhoff RC .30 .75
TT161 Boyd Kane RC .25 .60
TT162 Tuomas Pihlman RC .30 .75
TT163 John-Michael Liles RC .30 .75
TT164 Anton Babchuk RC .25 .60
TT165 Owen Fussey RC .25 .60

2003-04 Topps Traded Blue

*TT1-TT84 VETS/500: 4X TO 10X
*TT85-TT165 ROOKIE/500: 1.5X TO 4X

2003-04 Topps Traded Gold

*TT1-TT84 VETS/50: 10X TO 25X
*TT85-TT165 ROOKIE/50: 4X TO 10X

2003-04 Topps Traded Red

*TT1-TT84 VETS/100: 8X TO 20X
*TT85-TT165 ROOKIE/100: 3X TO 8X

2003-04 Topps Traded Franchise Fabrics

Memorabilia in Topps Traded was inserted at an overall rate of 3:24. No further insertion info was made available.
FFJT Joe Thornton 5.00 12.00
FFIK Ilya Kovalchuk
FFMB Martin Brodeur 15.00 40.00
FFMG Marian Gaborik 5.00 12.00
FFML Mario Lemieux 20.00 50.00
FFJS Joe Sakic 5.00 12.00
FFAY Alexei Yashin 3.00 8.00
FFVL Vincent Lecavalier 5.00 12.00
FFPM Patrick Marleau 4.00 10.00
FFMT Marty Turco 3.00 8.00
FFDA Daniel Alfredsson 3.00 8.00
FFBG Bill Guerin 3.00 8.00
FFTV Tomas Vokoun 3.00 8.00
FFMR Mark Recchi 3.00 8.00
FFZP Zigmund Palffy 3.00 8.00
FFKP Keith Primeau 3.00 8.00
FFJSG Jean-Sebastien Giguere 3.00 8.00
FFTB Todd Bertuzzi
FFRL Roberto Luongo 5.00 12.00
FFJI Jarome Iginla 5.00 12.00
FFRN Rick Nash 5.00 12.00
FFJTH Jose Theodore 5.00 12.00
FFMS Mats Sundin 4.00 10.00

2003-04 Topps Traded Future Phenoms

Memorabilia in Topps Traded was inserted at an overall rate of 3:24. No further insertion info was made available.
FPRM Ryan Miller 5.00 12.00
FPMS Matthew Stajan 4.00 10.00
FPDA David Aebischer 4.00 10.00
FPNH Nathan Horton 4.00 10.00
FPAV Antoine Vermette 2.00 5.00
FPPS Peter Sejna 2.00 5.00
FPJOL Joffrey Lupul 4.00 10.00
FPJL Jordan Leopold 2.00 5.00
FPSB Sean Bergenheim 2.00 5.00
FPMR Mike Ribeiro 2.00 5.00
FPJLU Jamie Lundmark 2.00 5.00
FPMW Mattias Weinhandl 2.00 5.00
FPDH Dan Hamhuis 2.00 5.00
FPNB Nick Boynton 2.00 5.00
FPJB Jay Bouwmeester 4.00 10.00
FPJP Joni Pitkanen 2.00 5.00
FPAH Adam Hall 2.00 5.00
FPSC Stanislav Chistov 2.00 5.00
FPAM Antti Miettinen 2.00 5.00
FPSW Stephen Weiss 2.00 5.00
FPRR Robyn Regehr 2.00 5.00
FPAF Alexander Frolov 4.00 10.00
FPBR Brad Richards 5.00 12.00
FPAT Alex Tanguay 4.00 10.00
FPBJ Barret Jackman 2.00 5.00
FPPD Pavel Datsyuk 4.00 10.00

2014 Topps U.S. Olympic Team

COMPLETE SET (100) 10.00 25.00
51 Hilary Knight .25 .60
53 Jocelyne Lamoureux .15 .40
54 Monique Lamoureux .15 .40

2014 Topps U.S. Olympic Team Bronze

*BRONZE: .5X TO 1.2X BASIC CARDS
STATED ODDS ONE PER PACK

2014 Topps U.S. Olympic Team Gold

*GOLD: 1.5X TO 4X BASIC CARDS
STATED ODDS 1:8

2014 Topps U.S. Olympic Team Silver

*SILVER: .6X TO 1.5X BASIC CARDS
STATED ODDS 1:2

2014 Topps U.S. Olympic Team Autographs

OVERALL AUTO ODDS ONE PER BOX
51 Hilary Knight 20.00 50.00

2014 Topps U.S. Olympic Team Autographs Bronze

*BRONZE/50: SAME AS BASIC AUTO
STATED ODDS 1:126

2014 Topps U.S. Olympic Team Autographs Gold

*GOLD/15: .6X TO 1.5X BASIC AUTO
STATED ODDS 1:418

2014 Topps U.S. Olympic Team Autographs Silver

*SILVER/30: .5X TO 1.2X BASIC AUTO
STATED ODDS 1:209

2014 Topps U.S. Olympic Team Champions Autographs

STATED ODDS 1:72 15.00 40.00
UOCJC Jim Craig 20.00 50.00
UOCME Mike Eruzione 35.00 70.00

2014 Topps U.S. Olympic Team Commemorative Pins

STATED ODDS 1:267
USPML Monique Lamoureux 8.00 20.00

2014 Topps U.S. Olympic Team Games of the XXII Olympiad

COMPLETE SET (15) 10.00 25.00
STATED ODDS 1:8
OLYHK Hilary Knight 1.50 4.00
Ice Hockey

2014 Topps U.S. Olympic Team Relics

STATED ODDS 1:26
ORHKN Hilary Knight 8.00 20.00

2014 Topps U.S. Olympic Team Relics Bronze

*BRONZE/75: SAME PRICE AS BASIC CARD
STATED ODDS 1:87

2014 Topps U.S. Olympic Team Relics Gold

GOLD/25: .6X TO 1.5X BASIC CARDS
STATED ODDS 1:261

2014 Topps U.S. Olympic Team Relics Silver

*SILVER/50: .5X TO 1.2X BASIC CARDS
STATED ODDS 1:131

2014 Topps U.S. Olympic Team Sochi Patch

STATED ODDS 1:133
USPJL Jocelyne Lamoureux 6.00 15.00
USPML Monique Lamoureux 6.00 15.00

1963-64 Toronto Star

This set of 42 photos was distributed one per week with the Toronto Star and was also available as a complete set directly. The photos measure approximately 4 3/4" by 6 3/4" and are entitled, "Hockey Stars in Action." There is a short write-up on the back of each photo. The player's team is identified in the checklist below, Boston Bruins (BB), Chicago Blackhawks (CBH), Detroit Red Wings (DRW), Montreal Canadiens (MC), New York Rangers (NYR), and Toronto Maple Leafs (TML). Since the photos are unnumbered, they are listed below in alphabetical order.
COMPLETE SET (42) 150.00 300.00
1 George Armstrong TML 4.00 8.00
2 Andy Bathgate NYR 4.00 8.00
3 Bob Baun TML 2.50 5.00
4 Jean Beliveau MC 7.50 15.00
5 Leo Boivin BB 2.50 5.00
6 Johnny Bower TML 5.00 10.00
7 Carl Brewer TML 2.50 5.00
8 Johnny Bucyk BB 4.00 8.00
9 Alex Delvecchio DRW 5.00 10.00
10 Kent Douglas TML 2.00 4.00
11 Dick Duff TML 2.50 5.00
12 Bill Gadsby DRW 3.00 6.00
13 Jean-Guy Gendron BB 2.00 4.00
14 BoomBoom Geoffrion MC 7.50 15.00
15 Glenn Hall CBH 6.00 12.00
16 Doug Harvey NYR 5.00 10.00
17 Bill Hay CBH 2.50 5.00
18 Camille Henry NYR 2.50 5.00
19 Tim Horton TML 7.50 15.00
20 Gordie Howe DRW 25.00 50.00
21 Bobby Hull CBH 15.00 30.00
22 Red Kelly TML 5.00 10.00
23 Dave Keon TML 7.50 15.00
24 Parker MacDonald DRW 2.00 4.00
25 Frank Mahovlich TML 7.50 15.00
26 Stan Mikita CBH 7.50 15.00
27 Dickie Moore MC 5.00 10.00
28 Eric Nesterenko CBH 2.50 5.00
29 Marcel Pronovost DRW 2.50 5.00
30 Claude Provost MC 2.50 5.00
31 Bob Pulford TML 3.00 6.00
32 Henri Richard MC 7.50 15.00
33 Terry Sawchuk DRW 10.00 20.00
34 Eddie Shack TML 5.00 10.00
35 Allan Stanley TML 3.00 6.00
36 Ron Stewart TML 2.00 4.00
37 Jean-Guy Talbot MC 2.50 5.00
38 Gilles Tremblay MC 2.00 4.00
39 J.C. Tremblay MC 2.50 5.00
40 Norm Ullman DRW 4.00 8.00
41 Elmer Vasko CBH 2.00 4.00
42 Ken Wharram CBH 2.50 5.00

1964-65 Toronto Star

This set of 48 photos was distributed one per week with the Toronto Star and was also available as a complete set directly. The direct complete sets also included a booklet and glossy photo of Dave Keon in the mail-away package. These blank-backed photos measure approximately 4 1/8" by 5 1/8". The player's team is identified in the checklist below, Boston Bruins (BB), Chicago Blackhawks (CBH), Detroit Red Wings (DRW), Montreal Canadiens (MC), New York Rangers (NYR), and Toronto Maple Leafs (TML). Since the photos are unnumbered, they are listed below in alphabetical order. There was an album (actually a folder) available for each team to slot in cards. However when the cards were placed in the album it rendered the card's caption unreadable as only the action photo was visible.
COMPLETE SET (48) 150.00 300.00
1 Dave Balon MC 2.00 4.00
2 Andy Bathgate TML 4.00 8.00
3 Bob Baun TML 3.00 6.00
4 Jean Beliveau MC 7.50 15.00
5 Red Berenson MC 2.50 5.00
6 Leo Boivin BB 3.00 6.00
7 Carl Brewer TML 2.50 5.00
8 Alex Delvecchio DRW 4.00 8.00
9 Rod Gilbert NYR 4.00 8.00
10 Ted Green BB 2.50 5.00
11 Glenn Hall CBH 5.00 10.00
12 Billy Harris TML 2.00 4.00
13 Bill Hay CBH 2.00 4.00
14 Paul Henderson DRW 3.00 6.00
15 Wayne Hillman CBH 2.00 4.00
16 Charlie Hodge MC 3.00 6.00
17 Tim Horton TML 7.50 15.00
18 Gordie Howe DRW 20.00 40.00
19 Harry Howell NYR 3.00 6.00
20 Bobby Hull CBH 12.50 25.00
21 Larry Jeffrey DRW 2.00 4.00
22 Tom Johnson BB 3.00 6.00
23 Forbes Kennedy BB 2.00 4.00
24 Dave Keon TML 6.00 12.00
25 Orland Kurtenbach BB 2.50 5.00
26 Jacques Laperriere MC 2.50 5.00
27 Parker MacDonald DRW 2.00 4.00
28 Al MacNeil CBH 2.00 4.00
29 Frank Mahovlich TML 6.00 12.00
30 Chico Maki CBH 2.00 4.00
31 Don McKenney TML 2.00 4.00
32 John McKenzie CBH 2.50 5.00
33 Stan Mikita CBH 6.00 12.00
34 Jim Neilson NYR 2.00 4.00
35 Jim Pappin TML 2.00 4.00
36 Pierre Pilote CBH 3.00 6.00
37 Jacques Plante NYR 10.00 20.00
38 Marcel Pronovost DRW 3.00 6.00
39 Claude Provost MC 2.50 5.00
40 Bob Pulford TML 3.00 6.00
41 Henri Richard MC 6.00 12.00
42 Wayne Rivers BB 2.00 4.00
43 Floyd Smith DRW 2.00 4.00
44 Allan Stanley TML 4.00 8.00
45 Ron Stewart TML 2.00 4.00
46 J.C. Tremblay MC 2.50 5.00
47 Norm Ullman DRW 4.00 8.00
48 Elmer Vasko CBH 2.00 4.00
xx Album 12.50 25.00
Folder

1971-72 Toronto Sun

This set of 294 photo cards with two punch holes has never been very popular with collectors. The photos are quite fragile, printed on thin paper, and measure approximately 5" by 7". The checklist below is in team order as follows: Boston Bruins (1-21), Buffalo Sabres (22-41), California Golden Seals (42-61), Chicago Blackhawks (62-82), Detroit Red Wings (83-103), Los Angeles Kings (104-124), Minnesota North Stars (125-145), Montreal Canadiens (146-166), New York Rangers (167-186), Philadelphia Flyers (187-208), Pittsburgh Penguins (209-230), St. Louis Blues (231-252), Toronto Maple Leafs (253-274), and Vancouver Canucks (275-294). The cards were intended to fit in a two-ring binder specially made to hold the cards. Also included was and introduction photo, with text by Scott Young.
COMPLETE SET (294) 300.00 600.00
1 Boston Bruins 1.50 3.00
2 Don Awrey .50 1.00
3 Garnet Bailey .50 1.00
4 Ivan Boldirev .50 1.00
5 Johnny Bucyk 3.00 6.00
6 Wayne Cashman .75 1.50
7 Gerry Cheevers 4.00 8.00
8 Phil Esposito 10.00 20.00
9 Ted Green .75 1.50
10 Ken Hodge .75 1.50
11 Ed Johnston 1.50 3.00
12 Reggie Leach 1.50 3.00
13 Don Marcotte .50 1.00
14 John McKenzie .50 1.00
15 Bobby Orr 30.00 60.00
16 Derek Sanderson 4.00 8.00
17 Dallas Smith .50 1.00
18 Richard Allan Smith .50 1.00
19 Fred Stanfield .50 1.00
20 Mike Walton .75 1.50
21 Ed Westfall .75 1.50
22 Buffalo Sabres 1.00 2.00
23 Doug Barrie .50 1.00
24 Roger Crozier 2.00 4.00
25 Dave Dryden 1.00 2.00
26 Dick Duff .75 1.50
27 Phil Goyette .50 1.00
28 Al Hamilton .50 1.00
29 Larry Keenan .50 1.00
30 Danny Lawson .50 1.00
31 Don Luce .50 1.00
32 Richard Martin 1.00 2.00
33 Ray McKay .50 1.00
34 Gerry Meehan .75 1.50
35 Kevin O'Shea .50 1.00
36 Gilbert Perreault 4.00 8.00
37 Tracy Pratt .50 1.00
38 Mike Robitaille .50 1.00
39 Eddie Shack 2.00 4.00
40 Jim Watson .50 1.00
41 Rod Zaine .50 1.00
42 California Seals 1.50 3.00
43 Wayne Carleton .50 1.00
44 Lyle Carter .50 1.00
45 Gary Croteau .50 1.00
46 Norm Ferguson .50 1.00
47 Stan Gilbertson .50 1.00
48 Ernie Hicke .50 1.00
49 Gary Jarrett 1.00 2.00
50 Joey Johnston .50 1.00
51 Marshall Johnston .50 1.00
52 Bert Marshall .50 1.00
53 Walt McKechnie .50 1.00
54 Don O'Donoghue .50 1.00
55 Gerry Pinder .75 1.50
56 Dick Redmond .50 1.00
57 Robert Sheehan .50 1.00
58 Paul Shmyr .50 1.00
59 Ron Stackhouse SP 6.00 12.00
60 Carol Vadnais .50 1.00
61 Tom Williams .50 1.00
62 Chicago Blackhawks 1.50 3.00
63 Lou Angotti .50 1.00
64 Bryan Campbell .50 1.00
65 Tony Esposito 10.00 20.00
66 Bobby Hull 15.00 30.00
67 Dennis Hull 1.00 2.00
68 Doug Jarrett .50 1.00
69 Jerry Korab .50 1.00
70 Cliff Koroll .50 1.00
71 Darryl Maggs .50 1.00
72 Keith Magnuson .75 1.50
73 Chico Maki .75 1.50
74 Dan Maloney .50 1.00
75 Pit Martin .75 1.50
76 Stan Mikita 6.00 12.00
77 Eric Nesterenko .50 1.00
78 Danny O'Shea .50 1.00
79 Jim Pappin .50 1.00
80 Gary Smith 1.00 2.00
81 Pat Stapleton .50 1.00
82 Bill White .50 1.00
83 Detroit Red Wings 1.50 3.00
84 Red Berenson .75 1.50
85 Gary Bergman .75 1.50
86 Arnie Brown .50 1.00
87 Guy Charron .50 1.00
88 Bill Collins .50 1.00
89 Brian Conacher .50 1.00
90 Joe Daley 1.50 3.00
91 Alex Delvecchio 3.00 6.00
92 Marcel Dionne 7.50 15.00
93 Tim Ecclestone .50 1.00
94 Ron Harris .50 1.00
95 Gerry Hart .50 1.00
96 Gordie Howe 25.00 50.00
97 Al Karlander .50 1.00
98 Nick Libett .75 1.50
99 Ab McDonald .50 1.00
100 James Niekamp .50 1.00
101 Mickey Redmond 2.00 4.00
102 Leon Rochefort .50 1.00
103 Al Smith .75 1.50
104 Los Angeles Kings 1.00 2.00
105 Ralph Backstrom .75 1.50
106 Bob Berry .75 1.50
107 Mike Byers .50 1.00
108 Larry Cahan .50 1.00
109 Paul Curtis .50 1.00
110 Denis DeJordy 1.50 3.00
111 Gary Edwards 1.00 2.00
112 Bill Flett .50 1.00
113 Butch Goring .75 1.50
114 Lucien Grenier .50 1.00
115 Larry Hillman .50 1.00
116 Dale Hoganson .50 1.00
117 Harry Howell 1.50 3.00
118 Eddie Joyal .50 1.00
119 Real Lemieux .50 1.00
120 Ross Lonsberry .50 1.00
121 Al McDonough .50 1.00
122 Jean Potvin .50 1.00
123 Bob Pulford 1.50 3.00
124 Juha Widing .75 1.50
125 Minnesota North Stars 1.00 2.00
126 Fred Barrett .50 1.00
127 Charlie Burns .50 1.00
128 Jude Drouin .50 1.00
129 Barry Gibbs .50 1.00
130 Gilles Gilbert 2.00 4.00
131 Bill Goldsworthy 1.00 2.00
132 Danny Grant .75 1.50
133 Ted Hampson .50 1.00
134 Ted Harris .50 1.00
135 Fred Harvey .50 1.00
136 Cesare Maniago 2.00 4.00
137 Doug Mohns .75 1.50
138 Lou Nanne .75 1.50
139 Bob Nevin .75 1.50
140 Dennis O'Brien .50 1.00
141 Murray Oliver .50 1.00
142 Jean-Paul Parise .75 1.50
143 Dean Prentice .75 1.50
144 Tom Reid .50 1.00
145 Gump Worsley 3.00 6.00
146 Montreal Canadiens 1.50 3.00
147 Pierre Bouchard .50 1.00
148 Yvan Cournoyer 3.00 6.00
149 Ken Dryden 25.00 50.00
150 Terry Harper .75 1.50
151 Rejean Houle .75 1.50
152 Guy Lafleur 15.00 30.00
153 Jacques Laperriere 1.00 2.00
154 Guy Lapointe 1.50 3.00
155 Claude Larose .50 1.00
156 Jacques Lemaire 2.00 4.00
157 Frank Mahovlich 6.00 12.00
158 Pete Mahovlich .75 1.50
159 Phil Myre 1.50 3.00
160 Larry Pleau .75 1.50
161 Henri Richard 6.00 12.00
162 Phil Roberto .50 1.00
163 Serge Savard 1.50 3.00
164 Marc Tardif .75 1.50
165 J.C. Tremblay .75 1.50
166 Rogatien Vachon 3.00 6.00
167 New York Rangers 1.50 3.00
168 Dave Balon .50 1.00
169 Ab DeMarco .50 1.00
170 Jack Egers .50 1.00
171 Bill Fairbairn .50 1.00
172 Ed Giacomin 4.00 8.00
173 Rod Gilbert 2.00 4.00
174 Vic Hadfield .75 1.50
175 Ted Irvine .50 1.00
176 Bruce MacGregor .50 1.00
177 Jim Neilson .50 1.00
178 Brad Park 3.00 6.00
179 Jean Ratelle 2.00 4.00
180 Dale Rolfe .50 1.00
181 Bobby Rousseau .75 1.50
182 Glen Sather 1.50 3.00
183 Rod Seiling .50 1.00
184 Pete Stemkowski .75 1.50
185 Walt Tkaczuk .75 1.50
186 Gilles Villemure 1.50 3.00
187 Philadelphia Flyers 1.50 3.00
188 Barry Ashbee 1.00 2.00
189 Serge Bernier .50 1.00
190 Larry Brown .50 1.00
191 Bobby Clarke 10.00 20.00
192 Gary Dornhoefer .75 1.50
193 Doug Favell 1.50 3.00
194 Bruce Gamble 2.00 4.00
195 Jean-Guy Gendron .50 1.00
196 Larry Hale .50 1.00
197 Wayne Hillman .50 1.00
198 Brent Hughes .50 1.00
199 Jim Johnson .50 1.00
200 Bob Kelly .50 1.00
201 Andre Lacroix .75 1.50
202 Bill Lesuk .50 1.00
203 Rick MacLeish 1.00 2.00
204 Larry Mickey .50 1.00
205 Simon Nolet .50 1.00
206 Pierre Plante .50 1.00
207 Ed Van Impe .50 1.00
208 Joe Watson .50 1.00
209 Pittsburgh Penguins 1.00 2.00
210 Syl Apps .75 1.50
211 Les Binkley 1.50 3.00
212 Wally Boyer .50 1.00
213 Darryl Edestrand .50 1.00
214 Roy Edwards 1.50 3.00
215 Nick Harbaruk .50 1.00
216 Bryan Hextall .75 1.50
217 Bill Hicke .50 1.00
218 Tim Horton 5.00 10.00
219 Sheldon Kannegiesser .50 1.00
220 Bob Leiter .50 1.00
221 Keith McCreary .50 1.00
222 Joe Noris .50 1.00
223 Greg Polis .50 1.00
224 Jean Pronovost .75 1.50
225 Rene Robert .75 1.50
226 Duane Rupp .50 1.00
227 Ken Schinkel .50 1.00
228 Ron Schock .50 1.00
229 Bryan Watson .75 1.50
230 Bob Woytowich .50 1.00
231 St. Louis Blues 1.00 2.00
232 Al Arbour 1.50 3.00
233 John Arbour .50 1.00
234 Chris Bordeleau .50 1.00
235 Carl Brewer .75 1.50
236 Gene Carr .50 1.00
237 Wayne Connelly .50 1.00
238 Terry Crisp .75 1.50
239 Jim Lorentz .50 1.00
240 Peter McDuffe 1.00 2.00
241 George Morrison .50 1.00
242 Michel Parizeau .50 1.00
243 Noel Picard .50 1.00
244 Barclay Plager .75 1.50
245 Bob Plager .75 1.50
246 Jim Roberts .50 1.00
247 Gary Sabourin .50 1.00
248 Jim Shires .50 1.00
249 Frank St.Marseille .50 1.00
250 Bill Sutherland .50 1.00
251 Garry Unger 1.00 2.00
252 Ernie Wakely 1.50 3.00
253 Toronto Maple Leafs 1.50 3.00
254 Bob Baun .75 1.50
255 Jim Dorey .50 1.00
256 Denis Dupere .50 1.00
257 Ron Ellis .75 1.50
258 Brian Glennie .50 1.00
259 Jim Harrison .50 1.00
260 Paul Henderson 1.00 2.00
261 Dave Keon 3.00 6.00
262 Rick Ley .50 1.00
263 Billy MacMillan .50 1.00
264 Don Marshall .50 1.00
265 Jim McKenny .50 1.00
266 Garry Monahan .50 1.00
267 Bernie Parent 6.00 12.00
268 Mike Pelyk .50 1.00
269 Jacques Plante 10.00 20.00
270 Brad Selwood .50 1.00
271 Darryl Sittler 6.00 12.00
272 Brian Spencer 1.00 2.00
273 Guy Trottier .50 1.00
274 Norm Ullman 2.50 5.00
275 Vancouver Canucks 1.00 2.00
276 Andre Boudrias .50 1.00
277 George Gardiner .50 1.00
278 Jocelyn Guevremont .75 1.50
279 Murray Hall .50 1.00
280 Danny Johnson .50 1.00
281 Dennis Kearns .50 1.00
282 Orland Kurtenbach .75 1.50
283 Bobby Lalonde .50 1.00
284 Wayne Maki .50 1.00
285 Rosaire Paiement .75 1.50
286 Paul Popiel .50 1.00
287 Pat Quinn 1.00 2.00
288 John Schella .50 1.00
289 Bobby Schmautz .75 1.50
290 Fred Speck .50 1.00
291 Dale Tallon .75 1.50
292 Ron Ward .50 1.00
293 Barry Wilkins .50 1.00
294 Dunc Wilson 1.50 3.00
xx Binder 12.50 25.00
NNO Introduction Card 2.00 4.00

2017-18 Toronto Maple Leafs Centennial

1 Rick Vaive .40 1.00
2 Ace Bailey .50 1.25
3 Eddie Shack .50 1.25
4 Johnny Bower .50 1.25
5 Rick Kehoe .40 1.00
6 Errol Thompson .40 1.00
7 Glenn Anderson .50 1.25
8 Alyn McCauley .40 1.00
9 Barry Melrose .40 1.00
10 Bob Rouse .40 1.00
11 Auston Matthews 2.00 5.00
12 Bob Neely .40 1.00
13 Ed Belfour .60 1.50
14 John Anderson .40 1.00
15 Brian Glennie .40 1.00
16 Bryan Berard .40 1.00
17 Red Horner .40 1.00
18 Mitch Marner .75 2.00
19 Red Kelly .40 1.00
20 King Clancy .40 1.00

21 Bruce Boudreau .40 1.00
22 Syl Apps .40 1.00
23 Bill Barilko .40 1.00
24 Nick Metz .40 1.00
25 Vincent Damphousse .40 1.00
26 Grant Fuhr .60 1.50
27 Jonas Hoglund .40 1.00
28 Gary Leeman .40 1.00
29 Doug Gilmour .60 1.50
30 Allan Bester .40 1.00
31 Dick Irvin .40 1.00
32 Dan Maloney .40 1.00
33 Dmitry Yushkevich .40 1.00
34 Lanny McDonald .50 1.25
35 Dave Hannan .30 .75
36 Dave Reid .30 .75
37 Bob Baun .40 1.00
38 Daniel Marois .40 1.00
39 Phil Kessel .60 1.50
40 Fredrik Modin .40 1.00
41 Norm Ullman .50 1.25
42 Ken Baumgartner .40 1.00
43 Gary Roberts .50 1.25
44 Ian Turnbull .40 1.00
45 King Clancy .40 1.00
46 Mike Foligno .40 1.00
47 Jamie Macoun .40 1.00
48 Robert Reichel .40 1.00
49 Jim McKenny .40 1.00
50 Darryl Sittler .50 1.25
51 Jim Morrison .40 1.00
52 Garry Valk .40 1.00
53 Bill Berg .30 .75
54 Jason Blake .30 .75
55 Nik Antropov .40 1.00
56 Jim Dorey .40 1.00
57 Terry Sawchuk .40 1.00
58 Gordie Drillon .40 1.00
59 James van Riemsdyk .50 1.25
60 Peter Ihnacak .40 1.00
61 Nazem Kadri .40 1.00
62 Morgan Rielly .50 1.25
63 Wilf Paiement .40 1.00
64 Frank Mahovlich .50 1.25
65 Bill Derlago .40 1.00
66 Pete Stemkowski .40 1.00
67 Jake Gardiner .40 1.00
68 Wendel Clark .60 1.50
69 Russ Courtnall .40 1.00
70 Howie Meeker .40 1.00
71 Leo Komarov .30 .75
72 Harry Lumley .40 1.00
73 Pat Boutette .40 1.00
74 Mike Krushelnyski .40 1.00
75 Tom Fergus .40 1.00
76 Charlie Conacher .40 1.00
77 Todd Warriner .40 1.00
78 Ed Olczyk .40 1.00
79 Terry Martin .40 1.00
80 Frederik Andersen .40 1.00
81 Shayne Corson .40 1.00
82 Felix Potvin .50 1.25
83 Dion Phaneuf .40 1.00
84 Miroslav Frycer .40 1.00
85 Kyle Wellwood .40 1.00
86 Mark Osborne .40 1.00
87 Al Iafrate .40 1.00
88 Don Metz .40 1.00
89 William Nylander .75 2.00
90 Borje Salming .40 1.00
91 Dave Andreychuk .50 1.25
92 Mike Gartner .50 1.25
93 Laurie Boschman .40 1.00
94 Sergei Berezin .40 1.00
95 Tyler Bozak .40 1.00
96 Mike Walton .40 1.00
97 Tomas Kaberle .40 1.00
98 Ron Ellis .40 1.00
99 Mike Johnson .40 1.00
100 Carlton .40 1.00
101 Charlie Conacher CAP .60 1.50
102 Red Horner CAP .60 1.50
103 Syl Apps CAP .60 1.50
104 Bob Davidson CAP .60 1.50
105 Darryl Sittler CAP .75 2.00
106 Rick Vaive CAP .60 1.50
107 Wendel Clark CAP 1.00 2.50
108 Doug Gilmour CAP 1.00 2.50
109 Dion Phaneuf CAP .60 1.50
110 Syl Apps TW .60 1.50
111 Gordie Drillon TW .60 1.50
112 Syl Apps TW .60 1.50
113 Howie Meeker TW .60 1.50
114 Harry Lumley TW .60 1.50
115 Frank Mahovlich TW .75 2.00
116 Red Kelly TW .60 1.50
117 Johnny Bower TW .75 2.00
118 Terry Sawchuk TW .60 1.50
119 Johnny Bower TW .75 2.00
120 Doug Gilmour TW 1.00 2.50
121 Jason Blake TW .50 1.25
122 Auston Matthews TW 3.00 8.00
123 Johnny Bower RN .75 2.00
124 Red Kelly RN .60 1.50
125 Bill Barilko RN .60 1.50
126 Ace Bailey RN .75 2.00
127 King Clancy RN .60 1.50
128 Charlie Conacher RN .60 1.50
129 Syl Apps RN .60 1.50
130 Wendel Clark RN 1.00 2.50
131 Borje Salming RN .60 1.50
132 Frank Mahovlich RN .75 2.00
133 Darryl Sittler RN .75 2.00
134 Doug Gilmour RN 1.00 2.50
135 Felix Potvin RH .75 2.00
136 Ed Belfour RH 1.00 2.50
137 Doug Gilmour RH 1.00 2.50
138 Borje Salming RH .60 1.50
139 Darryl Sittler RH .75 2.00
140 Gary Roberts RH .75 2.00
141 Felix Potvin RH .75 2.00
142 Rick Vaive RH .60 1.50
143 Darryl Sittler RH .75 2.00
144 Felix Potvin RH .75 2.00
145 Wendel Clark RH 1.00 2.50
146 Harry Lumley RH .60 1.50
147 Borje Salming RH .60 1.50
148 Mitch Marner RH 1.25 3.00
149 Auston Matthews RH 3.00 8.00
150 King Clancy HOF .60 1.50
151 Dick Irvin HOF .60 1.50
152 Syl Apps HOF .60 1.50
153 Charlie Conacher HOF .60 1.50
154 Red Horner HOF .60 1.50
155 Red Kelly HOF .60 1.50
156 Terry Sawchuk HOF .60 1.50
157 Ace Bailey HOF .75 2.00
158 Gordie Drillon HOF .60 1.50
159 Johnny Bower HOF .75 2.00
160 Harry Lumley HOF .60 1.50
161 Frank Mahovlich HOF .75 2.00
162 Norm Ullman HOF .75 2.00
163 Darryl Sittler HOF .75 2.00
164 Lanny McDonald HOF .75 2.00
165 Borje Salming HOF .60 1.50
166 Howie Meeker HOF .60 1.50
167 Doug Gilmour HOF 1.00 2.50
168 Ed Belfour HOF 1.00 2.50
169 Ace Bailey MM .75 2.00
170 Syl Apps MM .60 1.50
171 Howie Meeker MM .60 1.50
172 Howie Meeker MM .60 1.50
173 Don Metz MM .60 1.50
174 Bill Barilko MM .60 1.50
175 Harry Lumley MM .60 1.50
176 Red Kelly MM .60 1.50
177 Bob Baun MM .60 1.50
178 Terry Sawchuk MM .60 1.50
179 Red Kelly MM .60 1.50
180 Norm Ullman MM .75 2.00
181 Darryl Sittler MM .75 2.00
182 Darryl Sittler MM .75 2.00
183 Ian Turnbull MM .60 1.50
184 Ian Turnbull MM .60 1.50
185 Lanny McDonald MM .75 2.00
186 Rick Vaive MM .60 1.50
187 Wendel Clark MM 1.00 2.50
188 Wendel Clark MM 1.00 2.50
189 Gary Leeman MM .60 1.50
190 Doug Gilmour MM 1.00 2.50
191 Doug Gilmour MM 1.00 2.50
192 Felix Potvin MM .75 2.00
193 Dave Andreychuk MM .75 2.00
194 Gary Roberts MM .75 2.00
195 Ed Belfour MM 1.00 2.50
196 Ed Belfour MM 1.00 2.50
197 James van Riemsdyk MM .75 2.00
198 Auston Matthews MM 3.00 8.00
199 Auston Matthews MM 3.00 8.00
200 Auston Matthews MM 3.00 8.00

2017-18 Toronto Maple Leafs Centennial Gold

1 Rick Vaive 5.00 12.00
11 Auston Matthews 30.00 80.00
18 Mitch Marner 20.00 50.00

2017-18 Toronto Maple Leafs Centennial Green

*GREEN/25: 8X TO 20X BASIC CARDS
*SP.GREEN: 8X TO 20X BASIC CARDS
11 Auston Matthews 80.00 200.00
122 Auston Matthews TW 80.00 200.00
149 Auston Matthews RH 80.00 200.00
198 Auston Matthews MM 80.00 200.00
199 Auston Matthews MM 80.00 200.00
200 Auston Matthews MM 80.00 200.00

2017-18 Toronto Maple Leafs Centennial AKA Autographs

AKAAI Al Iafrate B 50.00 125.00
AKABB Bob Baun B 50.00 125.00
AKABO Bruce Boudreau B 50.00 125.00
AKADA Dave Andreychuk B 60.00 150.00
AKADG Doug Gilmour A 250.00 450.00
AKAEB Ed Belfour A 200.00 300.00
AKAES Eddie Shack B 50.00 125.00
AKAFP Felix Potvin B 80.00 200.00
AKAPS Pete Stemkowski B 50.00 125.00
AKARV Rick Vaive A
AKAWC Wendel Clark B 100.00 200.00

2017-18 Toronto Maple Leafs Centennial Blue Die Cut

*BLUE DIE-CUT: .75X TO 2X BASIC CARDS
11 Auston Matthews 8.00 20.00

2017-18 Toronto Maple Leafs Centennial Championship Banners

COMMON CARD 6.00 15.00
191718 1917-18 Maple Leafs 6.00 15.00
192122 1921-22 Maple Leafs 6.00 15.00
193132 1931-32 Maple Leafs 6.00 15.00
194142 1941-42 Maple Leafs 6.00 15.00
194445 1944-45 Maple Leafs 6.00 15.00
194647 1946-47 Maple Leafs 6.00 15.00
194748 1947-48 Maple Leafs 6.00 15.00
194849 1948-49 Maple Leafs 6.00 15.00
195051 1950-51 Maple Leafs 6.00 15.00
196162 1961-62 Maple Leafs 6.00 15.00
196263 1962-63 Maple Leafs 6.00 15.00
196364 1963-64 Maple Leafs 6.00 15.00
196667 1966-67 Maple Leafs 6.00 15.00

2017-18 Toronto Maple Leafs Centennial Maple Leaf Marks

COMMON CARD 12.00 30.00
SEMISTARS 15.00 40.00
UNLISTED STARS 20.00 50.00
MLMAB Allan Bester D 15.00 40.00
MLMAI Al Iafrate F 15.00 40.00
MLMAL Alyn McCauley D 15.00 40.00
MLMAM Auston Matthews A 1000.00 1500.00
MLMAN Glenn Anderson C 80.00 200.00
MLMBB Bob Baun G 15.00 40.00
MLMBD Bill Derlago F 15.00 40.00
MLMBE Bryan Berard E 15.00 40.00
MLMBG Brian Glennie F 15.00 40.00
MLMBI Bill Berg G 12.00 30.00
MLMBL Jason Blake G 12.00 30.00
MLMBN Bob Neely E 40.00 100.00
MLMBO Bruce Boudreau F 15.00 40.00
MLMBR Bob Rouse F 15.00 40.00
MLMBS Borje Salming B 150.00 250.00
MLMCB Connor Brown E 20.00 50.00
MLMDA Dave Andreychuk C 80.00 200.00
MLMDG Doug Gilmour A 250.00 400.00
MLMDH Dave Hannan F 12.00 30.00
MLMDM Dan Maloney G 30.00 80.00
MLMDR Dave Reid G 12.00 30.00
MLMDS Darryl Sittler B 150.00 300.00
MLMEB Ed Belfour A 200.00 300.00
MLMEO Ed Olczyk F 15.00 40.00
MLMES Eddie Shack E 15.00 40.00
MLMET Errol Thompson F 15.00 40.00
MLMFA Frederik Andersen F 15.00 40.00
MLMFM Frank Mahovlich B 200.00 300.00
MLMFO Mike Foligno F 15.00 40.00
MLMFP Felix Potvin C 60.00 150.00
MLMFR Fredrik Modin D 15.00 40.00
MLMGF Grant Fuhr A 500.00 700.00
MLMGL Gary Leeman G 15.00 40.00
MLMGR Gary Roberts F 20.00 50.00
MLMGV Garry Valk G 15.00 40.00
MLMHL Larry Hillman G 15.00 40.00
MLMHM Howie Meeker D 150.00 250.00
MLMIT Ian Turnbull F 15.00 40.00
MLMJA John Anderson E 15.00 40.00
MLMJB Johnny Bower B 250.00 400.00
MLMJD Jim Dorey E 15.00 40.00
MLMJH Jonas Hoglund G 15.00 40.00
MLMJI Jim Morrison F 15.00 40.00
MLMJM Jamie Macoun E 15.00 40.00
MLMJV Jack Valiquette F 15.00 40.00
MLMKB Ken Baumgartner F 15.00 40.00
MLMKE Rick Kehoe G 15.00 40.00
MLMKM Kirk Muller E 15.00 40.00
MLMKO Mike Komisarek F 15.00 40.00
MLMLB Laurie Boschman F 15.00 40.00
MLMLM Lanny McDonald B 100.00 200.00
MLMMA Daniel Marois G 15.00 40.00
MLMMC Jim McKenny G 15.00 40.00
MLMME Barry Melrose F 15.00 40.00
MLMMF Miroslav Frycer E 15.00 40.00
MLMMG Mike Gartner E 20.00 50.00
MLMMJ Mike Johnson F 15.00 40.00
MLMMK Mike Krushelnyski G 15.00 40.00
MLMMM Mitch Marner A 350.00 500.00
MLMMO Mark Osborne F 15.00 40.00
MLMMR Morgan Rielly B 80.00 200.00
MLMMU Larry Murphy E 100.00 250.00
MLMMW Mike Walton F 15.00 40.00
MLMNA Nik Antropov F 15.00 40.00
MLMON Owen Nolan D 80.00 200.00
MLMPB Pat Boutette F 15.00 40.00
MLMPH Pat Hickey F 15.00 40.00
MLMPI Peter Ihnacak F 15.00 40.00
MLMPS Pete Stemkowski G 15.00 40.00
MLMRC Russ Courtnall F 15.00 40.00
MLMRE Ron Ellis G 15.00 40.00
MLMRK Red Kelly A 250.00 400.00
MLMRL Rick Ley F 15.00 40.00
MLMRP Rob Pearson F 15.00 40.00
MLMRR Robert Reichel F 15.00 40.00
MLMRV Rick Vaive D 25.00 60.00
MLMRW Ron Wilson F 15.00 40.00
MLMSB Sergei Berezin F 15.00 40.00
MLMSC Shayne Corson F 15.00 40.00
MLMTF Tom Fergus G 15.00 40.00
MLMTK Tomas Kaberle D 15.00 40.00
MLMTM Terry Martin F 15.00 40.00
MLMTW Todd Warriner F 15.00 40.00
MLMVD Vincent Damphousse D 40.00 100.00
MLMWC Wendel Clark C 150.00 250.00
MLMWE Kyle Wellwood G 15.00 40.00
MLMWP Wilf Paiement F 15.00 40.00

2017-18 Toronto Maple Leafs Centennial Maple Leafs Materials

MLAM Auston Matthews C 50.00 125.00
MLBE Jonathan Bernier D 10.00 25.00
MLCB Connor Brown C 12.00 30.00
MLDG Doug Gilmour A 200.00 400.00
MLDP Dion Phaneuf D 10.00 25.00
MLEB Ed Belfour B 25.00 60.00
MLES Eddie Shack B 15.00 40.00
MLFA Frederik Andersen D 10.00 25.00
MLFP Felix Potvin C 12.00 30.00
MLJB Johnny Bower B 30.00 80.00
MLJG Jake Gardiner C 10.00 25.00
MLJV James van Riemsdyk C 12.00 30.00
MLKU Nikolay Kulemin C 12.00 30.00
MLLM Lanny McDonald A 80.00 150.00
MLMG Mike Gartner C 12.00 30.00
MLMM Mitch Marner C 20.00 50.00
MLMR Morgan Rielly D 12.00 30.00
MLNA Nik Antropov D 10.00 25.00
MLNK Nazem Kadri C 10.00 25.00
MLNZ Nikita Zaitsev C 10.00 25.00
MLPK Phil Kessel D 15.00 40.00
MLRV Rick Vaive C 10.00 25.00
MLTB Tyler Bozak D 10.00 25.00
MLTK Tomas Kaberle C 10.00 25.00
MLWN William Nylander C 15.00 40.00

2017-18 Toronto Maple Leafs Centennial Maple Leafs Materials Duos

ML2AR F.Andersen/M.Rielly 30.00 80.00
ML2BP E.Belfour/F.Potvin 50.00 125.00
ML2BV T.Bozak/J.van Riemsdyk 15.00 40.00
ML2GK J.Gardiner/T.Kaberle 40.00 100.00
ML2KB N.Kadri/C.Brown 30.00 80.00
ML2MM A.Matthews/M.Marner
ML2SB E.Shack/J.Bower

2017-18 Toronto Maple Leafs Centennial Maple Leafs Materials Trios

ML3BBA Belfour/Bower/Andersen 150.00 250.00
ML3NMM Nylander/Matthews/Marner 300.00 450.00
ML3VBK van Riemsdyk/Bozak/Kadri 60.00 150.00

2017-18 Toronto Maple Leafs Centennial Treasured Relics

TRBB Bob Baun/25 100.00 250.00
TRBS Borje Salming/15 80.00 200.00
TRDP Dion Phaneuf/25 80.00 150.00
TRFP Felix Potvin/15
TRGF Grant Fuhr/25 350.00 450.00
TRGR Gary Roberts/25
TRNK Nazem Kadri/25 250.00 350.00
TRTS Terry Sawchuk/10

2013-14 Totally Certified

ONE ROOKIE PER PACK
1 Taylor Hall 1.00 2.50
2 Jordan Eberle .50 1.25
3 David Perron .30 .75
4 Sam Gagner .40 1.00
5 Ryan Nugent-Hopkins .50 1.25
6 Roberto Luongo .50 1.25
7 Henrik Sedin .50 1.25
8 Kevin Bieksa .40 1.00
9 Daniel Sedin .50 1.25
10 Chris Tanev .40 1.00
11 Curtis Glencross .30 .75
12 Dennis Wideman .30 .75
13 Mike Cammalleri .40 1.00
14 T.J. Brodie .30 .75
15 Mikael Backlund .40 1.00
16 P.K. Subban .75 2.00
17 Andrei Markov .50 1.25
18 Carey Price 1.50 4.00
19 Max Pacioretty .50 1.25
20 Tomas Plekanec .50 1.25
21 Evander Kane .50 1.25
22 Andrew Ladd .50 1.25
23 Zach Bogosian .40 1.00
24 Ondrej Pavelec .50 1.25
25 Al Montoya .30 .75
26 Jason Spezza .50 1.25
27 Milan Michalek .30 .75
28 Erik Karlsson 1.00 2.50
29 Craig Anderson .50 1.25
30 Kyle Turris .30 .75
31 Phil Kessel .60 1.50
32 Nazem Kadri .50 1.25
33 Joffrey Lupul .40 1.00
34 James van Riemsdyk .50 1.25
35 Dion Phaneuf .50 1.25
36 Niklas Backstrom .40 1.00
37 Mikko Koivu .40 1.00
38 Zach Parise .50 1.25
39 Jason Pominville .40 1.00
40 Josh Harding .50 1.25
41 Brad Marchand .60 1.50
42 Tuukka Rask .50 1.25
43 Patrice Bergeron .60 1.50
44 David Krejci .50 1.25
45 Loui Eriksson .40 1.00
46 Drew Stafford .50 1.25
47 Tyler Ennis .40 1.00
48 Ryan Miller .50 1.25
49 Tyler Myers .40 1.00
50 Thomas Vanek .50 1.25
51 John Tavares 1.00 2.50
52 Kyle Okposo .50 1.25
53 Lubomir Visnovsky .30 .75
54 Matt Moulson .40 1.00
55 Evgeni Nabokov .40 1.00
56 Martin Brodeur 1.00 2.50
57 Cory Schneider .40 1.00
58 Patrik Elias .50 1.25
59 Jaromir Jagr 1.25 3.00
60 Travis Zajac .40 1.00
61 Rick Nash .50 1.25
62 Carl Hagelin .50 1.25
63 Ryan Callahan .50 1.25
64 Dan Girardi .30 .75
65 Henrik Lundqvist .60 1.50
66 Henrik Zetterberg .60 1.50
67 Brendan Smith .40 1.00
68 Jimmy Howard .50 1.25
69 Daniel Alfredsson .50 1.25
70 Pavel Datsyuk .60 1.50
71 Jonathan Toews 1.00 2.50
72 Patrick Sharp .50 1.25
73 Patrick Kane 1.00 2.50
74 Brent Seabrook .50 1.25
75 Corey Crawford .60 1.50
76 Evgeni Malkin 1.50 4.00
77 Rob Scuderi .30 .75
78 Sidney Crosby 2.00 5.00
79 Chris Kunitz .50 1.25
80 Marc-Andre Fleury .75 2.00
81 Scott Hartnell .50 1.25
82 Claude Giroux .50 1.25
83 Sean Couturier .50 1.25
84 Brayden Schenn .50 1.25
85 Braydon Coburn .30 .75
86 Braden Holtby .75 2.00
87 Karl Alzner .30 .75
88 Alex Ovechkin 2.00 5.00
89 Martin Erat .30 .75
90 Nicklas Backstrom .75 2.00
91 Jack Johnson .30 .75
92 Sergei Bobrovsky .50 1.25
93 R.J. Umberger .30 .75
94 Nathan Horton .50 1.25
95 Marian Gaborik .50 1.25
96 Joe Pavelski .50 1.25
97 Antti Niemi .40 1.00
98 Logan Couture .50 1.25
99 Brent Burns .60 1.50
100 Joe Thornton .50 1.25
101 Semyon Varlamov .50 1.25
102 Gabriel Landeskog .40 1.00
103 Paul Stastny .50 1.25
104 Matt Duchene .50 1.25
105 Alex Tanguay .30 .75
106 Alexander Steen .50 1.25
107 David Backes .50 1.25
108 T.J. Oshie .75 2.00
109 Alex Pietrangelo .40 1.00
110 Kevin Shattenkirk .50 1.25
111 Eric Staal .60 1.50
112 Jordan Staal .50 1.25
113 Jeff Skinner .40 1.00
114 Tuomo Ruutu .40 1.00
115 Cam Ward .50 1.25
116 David Legwand .40 1.00
117 Mike Fisher .40 1.00
118 Shea Weber .40 1.00
119 Roman Josi .50 1.25
120 Pekka Rinne .60 1.50
121 Dustin Brown .50 1.25
122 Jeff Carter .50 1.25
123 Justin Williams .40 1.00
124 Slava Voynov .40 1.00
125 Jonathan Quick .75 2.00
126 Teemu Selanne 1.00 2.50
127 Ryan Getzlaf .75 2.00
128 Francois Beauchemin .30 .75
129 Jonas Hiller .40 1.00
130 Corey Perry .50 1.25
131 Antoine Vermette .30 .75
132 Mike Ribeiro .40 1.00
133 Mike Smith .50 1.25
134 Shane Doan .40 1.00
135 Martin Hanzal .30 .75
136 Jamie Benn .60 1.50
137 Stephane Robidas .30 .75
138 Kari Lehtonen .40 1.00
139 Shawn Horcoff .30 .75
140 Tyler Seguin .75 2.00
141 Martin St. Louis .50 1.25
142 Ryan Malone .30 .75
143 Steven Stamkos 1.00 2.50
144 Anders Lindback .30 .75
145 Ben Bishop .50 1.25
146 Shawn Matthias .30 .75
147 Brian Campbell .30 .75
148 Scottie Upshall .30 .75
149 Erik Gudbranson .50 1.25
150 Jacob Markstrom .40 1.00
151 Drew Shore RC .75 2.00
152 Cristopher Nilstorp RC .75 2.00
153 Charlie Coyle RC 1.00 2.50
154 Sami Vatanen RC 1.00 2.50
155 Michael Sgarbossa RC .75 2.00
156 Danny DeKeyser RC 1.25 3.00
157 Tyler Toffoli RC 2.00 5.00
158 Ben Street RC .60 1.50
159 Thomas Hickey RC .75 2.00
160 Cory Conacher RC .60 1.50
161 Jack Campbell RC .75 2.00
162 Filip Forsberg RC 2.50 6.00
163 Edward Pasquale RC .60 1.50
164 Max Reinhart RC 1.00 2.50
165 Alex Killorn RC 1.00 2.50
166 Calvin Pickard RC 1.00 2.50
167 Jared Staal RC 1.00 2.50
168 J.T. Miller RC 1.00 2.50
169 Emerson Etem RC 1.00 2.50
170 Ryan Murphy RC 1.00 2.50
171 Nicklas Jensen RC .75 2.00
172 Mikhail Grigorenko RC 1.25 3.00
173 Nikita Kucherov RC 2.50 6.00
174 Richard Panik RC 1.00 2.50
175 Brock Nelson RC 1.00 2.50
176 Tom Wilson RC 1.50 4.00
177 Michael Caruso RC .60 1.50
178 Justin Schultz RC 1.00 2.50
179 Antoine Roussel RC 1.00 2.50
180 Eric Hartzell RC 1.00 2.50
181 Austin Watson RC .75 2.00
182 Vladimir Tarasenko RC 4.00 10.00
183 Anthony Peluso RC .60 1.50
184 Brendan Gallagher RC 3.00 8.00
185 Michal Jordan RC .60 1.50
186 Petr Mrazek RC 2.00 5.00
187 Stefan Matteau RC .75 2.00
188 Tye McGinn RC 1.00 2.50
189 Jarred Tinordi RC 1.00 2.50
190 Nail Yakupov RC 3.00 8.00
191 Frederik Andersen RC 1.50 4.00
192 Mark Arcobello RC 1.00 2.50
193 Ryan Spooner RC 1.00 2.50
194 Zach Redmond RC .75 2.00
195 Carl Soderberg RC 1.00 2.50
196 Jordan Schroeder RC 1.00 2.50
197 Nick Bjugstad RC 1.25 3.00
198 Philipp Grubauer RC 1.00 2.50
199 Jamie Oleksiak RC .75 2.00
200 Eric Gryba RC .75 2.00
201 Scott Laughton RC 1.00 2.50
202 Dmitrij Jaskin RC 1.00 2.50
203 Quinton Howden RC .75 2.00
204 Nathan Beaulieu RC .75 2.00
205 Mikael Granlund RC 1.50 4.00
206 Jonathan Huberdeau RC 2.50 6.00
207 Tanner Pearson RC 1.00 2.50
208 Viktor Fasth RC 1.00 2.50
209 Jonas Brodin RC .75 2.00
210 Brian Flynn RC .75 2.00
211 Rickard Rakell RC 1.00 2.50
212 Nick Petrecki RC .60 1.50
213 Beau Bennett RC 1.25 3.00
214 Brian Lashoff RC .75 2.00
215 Alex Chiasson RC 1.00 2.50
216 Dougie Hamilton RC 2.00 5.00
217 Alex Galchenyuk RC 3.00 8.00
218 Matt Irwin RC .75 2.00
219 Johan Larsson RC .75 2.00
220 Christian Thomas RC .75 2.00
221 Michael Kostka RC .75 2.00
222 Kevin Connauton RC .75 2.00
223 Darcy Kuemper RC 1.00 2.50
224 Frank Corrado RC .60 1.50
225 Mark Pysyk RC 1.00 2.50
226 Rasmus Ristolainen RC 1.50 4.00
227 Marek Mazanec RC 1.00 2.50
228 Jon Merrill RC 1.00 2.50
229 Nathan MacKinnon RC 8.00 20.00
230 Zemgus Girgensons RC 2.00 5.00
231 Joakim Nordstrom RC .75 2.00
232 Jacob Trouba RC 1.50 4.00
233 Tomas Hertl RC 1.25 3.00
234 Aleksander Barkov RC 2.50 6.00
235 Jesper Fast RC .75 2.00
236 Elias Lindholm RC 1.50 4.00
237 Xavier Ouellet RC 1.00 2.50
238 Matt Nieto RC .75 2.00
239 Olli Maatta RC 5.00 12.00
240 Sean Monahan RC 1.50 4.00
241 Seth Jones RC 1.00 2.50
242 Valeri Nichushkin RC 1.00 2.50
243 Boone Jenner RC 1.00 2.50
244 Ryan Murray RC 1.50 4.00
245 Matt Dumba RC 1.00 2.50
246 Morgan Rielly RC 2.50 6.00
247 Hampus Lindholm RC 1.50 4.00
248 Magnus Hellberg RC 1.00 2.50
249 Michael Bournival RC 1.00 2.50
250 Nikita Zadorov RC 1.00 2.50

2013-14 Totally Certified Mirror Platinum Blue

*1-150 VETS/10: 5X TO 12X BASIC CARDS
*151-250 ROOKIE/10: 2.5X TO 6X BASIC RC
75 Corey Crawford 8.00 20.00
90 Nicklas Backstrom 10.00 25.00
229 Nathan MacKinnon 125.00 200.00
239 Olli Maatta 60.00 100.00

2013-14 Totally Certified Mirror Platinum Purple

*1-150 VETS/35: 2.5X TO 6X BASIC CARDS
*151-250 ROOKIE/35: 1.5X TO 4X BASIC RC
75 Corey Crawford 4.00 10.00
90 Nicklas Backstrom 5.00 12.00

2013-14 Totally Certified Mirror Platinum Red

*1-150 VETS/25: 3X TO 8X BASIC CARDS
*151-250 ROOKIE/25: 2X TO 5X BASIC RC
75 Corey Crawford 5.00 12.00
90 Nicklas Backstrom 6.00 15.00
229 Nathan MacKinnon 75.00 135.00

2013-14 Totally Certified Platinum Blue

*1-150 VETS/50: X TO X BASIC CARDS
*151-250 ROOKIE/50: X TO X BASIC RC
75 Corey Crawford 3.00 8.00
90 Nicklas Backstrom 4.00 10.00

2013-14 Totally Certified Platinum Gold

*1-150 VETS/25: 3X TO 8X BASIC CARDS
*151-250 ROOKIE/25: 2X TO 5X BASIC RC
75 Corey Crawford 5.00 12.00
90 Nicklas Backstrom 6.00 15.00
229 Nathan MacKinnon 75.00 135.00

2013-14 Totally Certified Platinum Red

*1-150 VETS/100: 1.5X TO 4X BASIC CARDS
*151-250 ROOKIE/100: 1X TO 2.5X BASIC RC
75 Corey Crawford 2.50 6.00
90 Nicklas Backstrom 3.00 8.00

2013-14 Totally Certified Clear Cloth Jerseys Prime Blue

*BLUE/25: .8X TO 2X RED JSY/100
*BLUE/25: .6X TO 1.5X RED JSY/50
CLNMK Nathan MacKinnon/25 50.00 100.00

2013-14 Totally Certified Clear Cloth Jerseys Red

CLAB Aleksander Barkov/100 6.00 15.00
CLAF Adam Foote/100 2.50 6.00
CLAG Alex Galchenyuk/100 10.00 25.00
CLAH Adam Henrique/100 3.00 8.00
CLBC Bobby Clarke/50 8.00 20.00
CLBH Brett Hull/100 6.00 15.00
CLBR Bobby Ryan/100 4.00 10.00
CLBS Brendan Shanahan/100 4.00 10.00
CLBW Blake Wheeler/100 3.00 8.00
CLCC Cory Conacher/100 2.00 5.00
CLCN Cam Neely/50 6.00 15.00
CLCP Carey Price/100 8.00 20.00
CLDB David Backes/100 3.00 8.00
CLDG Doug Gilmour/100 5.00 12.00
CLDH Dougie Hamilton/100 4.00 10.00
CLEL Eric Lindros/100 8.00 20.00
CLEM Evgeni Malkin/100 6.00 15.00
CLFF Filip Forsberg/100 8.00 20.00
CLGF Grant Fuhr/100 4.00 10.00
CLHL Henrik Lundqvist/100 5.00 12.00
CLHS Henrik Sedin/100 3.00 8.00
CLHZ Henrik Zetterberg/100 4.00 10.00
CLJB Jonas Brodin/100 2.50 6.00
CLJH Jonathan Huberdeau/100 5.00 12.00
CLJJ Jaromir Jagr/100 6.00 15.00
CLJQ Jonathan Quick/100 5.00 12.00
CLJR Jeremy Roenick/100 3.00 8.00
CLJS Joe Sakic/50 8.00 20.00
CLJT John Tavares/100 6.00 15.00
CLKO Kyle Okposo/100 3.00 8.00
CLKY Keith Yandle/100 3.00 8.00
CLLC Logan Couture/100 3.00 8.00
CLLE Loui Eriksson/100 2.50 6.00
CLLU Roberto Luongo/100 3.00 8.00
CLMB Martin Brodeur/100 8.00 20.00
CLMG Marian Gaborik/100 5.00 12.00
CLMI Mikhail Grigorenko/100 2.50 6.00
CLML Mario Lemieux/100 10.00 25.00
CLMO Mike Modano/100 6.00 15.00
CLMP Max Pacioretty/100 3.00 8.00
CLNK Nazem Kadri/100 3.00 8.00
CLNL Nicklas Lidstrom/100 4.00 10.00
CLNY Nail Yakupov/100 6.00 15.00
CLOM Olli Maatta/100 12.00 30.00
CLPB Pavel Bure/50 6.00 15.00
CLPC Paul Coffey/100 4.00 10.00
CLPK Patrick Kane/100 6.00 15.00
CLRB Ray Bourque/100 6.00 15.00
CLRF Ron Francis/100 5.00 12.00
CLRN Rick Nash/100 3.00 8.00
CLSC Sidney Crosby/100 10.00 25.00
CLSD Shane Doan/100 2.50 6.00
CLSJ Seth Jones/100 2.00 5.00
CLSK Saku Koivu/100 5.00 12.00
CLSM Stan Mikita/100 5.00 12.00
CLSS Steven Stamkos/100 6.00 15.00
CLSW Shea Weber/100 2.50 6.00
CLSY Steve Yzerman/100 8.00 20.00
CLTH Taylor Hall/100 6.00 15.00
CLTS Tyler Seguin/100 5.00 12.00
CLVN Valeri Nichushkin/100 2.00 5.00
CLVT Vladimir Tarasenko/100 8.00 20.00
CLWC Wendel Clark/100 4.00 10.00
CLABU Alexandre Burrows/100 3.00 8.00
CLACO Andrew Cogliano/100 2.00 5.00
CLBHY Braden Holtby/100 5.00 12.00
CLBLI Bryan Little/100 3.00 8.00
CLCGX Claude Giroux/100 5.00 12.00
CLDAL Daniel Alfredsson/100 3.00 8.00
CLJLU Joffrey Lupul/100 2.50 6.00
CLJOS Jordan Staal/100 3.00 8.00
CLJTH Joe Thornton/100 4.00 10.00
CLJTO Jonathan Toews/50 8.00 20.00
CLJTR Jacob Trouba/100 3.00 8.00
CLLEL Lars Eller/100 4.00 10.00
CLLUC Luc Robitaille/100 4.00 10.00
CLMAF Marc-Andre Fleury/100 4.00 10.00
CLMBA Mikael Backlund/100 2.50 6.00
CLMBO Mikkel Boedker/100 2.00 5.00
CLMDB Matt Dumba/100 3.00 8.00
CLMGR Mikael Granlund/100 5.00 12.00
CLMRE Matt Read/100 2.00 5.00
CLMRI Mike Richards/100 4.00 10.00
CLMSL Martin St. Louis/100 3.00 8.00
CLNBO Nick Bonino/100 2.00 5.00
CLNMK Nathan MacKinnon/100 15.00 40.00
CLOVI Alex Ovechkin/50 15.00 40.00
CLPKS P.K. Subban/100 5.00 12.00
CLPLF Pat LaFontaine/100 4.00 10.00
CLPMR Petr Mrazek/100 8.00 20.00
CLRBL Rob Blake/100 4.00 10.00
CLRLY Morgan Rielly/100 5.00 12.00
CLRMP Ryan Murphy/100 3.00 8.00
CLRMR Ryan Murray/100 3.00 8.00
CLRNH Ryan Nugent-Hopkins/50 4.00 10.00
CLTHE Tomas Hertl/100 2.50 6.00
CLTMU Teemu Selanne/100 8.00 20.00
CLTTH Tim Thomas/100 3.00 8.00
CLTVA Thomas Vanek/100 3.00 8.00

2013-14 Totally Certified Certified Competitors Jerseys Red

*BLUE/50: .8X TO 2X RED JSY
*BLUE/25: 1X TO 2.5X RED JSY
*PATCH GOLD/15-25: 1.2X TO 3X JSY RED
CCBL M.Brodeur/Lundqvist 6.00 15.00
CCBP D.Brown/C.Perry 3.00 8.00
CCBT D.Backes/J.Toews 6.00 15.00
CCBY D.Byfuglien/K.Yandle 3.00 8.00
CCEP E.Etem/T.Pearson 3.00 8.00
CCFV A.Foote/Vanbiesbrouck 5.00 12.00
CCGC Granlund/A.Chiasson 3.00 8.00
CCGD R.Getzlaf/S.Doan 5.00 12.00
CCGF C.Giroux/M.Fleury 5.00 12.00
CCGM M.Gaborik/E.Malkin 10.00 25.00
CCGN C.Glencross/RNH 3.00 8.00
CCHC J.Howard/C.Crawford 4.00 10.00
CCKA P.Kessel/C.Anderson 4.00 10.00
CCKB N.Kadri/P.Bergeron 4.00 10.00
CCKN T.Kerr/C.Neely 4.00 10.00
CCKP R.Kesler/J.Pavelski 3.00 8.00
CCKR P.Kane/T.Rask 6.00 15.00
CCKS D.Keith/D.Sedin 3.00 8.00
CCLM E.Lindros/M.Messier 6.00 15.00
CCLS J.LeClair/B.Shanahan 4.00 10.00
CCMB S.Matteau/B.Bennett 2.50 6.00
CCMJ S.Jones/N.MacKinnon 8.00 20.00
CCOK A.Ovechkin/C.Kunitz 12.00 30.00
CCPB D.Potvin/B.Barber 4.00 10.00
CCPH D.Phaneuf/C.Hodgson 3.00 8.00
CCRL P.Rinne/K.Lehtonen 4.00 10.00
CCSB J.Schultz/Beauchemin 2.00 5.00
CCSC Z.Chara/P.Subban 5.00 12.00
CCSG B.Salming/B.Gainey 3.00 8.00
CCSH S.Stamkos/Huberdeau 5.00 12.00
CCSP J.Staal/R.Panik 3.00 8.00
CCTB J.Thornton/J.Benn 4.00 10.00
CCTR J.Tavares/B.Richards 6.00 15.00
CCWJ S.Weber/B.Jackman 2.50 6.00
CCYS S.Yzerman/J.Sakic 5.00 12.00

2013-14 Totally Certified EPIX Memorabilia Red Play

*BLUE/50: .6X TO 1.5X RED PLAY
*GOLD/25: .8X TO 2X RED PLAY
EBH Brett Hull 5.00 12.00
EEL Eric Lindros 8.00 20.00
EHL Henrik Lundqvist 5.00 12.00
EJI Jarome Iginla 4.00 10.00
EJJ Jaromir Jagr 10.00 25.00
EJQ Jonathan Quick 6.00 15.00
EJS Joe Sakic 8.00 20.00
EMB Martin Brodeur 10.00 25.00
EML Mario Lemieux 15.00 40.00
EMM Mark Messier 6.00 15.00
EMRI Mike Richards 4.00 10.00
ENY Nail Yakupov 5.00 12.00
EOVI Alex Ovechkin 15.00 40.00
EPB Pavel Bure 8.00 20.00
EPD Pavel Datsyuk 5.00 12.00
EPK Patrick Kane 6.00 15.00
EPKS P.K. Subban 6.00 15.00
EPR Patrick Roy 12.00 30.00
ERB Ray Bourque 8.00 20.00
ERF Ron Francis 6.00 15.00
ESC Sidney Crosby 15.00 40.00
ESS Steven Stamkos 8.00 20.00
ESY Steve Yzerman 8.00 20.00
ETMU Teemu Selanne 8.00 20.00
EZC Zdeno Chara 4.00 10.00

2013-14 Totally Certified HRX

STATED PRINT RUN 25 SER.#'d SETS
HGH Gordie Howe 50.00 100.00
HMM Mark Messier 30.00 60.00
HNY Nail Yakupov 60.00 120.00
HRNH Ryan Nugent-Hopkins 20.00 50.00
HOVI Alex Ovechkin 75.00 135.00

2013-14 Totally Certified Jerseys Red

*BLUE/50: .6X TO 1.5X RED JSY
*BLUE/25: .8X TO 2X RED JSY
*GOLD/25: .8X TO 2X RED JSY
TCAGR Adam Graves 3.00 8.00
TCAKO Anze Kopitar 5.00 12.00
TCALA Adam Larsson 3.00 8.00
TCAT Alex Tanguay 2.50 6.00
TCAVO Anton Volchenkov 2.00 5.00
TCBE Brian Elliott 2.50 6.00
TCBLI Bryan Little 3.00 8.00
TCBN Bernie Nicholls 3.00 8.00
TCBRM Brad Marchand 4.00 10.00
TCBW Blake Wheeler 3.00 8.00
TCBY Brandon Yip 2.00 5.00
TCCCH Chris Chelios 3.00 8.00
TCCCR Corey Crawford 4.00 10.00
TCCPE Corey Perry 3.00 8.00
TCCTA Chris Tanev 6.00 15.00
TCDA Dave Andreychuk 4.00 10.00
TCDD Drew Doughty 3.00 8.00
TCDE Dan Ellis 2.50 6.00
TCDHA Dan Hamhuis 2.50 6.00
TCDK Duncan Keith 3.00 8.00
TCDS Daniel Sedin 3.00 8.00
TCDST Derek Stepan 3.00 8.00
TCFB Francois Beauchemin 2.00 5.00
TCFN Frans Nielsen 2.00 5.00
TCGB Gabriel Bourque 2.50 6.00
TCGH Gordie Howe 8.00 20.00
TCGL Gabriel Landeskog 2.50 6.00
TCGRN Mike Green 3.00 8.00
TCIL Igor Larionov 5.00 12.00
TCJBO Jay Bouwmeester 3.00 8.00
TCJEN Jhonas Enroth 3.00 8.00
TCJG Josh Gorges 2.50 6.00
TCJHI Jonas Hiller 2.50 6.00
TCJHO Jimmy Howard 3.00 8.00
TCJLC John LeClair 3.00 8.00
TCJLU Joffrey Lupul 2.50 6.00
TCJN Joe Nieuwendyk 4.00 10.00
TCJPE Justin Peters 2.00 5.00
TCJPO Jason Pominville 2.50 6.00
TCKP Keith Primeau 3.00 8.00
TCMBA Mikael Backlund 2.50 6.00
TCMGI Mark Giordano 2.50 6.00
TCMHO Mark Howe 4.00 10.00
TCMMI Milan Michalek 2.00 5.00
TCMN Michal Neuvirth 2.50 6.00
TCMP Max Pacioretty 3.00 8.00
TCMXT Maxime Talbot 2.50 6.00
TCNH Nathan Horton 3.00 8.00
TCNKR Niklas Kronwall 2.50 6.00
TCOVI Alex Ovechkin 12.00 30.00
TCPAP P.A. Parenteau 2.00 5.00
TCPAS Paul Stastny 3.00 8.00
TCPB Pavel Bure 4.00 10.00
TCPBI Paul Bissonnette 2.00 5.00
TCPC Paul Coffey 4.00 10.00
TCPD Pavel Datsyuk 4.00 10.00
TCPRI Pekka Rinne 4.00 10.00
TCPT Pierre Turgeon 3.00 8.00
TCREB Rene Bourque 2.00 5.00
TCRJO Roman Josi 3.00 8.00
TCSC Sidney Crosby 12.00 30.00
TCSH Shawn Horcoff 2.00 5.00
TCSJN Matt Stajan 2.50 6.00
TCSSO Sheldon Souray 2.00 5.00
TCSTM Steve Mason 3.00 8.00
TCTTH Tim Thomas 3.00 8.00
TCTVA Thomas Vanek 3.00 8.00
TCTZ Travis Zajac 2.50 6.00
TCVFI Valtteri Filppula 3.00 8.00
TCZB Zach Boychuk 2.00 5.00

2013-14 Totally Certified Rookie Autograph Jerseys

ANNOUNCED PRINT RUN LESS THAN 250
SP ANNOUNCED PRINT RUN LESS THAN 100
EXCH EXPIRATION: 8/19/2015
*BLUE/25: .6X TO 1.5X BASIC INSERTS
*BLUE/25: .5X TO 1.2X BASIC SP
*PLAT.RED/25: .6X TO 1.5X BASIC INSERTS
*PLAT.RED/25: .5X TO 1.2X BASIC SP
*RED/50: .5X TO 1.2X BASIC INSERTS
*RED/50: .4X TO 1X BASIC SP
151 Drew Shore/250 4.00 10.00
152 Cristopher Nilstorp/250 4.00 10.00
153 Charlie Coyle/250 5.00 12.00
154 Sami Vatanen/250 5.00 12.00
155 Michael Sgarbossa/250 4.00 10.00
156 Danny DeKeyser/250 10.00 25.00
157 Tyler Toffoli/100 12.00 30.00
158 Ben Street/250 3.00 8.00
159 Thomas Hickey/250 4.00 10.00
160 Cory Conacher/250 3.00 8.00
161 Jack Campbell/250 4.00 10.00
162 Filip Forsberg/250 12.00 30.00
163 Edward Pasquale/250 3.00 8.00
164 Max Reinhart/250 5.00 12.00
165 Alex Killorn/100 6.00 15.00
166 Calvin Pickard/250 5.00 12.00
167 Jared Staal/250 5.00 12.00
168 J.T. Miller/100 6.00 15.00
169 Emerson Etem/250 5.00 12.00
170 Ryan Murphy/250 5.00 12.00
171 Nicklas Jensen/250 4.00 10.00
172 Mikhail Grigorenko/250 6.00 15.00
174 Richard Panik/250 5.00 12.00
175 Brock Nelson/250 5.00 12.00
176 Tom Wilson/250 8.00 20.00
177 Michael Caruso/250 3.00 8.00
178 Justin Schultz/250 5.00 12.00
179 Antoine Roussel/250 5.00 12.00
180 Eric Hartzell/250 5.00 12.00
181 Austin Watson/250 4.00 10.00
182 Vladimir Tarasenko/100 25.00 60.00
183 Anthony Peluso/250 3.00 8.00

4 Brendan Gallagher/100 25.00 50.00
5 Michal Jordan/250 3.00 8.00
6 Petr Mrazek/250 8.00 20.00
7 Stefan Matteau/100
8 Tye McGinn/250 5.00 12.00
9 Jarred Tinordi/100 6.00 15.00
0 Nail Yakupov/250 10.00 25.00
1 Frederik Andersen/100
2 Mark Arcobello/250 5.00 12.00
3 Ryan Spooner/100 6.00 15.00
4 Zach Redmond/250 4.00 10.00
5 Carl Soderberg/100 8.00 20.00
6 Jordan Schroeder/250 5.00 12.00
7 Nick Bjugstad/250 6.00 15.00
8 Philipp Grubauer/250 5.00 12.00
9 Jamie Oleksiak/250 4.00 10.00
0 Eric Gryba/250 4.00 10.00
1 Scott Laughton/250 5.00 12.00
2 Dmitrij Jaskin/250 5.00 12.00
3 Quinton Howden/250 4.00 10.00
4 Nathan Beaulieu/250 5.00 12.00
5 Mikael Granlund/250 8.00 20.00
6 Jonathan Huberdeau/100 15.00 30.00
7 Tanner Pearson/250 4.00 10.00
8 Viktor Fasth/250 5.00 12.00
9 Jonas Brodin/100
0 Brian Flynn/250 4.00 10.00
1 Rickard Rakell/250 5.00 12.00
2 Nick Petrecki/250 3.00 8.00
3 Beau Bennett/250 6.00 15.00
4 Brian Lashoff/250 4.00 10.00
5 Alex Chiasson/250 5.00 12.00
6 Dougie Hamilton/250 10.00 25.00
7 Alex Galchenyuk/100 20.00 50.00
8 Matt Irwin/250 4.00 10.00
9 Johan Larsson/250 4.00 10.00
0 Christian Thomas/250 4.00 10.00
1 Michael Kostka/250 4.00 10.00
4 Frank Corrado/250 4.00 10.00
5 Mark Pysyk/250 5.00 12.00
6 Rasmus Ristolainen/100
7 Marek Mazanec/250 5.00 12.00
8 Jon Merrill/250 8.00 20.00
9 Nathan MacKinnon/250 40.00 100.00
0 Joakim Nordstrom/250 4.00 10.00
1 Zemgus Girgensons/100 12.00 30.00
2 Jacob Trouba/250 12.00 30.00
3 Tomas Hertl/250 8.00 20.00
4 Aleksander Barkov/250 8.00 20.00
6 Elias Lindholm/250 6.00 15.00
7 Xavier Ouellet/100 6.00 15.00
8 Matt Nieto/250 4.00 10.00
9 Olli Maatta/100 EXCH 30.00 80.00
0 Sean Monahan/250 10.00 25.00
1 Seth Jones/250 8.00 20.00
2 Valeri Nichushkin/250 10.00 25.00
3 Boone Jenner/250 5.00 12.00
4 Ryan Murray/250 6.00 15.00
5 Matt Dumba/250 5.00 12.00
6 Morgan Rielly/250 12.00 30.00
7 Hampus Lindholm/250 6.00 15.00
8 Magnus Hellberg/250 5.00 12.00
9 Michael Bournival/250 5.00 12.00
0 Nikita Zadorov/250 5.00 12.00

013-14 Totally Certified Rookie Roll Call Jerseys Patch Gold

OLD/25: .8X TO 2X RED JSY
NMK Nathan MacKinnon 60.00 120.00

013-14 Totally Certified Rookie Roll Call Jerseys Red

LUE/50: .6X TO 1.5X RED JSY
AB Aleksander Barkov 6.00 15.00
AC Alex Chiasson 3.00 8.00
AG Alex Galchenyuk 6.00 15.00
AK Alex Killorn 3.00 8.00
ANP Anthony Peluso 2.00 5.00
AR Antoine Roussel 3.00 8.00
AW Austin Watson 2.50 6.00
BB Beau Bennett 5.00 12.00
BG Brendan Gallagher 6.00 15.00
BJE Boone Jenner 3.00 8.00
BNE Brock Nelson 3.00 8.00
BST Ben Street 3.00 8.00
CB Chris Brown 2.00 5.00
CC Cory Conacher 2.00 5.00
CM Connor Murphy 2.50 6.00
COY Charlie Coyle 3.00 8.00
CSO Carl Soderberg 3.00 8.00
DDK Danny DeKeyser 4.00 10.00
DH Dougie Hamilton 5.00 12.00
EE Emerson Etem 3.00 8.00
FF Filip Forsberg 8.00 20.00
HLI Hampus Lindholm 4.00 10.00
JAS Jared Staal 3.00 8.00
JB Jonas Brodin 2.50 6.00
JC Jack Campbell 2.50 6.00
JH Jonathan Huberdeau 5.00 12.00
JTM J.T. Miller 3.00 8.00
JTR Jacob Trouba 5.00 12.00
JUS Justin Schultz 3.00 8.00
MDB Matt Dumba 3.00 8.00
MGH Magnus Hellberg 3.00 8.00
MGR Mikael Granlund 5.00 12.00
MI Matt Irwin 2.50 6.00
MIK Mikhail Grigorenko 4.00 10.00
MNI Matt Nieto 2.50 6.00
NBE Nathan Beaulieu 2.50 6.00
NBJ Nick Bjugstad 4.00 10.00
NJ Nicklas Jensen 2.50 6.00
NMK Nathan MacKinnon 10.00 25.00
NP Nick Petrecki 2.00 5.00
NY Nail Yakupov 5.00 12.00
OM Olli Maatta 10.00 25.00
PMR Petr Mrazek 6.00 15.00
QH Quinton Howden 2.50 6.00
RLY Morgan Rielly 5.00 12.00
RMP Ryan Murphy 3.00 8.00
RMR Ryan Murray 4.00 10.00
RR Rickard Rakell 3.00 8.00
SJ Seth Jones 5.00 12.00
SL Scott Laughton 3.00 8.00
SMA Stefan Matteau 2.50 6.00
SMO Sean Monahan 5.00 12.00
SV Sami Vatanen 3.00 8.00
THE Tomas Hertl 6.00 15.00
THI Thomas Hickey 2.50 6.00
TMG Tye McGinn 3.00 8.00
TP Tanner Pearson 3.00 8.00
TT Tyler Toffoli 6.00 15.00
TW Tom Wilson 4.00 10.00
VF Viktor Fasth 3.00 8.00
VN Valeri Nichushkin 5.00 12.00
VT Vladimir Tarasenko 12.00 30.00
ZG Zemgus Girgensons 6.00 15.00
ZR Zach Redmond 2.50 6.00

013-14 Totally Certified Rookie Signatures

AB Aleksander Barkov 6.00 15.00
LE Anders Lee 5.00 12.00
TRANP Anthony Peluso 2.00 5.00
TRAPE Alex Petrovic 2.50 6.00
TRAR Antoine Roussel 3.00 8.00
TRBG Brendan Gallagher 15.00 40.00
TRBJE Boone Jenner 3.00 8.00
TRCB Chris Brown 2.00 5.00
TRCC Cory Conacher 2.00 5.00
TRCSC Cameron Schilling 2.00 5.00
TRDBA Daniel Bang 2.50 6.00
TRDDK Danny DeKeyser 6.00 15.00
TRDH Dougie Hamilton 6.00 15.00
TRFC Frank Corrado 2.50 6.00
TRFF Filip Forsberg 8.00 20.00
TRHLI Hampus Lindholm 5.00 12.00
TRIB Igor Bobkov 2.50 6.00
TRJCN Joe Cannata 2.50 6.00
TRJMU John Muse 3.00 8.00
TRJOO Joonas Rask 3.00 8.00
TRJSD Jordan Schroeder 3.00 8.00
TRJTM J.T. Miller 3.00 8.00
TRJTR Jacob Trouba 8.00 20.00
TRMDB Matt Dumba 3.00 8.00
TRMGR Mikael Granlund 5.00 12.00
TRMIK Mikhail Grigorenko 4.00 10.00
TRNBJ Nick Bjugstad 5.00 12.00
TRNJ Nicklas Jensen 2.50 6.00
TRNMK Nathan MacKinnon 50.00 100.00
TRNY Nail Yakupov 8.00 20.00
TRPMR Petr Mrazek 10.00 25.00
TRRLY Morgan Rielly 6.00 15.00
TRRMR Ryan Murray
TRRR Rickard Rakell 3.00 8.00
TRSEC Sean Collins 2.50 6.00
TRSJ Seth Jones 3.00 8.00
TRSL Scott Laughton 3.00 8.00
TRSMA Stefan Matteau 2.50 6.00
TRTB Taylor Beck 2.50 6.00
TRTHE Tomas Hertl 15.00 30.00
TRTP Tanner Pearson 3.00 8.00
TRTW Tom Wilson 5.00 12.00
TRVF Viktor Fasth 3.00 8.00
TRVN Valeri Nichushkin 3.00 8.00

2013-14 Totally Certified Rookie Slideshow

RSAG Alex Galchenyuk 25.00 50.00
RSAW Austin Watson 4.00 10.00
RSBB Beau Bennett 6.00 15.00
RSBG Brendan Gallagher 15.00 40.00
RSBNE Brock Nelson 5.00 12.00
RSCK Chris Kreider 5.00 12.00
RSCOY Charlie Coyle 5.00 12.00
RSDH Dougie Hamilton 10.00 25.00
RSEE Emerson Etem 5.00 12.00
RSFF Filip Forsberg 10.00 25.00
RSJC Jack Campbell 4.00 10.00
RSJO Jamie Oleksiak 4.00 10.00
RSJSC Jaden Schwartz 6.00 15.00
RSJTI Jarred Tinordi 5.00 12.00
RSJUS Justin Schultz 5.00 12.00
RSMIK Mikhail Grigorenko 6.00 15.00
RSNBE Nathan Beaulieu 4.00 10.00
RSNMK Nathan MacKinnon 20.00 50.00
RSNY Nail Yakupov 15.00 40.00
RSQH Quinton Howden 4.00 10.00
RSRLY Morgan Rielly 12.00 30.00
RSRMP Ryan Murphy 5.00 12.00
RSRMR Ryan Murray 8.00 20.00
RSRSM Reilly Smith 8.00 20.00
RSRSP Ryan Spooner 5.00 12.00
RSSJ Seth Jones 5.00 12.00
RSSL Scott Laughton 10.00 25.00
RSTBA Tyson Barrie 5.00 12.00
RSTT Tyler Toffoli 10.00 25.00
RSVT Vladimir Tarasenko 15.00 40.00

2013-14 Totally Certified Rookie Slideshow Autographs

RSAG Alex Galchenyuk/20 40.00 80.00
RSBG Brendan Gallagher/20
RSCK Chris Kreider/20 15.00 40.00
RSCOY Charlie Coyle/20 15.00 40.00
RSDH Dougie Hamilton/20
RSEE Emerson Etem/20 10.00 25.00
RSFF Filip Forsberg/20
RSJSC Jaden Schwartz/20 20.00 50.00
RSJUS Justin Schultz/20 20.00 50.00
RSMIK Mikhail Grigorenko/20 20.00 50.00
RSNMK Nathan MacKinnon/20 75.00 150.00
RSNY Nail Yakupov/20
RSRLY Morgan Rielly/20
RSRMP Ryan Murphy/20 15.00 40.00
RSRMR Ryan Murray/20 20.00 50.00
RSRSP Ryan Spooner/20 15.00 40.00
RSSJ Seth Jones/20
RSTBA Tyson Barrie/20 15.00 40.00
RSVT Vladimir Tarasenko/20

2013-14 Totally Certified Signatures

EXCH EXPIRATION: 8/19/2015
TSAA Akim Aliu 4.00 10.00
TSAH Adam Henrique 6.00 15.00
TSAL Andrew Ladd 6.00 15.00
TSAN Antti Niemi 5.00 12.00
TSBH Brett Hull 25.00 40.00
TSBM Brenden Morrow 5.00 12.00
TSBR Bobby Ryan 6.00 15.00
TSBSD Brandon Saad 8.00 20.00
TSCHO Cody Hodgson 4.00 10.00
TSCHP Chet Pickard 4.00 10.00
TSCK Chris Kreider 6.00 15.00
TSDBR Daniel Briere 6.00 15.00
TSDCA Daniel Carcillo 4.00 10.00
TSDPH Dion Phaneuf 6.00 15.00
TSEB Ed Belfour 20.00 50.00
TSERS Eric Staal 5.00 12.00
TSGH Gordie Howe 90.00 150.00
TSGL Gabriel Landeskog 5.00 12.00
TSHL Henrik Lundqvist 10.00 25.00
TSJI Jarome Iginla 15.00 30.00
TSJJ Jaromir Jagr 40.00 80.00
TSJP Joe Pavelski 6.00 15.00
TSJQ Jonathan Quick EXCH 30.00 60.00
TSJRE James Reimer 6.00 15.00
TSJSC Jaden Schwartz 5.00 12.00
TSJSI Jakob Silfverberg 5.00 12.00
TSJT John Tavares 12.00 30.00
TSJTB J.T. Brown 4.00 10.00
TSJZU Jason Zucker 5.00 12.00
TSLE Loui Eriksson 15.00 30.00
TSMAF Marc-Andre Fleury 10.00 25.00
TSMBA Mikael Backlund 5.00 12.00
TSMG Marian Gaborik 6.00 15.00
TSMM Mark Messier
TSMS Mike Smith 6.00 15.00
TSNL Nicklas Lidstrom 10.00 25.00
TSOVI Alex Ovechkin 25.00 50.00
TSPR Patrick Roy
TSRJO Roman Josi 6.00 15.00
TSRK Ryan Kesler 6.00 15.00
TSRNH Ryan Nugent-Hopkins 8.00 20.00
TSSB Sven Baertschi 5.00 12.00
TSSC Sidney Crosby
TSSDE Simon Despres 4.00 10.00
TSSWE Stephen Weiss 5.00 12.00
TSTS Tyler Seguin 10.00 25.00
TSVL Vincent Lecavalier 10.00 25.00

1972 Tower Hockey Instructions Booklets

Sponsored by Towers and Donimart stores, we have very little information about these oddball hockey instruction booklets.
1 Skating Skills 10.00 20.00

1936 Triumph Postcards

This eleven-card set was issued as a supplement to The Triumph (a newspaper). The cards measure approximately 3 1/2" by 5 1/2" and are in the postcard format. The borderless fronts feature full-length black and white posed action shots. The player's name and team name appear in the lower left corner. The back carries the typical postcard design with each player's name and biographical information in the upper corner. Different dates appear on the back of the cards, which represent the date each card was distributed. The cards were issued three the first week with The Triumph, then one per week thereafter. The cards are unnumbered and checklisted below in alphabetical order. The date mentioned below is the issue date as noted on the card back in Canadian style, day/month/year.
COMPLETE SET (11) 650.00 1300.00
1 Lionel Conacher/22/2/36 125.00 250.00
2 Harvey Jackson 125.00 250.00
Toronto Maple Leafs/18/1/36
3 Ivan Johnson 62.50 125.00
New York Rangers/8/2/36
4 Herbie Lewis/7/3/36 40.00 80.00
5 Sylvio Mantha 62.50 125.00
Montreal Canadiens/18/1/36
6 Nick Metz 40.00 80.00
Toronto Maple Leafs/15/2/36
7 Baldy Northcott 45.00 90.00
Montreal Maroons/1/2/36
8 Eddie Shore 250.00 500.00
Boston Bruins/25/1/36
9 Paul Thompson 40.00 80.00
Chicago Blackhawks/29/2/36
10 Roy Worters 62.50 125.00
New York Americans/18/1/36
11 Charley Conacher 40.00 80.00

1993 UDA Commemorative Cards

99 Wayne Gretzky AU/500 100.00 200.00
(1993-94 Upper Deck jumbo)
G5 Wayne Gretzky/2500 4.00 10.00
Gordie Howe Selects Jumbo

1994 UDA Commemorative Cards

WG Wayne Gretzky/10,000 3.00 8.00
802 goals
WGA Wayne Gretzky AU/500 100.00 200.00
802 goals
UDHC Wayne Gretzky/45,000 3.00 8.00
Happy Holidays

1995 UDA Commemorative Cards

WG Wayne Gretzky 2500 points 3.00 8.00

1996 UDA Commemorative Cards

AV Avalanche Stanley Cup Champs 5.00

1997 UDA Commemorative Cards

COMPLETE SET
WG2 Wayne Gretzky 3.00 8.00
16 Time AS/5000
WG1 1996 Wayne Gretzky 3.00 8.00
The Great One/5000

1998 UDA Commemorative Cards

RW 1997 Red Wings Stanley Cup/5000 2.50 6.00
RW 1997 Red Wings Stanley Cup/200 40.00 80.00
Steve Yzerman AUTO

1999 UDA Commemorative Cards

WG Wayne Gretzky Retires/9900 3.00 8.00

2000 UDA Commemorative Cards

WG Wayne Gretzky HOF/5000 3.00

2004-05 UD All-World

Released in June, this 120-card set featured NHL players who spent the lockout season playing in Europe as well as European legends. Two subsets, "Up Close and Personal" and "Euro-Legends" were inserted at 1:8 odds. Please note that cards #'s 108 and 119 do not exist and that card #110 is used on three different cards. Those cards are noted below with "A,B and C" suffixes.
COMPLETE SET (120)
1 Roman Turek .20 .50
2 Jiri Fischer .20 .50
3 Martin Rucinsky .20 .50
4 Ales Hemsky .25 .60
5 Milan Hejduk .20 .50
6 Zigmund Palffy .25 .60
7 Peter Stastny .20 .50
8 Petr Nedved .15 .40
9 Radek Bonk .20 .50
10 Roman Hamrlik .20 .50
11 Martin Havlat .25 .60
12 Jarkko Ruutu .20 .50
13 Matti Hagman .20 .50
14 Tomas Vokoun .20 .50
15 Mika Noronen .20 .50
16 Jari Kurri .25 .60
17 Teemu Selanne .50 1.25
18 Dwayne Roloson .20 .50
19 Saku Koivu .25 .60
20 Erik Cole .20 .50
21 Marco Sturm .15 .40
22 Mike York .15 .40
23 Ryan Malone .15 .40
24 Alex Kovalev .15 .40
25 Brad Richards .25 .60
26 Ilya Kovalchuk .25 .60
27 Nikolai Khabibulin .25 .60
28 Vincent Lecavalier .20 .50
29 Jaromir Jagr .60 1.50
30 Alexander Frolov .20 .50
31 Nikolai Zherdev .20 .50
32 Maxim Afinogenov .15 .40
33 Pavel Datsyuk .30 .75
34 Nikolai Antropov .20 .50
35 Evgeni Nabokov .20 .50
36 Patrik Elias .25 .60
37 Petr Sykora .20 .50
38 Sergei Gonchar .20 .50
39 Michael Nylander .15 .40
40 Fedor Fedorov .20 .50
41 Alexei Zhamnov .20 .50
42 Pavol Demitra .30 .75
43 Miroslav Satan .20 .50
44 Borje Salming .25 .60
45 Ulf Nilsson .20 .50
46 Tyler Arnason .15 .40
47 Mats Naslund .20 .50
48 Jose Theodore .25 .60
49 Marty Turco .25 .60
50 Kent Nilsson .20 .50
51 Marian Gaborik .40 1.00
52 Mike Comrie .20 .50
53 Sheldon Souray .15 .40
54 Zdeno Chara .25 .60
55 Hakan Loob .20 .50
56 Thomas Steen .20 .50
57 Daniel Alfredsson .25 .60
58 Jonathan Cheechoo .20 .50
59 Michael Ryder .20 .50
60 Brendan Morrison .20 .50
61 Justin Williams .15 .40
62 Tomas Holmstrom .20 .50
63 Adrian Aucoin .15 .40
64 Daniel Sedin .25 .60
65 Henrik Sedin .25 .60
66 Markus Naslund .25 .60
67 Peter Forsberg .30 .75
68 Anders Hedberg .15 .40
69 Ladislav Nagy .15 .40
70 Marcel Hossa .15 .40
71 Marian Hossa .20 .50
72 Trent Hunter .15 .40
73 Dick Tarnstrom .15 .40
74 Olli Jokinen .20 .50
75 Fredrik Modin .15 .40
76 Henrik Zetterberg .30 .75
77 Miikka Kiprusoff .20 .50
78 Joe Thornton .30 .75
79 Rick Nash .25 .60
80 Martin St. Louis .25 .60
81 Alex Tanguay .20 .50
82 David Aebischer .20 .50
83 Martin Gelinas .15 .40
84 Daniel Briere .25 .60
85 Dany Heatley .25 .60
86 Niko Kapanen .15 .40
87 Igor Larionov .25 .60
88 Richard Zednik .15 .40
89 Jochen Hecht .15 .40
90 Vladislav Tretiak .25 .60
91 Wayne Gretzky UCP 5.00 12.00
92 Gordie Howe UCP 3.00 8.00
93 Patrick Roy UCP 2.50 6.00
94 Joe Thornton UCP 1.25 3.00
95 Rick Nash UCP 1.00 2.50
96 Martin Brodeur UCP 2.00 5.00
97 Marty Turco UCP 1.00 2.50
98 Jarome Iginla UCP 1.00 2.50
99 Joe Sakic UCP 1.50 4.00
100 Peter Forsberg UCP 1.25 3.00
101 Mario Lemieux UCP 3.00 8.00
102 Markus Naslund UCP 1.00 2.50
103 Martin St. Louis UCP 1.00 2.50
104 Mike Bossy UCP 1.00 2.50
105 Jose Theodore UCP 1.00 2.50
106 Matti Hagman EL .75 2.00
107 Teemu Selanne EL 2.00 5.00
109 Borje Salming EL 1.00 2.50
110A Ulf Nilsson EL .75 2.00
110B Jari Kurri EL 1.00 2.50
110C Igor Larionov EL 1.00 2.50
111 Anders Hedberg EL .60 1.50
112 Vladislav Tretiak EL 1.00 2.50
113 Mats Naslund EL .75 2.00
114 Peter Stastny EL .75 2.00
115 Thomas Steen EL .75 2.00
116 Hakan Loob EL .75 2.00
117 Kent Nilsson EL .75 2.00
118 Saku Koivu EL 1.00 2.50
120 Jaromir Jagr EL 2.50 6.00

2004-05 UD All-World Gold

*GOLD/50: 6X TO 15X BASIC CARDS
STATED PRINT RUN 50 SER.#'d SETS
65 Henrik Sedin 5.00 12.00

2004-05 UD All-World Autographs

1-90 STATED ODDS 1:24
91-119 PRINT RUN 10 SER.#'d SETS
91-119 NOT PRICED DUE TO SCARCITY
SKIP NUMBERED SET
1 Roman Turek 6.00 15.00
4 Ales Hemsky 8.00 20.00
5 Milan Hejduk 8.00 20.00
6 Zigmund Palffy SP
7 Peter Stastny 8.00 20.00
11 Martin Havlat 10.00 25.00
12 Jarkko Ruutu 6.00 15.00
13 Matti Hagman 6.00 10.00
15 Mika Noronen 6.00 10.00
16 Jari Kurri 8.00 20.00
18 Dwayne Roloson 12.00 30.00
20 Erik Cole 8.00 15.00
26 Ilya Kovalchuk SP
27 Nikolai Khabibulin SP 40.00 80.00
28 Vincent Lecavalier SP
30 Alexander Frolov 6.00 15.00
31 Nikolai Zherdev 8.00 15.00
32 Maxim Afinogenov 6.00 15.00
44 Borje Salming 12.00 30.00
45 Ulf Nilsson 8.00 20.00
46 Tyler Arnason 6.00 10.00
47 Mats Naslund 15.00 40.00
48 Jose Theodore SP
50 Kent Nilsson 6.00 15.00
51 Marian Gaborik 20.00 50.00
52 Mike Comrie 6.00 15.00
53 Sheldon Souray 6.00 15.00
54 Zdeno Chara 10.00 25.00
55 Hakan Loob 12.00 30.00
56 Thomas Steen 6.00 15.00
57 Daniel Alfredsson SP
58 Jonathan Cheechoo 10.00 25.00
59 Michael Ryder SP 15.00 40.00
60 Brendan Morrison 6.00 15.00
61 Justin Williams 8.00 15.00
66 Markus Naslund SP
68 Anders Hedberg 6.00 15.00
69 Ladislav Nagy 6.00 10.00
70 Marcel Hossa 6.00 10.00
71 Marian Hossa SP
72 Trent Hunter 6.00 15.00
76 Henrik Zetterberg SP 25.00 60.00
78 Joe Thornton 15.00 40.00
79 Rick Nash SP 60.00 150.00
80 Martin St. Louis SP
81 Alex Tanguay SP
82 David Aebischer SP 15.00 40.00
84 Daniel Briere 12.00 30.00
85 Dany Heatley SP
87 Igor Larionov 10.00 25.00
88 Richard Zednik 6.00 15.00
90 Vladislav Tretiak 20.00 50.00

2004-05 UD All-World Dual Autographs

PRINT RUN 25 SER.#'d SETS
ADHN M.Hagman/M.Noronen 25.00 60.00
ADPS Z.Palffy/P.Stastny 25.00 60.00
ADHH M.Hejduk/A.Hemsky 30.00 80.00
ADAF M.Afinogenov/A. Frolov 20.00 50.00
ADFZ A.Frolov/N.Zherdev 30.00 80.00
ADJA J.Thornton/A.Tanguay 75.00 150.00
ADKK J.Kurri/S.Koivu 100.00 200.00
ADKL J.Kurri/H.Loob 30.00 80.00
ADLK V.Lecavalier/N.Khabibulin 75.00 150.00
ADLS H.Loob/T.Steen 30.00 80.00
ADMM M. Hossa/M. Hossa
ADNN M. Naslund/M.Naslund
ADNT R.Nash/J.Thornton 125.00 250.00
ADSC S.Souray/Z.Chara 25.00 60.00
ADSN B.Salming/K.Nilsson 30.00 80.00

2004-05 UD All-World Triple Autographs

STATED PRINT RUN 20 SER.#'d SETS
ATCWR Cheech/J.Will/J.Ruutu 40.00 80.00
ATKHK Kurri/Hagm/Koivu
ATKSN Kurri/P.Stats/Naslund 40.00 80.00
ATLTZ Larion/Tretiak/Zherd 100.00 175.00
ATNLN Naslung/Loob/Nilsson
ATRCM Ryder/Cheech/Morrison 50.00 100.00
ATSHH P.Stats/Hejd/Hemsky
ATSLN Steen/Loob/Nilsson 30.00 60.00
ATTAR Theod/Aebis/Roloson 50.00 100.00
ATZFA Zherd/Frolov/Afinog 30.00 60.00

2002-03 UD Artistic Impressions

Released in mid-April 2003, this 135-card set featured artist renderings of the featured player's on the card fronts. Rookies in this set were inserted at 1:4.
COMPLETE SET (135) 40.00 100.00
COMP.SET w/o SP's (90) 20.00 40.00
1 Jean-Sebastien Giguere .30 .75
2 Paul Kariya .40 1.00
3 Dany Heatley .30 .75
4 Ilya Kovalchuk .40 1.00
5 Ray Bourque .50 1.25
6 Joe Thornton .40 1.00
7 Bobby Orr 1.00 2.50
8 Sergei Samsonov .25 .60
9 Maxim Afinogenov .20 .50
10 Martin Biron .25 .60
11 Miroslav Satan .30 .75
12 Roman Turek .30 .75
13 Jarome Iginla .30 .75
14 Arturs Irbe .25 .60
15 Ron Francis .40 1.00
16 Jeff O'Neill .20 .50
17 Alexei Zhamnov .25 .60
18 Eric Daze .20 .50
19 Jocelyn Thibault .25 .60
20 Rob Blake .30 .75
21 Patrick Roy .75 2.00
22 Joe Sakic .50 1.25
23 Peter Forsberg .40 1.00
24 Ray Bourque .50 1.25
25 Marc Denis .25 .60
26 Espen Knutsen .20 .50
27 Rostislav Klesla .20 .50
28 Marty Turco .30 .75
29 Bill Guerin .30 .75
30 Mike Modano .50 1.25
31 Steve Yzerman .60 1.50
32 Nicklas Lidstrom .30 .75
33 Sergei Fedorov .50 1.25
34 Curtis Joseph .30 .75
35 Brendan Shanahan .40 1.00
36 Gordie Howe 1.00 2.50
37 Mike Comrie .30 .75
38 Tommy Salo .25 .60
39 Wayne Gretzky 1.50 4.00
40 Roberto Luongo .50 1.25
41 Kristian Huselius .20 .50
42 Zigmund Palffy .30 .75
43 Felix Potvin .50 1.25
44 Jason Allison .25 .60
45 Manny Fernandez .25 .60
46 Marian Gaborik .50 1.25
47 Saku Koivu .30 .75
48 Doug Gilmour .40 1.00
49 Jose Theodore .30 .75
50 David Legwand .25 .60
51 Tomas Vokoun .25 .60
52 Martin Brodeur .60 1.50
53 Patrik Elias .30 .75
54 Joe Nieuwendyk .30 .75
55 Alexei Yashin .25 .60
56 Michael Peca .25 .60
57 Chris Osgood .30 .75
58 Eric Lindros .50 1.25
59 Pavel Bure .40 1.00
60 Brian Leetch .30 .75
61 Martin Havlat .25 .60
62 Marian Hossa .25 .60
63 Daniel Alfredsson .30 .75
64 John LeClair .30 .75
65 Jeremy Roenick .30 .75
66 Simon Gagne .30 .75
67 Tony Amonte .25 .60
68 Sean Burke .20 .50
69 Daniel Briere .25 .60
70 Alex Kovalev .30 .75
71 Johan Hedberg .30 .75
72 Mario Lemieux 1.00 2.50
73 Teemu Selanne .60 1.50
74 Evgeni Nabokov .25 .60
75 Owen Nolan .30 .75
76 Chris Pronger .25 .60
77 Doug Weight .30 .75
78 Keith Tkachuk .30 .75
79 Brad Richards .30 .75
80 Nikolai Khabibulin .30 .75
81 Vincent Lecavalier .25 .60
82 Mats Sundin .30 .75
83 Ed Belfour .30 .75
84 Alexander Mogilny .25 .60
85 Todd Bertuzzi .30 .75
86 Dan Cloutier .25 .60
87 Markus Naslund .25 .60
88 Jaromir Jagr .75 2.00
89 Peter Bondra .30 .75
90 Olaf Kolzig .30 .75
91 Jonathan Hedstrom RC .50 1.25
92 Henrik Zetterberg RC 5.00 12.00
93 Steve Ott RC 1.00 2.50
94 Jay Bouwmeester RC 1.50 4.00
95 Rick Nash RC 4.00 10.00
96 Pascal LeClaire RC .60 1.50
97 Jason Spezza RC 3.00 8.00
98 Dick Tarnstrom RC .50 1.25
99 Alexei Smirnov RC .60 1.50
100 Ron Hainsey RC .50 1.25
101 Michael Leighton RC .75 2.00
102 Ian MacNeil RC .50 1.25
103 Anton Volchenkov RC .50 1.25
104 Ales Hemsky RC 2.00 5.00
105 Steve Eminger RC .50 1.25
106 Shaone Morrisonn RC .50 1.25
107 Levente Szuper RC .75 2.00
108 Brooks Orpik RC .75 2.00
109 Curtis Sanford RC .75 2.00
110 Jared Aulin RC .50 1.25
111 Eric Godard RC .50 1.25
112 Jim Fahey RC .50 1.25
113 Rickard Wallin RC .50 1.25
114 Mike Cammalleri RC 1.50 4.00
115 Mikael Tellqvist RC .50 1.25
116 Chuck Kobasew RC .60 1.50
117 Scottie Upshall RC .60 1.50
118 Jerred Smithson RC .50 1.25
119 Jeff Taffe RC .50 1.25
120 Cody Rudkowsky RC .50 1.25
121 Alexander Frolov RC 1.00 2.50
122 Alexander Svitov RC .50 1.25
123 Stanislav Chistov RC .50 1.25
124 P-M Bouchard RC .75 2.00
125 Patrick Sharp RC 1.50 4.00
126 Ryan Miller RC 3.00 8.00
127 Tomas Malec RC .50 1.25
128 Curtis Murphy RC .50 1.25
129 Jordan Leopold RC .75 2.00
130 Carlo Colaiacovo RC .75 2.00
131 Alexei Semenov RC .50 1.25
132 Craig Andersson RC 1.50 4.00
133 Jim Vandermeer RC .50 1.25
134 Ray Emery RC 1.50 4.00
135 Paul Manning RC .50 1.25
SC1 Joe Thornton Sample .75 2.00

2002-03 UD Artistic Impressions Gold

*1-90 VETS/199: 2.5X TO 6X BASIC CARDS
1-90 VETERAN PRINT RUN 199
*91-135 ROOK/75: 1.2X TO 3X BASIC RC
91-135 ROOKIE PRINT RUN 75

2002-03 UD Artistic Impressions Artist's Touch Jerseys

Singles in this 25-card memorabilia set were serial-numbered to 499 copies each.
STATED PRINT RUN 499 SER.#'d SETS
*GOLD/199: .5X TO 1.2X JSY/499
ATBS Brendan Shanahan 3.00 8.00
ATCJ Curtis Joseph 3.00 8.00
ATDH Dany Heatley 4.00 10.00
ATFP Felix Potvin 4.00 10.00
ATIK Ilya Kovalchuk 5.00 12.00
ATJI Jarome Iginla 4.00 10.00
ATJJ Jaromir Jagr 4.00 10.00
ATJR Jeremy Roenick 4.00 10.00
ATJS Joe Sakic 5.00 12.00
ATJT Joe Thornton 5.00 12.00
ATMB Martin Brodeur 8.00 20.00
ATMD Mike Dunham 3.00 8.00
ATML Mario Lemieux 10.00 25.00
ATMM Mike Modano 5.00 12.00
ATMS Mats Sundin 3.00 8.00
ATOK Olaf Kolzig 3.00 8.00
ATPF Peter Forsberg 5.00 12.00
ATPK Paul Kariya 3.00 8.00
ATPR Patrick Roy 10.00 25.00
ATRB Ray Bourque 5.00 12.00
ATSB Sean Burke 3.00 8.00
ATSF Sergei Fedorov 4.00 10.00
ATSG Simon Gagne 4.00 10.00
ATTH Jose Theodore 4.00 10.00
ATZP Zigmund Palffy 3.00 8.00

2002-03 UD Artistic Impressions Artwork Signatures

Inserted at one per case, these framed prints of the artwork used for the set carried certified player autographs under the print in the frame.
AI1 Ray Bourque 60.00 150.00
AI2 Martin Brodeur 80.00 200.00
AI3 Pavel Bure 30.00 80.00
AI4 Mike Comrie 20.00 50.00
AI5 Dany Heatley 50.00 100.00
AI6 Gordie Howe SP 200.00 400.00
AI7 Jarome Iginla 30.00 80.00
AI8 Curtis Joseph 50.00 120.00
AI9 Ilya Kovalchuk 60.00 150.00
AI10 John LeClair 25.00 60.00
AI11 Markus Naslund 25.00 60.00
AI12 Bobby Orr SP 300.00 600.00
AI13 Patrick Roy 100.00 250.00
AI14 Sergei Samsonov 25.00 60.00
AI15 Jose Theodore 40.00 100.00
AI16 Joe Thornton 60.00 150.00
AI17 Steve Yzerman 60.00 150.00

2002-03 UD Artistic Impressions UD Promos

Inserted into copies of the June 2003 issue of Beckett Hockey Collector, this 90-card set parallels the base set but carried a silver foil "UD Promo" stamp across the card fronts.
*UD PROMOS: .8X TO 2X BASIC CARDS

2002-03 UD Artistic Impressions Common Ground

COMPLETE SET (22) 20.00 40.00
STATED ODDS 1:8
*GOLD/75: 1X TO 2.5X BASIC INSERTS
CG1 P.Roy 2.00 5.00
P.LeClaire
CG2 A.Hemsky/J.Jagr 1.50 4.00
CG3 W.Gretzky/J.Spezza 4.00 10.00
CG4 J.Bouwmeester/N.Lidstrom 1.25 3.00
CG5 R.Cechmanek/L.Szuper 1.00 2.50
CG6 R.Nash/M.Lemieux 3.00 8.00
CG7 R.Bourque/J.Bouwmeester 1.50 4.00
CG8 P.Bouchard/S.Koivu 1.25 3.00
CG9 G.Howe/R.Nash 2.00 5.00
CG10 A.Frolov/P.Bure 1.25 3.00
CG11 R.Blake/B.Orpik 1.25 3.00
CG12 H.Zetterberg/M.Sundin 1.50 4.00
CG13 S.Samsonov/S.Chistov 1.00 2.50
CG14 J.Leopold/R.Bourque 1.25 3.00
CG15 B.Guerin/C.Kobasew 1.00 2.50
CG16 A.Svitov/S.Federov 1.50 4.00
CG17 J.Roenick/S.Upshall 1.50 4.00
CG18 C.Colaiacovo/N.Lidstrom 1.25 3.00
CG19 S.Yzerman/S.Ott 1.50 4.00
CG20 J.Taffe/M.Modano 1.25 3.00
CG21 P.Forsberg/H.Zetterberg 2.00 5.00
CG22 P.LeClaire/M.Brodeur 2.00 5.00

2002-03 UD Artistic Impressions Flashbacks

COMPLETE SET (9) 15.00 30.00
STATED ODDS 1:20
*GOLD/75: 1.2X TO 3X BASIC INSERTS
UD1 Joe Sakic 2.00 5.00
UD2 Mike Modano 1.25 3.00
UD3 Mario Lemieux 2.50 6.00
UD4 Brian Leetch .75 2.00
UD5 Ron Francis .75 2.00
UD6 Pavel Bure 1.00 2.50
UD7 Ray Bourque 2.00 5.00
UD8 Sergei Fedorov 1.50 4.00
UD9 Jaromir Jagr 1.50 4.00
UD10 Jeremy Roenick 1.00 2.50
UD11 Gordie Howe 2.50 6.00

2002-03 UD Artistic Impressions Great Depictions

COMPLETE SET (12) 12.00 30.00
STATED ODDS 1:20
*GOLD/75: 1.2X TO 3X BASIC INSERTS
GD1 Wayne Gretzky 3.00 8.00
GD2 Patrick Roy 2.50 6.00
GD3 Martin Brodeur 2.50 6.00
GD4 Bobby Orr 3.00 8.00
GD5 Ilya Kovalchuk 1.00 2.50
GD6 Mario Lemieux 3.00 8.00
GD7 Ray Bourque 2.00 5.00
GD8 Steve Yzerman 2.50 6.00
GD9 Gordie Howe 2.00 5.00
GD10 Pavel Bure .75 2.00
GD11 Marian Gaborik 1.00 2.50
GD12 Joe Thornton 1.00 2.50

2002-03 UD Artistic Impressions Performers Jerseys

Singles in this 6-card memorabilia set were serial-numbered to 199.
*GOLD/75: .5X TO 1.2X BASIC JSY/199
SSJJ Jaromir Jagr 4.00 10.00
SSJL John LeClair 3.00 8.00
SSMB Martin Brodeur 10.00 25.00
SSMM Mark Messier 3.00 8.00
SSPR Patrick Roy 12.00 30.00
SSSY Steve Yzerman 12.00 30.00

2002-03 UD Artistic Impressions Retrospectives

This 100-card set was inserted one per pack. These cards were smaller versions of the first 90 base cards with colored borders. The final 10 cards (rookies in the base set) were replaced with different players.
COMPLETE SET (100) 30.00 60.00
STATED ODDS 1:1
*SILVER/99: 2X TO 5X BASIC INSERT
*GOLD/25: 8X TO 20X BASIC INSERT
R1 Jean-Sebastien Giguere .25 .60
R2 Paul Kariya .30 .75
R3 Dany Heatley .40 1.00
R4 Ilya Kovalchuk .40 1.00
R5 Ray Bourque .40 1.00
R6 Joe Thornton .40 1.00
R7 Bobby Orr 1.25 3.00
R8 Sergei Samsonov .25 .60
R9 Maxim Afinogenov .20 .50
R10 Martin Biron .20 .50
R11 Miroslav Satan .25 .60
R12 Roman Turek .25 .60
R13 Jarome Iginla .40 1.00
R14 Arturs Irbe .25 .60
R15 Ron Francis .25 .60
R16 Jeff O'Neill .20 .50
R17 Alexei Zhamnov .25 .60
R18 Eric Daze .20 .50
R19 Jocelyn Thibault .25 .60
R20 Rob Blake .25 .60
R21 Patrick Roy 1.25 3.00
R22 Joe Sakic .40 1.00
R23 Peter Forsberg .30 .75
R24 Ray Bourque .40 1.00
R25 Marc Denis .20 .50
R26 Espen Knutsen .20 .50
R27 Rostislav Klesla .20 .50
R28 Marty Turco .25 .60
R29 Bill Guerin .25 .60
R30 Mike Modano .40 1.00
R31 Steve Yzerman 1.00 2.50
R32 Nicklas Lidstrom .30 .75
R33 Sergei Fedorov .40 1.00
R34 Curtis Joseph .30 .75
R35 Brendan Shanahan .30 .75
R36 Gordie Howe 1.25 3.00
R37 Mike Comrie .20 .50
R38 Tommy Salo .25 .60
R39 Wayne Gretzky 1.50 4.00
R40 Roberto Luongo .50 1.25
R41 Kristian Huselius .20 .50
R42 Zigmund Palffy .25 .60
R43 Felix Potvin .40 1.00
R44 Jason Allison .20 .50
R45 Manny Fernandez .25 .60
R46 Marian Gaborik .30 .75
R47 Saku Koivu .30 .75
R48 Doug Gilmour .25 .60
R49 Jose Theodore .30 .75
R50 David Legwand .20 .50
R51 Tomas Vokoun .25 .60
R52 Martin Brodeur 1.00 2.50
R53 Patrik Elias .25 .60
R54 Joe Nieuwendyk .25 .60
R55 Alexei Yashin .25 .60
R56 Michael Peca .20 .50
R57 Chris Osgood .30 .75
R58 Eric Lindros .30 .75
R59 Pavel Bure .30 .75
R60 Brian Leetch .25 .60
R61 Martin Havlat .25 .60
R62 Marian Hossa .30 .75
R63 Daniel Alfredsson .25 .60
R64 John LeClair .30 .75
R65 Jeremy Roenick .40 1.00
R66 Simon Gagne .30 .75
R67 Tony Amonte .25 .60
R68 Sean Burke .20 .50
R69 Daniel Briere .25 .60
R70 Alexei Kovalev .25 .60

R71 Johan Hedberg .25 .60
R72 Mario Lemieux 1.25 3.00
R73 Teemu Selanne .30 .75
R74 Evgeni Nabokov .25 .60
R75 Owen Nolan .20 .50
R76 Chris Pronger .20 .50
R77 Doug Weight .25 .60
R78 Keith Tkachuk .30 .75
R79 Brad Richards .25 .60
R80 Nikolai Khabibulin .30 .75
R81 Vincent Lecavalier .30 .75
R82 Mats Sundin .30 .75
R83 Ed Belfour .30 .75
R84 Alexander Mogilny .25 .60
R85 Todd Bertuzzi .30 .75
R86 Dan Cloutier .25 .60
R87 Markus Naslund .30 .75
R88 Jaromir Jagr .40 1.00
R89 Peter Bondra .25 .60
R90 Olaf Kolzig .25 .60
R91 Jason Spezza .75 2.00
R92 Rick Nash 1.25 3.00
R93 Jay Bouwmeester .50 1.25
R94 Stanislav Chistov .40 1.00
R95 P-M Bouchard .40 1.00
R96 Pascal LeClaire .40 1.00
R97 Brooks Orpik .40 1.00
R98 Steve Ott .40 1.00
R99 Alexander Frolov .60 1.50
R100 Alexander Svitov .30 .75

2002-03 UD Artistic Impressions Retrospectives Autographs

This autographed partial parallel set was serial-numbered to 10-25 copies each.
STATED PRINT RUN 10-25
R3 Dany Heatley
R4 Ilya Kovalchuk 40.00 80.00
R5 Ray Bourque 40.00 80.00
R6 Joe Thornton 30.00 60.00
R7 Bobby Orr 125.00 200.00
R9 Maxim Afinogenov 10.00 25.00
R13 Jarome Iginla 15.00 40.00
R24 Ray Bourque/10
R34 Curtis Joseph 30.00 60.00
R36 Gordie Howe/10
R37 Mike Comrie 15.00 40.00
R39 Wayne Gretzky 125.00 200.00
R49 Jose Theodore 12.00 30.00
R52 Martin Brodeur 75.00 150.00
R87 Markus Naslund/10
R91 Jason Spezza 40.00 80.00
R92 Rick Nash 50.00 100.00
R93 Jay Bouwmeester 10.00 25.00
R94 Stanislav Chistov 15.00 40.00
R95 P-M Bouchard 12.00 30.00
R96 Pascal LeClaire 12.00 30.00
R97 Brooks Orpik 10.00 25.00
R98 Steve Ott 12.00 30.00
R99 Alexander Frolov 15.00 40.00
R100 Alexander Svitov 12.00 30.00

2002-03 UD Artistic Impressions Right Track

*GOLD/175: .5X TO 1.2X BASIC INSERTS
RTAF Alexander Frolov 5.00 12.00
RTDB Daniel Briere 3.00 8.00
RTDH Dany Heatley 4.00 10.00
RTJA Jared Aulin 2.50 6.00
RTJL Jamie Lundmark 3.00 8.00
RTJW Justin Williams 3.00 8.00
RTKC Kyle Calder 2.50 6.00
RTMA Maxim Afinogenov 2.50 6.00
RTME Martin Erat 2.50 6.00
RTSC Stanislav Chistov 2.50 6.00
RTSR Steve Reinprecht 2.50 6.00

2008-09 UD Black

Cards #103-#124 were Rookie Cards issued as exchange cards. All of these were signed and numbered to 99 copies.
1 Alexander Ovechkin 30.00 80.00
2 Cam Neely 8.00 20.00
3 Saku Koivu 8.00 20.00
4 Dany Heatley 8.00 20.00
5 Dino Ciccarelli 8.00 20.00
6 Dominik Hasek 10.00 25.00
7 Eric Staal 10.00 25.00
8 Evgeni Malkin 25.00 60.00
9 Henrik Lundqvist 10.00 25.00
10 Henrik Zetterberg 10.00 25.00
11 Ilya Kovalchuk 8.00 20.00
12 Peter Forsberg 10.00 25.00
13 Jarome Iginla 8.00 20.00
14 Jaromir Jagr 20.00 50.00
15 Sidney Crosby 30.00 80.00
16 Roberto Luongo 10.00 25.00
17 Joe Sakic 12.00 30.00
18 Joe Thornton 10.00 25.00
19 Jonathan Cheechoo 8.00 20.00
20 Jordan Staal 8.00 20.00
21 Lanny McDonald 8.00 20.00
22 Jason Spezza 8.00 20.00
23 Luc Robitaille 8.00 20.00
24 Marian Gaborik 10.00 25.00
25 Ryan Miller 8.00 20.00
26 Mario Lemieux 25.00 60.00
27 Mark Messier 10.00 25.00
28 Markus Naslund 6.00 15.00
29 Martin Brodeur 15.00 40.00
30 Martin St. Louis 8.00 20.00
31 Mats Sundin 8.00 20.00
32 Michael Ryder 5.00 12.00
33 Miikka Kiprusoff 6.00 15.00
34 Mike Modano 12.00 30.00
35 Nicklas Lidstrom 8.00 20.00
36 Patrice Bergeron 10.00 25.00
37 Simon Gagne 8.00 20.00
38 Patrick Roy 20.00 50.00
39 Paul Kariya 10.00 25.00
40 Vincent Lecavalier 6.00 15.00
41 Ray Bourque 12.00 30.00
42 Daniel Alfredsson 8.00 20.00
43 Derick Brassard AU RC 6.00 15.00
44 Mark Fistric AU RC 8.00 20.00
45 Alex Goligoski AU RC 12.00 30.00
46 Claude Giroux AU RC 20.00 50.00
47 Jon Filewich AU RC 8.00 20.00
48 Robbie Earl AU RC 6.00 15.00
49 Ilya Zubov AU RC 8.00 20.00
50 Steve Mason AU RC 15.00 40.00
51 Brian Boyle AU RC 8.00 20.00
52 Shawn Matthias AU RC 10.00 25.00
53 Ryan Stone AU RC 6.00 15.00
54 Teddy Purcell AU RC 12.00 30.00
55 Tom Cavanagh AU RC EXCH 8.00 20.00
56 Kyle Okposo AU RC 10.00 25.00
57 Marc-Andre Gragnani AU RC 8.00 20.00
58 Jonathan Ericsson AU RC 10.00 25.00
59 Kyle Turris AU RC 15.00 40.00
60 Brian Lee RC 8.00 20.00
61 Justin Abdelkader RC 15.00 40.00
62 Theo Peckham RC 10.00 25.00
63 Adam Pineault RC 8.00 20.00
64 Boris Valabik RC 10.00 25.00
65 Darren Helm RC 10.00 25.00
66 Mike Iggulden RC 8.00 20.00
67 Tim Ramholt RC 8.00 20.00
68 Matt D'Agostini RC 8.00 20.00
69 Andrew Ebbett RC 6.00 15.00
70 Sami Lepisto RC 8.00 20.00
71 Tyler Plante RC 8.00 20.00
72 Niklas Hjalmarsson RC 15.00 40.00
73 Alex Foster RC 8.00 20.00
74 Clay Wilson RC 6.00 15.00
75 Zach Fitzgerald RC 10.00 25.00
76 Kyle Greentree RC 10.00 25.00
77 Joe Jensen RC 10.00 25.00
78 David Brine RC 6.00 15.00
79 B.J. Crombeen RC 6.00 15.00
80 Mike Brown RC 12.00 30.00
81 Jordan Hendry RC 8.00 20.00
82 Corey Locke RC 8.00 20.00
83 Cody McLeod RC 8.00 20.00
84 Jesse Winchester RC 6.00 15.00
85 Lauri Korpikoski RC 6.00 15.00
86 Jack Hillen RC 8.00 20.00
87 Mike Mole RC 8.00 20.00
88 Jordan LaVallee RC 10.00 25.00
89 Erik Ersberg RC 8.00 20.00
90 Darryl Boyce RC 8.00 20.00
91 Tom Sestito RC 10.00 25.00
92 Joey Mormina RC 8.00 20.00
93 Chris Minard RC 10.00 25.00
94 Pascal Pelletier RC 6.00 15.00
95 Tim Conboy RC 8.00 20.00
96 Kevin Doell RC 6.00 15.00
97 Andrew Murray RC 8.00 20.00
98 Brandon Nolan RC 8.00 20.00
99 Colin Stuart RC 8.00 20.00
100 Danny Taylor RC 8.00 20.00
101 Dan LaCosta RC 10.00 25.00
102 Mattias Ritola RC 8.00 20.00
103 Steven Stamkos AU RC 100.00 250.00
104 Nikita Filatov AU RC 15.00 40.00
105 Jakub Voracek AU RC 30.00 80.00
106 Fabian Brunnstrom AU RC 12.00 30.00
107 Michael Frolik AU RC 15.00 40.00
108 Drew Doughty AU RC 100.00 250.00
109 Colton Gillies AU RC 12.00 30.00
110 Patric Hornqvist AU RC 15.00 40.00
111 Petr Vrana AU RC 10.00 25.00
112 Luca Sbisa AU RC 10.00 25.00
113 Mikkel Boedker AU RC 20.00 50.00
114 Viktor Tikhonov AU RC 12.00 30.00
115 T.J. Oshie AU RC 30.00 80.00
116 Patrik Berglund AU RC 12.00 30.00
117 Alex Pietrangelo AU RC 20.00 50.00
118 Nikolai Kulemin AU RC 15.00 40.00
119 Luke Schenn AU RC 20.00 50.00
120 Blake Wheeler AU RC 40.00 100.00
121 Brandon Sutter AU RC 15.00 40.00
122 Zach Bogosian AU RC 15.00 40.00
123 James Neal AU RC 30.00 80.00
124 Zach Boychuk AU RC 15.00 40.00

2008-09 UD Black Autographs Jerseys

STATED PRINT RUN 25 SERIAL #'d SETS
BAJAF Alexander Frolov
BAJAH Ales Hemsky
BAJAK Anze Kopitar 30.00 80.00
BAJAM Al MacInnis 15.00 40.00
BAJAO Alexander Ovechkin 50.00 120.00
BAJBL Brian Leetch 20.00 50.00
BAJBS Borje Salming 20.00 50.00
BAJDH Dominik Hasek 25.00 60.00
BAJES Eric Staal 25.00 60.00
BAJHA Dale Hawerchuk 25.00 60.00
BAJHE Dany Heatley 12.00 30.00
BAJHJ Milan Hejduk 15.00 40.00
BAJHZ Henrik Zetterberg 25.00 60.00
BAJIK Ilya Kovalchuk 20.00 50.00
BAJJG Jean-Sebastien Giguere 20.00 50.00
BAJJI Jarome Iginla 20.00 50.00
BAJJJ Jack Johnson 12.00 30.00
BAJJT Jonathan Toews 60.00 120.00
BAJLR Luc Robitaille 20.00 50.00
BAJMB Martin Brodeur 60.00 120.00
BAJMF Marc-Andre Fleury 40.00 80.00
BAJMG Marian Gaborik
BAJMM Mike Modano 30.00 80.00
BAJMN Markus Naslund 15.00 40.00
BAJMR Michael Ryder 12.00 30.00
BAJMS Martin St. Louis 15.00 40.00
BAJMT Marty Turco 20.00 50.00
BAJMU Peter Mueller 15.00 40.00
BAJPB Patrice Bergeron 25.00 60.00
BAJPK Patrick Kane 50.00 100.00
BAJPR Patrick Roy 100.00 200.00
BAJPS Paul Stastny 20.00 50.00
BAJRB Ray Bourque 30.00 80.00
BAJRG Ryan Getzlaf 30.00 80.00
BAJRL Rod Langway 15.00 40.00
BAJRM Ryan Miller 20.00 50.00
BAJRV Alexander Radulov
BAJSC Sidney Crosby 175.00 300.00
BAJSG Simon Gagne 20.00 50.00
BAJST Peter Stastny 40.00 80.00
BAJTH Joe Thornton 25.00 60.00
BAJVL Vincent Lecavalier 15.00 40.00

2008-09 UD Black Game Night Autographs Tickets

STATED PRINT RUN 25 SERIAL #'d SETS
GNAO Alexander Ovechkin 75.00 150.00
GNBC Bobby Clarke 20.00 50.00
GNBO Bobby Orr 75.00 150.00
GNCN Cam Neely 15.00 40.00
GNCP Carey Price 100.00 175.00
GNDC Dino Ciccarelli 20.00 50.00
GNDH Dale Hawerchuk 25.00 60.00
GNDS Devin Setoguchi 15.00 40.00
GNEM Evgeni Malkin 60.00 150.00
GNFM Frank Mahovlich 20.00 50.00
GNGF Grant Fuhr 20.00 50.00
GNGH Gordie Howe 100.00 175.00
GNGL Guy Lafleur 25.00 60.00
GNHA Dominik Hasek 60.00 120.00
GNHE Dany Heatley 50.00 100.00
GNIK Ilya Kovalchuk 20.00 50.00
GNJB Johnny Bucyk 20.00 50.00
GNJI Jarome Iginla 30.00 80.00
GNJJ Jack Johnson 12.00 30.00
GNJK Jari Kurri 25.00 60.00
GNJS James Sheppard 12.00 30.00
GNJT Jiri Tlusty 30.00 60.00
GNLM Lanny McDonald 15.00 40.00
GNLR Larry Robinson 20.00 50.00
GNMB Mike Bossy 20.00 50.00
GNMM Mark Messier 60.00 120.00
GNMN Markus Naslund 15.00 40.00
GNMO Mike Modano 30.00 80.00
GNMS Marc Staal 20.00 50.00
GNMT Marty Turco 20.00 50.00
GNNB Nicklas Backstrom 30.00 80.00
GNNF Nick Foligno 20.00 50.00
GNNL Nicklas Lidstrom 40.00 80.00
GNPK Patrick Kane 75.00 150.00
GNPM Peter Mueller 15.00 40.00
GNPS Paul Stastny 20.00 50.00
GNRB Ray Bourque 30.00 80.00
GNRL Rod Langway 15.00 40.00
GNRN Rick Nash 30.00 60.00
GNRO Luc Robitaille 20.00 50.00
GNRS Ryan Smyth 15.00 40.00
GNSC Sidney Crosby 100.00 200.00
GNSG Sam Gagner 30.00 80.00
GNSS Steve Shutt 20.00 50.00
GNST Peter Stastny 30.00 60.00
GNTH Joe Thornton 25.00 60.00
GNTL Ted Lindsay 20.00 50.00
GNTO Jonathan Toews 75.00 150.00
GNVL Vincent Lecavalier 20.00 50.00
GNWG Wayne Gretzky 200.00 300.00

2008-09 UD Black Foursomes Jerseys

STATED PRINT RUN 25 SERIAL #'d SETS
UBJ4EHMS Hull/Sav/Wils/Espo 20.00 50.00
UBJ4ENBB Espo/Bcyk/Brq/Cam 20.00 50.00
UBJ4FKAM Messi/Kurri/Fhr/Andr 40.00 80.00
UBJ4HMMH Hwe/Hull/Mahv/Mikt 50.00 100.00
UBJ4IGSK Ignl/St.L/Ggne/Kane
UBJ4KTHN Htly/Nash/Karya/Tng 15.00 40.00
UBJ4LCGM Grtz/Mario/Mssi/Sid 60.00 120.00
UBJ4LDBP Mrio/Dnne/Perrlt/Belv 30.00 60.00
UBJ4LZKM Mess/Ltch/Kvalv/Zbv 25.00 60.00
UBJ4MRTM Mdno/Rnik/Mlln/Tkac 20.00 50.00
UBJ4NBLH Howe/Laflr/Bosy/Nly 30.00 80.00
UBJ4PPBR Brq/Rbnsn/Ptvn/Phnf 20.00 50.00
UBJ4PPJJ Prong/Phnf/Jhnsn/Jhns 12.00 30.00
UBJ4RBFE Roy/Fuhr/Espo/Brodr 30.00 80.00
UBJ4RBLF Roy/Brdur/Flry/Lungo 30.00 80.00
UBJ4RNGW Nder/Wrd/Rchrd/Gig 12.00 30.00
UBJ4SLTS Sakc/Thrnt/Lecv/Spz 20.00 50.00
UBJ4SNAZ Sund/Alfrd/Nslnd/Zett 15.00 40.00
UBJ4SRBH Hull/Bcyk/Robit/Shnh 25.00 50.00
UBJ4TPKG Tws/Kane/Ggnr/Price

2008-09 UD Black Jerseys Duals

STATED PRINT RUN 50 SERIAL #'d SETS
*GOLD/25: .5X TO 1.2X BASIC DUAL
BDJ2AS J.Spezza/D.Alfredsson 10.00 25.00
BDJ2BJ B.Shanahan/J.Sakic 15.00 40.00
BDJ2BP M.Brodeur/Z.Parise 12.00 30.00
BDJ2BS E.Staal/R.Brind'Amour 12.00 30.00
BDJ2CG W.Gretzky/S.Crosby 50.00 100.00
BDJ2DD P.Datsyuk/K.Draper 12.00 30.00
BDJ2DZ H.Zetterberg/P.Datsyuk 12.00 30.00
BDJ2FB P.Bergeron/M.Fernandez 15.00 40.00
BDJ2GD R.DiPietro/B.Guerin 10.00 25.00
BDJ2GK M.Gaborik.M.Koivu 10.00 25.00
BDJ2HG M.Gaborik/M.Hossa 12.00 30.00
BDJ2IK M.Kiprusoff/J.Iginla 10.00 25.00
BDJ2JL J.Jagr/H.Lundqvist 25.00 60.00
BDJ2JP J.Sakic/P.Roy 30.00 60.00
BDJ2JR J.Sakic/R.Smyth 15.00 40.00
BDJ2KB P.Kariya/B.Boyes 12.00 30.00
BDJ2KL I.Kovalchuk/K.Lehtonen 10.00 25.00
BDJ2KP D.Phaneuf/M.Kiprusoff 10.00 25.00
BDJ2LC S.Crosby/M.Lemieux 40.00 80.00
BDJ2LK R.Luongo/M.Kiprusoff 12.00 30.00
BDJ2LM M.Lemieux/L.Murphy 20.00 50.00
BDJ2LN R.Luongo/M.Naslund 12.00 30.00
BDJ2LS V.Lecavalier/J.Spezza 10.00 25.00
BDJ2MA M.Sundin/A.Steen 10.00 25.00
BDJ2MH E.Malkin/M.Hossa 30.00 80.00
BDJ2MM L.McDonald/J.Mullen 10.00 25.00
BDJ2MR M.Modano/J.Roenick 15.00 40.00
BDJ2MT J.Thornton/P.Marleau 12.00 30.00
BDJ2NL M.Naslund/T.Linden 10.00 25.00
BDJ2PG J.Giguere/C.Pronger 10.00 25.00
BDJ2PM P.Roy/M.Brodeur 40.00 80.00
BDJ2PN S.Niedermayer/C.Pronger 10.00 25.00
BDJ2RB L.Robitaille/R.Blake 10.00 25.00
BDJ2RH D.Roloson/A.Hemsky 8.00 20.00
BDJ2RP R.Nash/P.Leclaire 10.00 25.00
BDJ2RS R.Langway/S.Shutt 10.00 25.00
BDJ2RT V.Toskala/A.Raycroft 15.00 40.00
BDJ2SN R.Nash/B.Shanahan 12.00 30.00
BDJ2SR L.Robitaille/B.Shanahan 12.00 30.00
BDJ2SS J.Sakic/P.Stastny 15.00 40.00
BDJ2VJ T.Vokoun/O.Jokinen 8.00 20.00
BDJ2VM V.Lecavalier/M.St. Louis 10.00 25.00

2008-09 UD Black Lustrous Materials Autographs Jerseys

STATED PRINT RUN 25 SERIAL #'d SETS
LM2AH Ales Hemsky 40.00 80.00
LM2AO Alexander Ovechkin 75.00 150.00
LM2AR Alexander Radulov
LM2BC Bobby Clarke 25.00 60.00
LM2BF Bernie Federko 12.00 30.00
LM2BL Brian Leetch 15.00 40.00
LM2CD Chris Drury 25.00 60.00
LM2CN Cam Neely 25.00 60.00
LM2DH Dany Heatley 15.00 40.00
LM2DR Dwayne Roloson 12.00 30.00
LM2EJ Erik Johnson 12.00 30.00
LM2EM Evgeni Malkin 40.00 80.00
LM2ES Eric Staal 20.00 50.00
LM2GA Simon Gagne 15.00 40.00
LM2HZ Henrik Zetterberg 50.00 100.00
LM2IK Ilya Kovalchuk 15.00 30.00
LM2JG Jean-Sebastien Giguere 15.00 40.00
LM2JI Jarome Iginla 50.00 100.00
LM2JJ Jack Johnson 10.00 25.00
LM2JT Jonathan Toews 60.00 120.00
LM2KO Anze Kopitar 25.00 60.00
LM2MB Martin Brodeur 75.00 150.00
LM2MC Mike Cammalleri 12.00 30.00
LM2ME Mark Messier 60.00 150.00
LM2MG Marian Gaborik
LM2MM Mike Modano 25.00 60.00
LM2MN Markus Naslund 12.00 30.00
LM2MR Michael Ryder 10.00 25.00
LM2MS Miroslav Satan 15.00 40.00
LM2PK Patrick Kane 50.00 100.00
LM2PM Peter Mueller 40.00 80.00
LM2PR Patrick Roy 75.00 150.00
LM2PS Paul Stastny 12.00 30.00
LM2RB Ray Bourque 30.00 60.00
LM2RG Ryan Getzlaf 25.00 60.00
LM2RN Rick Nash 15.00 40.00
LM2SC Sidney Crosby 100.00 200.00
LM2SG Sam Gagner 50.00 100.00
LM2TH Joe Thornton 25.00 60.00
LM2TV Thomas Vanek 15.00 40.00
LM2VO Tomas Vokoun 12.00 30.00
LM2WG Wayne Gretzky 175.00 350.00

2008-09 UD Black Marks of Obsidian Autographs Patches

STATED PRINT RUN 35 SERIAL #'d SETS
MOAM Al MacInnis
MOAO Alexander Ovechkin 60.00 120.00
MOAT Alex Tanguay 8.00 20.00
MOBC Bobby Clarke 12.00 30.00
MOBH Bobby Hull 20.00 50.00
MOBL Brian Leetch 12.00 30.00
MOBO Mike Bossy 12.00 30.00
MOBS Borje Salming 12.00 30.00
MOCN Cam Neely 12.00 30.00
MODC Dino Ciccarelli 12.00 30.00
MODH Dany Heatley 12.00 30.00
MODO Dominik Hasek 20.00 50.00
MOEM Evgeni Malkin 30.00 80.00
MOES Eric Staal 15.00 40.00
MOGF Grant Fuhr 20.00 50.00
MOGL Guy Lafleur 15.00 40.00
MOGP Gilbert Perreault 12.00 30.00
MOHA Dale Hawerchuk 15.00 40.00
MOHE Milan Hejduk 10.00 25.00
MOHZ Henrik Zetterberg 30.00 60.00
MOIK Ilya Kovalchuk 12.00 30.00
MOJB Johnny Bucyk 12.00 30.00
MOJC Jonathan Cheechoo 12.00 30.00
MOJG Jean-Sebastien Giguere 15.00 40.00
MOJK Jari Kurri 15.00 40.00
MOJM Joe Mullen 10.00 25.00
MOJT Joe Thornton 15.00 40.00
MOLM Lanny McDonald 12.00 30.00
MOLR Luc Robitaille 12.00 30.00
MOMB Martin Brodeur 50.00 100.00
MOMD Marcel Dionne 15.00 40.00
MOMG Marian Gaborik
MOMH Marian Hossa 25.00 60.00
MOMM Mike Modano 20.00 50.00
MOMN Markus Naslund 10.00 25.00
MOMR Michael Ryder 8.00 20.00
MOMT Marty Turco 12.00 30.00
MONL Nicklas Lidstrom 15.00 40.00
MOOA Adam Oates 12.00 30.00
MOPK Phil Kessel 15.00 40.00
MOPS Peter Stastny 12.00 30.00
MORB Ray Bourque 20.00 50.00
MORH Ron Hextall 20.00 50.00
MORO Larry Robinson 12.00 30.00
MORS Ryan Smyth 10.00 25.00
MOSC Sidney Crosby 100.00 200.00
MOSG Simon Gagne 15.00 40.00
MOSK Saku Koivu 15.00 40.00
MOSM Stan Mikita 20.00 50.00
MOVL Vincent Lecavalier 25.00 60.00

2008-09 UD Black Marks of Obsidian Autographs Patches Duals

STATED PRINT RUN 25 SERIAL #'d SETS
MO2BG Bossy/Gillies 15.00 40.00
MO2BP Bucyk/Perreault 15.00 40.00
MO2CG S.Gagner/A.Cogliano 12.00 30.00
MO2DV M.Dionne/R.Vachon 20.00 50.00
MO2EH B.Hull/T.Esposito 25.00 60.00
MO2EJ E.Staal/J.Staal 12.00 30.00
MO2EO B.Orr/P.Esposito 150.00 250.00
MO2FJ F.Mahovlich/J.Bower 25.00 60.00
MO2FK G.Fuhr/J.Kurri 40.00 80.00
MO2FM E.Malkin/M.Fleury 50.00 100.00
MO2FT Tlusty/Foligno 15.00 40.00
MO2GB M.Gaborik/P.Bouchard 20.00 50.00
MO2GG J.Giguere/R.Getzlaf 15.00 40.00
MO2HN D.Heatley/R.Nash 30.00 80.00
MO2HS Stastny/Nash 15.00 40.00
MO2IT J.Iginla/A.Tanguay 15.00 40.00
MO2JJ J.Johnson/E.Johnson 12.00 30.00
MO2JM J.Staal/M.Staal 15.00 40.00
MO2KK Kurri/S.Koivu 15.00 40.00
MO2LH G.Howe/T.Lindsay 40.00 100.00
MO2LM M.Lemieux/M.Messier 100.00 200.00
MO2LS G.Lafleur/S.Shutt 20.00 50.00
MO2LZ Zetterberg/Lidstrom 40.00 100.00
MO2ML M.Messier/B.Leetch 100.00 200.00
MO2MM M.Modano/J.Mullen 20.00 50.00
MO2MS McDonald/Salming 20.00 50.00
MO2NB R.Bourque/C.Neely 25.00 60.00
MO2NO C.Neely/A.Oates 15.00 40.00
MO2NZ Zetterberg/Naslund 20.00 50.00
MO2OM A.Ovechkin/E.Malkin 100.00 200.00
MO2PH C.Price/J.Harding 125.00 250.00
MO2PP P.Stastny/P.Stastny 50.00 100.00
MO2PR C.Price/T.Rask 100.00 200.00
MO2RB M.Brodeur/P.Roy 125.00 250.00
MO2RC J.Carter/M.Richards 30.00 80.00
MO2RP M.Ryder/C.Price 60.00 150.00
MO2SS D.Sedin/H.Sedin 15.00 40.00
MO2TB J.Toews/Backstrom 60.00 125.00
MO2TC Thornton/Cheechoo 100.00 200.00
MO2TK P.Kane/J.Toews 75.00 175.00

2008-09 UD Black Trios Jerseys

STATED PRINT RUN 50 SERIAL #'d SETS
UBP3ASH Heatley/Spezza/Alfrd 10.00 25.00
UBP3ASR Radulv/Arntt/Sullvn 10.00 25.00
UBP3BEP Brodeur/Parise/Elias 20.00 50.00
UBP3BML Lngwy/Bourq/MacIns 15.00 40.00
UBP3BSW Staal/Ward/Brind 12.00 30.00
UBP3CLO Ciccrlli/Lngwy/Oates 10.00 25.00
UBP3DGS DiPtro/Guern/Satan 20.00 50.00
UBP3EBC Bcyk/P.Espo/Chvers 15.00 40.00
UBP3EKL Kvalck/Enstrm/Lhtn 10.00 25.00
UBP3FCM Crosby/Fleury/Malkin 40.00 80.00
UBP3FKM Messier/Fuhr/Kurri 12.00 30.00
UBP3GBC Gagne/Briere/Carter 10.00 25.00
UBP3HDZ Zetter/Hask/Datsyk 12.00 30.00
UBP3IGN Nash/Iginla/Gagne 10.00 25.00
UBP3IHN Nash/Heatley/Iginla 10.00 25.00
UBP3IKP Iginla/Kiprsff/Phneuf 10.00 25.00
UBP3KBT Kariya/Byes/Tkchk 15.00 40.00
UBP3KOM Ovech/Malkin/Kvlck 40.00 100.00
UBP3KRK Koivu/Ryder/Kovlev 12.00 30.00
UBP3LCG Grtzky/Lemux/Crsby 60.00 120.00
UBP3LJS Lecav/Jokin/St.Lou 10.00 25.00
UBP3LKM Messier/Ltch/Kovlv 10.00 25.00
UBP3LSR Lafleur/Robnsn/Sht 12.00 30.00
UBP3MMM McDnld/McIns/Mln 10.00 25.00
UBP3MRM Modano/Rnick/Mln 15.00 40.00
UBP3MSS Sittler/McDnld/Slmg 10.00 25.00
UBP3MTC Thrntn/Marl/Chcho 12.00 30.00
UBP3MTM Modano/Trco/Mrrw 15.00 40.00
UBP3NBO Bourque/Nly/Otes 10.00 25.00
UBP3NGG Gig/Getz/Nieder 15.00 40.00
UBP3NLM Lungo/Nslnd/Mrsn 12.00 30.00
UBP3RBL Roy/Brodr/Lungo 25.00 60.00
UBP3RSB Sakic/Brque/Roy 25.00 60.00
UBP3RVG Grtzky/Rbitle/Vchn 50.00 100.00
UBP3RWH Roy/Hextall/Ward 20.00 50.00
UBP3SBK Bergeron/Kesl/Svrd 12.00 30.00
UBP3SJL Jagr/Shanhn/Lndq 12.00 30.00
UBP3SNA Sundin/Nslnd/Alfrd 15.00 40.00
UBP3SSS Sakic/Stastny/Smyth 15.00 40.00
UBP3STS Sundin/Tuckr/Steen 15.00 40.00

2008-09 UD Black Pride of a Nation Autographs Patches

STATED PRINT RUN 25 SERIAL #'d SETS
PNAK Anze Kopitar 30.00 80.00
PNAO Alexander Ovechkin 150.00 300.00
PNAR Alexander Radulov
PNBC Bobby Clarke 30.00 80.00
PNBL Brian Leetch 30.00 80.00
PNBO Bobby Orr 200.00 400.00
PNCP Carey Price 150.00 250.00
PNDH Dominik Hasek 40.00 100.00
PNDR Dwayne Roloson 25.00 60.00
PNDS Devin Setoguchi 25.00 60.00
PNEM Evgeni Malkin 75.00 150.00
PNES Eric Staal 40.00 100.00
PNGH Gordie Howe 125.00 200.00
PNGL Guy Lafleur 40.00 100.00
PNGP Gilbert Perreault 30.00 80.00
PNHA Dale Hawerchuk 40.00 100.00
PNHE Dany Heatley 30.00 80.00
PNHL Henrik Lundqvist
PNHZ Henrik Zetterberg 40.00 100.00
PNIK Ilya Kovalchuk 30.00 80.00
PNJC Jonathan Cheechoo 30.00 80.00
PNJG Jean-Sebastien Giguere 30.00 80.00
PNJI Jarome Iginla 30.00 80.00
PNJK Jari Kurri 30.00 80.00
PNJM Joe Mullen 25.00 60.00
PNJS Jordan Staal 40.00 100.00
PNJT Joe Thornton 40.00 100.00
PNKE Phil Kessel 25.00 60.00
PNLR Larry Robinson 30.00 80.00
PNMB Martin Brodeur 100.00 200.00
PNMF Marc-Andre Fleury 75.00 150.00
PNMG Marian Gaborik
PNMH Marian Hossa 25.00 60.00
PNMI Milan Hejduk 25.00 60.00
PNMN Markus Naslund
PNMO Mike Modano 50.00 120.00
PNMR Mike Richards 75.00 150.00
PNMS Miroslav Satan 60.00 120.00
PNMT Marty Turco 30.00 80.00
PNNB Nicklas Backstrom 50.00 125.00
PNNL Nicklas Lidstrom 30.00 80.00
PNPE Phil Esposito 40.00 100.00
PNPK Patrick Kane 75.00 150.00
PNPS Paul Stastny 30.00 80.00
PNRG Ryan Getzlaf 50.00 120.00
PNRM Ryan Miller 30.00 80.00
PNRN Rick Nash 30.00 80.00
PNRS Ryan Smyth
PNSC Sidney Crosby 200.00 350.00
PNSG Sam Gagner 60.00 120.00
PNSK Saku Koivu 40.00 80.00
PNST Martin St. Louis 30.00 80.00
PNTE Tony Esposito 30.00 80.00
PNTL Jiri Tlusty 25.00 60.00
PNTO Jonathan Toews 100.00 200.00
PNTR Tuukka Rask 50.00 120.00
PNTV Thomas Vanek 30.00 80.00
PNVL Vincent Lecavalier 25.00 60.00
PNVO Tomas Vokoun 25.00 60.00
PNZP Zach Parise

2009-10 UD Black

1-42 STATED PRINT RUN 99
43-60 STATED PRINT RUN 499
61-72 AU STATED PRINT RUN 499
73-93 AU STATED PRINT RUN 99
1 Ilya Kovalchuk 6.00 15.00
2 Cam Neely 6.00 15.00
3 Phil Esposito 10.00 25.00
4 Ray Bourque 10.00 25.00
5 Jarome Iginla 6.00 15.00
6 Miikka Kiprusoff 5.00 12.00
7 Eric Staal 8.00 20.00
8 Tony Esposito 10.00 25.00
9 Jonathan Toews 12.00 30.00
10 Patrick Kane 12.00 30.00
11 Rick Nash 5.00 12.00
12 Marty Turco 6.00 15.00
13 Mike Modano 10.00 25.00
14 Gordie Howe 15.00 40.00
15 Henrik Zetterberg 8.00 20.00
16 Nicklas Lidstrom 6.00 15.00
17 Pavel Datsyuk 8.00 20.00
18 Grant Fuhr 6.00 15.00
19 Jari Kurri 6.00 15.00
20 Wayne Gretzky 30.00 80.00
21 Marian Gaborik 8.00 20.00
22 Carey Price 25.00 60.00
23 Larry Robinson 6.00 15.00
24 Patrick Roy 15.00 40.00
25 Martin Brodeur 12.00 30.00
26 Mike Bossy 6.00 15.00
27 Henrik Lundqvist 10.00 25.00
28 Mark Messier 8.00 20.00
29 Markus Naslund 5.00 12.00
30 Ron Hextall 10.00 25.00
31 Peter Mueller 5.00 12.00
32 Evgeni Malkin 20.00 50.00
33 Sidney Crosby 25.00 60.00
34 Mario Lemieux 20.00 50.00
35 Marc-Andre Fleury 10.00 25.00
36 Joe Thornton 6.00 15.00
37 Vincent Lecavalier 5.00 12.00
38 Borje Salming 6.00 15.00
39 Mats Sundin 6.00 15.00
40 Roberto Luongo 8.00 20.00
41 Alexander Ovechkin 25.00 60.00
42 Dale Hawerchuk 8.00 20.00
43 John Negrin RC 6.00 15.00
44 Tom Wandell RC 6.00 15.00
45 Ray Macias RC 5.00 12.00
46 Jay Beagle RC 8.00 20.00
47 Jakub Petruzalek RC 6.00 15.00
48 Alexander Sulzer RC 4.00 10.00
49 Taylor Chorney RC 6.00 15.00
50 Yannick Weber RC 6.00 15.00
51 Cal O'Reilly RC 5.00 12.00
52 Tim Wallace RC 4.00 10.00
53 Kevin Quick RC 4.00 10.00
54 Jesse Joensuu RC 5.00 12.00
55 Spencer Machacek RC 6.00 15.00
56 T.J. Galiardi RC 6.00 15.00
57 Michael Sauer RC 5.00 12.00
58 Matt Beleskey RC 5.00 12.00
59 Tim Stapleton RC 6.00 15.00
60 Grant Lewis RC 5.00 12.00
61 Mikael Backlund AU RC 12.00 30.00
62 Riku Helenius AU RC 8.00 20.00
63 Ville Leino AU RC 6.00 15.00
64 Michal Neuvirth AU RC 12.00 30.00
65 Artem Anisimov AU RC 10.00 25.00
66 Jhonas Enroth AU RC 12.00 30.00
67 Kris Chucko AU RC 6.00 15.00
68 Luca Caputi AU RC 10.00 25.00
69 Christian Hanson AU RC 8.00 20.00
70 Matt Pelech AU RC 8.00 20.00
71 Brian Salcido AU RC 6.00 15.00
72 Ivan Vishnevskiy AU RC 6.00 15.00
73 John Tavares AU RC 80.00 200.00
74 Matt Duchene AU RC 60.00 120.00
75 Victor Hedman AU RC 25.00 60.00
76 Evander Kane AU RC 30.00 80.00
77 James van Riemsdyk AU RC 60.00 120.00
78 Jonas Gustavsson AU RC 30.00 80.00
79 Logan Couture AU RC 30.00 80.00
80 Brad Marchand AU RC 40.00 100.00
81 Tyler Myers AU RC 20.00 50.00
82 Jamie Benn AU RC 50.00 100.00
83 Colin Wilson AU RC 15.00 40.00
84 Michael Del Zotto AU RC 15.00 40.00
85 Viktor Stalberg AU RC 20.00 50.00
86 Michael Grabner AU RC 50.00 100.00
87 Tyler Bozak AU RC 30.00 80.00
88 Erik Karlsson AU RC 75.00 150.00
89 Matt Gilroy AU RC 15.00 40.00
90 Ryan O'Reilly AU RC 30.00 80.00
91 Dmitry Kulikov AU RC 15.00 40.00
92 Sergei Shirokov AU RC 10.00 25.00
93 Cody Franson AU RC 15.00 40.00

2009-10 UD Black Foursomes Jerseys

STATED PRINT RUN 25 SER.#'d SETS
T4JBDLM Brod/Lundq/Miller/DiPiet 20.00 50.00
T4JDKOM Malkn/Kovl/Dtsyk/Ovch
T4JDSSB Stmk/Schn/Douty/Boed 20.00 40.00
T4JECMP Perrlt/Mahv/Clrke/Espo 30.00 60.00
T4JHLDZ Datsyk/Zettr/Lids/Hssa 30.00 60.00
T4JISCN St.L/Chech/Ignla/Nash 30.00 60.00
T4JKTKP Kovlv/Koivu/Tng/Price 25.00 50.00
T4JLGHM Messi/Grtz/Howe/Mario 125.00 200.00
T4JRBLF Flry/Luongo/Brodr/Roy 40.00 80.00
T4JSKJK Koivu/Kurri/Jokin/Selan 20.00 50.00
T4JSKTK Shrp/Toews/Khab/Kne 25.00 60.00
T4JSLTC Lecav/Crsby/Skic/Thorn 40.00 80.00

2009-10 UD Black Game Night Ticket Autographs

STATED PRINT RUN 35 SER.#'d SETS
GNAP Alex Pietrangelo 12.00 30.00
GNBC Bobby Clarke 25.00 50.00
GNBM Brendan Mikkelson 10.00 25.00
GNBO Bobby Orr 125.00 200.00
GNBS Brandon Sutter 15.00 40.00
GNBW Blake Wheeler 15.00 40.00
GNCG Colton Gillies 12.00 30.00
GNCP Carey Price 60.00 120.00
GNCS Cory Schneider 25.00 50.00
GNDD Drew Doughty 30.00 60.00
GNDG Doug Gilmour 30.00 60.00
GNEM Evgeni Malkin 50.00 100.00
GNFB Fabian Brunnstrom 10.00 25.00
GNHL Henrik Lundqvist 20.00 50.00
GNHZ Henrik Zetterberg 40.00 80.00
GNIK Ilya Kovalchuk 20.00 50.00
GNJI Jarome Iginla 40.00 80.00
GNJK Jari Kurri 30.00 60.00
GNJP Justin Pogge 12.00 30.00
GNJS Jordan Staal 25.00 50.00
GNJT Jonathan Toews 40.00 80.00
GNKA Karl Alzner 15.00 40.00
GNLS Luke Schenn 25.00 60.00
GNMB Mike Bossy 25.00 50.00
GNMG Marian Gaborik 25.00 50.00
GNMM Mark Messier 30.00 80.00
GNMP Max Pacioretty 20.00 50.00
GNMR Mike Richards 20.00 50.00
GNNB Nicklas Backstrom 30.00 60.00
GNRH Ron Hextall 35.00 80.00
GNRN Rick Nash 25.00 50.00
GNSC Sidney Crosby 150.00 250.00
GNSM Steve Mason 40.00 80.00
GNSS Steven Stamkos 40.00 80.00
GNTH Joe Thornton 30.00 60.00
GNTK Tim Kennedy 15.00 40.00
GNTV Thomas Vanek 25.00 50.00
GNZB Zach Bogosian 25.00 50.00

2009-10 UD Black Game Night Ticket Autographs Duals

STATED PRINT RUN 25 SER.#'d SETS
GN2BH R.Hextall/R.Bourque
GN2CP B.Clarke/G.Perreault 25.00 60.00
GN2DT P.Datsyuk/J.Toews 25.00 60.00
GN2EB Esposito/Beliveau 50.00 100.00
GN2ES P.Esposito/B.Salming 20.00 50.00
GN2GH Heatley/Giguere 15.00 40.00
GN2KP P.Kessel/C.Price
GN2KS I.Kovalchuk/E.Staal 20.00 50.00
GN2LI J.Iginla/V.Lecavalier 20.00 50.00
GN2LK V.Lecavalier/I.Kovalchuk 20.00 50.00
GN2LM N.Lidstrom/E.Malkin 40.00 100.00
GN2NK Kane/Nash 25.00 60.00
GN2NM Nash/Mueller 25.00 60.00
GN2NT E.Nabokov/M.Turco 25.00 60.00
GN2RB Brodeur/Roy 100.00 200.00
GN2RM E.Malkin/M.Richards 30.00 80.00
GN2TM R.Miller/J.Thornton 40.00 100.00

2009-10 UD Black Generations Jerseys

STATED PRINT RUN 25 SER.#'d SETS
GLW Left Wingers 60.00 120.00
GCEN Centers 60.00 120.00
GDEF Defensemen 50.00 120.00
GEDM Edmonton 150.00 300.00
GGOL Goalies 100.00 200.00
GSTR Superstars 250.00 500.00

2009-10 UD Black Jerseys Autographs

STATED PRINT RUN 25 SER.#'d SETS
AJAK Anze Kopitar 20.00 40.00
AJBL Brian Leetch 20.00 40.00
AJBS Borje Salming 20.00 40.00
AJBW Blake Wheeler 25.00 50.00
AJCN Cam Neely 20.00 40.00
AJCP Carey Price 40.00 80.00
AJDD Drew Doughty 25.00 50.00
AJDH Dale Hawerchuk 12.00 30.00
AJDP Dion Phaneuf 20.00 40.00
AJEM Evgeni Malkin 60.00 120.00
AJES Eric Staal 12.00 30.00
AJGP Gilbert Perreault 12.00 30.00
AJHL Henrik Lundqvist 30.00 60.00
AJHZ Henrik Zetterberg 30.00 60.00
AJIK Ilya Kovalchuk 25.00 50.00
AJJI Jarome Iginla 25.00 60.00
AJJN James Neal 25.00 50.00
AJJS Jordan Staal 25.00 50.00
AJJT Jonathan Toews 40.00 80.00
AJLS Luke Schenn 12.00 30.00
AJMG Marian Gaborik 12.00 30.00
AJMH Marian Hossa 20.00 40.00
AJMN Markus Naslund 12.00 30.00
AJNB Nicklas Backstrom 20.00 40.00
AJPK Patrick Kane 25.00 50.00
AJRB Ray Bourque 40.00 80.00
AJRN Rick Nash 25.00 50.00
AJSC Sidney Crosby 125.00 250.00
AJSS Steven Stamkos 30.00 60.00

2009-10 UD Black Jerseys Black Ice

QJAK Alex Kovalev 8.00 20.00
QJAO Alexander Ovechkin 20.00 50.00
QJBL Brian Leetch 8.00 20.00
QJBS Borje Salming 8.00 20.00
QJCN Cam Neely 8.00 20.00
QJCP Carey Price 30.00 80.00
QJEM Evgeni Malkin 25.00 60.00
QJES Eric Staal 10.00 25.00
QJGH Gordie Howe 20.00 50.00
QJGP Gilbert Perreault 8.00 20.00
QJHZ Henrik Zetterberg 10.00 25.00
QJIK Ilya Kovalchuk 8.00 20.00
QJJK Jari Kurri 8.00 20.00
QJJS Jason Spezza 8.00 20.00
QJJT Jonathan Toews 15.00 40.00
QJKL Kari Lehtonen 6.00 15.00
QJKO Anze Kopitar 12.00 30.00
QJLR Larry Robinson 8.00 20.00
QJMB Martin Brodeur 12.00 30.00
QJMG Marian Gaborik 10.00 25.00
QJML Mario Lemieux 12.00 30.00
QJMM Mark Messier 10.00 25.00
QJMS Mats Sundin 8.00 20.00
QJNL Nicklas Lidstrom 8.00 20.00
QJPD Pavel Datsyuk 8.00 20.00
QJPK Paul Kariya 10.00 25.00
QJPM Patrick Marleau
QJPR Patrick Roy 20.00 50.00
QJPS Paul Stastny 8.00 20.00
QJRB Ray Bourque 12.00 30.00
QJRL Roberto Luongo 10.00 25.00
QJRN Rick Nash 6.00 15.00
QJSA Joe Sakic 12.00 30.00
QJSC Sidney Crosby 20.00 50.00
QJSK Saku Koivu 6.00 15.00
QJSS Steven Stamkos 15.00 40.00
QJST Jordan Staal 8.00 20.00
QJTS Teemu Selanne 15.00 40.00
QJVL Vincent Lecavalier 6.00 15.00
QJWG Wayne Gretzky 40.00 80.00
QJZP Zach Parise 8.00 20.00

2009-10 UD Black Jerseys Black Ice Autographs

STATED PRINT RUN 25 SER.#'d SETS
QJBL Brian Leetch 20.00 40.00
QJBS Borje Salming 20.00 40.00
QJCN Cam Neely 20.00 40.00
QJCP Carey Price 40.00 80.00
QJEM Evgeni Malkin 50.00 100.00
QJES Eric Staal 10.00 25.00
QJGH Gordie Howe 75.00 125.00
QJGP Gilbert Perreault 12.00 30.00
QJHZ Henrik Zetterberg 30.00 60.00
QJIK Ilya Kovalchuk 25.00 50.00
QJJK Jari Kurri 20.00 40.00
QJJT Jonathan Toews 40.00 100.00
QJKO Anze Kopitar 20.00 40.00
QJLR Larry Robinson 12.00 30.00
QJMB Martin Brodeur 40.00 80.00
QJMG Marian Gaborik 25.00 50.00
QJML Mario Lemieux 50.00 100.00
QJMM Mark Messier 40.00 80.00
QJNL Nicklas Lidstrom 20.00 40.00
QJPD Pavel Datsyuk 25.00 50.00
QJPR Patrick Roy
QJPS Paul Stastny 20.00 40.00
QJRB Ray Bourque 30.00 60.00
QJRN Rick Nash 20.00 50.00
QJSC Sidney Crosby 125.00 250.00
QJSK Saku Koivu 20.00 40.00
QJSS Steven Stamkos 30.00 60.00
QJST Jordan Staal 12.00 30.00
QJVL Vincent Lecavalier 12.00 30.00
QJWG Wayne Gretzky 150.00 300.00

2009-10 UD Black Lustrous Materials Jersey Autographs

STATED PRINT RUN 50 SER.#'d SETS
LMAK Anze Kopitar 15.00 40.00
LMAO Adam Oates 12.00 30.00
LMBL Brian Leetch 15.00 40.00
LMBS Borje Salming 10.00 25.00
LMCD Chris Drury 12.00 30.00
LMCN Cam Neely 20.00 40.00
LMCP Carey Price 40.00 80.00
LMDC Dino Ciccarelli
LMDD Drew Doughty 12.00 30.00
LMDG Doug Gilmour 15.00 40.00
LMDH Dale Hawerchuk 12.00 30.00
LMDP Dion Phaneuf 20.00 40.00
LMEM Evgeni Malkin 30.00 80.00
LMES Eric Staal 12.00 30.00
LMGF Grant Fuhr 20.00 40.00
LMGP Gilbert Perreault 12.00 30.00
LMHE Dany Heatley 12.00 30.00
LMHL Henrik Lundqvist 20.00 50.00
LMHZ Henrik Zetterberg 25.00 50.00
LMIK Ilya Kovalchuk 15.00 40.00
LMJJ Jack Johnson 12.00 30.00
LMJN James Neal 12.00 30.00
LMJS Jordan Staal 15.00 40.00
LMJT Joe Thornton 25.00 50.00
LMLR Larry Robinson 10.00 25.00
LMMG Marian Gaborik 25.00 50.00
LMMM Mike Modano 12.00 30.00
LMMN Markus Naslund 10.00 25.00
LMMR Mike Richards 20.00 40.00
LMMT Marty Turco 12.00 30.00
LMNB Nicklas Backstrom 15.00 40.00
LMPB Patrik Berglund 12.00 30.00
LMPE Patrik Elias 12.00 30.00
LMPM Peter Mueller 10.00 25.00
LMPS Paul Stastny 12.00 30.00
LMRB Ray Bourque 30.00 60.00
LMRG Ryan Getzlaf 15.00 40.00
LMRN Rick Nash 20.00 40.00
LMTO Jonathan Toews 25.00 50.00
LMWG Wayne Gretzky 125.00 250.00

2009-10 UD Black Pride of a Nation Patches Autographs

STATED PRINT RUN 35 SER.#'d SETS
PNAK Anze Kopitar 30.00 60.00
PNBL Brian Leetch 20.00 50.00
PNBO Bobby Orr 175.00 300.00
PNBR Martin Brodeur 60.00 120.00
PNCD Chris Drury 15.00 40.00
PNCW Cam Ward 25.00 60.00
PNDD Drew Doughty 30.00 80.00
PNDH Dany Heatley 20.00 50.00
PNDP Dion Phaneuf 40.00 80.00
PNEM Evgeni Malkin 50.00 100.00

NEN Evgeni Nabokov 15.00 40.00
NFB Fabian Brunnstrom 15.00 40.00
NGA Simon Gagne 20.00 50.00
NGH Gordie Howe 100.00 175.00
NGP Gilbert Perreault 20.00 50.00
NHZ Henrik Zetterberg 50.00 100.00
NIK Ilya Kovalchuk 25.00 60.00
NJI Jarome Iginla 40.00 80.00
NJS Jordan Staal 20.00 50.00
NKO Saku Koivu 20.00 50.00
NLS Luke Schenn 15.00 40.00
NMB Mikkel Boedker 12.00 30.00
NME Mark Messier 60.00 120.00
NMG Marian Gaborik 40.00 80.00
NMM Mike Modano 25.00 60.00
NMR Mike Richards 40.00 80.00
NMT Marty Turco 20.00 50.00
NNF Nikita Filatov 15.00 40.00
NPD Pavel Datsyuk 40.00 80.00
NPE Patrik Elias 20.00 50.00
NPK Patrick Kane 75.00 150.00
NSC Sidney Crosby 100.00 200.00
NSG Scott Gomez 15.00 40.00
NSM Stan Mikita 25.00 60.00
NSS Steven Stamkos 100.00 200.00
NTE Tony Esposito 20.00 50.00
NTV Thomas Vanek 20.00 50.00

2009-10 UD Black Pride of a Nation Patches Autographs Dual

TATED PRINT RUN 25 SER.#'d SETS
N2AD K.Alzner/D.Doughty 50.00 100.00
N2CP B.Clarke/G.Perreault 30.00 60.00
N2DM E.Malkin/P.Datsyuk 60.00 120.00
N2EE P.Esposito/T.Esposito 60.00 120.00
N2EO B.Orr/P.Esposito 175.00 300.00
N2FH R.Hextall/G.Fuhr 60.00 120.00
N2FT V.Tikhonov/N.Filatov 25.00 50.00
N2FV J.Voracek/M.Frolik 60.00 120.00
N2HG M.Gaborik/M.Hossa 40.00 80.00
N2JS S.Koivu/J.Kurri 50.00 100.00
N2KK P.Kane/P.Kessel 50.00 100.00
N2LE E.Ersberg/H.Lundqvist 30.00 60.00
N2LI V.Lecavalier/J.Iginla 50.00 100.00
N2LS N.Lidstrom/B.Salming 30.00 60.00
N2MM M.Modano/J.Mullen 30.00 60.00
N2PM S.Mason/C.Price 60.00 120.00
N2RB Brodeur/Roy EXCH 150.00 250.00
N2SP J.Pogge/L.Schenn 25.00 50.00
N2ZB F.Brunnstrom/H.Zetterberg 30.00 60.00

2009-10 UD Black Rivals 6 on 6 Jerseys

TATED PRINT RUN 25 SER.#'d SETS
NALAK Ducks/Kings 60.00 120.00
NASJS Ducks/Sharks 40.00 80.00
OSNYR Bruins/Rangers 50.00 100.00
ARNJD Hurricanes/Devils 75.00 150.00
GYEDM Flames/Oilers 75.00 150.00
HIDET Hawks/Wings 100.00 200.00
HISTL Hawks/Blues 75.00 150.00
LBDET Jackets/Wings 50.00 100.00
OLDET Avs/Wings 125.00 250.00
LATBL Panthers/Lightning 60.00 120.00
TLBUF Canadiens/Sabres 50.00 100.00
YINYR Islanders/Rangers 75.00 150.00
YRNJD Rangers/Devils 60.00 120.00
TPHI Pens/Flyers 150.00 250.00
TWAS Pens/Caps 125.00 250.00
SLAK Sharks/Kings 40.00 100.00
NCGY Canucks/Flames 75.00 150.00
ASPHI Caps/Flyers 150.00 250.00
OSMTL1 Bruins/Canadians 1 75.00 150.00
OSMTL2 Bruins/Canadians 2 100.00 200.00
RMTL2 Leafs/Canadians 75.00 150.00

2009-10 UD Black Trios Jerseys

TATED PRINT RUN 50 SER.#'d SETS
JBEP Elias/Parise/Brodeur 20.00 40.00
JBGW Bouwmstr/Green/Webr 10.00 25.00
JCOM Ovech/Malkin/Crosby 40.00 80.00
JDKO Datsyuk/Ovech/Koval 20.00 40.00
JFBK Brown/Kopitar/Frolov 15.00 30.00
JGRC Gagne/Richards/Carter 15.00 30.00
JHDZ Datsyuk/Zetter/Hossa 20.00 40.00
JIKP Phaneuf/Kiprusf/Iginla 20.00 40.00
JKJS Johnson/Stamkos/Kane 20.00 40.00
JKKP Price/Kovalev/Koivu 15.00 30.00
JLGF Luongo/Fleury/Giguere 20.00 40.00
JLGM Lemieux/Gretz/Mess 40.00 80.00
JLSS Stamks/St.Lou/Lecav 15.00 30.00
JMCP Clarke/McDonld/Perre 15.00 30.00
JMDH Sedin/Sundin/Sedin 15.00 30.00
JNBO Oates/Bourque/Neely 15.00 30.00
JNLZ Zherdev/Lundq/Naslnd 15.00 30.00
JPDS Schenn/Dougty/Phanf 15.00 30.00
JPKK Parise/Kessel/Kane 12.00 30.00
JPMR Robnsn/MacIns/Potvn 10.00 25.00
JRBH Brodeur/Roy/Hextall 30.00 60.00
JSBK Kessel/Savrd/Bergrn 10.00 25.00
JSGH Savard/Hawer/Gilmr 20.00 40.00
JSKN Shanahan/Kariya/Nash 20.00 40.00
JSNG Nieder/Getzlaf/Selann 10.00 25.00
JSSS Staal/Staal/Staal 15.00 30.00
JSTT Toews/Sakic/Thorntn 15.00 30.00
JTKL Kiprusff/Lehton/Toskl 15.00 30.00

2014-15 UD Black

30 VETERAN STATED PRINT RUN 99
-60 ROOKIE STATED PRINT RUN 199
SERTS IN 2014-15 UPPER DECK ICE
Alexander Ovechkin 8.00 20.00
Pavel Datsyuk 2.50 6.00
Ryan Getzlaf 3.00 8.00
Evgeni Malkin 6.00 15.00
Duncan Keith 2.00 5.00
Anze Kopitar 3.00 8.00
Sidney Crosby 8.00 20.00
Steven Stamkos 4.00 10.00
Jonathan Bernier 2.00 5.00
P.K. Subban 3.00 8.00
Patrice Bergeron 2.50 6.00
Henrik Lundqvist 2.50 6.00
Tuukka Rask 2.00 5.00
Carey Price 6.00 15.00
Jonathan Toews 4.00 10.00
Shea Weber 1.50 4.00
Matt Duchene 2.00 5.00
Taylor Hall 4.00 10.00
Claude Giroux 2.00 5.00
John Tavares 4.00 10.00
Marcel Dionne 2.50 6.00
Bobby Orr 6.00 15.00
Mark Messier 2.00 5.00
Mats Sundin 2.00 5.00
Tony Esposito 2.00 5.00
Patrick Roy 5.00 12.00
Wayne Gretzky 12.00 30.00
Jean Beliveau 2.00 5.00
Mario Lemieux 6.00 15.00
Dominik Hasek 2.50 6.00
Adam Lowry RC 2.00 5.00
32 Victor Rask RC 2.00 5.00
33 Bo Horvat RC 6.00 15.00
34 Seth Griffith RC 2.50 6.00
35 William Karlsson RC 8.00 20.00
36 Chris Tierney RC 2.00 5.00
37 Evgeny Kuznetsov RC 8.00 20.00
38 Shayne Gostisbehere RC 8.00 20.00
39 Kevin Hayes RC 6.00 15.00
40 Griffin Reinhart RC 2.50 6.00
41 Damon Severson RC 2.00 5.00
42 Andrei Vasilevskiy RC 6.00 15.00
43 Alexander Wennberg RC 4.00 10.00
44 Marko Dano RC 2.00 5.00
45 Johnny Gaudreau RC 15.00 40.00
46 Teuvo Teravainen RC 3.00 8.00
47 Calle Jarnkrok RC 2.00 5.00
48 Jiri Sekac RC 2.00 5.00
49 Jori Lehtera RC 2.50 6.00
50 Sam Reinhart RC 6.00 15.00
51 Stuart Percy RC 2.00 5.00
52 Vladislav Namestnikov RC 3.00 8.00
53 Darnell Nurse RC 6.00 15.00
54 Derrick Pouliot RC 2.50 6.00
55 Anthony Duclair RC 3.00 8.00
56 Andre Burakovsky RC 3.00 8.00
57 Aaron Ekblad RC 8.00 20.00
58 Leon Draisaitl RC 10.00 25.00
59 Curtis Lazar RC 2.50 6.00
60 Jonathan Drouin RC 5.00 12.00

2014-15 UD Black Lustrous Materials

STATED ODDS 1:42 UPPER DECK ICE
LMAO Alexander Ovechkin 25.00 60.00
LMBH Brett Hull 6.00 15.00
LMCP Carey Price 20.00 50.00
LMMB Mike Bossy 6.00 15.00
LMMG Mike Gartner 6.00 15.00
LMML Mario Lemieux 20.00 50.00
LMMM Mark Messier 6.00 15.00
LMPR Patrick Roy 15.00 40.00
LMRB Rob Blake 6.00 15.00
LMRF Ron Francis 8.00 20.00
LMSC Sidney Crosby 25.00 60.00
LMSY Steve Yzerman 12.00 30.00
LMTA John Tavares 12.00 30.00
LMTH Taylor Hall 12.00 30.00
LMWG Wayne Gretzky 20.00 50.00

2014-15 UD Black Lustrous Rookies Autographs

INSERTS IN 2014-15 UPPER DECK ICE
LRBG Brandon Gormley 5.00 12.00
LREK Evgeny Kuznetsov 20.00 50.00
LRJD Jonathan Drouin 12.00 30.00
LRJG Johnny Gaudreau 30.00 80.00
LRLD Leon Draisaitl 25.00 60.00
LRSR Sam Reinhart 15.00 40.00
LRTR Ty Rattie 6.00 15.00
LRTT Teuvo Teravainen 15.00 30.00

2014-15 UD Black Lustrous Signatures

INSERTS IN 2014-15 UPPER DECK ICE
BSDS Darryl Sittler/99 10.00 25.00
BSEM Evgeni Malkin/99 30.00 60.00
BSJI Jarome Iginla/99 10.00 25.00
BSJJ Jaromir Jagr/49 30.00 60.00
BSJT John Tavares/99 25.00 50.00
BSML Mario Lemieux/25 60.00 100.00
BSMS Martin St. Louis/49 10.00 25.00
BSPD Pavel Datsyuk/99 20.00 40.00
BSPR Patrick Roy/25 50.00 100.00
BSPS Patrick Sharp/99 10.00 25.00
BSRN Rick Nash/99 12.00 30.00
BSSC Sidney Crosby/49 90.00 150.00
BSTS Teemu Selanne/49 20.00 50.00
BSWG Wayne Gretzky/25 150.00 250.00
BSZP Zach Parise/49 12.00 30.00

2015-16 UD Black

1 Ryan Getzlaf 6.00 15.00
2 Oliver Ekman-Larsson 3.00 8.00
3 Tuukka Rask 4.00 10.00
4 Ryan O'Reilly 4.00 10.00
5 Sean Monahan 4.00 10.00
6 Justin Faulk 4.00 10.00
7 Jonathan Toews 8.00 20.00
8 Nathan MacKinnon 8.00 20.00
9 Nick Foligno 3.00 8.00
10 Tyler Seguin 6.00 15.00
11 Henrik Zetterberg 5.00 12.00
12 Taylor Hall 8.00 20.00
13 Aaron Ekblad 4.00 10.00
14 Jonathan Quick 6.00 15.00
15 Zach Parise 4.00 10.00
16 P.K. Subban 6.00 15.00
17 Filip Forsberg 5.00 12.00
18 Cory Schneider 3.00 8.00
19 John Tavares 8.00 20.00
20 Henrik Lundqvist 5.00 12.00
21 Erik Karlsson 8.00 20.00
22 Claude Giroux 4.00 10.00
23 Sidney Crosby 15.00 40.00
24 Joe Pavelski 4.00 10.00
25 Vladimir Tarasenko 6.00 15.00
26 Steven Stamkos 8.00 20.00
27 Nazem Kadri 3.00 8.00
28 Daniel Sedin 4.00 10.00
29 Alexander Ovechkin 15.00 40.00
30 Andrew Ladd 4.00 10.00
31 Wayne Gretzky 20.00 50.00
32 Bobby Orr 12.00 30.00
33 Mario Lemieux 12.00 30.00
34 Steve Yzerman 6.00 15.00
35 Patrick Roy 10.00 25.00
36 Anton Slepyshev AU/299 RC 6.00 15.00
37 Nick Shore AU/299 RC 8.00 20.00
38 Kevin Fiala AU/299 RC 8.00 20.00
39 Ryan Hartman AU/299 RC 10.00 25.00
40 Daniel Sprong AU/299 RC 30.00 80.00
41 Sergei Plotnikov AU/299 RC 6.00 15.00
42 Jared McCann AU/299 RC 8.00 20.00
43 Radek Faksa AU/299 RC 8.00 20.00
44 Matt Puempel AU/299 RC 6.00 15.00
45 Chandler Stephenson AU/299 RC 8.00 20.00
46 Henrik Samuelsson AU/299 RC 6.00 15.00
47 Nikolay Goldobin AU/299 RC 8.00 20.00
48 Connor Hellebuyck AU/299 RC 20.00 50.00
49 Devin Shore AU/299 RC 8.00 20.00
50 Colton Parayko AU/299 RC 10.00 25.00
51 Nick Cousins AU/299 RC 8.00 20.00
52 Oscar Lindberg AU/299 RC 8.00 20.00
53 Antoine Bibeau AU/299 RC 8.00 20.00
54 Brock McGinn AU/299 RC 8.00 20.00
55 Nick Ritchie AU/299 RC 8.00 20.00
56 Jordan Weal AU/299 RC 8.00 20.00
57 Viktor Arvidsson AU/299 RC 10.00 25.00
58 Emile Poirier AU/299 RC 8.00 20.00
59 Malcolm Subban AU/299 RC 20.00 50.00
60 Vincent Hinostroza AU/299 RC 5.00 12.00
61 Hunter Shinkaruk AU/299 RC 8.00 20.00
62 Jacob de la Rose AU/299 RC 8.00 20.00
63 Ronalds Kenins AU/299 RC 8.00 20.00
64 Colin Miller AU/299 RC 6.00 15.00
65 Nicolas Petan AU/299 RC 8.00 20.00
66 Sam Brittain AU/299 RC 8.00 20.00
67 Dylan DeMelo AU/299 RC 6.00 15.00
68 Robby Fabbri AU/299 RC 10.00 25.00
69 Ben Hutton AU/299 RC 8.00 20.00
70 Mattias Janmark AU/299 RC 8.00 20.00
71 Shane Prince AU/299 RC 6.00 15.00
72 Andrew Copp AU/299 RC 8.00 20.00
73 Joel Edmundson AU/299 RC 6.00 15.00
74 Andreas Athanasiou AU/299 RC 20.00 50.00
75 Derek Forbort AU/299 RC 6.00 15.00
76 Artemi Panarin AU/199 RC 40.00 100.00
77 Jack Eichel/199 RC 50.00 125.00
78 Max Domi AU/199 RC 25.00 60.00
79 Sam Bennett AU/199 RC 15.00 40.00
80 Mikko Rantanen AU/199 RC 25.00 60.00
81 Noah Hanifin AU/199 RC 15.00 40.00
82 Dylan Larkin AU/199 RC 40.00 100.00
83 Jake Virtanen AU/199 RC 15.00 40.00
84 Nikolaj Ehlers AU/199 RC 25.00 60.00
85 Connor McDavid AU/199 RC 350.00 800.00
86 Matt Murray AU/199 RC 80.00 200.00

2015-16 UD Black Gold Spectrum

*VETS/25: .6X TO 1.5X BASIC CARDS
*RC/25: .6X TO 1.5X BASIC CARDS
40 Daniel Sprong AU 30.00 80.00
76 Artemi Panarin AU 100.00 200.00
81 Noah Hanifin AU 20.00 50.00
85 Connor McDavid AU 800.00 1200.00

2015-16 UD Black Black Ice Signatures

BIBB Brent Burns/49 20.00 50.00
BIBC Bobby Clarke/49 15.00 40.00
BIBO Bobby Orr/10
BICM Connor McDavid/25
BICP Carey Price/25 80.00 200.00
BIFP Felix Potvin/49 15.00 40.00
BIGH Glenn Hall/25 30.00 80.00
BIGL Guy Lafleur/25 25.00 60.00
BIJA Jake Allen/49
BIJV John Vanbiesbrouck/49 25.00 60.00
BIMM Mark Messier/10
BIMS Mark Stone/49 5.00 12.00
BINK Nikita Kucherov/49 8.00 20.00
BIRF Robby Fabbri/49 15.00 40.00
BITB Tom Barrasso/49
BITF Theoren Fleury/25
BITH Taylor Hall/49 10.00 25.00
BIVJ Jakub Voracek/49 15.00 40.00

2015-16 UD Black Cup Coronations Autographs

CCDG Doug Gilmour/25 25.00 60.00
CCDK David Krejci/99 12.00 30.00
CCGC Gerry Cheevers/99 12.00 30.00
CCGL Guy Lafleur/25 20.00 50.00
CCJS Joe Sakic/25
CCJT Jonathan Toews/25 60.00 150.00
CCLR Larry Robinson/99 8.00 20.00
CCMB Martin Brodeur/25 60.00 150.00
CCMS Martin St. Louis/99 15.00 40.00
CCNL Nicklas Lidstrom/25 25.00 60.00
CCRB Rod Brind'Amour/99 10.00 25.00
CCSC Sidney Crosby/25 150.00 350.00
CCTT Tyler Toffoli/99 15.00 40.00
CCWG Wayne Gretzky/25 350.00 600.00

2015-16 UD Black Lustrous Ink

LIAB Aleksander Barkov/50 15.00 40.00
LIAL Andrew Ladd/199 10.00 25.00
LIAO Alexander Ovechkin/25 50.00 120.00
LIBG Brendan Gallagher/50 20.00 50.00
LIBH Bo Horvat/199 15.00 40.00
LIBN Bob Nystrom/199 8.00 20.00
LICM Connor McDavid/35 700.00 1200.00
LIDH Dominik Hasek/50 20.00 50.00
LIGA Glenn Anderson/25 20.00 50.00
LIGH Glenn Hall/25 12.00 30.00
LIJA Jake Allen/199 12.00 30.00
LIJH Jiri Hudler/199 8.00 20.00
LIJI Jarome Iginla/50 15.00 40.00
LIJV Jake Virtanen/199 12.00 30.00
LIKF Kevin Fiala/199 10.00 25.00
LILC Logan Couture/50 15.00 40.00
LIMD Marcel Dionne/50 20.00 50.00
LIMS Martin St. Louis/50 15.00 40.00
LINK Nikita Kucherov/199 15.00 40.00
LINP Nicolas Petan/199 10.00 25.00
LIPD Pavel Datsyuk/25 30.00 80.00
LIPR Patrick Roy/25 75.00 150.00
LIRA Rod Brind'Amour/199 8.00 20.00
LIRB Ray Bourque/25 30.00 80.00
LISM Sean Monahan/199 10.00 25.00
LISY Steve Yzerman/25 75.00 150.00

2015-16 UD Black Lustrous Ink Spectrum Jerseys

LIAB Aleksander Barkov/99 20.00 50.00
LIAL Andrew Ladd/99 10.00 25.00
LIAO Alexander Ovechkin/10
LIBG Brendan Gallagher/99 12.00 30.00
LIBH Bo Horvat/99 15.00 40.00
LIBN Bob Nystrom/99 8.00 20.00
LICM Connor McDavid/10
LIDH Dominik Hasek/10
LIGA Glenn Anderson/14
LIGH Glenn Hall/25 12.00 30.00
LIJA Jake Allen/99 12.00 30.00
LIJH Jiri Hudler/99 8.00 20.00
LIJI Jarome Iginla/25 15.00 40.00
LIJV Jake Virtanen/99 12.00 30.00
LIKF Kevin Fiala/99 10.00 25.00
LILC Logan Couture/99 10.00 25.00
LIMD Marcel Dionne/25 20.00 50.00
LIMS Martin St. Louis/25 25.00 60.00
LINK Nikita Kucherov/99 15.00 40.00
LINP Nicolas Petan/99 10.00 25.00
LIPD Pavel Datsyuk/25 25.00 60.00
LIPR Patrick Roy/10
LIRB Ray Bourque/10
LISM Sean Monahan/50 15.00 40.00
LISY Steve Yzerman/10

2015-16 UD Black Pride of a Nation

PNAB Aleksander Barkov/99 15.00 40.00
PNAE Aaron Ekblad/99 15.00 40.00
PNAI Arturs Irbe/99 12.00 30.00
PNAK Anze Kopitar/25 80.00 150.00
PNAM Al MacInnis/25 30.00 80.00
PNAO Alexander Ovechkin/10
PNBO Bobby Orr/25 150.00 300.00
PNCC Chris Chelios/25 15.00 40.00
PNCM Connor McDavid/25 450.00 650.00
PNCP Carey Price/25 100.00 250.00
PNDG Doug Gilmour/10
PNGC Gerry Cheevers/99 15.00 40.00
PNGH Glenn Hall/25 40.00 100.00
PNGL Guy Lafleur/25 20.00 50.00
PNJH Jiri Hudler/99 12.00 30.00
PNJJ Jaromir Jagr/10
PNJK John Klingberg/99 12.00 30.00
PNJP Joe Pavelski/99 15.00 40.00
PNJT Jonathan Toews/25 60.00 150.00
PNJV Jakub Voracek/99 15.00 40.00
PNKH Kevin Hayes/99 15.00 40.00
PNKU Jari Kurri/99 15.00 40.00
PNLA Gabriel Landeskog/99 15.00 40.00
PNMM Mark Messier/10
PNMO Mike Modano/25 30.00 80.00
PNMZ Mats Zuccarello/99 12.00 30.00
PNNL Nicklas Lidstrom/25 25.00 60.00
PNOP Ondrej Palat/99 12.00 30.00
PNPF Peter Forsberg/10
PNPR Patrick Roy/10
PNRI Pekka Rinne/99 20.00 50.00
PNSB Sergei Bobrovsky/99 15.00 40.00
PNSC Sidney Crosby/10
PNTS Teemu Selanne/10
PNTT Tomas Tatar/99 12.00 30.00
PNWG Wayne Gretzky/10

2015-16 UD Black Pro Penmanship

PENAD Andrew Ladd E 8.00 20.00
PENBH Bo Horvat E 12.00 30.00
PENBL Brian Leetch C 12.00 30.00
PENBO Bobby Orr C 90.00 150.00
PENCM Connor McDavid A 400.00 650.00
PENCS Cory Schneider D 6.00 15.00
PENDL Dylan Larkin E 25.00 60.00
PENGP Gilbert Perreault D 8.00 20.00
PENJB Jamie Benn C 15.00 40.00
PENJC John Carlson E 15.00 40.00
PENJH Jiri Hudler E 6.00 15.00
PENJP Joe Pavelski D 8.00 20.00
PENJR Jeremy Roenick B 20.00 50.00
PENJT Jonathan Toews B 40.00 100.00
PENKY Keith Yandle E 8.00 20.00
PENML Mario Lemieux B 60.00 150.00
PENMR Morgan Rielly D 6.00 15.00
PENMS Mark Stone D 6.00 15.00
PENNG Nikolay Goldobin D 8.00 20.00
PENNM Nathan MacKinnon C 15.00 40.00
PENOP Ondrej Palat E 6.00 15.00
PENPC Paul Coffey B 20.00 50.00
PENTA John Tavares D 20.00 50.00
PENZP Zach Parise C 12.00 30.00

2015-16 UD Black Pro Penmanship Combos

PEN2DL P.Datsyuk/N.Lidstrom/15 40.00 100.00
PEN2FW J.Faulk/C.Ward/49 8.00 20.00
PEN2GM Wayne Gretzky
Connor McDavid/5
PEN2NS O.Nolan/J.Sakic/25
PEN2OB Bobby Orr
Ray Bourque/5
PEN2OC A.Ovechkin/J.Carlson/15
PEN2PG C.Price/A.Galchenyuk/15
PEN2TH K.Turris/M.Hoffman/49 8.00 20.00

2015-16 UD Black Pro Penmanship Trios

PEN31ST McDavid/Ekblad/MacKinnon
PEN3NYI Tavares/Strome/Lee
PEN3RC2 Panarin/Lindberg/McCann
PEN3SJS Pavelski/Marleau/Burns 90.00 150.00
PEN3TBL Kucherov/Johnson/Palat 50.00 120.00
PEN3HABS Price/Gallagher/Galchenyuk

2015-16 UD Black Rookie Coverage Autograph Relics Gold

RCOVAB Antoine Bibeau 8.00 20.00
RCOVBM Brock McGinn 8.00 20.00
RCOVCM Connor McDavid 200.00 400.00
RCOVDL Dylan Larkin 50.00 120.00
RCOVEP Emile Poirier 8.00 20.00
RCOVFA Robby Fabbri 15.00 40.00
RCOVHS Henrik Samuelsson 6.00 15.00
RCOVJD Jacob de la Rose 8.00 20.00
RCOVJE Jack Eichel (No Auto) 30.00 80.00
RCOVJM Jared McCann 8.00 20.00
RCOVJV Jake Virtanen 10.00 25.00
RCOVJW Jordan Weal 8.00 20.00
RCOVKF Kevin Fiala 8.00 20.00
RCOVMJ Mattias Janmark 8.00 20.00
RCOVMS Malcolm Subban 20.00 50.00
RCOVNC Nick Cousins 8.00 20.00
RCOVNE Nikolaj Ehlers 15.00 40.00
RCOVNG Nikolay Goldobin 8.00 20.00
RCOVNH Noah Hanifin 10.00 25.00
RCOVNS Nick Shore 8.00 20.00
RCOVOL Oscar Lindberg 8.00 20.00
RCOVRF Radek Faksa 8.00 20.00
RCOVRH Ryan Hartman 10.00 25.00
RCOVSP Shane Prince 6.00 15.00
RCOVZF Zachary Fucale 8.00 20.00

2015-16 UD Black Rookie Coverage Relics

RCOVAB Antoine Bibeau B 3.00 8.00
RCOVAP Artemi Panarin A 10.00 25.00
RCOVBM Brock McGinn A 3.00 8.00
RCOVCM Connor McDavid A 25.00 60.00
RCOVDL Dylan Larkin A 15.00 40.00
RCOVEP Emile Poirier B 3.00 8.00
RCOVFA Robby Fabbri B 4.00 10.00
RCOVHS Henrik Samuelsson B 2.50 6.00
RCOVJD Jacob de la Rose B 3.00 8.00
RCOVJE Jack Eichel A 15.00 40.00
RCOVJM Jared McCann B 3.00 8.00
RCOVJV Jake Virtanen B 4.00 10.00
RCOVJW Jordan Weal B 3.00 8.00
RCOVKF Kevin Fiala B 3.00 8.00
RCOVMD Max Domi B 6.00 15.00
RCOVMJ Mattias Janmark B 3.00 8.00
RCOVMR Mikko Rantanen B 6.00 15.00
RCOVNC Nick Cousins B 3.00 8.00
RCOVNE Nikolaj Ehlers B 6.00 15.00
RCOVNG Nikolay Goldobin B 3.00 8.00
RCOVNH Noah Hanifin B 4.00 10.00
RCOVNR Nick Ritchie B 3.00 8.00
RCOVNS Nick Shore B 3.00 8.00
RCOVOL Oscar Lindberg B 3.00 8.00
RCOVRF Radek Faksa B 3.00 8.00
RCOVRH Ryan Hartman B 4.00 10.00
RCOVSB Sam Bennett B 4.00 10.00
RCOVSP Shane Prince B 2.50 6.00
RCOVZF Zachary Fucale B 3.00 8.00

2015-16 UD Black Rookie Trademarks Relics

RTRAB Antoine Bibeau B 5.00 12.00
RTRAP Artemi Panarin A 15.00 40.00
RTRCM Connor McDavid A 40.00 100.00
RTRDF Nick Ritchie B 5.00 12.00
RTRDL Dylan Larkin A 15.00 40.00
RTREP Emile Poirier B 5.00 12.00
RTRFA Robby Fabbri B 6.00 15.00
RTRHS Henrik Samuelsson B 4.00 10.00
RTRJD Jacob de la Rose B 5.00 12.00
RTRJE Jack Eichel A 20.00 50.00
RTRJM Jared McCann B 5.00 12.00
RTRJV Jake Virtanen B 6.00 15.00
RTRJW Jordan Weal B 5.00 12.00
RTRKF Kevin Fiala B 5.00 12.00
RTRMD Max Domi B 10.00 25.00
RTRMJ Mattias Janmark B 5.00 12.00
RTRMR Mikko Rantanen B 10.00 25.00
RTRNC Nick Cousins B 5.00 12.00
RTRNE Nikolaj Ehlers B 10.00 25.00
RTRNG Nikolay Goldobin B 5.00 12.00
RTRNH Noah Hanifin B 6.00 15.00
RTRNS Nick Shore B 5.00 12.00
RTROL Oscar Lindberg B 5.00 12.00
RTRRF Radek Faksa B 5.00 12.00
RTRRH Ryan Hartman B 6.00 15.00
RTRSB Sam Bennett A 6.00 15.00
RTRSP Shane Prince B 4.00 10.00
RTRZF Zachary Fucale B 5.00 12.00

2015-16 UD Black Showcase Relics Patch

RSRAH Adam Henrique 8.00 20.00
RSRBC Brett Connolly 5.00 12.00
RSRBG Brendan Gallagher 25.00 60.00
RSRBH Bo Horvat 12.00 30.00
RSRBJ Boone Jenner 5.00 12.00
RSRCK Cody Eakin 5.00 12.00
RSRCM Connor McDavid 90.00 150.00
RSRDH Calvin de Haan 5.00 12.00
RSRDL Dylan Larkin 25.00 60.00
RSRDR David Rundblad 5.00 12.00
RSREB Jordan Eberle 8.00 20.00
RSREP Emile Poirier 8.00 20.00
RSRGB Brandon Gormley 5.00 12.00
RSRGL Gabriel Landeskog 8.00 20.00
RSRJA Jake Allen 10.00 25.00
RSRJE Jack Eichel 30.00 80.00
RSRJF Justin Faulk 8.00 20.00
RSRJG Jake Gardiner 8.00 20.00
RSRJH Jonathan Huberdeau 8.00 20.00
RSRJV Jake Virtanen 10.00 25.00
RSRKS Kevin Shattenkirk 6.00 15.00
RSRMG Mikhail Grigorenko 6.00 15.00
RSRMK Marcus Kruger 8.00 20.00
RSRMP Matt Puempel 6.00 15.00
RSRMS Malcolm Subban 20.00 50.00
RSRMZ Mika Zibanejad 8.00 20.00
RSRNG Nikolay Goldobin 8.00 20.00
RSRNH Noah Hanifin 10.00 25.00
RSRNK Nazem Kadri 6.00 15.00
RSRNM Nathan MacKinnon 15.00 40.00
RSRNP Nicolas Petan 8.00 20.00
RSRNR Nick Ritchie 8.00 20.00
RSRPM Petr Mrazek 10.00 25.00
RSRRE Ryan Ellis 5.00 12.00
RSRRF Robby Fabbri 10.00 25.00
RSRRJ Ryan Johansen 10.00 25.00
RSRRN Ryan Nugent-Hopkins 8.00 20.00
RSRRS Ryan Strome 6.00 15.00
RSRSB Brendan Smith 6.00 15.00
RSRSD Simon Despres 5.00 12.00
RSRSK Slater Koekkoek 6.00 15.00
RSRSM Sean Monahan 8.00 20.00
RSRSP Shane Prince 6.00 15.00
RSRTH Tomas Hertl 12.00 30.00
RSRTP Tanner Pearson 5.00 12.00
RSRTW Tom Wilson 8.00 20.00
RSRZF Zachary Fucale 8.00 20.00
RSRZK Zack Kassian 5.00 12.00

2015-16 UD Black Signature Rookies

SRAC Andrew Copp/249 10.00 25.00
SRAP Artemi Panarin/49 50.00 120.00
SRCM Connor McDavid/49
SRDL Dylan Larkin/149 40.00 100.00
SREP Emile Poirier/249 10.00 25.00
SRJM Jared McCann/149 15.00 40.00
SRNE Nikolaj Ehlers/49 40.00 100.00
SRNG Nikolay Goldobin/149 15.00 40.00
SROL Oscar Lindberg/149 15.00 40.00
SRSP Sergei Plotnikov/249 8.00 20.00
SRVA Viktor Arvidsson/249 12.00 30.00

2015-16 UD Black Sixes Relic Booklets

6RG1 Brodeur/Roy/Esposito 25.00 60.00
Hasek/Fuhr/Hall
6RG2 Lundqvist/Price/Fleury 30.00 80.00
Holtby/Quick/Rinne
6RRC1 McDavid/Eichel/Larkin 80.00 200.00
Domi/Panarin/Bennett
6RRC2 Rantanen/McGinn/Sprong 20.00 50.00
Poirier/Petan/Virtanen
6RRC3 Ehlers/Fiala/Goldobin 20.00 50.00
Hanifin/Fabbri/Ritchie
6RRC4 Bibeau/Hellebuyck 25.00 60.00
Samuelsson/Lindberg/Weal/Subban
6RVCCF Naslund/Bure/Sedin 15.00 40.00
Fleury/Iginla/McDonald
6RAVALA Colorado 20.00 50.00
6RBLUES St. Louis 15.00 40.00
6RBOLTS Tampa Bay 20.00 50.00
6RBRUIN Boston 15.00 40.00
6RCANES Carolina 12.00 30.00
6RCAPIT Washington 40.00 100.00
6RHAWKS Chicago 20.00 50.00
6RISLAN N.Y. Islanders 20.00 50.00
6RKINGS L.A Kings 15.00 40.00
6RLEGEN Legends 15.00 40.00
6ROILER Edmonton 20.00 50.00
6RPENGU Pittsburgh 30.00 80.00
6RPREDA Nashville 12.00 30.00
6RRANGE N.Y. Rangers 12.00 30.00
6RSHARK San Jose 12.00 30.00
6RSTARS Dallas 15.00 40.00
6RWINGS Detroit 30.00 80.00

2015-16 UD Black Star Coverage Autograph Relics Gold

SCOVAB Aleksander Barkov 15.00 40.00
SCOVAK Anze Kopitar 25.00 60.00
SCOVBB Brent Burns 20.00 50.00
SCOVBR Bobby Ryan 12.00 30.00
SCOVCW Cam Ward 15.00 40.00
SCOVDG Doug Gilmour 20.00 50.00
SCOVDH Dale Hawerchuk 20.00 50.00
SCOVDK David Krejci 12.00 30.00
SCOVGH Glenn Hall 12.00 30.00
SCOVJG Johnny Gaudreau 25.00 60.00
SCOVJS Joe Sakic 25.00 60.00
SCOVMB Martin Brodeur 30.00 80.00
SCOVMF Marc-Andre Fleury 25.00 60.00
SCOVNM Nathan MacKinnon 30.00 80.00
SCOVSC Sidney Crosby 60.00 150.00

2016-17 UD Black

1 Corey Perry 4.00 10.00
2 Max Domi 5.00 12.00
3 Patrice Bergeron 5.00 12.00
4 Jack Eichel 8.00 20.00
5 Sam Bennett 5.00 12.00
6 Jeff Skinner 4.00 10.00
7 Corey Crawford 5.00 12.00
8 Matt Duchene 4.00 10.00
9 Brandon Saad 4.00 10.00
10 John Klingberg 4.00 10.00
11 Dylan Larkin 6.00 15.00
12 Connor McDavid 20.00 50.00
13 Aleksander Barkov 4.00 10.00
14 Anze Kopitar 6.00 15.00
15 Mikko Koivu 3.00 8.00
16 Shea Weber 3.00 8.00
17 P.K. Subban 6.00 15.00
18 Taylor Hall 8.00 20.00
19 Andrew Ladd 4.00 10.00
20 Mats Zuccarello 4.00 10.00
21 Mark Stone 4.00 10.00
22 Shayne Gostisbehere 5.00 12.00
23 Phil Kessel 5.00 12.00
24 Joe Thornton 4.00 10.00
25 Jake Allen 5.00 12.00
26 Victor Hedman 5.00 12.00
27 Morgan Rielly 3.00 8.00
28 Henrik Sedin 4.00 10.00
29 Braden Holtby 6.00 15.00
30 Mark Scheifele 5.00 12.00
31 Chris Chelios 4.00 10.00
32 Joe Sakic 6.00 15.00
33 Phil Housley 4.00 10.00
34 Igor Larionov 4.00 10.00
35 Teemu Selanne 8.00 20.00
36 Dave Andreychuk 4.00 10.00
37 Pat LaFontaine 4.00 10.00
38 Mark Messier 5.00 12.00
39 Tony Esposito 4.00 10.00
40 Doug Gilmour 5.00 12.00
41 Hudson Fasching AU/299 RC 8.00 20.00
42 Oliver Bjorkstrand AU/299 RC 6.00 15.00
43 Kasperi Kapanen AU/299 RC 15.00 40.00
44 Michael Matheson AU/299 RC 8.00 20.00
45 Sonny Milano AU/299 RC 10.00 25.00
46 Esa Lindell AU/299 RC 8.00 20.00
47 Connor Brown AU/299 RC 12.00 30.00
48 Danton Heinen AU/299 RC 12.00 30.00
49 Tyler Motte AU/299 RC 8.00 20.00
50 Sebastian Aho AU/299 RC 15.00 40.00
51 Christian Dvorak AU/299 RC 8.00 20.00
52 Nick Schmaltz AU/299 RC 8.00 20.00
53 Anthony Beauvillier AU/299 RC 8.00 20.00
54 Artturi Lehkonen AU/299 RC 8.00 20.00
55 Joel Eriksson Ek AU/299 RC 8.00 20.00
56 Brayden Point AU/299 RC 20.00 50.00
57 Zach Werenski AU/299 RC 15.00 40.00
58 Pavel Buchnevich AU/299 RC 12.00 30.00
59 Jakob Chychrun AU/299 RC 8.00 20.00
60 Travis Konecny AU/299 RC 15.00 40.00
61 Mathew Barzal AU/299 RC 40.00 100.00
62 Jimmy Vesey AU/299 RC 15.00 40.00
63 Thomas Chabot AU/299 RC 15.00 40.00
64 Kevin Labanc AU/299 RC 8.00 20.00
65 Matthew Tkachuk AU/299 RC 25.00 60.00
66 Jesse Puljujarvi AU/299 RC 20.00 50.00
67 Pavel Zacha AU/299 RC 10.00 25.00
68 Anthony Mantha AU/299 RC 20.00 50.00
69 Ivan Provorov AU/299 RC 15.00 40.00
70 Kyle Connor AU/299 RC 20.00 50.00
71 William Nylander AU/199 RC 30.00 80.00
72 Dylan Strome AU/199 RC 15.00 40.00
73 Mitch Marner AU/99 RC 150.00 350.00
74 Patrik Laine AU/199 RC 80.00 200.00
75 Auston Matthews AU/99 RC 650.00 800.00

2016-17 UD Black Gold Spectrum

*VETS/35: .50X TO 1.25X BASIC CARDS
*RC/35: .6X TO 1.5X BASIC CARDS
12 Connor McDavid 30.00 80.00
35 Teemu Selanne 15.00 40.00
74 Patrik Laine AU/35 100.00 200.00

2016-17 UD Black Lustrous INK

LIBE Brian Elliott/175 6.00 15.00
LIBH Brett Hull/25 25.00 60.00
LIBJ Boone Jenner/175 8.00 20.00
LIBL Brian Leetch/125 8.00 20.00
LIBS Billy Smith/125 8.00 20.00
LICC Chris Chelios/49 15.00 40.00
LICN Cam Neely/49 20.00 50.00
LIDA Dave Andreychuk/125 8.00 20.00
LIHL Henrik Lundqvist/25 40.00 100.00
LIJJ Joe Thornton/25
LIJT Jonathan Toews/25
LIJV Jimmy Vesey/175 15.00 40.00
LIKL Kevin Labanc/175 8.00 20.00
LIKM Kirk McLean/49
LILD Leon Draisaitl/175 30.00 80.00
LILE Loui Eriksson/175 8.00 20.00
LIMG Marian Gaborik/175 8.00 20.00
LIMH Mike Hoffman/175 6.00 15.00
LIMM Mike Modano/49
LIMP Max Pacioretty/175 8.00 20.00
LIMR Mike Richter/125 8.00 20.00
LINE Nikolaj Ehlers/175 8.00 20.00
LIPB Peter Bondra/175 8.00 20.00
LIPK Patrick Kane/25 60.00 150.00
LIPL Patrik Laine/49 60.00 150.00
LIRJ Roman Josi/175 8.00 20.00
LIRK Ryan Kesler/175 8.00 20.00
LIRL Roberto Luongo/125 8.00 20.00
LITA John Tavares/125 15.00 40.00
LIZP Zach Parise/125 8.00 20.00

2016-17 UD Black Obsidian Signature Combos

OS2GP John Gibson 12.00 30.00
Corey Perry B
OS2OG Bobby Orr
Wayne Gretzky A
OS2SH Mark Stone 15.00 40.00
Mike Hoffman C
OS2TK Jonathan Toews 60.00 150.00
Patrick Kane B

2016-17 UD Black Obsidian Signature Jersey Combos

OS2GP J.Gibson/C.Perry 12.00 30.00
OS2SH M.Stone/M.Hoffman 20.00 50.00
OS2TK J.Toews/P.Kane

2016-17 UD Black Obsidian Signature Jerseys

OSAE Aaron Ekblad/25
OSAH Adam Henrique/50 8.00 20.00
OSAV Andrei Vasilevskiy/50 25.00 60.00
OSHZ Henrik Zetterberg/25 15.00 40.00
OSIP Ivan Provorov/50 20.00 50.00
OSJE Joel Eriksson Ek/50
OSJT Joe Thornton/25
OSPL Patrik Laine/50 40.00 100.00
OSRL Roberto Luongo/25
OSSE Tyler Seguin/25 10.00 25.00

2016-17 UD Black Obsidian Signatures

OSAE Aaron Ekblad D 8.00 20.00
OSAH Adam Henrique D 8.00 20.00
OSAM Auston Matthews A 250.00 350.00
OSAO Alexander Ovechkin C 30.00 80.00
OSAV Andrei Vasilevskiy D 10.00 25.00
OSBO Bobby Orr B 60.00 150.00
OSCM Connor McDavid B 150.00 250.00
OSEM Evgeni Malkin B 25.00 60.00
OSHZ Henrik Zetterberg C 10.00 25.00
OSIP Ivan Provorov D 15.00 40.00
OSJE Joel Eriksson Ek D 8.00 20.00
OSJS Joe Sakic C 20.00 50.00
OSJT Joe Thornton C 8.00 20.00
OSJV Jimmy Vesey D 15.00 40.00
OSPL Patrik Laine D 30.00 80.00
OSRL Roberto Luongo C 8.00 20.00
OSSC Sidney Crosby B 200.00 300.00
OSSE Tyler Seguin C 12.00 30.00
OSTS Teemu Selanne C 15.00 40.00

2016-17 UD Black Pro Penmanship

PENAD Anthony DeAngelo F 8.00 20.00
PENAH Adam Henrique E 8.00 20.00
PENAK Anze Kopitar B 30.00 80.00
PENAS Andrew Shaw E 8.00 20.00
PENCN Cam Neely C 15.00 40.00
PENCP Carey Price A 40.00 100.00
PENDG Doug Gilmour A 40.00 100.00
PENDT Dave Taylor E 8.00 20.00
PENEM Evgeni Malkin A 25.00 60.00
PENFA Frederik Andersen E 6.00 15.00
PENGF Grant Fuhr B 12.00 30.00
PENHF Hudson Fasching F 8.00 20.00
PENJG John Gibson F 8.00 20.00
PENKL Kevin Labanc F 8.00 20.00
PENKP Kyle Palmieri F 6.00 15.00
PENLA Patrik Laine D 30.00 80.00
PENLM Larry Murphy C 20.00 50.00
PENLR Luc Robitaille C 20.00 50.00
PENMD Matt Duchene D 8.00 20.00
PENMF Marc-Andre Fleury B 25.00 60.00
PENMH Mike Hoffman E 6.00 15.00
PENMS Mark Scheifele E 10.00 25.00
PENNB Nick Bjugstad F 6.00 15.00
PENNK Nikita Kucherov E 12.00 30.00
PENRJ Ryan Johansen D 10.00 25.00
PENSA Derek Sanderson C 20.00 50.00
PENWG Wayne Gretzky A 200.00 300.00

2016-17 UD Black Pro Penmanship Combos

PEN2CL K.Connor/P.Laine/49 80.00 150.00
PEN2HS T.Hall/C.Schneider/49 15.00 40.00
PEN2JJ R.Josi/R.Johansen/49 12.00 30.00
PEN2LH P.LaFontaine/D.Hawerchuk/25 100.00200.00
PEN2LR B.Leetch/M.Richter/25 80.00 150.00
PEN2LT A.Ladd/J.Tavares/49

2016-17 UD Black Quad Relics

4RACR ACR 10.00 25.00
4RARI ARI 6.00 15.00
4RBUF BUF 10.00 25.00
4RCAL CAL 15.00 40.00
4RCBL CBL 10.00 25.00
4REDM EDM 25.00 60.00
4RFLA FLA 12.00 30.00
4RLAK LAK 8.00 20.00
4RMIN MIN 5.00 12.00
4RMLR MLR 20.00 50.00
4RPEN PEN 15.00 40.00
4RPHI PHI 10.00 25.00
4RRC1 RC1 12.00 30.00
4RSEN SEN 10.00 25.00
4RSJS SJS 6.00 15.00
4RSTL STL 8.00 20.00
4RVAN VAN 5.00 12.00
4RWAS WAS 20.00 50.00
4RWIN WIN 20.00 50.00
4RWJR WJR 20.00 50.00

2016-17 UD Black Rookie Trademarks Relics

RTRAM Auston Matthews A 20.00 50.00
RTRCD Christian Dvorak C 3.00 8.00
RTRDS Dylan Strome C 6.00 15.00
RTRIP Ivan Provorov C 6.00 15.00
RTRJE Joel Eriksson Ek C 3.00 8.00
RTRJP Jesse Puljujarvi C 8.00 20.00
RTRJV Jimmy Vesey C 6.00 15.00
RTRKC Kyle Connor C 8.00 20.00
RTRKK Kasperi Kapanen C 6.00 15.00
RTRMB Mathew Barzal C 10.00 25.00
RTRMM Mitch Marner B 15.00 40.00
RTRMT Matthew Tkachuk C 10.00 25.00
RTRNS Nick Schmaltz C 3.00 8.00
RTRPL Patrik Laine A 12.00 30.00
RTRPZ Pavel Zacha C 4.00 10.00
RTRSA Sebastian Aho C 6.00 15.00
RTRTC Thomas Chabot C 6.00 15.00
RTRTK Travis Konecny C 6.00 15.00
RTRWN William Nylander B 12.00 30.00

2016-17 UD Black Signature Rookies

SRAB Anthony Beauvillier/149 15.00 40.00
SRAL Artturi Lehkonen/249 10.00 25.00
SRAM Auston Matthews/25 300.00 400.00
SRDS Dylan Strome/149 10.00 25.00
SRIP Ivan Provorov/249 10.00 25.00
SRJE Joel Eriksson Ek/249 6.00 15.00
SRJP Jesse Puljujarvi/149 20.00 50.00
SRJV Jimmy Vesey/249 15.00 40.00
SRKC Kyle Connor/249 10.00 25.00
SRPL Patrik Laine/149 50.00 120.00

2016-17 UD Black Star Trademarks Relic Autographs

TRAE Aaron Ekblad/35 12.00 30.00
TRHZ Henrik Zetterberg/20 12.00 30.00
TRJG John Gibson/35 12.00 30.00
TRJM Jake Muzzin/35 6.00 15.00
TRLE Loui Eriksson/35 15.00 40.00
TRMG Mark Giordano/20 8.00 20.00
TRRK Ryan Kesler/20 12.00 30.00
TRTB Tyson Barrie/35 6.00 15.00

2016-17 UD Black Star Trademarks Relics

TRAE Aaron Ekblad B 3.00 8.00
TRDH Dale Hawerchuk A 6.00 15.00
TREK Erik Karlsson B 6.00 15.00
TRHZ Henrik Zetterberg B 4.00 10.00
TRJE Jack Eichel B 6.00 15.00
TRJG John Gibson C 3.00 8.00
TRJM Jake Muzzin B 2.50 6.00
TRLE Loui Eriksson C 3.00 8.00
TRMB Martin Brodeur A 12.00 30.00
TRMG Mark Giordano C 2.50 6.00
TRRK Ryan Kesler C 3.00 8.00

TRSC Sidney Crosby A	12.00	30.00
TRSM Sean Monahan C	3.00	8.00
TRTB Tyson Barrie C	3.00	8.00
TRWS Wayne Simmonds C	4.00	10.00

2017-18 UD Black Lustrous Rookies

LRAB Anders Bjork	5.00	12.00
LRAD Alex DeBrincat	10.00	25.00
LRAK Adrian Kempe	5.00	12.00
LRAN Alexander Nylander	6.00	15.00
LRAT Alex Tuch	10.00	25.00
LRBB Brock Boeser	40.00	100.00
LRCF Christian Fischer	5.00	12.00
LRCK Clayton Keller	10.00	25.00
LRCM Charlie McAvoy	12.00	30.00
LRCW Colin White	4.00	10.00
LRDG Denis Gurianov	4.00	10.00
LRES Evgeny Svechnikov	8.00	20.00
LRFK Jakob Forsbacka-Karlsson	4.00	10.00
LRIB Ivan Barbashev	4.00	10.00
LRJG Jon Gillies	4.00	10.00
LRJH Josh Ho-Sang	5.00	12.00
LRJR Jack Roslovic	5.00	12.00
LRJT J.T. Compher	5.00	12.00
LRLK Luke Kunin	4.00	10.00
LRMB Madison Bowey	3.00	8.00
LRMV Mike Vecchione	3.00	8.00
LRNH Nico Hischier	12.00	30.00
LRNP Nolan Patrick	8.00	20.00
LRNS Nikita Scherbak	8.00	20.00
LROT Owen Tippett	8.00	20.00
LRPD Pierre-Luc Dubois	8.00	20.00
LRTJ Tyson Jost	8.00	20.00
LRTS Travis Sanheim	4.00	10.00
LRVS Vadim Shipachyov	12.00	30.00
LRVZ Valentin Zykov	4.00	10.00

2017-18 UD Black Lustrous Rookies Jerseys

LRAD Alex DeBrincat B	5.00	12.00
LRAK Adrian Kempe C	2.50	6.00
LRAN Alexander Nylander B	3.00	8.00
LRAT Alex Tuch B	6.00	15.00
LRBB Brock Boeser A	30.00	80.00
LRCF Christian Fischer B	6.00	15.00
LRCK Clayton Keller A	5.00	12.00
LRCM Charlie McAvoy A	6.00	15.00
LRCW Colin White B	2.00	5.00
LRES Evgeny Svechnikov A	4.00	10.00
LRIB Ivan Barbashev C	2.00	5.00
LRJG Jon Gillies C	2.00	5.00
LRJH Josh Ho-Sang A	2.50	6.00
LRJR Jack Roslovic C	2.50	6.00
LRMB Madison Bowey C	1.50	4.00
LRNH Nico Hischier A	6.00	15.00
LRNP Nolan Patrick A	4.00	10.00
LRNS Nikita Scherbak C	4.00	10.00
LRPD Pierre-Luc Dubois B	4.00	10.00
LRTJ Tyson Jost A	4.00	10.00
LRTS Travis Sanheim C	2.00	5.00

2017-18 UD Black Lustrous Rookies Jerseys Onyx Patch

*PATCH/35: 1X TO 2.5X BASIC INSERTS

LRAN Alexander Nylander	20.00	50.00
LRBB Brock Boeser	200.00	300.00

2017-18 UD Black Lustrous Rookies Onyx

*ONYX/25: .75X TO 2X BASIC INSERTS

LRAT Alex Tuch	30.00	80.00
LRBB Brock Boeser	40.00	100.00

2017-18 UD Black Obsidian Scripts

OSAW Alexander Wennberg C	5.00	12.00
OSCS Conor Sheary D	8.00	20.00
OSDH Dale Hawerchuk B	25.00	60.00
OSFP Felix Potvin B	25.00	60.00
OSJC John Carlson D	8.00	20.00
OSJP Joe Pavelski B	6.00	15.00
OSMM Matt Murray C	20.00	50.00
OSNE Nikolaj Ehlers D	6.00	15.00
OSPR Patrick Roy A	40.00	100.00
OSRB Rod Brind'Amour C	6.00	15.00
OSSS Steven Stamkos B	12.00	30.00
OSSY Steve Yzerman A		
OSTB Tom Barrasso C	5.00	12.00
OSWG Wayne Gretzky A		

2017-18 UD Black Obsidian Scripts Onyx

*ONYX/25: .75X TO 2X BASIC INSERTS

OSPR Patrick Roy	50.00	125.00

2017-18 UD Black Obsidian Scripts Rookies

OSBB Brock Boeser B		
OSCK Clayton Keller B	20.00	50.00
OSCM Charlie McAvoy A		
OSCW Colin White B	8.00	20.00
OSJH Josh Ho-Sang A	15.00	40.00

2017-18 UD Black Rookie Trademarks Jerseys

RTAB Anders Bjork	4.00	10.00
RTAD Alex DeBrincat	8.00	20.00
RTAN Alexander Nylander	5.00	12.00
RTBB Brock Boeser	15.00	40.00
RTCK Clayton Keller	8.00	20.00
RTCM Charlie McAvoy	10.00	25.00
RTCW Colin White	3.00	8.00
RTES Evgeny Svechnikov	6.00	15.00
RTFC Filip Chytil	3.00	8.00
RTJH Josh Ho-Sang	4.00	10.00
RTLB Logan Brown	3.00	8.00
RTLK Luke Kunin	3.00	8.00
RTNH Nico Hischier	10.00	25.00
RTNP Nolan Patrick	6.00	15.00
RTOT Owen Tippett	6.00	15.00
RTPD Pierre-Luc Dubois	6.00	15.00
RTTJ Tyson Jost	6.00	15.00
RTTT Tage Thompson	5.00	12.00

2017-18 UD Black Star Trademarks Jerseys

STAM Auston Matthews	12.00	30.00
STAW Alexander Wennberg	1.50	4.00
STCA Craig Anderson	2.00	5.00
STJC Jeff Carter	2.00	5.00
STMB Martin Brodeur	8.00	20.00
STPB Patrice Bergeron	2.50	6.00
STPK Patrick Kane	4.00	10.00
STPL Patrik Laine	3.00	8.00
STRJ Ryan Johansen	2.00	5.00
STTS Tyler Seguin	3.00	8.00

2017-18 UD Black Star Trademarks Patch Autographs

STPL Patrik Laine/15		
STTS Tyler Seguin/35	15.00	40.00

2001-02 UD Challenge for the Cup

Released in mid-March 2002, this 135-card set carried an SRP of $4.99 per 5-card pack. Cards 91-135 were short printed to 1000 copies each of which 320 copies of each card were graded by Beckett Grading Services.

COMP.SET w/o SP's (90)	12.00	30.00
1 Paul Kariya	.50	1.25
2 Jeff Friesen	.25	.60
3 Dany Heatley	.40	1.00
4 Milan Hnilicka	.30	.75
5 Joe Thornton	.50	1.25
6 Bill Guerin	.40	1.00
7 Miroslav Satan	.30	.75
8 Martin Biron	.30	.75
9 Jarome Iginla	.40	1.00
10 Roman Turek	.30	.75
11 Craig Conroy	.25	.60
12 Jeff O'Neill	.25	.60
13 Arturs Irbe	.30	.75
14 Tony Amonte	.30	.75
15 Steve Sullivan	.25	.60
16 Rob Blake	.40	1.00
17 Joe Sakic	.60	1.50
18 Milan Hejduk	.30	.75
19 Chris Drury	.30	.75
20 Patrick Roy	1.00	2.50
21 Espen Knutsen	.25	.60
22 Ray Whitney	.25	.60
23 Pierre Turgeon	.40	1.00
24 Ed Belfour	.40	1.00
25 Mike Modano	.60	1.50
26 Sergei Zubov	.30	.75
27 Dominik Hasek	.60	1.50
28 Steve Yzerman	1.25	3.00
29 Brendan Shanahan	.50	1.25
30 Nicklas Lidstrom	.40	1.00
31 Luc Robitaille	.40	1.00
32 Mike Comrie	.30	.75
33 Ryan Smyth	.30	.75
34 Tommy Salo	.30	.75
35 Roberto Luongo	.60	1.50
36 Valeri Bure	.25	.60
37 Pavel Bure	.50	1.25
38 Felix Potvin	.60	1.50
39 Jason Allison	.30	.75
40 Zigmund Palffy	.40	1.00
41 Manny Fernandez	.30	.75
42 Marian Gaborik	.60	1.50
43 Andrew Brunette	.25	.60
44 Brian Savage	.25	.60
45 Jeff Hackett	.30	.75
46 Oleg Petrov	.25	.60
47 Cliff Ronning	.25	.60
48 Mike Dunham	.30	.75
49 Scott Walker	.25	.60
50 Martin Brodeur	.75	2.00
51 Scott Niedermayer	.40	1.00
52 Scott Gomez	.30	.75
53 Patrik Elias	.40	1.00
54 Alexei Yashin	.30	.75
55 Chris Osgood	.40	1.00
56 Mike Peca	.30	.75
57 Mark Messier	.60	1.50
58 Theo Fleury	.50	1.25
59 Eric Lindros	.60	1.50
60 Brian Boucher	.30	.75
61 John LeClair	.40	1.00
62 Jeremy Roenick	.40	1.00
63 Keith Primeau	.30	.75
64 Michal Handzus	.25	.60
65 Claude Lemieux	.30	.75
66 Sean Burke	.25	.60
67 Alexei Kovalev	.30	.75
68 Mario Lemieux	1.25	3.00
69 Johan Hedberg	.30	.75
70 Martin Straka	.25	.60
71 Owen Nolan	.40	1.00
72 Evgeni Nabokov	.30	.75
73 Teemu Selanne	.75	2.00
74 Doug Weight	.40	1.00
75 Brent Johnson	.30	.75
76 Pavol Demitra	.50	1.25
77 Chris Pronger	.30	.75
78 Keith Tkachuk	.40	1.00
79 Vincent Lecavalier	.30	.75
80 Brad Richards	.40	1.00
81 Nikolai Khabibulin	.40	1.00
82 Curtis Joseph	.40	1.00
83 Alexander Mogilny	.30	.75
84 Mats Sundin	.40	1.00
85 Trevor Linden	.40	1.00
86 Markus Naslund	.40	1.00
87 Brendan Morrison	.30	.75
88 Jaromir Jagr	1.00	2.50
89 Olaf Kolzig	.40	1.00
90 Peter Bondra	.40	1.00
91 Ilja Bryzgalov RC	3.00	8.00
92 Timo Parssinen RC	1.50	4.00
93 Kevin Sawyer RC	1.25	3.00
94 Brian Pothier RC	1.25	3.00
95 Ilya Kovalchuk RC	6.00	15.00
96 Kamil Piros RC	1.25	3.00
97 Ivan Huml RC	1.25	3.00
98 Jukka Hentunen RC	1.25	3.00
99 Scott Nichol RC	1.25	3.00
100 Erik Cole RC	2.50	6.00
101 Jaroslav Obsut RC	1.25	3.00
102 Vaclav Nedorost RC	1.25	3.00
103 Martin Spanhel RC	1.25	3.00
104 Niko Kapanen RC	2.00	5.00
105 Pavel Datsyuk RC	6.00	15.00
106 Ty Conklin RC	2.00	5.00
107 Niklas Hagman RC	1.50	4.00
108 Kristian Huselius RC	2.00	5.00
109 Jaroslav Bednar RC	1.25	3.00
110 Pascal Dupuis RC	2.00	5.00
111 Mike Matteucci RC	1.25	3.00
112 Nick Schultz RC	1.25	3.00
113 Travis Roche RC	1.25	3.00
114 Martti Jarventie	1.25	3.00
115 Martin Erat RC	2.00	5.00
116 Pavel Skrbek RC	1.25	3.00
117 Josef Boumedienne RC	1.25	3.00
118 Andreas Salomonsson RC	1.25	3.00
119 Scott Clemmensen RC	1.25	3.00
120 Mikael Samuelsson RC	1.50	4.00
121 Dan Blackburn RC	1.50	4.00
122 Richard Scott RC	1.25	3.00
123 Radek Martinek RC	1.25	3.00
124 Raffi Torres RC	2.00	5.00
125 Ivan Ciernik RC	1.25	3.00
126 Jiri Dopita RC	1.25	3.00
127 Vaclav Pletka RC	1.25	3.00
128 Krys Kolanos RC	1.25	3.00
129 David Cullen RC	1.25	3.00
130 Jeff Jillson RC	1.25	3.00
131 Mark Rycroft RC	1.50	4.00
132 Ryan Tobler RC	1.50	4.00
133 Nikita Alexeev RC	1.25	3.00
134 Brian Sutherby RC	1.25	3.00
135 Chris Corrinet RC	1.25	3.00

2001-02 UD Challenge for the Cup 500 Game Winner

This 2-card set highlighted the career wins of Patrick Roy. Each card carried a swatch of game-worn jersey. One card also carried an authentic autograph and was serial-numbered to 25. The jersey only card was serial-numbered out of 300. Please note that both cards are numbered 500PR, the "A" on the autograph card is for checklisting only.

500PR Patrick Roy/300	60.00	150.00
500PRA Patrick Roy AU/25	400.00	800.00

2001-02 UD Challenge for the Cup Backstops

Cards from this 10-card goalie set were serial-numbered out of 35 each.

BB1 Roman Turek	12.00	30.00
BB2 Arturs Irbe	12.00	30.00
BB3 Patrick Roy	40.00	100.00
BB4 Dominik Hasek	25.00	60.00
BB5 Tommy Salo	12.00	30.00
BB6 Martin Brodeur	30.00	80.00
BB7 Roman Cechmanek	12.00	30.00
BB8 Evgeni Nabokov	12.00	30.00
BB9 Curtis Joseph	15.00	40.00
BB10 Olaf Kolzig	12.00	30.00

2001-02 UD Challenge for the Cup Century Men

Cards from this 10-card set were serial-numbered to just 100 copies each.

CM1 Jeremy Roenick	8.00	20.00
CM2 Joe Sakic	10.00	25.00
CM3 Steve Yzerman	12.50	30.00
CM4 Sergei Fedorov	8.00	20.00
CM5 Luc Robitaille	6.00	15.00
CM6 Mark Messier	6.00	15.00
CM7 Jaromir Jagr	10.00	25.00
CM8 Mario Lemieux	15.00	40.00
CM9 Brett Hull	8.00	20.00
CM10 Pavel Bure	6.00	15.00

2001-02 UD Challenge for the Cup Cornerstones

Cards from this 10-card set were serial-numbered to just 250.

COMPLETE SET (10)	75.00	150.00
CR1 Paul Kariya	1.50	4.00
CR2 Ilya Kovalchuk	8.00	20.00
CR3 Joe Sakic	3.00	8.00
CR4 Mike Modano	2.50	6.00
CR5 Steve Yzerman	6.00	15.00
CR6 Pavel Bure	2.00	5.00
CR7 Mario Lemieux	10.00	25.00
CR8 Chris Pronger	1.25	3.00
CR9 Mats Sundin	1.50	4.00
CR10 Jaromir Jagr	2.50	6.00

2001-02 UD Challenge for the Cup Future Famers

Cards in this 6-card set were serial-numbered to just 25.

FF1 Joe Sakic	25.00	60.00
FF2 Patrick Roy	50.00	120.00
FF3 Brett Hull	30.00	80.00
FF4 Luc Robitaille	25.00	60.00
FF5 Steve Yzerman	40.00	100.00
FF6 Mark Messier	30.00	80.00

2001-02 UD Challenge for the Cup Jerseys

Inserted at odds of 1:36, this 23-card set consisted of 4 different subsets: Terrific 200, Franchise Players, Then & Now, and Unstoppable Combos. The Then & Now and the Unstoppable Combos subsets featured two swatches of game used jerseys while the other subsets featured one swatch.

TCJ Curtis Joseph	4.00	10.00
TCO Chris Osgood	4.00	10.00
TDH Dominik Hasek	8.00	20.00
TEB Ed Belfour	6.00	15.00
TFP Felix Potvin	5.00	12.00
TMB Martin Brodeur	12.00	30.00
TMR Mike Richter	4.00	10.00
TPR Patrick Roy SP	20.00	50.00
TSB Sean Burke	4.00	10.00
TTB Tom Barrasso	4.00	10.00
FPDW Doug Weight	4.00	10.00
FPEL Eric Lindros SP	5.00	12.00
FPJA Jason Allison	5.00	12.00
FPJL John LeClair	5.00	12.00
FPML Mario Lemieux	10.00	25.00
FPNL Nicklas Lidstrom	5.00	12.00
FPPF Peter Forsberg	8.00	20.00
FPRB Ray Bourque	8.00	20.00
FPSY Steve Yzerman	10.00	25.00
FPTA Tony Amonte	4.00	10.00
TNAM Al MacInnis Dual	8.00	20.00
TNBS Brendan Shanahan Dual	8.00	20.00
TNCJ Curtis Joseph Dual	8.00	20.00
TNJS Joe Sakic Dual	10.00	25.00
TNKP Keith Primeau Dual	8.00	20.00
TNPR Patrick Roy Dual	12.00	30.00
TNRB Ray Bourque Dual	10.00	25.00
UCLB J.LeClair/B.Boucher	6.00	15.00
UCLL E.Lindros/B.Leetch	6.00	15.00
UCMB M.Modano/E.Belfour	8.00	20.00
UCPD Z.Palffy/A.Deadmarsh	6.00	15.00
UCSH J.Sakic/M.Hejduk SP	15.00	40.00
UCSJ M.Sundin/C.Joseph	8.00	20.00
UCSY B.Shanahan/S.Yzerman	10.00	25.00

2001-02 UD Challenge for the Cup Jersey Autographs

This 15-card set partially paralleled the base jersey set but also included authentic autographs from the featured players. Single jersey cards were serial-numbered to 75 while dual jersey cards were serial-numbered to 25.

TBE Ed Belfour	20.00	50.00
TBR Martin Brodeur	40.00	100.00
TJO Curtis Joseph	15.00	40.00
TPO Felix Potvin	15.00	40.00
TPR Patrick Roy	75.00	150.00
TRI Mike Richter	15.00	40.00
FPAL Jason Allison	15.00	40.00
FPBO Ray Bourque	25.00	60.00
FPJI Jarome Iginla	25.00	60.00
FPPB Pavel Bure	60.00	120.00
FPWE Doug Weight	15.00	40.00
FPYZ Steve Yzerman	30.00	80.00
TNBO Ray Bourque Dual	40.00	100.00
TNEB Ed Belfour Dual	40.00	100.00
TNJO Curtis Joseph Dual	30.00	80.00
TNKP Keith Primeau Dual	30.00	80.00
TNMA Al MacInnis Dual	30.00	80.00
UCAP J.Allison/Z.Palffy	60.00	120.00
UCBB R.Bourque/R.Blake	125.00	250.00
UCLG J.LeClair/S.Gagne	40.00	100.00
UCST S.Samsonov/J.Thornton	40.00	100.00

1998-99 UD Choice

The 1998-99 Upper Deck UD Choice set was issued with a total of 310 cards. The 12-card packs retail for $1.29 each. The set contains the subsets: GM's Choice (221-242), Crease Lightning (244-252), and Jr. Showcase (253-307). The fronts feature color action photos surrounded by a white border.

COMPLETE SET (310)	15.00	30.00
1 Guy Hebert	.08	.25
2 Mikhail Shtalenkov	.05	.15
3 Josef Marha	.05	.15
4 Paul Kariya	.10	.30
5 Travis Green	.05	.15
6 Steve Rucchin	.05	.15
7 Matt Cullen	.05	.15
8 Teemu Selanne	.10	.30
9 Antti Aalto	.05	.15
10 Byron Dafoe	.08	.25
11 Ted Donato	.05	.15
12 Dimitri Khristich	.05	.15
13 Sergei Samsonov	.08	.25
14 Jason Allison	.05	.15
15 Ray Bourque	.20	.50
16 Kyle McLaren	.05	.15
17 Cameron Mann	.05	.15
18 Shawn Bates	.05	.15
19 Joe Thornton	.20	.50
20 Vaclav Varada	.05	.15
21 Brian Holzinger	.05	.15
22 Miroslav Satan	.08	.25
23 Dominik Hasek	.25	.60
24 Michael Peca	.05	.15
25 Erik Rasmussen	.05	.15
26 Alexei Zhitnik	.05	.15
27 Geoff Sanderson	.08	.25
28 Donald Audette	.05	.15
29 Derek Morris	.05	.15
30 German Titov	.05	.15
31 Valeri Bure	.05	.15
32 Michael Nylander	.05	.15
33 Cory Stillman	.05	.15
34 Theo Fleury	.05	.15
35 Jarome Iginla	.15	.40
36 Gary Roberts	.05	.15
37 Jeff O'Neill	.05	.15
38 Bates Battaglia	.08	.25
39 Keith Primeau	.05	.15
40 Sami Kapanen	.05	.15
41 Glen Wesley	.05	.15
42 Trevor Kidd	.08	.25
43 Nelson Emerson	.05	.15
44 Daniel Cleary	.05	.15
45 Eric Daze	.08	.25
46 Chris Chelios	.10	.30
47 Gary Suter	.05	.15
48 Alexei Zhamnov	.05	.15
49 Jeff Hackett	.08	.25
50 Dmitri Nabokov	.05	.15
51 Tony Amonte	.08	.25
52 Jean-Yves Leroux	.05	.15
53 Eric Messier	.05	.15
54 Patrick Roy	.60	1.50
55 Claude Lemieux	.05	.15
56 Peter Forsberg	.30	.75
57 Adam Deadmarsh	.05	.15
58 Valeri Kamensky	.05	.15
59 Joe Sakic	.25	.60
60 Sandis Ozolinsh	.05	.15
61 Jamie Langenbrunner	.05	.15
62 Joe Nieuwendyk	.08	.25
63 Ed Belfour	.10	.30
64 Juha Lind	.05	.15
65 Derian Hatcher	.05	.15
66 Sergei Zubov	.05	.15
67 Darryl Sydor	.05	.15
68 Jere Lehtinen	.05	.15
69 Mike Modano	.20	.50
70 Larry Murphy	.08	.25
71 Igor Larionov	.05	.15
72 Darren McCarty	.05	.15
73 Steve Yzerman	.60	1.50
74 Chris Osgood	.08	.25
75 Sergei Fedorov	.20	.50
76 Brendan Shanahan	.10	.30
77 Nicklas Lidstrom	.10	.30
78 Vyacheslav Kozlov	.05	.15
79 Dean McAmmond	.05	.15
80 Roman Hamrlik	.05	.15
81 Curtis Joseph	.10	.30
82 Ryan Smyth	.08	.25
83 Boris Mironov	.05	.15
84 Bill Guerin	.08	.25
85 Doug Weight	.08	.25
86 Janne Niinimaa	.05	.15
87 Ray Whitney	.05	.15
88 Robert Svehla	.05	.15
89 John Vanbiesbrouck	.08	.25
90 Scott Mellanby	.05	.15
91 Ed Jovanovski	.05	.15
92 Dave Gagner	.05	.15
93 Dino Ciccarelli	.08	.25
94 Rob Niedermayer	.05	.15
95 Rob Blake	.08	.25
96 Yanic Perreault	.05	.15
97 Stephane Fiset	.08	.25
98 Luc Robitaille	.08	.25
99 Glen Murray	.05	.15
100 Jozef Stumpel	.08	.25
101 Vladimir Tsyplakov	.05	.15
102 Donald MacLean	.05	.15
103 Shayne Corson	.05	.15
104 Vladimir Malakhov	.05	.15
105 Saku Koivu	.10	.30
106 Andy Moog	.08	.25
107 Matt Higgins RC	.08	.25
108 Dave Manson	.05	.15
109 Mark Recchi	.08	.25
110 Vincent Damphousse	.05	.15
111 Brian Savage	.05	.15
112 Petr Sykora	.05	.15
113 Scott Stevens	.08	.25
114 Patrik Elias	.08	.25
115 Bobby Holik	.05	.15
116 Martin Brodeur	.40	1.00
117 Doug Gilmour	.08	.25
118 Jason Arnott	.05	.15
119 Scott Niedermayer	.05	.15
120 Brendan Morrison	.08	.25
121 Zigmund Palffy	.08	.25
122 Trevor Linden	.08	.25
123 Bryan Berard	.08	.25
124 Zdeno Chara	.15	.30
125 Kenny Jonsson	.05	.15
126 Robert Reichel	.05	.15
127 Bryan Smolinski	.05	.15
128 Wayne Gretzky	.75	2.00
129 Brian Leetch	.10	.30
130 Pat Lafontaine	.10	.30
131 Dan Cloutier	.05	.15
132 Niklas Sundstrom	.05	.15
133 Marc Savard	.08	.25
134 Adam Graves	.05	.15
135 Mike Richter	.10	.30
136 Jeff Beukeboom	.05	.15
137 Daniel Goneau	.05	.15
138 Shawn McEachern	.05	.15
139 Damian Rhodes	.08	.25
140 Wade Redden	.05	.15
141 Alexei Yashin	.05	.15
142 Marian Hossa	.10	.30
143 Chris Phillips	.05	.15
144 Daniel Alfredsson	.08	.25
145 Vaclav Prospal	.05	.15
146 Andreas Dackell	.05	.15
147 Sean Burke	.05	.15
148 Alexandre Daigle	.05	.15
149 Rod Brind'Amour	.08	.25
150 Chris Gratton	.08	.25
151 Paul Coffey	.10	.30
152 Eric Lindros	.10	.30
153 John LeClair	.10	.30
154 Chris Therien	.05	.15
155 Keith Carney	.05	.15
156 Craig Janney	.05	.15
157 Teppo Numminen	.05	.15
158 Jeremy Roenick	.15	.40
159 Oleg Tverdovsky	.05	.15
160 Keith Tkachuk	.10	.30
161 Brad Isbister	.05	.15
162 Nikolai Khabibulin	.08	.25
163 Daniel Briere	.05	.15
164 Juha Ylonen	.05	.15
165 Tom Barrasso	.08	.25
166 Alexei Morozov	.05	.15
167 Stu Barnes	.05	.15
168 Jaromir Jagr	.20	.50
169 Ron Francis	.08	.25
170 Peter Skudra	.05	.15
171 Robert Dome	.05	.15
172 Kevin Hatcher	.05	.15
173 Patrick Marleau	.08	.20
174 Jeff Friesen	.05	.15
175 Owen Nolan	.08	.25
176 John MacLean	.05	.15
177 Mike Vernon	.08	.25
178 Marcus Ragnarsson	.05	.15
179 Andrei Zyuzin	.05	.15
180 Mike Ricci	.08	.25
181 Marco Sturm	.05	.15
182 Steve Duchesne	.05	.15
183 Brett Hull	.15	.40
184 Pierre Turgeon	.08	.25
185 Chris Pronger	.08	.25
186 Pavol Demitra	.08	.25
187 Jamie McLennan	.08	.25
188 Al MacInnis	.08	.25
189 Jim Campbell	.05	.15
190 Geoff Courtnall	.05	.15
191 Daren Puppa	.08	.25
192 Daymond Langkow	.08	.25
193 Stephane Richer	.08	.25
194 Paul Ysebaert	.05	.15
195 Alexander Selivanov	.05	.15
196 Rob Zamuner	.05	.15
197 Mikael Renberg	.08	.25
198 Mathieu Schneider	.05	.15
199 Mike Johnson	.05	.15
200 Alyn McCauley	.05	.15
201 Sergei Berezin	.08	.25
202 Wendel Clark	.08	.25
203 Mats Sundin	.10	.30
204 Tie Domi	.08	.25
205 Jyrki Lumme	.05	.15
206 Mattias Ohlund	.08	.25
207 Garth Snow	.08	.25
208 Pavel Bure	.10	.30
209 Dave Scatchard	.05	.15
210 Alexander Mogilny	.08	.25
211 Mark Messier	.10	.30
212 Todd Bertuzzi	.10	.30
213 Peter Bondra	.08	.25
214 Joe Juneau	.08	.25
215 Olaf Kolzig	.08	.25
216 Jan Bulis	.05	.15
217 Adam Oates	.08	.25
218 Richard Zednik	.05	.15
219 Calle Johansson	.05	.15
220 Phil Housley	.05	.15
221 Dominik Hasek GM	.10	.30
222 Ray Bourque GM	.10	.30
223 Chris Chelios GM	.08	.25
224 Paul Kariya GM	.10	.30
225 Wayne Gretzky GM	.40	1.00
226 Jaromir Jagr GM	.10	.30
227 Rob Blake GM	.05	.15
228 Adam Foote GM	.05	.15
229 Peter Forsberg GM	.10	.30
230 Joe Sakic GM	.10	.30
231 Mark Recchi GM	.05	.15
232 Patrick Roy GM	.10	.30
233 Nicklas Lidstrom GM	.08	.25
234 Rob Blake GM	.05	.15
235 John LeClair GM	.10	.30
236 Wayne Gretzky GM	.40	1.00
237 Eric Lindros GM	.10	.30
238 Brian Leetch GM	.05	.15
239 Scott Stevens GM	.08	.25
240 Paul Kariya GM	.10	.30
241 Peter Forsberg GM	.10	.30
242 Teemu Selanne GM	.10	.30
243 Patrick Roy CRL	.10	.30
244 Dominik Hasek CRL	.10	.30
245 Martin Brodeur CRL	.10	.30
246 Mike Richter CRL	.08	.25
247 John Vanbiesbrouck CRL	.08	.25
248 Chris Osgood CRL	.08	.25
249 Ed Belfour CRL	.10	.30
250 Tom Barrasso CRL	.05	.15
251 Curtis Joseph CRL	.10	.30
252 Sean Burke CRL	.05	.15
253 Josh Holden	.05	.15
254 Daniel Tkaczuk	.05	.15
255 Manny Malhotra	.05	.15
256 Eric Brewer	.05	.15
257 Alex Tanguay	.08	.25
258 Roberto Luongo	.30	.75
259 Vincent Lecavalier	.15	.40
260 Mathieu Garon	.08	.25
261 Brad Ference RC	.10	.30
262 Jesse Wallin	.05	.15
263 Zenith Komarniski	.05	.15
264 Sean Blanchard RC	.08	.25
265 Cory Sarich	.05	.15
266 Mike Van Ryn	.05	.15
267 Steve Begin	.05	.15
268 Matt Cooke RC	.10	.30
269 Daniel Corso	.05	.15
270 Brett McLean	.05	.15
271 J-P Dumont	.05	.15
272 Jason Ward	.05	.15
273 Brian Willsie RC	.08	.25
274 Matt Bradley RC	.05	.15
275 Olli Jokinen	.08	.25
276 Teemu Elomo	.05	.15
277 Timo Vertala	.05	.15
278 Mika Noronen	.08	.25
279 Pasi Petrilainen	.05	.15
280 Timo Ahmaoja	.05	.15
281 Eero Somervuori	.05	.15
282 Maxim Afinogenov	.25	.60
283 Maxim Balmochnykh	.05	.15
284 Artem Chubarov	.05	.15
285 Vitali Vishnevsky	.05	.15
286 Denis Shvidki	.05	.15
287 Dmitri Vlasenkov	.05	.15
288 Magnus Nilsson RC	.08	.25
289 Mikael Holmqvist RC	.08	.25
290 Mattias Karlin RC	.05	.15
291 Pierre Hedin	.05	.15
292 Henrik Petre	.05	.15
293 Johan Forsander	.05	.15
294 Daniel Sedin	.15	.40
295 Henrik Sedin	.15	.40
296 Marcus Nilsson	.05	.15
297 Paul Mara	.05	.15
298 Brian Gionta RC	.75	2.00
299 Chris Hajt RC	.08	.25
300 Mike Mottau RC	.12	.30
301 Jean-Marc Pelletier RC	.12	.30
302 David Legwand	.15	.40
303 Ty Jones	.05	.15
304 Nikos Tselios	.05	.15
305 Jesse Boulerice	.05	.15
306 Jeff Farkas	.05	.15
307 Toby Petersen	.05	.15
308 Wayne Gretzky CL	.10	.30
309 Patrick Roy CL	.08	.25
310 Steve Yzerman CL	.08	.25

1998-99 UD Choice Blow-Ups

Inserted as box-toppers in UD choice, these oversized cards resembled the base set but were approximately 5" x 7". Cards were numbered "X of 5".

COMPLETE SET (5)	6.00	15.00
1 Patrick Roy	2.00	5.00
2 Steve Yzerman	2.00	5.00
3 John LeClair	.75	2.00
4 Martin Brodeur	1.25	3.00
5 Peter Forsberg	1.50	4.00

1998-99 UD Choice Draw Your Own Trading Card

Inserted one in every pack, this insert asks collectors to submit an 8.5" x 11" piece of paper, their rendering of a trading card of their favorite NHL star. The selected winners' works were featured in the next season's UD Choice Hockey product.

DW1 Wayne Gretzky	.20	.50

1998-99 UD Choice Hometeam Heroes

This set of 20-cards features members of the Detroit Red Wings. The cards were inserted one-per-pack of UD Choice throughout Michigan at retail outlets.

COMPLETE SET(20)	6.00	12.00
RW1 Steve Yzerman	2.00	5.00
RW2 Sergei Fedorov	1.25	3.00
RW3 Nicklas Lidstrom	.40	1.00
RW4 Vyacheslav Kozlov	.40	1.00
RW5 Chris Osgood	.75	2.00
RW6 Darren McCarty	.40	1.00
RW7 Brendan Shanahan	1.25	3.00
RW8 Igor Larionov	.20	.50
RW9 Martin Lapointe	.20	.50
RW10 Doug Brown	.20	.50
RW11 Kirk Maltby	.20	.50
RW12 Kris Draper	.20	.50
RW13 Tomas Holmstrom	.20	.50
RW14 Larry Murphy	.20	.50
RW15 Slave Fetisov	.20	.50
RW16 Anders Eriksson	.20	.50
RW17 Brent Gilchrist	.20	.50
RW18 Joey Kocur	.20	.50
RW19 Mike Knuble	.20	.50
RW20 Kevin Hodson	.20	.50

1998-99 UD Choice Mini Bobbing Head

Randomly inserted in packs at a rate of 1:4, this 30-card insert features specially enhanced miniatures that fold into a stand-up figure with a removable bobbing head.

COMPLETE SET (30)	10.00	25.00
BH1 Wayne Gretzky	2.00	5.00
BH2 Keith Tkachuk	.30	.75
BH3 Ray Bourque	.50	1.25
BH4 Brett Hull	.40	1.00
BH5 Jaromir Jagr	.50	1.25
BH6 John Leclair	.30	.75
BH7 Martin Brodeur	.75	2.00
BH8 Eric Lindros	.30	.75
BH9 Mark Messier	.30	.75
BH10 John Vanbiesbrouck	.25	.60
BH11 Paul Kariya	.30	.75
BH12 Luc Robitaille	.25	.60
BH13 Zigmund Palffy	.25	.60
BH14 Peter Forsberg	.75	2.00
BH15 Teemu Selanne	.30	.75
BH16 Mike Modano	.50	1.25
BH17 Mats Sundin	.30	.75
BH18 Dominik Hasek	.60	1.50
BH19 Joe Sakic	.60	1.50
BH20 Rob Blake	.25	.60
BH21 Patrick Roy	1.50	4.00
BH22 Sergei Samsonov	.25	.60
BH23 Chris Chelios	.30	.75
BH24 Brendan Shanahan	.30	.75
BH25 Theo Fleury	.25	.60
BH26 Ed Belfour	.30	.75
BH27 Steve Yzerman	1.50	4.00
BH28 Saku Koivu	.30	.75
BH29 Brian Leetch	.30	.75
BH30 Pavel Bure	.30	.75

1998-99 UD Choice Preview

The 1998-99 UD Choice Preview set was issued in tw series totaling 110 cards. The 6-card packs retail for $.79 each. Set is skip numbered.

COMPLETE SET (110)	6.00	15.0
1 Guy Hebert	.20	.5
3 Josef Marha	.07	.2
5 Travis Green	.07	.2
7 Matt Cullen	.07	.2
9 Antti Aalto	.07	.2
11 Ted Donato	.07	.2
13 Sergei Samsonov	.20	.5
15 Ray Bourque	.40	1.0
17 Cameron Mann	.07	.2
19 Joe Thornton	.40	1.0
21 Brian Holzinger	.07	.2
23 Dominik Hasek	.50	1.2
25 Erik Rasmussen	.07	.2
27 Geoff Sanderson	.07	.2
29 Derek Morris	.07	.2
31 Valeri Bure	.07	.2
33 Cory Stillman	.07	.2
35 Jarome Iginla	.30	.7
37 Jeff O'Neill	.07	.2
39 Keith Primeau	.07	.2
41 Glen Wesley	.07	.2
43 Nelson Emerson	.07	.2
45 Eric Daze	.20	.5
47 Gary Suter	.07	.2
49 Jeff Hackett	.20	.5
51 Tony Amonte	.20	.5
53 Eric Messier	.07	.2
55 Claude Lemieux	.07	.2
57 Adam Deadmarsh	.07	.2
59 Joe Sakic	.50	1.2
61 Jamie Langenbrunner	.07	.2
63 Ed Belfour	.25	.6
65 Derian Hatcher	.07	.2
67 Daryl Sydor	.20	.5
69 Mike Modano	.40	1.0
71 Igor Larionov	.07	.2
73 Steve Yzerman	1.25	3.0
75 Sergei Fedorov	.40	1.0
77 Nicklas Lidstrom	.25	.6
78 Slava Kozlov	.20	.5
79 Dean McAmmond	.07	.2
81 Curtis Joseph	.25	.6
83 Boris Mironov	.07	.2
85 Doug Weight	.20	.5
87 Ray Whitney	.07	.2
89 John Vanbiesbrouck	.20	.5
90 Scott Mellanby	.07	.2
91 Ed Jovanovksi	.07	.2
93 Dino Ciccarelli	.20	.5
95 Rob Blake	.20	.5
97 Stephane Fiset	.20	.5
99 Glen Murray	.07	.2
101 Vladimir Tsyplakov	.07	.2
103 Shayne Corson	.07	.2
105 Saku Koivu	.25	.6
107 Matt Higgins	.07	.2
109 Mark Recchi	.20	.5
111 Brian Savage	.07	.2
113 Scott Stevens	.20	.5
115 Bobby Holik	.07	.2
117 Doug Gilmour	.20	.5
119 Scott Niedermayer	.07	.2
121 Zigmund Palffy	.20	.5
123 Bryan Berard	.07	.2
125 Kenny Jonsson	.07	.2
127 Bryan Smolinski	.20	.5
129 Brian Leetch	.25	.6
131 Dan Cloutier	.20	.5
133 Marc Savard	.07	.2
135 Mike Richter	.25	.6
137 Daniel Goneau	.07	.2
139 Damian Rhodes	.20	.5
141 Alexei Yashin	.07	.2
143 Chris Phillips	.07	.2
147 Sean Burke	.20	.5
149 Rod Brind'Amour	.20	.5
151 Paul Coffey	.25	.6
153 John LeClair	.25	.6
157 Teppo Numminen	.07	.2
159 Oleg Tverdovsky	.07	.2
161 Brad Isbister	.07	.2
163 Daniel Briere	.07	.2
165 Tom Barrasso	.20	.5
167 Stu Barnes	.07	.2
169 Ron Francis	.07	.2
171 Robert Dome	.07	.2
173 Patrick Marleau	.25	.6
175 Owen Nolan	.20	.5
177 Mike Vernon	.20	.5
179 Andrei Zyuzin	.07	.2
181 Marco Sturm	.20	.5
183 Brett Hull	.30	.7
185 Chris Pronger	.20	.5
187 Jamie McLennan	.20	.5
189 Jim Campbell	.20	.5
190 Geoff Courtnall	.07	.2
191 Daren Puppa	.20	.5
193 Stephane Richer	.20	.5
195 Alexander Selivanov	.07	.2
197 Mikael Renberg	.20	.5
199 Mike Johnson	.07	.2
201 Sergei Berezin	.20	.5
203 Mats Sundin	.25	.6
205 Jyrki Lumme	.07	.2
207 Garth Snow	.20	.5
209 Dave Scatchard	.07	.2
211 Mark Messier	.25	.6
213 Peter Bondra	.20	.5
215 Olaf Kolzig	.07	.2
217 Adam Oates	.20	.5
219 Calle Johansson	.07	.2

1998-99 UD Choice Prime Choic Reserve

This hobby-only parallel showcases the same player found in the UD Choice base set, except each card is foil-stamped with the words "Prime Choice Reserve" The set is sequentially numbered to 100.

*VETS: 25X TO 60X BASIC CARDS
*ROOKIES: 25X TO 60X

1998-99 UD Choice Reserve

Randomly inserted in packs at a rate of 1:6, this 310-card parallel showcases the same players found in the UD Choice base set, except each card sports a distinctive foil treatment.
*VETS: 2.5X TO 6X BASIC CARDS
*ROOKIES: 1.5X TO 4X BASIC CARDS
STATED ODDS 1:6

1998-99 UD Choice StarQuest Blue

The 1998-99 UD Choice StarQuest insert set salutes 30 of the NHL's top players with each of four 30-card tiers representing a different insert ratio. The cards feature color action player photos in different colored borders and with a different number of stars in the left bottom corner according to which tier the card is from. StarQuest Blue has one star and is inserted two per pack; StarQuest Green has two stars with an insertion rate of 1:7; StarQuest Red features three stars and an insertion rate of 1:23; StarQuest Gold is a limited-edition set and displays four stars. Only 100 sequentially numbered Gold sets were made.

COMPLETE SET (30) 8.00 15.00
SQ1 Wayne Gretzky 1.50 4.00
SQ2 Pavel Bure .40 1.00
SQ3 Patrick Roy .75 2.00
SQ4 Dominik Hasek .60 1.50
SQ5 Teemu Selanne .60 1.50
SQ6 Sergei Samsonov .25 .60
SQ7 Brian Leetch .30 .75
SQ8 Saku Koivu .30 .75
SQ9 Brendan Shanahan .40 1.00
SQ10 Alexei Yashin .25 .60
SQ11 Joe Sakic .50 1.25
SQ12 Patrik Elias .30 .75
SQ13 Theo Fleury .40 1.00
SQ14 Peter Bondra .25 .60
SQ15 John LeClair .30 .75
SQ16 Jaromir Jagr 1.00 2.50
SQ17 Ed Belfour .30 .75
SQ18 Steve Yzerman 1.00 2.50
SQ19 Mats Sundin .30 .75
SQ20 Peter Forsberg .50 1.25
SQ21 Ray Bourque .50 1.25
SQ22 Brett Hull .50 1.25
SQ23 Martin Brodeur .60 1.50
SQ24 Mike Modano .50 1.25
SQ25 Paul Kariya .40 1.00
SQ26 Tony Amonte .25 .60
SQ27 Mike Johnson .20 .50
SQ28 Eric Lindros .50 1.25
SQ29 Mark Messier .50 1.25
SQ30 Keith Tkachuk .30 .75

1998-99 UD Choice StarQuest Gold

Randomly inserted into packs, this 30-card set is a gold parallel version of the Blue one star insert set. These cards display four stars. Only 100 sequentially numbered sets were made.
*GOLD/100: 75X TO 150X BLUE INSERTS
GOLD STATED PRINT RUN 100
SQ29 Mark Messier 50.00 120.00

1998-99 UD Choice StarQuest Green

Randomly inserted into packs at the rate of 1:7, this 30-card set is a green parallel version of the Blue one star insert set. These cards display two stars.
*GREEN: 1.2X TO 3X BLUE INSERTS
SQ29 Mark Messier 1.50 4.00

1998-99 UD Choice StarQuest Red

Randomly inserted into packs at the rate of 1:23, this 30-card set is a red parallel version of the Blue one star insert set. These cards display three stars.
*RED: 3X TO 8X BLUE INSERTS
SQ29 Mark Messier 4.00 10.00

2004-05 UD Legendary Signatures

Released in late-summer 2004, this 100-card set featured some of the more colorful greats of the past. The base set cards were not autographed.

COMPLETE SET (100) 40.00 80.00
1 Al Iafrate .25 .60
2 Butch Goring .20 .50
3 Bernie Federko .20 .50
4 Bernie Geoffrion .30 .75
5 Bill Barber .25 .60
6 Bill White .20 .50
7 Bob Nystrom .20 .50
8 Bobby Clarke .30 .75
9 Bobby Hull .50 1.25
10 Borje Salming .30 .75
11 Brad Marsh .20 .50
12 Brad Park .25 .60
13 Brian Bellows .25 .60
14 Brian Sutter .20 .50
15 Bryan Trottier .40 1.00
16 Cam Neely .30 .75
17 Charlie Simmer .20 .50
18 Clark Gillies .30 .75
19 Craig Hartsburg .20 .50
20 Darryl Sittler .30 .75
21 Billy Smith .25 .60
22 Dave Schultz .25 .60
23 Dave Taylor .25 .60
24 Tiger Williams .25 .60
25 Denis Potvin .30 .75
26 Dennis Hull .25 .60
27 Denis Savard .40 1.00
28 Dino Ciccarelli .30 .75
29 Don Cherry .60 1.50
30 Don Marcotte .20 .50
31 Doug Gilmour .40 1.00
32 Doug Wilson .20 .50
33 Tony Twist .25 .60
34 Errol Thompson .20 .50
35 Frank Mahovlich .30 .75
36 Gerry Cheevers .30 .75
37 Gilbert Perreault .30 .75
38 Glenn Anderson .30 .75
39 Glenn Hall .30 .75
40 Gordie Howe 1.00 2.50
41 Grant Fuhr .30 .75
42 Guy Lafleur .40 1.00
43 Guy Lapointe .25 .60
44 Henri Richard .30 .75
45 Ian Turnbull .20 .50
46 Jari Kurri .30 .75
47 Jean Beliveau .40 1.00
48 Brian Propp .25 .60
49 Johnny Bower .30 .75
50 Johnny Bucyk .30 .75
51 Ken Hodge .25 .60
52 Ken Morrow .25 .60
53 Lanny McDonald .25 .60
54 Gump Worsley .30 .75
55 Marcel Dionne .40 1.00
56 Mark Howe .30 .75
57 Mike Bossy .30 .75
58 Mike Ramsey .20 .50
59 Neal Broten .25 .60
60 Pat Stapleton .20 .50
61 Richard Brodeur .25 .60
62 Paul Coffey .30 .75
63 Paul Henderson .25 .60
64 Peter Mahovlich .20 .50
65 Phil Esposito .50 1.25
66 Randy Gregg .20 .50
67 Red Berenson .20 .50
68 Reggie Leach .25 .60
69 Rene Robert .20 .50
70 Rick Martin .20 .50
71 Wayne Babych .20 .50
72 Willi Plett .20 .50
73 Rod Seiling .20 .50
74 Ron Ellis .20 .50
75 Ron Duguay .25 .60
76 Rogie Vachon .30 .75
77 Stan Jonathan .25 .60
78 Stan Mikita .40 1.00
79 Steve Larmer .20 .50
80 Steve Shutt .25 .60
81 Stu Grimson .20 .50
82 Ted Lindsay .30 .75
83 Terry O'Reilly .25 .60
84 Tony Esposito .30 .75
85 Tony Tanti .20 .50
86 Vic Hadfield .20 .50
87 Wayne Cashman .20 .50
88 Wayne Gretzky 1.50 4.00
89 Rob McClanahan .20 .50
90 Yvan Cournoyer .30 .75
91 Chris Nilan .20 .50
92 Dave Christian .20 .50
93 Don Awrey .20 .50
94 J.P. Parise .20 .50
95 Jim Craig .30 .75
96 Keith Brown .20 .50
97 Ken Linseman .25 .60
98 Mark Tinordi .20 .50
99 Harold Snepsts .20 .50
100 Michel Goulet .20 .50

2004-05 UD Legendary Signatures AKA Autographs

This 24-card set featured signatures of past greats along with their nicknames. Each card was serial-numbered out of 100.

AKAGH G.Howe Mr.Hockey 75.00 150.00
AKATE T.Esposito Tony O 40.00 80.00
AKADG D.Gilmour Killer 50.00 100.00
AKAJE J.Beliveau LeGros Bill 75.00 150.00
AKABH B.Hull Golden Jet 75.00 125.00
AKADC D.Cherry Grapes 60.00 125.00
AKAYC Y.Cournoyer Road 50.00 100.00
AKABO J.Bower China Wall 50.00 100.00
AKACN C.Nilan Knuckles 20.00 50.00
AKAJB J.Bucyk Chief 20.00 50.00
AKAHS D.Schultz Hammer 30.00 80.00
AKAMJ M.Johnson 30.00 80.00
AKAGE B.Geoffrion Boom 50.00 100.00
AKARD R.Brodeur King 20.00 50.00
AKAGC G.Cheevers Cheesy 25.00 60.00
AKAHA G.Hall Mr.Goalie 30.00 80.00
AKALW L.Worsley Gump 40.00 80.00
AKAGL G.Lafleur The Flower 40.00 80.00
AKAFM F.Mahovlich Big M 50.00 100.00
AKAAI A.Iafrate Wild Thing 25.00 60.00
AKATO T.O'Reilly Taz 40.00 80.00
AKASG S.Grimson Grim Reaper 20.00 50.00
AKATW T.Twist Twister 20.00 50.00
AKABN B.Nystrom Thor 20.00 50.00

2004-05 UD Legendary Signatures Autographs

This 100-card autograph set paralleled the base set with certified player signatures and were inserted one per pack. Known short-print numbers are listed below.

AI Al Iafrate 10.00 25.00
BB Bill Barber 5.00 12.00
BC Bobby Clarke/34 50.00 120.00
BE Brian Bellows 5.00 12.00
BF Bernie Federko 6.00 15.00
BG Butch Goring 6.00 15.00
BH Bobby Hull/81 50.00 120.00
BI Billy Smith 10.00 25.00
BM Brad Marsh 5.00 12.00
BN Bob Nystrom 5.00 12.00
BO Johnny Bower 8.00 20.00
BP Brian Propp 6.00 15.00
BR Brian Sutter 5.00 12.00
BS Borje Salming 10.00 25.00
BT Bryan Trottier 12.00 30.00
BW Bill White 5.00 12.00
CA Cam Neely 15.00 40.00
CG Clark Gillies 5.00 12.00
CH Craig Hartsburg 5.00 12.00
CI Dino Ciccarelli 15.00 40.00
CN Chris Nilan 6.00 15.00
CS Charlie Simmer 6.00 15.00
DC Don Cherry 20.00 50.00
DE Denis Savard 6.00 15.00
DG Doug Gilmour/84 40.00 100.00
DH Dennis Hull 6.00 15.00
DM Don Marcotte 5.00 12.00
DP Denis Potvin 6.00 15.00
DS Darryl Sittler/91 20.00 50.00
DT Dave Taylor 5.00 12.00
DU Ron Duguay 6.00 15.00
DV Dave Christian 5.00 12.00
DW Doug Wilson 5.00 12.00
ET Errol Thompson 5.00 12.00
FM Frank Mahovlich/41 125.00 250.00
GA Glenn Anderson 6.00 15.00
GC Gerry Cheevers 15.00 40.00
GE Bernie Geoffrion 12.00 30.00
GF Grant Fuhr 15.00 40.00
GH Gordie Howe 50.00 100.00
GL Guy Lafleur/25 300.00 500.00
GP Gilbert Perreault/34 100.00 200.00
HA Glenn Hall 12.50 30.00
HR Henri Richard 10.00 25.00
HS Dave Schultz 6.00 15.00
IT Ian Turnbull 5.00 12.00
JB Johnny Bucyk 6.00 15.00
JC Jim Craig 15.00 40.00
JE Jean Beliveau/98 60.00 120.00
JK Jari Kurri 8.00 20.00
JP J.P. Parise 6.00 15.00
KB Keith Brown 5.00 12.00
KH Ken Hodge 5.00 12.00
KL Ken Linseman 6.00 15.00
KM Ken Morrow 5.00 12.00
LA Guy Lapointe 8.00 20.00
LM Lanny McDonald 8.00 20.00
LW Gump Worsley 20.00 50.00
LY Rod Langway 12.00 30.00
MB Mike Bossy 8.00 20.00
MD Marcel Dionne 10.00 25.00
MG Michel Goulet 5.00 12.00
MH Mark Howe 5.00 12.00
MT Mark Tinordi 5.00 12.00
NB Neal Broten 6.00 15.00
PC Paul Coffey 12.50 30.00
PE Phil Esposito/37 100.00 250.00
PH Paul Henderson 20.00 50.00
PM Peter Mahovlich 6.00 15.00
PS Pat Stapleton 5.00 12.00
RA Mike Ramsey 5.00 12.00
RB Red Berenson 5.00 12.00
RD Richard Brodeur 8.00 20.00
RE Ron Ellis 6.00 15.00
RG Randy Gregg 5.00 12.00
RL Reggie Leach 6.00 15.00
RM Rick Martin 8.00 20.00
RR Rene Robert 6.00 15.00
RS Rod Seiling 5.00 12.00
RV Rogie Vachon 10.00 25.00
SC Steve Shutt 6.00 15.00
SG Stu Grimson 5.00 12.00
SJ Stan Jonathan 6.00 15.00
SL Steve Larmer 5.00 12.00
SM Stan Mikita/91 20.00 50.00
SN Harold Snepsts 5.00 12.00
SS Stan Smyl 5.00 12.00
TE Tony Esposito/62 40.00 100.00
TI Tiger Williams 6.00 15.00
TL Ted Lindsay 12.00 30.00
TO Terry O'Reilly/96 25.00 60.00
TT Tony Tanti 5.00 12.00
TW Tony Twist 5.00 12.00
VH Vic Hadfield 5.00 12.00
VP Brad Park 6.00 15.00
WB Wayne Babych 5.00 12.00
WC Wayne Cashman 6.00 15.00
WG Wayne Gretzky 100.00 175.00
WP Willi Plett 5.00 12.00
YC Yvan Cournoyer 12.00 30.00

2004-05 UD Legendary Signatures Buybacks

This 195-card set featured past Upper Deck cards that were "bought back" by UD and autographed by the given player. The original set and print runs are listed below.

8 B.Smith Vin Jsy/38 20.00 50.00
52 D.Potvin UD Leg Miles/22 25.00 50.00
75 G.Cheevers Vin Jsy/27
81 G.Perreault UD Leg Miles/21
159 N.Broten Leg Miles/37 25.00 50.00
178 P.Esposito Vin Jsy/35
179 R.Vachon Vin Jsy/30 40.00 80.00
180 S.Shutt UD Leg Miles/20 40.00 100.00
181 S.Shutt Vin SoH/35 40.00 80.00

2004-05 UD Legendary Signatures HOF Inks

This 14-card set celebrated past great who have been inducted into the Hall of Fame. Each card was serial-numbered to the year in which the star was inducted and those print runs are listed below.

HOFGH Gordie Howe/72 125.00 250.00
HOFBC Bobby Clarke/87 25.00 50.00
HOFMD Marcel Dionne/92 20.00 50.00
HOFHR Henri Richard/79 20.00 50.00
HOFBO Johnny Bower/76 20.00 50.00
HOFGF Grant Fuhr/103 15.00 40.00
HOFDS Darryl Sittler/89 20.00 50.00
HOFTE Tony Esposito/88 20.00 50.00
HOFCG Clarke Gillies/102 15.00 40.00
HOFJB Johnny Bucyk/81 15.00 40.00
HOFGP Gilbert Perreault/90 15.00 40.00
HOFHA Glenn Hall/75 30.00 60.00
HOFMB Mike Bossy/91 15.00 40.00
HOFBI Billy Smith/93 15.00 40.00

2004-05 UD Legendary Signatures Linemates

This 13-card set featured triple auotgraphs of great lines from the past. Each card was serial-numbered to just 50 copioes.

BBBCRL Barber/Clarke/Leach 75.00 150.00
BENBCI Bellows/Brotn/Cicrlli 40.00 100.00
BRBFWB Sutter/Fedrko/Babych 40.00 100.00
CGBTMB Gillies/Trottier/Bossy 75.00 200.00
CSMDDT Simmer/Dionne/Taylor 75.00 175.00
ETDSLM Thmpsn/Sittlr/McDnld 50.00 125.00
GAWGJK Anderson/Gretzky/Kurri 250.00 400.00
RMGPRR Martin/Perreault/Robert 75.00 200.00
SCPMGL Shutt/P.Mahov/Laflr 40.00 100.00
SJDMTO Jonthn/Marcte/O'Rlly 60.00 120.00
SLDEMG Larmer/Savard/Goulet 40.00 100.00
TISSTT Williams/Smyl/Tanti 40.00 100.00
WCPEKH Cshmn/P.Espo/Hdge 75.00 200.00

2004-05 UD Legendary Signatures Miracle Men

This 18-card set highlighted the 1980 USA Olympic hockey team. Cards were inserted one per US pack.

COMPLETE SET (18) 12.00 30.00
STATED ODDS 1:1 US
USA1 Mike Eruzione 1.50 4.00
USA2 Jim Craig 1.25 3.00
USA3 Rob McClanahan .50 1.25
USA4 Buzz Schneider .50 1.25
USA5 Mark Johnson .75 2.00
USA6 Neal Broten .60 1.50
USA7 Mark Pavelich .50 1.25
USA8 Dave Christian .60 1.50
USA9 Mike Ramsey .50 1.25
USA10 Ken Morrow .60 1.50
USA11 Steve Christoff .50 1.25
USA12 Bill Baker .50 1.25
USA13 Marc Wells .50 1.25
USA14 John Harrington .50 1.25
USA15 Dave Silk .50 1.25
USA16 Steve Janaszak .50 1.25
USA17 Eric Strobel .50 1.25
USA18 Bob Suter .50 1.25

2004-05 UD Legendary Signatures Miracle Men Autographs

Inserted at 1:5 packs, this 18-card set featured certified autographs from the 1980 USA Olympic Hockey team. The Mark Johnson card was issued as a redemption.

USAME Mike Eruzione 40.00 80.00
USAJC Jim Craig/73 400.00 600.00
USANB Neal Broten/73 500.00 700.00
USARA Mike Ramsey/97 200.00 300.00
USADV Dave Christian 40.00 80.00
USAJA Steve Janaszak 15.00 40.00
USAKM Ken Morrow 20.00 50.00
USABZ Buzz Schneider 12.00 30.00
USAES Eric Strobel 10.00 25.00
USAOB Bob Suter 10.00 25.00
USAST Steve Christoff 10.00 25.00
USABI Bill Baker 10.00 25.00
USAJH John Harrington 12.00 30.00
USAMW Marc Wells 10.00 25.00
USARO Rob McClanahan 10.00 25.00
USASI Dave Silk 12.00 30.00
USAMP Mark Pavelich 12.00 30.00
USAMJ Mark Johnson 25.00 50.00

2004-05 UD Legendary Signatures Rearguard Retrospectives

This 6-card se featured great defensive combinations from the past. Each card carried dual autographs and was limited to 100 copies each.

BMMH B.Marsh/M.Hower 12.50 30.00
BSIT B.Salming/I.Turnbull 15.00 40.00
CHMT C.Hartsburg/M.Tinordi 10.00 25.00
DPKM D.Potvin/K.Morrow 20.00 50.00
DWKB D.Wilson/K.Brown 12.50 30.00
PCRG P.Coffey/R.Gregg 20.00 50.00

2004-05 UD Legendary Signatures Summit Stars

This 20-card set highlighted the 1972 Canada Cup Canadian team.

COMPLETE SET (20) 10.00 20.00
STATED ODDS 1:1 CANADIAN
CDN1 Phil Esposito 1.00 2.50
CDN2 Paul Henderson .75 2.00
CDN3 Bobby Clarke .60 1.50
CDN4 Yvan Cournoyer .60 1.50
CDN5 Brad Park .50 1.25
CDN6 Dennis Hull .50 1.25
CDN7 J.P. Parise .50 1.25
CDN8 Ron Ellis .50 1.25
CDN9 Gilbert Perreault .60 1.50
CDN10 Frank Mahovlich .60 1.50
CDN11 Peter Mahovlich .50 1.25
CDN12 Bill White .50 1.25
CDN13 Wayne Cashman .50 1.25
CDN14 Stan Mikita .60 1.50
CDN15 Red Berenson .50 1.25
CDN16 Don Awrey .50 1.25
CDN17 Vic Hadfield .50 1.25
CDN18 Rod Seiling .50 1.25
CDN19 Pat Stapleton .50 1.25
CDN20 Tony Esposito .60 1.50

2004-05 UD Legendary Signatures Summit Stars Autographs

This 20-card set paralleled the basic insert set but carried certified player autographs. Known short-print numbers are listed below.

STATED ODDS 1:5 CANADIAN
CDNBC Bobby Clarke/73 75.00 150.00
CDNPH Paul Henderson 25.00 40.00
CDNTE Tony Esposito/24 250.00 500.00
CDNFM Frank Mahovlich/48 100.00 200.00
CDNGP Gilbert Perreault/48 60.00 150.00
CDNPE Phil Esposito/48 200.00 350.00
CDNSM Stan Mikita/97 50.00 125.00
CDNBP Brad Park 12.50 30.00
CDNYC Yvan Cournoyer 15.00 40.00
CDNJP J.P. Parise 8.00 20.00
CDNDH Dennis Hull 8.00 20.00
CDNRB Red Berenson 8.00 20.00
CDNPM Pete Mahovlich 8.00 20.00
CDNRS Rod Seiling 8.00 20.00
CDNPS Pat Stapleton 8.00 20.00
CDNDA Don Awrey 8.00 20.00
CDNRE Ron Ellis 8.00 20.00
CDNBW Bill White 8.00 20.00
CDNWC Wayne Cashman 8.00 20.00
CDNVH Vic Hadfield 8.00 20.00

2004-05 UD Legends Classics

Released in late-2004, this 100-card set featured past greats of the NHL.

COMPLETE SET (100) 15.00 40.00
1 Al Iafrate .25 .60
2 Andy Bathgate .30 .75
3 Bernie Geoffrion .30 .75
4 Bill Barber .25 .60
5 Bob Cole .20 .50
6 Bob Nystrom .20 .50
7 Bobby Clarke .30 .75
8 Bobby Hull .50 1.25
9 Brad Park .25 .60
10 Bryan Trottier .40 1.00
11 Butch Goring .20 .50
12 Cam Neely .30 .75
13 Clark Gillies .30 .75
14 Tiger Williams .25 .60
15 Dave Schultz .25 .60
16 Dave Taylor .25 .60
17 Derek Sanderson .20 .50
18 Dickie Moore .20 .50
19 Don Cherry .60 1.50
20 Doug Wilson .20 .50
21 Frank Mahovlich .30 .75
22 Fred Cusick .20 .50
23 Gerry Cheevers .30 .75
24 Gilbert Perreault .30 .75
25 Glenn Anderson .30 .75
26 Glenn Hall .30 .75
27 Gordie Howe 1.00 2.50
28 Grant Fuhr .30 .75
29 Guy Lafleur .40 1.00
30 Jari Kurri .30 .75
31 Jean Beliveau .40 1.00
32 Johnny Bower .30 .75
33 Johnny Bucyk .30 .75
34 Ken Hodge .25 .60
35 Ken Morrow .25 .60
36 Lanny McDonald .25 .60
37 Larry Murphy .25 .60
38 Gump Worsley .30 .75
39 Marcel Dionne .40 1.00
40 Mike Bossy .30 .75
41 Patrick Roy .75 2.00
42 Paul Coffey .30 .75
43 Paul Henderson .25 .60
44 Phil Esposito .50 1.25
45 Phil Esposito .50 1.25
46 Red Kelly .30 .75
47 Reggie Leach .25 .60
48 Rene Robert .20 .50
49 Rick Martin .20 .50
50 Stan Mikita .40 1.00
51 Ted Lindsay .30 .75
52 Tony Esposito .30 .75
53 Wayne Cashman .20 .50
54 Wayne Gretzky 1.50 4.00
55 Darryl Sittler .30 .75
56 Gordie Howe 1.00 2.50
57 Gordie Howe 1.00 2.50
58 Paul Henderson .25 .60
59 Darryl Sittler .30 .75
60 Mike Bossy .30 .75
61 Tiger Williams .25 .60
62 Patrick Roy .75 2.00
63 Paul Coffey .30 .75
64 Marcel Dionne .40 1.00
65 Mike Bossy .30 .75
66 Bobby Hull .50 1.25
67 Jari Kurri .30 .75
68 Bryan Trottier .40 1.00
69 Phil Esposito .50 1.25
70 Bobby Clarke .30 .75
71 Jean Beliveau .40 1.00
72 Stan Mikita .40 1.00
73 Gilbert Perreault .30 .75
74 Glenn Hall .30 .75
75 Guy Lafleur .40 1.00
76 Ken Morrow .25 .60
77 Tony Esposito .30 .75
78 Johnny Bower .30 .75
79 Wayne Gretzky 1.50 4.00
80 Wayne Gretzky 1.50 4.00
81 Gordie Howe 1.00 2.50
82 Wayne Gretzky 1.50 4.00
83 Bobby Hull .50 1.25
84 Bobby Clarke .30 .75
85 Gilbert Perreault .30 .75
86 Darryl Sittler .30 .75
87 Guy Lafleur .40 1.00
88 Glenn Hall .30 .75
89 Andy Bathgate .30 .75
90 Red Kelly .30 .75
91 Tony Esposito .30 .75
92 Jean Beliveau .40 1.00
93 Grant Fuhr .30 .75
94 Frank Mahovlich .30 .75
95 Gerry Cheevers .30 .75
96 Phil Esposito .50 1.25
97 Bryan Trottier .40 1.00
98 Dickie Moore .20 .50
99 Stan Mikita .40 1.00
100 Marcel Dionne .40 1.00

2004-05 UD Legends Classics Gold

*GOLD/25: 10X TO 25X BASIC CARDS
GOLD PRINT RUN 25 SER.'d SETS

2004-05 UD Legends Classics Silver

*SILVER/75: 5X TO 12X BASIC CARDS
SILVER PRINT RUN 75 SER.#'d SETS

2004-05 UD Legends Classics Jacket Redemptions

Cards from this set were redeemable for Mitchell & Ness throwback jackets of the teams represented on the card.

STATED ODDS 1:384
JK1 Boston Bruins
JK2 Chicago Blackhawks 150.00 300.00
JK3 Detroit Red Wings
JK4 Montreal Canadiens 125.00 250.00
JK5 Toronto Maple Leafs 150.00 300.00

2004-05 UD Legends Classics Jersey Redemptions

Cards from this set were redeemable for Mitchell & Ness throwback jerseys of the players represented on the card. Please note, some cards have yet to be verified.

STATED ODDS 1:384
JY1 Henri Richard 60.00 150.00
JY2 Jean Beliveau 150.00 300.00
JY3 Maurice Richard 150.00 300.00
JY4 Dickie Moore
JY5 Doug Harvey 60.00 150.00
JY6 Jacques Plante 125.00 250.00
JY7 Bernie Geoffrion 60.00 150.00
JY8 Frank Mahovlich
JY9 T.Sawchuk TOR 175.00 350.00
JY10 Tim Horton 150.00 300.00
JY11 Johnny Bower 60.00 150.00
JY12 Red Kelly 75.00 150.00
JY13 Eddie Shack 60.00 150.00
JY14 Dave Keon 60.00 150.00
JY15 Marcel Pronovost 60.00 150.00
JY16 W.Gretzky EDM 300.00 700.00
JY17 Stan Mikita
JY18 Bobby Orr 250.00 500.00
JY19 Gordie Howe 250.00 500.00
JY20 T.Sawchuk DET 150.00 300.00
JY21 Bobby Clarke 125.00 250.00
JY22 Tony Esposito
JY23 P.Esposito BOS
JY24 P.Esposito NYR
JY25 Guy Lafleur 60.00 150.00
JY26 W.Gretzky AS 350.00 700.00
JY27 Bill Barber
JY28 Tiger Williams
JY29 Dave Schultz 60.00 150.00
JY30 Grant Fuhr 60.00 150.00
JY31 Reggie Leach

2004-05 UD Legends Classics Pennants

Inserted one per box, these team pennants were produced by Mitchell & Ness for UD. Numbers P1-P12 were limited to 158 copies and numbers P13-P19 were limited to 88 copies.

P1 The Dynamite Line 20.00 50.00
P2 The Kid Line 12.50 30.00
P3 The Punch Line 10.00 25.00
P4 The Pony Line 12.50 30.00
P5 The Kraut Line 10.00 25.00
P6 The Production Line 20.00 50.00
P7 The Uke Line 15.00 40.00
P8 The LCB Line 10.00 25.00
P9 The Big Three 10.00 25.00
P10 The GAG Line 12.50 30.00
P11 The Triple Crown Line
P12 The French Connection 12.50 30.00
P13 Kansas City Scouts 30.00 80.00
P14 California Golden Seals 20.00 50.00
P15 Colorado Rockies 12.50 30.00
P16 Atlanta Flames 6.00 15.00
P17 Hartford Whalers 15.00 40.00
P18 Quebec Nordiques 10.00 25.00
P19 Winnipeg Jets 15.00 40.00
P20 Boston Bruins 10.00 25.00
P21 NY Rangers 6.00 15.00
P22 Chicago Blackhawks 6.00 15.00
P23 Detroit Red Wings 10.00 25.00
P24 Toronto Maple Leafs 8.00 20.00
P25 Montreal Canadiens 6.00 15.00
P26 Philadelphia Flyers 6.00 15.00
P27 LA Kings 6.00 15.00
P28 St.Louis Blues 8.00 20.00
P29 Minnesota North Stars 10.00 25.00
P30 Pittsburgh Penguins 6.00 15.00
P31 Oakland Seals 6.00 15.00
P32 Detroit Cougars 6.00 15.00
P33 Toronto St.Pats 6.00 15.00

2004-05 UD Legends Classics Signature Moments

STATED PRINT RUN 125 SER.#'d SETS
M1 Wayne Gretzky 125.00 250.00
M2 Gordie Howe 75.00 150.00
M3 Don Cherry 25.00 50.00
M4 Red Kelly 10.00 25.00
M5 Dickie Moore 12.00 30.00
M6 Andy Bathgate 10.00 25.00
M7 Terry O'Reilly 12.50 30.00
M8 Wayne Cashman 12.00 30.00
M9 Tony Esposito 15.00 40.00
M10 Ted Lindsay 15.00 40.00
M11 Stan Mikita 10.00 25.00
M12 Reggie Leach 8.00 20.00
M13 Rene Robert 8.00 20.00
M14 Rick Martin 10.00 25.00
M15 Phil Esposito 20.00 50.00
M16 Paul Henderson 8.00 20.00
M17 Paul Coffey 12.50 30.00
M18 Mike Bossy 15.00 40.00
M19 Lanny McDonald 12.50 30.00
M20 Gump Worsley 10.00 25.00
M21 Marcel Dionne 10.00 25.00
M22 Ken Morrow 6.00 15.00
M23 Ken Hodge 12.00 30.00
M24 Johnny Bucyk 10.00 25.00
M25 Johnny Bower 15.00 30.00
M26 Jari Kurri 12.50 30.00
M27 Cam Neely 15.00 40.00
M28 Jean Beliveau 30.00 60.00
M29 Guy Lafleur 20.00 50.00
M30 Gerry Cheevers 12.50 30.00
M31 Gilbert Perreault 12.50 30.00
M32 Glenn Anderson 8.00 20.00
M33 Glenn Hall 10.00 25.00
M34 Dave Taylor 6.00 15.00
M35 Grant Fuhr 20.00 50.00
M36 Frank Mahovlich 15.00 40.00
M37 Don Cherry 20.00 50.00
M38 Doug Wilson 8.00 20.00
M39 Dave Schultz 8.00 20.00
M40 Tiger Williams 10.00 25.00
M41 Dave Taylor 6.00 15.00
M42 Clark Gillies 10.00 25.00
M43 Bryan Trottier 12.50 30.00
M44 Butch Goring 6.00 15.00
M45 Bernie Geoffrion 15.00 40.00
M46 Al Iafrate 12.50 30.00
M47 Bill Barber 10.00 25.00
M48 Bob Nystrom 8.00 20.00
M49 Bobby Clarke 15.00 40.00
M50 Bobby Hull 30.00 60.00
M51 Brad Park 8.00 20.00
M52 Patrick Roy 40.00 100.00
M53 Ray Bourque 30.00 60.00
M54 Derek Sanderson 15.00 40.00
M55 Reggie Leach 8.00 20.00
M56 Jari Kurri 12.50 30.00
M57 Marcel Dionne 10.00 25.00
M58 Ken Hodge 12.00 30.00
M59 Dave Schultz 8.00 20.00
M60 Brad Park 8.00 20.00
M61 Gilbert Perreault 15.00 40.00
M62 Ken Morrow 6.00 15.00
M63 Gerry Cheevers 15.00 40.00
M64 Ted Lindsay 10.00 25.00
M65 Dave Taylor 6.00 15.00
M66 Cam Neely 20.00 50.00
M67 Johnny Bucyk 12.00 30.00
M68 Larry Murphy 8.00 20.00
M69 Fred Cusick 8.00 20.00
M70 Bob Cole 8.00 20.00

2004-05 UD Legends Classics Signatures

This 98-card set featured 4 different levels including single, dual, triple and quadruple autographs. Overall odds were 1:12 packs.

SP PRINT RUN 200 OR FEWER
SSP PRINT RUN 100 OR FEWER
XSP PRINT RUN 55 OR FEWER
DUAL AU SER.#'d TO 75
TRIPLE AU SER.#'d TO 25
CS1 Wayne Gretzky XSP 125.00 250.00
CS2 Gordie Howe SSP 75.00 150.00
CS3 Don Cherry 15.00 40.00
CS4 Red Kelly 10.00 25.00
CS5 Dickie Moore 12.00 30.00
CS6 Andy Bathgate 10.00 25.00
CS7 Terry O'Reilly 15.00 40.00
CS8 Wayne Cashman 8.00 20.00
CS9 Tony Esposito XSP 40.00 100.00
CS10 Ted Lindsay XSP 20.00 50.00
CS11 Stan Mikita XSP 25.00 60.00
CS12 Reggie Leach 6.00 15.00
CS13 Rene Robert 8.00 20.00
CS14 Rick Martin 8.00 20.00
CS15 Phil Esposito XSP 75.00 125.00
CS16 Paul Henderson 10.00 25.00
CS17 Paul Coffey SSP 20.00 50.00
CS18 Mike Bossy 10.00 25.00
CS19 Lanny McDonald SP 12.50 30.00
CS20 Gump Worsley 15.00 40.00
CS21 Marcel Dionne SSP 15.00 40.00
CS22 Ken Morrow 6.00 15.00
CS23 Ken Hodge 6.00 15.00
CS24 Johnny Bucyk SP 10.00 25.00
CS25 Johnny Bower 10.00 25.00
CS26 Jari Kurri 10.00 25.00
CS27 Cam Neely SP 15.00 40.00
CS28 Jean Beliveau SSP 50.00 100.00
CS29 Guy Lafleur XSP 40.00 100.00
CS30 Gerry Cheevers 12.50 30.00
CS31 Gilbert Perreault XSP 30.00 80.00
CS32 Glenn Anderson 6.00 15.00
CS33 Glenn Hall 10.00 25.00
CS34 Grant Fuhr XSP 25.00 60.00
CS35 Frank Mahovlich XSP 25.00 60.00
CS36 Doug Wilson 6.00 15.00
CS37 Dave Schultz 8.00 20.00
CS38 Tiger Williams 8.00 20.00
CS39 Dave Taylor 6.00 15.00
CS40 Clark Gillies 6.00 15.00
CS41 Bryan Trottier/56* 15.00 40.00
CS42 Butch Goring 6.00 15.00
CS43 Bernie Geoffrion SP 25.00 60.00
CS44 Al Iafrate 6.00 15.00
CS45 Bill Barber 6.00 15.00
CS46 Bob Nystrom 6.00 15.00
CS47 Bobby Clarke SP 20.00 50.00
CS48 Bobby Hull XSP 50.00 100.00
CS49 Brad Park 10.00 25.00
CS50 Patrick Roy SSP 50.00 100.00
CS51 Ray Bourque/25 150.00 400.00
CS52 Derek Sanderson 12.00 30.00
CS53 Fred Cusick 6.00 15.00
CS54 Bob Cole 6.00 15.00
CS55 Larry Murphy 8.00 20.00
DC1 T.Esposito/P.Esposito 50.00 100.00
DC2 J.Beliveau/G.Lafleur 40.00 100.00
DC3 S.Mikita/B.Hull 30.00 80.00
DC4 R.Bourque/C.Neely 30.00 80.00
DC5 M.Bossy/B.Trottier 30.00 80.00
DC6 D.Sanderson/J.Bucyk 25.00 60.00
DC7 R.Robert/G.Perreault 25.00 60.00
DC8 C.Neely/J.Bucyk 25.00 60.00
DC9 J.Beliveau/D.Moore 40.00 100.00
DC10 B.Park/R.Bourque 40.00 100.00
DC11 D.Sanderson/P.Esposito 25.00 60.00
DC12 T.Esposito/G.Hall 40.00 100.00
DC13 M.Dionne/G.Lafleur 30.00 80.00
DC14 G.Howe/B.Hull 100.00 250.00
DC15 D.Schultz/D.Williams 15.00 40.00
DC16 L.Murphy/D.Taylor 20.00 50.00
DC17 M.Dionne/D.Taylor 15.00 40.00
DC18 B.Clarke/G.Perreault 40.00 100.00
DC19 F.Cusick/B.Cole 15.00 40.00
DC20 B.Clarke/B.Barber 30.00 80.00
DC21 A.Bathgate/J.Bower 40.00 100.00
DC22 S.Mikita/D.Wilson 25.00 60.00
TC1 T.Espo/Worsley/Roy 125.00 250.00
TC2 Mahov/Hndrsn/Bower 100.00 250.00
TC3 Chvers/P.Espo/Sandr 100.00 200.00
TC4 Hall/T.Espo/Cheevers 100.00 200.00
TC5 Gillies/Trottier/Bossy 60.00 150.00
TC6 Barber/Clarke/Leach 75.00 200.00
TC7 Geoffrion/Howe/Beliveau 250.00 500.00
TC8 Hodge/Park/P.Espo 30.00 80.00
TC9 Coffey/Murphy/Bourque 60.00 150.00
TC10 Martin/Perreault/Robert 60.00 150.00
TC11 Anderson/Gretzky/Kurri 350.00 500.00
TC12 Worsley/Beliveau/Moore 60.00 150.00
TC13 Howe/Kelly/Lindsay 200.00 400.00
TC14 Gretzky/Dionne/Lafleur 300.00 600.00
TC15 T.Esposito/Mikita/Wilson 75.00 200.00
QC1 Roy/T.Espo /Hall/Chvers
QC2 Howe/Lafleur/Bossy/Kurri
QC3 Hull/Mahvl/Lindsay/Bucyk
QC4 Gretz/Trottier/Perrlt/Dionne
QC5 P.Espo/O'Rlly/Neely/Cshmn EX
QC6 Howe/Clarke/Neely/Gillies

2001-02 UD Mask Collection

Released in June, this 190-card had a SRP of $3.99. The set featured 100 regular base cards, 40 Precious Gems rookie cards, 30 Manning the Nets subset cards and 20 Unmasked Warriors subset cards. The Precious Gems cards were serial-numbered out of 1500, the Unmasked Warriors cards were serial-numbered out of 1250, and the Manning the Nets cards were inserted at a rate of 1:3.

COMP.SET w/o SP's (100) 15.00 40.00
1 Paul Kariya .40 1.00
2 Jeff Friesen .20 .50
3 Matt Cullen .20 .50
4 Dany Heatley .30 .75
5 Lubos Bartecko .20 .50
6 Tony Hrkac .20 .50
7 Sergei Samsonov .25 .60
8 Joe Thornton .40 1.00
9 Bill Guerin .30 .75
10 P.J. Stock .20 .50
11 Stu Barnes .25 .60
12 Tim Connolly .20 .50
13 Jarome Iginla .30 .75
14 Craig Conroy .20 .50
15 Sami Kapanen .20 .50
16 Ron Francis .40 1.00
17 Tony Amonte .25 .60
18 Mark Bell .20 .50
19 Steve Sullivan .20 .50
20 Chris Drury .25 .60
21 Milan Hejduk .25 .60
22 Joe Sakic .50 1.25
23 Rob Blake .30 .75
24 Alex Tanguay .25 .60
25 Mike Sillinger .20 .50
26 Ray Whitney .20 .50
27 Rostislav Klesla .20 .50
28 Pierre Turgeon .30 .75
29 Jere Lehtinen .25 .60
30 Mike Modano .50 1.25
31 Sergei Zubov .25 .60
32 Brendan Shanahan .40 1.00
33 Steve Yzerman 1.00 2.50
34 Brett Hull .40 1.00
35 Sergei Fedorov .50 1.25
36 Mike Comrie .25 .60
37 Ryan Smyth .25 .60
38 Anson Carter .25 .60
39 Viktor Kozlov .20 .50
40 Marcus Nilsson .20 .50
41 Sandis Ozolinsh .20 .50
42 Adam Deadmarsh .25 .60
43 Jason Allison .25 .60
44 Zigmund Palffy .30 .75
45 Andrew Brunette .20 .50
46 Marian Gaborik .50 1.25
47 Jim Dowd .20 .50
48 Yanic Perreault .20 .50
49 Sergei Berezin .20 .50
50 Donald Audette .20 .50
51 Francois Bouillon .20 .50
52 Karlis Skrastins .20 .50
53 David Legwand .25 .60
54 Scott Hartnell .30 .75
55 Bobby Holik .20 .50
56 Joe Nieuwendyk .30 .75
57 Patrik Elias .30 .75
58 Brian Rafalski .20 .50
59 Mark Parrish .20 .50
60 Michael Peca .25 .60
61 Alexei Yashin .25 .60
62 Petr Nedved .25 .60
63 Theo Fleury .40 1.00
64 Pavel Bure .40 1.00
65 Eric Lindros .50 1.25
66 Martin Havlat .25 .60
67 Daniel Alfredsson .30 .75
68 Marian Hossa .25 .60
69 Radek Bonk .20 .50
70 Simon Gagne .30 .75
71 John LeClair .30 .75
72 Jeremy Roenick .30 .75
73 Mark Recchi .40 1.00
74 Michal Handzus .20 .50
75 Claude Lemieux .25 .60

76 Shane Doan .25 .60
77 Jamie Pushor .20 .50
78 Alexei Kovalev .25 .60
79 Mario Lemieux 1.00 2.50
80 Vincent Damphousse .25 .60
81 Owen Nolan .30 .75
82 Teemu Selanne .60 1.50
83 Keith Tkachuk .30 .75
84 Chris Pronger .25 .60
85 Doug Weight .30 .75
86 Pavol Demitra .40 1.00
87 Fredrik Modin .20 .50
88 Brad Richards .30 .75
89 Vincent Lecavalier .25 .60
90 Darcy Tucker .20 .50
91 Alexander Mogilny .25 .60
92 Mats Sundin .30 .75
93 Brendan Morrison .25 .60
94 Todd Bertuzzi .30 .75
95 Markus Naslund .30 .75
96 Ed Jovanovski .25 .60
97 Drake Berehowsky .20 .50
98 Ulf Dahlen .20 .50
99 Peter Bondra .30 .75
100 Jaromir Jagr .75 2.00
101 Jean-Sebastien Giguere MTN .75 2.00
102 Milan Hnilicka MTN .75 2.00
103 Byron Dafoe MTN .75 2.00
104 Martin Biron MTN .75 2.00
105 Roman Turek MTN .75 2.00
106 Arturs Irbe MTN .75 2.00
107 Jocelyn Thibault MTN .75 2.00
108 Patrick Roy MTN 2.50 6.00
109 Ron Tugnutt MTN .75 2.00
110 Ed Belfour MTN 1.00 2.50
111 Dominik Hasek MTN 1.50 4.00
112 Tommy Salo MTN .75 2.00
113 Roberto Luongo MTN 1.50 4.00
114 Felix Potvin MTN 1.50 4.00
115 Manny Fernandez MTN .75 2.00
116 Jose Theodore MTN 1.00 2.50
117 Mike Dunham MTN .75 2.00
118 Martin Brodeur MTN 2.00 5.00
119 Chris Osgood MTN 1.00 2.50
120 Mike Richter MTN 1.00 2.50
121 Patrick Lalime MTN .75 2.00
122 Roman Cechmanek MTN .75 2.00
123 Sean Burke MTN .60 1.50
124 Johan Hedberg MTN .75 2.00
125 Evgeni Nabokov MTN .75 2.00
126 Brent Johnson MTN .75 2.00
127 Nikolai Khabibulin MTN 1.00 2.50
128 Curtis Joseph MTN 1.00 2.50
129 Dan Cloutier MTN .75 2.00
130 Olaf Kolzig MTN 1.00 2.50
131 Frederic Cassivi RC 1.50 4.00
132 Ilya Kovalchuk RC 8.00 20.00
133 Pasi Nurminen RC 1.50 4.00
134 Mark Hartigan RC 1.50 4.00
135 Francis Lessard RC 1.50 4.00
136 Ivan Huml RC 1.50 4.00
137 Chris Kelleher RC 1.50 4.00
138 Erik Cole RC 3.00 8.00
139 Mike Peluso RC 1.50 4.00
140 Vaclav Nedorost RC 1.50 4.00
141 Jeff Daw RC 1.50 4.00
142 Andrej Nedorost RC 1.50 4.00
143 Sean Avery RC 1.50 4.00
144 Pavel Datsyuk RC 8.00 20.00
145 Stephen Weiss RC 4.00 10.00
146 Niklas Hagman RC 2.00 5.00
147 Kristian Huselius RC 2.50 6.00
148 Lukas Krajicek RC 1.50 4.00
149 Tony Virta RC 1.50 4.00
150 Olivier Michaud RC 2.50 6.00
151 Marcel Hossa RC 2.50 6.00
152 Martin Erat RC 2.50 6.00
153 Christian Berglund RC 2.00 5.00
154 Raffi Torres RC 2.50 6.00
155 Dan Blackburn RC 2.00 5.00
156 Martin Prusek RC 1.50 4.00
157 Chris Bala RC 1.50 4.00
158 Josh Langfeld RC 1.50 4.00
159 Jiri Dopita RC 1.50 4.00
160 Neil Little RC 1.50 4.00
161 Guillaume Lefebvre RC 1.50 4.00
162 Krys Kolanos RC 1.50 4.00
163 Branko Radivojevic RC 1.50 4.00
164 Shane Endicott RC 1.50 4.00
165 Hannes Hyvonen RC 1.50 4.00
166 Jeff Jillson RC 1.50 4.00
167 Nikita Alexeev RC 1.50 4.00
168 Gaetan Royer RC 1.50 4.00
169 Karel Pilar RC 1.50 4.00
170 Brian Sutherby RC 1.50 4.00
171 Byron Dafoe UW 1.50 4.00
172 Martin Biron UW 1.50 4.00
173 Roman Turek UW 1.50 4.00
174 Arturs Irbe UW 1.50 4.00
175 Patrick Roy UW 5.00 12.00
176 Ed Belfour UW 2.00 5.00
177 Dominik Hasek UW 3.00 8.00
178 Tommy Salo UW 1.50 4.00
179 Felix Potvin UW 3.00 8.00
180 Mike Dunham UW 1.50 4.00
181 Martin Brodeur UW 4.00 10.00
182 Chris Osgood UW 2.00 5.00
183 Mike Richter UW 2.00 5.00
184 Roman Cechmanek UW 1.50 4.00
185 Sean Burke UW 1.25 3.00
186 Johan Hedberg UW 1.50 4.00
187 Evgeni Nabokov UW 1.50 4.00
188 Nikolai Khabibulin UW 2.00 5.00
189 Curtis Joseph UW 2.00 5.00
190 Olaf Kolzig UW 2.00 5.00

2001-02 UD Mask Collection Gold

This 190-card set paralleled the base set. Each card was serial-numbered to just 50 copies each.
*1-100 VETS/50: 5X TO 12X BASIC CARDS
*101-130 MTN/50: 2.5X TO 6X BASIC MTN
*131-170 ROOKIE/50: 1.5X TO 4X BASIC RC
*171-190 UW/50: 1.2X TO 3X BASIC UW

2001-02 UD Mask Collection Dual Jerseys

Inserted at a rate of 1:288, this 14-card set featured two game-worn swatches of the players featured. There was two subsets, Premier Matchups and Behind the Mask. Card prefixes denote subset. Swatches were affixed beside a full-color action photo on the card front. Card backs carried a congratulatory message.
MBBC B.Boucher/R.Cechmanek 10.00 25.00
MBBT M.Brodeur/J.Theodore 15.00 40.00
MBCJ Curtis Joseph Dual 10.00 25.00
MBFP Felix Potvin Dual 10.00 25.00
MBPR Patrick Roy Dual 40.00 80.00
MBRD M.Richter/M.Dunham 10.00 25.00
MBTB J.Thibault/E.Belfour 10.00 25.00
PMAD T.Amonte/M.Dunham 10.00 25.00
PMAJ J.Arnott/C.Joseph 10.00 25.00
PMFT S.Fedorov/J.Thibault 10.00 25.00
PMGB S.Gagne/M.Biron 10.00 25.00
PMMJ M.Modano/B.Johnson 10.00 25.00
PMSB J.Sakic/M.Brodeur 12.50 30.00
PMYR S.Yzerman/P.Roy 25.00 60.00

2001-02 UD Mask Collection Gloves

Inserted at a rate of 1:144, this 13-card set featured game-used glove swatches of the featured player. Swatches were affixed beside a full-color action photo on the card front. Card backs carried a congratulatory message.
GGAM Alexander Mogilny 8.00 20.00
GGBD Byron Dafoe 8.00 20.00
GGBH Brett Hull 12.00 30.00
GGBS Brendan Shanahan 10.00 25.00
GGCD Chris Drury 8.00 20.00
GGEB Ed Belfour 10.00 25.00
GGJR Jeremy Roenick 12.00 30.00
GGMM Mark Messier 15.00 40.00
GGRB Ray Bourque 12.00 30.00
GGRD Rick DiPietro 10.00 25.00
GGSF Sergei Fedorov 10.00 25.00
GGSK Sami Kapanen 8.00 20.00
GGTK Keith Tkachuk 10.00 25.00

2001-02 UD Mask Collection Goalie Jerseys

This 39-card set featured game-worn jersey swatches of NHL goalies. There were five different subsets: Masked Marvels (inserted at 1:96), Super Stoppers and Styling Tenders (inserted at 1:168), View from the Cage (inserted at 1:144), and Caged Greats (inserted at 1:288). Card prefixes denote subset. Swatches were affixed beside a full-color action photo on the card front. Card backs carried a congratulatory message.
MMBB Brian Boucher MM 4.00 10.00
MMBD Byron Dafoe MM 4.00 10.00
MMDA David Aebischer MM 6.00 15.00
MMJT Jocelyn Thibault MM 4.00 10.00
MMMD Mike Dunham MM 4.00 10.00
MMMT Marty Turco MM 6.00 15.00
MMRT Ron Tugnutt MM 4.00 10.00
MMSB Sean Burke MM 4.00 10.00
SSBD Byron Dafoe SS 6.00 15.00
SSBJ Brent Johnson SS 6.00 15.00
SSFP Felix Potvin SS 10.00 25.00
SSJT Jocelyn Thibault SS 6.00 15.00
SSMB Martin Biron SS 6.00 15.00
SSRL Roberto Luongo SS 10.00 25.00
SSRT Ron Tugnutt SS 6.00 15.00
SSTH Jose Theodore SS 10.00 25.00
SYBB Brian Boucher ST 6.00 15.00
SYDA David Aebischer ST 6.00 15.00
SYEB Ed Belfour ST 12.50 30.00
SYJG Jean-Sebastien Giguere ST 6.00 15.00
SYMD Mike Dunham ST 6.00 15.00
SYMN Mika Noronen ST 6.00 15.00
SYPR Patrick Roy ST 15.00 40.00
SYRC Roman Cechmanek ST 6.00 15.00
VCEB Ed Belfour VC 15.00 40.00
VCFP Felix Potvin VC 10.00 25.00
VCMB Martin Brodeur VC 12.50 30.00
VCMD Mike Dunham VC 6.00 15.00
VCMT Marty Turco VC 8.00 20.00
VCPR Patrick Roy VC 15.00 40.00
VCRC Roman Cechmanek VC 6.00 15.00
VCSB Sean Burke VC 10.00 25.00
CGCJ Curtis Joseph CG 8.00 20.00
CGCO Chris Osgood CG 8.00 20.00
CGDH Dominik Hasek CG 12.50 30.00
CGMB Martin Brodeur CG 12.50 30.00
CGMR Mike Richter CG 8.00 20.00
CGPR Patrick Roy CG 15.00 40.00
CGSB Sean Burke CG 8.00 20.00

2001-02 UD Mask Collection Goalie Pads

Inserted at a rate of 1:66, this 8-card set featured game-worn goalie pad swatches of the featured goalie. Swatches were affixed beside a full-color action photo on the card front. Card backs carried a congratulatory message.
GPBD Byron Dafoe 5.00 12.00
GPDH Dominik Hasek 8.00 20.00
GPJH Johan Hedberg 5.00 12.00
GPJT Jose Theodore 6.00 15.00
GPMB Martin Biron 5.00 12.00
GPMD Marc Denis 5.00 12.00
GPOK Olaf Kolzig 5.00 12.00
GPPR Patrick Roy 8.00 20.00

2001-02 UD Mask Collection Jerseys

This 60-card set featured a game-worn jersey swatch of the featured player. Swatches were affixed beside a full-color action photo on the card front. Card backs carry a congratulatory message.
STATED PRINT RUN 150 SER.#'d SETS
*DUAL PATCH/500: 2X TO 5X JSY/150
*JSY-PATCH/100: 1X TO 2.5X JSY/150
JAD Adam Deadmarsh 4.00 10.00
JAT Alex Tanguay 4.00 10.00
JBB Brian Boucher 4.00 10.00
JBE Mark Bell 4.00 10.00
JBJ Brent Johnson 4.00 10.00
JBL Rob Blake 4.00 10.00
JBS Brendan Shanahan 6.00 15.00
JCD Chris Drury 4.00 10.00
JDA David Aebischer 6.00 15.00
JDB Daniel Briere 4.00 10.00
JEB Ed Belfour 6.00 15.00
JEK Espen Knutsen 4.00 10.00
JFP Felix Potvin 8.00 20.00
JGS Geoff Sanderson 4.00 10.00
JJA Jason Allison 4.00 10.00
JJD J-P Dumont 4.00 10.00
JJF Jeff Friesen 4.00 10.00
JJG Jean-Sebastien Giguere 4.00 10.00
JJI Jarome Iginla 8.00 20.00
JJJ Jaromir Jagr 8.00 20.00
JJN Joe Nieuwendyk 4.00 10.00
JJT Jocelyn Thibault 4.00 10.00
JJW Justin Williams 4.00 10.00
JKO Slava Kozlov 4.00 10.00
JKP Keith Primeau 4.00 10.00
JMA Maxim Afinogenov 4.00 10.00
JMB Martin Biron 4.00 10.00
JMD Marc Denis 4.00 10.00
JMH Milan Hejduk 6.00 15.00
JML Mario Lemieux 10.00 25.00
JMM Mike Modano 8.00 20.00
JMR Mike Richter 6.00 15.00
JMS Miroslav Satan 4.00 10.00
JMS Mats Sundin 6.00 15.00
JMT Marty Turco 4.00 10.00
JMY Mike York 4.00 10.00
JNL Nicklas Lidstrom 8.00 20.00
JPD Pavol Demitra 4.00 10.00
JPF Peter Forsberg 10.00 25.00
JPK Paul Kariya 6.00 15.00
JPR Patrick Roy 15.00 40.00
JRB Ray Bourque 10.00 25.00
JRF Ruslan Fedotenko 4.00 10.00
JRK Rostislav Klesla 4.00 10.00
JRT Ron Tugnutt 4.00 10.00
JRW Ray Whitney 4.00 10.00
JSA Marc Savard 4.00 10.00
JSD Shane Doan 4.00 10.00
JSF Sergei Fedorov 8.00 20.00
JSG Simon Gagne 6.00 15.00
JSK Saku Koivu 6.00 15.00
JSS Steve Sullivan 4.00 10.00
JSY Steve Yzerman 15.00 40.00
JTA Tony Amonte 4.00 10.00
JTC Tim Connolly 4.00 10.00
JTH Jose Theodore 8.00 20.00
JTL Trevor Linden 4.00 10.00
JTS Teemu Selanne 6.00 15.00
JVN Ville Nieminen 4.00 10.00
JZP Zigmund Palffy 4.00 10.00

2001-02 UD Mask Collection Mini Masks

Inserted one per box, these miniature masks feature the artwork sported by some of the league's top goalies. A chrome cage parallel was also created.
*CHROME MASK: .6X TO 1.5X
CJ Curtis Joseph 15.00 40.00
EBGD Ed Belfour Gold 25.00 60.00
EBGN Ed Belfour Green 15.00 40.00
EN Evgeni Nabokov 12.00 30.00
JH Johan Hedberg 12.00 30.00
JT Jose Theodore 15.00 40.00
MB Martin Brodeur 20.00 50.00
PRA Patrick Roy Col. 25.00 60.00
PRC Patrick Roy Mon. 50.00 120.00

2001-02 UD Mask Collection Signed Patches

This 8-card set featured game-worn jersey swatches that were signed by the featured player. Cards were serial-numbered out of 25. Swatches were affixed below a full-color action photo on the card front.
SPBI Martin Biron 100.00 200.00
SPCJ Curtis Joseph 150.00 300.00
SPEB Ed Belfour 150.00 300.00
SPFP Felix Potvin 150.00 300.00
SPJT Jose Theodore 200.00 500.00
SPMB Martin Brodeur 300.00 500.00
SPMR Mike Richter 150.00 300.00
SPPR Patrick Roy 300.00 600.00

2001-02 UD Mask Collection Sticks

Inserted at a rate of 1:288, this 7-card set featured game-used stick swatches of some of the premier goalies in the league. Swatches were affixed beside a full-color action photo on the card front.
SSBB Brian Boucher 8.00 20.00
SSDH Dominik Hasek 15.00 40.00
SSFP Felix Potvin 12.50 30.00
SSJT Jose Theodore 12.50 30.00
SSMB Martin Brodeur 15.00 40.00
SSOK Olaf Kolzig 8.00 20.00
SSTS Tommy Salo 8.00 20.00

2002-03 UD Mask Collection

Released in May 2003, this 180-card set featured 90 base cards and two subsets. Cards 1-90 carried a color player photo on the card front with a smaller black and white photo of a teammate in the background. Card backs carried stats of both players. Cards 91-115 were a "Team Saviours" subset and each card was serial-numbered to the featured goalies 2001-02 saves total. Cards 116-180 made up a "Potential Gems" subset. Cards 116-157 were serial-numbered to 1750 and cards 158-180 were serial-numbered to 1250.
COMPLETE SET (180)
COMP.SET w/o SP's (90) 8.00 20.00
1 J.Giguere/M.Gerber .25 .60
2 P.Kariya/J.Giguere .30 .75
3 B.Dafoe/M.Hnilicka .20 .50
4 M.Hnilicka/B.Dafoe .20 .50
5 D.Heatley/B.Dafoe .25 .60
6 I.Kovalchuk/B.Dafoe .30 .75
7 P.Nurminen/B.Dafoe .20 .50
8 J.Hackett/S.Shields .20 .50
9 S.Shields/J.Hackett .20 .50
10 J.Thornton/J.Hackett .30 .75
11 M.Biron/M.Noronen .20 .50
12 M.Noronen/M.Biron .20 .50
13 R.Turek/J.McLennan .25 .60
14 J.McLennan/R.Turek .25 .60
15 C.Drury/R.Turek .25 .60
16 J.Iginla/R.Turek .25 .60
17 K.Weekes/A.Irbe .20 .50
18 A.Irbe/K.Weekes .20 .50
19 J.Thibault/S.Passmore .20 .50
20 S.Passmore/J.Thibault .20 .50
21 P.Roy/D.Aebischer .60 1.50
22 D.Aebischer/P.Roy .60 1.50
23 J.Sakic/P.Roy .60 1.50
24 M.Denis/J.Labbe .20 .50
25 J.Labbe/M.Denis .20 .50
26 M.Turco/R.Tugnutt .25 .60
27 R.Tugnutt/M.Turco .25 .60
28 M.Modano/M.Turco .40 1.00
29 B.Guerin/M.Turco .25 .60
30 C.Joseph/M.Legace .25 .60
31 M.Legace/C.Joseph .25 .60
32 S.Yzerman/C.Joseph .50 1.25
33 B.Shanahan/C.Joseph .30 .75
34 T.Salo/J.Markkanen .20 .50
35 J.Markkanen/T.Salo .20 .50
36 M.Comrie/T.Salo .25 .60
37 R.Luongo/J.Hurme .40 1.00
38 J.Hurme/R.Luongo .40 1.00
39 F.Potvin/J.Storr .40 1.00
40 J.Storr/F.Potvin .40 1.00
41 Z.Palffy/F.Potvin .25 .60
42 M.Fernandez/D.Roloson .20 .50
43 D.Roloson/M.Fernandez .15 .40
44 M.Gaborik/M.Fernandez .40 1.00
45 J.Theodore/M.Garon .25 .60
46 M.Garon/J.Theodore .25 .60
47 S.Koivu/J.Theodore .25 .60
48 J.Lasak/T.Vokoun .20 .50
49 T.Vokoun/J.Lasak .20 .50
50 M.Brodeur/C.Schwab .50 1.25
51 C.Schwab/M.Brodeur .50 1.25
52 G.Snow/C.Osgood .25 .60
53 C.Osgood/G.Snow .25 .60
54 M.Dunham/D.Blackburn .20 .50
55 D.Blackburn/M.Dunham .20 .50
56 J.Labarbera/D.Blackburn .20 .50
57 P.Bure/M.Dunham .30 .75
58 P.Lalime/M.Prusek .20 .50
59 M.Prusek/P.Lalime .20 .50
60 R.Cechmanek/R.Esche .20 .50
61 R.Esche/R.Cechmanek .20 .50
62 J.Roenick/R.Cechmanek .25 .60
63 J.LeClair/R.Cechmanek .25 .60
64 B.Boucher/S.Burke .20 .50
65 S.Burke/B.Boucher .20 .50
66 J.Pelletier/B.Boucher .20 .50
67 T.Amonte/S.Burke .20 .50
68 J.Hedberg/J.Aubin .25 .60
69 J.Aubin/J.Hedberg .25 .60
70 M.Lemieux/J.Hedberg .75 2.00
71 S.Caron/J.Hedberg .25 .60
72 E.Nabokov/M.Kiprusoff .20 .50
73 V.Toskala/E.Nabokov .20 .50
74 M.Kiprusoff/E.Nabokov .20 .50
75 B.Johnson/Fred Brathwaite .20 .50
76 T.Barrasso/B.Johnson .20 .50
77 F.Brathwaite/B. Johnson .20 .50
78 R.Divis/B.Johnson .20 .50
79 N.Khabibulin/K.Hodson .25 .60
80 K.Hodson/N.Khabibulin .25 .60
81 E.Konstantinov/N.Khabibulin .25 .60
82 E.Belfour/T.Kidd .25 .60
83 T.Kidd/E.Belfour .25 .60
84 M.Sundin/E.Belfour .25 .60
85 D.Cloutier/P.Skudra .20 .50
86 P.Skudra/D.Cloutier .20 .50
87 J.Jagr/O.Kolzig .60 1.50
88 O.Kolzig/C.Billington .25 .60
89 C.Billington/O.Kolzig .25 .60
90 S.Charpentier/O.Kolzig .25 .60
91 Martin Brodeur/1499 4.00 10.00
92 Patrick Roy/1475 5.00 12.00
93 Curtis Joseph/1096 2.00 5.00
94 Roman Cechmanek/1042 1.50 4.00
95 Marty Turco/590 2.50 6.00
96 Jocelyn Thibault/1439 1.50 4.00
97 Jose Theodore/1836 2.00 5.00
98 Jean-Sebastien Giguere/1260 2.00 5.00
99 Ed Belfour/1305 2.00 5.00
100 Steve Shields/771 2.00 5.00
101 Johan Hedberg/1673 2.00 5.00
102 Martin Biron/1630 1.50 4.00
103 Dan Cloutier/1298 1.50 4.00
104 Evgeni Nabakov/1669 1.50 4.00
105 Sean Burke/1574 1.25 3.00
106 Nikolai Khabibulin/1733 2.00 5.00
107 Olaf Kolzig/1785 2.00 5.00
108 Byron Dafoe/1379 1.50 4.00
109 David Aebischer/501 2.00 5.00
110 Manny Fernandez/1032 1.50 4.00
111 Dan Blackburn/840 2.00 5.00
112 Felix Potvin/1529 3.00 8.00
113 Patrick Lalime/1373 1.50 4.00
114 Brent Johnson/1166 1.50 4.00
115 Marc Denis/1046 1.50 4.00
116 Micki Dupont RC 1.00 2.50
117 Cody Rudkowsky RC 1.00 2.50
118 Shawn Thornton RC 1.25 3.00
119 Lasse Pirjeta RC 1.00 2.50
120 Radovan Somik RC 1.00 2.50
121 Tomi Pettinen RC 1.00 2.50
122 Jonathan Hedstrom RC 1.00 2.50
123 Sylvain Blouin RC 1.00 2.50
124 Stephane Veilleux RC 1.00 2.50
125 Curtis Sanford RC 1.50 4.00
126 Kurt Sauer RC 1.00 2.50
127 Vernon Fiddler RC 1.25 3.00
128 Patrick Sharp RC 3.00 8.00
129 Greg Koehler RC 1.00 2.50
130 Dany Sabourin RC 1.00 2.50
131 Dmitri Bykov RC 1.00 2.50
132 Ivan Majesky RC 1.00 2.50
133 Ray Schultz RC 1.00 2.50
134 Matt Henderson RC 1.00 2.50
135 Tom Koivisto RC 1.00 2.50
136 Ian MacNeil RC 1.00 2.50
137 Eric Godard RC 1.00 2.50
138 Dick Tarnstrom RC 1.00 2.50
139 Jeff Paul RC 1.00 2.50
140 Darren Haydar RC 1.00 2.50
141 Levente Szuper RC 1.50 4.00
142 Dennis Seidenberg RC 1.50 4.00
143 Tim Thomas RC 4.00 10.00
144 Fernando Pisani RC 1.00 2.50
145 Alex Henry RC 1.25 3.00
146 Craig Andersson RC 3.00 8.00
147 Kari Haakana RC 1.00 2.50
148 Jared Aulin RC 1.00 2.50
149 Adam Hall RC 1.00 2.50
150 Carlo Colaiacovo RC 1.50 4.00
151 Martin Gerber RC 1.50 4.00
152 Jamie Hodson RC 1.00 2.50
153 Ray Emery RC 3.00 8.00
154 Ari Ahonen RC 1.00 2.50
155 Michael Leighton RC 1.50 4.00
156 Kris Vernarsky RC 1.00 2.50
157 Jim Vandermeer RC 1.00 2.50
158 Chuck Kobasew RC 1.25 3.00
159 Ron Hainsey RC 1.00 2.50
160 P-M Bouchard RC 1.50 4.00
161 Alexander Frolov RC 2.00 5.00
162 Henrik Zetterberg RC 10.00 25.00
163 Alexander Svitov RC 1.00 2.50
164 Mike Cammalleri RC 3.00 8.00
165 Ryan Miller RC 6.00 15.00
166 Anton Volchenkov RC 1.00 2.50
167 Brooks Orpik RC 1.50 4.00
168 Ales Hemsky RC 4.00 10.00
169 Stanislav Chistov RC 1.00 2.50
170 Shaone Morrisonn RC 1.00 2.50
171 Jason Spezza RC 6.00 15.00
172 Jay Bouwmeester RC 3.00 8.00
173 Jordan Leopold RC 1.50 4.00
174 Jeff Taffe RC 1.00 2.50
175 Pascal LeClaire RC 1.25 3.00
176 Scottie Upshall RC 1.25 3.00
177 Alexei Smirnov RC 1.25 3.00
178 Rick Nash RC 8.00 20.00
179 Mikael Tellqvist RC 1.00 2.50
180 Steve Eminger RC 1.00 2.50

2002-03 UD Mask Collection UD Promos

Inserted into copies of the May 2003 issue of Beckett Hockey Collector, this 90-card set parallels the base set but carried a silver foil "UD Promo" stamp across the card fronts.
*UD PROMO: .8X TO 2X BASIC CARDS

2002-03 UD Mask Collection Behind the Mask Jersey

Inserted at a rate of 1:60 hobby packs, this 18-card set featured swatches of game-worn jerseys.
BMAM Andy Moog SP 15.00 40.00
BMBI Martin Biron 6.00 15.00
BMBJ Brent Johnson 6.00 15.00
BMCJ Curtis Joseph 6.00 15.00
BMDU Mike Dunham 6.00 15.00
BMEB Ed Belfour 8.00 20.00
BMFP Felix Potvin 20.00 20.00
BMJG J-S Giguere 6.00 15.00
BMJH Johan Hedberg 6.00 15.00
BMJT Jose Theodore 6.00 15.00
BMMB Martin Brodeur 10.00 25.00
BMMD Marc Denis 6.00 15.00
BMMN Mika Noronen 6.00 15.00
BMMT Marty Turco 6.00 15.00
BMOK Olaf Kolzig 6.00 15.00
BMPR Patrick Roy 12.50 30.00
BMRC Roman Cechmanek 6.00 15.00
BMRD Rick DiPietro 6.00 15.00

2002-03 UD Mask Collection Career Wins Jersey

This 17-card set featured swatches of game-worn jerseys. Each card was serial-numbered to the given goalies career wins total as of press time.
STATED PRINT RUN 92-372
CWAM Andy Moog/372 8.00 20.00
CWBD Byron Dafoe/162 6.00 15.00
CWCJ Curtis Joseph/346 8.00 20.00
CWCO Chris Osgood/253 8.00 20.00
CWEB Ed Belfour/364 8.00 20.00
CWFP Felix Potvin/237 10.00 25.00
CWJT Jocelyn Thibault/196 8.00 20.00
CWMB Martin Brodeur/324 12.00 30.00
CWMD Mike Dunham/92 6.00 15.00
CWMR Mike Richter/296 10.00 25.00
CWOK Olaf Kolzig/182 8.00 20.00
CWPR Patrick Roy/227 12.00 30.00
CWRT Ron Tugnutt/168 8.00 20.00
CWRY Patrick Roy/289 12.00 30.00
CWSB Sean Burke/281 5.00 12.00
CWTS Tommy Salo/168 6.00 15.00
CWTU Roman Turek/126 8.00 20.00

2002-03 UD Mask Collection Great Gloves

Inserted at a rate of 1:60 hobby packs, this 18-card set featured swatches of game-worn jerseys.
STATED ODDS 1:60
GGBB Brian Boucher 5.00 12.00
GGBR Martin Brodeur 10.00 25.00
GGCJ Curtis Joseph 6.00 15.00
GGDB Dan Blackburn 5.00 12.00
GGDU Mike Dunham 5.00 12.00
GGEB Ed Belfour 6.00 15.00
GGFP Felix Potvin 6.00 15.00
GGJG Jean-Sebastien Giguere 6.00 15.00
GGJT Jose Theodore 6.00 15.00
GGMB Martin Biron 5.00 12.00
GGMD Marc Denis 5.00 12.00
GGMR Mike Richter 6.00 15.00
GGMT Marty Turco 5.00 12.00
GGOK Olaf Kolzig SP 10.00 25.00
GGPR Patrick Roy 12.50 30.00
GGRC Roman Cechmanek 5.00 12.00
GGRL Roberto Luongo 8.00 20.00
GGRT Roman Turek 5.00 12.00

2002-03 UD Mask Collection Instant Offense Jerseys

Serial-numbered out of 250, this 25-card set featured swatches of game-worn jerseys.
IOAY Alexei Yashin 4.00 10.00
IOBS Brendan Shanahan 5.00 12.00
IOCD Chris Drury 4.00 10.00
IOED Eric Daze 4.00 10.00
IOEL Eric Lindros 5.00 12.00
IOJA Jason Allison 4.00 10.00
IOJI Jarome Iginla 6.00 15.00
IOJJ Jaromir Jagr 8.00 20.00
IOJR Jeremy Roenick 6.00 15.00
IOJS Joe Sakic 8.00 25.00
IOJT Joe Thornton 8.00 20.00
IOML Mario Lemieux 10.00 25.00
IOMM Mike Modano 8.00 20.00
IOMN Markus Naslund 5.00 12.00
IOMS Miroslav Satan 4.00 10.00
IOPB Pavel Bure 5.00 12.00
IOPE Patrik Elias 4.00 10.00
IOPF Peter Forsberg 10.00 25.00
IOPK Paul Kariya 5.00 12.00
IOSG Simon Gagne 5.00 12.00
IOSK Saku Koivu 5.00 12.00
IOSS Sergei Samsonov 4.00 10.00
IOSU Mats Sundin 5.00 12.00
IOSY Steve Yzerman 12.50 30.00
IOZP Zigmund Palffy 4.00 10.00

2002-03 UD Mask Collection Masked Marvels Jerseys

Inserted at a rate of 1:60 hobby packs, this 17-card set featured swatches of game-worn jerseys.
MMBI Martin Biron 4.00 10.00
MMCO Chris Osgood 4.00 10.00
MMFP Felix Potvin 4.00 10.00
MMJG Jean-Sebastien Giguere 6.00 15.00
MMJH Johan Hedberg 4.00 10.00
MMJT Jocelyn Thibault 4.00 10.00
MMMB Martin Brodeur 6.00 15.00
MMMD Mike Dunham 4.00 10.00
MMMR Mike Richter 6.00 15.00
MMMT Marty Turco 5.00 12.00
MMOK Olaf Kolzig SP 5.00 12.00
MMPR Patrick Roy 12.50 30.00
MMRC Roman Cechmanek 4.00 10.00
MMRL Roberto Luongo 6.00 15.00
MMRM Ryan Miller 8.00 20.00
MMRT Roman Turek 4.00 10.00
MMTH Jose Theodore SP 8.00 20.00

2002-03 UD Mask Collection Mini Masks

Inserted one per box, these miniature masks feature the artwork sported by some of the league's top goalies. A glitter effect parallel was also created and values can be found by using the multiplier below. Glitter parallels were limited to 25 copies each.
*GLITTER: 1.25X TO 3X
GLITTER PRINT RUN 25 SETS
AM Andy Moog 20.00 50.00
CJ Curtis Joseph 25.00 60.00
CR Glenn Resch 12.50 30.00
EB Ed Belfour 20.00 50.00
EN Evgeni Nabokov 12.50 30.00
FP Felix Potvin 20.00 50.00
GC Gerry Cheevers 60.00 120.00
GF1 Grant Fuhr Sabres 12.50 30.00
GF2 Grant Fuhr Blues SP 25.00 60.00
JH Johan Hedberg 12.50 30.00
JP1 Jacques Plante Pretzel 15.00 40.00
JP2 Jacques Plante Alien SP 90.00 150.00
JT Jose Theodore 15.00 40.00
MB Martin Brodeur 20.00 50.00
NK Nikolai Khabibulin 25.00 60.00
PR Patrick Roy 25.00 60.00
TE Tony Esposito 20.00 50.00
TS Terry Sawchuk 15.00 40.00

2002-03 UD Mask Collection Mini Masks Autographs

CJ Curtis Joseph 75.00 150.00
EB Ed Belfour 125.00 250.00
EN Evgeni Nabokov 40.00 80.00
GC Gerry Cheevers 30.00 80.00
GF1 Grant Fuhr Sabres 30.00 80.00
GF2 Grant Fuhr Blues SP 50.00 125.00
JT Jose Theodore 40.00 100.00
MB Martin Brodeur 100.00 250.00
NK Nikolai Khabibulin 40.00 100.00
PR Patrick Roy 100.00 250.00
TE Tony Esposito 60.00 150.00

2002-03 UD Mask Collection Nation's Best Jerseys

Inserted at 1:280, thi 6-card set featured jersey swatches from each of the goalies featured on the card fronts.
NDBJ Boucher/Johnson/DiPietro 15.00 40.00
NJBT Turco/Burke/Joseph 10.00 25.00
NLBT Theodore/Luongo/Biron 30.00 80.00
NOBB Osgood/Blackburn/Belfour 12.50 30.00
NRBP Brodeur/Roy/Potvin 30.00 80.00
NRDM Richter/Dunham/Miller 12.50 30.00

2002-03 UD Mask Collection Patches

Serial-numbered to the total of goals for forwards and wins for goalies, this 42-card set featured swatches of game-worn jersey patches. Print runs under 25 are not priced due to scarcity.
PGBS Brendan Shanahan/37 40.00 100.00
PGDB Daniel Briere/32 25.00 60.00
PGED Eric Daze/37 25.00 60.00
PGEL Eric Lindros/37 25.00 60.00
PGGM Glen Murray/41 25.00 60.00
PGIK Ilya Kovalchuk/29 40.00 100.00
PGJA Jason Allison/19
PGJI Jarome Iginla/52 40.00 100.00
PGJJ Jaromir Jagr/31 40.00 100.00
PGJS Joe Sakic/26 40.00 100.00
PGMM Mike Modano/34 40.00 100.00
PGMN Markus Naslund/40 25.00 60.00
PGMS Mats Sundin/41 25.00 60.00
PGPB Peter Bondra/39 30.00 80.00
PGPE Patrik Elias/29 25.00 60.00
PGPK Paul Kariya/32 30.00 80.00
PGSF Sergei Fedorov/30 25.00 60.00
PGSG Simon Gagne/33 25.00 60.00
PGSY Steve Yzerman/13
PGZP Zigmund Palffy/31 20.00 50.00
PWBJ Brent Johnson/34 20.00 50.00
PWBR Martin Brodeur/38 60.00 150.00
PWCJ Curtis Joseph/29 40.00 100.00
PWCO Chris Osgood/31 20.00 50.00
PWDB Dan Blackburn/12
PWEB Ed Belfour/21 25.00 60.00
PWFP Felix Potvin/31 25.00 60.00
PWJG Jean-Sebastien Giguere/20 20.00 50.00
PWJH Johan Hedberg/25 20.00 50.00
PWJT Jocelyn Thibault/32 25.00 60.00
PWMB Martin Biron/31 20.00 50.00
PWMD Mike Dunham/23 20.00 50.00
PWMR Mike Richter/24
PWMT Marty Turco/15
PWOK Olaf Kolzig/31 20.00 50.00
PWPR Patrick Roy/32 125.00 250.00
PWRC Roman Cechmanek/24 15.00 40.00
PWRL Roberto Luongo/16
PWRT Roman Turek/30 20.00 50.00
PWSB Sean Burke/33 20.00 50.00
PWTH Jose Theodore/31 60.00 120.00
PWTS Tommy Salo/30 25.00 60.00

2002-03 UD Mask Collection Super Stoppers Jerseys

Inserted at a rate of 1:60 hobby packs, this 8-card set featured swatches of game-worn jerseys.
SSCJ Curtis Joseph 5.00 12.00
SSCO Chris Osgood 5.00 12.00
SSJT Jose Theodore 5.00 12.00
SSMB Martin Brodeur 8.00 20.00
SSOK Olaf Kolzig 5.00 12.00
SSPR Patrick Roy 10.00 25.00
SSRC Roman Cechmanek 4.00 10.00
SSRT Roman Turek 5.00 12.00

2002-03 UD Mask Collection View from the Cage Jerseys

Inserted at a rate of 1:140 hobby packs, this 17-card set featured swatches of game-worn jerseys.
VBI Martin Biron 5.00 12.00
VCJ Curtis Joseph 6.00 15.00
VEB Ed Belfour 6.00 15.00
VJG Jean-Sebastien Giguere 6.00 15.00
VJH Johan Hedberg 6.00 15.00
VJT Jocelyn Thibault 5.00 12.00
VMB Martin Brodeur 10.00 25.00
VMR Mike Richter 6.00 15.00
VMT Marty Turco 6.00 15.00
VOK Olaf Kolzig 6.00 15.00
VPR Patrick Roy 10.00 25.00
VRC Roman Cechmanek 5.00 12.00
VRL Roberto Luongo 10.00 25.00
VRT Roman Turek 6.00 15.00
VSB Sean Burke 4.00 10.00
VTH Jose Theodore 6.00 15.00
VTS Tommy Salo 5.00 12.00

2008-09 UD Masterpieces

This set was released on September 9, 2008. The base set consists of 87 cards, which are all veterans and legends.
COMPLETE SET (87) 20.00 50.00
1 Lord Stanley .50 1.25
2 Lester B. Pearson .40 1.00
3 Lady Byng .30 .75
4 Bill Barilko .30 .75
5 Jari Kurri .50 1.25
6 Syl Apps .75 2.00
7 Patrick Roy 1.25 3.00
8 Ron Hextall .75 2.00
9 Richard Brodeur .40 1.00
10 Mark Messier .60 1.50
11 Mario Lemieux 1.50 4.00
12 Mario Lemieux 1.50 4.00
13 Lester Patrick .50 1.25
14 Ray Bourque .75 2.00
15 Ray Bourque .75 2.00
16 Theoren Fleury .60 1.50
17 Wayne Gretzky 2.50 6.00
18 Dale Hawerchuk .60 1.50
19 Darryl Evans .30 .75
20 Wayne Gretzky 2.50 6.00
21 Patrick Roy 1.25 3.00
22 Cam Neely .50 1.25
23 Mike Bossy .50 1.25
24 Pat LaFontaine .50 1.25
25 Lanny McDonald .50 1.25
26 Denis Savard .60 1.50
27 Bobby Hull .75 2.00
28 B.Hull/G.Howe 1.25 3.00
29 Georges Vezina .75 2.00
30 George Hainsworth .60 1.50
31 Tony Esposito .50 1.25
32 Phil Esposito .75 2.00
33 Bobby Orr 1.50 4.00
34 Bobby Orr 1.50 4.00
35 Jari Kurri .50 1.25
36 Turk Broda .50 1.25
37 Foster Hewitt .30 .75
38 Wayne Gretzky 2.50 6.00
39 Luc Robitaille .50 1.25
40 Rick Vaive .30 .75
41 Borje Salming .50 1.25
42 Darryl Sittler .50 1.25
43 Clark Gillies .50 1.25
44 Scotty Bowman .50 1.25
45 Glenn Anderson .50 1.25
46 Bobby Hull .75 2.00
47 Grant Fuhr .50 1.25
48 Ray Bourque .75 2.00
49 Brian Leetch .50 1.25
50 Joe Mullen .40 1.00
51 Johnny Bower .60 1.50
52 Bob Baun .50 1.25
53 Guy Lafleur .60 1.50
54 Stan Mikita .60 1.50
55 Jean Beliveau .50 1.25
56 Dino Ciccarelli .50 1.25
57 Frank Mahovlich .50 1.25
58 Peter Stastny .50 1.25
59 Marcel Dionne .60 1.50
60 Rod Langway .40 1.00
61 Bobby Clarke .50 1.25
62 Sutter/Sutter/Sutter/Sutter Sutter/Sutter .50 1.25
63 Steve Shutt .50 1.25
64 Rick McLeish .30 .75
65 Manon Rheaume 1.00 2.50
66 Marty McSorley .40 1.00
67 Alex Delvecchio .60 1.50
68 Dale Hawerchuk .60 1.50
69 Gilbert Perreault .50 1.25
70 Rogie Vachon .60 1.50
71 Doug Wilson .40 1.00
72 Eddie Shack .50 1.25
73 Willie O'Ree .50 1.25
74 Guy Lafleur .60 1.50
75 Bernie Parent .50 1.25
76 Andy Bathgate .50 1.25
77 Craig MacTavish .40 1.00
78 Wayne Gretzky 2.50 6.00
79 Mark Messier .60 1.50
80 Gordie Howe 1.25 3.00
81 Mario Lemieux 1.50 4.00
82 Bobby Orr 1.50 4.00
83 Phil Esposito .75 2.00
84 Mark Messier .60 1.50
85 Gordie Howe 1.25 3.00
86 Mario Lemieux 1.50 4.00
87 Mark Messier .60 1.50

2008-09 UD Masterpieces Blue

*BLUE: 3X TO 8X BASE
STATED PRINT RUN 50 SERIAL #'d SETS

2008-09 UD Masterpieces Green

*GREEN: 2.5X TO 6X BASE
STATED PRINT RUN 99 SERIAL #'d SETS

2008-09 UD Masterpieces Red

*RED: 5X TO 12X BASE
STATED PRINT RUN 25 SERIAL #'d SETS

2008-09 UD Masterpieces 5x7

COMPLETE SET (24) 40.00 100.00
STATED ODDS 1 PER BOX
XLBH Bobby Hull 3.00 8.00
XLBP Bernie Parent 2.00 5.00
XLBR Richard Brodeur 1.50 4.00
XLBS Borje Salming 2.00 5.00
XLDC Dino Ciccarelli 2.00 5.00
XLDH Dale Hawerchuk 2.50 6.00
XLDS Darryl Sittler 2.00 5.00
XLFM Frank Mahovlich 2.00 5.00
XLGF Grant Fuhr 2.00 5.00
XLGH Gordie Howe 5.00 12.00
XLGL Guy Lafleur 2.50 6.00
XLGP Gilbert Perreault 2.00 5.00
XLLM Lanny McDonald 2.00 5.00
XLMB Mike Bossy 2.00 5.00
XLML Mario Lemieux 6.00 15.00
XLMM Mark Messier 2.50 6.00
XLPE Phil Esposito 3.00 8.00
XLPR Patrick Roy 5.00 12.00
XLRB Ray Bourque 3.00 8.00
XLRL Rod Langway 1.50 4.00
XLSB Scotty Bowman 2.00 5.00
XLVT Vladislav Tretiak 1.50 4.00
XLWG Wayne Gretzky 10.00 25.00
XLWO Willie O'Ree 2.00 5.00

2008-09 UD Masterpieces 5x7 Autographs

XLABB Bob Baun 20.00 50.00
XLABL Brian Leetch 15.00 40.00
XLABO Ray Bourque
XLACN Cam Neely 25.00 50.00
XLAGA Glenn Anderson 10.00 25.00
XLAHH G.Howe/B.Hull 100.00 200.00
XLAJB Johnny Bower 12.00 30.00
XLAJM Joe Mullen 15.00 40.00
XLALR Luc Robitaille 20.00 50.00
XLAMB Mike Bossy 15.00 40.00
XLAML Mario Lemieux
XLAMM Mark Messier
XLAOR Bobby Orr 75.00 150.00
XLAPR Patrick Roy
XLARH Ron Hextall 15.00 40.00
XLATE Tony Esposito
XLATF Theoren Fleury 15.00 40.00
XLAWG Wayne Gretzky 150.00 300.00

2008-09 UD Masterpieces Brushstrokes Blue

*BLUE: .5X TO 1.2X BROWN
STATED PRINT RUN 25 SERIAL #'d SETS
MBDH Dale Hawerchuk 50.00 100.00

2008-09 UD Masterpieces Brushstrokes Brown

STATED ODDS 1:10
MBAB Andy Bathgate 8.00 20.00
MBAD Alex Delvecchio 10.00 25.00
MBAM Al MacInnis 8.00 20.00
MBAO Adam Oates 8.00 20.00
MBBB Bob Bourne 5.00 12.00
MBBC Bobby Clarke 12.00 30.00
MBBD Bill Dineen 8.00 20.00
MBBF Bernie Federko 6.00 15.00
MBBH Bobby Hull 25.00 60.00
MBBK Johnny Bucyk 8.00 20.00
MBBL Brian Leetch 8.00 20.00
MBBN Bernie Nicholls 6.00 15.00
MBBO Bob Baun 8.00 20.00
MBBR Brian Sutter 8.00 20.00
MBBS Borje Salming 12.00 30.00
MBBU Butch Bouchard 15.00 40.00

CA Guy Carbonneau 8.00 20.00
CG Clark Gillies 8.00 20.00
CH Don Cherry 20.00 50.00
CN Cam Neely 20.00 50.00
DA Darryl Sutter 5.00 12.00
DC Dino Ciccarelli 8.00 20.00
DD Dick Duff 6.00 15.00
DG Doug Gilmour 10.00 25.00
DH Dale Hawerchuk
DP Denis Potvin 8.00 20.00
DU Duane Sutter 5.00 12.00
DW Doug Wilson 6.00 15.00
EL Ron Ellis 5.00 12.00
ES Eddie Shack 8.00 20.00
FM Frank Mahovlich 60.00 120.00
GA Glenn Anderson 8.00 20.00
GF Grant Fuhr 8.00 20.00
GH Gordie Howe 50.00 100.00
GL Guy Lafleur 10.00 25.00
GP Gilbert Perreault 8.00 20.00
HH Harry Howell 8.00 20.00
HO Mark Howe 8.00 20.00
HX Ron Hextall 15.00 40.00
JB Jean Beliveau 40.00 100.00
JK Jari Kurri 8.00 20.00
JM Joe Mullen 6.00 15.00
JO Johnny Bower 10.00 25.00
LA Rod Langway 6.00 15.00
LM Lanny McDonald 15.00 40.00
LR Larry Robinson 8.00 20.00
MB Mike Bossy 8.00 20.00
MC Craig MacTavish 6.00 15.00
MD Marcel Dionne 10.00 25.00
MF Mike Foligno 5.00 12.00
ML Mario Lemieux
MM Marty McSorley 6.00 15.00
MS Mark Messier 75.00 150.00
OR Bobby Orr 75.00 200.00
PE Phil Esposito 30.00 80.00
PL Pat LaFontaine
PR Patrick Roy 200.00 350.00
PS Peter Stastny 8.00 20.00
RB Ray Bourque 50.00 100.00
RD Ron Duguay 6.00 15.00
RG Rod Gilbert
RH Manon Rheaume 15.00 40.00
RI Richard Brodeur 6.00 15.00
RK Red Kelly 10.00 25.00
RL Rejean Lemelin 5.00 12.00
RM Rick McLeish 5.00 12.00
RO Luc Robitaille 8.00 20.00
RS Rich Sutter 5.00 12.00
RV Rogie Vachon 10.00 25.00
SA Denis Savard 10.00 25.00
SB Scotty Bowman 40.00 100.00
SC Dave Schultz 8.00 20.00
SM Stan Mikita 40.00 80.00
SR Ron Sutter 6.00 15.00
SS Steve Shutt 8.00 20.00
SU Brent Sutter 5.00 12.00
TE Tony Esposito 15.00 40.00
TF Theoren Fleury 12.50 30.00
TL Ted Lindsay 8.00 20.00
TO Terry O'Reilly 6.00 15.00
VT Vladislav Tretiak 25.00 50.00
WG Wayne Gretzky 200.00 300.00
WO Willie O'Ree 8.00 20.00
WT Walt Tkaczuk 5.00 12.00

2008-09 UD Masterpieces Brushstrokes Green

EEN/35: .5X TO 1.2X BROWN
TED PRINT RUN 15-35
DH Dale Hawerchuk 50.00 100.00

08-09 UD Masterpieces Brown

OWN: 1.2X TO 3X

2008-09 UD Masterpieces Canvas Clippings Brown

TED ODDS 1:10
JE: .5X TO 1.2X BROWN
EEN/85: .4X TO 1X BROWN
AM1 Al MacInnis 5.00 12.00
AM2 Al MacInnis 5.00 12.00
AO1 Adam Oates 5.00 12.00
AO2 Adam Oates 5.00 12.00
BC Bobby Clarke 5.00 12.00
BF Bernie Federko 4.00 10.00
BL Brian Leetch 5.00 12.00
BN1 Bernie Nicholls 4.00 10.00
BN2 Bernie Nicholls 4.00 10.00
BO Bob Bourne 3.00 8.00
BR Richard Brodeur 4.00 10.00
BS Billy Smith 5.00 12.00
BT Bryan Trottier 6.00 15.00
BU Johnny Bucyk 5.00 12.00
CN Cam Neely 5.00 12.00
DC1 Dino Ciccarelli 5.00 12.00
DC2 Dino Ciccarelli 5.00 12.00
DH Dale Hawerchuk 6.00 15.00
DS Darryl Sittler 5.00 12.00
FM1 Frank Mahovlich 6.00 15.00
FM2 Frank Mahovlich 6.00 15.00
GA1 Glenn Anderson 5.00 12.00
GA2 Glenn Anderson 5.00 12.00
GF Grant Fuhr 5.00 12.00
GH Gordie Howe 12.00 30.00
GP Gilbert Perreault 5.00 12.00
JB Jean Beliveau 10.00 25.00
JK Jari Kurri 5.00 12.00
JM1 Joe Mullen 4.00 10.00
JM2 Joe Mullen 4.00 10.00
LM1 Lanny McDonald 5.00 12.00
LM2 Lanny McDonald 5.00 12.00
LR Larry Robinson 5.00 12.00
MD Marcel Dionne 6.00 15.00
ML Mario Lemieux 15.00 40.00
MM1 Mark Messier 6.00 15.00
MM2 Mark Messier 6.00 15.00
MR Mike Richter 5.00 12.00
PE1 Phil Esposito 8.00 20.00
PE2 Phil Esposito 8.00 20.00
PL Pat LaFontaine 5.00 12.00
PR1 Patrick Roy 12.00 30.00
PR2 Patrick Roy 12.00 30.00
PS Peter Stastny 5.00 12.00
RB1 Ray Bourque 8.00 20.00

CCRB2 Ray Bourque 8.00 20.00
CCRE Ron Ellis 3.00 8.00
CCRH Ron Hextall 8.00 20.00
CCRL Rod Langway 4.00 10.00
CCRO Luc Robitaille 5.00 12.00
CCRV1 Rogie Vachon 6.00 15.00
CCRV2 Rogie Vachon 6.00 15.00
CCSA1 Denis Savard 6.00 15.00
CCSA2 Denis Savard 6.00 15.00
CCSB1 Scotty Bowman 5.00 12.00
CCSB2 Scotty Bowman 5.00 12.00
CCSB3 Scotty Bowman 5.00 12.00
CCSG Borje Salming 5.00 12.00
CCSM Stan Mikita 6.00 15.00
CCSS Steve Shutt 5.00 12.00
CCSU Brent Sutter 3.00 8.00
CCTE Tony Esposito 5.00 12.00
CCTF Theoren Fleury 6.00 15.00
CCTW Tiger Williams 4.00 10.00
CCWC1 Wendel Clark 5.00 12.00
CCWC2 Wendel Clark 5.00 12.00
CCWG Wayne Gretzky 40.00 80.00

2014-15 UD Masterpieces

91-150 STATED ODDS 1:2 HOBBY
151-180 STATED ODDS 1:6 HOBBY
181-230 STATED ODDS 1:5 HOBBY
231-240 STATED ODDS 1:23 HOBBY
1 Corey Perry .75 2.00
2 Evander Kane .75 2.00
3 Zdeno Chara .75 2.00
4 Cody Hodgson .75 2.00
5 Mark Scheifele 1.00 2.50
6 Dustin Byfuglien .75 2.00
7 Eric Staal 1.00 2.50
8 Patrick Kane 1.50 4.00
9 Blake Wheeler .75 2.00
10 Matt Duchene .75 2.00
11 Sergei Bobrovsky .75 2.00
12 Tyler Seguin 1.25 3.00
13 Daniel Alfredsson .75 2.00
14 Taylor Hall 1.50 4.00
15 Ryan Getzlaf 1.25 3.00
16 Jonathan Quick 1.25 3.00
17 Jason Pominville .60 1.50
18 Max Pacioretty .75 2.00
19 Shea Weber .60 1.50
20 Martin Brodeur 1.50 4.00
21 Kyle Okposo .75 2.00
22 Mats Zuccarello .75 2.00
23 Erik Karlsson 1.50 4.00
24 Kyle Turris .75 2.00
25 Keith Yandle .75 2.00
26 Evgeni Malkin 2.50 6.00
27 Joe Thornton .75 2.00
28 Alexander Steen .75 2.00
29 Pekka Rinne 1.00 2.50
30 James van Riemsdyk .75 2.00
31 Alexander Ovechkin 3.00 8.00
32 Tuukka Rask .75 2.00
33 Marian Hossa .60 1.50
34 Valeri Nichushkin .60 1.50
35 Sam Gagner .60 1.50
36 Alex Galchenyuk 1.25 3.00
37 Brad Richards .75 2.00
38 Marc-Andre Fleury 1.25 3.00
39 Ben Bishop .75 2.00
40 Phil Kessel 1.00 2.50
41 Nicklas Backstrom 1.25 3.00
42 Paul Stastny .75 2.00
43 Pavel Datsyuk 1.00 2.50
44 Gabriel Landeskog .60 1.50
45 Jonas Hiller .60 1.50
46 Seth Jones .60 1.50
47 Tomas Hertl .75 2.00
48 Zach Parise .75 2.00
49 Jim Howard .75 2.00
50 Ryan Johansen 1.00 2.50
51 Cam Ward .75 2.00
52 Corey Crawford 1.00 2.50
53 Aleksander Barkov .75 2.00
54 Patrik Elias .75 2.00
55 Wayne Gretzky 2.50 6.00
56 Ryan Strome .60 1.50
57 Logan Couture .75 2.00
58 Jonathan Bernier .75 2.00
59 Rick Nash .75 2.00
60 Tomas Plekanec .75 2.00
61 Ryan Nugent-Hopkins .75 2.00
62 Jamie Benn 1.00 2.50
63 Jeff Skinner .75 2.00
64 Duncan Keith .75 2.00
65 Brendan Gallagher .75 2.00
66 Patrick Marleau .75 2.00
67 Scott Laughton .50 1.25
68 Kari Lehtonen .60 1.50
69 Mikko Koivu .60 1.50
70 Anze Kopitar 1.25 3.00
71 David Perron .50 1.25
72 Jason Spezza .75 2.00
73 Shane Doan .60 1.50
74 Scott Hartnell .75 2.00
75 David Backes .75 2.00
76 Wayne Gretzky 2.50 6.00
77 Patrick Sharp .75 2.00
78 Vincent Lecavalier .60 1.50
79 T.J. Oshie 1.25 3.00
80 Radim Vrbata .60 1.50
81 James Neal .75 2.00
82 Dion Phaneuf .75 2.00
83 Chris Kunitz .75 2.00
84 Adam Henrique .75 2.00
85 Gustav Nyquist .60 1.50
86 Mikael Granlund .60 1.50
87 Bobby Ryan .75 2.00
88 Drew Doughty .75 2.00
89 Jonathan Huberdeau .75 2.00
90 Tyler Ennis .60 1.50
91 Roberto Luongo SP 1.00 2.50
92 Wayne Gretzky SP 5.00 12.00
93 Peter Forsberg SP 1.00 2.50
94 Bill Guerin SP 1.00 2.50
95 Theoren Fleury SP 1.25 3.00
96 Jarome Iginla SP 1.00 2.50
97 Steven Stamkos SP 2.00 5.00
98 Claude Giroux SP 1.00 2.50
99 Phil Esposito SP 1.50 4.00
100 Sidney Crosby SP 4.00 10.00
101 Guy Carbonneau SP 1.00 2.50
102 Mike Gartner SP 1.00 2.50
103 Bill Barber SP 1.00 2.50
104 Bobby Orr SP 3.00 8.00
105 Patrice Bergeron SP 1.25 3.00
106 Bill Ranford SP 1.00 2.50
107 Mike Bossy SP 1.00 2.50
108 Sean Monahan SP 1.00 2.50
109 Dale Hawerchuk SP 1.25 3.00
110 Jaromir Jagr SP 2.50 6.00
111 Joe Sakic SP 1.50 4.00
112 Henrik Zetterberg SP 1.25 3.00
113 Jordan Eberle SP 1.00 2.50
114 Grant Fuhr SP 1.00 2.50
115 Dominik Hasek SP 1.25 3.00
116 Brett Hull SP 1.00 2.50
117 Mike Richter SP 1.00 2.50
118 Doug Gilmour SP 1.25 3.00
119 Jonathan Toews SP 2.00 5.00
120 Mario Lemieux SP 3.00 8.00
121 Marcel Dionne SP 1.25 3.00
122 Mats Sundin SP 1.00 2.50
123 Adam Oates SP 1.00 2.50
124 Bobby Hull SP 1.00 2.50
125 Nathan MacKinnon SP 2.00 5.00
126 Guy Lafleur SP 1.25 3.00
127 Jeff Carter SP 1.00 2.50
128 Jeremy Roenick SP 1.00 2.50
129 Steve Yzerman SP 2.00 5.00
130 Martin St. Louis SP 1.00 2.50
131 Patrick Roy SP 2.50 6.00
132 Ray Bourque SP 1.50 4.00
133 Trevor Linden SP 1.00 2.50
134 Larry Robinson SP 1.00 2.50
135 Joe Pavelski SP 1.00 2.50
136 Pierre Turgeon SP 1.00 2.50
137 Nicklas Lidstrom SP 1.00 2.50
138 Nail Yakupov SP .75 2.00
139 Bobby Clarke SP 1.00 2.50
140 Stan Mikita SP 1.25 3.00
141 P.K. Subban SP 1.50 4.00
142 John Tavares SP 2.00 5.00
143 Jari Kurri SP 1.00 2.50
144 Mark Messier SP 1.00 2.50
145 Henrik Lundqvist SP 1.25 3.00
146 Jean Beliveau SP 1.00 2.50
147 Carey Price SP 3.00 8.00
148 Pelle Lindbergh SP 1.00 2.50
149 Chris Chelios SP 1.00 2.50
150 Wayne Gretzky SP 5.00 12.00
151 Bobby Orr BW 4.00 10.00
152 Patrick Kane BW 2.50 6.00
153 Mario Lemieux BW 4.00 10.00
154 Sidney Crosby BW 5.00 12.00
155 Mats Sundin BW 1.25 3.00
156 Alexander Ovechkin BW 5.00 12.00
157 Phil Kessel BW 1.50 4.00
158 Steve Yzerman BW 2.50 6.00
159 Evgeni Malkin BW 4.00 10.00
160 Pavel Datsyuk BW 1.50 4.00
161 Joe Sakic BW 2.00 5.00
162 Nathan MacKinnon BW 2.50 6.00
163 Mark Messier BW 1.25 3.00
164 Terry Sawchuk BW 1.25 3.00
165 Wayne Gretzky BW 6.00 15.00
166 Teuvo Teravainen RC 2.00 5.00
167 Evgeny Kuznetsov RC 5.00 12.00
168 Brandon Gormley RC 1.25 3.00
169 Ty Rattie RC 1.50 4.00
170 Johnny Gaudreau RC 4.00 10.00
171 Jonathan Drouin RC 3.00 8.00
172 Aaron Ekblad RC 5.00 12.00
173 Vladislav Namestnikov RC 2.00 5.00
174 Bo Horvat RC 4.00 10.00
175 Curtis Lazar RC 1.50 4.00
176 Alexander Khokhlachev RC 1.25 3.00
177 Joey Hishon RC 1.50 4.00
178 Calle Jarnkrok RC 1.25 3.00
179 Sam Reinhart RC 4.00 10.00
180 Leon Draisaitl RC 6.00 15.00
181 Guy Lafleur WP 1.50 4.00
182 Steve Shutt WP 1.00 2.50
183 Alex Galchenyuk WP 2.00 5.00
184 Nathan MacKinnon WP 2.50 6.00
185 Jonathan Toews WP 2.50 6.00
186 Teemu Selanne WP 2.50 6.00
187 Phil Kessel WP 1.50 4.00
188 Martin St. Louis WP 1.25 3.00
189 Joe Pavelski WP 1.25 3.00
190 Alexander Ovechkin WP 5.00 12.00
191 John Tavares WP 2.50 6.00
192 Mike Richter WP 1.25 3.00
193 Sidney Crosby WP 5.00 12.00
194 Wayne Gretzky WP 6.00 15.00
195 Sean Monahan WP 1.25 3.00
196 Mike Smith WP 1.25 3.00
197 John LeClair WP 1.25 3.00
198 Patrick Sharp WP 1.25 3.00
199 Tyler Seguin WP 2.00 5.00
200 Tomas Hertl WP 1.25 3.00
201 Matt Duchene WP 1.25 3.00
202 Corey Perry WP 1.25 3.00
203 Anze Kopitar WP 2.00 5.00
204 Bobby Orr WP 4.00 10.00
205 Jean Beliveau WP 1.25 3.00
206 Max Pacioretty WP 1.25 3.00
207 T.J. Oshie WP 2.00 5.00
208 Tyler Toffoli WP 1.25 3.00
209 Wayne Gretzky WP 6.00 15.00
210 Logan Couture WP 1.25 3.00
211 Mats Sundin WP 1.25 3.00
212 Bill Guerin WP 1.25 3.00
213 Dave Schultz WP 1.25 3.00
214 Brad Park WP 1.00 2.50
215 Pavel Datsyuk WP 1.50 4.00
216 Blake Wheeler WP 1.25 3.00
217 Doug Gilmour WP 1.50 4.00
218 James van Riemsdyk WP 1.25 3.00
219 Marian Gaborik WP 1.25 3.00
220 Valeri Nichushkin WP 1.00 2.50
221 Pete Peeters WP 1.00 2.50
222 Carey Price WP 4.00 10.00
223 Seth Jones WP 1.00 2.50
224 Ondrej Palat WP 1.00 2.50
225 Sergei Bobrovsky WP 1.25 3.00
226 Ryan O'Reilly WP 1.25 3.00
227 Jaromir Jagr WP 3.00 8.00
228 Brendan Gallagher WP 1.25 3.00
229 John Gibson WP 1.50 4.00
230 Nicklas Lidstrom WP 1.25 3.00
231 B.Gallagher/T.Plekanec WP 1.50 4.00
232 Joe Pavelski/Logan Couture WP 1.50 4.00
233 Martin St. Louis/Brad Richards WP 1.50 4.00
234 J.van Riemsdyk/P.Kessel WP 2.00 5.00
235 Ray Bourque/Rob Blake WP 2.50 6.00
236 Seth Jones/N.MacKinnon WP 3.00 8.00
237 Patrick Kane/Patrick Sharp WP 3.00 8.00
238 Dustin Brown/Anze Kopitar WP 2.50 6.00
239 Guy Lafleur/Steve Shutt WP 2.00 5.00
240 Aaron Ekblad/Sam Reinhart WP 6.00 15.00

2014-15 UD Masterpieces Framed Black Leather

*1-90 BLACK/50: 2X TO 5X BASIC CARDS
*91-150 BLACK/50: 1.5X TO 4X BASIC CARDS
*151-165 BLACK/50: 1.2X TO 3X BASIC CARDS
*166-180 BLACK/50: 1X TO 2.5X BASIC RC
41 Nicklas Backstrom 6.00 15.00
52 Corey Crawford 5.00 12.00
150 Wayne Gretzky 25.00 50.00

2014-15 UD Masterpieces Framed Red Cloth

*RED/100: 1.25X TO 3X BASIC CARDS 1-90
*RED/100: 1X TO 2.5X BASIC CARDS 91-150
*RED/100: .75X TO 2X BASIC CARDS 151-180
41 Nicklas Backstrom 4.00 10.00
52 Corey Crawford 3.00 8.00

2014-15 UD Masterpieces Autographs

GROUP A STATED ODDS 1:16,590
GROUP B STATED ODDS 1:388
GROUP C STATED ODDS 1:428
GROUP D STATED ODDS 1:148
GROUP E STATED ODDS 1:83
GROUP F STATED ODDS 1:76
GROUP A BW STATED ODDS 1:3,130
GROUP B BW STATED ODDS 1:5,925
GROUP C BW STATED ODDS 1:1,508
ROOK AU STATED ODDS 1:120
GROUP A BW STATED ODDS 1:3,130
GROUP B STATED ODDS 1:5,925
GROUP C STATED ODDS 1:1,508
GROUP D STATED ODDS 1:148
DUAL AU STATED ODDS 1:2,000
1 Corey Perry D 4.00 10.00
4 Cody Hodgson E 3.00 8.00
10 Matt Duchene D 4.00 10.00
11 Sergei Bobrovsky E 4.00 10.00
14 Taylor Hall D 8.00 20.00
17 Jason Pominville E 2.50 6.00
18 Max Pacioretty E 6.00 15.00
19 Shea Weber D 3.00 8.00
20 Martin Brodeur C 50.00 120.00
21 Kyle Okposo E 3.00 8.00
24 Kyle Turris 3.00 8.00
Issued in '15-16 UD2
26 Evgeni Malkin C EXCH 30.00 80.00
31 Alexander Ovechkin B EXCH
38 Marc-Andre Fleury D 10.00 25.00
39 Ben Bishop F 5.00 12.00
43 Pavel Datsyuk D 5.00 12.00
46 Seth Jones E 2.50 6.00
47 Tomas Hertl F 3.00 8.00
48 Zach Parise C 12.00 30.00
49 Jim Howard E 3.00 8.00
50 Ryan Johansen 12.00 30.00
Issued in '15-16 UD2
54 Patrik Elias E 3.00 8.00
55 Wayne Gretzky B 175.00 300.00
57 Logan Couture D 4.00 10.00
58 Jonathan Bernier D 4.00 10.00
60 Tomas Plekanec E 5.00 12.00
62 Jamie Benn D 5.00 12.00
63 Jeff Skinner D 4.00 10.00
65 Brendan Gallagher E 8.00 20.00
66 Patrick Marleau D 4.00 10.00
67 Scott Laughton F 2.50 6.00
72 Jason Spezza D 4.00 10.00
74 Scott Hartnell E 3.00 8.00
75 David Backes D 4.00 10.00
76 Wayne Gretzky C 150.00 300.00
83 Chris Kunitz F 3.00 8.00
84 Adam Henrique E 3.00 8.00
85 Gustav Nyquist F 4.00 10.00
86 Mikael Granlund F 2.50 6.00
87 Bobby Ryan D 4.00 10.00
89 Jonathan Huberdeau E 5.00 12.00
92 Wayne Gretzky B 175.00 300.00
94 Bill Guerin F 3.00 8.00
95 Theoren Fleury C 15.00 40.00
96 Jarome Iginla B 20.00 50.00
100 Sidney Crosby B EXCH 100.00 200.00
101 Guy Carbonneau F 3.00 8.00
102 Mike Gartner E 5.00 12.00
104 Bobby Orr E 60.00 120.00
106 Bill Ranford F 3.00 8.00
110 Jaromir Jagr B 50.00 120.00
111 Joe Sakic B 30.00 80.00
114 Grant Fuhr C 12.00 30.00
115 Dominik Hasek B 25.00 60.00
116 Brett Hull B 20.00 50.00
119 Jonathan Toews B 40.00 100.00
120 Mario Lemieux B 60.00 150.00
122 Mats Sundin B 20.00 50.00
123 Adam Oates F 6.00 15.00
125 Nathan MacKinnon C 25.00 60.00
129 Steve Yzerman B 40.00 100.00
130 Martin St. Louis C 12.00 30.00
131 Patrick Roy B 50.00 120.00
133 Trevor Linden D 4.00 10.00
135 Joe Pavelski E 3.00 8.00
136 Pierre Turgeon E 12.00 30.00
137 Nicklas Lidstrom B EXCH 20.00 50.00
138 Nail Yakupov E 5.00 12.00
142 John Tavares E 8.00 20.00
143 Jari Kurri E 5.00 12.00
144 Mark Messier B 20.00 50.00
147 Carey Price B 60.00 150.00
149 Chris Chelios B 20.00 50.00
150 Wayne Gretzky A
151 Bobby Orr C 90.00 150.00
153 Mario Lemieux A
154 Sidney Crosby A
155 Mats Sundin B 20.00 50.00
156 Alexander Ovechkin A
158 Steve Yzerman A
159 Evgeni Malkin C 40.00 100.00
160 Pavel Datsyuk C 15.00 40.00
161 Joe Sakic A
162 Nathan MacKinnon C 25.00 60.00
163 Mark Messier A
165 Wayne Gretzky B 100.00 250.00
166 Teuvo Teravainen 8.00 20.00
167 Evgeny Kuznetsov 20.00 50.00
168 Brandon Gormley 5.00 12.00
169 Ty Rattie 6.00 15.00
170 Johnny Gaudreau EXCH 40.00 100.00
171 Jonathan Drouin 25.00 50.00
172 Aaron Ekblad 20.00 50.00
173 Vladislav Namestnikov 8.00 20.00
174 Bo Horvat 15.00 40.00
175 Curtis Lazar 6.00 15.00
177 Alexander Khokhlachev 6.00 15.00
178 Joey Hishon 5.00 12.00
179 Sam Reinhart 15.00 40.00
180 Leon Draisaitl 12.00 30.00
183 Alex Galchenyuk WP B 30.00 80.00
184 Nathan MacKinnon WP B EXCH 20.00 50.00
185 Jonathan Toews WP A
186 Teemu Selanne WP A 40.00 80.00
188 Martin St. Louis WP B 20.00 50.00
189 Joe Pavelski WP D 10.00 25.00
190 Alexander Ovechkin WP A
191 John Tavares WP C 30.00 80.00
193 Sidney Crosby WP A
194 Wayne Gretzky WP B 100.00 250.00
195 Sean Monahan WP D 10.00 25.00
197 John LeClair WP B 20.00 50.00
200 Tomas Hertl WP D 10.00 25.00
201 Matt Duchene WP C 15.00 40.00
202 Corey Perry WP B 20.00 50.00
203 Anze Kopitar WP B 30.00 80.00
204 Bobby Orr WP C 90.00 150.00
206 Max Pacioretty WP C 15.00 40.00
208 Tyler Toffoli WP D EXCH 10.00 25.00
209 Wayne Gretzky WP A
210 Logan Couture WP C 15.00 40.00
211 Mats Sundin WP A
212 Bill Guerin WP D 10.00 25.00
213 Dave Schultz WP D 10.00 25.00
214 Brad Park WP C 12.00 30.00
215 Pavel Datsyuk WP B 25.00 60.00
221 Pete Peeters WP D 8.00 20.00
222 Carey Price WP A
223 Seth Jones WP C 12.00 30.00
224 Ondrej Palat WP D 8.00 20.00
225 Sergei Bobrovsky WP C 15.00 40.00
226 Ryan O'Reilly WP D 10.00 25.00
227 Jaromir Jagr WP A
228 Brendan Gallagher WP C 15.00 40.00
230 Nicklas Lidstrom WP B EXCH 15.00 40.00
232 L.Couture/J.Pavelski WP
235 R.Bourque/R.Blake WP 40.00 80.00
238 D.Brown/A.Kopitar WP 50.00 100.00
240 A.Ekblad/S.Reinhart WP

2014-15 UD Masterpieces Autographs Framed Red Cloth

*RED/30: 1.5X TO 4X F-F AU
*RED/30: 1.25X TO 3X D AU
STATED PRINT RUN 5-30
55 Wayne Gretzky/30 150.00 250.00
92 Wayne Gretzky/15 200.00 350.00
104 Bobby Orr/30 60.00 120.00
136 Pierre Turgeon/30 25.00 60.00
150 Wayne Gretzky/15 200.00 350.00
170 Johnny Gaudreau/30 EXCH 100.00 200.00
171 Jonathan Drouin/30 40.00 80.00

2014-15 UD Masterpieces Gretzky Jumbos

150 Wayne Gretzky 5.00 10.00

2014-15 UD Masterpieces Memorabilia

GROUP A STATED ODDS 1:1327 H
GROUP B STATED ODDS 1:27 H
GROUP C STATED ODDS 1:33 H
UNPRICED GROUP A BW STATED ODDS 1:16,400 H
GROUP B BW STATED ODDS 1:410 H
OVERALL STATED ODDS 1:15 H
OVERALL BW STATED ODDS 1:410 H
1 Corey Perry B 2.50 6.00
2 Evander Kane C 2.50 6.00
3 Zdeno Chara B 2.50 6.00
4 Cody Hodgson C 2.50 6.00
5 Mark Scheifele C 3.00 8.00
6 Dustin Byfuglien C 2.50 6.00
7 Eric Staal B 3.00 8.00
8 Patrick Kane B 5.00 12.00
9 Blake Wheeler C 2.50 6.00
10 Matt Duchene B 2.50 6.00
11 Sergei Bobrovsky B 2.50 6.00
12 Tyler Seguin B 4.00 10.00
13 Daniel Alfredsson B 2.50 6.00
14 Taylor Hall B 5.00 12.00
15 Ryan Getzlaf B 4.00 10.00
16 Jonathan Quick B 4.00 10.00
17 Jason Pominville C 2.00 5.00
18 Max Pacioretty C 2.50 6.00
19 Shea Weber B 2.00 5.00
20 Martin Brodeur B 8.00 20.00
21 Kyle Okposo C 2.50 6.00
22 Mats Zuccarello C 2.50 6.00
23 Erik Karlsson B 5.00 12.00
24 Kyle Turris C 2.50 6.00
25 Keith Yandle B 2.50 6.00
26 Evgeni Malkin B 8.00 20.00
27 Joe Thornton B 2.50 6.00
29 Pekka Rinne B 3.00 8.00
30 James van Riemsdyk C 2.50 6.00
31 Alexander Ovechkin B 6.00 15.00
32 Tuukka Rask B 2.50 6.00
33 Marian Hossa B 2.00 5.00
34 Valeri Nichushkin C 2.00 5.00
35 Sam Gagner C 2.00 5.00
36 Alex Galchenyuk C 4.00 10.00
37 Brad Richards C 2.50 6.00
38 Marc-Andre Fleury C 4.00 10.00
39 Ben Bishop C 2.50 6.00
40 Phil Kessel B 3.00 8.00
41 Nicklas Backstrom B 4.00 10.00
42 Paul Stastny C 2.50 6.00
43 Pavel Datsyuk B 3.00 8.00
44 Gabriel Landeskog C 2.00 5.00
45 Jonas Hiller C 2.00 5.00
46 Seth Jones B 2.00 5.00
47 Tomas Hertl C 2.50 6.00
48 Zach Parise B 2.50 6.00
49 Jim Howard C 2.50 6.00
50 Ryan Johansen B 3.00 8.00
51 Cam Ward B 2.50 6.00
52 Corey Crawford B 3.00 8.00
53 Aleksander Barkov C 2.50 6.00
55 Wayne Gretzky A 40.00 80.00
56 Ryan Strome C 2.00 5.00
57 Logan Couture B 2.50 6.00
58 Jonathan Bernier B 2.50 6.00
59 Rick Nash B 2.50 6.00
61 Ryan Nugent-Hopkins B 2.50 6.00
62 Jamie Benn B 3.00 8.00
63 Jeff Skinner C 2.50 6.00
64 Duncan Keith B 2.50 6.00
65 Brendan Gallagher C 2.50 6.00
66 Patrick Marleau B 2.50 6.00
67 Scott Laughton C 1.50 4.00
68 Kari Lehtonen C 2.00 5.00
69 Mikko Koivu B 2.00 5.00
70 Anze Kopitar C 4.00 10.00
71 David Perron B 1.50 4.00
72 Jason Spezza C 2.50 6.00
73 Shane Doan C 2.00 5.00
74 Scott Hartnell C 2.50 6.00
75 David Backes C 2.50 6.00
76 Wayne Gretzky A
77 Patrick Sharp B 2.50 6.00
78 Vincent Lecavalier B 2.00 5.00
79 T.J. Oshie C 4.00 10.00
81 James Neal B 2.50 6.00
82 Dion Phaneuf C 2.50 6.00
83 Chris Kunitz C 2.50 6.00
85 Gustav Nyquist C 2.00 5.00
86 Mikael Granlund C 2.00 5.00
87 Bobby Ryan B 2.50 6.00
88 Drew Doughty B 2.50 6.00
89 Jonathan Huberdeau C 2.50 6.00
90 Tyler Ennis C 2.00 5.00
91 Roberto Luongo B 2.50 6.00
92 Wayne Gretzky A 40.00 80.00
93 Peter Forsberg B 2.50 6.00
94 Bill Guerin B 2.50 6.00
95 Theoren Fleury B 3.00 8.00
96 Jarome Iginla B 2.50 6.00
97 Steven Stamkos B 5.00 12.00
98 Claude Giroux B 2.50 6.00
99 Phil Esposito B 4.00 10.00
100 Sidney Crosby B 10.00 25.00
101 Guy Carbonneau B 2.50 6.00
102 Mike Gartner B 2.50 6.00
105 Patrice Bergeron C 3.00 8.00
106 Bill Ranford B 2.50 6.00
107 Mike Bossy B 2.50 6.00
108 Sean Monahan C 2.50 6.00
109 Dale Hawerchuk B 3.00 8.00
110 Jaromir Jagr B 6.00 15.00
111 Joe Sakic B 4.00 10.00
112 Henrik Zetterberg B 3.00 8.00
113 Jordan Eberle B 2.50 6.00
114 Grant Fuhr B 2.50 6.00
115 Dominik Hasek B 3.00 8.00
116 Brett Hull B 2.50 6.00
118 Doug Gilmour B 3.00 8.00
119 Jonathan Toews B 5.00 12.00
120 Mario Lemieux B 8.00 20.00
121 Marcel Dionne B 3.00 8.00
122 Mats Sundin B 2.50 6.00
123 Adam Oates B 2.50 6.00
125 Nathan MacKinnon C 5.00 12.00
127 Jeff Carter C 2.50 6.00
128 Jeremy Roenick B 2.50 6.00
129 Steve Yzerman B 6.00 15.00
130 Martin St. Louis C 2.50 6.00
131 Patrick Roy B 8.00 20.00
132 Ray Bourque B 4.00 10.00
133 Trevor Linden B 2.50 6.00
135 Joe Pavelski C 2.50 6.00
136 Pierre Turgeon B 2.50 6.00
137 Nicklas Lidstrom B 2.50 6.00
138 Nail Yakupov C 2.00 5.00
140 Stan Mikita A 20.00 40.00
141 P.K. Subban C 4.00 10.00
142 John Tavares C 5.00 12.00
144 Mark Messier B 2.50 6.00
145 Henrik Lundqvist B 3.00 8.00
147 Carey Price C 8.00 20.00
148 Pelle Lindbergh B 40.00 80.00
149 Chris Chelios B 2.50 6.00
150 Wayne Gretzky A 50.00 100.00
152 Patrick Kane BW B
153 Mario Lemieux BW B
154 Sidney Crosby BW B 15.00 40.00
155 Mats Sundin BW B 4.00 10.00
156 Alexander Ovechkin BW B 15.00 40.00
157 Phil Kessel BW B 5.00 12.00
158 Steve Yzerman BW B 8.00 20.00
159 Evgeni Malkin BW B 12.00 30.00
160 Pavel Datsyuk BW B 5.00 12.00
162 Nathan MacKinnon BW B
163 Mark Messier BW B 4.00 10.00
164 Terry Sawchuk BW B 20.00 40.00
165 Wayne Gretzky BW A

2014-15 UD Masterpieces Memorabilia Framed Black Leather

*BLACK/35: .75X TO 2X B-C JSY
*BLACK/25: 1X TO 2.5X B-C JSY
*BLACK/15: 1.25X TO 3X B-C JSY
*BLACK/15: 1X TO 2.5X A JSY
41 Nicklas Backstrom/35 8.00 20.00
52 Corey Crawford/25 8.00 20.00
55 Wayne Gretzky/15 50.00 100.00
76 Wayne Gretzky/25 50.00 100.00
92 Wayne Gretzky/15 50.00 100.00
148 Pelle Lindbergh/25 75.00 150.00
150 Wayne Gretzky/25 50.00 100.00
165 Wayne Gretzky/15 BW 50.00 100.00

2014-15 UD Masterpieces Memorabilia Framed Red Cloth

*RED/85: .6X TO 1.5X B-C MEM
*RED/35-50: .75X TO 2X B-C MEM
*RED BW/35: .5X TO 1.2X B-C MEM
41 Nicklas Backstrom/85 6.00 15.00
52 Corey Crawford/85 5.00 12.00
55 Wayne Gretzky/15 50.00 100.00
76 Wayne Gretzky/15 50.00 100.00
92 Wayne Gretzky/15 50.00 100.00
150 Wayne Gretzky/15 50.00 100.00

2006-07 UD Mini Jersey Collection

This 130-card set was issued into the hobby in four-card packs, with an $6.99 SRP, which came 18 to a box. Cards numbered 1-100 feature veterans while cards 101-130 feature 2006-07 NHL rookies.

COMPLETE SET (130) 40.00 100.00
1 Teemu Selanne .75 2.00
2 Jean-Sebastien Giguere .40 1.00
3 Chris Pronger .30 .75
4 Ilya Kovalchuk .40 1.00
5 Kari Lehtonen .30 .75
6 Marian Hossa .30 .75
7 Patrice Bergeron .50 1.25
8 Brad Boyes .25 .60
9 Zdeno Chara .40 1.00
10 Thomas Vanek .50 1.25
11 Ryan Miller .40 1.00
12 Chris Drury .30 .75
13 Alex Tanguay .25 .60
14 Miikka Kiprusoff .30 .75
15 Dion Phaneuf .40 1.00
16 Jarome Iginla .40 1.00
17 Eric Staal .50 1.25
18 Cam Ward .40 1.00
19 Erik Cole .30 .75
20 Rod Brind`Amour .40 1.00
21 Martin Havlat .25 .60
22 Nikolai Khabibulin .40 1.00
23 Tuomo Ruutu .40 1.00
24 Joe Sakic .60 1.50
25 Marek Svatos .25 .60
26 Milan Hejduk .30 .75
27 Jose Theodore .40 1.00
28 Fredrik Modin .25 .60
29 Rick Nash .40 1.00
30 Sergei Fedorov .60 1.50
31 Nikolai Zherdev .25 .60
32 Eric Lindros .60 1.50
33 Mike Modano .60 1.50
34 Marty Turco .40 1.00
35 Brenden Morrow .30 .75
36 Henrik Zetterberg .50 1.25
37 Nicklas Lidstrom .40 1.00
38 Dominik Hasek .50 1.25
39 Gordie Howe .75 2.00
40 Pavel Datsyuk .50 1.25
41 Joffrey Lupul .30 .75
42 Fernando Pisani .25 .60
43 Ales Hemsky .30 .75
44 Ryan Smyth .30 .75
45 Dwayne Roloson .30 .75
46 Todd Bertuzzi .40 1.00
47 Olli Jokinen .40 1.00
48 Ed Belfour .40 1.00
49 Rob Blake .40 1.00
50 Alexander Frolov .25 .60
51 Marian Gaborik .50 1.25
52 Manny Fernandez .30 .75
53 Pavol Demitra .50 1.25
54 Saku Koivu .40 1.00
55 Michael Ryder .25 .60
56 Patrick Roy 1.00 2.50
57 Sergei Samsonov .30 .75
58 Paul Kariya .50 1.25
59 Tomas Vokoun .30 .75
60 Martin Brodeur .75 2.00
61 Patrik Elias .40 1.00
62 Alexei Yashin .30 .75
63 Miroslav Satan .30 .75
64 Rick DiPietro .30 .75
65 Jaromir Jagr 1.00 2.50
66 Henrik Lundqvist .75 2.00
67 Brendan Shanahan .50 1.25
68 Martin Gerber .30 .75
69 Jason Spezza .40 1.00
70 Dany Heatley .40 1.00
71 Daniel Alfredsson .40 1.00
72 Mike Richards .40 1.00
73 Peter Forsberg .50 1.25
74 Simon Gagne .40 1.00
75 Antero Niittymaki .30 .75
76 Jeff Carter .40 1.00
77 Shane Doan .30 .75
78 Jeremy Roenick .40 1.00
79 Curtis Joseph .40 1.00
80 Sidney Crosby 1.50 4.00
81 Marc-Andre Fleury .60 1.50
82 Jonathan Cheechoo .40 1.00
83 Vesa Toskala .30 .75
84 Patrick Marleau .40 1.00
85 Joe Thornton .50 1.25
86 Keith Tkachuk .40 1.00
87 Vincent Lecavalier .30 .75
88 Martin St. Louis .40 1.00
89 Brad Richards .40 1.00
90 Mats Sundin .40 1.00
91 Alexander Steen .40 1.00
92 Bryan McCabe .25 .60
93 Andrew Raycroft .30 .75
94 Darcy Tucker .30 .75
95 Markus Naslund .30 .75
96 Roberto Luongo .60 1.50
97 Henrik Sedin .40 1.00
98 Brendan Morrison .25 .60
99 Olaf Kolzig .40 1.00
100 Alexander Ovechkin 1.50 4.00
101 Yan Stastny RC 2.00 5.00
102 Mark Stuart RC 2.00 5.00
103 Phil Kessel RC 3.00 8.00
104 Ryan Shannon RC 2.00 5.00
105 Tomas Kopecky RC 2.50 6.00
106 M-A Pouliot RC 2.00 5.00
107 K.Pushkarev RC 2.50 6.00
108 Patrick O'Sullivan RC 2.50 6.00
109 Anze Kopitar RC 5.00 12.00
110 Shea Weber RC 5.00 12.00
111 Travis Zajac RC 4.00 10.00
112 G. Latendresse RC 2.00 5.00
113 M-E Vlasic RC 2.00 5.00
114 Ladislav Smid RC 2.00 5.00
115 Loui Eriksson RC 1.50 4.00
116 Kristopher Letang RC 6.00 15.00
117 Jarkko Immonen RC 2.00 5.00
118 Nigel Dawes RC 2.00 5.00
119 Luc Bourdon RC 3.00 8.00
120 Ryan Potulny RC 2.00 5.00
121 Keith Yandle RC 4.00 10.00
122 Patrick Thoresen RC 2.00 5.00
123 Noah Welch RC 2.00 5.00
124 Jordan Staal RC 4.00 10.00
125 Matt Carle RC 2.00 5.00
126 Evgeni Malkin RC 10.00 25.00
127 Brendan Bell RC 2.00 5.00
128 Ian White RC 2.50 6.00
129 Jeremy Williams RC 2.00 5.00
130 Eric Fehr RC 2.00 5.00

2006-07 UD Mini Jersey Collection Home Jerseys

COMPLETE SET (21) 125.00 200.00
ONE PER PACK OVERALL
*AWAY JERSEY: 1X TO 2.5X HOME JERSEY
*AWAY JERSEY: .6X TO 1.5X HOME JRSY SP
AF Alexander Frolov 1.50 4.00
AO Alexander Ovechkin 10.00 25.00
DH Dany Heatley 2.50 6.00
DP Dion Phaneuf 2.50 6.00
EM Evgeni Malkin 6.00 15.00
ES Eric Staal 3.00 8.00
GH Gordie Howe SP 60.00 100.00
HL Henrik Lundqvist 5.00 12.00
IK Ilya Kovalchuk 2.50 6.00
JS Joe Sakic 4.00 10.00
JT Joe Thornton 3.00 8.00
MN Markus Naslund 2.00 5.00
MR Michael Ryder 1.50 4.00
MS Mats Sundin 2.50 6.00
MT Marty Turco 2.50 6.00
PB Patrice Bergeron 3.00 8.00
PF Peter Forsberg 3.00 8.00
PR Patrick Roy 6.00 15.00
RN Rick Nash 2.50 6.00
SC Sidney Crosby 8.00 20.00
TV Thomas Vanek 3.00 8.00

2006-07 UD Mini Jersey Collection Jersey Autographs

STATED ODDS 1 PER CASE
1 Patrice Bergeron SP 50.00 100.00
2 Sidney Crosby SP 300.00 500.00
3 Alexander Frolov 25.00 60.00
4 Dany Heatley SP
5 Gordie Howe SP 250.00 400.00
6 Ilya Kovalchuk SP 75.00 150.00
7 Markus Naslund 25.00 60.00
8 Alexander Ovechkin SP 75.00 150.00
9 Dion Phaneuf 30.00 80.00
10 Michael Ryder 20.00 50.00
11 Eric Staal 40.00 80.00
12 Joe Thornton SP 75.00 150.00
13 Marty Turco 15.00 40.00
14 Thomas Vanek 30.00 60.00

2007-08 UD Mini Jersey Collection

This set was released on March 24, 2008. The base set consists of 150 cards. Cards 1-100 feature veterans, and cards 101-150 are rookies.

COMPLETE SET (150) 125.00 250.00
COMP.SET w/o SPs (100) 12.00 30.00
1 Jean-Sebastien Giguere .40 1.00
2 Ryan Getzlaf .60 1.50
3 Scott Niedermayer .40 1.00
4 Chris Pronger .30 .75

5 Ilya Kovalchuk .40 1.00
6 Marian Hossa .30 .75
7 Kari Lehtonen .30 .75
8 Patrice Bergeron .50 1.25
9 Phil Kessel .50 1.25
10 Zdeno Chara .40 1.00
11 Ryan Miller .40 1.00
12 Thomas Vanek .50 1.25
13 Jason Pominville .40 1.00
14 Derek Roy .25 .60
15 Miikka Kiprusoff .30 .75
16 Jarome Iginla .40 1.00
17 Alex Tanguay .25 .60
18 Dion Phaneuf .40 1.00
19 Eric Staal .50 1.25
20 Cam Ward .40 1.00
21 Justin Williams .30 .75
22 Martin Havlat .40 1.00
23 Nikolai Khabibulin .40 1.00
24 Duncan Keith .40 1.00
25 Joe Sakic .60 1.50
26 Milan Hejduk .30 .75
27 Peter Budaj .30 .75
28 Paul Stastny .40 1.00
29 Marty Turco .40 1.00
30 Mike Modano .60 1.50
31 Mike Ribeiro .30 .75
32 Henrik Zetterberg .50 1.25
33 Nicklas Lidstrom .40 1.00
34 Pavel Datsyuk .50 1.25
35 Dominik Hasek .50 1.25
36 Ales Hemsky .30 .75
37 Dwayne Roloson .30 .75
38 Jarret Stoll .30 .75
39 Shawn Horcoff .25 .60
40 Tomas Vokoun .30 .75
41 Olli Jokinen .30 .75
42 Nathan Horton .40 1.00
43 Anze Kopitar .60 1.50
44 Alexander Frolov .25 .60
45 Rob Blake .40 1.00
46 Mike Cammalleri .30 .75
47 Marian Gaborik .50 1.25
48 Niklas Backstrom .40 1.00
49 Pierre-Marc Bouchard .40 1.00
50 Saku Koivu .40 1.00
51 Michael Ryder .25 .60
52 Guillaume Latendresse .30 .75
53 Cristobal Huet .30 .75
54 Alexander Radulov .40 1.00
55 Chris Mason .30 .75
56 Jason Arnott .30 .75
57 Martin Brodeur .75 2.00
58 Patrik Elias .40 1.00
59 Zach Parise .50 1.25
60 Miroslav Satan .30 .75
61 Bill Guerin .40 1.00
62 Rick DiPietro .30 .75
63 Jaromir Jagr 1.00 2.50
64 Henrik Lundqvist .50 1.25
65 Martin Straka .25 .60
66 Dany Heatley .40 1.00
67 Ray Emery .30 .75
68 Daniel Alfredsson .40 1.00
69 Jason Spezza .40 1.00
70 Simon Gagne .40 1.00
71 Jeff Carter .40 1.00
72 Martin Biron .30 .75
73 Shane Doan .30 .75
74 Ed Jovanovski .30 .75
75 Keith Ballard .25 .60
76 Sidney Crosby 1.50 4.00
77 Evgeni Malkin 1.25 3.00
78 Marc-Andre Fleury .60 1.50
79 Jordan Staal .40 1.00
80 Joe Thornton .50 1.25
81 Patrick Marleau .40 1.00
82 Jonathan Cheechoo .40 1.00
83 Evgeni Nabokov .30 .75
84 Doug Weight .40 1.00
85 Manny Legace .30 .75
86 Brad Boyes .25 .60
87 Vincent Lecavalier .30 .75
88 Brad Richards .40 1.00
89 Martin St. Louis .40 1.00
90 Mats Sundin .40 1.00
91 Vesa Toskala .30 .75
92 Alexander Steen .40 1.00
93 Darcy Tucker .30 .75
94 Roberto Luongo .50 1.25
95 Markus Naslund .40 1.00
96 Henrik Sedin .40 1.00
97 Daniel Sedin .40 1.00
98 Alexander Ovechkin 1.50 4.00
99 Olaf Kolzig .40 1.00
100 Alexander Semin .40 1.00
101 Bobby Ryan RC 2.50 6.00
102 Drew Miller RC 1.25 3.00
103 Bryan Little RC 1.50 4.00
104 Ondrej Pavelec RC 2.00 5.00
105 Tuukka Rask RC 4.00 10.00
106 Vladimir Sobotka RC 1.25 3.00
107 Milan Lucic RC 5.00 12.00
108 Curtis McElhinney RC 1.50 4.00
109 Matt Keetley RC 1.25 3.00
110 Jonathan Toews RC 8.00 20.00
111 Patrick Kane RC 6.00 15.00
112 Tyler Weiman RC 1.25 3.00
113 T.J. Hensick RC 1.25 3.00
114 Kris Russell RC 1.25 3.00
115 Jared Boll RC 1.25 3.00
116 Matt Niskanen RC 1.50 4.00
117 Sam Gagner RC 2.00 5.00
118 Andrew Cogliano RC 1.50 4.00
119 Rob Schremp RC 1.25 3.00
120 Stefan Meyer RC 1.25 3.00
121 Jack Johnson RC 1.25 3.00
122 Jonathan Bernier RC 2.50 6.00
123 Petr Kalus RC 1.00 2.50
124 James Sheppard RC 1.00 2.50
125 Cal Clutterbuck RC 1.50 4.00
126 Carey Price RC 8.00 20.00
127 Kyle Chipchura RC 1.50 4.00
128 Nicklas Bergfors RC 1.00 2.50
129 Andy Greene RC 1.25 3.00
130 Frans Nielsen RC 1.50 4.00
131 Marc Staal RC 1.50 4.00
132 Ryan Callahan RC 2.00 5.00
133 Alexander Nikulin RC 1.25 3.00
134 Nick Foligno RC 2.00 5.00
135 Steve Downie RC 1.25 3.00
136 Peter Mueller RC 1.25 3.00
137 Martin Hanzal RC 1.25 3.00
138 Tyler Kennedy RC 1.50 4.00
139 Thomas Greiss RC 2.00 5.00
140 Devin Setoguchi RC 1.50 4.00
141 Torrey Mitchell RC 1.25 3.00
142 Erik Johnson RC 1.50 4.00
143 David Perron RC 1.50 4.00
144 Matt Smaby RC 1.00 2.50
145 Anton Stralman RC 1.00 2.50
146 Jiri Tlusty RC 1.50 4.00
147 Mason Raymond RC 1.50 4.00
148 Jannik Hansen RC 1.25 3.00
149 Chris Bourque RC 1.25 3.00
150 Nicklas Backstrom RC 3.00 8.00

2007-08 UD Mini Jersey Collection Home Jerseys

COMPLETE SET (30) 75.00 150.00
ONE PER PACK OVERALL
*AWAY JERSEY: .6X TO 1.5X HOME JERSEY
MINI1 Teemu Selanne 5.00 12.00
MINI2 Kari Lehtonen 2.00 5.00
MINI3 Phil Kessel 3.00 8.00
MINI4 Ryan Miller 2.50 6.00
MINI5 Jarome Iginla 2.50 6.00
MINI6 Cam Ward 2.50 6.00
MINI7 Martin Havlat 2.50 6.00
MINI8 Joe Sakic 4.00 10.00
MINI9 Sergei Fedorov 4.00 10.00
MINI10 Mike Modano 4.00 10.00
MINI11 Henrik Zetterberg 3.00 8.00
MINI12 Dwayne Roloson 2.00 5.00
MINI13 Olli Jokinen 2.00 5.00
MINI14 Anze Kopitar 4.00 10.00
MINI15 Marian Gaborik 3.00 8.00
MINI16 Saku Koivu 2.50 6.00
MINI17 Alexander Radulov 2.50 6.00
MINI18 Martin Brodeur 5.00 12.00
MINI19 Rick DiPietro 2.00 5.00
MINI20 Jaromir Jagr 6.00 15.00
MINI21 Jason Spezza 2.50 6.00
MINI22 Simon Gagne 2.50 6.00
MINI23 Shane Doan 2.00 5.00
MINI24 Sidney Crosby 10.00 25.00
MINI25 Jonathan Cheechoo 2.00 5.00
MINI26 Doug Weight 2.50 6.00
MINI27 Vincent Lecavalier 2.00 5.00
MINI28 Mats Sundin 2.50 6.00
MINI29 Roberto Luongo 3.00 8.00
MINI30 Alexander Ovechkin 10.00 25.00
NNO Checklist Card .05 .15

2007-08 UD Mini Jersey Collection Jerseys Autographs

STATED ODDS 1:360
1 Martin Brodeur 60.00 150.00
2 Jonathan Cheechoo 30.00 80.00
3 Sidney Crosby 125.00 300.00
4 Marian Gaborik
5 Simon Gagne
6 Martin Havlat 25.00 60.00
7 Jarome Iginla 30.00 80.00
8 Phil Kessel 40.00 100.00
9 Saku Koivu
10 Anze Kopitar 50.00 125.00
11 Vincent Lecavalier 40.00 80.00
12 Ryan Miller 30.00 80.00
13 Mike Modano 50.00 125.00
14 Alexander Ovechkin 125.00 300.00
15 Alexander Radulov 25.00 60.00
16 Dwayne Roloson 25.00 60.00
17 Cam Ward 30.00 80.00
18 Checklist Card .30 .75

2002-03 UD Piece of History

This 150-card set consisted of 90 regular base cards, 18 "Season to Remember subset cards, 12 "Tribute to Greatness" subset cards and 30 shortprinted "History in the Making" rookie cards. Subset cards were serial-numbered to 2999 and rookie cards were serial-numbered to 1500.

COMP.SET w/o SP's (90) 15.00 30.00
1 Paul Kariya .30 .75
2 Jean-Sebastien Giguere .25 .60
3 Ilya Kovalchuk .30 .75
4 Dany Heatley .25 .60
5 Joe Thornton .30 .75
6 Sergei Samsonov .20 .50
7 Glen Murray .20 .50
8 Miroslav Satan .25 .60
9 Tim Connolly .15 .40
10 Martin Biron .20 .50
11 Jeff O'Neill .15 .40
12 Erik Cole .20 .50
13 Ron Francis .30 .75
14 Arturs Irbe .20 .50
15 Roman Turek .25 .60
16 Marc Savard .15 .40
17 Jarome Iginla .25 .60
18 Eric Daze .15 .40
19 Steve Sullivan .15 .40
20 Jocelyn Thibault .20 .50
21 Espen Knutsen .15 .40
22 Rostislav Klesla .15 .40
23 Marc Denis .20 .50
24 Patrick Roy .60 1.50
25 Chris Drury .25 .60
26 Joe Sakic .40 1.00
27 Peter Forsberg .30 .75
28 Alex Tanguay .20 .50
29 Mike Modano .40 1.00
30 Marty Turco .25 .60
31 Jason Arnott .20 .50
32 Steve Yzerman .50 1.25
33 Sergei Fedorov .40 1.00
34 Nicklas Lidstrom .25 .60
35 Brett Hull .30 .75
36 Curtis Joseph .25 .60
37 Brendan Shanahan .30 .75
38 Mike Comrie .25 .60
39 Tommy Salo .20 .50
40 Ryan Smyth .20 .50
41 Roberto Luongo .40 1.00
42 Kristian Huselius .15 .40
43 Jason Allison .20 .50
44 Felix Potvin .40 1.00
45 Zigmund Palffy .25 .60
46 Marian Gaborik .40 1.00
47 Manny Fernandez .20 .50
48 Jose Theodore .25 .60
49 Saku Koivu .25 .60
50 Patrik Elias .25 .60
51 Martin Brodeur .50 1.25
52 Joe Nieuwendyk .25 .60
53 Scott Hartnell .25 .60
54 Mike Dunham .20 .50
55 Alexei Yashin .20 .50
56 Chris Osgood .25 .60
57 Michael Peca .20 .50
58 Eric Lindros .40 1.00
59 Mike Richter .25 .60
60 Pavel Bure .30 .75
61 Brian Leetch .25 .60
62 Patrick Lalime .20 .50
63 Marian Hossa .20 .50
64 Daniel Alfredsson .25 .60
65 Jeremy Roenick .25 .60
66 Simon Gagne .25 .60
67 Roman Cechmanek .20 .50
68 Sean Burke .15 .40
69 Daniel Briere .20 .50
70 Tony Amonte .20 .50
71 Alexei Kovalev .25 .60
72 Mario Lemieux .75 2.00
73 Johan Hedberg .25 .60
74 Patrick Marleau .25 .60
75 Owen Nolan .25 .60
76 Evgeni Nabokov .20 .50
77 Keith Tkachuk .25 .60
78 Chris Pronger .20 .50
79 Brent Johnson .20 .50
80 Nikolai Khabibulin .25 .60
81 Vincent Lecavalier .20 .50
82 Alexander Mogilny .20 .50
83 Mats Sundin .25 .60
84 Ed Belfour .25 .60
85 Todd Bertuzzi .25 .60
86 Dan Cloutier .20 .50
87 Markus Naslund .20 .50
88 Olaf Kolzig .25 .60
89 Peter Bondra .25 .60
90 Jaromir Jagr .60 1.50
91 Wayne Gretzky SR 5.00 12.00
92 Wayne Gretzky SR 5.00 12.00
93 Mario Lemieux SR 3.00 8.00
94 Patrick Roy SR 2.50 6.00
95 Steve Yzerman SR 2.00 5.00
96 Gordie Howe SR 3.00 8.00
97 Bobby Orr SR 3.00 8.00
98 Ray Bourque SR 1.50 4.00
99 Brett Hull SR 1.25 3.00
100 Teemu Selanne SR 2.00 5.00
101 Martin Brodeur SR 2.00 5.00
102 Jaromir Jagr SR 2.50 6.00
103 Eric Lindros SR 1.50 4.00
104 Joe Sakic SR 1.50 4.00
105 Mike Richter SR 1.00 2.50
106 Sergei Fedorov SR 1.50 4.00
107 Peter Forsberg SR 1.25 3.00
108 Mark Messier SR 1.50 4.00
109 Wayne Gretzky TG 5.00 12.00
110 Wayne Gretzky TG 5.00 12.00
111 Wayne Gretzky TG 5.00 12.00
112 Gordie Howe TG 3.00 8.00
113 Gordie Howe TG 3.00 8.00
114 Gordie Howe TG 3.00 8.00
115 Bobby Orr TG 3.00 8.00
116 Bobby Orr TG 3.00 8.00
117 Bobby Orr TG 3.00 8.00
118 Ray Bourque TG 1.50 4.00
119 Ray Bourque TG 1.50 4.00
120 Ray Bourque TG 1.50 4.00
121 Stanislav Chistov HM RC .75 2.00
122 Alexei Smirnov HM RC 1.00 2.50
123 Henrik Tallinder HM .75 2.00
124 Micki Dupont HM RC .75 2.00
125 Chuck Kobasew HM RC 1.00 2.50
126 Andrej Nedorost HM .75 2.00
127 Rick Nash HM RC 6.00 15.00
128 Henrik Zetterberg HM RC 8.00 20.00
129 Ales Hemsky HM RC 3.00 8.00
130 Jani Rita HM .75 2.00
131 Stephen Weiss HM 1.25 3.00
132 Jay Bouwmeester HM RC 2.50 6.00
133 Alexander Frolov HM RC 1.50 4.00
134 P-M Bouchard HM RC 1.25 3.00
135 Sylvain Blouin HM RC .75 2.00
136 Ron Hainsey HM RC .75 2.00
137 Adam Hall HM RC .75 2.00
138 Jan Lasak HM 1.00 2.50
139 Ray Schultz HM RC .75 2.00
140 Trent Hunter HM .75 2.00
141 Martin Prusek HM .75 2.00
142 Anton Volchenkov HM RC .75 2.00
143 Patrick Sharp HM RC 2.50 6.00
144 Dennis Seidenberg HM RC 1.25 3.00
145 Branko Radivojevic HM .75 2.00
146 Shane Endicott HM .75 2.00
147 Alexander Svitov HM RC .75 2.00
148 Sebastien Centomo HM .75 2.00
149 Karel Pilar HM .75 2.00
150 Steve Eminger HM RC .75 2.00

2002-03 UD Piece of History Awards Collection

COMPLETE SET (28) 25.00 50.00
STAT.ODDS 1:5 HBBY/1:6 RETAIL
AC1 Paul Kariya .50 1.25
AC2 Ray Bourque 1.00 2.50
AC3 Sergei Samsonov .40 1.00
AC4 Jarome Iginla .60 1.50
AC5 Chris Drury .40 1.00
AC6 Joe Sakic 1.00 2.50
AC7 Rob Blake .40 1.00
AC8 Peter Forsberg 1.25 3.00
AC9 Patrick Roy 2.00 5.00
AC10 Luc Robitaille .40 1.00
AC11 Brett Hull .60 1.50
AC12 Steve Yzerman 2.00 5.00
AC13 Dominik Hasek 1.00 2.50
AC14 Nicklas Lidstrom .50 1.25
AC15 Sergei Fedorov 1.00 2.50
AC16 Wayne Gretzky 3.00 8.00
AC17 Joe Nieuwendyk .40 1.00
AC18 Martin Brodeur 1.50 4.00
AC19 Brian Leetch .40 1.00
AC20 Pavel Bure .60 1.50
AC21 Claude Lemieux .40 1.00
AC22 Mario Lemieux 2.50 6.00
AC23 Evgeni Nabokov .40 1.00
AC24 Teemu Selanne .50 1.25
AC25 Chris Pronger .40 1.00
AC26 Al MacInnis .40 1.00
AC27 Jaromir Jagr .75 2.00
AC28 Olaf Kolzig .40 1.00

2002-03 UD Piece of History Exquisite Combos

ODDS 1:168 HOBBY ONLY
ECBM P.Bure/M.Messier 12.50 30.00
ECBR R.Blake/P.Roy 10.00 25.00
ECLK M.Lemieux/A.Kovalev 20.00 50.00
ECLM E.Lindros/M.Messier 10.00 25.00
ECNB C.Neely/R.Bourque 12.50 30.00

2002-03 UD Piece of History Heroes Jerseys

STATED ODDS 1:48
HHBS Borje Salming 4.00 10.00
HHGP Gilbert Perreault 3.00 8.00
HHJK Jari Kurri 5.00 12.00
HHMG Mike Gartner 3.00 8.00
HHPS Peter Stastny 3.00 8.00

2002-03 UD Piece of History Historical Swatches Jerseys

STATED ODDS 1:96
HSBS Borje Salming 6.00 15.00
HSBT Bryan Trottier 5.00 12.00
HSCN Cam Neely 12.50 30.00
HSGL Guy Lafleur 5.00 12.00
HSJB Johnny Bucyk 5.00 12.00
HSMB Mike Bossy 5.00 12.00
HSMG Michel Goulet 6.00 15.00
HSMG Mike Gartner 5.00 12.00
HSRB Ray Bourque 15.00 40.00
HSWG Wayne Gretzky 30.00 80.00

2002-03 UD Piece of History Hockey Beginnings

COMPLETE SET (8) 20.00 40.00
STATED ODDS 1:20
HB1 Bobby Orr 2.50 6.00
HB2 Ray Bourque .75 2.00
HB3 Steve Yzerman 2.00 5.00
HB4 Gordie Howe 2.00 5.00
HB5 Wayne Gretzky 2.50 6.00
HB6 Patrick Roy 2.00 5.00
HB7 Mike Bossy .60 1.50
HB8 Wayne Gretzky 2.50 6.00

2002-03 UD Piece of History Marks of Distinction

This 31-card autograph set was inserted at a rate of 1:168 hobby packs. Print runs listed below were provided by Upper Deck. Print runs of 25 or less not priced due to scarcity.

STATED ODDS 1:168 HOBBY PACKS
BO Bobby Orr/24 125.00 200.00
BR Rod Brind'Amour 6.00 15.00
BT Bryan Trottier/25
CN Cam Neely/25
DH Dany Heatley 12.50 30.00
DS Daniel Sedin 8.00 20.00
GA Mike Gartner/25 15.00 40.00
GH Gordie Howe/24 75.00 150.00
GL Guy Lafleur/25 75.00 100.00
GP Gilbert Perreault/25 20.00 40.00
HS Henrik Sedin 8.00 20.00
JB Johnny Bucyk/25
JI Jarome Iginla SP 12.50 30.00
JK Jari Kurri/25 15.00 40.00
JT Joe Thornton/24
MB Mike Bossy/25
MC Mike Comrie SP 12.50 30.00
MG Michel Goulet/25
MN Markus Naslund 8.00 20.00
MR Mike Richter 6.00 15.00
PA Pavel Brendl 6.00 15.00
PB Pavel Bure/24
PR Patrick Roy/24
PS Peter Stastny/25
RA Ray Bourque/24
SG Simon Gagne SP 12.50 30.00
SS Sergei Samsonov SP 12.50 30.00
SY Steve Yzerman 40.00 100.00
TS Teemu Selanne 12.00 30.00
VN Vaclav Nedorost 6.00 15.00
WG Wayne Gretzky/24 250.00 500.00

2002-03 UD Piece of History Patches

This 28-card memorabilia set had a stated print run of 25 serial-numbered sets.

PHBA Rob Blake 20.00 50.00
PHBL Brian Leetch 20.00 50.00
PHBS Brendan Shanahan 20.00 50.00
PHEL Eric Lindros 20.00 50.00
PHFP Felix Potvin 25.00 60.00
PHJS Joe Sakic 50.00 125.00
PHJT Jose Theodore 25.00 60.00
PHKP Keith Primeau 20.00 50.00
PHMA Maxim Afinogenov 20.00 50.00
PHMD Mike Dunham 20.00 50.00
PHMM Mike Modano 30.00 80.00
PHMN Markus Naslund 20.00 50.00
PHMS Mats Sundin 20.00 50.00
PHMT Marty Turco 20.00 50.00
PHPK Paul Kariya 20.00 50.00
PHPR Patrick Roy 75.00 200.00
PHRB Ray Bourque 40.00 100.00
PHRT Ron Tugnutt 20.00 50.00
PHSA Sergei Samsonov 20.00 50.00
PHSB Sean Burke 20.00 50.00
PHSF Sergei Fedorov 30.00 80.00
PHSG Simon Gagne 20.00 50.00
PHSS Steve Sullivan 20.00 50.00
PHSY Steve Yzerman 50.00 120.00
PHTH Joe Thornton 30.00 80.00
PHTS Teemu Selanne 20.00 50.00
PHWG Wayne Gretzky 125.00 300.00
PHZP Zigmund Palffy 20.00 50.00

2002-03 UD Piece of History Simply the Best

COMPLETE SET (6) 20.00 40.00
STATED ODDS 1:24
SB1 Ray Bourque 1.25 3.00
SB2 Bobby Orr 4.00 10.00
SB3 Patrick Roy 3.00 8.00
SB4 Steve Yzerman 3.00 8.00
SB5 Gordie Howe 3.00 8.00
SB6 Wayne Gretzky 4.00 10.00

2002-03 UD Piece of History Stellar Stitches Jerseys

STATED ODDS 1:168 HOBBY PACKS
SSJS Joe Sakic 6.00 15.00
SSJT Joe Thornton 8.00 20.00
SSMM Mike Modano 8.00 20.00
SSMS Mats Sundin 8.00 20.00
SSPK Paul Kariya 10.00 25.00
SSSY Steve Yzerman 15.00 40.00

2002-03 UD Piece of History Threads Jerseys

STATED ODDS 1:96 RETAIL PACKS
TTCD Chris Drury 4.00 10.00
TTCL Claude Lemieux 5.00 12.00
TTJT Jose Theodore 6.00 15.00
TTSF Sergei Fedorov 8.00 20.00
TTSG Simon Gagne 5.00 12.00
TTSH Scott Hartnell 5.00 12.00

2001-02 UD Playmakers

This 145-card set was released in early April and had a SRP of $2.99. The card front featured the a color photo of the player with his name, number and team in team colors in the lower right corner. The left side of the card fronts also were colored the featured team's color. Rookies in this set were short printed out of 1250.

COMP.SET w/o SP's (100) 8.00 20.00
1 Steve Shields .12 .30
2 Jeff Friesen .10 .25
3 Paul Kariya .20 .50
4 Ray Ferraro .10 .25
5 Milan Hnilicka .12 .30
6 Dany Heatley .15 .40
7 Sergei Samsonov .12 .30
8 Joe Thornton .20 .50
9 Byron Dafoe .12 .30
10 Hal Gill .10 .25
11 Miroslav Satan .12 .30
12 Stu Barnes .12 .30
13 Martin Biron .12 .30
14 Marc Savard .10 .25
15 Roman Turek .12 .30
16 Jarome Iginla .15 .40
17 Jeff O'Neill .10 .25
18 Sami Kapanen .10 .25
19 Arturs Irbe .12 .30
20 Steve Sullivan .10 .25
21 Jocelyn Thibault .12 .30
22 Tony Amonte .12 .30
23 Joe Sakic .25 .60
24 Milan Hejduk .12 .30
25 Chris Drury .12 .30
26 Patrick Roy .40 1.00
27 Rob Blake .15 .40
28 Marc Denis .12 .30
29 Ray Whitney .10 .25
30 Rostislav Klesla .10 .25
31 Ed Belfour .15 .40
32 Pierre Turgeon .15 .40
33 Mike Modano .25 .60
34 Brett Hull .20 .50
35 Dominik Hasek .25 .60
36 Brendan Shanahan .20 .50
37 Luc Robitaille .15 .40
38 Steve Yzerman .50 1.25
39 Mike Comrie .12 .30
40 Tommy Salo .12 .30
41 Ryan Smyth .12 .30
42 Anson Carter .12 .30
43 Valeri Bure .10 .25
44 Roberto Luongo .25 .60
45 Pavel Bure .20 .50
46 Felix Potvin .25 .60
47 Jason Allison .12 .30
48 Zigmund Palffy .15 .40
49 Manny Fernandez .12 .30
50 Marian Gaborik .25 .60
51 Andrew Brunette .10 .25
52 Yanic Perreault .10 .25
53 Jose Theodore .15 .40
54 Brian Savage .10 .25
55 David Legwand .12 .30
56 Mike Dunham .12 .30
57 Cliff Ronning .10 .25
58 Martin Brodeur .30 .75
59 Patrik Elias .15 .40
60 Jason Arnott .12 .30
61 Alexei Yashin .12 .30
62 Chris Osgood .15 .40
63 Mark Parrish .10 .25
64 Theo Fleury .20 .50
65 Brian Leetch .15 .40
66 Mark Messier .25 .60
67 Eric Lindros .25 .60
68 Radek Bonk .10 .25
69 Marian Hossa .12 .30
70 Martin Havlat .12 .30
71 John LeClair .15 .40
72 Mark Recchi .20 .50
73 Roman Cechmanek .12 .30
74 Jeremy Roenick .15 .40
75 Michal Handzus .10 .25
76 Shane Doan .12 .30
77 Sean Burke .10 .25
78 Alexei Kovalev .12 .30
79 Mario Lemieux .50 1.25
80 Johan Hedberg .12 .30
81 Owen Nolan .15 .40
82 Teemu Selanne .30 .75
83 Evgeni Nabokov .12 .30
84 Chris Pronger .12 .30
85 Pavol Demitra .20 .50
86 Keith Tkachuk .15 .40
87 Doug Weight .15 .40
88 Vincent Lecavalier .12 .30
89 Brad Richards .15 .40
90 Nikolai Khabibulin .15 .40
91 Wade Belak .12 .30
92 Alexander Mogilny .12 .30
93 Mats Sundin .15 .40
94 Curtis Joseph .15 .40
95 Brendan Morrison .12 .30
96 Trevor Linden .15 .40
97 Markus Naslund .15 .40
98 Peter Bondra .15 .40
99 Olaf Kolzig .15 .40
100 Jaromir Jagr .40 1.00
101 Timo Parssinen RC 1.25 3.00
102 Ilja Bryzgalov RC 2.50 6.00
103 Mike Weaver RC 1.00 2.50
104 Ilya Kovalchuk RC 5.00 12.00
105 Ivan Huml RC 1.00 2.50
106 Tony Tuzzolino RC 1.00 2.50
107 Jukka Hentunen RC 1.00 2.50
108 Scott Nichol RC 1.00 2.50
109 Erik Cole RC 2.00 5.00
110 Mike Peluso RC 1.00 2.50
111 Riku Hahl RC 1.00 2.50
112 Vaclav Nedorost RC 1.00 2.50
113 Blake Bellefeuille RC 1.00 2.50
114 Niko Kapanen RC 1.50 4.00
115 John Erskine RC 1.00 2.50
116 Pavel Datsyuk RC 5.00 12.00
117 Ty Conklin RC 1.50 4.00
118 Jason Chimera RC 1.00 2.50
119 Niklas Hagman RC 1.25 3.00
120 Kristian Huselius RC 1.50 4.00
121 Kip Brennan RC 1.00 2.50
122 Pascal Dupuis RC 1.50 4.00
123 Marcel Hossa RC 1.50 4.00
124 Olivier Michaud RC 1.50 4.00
125 Martin Erat RC 1.50 4.00
126 Christian Berglund RC 1.25 3.00
127 Andreas Salomonsson RC 1.00 2.50
128 Raffi Torres RC 1.50 4.00
129 Radek Martinek RC 1.00 2.50
130 Mikael Samuelsson RC 1.25 3.00
131 Dan Blackburn RC 1.25 3.00
132 Toni Dahlman RC 1.00 2.50
133 Bruno St. Jacques RC 1.00 2.50
134 Tomas Divisek RC 1.25 3.00
135 Jiri Dopita RC 1.00 2.50
136 Krys Kolanos RC 1.00 2.50
137 Eric Meloche RC 1.00 2.50
138 Tom Kostopoulos RC 1.00 2.50
139 Jeff Jillson RC 1.00 2.50
140 Mark Rycroft RC 1.25 3.00
141 Josef Boumedienne RC 1.00 2.50
142 Nikita Alexeev RC 1.00 2.50
143 Mike Farrell RC 1.00 2.50
144 Todd Rohloff RC 1.00 2.50
145 Brian Sutherby RC 1.00 2.50

2001-02 UD Playmakers Bobble Heads

Inserted at one per hobby box, this 24-figure set featured 12 players in both home and away jerseys.

CJA Curtis Joseph 5.00 12.00
CJH Curtis Joseph 5.00 12.00
DHA Dominik Hasek 5.00 12.00
DHH Dominik Hasek 5.00 12.00
DWA Doug Weight 5.00 12.00
DWH Doug Weight 5.00 12.00
ELA Eric Lindros 5.00 12.00
ELH Eric Lindros 5.00 12.00
IKA Ilya Kovalchuk 10.00 25.00
IKH Ilya Kovalchuk 10.00 25.00
JJA Jaromir Jagr 5.00 12.00
JJH Jaromir Jagr 5.00 12.00
JSA Joe Sakic 5.00 12.00
JSH Joe Sakic 5.00 12.00
MBA Martin Brodeur 5.00 12.00
MBH Martin Brodeur 5.00 12.00
MMA Mike Modano 5.00 12.00
MMH Mike Modano 5.00 12.00
PBA Pavel Bure 5.00 12.00
PBH Pavel Bure 5.00 12.00
PRA Patrick Roy 10.00 25.00
PRH Patrick Roy 10.00 25.00
SYA Steve Yzerman 10.00 25.00
SYH Steve Yzerman 10.00 25.00

2001-02 UD Playmakers Bobble Heads Autographed

Inserted at one per case, these bobble head figures parallel the regular set but also include authentic player autographs on the base.

EACH PLAYER HAS HOME/AWAY FIGURES
CJA Curtis Joseph 30.00 80.00
CJH Curtis Joseph 30.00 80.00
DWA Doug Weight 12.50 30.00
DWH Doug Weight 12.50 30.00
IKA Ilya Kovalchuk 30.00 80.00
IKH Ilya Kovalchuk 30.00 80.00
MBA Martin Brodeur 40.00 100.00
MBH Martin Brodeur 40.00 100.00
PBA Pavel Bure 25.00 60.00
PBH Pavel Bure 25.00 60.00
SYA Steve Yzerman 30.00 80.00
SYH Steve Yzerman 30.00 80.00

2001-02 UD Playmakers Combo Jerseys

Serial-numbered to 100 copies each, this 10-card set featured dual game-worn jersey swatches of the given player. A gold parallel was also created and serial-numbered to 50.

*GOLD/50: .8X TO 2X BASIC COMBO
CJJI Jarome Iginla 12.50 30.00
CJJL John LeClair 10.00 25.00
CJMA Maxim Afinogenov 10.00 25.00
CJMD Mike Dunham 10.00 25.00
CJMH Milan Hejduk 10.00 25.00
CJMR Mark Recchi 10.00 25.00
CJPK Paul Kariya 10.00 25.00
CJPR Patrick Roy 25.00 60.00
CJRB Rob Blake 10.00 25.00
CJSG Simon Gagne 12.50 30.00

2001-02 UD Playmakers Jerseys

Inserted at 1:72, this 10-card set featured swatches of game-used jerseys of the featured players. A gold parallel was also created and serial-numbered out of 100.

*GOLD/100: .6X TO 1.5X BASIC JSY
JJI Jarome Iginla 6.00 15.00
JMA Maxim Afinogenov 5.00 12.00
JMB Martin Brodeur 8.00 20.00
JML Mario Lemieux 12.00 30.00
JMR Mark Recchi 5.00 12.00
JPF Peter Forsberg 6.00 15.00
JRT Ron Tugnutt 5.00 12.00
JSG Simon Gagne 5.00 12.00
JTS Teemu Selanne 5.00 12.00
JZP Zigmund Palffy 5.00 12.00

2001-02 UD Playmakers Practice Jerseys

Inserted at 1:48, this 10-card set featured swatches of practice jerseys from the given player. A gold parallel was also created and serial-numbered to 200 copies each.

*GOLD/200: .6X TO 1.5X BASIC JSY
PJEB Ed Belfour 6.00 15.00
PJJI Jarome Iginla 8.00 20.00
PJJL John LeClair 6.00 15.00
PJMH Milan Hejduk 6.00 15.00
PJMO Maxime Ouellet 5.00 12.00
PJMS Miroslav Satan 5.00 12.00
PJRB Rod Brind'Amour 5.00 12.00
PJRF Rico Fata 5.00 12.00
PJSG Simon Gagne 6.00 15.00
PJTB Tyler Bouck 5.00 12.00

2001-02 UD Premier Collection

Released in early June, Premier Collection carried a SRP of $100 per pack. Each pack contained a memorabilia card, an autographed card, a serial-numbered rookie card as well as serial-numbered base cards. The base set was made up of 114 cards total, cards 1-87 were serial-numbered to 399, cards 88-108 were serial-numbered to 250 and cards 109-114 were serial-numbered to 199.

1 Paul Kariya 1.25 3.00
2 Dany Heatley 1.00 2.50
3 Joe Thornton 1.25 3.00
4 Ray Bourque 1.50 4.00
5 Bobby Orr 3.00 8.00
6 Sergei Samsonov .75 2.00
7 Tim Connolly .60 1.50
8 Jarome Iginla 1.00 2.50
9 Arturs Irbe .75 2.00
10 Jocelyn Thibault .75 2.00
11 Joe Sakic 1.50 4.00
12 Patrick Roy 2.50 6.00
13 Peter Forsberg 1.25 3.00
14 Chris Drury .75 2.00
15 Milan Hejduk .75 2.00
16 Rostislav Klesla .60 1.50
17 Mike Modano 1.50 4.00
18 Ed Belfour 1.00 2.50
19 Gordie Howe 3.00 8.00
20 Brendan Shanahan 1.25 3.00
21 Steve Yzerman 3.00 8.00
22 Brett Hull 1.25 3.00
23 Dominik Hasek 1.50 4.00
24 Sergei Fedorov 1.50 4.00
25 Wayne Gretzky 5.00 12.00
26 Tommy Salo .75 2.00
27 Roberto Luongo 1.50 4.00
28 Felix Potvin 1.50 4.00
29 Marian Gaborik 1.50 4
30 Jose Theodore 1.00 2
31 Mike Dunham .75 2
32 Martin Brodeur 2.00 5
33 Alexei Yashin .75 2
34 Eric Lindros 1.50 4
35 Pavel Bure 1.25 3
36 Marian Hossa .75 2
37 Jeremy Roenick 1.00 2
38 John LeClair 1.00 2
39 Simon Gagne 1.00 2
40 Sean Burke .60 1
41 Mario Lemieux 3.00 8
42 Evgeni Nabokov .75 2
43 Teemu Selanne 2.00 5
44 Keith Tkachuk 1.00 2
45 Chris Pronger .75 2
46 Brad Richards 1.00 2
47 Curtis Joseph 1.00 2
48 Mats Sundin 1.00 2
49 Markus Naslund 1.00 2
50 Jaromir Jagr 2.50 6
51 Timo Parssinen RC 4.00 10
52 Ben Simon RC 4.00 10
53 Frederic Cassivi RC 3.00 8
54 Ales Kotalik RC 6.00 15
55 Mike Peluso RC 3.00 8
56 Steve Moore RC 5.00 12
57 Martin Spanhel RC 3.00 8
58 Matt Davidson RC 3.00 8
59 Mathieu Darche RC 5.00 12
60 Duvie Westcott RC 3.00 8
61 Blake Bellefeuille RC 3.00 8
62 Ty Conklin RC 5.00 12
63 Stephen Weiss RC 8.00 20
64 Jaroslav Bednar RC 3.00 8
65 Pascal Dupuis RC 5.00 12
66 Nick Schultz RC 3.00 8
67 Travis Roche RC 3.00 8
68 Nathan Perrott RC 3.00 8
69 Scott Clemmensen RC 3.00 8
70 Andreas Salomonsson RC 3.00 8
71 Stanislav Gron RC 3.00 8
72 Radek Martinek RC 3.00 8
73 Mikael Samuelsson RC 4.00 10
74 Toni Dahlman RC 3.00 8
75 Bruno St. Jacques RC 3.00 8
76 Tomas Divisek RC 4.00 10
77 Vaclav Pletka RC 3.00 8
78 Eric Meloche RC 3.00 8
79 Tom Kostopoulos RC 3.00 8
80 Mark Rycroft RC 4.00 10
81 Martin Cibak RC 3.00 8
82 Josef Boumedienne RC 3.00 8
83 Karel Pilar RC 3.00 8
84 Sebastien Centomo RC 3.00 8
85 Justin Kurtz RC 5.00 12
86 Ivan Ciernik RC 3.00 8
87 Chris Corrinet RC 3.00 8
88 Ilja Bryzgalov RC 10.00 25
89 Pasi Nurminen RC 4.00 10
90 Ivan Huml RC 4.00 10
91 Erik Cole RC 8.00 20
92 Tyler Arnason RC 5.00 12
93 Riku Hahl RC 4.00 10
94 Niko Kapanen RC 6.00 15
95 Pavel Datsyuk RC 150.00 225
96 Sean Avery RC 4.00 10
97 Niklas Hagman RC 5.00 12
98 Olivier Michaud RC 6.00 15
99 Marcel Hossa RC 6.00 15
100 Martin Erat RC 6.00 15
101 Christian Berglund RC 5.00 12
102 Lukas Krajicek RC 4.00 10
103 Jiri Dopita RC 4.00 10
104 Branko Radivojevic RC 4.00 10
105 Shane Endicott RC 4.00 10
106 Jeff Jillson RC 4.00 10
107 Nikita Alexeev RC 4.00 10
108 Brian Sutherby RC 4.00 10
109 Ilya Kovalchuk AU RC 250.00 400
110 Vaclav Nedorost AU RC 8.00 20
111 Kristian Huselius AU RC 12.00 30
112 Raffi Torres AU RC 12.00 30
113 Dan Blackburn AU RC 10.00 25
114 Krys Kolanos AU RC 8.00 20

2001-02 UD Premier Collectio Dual Jerseys

Serial-numbered to just 100 copies each, this 35-c set featured dual-swatches of game-worn jerseys fr the pictured players. A black parallel to this set was also created and serial-numbered to 50 copies each Black parallels could be identified by both numberi and a small black square in the lower right hand sic each card front.

*BLACK/50: .5X TO 1.2X BASIC DUAL
DAT T.Amonte/J.Thibault 8.00 20
DBA P.Bure/M.Afinogenov 8.00 20
DBB R.Bourque/R.Blake 15.00 40
DBP R.Blake/C.Pronger 8.00 20
DCB R.Cechmanek/B.Boucher 8.00 20
DDM C.Drury/M.Modano 12.00 30
DDP A.Deadmarsh/F.Potvin 15.00 40
DFB S.Fedorov/P.Bure 12.00 30
DFD P.Forsberg/C.Drury 15.00 40
DGH W.Gretzky/B.Hull 30.00 80
DGK W.Gretzky/P.Kariya 25.00 60
DGL W.Gretzky/M.Lemieux 50.00 125
DGM W.Gretzky/M.Messier 50.00 125
DHC D.Hasek/R.Cechmanek 12.00 30
DHG G.Howe/W.Gretzky 50.00 125
DHJ M.Hejduk/J.Jagr 12.00 30
DJB J. Jagr/P.Bondra 12.00 30
DJP C.Joseph/F.Potvin 8.00 20
DKI P.Kariya/J.Iginla 12.00 30
DKS P.Kariya/J.Sakic 12.00 30
DLH N.Lidstrom/D.Hasek 15.00 40
DLK M.Lemieux/P.Kariya 15.00 40
DLR B.Leetch/M.Richter 8.00 20
DMB M.Modano/E.Belfour 12.50 30
DRB P.Roy/M.Brodeur 30.00 80
DRJ M.Richter/C.Joseph 8.00 20
DSN T.Selanne/V.Nieminen 8.00 20
DSP T.Selanne/Z.Palffy 8.00 20
DSR J.Sakic/P.Roy 20.00 50
DST S.Samsonov/J.Thornton 12.00 30
DSY B.Shanahan/S.Yzerman 20.00 50
DTB J.Thibault/S.Burke 8.00 20
DTN J.Thornton/J.Nieuwendyk 12.00 30
DBTE M.Brodeur/J.Theodore 15.00 40
DBTO R.Bourque/J.Thornton 12.50 30

2001-02 UD Premier Collectio Jerseys

This 44-card set featured game-worn jersey swatch of the pictured players. Bronze cards carried a bron logo and were serial-numbered to 300 copies each Silver cards carried a silver logo and were serial-numbered to 150 copies each. Gold cards carried a gold logo and were serial-numbered to 50 each.

LACK BRNZ/150: .5X TO 1.2X BASIC JSY
LACK SILVER/75: .5X TO 1.2X BASIC JSY
S Brendan Shanahan B 5.00 12.00
U Pavel Bure B 5.00 12.00
D Chris Drury B 5.00 12.00
B Ed Belfour B 5.00 12.00
L Eric Lindros B 5.00 12.00
K Ilya Kovalchuk B 8.00 20.00
A Jaromir Jagr B 8.00 20.00
I Jarome Iginla B 6.00 15.00
J Jaromir Jagr B 8.00 20.00
L John LeClair B 5.00 12.00
S Joe Sakic B 8.00 20.00
T Jose Theodore B 6.00 15.00
H Milan Hejduk B 5.00 12.00
R Mike Richter B 5.00 12.00
S Mats Sundin B 5.00 12.00
K Olaf Kolzig B 5.00 12.00
B Peter Bondra B 5.00 12.00
F Peter Forsberg B 8.00 20.00
K Paul Kariya B 5.00 12.00
R Patrick Roy B 12.00 30.00
B Ray Bourque B 10.00 25.00
F Sergei Fedorov B 6.00 15.00
G Simon Gagne B 5.00 12.00
K Saku Koivu B 5.00 12.00
S Sergei Samsonov B 5.00 12.00
A Tony Amonte B 5.00 12.00
F Theo Fleury B 5.00 12.00
S Teemu Selanne B 5.00 12.00
G Wayne Gretzky B 25.00 60.00
P Zigmund Palffy B 5.00 12.00
J Curtis Joseph S 10.00 25.00
H Dominik Hasek S 12.00 30.00
S Joe Sakic S 15.00 40.00
T Joe Thornton S 12.50 30.00
B Martin Brodeur S 15.00 40.00
M Mike Modano S 12.50 30.00
K Paul Kariya S 12.00 30.00
H Bobby Hull G 15.00 40.00
H Gordie Howe G 30.00 80.00
L Mario Lemieux G 30.00 80.00
R Patrick Roy G 15.00 40.00
B Ray Bourque G 25.00 60.00
Y Steve Yzerman G 30.00 80.00
G Wayne Gretzky G 50.00 125.00

2001-02 UD Premier Collection Signatures

erted with overall odds of 1 per pack, this 40 card featured authentic player autographs under full or action photos. Bronze, silver and gold subsets ld be identified by the color of the foil in the Upper k logo and a small rectangle at the bottom of each d front. Though not explicitly stated, the silver and d versions are thought to be more scarce than the nze.

LACK BRNZ/100: .6X TO 1.5X BASIC AU
LACK SLVR/50: 1X TO 2.5X BASIC AU
rturs Irbe B 4.00 10.00
Alexei Kovalev B 4.00 10.00
Martin Biron B 4.00 10.00
Marian Hossa B 6.00 15.00
Johan Hedberg B 4.00 10.00
Jose Theodore B 10.00 25.00
Mike Comrie B 5.00 12.00
Marian Gaborik B 6.00 15.00
Martin Havlat B 4.00 10.00
Markus Naslund B 6.00 15.00
Rostislav Klesla B 4.00 10.00
Raffi Torres B 5.00 12.00
Tommy Salo B 4.00 10.00
Tony Amonte B 4.00 10.00
Rob Blake S 6.00 15.00
Cam Neely S 15.00 40.00
Dany Heatley S 10.00 25.00
Doug Weight S 8.00 20.00
Felix Potvin S 10.00 25.00
Milan Hejduk S 8.00 20.00
arome Iginla S 10.00 25.00
ohn LeClair S 12.00 30.00
Mike Bossy S 10.00 25.00
Olaf Kolzig S 6.00 15.00
Peter Bondra S 8.00 20.00
Simon Gagne S 8.00 20.00
Zigmund Palffy S 6.00 15.00
Bobby Hull G 20.00 50.00
Bobby Orr G 125.00 250.00
D.Blackburn/M.Richter G 10.00 25.00
Curtis Joseph G 10.00 25.00
Gordie Howe G 40.00 100.00
Wayne Gretzky G 125.00 250.00
ya Kovalchuk G 10.00 25.00
Thornton/S.Samsonov G 20.00 50.00
Patrick Roy G 40.00 80.00
Ray Bourque G 20.00 50.00
Steve Yzerman G 30.00 80.00
eemu Selanne G 10.00 25.00
Wayne Gretzky G 125.00 250.00

001-02 UD Premier Collection Tribute to 500

ited to just 50 copies, this single-card set lighted the career wins of Patrick Roy. Each card ed a swatch of game jersey from both Montreal Colorado.

trick Roy Col./Mon. 75.00 200.00

002-03 UD Premier Collection

ased in April, this 103-card set featured serial-bered base cards and three different levels of le cards. Due to printing errors, several card bers were duplicated or excluded. Duplicate card bers are denoted below with a an "A" or "B" suffix, gh those letters did not appear on the cards. Cards 2 and 88-98 were serial-numbered to 399 sets. s #73-77 and 99-103 carried certified player graphs and were serial-numbered to 199. Cards -84 carried certified autographs and swatches of y patches. Patch/auto cards were serial-numbered copies each.

ul Kariya 2.00 5.00
a Kovalchuk 2.00 5.00
ny Heatley 1.50 4.00
ron Dafoe 1.25 3.00
e Thornton 2.00 5.00
f Hackett 1.25 3.00
rgei Samsonov 1.25 3.00
8 Miroslav Satan 1.50 4.00
9 Jarome Iginla 1.50 4.00
10 Ron Francis 2.00 5.00
11 Tyler Arnason 1.50 4.00
12 Jocelyn Thibault 1.25 3.00
13 Peter Forsberg 2.00 5.00
14 Joe Sakic 2.50 6.00
15 Patrick Roy 4.00 10.00
16 Milan Hejduk 1.25 3.00
17 Marc Denis 1.25 3.00
18 Mike Modano 2.50 6.00
19 Bill Guerin 1.50 4.00
20 Marty Turco 1.50 4.00
21 Steve Yzerman 3.00 8.00
22 Curtis Joseph 1.50 4.00
23 Brendan Shanahan 2.00 5.00
24 Nicklas Lidstrom 1.50 4.00
25 Mike Comrie 1.50 4.00
26 Stephen Weiss 1.50 4.00
27 Roberto Luongo 2.50 6.00
28 Zigmund Palffy 1.50 4.00
29 Marian Gaborik 2.50 6.00
30 Saku Koivu 1.50 4.00
31 Jose Theodore 1.50 4.00
32 David Legwand 1.25 3.00
33 Martin Brodeur 3.00 8.00
34 Michael Peca 1.25 3.00
35 Alexei Kovalev 1.50 4.00
36 Eric Lindros 2.50 6.00
37 Pavel Bure 2.00 5.00
38 Mike Dunham 1.25 3.00
39 Marian Hossa 1.25 3.00
40 Jeremy Roenick 1.50 4.00
41 John LeClair 1.50 4.00
42 Tony Amonte 1.25 3.00
43 Mario Lemieux 5.00 12.00
44A Sebastien Caron 1.25 3.00
44B Martin Gerber RC 4.00 10.00
45A Evgeni Nabokov 1.25 3.00
45B Tim Thomas RC 10.00 25.00
46A Kyle McLaren 1.00 2.50
46B Ryan Miller RC 15.00 40.00
47A Keith Tkachuk 1.50 4.00
47B Jordan Leopold RC 4.00 10.00
48A Vincent Lecavalier 1.25 3.00
48B Shaone Morrisonn RC 2.50 6.00
49A Nikolai Khabibulin 1.50 4.00
49B Levente Szuper RC 4.00 10.00
50 Mats Sundin 1.50 4.00
51A Ed Belfour 1.50 4.00
51B Jim Fahey RC 2.50 6.00
52A Todd Bertuzzi 1.50 4.00
52B Dmitri Bykov RC 2.50 6.00
53 Markus Naslund 1.25 3.00
54 Jaromir Jagr 4.00 10.00
55 Olaf Kolzig 1.50 4.00
56A Wayne Gretzky/299 8.00 20.00
56B Mike Cammalleri RC 8.00 20.00
57A Bobby Orr/299 12.50 30.00
57B Stephane Veilleux RC 2.50 6.00
58A Gordie Howe/299 5.00 12.00
58B Rickard Wallin RC 2.50 6.00
59A Ray Bourque/299 2.50 6.00
59B Vernon Fiddler RC 3.00 8.00
60A Alexei Semenov RC 2.50 6.00
60B Darren Haydar RC 2.50 6.00
61 Anton Volchenkov RC 2.50 6.00
62 Patrick Sharp RC 8.00 20.00
63 Dennis Seidenberg RC 4.00 10.00
64 Tomas Malec RC 2.50 6.00
65 Craig Andersson RC 8.00 20.00
66 Cody Rudkowsky RC 2.50 6.00
67A Ari Ahonen RC 2.50 6.00
67B Curtis Sanford RC 4.00 10.00
68 Adam Hall RC 2.50 6.00
69 Carlo Colaiacovo RC 4.00 10.00
70A Dick Tarnstrom RC 2.50 6.00
70B Steve Eminger RC 2.50 6.00
71A Jamie Hodson RC 2.50 6.00
71B Alexei Smirnov AU RC 8.00 20.00
72A Jarret Stoll RC 10.00 25.00
72B P-M Bouchard AU RC 12.50 30.00
73 Ron Hainsey AU RC 6.00 15.00
74 Pascal Leclaire AU RC 10.00 25.00
75 Scottie Upshall AU RC 8.00 20.00
76 Jeff Taffe AU RC 6.00 15.00
77 Mikael Tellqvist AU RC 6.00 15.00
78 S.Chistov JSY AU RC 15.00 40.00
79 C.Kobasew JSY AU RC 20.00 50.00
80 Rick Nash JSY AU RC 250.00 450.00
81 H.Zetterberg JSY AU RC 250.00 450.00
82 Bouwmeester JSY AU RC 50.00 125.00
83 J.Spezza JSY AU RC 80.00 200.00
84 A.Svitov JSY AU RC 15.00 40.00
88 Jerred Smithson RC 2.50 6.00
89 Jim Vandermeer RC 2.50 6.00
90 Michael Leighton RC 4.00 10.00
91 Ray Emery RC 8.00 20.00
92 Tomas Zizka RC 2.50 6.00
93 Bobby Allen RC 2.50 6.00
94 Kris Vernarsky RC 2.50 6.00
95 Cristobal Huet RC 5.00 12.00
96 Fernando Pisani RC 2.50 6.00
97 Jonathan Hedstrom RC 2.50 6.00
98 Konstantin Koltsov RC 3.00 8.00
99 Ales Hemsky AU RC 25.00 60.00
100 Steve Ott AU RC 12.00 30.00
101 Alexander Frolov AU RC 20.00 50.00
102 Brooks Orpik AU RC 10.00 25.00
103 Jared Aulin AU RC 6.00 15.00

2002-03 UD Premier Collection Gold

This 58-card skip-numbered set paralleled the rookie checklist of the base set but carried gold highlights and different serial-numbering. Cards #44-70, 71A, 72A and 88-98 were serial-numbered to 199. Autographed cards #71B, 72B, 73-77 and 99-103 were serial-numbered to 25. Patch autographs cards 78-84 were serial-numbered to just 15 copies.

*GOLD: .5X TO 1.2X BASIC RC
*71B,72B/73-77/99-103 AU/25: .6X TO 1.5X
*78-84 JSY AU/15: .6X TO 1.5X

2002-03 UD Premier Collection Jerseys Bronze

Single swatch jersey cards in this 58-card set were serial-numbered to 299. Dual jersey cards were serial numbered to 99.

AA Ari Ahonen 2.00 5.00
AK Alexei Kovalev 2.00 5.00
AS Alexander Svitov 2.00 5.00
AV Anton Volchenkov 2.00 5.00
AX Alexei Semenov 2.00 5.00
BO Brooks Orpik 3.00 8.00
BS Brendan Shanahan 3.00 8.00
CD Chris Drury 3.00 8.00
CJ Curtis Joseph 6.00 15.00
EL Eric Lindros 4.00 10.00
GM Glen Murray 3.00 8.00
IK Ilya Kovalchuk 6.00 15.00
JG Jaromir Jagr 8.00 20.00
JI Jarome Iginla 6.00 15.00
JJ Jaromir Jagr 8.00 20.00
JK Jeremy Roenick 6.00 15.00
JR Jeremy Roenick 6.00 15.00
JS Joe Sakic 8.00 20.00
JT Jose Theodore 6.00 15.00
MB Martin Brodeur 12.50 30.00
MC Mike Comrie 2.00 5.00
MH Milan Hejduk 4.00 10.00
ML Mario Lemieux 15.00 30.00
MM Mike Modano 6.00 15.00
MO Mike Modano 6.00 15.00
MS Mats Sundin 4.00 10.00
OK Olaf Kolzig 4.00 10.00
PB Pavel Bure 4.00 10.00
PF Peter Forsberg 8.00 20.00
PG Peter Forsberg 8.00 20.00
PK Paul Kariya 4.00 10.00
PL Pascal Leclaire 8.00 20.00
PR Patrick Roy 15.00 30.00
RB Ray Bourque 6.00 15.00
SF Sergei Fedorov 6.00 15.00
SG Simon Gagne 4.00 10.00
SK Saku Koivu 4.00 10.00
SO Steve Ott 2.00 5.00
SS Sergei Samsonov 2.00 5.00
SV Sergei Fedorov 6.00 15.00
SY Steve Yzerman 12.50 30.00
TF Theo Fleury 3.00 8.00
TH Joe Thornton 8.00 20.00
WG Wayne Gretzky 25.00 60.00
BL P.Bure/E.Lindros 10.00 25.00
BR R.Blake/P.Roy 12.50 30.00
FH P.Forsberg/M.Hejduk 12.00 30.00
FJ S.Fedorov/C.Joseph 10.00 25.00
GL W.Gretzky/M.Lemieux 50.00 125.00
JK J.Jagr/O.Kolzig 10.00 25.00
JR J.Spezza/R.Nash 25.00 60.00
KG P.Kariya/J.Giguere 10.00 25.00
PA P.Leclaire/A.Ahonen 10.00 25.00
RG J.Roenick/S.Gagne 10.00 25.00
SR J.Sakic/S.Reinprecht 12.50 30.00
ST S.Samsonov/J.Thornton 10.00 25.00
SY B.Shanahan/S.Yzerman 15.00 40.00
TK J.Theodore/S.Koivu 10.00 25.00

2002-03 UD Premier Collection Jerseys Gold

*SNGL.JSY: .6X TO 1.5X BRONZE
SNGL.JSY PRINT RUN 50 SER.#'d SETS
*DUAL JSY: .6X TO 1.5X BRONZE
DUAL JSY PRINT RUN 25 SER.#'d SETS

2002-03 UD Premier Collection Jerseys Silver

*SNGL.JSY: .5X TO 1.25X BRONZE
SNGL.JSY PRINT RUN 99 SER.#'d SETS
*DUAL JSY: .5X TO 1.25X BRONZE
DUAL JSY PRINT RUN 50 SER.#'d SETS

2002-03 UD Premier Collection Patches

This 32-card memorabilia set was limited to 25 serial-numbered sets.

PBO Ray Bourque 75.00 200.00
PBS Brendan Shanahan 50.00 120.00
PCD Chris Drury 50.00 120.00
PCJ Curtis Joseph 50.00 120.00
PEL Eric Lindros 50.00 120.00
PGR Wayne Gretzky 200.00 350.00
PIK Ilya Kovalchuk 60.00 150.00
PJI Jarome Iginla 60.00 150.00
PJJ Jaromir Jagr 75.00 200.00
PJR Jeremy Roenick 100.00 200.00
PJS Joe Sakic 75.00 200.00
PJT Jose Theodore 60.00 150.00
PMB Martin Brodeur 125.00 300.00
PMC Mike Comrie 50.00 120.00
PMH Milan Hejduk 50.00 120.00
PML Mario Lemieux 150.00 400.00
PMM Mike Modano 60.00 150.00
PMS Mats Sundin 50.00 120.00
POK Olaf Kolzig 50.00 120.00
PPB Pavel Bure 75.00 150.00
PPF Peter Forsberg 75.00 200.00
PPK Paul Kariya 50.00 120.00
PPR Patrick Roy 125.00 300.00
PRB Ray Bourque 75.00 200.00
PSF Sergei Fedorov 60.00 150.00
PSG Simon Gagne 50.00 120.00
PSK Saku Koivu 50.00 120.00
PSS Sergei Samsonov 25.00 60.00
PSY Steve Yzerman 125.00 300.00
PTH Joe Thornton 75.00 200.00
PTS Teemu Selanne 40.00 100.00
PWG Wayne Gretzky 200.00 350.00

2002-03 UD Premier Collection Signatures Bronze

This 48-card autograph set was inserted at a rate of 1:2 packs.

SAH Adam Hall SP 5.00 12.00
SAS Alexei Smirnov 5.00 12.00
SBO Bobby Orr 60.00 120.00
SBR Pavel Brendl 5.00 12.00
SBW Jay Bouwmeester 8.00 20.00
SCK Chuck Kobasew 5.00 12.00
SDH Dany Heatley 8.00 20.00
SEB Ed Belfour 10.00 25.00
SEC Erik Cole 5.00 12.00
SGH Gordie Howe 50.00 125.00
SHZ Henrik Zetterberg 12.00 30.00
SIK Ilya Kovalchuk 12.00 30.00
SJB Jay Bouwmeester 10.00 25.00
SJI Jarome Iginla 8.00 20.00
SJL John LeClair 6.00 15.00
SJT Joe Thornton 8.00 20.00
SJW Justin Williams 5.00 12.00
SMA Maxim Afinogenov 5.00 12.00
SMB Martin Brodeur SP 30.00 80.00
SMC Mike Comrie 5.00 12.00
SMF Manny Fernandez 5.00 12.00
SMH Martin Havlat 5.00 12.00
SMN Markus Naslund 6.00 15.00
SMT Mikael Tellqvist SP 8.00 20.00
SNA Rick Nash 20.00 50.00
SNK Nikolai Khabibulin 6.00 15.00
SPB Pavel Bure SP 6.00 15.00
SPM P-M Bouchard 6.00 15.00
SPR Patrick Roy 40.00 100.00
SRA Ray Bourque 15.00 40.00
SRB Ray Bourque 15.00 40.00
SRH Ron Hainsey SP 5.00 12.00
SRN Rick Nash 15.00 40.00
SSC Stanislav Chistov 5.00 12.00
SSG Simon Gagne 6.00 15.00
SSH Scott Hartnell 6.00 15.00
SSP Jason Spezza 25.00 60.00
SSS Sergei Samsonov 5.00 12.00
SSU Scottie Upshall SP 8.00 20.00
SSV Alexander Svitov 5.00 12.00
SSY Steve Yzerman 25.00 60.00
STA Jeff Taffe SP 5.00 12.00
SWG Wayne Gretzky SP 100.00 200.00
ASJT Joe Thornton 10.00 25.00
ASDH Dany Heatley 10.00 25.00
ASJI Jarome Iginla 8.00 20.00
ASMB Martin Brodeur 30.00 80.00
ASPR Patrick Roy SP 40.00 100.00

2002-03 UD Premier Collection Signatures Gold

*GOLD: .6X TO 1.5X BRONZE
GOLD PRINT RUN 50 SER.#'d SETS

2002-03 UD Premier Collection Signatures Silver

*SILVER: .5X TO 1.2X BRONZE
SILVER PRINT RUN 125 SER.#'d SETS

2003-04 UD Premier Collection

This 121-card set featured 59 veteran base cards; 48 short-printed rookie cards (#60-104 and #118-121) serial-numbered out of 399 each and 13 rookie autograph patch cards (#105-117). Cards 105-111 were serial-numbered to 199 and cards 112-117 were serial-numbered to 99 copies each.

COMP.SET w/o SP's (59) 50.00 100.00
1 Jean-Sebastien Giguere 1.25 3.00
2 Sergei Fedorov 2.00 5.00
3 Dany Heatley 1.25 3.00
4 Ilya Kovalchuk 1.25 3.00
5 Sergei Samsonov 1.00 2.50
6 Joe Thornton 1.50 4.00
7 Andrew Raycroft 1.00 2.50
8 Chris Drury 1.00 2.50
9 Jarome Iginla 1.25 3.00
10 Justin Williams 1.00 2.50
11 Jocelyn Thibault 1.00 2.50
12 Bryan Berard 1.00 2.50
13 David Aebischer 1.00 2.50
14 Joe Sakic 2.00 5.00
15 Paul Kariya 1.50 4.00
16 Peter Forsberg 1.50 4.00
17 Rick Nash 1.25 3.00
18 Marty Turco 1.25 3.00
19 Mike Modano 2.00 5.00
20 Brett Hull 1.50 4.00
21 Pavel Datsyuk 1.50 4.00
22 Steve Yzerman 3.00 8.00
23 Raffi Torres .75 2.00
24 Ales Hemsky 1.25 3.00
25 Roberto Luongo 2.00 5.00
26 Zigmund Palffy 1.25 3.00
27 Marian Gaborik 2.00 5.00
28 Jose Theodore 1.25 3.00
29 Saku Koivu 1.25 3.00
30 Tomas Vokoun 1.00 2.50
31 Scott Stevens 1.25 3.00
32 Martin Brodeur 2.50 6.00
33 Alexei Yashin 1.00 2.50
34 Rick DiPietro 1.00 2.50
35 Jaromir Jagr 3.00 8.00
36 Mark Messier 2.00 5.00
37 Eric Lindros 2.00 5.00
38 Jason Spezza 1.25 3.00
39 Marian Hossa 1.00 2.50
40 Patrick Lalime 1.00 2.50
41 Jeremy Roenick 1.25 3.00
42 Tony Amonte 1.00 2.50
43 Mike Comrie 1.00 2.50
44 Brian Boucher 1.00 2.50
45 Mario Lemieux 4.00 10.00
46 Evgeni Nabokov 1.00 2.50
47 Chris Osgood 1.25 3.00
48 Doug Weight 1.25 3.00
49 Keith Tkachuk 1.25 3.00
50 Nikolai Khabibulin 1.25 3.00
51 Mats Sundin 1.25 3.00
52 Owen Nolan 1.00 2.50
53 Ed Belfour 1.25 3.00
54 Ron Francis 1.50 4.00
55 Ed Jovanovski 1.00 2.50
56 Markus Naslund 1.25 3.00
57 Todd Bertuzzi 1.25 3.00
58 Brendan Morrison 1.00 2.50
59 Olaf Kolzig 1.25 3.00
60 Niklas Kronwall RC 5.00 12.00
61 Derek Roy RC 4.00 10.00
62 Tim Jackman RC 3.00 8.00
63 Timofei Shishkanov RC 2.50 6.00
64 Tomas Plekanec RC 8.00 20.00
65 Aleksander Suglobov RC 2.50 6.00
66 Kyle Wellwood RC 4.00 10.00
67 Mike Smith RC 8.00 20.00
68 Anton Babchuk RC 2.50 6.00
69 Ryan Barnes RC 2.50 6.00
70 Jason Pominville RC 6.00 15.00
71 Pavel Vorobiev RC 3.00 8.00
72 Dustin Brown RC 5.00 12.00
73 Chris Higgins RC 5.00 12.00
74 Dan Hamhuis RC 3.00 8.00
75 Marek Zidlicky RC 2.50 6.00
76 Sean Bergenheim RC 3.00 8.00
77 Antoine Vermette RC 5.00 12.00
78 Milan Michalek RC 5.00 12.00
79 Brad Boyes RC 4.00 10.00
80 Alexander Semin RC 8.00 20.00
81 Carl Corazzini RC 2.50 6.00
82 Sergei Zinovjev RC 2.50 6.00
83 Julien Vauclair RC 2.50 6.00
84 John Pohl RC 2.50 6.00
85 Benoit Dusablon RC 2.50 6.00
86 Tony Salmelainen RC 2.50 6.00
87 Bryce Lampman RC 3.00 8.00
88 Trevor Daley RC 4.00 10.00
89 Dan Ellis RC 3.00 8.00
90 Zbynek Michalek RC 2.50 6.00
91 Goran Bezina RC 2.50 6.00
92 Erik Westrum RC 2.50 6.00
93 Ryan Kesler RC 12.00 30.00
94 Owen Fussey RC 2.50 6.00
95 Josh Olson RC 2.50 6.00
96 Dan Fritsche RC 2.50 6.00
97 Michal Barinka RC 2.50 6.00
98 Kari Lehtonen RC 12.00 30.00
99 Mike Stutzel RC 2.50 6.00
100 Matt Hussey RC 2.50 6.00
101 Roman Tvrdon RC 2.50 6.00
102 Matthew Yeats RC 2.50 6.00
103 Brett Lysak 2.50 6.00
104 Thomas Pock RC 3.00 8.00
105 F.Sjostrom PATCH AU RC 20.00 50.00
106 P.Sejna PATCH AU RC 15.00 40.00
107 M.Stajan PATCH AU RC 20.00 50.00
108 N.Zherdev PATCH AU RC 25.00 60.00
109 P.Bergeron PATCH AU RC 100.00 175.00
110 J.Pitkanen PATCH AU RC 15.00 40.00
111 J.Lupul PATCH AU RC 40.00 80.00
112 J.Tootoo PATCH AU RC 40.00 100.00
113 N.Horton PATCH AU RC 40.00 100.00
114 E.Staal PATCH AU RC 100.00 200.00
115 J.Hudler PATCH AU RC 30.00 80.00
116 T.Ruutu PATCH AU RC 40.00 100.00
117 M.Fleury PATCH AU RC 200.00 400.00
118 Fedor Tyutin RC 2.50 6.00
119 Denis Grebeshkov RC 2.50 6.00
120 Cory Larose RC 2.50 6.00
121 Andy Chiodo RC 2.50 6.00

2003-04 UD Premier Collection Legends Jerseys

This 6-card set featured oversized swatches of jersey from past greats. Each card was serial-numbered out of 25.

PLGL Guy Lafleur 20.00 50.00
PLMB Mike Bossy 15.00 40.00
PLMH Gordie Howe 40.00 100.00
PLPR Patrick Roy 50.00 125.00
PLSB Scotty Bowman 25.00 60.00
PLWG Wayne Gretzky 150.00 250.00

2003-04 UD Premier Collection Matchups Jerseys

This 6-card set featured dual jersey swatches of two current players. Each card was serial-numbered out of 25.

PMBT Ed Belfour 20.00 50.00
Jose Theodore
PMGB M.Gaborik/T.Bertuzzi 15.00 40.00
PMHM A.Hemsky/M.Modano 20.00 50.00
PMHR M.Hossa/J.Roenick 20.00 50.00
PMRH P.Roy/D.Hasek 25.00 60.00
PMTB J.Thornton/M.Brodeur 25.00 60.00

2003-04 UD Premier Collection Signatures

This 41-card set featured player autographs in silver paint pen on black puck-like backgrounds below a full-color player photo. Cards were inserted one per pack.

PSAC Anson Carter 6.00 15.00
PSAH Ales Hemsky 6.00 15.00
PSBO Pavel Bure SP 30.00 60.00
PSBY Mike Bossy 10.00 25.00
PSCJ Curtis Joseph 8.00 20.00
PSDA David Aebischer 6.00 15.00
PSDC Don Cherry 15.00 40.00
PSEL Eric Lindros 8.00 20.00
PSES Eric Staal 10.00 25.00
PSGL Guy Lafleur SP 20.00 50.00
PSG1 Wayne Gretzky 75.00 150.00
PSHZ Henrik Zetterberg 10.00 25.00
PSIK Ilya Kovalchuk 10.00 25.00
PSJH Jiri Hudler 6.00 15.00
PSJI Jarome Iginla 10.00 25.00
PSJR Jeremy Roenick 8.00 20.00
PSJS Jason Spezza 12.00 30.00
PSJT Joe Thornton 10.00 25.00
PSJSG Jean-Sebastien Giguere 6.00 15.00
PSJTH Jose Theodore 10.00 25.00
PSMB Martin Brodeur 40.00 100.00
PSMG Marian Gaborik 10.00 25.00
PSMH Gordie Howe 50.00 100.00
PSMT Marty Turco 6.00 15.00
PSMAF Marc-Andre Fleury 15.00 40.00
PSMAH Marian Hossa 6.00 15.00
PSMCH Marcel Hossa 6.00 15.00
PSMNH Markus Naslund 6.00 15.00
PSNH Nathan Horton 6.00 15.00
PSON Owen Nolan 6.00 15.00
PSPB Patrice Bergeron SP 20.00 50.00
PSPR Patrick Roy 60.00 125.00
PSRL Roberto Luongo 10.00 25.00
PSRN Rick Nash 12.00 30.00
PSROY Patrick Roy SP 125.00 250.00
PSSK Saku Koivu 10.00 25.00
PSTB Todd Bertuzzi 6.00 15.00
PSTR Tuomo Ruutu 5.00 12.00
PSTOO Jordin Tootoo 10.00 25.00
PSWG Wayne Gretzky 100.00 200.00
PSZP Zigmund Palffy 6.00 15.00

2003-04 UD Premier Collection Skills Jerseys

This 6-card set featured dual jersey swatches from two current players. Each card was serial-numbered out of 50.

SKBF M.Brodeur/M.Fleury 25.00 50.00
SKBT T.Bertuzzi/K.Tkachuk 12.00 30.00
SKFT P.Forsberg/J.Thornton 12.00 30.00
SKLT M.Lemieux/J.Thornton 20.00 50.00
SKRR J.Roenick/T.Ruutu 12.00 30.00
SKSY J.Sakic/S.Yzerman 25.00 60.00

2003-04 UD Premier Collection Stars Jerseys

This 35-card set featured jersey swatches inset in the die-cut letter "e" of the word Premier across the card front. Each card was serial-numbered out of 250.

*PATCH/100: 1.2X TO 3X BASIC JSY/250
STAM Alexander Mogilny 3.00 8.00
STBH Brett Hull 4.00 10.00
STDH Dan Hamhuis 3.00 8.00
STDW Doug Weight 3.00 8.00
STES Eric Staal 8.00 20.00
STGM Glenn Murray 3.00 8.00
STIK Ilya Kovalchuk 4.00 10.00
STJH Jiri Hudler 3.00 8.00
STJI Jarome Iginla 4.00 10.00
STJL Joffrey Lupul 3.00 8.00
STJS Joe Sakic 6.00 15.00
STJT Jordin Tootoo 4.00 10.00
STJSG Jean-Sebastien Giguere 3.00 8.00
STLR Luc Robitaille 3.00 8.00
STMD Marc Denis 3.00 8.00
STMF Manny Fernandez 3.00 8.00
STMH Milan Hejduk 3.00 8.00
STMN Markus Naslund 3.00 8.00
STMR Mark Recchi 3.00 8.00
STMR Mike Ribeiro 3.00 8.00
STMS Martin Straka 3.00 8.00
STMAF Marc-Andre Fleury 10.00 25.00
STNH Nathan Horton 3.00 8.00
STNZ Nikolai Zherdev 3.00 8.00
STPB Patrice Bergeron 3.00 8.00
STPD Pavol Demitra 3.00 8.00
STPK Paul Kariya 3.00 8.00
STRC Roman Cechmanek 3.00 8.00
STRL Roberto Luongo 4.00 10.00
STSF Sergei Fedorov 5.00 12.00
STSS Sergei Samsonov 3.00 8.00
STSY Steve Yzerman 6.00 15.00
STTB Todd Bertuzzi 3.00 8.00
STTR Tuomo Ruutu 3.00 8.00
STVL Vincent Lecavalier 3.00 8.00

2003-04 UD Premier Collection Super Stars Jerseys

This 6-card set featured jersey swatches of current super stars serial-numbered to 100.

*PATCH/25: 1.2X TO 3X BASIC JSY/100
SSJS Jason Spezza 12.50 30.00
SSJT Joe Thornton 12.50 30.00
SSMB Martin Brodeur 25.00 60.00
SSMG Marian Gaborik 8.00 20.00
SSML Mario Lemieux 20.00 50.00
SSPF Peter Forsberg 12.50 30.00

2003-04 UD Premier Collection Teammates Jerseys

Serial-numbered out of 100, this 30-card set featured prominent players on the 30 NHL franchises and swatches of their jerseys.

PTAM J.Giguere/S.Fedorov 8.00 20.00
PTBB1 J.Thornton/S.Samsonov 10.00 25.00
PTBB2 J.Thornton/P.Bergeron 10.00 25.00
PTCB J.Thibault/T.Ruutu 8.00 20.00
PTCH R.Francis/E.Staal 12.50 30.00
PTCA1 P.Forsberg/J.Sakic 12.50 30.00
PTCA2 T.Selanne/P.Kariya 8.00 20.00
PTCB1 R.Nash/M.Denis 8.00 20.00
PTCB2 R.Nash/N.Zherdev 8.00 20.00
PTDR1 S.Yzerman/D.Hasek 15.00 40.00
PTDR2 S.Yzerman/B.Hull 12.00 30.00
PTDS1 M.Modano/M.Turco 8.00 20.00
PTDS2 B.Guerin/M.Modano 8.00 20.00
PTEO1 W.Gretzky/M.Messier 60.00 150.00
PTEO2 R.Torres/A.Hemsky 8.00 20.00
PTFP R.Luongo/O.Jokinen 10.00 25.00
PTLK Z.Palffy/R.Cechmanek 8.00 20.00
PTMC J.Theodore/S.Koivu 10.00 25.00
PTMW M.Gaborik/M.Fernandez 8.00 20.00
PTND M.Brodeur/S.Stevens 12.50 30.00
PTNR E.Lindros/M.Messier 10.00 25.00
PTOS J.Spezza/M.Hossa 10.00 25.00
PTPP M.Lemieux/M.Fleury 25.00 60.00
PTPF1 J.Roenick/T.Amonte 8.00 20.00
PTPF2 J.Roenick/J.Pitkanen 8.00 20.00
PTSB K.Tkachuk/D.Weight 8.00 20.00
PTTL V.Lecavalier/N.Khabibulin 10.00 25.00
PTTM1 M.Sundin/O.Nolan 8.00 20.00
PTTM2 E.Belfour/M.Sundin 8.00 20.00
PTVC T.Bertuzzi/M.Naslund 10.00 25.00

2003-04 UD Premier Collection Teammates Jerseys Patches

This set paralleled the basic insert set with authentic patches. This set was serial-numbered out of 25.

*PATCHES/25: 1.5X TO 4X BASIC JSY

2000-01 UD Reserve

The 2000-01 UD Reserve complete set consisted of 120 cards - 30 of which were rookies and 2 were checklists. The base set design used silver foil for the Upper Deck logo and for highlights on the cards, and they had a light blue border on the left side of the card front. The card backs had a small photo of the player on the top half and statistics below for the past couple seasons and also contained a career statistics line. The card backs also had the UD hologram on the bottom right corner.

1 Paul Kariya .25 .60
2 Steve Rucchin .12 .30
3 Teemu Selanne .40 1.00
4 Damian Rhodes .12 .30
5 Patrik Stefan .15 .40
6 Byron Dafoe .15 .40
7 Jason Allison .15 .40
8 Joe Thornton .30 .75
9 Doug Gilmour .25 .60
10 Dominik Hasek .30 .75
11 Miroslav Satan .12 .30
12 Jarome Iginla .20 .50
13 Oleg Saprykin .12 .30
14 Valeri Bure .15 .40
15 Sandis Ozolinsh .15 .40
16 Ron Francis .25 .60
17 Sami Kapanen .12 .30
18 Steve Sullivan .12 .30
19 Alexei Zhamnov .15 .40
20 Tony Amonte .15 .40
21 Ray Bourque .30 .75
22 Patrick Roy .50 1.25
23 Peter Forsberg .25 .60
24 Joe Sakic .30 .75
25 Ron Tugnutt .15 .40
26 Steve Heinze .12 .30
27 Mike Modano .30 .75
28 Brett Hull .30 .75
29 Ed Belfour .20 .50
30 Brendan Shanahan .25 .60
31 Sergei Fedorov .30 .75
32 Steve Yzerman .60 1.50
33 Ryan Smyth .15 .40
34 Tommy Salo .15 .40
35 Doug Weight .20 .50
36 Pavel Bure .25 .60
37 Ray Whitney .15 .40
38 Roberto Luongo .30 .75
39 Luc Robitaille .20 .50
40 Zigmund Palffy .20 .50
41 Jamie Storr .15 .40
42 Jamie McLennan .12 .30
43 Jim Dowd .12 .30
44 Brian Savage .12 .30
45 Jose Theodore .25 .60
46 Saku Koivu .20 .50
47 David Legwand .20 .50
48 Cliff Ronning .12 .30
49 Tomas Vokoun .15 .40
50 Scott Gomez .15 .40
51 Patrik Elias .20 .50
52 Martin Brodeur .40 1.00
53 Tim Connolly .12 .30
54 Roman Hamrlik .15 .40
55 John Vanbiesbrouck .15 .40
56 Theo Fleury .25 .60
57 Mark Messier .30 .75
58 Brian Leetch .20 .50
59 Marian Hossa .15 .40
60 Patrick Lalime .15 .40
61 Alexei Yashin .15 .40
62 John LeClair .20 .50
63 Mark Recchi .25 .60
64 Keith Primeau .15 .40
65 Jeremy Roenick .20 .50
66 Sean Burke .12 .30
67 Keith Tkachuk .20 .50
68 Jaromir Jagr .50 1.25
69 Milan Kraft .12 .30
70 Mario Lemieux .60 1.50
71 Owen Nolan .20 .50
72 Jeff Friesen .12 .30
73 Evgeni Nabokov .15 .40
74 Chris Pronger .15 .40
75 Scott Young .12 .30
76 Roman Turek .15 .40
77 Vincent Lecavalier .15 .40
78 Brad Richards .20 .50
79 Mike Johnson .12 .30
80 Curtis Joseph .25 .60
81 Mats Sundin .20 .50
82 Sergei Berezin .12 .30
83 Markus Naslund .15 .40
84 Daniel Sedin .40 1.00
85 Henrik Sedin .30 .75
86 Chris Simon .12 .30
87 Peter Bondra .15 .40
88 Olaf Kolzig .20 .50
89 Andrew Raycroft RC .50 1.25
90 Josef Vasicek RC .50 1.25
91 David Aebischer RC .40 1.00
92 Rostislav Klesla RC .50 1.25
93 Marty Turco RC .40 1.00
94 Tyler Bouck RC .20 .50
95 Shawn Horcoff RC .40 1.00
96 Eric Belanger RC .25 .60
97 Steven Reinprecht RC .30 .75
98 Marian Gaborik RC .60 1.50
99 Peter Bartos RC .25 .60
100 Scott Hartnell RC .50 1.25
101 Greg Classen RC .20 .50
102 Chris Mason RC .40 1.00
103 Willie Mitchell RC .30 .75
104 Rick DiPietro RC .75 2.00
105 Jason Labarbera RC .25 .60
106 Jani Hurme RC .20 .50
107 Martin Havlat RC .60 1.50
108 Ruslan Fedotenko RC .20 .50
109 Justin Williams RC .50 1.25
110 Petr Hubacek RC .20 .50
111 Roman Cechmanek RC .25 .60
112 Mark Smith RC .20 .50
113 Alexander Khavanov RC .20 .50
114 Alexander Kharitonov RC .20 .50
115 Marc-Andre Thinel RC .20 .50
116 Zdenek Blatny RC .20 .50
117 Jordan Krestanovich RC .20 .50
118 Jeff Bateman RC .20 .50
119 Mark Messier CL .30 .75
120 Curtis Joseph CL .25 .60

2000-01 UD Reserve Buyback Autographs

Randomly inserted in packs at a rate of 1:239, this set features 137 different original Upper Deck cards that Upper Deck bought back and had autographed. Please note these cards have print runs that vary. Cards with print runs of less than 25 are not priced due to scarcity. The Scott Gomez cards were only found in packs as exchange cards and the actual autographed buybacks have yet to be verified. For that reason only the exchange card is priced.

SER.#'d UNDER 25 NOT PRICED
23 S.Samsonov 99MVPSC/29 8.00 20.00
25 S.Gomez 99MVPSCSS/27 12.50 25.00
37 P.Brendl 99MVPSC/301 15.00 30.00
49 M.Ribiero 97UD/52 6.00 15.00
51 M.Ribiero 99UD/25 25.00 60.00
53 M.Modano 90UD46/56 20.00 50.00
56 M.Modano 92UD305/69 20.00 50.00
63 M.Modano 96UD43/39 40.00 100.00
100 K.Tkachuk 99UD/25 75.00 200.00
103 J.Theodore 99MVPSC/356 6.00 15.00
117 H.Sedin 99MVPSC/330 10.00 25.00
129 D.Sedin 99MVPSC/329 10.00 25.00

2000-01 UD Reserve Gold Strike

COMPLETE SET (10) 10.00 25.00
STATED ODDS 1:14
GS1 Teemu Selanne 2.00 5.00
GS2 Joe Sakic 1.50 4.00
GS3 Mike Modano 1.50 4.00
GS4 Sergei Fedorov 1.50 4.00
GS5 Pavel Bure 1.25 3.00
GS6 Scott Gomez .75 2.00
GS7 Theo Fleury 1.25 3.00
GS8 Mario Lemieux 3.00 8.00
GS9 Mats Sundin 1.00 2.50
GS10 Olaf Kolzig 1.00 2.50

2000-01 UD Reserve Golden Goalies

COMPLETE SET (10) 10.00 20.00
STATED ODDS 1:14
GG1 Guy Hebert .75 2.00
GG2 Dominik Hasek 1.50 4.00
GG3 Patrick Roy 2.50 6.00
GG4 Tommy Salo .75 2.00
GG5 Jose Theodore 1.25 3.00
GG6 Mike Dunham .60 1.50
GG7 Martin Brodeur 2.00 5.00
GG8 John Vanbiesbrouck .75 2.00
GG9 Roman Turek .75 2.00
GG10 Curtis Joseph 1.25 3.00

2000-01 UD Reserve On-Ice Success

COMPLETE SET (6) 6.00 12.00
STATED ODDS 1:23
OS1 Paul Kariya .75 2.00
OS2 Tony Amonte .75 2.00
OS3 Joe Sakic 1.50 4.00
OS4 Pavel Bure 1.00 2.50
OS5 Luc Robitaille .75 2.00
OS6 Mark Messier 1.00 2.50

2000-01 UD Reserve Power Portfolios

COMPLETE SET (6) 10.00 20.00
STATED ODDS 1:23
PP1 Patrick Roy 4.00 10.00
PP2 Brett Hull 1.00 2.50
PP3 Steve Yzerman 4.00 10.00
PP4 Martin Brodeur 2.00 5.00
PP5 Mark Messier 1.00 2.50
PP6 Jaromir Jagr 1.25 3.00

2000-01 UD Reserve Practice Session Jerseys

Randomly inserted in packs at a rate of 1:239, this 10-card set featured a swatch of a practice session jersey. The set used player initials for the card numbering. Autographed variations were also created and inserted at 1:479.

CO Chris Osgood 4.00 10.00
JJ Jaromir Jagr 6.00 15.00
JL John LeClair 4.00 10.00
JT Joe Thornton 6.00 15.00
MA Mark Messier 10.00 25.00
MM Mike Modano 6.00 15.00
MR Mark Recchi 4.00 10.00
PF Peter Forsberg 6.00 15.00
TF Theo Fleury 6.00 15.00
TS Teemu Selanne 5.00 12.00

2000-01 UD Reserve Practice Session Jerseys Autographs

Randomly inserted in packs at a rate of 1:479, this 10-card set featured a swatch of a practice session jersey and an autograph. The set used player initials for the card numbering.

CO Chris Osgood 15.00 40.00
JL John LeClair 15.00 40.00
JT Joe Thornton 20.00 50.00
MA Mark Messier 30.00 80.00
MM Mike Modano 20.00 50.00
MR Mark Recchi 15.00 40.00
TF Theo Fleury 15.00 40.00
TS Teemu Selanne 15.00 40.00

2000-01 UD Reserve The Big Ticket

COMPLETE SET (10) 15.00 30.00
STATED ODDS 1:14
BT1 Paul Kariya .75 2.00
BT2 Dominik Hasek 1.50 4.00
BT3 Ray Bourque 1.50 4.00
BT4 Steve Yzerman 4.00 10.00
BT5 Pavel Bure 1.00 2.50
BT6 Marian Gaborik 3.00 8.00
BT7 Martin Brodeur 2.00 5.00
BT8 John LeClair 1.00 2.50
BT9 Jaromir Jagr 1.25 3.00
BT10 Vincent Lecavalier .75 2.00

2005-06 UD Rookie Class

COMPLETE SET (50) 12.50 30.00
1 Sidney Crosby 4.00 10.00
2 Alexander Ovechkin 2.00 5.00
3 Henrik Lundqvist 1.00 2.50
4 Marek Svatos .20 .50
5 Thomas Vanek .50 1.25
6 Brad Boyes .20 .50
7 Petr Prucha .25 .60
8 Jussi Jokinen .25 .60
9 Dion Phaneuf .40 1.00
10 Alexander Steen .50 1.25
11 Alvaro Montoya .25 .60
12 Keith Ballard .20 .50
13 Jeff Carter .40 1.00
14 Michel Ouellet .20 .50
15 Andrej Meszaros .20 .50
16 Pavel Vorobiev .15 .40
17 Mike Richards .50 1.25
18 Milan Michalek .15 .40
19 Antti Miettinen .15 .40
20 Rene Bourque .25 .60
21 Chris Campoli .15 .40
22 Gilbert Brule .25 .60
23 Andrew Ladd .30 .75
24 R.J. Umberger .25 .60
25 Hannu Toivonen .25 .60
26 Ryan Miller .25 .60
27 Kyle Wellwood .20 .50
28 Fedor Tyutin .15 .40
29 Brent Seabrook .50 1.25
30 Jim Howard .60 1.50
31 Ryan Whitney .25 .60
32 Corey Perry 1.00 2.50
33 Alexander Perezhogin .20 .50
34 Zach Parise .60 1.50
35 Peter Budaj .30 .75
36 Mikko Koivu .30 .75
37 Rostislav Olesz .20 .50
38 Ryan Getzlaf .60 1.50
39 Yann Danis .20 .50
40 Wojtek Wolski .20 .50
41 Ryan Suter .30 .75
42 Patrick Eaves .25 .60
43 Anthony Stewart .20 .50
44 Brandon Bochenski .25 .60
45 Eric Nystrom .20 .50
46 Antero Niittymaki .20 .50
47 Johan Franzen .40 1.00
48 Andrei Kostitsyn .30 .75
49 Carlo Colaiacovo .15 .40
50 Cam Ward .30 .75

2005-06 UD Rookie Class Commemorative Boxtoppers

CC1 Sidney Crosby 6.00 15.00
CC2 Alexander Ovechkin 6.00 15.00
CC3 Henrik Lundqvist 5.00 12.00
CC4 Thomas Vanek 2.50 6.00
CC5 Dion Phaneuf 2.00 5.00
CC6 Alexander Steen 2.50 6.00
CC7 Jeff Carter 2.00 5.00

2001-02 UD Stanley Cup Champs

This 86-card set was available in 3-card packs that were inserted one pack per box of various Upper Deck products. The cards featured action photos of past Stanley Cup winners.

1 Phil Esposito 2.00 5.00
2 Bobby Orr 8.00 20.00
3 Glenn Hall 1.00 2.50
4 Bobby Hull 1.50 4.00
5 Ray Bourque 1.50 4.00
6 Gordie Howe 4.00 10.00
7 Ted Lindsay .40 1.00
8 Terry Sawchuk 2.00 5.00
9 Grant Fuhr .60 1.50
10 Wayne Gretzky 5.00 12.00
11 Jari Kurri .75 2.00
12 Bill Ranford .40 1.00
13 Jean Beliveau 1.00 2.50
14 Yvan Cournoyer .75 2.00
15 Guy Lafleur 1.50 4.00
16 Jacques Plante 1.25 3.00
17 Maurice Richard 1.50 4.00
18 Henri Richard .40 1.00
19 Mike Bossy 1.25 3.00
20 Bob Nystrom .40 1.00
21 Ken Morrow .40 1.00
22 Bryan Trottier .40 1.00
23 Bobby Clarke 1.25 3.00
24 Bernie Parent .60 1.50
25 Tim Horton .40 1.00
26 Frank Mahovlich .75 2.00
27 Mike Vernon .60 1.50
28 Theo Fleury .40 1.00
29 Al MacInnis .60 1.50
30 Peter Forsberg 2.00 5.00
31 Dan Hinote .40 1.00
32 Milan Hejduk .75 2.00
33 Alex Tanguay .60 1.50
34 David Aebischer .60 1.50
35 Chris Drury .60 1.50
36 Rob Blake .60 1.50
37 Joe Sakic 1.50 4.00
38 Patrick Roy 4.00 10.00
39 Ville Nieminen .40 1.00
40 Steven Reinprecht .40 1.00
41 Adam Foote .40 1.00
42 Adam Deadmarsh .40 1.00
43 Jon Klemm .40 1.00
44 Sandis Ozolinsh .40 1.00
45 Mike Keane .40 1.00
46 Mike Modano 1.25 3.00
47 Brett Hull 1.00 2.50
48 Joe Nieuwendyk .60 1.50
49 Sergei Zubov .40 1.00
50 Ed Belfour .75 2.00
51 Derian Hatcher .40 1.00
52 Jamie Langenbrunner .40 1.00
53 Grant Marshall .40 1.00
54 Jere Lehtinen .60 1.50
55 Darryl Sydor .40 1.00
56 Sergei Fedorov 1.25 3.00
57 Steve Yzerman 4.00 10.00
58 Nicklas Lidstrom .75 2.00
59 Mathieu Dandenault .40 1.00
60 Slava Kozlov .40 1.00
61 Chris Osgood .60 1.50
62 Darren McCarty .40 1.00
63 Kirk Maltby .40 1.00
64 Brendan Shanahan .75 2.00
65 Tomas Holmstrom .40 1.00
66 John LeClair .75 2.00
67 Patrick Roy 4.00 10.00
68 Eric Desjardins .40 1.00
69 Scott Stevens .60 1.50
70 Patrik Elias .60 1.50
71 Randy McKay .40 1.00
72 Jason Arnott .40 1.00
73 Alexander Mogilny .60 1.50
74 Petr Sykora .40 1.00
75 Scott Gomez .40 1.00
76 Sergei Brylin .40 1.00
77 Bobby Holik .40 1.00
78 Martin Brodeur 2.00 5.00
79 John Madden .40 1.00
80 Scott Niedermayer .40 1.00
81 Claude Lemieux .40 1.00
82 Brian Leetch .60 1.50
83 Mike Richter .75 2.00
84 Mark Messier .75 2.00
85 Jaromir Jagr 1.25 3.00
86 Mario Lemieux 5.00 12.00

2001-02 UD Stanley Cup Champs Jerseys

Randomly inserted in box topper packs, this 20-card set featured a game-worn jersey swatch of the featured player on the card front and a congratulatory message on the card back. Each card was numbered out of 200.

TBH Brett Hull 12.00 30.00
TBL Brian Leetch 8.00 20.00
TBS Brendan Shanahan 12.00 30.00
TBT Bryan Trottier 10.00 25.00
TEB Ed Belfour 12.00 30.00
TGL Guy Lafleur 10.00 25.00
TJJ Jaromir Jagr 12.00 30.00
TJS Joe Sakic 12.00 30.00
TKM Ken Morrow 10.00 25.00
TMB Mike Bossy 8.00 20.00
TME Mark Messier 12.00 30.00
TML Mario Lemieux 20.00 50.00
TMM Mike Modano 12.00 30.00
TPF Peter Forsberg 12.00 30.00
TPR Patrick Roy 20.00 50.00
TRB Ray Bourque 10.00 25.00
TRO Patrick Roy 20.00 50.00
TSF Sergei Fedorov 15.00 40.00
TSY Steve Yzerman 12.00 30.00
TTF Theo Fleury 12.00 30.00

2001-02 UD Stanley Cup Champs Pieces of Glory

Randomly inserted in box topper packs, this 30-card set featured pieces of a game-used jersey and stick from the featured player. Each card was serial numbered out of just 50.

GBG Bill Guerin 15.00 40.00
GBH Brett Hull 30.00 80.00
GBL Brian Leetch 15.00 40.00
GBO Mike Bossy 20.00 50.00
GBR Bill Ranford 15.00 40.00
GBS Brendan Shanahan 15.00 40.00
GBT Bryan Trottier 40.00 100.00
GCL Claude Lemieux 15.00 40.00
GCO Chris Osgood 15.00 40.00
GEB Ed Belfour 15.00 40.00
GGL Guy Lafleur 50.00 125.00
GJJ Jaromir Jagr 20.00 50.00
GJN Joe Nieuwendyk 15.00 40.00
GJS Joe Sakic 40.00 100.00
GLM Lanny McDonald 15.00 40.00
GMA Mark Messier 15.00 40.00
GMB Martin Brodeur 50.00 125.00
GML Mario Lemieux 60.00 150.00
GMM Mike Modano 20.00 50.00
GMR Mike Richter 15.00 40.00
GNL Nicklas Lidstrom 15.00 40.00
GPF Peter Forsberg 25.00 60.00
GPR Patrick Roy 60.00 150.00
GRB Ray Bourque 25.00 60.00
GRO Patrick Roy 40.00 100.00
GSF Sergei Fedorov 20.00 50.00
GSY Steve Yzerman 60.00 150.00
GTF Theo Fleury 15.00 40.00
GWG Wayne Gretzky 100.00 200.00

2001-02 UD Stanley Cup Champs Sticks

Randomly inserted into box topper packs, this 29-card set featured pieces of a game-used stick of the featured player on the card front and a congratulatory message on the card back. Each card was numbered out of 150.

SAM Al MacInnis 12.50 30.00
SAT Alex Tanguay 12.50 30.00
SBG Bill Guerin 12.50 30.00
SBH Brett Hull 15.00 40.00
SBK Rob Blake 12.50 30.00
SBL Brian Leetch 12.50 30.00
SBO Mike Bossy 20.00 50.00
SBS Brendan Shanahan 12.50 30.00
SBT Bryan Trottier 12.00 30.00
SCL Claude Lemieux 12.50 30.00
SEB Ed Belfour 12.50 30.00
SGH Gordie Howe 30.00 80.00
SGL Guy Lafleur 15.00 40.00
SJJ Jaromir Jagr 15.00 40.00
SJN Joe Nieuwendyk 12.50 30.00
SJS Joe Sakic 15.00 40.00
SMB Martin Brodeur 20.00 50.00
SML Mario Lemieux 40.00 100.00
SMM Mike Modano 15.00 40.00
SMO Alexander Mogilny 12.50 30.00
SMR Mike Richter 12.50 30.00
SPF Peter Forsberg 15.00 40.00
SPR Patrick Roy 15.00 40.00
SRB Ray Bourque 15.00 40.00
SRO Patrick Roy 20.00 50.00
SSF Sergei Fedorov 15.00 40.00
SSY Steve Yzerman 30.00 80.00
STF Theo Fleury 12.50 30.00
SWG Wayne Gretzky 50.00 100.00

2002-03 UD SuperStars

This 300 card set was released in March, 2003. This set was issued in five card packs with an $3 SRP. The packs were issued in 24 pack boxes which came 12 boxes to a case. The final 50 cards of the set featured two rookies from different sports.

COMPLETE SET (300) 30.00 80.00
6 Paul Kariya .40 1.00
11 Sean Burke .20 .50
22 Ilya Kovalchuk .40 1.00
36 Bobby Orr 1.00 2.50
37 Ray Bourque .40 1.00
41 Jarome Iginla .30 .75
53 Theoren Fleury .25 .60
67 Patrick Roy .75 2.00
68 Joe Sakic .40 1.00
69 Peter Forsberg .50 1.25
75 Mike Modano .40 1.00
81 Gordie Howe .75 2.00
82 Steve Yzerman .75 2.00
83 Curtis Joseph .25 .60
84 Wayne Gretzky 1.25 3.00
123 Zigmund Palffy .20 .50
138 Jose Theodore .30 .75
144 Martin Brodeur .40 1.00
165 Pavel Bure .30 .75
166 Michael Peca .15 .40
190 Jeremy Roenick .40 1.00
197 Mario Lemieux 1.00 2.50
216 Teemu Selanne .40 1.00
235 Keith Tkachuk .20 .50
244 Mats Sundin .15 .40
249 Jaromir Jagr .40 1.00
253 T.Duckett .40 1.00
I.Kovalchuk
254 S.Chistov .40 1.00
M.Ely
255 D.Heatley .40 1.00
J.Ennis
257 J.Peppers .75 2.00
E.Cole
261 A.Davis 1.50 4.00
R.Nash
268 H.Zetterberg 1.50 4.00
K.Edwards
269 J.Bouwmeester 1.00 2.50
C.Butler
276 D.Gooden .75 2.00
S.Upshall
283 P.Bouchard .20 .50
I.Rakocevic

2002-03 UD SuperStars Gold

Randomly inserted in packs, this is a parallel to the UD SuperStars set. These cards were issued to a stated print run of 250 serial numbered sets.

*GOLD 1-250: 2.5X TO 6X BASIC
*GOLD MATSUI: 6X TO 12X BASIC
*GOLD 251-300: 2X TO 5X BASIC

2002-03 UD SuperStars Benchmarks

Inserted at a stated rate of one in 20, these 10 cards feature two athletes from different sports with something in common. It could be being a legendary figure in the sport or playing in the same city.

B1 J.DiMaggio 3.00 8.00
W.Gretzky

2002-03 UD SuperStars City All-Stars Dual Jersey

Inserted at a stated rate of one in 32, these 43 cards featured two jersey swatches from star athletes from the same city. Some cards were issued in smaller quantities and we have notated that information with an SP in our database.

ABZP A.Beltre/Z.Palffy 4.00 10.00
BGJS B.Griese/J.Sakic 6.00 15.00
CDMS C.Delgado/M.Sundin 6.00 15.00
FPPL F.Potvin/P.Lo Duca 6.00 15.00
GAPK G.Anderson/P.Kariya 6.00 15.00
JLDS J.LeClair/D.Staley 6.00 15.00
KPBA K.Primeau/B.Abreu 4.00 10.00
MLBG M.Lemieux/B.Giles Pants 15.00 40.00
MMAR M.Modano/A.Rodriguez 6.00 15.00
MPEL M.Piazza/E.Lindros 6.00 15.00
RCPB R.Clemens/P.Bure 8.00 20.00
SSAW S.Samsonov/A.Walker 5.00 12.00
THRB T.Helton/R.Blake 6.00 15.00
WGJG W.Gretzky/J.Giambi 10.00 25.00

2002-03 UD SuperStars City All-Stars Triple Jersey

Randomly inserted in packs, these cards featured three game-used jersey swatches from all-stars from the same city. These cards were issued to a stated print run of 250 serial numbered sets.

DPE Erstad 10.00 25.00
Kariya
Brand
IMD I.Rod 15.00 40.00
Modano
Nowitzki
JKA Kendall/Stewart/Kovalev 15.00 30.00
JLP Giambi 6.00 15.00
Sprewell
Bure
JMK Drew/Faulk/Tkachuk 10.00 25.00
JSB Harrington 25.00 50.00
Yzer
Wallace
REA Clemens 15.00 30.00
Lind
Houston
RSS R.Johnson 6.00 15.00
Marion
Doan
SWK Green 40.00 80.00
Gretzky
Kobe

2002-03 UD SuperStars Keys to the City

Inserted at a stated rate of one in six. These 10 cards feature two star athletes from the same city.

COMPLETE SET (10) 10.00 25.00
K6 P.Roy 1.25 3.00
T.Helton
K9 S.Yzerman 1.25 3.00
J.Harrington

2002-03 UD SuperStars Legendary Leaders Dual Jersey

Inserted at a stated rate of one in 96, these 20 cards feature game-worn jersey pieces from two star athletes from the same city.

SYJH S.Yzerman/J.Harrington 10.00 25.00
ZPSG Z.Palffy/S.Green 6.00 15.00

2002-03 UD SuperStars Legendary Leaders Triple Jersey

Randomly inserted in packs, these 18 cards feature game-used jersey swatches from three athletes. This set is significant by the usage of game-worn swatches of soccer great David Beckham. Each card was issued to a stated print run of 250 serial numbered sets.

ADJ Iverson 20.00 50.00
McNabb
Roenick
AEM A.Rod/Emmitt/Modano 20.00 50.00
CJS Ripken/Jagr/Davis 12.50 30.00
JDM Giambi/Bledsoe/Messier 10.00 25.00
JWL DiMaggio 60.00 120.00
Gretzky
Bird
LBP Walker/Griese/Roy 15.00 40.00
MCA Piazza/C.Penn/Yashin 10.00 25.00
MPS McGwire/Manning/Yzer 30.00 80.00
RJM Clemens/Rice/Lemieux 30.00 60.00
SEB Sosa/Daze/Urlacher 10.00 25.00
SWK Green 40.00 80.00
Gretzky
Kobe
TEM Gwynn/Emmitt/Lemieux 12.50 30.00

2002-03 UD SuperStars Magic Moments

Inserted at a stated rate of one in five, this 20 card set featured a mix of active and retired players along with history about key moments in their career.

COMPLETE SET (20) 10.00 25.00
MM17 Bobby Orr 1.50 4.00
MM18 Wayne Gretzky 2.00 5.00
MM19 Patrick Roy 1.25 3.00

2002-03 UD SuperStars Rookie Review

Inserted at a stated rate of one in 20, these 10 cards feature two athletes who made their American professional debut in the same year.

R1 M.Messier 2.00 5.00
O.Smith

2002-03 UD SuperStars Spokesmen

Issued as a three-card pack topper, these 30 cards feature a mix of players who were also serving as spokesmen for Upper Deck.

*BLACK: 1.25X TO 3X BASIC SPOKESMEN
BLACK/GOLD INSERTS IN SPOKESMEN PACKS
BLACK PRINT RUN 250 SERIAL #'d SETS
*GOLD/25: 3X TO 8X BASIC INSERTS
GOLD PRINT RUN 25 SERIAL #'d SETS
UD12 Bobby Orr 2.00 5.00
UD13 Gordie Howe 1.50 4.00
UD14 Wayne Gretzky 2.50 6.00
UD27 Bobby Orr 2.00 5.00
UD28 Gordie Howe 1.50 4.00
UD29 Wayne Gretzky 2.50 6.00

2001-02 UD Top Shelf

Released in mid-October 2001, this 156-card set carried an SRP of $9.99. The original 97-card base set consisted of 45 veteran cards (1-45), 42 rookie cards (46-66) and 10-exchange rookie cards (67-76). Cards 46-66 were issued in two versions, both versions were serial-numbered to 900 each the only difference between the two versions was that the images on front and back were reversed. Cards 67-76 were redeemable for rookie players who made their debut during the season, and they were serial-numbered to 500 each. Cards 77-135 were available in random packs of UD Rookie Update and cards 122-135 were serial-numbered to 900 each. Cards 136-141 were available by redeeming cards TR1-TR6 of the Rookie Redemption set; they were serial-numbered to just 100 copies each.

COMP.SET w/o SP's (90) 30.00 60.00
1 Paul Kariya .75 2.00
2 Patrik Stefan .50 1.25
3 Joe Thornton .75 2.00
4 Miroslav Satan .50 1.25
5 Jarome Iginla .60 1.50
6 Jeff O'Neill .40 1.00
7 Tony Amonte .50 1.25
8 Joe Sakic 1.00 2.50
9 Peter Forsberg .75 2.00
10 Ray Bourque 1.00 2.50
11 Milan Hejduk .50 1.25
12 Patrick Roy 1.50 4.00
13 Rostislav Klesla .40 1.00
14 Mike Modano 1.00 2.50
15 Steve Yzerman 2.00 5.00
16 Luc Robitaille .60 1.50
17 Dominik Hasek 1.00 2.50
18 Tommy Salo .50 1.25
19 Pavel Bure .75 2.00
20 Zigmund Palffy .60 1.50
21 Brett Hull .75 2.00
22 Marian Gaborik 1.00 2.50
23 Saku Koivu .60 1.50
24 David Legwand .50 1.25
25 Martin Brodeur 1.25 3.00
26 Patrik Elias .60 1.50
27 Rick DiPietro .50 1.25
28 Eric Lindros 1.00 2.50
29 Marian Hossa .50 1.25
30 Jeremy Roenick .60 1.50
31 Roman Cechmanek .50 1.25
32 Sean Burke .40 1.00
33 Alexei Kovalev .50 1.25
34 Mario Lemieux 2.00 5.00
35 Johan Hedberg .50 1.25
36 Evgeni Nabokov .50 1.25
37 Teemu Selanne 1.25 3.00
38 Chris Pronger .50 1.25
39 Keith Tkachuk .60 1.50
40 Vincent Lecavalier .50 1.25
41 Curtis Joseph .60 1.50
42 Mats Sundin .60 1.50
43 Markus Naslund .60 1.50
44 Daniel Sedin .60 1.50
45 Jaromir Jagr 1.50 4.00
46A Mikael Samuelsson RC 2.50 6.00
(facing left)
46B Mikael Samuelsson RC 2.50 6.00
(facing right)
47A Dan Snyder RC 2.50 6.00
(skating)
47B Dan Snyder RC 2.50 6.00
(facing forward)
48A Zdenek Kutlak RC 2.00 5.00
(skating)
48B Zdenek Kutlak RC 2.00 5.00
(closeup)
49A Michel Larocque RC 2.00 5.00
(puck in glove)
49B Michel Larocque RC 2.00 5.00
(closeup)
50A Casey Hankinson RC 2.00 5.00
(stick to left)
50B Casey Hankinson RC 2.00 5.00
(closeup)
51A Bill Bowler RC 2.00 5.00
(stick to left)
51B Bill Bowler RC 2.00 5.00
(closeup)
52A Martin Spanhel RC 2.00 5.00
(highstick)
52B Martin Spanhel RC 2.00 5.00
(closeup)
53A Mathieu Darche RC 3.00 8.00
(stick to left)
53B Mathieu Darche RC 3.00 8.00
54A Jason Chimera RC 2.00 5.00
(stick to left)
54B Jason Chimera RC 2.00 5.00
(closeup)
55A Andrej Podkonicky RC 2.00 5.00
(stick on knees)
55B Andrej Podkonicky RC 2.00 5.00
(closeup)
56A Pascal Dupuis RC 3.00 8.00
(stick to right)
56B Pascal Dupuis RC 3.00 8.00
(closeup)
57A Francis Belanger RC 2.50 6.00
(stick at waist)
57B Francis Belanger RC 2.50 6.00
(closeup)
58A Mike Jefferson RC 2.00 5.00
(facing forward)
58B Mike Jefferson RC 2.00 5.00
(skating right)
59A Stanislav Gron RC#(white jersey) 2.00 5.00
59B Stanislav Gron RC 2.00 5.00
(red jersey)
60A Joel Kwiatkowski RC 2.00 5.00
(white jersey)
60B Joel Kwiatkowski RC 2.00 5.00
(red jersey)
61A Kirby Law RC 2.00 5.00
(skating right)
61B Kirby Law RC 2.00 5.00
(closeup)
62A Tomas Divisek RC 2.50 6.00
(skating right)
62B Tomas Divisek RC#(closeup) 2.50 6.00
63A Billy Tibbetts RC 2.00 5.00
(skating left)
63B Billy Tibbetts RC 2.00 5.00
(closeup)
64A Thomas Ziegler RC 2.50 6.00
(stick right hand)
64B Thomas Ziegler RC 2.50 6.00
(closeup)
65A Mike Brown 2.50 6.00
(facing forward)
65B Mike Brown 2.50 6.00
(closeup)
66A Pat Kavanagh RC 2.50 6.00
(standing up)
66B Pat Kavanagh RC 2.50 6.00
(closeup)
67 Ilja Bryzgalov RC 6.00 15.00
68 Ilya Kovalchuk RC 12.00 30.00
69 Vaclav Nedorost RC 2.50 6.00
70 Niko Kapanen RC 4.00 10.00
71 Kristian Huselius RC 4.00 10.00
72 Dan Blackburn RC 3.00 8.00
73 Krystofer Kolanos RC 2.50 6.00
74 Jiri Dopita RC 2.50 6.00
75 Nikita Alexeev RC 2.50 6.00
76 Brian Sutherby RC 2.50 6.00
77 Dany Heatley .60 1.50
78 Sergei Samsonov .50 1.25
79 Bill Guerin .60 1.50
80 Byron Dafoe .50 1.25
81 Martin Biron .50 1.25
82 Roman Turek .50 1.25
83 Arturs Irbe .50 1.25
84 Steve Sullivan .40 1.00
85 Mark Bell .40 1.00
86 Rob Blake .60 1.50
87 Alex Tanguay .50 1.25
88 Chris Drury .50 1.25
89 Espen Knutsen .40 1.00
90 Ed Belfour .60 1.50
91 Brendan Shanahan .75 2.00
92 Nicklas Lidstrom .60 1.50
93 Sergei Fedorov 1.00 2.50
94 Mike Comrie .50 1.25
95 Roberto Luongo 1.00 2.50
96 Felix Potvin 1.00 2.50
97 Jason Allison .50 1.25
98 Jose Theodore .60 1.50
99 Joe Nieuwendyk .60 1.50
100 Brian Gionta .50 1.25
101 Alexei Yashin .50 1.25
102 Michael Peca .50 1.25
103 Chris Osgood .60 1.50
104 Mark Parrish .40 1.00
105 Juraj Kolnik .40 1.00
106 Theo Fleury .75 2.00
107 Mike Richter .60 1.50
108 Brian Leetch .60 1.50
109 Pavel Bure .75 2.00
110 Martin Havlat .50 1.25
111 Adam Oates .60 1.50
112 John LeClair .60 1.50
113 Keith Primeau .50 1.25
114 Owen Nolan .60 1.50
115 Pavol Demitra .75 2.00
116 Brent Johnson .50 1.25
117 Doug Weight .60 1.50
118 Nikolai Khabibulin .60 1.50
119 Brad Richards .60 1.50
120 Peter Bondra .60 1.50
121 Olaf Kolzig .60 1.50
122 Pasi Nurminen RC 2.00 5.00
123 Ivan Huml RC 2.00 5.00
124 Erik Cole RC 4.00 10.00
125 Mike Peluso RC 2.00 5.00
126 Riku Hahl RC 2.00 5.00
127 Pavel Datsyuk RC 10.00 25.00
128 Niklas Hagman RC 2.50 6.00
129 Olivier Michaud RC 3.00 8.00
130 Marcel Hossa RC 3.00 8.00
131 Martin Erat RC 3.00 8.00
132 Christian Berglund RC 2.50 6.00
133 Raffi Torres RC 3.00 8.00
134 Branko Radivojevic RC 2.00 5.00
135 Jeff Jillson RC 2.00 5.00
136 Mark Hartigan RC 10.00 25.00
137 Stephen Weiss RC 25.00 60.00
138 Jan Lasak RC 10.00 25.00
139 Trent Hunter RC 20.00 50.00
140 Evgeny Konstantinov RC 10.00 25.00
141 Sebastien Charpentier RC 10.00 25.00

2001-02 UD Top Shelf All-Star Nets

Inserted at 1:287, this 6-card set featured a piece of All-Star game-used netting. Card fronts were team colored and the netting was affixed in an "X" design. Card backs carried a congratulatory message.

NDH Dominik Hasek 25.00 60.00
NEN Evgeni Nabokov 15.00 40.00
NMB Martin Brodeur 25.00 60.00
NPR Patrick Roy 30.00 80.00
NRC Roman Cechmanek 15.00 40.00
NSB Sean Burke 15.00 40.00

2001-02 UD Top Shelf Goalie Gear

This 14-card set featured game-used equipment from some of the top goalies of the NHL, past and present. Cards from this set were inserted at a rate of 1:12. Equipment used on each card is listed below beside the player's name. Card backs carried a congratulatory message.

BJH Johan Hedberg Blocker 5.00 12.00
SCO Chris Osgood Skate 5.00 12.00
GGJH Johan Hedberg Glove 5.00 12.00
LPBB Brian Boucher Pad 5.00 12.00
LPBD Byron Dafoe Pad 5.00 12.00
LPDH Dominik Hasek Pad 8.00 20.00
LPGC Gerry Cheevers Pad 5.00 12.00
LPJH Johan Hedberg Pad 5.00 12.00
LPJT Jose Theodore Pad 6.00 15.00
LPJV John Vanbiesbrouck Pad 5.00 12.00
LPMB Martin Biron Pad 5.00 12.00
LPRC Roman Cechmanek Pad 5.00 12.00
LPRL Roberto Luongo Pad 6.00 15.00
LPSS Steve Shields Pad 5.00 12.00

2001-02 UD Top Shelf Jerseys

This 30-card set featured swatches of game-worn jersey and color player photos on a mostly silver card front. Two subsets made up this set; Stanley Cup Champions jerseys and regular jerseys. Stanley Cup jerseys were inserted at 1:30 and are denoted below with an "SC" beside the player's name. Regular jerseys were inserted at 1:20. Card backs carried a congratulatory message. Cards found in UD Update packs carry a "TJ" prefix.

AY Alexei Yashin 4.00 10.00
BH Brett Hull SC 5.00 12.00
BS Brendan Shanahan SC 4.00 10.00
DS Daniel Sedin 4.00 10.00
DW Doug Weight 4.00 10.00
EB Ed Belfour SC 4.00 10.00
HS Henrik Sedin 4.00 10.00
JA Jason Allison 4.00 10.00
JI Jarome Iginla 5.00 12.00
JJ Jaromir Jagr SC 6.00 15.00
JL John LeClair SC 4.00 10.00
JO Jose Theodore 5.00 12.00
JS Joe Sakic SC 8.00 20.00
JT Joe Thornton 5.00 12.00
MH Marian Hossa 4.00 10.00
ML Mario Lemieux SC 20.00 50.00
MM Mike Modano SC 6.00 15.00
MR Mike Richter SC 4.00 10.00
MT Marty Turco 4.00 10.00
PB Peter Bondra 4.00 10.00
PF Peter Forsberg SC 10.00 25.00
PK Paul Kariya 4.00 10.00
PR Patrick Roy SC 12.50 30.00
PS Patrik Stefan 4.00 10.00
RB Ray Bourque SC 10.00 25.00
SF Sergei Fedorov SC 6.00 15.00
SY Steve Yzerman SC 12.50 30.00
TS Teemu Selanne 6.00 15.00
VB Valeri Bure 4.00 10.00
VL Vincent Lecavalier 4.00 10.00
TJBS Brendan Shanahan Upd 4.00 10.00
TJCD Chris Drury Upd 4.00 10.00
TJJI Jarome Iginla Upd 4.00 10.00
TJJW Justin Williams Upd 4.00 10.00
TJMH Milan Hejduk Upd 4.00 10.00
TJMN Markus Naslund Upd 4.00 10.00
TJMS Miroslav Satan Upd 4.00 10.00
TJPD Pavol Demitra Upd 4.00 10.00
TJPK Paul Kariya Upd 8.00 20.00
TJZP Zigmund Palffy Upd 4.00 10.00

2001-02 UD Top Shelf Jersey Autographs

This 18-card set paralleled the basic jersey set, but also incorporates an autograph of the featured player along with the jersey swatch. Each card was serial-numbered out of 100 copies. Card backs carried a congratulatory message.

DS Daniel Sedin 15.00 40.00
DW Doug Weight 15.00 40.00
EB Ed Belfour SC 15.00 40.00
HS Henrik Sedin 12.00 30.00
JA Jason Allison 15.00 40.00
JI Jarome Iginla 20.00 50.00
JL John LeClair SC 15.00 40.00
JO Jose Theodore 20.00 50.00
JT Joe Thornton 20.00 50.00
MH Marian Hossa 15.00 40.00
MM Mike Modano SC 25.00 60.00
MT Marty Turco 15.00 40.00
PS Patrik Stefan 15.00 40.00
RB Ray Bourque SC 40.00 100.00
SY Steve Yzerman SC 50.00 120.00
TS Teemu Selanne 25.00 60.00
VL Vincent Lecavalier 15.00 40.00

2001-02 UD Top Shelf Patches

Inserted at 1:287, this 6-card set partially parallels the base jersey set but each card carried a patch swatch on the card front. Please note that the Brodeur card does not have a parent card in the base jersey set. Card backs carried a congratulatory message.

PJJ Jaromir Jagr 15.00 40.00
PMB Martin Brodeur 30.00 80.00
PMM Mike Modano 15.00 40.00
PPF Peter Forsberg 20.00 50.00
PPR Patrick Roy 30.00 80.00
PSY Steve Yzerman 60.00 125.00

2001-02 UD Top Shelf Rookie Redemption

Available in random packs of UD Rookie Update, this set of exchange cards were redeemable for a rookie who made his debut late in the 2001/02 season or in the 2002/03 season. Each card was serial-numbered to 100. Shortly after the products release, Upper Deck announced the first six players in the set. Those first six cards can be found at the end of the base set as they were numbered #136-141. The remaining 4 players were not announced until March of 2003 and carry a "TS" prefix.

TS1 Stanislav Chistov 10.00 25.0
TS2 Rick Nash 30.00 80.0
TS3 Henrik Zetterberg 30.00 80.0
TS4 Jason Spezza 25.00 60.0

2001-02 UD Top Shelf Sticks

Inserted at overall odds of 1:12, this 29-card set featured dime-sized pieces of game-used sticks from the featured player(s). Card fronts were silver-toned and carried a color picture of the featured player. Card backs carried a congratulatory message.

SBH Brett Hull 8.00 20.0
SBS Brendan Shanahan 6.00 15.0
SCP Chris Pronger 6.00 15.0
SDH Dominik Hasek 8.00 20.0
SJL John LeClair 6.00 15.0
SJR Jeremy Roenick 8.00 20.0
SJS Joe Sakic 10.00 25.0
SKT Keith Tkachuk 6.00 15.0
SMB Martin Brodeur 15.00 40.0
SML Mario Lemieux 12.00 30.0
SMM Mark Messier 6.00 15.0
SNL Nicklas Lidstrom 6.00 15.0
SPB Peter Bondra 6.00 15.0
SPF Peter Forsberg 8.00 20.
SPK Paul Kariya 6.00 15.
SPR Patrick Roy 15.00 40.
SRB Ray Bourque 8.00 20.
SSF Sergei Fedorov 6.00 15.
SSO Sandis Ozolinsh 6.00 15.
SSY Steve Yzerman 12.50 30.
STF Theo Fleury 6.00 15.
SWG Wayne Gretzky 40.00 80.
SZP Zigmund Palffy 6.00 15.
SPBU Pavel Bure 6.00 15.
BFJ Bure/Forsberg/Jagr 50.00 125.
BPR Bourque/Pronger/Roy 60.00 150.
KSF Kariya/Sakic/Fleury 40.00 100.
LOH Lidstrom/Ozolinsh/Hasek 30.00 80.
RSF Roy/Sakic/Forsberg 40.00 100.

2002-03 UD Top Shelf

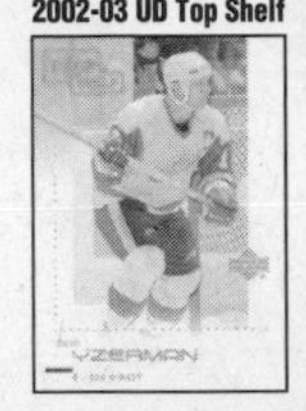

Released in August 2002 at an SRP of $4.99, this 16 card set featured 90 regular base cards and 45 rooki redemptions cards. Rookie redemption cards were redeemable for rookies who made their debut in the 2002-03 season. Cards 91-120 were serial-numbere to 1125 and cards 121-135 were serial-numbered to 500.

COMP.SET w/o SP's (90) 15.00 40.
1 Jean-Sebastien Giguere .50 1.
2 Jeff Friesen .30 .
3 Paul Kariya .60 1.
4 Ilya Kovalchuk .60 1.
5 Dany Heatley .50 1.
6 Joe Thornton .60 1.
7 Sergei Samsonov .40 1.
8 Bill Guerin .50 1.
9 Martin Biron .40 1.
10 Miroslav Satan .50 1.
11 Maxim Afinogenov .30 .
12 Jarome Iginla .50 1.
13 Roman Turek .50 1.
14 Craig Conroy .30 .
15 Jeff O'Neill .30 .
16 Arturs Irbe .40 1
17 Sami Kapanen .30
18 Jocelyn Thibault .40 1.
19 Eric Daze .30 .
20 Alexei Zhamnov .40 1.
21 Patrick Roy 1.25 3.
22 Joe Sakic .75 2.
23 Peter Forsberg .60 1.
24 Marc Denis .40 1.
25 Espen Knutsen .30 .
26 Mike Modano .75 2.
27 Jason Arnott .40 1.
28 Marty Turco .50 1.
29 Steve Yzerman 1.00 2.
30 Sergei Fedorov .75 2.
31 Dominik Hasek .75 2.
32 Brendan Shanahan .60 1.
33 Ryan Smyth .40 1.
34 Tommy Salo .40 1.
35 Mike Comrie .50 1.
36 Roberto Luongo .75 2
37 Kristian Huselius .30
38 Sandis Ozolinsh .40 1.
39 Zigmund Palffy .50 1.
40 Jason Allison .40 1.
41 Felix Potvin .75 2.
42 Manny Fernandez .40 1.
43 Marian Gaborik .75 2.
44 Andrew Brunette .30 .
45 Jose Theodore .50 1
46 Saku Koivu .50 1
47 Richard Zednik .30
48 Mike Dunham .40 1
49 David Legwand .40 1.
50 Patrik Elias .50 1.
51 Joe Nieuwendyk .50 1
52 Martin Brodeur 1.00 2.
53 Scott Niedermayer .50 1.
54 Alexei Yashin .40 1
55 Michael Peca .40 1.
56 Chris Osgood .50 1
57 Mike Richter .50 1.
58 Pavel Bure .60 1.
59 Eric Lindros .75 2.
60 Martin Havlat .40 1.
61 Patrick Lalime .40 1.
62 Marian Hossa .40 1.
63 Jeremy Roenick .50 1.
64 Roman Cechmanek .40 1
65 John LeClair .50 1
66 Simon Gagne .50 1
67 Ladislav Nagy .30
68 Sean Burke .30
69 Daniel Briere .40 1.
70 Johan Hedberg .50 1
71 Mario Lemieux 1.50 4
72 Alexei Kovalev .50 1
73 Evgeni Nabokov .40 1
74 Owen Nolan .50 1

5 Teemu Selanne 1.00 2.50
6 Brent Johnson .40 1.00
7 Keith Tkachuk .50 1.25
8 Chris Pronger .40 1.00
9 Brad Richards .50 1.25
0 Vincent Lecavalier .40 1.00
1 Nikolai Khabibulin .50 1.25
2 Alexander Mogilny .40 1.00
3 Mats Sundin .50 1.25
4 Curtis Joseph .50 1.25
5 Todd Bertuzzi .50 1.25
6 Brendan Morrison .40 1.00
7 Markus Naslund .40 1.00
8 Jaromir Jagr 1.25 3.00
9 Peter Bondra .50 1.25
0 Olaf Kolzig .50 1.25
1 Tim Thomas RC 5.00 12.00
2 Ivan Majesky RC 1.25 3.00
3 Jay Bouwmeester RC 4.00 10.00
4 Ron Hainsey RC 1.25 3.00
5 Ray Schultz RC 1.25 3.00
6 Tomi Pettinen RC 1.25 3.00
7 Eric Godard RC 1.25 3.00
8 Anton Volchenkov RC 1.25 3.00
9 Dennis Seidenberg RC 2.00 5.00
00 Radovan Somik RC 1.25 3.00
01 Patrick Sharp RC 4.00 10.00
02 Carlo Colaiacovo RC 2.00 5.00
03 Mikael Tellqvist RC 1.25 3.00
04 Steve Eminger RC 1.25 3.00
05 Alex Henry RC 1.50 4.00
06 Kurt Sauer RC 1.25 3.00
07 Micki Dupont RC 1.25 3.00
08 Shawn Thornton RC 1.50 4.00
09 Matt Henderson RC 1.25 3.00
0 Jeff Paul RC 1.25 3.00
1 Lasse Pirjeta RC 1.25 3.00
2 Dmitri Bykov RC 1.25 3.00
3 Kari Haakana RC 1.25 3.00
4 Sylvain Blouin RC 1.25 3.00
5 Stephane Veilleux RC 1.25 3.00
6 Greg Koehler RC 1.25 3.00
7 Lynn Loyns RC 1.25 3.00
8 Tom Koivisto RC 1.25 3.00
9 Curtis Sanford RC 2.00 5.00
0 Cody Rudkowsky RC 1.25 3.00
1 Martin Gerber RC 4.00 10.00
2 Alexei Smirnov RC 3.00 8.00
3 Stanislav Chistov RC 2.50 6.00
4 Jordan Leopold RC 4.00 10.00
5 Chuck Kobasew RC 3.00 8.00
6 Rick Nash RC 15.00 40.00
7 Henrik Zetterberg RC 12.00 30.00
8 Ales Hemsky RC 10.00 25.00
9 Alexander Frolov RC 5.00 12.00
0 P-M Bouchard RC 4.00 10.00
1 Adam Hall RC 2.50 6.00
2 Scottie Upshall RC 3.00 8.00
3 Jason Spezza RC 15.00 40.00
4 Jeff Taffe RC 2.50 6.00
5 Alexander Svitov RC 2.50 6.00

2002-03 UD Top Shelf All-Stars Jerseys

INT RUN 50 SER.#'d SETS
GR Wayne Gretzky 60.00 120.00
JJ Jaromir Jagr 12.00 30.00
JS Joe Sakic 12.00 30.00
KT Keith Tkachuk 8.00 20.00
MS Mats Sundin 8.00 20.00
PK Paul Kariya 10.00 25.00
SF Sergei Fedorov 12.00 30.00
SS Scott Stevens 8.00 20.00
TA Tony Amonte 6.00 15.00
TF Theo Fleury 10.00 25.00
TS Teemu Selanne 10.00 25.00
WG Wayne Gretzky 60.00 120.00

2002-03 UD Top Shelf Clutch Performers Jerseys

ATED PRINT RUN 75 SER.#'d SETS
AD Adam Deadmarsh 5.00 12.00
AM Al MacInnis 6.00 15.00
BG Bill Guerin 6.00 15.00
BL Brian Leetch 6.00 15.00
BO Peter Bondra 6.00 15.00
BS Brendan Shanahan 8.00 20.00
CD Chris Drury 6.00 15.00
CJ Curtis Joseph 6.00 15.00
CL Claude Lemieux 5.00 12.00
DW Doug Weight 6.00 15.00
EB Ed Belfour 6.00 15.00
EL Eric Lindros 10.00 25.00
IK Ilya Kovalchuk 8.00 20.00
JI Jarome Iginla 6.00 15.00
JJ Jaromir Jagr 15.00 40.00
JN Joe Nieuwendyk 6.00 15.00
JR Jeremy Roenick 6.00 15.00
JS Joe Sakic 10.00 25.00
JT Joe Thornton 8.00 20.00
KT Keith Tkachuk 6.00 15.00
LR Luc Robitaille 6.00 15.00
MB Martin Brodeur 12.00 30.00
MH Milan Hejduk 5.00 12.00
ML Mario Lemieux 20.00 50.00
MM Mike Modano 10.00 25.00
MR Mike Richter 6.00 15.00
MS Mats Sundin 6.00 15.00
NL Nicklas Lidstrom 6.00 15.00
PB Pavel Bure 8.00 20.00
PK Paul Kariya 8.00 20.00
PR Patrick Roy 15.00 40.00
RB Ray Bourque 10.00 25.00
SB Sean Burke 4.00 10.00
SF Sergei Fedorov 10.00 25.00
SGA Simon Gagne 6.00 15.00
SGO Sergei Gonchar 5.00 12.00
SSA Sergei Samsonov 5.00 12.00
SSU Steve Sullivan 4.00 10.00
SY Steve Yzerman 12.00 30.00
TS Teemu Selanne 12.00 30.00
WG Wayne Gretzky 30.00 80.00
ZP Zigmund Palffy 6.00 15.00

2002-03 UD Top Shelf Dual Player Jerseys

gles in this 42-card memorabilia set were serial-numbered out of 99.
M.Denis/E.Belfour 8.00 20.00
P.Bure/I.Kovalchuk 10.00 25.00
R.Blake/C.Pronger 8.00 20.00
S.Samsonov/P.Bure 10.00 25.00
P.Bondra/Z.Palffy 8.00 20.00
Fedorov/Afinogenov 12.00 30.00
J.Iginla/J.Williams 8.00 20.00
S.Gagne/P.Kariya 10.00 25.00
R.Klesla/N.Lidstrom 8.00 20.00
T.Connolly/M.Modano 12.00 30.00
Legwand/Nieuwendyk 8.00 20.00
F.Potvin/M.Biron 12.00 30.00
J.Thornton/K.Primeau 10.00 25.00
P.Roy/J.Theodore 20.00 50.00

RSF R.Fedotenko/M.Satan 8.00 20.00
RSH S.Hartnell/B.Shanahan 10.00 25.00
RSR Reinprecht/S.Sullivan 5.00 12.00
RYK K.Kolanos/S.Yzerman 15.00 40.00
STAB E.Belanger/J.Allison 6.00 15.00
STBB R.Bourque/R.Blake 12.00 30.00
STBD D.Briere/S.Doan 6.00 15.00
STBE B.Leetch/P.Bure 10.00 25.00
STBJ J.Jagr/P.Bondra 20.00 50.00
STBL R.Luongo/V.Bure 12.00 30.00
STBN M.Biron/M.Noronen 6.00 15.00
STBS M.Brodeur/S.Stevens 15.00 40.00
STBT J.Thornton/R.Bourque 12.00 30.00
STDE M.Erat/M.Dunham 6.00 15.00
STDT E.Daze/J.Thibault 6.00 15.00
STFL N.Lidstrom/S.Fedorov 12.00 30.00
STFP K.Primeau/R.Fedotenko 8.00 20.00
STFR M.Richter/T.Fleury 10.00 25.00
STGB B.Boucher/S.Gagne 8.00 20.00
STGD B.Guerin/B.Dafoe 8.00 20.00
STGK O.Kolzig/S.Gonchar 8.00 20.00
STGM M.Messier/W.Gretzky 50.00 100.00
STGR M.Recchi/S.Gagne 10.00 25.00
STGS J.Giguere/S.Shields 8.00 20.00
STHL D.Legwand/S.Hartnell 8.00 20.00
STHR M.Hejduk/Reinprecht 6.00 15.00
STIS J.Iginla/M.Savard 8.00 20.00
STJK J.Jagr/O.Kolzig 20.00 50.00
STKB K.Kolanos/S.Burke 5.00 12.00
STKF J.Friesen/P.Kariya 10.00 25.00
STKT J.Theodore/S.Koivu 8.00 20.00
STKW R.Whitney/R.Klesla 6.00 15.00
STLD C.Lemieux/S.Doan 6.00 15.00
STMA J. Arnott/M.Modano 12.00 30.00
STMM B.Morrow/M.Modano 12.00 30.00
STNL M.Naslund/T.Linden 10.00 25.00
STPD A.Deadmarsh/Z.Palffy 8.00 20.00
STSA M.Afinogenov/M.Satan 8.00 20.00
STSH D.Hinote/J.Sakic 12.00 30.00
STSM S.Sullivan/T.Amonte 6.00 15.00
STSN O.Nolan/T.Selanne 10.00 25.00
STST J.Thornton/S.Samsonov 10.00 25.00
STTD M.Denis/R.Tugnutt 6.00 15.00
STTG B.Guerin/J.Thornton 10.00 25.00
STYH J.Hecht/M.York 5.00 12.00
STYS B.Shanahan/S.Yzerman 20.00 50.00

2002-03 UD Top Shelf Goal Oriented Jerseys

PRINT RUN 75 SER.#'d SETS
GOAD Adam Deadmarsh 5.00 12.00
GOAT Alex Tanguay 5.00 12.00
GOBG Bill Guerin 6.00 15.00
GOBO Peter Bondra 6.00 15.00
GODA Denis Arkhipov 4.00 10.00
GODB Daniel Briere 5.00 12.00
GOED Eric Daze 4.00 10.00
GOGM Glen Murray 5.00 12.00
GOIK Ilya Kovalchuk 8.00 20.00
GOJJ Jaromir Jagr 15.00 40.00
GOJS Joe Sakic 10.00 25.00
GOJT Joe Thornton 8.00 20.00
GOMA Mats Sundin 6.00 15.00
GOMH Milan Hejduk 5.00 12.00
GOMM Mike Modano 10.00 25.00
GOMS Miroslav Satan 6.00 15.00
GOMY Mike York 4.00 10.00
GOPB Pavel Bure 8.00 20.00
GOPK Paul Kariya 8.00 20.00
GORD Radek Dvorak 5.00 12.00
GORL Robert Lang 4.00 10.00
GOSF Sergei Fedorov 10.00 25.00
GOSG Simon Gagne 6.00 15.00
GOSR Steven Reinprecht 4.00 10.00
GOSS Sergei Samsonov 5.00 12.00
GOSU Steve Sullivan 4.00 10.00
GOSY Steve Yzerman 12.00 30.00
GOTA Tony Amonte 5.00 12.00
GOTS Teemu Selanne 8.00 20.00
GOZP Zigmund Palffy 6.00 15.00

2002-03 UD Top Shelf Milestones Jerseys

This 10-card memorabilia set featured quad jersey swatches. Each card was serial-numbered out of 25.
MBBRR Jeremy Roenick 50.00 100.00
Mark Recchi
Pavel Bure
Peter Bondra
MBMBS Brque/Bure/Slnne/Mdno 100.00 200.00
MGBYM Grtz./Brqe/Mess./Yze. 250.00 400.00
MGHLY Grtz./Lem./Hwe/Yze. 250.00 400.00
MHPBJ Brke/Ptvin/Brrsso/Hasek 50.00 100.00
MLNLA Amnte/LClr/Lndrs/Noln 50.00 100.00
MMHYR Mess./Hull/Robit./Yze. 200.00 350.00
MRBRJ Roy/Brodr./Cujo/Richt. 150.00 300.00
MSFRM Fleury/Shan./Roe./Mess. 75.00 150.00
MSYVR Shan./Yze./Vbeek/Robit. 125.00 250.00

2002-03 UD Top Shelf Shooting Stars Jerseys

SHAR Jason Arnott 5.00 12.00
SHAT Alex Tanguay 5.00 12.00
SHBG Bill Guerin 6.00 15.00
SHBH Brett Hull 8.00 20.00
SHBL Brian Leetch 6.00 15.00
SHBM Brenden Morrow 5.00 12.00
SHBO Peter Bondra 6.00 15.00
SHBS Brendan Shanahan 8.00 20.00
SHDB Daniel Briere 5.00 12.00
SHEK Espen Knutsen 4.00 10.00
SHGM Glen Murray 5.00 12.00
SHJA Jason Allison 5.00 12.00
SHJJ Jaromir Jagr 15.00 40.00
SHJN Joe Nieuwendyk 6.00 15.00
SHKK Krys Kolanos 4.00 10.00
SHLE Rob Blake 6.00 15.00
SHMA Maxim Afinogenov 4.00 10.00
SHMH Milan Hejduk 5.00 12.00
SHML Mario Lemieux 20.00 50.00
SHMM Mike Modano 10.00 25.00
SHMSA Miroslav Satan 6.00 15.00
SHMSU Mats Sundin 6.00 15.00
SHMY Mike York 4.00 10.00
SHNA Nikolai Antropov 5.00 12.00
SHNL Nicklas Lidstrom 6.00 15.00
SHPB Pavel Bure 8.00 20.00
SHPF Peter Forsberg 8.00 20.00
SHPK Paul Kariya 8.00 20.00
SHRB Ray Bourque 10.00 25.00
SHRL Robert Lang 4.00 10.00
SHSD Shane Doan 5.00 12.00
SHSF Sergei Fedorov 10.00 25.00
SHSG Simon Gagne 6.00 15.00
SHSH Scott Hartnell 6.00 15.00
SHSK Saku Koivu 6.00 15.00
SHSR Steven Reinprecht 4.00 10.00
SHSS Steve Sullivan 4.00 10.00
SHSY Steve Yzerman 12.00 30.00
SHTA Tony Amonte 5.00 12.00
SHTF Theo Fleury 8.00 20.00
SHTS Teemu Selanne 8.00 20.00

SHZP Zigmund Palffy 6.00 15.00

2002-03 UD Top Shelf Signatures

Inserted at one per box, this 36-card set featured authentic autographs of the featured players. The Yzerman card was a redemption in pack.
AK Alexei Kovalev 5.00 12.00
BB Brian Boucher SP 8.00 20.00
BG Bill Guerin 5.00 12.00
BL Rob Blake 5.00 12.00
BO Bobby Orr/96 100.00 200.00
DH Dany Heatley 10.00 25.00
DS Daniel Sedin 8.00 20.00
DW Doug Weight/92 12.50 30.00
GH Gordie Howe/27 150.00 300.00
HA Martin Havlat 8.00 20.00
HS Henrik Sedin 8.00 20.00
JA Jason Allison SP 5.00 12.00
JH Johan Hedberg SP 5.00 12.00
JI Jarome Iginla 10.00 25.00
JL John LeClair 6.00 15.00
MB Martin Biron SP 5.00 12.00
MC Mike Comrie 5.00 12.00
MH Milan Hejduk 6.00 15.00
MN Markus Naslund 6.00 15.00
MO Maxime Ouellet 5.00 12.00
PA Pavel Brendl 5.00 12.00
PB Pavel Bure 10.00 25.00
PE Peter Bondra 5.00 12.00
PR Patrick Roy SP 40.00 100.00
RB Ray Bourque SP 12.00 30.00
RD Rick DiPietro 5.00 12.00
RK Rostislav Klesla SP 6.00 15.00
RT Raffi Torres 5.00 12.00
SG Simon Gagne 8.00 20.00
SH Scott Hartnell 6.00 15.00
SS Sergei Samsonov 5.00 12.00
SY Steve Yzerman/53 60.00 120.00
TH Jose Theodore 10.00 25.00
TS Tommy Salo 5.00 12.00
WG Wayne Gretzky/95 150.00 300.00
ZP Zigmund Palffy 5.00 12.00

2002-03 UD Top Shelf Stopper Jerseys

Singles in this 54-card memorabilia set were serial-numbered out of 99.
SSBB Brian Boucher 5.00 12.00
SSBD Byron Dafoe 5.00 12.00
SSBI Martin Biron 5.00 12.00
SSBJ Brent Johnson 5.00 12.00
SSCJ Curtis Joseph 6.00 15.00
SSDA David Aebischer 5.00 12.00
SSDB Dan Blackburn 5.00 12.00
SSDH Dominik Hasek 10.00 25.00
SSDU Mike Dunham 5.00 12.00
SSEB Ed Belfour 6.00 15.00
SSFP Felix Potvin 10.00 25.00
SSJGO Jean-Sebastien Giguere 6.00 15.00
SSJTO Jocelyn Thibault 5.00 12.00
SSMB Martin Brodeur 12.00 30.00
SSMD Marc Denis 5.00 12.00
SSMN Mika Noronen 5.00 12.00
SSMR Mike Richter 8.00 20.00
SSOK Olaf Kolzig 6.00 15.00
SSPR Patrick Roy 15.00 40.00
SSRC Roman Cechmanek 5.00 12.00
SSRT Ron Tugnutt 5.00 12.00
SSSB Sean Burke 4.00 10.00
SSSS Steve Shields 5.00 12.00
SSTH Jose Theodore 6.00 15.00

2002-03 UD Top Shelf Sweet Sweaters

PRINT RUN 50 SER.#'d SETS
SWAD Adam Deadmarsh 6.00 15.00
SWAT Alex Tanguay 6.00 15.00
SWBE Mark Bell 5.00 12.00
SWBG Bill Guerin 8.00 20.00
SWBH Brett Hull 10.00 25.00
SWCD Chris Drury 8.00 20.00
SWCJ Curtis Joseph 8.00 20.00
SWCL Claude Lemieux 6.00 15.00
SWDB Daniel Briere 6.00 15.00
SWDE Marc Denis 6.00 15.00
SWDG Doug Gilmour 10.00 25.00
SWFP Felix Potvin 12.00 30.00
SWJA Jason Allison 6.00 15.00
SWJF Jeff Friesen 5.00 12.00
SWJJ Jaromir Jagr 20.00 50.00
SWJO Joe Thornton 10.00 25.00
SWJS Joe Sakic 12.00 30.00
SWJT Jocelyn Thibault 6.00 15.00
SWKP Keith Primeau 8.00 20.00
SWKT Keith Tkachuk 8.00 20.00
SWMA Maxim Afinogenov 5.00 12.00
SWMB Martin Biron 6.00 15.00
SWMD Mike Dunham 6.00 15.00
SWMM Mike Modano 12.00 30.00
SWMS Mats Sundin 8.00 20.00
SWOK Olaf Kolzig 8.00 20.00
SWPB Pavel Bure 10.00 25.00
SWPK Paul Kariya 10.00 25.00
SWRB Ray Bourque 12.00 30.00
SWRK Rostislav Klesla 5.00 12.00
SWSA Miroslav Satan 8.00 20.00
SWSF Sergei Fedorov 12.00 30.00
SWSK Saku Koivu 8.00 20.00
SWSR Steven Reinprecht 5.00 12.00
SWSS Sergei Samsonov 6.00 15.00
SWSU Steve Sullivan 5.00 12.00
SWSY Steve Yzerman 15.00 40.00
SWTH Jose Theodore 8.00 20.00
SWTS Teemu Selanne 10.00 25.00
SWVN Ville Nieminen 5.00 12.00
SWWG Wayne Gretzky 40.00 100.00
SWZP Zigmund Palffy 8.00 20.00

2002-03 UD Top Shelf Triple Jerseys

These triple jersey memorabilia cards were randomly inserted into packs. The " Hat Trick" subset cards were serial-numbered out of 25 and the "Three Stars" subset was serial-numbered to just 10 sets and was not priced due to scarcity.
HTAPS Amonte/Palffy/Selanne 40.00 100.00
HTBSB Bondra/Bure/Satan 40.00 100.00
HTGHB Guerin/Bondra/Hossa 40.00 100.00
HTGLB Gretzky/Lemieux/Bure 250.00 400.00
HTJHS Hejduk/Jagr/Selanne 40.00 100.00
HTKGF Gagne/Kariya/Fleury 40.00 100.00
HTKYI Iginla/Kariya/Yzerman 150.00 300.00
HTLJT Thornton/Jagr/Lemieux 100.00 200.00
HTLRR Roenick/LeClair/Recchi 75.00 150.00
HTNTH Hejduk/Thornton/Naslund 40.00 100.00
HTSHR Shanahan/Hull/Robitaille 75.00 150.00
HTSIG Sakic/Iginla/Gagne 40.00 100.00

1998-99 UD3

The 1998-99 UD3 set is comprised of six 30-card subsets each printed with three different technologies and features color action player photos. The Embossed technology subsets include New Era (1-30) inserted 1:1 and Three Star Spotlight (151-180) inserted 1:23. The Light F/X technology subsets include new Era (61-90) inserted 1:1 and Three Star Spotlight (91-120). The Rainbow Foil technology subsets include New Era (121-150) inserted 1:5 and Three Star Spotlight (31-60) inserted 1:1. Each card features three card numbers on the back for sorting the cards together by: printing technology featured first, followed by overall card number, and third is the subset numbering. We've cataloged the cards according to their overall card number, called "set" on the backs.
COMPLETE SET (180) 300.00 500.00
1 Sergei Samsonov NE .40 1.00
2 Ryan Johnson NE RC .30 .75
3 Josef Marha NE .30 .75
4 Patrick Marleau NE .30 .75
5 Derek Morris NE .30 .75
6 Jamie Storr NE .40 1.00
7 Richard Zednik NE .30 .75
8 Alyn McCauley NE .30 .75
9 Robert Dome NE .30 .75
10 Patrik Elias NE .40 1.00
11 Olli Jokinen NE .40 1.00
12 Warren Luhning NE .30 .75
13 Chris Phillips NE .30 .75
14 Mattias Ohlund NE .40 1.00
15 Joe Thornton NE .75 2.00
16 Matt Cullen NE .30 .75
17 Bates Battaglia NE .30 .75
18 Andrei Zyuzin NE .30 .75
19 Cameron Mann NE .30 .75
20 Zdeno Chara NE .30 .75
21 Marc Savard NE .30 .75
22 Alexei Morozov NE .30 .75
23 Mike Johnson NE .40 1.00
24 Vaclav Varada NE .30 .75
25 Dan Cloutier NE .30 .75
26 Brad Isbister NE .30 .75
27 Marco Sturm NE .30 .75
28 Anders Eriksson NE .30 .75
29 Jan Bulis NE .30 .75
30 Brendan Morrison NE .40 1.00
31 Wayne Gretzky TSS 2.50 6.00
32 Jaromir Jagr TSS .60 1.50
33 Peter Forsberg TSS 1.00 2.50
34 Paul Kariya TSS .40 1.00
35 Brett Hull TSS .50 1.25
36 Martin Brodeur TSS 1.00 2.50
37 Eric Lindros TSS .50 1.25
38 Peter Bondra TSS .40 1.00
39 Mike Modano TSS .60 1.50
40 Theo Fleury TSS .40 1.00
41 Curtis Joseph TSS .40 1.00
42 Sergei Fedorov TSS .60 1.50
43 Saku Koivu TSS .40 1.00
44 Zigmund Palffy TSS .40 1.00
45 Ed Belfour TSS .40 1.00
46 Patrick Roy TSS 2.00 5.00
47 Brendan Shanahan TSS .40 1.00
48 Mats Sundin TSS .40 1.00
49 Alexei Yashin TR .40 1.00
50 Doug Gilmour TSS .40 1.00
51 Chris Osgood TSS .40 1.00
52 Keith Tkachuk TSS .40 1.00
53 Mark Messier TSS .50 1.25
54 John Vanbiesbrouck TSS .40 1.00
55 Ray Bourque TSS .60 1.50
56 John LeClair TSS .50 1.25
57 Dominik Hasek TSS .75 2.00
58 Teemu Selanne TSS .40 1.00
59 Joe Sakic TSS .75 2.00
60 Steve Yzerman TSS 2.00 5.00
61 Sergei Samsonov NE .40 1.00
62 Ryan Johnson NE .30 .75
63 Josef Marha NE .30 .75
64 Patrick Marleau NE .30 .75
65 Derek Morris NE .30 .75
66 Jamie Storr NE .40 1.00
67 Richard Zednik NE .30 .75
68 Alyn McCauley NE .30 .75
69 Robert Dome NE .30 .75
70 Patrik Elias NE .40 1.00
71 Olli Jokinen NE .40 1.00
72 Warren Luhning NE .30 .75
73 Chris Phillips NE .30 .75
74 Mattias Ohlund NE .40 1.00
75 Joe Thornton NE .75 2.00
76 Matt Cullen NE .30 .75
77 Bates Battaglia NE .30 .75
78 Andrei Zyuzin NE .30 .75
79 Cameron Mann NE .40 1.00
80 Zdeno Chara NE .50 1.25
81 Marc Savard NE .30 .75
82 Alexei Morozov NE .40 1.00
83 Mike Johnson NE .40 1.00
84 Vaclav Varada NE .30 .75
85 Dan Cloutier NE .30 .75
86 Brad Isbister NE .30 .75
87 Marco Sturm NE .40 1.00
88 Anders Eriksson NE .30 .75
89 Jan Bulis NE .30 .75
90 Brendan Morrison NE .40 1.00
91 Wayne Gretzky TSS 4.00 10.00
92 Jaromir Jagr TSS 1.00 2.50
93 Peter Forsberg TSS 1.50 4.00
94 Paul Kariya TSS .75 2.00
95 Brett Hull TSS .75 2.00
96 Martin Brodeur TSS 1.50 4.00
97 Eric Lindros TSS .75 2.00
98 Peter Bondra TSS .75 2.00
99 Mike Modano TSS 1.00 2.50
100 Theo Fleury TSS .60 1.50
101 Curtis Joseph TSS .75 2.00
102 Sergei Fedorov TSS 1.00 2.50
103 Saku Koivu TSS .75 2.00
104 Zigmund Palffy TSS .75 2.00
105 Ed Belfour TSS .75 2.00
106 Patrick Roy TSS 3.00 8.00
107 Brendan Shanahan TSS .75 2.00
108 Mats Sundin TSS .75 2.00
109 Alexei Yashin TSS .60 1.50
110 Doug Gilmour TSS .75 2.00
111 Chris Osgood TSS .75 2.00
112 Keith Tkachuk TSS .75 2.00
113 Mark Messier TSS .75 2.00
114 John Vanbiesbrouck TSS .60 1.50
115 Ray Bourque TSS 1.00 2.50
116 John LeClair TSS .50 1.25
117 Dominik Hasek TSS 1.25 3.00
118 Teemu Selanne TSS .75 2.00
119 Joe Sakic TSS 1.25 3.00
120 Steve Yzerman TSS 3.00 8.00
121 Sergei Samsonov NE 1.25 3.00
122 Ryan Johnson NE 1.00 2.50
123 Josef Marha NE 1.00 2.50
124 Patrick Marleau NE 1.00 2.50
125 Derek Morris NE 1.00 2.50
126 Jamie Storr NE 1.25 3.00
127 Richard Zednik NE 1.00 2.50
128 Alyn McCauley NE 1.00 2.50
129 Robert Dome NE 1.00 2.50
130 Patrik Elias NE 1.25 3.00
131 Olli Jokinen NE 1.25 3.00
132 Warren Luhning NE 1.00 2.50
133 Chris Phillips NE 1.00 2.50
134 Mattias Ohlund NE 1.25 3.00
135 Joe Thornton NE 2.50 6.00
136 Matt Cullen NE 1.00 2.50
137 Bates Battglia NE 1.00 2.50
138 Andrei Zyuzin NE 1.00 2.50
139 Cameron Mann NE 1.00 2.50
140 Zdeno Chara NE 1.00 2.50
141 Marc Savard NE 1.00 2.50
142 Alexei Morozov NE 1.25 3.00
143 Mike Johnson NE 1.25 3.00
144 Vaclav Varada NE 1.00 2.50
145 Dan Cloutier NE 1.00 2.50
146 Brad Isbister NE 1.00 2.50
147 Marco Sturm NE 1.25 3.00
148 Anders Eriksson NE 1.00 2.50
149 Jan Bulis NE 1.00 2.50
150 Brendan Morrison NE 1.50 4.00
151 Wayne Gretzky TSS 25.00 60.00
152 Jaromir Jagr TSS 6.00 15.00
153 Peter Forsberg TSS 5.00 12.00
154 Paul Kariya TSS 4.00 10.00
155 Brett Hull TSS 5.00 12.00
156 Martin Brodeur TSS 15.00 40.00
157 Eric Lindros TSS 4.00 10.00
158 Peter Bondra TSS 4.00 10.00
159 Mike Modano TSS 6.00 15.00
160 Theo Fleury TSS 3.00 8.00
161 Curtis Joseph TSS 4.00 10.00
162 Sergei Fedorov TSS 6.00 15.00
163 Saku Koivu TSS 4.00 10.00
164 Zigmund Palffy TSS 3.00 8.00
165 Ed Belfour TSS 4.00 10.00
166 Patrick Roy TSS 15.00 40.00
167 Brendan Shanahan TSS 4.00 10.00
168 Mats Sundin TSS 4.00 10.00
169 Alexei Yashin TSS 3.00 8.00
170 Doug Gilmour TSS 4.00 10.00
171 Chris Osgood TSS 4.00 10.00
172 Keith Tkachuk TSS 4.00 10.00
173 Mark Messier TSS 5.00 12.00
174 John Vanbiesbrouck TSS 4.00 10.00
175 Ray Bourque TSS 6.00 15.00
176 John LeClair TSS 4.00 10.00
177 Dominik Hasek TSS 8.00 20.00
178 Teemu Selanne TSS 4.00 10.00
179 Joe Sakic TSS 8.00 20.00
180 Steve Yzerman TSS 20.00 50.00

1998-99 UD3 Die-Cuts

This 180-card set is a limited edition die-cut parallel version of the base set. The New Era and Three Star Spotlight SE Light F/X card versions (61-120) are sequentially numbered to 1000. The New Era Embossed cards (1-30) are sequentially numbered to 200 with the Three Star Spotlight Embossed (151-180) sequentially numbered to 100. The New Era Rainbow cards (121-150) are sequentially numbered to 50. The Three Star Spotlight Rainbow ones (31-60) are numbered 1 of 1.
*1-30 EMB.DIE-CUT/200: 6X TO 15X
31-60 UNPRICED RAINBOW PRINT RUN 1
*61-90 DIE-CUT/1000: 2X TO 5X
*91-120 DIE-CUT/1000: 2X TO 5X
*121-150 DIE-CUT/50: 5X TO 15X
*151-180 DIE-CUT/100: 1.5X TO 4X

2004-05 Ultimate Collection

Released in early-summer 2005, this 84-card set is was packaged in 4-card packs that contained 1 serial-numbered base card, 1 autograph card, 1 memorabilia card and 1 serial-numbered subset card or extra base card. Cards 1-48 were serial-numbered to 350 and the World Cup subset cards (#59-84) were serial-numbered to 299.
1 Jean-Sebastien Giguere 1.00 2.50
2 Dany Heatley 1.00 2.50
3 Ilya Kovalchuk 1.00 2.50
4 Joe Thornton 1.25 3.00
5 Chris Drury .75 2.00
6 Jarome Iginla 1.00 2.50
7 Miikka Kiprusoff .75 2.00
8 Eric Staal 1.25 3.00
9 Jocelyn Thibault .75 2.00
10 Peter Forsberg 1.25 3.00
11 Joe Sakic 1.50 4.00
12 Rick Nash 1.00 2.50
13 Mike Modano 1.50 4.00
14 Pavel Datsyuk 1.25 3.00
15 Gordie Howe 3.00 8.00
16 Steve Yzerman 3.00 8.00
17 Wayne Gretzky 5.00 12.00
18 Ryan Smyth .75 2.00
19 Roberto Luongo 1.50 4.00
20 Luc Robitaille 1.00 2.50
21 Marian Gaborik 1.50 4.00
22 Patrick Roy 2.50 6.00
23 Jose Theodore 1.00 2.50
24 Tomas Vokoun .75 2.00
25 Martin Brodeur 2.00 5.00
26 Jaromir Jagr 2.50 6.00
27 Mark Messier 2.50 6.00
28 Michael Peca .75 2.00
29 Dominik Hasek 1.50 4.00
30 Jason Spezza 1.00 2.50
31 Jeremy Roenick 1.00 2.50
32 Simon Gagne 1.00 2.50
33 Brett Hull 1.25 3.00
34 Mario Lemieux 3.00 8.00
35 Evgeni Nabokov .75 2.00
36 Keith Tkachuk 1.00 2.50
37 Vincent Lecavalier .75 2.00
38 Martin St. Louis 1.00 2.50
39 Mats Sundin 1.00 2.50
40 Ed Belfour 1.00 2.50
41 Markus Naslund 1.00 2.50
42 Olaf Kolzig 1.00 2.50
43 Brad Fast RC .75 2.00
44 Brennan Evans RC .75 2.00
45 Layne Ulmer RC .60 1.50
46 Mel Angelstad RC .60 1.50
47 Garret Stroshein RC .60 1.50
48 Marcel Goc RC 1.00 2.50
49 Alexander Ragulin RC 1.00 2.50
50 Herb Brooks 1.00 2.50
51 Cammie Granato RC 1.00 2.50
52 Foster Hewitt .75 2.00
53 Mike Keenan 1.00 2.50
54 Bob Cole .60 1.50
55 Lord Stanley .75 2.00
56 James Norris .75 2.00
57 Ken Hitchcock .75 2.00
58 Dave Reece 1.50 4.00
59 Mario Lemieux WC 3.00 8.00
60 Joe Thornton WC 1.25 3.00
61 Dany Heatley WC 1.00 2.50
62 Jarome Iginla WC 1.00 2.50
63 Joe Sakic WC 1.50 4.00
64 Vincent Lecavalier WC .75 2.00
65 Martin Brodeur WC 2.00 5.00
66 Jaromir Jagr WC 2.50 6.00
67 Milan Hejduk WC .75 2.00
68 Miikka Kiprusoff WC .75 2.00
69 Tuomo Ruutu WC .75 2.00
70 Teemu Selanne WC 2.00 5.00
71 Marco Sturm WC .60 1.50
72 Olaf Kolzig WC 1.00 2.50
73 Ilya Kovalchuk WC 1.00 2.50
74 Sergei Samsonov WC .75 2.00
75 Marian Hossa WC .75 2.00
76 Marian Gaborik WC 1.50 4.00
77 Nicklas Lidstrom WC 1.00 2.50
78 Mats Sundin WC 1.00 2.50
79 Peter Forsberg WC 1.25 3.00
80 Robert Esche WC .75 2.00
81 Mike Modano WC 1.50 4.00
82 Bill Guerin WC 1.00 2.50
83 Tony Amonte WC .75 2.00
84 Keith Tkachuk WC 1.00 2.50

2004-05 Ultimate Collection Buybacks

This 96-cards set featured cards that were "bought back" by UD, signed by the players, serial-numbered and then re-inserted into this product. Each card carried a UD hologram and a "Buyback" certificate card.
1 A.Tanguay MVP Souv/28 15.00 40.00
4 C.Drury MVP Jsy/32 12.50 30.00
26 J.Spezza Prospects Jsy/51 25.00 60.00
28 J.Bouwmster Prospects Jsy/56 15.00 40.00
37 J.Thornton Ice Jsy/22 25.00 60.00
40 J.Thornton MVP Jsy/24 25.00 60.00
45 J.Theodore Mask Col Pad/23 40.00 100.00
46 J.Theodore Top Shelf Gear/18 40.00 100.00
57 M.Naslund Top Shelf Jsy/17 15.00 40.00
61 M.Turco MVP Souv/26 20.00 50.00
63 M.Noronen SPGU Auth Fab/21
64 M.Noronen Mask Col Jsy/22 12.50 30.00
66 M.Hejduk MVP Jsy/20 12.50 30.00
69 M.Hejduk Top Shelf Jsy/22 15.00 40.00
87 Z.Palffy SPGU Auth Fab/23
92 Z.Palffy UD Phenom Finish/19 15.00 40.00
94 Z.Palffy MVP Souv/26 12.50 30.00
96 Z.Palffy Top Shelf Jsy/23 12.50 30.00

2004-05 Ultimate Collection Jerseys

PRINT RUN 250 SER.#'d SETS
UGJAT Alex Tanguay 4.00 10.00
UGJBC Bobby Clarke 5.00 12.00
UGJBH Bobby Hull 8.00 20.00
UGJBO Mike Bossy 6.00 15.00
UGJBT Bryan Trottier 4.00 10.00
UGJCJ Curtis Joseph 6.00 15.00
UGJDH Dany Heatley 6.00 15.00
UGJDO Dominik Hasek 8.00 20.00
UGJGH Gordie Howe 12.00 30.00
UGJGL Guy Lafleur 8.00 20.00
UGJHE Milan Hejduk 4.00 10.00
UGJJB Johnny Bucyk 4.00 10.00
UGJJI Jarome Iginla 8.00 20.00
UGJJJ Jaromir Jagr 10.00 25.00
UGJJK Jari Kurri 5.00 12.00
UGJJO Jose Theodore 5.00 12.00
UGJJR Jeremy Roenick 5.00 12.00
UGJJS Joe Sakic 10.00 25.00
UGJJT Joe Thornton 8.00 20.00
UGJMB Martin Brodeur 10.00 25.00
UGJMH Marian Hossa 4.00 10.00
UGJML Mario Lemieux 15.00 40.00
UGJMM Mark Messier 8.00 20.00
UGJMN Markus Naslund 4.00 10.00
UGJMO Mike Modano 5.00 12.00
UGJMS Martin St.Louis 4.00 10.00
UGJNK Nikolai Khabibulin 4.00 10.00
UGJNZ Nikolai Zherdev 4.00 10.00
UGJPF Peter Forsberg 6.00 15.00
UGJPK Paul Kariya 4.00 10.00
UGJRB Ray Bourque 5.00 12.00
UGJRN Rick Nash 5.00 12.00
UGJSK Saku Koivu 4.00 10.00
UGJSP Jason Spezza 6.00 15.00
UGJSU Mats Sundin 5.00 12.00
UGJSY Steve Yzerman 10.00 25.00
UGJVL Vincent Lecavalier 4.00 10.00
UGJPR1 Patrick Roy 10.00 25.00
UGJPR2 Patrick Roy 10.00 25.00
UGJWG1 Wayne Gretzky AS 30.00 80.00
UGJWG2 Wayne Gretzky EDM 20.00 50.00

2004-05 Ultimate Collection Jerseys Gold

*GOLD: .75X TO 2X JSY HI
PRINT RUN 75 SER.#'d SETS

2004-05 Ultimate Collection Patches

STATED PRINT RUN 9-35
UPMH Marian Hossa 50.00 100.00
UPJT Joe Thornton 50.00 100.00
UPMB Martin Brodeur 100.00 200.00
UPJJ Jaromir Jagr 60.00 120.00
UPJO Jose Theodore 50.00 100.00
UPJR Jeremy Roenick 40.00 80.00
UPJS Joe Sakic 75.00 150.00
UPJG Jean-Sebastien Giguere 60.00 120.00
UPHE Milan Hejduk 40.00 80.00
UPMO Mike Modano 50.00 100.00
UPMS Martin St.Louis 40.00 80.00
UPNK Nikolai Khabibulin 40.00 80.00
UPBH Brett Hull 50.00 100.00
UPBL Brian Leetch 50.00 100.00
UPMM Mark Messier 100.00 200.00
UPSK Saku Koivu 50.00 100.00
UPSP Jason Spezza 100.00 200.00
UPSU Mats Sundin 75.00 200.00
UPML Mario Lemieux 200.00 400.00
UPHA Dominik Hasek 60.00 120.00
UPIK Ilya Kovalchuk 60.00 120.00
UPSY Steve Yzerman 125.00 250.00
UPVL Vincent Lecavalier 50.00 100.00
UPNZ Nikolai Zherdev 40.00 80.00
UPPF Peter Forsberg 60.00 120.00
UPRN Rick Nash 50.00 100.00
UPSF Sergei Fedorov 30.00 60.00
UPBS Brendan Shanahan 50.00 100.00
UPBT Bryan Trottier 50.00 100.00
UPPK Paul Kariya/9
UPCJ Curtis Joseph 60.00 120.00
UPEB Ed Belfour 30.00 80.00
UPTK Keith Tkachuk 40.00 80.00
UPRB1 Ray Bourque BOS 75.00 150.00
UPPR1 Patrick Roy COL 100.00 250.00
UPWG1 W.Gretzky LA/25 300.00 600.00
UPRB2 Ray Bourque COL 75.00 150.00
UPPR2 Patrick Roy MTL 100.00 200.00
UPWG2 W.Gretzky AS/25 250.00 500.00
UPDHA D. Heatley JSY 40.00 80.00
UPDHB D. Heatley PATCH 50.00 100.00
UPMNA M. Naslund JSY 30.00 60.00
UPMNB M. Naslund PATCH 40.00 80.00

2004-05 Ultimate Collection Patch Autographs

SINGLE AUTO PRINT RUN 50
UPAAT Alex Tanguay 30.00 80.00
UPABR Brad Richards 25.00 60.00
UPACD Chris Drury 25.00 60.00
UPADH Dany Heatley 60.00 150.00
UPADO Dominik Hasek 75.00 150.00
UPAEJ Ed Jovanovski 30.00 80.00
UPAJB Jay Bouwmeester 25.00 60.00
UPAJI Jarome Iginla 50.00 100.00
UPAJK Jari Kurri 50.00 100.00
UPAJO Jose Theodore 50.00 100.00
UPAJR Jeremy Roenick 30.00 80.00
UPAJT Joe Thornton 60.00 150.00
UPAMB Martin Brodeur 125.00 250.00
UPAMD Marcel Dionne 30.00 80.00
UPAMH Milan Hejduk 25.00 60.00
UPAMN Markus Naslund 25.00 60.00
UPAMS Martin St.Louis 30.00 80.00
UPAMT Marty Turco 15.00 40.00
UPANK Nikolai Khabibulin 50.00 100.00
UPANZ Nikolai Zherdev 20.00 50.00
UPAPR Patrick Roy 150.00 300.00
UPARB Ray Bourque 60.00 150.00
UPARL Roberto Luongo 40.00 100.00
UPARN Rick Nash 60.00 150.00
UPASK Saku Koivu 30.00 80.00
UPASP Jason Spezza 75.00 150.00
UPAVL Vincent Lecavalier 50.00 100.00
UPAWG1 Wayne Gretzky AS 200.00 400.00
UPAWG2 Wayne Gretzky LA 200.00 400.00

2004-05 Ultimate Collection Signatures

This 42-card set was seeded at one per pack. Known shortprints are listed below.
USAR Andrew Raycroft 6.00 15.00
USAT Alex Tanguay 6.00 15.00
USBB Brad Boyes 6.00 15.00
USBC Bobby Clarke 10.00 25.00
USBH Bobby Hull SP 40.00 80.00
USBL Brian Leetch 10.00 25.00
USBR Brad Richards 6.00 15.00
USBT Bryan Trottier SP 12.50 30.00
USCD Chris Drury 4.00 10.00
USDH Dany Heatley 10.00 25.00
USEJ Ed Jovanovski 4.00 10.00
USES Eric Staal 10.00 25.00
USGH Gordie Howe 50.00 100.00
USHA Dominik Hasek SP 30.00 80.00
USHZ Henrik Zetterberg 10.00 25.00
USIK Ilya Kovalchuk 12.00 30.00
USJB Jay Bouwmeester 6.00 15.00
USJI Jarome Iginla 8.00 20.00
USJK Jari Kurri 10.00 25.00
USJO Jose Theodore SP 15.00 40.00
USJT Joe Thornton 12.50 30.00
USKD Kris Draper 4.00 10.00
USKL Kari Lehtonen 8.00 20.00
USMA Marc-Andre Fleury 15.00 30.00
USMB Martin Brodeur SP 40.00 80.00
USMH Milan Hejduk 4.00 10.00
USMN Markus Naslund 6.00 15.00
USMR Michael Ryder 8.00 20.00
USMS Martin St. Louis 6.00 15.00
USMT Marty Turco 4.00 10.00
USNH Nathan Horton 4.00 10.00
USNK Nikolai Khabibulin 8.00 20.00
USNZ Nikolai Zherdev 6.00 15.00
USPR1 Patrick Roy SP 125.00 250.00
USRB1 Ray Bourque SP 25.00 60.00
USRL Roberto Luongo SP 10.00 25.00
USRN Rick Nash SP 20.00 50.00
USSK Saku Koivu SP 12.50 30.00
USSP Jason Spezza 12.50 30.00
USVL Vincent Lecavalier SP 20.00 50.00
USWG1 Wayne Gretzky 100.00 200.00
USZP Zigmund Palffy 4.00 10.00

2005-06 Ultimate Collection

This 232-card set was issued into the hobby in four-card packs, with an $100 SRP, which came four packs to a box and four boxes to a case. Every card in this set is serial numbered. Cards numbered 1-90 feature veterans and those cards were issued to a stated print run of 599 serial numbered sets. The rest of the set features Rookie Cards: Cards numbered 91-118 were signed by the player. Cards numbered 91-100 were issued to a stated print run of 299 serial numbered sets, while cards 101-132 were issued to a stated print run of 399 serial numbered sets and cards numbered 133-232 were issued to a stated print run of 599 serial numbered sets.
1 Teemu Selanne 4.00 10.00
2 Jean-Sebastien Giguere 2.00 5.00
3 Joffrey Lupul 1.50 4.00
4 Ilya Kovalchuk 2.00 5.00
5 Marian Hossa 1.50 4.00
6 Kari Lehtonen 1.50 4.00
7 Andrew Raycroft 1.50 4.00
8 Brad Boyes 1.50 4.00
9 Patrice Bergeron 2.50 6.00
10 Brian Leetch 2.00 5.00
11 Glen Murray 1.50 4.00
12 Chris Drury 1.50 4.00
13 Martin Biron 1.50 4.00
14 Daniel Briere 2.00 5.00
15 Jarome Iginla 2.00 5.00
16 Miikka Kiprusoff 1.50 4.00
17 Doug Weight 2.00 5.00
18 Eric Staal 2.50 6.00
19 Nikolai Khabibulin 2.00 5.00
20 Tuomo Ruutu 2.00 5.00
21 Marek Svatos 1.50 4.00
22 Joe Sakic 3.00 8.00
23 Jose Theodore 2.00 5.00
24 Rob Blake 2.00 5.00
25 Alex Tanguay 2.00 5.00
26 Milan Hejduk 1.50 4.00
27 Rick Nash 2.00 5.00
28 Sergei Fedorov 3.00 8.00
29 Mike Modano 3.00 8.00
30 Bill Guerin 2.00 5.00
31 Marty Turco 2.00 5.00

32 Steve Yzerman 5.00 12.00
33 Nicklas Lidstrom 2.00 5.00
34 Gordie Howe 6.00 15.00
35 Brendan Shanahan 2.50 6.00
36 Pavel Datsyuk 2.50 6.00
37 Henrik Zetterberg 2.50 6.00
38 Ryan Smyth 1.50 4.00
39 Chris Pronger 1.50 4.00
40 Ales Hemsky 1.50 4.00
41 Wayne Gretzky 10.00 25.00
42 Roberto Luongo 3.00 8.00
43 Olli Jokinen 2.00 5.00
44 Jeremy Roenick 2.00 5.00
45 Pavol Demitra 2.50 6.00
46 Luc Robitaille 2.00 5.00
47 Marian Gaborik 3.00 8.00
48 David Aebischer 1.50 4.00
49 Michael Ryder 1.50 4.00
50 Saku Koivu 2.00 5.00
51 Mike Ribeiro 1.50 4.00
52 Tomas Vokoun 1.50 4.00
53 Paul Kariya 2.50 6.00
54 Martin Brodeur 4.00 10.00
55 Patrik Elias 2.00 5.00
56 Rick DiPietro 1.50 4.00
57 Alexei Yashin 1.50 4.00
58 Miroslav Satan 1.50 4.00
59 Jaromir Jagr 5.00 12.00
60 Dominik Hasek 3.00 8.00
61 Dany Heatley 2.00 5.00
62 Jason Spezza 2.00 5.00
63 Martin Havlat 2.00 5.00
64 Daniel Alfredsson 2.00 5.00
65 Peter Forsberg 2.50 6.00
66 Simon Gagne 2.00 5.00
67 Robert Esche 1.50 4.00
68 Keith Primeau 2.00 5.00
69 Curtis Joseph 2.00 5.00
70 Shane Doan 1.50 4.00
71 Mario Lemieux 6.00 15.00
72 Ryan Malone 1.25 3.00
73 Marc-Andre Fleury 3.00 8.00
74 Joe Thornton 2.50 6.00
75 Evgeni Nabokov 1.50 4.00
76 Jonathan Cheechoo 2.00 5.00
77 Patrick Marleau 2.00 5.00
78 Keith Tkachuk 2.00 5.00
79 Brad Richards 2.00 5.00
80 Martin St. Louis 2.00 5.00
81 Vincent Lecavalier 1.50 4.00
82 Bryan McCabe 1.25 3.00
83 Eric Lindros 3.00 8.00
84 Ed Belfour 2.00 5.00
85 Mats Sundin 2.00 5.00
86 Markus Naslund 2.00 5.00
87 Brendan Morrison 1.25 3.00
88 Todd Bertuzzi 2.00 5.00
89 Ed Jovanovski 1.50 4.00
90 Olaf Kolzig 2.00 5.00
91 Sidney Crosby AU RC 500.00 800.00
92 Alexander Ovechkin AU RC 200.00 400.00
93 Gilbert Brule AU RC 10.00 25.00
94 Corey Perry AU RC 25.00 60.00
95 Jeff Carter AU RC 12.00 30.00
96 Alexander Steen AU RC 12.00 30.00
97 Henrik Lundqvist AU RC 40.00 80.00
98 Hannu Toivonen AU RC 10.00 25.00
99 Alexander Perezhogin AU RC 8.00 20.00
100 Thomas Vanek AU RC 15.00 40.00
101 Ryan Getzlaf AU RC 25.00 50.00
102 Braydon Coburn AU RC 10.00 25.00
103 Milan Jurcina AU RC 8.00 20.00
104 Andrew Alberts AU RC 6.00 15.00
105 Dion Phaneuf AU RC 15.00 40.00
106 Eric Nystrom AU RC 8.00 20.00
107 Cam Ward AU RC 15.00 40.00
108 Cam Barker AU RC 8.00 20.00
109 Brent Seabrook AU RC 20.00 50.00
110 Rene Bourque AU RC 10.00 25.00
111 Peter Budaj AU RC 12.00 30.00
112 Wojtek Wolski AU RC 8.00 20.00
113 Jussi Jokinen AU RC 10.00 25.00
114 Jim Howard AU RC 12.00 30.00
115 Johan Franzen AU RC 12.00 30.00
116 Brad Winchester AU RC 10.00 25.00
117 Rostislav Olesz AU RC 8.00 20.00
118 Anthony Stewart AU RC 8.00 20.00
119 Matt Foy AU RC 6.00 15.00
120 Yann Danis AU RC 8.00 20.00
121 Ryan Suter AU RC 12.00 30.00
122 Zach Parise AU RC 30.00 60.00
123 Robert Nilsson AU RC 10.00 25.00
124 Alvaro Montoya AU RC 6.00 15.00
125 Petr Prucha AU RC 10.00 25.00
126 Brandon Bochenski AU RC 10.00 25.00
127 Andrej Meszaros AU RC 8.00 20.00
128 Patrick Eaves AU RC 10.00 25.00
129 Mike Richards AU RC 12.00 30.00
130 Keith Ballard AU RC 8.00 20.00
131 Ryane Clowe AU RC 12.00 30.00
132 Jeff Woywitka AU RC 6.00 15.00
133 Michael Wall RC 3.00 8.00
134 Zenon Konopka RC 2.50 6.00
135 Jim Slater RC 3.00 8.00
136 Adam Berkhoel RC 3.00 8.00
137 Daniel Paille RC 4.00 10.00
138 Jordan Sigalet RC 2.50 6.00
139 Niklas Nordgren RC 4.00 10.00
140 Kevin Nastiuk RC 2.50 6.00
141 Duncan Keith RC 8.00 20.00
142 Jaroslav Balastik RC 2.50 6.00
143 Steven Goertzen RC 2.50 6.00
144 Alexandre Picard RC 2.50 6.00
145 Junior Lessard RC 2.50 6.00
146 Vojtech Polak RC 2.50 6.00
147 Brett Lebda RC 2.50 6.00
148 Valtteri Filppula RC 5.00 12.00
149 Kyle Brodziak RC 2.50 6.00
150 Matt Greene RC 2.50 6.00
151 Derek Boogaard RC 5.00 12.00
152 Brad Richardson RC 4.00 10.00
153 Mark Streit RC 2.50 6.00
154 Chris Campoli RC 2.50 6.00
155 Petteri Nokelainen RC 2.50 6.00
156 Kevin Colley RC 3.00 8.00
157 Ryan Hollweg RC 2.50 6.00
158 Jeremy Colliton RC 2.50 6.00
159 Brian McGrattan RC 2.50 6.00
160 Christoph Schubert RC 2.50 6.00
161 R.J. Umberger RC 4.00 10.00
162 Ben Eager RC 3.00 8.00
163 David Leneveu RC 3.00 8.00
164 Maxime Talbot RC 4.00 10.00
165 Josh Gorges RC 3.00 8.00
166 Dimitri Patzold RC 2.50 6.00
167 Jay McClement RC 2.50 6.00
168 Jeff Hoggan RC 2.50 6.00
169 Lee Stempniak RC 4.00 10.00
170 Andrei Kostitsyn RC 5.00 12.00
171 Timo Helbling RC 2.50 6.00
172 Paul Ranger RC 2.50 6.00
173 Ryan Craig RC 2.50 6.00
174 Evgeny Artyukhin RC 3.00 8.00
175 Andrew Wozniewski RC 3.00 8.00
176 Staffan Kronwall RC 2.50 6.00
177 Yanick Lehoux RC 4.00 10.00
178 Ryan Whitney RC 4.00 10.00
179 Erik Christensen RC 2.50 6.00
180 Andrew Ladd RC 5.00 12.00
181 Rob McVicar RC 3.00 8.00
182 Tomas Fleischmann RC 4.00 10.00
183 Jakub Klepis RC 2.50 6.00
184 Mike Green RC 5.00 12.00
185 Corey Crawford RC 15.00 30.00
186 Mikko Koivu RC 5.00 12.00
187 Steve Bernier RC 4.00 10.00
188 Cam Janssen RC 3.00 8.00
189 Barry Tallackson RC 3.00 8.00
190 Jeff Tambellini RC 2.50 6.00
191 Maxim Lapierre RC 4.00 10.00
192 Danny Richmond RC 2.50 6.00
193 Dustin Penner RC 4.00 10.00
194 Ben Walter RC 2.50 6.00
195 Chris Thorburn RC 3.00 8.00
196 Jiri Novotny RC 3.00 8.00
197 Richie Regehr RC 2.50 6.00
198 Chad Larose RC 2.50 6.00
199 James Wisniewski RC 3.00 8.00
200 Vitaly Kolesnik RC 3.00 8.00
201 Joakim Lindstrom RC 2.50 6.00
202 Ole-Kristian Tollefsen RC 3.00 8.00
203 Kyle Quincey RC 3.00 8.00
204 Danny Syvret RC 2.50 6.00
205 Jean-Francois Jacques RC 2.50 6.00
206 Greg Jacina RC 2.50 6.00
207 Petr Taticek RC 3.00 8.00
208 Rob Globke RC 2.50 6.00
209 George Parros RC 2.50 6.00
210 Petr Kanko RC 3.00 8.00
211 Richard Petiot RC 3.00 8.00
212 Jean-Philippe Cote RC 2.50 6.00
213 Kevin Klein RC 2.50 6.00
214 Pekka Rinne RC 15.00 40.00
215 Jason Ryznar RC 2.50 6.00
216 Bruno Gervais RC 2.50 6.00
217 Alexandre Picard RC 2.50 6.00
218 Stefan Ruzicka RC 2.50 6.00
219 Matt Jones RC 2.50 6.00
220 Colby Armstrong RC 4.00 10.00
221 Doug Murray RC 2.50 6.00
222 Grant Stevenson RC 2.50 6.00
223 Colin Hemingway RC 2.50 6.00
224 Kevin Dallman RC 3.00 8.00
225 Dennis Wideman RC 2.50 6.00
226 Darren Reid RC 2.50 6.00
227 Doug O'Brien RC 2.50 6.00
228 Gerald Coleman RC 3.00 8.00
229 Nick Tarnasky RC 2.50 6.00
230 Jay Harrison RC 3.00 8.00
231 Kevin Bieksa RC 5.00 12.00
232 Tomas Mojzis RC 2.50 6.00

2005-06 Ultimate Collection Gold

*1-90 VETS: 1.5X TO 4X BASIC CARDS
*ROOKIES: .8X TO 2X BASIC RC
STATED PRINT RUN 25 SER.#'d SETS

1 Teemu Selanne 15.00 40.00
2 Jean-Sebastien Giguere 8.00 20.00
3 Joffrey Lupul 6.00 15.00
4 Ilya Kovalchuk 8.00 20.00
5 Marian Hossa 6.00 15.00
6 Kari Lehtonen 6.00 15.00
7 Andrew Raycroft 6.00 15.00
8 Brad Boyes 6.00 15.00
9 Patrice Bergeron 10.00 25.00
10 Brian Leetch 8.00 20.00
11 Glen Murray 6.00 15.00
12 Chris Drury 6.00 15.00
13 Martin Biron 6.00 15.00
14 Daniel Briere 8.00 20.00
15 Jarome Iginla 8.00 20.00
16 Miikka Kiprusoff 6.00 15.00
17 Doug Weight 8.00 20.00
18 Eric Staal 10.00 25.00
19 Nikolai Khabibulin 8.00 20.00
20 Tuomo Ruutu 8.00 20.00
21 Marek Svatos 6.00 15.00
22 Joe Sakic 12.00 30.00
23 Jose Theodore 8.00 20.00
24 Rob Blake 8.00 20.00
25 Alex Tanguay 8.00 20.00
26 Milan Hejduk 6.00 15.00
27 Rick Nash 8.00 20.00
28 Sergei Fedorov 12.00 30.00
29 Mike Modano 12.00 30.00
30 Bill Guerin 8.00 20.00
31 Marty Turco 8.00 20.00
32 Steve Yzerman 20.00 50.00
33 Nicklas Lidstrom 8.00 20.00
34 Gordie Howe 25.00 60.00
35 Brendan Shanahan 10.00 25.00
36 Pavel Datsyuk 10.00 25.00
37 Henrik Zetterberg 10.00 25.00
38 Ryan Smyth 6.00 15.00
39 Chris Pronger 6.00 15.00
40 Ales Hemsky 6.00 15.00
41 Wayne Gretzky 40.00 100.00
42 Roberto Luongo 12.00 30.00
43 Olli Jokinen 8.00 20.00
44 Jeremy Roenick 8.00 20.00
45 Pavol Demitra 10.00 25.00
46 Luc Robitaille 8.00 20.00
47 Marian Gaborik 12.00 30.00
48 David Aebischer 6.00 15.00
49 Michael Ryder 6.00 15.00
50 Saku Koivu 8.00 20.00
51 Mike Ribeiro 6.00 15.00
52 Tomas Vokoun 6.00 15.00
53 Paul Kariya 10.00 25.00
54 Martin Brodeur 15.00 40.00
55 Patrik Elias 8.00 20.00
56 Rick DiPietro 6.00 15.00
57 Alexei Yashin 6.00 15.00
58 Miroslav Satan 6.00 15.00
59 Jaromir Jagr 20.00 50.00
60 Dominik Hasek 12.00 30.00
61 Dany Heatley 8.00 20.00
62 Jason Spezza 8.00 20.00
63 Martin Havlat 8.00 20.00
64 Daniel Alfredsson 8.00 20.00
65 Peter Forsberg 10.00 25.00
66 Simon Gagne 8.00 20.00
67 Robert Esche 6.00 15.00
68 Keith Primeau 8.00 20.00
69 Curtis Joseph 8.00 20.00
70 Shane Doan 6.00 15.00
71 Mario Lemieux 25.00 60.00
72 Ryan Malone 5.00 12.00
73 Marc-Andre Fleury 12.00 30.00
74 Joe Thornton 10.00 25.00
75 Evgeni Nabokov 6.00 15.00
76 Jonathan Cheechoo 8.00 20.00
77 Patrick Marleau 8.00 20.00
78 Keith Tkachuk 8.00 20.00
79 Brad Richards 8.00 20.00
80 Martin St. Louis 8.00 20.00
81 Vincent Lecavalier 6.00 15.00
82 Bryan McCabe 5.00 12.00
83 Eric Lindros 12.00 30.00
84 Ed Belfour 8.00 20.00
85 Mats Sundin 8.00 20.00
86 Markus Naslund 8.00 20.00
87 Brendan Morrison 5.00 12.00
88 Todd Bertuzzi 8.00 20.00
89 Ed Jovanovski 6.00 15.00
90 Olaf Kolzig 8.00 20.00
133 Michael Wall 6.00 15.00
134 Zenon Konopka 5.00 12.00
135 Jim Slater 6.00 15.00
136 Adam Berkhoel 6.00 15.00
137 Daniel Paille 8.00 20.00
138 Jordan Sigalet 5.00 12.00
139 Niklas Nordgren 8.00 20.00
140 Kevin Nastiuk 5.00 12.00
141 Duncan Keith 15.00 40.00
142 Jaroslav Balastik 5.00 12.00
143 Steven Goertzen 5.00 12.00
144 Alexandre Picard 5.00 12.00
145 Junior Lessard 5.00 12.00
146 Vojtech Polak 5.00 12.00
147 Brett Lebda 5.00 12.00
148 Valtteri Filppula 10.00 25.00
149 Kyle Brodziak 5.00 12.00
150 Matt Greene 5.00 12.00
151 Derek Boogaard 10.00 25.00
152 Brad Richardson 8.00 20.00
153 Mark Streit 5.00 12.00
154 Chris Campoli 5.00 12.00
155 Petteri Nokelainen 5.00 12.00
156 Kevin Colley 6.00 15.00
157 Ryan Hollweg 5.00 12.00
158 Jeremy Colliton 5.00 12.00
159 Brian McGrattan 5.00 12.00
160 Christoph Schubert 5.00 12.00
161 R.J. Umberger 8.00 20.00
162 Ben Eager 6.00 15.00
163 David Leneveu 6.00 15.00
164 Maxime Talbot 8.00 20.00
165 Josh Gorges 6.00 15.00
166 Dimitri Patzold 5.00 12.00
167 Jay McClement 5.00 12.00
168 Jeff Hoggan 5.00 12.00
169 Lee Stempniak 8.00 20.00
170 Andrei Kostitsyn 10.00 25.00
171 Timo Helbling 5.00 12.00
172 Paul Ranger 5.00 12.00
173 Ryan Craig 5.00 12.00
174 Evgeny Artyukhin 6.00 15.00
175 Andrew Wozniewski 6.00 15.00
176 Staffan Kronwall 5.00 12.00
177 Yanick Lehoux 8.00 20.00
178 Ryan Whitney 8.00 20.00
179 Erik Christensen 5.00 12.00
180 Andrew Ladd 10.00 25.00
181 Rob McVicar 6.00 15.00
182 Tomas Fleischmann 8.00 20.00
183 Jakub Klepis 5.00 12.00
184 Mike Green 10.00 25.00
186 Mikko Koivu 10.00 25.00
187 Steve Bernier 8.00 20.00
188 Cam Janssen 6.00 15.00
189 Barry Tallackson 6.00 15.00
190 Jeff Tambellini 5.00 12.00
191 Maxim Lapierre 8.00 20.00
192 Danny Richmond 5.00 12.00
193 Dustin Penner 8.00 20.00
194 Ben Walter 5.00 12.00
195 Chris Thorburn 6.00 15.00
196 Jiri Novotny 6.00 15.00
197 Richie Regehr 5.00 12.00
198 Chad Larose 5.00 12.00
199 James Wisniewski 6.00 15.00
200 Vitaly Kolesnik 6.00 15.00
201 Joakim Lindstrom 5.00 12.00
202 Ole-Kristian Tollefsen 6.00 15.00
203 Kyle Quincey 6.00 15.00
204 Danny Syvret 5.00 12.00
205 Jean-Francois Jacques 5.00 12.00
206 Greg Jacina 5.00 12.00
207 Petr Taticek 6.00 15.00
208 Rob Globke 5.00 12.00
209 George Parros 5.00 12.00
210 Petr Kanko 6.00 15.00
211 Richard Petiot 6.00 15.00
212 Jean-Philippe Cote 5.00 12.00
213 Kevin Klein 5.00 12.00
214 Pekka Rinne 30.00 80.00
215 Jason Ryznar 5.00 12.00
216 Bruno Gervais 5.00 12.00
217 Alexandre Picard 5.00 12.00
218 Stefan Ruzicka 5.00 12.00
219 Matt Jones 5.00 12.00
220 Colby Armstrong 8.00 20.00
221 Doug Murray 5.00 12.00
222 Grant Stevenson 5.00 12.00
223 Colin Hemingway 5.00 12.00
224 Kevin Dallman 6.00 15.00
225 Dennis Wideman 5.00 12.00
226 Darren Reid 5.00 12.00
227 Doug O'Brien 5.00 12.00
228 Gerald Coleman 6.00 15.00
229 Nick Tarnasky 5.00 12.00
230 Jay Harrison 6.00 15.00
231 Kevin Bieksa 10.00 25.00
232 Tomas Mojzis 5.00 12.00

2005-06 Ultimate Collection Autographed Patches

STATED PRINT RUN 25 SER.#'d SETS

91 Sidney Crosby 800.00 1200.00
92 Alexander Ovechkin 400.00 700.00
93 Gilbert Brule 150.00 250.00
94 Corey Perry 75.00 150.00
95 Jeff Carter 60.00 120.00
96 Alexander Steen 30.00 80.00
97 Henrik Lundqvist 125.00 250.00
98 Hannu Toivonen 25.00 60.00
99 Alexander Perezhogin
100 Thomas Vanek 75.00 150.00
101 Ryan Getzlaf 50.00 100.00
102 Braydon Coburn 25.00 60.00
103 Milan Jurcina 20.00 50.00
104 Andrew Alberts 15.00 40.00
105 Dion Phaneuf 150.00 250.00
106 Eric Nystrom
107 Cam Ward 100.00 200.00
108 Cam Barker 20.00 50.00
109 Brent Seabrook 50.00 125.00
110 Rene Bourque 25.00 60.00
111 Peter Budaj 30.00 80.00
112 Wojtek Wolski
113 Jussi Jokinen 25.00 60.00
114 Jim Howard 60.00 120.00
115 Johan Franzen 40.00 100.00
116 Brad Winchester 25.00 60.00
117 Rostislav Olesz 20.00 50.00
119 Matt Foy 15.00 40.00
120 Yann Danis
121 Ryan Suter 30.00 80.00
122 Zach Parise 75.00 150.00
123 Robert Nilsson 25.00 60.00
124 Alvaro Montoya 25.00 60.00
126 Brandon Bochenski 25.00 60.00
127 Andrej Meszaros 20.00 50.00
129 Mike Richards 50.00 100.00
130 Keith Ballard 20.00 50.00
131 Ryane Clowe 30.00 80.00
132 Jeff Woywitka 15.00 40.00

2005-06 Ultimate Collection Endorsed Emblems

STATED PRINT RUN 35

EEAT Alex Tanguay 15.00 40.00
EEAY Alexei Yashin 15.00 40.00
EEBC Bobby Clarke 30.00 80.00
EEBI Martin Biron 25.00 60.00
EEBK Rob Blake 25.00 60.00
EEBL Brian Leetch 25.00 60.00
EEBM Brendan Morrison 15.00 40.00
EEBU Johnny Bucyk 25.00 60.00
EEBY Mike Bossy 50.00 100.00
EECD Chris Drury 25.00 60.00
EECN Cam Neely 60.00 125.00
EEDA David Aebischer 20.00 50.00
EEDB Dustin Brown 15.00 40.00
EEDG Doug Gilmour EXCH 75.00 125.00
EEDH Dany Heatley 40.00 100.00
EEDL David Legwand 25.00 60.00
EEDP Denis Potvin 50.00 100.00
EEDR Dwayne Roloson 25.00 60.00
EEDS Darryl Sittler 25.00 60.00
EEDW Doug Weight 15.00 40.00
EEEB Ed Belfour 75.00 150.00
EEES Eric Staal 20.00 50.00
EEGE Martin Gerber 25.00 60.00
EEGF Grant Fuhr 40.00 100.00
EEGL Guy Lafleur 25.00 60.00
EEGM Glen Murray 15.00 40.00
EEHJ Milan Hejduk 20.00 50.00
EEHK Dominik Hasek 75.00 150.00
EEHO Marian Hossa EXCH 40.00 100.00
EEHV Martin Havlat 30.00 80.00
EEHZ Henrik Zetterberg 50.00 125.00
EEIK Ilya Kovalchuk 90.00 150.00
EEJC Jonathan Cheechoo 25.00 60.00
EEJI Jarome Iginla 25.00 60.00
EEJO Joe Thornton 40.00 100.00
EEJP Joni Pitkanen 20.00 50.00
EEJR Jeremy Roenick 25.00 60.00
EEJS Jean-Sebastien Giguere 25.00 60.00
EEJT Jose Theodore 25.00 60.00
EEKL Kari Lehtonen 25.00 60.00
EEKP Keith Primeau 15.00 40.00
EELM Lanny McDonald 30.00 80.00
EELR Luc Robitaille 50.00 100.00
EELU Joffrey Lupul 25.00 60.00
EEMB Martin Brodeur 150.00 300.00
EEMC Bryan McCabe 15.00 40.00
EEML Manny Legace 15.00 40.00
EEMM Mike Modano 50.00 100.00
EEMN Markus Naslund 25.00 60.00
EEMS Matt Stajan 15.00 40.00
EEMT Marty Turco 25.00 60.00
EEMU Larry Murphy 20.00 50.00
EEMW Brenden Morrow 25.00 60.00
EENZ Nikolai Zherdev 15.00 40.00
EEOK Olaf Kolzig 30.00 80.00
EEPA Mark Parrish 15.00 40.00
EEPB Patrice Bergeron 30.00 80.00
EEPM Patrick Marleau 25.00 60.00
EEPR Patrick Roy 125.00 250.00
EERB Ray Bourque 75.00 150.00
EERE Robert Esche 15.00 40.00
EERL Roberto Luongo 50.00 100.00
EERM Ryan Miller 40.00 100.00
EERN Rick Nash 50.00 120.00
EERS Ryan Smyth 15.00 40.00
EERY Michael Ryder 30.00 80.00
EERZ Richard Zednik 15.00 40.00
EESG Simon Gagne 20.00 50.00
EESK Saku Koivu 30.00 80.00
EESL Martin St. Louis 25.00 60.00
EESP Jason Spezza 50.00 100.00
EESV Denis Savard 30.00 80.00
EETC Ty Conklin EXCH 15.00 40.00
EEWG Wayne Gretzky 300.00 450.00

2005-06 Ultimate Collection Jerseys

PRINT RUN 250 #'d COPIES, UNLESS NOTED

JAO Alexander Ovechkin 15.00 40.00
JAS Alexander Steen 6.00 15.00
JAY Alexei Yashin 3.00 8.00
JBT Bryan Trottier 4.00 10.00
JCO Corey Perry 4.00 10.00
JCP Chris Pronger 3.00 8.00
JDH Dominik Hasek 6.00 15.00
JDP Dion Phaneuf 10.00 25.00
JDW Doug Weight 3.00 8.00
JEL Eric Lindros 5.00 12.00
JES Eric Staal 4.00 10.00
JGB Gilbert Brule 3.00 8.00
JGH Gordie Howe 15.00 40.00
JHE Dany Heatley 5.00 12.00
JHL Henrik Lundqvist 10.00 25.00
JHT Hannu Toivonen 3.00 8.00
JIK Ilya Kovalchuk 6.00 15.00
JJB Jean Beliveau 8.00 20.00
JJC Jeff Carter 6.00 15.00
JJI Jarome Iginla 5.00 12.00
JJJ Jaromir Jagr/200 6.00 15.00
JJO Joe Thornton 6.00 15.00
JJS Joe Sakic 6.00 15.00
JJT Jose Theodore 5.00 12.00
JKL Kari Lehtonen 3.00 8.00
JLR Luc Robitaille 3.00 8.00
JMA Martin St. Louis 3.00 8.00
JMB Martin Brodeur 8.00 20.00
JMG Marian Gaborik 5.00 12.00
JMH Milan Hejduk 3.00 8.00
JML Mario Lemieux 15.00 40.00
JMM Mike Modano 5.00 12.00
JMN Markus Naslund 3.00 8.00
JMS Mats Sundin 3.00 8.00
JMT Marty Turco 3.00 8.00
JPB Patrice Bergeron 3.00 8.00
JPD Pavel Datsyuk 3.00 8.00
JPE Phil Esposito 5.00 12.00
JPF Peter Forsberg 5.00 12.00
JPK Paul Kariya 3.00 8.00
JPM Patrick Marleau 3.00 8.00
JPR Patrick Roy 12.00 30.00
JRB Ray Bourque 5.00 12.00
JRG Ryan Getzlaf 5.00 12.00
JRL Roberto Luongo 5.00 12.00
JSC Sidney Crosby 30.00 60.00
JSG Simon Gagne 3.00 8.00
JSK Saku Koivu/125 8.00 20.00
JSP Jason Spezza 4.00 10.00
JSY Steve Yzerman 10.00 25.00
JTB Todd Bertuzzi 3.00 8.00
JTS Teemu Selanne 3.00 8.00
JTV Tomas Vokoun 3.00 8.00
JVA Thomas Vanek 6.00 15.00
JVL Vincent Lecavalier 3.00 8.00
JWG Wayne Gretzky 30.00 60.00

2005-06 Ultimate Collection Jerseys Dual

PRINT RUN 75 #'d COPIES

DJAL Allison/Lindros 8.00 20.00
DJBR Bergeron/Raycroft 8.00 20.00
DJCR Carter/Richards 15.00 40.00
DJFP Forsberg/Primeau 10.00 25.00
DJFZ Franzen/Zetterberg 10.00 25.00
DJGC Gretzky/Crosby 75.00 150.00
DJHC Hasek/Chara 10.00 25.00
DJHY Howe/Yzerman 60.00 150.00
DJJD Spezza/Heatley 12.00 30.00
DJJL Joseph/Leneveu
DJKH Kovalchuk/Hossa 10.00 25.00
DJKP Koivu/Perezhogin 8.00 20.00
DJKV Kariya/Vokoun 8.00 20.00
DJLC Lemieux/Crosby 90.00 150.00
DJLS Lupul/Selanne 8.00 20.00
DJML Montoya/Lundqvist 15.00 40.00
DJNB Nash/Brule/30 12.00 30.00
DJOC Ovechkin/Crosby 100.00 200.00
DJPG Perry/Getzlaf 10.00 25.00
DJPI Phaneuf/Iginla 20.00 50.00
DJRT Roy/Theodore 20.00 50.00
DJSB Seabrook/Barker 6.00 15.00
DJSH Sakic/Hejduk 10.00 25.00
DJSL St. Louis/Lecavalier 10.00 25.00
DJTD Theodore/Danis 8.00 20.00
DJTL Toivonen/Lehtonen 6.00 15.00
DJWN Ward/Nastiuk 12.00 30.00

2005-06 Ultimate Collection Jerseys Triple

PRINT RUN 25 SER.#'d SETS

TJFGC Forsberg/Gagne/Carter 40.00 80.00
TJGLC Gretzky/Lemieux/Sid 250.00 400.00
TJHSH Heatley/Spezza/Hasek 50.00 100.00
TJKTP Koivu/Theodore/Pere. 20.00 50.00
TJLVR St. L./Lecav/Richards 30.00 60.00
TJNOC Nash/Ovechkin/Crosby 200.00 350.00
TJPGL Perry/Getzlaf/Lupul 20.00 50.00
TJRTB Roy/Theodore/Brodeur 40.00 80.00
TJSLA Sundin/Lindros/Allison 40.00 80.00

2005-06 Ultimate Collection Marquee Attractions

PRINT RUN 250 #'d SETS

MA1 Corey Perry 3.00 8.00
MA2 Ryan Getzlaf 3.00 8.00
MA3 Jean-Sebastien Giguere 2.50 6.00
MA4 Ilya Kovalchuk 4.00 10.00
MA5 Marian Hossa 2.50 6.00
MA6 Hannu Toivonen 2.50 6.00
MA7 Patrice Bergeron 3.00 8.00
MA8 Andrew Raycroft 1.50 4.00
MA9 Thomas Vanek 3.00 8.00
MA10 Dion Phaneuf 8.00 20.00
MA11 Jarome Iginla 4.00 10.00
MA12 Eric Staal 3.00 8.00
MA13 Nikolai Khabibulin 2.50 6.00
MA14 Alex Tanguay 1.50 4.00
MA15 Milan Hejduk 2.50 6.00
MA16 Rick Nash 3.00 8.00
MA17 Mike Modano 3.00 8.00
MA18 Brenden Morrow 2.50 6.00
MA19 Marty Turco 2.50 6.00
MA20 Johan Franzen 1.50 4.00
MA21 Henrik Zetterberg 3.00 8.00
MA22 Chris Pronger 1.50 4.00
MA23 Roberto Luongo 4.00 10.00
MA24 Jeremy Roenick 3.00 8.00
MA25 Mikko Koivu 2.50 6.00
MA26 Alexander Perezhogin 1.50 4.00
MA27 Saku Koivu 3.00 8.00
MA28 Jose Theodore 3.00 8.00
MA29 Martin Brodeur 6.00 15.00
MA30 Miroslav Satan 2.50 6.00
MA31 Henrik Lundqvist 8.00 20.00
MA32 Dominik Hasek 4.00 10.00
MA33 Dany Heatley 4.00 10.00
MA34 Jason Spezza 3.00 8.00
MA35 Jeff Carter 4.00 10.00
MA36 Mike Richards 3.00 8.00
MA37 Keith Primeau 1.50 4.00
MA38 Shane Doan 1.50 4.00
MA39 Sidney Crosby 20.00 50.00
MA40 Mark Recchi 1.50 4.00
MA41 Joe Thornton 5.00 12.00
MA42 Martin St. Louis 1.50 4.00
MA43 Vincent Lecavalier 3.00 8.00
MA44 Alexander Steen 5.00 12.00
MA45 Mats Sundin 2.50 6.00
MA46 Ed Belfour 2.50 6.00
MA47 Markus Naslund 2.50 6.00
MA48 Alexander Ovechkin 12.00 30.00
MA49 Gilbert Brule 2.50 6.00
MA50 Olaf Kolzig 3.00 8.00

2005-06 Ultimate Collection National Heroes Jerseys

STATED PRINT RUN 200-225
*PATCH/25: .8X TO 2X BASIC JSY

NHJAF Alexander Frolov 3.00 8.00
NHJAK Alexei Kovalev 5.00 12.00
NHJAL Daniel Alfredsson 5.00 12.00
NHJAO Alexander Ovechkin 25.00 60.00
NHJAY Alexei Yashin 4.00 10.00
NHJBG Bill Guerin 5.00 12.00
NHJBR Brian Rolston 4.00 10.00
NHJCC Chris Chelios 5.00 12.00
NHJCD Chris Drury 4.00 10.00
NHJCP Chris Pronger/200 4.00 10.00
NHJDA David Aebischer 4.00 10.00
NHJDW Doug Weight 5.00 12.00
NHJFO Adam Foote 3.00 8.00
NHJFT Fedor Tyutin 3.00 8.00
NHJGA Marian Gaborik 8.00 20.00
NHJHA Michal Handzus 4.00 10.00
NHJHJ Milan Hejduk 4.00 10.00
NHJHK Dominik Hasek/200 8.00 20.00
NHJHO Marian Hossa 4.00 10.00
NHJHS Marcel Hossa 3.00 8.00
NHJHZ Henrik Zetterberg 6.00 15.00
NHJIK Ilya Kovalchuk 5.00 12.00
NHJJB Jay Bouwmeester 5.00 12.00
NHJJI Jarome Iginla 5.00 12.00
NHJJJ Jaromir Jagr 12.00 30.00
NHJJL Jere Lehtinen 4.00 10.00
NHJJO Joe Thornton 6.00 15.00
NHJJP Joni Pitkanen/200 3.00 8.00
NHJJS Joe Sakic 8.00 20.00
NHJKD Kris Draper 6.00 15.00
NHJKT Keith Tkachuk 5.00 12.00
NHJLE Jordan Leopold 3.00 8.00
NHJMB Martin Brodeur 10.00 25.00
NHJMC Bryan McCabe 3.00 8.00
NHJMG Martin Gerber/200 4.00 10.00
NHJMM Mike Modano 8.00 20.00
NHJMO Mattias Ohlund 3.00 8.00
NHJMP Mark Parrish 3.00 8.00
NHJMS Martin Straka/200 3.00 8.00
NHJMT Marty Turco 5.00 12.00
NHJNA Nik Antropov 4.00 10.00
NHJNL Nicklas Lidstrom 5.00 12.00
NHJOJ Olli Jokinen/200 5.00 12.00
NHJOK Olaf Kolzig 5.00 12.00
NHJPA Pavol Demitra 5.00 12.00
NHJPB Peter Bondra 4.00 10.00
NHJPD Pavel Datsyuk 6.00 15.00
NHJPE Patrik Elias 5.00 12.00
NHJPF Peter Forsberg 6.00 15.00
NHJRA Brian Rafalski/200 4.00 10.00
NHJRB Rob Blake 5.00 12.00
NHJRD Rick DiPietro 4.00 10.00
NHJRE Robert Esche 4.00 10.00
NHJRI Brad Richards 5.00 12.00
NHJRL Roberto Luongo 8.00 20.00
NHJRS Ryan Smyth/200 4.00 10.00
NHJSA Miroslav Satan 4.00 10.00
NHJSG Simon Gagne 5.00 12.00
NHJSO Sandis Ozolinsh 3.00 8.00
NHJSU Mats Sundin 5.00 12.00
NHJSV Marek Svatos/200 4.00 10.00
NHJTB Todd Bertuzzi/200 5.00 12.00
NHJTS Teemu Selanne 10.00 25.00
NHJTV Tomas Vokoun 4.00 10.00
NHJVK Viktor Kozlov 3.00 8.00
NHJVL Vincent Lecavalier 4.00 10.00
NHJWR Wade Redden 3.00 8.00
NHJZC Zdeno Chara 5.00 12.00

2005-06 Ultimate Collection Premium Patches

STATED PRINT RUN 15-35

PPAO Alexander Ovechkin 75.00 150.00
PPAP Alexander Perezhogin 15.00 40.00
PPAS Alexander Steen 25.00 60.00
PPAY Alexei Yashin 20.00 50.00
PPBS Brendan Shanahan 20.00 50.00
PPCP Chris Pronger 20.00 50.00
PPCW Cam Ward 20.00 50.00
PPDH Dany Heatley/30 25.00 60.00
PPDP Dion Phaneuf 30.00 80.00
PPDW Doug Weight 15.00 40.00
PPEL Eric Lindros 40.00 80.00
PPES Eric Staal 25.00 60.00
PPGB Gilbert Brule 15.00 40.00
PPHK Dominik Hasek 25.00 60.00
PPHL Henrik Lundqvist 40.00 100.00
PPHT Hannu Toivonen 15.00 40.00
PPIK Ilya Kovalchuk 30.00 80.00
PPJC Jeff Carter 30.00 80.00
PPJF Johan Franzen 20.00 50.00
PPJI Jarome Iginla 30.00 80.00
PPJJ Jaromir Jagr 50.00 125.00
PPJO Joe Thornton 30.00 80.00
PPJR Jeremy Roenick 25.00 60.00
PPJS Joe Sakic 60.00 120.00
PPJT Jose Theodore 25.00 60.00
PPKL Kari Lehtonen 25.00 60.00
PPLR Luc Robitaille 20.00 50.00
PPMB Martin Brodeur 75.00 150.00
PPMG Marian Gaborik 50.00 100.00
PPMH Milan Hejduk 25.00 60.00
PPML Mario Lemieux 100.00 200.00
PPMM Mike Modano 30.00 60.00
PPMN Markus Naslund 15.00 40.00
PPMR Mike Richards 50.00 100.00
PPMS Mats Sundin 40.00 100.00
PPMT Marty Turco 15.00 40.00
PPPB Patrice Bergeron 20.00 50.00
PPPD Pavel Datsyuk 20.00 50.00
PPPE Corey Perry 20.00 50.00
PPPF Peter Forsberg 30.00 80.00
PPPK Paul Kariya 20.00 50.00
PPPM Patrick Marleau 20.00 50.00
PPPR Patrick Roy 100.00 200.00
PPPS Jason Spezza 20.00 50.00
PPRB Ray Bourque 30.00 80.00
PPRG Ryan Getzlaf 30.00 80.00
PPRL Roberto Luongo 30.00 80.00
PPRN Rick Nash/15
PPSC Sidney Crosby 125.00 250.00
PPSF Sergei Fedorov 20.00 50.00
PPSG Simon Gagne 20.00 50.00
PPSY Steve Yzerman 75.00 150.00
PPTB Todd Bertuzzi 15.00 40.00
PPTS Teemu Selanne 25.00 60.00
PPTV Thomas Vanek 25.00 60.00
PPVL Vincent Lecavalier 30.00 80.00
PPVO Tomas Vokoun 40.00 100.00
PPWG Wayne Gretzky 75.00 150.00

2005-06 Ultimate Collection Premium Swatches

STATED PRINT RUN 35-75

PSAO Alexander Ovechkin 30.00 80.00
PSAP Alexander Perezhogin 4.00 10.00
PSAS Alexander Steen 10.00 25.00
PSAY Alexei Yashin 3.00 8.00
PSBS Brendan Shanahan 6.00 15.00
PSCP Chris Pronger 3.00 8.00
PSCW Cam Ward 8.00 20.00
PSDH Dany Heatley/35 12.00 30.00
PSDP Dion Phaneuf 10.00 25.00
PSDW Doug Weight 3.00 8.00
PSEL Eric Lindros 8.00 20.00
PSES Eric Staal 6.00 15.00
PSGB Gilbert Brule 5.00 12.00
PSHL Henrik Lundqvist 10.00 25.00
PSHT Hannu Toivonen 4.00 10.00
PSIK Ilya Kovalchuk 8.00 20.00
PSJC Jeff Carter 8.00 20.00
PSJF Johan Franzen 3.00 8.00
PSJI Jarome Iginla 6.00 15.00
PSJJ Jaromir Jagr/50 15.00 30.00
PSJO Joe Thornton 8.00 20.00
PSJR Jeremy Roenick 4.00 10.00
PSJS Joe Sakic 10.00 25.00
PSJT Jose Theodore 6.00 15.00
PSKL Kari Lehtonen 4.00 10.00
PSLR Luc Robitaille 4.00 10.00
PSMB Martin Brodeur/50 15.00 40.00
PSMG Marian Gaborik 6.00 15.00
PSMH Milan Hejduk 4.00 10.00
PSML Mario Lemieux 20.00 50.00
PSMM Mike Modano 4.00 10.00
PSMN Markus Naslund 4.00 10.00
PSMR Mike Richards 4.00 10.00
PSMS Mats Sundin 4.00 10.0
PSMT Marty Turco 4.00 10.0
PSPB Patrice Bergeron 4.00 10.0
PSPD Pavel Datsyuk 6.00 15.0
PSPE Corey Perry 4.00 10.0
PSPF Peter Forsberg 8.00 20.0
PSPM Patrick Marleau 3.00 8.0
PSPR Patrick Roy 20.00 50.0
PSPS Jason Spezza 5.00 12.0
PSRB Ray Bourque 5.00 12.0
PSRG Ryan Getzlaf 8.00 20.0
PSRL Roberto Luongo 6.00 15.0
PSSC Sidney Crosby 40.00 100.0
PSSK Saku Koivu 4.00 10.0
PSSL Martin St. Louis 4.00 10.0
PSSY Steve Yzerman 15.00 40.0
PSTB Todd Bertuzzi 4.00 10.0
PSTS Teemu Selanne 6.00 15.0
PSTV Thomas Vanek 6.00 15.0
PSVL Vincent Lecavalier 4.00 10.0
PSVO Tomas Vokoun 4.00 10.0
PSWG Wayne Gretzky 40.00 100.0

2005-06 Ultimate Collection Ultimate Achievements

UAAR Andrew Raycroft/29 15.00 30.0
UADH Dany Heatley/26 25.00 60.0
UAHZ Henrik Zetterberg/22 25.00 50.0
UAIK Ilya Kovalchuk/41 20.00 50.0
UAJC Jonathan Cheechoo/28 25.00 50.0
UAJG Jean-Sebastien Giguere/15 20.00 50.0
UAJI Jarome Iginla/41 20.00 50.0
UAJT Jose Theodore/23
UARL Roberto Luongo/23 30.00 60.0
UARN Rick Nash/41 15.00 40.0
UASL Martin St. Louis/24 12.50 30.0
UASN Scott Niedermayer/18

2005-06 Ultimate Collection Ultimate Debut Threads Jersey

PRINT RUN 250 #'d SETS

DTJAA Andrew Alberts 3.00 8.0
DTJAK Andrei Kostsitsyn 4.00 10.0
DTJAL Andrew Ladd 4.00 10.0
DTJAM Andrej Meszaros 3.00 8.0
DTJAO Alexander Ovechkin 15.00 40.0
DTJAP Alexander Perezhogin 3.00 8.0
DTJAS Alexander Steen 6.00 15.0
DTJBB Brandon Bochenski 3.00 8.0
DTJBC Braydon Coburn 3.00 8.0
DTJBS Brent Seabrook 3.00 8.0
DTJBT Barry Tallackson 3.00 8.0
DTJBW Brad Winchester 3.00 8.0
DTJCB Cam Barker 3.00 8.0
DTJCC Chris Campoli 3.00 8.0
DTJCP Corey Perry 4.00 10.0
DTJCS Christoph Schubert 3.00 8.0
DTJCW Cam Ward 6.00 15.0
DTJDB Derek Boogaard 3.00 8.0
DTJDL David Leneveu 3.00 8.0
DTJDP Dion Phaneuf 10.00 25.0
DTJEA Evgeny Artyukhin 3.00 8.0
DTJEN Eric Nystrom 3.00 8.0
DTJGB Gilbert Brule 4.00 10.0
DTJHL Henrik Lundqvist 10.00 25.0
DTJHT Hannu Toivonen 3.00 8.0
DTJJC Jeff Carter 6.00 15.0
DTJJF Johan Franzen 3.00 8.0
DTJJH Jim Howard 5.00 12.0
DTJJJ Jussi Jokinen 4.00 10.0
DTJJK Jakub Klepis 3.00 8.0
DTJJM Jay McClement 3.00 8.0
DTJJS Jim Slater 3.00 8.0
DTJJT Jeff Tambellini 3.00 8.0
DTJJW Jeff Woywitka 3.00 8.0
DTJKB Keith Ballard 3.00 8.0
DTJMJ Milan Jurcina 3.00 8.0
DTJMK Mikko Koivu 4.00 10.0
DTJML Maxim Lapierre 3.00 8.0
DTJMO Alvaro Montoya 4.00 10.0
DTJMR Mike Richards 4.00 10.0
DTJMT Maxime Talbot 3.00 8.0
DTJPP Petr Prucha 4.00 10.0
DTJRB Rene Bourque 3.00 8.0
DTJRC Ryane Clowe 5.00 12.0
DTJRG Ryan Getzlaf 5.00 12.0
DTJRJ R.J. Umberger 3.00 8.0
DTJRN Robert Nilsson 3.00 8.0
DTJRO Rostislav Olesz 4.00 10.0
DTJRS Ryan Suter 3.00 8.0
DTJRW Ryan Whitney 3.00 8.0
DTJSB Steve Bernier 4.00 10.
DTJSC Sidney Crosby 40.00 80.
DTJSI Jordan Sigalet 4.00 10.
DTJTF Tomas Fleischmann 3.00 8.
DTJTV Thomas Vanek 8.00 20.
DTJWW Wojtek Wolski 4.00 10.
DTJYD Yann Danis 3.00 8.
DTJZP Zach Parise 4.00 10.

2005-06 Ultimate Collection Ultimate Debut Threads Jersey Autographs

STATED PRINT RUN 25 SER.#'d CARDS

DAJAO Alexander Ovechkin 300.00 450.
DAJAS Alexander Steen 30.00 80.
DAJBB Brandon Bochenski 25.00 60.
DAJBC Braydon Coburn 15.00 40.
DAJBS Brent Seabrook 30.00 80.
DAJBW Brad Winchester 15.00 40.
DAJCP Corey Perry 40.00 100.
DAJDP Dion Phaneuf 30.00 80.
DAJGB Gilbert Brule 15.00 40.
DAJHL Henrik Lundqvist 100.00 175.
DAJJJ Jussi Jokinen 15.00 40.
DAJJS Jim Slater 10.00 25.
DAJKB Keith Ballard 10.00 25.
DAJMJ Milan Jurcina 12.00 30.
DAJMO Alvaro Montoya 10.00 25.
DAJMR Mike Richards 50.00 100.
DAJMT Maxime Talbot 12.00 30.
DAJPB Peter Budaj 20.00 50.
DAJPE Patrick Eaves 12.00 30.
DAJRB Rene Bourque 15.00 40.
DAJRG Ryan Getzlaf 40.00 100.
DAJSC Sidney Crosby 500.00 800.
DAJTV Thomas Vanek 30.00 60.
DAJYD Yann Danis 40.00 80.

2005-06 Ultimate Collection Ultimate Debut Threads Patches

PRINT RUN 60 #'d COPIES UNLESS NOTED

DTPAA Andrew Alberts 10.00 25.
DTPAL Andrew Ladd 15.00 40.
DTPAO Alexander Ovechkin 100.00 250.
DTPAP Alexander Perezhogin 15.00 40.
DTPBB Brandon Bochenski 15.00 40.
DTPBC Braydon Coburn 15.00 40.
DTPBS Brent Seabrook 25.00 60.
DTPBT Barry Tallackson 10.00 25.
DTPBW Brad Winchester 10.00 25.
DTPCB Cam Barker 15.00 40.

TPCC Chris Campoli/40 15.00 40.00
TPCP Corey Perry 30.00 80.00
TPCW Cam Ward 30.00 80.00
TPDB Derek Boogaard 20.00 50.00
TPDL David Leneveu 15.00 40.00
TPDP Dion Phaneuf 50.00 125.00
TPEA Evgeny Artyukhin/25 25.00 60.00
TPEN Eric Nystrom 15.00 40.00
TPGB Gilbert Brule/50 20.00 50.00
TPHL Henrik Lundqvist 50.00 125.00
TPHT Hannu Toivonen 20.00 50.00
TPJC Jeff Carter 40.00 100.00
TPJF Johan Franzen 10.00 25.00
TPJH Jim Howard 25.00 60.00
TPJJ Jussi Jokinen 15.00 40.00
TPJK Jakub Klepis 10.00 25.00
TPJM Jay McClement/15
TPJS Jim Slater 12.00 30.00
TPJT Jeff Tambellini/30 15.00 40.00
TPJW Jeff Woywitka 10.00 25.00
TPKB Keith Ballard 10.00 25.00
TPMJ Milan Jurcina/30 20.00 50.00
TPMK Mikko Koivu 15.00 40.00
TPMO Alvaro Montoya 20.00 50.00
TPMR Mike Richards 25.00 60.00
TPMT Maxime Talbot 10.00 25.00
TPPB Peter Budaj 20.00 50.00
TPPP Petr Prucha/30 30.00 60.00
TPRB Rene Bourque 15.00 40.00
TPRG Ryan Getzlaf 30.00 80.00
TPRJ R.J. Umberger/35 15.00 40.00
TPRN Robert Nilsson 15.00 40.00
TPRO Rostislav Olesz 15.00 40.00
TPRS Ryan Suter 15.00 40.00
TPRW Ryan Whitney 15.00 40.00
TPSB Steve Bernier/25 30.00 80.00
TPSC Sidney Crosby/1
TPSI Jordan Sigalet/35 25.00 50.00
TPTF Tomas Fleischmann 10.00 25.00
TPTV Thomas Vanek 30.00 80.00
TPWW Wojtek Wolski 15.00 40.00
TPYD Yann Danis 15.00 40.00
TPZP Zach Parise 30.00 80.00

2005-06 Ultimate Collection Ultimate Patches

ATED PRINT RUN 10-75
AO Alexander Ovechkin 40.00 100.00
AY Alexei Yashin 10.00 25.00
BS Brendan Shanahan 12.00 30.00
BT Bryan Trottier 15.00 40.00
CO Corey Perry 10.00 25.00
CP Chris Pronger 10.00 25.00
DH Dominik Hasek 15.00 40.00
DP Dion Phaneuf 20.00 50.00
DW Doug Weight 8.00 20.00
EL Eric Lindros 10.00 25.00
ES Eric Staal 12.00 30.00
GB Gilbert Brule 12.00 30.00
GH Gordie Howe/10
HE Dany Heatley 15.00 40.00
HL Henrik Lundqvist 20.00 50.00
HT Hannu Toivonen 10.00 25.00
IK Ilya Kovalchuk 15.00 40.00
JC Jeff Carter 12.00 40.00
JI Jarome Iginla 15.00 40.00
JJ Jaromir Jagr 20.00 50.00
JO Joe Thornton 20.00 50.00
JR Jeremy Roenick 15.00 40.00
JS Joe Sakic 20.00 50.00
JT Jose Theodore 12.00 30.00
KL Kari Lehtonen 10.00 25.00
LR Luc Robitaille 10.00 25.00
MA Martin St. Louis 8.00 20.00
MB Martin Brodeur 25.00 60.00
MG Marian Gaborik 15.00 40.00
MH Milan Hejduk 10.00 25.00
ML Mario Lemieux 30.00 80.00
MM Mike Modano 15.00 40.00
MN Markus Naslund 12.00 30.00
MS Mats Sundin 12.00 30.00
MT Marty Turco 10.00 25.00
PB Patrice Bergeron 12.00 30.00
PD Pavel Datsyuk 20.00 40.00
PE Phil Esposito 12.00 30.00
PF Peter Forsberg/35 20.00 50.00
PK Paul Kariya 10.00 25.00
PM Patrick Marleau 8.00 20.00
PR Patrick Roy 30.00 80.00
RB Ray Bourque 15.00 40.00
RG Ryan Getzlaf 15.00 40.00
RL Roberto Luongo 15.00 40.00
SC Sidney Crosby 75.00 150.00
SF Sergei Fedorov 10.00 25.00
SG Simon Gagne 8.00 20.00
SK Saku Koivu 10.00 25.00
SP Jason Spezza 12.00 30.00
SY Steve Yzerman 25.00 50.00
TB Todd Bertuzzi 10.00 25.00
TS Teemu Selanne 10.00 25.00
TV Tomas Vokoun 12.00 30.00
VA Thomas Vanek 15.00 40.00
VL Vincent Lecavalier 12.00 30.00

2005-06 Ultimate Collection Ultimate Patches Dual

ATED PRINT RUN 25 SER.#'d SETS
AL Allison/Lindros 20.00 50.00
BR Bergeron/Raycroft 25.00 60.00
CR Carter/Richards 30.00 80.00
FP Forsberg/Primeau
FZ Franzen/Zetterberg 25.00 60.00
HC Hasek/Chara 30.00 80.00
HY Howe/Yzerman 150.00 300.00
JD Spezza/Heatley 30.00 80.00
JL Joseph/Leneveu 15.00 40.00
KH Kovalchuk/Hossa 30.00 80.00
KP Koivu/Perezhogin 15.00 40.00
KV Kariya/Vokoun 15.00 40.00
LC Lemieux/Crosby 175.00 350.00
LS Lupul/Selanne 25.00 60.00
ML Montoya/Lundqvist 30.00 80.00
NB Nash/Brule 20.00 50.00
OC Ovechkin/Crosby 250.00 500.00
PG Perry/Getzlaf 40.00 80.00
PI Phaneuf/Iginla 60.00 120.00
RT Roy/Theodore 100.00 200.00
SB Seabrook/Barker 15.00 40.00
SH Sakic/Hejduk 25.00 60.00
SL St. Louis/Lecavalier 20.00 50.00
SY Shanahan/Yzerman 50.00 100.00
TD Theodore/Danis 15.00 40.00
TL Toivonen/Lehtonen 20.00 50.00
WN Ward/Nastiuk 25.00 50.00

2005-06 Ultimate Collection Ultimate Signatures

AO Alexander Ovechkin 80.00 150.00
AP Alexander Perezhogin 5.00 12.00
AR Andrew Raycroft 5.00 12.00
AT Alex Tanguay SP 15.00 40.00
AY Alexei Yashin 5.00 12.00
USBC Bobby Clarke 12.00 30.00
USBL Brian Leetch 6.00 15.00
USBM Brenden Morrow 5.00 12.00
USBP Bernie Parent 8.00 20.00
USBR Brad Richards 8.00 20.00
USCH Jonathan Cheechoo 6.00 15.00
USCN Cam Neely 12.00 30.00
USCW Cam Ward 6.00 15.00
USDH Dany Heatley SP 20.00 50.00
USDW Doug Weight 5.00 12.00
USEB Ed Belfour 10.00 25.00
USEC Erik Cole 5.00 12.00
USEN Eric Nystrom 5.00 12.00
USES Eric Staal EXCH 10.00 25.00
USGB Gilbert Brule 6.00 15.00
USGH Gordie Howe 40.00 80.00
USGP Gilbert Perreault 6.00 15.00
USHK Dominik Hasek 15.00 40.00
USHL Henrik Lundqvist 15.00 40.00
USHO Marian Hossa 5.00 12.00
USHT Hannu Toivonen 5.00 12.00
USHV Martin Havlat 5.00 12.00
USHZ Henrik Zetterberg 12.00 30.00
USIK Ilya Kovalchuk 15.00 40.00
USJB Jean Beliveau 25.00 50.00
USJC Jeff Carter 8.00 20.00
USJG Jean-Sebastien Giguere 5.00 12.00
USJH Jim Howard 8.00 20.00
USJI Jarome Iginla 8.00 20.00
USJO Joe Thornton 10.00 25.00
USJS Jason Spezza 10.00 25.00
USJT Jose Theodore 6.00 15.00
USKL Kari Lehtonen 6.00 15.00
USLR Luc Robitaille 8.00 20.00
USMB Martin Brodeur 40.00 80.00
USMF Marc-Andre Fleury 12.00 30.00
USMH Milan Hejduk 5.00 12.00
USML Manny Legace 5.00 12.00
USMM Mike Modano 10.00 25.00
USMN Markus Naslund 5.00 12.00
USMS Miroslav Satan 6.00 15.00
USMT Marty Turco 5.00 12.00
USNA Evgeni Nabokov 5.00 12.00
USNK Nikolai Khabibulin 6.00 15.00
USNZ Nikolai Zherdev 5.00 12.00
USON Jeff O'Neill 5.00 12.00
USPB Patrice Bergeron 8.00 20.00
USPE Phil Esposito SP 15.00 40.00
USPR Patrick Roy SP 75.00 150.00
USPY Corey Perry 8.00 20.00
USRB Ray Bourque SP 20.00 50.00
USRG Ryan Getzlaf 8.00 20.00
USRL Roberto Luongo 10.00 25.00
USRN Rick Nash 6.00 15.00
USRO Rostislav Olesz 5.00 12.00
USRS Ryan Suter 5.00 12.00
USRW Ryan Whitney 5.00 12.00
USRY Michael Ryder 5.00 12.00
USSC Sidney Crosby 250.00 400.00
USSG Simon Gagne 5.00 12.00
USSK Saku Koivu 8.00 20.00
USSL Martin St. Louis SP 15.00 40.00
USSM Ryan Smyth 8.00 20.00
USSN Scott Niedermayer 5.00 12.00
USST Alexander Steen 8.00 20.00
USSV Marek Svatos 5.00 12.00
USTB Todd Bertuzzi 5.00 12.00
USTE Tony Esposito 12.00 30.00
USTR Tuomo Ruutu 5.00 12.00
USTV Thomas Vanek 10.00 25.00
USVL Vincent Lecavalier 8.00 20.00
USWG Wayne Gretzky SP 150.00 350.00
USWW Wojtek Wolski 5.00 12.00
USYD Yann Danis 6.00 15.00

2005-06 Ultimate Collection Ultimate Signatures Pairings

PRINT RUN 25 SER.#'d SETS
UPBR Bourque/Roy
UPCP Clarke/Parent 40.00 80.00
UPCR Carter/Richards 100.00 200.00
UPEE P.Esposito/T.Espo
UPHE Bob.Hull/T.Esposito 60.00 120.00
UPHG Howe/Gretzky
UPHH Hasek/Havlat 60.00 120.00
UPHS Heatley/Spezza
UPIN Iginla/Nystrom 40.00 80.00
UPKH Kovalchuk/Hossa 40.00 80.00
UPKP Koivu/Perezhogin 30.00 60.00
UPLA Roenick/Robitaille
UPLM Lundqvist/Montoya 25.00 50.00
UPLT Lundqvist/Toivonen 40.00 80.00
UPMM Lanny/J. Mullen 25.00 50.00
UPPG Perry/Getzlaf 50.00 100.00
UPPV Perreault/Vanek 30.00 60.00
UPRB Roy/Brodeur 100.00 200.00
UPRG Nash/Brule 30.00 80.00
UPSL St. Louis/Lecavalier 15.00 40.00
UPTC Thornton/Cheechoo
UPZF Zetterberg/Franzen 50.00 100.00

2006-07 Ultimate Collection

1-60 STATED PRINT RUN 699
61-102 ROOKIE PRINT RUN 699
103-132 ROOKIE AU PRINT RUN 299
1 Teemu Selanne 4.00 10.00
2 Ilya Kovalchuk 2.00 5.00
3 Kari Lehtonen 1.50 4.00
4 Patrice Bergeron 2.50 6.00
5 Bobby Orr 6.00 15.00
6 Ray Bourque 3.00 8.00
7 Phil Esposito 3.00 8.00
8 Ryan Miller 2.00 5.00
9 Gilbert Perreault 2.00 5.00
10 Miikka Kiprusoff 1.50 4.00
11 Jarome Iginla 2.00 5.00
12 Dion Phaneuf 2.00 5.00
13 Eric Staal 2.50 6.00
14 Cam Ward 2.00 5.00
15 Martin Havlat 1.25 3.00
16 Bobby Hull 3.00 8.00
17 Joe Sakic 3.00 8.00
18 Jose Theodore 2.00 5.00
19 Rick Nash 2.00 5.00
20 Mike Modano 3.00 8.00
21 Marty Turco 2.00 5.00
22 Henrik Zetterberg 2.50 6.00
23 Dominik Hasek 2.50 6.00
24 Nicklas Lidstrom 2.00 5.00
25 Gordie Howe 6.00 15.00
26 Ales Hemsky 1.50 4.00
27 Wayne Gretzky 10.00 25.00
28 Jari Kurri 2.00 5.00
29 Ed Belfour 2.00 5.00
30 Rob Blake 2.00 5.00
31 Marian Gaborik 2.50 6.00
32 Saku Koivu 2.00 5.00
33 Michael Ryder 1.25 3.00
34 Patrick Roy 5.00 12.00
35 Tomas Vokoun 1.50 4.00
36 Paul Kariya 2.50 6.00
37 Martin Brodeur 4.00 10.00
38 Alexei Yashin 1.50 4.00
39 Mike Bossy 2.00 5.00
40 Jaromir Jagr 5.00 12.00
41 Brendan Shanahan 2.50 6.00
42 Henrik Lundqvist 4.00 10.00
43 Dany Heatley 2.00 5.00
44 Jason Spezza 2.00 5.00
45 Peter Forsberg 2.50 6.00
46 Shane Doan 1.50 4.00
47 Sidney Crosby 8.00 20.00
48 Marc-Andre Fleury 3.00 8.00
49 Mario Lemieux 6.00 15.00
50 Joe Thornton 2.50 6.00
51 Jonathan Cheechoo 2.00 5.00
52 Patrick Marleau 2.00 5.00
53 Brad Richards 2.00 5.00
54 Vincent Lecavalier 1.50 4.00
55 Martin St. Louis 2.00 5.00
56 Mats Sundin 2.00 5.00
57 Andrew Raycroft 1.50 4.00
58 Markus Naslund 1.50 4.00
59 Roberto Luongo 3.00 8.00
60 Alexander Ovechkin 8.00 20.00
61 David McKee RC 4.00 10.00
62 Ryan Shannon RC 4.00 10.00
63 Clarke MacArthur RC 5.00 12.00
64 Andrej Sekera RC 5.00 12.00
65 Michael Funk RC 4.00 10.00
66 Adam Dennis RC 4.00 10.00
67 Mike Card RC 4.00 10.00
68 Brandon Prust RC 4.00 10.00
69 Troy Brouwer RC 5.00 12.00
70 Adam Burish RC 6.00 15.00
71 Fredrik Norrena RC 4.00 10.00
72 Stefan Liv RC 4.00 10.00
73 Tomas Kopecky RC 5.00 12.00
74 Jeff Drouin-Deslauriers RC 4.00 10.00
75 David Booth RC 5.00 12.00
76 Janis Sprukts RC 4.00 10.00
77 Barry Brust RC 5.00 12.00
78 Konstantin Pushkarev RC 5.00 12.00
79 Shawn Belle RC 4.00 10.00
80 Niklas Backstrom RC 8.00 20.00
81 Mikhail Grabovski RC 8.00 20.00
82 Johnny Oduya RC 6.00 15.00
83 Blake Comeau RC 6.00 15.00
84 Jarkko Immonen RC 4.00 10.00
85 Josh Hennessy RC 4.00 10.00
86 Kelly Guard RC 5.00 12.00
87 Jussi Timonen RC 5.00 12.00
88 Martin Houle RC 5.00 12.00
89 Michel Ouellet RC 5.00 12.00
90 Yan Stastny RC 4.00 10.00
91 Roman Polak RC 5.00 12.00
92 Marek Schwarz RC 6.00 15.00
93 David Backes RC 15.00 40.00
94 Blair Jones RC 4.00 10.00
95 Karri Ramo RC 4.00 10.00
96 Ian White RC 5.00 12.00
97 Brendan Bell RC 4.00 10.00
98 Kris Newbury RC 4.00 10.00
99 Jean-Francois Racine RC 5.00 12.00
100 Jesse Schultz RC 4.00 10.00
101 Alexander Edler RC 6.00 15.00
102 Daren Machesney RC 4.00 10.00
103 Matt Lashoff AU RC 8.00 20.00
104 Phil Kessel AU/99 RC 50.00 100.00
105 Mark Stuart AU RC 8.00 20.00
106 Michael Blunden AU RC 8.00 20.00
107 Dave Bolland AU RC 12.00 30.00
108 Paul Stastny AU RC 15.00 40.00
109 Loui Eriksson AU RC 12.00 30.00
110 Niklas Grossman AU RC 12.00 30.00
111 Ladislav Smid AU RC 8.00 20.00
112 Patrick Thoresen AU RC 8.00 20.00
113 Marc-Antoine Pouliot AU RC 8.00 20.00
114 Anze Kopitar AU RC 25.00 50.00
115 Patrick O'Sullivan AU RC 12.00 30.00
116 G. Latendresse AU RC 12.00 30.00
117 Alexander Radulov AU RC 15.00 40.00
118 Shea Weber AU RC 20.00 40.00
119 Travis Zajac AU RC 15.00 40.00
120 Nigel Dawes AU RC 8.00 20.00
121 Dustin Boyd AU RC 8.00 20.00
122 Ryan Potulny AU RC 8.00 20.00
123 Benoit Pouliot AU RC 10.00 25.00
124 Keith Yandle AU RC 15.00 40.00
125 Evgeni Malkin AU/99 RC 200.00 400.00
126 Kristopher Letang AU RC 20.00 50.00
127 Jordan Staal AU/99 RC 25.00 60.00
128 Noah Welch AU RC 8.00 20.00
129 Marc-Edouard Vlasic AU RC 8.00 20.00
130 Matt Carle AU RC 8.00 20.00
131 Drew Stafford AU RC 12.00 30.00
132 Eric Fehr AU RC 12.00 30.00

2006-07 Ultimate Collection Autographed Jerseys

STATED PRINT RUN 50 SER.#'d SETS
AJAF Alexander Frolov 8.00 20.00
AJAH Ales Hemsky 10.00 25.00
AJAR Andrew Raycroft 10.00 25.00
AJBB Brad Boyes 8.00 20.00
AJBH Bobby Hull 20.00 50.00
AJBM Brenden Morrow 10.00 25.00
AJBO Mike Bossy 12.00 30.00
AJBP Brad Park 10.00 25.00
AJBS Billy Smith 12.00 30.00
AJCN Cam Neely 12.00 30.00
AJCW Cam Ward 12.00 30.00
AJDH Dany Heatley 12.00 30.00
AJDP Denis Potvin 12.00 30.00
AJDT Dave Taylor 10.00 25.00
AJEL Patrik Elias 12.00 30.00
AJEM Evgeni Malkin 50.00 100.00
AJES Eric Staal 15.00 40.00
AJGC Gerry Cheevers 12.00 30.00
AJGF Grant Fuhr 20.00 50.00
AJGL Guy Lafleur 15.00 40.00
AJGP Gilbert Perreault 12.00 30.00
AJHA Dominik Hasek 20.00 50.00
AJIK Ilya Kovalchuk 12.00 30.00
AJJB Jean Beliveau 25.00 50.00
AJJG Jean-Sebastien Giguere 12.00 30.00
AJJI Jarome Iginla 12.00 30.00
AJJK Jari Kurri 12.00 30.00
AJJR Jeremy Roenick 12.00 30.00
AJJS Jordan Staal 30.00 60.00
AJJT Joe Thornton 15.00 40.00
AJKL Kari Lehtonen 10.00 25.00
AJLM Lanny McDonald 12.00 30.00
AJLR Larry Robinson 12.00 30.00
AJMB Martin Brodeur 50.00 100.00
AJMG Marian Gaborik 15.00 40.00
AJMK Miikka Kiprusoff 10.00 25.00
AJML Mario Lemieux 50.00 120.00
AJMM Mike Modano 20.00 50.00
AJMT Marty Turco 12.00 30.00
AJNL Nicklas Lidstrom 20.00 50.00
AJPE Phil Esposito 20.00 50.00
AJPH Dion Phaneuf 12.00 30.00
AJPK Phil Kessel 15.00 40.00
AJPM Patrick Marleau 12.00 30.00
AJPR Patrick Roy 60.00 120.00
AJRB Ray Bourque 25.00 60.00
AJRM Ryan Miller 12.00 30.00
AJRN Rick Nash 12.00 30.00
AJRV Rogie Vachon 12.00 30.00
AJRY Michael Ryder 8.00 20.00
AJSA Borje Salming 12.00 30.00
AJSC Sidney Crosby 75.00 150.00
AJSG Simon Gagne 12.00 30.00
AJTE Tony Esposito 12.00 30.00
AJTH Jose Theodore 12.00 30.00
AJTV Tomas Vokoun 10.00 25.00
AJVL Vincent Lecavalier 10.00 25.00
AJWG Wayne Gretzky 150.00 250.00

2006-07 Ultimate Collection Jerseys

STATED PRINT RUN 200 SER.#'d SETS
*PATCH/75: .8X TO 2X JERSEY/200
*PREM.PATCH/25: 1.2X TO 3X JERSEY/200
UJAO Alexander Ovechkin 10.00 25.00
UJBC Bobby Clarke 5.00 12.00
UJBI Billy Smith 5.00 12.00
UJBR Martin Brodeur 10.00 25.00
UJBS Brendan Shanahan 6.00 15.00
UJCN Cam Neely 5.00 12.00
UJCW Cam Ward 5.00 12.00
UJDA Daniel Alfredsson 5.00 12.00
UJDH Dominik Hasek 6.00 15.00
UJDP Dion Phaneuf 5.00 12.00
UJDT Dave Taylor 4.00 10.00
UJEL Eric Lindros 8.00 20.00
UJEM Evgeni Malkin 12.00 30.00
UJES Eric Staal 6.00 15.00
UJGC Gerry Cheevers 5.00 12.00
UJGF Grant Fuhr 5.00 12.00
UJGL Guy Lafleur 6.00 15.00
UJGP Gilbert Perreault 5.00 12.00
UJGW Gump Worsley 5.00 12.00
UJHE Dany Heatley 5.00 12.00
UJHL Henrik Lundqvist 10.00 25.00
UJHZ Henrik Zetterberg 6.00 15.00
UJIK Ilya Kovalchuk 5.00 12.00
UJJB Jean Beliveau 5.00 12.00
UJJI Jarome Iginla 5.00 12.00
UJJJ Jaromir Jagr 12.00 30.00
UJJK Jari Kurri 5.00 12.00
UJJS Joe Sakic 8.00 20.00
UJJT Joe Thornton 8.00 20.00
UJKL Kari Lehtonen 4.00 10.00
UJLM Lanny McDonald 5.00 12.00
UJLR Larry Robinson 5.00 12.00
UJMB Mike Bossy 5.00 12.00
UJMD Marcel Dionne 6.00 15.00
UJMG Marian Gaborik 6.00 15.00
UJMH Milan Hejduk 4.00 10.00
UJML Mario Lemieux 15.00 40.00
UJMM Mike Modano 8.00 20.00
UJMN Markus Naslund 4.00 10.00
UJMR Michael Ryder 3.00 8.00
UJMS Mats Sundin 5.00 12.00
UJNL Nicklas Lidstrom 5.00 12.00
UJPB Patrice Bergeron 6.00 15.00
UJPF Peter Forsberg 6.00 15.00
UJPK Paul Kariya 6.00 15.00
UJPO Denis Potvin 5.00 12.00
UJPR Patrick Roy 12.00 30.00
UJPS Peter Stastny 5.00 12.00
UJRB Ray Bourque 8.00 20.00
UJRL Roberto Luongo 8.00 20.00
UJRN Rick Nash 5.00 12.00
UJSA Borje Salming 5.00 12.00
UJSC Sidney Crosby 15.00 40.00
UJSM Stan Mikita 6.00 15.00
UJSP Jason Spezza 5.00 12.00
UJSS Scott Stevens 5.00 12.00
UJST Martin St. Louis 5.00 12.00
UJTS Teemu Selanne 10.00 25.00
UJTV Tomas Vokoun 4.00 10.00
UJVL Vincent Lecavalier 4.00 10.00

2006-07 Ultimate Collection Jerseys Dual

STATED PRINT RUN 50 SER.#'d SETS
UJ2CM S.Crosby/E.Malkin 30.00 80.00
UJ2CP B.Clarke/G.Perreault 15.00 40.00
UJ2DB D.Sittler/B.Salming 8.00 20.00
UJ2DV M.Dionne/R.Vachon 8.00 20.00
UJ2EE P.Esposito/T.Esposito 12.00 30.00
UJ2FG P.Forsberg/S.Gagne 12.00 30.00
UJ2GL M.Lemieux/W.Gretzky 50.00 125.00
UJ2HL D.Hasek/N.Lidstrom 10.00 25.00
UJ2HS R.Smyth/A.Hemsky 8.00 20.00
UJ2JL J.Jagr/H.Lundqvist 20.00 50.00
UJ2KA P.Kariya/J.Arnott 10.00 25.00
UJ2KI J.Iginla/M.Kiprusoff 15.00 40.00
UJ2KS T.Selanne/J.Kurri 8.00 20.00
UJ2LN M.Naslund/R.Luongo 10.00 25.00
UJ2LS V.Lecavalier/M.St. Louis 10.00 25.00
UJ2ME L.McDonald/R.Ellis 6.00 15.00
UJ2ML M.Modano/E.Lindros 10.00 25.00
UJ2MM J.Mullen/A.MacInnis 6.00 15.00
UJ2NB C.Neely/P.Bergeron 12.00 30.00
UJ2NL P.LeClaire/R.Nash 8.00 20.00
UJ2RB P.Roy/R.Bourque 15.00 40.00
UJ2RD J.Roenick/S.Doan 6.00 15.00
UJ2RP D.Potvin/L.Robinson 10.00 25.00
UJ2SH J.Spezza/D.Heatley 10.00 25.00
UJ2SS J.Sakic/P.Stastny 15.00 40.00
UJ2SW E.Staal/C.Ward 8.00 20.00
UJ2TC J.Thornton/J.Cheechoo 12.00 30.00
UJ2TH M.Hejduk/J.Theodore 6.00 15.00
UJ2ZD P.Datsyuk/H.Zetterberg 10.00 25.00

2006-07 Ultimate Collection Jerseys Triple

STATED PRINT RUN 25 SER.#'d SETS
UJ3CMS Crosby/Malkin/Staal 100.00 200.00
UJ3ENK Esposito/Neely/Kessel 50.00 100.00
UJ3GHL Lemieux/Gretzky/Howe 125.00 250.00
UJ3LRS Lafleur/Shutt/Robinson 25.00 60.00
UJ3OMK Koval/Ovechkin/Malkin 50.00 120.00
UJ3RBL Roy/Brodeur/Luongo 75.00 150.00
UJ3SBG Bossy/Potvin/Smith 40.00 80.00
UJ3SFL Lidstrom/Forsberg/Sundin 30.00 80.00
UJ3SSH Sittler/Salming/Henderson 25.00 60.00
UJ3STS Sakic/Thornton/Staal 50.00 100.00

2006-07 Ultimate Collection Patches Dual

STATED PRINT RUN 25 SER.#'d SETS
UJ2CM Crosby/Malkin 175.00 300.00
UJ2CP Clarke/Perreault 25.00 60.00
UJ2DB Sittler/Salming 20.00 50.00
UJ2DV Dionne/Vachon/15 30.00 80.00
UJ2EE P.Espo/T.Espo 30.00 80.00
UJ2FG Forsberg/Gagne 20.00 50.00
UJ2GL Lemieux/Gretzky 150.00 300.00
UJ2HL Hasek/Lidstrom 25.00 60.00
UJ2HS Smyth/Hemsky 15.00 40.00
UJ2JL Jagr/Lundqvist 30.00 80.00
UJ2KA Kariya/Arnott 20.00 50.00
UJ2KI Iginla/Kiprusoff 25.00 60.00
UJ2KS Selanne/Kurri 60.00 150.00
UJ2LN Naslund/Luongo 25.00 60.00
UJ2LS Lecavalier/St. Louis 30.00 80.00
UJ2ME McDonald/Ellis 12.00 30.00
UJ2ML Modano/Lindros 25.00 60.00
UJ2MM Mullen/MacInnis 15.00 40.00
UJ2NB Neely/Bergeron 25.00 60.00
UJ2NL LeClaire/Nash 25.00 60.00
UJ2RB Roy/Bourque 60.00 150.00
UJ2RD Roenick/Doan 20.00 50.00
UJ2SH Spezza/Heatley 15.00 40.00
UJ2SS Sakic/Stastny 25.00 60.00
UJ2SW Staal/Ward 12.00 30.00
UJ2TC Thornton/Cheechoo 25.00 - 60.00
UJ2TH Hejduk/Theodore 15.00 40.00
UJ2ZD Datsyuk/Zetterberg 40.00 100.00

2006-07 Ultimate Collection Premium Swatches

STATED PRINT RUN 50 SER.#'d SETS
*PREM.PATCH/25: .8X TO 2X SWATCH/50
PSAF Alexander Frolov 6.00 15.00
PSAH Ales Hemsky 8.00 20.00
PSAK Alexei Kovalev 8.00 20.00
PSAM Al MacInnis 10.00 25.00
PSAR Andrew Raycroft 8.00 20.00
PSAS Alexander Steen 10.00 25.00
PSAT Alex Tanguay 6.00 15.00
PSAY Alexei Yashin 8.00 20.00
PSBL Rob Blake 10.00 25.00
PSBO Mike Bossy 10.00 25.00
PSBS Borje Salming 10.00 25.00
PSCD Chris Drury 8.00 20.00
PSCJ Curtis Joseph 10.00 25.00
PSCN Cam Neely 12.00 30.00
PSCW Cam Ward 10.00 25.00
PSDB Daniel Briere 10.00 25.00
PSDG Doug Gilmour 12.00 30.00
PSDH Dominik Hasek 15.00 40.00
PSEL Eric Lindros 15.00 40.00
PSES Eric Staal 12.00 30.00
PSGW Gump Worsley 12.00 30.00
PSHA Martin Havlat 6.00 15.00
PSHE Milan Hejduk 8.00 20.00
PSHT Hannu Toivonen 8.00 20.00
PSIK Ilya Kovalchuk 10.00 25.00
PSJB Jay Bouwmeester 10.00 25.00
PSJG Jean-Sebastien Giguere 10.00 25.00
PSJJ Jaromir Jagr 25.00 60.00
PSJL Jere Lehtinen 6.00 15.00
PSJM Joe Mullen 8.00 20.00
PSJP Joni Pitkanen 6.00 15.00
PSJR Jeremy Roenick 10.00 25.00
PSJT Joe Thornton 12.00 30.00
PSKL Kari Lehtonen 8.00 20.00
PSLM Lanny McDonald 10.00 25.00
PSMA Maxim Afinogenov 6.00 15.00
PSMB Martin Brodeur 20.00 50.00
PSMG Marian Gaborik 12.00 30.00
PSMH Marian Hossa 8.00 20.00
PSMK Miikka Kiprusoff 12.00 30.00
PSMM Mike Modano 15.00 40.00
PSMN Markus Naslund 8.00 20.00
PSMP Michael Peca 8.00 20.00
PSMR Mark Recchi 12.00 30.00
PSMS Miroslav Satan 8.00 20.00
PSMT Marty Turco 10.00 25.00
PSMU Larry Murphy 8.00 20.00
PSOK Olaf Kolzig 10.00 25.00
PSPD Pavel Datsyuk 12.00 30.00
PSPE Patrik Elias 10.00 25.00
PSPL Pascal LeClaire 8.00 20.00
PSPM Patrick Marleau 10.00 25.00
PSRB Ray Bourque 15.00 40.00
PSRE Ron Ellis 6.00 15.00
PSRM Ryan Miller 10.00 25.00
PSRS Ryan Smyth 8.00 20.00
PSSF Sergei Fedorov 15.00 40.00
PSSS Scott Stevens 10.00 25.00
PSSZ Sergei Zubov 8.00 20.00
PSZC Zdeno Chara 10.00 25.00

2006-07 Ultimate Collection Rookies Autographed Patches

STATED PRINT RUN 25 #'d SETS
103 Matt Lashoff 12.00 30.00
104 Phil Kessel 75.00 150.00
105 Mark Stuart 12.00 30.00
106 Michael Blunden 12.00 30.00
107 Dave Bolland 20.00 50.00
108 Paul Stastny 30.00 80.00
109 Loui Eriksson 20.00 50.00
110 Niklas Grossman 20.00 50.00
111 Ladislav Smid 12.00 30.00
112 Patrick Thoresen 12.00 30.00
113 Marc-Antoine Pouliot 12.00 30.00
114 Anze Kopitar 100.00 200.00
115 Patrick O'Sullivan 20.00 50.00
116 Guillaume Latendresse 20.00 50.00
117 Alexander Radulov 25.00 60.00
118 Shea Weber 30.00 80.00
119 Travis Zajac 25.00 60.00
120 Nigel Dawes 12.00 30.00
121 Dustin Boyd 12.00 30.00
122 Ryan Potulny 12.00 30.00
123 Benoit Pouliot 15.00 40.00
124 Keith Yandle 25.00 60.00
125 Evgeni Malkin 200.00 400.00
126 Kristopher Letang 60.00 120.00
127 Jordan Staal 60.00 120.00
128 Noah Welch 12.00 30.00
129 Marc-Edouard Vlasic 12.00 30.00
130 Matt Carle 12.00 30.00
131 Drew Stafford 20.00 50.00
132 Eric Fehr 20.00 50.00

2006-07 Ultimate Collection Signatures

USAF Alexander Frolov 4.00 10.00
USAH Ales Hemsky 5.00 12.00
USAK Anze Kopitar 12.00 30.00
USAM Al MacInnis 8.00 20.00
USAR Andrew Raycroft 5.00 12.00
USAT Alex Tanguay 4.00 10.00
USBB Brad Boyes 4.00 10.00
USBC Bobby Clarke 8.00 20.00
USBF Bernie Federko 5.00 12.00
USBH Bobby Hull SP 20.00 50.00
USBM Mike Bossy SP 20.00 50.00
USBO Pierre-Marc Bouchard 6.00 15.00
USBP Bernie Parent 10.00 25.00
USBR Richard Brodeur 5.00 12.00
USBU Johnny Bucyk 6.00 15.00
USCA Colby Armstrong 5.00 12.00
USCH Jonathan Cheechoo 6.00 15.00
USCI Dino Ciccarelli 6.00 15.00
USCN Cam Neely 8.00 20.00
USCW Cam Ward 6.00 15.00
USDC Don Cherry 15.00 40.00
USDH Dominik Hasek SP 20.00 50.00
USDR Dwayne Roloson 5.00 12.00
USDS Denis Savard 8.00 20.00
USEM Evgeni Malkin 40.00 80.00
USES Eric Staal 8.00 20.00
USGB Gilbert Brule 5.00 12.00
USGC Gerry Cheevers 10.00 25.00
USGF Grant Fuhr SP 12.00 30.00
USGH Gordie Howe 40.00 80.00
USGL G. Latendresse 6.00 15.00
USGP Gilbert Perreault 6.00 15.00
USHA Dale Hawerchuk 6.00 15.00
USHE D. Heatley SP EXCH 12.50 30.00
USHL Henrik Lundqvist 12.00 30.00
USIK Ilya Kovalchuk 8.00 20.00
USJA Jason Arnott 5.00 12.00
USJB Jean Beliveau SP 50.00 100.00
USJG Jean-Sebastien Giguere 6.00 15.00
USJI Jarome Iginla SP 10.00 25.00
USJK Jari Kurri 6.00 15.00
USJM Joe Mullen 5.00 12.00
USJO Johnny Bower 10.00 25.00
USKL Kari Lehtonen 5.00 12.00
USLR Larry Robinson 8.00 20.00
USMB Martin Brodeur SP 60.00 120.00
USMC Matt Carle 4.00 10.00
USMD Marcel Dionne 12.00 30.00
USMF Marc-Andre Fleury 10.00 25.00
USMG Marian Gaborik 8.00 20.00
USMH Martin Havlat 4.00 10.00
USMI Milan Hejduk 5.00 12.00
USML Mario Lemieux SP 100.00 200.00
USMM Mike Modano 10.00 25.00
USMR Michael Ryder 6.00 15.00
USMS Marek Svatos 4.00 10.00
USMT Marty Turco 6.00 15.00
USNL Nicklas Lidstrom 15.00 30.00
USOR Bobby Orr 60.00 120.00
USPB Patrice Bergeron 8.00 20.00
USPE Patrik Elias 6.00 15.00
USPH Phil Esposito SP 10.00 25.00
USPK Phil Kessel 10.00 25.00
USPM Patrick Marleau SP 8.00 20.00
USPO Denis Potvin 6.00 15.00
USPR Patrick Roy SP 75.00 150.00
USPS Paul Stastny 12.50 30.00
USRA Alexander Radulov 10.00 25.00
USRB Ray Bourque SP 25.00 60.00
USRH Ron Hextall 10.00 25.00
USRM Ryan Miller 8.00 20.00
USRN Rick Nash 10.00 25.00
USRS Ryan Smyth 5.00 12.00
USSB Steve Bernier 4.00 10.00
USSC Sidney Crosby 60.00 120.00
USSG Simon Gagne 6.00 15.00
USSK Saku Koivu SP 25.00 50.00
USSP Peter Stastny 6.00 15.00
USSS Scott Stevens 8.00 20.00
USST Jordan Staal 15.00 40.00
USTE Tony Esposito SP 12.00 30.00
USTH Joe Thornton SP 20.00 50.00
USTL Ted Lindsay 8.00 20.00
USTO Terry O'Reilly 8.00 20.00
USTV Tomas Vokoun 5.00 12.00
USVL Vincent Lecavalier SP 20.00 50.00
USVT Vesa Toskala 5.00 12.00
USWG Wayne Gretzky 100.00 200.00

2006-07 Ultimate Collection Ultimate Achievements Autographs

UABC Bobby Clarke/89 12.00 30.00
UABH Bobby Hull/58 15.00 40.00
UABO Bobby Orr/6
UABP Bernie Parent/47 15.00 40.00
UACN Cam Neely/9
UACW Cam Ward/15 40.00 100.00
UADH Dany Heatley/50 15.00 40.00
UAEM Evgeni Malkin/6
UAES Eric Staal/28 15.00 40.00
UAGF Grant Fuhr/23 30.00 60.00
UAGH Gordie Howe/26 60.00 125.00
UAGL Guy Lafleur/60 20.00 50.00
UAGP Gilbert Perreault/72 10.00 25.00
UAHA Dominik Hasek/41 20.00 50.00
UAIK Ilya Kovalchuk/52 12.00 30.00
UAJB Jean Beliveau/10 75.00 150.00
UAJC Jonathan Cheechoo/56 10.00 25.00
UAJI Jarome Iginla/52 15.00 40.00
UAJK Jari Kurri/68 10.00 25.00
UAJT Joe Thornton/96 12.00 30.00
UALR Luc Robitaille/63 20.00 50.00
UAMB Martin Brodeur/43 50.00 100.00
UAMD Marcel Dionne/53 12.00 30.00
UAMF Marc-Andre Fleury/40 20.00 40.00
UAMG Marian Gaborik/38 20.00 50.00
UAMH Milan Hejduk/50 6.00 15.00
UAMI Mike Bossy/9 125.00 200.00
UAMK Miikka Kiprusoff/42 20.00 50.00
UAML Mario Lemieux/8
UAMM Mike Modano/23 25.00 50.00
UANL Nicklas Lidstrom/80 15.00 40.00
UAPE Phil Esposito/76 12.00 30.00
UAPR Patrick Roy/23 100.00 200.00
UAPS Peter Stastny/70 8.00 20.00
UARN Rick Nash/41 15.00 40.00
UASC Sidney Crosby/39 100.00 200.00
UASK Saku Koivu/71 12.00 30.00
UATV Tomas Vokoun/36 12.00 30.00
UAVL Vincent Lecavalier/78 12.00 30.00
UAWG Wayne Gretzky/10 750.00 1000.00

2006-07 Ultimate Collection Ultimate Debut Threads Jerseys

STATED PRINT RUN 150 SER.#'d SETS
*PATCH/25: 1.5X TO 4X BASIC JSY
DJAK Anze Kopitar 12.00 30.00
DJAR Alexander Radulov 6.00 15.00
DJBB Brendan Bell 3.00 8.00
DJBO Dave Bolland 5.00 12.00
DJBP Benoit Pouliot 4.00 10.00
DJBT Billy Thompson 3.00 8.00
DJCG Carsen Germyn 3.00 8.00
DJDB Dustin Byfuglien 8.00 20.00
DJDK D.J. King 3.00 8.00
DJDP David Printz 3.00 8.00
DJDS Drew Stafford 5.00 12.00
DJDU Dustin Boyd 3.00 8.00
DJEF Eric Fehr 5.00 12.00
DJEM Evgeni Malkin 50.00 100.00
DJFD Frank Doyle 4.00 10.00
DJFN Filip Novak 3.00 8.00
DJGL Guillaume Latendresse 5.00 12.00
DJIW Ian White 4.00 10.00
DJJI Jarkko Immonen 3.00 8.00
DJJJ Jonas Johansson 3.00 8.00
DJJO John Oduya 5.00 12.00
DJJW Jeremy Williams 3.00 8.00
DJKL Kristopher Letang 10.00 25.00
DJKP Konstantin Pushkarev 4.00 10.00
DJKY Keith Yandle 6.00 15.00
DJLB Luc Bourdon 5.00 12.00
DJLE Loui Eriksson 5.00 12.00
DJLS Ladislav Smid 3.00 8.00
DJMB Michael Blunden 3.00 8.00
DJMC Matt Carle 3.00 8.00
DJMI Mikko Lehtonen 4.00 10.00
DJMK Miroslav Kopriva 3.00 8.00
DJML Matt Lashoff 3.00 8.00
DJMM Masi Marjamaki 3.00 8.00
DJMO Michel Ouellet 4.00 10.00
DJMP Marc-Antoine Pouliot 3.00 8.00
DJMS Mark Stuart 3.00 8.00
DJMV Marc-Edouard Vlasic 3.00 8.00
DJNB Niklas Backstrom 6.00 15.00
DJND Nigel Dawes 3.00 8.00
DJNO Fredrik Norrena 3.00 8.00
DJNW Noah Welch 3.00 8.00
DJON Ben Ondrus 3.00 8.00
DJPK Phil Kessel 8.00 20.00
DJPO Patrick O'Sullivan 5.00 12.00
DJPR Brandon Prust 3.00 8.00
DJPS Paul Stastny 8.00 20.00
DJPT Patrick Thoresen 3.00 8.00
DJRO Roman Polak 4.00 10.00
DJRP Ryan Potulny 3.00 8.00
DJRS Ryan Shannon 3.00 8.00
DJSO Shane O'Brien 3.00 8.00
DJST Jordan Staal 8.00 20.00
DJSW Shea Weber 8.00 20.00
DJTK Tomas Kopecky 4.00 10.00
DJTZ Travis Zajac 6.00 15.00
DJYS Yan Stastny 3.00 8.00

2006-07 Ultimate Collection Ultimate Debut Threads Jerseys Autographs

STATED PRINT RUN 35 SER.#'d SETS
DJAK Anze Kopitar 40.00 100.00
DJAR Alexander Radulov 20.00 50.00
DJBB Brendan Bell 10.00 25.00
DJBO Dave Bolland 15.00 40.00
DJBP Benoit Pouliot 12.00 30.00
DJBT Billy Thompson 10.00 25.00
DJCG Carsen Germyn 10.00 25.00
DJDB Dustin Byfuglien 25.00 60.00
DJDK D.J. King 10.00 25.00
DJDP David Printz 10.00 25.00
DJDS Drew Stafford 15.00 40.00
DJDU Dustin Boyd 10.00 25.00
DJEF Eric Fehr 15.00 40.00
DJEM Evgeni Malkin 75.00 150.00
DJFD Frank Doyle 12.00 30.00
DJFN Filip Novak 10.00 25.00
DJGL G. Latendresse 15.00 40.00
DJIW Ian White 12.00 30.00
DJJI Jarkko Immonen 10.00 25.00
DJJJ Jonas Johansson 10.00 25.00
DJJO John Oduya 15.00 40.00
DJJW Jeremy Williams 10.00 25.00
DJKL Kristopher Letang 30.00 80.00
DJKP Konstantin Pushkarev 12.00 30.00
DJKY Keith Yandle 15.00 40.00
DJLB Luc Bourdon 15.00 40.00
DJLE Loui Eriksson 15.00 40.00
DJLS Ladislav Smid 10.00 25.00
DJMB Michael Blunden 10.00 25.00
DJMC Matt Carle 10.00 25.00
DJMI Mikko Lehtonen 12.00 30.00
DJMK Miroslav Kopriva 10.00 25.00
DJML Matt Lashoff 10.00 25.00
DJMM Masi Marjamaki 10.00 25.00
DJMO Michel Ouellet 12.00 30.00
DJMP Marc-Antoine Pouliot 10.00 25.00
DJMS Mark Stuart 10.00 25.00
DJMV Marc-Edouard Vlasic 10.00 25.00
DJNB Niklas Backstrom 20.00 50.00
DJND Nigel Dawes 10.00 25.00
DJNO Fredrik Norrena 10.00 25.00
DJNW Noah Welch 10.00 25.00
DJON Ben Ondrus 10.00 25.00
DJPK Phil Kessel 25.00 60.00
DJPO Patrick O'Sullivan 15.00 40.00
DJPR Brandon Prust 10.00 25.00
DJPS Paul Stastny 25.00 60.00
DJPT Patrick Thoresen 10.00 25.00
DJRO Roman Polak 12.00 30.00
DJRP Ryan Potulny 10.00 25.00
DJRS Ryan Shannon 10.00 25.00
DJSO Shane O'Brien 10.00 25.00
DJST Jordan Staal 25.00 60.00
DJSW Shea Weber 25.00 60.00
DJTK Tomas Kopecky 12.00 30.00
DJTZ Travis Zajac 20.00 50.00
DJYS Yan Stastny 10.00 25.00

2007-08 Ultimate Collection

COMP.SET w/o SP's (60) 100.00 200.00
STATED PRINT RUN 499 SER.#'d SETS
STATED PRINT RUN 499 SER.#'d SETS
STATED PRINT RUN 399 SER.#'d SETS
STATED PRINT RUN 99 SER.#'d SETS
1 Alexander Ovechkin 5.00 12.00
2 Roberto Luongo 1.50 4.00
3 Markus Naslund 1.25 3.00
4 Mats Sundin 1.25 3.00
5 Darcy Tucker 1.00 2.50
6 Darryl Sittler 1.00 2.50
7 Frank Mahovlich 1.50 4.00
8 Vincent Lecavalier 1.00 2.50
9 Martin St. Louis 1.25 3.00
10 Paul Kariya 1.50 4.00
11 Keith Tkachuk 1.25 3.00
12 Joe Thornton 1.50 4.00
13 Jonathan Cheechoo 1.25 3.00
14 Patrick Marleau 1.25 3.00
15 Mario Lemieux 4.00 10.00
16 Sidney Crosby 5.00 12.00
17 Marc-Andre Fleury 2.00 5.00
18 Evgeni Malkin 4.00 10.00
19 Shane Doan 1.00 2.50
20 Ron Hextall 2.00 5.00
21 Simon Gagne 1.25 3.00
22 Daniel Briere 1.25 3.00
23 Dany Heatley 1.25 3.00
24 Jason Spezza 1.25 3.00

25 Ray Emery 1.00 2.50
26 Jaromir Jagr 3.00 8.00
27 Brendan Shanahan 1.50 4.00
28 Henrik Lundqvist 1.50 4.00
29 Mike Bossy 1.25 3.00
30 Rick DiPietro 1.00 2.50
31 Martin Brodeur 2.50 6.00
32 Zach Parise 1.50 4.00
33 Alexander Radulov 1.25 3.00
34 Saku Koivu 1.25 3.00
35 Michael Ryder .75 2.00
36 Larry Robinson 1.25 3.00
37 Marian Gaborik 1.50 4.00
38 Wayne Gretzky 6.00 15.00
39 Anze Kopitar 2.00 5.00
40 Tomas Vokoun 1.00 2.50
41 Mark Messier 2.00 5.00
42 Dwayne Roloson 1.00 2.50
43 Dominik Hasek 1.50 4.00
44 Henrik Zetterberg 1.50 4.00
45 Gordie Howe 3.00 8.00
46 Mike Modano 2.00 5.00
47 Rick Nash 1.25 3.00
48 Joe Sakic 2.00 5.00
49 Patrick Roy 3.00 8.00
50 Paul Stastny 1.25 3.00
51 Bobby Hull 2.00 5.00
52 Eric Staal 1.50 4.00
53 Jarome Iginla 1.25 3.00
54 Miikka Kiprusoff 1.00 2.50
55 Thomas Vanek 1.50 4.00
56 Ryan Miller 1.25 3.00
57 Patrice Bergeron 1.50 4.00
58 Bobby Orr 4.00 10.00
59 Ilya Kovalchuk 1.25 3.00
60 Jean-Sebastien Giguere 1.25 3.00
61 T.J. Hensick RC 4.00 10.00
62 Jannik Hansen RC 4.00 10.00
63 Jaroslav Halak RC 15.00 40.00
64 Tom Gilbert RC 4.00 10.00
65 Jason Jaffray RC 3.00 8.00
66 Ryan O'Byrne RC 5.00 12.00
67 Steve Downie RC 4.00 10.00
68 David Moss RC 5.00 12.00
69 Mike Weber RC 3.00 8.00
70 Tomas Popperle RC 4.00 10.00
71 Daniel Girardi RC 4.00 10.00
72 Matt Keetley RC 4.00 10.00
73 Cal Clutterbuck RC 5.00 12.00
74 Tobias Stephan RC 4.00 10.00
75 Marc Methot RC 3.00 8.00
76 Matt Hunwick RC 4.00 10.00
77 Mike Lundin RC 3.00 8.00
78 Ryan Carter RC 3.00 8.00
79 Casey Borer RC 3.00 8.00
80 Martin Lojek RC 3.00 8.00
81 Mark Mancari RC 4.00 10.00
82 Jared Boll RC 4.00 10.00
83 Thomas Greiss RC 6.00 15.00
84 Bryan Young RC 3.00 8.00
85 Patrick Kaleta RC 3.00 8.00
86 Rod Pelley RC 3.00 8.00
87 Jonas Hiller RC 6.00 15.00
88 Magnus Johansson RC 3.00 8.00
89 Cory Murphy RC 3.00 8.00
90 Cody Bass RC 4.00 10.00
91 Craig Weller RC 3.00 8.00
92 Steve Wagner RC 3.00 8.00
93 Johnny Boychuk RC 5.00 12.00
94 Matt Ellis RC 4.00 10.00
95 Joel Lundqvist RC 3.00 8.00
96 Jonathan Quick RC 60.00 150.00
97 Daniel Winnik RC 4.00 10.00
98 Drew MacIntyre RC 4.00 10.00
99 Daniel Carcillo RC 4.00 10.00
100 John Zeiler RC 3.00 8.00
101 Brandon Dubinsky RC 6.00 15.00
102 Liam Reddox RC 3.00 8.00
103 Tomas Plihal RC 4.00 10.00
104 Frans Nielsen RC 5.00 12.00
105 Chris Conner RC 3.00 8.00
106 Jack Skille RC 4.00 10.00
107 Tyler Kennedy RC 5.00 12.00
108 Matt Moulson RC 5.00 12.00
109 Sergei Kostitsyn RC 4.00 10.00
110 Tanner Glass RC 3.00 8.00
111 Kent Huskins RC 3.00 8.00
112 Riley Cote RC 4.00 10.00
113 Antti Pihlstrom RC 4.00 10.00
114 Chris Bourque RC 4.00 10.00
115 David Jones RC 3.00 8.00
116 Lukas Kaspar RC 3.00 8.00
117 Nathan Guenin RC 4.00 10.00
118 Kris Russell RC 4.00 10.00
119 Tobias Enstrom RC 5.00 12.00
120 Anton Stralman RC 3.00 8.00
121 Bobby Ryan AU RC 12.00 30.00
122 Sam Gagner AU RC 10.00 25.00
123 Nicklas Bergfors AU RC 5.00 12.00
124 Erik Johnson AU RC 8.00 20.00
125 Jack Johnson AU RC 6.00 15.00
126 Jonathan Bernier AU RC 15.00 40.00
127 Bryan Little AU RC 8.00 20.00
129 Matt Niskanen AU RC 8.00 20.00
130 Andrew Cogliano AU RC 8.00 20.00
131 Marc Staal AU RC 8.00 20.00
132 Nick Foligno AU RC 10.00 25.00
133 Brett Sterling AU RC 5.00 12.00
134 Martin Hanzal AU RC 6.00 15.00
135 Matt Smaby AU RC 5.00 12.00
136 Petr Kalus AU RC 5.00 12.00
137 Andy Greene AU RC 6.00 15.00
138 Ondrej Pavelec AU RC 10.00 25.00
139 Rob Schremp AU RC 6.00 15.00
140 Kyle Chipchura AU RC 8.00 20.00
141 Ryan Parent AU RC 5.00 12.00
142 David Krejci AU RC 20.00 35.00
143 Lauri Tukonen AU RC 5.00 12.00
144 James Sheppard AU RC 5.00 12.00
145 Mason Raymond AU RC 8.00 20.00
146 Devin Setoguchi AU RC 8.00 20.00
147 Curtis McElhinney AU RC 8.00 20.00
148 Brian Elliott AU RC 10.00 25.00
149 Drew Miller AU RC 6.00 15.00
150 Ryan Callahan AU RC 10.00 25.00
151 Ville Koistinen AU RC 5.00 12.00
152 Torrey Mitchell AU RC 6.00 15.00
153 David Perron AU RC 8.00 20.00
154 Milan Lucic AU RC 12.00 30.00
155 Jaroslav Hlinka AU RC 6.00 15.00
156 Tyler Weiman AU RC 6.00 15.00
157 Jonathan Toews AU/99 RC 250.00 450.00
158 Carey Price AU/99 RC 250.00 400.00
159 Patrick Kane AU/99 RC 250.00 400.00
160 Nicklas Backstrom AU/99 RC 75.00 125.00
161 Peter Mueller AU/99 RC 15.00 40.00
162 Jiri Tlusty AU/99 RC 20.00 50.00

2007-08 Ultimate Collection Autographed Jerseys

STATED PRINT RUN 25-50 SERIAL #'d SETS
AJAK Anze Kopitar/50 20.00 50.00
AJAO Alexander Ovechkin/25 100.00 175.00
AJAT Alex Tanguay/50 8.00 20.00
AJBS Borje Salming/50 12.00 30.00
AJCN Cam Neely/25 20.00 50.00
AJCW Cam Ward/50 12.00 30.00
AJEM Evgeni Malkin/25 75.00 150.00
AJES Eric Staal/50 15.00 40.00
AJGF Grant Fuhr/25
AJGL Guy Lafleur/25 30.00 60.00
AJGP Gilbert Perreault/50 12.00 30.00
AJIK Ilya Kovalchuk/50 10.00 25.00
AJJG Jean-Sebastien Giguere/50 12.00 30.00
AJJI Jarome Iginla/25 20.00 50.00
AJJT Joe Thornton/25 20.00 50.00
AJLR Larry Robinson/50 12.00 30.00
AJMB Martin Brodeur/25 60.00 120.00
AJMF Marc-Andre Fleury/50 30.00 60.00
AJMG Marian Gaborik/25 20.00 50.00
AJMH Milan Hejduk/50 10.00 25.00
AJML Mario Lemieux/25 125.00 200.00
AJMM Mark Messier/25 60.00 120.00
AJMN Markus Naslund/50 12.00 30.00
AJMO Mike Modano/50 20.00 50.00
AJMR Michael Ryder/50 8.00 20.00
AJNL Nicklas Lidstrom/50 20.00 50.00
AJPR Patrick Roy/25 75.00 150.00
AJPS Peter Stastny/50 10.00 25.00
AJSC Sidney Crosby/25 100.00 200.00
AJSM Stan Mikita/50 20.00 50.00
AJTV Tomas Vokoun/50 10.00 25.00
AJVL Vincent Lecavalier/50 10.00 25.00
AJWG Wayne Gretzky/25 175.00 300.00

2007-08 Ultimate Collection Autographed Patches

STATED PRINT RUN 10-25
AJAK Anze Kopitar/25 40.00 100.00
AJAT Alex Tanguay/25 15.00 40.00
AJBS Borje Salming/25 20.00 50.00
AJCW Cam Ward/25 30.00 60.00
AJES Eric Staal/25 25.00 50.00
AJGP Gilbert Perreault/25 15.00 40.00
AJIK Ilya Kovalchuk/25 25.00 60.00
AJJG Jean-Sebastien Giguere/25 60.00 120.00
AJLR Larry Robinson/25 20.00 50.00
AJMF Marc-Andre Fleury/25 75.00 150.00
AJMH Milan Hejduk/25 15.00 40.00
AJMM Mike Modano/25 20.00 50.00
AJMN Markus Naslund/25 15.00 40.00
AJMR Michael Ryder/25 15.00 40.00
AJMS Martin St. Louis/25 15.00 40.00
AJNL Nicklas Lidstrom/25 60.00 120.00
AJPS Peter Stastny/25 20.00 50.00
AJRG Ryan Getzlaf/25 12.00 30.00
AJSM Stan Mikita/25 25.00 50.00
AJTV Tomas Vokoun/25 20.00 50.00
AJVL Vincent Lecavalier/25 30.00 80.00

2007-08 Ultimate Collection Jerseys

STATED PRINT RUN 100 SER.#'d SETS
UJAH Ales Hemsky 4.00 10.00
UJAK Anze Kopitar 8.00 20.00
UJAO Alexander Ovechkin 20.00 50.00
UJAT Alex Tanguay 3.00 8.00
UJBC Bobby Clarke 5.00 12.00
UJBL Brian Leetch 5.00 12.00
UJBO Mike Bossy 5.00 12.00
UJBR Brad Richards 5.00 12.00
UJBS Billy Smith 5.00 12.00
UJCN Cam Neely 5.00 12.00
UJCW Cam Ward 5.00 12.00
UJDA Daniel Alfredsson 5.00 12.00
UJDB Daniel Briere 5.00 12.00
UJDH Dale Hawerchuk 6.00 15.00
UJDS Darryl Sittler 4.00 10.00
UJEM Evgeni Malkin 10.00 25.00
UJES Eric Staal 6.00 15.00
UJGP Gilbert Perreault 5.00 12.00
UJHA Dominik Hasek 6.00 15.00
UJHE Dany Heatley 5.00 12.00
UJHL Henrik Lundqvist 6.00 15.00
UJHZ Henrik Zetterberg 6.00 15.00
UJIK Ilya Kovalchuk 5.00 12.00
UJJC Jonathan Cheechoo 5.00 12.00
UJJG Jean-Sebastien Giguere 5.00 12.00
UJJI Jarome Iginla 5.00 12.00
UJJJ Jaromir Jagr 12.00 30.00
UJJO Joe Sakic 8.00 20.00
UJJS Jason Spezza 5.00 12.00
UJJT Joe Thornton 6.00 15.00
UJKL Kari Lehtonen 4.00 10.00
UJMB Martin Brodeur 10.00 25.00
UJMG Marian Gaborik 6.00 15.00
UJMK Miikka Kiprusoff 4.00 10.00
UJML Mario Lemieux 12.00 30.00
UJMM Mike Modano 8.00 20.00
UJMN Markus Naslund 5.00 12.00
UJMR Michael Ryder 3.00 8.00
UJMS Mats Sundin 5.00 12.00
UJPB Patrice Bergeron 6.00 15.00
UJPD Pavel Datsyuk 6.00 15.00
UJPF Peter Forsberg 6.00 15.00
UJPH Dion Phaneuf 5.00 12.00
UJPK Paul Kariya 6.00 15.00
UJPM Patrick Marleau 5.00 12.00
UJPR Patrick Roy 12.00 30.00
UJRB Ray Bourque 8.00 20.00
UJRL Roberto Luongo 6.00 15.00
UJRN Rick Nash 5.00 12.00
UJRS Ryan Smyth 4.00 10.00
UJSA Borje Salming 5.00 12.00
UJSC Sidney Crosby 25.00 50.00
UJSD Shane Doan 4.00 10.00
UJSG Simon Gagne 5.00 12.00
UJSH Brendan Shanahan 6.00 15.00
UJSK Saku Koivu 5.00 12.00
UJSS Scott Stevens 5.00 12.00
UJVL Vincent Lecavalier 4.00 10.00
UJWG Wayne Gretzky 25.00 50.00

2007-08 Ultimate Collection Jerseys Duos

STATED PRINT RUN 50 SERIAL #'d SETS
UJ2BB J.Bucyk/P.Bergeron 8.00 20.00
UJ2BS M.Brodeur/S.Stevens 6.00 15.00
UJ2CG W.Gretzky/S.Crosby 60.00 120.00
UJ2CS S.Crosby/J.Staal 25.00 60.00
UJ2DJ J.Spezza/D.Heatley 6.00 15.00
UJ2FK A.Frolov/A.Kopitar 10.00 25.00
UJ2FR G.Fuhr/D.Roloson 12.00 30.00
UJ2GB S.Gagne/D.Briere 10.00 25.00
UJ2GK M.Gaborik/M.Koivu 8.00 20.00
UJ2HD D.Hasek/P.Datsyuk 10.00 25.00
UJ2HK M.Hossa/I.Kovalchuk 6.00 15.00
UJ2IK J.Iginla/M.Kiprusoff 12.00 30.00
UJ2JL J.Jagr/H.Lundqvist 12.00 30.00
UJ2JP P.Marleau/J.Thornton 8.00 20.00
UJ2KW P.Kariya/D.Weight 8.00 20.00
UJ2LM M.Lemieux/M.Messier 25.00 50.00
UJ2LR G.Lafleur/M.Ryder
UJ2LZ N.Lidstrom/H.Zetterberg 8.00 20.00
UJ2ME M.Lemieux/E.Malkin 25.00 60.00
UJ2MH S.Mikita/M.Havlat 12.00 30.00
UJ2MT M.Modano/M.Turco 10.00 25.00
UJ2NF R.Nash/S.Fedorov 12.00 30.00
UJ2NK C.Neely/P.Kessel 12.00 30.00
UJ2NL M.Naslund/R.Luongo 8.00 20.00
UJ2OM A.Ovechkin/E.Malkin 20.00 50.00
UJ2PV G.Perreault/T.Vanek 10.00 25.00
UJ2SH J.Sakic/M.Hejduk 10.00 25.00
UJ2SS M.Sundin/B.Salming 6.00 15.00
UJ2VB V.Lecavalier/B.Richards 6.00 15.00
UJ2VH T.Vokoun/N.Horton 6.00 15.00

2007-08 Ultimate Collection Jerseys Trios

STATED PRINT RUN 25 SERIAL #'d SETS
UJ3BCP Clarke/Bucyk/Perrlt 30.00 60.00
UJ3BLS Lafleur/Bossy/Sittler 25.00 50.00
UJ3ISH St.L/Htley/Iginla 15.00 40.00
UJ3LCG Lemx/Crsby/Grtzky 125.00 200.00
UJ3LPB Lidst/Brque/Phanf 30.00 60.00
UJ3OMR Malkin/Ovech/Rdulv
UJ3RBF Brodeur/Fleury/Roy 50.00 100.00
UJ3SKK Selanne/Koivu/Kurri 60.00 120.00
UJ3SLT Lecav/Sakc/Thrntn
UJ3SNZ Sndin/Zettr/Nslund 40.00 80.00

2007-08 Ultimate Collection Patches

STATED PRINT RUN 25 SERIAL #'d SETS
UPAH Ales Hemsky 10.00 25.00
UPAK Anze Kopitar 20.00 50.00
UPAO Alexander Ovechkin 125.00 250.00
UPAR Alexander Radulov 12.00 30.00
UPAS Alexander Steen 12.00 30.00
UPAT Alex Tanguay 8.00 20.00
UPBR Brad Richards 30.00 60.00
UPBS Borje Salming 12.00 30.00
UPCN Cam Neely 12.00 30.00
UPCW Cam Ward 30.00 60.00
UPDA Daniel Alfredsson 20.00 50.00
UPDH Dale Hawerchuk 30.00 60.00
UPDR Dwayne Roloson
UPDW Doug Weight 12.00 30.00
UPES Eric Staal 20.00 50.00
UPHA Dominik Hasek 20.00 50.00
UPHE Dany Heatley 12.00 30.00
UPHL Henrik Lundqvist 30.00 60.00
UPHZ Henrik Zetterberg 15.00 40.00
UPIK Ilya Kovalchuk 20.00 50.00
UPJG Jean-Sebastien Giguere 12.00 30.00
UPJI Jarome Iginla 15.00 40.00
UPJJ Jaromir Jagr 30.00 60.00
UPJS Jason Spezza 12.00 30.00
UPJT Joe Thornton 15.00 40.00
UPKE Phil Kessel 30.00 60.00
UPKL Kari Lehtonen 10.00 25.00
UPLM Lanny McDonald 12.00 30.00
UPLR Larry Robinson 12.00 30.00
UPMB Martin Brodeur 30.00 60.00
UPMG Marian Gaborik 20.00 50.00
UPMH Marian Hossa 20.00 50.00
UPMI Milan Hejduk 10.00 25.00
UPMK Mikko Koivu 10.00 25.00
UPML Mario Lemieux 50.00 100.00
UPMM Mike Modano 20.00 50.00
UPMN Markus Naslund 12.00 30.00
UPMR Mark Recchi 15.00 40.00
UPMS Martin St. Louis 12.00 30.00
UPMT Marty Turco 12.00 30.00
UPNL Nicklas Lidstrom 12.00 30.00
UPPB Patrice Bergeron 20.00 50.00
UPPF Peter Forsberg 15.00 40.00
UPPK Paul Kariya 15.00 40.00
UPPR Patrick Roy 50.00 100.00
UPPS Peter Stastny
UPRB Ray Bourque 20.00 50.00
UPRG Ryan Getzlaf 20.00 50.00
UPRL Roberto Luongo 15.00 30.00
UPRN Rick Nash 30.00 60.00
UPRS Ryan Smyth 10.00 25.00
UPSA Joe Sakic 20.00 50.00
UPSC Sidney Crosby 150.00 300.00
UPSD Shane Doan 10.00 25.00
UPSF Sergei Fedorov 20.00 50.00
UPSG Simon Gagne 12.00 30.00
UPSH Brendan Shanahan 15.00 40.00
UPSK Saku Koivu 12.00 30.00
UPSU Mats Sundin 12.00 30.00
UPVL Vincent Lecavalier 10.00 25.00

2007-08 Ultimate Collection Premium Patches

STATED PRINT RUN 25 SERIAL #'d SETS
PSAS Alexander Steen
PSBO Borje Salming 40.00 100.00
PSBS Billy Smith 40.00 80.00
PSBU Johnny Bucyk 20.00 50.00
PSCJ Jonathan Cheechoo 20.00 50.00
PSCN Cam Neely 30.00 60.00
PSCP Chris Pronger 30.00 60.00
PSDA Daniel Alfredsson 50.00 100.00
PSDC Dino Ciccarelli 12.00 30.00
PSDG Doug Gilmour 12.00 30.00
PSDH Dale Hawerchuk
PSEL Patrik Elias 12.00 30.00
PSGF Grant Fuhr 40.00 80.00
PSGP Gilbert Perreault 30.00 60.00
PSHE Dany Heatley 30.00 60.00
PSHL Henrik Lundqvist 40.00 80.00
PSHZ Henrik Zetterberg 30.00 60.00
PSIK Ilya Kovalchuk 50.00 100.00
PSJG Jean-Sebastien Giguere 15.00 40.00
PSJI Jarome Iginla 15.00 40.00
PSJJ Jaromir Jagr 75.00 150.00
PSJM Joe Mullen 15.00 40.00
PSJO Joe Sakic 25.00 60.00
PSJS Jason Spezza 30.00 60.00
PSJT Joe Thornton 20.00 50.00
PSLM Lanny McDonald 12.00 30.00
PSMA Al MacInnis 20.00 50.00
PSMB Martin Brodeur 40.00 80.00
PSMG Marian Gaborik 40.00 80.00
PSMH Marian Hossa 20.00 50.00
PSML Mario Lemieux 60.00 120.00
PSMM Mike Modano 20.00 50.00
PSMN Markus Naslund 15.00 40.00
PSMS Martin St. Louis 15.00 40.00
PSMT Marty Turco 15.00 40.00
PSNL Nicklas Lidstrom 20.00 50.00
PSOV Alexander Ovechkin 60.00 120.00
PSPB Patrice Bergeron 15.00 40.00
PSPD Pavel Datsyuk 50.00 100.00
PSPK Paul Kariya 20.00 50.00
PSPM Patrick Marleau 15.00 40.00
PSPR Patrick Roy 75.00 150.00
PSPS Peter Stastny
PSRB Ray Bourque 25.00 60.00
PSRL Roberto Luongo 30.00 60.00
PSRN Rick Nash 60.00 120.00
PSSC Sidney Crosby 100.00 200.00
PSSG Simon Gagne 20.00 50.00
PSSH Brendan Shanahan 20.00 50.00
PSSI Darryl Sittler 15.00 40.00
PSST Jordan Staal 15.00 40.00
PSSU Mats Sundin 15.00 40.00
PSVL Vincent Lecavalier 20.00 50.00
PSWG Wayne Gretzky 150.00 250.00

2007-08 Ultimate Collection Premium Swatches

STATED PRINT RUN 50 SERIAL #'d SETS
PSAS Alexander Steen 8.00 20.00
PSBO Borje Salming 8.00 20.00
PSBS Billy Smith 8.00 20.00
PSBU Johnny Bucyk 6.00 15.00
PSCJ Jonathan Cheechoo 8.00 20.00
PSCN Cam Neely 8.00 20.00
PSCP Chris Pronger 6.00 15.00
PSDA Daniel Alfredsson 8.00 20.00
PSDC Dino Ciccarelli 8.00 20.00
PSDG Doug Gilmour 10.00 25.00
PSDH Dale Hawerchuk
PSDS Denis Savard 10.00 25.00
PSEL Patrik Elias 8.00 20.00
PSGF Grant Fuhr 8.00 20.00
PSGP Gilbert Perreault 8.00 20.00
PSHE Dany Heatley 8.00 20.00
PSHL Henrik Lundqvist 10.00 25.00
PSHZ Henrik Zetterberg 10.00 25.00
PSIK Ilya Kovalchuk 8.00 20.00
PSJB Jean Beliveau 10.00 25.00
PSJG Jean-Sebastien Giguere 8.00 20.00
PSJI Jarome Iginla 12.00 30.00
PSJJ Jaromir Jagr 20.00 50.00
PSJM Joe Mullen 6.00 15.00
PSJO Joe Sakic 12.00 30.00
PSJS Jason Spezza 8.00 20.00
PSJT Joe Thornton 10.00 25.00
PSLM Lanny McDonald 8.00 20.00
PSMA Al MacInnis 8.00 20.00
PSMB Martin Brodeur 15.00 40.00
PSMG Marian Gaborik 10.00 25.00
PSMH Marian Hossa 6.00 15.00
PSML Mario Lemieux 15.00 40.00
PSMM Mike Modano 12.00 30.00
PSMN Markus Naslund 8.00 20.00
PSMS Martin St. Louis 8.00 20.00
PSMT Marty Turco 8.00 20.00
PSNL Nicklas Lidstrom 8.00 20.00
PSOV Alexander Ovechkin 30.00 60.00
PSPB Patrice Bergeron 10.00 25.00
PSPD Pavel Datsyuk 10.00 25.00
PSPK Paul Kariya 10.00 25.00
PSPM Patrick Marleau 8.00 20.00
PSPR Patrick Roy 20.00 50.00
PSPS Peter Stastny 6.00 15.00
PSRB Ray Bourque 12.00 30.00
PSRH Ron Hextall 12.00 30.00
PSRL Roberto Luongo 10.00 25.00
PSRM Ryan Miller 8.00 20.00
PSRN Rick Nash 8.00 20.00
PSRY Michael Ryder 5.00 12.00
PSSC Sidney Crosby 30.00 60.00
PSSG Simon Gagne
PSSH Brendan Shanahan 10.00 25.00
PSSI Darryl Sittler 6.00 15.00
PSSK Saku Koivu 8.00 20.00
PSST Jordan Staal 8.00 20.00
PSSU Mats Sundin 8.00 20.00
PSVL Vincent Lecavalier 6.00 15.00
PSWG Wayne Gretzky 40.00 80.00

2007-08 Ultimate Collection Rookies Autographed Patches

STATED PRINT RUN 25 SERIAL #'d SETS
121 Bobby Ryan 40.00 100.00
122 Sam Gagner 30.00 80.00
123 Nicklas Bergfors 15.00 40.00
124 Erik Johnson 25.00 60.00
125 Jack Johnson 20.00 50.00
126 Jonathan Bernier 75.00 150.00
127 Bryan Little 20.00 50.00
129 Matt Niskanen 25.00 60.00
130 Andrew Cogliano 25.00 60.00
131 Marc Staal 25.00 60.00
132 Nick Foligno 30.00 80.00
133 Brett Sterling 15.00 40.00
134 Martin Hanzal 20.00 50.00
135 Matt Smaby 15.00 40.00
136 Petr Kalus 15.00 40.00
137 Andy Greene 20.00 50.00
138 Ondrej Pavelec 25.00 60.00
139 Rob Schremp 20.00 50.00
140 Kyle Chipchura 25.00 60.00
141 Ryan Parent 15.00 40.00
142 David Krejci 75.00 125.00
143 Lauri Tukonen 15.00 40.00
144 James Sheppard 15.00 40.00
145 Mason Raymond 25.00 60.00
146 Devin Setoguchi 25.00 60.00
147 Curtis McElhinney 25.00 60.00
148 Brian Elliott 30.00 80.00
149 Drew Miller 20.00 50.00
150 Ryan Callahan 30.00 80.00
151 Ville Koistinen 15.00 40.00
152 Torrey Mitchell 20.00 50.00
153 David Perron 25.00 60.00
154 Milan Lucic 125.00 200.00
155 Jaroslav Hlinka 20.00 50.00
156 Tyler Weiman 20.00 50.00
157 Jonathan Toews 350.00 500.00
158 Carey Price 350.00 500.00
159 Patrick Kane 250.00 400.00
160 Nicklas Backstrom 90.00 150.00
161 Peter Mueller 60.00 120.00
162 Jiri Tlusty 30.00 80.00

2007-08 Ultimate Collection Signatures

USAC Andrew Cogliano 6.00 15.00
USAO Alexander Ovechkin 25.00 60.00
USAT Alex Tanguay 4.00 10.00
USBO Bobby Orr 75.00 150.00
USBP Bernie Parent 12.00 30.00
USCP Carey Price 20.00 50.00
USEM Evgeni Malkin 30.00 60.00
USES Eric Staal 8.00 20.00
USGF Grant Fuhr 8.00 20.00
USGH Gordie Howe 50.00 100.00
USIK Ilya Kovalchuk 8.00 20.00
USJG Jean-Sebastien Giguere 6.00 15.00
USJJ Jack Johnson 5.00 12.00
USJK Jari Kurri 6.00 15.00
USJM Joe Mullen 5.00 12.00
USJS James Sheppard 4.00 10.00
USJT Joe Thornton 8.00 20.00
USLM Lanny McDonald 8.00 20.00
USMA Martin St. Louis 6.00 15.00
USMB Martin Brodeur 30.00 60.00
USMF Marc-Andre Fleury 15.00 40.00
USMG Marian Gaborik 8.00 20.00
USML Mario Lemieux 75.00 150.00
USMM Mark Messier 40.00 100.00
USMN Markus Naslund 6.00 15.00
USMR Michael Ryder 4.00 10.00
USMS Marc Staal 6.00 15.00
USNB Nicklas Backstrom 12.00 30.00
USNF Nick Foligno 8.00 20.00
USNL Nicklas Lidstrom 10.00 25.00
USPE Corey Perry 6.00 15.00
USPK Patrick Kane 30.00 60.00
USPM Peter Mueller 5.00 12.00
USPR Patrick Roy 60.00 120.00
USPS Paul Stastny 6.00 15.00
USRB Ray Bourque 15.00 40.00
USRH Ron Hextall 10.00 25.00
USRM Ryan Miller 6.00 15.00
USSC Sidney Crosby 100.00 175.00
USSG Sam Gagner 8.00 20.00
USST Jordan Staal 12.00 30.00
USTO Jonathan Toews 60.00 100.00
USTV Tomas Vokoun 5.00 12.00
USVL Vincent Lecavalier 8.00 20.00
USWG Wayne Gretzky 175.00 300.00

2007-08 Ultimate Collection Ultimate Debut Threads Jerseys

STATED PRINT RUN 200 SERIAL #'d SETS
DTAC Andrew Cogliano 6.00 15.00
DTAG Andy Greene 5.00 12.00
DTBA Nicklas Backstrom 8.00 20.00
DTBD Brandon Dubinsky 8.00 20.00
DTBE Brian Elliott 8.00 20.00
DTBL Bryan Little 4.00 10.00
DTBR Bobby Ryan 10.00 25.00
DTBS Brett Sterling 4.00 10.00
DTCM Curtis McElhinney 6.00 15.00
DTCP Carey Price 25.00 50.00
DTDK David Krejci 12.00 30.00
DTDP David Perron 6.00 15.00
DTEJ Erik Johnson 6.00 15.00
DTFN Frans Nielsen 6.00 15.00
DTHA Jannik Hansen 5.00 12.00
DTJB Jonathan Bernier 8.00 20.00
DTJH Jaroslav Hlinka 5.00 12.00
DTJJ Jack Johnson 5.00 12.00
DTJS James Sheppard 4.00 10.00
DTJT Jonathan Toews 20.00 50.00
DTKC Kyle Chipchura 6.00 15.00
DTKR Kris Russell 5.00 12.00
DTMH Martin Hanzal 5.00 12.00
DTML Milan Lucic 20.00 50.00
DTMN Matt Niskanen 6.00 15.00
DTMR Mason Raymond 6.00 15.00
DTMS Marc Staal 6.00 15.00
DTNB Nicklas Bergfors 4.00 10.00
DTNF Nick Foligno 8.00 20.00
DTPK Patrick Kane 15.00 40.00
DTPM Peter Mueller 5.00 12.00
DTRC Ryan Callahan 8.00 20.00
DTRP Ryan Parent 4.00 10.00
DTRS Rob Schremp 6.00 15.00
DTSG Sam Gagner 6.00 15.00
DTSM Matt Smaby 4.00 10.00
DTTM Torrey Mitchell 5.00 12.00
DTTS Tobias Stephan 5.00 12.00
DTTW Tyler Weiman 5.00 12.00

2007-08 Ultimate Collection Ultimate Debut Threads Jerseys Autographs

STATED PRINT RUN 35 SERIAL #'d SETS
DTAC Andrew Cogliano 12.00 30.00
DTAG Andy Greene 10.00 25.00
DTBA Nicklas Backstrom 40.00 80.00
DTBD Brandon Dubinsky 15.00 40.00
DTBE Brian Elliott 15.00 40.00
DTBL Bryan Little 10.00 25.00
DTBR Bobby Ryan 20.00 50.00
DTBS Brett Sterling 8.00 20.00
DTCM Curtis McElhinney 12.00 30.00
DTCP Carey Price 75.00 150.00
DTDK David Krejci 20.00 50.00
DTDP David Perron 12.00 30.00
DTEJ Erik Johnson 12.00 30.00
DTFN Frans Nielsen 12.00 30.00
DTHA Jannik Hansen 10.00 25.00
DTJB Jonathan Bernier 40.00 80.00
DTJH Jaroslav Hlinka 10.00 25.00
DTJJ Jack Johnson 30.00 60.00
DTJS James Sheppard 8.00 20.00
DTJT Jonathan Toews 75.00 150.00
DTKC Kyle Chipchura 12.00 30.00
DTLT Lauri Tukonen 8.00 20.00
DTMH Martin Hanzal 10.00 25.00
DTML Milan Lucic 40.00 100.00
DTMN Matt Niskanen 12.00 30.00
DTMR Mason Raymond 12.00 30.00
DTMS Marc Staal 12.00 30.00
DTNB Nicklas Bergfors
DTNF Nick Foligno 15.00 40.00
DTPK Patrick Kane 75.00 150.00
DTPM Peter Mueller 15.00 40.00
DTRC Ryan Callahan 15.00 40.00
DTRP Ryan Parent 8.00 20.00
DTRS Rob Schremp 10.00 25.00
DTSG Sam Gagner 30.00 60.00
DTSM Matt Smaby 8.00 20.00
DTTM Torrey Mitchell
DTTS Tobias Stephan 10.00 25.00
DTTW Tyler Weiman 10.00 25.00

2007-08 Ultimate Collection Ultimate Debut Threads Patches

STATED PRINT RUN 50 SERIAL #'d SETS
DTAC Andrew Cogliano 15.00 40.00
DTAG Andy Greene 12.00 30.00
DTBA Nicklas Backstrom 40.00 80.00
DTBD Brandon Dubinsky 20.00 50.00
DTBE Brian Elliott 20.00 50.00
DTBL Bryan Little 8.00 20.00
DTBR Bobby Ryan 25.00 60.00
DTBS Brett Sterling 10.00 25.00
DTCM Curtis McElhinney 15.00 40.00
DTCP Carey Price 100.00 200.00
DTDK David Krejci 30.00 80.00
DTDM Drew Miller 12.00 30.00
DTDP David Perron 15.00 40.00
DTEJ Erik Johnson 12.00 30.00
DTFN Frans Nielsen 15.00 40.00
DTHA Jannik Hansen 12.00 30.00
DTJB Jonathan Bernier 25.00 60.00
DTJH Jaroslav Hlinka 12.00 30.00
DTJJ Jack Johnson 12.00 30.00
DTJS James Sheppard 10.00 25.00
DTJT Jonathan Toews 100.00 200.00
DTKA Petr Kalus 10.00 25.00
DTKC Kyle Chipchura 15.00 40.00
DTKR Kris Russell 12.00 30.00
DTLT Lauri Tukonen 10.00 25.00
DTMH Martin Hanzal 12.00 30.00
DTML Milan Lucic 40.00 80.00
DTMN Matt Niskanen 15.00 40.00
DTMR Mason Raymond 15.00 40.00
DTMS Marc Staal 15.00 40.00
DTNB Nicklas Bergfors 10.00 25.00
DTNF Nick Foligno 20.00 50.00
DTPK Patrick Kane 100.00 200.00
DTPM Peter Mueller 12.00 30.00
DTRC Ryan Callahan 20.00 50.00
DTRP Ryan Parent 10.00 25.00
DTRS Rob Schremp 12.00 30.00
DTSG Sam Gagner 20.00 50.00
DTSM Matt Smaby 10.00 25.00
DTTM Torrey Mitchell 40.00 80.00
DTTS Tobias Stephan 12.00 30.00
DTTW Tyler Weiman 20.00 50.00

2008-09 Ultimate Collection

This 102-card set was released in May, 2009. It included 42 veterans and 60 rookies. The veterans were serial numbered to 299 along with 18 of the rookies. The next 36 rookies were serial numbered to 399 and included an on-card autograph. The final six rookies in the set were serial numbered to 99 and also included an on-card autograph. The Fabian Brunnstrom was released with two versions available. The serial numbering on 51 of the cards was set to 399, whil 48 of these cards were serial numbered to 99. Upper Deck can confirm there are only 99 of the cards in these cards in the market. Worthy of note, Brunnstrom signed the first 48 cards without damage in black ink, the remaining 51 were numbered to 399 and were signed in blue ink.

COMP.SET w/o SPs (42) 100.00 200.00
(43-60) PRINT RUN 299 SER.#'d SETS
(61-96) PRINT RUN 399 SER.#'d SETS
(97-102) PRINT RUN 99 SER.#'d SETS
BRUNSTROM BLACK INK #'d TO 99
BRUNSTROM BLUE INK #'d TO 399
1 Ilya Kovalchuk 1.50 4.00
2 Bobby Orr 5.00 12.00
3 Thomas Vanek 1.50 4.00
4 Jarome Iginla 1.50 4.00
5 Miikka Kiprusoff 1.25 3.00
6 Eric Staal 2.00 5.00
7 Patrick Kane 3.00 8.00
8 Jonathan Toews 4.00 10.00
9 Joe Sakic 2.50 6.00
10 Paul Stastny 1.50 4.00
11 Rick Nash 1.50 4.00
12 Mike Modano 2.50 6.00
13 Henrik Zetterberg 2.00 5.00
14 Wayne Gretzky 8.00 20.00
15 Mark Messier 2.00 5.00
16 Ray Bourque 2.50 6.00
17 Gordie Howe 4.00 10.00
18 Marian Gaborik 2.00 5.00
19 Carey Price 6.00 15.00
20 Saku Koivu 1.50 4.00
21 Patrick Roy 4.00 10.00
22 Martin Brodeur 3.00 8.00
23 Rick DiPietro 1.25 3.00
24 Markus Naslund 1.25 3.00
25 Henrik Lundqvist 2.00 5.00
26 Dany Heatley 1.50 4.00
27 Jason Spezza 1.50 4.00
28 Mike Richards 1.50 4.00
29 Shane Doan 1.25 3.00
30 Peter Mueller 1.25 3.00
31 Mario Lemieux 5.00 12.00
32 Sidney Crosby 6.00 15.00
33 Marc-Andre Fleury 2.50 6.00
34 Evgeni Malkin 5.00 12.00
35 Joe Thornton 2.00 5.00
36 Paul Kariya 2.00 5.00
37 Vincent Lecavalier 1.25 3.00
38 Martin St. Louis 1.50 4.00
39 Vesa Toskala 1.25 3.00
40 Pavel Datsyuk 2.00 5.00
41 Roberto Luongo 2.00 5.00
42 Alexander Ovechkin 6.00 15.00
43 Max Pacioretty RC 15.00 30.00
44 Justin Pogge RC 3.00 8.00
45 Tim Kennedy RC 3.00 8.00
46 Ben Bishop RC 5.00 12.00
47 Michal Repik RC 3.00 8.00
48 Brian Boyle RC 2.50 6.00
49 Brian Lee RC 2.50 6.00
50 John Curry RC 3.00 8.00
51 Ben Maxwell RC 3.00 8.00
52 Jamie McGinn RC 3.00 8.00
53 Jonas Frogren RC 2.00 5.00
54 Brendan Mikkelson RC 2.00 5.00
55 Ty Wishart RC 2.50 6.00
56 Mark Fistric RC 2.50 6.00
57 Matt D'Agostini RC 2.50 6.00
58 Trevor Lewis RC 3.00 8.00
59 Simeon Varlamov RC 15.00 40.00
60 Wayne Simmonds RC 5.00 12.00
61 Adam Pineault AU RC 5.00 12.00
62 Alex Goligoski AU RC 8.00 20.00
63 Alex Pietrangelo AU RC 8.00 20.00
64 Chris Stewart AU RC 6.00 15.00
65 Brandon Sutter AU RC 6.00 15.00
66 Claude Giroux AU RC 30.00 60.00
67 Colton Gillies AU RC 5.00 12.00
68 Darren Helm AU RC 10.00 25.00
69 Derick Brassard AU RC 5.00 12.00
70 Drew Doughty AU RC 25.00 50.00
71 Kenndal McArdle AU RC 5.00 12.00
72 Josh Bailey AU RC 8.00 20.00
73 James Neal AU RC 12.00 30.00
74 Justin Abdelkader AU RC 10.00 25.00
75 Nathan Gerbe AU RC 6.00 15.00
76 Kyle Okposo AU RC 6.00 15.00
77 Luca Sbisa AU RC 4.00 10.00
78 Luke Schenn AU RC 8.00 20.00
79 Mattias Ritola AU RC 5.00 12.00
80 Michael Frolik AU RC 6.00 15.00
81 Mikkel Boedker AU RC 8.00 20.00
82 Cory Schneider AU RC 15.00 40.00
83 Nikolai Kulemin AU RC 6.00 15.0
84 Oscar Moller AU RC 5.00 12.0
85 Patric Hornqvist AU RC 6.00 15.0
86 Patrik Berglund AU RC 5.00 12.0
87 Petr Vrana AU RC 4.00 10.0
88 Robbie Earl AU RC 4.00 10.0
89 Karl Alzner AU RC 4.00 10.0
90 Shawn Matthias AU RC 6.00 15.0
91 Steve Mason AU RC 15.00 40.0
92 T.J. Oshie AU RC 20.00 50.0
93 Viktor Tikhonov AU RC 5.00 12.0
94 Vladimir Mihalik AU RC 4.00 10.0
95 Zach Bogosian AU RC 6.00 15.0
96 Zach Boychuk AU RC 6.00 15.0
97 Nikita Filatov AU RC/99 12.00 30.0
98 Jakub Voracek AU RC/99 25.00 60.0
99 Brunstrm AU RC/51* blu ink 10.00 25.0
99B Brunstrm AU RC/48* blk ink 10.00 25.0
100 Blake Wheeler AU RC/99 25.00 50.0
101 Kyle Turris AU RC/99 30.00 80.0
102 Steven Stamkos AU RC/99 350.00 600.0

2008-09 Ultimate Collection Debut Threads

*PATCH/50: .8X TO 2X BASIC JSY/200
DTAG Alex Goligoski 5.00 12.0
DTAN Andreas Nodl 2.50 6.0
DTAP Adam Pineault 3.00 8.0
DTBB Brian Boyle 3.00 8.0
DTBO Zach Boychuk 4.00 10.0
DTBP Ben Bishop 5.00 12.0
DTBS Brandon Sutter 4.00 10.0
DTBW Blake Wheeler 10.00 25.0
DTCG Colton Gillies 3.00 8.0
DTDB Derick Brassard 3.00 8.0
DTDD Drew Doughty 10.00 25.0
DTDH Darren Helm 4.00 10.0
DTEE Erik Ersberg 3.00 8.0
DTFB Fabian Brunnstrom 3.00 8.0
DTFR Michael Frolik 4.00 10.0
DTGI Claude Giroux 10.00 25.0
DTIZ Ilya Zubov 3.00 8.0
DTJA Justin Abdelkader 6.00 15.0
DTJE Jonathan Ericsson 4.00 10.0
DTJN James Neal 5.00 12.0
DTJV Jakub Voracek 5.00 12.0
DTKO Kyle Okposo 4.00 10.0
DTKP Kevin Porter 3.00 8.0
DTKT Kyle Turris 6.00 15.0
DTLK Lauri Korpikoski 2.50 6.0
DTLS Luca Sbisa 2.50 6.0
DTMA Shawn Matthias 4.00 10.0
DTMB Mikkel Boedker 5.00 12.0
DTMD Matt D'Agostini 3.00 8.0
DTMF Mark Fistric 3.00 8.0
DTMR Mattias Ritola 3.00 8.0
DTNF Nikita Filatov 4.00 10.0
DTNK Nikolai Kulemin 4.00 10.0
DTNO Nathan Oystrick 4.00 10.0
DTOM Oscar Moller 3.00 8.0
DTPB Patrik Berglund 3.00 8.0
DTPH Patric Hornqvist 4.00 10.0
DTPI Alex Pietrangelo 5.00 12.0
DTPV Petr Vrana 2.50 6.0
DTRE Robbie Earl 2.50 6.0
DTRJ Ryan Jones 4.00 10.0
DTRS Ryan Stone 2.50 6.0
DTSC Luke Schenn 5.00 12.0
DTSM Steve Mason 6.00 15.0
DTSS Steven Stamkos 30.00 60.0
DTTO T.J. Oshie 8.00 20.0
DTTS Tom Sestito 4.00 10.0
DTVM Vladimir Mihalik 2.50 6.0
DTVT Viktor Tikhonov 3.00 8.0
DTZB Zach Bogosian 4.00 10.0

2008-09 Ultimate Collection Debut Threads Autographs

STATED PRINT RUN 35 SER.#'d SETS
SDTAG Alex Goligoski
SDTAN Andreas Nodl 6.00 15.0
SDTAP Adam Pineault 8.00 20.0
SDTBB Brian Boyle
SDTBO Zach Boychuk
SDTBP Ben Bishop 15.00 40.0
SDTBS Brandon Sutter
SDTBW Blake Wheeler 20.00 50.0
SDTCG Colton Gillies 8.00 20.0
SDTDB Derick Brassard
SDTDD Drew Doughty 30.00 60.0
SDTDH Darren Helm 10.00 25.0
SDTEE Erik Ersberg 8.00 20.0
SDTFB Fabian Brunnstrom 8.00 20.0
SDTFR Michael Frolik 10.00 25.0
SDTGI Claude Giroux 20.00 50.0
SDTIZ Ilya Zubov 8.00 20.0
SDTJA Justin Abdelkader 15.00 40.0
SDTJE Jonathan Ericsson 10.00 25.0
SDTJN James Neal 20.00 50.0
SDTJV Jakub Voracek 20.00 50.0
SDTKO Kyle Okposo
SDTKP Kevin Porter 8.00 20.
SDTKT Kyle Turris 15.00 40.
SDTLK Lauri Korpikoski 6.00 15.
SDTLS Luca Sbisa 6.00 15.
SDTMA Shawn Matthias 10.00 25.
SDTMB Mikkel Boedker 12.00 30.
SDTMD Matt D'Agostini
SDTMF Mark Fistric
SDTMR Mattias Ritola 8.00 20.
SDTNF Nikita Filatov 10.00 25.
SDTNK Nikolai Kulemin 10.00 25.
SDTNO Nathan Oystrick 10.00 25.
SDTOM Oscar Moller 8.00 20.
SDTPB Patrik Berglund 8.00 20.
SDTPH Patric Hornqvist 10.00 25.
SDTPI Alex Pietrangelo 12.00 30.
SDTPV Petr Vrana 6.00 15.
SDTRE Robbie Earl 6.00 15.
SDTRJ Ryan Jones 10.00 25.
SDTRS Ryan Stone 6.00 15.
SDTSC Luke Schenn 12.00 30.
SDTSM Steve Mason 40.00 100.
SDTSS Steven Stamkos 60.00 120.
SDTTO T.J. Oshie 20.00 50.
SDTTS Tom Sestito
SDTVM Vladimir Mihalik 6.00 15.
SDTVT Viktor Tikhonov 8.00 20.
SDTZB Zach Bogosian 10.00 25.

2008-09 Ultimate Collection Premium Patches

STATED PRINT RUN 25 SER.#'d SETS
PSAO Alexander Ovechkin
PSCP Carey Price 60.00 120
PSDH Dale Hawerchuk 15.00 40
PSDP Dion Phaneuf 12.00 30
PSEM Evgeni Malkin
PSHZ Henrik Zetterberg 15.00 40
PSIK Ilya Kovalchuk 12.00 30
PSJC Jonathan Cheechoo
PSJI Jarome Iginla 12.00 30

Joe Sakic 50.00 100.00
Joe Thornton 15.00 40.00
) Anze Kopitar
M Lanny McDonald
B Martin Brodeur 40.00 100.00
G Marian Gaborik 15.00 40.00
M Mike Modano 15.00 40.00
R Mike Richards 20.00 50.00
S Marc Savard 40.00 80.00
3 Nicklas Backstrom
Nicklas Lidstrom 12.00 30.00
Olli Jokinen 10.00 25.00
3 Patrice Bergeron 15.00 40.00
) Pavel Datsyuk 15.00 40.00
(Patrick Kane
M Peter Mueller 10.00 25.00
Paul Stastny 12.00 30.00
3 Ray Bourque 20.00 50.00
G Ryan Getzlaf 20.00 50.00
M Ryan Miller 25.00 60.00
Rick Nash
C Sidney Crosby 100.00 200.00
) Shane Doan
Simon Gagne 20.00 50.00
(Saku Koivu 20.00 50.00
Steve Shutt 12.00 30.00
Jason Spezza 12.00 30.00
) Jonathan Toews 50.00 100.00
Teemu Selanne 25.00 60.00
Thomas Vanek
Vincent Lecavalier

2008-09 Ultimate Collection Rookie Patch Autographs

ED PRINT RUN 25 SER.#'d SETS
dam Pineault 12.00 30.00
lex Goligoski 20.00 50.00
lex Pietrangelo 20.00 50.00
hris Stewart 20.00 50.00
randon Sutter
laude Giroux 125.00 200.00
olton Gillies 12.00 30.00
arren Helm 15.00 40.00
erick Brassard 15.00 40.00
rew Doughty 50.00 125.00
enndal McArdle 12.00 30.00
osh Bailey
ames Neal 30.00 80.00
ustin Abdelkader 25.00 60.00
athan Gerbe 15.00 40.00
yle Okposo
uca Sbisa 10.00 25.00
uke Schenn 20.00 50.00
attias Ritola 12.00 30.00
ichael Frolik 15.00 40.00
ikkel Boedker 20.00 50.00
ory Schneider 40.00 100.00
ikolai Kulemin 30.00 80.00
scar Moller 12.00 30.00
atric Hornqvist 15.00 40.00
atrik Berglund 12.00 30.00
etr Vrana 10.00 25.00
obbie Earl 10.00 25.00
hawn Matthias 15.00 40.00
teve Mason 40.00 100.00
.J. Oshie 30.00 80.00
iktor Tikhonov 12.00 30.00
ladimir Mihalik 10.00 25.00
ach Bogosian 15.00 40.00
ach Boychuk 15.00 40.00
ikita Filatov 15.00 40.00
akub Voracek 30.00 80.00
abian Brunnstrom 12.00 30.00
lake Wheeler 40.00 80.00
yle Turris 25.00 60.00
teven Stamkos 200.00 350.00

008-09 Ultimate Collection Ultimate Jerseys

ED PRINT RUN 100 SER.#'d SETS
H/25: .8X TO 2X BASIC JSY/100
Alexander Ovechkin 12.00 30.00
Cam Neely 6.00 15.00
Carey Price 10.00 25.00
Evgeni Malkin
Henrik Lundqvist 8.00 20.00
Henrik Zetterberg 8.00 20.00
lya Kovalchuk 6.00 15.00
arome Iginla 6.00 15.00
Joe Sakic 10.00 25.00
Martin Brodeur 12.00 30.00
Mark Messier 8.00 20.00
Mario Lemieux 20.00 50.00
Pavel Datsyuk 8.00 20.00
Patrick Roy 15.00 40.00
Ray Bourque 10.00 25.00
Roberto Luongo 8.00 20.00
Rick Nash 6.00 15.00
Sidney Crosby 20.00 50.00
Vincent Lecavalier 5.00 12.00
Wayne Gretzky 20.00 50.00

008-09 Ultimate Collection ltimate Jerseys Autographs

D PRINT RUN 25-50
Anze Kopitar 15.00 40.00
Adam Oates
Brian Leetch 10.00 25.00
Martin Brodeur/25 50.00 100.00
Cam Neely/25
Carey Price 40.00 100.00
Dale Hawerchuk 12.00 30.00
Evgeni Malkin/25 50.00 100.00
Eric Staal 12.00 30.00
Grant Fuhr/25 25.00 50.00
Gilbert Perreault 10.00 25.00
Marian Hossa 8.00 20.00
Henrik Zetterberg/25 15.00 40.00
ya Kovalchuk/25
arome Iginla/25 12.00 30.00
ordan Staal 10.00 25.00
oe Thornton/25 15.00 40.00
arry Robinson 10.00 25.00
Marc-Andre Fleury 15.00 40.00
Mario Lemieux/25 50.00 100.00
Mark Messier/25 50.00 100.00
Mike Modano 15.00 40.00
Marty Turco
Nicklas Lidstrom 25.00 50.00
Patrice Bergeron 12.00 30.00
Patrick Kane 20.00 50.00
Patrick Roy/25 60.00 120.00
Ryan Getzlaf
Rick Nash
Sidney Crosby/25 250.00 400.00
Sam Gagner 8.00 20.00
Vincent Lecavalier 8.00 20.00
Wayne Gretzky/25 175.00 300.00

2008-09 Ultimate Collection Ultimate Jerseys Duos

STATED PRINT RUN 50 SER.#'d SETS
UJ2HD Datsyuk/Zetterberg 6.00 15.00
UJ2IK Iginla/Kiprusoff 5.00 12.00
UJ2KM Kovalchuk/Malkin 15.00 40.00
UJ2LM Lemieux/Malkin 15.00 40.00
UJ2LN Lundqvist/Naslund 6.00 15.00
UJ2LZ Lidstrom/Zetterberg 6.00 15.00
UJ2MT Turco/Modano
UJ2OB Ovechkin/Backstrom 20.00 50.00
UJ2RB Roy/Brodeur 12.00 30.00

2008-09 Ultimate Collection Ultimate Jerseys Duos Autographs

STATED PRINT RUN 10-20
2UJHY Howe/Yzerman/10
2UJBN Bourque/Neely/20 60.00 100.00
2UJDM Doan/Mueller/20 15.00 30.00
2UJGM Gretzky/Messier/10
2UJHM Hasek/Miller/20 40.00 80.00
2UJLM Lemieux/Malkin/10
2UJMF Malkin/Fleury/20
2UJMK Malkin/Kovalchuk/20 30.00 60.00
2UJRB Roy/Brodeur/10
2UJSS Pa.Stastny/Pe.Stastny/20 15.00 40.00
2UJTB Toews/Backstrom/20 50.00 100.00
2UJZD Zetterberg/Datsyuk/20 40.00 80.00

2008-09 Ultimate Collection Ultimate Jerseys Trios

STATED PRINT RUN 25 SER.#'d SETS
UJ3FWD Lecav/Thornton/Iginla 10.00 25.00
UJ3HOF Gretzky/Messier/Lemieux 40.00 100.00
UJ3NET Roy/Brodeur/Price 15.00 40.00
UJ3RSN Malkin/Koval/Ovech 30.00 80.00
UJ3SWD Zett/Lids/Lundq 10.00 25.00

2008-09 Ultimate Collection Ultimate Patches Autographs

STATED PRINT RUN 10-25
AJAK Anze Kopitar 30.00 80.00
AJBL Brian Leetch 40.00 80.00
AJCP Carey Price 50.00 100.00
AJDH Dale Hawerchuk 15.00 40.00
AJES Eric Staal 25.00 60.00
AJGF Grant Fuhr 25.00 60.00
AJGP Gilbert Perreault
AJHO Marian Hossa 20.00 50.00
AJJS Jordan Staal 15.00 40.00
AJLR Larry Robinson
AJMF Marc-Andre Fleury 40.00 100.00
AJMO Mike Modano
AJNL Nicklas Lidstrom 40.00 80.00
AJPB Patrice Bergeron
AJPK Patrick Kane 40.00 100.00
AJSG Sam Gagner
AJVL Vincent Lecavalier 15.00 40.00

2008-09 Ultimate Collection Ultimate Patches Duos

STATED PRINT RUN 15 SER.#'d SETS
UJ2HD Datsyuk/Zetterberg 20.00 50.00
UJ2IK Iginla/Kiprusoff 30.00 80.00
UJ2KM Kovalchuk/Malkin 50.00 125.00
UJ2LM Lemieux/Malkin 50.00 120.00
UJ2LN Lundqvist/Naslund
UJ2LZ Lidstrom/Zetterberg 20.00 50.00
UJ2MT Turco/Modano 25.00 60.00
UJ2OB Ovechkin/Backstrom
UJ2RB Roy/Brodeur 40.00 100.00

2008-09 Ultimate Collection Ultimate Signatures

OVERALL AU ODDS 1 PER PACK
USBK Mikkel Boedker 8.00 20.00
USBL Brian Leetch 6.00 15.00
USBO Bobby Orr 60.00 120.00
USBR Martin Brodeur 50.00 100.00
USBW Blake Wheeler 15.00 40.00
USCA Carey Price 25.00 60.00
USCG Claude Giroux 12.00 30.00
USDH Dany Heatley 6.00 15.00
USEM Evgeni Malkin 20.00 50.00
USES Eric Staal 8.00 20.00
USFB Fabian Brunnstrom 5.00 12.00
USGH Gordie Howe 50.00 100.00
USJI Jarome Iginla 6.00 15.00
USJM Joe Mullen 5.00 12.00
USJS Jordan Staal 6.00 15.00
USJV Jakub Voracek 10.00 25.00
USKT Kyle Turris 15.00 40.00
USLE Brian Lee 5.00 12.00
USMB Mike Bossy 10.00 25.00
USMG Marian Gaborik 8.00 20.00
USML Mario Lemieux 50.00 100.00
USMM Mark Messier 40.00 80.00
USMS Martin St. Louis 6.00 15.00
USNF Nikita Filatov 8.00 20.00
USNL Nicklas Lidstrom 12.00 30.00
USPK Patrick Kane 15.00 40.00
USPR Patrick Roy 60.00 120.00
USPS Paul Stastny 6.00 15.00
USRB Ray Bourque 15.00 40.00
USRH Ron Hextall 12.00 30.00
USSC Sidney Crosby 75.00 150.00
USSS Steven Stamkos 30.00 60.00
USTH Joe Thornton 8.00 20.00
USVL Vincent Lecavalier 10.00 25.00
USWG Wayne Gretzky 100.00 200.00

2009-10 Ultimate Collection

1-60 STATED PRINT RUN 399
131-170 STATED PRINT RUN 399
101-136 STATED PRINT RUN 299
137-142 STATED PRINT RUN 99
1 Alexander Ovechkin 6.00 15.00
2 Eric Staal 2.00 5.00
3 Marty Turco 1.50 4.00
4 Jarome Iginla 1.50 4.00
5 Martin St. Louis 1.50 4.00
6 Jonathan Toews 3.00 8.00
7 Thomas Vanek 1.50 4.00
8 Gordie Howe 4.00 10.00
9 Jeff Carter 1.50 4.00
10 Rick Nash 1.25 3.00
11 Jason Spezza 1.50 4.00
12 Carey Price 6.00 15.00
13 Devin Setoguchi 1.25 3.00
14 Tim Thomas 1.50 4.00
15 Paul Stastny 1.50 4.00
16 Mario Lemieux 5.00 12.00
17 Shea Weber 1.25 3.00
18 Zach Parise 1.50 4.00
19 Sam Gagner 1.25 3.00
20 Evgeni Malkin 5.00 12.00
21 Marian Gaborik 2.00 5.00
22 Henrik Zetterberg 2.00 5.00
23 Miikka Kiprusoff 1.25 3.00
24 Mark Messier 2.00 5.00
25 Zdeno Chara 1.50 4.00
26 Mike Richards 1.50 4.00
27 Luke Schenn 1.25 3.00
28 Ilya Kovalchuk 1.50 4.00
29 David Perron 1.00 2.50
30 Marc-Andre Fleury 2.50 6.00
31 Nicklas Lidstrom 1.50 4.00
32 Bobby Orr 5.00 12.00
33 Dany Heatley 1.50 4.00
34 Steven Stamkos 3.00 8.00
35 Roberto Luongo 2.00 5.00
36 Mike Modano 2.50 6.00
37 Bobby Ryan 1.50 4.00
38 Patrick Marleau 1.50 4.00
39 Patrick Roy 4.00 10.00
40 Cam Neely 1.50 4.00
41 Steve Mason 1.25 3.00
42 Vincent Lecavalier 1.25 3.00
43 Andrew Cogliano 1.25 3.00
44 Pavel Datsyuk 2.00 5.00
45 Ryan Miller 1.50 4.00
46 Wayne Gretzky 8.00 20.00
47 Saku Koivu 1.50 4.00
48 Patrick Kane 3.00 8.00
49 Henrik Lundqvist 2.50 6.00
50 Joe Thornton 1.50 4.00
51 Doug Gilmour 2.00 5.00
52 Teemu Selanne 3.00 8.00
53 Phil Kessel 2.00 5.00
54 Steve Yzerman 4.00 10.00
55 T.J. Oshie 2.50 6.00
56 Shane Doan 1.25 3.00
57 Martin Brodeur 3.00 8.00
58 Mike Bossy 1.50 4.00
59 Mikko Koivu 1.50 4.00
60 Sidney Crosby 6.00 15.00
101 Matt Beleskey AU RC 4.00 10.00
102 Sergei Shirokov AU RC 3.00 8.00
103 Logan Couture AU RC 15.00 40.00
104 Matt Gilroy AU RC 5.00 12.00
105 Mikael Backlund AU RC 5.00 12.00
106 Dmitry Kulikov AU RC 5.00 12.00
107 Christian Hanson AU RC 5.00 12.00
108 Kris Chucko AU RC 4.00 10.00
109 Perttu Lindgren AU RC 4.00 10.00
110 Artem Anisimov AU RC 5.00 12.00
111 Tyler Myers AU RC 10.00 25.00
112 Tyler Bozak AU RC 8.00 20.00
113 Yannick Weber AU RC 5.00 12.00
114 Viktor Stalberg AU RC 5.00 12.00
115 Ivan Vishnevskiy AU RC 4.00 10.00
116 Ryan O'Reilly AU RC 8.00 20.00
117 Brad Marchand AU RC 12.50 25.00
118 Cody Franson AU RC 5.00 12.00
119 Michael Del Zotto AU RC 5.00 12.00
120 Ville Leino AU RC 4.00 10.00
121 Jamie Benn AU RC 20.00 40.00
122 Antti Niemi AU RC 8.00 20.00
123 Devan Dubnyk AU RC 10.00 25.00
124 Erik Karlsson AU RC 30.00 60.00
125 Michael Grabner AU RC 12.00 30.00
126 Spencer Machacek AU RC 5.00 12.00
127 Colin Wilson AU RC 5.00 12.00
128 Jakub Kindl AU RC 5.00 12.00
129 Brian Salcido AU RC 4.00 10.00
130 Riku Helenius AU RC 5.00 12.00
131 Matt Pelech AU RC 5.00 12.00
131B Michal Neuvirth RC 5.00 12.00
132 Benn Ferriero AU RC 5.00 12.00
132B Mikko Lehtonen RC 5.00 12.00
133 Bobby Sanguinetti AU RC 3.00 8.00
133B Andrei Loktionov RC 4.00 10.00
134 Matthew Corrente AU RC 4.00 10.00
134B Colin McDonald RC 2.50 6.00
135 Alec Martinez AU RC 6.00 15.00
135B John Carlson RC 5.00 12.00
136 Lars Eller AU RC 5.00 12.00
136B MacGregor Sharp RC 3.00 8.00
137 Matt Duchene AU RC/99 60.00 120.00
137B Tyler Eckford RC 2.50 6.00
138 Victor Hedman AU RC/99 30.00 80.00
138B Daniel Larsson RC 2.50 6.00
139 John Tavares AU RC/99 200.00 350.00
139B Tyler Ennis RC 4.00 10.00
140 J.van Riemsdyk AU RC/99 75.00 150.00
140B Tom Pyatt RC 3.00 8.00
141 Evander Kane AU RC/99 30.00 80.00
141B Peter Olvecky RC 3.00 8.00
142 J.Gustavsson AU RC/99 20.00 50.00
142B Anton Khudobin RC 3.00 8.00
143 Steven Zalewski RC 2.50 6.00
144 T.J. Galiardi RC 3.00 8.00
145 John Negrin RC 3.00 8.00
146 Oskars Bartulis RC 3.00 8.00
147 Carl Gunnarsson RC 2.50 6.00
148 David Laliberte RC 2.50 6.00
149 Scott Parse RC 3.00 8.00
150 Andreas Thuresson RC 2.50 6.00
151 Dan Sexton RC 4.00 10.00
152 James Reimer RC 8.00 20.00
153 Ryan Vesce RC 2.50 6.00
154 James Wright RC 3.00 8.00
155 Mathieu Perreault RC 5.00 12.00
156 Phil Oreskovic RC 3.00 8.00
157 Ryan O'Marra RC 2.00 5.00
158 Vladimir Zharkov RC 3.00 8.00
159 Mario Bliznak RC 3.00 8.00
160 Alexander Salak RC 2.50 6.00
161 Chad Johnson RC 3.00 8.00
162 Danny Irmen RC 2.00 5.00
163 Jesse Joensuu RC 2.50 6.00
164 Ryan Wilson RC 3.00 8.00
165 Frazer McLaren RC 2.50 6.00
166 Mathieu Carle RC 3.00 8.00
167 Teemu Laakso RC 2.00 5.00
168 Braden Holtby RC 12.00 30.00
169 Mike Santorelli RC 3.00 8.00
170 Aaron Gagnon RC 2.00 5.00

2009-10 Ultimate Collection Debut Threads

STATED PRINT RUN 200 SER.#'d SETS
UDTAA Artem Anisimov 3.00 8.00
UDTAN Antti Niemi 5.00 12.00
UDTBM Brad Marchand 8.00 20.00
UDTCA Luca Caputi 3.00 8.00
UDTCF Cody Franson 3.00 8.00
UDTCH Christian Hanson 3.00 8.00
UDTCW Colin Wilson 3.00 8.00
UDTDE Michael Del Zotto 3.00 8.00
UDTDK Dmitry Kulikov 3.00 8.00
UDTEK Evander Kane 6.00 15.00
UDTGR Michael Grabner 3.00 8.00
UDTIV Ivan Vishnevskiy 2.50 6.00
UDTJB Jamie Benn 10.00 25.00
UDTJE Jhonas Enroth 8.00 20.00
UDTJG Jonas Gustavsson 4.00 10.00
UDTJT John Tavares 15.00 40.00
UDTJV James van Riemsdyk 6.00 15.00
UDTKA Erik Karlsson 10.00 25.00
UDTLC Logan Couture 6.00 15.00
UDTMB Mikael Backlund 3.00 8.00
UDTMD Matt Duchene 6.00 15.00
UDTMG Matt Gilroy 3.00 8.00
UDTPL Perttu Lindgren 2.50 6.00
UDTSS Sergei Shirokov 2.00 5.00
UDTTB Tyler Bozak 5.00 12.00
UDTTM Tyler Myers 5.00 12.00
UDTVH Victor Hedman 6.00 15.00
UDTVL Ville Leino 2.50 6.00
UDTVS Viktor Stalberg 3.00 8.00
UDTYW Yannick Weber 3.00 8.00

2009-10 Ultimate Collection Debut Threads Autographs

STATED PRINT RUN 50 SER.#'d SETS
SDTAA Artem Anisimov 8.00 20.00
SDTAN Antti Niemi 12.00 30.00
SDTCA Luca Caputi 8.00 20.00
SDTCF Cody Franson 8.00 20.00
SDTCH Christian Hanson 8.00 20.00
SDTCW Colin Wilson 8.00 20.00
SDTDE Michael Del Zotto 8.00 20.00
SDTDK Dmitry Kulikov 8.00 20.00
SDTEK Evander Kane 15.00 40.00
SDTGR Michael Grabner 8.00 20.00
SDTJB Jamie Benn 25.00 50.00
SDTJE Jhonas Enroth 10.00 25.00
SDTJG Jonas Gustavsson 10.00 25.00
SDTJT John Tavares 40.00 100.00
SDTJV James van Riemsdyk 15.00 40.00
SDTKA Erik Karlsson 40.00 80.00
SDTLC Logan Couture 15.00 40.00
SDTMB Mikael Backlund 8.00 20.00
SDTMD Matt Duchene 15.00 40.00
SDTMG Matt Gilroy 8.00 20.00
SDTTB Tyler Bozak 12.00 30.00
SDTTM Tyler Myers 12.00 30.00
SDTVL Ville Leino 6.00 15.00
SDTVS Viktor Stalberg 8.00 20.00
SDTYW Yannick Weber 8.00 20.00

2009-10 Ultimate Collection Debut Threads Patches

*SINGLES: 1X TO 2.5X THREADS
STATED PRINT RUN 35 SER.#'d SETS
UDTAN Antti Niemi 15.00 40.00
UDTCA Luca Caputi 8.00 20.00

2009-10 Ultimate Collection Debut Threads Patches Autographs

STATED PRINT RUN 25 SER.#'d SETS
SDTAA Artem Anisimov 30.00 60.00
SDTAN Antti Niemi 20.00 50.00
SDTCA Luca Caputi 12.00 30.00
SDTCF Cody Franson 15.00 40.00
SDTCH Christian Hanson 12.00 30.00
SDTCW Colin Wilson 12.00 30.00
SDTDE Michael Del Zotto 12.00 30.00
SDTDK Dmitry Kulikov 12.00 30.00
SDTEK Evander Kane 25.00 60.00
SDTGR Michael Grabner 50.00 100.00
SDTIV Ivan Vishnevskiy 10.00 25.00
SDTJB Jamie Benn 30.00 60.00
SDTJE Jhonas Enroth 15.00 40.00
SDTJG Jonas Gustavsson 50.00 100.00
SDTJT John Tavares 125.00 250.00
SDTJV James van Riemsdyk 25.00 60.00
SDTKA Erik Karlsson 60.00 120.00
SDTLC Logan Couture 40.00 80.00
SDTMB Mikael Backlund 25.00 60.00
SDTMD Matt Duchene 75.00 150.00
SDTMG Matt Gilroy 12.00 30.00
SDTTB Tyler Bozak 15.00 40.00
SDTTM Tyler Myers 75.00 150.00
SDTVL Ville Leino 25.00 60.00
SDTVS Viktor Stalberg 12.00 30.00
SDTYW Yannick Weber 12.00 30.00

2009-10 Ultimate Collection Premium Patches

STATED PRINT RUN 25 SER.#'d SETS
PSAC Andrew Cogliano 10.00 25.00
PSAO Alexander Ovechkin 50.00 125.00
PSBC Brian Campbell 10.00 25.00
PSBS Borje Salming 12.00 30.00
PSCN Cam Neely 12.00 30.00
PSDB Derick Brassard 12.00 30.00
PSDD Drew Doughty 30.00 60.00
PSDH Dale Hawerchuk 15.00 40.00
PSDP Dion Phaneuf 15.00 40.00
PSEM Evgeni Malkin 40.00 100.00
PSGA Glenn Anderson 12.00 30.00
PSHZ Henrik Zetterberg 15.00 40.00
PSIK Ilya Kovalchuk 12.00 30.00
PSJB Jay Bouwmeester 12.00 30.00
PSJC Jeff Carter 12.00 30.00
PSJI Jarome Iginla 12.00 30.00
PSJS Jordan Staal 12.00 30.00
PSJT Jonathan Toews 25.00 60.00
PSJV Jakub Voracek 12.00 30.00
PSKA Patrick Kane 30.00 80.00
PSKI Miikka Kiprusoff 10.00 25.00
PSLM Lanny McDonald 12.00 30.00
PSMB Martin Brodeur 25.00 60.00
PSMG Marian Gaborik 15.00 40.00
PSMK Mikko Koivu 12.00 30.00
PSMM Mike Modano 20.00 50.00
PSMR Mike Richards 12.00 30.00
PSNB Nicklas Backstrom 20.00 50.00
PSNL Nicklas Lidstrom 12.00 30.00
PSOJ Olli Jokinen 10.00 25.00
PSPB Patrice Bergeron 15.00 40.00
PSPD Pavel Datsyuk 15.00 40.00
PSPK Phil Kessel 15.00 40.00
PSPS Peter Stastny 12.00 30.00
PSRL Roberto Luongo 15.00 40.00
PSRM Ryan Miller 12.00 30.00
PSRN Rick Nash 10.00 25.00
PSRS Ryan Smyth 10.00 25.00
PSSC Sidney Crosby 30.00 80.00
PSSD Shane Doan 10.00 25.00
PSSG Sam Gagner 10.00 25.00
PSSH Steve Shutt 12.00 30.00
PSSK Saku Koivu 12.00 30.00
PSSP Jason Spezza 12.00 30.00
PSSS Steven Stamkos 25.00 60.00
PSST Paul Stastny 12.00 30.00
PSSY Steve Yzerman 30.00 80.00
PSTH Joe Thornton 12.00 30.00
PSTV Tomas Vokoun 10.00 25.00
PSZP Zach Parise 12.00 30.00

2009-10 Ultimate Collection Premium Swatches

STATED PRINT RUN 35 SER.#'d SETS
PSAO Alexander Ovechkin 25.00 60.00
PSCN Cam Neely 6.00 15.00
PSDB Derick Brassard 6.00 15.00
PSDD Drew Doughty 8.00 20.00
PSDG Doug Gilmour 8.00 20.00
PSDH Dale Hawerchuk 8.00 20.00
PSEM Evgeni Malkin 20.00 50.00
PSES Eric Staal 8.00 20.00
PSIK Ilya Kovalchuk 6.00 15.00
PSJC Jeff Carter 6.00 15.00
PSJV Jakub Voracek 6.00 15.00
PSKA Patrick Kane 15.00 40.00
PSKI Miikka Kiprusoff 5.00 12.00
PSLM Lanny McDonald 6.00 15.00
PSMB Martin Brodeur 12.00 30.00
PSMG Marian Gaborik 8.00 20.00
PSMM Mike Modano 10.00 25.00
PSMR Mike Richards 6.00 15.00
PSNB Nicklas Backstrom 10.00 25.00
PSNL Nicklas Lidstrom 6.00 15.00
PSPD Pavel Datsyuk 8.00 20.00
PSPK Phil Kessel 8.00 20.00
PSPS Peter Stastny 6.00 15.00
PSRL Roberto Luongo 8.00 20.00
PSRM Ryan Miller 6.00 15.00
PSRN Rick Nash 5.00 12.00
PSRS Ryan Smyth 5.00 12.00
PSSD Shane Doan 5.00 12.00
PSSG Sam Gagner 5.00 12.00
PSSH Steve Shutt 6.00 15.00
PSSK Saku Koivu 6.00 15.00
PSST Paul Stastny 6.00 15.00
PSSY Steve Yzerman 15.00 40.00
PSTV Tomas Vokoun 5.00 12.00
PSVL Vincent Lecavalier 5.00 12.00
PSWG Wayne Gretzky 30.00 80.00
PSZP Zach Parise 6.00 15.00

2009-10 Ultimate Collection Rookie Patch Autographs

STATED PRINT RUN 25 SER.#'d SETS
101 Matt Beleskey 10.00 25.00
103 Logan Couture 25.00 60.00
104 Matt Gilroy 12.00 30.00
105 Mikael Backlund 12.00 30.00
106 Dmitry Kulikov 12.00 30.00
107 Christian Hanson 12.00 30.00
108 Kris Chucko 10.00 25.00
110 Artem Anisimov 12.00 30.00
111 Tyler Myers 20.00 50.00
112 Tyler Bozak 20.00 50.00
113 Yannick Weber 12.00 30.00
114 Viktor Stalberg 12.00 30.00
115 Ivan Vishnevskiy 10.00 25.00
117 Brad Marchand 40.00 80.00
118 Cody Franson 12.00 30.00
119 Michael Del Zotto 12.00 30.00
120 Ville Leino 10.00 25.00
121 Jamie Benn 50.00 100.00
122 Antti Niemi 30.00 80.00
123 Devan Dubnyk 25.00 60.00
124 Erik Karlsson 100.00 175.00
125 Michael Grabner 12.00 30.00
126 Spencer Machacek 12.00 30.00
127 Colin Wilson 12.00 30.00
128 Jakub Kindl 12.00 30.00
129 Brian Salcido 10.00 25.00
131 Matt Pelech 12.00 30.00
132 Benn Ferriero 12.00 30.00
133 Bobby Sanguinetti 8.00 20.00
134 Matthew Corrente 10.00 25.00
135 Alec Martinez 15.00 40.00
136 Lars Eller 12.00 30.00
137 Matt Duchene 25.00 60.00
138 Victor Hedman 25.00 60.00
139 John Tavares 150.00 300.00
140 James van Riemsdyk 25.00 60.00
141 Evander Kane 25.00 60.00
142 Jonas Gustavsson 15.00 40.00

2009-10 Ultimate Collection Ultimate Achievements

STATED PRINT RUN 25 SER.#'d SETS
UAAO Alexander Ovechkin 40.00 100.00
UABO Bobby Orr 100.00 200.00
UACN Cam Neely 15.00 40.00
UAEM Evgeni Malkin 40.00 80.00
UAGH Gordie Howe 60.00 120.00
UAJB Jean Beliveau 40.00 80.00
UAJI Jarome Iginla 25.00 60.00
UAJT Jonathan Toews 40.00 80.00
UAMB Martin Brodeur 60.00 120.00
UAMI Mike Bossy 15.00 40.00
UAML Mario Lemieux 60.00 120.00
UAPD Pavel Datsyuk 20.00 50.00
UAPE Phil Esposito 15.00 40.00
UAPR Patrick Roy 50.00 100.00
UARH Ron Hextall 25.00 50.00
UASC Sidney Crosby 100.00 200.00
UASM Steve Mason 12.00 30.00
UASY Steve Yzerman 50.00 125.00
UAWG Wayne Gretzky 150.00 250.00

2009-10 Ultimate Collection Ultimate Jerseys

STATED PRINT RUN 100 SER.#'d SETS
UJAO Alexander Ovechkin 10.00 25.00
UJBC Bobby Clarke 5.00 12.00
UJBL Brian Leetch 4.00 10.00
UJCN Cam Neely 4.00 10.00
UJCW Cam Ward 4.00 10.00
UJDG Doug Gilmour
UJDH Dany Heatley
UJEM Evgeni Malkin 12.00 30.00
UJES Eric Staal 5.00 12.00
UJGF Grant Fuhr 4.00 10.00
UJGH Gordie Howe 10.00 25.00
UJGP Gilbert Perreault 4.00 10.00
UJHA Dale Hawerchuk 5.00 12.00
UJIK Ilya Kovalchuk 4.00 10.00
UJJB Jean Beliveau 4.00 10.00
UJJC Jeff Carter
UJJK Jari Kurri 4.00 10.00
UJJT Jonathan Toews 8.00 20.00
UJLM Lanny McDonald 4.00 10.00
UJMB Martin Brodeur 8.00 20.00
UJMD Marcel Dionne 5.00 12.00
UJMG Marian Gaborik 5.00 12.00
UJMK Miikka Kiprusoff 3.00 8.00
UJMM Mike Modano 6.00 15.00
UJMR Mike Richards 4.00 10.00
UJMT Marty Turco 4.00 10.00
UJNB Nicklas Backstrom 6.00 15.00
UJPD Pavel Datsyuk 5.00 12.00
UJPE Phil Esposito 6.00 15.00
UJPK Patrick Kane 8.00 20.00
UJPR Patrick Roy 10.00 25.00
UJPS Peter Stastny 4.00 10.00
UJRB Ray Bourque 6.00 15.00
UJRL Roberto Luongo 5.00 12.00
UJRN Rick Nash 3.00 8.00
UJSA Borje Salming 4.00 10.00
UJSC Sidney Crosby 15.00 40.00
UJST Jordan Staal 4.00 10.00
UJSY Steve Yzerman 10.00 25.00
UJTE Tony Esposito 6.00 15.00
UJVL Vincent Lecavalier 3.00 8.00
UJWG Wayne Gretzky 20.00 50.00
UJZP Zach Parise 4.00 10.00

2009-10 Ultimate Collection Ultimate Jerseys Autographs

STATED PRINT RUN 25 SER.#'d SETS
AJAO Alexander Ovechkin 40.00 100.00
AJBL Brian Leetch 12.00 30.00
AJCN Cam Neely 25.00 50.00
AJCP Carey Price 40.00 80.00
AJCW Cam Ward 12.00 30.00
AJEM Evgeni Malkin EXCH 40.00 100.00
AJGH Gordie Howe 75.00 150.00
AJGP Gilbert Perreault 12.00 30.00
AJHZ Henrik Zetterberg 20.00 50.00
AJJI Jarome Iginla 12.00 30.00
AJJK Jari Kurri 12.00 30.00
AJMB Martin Brodeur 50.00 100.00
AJPD Pavel Datsyuk 25.00 60.00
AJPK Patrick Kane 25.00 60.00
AJPR Patrick Roy 60.00 120.00
AJRB Ray Bourque 20.00 50.00
AJRN Rick Nash 10.00 25.00
AJSC Sidney Crosby 100.00 200.00
AJSY Steve Yzerman 75.00 150.00
AJTE Tony Esposito 40.00 80.00
AJTO Jonathan Toews 25.00 60.00
AJWG Wayne Gretzky 150.00 300.00

2009-10 Ultimate Collection Ultimate Jerseys Duos

STATED PRINT RUN 50 SER.#'d SETS
UJ2AS Spezza/Alfredsson 8.00 20.00
UJ2BL Brodeur/Luongo 15.00 40.00
UJ2CO Ovechkin/Crosby 20.00 50.00
UJ2DP Dionne/Perreault 8.00 20.00
UJ2EE Esposito/Esposito 12.00 30.00
UJ2EH Emery/Hextall 12.00 30.00
UJ2FC Crosby/Fleury 15.00 40.00
UJ2GL Gaborik/Lundqvist 12.00 30.00
UJ2HN Nash/Heatley 8.00 20.00
UJ2HT Hossa/Toews 15.00 40.00
UJ2KA Anderson/Kurri 8.00 20.00
UJ2KO Kovalchuk/Ovechkin 20.00 50.00
UJ2LM Messier/Leetch 10.00 25.00
UJ2LT Lecavalier/Thornton 8.00 20.00
UJ2LY Lemieux/Yzerman 25.00 60.00
UJ2MP Modano/Parise 12.00 30.00
UJ2PK Parise/Kane 15.00 40.00
UJ2RB Brodeur/Roy 20.00 50.00
UJ2RD Robinson/Doughty 10.00 25.00
UJ2RH Robitaille/Hull 10.00 25.00
UJ2RP Roy/Price 30.00 80.00
UJ2SK Selanne/Koivu 15.00 40.00
UJ2SS Stastny/Stastny 8.00 20.00
UJ2YH Howe/Yzerman 20.00 50.00
UJ2ZB Backstrom/Zetterberg 12.00 30.00

2009-10 Ultimate Collection Ultimate Jerseys Trios

STATED PRINT RUN 25 SER.#'d SETS
UJ3CRT Toews/Richrds/Crosby 30.00 80.00
UJ3DOM Malkin/Datsyuk/Ovech 40.00 100.00
UJ3ICO Ovech/Crosby/Iginla 40.00 100.00
UJ3LTS Lecav/Spezza/Thrntn 10.00 25.00
UJ3MPK Parise/Modano/Kane 20.00 50.00
UJ3RBL Roy/Brodeur/Luongo 25.00 60.00
UJ3YZH Zettrbrg/Howe/Yzermn 25.00 60.00

2009-10 Ultimate Collection Ultimate Nicknames

STATED PRINT RUN 25 SER.#'d SETS
UNAO Alexander Ovechkin 75.00 150.00
UNBE Jean Beliveau 40.00 80.00
UNBH Bobby Hull 40.00 80.00
UNCN Cam Neely 25.00 60.00
UNDC Don Cherry 40.00 100.00
UNDG Doug Gilmour 25.00 60.00
UNDH Dale Hawerchuk 15.00 40.00
UNEM Evgeni Malkin 25.00 60.00
UNGH Gordie Howe 75.00 150.00
UNJB Johnny Bucyk 15.00 40.00
UNJI Jarome Iginla 25.00 50.00
UNJT Joe Thornton 20.00 50.00
UNLR Luc Robitaille 12.00 30.00
UNMD Marcel Dionne 15.00 40.00
UNMF Marc-Andre Fleury 20.00 50.00
UNML Mario Lemieux 50.00 100.00
UNPR Patrick Roy 60.00 120.00
UNSC Sidney Crosby 125.00 200.00
UNSY Steve Yzerman 100.00 175.00
UNTE Tony Esposito 25.00 50.00

2009-10 Ultimate Collection Ultimate Patches

STATED PRINT RUN 35 SER.#'d SETS
UJAO Alexander Ovechkin 40.00 100.00
UJBH Bobby Hull 12.00 30.00
UJBL Brian Leetch 10.00 25.00
UJCW Cam Ward 10.00 25.00
UJDH Dany Heatley 10.00 25.00
UJEM Evgeni Malkin 30.00 80.00
UJHZ Henrik Zetterberg 12.00 30.00
UJIK Ilya Kovalchuk 10.00 25.00
UJJC Jeff Carter 10.00 25.00
UJJI Jarome Iginla 10.00 25.00
UJJK Jari Kurri 10.00 25.00
UJJS Jason Spezza 10.00 25.00
UJJT Jonathan Toews 20.00 50.00
UJKO Mikko Koivu 10.00 25.00
UJMB Martin Brodeur 20.00 50.00
UJME Mark Messier 12.00 30.00
UJMG Marian Gaborik 12.00 30.00
UJMK Miikka Kiprusoff 8.00 20.00
UJML Mario Lemieux 30.00 80.00
UJMM Mike Modano 15.00 40.00
UJMR Mike Richards 10.00 25.00
UJMS Martin St. Louis 10.00 25.00
UJMT Marty Turco 10.00 25.00
UJNB Nicklas Backstrom 15.00 40.00
UJPD Pavel Datsyuk 12.00 30.00
UJPE Phil Esposito 15.00 40.00
UJPK Patrick Kane 20.00 50.00
UJPR Patrick Roy 25.00 60.00
UJPS Peter Stastny 10.00 25.00
UJRB Ray Bourque 15.00 40.00
UJRL Roberto Luongo 10.00 25.00
UJRN Rick Nash 8.00 20.00
UJSA Borje Salming 10.00 25.00
UJSC Sidney Crosby 40.00 100.00
UJSN Scott Niedermayer 10.00 25.00
UJST Jordan Staal 10.00 25.00
UJSY Steve Yzerman 25.00 60.00
UJTH Joe Thornton 10.00 25.00
UJTS Teemu Selanne 12.00 30.00
UJWG Wayne Gretzky 50.00 100.00
UJZP Zach Parise 12.00 30.00

2009-10 Ultimate Collection Ultimate Patches Duos

STATED PRINT RUN 25 SER.#'d SETS
UJ2AS Spezza/Alfredsson 15.00 40.00
UJ2BL Brodeur/Luongo 30.00 80.00
UJ2CO Ovechkin/Crosby 125.00 200.00
UJ2CR Clarke/Richards 40.00 80.00
UJ2EH Hextall/Emery 25.00 60.00
UJ2FC Crosby/Fleury 60.00 120.00
UJ2GL Gaborik/Lundqvist 20.00 50.00
UJ2HN Nash/Heatley 15.00 40.00
UJ2HT Hossa/Toews 30.00 80.00
UJ2IK Iginla/Kiprusoff 25.00 60.00
UJ2IS Iginla/St. Louis 15.00 40.00
UJ2KA Kurri/Anderson 15.00 40.00
UJ2KO Kovalchuk/Ovechkin 30.00 80.00
UJ2LG Gretzky/Lemieux 100.00 200.00
UJ2LM Messier/Leetch 20.00 50.00
UJ2LT Lecavalier/Thornton 15.00 40.00
UJ2LY Lemieux/Yzerman 60.00 120.00
UJ2MP Modano/Parise 25.00 60.00
UJ2PK Parise/Kane 30.00 80.00
UJ2RB Brodeur/Roy 40.00 100.00
UJ2RD Doughty/Robinson 20.00 50.00
UJ2RH Robitaille/Hull 20.00 50.00
UJ2SK Selanne/Koivu 20.00 50.00
UJ2SS Stastny/Stastny 15.00 40.00
UJ2ZB Backstrom/Zetterberg 40.00 100.00

2009-10 Ultimate Collection Ultimate Signatures

USAA Artem Anisimov 6.00 15.00
USAN Antti Niemi 10.00 25.00
USAO Alexander Ovechkin 30.00 80.00
USBH Bobby Hull 12.00 30.00
USBO Bobby Orr 60.00 120.00
USCF Cody Franson 6.00 15.00
USCP Carey Price 12.00 30.00
USCW Colin Wilson 8.00 20.00
USDE Michael Del Zotto 6.00 15.00
USDH Dany Heatley 11-12 4.00 10.00
USEK Evander Kane 10.00 25.00
USES Eric Staal 6.00 15.00
USGF Grant Fuhr 8.00 20.00
USGH Gordie Howe 90.00 150.00
USHL Henrik Lundqvist 15.00 30.00
USHZ Henrik Zetterberg 10.00 25.00
USJB Jamie Benn 12.00 30.00
USJC Jeff Carter 6.00 15.00
USJI Jarome Iginla 10.00 25.00
USJK Jari Kurri 6.00 15.00
USJT Jonathan Toews 25.00 50.00
USJV James van Riemsdyk 10.00 25.00
USKA Erik Karlsson 12.00 30.00
USMB Mikael Backlund 6.00 15.00
USMB Martin Brodeur 40.00 100.00
USMD Matt Duchene 12.00 30.00
USMF Marc-Andre Fleury 10.00 25.00
USMG Michael Grabner 6.00 15.00
USMG Marian Gaborik 20.00 50.00
USMI Mike Bossy 6.00 15.00
USML Mario Lemieux 50.00 100.00
USMO Mike Modano 8.00 20.00
USMR Mike Richards 11-12 5.00 12.00
USPD Pavel Datsyuk 20.00 50.00
USPE Phil Esposito 15.00 40.00
USPK Phil Kessel 8.00 20.00
USPR Patrick Roy 50.00 100.00
USRM Ryan Miller 8.00 20.00
USRN Rick Nash 5.00 12.00
USRY Bobby Ryan 6.00 15.00
USSC Sidney Crosby 75.00 135.00
USSM Steve Mason 8.00 20.00
USSS Steven Stamkos 20.00 50.00
USSY Steve Yzerman 50.00 100.00
USTA John Tavares 20.00 50.00
USTB Tyler Bozak 8.00 20.00
USTE Tony Esposito 10.00 25.00
USTH Joe Thornton 6.00 15.00
USTM Tyler Myers 10.00 25.00
USVH Victor Hedman 11-12 4.00 10.00
USVL Ville Leino 5.00 12.00
USVS Viktor Stalberg 6.00 15.00
USWG Wayne Gretzky

2010-11 Ultimate Collection

(1-100) PRINT RUN 399 SER.#'d SETS
(101-137) PRINT RUN 299 SER.#'d SETS
(138-142) PRINT RUN 99 SER.#'d SETS
1 Teemu Selanne 3.00 8.00
2 Saku Koivu 1.50 4.00
3 Ryan Getzlaf 2.50 6.00
4 Cam Neely 1.50 4.00
5 Bobby Orr 5.00 12.00
6 Thomas Vanek 1.50 4.00
7 Ryan Miller 1.50 4.00
8 Jarome Iginla 1.50 4.00
9 Eric Staal 2.00 5.00
10 Jonathan Toews 3.00 8.00
11 Bobby Hull 1.50 4.00
12 Tony Esposito 1.50 4.00
13 Phil Esposito 2.50 6.00
14 Patrick Kane 3.00 8.00
15 Matt Duchene 1.50 4.00
16 Ray Bourque 2.50 6.00
17 Paul Stastny 1.50 4.00
18 Rick Nash 1.50 4.00
19 Ted Lindsay 1.50 4.00
20 Igor Larionov 1.50 4.00
21 Pavel Datsyuk 2.00 5.00
22 Terry Sawchuk 2.00 5.00
23 Nicklas Lidstrom 1.50 4.00
24 Wayne Gretzky 8.00 20.00
25 Jari Kurri 1.50 4.00
26 Grant Fuhr 1.50 4.00
27 Gordie Howe 4.00 10.00
28 Luc Robitaille 1.50 4.00
29 Anze Kopitar 2.50 6.00
30 Guy Lafleur 2.00 5.00
31 Carey Price 6.00 15.00
32 Patrick Roy 4.00 10.00
33 Martin Brodeur 3.00 8.00
34 Zach Parise 1.50 4.00
35 Ilya Kovalchuk 1.50 4.00
36 John Tavares 3.00 8.00
37 Mark Messier 2.50 6.00
38 Marian Gaborik 2.00 5.00
39 Jason Spezza 1.00 2.50
40 Ron Hextall 2.00 5.00
41 Jeff Carter 1.50 4.00
42 Mike Richards 1.50 4.00
43 Mario Lemieux 5.00 12.00
44 Marc-Andre Fleury 2.50 6.00
45 Ron Francis 2.00 5.00
46 Evgeni Malkin 5.00 12.00

47 Sidney Crosby 6.00 15.00
48 Joe Sakic 2.50 6.00
49 Dany Heatley 1.25 3.00
50 Jaroslav Halak 1.50 4.00
51 Steven Stamkos 3.00 8.00
52 Martin St. Louis 1.50 4.00
53 Doug Gilmour 2.00 5.00
54 Frank Mahovlich 1.50 4.00
55 Markus Naslund 1.25 3.00
56 Roberto Luongo 1.50 4.00
57 Nicklas Backstrom 2.50 6.00
58 Alexander Ovechkin 6.00 15.00
59 Alexander Semin 1.50 4.00
60 Dale Hawerchuk 2.00 5.00
61 Brandon McMillan RC 2.50 6.00
62 Patrice Cormier RC 3.00 8.00
63 Jamie Arniel RC 2.50 6.00
64 Colby Cohen RC 2.50 6.00
65 Jon Matsumoto RC 2.50 6.00
66 Ben Smith RC 2.50 6.00
67 Brandon Pirri RC 2.50 6.00
68 Jeremy Morin RC 2.50 6.00
69 Mark Olver RC 2.50 6.00
70 Jonas Holos RC 2.50 6.00
71 Richard Bachman RC 3.00 8.00
72 Tomas Tatar RC 6.00 15.00
73 Jan Mursak RC 5.00 12.00
74 Linus Omark RC 6.00 15.00
75 Dean Arsene RC 2.50 6.00
76 Jake Muzzin RC 2.50 6.00
77 Maxim Noreau RC 2.00 5.00
78 Nate Prosser RC 2.50 6.00
79 Matt Hackett RC 4.00 10.00
80 Casey Wellman RC 2.50 6.00
81 Matt Kassian RC 2.50 6.00
82 J.T. Wyman RC 2.50 6.00
83 Linus Klasen RC 2.50 6.00
84 Mark Dekanich RC 2.50 6.00
85 Alexander Vasyunov RC 2.50 6.00
86 Alexander Urbom RC 2.50 6.00
87 Ryan McDonagh RC 6.00 15.00
88 Mats Zuccarello-Aasen RC 4.00 10.00
89 Kevin Poulin RC 3.00 8.00
90 Nathan Lawson RC 2.50 6.00
91 Travis Hamonic RC 3.00 8.00
92 Derek Smith RC 2.50 6.00
93 Kaspars Daugavins RC 3.00 8.00
94 Robin Lehner RC 5.00 12.00
95 Alexander Pechurskiy RC 3.00 8.00
96 Brett MacLean RC 3.00 8.00
97 Ryan Reaves RC 3.00 8.00
98 Ian Cole RC 2.50 6.00
99 Nikita Nikitin RC 2.50 6.00
100 Christopher Tanev RC 6.00 15.00
101 Cam Fowler AU/299 RC 5.00 12.00
102 Kyle Palmieri AU/299 RC 8.00 20.00
103 A.Burmistrov AU/299 RC 4.00 10.00
104 Jordan Caron AU/299 RC 6.00 15.00
105 Zach Hamill AU/299 RC 4.00 10.00
106 Henrik Karlsson AU/299 RC 4.00 10.00
107 Jamie McBain AU/299 RC 4.00 10.00
108 Zac Dalpe AU/299 RC 4.00 10.00
109 Jeff Skinner AU/99 RC 30.00 60.00
110 Nick Leddy AU/299 RC 4.00 10.00
111 Brandon Yip AU/299 RC 4.00 10.00
112 K.Shattenkirk AU/299 RC 8.00 20.00
113 Philip Larsen AU/299 RC 4.00 10.00
114 Alex Plante AU/299 RC 4.00 10.00
115 Magnus Paajarvi AU/299 RC 20.00 50.00
116 Brayden Schenn AU/299 RC 15.00 40.00
117 Kyle Clifford AU/299 RC 4.00 10.00
118 Justin Falk AU/299 RC 3.00 8.00
119 M.Scandella AU/299 RC 4.00 10.00
120 Cody Almond AU/299 RC 4.00 10.00
121 A.Lindback AU/299 RC 4.00 10.00
122 Jacob Josefson AU/299 RC 4.00 10.00
123 Nick Palmieri AU/299 RC 4.00 10.00
124 N.Niederreiter AU/299 RC 5.00 12.00
125 E.Grachev AU/299 RC 4.00 10.00
126 Luke Adam AU/299 RC 4.00 10.00
127 Jared Cowen AU/299 RC 4.00 10.00
128 S.Bobrovsky AU/299 RC 10.00 25.00
129 Ekman-Larsson AU/299 RC 6.00 15.00
130 Eric Wellwood AU/299 RC 5.00 12.00
131 Eric Tangradi AU/299 RC 4.00 10.00
132 Nick Johnson AU/299 RC 3.00 8.00
133 M.Tedenby AU/299 RC 3.00 8.00
134 Dustin Tokarski AU/299 RC 4.00 10.00
135 Dana Tyrell AU/299 RC 4.00 10.00
136 M.Johansson AU/299 RC 6.00 15.00
137 Derek Stepan AU/299 RC 8.00 20.00
138 Nazem Kadri AU/99 RC 30.00 60.00
139 P.K. Subban AU/99 RC 75.00 150.00
140 Jordan Eberle AU/99 RC 100.00 200.00
141 Tyler Seguin AU/99 RC 150.00 250.00
142 Taylor Hall AU/99 RC 150.00 250.00
143 Thomas McCollum AU/99 RC
144 Jacob Markstrom AU/99 RC 20.00 40.00

2010-11 Ultimate Collection Debut Threads

STATED PRINT RUN 200 SER.#'d SETS
*PATCH/35: 1X TO 2.5X THREADS
DTAL Anders Lindback 2.50 6.00
DTBP Brandon Pirri 2.50 6.00
DTBS Brayden Schenn 4.00 10.00
DTBU Alexander Burmistrov 2.50 6.00
DTBY Brandon Yip 2.50 6.00
DTCA Cody Almond 2.50 6.00
DTCC Colby Cohen 2.50 6.00
DTCF Cam Fowler 3.00 8.00
DTDS Derek Stepan 5.00 12.00
DTDT Dustin Tokarski 2.50 6.00
DTEG Evgeny Grachev 2.50 6.00
DTET Eric Tangradi 2.50 6.00
DTEW Eric Wellwood 3.00 8.00
DTHK Henrik Karlsson 2.50 6.00
DTIC Ian Cole 2.50 6.00
DTJC Jared Cowen 2.50 6.00
DTJE Jordan Eberle 8.00 20.00
DTJF Justin Falk 2.00 5.00
DTJJ Jacob Josefson 2.50 6.00
DTJO Jordan Caron 4.00 10.00
DTJS Jeff Skinner 5.00 12.00
DTKC Kyle Clifford 2.50 6.00
DTKP Kyle Palmieri 5.00 12.00
DTKS Kevin Shattenkirk 5.00 12.00
DTLA Philip Larsen 2.50 6.00
DTLK Luke Adam 2.50 6.00
DTMC Jamie McBain 2.50 6.00
DTMJ Marcus Johansson 4.00 10.00
DTMN Maxim Noreau 2.00 5.00
DTMO Mark Olver 2.50 6.00
DTMP Magnus Paajarvi 3.00 8.00
DTMS Marco Scandella 2.50 6.00
DTMT Mattias Tedenby 2.00 5.00
DTNJ Nick Johnson 2.00 5.00
DTNK Nazem Kadri 5.00 12.00
DTNL Nick Leddy 4.00 10.00
DTNN Nino Niederreiter 3.00 8.00
DTNP Nick Palmieri 2.50 6.00
DTNS Nick Spaling 2.50 6.00
DTOE Oliver Ekman-Larsson 5.00 12.00
DTPL Alex Plante 2.50 6.00
DTPS P.K. Subban 8.00 20.00
DTSB Sergei Bobrovsky 6.00 15.00
DTTB T.J. Brodie 2.50 6.00
DTTH Taylor Hall 12.00 30.00
DTTS Tyler Seguin 8.00 20.00
DTTY Dana Tyrell 2.50 6.00
DTZD Zac Dalpe 2.50 6.00
DTZH Zach Hamill 2.50 6.00

2010-11 Ultimate Collection Debut Threads Autographs

STATED PRINT RUN 50 SER.#'d SETS
*PATCH/25: .8X TO 2X JSY AU/50
SDTAL Anders Lindback 6.00 15.00
SDTBP Brandon Pirri 6.00 15.00
SDTBS Brayden Schenn 10.00 25.00
SDTBU Alexander Burmistrov 6.00 15.00
SDTBY Brandon Yip 6.00 15.00
SDTCA Cody Almond 6.00 15.00
SDTCC Colby Cohen 6.00 15.00
SDTCF Cam Fowler 8.00 20.00
SDTDS Derek Stepan 12.00 30.00
SDTDT Dustin Tokarski 6.00 15.00
SDTEG Evgeny Grachev 6.00 15.00
SDTET Eric Tangradi 10.00 25.00
SDTEW Eric Wellwood 10.00 25.00
SDTHK Henrik Karlsson 6.00 15.00
SDTIC Ian Cole 6.00 15.00
SDTJC Jared Cowen 6.00 15.00
SDTJE Jordan Eberle 50.00 100.00
SDTJF Justin Falk 5.00 12.00
SDTJJ Jacob Josefson 6.00 15.00
SDTJO Jordan Caron 10.00 25.00
SDTJS Jeff Skinner 15.00 40.00
SDTKC Kyle Clifford 6.00 15.00
SDTKS Kevin Shattenkirk 12.00 30.00
SDTLA Philip Larsen 6.00 15.00
SDTLK Luke Adam 6.00 15.00
SDTMC Jamie McBain 6.00 15.00
SDTMJ Marcus Johansson 10.00 25.00
SDTMN Maxim Noreau 5.00 12.00
SDTMO Mark Olver 6.00 15.00
SDTMP Magnus Paajarvi 12.00 30.00
SDTMS Marco Scandella 6.00 15.00
SDTMT Mattias Tedenby 5.00 12.00
SDTNJ Nick Johnson 5.00 12.00
SDTNK Nazem Kadri 20.00 50.00
SDTNL Nick Leddy 12.00 30.00
SDTNN Nino Niederreiter 8.00 20.00
SDTNP Nick Palmieri 6.00 15.00
SDTNS Nick Spaling 6.00 15.00
SDTOE Oliver Ekman-Larsson 10.00 25.00
SDTPL Alex Plante 6.00 15.00
SDTPS P.K. Subban 40.00 100.00
SDTSB Sergei Bobrovsky 15.00 40.00
SDTTB T.J. Brodie 6.00 15.00
SDTTH Taylor Hall 40.00 100.00
SDTTS Tyler Seguin 40.00 100.00
SDTTY Dana Tyrell 6.00 15.00
SDTZD Zac Dalpe 8.00 20.00
SDTZH Zach Hamill 8.00 20.00

2010-11 Ultimate Collection Debut Threads Patches

STATED PRINT RUN 35 SER.#'d SETS
DTAL Anders Lindback 6.00 15.00
DTBP Brandon Pirri 6.00 15.00
DTBS Brayden Schenn 10.00 25.00
DTBU Alexander Burmistrov 6.00 15.00
DTBY Brandon Yip 6.00 15.00
DTCA Cody Almond 6.00 15.00
DTCC Colby Cohen 6.00 15.00
DTCF Cam Fowler 8.00 20.00
DTDS Derek Stepan 12.00 30.00
DTDT Dustin Tokarski 6.00 15.00
DTEG Evgeny Grachev 6.00 15.00
DTET Eric Tangradi 6.00 15.00
DTEW Eric Wellwood 8.00 20.00
DTHK Henrik Karlsson 6.00 15.00
DTIC Ian Cole 6.00 15.00
DTJC Jared Cowen 6.00 15.00
DTJE Jordan Eberle 20.00 50.00
DTJF Justin Falk 5.00 12.00
DTJJ Jacob Josefson 6.00 15.00
DTJO Jordan Caron 10.00 25.00
DTJS Jeff Skinner 12.00 30.00
DTKC Kyle Clifford 6.00 15.00
DTKP Kyle Palmieri 12.00 30.00
DTKS Kevin Shattenkirk 15.00 40.00
DTLA Philip Larsen 6.00 15.00
DTLK Luke Adam 6.00 15.00
DTMC Jamie McBain 6.00 15.00
DTMJ Marcus Johansson 10.00 25.00
DTMN Maxim Noreau 5.00 12.00
DTMO Mark Olver 6.00 15.00
DTMP Magnus Paajarvi 8.00 20.00
DTMS Marco Scandella 6.00 15.00
DTMT Mattias Tedenby 5.00 12.00
DTNJ Nick Johnson 5.00 12.00
DTNL Nick Leddy 10.00 25.00
DTNN Nino Niederreiter 8.00 20.00
DTNP Nick Palmieri 6.00 15.00
DTNS Nick Spaling 6.00 15.00
DTOE Oliver Ekman-Larsson 12.00 30.00
DTPL Alex Plante 6.00 15.00
DTPS P.K. Subban 20.00 50.00
DTSB Sergei Bobrovsky 15.00 40.00
DTTB T.J. Brodie 6.00 15.00
DTTH Taylor Hall 25.00 60.00
DTTS Tyler Seguin 20.00 50.00
DTTY Dana Tyrell 15.00 40.00
DTZD Zac Dalpe 6.00 15.00
DTZH Zach Hamill 8.00 20.00

2010-11 Ultimate Collection Debut Threads Patches Autographs

*PATCH/25: .8X TO 2X JSY AU/50
STATED PRINT RUN 25 SER.#'d SETS
SDTAL Anders Lindback 12.00 30.00
SDTBP Brandon Pirri 12.00 30.00
SDTBS Brayden Schenn 20.00 50.00
SDTBU Alexander Burmistrov 12.00 30.00
SDTBY Brandon Yip 12.00 30.00
SDTCA Cody Almond 12.00 30.00
SDTCC Colby Cohen 12.00 30.00
SDTCF Cam Fowler 25.00 50.00
SDTDS Derek Stepan 25.00 60.00
SDTDT Dustin Tokarski 12.00 30.00
SDTEG Evgeny Grachev 12.00 30.00
SDTET Eric Tangradi 20.00 50.00
SDTEW Eric Wellwood 20.00 50.00
SDTHK Henrik Karlsson 12.00 30.00
SDTIC Ian Cole 12.00 30.00
SDTJC Jared Cowen 12.00 30.00
SDTJE Jordan Eberle 75.00 200.00
SDTJF Justin Falk 10.00 25.00
SDTJJ Jacob Josefson 12.00 30.00
SDTJO Jordan Caron 15.00 40.00
SDTJS Jeff Skinner 30.00 80.00
SDTKC Kyle Clifford 12.00 30.00
SDTKS Kevin Shattenkirk 25.00 50.00
SDTLA Philip Larsen 12.00 30.00
SDTLK Luke Adam 12.00 30.00
SDTMC Jamie McBain 12.00 30.00
SDTMJ Marcus Johansson 20.00 50.00
SDTMN Maxim Noreau 10.00 25.00
SDTMO Mark Olver 12.00 30.00
SDTMP Magnus Paajarvi 25.00 60.00
SDTMS Marco Scandella 12.00 30.00
SDTMT Mattias Tedenby 10.00 25.00
SDTNJ Nick Johnson 10.00 25.00
SDTNL Nick Leddy 25.00 60.00
SDTNN Nino Niederreiter 15.00 40.00
SDTNP Nick Palmieri 12.00 30.00
SDTNS Nick Spaling 12.00 30.00
SDTOE Oliver Ekman-Larsson 20.00 50.00
SDTPL Alex Plante 12.00 30.00
SDTPS P.K. Subban 125.00 250.00
SDTSB Sergei Bobrovsky 30.00 80.00
SDTTB T.J. Brodie 12.00 30.00
SDTTH Taylor Hall 100.00 200.00
SDTTS Tyler Seguin EXCH 100.00 250.00
SDTTY Dana Tyrell 12.00 30.00
SDTZD Zac Dalpe 12.00 30.00
SDTZH Zach Hamill 15.00 40.00

2010-11 Ultimate Collection Premium Patches

STATED PRINT RUN 25 SER.#'d SETS
PAH Ales Hemsky 40.00 100.00
PAK Anze Kopitar 20.00 50.00
PAO Alexander Ovechkin 40.00 80.00
PBR Brad Richards 12.00 30.00
PCG Claude Giroux 12.00 30.00
PDA Daniel Alfredsson 30.00 60.00
PDC Dino Ciccarelli 12.00 30.00
PDD Drew Doughty 25.00 60.00
PDH Dany Heatley 10.00 25.00
PDK Duncan Keith
PDP Dion Phaneuf 20.00 50.00
PDS Devin Setoguchi 10.00 25.00
PEM Evgeni Malkin 40.00 80.00
PHL Henrik Lundqvist 20.00 50.00
PHO Marian Hossa 20.00 50.00
PHZ Henrik Zetterberg 15.00 40.00
PJA Jakub Voracek 12.00 30.00
PJC Jeff Carter 25.00 60.00
PJG Jean-Sebastien Giguere 15.00 40.00
PJI Jarome Iginla 12.00 30.00
PJS Joe Sakic 20.00 50.00
PJT Joe Thornton 25.00 60.00
PJV James van Riemsdyk 20.00 50.00
PKE Phil Kessel
PKO Mikko Koivu 12.00 30.00
PMB Martin Brodeur 25.00 60.00
PMD Matt Duchene 12.00 30.00
PMG Marian Gaborik 30.00 80.00
PMH Milan Hejduk 15.00 40.00
PMK Miikka Kiprusoff 10.00 25.00
PML Mario Lemieux 40.00 100.00
PMS Martin St. Louis 15.00 40.00
PNB Nicklas Backstrom 20.00 50.00
PNL Nicklas Lidstrom 15.00 40.00
PPD Pavel Datsyuk 40.00 100.00
PPK Patrick Kane 25.00 60.00
PPS Patrick Sharp 12.00 30.00
PRG Ryan Getzlaf 25.00 60.00
PRK Ryan Kesler 12.00 30.00
PRL Roberto Luongo 12.00 30.00
PRM Ryan Miller 40.00 80.00
PRN Rick Nash 25.00 60.00
PSC Sidney Crosby 50.00 125.00
PSD Shane Doan 15.00 40.00
PSP Jason Spezza 15.00 40.00
PSS Steven Stamkos 25.00 60.00
PST Jordan Staal 12.00 30.00
PTA John Tavares 40.00 80.00
PTV Thomas Vanek 20.00 50.00
PVO Tomas Vokoun 10.00 25.00
PYZ Steve Yzerman 30.00 80.00

2010-11 Ultimate Collection Premium Swatches

STATED PRINT RUN 35 SER.#'d SETS
PAK Anze Kopitar 8.00 20.00
PAO Alexander Ovechkin 20.00 50.00
PBR Brad Richards 5.00 12.00
PCG Claude Giroux 5.00 12.00
PCP Carey Price 20.00 50.00
PDD Drew Doughty 8.00 20.00
PDH Dany Heatley 4.00 10.00
PDP Dion Phaneuf 5.00 12.00
PHL Henrik Lundqvist 8.00 20.00
PHO Marian Hossa 4.00 10.00
PHZ Henrik Zetterberg 10.00 25.00
PJC Jeff Carter 5.00 12.00
PJG Jean-Sebastien Giguere 8.00 20.00
PJI Jarome Iginla 10.00 25.00
PJS Joe Sakic 8.00 20.00
PJT Joe Thornton 12.00 30.00
PJV James van Riemsdyk 8.00 20.00
PKE Phil Kessel 6.00 15.00
PKO Mikko Koivu 5.00 12.00
PMB Martin Brodeur 10.00 25.00
PMD Matt Duchene 5.00 12.00
PMG Marian Gaborik 6.00 15.00
PMH Milan Hejduk 4.00 10.00
PMK Miikka Kiprusoff 4.00 10.00
PML Mario Lemieux/10
PMM Mark Messier 8.00 20.00
PMS Martin St. Louis 5.00 12.00
PNB Nicklas Backstrom 8.00 20.00
PNL Nicklas Lidstrom 5.00 12.00
PPD Pavel Datsyuk 8.00 20.00
PPK Patrick Kane 10.00 25.00
PPS Patrick Sharp 5.00 12.00
PRG Ryan Getzlaf 8.00 20.00
PRK Ryan Kesler 5.00 12.00
PRL Roberto Luongo 5.00 12.00
PRM Ryan Miller
PRN Rick Nash 8.00 20.00
PSC Sidney Crosby 20.00 50.00
PSD Shane Doan 4.00 10.00
PSM Steve Mason 4.00 10.00
PSP Jason Spezza 3.00 8.00
PSS Steven Stamkos 10.00 25.00
PST Jordan Staal 5.00 12.00
PTA John Tavares 12.00 30.00
PTO Jonathan Toews 10.00 25.00
PTV Thomas Vanek
PVO Tomas Vokoun 6.00 15.00
PWG Wayne Gretzky 25.00 60.00
PYZ Steve Yzerman 12.00 30.00
PZP Zach Parise 8.00 20.00

2010-11 Ultimate Collection Rookie Patch Autographs

STATED PRINT RUN 25-35
101 Cam Fowler/35 30.00 80.00
102 Kyle Palmieri/35 25.00 60.00
103 Alexander Burmistrov/35 12.00 30.00
104 Jordan Caron/35 20.00 50.00
105 Zach Hamill/35 12.00 30.00
106 Henrik Karlsson/35 12.00 30.00
107 Jamie McBain/35 12.00 30.00
108 Zac Dalpe/35 12.00 30.00
109 Jeff Skinner/25 75.00 150.00
110 Nick Leddy/35 12.00 30.00
111 Brandon Yip/35 12.00 30.00
112 Kevin Shattenkirk/35 25.00 60.00
113 Philip Larsen/35 12.00 30.00
114 Alex Plante/35 12.00 30.00
115 Magnus Paajarvi/35 15.00 40.00
116 Brayden Schenn/35 20.00 50.00
117 Kyle Clifford/35 12.00 30.00
118 Justin Falk/35 10.00 25.00
119 Marco Scandella/35 12.00 30.00
120 Cody Almond/35 12.00 30.00
121 Anders Lindback/35 12.00 30.00
122 Jacob Josefson/35 12.00 30.00
123 Nick Palmieri/35 12.00 30.00
124 Nino Niederreiter/35 15.00 40.00
125 Evgeny Grachev/35 12.00 30.00
126 Luke Adam/35 12.00 30.00
127 Jared Cowen/35 12.00 30.00
128 Sergei Bobrovsky/35 30.00 80.00
129 Oliver Ekman-Larsson/35 20.00 50.00
130 Eric Wellwood/35 15.00 40.00
131 Eric Tangradi/35 12.00 30.00
132 Nick Johnson/35 10.00 25.00
133 Mattias Tedenby/35 10.00 25.00
134 Dustin Tokarski/35 12.00 30.00
135 Dana Tyrell/35 12.00 30.00
136 Marcus Johansson/35 20.00 50.00
137 Derek Stepan/35 30.00 80.00
138 Nazem Kadri/25 75.00 150.00
139 P.K. Subban/25 75.00 150.00
140 Jordan Eberle/25 200.00 350.00
141 Tyler Seguin/25 125.00 250.00
142 Taylor Hall/25 200.00 400.00
144 Jacob Markstrom/25 20.00 50.00

2010-11 Ultimate Collection Ultimate Achievements Autographs

STATED PRINT RUN 25 SER.#'d SETS
UAAN Antti Niemi 12.00 30.00
UAAO Alexander Ovechkin 40.00 80.00
UABO Bobby Orr 125.00 250.00
UAEM Evgeni Malkin 25.00 60.00
UAGH Gordie Howe 75.00 150.00
UAGL Guy Lafleur 20.00 50.00
UAJT John Tavares 25.00 60.00
UAMB Martin Brodeur 40.00 80.00
UAML Mario Lemieux 50.00 100.00
UAMM Mark Messier 40.00 80.00
UAPD Pavel Datsyuk 15.00 40.00
UAPE Phil Esposito 15.00 40.00
UAPK Patrick Kane 20.00 50.00
UAPR Patrick Roy 60.00 120.00
UARM Ryan Miller 15.00 40.00
UASC Sidney Crosby 100.00 175.00
UASS Steven Stamkos 40.00 80.00
UATM Tyler Myers
UATO Jonathan Toews 25.00 60.00
UAWG Wayne Gretzky 175.00 300.00

2010-11 Ultimate Collection Ultimate Jerseys

STATED PRINT RUN 100 SER.#'d SETS
UJAK Alex Kovalev 4.00 10.00
UJAO Alexander Ovechkin 15.00 40.00
UJBL Brian Leetch 4.00 10.00
UJCA Craig Anderson 4.00 10.00
UJCN Cam Neely 4.00 10.00
UJCW Cam Ward 4.00 10.00
UJDB David Backes 4.00 10.00
UJDG Doug Gilmour 5.00 12.00
UJDH Dany Heatley 3.00 8.00
UJDS Daniel Sedin 4.00 10.00
UJEM Evgeni Malkin 12.00 30.00
UJES Eric Staal 5.00 12.00
UJGH Gordie Howe 10.00 25.00
UJHS Henrik Sedin 4.00 10.00
UJIK Ilya Kovalchuk 4.00 10.00
UJJC Jeff Carter 4.00 10.00
UJJH Jaroslav Halak 4.00 10.00
UJJI Jarome Iginla 4.00 10.00
UJJK Jari Kurri 4.00 10.00
UJJS Jason Spezza 2.50 6.00
UJJT Jonathan Toews 8.00 20.00
UJLE Loui Eriksson 3.00 8.00
UJMB Martin Brodeur 8.00 20.00
UJMD Matt Duchene 4.00 10.00
UJMF Marc-Andre Fleury 6.00 15.00
UJMG Marian Gaborik 5.00 12.00
UJMK Miikka Kiprusoff 3.00 8.00
UJML Mario Lemieux 12.00 30.00
UJMM Mike Modano 6.00 15.00
UJMR Mike Richards 4.00 10.00
UJMT Marty Turco 4.00 10.00
UJNB Nicklas Backstrom 6.00 15.00
UJPB Patrice Bergeron 5.00 12.00
UJPD Pavel Datsyuk 5.00 12.00
UJPK Patrick Kane 8.00 20.00
UJPM Patrick Marleau 4.00 10.00
UJPR Patrick Roy 10.00 25.00
UJRB Ray Bourque 6.00 15.00
UJRG Ryan Getzlaf 6.00 15.00
UJRI Brad Richards 4.00 10.00
UJRL Roberto Luongo 4.00 10.00
UJRM Ryan Miller 4.00 10.00
UJRN Rick Nash 4.00 10.00
UJSC Sidney Crosby 15.00 40.00
UJSY Steve Yzerman 10.00 25.00
UJTA John Tavares 8.00 20.00
UJTH Joe Thornton 4.00 10.00
UJVL Vincent Lecavalier 3.00 8.00
UJWG Wayne Gretzky 20.00 50.00
UJZC Zdeno Chara 3.00 8.00
UJZP Zach Parise 4.00 10.00

2010-11 Ultimate Collection Ultimate Jerseys Autographs

STATED PRINT RUN 25 SER.#'d SETS
UAJAK Anze Kopitar 15.00 40.00
UAJAO Alexander Ovechkin 50.00 100.00
UAJBR Brad Richards 12.00 30.00
UAJDD Drew Doughty 12.00 30.00
UAJDH Dany Heatley 10.00 25.00
UAJJC Jeff Carter 12.00 30.00
UAJJI Jarome Iginla 12.00 30.00
UAJJV James van Riemsdyk 20.00 50.00
UAJMB Martin Brodeur 25.00 60.00
UAJMD Matt Duchene 12.00 30.00
UAJML Mario Lemieux 75.00 150.00
UAJMM Mark Messier 40.00 80.00
UAJMR Mike Richards
UAJNB Nicklas Backstrom 20.00 50.00
UAJPK Patrick Kane 30.00 60.00
UAJPR Patrick Roy 60.00 125.00
UAJRM Ryan Miller 15.00 40.00
UAJSC Sidney Crosby 100.00 175.00
UAJSS Steven Stamkos 30.00 80.00
UAJTA John Tavares 25.00 60.00
UAJTM Tyler Myers
UAJTO Jonathan Toews 25.00 60.00
UAJVL Vincent Lecavalier 10.00 25.00
UAJWG Wayne Gretzky 200.00 300.00

2010-11 Ultimate Collection Ultimate Jerseys Duos

STATED PRINT RUN 50 SER.#'d SETS
UDJBK M.Koivu/N.Backstrom
UDJBP Z.Parise/M.Brodeur 15.00 40.00
UDJCM S.Crosby/E.Malkin 15.00 40.00
UDJCO S.Crosby/A.Ovechkin 20.00 50.00
UDJCR Z.Chara/T.Rask 8.00 20.00
UDJCS S.Stamkos/S.Crosby
UDJCV J.Carter/J.van Riemsdyk 8.00 20.00
UDJGL M.Gaborik/H.Lundqvist 8.00 20.00
UDJGP J.Giguere/D.Phaneuf 8.00 20.00
UDJGR W.Gretzky/L.Robitaille 40.00 100.00
UDJGV M.Green/S.Varlamov 8.00 20.00
UDJHD M.Duchene/M.Hejduk 8.00 20.00
UDJHP D.Penner/A.Hemsky 6.00 15.00
UDJHT M.Hossa/J.Toews 15.00 40.00
UDJIK J.Iginla/M.Kiprusoff 8.00 20.00
UDJKB R.Kesler/D.Backes
UDJKD A.Kopitar/D.Doughty 12.00 30.00
UDJKK P.Kane/D.Keith
UDJKM J.Kurri/M.Messier 12.00 30.00
UDJLM R.Luongo/R.Miller 8.00 20.00
UDJMH P.Marleau/D.Heatley 8.00 20.00
UDJMV R.Miller/T.Vanek 8.00 20.00
UDJNB R.Bourque/C.Neely 12.00 30.00
UDJNV R.Nash/J.Voracek 8.00 20.00
UDJOB A.Ovechkin/N.Backstrom 30.00 80.00
UDJRG M.Richards/C.Giroux 8.00 20.00
UDJRS P.Roy/J.Sakic 20.00 50.00
UDJSM M.St. Louis/S.Stamkos
UDJSS H.Sedin/D.Sedin 8.00 20.00
UDJTD J.Tavares/M.Duchene 15.00 40.00

2010-11 Ultimate Collection Ultimate Jerseys Trios

STATED PRINT RUN 25 SER.#'d SETS
UTJ1 Lemieux/Yzerman/Gretzky 50.00 125.00
UTJ2 Yzerman/Lemieux/Messier 30.00 80.00
UTJ3 Green/Backstrom/Ovechkin 40.00 100.00
UTJ4 Phaneuf/Kessel/Giguere
UTJ5 Staal/Malkin/Fleury 30.00 80.00
UTJ6 Roy/Brodeur/Price 25.00 60.00
UTJ7 Kane/Toews/Hossa 40.00 100.00
UTJ8 Lecavalier/St. Louis/Stamkos
UTJ9 Myers/Miller/Vanek 10.00 25.00
UTJ10 Heatley/Marleau/Thornton

2010-11 Ultimate Collection Ultimate Nicknames Autographs

STATED PRINT RUN 25 SER.#'d SETS
UNAD Alex Delvecchio 10.00 25.00
UNAN Antti Niemi 25.00 50.00
UNAO Alexander Ovechkin 75.00 125.00
UNEM Evgeni Malkin 20.00 50.00
UNGH Gordie Howe 60.00 120.00
UNGJ Bobby Hull 25.00 60.00
UNGL Guy Lafleur 25.00 60.00
UNHZ Henrik Zetterberg
UNJG Jean-Sebastien Giguere 15.00 40.00
UNJH Jaroslav Halak 15.00 40.00
UNJI Jarome Iginla 15.00 40.00
UNJT Jonathan Toews 20.00 50.00
UNMB Martin Brodeur 40.00 80.00
UNMF Marc-Andre Fleury 25.00 60.00
UNML Mario Lemieux 60.00 120.00
UNMM Mark Messier 30.00 60.00
UNNL Nicklas Lidstrom 25.00 60.00
UNPR Patrick Roy 75.00 125.00
UNRM Ryan Miller 30.00 60.00
UNRS Ryan Smyth 30.00 60.00

2010-11 Ultimate Collection Ultimate Patches

STATED PRINT RUN 35 SER.#'d SETS
UJAK Alex Kovalev 10.00 25.00
UJAO Alexander Ovechkin 40.00 100.00
UJBL Brian Leetch 10.00 25.00
UJCA Craig Anderson 10.00 25.00
UJCN Cam Neely 10.00 25.00
UJCW Cam Ward 10.00 25.00
UJDB David Backes 10.00 25.00
UJDH Dany Heatley 8.00 20.00
UJDS Daniel Sedin 10.00 25.00
UJEM Evgeni Malkin 30.00 80.00
UJES Eric Staal 12.00 30.00
UJHL Henrik Lundqvist 15.00 40.00
UJHS Henrik Sedin 10.00 25.00
UJHZ Henrik Zetterberg 12.00 30.00
UJIK Ilya Kovalchuk 10.00 25.00
UJJC Jeff Carter 10.00 25.00
UJJI Jarome Iginla 10.00 25.00
UJJS Jason Spezza 6.00 15.00
UJJT Jonathan Toews 20.00 50.00
UJKO Mikko Koivu 10.00 25.00
UJLE Loui Eriksson 8.00 20.00
UJLR Luc Robitaille 10.00 25.00
UJMB Martin Brodeur 20.00 50.00
UJMF Marc-Andre Fleury 15.00 40.00
UJMG Marian Gaborik 12.00 30.00
UJMK Miikka Kiprusoff 8.00 20.00
UJML Mario Lemieux 30.00 80.00
UJMM Mike Modano 15.00 40.00
UJMS Martin St. Louis 10.00 25.00
UJMT Marty Turco 10.00 25.00
UJNB Nicklas Backstrom 15.00 40.00
UJPB Patrice Bergeron 12.00 30.00
UJPD Pavel Datsyuk 20.00 50.00
UJPK Patrick Kane 20.00 50.00
UJPM Patrick Marleau 10.00 25.00
UJPR Patrick Roy 25.00 60.00
UJRB Ray Bourque 15.00 40.00
UJRG Ryan Getzlaf 15.00 40.00
UJRI Brad Richards 10.00 25.00
UJRL Roberto Luongo 10.00 25.00
UJRM Ryan Miller 10.00 25.00
UJRN Rick Nash 10.00 25.00
UJSC Sidney Crosby 40.00 100.00
UJSY Steve Yzerman 25.00 60.00
UJTA John Tavares 20.00 50.00
UJVL Vincent Lecavalier 8.00 20.00
UJJT Joe Thornton 10.00 25.00
UJZC Zdeno Chara 8.00 20.00

2010-11 Ultimate Collection Ultimate Patches Duos

STATED PRINT RUN 25 SER.#'d SETS
UDJBK M.Koivu/N.Backstrom
UDJBP Z.Parise/M.Brodeur
UDJCM S.Crosby/E.Malkin 60.00 150.00
UDJCO S.Crosby/A.Ovechkin 100.00 200.00
UDJCR Z.Chara/T.Rask 25.00 60.00
UDJCS S.Stamkos/S.Crosby
UDJCV J.Carter/J.van Riemsdyk 15.00 40.00
UDJGL M.Gaborik/H.Lundqvist 25.00 60.00
UDJGP J.Giguere/D.Phaneuf 15.00 40.00
UDJGR W.Gretzky/L.Robitaille
UDJGV M.Green/S.Varlamov
UDJHD M.Duchene/M.Hejduk 15.00 40.00
UDJHP D.Penner/A.Hemsky
UDJHT M.Hossa/J.Toews 40.00 100.00
UDJIK J.Iginla/M.Kiprusoff 15.00 40.00
UDJKB R.Kesler/D.Backes 25.00 60.00
UDJKD A.Kopitar/D.Doughty 30.00 80.00
UDJKK P.Kane/D.Keith 30.00 80.00
UDJKM J.Kurri/M.Messier
UDJLM R.Luongo/R.Miller 15.00 40.00
UDJMH P.Marleau/D.Heatley 15.00 40.00
UDJMV R.Miller/T.Vanek 15.00 40.00
UDJNB R.Bourque/C.Neely 25.00 60.00
UDJNV R.Nash/J.Voracek 15.00 40.00
UDJOB A.Ovechkin/N.Backstrom 40.00 100.00
UDJRG M.Richards/C.Giroux
UDJRS P.Roy/J.Sakic 40.00 100.00
UDJSM M.St. Louis/S.Stamkos
UDJSS H.Sedin/D.Sedin 15.00 40.00
UDJTD J.Tavares/M.Duchene 30.00 80.00

2010-11 Ultimate Collection Ultimate Signatures

USAO Alexander Ovechkin 40.00 100.00
USBA Mikael Backlund
USBC Bobby Clarke 12.00 30.00
USBD Brandon Dubinsky 5.00 12.00
USBH Bobby Hull 15.00 40.00
USBO Bobby Orr 60.00 120.00
USBR Bobby Ryan 6.00 15.00
USBS Brayden Schenn 12.00 30.00
USBY Brandon Yip 5.00 12.00
USCS Chris Stewart 5.00 12.00
USDD Drew Doughty 10.00 25.00
USDS Derek Stepan 8.00 20.00
USEG Evgeny Grachev 5.00 12.00
USEK Evander Kane 6.00 15.00
USEM Evgeni Malkin 20.00 50.00
USET Eric Tangradi 5.00 12.00
USGH Gordie Howe 60.00 120.00
USGL Guy Lafleur 20.00 50.00
USGU Guillaume Latendresse 5.00 12.00
USJC Jared Cowen 5.00 12.00
USJE Jordan Eberle 12.00 30.00
USJF Jeff Skinner 10.00 25.00
USJH Jaroslav Halak 6.00 15.00
USJI Jarome Iginla 6.00 15.00
USJK Jari Kurri 12.00 30.00
USJM Jamie McBain 5.00 12.00
USJS Joe Sakic 25.00 60.00
USMB Martin Brodeur 40.00 80.00
USMD Matt Duchene 6.00 15.00
USMH Milan Hejduk 5.00 12.00
USMI Mike Bossy 8.00 20.00
USMJ Marcus Johansson 8.00 20.00
USML Mario Lemieux 60.00 120.00
USMM Mark Messier 40.00 80.00
USMP Magnus Paajarvi
USMT Mattias Tedenby 4.00 10.00
USNF Nick Foligno 5.00 12.00
USNK Nazem Kadri 15.00 40.00
USNL Nicklas Lidstrom 12.00 30.00
USNN Nino Niederreiter 6.00 15.00
USPD Pavel Datsyuk 20.00 50.00
USPE Phil Esposito 15.00 40.00
USPK Patrick Kane 50.00 100.00
USPR Patrick Roy 60.00 120.00
USPS P.K. Subban 8.00 20.00
USRM Ryan Miller 10.00 25.00
USSB Sergei Bobrovsky 8.00 20.00
USSC Sidney Crosby 75.00 150.00
USSS Steven Stamkos 15.00 40.00
USTA John Tavares 15.00 40.00
USTH Taylor Hall 20.00 50.00
USTM Tyler Myers
USTO Jonathan Toews 30.00 60.00
USTS Tyler Seguin 20.00 50.00
USWG Wayne Gretzky 200.00 400.00
USZH Zach Hamill 5.00 12.00
USPEI Brad Richards 6.00 15.00

2011-12 Ultimate Collection

1-110 STATED PRINT RUN 399
111-15 ROOKIE AU PRINT RUN 99-299
EXCH EXPIRATION: 7/20/2014
1 Corey Perry 1.50 4.00
2 Ryan Getzlaf 2.50 6.00
3 Cam Neely 1.50 4.00
4 Bobby Orr 5.00 12.00
5 Phil Esposito 2.50 6.00
6 Ray Bourque 2.50 6.00
7 Thomas Vanek 1.50 4.00
8 Ryan Miller 1.50 4.00
9 Jarome Iginla 1.50 4.00
10 Miikka Kiprusoff 1.50 4.00
11 Eric Staal 2.00 5.00
12 Jeff Skinner 1.50 4.00
13 Jonathan Toews 3.00 8.00
14 Bobby Hull 1.50 4.00
15 Patrick Kane 3.00 8.00
16 Matt Duchene 1.50 4.00
17 Joe Sakic 2.50 6.00
18 Rick Nash 1.50 4.00
19 Jeff Carter 1.50 4.00
20 Igor Larionov 1.50 4.00
21 Pavel Datsyuk 2.00 5.00
22 Nicklas Lidstrom 1.50 4.00
23 Jordan Eberle 1.50 4.00
24 Taylor Hall 3.00 8.00
25 Jari Kurri 1.50 4.00
26 Paul Coffey 1.50 4.00
27 Brendan Shanahan 2.00 5.00
28 Ron Francis 2.00 5.00
29 Wayne Gretzky 8.00 20.00
30 Luc Robitaille 1.50 4.00
31 Mike Richards 1.50 4.00
32 P.K. Subban 3.00 8.00
33 Jean Beliveau 2.00 5.00
34 Carey Price 5.00 12.00
35 Patrick Roy 6.00 15.00
36 Martin Brodeur 4.00 10.00
37 Zach Parise 1.50 4.00
38 Ilya Kovalchuk 1.50 4.00
39 John Tavares 3.00 8.00
40 Mark Messier 2.00 5.00
41 Henrik Lundqvist 2.50 6.00
42 Jason Spezza 1.50 4.00
43 Brayden Schenn 1.50 4.00
44 Jaromir Jagr 4.00 10.00
45 Ron Hextall 2.00 5.00
46 Mario Lemieux 5.00 12.00
47 Marc-Andre Fleury 2.50 6.00
48 Evgeni Malkin 5.00 12.00
49 Sidney Crosby 5.00 12.00
50 Patrick Marleau 1.50 4.00
51 Joe Thornton 1.50 4.00
52 Jaroslav Halak 1.50
53 Steven Stamkos 3.00
54 Phil Kessel 2.00
55 Markus Naslund 1.25
56 Roberto Luongo 1.50
57 Trevor Linden 1.50
58 Mike Gartner 1.50
59 Alexander Ovechkin 6.00
60 Dale Hawerchuk 2.00
61 Pat Maroon RC 2.50
62 Peter Holland RC 2.50
63 Iiro Tarkki RC 3.00
64 Marcus Foligno RC 4.00
65 Corey Tropp RC 2.50
66 Derek Whitmore RC 6.00
67 Brayden McNabb RC 2.50
68 Joe Finley RC 2.50
69 Riley Nash RC 2.50
70 Dylan Olsen RC 3.00
71 Andrew Shaw RC 6.00
72 Jimmy Hayes RC 5.00
73 Jordie Benn RC 2.50
74 Brendan Smith RC 2.50
75 Joakim Andersson RC 2.50
76 Milan Kytnar RC 3.00
77 Bracken Kearns RC 2.50
78 Jarod Palmer RC 2.50
79 Kris Fredheim RC 2.50
80 David McIntyre RC 2.50
81 Frederic St. Denis RC 2.50
82 Mattias Ekholm RC 2.50
83 Ryan Ellis RC 2.50
84 Roman Josi RC 4.00
85 Keith Kinkaid RC 2.50
86 David Ullstrom RC 2.50
87 Mikko Koskinen RC 3.00
88 Anders Nilsson RC 2.50
89 Stu Bickel RC 2.50
90 Carl Hagelin RC 5.00
91 Andre Petersson RC 3.00
92 Mike Hoffman RC 15.00
93 Zac Rinaldo RC 2.50
94 Harry Zolnierczyk RC 2.50
95 Marc-Andre Bourdon RC 2.50
96 Robert Bortuzzo RC 2.50
97 Carl Sneep RC 2.50
98 Cade Fairchild RC 2.00
99 Kevin Marshall RC 2.50
100 Dmitry Orlov RC 3.00
101 Ben Holmstrom RC 2.50
102 Cam Atkinson RC 6.00
103 David Rundblad RC 2.50
104 Erik Gustafsson RC 3.00
105 Joe Vitale RC 2.50
106 Patrick Wiercioch RC 2.50
107 Roman Horak RC 3.00
108 Roman Wick RC 3.00
109 Stephane Da Costa RC 2.50
110 Tomas Vincour RC 2.50
111 Voynov AU/299 RC 4.00
112 Gustav Nyquist AU/299 RC 20.00
113 Brendan Smith AU/299 RC 4.00
114 Alexei Emelin AU/299 RC 4.00
115 Harri Sateri AU/299 RC 6.00
116 Carl Klingberg AU/299 RC 4.00
117 Raphael Diaz AU/299 RC 4.00
118 Colin Greening AU/299 RC 4.00
119 Justin Faulk AU/299 RC 6.00
120 Tim Erixon AU/299 RC 4.00
121 Nugent-Hopkins AU/99 RC 150.00
122 G.Landeskog AU/99 RC 75.00
123 Anton Lander AU/299 RC 4.00
124 Devante Smith-Pelly AU/299 RC 6.00
125 Leland Irving AU/99 RC 10.00
126 Zack Kassian AU/99 RC 30.00
127 Marcus Kruger AU/299 RC 6.00
128 Louis Leblanc AU/99 RC 20.00
129 Ryan Johansen AU/99 RC 40.00
130 Hartikainen AU/299 RC 8.00
131 Lennart Petrell AU/299 RC 6.00
132 E.Gudbranson AU/99 RC 15.00
133 Matt Frattin AU/299 RC 4.00
134 Calvin de Haan AU/99 RC 15.00
135 Palushaj AU/299 RC EXCH 4.00
136 Adam Henrique AU/99 RC 50.00
137 Adam Larsson AU/99 RC 25.00
138 Mika Zibanejad AU/99 RC 25.00
139 Sean Couturier AU/99 RC 30.00
140 Matt Read AU/99 RC 30.00
141 Blake Geoffrion AU/299 RC 4.00
142 Andy Miele AU/291 RC 4.00
143 Cody Eakin AU/99 RC 20.00
144 Brett Connolly AU/99 RC 15.00
145 Joe Colborne AU/99 RC 15.00
146 Jake Gardiner AU/99 RC 40.00
147 Cody Hodgson AU/99 RC 25.00
148 Craig Smith AU/99 RC 12.00
149 Jonathon Blum AU/299 RC 4.00
150 Mark Scheifele AU/99 RC 30.00

2011-12 Ultimate Collection 1997 Legends Autographs

GROUP A ODDS 1:82
GROUP B ODDS 1:69
GROUP C ODDS 1:22
OVERALL STATED ODDS 1:15
AL1 Bobby Hull A 40.00
AL2 Stan Mikita A 30.00
AL3 Tony Esposito A 30.00
AL4 Alex Delvecchio C 10.00
AL5 Red Kelly C 10.00
AL6 Ted Lindsay B 15.00
AL7 Bill Ranford C 10.00
AL8 Glenn Anderson B 15.00
AL9 Grant Fuhr B 15.00
AL10 Jari Kurri C 12.00
AL11 Marty McSorley C 12.00
AL12 Mark Messier A 50.00
AL13 Paul Coffey A 25.00
AL14 Wayne Gretzky A 300.00
AL15 Guy Lafleur A 30.00
AL16 Jean Beliveau A 100.00
AL17 Larry Robinson B 20.00
AL18 Patrick Roy A 125.00
AL19 Bill Barber C 12.00
AL20 Bobby Clarke B 20.00
AL21 Dave Schultz C 10.00
AL22 Eric Lindros A 50.00
AL23 Ron Hextall B 20.00
AL24 Reggie Leach C 10.00
AL25 Rick MacLeish C 12.00
AL26 Tim Kerr C 8.00
AL27 Adam Oates C 15.00
AL28 Brett Hull A 75.00
AL29 Doug Gilmour A 75.00
AL30 Wendel Clark B 15.00

2011-12 Ultimate Collection Debut Threads Autographs

STATED PRINT RUN 50 SER.#'d SETS
DTAH Adam Henrique 15.00

L Anton Lander 6.00 15.00
M Andy Miele 6.00 15.00
P Aaron Palushaj 6.00 15.00
Y Alexei Emelin 6.00 15.00
B Brett Bulmer 6.00 15.00
nserted in 2013-14 Ultimate Collection)
C Brett Connolly 6.00 15.00
G Blake Geoffrion 6.00 15.00
S Brendan Smith 6.00 15.00
E Cody Eakin 12.00 30.00
G Colin Greening 6.00 15.00
H Cody Hodgson 12.00 30.00
K Carl Klingberg 6.00 15.00
S Craig Smith 10.00 25.00
V Calvin de Haan 6.00 15.00
S Devante Smith-Pelly 10.00 25.00
G Erik Gudbranson 8.00 20.00
O Marcus Foligno 20.00 50.00
L Gabriel Landeskog 20.00 50.00
N Greg Nemisz 6.00 15.00
S Harri Sateri 6.00 15.00
B Jonathon Blum 12.00 30.00
C Joe Colborne 6.00 15.00
F Justin Faulk 10.00 25.00
G Jake Gardiner 15.00 40.00
V Joe Vitale 6.00 15.00
A Adam Larsson 15.00 40.00
I Leland Irving 6.00 15.00
L Louis Leblanc 6.00 15.00
P Lennart Petrell 8.00 20.00
MF Matt Frattin 6.00 15.00
MK Marcus Kruger 10.00 25.00
MR Matt Read 12.00 30.00
MS Mark Scheifele 15.00 40.00
MZ Mika Zibanejad 10.00 25.00
Y Gustav Nyquist 15.00 40.00
W Patrick Wiercioch 6.00 15.00
D Raphael Diaz 6.00 15.00
E Ryan Ellis 6.00 15.00
J Ryan Johansen 12.00 30.00
N Ryan Nugent-Hopkins 25.00 60.00
A David Savard 6.00 15.00
C Sean Couturier 12.00 30.00
D Stephane Da Costa 6.00 15.00
E Tim Erixon 6.00 15.00
H Teemu Hartikainen 12.00 30.00
V Viatcheslav Voynov 6.00 15.00
K Zack Kassian 8.00 20.00

2011-12 Ultimate Collection Debut Threads Patches

TED PRINT RUN 100 SER.#'d SETS
H Adam Henrique 15.00 40.00
L Anton Lander 6.00 15.00
M Andy Miele 6.00 15.00
P Aaron Palushaj 6.00 15.00
Y Alexei Emelin 6.00 15.00
B Brett Bulmer 6.00 15.00
C Brett Connolly 6.00 15.00
G Blake Geoffrion 6.00 15.00
S Brendan Smith 6.00 15.00
E Cody Eakin 8.00 20.00
G Colin Greening 6.00 15.00
H Cody Hodgson 12.00 30.00
S Craig Smith 8.00 20.00
V Calvin de Haan 12.00 30.00
R David Rundblad 6.00 15.00
S Devante Smith-Pelly 10.00 25.00
G Erik Gudbranson 8.00 20.00
O Marcus Foligno 10.00 25.00
L Gabriel Landeskog 15.00 40.00
N Greg Nemisz 6.00 15.00
S Harri Sateri 6.00 15.00
B Jonathon Blum 6.00 15.00
C Joe Colborne 6.00 15.00
F Justin Faulk 10.00 25.00
G Jake Gardiner 10.00 25.00
V Joe Vitale 6.00 15.00
A Adam Larsson 8.00 20.00
I Leland Irving 6.00 15.00
L Louis Leblanc 6.00 15.00
P Lennart Petrell 8.00 20.00
F Matt Frattin 6.00 15.00
K Marcus Kruger 8.00 20.00
R Matt Read 12.00 30.00
Z Mika Zibanejad 15.00 40.00
Y Gustav Nyquist 15.00 40.00
W Patrick Wiercioch 6.00 15.00
D Raphael Diaz 6.00 15.00
E Ryan Ellis 8.00 20.00
J Ryan Johansen 12.00 30.00
N Ryan Nugent-Hopkins 25.00 60.00
A David Savard 6.00 15.00
C Sean Couturier 12.00 30.00
D Stephane Da Costa 6.00 15.00
E Tim Erixon 6.00 15.00
H Teemu Hartikainen 6.00 15.00
V Viatcheslav Voynov 6.00 15.00
K Zack Kassian 8.00 20.00

2011-12 Ultimate Collection Premium Patches

TED PRINT RUN 25 SER.#'d SETS
K Andrei Kostitsyn 10.00 25.00
M Andrei Markov 12.00 30.00
S Brendan Shanahan 15.00 40.00
P Chris Pronger 10.00 25.00
A Daniel Alfredsson 12.00 30.00
B Dustin Brown 12.00 30.00
P David Perron 8.00 20.00
R Derek Roy 10.00 25.00
Eric Lindros 20.00 50.00
R Mike Green 12.00 30.00
Jonas Hiller 10.00 25.00
S Henrik Sedin 12.00 30.00
Z Henrik Zetterberg 15.00 40.00
Ilya Bryzgalov 12.00 30.00
Ilya Kovalchuk 12.00 30.00
Jaromir Jagr 30.00 80.00
Jeff Carter 12.00 30.00
Johan Franzen 12.00 30.00
Jean-Sebastien Giguere 10.00 25.00
Jim Howard 12.00 30.00
Jarome Iginla 12.00 30.00
Jaromir Jagr 30.00 60.00
Jordan Staal 12.00 30.00
Jason Pominville 10.00 25.00
Jason Spezza 12.00 30.00
Lars Eller 10.00 25.00
Linus Omark 12.00 30.00
C Michael Cammalleri 10.00 25.00
D Matt Duchene 12.00 30.00
K Miikka Kiprusoff 12.00 30.00
M Mike Modano 20.00 50.00
R Mike Richards 12.00 30.00
T Matt Moulson 10.00 25.00
Nicklas Backstrom 20.00 50.00
Nikita Filatov 8.00 20.00
Ondrej Pavelec 20.00 50.00
Dustin Penner 10.00 25.00
Patric Hornqvist 10.00 25.00

PSPR Pekka Rinne 30.00 60.00
PSRL Roberto Luongo 12.00 30.00
PSRM Ryan Miller 12.00 30.00
PSSA Joe Sakic 20.00 50.00
PSSE Daniel Sedin 12.00 30.00
PSSH Brendan Shanahan 15.00 40.00
PSSM Steve Mason 12.00 30.00
PSSN Scott Niedermayer 12.00 30.00
PSST Drew Stafford 12.00 30.00
PSSV Semyon Varlamov 12.00 30.00
PSSW Shea Weber 15.00 30.00
PSTE Tyler Ennis 10.00 25.00
PSTM Tyler Myers 12.00 30.00
PSTR Tuukka Rask 12.00 30.00
PSTS Teemu Selanne 25.00 60.00
PSTT Tim Thomas 15.00 30.00
PSTV Thomas Vanek 12.00 30.00
PSTY Tyler Seguin 15.00 40.00
PSVF Valtteri Filppula 12.00 30.00
PSZC Zdeno Chara 12.00 30.00
PSZP Zach Parise 12.00 30.00

2011-12 Ultimate Collection Premium Swatches

*SWATCH/35: .15X TO .4X PATCH/25
STATED PRINT RUN 35 SER.#'d SETS
PSNB Nicklas Backstrom 8.00 20.00
PSWG Wayne Gretzky 30.00 80.00

2011-12 Ultimate Collection Rookie Patch Autographs

STATED PRINT RUN 25-35
111 Viatcheslav Voynov/35 12.00 30.00
112 Gustav Nyquist/35 30.00 80.00
113 Brendan Smith/35 12.00 30.00
114 Alexei Emelin/35 12.00 30.00
115 Harri Sateri/35 25.00 50.00
116 Carl Klingberg/35 15.00 40.00
117 Raphael Diaz/35 12.00 30.00
118 Colin Greening/35 15.00 40.00
119 Justin Faulk/35 20.00 50.00
120 Tim Erixon/35 12.00 30.00
121 Ryan Nugent-Hopkins/25 125.00 250.00
122 Gabriel Landeskog/25 60.00 120.00
123 Anton Lander/25 25.00 50.00
124 Devante Smith-Pelly/25 15.00 40.00
125 Leland Irving/25 12.00 30.00
126 Zack Kassian/25 15.00 40.00
127 Marcus Kruger/25 15.00 40.00
128 Louis Leblanc/25 20.00 50.00
129 Ryan Johansen/25 40.00 80.00
130 Teemu Hartikainen/25 30.00 60.00
131 Lennart Petrell/25 25.00 50.00
132 Erik Gudbranson/25 15.00 40.00
133 Matt Frattin/25 30.00 60.00
134 Calvin de Haan/25 12.00 30.00
135 Aaron Palushaj/25 12.00 30.00
136 Adam Henrique/25 30.00 80.00
137 Adam Larsson/25 15.00 40.00
138 Mika Zibanejad/25 40.00 80.00
139 Sean Couturier/25 40.00 100.00
140 Matt Read/25 25.00 60.00
141 Blake Geoffrion/25 12.00 30.00
142 Andy Miele/25 20.00 50.00
143 Cody Eakin/25 15.00 40.00
144 Brett Connolly/25 25.00 50.00
145 Joe Colborne/25 12.00 30.00
146 Jake Gardiner/25 30.00 75.00
147 Cody Hodgson/25 30.00 80.00
148 Craig Smith/25 20.00 50.00
149 Jonathon Blum/25 12.00 30.00
150 Mark Scheifele/25 75.00 150.00

2011-12 Ultimate Collection Ultimate Jerseys

STATED PRINT RUN 100 SER.#'d SETS
*PATCH/35: 1X TO 2.5X JSY/100
UJAK Anze Kopitar 6.00 15.00
UJAO Alexander Ovechkin 5.00 12.00
UJBC Brett Connolly 3.00 8.00
UJCU Sean Couturier 6.00 15.00
UJDD Drew Doughty 4.00 10.00
UJDR Derek Roy 3.00 8.00
UJDS Daniel Sedin 4.00 10.00
UJEL Eric Lindros 8.00 20.00
UJES Eddie Shack 4.00 10.00
UJHL Henrik Lundqvist 5.00 12.00
UJHS Henrik Sedin 4.00 10.00
UJHZ Henrik Zetterberg 5.00 12.00
UJIK Ilya Kovalchuk 4.00 10.00
UJJB Johnny Bower 6.00 15.00
UJJC Jeff Carter 4.00 10.00
UJJK Jari Kurri 4.00 10.00
UJJS Jordan Staal 4.00 10.00
UJLR Luc Robitaille 4.00 10.00
UJMB Martin Brodeur 8.00 20.00
UJMD Matt Duchene 4.00 10.00
UJMF Marc-Andre Fleury 6.00 15.00
UJMK Miikka Kiprusoff 4.00 10.00
UJML Mario Lemieux 10.00 25.00
UJMM Mike Modano 6.00 15.00
UJMR Mike Richards 4.00 10.00
UJNB Nicklas Backstrom 6.00 15.00
UJPD Pavel Datsyuk 5.00 12.00
UJPE Phil Esposito 5.00 12.00
UJPK P.K. Subban 6.00 15.00
UJPM Patrick Marleau 4.00 10.00
UJRJ Ryan Johansen 6.00 15.00
UJRL Roberto Luongo 4.00 10.00
UJRM Ryan Miller 4.00 10.00
UJSC Sidney Crosby 15.00 40.00
UJTO Jonathan Toews 8.00 20.00
UJTT Tim Thomas 4.00 10.00
UJTV Thomas Vanek 4.00 10.00
UJVL Vincent Lecavalier 3.00 8.00
UJWG Wayne Gretzky 20.00 50.00
UJZP Zach Parise 4.00 10.00

2011-12 Ultimate Collection Ultimate Jerseys Autographs

STATED PRINT RUN 25 SER.#'d SETS
UJAK Anze Kopitar 20.00 50.00
UJBC Brett Connolly 10.00 25.00
UJCU Sean Couturier 25.00 50.00
UJDD Drew Doughty 12.00 30.00
UJDR Derek Roy 8.00 20.00
UJEL Eric Lindros 30.00 60.00
UJHL Henrik Lundqvist 15.00 40.00
UJJB Johnny Bower 30.00 80.00
UJJK Jari Kurri 12.00 30.00
UJJS Jordan Staal 12.00 30.00
UJLR Luc Robitaille 20.00 40.00
UJMB Martin Brodeur 40.00 80.00
UJMD Matt Duchene 15.00 40.00
UJMF Marc-Andre Fleury 20.00 50.00
UJML Mario Lemieux 60.00 120.00
UJMM Mike Modano 15.00 40.00
UJNB Nicklas Backstrom
UJNB Nicklas Backstrom 20.00 50.00
(inserted in 2013-14 Ultimate Collection)
UJPD Pavel Datsyuk 15.00 40.00
UJPE Phil Esposito 15.00 40.00
UJPK P.K. Subban 25.00 60.00
UJPM Patrick Marleau 12.00 30.00
UJRJ Ryan Johansen
UJRM Ryan Miller 12.00 30.00
UJSC Sidney Crosby 90.00 150.00
UJTO Jonathan Toews 30.00 60.00
UJTV Thomas Vanek 12.00 30.00
UJVL Vincent Lecavalier 12.00 30.00
UJWG Wayne Gretzky 175.00 300.00

2011-12 Ultimate Collection Ultimate Jerseys Duos

STATED PRINT RUN 50 SER.#'d SETS
*PATCH/25: .8X TO 2X JSY DUO/50
UDJBF M.Brodeur/M.Fleury 12.00 30.00
UDJCC B.Connolly/S.Couturier 10.00 25.00
UDJEE P.Esposito/T.Esposito 8.00 20.00
UDJEH T.Hall/J.Eberle 12.00 30.00
UDJFS M.Fleury/J.Staal 10.00 25.00
UDJGL W.Gretzky/M.Lemieux 30.00 80.00
UDJGV R.Luongo/M.Kiprusoff 6.00 15.00
UDJIK R.Kesler/J.Iginla 6.00 15.00
UDJJC J.Eberle/C.Hodgson 10.00 25.00
UDJJF J.Jagr/R.Francis 15.00 40.00
UDJKP I.Kovalchuk/Z.Parise 6.00 15.00
UDJLD N.Lidstrom/P.Datsyuk 8.00 20.00
UDJMR R.Miller/D.Roy 6.00 15.00
UDJOG A.Ovechkin/M.Green 8.00 20.00
UDJOS A.Ovechkin/A.Semin 10.00 25.00
UDJSK J.Spezza/E.Karlsson 12.00 30.00
UDJTK J.Toews/P.Kane 12.00 30.00
UDJTZ T.Thomas/Z.Chara 6.00 15.00

2011-12 Ultimate Collection Ultimate Jerseys Trios

STATED PRINT RUN 25 SER.#'d SETS
U3CCJ Couturr/Connlly/Johnsn 12.00 30.00
U3BEES Thomas/Chara/Krejci 15.00 40.00
U3CAPS Ovchkn/Bckstrm/Semn 30.00 80.00
U3GOLD Toews/Perry/Getzlaf 15.00 40.00
U3PENS Fleury/Malkin/Staal 10.00 25.00
U3HAWKS Toews/Kane/Sharp 15.00 40.00
U3WINGS Shanhn/Lidstrm/Hask 10.00 25.00
U3FLYERS Giroux/Brier/vanRms 8.00 20.00
U3OILERS Hall/Ebrl/Paajarvi 15.00 40.00
U3QGFGOLD Luong/Brodr/Flury 15.00 40.00

2011-12 Ultimate Collection Ultimate Nicknames Autographs

STATED PRINT RUN 25 SER.#'d SETS
EXCH EXPIRATION: 7/23/2014
NBH Brett Hull 50.00 100.00
NBM Brad Marchand 15.00 40.00
(inserted in 2013-14 Ultimate Collection)
NBO Bobby Orr 150.00 250.00
NDS Dave Schultz 25.00 50.00
NEL Eric Lindros 40.00 80.00
NIL Igor Larionov 12.00 30.00
NJF Johan Franzen 12.00 30.00
NJP Joe Pavelski 12.00 30.00
NJT Jonathan Toews 40.00 80.00
NMM Mark Messier 40.00 80.00
NPR Patrick Roy 60.00 120.00
NRL Reggie Leach 20.00 50.00
NRN Ryan Nugent-Hopkins 175.00 300.00
NSC Sidney Crosby EXCH 75.00 150.00

2011-12 Ultimate Collection Ultimate Rookie Jerseys

STATED PRINT RUN 200 SER.#'d SETS
*PATCH/65: .8X TO 2X BASIC JSY/200
URJAH Adam Henrique 6.00 15.00
URJBC Brett Connolly 2.50 6.00
URJBS Brendan Smith 2.50 6.00
URJCE Cody Eakin 4.00 10.00
URJCH Cody Hodgson 5.00 12.00
URJGL Gabriel Landeskog 8.00 20.00
URJJC Joe Colborne 2.50 6.00
URJJG Jake Gardiner 4.00 10.00
URJLA Adam Larsson 3.00 8.00
URJLL Louis Leblanc 2.50 6.00
URJMF Matt Frattin 2.50 6.00
URJMR Matt Read 5.00 12.00
URJMS Mark Scheifele 6.00 15.00
URJRJ Ryan Johansen 5.00 12.00
URJRN Ryan Nugent-Hopkins 10.00 25.00
URJSC Sean Couturier 5.00 12.00
URJTH Teemu Hartikainen 2.50 6.00
URJZK Zack Kassian 3.00 8.00

2011-12 Ultimate Collection Ultimate Rookie Jerseys Duos

STATED PRINT RUN 100 SER.#'d SETS
*PATCH/35: .8X TO 2X JSY DUO/100
URJ2CF J.Colborne/M.Frattin 3.00 8.00
URJ2CR S.Couturier/M.Read 6.00 15.00
URJ2HC Hodgson/B.Connolly 6.00 15.00
URJ2HL A.Larsson/Henrique 8.00 20.00
URJ2KS Scheifele/C.Klingberg 8.00 20.00
URJ2LD L.Leblanc/R.Diaz 8.00 20.00
URJ2NL RNH/G.Landeskog 12.00 30.00
URJ2ZG Zibanejad/Greening 15.00 40.00

2011-12 Ultimate Collection Ultimate Rookie Jerseys Trios

STATED PRINT RUN 50 SER.#'d SETS
*PATCH/15: 1X TO 2.5X JSY TRIO/50
URJ3EDM RNH/Lander/Hartikain 25.00 60.00
URJ3NLL RNH/Landskg/Leblanc 25.00 60.00
URJ3TML Colborne/Frattn/Gardnr 5.00 12.00
URJ3CANF Scheifl/Connlly/Coutur 12.50 30.00

2011-12 Ultimate Collection Ultimate Signatures

GROUP A ODDS 1:141
GROUP B ODDS 1:50
GROUP C ODDS 1:24
GROUP D ODDS 1:9
GROUP E ODDS 1:3
OVERALL STATED ODDS 1:2
EXCH EXPIRATION: 7/23/2014
USAH Adam Henrique B 12.00 30.00
USAL Adam Larsson B 5.00 12.00
USBC Brett Connolly TBL E 5.00 12.00
USBM Brad Marchand A 6.00 15.00
USBO Bobby Orr D 60.00 100.00
USBR Bobby Ryan E 5.00 12.00
USBS Brayden Schenn E 6.00 15.00
USCH Cody Hodgson E 6.00 15.00
USCN B.Connolly Canada B 15.00 30.00
USCP Carey Price C 20.00 50.00
USCR Sidney Crosby B EXCH 75.00 125.00
USCU S.Couturier Canada B 20.00 40.00
USDH Dany Heatley C 5.00 12.00
USEL Eric Lindros A 25.00 50.00
USEM Evgeni Malkin D 15.00 40.00
USGC Guy Carbonneau D 6.00 15.00
USGL Gabriel Landeskog D 8.00 20.00
USGR W.Gretzky Canada A 300.00 500.00
USJC Joe Colborne E 6.00 15.00
USJE Jordan Eberle B 10.00 25.00
USJM Jacob Markstrom B 5.00 12.00
USJP Joe Pavelski E 5.00 12.00
USJS Jeff Skinner C 10.00 25.00
USJT John Tavares E 12.00 30.00
USKN Patrick Kane C 15.00 30.00
USLC Logan Couture E 5.00 12.00
USMD Matt Duchene E 6.00 15.00
USMF Matt Frattin E 6.00 15.00
USML Mario Lemieux A 60.00 120.00
USMM Mark Messier A 40.00 80.00
USMS Mark Scheifele Jets E 6.00 15.00
USNH Nathan Horton C 8.00 20.00
USNU Nugent-Hopkins Can B 60.00 120.00
USPK P.K. Subban D 12.00 30.00
USPR Pekka Rinne A 5.00 12.00
USRG Ryan Getzlaf D 5.00 12.00
USRK Ryan Kesler C 8.00 20.00
USRL Reggie Leach E 5.00 12.00
USRM Rick MacLeish E 5.00 12.00
USRN R.Nugent-Hopkins Oilr D 15.00 40.00
USRY Patrick Roy C 40.00 80.00
USSA Joe Sakic A 40.00 80.00
USSC S.Couturier Flyers E 8.00 20.00
USSD Sidney Crosby Can A 100.00 175.00
USSF M.Scheifele Canada B 12.00 30.00
USSS Steven Stamkos A 30.00 80.00
USST Jordan Staal C 6.00 15.00
USTH Taylor Hall C 20.00 40.00
USTO Jonathan Toews C 20.00 40.00
USTS Tyler Seguin D 12.00 30.00
USTV Tomas Vokoun E 5.00 12.00
USWG W.Gretzky Oilers B 150.00 300.00

2012-13 Ultimate Collection

EXCH EXPIRATION: 9/27/2015
1 Teemu Selanne 3.00 8.00
2 Tyler Seguin 2.50 6.00
3 Thomas Vanek 1.50 4.00
4 Patrick Kane 3.00 8.00
5 Jonathan Toews 3.00 8.00
6 Ryan Nugent-Hopkins 1.50 4.00
7 Wayne Gretzky 8.00 20.00
8 Drew Doughty 1.50 4.00
9 Jonathan Quick 2.50 6.00
10 Zach Parise 1.50 4.00
11 Patrick Roy 4.00 10.00
12 Carey Price 5.00 12.00
13 Pekka Rinne 2.00 5.00
14 Martin Brodeur 3.00 8.00
15 Ilya Kovalchuk 1.50 4.00
16 John Tavares 3.00 8.00
17 Henrik Lundqvist 2.00 5.00
18 Jason Spezza 1.50 4.00
19 Eric Lindros 2.50 6.00
20 Evgeni Malkin 5.00 12.00
21 Sidney Crosby 6.00 15.00
22 Mario Lemieux 5.00 12.00
23 Steven Stamkos 3.00 8.00
24 Mats Sundin 1.50 4.00
25 Pavel Bure 2.00 5.00
26 Alexander Ovechkin 6.00 15.00
27 Ondrej Pavelec 1.50 4.00
28 Maxime Sauve AU RC 8.00 20.00
29 Sven Baertschi AU RC 10.00 25.00
30 Brandon Bollig AU RC 12.00 30.00
31 Tyson Barrie AU RC 15.00 40.00
32 Reilly Smith AU RC 15.00 40.00
33 Scott Glennie AU RC EXCH 10.00 25.00
34 Riley Sheahan AU RC 8.00 20.00
35 Jordan Nolan AU RC 8.00 20.00
36 Jason Zucker AU RC 10.00 25.00
37 Chet Pickard AU RC 8.00 20.00
38 Casey Cizikas AU RC 15.00 30.00
39 Chris Kreider AU RC 30.00 60.00
40 Jakob Silfverberg AU RC 20.00 40.00
41 Mark Stone AU RC 40.00 80.00
42 Jake Allen AU RC 25.00 60.00
43 Jaden Schwartz AU RC 25.00 50.00
44 Carter Ashton AU RC 6.00 15.00
45 Jussi Rynnas AU RC 10.00 25.00

2012-13 Ultimate Collection 1997 Legends Autographs

GROUP A ODDS 1:42
GROUP B ODDS 1:20
GROUP C ODDS 1:31
OVERALL ODDS 1:9
AL32 Brad Park C 15.00 40.00
AL33 Ray Bourque A 40.00 80.00
AL34 Milt Schmidt C 15.00 40.00
AL36 Phil Esposito A 125.00 225.00
AL37 Bobby Orr C 90.00 150.00
AL38 Brett Hull A 50.00 120.00
AL39 Mike Modano B 30.00 60.00
AL40 Ed Belfour B 30.00 80.00
AL41 Marcel Dionne B 12.00 30.00
AL42 Jari Kurri C 15.00 40.00
AL43 Luc Robitaille B 15.00 40.00
AL44 Wayne Gretzky A 250.00 400.00
AL46 Denis Potvin B 20.00 50.00
AL47 Clark Gillies B 20.00 50.00
AL48 Mike Bossy B 25.00 60.00
AL49 Ron Francis B 20.00 50.00
AL50 Mario Lemieux A 175.00 300.00
AL51 Jaromir Jagr A 60.00 120.00

2012-13 Ultimate Collection Debut Threads Patches

UDTPCA Carter Ashton 5.00 12.00
UDTPCC Casey Cizikas 10.00 25.00
UDTPCG Cody Goloubef 8.00 20.00
UDTPCK Chris Kreider 12.00 30.00
UDTPCP Chet Pickard 6.00 15.00
UDTPJA Jake Allen 20.00 50.00
UDTPJN Jordan Nolan 6.00 15.00
UDTPJR Jussi Rynnas 6.00 15.00
UDTPJS Jakob Silfverberg 12.00 30.00
UDTPJZ Jason Zucker 8.00 20.00
UDTPMS Mark Stone 12.00 30.00
UDTPRS Reilly Smith 12.00 30.00
UDTPSB Sven Baertschi 8.00 20.00
UDTPSC Jaden Schwartz 12.00 30.00
UDTPSG Scott Glennie 6.00 15.00
UDTPSH Riley Sheahan 6.00 15.00
UDTPTB Tyson Barrie 12.00 30.00
UDTPTC Tyler Cuma 6.00 15.00

2012-13 Ultimate Collection Rookie Patch Autographs

28 Maxime Sauve 12.00 30.00
29 Sven Baertschi 15.00 40.00
30 Brandon Bollig 15.00 40.00
(inserted in 2013-14 Ultimate Collection)
31 Tyson Barrie 25.00 60.00
32 Reilly Smith 30.00 60.00
34 Riley Sheahan 12.00 30.00
35 Jordan Nolan 12.00 30.00
37 Chet Pickard 12.00 30.00
39 Chris Kreider 30.00 60.00
40 Jakob Silfverberg 25.00 60.00
41 Mark Stone 25.00 60.00
42 Jake Allen 40.00 100.00
43 Jaden Schwartz 30.00 60.00
44 Carter Ashton 12.00 30.00
45 Jussi Rynnas 15.00 40.00

2012-13 Ultimate Collection Ultimate Rookie Patches

STATED PRINT RUN 65 SER.#'d SETS
URPCA Carter Ashton 8.00 20.00
URPCK Chris Kreider 10.00 25.00
URPCP Chet Pickard 10.00 25.00
URPJA Jake Allen 15.00 40.00
URPJR Jussi Rynnas 5.00 12.00
URPJS Jaden Schwartz 12.00 30.00
URPJZ Jason Zucker 6.00 15.00
URPRS Riley Sheahan 10.00 25.00
URPSB Sven Baertschi 6.00 15.00
URPSG Scott Glennie 5.00 12.00
URPSI Jakob Silfverberg 10.00 25.00
URPTB Tyson Barrie 10.00 25.00

2012-13 Ultimate Collection Ultimate Rookie Patches Duos

STATED PRINT RUN 35 SER.#'d SETS
DRPAR J.Rynnas/C.Ashton 8.00 20.00
DRPAS J.Schwartz/J.Allen 20.00 50.00
DRPBK C.Kreider/S.Baertschi 12.00 30.00
DRPSK C.Kreider/J.Schwartz 12.00 30.00
DRPSS J.Silfverberg/M.Stone 12.00 30.00

2012-13 Ultimate Collection Ultimate Rookie Patches Trios

STATED PRINT RUN 25 SER.#'d SETS
TRPBKS Baertschi/Kreider/Silfverberg 20.00 50.00
TRPPAR Allen/Rynnas/Pickard 20.00 50.00
TRPSBK Kreider/Baertschi/Schwartz 20.00 50.00

2012-13 Ultimate Collection Ultimate Signature Masterpieces

GROUP A ODDS 1:86
GROUP A ODDS 1:80
GROUP A ODDS 1:12
OVERALL ODDS 1:9
USMAH Adam Henrique C 12.00 30.00
USMBO Bobby Orr B 75.00 135.00
USMCK Chris Kreider C 12.00 30.00
USMCS Cory Schneider C 8.00 20.00
USMDP Dion Phaneuf B 25.00 50.00
USMJA Jaden Schwartz C 12.00 30.00
USMJJ Jaromir Jagr A 60.00 120.00
USMJS Jeff Skinner C 12.00 30.00
USMMD Matt Duchene C 15.00 40.00
USMML Mario Lemieux A 100.00 175.00
USMOV Alexander Ovechkin A 60.00 120.00
USMSC Sidney Crosby A 150.00 250.00
USMWG Wayne Gretzky A 300.00 450.00

2012-13 Ultimate Collection Ultimate Signatures

USAH Adam Henrique B 8.00 20.00
USBO Bobby Orr C 60.00 150.00
USBS Brayden Schenn A 8.00 20.00
USCH Cody Hodgson B 8.00 20.00
USCK Chris Kreider C 12.00 30.00
USCP Carey Price A 30.00 80.00
USEL Eric Lindros B 25.00 60.00
USGL Guy Lafleur B 20.00 50.00
USGR Wayne Gretzky B 150.00 250.00
USJA Jake Allen B 10.00 25.00
USJJ Jaromir Jagr B 30.00 80.00
USJR Jussi Rynnas C 6.00 15.00
USJS Jakob Silfverberg C 12.00 30.00
USLE Mario Lemieux B 80.00 200.00
USME Mark Messier B 25.00 60.00
USOR Bobby Orr A 60.00 150.00
USPB Pavel Bure A 30.00 80.00
USPI Chet Pickard B 6.00 15.00
USPR Carey Price A 25.00 60.00
USRI Pekka Rinne B 10.00 25.00
USRN Ryan Nugent-Hopkins 8.00 20.00
(inserted in 2016-17 Ultimate Collection)
USRO Patrick Roy A 40.00 100.00
USSG Scott Glennie B 6.00 15.00
USSJ Jaden Schwartz B 12.00 30.00
USWG Wayne Gretzky A 200.00 350.00

2013-14 Ultimate Collection

1 Logan Couture 1.50 4.00
2 Pavel Datsyuk 2.00 5.00
3 Jeremy Roenick 1.50 4.00
4 Jonathan Toews 3.00 8.00
5 Joe Sakic 2.50 6.00
6 Jaromir Jagr 4.00 10.00
7 Drew Doughty 1.50 4.00
8 Matt Duchene 1.50 4.00
9 Jari Kurri 1.50 4.00
10 Jim Howard 1.50 4.00
11 Wayne Gretzky 8.00 20.00
12 Jordan Eberle 1.50 4.00
13 Evander Kane 1.50 4.00
14 Chris Kunitz 1.50 4.00
15 David Backes 1.50 4.00
16 Nicklas Backstrom 2.50 6.00
17 Tyler Seguin 2.50 6.00
18 Ryan Nugent-Hopkins 1.50 4.00
19 Matt Moulson 1.25 3.00
20 Tuukka Rask 1.50 4.00
21 Antti Niemi 1.25 3.00
22 Bobby Clarke 1.50 4.00
23 Ryan Kesler 1.50 4.00
24 Bobby Ryan 1.50 4.00
25 Zach Parise 1.50 4.00
26 Henrik Sedin 1.50 4.00
27 Ben Bishop 1.50 4.00
28 Ryan Miller 1.50 4.00
29 Ryan Getzlaf 2.50 6.00
30 Alexander Ovechkin 6.00 15.00
31 Mike Ribeiro 1.25 3.00
32 Mike Bossy 1.50 4.00
33 Steven Stamkos 3.00 8.00
34 Sergei Bobrovsky 1.50 4.00
35 Ron Francis 2.00 5.00
36 Carey Price 5.00 12.00
37 Evgeni Malkin 5.00 12.00
38 Phil Kessel 2.00 5.00
39 David Krejci 1.50 4.00
40 Nazem Kadri 1.50 4.00
41 Jamie Benn 2.00 5.00
42 Marian Gaborik 1.50 4.00
43 Jonathan Quick 2.50 6.00
44 Henrik Lundqvist 2.00 5.00
45 Eric Staal 2.00 5.00
46 Jiri Hudler 1.25 3.00
47 Kyle Okposo 1.50 4.00
48 John Tavares 3.00 8.00
49 Mike Gartner 1.50 4.00
50 Alexander Steen 1.50 4.00
51 P.K. Subban 2.50 6.00
52 Pekka Rinne 2.00 5.00
53 Patrick Kane 3.00 8.00
54 Mario Lemieux 5.00 12.00
55 Adam Henrique 1.50 4.00
56 Marcel Dionne 2.00 5.00
57 Vincent Lecavalier 1.25 3.00
58 Sidney Crosby 6.00 15.00
59 Guy Carbonneau 1.50 4.00
60 Erik Karlsson 3.00 8.00
61 Michael Latta/499 RC 2.50 6.00
62 Ryan Stanton/499 RC 3.00 8.00
63 Carl Soderberg/499 RC 3.00 8.00
64 Darcy Kuemper/499 RC 3.00 8.00
65 Tyler Johnson/499 RC 8.00 20.00
65A Tyler Johnson AU/99 RC 100.00 200.00
66 Jack Campbell/499 RC 2.50 6.00
67 Thomas Hickey/499 RC 2.50 6.00
68 Tomas Jurco/499 RC 5.00 12.00
68A Tomas Jurco AU/99 RC 20.00 50.00
69 Jason Missiaen/499 RC 3.00 8.00
70 Eric Hartzell/499 RC 3.00 8.00
71 Anton Belov/499 RC 3.00 8.00
72 Tye McGinn/499 RC 3.00 8.00
73 Reid Boucher/499 RC 3.00 8.00
74 Josh Leivo/499 RC 3.00 8.00
75 Jordan Szwarz/499 RC 3.00 8.00
76 Jamie Oleksiak/499 RC 2.50 6.00
77 Dylan McIlrath/499 RC 2.00 5.00
78 Jon Merrill/499 RC 3.00 8.00
79 Nikita Zadorov/499 RC 3.00 8.00
80 Zach Redmond/499 RC 2.50 6.00
81 Jamie Devane/499 RC 2.50 6.00
82 Xavier Ouellet/499 RC 3.00 8.00
83 Sami Vatanen/499 RC 3.00 8.00
84 Michael Raffl/499 RC 2.50 6.00
85 Ryan Strome/499 RC 6.00 15.00
85A Ryan Strome AU/99 RC 40.00 80.00
86 Jonas Brodin/499 RC 2.50 6.00
87 Linden Vey/499 RC 2.00 5.00
88 Nathan Beaulieu/499 RC 2.50 6.00
89 Antti Raanta/499 RC 4.00 10.00
90 Spencer Abbott/499 RC 2.50 6.00
91 J.T. Miller/499 RC 3.00 8.00
92 Lucas Lessio/499 RC 2.00 5.00
93 Nick Bjugstad/499 RC 4.00 10.00
94 Austin Watson/499 RC 2.50 6.00
95 Mark Barberio/499 RC 2.00 5.00
96 Brian Lashoff/499 RC 2.50 6.00
97 Antoine Roussel/499 RC 3.00 8.00
98 Dmitrij Jaskin/499 RC 3.00 8.00
99 Marek Mazanec/499 RC 3.00 8.00
100 Drew LeBlanc/499 RC 2.00 5.00
101 Eric Gelinas/499 RC 2.50 6.00
102 Reto Berra/499 RC 3.00 8.00
103 Andrej Sustr/499 RC 2.00 5.00
104 Quinton Howden/499 RC 2.50 6.00
105 Nate Schmidt/499 RC 2.50 6.00
106 Frank Corrado/499 RC 2.00 5.00
107 Eric Gryba/499 RC 2.50 6.00
108 Johan Gustafsson/499 RC 4.00 10.00
109 Jeff Zatkoff/499 RC 3.00 8.00
110 Alex Chiasson/499 RC 3.00 8.00
111 Martin Jones/499 RC 5.00 12.00
112 Stefan Matteau/499 RC 2.50 6.00
113 Joakim Nordstrom/499 RC 2.50 6.00
114 Freddie Hamilton/499 RC 3.00 8.00
115 Jason Akeson/499 RC 2.50 6.00
116 John Gibson/499 RC 10.00 25.00
116A John Gibson AU/99 RC 50.00 100.00
117 Patrick Holland/499 RC 5.00 12.00
118 Ondrej Palat/499 RC 4.00 10.00
118A Ondrej Palat AU/99 RC EXCH 25.00 50.00
119 Cody Ceci/499 RC 2.50 6.00
120 David Broll/499 RC 3.00 8.00
121 Frederik Andersen AU/399 RC 8.00 20.00
122 Brock Nelson AU/399 RC 5.00 12.00
123 Chris Brown AU/399 RC 3.00 8.00
124 Matt Nieto AU/399 RC 4.00 10.00
125 Nicklas Jensen AU/399 RC 4.00 10.00
126 Radko Gudas AU/399 RC 5.00 12.00
127 Mark Arcobello AU/399 RC 4.00 10.00
128 Drew Shore AU/399 RC 4.00 10.00
129 Richard Panik AU/399 RC 5.00 12.00
130 Max Reinhart AU/399 RC 5.00 12.00
131 Scott Laughton AU/399 RC 5.00 12.00
132 Alex Killorn AU/399 RC 5.00 12.00
133 Jordan Schroeder AU/399 RC 6.00 15.00
134 Will Acton AU/399 RC 4.00 10.00
135 Jarred Tinordi AU/399 RC 5.00 12.00
136 Jacob Trouba AU/299 RC 8.00 20.00
137 Matt Irwin AU/299 RC 4.00 10.00
138 Mathew Dumba AU/299 RC 5.00 12.00
139 Olli Maatta AU/299 RC 10.00 25.00
140 Tom Wilson AU/299 RC 8.00 20.00
141 Viktor Fasth AU/299 RC 5.00 12.00
142 Michael Bournival AU/299 RC 5.00 12.00
143 Connor Carrick AU/299 RC 4.00 10.00
144 Mikael Granlund AU/299 RC 8.00 20.00
145 Danny DeKeyser AU/299 RC 6.00 15.00
146 Filip Forsberg AU/299 RC 25.00 60.00
147 Beau Bennett AU/299 RC 8.00 20.00
148 Emerson Etem AU/299 RC 8.00 20.00
149 Justin Fontaine AU/299 RC 5.00 12.00
150 Jesper Fast AU/299 RC 4.00 10.00
151 Tanner Pearson AU/299 RC 12.00 30.00
152 Ryan Murphy AU/299 RC 5.00 12.00
153 Jean-Gabriel Pageau AU/299 RC 4.00 10.00
154 Zemgus Girgensons AU/299 RC 10.00 25.00
155 Tyler Toffoli AU/299 RC 15.00 30.00
156 Damien Brunner AU/99 RC 10.00 25.00
157 Seth Jones AU/99 RC 40.00 80.00
158 Brian Flynn AU/99 RC 10.00 25.00
159 Charlie Coyle AU/99 RC 12.00 30.00
160 Hampus Lindholm AU/99 RC 20.00 50.00
161 Petr Mrazek AU/99 RC 25.00 60.00
162 Morgan Rielly AU/99 RC 40.00 50.00
163 Boone Jenner AU/99 RC 20.00 50.00
164 Rasmus Ristolainen AU/99 RC 20.00 50.00
165 Cory Conacher AU/99 RC 8.00 20.00
166 Valeri Nichushkin AU/99 RC 50.00 100.00
167 Ryan Murray AU/99 RC 20.00 50.00
168 Tomas Hertl AU/99 RC 15.00 40.00
169 Mikhail Grigorenko AU/99 RC 15.00 40.00
170 Justin Schultz AU/99 RC 25.00 60.00
171 Nathan MacKinnon AU/99 RC 250.00 450.00
172 Vladimir Tarasenko AU/99 RC 90.00 150.00
173 Sean Monahan AU/99 RC 50.00 100.00
174 Jonathan Huberdeau AU/99 RC 50.00 100.00
175 Brendan Gallagher AU/99 RC 60.00 120.00
176 Nail Yakupov AU/99 RC 40.00 100.00
177 Alex Galchenyuk AU/99 RC 100.00 200.00
178 Aleksander Barkov AU/99 RC 50.00 100.00
179 Elias Lindholm AU/99 RC 20.00 50.00
180 Dougie Hamilton AU/99 RC 50.00 100.00

2013-14 Ultimate Collection '97 Legends Autographs

GROUP A ODDS 1:125
GROUP B ODDS 1:60
GROUP C ODDS 1:78
GROUP D ODDS 1:20
OVERALL ODDS 1:15
AL31 Cam Neely B 125.00 200.00
AL35 Johnny Bucyk B 30.00 60.00
AL45 Michel Goulet C 12.00 30.00
AL52 Doug Wilson D 6.00 15.00
AL53 Denis Savard D 10.00 25.00
AL54 Ray Bourque B 40.00 100.00
AL55 Patrick Roy A
AL56 Joe Sakic A
AL57 Peter Forsberg A 150.00 250.00
AL58 Nicklas Lidstrom D 15.00 30.00
AL59 Dominik Hasek B 40.00 80.00
AL60 Steve Yzerman A 125.00 200.00
AL61 Vincent Damphousse D 12.00 30.00
AL62 Martin Brodeur B 75.00 135.00
AL64 Glenn Anderson D 8.00 20.00
AL65 Wayne Gretzky A
AL66 Theoren Fleury B 25.00 60.00
AL67 Pavel Bure
(inserted in 2015-16 Ultimate Collection)
AL68 Brian Leetch B 25.00 50.00
AL69 Markus Naslund D 8.00 20.00
AL70 Mark Messier A
AL71 Mike Gartner D 8.00 20.00
AL72 Richard Brodeur D 15.00 30.00
AL74 Paul Coffey B 20.00 50.00
AL75 Joe Sakic A 40.00 100.00
AL76 Mats Sundin A 75.00 125.00
AL77 Wayne Gretzky A 350.00 500.00
AL78 Chris Pronger A 75.00 150.00
AL79 Mats Sundin A 50.00 100.00
AL80 Pavel Bure
(inserted in 2015-16 Ultimate Collection)
AL81 Alexander Ovechkin A 125.00 200.00
AL83 John LeClair B 15.00 40.00
AL84 Jeremy Roenick D 15.00 40.00
AL85 Gilbert Perreault D 10.00 25.00
AL86 Arturs Irbe C 30.00 60.00
AL87 Dale Hawerchuk B 25.00 60.00
AL88 Curtis Joseph C 25.00 50.00
AL89 Grant Fuhr C 15.00 40.00
AL90 Trevor Linden C 20.00 40.00

2013-14 Ultimate Collection Debut Threads Patches

UDTAB Aleksander Barkov 15.00 40.00
UDTAG Alex Galchenyuk 20.00 50.00
UDTAK Alex Killorn 8.00 20.00
UDTBB Beau Bennett 10.00 25.00
UDTBF Brian Flynn 6.00 15.00
UDTBG Brendan Gallagher 20.00 50.00
UDTBJ Boone Jenner 8.00 20.00
UDTBN Brock Nelson 8.00 20.00
UDTCA Connor Carrick 6.00 15.00
UDTCB Chris Brown 5.00 12.00
UDTCC Cory Conacher 5.00 12.00
UDTCO Charlie Coyle 8.00 20.00
UDTDB Damien Brunner 6.00 15.00
UDTDD Danny DeKeyser 10.00 25.00
UDTDH Dougie Hamilton 15.00 40.00
UDTDS Drew Shore 6.00 15.00
UDTEE Emerson Etem 8.00 20.00
UDTEL Elias Lindholm 12.00 30.00
UDTFA Frederik Andersen 12.00 30.00
UDTFF Filip Forsberg 20.00 50.00
UDTGR Mikhail Grigorenko 10.00 25.00
UDTHL Hampus Lindholm 10.00 25.00
UDTJE Jesper Fast 8.00 20.00
UDTJF Justin Fontaine 8.00 20.00
UDTJH Jonathan Huberdeau 15.00 40.00
UDTJP Jean-Gabriel Pageau 6.00 15.00
UDTJS Jordan Schroeder 8.00 20.00
UDTJT Jarred Tinordi 8.00 20.00
UDTMA Mark Arcobello 8.00 20.00
UDTMB Michael Bournival 8.00 20.00
UDTMD Mathew Dumba 8.00 20.00
UDTMG Mikael Granlund 10.00 25.00
UDTMI Matt Irwin 6.00 15.00
UDTMN Matt Nieto 6.00 15.00
UDTMR Max Reinhart 8.00 20.00
UDTMU Ryan Murray 12.00 30.00
UDTNJ Nicklas Jensen 8.00 20.00
UDTNM Nathan MacKinnon 30.00 80.00
UDTNY Nail Yakupov 12.00 30.00
UDTOM Olli Maatta 12.00 30.00
UDTPM Petr Mrazek 12.00 30.00
UDTRG Radko Gudas 10.00 25.00
UDTRI Morgan Rielly 15.00 40.00
UDTRM Ryan Murphy 8.00 20.00
UDTRP Richard Panik 8.00 20.00
UDTRR Rasmus Ristolainen 12.00 30.00
UDTSC Justin Schultz 6.00 15.00
UDTSJ Seth Jones 12.00 30.00
UDTSL Scott Laughton 8.00 20.00
UDTSM Sean Monahan 15.00 40.00
UDTTH Tomas Hertl 15.00 40.00
UDTTP Tanner Pearson 8.00 20.00
UDTTR Jacob Trouba 12.00 30.00
UDTTT Tyler Toffoli 12.00 30.00
UDTTW Tom Wilson 15.00 40.00
UDTVF Viktor Fasth 8.00 20.00
UDTVN Valeri Nichushkin 15.00 40.00
UDTVT Vladimir Tarasenko 25.00 50.00
UDTWA Will Acton 6.00 15.00
UDTZG Zemgus Girgensons 10.00 25.00

2013-14 Ultimate Collection Premium Patches

PSAK Anze Kopitar 20.00 50.00
PSAN Antti Niemi 10.00 25.00
PSBB Brian Boyle 8.00 20.00
PSCC Corey Crawford 25.00 50.00
PSCH Carl Hagelin 12.00 30.00
PSCJ Curtis Joseph 12.00 30.00
PSCP Chris Pronger 10.00 25.00
PSDB Dustin Brown 12.00 30.00
PSDC David Clarkson 8.00 20.00
PSDD Drew Doughty 12.00 30.00
PSDE Devan Dubnyk 12.00 30.00
PSDH Dominik Hasek 15.00 40.00
PSDK David Krejci 12.00 30.00
PSDU Duncan Keith 12.00 30.00
PSEB Ed Belfour 12.00 30.00
PSGL Georges Laraque 8.00 20.00
PSGM Glen Murray 10.00 25.00
PSHS Henrik Sedin 12.00 30.00
PSHZ Henrik Zetterberg 15.00 40.00
PSJE Jordan Eberle 12.00 30.00
PSJQ Jonathan Quick 20.00 50.00
PSJS Jason Spezza 12.00 30.00
PSKA Nazem Kadri 12.00 30.00
PSKL Kari Lehtonen 10.00 25.00
PSKO Kyle Okposo 12.00 30.00
PSLC Logan Couture 12.00 30.00
PSMF Marc-Andre Fleury 20.00 50.00
PSMG Michael Grabner 10.00 25.00
PSML Milan Lucic 12.00 30.00
PSMN Markus Naslund 12.00 30.00
PSNB Nicklas Backstrom 20.00 50.00
PSNK Nikolai Kulemin 10.00 25.00
PSPA Patrick Sharp 12.00 30.00
PSPB Patrik Berglund 8.00 20.00
PSPF Peter Forsberg 12.00 30.00
PSPS Paul Stastny 12.00 30.00
PSPU P.A. Parenteau 8.00 20.00
PSRG Ryan Getzlaf 20.00 50.00

PSRJ Ryan Johansen 15.00 40.00
PSRM Ryan Miller 12.00 30.00
PSRN Ryan Nugent-Hopkins 12.00 30.00
PSST Martin St. Louis 12.00 30.00
PSSW Shea Weber 10.00 25.00
PSSY Steve Yzerman 25.00 60.00
PSTH Taylor Hall 25.00 60.00
PSTM Tyler Myers 10.00 25.00
PSTS Tyler Seguin 20.00 50.00
PSTV Thomas Vanek 12.00 30.00

2013-14 Ultimate Collection Premium Swatches

PSAK Anze Kopitar 10.00 25.00
PSAN Antti Niemi 5.00 12.00
PSBB Brian Boyle 4.00 10.00
PSCC Corey Crawford 8.00 20.00
PSCH Carl Hagelin 6.00 15.00
PSCJ Curtis Joseph 8.00 20.00
PSCN Cam Neely 6.00 15.00
PSDB Dustin Brown 6.00 15.00
PSDC David Clarkson 4.00 10.00
PSDD Drew Doughty 6.00 15.00
PSDE Devan Dubnyk 6.00 15.00
PSDH Dominik Hasek 8.00 20.00
PSDK David Krejci 6.00 15.00
PSDS Derek Stepan 6.00 15.00
PSDU Duncan Keith 6.00 15.00
PSEB Ed Belfour 6.00 15.00
PSGM Glen Murray 5.00 12.00
PSHZ Henrik Zetterberg 8.00 20.00
PSIK Ilya Kovalchuk 6.00 15.00
PSJE Jordan Eberle 5.00 12.00
PSJQ Jonathan Quick 10.00 25.00
PSJS Jason Spezza 6.00 15.00
PSKA Nazem Kadri 6.00 15.00
PSKL Kari Lehtonen 5.00 12.00
PSKO Kyle Okposo 6.00 15.00
PSMB Martin Brodeur 12.00 30.00
PSMF Marc-Andre Fleury 10.00 25.00
PSMG Michael Grabner 5.00 12.00
PSMH Milan Hejduk 5.00 12.00
PSML Milan Lucic 6.00 15.00
PSMN Markus Naslund 5.00 12.00
PSNB Nicklas Backstrom 10.00 25.00
PSNK Nikolai Kulemin 5.00 12.00
PSPA Patrick Sharp 6.00 15.00
PSPB Patrik Berglund 4.00 10.00
PSPU P.A. Parenteau 4.00 10.00
PSRG Ryan Getzlaf 10.00 25.00
PSRN Ryan Nugent-Hopkins 8.00 20.00
PSST Martin St. Louis 6.00 15.00
PSSU P.K. Subban 10.00 25.00
PSSW Shea Weber 5.00 12.00
PSSY Steve Yzerman 12.00 30.00
PSTH Taylor Hall 12.00 30.00
PSTM Tyler Myers 5.00 12.00
PSTS Tyler Seguin 10.00 25.00
PSTV Thomas Vanek 6.00 15.00

2013-14 Ultimate Collection Rookie Patch Autographs

EXCH EXPIRATION: 7/22/2016
65 Tyler Johnson 100.00 200.00
68 Tomas Jurco 20.00 50.00
85 Ryan Strome 15.00 40.00
116 John Gibson 75.00 135.00
121 Frederik Andersen 20.00 50.00
122 Brock Nelson 12.00 30.00
123 Chris Brown 8.00 20.00
124 Matt Nieto 10.00 25.00
125 Nicklas Jensen 10.00 25.00
126 Radko Gudas 12.00 30.00
127 Mark Arcobello 12.00 30.00
128 Drew Shore 12.00 30.00
129 Richard Panik 15.00 40.00
130 Max Reinhart 12.00 30.00
131 Scott Laughton 12.00 30.00
132 Alex Killorn 12.00 30.00
133 Jordan Schroeder 12.00 30.00
134 Will Acton 10.00 25.00
135 Jarred Tinordi 12.00 30.00
136 Jacob Trouba 20.00 50.00
138 Mathew Dumba 12.00 30.00
139 Olli Maatta 40.00 80.00
140 Tom Wilson 40.00 80.00
141 Viktor Fasth 12.00 30.00
142 Michael Bournival 12.00 30.00
143 Connor Carrick 10.00 25.00
144 Mikael Granlund 20.00 50.00
145 Danny DeKeyser 15.00 40.00
146 Filip Forsberg 50.00 100.00
147 Beau Bennett 20.00 50.00
148 Emerson Etem 15.00 40.00
149 Justin Fontaine 12.00 30.00
150 Jesper Fast 10.00 25.00
151 Tanner Pearson 15.00 40.00
152 Ryan Murphy 12.00 30.00
153 Jean-Gabriel Pageau 15.00 40.00
154 Zemgus Girgensons 25.00 60.00
155 Tyler Toffoli 40.00 80.00
156 Damien Brunner 10.00 25.00
157 Seth Jones 12.00 30.00
158 Brian Flynn 10.00 25.00
159 Charlie Coyle 12.00 30.00
160 Hampus Lindholm 20.00 50.00
161 Petr Mrazek 30.00 80.00
162 Morgan Rielly 30.00 80.00
163 Boone Jenner 15.00 40.00
164 Rasmus Ristolainen 20.00 50.00
165 Cory Conacher 8.00 20.00
166 Valeri Nichushkin 25.00 60.00
167 Ryan Murray EXCH 30.00 60.00
168 Tomas Hertl 15.00 40.00
169 Mikhail Grigorenko 15.00 40.00
170 Justin Schultz 12.00 30.00
171 Nathan MacKinnon 250.00 500.00
172 Vladimir Tarasenko 100.00 175.00
173 Sean Monahan 40.00 80.00
174 Jonathan Huberdeau 75.00 125.00
175 Brendan Gallagher 75.00 150.00
176 Nail Yakupov 75.00 135.00
177 Alex Galchenyuk 125.00 200.00
178 Aleksander Barkov 30.00 80.00
179 Elias Lindholm 20.00 50.00
180 Dougie Hamilton 25.00 60.00

2013-14 Ultimate Collection Ultimate Dual Patch Autographs

UDPAF Marc-Andre Fleury/25 20.00 40.00
UDPAH Adam Henrique/25 10.00 25.00
UDPAN Antti Niemi/25 15.00 40.00
UDPCH Carl Hagelin/25 10.00 25.00
UDPCP Corey Perry/25
UDPDB Dustin Brown/25 15.00 40.00
UDPDR Dwayne Roloson/25 8.00 20.00
UDPES Eric Staal/25 12.00 30.00
UDPGC Claude Giroux/25 25.00 50.00
UDPGL Gabriel Landeskog/25 8.00 20.00
UDPGM Glen Murray/25 8.00 20.00
UDPJH Jim Howard/25 10.00 25.00
UDPKL Kris Letang/25 35.00 60.00
UDPMH Milan Hejduk/25 8.00 20.00
UDPRK Ryan Kesler/25 10.00 25.00
UDPST Paul Stastny/25 10.00 25.00
UDPSW Shea Weber/25 8.00 20.00

2013-14 Ultimate Collection Ultimate Duos Jerseys

UDJCP L.Couture/C.Perry 6.00 15.00
UDJCR C.Crawford/T.Rask 8.00 20.00
UDJDV D.Doughty/S.Voynov 6.00 15.00
UDJHH T.Hall/A.Hemsky 6.00 15.00
UDJPS C.Price/P.Subban 10.00 25.00
UDJSK J.Spezza/E.Karlsson 12.00 30.00
UDJVR J.Voracek/M.Read 6.00 15.00

2013-14 Ultimate Collection Ultimate Duos Patches

*PATCH: .8X TO 2X JERSEYS/65
UDJCR Corey Crawford 15.00 40.00
Tuukka Rask
UDJEZ Patrik Elias 12.00 30.00
Travis Zajac

2013-14 Ultimate Collection Ultimate Jerseys

GROUP A ODDS 1:220
GROUP B ODDS 1:10
OVERALL ODDS 1:10
UJCJ Curtis Joseph B 4.00 10.00
UJCK Chris Kreider B 4.00 10.00
UJCP Carey Price B 12.00 30.00
UJDB Dustin Brown B 4.00 10.00
UJDD Drew Doughty B 4.00 10.00
UJDK Duncan Keith B 4.00 10.00
UJEB Ed Belfour B 4.00 10.00
UJJE Jordan Eberle B 4.00 10.00
UJJS Jason Spezza B 4.00 10.00
UJJV Jakub Voracek B 4.00 10.00
UJLR Luc Robitaille B 4.00 10.00
UJNK Niklas Kronwall B 3.00 8.00
UJPE Corey Perry B 4.00 10.00
UJPF Peter Forsberg A 15.00 40.00
UJPK P.K. Subban B 6.00 15.00
UJPS Paul Stastny A 6.00 15.00
UJSU Mats Sundin B 4.00 10.00
UJSV Slava Voynov B 3.00 8.00

2013-14 Ultimate Collection Ultimate Patches

*PATCH/35: 1X TO 2.5X JERSEY
UJEL Patrik Elias 10.00 25.00
UJPF Peter Forsberg 12.00 30.00
UJSK Jeff Skinner 8.00 20.00
UJSM Steve Mason 8.00 20.00

2013-14 Ultimate Collection Ultimate Quad Jerseys

UJ4TOR Jsph/Blfr/Sndn/Lndrs 15.00 40.00
UJ4BEES Brgrn/Chra/Rsk/Lcc 15.00 30.00
UJ4KINGS Dghty/Vynv/Brwn/Rchrds 15.00 30.00

2013-14 Ultimate Collection Ultimate Rookie Jerseys

*PATCH/75: .6X TO 1.5X JERSEY
URJAB Aleksander Barkov 5.00 12.00
URJAC Alex Chiasson 2.50 6.00
URJAK Alex Killorn 2.50 6.00
URJBJ Boone Jenner 2.50 6.00
URJEL Elias Lindholm 4.00 10.00
URJFA Jesper Fast 2.00 5.00
URJHL Hampus Lindholm 4.00 10.00
URJJF Justin Fontaine 2.50 6.00
URJJG John Gibson 5.00 12.00
URJJN Joakim Nordstrom 2.00 5.00
URJJT Jacob Trouba 4.00 10.00
URJLL Lucas Lessio 1.50 4.00
URJMA Mark Arcobello 2.50 6.00
URJMD Mathew Dumba 2.50 6.00
URJMN Matt Nieto 2.00 5.00
URJMR Morgan Rielly 4.00 10.00
URJNM Nathan MacKinnon 12.00 30.00
URJOM Olli Maatta 5.00 12.00
URJRM Ryan Murray 4.00 10.00
URJRR Rasmus Ristolainen 4.00 10.00
URJSJ Seth Jones 2.50 6.00
URJSM Sean Monahan 5.00 12.00
URJTH Tomas Hertl 5.00 12.00
URJVN Valeri Nichushkin 4.00 10.00
URJZG Zemgus Girgensons 5.00 12.00

2013-14 Ultimate Collection Ultimate Rookie Jerseys Duos

*PATCH/35: .8X TO 2X DUAL JSY/75
URJ2D M.Rielly/S.Jones 8.00 20.00
URJ2TB A.Killorn/T.Johnson 5.00 12.00
URJ21ST N.MacKinnon/N.Yakupov 12.00 30.00
URJ2CBJ B.Jenner/R.Murray 5.00 12.00
URJ2DAL V.Nichushkin/A.Chiasson 4.00 10.00
URJ2FLO A.Barkov/J.Huberdeau 5.00 12.00
URJ2NYR J.Miller/D.McIlrath 4.00 10.00
URJ2BUFF R.Ristolainen/N.Zadorov 6.00 15.00
URJ2WILD J.Brodin/M.Dumba 4.00 10.00

2013-14 Ultimate Collection Ultimate Rookie Jerseys Quad

URJ4RUS Ykv/Nch/Grnk/Trsn 20.00 50.00
URJ4USA Jns/Glchk/Bntt/Mllr 12.00 30.00
URJ4CAND Hmln/Rly/Schlt/Mry 12.00 30.00
URJ4CANO McKn/Glhr/Mhn/Hbr 15.00 40.00

2013-14 Ultimate Collection Ultimate Rookie Jerseys Six

URJ6EAST Bar/Hub/Gal/Rlly/Lin/Cnr 15.00 40.00
URJ6WEST McK/Mn/Yk/Jns/Hrt/Nch 40.00 80.00

2013-14 Ultimate Collection Ultimate Rookie Jerseys Trios

*PATCH/25: .6X TO 1.5X BASIC TRIO/65
URJ3C Brkv/Arcbllo/Jnnr 10.00 25.00
URJ3D Mrry/Jns/Rlly 8.00 20.00
URJ3RW Ykpv/Nchshkn/Gllghr 12.00 30.00
URJ3DEF Rstlnn/Trba/Dmba 6.00 15.00
URJ3FWD McKnnn/Hbrdau/Glchnk 15.00 40.00
URJ32013 McKnnn/Brkv/Jns 15.00 40.00
URJ3GOALS Hrtl/Mnhn/Chssn 6.00 15.00
URJ3WING Nto/Fst/Fntne 4.00 10.00

2013-14 Ultimate Collection Ultimate Rookie Patches Quad

*PATCH/15: .8X TO 2X JERSEY/50
URJ4CANO McKn/Glgh/Mnh/Hbrd 100.00 200.00

2013-14 Ultimate Collection Ultimate Rookie Signatures

GROUP A STATED ODDS 1:16
GROUP B STATED ODDS 1:8
OVERALL STATED ODDS 1:6
USRAG Alex Galchenyuk A 15.00 40.00
USRBB Beau Bennett B 4.00 10.00
USRBG Brendan Gallagher B 20.00 50.00
USRBJ Boone Jenner B 5.00 12.00
USRCO Cory Conacher B 4.00 10.00
USRDH Dougie Hamilton B 12.50 25.00
USREE Emerson Etem B 3.00 8.00
USREL Elias Lindholm B 5.00 12.00
USRFF Filip Forsberg B 12.00 30.00
USRJC Jack Campbell A 3.00 8.00
USRJH Jonathan Huberdeau A 8.00 20.00
USRJS Justin Schultz B 3.00 8.00
USRMD Mathew Dumba A 4.00 10.00
USRMR Morgan Rielly A 8.00 20.00
USRNM Nathan MacKinnon A 20.00 50.00
USRNY Nail Yakupov A 12.00 30.00
USRPM Petr Mrazek B 12.50 25.00
USRSC Jordan Schroeder B 3.00 8.00
USRSJ Seth Jones A 4.00 10.00
USRSM Sean Monahan A 6.00 15.00
USRTH Tomas Hertl B 4.00 10.00
USRTT Tyler Toffoli B 8.00 20.00
USRVF Viktor Fasth B 3.00 8.00
USRVN Valeri Nichushkin B 3.00 8.00

2013-14 Ultimate Collection Ultimate Signature Masterpiece

GROUP A ODDS 1:492
GROUP B ODDS 1:134
GROUP C ODDS 1:187
GROUP D ODDS 1:65
GROUP E ODDS 1:21
OVERALL STATED ODDS 1:15
USMAB Alexandre Burrows E 8.00 20.00
USMAG Alex Galchenyuk E 20.00 50.00
USMAP Alex Pietrangelo C 10.00 25.00
USMBC Bobby Clarke E 12.00 30.00
USMBG Brendan Gallagher E 25.00 50.00
USMBH Brett Hull B 40.00 80.00
USMCP Carey Price A 75.00 150.00
USMDH Dominik Hasek B 30.00 60.00
USMEM Evgeni Malkin B 40.00 80.00
USMJB Jamie Benn C 15.00 40.00
USMJH Jonathan Huberdeau E 12.00 30.00
USMJN James Neal E 10.00 25.00
USMJT Jonathan Toews B 40.00 80.00
USMJTA John Tavares D 20.00 50.00
USMMS Mats Sundin B 20.00 50.00
USMNM Nathan MacKinnon E 60.00 120.00
USMNY Nail Yakupov D 25.00 60.00
USMPF Peter Forsberg B 40.00 80.00
USMPK Patrick Kane A
USMPR Patrick Roy A 125.00 200.00
USMPV Pavel Bure A 75.00 150.00
USMRI Pekka Rinne C 10.00 25.00
USMRN Ryan Nugent-Hopkins D 15.00 40.00
USMSH Scott Hartnell E 8.00 20.00
USMSJ Seth Jones E 12.00 30.00
USMSW Shea Weber D 8.00 20.00
USMSY Steve Yzerman B 40.00 80.00
USMTF Theoren Fleury B 25.00 60.00
USMTH Taylor Hall D 25.00 50.00
USMTS Tyler Seguin C 25.00 50.00
USMVT Vladimir Tarasenko E 25.00 50.00
USMWG Wayne Gretzky B
USMZP Zach Parise D 15.00 30.00

2013-14 Ultimate Collection Ultimate Signatures

GROUP A ODDS 1:203
GROUP B ODDS 1:97
GROUP C ODDS 1:39
GROUP D ODDS 1:37
GROUP E ODDS 1:13
OVERALL STATED ODDS 1:5
USAI Arturs Irbe D 6.00 15.00
USAS Andrew Shaw E 5.00 12.00
USBO Bobby Orr B 60.00 100.00
USCH Cody Hodgson E 5.00 12.00
USCO Chris Osgood C 5.00 12.00
USCP Carey Price A 20.00 50.00
USDW Doug Wilson E 5.00 12.00
USGL Gabriel Landeskog E 4.00 10.00
USGR Wayne Gretzky A 175.00 300.00
USJJ Jaromir Jagr A 40.00 80.00
USJS Jeff Skinner A 20.00 40.00
USJT Jonathan Toews A 40.00 80.00
USLE Loui Eriksson E 4.00 10.00
USMK Mikko Koivu D 4.00 10.00
USOR Bobby Orr B 60.00 120.00
USPB Patrice Bergeron C 12.00 30.00
USPK Patrick Kane C 25.00 50.00
USRE Ryan Ellis E 3.00 8.00
USSA Joe Sakic A 30.00 80.00
USSK Saku Koivu D 5.00 12.00
USST Jarret Stoll D 6.00 15.00
USSW Shea Weber C 4.00 10.00
USTH Taylor Hall C 8.00 20.00
USTS Tyler Seguin C 10.00 25.00
USWG Wayne Gretzky B 150.00 250.00

2013-14 Ultimate Collection Ultimate Six Jerseys

UJ6LAK Rds/Bn/Ctr/Dgh/Vn/Kp 20.00 40.00
UJ6NET Qk/Rk/Cfd/Nm/Sch/Hd 10.00 25.00
UJ6STLDET St/Ptg/Hk/Hd/Ztr/Frn 10.00 25.00

2013-14 Ultimate Collection Ultimate Threads Autographs

EXCH EXPIRATION: 7/22/2016
UATAN Antti Niemi/99 6.00 15.00
UATAO Alexander Ovechkin/25
UATBH Brett Hull/25 20.00 40.00
UATBU Pavel Bure/25
(inserted in 2015-16 Ultimate Collection)
UATCP Carey Price/25 25.00 50.00
UATCS Cory Schneider/99 6.00 15.00
UATDH Dale Hawerchuk/99 10.00 25.00
UATEK Evander Kane/99 6.00 15.00
UATEM Evgeni Malkin/25 25.00 50.00
UATGL Gabriel Landeskog/99 8.00 20.00
UATJH Jonas Hiller/99 6.00 15.00
UATJS Jeff Skinner/99 6.00 15.00
UATJT Jonathan Toews/25 30.00 60.00
UATMD Matt Duchene/99 8.00 20.00
UATML Mario Lemieux/25 40.00 80.00
UATPB Patrice Bergeron/25
UATPE Corey Perry/25 12.00 30.00
UATSA Joe Sakic/25 25.00 50.00
UATSH Scott Hartnell/99 6.00 15.00
UATSU Mats Sundin/25
UATSY Steve Yzerman/25 30.00 60.00
UATTF Theoren Fleury/25 30.00 60.00
UATTH Taylor Hall/25 EXCH 25.00 60.00
UATTS Tyler Seguin/25 25.00 60.00
UATWG Wayne Gretzky/25 175.00 300.00

2013-14 Ultimate Collection Ultimate Trios Jerseys

U3LAK Dghty/Rchrds/Brwn 5.00 12.00
U3NET Rsk/Crwfrd/Qck 8.00 20.00
U3BEES Nly/Rsk/Mrry 5.00 12.00
U3WINGS Hwrd/Yzrmn/Zttrbrg 6.00 15.00

2013-14 Ultimate Collection Ultimate Trios Patches

U3NJD Brodeur/Elias/Schndr
U3OTT Karlsn/Spezza/Lehner
U3WEST Couture/Perry/Dghty 30.00 60.00

2014-15 Ultimate Collection

1-50 STATED PRINT RUN 299
51-75 JSY STATED PRINT RUN 99
76-125 ROOKIE AU PRINT RUN 99-299
EXCH EXPIRATION: 7/10/2017
1 Jordan Eberle 2.00 5.00
2 Jamie Benn 2.50 6.00
3 Jiri Hudler 1.50 4.00
4 Nathan MacKinnon 4.00 10.00
5 Drew Doughty 2.00 5.00
6 Jason Spezza 2.00 5.00
7 Ryan Miller 2.00 5.00
8 Jonathan Bernier 2.00 5.00
9 David Backes 2.00 5.00
10 Corey Crawford 2.50 6.00
11 Henrik Sedin 2.00 5.00
12 Aleksander Barkov 2.00 5.00
13 Joe Pavelski 2.00 5.00
14 Kyle Turris 2.00 5.00
15 Tomas Hertl 2.00 5.00
16 Martin St. Louis 2.00 5.00
17 Ryan Nugent-Hopkins 2.00 5.00
18 Jakub Voracek 2.00 5.00
19 Jason Pominville 1.50 4.00
20 Kari Lehtonen 1.50 4.00
21 Jonathan Toews 4.00 10.00
22 Alexander Ovechkin 8.00 20.00
23 Corey Perry 2.00 5.00
24 Evgeni Malkin 6.00 15.00
25 Patrick Sharp 2.00 5.00
26 Max Pacioretty 2.00 5.00
27 Pavel Datsyuk 2.50 6.00
28 Tuukka Rask 2.00 5.00
29 Henrik Zetterberg 2.50 6.00
30 Blake Wheeler 2.00 5.00
31 Shane Doan 1.50 4.00
32 Cody Hodgson 2.00 5.00
33 Sergei Bobrovsky 2.00 5.00
34 Alex Galchenyuk 3.00 8.00
35 Zdeno Chara 2.00 5.00
36 Phil Kessel 2.50 6.00
37 Shea Weber 1.50 4.00
38 Henrik Lundqvist 2.50 6.00
39 Gabriel Landeskog 1.50 4.00
40 Milan Lucic 2.00 5.00
41 Kyle Okposo 2.00 5.00
42 Erik Karlsson 4.00 10.00
43 Eric Staal 2.50 6.00
44 Jonathan Quick 3.00 8.00
45 Seth Jones 1.50 4.00
46 P.K. Subban 3.00 8.00
47 Jaromir Jagr 5.00 12.00
48 Jeff Carter 2.00 5.00
49 Roberto Luongo 2.00 5.00
50 Cory Schneider 1.50 4.00
51 Tyler Seguin JSY 6.00 15.00
52 Rick Nash JSY 4.00 10.00
53 T.J. Oshie JSY 6.00 15.00
54 Charlie Coyle JSY 3.00 8.00
55 Patrice Bergeron JSY 5.00 12.00
56 Pekka Rinne JSY 5.00 12.00
57 Patrick Kane JSY 8.00 20.00
58 Taylor Hall JSY 8.00 20.00
59 John Tavares JSY 8.00 20.00
60 Matt Duchene JSY 4.00 10.00
61 Daniel Sedin JSY 4.00 10.00
62 Claude Giroux JSY 4.00 10.00
63 Steven Stamkos JSY 8.00 20.00
64 Alexander Semin JSY 4.00 10.00
65 Zach Parise JSY 4.00 10.00
66 Nicklas Backstrom JSY 6.00 15.00
67 Sean Monahan JSY 4.00 10.00
68 Sidney Crosby JSY 15.00 40.00
69 Vladimir Tarasenko JSY 6.00 15.00
70 Jonathan Huberdeau JSY 4.00 10.00
71 Zemgus Girgensons JSY 4.00 10.00
72 Ryan Kesler JSY 4.00 10.00
73 Ryan Getzlaf JSY 6.00 15.00
74 Carey Price JSY 12.00 30.00
75 Anze Kopitar JSY 6.00 15.00
76 Bogdan Yakimov AU/299 RC 5.00 12.00
77 Patrick Brown AU/299 RC 4.00 10.00
78 P-E Bellemare AU/299 RC 4.00 10.00
79 Sven Andrighetto AU/299 RC 5.00 12.00
80 Christian Folin AU/299 RC 4.00 10.00
81 John Klingberg AU/299 RC 12.00 30.00
82 Justin Hodgman AU/299 RC 3.00 8.00
83 Rocco Grimaldi AU/299 RC 4.00 10.00
84 Josh Jooris AU/299 RC 4.00 10.00
85 B.Goodrow AU/299 RC 4.00 10.00
86 Joe Morrow AU/299 RC 5.00 12.00
87 David Pastrnak AU/99 RC 60.00 150.00
88 D.Everberg AU/299 RC 4.00 10.00
89 M.Granlund AU/299 RC 6.00 15.00
90 A.Vasilevskiy AU/299 RC 12.00 30.00
91 Brandon Kozun AU/299 RC 3.00 8.00
92 Seth Helgeson AU/299 RC 3.00 8.00
93 Brett Ritchie AU/299 RC 4.00 10.00
94 C.McKenzie AU/299 RC 3.00 8.00
95 Hammond AU/99 RC EXCH 15.00 40.00
96 Kevin Hayes AU/299 RC 12.00 30.00
97 Mirco Mueller AU/299 RC 4.00 10.00
98 T.van Riemsdyk AU/299 RC 6.00 15.00
99 Victor Rask AU/299 RC 4.00 10.00
100 V.Namestnikov AU/299 RC 6.00 15.00
101 W.Karlsson AU/299 RC 15.00 40.00
102 Chris Tierney AU/299 RC 4.00 10.00
103 Curtis Lazar AU/299 RC 5.00 12.00
104 Adam Lowry AU/299 RC 4.00 10.00
105 Ryan Sproul AU/299 RC 4.00 10.00
106 Marko Dano AU/299 RC 4.00 10.00
107 Stuart Percy AU/299 RC 4.00 10.00
108 Darnell Nurse AU/299 RC 12.00 30.00
109 Griffin Reinhart AU/299 RC 5.00 12.00
110 S.Gostisbehere AU/299 RC 15.00 40.00
111 D.Severson AU/299 RC 4.00 10.00
112 Jiri Sekac AU/99 RC 10.00 25.00
113 Seth Griffith AU/299 RC 6.00 15.00
114 A.Wennberg AU/299 RC 8.00 20.00
115 A.Duclair AU/99 RC EXCH 25.00 50.00
116 T.Teravainen AU/99 RC 15.00 40.00
117 Jori Lehtera AU/299 RC 5.00 12.00
118 E.Kuznetsov AU/299 RC 15.00 40.00
119 Bo Horvat AU/99 RC 30.00 80.00
120 A.Burakovsky AU/299 RC 6.00 15.00
121 J.Gaudreau AU/99 RC 80.00 150.00
122 Leon Draisaitl AU/99 RC 40.00 100.00
123 Sam Reinhart AU/99 RC 30.00 80.00
124 Aaron Ekblad AU/99 RC 30.00 80.00
125 Jonathan Drouin AU/99 RC 60.00 120.00

2014-15 Ultimate Collection Blue Spectrum

STATED PRINT RUN 25 SER.#'d SETS
55 Patrice Bergeron STK 12.00 30.00
57 Patrick Kane STK 20.00 50.00
59 John Tavares GLV 20.00 50.00
60 Matt Duchene STK 10.00 25.00
61 Daniel Sedin STK 10.00 25.00
62 Claude Giroux STK 10.00 25.00
64 Alexander Semin STK 10.00 25.00
66 Nicklas Backstrom STK 15.00 40.00
68 Sidney Crosby STK 40.00 100.00
70 Jonathan Huberdeau STK 10.00 25.00
73 Ryan Getzlaf STK 15.00 40.00
75 Anze Kopitar STK 15.00 40.00

2014-15 Ultimate Collection Gold Spectrum

*51-75 PATCH/35: .8X TO 2X BASIC JSY/99
66 Nicklas Backstrom PATCH 12.00 30.00

2014-15 Ultimate Collection Silver Spectrum

76 Bogdan Yakimov PATCH AU 12.00 30.00
77 Patrick Brown PATCH AU 12.00 30.00
78 P-E Bellemare PATCH AU 12.00 30.00
79 Sven Andrighetto PATCH AU 15.00 40.00
81 John Klingberg PATCH AU 100.00 175.00
82 Justin Hodgman PATCH AU 10.00 25.00
83 Rocco Grimaldi PATCH AU 12.00 30.00
85 Barclay Goodrow PATCH AU 12.00 30.00
86 Joe Morrow PATCH AU 15.00 40.00
87 David Pastrnak PATCH AU 75.00 150.00
90 Andrei Vasilevskiy PATCH AU 25.00 60.00
91 Brandon Kozun PATCH AU 10.00 25.00
92 Seth Helgeson PATCH AU 10.00 25.00
93 Brett Ritchie PATCH AU 12.00 30.00
94 Curtis McKenzie PATCH AU 10.00 25.00
95 A.Hmmond PATCH AU 40.00 80.00
97 Mirco Mueller PATCH AU 12.00 30.00
101 William Karlsson PATCH AU 50.00 120.00
102 Chris Tierney PATCH AU 12.00 30.00
103 Curtis Lazar PATCH AU 15.00 40.00
104 Adam Lowry PATCH AU 12.00 30.00
105 Ryan Sproul PATCH AU 15.00 40.00
106 Marko Dano PATCH AU 12.00 30.00
107 Stuart Percy PATCH AU 12.00 30.00
108 Darnell Nurse PATCH AU 40.00 100.00
109 Griffin Reinhart PATCH AU 15.00 40.00
110 S.Gostisbehere PATCH AU 75.00 125.00
111 Damon Severson PATCH AU 12.00 30.00
112 Jiri Sekac PATCH AU 12.00 30.00
114 Alexander Wennberg PATCH AU 25.00 60.00
116 T.Teravainen PATCH AU 75.00 150.00
117 Jori Lehtera PATCH AU 15.00 40.00
118 Evgeny Kuznetsov PATCH AU 75.00 125.00
119 Bo Horvat PATCH AU 40.00 80.00
120 Andre Burakovsky PATCH AU 20.00 50.00
121 J.Gaudreau PATCH AU 125.00 250.00
122 Leon Draisaitl PATCH AU 50.00 100.00
123 Sam Reinhart PATCH AU 50.00 100.00
124 Aaron Ekblad PATCH AU 60.00 120.00
125 Jonathan Drouin PATCH AU 60.00 120.00

2014-15 Ultimate Collection '04-05 Retro

1 Phil Kessel/150 2.00 5.00
2 Joe Pavelski/150 1.50 4.00
3 Chris Kunitz/150 1.50 4.00
4 Jonathan Toews/150 3.00 8.00
5 Sidney Crosby/150 6.00 15.00
6 Nathan MacKinnon/150 3.00 8.00
7 Pavel Datsyuk/150 2.00 5.00
8 Tuukka Rask/150 1.50 4.00
9 Ryan Getzlaf/150 2.50 6.00
10 Matt Duchene/150 1.50 4.00
11 Jaromir Jagr/150 4.00 10.00
12 Patrice Bergeron/150 2.00 5.00
13 Duncan Keith/150 1.50 4.00
14 Henrik Lundqvist/150 2.00 5.00
15 Joe Thornton/150 1.50 4.00
16 Claude Giroux/150 1.50 4.00
17 Patrick Kane/150 3.00 8.00
18 Steven Stamkos/150 3.00 8.00
19 Sergei Bobrovsky/150 1.50 4.00
20 Evgeni Malkin/150 5.00 12.00
21 Taylor Hall/150 3.00 8.00
22 Jarome Iginla/150 1.50 4.00
23 John Tavares/150 3.00 8.00
24 Carey Price/150 5.00 12.00
25 Anze Kopitar/150 2.50 6.00
26 Shea Weber/150 1.25 3.00
27 Max Pacioretty/150 1.50 4.00
28 Martin St. Louis/150 1.50 4.00
29 P.K. Subban/150 2.50 6.00
30 Jason Spezza/150 1.50 4.00
31 Henrik Zetterberg/150 2.00 5.00
32 Jamie Benn/150 2.00 5.00
33 Drew Doughty/150 1.50 4.00
34 Alexander Ovechkin/150 6.00 15.00
35 Tyler Seguin/150 2.50 6.00
36 Mario Lemieux/199 6.00 15.00
37 Pelle Lindbergh/199 2.00 5.00
38 Wayne Gretzky/199 12.50 25.00
39 Terry Sawchuk/199 2.00 5.00
40 Bobby Orr/199 6.00 15.00
41 Curtis Lazar/299 1.25 3.00
42 Anthony Duclair/299 1.50 4.00
43 Evgeny Kuznetsov/299 4.00 10.00
44 Johnny Gaudreau/299 3.00 8.00
45 Bo Horvat/299 3.00 8.00
46 Andre Burakovsky/299 1.50 4.00
47 Aaron Ekblad/299 4.00 10.00
48 Leon Draisaitl/299 5.00 12.00
49 Sam Reinhart/299 3.00 8.00
50 Jonathan Drouin/299 2.50 6.00

2014-15 Ultimate Collection '04-05 Retro Ultimate Memorabilia

STATED PRINT RUN 99 SER.#'d SETS
UGJDS Daniel Sedin 4.00 10.00
UGJJB Jonathan Bernier 4.00 10.00
UGJJE Jordan Eberle 4.00 10.00
UGJJS Jason Spezza 4.00 10.00
UGJJV James van Riemsdyk 4.00 10.00
UGJPR Pekka Rinne 5.00 12.00
UGJPS P.K. Subban 6.00 15.00
UGJRO Patrick Roy 10.00 25.00
UGJSH Patrick Sharp 4.00 10.00
UGJTR Tuukka Rask 4.00 10.00
UGJTS Teemu Selanne 8.00 20.00

2014-15 Ultimate Collection '04-05 Retro Ultimate Memorabilia Gold Spectrum

*GOLD SPECT/25: 1X TO 2.5X BASIC JSY/99
UGJPL Pelle Lindbergh 10.00 25.00

2014-15 Ultimate Collection '04-05 Retro Ultimate Signatures

GROUP A STATED ODDS 1:50
GROUP B STATED ODDS 1:30
GROUP C STATED ODDS 1:10
GROUP D STATED ODDS 1:8
OVERALL STATED ODDS 1:3
RUSAB Aleksander Barkov C 4.00 10.00
RUSAE Aaron Ekblad B 15.00 30.00
RUSAI Arturs Irbe B 10.00 25.00
RUSAO Alexander Ovechkin A 50.00 100.00
RUSAW Alexander Wennberg D 8.00 20.00
RUSBO Bobby Orr A 75.00 150.00
RUSBR Brett Ritchie D 4.00 10.00
RUSBU Andre Burakovsky C 6.00 15.00
RUSCL Curtis Lazar C 5.00 12.00
RUSCP Carey Price B 25.00 50.00
RUSDS Damon Severson D 4.00 10.00
RUSGJ Johnny Gaudreau C 25.00 50.00
RUSGN Gustav Nyquist C 3.00 8.00
RUSJD Jonathan Drouin C 10.00 25.00
RUSJG John Gibson D 6.00 15.00
RUSJI Jarome Iginla B 8.00 20.00
RUSJP Joe Pavelski D 4.00 10.00
RUSJT Jonathan Toews A
(inserted in 2015-16 Ultimate Collection)
RUSJV John Vanbiesbrouck D 8.00 20.00
RUSLD Leon Draisaitl C 20.00 50.00
RUSMB Martin Brodeur A
RUSMF Marc-Andre Fleury B 15.00 30.00
RUSML Mario Lemieux A 60.00 120.00
RUSMM Mark Messier A 20.00 40.00
RUSMP Max Pacioretty C 6.00 15.00
RUSPD Pavel Datsyuk B 15.00 30.00
RUSPP Pete Peeters C
(inserted in 2015-16 Ultimate Collection)
RUSPR Patrick Roy A 50.00 100.00
RUSRN Rick Nash B
(inserted in 2015-16 Ultimate Collection)
RUSSB Sergei Bobrovsky D
(inserted in 2015-16 Ultimate Collection)
RUSSC Sidney Crosby A
RUSSM Sean Monahan C 6.00 15.00
RUSSR Sam Reinhart D 12.00 30.00
RUSTA John Tavares C 10.00 25.00
RUSTS Tyler Seguin A
(inserted in 2015-16 Ultimate Collection)
RUSTT Teuvo Teravainen D 15.00 30.00
RUSVD Vincent Damphousse C 6.00 15.00
RUSWG Wayne Gretzky C 150.00 250.00

2014-15 Ultimate Collection Debut Threads Patches

DTAB Andre Burakovsky 6.00 15.00
DTAE Aaron Ekblad 15.00 40.00
DTAL Adam Lowry 4.00 10.00
DTAV Andrei Vasilevskiy 12.00 30.00
DTAW Alexander Wennberg 8.00 20.00
DTBA Barclay Goodrow 4.00 10.00
DTBH Bo Horvat 15.00 40.00
DTBK Brandon Kozun 3.00 8.00
DTBR Brett Ritchie 4.00 10.00
DTCL Curtis Lazar 5.00 12.00
DTCM Curtis McKenzie 3.00 8.00
DTCT Chris Tierney 4.00 10.00
DTDN Darnell Nurse 12.00 30.00
DTDP Derrick Pouliot 5.00 12.00
DTDS Damon Severson 4.00 10.00
DTEK Evgeny Kuznetsov 15.00 40.00
DTGO Shayne Gostisbehere 15.00 40.00
DTGR Griffin Reinhart 5.00 12.00
DTHE Seth Helgeson 3.00 8.00
DTHO Justin Hodgman 3.00 8.00
DTJB Jordan Binnington 4.00 10.00
DTJD Jonathan Drouin 10.00 25.00
DTJG Johnny Gaudreau 12.00 30.00
DTJK John Klingberg 12.00 30.00
DTJL Jori Lehtera 5.00 12.00
DTKR Kerby Rychel 3.00 8.00
DTLD Leon Draisaitl 20.00 50.00
DTMD Marko Dano 4.00 10.00
DTMM Mirco Mueller 4.00 10.00
DTMO Joe Morrow 5.00 12.00
DTPD Phillip Danault 4.00 10.00
DTPE Pierre-Edouard Bellemare 4.00 10.00
DTRG Rocco Grimaldi 4.00 10.00
DTRI Tobias Rieder 4.00 10.00
DTRZ Rob Zepp 6.00 15.00
DTSA Sven Andrighetto 5.00 12.00
DTSG Seth Griffith 5.00 12.00
DTSM Colin Smith 4.00 10.00
DTSP Stuart Percy 4.00 10.00
DTSR Sam Reinhart 12.00 30.00
DTTP Teemu Pulkkinen 5.00 12.00
DTTT Teuvo Teravainen 6.00 15.00
DTTV Trevor van Riemsdyk 6.00 15.00
DTVN Vladislav Namestnikov 6.00 15.00
DTVR Victor Rask 4.00 10.00

2014-15 Ultimate Collection Memorable Materials Dual Swatch Combos

STATED PRINT RUN 25 SER.#'d SETS
MM2AK C.Anderson/E.Karlsson 15.00 40.00
MM2BL M.Lucic/P.Bergeron 15.00 40.00
MM2BN J.Benn/V.Nichushkin 10.00 25.00
MM2BT D.Backes/Tarasenko
MM2CT J.Toews/C.Crawford 20.00 50.00
MM2DR J.Drouin/S.Reinhart 12.00 30.00
MM2EB Kuznetsov/Burakovsky 25.00 60.00
MM2EN Eberle/Nugent-Hopkins 10.00 25.00
MM2ER A.Ekblad/S.Reinhart 12.00 30.00
MM2GC C.Coyle/M.Granlund 6.00 15.00
MM2HB J.Huberdeau/A.Barkov 12.00 30.00
MM2HD S.Hartnell/B.Dubinsky 8.00 20.00
MM2IL J.Iginla/G.Landeskog 8.00 20.00
MM2JT J.Carter/T.Toffoli 8.00 20.00
MM2KG R.Getzlaf/R.Kesler 12.00 30.00
MM2KM E.Malkin/C.Kunitz 25.00 60.00
MM2KV J.van Rmsdyk/Kessel 10.00 25.00
MM2MH C.Hodgson/M.Moulson 8.00 20.00
MM2OB Ovechkin/N.Backstrom 30.00 80.00
MM2PC L.Couture/J.Pavelski 8.00 20.00
MM2PS M.Pacioretty/P.Subban 12.00 30.00
MM2RD L.Draisaitl/S.Reinhart 12.00 30.00
MM2SC R.Strome/C.Coyle 6.00 15.00
MM2SH S.Stamkos/V.Hedman 15.00 40.00
MM2SM R.Miller/H.Sedin 8.00 20.00
MM2SN R.Nash/M.St. Louis 10.00 25.00
MM2SS J.Skinner/A.Semin 8.00 20.00
MM2VG C.Giroux/J.Voracek 15.00 40.00
MM2WJ S.Weber/S.Jones 10.00 25.00
MM2WS B.Wheeler/M.Scheifele 10.00 25.00

2014-15 Ultimate Collection Memorable Materials Triple Swatch Combos

MM3BF P.Forsberg/R.Blake
MM3CB Z.Chara/R.Bourque 30.00 60.00
MM3GK A.Kopitar/M.Gaborik
MM3KB P.Kessel/J.Bernier
MM3MO A.Oates/G.Murray
MM3MT MacKinnon/Tarasenko 20.00 50.00
MM3RS P.Roy/J.Sakic
MM3SD J.Drouin/S.Stamkos
MM3SG W.Gretzky/J.Sakic

2014-15 Ultimate Collection Obsidian Script

GROUP A ODDS 1:220
GROUP B ODDS 1:115
GROUP D ODDS 1:19
GROUP E ODDS 1:14
GROUP F ODDS 1:9
OVERAL OBSIDIAN ODDS 1:3
OSAG Alex Galchenyuk F 10.00 25
OSEK Evgeny Kuznetsov E 15.00 30
OSGN Gustav Nyquist F 6.00 15
OSJG Johnny Gaudreau F 30.00 60
OSLD Leon Draisaitl D 40.00 100
OSMB Matt Beleskey F 4.00 10
OSMG Mike Gartner F 6.00 15
OSMS Mats Sundin A
(inserted in 2015-16 Ultimate Collection)
OSOV Alexander Ovechkin A 40.00 80
OSRF Ron Francis B 15.00 40
OSRK Ryan Kesler E 8.00 20
OSSB Sergei Bobrovsky B
(inserted in 2015-16 Ultimate Collection)

2014-15 Ultimate Collection Obsidian Script Inscribed

GROUP A ODDS 1:220
GROUP B ODDS 1:115
GROUP C ODDS 1:55
GROUP D ODDS 1:19
GROUP E ODDS 1:14
GROUP F ODDS 1:9
OVERAL OBSIDIAN ODDS 1:3
OSAE Aaron Ekblad D 25.00 60
OSAO Adam Oates D 10.00 25
OSAW Alexander Wennberg F 12.00 30
OSBH Brett Hull B 30.00 60
OSCC Chris Chelios C 20.00 40
OSCJ Curtis Joseph D 15.00 30
OSCL Curtis Lazar F 10.00 25
OSDA Damon Severson E 6.00 15
OSJD Jonathan Drouin D 12.00 30
OSJJ Jaromir Jagr A
OSMF Marc-Andre Fleury C 20.00 40
OSMM Mark Messier A
OSMR Morgan Rielly E 12.00 30
OSPM Patrick Marleau C 10.00 25
OSSG Shayne Gostisbehere E 25.00 60
OSSR Sam Reinhart D 30.00 60
OSSY Steve Yzerman A 50.00 100
OSTE Teuvo Teravainen E 30.00 60
OSWG Wayne Gretzky B 175.00 300

2014-15 Ultimate Collection Obsidian Script Materials

STATED PRINT RUN 25 SER.#'d SETS
OSAE Aaron Ekblad 75.00 135
OSAG Alex Galchenyuk 40.00 80
OSAO Adam Oates 25.00 60
OSAV Andrei Vasilevskiy 25.00 60
OSAW Alexander Wennberg 30.00 80
OSBH Brett Hull 40.00 80
OSCC Chris Chelios 20.00 50
OSCJ Curtis Joseph 25.00 60
OSCL Curtis Lazar 15.00 40
OSDA Damon Severson 15.00 40
OSDP Derrick Pouliot 20.00 50
OSEK Evgeny Kuznetsov 50.00 100
OSGN Gustav Nyquist 20.00 50
OSJD Jonathan Drouin 50.00 100
OSJG Johnny Gaudreau 10.00 175
OSJJ Jaromir Jagr 50.00 100
OSJL Jori Lehtera 20.00 50
OSLD Leon Draisaitl 25.00 60
OSMF Marc-Andre Fleury
OSMM Mark Messier 25.00 60
OSMR Morgan Rielly 25.00 60
OSMS Mats Sundin
(inserted in 2015-16 Ultimate Collection)
OSOV Alexander Ovechkin 100.00 175
OSRF Ron Francis 30.00 80
OSSB Sergei Bobrovsky
(inserted in 2015-16 Ultimate Collection)
OSSG Shayne Gostisbehere 60.00 150
OSSR Sam Reinhart 40.00 80
OSSY Steve Yzerman 125.00 200
OSTE Teuvo Teravainen 100.00 175
OSTS Tyler Seguin
(inserted in 2015-16 Ultimate Collection)
OSWG Wayne Gretzky 150.00 250

2014-15 Ultimate Collection Rare Materials

*BLUE/10: 1X TO 2.5X BASIC JSY/99
*GOLD/15: 1X TO 2.5X BASIC JSY/99
RMAS Alexander Semin 4.00 10
RMBB Ben Bishop 4.00 10
RMBW Blake Wheeler 4.00 10
RMCA Craig Anderson 4.00 10
RMCS Cory Schneider 3.00 8
RMDK David Krejci 4.00 10
RMEK Evander Kane 4.00 10
RMEM Evgeni Malkin 12.00 30
RMHI Jonas Hiller 3.00 8
RMHL Henrik Lundqvist 5.00 12
RMJG John Gibson 5.00 12
RMJH Jonathan Huberdeau 4.00 10
RMJJ Jaromir Jagr 10.00 25
RMJS Jason Spezza 4.00 10
RMJT Jonathan Toews 8.00 20
RMMM Matt Moulson 3.00 8
RMMS Mike Smith 4.00 10
RMNK Niklas Kronwall 3.00 8
RMNY Nail Yakupov 3.00 8
RMPS Paul Stastny 4.00 10
RMRN Rick Nash 4.00 10
RMSB Sergei Bobrovsky 4.00 10
RMSC Sean Couturier 4.00 10
RMSS Steven Stamkos 8.00 20
RMTT Tyler Toffoli 4.00 10

2014-15 Ultimate Collection Ultimate Foursomes

STATED ODDS 1:10
U4CAR Stl/Lndhlm/Sknnr/Smn 8.00 20
U4DEF Wbr/Kth/Dghty/Sbbn 10.00 25
U4NET Qck/Prce/Rsk/Bbrvsky 20.00 50
U4NYR Nsh/Krdr/St.Ls/Zccrllo 8.00 20
U4SOPH McKnn/Hrtl/Mnhn/Plt 12.00 30
U4WILD Prse/Cyle/Pmnvlle/Grnlnd 6.00 15
U4WINGS Zttrbrg/Dtsyk/Jrco/Nyqst 8.00 20

2014-15 Ultimate Collection Ultimate Gear

GROUP A ODDS 1:36
GROUP B ODDS 1:4
OVERALL STATED ODDS 1:3
*BLUE/15: .8X TO 2X JSY GROUP A
*BLUE/15: 1.2X TO 3X JSY GROUP B
*GOLD/25: .6X TO 1.5X JSY GROUP A
*GOLD/25: 1X TO 2.5X JSY GROUP B
UGAE Aaron Ekblad B 6.00 1
UGBE Jamie Benn B 5.00 1
UGBH Brett Hull A 6.00 1
UGBR Bobby Ryan B 4.00 1
UGCJ Curtis Joseph A 6.00 1
UGCL Curtis Lazar A 6.00 1
UGDB David Backes B 4.00 1
UGDK Duncan Keith B 4.00 1
UGDN Darnell Nurse B 8.00 2
UGDS Daniel Sedin B 4.00 1

GHL Henrik Lundqvist B 5.00 12.00
JB Jonathan Bernier B 4.00 10.00
JD Jonathan Drouin B 6.00 15.00
JN James Neal B 4.00 10.00
JS Jeff Skinner B 4.00 10.00
LD Leon Draisaitl B 12.00 30.00
MD Marcel Dionne A 8.00 20.00
MG Marian Gaborik B 4.00 10.00
ML Milan Lucic B 4.00 10.00
MS Martin St. Louis B 4.00 10.00
PS P.K. Subban B 6.00 15.00
VT Vladimir Tarasenko B 6.00 15.00

2014-15 Ultimate Collection Ultimate Signature Masterpieces

ROUP A ODDS 1:60
ROUP B ODDS 1:25
ROUP C ODDS 1:6
VERALL STATED ODDS 1:4
MAE Aaron Ekblad C 25.00 50.00
MAI Arturs Irbe A 12.00 30.00
MBR Brett Hull A 15.00 40.00
MBS Brandon Saad C
(inserted in 2015-16 Ultimate Collection)
MCJ Curtis Joseph C 10.00 25.00
MDB Dustin Brown C 6.00 15.00
MDS Dave Schultz B 12.00 30.00
MEK Evgeny Kuznetsov C 12.00 30.00
MGR Wayne Gretzky A 150.00 250.00
MHE Tomas Hertl C 8.00 20.00
MJD Jonathan Drouin C 20.00 50.00
MJG Johnny Gaudreau C 25.00 50.00
MLD Leon Draisaitl C 40.00 100.00
MMB Mike Bossy B 25.00 50.00
MMF Marc-Andre Fleury B 30.00 60.00
MMM Mark Messier A 15.00 30.00
MMP Max Pacioretty C 8.00 20.00
MNA Rick Nash B
(inserted in 2015-16 Ultimate Collection)
MRS Ryan Strome C
(inserted in 2015-16 Ultimate Collection)
MSA Joe Sakic A
(inserted in 2015-16 Ultimate Collection)
MSR Sam Reinhart B 25.00 60.00
MST Martin St. Louis B
(inserted in 2015-16 Ultimate Collection)
MTB Tom Barrasso B 12.00 30.00
MTT Teuvo Teravainen C 15.00 30.00

2014-15 Ultimate Collection Ultimate Signature Patches

PBL Rob Blake/25 25.00 50.00
PBR Dustin Brown/25 10.00 25.00
PCS Cory Schneider/25 10.00 25.00
PDB David Backes/25 12.00 30.00
PDK David Krejci/25 12.00 30.00
PDW Doug Weight/25 12.00 30.00
PGU Bill Guerin/25 12.00 30.00
PJB Jonathan Bernier/25 12.00 30.00
PJI Jarome Iginla/25 25.00 50.00
PLC Logan Couture/25
(inserted in 2015-16 Ultimate Collection)
PMG Marian Gaborik/25 40.00 80.00
PMR Morgan Rielly/25 12.00 30.00
PMS Mats Sundin/25
(inserted in 2015-16 Ultimate Collection)
PNA Rick Nash/25
(inserted in 2015-16 Ultimate Collection)
PTH Tomas Hertl/25 30.00 60.00
PVD Vincent Damphousse/25 30.00 60.00
PZP Zach Parise/25 12.00 30.00

2015-16 Ultimate Collection

Wayne Gretzky JSY/99 30.00 80.00
Taylor Hall JSY/199 10.00 25.00
Anthony Duclair JSY/199 4.00 10.00
Jakub Voracek JSY/199 5.00 12.00
Carey Price JSY/199 15.00 40.00
Jarome Iginla JSY/199 5.00 12.00
Jaromir Jagr JSY/199 12.00 30.00
Anze Kopitar JSY/199 8.00 20.00
John Tavares JSY/199 10.00 25.00
Joe Sakic JSY/99 15.00 40.00
Evgeni Malkin JSY/199 15.00 40.00
Jori Lehtera JSY/199 4.00 10.00
James van Riemsdyk JSY/199 5.00 12.00
P.K. Subban JSY/199 8.00 20.00
Henrik Lundqvist JSY/199 6.00 15.00
Henrik Zetterberg JSY/199 6.00 15.00
Joe Pavelski JSY/199 5.00 12.00
David Krejci JSY/199 4.00 10.00
Steven Stamkos JSY/199 10.00 25.00
Mark Messier JSY/99 15.00 40.00
Rick Nash JSY/199 5.00 12.00
Nathan MacKinnon JSY/199 10.00 25.00
Andrew Ladd JSY/199 5.00 12.00
Shea Weber JSY/199 4.00 10.00
Ryan Miller JSY/199 5.00 12.00
Corey Perry JSY/199 5.00 12.00
Jonathan Toews JSY/199 10.00 25.00
Jiri Hudler JSY/199 4.00 10.00
Jamie Benn JSY/199 6.00 15.00
Patrick Roy JSY/99 25.00 60.00
Sidney Crosby JSY/199 20.00 50.00
Kyle Okposo JSY/199 5.00 12.00
Patrick Marleau JSY/199 5.00 12.00
Daniel Sedin JSY/199 5.00 12.00
Sergei Bobrovsky JSY/199 5.00 12.00
Zach Parise JSY/199 5.00 12.00
Erik Karlsson JSY/199 10.00 25.00
Pekka Rinne JSY/199 6.00 15.00
Corey Crawford JSY/199 6.00 15.00
Ben Bishop JSY/199 5.00 12.00
Eric Staal JSY/199 6.00 15.00
Johnny Gaudreau JSY/199 8.00 20.00
Alexander Ovechkin JSY/199 20.00 50.00
Mike Hoffman JSY/199 4.00 10.00
Cory Schneider JSY/199 4.00 10.00
Tyler Seguin JSY/199 8.00 20.00
Nail Yakupov JSY/199 4.00 10.00
Pavel Datsyuk JSY/199 6.00 15.00
Matt Moulson JSY/199 4.00 10.00
Mike Bossy JSY/99 10.00 25.00
Brett Pesce AU/299 RC 6.00 15.00
Dylan DeMelo AU/299 RC 6.00 15.00
Anton Slepyshev AU/299 RC 6.00 15.00
Vincent Hinostroza AU/299 RC 5.00 12.00
Henrik Samuelsson AU/299 RC 6.00 15.00
Jean-Francois Berube AU/299 RC 6.00 15.00
Colin Miller AU/299 RC 6.00 15.00
Mike McCarron AU/299 RC 10.00 25.00
Mark Alt AU/299 RC 5.00 12.00
Joonas Donskoi AU/299 RC 8.00 20.00
Frank Vatrano AU/299 RC 15.00 40.00
Mackenzie Skapski AU/299 RC 8.00 20.00
Anthony Stolarz AU/299 RC 8.00 20.00
Derek Forbort AU/299 RC 6.00 15.00
Mattias Janmark AU/299 RC 8.00 20.00
Brock McGinn AU/299 RC 8.00 20.00
Viktor Arvidsson AU/299 RC 10.00 25.00
Josh Anderson AU/299 RC 8.00 20.00
69 Chandler Stephenson AU/299 RC 8.00 20.00
70 Matt Puempel AU/299 RC 6.00 15.00
71 Andreas Athanasiou AU/299 RC 20.00 50.00
72 Garret Sparks AU/299 RC 10.00 25.00
73 Antoine Bibeau AU/299 RC 8.00 20.00
74 Linus Ullmark AU/299 RC 10.00 25.00
75 Brendan Gaunce AU/299 RC 10.00 25.00
76 David Musil AU/299 RC 6.00 15.00
77 Brett Kulak AU/299 RC 6.00 15.00
78 Shane Prince AU/299 RC 6.00 15.00
79 Chris Wideman AU/299 RC 8.00 20.00
80 Sergei Plotnikov AU/299 RC 6.00 15.00
81 Devin Shore AU/299 RC 8.00 20.00
82 Ben Hutton AU/299 RC 8.00 20.00
83 Colton Parayko AU/299 RC 10.00 25.00
84 Mike Condon AU/299 RC 8.00 20.00
85 Oscar Lindberg AU/299 RC 8.00 20.00
86 Keegan Lowe AU/299 RC 8.00 20.00
87 Brady Skjei AU/299 RC 6.00 15.00
88 Kyle Baun AU/299 RC 8.00 20.00
89 Chris Driedger AU/299 RC 6.00 15.00
90 Radek Faksa AU/299 RC 8.00 20.00
91 Joel Edmundson AU/299 RC 6.00 15.00
92 Stanislav Galiev AU/299 RC 8.00 20.00
93 Slater Koekkoek AU/299 RC 6.00 15.00
94 Matt O'Connor AU/299 RC 6.00 15.00
95 Ronalds Kenins AU/299 RC 8.00 20.00
96 Charles Hudon AU/299 RC 8.00 20.00
97 Andrew Copp AU/299 RC 8.00 20.00
98 Nick Cousins AU/299 RC 8.00 20.00
99 Connor Brickley AU/299 RC 6.00 15.00
100 Ryan Hartman AU/299 RC 10.00 25.00
101 Nicolas Petan AU/299 RC 8.00 20.00
102 Matt Murray AU/99 RC 80.00 200.00
103 Kevin Fiala AU/299 RC 8.00 20.00
104 Emile Poirier AU/299 RC 8.00 20.00
105 Zachary Fucale AU/299 RC 8.00 20.00
106 Daniel Sprong AU/299 RC 15.00 40.00
107 Mikko Rantanen AU/299 RC 15.00 40.00
108 Nikolay Goldobin AU/299 RC 8.00 20.00
109 Connor McDavid AU/99 RC 500.00 1250.00
110 Sam Bennett AU/99 RC 30.00 80.00
111 Robby Fabbri AU/99 RC 25.00 60.00
112 Jared McCann AU/99 RC 10.00 25.00
113 Dylan Larkin AU/99 RC 50.00 125.00
114 Jake Virtanen AU/99 RC 20.00 50.00
115 Noah Hanifin AU/99 RC 15.00 40.00
116 Jacob de la Rose AU/99 RC 10.00 25.00
117 Artemi Panarin AU/99 RC 50.00 125.00
118 Nikolaj Ehlers AU/99 RC 40.00 100.00
119 Max Domi AU/99 RC 30.00 80.00
120 Jack Eichel/99 RC 60.00 150.00

2015-16 Ultimate Collection Gold

109 Connor McDavid PATCH 80.00 150.00

2015-16 Ultimate Collection '05-06 Ultimate Rookies

05AA Andreas Athanasiou AU/275 8.00 20.00
05BM Brock McGinn AU/275 3.00 8.00
05BS Brady Skjei AU/275 2.50 6.00
05CH Charles Hudon AU/275 3.00 8.00
05CM Connor McDavid AU/175 350.00 650.00
05CP Colton Parayko AU/275 4.00 10.00
05CS Chandler Stephenson AU/275 3.00 8.00
05DA Daniel Sprong AU/275 6.00 15.00
05DL Dylan Larkin AU/175 25.00 60.00
05EP Emile Poirier AU/275 3.00 8.00
05FA Radek Faksa AU/275 3.00 8.00
05FV Frank Vatrano AU/275 6.00 15.00
05HS Henrik Samuelsson AU/275 2.50 6.00
05JE Jack Eichel/175 12.00 30.00
05JM Jared McCann AU/275 3.00 8.00
05JV Jake Virtanen AU/175 6.00 15.00
05KF Kevin Fiala AU/275 3.00 8.00
05NC Nick Cousins AU/275 3.00 8.00
05NG Nikolay Goldobin AU/275 6.00 15.00
05NH Noah Hanifin AU/175 6.00 15.00
05NP Nicolas Petan AU/275 3.00 8.00
05OL Oscar Lindberg AU/275 3.00 8.00
05RF Robby Fabbri AU/175 4.00 10.00
05SB Sam Bennett AU/175 4.00 10.00
05ST Shea Theodore AU/275 6.00 15.00

2015-16 Ultimate Collection '05-06 Ultimate Rookies Silver

05AA Andreas Athanasiou JSY 6.00 15.00
05AP Artemi Panarin JSY 8.00 20.00
05BM Brock McGinn JSY 2.50 6.00
05BS Brady Skjei JSY 2.00 5.00
05CH Charles Hudon JSY 2.50 6.00
05CM Connor McDavid JSY 20.00 50.00
05CP Colton Parayko JSY 3.00 8.00
05CS Chandler Stephenson JSY 2.50 6.00
05DA Daniel Sprong JSY 5.00 12.00
05DL Dylan Larkin JSY 8.00 20.00
05EP Emile Poirier JSY 2.50 6.00
05FA Radek Faksa JSY 2.50 6.00
05FV Frank Vatrano JSY 5.00 12.00
05HS Henrik Samuelsson JSY 2.00 5.00
05JE Jack Eichel JSY 10.00 25.00
05JM Jared McCann JSY 2.50 6.00
05JV Jake Virtanen JSY 3.00 8.00
05KF Kevin Fiala JSY 2.50 6.00
05MD Max Domi JSY 5.00 12.00
05MR Mikko Rantanen JSY 5.00 12.00
05NC Nick Cousins JSY 2.50 6.00
05NE Nikolaj Ehlers JSY 5.00 12.00
05NG Nikolay Goldobin JSY 2.50 6.00
05NH Noah Hanifin JSY 3.00 8.00
05NP Nicolas Petan JSY 2.50 6.00
05OL Oscar Lindberg JSY 2.50 6.00
05RF Robby Fabbri JSY 3.00 8.00
05SB Sam Bennett JSY 3.00 8.00
05SP Sergei Plotnikov JSY 2.00 5.00
05ST Shea Theodore JSY 2.50 6.00

2015-16 Ultimate Collection '05-06 Ultimate Rookies Spectrum Silver

*SINGLES: .75X TO 2X BASIC INSERTS
05CM Connor McDavid JSY AU 450.00 600.00
05DL Dylan Larkin JSY AU 40.00 100.00

2015-16 Ultimate Collection Debut Threads

DTAP Artemi Panarin 6.00 15.00
DTBM Brock McGinn 2.00 5.00
DTCH Charles Hudon 2.00 5.00
DTCM Connor McDavid 20.00 50.00
DTDL Dylan Larkin 6.00 15.00
DTDS Daniel Sprong 4.00 10.00
DTEP Emile Poirier 2.00 5.00
DTFA Robby Fabbri 2.50 6.00
DTHS Henrik Samuelsson 1.50 4.00
DTJD Jacob de la Rose 2.00 5.00
DTJE Jack Eichel 8.00 20.00
DTJM Jared McCann 2.00 5.00
DTJV Jake Virtanen 2.50 6.00
DTJW Jordan Weal 2.00 5.00
DTKF Kevin Fiala 2.00 5.00
DTMC Mike Condon 2.00 5.00
DTMD Max Domi 4.00 10.00
DTMR Mikko Rantanen 4.00 10.00
DTMS Malcolm Subban 5.00 12.00
DTNE Nikolaj Ehlers 4.00 10.00
DTNG Nikolay Goldobin 2.00 5.00
DTNH Noah Hanifin 2.50 6.00
DTNP Nicolas Petan 2.00 5.00
DTNR Nick Ritchie 2.00 5.00
DTOL Oscar Lindberg 2.00 5.00
DTRF Radek Faksa 2.00 5.00
DTRH Ryan Hartman 2.50 6.00
DTSB Sam Bennett 2.50 6.00
DTSH Hunter Shinkaruk 2.00 5.00
DTZF Zachary Fucale 2.00 5.00

2015-16 Ultimate Collection Debut Threads Autographs

ADTBM Brock McGinn 6.00 15.00
ADTCH Charles Hudon 6.00 15.00
ADTCM Connor McDavid 250.00 500.00
ADTDL Dylan Larkin 25.00 60.00
ADTDO Joonas Donskoi 6.00 15.00
ADTDS Daniel Sprong 12.00 30.00
ADTEP Emile Poirier 6.00 15.00
ADTFA Robby Fabbri 8.00 20.00
ADTHS Henrik Samuelsson 5.00 12.00
ADTJD Jacob de la Rose 6.00 15.00
ADTJM Jared McCann 6.00 15.00
ADTJV Jake Virtanen 8.00 20.00
ADTJW Jordan Weal 6.00 15.00
ADTKF Kevin Fiala 6.00 15.00
ADTMC Mike Condon 6.00 15.00
ADTNE Nikolaj Ehlers 12.00 30.00
ADTNG Nikolay Goldobin 6.00 15.00
ADTNH Noah Hanifin 8.00 20.00
ADTNP Nicolas Petan 6.00 15.00
ADTNR Nick Ritchie 6.00 15.00
ADTOL Oscar Lindberg 6.00 15.00
ADTRF Radek Faksa 6.00 15.00
ADTRH Ryan Hartman 8.00 20.00
ADTSB Sam Bennett 8.00 20.00
ADTSH Hunter Shinkaruk 6.00 15.00
ADTZF Zachary Fucale 6.00 15.00

2015-16 Ultimate Collection Honoured Materials

HMAO Alexander Ovechkin 25.00 60.00
HMBH Brett Hull 6.00 15.00
HMBL Rob Blake 6.00 15.00
HMBO Mike Bossy 6.00 15.00
HMCM Connor McDavid 50.00 125.00
HMCP Carey Price 20.00 50.00
HMDH Dale Hawerchuk 8.00 20.00
HMGF Grant Fuhr 6.00 15.00
HMGL Guy Lafleur 8.00 20.00
HMHL Henrik Lundqvist 8.00 20.00
HMHZ Henrik Zetterberg 8.00 20.00
HMJE Jack Eichel 25.00 60.00
HMJK Jari Kurri 6.00 15.00
HMLR Luc Robitaille 8.00 20.00
HMMB Martin Brodeur 12.00 30.00
HMML Mario Lemieux 20.00 50.00
HMMM Mark Messier 10.00 25.00
HMPR Patrick Roy 15.00 40.00
HMRB Ray Bourque 10.00 25.00
HMRM Ryan Miller 6.00 15.00
HMSC Sidney Crosby 25.00 60.00
HMSS Steven Stamkos 12.00 30.00
HMSY Steve Yzerman 10.00 25.00
HMWG Wayne Gretzky 30.00 80.00

2015-16 Ultimate Collection Iconic Fabrics

IFCM Connor McDavid 30.00 80.00
IFEK Erik Karlsson 8.00 20.00
IFHL Henrik Lundqvist 5.00 12.00
IFJB Jamie Benn 5.00 12.00
IFJE Jack Eichel 15.00 40.00
IFJI Jarome Iginla 4.00 10.00
IFJJ Jaromir Jagr 10.00 25.00
IFJM Jared McCann 4.00 10.00
IFJQ Jonathan Quick 6.00 15.00
IFJT Jonathan Toews 8.00 20.00
IFJV Jake Virtanen 5.00 12.00
IFMR Mikko Rantanen 8.00 20.00
IFNH Noah Hanifin 5.00 12.00
IFNP Nicolas Petan 4.00 10.00
IFPK Patrick Kane 8.00 20.00
IFPS P.K. Subban 6.00 15.00
IFRF Robby Fabbri 5.00 12.00
IFSS Steven Stamkos 8.00 20.00
IFTS Tyler Seguin 6.00 15.00
IFZP Zach Parise 4.00 10.00

2015-16 Ultimate Collection Jumbo Material Autographs

AJMCM Connor McDavid/40 200.00 500.00
AJMCP Corey Perry/40 8.00 20.00
AJMDL Dylan Larkin/40 25.00 60.00
AJMDS Denis Savard/40 10.00 25.00
AJMEM Evgeni Malkin/40 25.00 60.00
AJMJB Jamie Benn/40 10.00 25.00
AJMJI Jarome Iginla/40 8.00 20.00
AJMJJ Jaromir Jagr/40 20.00 50.00
AJMJM Jared McCann/40 8.00 20.00
AJMJP Joe Pavelski/40 8.00 20.00
AJMJT Jonathan Toews/40 15.00 40.00
AJMJV Jake Virtanen/40 10.00 25.00
AJMKF Kevin Fiala/40 8.00 20.00
AJMML Mario Lemieux/15
AJMNM Nathan MacKinnon/40 15.00 40.00
AJMOL Oscar Lindberg/40 8.00 20.00
AJMPD Pavel Datsyuk/40 10.00 25.00
AJMPR Carey Price/40 25.00 60.00
AJMRB Ray Bourque/15
AJMRF Robby Fabbri/40 10.00 25.00
AJMRO Patrick Roy/15
AJMSA Joe Sakic/15
AJMSB Sam Bennett/40 10.00 25.00
AJMSC Sidney Crosby/15
AJMSP Daniel Sprong/40 15.00 40.00
AJMSY Steve Yzerman/15
AJMTA John Tavares/40 15.00 40.00
AJMTH Taylor Hall/40 15.00 40.00
(inserted in 2016-17 Ultimate Collection)
AJMTS Tyler Seguin/40 12.00 30.00
AJMVO Jakub Voracek/40 8.00 20.00
AJMZF Zachary Fucale/40 8.00 20.00
AJMZP Zach Parise/40 8.00 20.00

2015-16 Ultimate Collection Jumbo Materials

JMAH Adam Henrique 4.00 10.00
JMBH Braden Holtby 6.00 15.00
JMBW Blake Wheeler 4.00 10.00
JMCC Corey Crawford 5.00 12.00
JMCG Claude Giroux 4.00 10.00
JMCM Connor McDavid 30.00 80.00
JMDB Dustin Byfuglien 4.00 10.00
JMDD Drew Doughty 4.00 10.00
JMDK Duncan Keith 4.00 10.00
JMDL Dylan Larkin 12.00 30.00
JMDS Daniel Sedin 4.00 10.00
JMEB Jordan Eberle 4.00 10.00
JMEK Erik Karlsson 8.00 20.00
JMHL Henrik Lundqvist 5.00 12.00
JMHS Henrik Sedin 4.00 10.00
JMHU Brett Hull 4.00 10.00
JMHZ Henrik Zetterberg 5.00 12.00
JMJE Jack Eichel 15.00 40.00
JMJG Johnny Gaudreau 6.00 15.00
JMJQ Jonathan Quick 6.00 15.00
JMKE Phil Kessel 6.00 15.00
JMKL Kris Letang 4.00 10.00
JMMB Martin Brodeur 8.00 20.00
JMMD Max Domi 8.00 20.00
JMMF Marc-Andre Fleury 6.00 15.00
JMMJ Martin Jones 4.00 10.00
JMMP Max Pacioretty 4.00 10.00
JMMR Mikko Rantanen 8.00 20.00
JMNA Rick Nash 4.00 10.00
JMNB Nicklas Backstrom 6.00 15.00
JMNE Nikolaj Ehlers 8.00 20.00
JMNK Nazem Kadri 3.00 8.00
JMNR Nick Ritchie 4.00 10.00
JMPA Patrick Roy 10.00 25.00
JMPB Patrice Bergeron 5.00 12.00
JMPC Paul Coffey 4.00 10.00
JMPK Patrick Kane 8.00 20.00
JMPR Pekka Rinne 5.00 12.00
JMPS P.K. Subban 6.00 15.00
JMRF Robby Fabbri 5.00 12.00
JMRG Ryan Getzlaf 6.00 15.00
JMRJ Roman Josi 4.00 10.00
JMRL Roberto Luongo 4.00 10.00
JMRM Ryan Miller 4.00 10.00
JMRN Ryan Nugent-Hopkins 4.00 10.00
JMRO Ryan O'Reilly 4.00 10.00
JMSA Denis Savard 5.00 12.00
JMSB Sam Bennett 5.00 12.00
JMSS Steven Stamkos 8.00 20.00
JMTR Tuukka Rask 4.00 10.00
JMVH Victor Hedman 5.00 12.00
JMVT Vladimir Tarasenko 6.00 15.00
JMWS Wayne Simmonds 5.00 12.00
JMZF Zachary Fucale 4.00 10.00

2015-16 Ultimate Collection Material Achievements

MABB Bob Bourne 3.00 8.00
MABH Brett Hull 4.00 10.00
MADD Drew Doughty 4.00 10.00
MADH Dale Hawerchuk 5.00 12.00
MADS Denis Savard 5.00 12.00
MAGC Gerry Cheevers 4.00 10.00
MAGF Grant Fuhr 4.00 10.00
MAGL Guy Lafleur 5.00 12.00
MAHA Dominik Hasek 5.00 12.00
MAHL Henrik Lundqvist 5.00 12.00
MAHZ Henrik Zetterberg 5.00 12.00
MALR Luc Robitaille 5.00 12.00
MAMM Mark Messier 6.00 15.00
MAMS Martin St. Louis 4.00 10.00
MAPK Patrick Kane 8.00 20.00
MAPR Patrick Roy 10.00 25.00
MARL Roberto Luongo 4.00 10.00
MARO Larry Robinson 4.00 10.00
MASS Steven Stamkos 8.00 20.00
MASY Steve Yzerman 6.00 15.00

2015-16 Ultimate Collection Material Combos

MC2ANA R.Getzlaf/C.Perry B 5.00 12.00
MC2ARZ M.Domi/A.Duclair D 6.00 15.00
MC2CAL J.Gaudreau/S.Monahan C 5.00 12.00
MC2CAR E.Staal/J.Skinner C 4.00 10.00
MC2CHI J.Toews/M.Hossa A 6.00 15.00
MC2CLB N.Foligno/B.Saad D 3.00 8.00
MC2DET H.Zetterberg/G.Nyquist B 4.00 10.00
MC2EDM R.Nugent-Hopkins/J.Eberle C 3.00 8.00
MC2FLA A.Barkov/J.Jagr A 8.00 20.00
MC2LAK A.Kopitar/M.Gaborik C 5.00 12.00
MC2MIN M.Granlund/Z.Parise C 3.00 8.00
MC2NAS F.Forsberg/J.Neal D 4.00 10.00
MC2NJD M.Cammalleri/A.Henrique D 3.00 8.00
MC2NYI J.Tavares/K.Okposo B 6.00 15.00
MC2OTT K.Turris/M.Hoffman D 2.50 6.00
MC2PEN E.Malkin/P.Kessel B 10.00 25.00
MC2TBL S.Stamkos/T.Johnson B 6.00 15.00
MC2TCG M.Brodeur/R.Luongo A 6.00 15.00
MC2TCL W.Gretzky/J.Sakic A 15.00 40.00
MC2TOR J.van Riemsdyk/N.Kadri D 2.50 6.00
MC2WIN B.Wheeler/M.Scheifele D 4.00 10.00

2015-16 Ultimate Collection Material Quads

MC403DR Fleury/Parise/Getzlaf/Perry 10.00 25.00
MC404DR Ovechkin/Malkin Ladd/Wheeler 25.00 60.00
MC406DR Toews/Backstrom Kessel/Okposo 12.00 30.00
MC409DR Tavares/Hedman Duchene/Ekman-Larsson 12.00 30.00
MC410DR Hall/Seguin/Skinner Tarasenko 12.00 30.00
MC411DR Nugent-Hopkins/Landeskog Huberdeau/Zibanejad 6.00 15.00
MC413DR MacKinnon/Barkov Drouin/Monahan 12.00 30.00
MC414DR Ekblad/Reinhart Draisaitl/Bennett 8.00 20.00
MC415DR McDavid/Eichel Hanifin/Rantanen 50.00 125.00
MC497DR Thornton/Marleau Luongo/Hossa 6.00 15.00

2015-16 Ultimate Collection Material Sixes

MC6SC Keith/Kopitar/Kane Quick/Bergeron/Toews B 15.00 40.00
MC6VT Price/Rask/Bobrovsky Lundqvist/Miller/Brodeur B 25.00 60.00
MC6O6C Pacioretty/Phaneuf Chara/Zetterberg/Toews/McDonagh B 15.00 40.00
MC6O6L Lafleur/Gilmour/Bucyk Hasek/Savard/Messier A 12.00 30.00
MC6O6R Fucale/Sparks/Subban Larkin/Panarin/Lindberg B 25.00 60.00
MC6PRZ Lundqvist/Bergeron Toews/Sedin/Sedin/Ovechkin B 30.00 80.00

2015-16 Ultimate Collection Material Trios

MC3BOS Marchand/Bergeron/Eriksson C 8.00 20.00
MC3BUF Kane/Eichel/Reinhart C 25.00 60.00
MC3DAL Benn/Seguin/Sharp B 10.00 25.00
MC3NYR Kreider/Stepan/Hayes C 6.00 15.00
MC3PHI Schenn/Giroux/Simmonds C 8.00 20.00
MC3SJS Marleau/Thornton/Pavelski C 6.00 15.00
MC3STL Steen/Stastny/Tarasenko C 10.00 25.00
MC3TCS Toews/Iginla/Getzlaf D 12.00 30.00
MC3WAS Ovechkin/Backstrom/Oshie B 25.00 60.00
MC390DR Nolan/Jagr/Brodeur A 15.00 40.00

2015-16 Ultimate Collection Signature Honoured Materials

SHMAK Anze Kopitar/35 10.00 25.00
SHMCP Corey Perry/85 6.00 15.00
SHMDH Dominik Hasek/15
SHMDL Dylan Larkin/85 20.00 50.00
SHMEM Evgeni Malkin/35 20.00 50.00
SHMJI Jarome Iginla/35 6.00 15.00
SHMJT John Tavares/35 12.00 30.00
SHMJV Jake Virtanen/85 8.00 20.00
SHMNE Nikolaj Ehlers/85 12.00 30.00
SHMPR Patrick Roy/15
SHMSC Sidney Crosby/15
SHMTF Theoren Fleury/35 8.00 20.00
SHMZF Zachary Fucale/85 6.00 15.00

2015-16 Ultimate Collection Signature Iconic Fabrics

SIFAO Alexander Ovechkin/8
SIFCP Carey Price/31 50.00 125.00
SIFDL Dylan Larkin/71 25.00 60.00
SIFMD Max Domi/15
(inserted in 2016-17 Ultimate Collection)
SIFML Mario Lemieux/6
SIFNE Nikolaj Ehlers/27 12.00 30.00
SIFPR Patrick Roy/33 50.00 125.00
SIFSB Sam Bennett/93 15.00 40.00
SIFSY Steve Yzerman/19 50.00 125.00

2015-16 Ultimate Collection Signature Material Achievements

SMAAE Aaron Ekblad/40 8.00 20.00
SMAAO Alexander Ovechkin/25 30.00 80.00
SMACP Carey Price/40 25.00 60.00
SMAJB Jamie Benn/40 10.00 25.00
SMAJT Jonathan Toews/40 15.00 40.00
SMAMB Martin Brodeur/25 15.00 40.00
SMAPR Patrick Roy/10
SMATA John Tavares/40 15.00 40.00
SMAWG Wayne Gretzky/10

2015-16 Ultimate Collection Signature Material Laureates

SMLAE Aaron Ekblad/40 20.00 50.00
SMLAO Alexander Ovechkin/15
SMLBH Brett Hull/15
SMLCP Carey Price/40 75.00 150.00
SMLDK David Krejci/40 15.00 40.00
SMLDS Denis Savard/40 25.00 60.00
SMLEM Evgeni Malkin/40 60.00 150.00
SMLGF Grant Fuhr/40 20.00 50.00
SMLJB Jamie Benn/40 25.00 60.00
SMLJI Jarome Iginla/40 20.00 50.00
SMLJT John Tavares/40 40.00 100.00
SMLKT Kyle Turris/40 15.00 40.00
SMLMB Martin Brodeur/15
SMLMM Mark Messier/15
SMLMS Martin St. Louis/40 20.00 50.00
SMLPD Pavel Datsyuk/40 25.00 60.00
SMLPE Corey Perry/40 20.00 50.00
SMLSC Sidney Crosby/15
SMLZP Zach Parise/40 20.00 50.00

2015-16 Ultimate Collection Ultimate Dozen Relic Booklets

U12ALB Flames/Oilers 125.00 300.00
U12FWY Kings/Ducks 25.00 60.00
U12GOV Panthers/Lightning 40.00 100.00
U12HOF HOF 60.00 150.00
U12KEY Flyers/Penguins 50.00 125.00
U1214SC Kings/Rangers 30.00 80.00
U1215SC Blackhawks/Lightning 40.00 100.00
U12BHRW Blackhawks/RedWings 30.00 80.00
U12BRCA Bruins/Canadiens 50.00 125.00
U12CAFL Flames/Canucks 25.00 60.00
U12NYBR Islanders/Rangers 30.00 80.00
U12OIJE Oilers/Jets 125.00 300.00
U12OSIX Original Six 60.00 150.00
U12ROOK Rookies 125.00 300.00

2015-16 Ultimate Collection Ultimate Rookie Autograph Relic Booklets

RBRAP Artemi Panarin/49 100.00 200.00
RBRBM Brock McGinn/99 15.00 40.00
RBRCM Connor McDavid/49 400.00 600.00
RBRDL Dylan Larkin/49 75.00 150.00
RBRDS Daniel Sprong/99 30.00 80.00
RBREP Emile Poirier/99 15.00 40.00
RBRHS Henrik Samuelsson/99 12.00 30.00
RBRJM Jared McCann/99 15.00 40.00
RBRJV Jake Virtanen/99 20.00 50.00
RBRKF Kevin Fiala/99 15.00 40.00
RBRMP Matt Puempel/99 12.00 30.00
RBRNP Nicolas Petan/99 15.00 40.00
RBRNR Nick Ritchie/99 15.00 40.00
RBRRF Robby Fabbri/99 20.00 50.00
RBRSB Sam Bennett/49 30.00 80.00
RBRSH Hunter Shinkaruk/99 15.00 40.00
RBRZF Zachary Fucale/99 15.00 40.00

2015-16 Ultimate Collection Ultimate Signatures

USAE Aaron Ekblad C
USAO Alexander Ovechkin A 90.00 150.00
USBH Bobby Hull A
USBO Bobby Orr B
USBS Brady Skjei C
USCH Charles Hudon C
USCP Carey Price A 50.00 120.00
USDK David Krejci C 12.00 30.00
USDL Dylan Larkin C 40.00 100.00
USEM Evgeni Malkin A
USJI Jarome Iginla B 12.00 30.00
USJJ Jaromir Jagr B
USJP Joe Pavelski B
USJT Jonathan Toews A 60.00 150.00
USJV James van Riemsdyk C 10.00 25.00
USMC Mike McCarron C 8.00 20.00
USML Mario Lemieux A 80.00 150.00
USMM Mark Messier A
USMS Mark Stone C
USNM Nathan MacKinnon C 15.00 40.00
USPD Pavel Datsyuk B 20.00 50.00
USRF Robby Fabbri C 12.00 30.00
USSB Sam Bennett C 20.00 50.00
USSC Sidney Crosby A
USTH Taylor Hall
(inserted in 2016-17 Ultimate Collection)
USTJ Tyler Johnson C 6.00 15.00
USTS Tyler Seguin B
USVI Jake Virtanen C 12.00 30.00
USWG Wayne Gretzky A 200.00 500.00
USZF Zachary Fucale C 15.00 30.00
USZP Zach Parise B 15.00 30.00

2015-16 Ultimate Collection Ultimate Skills Jumbo Jerseys

USKAE Aaron Ekblad C 6.00 15.00
USKAK Anze Kopitar C 10.00 25.00
USKAO Alexander Ovechkin B 30.00 80.00
USKBB Brent Burns C 8.00 20.00
USKBE Brian Elliott C 5.00 12.00
USKBR Bobby Ryan A
USKCC Corey Crawford C 8.00 20.00
USKCG Claude Giroux C 6.00 15.00
USKCP Carey Price C 20.00 50.00
USKDD Drew Doughty C 6.00 15.00
USKDK Duncan Keith A
USKJF Justin Faulk C 6.00 15.00
USKJG Johnny Gaudreau C 10.00 25.00
USKJH Jaroslav Halak C 5.00 12.00
USKJS Jiri Sekac C 5.00 12.00
USKJV Jakub Voracek A
USKKE Phil Kessel C 10.00 25.00
USKMF Marc-Andre Fleury C 10.00 25.00
USKMG Mark Giordano B 8.00 20.00
USKMH Mike Hoffman C 5.00 12.00
USKOE Oliver Ekman-Larsson C 5.00 12.00
USKPB Patrice Bergeron C 8.00 20.00
USKPE Patrik Elias C 6.00 15.00
USKRJ Ryan Johansen C 8.00 20.00
USKRL Roberto Luongo C 6.00 15.00
USKRV Radim Vrbata C 5.00 12.00
USKTS Tyler Seguin B 12.00 30.00

2016-17 Ultimate Collection

1 John Tavares 4.00 10.00
2 Tyler Seguin 3.00 8.00
3 Mats Zuccarello 2.00 5.00
4 Mark Scheifele 2.50 6.00
5 Cory Schneider 1.50 4.00
6 Alexander Ovechkin 8.00 20.00
7 Mike Hoffman 1.50 4.00
8 Jakub Voracek 2.00 5.00
9 Andrew Ladd 2.00 5.00
10 Tyson Barrie 2.00 5.00
11 Henrik Zetterberg 2.50 6.00
12 Patrice Bergeron 2.50 6.00
13 Jake Muzzin 1.50 4.00
14 Steven Stamkos 4.00 10.00
15 P.K. Subban 3.00 8.00
16 Oliver Ekman-Larsson 1.50 4.00
17 James van Riemsdyk 2.00 5.00
18 Taylor Hall 4.00 10.00
19 David Backes 2.00 5.00
20 Boone Jenner 2.00 5.00
21 Erik Karlsson 4.00 10.00
22 Nikita Kucherov 3.00 8.00
23 Roberto Luongo 2.00 5.00
24 Drew Doughty 2.00 5.00
25 Frederik Andersen 1.50 4.00
26 Alex Galchenyuk 2.50 6.00
27 Loui Eriksson 2.00 5.00
28 Jaromir Jagr 5.00 12.00
29 Connor McDavid 15.00 40.00
30 Nikolaj Ehlers 2.00 5.00
31 Jaden Schwartz 2.50 6.00
32 Jamie Benn 2.50 6.00
33 Carey Price 6.00 15.00
34 Brian Elliott 1.50 4.00
35 Artem Anisimov 1.50 4.00
36 Corey Perry 2.00 5.00
37 Henrik Lundqvist 2.00 5.00
38 Patrick Kane 4.00 10.00
39 Ryan O'Reilly 2.00 5.00
40 Joe Thornton 2.00 5.00
41 Evgeni Malkin 6.00 15.00
42 Claude Giroux 2.00 5.00
43 Ryan Johansen 2.50 6.00
44 Brent Burns 2.50 6.00
45 Braden Holtby 3.00 8.00
46 Sidney Crosby 10.00 25.00
47 John Gibson 2.00 5.00
48 Sam Bennett 2.50 6.00
49 Nino Niederreiter 2.00 5.00
50 Teuvo Teravainen 2.00 5.00
51 Brandon Montour RC 2.00 5.00
52 Josh Morrissey RC 2.50 6.00
53 Jared Coreau RC 2.50 6.00
54 Jakub Vrana RC 2.00 5.00
55 Pontus Aberg RC 2.50 6.00
56 Nic Dowd RC 2.00 5.00
57 Chris Bigras RC 1.50 4.00
58 Jacob Larsson RC 3.00 8.00
59 Troy Stecher RC 2.00 5.00
60 Hudson Fasching RC 2.00 5.00
61 Thatcher Demko RC 4.00 10.00
62 Esa Lindell RC 2.00 5.00
63 Zach Sanford RC 2.00 5.00
64 Nick Baptiste RC 2.00 5.00
65 Alan Quine RC 2.00 5.00
66 Thomas Chabot RC 4.00 10.00
67 Michael Matheson RC 2.00 5.00
68 Matthew Benning RC 2.50 6.00
69 Stephen Johns RC 1.50 4.00
70 Sonny Milano RC 2.50 6.00
71 Mathew Barzal RC 6.00 15.00
72 Artturi Lehkonen RC 2.00 5.00
73 Brayden Point RC 5.00 12.00
74 Christian Dvorak RC 2.00 5.00
75 Connor Brown RC 3.00 8.00
76 Jakob Chychrun RC 2.00 5.00
77 Timo Meier RC 2.00 5.00
78 Nick Schmaltz RC 2.00 5.00
79 Pavel Buchnevich RC 3.00 8.00
80 Nikita Zaitsev RC 2.00 5.00
81 Tyler Motte RC 2.00 5.00
82 Brandon Carlo RC 2.00 5.00
83 Pavel Zacha RC 2.50 6.00
84 Kyle Connor RC 5.00 12.00
85 Anthony Mantha RC 5.00 12.00
86 Joel Eriksson Ek RC 2.00 5.00
87 Ivan Provorov RC 4.00 10.00
88 Anthony Beauvillier RC 2.00 5.00
89 Mikhail Sergachev RC 4.00 10.00
90 Sebastian Aho RC 4.00 10.00
91 Travis Konecny RC 4.00 10.00
92 Zach Werenski RC 4.00 10.00
93 Mitch Marner RC 15.00 40.00
94 Jimmy Vesey RC 8.00 20.00
95 Dylan Strome RC 12.00 30.00
96 Jesse Puljujarvi RC 5.00 12.00
97 William Nylander RC 15.00 40.00
98 Matthew Tkachuk RC 6.00 15.00
99 Patrik Laine RC 20.00 50.00
100 Auston Matthews RC 50.00 120.00
102 Christian Dvorak AU/299 6.00 15.00
104 Pavel Buchnevich AU/299 10.00 25.00
105 Trevor Carrick AU/299 6.00 15.00
106 Dominik Simon AU/299 6.00 15.00
107 Jakob Chychrun AU/299 6.00 15.00
108 Thomas Chabot AU/299 12.00 30.00
110 Anthony Beauvillier AU/299 6.00 15.00
111 Jakub Vrana AU/299 6.00 15.00
112 Ivan Provorov AU/299 12.00 30.00
113 Steven Santini AU/299 5.00 12.00
114 Mathew Barzal AU/299 20.00 50.00
115 Hudson Fasching AU/299 6.00 15.00
116 Timo Meier AU/299 6.00 15.00
117 Zach Werenski AU/299 12.00 30.00
119 Sergey Tolchinsky AU/299 5.00 12.00
121 Oliver Bjorkstrand AU/299 5.00 12.00
123 J.C. Lipon AU/299 6.00 15.00
125 Lawson Crouse AU/299 5.00 12.00
126 Mark McNeill AU/299 6.00 15.00
127 Chase De Leo AU/299 6.00 15.00
128 Justin Bailey AU/299 6.00 15.00
129 Esa Lindell AU/299 6.00 15.00
130 Charlie Lindgren AU/299 12.00 30.00
131 Sonny Milano AU/299 8.00 20.00
132 Ryan Pulock AU/299 6.00 15.00
133 Nikita Soshnikov AU/299 4.00 10.00
135 Oskar Sundqvist AU/299 6.00 15.00
136 Danton Heinen AU/299 10.00 25.00
139 Oliver Kylington AU/299 5.00 12.00
140 Dylan Strome AU/299 12.00 30.00
141 Josh Morrissey AU/299 8.00 20.00
142 Tom Kuhnhackl AU/299 5.00 12.00
143 Kasperi Kapanen AU/299 12.00 30.00
144 Tyler Motte AU/299 6.00 15.00
145 Jason Dickinson AU/299 5.00 12.00
147 Mikhail Sergachev AU/299 12.00 30.00
149 Mitch Marner AU/99 200.00 300.00
150 Sebastian Aho AU/99 40.00 100.00
151 Travis Konecny AU/99 30.00 80.00
152 Kyle Connor AU/99 20.00 50.00
153 Jimmy Vesey AU/99 30.00 80.00
154 Matthew Tkachuk AU/99 40.00 100.00
155 Pavel Zacha AU/99 15.00 40.00
156 William Nylander AU/99 80.00 200.00
157 Anthony Mantha AU/99 50.00 125.00
158 Jesse Puljujarvi AU/99 30.00 80.00
159 Patrik Laine AU/99 150.00 250.00
160 Auston Matthews AU/99 600.00 1200.00
161 Jake Guentzel AU/99 100.00 250.00
NNO Rookie Autograph Redemption 40.00 100.00

2016-17 Ultimate Collection Gold

*VETS: 1.25X TO 3X BASIC CARDS
*ROOKIES: .6X TO 1.5X BASIC CARDS
1 John Tavares AU/50 12.00 30.00
2 Tyler Seguin AU/50 12.00 30.00
23 Roberto Luongo AU/50 12.00 30.00
33 Carey Price AU/25 40.00 100.00
37 Henrik Lundqvist AU/25 30.00 80.00
40 Joe Thornton AU/50 12.00 30.00
41 Evgeni Malkin AU/25 30.00 80.00
140 Dylan Strome PATCH AU/49 40.00 100.00
150 Sebastian Aho PATCH AU/49 40.00 100.00
153 Jimmy Vesey PATCH AU/49 30.00 80.00
154 Matthew Tkachuk PATCH AU/49 80.00 150.00
156 William Nylander PATCH AU/49 80.00 200.00
157 Anthony Mantha PATCH AU/49 80.00 150.00
158 Jesse Puljujarvi PATCH AU/49 80.00 200.00
159 Patrik Laine PATCH AU/49 250.00 600.00
160 Auston Matthews PATCH AU/49 400.00 800.00

2016-17 Ultimate Collection Silver

COMMON CARD 1.00 3.00
SEMISTARS 1.50 4.00
UNLISTED STARS 2.00 5.00
159 Patrik Laine JSY 15.00 40.00
160 Auston Matthews JSY 30.00 80.00

2016-17 Ultimate Collection '06-07 Retro Rookie Autographs

RRAAB Anthony Beauvillier/199 5.00 12.00
RRAAM Auston Matthews/49 300.00 500.00
RRACD Christian Dvorak/199 5.00 12.00
RRADH Danton Heinen/199 8.00 20.00
RRADS Dylan Strome/199 15.00 40.00
RRAEL Esa Lindell/199 5.00 12.00
RRAHF Hudson Fasching/199 5.00 12.00
RRAIP Ivan Provorov/199 10.00 25.00
RRAJC Jakob Chychrun/199 5.00 12.00
RRAJP Jesse Puljujarvi/199 25.00 60.00
RRAJV Jimmy Vesey/199 10.00 25.00
RRAKC Kyle Connor/199 12.00 30.00
RRAKK Kasperi Kapanen/199 10.00 25.00
RRAKL Kevin Labanc/199 5.00 12.00
RRALC Lawson Crouse/199 4.00 10.00
RRAMA Anthony Mantha/49 50.00 120.00
RRAMB Mathew Barzal/199 15.00 40.00
RRAME Timo Meier/199 5.00 12.00
RRAMM Mitch Marner/49 60.00 150.00
RRAMT Matthew Tkachuk/49 40.00 100.00
RRAOB Oliver Bjorkstrand/199 4.00 10.00
RRAOK Oliver Kylington/199 4.00 10.00
RRAPB Pavel Buchnevich/199 8.00 20.00
RRAPL Patrik Laine/49 80.00 200.00
RRAPZ Pavel Zacha/49 12.00 30.00
RRASS Steven Santini/199 4.00 10.00
RRATC Thomas Chabot/199 10.00 25.00
RRATM Tyler Motte/199 5.00 12.00
RRAVR Jakub Vrana/199 5.00 12.00
RRAWN William Nylander/49 60.00 150.00

2016-17 Ultimate Collection '06-07 Retro Rookie Jerseys

RRJAB Anthony Beauvillier 2.00 5.00
RRJAM Auston Matthews 15.00 40.00
RRJBP Brayden Point 5.00 12.00
RRJCD Christian Dvorak 2.00 5.00
RRJDS Dylan Strome 4.00 10.00
RRJEL Esa Lindell 2.00 5.00
RRJHF Hudson Fasching 2.00 5.00
RRJIP Ivan Provorov 4.00 10.00
RRJJC Jakob Chychrun 2.00 5.00
RRJJE Joel Eriksson Ek 2.00 5.00
RRJJH Julius Honka 2.00 5.00
RRJJP Jesse Puljujarvi 5.00 12.00
RRJJV Jimmy Vesey 4.00 10.00
RRJKC Kyle Connor 5.00 12.00
RRJKK Kasperi Kapanen 4.00 10.00
RRJKL Kevin Labanc 2.00 5.00
RRJLC Lawson Crouse 1.50 4.00
RRJMA Anthony Mantha 5.00 12.00
RRJMB Mathew Barzal 6.00 15.00
RRJME Timo Meier 2.00 5.00
RRJMI Michael Matheson 2.00 5.00
RRJMM Mitch Marner 10.00 25.00
RRJMT Matthew Tkachuk 6.00 15.00
RRJMW Miles Wood 1.50 4.00
RRJNS Nick Schmaltz 2.00 5.00
RRJOB Oliver Bjorkstrand 1.50 4.00
RRJOK Oliver Kylington 1.50 4.00
RRJPB Pavel Buchnevich 3.00 8.00
RRJPL Patrik Laine 8.00 20.00
RRJPZ Pavel Zacha 2.50 6.00
RRJSA Sebastian Aho 4.00 10.00
RRJSS Steven Santini 1.50 4.00
RRJTC Thomas Chabot 4.00 10.00
RRJTD Thatcher Demko 4.00 10.00
RRJTK Travis Konecny 4.00 10.00
RRJTM Tyler Motte 2.00 5.00
RRJVR Jakub Vrana 2.00 5.00
RRJWN William Nylander 8.00 20.00
RRJZW Zach Werenski 4.00 10.00

2016-17 Ultimate Collection Debut Threads Patch Autographs

DTAB Anthony Beauvillier/99	12.00	30.00
DTAM Auston Matthews/25	350.00	800.00
DTCA Trevor Carrick/99	12.00	30.00
DTCD Christian Dvorak/99	12.00	30.00
DTCL Charlie Lindgren/99	25.00	60.00
DTDS Dylan Strome/99	25.00	60.00
DTEL Esa Lindell/99	12.00	30.00
DTHF Hudson Fasching/99	12.00	30.00
DTIP Ivan Provorov/99	25.00	60.00
DTJB Justin Bailey/99	12.00	30.00
DTJC Jakob Chychrun/99	12.00	30.00
DTJL J.C. Lipon/99	12.00	30.00
DTJP Jesse Puljujarvi/99	30.00	80.00
DTJV Jimmy Vesey/99	25.00	60.00
DTKC Kyle Connor/99	30.00	80.00
DTKK Kasperi Kapanen/99	25.00	60.00
DTKU Tom Kuhnhackl/99	10.00	25.00
DTLC Lawson Crouse/99	10.00	25.00
DTMA Anthony Mantha/99	30.00	80.00
DTMB Mathew Barzal/99	40.00	100.00
DTMC Mark McNeill/99	12.00	30.00
DTME Timo Meier/99	12.00	30.00
DTMM Mitch Marner/49	100.00	250.00
DTMR Mike Reilly/99	10.00	25.00
DTMT Matthew Tkachuk/49	50.00	120.00
DTOB Oliver Bjorkstrand/99	10.00	25.00
DTOK Oliver Kylington/99	10.00	25.00
DTPB Pavel Buchnevich/99	20.00	50.00
DTPE Brendan Perlini/99	12.00	30.00
DTPL Patrik Laine/49	250.00	500.00
DTPZ Pavel Zacha/99	15.00	40.00
DTRP Ryan Pulock/99	12.00	30.00
DTSM Sonny Milano/99	15.00	40.00
DTSS Steven Santini/99	10.00	25.00
DTTC Thomas Chabot/99	25.00	60.00
DTTM Tyler Motte/99	12.00	30.00
DTVR Jakub Vrana/99	12.00	30.00
DTWN William Nylander/49	60.00	150.00
DTZW Zach Werenski/99	25.00	60.00

2016-17 Ultimate Collection Keystone Fabrics

KFAK Anze Kopitar	4.00	10.00
KFAO Alexander Ovechkin	10.00	25.00
KFAP Alex Pietrangelo	2.00	5.00
KFBW Blake Wheeler	2.50	6.00
KFCG Claude Giroux	2.50	6.00
KFDD Drew Doughty	2.50	6.00
KFDG Doug Gilmour	3.00	8.00
KFDK Duncan Keith	2.50	6.00
KFDS Daniel Sedin	2.50	6.00
KFEK Erik Karlsson	5.00	12.00
KFEM Evgeni Malkin	8.00	20.00
KFHS Henrik Sedin	2.50	6.00
KFHZ Henrik Zetterberg	3.00	8.00
KFJB Jamie Benn	3.00	8.00
KFJQ Jonathan Quick	4.00	10.00
KFJT Jonathan Toews	5.00	12.00
KFKL Kris Letang	2.50	6.00
KFMB Martin Brodeur	5.00	12.00
KFPB Patrice Bergeron	3.00	8.00
KFPE Patrik Elias	2.50	6.00
KFPM Patrick Marleau	2.50	6.00
KFPR Pekka Rinne	3.00	8.00
KFRG Ryan Getzlaf	4.00	10.00
KFSC Sidney Crosby	10.00	25.00
KFSS Steven Stamkos	5.00	12.00
KFTA John Tavares	5.00	12.00
KFTR Tuukka Rask	2.50	6.00
KFVR Victor Rask	2.00	5.00

2016-17 Ultimate Collection Keystone Fabrics Autographs

SKFCP Carey Price/49	40.00	100.00
SKFDS Denis Savard/99	10.00	25.00
SKFEM Evgeni Malkin/49	30.00	80.00
SKFGC Gerry Cheevers/49	25.00	60.00
SKFHL Henrik Lundqvist/49	40.00	100.00
SKFIL Igor Larionov/15	20.00	50.00
SKFJP Joe Pavelski/99	10.00	25.00
SKFMG Mark Giordano/99	5.00	12.00
SKFML Mario Lemieux/15	90.00	150.00
SKFWG Wayne Gretzky/15		
SKFWS Wayne Simmonds/99	20.00	50.00

2016-17 Ultimate Collection Keystone Fabrics Autographs Gold

SKFCP Carey Price/15	90.00	150.00
SKFDT Dave Taylor/25	40.00	100.00
SKFEM Evgeni Malkin/15	90.00	150.00
SKFHL Henrik Lundqvist/15	80.00	150.00
SKFJP Joe Pavelski/25	20.00	50.00
SKFMG Mark Giordano/25	15.00	40.00
SKFWS Wayne Simmonds/25	60.00	150.00

2016-17 Ultimate Collection Numeric Excellence Materials

NEAM Auston Matthews	40.00	100.00
NEBB Brent Burns	8.00	20.00
NEBH Braden Holtby	10.00	25.00
NEBS Brandon Saad	6.00	15.00
NEDH Dominik Hasek	6.00	15.00
NEJE Jack Eichel	12.00	30.00
NEJG Johnny Gaudreau	10.00	25.00
NEJJ Jaromir Jagr	15.00	40.00
NEJV Jimmy Vesey	12.00	30.00
NEML Mario Lemieux	20.00	50.00
NEMM Mitch Marner	30.00	80.00
NEOE Oliver Ekman-Larsson	5.00	12.00
NEPL Patrik Laine	25.00	60.00
NEPS P.K. Subban	10.00	25.00
NERB Ray Bourque	10.00	25.00
NESC Sidney Crosby	25.00	60.00
NETK Travis Konecny	12.00	30.00
NETS Tyler Seguin	10.00	25.00
NEVH Victor Hedman	8.00	20.00
NEVT Vladimir Tarasenko	10.00	25.00

2016-17 Ultimate Collection Signature Laureates

SLBO Bobby Orr	100.00	200.00
SLCN Cam Neely	20.00	50.00
SLGL Guy Lafleur	25.00	60.00
SLMD Marcel Dionne	20.00	50.00
SLWG Wayne Gretzky	200.00	300.00

2016-17 Ultimate Collection Signature Material Laureates

SMLAL Andrew Ladd/99	10.00	25.00
SMLBE Brian Elliott/99	8.00	20.00
SMLCN Cam Neely/99	10.00	25.00
SMLDB David Backes/99	10.00	25.00
SMLHL Henrik Lundqvist/99	10.00	25.00
SMLJS Jaden Schwartz/99	12.00	30.00
SMLLE Loui Eriksson/99	10.00	25.00
SMLMG Marian Gaborik/99	10.00	25.00
SMLMS Mark Scheifele/99	12.00	30.00
SMLNB Nick Bjugstad/99	8.00	20.00
SMLNN Nino Niederreiter/99	10.00	25.00
SMLRK Ryan Kesler/99	10.00	25.00
SMLTS Tyler Seguin/99	15.00	40.00
SMLWS Wayne Simmonds/99	25.00	60.00

2016-17 Ultimate Collection Signature Material Phenoms

SMPAB Anthony Beauvillier/65	12.00	30.00
SMPCD Christian Dvorak/65	12.00	30.00
SMPDS Dylan Strome/15		
SMPHF Hudson Fasching/65	12.00	30.00
SMPIP Ivan Provorov/15		
SMPJP Jesse Puljujarvi/15		
SMPJV Jimmy Vesey/15		
SMPKC Kyle Connor/15		
SMPMB Mathew Barzal/65	40.00	100.00
SMPME Timo Meier/65	12.00	30.00
SMPPL Patrik Laine/15		
SMPTC Thomas Chabot/65	25.00	60.00
SMPTM Tyler Motte/65	12.00	30.00

2016-17 Ultimate Collection Ultimate Performers Material Autographs

UPACC Chris Chelios/50	10.00	25.00
UPACP Carey Price/25		
UPAGC Gerry Cheevers/25		
UPAJJ Joe Thornton/50		
UPAJT Jonathan Toews/50	30.00	80.00
UPATE Tony Esposito/25	25.00	60.00

2016-17 Ultimate Collection Ultimate Performers Materials

UPAO Alexander Ovechkin/99	20.00	50.00
UPBH Brett Hull/99	5.00	12.00
UPIL Igor Larionov/49	5.00	12.00
UPJI Jarome Iginla/99	5.00	12.00
UPJJ Jaromir Jagr/99	12.00	30.00
UPMB Martin Brodeur/99	10.00	25.00
UPMH Marian Hossa/99	4.00	10.00
UPML Mario Lemieux/49	15.00	40.00
UPMM Mark Messier/49	6.00	15.00
UPPC Paul Coffey/99	5.00	12.00
UPPR Patrick Roy/49	12.00	30.00
UPRL Roberto Luongo/99	5.00	12.00
UPSC Sidney Crosby/99	20.00	50.00
UPWG Wayne Gretzky/49	30.00	80.00

2017-18 Ultimate Collection

1 Auston Matthews	8.00	20.00
2 Brad Marchand	2.50	6.00
3 Logan Couture	2.00	5.00
4 Erik Karlsson	2.50	6.00
5 Marc-Andre Fleury	3.00	8.00
6 Kevin Shattenkirk	2.00	5.00
7 John Tavares	4.00	10.00
8 Jason Pominville	1.50	4.00
9 Anze Kopitar	3.00	8.00
10 Connor McDavid	8.00	20.00
11 Daniel Sedin	2.00	5.00
12 Steven Stamkos	4.00	10.00
13 Christian Dvorak	1.50	4.00
14 Patrik Laine	3.00	8.00
15 Nathan MacKinnon	4.00	10.00
16 Devan Dubnyk	2.00	5.00
17 Jonathan Drouin	2.00	5.00
18 Tyler Seguin	3.00	8.00
19 Filip Forsberg	2.50	6.00
20 Sidney Crosby	8.00	20.00
21 Jeff Skinner	1.50	4.00
22 Taylor Hall	4.00	10.00
23 Vincent Trocheck	1.50	4.00
24 Wayne Simmonds	2.50	6.00
25 Alexander Ovechkin	8.00	20.00
26 Vladimir Tarasenko	3.00	8.00
27 Rickard Rakell	1.50	4.00
28 Matthew Tkachuk	2.00	5.00
29 Sergei Bobrovsky	2.00	5.00
30 Patrick Kane	4.00	10.00
31 Henrik Zetterberg	2.00	5.00
32 Tuukka Rask	2.00	5.00
33 Nikita Kucherov	3.00	8.00
34 Leon Draisaitl	3.00	8.00
35 Carey Price	6.00	15.00
36 Aleksander Barkov	2.00	5.00
37 Jeff Carter	2.00	5.00
38 Roman Josi	2.00	5.00
39 Mitch Marner	3.00	8.00
40 Henrik Lundqvist	3.00	8.00
41 Johnny Gaudreau	3.00	8.00
42 Duncan Keith	2.00	5.00
43 Jack Eichel	3.00	8.00
44 Jake Guentzel	2.50	6.00
45 Anthony Mantha	2.00	5.00
46 Mark Scheifele	2.50	6.00
47 Cam Atkinson	2.00	5.00
48 Matt Murray	3.00	8.00
49 Patrick Marleau	2.00	5.00
50 Jonathan Toews	4.00	10.00
51 Christian Fischer AU/399 RC	8.00	20.00
52 Haydn Fleury/399 RC	6.00	15.00
53 Evgeny Svechnikov/399 RC	12.00	30.00
54 Jakob Forsbacka-Karlsson AU/399 RC	6.00	15.00
55 Filip Chlapik AU/399 RC	6.00	15.00
56 Samuel Morin AU/399 RC	6.00	15.00
57 Ivan Barbashev/399 RC	6.00	15.00
58 Jack Roslovic AU/399 RC	8.00	20.00
59 Martin Necas AU/399 RC	6.00	15.00
60 Ville Husso AU/399 RC	6.00	15.00
61 Nikita Scherbak AU/399 RC	12.00	30.00
62 J.T. Compher AU/399 RC	8.00	20.00
63 Calle Rosen/399 RC	6.00	15.00
64 Colin White AU/399 RC	6.00	15.00
65 Denis Gurianov AU/399 RC	6.00	15.00
66 Michael Amadio AU/399 RC	6.00	15.00
67 Vladislav Kamenev/399 RC	10.00	25.00
68 Lucas Wallmark/399 RC	6.00	15.00
69 Jon Gillies AU/399 RC	6.00	15.00
70 Vince Dunn AU/399 RC	6.00	15.00
71 Robert Hagg AU/399 RC	6.00	15.00
72 Alex Formenton AU/399 RC	6.00	15.00
73 Riley Barber/399 RC	5.00	12.00
74 Christian Djoos AU/399 RC	6.00	15.00
75 Madison Bowey AU/399 RC	5.00	12.00
76 Filip Chytil AU/399 RC	6.00	15.00
77 Alex Kerfoot AU/299 RC	6.00	15.00
78 Luke Kunin AU/299 RC	6.00	15.00
79 Jake DeBrusk AU/299 RC	10.00	25.00
80 Kailer Yamamoto AU/299 RC	15.00	40.00
81 Tage Thompson AU/299 RC	10.00	25.00
82 Victor Mete AU/299 RC	6.00	15.00
83 Travis Sanheim AU/299 RC	6.00	15.00
84 Logan Brown/399 RC	6.00	15.00
85 Adrian Kempe AU/299 RC	8.00	20.00
86 Anders Bjork/399 RC	8.00	20.00
87 Jesper Bratt AU/299 RC	10.00	25.00
88 Alex Tuch AU/299 RC	15.00	40.00
89 Pierre-Luc Dubois AU/99 RC	150.00	250.00
90 Clayton Keller AU/99 RC		
91 Alex DeBrincat AU/99 RC	80.00	150.00
92 Tyson Jost AU/99 RC	60.00	150.00
93 Brock Boeser AU/99 RC	350.00	450.00
94 Owen Tippett AU/99 RC		
95 Charlie McAvoy AU/99 RC	100.00	200.00
96 Josh Ho-Sang AU/99 RC	30.00	80.00
97 Alexander Nylander AU/99 RC		
98 Will Butcher AU/99 RC		
99 Nico Hischier/99 RC	50.00	120.00
100 Nolan Patrick/99 RC	40.00	100.00

2017-18 Ultimate Collection '07-08 Retro Debut Threads

RDTAB Anders Bjork	2.50	6.00
RDTAD Alex DeBrincat	5.00	12.00
RDTAK Adrian Kempe	2.50	6.00
RDTAN Alexander Nylander	3.00	8.00
RDTAT Alex Tuch	5.00	12.00
RDTBB Brock Boeser	15.00	40.00
RDTCK Clayton Keller	5.00	12.00
RDTCM Charlie McAvoy	6.00	15.00
RDTFC Filip Chytil	2.00	5.00
RDTJD Jake DeBrusk	3.00	8.00
RDTJH Josh Ho-Sang	2.50	6.00
RDTKY Kailer Yamamoto	5.00	12.00
RDTLB Logan Brown	2.00	5.00
RDTLK Luke Kunin	2.00	5.00
RDTMB Madison Bowey	1.50	4.00
RDTNH Nico Hischier	6.00	15.00
RDTNP Nolan Patrick	4.00	10.00
RDTOT Owen Tippett	4.00	10.00
RDTPD Pierre-Luc Dubois	4.00	10.00
RDTTJ Tyson Jost	4.00	10.00
RDTTT Tage Thompson	3.00	8.00
RDTVD Vince Dunn	2.00	5.00
RDTVM Victor Mete	2.00	5.00
RDTWB Will Butcher	2.50	6.00

2017-18 Ultimate Collection '07-08 Retro Debut Threads Patch Autographs

RDTAD Alex DeBrincat	50.00	125.00
RDTAK Adrian Kempe	25.00	60.00
RDTAN Alexander Nylander	30.00	80.00
RDTAT Alex Tuch	50.00	125.00
RDTBB Brock Boeser	100.00	250.00
RDTCK Clayton Keller	50.00	125.00
RDTCM Charlie McAvoy	60.00	150.00
RDTJD Jake DeBrusk	30.00	80.00
RDTJH Josh Ho-Sang	25.00	60.00
RDTKY Kailer Yamamoto	50.00	125.00
RDTLK Luke Kunin	20.00	50.00
RDTMB Madison Bowey	15.00	40.00
RDTNH Nico Hischier (No Auto)	60.00	150.00
RDTNP Nolan Patrick (No Auto)	40.00	100.00
RDTOT Owen Tippett	40.00	100.00
RDTPD Pierre-Luc Dubois	40.00	100.00
RDTTJ Tyson Jost	40.00	100.00
RDTTT Tage Thompson	30.00	80.00
RDTVD Vince Dunn	20.00	50.00
RDTVM Victor Mete	20.00	50.00
RDTWB Will Butcher	25.00	60.00

2017-18 Ultimate Collection Debut Threads Patch Autographs

DTAAD Alex DeBrincat/49	60.00	150.00
DTAAF Alex Formenton/149	15.00	40.00
DTAAK Adrian Kempe/149	20.00	50.00
DTAAN Alexander Nylander/149	25.00	60.00
DTAAT Alex Tuch/149	40.00	100.00
DTABB Brock Boeser/49	150.00	250.00
DTACF Christian Fischer/149	20.00	50.00
DTACK Clayton Keller/49	30.00	80.00
DTACM Charlie McAvoy/49	40.00	100.00
DTACW Colin White/149	15.00	40.00
DTADG Denis Gurianov/149	15.00	40.00
DTAFC Filip Chlapik/149	15.00	40.00
DTAJB Jesper Bratt/149	25.00	60.00
DTAJC J.T. Compher/149	20.00	50.00
DTAJF Jakob Forsbacka-Karlsson/149	15.00	40.00
DTAJG Jon Gillies/149	15.00	40.00
DTAJH Josh Ho-Sang/149	20.00	50.00
DTAJK Janne Kuokkanen/149	15.00	40.00
DTAJR Jack Roslovic/149	20.00	50.00
DTAKY Kailer Yamamoto/149	40.00	100.00
DTALK Luke Kunin/149	15.00	40.00
DTAMB Madison Bowey/149	12.00	30.00
DTANH Nico Hischier/49 (No Auto)	50.00	125.00
DTANP Nolan Patrick/49 (No Auto)	40.00	100.00
DTANS Nikita Scherbak/149	30.00	80.00
DTAOT Owen Tippett/149	30.00	80.00
DTAPD Pierre-Luc Dubois/149	30.00	80.00
DTARE Remi Elie/149	12.00	30.00
DTASM Samuel Morin/149	15.00	40.00
DTATJ Tyson Jost/149	30.00	80.00
DTATP Tucker Poolman/149	15.00	40.00
DTATS Travis Sanheim/149	15.00	40.00
DTATT Tage Thompson/149	25.00	60.00
DTAVD Vince Dunn/149	15.00	40.00
DTAVH Ville Husso/149	15.00	40.00
DTAVM Victor Mete/149	15.00	40.00
DTAVZ Valentin Zykov/149	15.00	40.00
DTAWB Will Butcher/149	20.00	50.00

2017-18 Ultimate Collection Future Legacy Jerseys

FLAB Anders Bjork	3.00	8.00
FLAD Alex DeBrincat	6.00	15.00
FLBB Brock Boeser	12.00	30.00
FLCK Clayton Keller	6.00	15.00
FLCM Charlie McAvoy	8.00	20.00
FLJH Josh Ho-Sang	3.00	8.00
FLNH Nico Hischier	8.00	20.00
FLNP Nolan Patrick	5.00	12.00
FLOT Owen Tippett	5.00	12.00
FLPD Pierre-Luc Dubois	5.00	12.00

2017-18 Ultimate Collection Patches

93 Brock Boeser AU/49	150.00	250.00

2017-18 Ultimate Collection Signature Laureates

SLBO Bobby Orr	80.00	150.00
SLMB Mike Bossy		
SLMM Mark Messier		
SLWG Wayne Gretzky	300.00	400.00

2017-18 Ultimate Collection Signature Material Laureates

SMLAO Alexander Ovechkin/10		
SMLCP Colton Parayko/99	12.00	30.00
SMLDH Dale Hawerchuk/99	15.00	40.00
SMLGF Grant Fuhr/99	15.00	40.00
SMLJC Jeff Carter/99	12.00	30.00
SMLJD Jonathan Drouin/99	12.00	30.00
SMLJG Jake Guentzel/99	15.00	40.00
SMLJP Jason Pominville/99	10.00	25.00
SMLKS Kevin Shattenkirk/99	12.00	30.00
SMLLC Logan Couture/99	12.00	30.00
SMLMB Martin Brodeur/10		
SMLNK Nikita Kucherov/99	20.00	50.00
SMLSB Sergei Bobrovsky/99	12.00	30.00
SMLSY Steve Yzerman/10		
SMLWG Wayne Gretzky/10		

2017-18 Ultimate Collection Signature Material Phenoms

SMPAD Alex DeBrincat/15		
SMPAK Adrian Kempe/65		
SMPAN Alexander Nylander/15		
SMPAT Alex Tuch/65	80.00	150.00
SMPBB Brock Boeser/15		
SMPCK Clayton Keller/15		
SMPCM Charlie McAvoy/15		
SMPJH Josh Ho-Sang/15		
SMPKY Kailer Yamamoto/65		
SMPOT Owen Tippett/65	25.00	60.00
SMPPD Pierre-Luc Dubois/15		
SMPTJ Tyson Jost/15		
SMPVM Victor Mete/65	8.00	20.00
SMPWB Will Butcher/65		

2017-18 Ultimate Collection Signature Ultimate Performers Jerseys

SUPCM Connor McDavid		
SUPHL Henrik Lundqvist	8.00	20.00
SUPJI Jarome Iginla	5.00	12.00
SUPJT John Tavares	10.00	25.00
SUPSS Steven Stamkos	10.00	25.00
SUPWG Wayne Gretzky		

2017-18 Ultimate Collection Ultimate Introductions

UI1 Henrik Haapala	2.00	5.00
UI2 J.T. Compher	2.50	6.00
UI3 Haydn Fleury	2.00	5.00
UI4 Nikita Scherbak	4.00	10.00
UI5 Carter Rowney	1.50	4.00
UI6 Vince Dunn	2.00	5.00
UI7 Christian Djoos	2.00	5.00
UI8 Samuel Girard	2.00	5.00
UI9 Calle Rosen	2.00	5.00
UI10 Evgeny Svechnikov	4.00	10.00
UI11 Colin White	2.00	5.00
UI12 Christian Jaros	2.00	5.00
UI13 Eric Comrie	1.50	4.00
UI14 Samuel Blais	2.00	5.00
UI15 Filip Chytil	2.00	5.00
UI16 Robert Hagg	2.00	5.00
UI17 Nick Merkley	2.00	5.00
UI18 Tage Thompson	3.00	8.00
UI19 Alex Tuch	5.00	12.00
UI20 Anders Bjork	2.50	6.00
UI21 Alex Kerfoot	2.00	5.00
UI22 Jesper Bratt	3.00	8.00
UI23 Martin Necas	2.00	5.00
UI24 Travis Sanheim	2.00	5.00
UI25 Luke Kunin	2.00	5.00
UI26 Victor Mete	2.00	5.00
UI27 Logan Brown	2.00	5.00
UI28 Christian Fischer	2.50	6.00
UI29 Tyson Jost	4.00	10.00
UI30 Josh Ho-Sang	2.50	6.00
UI31 Kailer Yamamoto	5.00	12.00
UI32 Alexander Nylander	3.00	8.00
UI33 Will Butcher	2.50	6.00
UI34 Jake DeBrusk	3.00	8.00
UI35 Owen Tippett	4.00	10.00
UI36 Adrian Kempe	2.50	6.00
UI37 Charlie McAvoy	6.00	15.00
UI38 Pierre-Luc Dubois	4.00	10.00
UI39 Brock Boeser	10.00	25.00
UI40 Nolan Patrick	4.00	10.00
UI41 Alex DeBrincat	5.00	12.00
UI42 Clayton Keller	5.00	12.00
UI43 Nico Hischier	6.00	15.00

2017-18 Ultimate Collection Ultimate Introductions Gold Spectrum Autographs

UI2 J.T. Compher	12.00	30.00
UI4 Nikita Scherbak	20.00	50.00
UI6 Vince Dunn	10.00	25.00
UI7 Christian Djoos	10.00	25.00
UI8 Samuel Girard	10.00	25.00
UI11 Colin White	10.00	25.00
UI15 Filip Chytil	10.00	25.00
UI16 Robert Hagg	10.00	25.00
UI17 Nick Merkley	10.00	25.00
UI18 Tage Thompson	15.00	40.00
UI19 Alex Tuch	25.00	60.00
UI21 Alex Kerfoot	10.00	25.00
UI22 Jesper Bratt	15.00	40.00
UI23 Martin Necas	10.00	25.00
UI24 Travis Sanheim	10.00	25.00
UI25 Luke Kunin	10.00	25.00
UI26 Victor Mete	10.00	25.00
UI28 Christian Fischer	12.00	30.00
UI29 Tyson Jost	20.00	50.00
UI30 Josh Ho-Sang	12.00	30.00
UI31 Kailer Yamamoto	25.00	60.00
UI32 Alexander Nylander	15.00	40.00
UI33 Will Butcher	12.00	30.00
UI34 Jake DeBrusk	15.00	40.00
UI35 Owen Tippett	20.00	50.00
UI36 Adrian Kempe	12.00	30.00
UI37 Charlie McAvoy	30.00	80.00
UI39 Brock Boeser	150.00	250.00
UI41 Alex DeBrincat	25.00	60.00
UI42 Clayton Keller	25.00	60.00

2017-18 Ultimate Collection Ultimate Legacy Jerseys

ULCP Carey Price C	10.00	25.00
ULEK Erik Karlsson D	4.00	10.00
ULJT Jonathan Toews D	6.00	15.00
ULML Mario Lemieux A	10.00	25.00
ULMM Mark Messier A	5.00	12.00
ULPD Pavel Datsyuk D	5.00	12.00
ULPF Peter Forsberg C	5.00	12.00
ULSC Sidney Crosby A	12.00	30.00
ULSS Steven Stamkos B	6.00	15.00
ULWG Wayne Gretzky A	15.00	40.00

2017-18 Ultimate Collection Ultimate Legacy Signatures

ULSBO Bobby Orr C	60.00	150.00
ULSEB Ed Belfour C	10.00	25.00
ULSHL Henrik Lundqvist B	40.00	100.00
ULSSS Steven Stamkos A		
ULSWG Wayne Gretzky A		

2017-18 Ultimate Collection Ultimate Performers Jerseys

UPCP Carey Price/99	10.00	25.00
UPDH Dominik Hasek/99	3.00	8.00
UPDS Daniel Sedin/99	3.00	8.00
UPEM Evgeni Malkin/99	10.00	25.00
UPJS Joe Sakic/99	4.00	10.00
UPJT Jonathan Toews/99	6.00	15.00
UPMB Martin Brodeur/49	12.00	30.00
UPPD Pavel Datsyuk/99	5.00	12.00
UPRB Ray Bourque/99	5.00	12.00
UPSY Steve Yzerman/49	20.00	50.00
UPWG Wayne Gretzky/49	25.00	60.00

1991-92 Ultimate Original Six Promos

53 Bobby Hull	.50	1.25
103 Bobby Baun Baun's Heroics	.30	.75

1991-92 Ultimate Original Six

Produced by the Ultimate Trading Card Company, this 100-card standard-size set celebrates the 75th anniversary of the NHL by featuring players from the original six teams in the NHL. The cards were available only in foil packs, with a production run reportedly of 25,000 foil cases. Each foil pack included a sweepstake card; prizes offered included 250 autographed Bobby Hull holograms and 500 sets autographed by those players living at the time. The fronts feature color action photos with white borders, with the player's name in a silver bar at the top and the left lower corner of the picture rolled back to allow space for the producer's logo. The backs have a career summary presented in the format of a newspaper article (with different headlines), with biography and career statistics appearing in a silver box toward the bottom of the card. The cards are numbered on the back and checklisted below as follows: Team Checklists (1-6), Montreal Canadiens (7-17), New York Rangers (18-29), Toronto Maple Leafs (30-46), Boston Bruins (47-56), Chicago Blackhawks (57-65), Detroit Red Wings (66-72), Ultimate Hall of Fame (73-78), All Ultimate Team (79-84), Referees (85-87), Bobby Hull (88-92), and Great Moments (93-97). The cards were produced in both English and French versions. Either version is valued the same.

COMPLETE SET (100)	2.50	6.00
*FRENCH: 4X TO 1X BASIC CARDS		
1 Montreal Canadiens	.02	.10
2 New York Rangers	.01	.05
3 Toronto Maple Leafs	.01	.05
4 Boston Bruins	.01	.05
5 Chicago Blackhawks	.01	.05
6 Detroit Red Wings	.01	.05
7 Ralph Backstrom	.01	.05
8 Butch Bouchard	.05	.15
9 John Ferguson	.02	.10
10 Boom Boom Geoffrion	.25	.60
11 Phil Goyette	.01	.05
12 Doug Harvey	.15	.40
13 Don Marshall	.02	.10
14 Henri Richard	.20	.50
15 Dollard St.Laurent	.01	.05
16 Jean-Guy Talbot	.02	.10
17 Gump Worsley	.15	.40
18 Andy Bathgate	.07	.20
19 Lou Fontinato	.01	.05
20 Ed Giacomin	.07	.20
21 Vic Hadfield	.02	.10
22 Camille Henry	.01	.05
23 Harry Howell	.05	.15
24 Orland Kurtenbach	.02	.10
25 Jim Neilson	.01	.05
26 Bob Nevin	.01	.05
27 Dean Prentice	.02	.10
28 Leo Reise Jr.	.01	.05
29 George Sullivan	.01	.05
30 Bob Baun	.08	.20
31 Gus Bodnar	.01	.05
32 Johnny Bower	.07	.20
33 Bob Davidson	.01	.05
34 Ron Ellis	.02	.10
35 Billy Harris	.01	.05
36 Larry Hillman	.01	.05
37 Tim Horton	.30	.75
38 Red Kelly	.10	.30
39 Dave Keon	.07	.20
40 Frank Mahovlich	.20	.50
41 Eddie Shack	.07	.20
42 Tod Sloan	.01	.05
43 Sid Smith	.02	.10
44 Allan Stanley	.07	.20
45 Gaye Stewart	.01	.05
46 Harry Watson	.05	.15
47 Wayne Carleton	.01	.05
48 Fern Flaman	.02	.10
49 Ken Hodge UER	.02	.10
50 Leo Labine	.01	.05
51 Harry Lumley	.07	.20
52 John McKenzie	.02	.10
53 Doug Mohns	.02	.10
54 Fred Stanfield	.01	.05
55 Jerry Toppazzini	.01	.05
56 Ed Westfall	.02	.10
57 Bobby Hull	.40	1.00
58 Ed Litzenberger	.01	.05
59 Gilles Marotte	.01	.05
60 Ab McDonald	.01	.05
61 Bill Mosienko	.05	.15
62 Jim Pappin	.01	.05
63 Pierre Pilote	.05	.15
64 Elmer Vasko	.01	.05
65 Johnny Wilson	.01	.05
66 Sid Abel	.07	.20
67 Gary Bergman	.01	.05
68 Alex Delvecchio	.10	.30
69 Bill Gadsby	.07	.20
70 Ted Lindsay	.15	.40
71 Marcel Pronovost	.05	.15
72 Norm Ullman	.07	.20
73 Boom Boom Geoffrion	.25	.60
74 Andy Bathgate	.07	.20
75 Allan Stanley	.07	.20
76 Fern Flaman	.05	.15
77 Bobby Hull	.40	1.00
78 Norm Ullman	.07	.20
79 Red Kelly	.10	.30
80 Johnny Bower	.10	.30
81 Henri Richard	.20	.50
82 Bobby Hull	.40	1.00
83 Boom Boom Geoffrion	.25	.60
84 Tim Horton	.30	.75
85 Bill Friday REF	.01	.05
86 Bruce Hood REF	.01	.05
87 Ron Wicks REF	.01	.05
88 Bobby Hull Electric Slap Shot	.20	.50
89 Bobby Hull The Point Race	.20	.50
90 Bobby Hull 1960-61 Stanley Cup	.20	.50
91 Bobby Hull The Curse of Muldoon is lifted	.20	.50
92 Bobby Hull Million Dollar Man	.20	.50
93 Bobby Baun Baun's Heroics	.01	.05
94 Ted Lindsay Lindsay's comeback	.05	.15
95 Henri Richard Richard's 99-year record	.05	.15
96 Bobby Hull Hull breaks 50 goal barrier	.20	.50
97 Tim Horton Tribute	.08	.25
98 Keith McCreary	.01	.05
99 Checklist 1	.01	.05
100 Checklist 2	.01	.05
NNO Bobby Hull Hologram	4.00	10.00

1991-92 Ultimate Original Six Box Bottoms

This four-card standard-size set was issued on the bottom of foil boxes. The cards feature on the fronts four-color or black and white action photos, with the lower left corner turned upward to allow space for the Ultimate logo. The player's name appears in black in a silver border at the top and the NHL logo is placed toward the end of the silver bar. Bobby Hull's card features red to black screened bars on two sides enclosing an artwork collage. The cards are unnumbered and checklisted below in alphabetical order.

COMPLETE SET (4)	.60	1.50
1 Ed Giacomin	.20	.50
2 Bobby Hull The Golden Jet	.40	1.00
3 Marcel Pronovost	.08	.25
4 Eddie Shack	.08	.25

1999-00 Ultimate Victory

The 1999-00 Upper Deck Ultimate Victory set was released as a 120-card set, which features 90 veteran cards, 20 short-printed prospects, and 10 Ultimate Hockey Legacy Wayne Gretzky cards on a front foil card-stock. This product was released in 5-card packs and 24-pack boxes.

COMPLETE SET (120)	60.00	125.00
COMP.SET w/o SP's (90)	10.00	20.00
1 Paul Kariya	.25	.60
2 Teemu Selanne	.25	.60
3 Jason Marshall	.08	.25
4 David Harlock	.08	.25
5 Ray Ferraro	.08	.25
6 Kelly Buchberger	.08	.25
7 Sergei Samsonov	.20	.50
8 Ray Bourque	.40	1.00
9 Darren Van Impe	.08	.25
10 Dominik Hasek	.50	1.25
11 Miroslav Satan	.20	.50
12 Geoff Sanderson	.20	.50
13 Valeri Bure	.08	.25
14 Cale Hulse	.08	.25
15 Cory Stillman	.08	.25
16 Ron Francis	.20	.50
17 Andrei Kovalenko	.08	.25
18 Sami Kapanen	.08	.25
19 Tony Amonte	.20	.50
20 Steve Sullivan	.08	.25
21 Doug Gilmour	.20	.50
22 Milan Hejduk	.25	.60
23 Joe Sakic	.50	1.25
24 Patrick Roy	1.25	3.00
25 Chris Drury	.20	.50
26 Peter Forsberg	.60	1.50
27 Mike Modano	.40	1.00
28 Brett Hull	.30	.75
29 Ed Belfour	.25	.60
30 Blake Sloan	.08	.25
31 Steve Yzerman	1.25	3.00
32 Chris Osgood	.20	.50
33 Brendan Shanahan	.25	.60
34 Larry Murphy	.20	.50
35 Doug Weight	.20	.50
36 Christian Laflamme	.08	.25
37 Alexander Selivanov	.08	.25
38 Pavel Bure	.25	.60
39 Jaroslav Spacek	.08	.25
40 Viktor Kozlov	.20	.50
41 Luc Robitaille	.20	.50
42 Zigmund Palffy	.20	.50
43 Rob Blake	.20	.50
44 Saku Koivu	.25	.60
45 Patrick Poulin	.08	.25
46 Brian Savage	.08	.25
47 David Legwand	.20	.50
48 Sergei Krivokrasov	.08	.25
49 Rob Valicevic RC	.08	.25
50 Martin Brodeur	.60	1.50
51 Scott Stevens	.20	.50
52 Krzysztof Oliwa	.08	.25
53 Jamie Heward	.08	.25
54 Mariusz Czerkawski	.08	.25
55 Kenny Jonsson	.08	.25
56 Mike Richter	.25	.60
57 Theo Fleury	.08	.25
58 Tim Taylor	.08	.25
59 Brian Leetch	.25	.60
60 Andreas Dackell	.08	.25
61 Marian Hossa	.25	.60
62 Ron Tugnutt	.20	.50
63 Craig Berube	.08	.25
64 Eric Lindros	.25	.60
65 John LeClair	.25	.60
66 Dallas Drake	.08	.25
67 Keith Tkachuk	.25	.60
68 Jeremy Roenick	.30	.75
69 Jaromir Jagr	.40	1.00
70 Martin Straka	.08	.25
71 Rob Brown	.08	.25
72 Marcus Ragnarsson	.08	.25
73 Steve Shields	.20	.50
74 Owen Nolan	.20	.50
75 Jeff Friesen	.08	.25
76 Pavol Demitra	.20	.50
77 Roman Turek	.20	.50
78 Mike Eastwood	.08	.25
79 Vincent Lecavalier	.25	[illegible]
80 Dan Cloutier	.20	[illegible]
81 Stan Drulia	.08	[illegible]
82 Mats Sundin	.25	[illegible]
83 Igor Korolev	.08	[illegible]
84 Curtis Joseph	.25	[illegible]
85 Mark Messier	.25	[illegible]
86 Harry York	.20	[illegible]
87 Peter Schaefer	.08	[illegible]
88 Olaf Kolzig	.20	[illegible]
89 Steve Konowalchuk	.08	[illegible]
90 Peter Bondra	.25	[illegible]
91 Patrik Stefan SP RC	1.25	3.0
92 Brian Campbell SP RC	1.25	3.0
93 Mikko Eloranta SP RC	1.25	3.0
94 Oleg Saprykin SP RC	1.25	3.0
95 Kyle Calder SP RC	1.50	4.0
96 Jon Sim SP RC	1.25	3.0
97 Marc Rodgers SP RC	1.25	3.0
98 Paul Comrie SP RC	1.25	3.0
99 Ivan Novoseltsev SP RC	1.25	3.0
100 Jason Blake SP RC	1.25	3.0
101 Brian Rafalski SP RC	2.00	5.0
102 Jorgen Jonsson SP RC	1.25	3.0
103 Nikolai Antropov SP RC	2.00	5.0
104 Steve Kariya SP RC	1.50	4.0
105 Glen Metropolit SP RC	1.25	3.0
106 Jochen Hecht SP RC	2.00	5.0
107 Sheldon Keefe SP RC	1.25	3.0
108 Branislav Mezei SP RC	1.25	3.0
109 Pavel Brendl SP RC	1.25	3.0
110 Milan Kraft SP RC	1.25	3.0
111 Wayne Gretzky	1.50	4.0
112 Wayne Gretzky	1.50	4.0
113 Wayne Gretzky	1.50	4.0
114 Wayne Gretzky	1.50	4.0
115 Wayne Gretzky	1.50	4.0
116 Wayne Gretzky	1.50	4.0
117 Wayne Gretzky	1.50	4.0
118 Wayne Gretzky	1.50	4.0
119 Wayne Gretzky	1.50	4.0
120 Wayne Gretzky	1.50	4.0

1999-00 Ultimate Victory Parallel 1/1

Randomly inserted in packs, this 120-card set featur[illegible] the base card in a one of one parallel.

1999-00 Ultimate Victory Foil Parallel

Randomly inserted in packs, this 120-card parallel s[illegible] features the base card etched with a vertical rainbow effect.

*VETS 1-90/111-120: 1.2X TO 3X BASIC CARDS
*ROOKIES 91-110: .6X TO 1.5X BASIC SP RC

1999-00 Ultimate Victory Parallel 100

Randomly inserted in packs, this 120-card parallel s[illegible] is printed on a bronze version of the base card and serial numbered to 100.

*VETS 1-90/111-120: 5X TO 12X BASIC CARDS
*ROOKIES 91-110: 2X TO 5X BASIC SP RC

1999-00 Ultimate Victory Frozen Fury

COMPLETE SET (10)	12.00	25.[illegible]
STATED ODDS 1:23		
FF1 Eric Lindros	1.25	3.[illegible]
FF2 Paul Kariya	.75	2.0
FF3 Pavel Bure	1.00	2.5
FF4 Steve Kariya	.40	1.0
FF5 Mike Modano	1.25	3.0
FF6 Patrik Stefan	.40	1.0
FF7 Martin Brodeur	2.00	5.0
FF8 Jaromir Jagr	1.25	3.0
FF9 Joe Sakic	1.50	4.0
FF10 Steve Yzerman	4.00	10.0

1999-00 Ultimate Victory Legendary Fabrics

Randomly inserted in packs, this five-card set feature[illegible] single and dual game-worn jersey swatches with the addition of certified autographs on two cards in the s[illegible] Lower print runs are not priced due to scarcity.

BOS Bobby Orr/4 AU		
LFBO Bobby Orr/99	50.00	120.0
LFWG Wayne Gretzky/99	50.00	120.0
UFS W.Gretzky/B.Orr/10 AU		
UF W.Gretzky/B.Orr/99	200.00	400.0

1999-00 Ultimate Victory Net Work

COMPLETE SET (10)	12.00	25.0
STATED ODDS 1:11		
NW1 Dominik Hasek	1.50	4.[illegible]
NW2 Patrick Roy	5.00	12.[illegible]
NW3 Chris Osgood	.75	2.[illegible]
NW4 Ed Belfour	1.00	2.[illegible]
NW5 Mike Richter	1.00	2.[illegible]
NW6 Roman Turek	.75	2.[illegible]
NW7 Steve Shields	.75	2.[illegible]
NW8 Curtis Joseph	.75	2.[illegible]
NW9 Guy Hebert	.75	2.[illegible]
NW10 Martin Brodeur	2.00	5.[illegible]

1999-00 Ultimate Victory Smokin Guns

COMPLETE SET (12)	8.00	15.[illegible]
STATED ODDS 1:11		
SG1 Jaromir Jagr	.75	2.[illegible]
SG2 Paul Kariya	.50	1.[illegible]
SG3 Sergei Fedorov	1.00	2.[illegible]
SG4 Steve Kariya	.30	[illegible]
SG5 Peter Forsberg	1.25	3.[illegible]
SG6 Marian Hossa	.50	1.[illegible]
SG7 Theo Fleury	.50	1.[illegible]
SG8 Patrik Stefan	.75	2.[illegible]
SG9 Pavel Bure	.60	1.[illegible]
SG10 Eric Lindros	.75	2.[illegible]
SG11 Brett Hull	.60	1.[illegible]
SG12 Teemu Selanne	.50	1.[illegible]

1999-00 Ultimate Victory Stature

COMPLETE SET (12)	6.00	12.[illegible]
STATED ODDS 1:6		
S1 Paul Kariya	.30	[illegible]
S2 Joe Sakic	.60	1.[illegible]

S3 Peter Forsberg .75 2.00
S4 Mike Modano .50 1.25
S5 Brendan Shanahan .50 1.25
S6 Pavel Bure .40 1.00
S7 Martin Brodeur .75 2.00
S8 Theo Fleury .30 .75
S9 Eric Lindros .50 1.25
S10 Keith Tkachuk .30 .75
S11 Jaromir Jagr .50 1.25
S12 Ray Bourque .50 1.25

1999-00 Ultimate Victory The Victors

COMPLETE SET (8) 10.00 20.00
STATED ODDS 1:23
V1 Mark Messier .75 2.00
V2 Brett Hull .75 2.00
V3 Steve Yzerman 3.00 8.00
V4 Jaromir Jagr 1.00 2.50
V5 Patrick Roy 3.00 8.00
V6 Martin Brodeur 1.50 4.00
V7 Peter Forsberg 1.50 4.00
V8 Theo Fleury .60 1.50

1999-00 Ultimate Victory UV Extra

COMPLETE SET (8) 12.00 25.00
STATED ODDS 1:23
UV1 Jaromir Jagr 1.00 2.50
UV2 Patrick Roy 3.00 8.00
UV3 Pavel Bure .60 1.50
UV4 Bobby Orr 4.00 10.00
UV5 Paul Kariya 1.25 3.00
UV6 Peter Forsberg 1.50 4.00
UV7 Steve Yzerman 3.00 8.00
UV8 Eric Lindros 1.00 2.50

1992-93 Ultra

The 1992-93 Ultra hockey set consists of 450 standard-size cards. The fronts have glossy color action player photos that are full-bleed except at the bottom where a diagonal gold-foil stripe edges a "blue ice" border. The player's name and team appear on two team color-coded bars that overlay the bottom border. The horizontally oriented backs display action and close-up cut-out player photos against a hockey rink background. The Roenick Harding promo was issued in advance of the series and pictures the two men (the latter, the president of Fleer) in front of the Chicago skyline.

1 Brent Ashton .10 .25
2 Ray Bourque .25 .60
3 Steve Heinze .10 .25
4 Joe Juneau .10 .25
5 Stephen Leach .10 .25
6 Andy Moog .12 .30
7 Cam Neely .15 .40
8 Adam Oates .15 .40
9 Dave Poulin .10 .25
10 Vladimir Ruzicka .10 .25
11 Glen Wesley .10 .25
12 Dave Andreychuk .15 .40
13 Keith Carney RC .30 .75
14 Tom Draper .10 .25
15 Dale Hawerchuk .20 .50
16 Pat LaFontaine .15 .40
17 Brad May .10 .25
18 Alexander Mogilny .12 .30
19 Mike Ramsey .10 .25
20 Ken Sutton .10 .25
21 Theo Fleury .25 .60
22 Gary Leeman .10 .25
23 Al MacInnis .12 .30
24 Sergei Makarov .10 .25
25 Joe Nieuwendyk .12 .30
26 Joel Otto .10 .25
27 Paul Ranheim .10 .25
28 Robert Reichel .10 .25
29 Gary Roberts .10 .25
30 Gary Suter .10 .25
31 Mike Vernon .12 .30
32 Ed Belfour .15 .40
33 Rob Brown .10 .25
34 Chris Chelios .15 .40
35 Michel Goulet .12 .30
36 Dirk Graham .10 .25
37 Mike Hudson .10 .25
38 Igor Kravchuk .10 .25
39 Steve Larmer .10 .25
40 Dean McAmmond RC .10 .25
41 Jeremy Roenick .25 .60
42 Steve Smith .10 .25
43 Brent Sutter .10 .25
44 Shawn Burr .10 .25
45 Jimmy Carson .10 .25
46 Tim Cheveldae .10 .25
47 Dino Ciccarelli .12 .30
48 Sergei Fedorov .25 .60
49 Vladimir Konstantinov .15 .40
50 Slava Kozlov .12 .30
51 Nicklas Lidstrom .12 .30
52 Brad McCrimmon .10 .25
53 Bob Probert .12 .30
54 Paul Ysebaert .10 .25
55 Steve Yzerman .40 1.00
56 Josef Beranek .10 .25
57 Shayne Corson .10 .25
58 Brian Glynn .10 .25
59 Petr Klima .10 .25
60 Kevin Lowe .12 .30
61 Norm Maciver .10 .25
62 Dave Manson .10 .25
63 Joe Murphy .10 .25
64 Bernie Nicholls .10 .25
65 Bill Ranford .12 .30
66 Craig Simpson .10 .25
67 Esa Tikkanen .10 .25
68 Sean Burke .12 .30
69 Adam Burt .10 .25
70 Andrew Cassels .10 .25
71 Murray Craven .10 .25
72 John Cullen .10 .25
73 Randy Cunneyworth .10 .25
74 Tim Kerr .10 .25
75 Geoff Sanderson .12 .30
76 Eric Weinrich .10 .25
77 Zarley Zalapski .10 .25
78 Peter Ahola .10 .25
79 Rob Blake .12 .30
80 Paul Coffey .15 .40
81 Mike Donnelly .10 .25
82 Tony Granato .10 .25
83 Wayne Gretzky .75 2.00
84 Kelly Hrudey .12 .30
85 Jari Kurri .15 .40
86 Corey Millen .10 .25
87 Luc Robitaille .12 .30
88 Tomas Sandstrom .12 .30
89 Neal Broten .12 .30
90 Jon Casey .10 .25
91 Russ Courtnall .10 .25
92 Ulf Dahlen .10 .25
93 Todd Elik .10 .25
94 Dave Gagner .12 .30
95 Jim Johnson .12 .30
96 Mike Modano UER .40 1.00
97 Bobby Smith .12 .30
98 Mark Tinordi .10 .25
99 Darcy Wakaluk .12 .30
100 Brian Bellows .12 .30
101 Benoit Brunet .10 .25
102 Guy Carbonneau .12 .30
103 Vincent Damphousse .12 .30
104 Eric Desjardins .12 .30
105 Gilbert Dionne .10 .25
106 Mike Keane .10 .25
107 Kirk Muller .10 .25
108 Patrick Roy .40 1.00
109 Denis Savard .20 .50
110 Mathieu Schneider .10 .25
111 Brian Skrudland .12 .30
112 Tom Chorske .12 .30
113 Zdeno Ciger .10 .25
114 Claude Lemieux .10 .25
115 John MacLean .12 .30
116 Scott Niedermayer .15 .40
117 Stephane Richer .12 .30
118 Peter Stastny .12 .30
119 Scott Stevens .15 .40
120 Chris Terreri .12 .30
121 Kevin Todd .10 .25
122 Valeri Zelepukin .10 .25
123 Ray Ferraro .10 .25
124 Mark Fitzpatrick .12 .30
125 Patrick Flatley .12 .30
126 Glenn Healy .12 .30
127 Benoit Hogue .10 .25
128 Derek King .10 .25
129 Uwe Krupp .10 .25
130 Scott Lachance .10 .25
131 Steve Thomas .12 .30
132 Pierre Turgeon .12 .30
133 Tony Amonte .12 .30
134 Paul Broten .10 .25
135 Mike Gartner .12 .30
136 Adam Graves .10 .25
137 Alexei Kovalev .12 .30
138 Brian Leetch .12 .30
139 Mark Messier .25 .60
140 Sergei Nemchinov .10 .25
141 James Patrick .10 .25
142 Mike Richter .15 .40
143 Darren Turcotte .10 .25
144 John Vanbiesbrouck .12 .30
145 Dominic Lavoie .12 .30
146 Lonnie Loach RC .10 .25
147 Andrew McBain .12 .30
148 Darren Rumble .10 .25
149 Sylvain Turgeon .10 .25
150 Peter Sidorkiewicz .10 .25
151 Brian Benning .10 .25
152 Rod Brind'Amour .10 .25
153 Viacheslav Butsayev RC .10 .25
154 Kevin Dineen .10 .25
155 Pelle Eklund .12 .30
156 Garry Galley .10 .25
157 Eric Lindros .50 1.25
158 Mark Recchi .20 .50
159 Dominic Roussel .12 .30
160 Tommy Soderstrom RC .12 .30
161 Dimitri Yushkevich RC .10 .25
162 Tom Barrasso .12 .30
163 Ron Francis .20 .50
164 Jaromir Jagr .40 1.00
165 Mario Lemieux .60 1.50
166 Joe Mullen .12 .30
167 Larry Murphy .12 .30
168 Jim Paek .12 .30
169 Kjell Samuelsson .12 .30
170 Ulf Samuelsson .10 .25
171 Kevin Stevens .10 .25
172 Rick Tocchet .12 .30
173 Alexei Gusarov .10 .25
174 Ron Hextall .12 .30
175 Mike Hough .12 .30
176 Claude Lapointe .10 .25
177 Owen Nolan .10 .25
178 Mike Ricci .12 .30
179 Joe Sakic .40 1.00
180 Mats Sundin .15 .40
181 Mikhail Tatarinov .10 .25
182 Bob Bassen .10 .25
183 Jeff Brown .12 .30
184 Garth Butcher .12 .30
185 Paul Cavallini .10 .25
186 Brett Hull .25 .60
187 Craig Janney .12 .30
188 Curtis Joseph .15 .40
189 Brendan Shanahan .20 .50
190 Ron Sutter .10 .25
191 David Bruce .10 .25
192 Dale Craigwell .10 .25
193 Dean Evason .10 .25
194 Pat Falloon .10 .25
195 Jeff Hackett .12 .30
196 Kelly Kisio .12 .30
197 Brian Lawton .12 .30
198 Neil Wilkinson .10 .25
199 Doug Wilson .12 .30
200 Marc Bergevin .12 .30
201 Roman Hamrlik RC .30 .75
202 Pat Jablonski .12 .30
203 Michel Mongeau .12 .30
204 Peter Taglianetti .12 .30
205 Steve Tuttle .12 .30
206 Wendell Young .12 .30
207 Glenn Anderson .15 .40
208 Wendel Clark .12 .30
209 Dave Ellett .10 .25
210 Grant Fuhr .15 .40
211 Doug Gilmour .20 .50
212 Jamie Macoun .12 .30
213 Felix Potvin .30 .75
214 Bob Rouse .12 .30
215 Joe Sacco .10 .25
216 Peter Zezel .10 .25
217 Greg Adams .10 .25
218 Dave Babych .12 .30
219 Pavel Bure .30 .75
220 Geoff Courtnall .10 .25
221 Doug Lidster .12 .30
222 Trevor Linden .12 .30
223 Jyrki Lumme .10 .25
224 Kirk McLean .10 .25
225 Sergio Momesso .10 .25
226 Petr Nedved .12 .30
227 Cliff Ronning .10 .25
228 Jim Sandlak .10 .25
229 Don Beaupre .12 .30
230 Peter Bondra .12 .30
231 Kevin Hatcher .10 .25
232 Dale Hunter .12 .30
233 Al Iafrate .12 .30
234 Calle Johansson .10 .25
235 Dimitri Khristich .10 .25
236 Kelly Miller .10 .25
237 Michal Pivonka .10 .25
238 Mike Ridley .10 .25
239 Luciano Borsato .10 .25
240 Bob Essensa .12 .30
241 Phil Housley .10 .25
242 Troy Murray .10 .25
243 Teppo Numminen .10 .25
244 Fredrik Olausson .10 .25
245 Ed Olczyk .10 .25
246 Darrin Shannon .10 .25
247 Thomas Steen .10 .25
248 Checklist 1 .10 .25
249 Checklist 2 .10 .25
250 Checklist 3 .10 .25
251 Ted Donato .10 .25
252 Dmitri Kvartalnov RC .10 .25
253 Gord Murphy .12 .30
254 Gregori Panteleyev RC .10 .25
255 Gordie Roberts .12 .30
256 David Shaw .12 .30
257 Don Sweeney .10 .25
258 Doug Bodger .10 .25
259 Gord Donnelly .12 .30
260 Yuri Khmylev RC .10 .25
261 Daren Puppa .12 .30
262 Richard Smehlik RC .10 .25
263 Petr Svoboda .12 .30
264 Bob Sweeney .10 .25
265 Randy Wood .10 .25
266 Kevin Dahl RC .10 .25
267 Chris Dahlquist .12 .30
268 Roger Johansson .12 .30
269 Chris Lindberg .10 .25
270 Frank Musil .12 .30
271 Ronnie Stern .12 .30
272 Carey Wilson .12 .30
273 Dave Christian .10 .25
274 Karl Dykhuis .10 .25
275 Greg Gilbert .12 .30
276 Sergei Krivokrasov .10 .25
277 Frantisek Kucera .12 .30
278 Bryan Marchment .12 .30
279 Stephane Matteau .10 .25
280 Brian Noonan .10 .25
281 Christian Ruuttu .10 .25
282 Steve Chiasson .10 .25
283 Dino Ciccarelli .12 .30
284 Gerard Gallant .10 .25
285 Mark Howe .15 .40
286 Keith Primeau .12 .30
287 Yves Racine .12 .30
288 Vincent Riendeau .12 .30
289 Ray Sheppard .10 .25
290 Mike Sillinger .10 .25
291 Kelly Buchberger .10 .25
292 Shayne Corson .10 .25
293 Brent Gilchrist .10 .25
294 Craig MacTavish .10 .25
295 Scott Mellanby .10 .25
296 Craig Muni .12 .30
297 Luke Richardson .12 .30
298 Ron Tugnutt .12 .30
299 Shaun Van Allen .12 .30
300 Steve Konroyd .12 .30
301 Nick Kypreos .10 .25
302 Robert Petrovicky RC .10 .25
303 Frank Pietrangelo .12 .30
304 Patrick Poulin .10 .25
305 Pat Verbeek .10 .25
306 Eric Weinrich .10 .25
307 Jim Hiller RC .10 .25
308 Charlie Huddy .12 .30
309 Lonnie Loach .10 .25
310 Marty McSorley .10 .25
311 Robb Stauber .12 .30
312 Darryl Sydor .10 .25
313 Dave Taylor .12 .30
314 Alexei Zhitnik .10 .25
315 Shane Churla .12 .30
316 Russ Courtnall .10 .25
317 Mike Craig .10 .25
318 Gaetan Duchesne .10 .25
319 Derian Hatcher .10 .25
320 Craig Ludwig .12 .30
321 Richard Matvichuk RC .12 .30
322 Mike McPhee .10 .25
323 Tommy Sjodin RC .10 .25
324 Brian Bellows .12 .30
325 Patrice Brisebois .10 .25
326 J.J.Daigneault .10 .25
327 Kevin Haller .10 .25
328 Sean Hill RC .10 .25
329 Stephan Lebeau .10 .25
330 John LeClair .25 .60
331 Lyle Odelein .12 .30
332 Andre Racicot .12 .30
333 Ed Ronan RC .10 .25
334 Craig Billington .12 .30
335 Ken Daneyko .10 .25
336 Bruce Driver .10 .25
337 Slava Fetisov .10 .25
338 Bill Guerin RC .30 .75
339 Bobby Holik .12 .30
340 Alexei Kasatonov .10 .25
341 Alexander Semak .10 .25
342 Tom Fitzgerald .10 .25
343 Travis Green RC .12 .30
344 Darius Kasparaitis .10 .25
345 Danny Lorenz RC .12 .30
346 Vladimir Malakhov .10 .25
347 Marty McInnis .10 .25
348 Brian Mullen .10 .25
349 Jeff Norton .12 .30
350 David Volek .10 .25
351 Jeff Beukeboom .10 .25
352 Phil Bourque .10 .25
353 Paul Broten .10 .25
354 Mark Hardy .12 .30
355 Steven King RC .10 .25
356 Kevin Lowe .12 .30
357 Ed Olczyk .10 .25
358 Doug Weight .30 .75
359 Sergei Zubov RC .25 .60
360 Jamie Baker .10 .25
361 Daniel Berthiaume .12 .30
362 Chris Luongo RC .10 .25
363 Norm Maciver .10 .25
364 Brad Marsh .12 .30
365 Mike Peluso .12 .30
366 Brad Shaw .10 .25
367 Peter Sidorkiewicz .10 .25
368 Keith Acton .12 .30
369 Stephane Beauregard .12 .30
370 Terry Carkner .12 .30
371 Brent Fedyk .10 .25
372 Andrei Lomakin .10 .25
373 Ryan McGill RC .10 .25
374 Ric Nattress .12 .30
375 Greg Paslawski .10 .25
376 Peter Ahola .10 .25
377 Jeff Daniels .10 .25
378 Troy Loney .10 .25
379 Shawn McEachern .10 .25
380 Mike Needham RC .10 .25
381 Paul Stanton .10 .25
382 Martin Straka RC .30 .75
383 Ken Wregget .12 .30
384 Steve Duchesne .10 .25
385 Ron Hextall .12 .30
386 Kerry Huffman .10 .25
387 Andrei Kovalenko RC .25 .60
388 Bill Lindsay RC .10 .25
389 Mike Ricci .12 .30
390 Martin Rucinsky .10 .25
391 Scott Young .10 .25
392 Philippe Bozon .10 .25
393 Nelson Emerson .10 .25
394 Guy Hebert RC .25 .60
395 Igor Korolev RC .10 .25
396 Kevin Miller .10 .25
397 Vitali Prokhorov RC .10 .25
398 Rich Sutter .10 .25
399 John Carter .12 .30
400 Johan Garpenlov .10 .25
401 Arturs Irbe .12 .30
402 Sandis Ozolinsh .10 .25
403 Tom Pederson RC .12 .30
404 Michel Picard .12 .30
405 Doug Zmolek RC .10 .25
406 Mikael Andersson .10 .25
407 Bob Beers .12 .30
408 Brian Bradley .10 .25
409 Adam Creighton .10 .25
410 Doug Crossman .12 .30
411 Ken Hodge Jr. .10 .25
412 Chris Kontos RC .10 .25
413 Rob Ramage .10 .25
414 John Tucker .10 .25
415 Rob Zamuner RC .12 .30
416 Ken Baumgartner .12 .30
417 Drake Berehowsky .10 .25
418 Nikolai Borschevsky RC .10 .25
419 John Cullen .10 .25
420 Mike Foligno .12 .30
421 Mike Krushelnyski .10 .25
422 Dmitri Mironov .10 .25
423 Rob Pearson .10 .25
424 Gerald Diduck .12 .30
425 Robert Dirk .12 .30
426 Tom Fergus .12 .30
427 Gino Odjick .12 .30
428 Adrien Plavsic .10 .25
429 Anatoli Semenov .10 .25
430 Jiri Slegr .10 .25
431 Dixon Ward RC .12 .30
432 Paul Cavallini .10 .25
433 Sylvain Cote .12 .30
434 Pat Elynuik .10 .25
435 Jim Hrivnak .12 .30
436 Keith Jones RC .15 .40
437 Steve Konowalchuk RC .12 .30
438 Todd Krygier .12 .30
439 Paul MacDermid .12 .30
440 Sergei Bautin RC .10 .25
441 Evgeny Davydov .10 .25
442 John Druce .10 .25
443 Troy Murray .10 .25
444 Teemu Selanne .30 .75
445 Rick Tabaracci .10 .25
446 Keith Tkachuk .15 .40
447 Alexei Zhamnov .12 .30
448 Checklist 4 .10 .25
449 Checklist 5 .10 .25
450 Checklist 6 .30 .75
NNO Jeremy Roenick Harding Promo .25 .60

1992-93 Ultra All-Stars

This 12-card standard-size set was randomly inserted in 1992-93 Ultra first series foil packs. The cards depict First Team All-Stars by conference. The glossy color action player photos on the fronts are full-bleed except at the bottom where a diagonal gold-foil stripe edges a beige marbleized border. A gold-foil insignia with a star is superimposed on the beige border.

COMPLETE SET (12) 8.00 20.00
1 Paul Coffey UER .50 1.25
2 Ray Bourque .75 2.00
3 Patrick Roy 1.50 4.00
4 Mario Lemieux 1.50 4.00
5 Kevin Stevens UER .15 .40
6 Jaromir Jagr .75 2.00
7 Chris Chelios .50 1.25
8 Al MacInnis .30 .75
9 Ed Belfour .50 1.25
10 Wayne Gretzky 2.00 5.00
11 Luc Robitaille .30 .75
12 Brett Hull .75 2.00

1992-93 Ultra Award Winners

This ten-card standard-size set was randomly inserted in 1992-93 Ultra first series foil packs. The cards feature 1991-92 award winners. The glossy color action player photos on the fronts are full-bleed except at the bottom where a gold-foil stripe edges into a marbleized border.

COMPLETE SET (10) 6.00 15.00
1 Mark Messier .60 1.50
2 Brian Leetch .50 1.25
3 Guy Carbonneau .30 .75
4 Patrick Roy 1.50 4.00
5 Mario Lemieux 1.50 4.00
6 Wayne Gretzky 2.00 5.00
7 Mark Fitzpatrick .30 .75
8 Ray Bourque .60 1.50
9 Pavel Bure .50 1.25
10 Mark Messier .60 1.50

1992-93 Ultra Imports

Randomly inserted in second series 1992-93 Ultra foil packs, this 25-card set measures the standard size. The cards depict foreign players in the National Hockey League. Fronts feature color action cut-out player photos against a purple surreal background showing the player on ice with a globe design in the distance. The player's name is silver foil stamped at the bottom. The horizontal backs carry a close-up of the player, the player's name, and player information. The background is similar to the front.

COMPLETE SET (25) 8.00 20.00
1 Nikolai Borschevsky .20 .50
2 Pavel Bure 1.00 2.50
3 Sergei Fedorov 1.00 2.50
4 Roman Hamrlik .20 .50
5 Arturs Irbe .50 1.25
6 Jaromir Jagr 1.25 3.00
7 Dimitri Khristich .20 .50
8 Petr Klima .20 .50
9 Andrei Kovalenko .20 .50
10 Alexei Kovalev .40 1.00
11 Jari Kurri .75 2.00
12 Dmitri Kvartalnov .20 .50
13 Nicklas Lidstrom .75 2.00
14 Vladimir Malakhov .20 .50
15 Dmitri Mironov .20 .50
16 Alexander Mogilny .50 1.25
17 Petr Nedved .20 .50
18 Fredrik Olausson .20 .50
19 Sandis Ozolinsh .20 .50
20 Ulf Samuelsson .20 .50
21 Teemu Selanne 2.00 5.00
22 Richard Smehlik .20 .50
23 Tommy Soderstrom .20 .50
24 Peter Stastny .40 1.00
25 Mats Sundin 1.00 2.50

1992-93 Ultra Jeremy Roenick

Randomly inserted in first series 1992-93 Ultra foil packs, this 12-card set measures the standard size. Two of the cards (11, 12) were available through a mail-in offer which was not available in Canada. The set, which features color action photos on front and career highlights on back, spotlights the career of Chicago Blackhawks' Jeremy Roenick. Roenick personally autographed more than 2,000 of his cards. Stated odds suggest the likelihood of pulling an autographed card at 1:8,000 packs.

COMPLETE SET (10) 10.00 20.00
COMMON ROENICK (1-10) .75 2.00
COMMON MAIL-IN (11-12) 1.25 3.00
13 Jeremy Roenick AU 30.00 80.00

1992-93 Ultra Rookies

This eight-card standard-size set was randomly inserted in 1992-93 Ultra series one foil packs. The card fronts feature color, action player photos. A brown marbleized border runs diagonally across the bottom. This border is separated from the photo by a thin gold foil stripe. The player's name and the words "Ultra Rookie" are printed in gold foil on the marbleized border. The backs show a close-up picture with a player profile against a gray marbleized background.

COMPLETE SET (8) 5.00 10.00
1 Tony Amonte .40 1.00
2 Donald Audette .40 1.00
3 Pavel Bure .75 2.00
4 Gilbert Dionne .40 1.00
5 Nelson Emerson .40 1.00
6 Pat Falloon .40 1.00
7 Nicklas Lidstrom .75 2.00
8 Kevin Todd .40 1.00

1993-94 Ultra

The 1993-94 Ultra hockey set consists of 500 standard-size cards. Both the first and second series contained 250 cards. The color action player photos on the fronts are full-bleed except at the bottom where a diagonal gold foil stripe separates the picture from a gray ice border. The player's name, team name, and position are gold foil-stamped on team color-coded bars.

1 Ray Bourque UER .15 .40
2 Andy Moog .10 .25
3 Brian Benning .05 .15
4 Brian Bellows .07 .20
5 Claude Lemieux .05 .15
6 Jamie Baker .05 .15
7 Steve Duchesne .05 .15
8 Ed Courtenay .05 .15
9 Glenn Anderson .10 .25
10 Sergei Bautin .05 .15
11 Al Iafrate .05 .15
12 Gary Shuchuk .05 .15
13 Matthew Barnaby .07 .20
14 Tim Cheveldae .07 .20
15 Sean Burke .05 .15
16 Ray Ferraro .05 .15
17 Josef Beranek .05 .15
18 Bob Beers .05 .15
19 Greg Adams .05 .15
20 John Cullen .05 .15
21 Kirk Muller .05 .15
22 Ed Belfour .10 .25
23 Kevin Dahl .05 .15
24 Rob Blake .07 .20
25 Mike Gartner .07 .20
26 Tom Barrasso .07 .20
27 Garth Butcher .05 .15
28 Don Beaupre .07 .20
29 Kirk McLean .07 .20
30 Felix Potvin .20 .50
31 Doug Bodger .05 .15
32 Dino Ciccarelli .07 .20
33 Andrew Cassels .05 .15
34 Patrick Flatley .05 .15
35 Jason Bowen RC .10 .25
36 Brian Bradley .05 .15
37 Pavel Bure .10 .25
38 Dave Ellett .05 .15
39 Patrick Roy .25 .60
40 Chris Chelios .10 .25
41 Theo Fleury .05 .15
42 Jimmy Carson .05 .15
43 Adam Graves .05 .15
44 Ron Francis .12 .30
45 Nelson Emerson .05 .15
46 Peter Bondra .07 .20
47 Sergio Momesso .05 .15
48 Teemu Selanne .20 .50
49 Joe Juneau .07 .20
50 Russ Courtnall .05 .15
51 Shayne Corson .05 .15
52 Patrice Brisebois .05 .15
53 John MacLean .07 .20
54 Daniel Berthiaume .05 .15
55 Stephane Fiset .07 .20
56 Pat Falloon .05 .15
57 Dave Andreychuk .10 .25
58 Evgeny Davydov .05 .15
59 Dimitri Khristich .05 .15
60 Darryl Sydor .05 .15
61 Dirk Graham .05 .15
62 Chris Lindberg .05 .15
63 Tony Granato .05 .15
64 Corey Hirsch .07 .20
65 Jaromir Jagr .25 .60
66 Bret Hedican .05 .15
67 Pat Elynuik .05 .15
68 Petr Nedved .05 .15
69 Thomas Steen .05 .15
70 Philippe Boucher .05 .15
71 Paul Coffey .10 .25
72 Mike Lenarduzzi RC .05 .15
73 Iain Fraser RC .10 .25
74 Rod Brind'Amour .07 .20
75 Shawn Chambers .05 .15
76 Geoff Courtnall .05 .15
77 Todd Gill .05 .15
78 Mathieu Schneider .05 .15
79 Vincent Damphousse .07 .20
80 Igor Kravchuk .05 .15
81 Ulf Dahlen .05 .15
82 Dmitri Kvartalnov .05 .15
83 Johan Garpenlov .05 .15
84 Valeri Kamensky .07 .20
85 Bob Kudelski .05 .15
86 Bernie Nicholls .05 .15
87 Alexei Zhitnik .05 .15
88 Kelly Miller .05 .15
89 Bob Essensa .07 .20
90 Drake Berehowsky .05 .15
91 Jon Casey .07 .20
92 Dave Gagner .07 .20
93 Dave Manson .05 .15
94 Eric Desjardins .07 .20
95 Scott Niedermayer .10 .25
96 Chris Luongo .05 .15
97 Dave Karpa .05 .15
98 Rob Gaudreau RC .10 .25
99 Nikolai Borschevsky .05 .15
100 Phil Housley .07 .20
101 Michal Pivonka .05 .15
102 Dixon Ward .05 .15
103 Grant Fuhr .10 .25
104 Dallas Drake RC .10 .25
105 Michael Nylander .05 .15
106 Glenn Healy .07 .20
107 Kevin Dineen .05 .15
108 Roman Hamrlik .05 .15
109 Trevor Linden .07 .20
110 Doug Gilmour .12 .30
111 Keith Tkachuk .10 .25
112 Sergei Krivokrasov .05 .15
113 Al MacInnis .07 .20
114 Wayne Gretzky .50 1.25
115 Alexei Kovalev .07 .20
116 Mario Lemieux .40 1.00
117 Brett Hull .15 .40
118 Kevin Hatcher .05 .15
119 Cliff Ronning .05 .15
120 Viktor Gordiouk .05 .15
121 Sergei Fedorov .15 .40
122 Patrick Poulin .05 .15
123 Benoit Hogue .05 .15
124 Garry Galley .05 .15
125 Pat Jablonski .05 .15
126 Jyrki Lumme .05 .15
127 Dimitri Mironov .05 .15
128 Alexei Zhamnov .07 .20
129 Steve Larmer .07 .20
130 Joe Nieuwendyk .07 .20
131 Kelly Hrudey .07 .20
132 Brian Leetch .10 .25
133 Shawn McEachern .05 .15
134 Craig Janney .07 .20
135 Dale Hunter .05 .15
136 Jiri Slegr .05 .15
137 Mats Sundin .07 .20
138 Cam Neely .10 .25
139 Derian Hatcher .05 .15
140 Shjon Podein RC .10 .25
141 Gilbert Dionne .05 .15
142 Scott Pellerin RC .10 .25
143 Norm Maciver .05 .15
144 Andrei Kovalenko .05 .15
145 Arturs Irbe .07 .20
146 Wendel Clark .07 .20
147 Fredrik Olausson .05 .15
148 Mike Ridley .05 .15
149 Dale Hawerchuk .12 .30
150 Vladimir Konstantinov .07 .20
151 Geoff Sanderson .07 .20
152 Stephane Richer .07 .20
153 Darren Rumble .05 .15
154 Owen Nolan .07 .20
155 Kelly Kisio .05 .15
156 Adam Oates .10 .25
157 Trent Klatt .05 .15
158 Bill Ranford .07 .20
159 Paul DiPietro .05 .15
160 Darius Kasparaitis .05 .15
161 Eric Lindros .30 .75
162 Chris Kontos .05 .15
163 Joe Murphy .05 .15
164 Robert Reichel .05 .15
165 Jari Kurri .10 .25
166 Alexander Semak .05 .15
167 Brad Shaw .05 .15
168 Mike Ricci .05 .15
169 Sandis Ozolinsh .05 .15
170 Joby Messier RC .10 .25
171 Joe Mullen .07 .20
172 Curtis Joseph .10 .25
173 Yuri Khmylev .05 .15
174 Slava Kozlov .07 .20
175 Pat Verbeek .05 .15
176 Derek King .05 .15
177 Ryan McGill .05 .15
178 Chris LiPuma RC .05 .15
179 Grigori Pantaleyev .05 .15
180 Richard Matvichuk .05 .15
181 Steven Rice .05 .15
182 Sean Hill .05 .15
183 Mark Messier .10 .25
184 Larry Murphy .07 .20
185 Igor Korolev .05 .15
186 Jeremy Roenick .15 .40
187 Gary Roberts .05 .15
188 Robert Lang .07 .20
189 Scott Stevens .10 .25
190 Sylvain Turgeon .05 .15
191 Martin Rucinsky .05 .15
192 J.F. Quintin .05 .15
193 Dave Poulin .05 .15
194 Mike Modano .15 .40
195 Doug Weight .07 .20
196 Mike Keane .05 .15
197 Pierre Turgeon .07 .20
198 Dimitri Yushkevich .05 .15
199 Rob Zamuner .05 .15
200 Richard Smehlik .05 .15
201 Steve Yzerman .25 .60
202 Tony Amonte .07 .20
203 Sergei Nemchinov .05 .15
204 Ulf Samuelsson .05 .15
205 Kevin Miehm .05 .15
206 Brent Sutter .05 .15
207 Mike Vernon .07 .20
208 Luc Robitaille .07 .20
209 Chris Terreri .07 .20
210 Philippe Bozon .05 .15
211 John Tucker .05 .15
212 Jozef Stumpel .05 .15
213 Mark Tinordi .05 .15
214 Bruce Driver .05 .15
215 John LeClair .10 .25
216 Steve Thomas .05 .15
217 Tommy Soderstrom .07 .20
218 Kevin Miller .05 .15
219 Pat LaFontaine .10 .25
220 Nicklas Lidstrom .10 .25
221 Terry Yake .05 .15
222 Valeri Zelepukin .05 .15
223 Jeff Brown .05 .15
224 Chris Simon RC .10 .25
225 Rick Tocchet .07 .20
226 Gary Suter .05 .15
227 Marty McSorley .05 .15
228 Mike Richter .10 .25
229 Kevin Stevens .05 .15
230 Doug Wilson .05 .15
231 Steve Smith .05 .15
232 Bryan Smolinski .05 .15
233 Tommy Sjodin .05 .15
234 Zarley Zalapski .05 .15
235 Vladimir Malakhov .05 .15
236 Mark Recchi .12 .30
237 David Littman RC .05 .15
238 Alexander Mogilny .07 .20
239 Keith Primeau .05 .15
240 Tyler Wright .05 .15
241 Stephan Lebeau .05 .15
242 Joe Sakic .25 .60
243 Sergei Zubov .05 .15
244 Martin Straka .05 .15
245 Brendan Shanahan .12 .30
246 Tomas Sandstrom .05 .15
247 Milan Tichy RC .05 .15
248 C.J. Young .05 .15
249 Eric Lindros CL .30 .75
250 Teemu Selanne CL .20 .50
251 Patrick Carnback RC .10 .25
252 Todd Ewen .05 .15
253 Stu Grimson .05 .15
254 Guy Hebert .07 .20
255 Sean Hill .05 .15
256 Bill Houlder .05 .15
257 Alexei Kasatonov .05 .15
258 Steven King .05 .15
259 Troy Loney .05 .15
260 Joe Sacco .05 .15
261 Anatoli Semenov .05 .15
262 Tim Sweeney .05 .15
263 Ron Tugnutt .07 .20
264 Shaun Van Allen .05 .15
265 Terry Yake .05 .15
266 Jon Casey .07 .20
267 Ted Donato .05 .15
268 Steve Leach .05 .15
269 David Reid .05 .15
270 Cam Stewart RC .10 .25
271 Don Sweeney .05 .15
272 Glen Wesley .05 .15
273 Donald Audette .05 .15
274 Dominik Hasek .20 .50
275 Sergei Petrenko .05 .15
276 Derek Plante RC .10 .25
277 Craig Simpson .05 .15
278 Bob Sweeney .05 .15
279 Randy Wood .05 .15
280 Ted Drury .05 .15
281 Trevor Kidd .07 .20
282 Kelly Kisio .05 .15
283 Frank Musil .05 .15
284 Jason Muzzatti RC .10 .25
285 Joel Otto .05 .15
286 Paul Ranheim .05 .15
287 Wes Walz .05 .15
288 Ivan Droppa RC .05 .15
289 Michel Goulet .05 .15
290 Stephane Matteau .05 .15
291 Brian Noonan .05 .15
292 Patrick Poulin .05 .15
293 Rich Sutter .05 .15
294 Kevin Todd .05 .15
295 Eric Weinrich .05 .15
296 Neal Broten .07 .20
297 Mike Craig .05 .15
298 Dean Evason .05 .15
299 Grant Ledyard .05 .15
300 Mike McPhee .05 .15
301 Andy Moog .10 .25
302 Jarkko Varvio .05 .15
303 Micah Aivazoff RC .10 .25
304 Terry Carkner .05 .15
305 Steve Chiasson .05 .15
306 Greg Johnson .05 .15
307 Darren McCarty RC .15 .40
308 Chris Osgood RC .60 1.50
309 Bob Probert .07 .20
310 Ray Sheppard .07 .20
311 Mike Sillinger .05 .15
312 Jason Arnott RC .20 .50
313 Fred Brathwaite RC .10 .25
314 Kelly Buchberger .05 .15
315 Zdeno Ciger .05 .15
316 Craig MacTavish .05 .15
317 Dean McAmmond .05 .15
318 Luke Richardson .05 .15
319 Vladimir Vujtek .05 .15
320 Jesse Belanger .05 .15
321 Brian Benning .05 .15
322 Keith Brown .05 .15
323 Evgeny Davydov .05 .15
324 Tom Fitzgerald .05 .15
325 Alexander Godynyuk .05 .15
326 Scott Levins RC .10 .25
327 Andrei Lomakin .05 .15
328 Scott Mellanby .07 .20
329 Gord Murphy .05 .15
330 Rob Niedermayer .07 .20
331 Brent Severyn RC .10 .25
332 Brian Skrudland .05 .15
333 John Vanbiesbrouck .07 .20
334 Mark Greig .05 .15
335 Bryan Marchment .05 .15
336 James Patrick .05 .15
337 Robert Petrovicky .05 .15
338 Frank Pietrangelo .07 .20
339 Chris Pronger .10 .25
340 Brian Propp .05 .15
341 Darren Turcotte .05 .15
342 Pat Conacher .05 .15
343 Mark Hardy .05 .15
344 Charlie Huddy .05 .15
345 Shawn McEachern .05 .15
346 Warren Rychel .05 .15
347 Robb Stauber .05 .15
348 Dave Taylor .05 .15
349 Benoit Brunet .05 .15

350 Guy Carbonneau .05 .15
351 J.J. Daigneault .05 .15
352 Kevin Haller .05 .15
353 Gary Leeman .05 .15
354 Lyle Odelein .05 .15
355 Andre Racicot .05 .15
356 Ron Wilson .05 .15
357 Martin Brodeur .25 .60
358 Ken Daneyko .05 .15
359 Bill Guerin .05 .15
360 Bobby Holik .05 .15
361 Corey Millen .05 .15
362 Jaroslav Modry RC .10 .25
363 Jason Smith RC .05 .15
364 Brad Dalgarno .05 .15
365 Travis Green .07 .20
366 Ron Hextall .07 .20
367 Steve Junker .10 .25
368 Tom Kurvers .05 .15
369 Scott Lachance .05 .15
370 Marty McInnis .05 .15
371 Glenn Healy .07 .20
372 Alexander Karpovtsev .05 .15
373 Steve Larmer .07 .20
374 Doug Lidster .05 .15
375 Kevin Lowe .05 .15
376 Mattias Norstrom RC .10 .25
377 Esa Tikkanen .05 .15
378 Craig Billington .07 .20
379 Robert Burakovsky RC .10 .25
380 Alexandre Daigle .05 .15
381 Dmitri Filimonov .05 .15
382 Darrin Madeley RC .10 .25
383 Vladimir Ruzicka .05 .15
384 Alexei Yashin .07 .20
385 Viacheslav Butsayev .05 .15
386 Pelle Eklund .05 .15
387 Brent Fedyk .05 .15
388 Greg Hawgood .05 .15
389 Milos Holan RC .10 .25
390 Stewart Malgunas RC .10 .25
391 Mikael Renberg .10 .25
392 Dominic Roussel .07 .20
393 Doug Brown .05 .15
394 Marty McSorley .05 .15
395 Markus Naslund .10 .25
396 Mike Ramsey .05 .15
397 Peter Taglianetti .05 .15
398 Bryan Trottier .12 .30
399 Ken Wregget .05 .15
400 Iain Fraser .10 .25
401 Martin Gelinas .05 .15
402 Kerry Huffman .05 .15
403 Claude Lapointe .05 .15
404 Curtis Leschyshyn .05 .15
405 Chris Lindberg .05 .15
406 Jocelyn Thibault RC .10 .25
407 Murray Baron .05 .15
408 Bob Bassen .05 .15
409 Phil Housley .07 .20
410 Jim Hrivnak .05 .15
411 Tony Hrkac .05 .15
412 Vitali Karamnov .05 .15
413 Jim Montgomery RC .10 .25
414 Vlastimil Kroupa RC .10 .25
415 Igor Larionov .05 .15
416 Sergei Makarov .05 .15
417 Jeff Norton .05 .15
418 Mike Rathje .05 .15
419 Jim Waite .07 .20
420 Ray Whitney .05 .15
421 Mikael Andersson .05 .15
422 Donald Dufresne .05 .15
423 Chris Gratton .07 .20
424 Brent Gretzky RC .10 .25
425 Petr Klima .05 .15
426 Bill McDougall RC .10 .25
427 Daren Puppa .05 .15
428 Denis Savard .12 .30
429 Ken Baumgartner .05 .15
430 Sylvain Lefebvre .05 .15
431 Jamie Macoun .05 .15
432 Matt Martin RC .10 .25
433 Mark Osborne .05 .15
434 Rob Pearson .05 .15
435 Damian Rhodes RC .10 .25
436 Peter Zezel .05 .15
437 Shawn Antoski .05 .15
438 Jose Charbonneau .10 .25
439 Murray Craven .05 .15
440 Gerald Diduck .05 .15
441 Dana Murzyn .05 .15
442 Gino Odjick .05 .15
443 Kay Whitmore .05 .15
444 Randy Burridge .05 .15
445 Sylvain Cote .05 .15
446 Keith Jones .05 .15
447 Olaf Kolzig .07 .20
448 Todd Krygier .05 .15
449 Pat Peake .05 .15
450 Dave Poulin .05 .15
451 Stephane Beauregard .05 .15
452 Luciano Borsato .05 .15
453 Nelson Emerson .05 .15
454 Boris Mironov .05 .15
455 Teppo Numminen .05 .15
456 Stephane Quintal .05 .15
457 Paul Ysebaert .05 .15
458 Adrian Aucoin RC .10 .25
459 Todd Brost RC .10 .25
460 Martin Gendron RC .07 .20
461 David Harlock .07 .20
462 Corey Hirsch .07 .20
463 Todd Hlushko RC .07 .20
464 Fabian Joseph RC .07 .20
465 Paul Kariya 2.00 5.00
466 Brett Lindros RC .15 .40
467 Ken Lovsin RC .07 .20
468 Jason Marshall .07 .20
469 Derek Mayer RC .05 .15
470 Dwayne Norris RC .05 .15
471 Russ Romaniuk .05 .15
472 Brian Savage RC .10 .25
473 Trevor Sim RC .10 .25
474 Chris Therien RC .10 .25
475 Brad Turner RC .07 .20
476 Todd Warriner RC .10 .25
477 Craig Woodcroft RC .10 .25
478 Mark Beaufait RC .10 .25
479 Jim Campbell .07 .20
480 Ted Crowley RC .10 .25
481 Mike Dunham .07 .20
482 Chris Ferraro RC .07 .20
483 Peter Ferraro .07 .20
484 Brett Hauer RC .07 .20
485 Darby Hendrickson RC .07 .20
486 Chris Imes RC .07 .20
487 Craig Johnson RC .07 .20
488 Peter Laviolette RC .07 .20
489 Jeff Lazaro .07 .20
490 John Lilley RC .07 .20
491 Todd Marchant .07 .20
492 Ian Moran RC .07 .20
493 Travis Richards RC .07 .20
494 Barry Richter RC .07 .20
495 David Roberts RC .07 .20
496 Brian Rolston .07 .20
497 David Sacco RC .07 .20
498 Checklist Card .05 .15
499 Checklist Card .05 .15
500 Checklist Card .05 .15
C3C Wayne Gretzky 2/10 6.00 15.00

1993-94 Ultra Adam Oates

As part of Ultra's Signature series, this 12-card standard-size set presents career highlights of Adam Oates. These cards were randomly inserted throughout all packs, and Oates autographed more than 2,000 of his cards. Stated odds suggest the likelihood of pulling an autographed card at 1:10,000 packs. Two additional cards (11, 12) were available only by mail for ten Ultra wrappers plus 1.00.

COMPLETE SET (10) 1.50 4.00
COMMON OATES (1-10) .20 .50
COMMON MAIL-IN (11-12) .75 2.00
NNO Adam Oates AU 12.00 30.00

1993-94 Ultra All-Rookies

Randomly inserted at a rate of 1:20 per 19-card first-series jumbo pack, this 10-card standard-size set features on its borderless fronts color player action cutouts "breaking out" of their simulated ice backgrounds. The player's name appears in gold-foil lettering at a lower corner. The blue back carries the player's name at the top in gold-foil lettering, followed below by career highlights and a color player action cutout. The cards are numbered on the back as "X of 10."

1 Philippe Boucher 3.00 8.00
2 Viktor Gordiouk 3.00 8.00
3 Corey Hirsch 5.00 12.00
4 Chris LiPuma 3.00 8.00
5 David Littman 3.00 8.00
6 Joby Messier 3.00 8.00
7 Chris Simon 3.00 8.00
8 Bryan Smolinski 3.00 8.00
9 Jozef Stumpel 3.00 8.00
10 Milan Tichy 3.00 8.00

1993-94 Ultra All-Stars

Randomly inserted into all first series packs, this 18-card standard-size set focuses on 18 of the NHL's best players. The set numbering is by conference All-Stars, Wales (1-9) and Campbell (10-18).

COMPLETE SET (18) 10.00 25.00
1 Patrick Roy 2.50 6.00
2 Ray Bourque .75 2.00
3 Pierre Turgeon .25 .60
4 Pat LaFontaine .50 1.25
5 Alexander Mogilny .25 .60
6 Kevin Stevens .15 .40
7 Adam Oates .25 .60
8 Al Iafrate .15 .40
9 Kirk Muller .15 .40
10 Ed Belfour .50 1.25
11 Teemu Selanne .50 1.25
12 Steve Yzerman 2.50 6.00
13 Luc Robitaille .25 .60
14 Chris Chelios .50 1.25
15 Wayne Gretzky 3.00 8.00
16 Doug Gilmour .25 .60
17 Pavel Bure .50 1.25
18 Phil Housley .25 .60

1993-94 Ultra Award Winners

Randomly inserted into all first series packs, this six-card standard-size set honors NHL award winners of the previous season. Each borderless front features the player with his award. The back has an action photo and career highlights. The cards are numbered "X of 6".

COMPLETE SET (6) 3.00 8.00
1 Ed Belfour .60 1.50
2 Chris Chelios .60 1.50
3 Doug Gilmour .30 .75
4 Mario Lemieux 2.00 5.00
5 Dave Poulin .20 .50
6 Teemu Selanne .60 1.50

1993-94 Ultra Premier Pivots

Randomly inserted in all series II packs, these ten standard-size cards feature some of the NHL's greatest centers. The borderless fronts have color player action shots on motion-streaked backgrounds. The player's name appears in silver foil at the upper right. The cards are numbered on the back as "X of 10."

COMPLETE SET (10) 8.00 20.00
1 Doug Gilmour .20 .50
2 Wayne Gretzky 2.50 6.00
3 Pat LaFontaine .40 1.00
4 Mario Lemieux 2.00 5.00
5 Eric Lindros .40 1.00
6 Mark Messier .40 1.00
7 Adam Oates .20 .50
8 Jeremy Roenick .50 1.25
9 Pierre Turgeon .20 .50
10 Steve Yzerman 2.00 5.00

1993-94 Ultra Promo Sheet

This (approximately) 11" by 8 1/2" sheet features some of the cards of the 1993-94 Ultra set. It is arranged in three rows with three cards each, the middle card in the middle row is not a player's card but a title card. The backs are also identical to the cards' backs.

NNO Uncut Panel 2.00 5.00
Joe Juneau
Sergei Fedorov
Mats Sundin
Mark Recchi
Cover Card
Jeremy Roenick
Felix Potvin
Alexei Kovalev
Doug Gilmour

1993-94 Ultra Prospects

Randomly inserted into first series foil packs, the Ultra Prospects set consists of ten standard-size cards. Borderless fronts feature the player emerging from a solid background. The backs contain a photo and career highlights. The cards are numbered as "X of 10".

COMPLETE SET (10) 5.00 10.00
1 Iain Fraser .40 1.00
2 Rob Gaudreau .40 1.00
3 Dave Karpa .40 1.00
4 Trent Klatt .40 1.00
5 Mike Lenarduzzi .40 1.00
6 Kevin Miehm .40 1.00
7 Michael Nylander .75 2.00
8 J.F. Quintin .40 1.00
9 Gary Shuchuk .40 1.00
10 Tyler Wright .40 1.00

1993-94 Ultra Red Light Specials

Randomly inserted in series 2 packs, this ten-card standard-size set highlights some of the NHL's best goal scorers. The borderless fronts feature two color player action shots, one superimposed upon the other. The player's name appears in red foil at the bottom. The horizontal back carries an on-ice close-up of the player set off to the right. The player's name appears in red foil at the upper left, followed below by the player's goal-scoring highlights, all on the red-screened background from the player close-up. The cards are numbered on the back as "X of 10."

COMPLETE SET (10) 6.00 15.00
1 Dave Andreychuk .40 1.00
2 Pavel Bure .75 2.00
3 Mike Gartner .40 1.00
4 Brett Hull 1.00 2.50
5 Jaromir Jagr 1.25 3.00
6 Mario Lemieux 2.00 5.00
7 Alexander Mogilny .40 1.00
8 Mark Recchi .40 1.00
9 Luc Robitaille .40 1.00
10 Teemu Selanne .75 2.00

1993-94 Ultra Scoring Kings

Randomly inserted into all first series packs, this six-card standard-size set showcases six of the NHL's top scorers. Borderless fronts have action player photos. Backs feature a player photo and career highlights. The player's name appears in gold at the top. The card are numbered "X of 6".

COMPLETE SET (6) 10.00 25.00
1 Pat LaFontaine .60 1.50
2 Wayne Gretzky 4.00 10.00
3 Brett Hull .75 2.00
4 Mario Lemieux 3.00 8.00
5 Pierre Turgeon .30 .75
6 Steve Yzerman 3.00 8.00

1993-94 Ultra Speed Merchants

Randomly inserted in second series jumbo packs, this 10-card standard-size set sports fronts of motion-streaked color player action cutouts set on borderless indigo backgrounds highlighted by ice spray. The cards are numbered on the back as "X of 10."

COMPLETE SET (10) 15.00 40.00
1 Pavel Bure 2.00 5.00
2 Russ Courtnall .75 2.00
3 Sergei Fedorov 2.00 5.00
4 Mike Gartner .75 2.00
5 Al Iafrate .75 2.00
6 Pat LaFontaine 1.50 4.00
7 Alexander Mogilny 1.50 4.00
8 Rob Niedermayer .75 2.00
9 Geoff Sanderson .75 2.00
10 Teemu Selanne 2.00 5.00

1993-94 Ultra Wave of the Future

Randomly inserted in series II packs, these 20 standard-size cards highlight players in their first or second NHL season. The borderless fronts feature color player action shots with "rippled" on-ice backgrounds. The player's name appears in gold foil at a lower corner.The cards are numbered on the back as "X of 20."

COMPLETE SET (20) 6.00 15.00
1 Jason Arnott .40 1.00
2 Martin Brodeur 2.00 5.00
3 Alexandre Daigle .20 .50
4 Ted Drury .20 .50
5 Chris Gratton .20 .50
6 Milos Holan .20 .50
7 Greg Johnson .20 .50
8 Boris Mironov .20 .50
9 Jaroslav Modry .20 .50
10 Markus Naslund .60 1.50
11 Rob Niedermayer .40 1.00
12 Chris Osgood .75 2.00
13 Derek Plante .20 .50
14 Chris Pronger .60 1.50
15 Mike Rathje .20 .50
16 Mikael Renberg .40 1.00
17 Jason Smith .20 .50
18 Jocelyn Thibault .60 1.50
19 Jarkko Varvio .20 .50
20 Alexei Yashin .20 .50

1994-95 Ultra

The 1994-95 Ultra hockey set consists of two series of 200 and 150 cards, for a total of 350 standard-size cards. The suggested retail price for 12-card packs was $1.99, and $2.69 for 15-card packs. Every pack included one insert card, and one "Hot Pack" consisting exclusively of insert cards was seeded once every two boxes (or 1:72 packs). Full-bleed card fronts have the player's name, team and Ultra logo in gold foil at the bottom. The backs also have a full-bleed photo with two smaller inset photos. Stats are at the bottom. Each series is arranged alphabetically by team and the player's within each team alphabetized. Rookie Cards include Mariusz Czerkawski and Eric Fichaud.

1 Bob Corkum .05 .15
2 Todd Ewen .05 .15
3 Guy Hebert .07 .20
4 Bill Houlder .05 .15
5 Stephan Lebeau .05 .15
6 Joe Sacco .05 .15
7 Anatoli Semenov .05 .15
8 Tim Sweeney .05 .15
9 Terry Yake .05 .15
10 Ray Bourque .15 .40
11 Mariusz Czerkawski RC .10 .25
12 Ted Donato .05 .15
13 Cam Neely .10 .25
14 Adam Oates .10 .25
15 Vincent Riendeau .05 .15
16 Bryan Smolinski .05 .15
17 Don Sweeney .05 .15
18 Glen Wesley .05 .15
19 Donald Audette .05 .15
20 Doug Bodger .05 .15
21 Jason Dawe .05 .15
22 Dominik Hasek .20 .50
23 Dale Hawerchuk .12 .30
24 Pat LaFontaine .10 .25
25 Brad May .05 .15
26 Alexander Mogilny .07 .20
27 Derek Plante .05 .15
28 Richard Smehlik .05 .15
29 Theo Fleury .10 .25
30 Trevor Kidd .07 .20
31 Frank Musil .05 .15
32 Michael Nylander .07 .20
33 James Patrick .05 .15
34 Robert Reichel .05 .15
35 Gary Roberts .05 .15
36 German Titov .05 .15
37 Wes Walz .05 .15
38 Zarley Zalapski .05 .15
39 Ed Belfour .10 .25
40 Chris Chelios .10 .25
41 Dirk Graham .05 .15
42 Bernie Nicholls .07 .20
43 Patrick Poulin .05 .15
44 Jeremy Roenick .20 .50
45 Steve Smith .05 .15
46 Gary Suter .05 .15
47 Brent Sutter .07 .20
48 Neal Broten .07 .20
49 Paul Cavallini .05 .15
50 Dean Evason .05 .15
51 Dave Gagner .07 .20
52 Derian Hatcher .05 .15
53 Trent Klatt .05 .15
54 Grant Ledyard .05 .15
55 Mike Modano .15 .40
56 Andy Moog .10 .25
57 Mark Tinordi .05 .15
58 Dino Ciccarelli .07 .20
59 Paul Coffey .10 .25
60 Sergei Fedorov .15 .40
61 Vladimir Konstantinov .07 .20
62 Nicklas Lidstrom .10 .25
63 Darren McCarty .05 .15
64 Chris Osgood .15 .40
65 Keith Primeau .10 .25
66 Ray Sheppard .07 .20
67 Steve Yzerman .25 .60
68 Jason Arnott .07 .20
69 Bob Beers .07 .20
70 Ilya Byakin .05 .15
71 Zdeno Ciger .05 .15
72 Igor Kravchuk .05 .15
73 Boris Mironov .05 .15
74 Fredrik Olausson .05 .15
75 Scott Pearson .05 .15
76 Bill Ranford .07 .20
77 Doug Weight .07 .20
78 Stu Barnes .05 .15
79 Jesse Belanger .05 .15
80 Bob Kudelski .05 .15
81 Andrei Lomakin .05 .15
82 Dave Lowry .05 .15
83 Gord Murphy .05 .15
84 Rob Niedermayer .07 .20
85 Brian Skrudland .05 .15
86 John Vanbiesbrouck .07 .20
87 Sean Burke .07 .20
88 Ted Drury .05 .15
89 Alexander Godynyuk .05 .15
90 Robert Kron .05 .15
91 Chris Pronger .10 .25
92 Brian Propp .05 .15
93 Geoff Sanderson .07 .20
94 Darren Turcotte .05 .15
95 Pat Verbeek .07 .20
96 Rob Blake .10 .25
97 Mike Donnelly .05 .15
98 John Druce .07 .20
99 Kelly Hrudey .07 .20
100 Jari Kurri .07 .20
101 Robert Lang .05 .15
102 Marty McSorley .05 .15
103 Luc Robitaille .10 .25
104 Alexei Zhitnik .07 .20
105 Brian Bellows .07 .20
106 Patrice Brisebois .05 .15
107 Vincent Damphousse .07 .20
108 Eric Desjardins .07 .20
109 Gilbert Dionne .05 .15
110 Mike Keane .05 .15
111 John LeClair .10 .25
112 Lyle Odelein .07 .20
113 Patrick Roy .25 .60
114 Mathieu Schneider .05 .15
115 Martin Brodeur .25 .60
116 Jim Dowd .05 .15
117 Bill Guerin .07 .20
118 Claude Lemieux .10 .25
119 John MacLean .07 .20
120 Corey Millen .05 .15
121 Scott Niedermayer .10 .25
122 Stephane Richer .07 .20
123 Scott Stevens .10 .25
124 Valeri Zelepukin .05 .15
125 Patrick Flatley .05 .15
126 Travis Green .07 .20
127 Ron Hextall .07 .20
128 Benoit Hogue .05 .15
129 Darius Kasparaitis .05 .15
130 Vladimir Malakhov .05 .15
131 Marty McInnis .05 .15
132 Steve Thomas .05 .15
133 Pierre Turgeon .07 .20
134 Dennis Vaske .05 .15
135 Glenn Anderson .10 .25
136 Jeff Beukeboom .05 .15
137 Adam Graves .05 .15
138 Steve Larmer .07 .20
139 Brian Leetch .10 .25
140 Mark Messier .10 .25
141 Petr Nedved .07 .20
142 Sergei Nemchinov .05 .15
143 Mike Richter .10 .25
144 Sergei Zubov .05 .15
145 Craig Billington .07 .20
146 Alexandre Daigle .05 .15
147 Evgeny Davydov .05 .15
148 Scott Levins .05 .15
149 Norm Maciver .05 .15
150 Troy Mallette .05 .15
151 Brad Shaw .05 .15
152 Alexei Yashin .10 .25
153 Josef Beranek .05 .15
154 Jason Bowen .05 .15
155 Rod Brind'Amour .07 .20
156 Kevin Dineen .05 .15
157 Garry Galley .05 .15
158 Mark Recchi .12 .30
159 Mikael Renberg .07 .20
160 Tommy Soderstrom .07 .20
161 Dimitri Yushkevich .05 .15
162 Tom Barrasso .07 .20
163 Ron Francis .12 .30
164 Jaromir Jagr .25 .60
165 Mario Lemieux .40 1.00
166 Shawn McEachern .05 .15
167 Joe Mullen .07 .20
168 Larry Murphy .07 .20
169 Ulf Samuelsson .05 .15
170 Kevin Stevens .05 .15
171 Martin Straka .05 .15
172 Wendel Clark .07 .20
173 Stephane Fiset .07 .20
174 Iain Fraser .05 .15
175 Andrei Kovalenko .05 .15
176 Sylvain Lefebvre .05 .15
177 Owen Nolan .10 .25
178 Mike Ricci .05 .15
179 Martin Rucinsky .05 .15
180 Joe Sakic .20 .50
181 Scott Young .05 .15
182 Steve Duchesne .05 .15
183 Brett Hull .20 .50
184 Curtis Joseph .15 .40
185 Al MacInnis .07 .20
186 Kevin Miller .05 .15
187 Jim Montgomery .05 .15
188 Vitali Prokhorov .05 .15
189 Brendan Shanahan .12 .30
190 Peter Stastny .07 .20
191 Esa Tikkanen .05 .15
192 Ulf Dahlen .05 .15
193 Todd Elik .05 .15
194 Johan Garpenlov .05 .15
195 Arturs Irbe .07 .20
196 Vlastimil Kroupa .05 .15
197 Igor Larionov .05 .15
198 Sergei Makarov .05 .15
199 Jeff Norton .05 .15
200 Sandis Ozolinsh .05 .15
201 Mike Rathje .05 .15
202 Brian Bradley .05 .15
203 Shawn Chambers .05 .15
204 Danton Cole .05 .15
205 Chris Gratton .05 .15
206 Roman Hamrlik .07 .20
207 Chris Joseph .05 .15
208 Petr Klima .05 .15
209 Daren Puppa .07 .20
210 John Tucker .05 .15
211 Dave Andreychuk .10 .25
212 Ken Baumgartner .07 .20
213 Dave Ellett .05 .15
214 Mike Gartner .10 .25
215 Todd Gill .05 .15
216 Doug Gilmour .12 .30
217 Jamie Macoun .05 .15
218 Dmitri Mironov .05 .15
219 Felix Potvin .10 .25
220 Mats Sundin .07 .20
221 Jeff Brown .05 .15
222 Pavel Bure .10 .25
223 Murray Craven .05 .15
224 Bret Hedican .05 .15
225 Nathan Lafayette .05 .15
226 Trevor Linden .07 .20
227 Jyrki Lumme .05 .15
228 Kirk McLean .07 .20
229 Gino Odjick .05 .15
230 Cliff Ronning .05 .15
231 Peter Bondra .07 .20
232 Sylvain Cote .05 .15
233 Kevin Hatcher .05 .15
234 Dale Hunter .05 .15
235 Calle Johansson .05 .15
236 Dimitri Khristich .05 .15
237 Pat Peake .05 .15
238 Michal Pivonka .07 .20
239 Rick Tabaracci .07 .20
240 Tim Cheveldae .07 .20
241 Dallas Drake .05 .15
242 Nelson Emerson .05 .15
243 Dave Manson .05 .15
244 Teppo Numminen .05 .15
245 Stephane Quintal .05 .15
246 Teemu Selanne .20 .50
247 Keith Tkachuk .10 .25
248 Checklist .05 .15
249 Checklist .07 .20
250 Checklist .05 .15
251 John Lilley .05 .15
252 Mikhail Shtalenkov .05 .15
253 Garry Valk .05 .15
254 John Gruden RC .05 .15
255 Brent Hughes .05 .15
256 Al Iafrate .05 .15
257 Alexei Kasatonov .05 .15
258 Mikko Makela .05 .15
259 Marc Potvin .05 .15
260 Jon Rohloff RC .10 .25
261 Jozef Stumpel .05 .15
262 Grant Fuhr .10 .25
263 Viktor Gordiouk .07 .20
264 Yuri Khmylev .05 .15
265 Craig Muni .05 .15
266 Craig Simpson .05 .15
267 Denis Tsygurov RC .10 .25
268 Steve Chiasson .05 .15
269 Phil Housley .07 .20
270 Joel Otto .05 .15
271 Andrei Trefilov .05 .15
272 Vesa Viitakoski .07 .20
273 Tony Amonte .07 .20
274 Brent Grieve .05 .15
275 Bernie Nicholls .07 .20
276 Christian Soucy RC .07 .20
277 Paul Ysebaert .05 .15
278 Shane Churla .05 .15
279 Russ Courtnall .05 .15
280 Craig Ludwig .05 .15
281 Jarkko Varvio .05 .15
282 Darcy Wakaluk .07 .20
283 Greg Johnson .05 .15
284 Slava Kozlov .07 .20
285 Martin Lapointe .05 .15
286 Tim Taylor RC .10 .25
287 Mike Vernon .07 .20
288 Jason York RC .05 .15
289 Fred Brathwaite .05 .15
290 Kelly Buchberger .05 .15
291 Shayne Corson .05 .15
292 Dean McAmmond .05 .15
293 Vladimir Vujtek .05 .15
294 Doug Barrault .05 .15
295 Keith Brown .05 .15
296 Mark Fitzpatrick .07 .20
297 Mike Hough .05 .15
298 Scott Mellanby .07 .20
299 Jimmy Carson .05 .15
300 Andrew Cassels .05 .15
301 Andrei Nikolishin .05 .15
302 Steven Rice .05 .15
303 Glen Wesley .05 .15
304 Rob Brown .05 .15
305 Tony Granato .05 .15
306 Wayne Gretzky .50 1.25
307 Dan Quinn .07 .20
308 Darryl Sydor .05 .15
309 Rick Tocchet .07 .20
310 Donald Brashear RC .05 .15
311 Valeri Bure .05 .15
312 Jim Montgomery .05 .15
313 Kirk Muller .05 .15
314 Oleg Petrov .05 .15
315 Peter Popovic .05 .15
316 Yves Racine .05 .15
317 Turner Stevenson .05 .15
318 Ken Daneyko .05 .15
319 David Emma .05 .15
320 Brian Rolston .05 .15
321 Alexander Semak .05 .15
322 Jason Smith .07 .20
323 Chris Terreri .07 .20
324 Ray Ferraro .05 .15
325 Derek King .05 .15
326 Scott Lachance .05 .15
327 Brett Lindros .05 .15
328 Jamie McLennan .07 .20
329 Zigmund Palffy .07 .20
330 Corey Hirsch .07 .20
331 Alexei Kovalev .05 .15
332 Stephane Matteau .05 .15
333 Petr Nedved .07 .20
334 Mattias Norstrom .05 .15
335 Mark Osborne .05 .15
336 Randy Cunneyworth .05 .15
337 Pavol Demitra .12 .30
338 Pat Elynuik .05 .15
339 Sean Hill .05 .15
340 Darrin Madeley .05 .15
341 Sylvain Turgeon .05 .15
342 Vladislav Boulin RC .10 .25
343 Ron Hextall .07 .20
344 Patrik Juhlin RC .05 .15
345 Eric Lindros .10 .25
346 Shjon Podein .05 .15
347 Chris Therien .05 .15
348 John Cullen .05 .15
349 Markus Naslund .10 .25
350 Luc Robitaille .10 .25
351 Kjell Samuelsson .05 .15
352 Tomas Sandstrom .05 .15
353 Ken Wregget .07 .20
354 Wendel Clark .07 .20
355 Adam Deadmarsh .05 .15
356 Peter Forsberg .25 .60
357 Valeri Kamensky .07 .20
358 Uwe Krupp .05 .15
359 Janne Laukkanen .07 .20
360 Sylvain Lefebvre .05 .15
361 Jocelyn Thibault .10 .25
362 Bill Houlder .05 .15
363 Craig Janney .07 .20
364 Pat Falloon .05 .15
365 Jeff Friesen .05 .15
366 Viktor Kozlov .05 .15
367 Andrei Nazarov .05 .15
368 Jeff Odgers .05 .15
369 Michal Sykora .05 .15
370 Mikael Andersson .05 .15
371 Eric Charron RC .10 .25
372 Chris LiPuma .05 .15
373 Denis Savard .12 .30
374 Jason Wiemer RC .05 .15
375 Nikolai Borschevsky .05 .15
376 Eric Fichaud RC .10 .25
377 Kenny Jonsson .05 .15
378 Mike Ridley .05 .15
379 Mats Sundin .07 .20
380 Greg Adams .05 .15
381 Shawn Antoski .05 .15
382 Geoff Cournall .05 .15
383 Martin Gelinas .05 .15
384 Sergio Momesso .10 .25
385 Jiri Slegr .05 .15
386 Jason Allison .07 .20
387 Don Beaupre .07 .20
388 Joe Juneau .07 .20
389 Steve Konowalchuk .05 .15
390 Kelly Miller .05 .15
391 Dave Poulin .05 .15
392 Tie Domi .07 .20
393 Michal Grosek RC .05 .15
394 Russ Romaniuk .05 .15
395 Darrin Shannon .05 .15
396 Thomas Steen .05 .15
397 Igor Ulanov .05 .15
398 Alexei Zhamnov .07 .20
399 Checklist .05 .15
400 Checklist .05 .15

1994-95 Ultra All-Rookies

Randomly inserted in first series jumbo packs, this 10-card standard-size set reflects top rookies from the 1993-94 campaign. On acetate stock, the player is on the right superimposed over an ice-like surface. The left side is clear with the set title. The left portion of the back has a brief write-up and photo. Two distinct versions of each card in this set exist; one version carries the words "All-Rookie 1994-95" in a dark, greyish silver tint; the other in a bright, sparkling silver tint.

COMPLETE SET (10) 15.00 40.00
1 Jason Arnott 1.25 3.00
2 Martin Brodeur 5.00 12.00
3 Alexandre Daigle 1.25 3.00
4 Chris Gratton .60 1.50
5 Boris Mironov .60 1.50
6 Derek Plante .60 1.50
7 Chris Pronger 1.25 3.00
8 Mikael Renberg .60 1.50
9 Bryan Smolinski .60 1.50
10 Alexei Yashin 1.25 3.00

1994-95 Ultra All-Stars

Randomly inserted into first series foil packs at a rate of 1:2, this standard-size set focuses on 12 players who participated in the 1994 NHL All-Star Game in New York. The set is arranged according to Eastern (1-6) and Western Conferences (7-12). Horizontally designed, the front features the player in his All-Star jersey. The background is colorful and flashy. The All-Star logo also appears on front. The backs are much the same with an up-close player photo.

COMPLETE SET (12) 4.00 10.00
1 Ray Bourque .30 .75
2 Brian Leetch .20 .50
3 Eric Lindros .30 .75
4 Mark Messier .20 .50
5 Alexander Mogilny .20 .50
6 Patrick Roy .75 2.00
7 Pavel Bure .20 .50
8 Chris Chelios .20 .50
9 Paul Coffey .20 .50
10 Wayne Gretzky 1.25 3.00
11 Brett Hull .30 .75
12 Felix Potvin .25 .60

1994-95 Ultra Award Winners

Randomly inserted into first series foil packs, this 8-card standard-size set honors NHL award winners of the previous season. Horizontally designed, the fronts have an action photo and, to the left, the player in his tux at the awards ceremony. The backs have a write-up and a player photo.

COMPLETE SET (8) 5.00 12.00
1 Ray Bourque .60 1.50
2 Martin Brodeur 1.00 2.50
3 Sergei Fedorov .60 1.50
4 Adam Graves .10 .30
5 Wayne Gretzky 2.50 6.00
6 Dominik Hasek .75 2.00
7 Brian Leetch .40 1.00
8 Cam Neely .40 1.00

1994-95 Ultra Global Greats

Randomly inserted in second series 15-card jumbo packs at a rate of 1:12, this 10-card standard-size set features superstars who hail from outside North America. On the front, a player photo is superimposed over a background of colorful globes. The back features a write-up and a photo over the same background.

COMPLETE SET (10) 25.00 50.00
1 Sergei Fedorov 6.00 15.00
2 Dominik Hasek 6.00 15.00
3 Arturs Irbe 1.25 3.00
4 Jaromir Jagr 6.00 15.00
5 Jari Kurri 3.00 8.00
6 Alexander Mogilny 1.25 3.00
7 Petr Nedved 1.25 3.00
8 Mikael Renberg 1.25 3.00
9 Teemu Selanne 8.00 20.00
10 Alexei Yashin 1.25 3.00

1994-95 Ultra Power

Randomly inserted in first series foil packs and distributed one set per hobby case, this 10-card standard-size set focuses on high scoring forwards. The card fronts contain a player photo superimposed over a glossy and circular background. The backs are horizontal with a player photo, highlights and a similar background.

COMPLETE SET (10) 3.00 8.00
1 Dave Andreychuk .30 .75
2 Jason Arnott .20 .50
3 Chris Gratton .20 .50
4 Adam Graves .20 .50
5 Eric Lindros .60 1.50
6 Cam Neely .60 1.50
7 Mikael Renberg .30 .75
8 Jeremy Roenick .60 1.50
9 Brendan Shanahan .60 1.50
10 Keith Tkachuk .60 1.50

1994-95 Ultra Premier Pad Men

Randomly inserted in first series foil packs at a rate of 1:37, this 6-card standard-size set spotlights leading goaltenders. On front, a gold embossed design serves as background to the player photo. The backs have a solid color background that coordinates with the player's team. A player photo and write-up are in the foreground.

COMPLETE SET (6) 10.00 20.00
1 Dominik Hasek 2.00 5.00
2 Arturs Irbe 1.00 2.50
3 Curtis Joseph 1.25 3.00
4 Felix Potvin 1.50 4.00
5 Mike Richter 1.25 3.00
6 Patrick Roy 5.00 12.00

1994-95 Ultra Premier Pivots

Randomly inserted in second series foil packs at a rate of 1:4, this 10-card standard-size set spotlights leading NHL centers. The fronts contain a player photo superimposed over a brown checkered background. The backs are similar except for the addition of some player highlights.

COMPLETE SET (10) 6.00 12.00
1 Jason Arnott .10 .30
2 Sergei Fedorov .60 1.50
3 Doug Gilmour .20 .50
4 Wayne Gretzky 2.50 6.00
5 Pat LaFontaine .40 1.00
6 Eric Lindros .60 1.50
7 Mark Messier .40 1.00
8 Mike Modano .60 1.50
9 Adam Oates .20 .50
10 Steve Yzerman 2.00 5.00

1994-95 Ultra Prospects

Randomly inserted in second series 12-card foil packs at a rate of 1:12, this 10-card standard-size set focuses on some of the rookie crop from the 1994-95 season. The fronts have an embossed player photo superimposed over a background containing the set name. The backs have a photo and write-up.

COMPLETE SET (10) 12.00 25.00
1 Peter Forsberg 5.00 12.00
2 Todd Harvey .75 2.00
3 Paul Kariya 2.00 5.00
4 Viktor Kozlov .75 2.00
5 Brett Lindros .75 2.00
6 Mike Peca .75 2.00
7 Brian Rolston .75 2.00
8 Jamie Storr 1.25 3.00
9 Oleg Tverdovsky .75 2.00
10 Jason Wiemer .75 2.00

1994-95 Ultra Red Light Specials

Randomly inserted in second series foil packs at a rate of 1:12, this 10-card standard-size set presents top goal scorers. The fronts are horizontally designed with a player photo superimposed over three action strips of the player. The set logo is in red foil at bottom left. The backs offer a photo and highlights.

COMPLETE SET (10) 1.50 4.00
1 Dave Andreychuk .10 .30
2 Pavel Bure .25 .60

Mike Gartner .10 .30
Adam Graves .07 .20
Brett Hull .30 .75
Cam Neely .25 .60
Gary Roberts .07 .20
Teemu Selanne .25 .60
Brendan Shanahan .25 .60
Kevin Stevens .07 .20

1994-95 Ultra Scoring Kings

andomly inserted in first series foil packs, this 7-card andard-size set showcases seven of the NHL's top corers. The fronts provide three player photos with a old foil set logo at bottom left. The backs have a ayer photo and write-up.

OMPLETE SET (7) 5.00 10.00
Pavel Bure .25 .60
Sergei Fedorov .40 1.00
Doug Gilmour .10 .30
Wayne Gretzky 1.50 4.00
Mario Lemieux 1.25 3.00
Eric Lindros .25 .60
Steve Yzerman 1.25 3.00

1994-95 Ultra Sergei Fedorov

easuring the standard-size, the first ten cards were ndomly inserted in first series foil packs. Card Nos. 1 and 12 were available through a mail-in offer. The et chronicles various stages of Fedorov's career and s abilities. The front offers a photo with a quote from opposing player, teammate or executive. In addition providing career information, horizontal backs ontain a player photo. An indeterminate number of ards were autographed by Fedorov, and randomly serted in series one packs.

OMPLETE SET (10) 5.00 10.00
OMMON FEDOROV (1-10) .60 1.50
OMMON FEDOROV AUTO 25.00 60.00
OMMON MAIL-IN (11-12) .75 2.00

1994-95 Ultra Speed Merchants

andomly inserted in second series foil packs at the te of 1:2, this 10-card standard-size set salutes the ague's fastest and hardest-to-defend skaters. A player hoto is superimposed over an action-oriented ackground with the player's name and set title in gold il at the bottom. The backs contain a checkered flag ackground with a photo and highlights.

OMPLETE SET (10) 2.50 6.00
Pavel Bure .20 .50
Russ Courtnall .05 .15
Sergei Fedorov .40 1.00
Al Iafrate .05 .15
Pat LaFontaine .20 .50
Brian Leetch .20 .50
Mike Modano .40 1.00
Alexander Mogilny .08 .25
Jeremy Roenick .25 .60
Geoff Sanderson .08 .25

1995-96 Ultra

hese 400 standard-size cards represent the two series elease of the 1995-96 Ultra issue. Issued in 12-card acks, the suggested retail price per pack was $2.49. ach series one pack contains two insert cards. One as a Gold Medallion parallel insert while the other as from one of the five series one Ultra insert sets. econd series packs did not guarantee an insert per ack. The cards are printed on 20-point stock. Key RCs the set include Daniel Alfredsson, Todd Bertuzzi, had Kilger and Kyle McLaren. The Cool Trade xchange card was randomly inserted 1:360 series two acks, making it the hardest to pull of the five vailable. The card could be redeemed, until the xpiration date of 3/1/97, for special Emotion cards of eremy Roenick, Paul Kariya, Saku Koivu and Martin rodeur.

OMPLETE SET (400) 20.00 50.00
OMP.SERIES 1 (200) 10.00 25.00
OMP.SERIES 2 (200) 10.00 25.00
Guy Hebert .05 .15
Milos Holan .02 .10
Paul Kariya .10 .30
Denny Lambert RC .02 .10
Stephan Lebeau .02 .10
Oleg Tverdovsky .02 .10
Shaun Van Allen .02 .10
Ray Bourque .20 .50
Mariusz Czerkawski .02 .10
Blaine Lacher .05 .15
1 Sandy Moger RC .02 .10
2 Cam Neely .10 .30
3 Adam Oates .05 .15
4 Bryan Smolinski .02 .10
5 Donald Audette .02 .10
Jason Dawe .02 .10
7 Garry Galley .02 .10
3 Dominik Hasek .25 .60
Brian Holzinger RC .05 .15
Pat Lafontaine .10 .30
1 Alexander Mogilny .05 .15
2 Alexei Zhitnik .02 .10
3 Steve Chiasson .02 .10
4 Theo Fleury .02 .10
5 Phil Housley .05 .15
Trevor Kidd .05 .15
7 Joel Otto .02 .10
3 Gary Roberts .02 .10
Zarley Zalapski .02 .10
Ed Belfour .10 .30
Chris Chelios .10 .30
2 Eric Daze .05 .15
3 Sergei Krivokrasov .02 .10
4 Bernie Nicholls .02 .10
5 Jeremy Roenick .15 .40
Gary Suter .02 .10
7 Todd Harvey .05 .15
3 Derian Hatcher .02 .10
Mike Kennedy .02 .10
Grant Ledyard .02 .10
Mike Modano .20 .50
2 Andy Moog .10 .30
3 Mike Torchia RC .05 .15
4 Paul Coffey .10 .30
5 Sergei Fedorov .20 .50
Vladimir Konstantinov .05 .15
7 Slava Kozlov .05 .15
3 Keith Primeau .02 .10
Ray Sheppard .02 .10
Mike Vernon .05 .15
Steve Yzerman .60 1.50
2 Jason Arnott .02 .10
3 Shayne Corson .02 .10
4 Igor Kravchuk .02 .10
5 Todd Marchant .02 .10
David Oliver .02 .10
7 Bill Ranford .05 .15
3 Doug Weight .05 .15
Stu Barnes .02 .10
Jesse Belanger .02 .10
Gord Murphy .02 .10
2 Rob Niedermayer .05 .15
3 Brian Skrudland .02 .10
64 John Vanbiesbrouck .05 .15
65 Sean Burke .05 .15
66 Andrew Cassels .02 .10
67 Frantisek Kucera .02 .10
68 Andrei Nikolishin .02 .10
69 Chris Pronger .10 .30
70 Geoff Sanderson .02 .10
71 Kevin Smyth .02 .10
72 Darren Turcotte .02 .10
73 Rob Blake .05 .15
74 Wayne Gretzky .75 2.00
75 Kelly Hrudey .05 .15
76 Marty McSorley .02 .10
77 Jamie Storr .05 .15
78 Darryl Sydor .05 .15
79 Rick Tocchet .05 .15
80 Vincent Damphousse .02 .10
81 Vladimir Malakhov .02 .10
82 Mark Recchi .05 .15
83 Patrick Roy .60 1.50
84 Brian Savage .02 .10
85 Pierre Turgeon .05 .15
86 Martin Brodeur .30 .75
87 Neal Broten .05 .15
88 Sergei Brylin .02 .10
89 John MacLean .05 .15
90 Scott Niedermayer .02 .10
91 Stephane Richer .05 .15
92 Scott Stevens .05 .15
93 Ray Ferraro .02 .10
94 Scott Lachance .02 .10
95 Brett Lindros .02 .10
96 Kirk Muller .02 .10
97 Zigmund Palffy .05 .15
98 Tommy Salo RC .20 .50
99 Mathieu Schneider .02 .10
100 Tommy Soderstrom .05 .15
101 Glenn Healy .05 .15
102 Darren Langdon RC .02 .10
103 Steve Larmer .05 .15
104 Brian Leetch .05 .15
105 Mark Messier .10 .30
106 Mattias Norstrom .02 .10
107 Pat Verbeek .02 .10
108 Sergei Zubov .02 .10
109 Don Beaupre .05 .15
110 Radek Bonk .02 .10
111 Alexandre Daigle .02 .10
112 Steve Larouche RC .02 .10
113 Stanislav Neckar .02 .10
114 Alexei Yashin .02 .10
115 Rod Brind'Amour .05 .15
116 Eric Desjardins .05 .15
117 Ron Hextall .05 .15
118 John LeClair .10 .30
119 Eric Lindros .10 .30
120 Mikael Renberg .05 .15
121 Chris Therien .02 .10
122 Ron Francis .05 .15
123 Jaromir Jagr .20 .50
124 Joe Mullen .05 .15
125 Larry Murphy .05 .15
126 Ulf Samuelsson .02 .10
127 Kevin Stevens .02 .10
128 Ken Wregget .05 .15
129 Wendel Clark .05 .15
130 Adam Deadmarsh .02 .10
131 Stephane Fiset .05 .15
132 Peter Forsberg .30 .75
133 Curtis Leschyshyn .02 .10
134 Owen Nolan .05 .15
135 Mike Ricci .05 .15
136 Joe Sakic .25 .60
137 Denis Chasse .02 .10
138 Steve Duchesne .02 .10
139 Brett Hull .15 .40
140 Curtis Joseph .10 .30
141 Ian Laperriere .02 .10
142 Brendan Shanahan .10 .30
143 Esa Tikkanen .02 .10
144 Ulf Dahlen .02 .10
145 Jeff Friesen .02 .10
146 Arturs Irbe .05 .15
147 Craig Janney .02 .10
148 Sergei Makarov .02 .10
149 Sandis Ozolinsh .02 .10
150 Ray Whitney .05 .15
151 Chris Gratton .02 .10
152 Roman Hamrlik .05 .15
153 Petr Klima .02 .10
154 Brantt Myhres RC .02 .10
155 Daren Puppa .05 .15
156 Jason Wiemer .02 .10
157 Paul Ysebaert .02 .10
158 Dave Andreychuk .05 .15
159 Tie Domi .05 .15
160 Doug Gilmour .05 .15
161 Kenny Jonsson .02 .10
162 Felix Potvin .10 .30
163 Mike Ridley .02 .10
164 Mats Sundin .10 .30
165 Jeff Brown .02 .10
166 Pavel Bure .10 .30
167 Geoff Courtnall .02 .10
168 Russ Courtnall .02 .10
169 Trevor Linden .05 .15
170 Kirk McLean .05 .15
171 Roman Oksiuta .02 .10
172 Peter Bondra .05 .15
173 Jim Carey .05 .15
174 Martin Gendron .02 .10
175 Dale Hunter .05 .15
176 Calle Johansson .02 .10
177 Michal Pivonka .02 .10
178 Mark Tinordi .02 .10
179 Nelson Emerson .02 .10
180 Nikolai Khabibulin .05 .15
181 Dave Manson .02 .10
182 Teppo Numminen .02 .10
183 Teemu Selanne .10 .30
184 Keith Tkachuk .10 .30
185 Alexei Zhamnov .05 .15
186 Martin Brodeur SC .30 .75
187 Neal Broten .05 .15
188 Bob Carpenter .02 .10
189 Ken Daneyko .02 .10
190 Bruce Driver .02 .10
191 Bill Guerin .05 .15
192 Claude Lemieux .02 .10
193 John MacLean .05 .15
194 Scott Niedermayer .02 .10
195 Stephane Richer .05 .15
196 Scott Stevens .05 .15
197 Stanley Cup Presentation .05 .15
198 Checklist (1-83) .02 .10
199 Checklist (84-169) .02 .10
200 Checklist (170-200) .02 .10
201 Todd Krygier .02 .10
202 Steve Rucchin .05 .15
203 Mike Sillinger .02 .10
204 Ted Donato .02 .10
205 Shawn McEachern .02 .10
206 Joe Mullen .05 .15
207 Kevin Stevens .02 .10
208 Don Sweeney .02 .10
209 Mark Astley .02 .10
210 Randy Burridge .02 .10
211 Jason Dawe .02 .10
212 Mike Peca .05 .15
213 Michael Nylander .02 .10
214 Cory Stillman .02 .10
215 Pavel Torgajev RC .02 .10
216 Tony Amonte .05 .15
217 Joe Murphy .02 .10
218 Bob Probert .05 .15
219 Denis Savard .05 .15
220 Stephane Fiset .05 .15
221 Valeri Kamensky .05 .15
222 Sylvain Lefebvre .02 .10
223 Claude Lemieux .02 .10
224 Sandis Ozolinsh .02 .10
225 Patrick Roy .60 1.50
226 Scott Young .02 .10
227 Greg Adams .02 .10
228 Guy Carbonneau .10 .30
229 Dave Gagner .02 .10
230 Kevin Hatcher .02 .10
231 Darcy Wakaluk .05 .15
232 Dino Ciccarelli .05 .15
233 Greg Johnson .02 .10
234 Igor Larionov .02 .10
235 Darren McCarty .02 .10
236 Chris Osgood .05 .15
237 Zdeno Ciger .02 .10
238 Bryan Marchment .02 .10
239 Boris Mironov .02 .10
240 Peter White .02 .10
241 Jody Hull .02 .10
242 Scott Mellanby .02 .10
243 Gord Murphy .02 .10
244 Jason Woolley .02 .10
245 Gerald Diduck .02 .10
246 Nelson Emerson .02 .10
247 Brendan Shanahan .10 .30
248 Glen Wesley .02 .10
249 Tony Granato .02 .10
250 Dimitri Khristich .02 .10
251 Jari Kurri .10 .30
252 Eric Lacroix .02 .10
253 Yanic Perreault .02 .10
254 Patrice Brisebois .02 .10
255 Benoit Brunet .02 .10
256 Valeri Bure .02 .10
257 Stephane Quintal .02 .10
258 Jocelyn Thibault .10 .30
259 Shawn Chambers .02 .10
260 Jim Dowd .02 .10
261 Bill Guerin .05 .15
262 Bobby Holik .02 .10
263 Steve Thomas .05 .15
264 Esa Tikkanen .02 .10
265 Wendel Clark .05 .15
266 Travis Green .05 .15
267 Brett Lindros .02 .10
268 Kirk Muller .02 .10
269 Zigmund Palffy .05 .15
270 Mathieu Schneider .02 .10
271 Alexander Semak .02 .10
272 Dennis Vaske .02 .10
273 Ray Ferraro .02 .10
274 Adam Graves .02 .10
275 Alexei Kovalev .02 .10
276 Mike Richter .10 .30
277 Luc Robitaille .05 .15
278 Ulf Samuelsson .02 .10
279 Steve Duchesne .02 .10
280 Trent McCleary RC .02 .10
281 Dan Quinn .02 .10
282 Martin Straka .02 .10
283 Karl Dykhuis .02 .10
284 Pat Falloon .02 .10
285 Joel Otto .02 .10
286 Kjell Samuelsson .02 .10
287 Garth Snow .05 .15
288 Mario Lemieux .60 1.50
289 Norm Maciver .02 .10
290 Dmitri Mironov .02 .10
291 Markus Naslund .10 .30
292 Petr Nedved .05 .15
293 Tomas Sandstrom .02 .10
294 Bryan Smolinski .02 .10
295 Sergei Zubov .02 .10
296 Shayne Corson .02 .10
297 Geoff Courtnall .02 .10
298 Grant Fuhr .10 .30
299 Dale Hawerchuk .10 .30
300 Al MacInnis .05 .15
301 Brian Noonan .02 .10
302 Chris Pronger .10 .30
303 Andrei Nazarov .02 .10
304 Owen Nolan .05 .15
305 Ray Sheppard .02 .10
306 Chris Terreri .05 .15
307 Brian Bellows .02 .10
308 Brian Bradley .02 .10
309 John Cullen .02 .10
310 Alexander Selivanov .02 .10
311 Mike Gartner .05 .15
312 Benoit Hogue .02 .10
313 Sergio Momesso .02 .10
314 Larry Murphy .05 .15
315 Dave Babych .02 .10
316 Bret Hedican .02 .10
317 Alexander Mogilny .05 .15
318 Mike Ridley .02 .10
319 Peter Bondra .05 .15
320 Jim Carey .05 .15
321 Sylvain Cote .02 .10
322 Sergei Gonchar .02 .10
323 Joe Juneau .02 .10
324 Steve Konowalchuk .02 .10
325 Pat Peake .02 .10
326 Dallas Drake .02 .10
327 Igor Korolev .02 .10
328 Darren Turcotte .02 .10
329 Daniel Alfredsson RC .50 1.25
330 Aki Berg RC .05 .15
331 Todd Bertuzzi RC .75 2.00
332 Jason Bonsignore .02 .10
333 Curtis Brown RC .10 .30
334 Byron Dafoe .05 .15
335 Eric Daze .05 .15
336 Shane Doan RC .30 .75
337 Jason Doig .02 .10
338 Radek Dvorak RC .20 .50
339 Joe Dziedzic .02 .10
340 Darby Hendrickson .02 .10
341 Brian Holzinger RC .10 .30
342 Ed Jovanovski .05 .15
343 Chad Kilger RC .02 .10
344 Saku Koivu .10 .30
345 Darren Langdon .02 .10
346 Jamie Langenbrunner .02 .10
347 Jere Lehtinen .05 .15
348 Bryan McCabe .02 .10
349 Kyle McLaren RC .02 .10
350 Marty Murray .02 .10
351 Jeff O'Neill .02 .10
352 Deron Quint .02 .10
353 Marcus Ragnarsson RC .05 .15
354 Tommy Salo .20 .50
355 Miroslav Satan RC .50 1.25
356 Jamie Storr .05 .15
357 Niklas Sundstrom .05 .15
358 Robert Svehla RC .02 .10
359 Denis Pederson .02 .10
360 Antti Tormanen .02 .10
361 Brendan Witt .02 .10
362 Vitali Yachmenev .02 .10
363 Stephane Yelle .02 .10
364 Tom Barrasso NE .05 .15
365 Ed Belfour NE .10 .30
366 Martin Brodeur NE .30 .75
367 Sean Burke NE .05 .15
368 Jim Carey NE .02 .10
369 Stephane Fiset NE .05 .15
370 Dominik Hasek NE .25 .60
371 Ron Hextall NE .05 .15
372 Nikolai Khabibulin NE .05 .15
373 Kirk McLean NE .05 .15
374 Chris Osgood NE .05 .15
375 Felix Potvin NE .05 .15
376 Daren Puppa NE .05 .15
377 Patrick Roy NE .60 1.50
378 John Vanbiesbrouck NE .05 .15
379 Pavel Bure UC .10 .30
380 Chris Chelios UC .10 .30
381 Sergei Fedorov UC .20 .50
382 Theo Fleury UC .02 .10
383 Peter Forsberg UC .30 .75
384 Ron Francis UC .05 .15
385 Wayne Gretzky UC .75 2.00
386 Brett Hull UC .15 .40
387 Jaromir Jagr UC .20 .50
388 Paul Kariya UC .10 .30
389 Pat LaFontaine UC .05 .15
390 Brian Leetch UC .05 .15
391 Mario Lemieux UC .60 1.50
392 Eric Lindros UC .20 .50
393 Mark Messier UC .10 .30
394 Mike Modano UC .10 .30
395 Adam Oates UC .05 .15
396 Jeremy Roenick UC .15 .40
397 Joe Sakic UC .25 .60
398 Alexei Zhamnov UC .05 .15
399 Checklist .02 .10
400 Checklist .02 .10

1995-96 Ultra Gold Medallion

This 200-card standard-size set is a parallel to the basic Ultra series one issue. These cards were issued one per series one pack. No Gold Medallion version exists for series two cards. The fronts have the same photos as the regular cards except the entire background is gold. The Ultra Gold Medallion logo is in the middle of the card and is embossed for effect. The words "Gold Medallion Edition" are located under the player's name. The backs are identical to the regular cards. Gold Medallion version also could be found for series one insert cards. Values for those are included under the appropriate insert header.

*VETS: 2.5X TO 6X BASIC CARDS
*ROOKIES: 1.2X TO 3X

1995-96 Ultra All-Rookie

These ten cards, which were randomly inserted at a rate of 1:4 series one retail packs, focus on the top rookies from the 1994-95 campaign. Gold Medallion parallel versions of these cards also were available, at indeterminate odds.

COMPLETE SET (10) 6.00 15.00
*GOLD MED: .8X TO 2X BASIC INSERTS
1 Jim Carey .40 1.00
2 Mariusz Czerkawski .40 1.00
3 Peter Forsberg 2.00 5.00
4 Jeff Friesen .40 1.00
5 Paul Kariya 1.50 4.00
6 Blaine Lacher .40 1.00
7 Ian Laperriere .40 1.00
8 Todd Marchant .40 1.00
9 Roman Oksiuta .40 1.00
10 David Oliver .40 1.00

1995-96 Ultra Crease Crashers

These twenty cards capture a goalie's worst nightmare -- a soft-handed forward with a propensity for invading a netminder's home turf. The cards were randomly inserted in series two retail packs only at a rate of 1:18.

COMPLETE SET (20) 30.00 80.00
1 Jason Arnott 2.00 5.00
2 Rod Brind'Amour 2.00 5.00
3 Theo Fleury 3.00 8.00
4 Todd Harvey 2.00 5.00
5 John LeClair 2.50 6.00
6 Claude Lemieux 2.50 6.00
7 Trevor Linden 2.50 6.00
8 Eric Lindros 5.00 12.00
9 Darren McCarty 2.00 5.00
10 Scott Mellanby 2.00 5.00
11 Mark Messier 3.00 8.00
12 Cam Neely 3.00 8.00
13 Owen Nolan 2.00 5.00
14 Keith Primeau 2.00 5.00
15 Jeremy Roenick 4.00 10.00
16 Tomas Sandstrom 2.00 5.00
17 Brendan Shanahan 2.50 6.00
18 Kevin Stevens 2.00 5.00
19 Rick Tocchet 2.00 5.00
20 Keith Tkachuk 2.50 6.00

1995-96 Ultra Extra Attackers

When pulling the goalie and down late in the game, these are the guys you'd love to tap on the shoulder. The cards were randomly inserted in series two hobby packs only at a rate of 1:18.

COMPLETE SET (20) 40.00 80.00
1 Peter Bondra 1.25 3.00
2 Eric Daze 1.25 3.00
3 Radek Dvorak 1.25 3.00
4 Sergei Fedorov 2.50 6.00
5 Peter Forsberg 3.00 8.00
6 Ron Francis 1.25 3.00
7 Wayne Gretzky 10.00 25.00
8 Brett Hull 2.00 5.00
9 Jaromir Jagr 3.00 8.00
10 Ed Jovanovski 1.25 3.00
11 Paul Kariya 1.50 4.00
12 Saku Koivu 1.50 4.00
13 Mario Lemieux 8.00 20.00
14 Mike Modano 2.50 6.00
15 Alexander Mogilny 2.00 5.00
16 Adam Oates 1.25 3.00
17 Joe Sakic 4.00 10.00
18 Niklas Sundstrom 1.25 3.00
19 Mats Sundin 1.50 4.00
20 Steve Yzerman 8.00 20.00

1995-96 Ultra High Speed

Young stars in a hurry to reach the upper echelon of the NHL pay scale, and some already there trying to prove they're worth it, are featured in this 20-card set. Collectors could find these cards randomly inserted at a rate of 1:5 series two packs.

COMPLETE SET (20) 10.00 20.00
1 Daniel Alfredsson .75 2.00
2 Jason Arnott .20 .50
3 Todd Bertuzzi .75 2.00
4 Radek Bonk .20 .50
5 Martin Brodeur 2.00 5.00
6 Alexandre Daigle .20 .50
7 Shane Doan .40 1.00
8 Peter Forsberg 1.50 4.00
9 Roman Hamrlik .20 .50
10 Todd Harvey .20 .50
11 Paul Kariya .75 2.00
12 Travis Green .20 .50
13 Chris Osgood .40 1.00
14 Zigmund Palffy .40 1.00
15 Marcus Ragnarsson .20 .50
16 Mikael Renberg .20 .50
17 Brian Savage .20 .50
18 Robert Svehla .20 .50
19 Jocelyn Thibault .40 1.00
20 Brendan Witt .20 .50

1995-96 Ultra Premier Pad Men

Cards from this 12-card standard-size set was inserted 1:36 series one packs. This set features leading NHL goaltenders on a special gold foil embossed design. There is also a Gold Medallion parallel version of each card that were inserted at 1:360. Multipliers can be found in the header to determine values for these.

COMPLETE SET (12) 30.00 60.00
*GOLD MED: 3X TO 6X BASIC INSERTS
1 Ed Belfour 2.50 6.00
2 Martin Brodeur 6.00 15.00
3 Sean Burke 2.00 5.00
4 Jim Carey 2.00 5.00
5 Dominik Hasek 3.00 8.00
6 Curtis Joseph 3.00 8.00
7 Blaine Lacher 2.00 5.00
8 Andy Moog 3.00 8.00
9 Felix Potvin 3.00 8.00
10 Patrick Roy 6.00 15.00
11 John Vanbiesbrouck 4.00 10.00
12 Mike Vernon 3.00 8.00

1995-96 Ultra Premier Pivots

These 10 standard-size cards were inserted into first series packs at a rate of 1:4. Leading NHL centers are showcased on these cards. There also are Gold Medallion versions of each of these cards which were inserted at 1:40. Multipliers can be found in the header to determine values for these.

COMPLETE SET (10) 6.00 12.00
*GOLD MED: .8X TO 2X BASIC INSERTS
1 Sergei Fedorov .60 1.50
2 Ron Francis .20 .50
3 Wayne Gretzky 2.50 6.00
4 Eric Lindros .40 1.00
5 Mark Messier .40 1.00
6 Adam Oates .20 .50
7 Jeremy Roenick .50 1.25
8 Joe Sakic .75 2.00
9 Mats Sundin .40 1.00
10 Alexei Zhamnov .20 .50

1995-96 Ultra Red Light Specials

These 10 standard-size cards were inserted into series one packs at a rate of 1:3. These cards feature players who lit the lamp on a regular basis during the '94-95 season. There is also a Gold Medallion parallel version of each card inserted at 1:30. Multipliers can be found in the header to determine values for these.

COMPLETE SET (10) 1.25 3.00
*GOLD MED: .75X TO 2X BASIC INSERTS
1 Peter Bondra .20 .50
2 Theo Fleury .15 .40
3 Brett Hull .30 .75
4 Jaromir Jagr .40 1.00
5 John LeClair .25 .60
6 Eric Lindros .30 .75
7 Cam Neely .25 .60
8 Owen Nolan .20 .50
9 Ray Sheppard .15 .40
10 Alexei Zhamnov .20 .50

1995-96 Ultra Rising Stars

These 10 standard-size cards were randomly inserted 1:4 series one packs. There are also Gold Medallion parallel versions of these cards which were randomly inserted at 1:40. Multipliers can be found in the header below to determine values for these.

COMPLETE SET (10) .75 2.00
*GOLD MED: .8X TO 2X BASIC INSERTS
1 Jason Arnott .15 .40
2 Alexandre Daigle .15 .40
3 Roman Hamrlik .20 .50
4 Trevor Kidd .20 .50
5 Scott Niedermayer .15 .40
6 Keith Primeau .15 .40
7 Mikael Renberg .20 .50
8 Jocelyn Thibault .30 .75
9 Alexei Yashin .15 .40
10 Alexei Zhitnik .15 .40

1995-96 Ultra Ultraview

This 10-card set features the NHL's best on clear acrylic. The cards were randomly inserted at a rate of 1:55 series two packs. A parallel version of these cards could be found in complete set form in randomly inserted Ultraview Hot Packs. These sets, which bore the Hot Pack logo, were found in 1:360 packs. Because they were found in complete set form, dealers tended to discount them slightly at time of sale. Multipliers can be found in the header to determine value for these.

COMPLETE SET (10) 20.00 40.00
*HOT PACK: .2X TO .5X BASIC INSERTS
1 Sergei Fedorov 1.25 3.00
2 Wayne Gretzky 6.00 15.00
3 Dominik Hasek 2.00 5.00
4 Jaromir Jagr 1.50 4.00
5 Brian Leetch .75 2.00
6 Mario Lemieux 5.00 12.00
7 Eric Lindros 1.00 2.50
8 Jeremy Roenick 1.25 3.00
9 Joe Sakic 2.00 5.00
10 Alexei Zhamnov .75 2.00

1996-97 Ultra

The 1996-97 Ultra set was issued in one series totaling 180 cards. Ten-card packs retailed for $2.49. Key rookies include Dainius Zubrus, Patrick Lalime, and Sergei Berezin. Card fronts feature a color action photo with player information on the back.

COMPLETE SET (180) 15.00 30.00
1 Guy Hebert .25 .60
2 Paul Kariya .40 1.00
3 Jari Kurri .30 .75
4 Roman Oksiuta .20 .50
5 Ruslan Salei RC .30 .75
6 Teemu Selanne .60 1.50
7 Darren Van Impe .20 .50
8 Ray Bourque .50 1.25
9 Kyle McLaren .20 .50
10 Adam Oates .30 .75
11 Bill Ranford .25 .60
12 Rick Tocchet .25 .60
13 Donald Audette .20 .50
14 Curtis Brown .20 .50
15 Jason Dawe .20 .50
16 Dominik Hasek .50 1.25
17 Pat LaFontaine .30 .75
18 Jay McKee RC .20 .50
19 Derek Plante .20 .50
20 Wayne Primeau .20 .50
21 Theo Fleury .60 1.50
22 Dave Gagner .30 .75
23 Jonas Hoglund .20 .50
24 Jarome Iginla .40 1.00
25 Trevor Kidd .20 .50
26 Robert Reichel .20 .50
27 German Titov .20 .50
28 Tony Amonte .25 .60
29 Ed Belfour .30 .75
30 Chris Chelios .30 .75
31 Eric Daze .25 .60
32 Ethan Moreau RC .30 .75
33 Gary Suter .20 .50
34 Adam Deadmarsh .20 .50
35 Peter Forsberg .50 1.25
36 Valeri Kamensky .25 .60
37 Claude Lemieux .20 .50
38 Sandis Ozolinsh .20 .50
39 Patrick Roy .75 2.00
40 Joe Sakic .50 1.25
41 Landon Wilson .20 .50
42 Derian Hatcher .20 .50
43 Jamie Langenbrunner .20 .50
44 Mike Modano .50 1.25
45 Andy Moog .30 .75
46 Joe Nieuwendyk .30 .75
47 Pat Verbeek .20 .50
48 Sergei Zubov .20 .50
49 Anders Eriksson .20 .50
50 Sergei Fedorov .50 1.25
51 Vladimir Konstantinov .25 .60
52 Slava Kozlov .20 .50
53 Nicklas Lidstrom .40 1.00
54 Chris Osgood .30 .75
55 Brendan Shanahan .40 1.00
56 Steve Yzerman .75 2.00
57 Jason Arnott .25 .60
58 Mike Grier RC .40 1.00
59 Curtis Joseph .30 .75
60 Rem Murray RC .30 .75
61 Jeff Norton .25 .60
62 Miroslav Satan .20 .50
63 Doug Weight .30 .75
64 Radek Dvorak .25 .60
65 Ed Jovanovski .25 .60
66 Scott Mellanby .25 .60
67 Rob Niedermayer .25 .60
68 Ray Sheppard .25 .60
69 Robert Svehla .20 .50
70 John Vanbiesbrouck .30 .75
71 Steve Washburn RC .30 .75
72 Jeff Brown .20 .50
73 Sean Burke .20 .50
74 Hnat Domenichelli .20 .50
75 Keith Primeau .20 .50
76 Geoff Sanderson .25 .60
77 Rob Blake .30 .75
78 Stephane Fiset .25 .60
79 Dimitri Khristich .20 .50
80 Mattias Norstrom .20 .50
81 Ed Olczyk .20 .50
82 Jamie Storr .20 .50
83 Jan Vopat .20 .50
84 Vitali Yachmenev .20 .50
85 Shayne Corson .20 .50
86 Vincent Damphousse .25 .60
87 Saku Koivu .30 .75
88 Mark Recchi .40 1.00
89 Stephane Richer .25 .60
90 Jocelyn Thibault .30 .75
91 David Wilkie .20 .50
92 Dave Andreychuk .30 .75
93 Martin Brodeur .60 1.50
94 Scott Niedermayer .30 .75
95 Scott Stevens .30 .75
96 Petr Sykora .20 .50
97 Steve Thomas .20 .50
98 Bryan Berard .30 .75
99 Todd Bertuzzi .30 .75
100 Eric Fichaud .25 .60
101 Travis Green .25 .60
102 Kenny Jonsson .20 .50
103 Zigmund Palffy .30 .75
104 Christian Dube .20 .50
105 Daniel Goneau RC .30 .75
106 Wayne Gretzky 1.50 4.00
107 Alexei Kovalev .20 .50
108 Brian Leetch .30 .75
109 Mark Messier .50 1.25
110 Mike Richter .30 .75
111 Luc Robitaille .30 .75
112 Niklas Sundstrom .20 .50
113 Daniel Alfredsson .30 .75
114 Radek Bonk .20 .50
115 Andreas Dackell RC .30 .75
116 Alexandre Daigle .20 .50
117 Steve Duchesne .20 .50
118 Wade Redden .20 .50
119 Damian Rhodes .25 .60
120 Alexei Yashin .25 .60
121 Rod Brind'Amour .30 .75
122 Paul Coffey .30 .75
123 Eric Desjardins .25 .60
124 Ron Hextall .25 .60
125 John LeClair .30 .75
126 Eric Lindros .50 1.25
127 Janne Niinimaa .30 .75
128 Mikael Renberg .25 .60
129 Dainius Zubrus RC .40 1.00
130 Mike Gartner .30 .75
131 Craig Janney .25 .60
132 Nikolai Khabibulin .25 .60
133 Dave Manson .20 .50
134 Teppo Numminen .20 .50
135 Jeremy Roenick .50 1.25
136 Keith Tkachuk .30 .75
137 Oleg Tverdovsky .25 .60
138 Tom Barrasso .25 .60
139 Ron Francis .40 1.00
140 Kevin Hatcher .20 .50
141 Jaromir Jagr .75 2.00
142 Patrick Lalime RC .40 1.00
143 Mario Lemieux 1.00 2.50
144 Jim Campbell .20 .50
145 Grant Fuhr .30 .75
146 Brett Hull 1.50 4.00
147 Al MacInnis .30 .75
148 Pierre Turgeon .30 .75
149 Harry York RC .30 .75
150 Kelly Hrudey .25 .60
151 Al Iafrate .20 .50
152 Bernie Nicholls .20 .50
153 Owen Nolan .30 .75
154 Darren Turcotte .20 .50
155 Brian Bradley .20 .50
156 Dino Ciccarelli .30 .75
157 Roman Hamrlik .25 .60
158 Daymond Langkow .25 .60
159 Daren Puppa .25 .60
160 Alexander Selivanov .20 .50
161 Sergei Berezin RC .50 1.25
162 Wendel Clark .25 .60
163 Doug Gilmour .40 1.00
164 Larry Murphy .25 .60
165 Felix Potvin .30 .75
166 Mats Sundin .30 .75
167 Pavel Bure .40 1.00
168 Trevor Linden .25 .60
169 Kirk McLean .25 .60
170 Alexander Mogilny .25 .60
171 Esa Tikkanen .20 .50
172 Peter Bondra .25 .60
173 Andrew Brunette RC .40 1.00
174 Jim Carey .30 .75
175 Sergei Gonchar .20 .50
176 Phil Housley .25 .60
177 Joe Juneau .20 .50
178 Michal Pivonka .20 .50
179 Checklist (1-143) .20 .50
180 Checklist (143-180 inserts) .20 .50
S125 John LeClair promo

1996-97 Ultra Gold Medallion

A one-per-pack parallel, these cards differ from the base cards by the use of gold foil to highlight the player's name on the card front. The words "Gold Medallion" are also included. Values for the cards can be determined by using the multipliers below on the corresponding base card.

*VETS: 2.5X TO 6X BASIC CARDS
*ROOKIES: 1.2X TO 3X

1996-97 Ultra Clear the Ice

Ten players recognized as some of the elite at their position are the subject of this set, which was randomly inserted in packs at the stingy rate of 1:350.

COMPLETE SET (10) 50.00 125.00
1 Jim Carey 5.00 12.00
2 Peter Forsberg 10.00 25.00
3 Dominik Hasek 8.00 20.00
4 Jaromir Jagr 8.00 20.00
5 John LeClair 5.00 12.00
6 Eric Lindros 8.00 20.00
7 Mark Messier 5.00 12.00
8 Patrick Roy 20.00 50.00
9 Brendan Shanahan 5.00 12.00
10 Keith Tkachuk 5.00 12.00

1996-97 Ultra Mr. Momentum

Randomly inserted in retail packs only at a rate of 1:36, these ten cards offer simple fronts and three-photo, text-laden backs.

COMPLETE SET (10) 20.00 40.00
1 Peter Bondra 1.00 2.50
2 Pavel Bure 2.00 5.00
3 Ron Francis 1.00 2.50
4 Brett Hull 2.50 6.00
5 Jaromir Jagr 3.00 8.00
6 Pat LaFontaine 2.00 5.00
7 Eric Lindros 2.00 5.00
8 Mark Messier 2.00 5.00
9 Mats Sundin 2.00 5.00
10 Steve Yzerman 6.00 15.00

1996-97 Ultra Power

The 16 cards in this set were randomly inserted in packs at a rate of 1:16. The cards feature fiery lettering and a glitter-enhanced design. Card fronts also feature a color action photo, with biographical info on the back. The checklist was mirrored in the Red Line and Blue Line sets, although photo choice and card numbering varied slightly.

COMPLETE SET (16) 25.00 60.00
1 Ray Bourque 2.00 5.00
2 Chris Chelios 1.25 3.00
3 Paul Coffey 1.25 3.00
4 Sergei Fedorov 2.00 5.00
5 Wayne Gretzky 8.00 20.00
6 Roman Hamrlik .60 1.50
7 Ed Jovanovski .60 1.50
8 Paul Kariya 1.25 3.00
9 Vladimir Konstantinov .60 1.50
10 Brian Leetch 1.25 3.00
11 Mario Lemieux 6.00 15.00
12 Nicklas Lidstrom 1.25 3.00
13 Alexander Mogilny .60 1.50
14 Adam Oates .60 1.50
15 Joe Sakic 2.50 6.00
16 Teemu Selanne 1.25 3.00

1996-97 Ultra Power Blue Line

Randomly inserted in hobby packs only at a rate of 1:90, this tough insert features eight top defensive players. The cards are sequentially numbered on the back out of 1,082.

COMPLETE SET (8) 10.00 25.00
1 Ray Bourque 4.00 10.00
2 Chris Chelios 2.50 6.00
3 Paul Coffey 2.50 6.00
4 Roman Hamrlik 1.25 3.00
5 Ed Jovanovski 1.25 3.00
6 Vladimir Konstantinov 1.25 3.00
7 Brian Leetch 2.50 6.00
8 Nicklas Lidstrom 2.50 6.00

1996-97 Ultra Power Red Line

Eight of the absolute best offensive weapons grace this tough insert set, randomly seeded only in hobby packs at a rate of 1:90. The cards are sequentially numbered on the back out of 1,082.

COMPLETE SET (8) 30.00 80.00
1 Sergei Fedorov 4.00 10.00
2 Wayne Gretzky 12.50 30.00
3 Paul Kariya 2.50 6.00
4 Mario Lemieux 12.50 30.00
5 Alexander Mogilny 1.25 3.00
6 Adam Oates 1.25 3.00
7 Joe Sakic 5.00 12.00
8 Teemu Selanne 2.50 6.00

1996-97 Ultra Rookies

Randomly inserted in packs at a rate of 1:9, these cards offer a single player photo with the player's name with "Rookie" written on the left-hand side. Flip sides give a smaller photo with several pieces of information about each athlete.

COMPLETE SET (20) 8.00 20.00
1 Bryan Berard .40 1.00
2 Sergei Berezin .40 1.00
3 Curtis Brown .40 1.00
4 Jim Campbell .40 1.00
5 Christian Dube .40 1.00
6 Anders Eriksson .40 1.00
7 Eric Fichaud .75 2.00
8 Daniel Goneau .40 1.00
9 Mike Grier .75 2.00
10 Jarome Iginla 3.00 8.00
11 Jamie Langenbrunner .40 1.00
12 Jay McKee .40 1.00
13 Ethan Moreau .40 1.00
14 Rem Murray .40 1.00
15 Janne Niinimaa .40 1.00
16 Wayne Primeau .40 1.00
17 Wade Redden .75 2.00
18 Jamie Storr .75 2.00
19 David Wilkie .40 1.00
20 Landon Wilson .40 1.00

2005-06 Ultra

This 271-card set was issued into the hobby in eight-card packs, with a $2.99 SRP, which came 24 packs to a box and 12 boxes to a case. Cards numbered 1-200 feature veterans in team alphabetical order while cards 201-271 feature Rookie Cards. Cards numbered 201-250 were issued at a stated rate of one in four and cards 251-271 were inserted at a stated rate of one in 24.

1 Jean-Sebastien Giguere .30 .75
2 Teemu Selanne .60 1.50
3 Petr Sykora .25 .60
4 Rob Niedermayer .25 .60
5 Scott Niedermayer .30 .75
6 Sandis Ozolinsh .20 .50
7 Joffrey Lupul .25 .60
8 Kari Lehtonen .25 .60
9 Ilya Kovalchuk .30 .75
10 Peter Bondra .25 .60
11 Marian Hossa .25 .60
12 Patrik Stefan .20 .50
13 Bobby Holik .20 .50
14 Marc Savard .20 .50
15 Andrew Raycroft .25 .60
16 Patrice Bergeron .40 1.00
17 Joe Thornton .40 1.00
18 Glen Murray .25 .60
19 Brian Leetch .30 .75
20 Nick Boynton .20 .50
21 Sergei Samsonov .25 .60
22 Shawn McEachern .20 .50
23 Martin Biron .25 .60
24 Chris Drury .25 .60
25 Daniel Briere .30 .75
26 Derek Roy .20 .50
27 Maxim Afinogenov .20 .50
28 J.P. Dumont .20 .50
29 Mika Noronen .25 .60
30 Miikka Kipruosoff .25 .60
31 Jarome Iginla .30 .75
32 Tony Amonte .25 .60
33 Matthew Lombardi .20 .50
34 Robyn Regehr .20 .50
35 Jordan Leopold .20 .50
36 Chuck Kobasew .20 .50
37 Phillippe Sauve .25 .60
38 Darren McCarty .20 .50
39 Martin Gerber .25 .60
40 Eric Staal .40 1.00
41 Erik Cole .25 .60
42 Justin Williams .25 .60
43 Glen Wesley .20 .50
44 Oleg Tverdovsky .20 .50
45 Cory Stillman .25 .60
46 Rod Brind'Amour .30 .75
47 Nikolai Khabibulin .30 .75
48 Tuomo Ruutu .30 .75
49 Eric Daze .25 .60
50 Tyler Arnason .20 .50
51 Adrian Aucoin .20 .50
52 Kyle Calder .20 .50
53 Mark Bell .20 .50
54 David Aebischer .25 .60
55 Joe Sakic .50 1.25
56 Milan Hejduk .25 .60
57 Alex Tanguay .30 .75
58 Rob Blake .30 .75
59 John-Michael Liles .20 .50
60 Pierre Turgeon .30 .75
61 Marc Denis .25 .60
62 Rick Nash .30 .75
63 Nikolai Zherdev .20 .50
64 Rostislav Klesla .20 .50
65 Bryan Berard .20 .50
66 Sergei Fedorov .50 1.25
67 Marty Turco .30 .75
68 Mike Modano .50 1.25
69 Brenden Morrow .25 .60
70 Bill Guerin .30 .75
71 Sergei Zubov .25 .60
72 Jere Lehtinen .25 .60
73 Manny Legace .30 .75
74 Steve Yzerman .75 2.00
75 Brendan Shanahan .40 1.00
76 Pavel Datsyuk .40 1.00
77 Nicklas Lidstrom .30 .75
78 Chris Chelios .30 .75
79 Henrik Zetterberg .40 1.00
80 Ty Conklin .25 .60
81 Michael Peca .25 .60
82 Ryan Smyth .25 .60
83 Raffi Torres .20 .50
84 Chris Pronger .25 .60
85 Ales Hemsky .25 .60
86 Roberto Luongo .50 1.25
87 Joe Nieuwendyk .30 .75
88 Stephen Weiss .20 .50
89 Olli Jokinen .30 .75
90 Jay Bouwmeester .30 .75
91 Nathan Horton .30 .75
92 Mathieu Garon .25 .60
93 Jeremy Roenick .30 .75
94 Luc Robitaille .30 .75
95 Pavol Demitra .40 1.00
96 Dustin Brown .30 .75
97 Alexander Frolov .20 .50
98 Dwayne Roloson .25 .60
99 Marian Gaborik .50 1.25
100 Alexandre Daigle .20 .50
101 Pierre-Marc Bouchard .30 .75
102 Filip Kuba .20 .50
103 Manny Fernandez .25 .60
104 Saku Koivu .30 .75
105 Jose Theodore .30 .75
106 Mike Ribeiro .25 .60
107 Michael Ryder .25 .60
108 Sheldon Souray .20 .50
109 Richard Zednik .20 .50
110 Tomas Vokoun .25 .60
111 Paul Kariya .40 1.00
112 Steve Sullivan .20 .50
113 David Legwand .25 .60
114 Kimmo Timonen .20 .50
115 Scott Walker .20 .50
116 Martin Brodeur .60 1.50
117 Scott Gomez .25 .60
118 Patrik Elias .30 .75
119 Alexander Mogilny .25 .60
120 Brian Rafalski .25 .60
121 John Madden .20 .50
122 Rick DiPietro .25 .60
123 Alexei Yashin .25 .60
124 Miroslav Satan .25 .60
125 Trent Hunter .20 .50
126 Brent Sopel .20 .50
127 Mark Parrish .20 .50
128 Kevin Weekes .25 .60
129 Jaromir Jagr .75 2.00
130 Marcel Hossa .20 .50
131 Steve Rucchin .20 .50
132 Tom Poti .20 .50
133 Dominik Hasek .50 1.25
134 Jason Spezza .30 .75
135 Dany Heatley .30 .75
136 Martin Havlat .30 .75
137 Wade Redden .20 .50
138 Zdeno Chara .30 .75
139 Daniel Alfredsson .30 .75
140 Robert Esche .25 .60
141 Peter Forsberg .40 1.00
142 Simon Gagne .30 .75
143 Keith Primeau .30 .75
144 Joni Pitkanen .20 .50
145 Kim Johnsson .20 .50
146 Sami Kapanen .20 .50
147 Curtis Joseph .30 .75
148 Shane Doan .25 .60
149 Jamie Lundmark .20 .50
150 Ladislav Nagy .20 .50
151 Mike Ricci .25 .60
152 Petr Nedved .20 .50
153 Jocelyn Thibault .25 .60
154 Mario Lemieux 1.00 2.50
155 Mark Recchi .40 1.00
156 Zigmund Palffy .30 .75
157 John LeClair .30 .75
158 Ryan Malone .20 .50
159 Marc-Andre Fleury .50 1.25
160 Evgeni Nabokov .25 .60
161 Patrick Marleau .30 .75
162 Jonathan Cheechoo .30 .75
163 Marco Sturm .20 .50
164 Brad Stuart .20 .50
165 Patrick Lalime .25 .60
166 Doug Weight .30 .75
167 Keith Tkachuk .30 .75
168 Mark Rycroft .20 .50
169 Barret Jackman .20 .50
170 Dallas Drake .20 .50
171 Sean Burke .20 .50
172 Martin St. Louis .30 .75
173 Vincent Lecavalier .25 .60
174 Brad Richards .30 .75
175 Ruslan Fedotenko .20 .50
176 Fredrik Modin .20 .50
177 Dave Andreychuk .30 .75
178 Pavel Kubina .20 .50
179 Ed Belfour .30 .75
180 Mats Sundin .30 .75
181 Eric Lindros .50 1.25
182 Jeff O'Neill .20 .50
183 Bryan McCabe .20 .50
184 Tie Domi .25 .60
185 Matt Stajan .25 .60
186 Nik Antropov .25 .60
187 Jason Allison .25 .60
188 Dan Cloutier .25 .60
189 Markus Naslund .30 .75
190 Brendan Morrison .20 .50
191 Todd Bertuzzi .30 .75
192 Ed Jovanovski .25 .60
193 Mattias Ohlund .20 .50
194 Trevor Linden .30 .75
195 Anson Carter .25 .60
196 Ryan Kesler .40 1.00
197 Olaf Kolzig .30 .75
198 Jeff Friesen .20 .50
199 Brian Willsie .20 .50
200 Brendan Witt .20 .50
201 Braydon Coburn RC 2.00 5.00
202 Jim Slater RC 1.50 4.00
203 Adam Berkhoel RC 1.50 4.00
204 Andrew Alberts RC 1.25 3.00
205 Kevin Dallman RC 1.50 4.00
206 Milan Jurcina RC 1.50 4.00
207 Niklas Nordgren RC 2.00 5.00
208 Kevin Nastiuk RC 1.25 3.00
209 Brent Seabrook RC 4.00 10.00
210 Rene Bourque RC 2.00 5.00
211 Duncan Keith RC 4.00 10.00
212 Cam Barker RC 1.50 4.00
213 Peter Budaj RC 2.50 6.00
214 Jaroslav Balastik RC 1.25 3.00
215 Jussi Jokinen RC 2.00 5.00
216 Brett Lebda RC 1.25 3.00
217 Johan Franzen RC 3.00 8.00
218 Brad Winchester RC 2.00 5.00
219 Kyle Brodziak RC 1.25 3.00
220 George Parros RC 1.25 3.00
221 Derek Boogaard RC 2.50 6.00
222 Matthew Foy RC 1.25 3.00
223 Yann Danis RC 1.50 4.00
224 Mark Streit RC 1.25 3.00
225 Raitis Ivanans RC 1.25 3.00
226 Ryan Suter RC 2.50 6.00
227 Petteri Nokelainen RC 1.25 3.00
228 Chris Campoli RC 1.25 3.00
229 Ryan Hollweg RC 1.25 3.00
230 Petr Prucha RC 2.00 5.00
231 Al Montoya RC 2.00 5.00
232 Chris Holt RC 1.25 3.00
233 Brandon Bochenski RC 2.00 5.00
234 Andrej Meszaros RC 1.50 4.00
235 Brian McGrattan RC 1.25 3.00
236 Patrick Eaves RC 2.00 5.00
237 Wade Skolney RC 1.25 3.00
238 Keith Ballard RC 1.50 4.00
239 David Leneveu RC 1.50 4.00
240 Maxime Talbot RC 2.00 5.00
241 Ryane Clowe RC 2.50 6.00
242 Josh Gorges RC 1.50 4.00
243 Jay McClement RC 1.25 3.00
244 Jeff Hoggan RC 1.25 3.00
245 Lee Stempniak RC 2.00 5.00
246 Andy Roach RC 1.25 3.00
247 Timo Helbling RC 1.25 3.00
248 Paul Ranger RC 1.25 3.00
249 Andrew Wozniewski RC 1.50 4.00
250 Anthony Stewart RC 1.50 4.00
251 Sidney Crosby RC 60.00 150.00
252 Alexander Ovechkin RC 15.00 40.00
253 Corey Perry RC 8.00 20.00
254 Jeff Carter RC 3.00 8.00
255 Gilbert Brule RC 2.00 5.00
256 Wojtek Wolski RC 1.50 4.00
257 Jeff Woywitka RC 1.25 3.00
258 Hannu Toivonen RC 2.00 5.00
259 Alexander Perezhogin RC 1.50 4.00
260 Zach Parise RC 5.00 12.00
261 Dion Phaneuf RC 3.00 8.00
262 Mike Richards RC 4.00 10.00
263 Cam Ward RC 3.00 8.00
264 Robert Nilsson RC 2.00 5.00
265 Eric Nystrom RC 1.50 4.00
266 Alexander Steen RC 4.00 10.00
267 Ryan Getzlaf RC 5.00 12.00
268 Rostislav Olesz RC 1.50 4.00
269 Henrik Lundqvist RC 6.00 15.00
270 Jim Howard RC 5.00 12.00
271 Thomas Vanek RC 4.00 10.00

2005-06 Ultra Gold

*1-200 VETS: 1.5X TO 4X BASIC CARDS
*201-250 ROOKIES: .3X TO .8X BASIC RC
*251-271 ROOKIES: 1X TO 2.5X BASIC RC
ONE PER NON-INSERT PACK
251 Sidney Crosby 125.00 250.00
252 Alexander Ovechkin 50.00 120.00

2005-06 Ultra Difference Makers

COMPLETE SET (12) 20.00 40.00
STATED ODDS 1:32
DM1 Rick Nash .60 1.50
DM2 Pavel Datsyuk .75 2.00
DM3 Steve Yzerman 1.25 3.00
DM4 Todd Bertuzzi .60 1.50
DM5 Jeff Carter 1.00 2.50
DM6 Sidney Crosby 6.00 15.00
DM7 Tuomo Ruutu .40 1.00
DM8 Patrice Bergeron .40 1.00
DM9 Alexander Ovechkin 3.00 8.00
DM10 Martin St. Louis .40 1.00
DM11 Jarome Iginla .60 1.50
DM12 Andrew Raycroft .40 1.00

2005-06 Ultra Difference Makers Jerseys

STATED ODDS 1:164
*PATCH/25: 1.5X TO 4X BASIC JSY
DMJAO Alexander Ovechkin 10.00 25.00
DMJAR Andrew Raycroft 4.00 10.00
DMJJC Jeff Carter 5.00 12.00
DMJJI Jarome Iginla 5.00 12.00
DMJPB Patrice Bergeron 4.00 10.00
DMJPD Pavel Datsyuk 4.00 10.00
DMJRN Rick Nash 8.00 20.00
DMJSC Sidney Crosby 15.00 40.00
DMJSL Martin St. Louis 4.00 10.00
DMJSY Steve Yzerman 8.00 20.00
DMJTB Todd Bertuzzi 4.00 10.00
DMJTR Tuomo Ruutu 4.00 10.00

2005-06 Ultra Fresh Ink

STATED ODDS 1:360
FIAM Al Montoya 10.00 25.00
FIAO Alexander Ovechkin 50.00 120.00
FIAP Alexander Perezhogin 5.00 12.00
FIAR Andrew Raycroft SP 12.50 25.00
FIAS Alexander Steen 12.00 30.00
FIAT Alex Tanguay SP 12.50 30.00
FIAW Andrew Wozniewski 5.00 12.00
FIAY Alexei Yashin 5.00 12.00
FIBG Boyd Gordon 4.00 10.00
FIBL Brett Lebda 4.00 10.00
FIBM Brenden Morrow 5.00 12.00
FIBO Derek Boogaard 8.00 20.00
FICA Mike Cammalleri 6.00 15.00
FICB Cam Barker 5.00 12.00
FICD Chris Drury 5.00 12.00
FICE Christian Ehrhoff 4.00 10.00
FICK Chris Kunitz 6.00 15.00
FICP Corey Perry SP 12.00 30.00
FICW Cam Ward 10.00 25.00
FIDB Dustin Brown 6.00 15.00
FIDL David Leneveu 5.00 12.00
FIDP Dion Phaneuf 20.00 50.00
FIDR Dwayne Roloson 5.00 12.00
FIDW Doug Weight 6.00 15.00
FIEJ Ed Jovanovski 5.00 12.00
FIEN Eric Nystrom 5.00 12.00
FIES Eric Staal SP 20.00 50.00
FIGB Gilbert Brule 6.00 15.00
FIGM Glen Murray 5.00 12.00
FIGP George Parros 4.00 10.00
FIHO Jeff Hoggan 4.00 10.00
FIHT Hannu Toivonen 6.00 15.00
FIHV Martin Havlat SP
FIHZ Henrik Zetterberg 15.00 30.00
FIIK Ilya Kovalchuk SP 25.00 60.00
FIIL Ian Laperriere 4.00 10.00
FIJA Jaroslav Balastik 4.00 10.00
FIJB Jay Bouwmeester SP 10.00 25.00
FIJC Jeff Carter 20.00 50.00
FIJG Josh Gorges 5.00 12.00
FIJH Jochen Hecht 4.00 10.00
FIJI Jarome Iginla 30.00 75.00
FIJI Jim Howard 12.50 25.00
FIJL Joffrey Lupul 5.00 12.00
FIJM Jay McClement 4.00 10.00
FIJN Jocelyn Thibault 5.00 12.00
FIJO Jeff O'Neill
FIJR Jeremy Roenick SP 20.00 50.00
FIJS Jason Spezza SP 20.00 50.00
FIJT Joe Thornton SP 25.00 60.00
FIJW Jeff Woywitka 4.00 10.00
FIKD Kevin Dallman 5.00 12.00
FIKP Keith Primeau 6.00 15.00
FIKW Kevin Weekes 5.00 12.00
FILN Ladislav Nagy SP 10.00 25.00
FIMB Martin Brodeur SP 75.00 125.00
FIMC Bryan McCabe 4.00 10.00
FIMO Brendan Morrison 4.00 10.00
FIMP Michael Peca 5.00 12.00
FIMR Mike Richards 15.00 30.00
FIMS Matt Stajan 10.00 25.00
FIMT Marty Turco SP 10.00 25.00
FINI Rob Niedermayer 5.00 12.00
FINN Niklas Nordgren 6.00 15.00
FINS Robert Nilsson 6.00 15.00
FINZ Nikolai Zherdev 4.00 10.00
FION Owen Nolan 5.00 12.00
FIPB Patrice Bergeron SP
FIPE Mark Popovic SP 6.00 15.00
FIRE Robert Esche 5.00 12.00
FIRF Ruslan Fedotenko 4.00 10.00
FIRG Ryan Getzlaf SP 15.00 40.00
FIRH Ryan Hollweg 4.00 10.00
FIRI Raitis Ivanans 4.00 10.00
FIRK Ryan Kesler 8.00 20.00
FIRL Roberto Luongo 10.00 25.00
FIRN Rick Nash SP
FIRO Rostislav Olesz 5.00 12.00
FIRS Ryan Smyth 5.00 12.00
FIRZ Richard Zednik 4.00 10.00
FISA Miroslav Satan 5.00 12.00
FISB Sean Burke 4.00 10.00
FISC Sidney Crosby SP 150.00 250.00
FISD Shane Doan 5.00 12.00
FISG Simon Gagne 12.00 30.00
FISK Saku Koivu SP 20.00 50.00
FISN Scott Niedermayer 6.00 15.00
FISS Sheldon Souray 4.00 10.00
FIST Anthony Stewart 5.00 12.00
FISU Ryan Suter 8.00 20.00
FITH Jose Theodore SP 20.00 50.00
FITI Timo Helbling 4.00 10.00
FITL Trevor Linden 25.00 50.00
FITR Tuomo Ruutu 6.00 15.00
FITS Timofei Shishkanov 4.00 10.00
FITV Thomas Vanek 12.00 30.00
FIVL Vincent Lecavalier 20.00 50.00
FIWW Wojtek Wolski 5.00 12.00
FIYD Yann Danis 5.00 12.00
FIZC Zdeno Chara 6.00 15.00
FIZP Zach Parise 15.00 40.00

2005-06 Ultra Fresh Ink Blue

*BLUE/25: .8X TO 2X BASIC AU
*BLUE/25: .5X TO 1.2X BASIC AU SP
FIJI Jarome Iginla 50.00 100.00
FISC Sidney Crosby 400.00 600.00

2005-06 Ultra Ice

*1-200 VETS/100: 4X TO 10X BASIC CARDS
1-200 VETERAN PRINT RUN 100
*201-250 ROOKIE/25: 1.5X TO 4X BASIC RC
*251-271 ROOKIE/25: 1.2X TO 3X BASIC RC
201-271 ROOKIE PRINT RUN 25
251 Sidney Crosby 400.00 650.00
252 Alexander Ovechkin 150.00 300.00

2005-06 Ultra Rookie Uniformity Jerseys

STATED ODDS 1:48
*PATCH/35: 1.2X TO 3X BASE JSY
RUAA Andrew Alberts 2.50 6.00
RUAM Andrej Meszaros 3.00 8.00
RUAO Alexander Ovechkin 12.00 30.00
RUAP Alexander Perezhogin 3.00 8.00
RUAS Alexander Steen 8.00 20.00
RUAW Andrew Wozniewski 3.00 8.00
RUBB Brandon Bochenski 4.00 10.00
RUBC Braydon Coburn 4.00 10.00
RUBL Brett Lebda 2.50 6.00
RUBS Brent Seabrook 8.00 20.00
RUBW Brad Winchester 4.00 10.00
RUCB Cam Barker 3.00 8.00
RUCP Corey Perry 15.00 40.00
RUCW Cam Ward 6.00 15.00
RUDK Duncan Keith 8.00 20.00
RUDL David Leneveu 3.00 8.00
RUDP Dion Phaneuf 6.00 15.00
RUEN Eric Nystrom 3.00 8.00
RUGB Gilbert Brule 4.00 10.00
RUGP George Parros 2.50 6.00
RUHL Henrik Lundqvist 10.00 25.00
RUHO Jeff Hoggan 2.50 6.00
RUHT Hannu Toivonen 4.00 10.00
RUJB Jaroslav Balastik 2.50 6.00
RUJC Jeff Carter 6.00 15.00
RUJF Johan Franzen 6.00 15.00
RUJG Josh Gorges 3.00 8.00
RUJH Jim Howard 10.00 25.00
RUJJ Jussi Jokinen 4.00 10.00
RUJM Jay McClement 2.50 6.00
RUJS Jim Slater 3.00 8.00
RUJW Jeff Woywitka 2.50 6.00
RUKB Keith Ballard 3.00 8.00
RUKD Kevin Dallman 3.00 8.00
RUKN Kevin Nastiuk 2.50 6.00
RUMF Matthew Foy 2.50 6.00
RUMJ Milan Jurcina 3.00 8.00
RUMO Al Montoya 4.00 10.00
RUMR Mike Richards 8.00 20.00
RUMT Maxime Talbot 4.00 10.00
RUNN Niklas Nordgren 4.00 10.00
RUPB Peter Budaj 5.00 12.00
RUPE Patrick Eaves 4.00 10.00
RUPN Petteri Nokelainen 2.50 6.00
RUPP Petr Prucha 4.00 10.00
RURB Rene Bourque 4.00 10.00
RURC Ryane Clowe 5.00 12.00
RURG Ryan Getzlaf 10.00 25.00
RURH Ryan Hollweg 2.50 6.00
RURI Raitis Ivanans 2.50 6.00
RURN Robert Nilsson 4.00 10.00
RURO Rostislav Olesz 3.00 8.00
RURS Ryan Suter 5.00 12.00
RUSC Sidney Crosby 30.00 80.00
RUST Anthony Stewart 3.00 8.00
RUTH Timo Helbling 2.50 6.00
RUTV Thomas Vanek 8.00 20.00
RUWW Wojtek Wolski 3.00 8.00
RUYD Yann Danis 3.00 8.00
RUZP Zach Parise 10.00 25.00

2005-06 Ultra Rookie Uniformity Jersey Autographs

STATED PRINT RUN 25 SER.#'d SETS
ARUAA Andrew Alberts 10.00 25.00
ARUAM Al Montoya 15.00 40.00
ARUAM Andrej Meszaros 12.00 30.00
ARUAO Alexander Ovechkin 250.00 400.00
ARUAP Alexander Perezhogin 30.00 80.00
ARUAS Alexander Steen 30.00 80.00
ARUAW Andrew Wozniewski 12.00 30.00
ARUBB Brandon Bochenski 15.00 40.00
ARUBC Braydon Coburn 15.00 40.00
ARUBL Brett Lebda 10.00 25.00
ARUBS Brent Seabrook 30.00 80.00
ARUBW Brad Winchester 15.00 40.00
ARUCB Cam Barker 12.00 30.00
ARUCP Corey Perry 40.00 100.00
ARUCW Cam Ward 40.00 80.00
ARUDK Duncan Keith 40.00 80.00
ARUDL David Leneveu 12.00 30.00
ARUDP Dion Phaneuf 75.00 150.00
ARUEN Eric Nystrom 12.00 30.00
ARUGB Gilbert Brule 15.00 40.00
ARUGP George Parros 10.00 25.00
ARUHL Henrik Lundqvist 75.00 150.00
ARUHO Jeff Hoggan 10.00 25.00
ARUHT Hannu Toivonen 15.00 40.00
ARUJB Jaroslav Balastik 10.00 25.00
ARUJC Jeff Carter 25.00 60.00
ARUJF Johan Franzen 25.00 60.00
ARUJG Josh Gorges 12.00 30.00
ARUJH Jim Howard 40.00 80.00
ARUJJ Jussi Jokinen 15.00 40.00
ARUJM Jay McClement 10.00 25.00
ARUJS Jim Slater 12.00 30.00
ARUJW Jeff Woywitka 10.00 25.00
ARUKB Keith Ballard 12.00 30.00
ARUKD Kevin Dallman 12.00 30.00
ARUKN Kevin Nastiuk 10.00 25.00
ARUMF Matthew Foy 10.00 25.00
ARUMJ Milan Jurcina 12.00 30.00
ARUMR Mike Richards 40.00 100.00
ARUMT Maxime Talbot 15.00 40.00
ARUNN Niklas Nordgren 15.00 40.00
ARUPB Peter Budaj 20.00 50.00
ARUPE Patrick Eaves 15.00 40.00
ARUPN Petteri Nokelainen 10.00 25.00
ARUPP Petr Prucha 15.00 40.00
ARURB Rene Bourque 15.00 40.00
ARURC Ryane Clowe 20.00 50.00
ARURG Ryan Getzlaf 30.00 80.00
ARURH Ryan Hollweg 10.00 25.00
ARURI Raitis Ivanans 10.00 25.00
ARURN Robert Nilsson 15.00 40.00
ARURO Rostislav Olesz 12.00 30.00
ARURS Ryan Suter 20.00 50.00
ARUSC Sidney Crosby 400.00 700.00
ARUST Anthony Stewart 12.00 30.00
ARUTH Timo Helbling 10.00 25.00
ARUTV Thomas Vanek 30.00 80.00
ARUWW Wojtek Wolski 12.00 30.00
ARUYD Yann Danis 12.00 30.00
ARUZP Zach Parise 25.00 60.00

2005-06 Ultra Scoring Kings

SK1 Mario Lemieux 2.50 6.00
SK2 Martin St. Louis .75 2.00
SK3 Joe Thornton 1.00 2.50
SK4 Mats Sundin .75 2.00
SK5 Jarome Iginla .75 2.00
SK6 Mike Modano 1.25 3.00
SK7 Steve Yzerman 2.00 5.00
SK8 Joe Sakic 1.25 3.00
SK9 Alex Tanguay .75 2.00
SK10 Dany Heatley .75 2.00
SK11 Sidney Crosby 8.00 20.00
SK12 Jeremy Roenick .75 2.00
SK13 Jason Spezza .75 2.00
SK14 Patrik Elias .75 2.00
SK15 Jaromir Jagr 2.00 5.00
SK16 Brad Richards .75 2.00
SK17 Markus Naslund .75 2.00
SK18 Alexander Ovechkin 4.00 10.00
SK19 Doug Weight .75 2.00
SK20 Ilya Kovalchuk .75 2.00
SK21 Peter Forsberg 1.00 2.50
SK22 Sergei Fedorov 1.25 3.00
SK23 Marian Hossa .60 1.50
SK24 Milan Hejduk .60 1.50
SK25 Bill Guerin .75 2.00
SK26 Shane Doan .60 1.50
SK27 Mike Ribiero .60 1.50
SK28 Martin Havlat .75 2.00
SK29 Corey Perry 3.00 8.00
SK30 Mike Richards 1.50 4.00
SK31 Ryan Getzlaf 2.00 5.00
SK32 Keith Tkachuk .75 2.00
SK33 Glen Murray .60 1.50
SK34 Brendan Shanahan 1.00 2.50
SK35 Paul Kariya 1.00 2.50
SK36 Marian Gaborik 1.25 3.00
SK37 Luc Robitaille .75 2.00
SK38 Daniel Alfredsson .75 2.00
SK39 Vincent Lecavalier .60 1.50
SK40 Eric Daze .60 1.50

2005-06 Ultra Scoring Kings Jerseys

SKJAO Alexander Ovechkin 10.00 25.00
SKJAT Alex Tanguay 2.00 5.00
SKJBG Bill Guerin 2.00 5.00
SKJBR Brad Richards 2.00 5.00
SKJBS Brendan Shanahan 2.50 6.00
SKJCP Corey Perry 8.00 20.00
SKJDA Daniel Alfredsson 2.00 5.00
SKJDH Dany Heatley 2.00 5.00
SKJDW Doug Weight 2.00 5.00
SKJED Eric Daze 1.50 4.00
SKJGM Glen Murray 1.50 4.00
SKJHO Marian Hossa 1.50 4.00
SKJHV Martin Havlat 2.00 5.00
SKJIK Ilya Kovalchuk 2.00 5.00
SKJJI Jarome Iginla 2.00 5.00
SKJJJ Jaromir Jagr 5.00 12.00
SKJJR Jeremy Roenick 2.00 5.00
SKJJS Jason Spezza 2.00 5.00
SKJJS Joe Sakic 3.00 8.00
SKJJT Joe Thornton 2.50 6.00
SKJKT Keith Tkachuk 2.00 5.00
SKJLR Luc Robitaille 2.00 5.00
SKJMG Marian Gaborik 3.00 8.00
SKJMH Milan Hejduk 1.50 4.00
SKJML Mario Lemieux 10.00 25.00
SKJMM Mike Modano 3.00 8.00
SKJMN Markus Naslund 2.00 5.00
SKJMR Mike Ribeiro 1.50 4.00
SKJMS Mats Sundin 2.00 5.00
SKJPE Patrik Elias 2.00 5.00
SKJPF Peter Forsberg 2.50 6.00
SKJPK Paul Kariya 2.50 6.00
SKJRG Ryan Getzlaf 5.00 12.00
SKJRI Mike Richards 4.00 10.00
SKJSC Sidney Crosby 15.00 40.00
SKJSD Shane Doan 1.50 4.00
SKJSF Sergei Fedorov 3.00 8.00
SKJSL Martin St. Louis 2.00 5.00
SKJSY Steve Yzerman 5.00 12.00
SKJVL Vincent Lecavalier 1.50 4.00

2005-06 Ultra Scoring Kings Jersey Autographs

STATED PRINT RUN 20 SER.#'d SETS
KAJAO Alexander Ovechkin 150.00 250.00
KAJAT Alex Tanguay 12.00 30.00
KAJBR Brad Richards
KAJCP Corey Perry 50.00 120.00
KAJDA Daniel Alfredsson
KAJDH Dany Heatley 12.00 30.00
KAJDW Doug Weight 12.00 30.00
KAJED Eric Daze 10.00 25.00
KAJGM Glen Murray 10.00 25.00
KAJHO Marian Hossa 25.00 50.00
KAJHV Martin Havlat 12.00 30.00
KAJIK Ilya Kovalchuk
KAJJI Jarome Iginla
KAJJR Jeremy Roenick 15.00 40.00
KAJJS Jason Spezza 15.00 40.00
KAJJT Joe Thornton
KAJMH Milan Hejduk 10.00 25.00
KAJMM Mike Modano 15.00 40.00
KAJMN Markus Naslund 12.00 30.00
KAJMR Mike Ribiero 10.00 25.00
KAJMS Mats Sundin
KAJRG Ryan Getzlaf 30.00 80.00
KAJRI Mike Richards 25.00 60.00
KAJSC Sidney Crosby 250.00 400.00
KAJSD Shane Doan
KAJSL Martin St. Louis
KAJVL Vincent Lecavalier 10.00 25.00

2005-06 Ultra Scoring Kings Patches

*PATCHES: 1.25X TO 3X BASE JSY
PRINT RUN 50 SER.#'d SETS
SKPAO Alexander Ovechkin 75.00 200.00
SKPSC Sidney Crosby 100.00 250.00

2005-06 Ultra Super Six

COMPLETE SET (8) 10.00 25.00
STATED ODDS 1:42
SS1 Mario Lemieux 2.00 5.00
SS2 Joe Thornton .75 2.00
SS3 Martin Brodeur 1.25 3.00
SS4 Ray Bourque 1.00 2.50
SS5 Joe Sakic 1.00 2.50
SS6 Patrick Roy 1.50 4.00
SS7 Ray Bourque 1.00 2.50
SS8 Patrick Roy 1.50 4.00

2005-06 Ultra Super Six Jerseys

STATED ODDS 1:288
SSJJS Joe Sakic 10.00 25.00
SSJJT Joe Thornton 8.00 20.00
SSJMB Martin Brodeur 8.00 20.00
SSJML Mario Lemieux 15.00 30.00
SSJPR1 Patrick Roy 15.00 30.00
SSJPR2 Patrick Roy 15.00 30.00
SSJRB1 Ray Bourque 6.00 15.00
SSJRB2 Ray Bourque 6.00 15.00

2006-07 Ultra

This 251-card set was issued to the hobby in eight-card packs, with a $2.99 SRP, which came 24 packs to a box and 20 boxes to a case. Cards numbered 1-200 feature players in team alphabetical order while Rookie Cards 201-230 were issued with the product and inserted at a stated rate of one in four. In addition, rookie redemptions were inserted at a stated rate of one in 24 and those turned out to be cards numbered 231-251 in this product.

COMPLETE SET (251) 100.00 250.00
COMP.SET w/o SPs (200) 15.00 40.00
1 Jean-Sebastien Giguere .30 .75
2 Chris Pronger .25 .60
3 Andy McDonald .25 .60
4 Corey Perry .30 .75
5 Teemu Selanne .60 1.50
6 Ryan Getzlaf .50 1.25
7 Scott Niedermayer .30 .75
8 Kari Lehtonen .25 .60
9 Steve Rucchin .20 .50
10 Marian Hossa .25 .60
11 Ilya Kovalchuk .30 .75
12 Slava Kozlov .20 .50
13 Bobby Holik .20 .50
14 Patrice Bergeron .40 1.00
15 Brad Boyes .20 .50
16 Marc Savard .20 .50
17 Brad Stuart .20 .50
18 Marco Sturm .20 .50
19 Glen Murray .25 .60
20 Zdeno Chara .30 .75
21 Thomas Vanek .40 1.00
22 Ryan Miller .30 .75
23 Maxim Afinogenov .20 .50
24 Ales Kotalik .20 .50
25 Chris Drury .25 .60
26 Martin Biron .25 .60
27 Daniel Briere .30 .75
28 Miikka Kiprusoff .25 .60
29 Jarome Iginla .30 .75
30 Chuck Kobasew .20 .50
31 Kristian Huselius .20 .50
32 Daymond Langkow .20 .50
33 Dion Phaneuf .30 .75
34 Alex Tanguay .20 .50
35 Cam Ward .30 .75
36 Andrew Ladd .30 .75
37 Eric Staal .40 1.00
38 Justin Williams .25 .60
39 Erik Cole .25 .60
40 Mike Commodore .20 .50
41 Rod Brind`Amour .30 .75
42 Nikolai Khabibulin .30 .75
43 Tuomo Ruutu .30 .75
44 Kyle Calder .20 .50
45 Martin Havlat .20 .50
46 Rene Bourque .20 .50
47 Duncan Keith .40 1.00
48 Jose Theodore .30 .75
49 Joe Sakic .50 1.25
50 Milan Hejduk .25 .60
51 Andrew Brunette .20 .50
52 Marek Svatos .20 .50
53 Pierre Turgeon .30 .75
54 Peter Budaj .25 .60
55 Fredrik Modin .20 .50
56 Nikolai Zherdev .20 .50
57 Rick Nash .30 .75
58 Sergei Fedorov .50 1.25
59 Rostislav Klesla .20 .5
60 Bryan Berard .20 .5
61 David Vyborny .20 .5
62 Marty Turco .30 .7
63 Mike Modano .50 1.2
64 Sergei Zubov .25 .6
65 Brenden Morrow .25 .6
66 Jussi Jokinen .25 .6
67 Eric Lindros .50 1.2
68 Jere Lehtinen .20 .5
69 Tomas Holmstrom .25 .6
70 Henrik Zetterberg .40 1.0
71 Nicklas Lidstrom .30 .7
72 Pavel Datsyuk .40 1.0
73 Chris Osgood .30 .7
74 Kris Draper .20 .5
75 Steve Yzerman .75 2.0
76 Ales Hemsky .25 .6
77 Jarret Stoll .25 .6
78 Joffrey Lupul .25 .6
79 Dwayne Roloson .25 .6
80 Ryan Smyth .25 .6
81 Shawn Horcoff .20 .5
82 Fernando Pisani .20 .5
83 Todd Bertuzzi .30 .7
84 Nathan Horton .30 .7
85 Alex Auld .20 .5
86 Olli Jokinen .30 .7
87 Jay Bouwmeester .30 .7
88 Rostislav Olesz .20 .5
89 Joe Nieuwendyk .30 .7
90 Alexander Frolov .20 .5
91 Mathieu Garon .25 .6
92 Mike Cammalleri .20 .5
93 Rob Blake .30 .7
94 Lubomir Visnovsky .20 .5
95 Dustin Brown .30 .7
96 Marian Gaborik .40 1.0
97 Manny Fernandez .25 .6
98 Mark Parrish .20 .5
99 Pierre-Marc Bouchard .30 .7
100 Brian Rolston .25 .6
101 Pavol Demitra .40 1.0
102 Saku Koivu .30 .7
103 Cristobal Huet .25 .6
104 Alex Kovalev .25 .6
105 Michael Ryder .20 .5
106 David Aebischer .25 .6
107 Mike Ribeiro .25 .6
108 Chris Higgins .20 .5
109 Tomas Vokoun .25 .6
110 Steve Sullivan .20 .5
111 David Legwand .25 .6
112 Paul Kariya .40 1.0
113 Jason Arnott .25 .6
114 Kimmo Timonen .20 .5
115 Martin Brodeur .60 1.5
116 Brian Rafalski .25 .6
117 Patrik Elias .30 .7
118 Brian Gionta .25 .6
119 Scott Gomez .25 .6
120 Zach Parise .40 1.0
121 Alexei Yashin .25 .6
122 Rick DiPietro .25 .6
123 Miroslav Satan .25 .6
124 Trent Hunter .20 .5
125 Jason Blake .20 .5
126 Mike Sillinger .20 .5
127 Henrik Lundqvist .60 1.5
128 Martin Straka .20 .5
129 Jaromir Jagr .75 2.0
130 Petr Prucha .25 .6
131 Brendan Shanahan .40 1.0
132 Matt Cullen .20 .5
133 Martin Gerber .25 .6
134 Jason Spezza .30 .7
135 Wade Redden .20 .5
136 Dany Heatley .30 .7
137 Daniel Alfredsson .30 .7
138 Patrick Eaves .20 .5
139 Ray Emery .25 .6
140 Peter Forsberg .40 1.0
141 Antero Niittymaki .25 .6
142 Joni Pitkanen .20 .5
143 Simon Gagne .30 .7
144 Keith Primeau .30 .7
145 Jeff Carter .30 .7
146 Robert Esche .25 .6
147 Mike Richards .30 .7
148 Ladislav Nagy .20 .5
149 Curtis Joseph .30 .7
150 Mike Comrie .25 .6
151 Shane Doan .25 .6
152 Ed Jovanovski .25 .6
153 Jeremy Roenick .30 .7
154 Sidney Crosby 1.25 3.0
155 Marc-Andre Fleury .50 1.2
156 Ryan Malone .20 .5
157 Colby Armstrong .25 .6
158 Ryan Whitney .25 .6
159 John LeClair .30 .7
160 Evgeni Nabokov .25 .6
161 Joe Thornton .40 1.0
162 Patrick Marleau .30 .7
163 Vesa Toskala .25 .6
164 Jonathan Cheechoo .30 .7
165 Steve Bernier .20 .5
166 Mark Bell .20 .5
167 Keith Tkachuk .30 .7
168 Curtis Sanford .25 .6
169 Doug Weight .30 .7
170 Bill Guerin .30 .7
171 Lee Stempniak .20 .5
172 Petr Cajanek .20 .5
173 Evgeni Artyukhin .20 .5
174 Brad Richards .30 .7
175 Martin St. Louis .30 .7
176 Vincent Lecavalier .25 .6
177 Vaclav Prospal .20 .5
178 Marc Denis .25 .6
179 Ruslan Fedotenko .20 .5
180 Andrew Raycroft .25 .6
181 Mats Sundin .30 .7
182 Bryan McCabe .20 .5
183 Alexander Steen .30 .7
184 Kyle Wellwood .25 .6
185 Darcy Tucker .25 .6
186 Tomas Kaberle .20 .5
187 Michael Peca .25 .6
188 Markus Naslund .25 .6
189 Roberto Luongo .50 1.2
190 Henrik Sedin .30 .7
191 Mattias Ohlund .20 .5
192 Brendan Morrison .20 .5
193 Ryan Kesler .40 1.0
194 Daniel Sedin .30 .7
195 Olaf Kolzig .30 .7
196 Alexander Ovechkin 1.25 3.0
197 Brian Pothier .20 .5
198 Dainius Zubrus .20 .5
199 Chris Clark .20 .5

200 Matt Pettinger .25 .60
201 Yan Stastny RC 1.25 3.00
202 Mark Stuart RC 1.25 3.00
203 Carsen Germyn RC 1.25 3.00
204 Dustin Byfuglien RC 3.00 8.00
205 Dan Jancevski RC 1.25 3.00
206 Tomas Kopecky RC 1.50 4.00
207 Marc-Antoine Pouliot RC 1.25 3.00
208 Konstantin Pushkarev RC 1.50 4.00
209 Erik Reitz RC 1.25 3.00
210 Miroslav Kopriva RC 1.25 3.00
211 Shea Weber RC 3.00 8.00
212 Frank Doyle RC 1.50 4.00
213 Rob Collins RC 1.25 3.00
214 Steve Regier RC 1.25 3.00
215 Ryan Caldwell RC 1.25 3.00
216 Masi Marjamaki RC 1.25 3.00
217 Jarkko Immonen RC 1.25 3.00
218 Billy Thompson RC 1.25 3.00
219 Filip Novak RC 1.25 3.00
220 Ryan Potulny RC 1.25 3.00
221 Bill Thomas RC 1.25 3.00
222 Joel Perrault RC 1.25 3.00
223 Noah Welch RC 1.25 3.00
224 Michel Ouellet RC 1.50 4.00
225 Matt Carle RC 1.25 3.00
226 Ben Ondrus RC 1.25 3.00
227 Brendan Bell RC 1.25 3.00
228 Ian White RC 1.50 4.00
229 Jeremy Williams RC 1.25 3.00
230 Eric Fehr RC 2.00 5.00
231 Patrick Thoreson RC 1.50 4.00
232 Ryan Shannon RC 1.50 4.00
233 Anze Kopitar RC 6.00 15.00
234 Travis Zajac RC 3.00 8.00
235 Nigel Dawes RC 1.50 4.00
236 Kris Letang RC 5.00 12.00
237 Marc Edouard Vlasic RC 1.50 4.00
238 Keith Yandle RC 3.00 8.00
239 Alexei Mikhnov RC 1.50 4.00
240 Ladislav Smid RC 1.50 4.00
241 Loui Eriksson RC 2.50 6.00
242 Luc Bourdon RC 2.50 6.00
243 Alexander Radulov RC 3.00 8.00
244 Alexei Kaigorodov RC 1.50 4.00
245 Enver Lisin RC 1.50 4.00
246 Patrick O'Sullivan RC 2.50 6.00
247 Jordan Staal RC 4.00 10.00
248 Paul Stastny RC 4.00 10.00
249 Guillaume Latendresse RC 2.50 6.00
250 Phil Kessel RC 4.00 10.00
251 Evgeni Malkin RC

2006-07 Ultra Gold Medallion

*STARS 2X to 5X BASE HI
*ROOKIES .75X to 2X BASE HI
ONE PER PACK
ROOKIE REDEMPTIONS: 1X to 1.5X HI

2006-07 Ultra Ice Medallion

*STARS: 6X to 15X BASE HI
ROOKIES: 1.5X to 3X BASE HI
STATED PRINT RUN 100 #'d SETS
ROOKIE REDEMPTIONS 1.5X to 3X HI
ROOKIE RED. PRINT RUN 25 #'d SETS
75 Steve Yzerman 12.00 30.00
154 Sidney Crosby 30.00 80.00
196 Alexander Ovechkin 20.00 50.00
233 Anze Kopitar 30.00 80.00
247 Jordan Staal 50.00 125.00
249 Guillaume Latendresse 25.00 60.00
251 Evgeni Malkin 150.00 250.00

2006-07 Ultra Action

STATED ODDS 1:12
UA1 Kari Lehtonen .75 2.00
UA2 Jarome Iginla 1.00 2.50
UA3 Dion Phaneuf 1.00 2.50
UA4 Eric Staal 1.25 3.00
UA5 Joe Sakic 1.50 4.00
UA6 Marek Svatos .60 1.50
UA7 Rick Nash 1.00 2.50
UA8 Mike Modano 1.50 4.00
UA9 Henrik Zetterberg 1.25 3.00
UA10 Brendan Shanahan 1.25 3.00
UA11 Chris Pronger .75 2.00
UA12 Roberto Luongo 1.50 4.00
UA13 Marian Gaborik 1.25 3.00
UA14 Saku Koivu 1.00 2.50
UA15 Paul Kariya 1.25 3.00
UA16 Martin Brodeur 2.00 5.00
UA17 Alexei Yashin .75 2.00
UA18 Jaromir Jagr 2.50 6.00
UA19 Dominik Hasek 1.25 3.00
UA20 Dany Heatley 1.00 2.50
UA21 Peter Forsberg 1.25 3.00
UA22 Shane Doan .75 2.00
UA23 Sidney Crosby 4.00 10.00
UA24 Joe Thornton 1.25 3.00
UA25 Evgeni Nabokov .75 2.00
UA26 Martin St. Louis 1.00 2.50
UA27 Vincent Lecavalier .75 2.00
UA28 Alexander Ovechkin 4.00 10.00
UA29 Mats Sundin 1.00 2.50
UA30 Markus Naslund .75 2.00

2006-07 Ultra Difference Makers

STATED ODDS 1:12
DM1 Ilya Bryzgalov .75 2.00
DM2 Ilya Kovalchuk .75 2.00
DM3 Patrice Bergeron 1.00 2.50
DM4 Ryan Miller .75 2.00
DM5 Jarome Iginla .75 2.00
DM6 Miikka Kiprusoff .60 1.50
DM7 Eric Staal 1.00 2.50
DM8 Markus Naslund .60 1.50
DM9 Alex Tanguay .50 1.25
DM10 Jose Theodore .75 2.00
DM11 Rick Nash .75 2.00
DM12 Marty Turco .75 2.00
DM13 Pavel Datsyuk 1.00 2.50
DM14 Henrik Zetterberg 1.00 2.50
DM15 Chris Pronger .60 1.50
DM16 Roberto Luongo 1.25 3.00
DM17 Michael Ryder .50 1.25
DM18 Saku Koivu .75 2.00
DM19 Mats Sundin .75 2.00
DM20 Martin Brodeur 1.50 4.00
DM21 Jaromir Jagr 2.00 5.00
DM22 Henrik Lundqvist 1.50 4.00
DM23 Daniel Alfredsson .75 2.00
DM24 Dany Heatley .75 2.00
DM25 Jason Spezza .75 2.00
DM26 Peter Forsberg 1.00 2.50
DM27 Alexander Ovechkin 3.00 8.00
DM28 Sidney Crosby 4.00 10.00
DM29 Joe Thornton 1.00 2.50
DM30 Vincent Lecavalier .60 1.50

2006-07 Ultra Fresh Ink

STATED ODDS 1:200
IAL Andrew Ladd SP
IAM Al Montoya 6.00 15.00
IAO Alexander Ovechkin SP 60.00 100.00
IBB Brad Boyes SP 8.00 20.00
IBL Brian Leetch SP 20.00 50.00
IBM Brenden Morrow SP
IBR Martin Brodeur SP
ICD Chris Drury SP 10.00 25.00
ICK Chuck Kobasew 4.00 10.00
ICO Chris Osgood SP 10.00 25.00
IDB Daniel Briere SP 10.00 25.00
IDC Dan Cloutier SP 10.00 25.00
IDL David Leneveu 6.00 15.00
IDR Dwayne Roloson 6.00 15.00
IEN Evgeni Nabokov 6.00 15.00
IGM Glen Murray SP 15.00 40.00
IHE Milan Hejduk SP 12.00 30.00
IJB Jay Bouwmeester SP 10.00 25.00
IJH Jeff Halpern 6.00 15.00
IJI Jarome Iginla SP 25.00 60.00
IJL Jason Labarbera 6.00 15.00
IJO Jeff O'Neill SP 8.00 20.00
IJT Jose Theodore SP 15.00 40.00
IJV Josef Vasicek 8.00 20.00
IMB Martin Biron 6.00 15.00
IMC Mike Cammalleri SP 8.00 20.00
IMG Marian Gaborik SP 15.00 40.00
IMH Michal Handzus 6.00 15.00
IMN Mika Noronen 5.00 12.00
IMR Michael Ryder SP 10.00 25.00
IMS Marc Savard 6.00 15.00
IMT Mikael Tellqvist 8.00 20.00
IMZ Marek Zidlicky SP 8.00 20.00
INA Nikolai Antropov SP 8.00 20.00
IOK Olaf Kolzig SP 12.00 30.00
IPS Philippe Sauve 4.00 10.00
IRF Ruslan Fedotenko SP 8.00 20.00
IRM Ryan Malone SP 10.00 25.00
IRS Ryan Smyth SP 12.00 30.00
ISC Sidney Crosby SP 150.00 250.00
ISG Scott Gomez SP 10.00 25.00
ISH Scott Hartnell SP 8.00 20.00
ISK Saku Koivu SP 12.00 30.00
ISS Sergei Samsonov SP 6.00 15.00
ISU Ryan Suter 8.00 20.00
ITB Todd Bertuzzi SP 15.00 40.00
ITC Ty Conklin SP 8.00 20.00
ITG Tim Gleason 5.00 12.00

2006-07 Ultra Scoring Kings

STATED ODDS 1:12
SK1 Alex Tanguay .50 1.25
SK2 Alexander Ovechkin 3.00 8.00
SK3 Brad Richards .75 2.00
SK4 Brendan Shanahan 1.00 2.50
SK5 Daniel Alfredsson .75 2.00
SK6 Dany Heatley .75 2.00
SK7 Eric Staal 1.00 2.50
SK8 Henrik Zetterberg 1.00 2.50
SK9 Ilya Kovalchuk .75 2.00
SK10 Jarome Iginla .75 2.00
SK11 Jaromir Jagr 2.00 5.00
SK12 Jason Spezza .75 2.00
SK13 Joe Sakic 1.25 3.00
SK14 Joe Thornton 1.00 2.50
SK15 Jonathan Cheechoo .75 2.00
SK16 Ryan Smyth .60 1.50
SK17 Marian Gaborik 1.00 2.50
SK18 Markus Naslund .60 1.50
SK19 Mats Sundin .75 2.00
SK20 Michael Ryder .50 1.25
SK21 Mike Modano 1.25 3.00
SK22 Patrice Bergeron 1.00 2.50
SK23 Paul Kariya 1.00 2.50
SK24 Pavel Datsyuk 1.00 2.50
SK25 Peter Forsberg 1.00 2.50
SK26 Rick Nash .75 2.00
SK27 Saku Koivu .75 2.00
SK28 Sidney Crosby 4.00 10.00
SK29 Simon Gagne .75 2.00
SK30 Vincent Lecavalier .60 1.50

2006-07 Ultra Uniformity

STATED ODDS 1:12
*PATCH/25: 1.5X TO 4X BASIC JSY
UAH Ales Hemsky 3.00 8.00
UAO Alexander Ovechkin 10.00 25.00
UBL Rob Blake 3.00 8.00
UBM Brendan Morrison 3.00 8.00
UBR Martin Brodeur 8.00 20.00
UBS Brad Stuart 3.00 8.00
UCC Carlo Colaiacovo 3.00 8.00
UCD Chris Drury 3.00 8.00
UCP Chris Pronger 4.00 10.00
UDE Pavol Demitra 3.00 8.00
UDH Dan Hamhuis 3.00 8.00
UDL David Legwand 3.00 8.00
UDM Darren McCarty 3.00 8.00
UEB Ed Belfour 4.00 10.00
UED Eric Daze 3.00 8.00
UEJ Ed Jovanovski 3.00 8.00
UEL Eric Lindros 4.00 10.00
UEN Evgeni Nabokov 4.00 10.00
UES Eric Staal 4.00 10.00
UFP Fernando Pisani 3.00 8.00
UGE Martin Gerber 3.00 8.00
UHA Dominik Hasek SP 8.00 20.00
UJA Jason Arnott 3.00 8.00
UJG Jean-Sebastien Giguere 3.00 8.00
UJK Jason King 3.00 8.00
UJL Jere Lehtinen 3.00 8.00
UJS Joe Sakic 8.00 20.00
UJT Joe Thornton 6.00 15.00
UJW Justin Williams 3.00 8.00
UKO Mikko Koivu 3.00 8.00
UKT Keith Tkachuk 3.00 8.00
ULN Ladislav Nagy 3.00 8.00
ULR Luc Robitaille 4.00 10.00
UMB Martin Biron 3.00 8.00
UMC Bryan McCabe 3.00 8.00
UMD Marc Denis 3.00 8.00
UMG Marian Gaborik 6.00 15.00
UMK Miikka Kiprusoff 5.00 12.00
UMM Mike Modano 5.00 12.00
UMN Markus Naslund 4.00 10.00
UMP Mark Parrish 3.00 8.00
UMR Michael Ryder 4.00 10.00
UMS Marek Svatos 3.00 8.00
UNA Nikolai Antropov 3.00 8.00
UPB Pierre-Marc Bouchard 3.00 8.00
UPD Pavel Datsyuk 4.00 10.00
UPE Michael Peca 3.00 8.00
UPF Peter Forsberg 6.00 15.00
UPL Patrick Lalime 3.00 8.00
UPP Petr Prucha 3.00 8.00
URB Radek Bonk 3.00 8.00
URE Robert Esche 3.00 8.00
URR Robyn Regehr 3.00 8.00
URZ Richard Zednik 3.00 8.00
USG Simon Gagne 4.00 10.00
USK Saku Koivu 4.00 10.00
UST Martin Straka 3.00 8.00
USU Mats Sundin 4.00 10.00
USW Stephen Weiss 3.00 8.00
UTS Teemu Selanne 4.00 10.00

2006-07 Ultra Uniformity Autographed Jerseys

STATED PRINT RUN 35 SER.#'d SETS
UAJA Jason Arnott 6.00 15.00
UAJT Joe Thornton 10.00 25.00
UAMK Miikka Kiprusoff 6.00 15.00
UAPB Pierre-Marc Bouchard 8.00 20.00
UAPE Michael Peca 6.00 15.00

2007-08 Ultra

This 271-card set was released in September, 2007. The set was issued into the hobby in eight-card packs which came 24 packs to a box and 12 boxes to a case. Cards numbered 1-200 feature veterans basically in reverse team alphabetical order and cards numbered 201-250 are Rookie Cards which were inserted at a stated rate of one in four. In addition, one rookie redemption card, which becames R251-R271, were inserted into packs at a stated rate of one in 24.

COMP.SET w/o RCs (200) 10.00 25.00
201-250 ROOKIE STATED ODDS 1:4
251-271 ROOKIE STATED ODDS 1:24
1 Alexander Ovechkin 1.25 3.00
2 Alexander Semin .30 .75
3 Chris Clark .20 .50
4 Matt Pettinger .20 .50
5 Olaf Kolzig .30 .75
6 Markus Naslund .30 .75
7 Roberto Luongo .40 1.00
8 Henrik Sedin .30 .75
9 Brendan Morrison .20 .50
10 Kevin Bieksa .25 .60
11 Daniel Sedin .30 .75
12 Andrew Raycroft .25 .60
13 Mats Sundin .30 .75
14 Bryan McCabe .20 .50
15 Alexander Steen .30 .75
16 Kyle Wellwood .25 .60
17 Darcy Tucker .25 .60
18 Tomas Kaberle .20 .50
19 Brad Richards .30 .75
20 Martin St. Louis .30 .75
21 Vincent Lecavalier .25 .60
22 Vaclav Prospal .20 .50
23 Johan Holmqvist .25 .60
24 Ruslan Fedotenko .20 .50
25 Doug Weight .30 .75
26 Brad Boyes .20 .50
27 Manny Legace .25 .60
28 Lee Stempniak .20 .50
29 Evgeni Nabokov .25 .60
30 Joe Thornton .40 1.00
31 Patrick Marleau .30 .75
32 Matt Carle .20 .50
33 Vesa Toskala .25 .60
34 Jonathan Cheechoo .30 .75
35 Steve Bernier .20 .50
36 Bill Guerin .30 .75
37 Sidney Crosby 1.25 3.00
38 Evgeni Malkin 1.00 2.50
39 Marc-Andre Fleury .50 1.25
40 Ryan Malone .20 .50
41 Colby Armstrong .20 .50
42 Ryan Whitney .25 .60
43 Jordan Staal .30 .75
44 Georges Laraque .25 .60
45 Zbynek Michalek .20 .50
46 Curtis Joseph .30 .75
47 Keith Ballard .20 .50
48 Shane Doan .25 .60
49 Ed Jovanovski .25 .60
50 Mike Richards .30 .75
51 R.J. Umberger .20 .50
52 Antero Niittymaki .25 .60
53 Joni Pitkanen .20 .50
54 Simon Gagne .30 .75
55 Jeff Carter .30 .75
56 Martin Biron .25 .60
57 Tom Preissing .20 .50
58 Jason Spezza .30 .75
59 Wade Redden .20 .50
60 Dany Heatley .30 .75
61 Daniel Alfredsson .30 .75
62 Andrej Meszaros .20 .50
63 Ray Emery .25 .60
64 Chris Neil .20 .50
65 Henrik Lundqvist .40 1.00
66 Martin Straka .20 .50
67 Jaromir Jagr .75 2.00
68 Petr Prucha .20 .50
69 Brendan Shanahan .40 1.00
70 Michael Nylander .20 .50
71 Sean Avery .20 .50
72 Rick DiPietro .25 .60
73 Miroslav Satan .25 .60
74 Ryan Smyth .25 .60
75 Jason Blake .20 .50
76 Mike Sillinger .20 .50
77 Alexei Yashin .25 .60
78 Jamie Langenbrunner .20 .50
79 Martin Brodeur .60 1.50
80 Brian Rafalski .25 .60
81 Patrik Elias .30 .75
82 Brian Gionta .25 .60
83 Scott Gomez .25 .60
84 Zach Parise .40 1.00
85 Peter Forsberg .40 1.00
86 Tomas Vokoun .25 .60
87 Steve Sullivan .20 .50
88 David Legwand .25 .60
89 Paul Kariya .40 1.00
90 J.P. Dumont .20 .50
91 Shea Weber .25 .60
92 Radek Bonk .20 .50
93 Saku Koivu .30 .75
94 Cristobal Huet .25 .60
95 Sheldon Souray .20 .50
96 Michael Ryder .20 .50
97 Guillaume Latendresse .25 .60
98 Tomas Plekanec .30 .75
99 Mikko Koivu .25 .60
100 Niklas Backstrom .30 .75
101 Pierre-Marc Bouchard .30 .75
102 Brian Rolston .25 .60
103 Pavol Demitra .40 1.00
104 Marian Gaborik .40 1.00
105 Manny Fernandez .25 .60
106 Alexander Frolov .20 .50
107 Mike Cammalleri .25 .60
108 Rob Blake .30 .75
109 Anze Kopitar .50 1.25
110 Dustin Brown .30 .75
111 Patrick O'Sullivan .25 .60
112 Nathan Horton .30 .75
113 Ed Belfour .30 .75
114 Olli Jokinen .25 .60
115 Jay Bouwmeester .30 .75
116 Noah Welch .20 .50
117 Ales Hemsky .25 .60
118 Jarret Stoll .25 .60
119 Shawn Horcoff .20 .50
120 Dwayne Roloson .25 .60
121 Petr Sykora .25 .60
122 Joffrey Lupul .25 .60
123 Raffi Torres .20 .50
124 Tomas Holmstrom .25 .60
125 Henrik Zetterberg .40 1.00
126 Nicklas Lidstrom .30 .75
127 Pavel Datsyuk .40 1.00
128 Dominik Hasek .40 1.00
129 Todd Bertuzzi .30 .75
130 Robert Lang .20 .50
131 Marty Turco .30 .75
132 Mike Modano .50 1.25
133 Sergei Zubov .25 .60
134 Brenden Morrow .25 .60
135 Jussi Jokinen .20 .50
136 Eric Lindros .50 1.25
137 Jere Lehtinen .20 .50
138 Philippe Boucher .20 .50
139 Fredrik Modin .20 .50
140 Nikolai Zherdev .20 .50
141 Rick Nash .30 .75
142 Sergei Fedorov .50 1.25
143 Gilbert Brule .25 .60
144 Fredrik Norrena .20 .50
145 David Vyborny .20 .50
146 Wojtek Wolski .25 .60
147 Jose Theodore .30 .75
148 Joe Sakic .50 1.25
149 Milan Hejduk .25 .60
150 Andrew Brunette .20 .50
151 Marek Svatos .20 .50
152 Paul Stastny .30 .75
153 Peter Budaj .25 .60
154 Nikolai Khabibulin .30 .75
155 Tuomo Ruutu .30 .75
156 Brent Seabrook .30 .75
157 Martin Havlat .30 .75
158 Patrick Sharp .30 .75
159 Duncan Keith .30 .75
160 Cam Ward .30 .75
161 Ray Whitney .25 .60
162 Eric Staal .40 1.00
163 Justin Williams .25 .60
164 Erik Cole .25 .60
165 Mike Commodore .20 .50
166 Rod Brind'Amour .30 .75
167 Dustin Boyd .20 .50
168 Miikka Kiprusoff .25 .60
169 Jarome Iginla .30 .75
170 Kristian Huselius .20 .50
171 Daymond Langkow .20 .50
172 Dion Phaneuf .30 .75
173 Alex Tanguay .20 .50
174 Thomas Vanek .40 1.00
175 Ryan Miller .30 .75
176 Maxim Afinogenov .20 .50
177 Jason Pominville .30 .75
178 Chris Drury .25 .60
179 Drew Stafford .25 .60
180 Daniel Briere .30 .75
181 Patrice Bergeron .40 1.00
182 Phil Kessel .40 1.00
183 Marc Savard .20 .50
184 Glen Murray .25 .60
185 Zdeno Chara .30 .75
186 Tim Thomas .40 1.00
187 Marco Sturm .20 .50
188 Kari Lehtonen .25 .60
189 Marian Hossa .25 .60
190 Ilya Kovalchuk .30 .75
191 Slava Kozlov .20 .50
192 Keith Tkachuk .30 .75
193 Jean-Sebastien Giguere .30 .75
194 Chris Pronger .25 .60
195 Andy McDonald .25 .60
196 Corey Perry .30 .75
197 Chris Kunitz .30 .75
198 Teemu Selanne .60 1.50
199 Ryan Getzlaf .50 1.25
200 Scott Niedermayer .30 .75
201 Aaron Rome RC 1.50 4.00
202 Andy Greene RC 1.50 4.00
203 Brandon Dubinsky RC 2.50 6.00
204 Bryan Bickell RC 2.50 6.00
205 Bryan Young RC 1.25 3.00
206 Colin Fraser RC 1.25 3.00
207 Daniel Girardi RC 1.50 4.00
208 Danny Bois RC 1.25 3.00
209 Curtis Glencross RC 2.00 5.00
210 David Clarkson RC 2.00 5.00
211 David Koci RC 1.25 3.00
212 David Krejci RC 4.00 10.00
213 David Moss RC 2.00 5.00
214 Drew Fata RC 1.25 3.00
215 Drew Miller RC 1.50 4.00
216 Duncan Milroy RC 1.25 3.00
217 Frans Nielsen RC 2.00 5.00
218 Gabe Gauthier RC 1.25 3.00
219 Jack Johnson RC 1.50 4.00
220 Jannik Hansen RC 1.50 4.00
221 Jaroslav Halak RC 3.00 8.00
222 Jeff Finger RC 1.25 3.00
223 Jeff Schultz RC 1.50 4.00
224 Joel Lundqvist RC 1.25 3.00
225 Jonathan Sigalet RC 1.25 3.00
226 Kent Huskins RC 1.25 3.00
227 Krys Barch RC 1.50 4.00
228 Lauri Tukonen RC 1.25 3.00
229 Marc Mothot RC 1.25 3.00
230 Mark Fraser RC 1.25 3.00
231 Mark Mancari RC 1.50 4.00
232 Mathieu Roy RC 1.25 3.00
233 Matt Ellis RC 1.50 4.00
234 Nathan Guenin RC 1.50 4.00
235 Patrick Kaleta RC 1.25 3.00
236 Petr Kalus RC 1.25 3.00
237 Rich Peverley RC 2.00 5.00
238 Riley Cote RC 1.50 4.00
239 Rob Schremp RC 1.50 4.00
240 Rod Pelley RC 1.25 3.00
241 Ryan Callahan RC 2.50 6.00
242 Ryan Parent RC 1.25 3.00
243 Scott Munroe RC 1.25 3.00
244 Shay Stephenson RC 1.25 3.00
245 Tobias Stephan RC 1.50 4.00
246 Tom Gilbert RC 1.50 4.00
247 Tomas Popperle RC 1.50 4.00
248 Tomi Maki RC 1.25 3.00
249 Yutaka Fukufuji RC 1.50 4.00
250 Zack Stortini RC 1.25 3.00
251 Carey Price RC 20.00 40.00
252 Jonathan Toews RC 20.00 40.00
253 Sam Gagner RC 3.00 8.00
254 Bobby Ryan RC 4.00 10.00
255 Niklas Bergfors RC 1.50 4.00
256 Erik Johnson RC 2.50 6.00
257 Nicklas Backstrom RC 5.00 12.00
258 Jonathan Bernier RC 4.00 10.00
259 Bryan Little RC 2.50 6.00
260 Patrick Kane RC 20.00 50.00
261 Andrew Cogliano RC 2.50 6.00
262 Marc Staal RC 2.50 6.00
263 Nick Foligno RC 3.00 8.00
264 Peter Mueller RC 2.00 5.00
265 Brett Sterling RC 1.50 4.00
266 Devon Setoguchi RC 2.50 6.00
267 David Perron RC 2.50 6.00
268 James Sheppard RC 1.50 4.00
269 Jiri Tlusty RC 2.50 6.00
270 Mason Raymond RC 2.50 6.00
271 Milan Lucic RC 8.00 20.00

2007-08 Ultra Gold Medallion

*1-200 VETS: 1.5X TO 4X BASIC CARDS
*201-250 ROOKIES: .5X TO 1.2X BASIC RC
*251-271 ROOKIES: .6X TO 1.5X BASIC RC
ONE PER HOBBY PACK

2007-08 Ultra Ice Medallion

*1-200 VETS/100: 5X TO 12X
*201-250 ROOKIES/100: 1.5X TO 4X
*251-271 ROOKIES/100: 1.5X TO 4X 10.00 25.00
STATED PRINT RUN 100 SER.#'d SETS
251 Carey Price 60.00 120.00
252 Jonathan Toews 60.00 120.00
260 Patrick Kane 60.00 120.00

2007-08 Ultra Oversized

1 Alexander Ovechkin 10.00 25.00
6 Markus Naslund 2.50 6.00
7 Roberto Luongo 3.00 8.00
12 Andrew Raycroft 2.00 5.00
13 Mats Sundin 2.50 6.00
20 Martin St. Louis 2.50 6.00
21 Vincent Lecavalier 2.00 5.00
30 Joe Thornton 3.00 8.00
37 Sidney Crosby 10.00 25.00
38 Evgeni Malkin 8.00 20.00
39 Marc-Andre Fleury 4.00 10.00
54 Simon Gagne 2.50 6.00
58 Jason Spezza 2.50 6.00
60 Dany Heatley 2.50 6.00
65 Henrik Lundqvist 3.00 8.00
67 Jaromir Jagr 6.00 15.00
79 Martin Brodeur 5.00 12.00
85 Peter Forsberg 3.00 8.00
93 Saku Koivu 2.50 6.00
96 Michael Ryder 1.50 4.00
104 Marian Gaborik 3.00 8.00
117 Ales Hemsky 2.00 5.00
120 Dwayne Roloson 2.00 5.00
125 Henrik Zetterberg 3.00 8.00
126 Nicklas Lidstrom 2.50 6.00
127 Pavel Datsyuk 3.00 8.00
131 Marty Turco 2.50 6.00
132 Mike Modano 4.00 10.00
141 Rick Nash 2.50 6.00
148 Joe Sakic 4.00 10.00
162 Eric Staal 3.00 8.00
168 Miikka Kiprusoff 2.00 5.00
169 Jarome Iginla 2.50 6.00
172 Dion Phaneuf 2.50 6.00
174 Thomas Vanek 3.00 8.00
175 Ryan Miller 2.50 6.00
181 Patrice Bergeron 3.00 8.00
189 Marian Hossa 2.00 5.00
190 Ilya Kovalchuk 2.50 6.00
194 Chris Pronger 2.00 5.00
198 Teemu Selanne 5.00 12.00
199 Ryan Getzlaf 4.00 10.00

2007-08 Ultra Action

COMPLETE SET (7) 10.00 25.00
STATED ODDS 1:12
UA1 Sidney Crosby 3.00 8.00
UA2 Joe Thornton 1.00 2.50
UA3 Alexander Ovechkin 3.00 8.00
UA4 Martin Brodeur 1.50 4.00
UA5 Roberto Luongo 1.00 2.50
UA6 Jarome Iginla .75 2.00
UA7 Daniel Briere .75 2.00

2007-08 Ultra All-Stars

COMPLETE SET (30) 100.00 200.00
RETAIL PACKS ONLY
UAS1 Roberto Luongo 4.00 10.00
UAS2 Nicklas Lidstrom 3.00 8.00
UAS3 Jonathan Cheechoo 3.00 8.00
UAS4 Joe Sakic 5.00 12.00
UAS5 Philippe Boucher 2.00 5.00
UAS6 Joe Thornton 4.00 10.00
UAS7 Teemu Selanne 6.00 15.00
UAS8 Patrick Marleau 3.00 8.00
UAS9 Bill Guerin 3.00 8.00
UAS10 Martin Havlat 3.00 8.00
UAS11 Miikka Kiprusoff 2.50 6.00
UAS12 Marty Turco 3.00 8.00
UAS13 Rick Nash 3.00 8.00
UAS14 Dion Phaneuf 3.00 8.00
UAS15 Yanic Perreault 2.00 5.00
UAS16 Alexander Ovechkin 12.00 30.00
UAS17 Ryan Miller 3.00 8.00
UAS18 Sheldon Souray 2.00 5.00
UAS19 Daniel Briere 3.00 8.00
UAS20 Brian Campbell 2.50 6.00
UAS21 Sidney Crosby 12.00 30.00
UAS22 Vincent Lecavalier 2.50 6.00
UAS23 Simon Gagne 3.00 8.00
UAS24 Brendan Shanahan 4.00 10.00
UAS25 Dany Heatley 3.00 8.00
UAS26 Marian Hossa 2.50 6.00
UAS27 Eric Staal 4.00 10.00
UAS28 Martin St. Louis 3.00 8.00
UAS29 Martin Brodeur 6.00 15.00
UAS30 Cristobal Huet 2.50 6.00

2007-08 Ultra Difference Makers

COMPLETE SET (14) 12.00 30.00
STATED ODDS 1:12
DM1 Ryan Miller .75 2.00
DM2 Jarome Iginla .75 2.00
DM3 Rick Nash .75 2.00
DM4 Pavel Datsyuk 1.00 2.50
DM5 Roberto Luongo 1.00 2.50
DM6 Saku Koivu .75 2.00
DM7 Mats Sundin .75 2.00
DM8 Martin Brodeur 1.50 4.00
DM9 Jaromir Jagr 2.00 5.00
DM10 Dany Heatley .75 2.00
DM11 Alexander Ovechkin 3.00 8.00
DM12 Sidney Crosby 3.00 8.00
DM13 Joe Thornton 1.00 2.50
DM14 Teemu Selanne 1.50 4.00

2007-08 Ultra Flair Showcase

COMPLETE SET (100) 200.00 350.00
1 Alex Tanguay 1.25 3.00
2 Alexander Steen 2.00 5.00
3 Andrej Meszaros 1.25 3.00
4 Andrew Raycroft 1.50 4.00
5 Bill Guerin 2.00 5.00
6 Brad Richards 2.00 5.00
7 Brendan Shanahan 2.50 6.00
8 Chris Drury 1.50 4.00
9 Chris Pronger 1.50 4.00
10 Daniel Alfredsson 2.00 5.00
11 Daniel Briere 2.00 5.00
12 Daniel Sedin 2.00 5.00
13 Dany Heatley 2.00 5.00
14 Dion Phaneuf 2.00 5.00
15 Doug Weight 2.00 5.00
16 Drew Stafford 1.50 4.00
17 Dwayne Roloson 1.50 4.00
18 Ed Belfour 2.00 5.00
19 Ed Jovanovski 1.50 4.00
20 Eric Staal 2.50 6.00
21 Evgeni Nabokov 1.50 4.00
22 Gilbert Brule 1.50 4.00
23 Guillaume Latendresse 1.50 4.00
24 Henrik Sedin 2.00 5.00
25 Ilya Kovalchuk 2.00 5.00
26 Jaroslav Halak 3.00 8.00
27 Jeff Carter 2.00 5.00
28 Jonathan Cheechoo 2.00 5.00
29 Jordan Staal 2.00 5.00
30 Kari Lehtonen 1.50 4.00
31 Lauri Tukonen 1.25 3.00
32 Manny Fernandez 1.50 4.00
33 Manny Legace 1.50 4.00
34 Marc-Andre Fleury 3.00 8.00
35 Michael Ryder 1.25 3.00
36 Miikka Kiprusoff 1.50 4.00
37 Mike Modano 3.00 8.00
38 Mike Ribeiro 1.50 4.00
39 Milan Hejduk 1.50 4.00
40 Miroslav Satan 1.50 4.00
41 Nicklas Lidstrom 2.00 5.00
42 Nikolai Khabibulin 2.00 5.00
43 Patrice Bergeron 2.50 6.00
44 Patrick Marleau 2.00 5.00
45 Patrik Elias 2.00 5.00
46 Pavel Datsyuk 2.50 6.00
47 Peter Forsberg 2.50 6.00
48 Petr Kalus 1.25 3.00
49 Ryan Parent 1.25 3.00
50 Ryan Smyth 1.50 4.00
51 Scott Niedermayer 2.00 5.00
52 Sergei Fedorov 3.00 8.00
53 Shane Doan 1.50 4.00
54 Eric Lindros 3.00 8.00
55 Thomas Vanek 2.50 6.00
56 Tomas Kaberle 1.25 3.00
57 Tomas Vokoun 1.50 4.00
58 Vincent Lecavalier 1.50 4.00
59 Wade Redden 1.25 3.00
60 Zdeno Chara 2.00 5.00
61 Evgeni Malkin 6.00 15.00
62 Henrik Zetterberg 2.50 6.00
63 Jean-Sebastien Giguere 2.00 5.00
64 Jarome Iginla 2.00 5.00
65 Rick Nash 2.00 5.00
66 Jason Spezza 2.00 5.00
67 Simon Gagne 2.00 5.00
68 Henrik Lundqvist 2.50 6.00
69 Jack Johnson 1.50 4.00
70 Rob Schremp 1.50 4.00
71 Anze Kopitar 3.00 8.00
72 Marian Gaborik 2.50 6.00
73 Marty Turco 2.00 5.00
74 Ales Hemsky 1.50 4.00
75 Olli Jokinen 1.50 4.00
76 Paul Kariya 2.50 6.00
77 Mats Sundin 2.00 5.00
78 Markus Naslund 2.00 5.00
79 Olaf Kolzig 2.00 5.00
80 Martin St. Louis 2.00 5.00
81 Joe Thornton 2.50 6.00
82 Phil Kessel 2.50 6.00
83 Marian Hossa 1.50 4.00
84 Ryan Miller 2.00 5.00
85 Martin Havlat 2.00 5.00
86 Cam Ward 2.00 5.00
87 Teemu Selanne 4.00 10.00
88 Rick DiPietro 1.50 4.00
89 Saku Koivu 2.00 5.00
90 Dominik Hasek 2.50 6.00
91 Gordie Howe 5.00 12.00
92 Bobby Orr 6.00 15.00
93 Mark Messier 3.00 8.00
94 Sidney Crosby 8.00 20.00
95 Mario Lemieux 6.00 15.00
96 Alexander Ovechkin 8.00 20.00
97 Roberto Luongo 2.50 6.00
98 Joe Sakic 3.00 8.00
99 Jaromir Jagr 5.00 12.00
100 Martin Brodeur 4.00 10.00

2007-08 Ultra Fresh Ink

FIAA Adrian Aucoin 3.00 8.00
FIAD Adam Dennis 4.00 10.00
FIAF Alexander Frolov 3.00 8.00
FIAK Andrei Kostitsyn 4.00 10.00
FIAL Andrew Ladd 5.00 12.00
FIAO Alexander Ovechkin 75.00 150.00
FIAP Alexandre Picard
FIAR Alexander Radulov 5.00 12.00
FIAT Alex Tanguay 3.00 8.00
FIAY Alexei Yashin 4.00 10.00
FIBB Brendan Bell 3.00 8.00
FIBM Brendan Morrison 3.00 8.00
FIBO Dave Bolland 5.00 12.00
FIBR Brad Richardson 4.00 10.00
FIBW Ben Walter 3.00 8.00
FICC Chris Campoli 3.00 8.00
FICH Chris Higgins 3.00 8.00
FICK Chuck Kobasew
FICO Chris Osgood 5.00 12.00
FIDA David Aebischer 4.00 10.00
FIDB Daniel Briere 5.00 12.00
FIDH Dany Heatley 8.00 20.00
FIDP Dion Phaneuf 5.00 12.00
FIDS Drew Stafford 4.00 10.00
FIDT Darcy Tucker 4.00 10.00
FIDW Doug Weight 5.00 12.00
FIEC Erik Christensen 3.00 8.00
FIEM Evgeni Malkin 25.00 60.00
FIEN Eric Nystrom 3.00 8.00
FIER Erik Cole 4.00 10.00
FIES Eric Staal 6.00 15.00
FIGL Guillaume Latendresse 4.00 10.00
FIHA Martin Havlat 5.00 12.00
FIHE Milan Hejduk 4.00 10.00
FIHL Henrik Lundqvist
FIHU Cristobal Huet 4.00 10.00
FIHZ Henrik Zetterberg 6.00 15.00
FIJA Jay Bouwmeester 5.00 12.00
FIJB Jaroslav Balastik 3.00 8.00
FIJC Jeff Carter 5.00 12.00
FIJE Jeremy Colliton 3.00 8.00
FIJJ Jussi Jokinen 3.00 8.00
FIJL Joffrey Lupul 4.00 10.00
FIJP Joel Perrault 3.00 8.00
FIJT Joe Thornton 6.00 15.00
FIJW Jeff Woywitka 3.00 8.00
FIKB Kevin Bieksa
FIKC Kyle Calder 3.00 8.00
FIKL Kari Lehtonen
FIKO Anze Kopitar 8.00 20.00
FILA Maxim Lapierre 3.00 8.00
FILN Ladislav Nagy 3.00 8.00
FIMH Marcel Hossa 3.00 8.00
FIMI Michal Handzus 4.00 10.00
FIMK Miikka Kiprusoff 4.00 10.00
FIML Mario Lemieux
FIMN Mika Noronen 3.00 8.00
FIMO Brenden Morrow 4.00 10.00
FIMS Martin St. Louis 5.00 12.00
FINA Evgeni Nabokov 4.00 10.00
FINL Nicklas Lidstrom
FINZ Nikolai Zherdev 3.00 8.00
FIPA Joe Pavelski 5.00 12.00
FIPE Michael Peca 4.00 10.00
FIPK Phil Kessel 6.00 15.00
FIPS Paul Stastny 6.00 15.00
FIPT Patrick Thoresen 3.00 8.00
FIRG Ryan Getzlaf 8.00 20.00
FIRH Ryan Hollweg 3.00 8.00
FIRK Rostislav Klesla 3.00 8.00
FIRN Rick Nash 5.00 12.00
FISG Scott Gomez 4.00 10.00
FITA Maxime Talbot 5.00 12.00
FITR Tuomo Ruutu 5.00 12.00
FIVT Vesa Toskala 4.00 10.00
FIWI Jeremy Williams 3.00 8.00
FIYS Yan Stastny 3.00 8.00
FIZC Zdeno Chara 6.00 15.00

2007-08 Ultra Generations

COMPLETE SET (21) 50.00 100.00
TARGET PACKS ONLY
G1 Lemieux/Fleury/Malkin 5.00 12.00
G2 Roy/Sakic/Stastny 4.00 10.00
G3 Robitaille/Blake/Kopitar 2.50 6.00
G4 Dionne/Frolov/O'Sullivan 2.00 5.00
G5 Stastny/Hejduk/Svatos 1.25 3.00
G6 Lemieux/Crosby/Staal 6.00 15.00
G7 Lafleur/Koivu/Latendresse 2.00 5.00
G8 Orr/Bergeron/Kessel 5.00 12.00
G9 Perreault/Vanek/Stafford 2.00 5.00
G10 Salming/Sundin/Steen 1.50 4.00
G11 Cheevers/Thomas/Toivonen 1.50 4.00
G12 Clarke/Gagne/Carter 1.50 4.00
G13 Kurri/Hemsky/Schremp 1.50 4.00
G14 Lafleur/Koivu/Kostitsyn 2.00 5.00
G15 Langway/Pothier/Green 1.50 4.00
G16 Howe/Zetterberg/Hudler 4.00 10.00
G17 Howe/Datsyuk/Filppula 4.00 10.00
G18 Stevens/Brodeur/Parise 1.50 4.00
G19 Roy/Huet/Halak 4.00 10.00
G20 Hull/Havlat/Barker 2.50 6.00
G21 McDonald/Iginla/Boyd 1.50 4.00

2007-08 Ultra Hot Gloves

COMPLETE SET (15) 75.00 150.00
HG1 Martin Brodeur 10.00 25.00
HG2 Roberto Luongo 6.00 15.00
HG3 Ryan Miller 5.00 12.00
HG4 Cristobal Huet 4.00 10.00
HG5 Miikka Kiprusoff 4.00 10.00
HG6 Marty Turco 5.00 12.00
HG7 Dominik Hasek 6.00 15.00
HG8 Ray Emery 4.00 10.00
HG9 Jean-Sebastien Giguere 5.00 12.00
HG10 Rick DiPietro 4.00 10.00
HG11 Marc-Andre Fleury 8.00 20.00
HG12 Evgeni Nabokov 4.00 10.00
HG13 Peter Budaj 4.00 10.00
HG14 Tomas Vokoun 4.00 10.00
HG15 Henrik Lundqvist 6.00 15.00

2007-08 Ultra Hot Numbers

COMPLETE SET (15) 100.00 200.00
STATED ODDS 1:288
HN1 Jarome Iginla 5.00 12.00
HN2 Mats Sundin 5.00 12.00
HN3 Martin St. Louis 5.00 12.00
HN4 Martin Brodeur 10.00 25.00
HN5 Dominik Hasek 6.00 15.00
HN6 Roberto Luongo 6.00 15.00
HN7 Daniel Briere 5.00 12.00
HN8 Vincent Lecavalier 4.00 10.00
HN9 Dany Heatley 5.00 12.00
HN10 Teemu Selanne 10.00 25.00
HN11 Evgeni Malkin 15.00 40.00
HN12 Alexander Ovechkin 20.00 50.00
HN13 Joe Thornton 6.00 15.00
HN14 Joe Sakic 8.00 20.00
HN15 Sidney Crosby 20.00 50.00

2007-08 Ultra Scoring Kings

COMPLETE SET (14) 12.00 30.00
STATED ODDS 1:12
SK1 Alexander Ovechkin 3.00 8.00
SK2 Dany Heatley .75 2.00
SK3 Jarome Iginla .75 2.00
SK4 Jaromir Jagr 2.00 5.00
SK5 Jason Spezza .75 2.00
SK6 Joe Sakic 1.25 3.00
SK7 Joe Thornton 1.00 2.50
SK8 Sidney Crosby 3.00 8.00
SK9 Vincent Lecavalier .60 1.50
SK10 Evgeni Malkin 2.50 6.00
SK11 Patrice Bergeron 1.00 2.50
SK12 Marian Hossa .60 1.50
SK13 Martin St. Louis .75 2.00
SK14 Thomas Vanek 1.00 2.50

2007-08 Ultra Season Crowns
COMPLETE SET (7) 6.00 15.00
STATED ODDS 1:12
SC1 Niklas Backstrom .75 2.00
SC2 Sidney Crosby 3.00 8.00
SC3 Martin Brodeur 1.50 4.00
SC4 Thomas Vanek 1.00 2.50
SC5 Ben Eager .50 1.25
SC6 Vincent Lecavalier .60 1.50
SC7 Joe Thornton 1.00 2.50

2007-08 Ultra Team Leaders
COMPLETE SET (30) 50.00 100.00
TL1 Vincent Lecavalier 1.50 4.00
TL2 Teemu Selanne 4.00 10.00
TL3 Simon Gagne 2.00 5.00
TL4 Sidney Crosby 8.00 20.00
TL5 Shane Doan 1.50 4.00
TL6 Saku Koivu 2.00 5.00
TL7 Ray Whitney 1.50 4.00
TL8 Pavel Datsyuk 2.50 6.00
TL9 Paul Kariya 2.50 6.00
TL10 Patrik Elias 2.00 5.00
TL11 Olli Jokinen 1.50 4.00
TL12 Mike Ribeiro 1.50 4.00
TL13 Mike Cammalleri 1.50 4.00
TL14 Mats Sundin 2.00 5.00
TL15 Martin Havlat 2.00 5.00
TL16 Marian Hossa 1.50 4.00
TL17 Marc Savard 1.25 3.00
TL18 Joe Thornton 2.50 6.00
TL19 Joe Sakic 3.00 8.00
TL20 Jason Blake 1.25 3.00
TL21 Jaromir Jagr 5.00 12.00
TL22 Jarome Iginla 2.00 5.00
TL23 Doug Weight 2.00 5.00
TL24 David Vyborny 1.25 3.00
TL25 Dany Heatley 2.00 5.00
TL26 Daniel Sedin 2.00 5.00
TL27 Daniel Briere 2.00 5.00
TL28 Brian Rolston 1.50 4.00
TL29 Alexander Ovechkin 8.00 20.00
TL30 Ales Hemsky 1.50 4.00

2007-08 Ultra Uniformity
*PATCH/25: 1.5X TO 3X BASIC JSY
UAA Alex Auld 2.50 6.00
UAF Alexander Frolov 2.50 6.00
UAH Ales Hemsky 3.00 8.00
UAK Alex Kovalev 3.00 8.00
UAL Andrew Ladd 4.00 10.00
UAM Andrej Meszaros 2.50 6.00
UAO Alexander Ovechkin 15.00 40.00
UAP Alexander Perezhogin 2.50 6.00
UAR Andrew Raycroft 3.00 8.00
UAS Alexander Steen 4.00 10.00
UAT Alex Tanguay 2.50 6.00
UAY Alexei Yashin 3.00 8.00
UBB Brad Boyes 2.50 6.00
UBG Bill Guerin 4.00 10.00
UBI Brandon Bochenski 2.50 6.00
UBJ Barret Jackman 2.50 6.00
UBM Brendan Morrison 2.50 6.00
UBO Jay Bouwmeester 4.00 10.00
UBR Brad Richards 4.00 10.00
UBS Brendan Shanahan 5.00 12.00
UBT Barry Tallackson 2.50 6.00
UBW Brendan Witt 2.50 6.00
UCH Chris Higgins 2.50 6.00
UCO Chris Osgood 4.00 10.00
UCP Chris Phillips 2.50 6.00
UCS Curtis Sanford 3.00 8.00
UDA Daniel Alfredsson 4.00 10.00
UDB Dustin Brown 4.00 10.00
UDC Dan Cloutier 3.00 8.00
UDH Dany Heatley 4.00 10.00
UDL David Legwand 3.00 8.00
UDM Dominic Moore 2.50 6.00
UDO Dominik Hasek 5.00 12.00
UDP Daniel Paille 2.50 6.00
UDR Dwayne Roloson 3.00 8.00
UDS Daniel Sedin 4.00 10.00
UDW Doug Weight 4.00 10.00
UEB Ed Belfour 4.00 10.00
UEC Erik Cole 3.00 8.00
UEJ Ed Jovanovski 3.00 8.00
UES Eric Staal 5.00 12.00
UFP Fernando Pisani 2.50 6.00
UGL Georges Laraque 3.00 8.00
UGM Glen Murray 3.00 8.00
UGR Gary Roberts 2.50 6.00
UHA Adam Hall 2.50 6.00
UHD Dan Hamhuis 3.00 8.00
UHS Henrik Sedin 4.00 10.00
UHT Hannu Toivonen 3.00 8.00
UIG Jarome Iginla 4.00 10.00
UIK Ilya Kovalchuk 4.00 10.00
UIW Ian White 2.50 6.00
UJA Jason Arnott 3.00 8.00
UJB Jason Blake 2.50 6.00
UJC Jeff Carter 4.00 10.00
UJF Jeff Friesen 2.50 6.00
UJG Jean-Sebastien Giguere 4.00 10.00
UJH Jeff Hoggan 2.50 6.00
UJI Jarkko Immonen 2.50 6.00
UJJ Jaromir Jagr 10.00 25.00
UJK Jakub Klepis 2.50 6.00
UJL Jere Lehtinen 2.50 6.00
UJP Joni Pitkanen 2.50 6.00
UJS Jarret Stoll 3.00 8.00
UJT Joe Thornton 5.00 12.00
UJW Jason Williams 2.50 6.00
UKC Kyle Calder 2.50 6.00
UKL Kari Lehtonen 3.00 8.00
UKO Andrei Kostitsyn 3.00 8.00
ULJ Jamie Lundmark 2.50 6.00
ULU Joffrey Lupul 3.00 8.00
UMB Martin Brodeur 8.00 20.00
UMC Bryan McCabe 2.50 6.00
UMD Marc Denis 3.00 8.00
UMF Manny Fernandez 3.00 8.00
UMG Martin Gerber 3.00 8.00
UMH Marian Hossa 3.00 8.00
UMK Miikka Kiprusoff 3.00 8.00
UMN Markus Naslund 4.00 10.00
UMR Michael Ryder 2.50 6.00
UMS Mats Sundin 4.00 10.00
UMT Marty Turco 4.00 10.00
UON Ben Ondrus 2.50 6.00
UPB Patrice Bergeron 5.00 12.00
UPE Corey Perry 4.00 10.00
UPK Paul Kariya 5.00 12.00
UPR Chris Pronger 3.00 8.00
URA Brian Rafalski 3.00 8.00
URO Brian Rolston 3.00 8.00
USA Joe Sakic 6.00 15.00
USC Sidney Crosby 15.00 40.00
USG Simon Gagne 4.00 10.00
USK Saku Koivu 4.00 10.00
USP Jason Spezza 4.00 10.00
UST Brad Stuart 2.50 6.00
UTH Billy Thompson 2.50 6.00
UTK Keith Tkachuk 4.00 10.00
UTV Tomas Vokoun 3.00 8.00
UWI Justin Williams 3.00 8.00

2008-09 Ultra
This set was released on October 21, 2008. The base set consists of 271 cards. Cards 1-200 feature veterans, and cards 201-271 are rookies. Cards 251-271 were issued as exchange cards and have all been redeemed.

COMP.SET w/o EXCH RC (250) 75.00 150.00
COMP.SET w/o RC's (200) 15.00 40.00
RC (201-250) STATED ODDS 1:4
RC (251-271) STATED ODDS 1:24
1 Ilya Kovalchuk .30 .75
2 Eric Perrin .20 .50
3 Colby Armstrong .20 .50
4 Kari Lehtonen .25 .60
5 Bryan Little .25 .60
6 Tobias Enstrom .20 .50
7 Patrice Bergeron .40 1.00
8 Marc Savard .20 .50
9 Tim Thomas .30 .75
10 Zdeno Chara .30 .75
11 Marco Sturm .20 .50
12 Phil Kessel .40 1.00
13 Glen Murray .25 .60
14 Michael Ryder .20 .50
15 Thomas Vanek .30 .75
16 Ryan Miller .30 .75
17 Derek Roy .20 .50
18 Jason Pominville .30 .75
19 Drew Stafford .25 .60
20 Daniel Paille .20 .50
21 Eric Staal .40 1.00
22 Rod Brind'Amour .30 .75
23 Cam Ward .30 .75
24 Justin Williams .25 .60
25 Ray Whitney .25 .60
26 Joni Pitkanen .20 .50
27 Tomas Vokoun .25 .60
28 Nathan Horton .25 .60
29 David Booth .20 .50
30 Stephen Weiss .20 .50
31 Jay Bouwmeester .30 .75
32 Saku Koivu .30 .75
33 Carey Price 1.25 3.00
34 Tomas Plekanec .30 .75
35 Alex Tanguay .20 .50
36 Alex Kovalev .25 .60
37 Chris Higgins .20 .50
38 Andrei Markov .30 .75
39 Guillaume Latendresse .20 .50
40 Martin Brodeur .60 1.50
41 Zach Parise .30 .75
42 Patrik Elias .30 .75
43 Brian Gionta .25 .60
44 John Madden .20 .50
45 Travis Zajac .25 .60
46 Rick DiPietro .25 .60
46 Brian Rolston .25 .60
47 Mike Comrie .25 .60
48 Bill Guerin .30 .75
49 Trent Hunter .20 .50
50 Mark Streit .20 .50
51 Wade Redden .20 .50
52 Michal Rozsival .20 .50
53 Henrik Lundqvist .40 1.00
54 Chris Drury .25 .60
55 Scott Gomez .25 .60
56 Markus Naslund .25 .60
57 Marc Staal .30 .75
58 Brandon Dubinsky .25 .60
59 Nikolai Zherdev .20 .50
60 Jason Spezza .30 .75
61 Andrej Meszaros .20 .50
62 Antoine Vermette .20 .50
63 Mike Fisher .20 .50
64 Daniel Alfredsson .30 .75
66 Martin Gerber .25 .60
67 Dany Heatley .30 .75
68 Martin Biron .25 .60
69 Daniel Briere .30 .75
70 Simon Gagne .30 .75
71 Mike Knuble .20 .50
72 Jeff Carter .30 .75
73 Mike Richards .30 .75
74 Sidney Crosby 1.25 3.00
75 Marc-Andre Fleury .50 1.25
76 Miroslav Satan .30 .75
77 Evgeni Malkin 1.00 2.50
78 Sergei Gonchar .20 .50
79 Ryan Whitney .30 .75
80 Jordan Staal .30 .75
81 Ryan Malone .20 .50
82 Vincent Lecavalier .25 .60
83 Mike Smith .30 .75
84 Jussi Jokinen .20 .50
85 Martin St. Louis .30 .75
86 Paul Ranger .20 .50
87 Karri Ramo .25 .60
88 Olaf Kolzig .30 .75
89 Mats Sundin .30 .75
90 Vesa Toskala .25 .60
91 Alexander Steen .30 .75
92 Tomas Kaberle .20 .50
93 Nikolai Antropov .25 .60
94 Matt Stajan .25 .60
95 Jiri Tlusty .25 .60
96 Alexander Ovechkin 1.25 3.00
97 Jose Theodore .30 .75
98 Nicklas Backstrom .50 1.25
99 Sergei Fedorov .50 1.25
100 Mike Green .30 .75
101 Alexander Semin .30 .75
102 Ryan Getzlaf .50 1.25
103 Jean-Sebastien Giguere .30 .75
104 Corey Perry .30 .75
105 Teemu Selanne .60 1.50
106 Chris Pronger .25 .60
107 Chris Kunitz .30 .75
108 Scott Niedermayer .30 .75
109 Miikka Kiprusoff .25 .60
110 Jarome Iginla .30 .75
111 Daymond Langkow .20 .50
112 Dion Phaneuf .30 .75
114 Todd Bertuzzi .30 .75
115 Matthew Lombardi .20 .50
116 Mike Cammalleri .25 .60
117 Patrick Kane .60 1.50
118 Nikolai Khabibulin .30 .75
119 Patrick Sharp .30 .75
120 Brent Seabrook .30 .75
121 Jonathan Toews .75 2.00
122 Martin Havlat .30 .75
123 Duncan Keith .30 .75
124 Brian Campbell .25 .60
125 Darcy Tucker .25 .60
126 Joe Sakic .50 1.25
127 Milan Hejduk .25 .60
128 Marek Svatos .20 .50
129 Paul Stastny .30 .75
130 Wojtek Wolski .25 .60
131 Peter Forsberg .40 1.00
132 Ryan Smyth .25 .60
132 Pascal Leclaire .25 .60
133 R.J. Umberger .20 .50
134 Rostislav Klesla .20 .50
135 Jared Boll .20 .50
136 Rick Nash .30 .75
137 Brad Richards .30 .75
138 Marty Turco .30 .75
139 Mike Ribeiro .25 .60
140 Brenden Morrow .25 .60
141 Jere Lehtinen .20 .50
142 Mike Modano .50 1.25
142 Marian Hossa .25 .60
143 Johan Franzen .30 .75
144 Nicklas Lidstrom .30 .75
145 Pavel Datsyuk .40 1.00
146 Chris Osgood .30 .75
147 Henrik Zetterberg .40 1.00
148 Dan Cleary .25 .60
149 Tomas Holmstrom .25 .60
150 Valtteri Filppula .30 .75
151 Sam Gagner .25 .60
152 Ales Hemsky .25 .60
153 Mathieu Garon .25 .60
154 Shawn Horcoff .20 .50
155 Dustin Penner .25 .60
156 Andrew Cogliano .25 .60
157 Dwayne Roloson .25 .60
158 Gilbert Brule .20 .50
159 Anze Kopitar .50 1.25
160 Alexander Frolov .20 .50
161 Dustin Brown .30 .75
162 Jonathan Bernier .40 1.00
163 Patrick O'Sullivan .25 .60
164 Marian Gaborik .40 1.00
165 Niklas Backstrom .30 .75
166 Pierre-Marc Bouchard .30 .75
168 Josh Harding .30 .75
169 Mikko Koivu .25 .60
170 Alexander Radulov .30 .75
171 Jason Arnott .25 .60
172 Dan Ellis .20 .50
173 Martin Erat .20 .50
174 J.P. Dumont .20 .50
175 David Legwand .25 .60
176 Peter Mueller .25 .60
177 Shane Doan .25 .60
178 Ilya Bryzgalov .25 .60
179 Ed Jovanovski .25 .60
180 Olli Jokinen .25 .60
181 Martin Hanzal .25 .60
182 Daniel Carcillo .20 .50
183 Evgeni Nabokov .25 .60
184 Jonathan Cheechoo .30 .75
185 Milan Michalek .20 .50
186 Rob Blake .30 .75
187 Patrick Marleau .30 .75
188 Joe Thornton .40 1.00
189 Manny Legace .30 .75
190 Erik Johnson .25 .60
191 Brad Boyes .20 .50
192 Lee Stempniak .20 .50
193 Keith Tkachuk .30 .75
194 Paul Kariya .40 1.00
195 Daniel Sedin .30 .75
196 Steve Bernier .20 .50
197 Ryan Kesler .40 1.00
198 Alexander Edler .20 .50
199 Roberto Luongo .40 1.00
200 Henrik Sedin .30 .75
201 Derick Brassard RC 1.50 4.00
202 Mark Fistric RC 1.50 4.00
203 Alex Goligoski RC 2.50 6.00
204 Claude Giroux RC 4.00 10.00
205 Jon Filewich RC 1.50 4.00
206 Robbie Earl RC 1.25 3.00
207 Ilya Zubov RC 1.50 4.00
208 Steve Mason RC 3.00 8.00
209 Brian Boyle RC 1.50 4.00
210 Shawn Matthias RC 2.00 5.00
211 Ryan Stone RC 1.25 3.00
212 Teddy Purcell RC 2.50 6.00
213 Mike Iggulden RC 1.50 4.00
214 Justin Abdelkader RC 3.00 8.00
215 Marc-Andre Gragnani RC 1.50 4.00
216 Jonathan Ericsson RC 2.00 5.00
217 Kyle Okposo RC 2.00 5.00
218 Kyle Turris RC 3.00 8.00
219 Brian Lee RC 1.50 4.00
220 Theo Peckham RC 2.00 5.00
221 Adam Pineault RC 1.50 4.00
222 Boris Valabik RC 2.00 5.00
223 Matt D'Agostini RC 1.50 4.00
224 Andrew Ebbett RC 1.25 3.00
225 Sami Lepisto RC 1.50 4.00
226 Mattias Ritola RC 1.50 4.00
227 Dan LaCosta RC 2.00 5.00
228 Danny Taylor RC 1.50 4.00
229 Cody McLeod RC 1.50 4.00
230 Corey Locke RC 1.50 4.00
231 Jordan Hendry RC 1.50 4.00
232 Mike Brown RC 2.50 6.00
233 B.J. Crombeen RC 1.25 3.00
234 David Brine RC 1.25 3.00
235 Joe Jensen RC 2.00 5.00
236 Kyle Greentree RC 2.00 5.00
237 Zack Fitzgerald RC 2.00 5.00
238 Clay Wilson RC 1.25 3.00
239 Alex Foster RC 1.50 4.00
240 Tom Cavanagh RC 1.50 4.00
241 Erik Ersberg RC 1.50 4.00
242 Tim Conboy RC 1.50 4.00
243 Jordan LaVallee RC 2.00 5.00
244 Mike Mole RC 1.50 4.00
245 Jesse Winchester RC 1.25 3.00
246 Garrett Stafford RC 2.00 5.00
247 Darryl Boyce RC 1.50 4.00
248 Chris Minard RC 2.00 5.00
249 Jack Hillen RC 1.50 4.00
250 Colin Stuart RC 1.50 4.00
251 Steven Stamkos RC 10.00 25.00
252 Fabian Brunnstrom RC 2.00 5.00
253 Jakub Voracek RC 5.00 12.00
254 Blake Wheeler RC 6.00 15.00
255 Brandon Sutter RC 2.50 6.00
256 Zach Boychuk RC 2.50 6.00
257 Alex Pietrangelo RC 3.00 8.00
258 Zach Bogosian RC 2.50 6.00
259 Drew Doughty RC 6.00 15.00
260 Luke Schenn RC 3.00 8.00
261 T.J. Oshie RC 5.00 12.00
262 Mikkel Boedker RC 3.00 8.00
263 Nikita Filatov RC 2.50 6.00
264 James Neal RC 5.00 12.00
265 Colton Gillies RC 2.00 5.00
266 Petr Vrana RC 1.50 4.00
267 Luca Sbisa RC 1.50 4.00
268 Patric Hornqvist RC 2.50 6.00
269 Andreas Nodl RC 1.50 4.00
270 Nikolai Kulemin RC 2.50 6.00
271 Michael Frolik RC 2.50 6.00

2008-09 Ultra Gold Medallion
*GOLD: 1X TO 2.5X BASE
*GOLD RCs: .6X TO 1.5X BASE RCs
*251-271 GOLD: .8X TO 2X BASE
STATED ODDS 1 PER PACK
98 Nicklas Backstrom 1.25 3.00

2008-09 Ultra Ice Medallion
*ICE: 4X TO 10X BASE
*ICE RCs: 1.5X TO 4X BASE
*ICE EXCH: .8X TO 2X BASE
STATED PRINT RUN 100 SERIAL #'d SETS
98 Nicklas Backstrom 5.00 12.00

2008-09 Ultra All-Star Royalty
COMPLETE SET (21) 25.00 60.00
OVERALL NON-AU/MEM ODDS 1:2
ASR1 Alexander Ovechkin 5.00 12.00
ASR2 Roberto Luongo 1.50 4.00
ASR3 Mats Sundin 1.25 3.00
ASR4 Vincent Lecavalier 1.00 2.50
ASR5 Martin St. Louis 1.25 3.00
ASR6 Joe Thornton 1.50 4.00
ASR7 Sidney Crosby 5.00 12.00
ASR8 Evgeni Malkin 4.00 10.00
ASR9 Dany Heatley 1.25 3.00
ASR10 Martin Brodeur 2.50 6.00
ASR11 Saku Koivu 1.25 3.00
ASR12 Marian Gaborik 1.50 4.00
ASR13 Anze Kopitar 2.00 5.00
ASR14 Nicklas Lidstrom 1.25 3.00
ASR15 Rick Nash 1.25 3.00
ASR16 Joe Sakic 2.00 5.00
ASR17 Eric Staal 1.50 4.00
ASR18 Miikka Kiprusoff 1.00 2.50
ASR19 Jarome Iginla 1.25 3.00
ASR20 Ilya Kovalchuk 1.25 3.00
ASR21 Ryan Getzlaf 2.00 5.00

2008-09 Ultra Difference Makers
COMPLETE SET 15.00 40.00
OVERALL NON-AU/MEM ODDS 1:2
DM1 Martin Brodeur 1.25 3.00
DM2 Alexander Ovechkin 2.50 6.00
DM3 Teemu Selanne 1.25 3.00
DM4 Paul Stastny .60 1.50
DM5 Nicklas Lidstrom .60 1.50
DM6 Ryan Miller .60 1.50
DM7 Joe Thornton .75 2.00
DM8 Peter Mueller .50 1.25
DM9 Miikka Kiprusoff .50 1.25
DM10 Martin St. Louis .60 1.50
DM11 Sidney Crosby 2.50 6.00
DM12 Patrick Kane 1.25 3.00
DM13 Jarome Iginla .60 1.50
DM14 Pavel Datsyuk .75 2.00
DM15 Peter Forsberg .75 2.00
DM16 Carey Price 2.50 6.00
DM17 Patrice Bergeron .75 2.00
DM18 Roberto Luongo .75 2.00
DM19 Evgeni Malkin 2.00 5.00
DM20 Mats Sundin .60 1.50

2008-09 Ultra EX Essential Credentials
COMPLETE SET 60.00 120.00
STATED ODDS 1:8
1 Alexander Ovechkin 5.00 12.00
2 Roberto Luongo 1.50 4.00
3 Mats Sundin 1.25 3.00
4 Vincent Lecavalier 1.00 2.50
5 Martin St. Louis 1.25 3.00
6 Paul Kariya 1.50 4.00
7 Joe Thornton 1.50 4.00
8 Sidney Crosby 5.00 12.00
9 Evgeni Malkin 4.00 10.00
10 Peter Mueller 1.00 2.50
11 Simon Gagne 1.25 3.00
12 Dany Heatley 1.25 3.00
13 Daniel Alfredsson 1.25 3.00
14 Jaromir Jagr 3.00 8.00
15 Brendan Shanahan 1.50 4.00
16 Martin Brodeur 2.50 6.00
17 Alexander Radulov 1.25 3.00
18 Carey Price 5.00 12.00
19 Saku Koivu 1.25 3.00
20 Marian Gaborik 1.50 4.00
21 Anze Kopitar 2.00 5.00
22 Tomas Vokoun 1.00 2.50
23 Sam Gagner 1.00 2.50
24 Henrik Zetterberg 1.50 4.00
25 Dominik Hasek 1.50 4.00
26 Nicklas Lidstrom 1.25 3.00
27 Mike Modano 2.00 5.00
28 Marty Turco 1.25 3.00
29 Rick Nash 1.25 3.00
30 Peter Forsberg 4.00 10.00
31 Joe Sakic 2.00 5.00
32 Paul Stastny 1.25 3.00
33 Patrick Kane 2.50 6.00
34 Jonathan Toews 3.00 8.00
35 Eric Staal 1.50 4.00
36 Jarome Iginla 1.25 3.00
37 Miikka Kiprusoff 1.00 2.50
38 Ryan Miller 1.25 3.00
39 Patrice Bergeron 1.50 4.00
40 Ilya Kovalchuk 1.25 3.00
41 Ryan Getzlaf 2.00 5.00
42 Teemu Selanne 2.50 6.00

2008-09 Ultra EX Essential Credentials Green
*GREEN: 1.2X TO 3X
1 Alexander Ovechkin/92 20.00 50.00
2 Roberto Luongo/99 6.00 15.00
3 Mats Sundin/87 5.00 12.00
4 Vincent Lecavalier/96 4.00 10.00
5 Martin St. Louis/74 5.00 12.00
6 Paul Kariya/91 6.00 15.00
7 Joe Thornton/81 6.00 15.00
9 Evgeni Malkin/29 15.00 40.00
11 Simon Gagne/88 5.00 12.00
12 Dany Heatley/85 5.00 12.00
13 Daniel Alfredsson/89 5.00 12.00
14 Jaromir Jagr/32 12.00 30.00
15 Brendan Shanahan/86 6.00 15.00
16 Martin Brodeur/70 10.00 25.00
17 Alexander Radulov/53 5.00 12.00
18 Carey Price/69 20.00 50.00
19 Saku Koivu/89 5.00 12.00
20 Marian Gaborik/90 6.00 15.00
21 Anze Kopitar/89 8.00 20.00
22 Tomas Vokoun/71 4.00 10.00
24 Henrik Zetterberg/60 6.00 15.00
25 Dominik Hasek/61 6.00 15.00
26 Nicklas Lidstrom/95 5.00 12.00
27 Mike Modano/91 8.00 20.00
28 Marty Turco/65 5.00 12.00
29 Rick Nash/39 5.00 12.00
30 Peter Forsberg/79 6.00 15.00
31 Joe Sakic/81 8.00 20.00
32 Paul Stastny/74 5.00 12.00
34 Jonathan Toews/81 12.00 30.00
35 Eric Staal/88 6.00 15.00
36 Jarome Iginla/88 5.00 12.00
37 Miikka Kiprusoff/66 4.00 10.00
38 Ryan Miller/70 5.00 12.00
39 Patrice Bergeron/63 6.00 15.00
40 Ilya Kovalchuk/83 5.00 12.00
41 Ryan Getzlaf/85 8.00 20.00
42 Teemu Selanne/92 10.00 25.00

2008-09 Ultra EX Essential Credentials Red
*RED: 1.2X TO 3X BASIC
5 Martin St. Louis/26 4.00 10.00
7 Joe Thornton/19 15.00 40.00
8 Sidney Crosby/87 15.00 40.00
9 Evgeni Malkin/71 12.00 30.00
10 Peter Mueller/88 3.00 8.00
14 Jaromir Jagr/68 10.00 25.00
16 Martin Brodeur/30 8.00 20.00
17 Alexander Radulov/47 4.00 10.00
18 Carey Price/31 15.00 40.00
22 Tomas Vokoun/29 3.00 8.00
23 Sam Gagner/89 3.00 8.00
24 Henrik Zetterberg/40 5.00 12.00
25 Dominik Hasek/39 5.00 12.00
28 Marty Turco/35 4.00 10.00
29 Rick Nash/61 4.00 10.00
30 Peter Forsberg/21 25.00 60.00
32 Paul Stastny/26 4.00 10.00
33 Patrick Kane/88 8.00 20.00
34 Jonathan Toews/19 25.00 60.00
37 Miikka Kiprusoff/34 3.00 8.00
38 Ryan Miller/30 4.00 10.00
39 Patrice Bergeron/37 5.00 12.00

2008-09 Ultra EX Jambalaya
STATED ODDS 1:864
JAM1 Wayne Gretzky
JAM2 Bobby Orr 60.00 120.00
JAM3 Gordie Howe 60.00 125.00
JAM4 Mark Messier 30.00 80.00
JAM5 Mario Lemieux 30.00 80.00
JAM6 Teemu Selanne 30.00 80.00
JAM7 Joe Sakic 25.00 60.00
JAM8 Mike Modano 25.00 60.00
JAM9 Sidney Crosby 75.00 150.00
JAM10 Alexander Ovechkin 50.00 100.00
JAM11 Evgeni Malkin 25.00 60.00
JAM12 Ilya Kovalchuk
JAM13 Vincent Lecavalier 12.00 30.00
JAM14 Jarome Iginla 30.00 80.00
JAM15 Marian Gaborik 20.00 50.00
JAM16 Dany Heatley
JAM17 Simon Gagne 15.00 40.00
JAM18 Jaromir Jagr 30.00 60.00
JAM19 Mats Sundin 15.00 40.00
JAM20 Jonathan Toews 50.00 100.00

2008-09 Ultra Franchise Players
COMPLETE SET (10) 10.00 25.00
OVERALL NON-AU/MEM ODDS 1:2
FP1 Jarome Iginla .60 1.50
FP2 Joe Thornton .75 2.00
FP3 Roberto Luongo .75 2.00
FP4 Patrick Kane 1.25 3.00
FP5 Joe Sakic 1.00 2.50
FP6 Martin Brodeur 1.25 3.00
FP7 Mats Sundin .60 1.50
FP8 Carey Price 2.50 6.00
FP9 Vincent Lecavalier .50 1.25
FP10 Sidney Crosby 2.50 6.00

2008-09 Ultra Fresh Ink
STATED ODDS 1:288
FIBB Brad Boyes 6.00 15.00
FIBD Brandon Dubinsky 10.00 25.00
FIBE Brendan Bell 5.00 12.00
FIBR Bobby Ryan 8.00 20.00
FICA Colby Armstrong 5.00 12.00
FICB Casey Borer 8.00 20.00
FICS Cory Stillman 5.00 12.00
FIDB David Booth 8.00 20.00
FIDM Drew Miller 6.00 15.00
FIDP Daniel Paille 8.00 20.00
FIEC Erik Christensen 5.00 12.00
FIES Eric Staal 40.00 80.00
FIFN Fredrik Norrena 8.00 20.00
FIGE Martin Gerber 6.00 15.00
FIHM Martin Havlat 5.00 12.00
FIHO Tomas Holmstrom 5.00 12.00
FIJH Jannik Hansen 6.00 15.00
FIJL John-Michael Liles 6.00 15.00
FIJO Joe Pavelski 5.00 12.00
FIJT Jiri Tlusty 15.00 40.00
FIJW Justin Williams 25.00 50.00
FIKC Kyle Calder 6.00 15.00
FIKN Mike Knuble 10.00 25.00
FIKQ Kyle Quincey 20.00 40.00
FIKY Kyle Chipchura 5.00 12.00
FILE Loui Eriksson 15.00 30.00
FIMI Michal Handzus 5.00 12.00
FIML Milan Lucic 20.00 40.00
FIMP Marc-Antoine Pouliot 8.00 20.00
FIMR Mason Raymond 40.00 80.00
FIMS Marek Schwarz 6.00 15.00
FIMT Maxime Talbot 8.00 20.00
FIND Nigel Dawes 6.00 15.00
FINI Nicklas Bergfors 6.00 15.00
FINW Noah Welch 5.00 12.00
FIPE Corey Perry 8.00 20.00
FIPH Chris Phillips 5.00 12.00
FIPK Patrick Kane 40.00 80.00
FIRC Ryane Clowe 12.00 30.00
FIRS Ryan Smyth 6.00 15.00
FISC Sidney Crosby 75.00 150.00
FISM Stefan Meyer 8.00 20.00
FISS Steve Sullivan 6.00 15.00
FISW Shea Weber 8.00 20.00
FITC Ty Conklin 8.00 20.00
FITE Tobias Enstrom 6.00 15.00
FITG Tom Gilbert 8.00 20.00
FITH Joe Thornton 6.00 15.00
FIVF Valtteri Filppula 8.00 20.00

2008-09 Ultra Oversized
COMPLETE SET (42) 40.00 100.00
TRU1 Ilya Kovalchuk 1.00 2.50
TRU2 Patrice Bergeron 1.25 3.00
TRU3 Ryan Miller 1.00 2.50
TRU4 Eric Staal 1.25 3.00
TRU5 Saku Koivu 1.00 2.50
TRU6 Carey Price 4.00 10.00
TRU7 Martin Brodeur 2.00 5.00
TRU8 Rick DiPietro .75 2.00
TRU9 Henrik Lundqvist 1.25 3.00
TRU10 Jason Spezza 1.00 2.50
TRU11 Dany Heatley 1.00 2.50
TRU12 Mike Richards 1.00 2.50
TRU13 Sidney Crosby 4.00 10.00
TRU14 Marc-Andre Fleury 1.50 4.00
TRU15 Evgeni Malkin 3.00 8.00
TRU16 Vincent Lecavalier .75 2.00
TRU17 Vesa Toskala .75 2.00
TRU18 Alexander Steen 1.00 2.50
TRU19 Alexander Ovechkin 4.00 10.00
TRU20 Ryan Getzlaf 1.50 4.00
TRU21 Jean-Sebastien Giguere 1.00 2.50
TRU22 Miikka Kiprusoff .75 2.00
TRU23 Jarome Iginla 1.00 2.50
TRU24 Patrick Kane 2.00 5.00
TRU25 Jonathan Toews 2.50 6.00
TRU26 Joe Sakic 1.50 4.00
TRU27 Peter Forsberg 1.25 3.00
TRU28 Rick Nash 1.00 2.50
TRU29 Marty Turco 1.00 2.50
TRU30 Mike Modano 1.50 4.00
TRU31 Nicklas Lidstrom 1.00 2.50
TRU32 Henrik Zetterberg 1.25 3.00
TRU33 Sam Gagner .75 2.00
TRU34 Andrew Cogliano .75 2.00
TRU35 Anze Kopitar 1.50 4.00
TRU36 Marian Gaborik 1.25 3.00
TRU37 Jason Arnott .75 2.00
TRU38 Peter Mueller .75 2.00
TRU39 Jonathan Cheechoo 1.00 2.50
TRU40 Joe Thornton 1.25 3.00
TRU41 Paul Kariya 1.25 3.00
TRU42 Roberto Luongo 1.25 3.00

2008-09 Ultra Rookie Sensations
COMPLETE SET (30) 40.00 100.00
OVERALL NON-AU/MEM ODDS 1:2
RS1 Jon Filewich 1.50 4.00
RS2 Alex Goligoski 2.50 6.00
RS3 Mark Fistric 1.50 4.00
RS4 Jonathan Ericsson 2.00 5.00
RS5 Marc-Andre Gragnani 1.50 4.00
RS6 Brian Lee 1.50 4.00
RS7 Theo Peckham 2.00 5.00
RS8 Ryan Stone 1.25 3.00
RS9 Adam Pineault 1.50 4.00
RS10 Boris Valabik 2.00 5.00
RS11 Darren Helm 2.00 5.00
RS12 Mike Iggulden 1.50 4.00
RS13 Niklas Hjalmarsson 3.00 8.00
RS14 Tom Sestito 2.00 5.00
RS15 Alex Foster 1.50 4.00
RS16 Tom Cavanagh 1.50 4.00
RS17 Jordan Hendry 1.50 4.00
RS18 Cody McLeod 1.50 4.00
RS19 Dan LaCosta 2.00 5.00
RS20 Justin Abdelkader 3.00 8.00
RS21 Steve Mason 3.00 8.00
RS22 Derick Brassard 1.50 4.00
RS23 Claude Giroux 4.00 10.00
RS24 Robbie Earl 1.25 3.00
RS25 Ilya Zubov 1.50 4.00
RS26 Brian Boyle 1.50 4.00
RS27 Shawn Matthias 2.00 5.00
RS28 Kyle Okposo 2.00 5.00
RS29 Kyle Turris 3.00 8.00
RS30 Tyler Plante 1.50 4.00

2008-09 Ultra Scoring Kings
COMPLETE SET (20) 12.00 30.00
OVERALL NON-AU/MEM ODDS 1:2
SK1 Sidney Crosby 2.50 6.00
SK2 Joe Thornton .75 2.00
SK3 Vincent Lecavalier .50 1.25
SK4 Jarome Iginla .60 1.50
SK5 Joe Sakic 1.00 2.50
SK6 Jaromir Jagr 1.50 4.00
SK7 Henrik Zetterberg .75 2.00
SK8 Daniel Alfredsson .60 1.50
SK9 Marc Savard .40 1.00
SK10 Henrik Sedin .60 1.50
SK11 Evgeni Malkin 2.00 5.00
SK12 Ilya Kovalchuk .60 1.50
SK13 Rick Nash .60 1.50
SK14 Marian Gaborik .75 2.00
SK15 Eric Staal .75 2.00
SK16 Mike Modano 1.00 2.50
SK17 Brendan Shanahan .75 2.00
SK18 Dany Heatley .60 1.50
SK19 Peter Forsberg .75 2.00
SK20 Alexander Ovechkin 2.50 6.00

2008-09 Ultra Season Crowns
COMPLETE SET (10) 6.00 15.00
OVERALL NON-AU/MEM ODDS 1:2
SC1 Alexander Ovechkin 3.00 8.00
SC2 Joe Thornton 1.00 2.50
SC3 Alexander Ovechkin 3.00 8.00
SC4 Evgeni Nabokov .60 1.50
SC5 Dan Ellis .50 1.25
SC6 Chris Osgood .75 2.00
SC7 Henrik Lundqvist 1.00 2.50
SC8 Pavel Datsyuk 1.00 2.50
SC9 Daniel Carcillo .50 1.25
SC10 Henrik Zetterberg 1.00 2.50

2008-09 Ultra Team Leaders
COMPLETE SET (30) 40.00 100.00
OVERALL NON-AU/MEM ODDS 1:2
TL1 Mike Richards 1.50 4.00
TL2 Rick DiPietro 1.25 3.00
TL3 Daniel Alfredsson 1.50 4.00
TL4 Carey Price 6.00 15.00
TL5 Marc Savard 1.00 2.50
TL6 Ryan Miller 1.50 4.00
TL7 Eric Staal 2.00 5.00
TL8 Ilya Kovalchuk 1.50 4.00
TL9 Tomas Vokoun 1.25 3.00
TL10 Henrik Zetterberg 2.00 5.00
TL11 J.P. Dumont 1.00 2.50
TL12 Rick Nash 1.50 4.00
TL13 Patrick Kane 3.00 8.00
TL14 Paul Kariya 2.00 5.00
TL15 Marian Gaborik 2.00 5.00
TL16 Ales Hemsky 1.25 3.00
TL17 Marty Turco 1.50 4.00
TL18 Jean-Sebastien Giguere 1.50 4.00
TL19 Shane Doan 1.25 3.00
TL20 Anze Kopitar 2.50 6.00
TL21 Martin Brodeur 3.00 8.00
TL22 Sidney Crosby 6.00 15.00
TL23 Jaromir Jagr 4.00 10.00
TL24 Mats Sundin 1.50 4.00
TL25 Alexander Ovechkin 6.00 15.00
TL26 Vincent Lecavalier 1.25 3.00
TL27 Jarome Iginla 1.50 4.00
TL28 Roberto Luongo 2.00 5.00
TL29 Paul Stastny 1.50 4.00
TL30 Joe Thornton 2.00 5.00

2008-09 Ultra Total D
COMPLETE SET (21) 25.00 60.00
OVERALL NON-AU/MEM ODDS 1:2
TD1 Jean-Sebastien Giguere 2.00 5.00
TD2 Kari Lehtonen 1.50 4.00
TD3 Ryan Miller 2.00 5.00
TD4 Miikka Kiprusoff 1.50 4.00
TD5 Cam Ward 2.00 5.00
TD6 Nikolai Khabibulin 2.00 5.00
TD7 Jose Theodore 2.00 5.00
TD8 Pascal Leclaire 1.50 4.00
TD9 Marty Turco 2.00 5.00
TD10 Vesa Toskala 1.50 4.00
TD11 Chris Osgood 2.00 5.00
TD12 Tomas Vokoun 1.50 4.00
TD13 Josh Harding 2.00 5.00
TD14 Carey Price 8.00 20.00
TD15 Martin Brodeur 4.00 10.00
TD16 Henrik Lundqvist 2.50 6.00
TD17 Martin Biron 1.50 4.00
TD18 Marc-Andre Fleury 3.00 8.00
TD19 Evgeni Nabokov 1.50 4.00
TD20 Manny Legace 2.00 5.00
TD21 Roberto Luongo 2.50 6.00

2008-09 Ultra Uniformity
STATED ODDS 1:12
UAAA Arron Asham 2.50 6.00
UAAE Alexander Edler 2.50 6.00
UAAK Alex Kovalev 3.00 8.00
UAAM Andrej Meszaros 2.50 6.00
UAAO Alexander Ovechkin/250* 15.00 40.00
UAAR Andrew Raycroft 3.00 8.00
UAAS Alexander Semin 4.00 10.00
UABB Brad Boyes 2.50 6.00
UABG Bill Guerin 4.00 10.00
UABJ Barret Jackman 2.50 6.00
UABM Brendan Morrison 2.50 6.00
UABO Brandon Bochenski 2.50 6.00
UABR Brad Richardson 3.00 8.00
UACA Colby Armstrong 2.50 6.00
UACC Carlo Colaiacovo 2.50 6.00
UACH Jonathan Cheechoo 4.00 10.00
UACJ Curtis Joseph 4.00 10.00
UACK Chuck Kobasew 2.50 6.00
UACM Matt Carle 2.50 6.00
UACS Cory Stillman 2.50 6.00
UACW Cam Ward 4.00 10.00
UADB Dustin Brown 4.00 10.00
UADO Donald Brashear 2.50 6.00
UADP Daniel Paille 2.50 6.00
UADS Daniel Sedin 4.00 10.00
UADT Darcy Tucker 3.00 8.00
UADV David Vyborny 2.50 6.00
UAEC Erik Cole 3.00 8.00
UAEJ Ed Jovanovski 3.00 8.00
UAEM Evgeni Malkin/250* 12.00 30.00
UAEN Evgeni Nabokov 3.00 8.00
UAES Eric Staal/250* 5.00 12.00
UAFP Fernando Pisani 2.50 6.00
UAGB Gilbert Brule 2.50 6.00
UAGE Martin Gerber 3.00 8.00
UAGI Brian Gionta 3.00 8.00
UAGM Glen Murray 3.00 8.00
UAHL Henrik Lundqvist 5.00 12.00
UAHS Henrik Sedin 4.00 10.00
UAHT Hannu Toivonen 3.00 8.00
UAIK Ilya Kovalchuk/250* 4.00 10.00
UAIW Ian White 2.50 6.00
UAJA Jason Arnott 3.00 8.00
UAJB Jay Bouwmeester 4.00 10.00
UAJC Jeff Carter
UAJI Jarome Iginla/250* 4.00 10.00
UAJJ Jaromir Jagr/250* 10.00 25.00
UAJL Jere Lehtinen 2.50 6.00
UAJO Erik Johnson 3.00 8.00
UAJP Joni Pitkanen 2.50 6.00
UAJR Jeremy Roenick 4.00 10.00
UAJS Joe Sakic/250* 6.00 15.00
UAJT Joe Thornton/250* 5.00 12.00
UAJU Jussi Jokinen 2.50 6.00
UAJW Justin Williams 3.00 8.00
UAKL Kari Lehtonen 3.00 8.00
UAKO Andrei Kostitsyn 3.00 8.00
UAKT Keith Tkachuk 4.00 10.00
UALE Kristopher Letang 4.00 10.00
UALS Lee Stempniak 2.50 6.00
UALU Joffrey Lupul 3.00 8.00
UAMA Martin Straka 2.50 6.00
UAMB Martin Brodeur/250* 8.00 20.00
UAMC Bryan McCabe 2.50 6.00
UAMF Manny Fernandez 3.00 8.00
UAMG Marian Gaborik 5.00 12.00
UAMI Milan Michalek 2.50 6.00
UAMK Mikko Koivu 3.00 8.00
UAML Manny Legace 4.00 10.00
UAMM Mike Modano 6.00 15.00
UAMN Markus Naslund 3.00 8.00
UAMO Brenden Morrow 3.00 8.00
UAMP Marc-Antoine Pouliot 2.50 6.00
UAMR Mark Recchi 5.00 12.00
UAMS Martin St. Louis 4.00 10.00
UAMT Marty Turco 4.00 10.00
UAMZ Marek Zidlicky 2.50 6.00
UANA Nikolai Antropov 3.00 8.00

JANL Nicklas Lidstrom 4.00 10.00
JANZ Nikolai Zherdev 2.50 6.00
JAOJ Olli Jokinen 3.00 8.00
JAON Owen Nolan 3.00 8.00
JAPB Patrice Bergeron 5.00 12.00
JAPD Pavol Demitra 5.00 12.00
JAPH Dion Phaneuf 4.00 10.00
JAPK Phil Kessel 5.00 12.00
JAPM Patrick Marleau 4.00 10.00
JARI Mike Richards 4.00 10.00
JARL Roberto Luongo 5.00 12.00
JARN Rick Nash 4.00 10.00
JARY Michael Ryder 2.50 6.00
JASA Miroslav Satan 4.00 10.00
JASC Sidney Crosby/250* 15.00 40.00
JASJ Jordan Staal 4.00 10.00
JASM Matt Stajan 3.00 8.00
JAST Drew Stafford 3.00 8.00
JASU Mats Sundin 4.00 10.00
JATH Jose Theodore 4.00 10.00
JATI Kimmo Timonen 2.50 6.00
JAWR Wade Redden 2.50 6.00

2009-10 Ultra

COMPLETE SET (250) 75.00 150.00
COMP.SET w/o SPS (200) 12.00 30.00
RC STATED ODDS 1:4
EXCH STATED ODDS 1:28
1 Ryan Getzlaf .50 1.25
2 Corey Perry .30 .75
3 Bobby Ryan .30 .75
4 Jonas Hiller .25 .60
5 Jean-Sebastien Giguere .30 .75
6 Ilya Kovalchuk .30 .75
7 Slava Kozlov .20 .50
8 Bryan Little .30 .75
9 Kari Lehtonen .25 .60
10 Marc Savard .20 .50
11 Patrice Bergeron .40 1.00
12 Tim Thomas .30 .75
13 David Krejci .30 .75
14 Phil Kessel .40 1.00
15 Blake Wheeler .30 .75
16 Thomas Vanek .30 .75
17 Derek Roy .25 .60
18 Ryan Miller .30 .75
19 Jason Pominville .30 .75
20 Drew Stafford .30 .75
21 Jarome Iginla .30 .75
22 Robyn Regehr .25 .60
23 Daymond Langkow .20 .50
24 Dion Phaneuf .40 1.00
25 Miikka Kiprusoff .25 .60
26 Olli Jokinen .25 .60
27 Ray Whitney .25 .60
28 Cam Ward .30 .75
29 Eric Staal .40 1.00
30 Rod Brind'Amour .30 .75
31 Patrick Kane .60 1.50
32 Kris Versteeg .30 .75
33 Jonathan Toews .60 1.50
34 Cristobal Huet .30 .75
35 Brian Campbell .25 .60
36 Patrick Sharp .30 .75
37 Ryan Smyth .25 .60
38 Peter Budaj .25 .60
39 Milan Hejduk .25 .60
40 Paul Stastny .30 .75
41 Wojtek Wolski .20 .50
42 Rick Nash .25 .60
43 Steve Mason .25 .60
44 Nikita Filatov .25 .60
45 Derick Brassard .30 .75
46 Jakub Voracek .30 .75
47 Brad Richards .30 .75
48 Loui Eriksson .25 .60
49 Mike Modano .50 1.25
50 James Neal .30 .75
51 Marty Turco .30 .75
52 Pavel Datsyuk .40 1.00
53 Dan Cleary .30 .75
54 Henrik Zetterberg .40 1.00
55 Nicklas Lidstrom .30 .75
56 Valtteri Filppula .30 .75
57 Ty Conklin .25 .60
58 Ales Hemsky .25 .60
59 Sheldon Souray .20 .50
60 Andrew Cogliano .25 .60
61 Ethan Moreau .20 .50
62 Sam Gagner .25 .60
63 David Booth .20 .50
64 Nathan Horton .30 .75
65 Craig Anderson .30 .75
66 Tomas Vokoun .25 .60
67 Michael Frolik .25 .60
68 Anze Kopitar .50 1.25
69 Dustin Brown .25 .60
70 Alexander Frolov .25 .60
71 Drew Doughty .40 1.00
72 Jonathan Quick .60 1.50
73 Mikko Koivu .30 .75
74 Niklas Backstrom .30 .75
75 Antti Miettinen .20 .50
76 Pierre-Marc Bouchard .30 .75
77 Andrew Brunette .20 .50
78 Andrei Markov .30 .75
79 Jaroslav Halak .30 .75
80 Andrei Kostitsyn .25 .60
81 Sergei Kostitsyn .20 .50
82 Carey Price 1.25 3.00
83 Tomas Plekanec .30 .75
84 J.P. Dumont .20 .50
85 Jason Arnott .25 .60
86 Pekka Rinne .40 1.00
87 Shea Weber .25 .60
88 Martin Brodeur .60 1.50
89 Zach Parise .30 .75
90 Patrik Elias .30 .75
91 Travis Zajac .25 .60
92 David Clarkson .25 .60
93 Doug Weight .30 .75
94 Kyle Okposo .30 .75
95 Rick DiPietro .25 .60
96 Josh Bailey .25 .60
97 Henrik Lundqvist .50 1.25
98 Brandon Dubinsky .25 .60
99 Chris Drury .25 .60
100 Nikolai Zherdev .20 .50
101 Scott Gomez .25 .60
102 Daniel Alfredsson .30 .75
103 Dany Heatley .30 .75
104 Jason Spezza .30 .75
105 Brian Elliott .25 .60
106 Jeff Carter .30 .75
107 Mike Richards .30 .75
108 Simon Gagne .30 .75
109 Daniel Carcillo .20 .50
110 Scott Hartnell .30 .75
111 Shane Doan .25 .60
112 Kyle Turris .30 .75
113 Peter Mueller .25 .60
114 Mikkel Boedker .20 .50
115 Ilya Bryzgalov .25 .60
116 Evgeni Malkin 1.00 2.50
117 Sidney Crosby 1.25 3.00
118 Jordan Staal .30 .75
119 Marc-Andre Fleury .50 1.25
120 Rob Scuderi .20 .50
121 Chris Kunitz .30 .75
122 Joe Thornton .30 .75
123 Patrick Marleau .30 .75
124 Evgeni Nabokov .25 .60
125 Devin Setoguchi .25 .60
126 Dan Boyle .25 .60
127 Brad Boyes .20 .50
128 Patrik Berglund .20 .50
129 David Perron .20 .50
130 David Backes .30 .75
131 T.J. Oshie .50 1.25
132 Martin St. Louis .30 .75
133 Vincent Lecavalier .25 .60
134 Vaclav Prospal .20 .50
135 Steven Stamkos .60 1.50
136 Luke Schenn .25 .60
137 Matt Stajan .25 .60
138 Justin Pogge .30 .75
139 Alexei Ponikarovsky .20 .50
140 Tomas Kaberle .20 .50
141 Pavol Demitra .40 1.00
142 Alexandre Burrows .30 .75
143 Willie Mitchell .20 .50
144 Roberto Luongo .40 1.00
145 Ryan Kesler .30 .75
146 Alexander Ovechkin 1.25 3.00
147 Nicklas Backstrom .50 1.25
148 Mike Green .30 .75
149 Alexander Semin .30 .75
150 Jose Theodore .30 .75
151 Simeon Varlamov .30 .75
152 David Steckel .20 .50
153 Steve Bernier .20 .50
154 Kyle Wellwood .25 .60
155 Mikhail Grabovski .30 .75
156 Niklas Hagman .20 .50
157 Ryan Malone .20 .50
158 Chris Mason .25 .60
159 Andy McDonald .25 .60
160 Joe Pavelski .30 .75
161 Brad Lukowich .20 .50
162 Sergei Gonchar .20 .50
163 Eric Godard .20 .50
164 Steven Reinprecht .20 .50
165 Keith Yandle .30 .75
166 Daniel Carcillo .20 .50
167 Riley Cote .20 .50
168 Filip Kuba .20 .50
169 Mike Fisher .20 .50
170 Sean Avery .25 .60
171 Nik Antropov .25 .60
172 Mark Streit .20 .50
173 Joey MacDonald .25 .60
174 Jamie Langenbrunner .20 .50
175 Scott Clemmensen .25 .60
176 Greg Zanon .20 .50
177 Ryan Suter .30 .75
178 Saku Koivu .30 .75
179 Alex Kovalev .30 .75
180 Brent Burns .40 1.00
181 Marian Gaborik .40 1.00
182 Jarret Stoll .25 .60
183 Jack Johnson .20 .50
184 Stephen Weiss .20 .50
185 Dustin Penner .20 .50
186 Shawn Horcoff .20 .50
187 Niklas Kronwall .25 .60
188 Tomas Holmstrom .25 .60
189 Brenden Morrow .25 .60
190 Mike Ribeiro .25 .60
191 Antoine Vermette .20 .50
192 Cody McLeod .20 .50
193 Patrick Sharp .30 .75
194 Erik Cole .25 .60
195 Rene Bourque .20 .50
196 Mike Cammalleri .25 .60
197 Tim Connolly .20 .50
198 Milan Lucic .25 .60
199 Todd White .20 .50
200 George Parros .20 .50
201 Alexander Sulzer RC 1.00 2.50
202 Andrew MacDonald RC 1.00 2.50
203 Antti Niemi RC 2.50 6.00
204 Artem Anisimov RC 1.50 4.00
205 Ben Lovejoy RC 1.50 4.00
206 Brandon Segal RC 1.25 3.00
207 Brian Salcido RC 1.25 3.00
208 Bryan Rodney RC 1.25 3.00
209 Byron Bitz RC 1.25 3.00
210 Cal O'Reilly RC 1.25 3.00
211 Chris Durno RC 1.25 3.00
212 David Schlemko RC 1.25 3.00
213 David Van Der Gulik RC 1.25 3.00
214 Davis Drewiske RC 1.50 4.00
215 Derek Peltier RC 1.00 2.50
216 Grant Lewis RC 1.25 3.00
217 Jakub Petruzalek RC 1.50 4.00
218 Jaime Sifers RC 1.25 3.00
219 Jay Beagle RC 2.00 5.00
220 Jesse Joensuu RC 1.25 3.00
221 Jhonas Enroth RC 2.00 5.00
222 Joel Rechlicz RC 1.00 2.50
223 John Scott RC 1.50 4.00
224 Kevin Quick RC 1.00 2.50
225 Kevin Westgarth RC 1.25 3.00
226 Kris Chucko RC 1.25 3.00
227 Kurtis McLean RC 1.25 3.00
228 Luca Caputi RC 1.50 4.00
229 Matt Beleskey RC 1.25 3.00
230 Matt Hendricks RC 1.25 3.00
231 Michael Vernace RC 1.25 3.00
232 Michal Neuvirth RC 2.50 6.00
233 Mikael Backlund RC 1.50 4.00
234 Mike McKenna RC 1.25 3.00
235 Mike Santorelli RC 1.50 4.00
236 Peter Regin RC 1.25 3.00
237 Phil Oreskovic RC 1.50 4.00
238 Riku Helenius RC 1.50 4.00
239 Riley Armstrong RC 1.25 3.00
240 Ryan Vesce RC 1.25 3.00
241 Scott Lehman RC 1.00 2.50
242 Christian Hanson RC 1.50 4.00
243 Spencer Machacek RC 1.50 4.00
244 T.J. Galiardi RC 1.50 4.00
245 Tim Stapleton RC 1.50 4.00
246 Tim Wallace RC 1.00 2.50
247 Tom Wandell RC 1.50 4.00
248 Troy Bodie RC 1.25 3.00
249 Ville Leino RC 1.25 3.00
250 Yannick Weber RC 1.50 4.00
251 John Tavares RC 12.00 30.00
252 Matt Duchene RC 10.00 25.00
253 Victor Hedman RC 5.00 12.00
254 Evander Kane RC 5.00 12.00
255 James van Riemsdyk RC 5.00 12.00
256 Jonas Gustavsson RC 3.00 8.00
257 Jamie Benn RC 8.00 20.00
258 Erik Karlsson RC 8.00 20.00
259 Tyler Myers RC 4.00 10.00
260 Ryan O'Reilly RC 4.00 10.00
261 Matt Gilroy RC 2.50 6.00
262 Michael Del Zotto RC 2.50 6.00
263 Viktor Stalberg RC 2.50 6.00
264 Tyler Bozak RC 4.00 10.00
265 Sergei Shirokov RC 1.50 4.00
266 Colin Wilson RC 2.50 6.00
267 Benn Ferriero RC 2.50 6.00
268 Michael Grabner RC 2.50 6.00
269 Dmitry Kulikov RC 2.50 6.00
270 Cody Franson RC 2.50 6.00

2009-10 Ultra Gold Medallion

COMP.SET w/o SPs (200) 40.00 100.00
*GOLD: 1X TO 2.5X BASIC CARDS
OVERALL GOLD MED ODDS 1 PER PACK
*GOLD ROOKIE 201-250: .6X TO 1.5X
201-250 ROOKIE ODDS 1:8
*GOLD ROOKIE 251-270: .6X TO 1.5X
251-270 EXCH ODDS 1:288
147 Nicklas Backstrom 1.25 3.00
251 John Tavares 60.00 120.00
252 Matt Duchene 20.00 50.00
259 Tyler Myers 6.00 15.00
262 Michael Del Zotto 12.00 30.00
263 Viktor Stalberg 4.00 10.00

2009-10 Ultra Ice Medallion

*1-200 ICE VETS: 3X TO 8X BASIC CARDS
*201-250 ICE ROOKIES: 1.5X TO 4X BASE RC
1-250 STATED PRINT RUN 100
*251-270 ICE ROOKIES: 1.5X TO 4X BASE RC
ICE EXCH PRINT RUN 25
147 Nicklas Backstrom 4.00 10.00

2009-10 Ultra Crowning Achievements

COMPLETE SET (10) 10.00 25.00
STATED ODDS 1:4
CA1 Steve Mason .60 1.50
CA2 Alexander Ovechkin 3.00 8.00
CA3 Sidney Crosby 3.00 8.00
CA4 Mike Green .75 2.00
CA5 Doug Weight .75 2.00
CA6 Keith Tkachuk .75 2.00
CA7 Eric Staal 1.00 2.50
CA8 Martin Brodeur 1.50 4.00
CA9 Jonas Hiller .60 1.50
CA10 Tim Thomas .75 2.00

2009-10 Ultra EX Hockey

COMPLETE SET (42) 40.00 100.00
STATED ODDS 1:8
EX1 Ryan Getzlaf 2.00 5.00
EX2 Ilya Kovalchuk 1.25 3.00
EX3 Phil Kessel 1.50 4.00
EX4 Thomas Vanek 1.25 3.00
EX5 Ryan Miller 1.25 3.00
EX6 Jarome Iginla 1.25 3.00
EX7 Miikka Kiprusoff 1.00 2.50
EX8 Eric Staal 1.50 4.00
EX9 Jonathan Toews 2.50 6.00
EX10 Patrick Kane 2.50 6.00
EX11 Joe Sakic 2.00 5.00
EX12 Paul Stastny 1.25 3.00
EX13 Rick Nash 1.00 2.50
EX14 Steve Mason 1.00 2.50
EX15 Mike Modano 2.00 5.00
EX16 Henrik Zetterberg 1.50 4.00
EX17 Pavel Datsyuk 1.50 4.00
EX18 Andrew Cogliano 1.00 2.50
EX19 Tomas Vokoun 1.00 2.50
EX20 Anze Kopitar 2.00 5.00
EX21 Drew Doughty 1.50 4.00
EX22 Marian Gaborik 1.50 4.00
EX23 Carey Price 5.00 12.00
EX24 Saku Koivu 1.25 3.00
EX25 Martin Brodeur 2.50 6.00
EX26 Zach Parise 1.25 3.00
EX27 Henrik Lundqvist 2.00 5.00
EX28 Jason Spezza 1.25 3.00
EX29 Mike Richards 1.25 3.00
EX30 Jeff Carter 1.25 3.00
EX31 Peter Mueller 1.00 2.50
EX32 Sidney Crosby 5.00 12.00
EX33 Evgeni Malkin 4.00 10.00
EX34 Joe Thornton 1.25 3.00
EX35 Patrick Marleau 1.25 3.00
EX36 Paul Kariya 1.50 4.00
EX37 Vincent Lecavalier 1.00 2.50
EX38 Martin St. Louis 1.25 3.00
EX39 Luke Schenn 1.00 2.50
EX40 Roberto Luongo 1.50 4.00
EX41 Alexander Ovechkin 5.00 12.00
EX42 Mike Green 1.25 3.00

2009-10 Ultra EX Hockey Jambalaya

STATED ODDS 1:288
JAM1 Alexander Ovechkin 60.00 150.00
JAM2 Roberto Luongo 20.00 50.00
JAM3 Vincent Lecavalier 15.00 40.00
JAM4 Patrick Marleau 20.00 50.00
JAM5 Evgeni Malkin 50.00 125.00
JAM6 Mario Lemieux 60.00 150.00
JAM7 Sidney Crosby 80.00 200.00
JAM8 Henrik Lundqvist 30.00 80.00
JAM9 Martin Brodeur 30.00 80.00
JAM10 Carey Price 60.00 150.00
JAM11 Patrick Roy 30.00 80.00
JAM12 Mark Messier 20.00 50.00
JAM13 Gordie Howe 50.00 125.00
JAM14 Henrik Zetterberg 25.00 60.00
JAM15 Joe Sakic 30.00 80.00
JAM16 Jonathan Toews 40.00 100.00
JAM17 Patrick Kane 40.00 100.00
JAM18 Jarome Iginla 20.00 50.00
JAM19 Bobby Orr 60.00 150.00
JAM20 Ilya Kovalchuk 20.00 50.00

2009-10 Ultra Fresh Ink

STATED ODDS 1:288
FIAC Andrew Cogliano 5.00 12.00
FIBA Josh Bailey 5.00 12.00
FIBL Brian Lee 6.00 15.00
FIBM Ben Maxwell 5.00 12.00
FIBS Brandon Sutter
FIBW Blake Wheeler 6.00 15.00
FICB Casey Borer
FICG Colton Gillies 6.00 15.00
FICK Chris Kunitz 6.00 15.00
FICL David Clarkson 5.00 12.00
FICP Carey Price
FICS Chris Stewart 5.00 12.00
FIDC Dan Cleary 6.00 15.00
FIDD Drew Doughty
FIDH Dany Heatley
FIDJ David Jones
FIDP Dion Phaneuf 8.00 20.00
FIDS Daniel Sedin
FIDU Dustin Penner 4.00 10.00
FIGR Mike Green 25.00 60.00
FIHL Henrik Lundqvist
FIHS Henrik Sedin
FIIK Ilya Kovalchuk 12.00 30.00
FIJD J.P. Dumont
FIJI Jarome Iginla
FIJN James Neal 12.00 30.00
FIJP Justin Pogge 6.00 15.00
FIJS Jack Skille 4.00 10.00
FIJT Joe Thornton
FIKA Karl Alzner 4.00 10.00
FIKE Tim Kennedy 5.00 12.00
FIKM Kenndal McArdle
FIKV Kris Versteeg 30.00 60.00
FILS Luke Schenn
FIMB Mikkel Boedker
FIMG Marian Gaborik
FIMP Max Pacioretty 8.00 20.00
FINF Nikita Filatov 5.00 12.00
FING Nathan Gerbe 5.00 12.00
FIPB Patrik Berglund 4.00 10.00
FIPD Pavel Datsyuk
FIPE Patrik Elias
FISB Steve Bernier 5.00 12.00
FISC Cory Schneider 20.00 50.00
FISG Simon Gagne
FISM Steve Mason
FISS Steven Stamkos 25.00 50.00
FISV Simeon Varlamov
FITK Tyler Kennedy 12.00 30.00
FITL Trevor Lewis 5.00 12.00
FITO T.J. Oshie 10.00 25.00
FITP Tomas Plihal
FITW Ty Wishart 5.00 12.00
FIVT Viktor Tikhonov 5.00 12.00
FIZB Zach Bogosian 5.00 12.00

2009-10 Ultra Go To Players

COMPLETE SET (5) 10.00 25.00
STATED ODDS 1:4
GT1 Alexander Ovechkin 3.00 8.00
GT2 Henrik Zetterberg 1.00 2.50
GT3 Ilya Kovalchuk .75 2.00
GT4 Sidney Crosby 3.00 8.00
GT5 Jonathan Toews 1.50 4.00

2009-10 Ultra Rookie Sensations

COMPLETE SET (30) 40.00 100.00
STATED ODDS 1:4
RS1 Alex Goligoski .60 1.50
RS2 Alex Pietrangelo .60 1.50
RS3 Blake Wheeler SP 1.50 4.00
RS4 Bobby Ryan SP 1.50 4.00
RS5 Brandon Sutter .60 1.50
RS6 Claude Giroux .75 2.00
RS7 Cody McLeod .50 1.25
RS8 Colton Gillies .75 2.00
RS9 Derick Brassard SP 1.50 4.00
RS10 Drew Doughty SP 4.00 10.00
RS11 Fabian Brunnstrom .60 1.50
RS12 Jakub Voracek .75 2.00
RS13 James Neal .75 2.00
RS14 Josh Bailey .60 1.50
RS15 Justin Pogge SP 1.50 4.00
RS16 Kris Versteeg SP 1.50 4.00
RS17 Kyle Okposo .75 2.00
RS18 Kyle Turris .75 2.00
RS19 Luke Schenn SP 1.25 3.00
RS20 Max Pacioretty 1.00 2.50
RS21 Michael Frolik .60 1.50
RS22 Mikkel Boedker SP 3.00 8.00
RS23 Nikita Filatov .60 1.50
RS24 Nikolai Kulemin .60 1.50
RS25 Patrik Berglund .50 1.25
RS26 Shawn Matthias .75 2.00
RS27 Steve Mason SP 1.25 3.00
RS28 Steven Stamkos SP 3.00 8.00
RS29 T.J. Oshie 1.25 3.00
RS30 Zach Bogosian .60 1.50

2009-10 Ultra Scoring Kings

COMPLETE SET (10) 12.00 30.00
STATED ODDS 1:4
SK1 Alexander Ovechkin 3.00 8.00
SK2 Martin St. Louis .75 2.00
SK3 Joe Thornton .75 2.00
SK4 Sidney Crosby 3.00 8.00
SK5 Evgeni Malkin 2.50 6.00
SK6 Zach Parise .75 2.00
SK7 Pavel Datsyuk 1.00 2.50
SK8 Jarome Iginla .75 2.00
SK9 Ilya Kovalchuk .75 2.00
SK10 Ryan Getzlaf 1.25 3.00

2009-10 Ultra Team Leaders

COMPLETE SET (30) 20.00 50.00
STATED ODDS 1:4
TL1 Ryan Getzlaf 1.25 3.00
TL2 Ilya Kovalchuk .75 2.00
TL3 Tim Thomas SP 1.25 3.00
TL4 Derek Roy .60 1.50
TL5 Jarome Iginla SP 1.25 3.00
TL6 Ray Whitney .60 1.50
TL7 Jonathan Toews SP 2.50 6.00
TL8 Ryan Smyth .60 1.50
TL9 Rick Nash .60 1.50
TL10 Steve Ott .50 1.25
TL11 Pavel Datsyuk SP 1.50 4.00
TL12 Ales Hemsky SP 1.00 2.50
TL13 David Booth .50 1.25
TL14 Anze Kopitar 1.25 3.00
TL15 Mikko Koivu .75 2.00
TL16 Alex Kovalev SP 1.25 3.00
TL17 J.P. Dumont .50 1.25
TL18 Zach Parise .75 2.00
TL19 Mark Streit .50 1.25
TL20 Henrik Lundqvist SP 2.00 5.00
TL21 Daniel Alfredsson .75 2.00
TL22 Jeff Carter SP 1.25 3.00
TL23 Shane Doan .60 1.50
TL24 Evgeni Malkin SP 4.00 10.00
TL25 Joe Thornton .75 2.00
TL26 David Backes .75 2.00
TL27 Martin St. Louis .75 2.00
TL28 Jason Blake .50 1.25
TL29 Roberto Luongo SP 1.50 4.00
TL30 Alexander Ovechkin 3.00 8.00

2009-10 Ultra Total O

COMPLETE SET (5) 6.00 15.00
STATED ODDS 1:4
TO1 Sidney Crosby 3.00 8.00
TO2 Alexander Ovechkin 3.00 8.00
TO3 Evgeni Malkin 2.50 6.00
TO4 Vincent Lecavalier .60 1.50
TO5 Pavel Datsyuk 1.00 2.50

2009-10 Ultra Uniformity

STATED ODDS 1:12
UUAF Adam Foote 3.00 8.00
UUAH Adam Hall 3.00 8.00
UUAK Alex Kovalev 5.00 12.00
UUAN Anze Kopitar 8.00 20.00
UUAO Alexander Ovechkin 20.00 50.00
UUAS Alexander Steen 5.00 12.00
UUBL Bryan Little 5.00 12.00
UUBR Dustin Brown 4.00 10.00
UUCP Carey Price 20.00 50.00
UUCS Cory Stillman 4.00 10.00
UUDB David Booth 3.00 8.00
UUDC David Clarkson 4.00 10.00
UUDD Drew Doughty 6.00 15.00
UUDM Dominic Moore 5.00 12.00
UUDP David Perron 3.00 8.00
UUDR Derek Roy 4.00 10.00
UUDS Drew Stafford 5.00 12.00
UUDT Darcy Tucker 4.00 10.00
UUEC Erik Cole 4.00 10.00
UUEM Evgeni Malkin 15.00 40.00
UUES Eric Staal 6.00 15.00
UUFL Marc-Andre Fleury 8.00 20.00
UUIK Ilya Kovalchuk 5.00 12.00
UUJB Jay Bouwmeester 5.00 12.00
UUJC Jonathan Cheechoo 5.00 12.00
UUJG Jean-Sebastien Giguere 5.00 12.00
UUJL Joffrey Lupul 4.00 10.00
UUJN James Neal 5.00 12.00
UUJP Jason Pominville 5.00 12.00
UUJS Jason Spezza 5.00 12.00
UUKL Kari Lehtonen 4.00 10.00
UUKO Andrei Kostitsyn 4.00 10.00
UULE Kristopher Letang 5.00 12.00
UUMF Manny Fernandez 4.00 10.00
UUMG Marian Gaborik 6.00 15.00
UUMI Ryan Miller 5.00 12.00
UUMM Mike Modano 8.00 20.00
UUMP Marc-Antoine Pouliot 4.00 10.00
UUMR Michael Ryder 3.00 8.00
UUMS Marc Savard 3.00 8.00
UUMU Peter Mueller 4.00 10.00
UUNA Nik Antropov 4.00 10.00
UUNB Nicklas Backstrom 8.00 20.00
UUNL Nicklas Lidstrom 5.00 12.00
UUPM Patrick Marleau 5.00 12.00
UUPO Patrick O'Sullivan 4.00 10.00
UUPR Chris Pronger 4.00 10.00
UURD Rick DiPietro 4.00 10.00
UURI Mike Richards 5.00 12.00
UURL Roberto Luongo 6.00 15.00
UURM Ryan Malone 3.00 8.00
UURN Rick Nash 4.00 10.00
UUSC Sidney Crosby 20.00 50.00
UUSD Shane Doan 4.00 10.00
UUSG Sam Gagner 4.00 10.00
UUSK Saku Koivu 5.00 12.00
UUST Marc Staal 5.00 12.00
UUSV Marek Svatos 3.00 8.00
UUSW Shea Weber 4.00 10.00

2014-15 Ultra

COMP.SET w/o SP's (200) 30.00 60.00
ROOKIE EXCH ODDS 1:18 HOB
*ROOKIE EXCH: .4X TO 1X RC
1 John Gibson .50 1.25
2 Cam Fowler .30 .75
3 Sami Vatanen .25 .60
4 Andrew Cogliano .25 .60
5A Ryan Getzlaf .60 1.50
5B R.Getzlaf SP org 10.00 25.00
6 Corey Perry .40 1.00
7A Hampus Lindholm .30 .75
7B H.Lindholm SP org 5.00 12.00
8 Daniel Paille .25 .60
9 David Krejci .40 1.00
10 Zdeno Chara .40 1.00
11 Brad Marchand .50 1.25
12 Torey Krug .40 1.00
13 Milan Lucic .40 1.00
14 Patrice Bergeron .50 1.25
15 Reilly Smith .40 1.00
16 Tuukka Rask .40 1.00
17 Michal Neuvirth .30 .75
18 Cody Hodgson .40 1.00
19 Tyler Ennis .30 .75
20 Johnny Gaudreau RC 2.50 6.00
21 Karri Ramo .30 .75
22 Jiri Hudler .30 .75
23 Sean Monahan .40 1.00
24 Alexander Semin .40 1.00
25 Cam Ward .40 1.00
26 Jeff Skinner .40 1.00
27 Eric Staal .50 1.25
28 Teuvo Teravainen RC 1.25 3.00
29 Antti Raanta .40 1.00
30 Brandon Saad .40 1.00
31 Marian Hossa .30 .75
32 Brent Seabrook .40 1.00
33 Andrew Shaw .40 1.00
34A Patrick Kane .75 2.00
34B P.Kane SP blk 12.00 30.00
35 Duncan Keith .40 1.00
36 Corey Crawford .50 1.25
37A Patrick Sharp .40 1.00
37B P.Sharp SP blk 6.00 15.00
38A Jonathan Toews .75 2.00
38B J.Toews SP blk 15.00 30.00
39 Ryan O'Reilly .40 1.00
40 Nathan MacKinnon .75 2.00
41 Semyon Varlamov .40 1.00
42 Jean-Sebastien Giguere .30 .75
43 Erik Johnson .25 .60
44 Matt Duchene .40 1.00
45 Gabriel Landeskog .30 .75
46 Ryan Johansen .50 1.25
47 Jack Johnson .25 .60
48 Sergei Bobrovsky .40 1.00
49 Cody Eakin .25 .60
50 Shawn Horcoff .25 .60
51 Jack Campbell .50 1.25
52 Kari Lehtonen .30 .75
53 Vernon Fiddler .25 .60
54 Rich Peverley .40 1.00
55 Tyler Seguin .60 1.50
56 Valeri Nichushkin .30 .75
57 Jamie Benn .50 1.25
58 Justin Abdelkader .30 .75
59 Petr Mrazek .40 1.00
60 Gustav Nyquist .30 .75
61 Darren Helm .30 .75
62 Jim Howard .40 1.00
63 Niklas Kronwall .30 .75
64A Henrik Zetterberg .50 1.25
64B H.Zetterberg SP 8.00 20.00
65 Johan Franzen .40 1.00
66 Daniel Alfredsson .40 1.00
67A Pavel Datsyuk .50 1.25
67B P.Datsyuk SP 8.00 20.00
68 Ben Scrivens .30 .75
69 Oscar Klefbom RC 1.50 4.00
70 David Perron .25 .60
71 Viktor Fasth .30 .75
72 Nail Yakupov .30 .75
73 Taylor Hall .75 2.00
74 Jordan Eberle .40 1.00
75 Ryan Nugent-Hopkins .40 1.00
76 Tomas Fleischmann .25 .60
77 Jonathan Huberdeau .40 1.00
78 Roberto Luongo .40 1.00
79 Justin Williams .30 .75
80 Mike Richards .40 1.00
81 Slava Voynov .40 1.00
82A Dustin Brown .30 .75
82B Dustin Brown SP 5.00 12.00
(Grey Jersey)
83 Marian Gaborik .40 1.00
84A Jonathan Quick .60 1.50
84B J.Quick SP 10.00 25.00
85 Drew Doughty .40 1.00
86A Anze Kopitar .60 1.50
86B A.Kopitar SP 10.00 25.00
87 Jeff Carter .40 1.00
88 Darcy Kuemper .30 .75
89 Mikael Granlund .30 .75
90 Erik Haula .30 .75
91 Jason Pominville .30 .75
92 Zach Parise .40 1.00
93 Mikko Koivu .30 .75
94 Ryan Suter .40 1.00
95 Nino Niederreiter .25 .60
96 David Desharnais .40 1.00
97 Tomas Plekanec .40 1.00
98 Andrei Markov .40 1.00
99 P.K. Subban .60 1.50
100 Carey Price 1.25 3.00
101 Alex Galchenyuk .60 1.50
102 Max Pacioretty .40 1.00
103 Seth Jones .30 .75
104 Mike Fisher .30 .75
105 Shea Weber .30 .75
106 Pekka Rinne .50 1.25
107 Marek Zidlicky .25 .60
108A Jaromir Jagr 1.00 2.50
108B J.Jagr SP 15.00 40.00
109 Patrik Elias .40 1.00
110 Adam Henrique .40 1.00
111 Cory Schneider .30 .75
112A Martin Brodeur .75 2.00
112B M.Brodeur SP 12.00 30.00
113 Ryan Strome .30 .75
114A Kyle Okposo .40 1.00
114B K.Okposo SP 6.00 15.00
115A John Tavares .75 2.00
115B J.Tavares SP 12.00 30.00
116A Chris Kreider .40 1.00
116B C.Kreider SP 6.00 15.00
117 Ryan McDonagh .40 1.00
118A Derek Stepan .40 1.00
118B D.Stepan SP 6.00 15.00
119A Rick Nash .40 1.00
119B R.Nash SP 6.00 15.00
120 Henrik Lundqvist .50 1.25
121A Mats Zuccarello .40 1.00
121B M.Zuccarello SP 8.00 20.00
122 Martin St. Louis .40 1.00
123 Kyle Turris .40 1.00
124 Mika Zibanejad .40 1.00
125 Clarke MacArthur .25 .60
126 Bobby Ryan .40 1.00
127A Cody Ceci .25 .60
127B C.Ceci SP 4.00 10.00
128A Craig Anderson .40 1.00
128B C.Anderson SP 6.00 15.00
129A Erik Karlsson .75 2.00
129B E.Karlsson SP 12.00 30.00
130 Brayden Schenn .40 1.00
131 Wayne Simmonds .50 1.25
132 Jakub Voracek .40 1.00
133 Steve Mason .30 .75
134 Matt Read .25 .60
135 Andrew MacDonald .25 .60
136 Claude Giroux .40 1.00
137 Vincent Lecavalier .30 .75
138 Oliver Ekman-Larsson .30 .75
139 Mike Smith .40 1.00
140 Keith Yandle .40 1.00
141 Martin Hanzal .25 .60
142 Antoine Vermette .25 .60
143 Brandon Gormley RC .75 2.00
144 Shane Doan .30 .75
145 Mark Visentin RC .75 2.00
146 Olli Maatta .40 1.00
147 Paul Martin .25 .60
148 Pascal Dupuis .25 .60
149A Evgeni Malkin 1.25 3.00
149B E.Malkin SP 20.00 50.00
150 Chris Kunitz .40 1.00
151 Marc-Andre Fleury .60 1.50
152 Kris Letang .40 1.00
153A Sidney Crosby 1.50 4.00
153B S.Crosby SP 25.00 60.00
154 Joe Pavelski .40 1.00
155 Tomas Hertl .40 1.00
156 Marc-Edouard Vlasic .25 .60
157 Patrick Marleau .40 1.00
158 Joe Thornton .40 1.00
159 Logan Couture .40 1.00
160 Antti Niemi .30 .75
161 T.J. Oshie .60 1.50
162 Jay Bouwmeester .40 1.00
163 Brian Elliott .30 .75
164 Patrik Berglund .25 .60
165 Kevin Shattenkirk .40 1.00
166 Ty Rattie RC 1.00 2.50
167 Alexander Steen .40 1.00
168 David Backes .40 1.00
169 Alex Pietrangelo .30 .75
170 Vladimir Tarasenko .60 1.50
171 Vladislav Namestnikov RC 1.25 3.00
172 Ben Bishop .40 1.00
173 Victor Hedman .50 1.25
174 Ondrej Palat .30 .75
175 Steven Stamkos .75 2.00
176 Ryan Callahan .40 1.00
177 Dion Phaneuf .40 1.00
178 Greg McKegg RC .60 1.50
179 Colton Orr .25 .60
180A James van Riemsdyk .40 1.00
180B J.Riemsdyk SP 6.00 15.00
181 Nazem Kadri .40 1.00
182 Phil Kessel .50 1.25
183A Jonathan Bernier .40 1.00
183B J.Bernier SP 6.00 15.00
184 Alexander Edler .25 .60
185 Alexandre Burrows .40 1.00
186A Eddie Lack .30 .75
186B E.Lack SP 5.00 12.00
187 Daniel Sedin .40 1.00
188 Henrik Sedin .40 1.00
189A Zack Kassian .30 .75
189B Z.Kassian SP 5.00 12.00
190 Joel Ward .25 .60
191 Evgeny Kuznetsov RC 8.00 20.00
192 Mike Green .40 1.00
193 Braden Holtby .60 1.50
194 Nicklas Backstrom .60 1.50
195 Alexander Ovechkin 1.50 4.00
196 Blake Wheeler .40 1.00
197 Bryan Little .40 1.00
198 Ondrej Pavelec .40 1.00
199 Andrew Ladd .40 1.00
200 Dustin Byfuglien .40 1.00
201 Jonathan Drouin RC 6.00 15.00
202 Aaron Ekblad RC 6.00 15.00
203 Sam Reinhart RC 8.00 20.00
204 Leon Draisaitl RC 12.00 30.00
205 Bo Horvat RC 8.00 20.00
206 Andre Burakovsky RC 4.00 10.00
207 Anthony Duclair RC 4.00 10.00
208 Curtis Lazar RC 3.00 8.00
209 Seth Griffith RC 3.00 8.00
210 Alexander Wennberg RC 5.00 12.00
211 Jiri Sekac RC 2.50 6.00
212 Damon Severson RC 2.50 6.00
213 Griffin Reinhart RC 3.00 8.00
214 Darnell Nurse RC 8.00 20.00
215 Marko Dano RC 2.50 6.00
216 Stuart Percy RC 2.50 6.00
217 Shayne Gostisbehere RC 10.00 25.00
218 Adam Lowry RC 2.50 6.00
219 Teemu Pulkkinen RC 3.00 8.00
220 Brandon Kozun RC 2.00 5.00
221 Joni Lehtera RC 3.00 8.00
222 David Pastrnak RC 6.00 15.00
223 Victor Rask RC 2.50 6.00
224 William Karlsson RC 10.00 25.00
225 Chris Tierney RC 2.50 6.00
226 Mirco Mueller RC 2.50 6.00
227 Josh Jooris RC 2.50 6.00
228 Kevin Hayes RC 8.00 20.00
229 Tobias Rieder RC 2.50 6.00
230 Trevor van Riemsdyk RC 4.00 10.00

2014-15 Ultra Gold Medallion

*VETS: .5X TO 1.2X BASIC CARDS
*ROOKIES: .5X TO 1.2X BASIC CARDS
*ROOKIE RED: .5X TO 1.2X BASIC CARDS
STATED ODDS 1:2 HOBBY
ROOK. RED. STATED ODDS 1:96 HOB
36 Corey Crawford .60 1.50
194 Nicklas Backstrom .75 2.00

2014-15 Ultra Platinum Medallion

*VETS/99: 3X TO 8X BASIC CARDS
*ROOKIES/99: .2X TO 5X BASIC CARDS
*ROOKIE RED/25: 1.2X TO 3X BASIC CARDS
ROOKIE RED ODDS 1:880 HOB
36 Corey Crawford 4.00 10.00
40 Nathan MacKinnon 20.00 40.00
194 Nicklas Backstrom 5.00 12.00

2014-15 Ultra Violet

EX1 Veteran Redemption Card 50.00 100.00
EX2 Rookie Redemption Card 100.00 200.00

2014-15 Ultra Buckets

STATED ODDS 1:9 HOBBY
BB1 Ryan Getzlaf 2.50 6.00
BB2 Shane Doan 1.25 3.00
BB3 Patrice Bergeron 2.00 5.00
BB4 Cody Hodgson 1.50 4.00
BB5 Sean Monahan 1.50 4.00
BB6 Eric Staal 2.00 5.00
BB7 Jonathan Toews 3.00 8.00
BB8 Matt Duchene 1.50 4.00
BB9 Brandon Dubinsky 1.25 3.00
BB10 Tyler Seguin 2.50 6.00
BB11 Pavel Datsyuk 2.00 5.00
BB12 Taylor Hall 3.00 8.00
BB13 Jonathan Huberdeau 1.50 4.00
BB14 Anze Kopitar 2.50 6.00
BB15 Ryan Suter 1.50 4.00
BB16 P.K. Subban 2.50 6.00
BB17 Shea Weber 1.25 3.00
BB18 Jaromir Jagr 4.00 10.00
BB19 John Tavares 3.00 8.00
BB20 Derek Stepan 1.50 4.00
BB21 Erik Karlsson 3.00 8.00
BB22 Claude Giroux 1.50 4.00
BB23 Sidney Crosby 6.00 15.00
BB24 Joe Pavelski 1.50 4.00
BB25 Alexander Steen 1.50 4.00
BB26 Steven Stamkos 3.00 8.00
BB27 Phil Kessel 2.00 5.00
BB28 Henrik Sedin 1.50 4.00
BB29 Alexander Ovechkin 6.00 15.00
BB30 Blake Wheeler 1.50 4.00

2014-15 Ultra EX

28-42 STATED PRINT RUN 249-299
1 Patrick Kane 3.00 8.00
2 Tyler Seguin 2.50 6.00
3 Jaromir Jagr 4.00 10.00
4 Ryan Getzlaf 2.50 6.00
5 Drew Doughty 1.50 4.00
6 Erik Karlsson 3.00 8.00
7 Evgeni Malkin 5.00 12.00
8 Alexander Ovechkin 6.00 15.00
9 Anze Kopitar 2.50 6.00
10 John Tavares 3.00 8.00
11 Phil Kessel 2.00 5.00
12 Steven Stamkos 3.00 8.00
13 Jonathan Bernier 1.50 4.00
14 Tuukka Rask 1.50 4.00
15 Jonathan Quick 2.50 6.00
16 Corey Perry 1.50 4.00
17 Claude Giroux 1.50 4.00
18 Patrice Bergeron 2.00 5.00
19 Duncan Keith 1.50 4.00
20 Carey Price 5.00 12.00
21 Alex Pietrangelo 1.25 3.00
22 Sidney Crosby 6.00 15.00
23 Henrik Lundqvist 2.00 5.00
24 Pavel Datsyuk 2.00 5.00
25 Jonathan Toews 3.00 8.00
26 Taylor Hall 3.00 8.00
27 P.K. Subban 2.50 6.00
28 Mark Messier 3.00 8.00
29 Patrick Roy 8.00 20.00
30 Joe Sakic 5.00 12.00
31 Wayne Gretzky 15.00 40.00
32 Mike Bossy 3.00 8.00
33 Mats Sundin 3.00 8.00
34 Bobby Orr 6.00 15.00
35 Mario Lemieux 10.00 25.00
36 Luc Robitaille 3.00 8.00
37 Calle Jarnkrok 4.00 10.00
38 Brandon Gormley 4.00 10.00
39 Johnny Gaudreau 12.00 30.00
40 Ty Rattie 5.00 12.00
41 Teuvo Teravainen 6.00 15.00
42 Evgeny Kuznetsov 15.00 40.00

2014-15 Ultra EX Essential Credentials Future

*FUTURE/30-42: 1.2X TO 3X BASIC EX
*FUTURE/20-29: 1.5X TO 4X BASIC EX
*FUTURE/16-19: 2X TO 5X BASIC EX

2014-15 Ultra EX Essential Credentials Now

*FUTURE/37-42: .6X TO 1.5X BASIC EX
*FUTURE/28-36: 1.2X TO 3X BASIC EX
*FUTURE/20-27: 1.5X TO 4X BASIC EX
*FUTURE/16-19: 2X TO 5X BASIC EX

2014-15 Ultra EX Jambalaya

RANDOMLY INSERTED IN BONUS PACKS
1 Jonathan Bernier 10.00 25.00
2 Corey Perry 10.00 25.00
3 Jeff Carter 10.00 25.00
4 Jaromir Jagr 25.00 60.00
5 Nathan MacKinnon 20.00 50.00
6 Ryan Getzlaf 15.00 40.00
7 Steven Stamkos 12.00 30.00
8 Alexander Ovechkin 20.00 50.00
9 Duncan Keith 10.00 25.00
10 Ryan Suter 10.00 25.00
11 Erik Karlsson 20.00 50.00
12 James van Riemsdyk 10.00 25.00
13 Jamie Benn 12.00 30.00
14 Antti Niemi 8.00 20.00
15 Taylor Hall 20.00 50.00
16 Matt Duchene 10.00 25.00
17 Shea Weber 8.00 20.00
18 Nicklas Backstrom 15.00 40.00
19 Max Pacioretty 10.00 25.00
20 Pavel Datsyuk 15.00 40.00
21 Tuukka Rask 10.00 25.00
22 Phil Kessel 12.00 30.00
23 Evgeni Malkin 30.00 80.00
24 Brad Marchand 12.00 30.00
25 Sidney Crosby 40.00 80.00
26 Claude Giroux 15.00 40.00
27 Tyler Seguin 15.00 40.00
28 Drew Doughty 10.00 25.00
29 Anze Kopitar 15.00 40.00
30 Carey Price 25.00 60.00
31 Jonathan Quick 15.00 40.00
32 Patrick Kane 15.00 40.00
33 Pekka Rinne 12.00 30.00
34 John Tavares 20.00 50.00
35 Henrik Zetterberg 12.00 30.00
36 Jonathan Toews 30.00 60.00
37 Patrice Bergeron 12.00 30.00
38 Martin St. Louis 10.00 25.00
39 Zach Parise 10.00 25.00
40 Henrik Lundqvist 12.00 30.00
41 P.K. Subban 15.00 40.00
42 Patrick Sharp 10.00 25.00

2014-15 Ultra Fresh Ink

STATED GROUP A ODDS 1:20,890
STATED GROUP B ODDS 1:2,500
STATED GROUP C ODDS 1:895
STATED GROUP D ODDS 1:144
OVERALL ODDS 1:120H, 1:1200R, 1:2400B
FIBH Braden Holtby C 6.00 15.00
FIBO Sergei Bobrovsky C 4.00 10.00
FIBS Brandon Sutter D 3.00 8.00
FIBU Johnny Bucyk C 3.00 8.00
FICK Chris Kreider C 4.00 10.00
FIDH Dany Heatley B 5.00 12.00
FIJB J.T. Brown D 2.50 6.00
FIJC Jared Cowen D 2.50 6.00
FIJF Jesper Fast D 3.00 8.00
FIJJ Jaromir Jagr A 40.00 80.00
FIJM Jacob Markstrom D 3.00 8.00
FIJO Jamie Oleksiak D 3.00 8.00
FIJP Joe Pavelski C 5.00 12.00
FIJS Jared Staal D 4.00 10.00
FIJT John Tavares B
FIKS Kevin Shattenkirk D 4.00 10.00
FILE Lars Eller D 4.00 10.00
FILR Larry Robinson C 4.00 10.00
FIMH Milan Hejduk B 8.00 20.00
FIMO John Moore D 2.50 6.00
FIMP Mark Pysyk D 2.50 6.00
FIRF Ron Francis B 10.00 25.00
FIRP Richard Panik D 2.50 6.00
FITO Terry O'Reilly C 3.00 8.00
FITW Tom Wilson D 4.00 10.00
FIVL Vincent Lecavalier B 6.00 15.00
FIZK Zenon Konopka D 3.00 8.00

2014-15 Ultra Gongshow Grinders

GG1 P.K. Subban 3.00 8.00
GG2 Zac Rinaldo 1.50 4.00
GG3 Matt Greene 1.25 3.00
GG4 Shea Weber 1.50 4.00
GG5 Niklas Kronwall 1.50 4.00
GG6 Brent Seabrook 2.00 5.00
GG7 Pat Maroon 1.25 3.00
GG8 Luke Schenn 1.25 3.00
GG9 Radko Gudas 1.25 3.00
GG10 Alexander Ovechkin 8.00 20.00
GG11 Ryan Callahan 2.00 5.00
GG12 David Backes 2.00 5.00
GG13 Cody Franson 1.25 3.00
GG14 Milan Lucic 2.00 5.00
GG15 Cal Clutterbuck 2.00 5.00
GG16 Chris Phillips 1.25 3.00
GG17 Jared Cowen 1.25 3.00
GG18 Matt Martin 1.25 3.00
GG19 Dion Phaneuf 2.00 5.00
GG20 Zdeno Chara 2.00 5.00

2014-15 Ultra National Heroes

STATED ODDS 1:30 HOBBY
NHAB Aleksander Barkov 4.00 10.00
NHAO Alexander Ovechkin 15.00 40.00
NHCP Carey Price 12.00 30.00
NHDA Daniel Alfredsson 4.00 10.00
NHDD Drew Doughty 4.00 10.00
NHEK Erik Karlsson 8.00 20.00
NHEM Evgeni Malkin 12.00 30.00
NHGL Gabriel Landeskog 3.00 8.00
NHHL Henrik Lundqvist 5.00 12.00
NHHZ Henrik Zetterberg 5.00 12.00
NHJB Jamie Benn 5.00 12.00
NHJC Jeff Carter 4.00 10.00
NHJP Joe Pavelski 4.00 10.00
NHJQ Jonathan Quick 6.00 15.00
NHJT Jonathan Toews 8.00 20.00
NHJV James van Riemsdyk 4.00 10.00
NHKA Patrick Kane 8.00 20.00
NHMG Mikael Granlund 3.00 8.00
NHMS Martin St. Louis 4.00 10.00
NHNK Niklas Kronwall 3.00 8.00
NHOM Olli Maatta 4.00 10.00
NHPB Patrice Bergeron 5.00 12.00
NHPD Pavel Datsyuk 5.00 12.00
NHPE Corey Perry 4.00 10.00
NHPK Phil Kessel 5.00 12.00
NHPS Patrick Sharp 4.00 10.00
NHRG Ryan Getzlaf 6.00 15.00
NHRS Ryan Suter 4.00 10.00
NHSB Sergei Bobrovsky 4.00 10.00
NHSC Sidney Crosby 15.00 40.00
NHSU P.K. Subban 6.00 15.00
NHSV Slava Voynov 4.00 10.00
NHSW Shea Weber 3.00 8.00
NHTA John Tavares 8.00 20.00
NHTO T.J. Oshie 6.00 15.00
NHTR Tuukka Rask 4.00 10.00
NHTS Teemu Selanne 8.00 20.00
NHVA Sami Vatanen 2.50 6.00
NHVN Valeri Nichushkin 3.00 8.00
NHZP Zach Parise 4.00 10.00

2014-15 Ultra National Heroes Autographs

NHAB Aleksander Barkov 12.00 30.00
NHAO Alexander Ovechkin 40.00 80.00
NHEM Evgeni Malkin 40.00 100.00
NHGL Gabriel Landeskog 10.00 25.00
NHJP Joe Pavelski 12.00 30.00
NHJT Jonathan Toews 30.00 80.00
NHJV James van Riemsdyk 12.00 30.00
NHKA Patrick Kane 25.00 50.00
NHMG Mikael Granlund 10.00 25.00
NHMS Martin St. Louis 12.00 30.00
NHNK Niklas Kronwall 10.00 25.00
NHPD Pavel Datsyuk 20.00 40.00
NHPE Corey Perry
NHPK Phil Kessel
NHPS Patrick Sharp 20.00 50.00
NHRS Ryan Suter 12.00 30.00
NHSB Sergei Bobrovsky 15.00 40.00
NHTA John Tavares 30.00 60.00
NHZP Zach Parise 12.00 30.00

2014-15 Ultra Photo Vault Film Slide

EACH PLAYER HAS FIVE CARDS PRICED EQUALLY
PVAI1 Arturs Irbe 8.00 20.00
PVAI2 Arturs Irbe 8.00 20.00
PVAI3 Arturs Irbe 8.00 20.00
PVAI4 Arturs Irbe 8.00 20.00
PVAI5 Arturs Irbe 8.00 20.00
PVBH1 Brett Hull 6.00 15.00
PVBH2 Brett Hull 6.00 15.00
PVBH3 Brett Hull 6.00 15.00
PVBH4 Brett Hull 6.00 15.00
PVBH5 Brett Hull 6.00 15.00
PVFP1 Felix Potvin 10.00 25.00
PVFP2 Felix Potvin 10.00 25.00
PVFP3 Felix Potvin 10.00 25.00
PVFP4 Felix Potvin 10.00 25.00
PVFP5 Felix Potvin 10.00 25.00
PVJJ1 Jaromir Jagr 15.00 40.00
PVJJ2 Jaromir Jagr 15.00 40.00
PVJJ3 Jaromir Jagr 15.00 40.00
PVJJ4 Jaromir Jagr 15.00 40.00
PVJJ5 Jaromir Jagr 15.00 40.00
PVJK1 Jari Kurri 6.00 15.00
PVJK2 Jari Kurri 6.00 15.00
PVJK3 Jari Kurri 6.00 15.00
PVJK4 Jari Kurri 6.00 15.00
PVJK5 Jari Kurri 6.00 15.00
PVJR1 Jeremy Roenick 6.00 15.00
PVJR2 Jeremy Roenick 6.00 15.00
PVJR3 Jeremy Roenick 6.00 15.00
PVJR4 Jeremy Roenick 6.00 15.00
PVJR5 Jeremy Roenick 6.00 15.00
PVLR1 Luc Robitaille 6.00 15.00
PVLR2 Luc Robitaille 6.00 15.00
PVLR3 Luc Robitaille 6.00 15.00
PVLR4 Luc Robitaille 6.00 15.00
PVLR5 Luc Robitaille 6.00 15.00
PVMB1 Martin Brodeur 12.00 30.00
PVMB2 Martin Brodeur 12.00 30.00
PVMB3 Martin Brodeur 12.00 30.00
PVMB4 Martin Brodeur 12.00 30.00
PVMB5 Martin Brodeur 12.00 30.00
PVMS1 Mats Sundin 6.00 15.00
PVMS2 Mats Sundin 6.00 15.00
PVMS3 Mats Sundin 6.00 15.00
PVMS4 Mats Sundin 6.00 15.00
PVMS5 Mats Sundin 6.00 15.00
PVPB1 Pavel Bure 8.00 20.00
PVPB2 Pavel Bure 8.00 20.00
PVPB3 Pavel Bure 8.00 20.00
PVPB4 Pavel Bure 8.00 20.00
PVPB5 Pavel Bure 8.00 20.00
PVPR1 Patrick Roy 12.00 30.00
PVPR2 Patrick Roy 12.00 30.00
PVPR3 Patrick Roy 12.00 30.00
PVPR4 Patrick Roy 12.00 30.00
PVPR5 Patrick Roy 12.00 30.00
PVRB1 Ray Bourque 10.00 25.00
PVRB2 Ray Bourque 10.00 25.00
PVRB3 Ray Bourque 10.00 25.00
PVRB4 Ray Bourque 10.00 25.00
PVRB5 Ray Bourque 10.00 25.00
PVSY1 Steve Yzerman 12.00 30.00
PVSY2 Steve Yzerman 12.00 30.00
PVSY3 Steve Yzerman 12.00 30.00
PVSY4 Steve Yzerman 12.00 30.00
PVSY5 Steve Yzerman 12.00 30.00
PVWG1 Wayne Gretzky 20.00 50.00
PVWG2 Wayne Gretzky 20.00 50.00
PVWG3 Wayne Gretzky 20.00 50.00
PVWG4 Wayne Gretzky 20.00 50.00
PVWG5 Wayne Gretzky 20.00 50.00

2014-15 Ultra Premier Pad Men

STATED ODDS 1:54 HOBBY
PP1 Sergei Bobrovsky 4.00 10.00
PP2 Cory Schneider 3.00 8.00
PP3 Pekka Rinne 5.00 12.00
PP4 Semyon Varlamov 4.00 10.00
PP5 Jonathan Bernier 4.00 10.00
PP6 Corey Crawford 5.00 12.00
PP7 Marc-Andre Fleury 6.00 15.00
PP8 Eddie Lack 3.00 8.00
PP9 Craig Anderson 4.00 10.00
PP10 Steve Mason 5.00 12.00
PP11 Philipp Grubauer 4.00 10.00
PP12 Mike Smith 4.00 10.00
PP13 Ben Bishop 4.00 10.00
PP14 Anders Nilsson 4.00 10.00
PP15 Antti Niemi 3.00 8.00
PP16 Ben Scrivens 3.00 8.00
PP17 Cam Ward 4.00 10.00
PP18 Tuukka Rask 4.00 10.00
PP19 Jhonas Enroth 4.00 10.00
PP20 Jim Howard 4.00 10.00
PP21 Karri Ramo 3.00 8.00
PP22 Kari Lehtonen 3.00 8.00
PP23 Brian Elliott 3.00 8.00
PP24 Josh Harding 3.00 8.00
PP25 Roberto Luongo 4.00 10.00
PP26 Henrik Lundqvist 5.00 12.00
PP27 John Gibson 6.00 15.00
PP28 Carey Price 12.00 30.00
PP29 Ondrej Pavelec 4.00 10.00
PP30 Jonathan Quick 6.00 15.00

2014-15 Ultra Red Light Views

STATED ODDS 1:36 HOBBY
RLV1 Wings vs. Leafs 3.00 8.00
RLV2 Devils vs. Rangers 4.00 10.00
RLV3 Hawks vs. Penguins 3.00 8.00
RLV4 Senators vs. Canucks 2.00 5.00
RLV5 Sharks vs. Kings 3.00 8.00
RLV6 Rangers vs. Penguins 2.50 6.00
RLV7 Ducks vs. Kings 3.00 8.00
RLV8 Kings vs. Rangers 2.50 6.00
RLV9 Rangers vs. Kings 3.00 8.00
RLV10 Canadiens vs. Rangers 1.25 3.00

2014-15 Ultra Road to the Championship

R1 STATED ODDS 1:30 HOBBY
R2 STATED ODDS 1:60 HOBBY
R3 STATED ODDS 1:180 HOBBY
R4 STATED ODDS 1:720 HOBBY
OVERALL STATED ODDS 1:18H, 1:36R, 1:72B
EACH HAS MULTIPLE CARDS OF EQUAL VALUE
RTCADAC1 A.Cogliano R1 (4/16/14) 1.50 4.00
RTCADAC2 A.Cogliano R1 (4/18/14) 1.50 4.00
RTCADAC3 A.Cogliano R1 (4/25/14) 1.50 4.00
RTCADAC4 A.Cogliano R2 (5/3/14) 2.00 5.00
RTCADAC5 A.Cogliano R2 (5/5/14) 2.00 5.00
RTCADAC6 A.Cogliano R2 (5/12/14) 2.00 5.00
RTCADAC7 A.Cogliano R2 (5/16/14) 2.00 5.00
RTCADCF1 C.Fowler R1 (4/16/14) 2.00 5.00
RTCADCF2 C.Fowler R1 (4/18/14) 2.00 5.00
RTCADCF3 C.Fowler R1 (4/25/14) 2.00 5.00
RTCADCF4 C.Fowler R2 (5/3/14) 2.50 6.00
RTCADCF5 C.Fowler R2 (5/5/14) 2.50 6.00
RTCADCF6 C.Fowler R2 (5/12/14) 2.50 6.00
RTCADCF7 C.Fowler R2 (5/16/14) 2.50 6.00
RTCADCP1 C.Perry R1 (4/16/14) 2.50 6.00
RTCADCP2 C.Perry R1 (4/18/14) 2.50 6.00
RTCADCP3 C.Perry R1 (4/25/14) 2.50 6.00
RTCADCP4 C.Perry R2 (5/3/14) 3.00 8.00
RTCADCP5 C.Perry R2 (5/5/14) 3.00 8.00
RTCADCP6 C.Perry R2 (5/12/14) 3.00 8.00
RTCADCP7 C.Perry R2 (5/16/14) 3.00 8.00
RTCADJG1 J.Gibson R2 (5/12/14) 4.00 10.00
RTCADJG2 J.Gibson R2 (5/16/14) 4.00 10.00
RTCADRG1 R.Getzlaf R1 (4/16/14) 4.00 10.00
RTCADRG2 R.Getzlaf R1 (4/18/14) 4.00 10.00
RTCADRG3 R.Getzlaf R1 (4/25/14) 4.00 10.00
RTCADRG4 R.Getzlaf R2 (5/3/14) 5.00 12.00
RTCADRG5 R.Getzlaf R2 (5/5/14) 5.00 12.00
RTCADRG6 R.Getzlaf R2 (5/12/14) 5.00 12.00
RTCADRG7 R.Getzlaf R2 (5/16/14) 5.00 12.00
RTCADTS1 T.Selanne R1 (4/16/14) 5.00 12.00
RTCADTS2 T.Selanne R1 (4/18/14) 5.00 12.00
RTCADTS3 T.Selanne R1 (4/25/14) 5.00 12.00
RTCADTS4 T.Selanne R2 (5/3/14) 6.00 15.00
RTCADTS5 T.Selanne R2 (5/5/14) 6.00 15.00
RTCADTS6 T.Selanne R2 (5/12/14) 6.00 15.00
RTCADTS7 T.Selanne R2 (5/16/14) 6.00 15.00
RTCBBBM1 B.Marchand R1 (4/18/14) 3.00 8.00
RTCBBBM2 B.Marchand R1 (4/20/14) 3.00 8.00
RTCBBBM3 B.Marchand R1 (4/26/14) 3.00 8.00
RTCBBBM4 B.Marchand R2 (5/1/14) 4.00 10.00
RTCBBBM5 B.Marshand R2 (5/3/14) 4.00 10.00
RTCBBBM6 B.Marchand R2 (5/10/14) 4.00 10.00
RTCBBBM7 B.Marchand R2 (5/14/14) 4.00 10.00
RTCBBDK1 D.Krejci R1 (4/18/14) 2.50 6.00
RTCBBDK2 D.Krejci R1 (4/20/14) 2.50 6.00
RTCBBDK3 D.Krejci R1 (4/26/14) 2.50 6.00
RTCBBDK4 D.Krejci R2 (5/1/14) 3.00 8.00
RTCBBDK5 D.Krejci R2 (5/3/14) 3.00 8.00
RTCBBDK6 D.Krejci R2 (5/10/14) 3.00 8.00
RTCBBDK7 D.Krejci R2 (5/14/14) 3.00 8.00
RTCBBJI1 J.Iginla R1 (4/18/14) 2.50 6.00
RTCBBJI2 J.Iginla R1 (4/20/14) 2.50 6.00
RTCBBJI3 J.Iginla R1 (4/26/14) 2.50 6.00
RTCBBJI4 J.Iginla R2 (5/1/14) 3.00 8.00
RTCBBJI5 J.Iginla R2 (5/3/14) 3.00 8.00
RTCBBJI6 J.Iginla R2 (5/10/14) 3.00 8.00
RTCBBJI7 J.Iginla R2 (5/14/14) 3.00 8.00
RTCBBML1 M.Lucic R1 (4/18/14) 2.50 6.00
RTCBBML2 M.Lucic R1 (4/20/14) 2.50 6.00
RTCBBML3 M.Lucic R1 (4/26/14) 2.50 6.00
RTCBBML4 M.Lucic R2 (5/1/14) 3.00 8.00
RTCBBML5 M.Lucic R2 (5/3/14) 3.00 8.00
RTCBBML6 M.Lucic R2 (5/10/14) 3.00 8.00
RTCBBML7 M.Lucic R2 (5/14/14) 3.00 8.00
RTCBBPB1 P.Bergeron R1 (4/18/14) 3.00 8.00
RTCBBPB2 P.Bergeron R1 (4/20/14) 3.00 8.00
RTCBBPB3 P.Bergeron R1 (4/26/14) 3.00 8.00
RTCBBPB4 P.Bergeron R2 (5/1/14) 4.00 10.00
RTCBBPB5 P.Bergeron R2 (5/3/14) 4.00 10.00
RTCBBPB6 P.Bergeron R2 (5/10/14) 4.00 10.00
RTCBBPB7 P.Bergeron R2 (5/14/14) 4.00 10.00
RTCBBRS1 R.Smith R1 (4/18/14) 2.50 6.00
RTCBBRS2 R.Smith R1 (4/20/14) 2.50 6.00
RTCBBRS3 R.Smith R1 (4/26/14) 2.50 6.00
RTCBBRS4 R.Smith R2 (5/1/14) 3.00 8.00
RTCBBRS5 R.Smith R2 (5/3/14) 3.00 8.00
RTCBBRS6 R.Smith R2 (5/10/14) 3.00 8.00
RTCBBRS7 R.Smith R2 (5/14/14) 3.00 8.00
RTCBBTK1 T.Krug R1 (4/18/14) 2.50 6.00
RTCBBTK2 T.Krug R1 (4/20/14) 2.50 6.00
RTCBBTK3 T.Krug R1 (4/26/14) 2.50 6.00
RTCBBTK4 T.Krug R2 (5/1/14) 3.00 8.00
RTCBBTK5 T.Krug R2 (5/3/14) 3.00 8.00
RTCBBTK6 T.Krug R2 (5/10/14) 3.00 8.00
RTCBBTK7 T.Krug R2 (5/14/14) 3.00 8.00
RTCBBTR1 T.Rask R1 (4/18/14) 2.50 6.00
RTCBBTR2 T.Rask R1 (4/20/14) 2.50 6.00
RTCBBTR3 T.Rask R1 (4/26/14) 2.50 6.00
RTCBBTR4 T.Rask R2 (5/1/14) 3.00 8.00
RTCBBTR5 T.Rask R2 (5/3/14) 3.00 8.00
RTCBBTR6 T.Rask R2 (5/10/14) 3.00 8.00
RTCBBTR7 T.Rask R2 (5/14/14) 3.00 8.00
RTCBBZC1 Z.Chara R1 (4/18/14) 2.50 6.00
RTCBBZC2 Z.Chara R1 (4/20/14) 2.50 6.00
RTCBBZC3 Z.Chara R1 (4/26/14) 2.50 6.00
RTCBBZC4 Z.Chara R2 (5/1/14) 3.00 8.00
RTCBBZC5 Z.Chara R2 (5/3/14) 3.00 8.00
RTCBBZC6 Z.Chara R2 (5/10/14) 3.00 8.00
RTCBBZC7 Z.Chara R2 (5/14/14) 3.00 8.00
RTCCAGL1 G.Landeskog R1 (4/17/14) 2.00 5.00
RTCCAGL2 G.Landeskog R1 (4/19/14) 2.00 5.00
RTCCAGL3 G.Landeskog R1 (4/26/14) 2.00 5.00
RTCCAGL4 G.Landeskog R1 (4/30/14) 2.00 5.00
RTCCAMD M.Duchene R1 (4/30/14) 2.50 6.00
RTCCANM1 MacKinnon R1 (4/17/14) 5.00 12.00
RTCCANM2 N.MacKinnon R1 (4/19/14) 5.00 12.00
RTCCANM3 N.MacKinnon R1 (4/26/14) 5.00 12.00
RTCCANM4 N.MacKinnon R1 (4/30/14) 5.00 12.00
RTCCAPS1 P.Stastny R1 (4/17/14) 2.50 6.00
RTCCAPS2 P.Stastny R1 (4/19/14) 2.50 6.00
RTCCAPS3 P.Stastny R1 (4/26/14) 2.50 6.00
RTCCAPS4 P.Stastny R1 (4/30/14) 2.50 6.00
RTCCASV1 S.Varlamov R1 (4/17/14) 2.50 6.00
RTCCASV2 S.Varlamov R1 (4/19/14) 2.50 6.00
RTCCASV3 S.Varlamov R1 (4/26/14) 2.50 6.00
RTCCASV4 S.Varlamov R1 (4/30/14) 2.50 6.00
RTCCBBS1 B.Seabrook R1 (4/27/14) 2.50 6.00
RTCCBBS2 B.Seabrook R2 (5/2/14) 3.00 8.00
RTCCBBS3 B.Seabrook R2 (5/4/14) 3.00 8.00
RTCCBBS4 B.Seabrook R2 (5/11/14) 3.00 8.00
RTCCBBS5 B.Seabrook R3 (5/18/14) 6.00 15.00
RTCCBBS6 B.Seabrook R3 (5/21/14) 6.00 15.00
RTCCBBS7 B.Seabrook R3 (5/28/14) 6.00 15.00
RTCCBBS8 B.Seabrook R3 (6/1/14) 6.00 15.00
RTCCBCC1 C.Crawford R1 (4/21/14) 3.00 8.00
RTCCBCC2 C.Crawford R1 (4/23/14) 3.00 8.00
RTCCBCC3 C.Crawford R1 (4/27/14) 3.00 8.00
RTCCBCC4 C.Crawford R2 (5/2/14) 4.00 10.00
RTCCBCC5 C.Crawford R2 (5/4/14) 4.00 10.00
RTCCBCC6 C.Crawford R2 (5/11/14) 4.00 10.00
RTCCBCC7 C.Crawford R3 (5/18/14) 8.00 20.00
RTCCBCC8 C.Crawford R3 (5/21/14) 8.00 20.00
RTCCBCC9 C.Crawford R3 (5/28/14) 8.00 20.00
RTCCBCC10 C.Crawford R3 (6/1/14) 8.00 20.00
RTCCBDK1 D.Keith R1 (4/21/14) 2.50 6.00
RTCCBDK2 D.Keith R1 (4/27/14) 2.50 6.00
RTCCBDK3 D.Keith R2 (5/2/14) 2.50 6.00
RTCCBDK4 D.Keith R2 (5/4/14) 3.00 8.00
RTCCBDK5 D.Keith R2 (5/11/14) 3.00 8.00
RTCCBDK6 D.Keith R3 (5/18/14) 3.00 8.00
RTCCBDK7 D.Keith R3 (5/21/14) 6.00 15.00
RTCCBDK8 D.Keith R3 (5/28/14) 6.00 15.00
RTCCBDK9 D.Keith R3 (6/1/14) 6.00 15.00
RTCCBDK10 D.Keith R1 (4/23/14) 6.00 15.00
RTCCBJBD1 B.Dubinsky R1 (4/21/14) 2.00 5.00
RTCCBJBD2 B.Dubinsky R1 (4/23/14) 2.00 5.00
RTCCBJBD3 B.Dubinsky R1 (4/28/14) 2.00 5.00
RTCCBJRJ1 R.Johansen R1 (4/21/14) 3.00 8.00
RTCCBJRJ2 R.Johansen R1 (4/23/14) 3.00 8.00
RTCCBJRJ3 R.Johansen R1 (4/28/14) 3.00 8.00
RTCCBJSB1 S.Bobrovsky R1 (4/21/14) 2.50 6.00
RTCCBJSB2 S.Bobrovsky R1 (4/23/14) 2.50 6.00
RTCCBJSB3 S.Bobrovsky R1 (4/28/14) 2.50 6.00
RTCCBJT1 J.Toews R1 (4/21/14) 5.00 12.00
RTCCBJT2 J.Toews R1 (4/23/14) 5.00 12.00
RTCCBJT3 J.Toews R1 (4/27/14) 8.00 20.00
RTCCBJT4 J.Toews R2 (5/2/14) 6.00 15.00
RTCCBJT5 J.Toews R2 (5/4/14) 6.00 15.00
RTCCBJT6 J.Toews R2 (5/11/14) 6.00 15.00
RTCCBJT7 J.Toews R3 (5/18/14) 15.00 40.00
RTCCBJT8 J.Toews R3 (5/21/14) 15.00 40.00
RTCCBJT9 J.Toews R3 (5/28/14) 15.00 40.00
RTCCBJT10 J.Toews R3 (6/1/14) 15.00 40.00
RTCCBMH1 M.Hossa R1 (4/21/14) 2.00 5.00
RTCCBMH2 M.Hossa R1 (4/23/14) 2.00 5.00
RTCCBMH3 M.Hossa R1 (4/27/14) 2.00 5.00
RTCCBMH4 M.Hossa R2 (5/2/14) 2.50 6.00
RTCCBMH5 M.Hossa R2 (5/4/14) 2.50 6.00
RTCCBMH6 M.Hossa R2 (5/11/14) 2.50 6.00
RTCCBMH7 M.Hossa R3 (5/18/14) 5.00 12.00
RTCCBMH8 M.Hossa R3 (5/21/14) 5.00 12.00
RTCCBMH9 M.Hossa R3 (5/28/14) 5.00 12.00
RTCCBMH10 M.Hossa R3 (6/1/14) 5.00 12.00
RTCCBPK1 P.Kane R1 (4/21/14) 5.00 12.00
RTCCBPK2 P.Kane R1 (4/23/14) 5.00 12.00
RTCCBPK3 P.Kane R1 (4/27/14) 5.00 12.00
RTCCBPK4 P.Kane R2 (5/2/14) 6.00 15.00
RTCCBPK5 P.Kane R2 (5/4/14) 6.00 15.00
RTCCBPK6 P.Kane R2 (5/11/14) 6.00 15.00
RTCCBPK7 P.Kane R3 (5/18/14) 12.00 30.00
RTCCBPK8 P.Kane R3 (5/21/14) 12.00 30.00
RTCCBPK9 P.Kane R3 (5/28/14) 12.00 30.00
RTCCBPK10 P.Kane R3 (6/1/14) 12.00 30.00
RTCCBPS1 P.Sharp R1 (4/21/14) 2.50 6.00
RTCCBPS2 P.Sharp R1 (4/23/14) 2.50 6.00
RTCCBPS3 P.Sharp R1 (4/27/14) 2.50 6.00
RTCCBPS4 P.Sharp R2 (5/2/14) 3.00 8.00
RTCCBPS5 P.Sharp R2 (5/4/14) 3.00 8.00
RTCCBPS6 P.Sharp R2 (5/11/14) 3.00 8.00
RTCCBPS7 P.Sharp R3 (5/18/14) 6.00 15.00
RTCCBPS8 P.Sharp R3 (5/21/14) 6.00 15.00
RTCCBPS9 P.Sharp R3 (5/28/14) 6.00 15.00
RTCCBPS10 P.Sharp R3 (6/1/14) 6.00 15.00
RTCCBSA1 B.Saad R1 (4/21/14) 2.50 6.00
RTCCBSA2 B.Saad R1 (4/23/14) 2.50 6.00
RTCCBSA3 B.Saad R1 (4/27/14) 2.50 6.00
RTCCBSA4 B.Saad R2 (5/2/14) 3.00 8.00
RTCCBSA5 B.Saad R2 (5/4/14) 3.00 8.00
RTCCBSA6 B.Saad R2 (5/11/14) 3.00 8.00
RTCCBSA7 B.Saad R3 (5/18/14) 6.00 15.00
RTCCBSA8 B.Saad R3 (5/21/14) 6.00 15.00
RTCCBSA9 B.Saad R3 (5/28/14) 6.00 15.00
RTCCBSA10 B.Saad R3 (6/1/14) 6.00 15.00
RTCDRWHZ Zetterberg R1 (4/24/14) 3.00 8.00
RTCDRWJF1 J.Franzen R1 (4/22/14) 2.50 6.00
RTCDRWJF2 J.Franzen R1 (4/24/14) 2.50 6.00
RTCDRWJH J.Howard R1 (4/22/14) 2.50 6.00
RTCDRWNK1 N.Kronwall R1 (4/22/14) 2.00 5.00
RTCDRWNK2 N.Kronwall R1 (4/24/14) 2.00 5.00
RTCDRWPD1 P.Datsyuk R1 (4/22/14) 3.00 8.00
RTCDRWPD2 P.Datsyuk R1 (4/24/14) 3.00 8.00
RTCDSJB1 J.Benn R1 (4/21/14) 3.00 8.00
RTCDSJB2 J.Benn R1 (4/23/14) 3.00 8.00
RTCDSJB3 J.Benn R1 (4/27/14) 3.00 8.00
RTCDSTS1 T.Seguin R1 (4/21/14) 4.00 10.00
RTCDSTS2 T.Seguin R1 (4/23/14) 4.00 10.00
RTCDSTS3 T.Seguin R1 (4/27/14) 4.00 10.00
RTCLAKAK1 A.Kopitar R1 (4/22/14) 4.00 10.00
RTCLAKAK2 A.Kopitar R1 (4/24/14) 4.00 10.00
RTCLAKAK3 A.Kopitar R1 (4/28/14) 4.00 10.00
RTCLAKAK4 A.Kopitar R2 (5/8/14) 5.00 12.00
RTCLAKAK5 A.Kopitar R2 (5/10/14) 5.00 12.00
RTCLAKAK6 A.Kopitar R2 (5/14/14) 5.00 12.00
RTCLAKAK7 A.Kopitar R3 (5/24/14) 10.00 25.00
RTCLAKAK8 A.Kopitar R3 (5/26/14) 10.00 25.00
RTCLAKAK9 A.Kopitar R3 (5/30/14) 10.00 25.00
RTCLAKAK10 A.Kopitar R4 (6/4/14) 20.00 50.00
RTCLAKAK11 A.Kopitar R4 (6/7/14) 20.00 50.00
RTCLAKAK12 A.Kopitar R4 (6/13/14) 20.00 50.00
RTCLAKAM1 A.Martinez R1 (4/22/14) 1.50 4.00
RTCLAKAM2 A.Martinez R1 (4/24/14) 1.50 4.00
RTCLAKAM3 A.Martinez R1 (4/28/14) 1.50 4.00
RTCLAKAM4 A.Martinez R2 (5/8/14) 2.00 5.00
RTCLAKAM5 A.Martinez R2 (5/10/14) 2.00 5.00
RTCLAKAM6 A.Martinez R2 (5/14/14) 2.00 5.00
RTCLAKAM7 A.Martinez R3 (5/24/14) 4.00 10.00
RTCLAKAM8 A.Martinez R3 (5/26/14) 4.00 10.00
RTCLAKAM9 A.Martinez R3 (5/30/14) 4.00 10.00
RTCLAKAM10 A.Martinez R4 (6/4/14) 8.00 20.00
RTCLAKAM11 A.Martinez R4 (6/7/14) 8.00 20.00
RTCLAKAM12 A.Martinez R4 (6/13/14) 8.00 20.00
RTCLAKDB1 D.Brown R1 (4/22/14) 2.00 5.00
RTCLAKDB2 D.Brown R1 (4/24/14) 2.00 5.00
RTCLAKDB3 D.Brown R1 (4/28/14) 2.00 5.00
RTCLAKDB4 D.Brown R2 (5/8/14) 2.50 6.00
RTCLAKDB5 D.Brown R2 (5/10/14) 2.50 6.00
RTCLAKDB6 D.Brown R2 (5/14/14) 2.50 6.00
RTCLAKDB7 D.Brown R3 (5/24/14) 5.00 12.00
RTCLAKDB8 D.Brown R3 (5/26/14) 5.00 12.00
RTCLAKDB9 D.Brown R3 (5/30/14) 5.00 12.00
RTCLAKDB10 D.Brown R4 (6/4/14) 10.00 25.00
RTCLAKDB11 D.Brown R4 (6/7/14) 10.00 25.00
RTCLAKDB12 D.Brown R4 (6/13/14) 10.00 25.00
RTCLAKDD1 D.Doughty R1 (4/22/14) 2.50 6.00
RTCLAKDD2 D.Doughty R1 (4/24/14) 2.50 6.00
RTCLAKDD3 D.Doughty R1 (4/28/14) 2.50 6.00
RTCLAKDD4 D.Doughty R2 (5/8/14) 3.00 8.00
RTCLAKDD5 D.Doughty R2 (5/10/14) 3.00 8.00
RTCLAKDD6 D.Doughty R2 (5/14/14) 3.00 8.00
RTCLAKDD7 D.Doughty R3 (5/24/14) 6.00 15.00
RTCLAKDD8 D.Doughty R3 (5/26/14) 6.00 15.00
RTCLAKDD9 D.Doughty R3 (5/30/14) 6.00 15.00
RTCLAKDD10 D.Doughty R4 (6/4/14) 15.00 40.00
RTCLAKDD11 D.Doughty R4 (6/7/14) 15.00 40.00
RTCLAKDD12 D.Doughty R4 (6/13/14) 15.00 40.00
RTCLAKJC1 J.Carter R1 (4/22/14) 2.50 6.00
RTCLAKJC2 J.Carter R1 (4/24/14) 2.50 6.00
RTCLAKJC3 J.Carter R1 (4/28/14) 2.50 6.00
RTCLAKJC4 J.Carter R2 (5/8/14) 3.00 8.00
RTCLAKJC5 J.Carter R2 (5/10/14) 3.00 8.00
RTCLAKJC6 J.Carter R2 (5/14/14) 3.00 8.00
RTCLAKJC7 J.Carter R3 (5/24/14) 6.00 15.00
RTCLAKJC8 J.Carter R3 (5/26/14) 6.00 15.00
RTCLAKJC9 J.Carter R3 (5/30/14) 6.00 15.00
RTCLAKJC10 J.Carter R4 (6/4/14) 12.00 30.00
RTCLAKJC11 J.Carter R4 (6/7/14) 12.00 30.00
RTCLAKJC12 J.Carter R4 (6/13/14) 12.00 30.00
RTCLAKJQ1 J.Quick R1 (4/22/14) 4.00 10.00
RTCLAKJQ2 J.Quick R1 (4/24/14) 4.00 10.00
RTCLAKJQ3 J.Quick R1 (4/28/14) 4.00 10.00
RTCLAKJQ4 J.Quick R2 (5/8/14) 5.00 12.00
RTCLAKJQ5 J.Quick R2 (5/10/14) 5.00 12.00
RTCLAKJQ6 J.Quick R2 (5/14/14) 5.00 12.00
RTCLAKJQ7 J.Quick R3 (5/24/14) 10.00 25.00
RTCLAKJQ8 J.Quick R3 (5/26/14) 10.00 25.00
RTCLAKJQ9 J.Quick R3 (5/30/14) 10.00 25.00
RTCLAKJQ10 J.Quick R4 (6/4/14) 20.00 50.00
RTCLAKJQ11 J.Quick R4 (6/7/14) 20.00 50.00
RTCLAKJQ12 J.Quick R4 (6/13/14) 20.00 50.00
RTCLAKJW1 J.Williams R1 (4/22/14) 2.00 5.00
RTCLAKJW2 J.Williams R1 (4/24/14) 2.00 5.00
RTCLAKJW3 J.Williams R1 (4/28/14) 2.00 5.00
RTCLAKJW4 J.Williams R2 (5/8/14) 2.50 6.00
RTCLAKJW5 J.Williams R2 (5/10/14) 2.50 6.00
RTCLAKJW6 J.Williams R2 (5/14/14) 2.50 6.00
RTCLAKJW7 J.Williams R3 (5/24/14) 5.00 12.00
RTCLAKJW8 J.Williams R3 (5/26/14) 5.00 12.00
RTCLAKJW9 J.Williams R3 (5/30/14) 5.00 12.00
RTCLAKJW10 J.Williams R4 (6/4/14) 10.00 25.00
RTCLAKJW11 J.Williams R4 (6/7/14) 10.00 25.00
RTCLAKJW12 J.Williams R4 (6/13/14) 10.00 25.00
RTCLAKMG1 M.Gaborik R1 (4/22/14) 2.50 6.00
RTCLAKMG2 M.Gaborik R1 (4/24/14) 2.50 6.00
RTCLAKMG3 M.Gaborik R1 (4/28/14) 2.50 6.00
RTCLAKMG4 M.Gaborik R2 (5/8/14) 3.00 8.00
RTCLAKMG5 M.Gaborik R2 (5/10/14) 3.00 8.00
RTCLAKMG6 M.Gaborik R2 (5/14/14) 3.00 8.00
RTCLAKMG7 M.Gaborik R3 (5/24/14) 6.00 15.00
RTCLAKMG8 M.Gaborik R3 (5/26/14) 6.00 15.00
RTCLAKMG9 M.Gaborik R3 (5/30/14) 6.00 15.00
RTCLAKMG10 M.Gaborik R4 (6/4/14) 12.00 30.00
RTCLAKMG11 M.Gaborik R4 (6/7/14) 12.00 30.00
RTCLAKMG12 M.Gaborik R4 (6/13/14) 12.00 30.00
RTCLAKTP1 T.Pearson R1 (4/22/14) 1.50 4.00
RTCLAKTP2 T.Pearson R1 (4/24/14) 1.50 4.00
RTCLAKTP3 T.Pearson R1 (4/28/14) 1.50 4.00
RTCLAKTP4 T.Pearson R2 (5/8/14) 2.00 5.00
RTCLAKTP5 T.Pearson R2 (5/10/14) 2.00 5.00
RTCLAKTP6 T.Pearson R2 (5/14/14) 2.00 5.00
RTCLAKTP7 T.Pearson R3 (5/24/14) 4.00 10.00
RTCLAKTP8 T.Pearson R3 (5/26/14) 4.00 10.00
RTCLAKTP9 T.Pearson R3 (5/30/14) 4.00 10.00
RTCLAKTP10 T.Pearson R4 (6/4/14) 8.00 20.00
RTCLAKTP11 T.Pearson R4 (6/7/14) 8.00 20.00
RTCLAKTP12 T.Pearson R4 (6/13/14) 8.00 20.00
RTCLAKTT1 T.Toffoli R1 (4/22/14) 2.50 6.00
RTCLAKTT2 T.Toffoli R1 (4/24/14) 2.50 6.00
RTCLAKTT3 T.Toffoli R1 (4/28/14) 2.50 6.00
RTCLAKTT4 T.Toffoli R2 (5/8/14) 3.00 8.00
RTCLAKTT5 T.Toffoli R2 (5/10/14) 3.00 8.00
RTCLAKTT6 T.Toffoli R2 (5/14/14) 3.00 8.00
RTCLAKTT7 T.Toffoli R3 (5/24/14) 6.00 15.00
RTCLAKTT8 T.Toffoli R3 (5/26/14) 6.00 15.00
RTCLAKTT9 T.Toffoli R3 (5/30/14) 6.00 15.00
RTCLAKTT10 T.Toffoli R4 (6/4/14) 12.00 30.00
RTCLAKTT11 T.Toffoli R4 (6/7/14) 12.00 30.00
RTCLAKTT12 T.Toffoli R4 (6/13/14) 12.00 30.00
RTCMCBG1 B.Gallagher R1 (4/20/14) 2.50 6.00
RTCMCBG2 B.Gallagher R1 (4/22/14) 2.50 6.00
RTCMCBG3 B.Gallagher R2 (5/6/14) 3.00 8.00
RTCMCBG4 B.Gallagher R2 (5/8/14) 3.00 8.00
RTCMCBG5 B.Gallagher R2 (5/12/14) 3.00 8.00
RTCMCBG6 Gallagher R3 (5/17/14) 6.00 15.00
RTCMCBG7 B.Gallagher R3 (5/19/14) 6.00 15.00
RTCMCBG8 B.Gallagner R3 (5/27/14) 6.00 15.00
RTCMCCP1 C.Price R1 (4/20/14) 8.00 20.00
RTCMCCP2 C.Price R1 (4/22/14) 8.00 20.00
RTCMCCP3 C.Price R2 (5/6/14) 10.00 25.00
RTCMCCP4 C.Price R2 (5/8/14) 10.00 25.00
RTCMCCP5 C.Price R2 (5/12/14) 10.00 25.00
RTCMCCP6 C.Price R3 (5/17/14) 20.00 50.00
RTCMCDT1 D.Tokarski R3 (5/17/14) 4.00 10.00
RTCMCDT2 D.Tokarski R3 (5/19/14) 4.00 10.00
RTCMCDT3 D.Tokarski R3 (5/27/14) 4.00 10.00
RTCMCLE1 L.Eller R1 (4/20/14) 2.00 5.00
RTCMCLE2 L.Eller R1 (4/22/14) 2.00 5.00
RTCMCLE3 L.Eller R2 (5/6/14) 2.50 6.00
RTCMCLE4 L.Eller R2 (5/8/14) 2.50 6.00
RTCMCLE5 L.Eller R2 (5/12/14) 2.50 6.00
RTCMCLE6 L.Eller R3 (5/17/14) 5.00 12.00
RTCMCLE7 L.Eller R3 (5/19/14) 5.00 12.00
RTCMCLE8 L.Eller R3 (5/27/14) 5.00 12.00
RTCMCMP1 M.Pacioretty R1 (4/20/14) 2.50 6.00
RTCMCMP2 M.Pacioretty R1 (4/22/14) 2.50 6.00
RTCMCMP3 M.Pacioretty R2 (5/6/14) 3.00 8.00
RTCMCMP4 M.Pacioretty R2 (5/8/14) 3.00 8.00
RTCMCMP5 M.Pacioretty R2 (5/12/14) 3.00 8.00
RTCMCMP6 M.Pacioretty R3 (5/17/14) 6.00 15.00
RTCMCMP7 M.Pacioretty R3 (5/19/14) 6.00 15.00
RTCMCMP8 M.Pacioretty R3 (5/27/14) 6.00 15.00
RTCMCPS1 P.Subban R1 (4/20/14) 4.00 10.00
RTCMCPS2 P.Subban R1 (4/22/14) 4.00 10.00
RTCMCPS3 P.Subban R2 (5/6/14) 5.00 12.00
RTCMCPS4 P.Subban R2 (5/8/14) 5.00 12.00
RTCMCPS5 P.Subban R2 (5/12/14) 5.00 12.00
RTCMCPS6 P.Subban R3 (5/17/14) 10.00 25.00
RTCMCPS7 P.Subban R3 (5/19/14) 10.00 25.00
RTCMCPS8 P.Subban R3 (5/27/14) 10.00 25.00
RTCMCTP1 T.Plekanec R1 (4/20/14) 2.50 6.00
RTCMCTP2 T.Plekanec R1 (4/22/14) 2.50 6.00
RTCMCTP3 T.Plekanec R2 (5/6/14) 3.00 8.00
RTCMCTP4 T.Plekanec R2 (5/8/14) 3.00 8.00
RTCMCTP5 T.Plekanec R2 (5/12/14) 3.00 8.00
RTCMCTP6 T.Plekanec R3 (5/17/14) 6.00 15.00
RTCMCTP7 T.Plekanec R3 (5/19/14) 6.00 15.00
RTCMCTP8 T.Plekanec R3 (5/27/14) 6.00 15.00
RTCMCTV1 T.Vanek R1 (4/20/14) 2.50 6.00
RTCMCTV2 T.Vanek R1 (4/22/14) 2.50 6.00
RTCMCTV3 T.Vanek R2 (5/6/14) 3.00 8.00
RTCMCTV4 T.Vanek R2 (5/8/14) 3.00 8.00
RTCMCTV5 T.Vanek R2 (5/12/14) 3.00 8.00
RTCMCTV6 T.Vanek R3 (5/17/14) 6.00 15.00
RTCMCTV7 T.Vanek R3 (5/19/14) 6.00 15.00
RTCMCTV8 T.Vanek R3 (5/27/14) 6.00 15.00
RTCMWDK1 D.Kuemper R1 (4/21/14) 2.00 5.00
RTCMWDK2 D.Kuemper R1 (4/24/14) 2.00 5.00
RTCMWDK3 D.Kuemper R1 (4/28/14) 2.00 5.00
RTCMWJP1 J.Pominville R1 (4/21/14) 2.00 5.00
RTCMWJP2 J.Pominville R1 (4/24/14) 2.00 5.00
RTCMWJP3 J.Pominville R1 (4/28/14) 2.00 5.00
RTCMWJP4 J.Pominville R2 (5/6/14) 2.50 6.00
RTCMWJP5 J.Pominville R2 (5/9/14) 2.50 6.00
RTCMWJP6 J.Pominville R2 (5/13/14) 2.50 6.00
RTCMWMG1 M.Granlund R1 (4/21/14) 2.00 5.00
RTCMWMG2 M.Granlund R1 (4/24/14) 2.00 5.00
RTCMWMG3 M.Granlund R1 (4/28/14) 2.00 5.00
RTCMWMG4 M.Granlund R2 (5/6/14) 2.50 6.00
RTCMWMG5 M.Granlund R2 (5/9/14) 2.50 6.00
RTCMWMG6 M.Granlund R2 (5/13/14) 2.50 6.00
RTCMWMK1 M.Koivu R1 (4/21/14) 2.00 5.00
RTCMWMK2 M.Koivu R1 (4/24/14) 2.00 5.00
RTCMWMK3 M.Koivu R1 (4/28/14) 2.00 5.00
RTCMWMK4 M.Koivu R2 (5/6/14) 2.50 6.00
RTCMWMK5 M.Koivu R2 (5/9/14) 2.50 6.00
RTCMWMK6 M.Koivu R2 (5/13/14) 2.50 6.00
RTCMWNN1 N.Niederreiter R1 (4/21/14) 1.50 4.00
RTCMWNN2 N.Niederreiter R1 (4/24/14) 1.50 4.00
RTCMWNN3 N.Niederreiter R1 (4/28/14) 1.50 4.00
RTCMWNN4 N.Niederreiter R2 (5/6/14) 2.00 5.00
RTCMWNN5 N.Niederreiter R2 (5/9/14) 2.00 5.00
RTCMWNN6 N.Niederreiter R2 (5/13/14) 2.00 5.00
RTCMWRS1 R.Suter R1 (4/21/14) 2.50 6.00
RTCMWRS2 R.Suter R1 (4/24/14) 2.50 6.00
RTCMWRS3 R.Suter R1 (4/28/14) 2.50 6.00
RTCMWRS4 R.Suter R2 (5/6/14) 3.00 8.00
RTCMWRS5 R.Suter R2 (5/9/14) 3.00 8.00
RTCMWRS6 R.Suter R2 (5/13/14) 3.00 8.00
RTCMWZP1 Z.Parise R1 (4/21/14) 4.00 10.00
RTCMWZP2 Z.Parise R1 (4/24/14) 4.00 10.00
RTCMWZP3 Z.Parise R1 (4/28/14) 4.00 10.00
RTCMWZP4 Z.Parise R2 (5/6/14) 5.00 12.00
RTCMWZP5 Z.Parise R2 (5/9/14) 5.00 12.00
RTCMWZP6 Z.Parise R2 (5/13/14) 5.00 12.00
RTCNYRBP1 B.Pouliot R1 (4/17/14) 1.50 4.00
RTCNYRBP2 B.Pouliot R1 (4/20/14) 1.50 4.00
RTCNYRBP3 B.Pouliot R1 (4/27/14) 1.50 4.00
RTCNYRBP4 B.Pouliot R1 (4/30/14) 1.50 4.00
RTCNYRBP5 B.Pouliot R2 (5/5/14) 2.00 5.00
RTCNYRBP6 B.Pouliot R2 (5/7/14) 2.00 5.00
RTCNYRBP7 B.Pouliot R2 (5/11/14) 2.00 5.00
RTCNYRBP8 B.Pouliot R3 (5/22/14) 4.00 10.00
RTCNYRBP9 B.Pouliot R3 (5/25/14) 4.00 10.00
RTCNYRBP10 B.Pouliot R3 (5/29/14) 4.00 10.00
RTCNYRBP11 B.Pouliot R4 (6/9/14) 8.00 20.00
RTCNYRBP12 B.Pouliot R4 (6/11/14) 8.00 20.00
RTCNYRBR1 B.Richards R1 (4/17/14) 2.50 6.00
RTCNYRBR2 B.Richards R1 (4/20/14) 2.50 6.00
RTCNYRBR3 B.Richards R1 (4/27/14) 2.50 6.00
RTCNYRBR4 B.Richards R1 (4/30/14) 2.50 6.00
RTCNYRBR5 B.Richards R2 (5/5/14) 3.00 8.00
RTCNYRBR6 B.Richards R2 (5/7/14) 3.00 8.00
RTCNYRBR7 B.Richards R2 (5/11/14) 3.00 8.00
RTCNYRBR8 B.Richards R3 (5/22/14) 6.00 15.00
RTCNYRBR9 B.Richards R3 (5/25/14) 6.00 15.00
RTCNYRBR10 B.Richards R3 (5/29/14) 6.00 15.00
RTCNYRBR11 B.Richards R4 (6/9/14) 12.00 30.00
RTCNYRBR12 B.Richards R4 (6/11/14) 12.00 30.00
RTCNYRCH1 C.Hagelin R1 (4/17/14) 2.50 6.00
RTCNYRCH2 C.Hagelin R1 (4/20/14) 2.50 6.00
RTCNYRCH3 C.Hagelin R1 (4/27/14) 2.50 6.00
RTCNYRCH4 C.Hagelin R1 (4/30/14) 2.50 6.00
RTCNYRCH5 C.Hagelin R2 (5/5/14) 3.00 8.00
RTCNYRCH6 C.Hagelin R2 (5/7/14) 3.00 8.00
RTCNYRCH7 C.Hagelin R2 (5/11/14) 3.00 8.00
RTCNYRCH8 C.Hagelin R3 (5/22/14) 6.00 15.00
RTCNYRCH9 C.Hagelin R3 (5/25/14) 6.00 15.00
RTCNYRCH10 C.Hagelin R3 (5/29/14) 6.00 15.00
RTCNYRCH11 C.Hagelin R4 (6/9/14) 12.00 30.00
RTCNYRCH12 C.Hagelin R4 (6/11/14) 12.00 30.00
RTCNYRCK1 C.Kreider R2 (5/7/14) 3.00 8.00
RTCNYRCK2 C.Kreider R2 (5/11/14) 3.00 8.00
RTCNYRCK3 C.Kreider R3 (5/22/14) 6.00 15.00
RTCNYRCK4 C.Kreider R3 (5/25/14) 6.00 15.00
RTCNYRCK5 C.Kreider R3 (5/29/14) 6.00 15.00
RTCNYRCK6 C.Kreider R4 (6/9/14) 12.00 30.00
RTCNYRCK7 C.Kreider R4 (6/11/14) 12.00 30.00
RTCNYRDS1 D.Stepan R1 (4/17/14) 2.50 6.00
RTCNYRDS2 D.Stepan R1 (4/20/14) 2.50 6.00
RTCNYRDS3 D.Stepan R1 (4/27/14) 2.50 6.00
RTCNYRDS4 D.Stepan R1 (4/30/14) 2.50 6.00
RTCNYRDS5 D.Stepan R2 (5/5/14) 3.00 8.00
RTCNYRDS6 D.Stepan R2 (5/7/14) 3.00 8.00
RTCNYRDS7 D.Stepan R2 (5/11/14) 3.00 8.00
RTCNYRDS8 D.Stepan R3 (5/22/14) 8.00 20.00
RTCNYRDS9 D.Stepan R3 (5/29/14) 8.00 20.00
RTCNYRDS10 D.Stepan R4 (6/9/14) 12.00 30.00
RTCNYRDS11 D.Stepan R4 (6/11/14) 12.00 30.00
RTCNYRHL1 Lundqvist R1 (4/17/14) 3.00 8.00
RTCNYRHL2 H.Lundqvist R1 (4/20/14) 3.00 8.00
RTCNYRHL3 H.Lundqvist R1 (4/27/14) 3.00 8.00
RTCNYRHL4 H.Lundqvist R1 (4/30/14) 3.00 8.00
RTCNYRHL5 H.Lundqvist R2 (5/5/14) 4.00 10.00
RTCNYRHL6 H.Lundqvist R2 (5/7/14) 4.00 10.00
RTCNYRHL7 H.Lundqvist R2 (5/11/14) 4.00 10.00
RTCNYRHL8 Lundqvist R3 (5/22/14) 8.00 20.00
RTCNYRHL9 H.Lundqvist R3 (5/25/14) 8.00 20.00
RTCNYRHL10 H.Lundqvist R3 (5/29/14) 8.00 20.00
RTCNYRHL11 H.Lundqvist R4 (6/9/14) 15.00 40.00
RTCNYRHL12 H.Lundqvist R4 (6/11/14) 15.00 40.00
RTCNYRMS1 M.St.Louis R1 (4/17/14) 5.00 12.00
RTCNYRMS2 M.St.Louis R1 (4/20/14) 2.50 6.00
RTCNYRMS3 M.St.Louis R1 (4/27/14) 2.50 6.00
RTCNYRMS4 M.St.Louis R1 (4/30/14) 2.50 6.00
RTCNYRMS5 M.St.Louis R2 (5/5/14) 3.00 8.00
RTCNYRMS6 M.St.Louis R2 (5/7/14) 3.00 8.00
RTCNYRMS7 M.St.Louis R2 (5/11/14) 3.00 8.00
RTCNYRMS8 M.St.Louis R3 (5/22/14) 6.00 15.00
RTCNYRMS9 M.St.Louis R3 (5/25/14) 6.00 15.00
RTCNYRMS10 M.St.Louis R3 (5/29/14) 6.00 15.00
RTCNYRMS11 M.St.Louis R4 (6/9/14) 12.00 30.00
RTCNYRMS12 M.St.Louis R4 (6/11/14) 12.00 30.00
RTCNYRMZ1 M.Zuccarello R1 (4/17/14) 2.50 6.00
RTCNYRMZ2 M.Zuccarello R1 (4/20/14) 2.50 6.00
RTCNYRMZ3 M.Zuccarello R1 (4/27/14) 2.50 6.00
RTCNYRMZ4 M.Zuccarello R1 (4/30/14) 2.50 6.00
RTCNYRMZ5 M.Zuccarello R2 (5/5/14) 3.00 8.00
RTCNYRMZ6 M.Zuccarello R2 (5/7/14) 3.00 8.00
RTCNYRMZ7 M.Zuccarello R2 (5/11/14) 3.00 8.00
RTCNYRMZ8 M.Zuccarello R3 (5/22/14) 6.00 15.00
RTCNYRMZ9 M.Zuccarello R3 (5/25/14) 6.00 15.00
RTCNYRMZ10 M.Zuccarello R3 (5/29/14) 6.00 15.00
RTCNYRMZ11 M.Zuccarello R4 (6/9/14) 12.00 30.00
RTCNYRMZ12 M.Zuccarello R4 (6/11/14) 12.0030.00
RTCNYRRM1 R.McDonagh R1 (4/17/14) 2.50 6.00
RTCNYRRM2 R.McDonagh R1 (4/20/14) 2.50 6.00
RTCNYRRM3 R.McDonagh R1 (4/27/14) 2.50 6.00
RTCNYRRM4 R.McDonagh R1 (4/30/14) 2.50 6.00
RTCNYRRM5 R.McDonagh R2 (5/5/14) 3.00 8.00
RTCNYRRM6 R.McDonagh R2 (5/7/14) 3.00 8.00
RTCNYRRM7 R.McDonagh R2 (5/11/14) 3.00 8.00
RTCNYRRM8 R.McDonagh R3 (5/22/14) 6.00 15.00
RTCNYRRM9 R.McDonagh R3 (5/25/14) 6.00 15.00
RTCNYRRM10 R.McDonagh R3 (5/29/14) 6.00 15.00
RTCNYRRM11 R.McDonagh R4 (6/9/14) 12.00 30.00
RTCNYRRM12 R.McDonagh R4 (6/11/14) 12.0030.00
RTCNYRRN1 R.Nash R1 (4/17/14) 2.50 6.00
RTCNYRRN2 R.Nash R1 (4/20/14) 2.50 6.00
RTCNYRRN3 R.Nash R1 (4/27/14) 2.50 6.00
RTCNYRRN4 R.Nash R1 (4/30/14) 2.50 6.00
RTCNYRRN5 R.Nash R2 (5/5/14) 3.00 8.00
RTCNYRRN6 R.Nash R2 (5/7/14) 3.00 8.00
RTCNYRRN7 R.Nash R2 (5/11/14) 3.00 8.00
RTCNYRRN8 R.Nash R3 (5/22/14) 6.00 15.00
RTCNYRRN9 R.Nash R3 (5/25/14) 6.00 15.00
RTCNYRRN10 R.Nash R3 (5/29/14) 6.00 15.00
RTCNYRRN11 R.Nash R4 (6/9/14) 12.00 30.00
RTCNYRRN12 R.Nash R4 (6/11/14) 12.00 30.00
RTCPFCG1 C.Giroux R1 (4/22/14) 2.50 6.00
RTCPFCG2 C.Giroux R1 (4/25/14) 2.50 6.00
RTCPFCG3 C.Giroux R1 (4/29/14) 2.50 6.00
RTCPFJV1 J.Voracek R1 (4/22/14) 2.50 6.00
RTCPFJV2 J.Voracek R1 (4/25/14) 2.50 6.00
RTCPFJV3 J.Voracek R1 (4/29/14) 2.50 6.00
RTCPFSM1 S.Mason R1 (4/22/14) 2.00 5.00
RTCPFSM2 S.Mason R1 (4/25/14) 2.00 5.00
RTCPFSM3 S.Mason R1 (4/29/14) 2.00 5.00
RTCPFWS1 W.Simmonds R1 (4/22/14) 3.00 8.00
RTCPFWS2 W.Simmonds R1 (4/25/14) 3.00 8.00
RTCPFWS3 W.Simmonds R1 (4/29/14) 3.00 8.00
RTCPPCK1 C.Kunitz R1 (4/16/14) 2.50 6.00
RTCPPCK2 C.Kunitz R1 (4/19/14) 2.50 6.00
RTCPPCK3 C.Kunitz R1 (4/26/14) 2.50 6.00
RTCPPCK4 C.Kunitz R2 (5/2/14) 3.00 8.00
RTCPPCK5 C.Kunitz R2 (5/4/14) 3.00 8.00
RTCPPCK6 C.Kunitz R2 (5/9/14) 3.00 8.00
RTCPPCK7 C.Kunitz R2 (5/13/14) 3.00 8.00
RTCPPEM1 E.Malkin R1 (4/16/14) 8.00 20.00
RTCPPEM2 E.Malkin R1 (4/19/14) 8.00 20.00
RTCPPEM3 E.Malkin R1 (4/26/14) 8.00 20.00
RTCPPEM4 E.Malkin R2 (5/2/14) 10.00 25.00
RTCPPEM5 E.Malkin R2 (5/4/14) 10.00 25.00
RTCPPEM6 E.Malkin R2 (5/9/14) 10.00 25.00
RTCPPEM7 E.Malkin R2 (5/13/14) 10.00 25.00
RTCPPJJ1 J.Jokinen R1 (4/16/14) 1.50 4.00
RTCPPJJ2 J.Jokinen R1 (4/19/14) 1.50 4.00
RTCPPJJ3 J.Jokinen R1 (4/26/14) 1.50 4.00
RTCPPJJ4 J.Jokinen R2 (5/2/14) 2.00 5.00
RTCPPJJ5 J.Jokinen R2 (5/4/14) 2.00 5.00
RTCPPJJ6 J.Jokinen R2 (5/9/14) 2.00 5.00
RTCPPJJ7 J.Jokinen R2 (5/13/14) 2.00 5.00
RTCPPJN1 J.Neal R1 (4/16/14) 2.50 6.00
RTCPPJN2 J.Neal R1 (4/19/14) 2.50 6.00
RTCPPJN3 J.Neal R1 (4/26/14) 2.50 6.00
RTCPPJN4 J.Neal R2 (5/2/14) 3.00 8.00
RTCPPJN5 J.Neal R2 (5/4/14) 3.00 8.00
RTCPPJN6 J.Neal R2 (5/9/14) 3.00 8.00
RTCPPJN7 J.Neal R2 (5/13/14) 3.00 8.00
RTCPPKL1 K.Letang R1 (4/16/14) 2.50 6.00
RTCPPKL2 K.Letang R1 (4/19/14) 2.50 6.00
RTCPPKL3 K.Letang R1 (4/26/14) 2.50 6.00
RTCPPKL4 K.Letang R2 (5/2/14) 3.00 8.00
RTCPPKL5 K.Letang R2 (5/4/14) 3.00 8.00
RTCPPKL6 K.Letang R2 (5/9/14) 3.00 8.00
RTCPPKL7 K.Letang R2 (5/13/14) 3.00 8.00
RTCPPMF1 M.Fleury R1 (4/16/14) 4.00 10.00
RTCPPMF2 M.Fleury R1 (4/19/14) 4.00 10.00
RTCPPMF3 M.Fleury R1 (4/26/14) 4.00 10.00
RTCPPMF4 M.Fleury R2 (5/2/14) 5.00 12.00
RTCPPMF5 M.Fleury R2 (5/4/14) 5.00 12.00
RTCPPMF6 M.Fleury R2 (5/9/14) 5.00 12.00
RTCPPMF7 M.Fleury R2 (5/13/14) 5.00 12.00
RTCPPOM1 O.Maatta R1 (4/16/14) 2.50 6.00
RTCPPOM2 O.Maatta R1 (4/19/14) 2.50 6.00
RTCPPOM3 O.Maatta R1 (4/26/14) 2.50 6.00
RTCPPOM4 O.Maatta R2 (5/2/14) 3.00 8.00
RTCPPOM5 O.Maatta R2 (5/4/14) 3.00 8.00
RTCPPOM6 O.Maatta R2 (5/9/14) 3.00 8.00
RTCPPOM7 O.Maatta R2 (5/13/14) 3.00 8.00
RTCPPSC1 S.Crosby R1 (4/16/14) 10.00 25.00
RTCPPSC2 S.Crosby R1 (4/19/14) 10.00 25.00
RTCPPSC3 S.Crosby R1 (4/26/14) 10.00 25.00
RTCPPSC4 S.Crosby R2 (5/2/14) 12.00 30.00
RTCPPSC5 S.Crosby R2 (5/4/14) 12.00 30.00
RTCPPSC6 S.Crosby R2 (5/9/14) 12.00 30.00
RTCPPSC7 S.Crosby R2 (5/13/14) 12.00 30.00
RTCSJSAN1 A.Niemi R1 (4/17/14) 2.00 5.00
RTCSJSAN2 A.Niemi R1 (4/20/14) 2.00 5.00
RTCSJSAN3 A.Niemi R1 (4/26/14) 2.00 5.00
RTCSJSAN4 A.Niemi R1 (4/30/14) 2.00 5.00
RTCSJSBB1 B.Burns R1 (4/17/14) 3.00 8.00
RTCSJSBB2 B.Burns R1 (4/20/14) 3.00 8.00
RTCSJSBB3 B.Burns R1 (4/26/14) 3.00 8.00
RTCSJSBB4 B.Burns R1 (4/30/14) 3.00 8.00
RTCSJSJP1 J.Pavelski R1 (4/17/14) 2.50 6.00
RTCSJSJP2 J.Pavelski R1 (4/20/14) 2.50 6.00
RTCSJSJP3 J.Pavelski R1 (4/26/14) 2.50 6.00
RTCSJSJP4 J.Pavelski R1 (4/30/14) 2.50 6.00
RTCSJSJT1 J.Thornton R1 (4/17/14) 2.50 6.00
RTCSJSJT2 J.Thornton R1 (4/20/14) 2.50 6.00
RTCSJSJT3 J.Thornton R1 (4/26/14) 2.50 6.00
RTCSJSJT4 J.Thornton R1 (4/30/14) 2.50 6.00
RTCSJSLC1 L.Couture R1 (4/17/14) 2.50 6.00
RTCSJSLC2 L.Couture R1 (4/20/14) 2.50 6.00
RTCSJSLC3 L.Couture R1 (4/26/14) 2.50 6.00
RTCSJSLC4 L.Couture R1 (4/30/14) 2.50 6.00
RTCSJSPM1 P.Marleau R1 (4/17/14) 2.50 6.00
RTCSJSPM2 P.Marleau R1 (4/20/14) 2.50 6.00
RTCSJSPM3 P.Marleau R1 (4/26/14) 2.50 6.00
RTCSJSPM4 P.Marleau R1 (4/30/14) 2.50 6.00
RTCSJSTH1 T.Hertl R1 (4/17/14) 2.50 6.00
RTCSJSTH2 T.Hertl R1 (4/20/14) 2.50 6.00
RTCSJSTH3 T.Hertl R1 (4/26/14) 2.50 6.00
RTCSJSTH4 T.Hertl R1 (4/30/14) 2.50 6.00
RTCSTLAP1 A.Pietrangelo R1 (4/17/14) 2.00 5.00
RTCSTLAP2 A.Pietrangelo R1 (4/19/14) 2.00 5.00
RTCSTLAP3 A.Pietrangelo R1 (4/25/14) 2.00 5.00
RTCSTLAS1 A.Steen R1 (4/17/14) 2.50 6.00
RTCSTLAS2 A.Steen R1 (4/19/14) 2.50 6.00
RTCSTLAS3 A.Steen R1 (4/25/14) 2.50 6.00
RTCSTLDB1 D.Backes R1 (4/17/14) 2.50 6.00
RTCSTLDB2 D.Backes R1 (4/19/14) 2.50 6.00
RTCSTLDB3 D.Backes R1 (4/25/14) 2.50 6.00
RTCSTLRM1 R.Miller R1 (4/17/14) 2.50 6.00
RTCSTLRM2 R.Miller R1 (4/19/14) 2.50 6.00
RTCSTLRM3 R.Miller R1 (4/25/14) 2.50 6.00
RTCSTLTO1 T.Oshie R1 (4/19/14) 4.00 10.00
RTCSTLTO2 T.Oshie R1 (4/25/14) 4.00 10.00
RTCTBLOP O.Palat R1 (4/16/14) 2.00 5.00
RTCTBLSS1 S.Stamkos R1 (4/16/14) 5.00 12.00
RTCTBLSS2 S.Stamkos R1 (4/18/14) 5.00 12.00

2014-15 Ultra Rookie Buyback Autographs

20 Johnny Gaudreau 30.00 60.00
28 Teuvo Teravainen 15.00 30.00
143 Brandon Gormley 5.00 12.00
145 Mark Visentin 5.00 12.00
166 Ty Rattie 6.00 15.00
171 Vladislav Namestnikov 8.00 20.00
178 Greg McKegg 4.00 10.00
191 Evgeny Kuznetsov 20.00 50.00

2014-15 Ultra Rule 76

STATED ODDS 1:108 HOBBY
F01 J.Tavares/D.Stepan 6.00 15.00
F02 W.Gretzky/M.Lemieux 10.00 25.00
F03 S.Yzerman/J.Sakic 6.00 15.00
F04 C.Giroux/E.Malkin 10.00 25.00
F05 P.Bergeron/T.Plekanec 4.00 10.00
F06 T.Bozak/D.Desharnais 3.00 8.00

D7 N.Kadri/R.Nugent-Hopkins 3.00 8.00
D8 A.Kopitar/R.Getzlaf 5.00 12.00
D9 E.Staal/N.Backstrom 5.00 12.00
D10 J.Toews/D.Backes 6.00 15.00

1961-62 Union Oil WHL

This 12-drawing set features players from the Los Angeles Blades (1-8) and the San Francisco Seals (9-12) of the Western Hockey League. The black-and-white drawings by artist Sam Patrick measure approximately 6" by 8" and are printed on textured white paper. The back of each drawing carries the player's career highlights and biographical information. The Union Oil name and logo at the bottom round out the backs. The cards are unnumbered and listed below alphabetically within teams. Reportedly only eight cards were issued to the public, making four of the cards extremely scarce.

COMPLETE SET (12) 50.00 100.00
Jack Bowness 3.00 6.00
Ed Diachuk 3.00 6.00
Leo LaBine 5.00 10.00
Willie O'Ree 20.00 40.00
Bruce Carmichael 3.00 6.00
Gordon Haworth 4.00 8.00
Fleming Mackell 5.00 10.00
Robert Solinger 3.00 6.00
Gary Edmundson 3.00 6.00
0 Al Nicholson 3.00 6.00
1 Orland Kurtenbach 7.50 15.00
2 Tom Thurlby 3.00 6.00

1990-91 Upper Deck

The 1990-91 Upper Deck Hockey set contains 550 standard-size cards released in two series of 400 and 150 cards, respectively. The card fronts feature color action photos while the backs feature biographical information, a card number, career statistics and a small Upper Deck authenticity hologram. This small hologram features the words "Upper Deck" in the foreground with "90" and a pair of hockey sticks printed in the background. This is considered the standard hologram for both Series One and Series Two. Series One cards can also be found printed with two other Upper Deck Hologram types on the back: the 1990 Upper Deck Comic Ball hologram that features the words "Upper Deck" in the foreground and "90" and an image of carrots (in honor of Bugs Bunny) in the background, and the 1990 Upper Deck Baseball hologram that features the words" Upper Deck" in the foreground and an image of a baseball in the background. Series Two cards can also be found with the 1991-92 Upper Deck Hockey hologram that features "Upper Deck" in a stacked layout in the foreground and "19" upside down in the background without any hockey stick images. Finally, there was also a French language version that was produced in slightly smaller quantities compared to the English version featuring the same 1990-91 Hockey hologram. Series Two French cards can be found with a variation hologram attached to the cardbacks that was primarily used for 1991 Upper Deck Baseball.

COMPLETE SET (550) 15.00 40.00
COMP.LO SERIES (400) 10.00 25.00
COMP.HI SERIES (150) 6.00 15.00
COMP.HI FACT.SET (150) 6.00 15.00
*1990 BASEBALL HOLOGRAM BACK: .5X TO 1.25X
*1990 COMIC BALL HOLOGRAM BACK: ..5X TO 1.25X
*91-92 HOLOGRAM BACK: ..5X TO 1.25X
1 David Volek .20 .50
2 Brian Propp .20 .50
3 Wendel Clark .20 .50
4 Adam Creighton .12 .30
5 Mark Osborne .15 .40
6 Murray Craven .20 .50
7 Doug Crossman .15 .40
8 Mario Marois .15 .40
9 Curt Giles .15 .40
10 Rick Wamsley .20 .50
11 Troy Mallette RC .15 .40
12 John Cullen .20 .50
13 Miloslav Horava RC .15 .40
14 Kevin Stevens RC .40 1.00
15 David Shaw .20 .50
16 Randy Wood .12 .30
17 Peter Zezel .20 .50
18 Glenn Healy RC .40 1.00
19 Sergio Momesso RC .15 .40
20 Don Maloney .20 .50
21 Craig Muni .15 .40
22 Phil Housley .15 .40
23 Martin Gelinas RC .40 1.00
24 Alexander Mogilny RC .60 1.50
25 John Byce RC .15 .40
26 Joe Nieuwendyk .12 .30
27 Ron Tugnutt .15 .40
28 Don Barber RC .15 .40
29 Gary Roberts .20 .50
30 Basil McRae .15 .40
31 Phil Bourque .15 .40
32 Mike Richter RC .60 1.50
33 Zarley Zalapski .15 .40
34 Bernie Nicholls .20 .50
35 Bob Corkum RC .12 .30
36 Rod Brind'Amour RC .40 1.00
37 Mark Fitzpatrick RC .15 .40
38 Gino Cavallini .20 .50
39 Mick Vukota RC .20 .50
40 Mike Lalor RC .15 .40
41 Dave Andreychuk .20 .50
42 Bill Ranford .15 .40
43 Pierre Turgeon .15 .40
44 Mark Messier .40 1.00
45 Rob Blake RC .30 .75
46 Mike Modano RC 1.00 2.50
47 Theo Fleury .25 .60
40 Neal Broten .12 .30
49 Paul Gillis .15 .40
50 Doug Bodger UER .15 .40
51 Stephan Lebeau RC .15 .40
52 Larry Robinson .15 .40
53 Dale Hawerchuk .25 .60
54 Wayne Gretzky 1.00 2.50
55 Ed Belfour RC .60 1.50
56 Steve Yzerman .60 1.50
57 Rod Langway .20 .50
58 Bernie Federko .15 .40
59 Mario Lemieux Streak .75 2.00
60 Doug Lidster .20 .50
61 Dave Christian .15 .40
62 Rob Ramage .20 .50
63 Jeremy Roenick RC .60 1.50
64 Ray Bourque .30 .75
65 Jon Morris RC .12 .30
66 Sean Burke .15 .40
67 Ron Francis .25 .60
68 Ron Sutter .15 .40
69 Peter Sidorkiewicz .20 .50
70 Sylvain Turgeon .15 .40
71 Dave Ellett .12 .30
72 Bobby Smith .15 .40
73 Luc Robitaille .20 .50
74 Pat Elynuik .15 .40
75 Jason Soules RC .12 .30
76 Dino Ciccarelli .20 .50
77 Vladimir Krutov RC .40 1.00
78 Lee Norwood .15 .40
79 Brian Bradley .15 .40
80 Michal Pivonka RC .15 .40
81 Mark LaForest RC .12 .30
82 Trent Yawney .20 .50
83 Tom Fergus .15 .40
84 Andy Brickley .12 .30
85 Dave Manson .20 .50
86 Gord Murphy RC .20 .50
87 Scott Young .12 .30
88 Tommy Albelin .12 .30
89 Ken Wregget .20 .50
90 Brad Shaw RC .15 .40
91 Mario Gosselin .15 .40
92 Paul Fenton .20 .50
93 Brian Skrudland .15 .40
94 Thomas Steen .15 .40
95 John Tonelli .15 .40
96 Steve Chiasson UER .12 .30
97 Mike Ridley .12 .30
98 Garth Butcher .15 .40
99 Daniel Shank RC .20 .50
100 Checklist 1-100 .12 .30
101 Jamie Macoun .15 .40
102 Wendell Young RC .20 .50
103 Laurie Boschman .15 .40
104 Paul Ranheim RC .20 .50
105 Doug Smail .15 .40
106 Shawn Chambers .15 .40
107 Steve Weeks .20 .50
108 Gaetan Duchesne .20 .50
109 Kevin Hatcher .15 .40
110 Paul Reinhart .20 .50
111 Shawn Burr .15 .40
112 Troy Murray .15 .40
113 John Chabot .20 .50
114 Jacques Cloutier RC .15 .40
115 Rick Zombo RC .20 .50
116 Kjell Samuelsson .15 .40
117 Tim Watters .12 .30
118 Pat Flatley .20 .50
119 Tom Laidlaw .20 .50
120 Ilkka Sinisalo .15 .40
121 Tom Barrasso .15 .40
122 Bob Essensa RC .30 .75
123 Sergei Makarov RC .40 1.00
124 Paul Coffey .20 .50
125 Bob Beers RC .15 .40
126 Brian Bellows .15 .40
127 Mike Liut .15 .40
128 Igor Larionov RC .40 1.00
129 Craig Simpson .15 .40
130 Kelly Miller .12 .30
131 Dirk Graham .15 .40
132 Jimmy Carson .15 .40
133 Michel Goulet .12 .30
134 Gerard Gallant .12 .30
135 Bruce Hoffort RC .20 .50
136 Steve Duchesne .12 .30
137 Bryan Trottier .25 .60
138 Pelle Eklund .12 .30
139 Gary Nylund .15 .40
140 Steve Kasper .15 .40
141 Joel Otto .15 .40
142 Rob Brown .40 1.00
143 Al MacInnis .15 .40
144 Mario Lemieux .75 2.00
145 Peter Eriksson RC UER .12 .30
146 Jari Kurri .25 .60
147 Petri Skriko .20 .50
148 Steve Smith .15 .40
149 Calle Johansson .20 .50
150 Stewart Gavin .20 .50
151 Randy Ladouceur .20 .50
152 Vincent Riendeau RC .20 .50
153 Patrick Roy .50 1.25
154 Brett Hull .40 1.00
155 Craig Fisher RC .20 .50
156 Cam Neely .20 .50
157 Al Iafrate .12 .30
158 Bob Carpenter .15 .40
159 Doug Brown .15 .40
160 Tom Kurvers .20 .50
161 John MacLean .15 .40
162 Guy Lafleur .25 .60
163 Peter Stastny .15 .40
164 Joe Sakic .60 1.50
165 Robb Stauber RC .20 .50
166 Daren Puppa .15 .40
167 Esa Tikkanen .15 .40
168 Mike Ramsey .12 .30
169 Craig MacTavish .15 .40
170 Christian Ruuttu .15 .40
171 Brian Hayward .20 .50
172 Pat Verbeek .15 .40
173 Adam Oates .20 .50
174 Chris Chelios .20 .50
175 Curtis Joseph RC .60 1.50
176 Slava Fetisov RC .40 1.00
177 Dave Poulin .20 .50
178 Mark Recchi RC .60 1.50
179 Daniel Marois .15 .40
180 Mark Johnson .15 .40
181 Michel Petit .15 .40
182 Brian Mullen .20 .50
183 Chris Terreri RC .40 1.00
184 Tony Hrkac .12 .30
185 James Patrick .20 .50
186 Craig Ludwig .20 .50
187 Uwe Krupp .20 .50
188 Guy Carbonneau .12 .30
189 Dave Snuggerud RC .15 .40
190 Joe Murphy RC .15 .40
191 Jeff Brown .20 .50
192 Dean Evason .15 .40
193 Petr Svoboda .15 .40
194 Dave Babych .12 .30
195 Steve Tuttle .15 .40
196 Randy Burridge .15 .40
197 Tony Tanti .15 .40
198 Bob Sweeney .12 .30
199 Brad Marsh .15 .40
200 Checklist 101-200 .12 .30
201 B.Ranford Conn Smythe .15 .40
202 Sergei Makarov Calder .40 1.00
203 Brett Hull Byng .40 1.00
204 Ray Bourque Norris .30 .75
205 Wayne Gretzky Ross 1.00 2.50
206 Mark Messier Hart .40 1.00
207 Patrick Roy Vezina .50 1.25
208 Rick Meagher Selke .15 .40
209 William Jennings Trophy .20 .50
Andy Moog
Reggie Lemelin
210 Aaron Broten .15 .40
211 John Carter RC .15 .40
212 Marty McSorley .20 .50
213 Greg Millen .15 .40
214 Dave Taylor .20 .50
215 Rejean Lemelin .15 .40
216 Dave McLlwain .20 .50
217 Don Beaupre .12 .30
218 Paul MacDermid .15 .40
219 Dale Hunter .20 .50
220 Brent Ashton .20 .50
221 Steve Thomas .12 .30
222 Ed Olczyk .20 .50
223 Doug Wilson .20 .50
224 Vincent Damphousse .15 .40
225 Rob DiMaio RC .20 .50
226 Hubie McDonough RC .15 .40
227 Ron Hextall .15 .40
220 Dave Chyzowski RC .15 .40
229 Larry Murphy .15 .40
230 Mike Bullard .15 .40
231 Kelly Hrudey .12 .30
232 Andy Moog .20 .50
233 Todd Elik RC .20 .50
234 Craig Janney .20 .50
235 Peter Lappin RC .15 .40
236 Scott Stevens .20 .50
237 Fredrik Olausson .15 .40
238 Geoff Courtnall .15 .40
239 Greg Paslawski .15 .40
240 Alan May RC .12 .30
241 Allan Bester .20 .50
242 Steve Larmer .15 .40
243 Gary Leeman .15 .40
244 Denis Savard .25 .60
245 Eric Weinrich RC .20 .50
246 Pat LaFontaine .20 .50
247 Tim Kerr .20 .50
248 Dave Gagner .20 .50
249 Brent Sutter .15 .40
250 Claude Vilgrain RC .12 .30
251 Tomas Sandstrom .20 .50
252 Joe Mullen .15 .40
253 Brian Leetch .25 .60
254 Mike Vernon .20 .50
255 Daniel Dore RC .12 .30
256 Trevor Linden .15 .40
257 Dave Barr .20 .50
258 John Ogrodnick .20 .50
259 Russ Courtnall .20 .50
260 Dan Quinn .15 .40
261 Mark Howe .20 .50
262 Kevin Lowe .20 .50
263 Rick Tocchet .20 .50
264 Grant Fuhr .20 .50
265 Andrew Cassels RC .12 .30
266 Kevin Dineen .20 .50
267 Kirk Muller .15 .40
268 Randy Cunneyworth .15 .40
269 Brendan Shanahan .25 .60
270 Dave Tippett .15 .40
271 Doug Gilmour .25 .60
272 Tony Granato .15 .40
273 Gary Suter .20 .50
274 Darren Turcotte RC .15 .40
275 Murray Baron RC .15 .40
276 Stephane Richer .20 .50
277 Mike Gartner .20 .50
278 Kirk McLean .12 .30
279 John Vanbiesbrouck .15 .40
280 Shayne Corson .15 .40
281 Paul Cavallini .15 .40
282 Petr Klima .12 .30
283 Ulf Dahlen .20 .50
284 Glenn Anderson .20 .50
285 Rick Meagher .15 .40
286 Alexei Kasatonov RC .20 .50
287 Ulf Samuelsson .20 .50
288 Patrik Sundstrom .20 .50
289 Ray Ferraro .15 .40
290 Janne Ojanen RC .20 .50
291 Jeff Jackson .15 .40
292 Jiri Hrdina RC .15 .40
293 Joe Cirella .12 .30
294 Brad McCrimmon .20 .50
295 Curtis Leschyshyn RC .15 .40
296 Kelly Kisio .15 .40
297 Jyrki Lumme RC .12 .30
298 Mark Janssens RC .20 .50
299 Stan Smyl .12 .30
300 Checklist 201-300 .12 .30
301 Joe Sakic TC .60 1.50
302 Petri Skriko TC .20 .50
303 Steve Yzerman TC .60 1.50
304 Tim Kerr TC .20 .50
305 Mario Lemieux TC .75 2.00
306 Pat LaFontaine TC .20 .50
307 Wayne Gretzky TC 1.00 2.50
308 Brian Bellows TC .15 .40
309 Rod Langway TC .20 .50
310 Gary Leeman TC .15 .40
311 Kirk Muller TC .15 .40
312 Brett Hull TC .40 1.00
313 Thomas Steen TC .15 .40
314 Ron Francis TC .25 .60
315 Brian Leetch TC .25 .60
316 Jeremy Roenick TC .60 1.50
317 Patrick Roy TC .50 1.25
318 Pierre Turgeon TC .15 .40
319 Al MacInnis TC .15 .40
320 Ray Bourque TC .30 .75
321 Mark Messier TC .40 1.00
322 Jody Hull RC .20 .50
323 Chris Joseph RC .12 .30
324 Adam Burt RC .15 .40
325 Jason Herter RC .12 .30
326 Geoff Smith ART RC .20 .50
327 Brad Shaw ART .15 .40
328 Rich Sutter .20 .50
329 Barry Pederson .15 .40
330 Paul MacLean .15 .40
331 Randy Carlyle .15 .40
332 Donald Dufresne RC UER .12 .30
333 Brent Hughes RC .12 .30
334 Mathieu Schneider RC .15 .40
335 Jason Miller RC .12 .30
336 Sergei Makarov ART .40 1.00
337 Bob Essensa ART .30 .75
338 Claude Loiselle RC .12 .30
339 Wayne Presley .12 .30
340 Tony McKegney .12 .30
341 Charlie Huddy .15 .40
342 Greg Adams UER .12 .30
Front photo is Igor Larionov
343 Mike Tomlak RC .20 .50
344 Adam Graves RC .40 1.00
345 Michel Mongeau RC .15 .40
346 Mike Modano ART UER .60 1.50
347 Rod Brind'Amour ART .40 1.00
348 Dana Murzyn .20 .50
349 Dave Lowry RC .15 .40
350 Star Rookie CL .12 .30
351 Nol/Prim/Nedv/Ric CL .60 1.50
352 Owen Nolan RC .60 1.50
353 Petr Nedved RC .20 .50
354 Keith Primeau RC .30 .75
355 Mike Ricci RC .20 .50
356 Jaromir Jagr RC 2.50 6.00
357 Scott Scissons RC .15 .40
358 Darryl Sydor RC .20 .50
359 Derian Hatcher RC .15 .40
360 John Slaney RC .12 .30
361 Drake Berehowsky RC .15 .40
362 Luke Richardson .15 .40
363 Lucien DeBlois .15 .40
364 Dave Reid RC .20 .50
365 Mats Sundin RC .75 2.00
366 Jan Erixon .20 .50
367 Troy Loney RC .20 .50
368 Chris Nilan .12 .30
369 Gord Dineen .15 .40
370 Jeff Bloemberg RC .15 .40
371 John Druce RC .20 .50
372 Brian MacLellan .15 .40
373 Bruce Driver .20 .50
374 Marc Habscheid .15 .40
375 Paul Ysebaert RC .15 .40
376 Rick Vaive .15 .40
377 Glen Wesley .15 .40
378 Mike Foligno .15 .40
379 Garry Galley RC .12 .30
380 Dean Kennedy RC .12 .30
381 Daniel Berthiaume .15 .40
382 Mike Keane RC .12 .30
383 Frank Musil .12 .30
384 Mike McPhee .15 .40
385 Jon Casey .20 .50
386 Jeff Norton .20 .50
387 John Tucker .15 .40
388 Alan Kerr .15 .40
389 Bob Rouse .12 .30
390 Gerald Diduck .15 .40
391 Greg Hawgood .15 .40
392 Randy Velischek .12 .30
393 Tim Cheveldae RC .15 .40
394 Mike Krushelnyski .20 .50
395 Glen Hanlon .15 .40
396 Lou Franceschetti RC .20 .50
397 Scott Arniel .12 .30
398 Terry Carkner .15 .40
399 Clint Malarchuk .15 .40
400 Checklist 301-400 .12 .30
401 Mikhail Tatarinov RC .12 .30
402 Benoit Hogue .20 .50
403 Frank Pietrangelo RC .12 .30
404 Paul Stanton RC .20 .50
405 Anatoli Semenov RC .15 .40
406 Bobby Smith .15 .40
407 Derek King .20 .50
408 J.C. Bergeron RC .20 .50
409 Brian Propp .20 .50
410 Jiri Latal RC .20 .50
411 Joey Kocur RC .40 1.00
412 Daniel Berthiaume .15 .40
413 Dave Ellett .12 .30
414 Jay Miller RC .12 .30
415 Steph Beauregard RC .15 .40
416 Mark Hardy .12 .30
417 Todd Krygier RC .15 .40
418 Randy Moller .20 .50
419 Doug Crossman .15 .40
420 Ray Sheppard .12 .30
421 Sylvain Lefebvre RC .15 .40
422 Chris Chelios .20 .50
423 Joe Mullen .15 .40
424 Pete Peeters .12 .30
425 Bryan Trottier .25 .60
426 Denis Savard .25 .60
427 Ken Daneyko .12 .30
428 Eric Desjardins RC .40 1.00
429 Zdeno Ciger RC .20 .50
430 Brad McCrimmon .20 .50
431 Ed Olczyk .20 .50
432 Peter Ing RC .20 .50
433 Bob Kudelski RC .15 .40
434 Troy Gamble RC .20 .50
435 Phil Housley .15 .40
436 Scott Stevens .20 .50
437 Normand Rochefort .12 .30
438 Geoff Courtnall .15 .40
439 Ken Baumgartner RC .20 .50
440 Kris King RC .20 .50
441 Troy Crowder RC .12 .30
442 Chris Nilan .12 .30
443 Dale Hawerchuk .25 .60
444 Kevin Miller RC .20 .50
445 Keith Acton .20 .50
446 Jeff Chychrun RC .15 .40
447 Claude Lemieux .12 .30
448 Bob Probert .20 .50
449 Brian Hayward .20 .50
450 Craig Berube RC .12 .30
451 Team Canada Juniors 1.25 3.00
452 Mike Sillinger RC .20 .50
453 Jason Marshall RC .12 .30
454 Patrice Brisebois RC .12 .30
455 Brad May RC .15 .40
456 Pierre Sevigny RC .12 .30
457 John Slaney .12 .30
458 Felix Potvin RC .75 2.00
459 Scott Thornton RC .12 .30
460 Greg Johnson RC .12 .30
461 Scott Niedermayer RC .30 .75
462 Steven Rice RC .20 .50
463 Trevor Kidd RC .15 .40
464 Dale Craigwell RC .12 .30
465 Kent Manderville RC .12 .30
466 Kris Draper RC .15 .40
467 Martin Lapointe RC .20 .50
468 Chris Snell RC .12 .30
469 Pat Falloon RC .12 .30
470 David Harlock RC .12 .30
471 Karl Dykhuis RC .15 .40
472 Mike Craig RC .20 .50
473 Canada's Captains 1.25 3.00
474 Brett Hull AS .40 1.00
475 Darren Turcotte AS .15 .40
476 Wayne Gretzky AS 1.00 2.50
477 Steve Yzerman AS .60 1.50
478 Theo Fleury AS .25 .60
479 Pat LaFontaine AS .20 .50
480 Trevor Linden AS .15 .40
481 Jeremy Roenick AS .60 1.50
482 Scott Stevens AS .20 .50
483 Adam Oates AS .20 .50
484 Vincent Damphousse AS .15 .40
485 Brian Leetch AS .25 .60
486 Kevin Hatcher AS .15 .40
487 Mark Recchi AS .60 1.50
488 Rick Tocchet AS .20 .50
489 Ray Bourque AS .30 .75
490 Joe Sakic AS .60 1.50
491 Chris Chelios AS .20 .50
492 John Cullen AS .20 .50
493 Cam Neely AS .20 .50
494 Mark Messier AS .40 1.00
495 Mike Vernon AS .20 .50
496 Patrick Roy AS .50 1.25
497 Al MacInnis AS .15 .40
498 Paul Coffey AS .20 .50
499 Steve Larmer AS .15 .40
500 Checklist 401-500 .12 .30
501 Heroes Checklist .12 .30
502 Red Kelly HERO .20 .50
503 Eric Nesterenko HERO .20 .50
504 Darryl Sittler HERO .20 .50
505 Jim Schoenfeld HERO .20 .50
506 Serge Savard HERO .20 .50
507 Glenn Resch HERO .20 .50
508 Lanny McDonald HERO .20 .50
509 Bobby Clarke HERO .20 .50
510 Phil Esposito HERO .30 .75
511 Harry Howell HERO .20 .50
512 Rod Gilbert HERO .20 .50
513 Pit Martin HERO .20 .50
514 Jimmy Watson HERO .12 .30
515 Denis Potvin HERO .12 .30
516 Robert Ray RC .20 .50
517 Danton Cole RC .20 .50
518 Gino Odjick RC .12 .30
519 Donald Audette RC .20 .50
520 Rick Tabaracci RC .12 .30
521 Young Guns CL/Federov .40 1.00
522 Kip Miller YG RC .15 .40
523 Johan Garpenlov YG RC .20 .50
524 Stephane Morin YG RC .12 .30
525 Sergei Fedorov YG RC UER 1.50 4.00
526 Pavel Bure YG RC 2.00 5.00
527 Wes Walz YG RC .20 .50
528 Robert Kron YG RC .20 .50
529 Ken Hodge Jr. YG RC .12 .30
530 Garry Valk YG RC .12 .30
531 Tim Sweeney YG RC .20 .50
532 Mark Pederson YG RC .20 .50
533 Robert Reichel YG RC .20 .50
534 Bobby Holik YG RC .20 .50
535 Stephane Matteau YG RC .20 .50
536 Peter Bondra YG RC .60 1.50
537 Dimitri Khristich RC .12 .30
538 Vladimir Ruzicka RC .20 .50
539 Al Iafrate .12 .30
540 Rick Bennett RC .12 .30
541 Daryl Reaugh RC .12 .30
542 Martin Hostak RC .20 .50
543 Kari Takko RC .12 .30
544 Jocelyn Lemieux RC .15 .40
545 W.Gretzky 2000th 1.00 2.50
546 Brett Hull 50/50 .40 1.00
547 Neil Wilkinson RC .15 .40
548 Bryan Fogarty RC .12 .30
549 Zamboni Machine .12 .30
550 Checklist 501-550 .12 .30

1990-91 Upper Deck Holograms

The nine standard-size cards in this set were randomly inserted in 1990-91 Upper Deck foil packs (low and high series). The cards are best described as stereograms because the players show movement when the cards are slowly rotated. On the fronts, the stereograms are enclosed by a frame with rounded corners. The Upper Deck logo and title line "Hockey Superstars" appear in a bar at the top. The backs are blank and can be peeled off to stick the stereogram on a surface. The cards are unnumbered and checklisted below in alphabetical order.

1 Wayne Gretzky 1.00 2.50
2 Wayne Gretzky 1.00 2.50
3 Wayne Gretzky 1.00 2.50
4 Brett Hull .40 1.00
5 Mark Messier .40 1.00
6 M.Messier/B.Hull .40 1.00
7 M.Messier/S.Yzerman .60 1.50
8 Steve Yzerman .60 1.50
9 Steve Yzerman .60 1.50

1990-91 Upper Deck Promos

The 1990-91 Upper Deck Promo set is a two-card set featuring Wayne Gretzky and Patrick Roy both numbered as card number 241. The cards were first handed out as samples at the 1990 National Sports Collectors Convention in Arlington. The Arlington National promos were issued as a set in a special screw-down holder commemorating the National; these sets are much more limited and are rarely offered for sale. The photos on the front and back of both of the cards were changed in the regular set, as were the card numbers.

COMPLETE SET (2) 20.00 50.00
241A Wayne Gretzky UER 8.00 20.00
Wrong height, feet
and inches reversed)
241B Patrick Roy UER 6.00 15.00
Wrong height, feet
and inches reversed)

1990-91 Upper Deck Sheets

As an advertising promotion, Upper Deck produced hockey commemorative sheets that were given away during the 1990-91 season at selected games in large arenas. Each sheet measures 8 1/2" by 11" and is printed on card stock. The fronts of the team commemorative sheets feature the team logo and a series of Upper Deck cards of star players on that team. Some of these sheets have a brief history of the team, which is tied in with an Upper Deck advertisement. The All-Star game sheet is distinguished by a hockey stick facsimile autographed by those All-Star players whose cards are displayed. All the sheets have an Upper Deck stamp indicating the production quota; in addition, some of the sheets have the serial number. The backs are blank. The sheets are listed below in chronological order.

COMPLETE SET (11) 64.00 160.00
1 Toronto Maple Leafs 10.00 25.00
vs. Detroit Red Wings
Nov. 17, 1990 (20,000)
Al Iafrate
Ed Olcyzk
Vincent Damphousse
Wendel Clark
Gary Leeman
Drake Berehowsky
2 Detroit Red Wings I 6.00 15.00
vs. Boston Bruins
Dec. 4, 1990 (22,000)
Keith Primeau
Shawn Burr
Steve Yzerman
Jimmy Carson
Tim Cheveldae
Steve Chiasson
3 Los Angeles Kings 6.00 15.00
vs. Calgary Flames
Dec. 13, 1990 (19,500)
Steve Duchesne
Luc Robitaille
Rob Blake
Wayne Gretzky
Tony Granato
Tomas Sandstrom
4 New York Rangers I 4.00 10.00
vs. Hartford Whalers
Jan. 13, 1991 (25,700)
Mike Richter
Ray Sheppard
Troy Mallette
Normand Rochefort
Mark Janssens
Dennis Vial
John Ogrodnick
Lindy Ruff
Brian Leetch
5 New York Rangers II 5.00 12.00
vs. Chicago Blackhawks
Jan. 17, 1991 (25,700)
David Shaw
Miloslav Horava
Darren Turcotte
Jan Erixon
Kelly Kisio
Brian Mullen
Bernie Nicholls
John Vanbiesbrouck
James Patrick
6 Campbell All-Stars 12.00 30.00
Chicago Stadium
Jan. 19, 1991 (15,100)
Wayne Gretzky
Chris Chelios
Luc Robitaille
Brett Hull
Al MacInnis
Mike Vernon
7 Wales All-Stars 10.00 25.00
Chicago Stadium
Jan. 19, 1991 (15,100)
Ray Bourque
Rick Tocchet
Joe Sakic
Paul Coffey
Cam Neely
Patrick Roy
8 St. Louis Blues 4.00 10.00
vs. Buffalo Sabres
Jan. 29, 1991 (21,000)
Jeff Brown
Vincent Riendeau
Brent Hull
Paul Cavallini
Curtis Joseph
Gino Cavallini
Adam Oates
Scott Stevens
Rod Brind'Amour
9 Detroit Red Wings II 5.00 12.00
vs. Minnesota North Stars
Feb. 16, 1991 (23,000)
Joey Kocur
Rick Zombo
Sergei Fedorov
Gerard Gallant
Johan Garpenlov
Glen Hanlon
Dave Barr
John Chabot
Bob Probert
10 New York Rangers III 4.00 10.00
vs. New York Islanders
Feb. 18, 1991 (25,700)
Tie Domi
Randy Moller
Mike Gartner
Kevin Miller
Mark Hardy
Jody Hull
Kris King
Bob Froese
Paul Broten
11 All-Rookie Team 8.00 20.00
June 21, 1991 (16,000)
Eric Weinrich
Jaromir Jagr
Ed Belfour
Sergei Fedorov
Rob Blake
Ken Hodge

1991-92 Upper Deck

The 1991-92 UD set was released in two series of 500 and 200 cards, respectively. The front design features action photos with white borders. The player's name and position appear in the top white border, while the team name is given in the bottom white border. Biographical information, statistics, or player profile are displayed on the back alongside a second color photo. The All-Rookie Team and the Star Rookies are marked by the abbreviations ART and SR respectively in the list below. A randomly inserted Glasnost card (SP1) featuring Wayne Gretzky, Brett Hull and Valeri Kamensky and ballots by which fans could vote for their favorite NHL All-Stars were included in foil packs. Special subsets include members of the teams that participated in the IIHF World Junior Championships (650--699).

1 Vladimir Malakhov SS RC .07 .20
2 Alexei Zhamnov SS RC .07 .20
3 Dimitri Filiminov SS RC .07 .20
4 Alexander Semak SS RC .10 .25
5 Slava Kozlov RC .10 .25
6 Sergei Fedorov SS .15 .40
7 E.Lindros/B.Hull CC CL .15 .40
8 Al MacInnis CC .07 .20
9 Eric Lindros CC .07 .20
10 Bill Ranford CC .07 .20
11 Paul Coffey CC .07 .20
12 Dale Hawerchuk CC .12 .30
13 Wayne Gretzky CC .50 1.25
14 Mark Messier CC .25 .60
15 Steve Larmer CC .07 .20
16 Zigmund Palffy CC RC .60 1.50
17 Josef Beranek CC RC .10 .25
18 Jiri Slegr CC RC .05 .15
19 Martin Rucinsky CC RC .07 .20
20 Jaromir Jagr CC .25 .60
21 Teemu Selanne CC RC 1.25 3.00
22 Janne Laukkanen CC RC .05 .15
23 Markus Ketterer CC RC .05 .15
24 Jari Kurri CC .07 .20
25 Janne Ojanen CC .05 .15
26 Nicklas Lidstrom CC RC 1.25 3.00
27 Tomas Forslund CC RC .10 .25
28 Johan Garpenlov CC .07 .20
29 Niclas Andersson CC RC .05 .15
30 Tomas Sandstrom CC .07 .20
31 Mats Sundin CC .10 .25
32 Mike Modano CC .20 .50
33 Brett Hull CC .15 .40
34 Mike Richter CC .10 .25
35 Brian Leetch CC .07 .20
36 Jeremy Roenick CC .25 .60
37 Chris Chelios CC .10 .25
38 Wayne Gretzky 99 .50 1.25
39 Ed Belfour ART .25 .60
40 Sergei Fedorov ART .15 .40
41 Ken Hodge Jr. ART .10 .25
42 Jaromir Jagr ART .25 .60
43 Rob Blake ART .10 .25
44 Eric Weinrich ART .10 .25
45 The 50/50 Club .50 1.25
46 Russ Romaniuk RC .10 .25
47 M.Lemieux/G.Bush .40 1.00
48 Michel Picard RC .10 .25
49 Dennis Vaske .07 .20
50 Eric Murano RC .05 .15
51 Enrico Ciccone RC .05 .15
52 Shaun Van Allen RC .07 .20
53 Stu Barnes .07 .20
54 Pavel Bure .07 .20
55 Neil Wilkinson .07 .20
56 Tony Hrkac .07 .20
57 Brian Mullen .07 .20
58 Jeff Hackett .07 .20
59 Brian Hayward .07 .20
60 Craig Coxe .05 .15
61 Rob Zettler .07 .20
62 Bob McGill .07 .20
63 Lapointe .07 .20
Pushor CL
64 Peter Forsberg RC 1.50 4.00
65 Patrick Poulin RC .05 .15
66 Martin Lapointe .07 .20
67 Tyler Wright RC .05 .15
68 Philippe Boucher RC .05 .15
69 Glen Murray RC .10 .25
70 Martin Rucinsky RC .07 .20
71 Zigmund Palffy RC .60 1.50
72 Jassen Cullimore RC .05 .15
73 Jamie Pushor RC .05 .15
74 Andrew Verner RC .05 .15
75 Jason Dawe RC .05 .15
76 Jamie Matthews RC .05 .15
77 Sandy McCarthy RC .07 .20
78 Cam Neely .10 .25
(Boston Bruins TC)
79 Dale Hawerchuk .12 .30
(Buffalo Sabres TC)
80 Theo Fleury TC .07 .20
81 Ed Belfour TC .25 .60
82 Sergei Fedorov TC .15 .40
83 Esa Tikkanen .07 .20
(Edmonton Oilers TC)
84 John Cullen .07 .20
(Hartford Whalers TC)
85 Tomas Sandstrom .07 .20
(Los Angeles Kings TC)
86 Dave Gagner .07 .20
(Minnesota North Stars TC)
87 Russ Courtnall .07 .20
(Montreal Canadiens TC)
88 John MacLean .07 .20
(New Jersey Devils TC)
89 David Volek .07 .20
(New York Islanders TC)
90 Darren Turcotte .07 .20
(New York Rangers TC)
91 Rick Tocchet .07 .20
(Philadelphia Flyers TC)
92 Mark Recchi TC .12 .30
93 Mats Sundin TC .10 .25
94 Adam Oates TC .10 .25
95 Neil Wilkinson TC .07 .20
96 Dave Ellett .07 .20
(Toronto Maple Leafs TC)
97 Trevor Linden TC .07 .20
98 Kevin Hatcher .07 .20
(Washington Capitals TC)
99 Ed Olczyk .07 .20
(Winnipeg Jets TC)
100 Checklist 1-100 .05 .15
101 Bob Essensa .07 .20
102 Uwe Krupp .07 .20
103 Pelle Eklund .07 .20
104 Christian Ruuttu .07 .20
105 Kevin Dineen .07 .20
106 Phil Housley .07 .20
107 Pat Jablonski RC .07 .20
108 Jarmo Kekalainen RC .05 .15
109 Pat Elynuik .07 .20
110 Corey Millen RC .10 .25
111 Petr Klima .07 .20
112 Mike Ridley .07 .20
113 Peter Stastny .07 .20
114 Jyrki Lumme .07 .20
115 Chris Terreri .07 .20
116 Tom Barrasso .07 .20
117 Bill Ranford .07 .20
118 Peter Ing .07 .20
119 John Tanner .05 .15
120 Troy Gamble .05 .15
121 Stephane Matteau .07 .20
122 Rick Tocchet .07 .20
123 Wes Walz .07 .20
124 Dave Andreychuk .10 .25
125 Mike Craig .07 .20
126 Dale Hawerchuk .12 .30
127 Dean Evason .07 .20
128 Craig Janney .07 .20
129 Tim Cheveldae .07 .20
130 Rick Wamsley .05 .15
131 Peter Bondra .07 .20

132 Scott Stevens .10 .25
133 Kelly Miller .07 .20
134 Mats Sundin .10 .25
135 Mick Vukota .07 .20
136 Vincent Damphousse .07 .20
137 Patrick Roy .25 .60
138 Hubie McDonough .07 .20
139 Curtis Joseph .07 .20
140 Brent Sutter .07 .20
141 Tomas Sandstrom .07 .20
142 Kevin Miller .07 .20
143 Mike Ricci .10 .25
144 Sergei Fedorov .15 .40
145 Luc Robitaille .07 .20
146 Steve Yzerman .30 .75
147 Andy Moog .07 .20
148 Rob Blake .10 .25
149 Kirk Muller .05 .15
150 Daniel Berthiaume .07 .20
151 John Druce .07 .20
152 Garry Valk .07 .20
153 Brian Leetch .07 .20
154 Kevin Stevens .07 .20
155 Darren Turcotte .07 .20
156 Mario Lemieux .40 1.00
157 Dimitri Khristich .07 .20
158 Brian Glynn .07 .20
159 Benoit Hogue UER .07 .20
160 Mike Modano .20 .50
161 Jimmy Carson .07 .20
162 Steve Thomas .07 .20
163 Mike Vernon .07 .20
164 Ed Belfour .25 .60
165 Joel Otto .07 .20
166 Jeremy Roenick .25 .60
167 Johan Garpenlov .07 .20
168 Russ Courtnall .07 .20
169 John MacLean .07 .20
170 J.J. Daigneault .05 .15
171 Sylvain Lefebvre .07 .20
172 Tony Granato .07 .20
173 David Volek .07 .20
174 Trevor Linden .07 .20
175 Mike Richter .10 .25
176 Pierre Turgeon .07 .20
177 Paul Coffey .07 .20
178 Jan Erixon .07 .20
179 Rick Vaive .05 .15
180 Dave Gagner .07 .20
181 Thomas Steen .07 .20
182 Esa Tikkanen .07 .20
183 Sean Burke .10 .25
184 Paul Cavallini .07 .20
185 Alexei Kasatonov .05 .15
186 Kevin Lowe .07 .20
187 Gino Cavallini .07 .20
188 Doug Gilmour .20 .50
189 Rod Brind'Amour .07 .20
190 Gary Roberts .07 .20
191 Kirk McLean .07 .20
192 Kevin Haller RC .10 .25
193 Pat Verbeek .07 .20
194 Dave Snuggerud .05 .15
195 Gino Odjick .07 .20
196 Dave Ellett .07 .20
197 Don Beaupre .07 .20
198 Rob Brown .07 .20
199 Marty McSorley .07 .20
200 Checklist 101-200 .05 .05
201 Joe Mullen .07 .20
202 Dave Capuano .07 .20
203 Paul Stanton .07 .20
204 Terry Carkner .07 .20
205 Jon Casey .07 .20
206 Ken Wregget .07 .20
207 Gaetan Duchesne .05 .15
208 Cliff Ronning .07 .20
209 Dale Hunter .07 .20
210 Danton Cole .05 .15
211 Jeff Brown .07 .20
212 Mike Foligno .10 .25
213 Michel Mongeau .05 .15
214 Doug Brown .07 .20
215 Todd Krygier .07 .20
216 Jon Morris .07 .20
217 David Reid .05 .15
218 John McIntyre .07 .20
219 Guy Lafleur's Farewell .12 .30
220 Vincent Riendeau .07 .20
221 Tim Hunter .07 .20
222 Dave McLlwain .07 .20
223 Robert Reichel .20 .50
224 Glenn Healy .10 .25
225 Robert Kron .07 .20
226 Patrick Flatley .07 .20
227 Petr Nedved .07 .20
228 Mark Janssens .07 .20
229 Michal Pivonka .07 .20
230 Ulf Samuelsson .07 .20
231 Zarley Zalapski .07 .20
232 Neal Broten .07 .20
233 Bobby Holik .10 .25
234 Cam Neely .10 .25
235 John Cullen .07 .20
236 Brian Bellows .07 .20
237 Chris Nilan .07 .20
238 Mikael Andersson .07 .20
239 Bob Probert .07 .20
240 Teppo Numminen .07 .20
241 Peter Zezel .05 .15
242 Denis Savard .12 .30
243 Al MacInnis .07 .20
244 Stephane Richer .07 .20
245 Theo Fleury .07 .20
246 Mark Messier .25 .60
247 Mike Gartner .07 .20
248 Daren Puppa .07 .20
249 Louie DeBrusk RC .10 .25
250 Glenn Anderson .10 .25
251 Ken Hodge Jr. .10 .25
252 Adam Oates .10 .25
253 Pat LaFontaine .10 .25
254 Adam Creighton .07 .20
255 Ray Bourque .15 .40
256 Jaromir Jagr .25 .60
257 Steve Larmer .07 .20
258 Keith Primeau .07 .20
259 Mike Liut .07 .20
260 Brian Propp .07 .20
261 Stephan Lebeau .07 .20
262 Kelly Hrudey .07 .20
263 Joe Nieuwendyk .07 .20
264 Grant Fuhr .10 .25
265 Guy Carbonneau .07 .20
266 Martin Gelinas .07 .20
267 Alexander Mogilny .07 .20
268 Adam Graves .07 .20
269 Anatoli Semenov .07 .20
270 Dave Taylor .07 .20
271 Dirk Graham .07 .20
272 Gary Leeman .07 .20
273 Valeri Kamensky RC .25 .60
274 Marc Bureau .07 .20
275 James Patrick .07 .20
276 Dino Ciccarelli .07 .20
277 Ron Tugnutt .07 .20
278 Paul Ysebaert .07 .20
279 Laurie Boschman .07 .20
280 Dave Manson .07 .20
281 Dave Chyzowski .05 .15
282 Shayne Corson .07 .20
283 Steve Chiasson .07 .20
284 Craig MacTavish .07 .20
285 Petr Svoboda .07 .20
286 Craig Simpson .05 .15
287 Ron Hoover RC .05 .15
288 Vladimir Ruzicka .07 .20
289 Randy Wood .07 .20
290 Doug Lidster .07 .20
291 Kay Whitmore .07 .20
292 Bruce Driver .07 .20
293 Bobby Smith .07 .20
294 Claude Lemieux .07 .20
295 Mark Tinordi .07 .20
296 Mark Osborne .07 .20
297 Brad Shaw .05 .15
298 Igor Larionov .07 .20
299 Ron Francis .12 .30
300 Checklist 201-300 .05 .05
301 Bob Kudelski .05 .15
302 Larry Murphy .07 .20
303 Brent Ashton .07 .20
304 Brad Jones .07 .20
305 Gord Donnelly .07 .20
306 Murray Craven .07 .20
307 Chris Dahlquist .07 .20
308 Jim Paek RC .10 .25
309 Ron Sutter .07 .20
310 Mike Tomlak .07 .20
311 Ray Ferraro .07 .20
312 Dave Hannan .07 .20
313 Randy McKay .07 .20
314 Rod Langway .07 .20
315 Shawn Burr .07 .20
316 Calle Johansson .07 .20
317 Rich Sutter .07 .20
318 Al Iafrate .07 .20
319 Bob Bassen .07 .20
320 Mike Krushelnyski .07 .20
321 Sergei Makarov .07 .20
322 Darrin Shannon .07 .20
323 Terry Yake .07 .20
324 John Vanbiesbrouck .07 .20
325 Peter Sidorkiewicz .07 .20
326 Troy Mallette .07 .20
327 Ron Hextall .10 .25
328 Mathieu Schneider .07 .20
329 Bryan Trottier .12 .30
330 Kris King .07 .20
331 Daniel Marois .07 .20
332 Shayne Stevenson .07 .20
333 Joe Sakic .30 .75
334 Petri Skriko .05 .15
335 Dominik Hasek RC 1.50 4.00
336 Scott Pearson .07 .20
337 Bryan Fogarty .07 .20
338 Don Sweeney .07 .20
339 Rick Tabaracci .07 .20
340 Steven Finn .07 .20
341 Gary Suter .07 .20
342 Troy Crowder .07 .20
343 Jim Hrivnak .07 .20
344 Eric Weinrich .10 .25
345 John LeClair RC .50 1.25
346 Mark Recchi .12 .30
347 Dan Currie RC .05 .15
348 Ulf Dahlen .07 .20
349 Robert Ray .07 .20
350 Steve Smith .10 .25
351 Shawn Antoski .07 .20
352 Cam Russell .05 .15
353 Scott Thornton .07 .20
354 Chris Chelios .10 .25
355 Sergei Nemchinov FUDC .07 .20
356 Bernie Nicholls .07 .20
357 Jeff Norton .07 .20
358 Dan Quinn .07 .20
359 Michel Petit .07 .20
360 Eric Desjardins .10 .25
361 Kevin Hatcher .07 .20
362 Jiri Sejba .07 .20
363 Mark Pederson .07 .20
364 Jeff Lazaro RC .07 .20
365 Alexei Gusarov RC .07 .20
366 Jari Kurri .07 .20
367 Owen Nolan .10 .25
368 Clint Malarchuk .07 .20
369 Patrik Sundstrom .07 .20
370 Glen Wesley .07 .20
371 Wayne Presley .07 .20
372 Craig Muni .07 .20
373 Brent Fedyk FUDC .07 .20
374 Michel Goulet .07 .20
375 Tim Sweeney .07 .20
376 Gary Shuchuk .07 .20
377 Andre Racicot RC .07 .20
378 Jay Mazur RC .05 .15
379 Andrew Cassels .07 .20
380 Brian Noonan .05 .15
381 Sergei Kharin RC .07 .20
382 Derek King .05 .15
383 Fredrik Olausson .07 .20
384 Tom Fergus .07 .20
385 Zdeno Ciger .07 .20
386 Wendel Clark .10 .25
387 Ed Olczyk .07 .20
388 Basil McRae .07 .20
389 Tom Fitzgerald .07 .20
390 Ray Sheppard .07 .20
391 Bob Sweeney .07 .20
392 Gord Murphy .07 .20
393 John Chabot .05 .15
394 Jeff Beukeboom .07 .20
395 Rick Zombo .07 .20
396 Kjell Samuelsson .07 .20
397 Garth Butcher .07 .20
398 Phil Bourque .07 .20
399 Lou Franceschetti .07 .20
400 Checklist 301-400 .05 .05
401 Kevin Todd RC .10 .25
402 Ken Baumgartner .07 .20
403 Peter Douris .07 .20
404 Jiri Latal .05 .15
405 Marc Potvin RC .05 .15
406 Gary Nylund .07 .20
407 Yvon Corriveau .05 .15
408 Sheldon Kennedy FUDC .07 .20
409 David Shaw .07 .20
410 Slava Fetisov .07 .20
411 Mario Doyon RC .05 .15
412 Jamie Macoun .07 .20
413 Curtis Leschyshyn .07 .20
414 Mike Peluso .07 .20
415 Brian Benning .07 .20
416 Stu Grimson RC .05 .15
417 Ken Sabourin .07 .20
418 Luke Richardson .07 .20
419 Ken Quinney RC .05 .15
420 Mike Donnelly RC .10 .25
421 Darcy Loewen RC .05 .15
422 Brian Skrudland .07 .20
423 Joel Savage RC .05 .15
424 Adrien Plavsic .07 .20
425 Jergus Baca .07 .20
426 Greg Adams .07 .20
427 Tom Chorske .07 .20
428 Scott Scissons .05 .15
429 Dale Kushner .07 .20
430 Todd Richards RC .05 .15
431 Kip Miller .07 .20
432 Jason Prosofsky RC .05 .15
433 Stephane Morin .07 .20
434 Brian McReynolds .05 .15
435 Ken Daneyko .07 .20
436 Chris Joseph .07 .20
437 Wayne Gretzky .50 1.25
438 Jocelyn Lemieux .07 .20
439 Garry Galley .07 .20
440 Amon/Weig/Rice SR CL .25 .60
441 Steven Rice SR .07 .20
442 Patrice Brisebois SR .05 .15
443 Jim Waite FUDC .07 .20
444 Doug Weight SR RC .25 .60
445 Nelson Emerson SR .07 .20
446 Jarrod Skalde SR RC .07 .20
447 Jamie Leach SR .07 .20
448 Gilbert Dionne SR RC .10 .25
449 Trevor Kidd SR .07 .20
450 Tony Amonte SR RC .25 .60
451 Pat Murray SR .07 .20
452 Stephane Fiset SR .05 .15
453 Patrick Lebeau RC .07 .20
454 Chris Taylor RC .05 .15
455 Chris Tancill RC .07 .20
456 Mark Greig SR .07 .20
457 Mike Sillinger .07 .20
458 Ken Sutton RC .10 .25
459 Len Barrie RC .05 .15
460 Felix Potvin SR .20 .50
461 Brian Sakic RC .05 .15
462 Slava Kozlov RC .10 .25
463 Matt DelGuidice RC .10 .25
464 Brett Hull .15 .40
465 Norm Foster .05 .15
466 Alexander Godynyuk RC .10 .25
467 Geoff Courtnall .07 .20
468 Frantisek Kucera .07 .20
469 Benoit Brunet RC .05 .15
470 Mark Vermette .05 .15
471 Tim Watters .05 .15
472 Paul Ranheim .10 .25
473 Martin Hostak .05 .15
474 Joe Murphy .07 .20
475 Claude Boivin RC .05 .15
476 John Ogrodnick .07 .20
477 Doug Bodger .07 .20
478 Shawn Cronin .07 .20
479 Mark Hunter .07 .20
480 Dave Tippett .07 .20
481 Rob DiMaio .07 .20
482 Lyle Odelein .07 .20
483 Joe Reekie .07 .20
484 Randy Velischek .07 .20
485 Myles O'Connor RC .07 .20
486 Craig Wolanin .07 .20
487 Mike McPhee .07 .20
488 Claude Lapointe RC .07 .20
489 Troy Loney .05 .15
490 Bob Beers .07 .20
491 Sylvain Couturier .05 .15
492 Kimbi Daniels .10 .25
493 Darryl Shannon .10 .25
494 Jim McKenzie RC .10 .25
495 Don Gibson RC .05 .15
496 Ralph Barahona RC .05 .15
497 Murray Baron .07 .20
498 Yves Racine .07 .20
499 Larry Robinson .05 .15
500 Checklist 401-500 .05 .05
501 P.Coffey/Gretzky CC CL .50 1.25
502 Dirk Graham CC .07 .20
503 Rick Tocchet CC .07 .20
504 Eric Desjardins CC .10 .25
505 Shayne Corson CC .07 .20
506 Theo Fleury CC .07 .20
507 Luc Robitaille CC .07 .20
508 Tony Granato CC .07 .20
509 Eric Weinrich CC .10 .25
510 Gary Suter CC .07 .20
511 Kevin Hatcher CC .07 .20
512 Craig Janney CC .07 .20
513 Darren Turcotte CC .07 .20
514 Chris Winnes RC .07 .20
515 Kelly Kisio .07 .20
516 Joe Day RC .05 .15
517 Ed Courtenay RC .05 .15
518 Andrei Lomakin FUDC .07 .20
519 Kirk Muller .05 .15
520 Rick Lessard RC .07 .20
521 Scott Thornton .07 .20
522 Luke Richardson .07 .20
523 Mike Eagles .07 .20
524 Mike McNeill .07 .20
525 Ken Priestlay .07 .20
526 Louie DeBrusk .10 .25
527 Dave McLlwain .07 .20
528 Gary Leeman .07 .20
529 Adam Foote RC .20 .50
530 Kevin Dineen .07 .20
531 David Reid .05 .15
532 Arturs Irbe .07 .20
533 Mark Osiecki RC .07 .20
534 Steve Thomas .07 .20
535 Vincent Damphousse .07 .20
536 Stephane Richer .07 .20
537 Jarmo Myllys .07 .20
538 Carey Wilson .07 .20
539 Scott Stevens .10 .25
540 Uwe Krupp .07 .20
541 Dave Christian .07 .20
542 Scott Mellanby .07 .20
543 Peter Ahola RC .10 .25
544 Todd Elik .07 .20
545 Mark Messier .25 .60
546 Derian Hatcher .07 .20
547 Rod Brind'Amour .07 .20
548 Dave Manson .07 .20
549 Darryl Sydor .07 .20
550 Paul Broten .05 .15
551 Andrew Cassels .07 .20
552 Tom Draper RC .10 .25
553 Grant Fuhr .10 .25
554 Pierre Turgeon .07 .20
555 Pavel Bure .07 .20
556 Pat LaFontaine .10 .25
557 Dave Thomlinson .05 .15
558 Doug Gilmour .20 .50
559 Craig Billington RC .10 .25
560 Dean Evason .07 .20
561 Brendan Shanahan .12 .30
562 Mike Hough .07 .20
563 Dan Quinn .07 .20
564 Jeff Daniels RC .07 .20
565 Troy Murray .07 .20
566 Bernie Nicholls .07 .20
567 Randy Burridge .07 .20
568 Todd Hartje RC .05 .15
569 Charlie Huddy .07 .20
570 Steve Duchesne .05 .15
571 Sergio Momesso .07 .20
572 Brian Lawton .07 .20
573 Ray Sheppard .07 .20
574 Adam Graves .07 .20
575 Rollie Melanson .05 .15
576 Steve Kasper .07 .20
577 Jim Sandlak .07 .20
578 Pat MacLeod RC .10 .25
579 Sylvain Turgeon .07 .20
580 James Black RC .05 .15
581 Darrin Shannon .07 .20
582 Todd Krygier .07 .20
583 Dominic Roussel RC .10 .25
584 Nicklas Lidstrom YG CL .40 1.00
585 Donald Audette .07 .20
586 Tomas Forslund .10 .25
587 Nicklas Lidstrom .40 1.00
588 Geoff Sanderson RC .10 .25
589 Valeri Zelepukin RC .10 .25
590 Igor Ulanov RC .10 .25
591 Corey Foster RC .10 .25
592 Dan Lambert RC .07 .20
593 Pat Falloon .07 .20
594 Vladimir Konstantinov RC .25 .60
595 Josef Beranek .10 .25
596 Brad May .07 .20
597 Jeff Odgers RC .10 .25
598 Rob Pearson RC .10 .25
599 Luciano Borsato RC .10 .25
600 Checklist 501-600 .05 .05
601 Peter Douris .07 .20
602 Mark Fitzpatrick .07 .20
603 Randy Gilhen .07 .20
604 Corey Millen .10 .25
605 Jason Cirone RC .05 .15
606 Kyosti Karjalainen RC .10 .25
607 Garry Galley .07 .20
608 Brent Thompson RC .05 .15
609 Alexander Godynyuk .10 .25
610 Leetch/Richt/Mess CL .25 .60
611 Mario Lemieux AS .40 1.00
612 Brian Leetch AS .07 .20
613 Kevin Stevens AS .07 .20
614 Patrick Roy AS .25 .60
615 Paul Coffey AS .07 .20
616 Joe Sakic AS .30 .75
617 Jaromir Jagr AS .25 .60
618 Alexander Mogilny AS .07 .20
619 Owen Nolan AS .10 .25
620 Mark Messier AS .25 .60
621 Wayne Gretzky AS .50 1.25
622 Brett Hull AS .15 .40
623 Luc Robitaille AS .07 .20
624 Phil Housley AS .07 .20
625 Ed Belfour AS .25 .60
626 Steve Yzerman AS .30 .75
627 Adam Oates AS .10 .25
628 Trevor Linden AS .07 .20
629 Jeremy Roenick AS .25 .60
630 Theo Fleury AS .07 .20
631 Sergei Fedorov AS .15 .40
632 Al MacInnis AS .07 .20
633 Ray Bourque AS .15 .40
634 Mike Richter AS .10 .25
635 Al Secord HERO .05 .15
636 Marcel Dionne HERO .12 .30
637 Ken Morrow HERO .05 .15
638 Guy Lafleur HERO .12 .30
639 Ed Mio HERO .05 .15
640 Clark Gillies HERO .10 .25
641 Bob Nystrom HERO .05 .15
642 Pete Peeters HERO .05 .15
643 Ulf Nilsson HERO .05 .15
644 Lebeau Bros. .07 .20
645 Sutter Bros. .07 .20
646 Cavallini Bros. .07 .20
647 Bure Bros. .07 .20
648 Ferraro Bros. .07 .20
649 World Jr. CCCP Team CL .05 .25
650 Darius Kasparaitis RC .10 .25
651 Alexei Yashin RC .30 .75
652 Nikolai Khabibulin RC .25 .60
653 Denis Metlyuk RC .05 .15
654 Konstantin Korotkov RC .05 .15
655 Alexei Kovalev RC .60 1.50
656 Alexander Kuzminsky RC .05 .15
657 Alexander Cherbayev RC .05 .15
658 Sergei Krivokrasov RC .05 .15
659 Sergei Zholtok RC .05 .15
660 Alexei Zhitnik RC .05 .15
661 Sandis Ozolinsh RC .10 .25
662 Boris Mironov RC .05 .15
663 Pauli Jaks RC .05 .15
664 Gaetan Voisard RC .05 .15
665 Nicola Celio RC .05 .15
666 Marc Weber RC .05 .15
667 Bernhard Schumperli RC .05 .15
668 Laurent Bucher RC .05 .15
669 Michael Blaha RC .05 .15
670 Tiziano Gianini RC .05 .15
671 Marko Kiprusoff RC .05 .15
672 Janne Gronvall RC .05 .15
673 Juha Ylonen RC .05 .15
674 Sami Kapanen RC .10 .25
675 Marko Tuomainen RC .05 .15
676 Jarkko Varvio RC .07 .20
677 Tomas Gronman RC .07 .20
678 Andreas Naumann RC .07 .20
679 Steffen Ziesche RC .07 .20
680 Jens Schwabe RC .07 .20
681 Thomas Schubert RC .07 .20
682 Hans-Jorg Mayer RC .05 .15
683 Marc Seliger RC .07 .20
684 Trevor Kidd .07 .20
685 Martin Lapointe .07 .20
686 Tyler Wright RC .05 .15
687 Kimbi Daniels RC .10 .25
688 Karl Dykhuis .07 .20
689 Jeff Nelson RC .07 .20
690 Jassen Cullimore RC .05 .15
691 Turner Stevenson .05 .15
692 Scott Lachance RC .10 .25
693 Mike Dunham RC .10 .25
694 Brent Bilodeau RC .07 .20
695 Ryan Sittler RC .07 .20
696 Peter Ferraro RC .07 .20
697 Pat Peake RC .07 .20
698 Keith Tkachuk RC .10 .25
699 Brian Rolston RC .07 .20
700 Checklist 601-700 .05 .05
SP1 Gretzky/Hull/Kamensky .50 1.25

1991-92 Upper Deck French

COMPLETE SET (700) 20.00 40.00
COMPLETE LO SET (500) 15.00 30.00
COMPLETE HI SET (200) 5.00 12.00
COMPLETE HI FACT.SET (200) 5.00 12.00
*FRENCH VERSION: SAME VALUE

1991-92 Upper Deck Award Winner Holograms

This nine-card standard-size hologram set features award-winning hockey players with their respective trophies for most outstanding performance. The name of the award appears in the left border stripe, while the player's name and position are printed in the bottom border stripe. The backs have a color photo of the player with the trophy as well as biographical information. The holograms were randomly inserted into foil packs and subdivided into three groups: AW1-AW3 (low series); AW5-AW7 (late winter, low series); and AW4, AW8, and AW9 (high series).

COMPLETE SET (9) 5.00 12.00
AW1 Wayne Gretzky 1.00 2.50
AW2 Ed Belfour .40 1.00
AW3 Brett Hull .40 1.00
AW4 Ed Belfour .40 1.00
AW5A Ray Bourque ERR .40 1.00
AW5B Ray Bourque COR .40 1.00
AW6 Wayne Gretzky 1.00 2.50
AW7 Ed Belfour .40 1.00
AW8 Dirk Graham .30 .75
AW9 Mario Lemieux .75 2.00

1991-92 Upper Deck Box Bottoms

These five box bottoms are printed on glossy cover stock and measure approximately 5 1/2" by 9". Though they were issued with both French and English hockey sets, the New York Rangers' Mark Messier box bottom was available only with the high series. Each bottom features a four-color action photo enclosed by white borders. The Upper Deck logo, player's name, and position appear above the photo while the team name and the 75th NHL Anniversary logo appear beneath the picture superimposed on small black lines. The box bottoms are unnumbered and checklisted below alphabetically.

COMPLETE SET (5) 2.00 5.00
1 Wayne Gretzky .75 2.00
2 Brett Hull .25 .60
3 Mark Messier .25 .60
4 Mark Messier .40 1.00
5 Steve Yzerman .60 1.50
Detroit R

1991-92 Upper Deck Brett Hull Heroes

This ten-card standard-size set was inserted in 1991-92 Upper Deck low series foil packs (French as well as English editions). On a light gray textured background, the fronts have color player photos cut out and superimposed on an emblem. The textured background is enclosed by thin tan border stripes. On the same textured background, the backs summarize various moments in Hull's career. Brett Hull personally signed and numbered 2,500 of the checklist card number 9; these autographed cards were randomly inserted in packs. The signed cards are numbered by hand on the front.

COMPLETE SET (10) 6.00 15.00
COMMON HULL HEROES (1-9) .40 1.00
*FRENCH: .4X TO 1X BASIC INSERTS
9AU Brett Hull AU/2500 100.00 200.00
NNO Hull Header SP 2.00 5.00

1991-92 Upper Deck Czech World Juniors

This 100 card standard-size set featured players from the 1991 World Junior Championships. Two Wayne Gretzky Holograms were inserted into the set. They are priced at the end of the listings but are not included in the set price. Inside white borders, the fronts display glossy color action photos of the players in their national team uniforms. The player's name and position appear on the top, while the World Junior Tournament logo and an emblem of their national flag overlay the bottom. The backs have a second color player photo; alongside in a gray box, the player's position and a brief profile are printed in English and Czech. The cards are sequenced in this way: C.I.S. (1-23), Switzerland (24-31), Finland (32-40), Germany (41-46), Canada (47-65), U.S.A. (66-86), Czechoslovakia (87-99). These cards were designed for distribution in Eastern Europe. An album (valued at about $5) was also made to house the set.

COMPLETE SET (100) 10.00 25.00
1 Description Card .05 .15
2 Vladislav Boulin .05 .15
3 Ravil Gusmanov .05 .15
4 Denis Vinokurov .05 .15
5 Mikhail Volkov .05 .15
6 Alexei Troschinsky .05 .15
7 Andrei Nikolishin .20 .50
8 Alexander Sverztov .05 .15
9 Artem Kopot .05 .15
10 Ildar Mukhometov .05 .15
11 Darius Kasparaitis .20 .50
12 Alexei Yashin .30 .75
13 Nikolai Khabibulin .60 1.50
14 Denis Metlyuk .05 .15
15 Konstantin Korotkov .05 .15
16 Alexei Kovalev .60 1.50
17 Alexander Kuzminsky .05 .15
18 Alexander Cherbayev .05 .15
19 Sergei Krivokrasov .20 .50
20 Sergei Zholtok .20 .50
21 Alexei Zhitnik .30 .75
22 Sandis Ozolinsh .30 .75
23 Boris Mironov .30 .75
24 Pauli Jaks .05 .15
25 Gaetan Voisard .05 .15
26 Nicola Celio .05 .15
27 Marc Weber .05 .15
28 Bernhard Schumperli .05 .15
29 Laurent Bucher .05 .15
30 Michael Blaha .05 .15
31 Tiziano Gianini .05 .15
32 Tero Lehtera .05 .15
33 Mikko Luovi .05 .15
34 Marko Kiprusoff .05 .15
35 Janne Gronvall .05 .15
36 Juha Ylonen .20 .50
37 Sami Kapanen .20 .50
38 Marko Tuomainen .05 .15
39 Jarkko Varvio .05 .15
40 Tuomas Gronman .05 .15
41 Andreas Naumann .05 .15
42 Steffen Ziesche .05 .15
43 Jens Schwabe .05 .15
44 Thomas Schubert .05 .15
45 Hans-Jorg Mayer .05 .15
46 Marc Seliger .20 .50
47 Ryan Hughes .05 .15
48 Richard Matvichuk .20 .50
49 David St. Pierre .05 .15
50 Paul Kariya 2.00 5.00
51 Patrick Poulin .20 .50
52 Mike Fountain .20 .50
53 Scott Niedermayer .20 .50
54 John Slaney .05 .15
55 Brad Bombardir .05 .15
56 Andy Schneider .05 .15
57 Steve Junker .05 .15
58 Trevor Kidd .40 1.00
59 Martin Lapointe .40 1.00
60 Tyler Wright .20 .50
61 Kimbi Daniels .05 .15
62 Karl Dykhuis .20 .50
63 Jeff Nelson .05 .15
64 Jassen Cullimore .05 .15
65 Turner Stevenson .20 .50
66 Brian Mueller .05 .15
67 Chris Tucker .05 .15
68 Marty Schriner .05 .15
69 Mike Prendergast .05 .15
70 John Lilley .05 .15
71 Jim Campbell .20 .50
72 Brian Holzinger .20 .50
73 Steve Konowalchuk .20 .50
74 Chris Ferraro .05 .15
75 Chris Imes .05 .15
76 Rich Brennan .05 .15
77 Todd Hall .05 .15
78 Brian Rafalski .20 .50
79 Scott Lachance .20 .50
80 Mike Dunham .40 1.00
81 Brent Bilodeau .05 .15
82 Ryan Sittler .05 .15
83 Peter Ferraro .05 .15
84 Pat Peake .05 .15
85 Keith Tkachuk .75 2.00
86 Brian Rolston .40 1.00
87 Milan Hnilicka .20 .50
88 Roman Hamrlik .20 .50
89 Milan Nedoma .05 .15
90 Patrik Luza .05 .15
91 Jan Caloun .20 .50
92 Viktor Ujcik .05 .15
93 Robert Petrovicky .20 .50
94 Roman Meluzin .05 .15
95 Jan Vopat .05 .15
96 Martin Prochazka .20 .50
97 Zigmund Palffy .50 1.25
98 Ivan Droppa .05 .15
99 Martin Straka .20 .50
100 Checklist 1-100 .05 .15
NNO W.Gretzky Hologram 1.50 4.00
NNO W.Gretzky Hologram 1.50 4.00

1991-92 Upper Deck Euro-Stars

This 18-card standard-size set spotlights NHL players from Finland, the former Soviet Union, Czechoslovakia, and Sweden. One Euro-Star card was inserted in each 1991-92 Upper Deck Hockey jumbo pack in both English and French editions. The front design of the cards is the same as the regular issue except that a Euro-Stars emblem featuring a segment of the player's homeland flag, appears in the lower right corner. On a textured background, the backs present career summary.

COMPLETE SET (18) 5.00 12.00
*FRENCH: .4X TO 1X BASIC INSERTS
E1 Jarmo Kekalainen .08 .25
E2 Alexander Mogilny .30 .75
E3 Bobby Holik .20 .50
E4 Anatoli Semenov .08 .25
E5 Petr Nedved .20 .50
E6 Jaromir Jagr .60 1.50
E7 Tomas Sandstrom .20 .50
E8 Robert Kron .08 .25
E9 Sergei Fedorov .60 1.50
E10 Esa Tikkanen .20 .50
E11 Christian Ruuttu .08 .25
E12 Peter Bondra .30 .75
E13 Mats Sundin .50 1.25
E14 Dominik Hasek 1.25 3.00
E15 Johan Garpenlov .08 .25
E16 Alexander Godynyuk .08 .25
E17 Ulf Samuelsson .08 .25
E18 Igor Larionov .20 .50

1991-92 Upper Deck Sheets

For the second straight year, Upper Deck produced hockey commemorative sheets that were given away during the 1991-92 season at selected games in large arenas. Each sheet measures approximately 8 1/2" by 11" and is printed on card stock. The fronts of the team commemorative sheets feature the team logo and a series of Upper Deck cards of star players on that team. The Alumni sheet features player portraits by sports artist Alan Studt. All the sheets have an Upper Deck stamp indicating the production quota and the serial number. The backs are blank. The sheets are listed below in chronological order.

COMPLETE SET (19) 90.00 225.00
1 Los Angeles Kings 6.00 15.00
2 New York Rangers 4.00 10.00
3 St. Louis Blues 4.00 10.00
4 New Jersey Devils 4.00 10.00
5 Calgary Flames 5.00 12.00
6 New York Rangers 4.00 10.00
7 Philadelphia Flyers 4.00 10.00
8 Campbell All-Stars 10.00 25.00
9 Wales All-Stars 10.00 25.00
10 Detroit Red Wings 5.00 12.00
11 Washington Capitals 4.00 10.00
12 Minnesota North Stars 8.00 20.00
13 Pittsburgh Penguins 8.00 20.00
14 New York Rangers 4.00 10.00
15 Edmonton Oilers 5.00 12.00
16 Minnesota North Stars 8.00 20.00
17 Calgary Flames 5.00 12.00
18 Detroit Red Wings 4.00 10.00
19 Philadelphia Flyers 4.00 10.00

1992-93 Upper Deck

The 1992-93 Upper Deck hockey set contains 640 standard-size cards. The set was released in two series of 440 and 200 cards, respectively. Action photos on the fronts are bordered by the player's name and team logo at the bottom. Special subsets featured include Team Checklists (1-24), Bloodlines (35-39), '92 World Juniors (222-236), Russian Stars from Moscow Dynamo (333-353), Rookie Report (354-368), '92 World Championships (369-386), Team USA (392-397), Star Rookies (398-422), and Award Winners (431-440). Pavel Bure is showcased on a special card (SP2) that was randomly inserted in first series foil and jumbo packs. Another special card (SP3) titled "World Champions", honors Canada's 1993 IIHF World Junior Champions team. High series subsets featured are Lethal Lines (453-456), Young Guns (554-583), and World Junior Champions (584-619). The World Junior Champions subset is grouped according to national teams as follows: Canada (585-594), Sweden (595-599), Czechoslovakia (600-604), USA (605-609), Russia (610-614), and Finland (615-619). An Upper Deck Profiles (620-640) subset closes out the set. Card No. 88, Eric Lindros, was short-printed (SP) as it was not included in second series packaging. This was brought about because of a controversy over Lindros' head being superimposed on a teammate's body.

1 Andy Moog TC .07 .20
2 Donald Audette TC .07 .20
3 Tomas Forslund TC .05 .15
4 Steve Larmer TC .05 .15
5 Tim Cheveldae TC .05 .15
6 Vincent Damphousse TC .07 .20
7 Pat Verbeek TC .05 .15
8 Luc Robitaille TC .07 .20
9 Mike Modano TC .25 .60
10 Denis Savard TC .12 .30
11 Kevin Todd TC .05 .15
12 Ray Ferraro TC .05 .15
13 Tony Amonte TC .05 .15
14 Peter Sidorkiewicz TC .05 .15
15 Rod Brind'Amour TC .05 .15
16 Jaromir Jagr TC .25 .60
17 Owen Nolan TC .05 .15
18 Nelson Emerson TC .05 .15
19 Pat Falloon TC .05 .15
20 Anatoli Semenov TC .05 .15
21 Doug Gilmour TC .12 .30
22 Kirk McLean TC .05 .15
23 Don Beaupre TC .07 .20
24 Phil Housley TC .05 .15
25 Wayne Gretzky .50 1.25
26 Mario Lemieux .40 1.00
27 Valeri Kamensky .05 .15
28 Jaromir Jagr .25 .60
29 Brett Hull .15 .40
30 Neil Wilkinson .05 .15
31 Dominic Roussel .07 .20
32 Kent Manderville .05 .15
33 Wayne Gretzky 1500 .50 1.25
34 Presidents Trophy .15 .40
Rangers
35 Miller Bros. .05 .15
36 Sakic Bros. .25 .60
37 Gretkzy Bros. .50 1.25
38 Linden Bros. .07 .20
39 Courtnall Bros. .05 .15
40 Dale Craigwell .05 .15
41 Peter Ahola .05 .15
42 Robert Reichel .05 .15
43 Chris Terreri .07 .20
44 John Vanbiesbrouck .07 .20
45 Alexander Semak .05 .15
46 Mike Sullivan .05 .15
47 Bob Sweeney .05 .15
48 Corey Millen .05 .15
49 Murray Craven .05 .15
50 Dennis Vaske .05 .15
51 David Williams RC .05 .15
52 Tom Fitzgerald .05 .15
53 Corey Foster .05 .15
54 Al Iafrate .07 .20
55 John LeClair .15 .40
56 Stephane Richer .07 .20
57 Claude Boivin .05 .15
58 Rick Tabaracci .05 .15
59 Johan Garpenlov .05 .15
60 Checklist 1-110 .05 .15
61 Steve Leach .05 .15
62 Trent Klatt RC .07 .20
63 Darryl Sydor .05 .15
64 Brian Glynn .05 .15
65 Mike Craig .05 .15
66 Gary Leeman .05 .15
67 Jim Waite .07 .20
68 Jason Marshall .05 .15
69 Robert Kron .05 .15
70 Yanic Perreault RC .25 .60
71 Daniel Marois .05 .15
72 Mark Osborne .05 .15
73 Mark Tinordi .05 .15
74 Brad May .05 .15
75 Kimbi Daniels .05 .15
76 Kay Whitmore .07 .20
77 Luciano Borsato .05 .15
78 Kris King .05 .15
79 Felix Potvin .20 .50
80 Benoit Brunet .05 .15
81 Shawn Antoski .05 .15
82 Randy Gilhen .05 .15
83 Dmitri Mironov .05 .15
84 Dave Manson .05 .15
85 Sergio Momesso .05 .15
86 Cam Neely .10 .25
87 Mike Krushelnyski .05 .15
88 Eric Lindros SP .30 .75
89 Wendel Clark .07 .20
90 Enrico Ciccone .05 .15
91 Jarrod Skalde .05 .15
92 Dominik Hasek .20 .50
93 Dave McLlwain .05 .15
94 Russ Courtnall .05 .15
95 Tim Sweeney .05 .15
96 Alexei Kasatonov .05 .15
97 Chris Lindberg .05 .15
98 Steven Rice .05 .15
99 Tie Domi .10 .25

100 Paul Stanton .05 .15
101 Brad Schlegel .05 .15
102 David Bruce .05 .15
103 Mikael Andersson .05 .15
104 Shawn Chambers .05 .15
105 Rob Ramage .05 .15
106 Joe Reekie .05 .15
107 Sylvain Turgeon .05 .15
108 Rob Murphy .05 .15
109 Brad Shaw .05 .15
110 Darren Rumble RC .05 .15
111 Kyosti Karjalainen .05 .15
112 Mike Vernon .07 .20
113 Michel Goulet .07 .20
114 Garry Valk .05 .15
115 Peter Bondra .07 .20
116 Paul Coffey .10 .25
117 Brian Noonan .05 .15
118 John McIntyre .05 .15
119 Scott Mellanby .05 .15
120 Jim Sandlak .05 .15
121 Mats Sundin .10 .25
122 Brendan Shanahan .12 .30
123 Kelly Buchberger .05 .15
124 Doug Smail .05 .15
125 Craig Janney .07 .20
126 Mike Gartner .07 .20
127 Alexei Gusarov .05 .15
128 Joe Nieuwendyk .07 .20
129 Troy Murray .05 .15
130 Jamie Baker .05 .15
131 Dale Hunter .07 .20
132 Darrin Shannon .05 .15
133 Adam Oates .10 .25
134 Trevor Kidd .07 .20
135 Steve Larmer .05 .15
136 Fredrik Olausson .05 .15
137 Jyrki Lumme .05 .15
138 Tony Amonte .07 .20
139 Calle Johansson .05 .15
140 Rob Blake .07 .20
141 Phil Bourque .05 .15
142 Yves Racine .05 .15
143 Rich Sutter .05 .15
144 Joe Mullen .07 .20
145 Mike Richter .10 .25
146 Pat MacLeod .05 .15
147 Claude Lapointe .05 .15
148 Paul Broten .05 .15
149 Patrick Roy .25 .60
150 Doug Wilson .07 .20
151 Jim Hrivnak .07 .20
152 Joe Murphy .05 .15
153 Randy Burridge .05 .15
154 Thomas Steen .05 .15
155 Steve Yzerman .25 .60
156 Pavel Bure .20 .50
157 Sergei Fedorov .15 .40
158 Trevor Linden .07 .20
159 Chris Chelios .10 .25
160 Cliff Ronning .05 .15
161 Jeff Beukeboom .05 .15
162 Denis Savard .12 .30
163 Claude Lemieux .05 .15
164 Mike Keane .05 .15
165 Pat LaFontaine .10 .25
166 Nelson Emerson .05 .15
167 Alexander Mogilny .07 .20
168 Jamie Leach .05 .15
169 Darren Turcotte .05 .15
170 Checklist 111-220 .05 .15
171 Steve Thomas .07 .20
172 Brian Bellows .07 .20
173 Mike Ridley .05 .15
174 Dave Gagner .07 .20
175 Pierre Turgeon .07 .20
176 Paul Ysebaert .05 .15
177 Brian Propp .05 .15
178 Nicklas Lidstrom .07 .20
179 Kelly Miller .05 .15
180 Kirk Muller .05 .15
181 Bob Bassen .05 .15
182 Tony Tanti .05 .15
183 Mikhail Tatarinov .05 .15
184 Ron Sutter .05 .15
185 Tony Granato .05 .15
186 Curtis Joseph .10 .25
187 Uwe Krupp .05 .15
188 Esa Tikkanen .05 .15
189 Ulf Samuelsson .05 .15
190 Jon Casey .05 .15
191 Derek King .05 .15
192 Greg Adams .05 .15
193 Ray Ferraro .05 .15
194 Dave Christian .05 .15
195 Eric Weinrich .05 .15
196 Josef Beranek .05 .15
197 Tim Cheveldae .05 .15
198 Kevin Hatcher .05 .15
199 Brent Sutter .05 .15
200 Bruce Driver .05 .15
201 Tom Draper .05 .15
202 Ted Donato .05 .15
203 Ed Belfour .10 .25
204 Pat Verbeek .05 .15
205 John Druce .05 .15
206 Neal Broten .07 .20
207 Doug Bodger .05 .15
208 Troy Loney .05 .15
209 Mark Pederson .05 .15
210 Todd Elik .05 .15
211 Ed Olczyk .05 .15
212 Paul Cavallini .05 .15
213 Stephan Lebeau .05 .15
214 Dave Ellett .05 .15
215 Doug Gilmour .12 .30
216 Luc Robitaille .07 .20
217 Bob Essensa .07 .20
218 Jari Kurri .10 .25
219 Dimitri Khristich .05 .15
220 Joel Otto .05 .15
221 Checklist 221-280 .05 .15
222 Jonas Hoglund RC .10 .25
223 Rolf Wanhainen RC .05 .15
224 Stefan Klockare RC .05 .15
225 Johan Norgren RC .05 .15
226 Rogor Kyro RC .05 .15
227 Niklas Sundblad RC .05 .15
228 Calle Carlsson RC .05 .15
229 Jakob Karlsson RC .05 .15
230 Fredrik Jax RC .05 .15
231 Bjorn Nord RC .05 .15
232 Kristian Gahn RC .05 .15
233 Mikael Renberg RC .25 .60
234 Markus Naslund RC 1.00 2.50
235 Peter Forsberg .10 .25
236 Michael Nylander RC .05 .15
237 Stanley Cup Centennial .05 .15
238 Rick Tocchet .07 .20
239 Igor Kravchuk .05 .15
240 Geoff Courtnall .05 .15
241 Larry Murphy .07 .20
242 Mark Messier .15 .40
243 Tom Barrasso .07 .20
244 Glen Wesley .05 .15
245 Randy Wood .05 .15
246 Gerard Gallant .05 .15
247 Kip Miller .05 .15
248 Bob Probert .07 .20
249 Gary Suter .05 .15
250 Ulf Dahlen .05 .15
251 Dan Lambert .05 .15
252 Bobby Holik .07 .20
253 Jimmy Carson .05 .15
254 Ken Hodge Jr. .05 .15
255 Joe Sakic .25 .60
256 Kevin Dineen .05 .15
257 Al MacInnis .07 .20
258 Vladimir Ruzicka .05 .15
259 Ken Daneyko .05 .15
260 Guy Carbonneau .07 .20
261 Michal Pivonka .05 .15
262 Bill Ranford .07 .20
263 Petr Nedved .07 .20
264 Rod Brind'Amour .05 .15
265 Ray Bourque .15 .40
266 Joe Sacco .05 .15
267 Vladimir Konstantinov .10 .25
268 Eric Desjardins .07 .20
269 Dave Andreychuk .10 .25
270 Kelly Hrudey .07 .20
271 Grant Fuhr .10 .25
272 Dirk Graham .05 .15
273 Frank Pietrangelo .07 .20
274 Jeremy Roenick .15 .40
275 Kevin Stevens .05 .15
276 Phil Housley .05 .15
277 Patrice Brisebois .05 .15
278 Slava Fetisov .05 .15
279 Doug Weight .20 .50
280 Checklist 281-330 .05 .15
281 Dean Evason .05 .15
282 Martin Gelinas .05 .15
283 Philippe Bozon .05 .15
284 Brian Leetch .07 .20
285 Theo Fleury .15 .40
286 Pat Falloon .05 .15
287 Derian Hatcher .05 .15
288 Andrew Cassels .05 .15
289 Gary Roberts .05 .15
290 Bernie Nicholls .05 .15
291 Ron Francis .12 .30
292 Tom Kurvers .05 .15
293 Geoff Sanderson .07 .20
294 Slava Kozlov .07 .20
295 Valeri Zelepukin .05 .15
296 Ray Sheppard .05 .15
297 Scott Stevens .10 .25
298 Sergei Nemchinov .05 .15
299 Kirk McLean .05 .15
300 Igor Ulanov .05 .15
301 Brian Benning .05 .15
302 Dale Hawerchuk .12 .30
303 Kevin Todd .05 .15
304 John Cullen .05 .15
305 Mike Modano .25 .60
306 Donald Audette .07 .20
307 Vincent Damphousse .07 .20
308 Jeff Hackett .07 .20
309 Craig Simpson .05 .15
310 Don Beaupre .07 .20
311 Adam Creighton .05 .15
312 Pat Elynuik .05 .15
313 David Volek .05 .15
314 Sergei Makarov .05 .15
315 Craig Billington .07 .20
316 Zarley Zalapski .05 .15
317 Brian Mullen .05 .15
318 Rob Pearson .05 .15
319 Garry Galley .05 .15
320 James Patrick .05 .15
321 Owen Nolan .05 .15
322 Marty McSorley .05 .15
323 James Black .05 .15
324 Jacques Cloutier .07 .20
325 Benoit Hogue .05 .15
326 Teppo Numminen .05 .15
327 Mark Recchi .12 .30
328 Paul Ranheim .05 .15
329 Andy Moog .07 .20
330 Shayne Corson .05 .15
331 J.J. Daigneault .05 .15
332 Mark Fitzpatrick .07 .20
333 Moscow Dynamo CL .05 .15
334 Alexei Yashin RS .07 .20
335 Darius Kasparaitis RS .05 .15
336 Alexander Yudin RS RC .05 .15
337 Sergei Bautin RS RC .05 .15
338 Igor Korolev RS RC .05 .15
339 Sergei Klimovich RS RC .07 .20
340 Andrei Nikolishin RS RC .05 .15
341 Vitali Karamnov RS RC .05 .15
342 Alex Andriyevski RS RC .05 .15
343 Sergei Sorokin RS RC .05 .15
344 Yan Kaminsky RS RC .05 .15
345 Andrei Trefilov RS RC .05 .15
346 Sergei Petrenko RS RC .05 .15
347 Ravil Khaidarov RS RC .05 .15
348 Dmitri Frolov RS .05 .15
349 Ravil Yakubov RS RC .05 .15
350 Dimitri Yushkevich RS RC .05 .15
351 Alex Karpovtsev RS RC .07 .20
352 Igor Dorofeyev RS RC .05 .15
353 Alex Galchenyuk RS RC .05 .15
354 Joe Juneau RR .05 .15
355 Pat Falloon RR .05 .15
356 Gilbert Dionne RR .05 .15
357 Vladimir Konstantinov RR .10 .25
358 Rick Tabaracci RR .05 .15
359 Tony Amonte RR .05 .15
360 Scott Lachance RR .05 .15
361 Tom Draper RR .05 .15
362 Pavel Bure RR .07 .20
363 Nicklas Lidstrom RR .07 .20
364 Keith Tkachuk RR .10 .25
365 Kevin Todd RR .05 .15
366 Dominik Hasek RR .20 .50
367 Igor Kravchuk RR .05 .15
368 Shawn McEachern RR .05 .15
369 Blomsten/Forsberg CL .10 .25
370 Dieter Hegen RC .05 .15
371 Stefan Ustorf RC .05 .15
372 Ernst Kopf RC .05 .15
373 Raimond Hilger RC .05 .15
374 Mats Sundin .10 .25
375 Peter Forsberg .10 .25
376 Arto Blomsten RC .05 .15
377 Tommy Soderstrom RC .07 .20
378 Michael Nylander RC .05 .15
379 David Jensen RC .05 .15
380 Chris Winnes .05 .15
381 Ray LeBlanc .07 .20
382 Joe Sacco .05 .15
383 Dennis Vaske .05 .15
384 Jorg Eberle RC .05 .15
385 Trevor Kidd .07 .20
386 Pat Falloon .05 .15
387 Rob Brown .05 .15
388 Adam Graves .05 .15
389 Peter Zezel .05 .15
390 Checklist 391-440 .05 .15
391 Don Sweeney .05 .15
392 Sean Hill RC .05 .15
393 Ted Donato .05 .15
394 Marty McInnis .05 .15
395 C.J. Young RC .05 .15
396 Ted Drury RC .05 .15
397 Scott Young .05 .15
398 S.Lachance/K.Tkachuk CL .10 .25
399 Joe Juneau SR .05 .15
400 Steve Heinze SR .05 .15
401 Glen Murray SR .05 .15
402 Keith Carney SR RC .20 .50
403 Dean McAmmond SR RC .05 .15
404 Karl Dykhuis SR .05 .15
405 Martin Lapointe SR .05 .15
406 Scott Niedermayer SR .10 .25
407 Ray Whitney SR RC .15 .40
408 Martin Brodeur SR .25 .60
409 Scott Lachance SR .05 .15
410 Marty McInnis SR .05 .15
411 Bill Guerin SR RC .20 .50
412 Shawn McEachern SR .05 .15
413 Denny Felsner SR RC .07 .20
414 Bret Hedican SR RC .07 .20
415 Drake Berehowsky SR .05 .15
416 Patrick Poulin SR .05 .15
417 Vladimir Vujtek SR RC .05 .15
418 Steve Konowalchuk SR RC .07 .20
419 Keith Tkachuk SR .10 .25
420 Evgeny Davydov SR .05 .15
421 Yanick Dupre SR .05 .15
422 Jason Woolley RC .05 .15
423 B.Hull/W.Gretzky .50 1.25
424 Tomas Sandstrom .07 .20
425 Craig MacTavish .05 .15
426 Stu Barnes .05 .15
427 Gilbert Dionne .05 .15
428 Andrei Lomakin .05 .15
429 Tomas Forslund .05 .15
430 Andre Racicot .07 .20
431 Pavel Bure AW .20 .50
432 Mark Messier AW .15 .40
433 Mario Lemieux AW .40 1.00
434 Brian Leetch AW .07 .20
435 Wayne Gretzky AW .50 1.25
436 Mario Lemieux AW .40 1.00
437 Mark Messier AW .07 .20
438 Patrick Roy AW .25 .60
439 Guy Carbonneau AW .07 .20
440 Patrick Roy AW .25 .60
441 Russ Courtnall .05 .15
442 Jeff Reese .05 .15
443 Brent Fedyk .05 .15
444 Kerry Huffman .05 .15
445 Mark Freer .05 .15
446 Christian Ruuttu .05 .15
447 Nick Kypreos .05 .15
448 Mike Hurlbut RC .05 .15
449 Bob Sweeney .05 .15
450 Checklist 491-540 .05 .15
451 Perry Berezan .05 .15
452 Phil Bourque .05 .15
453 Messier/Amonte/Graves LL .15 .40
454 Lemieux/Stev/Tocch LL .40 1.00
455 Oates/Juneau/Kvartal LL .10 .25
456 LaFont/Andrey/Mogil LL .10 .25
457 Zdeno Ciger .05 .15
458 Pat Jablonski .07 .20
459 Brent Gilchrist .05 .15
460 Yvon Corriveau .05 .15
461 Dino Ciccarelli .07 .20
462 David Emma .05 .15
463 Corey Hirsch RC .10 .25
464 Jamie Baker .05 .15
465 John Cullen .05 .15
466 Lonnie Loach RC .05 .15
467 Louie DeBrusk .05 .15
468 Brian Mullen .05 .15
469 Gaeten Duchesne .05 .15
470 Eric Lindros .30 .75
471 Brian Bellows .07 .20
472 Bill Lindsay RC .05 .15
473 Dave Archibald .05 .15
474 Reggie Savage .05 .15
475 Tommy Soderstrom .07 .20
476 Vincent Damphousse .07 .20
477 Mike Ricci .07 .20
478 Bob Carpenter .05 .15
479 Kevin Haller .05 .15
480 Peter Sidorkiewicz .05 .15
481 Peter Andersson RC .05 .15
482 Kevin Miller .05 .15
483 Jean-Francois Quintin RC .05 .15
484 Philippe Boucher .05 .15
485 Jozef Stumpel .05 .15
486 Vitali Prokhorov RC .05 .15
487 Stan Drulia RC .05 .15
488 Jay More .05 .15
489 Mike Needham RC .05 .15
490 Glenn Mulvenna RC .05 .15
491 Ed Ronan RC .05 .15
492 Grigori Panteleyev RC .05 .15
493 Kevin Dahl RC .05 .15
494 Ryan McGill RC .05 .15
495 Robb Stauber .07 .20
496 Vladimir Vujtek RC .05 .15
497 Tomas Jelinek RC .05 .15
498 Patrik Kjellberg RC .10 .25
499 Sergei Bautin .05 .15
500 Bobby Holik .07 .20
501 Guy Hebert RC .15 .40
502 Chris Kontos RC .05 .15
503 Vyatcheslav Butsayev RC .05 .15
504 Yuri Khymlev RC .05 .15
505 Richard Matvichuk RC .07 .20
506 Dominik Hasek .20 .50
507 Ed Courtenay .05 .15
508 Jeff Daniels .05 .15
509 Doug Zmolek RC .05 .15
510 Vitali Karamnov .05 .15
511 Norm MacIver .05 .15
512 Terry Yake .05 .15
513 Steve Duchesne .05 .15
514 Andrei Trefilov .05 .15
515 Jiri Slegr .05 .15
516 Sergei Zubov RC .15 .40
517 Dave Karpa RC .05 .15
518 Sean Burke .07 .20
519 Adrien Plavsic .05 .15
520 Michael Nylander .05 .15
521 John MacLean .07 .20
522 Jason Ruff RC .05 .15
523 Sean Hill .05 .15
524 Mike Sillinger .05 .15
525 Daniel Laperriere RC .05 .15
526 Peter Ahola .05 .15
527 Guy Larose .05 .15
528 Tommy Sjodin RC .05 .15
529 Rob DiMaio .05 .15
530 Mark Howe .10 .25
531 Greg Paslawski .05 .15
532 Ron Hextall .07 .20
533 Keith Jones RC .10 .25
534 Chris Luongo RC .05 .15
535 Anatoli Semenov .05 .15
536 Stephane Beauregard .07 .20
537 Pat Elynuik .05 .15
538 Mike McPhee .05 .15
539 Jody Hull .05 .15
540 Stephane Matteau .05 .15
541 Shayne Corson .05 .15
542 Mikhail Kravets RC .05 .15
543 Kevin Miehm RC .05 .15
544 Brian Bradley .05 .15
545 Mathieu Schneider .05 .15
546 Steve Chiasson .05 .15
547 Warren Rychel RC .05 .15
548 John Tucker .05 .15
549 Todd Ewen .05 .15
550 Checklist 591-640 .05 .15
551 Petr Klima .05 .15
552 Robert Lang RC .05 .15
553 Eric Weinrich .05 .15
554 Kasparaitis/Malakhov CL .05 .15
555 Roman Hamrlik RC .20 .50
556 Martin Rucinsky YG .05 .15
557 Patrick Poulin YG .05 .15
558 Tyler Wright YG .05 .15
559 Martin Straka YG RC .20 .50
560 Jim Hiller YG RC .05 .15
561 Dmitri Kvartalnov YG RC .05 .15
562 Scott Niedermayer YG .10 .25
563 Darius Kasparaitis YG .05 .15
564 Richard Smehlik RC .05 .15
565 Shawn McEachern YG .05 .15
566 Alexei Zhitnik YG .05 .15
567 Andrei Kovalenko YG RC .15 .40
568 Sandis Ozolinsh YG .05 .15
569 Robert Petrovicky RC .05 .15
570 Dimitri Yushkevich YG .05 .15
571 Scott Lachance YG .05 .15
572 Nikolai Borschevsky YG .05 .15
573 Alexei Kovalev YG .07 .20
574 Teemu Selanne YG .20 .50
575 Steven King RC .05 .15
576 Guy Leveque YG RC .05 .15
577 Vladimir Malakhov YG .05 .15
578 Alexei Zhamnov YG .07 .20
579 Viktor Gordiouk YG RC .05 .15
580 Dixon Ward YG RC .07 .20
581 Igor Korolev YG .05 .15
582 Sergei Krivokrasov YG .05 .15
583 Rob Zamuner RC .07 .20
584 Aucoin/Lapnte/Wright CL .05 .15
585 Manny Legace RC .10 .25
586 Paul Kariya RC 3.00 8.00
587 Alexandre Daigle RC .10 .25
588 Nathan Lafeyette RC .07 .20
589 Mike Rathje RC .05 .15
590 Chris Gratton RC .10 .25
591 Chris Pronger RC 2.00 5.00
592 Brent Tully RC .05 .15
593 Rob Niedermayer RC .10 .25
594 Darcy Werenka RC .05 .15
595 Peter Forsberg .10 .25
596 Kenny Jonsson RC .10 .25
597 Niklas Sundstrom RC .10 .25
598 Reine Rauhala RC .05 .15
599 Daniel Johansson RC .05 .15
600 David Vyborny RC .10 .25
601 Jan Vopat RC .07 .20
602 Pavol Demitra RC .20 .50
603 Michal Cerny RC .05 .15
604 Ondrej Steiner RC .05 .15
605 Jim Campbell RC .07 .20
606 Todd Marchant RC .07 .20
607 Mike Pomichter RC .07 .20
608 John Emmons RC .05 .15
609 Adam Deadmarsh RC .10 .25
610 Nikolai Semin RC .05 .15
611 Igor Alexandrov RC .05 .15
612 Vadim Sharifjanov RC .10 .25
613 Viktor Kozlov RC .10 .25
614 Nikolai Tsulygin RC .05 .15
615 Jere Lehtinen RC .10 .25
616 Ville Peltonen RC .07 .20
617 Saku Koivu RC 1.50 4.00
618 Kimmo Rintanen RC .05 .15
619 Jonni Vauhkonen RC .05 .15
620 Brett Hull PRO .15 .40
621 Wayne Gretzky PRO .50 1.25
622 Jaromir Jagr PRO .25 .60
623 Darius Kasparaitis PRO .05 .15
624 Bernie Nicholls .05 .15
625 Gilbert Dionne .05 .15
626 Ray Bourque .15 .40
627 Mike Ricci .07 .20
628 Phil Housley .05 .15
629 Chris Chelios .10 .25
630 Kevin Stevens PRO .05 .15
631 Roman Hamrlik PRO .20 .50
632 Sergei Fedorov PRO .15 .40
633 Alexei Kovalev PRO .07 .20
634 Shawn McEachern PRO .05 .15
635 Tony Amonte PRO .05 .15
636 Brian Bellows .07 .20
637 Adam Oates .10 .25
638 Denis Savard .12 .30
639 Doug Gilmour PRO .12 .30
640 Brian Leetch PRO .07 .20
SP2 Pavel Bure ART .20 .50
SP3 World Jr.Gold Medal .30 .75

1992-93 Upper Deck All-Rookie Team

This seven-card set was inserted only in low series U.S. foil packs and features six of the NHL's brightest rookies from the 1991-92 season. The fronts show a triple-pose player photo and have a diagonal silver foil stripe in the lower right corner with the words "All-Rookie Team". The backs provide biographical information and a color photo of the player in civilian dress. The checklist card has a group photo of all six players. The cards are numbered on the back with an "AR" prefix.

COMPLETE SET (7) 6.00 15.00
AR1 Tony Amonte .40 1.00
AR2 Gilbert Dionne .40 1.00
AR3 Kevin Todd .40 1.00
AR4 Nicklas Lidstrom 2.00 5.00
AR5 Vladimir Konstantinov 2.00 5.00
AR6 Dominik Hasek 2.00 5.00
AR7 Team .75 2.00
Photo Checklist

1992-93 Upper Deck All-World Team

This six-card set was randomly inserted only in Canadian low series foil packs. These standard size cards are full bleed with a gold "All-World Team" logo at the bottom of the card. The cards are numbered on the back with a "W" prefix.

COMPLETE SET (6) 8.00 20.00
W1 Wayne Gretzky 4.00 10.00
W2 Brett Hull 1.00 2.50
W3 Jaromir Jagr 1.00 2.50
W4 Nicklas Lidstrom .60 1.50
W5 Vladimir Konstantinov .60 1.50
W6 Patrick Roy 3.00 8.00

1992-93 Upper Deck Ameri/Can Holograms

Randomly inserted in high series foil packs, this six-card hologram standard-size set spotlights the top rookies of either U.S. or Canadian heritage at each position. The cards have the photo superimposed over the hologram.

COMPLETE SET (6) 2.00 5.00
AC1 Joe Juneau .30 .75
AC2 Keith Tkachuk .50 1.25
AC3 Steve Heinze .30 .75
AC4 Scott Lachance .30 .75
AC5 Scott Niedermayer .30 .75
AC6 Dominic Roussel .40 1.00

1992-93 Upper Deck Calder Candidates

Randomly inserted into 1992-93 Upper Deck U.S. high series retail foil packs only, this 20-card standard-size set spotlights top rookies eligible to win the Calder Memorial Trophy for the 1992-93 season. The full-bleed photos on the front are bordered on the top by a gold foil stripe. The team name and player's name appears in bar that shades from black to white. On a background consisting of a stone slab carved with an image of the Calder trophy, the backs present a career summary. The card number appears in a white stripe that cuts across the top of the card. The cards are numbered with a "CC" prefix.

COMPLETE SET (20) 10.00 25.00
CC1 Dixon Ward .40 1.00
CC2 Igor Korolev .40 1.00
CC3 Felix Potvin 1.50 4.00
CC4 Rob Zamuner .40 1.00
CC5 Scott Niedermayer .75 2.00
CC6 Eric Lindros 2.00 5.00
CC7 Alexei Zhitnik .40 1.00
CC8 Roman Hamrlik .40 1.00
CC9 Joe Juneau 1.00 2.50
CC10 Teemu Selanne 2.00 5.00
CC11 Alexei Kovalev .75 2.00
CC12 Vladimir Malakhov .40 1.00
CC13 Darius Kasparaitis .40 1.00
CC14 Shawn McEachern .40 1.00
CC15 Keith Tkachuk 1.50 4.00
CC16 Scott Lachance .40 1.00
CC17 Andrei Kovalenko .40 1.00
CC18 Patrick Poulin .40 1.00
CC19 Evgeny Davydov .40 1.00
CC20 Dimitri Yushkevich .40 1.00

1992-93 Upper Deck Euro-Rookie Team

This six-card standard-size set was randomly inserted in 1992-93 Upper Deck low series packs. The cards feature cut-out color player photos superimposed on a hologram that shows the player in action. The horizontal fronts are bordered on the left and top by gray wood-textured panels. The team logo appears at the top left on a tan wood-textured panel. The horizontal backs feature a player profile on a tan background bordered by gray wood-textured panels. The cards are numbered on the back with an "ERT" prefix.

COMPLETE SET (6) 4.00 10.00
ERT1 Pavel Bure .75 2.00
ERT2 Nicklas Lidstrom 1.00 2.50
ERT3 Dominik Hasek 2.00 5.00
ERT4 Peter Ahola .20 .50
ERT5 Alexander Semak .20 .50
ERT6 Tomas Forslund .20 .50

1992-93 Upper Deck Euro-Rookies

One per high series jumbo pack, this 20-card standard-size set spotlights European born rookies. The color action player photos on the fronts are full-bleed except on the right side, where a black stripe carries the player's name in bronze foil lettering. At the upper right corner appears a bronze foil "Euro-Rookies" seal, with the flag of the player's country immediately to the right. The cards are numbered on the back with an "ER" prefix.

COMPLETE SET (20) 4.00 10.00
ER1 Richard Smehlik .20 .50
ER2 Michael Nylander .30 .75
ER3 Igor Korolev .20 .50
ER4 Robert Lang .20 .50
ER5 Sergei Krivokrasov .20 .50
ER6 Teemu Selanne .75 2.00
ER7 Darius Kasparaitis .20 .50
ER8 Alexei Zhamnov .30 .75
ER9 Jiri Slegr .20 .50
ER10 Alexei Kovalev .60 1.50
ER11 Roman Hamrlik .40 1.00
ER12 Dimitri Yushkevich .20 .50
ER13 Alexei Zhitnik .20 .50
ER14 Andrei Kovalenko .20 .50
ER15 Vladimir Malakhov .20 .50
ER16 Sandis Ozolinsh .40 1.00
ER17 Evgeny Davydov .20 .50
ER18 Victor Gordijuk .20 .50
ER19 Martin Straka .30 .75
ER20 Robert Petrovicky .20 .50

1992-93 Upper Deck Euro-Stars

This 20-card standard-size set, issued one per low series jumbo pack, features action color player photos with a silver foil border. The borders are prone to chipping. The pictures are silver-foil stamped with the player's name and with the "Euro Stars" emblem which hangs down from a white, red, and blue ribbon at the upper right corner. The backs display player profile information against a light gray panel with a black, silver, and gold frame design. The cards are numbered on the back with an "E" prefix.

COMPLETE SET (20) 4.00 10.00
E1 Sergei Fedorov .75 2.00
E2 Pavel Bure .40 1.00
E3 Dominik Hasek 1.00 2.50
E4 Vladimir Ruzicka .20 .50
E5 Peter Ahola .20 .50
E6 Kyosti Karjalainen .20 .50
E7 Igor Kravchuk .20 .50
E8 Evgeny Davydov .20 .50
E9 Nicklas Lidstrom .40 1.00
E10 Vlad. Konstantinov .40 1.00
E11 Josef Beranek .20 .50
E12 Valeri Zelepukin .20 .50
E13 Sergei Nemchinov .20 .50
E14 Jaromir Jagr 1.00 2.50
E15 Igor Ulanov .20 .50
E16 Sergei Makarov .20 .50
E17 Andrei Lomakin .20 .50
E18 Mats Sundin .40 1.00
E19 Jarmo Myllys .20 .50
E20 Valeri Kamensky .20 .50

1992-93 Upper Deck Gordie Howe Heroes

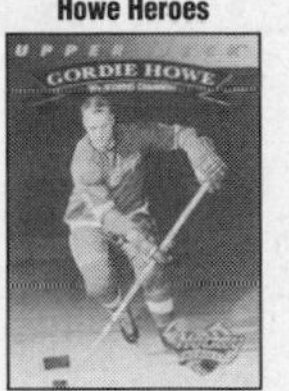

Randomly inserted in high series foil packs, this 10-card "Hockey Heroes" standard-size set showcases Gordie Howe, the NHL's former all-time leader in goals, assists, and points. The backs capture highlights in Howe's career. The cards are numbered on the back and continue from where the Gretzky Heroes left off.

COMPLETE SET (10) 8.00 20.00
COMMON HOWE (19-27) 1.00 2.50
NNO G.Howe Header SP 1.00 3.00

1992-93 Upper Deck Gordie Howe Selects

Randomly inserted throughout U.S. high series hobby packs only, this 20-card set standard-size features Gordie Howe's selections of ten current NHL superstars and ten rookies who he believes are the NHL's best. The fronts carry full-bleed color player photos. Howe's signature in gold foil sits on top of a black bar (carrying the word "Selects") toward the bottom of the picture, with the player's name and position immediately below. The backs have a color head shot in an oval and a quote of Howe's evaluation of the player's strengths. A small color player cut-out of Howe and the player's statistics complete the back. The cards are numbered on the back with a "G" prefix.

COMPLETE SET (20) 10.00 25.00
G1 Brian Bellows .15 .40
G2 Luc Robitaille .30 .75
G3 Pat LaFontaine .60 1.50
G4 Kevin Stevens .15 .40
G5 Wayne Gretzky 3.00 8.00
G6 Steve Larmer .30 .75
G7 Brett Hull 1.25 3.00
G8 Jeremy Roenick 1.00 2.50
G9 Mario Lemieux 3.00 8.00
G10 Steve Yzerman 3.00 8.00
G11 Joe Juneau .15 .40
G12 Vladimir Malakhov .15 .40
G13 Alexei Kovalev .30 .75
G14 Eric Lindros .75 2.00
G15 Teemu Selanne 1.50 4.00
G16 Patrick Poulin .15 .40
G17 Shawn McEachern .15 .40
G18 Keith Tkachuk .75 2.00
G19 Andrei Kovalenko .15 .40
G20 Ted Donato .15 .40

1992-93 Upper Deck Sheets

For the third straight year, Upper Deck produced hockey commemorative sheets that were given away during the 1992-93 season at selected games in large arenas. Each sheet measures 8 1/2" by 11" and is printed on card stock. The fronts of the team commemorative sheets feature a series of Upper Deck cards of star players on a particular team and the team logo. The 1993 All-Star Game sheets feature a series of Upper Deck cards of players that participated in the All-Star Game. Most the sheets have an Upper Deck stamp indicating the production quota and the serial number and the backs are blank. The players are listed as they appear from left to right.

COMPLETE SET (17) 60.00 150.00
1 1991-92 All-Rookie Team/17,000 4.00 10.00
June 1992
Gilbert Dionne
Kevin Todd
Vladimir Konstantinov
Tony Amonte
Nicklas Lidstrom
Dominik Hasek
2 New York Rangers/18,000 4.00 10.00
Defending Season Champs
Peter Andersson
Phil Bourque
Joe Kocur
Doug Weight
Randy Gilhen
John Vanbiesbrouck
Adam Graves
Mark Messier
3 Gordie Howe 65th Birthday 4.00 10.00
Celebration Tour
(Nine Howe Hockey Heroes cards)
4 Gordie Howe Birthday 4.00 10.00
(Hamilton McDonald's)
5 Wayne Gretzky 6.00 15.00
Heroes Mail-In
6 New York Rangers/18,000 2.00 5.00
Quebec Nordiques, Oct. 29, 1992
Paul Broten
Mike Richter
Sergei Nemchinov
Tie Domi
Kris King
Jeff Beukeboom
Brian Leetch Norris
Tony Amonte
7 Los Angeles Kings/18,000 4.00 10.00
Vancouver Canucks, Nov. 12, 1992
Luc Robitaille
Paul Coffey
Tony Granato
Rob Blake
Tomas Sandstrom
Kelly Hrudey
8 Minnesota North Stars/16,500 6.00 15.00
San Jose Sharks, Nov. 28, 1992
9 Edmonton Oilers/18,500 2.00 5.00
Calgary Flames, Dec. 8, 1992
Brian Glynn
Scott Mellanby
Dave Manson
Craig MacTavish
Bernie Nicholls
Bill Ranford
10 Philadelphia Flyers/19,000 2.00 5.00
Pittsburgh Penguins, Dec. 17, 1992
Kevin Dineen
Mark Recchi
Garry Galley
Dominic Roussel
Brian Benning
Rod Brind'Amour
11 Minnesota North Stars/16,500 6.00 15.00
Tampa Bay Lightning, Jan. 30, 1993
Dave Gagner
Neal Broten
Ulf Dahlen
Todd Elik
Tommy Sjodin
Gaetan Duchesne
12 Campbell All-Stars 4.00 10.00
Montreal Forum, Feb. 6, 1993
13 Wales All-Stars 4.00 10.00
Montreal Forum, Feb. 6, 1993
Patrick Roy
Brian Leetch
Ray Bourque
Kevin Stevens
Mario Lemieux
Jaromir Jagr
14 Washington Capitals/17,000 4.00 10.00
St. Louis Blues, Feb. 21, 1993
Jim Hrivnak
Mike Ridley
Peter Bondra
Dale Hunter
Kelly Miller
Don Beaupre
15 Los Angeles Kings/18,000 4.00 10.00
Ottawa Senators, Mar.4, 1993
Jari Kurri
Corey Millen
Marty McSorley
Darryl Sydor
Wayne Gretzky
Robb Stauber
16 Quebec Nordiques/15,000 6.00 15.00
Hartford Whalers, Mar. 8, 1993
17 St.Louis Blues/17,500 2.00 5.00
Vancouver Canucks, Mar. 30, 1993

1992-93 Upper Deck Wayne Gretzky Heroes

Randomly inserted in low series foil packs, this ten-card "Hockey Heroes" standard-size set pays tribute to Wayne Gretzky by chronicling his career. Inside white borders on a gray ice background, the fronts display color photos that are cut out to fit a emblem design. On a gray ice background accented by black, the backs (which continue the numbering from where the Hull Heroes left off) capture highlights in Gretzky's career.

COMPLETE SET (10) 10.00 25.00
COMMON GRETZKY (10-18) 2.00 5.00
NNO W.Gretzky Header SP 5.00 10.00

1992-93 Upper Deck World Junior Grads

Randomly inserted in Canadian high series foil packs, this 20-card standard-size set features top players in the world who have participated in the IIHF Junior Championships. Beneath a black stripe carrying the player's name, the fronts display full-bleed color action player photos. The top portion of a globe and the words "World Junior Grads" are silver foil-stamped at the bottom of the picture. On the backs, a full-size globe serves as a panel for displaying a career summary and a color action player cut-out. The back also includes the year the player participated in the IIHF World Junior Championships. The cards are numbered on the back with a "WG" prefix.

COMPLETE SET (20) 20.00 50.00
WG1 Scott Niedermayer .40 1.00
WG2 Slava Kozlov .40 1.00
WG3 Chris Chelios .75 2.00
WG4 Jari Kurri .75 2.00
WG5 Pavel Bure 1.50 4.00
WG6 Jaromir Jagr 2.00 5.00
WG7 Steve Yzerman 6.00 15.00
WG8 Joe Sakic 2.00 5.00
WG9 Alexei Kovalev .40 1.00
WG10 Wayne Gretzky 8.00 20.00
WG11 Mario Lemieux 6.00 15.00
WG12 Eric Lindros 1.50 4.00
WG13 Pat Falloon .40 1.00
WG14 Trevor Linden .40 1.00
WG15 Brian Leetch .75 2.00
WG16 Sergei Fedorov 3.00 8.00
WG17 Mats Sundin .75 2.00
WG18 Alexander Mogilny .40 1.00
WG19 Jeremy Roenick 1.50 4.00
WG20 Luc Robitaille .75 2.00

1993 Upper Deck Locker All-Stars

This 60-card standard-size set was issued as the 1992-93 Upper Deck NHL All-Star Locker Series. The set came in a plastic locker box. Personally signed Gordie Howe "Hockey Heroes" cards were randomly inserted throughout the locker boxes; the odds of finding one are one in 120 boxes. The fronts feature full-bleed, color, action player photos. The player's name is printed in gold foil above a blue and gold-foil curving stripe at the bottom. The 44th NHL All-Star game logo overlaps the stripe and is printed in the lower right corner. The backs carry a small, close-up picture within a bright blue rough-edged border that gives the effect of torn paper. This photo overlaps a gray panel with the same rough-edge look. This panel carries player profile information. After presenting the NHL All-Stars by conference, Campbell Conference All-Stars (1-18) and Wales Conference All-Stars (19-36), the set features the following special subsets, All-Star Skills Winners (37-40), All-Star Heroes (41-50), and Future All-Stars (51-60). The card pictures for this set were taken during the 1993 NHL All-Star Weekend in Montreal.

COMPLETE SET (60) 6.00 15.00
1 Peter Bondra .20 .50

2 Steve Duchesne .01 .05
3 Jaromir Jagr .60 1.50
4 Pat LaFontaine .20 .50
5 Brian Leetch .20 .50
6 Mario Lemieux 1.00 2.50
7 Mark Messier .25 .60
8 Alexander Mogilny .08 .25
9 Kirk Muller .01 .05
10 Adam Oates .08 .25
11 Mark Recchi .08 .25
12 Patrick Roy 1.00 2.50
13 Joe Sakic .40 1.00
14 Kevin Stevens .01 .05
15 Scott Stevens .08 .25
16 Rick Tocchet .01 .05
17 Pierre Turgeon .08 .25
18 Zarley Zalapski .01 .05
19 Ed Belfour .20 .50
20 Brian Bradley .01 .05
21 Pavel Bure .40 1.00
22 Chris Chelios .20 .50
23 Paul Coffey .20 .50
24 Doug Gilmour .20 .50
25 Wayne Gretzky 1.25 3.00
26 Phil Housley .08 .25
27 Brett Hull .25 .60
28 Kelly Kisio .01 .05
29 Jari Kurri .20 .50
30 Dave Manson .01 .05
31 Mike Modano .25 .60
32 Gary Roberts .08 .25
33 Luc Robitaille .08 .25
34 Jeremy Roenick .20 .50
35 Teemu Selanne .40 1.00
36 Steve Yzerman .60 1.50
37 Al Iafrate .08 .25
38 Mike Gartner .08 .25
39 Ray Bourque .25 .60
40 Jon Casey .08 .25
41 Bob Gainey .08 .25
42 Gordie Howe .40 1.00
43 Bobby Hull .30 .75
44 Frank Mahovlich .20 .50
45 Lanny McDonald .08 .25
46 Stan Mikita .15 .40
47 Henri Richard .10 .30
48 Larry Robinson .20 .50
49 Glen Sather .08 .25
50 Bryan Trottier .08 .25
51 Tony Amonte .08 .25
52 Pat Falloon .01 .05
53 Joe Juneau .08 .25
54 Alexei Kovalev .08 .25
55 Dmitri Kvartalnov .01 .05
56 Eric Lindros .50 1.25
57 Vladimir Malakhov .01 .05
58 Felix Potvin .20 .50
59 Mats Sundin .20 .50
60 Alexei Zhamnov .08 .25
AU Gordie Howe AU 60.00 125.00

1993-94 Upper Deck

The 1993-94 Upper Deck hockey set contains 575 standard-size cards. The set was released in two series of 310 and 265 cards, respectively. The fronts feature a photo with team color-coded inner borders. The player's name, position and team name are at the bottom. The backs have a photo in the upper half with yearly statistics in the bottom portion. The following subsets are included: 100-Point Club (220-235), NHL Star Rookies (236-249), World Jr. Championships - which include Canada (250-260/531-550), Czechoslovakia (261-267/573), Finland (268-271), Russia (272-279/571/574) and USA (551-568) - All-Rookie Team (280-285) and Team Point Leaders (286-309). The set closes with an All-World Junior Team subset (569-574). A special card (SP4) was randomly inserted in Upper Deck series one packs commemorating Teemu Selanne's record-breaking 76 goal rookie season. A Wayne Gretzky card commemorating his 802nd NHL goal was randomly inserted at a rate of 1:36 Parkhurst series two packs. This card is identical to his regular Upper Deck card for '93-94, with the exception of a gold foil stamp that indicates his 602nd goal. The silver version of this card was handed out to Canadian dealers as a promotion for Parkhurst series two, and also given to each of the 16,005 fans attending the next game at the Great Western Forum following the event.

1 Guy Hebert .07 .20
2 Bob Bassen .05 .15
3 Theo Fleury .05 .15
4 Ray Whitney .05 .15
5 Donald Audette .05 .15
6 Martin Rucinsky .05 .15
7 Lyle Odelein .05 .15
8 John Vanbiesbrouck .07 .20
9 Tim Cheveldae .07 .20
10 Jock Callander .05 .15
11 Nick Kypreos .05 .15
12 Jarrod Skalde .05 .15
13 Gary Shuchuk .05 .15
14 Kris King .05 .15
15 Josef Beranek .05 .15
16 Sean Hill .05 .15
17 Bob Kudelski .05 .15
18 Jiri Slegr .05 .15
19 Dmitri Kvartalnov .05 .15
20 Drake Berehowsky .05 .15
21 Jean-Francois Quintin .05 .15
22 Randy Wood .05 .15
23 Jim McKenzie .05 .15
24 Steven King .05 .15
25 Scott Niedermayer .10 .25
26 Alexander Andrijevski .05 .15
27 Alexei Kovalev .07 .20
28 Steve Konowalchuk .05 .15
29 Vladimir Malakhov .05 .15
30 Eric Lindros .30 .75
31 Mathieu Schneider .05 .15
32 Russ Courtnall .05 .15
33 Ron Sutter .05 .15
34 Radek Hamr RC .10 .25
35 Pavel Bure .10 .25
36 Joe Sacco .05 .15
37 Robert Petrovicky .05 .15
38 Anatoli Fedotov RC .10 .25
39 Pat Falloon .05 .15
40 Martin Straka .05 .15
41 Brad Werenka .05 .15
42 Mike Richter .10 .25
43 Mike McPhee .05 .15
44 Sylvain Turgeon .05 .15
45 Tom Barrasso .07 .20
46 Anatoli Semenov .05 .15
47 Joe Murphy .05 .15
48 Rob Pearson .05 .15
49 Patrick Roy .25 .60
50 Dallas Drake RC .10 .25
51 Mark Messier .10 .25
52 Scott Pellerin RC .10 .25
53 Teppo Numminen .05 .15
54 Chris Kontos .05 .15
55 Richard Matvichuk .05 .15
56 Dale Craigwell .05 .15
57 Mike Eastwood .05 .15
58 Bernie Nicholls .05 .15
59 Travis Green .07 .20
60 Shjon Podein RC .10 .25
61 Darrin Madeley RC .10 .25
62 Dixon Ward .05 .15
63 Andre Faust .05 .15
64 Tony Amonte .07 .20
65 Joe Cirella .05 .15
66 Michel Petit .05 .15
67 David Lowry .05 .15
68 Shawn Chambers .05 .15
69 Joe Sakic .25 .60
70 Michael Nylander .05 .15
71 Peter Andersson .05 .15
72 Sandis Ozolinsh .05 .15
73 Joby Messier RC .10 .25
74 John Blue .07 .20
75 Pat Elynuik .05 .15
76 Keith Osborne RC .10 .25
77 Greg Adams .05 .15
78 Chris Gratton .07 .20
79 Louie DeBrusk .05 .15
80 Todd Harkins RC .10 .25
81 Neil Brady .05 .15
82 Philippe Boucher .05 .15
83 Darryl Sydor .05 .15
84 Oleg Petrov .05 .15
85 Andrei Kovalenko .05 .15
86 Dave Andreychuk .10 .25
87 Jeff Daniels .05 .15
88 Kevin Todd .05 .15
89 Mark Tinordi .05 .15
90 Garry Galley .05 .15
91 Shawn Burr .05 .15
92 Tom Pederson .05 .15
93 Warren Rychel .05 .15
94 Stu Barnes .05 .15
95 Peter Bondra .07 .20
96 Brian Skrudland .05 .15
97 Doug MacDonald RC .10 .25
98 Rob Niedermayer .07 .20
99 Wayne Gretzky .50 1.25
100 Peter Taglianetti .05 .15
101 Don Sweeney .05 .15
102 Andrei Lomakin .05 .15
103 Checklist 1-103 .05 .15
104 Sergio Momesso .05 .15
105 Dave Archibald .05 .15
106 Karl Dykhuis .05 .15
107 Scott Mellanby .07 .20
108 Paul DiPietro .05 .15
109 Neal Broten .07 .20
110 Chris Terreri .07 .20
111 Craig MacTavish .05 .15
112 Jody Hull .05 .15
113 Philippe Bozon .05 .15
114 Geoff Courtnall .05 .15
115 Ed Olcyzk .05 .15
116 Ray Bourque .15 .40
117 Gilbert Dionne .05 .15
118 Valeri Kamensky .07 .20
119 Scott Stevens .10 .25
120 Pelle Eklund .05 .15
121 Brian Bradley .05 .15
122 Steve Thomas .05 .15
123 Don Beaupre .07 .20
124 Joel Otto .05 .15
125 Arturs Irbe .07 .20
126 Kevin Stevens .05 .15
127 Dimitri Yushkevich .05 .15
128 Adam Graves .05 .15
129 Chris Chelios .10 .25
130 Jeff Brown .05 .15
131 Paul Ranheim .05 .15
132 Shayne Corson .05 .15
133 Curtis Leschyshyn .05 .15
134 John MacLean .07 .20
135 Dimitri Khristich .05 .15
136 Dino Ciccarelli .07 .20
137 Pat LaFontaine .10 .25
138 Patrick Poulin .05 .15
139 Jaromir Jagr .25 .60
140 Kevin Hatcher .05 .15
141 Christian Ruuttu .05 .15
142 Ulf Samuelsson .05 .15
143 Ted Donato .05 .15
144 Bob Essensa .07 .20
145 Dave Gagner .07 .20
146 Tony Granato .05 .15
147 Ed Belfour .10 .25
148 Kirk Muller .05 .15
149 Rob Gaudreau RC .10 .25
150 Nicklas Lidstrom .10 .25
151 Gary Roberts .05 .15
152 Trent Klatt .05 .15
153 Ray Ferraro .05 .15
154 Michal Pivonka .05 .15
155 Mike Foligno .05 .15
156 Kirk McLean .07 .20
157 Curtis Joseph .10 .25
158 Roman Hamrlik .05 .15
159 Felix Potvin .20 .50
160 Brett Hull .15 .40
161 Alexei Zhitnik .05 .15
162 Alexei Zhamnov .07 .20
163 Grant Fuhr .10 .25
164 Nikolai Borschevsky .05 .15
165 Tomas Jelinek .05 .15
166 Thomas Steen .05 .15
167 John LeClair .10 .25
168 Vladimir Vujtek .05 .15
169 Richard Smehlik .05 .15
170 Alexandre Daigle .05 .15
171 Sergei Fedorov .15 .40
172 Steve Larmer .07 .20
173 Darius Kasparaitis .05 .15
174 Igor Kravchuk .05 .15
175 Owen Nolan .07 .20
176 Rob DiMaio .05 .15
177 Mike Vernon .07 .20
178 Alexander Semak .05 .15
179 Rick Tocchet .07 .20
180 Bill Ranford .07 .20
181 Sergei Zubov .05 .15
182 Tommy Soderstrom .07 .20
183 Al Iafrate .05 .15
184 Eric Desjardins .07 .20
185 Bret Hedican .05 .15
186 Joe Mullen .07 .20
187 Doug Bodger .05 .15
188 Tomas Sandstrom .05 .15
189 Glen Murray .05 .15
190 Chris Pronger .10 .25
191 Mike Craig .05 .15
192 Jim Paek .05 .15
193 Doug Zmolek .05 .15
194 Yves Racine .05 .15
195 Keith Tkachuk .10 .25
196 Chris Lindberg .05 .15
197 Kelly Buchberger .05 .15
198 Mark Janssens .05 .15
199 Peter Zezel .05 .15
200 Bob Probert .07 .20
201 Brad May .07 .20
202 Rob Zamuner .05 .15
203 Stephane Fiset .07 .20
204 Derian Hatcher .05 .15
205 Mike Gartner .07 .20
206 Checklist 104-206 .05 .05
207 Todd Krygier .05 .15
208 Glen Wesley .05 .15
209 Fredrik Olausson .05 .15
210 Patrick Flatley .05 .15
211 Cliff Ronning .05 .15
212 Kevin Dineen .05 .15
213 Zarley Zalapski .05 .15
214 Stephane Matteau .05 .15
215 Dave Ellett .05 .15
216 Kelly Hrudey .07 .20
217 Steve Duchesne .05 .15
218 Bobby Holik .05 .15
219 Brad Dalgarno .05 .15
220 Mats Sundin 100 CL .07 .20
221 Pat LaFontaine 100 .10 .25
222 Mark Recchi 100 .12 .30
223 Joe Sakic 100 .25 .60
224 Pierre Turgeon 100 .07 .20
225 Craig Janney 100 .07 .20
226 Adam Oates 100 .10 .25
227 Steve Yzerman 100 .25 .60
228 Mats Sundin 100 .07 .20
229 Theo Fleury 100 .05 .15
230 Kevin Stevens 100 .05 .15
231 Luc Robitaille 100 .07 .20
232 Brett Hull 100 .15 .40
233 Rick Tocchet 100 .07 .20
234 Alexander Mogilny 100 .07 .20
235 Jeremy Roenick 100 .15 .40
236 G.Leveque/T.Stevenson .05 .15
237 Adam Bennett SR RC .10 .25
238 Dody Wood SR RC .10 .25
239 Niclas Andersson SR .05 .15
240 Jason Bowen SR RC .10 .25
241 Steve Junker SR RC .10 .25
242 Bryan Smolinski SR .05 .15
243 Chris Simon SR RC .10 .25
244 Sergei Zholtok SR .05 .15
245 Dan Ratushny SR RC .10 .25
246 Guy Leveque SR .05 .15
247 Scott Thomas RC .10 .25
248 Turner Stevenson SR .05 .15
249 Dan Keczmer SR .05 .15
250 Alexandre Daigle WJC CL .05 .15
251 Adrian Aucoin WJC RC .10 .25
252 Jason Smith WJC .05 .15
253 Ralph Intranouvo WJC RC .10 .25
254 Jason Dawe WJC .05 .15
255 Jeff Bes WJC RC .10 .25
256 Tyler Wright WJC .05 .15
257 Martin Lapointe WJC .05 .15
258 Jeff Shantz WJC RC .05 .15
259 Martin Gendron WJC RC .07 .20
260 Philippe DeRouville WJC RC .10 .25
261 Frantisek Kaberle WJC RC .10 .25
262 Radim Bicanek WJC RC .10 .25
263 Tomas Klimt WJC RC .10 .25
264 Tomas Nemcicky WJC RC .10 .25
265 Richard Kapus WJC RC .10 .25
266 Patrik Krisak WJC RC .10 .25
267 Roman Kadera WJC RC .10 .25
268 Kimmo Timonen WJC RC .10 .25
269 Jukka Ollila WJC RC .10 .25
270 Tuomas Gronman WJC .05 .15
271 Mikko Luovi WJC RC .10 .25
272 Sergei Gonchar WJC RC .10 .25
273 Maxim Golanov WJC RC .10 .25
274 Oleg Belov WJC RC .10 .25
275 Sergei Klimovich WJC .10 .25
276 Sergei Brylin WJC RC .10 .25
277 Alexei Yashin WJC .07 .20
278 Vitali Tomilin WJC RC .10 .25
279 Alexander Cherbaev WJC .05 .15
280 Eric Lindros ART .30 .75
281 Teemu Selanne ART .20 .50
282 Joe Juneau ART .07 .20
283 Vladimir Malakhov ART .05 .15
284 Scott Niedermayer ART .10 .25
285 Felix Potvin ART .20 .50
286 Adam Oates TL .10 .25
287 Pat LaFontaine TL .10 .25
288 Theo Fleury TL .05 .15
289 Jeremy Roenick TL .15 .40
290 Steve Yzerman TL .25 .60
291 P.Klima/D.Weight TL .05 .15
292 Geoff Sanderson TL .07 .20
293 Luc Robitaille TL .07 .20
294 Mike Modano TL .15 .40
295 Vincent Damphousse TL .07 .20
296 Claude Lemieux TL .05 .15
297 Pierre Turgeon TL .07 .20
298 Mark Messier TL .10 .25
299 Norm Maciver TL .05 .15
300 Mark Recchi TL .12 .30
301 Mario Lemieux TL .40 1.00
302 Mats Sundin TL .07 .20
303 Craig Janney TL .07 .20
304 Kelly Kisio TL .05 .15
305 Brian Bradley TL .05 .15
306 Doug Gilmour TL .12 .30
307 Pavel Bure TL .10 .25
308 Peter Bondra TL .07 .20
309 Teemu Selanne TL .20 .50
310 Checklist 207-310 .05 .05
311 Terry Yake .05 .15
312 Bob Sweeney .05 .15
313 Robert Reichel .05 .15
314 Jeremy Roenick .15 .40
315 Paul Coffey .10 .25
316 Geoff Sanderson .07 .20
317 Rob Blake .07 .20
318 Patrice Brisebois .05 .15
319 Jaroslav Modry RC .10 .25
320 Scott Lachance .05 .15
321 Glenn Healy .07 .20
322 Martin Gelinas .05 .15
323 Craig Janney .07 .20
324 Bill McDougall RC .10 .25
325 Shawn Antoski .05 .15
326 Olaf Kolzig .07 .20
327 Adam Oates .10 .25
328 Dirk Graham .05 .15
329 Brent Gilchrist .05 .15
330 Zdeno Ciger .05 .15
331 Pat Verbeek .05 .15
332 Jari Kurri .10 .25
333 Kevin Haller .05 .15
334 Martin Brodeur .25 .60
335 Norm Maciver .05 .15
336 Dominic Roussel .07 .20
337 Iain Fraser RC .10 .25
338 Vitali Karamnov .05 .15
339 Rene Corbet RC .10 .25
340 Wendel Clark .07 .20
341 Mike Ridley .05 .15
342 Nelson Emerson .05 .15
343 Joe Juneau .07 .20
344 Vesa Viitakoski RC .10 .25
345 Steve Chiasson .05 .15
346 Andrew Cassels .05 .15
347 Pierre Turgeon .07 .20
348 Brian Leetch .10 .25
349 Alexei Yashin .07 .20
350 Mark Recchi .12 .30
351 Ron Francis .12 .30
352 Mike Ricci .05 .15
353 Igor Korolev .05 .15
354 Brent Gretzky RC .10 .25
355 Dave Poulin .05 .15
356 Cam Neely .10 .25
357 Gary Suter .05 .15
358 Dave Manson .05 .15
359 Robert Kron .05 .15
360 Ulf Dahlen .05 .15
361 Rod Brind'Amour .07 .20
362 Alexei Gusarov .05 .15
363 Vitali Prokhorov .05 .15
364 Damian Rhodes RC .10 .25
365 Paul Ysebaert .05 .15
366 Vladimir Konstantinov .07 .20
367 Steven Rice .05 .15
368 Brian Propp .05 .15
369 Valeri Zelepukin .05 .15
370 David Volek .05 .15
371 Sergei Nemchinov .05 .15
372 Pavol Demitra .12 .30
373 Brent Fedyk .05 .15
374 Larry Murphy .07 .20
375 Dave Karpa .05 .15
376 Dave Babych .05 .15
377 Keith Jones .05 .15
378 Neil Wilkinson .05 .15
379 Jozef Stumpel .05 .15
380 Vincent Damphousse .07 .20
381 Tom Kurvers .05 .15
382 Doug Gilmour .12 .30
383 Trevor Linden .07 .20
384 Kelly Miller .05 .15
385 Tim Sweeney .05 .15
386 Mikhail Tatarinov .05 .15
387 Dominik Hasek .20 .50
388 Steve Yzerman .25 .60
389 Scott Pearson .05 .15
390 Brian Bellows .07 .20
391 Claude Lemieux .05 .15
392 Marty McInnis .05 .15
393 Jim Sandlak .05 .15
394 Jocelyn Thibault RC .10 .25
395 John Cullen .05 .15
396 Joe Nieuwendyk .07 .20
397 Mike Modano .15 .40
398 Ray Sheppard .07 .20
399 Trevor Kidd .07 .20
400 Checklist .05 .15
401 Frank Pietrangelo .07 .20
402 Stephan Lebeau .05 .15
403 Stephane Richer .07 .20
404 Greg Gilbert .05 .15
405 Dmitri Filimonov .05 .15
406 Vyacheslav Butsayev .05 .15
407 Mario Lemieux .40 1.00
408 Kevin Miller .05 .15
409 John Tucker .05 .15
410 Murray Craven .05 .15
411 Dale Hawerchuk .12 .30
412 Al MacInnis .07 .20
413 Keith Primeau .05 .15
414 Luc Robitaille .07 .20
415 Benoit Brunet .05 .15
416 Tom Chorske .05 .15
417 Derek King .05 .15
418 Troy Mallette .05 .15
419 Mats Sundin .07 .20
420 Kent Manderville .05 .15
421 Kip Miller .05 .15
422 Jarkko Varvio .05 .15
423 Jason Arnott RC .20 .50
424 Craig Billington .07 .20
425 Stewart Malgunas RC .10 .25
426 Ron Tugnutt .07 .20
427 Alexei Kudashov RC .10 .25
428 Harijs Vitolinsh .05 .15
429 Bill Houlder .05 .15
430 Craig Simpson .05 .15
431 Wes Walz .05 .15
432 Micah Aivazoff RC .10 .25
433 Scott Levins RC .10 .25
434 Ron Hextall .07 .20
435 Fred Brathwaite RC .10 .25
436 Chad Penney RC .10 .25
437 Vlastimil Kroupa RC .10 .25
438 Troy Loney .05 .15
439 Matthew Barnaby .07 .20
440 Kevin Todd .05 .15
441 Paul Cavallini .05 .15
442 Doug Weight .07 .20
443 Egeny Davydov .05 .15
444 Dominic Lavoie .05 .15
445 Peter Popovic RC .10 .25
446 Sergei Makarov .05 .15
447 Matt Martin RC .10 .25
448 Teemu Selanne .20 .50
449 Todd Ewen .05 .15
450 Sergei Petrenko .05 .15
451 Jeff Shantz .05 .15
452 Greg Johnson .05 .15
453 Brent Severyn RC .10 .25
454 Shawn McEachern .05 .15
455 Pierre Sevigny .05 .15
456 Benoit Hogue .05 .15
457 Esa Tikkanen .05 .15
458 Brian Glynn .05 .15
459 Doug Brown .05 .15
460 Mike Rathje .05 .15
461 Rudy Poeschek .05 .15
462 Jason Woolley .05 .15
463 Patrick Carnback RC .10 .25
464 Cam Stewart RC .10 .25
465 Petr Svoboda .05 .15
466 Ted Drury .05 .15
467 Ladislav Karabin RC .10 .25
468 Paul Broten .05 .15
469 Alexander Godynyuk .05 .15
470 Bob Jay RC .10 .25
471 Steve Larmer .07 .20
472 Jim Montgomery RC .10 .25
473 Darren Puppa .05 .15
474 Alexei Kasatonov .05 .15
475 Derek Plante RC .10 .25
476 German Titov RC .10 .25
477 Steve Dubinsky RC .10 .25
478 Andy Moog .10 .25
479 Aaron Ward RC .10 .25
480 Dean McAmmond .05 .15
481 Randy Gilhen .05 .15
482 Jason Muzzatti RC .10 .25
483 Corey Millen .05 .15
484 Alexander Karpovtsev .05 .15
485 Bill Huard RC .10 .25
486 Mikael Renberg .10 .25
487 Marty McSorley .05 .15
488 Alexander Mogilny .07 .20
489 Michal Sykora RC .10 .25
490 Checklist .05 .05
491 Tom Tilley .05 .15
492 Boris Mironov .05 .15
493 Sandy McCarthy .05 .15
494 Mark Astley RC .10 .25
495 Slava Kozlov .07 .20
496 Brian Benning .05 .15
497 Eric Weinrich .05 .15
498 Robert Burakovsky RC .10 .25
499 Patrick Lebeau .05 .15
500 Markus Naslund .10 .25
501 Jimmy Waite .07 .20
502 Denis Savard .12 .30
503 Jose Charbonneau RC .10 .25
504 Randy Burridge .05 .15
505 Arto Blomsten .05 .15
506 Shaun Van Allen .05 .15
507 Jon Casey .07 .20
508 Darren McCarty RC .15 .40
509 Roman Oksiuta RC .10 .25
510 Jody Hull .05 .15
511 Scott Scissons .05 .15
512 Jeff Norton .05 .15
513 Dmitri Mironov .05 .15
514 Sergei Bautin .05 .15
515 Garry Valk .05 .15
516 Keith Carney .05 .15
517 James Black .05 .15
518 Pat Peake .05 .15
519 Chris Osgood RC 1.50 4.00
520 Kirk Maltby RC .10 .25
521 Gord Murphy .05 .15
522 Mattias Norstrom RC .10 .25
523 Milos Holan RC .10 .25
524 Dave McLlwain .05 .15
525 Phil Housley .07 .20
526 Petr Klima .05 .15
527 John McIntyre .05 .15
528 Enrico Ciccone .05 .15
529 Stephane Quintal .05 .15
530 World Juniors CL .07 .20
Brent Tully
531 Anson Carter WJC RC .10 .25
532 Jeff Friesen WJC RC .10 .25
533 Yanick Dube WJC RC .10 .25
534 Jason Botterill WJC RC .10 .25
535 Todd Harvey WJC RC .10 .25
536 Manny Fernandez WJC RC .10 .25
537 Jason Allison WJC RC .10 .25
538 Jamie Storr WJC RC .10 .25
539 Rick Girard WJC RC .10 .25
540 Martin Gendron WJC .07 .20
541 Joel Bouchard WJC RC .10 .25
542 Mike Peca WJC RC .10 .25
543 Nick Stajduhar WJC RC .10 .25
544 Brendan Witt WJC RC .10 .25
545 Aaron Gavey WJC RC .10 .25
546 Chris Armstrong WJC RC .10 .25
547 Curtis Bowen WJC RC .10 .25
548 Brandon Convery WJC RC .10 .25
549 Bryan McCabe WJC RC .10 .25
550 Marty Murray WJC RC .10 .25
551 Ryan Sittler WJC .05 .15
552 Jason McBain WJC RC .10 .25
553 Richard Park WJC RC .10 .25
554 Aaron Ellis WJC RC .10 .25
555 Toby Kvalevog WJC RC .10 .25
556 Jay Pandolfo WJC RC .10 .25
557 John Emmons WJC .05 .15
558 David Wilkie WJC RC .10 .25
559 John Varga WJC RC .10 .25
560 Jason Bonsignore WJC RC .10 .25
561 Deron Quint WJC RC .10 .25
562 Adam Deadmarsh WJC .05 .15
563 Jon Coleman WJC RC .10 .25
564 Bob Lachance WJC RC .10 .25
565 Chris O'Sullivan WJC RC .10 .25
566 J.Langenbrunner WJC RC .10 .25
567 Kevin Hilton WJC RC .10 .25
568 Kevyn Adams WJC RC .10 .25
569 Saku Koivu WJC .10 .25
570 Mats Lindgren WJC RC .10 .25
571 Valeri Bure WJC RC .10 .25
572 Edvin Frylen WJC RC .10 .25
573 Jaroslav Miklenda WJC RC .10 .25
574 Vadim Sharifijanov WJC .07 .20
575 Checklist Card .05 .15
99B1 W.Gretzky 802 Silver 6.00 15.00
99B2 W.Gretzky 802 Gold 4.00 10.00
SP4 Teemu Selanne Hologram .20 .50

1993-94 Upper Deck Award Winners

Randomly inserted at a rate of 1:30 Canadian first-series foil packs, this eight-card set measures the standard size. The fronts feature a black-and-white photo of the player and his trophy. The player's name appears at the bottom and in silver-foil letters on the left side.

COMPLETE SET (8) 5.00 12.00
AW1 Mario Lemieux 1.50 4.00
AW2 Teemu Selanne .30 .75
AW3 Ed Belfour .30 .75
AW4 Patrick Roy 1.50 4.00
AW5 Chris Chelios .30 .75
AW6 Doug Gilmour .15 .40
AW7 Pierre Turgeon .15 .40
AW8 Dave Poulin .08 .25

1993-94 Upper Deck Future Heroes

Randomly inserted at a rate of 1:30 first-series U.S. hobby packs, this 10-card set measures the standard size. The tan-bordered fronts feature sepia-toned action player photos with the player's name in white lettering within a black bar above the photo. The set's title appears below the photo, with the word "Heroes" printed in copper foil. On a gray background, the back carries a player profile. The cards are numbered on the back and continue where the Howe Heroes left off.

COMPLETE SET (10) 6.00 15.00
28 Felix Potvin .50 1.25
29 Pat Falloon .15 .40
30 Pavel Bure .40 1.00
31 Eric Lindros .40 1.00
32 Teemu Selanne .30 .75
33 Jaromir Jagr .50 1.25
34 Alexander Mogilny .20 .50
35 Joe Juneau .15 .40
36 Checklist 2.00 5.00
NNO Header Card .75 2.00

1993-94 Upper Deck Gretzky's Great Ones

Randomly inserted in series one packs and one per series one jumbo, this 10-card set measures the standard size. The fronts feature color player photos with blue and gray bars above, below, and to the left. The player's name and the words "Gretzky's Great Ones" in copper-foil letters appear below and above the photo, respectively.The cards are numbered on the back with a "GG" prefix.

COMPLETE SET (10) 4.00 10.00
GG1 Denis Savard .30 .75
GG2 Chris Chelios .40 1.00
GG3 Brett Hull .50 1.25
GG4 Mario Lemieux 1.25 3.00
GG5 Mark Messier .50 1.25
GG6 Paul Coffey .40 1.00
GG7 Theo Fleury .40 1.00
GG8 Luc Robitaille .30 .75
GG9 Marty McSorley .30 .75
GG10 Grant Fuhr .30 .75

1993-94 Upper Deck Gretzky Box Bottom

Issued on the bottom of Upper Deck boxes, this card measures approximately 5" by 7" and features Wayne Gretzky on the front. The design is the same as his regular issue card. The back is blank. The card is unnumbered.

1 Wayne Gretzky .40 1.00

1993-94 Upper Deck Gretzky Sheet

This sheet was mailed to collectors who ordered Wayne Gretzky's 24-Karat Gold Card commemorating his NHL record breaking 802nd goal after Upper Deck had unexpected production difficulties. It could also be ordered through the Upper Deck Authenticated catalog. It measures 8 1/2" by 11". The front features a white border and three color action photos of Wayne Gretzky set against a background with the number "802". A seal on the front carries the serial number and the production figure (30,000). The back is blank.

1 Wayne Gretzky 8.00 20.00

1993-94 Upper Deck Hat Tricks

Inserted one per series one jumbo pack, this 20-card set measures the standard size. The fronts feature color player photos that are borderless, except on the right, where a strip that fades from brown to black carries the player's name. The cards are numbered on the back with an "HT" prefix.

COMPLETE SET (20) 2.00 5.00
HT1 Adam Graves .08 .25
HT2 Geoff Sanderson .02 .10
HT3 Gary Roberts .08 .25
HT4 Robert Reichel .02 .10
HT5 Adam Oates .08 .25
HT6 Steve Yzerman 1.00 2.50
HT7 Alexei Kovalev .08 .25
HT8 Vincent Damphousse .02 .10
HT9 Rob Gaudreau .02 .10
HT10 Pat LaFontaine .08 .25
HT11 Pierre Turgeon .08 .25
HT12 Rick Tocchet .08 .25
HT13 Michael Nylander .02 .10
HT14 Steve Larmer .08 .25
HT15 Alexander Mogilny .08 .25
HT16 Owen Nolan .08 .25
HT17 Luc Robitaille .20 .50
HT18 Jeremy Roenick .25 .60
HT19 Kevin Stevens .02 .10
HT20 Mats Sundin .20 .50

1993-94 Upper Deck Next In Line

Randomly inserted in all first-series packs, this six-card set measures the standard-size. The horizontal metallic and prismatic fronts feature photos of two NHL players, diagonally divided in the middle. The players' names appear under the photos. The cards are numbered on the back with an "NL" prefix.

COMPLETE SET (6) 7.50 15.00
NL1 W.Gretzky/M.Nylander 2.50 6.00
NL2 B.Hull/P.Poulin .75 2.00
NL3 S.Yzerman/J.Sakic 2.50 6.00
NL4 R.Bourque/B.Leetch 2.00 5.00
NL5 D.Gilmour/K.Tkachuk 1.00 2.50
NL6 P.Roy/F.Potvin 1.25 3.00

1993-94 Upper Deck NHL's Best

Randomly inserted at a rate of 1:30 first-series U.S. retail packs, this 10-card set measures the standard size. The fronts feature color action player photos that are borderless, except at the bottom, where a black bar carries the player's name. The cards are numbered on the back with an "HB" prefix.

COMPLETE SET (10) 5.00 10.00
HB1 Alexander Mogilny .10 .30
HB2 Rob Gaudreau .05 .15
HB3 Brett Hull .40 1.00
HB4 Dallas Drake .05 .15
HB5 Pavel Bure .30 .75
HB6 Alexei Kovalev .10 .30
HB7 Mario Lemieux 1.50 4.00
HB8 Eric Lindros .30 .75
HB9 Wayne Gretzky 2.00 5.00
HB10 Joe Juneau .10 .30

1993-94 Upper Deck NHLPA/Roots

Teamed with the NHL Players Association, Upper Deck issued these clothing tags as a promotion for a new line of clothing produced by the clothing manufacturer, Roots Canada. Called "Hang Out," each article of clothing came with one of ten "hang tag" cards featuring on their fronts a full-bleed photo of the NHL player wearing the clothing. The clothing tags measure the standard size and are punch holed in the upper left corner. Versions of these cards without the punch hole also exist. With a faded and enlarged Upper Deck logo, the backs carry the player's name and an advertisement for the NHLPA apparel. The cards are numbered on the back. The entire set could also be purchased by mail. The first series came out in 1993, while the second series came out in 1994. Reportedly 5,000 sets of the third series were produced. The backs of cards 21-30 also have a NHLPA apparel advertisement but sport a different design than cards 1-20.

COMPLETE SET (30) 16.00 40.00
COMPLETE SERIES 1 (10) 6.00 15.00
COMPLETE SERIES 2 (10) 6.00 15.00
COMPLETE SERIES 3 (10) 6.00 15.00
1 Trevor Linden .50 1.25
2 Patrick Roy 4.00 10.00
Montreal Ca
3 Felix Potvin .75 2.00
4 Steve Yzerman 4.00 10.00
5 Doug Gilmour .60 1.50
Toronto Ma
6 Wendel Clark .50 1.25
7 Kirk McLean .50 1.25
8 Larry Murphy .15 .40
9 Guy Carbonneau .15 .40
10 Mike Ricci .50 1.25
11 Doug Gilmour .60 1.50
Toronto Ma
12 Sergei Fedorov 1.25 3.00
Detroit
13 Shayne Corson .15 .40
14 Alexei Yashin .50 1.25
15 Pavel Bure 1.50 4.00
16 Joe Sakic 1.50 4.00
17 Teemu Selanne 1.25 3.00
Winnipeg
18 Dave Andreychuk .50 1.25
Toronto
19 Al MacInnis .50 1.25
Calgary Fla
20 Rob Blake .50 1.25
Los Angeles K
21 Doug Gilmour .60 1.50
22 Steve Larmer .15 .40
23 Eric Lindros 1.50 4.00
24 Mike Modano .75 2.00
25 Vincent Damphousse .50 1.25
26 Mike Gartner .50 1.25
27 John Vanbiesbrouck .60 1.50
28 Theo Fleury .60 1.50
29 Ken Baumgartner .15 .40
30 Jeremy Roenick .60 1.50

1993-94 Upper Deck Program of Excellence

Randomly inserted at a rate of 1:30 Canadian second series packs, this 15-card set measures the standard size. The fronts feature color action player photos that are borderless, except at the right, where the margin carries the player's name in silver-foil letters. The silver-foil "Program of Excellence" logo rests at the lower right. The cards are numbered on the back with an "E" prefix.

COMPLETE SET (15) 40.00 80.00
E1 Adam Smith 1.00 2.50
E2 Jason Podollan 1.00 2.50
E3 Jason Wiemer 1.00 2.50
E4 Jeff O'Neill 4.00 10.00
E5 Daniel Goneau 1.00 2.50
E6 Christian Laflamme 1.00 2.50
E7 Daymond Langkow 1.50 4.00
E8 Jeff Friesen 1.50 4.00
E9 Wayne Primeau 1.00 2.50
E10 Paul Kariya 8.00 20.00
E11 Rob Niedermayer 4.00 10.00
E12 Eric Lindros 6.00 15.00
E13 Mario Lemieux 8.00 20.00
E14 Steve Yzerman 8.00 20.00
E15 Alexandre Daigle 1.50 4.00

1993-94 Upper Deck Silver Skates

The first ten standard-size die-cut cards (H1-H10) listed below were randomly inserted in U.S. second-series hobby packs, while the second ten (R1-R10) were inserted in U.S. retail packs. The fronts feature color player action cutouts set on red and black backgrounds. The trade cards were randomly inserted in both hobby and jumbo packs and could be redeemed for a silver or gold retail set. These cards picture Gretzky, and because the majority were redeemed, they have become highly sought after in their own right.

COMPLETE HOBBY SET (10) 2.50 6.00
COMPLETE RETAIL SET (10) 5.00 12.00
*RETAIL GOLD EXCH: .75X TO 1.5X BASIC INSERTS
H1 Mario Lemieux 1.50 4.00
H2 Pavel Bure .30 .75
H3 Eric Lindros .30 .75
H4 Rob Niedermayer .20 .50
H5 Chris Pronger .08 .25
H6 Adam Oates .08 .25
H7 Pierre Turgeon .20 .50
H8 Alexei Yashin .08 .25
H9 Joe Sakic .60 1.50
H10 Alexander Mogilny .20 .50
R1 Wayne Gretzky 3.00 8.00
R2 Teemu Selanne .30 .75
R3 Alexandre Daigle .08 .25
R4 Chris Gratton .08 .25
R5 Brett Hull .40 1.00
R6 Steve Yzerman 1.50 4.00
R7 Doug Gilmour .08 .25
R8 Jaromir Jagr .50 1.25
R9 Jason Arnott .60 1.50
R10 Jeremy Roenick .40 1.00
EXG W.Gretzky Gold EXCH 20.00 50.00
EXS W.Gretzky Silver EXCH 15.00 40.00

1993-94 Upper Deck SP Inserts

Inserted one per second-series pack and two per second-series jumbo, these 180 standard-size cards feature color player action shots on their fronts. The photos are borderless, except at the bottom, where a team color-coded margin carries the player's name and position in white lettering. The player's team name appears in a silver-foil arc above him.

COMPLETE SET (180) 20.00 50.00
1 Sean Hill .12 .30
2 Troy Loney .12 .30
3 Joe Sacco .12 .30
4 Anatoli Semenov .12 .30
5 Ron Tugnutt .30 .75
6 Terry Yake .12 .30
7 Ray Bourque .75 2.00
8 Jon Casey .30 .75
9 Joe Juneau .30 .75
10 Cam Neely .40 1.00
11 Adam Oates .30 .75
12 Bryan Smolinski .12 .30
13 Matthew Barnaby .20 .50
14 Philippe Boucher .12 .30
15 Grant Fuhr .30 .75
16 Dale Hawerchuk .20 .50
17 Pat LaFontaine .40 1.00
18 Alexander Mogilny .20 .50
19 Craig Simpson .12 .30
20 Ted Drury .12 .30
21 Theo Fleury .12 .30
22 Al MacInnis .20 .50
23 Joe Nieuwendyk .20 .50
24 Joel Otto .12 .30
25 Gary Roberts .12 .30
26 Vesa Viitakoski .12 .30
27 Ed Belfour .60 1.50
28 Chris Chelios .40 1.00
29 Joe Murphy .12 .30
30 Patrick Poulin .12 .30
31 Jeremy Roenick .75 2.00
32 Jeff Shantz .12 .30
33 Kevin Todd .12 .30

4 Neal Broten .20 .50
5 Paul Cavallini .12 .30
6 Russ Courtnall .12 .30
7 Derian Hatcher .12 .30
8 Mike Modano 1.00 2.50
9 Andy Moog .20 .50
0 Jarkko Varvio .12 .30
1 Dino Ciccarelli .20 .50
2 Paul Coffey .40 1.00
3 Dallas Drake .12 .30
4 Sergei Fedorov .60 1.50
5 Keith Primeau .12 .30
6 Bob Probert .30 .75
7 Steve Yzerman 2.00 5.00
8 Jason Arnott .30 .75
9 Shayne Corson .12 .30
0 Dave Manson .12 .30
1 Dean McAmmond .12 .30
2 Bill Ranford .30 .75
3 Doug Weight .20 .50
4 Brad Werenka .12 .30
5 Evgeny Davydov .12 .30
6 Scott Levins .12 .30
7 Scott Mellanby .20 .50
8 Rob Niedermayer .20 .50
9 Brian Skrudland .12 .30
0 John Vanbiesbrouck .20 .50
1 Robert Kron .12 .30
2 Michael Nylander .12 .30
3 Robert Petrovicky .12 .30
4 Chris Pronger .20 .50
5 Geoff Sanderson .20 .50
6 Darren Turcotte .12 .30
7 Pat Verbeek .12 .30
8 Rob Blake .20 .50
9 Tony Granato .12 .30
70 Wayne Gretzky 3.00 8.00
71 Kelly Hrudey .20 .50
72 Shawn McEachern .12 .30
73 Luc Robitaille .30 .75
74 Darryl Sydor .12 .30
75 Alexei Zhitnik .12 .30
76 Brian Bellows .12 .30
77 Vincent Damphousse .12 .30
78 Stephan Lebeau .12 .30
79 John LeClair .40 1.00
80 Kirk Muller .12 .30
81 Patrick Roy 2.00 5.00
82 Pierre Sevigny .12 .30
83 Claude Lemieux .12 .30
84 Corey Millen .12 .30
85 Bernie Nicholls .12 .30
86 Scott Niedermayer .12 .30
87 Stephane Richer .20 .50
88 Alexander Semak .12 .30
89 Scott Stevens .20 .50
90 Ray Ferraro .12 .30
91 Darius Kasparaitis .12 .30
92 Scott Lachance .12 .30
93 Vladimir Malakhov .12 .30
94 Marty McInnis .12 .30
95 Steve Thomas .12 .30
96 Pierre Turgeon .20 .50
97 Tony Amonte .20 .50
98 Mike Gartner .30 .75
99 Adam Graves .12 .30
100 Alexander Karpovtsev .12 .30
101 Alexei Kovalev .20 .50
102 Brian Leetch .40 1.00
103 Mark Messier .60 1.50
104 Esa Tikkanen .12 .30
105 Craig Billington .20 .50
106 Robert Burakovsky .12 .30
107 Alexandre Daigle .12 .30
108 Pavol Demitra .20 .50
109 Dmitri Filimonov .12 .30
110 Bob Kudelski .12 .30
111 Norm Maciver .12 .30
112 Alexei Yashin .12 .30
113 Josef Beranek .12 .30
114 Rod Brind'Amour .20 .50
115 Milos Holan .12 .30
116 Eric Lindros .75 2.00
117 Mark Recchi .20 .50
118 Mikael Renberg .20 .50
119 Dimitri Yushkevich .12 .30
120 Tom Barrasso .20 .50
121 Jaromir Jagr 1.25 3.00
122 Mario Lemieux 2.00 5.00
123 Markus Naslund .40 1.00
124 Kevin Stevens .12 .30
125 Martin Straka .12 .30
126 Rick Tocchet .30 .75
127 Martin Gelinas .12 .30
128 Owen Nolan .30 .75
129 Mike Ricci .12 .30
130 Joe Sakic 1.25 3.00
131 Chris Simon .30 .75
132 Mats Sundin .60 1.50
133 Jocelyn Thibault .40 1.00
134 Philippe Bozon .12 .30
135 Jeff Brown .12 .30
136 Phil Housley .30 .75
137 Brett Hull .75 2.00
138 Craig Janney .30 .75
139 Curtis Joseph .60 1.50
140 Brendan Shanahan .60 1.50
141 Pat Falloon .12 .30
142 Johan Garpenlov .12 .30
143 Rob Gaudreau .12 .30
144 Vlastimil Kroupa .12 .30
145 Sergei Makarov .12 .30
146 Sandis Ozolinsh .12 .30
147 Mike Rathje .12 .30
148 Brian Bradley .12 .30
149 Chris Gratton .30 .75
150 Brent Gretzky .12 .30
151 Roman Hamrlik .12 .30
152 Petr Klima .12 .30
153 Denis Savard .30 .75
154 Rob Zamuner .12 .30
155 Dave Andreychuk .30 .75
156 Nikolai Borschevsky .12 .30
157 Dave Ellett .12 .30
158 Doug Gilmour .30 .75
159 Alexei Kudashov .12 .30
160 Felix Potvin .75 2.00
161 Greg Adams .12 .30
162 Pavel Bure .60 1.50
163 Geoff Courtnall .12 .30
164 Trevor Linden .30 .75
165 Kirk McLean .30 .75
166 Jiri Slegr .12 .30
167 Dixon Ward .12 .30
168 Peter Bondra .30 .75
169 Kevin Hatcher .12 .30
170 Al Iafrate .12 .30
171 Dimitri Khristich .12 .30
172 Pat Peake .12 .30
173 Mike Ridley .12 .30
174 Arlo Blomsten .12 .30
175 Nelson Emerson .12 .30
176 Boris Mironov .12 .30
177 Teemu Selanne .60 1.50
178 Keith Tkachuk .40 1.00
179 Paul Ysebaert .12 .30
180 Alexei Zhamnov .30 .75

1994 Upper Deck Gretzky 24K Gold

Issued in a heavy Plexiglas holder, this card measures the standard size and commemorates Wayne Gretzky's record-breaking 802nd goal. On a black background, the horizontal front features a 24-karat gold photo and a facsimile autograph of Gretzky, along with "802" printed in large silver numbers on the left. On the same black background, the horizontal back carries Gretzky's biography and stats in gold print. The card's serial number and the production run figure (3,500) round out the back.

1 Wayne Gretzky 40.00 100.00
Los Angel

1994 Upper Deck NHLPA/Be A Player

This special 45-card set features the NHL's top players in unique settings. Upper Deck sent three top photographers, including Walter Iooss, to capture on film players in off-ice situations. The first 18 cards bear Iooss' photos (Walter Iooss Collection) and are arranged alphabetically. Cards 19-40 are also arranged alphabetically and carry photos of the other photographers. The final five cards feature Doug Gilmour: A Canadian Hero (41-45).

COMPLETE SET (45) 12.00 30.00
1 Tony Amonte .20 .50
New York Ra
2 Chris Chelios .30 .75
3 Alexandre Daigle .08 .25
Ottawa
4 Dave Ellett .08 .25
5 Sergei Fedorov .60 1.50
Detroit
6 Chris Gratton .08 .25
Tampa Bay
7 Wayne Gretzky 2.00 5.00
Los Angel
8 Brett Hull .40 1.00
St. Louis Bl
9 Brian Leetch .30 .75
New York R
10 Rob Niedermayer .20 .50
11 Felix Potvin .30 .75
Toronto Ma
12 Luc Robitaille .20 .50
Los Ange
13 Jeremy Roenick .30 .75
Chicago
14 Joe Sakic .60 1.50
Quebec Nordiq
15 Teemu Selanne .60 1.50
Winnipeg
16 Brendan Shanahan .40 1.00
17 Alexei Yashin .20 .50
18 Steve Yzerman 1.50 4.00
Detroit R
19 Jason Arnott .20 .50
Edmonton O
20 Pavel Bure .60 1.50
Vancouver Ca
21 Theo Fleury .30 .75
22 Mike Gartner .20 .50
23 Kevin Haller .08 .25
24 Derian Hatcher .08 .25
25 Mark Howe .30 .75
Gordie Howe
26 Al Iafrate .08 .25
27 Joe Juneau .20 .50
Boston Bruin
28 Pat LaFontaine .20 .50
Buffalo
29 Eric Lindros .60 1.50
Philadelph
30 Dave Manson .08 .25
31 Mike Modano .40 1.00
32 Scott Niedermayer .20 .50
33 Owen Nolan .20 .50
Quebec Nordi
34 Joel Otto .08 .25
35 Chris Pronger .20 .50
Hartford
36 Scott Stevens .20 .50
37 Pierre Turgeon .20 .50
38 Pat Verbeek .08 .25
39 Doug Weight .20 .50
Edmonton Oi
40 Terry Yake .08 .25
41 Doug Gilmour .30 .75
(Two-Year
42 Doug Gilmour .30 .75
(Nine-Year
43 Doug Gilmour .30 .75
(Standing
44 Doug Gilmour .30 .75
(Sitting O
45 Doug Gilmour .30 .75
(With Fish

1994-95 Upper Deck

The 1994-95 Upper Deck set was issued in two series of 270 and 300 cards for a total of 570 standard-size cards. The product was available in three packaging versions per series: US Hobby, US Retail and Canadian. The fronts have a team color coded bar on the left border. The team name, position and player name are within the bar in gold foil. Due to a printing error, card numbers 22, 65, 85 and 200 each appear with two different numbers. Each variation was printed in the same quantity, so neither version carries a premium. Subsets include Shooter's Edge (227-234), Super Rookies (235-270), World Junior Championship teams including Canada (496-505), Czech Republic (506-509), Finland (510-512), Russia (513-517), Sweden (518-521) and USA (522-525), as well as Calder Candidates (526-540), and 1994 World Tour (541-570).

1 Wayne Gretzky 1.00 2.50
2 German Titov .12 .30
3 Guy Hebert .15 .40
4 Tony Amonte .15 .40
5 Dino Ciccarelli .15 .40
6 Geoff Sanderson .15 .40
7 Alexei Zhamnov .15 .40
8 John MacLean .15 .40
9 Brent Fedyk .12 .30
10 Adam Graves .12 .30
11 Adam Oates .20 .50
12 Ron Francis .25 .60
13 Bobby Dollas .12 .30
14 Ray Ferraro .12 .30
15 Paul Broten .12 .30
16 Ulf Dahlen .12 .30
17 Pat LaFontaine .20 .50
18 Craig Janney .15 .40
19 Garry Galley .12 .30
20 Gary Roberts .12 .30
21 Bill Ranford .15 .40
22 Mario Lemieux .75 2.00
22B Mike Sillinger ERR .12 .30
23 Glen Murray .12 .30
24 Paul Coffey .20 .50
25 Corey Millen .12 .30
26 Chris Chelios .20 .50
27 Ronnie Stern .12 .30
28 Zdeno Ciger .12 .30
29 Tony Granato .12 .30
30 Donald Audette .12 .30
31 Russ Courtnall .12 .30
32 Mike Gartner .20 .50
33 Marty McSorley .12 .30
34 Jeff Brown .12 .30
35 Mark Janssens .12 .30
36 Patrick Poulin .12 .30
37 Sergei Fedorov .30 .75
38 Tim Sweeney .12 .30
39 John Slaney .12 .30
40 Steve Larmer .15 .40
41 Dave Karpa .12 .30
42 Esa Tikkanen .12 .30
43 Joel Otto .12 .30
44 Doug Weight .15 .40
45 Murray Craven .12 .30
46 John Vanbiesbrouck .15 .40
47 Nelson Emerson .12 .30
48 Dean Evason .12 .30
49 Evgeny Davydov .12 .30
50 Craig Simpson .12 .30
51 Mats Sundin .15 .40
52 Chris Pronger .20 .50
53 Stephan Lebeau .12 .30
54 Martin Gelinas .12 .30
55 Bob Rouse .12 .30
56 Christian Ruuttu .12 .30
57 Gilbert Dionne .12 .30
58 Mike Modano .30 .75
59 Derek King .12 .30
60 Peter Stastny .15 .40
61 Ted Donato .12 .30
62 Mark Messier .20 .50
63 Dave Manson .12 .30
64 Johan Garpenlov .12 .30
65 Igor Larionov .12 .30
65B Sergio Momesso ERR .20 .50
66 Kirk Muller .12 .30
67 Dave Ellett .12 .30
68 Dale Hunter .12 .30
69 Brent Gretzky .12 .30
70 Tom Barrasso .15 .40
71 Philippe Boucher .12 .30
72 Jesse Belanger .12 .30
73 Scott Stevens .20 .50
74 Gary Suter .12 .30
75 Tim Cheveldae .15 .40
76 Dimitri Khristich .12 .30
77 Pierre Turgeon .15 .40
78 Mike Richter .20 .50
79 Michael Nylander .15 .40
80 Sergei Krivokrasov .12 .30
81 Andy Moog UER .20 .50
82 Al Iafrate .12 .30
83 Bernie Nicholls .15 .40
84 Darren Turcotte .12 .30
85 Sergio Momesso .20 .50
85B Igor Larionov ERR .12 .30
86 Petr Klima .12 .30
87 Alexandre Daigle .12 .30
88 Joe Juneau .15 .40
89 Glen Wesley .12 .30
90 Teemu Selanne .40 1.00
91 Curtis Joseph .30 .75
92 Scott Mellanby .15 .40
93 Jaromir Jagr .50 1.25
94 Mark Recchi .25 .60
95 Jiri Slegr .12 .30
96 Martin Brodeur .50 1.25
97 Scott Pearson .12 .30
98 Eric Lindros .20 .50
99 Larry Murphy .15 .40
100 Sergei Zubov .12 .30
101 Mathieu Schneider .12 .30
102 Dale Hawerchuk .25 .60
103 Owen Nolan .20 .50
104 Darryl Sydor .12 .30
105 Anatoli Semenov .12 .30
106 Marty McInnis .12 .30
107 Derek Mayer .12 .30
108 Steve Duchesne .12 .30
109 Geoff Smith .12 .30
110 Zarley Zalapski .12 .30
111 Rod Brind'Amour .15 .40
112 Nicklas Lidstrom .20 .50
113 Teppo Numminen .12 .30
114 Denny Felsner .12 .30
115 Wendel Clark .15 .40
116 Arturs Irbe .15 .40
117 Josef Beranek .12 .30
118 Brian Bradley .12 .30
119 Eric Weinrich .12 .30
120 Kevin Todd .12 .30
121 Patrick Roy .50 1.25
122 Guy Carbonneau .12 .30
123 Tom Kurvers .12 .30
124 Sergei Makarov .12 .30
125 Pat Peake .12 .30
126 Danton Cole .12 .30
127 Derian Hatcher .12 .30
128 Kjell Samuelsson .12 .30
129 Alexei Yashin .20 .50
130 Chris Osgood .30 .75
131 Kent Manderville .12 .30
132 Jim Montgomery .12 .30
133 Kirk McLean .15 .40
134 Kelly Buchberger .12 .30
135 Peter Bondra .15 .40
136 Stephane Matteau .12 .30
137 Oleg Petrov .12 .30
138 Doug Gilmour .25 .60
139 Vladimir Malakhov .12 .30
140 Peter Zezel .12 .30
141 Mike Vernon .15 .40
142 Derek Plante .12 .30
143 Valeri Zelepukin .12 .30
144 Kevin Haller .12 .30
145 Keith Tkachuk .20 .50
146 Claude Boivin .12 .30
147 Jocelyn Thibault .20 .50
148 Jyrki Lumme .12 .30
149 Ray Whitney .12 .30
150 Al MacInnis .15 .40
151 Kelly Miller .12 .30
152 Ray Sheppard .15 .40
153 Aaron Ward .12 .30
154 Damian Rhodes .15 .40
155 Jozef Stumpel .12 .30
156 Sergei Nemchinov .12 .30
157 Richard Matvichuk .12 .30
158 Sean Burke .15 .40
159 Todd Marchant .12 .30
160 Ryan McGill .12 .30
161 Sean Hill .12 .30
162 Iain Fraser .12 .30
163 Shawn McEachern .12 .30
164 Petr Nedved .15 .40
165 John Lilley .12 .30
166 Joe Sacco .12 .30
167 Jason Dawe .12 .30
168 Mike Rathje .12 .30
169 Phil Housley .15 .40
170 Ron Hextall .15 .40
171 Yves Racine .12 .30
172 Boris Mironov .12 .30
173 Vitali Prokhorov .12 .30
174 Roman Hamrlik .15 .40
175 Robert Lang .12 .30
176 Jody Hull .12 .30
177 Mike Ridley .12 .30
178 Dmitri Filimonov .12 .30
179 Rene Corbet .12 .30
180 Rob Pearson .12 .30
181 Richard Smehlik .12 .30
182 Rob Gaudreau .12 .30
183 Bill Houlder .12 .30
184 Igor Korolev .12 .30
185 Chris Joseph .12 .30
186 Shane Churla .12 .30
187 Rick Tabaracci .15 .40
188 Alexander Godynyuk .12 .30
189 Vladimir Konstantinov .15 .40
190 Markus Naslund .20 .50
191 Tom Chorske .12 .30
192 Thomas Steen .12 .30
193 Patrice Brisebois .12 .30
194 Luc Robitaille .20 .50
195 Michal Sykora .12 .30
196 Troy Mallette .12 .30
197 Steve Chiasson .12 .30
198 Jimmy Carson .12 .30
199 Mike Donnelly .12 .30
200 Mike Sillinger .12 .30
200B Mario Lemieux ERR .75 2.00
201 Martin Rucinsky .12 .30
202 Adam Bennett .12 .30
203 Matt Johnson RC .12 .30
204 Daren Puppa .15 .40
205 Ted Drury .12 .30
206 Jon Casey .15 .40
207 Alexei Kovalev .12 .30
208 Alexei Kasatonov .12 .30
209 Ulf Samuelsson .12 .30
210 Justin Hocking RC .12 .30
211 Greg Adams .12 .30
212 Greg Johnson .12 .30
213 Mike Craig .12 .30
214 Steve Konowalchuk .12 .30
215 Luke Richardson .12 .30
216 Pavol Demitra .25 .60
217 Brian Benning .12 .30
218 Corey Hirsch .15 .40
219 Alexander Semak .12 .30
220 Travis Green .15 .40
221 Turner Stevenson .12 .30
222 Dimitri Mironov .12 .30
223 Christian Soucy RC .15 .40
224 Rick Tocchet .15 .40
225 Craig MacTavish .12 .30
226 Wayne Gretzky RB 802 1.00 2.50
227 Pavel Bure SE .20 .50
228 Wayne Gretzky SE 1.00 2.50
229 Brett Hull SE .40 1.00
230 Mike Gartner .20 .50
231 Brian Leetch .20 .50
232 Al MacInnis .15 .40
233 Dominik Hasek SE .40 1.00
234 Mark Messier SE .20 .50
235 Paul Kariya SR .25 .60
236 Jamie Storr SR .15 .40
237 Jeff Friesen SR .12 .30
238 Kenny Jonsson SR .12 .30
239 Mariusz Czerkawski SR RC .20 .50
240 Brett Lindros SR .12 .30
241 Andrei Nikolishin .12 .30
242 Jason Allison SR .15 .40
243 Oleg Tverdovsky SR .15 .40
244 Brian Savage .12 .30
245 Peter Forsberg SR .50 1.25
246 Patrik Juhlin RC .12 .30
247 Jassen Cullimore .12 .30
248 Chris Therien .12 .30
249 Kevin Brown SR RC .20 .50
250 Jeff Nelson .12 .30
251 Janne Laukkanen .15 .40
252 Jamie McLennan .15 .40
253 Craig Johnson .12 .30
254 Ravil Gusmanov SR RC .12 .30
255 Valeri Bure SR .12 .30
256 Valeri Karpov SR RC .12 .30
257 Mike Peca .15 .40
258 Brian Rolston .12 .30
259 Brandon Convery .12 .30
260 Mark Lawrence SR RC .12 .30
261 Adam Deadmarsh .12 .30
262 Jason Wiemer RC .12 .30
263 Alexander Cherbayev .12 .30
264 Sergei Gonchar .12 .30
265 Viktor Kozlov SR .12 .30
266 Vladislav Boulin RC .20 .50
267 Todd Harvey SR .12 .30
268 Cory Stillman SR RC .12 .30
269 David Oliver SR RC .12 .30
270 Andrei Nazarov .12 .30
271 Mikael Renberg .15 .40
272 Andrei Kovalenko .12 .30
273 Neal Broten .15 .40
274 Ed Olczyk .12 .30
275 Steve Thomas .12 .30
276 Joe Nieuwendyk .20 .50
277 Rob Gaudreau .12 .30
278 Pat Verbeek .15 .40
279 Eric Desjardins .15 .40
280 Vincent Damphousse .15 .40
281 John Cullen .12 .30
282 Garry Valk .12 .30
283 Daniel Lacroix .12 .30
284 Mike Ricci .12 .30
285 Dominik Hasek .40 1.00
286 Geoff Courtnall .12 .30
287 Rob Niedermayer .15 .40
288 Alexander Karpovtsev .12 .30
289 Martin Straka .12 .30
290 Ed Belfour .20 .50
291 Dave Lowry .12 .30
292 Brendan Shanahan .25 .60
293 Jari Kurri .15 .40
294 Steven Rice .12 .30
295 Scott Levins .12 .30
296 Ray Bourque .30 .75
297 Mikael Andersson .12 .30
298 Darius Kasparaitis .12 .30
299 Chris Simon .12 .30
300 Steve Yzerman .50 1.25
301 Don McSween .12 .30
302 Brian Noonan .12 .30
303 Claude Lemieux .20 .50
304 Radek Bonk RC .12 .30
305 Jason Arnott .15 .40
306 Ian Laperriere RC .20 .50
307 Pat Falloon .12 .30
308 Kris King .12 .30
309 Brian Bellows .15 .40
310 Uwe Krupp .12 .30
311 Paul Cavallini .12 .30
312 Shaun Van Allen .12 .30
313 Dave Andreychuk .20 .50
314 Bobby Holik .12 .30
315 Theo Fleury .20 .50
316 Mark Osborne .12 .30
317 Andrew Cassels .12 .30
318 Chris Tamer .12 .30
319 Trevor Linden .15 .40
320 Tom Fitzgerald .12 .30
321 Ron Tugnutt .15 .40
322 Jeremy Roenick .40 1.00
323 Todd Marchant .12 .30
324 Scott Niedermayer .20 .50
325 Tim Taylor RC .20 .50
326 Mike Kennedy RC .20 .50
327 Steve Heinze .12 .30
328 David Sacco .12 .30
329 Sergei Brylin .12 .30
330 John LeClair .20 .50
331 Brian Skrudland .12 .30
332 Kevin Hatcher .12 .30
333 Brett Hull .40 1.00
334 Alexander Mogilny .15 .40
335 Sylvain Lefebvre .12 .30
336 Sylvain Turgeon .12 .30
337 Keith Primeau .20 .50
338 Eric Fichaud RC .20 .50
339 Jeff Beukeboom .12 .30
340 Cory Cross RC .12 .30
341 J.J. Daigneault .12 .30
342 Stephen Leach .12 .30
343 Zigmund Palffy .15 .40
344 Igor Korolev .12 .30
345 Chris Gratton .12 .30
346 Joe Mullen .15 .40
347 Brent Gilchrist .12 .30
348 Adam Creighton .12 .30
349 Dimitri Yushkevich .12 .30
350 Wes Walz .12 .30
351 Shayne Corson .12 .30
352 Eric Lacroix RC .20 .50
353 Maxim Bets .12 .30
354 Sylvain Cote .12 .30
355 Valeri Kamensky .15 .40
356 Shjon Podein .12 .30
357 Robert Reichel .12 .30
358 Cliff Ronning .12 .30
359 Bill Guerin .15 .40
360 Dallas Drake .12 .30
361 Robert Petrovicky .12 .30
362 Ken Wregget .15 .40
363 Todd Elik .12 .30
364 Cam Neely .20 .50
365 Darren McCarty .12 .30
366 Shean Donovan RC .20 .50
367 Felix Potvin .20 .50
368 Yuri Khmylev .12 .30
369 Mark Tinordi .12 .30
370 Craig Billington .15 .40
371 Patrick Flatley .12 .30
372 Jocelyn Lemieux .12 .30
373 Slava Kozlov .15 .40
374 Trent Klatt .12 .30
375 Geoff Sarjeant RC .20 .50
376 Bob Kudelski .12 .30
377 Stanislav Neckar RC .20 .50
378 Jon Rohloff RC .20 .50
379 Jeff Shantz .12 .30
380 Dale Craigwell .12 .30
381 Adrien Plavsic .12 .30
382 Dave Gagner .15 .40
383 Dave Archibald .12 .30
384 Gilbert Dionne .12 .30
385 Troy Loney .12 .30
386 Dean McAmmond .12 .30
387 Pauli Jaks .15 .40
388 Stephane Richer .15 .40
389 Don Beaupre .15 .40
390 Kevin Stevens .12 .30
391 Brad May .12 .30
392 Neil Wilkinson .12 .30
393 Kevin Lowe .12 .30
394 Frederik Olausson .12 .30
395 Trevor Kidd .15 .40
396 Brent Grieve .12 .30
397 Dominic Roussel .15 .40
398 Bret Hedican .12 .30
399 Bryan Smolinski .12 .30
400 Doug Lidster .12 .30
401 Bob Errey .12 .30
402 Pierre Sevigny .12 .30
403 Rob Brown .12 .30
404 Joe Sakic .40 1.00
405 Nikolai Borschevsky .12 .30
406 Martin Lapointe .12 .30
407 Jean-Yves Roy RC .20 .50
408 Robert Kron .12 .30
409 Tie Domi .15 .40
410 Jim Dowd .12 .30
411 Keith Jones .12 .30
412 Scott Lachance .12 .30
413 Bob Corkum .12 .30
414 Denis Chasse RC .20 .50
415 Denis Savard .25 .60
416 Joe Murphy .12 .30
417 Vyacheslav Butsayev .12 .30
418 Mattias Norstrom .12 .30
419 Sergei Zholtok .12 .30
420 Nikolai Khabibulin .15 .40
421 Pat Elynuik .12 .30
422 Doug Brown .12 .30
423 Dave McLlwain .12 .30
424 James Patrick .12 .30
425 Alexander Selivanov RC .15 .40
426 Scott Thornton .12 .30
427 Todd Ewen .12 .30
428 Peter Popovic .12 .30
429 Jarkko Varvio .12 .30
430 Paul Ranheim .12 .30
431 Kevin Dineen .12 .30
432 Kelly Hrudey .15 .40
433 Michal Grosek RC .12 .30
434 Slava Fetisov .12 .30
435 Ivan Droppa .12 .30
436 Benoit Hogue .12 .30
437 Sheldon Kennedy .12 .30
438 Gord Murphy .12 .30
439 Jamie Baker .12 .30
440 Todd Gill .12 .30
441 Mark Recchi .25 .60
442 Ted Crowley .12 .30
443 Ryan Smyth RC .60 1.50
444 Brian Leetch .20 .50
445 Bob Sweeney .12 .30
446 Don Sweeney .12 .30
447 Byron Dafoe RC .60 1.50
448 Nathan Lafayette .12 .30
449 Keith Carney .12 .30
450 Stephane Fiset .15 .40
451 Kevin Miller .12 .30
452 Craig Darby RC .20 .50
453 Vlastimil Kroupa .12 .30
454 Rob Zettler .12 .30
455 Glenn Healy .15 .40
456 Todd Simon .12 .30
457 Mark Fitzpatrick .15 .40
458 Drake Berehowsky .12 .30
459 Darcy Wakaluk .15 .40
460 Enrico Ciccone .12 .30
461 Tomas Sandstrom .12 .30
462 Mikhail Shtalenkov .12 .30
463 Igor Kravchuk .12 .30
464 Jamie Allison RC .20 .50
465 Gino Odjick .12 .30
466 Norm Maciver .12 .30
467 Terry Carkner .12 .30
468 Rob Zamuner .12 .30
469 Pavel Bure .20 .50
470 Patrice Tardif RC .20 .50
471 Andrei Lomakin .12 .30
472 Kirk Maltby .12 .30
473 Jaroslav Modry .12 .30
474 Tommy Soderstrom .15 .40
475 Patrik Carnback .12 .30
476 Jeff Reese .12 .30
477 Todd Krygier .12 .30
478 John McIntyre .12 .30
479 Joey Kocur .12 .30
480 Steve Rucchin RC .60 1.50
481 Bob Bassen .12 .30
482 Marek Malik RC .12 .30
483 Darrin Shannon .12 .30
484 Shawn Burr .12 .30
485 Louie DeBrusk .12 .30
486 Olaf Kolzig .15 .40
487 Cam Stewart .12 .30
488 Rob Blake .20 .50
489 Eric Charron RC .20 .50
490 Sandis Ozolinsh .12 .30
491 Paul Ysebaert .12 .30
492 Kris Draper .12 .30
493 Stu Barnes .12 .30
494 Doug Bodger .12 .30
495 Blaine Lacher RC .15 .40
496 Ed Jovanovski RC .30 .75
497 Eric Daze RC .30 .75
498 Dan Cloutier RC .30 .75
499 Chad Allan RC .20 .50
500 Todd Harvey .12 .30
501 Jamie Rivers RC .20 .50
502 Bryan McCabe .12 .30
503 Darcy Tucker RC .30 .75
504 Wade Redden RC .30 .75
505 Nolan Baumgartner RC .20 .50
506 Marek Malik RC .12 .30
507 Petr Cajanek RC .30 .75
508 Jan Hlavac RC .30 .75
509 Ladislav Kohn RC .20 .50
510 Kimmo Timonen .15 .40
511 Antti Aalto RC .15 .40
512 Tommi Rajamaki RC .15 .40
513 Vitali Yachmenev RC .20 .50
514 Vadim Epantchinsev RC .15 .40
515 Dmitri Klevakin RC .15 .40
516 Nikolai Zavarukhin RC .20 .50
517 Alexander Korolyuk RC .20 .50
518 Anders Eriksson .15 .40
519 Jesper Mattsson RC .15 .40
520 Mattias Ohlund RC .30 .75
521 Anders Soderberg RC .15 .40
522 Bryan Berard RC .30 .75
523 Jason Bonsignore .20 .50
524 Deron Quint .12 .30
525 Richard Park .12 .30
526 Jeff Friesen CC .12 .30
527 Paul Kariya CC .25 .60
528 Peter Forsberg CC .50 1.25
529 Zigmund Palffy CC .15 .40
530 Kenny Jonsson CC .12 .30
531 Jamie Storr CC .15 .40
532 Alexander Selivanov CC .15 .40
533 Mike Peca CC .15 .40
534 Mariusz Czerkawski CC .20 .50
535 Jason Allison CC .15 .40
536 Todd Harvey CC .12 .30
537 Brett Lindros CC .12 .30
538 Radek Bonk CC .12 .30
539 Blaine Lacher CC .15 .40
540 Oleg Tverdovsky CC .15 .40
541 Wayne Gretzky WT 1.00 2.50
542 Radek Bonk WT .12 .30
543 Mariusz Czerkawski WT .20 .50
544 Jaromir Jagr WT .50 1.25
545 Dominik Hasek WT .40 1.00
546 Todd Harvey WT .12 .30
547 Mike Peca WT .15 .40
548 Mats Sundin WT .15 .40
549 Doug Weight WT .15 .40
550 Steve Yzerman WT .50 1.25
551 Brett Lindros WT .12 .30
552 Alexander Mogilny WT .15 .40
553 Patrik Juhlin WT .12 .30
554 Alexei Yashin WT .20 .50
555 Peter Forsberg WT .50 1.25
556 Michael Nylander WT .15 .40
557 Teemu Selanne WT .40 1.00
558 Marek Malik WT .12 .30
559 Jari Kurri WT .15 .40
560 Kenny Jonsson WT .12 .30
561 Mikael Renberg WT .15 .40
562 Adam Deadmarsh WT .12 .30
563 Mark Messier WT .20 .50
564 Rob Blake WT .20 .50
565 Janne Laukkanen WT .15 .40
566 Theo Fleury WT .20 .50
567 Alexei Kovalev WT .12 .30
568 Jamie Storr WT .15 .40
569 Brett Hull WT .40 1.00
570 Valeri Karpov WT .12 .30
1P Wayne Gretzky Jumbo Promo 1.00 2.50

1994-95 Upper Deck Electric Ice

This is a parallel set to the regular Upper Deck issue and is inserted in packs at the rate of 1:35. The backs are identical to the regular set. The only difference on the front is that the words "Electric Ice" are at the bottom which, along with the player's name and bar enclosing his position, are all in electric foil.

*VETS: 8X TO 20X BASIC CARDS
*ROOKIES: 4X TO 10X BASIC CARDS

1994-95 Upper Deck Ice Gallery

This 15-card set features some of the NHL's top players, along with a few journeymen. The cards were inserted 1:25 packs in Upper Deck series one. The cards feature a close-up headshot with a wide black and gray border. An action photo and text appear on the back. The cards are numbered with an "IG" prefix.

COMPLETE SET (15) 15.00 40.00
IG1 Steve Yzerman 5.00 12.00
IG2 Jason Arnott .30 .75
IG3 Jeremy Roenick 1.25 3.00
IG4 Brendan Shanahan 1.00 2.50
IG5 Scott Stevens .50 1.25
IG6 Scott Niedermayer .30 .75
IG7 Adam Graves .30 .75
IG8 Mike Modano 1.50 4.00
IG9 Kirk Muller .30 .75
IG10 Alexandre Daigle .30 .75
IG11 Martin Brodeur 2.50 6.00
IG12 Garry Valk .30 .75
IG13 Teemu Selanne 1.00 2.50
IG14 Pat LaFontaine 1.00 2.50
IG15 Wayne Gretzky 6.00 15.00

1994-95 Upper Deck Predictor Canadian

The Calder Predictors (C1-C15) were inserted at a rate of 1:20 first series Canadian packs, while the Pearson/Norris cards (C16-C35) were inserted at a rate of 1:20 series two Canadian packs. C1 (Peter Forsberg) was the winning card that could be redeemed for a gold foil Calder set, while C15 (Long Shot) could be redeemed for a silver version. Either C23 (Eric Lindros) or C31 (Paul Coffey) could be redeemed for a 20-card gold foil Pearson/Norris set, while C24 (Jaromir Jagr) netted the collector a silver version of cards C16-C25, and C29 (Chris Chelios) could be redeemed for a silver version of cards C26-C35.

COMPLETE SET (35) 30.00 80.00
*GOLD PRIZE: .2X TO .5X BASIC INSERTS
*SILVER PRIZE: .2X TO .5X BASIC INSERTS
C1 Peter Forsberg WIN 3.00 8.00
C2 Paul Kariya 1.25 3.00
C3 Viktor Kozlov .40 1.00
C4 Jason Allison .40 1.00
C5 Mariusz Czerkawski 1.50 4.00
C6 Valeri Karpov .40 1.00
C7 Brett Lindros .40 1.00
C8 Valeri Bure .40 1.00
C9 Andrei Nikolishin .40 1.00
C10 Mike Peca .40 1.00
C11 Kenny Jonsson .40 1.00
C12 Alexander Cherbayev .40 1.00
C13 Brian Rolston .40 1.00
C14 Oleg Tverdovsky .60 1.50
C15 Calder Long Shot WIN .40 1.00
C16 Wayne Gretzky 5.00 12.00
C17 Brett Hull 1.50 4.00
C18 Doug Gilmour .60 1.50
C19 Jeremy Roenick 1.50 4.00
C20 John Vanbiesbrouck .60 1.50
C21 Sergei Fedorov 2.00 5.00
C22 Mark Messier 1.25 3.00
C23 Eric Lindros WIN 1.25 3.00
C24 Jaromir Jagr WIN 2.00 5.00
C25 Pearson Long Shot .40 1.00
C26 Ray Bourque 2.00 5.00
C27 Sandis Ozolinsh .40 1.00
C28 Brian Leetch 1.25 3.00
C29 Chris Chelios WIN 1.25 3.00
C30 Scott Stevens .60 1.50
C31 Paul Coffey WIN 1.25 3.00
C32 Rob Blake .60 1.50
C33 Al MacInnis .60 1.50
C34 Scott Niedermayer .40 1.00
C35 Norris Long Shot .40 1.00

1994-95 Upper Deck Predictor Hobby

The Hart Predictors (H1-H15) were inserted at a rate of 1:20 first series U.S. hobby packs, while the Art Ross/Vezina cards (H16-H35) were inserted at a rate of 1:20 second series U.S. hobby packs. H8 (Eric Lindros) was redeemable for a gold foil version of the Hart set, while card H15 (Long Shot) was redeemable for a silver version. Either H24 (Jaromir Jagr) or H31 (Dominik Hasek) could be redeemed for a 20-card gold foil version of the Art Ross/Vezina set, while H23 (Eric Lindros) and H27 (Ed Belfour) won gold foil versions of cards H16-H25, and H26-H35, respectively.

COMPLETE SET (35) 40.00 100.00
*GOLD PRIZE: .2X TO .5X BASIC INSERTS
*SILVER PRIZE: .2X TO .5X BASIC INSERTS
H1 Wayne Gretzky 5.00 12.00
H2 Pavel Bure 1.25 3.00
H3 Doug Gilmour .60 1.50
H4 Mark Messier 1.25 3.00
H5 Patrick Roy 4.00 10.00
H6 Sergei Fedorov 2.00 5.00
H7 Chris Chelios 1.25 3.00
H8 Eric Lindros 1.25 3.00
H9 Alexander Mogilny .60 1.50
H10 Peter Forsberg 3.00 8.00
H11 Brian Leetch 1.25 3.00
H12 Martin Brodeur 3.00 8.00
H13 Jeremy Roenick 1.50 4.00
H14 Paul Kariya 1.25 3.00
H15 Hart Long Shot .40 1.00

H16 Wayne Gretzky 5.00 12.00
H17 Joe Sakic 2.50 6.00
H18 Sergei Fedorov 2.00 5.00
H19 Pavel Bure 1.25 3.00
H20 Adam Oates .60 1.50
H21 Doug Gilmour .60 1.50
H22 Steve Yzerman 4.00 10.00
H23 Eric Lindros 1.25 3.00
H24 Jaromir Jagr 2.00 5.00
H25 Art Ross Long Shot .40 1.00
H26 Patrick Roy 4.00 10.00
H27 Ed Belfour 1.25 3.00
H28 Felix Potvin 1.25 3.00
H29 Martin Brodeur 3.00 8.00
H30 Mike Richter 1.25 3.00
H31 Dominik Hasek 2.50 6.00
H32 John Vanbiesbrouck .60 1.50
H33 Curtis Joseph 1.25 3.00
H34 Kirk McLean .60 1.50
H35 Vezina Long Shot .40 1.00

1994-95 Upper Deck Predictor Retail

The Scoring Predictors (R1-R30) were inserted at a rate of 1:20 series one U.S. retail packs, while the Playoff Scoring cards (R31-R60) were inserted at a rate of 1:20 series two U.S. retail packs. Cards R10 (Goals Long Shot), R20 (Assists Long Shot), R28 (Eric Lindros), R29 (Jaromir Jagr), and R30 (Points Long Shot) were all redeemable for a 30 card gold foil version of Scoring Predictors. Cards R40 (Goals Long Shot), R50 (Assists Long Shot), and R52 (Sergei Fedorov) were all redeemable for a 30 card gold foil version of the Playoff Scoring Predictors. Cards R39 (Jaromir Jagr), and R60 (Points Long Shot) won gold foil versions of cards R31-40, and R51-60, respectively.

COMPLETE SET (60) 40.00 100.00
*EXCH.CARDS: .2X TO .5X BASIC INSERTS
ONE EXCH.SET VIA MAIL PER PRED.WINNER
R1 Pavel Bure 1.25 3.00
R2 Brett Hull 1.50 4.00
R3 Teemu Selanne 1.25 3.00
R4 Sergei Fedorov 2.00 5.00
R5 Adam Graves .40 1.00
R6 Dave Andreychuk .60 1.50
R7 Brendan Shanahan 1.25 3.00
R8 Jeremy Roenick 1.50 4.00
R9 Eric Lindros 1.25 3.00
R10 Goals Long Shot .40 1.00
R11 Doug Gilmour .60 1.50
R12 Adam Oates .60 1.50
R13 Brian Leetch 1.25 3.00
R14 Ray Bourque 2.00 5.00
R15 Joe Juneau .60 1.50
R16 Craig Janney .60 1.50
R17 Pat LaFontaine 1.25 3.00
R18 Jaromir Jagr 2.00 5.00
R19 Wayne Gretzky 5.00 12.00
R20 Assists Long Shot .40 1.00
R21 Wayne Gretzky 5.00 12.00
R22 Pat LaFontaine 1.25 3.00
R23 Sergei Fedorov 2.00 5.00
R24 Steve Yzerman 4.00 10.00
R25 Pavel Bure 1.25 3.00
R26 Adam Oates .60 1.50
R27 Doug Gilmour .60 1.50
R28 Eric Lindros 1.25 3.00
R29 Jaromir Jagr 2.00 5.00
R30 Points Long Shot .40 1.00
R31 Pavel Bure 1.25 3.00
R32 Brett Hull 1.50 4.00
R33 Cam Neely 1.25 3.00
R34 Mark Messier 1.25 3.00
R35 Dave Andreychuk .60 1.50
R36 Sergei Fedorov 2.00 5.00
R37 Mike Modano 2.00 5.00
R38 Adam Graves .40 1.00
R39 Jaromir Jagr 2.00 5.00
R40 Playoff Goals .40 1.00
R41 Theo Fleury .40 1.00
R42 Wayne Gretzky 5.00 12.00
R43 Steve Yzerman 4.00 10.00
R44 Adam Oates .60 1.50
R45 Brian Leetch 1.25 3.00
R46 Al MacInnis .60 1.50
R47 Pat LaFontaine 1.25 3.00
R48 Scott Stevens .60 1.50
R49 Doug Gilmour .60 1.50
R50 Playoff Assists .40 1.00
R51 Brian Leetch 1.25 3.00
R52 Sergei Fedorov 2.00 5.00
R53 Pavel Bure 1.25 3.00
R54 Mark Messier 1.25 3.00
R55 Pat LaFontaine 1.25 3.00
R56 Doug Gilmour .60 1.50
R57 Brett Hull 1.50 4.00
R58 Theo Fleury .40 1.00
R59 Wayne Gretzky 5.00 12.00
R60 Playoff Points .40 1.00

1994-95 Upper Deck SP Inserts

The 1994-95 Upper Deck SP Insert set was released in two series of 90 cards for a total of 180. One SP Insert was found in each Upper Deck hobby pack, with two per retail pack.

SP1 Maxim Bets .20 .50
SP2 Stephan Lebeau .20 .50
SP3 Garry Valk .20 .50
SP4 Ray Bourque .50 1.25
SP5 Mariusz Czerkawski .30 .75
SP6 Cam Neely .30 .75
SP7 Adam Oates .30 .75
SP8 Dominik Hasek .60 1.50
SP9 Dale Hawerchuk .40 1.00
SP10 Alexander Mogilny .25 .60
SP11 Theo Fleury .30 .75
SP12 Trevor Kidd .25 .60
SP13 Joe Nieuwendyk .30 .75
SP14 Gary Roberts .20 .50
SP15 Ed Belfour .30 .75
SP16 Chris Chelios .30 .75
SP17 Jeremy Roenick .60 1.50
SP18 Neal Broten .25 .60
SP19 Russ Courtnall .20 .50
SP20 Derian Hatcher .20 .50
SP21 Mike Modano .50 1.25
SP22 Paul Coffey .30 .75
SP23 Slava Kozlov .25 .60
SP24 Keith Primeau .30 .75
SP25 Steve Yzerman .75 2.00
SP26 Jason Arnott .25 .60
SP27 Bill Ranford .25 .60
SP28 Doug Weight .25 .60
SP29 Bob Kudelski .20 .50
SP30 Rob Niedermayer .25 .60
SP31 John Vanbiesbrouck .25 .60
SP32 Andrew Cassels .20 .50
SP33 Chris Pronger .30 .75
SP34 Geoff Sanderson .25 .60
SP35 Rob Blake .30 .75
SP36 Wayne Gretzky 1.50 4.00
SP37 Jari Kurri .25 .60
SP38 Alexei Zhitnik .25 .60
SP39 Vincent Damphousse .25 .60
SP40 Kirk Muller .20 .50
SP41 Oleg Petrov .20 .50
SP42 Patrick Roy .75 2.00
SP43 Martin Brodeur .75 2.00
SP44 Stephane Richer .25 .60
SP45 Scott Stevens .30 .75
SP46 Darius Kasparaitis .20 .50
SP47 Vladimir Malakhov .20 .50
SP48 Pierre Turgeon .25 .60
SP49 Alexei Kovalev .20 .50
SP50 Brian Leetch .30 .75
SP51 Mark Messier .30 .75
SP52 Mike Richter .30 .75
SP53 Craig Billington .25 .60
SP54 Alexandre Daigle .20 .50
SP55 Alexei Yashin .30 .75
SP56 Josef Beranek .20 .50
SP57 Rod Brind'Amour .25 .60
SP58 Mark Recchi .40 1.00
SP59 Mikael Renberg .25 .60
SP60 Jaromir Jagr .75 2.00
SP61 Mario Lemieux 1.25 3.00
SP62 Kevin Stevens .20 .50
SP63 Owen Nolan .30 .75
SP64 Mike Ricci .20 .50
SP65 Joe Sakic .60 1.50
SP66 Brett Hull .60 1.50
SP67 Craig Janney .25 .60
SP68 Curtis Joseph .50 1.25
SP69 Brendan Shanahan .40 1.00
SP70 Ulf Dahlen .20 .50
SP71 Arturs Irbe .25 .60
SP72 Sergei Makarov .20 .50
SP73 Sandis Ozolinsh .20 .50
SP74 Brian Bradley .20 .50
SP75 Chris Gratton .20 .50
SP76 Denis Savard .40 1.00
SP77 Dave Andreychuk .30 .75
SP78 Mike Gartner .30 .75
SP79 Dimitri Mironov .20 .50
SP80 Felix Potvin .30 .75
SP81 Jeff Brown .20 .50
SP82 Geoff Courtnall .20 .50
SP83 Trevor Linden .25 .60
SP84 Kirk McLean .25 .60
SP85 Peter Bondra .25 .60
SP86 Kevin Hatcher .20 .50
SP87 Dimitri Khristich .20 .50
SP88 Teemu Selanne .60 1.50
SP89 Keith Tkachuk .30 .75
SP90 Alexei Zhamnov .25 .60
SP91 Paul Kariya .40 1.00
SP92 Valeri Karpov .20 .50
SP93 Oleg Tverdovsky .25 .60
SP94 Al Iafrate .20 .50
SP95 Blaine Lacher .25 .60
SP96 Bryan Smolinski .20 .50
SP97 Donald Audette .20 .50
SP98 Yuri Khymlev .20 .50
SP99 Pat LaFontaine .30 .75
SP100 Derek Plante .20 .50
SP101 Steve Chiasson .20 .50
SP102 Phil Housley .25 .60
SP103 Michael Nylander .25 .60
SP104 Robert Reichel .20 .50
SP105 Tony Amonte .25 .60
SP106 Bernie Nicholls .25 .60
SP107 Gary Suter .20 .50
SP108 Paul Cavallini .20 .50
SP109 Todd Harvey .20 .50
SP110 Kevin Hatcher .20 .50
SP111 Andy Moog .30 .75
SP112 Dino Ciccarelli .25 .60
SP113 Sergei Fedorov .50 1.25
SP114 Nicklas Lidstrom .30 .75
SP115 Mike Vernon .25 .60
SP116 Shayne Corson .20 .50
SP117 David Oliver .20 .50
SP118 Ryan Smyth 1.00 2.50
SP119 Jesse Belanger .20 .50
SP120 Mark Fitzpatrick .25 .60
SP121 Scott Mellanby .25 .60
SP122 Andrei Nikolishin .20 .50
SP123 Darren Turcotte .20 .50
SP124 Pat Verbeek .25 .60
SP125 Glen Wesley .20 .50
SP126 Tony Granato .20 .50
SP127 Marty McSorley .20 .50
SP128 Jamie Storr .25 .60
SP129 Rick Tocchet .25 .60
SP130 Brian Bellows .25 .60
SP131 Valeri Bure .20 .50
SP132 Turner Stevenson .20 .50
SP133 John MacLean .25 .60
SP134 Scott Niedermayer .30 .75
SP135 Brian Rolston .20 .50
SP136 Brett Lindros .20 .50
SP137 Jamie McLennan .25 .60
SP138 Zigmund Palffy .25 .60
SP139 Steve Thomas .20 .50
SP140 Adam Graves .20 .50
SP141 Petr Nedved .25 .60
SP142 Sergei Zubov .20 .50
SP143 Don Beaupre .25 .60
SP144 Radek Bonk .20 .50
SP145 Pavol Demitra .40 1.00
SP146 Sylvain Turgeon .20 .50
SP147 Ron Hextall .25 .60
SP148 Patrik Juhlin .20 .50
SP149 Eric Lindros .30 .75
SP150 Ron Francis .40 1.00
SP151 Markus Naslund .30 .75
SP152 Luc Robitaille .30 .75
SP153 Martin Straka .20 .50
SP154 Wendel Clark .25 .60
SP155 Adam Deadmarsh .20 .50
SP156 Peter Forsberg .75 2.00
SP157 Janne Laukkanen .25 .60
SP158 Steve Duchesne .20 .50
SP159 Al MacInnis .25 .60
SP160 Esa Tikkanen .20 .50
SP161 Jeff Friesen .20 .50
SP162 Viktor Kozlov .20 .50
SP163 Ray Whitney .20 .50
SP164 Roman Hamrlik .25 .60
SP165 Alexander Selivanov .25 .60
SP166 Jason Wiemer .20 .50
SP167 Doug Gilmour .40 1.00
SP168 Kenny Jonsson .20 .50
SP169 Mike Ridley .20 .50
SP170 Mats Sundin .25 .60
SP171 Pavel Bure .30 .75
SP172 Martin Gelinas .20 .50
SP173 Mike Peca .25 .60
SP174 Jason Allison .25 .60
SP175 Joe Juneau .25 .60
SP176 Pat Peake .20 .50
SP177 Mark Tinordi .20 .50
SP178 Tim Cheveldae .25 .60
SP179 Nelson Emerson .20 .50
SP180 Dave Manson .20 .50

1995 Upper Deck World Junior Alumni

Produced by Upper Deck in conjunction with the Canadian Amateur Hockey Association, this 15-card set features players from the 1992, 1993, and 1994 Canadian World Junior Championship teams. The sets were offered at Esso service stations in Alberta, Canada for 2.99 with a gasoline purchase. The offer ran from December 20, 1994 through January 4, 1995, during the 1995 World Junior Hockey Championships, which were headquartered in Red Deer, Alberta. The fronts display color action shots that are full-bleed except on the left, where a white stripe carries player identification, year and the set title. The backs present a second color action shot and a player profile.

1 World Junior Championsh .01
2 Manny Legace .40 1.00
3 Jeff Nelson .08 .25
4 Alexandre Daigle .15 .40
5 Paul Kariya 2.00 5.00
6 Turner Stevenson .08 .25
7 Mike Peca .40 1.00
8 Tyler Wright .08 .25
9 Brent Tully .08 .25
10 Trevor Kidd .20 .50
11 Martin Lapointe .20 .50
12 Scott Niedermayer .20 .50
13 Jeff Friesen .30 .75
14 Todd Harvey .20 .50
15 Jamie Storr .20 .50

1995-96 Upper Deck

The 1995-96 Upper Deck set was issued in two series totaling 570 cards. The set is distinguished primarily through the inclusion of a number of noteworthy rookie cards in the Star Rookie (496-507) and Program of Excellence (508-525) subsets. The Cool Trade Exchange card was randomly inserted in 1:82 series 2 packs. The card could be redeemed for special die-cut cards of Wayne Gretzky, Sergei Fedorov, Peter Forsberg and Doug Gilmour.

1 Cam Neely .10 .25
2 Donald Audette .07 .20
3 Derian Hatcher .07 .20
4 Mike Vernon .07 .20
5 Darryl Sydor .07 .20
6 Patrice Brisebois .05 .15
7 John LeClair .10 .25
8 Luc Robitaille .10 .25
9 Todd Krygier .05 .15
10 Steve Chiasson .05 .15
11 Sergei Krivokrasov .05 .15
12 Marko Tuomainen .05 .15
13 Paul Ranheim .05 .15
14 Brian Rolston .05 .15
15 Alexei Yashin .07 .20
16 Joe Mullen .07 .20
17 Dallas Drake .05 .15
18 Tony Amonte .07 .20
19 Gary Roberts .05 .15
20 Geoff Sanderson .05 .15
21 Gord Murphy .05 .15
22 Dean Evason .05 .15
23 Brantt Myhres RC .05 .15
24 Sergei Makarov .05 .15
25 Joe Juneau .07 .20
26 Greg Adams .05 .15
27 Yuri Khmylev .05 .15
28 Yanic Perreault .05 .15
29 Jason Arnott .07 .20
30 Glenn Healy .07 .20
31 Sergei Brylin .05 .15
32 Ian Laperriere .05 .15
33 Trevor Linden .10 .25
34 Nicklas Lidstrom .10 .25
35 Don Sweeney .05 .15
36 Brian Savage .05 .15
37 Richard Matvichuk .07 .20
38 Dale Hawerchuk .12 .30
39 Patrick Roy .25 .60
40 Alexander Semak .05 .15
41 Kirk Maltby .07 .20
42 Jiri Slegr .05 .15
43 Joe Sacco .05 .15
44 Claude Lemieux .10 .25
45 Eric Weinrich .05 .15
46 Ron Francis .12 .30
47 Jamie Storr .07 .20
48 Felix Potvin .10 .25
49 Steve Duchesne .05 .15
50 Jody Hull .05 .15
51 Dave Manson .05 .15
52 Marty McInnis .05 .15
53 James Patrick .05 .15
54 Joe Sakic .15 .40
55 Andrei Nikolishin .05 .15
56 Adrian Aucoin .05 .15
57 Wade Flaherty RC .07 .20
58 Marek Malik .05 .15
59 Jason Allison .07 .20
60 Stephane Matteau .05 .15
61 Jason Dawe .05 .15
62 Ray Whitney .07 .20
63 Bill Lindsay .05 .15
64 Alexei Zhamnov .10 .25
65 Adam Deadmarsh .05 .15
66 Vincent Damphousse .07 .20
67 Josef Beranek .05 .15
68 Stanislav Neckar .05 .15
69 Alexei Kasatonov .05 .15
70 Jon Casey .07 .20
71 Todd Marchant .05 .15
72 Mike Sillinger .05 .15
73 Markus Naslund .10 .25
74 John MacLean .07 .20
75 Mike Ridley .05 .15
76 Petr Svoboda .05 .15
77 Milos Holan .05 .15
78 John Tucker .05 .15
79 Doug Brown .05 .15
80 Ted Donato .05 .15
81 Dimitri Yushkevich .05 .15
82 Brett Lindros .05 .15
83 Brian Bradley .07 .20
84 Mario Lemieux .30 .75
85 Nikolai Khabibulin .07 .20
86 Larry Murphy .10 .25
87 Mike Donnelly .05 .15
88 Brian Holzinger RC .20 .50
89 Steve Larouche RC .05 .15
90 Ray Ferraro .05 .15
91 Mikhail Shtalenkov .05 .15
92 Viktor Kozlov .07 .20
93 Jon Klemm .05 .15
94 Mark Tinordi .05 .15
95 Bret Hedican .05 .15
96 Kevin Stevens .07 .20
97 Bernie Nicholls .05 .15
98 Pat Verbeek .07 .20
99 Wayne Gretzky .50 1.25
100 Rene Corbet .05 .15
101 Shayne Corson .05 .15
102 Cliff Ronning .05 .15
103 Olaf Kolzig .07 .20
104 Dominik Hasek .12 .30
105 Corey Millen .05 .15
106 Patrick Flatley .05 .15
107 Chris Therien .05 .15
108 Ken Wregget .07 .20
109 Paul Ysebaert .05 .15
110 Mike Gartner .10 .25
111 Michal Grosek .05 .15
112 Craig Billington .07 .20
113 Steve Yzerman .12 .30
114 Neal Broten .07 .20
115 Tom Barrasso .07 .20
116 Brent Fedyk .05 .15
117 Todd Gill .05 .15
118 Petr Klima .05 .15
119 Dave Karpa .05 .15
120 Geoff Courtnall .05 .15
121 Kelly Buchberger .05 .15
122 Eric LaCroix .05 .15
123 Janne Laukkanen .05 .15
124 Radek Bonk .05 .15
125 Sergio Momesso .05 .15
126 Esa Tikkanen .05 .15
127 Jon Rohloff .05 .15
128 Ken Klee RC .05 .15
129 Johan Garpenlov .05 .15
130 Sean Burke .05 .15
131 Shean Donovan .05 .15
132 Alexei Kovalev .05 .15
133 Sylvain Cote .05 .15
134 Jeff Friesen .05 .15
135 Scott Pearson .05 .15
136 Kirk McLean .07 .20
137 Glen Wesley .05 .15
138 Bob Kudelski .05 .15
139 Craig Johnson .05 .15
140 Zigmund Palffy .10 .25
141 Kris King .05 .15
142 Rusty Fitzgerald RC .05 .15
143 Trevor Kidd .07 .20
144 Dave Ellett .05 .15
145 Kelly Hrudey .07 .20
146 Igor Kravchuk .05 .15
147 Mats Sundin .10 .25
148 Shawn Chambers .05 .15
149 Bob Corkum .05 .15
150 Shjon Podein .05 .15
151 Murray Craven .05 .15
152 Roman Hamrlik .05 .15
153 Lyle Odelein .05 .15
154 Vyacheslav Kozlov .07 .20
155 David Emma .05 .15
156 Benoit Brunet .05 .15
157 Jozef Stumpel .05 .15
158 Darrin Madeley .05 .15
159 Keith Primeau .05 .15
160 Jeff Norton .05 .15
161 Mathieu Schneider .05 .15
162 Trent Klatt .05 .15
163 Pat Peake .05 .15
164 Rob Gaudreau .05 .15
165 Doug Bodger .05 .15
166 Sergei Nemchinov .05 .15
167 David Oliver .05 .15
168 Sandis Ozolinsh .07 .20
169 Mark Messier .15 .40
170 Chris Chelios .10 .25
171 Teemu Selanne .20 .50
172 Robert Svehla RC .05 .15
173 Nikolai Borschevsky .05 .15
174 Chris Pronger .10 .25
175 Dave Lowry .05 .15
176 Owen Nolan .10 .25
177 Sylvain Turgeon .05 .15
178 Nelson Emerson .05 .15
179 Theo Fleury .12 .30
180 Patrik Carnback .05 .15
181 Kevin Smyth .05 .15
182 Jeff Shantz .05 .15
183 Bob Carpenter .05 .15
184 Brendan Shanahan .12 .30
185 Tomas Sandstrom .07 .20
186 Eric Desjardins .07 .20
187 Alexei Zhitnik .05 .15
188 Alexander Mogilny .07 .20
189 Mariusz Czerkawski .05 .15
190 Vladimir Konstantinov .07 .20
191 Andy Moog .10 .25
192 Peter Popovic .05 .15
193 Marty McSorley .05 .15
194 Mikael Renberg .07 .20
195 Alek Stojanov RC .05 .15
196 Rick Tabaracci .07 .20
197 Adam Oates .10 .25
198 Garry Galley .05 .15
199 Todd Harvey .05 .15
200 Martin Lapointe .05 .15
201 Tony Granato .05 .15
202 Turner Stevenson .05 .15
203 Jeff Beukeboom .05 .15
204 Adam Foote .07 .20
205 Daren Puppa .07 .20
206 Paul Kariya .12 .30
207 German Titov .07 .20
208 Patrick Poulin .05 .15
209 Jesse Belanger .05 .15
210 Steven Rice .05 .15
211 Martin Brodeur .25 .60
212 Rob Pearson .05 .15
213 Igor Larionov .05 .15
214 Pavel Bure 5 .12 .30
215 Sergei Fedorov 5 .15 .40
216 Ed Belfour 5 .07 .20
217 Mark Messier 5 .15 .40
218 Steve Yzerman 5 .12 .30
219 Mats Sundin 5 .10 .25
220 Mike Modano .15 .40
221 Alexander Mogilny .07 .20
222 Wayne Gretzky 5 .50 1.25
223 Keith Primeau .05 .15
224 Adam Graves .07 .20
225 Owen Nolan .10 .25
226 Paul Coffey .10 .25
227 Jeremy Roenick 5 .12 .30
228 Felix Potvin 5 .10 .25
229 Trevor Kidd .07 .20
230 Ray Bourque .15 .40
231 Mario Lemieux 5 .30 .75
232 Peter Bondra .10 .25
233 Brett Hull 5 .12 .30
234 Alexei Zhamnov .10 .25
235 Theo Fleury .12 .30
236 Brian Leetch .10 .25
237 Cam Neely MM .10 .25
238 Chris Chelios .10 .25
239 Adam Graves .07 .20
240 Doug Gilmour MM .12 .30
241 Jeremy Roenick MM .12 .30
242 Joe Sakic MM .15 .40
243 Keith Tkachuk .10 .25
244 Luc Robitaille .10 .25
245 Paul Kariya MM .12 .30
246 Owen Nolan .10 .25
247 John LeClair .10 .25
248 Paul Coffey .10 .25
249 Peter Bondra .10 .25
250 Ray Bourque .15 .40
251 Brett Hull MM .12 .30
252 Wayne Gretzky MM .50 1.25
253 Teemu Selanne MM .20 .50
254 Ray Sheppard .07 .20
255 Ron Francis .12 .30
256 Kevin Hatcher .07 .20
257 Brett Lindros .05 .15
258 Claude Lemieux .10 .25
259 Saku Koivu .10 .25
260 Radek Dvorak RC .12 .30
261 Niklas Sundstrom .10 .25
262 Chad Kilger RC .10 .25
263 Vitali Yachmenev .10 .25
264 Jeff O'Neill .10 .25
265 Brendan Witt .10 .25
266 Jason Bonsignore .05 .15
267 Aki Berg RC .10 .25
268 Eric Daze .20 .50
269 Shane Doan RC .30 .75
270 Daymond Langkow RC .10 .25
271 Alexandre Daigle .05 .15
272 Brian Noonan .05 .15
273 Guy Carbonneau .10 .25
274 Rick Tocchet .07 .20
275 Teppo Numminen .05 .15
276 Brian Skrudland .05 .15
277 Andrei Trefilov .05 .15
278 Joe Murphy .05 .15
279 Sergei Fedorov .15 .40
280 Doug Weight .10 .25
281 Robert Lang .05 .15
282 Darryl Shannon .05 .15
283 Cory Stillman .05 .15
284 Gary Suter .07 .20
285 Joe Nieuwendyk .10 .25
286 Terry Carkner .05 .15
287 Dimitri Khristich .05 .15
288 Alexander Karpovtsev .05 .15
289 Garth Snow .07 .20
290 Al MacInnis .10 .25
291 Doug Gilmour .12 .30
292 Mike Eastwood .05 .15
293 Steve Heinze .05 .15
294 Phil Housley .07 .20
295 Tim Taylor .05 .15
296 Curtis Joseph .10 .25
297 Patrick Roy .25 .60
298 Ted Drury .05 .15
299 Igor Korolev .05 .15
300 Ray Bourque .15 .40
301 Darren McCarty .05 .15
302 Miroslav Satan RC .12 .30
303 Adam Burt .05 .15
304 Valeri Bure .05 .15
305 Sergei Gonchar .05 .15
306 Jason York .05 .15
307 Brent Grieve .05 .15
308 Greg Johnson .05 .15
309 Kevin Hatcher .07 .20
310 Rob Niedermayer .07 .20
311 Nelson Emerson .05 .15
312 Mark Janssens .05 .15
313 Tommy Soderstrom .07 .20
314 Joey Kocur .07 .20
315 Craig Janney .05 .15
316 Alexander Selivanov .07 .20
317 Russ Courtnall .05 .15
318 Petr Sykora RC .25 .60
319 Rick Zombo .05 .15
320 Randy Burridge .05 .15
321 John Vanbiesbrouck .07 .20
322 Dmitri Mironov .05 .15
323 Sean Hill .05 .15
324 Rod Brind'Amour .10 .25
325 Wendel Clark .10 .25
326 Brent Gilchrist .05 .15
327 Tyler Wright .05 .15
328 Scott Daniels RC .05 .15
329 Adam Graves .07 .20
330 Dean Malkoc RC .05 .15
331 Jamie Macoun .05 .15
332 Sandy Moger RC .05 .15
333 Mike Peca .07 .20
334 Greg Johnson .05 .15
335 Jason Woolley .05 .15
336 Rob Dimaio .05 .15
337 Damian Rhodes .07 .20
338 Gino Odjick .05 .15
339 Peter Bondra .10 .25
340 Todd Ewen .05 .15
341 Matthew Barnaby .10 .25
342 Sylvain Lefebvre .05 .15
343 Oleg Petrov .05 .15
344 Jim Carey .07 .20
345 Stu Barnes .05 .15
346 Kelly Miller .05 .15
347 Antti Tormanen RC .05 .15
348 Ray Sheppard .07 .20
349 Igor Larionov .05 .15
350 Kjell Samuelsson .05 .15
351 Benoit Hogue .05 .15
352 Jeff Brown .07 .20
353 Nolan Baumgartner .05 .15
354 Denis Pederson .05 .15
355 Shawn Burr .05 .15
356 Jyrki Lumme .05 .15
357 Kevin Haller .05 .15
358 John Cullen .05 .15
359 Martin Gelinas .05 .15
360 Shawn McEachern .05 .15
361 Sandy McCarthy .05 .15
362 Grant Marshall .05 .15
363 Dean McAmmond .05 .15
364 Kevin Todd .05 .15
365 Bobby Holik .05 .15
366 Joel Otto .05 .15
367 Dave Andreychuk .10 .25
368 Ronnie Stern .05 .15
369 Jocelyn Thibault .07 .20
370 Dave Gagner .05 .15
371 Bryan Marchment .05 .15
372 Jari Kurri .10 .25
373 Bill Guerin .07 .20
374 Eric Lindros .15 .40
375 Adam Creighton .05 .15
376 Dimitri Yushkevich .05 .15
377 Peter Zezel .05 .15
378 Valeri Karpov .05 .15
379 Patrick Labrecque RC .05 .15
380 Mick Vukota .05 .15
381 Ulf Dahlen .05 .15
382 Enrico Ciccone .05 .15
383 Scott Niedermayer .10 .25
384 Ville Peltonen .05 .15
385 Blaine Lacher .07 .20
386 Pat LaFontaine .10 .25
387 Jeff Hackett .07 .20
388 Mike Keane .05 .15
389 Pierre Turgeon .10 .25
390 Scott Lachance .05 .15
391 Jason Wiemer .05 .15
392 Michal Pivonka .05 .15
393 Dennis Bonvie RC .05 .15
394 Glen Murray .05 .15
395 Bobby Dollas .05 .15
396 Paul Coffey .10 .25
397 Stephane Fiset .07 .20
398 Jere Lehtinen .07 .20
399 Scott Mellanby .07 .20
400 Robert Kron .05 .15
401 Doug Lidster .05 .15
402 Don Beaupre .07 .20
403 Arturs Irbe .07 .20
404 Brian Bellows .07 .20
405 Corey Hirsch .07 .20
406 Pavel Bure .12 .30
407 Chris Gratton .05 .15
408 Oleg Tverdovsky .10 .25
409 Derek Plante .05 .15
410 Dan Keczmer .05 .15
411 Donald Brashear .07 .20
412 Andrei Vasilyev RC .05 .15
413 Tommy Salo RC .15 .40
414 Kevin Lowe .07 .20
415 Dody Wood .05 .15
416 Denis Chasse .05 .15
417 Aaron Gavey .05 .15
418 Scott Walker .05 .15
419 Richard Park .10 .25
420 Mike Modano .15 .40
421 Kyle McLaren RC .05 .15
422 Jeremy Roenick .12 .30
423 Mark Fitzpatrick .07 .20
424 Landon Wilson RC .05 .15
425 Steve Rucchin .07 .20
426 Stephane Richer .07 .20
427 Martin Straka .05 .15
428 Ron Hextall .10 .25
429 Joe Dziedzic RC .05 .15
430 Peter Forsberg .25 .60
431 Dino Ciccarelli .07 .20
432 Robert Dirk .05 .15
433 Wayne Primeau RC .05 .15
434 Denis Savard .12 .30
435 Keith Carney .05 .15
436 Tom Fitzgerald .05 .15
437 Cale Hulse .05 .15
438 Mike Richter .10 .25
439 Marcus Ragnarsson RC .12 .30
440 Roman Vopat .05 .15
441 Zdenek Nedved .05 .15
442 Dale Hunter .07 .20
443 Bob Sweeney .05 .15
444 Randy McKay .05 .15
445 Chris Osgood .07 .20
446 Andrei Kovalenko .05 .15
447 Darius Kasparaitis .05 .15
448 Ulf Samuelsson .05 .15
449 Chris Joseph .05 .15
450 Chris Terreri .07 .20
451 Keith Jones .07 .20
452 Tim Cheveldae .07 .20
453 Stephen Leach .05 .15
454 Michael Nylander .05 .15
455 Ed Belfour .07 .20
456 Claude Lemieux .10 .25
457 Mike Ricci .07 .20
458 Shane Churla .05 .15
459 Kris Draper .10 .25
460 Byron Dafoe .07 .20
461 Troy Mallette .05 .15
462 Petr Nedved .07 .20
463 Kenny Jonsson .10 .25
464 Keith Tkachuk .10 .25
465 Jaromir Jagr .25 .60
466 Vladimir Malakhov .05 .15
467 Guy Hebert .07 .20
468 Brad May .05 .15
469 Bob Probert .07 .20
470 Sandis Ozolinsh .07 .20
471 Oleg Mikulchik RC .05 .15
472 Steve Thomas .07 .20
473 Travis Green .07 .20
474 Sergei Zubov .07 .20
475 Bill Houlder .05 .15
476 Roman Oksiuta .05 .15
477 Jamie Rivers .05 .15
478 Rob Blake .07 .20
479 Todd Elik .05 .15
480 Zarley Zalapski .05 .15
481 Darren Turcotte .05 .15
482 Scott Stevens .10 .25
483 Pat Falloon .05 .15
484 Grant Fuhr .10 .25
485 Martin Rucinsky .05 .15
486 Brett Hull .12 .30
487 Brian Leetch .10 .25
488 Shaun Van Allen .05 .15
489 Valeri Kamensky .07 .20
490 Mark Recchi .12 .30
491 Jason Muzzatti .07 .20
492 Andrew Cassels .05 .15
493 Nick Kypreos .05 .15
494 Bryan Smolinski .05 .15
495 Owen Nolan .10 .25
496 Bryan McCabe .10 .25
497 Mathieu Dandenault RC .20 .50
498 Deron Quint .07 .20
499 Jason Doig .10 .25
500 Marty Murray .10 .25
501 Ed Jovanovski .10 .25
502 Stefan Ustorf .05 .15
503 Jamie Langenbrunner .05 .15
504 Daniel Alfredsson RC .50 1.25
505 Darby Hendrickson .05 .15
506 Brett McLean RC .07 .20
507 Daniel Cleary RC .07 .20
508 Todd Robinson .05 .15
509 Arron Asham RC .07 .20
510 Daniel Corso RC .20 .50
511 Darren Van Oene RC .05 .15
512 Trevor Wasyluk RC .10 .25
513 Josh Holden RC .05 .15
514 Etienne Drapeau RC .07 .20
515 Matt Osborne .05 .15
516 Zenith Komarniski RC .07 .20
517 Chris Phillips RC .10 .25
518 Chris Fleury RC .10 .25
519 Cory Sarich RC .07 .20
520 Glenn Crawford RC .05 .15
521 Francois Methot RC .05 .15
522 Geoff Peters RC .05 .15
523 Joey Tetarenko .07 .20
524 Randy Petruk RC .07 .20
525 Mathieu Garon RC .25 .60
526 Daymond Langkow .10 .25
527 Craig Mills RC .05 .15
528 Rhett Warrener .05 .15
529 Marc Denis RC .30 .75
530 Jose Theodore RC .30 .75
531 Curtis Brown RC .10 .25
532 Chad Allen .05 .15
533 Denis Gauthier RC .05 .15
534 Brad Larsen .05 .15
535 Jamie Wright RC .10 .25
536 Mike Watt RC .10 .25
537 Jason Holland RC .10 .25
538 Robb Gordon RC .10 .25
539 Hnat Domenichelli RC .10 .25
540 Ondrej Kratena RC .10 .25
541 Michal Bros RC .10 .25
542 Marek Posmyk RC .10 .25
543 Marek Melanovsky RC .10 .25
544 Jan Tomajko .10 .25
545 Ales Pisa RC .10 .25
546 Miika Elomo .10 .25
547 Timo Salonen .10 .25
548 Teemu Riihijarvi RC .10 .25
549 Antti-Jussi Niemi .10 .25
550 Pasi Petrilainen RC .10 .25
551 Toni Lydman RC .10 .25
552 Dmitri Nabokov .10 .25
553 Alexei Morozov .10 .25
554 Sergei Samsonov .10 .25
555 Alexei Vasilyev RC .10 .25
556 Andrei Petrunin .05 .15
557 Dimitri Rjabykin .10 .25
558 Sergei Zimakov RC .10 .25
559 Peter Nylander RC .10 .25
560 Marcus Nilsson UER RC .20 .50
561 Niklas Anger RC .10 .25
562 Per Anton Lundstrom RC .10 .25
563 Patrik Wallenberg RC .10 .25
564 Per Ragnar Bergkvist RC .10 .25
565 Mike Sylvia .10 .25
566 Marty Reasoner .10 .25
567 Reg Berg RC .10 .25
568 Tom Poti RC .10 .25
569 Chris Drury RC .30 .75
570 Michael McBain .10 .25

1995-96 Upper Deck Electric Ice

The Electric Ice cards were inserted one per retail pack, or two per jumbo. These cards featured the Electric Ice logo on a silver foil background.

*VETS: 4X TO 10X BASIC CARDS
*ROOKIES: 1X TO 2.5X

1995-96 Upper Deck Electric Ice Gold

These cards were inserted at the rate of 1:35 retail packs only, and could be differentiated from basic UD cards by the inclusion of the words Electric Ice embossed in gold down the side of the card front. The card J-171 is a recently confirmed jumbo version of the Electric Ice Gold Selanne card. The J prefix was added for checklisting purposes. It is not known whether other jumbo versions exist for Electric Ice Gold cards.

*VETS: 20X TO 50X BASIC CARDS
*ROOKIES: 8X TO 20X
J171 Teemu Selanne 2.00 5.00

1995-96 Upper Deck All-Star Game Predictors

The thirty cards in this set were handed out one per person at the Upper Deck booth at the All-Star FanFest in Boston. The winning card, no. 21 Ray Bourque, was redeemable for a full thirty card set of All-Star Game Predictors that contained different photos than the original give-aways. Prices below are for the cards handed out at the All-Star game. Separate multipliers to determine values for the redeemed versions can be found in the header below. The redeemed Bourque card is actually worth about 33 percent of the game card; this is due to the mass redemption of the Bourque game card, making it extremely difficult to locate in the secondary market.

*REDEEMED CARDS: 2X TO 3X BASIC PREDICTORS
1 Wayne Gretzky 75.00 200.00
2 Sergei Fedorov 20.00 50.00
3 Brett Hull 15.00 40.00
4 Alexander Mogilny 6.00 15.00
5 Joe Sakic 20.00 50.00
6 Paul Kariya 30.00 75.00
7 Teemu Selanne 20.00 50.00
8 Paul Coffey 10.00 25.00
9 Chris Chelios 15.00 40.00
10 Doug Gilmour 10.00 25.00
11 Peter Forsberg 25.00 60.00
12 Jeremy Roenick 15.00 40.00
13 Theo Fleury 10.00 25.00
14 Mike Modano 15.00 40.00
15 Steve Yzerman 50.00 125.00
16 Mario Lemieux 60.00 150.00
17 Jaromir Jagr 25.00 60.00
18 Eric Lindros 20.00 50.00
19 Mark Messier 15.00 40.00
20 Brendan Shanahan 15.00 40.00
21 Ray Bourque 75.00 200.00
22 Cam Neely 15.00 40.00
23 Ron Francis 6.00 15.00
24 John LeClair 15.00 40.00
25 Brian Leetch 10.00 25.00
26 Peter Bondra 10.00 25.00
27 Scott Stevens 6.00 15.00
28 Adam Oates 6.00 15.00
29 Martin Brodeur 25.00 60.00
30 Longshot 2.00 5.00

1995-96 Upper Deck Freeze Frame

Twenty top stars are featured in this multiple photo insert set which utilizes Upper Deck's Light FX foil printing technology. The cards were randomly inserted at a rate of 1:34 series one packs. Jumbo versions of these cards, measuring 3 1/2" by 6", were inserted one per series one box. Multipliers can be found in the header below to determine values for these.

COMPLETE SET (20) 25.00 60.00
*JUMBOS: .8X TO 2X BASIC INSERTS
F1 Peter Forsberg 2.50 6.00
F2 Wayne Gretzky 6.00 15.00
F3 Eric Lindros 1.50 4.00
F4 Jaromir Jagr 2.00 5.00
F5 Cam Neely 1.25 3.00
F6 Jeremy Roenick 1.25 3.00
F7 Mark Messier 1.25 3.00
F8 Sergei Fedorov 1.25 3.00
F9 Paul Kariya 1.25 3.00

10 Pavel Bure 1.25 3.00
11 Dominik Hasek 2.50 5.00
12 Theo Fleury .75 2.00
13 Alexei Zhamnov .40 1.00
14 Martin Brodeur 3.00 8.00
15 Brett Hull 1.25 3.00
16 Mario Lemieux 4.00 10.00
17 Paul Coffey .60 1.50
18 Brian Leetch .60 1.50
19 Ray Bourque 1.25 3.00
20 Jim Carey .75 1.50

1995-96 Upper Deck Gretzky Collection

This 24 card set, which focuses on the many remarkable achievements in the career of Wayne Gretzky, was released through four separate products. Cards G1-G9, along with a header card, could be found in 1995-96 Collector's Choice retail and hobby packs at a rate of 1:11. Cards G10-G13 and a header card were randomly inserted in packs of Upper Deck series 1 at a rate of 1:29. Cards G14-17 along with a header card were randomly inserted in packs of Upper Deck series 2 at a rate of 1:29. Finally, cards G18-G20, along with an NNO header card, were randomly inserted at a rate of 1:45 packs of SP. The cards share a similar design element, but with added foil enhancements for each step up the premium ladder. A jumbo version of cards G1-G9 and the CC header were produced and inserted into some Collector's Choice boxes.

COMPLETE SET (24) 60.00 120.00
COMP.CC SET (10) 12.00 30.00
COMP.SP SET (4) 30.00 80.00
COMP.UD SER.1 (5) 15.00 40.00
COMP.UD SER.2 (4) 15.00 40.00
COMMON CC (G1-G9/HDR) 2.00 5.00
COMMON UD (G10-G17/HUD) 4.00 10.00
COMMON SP (G18-G20/HSP) 12.50 30.00
*JUMBOS: .6X TO 1.5X BASIC INSERTS

1995-96 Upper Deck NHL All-Stars

Randomly inserted in packs at a rate of 1:34 series 2 packs, these twenty two-sided cards highlight the participants in the 1995-96 All-Star Game. The cards utilize the UD Light FX technology. Players from the Western Conference have a teal left border, while players from the Eastern Conference have purple left border. There also were jumbo version of these cards inserted one per series 2 box. Multipliers can be found in the header below to determine value for these.

COMPLETE SET (20) 25.00 50.00
*JUMBOS: .4X TO 1X BASIC INSERTS
AS1 R.Bourque/P.Coffey 1.00 2.50
AS2 Stevens/Chelios .75 2.00
AS3 J.Jagr/B.Hull 1.25 3.00
AS4 B.Shanahan/P.Bure .75 2.00
AS5 M.Lemieux/W.Gretzky 8.00 20.00
AS6 M.Brodeur/E.Belfour 2.00 5.00
AS7 Leetch/Lidstrom .75 2.00
AS8 Hamrlik/Suter .75 2.00
AS9 Desjardins/MacInnis .75 2.00
AS10 Neely/Mogilny .75 2.00
AS11 Bondra/Fleury .75 2.00
AS12 D.Alfredsson/T.Selanne .75 2.00
AS13 Verbeek/Nolan .75 2.00
AS14 J.LeClair/P.Kariya 2.00 5.00
AS15 P.Turgeon/S.Fedorov 1.00 2.50
AS16 M.Messier/D.Weight .75 2.00
AS17 E.Lindros/P.Forsberg 2.50 6.00
AS18 Francis/Sundin .75 2.00
AS19 J.Vanbies./C.Osgood .75 2.00
AS20 D.Hasek/F.Potvin 2.00 5.00

1995-96 Upper Deck Predictor Hobby

The 40 cards in this set were randomly inserted in series 1 hobby packs (H1-H20) at the rate of 1:30, and series 2 hobby packs (H21-H40) at the rate of 1:23. Each card was a potential winner in an interactive game based on season-end award recipients: if the player pictured on your card came in first or second in the voting for that award, you could redeem your card for a complete set of Predictors from that distribution category. Cards H1-H10 were contestants for the Hart Trophy, cards H11-H20 were goalies competing for the Vezina Trophy, cards H21-H30 were contestants for the Calder Trophy, and cards H31-H40 were vying for the James Norris Trophy. The cards of Mario Lemieux, Mark Messier, Jim Carey, Vezina Long Shot, Daniel Alfredsson, Eric Daze, Chris Chelios and Ray Bourque may be somewhat harder to locate now, because, as winners, many of them were redeemed and destroyed.

COMPLETE SET (40) 30.00 80.00
COMP.HART PRIZE SET (10) 6.00 15.00
COMP.VEZINA PRIZE (10) 5.00 12.00
COMP.CALDER PRIZE (10) 2.50 6.00
COMP.NORRIS PRIZE (10) 2.50 6.00
*PRIZE CARDS: .2X TO .5X BASIC INSERTS
ONE PRIZE SET PER PRED.WINNER
H1 Eric Lindros 1.00 2.50
H2 Jaromir Jagr 1.50 4.00
H3 Paul Coffey 1.00 2.50
H4 Mario Lemieux WIN 4.00 10.00
H5 Martin Brodeur 2.50 6.00
H6 Sergei Fedorov 1.00 2.50
H7 Wayne Gretzky 6.00 15.00
H8 Peter Forsberg 1.50 4.00
H9 Mark Messier WIN 1.25 3.00
H10 Hart Long Shot .40 1.00
H11 Martin Brodeur 2.50 6.00
H12 Mike Richter 1.00 2.50
H13 Dominik Hasek 2.00 5.00
H14 Patrick Roy 4.00 10.00
H15 Blaine Lacher .40 1.00
H16 Jim Carey WIN .40 1.00
H17 Felix Potvin 1.25 3.00
H18 Ed Belfour 1.25 3.00
H19 John Vanbiesbrouck .75 2.00
H20 Vezina Long Shot WIN .40 1.00
H21 Vitali Yachmenev .40 1.00
H22 Saku Koivu 1.00 2.50
H23 Daniel Alfredsson WIN 2.00 5.00
H24 Ed Jovanovski .40 1.00
H25 Aki Berg .40 1.00
H26 Radek Dvorak .40 1.00
H27 Shane Doan .75 2.00
H28 Nicklas Sundstrom .40 1.00
H29 Eric Daze WIN .40 1.00
H30 Calder Long Shot .40 1.00
H31 Paul Coffey .75 2.00
H32 Ray Bourque WIN 1.25 3.00
H33 Brian Leetch .75 2.00
H34 Chris Chelios WIN 1.25 3.00
H35 Scott Stevens .40 1.00
H36 Nicklas Lidstrom 1.00 2.50
H37 Sergei Zubov .40 1.00
H38 Larry Murphy .40 1.00
H39 Roman Hamrlik .40 1.00
H40 Norris Long Shot .40 1.00

1995-96 Upper Deck Predictor Retail

The 60 cards in this interactive set were randomly inserted in retail packs from both series. R1-R30 were inserted at a rate of 1:30 series 1 retail packs, and 1:17 Value Added retail packs, while cards R31-R60 were inserted at a rate of 1:23 retail series 2 packs. A card could be redeemed if the player pictured finished first or second in the race for the scoring category featured. Cards R1-R10 battled for the assists crown, R11-R20 aimed to be the most prolific snipers, R21-R30 aimed to reach the top of the point scoring heap, R31-R40 were shooting for Art Ross, R41-R50 were in search of Lester B. Pearson, and R51-R60 were players looking to be awarded the Conn Smythe. However, a printing error at the printing plant reversed the intended categories on cards R1-R10 and R11-R20. In light of this, Upper Deck decided to honour a card as a winner if the player pictured won in either category. The cards of Mario Lemieux (R32, R42), Jaromir Jagr, Patrick Roy, Ron Francis and the Long Shots in the Assists, Goals, Points, and Smythe categories may be somewhat harder to find, as many were redeemed as winners.

COMPLETE SET (60) 75.00 200.00
COMP.ASSIST PRIZE (10) 4.00 10.00
COMP.GOAL PRIZE (10) 6.00 15.00
COMP.POINT PRIZE (10) 6.00 15.00
COMP.ROSS PRIZE (10) 8.00 20.00
COMP.PEARSON PRIZE (10) 8.00 20.00
COMP.SMYTHE PRIZE (10) 10.00 25.00
*PRIZE CARDS: .2X TO .5X BASIC INSERTS
ONE PRIZE SET PER PRED.WINNER
R1 Cam Neely 1.25 3.00
R2 Eric Lindros 1.25 3.00
R3 Jaromir Jagr WIN 2.00 5.00
R4 Brendan Shanahan 1.25 3.00
R5 Brett Hull 1.50 4.00
R6 Alexander Mogilny .60 1.50
R7 Owen Nolan .60 1.50
R8 Theo Fleury .40 1.00
R9 Pavel Bure 1.25 3.00
R10 Assists Long Shot WIN .40 1.00
R11 Ron Francis WIN .60 1.50
R12 Paul Coffey 1.25 3.00
R13 Wayne Gretzky 6.00 15.00
R14 Joe Sakic 2.50 6.00
R15 Steve Yzerman 4.00 10.00
R16 Adam Oates .60 1.50
R17 Joe Juneau .40 1.00
R18 Brian Leetch .60 1.50
R19 Pat LaFontaine 1.25 3.00
R20 Goals Long Shot WIN .40 1.00
R21 Eric Lindros 1.25 3.00
R22 Jaromir Jagr WIN 2.00 5.00
R23 Wayne Gretzky 6.00 15.00
R24 Sergei Fedorov 1.50 4.00
R25 Peter Forsberg 2.00 5.00
R26 Pavel Bure 1.25 3.00
R27 Joe Sakic 2.50 6.00
R28 Alexei Zhamnov .40 1.00
R29 Pat LaFontaine 1.25 3.00
R30 Points Long Shot WIN .40 1.00
R31 Wayne Gretzky 6.00 15.00
R32 Mario Lemieux WIN 4.00 10.00
R33 Eric Lindros 1.25 3.00
R34 Sergei Fedorov 1.50 4.00
R35 Alexander Mogilny .60 1.50
R36 Joe Sakic 2.50 6.00
R37 Peter Forsberg 2.00 5.00
R38 Jaromir Jagr WIN 2.00 5.00
R39 Mark Messier 1.25 3.00
R40 Ross Long Shot .40 1.00
R41 Wayne Gretzky 6.00 15.00
R42 Mario Lemieux 4.00 10.00
R43 Paul Kariya 1.25 3.00
R44 Sergei Fedorov 1.50 4.00
R45 Joe Sakic 2.50 6.00
R46 Jaromir Jagr WIN 2.00 5.00
R47 Jeremy Roenick 1.50 4.00
R48 Ray Bourque 1.25 3.00
R49 Teemu Selanne 1.25 3.00
R50 Pearson Long Shot .40 1.00
R51 Wayne Gretzky 6.00 15.00
R52 Eric Lindros 1.25 3.00
R53 Mario Lemieux WIN 4.00 10.00
R54 Peter Forsberg 2.00 5.00
R55 Patrick Roy WIN 5.00 12.00
R56 Mark Messier 1.25 3.00
R57 Martin Brodeur 2.50 6.00
R58 Steve Yzerman 4.00 10.00
R59 Mike Modano 1.50 4.00
R60 Smythe Long Shot WIN .40 1.00

1995-96 Upper Deck Special Edition

This 180-card set was inserted one per hobby pack over both series of 1995-96 Upper Deck cards. Cards 1-90 were found in series 1 packs, while 91-180 were in series 2.

COMPLETE SET (180) 20.00 50.00
*GOLDS: 6X TO 15X BASIC INSERTS
SE1 Paul Kariya .25 .60
SE2 Oleg Tverdovsky .07 .20
SE3 Guy Hebert .10 .30
SE4 Ray Bourque .25 .60
SE5 Adam Oates .10 .30
SE6 Mariusz Czerkawski .07 .20
SE7 Blaine Lacher .10 .30
SE8 Garry Galley .07 .20
SE9 Donald Audette .07 .20
SE10 Pat LaFontaine .25 .60
SE11 Alexei Zhitnik .07 .20
SE12 Joe Nieuwendyk .10 .30
SE13 Phil Housley .10 .30
SE14 German Titov .07 .20
SE15 Trevor Kidd .10 .30
SE16 Bernie Nicholls .07 .20
SE17 Chris Chelios .25 .60
SE18 Tony Amonte .10 .30
SE19 Ed Belfour .25 .60
SE20 Jon Klemm .07 .20
SE21 Peter Forsberg .40 1.00
SE22 Adam Deadmarsh .07 .20
SE23 Stephane Fiset .10 .30
SE24 Dave Gagner .07 .20
SE25 Kevin Hatcher .07 .20
SE26 Mike Modano .30 .75
SE27 Keith Primeau .07 .20
SE28 Dino Ciccarelli .10 .30
SE29 Nicklas Lidstrom .25 .60
SE30 Steve Yzerman 1.25 3.00
SE31 Doug Weight .10 .30
SE32 Bill Ranford .10 .30
SE33 Stu Barnes .07 .20
SE34 Bob Kudelski .07 .20
SE35 Rob Niedermayer .10 .30
SE36 Andrew Cassels .07 .20
SE37 Darren Turcotte .07 .20
SE38 Andrei Nikolishin .07 .20
SE39 Sean Burke .10 .30
SE40 Rick Tocchet .10 .30
SE41 Jari Kurri .25 .60
SE42 Rob Blake .10 .30
SE43 Mark Recchi .10 .30
SE44 Pierre Turgeon .10 .30
SE45 Vladimir Malakhov .07 .20
SE46 Valeri Bure .07 .20
SE47 Stephane Richer .10 .30
SE48 Bill Guerin .10 .30
SE49 Scott Stevens .10 .30
SE50 Claude Lemieux .07 .20
SE51 Zigmund Palffy .10 .30
SE52 Kirk Muller .07 .20
SE53 Todd Bertuzzi .10 .30
SE54 Brett Lindros .07 .20
SE55 Brian Leetch .10 .30
SE56 Alexei Kovalev .07 .20
SE57 Adam Graves .07 .20
SE58 Mike Richter .25 .60
SE59 Alexei Yashin .07 .20
SE60 Alexandre Daigle .07 .20
SE61 Don Beaupre .10 .30
SE62 Radek Bonk .07 .20
SE63 John LeClair .25 .60
SE64 Rod Brind'Amour .10 .30
SE65 Ron Hextall .10 .30
SE66 Ron Francis .10 .30
SE67 Markus Naslund .25 .60
SE68 Tom Barrasso .10 .30
SE69 Ian Laperriere .07 .20
SE70 Esa Tikkanen .07 .20
SE71 Al MacInnis .10 .30
SE72 Ulf Dahlen .07 .20
SE73 Craig Janney .07 .20
SE74 Jeff Friesen .07 .20
SE75 Chris Gratton .07 .20
SE76 Roman Hamrlik .10 .30
SE77 Alexander Selivanov .07 .20
SE78 Daren Puppa .10 .30
SE79 Dave Andreychuk .10 .30
SE80 Doug Gilmour .10 .30
SE81 Kenny Jonsson .07 .20
SE82 Trevor Linden .10 .30
SE83 Kirk McLean .10 .30
SE84 Jeff Brown .07 .20
SE85 Keith Jones .10 .30
SE86 Joe Juneau .07 .20
SE87 Jim Carey .10 .30
SE88 Keith Tkachuk .25 .60
SE89 Teemu Selanne .25 .60
SE90 Igor Korolev .07 .20
SE91 Mike Sillinger .07 .20
SE92 Steve Rucchin .10 .30
SE93 Valeri Karpov .07 .20
SE94 Cam Neely .25 .60
SE95 Shawn McEachern .07 .20
SE96 Kevin Stevens .07 .20
SE97 Ted Donato .07 .20
SE98 Dominik Hasek .50 1.25
SE99 Randy Burridge .07 .20
SE100 Jason Dawe .07 .20
SE101 Theo Fleury .07 .20
SE102 Michael Nylander .07 .20
SE103 Rick Tabaracci .10 .30
SE104 Jeremy Roenick .30 .75
SE105 Bob Probert .10 .30
SE106 Patrick Poulin .07 .20
SE107 Gary Suter .07 .20
SE108 Claude Lemieux .07 .20
SE109 Sandis Ozolinsh .07 .20
SE110 Patrick Roy 1.25 3.00
SE111 Joe Sakic .50 1.25
SE112 Derian Hatcher .07 .20
SE113 Greg Adams .07 .20
SE114 Todd Harvey .10 .30
SE115 Sergei Fedorov .40 1.00
SE116 Chris Osgood .10 .30
SE117 Vyacheslav Kozlov .10 .30
SE118 Paul Coffey .25 .60
SE119 Jason Arnott .07 .20
SE120 David Oliver .07 .20
SE121 Todd Marchant .07 .20
SE122 John Vanbiesbrouck .10 .30
SE123 Jody Hull .07 .20
SE124 Jason Woolley .07 .20
SE125 Brendan Shanahan .25 .60
SE126 Nelson Emerson .07 .20
SE127 Geoff Sanderson .07 .20
SE128 Wayne Gretzky 3.00 8.00
SE129 Marty McSorley .07 .20
SE130 Yanic Perreault .07 .20
SE131 Jocelyn Thibault .25 .60
SE132 Brian Savage .07 .20
SE133 Vincent Damphousse .07 .20
SE134 John Mclean .10 .30
SE135 Martin Brodeur 1.50 4.00
SE136 Steve Thomas .10 .30
SE137 Scott Niedermayer .07 .20
SE138 Travis Green .10 .30
SE139 Wendel Clark .10 .30
SE140 Tommy Soderstrom .10 .30
SE141 Mark Messier .25 .60
SE142 Ulf Samuelsson .07 .20
SE143 Ray Ferraro .07 .20
SE144 Luc Robitaille .10 .30
SE145 Daniel Alfredsson 1.00 2.50
SE146 Martin Straka .07 .20
SE147 Steve Duschene .07 .20
SE148 Eric Lindros .25 .60
SE149 Mikael Renberg .10 .30
SE150 Eric Desjardins .10 .30
SE151 Joel Otto .07 .20
SE152 Mario Lemieux 1.25 3.00
SE153 Jaromir Jagr .40 1.00
SE154 Petr Nedved .10 .30
SE155 Sergei Zubov .07 .20
SE156 Tomas Sandstrom .07 .20
SE157 Brett Hull .30 .75
SE158 Grant Fuhr .25 .60
SE159 Shayne Corson .07 .20
SE160 Chris Pronger .25 .60
SE161 Ray Sheppard .07 .20
SE162 Arturs Irbe .10 .30
SE163 Owen Nolan .10 .30
SE164 Andrei Nazarov .07 .20
SE165 Paul Ysebaert .07 .20
SE166 Brian Bradley .07 .20
SE167 Petr Klima .07 .20
SE168 Felix Potvin .25 .60
SE169 Mats Sundin .25 .60
SE170 Larry Murphy .10 .30
SE171 Benoit Hogue .07 .20
SE172 Pavel Bure .25 .60
SE173 Alexander Mogilny .10 .30
SE174 Cliff Ronning .07 .20
SE175 Pat Peake .07 .20
SE176 Sylvain Cote .07 .20
SE177 Peter Bondra .10 .30
SE178 Dallas Drake .07 .20
SE179 Tim Cheveldae .10 .30
SE180 Darren Turcotte .07 .20

1996-97 Upper Deck

This two-series, 390-card set was distributed in 12-card packs with the suggested retail price of $2.49. The set was highlighted by the use of actual game dating for much of the photography, the selection of which included some of the most memorable moments of the '96 season. The set is noteworthy for including Wayne Gretzky in his new uniform as a New York Ranger both in the set and on all packaging. The set also contained a 15-card Star Rookie subset (#181-195), a 13-card Through the Glass subset (#196-208), a 10-card On-Ice Insight subset (359-368) and four checklist cards. Several key rookies appeared in this set, including Joe Thornton, Patrick Marleau, Daniel Tkaczuk, and Dainius Zubrus. The "Meet the Stars" promotion was continued in this set, which gave the collector an opportunity to win a chance to meet "The Great One" himself. Trivia cards were inserted one in every four packs and Instant Win cards one in every 56 packs. These cards are not widely traded, but are now worth about ten cents each.

1 Paul Kariya .25 .60
2 Guy Hebert .15 .40
3 J.F. Jomphe RC .20 .50
4 Joe Sacco .25 .60
5 Jason York .12 .30
6 Alex Hicks RC .20 .50
7 Mikhail Shtalenkov .12 .30
8 Bill Ranford .15 .40
9 Kyle McLaren .12 .30
10 Rick Tocchet .15 .40
11 Jon Rohloff .12 .30
12 Jozef Stumpel .12 .30
13 Cam Neely .20 .50
14 Ray Bourque .30 .75
15 Pat LaFontaine .20 .50
16 Brian Holzinger .15 .40
17 Alexei Zhitnik .12 .30
18 Donald Audette .12 .30
19 Jason Dawe .12 .30
20 Wayne Primeau .12 .30
21 Mike Peca .12 .30
22 Theo Fleury .40 1.00
23 Sandy McCarthy .12 .30
24 Zarley Zalapski .12 .30
25 Trevor Kidd .12 .30
26 Steve Chiasson .12 .30
27 Michael Nylander .12 .30
28 Ronnie Stern .12 .30
29 Eric Daze .15 .40
30 Jeff Hackett .15 .40
31 Chris Chelios .20 .50
32 Tony Amonte .15 .40
33 Bob Probert .15 .40
34 Eric Weinrich .12 .30
35 Jeremy Roenick .30 .75
36 Mike Ricci .12 .30
37 Sandis Ozolinsh .12 .30
38 Patrick Roy .75 2.00
39 Uwe Krupp .12 .30
40 Stephane Yelle .12 .30
41 Adam Deadmarsh .12 .30
42 Scott Young .12 .30
43 Mike Modano .30 .75
44 Derian Hatcher .12 .30
45 Todd Harvey .12 .30
46 Brent Fedyk .12 .30
47 Grant Marshall .12 .30
48 Jamie Langenbrunner .12 .30
49 Jere Lehtinen .12 .30
50 Steve Yzerman .75 2.00
51 Igor Larionov .20 .50
52 Vladimir Konstantinov .15 .40
53 Chris Osgood .20 .50
54 Jamie Pushor .12 .30
55 Darren McCarty .12 .30
56 Nicklas Lidstrom .25 .60
57 Jason Arnott .15 .40
58 Doug Weight .20 .50
59 Todd Marchant .12 .30
60 David Oliver .12 .30
61 Luke Richardson .12 .30
62 Jason Bonsignore .12 .30
63 John Vanbiesbrouck .20 .50
64 Stu Barnes .12 .30
65 Martin Straka .12 .30
66 Ed Jovanovski .15 .40
67 Robert Svehla .12 .30
68 Gord Murphy .12 .30
69 Tom Fitzgerald .12 .30
70 Jeff O'Neill .12 .30
71 Jason Muzzatti .15 .40
72 Sean Burke .12 .30
73 Jeff Brown .12 .30
74 Andrew Cassels .12 .30
75 Geoff Sanderson .15 .40
76 Dimitri Khristich .12 .30
77 Vitali Yachmenev .12 .30
78 Kevin Stevens .12 .30
79 Yanic Perreault .12 .30
80 Craig Johnson .12 .30
81 John Slaney .12 .30
82 Saku Koivu .20 .50
83 Jocelyn Thibault .20 .50
84 Vladimir Malakhov .12 .30
85 Turner Stevenson .12 .30
86 Vincent Damphousse .15 .40
87 Mark Recchi .25 .60
88 Patrice Brisebois .12 .30
89 Dave Andreychuk .20 .50
90 Bill Guerin .20 .50
91 Martin Brodeur .40 1.00
92 Scott Niedermayer .20 .50
93 Petr Sykora .12 .30
94 Stephane Richer .15 .40
95 John MacLean .15 .40
96 Eric Fichaud .15 .40
97 Zigmund Palffy .20 .50
98 Alexander Semak .12 .30
99 Bryan McCabe .12 .30
100 Darby Hendrickson .12 .30
101 Kenny Jonsson .12 .30
102 Marty McInnis .12 .30
103 Alexei Kovalev .12 .30
104 Ulf Samuelsson .12 .30
105 Jeff Beukeboom .12 .30
106 Marty McSorley .12 .30
107 Niklas Sundstrom .12 .30
108 W.Gretzky/M.Messier 1.00 2.50
109 Mike Richter .20 .50
110 Alexei Yashin .15 .40
111 Randy Cunneyworth .12 .30
112 Damian Rhodes .15 .40
113 Daniel Alfredsson .20 .50
114 Antti Tormanen .12 .30
115 Ted Drury .12 .30
116 Janne Laukkanen .12 .30
117 Sean Hill .12 .30
118 John LeClair .20 .50
119 Ron Hextall .15 .40
120 Dale Hawerchuk .25 .60
121 Rod Brind'Amour .20 .50
122 Pat Falloon .12 .30
123 Eric Desjardins .15 .40
124 Joel Otto .12 .30
125 Alexei Zhamnov .15 .40
126 Nikolai Khabibulin .15 .40
127 Craig Janney .15 .40
128 Deron Quint .12 .30
129 Oleg Tverdovsky .15 .40
130 Chad Kilger .12 .30
131 Teppo Numminen .12 .30
132 Tom Barrasso .15 .40
133 Ron Francis .25 .60
134 Petr Nedved .15 .40
135 Ken Wregget .15 .40
136 Joe Dziedzic .12 .30
137 Tomas Sandstrom .12 .30
138 Dmitri Mironov .12 .30
139 Shayne Corson .12 .30
140 Grant Fuhr .20 .50
141 Al MacInnis .20 .50
142 Stephen Leach .12 .30
143 Murray Baron .12 .30
144 Chris Pronger .15 .40
145 Jamie Rivers .12 .30
146 Owen Nolan .20 .50
147 Chris Terreri .15 .40
148 Marcus Ragnarsson .12 .30
149 Shean Donovan .12 .30
150 Ray Whitney .12 .30
151 Michal Sykora .12 .30
152 Viktor Kozlov .12 .30
153 Roman Hamrlik .15 .40
154 Bill Houlder .12 .30
155 Mikael Andersson .12 .30
156 Petr Klima .12 .30
157 Jason Wiemer .12 .30
158 Rob Zamuner .12 .30
159 Paul Ysebaert .12 .30
160 Mats Sundin .20 .50
161 Larry Murphy UER .15 .40
162 Doug Gilmour .25 .60
163 Todd Warriner .12 .30
164 Dimitri Yushkevich .12 .30
165 Kirk Muller .12 .30
166 Jamie Macoun .12 .30
167 Alexander Mogilny .15 .40
168 Corey Hirsch .15 .40
169 Trevor Linden .15 .40
170 Markus Naslund .20 .50
171 Martin Gelinas .12 .30
172 Jyrki Lumme .12 .30
173 Bret Hedican .12 .30
174 Jim Carey .20 .50
175 Sergei Gonchar .12 .30
176 Joe Juneau .12 .30
177 Brendan Witt .12 .30
178 Dale Hunter .15 .40
179 Steve Konowalchuk .12 .30
180 Peter Bondra .15 .40
181 Jarome Iginla .25 .60
182 Ralph Intranuovo .12 .30
183 Anders Eriksson .12 .30
184 Andrew Brunette RC .25 .60
185 Steve Sullivan RC .15 .40
186 Brandon Convery .12 .30
187 Ethan Moreau RC .20 .50
188 Marko Kiprusoff .12 .30
189 Jason McBain .12 .30
190 Mark Kolesar .12 .30
191 Greg DeVries RC .20 .50
192 Alexei Yegorov RC .20 .50
193 Sebastien Bordeleau RC .20 .50
194 Nick Stajduhar .12 .30
195 Jan Caloun RC .20 .50
196 Dino Ciccarelli TTG .20 .50
197 Ron Hextall TTG .15 .40
198 Murray Baron TTG .12 .30
199 Patrick Roy TTG .50 1.25
200 Scott Mellanby TTG .15 .40
201 Tie Domi TTG .15 .40
202 Glenn Healy TTG .15 .40
203 Keith Primeau .12 .30
204 Joe Sakic TTG .30 .75
205 Jeremy Roenick TTG .30 .75
206 Sergei Fedorov TTG .30 .75
207 Claude Lemieux TTG .12 .30
208 Theo Fleury TTG .40 1.00
209 Checklist (1-104) .10 .25
210 Checklist (105-210) .10 .25
211 Teemu Selanne .40 1.00
212 Jari Kurri .20 .50
213 Darren Van Impe .12 .30
214 Steve Rucchin .12 .30
215 Ruslan Salei RC .20 .50
216 Adam Oates .20 .50
217 Don Sweeney .12 .30
218 Steve Staios RC .20 .50
219 Barry Richter .12 .30
220 Mattias Timander RC .20 .50
221 Ted Donato .12 .30
222 Dominik Hasek .30 .75
223 Derek Plante .12 .30
224 Vaclav Varada RC .20 .50
225 Andrei Trefilov .12 .30
226 Curtis Brown .12 .30
227 German Titov .12 .30
228 Robert Reichel .12 .30
229 Cory Stillman .12 .30
230 Chris O'Sullivan .12 .30
231 Corey Millen .12 .30
232 Jonas Hoglund .12 .30
233 Alexei Zhamnov .15 .40
234 Ed Belfour .20 .50
235 Gary Suter .12 .30
236 Kevin Miller .12 .30
237 Tuomas Gronman .12 .30
238 Enrico Ciccone .12 .30
239 Peter Forsberg .30 .75
240 Joe Sakic .30 .75
241 Valeri Kamensky .15 .40
242 Landon Wilson .12 .30
243 Claude Lemieux .12 .30
244 Eric Lacroix .12 .30
245 Joe Nieuwendyk .20 .50
246 Sergei Zubov .12 .30
247 Benoit Hogue .12 .30
248 Arturs Irbe .15 .40
249 Pat Verbeek .12 .30
250 Sergei Fedorov .30 .75
251 Vyacheslav Kozlov .12 .30
252 Brendan Shanahan .25 .60
253 Kevin Hodson RC .20 .50
254 Greg Johnson .12 .30
255 Tomas Holmstrom RC .60 1.50
256 Curtis Joseph .20 .50
257 Dean McAmmond .12 .30
258 Ryan Smyth .15 .40
259 Mike Grier RC .25 .60
260 Miroslav Satan .12 .30
261 Rem Murray RC .20 .50
262 Rob Niedermayer .15 .40
263 Ray Sheppard .15 .40
264 Dave Lowry .12 .30
265 Scott Mellanby .15 .40
266 Rhett Warrener .12 .30
267 Per Gustafsson RC .20 .50
268 Paul Coffey .20 .50
269 Nelson Emerson .12 .30
270 Kevin Dineen .12 .30
271 Keith Primeau .12 .30
272 Hnat Domenichelli .12 .30
273 Ray Ferraro .12 .30
274 Stephane Fiset .15 .40
275 Kai Nurminen RC .20 .50
276 Dan Bylsma RC .20 .50
277 Mattias Norstrom .12 .30
278 Rob Blake .20 .50
279 Jose Theodore .25 .60
280 Martin Rucinsky .12 .30
281 Darcy Tucker .12 .30
282 David Wilkie .12 .30
283 Valeri Bure .12 .30
284 Steve Thomas .12 .30
285 Brian Rolston .15 .40
286 Scott Stevens .20 .50
287 Shawn Chambers .12 .30
288 Denis Pederson .12 .30
289 Lyle Odelein .12 .30
290 Travis Green .15 .40
291 Todd Bertuzzi .20 .50
292 Niclas Andersson .12 .30
293 Darius Kasparaitis .12 .30
294 Bryan Berard .20 .50
295 Daniel Goneau RC .20 .50
296 Christian Dube .12 .30
297 Adam Graves .12 .30
298 Sergei Nemchinov .12 .30
299 Mark Messier .30 .75
300 Brian Leetch .20 .50
301 Radek Bonk .12 .30
302 Alexandre Daigle .12 .30
303 Andreas Dackell RC .20 .50
304 Steve Duchesne .12 .30
305 Wade Redden .12 .30
306 Eric Lindros .30 .75
307 Mikael Renberg .15 .40
308 Shjon Podein .12 .30
309 Dainius Zubrus RC .25 .60
310 Janne Niinimaa .20 .50
311 Karl Dykhuis .12 .30
312 Jeremy Roenick .30 .75
313 Keith Tkachuk .20 .50
314 Shane Doan .15 .40
315 Cliff Ronning .12 .30
316 Mike Gartner .20 .50
317 Dave Manson .12 .30
318 Shawn Antoski .12 .30
319 Kevin Hatcher .12 .30
320 Jaromir Jagr .50 1.25
321 Mario Lemieux .75 2.00
322 Bryan Smolinski .12 .30
323 Stefan Bergkvist RC .20 .50
324 Brett Hull 1.00 2.50
325 Joe Murphy .12 .30
326 Stephane Matteau .12 .30
327 Geoff Courtnall .12 .30
328 Jim Campbell .12 .30
329 Harry York RC .20 .50
330 Kelly Hrudey .15 .40
331 Al Iafrate .12 .30
332 Jeff Friesen .12 .30
333 Darren Turcotte .12 .30
334 Bernie Nicholls .12 .30
335 Ville Peltonen .12 .30
336 Dino Ciccarelli .20 .50
337 Chris Gratton .15 .40
338 Daren Puppa .15 .40
339 Alexander Selivanov .12 .30
340 Daymond Langkow .15 .40
341 Felix Potvin .20 .50
342 Wendel Clark .15 .40
343 Mathieu Schneider .12 .30
344 Dave Ellet .12 .30
345 Fredrik Modin RC .50 1.25
346 Sergei Berezin RC .30 .75
347 Pavel Bure .25 .60
348 Kirk McLean .15 .40
349 Mike Sillinger .12 .30
350 Russ Courtnall .12 .30
351 Scott Walker .12 .30
352 Esa Tikkanen .12 .30
353 Pat Peake .12 .30
354 Olaf Kolzig .20 .50
355 Michal Pivonka .12 .30
356 Richard Zednik RC .25 .60
357 Phil Housley .15 .40
358 Anson Carter .15 .40
359 Eric Daze OII .15 .40
360 Felix Potvin OII .20 .50
361 Wayne Gretzky OII 1.00 2.50
362 Ed Jovanovski OII .15 .40
363 Mike Modano OII .30 .75
364 Peter Bondra OII .15 .40
365 Patrick Roy OII .50 1.25
366 Ray Bourque OII .30 .75
367 Roman Hamrlik OII .15 .40
368 John LeClair OII .20 .50
369 Adam Colagiacomo RC .20 .50
370 Joe Thornton RC 5.00 12.00
371 Patrick Desrochers RC .20 .50
372 Pierre-Luc Therrien RC .20 .50
373 Nick Boynton RC .20 .50
374 Andrew Ference RC .20 .50
375 Jean-Francois Fortin RC .20 .50
376 Daniel Tetrault RC .20 .50
377 Luc Theoret RC .20 .50
378 Mike Van Ryn RC .20 .50
379 Scott Barney RC .20 .50
380 Harold Druken RC .20 .50
381 Dylan Gyori RC .20 .50
382 Chris Heron RC .20 .50
383 Chad Hinz RC .20 .50
384 Patrick Marleau RC 3.00 8.00
385 Serge Payer RC .20 .50
386 Jeremy Reich RC .20 .50
387 Daniel Tkaczuk RC .20 .50
388 Jason Ward RC .20 .50
389 Checklist (211-298) .10 .25
390 Checklist (299-390) .10 .25
HK1 Wayne Gretzky 1.00 2.50

1996-97 Upper Deck Game Jerseys

Inserted 1:2500 packs, these highly popular inserts featured swatches of actual game-worn jerseys as part of the card stock. Five cards were inserted in series one packs, while the remaining eight cards were distributed with series two.

*MULT.COLOR SWATCH: .6X TO 1.5X
GJ1 Steve Yzerman 100.00 200.00
GJ2 Brett Hull 80.00 150.00
GJ3 Doug Gilmour 50.00 120.00
GJ4 Jaromir Jagr 80.00 200.00
GJ5 Ray Bourque 60.00 150.00
GJ6 Mario Lemieux 150.00 300.00
GJ7 John Vanbiesbrouck 50.00 120.00
GJ8 Eric Lindros 50.00 120.00
GJ9 Mike Modano 50.00 100.00
GJ10 Pavel Bure 80.00 150.00
GJ11 Mark Messier 50.00 120.00
GJ12 Theo Fleury 50.00 120.00
GJ13 Mats Sundin UER 30.00 80.00

1996-97 Upper Deck Generation Next

Randomly inserted in packs at a rate of 1:4, this double-fronted, series two insert paired up two top players on each card. Both sides were enhanced with silver and gold foil.

COMPLETE SET (40) 25.00 60.00
X1 P.Kariya/W.Gretzky 5.00 12.00
X2 T.Linden/P.Forsberg 1.50 4.00
X3 J.Sakic/R.Niedermayer 1.25 3.00
X4 C.O'Sullivan/E.Weinrich .40 1.00
X5 J.Thibault/P.Roy 3.00 8.00
X6 B.Hull/D.Alfredsson 1.25 3.00
X7 C.Osgood/J.Vanbiesbrouck .75 2.00
X8 R.Bourque/R.Hamrlik 1.25 3.00
X9 P.Coffey/S.Ozolinsh 1.25 3.00
X10 D.Gilmour/S.Fedorov 1.25 3.00
X11 C.Chelios/E.Jovanovski 1.25 3.00
X12 J.Arnott/J.Roenick 1.25 3.00
X13 D.Weight/S.Yzerman 3.00 8.00
X14 B.Shanahan/T.Bertuzzi 1.25 3.00
X15 W.Clark/K.Tkachuk 1.25 3.00
X16 S.Koivu/T.Selanne 1.25 3.00
X17 J.Jagr/Z.Palffy 1.25 3.00
X18 E.Belfour/M.Brodeur 1.50 4.00
X19 E.Daze/O.Nolan .75 2.00
X20 V.Kamensky/V.Yachmenev .40 1.00
X21 J.Iginla/M.Modano 1.50 4.00
X22 A.Eriksson/N.Lidstrom 1.25 3.00
X23 B.Leetch/B.Berard 1.25 3.00
X24 J.Kurri/N.Sundstrom .40 1.00
X25 A.Deadmarsh/S.Mellanby .40 1.00
X26 P.Bondra/P.Sykora .40 1.00
X27 C.Joseph/E.Fichaud 1.25 3.00
X28 D.Hasek/R.Turek 2.00 5.00
X29 A.Mogilny/V.Bure .40 1.00
X30 D.Langkow/T.Fleury .40 1.00
X31 B.Nicholls/S.Berezin .75 2.00
X32 C.Gratton/R.Tocchet .75 2.00
X33 F.Potvin/G.Fuhr 1.25 3.00
X34 K.Primeau/K.Stevens .40 1.00
X35 R.Blake/W.Redden .40 1.00
X36 C.Pronger/S.Stevens .75 2.00
X37 G.Suter/K.McLaren .40 1.00
X38 J.Hoglund/M.Sundin .75 2.00
X39 L.Murphy/S.Zubov .40 1.00
X40 A.Oates/J.Juneau .75 2.00

1996-97 Upper Deck Hart Hopefuls Bronze

Randomly inserted in packs at a rate of 1:30, this series two-only insert consisted of twenty players vying for the title of league MVP and the chance to take home the Hart Trophy. Cards were numbered "One of 5000" on the back. Silver and gold parallels were also created. Silver were inserted at 1:150 and only 1000 were printed. Gold were inserted at 1:1500 and only 100 were produced.

COMPLETE SET (20) 20.00 50.00
SILVER/1000: 1X TO 2.5X BRONZE
*GOLD/100: 4X TO 10X BRONZE
HH1 Wayne Gretzky 5.00 12.00
HH2 Mark Messier 1.50 4.00
HH3 Eric Lindros 2.00 5.00
HH4 Sergei Fedorov 2.50 6.00
HH5 Saku Koivu 1.25 3.00
HH6 John Vanbiesbrouck 1.50 4.00
HH7 Peter Forsberg 1.50 4.00
HH8 Keith Tkachuk 1.25 3.00
HH9 Paul Kariya 1.25 3.00
HH10 Martin Brodeur 2.50 6.00
HH11 Patrick Roy 3.00 8.00
HH12 Alexander Mogilny 1.25 3.00
HH13 Brett Hull 1.50 4.00
HH14 Pavel Bure 2.00 5.00
HH15 Teemu Selanne 1.50 4.00
HH16 Mario Lemieux 4.00 10.00
HH17 Jeremy Roenick 1.50 4.00
HH18 Jaromir Jagr 2.00 5.00
HH19 Steve Yzerman 3.00 8.00
HH20 Joe Sakic 2.00 5.00

1996-97 Upper Deck Lord Stanley's Heroes Quarterfinals

Randomly inserted in series one packs at a rate of 1:37, this 20-card set featured numbered inserts (one of 5,000) on cel chrome technology. A player's head photo was displayed on acetate in the middle of the trophy. Semifinals and finals parallel variations were also produced and inserted randomly. Semifinals parallels were inserted at 1:185 and only 1000 sets were produced. Finals parallels were inserted at 1:1850 and only 100 sets were produced.

COMPLETE SET (20) 30.00 80.00
*FINALS/100: 5X TO 12X QUARTER/5000
*SEMIFINAL/1000: 1X TO 2.5X QUART/5000
LS1 Wayne Gretzky 8.00 20.00
LS2 Mark Messier 3.00 8.00
LS3 Mario Lemieux 6.00 15.00
LS4 Jaromir Jagr 3.00 8.00
LS5 Martin Brodeur 5.00 12.00

LS6 Patrick Roy 6.00 15.00
LS7 Joe Sakic 4.00 10.00
LS8 Peter Forsberg 3.00 8.00
LS9 Theo Fleury 2.50 6.00
LS10 Paul Coffey 2.00 5.00
LS11 Doug Gilmour 2.00 5.00
LS12 Paul Kariya 2.00 5.00
LS13 Eric Lindros 3.00 8.00
LS14 Sergei Fedorov 2.50 6.00
LS15 Eric Daze 1.50 4.00
LS16 Teemu Selanne 2.50 6.00
LS17 Keith Tkachuk 2.00 5.00
LS18 Pavel Bure 2.50 6.00
LS19 Mats Sundin 2.50 6.00
LS20 Saku Koivu 2.00 5.00

1996-97 Upper Deck Power Performers

Randomly inserted in series two packs at a rate of 1:13, these cards featured a layered design on gold foil. Thirty of the league's toughest physical competitors were highlighted in the set.

COMPLETE SET (30) 15.00 40.00
P1 Brendan Shanahan 1.50 4.00
P2 Mikael Renberg .40 1.00
P3 John LeClair .75 2.00
P4 Keith Primeau .40 1.00
P5 Adam Graves .40 1.00
P6 Jason Arnott .40 1.00
P7 Todd Bertuzzi .75 2.00
P8 Ed Jovanovski .40 1.00
P9 Scott Stevens .40 1.00
P10 Chris Gratton .40 1.00
P11 Bill Guerin .40 1.00
P12 Vladimir Konstantinov .75 2.00
P13 Mike Grier .40 1.00
P14 Theo Fleury .75 2.00
P15 Chris Chelios .75 2.00
P16 Trevor Linden .75 2.00
P17 Claude Lemieux .40 1.00
P18 Owen Nolan .75 2.00
P19 Jarome Iginla 3.00 8.00
P20 Joe Nieuwendyk .75 2.00
P21 Kevin Hatcher .40 1.00
P22 Dino Ciccarelli .40 1.00
P23 Adam Deadmarsh .40 1.00
P24 Chris Pronger .75 2.00
P25 Mike Ricci .40 1.00
P26 Rod Brind'Amour .75 2.00
P27 Derian Hatcher .40 1.00
P28 Mats Sundin 1.50 4.00
P29 Doug Gilmour .75 2.00
P30 Todd Harvey .40 1.00

1996-97 Upper Deck Superstar Showdown

Randomly inserted in first series packs at a rate of 1:4, this 60-card set featured 30 different one-on-one match-ups of the NHL's top stars. Each of the card fronts displayed a single player photo with a die-cut design that enabled the cards to be matched together in pairs.

COMPLETE SET (60) 30.00 80.00
SS1A Pavel Bure .60 1.50
SS1B Paul Kariya .60 1.50
SS2A Patrick Roy 3.00 8.00
SS2B John Vanbiesbrouck .40 1.00
SS3A Eric Lindros .60 1.50
SS3B Ed Jovanovski .40 1.00
SS4A Theo Fleury .40 1.00
SS4B Doug Gilmour .40 1.00
SS5A Wayne Gretzky 4.00 10.00
SS5B Mario Lemieux 3.00 8.00
SS6A Keith Tkachuk .60 1.50
SS6B Brendan Shanahan .60 1.50
SS7A Ray Bourque 1.00 2.50
SS7B Brian Leetch .60 1.50
SS8A Peter Forsberg 1.00 2.50
SS8B Sergei Fedorov .60 1.50
SS9A Mark Messier .60 1.50
SS9B Scott Stevens .40 1.00
SS10A Teemu Selanne .60 1.50
SS10B Alexander Mogilny .40 1.00
SS11A Felix Potvin .60 1.50
SS11B Jocelyn Thibault .60 1.50
SS12A Martin Brodeur 1.50 4.00
SS12B Eric Fichaud .40 1.00
SS13A Roman Hamrlik .40 1.00
SS13B Jaromir Jagr 1.00 2.50
SS14A Jim Carey .60 1.50
SS14B Saku Koivu .60 1.50
SS15A Jeremy Roenick .75 2.00
SS15B Brett Hull .75 2.00
SS16A Joe Sakic 1.25 3.00
SS16B Steve Yzerman 3.00 8.00
SS17A Doug Weight .40 1.00
SS17B Pat LaFontaine .60 1.50
SS18A Daniel Alfredsson .40 1.00
SS18B Eric Daze .40 1.00
SS19A Mike Modano .75 2.00
SS19B Jason Arnott .15 .40
SS20A Paul Coffey .60 1.50
SS20B Sandis Ozolinsh .15 .40
SS21A Zigmund Palffy .40 1.00
SS21B Petr Sykora .15 .40
SS22A Ed Belfour .60 1.50
SS22B Ron Hextall .40 1.00
SS23A Mats Sundin .60 1.50
SS23B Mikael Renberg .40 1.00
SS24A Vitali Yachmenev .15 .40
SS24B Alexei Zhamnov .40 1.00
SS25A Oleg Tverdovsky .40 1.00
SS25B Kyle McLaren .15 .40
SS26A Dominik Hasek 1.25 3.00
SS26B Petr Nedved .40 1.00
SS27A Chris Chelios .60 1.50
SS27B Chris Pronger .40 1.00
SS28A Rob Niedermayer .40 1.00
SS28B Scott Niedermayer .15 .40
SS29A Keith Primeau .15 .40
SS29B Bob Probert .40 1.00
SS30A Bill Ranford .40 1.00
SS30B Chris Osgood .40 1.00

1997-98 Upper Deck

The 1997-98 Upper Deck set was issued in two series totaling 420 cards and was distributed in 12-card packs with a suggested retail price of $2.49. The fronts feature color player photos, while the backs carry player information and career statistics. Series 1 contains the following subsets: Star Rookie (181-195), Fan Favorites (196-208) and two checklists (209-210). Series 2 contains the following subsets: Physical Force (389-398), Program of Excellence (399-418) and two checklists (419-420). Card #229 was not printed. Two card number #239 were printed.

COMPLETE SET (420) 30.00 80.00
COMP.SERIES 1 (210) 10.00 20.00
COMP.SERIES 2 (210) 15.00 40.00
1 Teemu Selanne .30 .75
2 Steve Rucchin .12 .30
3 Kevin Todd .10 .25
4 Darren Van Impe .12 .30
5 Mark Janssens .12 .30
6 Guy Hebert .12 .30
7 Sean Pronger .10 .25
8 Jason Allison .12 .30
9 Ray Bourque .25 .60
10 Landon Wilson .10 .25
11 Anson Carter .10 .25
12 Jean-Yves Roy .10 .25
13 Kyle McLaren .10 .25
14 Don Sweeney .10 .25
15 Brian Holzinger .12 .30
16 Matthew Barnaby .12 .30
17 Wayne Primeau .12 .30
18 Steve Shields RC .15 .40
19 Jason Dawe .12 .30
20 Donald Audette .12 .30
21 Dixon Ward .12 .30
22 Hnat Domenichelli .12 .30
23 Trevor Kidd .10 .25
24 Jarome Iginla .15 .40
25 Sandy McCarthy .10 .25
26 Marty McInnis .10 .25
27 Jonas Hoglund .12 .30
28 Aaron Gavey .10 .25
29 Keith Primeau .12 .30
30 Geoff Sanderson .12 .30
31 Sean Burke .10 .25
32 Steven Rice .12 .30
33 Stu Grimson .12 .30
34 Jeff O'Neill .12 .30
35 Curtis Leschyshyn .10 .25
36 Chris Chelios .15 .40
37 Sergei Krivokrasov .10 .25
38 Jeff Hackett .10 .25
39 Bob Probert .10 .25
40 Chris Terreri .10 .25
41 Eric Daze .10 .25
42 Alexei Zhamnov .10 .25
43 Patrick Roy .40 1.00
44 Sandis Ozolinsh .12 .30
45 Eric Messier RC .15 .40
46 Adam Deadmarsh .10 .25
47 Claude Lemieux .12 .30
48 Mike Ricci .12 .30
49 Stephane Yelle .10 .25
50 Joe Nieuwendyk .15 .40
51 Derian Hatcher .12 .30
52 Jere Lehtinen .12 .30
53 Roman Turek .12 .30
54 Darryl Sydor .10 .25
55 Todd Harvey .12 .30
56 Mike Modano .25 .60
57 Steve Yzerman .30 .75
58 Martin Lapointe .10 .25
59 Darren McCarty .12 .30
60 Mike Vernon .12 .30
61 Kirk Maltby .10 .25
62 Kris Draper .10 .25
63 Vladimir Konstantinov .10 .25
64 Todd Marchant .12 .30
65 Doug Weight .15 .40
66 Jason Arnott .12 .30
67 Mike Grier .12 .30
68 Mats Lindgren .10 .25
69 Bryan Marchment .15 .40
70 Rem Murray .10 .25
71 Radek Dvorak .12 .30
72 John Vanbiesbrouck .15 .40
73 Robert Svehla .12 .30
74 Bill Lindsay .12 .30
75 Paul Laus .12 .30
76 Kirk Muller .10 .25
77 Dave Nemirovsky .10 .25
78 Roman Vopat .12 .30
79 Jan Vopat .10 .25
80 Dimitri Khristich .12 .30
81 Glen Murray .10 .25
82 Mattias Norstrom .12 .30
83 Ian Laperriere .10 .25
84 Mark Recchi .20 .50
85 Jose Theodore .15 .40
86 Vincent Damphousse .12 .30
87 Sebastien Bordeleau .12 .30
88 Darcy Tucker .15 .40
89 Martin Rucinsky .12 .30
90 Jocelyn Thibault .10 .25
91 Doug Gilmour .20 .50
92 Brian Rolston .12 .30
93 Jay Pandolfo .12 .30
94 John MacLean .10 .25
95 Scott Stevens .15 .40
96 Dave Andreychuk .15 .40
97 Denis Pederson .10 .25
98 Bryan Berard .10 .25
99 Zigmund Palffy .15 .40
100 Bryan McCabe .10 .25
101 Rich Pilon .12 .30
102 Eric Fichaud .12 .30
103 Todd Bertuzzi .15 .40
104 Robert Reichel .12 .30
105 Christian Dube .12 .30
106 Niklas Sundstrom .12 .30
107 Mike Richter .15 .40
108 Adam Graves .10 .25
109 Wayne Gretzky .75 2.00
110 Bruce Driver .12 .30
111 Esa Tikkanen .10 .25
112 Daniel Alfredsson .15 .40
113 Ron Tugnutt .15 .40
114 Steve Duchesne .10 .25
115 Bruce Gardiner RC .12 .30
116 Sergei Zholtok .12 .30
117 Alexandre Daigle .10 .25
118 Wade Redden .10 .25
119 Mikael Renberg .12 .30
120 Trent Klatt .12 .30
121 Rod Brind'Amour .15 .40
122 Dainius Zubrus .12 .30
123 John LeClair .15 .40
124 Janne Niinimaa .12 .30
125 Vaclav Prospal RC .12 .30
126 Keith Tkachuk .15 .40
127 Jeremy Roenick .20 .50
128 Mike Gartner .15 .40
129 Nikolai Khabibulin .15 .40
130 Chad Kilger .12 .30
131 Shane Doan .12 .30
132 Cliff Ronning .10 .25
133 Patrick Lalime .12 .30
134 Greg Johnson .10 .25
135 Ron Francis .20 .50
136 Darius Kasparaitis .12 .30
137 Petr Nedved .15 .40
138 Jason Woolley .12 .30
139 Fredrik Olausson .12 .30
140 Harry York .12 .30
141 Brett Hull .20 .50
142 Chris Pronger .12 .30
143 Jim Campbell .10 .25
144 Libor Zabransky RC .10 .25
145 Grant Fuhr .15 .40
146 Pavol Demitra .20 .50
147 Owen Nolan .15 .40
148 Stephen Guolla RC .10 .25
149 Marcus Ragnarsson .10 .25
150 Bernie Nicholls .12 .30
151 Todd Gill .12 .30
152 Shean Donovan .12 .30
153 Corey Schwab .12 .30
154 Dino Ciccarelli .15 .40
155 Chris Gratton .10 .25
156 Alexander Selivanov .10 .25
157 Roman Hamrlik .12 .30
158 Daymond Langkow .10 .25
159 Paul Ysebaert .12 .30
160 Steve Sullivan .12 .30
161 Sergei Berezin .12 .30
162 Fredrik Modin .12 .30
163 Todd Warriner .12 .30
164 Wendel Clark .15 .40
165 Jason Podollan .12 .30
166 Darby Hendrickson .10 .25
167 Martin Gelinas .10 .25
168 Pavel Bure .20 .50
169 Trevor Linden .12 .30
170 Mike Sillinger .10 .25
171 Corey Hirsch .12 .30
172 Lonny Bohonos .12 .30
173 Markus Naslund .12 .30
174 Steve Konowalchuk .12 .30
175 Dale Hunter .12 .30
176 Joe Juneau .12 .30
177 Adam Oates .15 .40
178 Bill Ranford .12 .30
179 Pat Peake .12 .30
180 Sergei Gonchar .10 .25
181 Mike Leclerc RC .20 .50
182 Randy Robitaille RC .20 .50
183 Paxton Schafer RC .10 .25
184 Rumun Ndur RC .15 .40
185 Christian Laflamme RC .15 .40
186 Wade Belak RC .15 .40
187 Mike Knuble RC .15 .40
188 Steve Kelly .12 .30
189 Patrik Elias RC 1.50 4.00
190 Ken Belanger RC .15 .40
191 Colin Forbes RC .15 .40
192 Juha Ylonen .12 .30
193 David Cooper RC .15 .40
194 D.J. Smith RC .15 .40
195 Jaroslav Svejkovsky .12 .30
196 Tie Domi .15 .40
197 Bob Probert .10 .25
198 Doug Gilmour .20 .50
199 Dino Ciccarelli .15 .40
200 Martin Gelinas .10 .25
201 Tony Twist .12 .30
202 Claude Lemieux .12 .30
203 Vladimir Konstantinov .10 .25
204 Ulf Samuelsson .15 .40
205 Chris Simon .12 .30
206 Gino Odjick .12 .30
207 Mike Grier .12 .30
208 Tony Amonte .12 .30
209 Wayne Gretzky CL .75 2.00
210 Patrick Roy CL .40 1.00
211 Paul Kariya .20 .50
212 J.J. Daigneault .12 .30
213 Dmitri Mironov .12 .30
214 Joe Sacco .12 .30
215 Richard Park .10 .25
216 Espen Knutsen RC .15 .40
217 Dave Karpa .10 .25
218 Joe Thornton .15 .40
219 Sergei Samsonov .10 .25
220 P.J. Axelsson RC .15 .40
221 Ted Donato .10 .25
222 Dean Chynoweth .12 .30
223 Rob Tallas RC .15 .40
224 Mattias Timander .12 .30
225 Dominik Hasek .25 .60
226 Erik Rasmussen .12 .30
227 Mike Peca .12 .30
228 Rob Ray .10 .25
239B Vaclav Varada .10 .25
230 Curtis Brown .10 .25
231 Jay McKee .10 .25
232 Theo Fleury .20 .50
233 Derek Morris RC .15 .40
234 Chris Dingman RC .15 .40
235 Chris O'Sullivan .12 .30
236 Rick Tabaracci .12 .30
237 Tommy Albelin .12 .30
238 Todd Simpson .12 .30
239A Sami Kapanen .12 .30
240 Gary Roberts .12 .30
241 Kevin Dineen .12 .30
242 Kevin Haller .12 .30
243 Nelson Emerson .12 .30
244 Glen Wesley .10 .25
245 Tony Amonte .12 .30
246 Eric Weinrich .10 .25
247 Daniel Cleary .12 .30
248 Jeff Shantz .12 .30
249 Jean-Yves Leroux RC .15 .40
250 Ethan Moreau .10 .25
251 Craig Mills .10 .25
252 Peter Forsberg .20 .50
253 Joe Sakic .25 .60
254 Valeri Kamensky .12 .30
255 Adam Foote .10 .25
256 Josef Marha .10 .25
257 Christian Matte RC .15 .40
258 Aaron Miller .10 .25
259 Ed Belfour .15 .40
260 Jamie Langenbrunner .12 .30
261 Juha Lind RC .15 .40
262 Pat Verbeek .12 .30
263 Sergei Zubov .12 .30
264 Dave Reid .10 .25
265 Greg Adams .12 .30
266 Sergei Fedorov .25 .60
267 Nicklas Lidstrom .15 .40
268 Brendan Shanahan .20 .50
269 Chris Osgood .15 .40
270 Aaron Ward .10 .25
271 Vyacheslav Kozlov .12 .30
272 Kevin Hodson .12 .30
273 Curtis Joseph .15 .40
274 Ryan Smyth .12 .30
275 Dean McAmmond .10 .25
276 Boris Mironov .10 .25
277 Dennis Bonvie .10 .25
278 Kelly Buchberger .12 .30
279 Kevin Lowe .10 .25
280 Ray Sheppard .12 .30
281 Rob Niedermayer .10 .25
282 Scott Mellanby .12 .30
283 Terry Carkner .12 .30
284 Ed Jovanovski .10 .25
285 Gord Murphy .10 .25
286 Tom Fitzgerald .10 .25
287 Jamie Storr .12 .30
288 Olli Jokinen RC .20 .50
289 Vladimir Tsyplakov .12 .30
290 Luc Robitaille .15 .40
291 Vitali Yachmenev .12 .30
292 Donald MacLean RC .15 .40
293 Saku Koivu .15 .40
294 Andy Moog .15 .40
295 Patrice Brisebois .12 .30
296 Brad Brown RC .15 .40
297 Turner Stevenson .12 .30
298 Shayne Corson .10 .25
299 Brian Savage .10 .25
300 Martin Brodeur .30 .75
301 Scott Niedermayer .15 .40
302 Krzysztof Oliwa RC .15 .40
303 Valeri Zelepukin .12 .30
304 Bobby Holik .10 .25
305 Ken Daneyko .12 .30
306 Lyle Odelein .10 .25
307 Travis Green .12 .30
308 Steve Webb RC .15 .40
309 Dan Plante .12 .30
310 Bryan Smolinski .12 .30
311 Claude Lapointe .12 .30
312 Kenny Jonsson .12 .30
313 Ulf Samuelsson .15 .40
314 Jeff Beukeboom .12 .30
315 Mike Keane .10 .25
316 Brian Leetch .15 .40
317 Shane Chrula .12 .30
318 Pat LaFontaine .15 .40
319 Alexei Kovalev .10 .25
320 Radek Bonk .10 .25
321 Alexei Yashin .12 .30
322 Damian Rhodes .12 .30
323 Andreas Dackell .12 .30
324 Magnus Arvedson RC .15 .40
325 Chris Phillips .12 .30
326 Marian Hossa RC 3.00 8.00
327 Chris Gratton .10 .25
328 Shjon Podein .10 .25
329 Paul Coffey .15 .40
330 Luke Richardson .10 .25
331 Eric Lindros .25 .60
332 Eric Desjardins .10 .25
333 Joel Otto .10 .25
334 Craig Janney .10 .25
335 Oleg Tverdovsky .12 .30
336 Teppo Numminen .12 .30
337 Jim McKenzie .12 .30
338 Dallas Drake .12 .30
339 Rick Tocchet .10 .25
340 Brad Isbister .12 .30
341 Alexei Morozov .12 .30
342 Jaromir Jagr .40 1.00
343 Kevin Hatcher .10 .25
344 Ken Wregget .10 .25
345 Chris Tamer .10 .25
346 Robert Dome .10 .25
347 Neil Wilkinson .10 .25
348 Chris McAlpine .10 .25
349 Joe Murphy .12 .30
350 Robert Petrovicky .12 .30
351 Marc Bergevin .12 .30
352 Al MacInnis .15 .40
353 Pierre Turgeon .15 .40
354 Patrick Marleau .20 .50
355 Marco Sturm RC .15 .40
356 Mike Vernon .12 .30
357 Al Iafrate .12 .30
358 Jeff Friesen .12 .30
359 Viktor Kozlov .12 .30
360 Tony Granato .12 .30
361 Mikael Renberg .12 .30
362 Daren Puppa .12 .30
363 Roman Hamrlik .12 .30
364 Rob Zamuner .10 .25
365 Cory Cross .10 .25
366 Patrick Poulin .10 .25
367 Felix Potvin .15 .40
368 Tie Domi .15 .40
369 Mats Sundin .15 .40
370 Jeff Ware .10 .25
371 Alyn McCauley .12 .30
372 Mathieu Schneider .12 .30
373 Craig Wolanin .12 .30
374 Mark Messier .25 .60
375 Kirk McLean .12 .30
376 Donald Brashear .12 .30
377 Arturs Irbe .12 .30
378 Jyrki Lumme .12 .30
379 Gino Odjick .12 .30
380 Mattias Ohlund .12 .30
381 Jan Bulis RC .15 .40
382 Andrew Brunette .12 .30
383 Calle Johansson .12 .30
384 Brendan Witt .12 .30
385 Mark Tinordi .12 .30
386 Ken Klee .12 .30
387 Chris Simon .12 .30
388 Richard Zednik .12 .30
389 Ed Jovanovski .10 .25
390 Darren McCarty .12 .30
391 Darius Kasparaitis .12 .30
392 Bryan Marchment .15 .40
393 Matthew Barnaby .12 .30
394 Chris Chelios .15 .40
395 Ulf Samuelsson .15 .40
396 Scott Stevens .15 .40
397 Derian Hatcher .12 .30
398 Chris Pronger .12 .30
399 Mathieu Chouinard RC .15 .40
400 Jake McCracken RC .20 .50
401 Bryan Allen RC .15 .40
402 Christian Chartier RC .20 .50
403 Jonathan Girard RC .15 .40
404 Abe Herbst RC .15 .40
405 Stephen Peat RC .15 .40
406 Robyn Regehr RC .15 .40
407 Blair Betts RC .15 .40
408 Eric Chouinard RC .20 .50
409 Brett DeCecco RC .15 .40
410 Rico Fata RC .20 .50
411 Simon Gagne RC 2.50 6.00
412 Vincent Lecavalier RC 3.00 8.00
413 Manny Malhotra RC .20 .50
414 Norm Milley RC .20 .50
415 Justin Papineau RC .20 .50
416 Garrett Prosofsky RC .15 .40
417 Mike Ribeiro RC .60 1.50
418 Brad Richards RC 1.50 4.00
419 Wayne Gretzky CL .75 2.00
420 Patrick Roy CL .40 1.00

1997-98 Upper Deck Jumbos 3x5

Inserted as box-toppers or in special retail packs, these oversized cards resembled the base set but were approximately 3 1/2" x 5". Cards were numbered X of 10. The suffixes below are for checklisting only and designate whether the cards were available in series 1 (A) or series 2 (B) packs.

COMPLETE SET (20) 15.00 40.00
1A Wayne Gretzky 4.00 10.00
2A Steve Yzerman 3.00 8.00
3A Bryan Berard .40 1.00
4A Owen Nolan .40 1.00
5A Pavel Bure .60 1.50
6A Patrick Roy 3.00 8.00
7A Teemu Selanne .60 1.50
8A Brett Hull .75 2.00
9A Keith Tkachuk .60 1.50
10A John Vanbiesbrouck .40 1.00
1B Paul Kariya .60 1.50
2B Joe Thornton 1.50 4.00
3B Joe Sakic 1.25 3.00
4B Martin Brodeur 1.50 4.00
5B Slava Kozlov .40 1.00
6B Mark Messier .60 1.50
7B Jaromir Jagr 1.00 2.50
8B Eric Lindros .60 1.50
9B Peter Forsberg 1.50 4.00
10B Sergei Samsonov .40 1.00

1997-98 Upper Deck Jumbos 5x7

Inserted as box-toppers in various distribution forms of Upper Deck, these oversized cards resembled the base set but were approximately 5" x 7". Cards were numbered "X of 5" (the suffixes below are for checklisting only).

COMPLETE SET (14) 10.00 25.00
1A Mark Messier .60 1.50
1B Patrick Roy 3.00 8.00
1C Paul Kariya .75 2.00
2A Jaromir Jagr 1.50 4.00
2B Teemu Selanne 1.25 3.00
3A Joe Sakic 1.25 3.00
3B Eric Lindros 1.00 2.50
4A Peter Forsberg 1.50 4.00
4B Martin Brodeur 1.50 4.00
4C Keith Tkachuk .75 2.00
5A Sergei Samsonov .60 1.50
5B Pavel Bure 1.25 3.00
5C Slava Kozlov .60 1.50
5D John Vanbiesbrouck .60 1.50

1997-98 Upper Deck Game Dated Moments Parallel

Randomly inserted in packs at the rate of 1:1500, this 60-card set features color player photos of their top moments of last year and printed on 24 pt. embossed Light F/X cards. The set is skip numbered. It is important to note that these cards are printed on card stock that is approximately 3X thicker than the base set and carry silver foil highlights that distinguish them from the base set cards that also carry the Game Dated stamp.

*GAME DATED: 60X TO 150X BASIC CARDS

1997-98 Upper Deck Game Jerseys

Randomly inserted in packs at the rate of 1:2,500, this 15-card set features color player photos with an actual piece of the player's game-worn jersey embedded in the card. Patrick Roy autographed 33 cards inserted in Series 1 packs, and Wayne Gretzky signed 99 cards containing remnants of his 1997 All-Star Game jersey inserted in Series 2 packs.

GJ1 Patrick Roy HOME 100.00 250.00
GJ2 Patrick Roy AWAY 125.00 300.00
GJ3 Dominik Hasek 50.00 125.00
GJ4 Jarome Iginla 40.00 100.00
GJ5 Sergei Fedorov 40.00 100.00
GJ6 Tony Amonte 20.00 50.00
GJ7 Joe Sakic 40.00 100.00
GJ8 Wayne Gretzky 150.00 400.00
GJ9 Saku Koivu 15.00 40.00
GJ11 Mike Richter 15.00 40.00
GJ12 Doug Weight 12.00 30.00
GJ13 Brendan Shanahan 20.00 50.00
GJ14 Brian Leetch 15.00 40.00
GJ1AU Patrick Roy AU/33 350.00 600.00
GJ8AU Wayne Gretzky AU/99 400.00 800.00

1997-98 Upper Deck Sixth Sense Masters

Randomly inserted in Series 2 packs, this 30-card set features color photos of the NHL's brightest stars. Only 2,000 of each card were produced and are sequentially numbered. A holographic die-cut parallel version labeled "Wizards" was alos produced and limited to 100 copies each.

COMPLETE SET (30) 125.00 250.00
*WIZARD/100: 2.5X TO 6X BASIC INSERTS
SS1 Wayne Gretzky 12.50 30.00
SS2 Jaromir Jagr 5.00 12.00
SS3 Sergei Fedorov 4.00 10.00
SS4 Brett Hull 4.00 10.00
SS5 Brian Leetch 2.00 5.00
SS6 Joe Thornton 5.00 12.00
SS7 Ray Bourque 4.00 10.00
SS8 Teemu Selanne 3.00 8.00
SS9 Paul Kariya 3.00 8.00
SS10 Doug Weight 2.00 5.00
SS11 Mark Messier 3.00 8.00
SS12 Adam Oates 2.00 5.00
SS13 Mats Sundin 3.00 8.00
SS14 Brendan Shanahan 3.00 8.00
SS15 Saku Koivu 3.00 8.00
SS16 Doug Gilmour 2.00 5.00
SS17 Eric Lindros 3.00 8.00
SS18 Tony Amonte 2.00 5.00
SS19 Joe Sakic 6.00 15.00
SS20 Steve Yzerman 10.00 25.00
SS21 Peter Forsberg 5.00 12.00
SS22 Geoff Sanderson 2.00 5.00
SS23 Keith Tkachuk 2.00 5.00
SS24 Pavel Bure 4.00 10.00
SS25 Ron Francis 2.00 5.00
SS26 Zigmund Palffy 2.00 5.00
SS27 Daniel Alfredsson 2.00 5.00
SS28 Bryan Berard 2.00 5.00
SS29 Mike Modano 5.00 12.00
SS30 Patrick Roy 10.00 25.00

1997-98 Upper Deck Smooth Grooves

COMPLETE SET (60) 30.00 80.00
STATED ODDS 1:4
SG1 Wayne Gretzky 5.00 12.00
SG2 Patrick Roy 4.00 10.00
SG3 Patrick Marleau 1.25 3.00
SG4 Martin Brodeur 2.00 5.00
SG5 Zigmund Palffy .50 1.25
SG6 Joe Thornton 2.00 5.00
SG7 Chris Chelios .75 2.00
SG8 Teemu Selanne .75 2.00
SG9 Paul Kariya .75 2.00
SG10 Tony Amonte .50 1.25
SG11 Mark Messier .75 2.00
SG12 Jarome Iginla 1.00 2.50
SG13 Mats Sundin .75 2.00
SG14 Brendan Shanahan .75 2.00
SG15 Ed Jovanovski .50 1.25
SG16 Brett Hull 1.00 2.50
SG17 Brian Rolston .20 .50
SG18 Saku Koivu .75 2.00
SG19 Steve Yzerman 4.00 10.00
SG20 Doug Weight .50 1.25
SG21 Peter Forsberg 2.00 5.00
SG22 Brian Leetch .75 2.00
SG23 Alexei Yashin .20 .50
SG24 Owen Nolan .50 1.25
SG25 Mike Grier .20 .50
SG26 Jere Lehtinen .20 .50
SG27 Vaclav Prospal .75 2.00
SG28 Sandis Ozolinsh .20 .50
SG29 Mike Modano 1.25 3.00
SG30 Sergei Samsonov .50 1.25
SG31 Curtis Joseph .75 2.00
SG32 Daymond Langkow .50 1.25
SG33 Doug Gilmour .50 1.25
SG34 Bryan Berard .50 1.25
SG35 Joe Sakic 1.50 4.00
SG36 Wade Redden .20 .50
SG37 Keith Tkachuk .75 2.00
SG38 Jaromir Jagr 1.25 3.00
SG39 Dominik Hasek 1.50 4.00
SG40 Patrick Lalime .50 1.25
SG41 Janne Niinima .20 .50
SG42 Oleg Tverdovsky .20 .50
SG43 Vitali Yachmenev .20 .50
SG44 Rob Niedermayer .20 .50
SG45 Nicklas Lidstrom .75 2.00
SG46 Jim Campbell .20 .50
SG47 Roman Hamrlik .50 1.25
SG48 Eric Lindros .75 2.00
SG49 Brian Holzinger .20 .50
SG50 John LeClair .75 2.00
SG51 Sergei Berezin .20 .50
SG52 Jaroslav Svejkovsky .50 1.25
SG53 Mike Richter .75 2.00
SG54 John Vanbiesbrouck .50 1.25
SG55 Keith Primeau .20 .50
SG56 Adam Oates .50 1.25
SG57 Jeremy Roenick 1.00 2.50
SG58 Pavel Bure .75 2.00
SG59 Dainius Zubrus .75 2.00
SG60 Jose Theodore 1.00 2.50

1997-98 Upper Deck The Specialists

Randomly inserted in Series 1 packs, this 30-card set features black-and-white action photos of the NHL brightest stars. Only 4,000 of each card were produced.

COMPLETE SET (30) 40.00 100.00
S1 Wayne Gretzky 5.00 12.00
S2 Patrick Roy 4.00 10.00
S3 Jaromir Jagr 2.00 5.00
S4 Joe Sakic 2.50 6.00
S5 Mark Messier 1.25 3.00
S6 Eric Lindros 1.25 3.00
S7 John Vanbiesbrouck 1.00 2.50
S8 Teemu Selanne 1.25 3.00
S9 Paul Kariya 1.25 3.00
S10 Pavel Bure 1.25 3.00
S11 Sergei Fedorov 2.00 5.00
S12 Peter Bondra 1.00 2.50
S13 Mats Sundin 1.25 3.00
S14 Brendan Shanahan 1.25 3.00
S15 Keith Tkachuk 1.25 3.00
S16 Brett Hull 1.50 4.00
S17 Jeremy Roenick 1.50 4.00
S18 Dominik Hasek 2.50 6.00
S19 Steve Yzerman 4.00 10.00
S20 John LeClair 1.25 3.00
S21 Peter Forsberg 3.00 8.00
S22 Zigmund Palffy 1.00 2.50
S23 Tony Amonte 1.00 2.50
S24 Jarome Iginla 1.25 3.00
S25 Curtis Joseph 1.25 3.00
S26 Mike Modano 2.00 5.00
S27 Ray Bourque 2.00 5.00
S28 Brian Leetch 1.25 3.00
S29 Bryan Berard 1.00 2.50
S30 Martin Brodeur 3.00 8.00

1997-98 Upper Deck Three Star Selects

Randomly inserted in Series 1 packs at the rate of 1:4, this 60-card set features color photos on die-cut cards of three top players that fit together to form 20 different sets.

COMPLETE SET (60) 30.00 80.00
T1A Eric Lindros .75 2.00
T1B Wayne Gretzky 5.00 12.00
T1C Peter Forsberg 2.00 5.00
2A Dominik Hasek 1.50 4.00
T2B Patrick Roy 3.00 8.00
T2C John Vanbiesbrouck .75 2.00
T3A Joe Sakic 1.50 4.00
T3B Steve Yzerman 3.00 8.00
T3C Paul Kariya .75 2.00
T4A Bryan Berard .20 .50
T4B Brian Leetch .40 1.00
T4C Chris Chelios .40 1.00
T5A Teemu Selanne .75 2.00
T5B Jaromir Jagr 1.25 3.00
T5C Pavel Bure .75 2.00
T6A Owen Nolan .40 1.00
T6B Brendan Shanahan .75 2.00
T6C Keith Tkachuk .40 1.00
T7A Sergei Fedorov 1.00 2.50
T7B Niklas Sundstrom .20 .50
T7C Mike Peca .20 .50
T8A Janne Niinimaa .20 .50
T8B Saku Koivu .75 2.00
T8C Jere Lehtinen .20 .50
T9A Tony Amonte .40 1.00
T9B John LeClair .40 1.00
T9C Brett Hull 1.00 2.50
T10A Martin Brodeur 2.00 5.00
T10B Curtis Joseph .75 2.00
T10C Mike Richter .75 2.00
T11A Ray Bourque 1.00 2.50
T11B Mark Messier .75 2.00
T11C Scott Stevens .20 .50
T12A Patrick Lalime .40 1.00
T12B Marc Denis .40 1.00
T12C Jose Theodore 1.00 2.50
T13A Adam Deadmarsh .20 .50
T13B Doug Weight .40 1.00
T13C Bill Guerin .20 .50
T14A Daniel Alfredsson .40 1.00
T14B Mats Sundin .75 2.00
T14C Nicklas Lidstrom .75 2.00
T15A Jim Campbell .20 .50
T15B Dainius Zubrus .40 1.00
T15C Daymond Langkow .20 .50
T16A Mike Grier .20 .50
T16B Mike Modano 1.25 3.00
T16C Jeremy Roenick 1.00 2.50
T17A Jason Arnott .20 .50
T17B Trevor Linden .40 1.00
T17C Rod Brind'Amour .40 1.00
T18A Adam Oates .40 1.00
T18B Doug Gilmour .40 1.00
T18C Joe Juneau .20 .50
T19A Sergei Berezin .20 .50
T19B Alexander Mogilny .40 1.00
T19C Alexei Zhamnov .20 .50
T20A Derian Hatcher .20 .50
T20B Wade Redden .20 .50
T20C Sandis Ozolinsh .20 .50

1997 Upper Deck Crash the All-Star Game

Distributed one per attendee of the 1997 NHL All-Star Game in San Jose, these one-off Crash the Game cards were redeemable for a special set if the player pictured scored a goal in the contest. The Western Conference cards (1-11) were rumored to be the only ones distributed, although a few copies of each of the Eastern Conference cards have surfaced as well. The complete set price below includes both conferences. The winners are numbered AR1 thru AR20, and feature gold foil and a record of the player's performance in the game.

1 Tony Amonte 8.00 20.00
2 Paul Kariya 50.00 125.00
3 Brett Hull 15.00 40.00
4 Teemu Selanne 25.00 60.00
5 Steve Yzerman 40.00 100.00
6 Owen Nolan 8.00 20.00
7 Mats Sundin 12.00 30.00
8 Pavel Bure 30.00 80.00
9 Brendan Shanahan 25.00 60.00
10 Sandis Ozolinsh 8.00 20.00
11 Keith Tkachuk 12.00 30.00
12 Ray Bourque 15.00 40.00
13 Eric Lindros 30.00 80.00
14 Mark Messier 15.00 40.00
15 John LeClair 20.00 50.00
16 Jaromir Jagr 40.00 100.00
17 Dino Ciccarelli 8.00 20.00
18 Peter Bondra 12.00 30.00
19 Brian Leetch 15.00 40.00
20 Wayne Gretzky 75.00 200.00
AR1 Tony Amonte 4.00 10.00
AR2 Paul Kariya 20.00 50.00
AR3 Brett Hull 6.00 15.00
AR4 Teemu Selanne 10.00 25.00
AR5 Steve Yzerman 15.00 40.00
AR6 Owen Nolan 6.00 15.00
AR7 Mats Sundin 8.00 20.00
AR8 Pavel Bure 10.00 25.00
AR9 Brendan Shanahan 10.00 25.00
AR10 Sandis Ozolinsh 4.00 10.00
AR11 Keith Tkachuk 6.00 15.00
AR12 Ray Bourque 4.00 10.00
AR13 Eric Lindros 20.00 50.00
AR14 Mark Messier 6.00 15.00
AR15 John LeClair 8.00 20.00
AR16 Jaromir Jagr 15.00 40.00
AR17 Dino Ciccarelli 4.00 10.00
AR18 Peter Bondra 5.00 12.00
AR19 Brian Leetch 5.00 12.00
AR20 Wayne Gretzky 30.00 80.00

1998-99 Upper Deck

The 1998-99 Upper Deck set was issued in two series of 210 cards each for a total of 420 cards and was distributed in 10-card packs with a suggested retail price of $2.49. The fronts feature a color action player photo with player information on the backs. Series 1 contains the following subsets: Star Rookies, Rookie Rewind, and three Checklist cards. Series 2 contains the subset Program of Excellence which consists of the top Canadian prospects, eight Calder Candidates, and three Checklist cards.

COMPLETE SET (420) 75.00 150.00
1 Antti Aalto SR .30 .75
2 Cameron Mann SR .30 .75
3 Norm Maracle SR RC .30 .75
4 Daniel Cleary SR .30 .75
5 Brendan Morrison SR .30 .75
6 Marian Hossa SR .40 1.00
7 Daniel Briere SR .40 1.00
8 Mike Crowley SR RC .40 1.00
9 Darryl Laplante SR RC .40 1.00
10 Sven Butenschon SR .40 1.00
11 Yan Golubovsky SR RC .40 1.00
12 Olli Jokinen SR .40 1.00
13 Jean-Sebastien Giguere SR .40 1.00
14 Mike Watt SR .30 .75
15 Ryan Johnson SR RC .30 .75
16 Teemu Selanne RR 1.00 2.50
17 Paul Kariya RR .60 1.50
18 Pavel Bure RR .60 1.50
19 Joe Thornton RR 1.50 4.00
20 Dominik Hasek RR 1.00 2.50
21 Bryan Berard RR .40 1.00
22 Chris Phillips RR .30 .75
23 Sergei Fedorov RR 1.00 2.50
24 Sergei Samsonov RR .40 1.00
25 Marc Denis RR .40 1.00
26 Patrick Marleau RR .50 1.25
27 Jaromir Jagr RR 1.50 4.00
28 Saku Koivu RR .50 1.25
29 Peter Forsberg RR 2.00 5.00
30 Mike Modano RR 1.00 2.50
31 Paul Kariya .20 .50

32 Matt Cullen .10 .25
33 Josef Marha .10 .25
34 Teemu Selanne .30 .75
35 Pavel Trnka .10 .25
36 Tom Askey RC .10 .25
37 Tim Taylor .10 .25
38 Ray Bourque .25 .60
39 Sergei Samsonov .12 .30
40 Don Sweeney .10 .25
41 Jason Allison .12 .30
42 Steve Heinze .10 .25
43 Erik Rasmussen .10 .25
44 Dominik Hasek .30 .75
45 Geoff Sanderson .10 .25
46 Michael Peca .10 .25
47 Brian Holzinger .10 .25
48 Vaclav Varada .10 .25
49 Steve Begin .10 .25
50 Denis Gauthier .10 .25
51 Derek Morris .10 .25
52 Valeri Bure .10 .25
53 Hnat Domenichelli .10 .25
54 Cory Stillman .10 .25
55 Jarome Iginla .30 .75
56 Tyler Moss .10 .25
57 Sami Kapanen .10 .25
58 Trevor Kidd .10 .25
59 Glen Wesley .10 .25
60 Nelson Emerson .10 .25
61 Jeff O'Neill .10 .25
62 Bates Battaglia .10 .25
63 Doug Gilmour .20 .50
64 Christian LaFlamme .10 .25
65 Chris Chelios .15 .40
66 Paul Coffey .15 .40
67 Eric Weinrich .10 .25
68 Eric Daze .12 .30
69 Peter Forsberg .25 .60
70 Eric Messier .10 .25
71 Eric Lacroix .10 .25
72 Adam Deadmarsh .10 .25
73 Claude Lemieux .12 .30
74 Patrick Roy .40 1.00
75 Marc Denis .12 .30
76 Brett Hull .25 .60
77 Mike Keane .10 .25
78 Joe Nieuwendyk .15 .40
79 Darryl Sydor .10 .25
80 Ed Belfour .15 .40
81 Jamie Langenbrunner .10 .25
82 Petr Buzek .10 .25
83 Nicklas Lidstrom .20 .50
84 Mathieu Dandenault .10 .25
85 Steve Yzerman .50 1.25
86 Martin Lapointe .10 .25
87 Brendan Shanahan .20 .50
88 Anders Erikkson .10 .25
89 Tomas Holmstrom .10 .25
90 Doug Weight .15 .40
91 Janne Niinimaa .10 .25
92 Bill Guerin .15 .40
93 Kelly Buchberger .10 .25
94 Mike Grier .10 .25
95 Craig Millar .10 .25
96 Roman Hamrlik .10 .25
97 Ray Whitney .10 .25
98 Viktor Kozlov .12 .30
99 Peter Worrell RC .12 .30
100 Kevin Weekes .12 .30
101 Ed Jovanovski .12 .30
102 Bill Lindsay .10 .25
103 Jozef Stumpel .12 .30
104 Luc Robitaille .15 .40
105 Yanic Perreault .10 .25
106 Donald MacLean .10 .25
107 Jamie Storr .12 .30
108 Ian Laperriere .10 .25
109 Jason Morgan RC .10 .25
110 Vincent Damphousse .12 .30
111 Mark Recchi .20 .50
112 Vladimir Malakhov .10 .25
113 Dave Manson .10 .25
114 Jose Theodore .20 .50
115 Brian Savage .10 .25
116 Jonas Hoglund .10 .25
117 Krzysztof Oliwa .10 .25
118 Martin Brodeur .30 .75
119 Patrik Elias .15 .40
120 Jason Arnott .12 .30
121 Scott Stevens .15 .40
122 Sheldon Souray RC .20 .50
123 Brian Rolston .12 .30
124 Trevor Linden .12 .30
125 Warren Luhning .10 .25
126 Zdeno Chara .15 .40
127 Bryan Berard .12 .30
128 Bryan Smolinski .10 .25
129 Jason Dawe .10 .25
130 Kevin Stevens .10 .25
131 P.J. Stock RC .30 .75
132 Marc Savard .12 .30
133 Pat LaFontaine .15 .40
134 Dan Cloutier .12 .30
135 Wayne Gretzky .75 2.00
136 Niklas Sundstrom .10 .25
137 Damian Rhodes .15 .40
138 Magnus Arvedson .10 .25
139 Alexei Yashin .12 .30
140 Chris Phillips .10 .25
141 Janne Laukkanen .10 .25
142 Shawn McEachern .10 .25
143 John LeClair .15 .40
144 Alexandre Daigle .10 .25
145 Dainius Zubrus .10 .25
146 Joel Otto .10 .25
147 Mike Sillinger .10 .25
148 John Vanbiesbrouck .12 .30
149 Chris Gratton .12 .30
150 Eric Desjardins .12 .30
151 Juha Ylonen .10 .25
152 Brad Isbister .10 .25
153 Oleg Tverdovsky .15 .40
154 Keith Tkachuk .15 .40
155 Teppo Numminen .10 .25
156 Cliff Ronning .10 .25
157 Nikolai Khabibulin .15 .40
158 Alexei Morozov .10 .25
159 Kevin Hatcher .10 .25
160 Darius Kasparaitis .10 .25
161 Jaromir Jagr .40 1.00
162 Tom Barrasso .12 .30
163 Tuomas Gronman .10 .25
164 Robert Dome .10 .25
165 Peter Skudra .10 .25
166 Marcus Ragnarsson .10 .25
167 Mike Vernon .12 .30
168 Andrei Zyuzin .10 .25
169 Marco Sturm .10 .25
170 Mike Ricci .10 .25
171 Patrick Marleau .15 .40
172 Pierre Turgeon .15 .40
173 Pavol Demitra .20 .50
174 Chris Pronger .12 .30
175 Pascal Rheaume .10 .25
176 Al MacInnis .15 .40
177 Tony Twist .10 .25
178 Jim Campbell .10 .25
179 Mikael Renberg .12 .30
180 Jason Bonsignore .10 .25
181 Zac Bierk RC .20 .50
182 Alexander Selivanov .10 .25
183 Stephane Richer .10 .25
184 Sandy McCarthy .10 .25
185 Alyn McCauley .10 .25
186 Sergei Berezin .12 .30
187 Mike Johnson .10 .25
188 Wendel Clark .12 .30
189 Tie Domi .12 .30
190 Yannick Tremblay .10 .25
191 Curtis Joseph .15 .40
192 Fredrik Modin .10 .25
193 Pavel Bure .20 .50
194 Todd Bertuzzi .15 .40
195 Mark Messier .25 .60
196 Bret Hedican .10 .25
197 Mattias Ohlund .10 .25
198 Garth Snow .12 .30
199 Adam Oates .15 .40
200 Peter Bondra .12 .30
201 Sergei Gonchar .10 .25
202 Jan Bulis .10 .25
203 Joe Juneau .12 .30
204 Brian Bellows .12 .30
205 Olaf Kolzig .15 .40
206 Richard Zednik .10 .25
207 Wayne Gretzky CL .75 2.00
208 Patrick Roy CL .40 1.00
209 Steve Yzerman CL .50 1.25
210 Mike Dunham .12 .30
211 Johan Davidsson .10 .25
212 Guy Hebert .12 .30
213 Mike Leclerc .10 .25
214 Steve Rucchin .10 .25
215 Travis Green .10 .25
216 Josef Marha .10 .25
217 Ted Donato .10 .25
218 Joe Thornton .30 .75
219 Kyle McLaren .10 .25
220 Peter Nordstrom RC .12 .30
221 Byron Dafoe .12 .30
222 Jonathon Girard .10 .25
223 Antti Laaksonen RC .30 .75
224 Jason Holland .10 .25
225 Miroslav Satan .12 .30
226 Alexei Zhitnik .10 .25
227 Donald Audette .10 .25
228 Matthew Barnaby .10 .25
229 Rumun Ndur .10 .25
230 Ken Wregget .12 .30
231 Andrew Cassels .10 .25
232 Theo Fleury .20 .50
233 Phil Housley .12 .30
234 Martin St. Louis RC 5.00 12.00
235 Mike Rucinski RC .10 .25
236 Gary Roberts .10 .25
237 Keith Primeau .10 .25
238 Martin Gelinas .10 .25
239 Nolan Pratt RC .10 .25
240 Ray Sheppard .10 .25
241 Ron Francis .20 .50
242 Ty Jones .10 .25
243 Tony Amonte .12 .30
244 Chad Kilger .10 .25
245 Alexei Zhamnov .10 .25
246 Remi Royer RC .10 .25
247 Milan Hejduk RC 1.00 2.50
248 Joe Sakic .25 .60
249 Valeri Kamensky .10 .25
250 Sandis Ozolinsh .10 .25
251 Shean Donovan .10 .25
252 Wade Belak .10 .25
253 Jamie Wright .10 .25
254 Sergei Zubov .10 .25
255 Richard Matvichuk .10 .25
256 Mike Modano .25 .60
257 Pat Verbeek .10 .25
258 Jere Lehtinen .12 .30
259 Derian Hatcher .10 .25
260 Jason Botterill .10 .25
261 Igor Larionov .15 .40
262 Sergei Fedorov .25 .60
263 Chris Osgood .15 .40
264 Vyacheslav Kozlov .12 .30
265 Larry Murphy .12 .30
266 Darren McCarty .10 .25
267 Doug Brown .10 .25
268 Kris Draper .10 .25
269 Uwe Krupp .10 .25
270 Fredrik Lindquist RC .10 .25
271 Dean McAmmond .10 .25
272 Ryan Smyth .12 .30
273 Boris Mironov .10 .25
274 Tom Poti .10 .25
275 Todd Marchant .10 .25
276 Sean Brown .10 .25
277 Rob Niedermayer .10 .25
278 Robert Svehla .10 .25
279 Scott Mellanby .10 .25
280 Radek Dvorak .10 .25
281 Jaroslav Spacek RC .10 .25
282 Mark Parrish RC .25 .60
283 Ryan Johnson .10 .25
284 Glen Murray .10 .25
285 Rob Blake .15 .40
286 Steve Duchesne .12 .30
287 Vladimir Tsyplakov .10 .25
288 Stephane Fiset .12 .30
289 Mattias Norstrom .10 .25
290 Saku Koivu .15 .40
291 Shayne Corson .12 .30
292 Brad Brown .10 .25
293 Patrice Brisebois .10 .25
294 Terry Ryan .10 .25
295 Jocelyn Thibault .12 .30
296 Miroslav Guren .10 .25
297 Darren Turcotte .12 .30
298 Sebastien Bordeleau .10 .25
299 Jan Vopat .10 .25
300 Blair Atcheynum .10 .25
301 Andrew Brunette .12 .30
302 Sergei Krivokrasov .10 .25
303 Marian Cisar .10 .25
304 Patrick Cote .10 .25
305 J.J. Daigneault .10 .25
306 Greg Johnson .10 .25
307 Chris Terreri .12 .30
308 Scott Niedermayer .15 .40
309 Vadim Sharifijanov .10 .25
310 Petr Sykora .10 .25
311 Sergei Brylin .10 .25
312 Denis Pederson .10 .25
313 Bobby Holik .10 .25
314 Bryan Muir RC .10 .25
315 Zigmund Palffy .15 .40
316 Mike Watt .10 .25
317 Tommy Salo .12 .30
318 Kenny Jonsson .10 .25
319 Dmitri Nabokov .10 .25
320 John MacLean .10 .25
321 Zarley Zalapski .10 .25
322 Brian Leetch .15 .40
323 Todd Harvey .10 .25
324 Mike Richter .15 .40
325 Mike Knuble .10 .25
326 Jeff Beukeboom .10 .25
327 Daniel Alfredsson .15 .40
328 Vaclav Prospal .10 .25
329 Wade Redden .10 .25
330 Igor Kravchuk .10 .25
331 Andreas Dackell .10 .25
332 Mike Maneluk RC .10 .25
333 Eric Lindros .25 .60
334 Rod Brind'Amour .15 .40
335 Colin Forbes .10 .25
336 Dimitri Tertyshny RC .10 .25
337 Shjon Podein .10 .25
338 Chris Therien .10 .25
339 Jeremy Roenick .25 .60
340 Jyrki Lumme .10 .25
341 Rick Tocchet .12 .30
342 Dallas Drake .10 .25
343 Keith Carney .10 .25
344 Greg Adams .10 .25
345 Jan Hrdina RC .20 .50
346 German Titov .10 .25
347 Stu Barnes .10 .25
348 Kevin Hatcher .10 .25
349 Martin Straka .10 .25
350 Jean-Sebastien Aubin RC .25 .60
351 Jeff Friesen .10 .25
352 Tony Granato .10 .25
353 Scott Hannan RC .10 .25
354 Owen Nolan .15 .40
355 Stephane Matteau .10 .25
356 Bryan Marchment .10 .25
357 Geoff Courtnall .12 .30
358 Brent Johnson RC .20 .50
359 Jamie Rivers .10 .25
360 Terry Yake .10 .25
361 Jamie McLennan .12 .30
362 Grant Fuhr .15 .40
363 Michal Handzus RC .20 .50
364 Bill Ranford .12 .30
365 John Cullen .10 .25
366 Craig Janney .10 .25
367 Daren Puppa .12 .30
368 Pavel Kubina RC .12 .30
369 Wendel Clark .12 .30
370 Mats Sundin .15 .40
371 Felix Potvin .15 .40
372 Daniil Markov RC .10 .25
373 Derek King .10 .25
374 Steve Thomas .10 .25
375 Tomas Kaberle RC .20 .50
376 Alexander Mogilny .12 .30
377 Bill Muckalt RC .10 .25
378 Brian Noonan .10 .25
379 Markus Naslund .15 .40
380 Brad May .10 .25
381 Matt Cooke RC .10 .25
382 Calle Johansson .10 .25
383 Dale Hunter .12 .30
384 Jaroslav Svejkovsky .10 .25
385 Dmitri Mironov .10 .25
386 Matt Herr RC .10 .25
387 Nolan Baumgartner .10 .25
388 Wayne Gretzky CL .75 2.00
389 Steve Yzerman CL .50 1.25
390 Wayne Gretzky CL .75 2.00
391 Brian Finley PE RC .40 1.00
392 Maxime Ouellet PE RC .40 1.00
393 Kurtis Foster PE RC .40 1.00
394 Barret Jackman PE RC .60 1.50
395 Ross Lupaschuk PE RC .40 1.00
396 Steven McCarthy PE RC .40 1.00
397 Peter Reynolds PE RC .40 1.00
398 Bart Rushmer PE RC .40 1.00
399 Jonathan Zion PE RC .40 1.00
400 Kris Beech PE RC .40 1.00
401 Brandin Cote PE RC .40 1.00
402 Scott Kelman PE RC .40 1.00
403 Jamie Lundmark PE RC .40 1.00
404 Derek MacKenzie PE RC .40 1.00
405 Rory McDade PE RC .40 1.00
406 David Morisset PE RC .40 1.00
407 Mirko Murovic PE RC .40 1.00
408 Taylor Pyatt PE RC .40 1.00
409 Charlie Stephens PE .40 1.00
410 Kyle Wanvig PE RC .40 1.00
411 Krzystof Wieckowski PE RC .40 1.00
412 Michael Zigomanis PE RC .40 1.00
413 Rico Fata CC .40 1.00
414 Vincent Lecavalier CC 1.00 2.50
415 Chris Drury CC .60 1.50
416 Oleg Kvasha CC RC .50 1.25
417 Eric Brewer CC .50 1.25
418 Josh Green CC RC .50 1.25
419 Marty Reasoner CC .50 1.25
420 Manny Malhotra CC .50 1.25

1998-99 Upper Deck Exclusives

Randomly inserted into hobby packs only, this 420-card set is parallel to the base set. Cards are serial numbered to only 100 copies. An exclusive 1 of 1 parallel also exists and randomly inserted into packs.
*1-30 SR/RR: 5X TO 12X BASIC CARDS
*1-30 SR/RR RCs: 4X TO 10X BASIC CARDS
*31-390 VETS: 25X TO 60X BASIC CARDS
*31-390 ROOKIES: 15X TO 30X
*391-412 PE: 3X TO 8X BASIC CARDS
*413-420 CC: 3X TO 8X BASIC CARDS

1998-99 Upper Deck Jumbos 5x7

Inserted as box-toppers in various distribution forms of Upper Deck, these oversized cards resembled differentr insert sets but were approximately 5" x 7". Cards were numbered the same as the basic insert card.
85 Steve Yzerman 3.00 8.00
Upper Deck
P3 Steve Yzerman 3.00 8.00
Profiles
FF20 Steve Yzerman 3.00 8.00
Fantastic Finishers
FT1 Steve Yzerman 3.00 8.00
Frozen in Time
LS14 Steve Yzerman 3.00 8.00
Lord Stanley's Heroes

1998-99 Upper Deck Fantastic Finishers

Randomly inserted into Series 1 packs at a rate of 1:12, this 30-card set features color action photos of players considered to be the more prolific and gifted finishers in the NHL. Three Tier Quantum parallel versions of this insert set were also produced and inserted into Series 1 packs. Tier 1 cards were sequentially numbered to 1,500; Tier 2 cards were sequentially numbered to 50; and Tier 3 cards were sequentially numbered to 1.
COMPLETE SET (30) 50.00 100.00
*QUANTUM ONE/1500: .8X TO 2X BASIC INSERTS
*QUANTUM TWO/50: 8X TO 20X BASIC INSERTS
FF1 Wayne Gretzky 6.00 15.00
FF2 Peter Bondra .75 2.00
FF3 Sergei Samsonov .75 2.00
FF4 Jaromir Jagr 1.50 4.00
FF5 Brendan Shanahan 1.00 2.50
FF6 Joe Sakic 2.00 5.00
FF7 Brett Hull 1.50 4.00
FF8 Paul Kariya 1.00 2.50
FF9 Keith Tkachuk 1.00 2.50
FF10 Zigmund Palffy .75 2.00
FF11 Eric Lindros 1.00 2.50
FF12 Mike Modano 1.50 4.00
FF13 Pavel Bure 1.00 2.50
FF14 Mats Sundin .75 2.00
FF15 Patrik Elias .75 2.00
FF16 Tony Amonte .75 2.00
FF17 Peter Forsberg 2.50 6.00
FF18 Alexei Yashin .75 2.00
FF19 Mark Recchi .75 2.00
FF20 Steve Yzerman 4.00 10.00
FF21 Doug Weight .75 2.00
FF22 Jeremy Roenick 1.25 3.00
FF23 Teemu Selanne 1.00 2.50
FF24 Owen Nolan .75 2.00
FF25 John LeClair 1.00 2.50
FF26 Jason Allison .75 2.00
FF27 Mike Johnson .75 2.00
FF28 Theo Fleury .75 2.00
FF29 Nicklas Lidstrom 1.00 2.50
FF30 Joe Nieuwendyk .75 2.00

1998-99 Upper Deck Frozen In Time

Randomly inserted in Series 1 packs at a rate of 1:23, this 30-card set features color action photos of some of the key moments throughout the careers of the highlighted players. Three Tier Quantum parallel versions of this insert set were also produced and inserted into Series 1 packs. Tier 1 cards were sequentially numbered to 1,000; Tier 2 cards were sequentially numbered to 25; and Tier 3 cards were numbered to 1.
COMPLETE SET (30) 50.00 100.00
*QUANTUM ONE/1000: .6X TO 1.5X BASIC INSERTS
*QUANTUM TWO/25: 5X TO 12X BASIC INSERTS
FT1 Steve Yzerman 4.00 10.00
FT2 Peter Forsberg 2.50 6.00
FT3 Sergei Samsonov 1.25 3.00
FT4 Martin Brodeur 2.50 6.00
FT5 Theo Fleury .75 2.00
FT6 Paul Kariya 1.50 4.00
FT7 Rob Blake 1.25 3.00
FT8 Jari Kurri .75 2.00
FT9 Eric Lindros 1.50 4.00
FT10 Dominik Hasek 2.00 5.00
FT11 Patrick Roy 4.00 10.00
FT12 Saku Koivu 1.50 4.00
FT13 Mike Modano 1.50 4.00
FT14 Alexei Morozov .75 2.00
FT15 Chris Osgood 1.25 3.00
FT16 Doug Gilmour 1.25 3.00
FT17 Owen Nolan 1.25 3.00
FT18 Mike Johnson 1.25 3.00
FT19 Keith Tkachuk 1.50 4.00
FT20 Adam Oates 1.25 3.00
FT21 Chris Chelios 1.50 4.00
FT22 Brendan Shanahan 1.50 4.00
FT23 Joe Sakic 2.00 5.00
FT24 Pavel Bure 1.50 4.00
FT25 Ray Bourque 2.00 5.00
FT26 Ed Belfour 1.50 4.00
FT27 John LeClair 1.50 4.00
FT28 Teemu Selanne 1.50 4.00
FT29 Jaromir Jagr 1.50 4.00
FT30 Wayne Gretzky 6.00 15.00

1998-99 Upper Deck Game Jerseys

Randomly inserted into Series 1 and Series 2 packs at the rate of one in 2,500 retail and 1:288 hobby, this 24-card set features color action player photos with a piece from an actual game-worn jersey embedded in the cards. Four of the player's autographed some of their cards. The number of cards each player autographed follow the player's name in the checklist below.
GJ1 Wayne Gretzky 40.00 100.00
GJ2 Vincent Lecavalier 15.00 40.00
GJ3 Bobby Hull 15.00 40.00
GJ4 Curtis Joseph 12.00 30.00
GJ5 Roberto Luongo 12.00 30.00
GJ6 Martin Brodeur 15.00 40.00
GJ8 Ed Belfour 12.00 30.00
GJ9 Al MacInnis 8.00 20.00
GJ10 Derian Hatcher 5.00 12.00
GJ11 Daniel Tkaczuk 5.00 12.00
GJ12 Manny Malhotra 6.00 15.00
GJ13 Eric Brewer 5.00 12.00
GJ14 Alex Tanguay 5.00 12.00
GJ15 Brendan Shanahan 12.00 30.00
GJ16 Jaromir Jagr 15.00 40.00
GJ16 Chris Osgood 12.00 30.00
GJ17 Dominik Hasek 25.00 60.00
GJ18 Doug Gilmour 10.00 25.00
GJ19 Mats Sundin 10.00 25.00
GJ20 Darryl Sydor 5.00 12.00
GJ21 Chris Therien 5.00 12.00
GJ22 Darius Kasparaitis 6.00 15.00
GJ23 Alexei Zhamnov 5.00 12.00
GJ24 Joe Nieuwendyk 6.00 15.00
GJA1 Bobby Hull AU/9
GJA2 W.Gretzky AU/99 250.00 500.00
GJA3 V.Lecavalier AU/100 60.00 150.00
GJA4 Gretzky JSY AU/99 250.00 600.00

1998-99 Upper Deck Generation Next

Randomly inserted in Series 2 packs at the rate of 1:23, this 30-card set features color action photos of ten of the top players in the NHL on one side with one of three heir apparent pictured on the other. Quantum parallels of this set were also produced and inserted into Series 2 packs. Three different Quantum parallel sets exist, and each Quantum set was broken into three levels or "tiers". Quantum 1 had tiers that featured ten cards sequentially numbered to 1,000; ten numbered to 500; and ten cards sequentially numbered to 250. Quantum 2 had tiers that contained ten cards sequentially numbered to 75; ten numbered to 25; and ten cards sequentially numbered to 10. Quantum 3 had tiers with ten cards sequentially numbered to 3; ten sequentially numbered to 2; and ten cards numbered to 1. The card numbers in each tier were the same for each set, the card numbers are listed below. Tiers were grouped by serial numbers in descending order. Quantum 2, Tier 3 and Quantum 3 cards are not priced due to their scarcity.
COMPLETE SET (30) 30.00 60.00
*QUANTUM ONE/1000: .6X TO 1.5
*QUANTUM ONE/500: 1.2X TO 3X
*QUANTUM ONE/250: 2X TO 5X
*QUANTUM TWO/75: 8X TO 20X
*QUANTUM TWO/25: 20X TO 50X
*QUANTUM TWO/10: 25X TO 60X
TIER 1 CARDS: 1,4,7,10,13,16,19,22,25,28
TIER 2 CARDS: 2,5,8,11,14,17,20,23,26,29
TIER 3 CARDS: 3,6,9,12,15,18,21,24,27,30
GN1 W.Gretzky/S.Samsonov 2.00 5.00
GN2 W.Gretzky/M.Hossa 2.00 5.00
GN3 W.Gretzky/V.Lecavalier 2.00 5.00
GN4 S.Yzerman/B.Morrison 1.00 2.50
GN5 S.Yzerman/M.Reasoner 1.50 4.00
GN6 S.Yzerman/M.Malhotra 1.50 4.00
GN7 P.Roy/Jean-Sebastien Giguere 1.50 4.00
GN8 P.Roy/J.Theodore 2.00 5.00
GN9 P.Roy/M.Denis 1.50 4.00
GN10 E.Lindros/P.Marleau .60 1.50
GN11 E.Lindros/B.Isbister .60 1.50
GN12 E.Lindros/J.Thornton .60 1.50
GN13 B.Shanahan/J.Green .60 1.50
GN14 B.Shanahan/T.Jones .60 1.50
GN15 B.Shanahan/M.Watt .60 1.50
GN16 R.Bourque/M.Ohlund .60 1.50
GN17 R.Bourque/T.Poti .60 1.50
GN18 R.Bourque/E.Brewer .75 2.00
GN19 P.Kariya/D.Briere .60 1.50
GN20 P.Kariya/R.Fata .60 1.50
GN21 P.Kariya/C.Drury .60 1.50
GN22 J.Jagr/R.Dome .60 1.50
GN23 J.Jagr/R.Zednik .60 1.50
GN24 J.Jagr/O.Kvasha .60 1.50
GN25 P.Forsberg/O.Jokinen 1.25 3.00
GN26 P.Forsberg/N.Sundstrom 1.00 2.50
GN27 P.Forsberg/B.Morrison 1.00 2.50
GN28 P.Bure/V.Sharifijanov .60 1.50
GN29 P.Bure/D.Nabokov .60 1.50
GN30 P.Bure/S.Samsonov .60 1.50

1998-99 Upper Deck Lord Stanley's Heroes

Randomly inserted into Series 1 packs at a rate of one in six, this 30-card set features color action photos of players vying for their chance at claiming the Stanley Cup. Three Tier Quantum parallel versions of this insert set were also produced and inserted into Series 1 packs. Tier 1 cards were sequentially numbered to 2,000; Tier 2 cards were sequentially numbered to 100; and Tier 3 cards were numbered to 1.
COMPLETE SET (30) 30.00 60.00
*QUANTUM ONE/2000: .6X TO 1.5X BASIC INSERTS
*QUANTUM TWO/100: 8X TO 20X BASIC INSERTS
LS1 Wayne Gretzky 4.00 10.00
LS2 Joe Sakic 1.25 3.00
LS3 Jaromir Jagr .75 2.00
LS4 Brendan Shanahan .60 1.50
LS5 Martin Brodeur 1.50 4.00
LS6 Theo Fleury .60 1.50
LS7 Doug Gilmour .40 1.00
LS8 Ron Francis .40 1.00
LS9 Sergei Fedorov 1.00 2.50
LS10 Patrick Roy 3.00 8.00
LS11 Mark Messier .60 1.50
LS12 Peter Forsberg 1.50 4.00
LS13 Brian Leetch .60 1.50
LS14 Steve Yzerman 3.00 8.00
LS15 Sergei Samsonov .40 1.00
LS16 Eric Lindros .60 1.50
LS17 Paul Kariya .60 1.50
LS18 Saku Koivu .60 1.50
LS19 Bryan Berard .40 1.00
LS20 Chris Pronger .40 1.00
LS21 Keith Tkachuk .60 1.50
LS22 Doug Weight .40 1.00
LS23 Ed Belfour .60 1.50
LS24 Mats Sundin .60 1.50
LS25 John LeClair .60 1.50
LS26 Pavel Bure .60 1.50
LS27 Dominik Hasek 1.25 3.00
LS28 Mike Modano 1.00 2.50
LS29 Curtis Joseph .60 1.50
LS30 Teemu Selanne .60 1.50

1998-99 Upper Deck Profiles

Randomly inserted into Series 2 packs at the rate of one in 12, this 30-card set features color action photos of some of the greatest current players in the NHL. Three Tier Quantum parallel versions of this insert set were also produced and inserted into Series 2 packs. Tier 1 cards were sequentially numbered to 1,500; Tier 2 cards were sequentially numbered to 50; and Tier 3 cards were numbered to 1.
COMPLETE SET (30) 20.00 50.00
*QUANTUM ONE/1500: .6X TO 1.5X BASIC INSERTS
*QUANTUM TWO/50: 10X TO 25X BASIC INSERTS
P1 Marty Reasoner .50 1.25
P2 Brett Hull 1.00 2.50
P3 Steve Yzerman 4.00 10.00
P4 Eric Lindros .75 2.00
P5 Eric Brewer .60 1.50
P6 Martin Brodeur 2.00 5.00
P7 John Vanbiesbrouck .50 1.25
P8 Teemu Selanne .75 2.00
P9 Wayne Gretzky 5.00 12.00
P10 Jaromir Jagr 1.25 3.00
P11 Peter Forsberg 2.00 5.00
P12 Manny Malhotra .50 1.25
P13 Sergei Samsonov .50 1.25
P14 Brendan Shanahan .75 2.00
P15 Doug Gilmour .50 1.25
P16 Vincent Lecavalier .75 2.00
P17 Dominik Hasek 1.50 4.00
P18 Mike Modano 1.25 3.00
P19 Saku Koivu .75 2.00
P20 Curtis Joseph .75 2.00
P21 Paul Kariya .75 2.00
P22 Doug Weight .60 1.50
P23 Ray Bourque 1.50 4.00
P24 Patrick Roy 4.00 10.00
P25 John LeClair .75 2.00
P26 Chris Drury .50 1.25
P27 Theo Fleury .60 1.50
P28 Mats Sundin .60 1.50
P29 Sergei Fedorov 1.00 2.50
P30 Rico Fata .60 1.50

1998-99 Upper Deck Wayne Gretzky Game Jersey Autographs

These cards could be found in packs of Black Diamond, Upper Deck MVP, SP Authentic, and SPx Top Prospects. Each product had one version of the card numbered to 40 sets. The cards contain an actual piece of a game worn Wayne Gretzy jersey embedded in the cards and an authentic autograph.
COMMON CARD 200.00 500.00

1998-99 Upper Deck Year of the Great One

Randomly inserted into Series 2 packs at the rate of 1:6, this 30-card set features color photos of Hockey great, Wayne Gretzky. Three Tier Quantum parallel versions of this insert set were also produced and inserted into Series 2 packs. Tier 1 cards were sequentially numbered to 1,999; Tier 2 cards were sequentially numbered to 99; and Tier 3 cards were numbered to 1.
COMPLETE SET (30) 20.00 50.00
COMMON GRETZKY (G01-G030) 1.50 4.00
*QUANTUM ONE/199: 1.5X TO 4X BASIC INSERTS
*QUANTUM TWO/99: 6X TO 15X BASIC INSERTS

1998-99 Upper Deck Arena Giveaway Pittsburgh Penguins

COMPLETE SET (4)
PIT1 Martin Straka
PIT2 Stu Barnes
PIT3 Tom Barrasso
PIT4 Jaromir Jagr

1998 Upper Deck Willie O'Ree Commemorative Card

This card was issued by Upper Deck of the 1998 NHL All-Stars game in Vancouver. It was available at All-Star activities throughout the weekend.
22 Willie O'Ree 5.00 10.00

1999-00 Upper Deck

Upper Deck was released as a 335-card two series set with 270 regular issue cards and 65 short prints. Series one is comprised of 135 regular cards and 35 short prints (Star Power and Young Guns) for a total of 170 cards, and series two was comprised of 135 regular cards and 30 short prints (Prospects 2000) for a total of 165 cards. Base cards have a blue and black border along the bottom edge of the card with enhanced bronze foil stamping. Upper Deck was released in 24-pack boxes with packs containing 10 cards and carried a suggested retail price of $2.99.
COMPLETE SET (335) 40.00 100.00
136-170/306-335 SP ODDS 1:4
1 Wayne Gretzky .60 1.50
2 Wayne Gretzky .60 1.50
3 Wayne Gretzky .60 1.50
4 Wayne Gretzky .60 1.50
5 Wayne Gretzky .60 1.50
6 Wayne Gretzky .60 1.50
7 Wayne Gretzky .60 1.50
8 Wayne Gretzky .60 1.50
9 Wayne Gretzky .60 1.50
10 Wayne Gretzky .60 1.50
11 Paul Kariya .25 .60
12 Matt Cullen .12 .30
13 Steve Rucchin .12 .30
14 Fredrik Olausson .12 .30
15 Damian Rhodes .12 .30
16 Jody Hull .12 .30
17 Ray Bourque .30 .75
18 Joe Thornton .30 .75
19 Jonathan Girard .12 .30
20 Shawn Bates .12 .30
21 Byron Dafoe .12 .30
22 Dominik Hasek .30 .75
23 Michael Peca .15 .40
24 Miroslav Satan .15 .40
25 Dixon Ward .12 .30
26 Valeri Bure .12 .30
27 Derek Morris .12 .30
28 Jarome Iginla .20 .50
29 Rico Fata .12 .30
30 Jean-Sebastien Giguere .20 .50
31 Arturs Irbe .15 .40
32 Sami Kapanen .12 .30
33 Gary Roberts .12 .30
34 Bates Battaglia .12 .30
35 J-P Dumont .15 .40
36 Ty Jones .12 .30
37 Tony Amonte .15 .40
38 Anders Eriksson .12 .30
39 Peter Forsberg .20 .50
40 Adam Foote .15 .40
41 Chris Drury .15 .40
42 Milan Hejduk .15 .40
43 Brett Hull .30 .75
44 Ed Belfour .20 .50
45 Jamie Langenbrunner .12 .30
46 Derian Hatcher .15 .40
47 Jon Sim RC .20 .50
48 Joe Nieuwendyk .20 .50
49 Steve Yzerman .60 1.50
50 Brendan Shanahan .25 .60
51 Nicklas Lidstrom .20 .50
52 Igor Larionov .20 .50
53 Vyacheslav Kozlov .12 .30
54 Bill Guerin .20 .50
55 Mike Grier .12 .30
56 Tommy Salo .15 .40
57 Tom Poti .12 .30
58 Mark Parrish .12 .30
59 Pavel Bure .25 .60
60 Scott Mellanby .12 .30
61 Chris Allen RC .12 .30
62 Rob Blake .20 .50
63 Pavel Rosa .12 .30
64 Donald Audette .12 .30
65 Vladimir Tsyplakov .12 .30
66 Manny Legace .12 .30
67 Saku Koivu .20 .50
68 Eric Weinrich .12 .30
69 Jeff Hackett .12 .30
70 Arron Asham .12 .30
71 Trevor Linden .20 .50
72 Cliff Ronning .12 .30
73 David Legwand .12 .30
74 Kimmo Timonen .12 .30
75 Sergei Krivokrasov .12 .30
76 Mike Dunham .12 .30
77 Martin Brodeur .40 1.00
78 Patrik Elias .20 .50
79 Petr Sykora .15 .40
80 Vadim Sharifijanov .12 .30
81 John Madden RC .20 .50
82 Eric Brewer .12 .30
83 Dmitri Nabokov .12 .30
84 Kenny Jonsson .12 .30
85 Zdeno Chara .20 .50
86 Wayne Gretzky 1.00 2.50
87 Mike Richter .20 .50
88 Adam Graves .15 .40
89 Manny Malhotra .15 .40
90 Alexei Yashin .15 .40
91 Sami Salo .15 .40
92 Marian Hossa .15 .40
93 Shawn McEachern .12 .30
94 Eric Lindros .30 .75
95 Jean-Marc Pelletier .12 .30
96 Rod Brind'Amour .20 .50
97 Mark Recchi .25 .60
98 Eric Desjardins .15 .40
99 Robert Reichel .12 .30
100 Keith Tkachuk .20 .50
101 Robert Esche RC .20 .50
102 Oleg Tverdovsky .12 .30
103 Trevor Letowski .12 .30
104 Jaromir Jagr .50 1.25
105 Tom Barrasso .20 .50
106 Jan Hrdina .12 .30
107 Matthew Barnaby .15 .40
108 Vincent Damphousse .15 .40
109 Jeff Friesen .15 .40
110 Patrick Marleau .20 .50
111 Mike Ricci .15 .40
112 Scott Hannan .12 .30
113 Pavol Demitra .25 .60
114 Al MacInnis .20 .50
115 Lubos Bartecko .12 .30
116 Jochen Hecht RC .30 .75
117 Vincent Lecavalier .15 .40
118 Paul Mara .12 .30
119 Kevin Hodson .12 .30
120 Dan Cloutier .12 .30
121 Mats Sundin .20 .50
122 Daniil Markov .12 .30
123 Sergei Berezin .12 .30
124 Steve Thomas .12 .30
125 Tomas Kaberle .12 .30
126 Mark Messier .30 .75
127 Bill Muckalt .12 .30
128 Kevin Weekes .12 .30
129 Josh Holden .12 .30
130 Jaroslav Svejkovsky .12 .30
131 Adam Oates .20 .50
132 Peter Bondra .15 .40
133 Jan Bulis .12 .30
134 Wayne Gretzky CL .60 1.50
135 Wayne Gretzky CL .60 1.50
136 Wayne Gretzky SP 1.50 4.00
137 Eric Lindros SP .50 1.25
138 Jaromir Jagr SP .75 2.00
139 Paul Kariya SP .40 1.00
140 Steve Yzerman SP 1.00 2.50
141 Patrick Roy SP 1.25 3.00
142 Chris Drury SP .25 .60
143 Sergei Samsonov SP .25 .60
144 Brett Hull SP .50 1.25
145 Dominik Hasek SP .50 1.25
146 Keith Tkachuk SP .30 .75
147 Alexei Yashin SP .25 .60
148 Martin Brodeur SP .60 1.50
149 Pavel Bure SP .40 1.00
150 Paul Mara SP .20 .50
151 Peter Bondra SP .25 .60
152 Mike Modano SP .50 1.25
153 Teemu Selanne SP .60 1.50
154 Peter Forsberg SP .30 .75
155 Brendan Shanahan SP .40 1.00
156 Ray Bourque SP .50 1.25
157 Saku Koivu SP .30 .75
158 John LeClair SP .30 .75
159 Joe Sakic SP .50 1.25
160 David Legwand SP .20 .50
161 Patrik Stefan YG RC .50 1.25
162 Nick Boynton YG .40 1.00
163 Roberto Luongo YG .60 1.50
164 Rico Fata SP .20 .50
165 Daniel Sedin YG 3.00 8.00
166 Henrik Sedin YG 3.00 8.00
167 Brad Stuart YG .40 1.00
168 Tony Amonte SP .40 1.00
169 Oleg Saprykin YG RC .50 1.25
170 Denis Shvidki YG .40 1.00
171 Guy Hebert .20 .50
172 Niclas Havelid RC .20 .50
173 Oleg Tverdovsky .12 .30
174 Teemu Selanne .40 1.00
175 Damian Rhodes .12 .30
176 Nelson Emerson .12 .30
177 Per Svartvadet RC .12 .30
178 Ray Ferraro .12 .30
179 Kelly Buchberger .12 .30
180 Norm Maracle .12 .30
181 Patrik Stefan .20 .50
182 Dave Andreychuk .20 .50
183 Sergei Samsonov .15 .40
184 John Grahame RC .15 .40
185 Jason Allison .15 .40
186 Kyle McLaren .12 .30
187 Anson Carter .15 .40
188 Martin Biron .15 .40
189 Brian Campbell RC .20 .50
190 Curtis Brown .12 .30
191 Alexei Zhitnik .12 .30
192 David Moravec RC .12 .30
193 Oleg Saprykin .20 .50
194 Grant Fuhr .20 .50
195 Phil Housley .12 .30
196 Marc Savard .12 .30
197 Robyn Regehr .12 .30
198 Martin Gelinas .12 .30
199 Ron Francis .25 .60
200 Jeff O'Neil .12 .30
201 Keith Primeau .12 .30
202 Paul Ranheim .12 .30
203 Kyle Calder RC .15 .40
204 Jocelyn Thibault .15 .40
205 Wendel Clark .15 .40
206 Doug Gilmour .25 .60
207 Josef Marha .12 .30
208 Alexei Zhamnov .12 .30
209 Dan Hinote RC .15 .40
210 Patrick Roy .75 2.00
211 Joe Sakic .30 .75
212 Alex Tanguay .15 .40
213 Sandis Ozolinsh .12 .30
214 Adam Deadmarsh .12 .30
215 Jere Lehtinen .15 .40
216 Mike Modano .30 .75
217 Darryl Sydor .15 .40
218 Sergei Zubov .12 .30
219 Pavel Patera RC .12 .30
220 Jamie Pushor .12 .30
221 Chris Osgood .20 .50
222 Tomas Holmstrom .12 .30
223 Chris Chelios .20 .50
224 Sergei Fedorov .30 .75
225 Jiri Fischer .12 .30
226 Paul Comrie RC .30 .75

227 Frantisek Musil .12 .30
228 Janne Niinimaa .12 .30
229 Doug Weight .20 .50
230 Trevor Kidd .12 .30
231 Oleg Kvasha .12 .30
232 Victor Kozlov .12 .30
233 Rob Niedermayer .12 .30
234 Luc Robitaille .20 .50
235 Aki Berg .12 .30
236 Bryan Smolinski .12 .30
237 Jozef Stumpel .12 .30
238 Zigmund Palffy .20 .50
239 Stephane Fiset .15 .40
240 Jason Blake RC .15 .40
241 Scott Lachance .12 .30
242 Vladimir Malakhov .12 .30
243 Mike Ribeiro .15 .40
244 Brian Savage .12 .30
245 Tomas Vokoun .20 .50
246 Randy Robitaille .12 .30
247 Sergei Nemchinov .12 .30
248 Brendan Morrison .15 .40
249 Scott Niedermayer .20 .50
250 Scott Stevens .20 .50
251 Scott Gomez .15 .40
252 Mark Lawrence .12 .30
253 Felix Potvin .30 .75
254 Olli Jokinen .15 .40
255 Tim Connolly .12 .30
256 Mariusz Czerkaswki .12 .30
257 Valeri Kamensky .12 .30
258 Brian Leetch .20 .50
259 Petr Nedved .12 .30
260 Theo Fleury .25 .60
261 Kevin Hatcher .12 .30
262 Mike York .12 .30
263 Ron Tugnutt .15 .40
264 Chris Phillips .12 .30
265 Daniel Alfredsson .20 .50
266 Radek Bonk .12 .30
267 Wade Redden .12 .30
268 John Vanbiesbrouck .15 .40
269 John LeClair .20 .50
270 Simon Gagne .20 .50
271 Nikolai Khabibulin .15 .40
272 Daniel Briere .15 .40
273 Jeremy Roenick .20 .50
274 Andrew Ference .12 .30
275 Alexei Kovalev .15 .40
276 Martin Straka .12 .30
277 Alexei Morozov .15 .40
278 Steve Shields .15 .40
279 Marco Sturm .15 .40
280 Niklas Sundstrom .12 .30
281 Brad Stuart .15 .40
282 Owen Nolan .20 .50
283 Roman Turek .15 .40
284 Chris Pronger .15 .40
285 Jim Campbell .12 .30
286 Michal Handzus .15 .40
287 Pierre Turgeon .20 .50
288 Darcy Tucker .12 .30
289 Andrei Zyuzin .12 .30
290 Stephen Guolla .12 .30
291 Curtis Joseph .20 .50
292 Jonas Hoglund .12 .30
293 Bryan Berard .12 .30
294 Mike Johnson .15 .40
295 Garth Snow .15 .40
296 Jason Strudwick .12 .30
297 Steve Kariya RC .20 .50
298 Markus Naslund .20 .50
299 Mattias Ohlund .15 .40
300 Alexander Mogilny .15 .40
301 Olaf Kolzig .20 .50
302 Alexei Tezikov RC .20 .50
303 Alexander Volchkov RC .12 .30
304 Steve Yzerman CL .40 1.00
305 Curtis Joseph CL .12 .30
306 Pavel Brendl PRO RC .75 2.00
307 Daniel Sedin PRO 1.25 3.00
308 Henrik Sedin PRO 1.25 3.00
309 Sheldon Keefe PRO RC .50 1.25
310 Ryan Jardine PRO RC .40 1.00
311 Maxime Ouellet PRO .50 1.25
312 Barret Jackman PRO .30 .75
313 Kristian Kudroc PRO RC .30 .75
314 Branislav Mezei PRO RC .30 .75
315 Denis Shvidki PRO .40 1.00
316 Brian Finley PRO .50 1.25
317 Jonathan Cheechoo PRO 1.50 4.00
318 Mark Bell PRO .30 .75
319 Taylor Pyatt PRO .30 .75
320 Norm Milley PRO .30 .75
321 Jamie Lundmark PRO .40 1.00
322 Alexander Buturlin PRO RC .40 1.00
323 Jaroslav Kristek PRO RC .40 1.00
324 Kris Beech PRO .30 .75
325 Scott Kelman PRO .30 .75
326 Milan Kraft PRO RC .40 1.00
327 Mattias Weinhandl PRO .30 .75
328 Alexei Volkov PRO .40 1.00
329 Andrei Shefer PRO RC .40 1.00
330 Mathieu Chouinard PRO .30 .75
331 Justin Papineau PRO .30 .75
332 Mike Van Ryn PRO .30 .75
333 Jeff Heerema PRO .30 .75
334 Michael Zigomanis PRO .30 .75
335 Bryan Kazarian PRO RC .40 1.00

1999-00 Upper Deck Exclusives

Randomly inserted in packs, this 335-card set parallels the base Upper Deck set with gold foil highlights. Each card is sequentially numbered to 100.
*1-305 EXCL/100: 12X TO 30X BASIC CARDS
*136-160 VET/100: 8X TO 20X BASIC SP
*161-170 YG/100: 5X TO 12X BASIC YG
*306-335 PRO/100: 5X TO 12X BASIC PRO

1999-00 Upper Deck A Piece of History 500 Goal Club

Randomly inserted in various Upper Deck products, these cards feature players who attained the 500-goal mark during their career. The front pictures the player and includes a swatch of game-worn jersey or game-used stick. An autographed version of each card, serial-numbered to 25, was also available. Michel Goulet and Stan Mikita were randomly available in Black Diamond with stated odds of 1:1788. Bobby Hull and Brett Hull were randomly available in SP Authentic with stated odds of 1:1339. Gordie Howe was randomly available in Upper Deck Series II packs with stated odds of 1:2989. Bryan Trottier and Mike Bossy were randomly available in Upper Deck MVP SC Edition with stated odds of 1:3995. Luc Robitaille and Marcel Dionne were randomly available in Upper Deck Ovation with stated odds of 1:947. Dino Ciccarelli and Steve Yzerman were randomly available in Upper Deck PowerDeck with stated odds of 1:330. Gilbert Perreault and Maurice Richard were randomly available in Upper Deck Ultimate Victory with stated odds of 1:1113. Guy Lafleur and Jean Beliveau were randomly available in Wayne Gretzky Hockey with stated odds of 1:1259.
500BHA Bobby Hull AU/25 350.00 550.00
500BH Bobby Hull 40.00 100.00
500BTA Bryan Trottier AU/25 200.00 400.00
500BT Bryan Trottier 15.00 40.00
500DCA Dino Ciccarelli AU/25 150.00 300.00
500DC Dino Ciccarelli 25.00 60.00
500GH Gordie Howe 75.00 150.00
500GHA Gordie Howe AU/25 600.00 800.00
500GLA Guy Lafleur AU/25 150.00 350.00
500GL Guy Lafleur 100.00 200.00
500GP Gilbert Perreault 15.00 40.00
500GPA Gilbert Perreault AU/25 400.00 600.00
500JBA Jean Beliveau AU/25 300.00 500.00
500JB Jean Beliveau 100.00 200.00
500LRA Luc Robitaille AU/25 350.00 500.00
500LR Luc Robitaille 15.00 40.00
500MB Mike Bossy 20.00 50.00
500MBA Mike Bossy AU/25 400.00 500.00
500MDAS Marcel Dionne AU/25 125.00 250.00
500MD Marcel Dionne 15.00 40.00
500MGA Michel Goulet AU/25 150.00 300.00
500MG Michel Goulet 15.00 40.00
500MR Maurice Richard 75.00 200.00
500MRA M. Richard AU/25 450.00 700.00
500SM Stan Mikita 25.00 60.00
500SMA Stan Mikita AU/25 200.00 400.00
500SY Steve Yzerman 75.00 150.00
500SYA Steve Yzerman AU/25 500.00 750.00
500BHUA Brett Hull AU/25 250.00 500.00
500BHU Brett Hull 25.00 60.00

1999-00 Upper Deck All-Star Class

Randomly inserted in Series Two packs at the rate of 1:23, this 20-card set features an all blue foil card stock with full color action player photos. Silver and gold parallels were also created and inserted randomly. Silver parallels were limited to 100 serial numbered sets. Gold parallels were numbered 1/1 and are not priced due to scarcity.
COMPLETE SET (20) 30.00 60.00
*SILVER/100: 10X TO 25X BASIC INSERTS
AS1 Dominik Hasek 2.00 5.00
AS2 Patrick Roy 5.00 12.00
AS3 Jaromir Jagr 1.50 4.00
AS4 Paul Kariya 1.00 2.50
AS5 Teemu Selanne 1.00 2.50
AS6 Keith Tkachuk 1.00 2.50
AS7 Pavel Bure 1.00 2.50
AS8 John LeClair 1.00 2.50
AS9 Mats Sundin 1.00 2.50
AS10 Steve Yzerman 5.00 12.00
AS11 Peter Forsberg 2.50 6.00
AS12 Eric Lindros 1.00 2.50
AS13 Steve Kariya 1.25 3.00
AS14 Ed Belfour 1.00 2.50
AS15 Nicklas Lidstrom .75 2.00
AS16 Ray Bourque 1.50 4.00
AS17 Sandis Ozolinsh .75 2.00
AS18 Al MacInnis .75 2.00
AS19 Martin Brodeur 2.50 6.00
AS20 Patrik Stefan 1.50 4.00

1999-00 Upper Deck Crunch Time

Randomly inserted in Series One packs at the rate of 1:4, this 30-card set features an all foil card stock with concentric laser rays coming out from behind an action player shot. Background foil color matches the respective player's team colors. Silver and gold parallels were also created and inserted randomly. Silver parallels were limited to 100 serial numbered sets. Unpriced gold parallels were numbered 1/1.
COMPLETE SET (30) 15.00 30.00
*SILVER/100: 25X TO 60X BASIC INSERTS
CT1 Vincent Lecavalier .40 1.00
CT2 Steve Yzerman 2.00 5.00
CT3 Peter Bondra .30 .75
CT4 Jean-Marc Pelletier .30 .75
CT5 Brendan Shanahan .40 1.00
CT6 Joe Sakic .75 2.00
CT7 Jean-Sebastien Giguere .30 .75
CT8 Brett Hull .50 1.25
CT9 Jaromir Jagr .60 1.50
CT10 Eric Brewer .30 .75
CT11 Sergei Samsonov .30 .75
CT12 Alexei Yashin .20 .50
CT13 Mats Sundin .40 1.00
CT14 Mike Modano .60 1.50
CT15 Al MacInnis .30 .75
CT16 Paul Mara .20 .50
CT17 David Legwand .30 .75
CT18 Eric Lindros .40 1.00
CT19 Peter Forsberg 1.00 2.50
CT20 Ray Bourque .60 1.50
CT21 Teemu Selanne .40 1.00
CT22 John LeClair .40 1.00
CT23 Dominik Hasek .75 2.00
CT24 Martin Brodeur 1.00 2.50
CT25 Tony Amonte .30 .75
CT26 Keith Tkachuk .40 1.00
CT27 Patrick Roy 2.00 5.00
CT28 Pavel Bure .40 1.00
CT29 Paul Kariya .40 1.00
CT30 Curtis Joseph .40 1.00

1999-00 Upper Deck Fantastic Finishers

Randomly inserted in Series One packs at the rate of 1:11, this 15-card set features a gray and white border and blue foil stamping. Silver and gold parallels were also created and inserted randomly. Silver parallels were limited to 100 serial numbered sets. Gold parallels were numbered 1/1 and are unpriced due to scarcity.
COMPLETE SET (15) 12.00 25.00
*SILVER/100: 20X TO 50X BASIC INSERTS
FF1 Brett Hull .60 1.50
FF2 John LeClair .50 1.25
FF3 Eric Lindros .50 1.25
FF4 Jaromir Jagr .75 2.00
FF5 Sergei Samsonov .40 1.00
FF6 Teemu Selanne .50 1.25
FF7 Alexei Yashin .40 1.00
FF8 Keith Tkachuk .50 1.25
FF9 Pavel Bure .50 1.25
FF10 Peter Forsberg 1.25 3.00
FF11 Brendan Shanahan .50 1.25
FF12 Tony Amonte .40 1.00
FF13 Paul Kariya .50 1.25
FF14 Steve Yzerman 2.50 6.00
FF15 Joe Sakic 1.00 2.50

1999-00 Upper Deck Game Jerseys

Randomly inserted in Series One packs at the rate of 1:287, this 18-card set features player action shots with a swatch of a game worn jersey in the shape of the NHL logo. A special Wayne Gretzky jersey card was released that features a swatch of an NHL jersey and a CHL jersey which are sequentially numbered to 99, and a special Nagano Olympic Gretzky jersey was issued as well. Several players have signed versions that are sequentially numbered to 25.
BH Brett Hull 10.00 25.00
DH Dominik Hasek 12.50 30.00
EL Eric Lindros 8.00 20.00
JJ Jaromir Jagr 12.50 30.00
JL John LeClair 8.00 20.00
JS Joe Sakic 15.00 40.00
MB Martin Brodeur 20.00 50.00
MM Mike Modano 10.00 25.00
PF Peter Forsberg 20.00 50.00
PR Patrick Roy 20.00 50.00
RB Ray Bourque 12.00 30.00
SF Sergei Fedorov 10.00 25.00
SS Sergei Samsonov 8.00 20.00
SY Steve Yzerman 15.00 40.00
TS Teemu Selanne 10.00 25.00
WG1 Wayne Gretzky 30.00 80.00
WG2 Wayne Gretzky Dual/99 300.00 600.00
WG3 Wayne Gretzky Nagano 125.00 300.00
BHS B.Hull AU/25 150.00 300.00
RBS R.Bourque AU/25 150.00 300.00
SYS S.Yzerman AU/25 250.00 500.00
WGS1 W.Gretzky AU/25 400.00 800.00

1999-00 Upper Deck Game Jerseys Series II

Randomly inserted in Series Two packs at the rate of 1:287, this 16-card set features player action photography coupled with a swatch of a game worn jersey. A special Canadian jersey card was issued for Steve Yzerman, and several players have autographed versions that are sequentially numbered to 25.
AM Al MacInnis 8.00 20.00
CJ Curtis Joseph 8.00 20.00
DH Dominik Hasek 15.00 40.00
EB Ed Belfour 8.00 20.00
JJ Jaromir Jagr 12.00 30.00
JL John LeClair 8.00 20.00
JR Jeremy Roenick 10.00 25.00
JT Joe Thornton 12.00 30.00
MB Martin Brodeur 20.00 50.00
PF Peter Forsberg 12.00 30.00
PK Paul Kariya 10.00 25.00
PR Patrick Roy 20.00 50.00
SF Sergei Fedorov 10.00 25.00
SY Steve Yzerman 20.00 50.00
TS Teemu Selanne 12.00 30.00
WG Wayne Gretzky 30.00 80.00
CJS C.Joseph AU/25 100.00 200.00
EBS E.Belfour AU/25 100.00 200.00
SYC Steve Yzerman CAN 15.00 40.00
SYS S.Yzerman AU/25 250.00 500.00
WGS W.Gretzky AU/25 400.00 800.00

1999-00 Upper Deck Game Jersey Patch

Randomly inserted in Series One packs, this 17-card set features premium swatches of game jersey patches. Unpriced 1/1 parallels also exist.
WG1P Wayne Gretzky 400.00 800.00
WG2P Wayne Gretzky 400.00 800.00
BHP Brett Hull 125.00 300.00
DHP Dominik Hasek 125.00 300.00
ELP Eric Lindros 75.00 200.00
JJP Jaromir Jagr 125.00 300.00
JLP John LeClair 75.00 200.00
JSP Joe Sakic 125.00 300.00
MBP Martin Brodeur 150.00 400.00
MMP Mike Modano 100.00 250.00
PFP Peter Forsberg 125.00 300.00
PRP Patrick Roy 150.00 400.00
RBP Ray Bourque 125.00 300.00
SFP Sergei Fedorov 125.00 300.00
SSP Sergei Samsonov 75.00 200.00
SYP Steve Yzerman 150.00 400.00
TSP Teemu Selanne 75.00 200.00

1999-00 Upper Deck Game Jersey Patch Series II

Randomly inserted in Series Two packs at a rate of 1:7500, this 14-card set features premium swatches of game used jersey patches. Unpriced 1/1 parallels also exist.
CJP Curtis Joseph 100.00 250.00
DHP Dominik Hasek 125.00 300.00
EBP Ed Belfour 100.00 250.00
JJP Jaromir Jagr 125.00 300.00
JLP John LeClair 60.00 150.00
JTP Joe Thornton 100.00 250.00
KTP Keith Tkachuk 60.00 150.00
MBP Martin Brodeur 150.00 350.00
PFP Peter Forsberg 100.00 250.00
PKP Paul Kariya 75.00 200.00
PRP Patrick Roy 150.00 400.00
SFP Sergei Fedorov 75.00 200.00
SYP Steve Yzerman 150.00 400.00
WGP Wayne Gretzky 400.00 800.00

1999-00 Upper Deck Game Pads

Randomly inserted in Series Two packs at the rate of 1:5000, this single card issue features a swatch of Curtis Joseph game used goalie pads.
CJGP Curtis Joseph 20.00 50.00

1999-00 Upper Deck Gretzky Profiles

Randomly inserted in Series One Hobby packs at the rate of 1:23, this 10-card set pays tribute to the career of Wayne Gretzky. Both silver and gold parallels were also created. Silver parallels were serial numbered to 100, and gold to 1/1.
COMPLETE SET (10) 20.00 50.00
COMMON GRETZKY (GP1-GP10) 2.50 6.00
*SILVER/100: 2.5X TO 6X BASIC INSERTS

1999-00 Upper Deck Headed for the Hall

Randomly seeded in Series Two pack, this 15-card set features top NHL players on an all silver foil card stock with foil stamp highlights. Silver and gold parallels were also created. Silver parallels were limited to 100 serial numbered sets. Unpriced gold parallels were numbered 1/1.
COMPLETE SET (15) 20.00 40.00
*SILVER/100: 8X TO 20X BASIC INSERTS
HOF1 Wayne Gretzky 5.00 12.00
HOF2 Dominik Hasek 1.50 4.00
HOF3 Ray Bourque 1.25 3.00
HOF4 Steve Yzerman 4.00 10.00
HOF5 Jaromir Jagr 1.25 3.00
HOF6 Brett Hull 1.00 2.50
HOF7 Eric Lindros .75 2.00
HOF8 Adam Oates .60 1.50
HOF9 Brian Leetch .75 2.00
HOF10 Patrick Roy 4.00 10.00
HOF11 Mark Messier .75 2.00
HOF12 Luc Robitaille .60 1.50
HOF13 Joe Sakic 1.50 4.00
HOF14 Chris Chelios .75 2.00
HOF15 Curtis Joseph .75 2.00

1999-00 Upper Deck Ice Gallery

Randomly inserted in Series Two packs at the rate of 1:72, this 10-card set features silver foil borders along the top and the two sided of the card with blue foil highlights. Silver and gold parallels were also created and inserted randomly. Silver parallels were limited to 100 serial numbered sets. Unpriced gold parallels were numbered 1/1.
COMPLETE SET (10) 40.00 80.00
*SILVER/100: 4X TO 10X BASIC INSERTS
IG1 Jaromir Jagr 4.00 10.00
IG2 Paul Kariya 3.00 8.00
IG3 Peter Forsberg 6.00 15.00
IG4 Dominik Hasek 5.00 12.00
IG5 Patrick Roy 12.50 30.00
IG6 Teemu Selanne 3.00 8.00
IG7 Eric Lindros 3.00 8.00
IG8 Patrik Stefan 4.00 10.00
IG9 Steve Kariya 3.00 8.00
IG10 Pavel Bure 3.00 8.00

1999-00 Upper Deck Marquee Attractions

Randomly seeded in Series One packs, this 15-card set features an all silver foil card stock with color player photography and blue foil highlights. Silver and gold parallels were also created. Silver parallels were limited to 100 serial numbered sets. Gold parallels were numbered 1/1 and are not priced.
COMPLETE SET (15) 12.00 25.00
*SILVER/100: 20X TO 50X BSIC INSERTS
MA1 Ray Bourque .75 2.00
MA2 Paul Kariya .50 1.25
MA3 Eric Lindros .50 1.25
MA4 Jaromir Jagr .75 2.00
MA5 Dominik Hasek 1.00 2.50
MA6 Patrick Roy 2.50 6.00
MA7 Alexei Yashin .40 1.00
MA8 Mats Sundin .50 1.25
MA9 Steve Yzerman 2.50 6.00
MA10 Pavel Bure .50 1.25
MA11 Vincent Lecavalier .50 1.25
MA12 Teemu Selanne .50 1.25
MA13 Mike Modano .75 2.00
MA14 Keith Tkachuk .50 1.25
MA15 Peter Forsberg 1.25 3.00

1999-00 Upper Deck New Ice Age

Randomly seeded in Series One packs, this 20-card set features foil card stock with color player photography and highlights several players ready to take the NHL in the 21st Century. Silver and gold parallels were also created. Silver parallels were limited to 100 serial numbered sets. Unpriced gold parallels were numbered 1/1.
COMPLETE SET (20) 20.00 40.00
*SILVER/100: 10X TO 25X BASIC INSERTS
N1 Jaromir Jagr 1.50 4.00
N2 Paul Kariya 1.00 2.50
N3 Sergei Samsonov .75 2.00
N4 Vadim Sharifijanov .40 1.00
N5 Ty Jones .40 1.00
N6 Teemu Selanne 1.00 2.50
N7 Martin Brodeur 2.50 6.00
N8 David Legwand .75 2.00
N9 Vincent Lecavalier 1.00 2.50
N10 Paul Mara .75 2.00
N11 Jean-Marc Pelletier .40 1.00
N12 Jean-Sebastien Giguere .75 2.00
N13 Marian Hossa 1.00 2.50
N14 Milan Hejduk 1.00 2.50
N15 Chris Drury .75 2.00
N16 Rico Fata .40 1.00
N17 Patrik Elias .75 2.00
N18 Eric Brewer .75 2.00
N19 Joe Thornton 1.50 4.00
N20 J-P Dumont .75 2.00

1999-00 Upper Deck NHL Scrapbook

Randomly seeded in Series Two packs, this 15-card set features a shadowed background with a full color player photograph and gold foil highlights. Silver and gold parallels were also created. Silver parallels were limited to 100 serial numbered sets. Gold parallels were numbered 1/1 and are not priced due to scarcity.
COMPLETE SET (15) 12.00 25.00
*SILVER/100: 10X TO 25X BASIC CARDS
SB1 Patrick Roy 2.50 6.00
SB2 Ray Bourque .75 2.00
SB3 Steve Yzerman 2.50 6.00
SB4 Jaromir Jagr .75 2.00
SB5 Paul Kariya .60 1.50
SB6 Peter Forsberg 1.25 3.00
SB7 Pavel Bure .60 1.50
SB8 Curtis Joseph .60 1.50
SB9 Brett Hull .60 1.50
SB10 Eric Lindros .60 1.50
SB11 Teemu Selanne .60 1.50
SB12 Brendan Shanahan .60 1.50
SB13 John LeClair .60 1.50
SB14 Steve Kariya .60 1.50
SB15 Patrik Stefan .75 2.00

1999-00 Upper Deck PowerDeck Inserts

Randomly inserted in Series 1 Hobby packs at the rate of 1:23 for base cards and one in 288 for Gretzky SP cards, this 9-card set is an actual CD-ROM that contains footage, interviews, and a photo gallery that can be viewed with a PC.
COMPLETE SET (9) 75.00 150.00
PD1 Dominik Hasek 3.00 8.00
PD2 Paul Kariya 2.00 5.00
PD3 Jaromir Jagr 2.50 6.00
PD4 Steve Yzerman 8.00 20.00
PD5 Patrick Roy 8.00 20.00
PD6 Brett Hull 2.00 5.00
PD7 Wayne Gretzky 12.50 25.00
PD8 Wayne Gretzky SP 30.00 80.00
PD9 Wayne Gretzky SP 30.00 80.00

1999-00 Upper Deck Sixth Sense

Randomly inserted in Series Two packs, this 20-card set highlights top players on a "framed" card stock with foil stamp highlights. Silver and gold parallels were also created. Silver parallels were limited to 100 serial numbered sets. Gold parallels were numbered 1/1 and are not priced due to scarcity.
COMPLETE SET (20) 10.00 25.00
*SILVER/100: 25X TO 60X BASIC INSERTS
SS1 Paul Kariya .40 1.00
SS2 Patrick Roy 2.00 5.00
SS3 Brett Hull .50 1.25
SS4 Eric Lindros .40 1.00
SS5 Sergei Samsonov .40 1.00
SS6 Peter Forsberg 1.00 2.50
SS7 Patrik Stefan .60 1.50
SS8 Steve Yzerman 2.00 5.00
SS9 Jaromir Jagr .60 1.50
SS10 David Legwand .40 1.00
SS11 Steve Kariya .50 1.25
SS12 Tim Connolly .40 1.00
SS13 Pavel Bure .40 1.00
SS14 Brendan Shanahan .40 1.00
SS15 Martin Brodeur 1.00 2.50
SS16 Dominik Hasek .75 2.00
SS17 Mats Sundin .40 1.00
SS18 Vincent Lecavalier .40 1.00
SS19 Keith Tkachuk .40 1.00
SS20 Mike Modano .60 1.50

1999-00 Upper Deck Ultimate Defense

Randomly inserted in Series Two packs, this 10-card set features top goalies on an all foil card with color borders to match each respective goalie's team colors and blue foil highlights. Silver and gold parallels were also created. Silver parallels were limited to 100 serial numbered sets. Gold parallels were numbered 1/1 and are not priced due to scarcity.
COMPLETE SET (10) 10.00 20.00
*SILVER/100: 12X TO 30X BASIC INSERTS
UD1 Byron Dafoe .60 1.50
UD2 Dominik Hasek 1.50 4.00
UD3 Patrick Roy 1.25 3.00
UD4 Chris Osgood .60 1.50
UD5 Ed Belfour .75 2.00
UD6 Roman Turek .60 1.50
UD7 Mike Richter .75 2.00
UD8 Nikolai Khabibulin .60 1.50
UD9 Martin Brodeur 2.00 5.00
UD10 Curtis Joseph .60 1.50

1999-00 Upper Deck Sobey's Memorial Cup

Released by Upper Deck in conjunction with Sobey's grocery stores and Kraft, this 16-card set features players and designs from the 1999-2000 Upper Deck NHL Prospects set and pays tribute the 2000 Memorial Cup tournament. The cards were available in 4-card cello packs over a four-week period at Sobey's stores in the Halifax area. The cards mirror the UD CHL series issued earlier that year, but feature several small design changes, including the addition of a Sobey's logo.
COMPLETE SET (16) 16.00 25.00
1 Alexei Volkov .75 2.00
2 Justin Papineau .75 2.00
3 Michael Henrich .40 1.00
4 Kris Beech .75 2.00
5 Mark Bell 1.50 4.00
6 Andrei Shefer .40 1.00
7 Pavel Brendl .75 2.00
8 Blake Robson .40 1.00
9 Ben Knopp .40 1.00
10 Maxime Ouellet 1.50 4.00
11 Thatcher Bell .40 1.00
12 Brian Finley .75 2.00
13 Jared Aulin 1.50 4.00
14 Jared Newman .40 1.00
15 Brad Boyes 4.00 10.00
16 Miguel Delisle .40 1.00

2000-01 Upper Deck

Released as a 440-card set, Upper Deck is comprised of 180 veteran cards and 50 short printed prospect cards (181-230) in series one, and 180 veteran cards and 30 short printed prospect cards (411-440) in series two. Base cards have full color action photography and foil highlights. Upper Deck was packaged in 24-pack boxes with packs containing 10 cards and carried a suggested retail price of $2.99.
COMPLETE SET (440) 200.00 400.00
COMP.SET w/o YG's (360) 20.00 50.00
COMP.SER.1 (230) 125.00 250.00
COMP.SER.1 w/o YG's (180) 15.00 30.00
COMP.SER.2 (210) 100.00 200.00
COMP.SER.2 w/o YG's (180) 10.00 25.00
1 Paul Kariya .25 .60
2 Steve Rucchin .12 .30
3 Oleg Tverdovsky .12 .30
4 Mike Leclerc .12 .30
5 Ladislav Kohn .12 .30
6 Guy Hebert .15 .40
7 Dean Sylvester .12 .30
8 Andrew Brunette .12 .30
9 Ray Ferraro .12 .30
10 Donald Audette .15 .40
11 Damian Rhodes .12 .30
12 Patrik Stefan .15 .40
13 Joe Thornton .30 .75
14 Brian Rolston .15 .40
15 John Grahame .12 .30
16 Jason Allison .15 .40
17 Kyle McLaren .12 .30
18 Andre Savage .12 .30
19 Martin Biron .15 .40
20 Doug Gilmour .25 .60
21 Chris Gratton .12 .30
22 Miroslav Satan .12 .30
23 Maxim Afinogenov .12 .30
24 Dimitri Kalinin .12 .30
25 Oleg Saprykin .12 .30
26 Valeri Bure .15 .40
27 Derek Morris .12 .30
28 Marc Savard .15 .40
29 Clarke Wilm .12 .30
30 Fred Brathwaite .15 .40
31 Ron Francis .25 .60
32 Sami Kapanen .12 .30
33 Bates Battaglia .12 .30
34 Arturs Irbe .15 .40
35 Dave Tanabe .12 .30
36 Rod Brind'Amour .20 .50
37 Michal Grosek .12 .30
38 Steve Sullivan .12 .30
39 Eric Daze .15 .40
40 Bryan McCabe .12 .30
41 Michael Nylander .12 .30
42 Alexei Zhamnov .15 .40
43 Milan Hejduk .15 .40
44 Ray Bourque .30 .75
45 Patrick Roy .50 1.25
46 Peter Forsberg .25 .60
47 Martin Skoula .15 .40
48 Shjon Podein .12 .30
49 Aaron Miller .12 .30
50 Espen Knutsen .12 .30
51 Jamie Pushor .12 .30
52 Kevyn Adams .12 .30
53 Marc Denis .15 .40
54 Ron Tugnutt .15 .40
55 Mike Modano .30 .75
56 Joe Nieuwendyk .20 .50
57 Mike Keane .15 .40
58 Darryl Sydor .15 .40
59 Brenden Morrow .15 .40
60 Jere Lehtinen .15 .40
61 Derian Hatcher .15 .40
62 Brendan Shanahan .25 .60
63 Sergei Fedorov .30 .75
64 Darren McCarty .12 .30
65 Tomas Holmstrom .15 .40
66 Chris Osgood .20 .50
67 Nicklas Lidstrom .20 .50
68 Ryan Smyth .15 .40
69 Igor Ulanov .12 .30
70 Tommy Salo .15 .40
71 Ethan Moreau .12 .30
72 Daniel Cleary .15 .40
73 Bill Guerin .20 .50
74 Pavel Bure .25 .60
75 Ray Whitney .15 .40
76 Lance Pitlick .12 .30
77 Trevor Kidd .12 .30
78 Mike Wilson .12 .30
79 Ivan Novoseltsev .12 .30
80 Luc Robitaille .20 .50
81 Stephane Fiset .12 .30
82 Rob Blake .20 .50
83 Jozef Stumpel .12 .30
84 Craig Johnson .12 .30
85 Glen Murray .12 .30
86 Kelly Buchberger .15 .40
87 Manny Fernandez .15 .40
88 Stacy Roest .12 .30
89 Andy Sutton .12 .30
90 Scott Pellerin .12 .30
91 Jim Dowd .12 .30
92 Dainius Zubrus .12 .30
93 Brian Savage .12 .30
94 Martin Rucinsky .12 .30
95 Craig Darby .12 .30
96 Jose Theodore .25 .60
97 David Legwand .20 .50
98 Rob Valicevic .12 .30
99 Randy Robitaille .12 .30
100 Mike Dunham .12 .30
101 Kimmo Timonen .12 .30
102 Scott Gomez .15 .40
103 Petr Sykora .15 .40
104 Alexander Mogilny .15 .40
105 John Madden .15 .40
106 Jason Arnott .15 .40
107 Sergei Brylin .12 .30
108 Scott Stevens .20 .50
109 Tim Connolly .12 .30
110 Mariusz Czerkawski .12 .30
111 Zdeno Chara .20 .50
112 Kenny Jonsson .12 .30
113 Claude Lapointe .12 .30
114 Theo Fleury .25 .60
115 Mike Richter .20 .50
116 Mike York .12 .30
117 Jan Hlavac .12 .30
118 Adam Graves .15 .40
119 Mark Messier .30 .75
120 Marian Hossa .15 .40
121 Daniel Alfredsson .20 .50
122 Mike Fisher .15 .40
123 Patrick Lalime .15 .40
124 Wade Redden .12 .30
125 Shawn McEachern .12 .30
126 John LeClair .20 .50
127 Mark Recchi .25 .60
128 Brian Boucher .15 .40
129 Simon Gagne .20 .50
130 Eric Desjardins .15 .40
131 Rick Tocchet .15 .40
132 Jeremy Roenick .20 .50
133 Travis Green .12 .30
134 Trevor Letowski .12 .30
135 Teppo Numminen .12 .30
136 Shane Doan .15 .40
137 Mike Sullivan .12 .30
138 Jaromir Jagr .50 1.25
139 Robert Lang .12 .30
140 Jan Hrdina .12 .30
141 Matthew Barnaby .15 .40
142 Jean-Sebastien Aubin .15 .40
143 Jiri Slegr .12 .30
144 Owen Nolan .20 .50
145 Jeff Friesen .12 .30
146 Patrick Marleau .20 .50
147 Brad Stuart .15 .40
148 Steve Shields .12 .30
149 Todd Harvey .15 .40
150 Pavol Demitra .25 .60
151 Chris Pronger .15 .40
152 Scott Young .12 .30
153 Todd Reirden .12 .30
154 Roman Turek .15 .40
155 Marty Reasoner .12 .30
156 Mike Johnson .12 .30
157 Todd Warriner .12 .30
158 Paul Mara .12 .30
159 Dan Cloutier .15 .40
160 Fredrik Modin .12 .30
161 Curtis Joseph .25 .60
162 Steve Thomas .12 .30
163 Darcy Tucker .12 .30
164 Yanic Perreault .12 .30
165 Sergei Berezin .12 .30
166 Dimitri Yushkevich .12 .30
167 Markus Naslund .15 .40
168 Andrew Cassels .12 .30
169 Todd Bertuzzi .15 .40
170 Felix Potvin .30 .75
171 Ed Jovanovski .15 .40
172 Trent Klatt .12 .30
173 Adam Oates .20 .50
174 Chris Simon .12 .30
175 Richard Zednik .12 .30
176 Calle Johansson .12 .30
177 Andrei Nikolishin .12 .30
178 Jeff Halpern .12 .30
179 Steve Yzerman CL .40 1.00
180 Curtis Joseph CL .15 .40
181 Eric Nickulas YG RC 1.50 4.00
182 Serge Aubin YG RC 2.00 5.00
183 Keith Aldridge YG RC 1.50 4.00
184 Mike Minard YG RC 2.50 6.00
185 Steven Reinprecht YG RC 2.50 6.00
186 David Gosselin YG RC 2.00 5.00
187 Andrew Berenzweig YG 1.50 4.00
188 Willie Mitchell YG RC 2.50 6.00
189 Colin White YG RC 1.50 4.00
190 Petr Mika YG RC 1.50 4.00
191 Steve Valiquette YG RC 2.00 5.00
192 Kyle Freadrich YG RC 1.50 4.00
193 Rich Parent YG RC 2.00 5.00
194 Greg Andrusak YG RC 2.00 5.00
195 Brent Sopel YG RC 2.50 6.00
196 Matt Pettinger YG RC 1.50 4.00
197 Chris Nielsen YG RC 1.50 4.00
198 Dany Heatley YG RC 10.00 25.00
199 Matt Zultek YG RC 1.50 4.00
200 Dmitri Afanasenkov YG RC 1.50 4.00
201 Tyler Bouck YG RC 1.50 4.00
202 Jonas Andersson YG RC 1.50 4.00
203 Marc-Andre Thinel YG RC 1.50 4.00
204 Jaroslav Svoboda YG RC 1.50 4.00
205 Josef Vasicek YG RC 4.00 10.00
206 Andrew Raycroft YG RC 4.00 10.00
207 Juraj Kolnik YG RC 1.50 4.00
208 Zdenek Blatny YG RC 1.50 4.00
209 Sebastien Caron YG RC 2.00 5.00
210 Michael Ryder YG RC 4.00 10.00
211 Jason Jaspers YG RC 1.50 4.00
212 Pavel Brendl YG 1.50 4.00
213 Milan Kraft YG 1.50 4.00
214 Justin Williams YG RC 12.00 30.00
215 Andreas Karlsson YG 1.50 4.00
216 Herbert Vasilijevs YG RC 1.50 4.00
217 Sergei Vyshedkevich YG RC 1.50 4.00
218 Johnathan Aitken YG RC 1.50 4.00
219 Brandon Smith YG RC 1.50 4.00
220 Jeff Cowan YG RC 1.50 4.00
221 Steve Brule YG RC 1.50 4.00
222 Johan Witehall YG RC 1.50 4.00
223 Jani Hurme YG RC 1.50 4.00
224 Jean-Guy Trudel YG RC 1.50 4.00
225 Kaspars Astashenko YG RC 1.50 4.00
226 Scott Hartnell YG RC 8.00 20.00
227 Dieter Kochan YG RC 1.50 4.00
228 Rostislav Klesla YG RC 4.00 10.00
229 Marian Gaborik YG RC 15.00 40.00
230 Alfie Michaud YG 2.50 6.00
231 Teemu Selanne .40 1.00
232 Matt Cullen .12 .30
233 German Titov .12 .30
234 Vitali Vishnevski .12 .30
235 Pavel Trnka .12 .30
236 Marty McInnis .15 .40
237 Hnat Domenichelli .12 .30
238 Per Svartvadet .12 .30
239 Steve Guolla .12 .30
240 Frantisek Kaberle .12 .30
241 Steve Staios .12 .30
242 Byron Dafoe .15 .40
243 Peter Popovic .12 .30
244 Paul Coffey .20 .50
245 Sergei Samsonov .15 .40
246 Andrei Kovalenko .12 .30
247 Shawn Bates .12 .30
248 Dominik Hasek .30 .75
249 Stu Barnes .15 .40
250 Curtis Brown .12 .30
251 Alexei Zhitnik .15 .40
252 Jay McKee .12 .30
253 Vaclav Varada .12 .30
254 Jarome Iginla .20 .50
255 Phil Housley .15 .40
256 Cory Stillman .12 .30
257 Mike Vernon .15 .40
258 Jeff Shantz .12 .30
259 Brad Werenka .12 .30
260 Jeff O'Neill .15 .40
261 Martin Gelinas .12 .30
262 Tommy Westlund .12 .30
263 Steve Halko .12 .30
264 Sandis Ozolinsh .15 .40
265 Rob DiMaio .12 .30
266 Tony Amonte .15 .40
267 Jocelyn Thibault .15 .40
268 Boris Mironov .12 .30
269 Dean McAmmond .12 .30
270 Jean-Yves Leroux .12 .30
271 Valeri Zelepukin .12 .30
272 Nolan Pratt .12 .30
273 Joe Sakic .30 .75
274 Chris Drury .15 .40
275 Alex Tanguay .15 .40
276 Adam Deadmarsh .15 .40
277 Stephane Yelle .12 .30
278 Ron Tugnutt .15 .40
279 Geoff Sanderson .15 .40
280 Steve Heinze .12 .30
281 Jean-Luc Grand-Pierre .12 .30
282 Robert Kron .12 .30
283 Kevin Dineen .12 .30
284 Brett Hull .30 .75
285 Sergei Zubov .15 .40
286 Jamie Langenbrunner .15 .40
287 Ed Belfour .20 .50
288 Roman Lyashenko .12 .30
289 Ted Donato .12 .30
290 Martin LaPointe .15 .40
291 Chris Chelios .20 .50
292 Slava Kozlov .15 .40
293 Steve Yzerman .60 1.50
294 Larry Murphy .15 .40
295 Brent Gilchrist .12 .30
296 Doug Weight .20 .50
297 Eric Brewer .12 .30
298 Todd Marchant .12 .30
299 Tom Poti .12 .30
300 Mike Grier .12 .30
301 Georges Laraque .15 .40
302 Igor Larionov .20 .50
303 Roberto Luongo .30 .75
304 Olli Jokinen .15 .40
305 Viktor Kozlov .15 .40
306 Robert Svehla .12 .30
307 Mike Sillinger .12 .30
308 Jere Karalahti .12 .30
309 Zigmund Palffy .20 .50
310 Mattias Norstrom .12 .30
311 Bryan Smolinski .15 .40
312 Jamie Storr .15 .40
313 Ian Laperriere .12 .30
314 Manny Fernandez .15 .40
315 Sergei Krivokrasov .12 .30
316 Darryl Laplante .12 .30
317 Sean O'Donnell .12 .30
318 Scott Pellerin .12 .30
319 Saku Koivu .20 .50
320 Sergei Zholtok .12 .30
321 Jeff Hackett .12 .30
322 Eric Weinrich .12 .30
323 Karl Dykhuis .12 .30
324 Benoit Brunet .12 .30
325 Cliff Ronning .12 .30
326 Patric Kjellberg .12 .30
327 Drake Berehowsky .12 .30
328 Vitali Yachmenev .12 .30
329 Tomas Vokoun .15 .40
330 Greg Johnson .12 .30
331 Patrik Elias .20 .50
332 Bobby Holik .12 .30

333 Randy McKay .12 .30
334 Brian Rafalski .12 .30
335 Martin Brodeur .40 1.00
336 Sergei Brylin .12 .30
337 Brad Isbister .12 .30
338 Roman Hamrlik .15 .40
339 John Vanbiesbrouck .15 .40
340 Dave Scatchard .12 .30
341 Oleg Kvasha .12 .30
342 Mark Parrish .12 .30
343 Petr Nedved .15 .40
344 Brian Leetch .20 .50
345 Radek Dvorak .15 .40
346 Vladimir Malakhov .12 .30
347 Valeri Kamensky .12 .30
348 Rich Pilon .12 .30
349 Radek Bonk .15 .40
350 Vaclav Prospal .12 .30
351 Jason York .12 .30
352 Andreas Dackell .12 .30
353 Magnus Arvedson .12 .30
354 Rob Zamuner .12 .30
355 Daymond Langkow .12 .30
356 Keith Primeau .15 .40
357 Dan McGillis .12 .30
358 Andy Delmore .12 .30
359 Jody Hull .12 .30
360 Luke Richardson .12 .30
361 Joe Juneau .15 .40
362 Mika Alatalo .12 .30
363 Keith Tkachuk .20 .50
364 Radoslav Suchy .12 .30
365 Louie DeBrusk .12 .30
366 Sean Burke .12 .30
367 Martin Straka .15 .40
368 Alexei Kovalev .15 .40
369 Alexei Morozov .12 .30
370 Josef Beranek .12 .30
371 Milan Kraft .12 .30
372 Darius Kasparaitis .15 .40
373 Vincent Damphousse .15 .40
374 Mike Ricci .15 .40
375 Scott Thornton .15 .40
376 Niklas Sundstrom .12 .30
377 Marco Sturm .15 .40
378 Jeff Norton .12 .30
379 Pierre Turgeon .20 .50
380 Al MacInnis .20 .50
381 Jochen Hecht .12 .30
382 Sean Hill .12 .30
383 Pavol Demitra .25 .60
384 Michal Handzus .12 .30
385 Mike Eastwood .12 .30
386 Vincent Lecavalier .15 .40
387 Brian Holzinger .12 .30
388 Pavel Kubina .12 .30
389 Andrei Zyuzin .12 .30
390 Wayne Primeau .12 .30
391 Mats Sundin .20 .50
392 Gary Roberts .12 .30
393 Igor Korolev .12 .30
394 Shayne Corson .12 .30
395 Tomas Kaberle .12 .30
396 Cory Cross .12 .30
397 Peter Schaefer .12 .30
398 Adrian Aucoin .12 .30
399 Brendan Morrison .20 .50
400 Daniel Sedin .40 1.00
401 Donald Brashear .12 .30
402 Henrik Sedin .30 .75
403 Joe Murphy .15 .40
404 Steve Konowalchuk .12 .30
405 Joe Reekie .12 .30
406 Sergei Gonchar .12 .30
407 Peter Bondra .15 .40
408 Olaf Kolzig .20 .50
409 Steve Yzerman CL .40 1.00
410 Mark Messier CL .20 .50
411 Rick DiPietro YG RC 6.00 15.00
412 Michel Riesen YG RC 2.00 5.00
413 Reto Von Arx YG RC 2.00 5.00
414 Martin Havlat YG RC 5.00 12.00
415 Matt Elich YG RC 2.00 5.00
416 Jonas Ronnqvist YG RC 1.50 4.00
417 Jason Labarbera YG RC 2.00 5.00
418 Marc Moro YG RC 1.50 4.00
419 Mark Smith YG RC 1.50 4.00
420 Petr Hubacek YG RC 1.50 4.00
421 Niclas Wallin YG RC 2.00 5.00
422 Brian Swanson YG RC 1.50 4.00
423 Petteri Nummelin YG RC 1.50 4.00
424 Alexandre Boikov YG RC 1.50 4.00
425 Ossi Vaananen YG RC 2.00 5.00
426 Roman Simicek YG RC 1.50 4.00
427 Greg Classen YG RC 1.50 4.00
428 Marty Turco YG RC 6.00 15.00
429 Shane Hnidy YG RC 1.50 4.00
430 Lubomir Visnovsky YG RC 3.00 8.00
431 Bryce Salvador YG RC 2.00 5.00
432 Lubomir Sekeras YG RC 1.50 4.00
433 David Aebischer YG RC 3.00 8.00
434 Peter Ratchuk YG RC 2.00 5.00
435 Roman Cechmanek YG RC 2.00 5.00
436 Eric Belanger YG RC 2.00 5.00
437 Alexander Kharitonov YG RC 1.50 4.00
438 Jeff Bateman YG RC 1.50 4.00
439 Damian Surma YG RC 1.50 4.00
440 Jordan Krestanovich YG RC 1.50 4.00

2000-01 Upper Deck Exclusives Tier 1

Randomly inserted in Hobby packs, this 440-card set parallels the base set enhanced with silver foil. Each card is sequentially numbered to 100.
*VETS/100: 10X TO 25X BASIC CARDS
*YOUNG GUNS/100: 1X TO 2.5X BASIC YG
119 Mark Messier 8.00 20.00
229 Marian Gaborik YG 50.00 100.00
410 Mark Messier CL 6.00 15.00

2000-01 Upper Deck Exclusives Tier 2

Randomly inserted in Hobby packs, this 440-card set parallels the base set enhanced with gold foil. Each card is sequentially numbered to 25.
*VETS/25: 25X TO 60X BASIC CARDS
*YOUNG GUNS/25: 2X TO 5X BASIC YG
119 Mark Messier 20.00 50.00
410 Mark Messier CL 15.00 40.00

2000-01 Upper Deck 500 Goal Club

Randomly inserted in various Upper Deck product packs, this set pays tribute to the members of the esteemed 500-goal club. Each card contains a swatch of a game worn jersey or stick in the shape of the NHL logo. Card numbers on the back carry a "500" prefix. Dale Hawerchuk and Mike Gartner were randomly found in Black Diamond and only 650 unsigned versions were produced. Pat Verbeek and Mario Lemieux were randomly available in SPx with a total of 800 unsigned cards produced of each and 25 serial-numbered autographed versions. Phil Esposito was randomly available in Upper Deck Ice with 450 unsigned cards and 25 serial-numbered signed cards produced. Dave Andreychuk and John Bucyk were randomly available in Upper Deck Legends with a total of 900 unsigned cards produced between the two players and 25 serial-numbered autographed versions of each. Frank Mahovlich and Lanny McDonald were randomly available in Upper Deck MVP with 600 unsigned cards produced and 25 serial-numbered autographed versions. Mark Messier was available in Upper Deck Vintage, 300 total cards were issued for the unsigned version, and 25 autographed copies were issued. Jari Kurri, Joe Mullen, Mark Messier, and Wayne Gretzky were all randomly available in Upper Deck Series I packs. A serial-numbered autographed version of each was also produced. Mark Messier was the only player inserted in series 2 packs.
500DA Dave Andreychuk J 12.00 30.00
500DA D.Andreychuk J AU/25 150.00 300.00
500DH Dale Hawerchuk J 12.00 30.00
500DH D.Hawerchuk J AU/25 150.00 300.00
500FM F. Mahovlich S 20.00 50.00
500FM F. Mahovlich S AU/25 200.00 400.00
500JK Jari Kurri J 30.00 80.00
500JK Jarri Kurri J AU/25 400.00 600.00
500JM Joe Mullen J 20.00 50.00
500JM Joe Mullen J AU/25 100.00 250.00
500LM L.McDonald S AU/25 350.00 500.00
500LM Lanny McDonald S 15.00 40.00
500MG Michel Goulet S AU/25 100.00 250.00
500MG Michel Goulet S 12.50 30.00
500ML Mario Lemieux J 100.00 200.00
500ML Mario Lemieux J AU/25 800.00 1200.00
500MM Mark Messier J 30.00 80.00
500MM Mark Messier J AU/25 400.00 600.00
500PE Phil Esposito S 15.00 40.00
500PE Phil Esposito S AU/25 200.00 400.00
500PV Pat Verbeek J 12.50 30.00
500PV Pat Verbeek J AU/25 125.00 250.00
500WG Wayne Gretzky J 75.00 200.00
500WG Wayne Gretzky J AU/25 1000.00 2000.00
500JBU John Bucyk S AU/25 200.00 400.00
500JBU John Bucyk S 12.50 30.00
500MGA Mike Gartner J AU/25 300.00 500.00
500MGA Mike Gartner J 12.50 30.00

2000-01 Upper Deck All-Star Class

COMPLETE SET (10) 8.00 15.00
STATED ODDS 1:23 SER.2
A1 Teemu Selanne .60 1.50
A2 Valeri Bure .60 1.50
A3 Milan Hejduk .60 1.50
A4 Mike Modano 1.00 2.50
A5 Pavel Bure 1.00 2.50
A6 Marian Hossa .60 1.50
A7 Brian Boucher .60 1.50
A8 Keith Tkachuk .60 1.50
A9 Jaromir Jagr 1.25 3.00
A10 Curtis Joseph .60 1.50

2000-01 Upper Deck Dignitaries

COMPLETE SET (10) 20.00 40.00
STATED ODDS 1:23 SERIES 1
D1 Paul Kariya 1.50 4.00
D2 Ray Bourque 2.00 5.00
D3 Patrick Roy 3.00 8.00
D4 Brett Hull 2.00 5.00
D5 Steve Yzerman 4.00 10.00
D6 Pavel Bure 1.50 4.00
D7 Luc Robitaille 1.25 3.00
D8 Brian Leetch 1.25 3.00
D9 Jaromir Jagr 3.00 8.00
D10 Mark Messier 2.00 5.00

2000-01 Upper Deck e-Cards

Randomly inserted in packs at the rate of 1:12, this twelve card set features an interactive number that can be entered at the Upper Deck website to see if it evolves. Cards can evolve into Game Jersey Cards sequentially numbered to 300, Autographed Cards sequentially numbered to 200, or Autographed Game Jersey Cards sequentially numbered to 50.
EC1 Sergei Samsonov .20 .50
EC2 Brett Hull .30 .75
EC3 Steve Yzerman 1.25 3.00
EC4 Pavel Bure .40 1.00
EC5 John LeClair .30 .75
EC6 Curtis Joseph .25 .60
EC7 Martin Brodeur .60 1.50
EC8 Mark Messier .30 .75
EC9 Chris Osgood .20 .50
EC10 Mike Richter .25 .60
EC11 Ray Bourque .50 1.25
EC12 Jeremy Roenick .30 .75

2000-01 Upper Deck e-Card Prizes

Winning e-Cards may be redeemed for Game Jersey Cards sequentially numbered to 300, Autographed Cards sequentially numbered to 200, or Autographed Game Jersey Cards sequentially numbered to 50. The original checklist contained a Mark Messier jersey card which was later found to be non-existent.
ABH Brett Hull AU 20.00 50.00
ACJ Curtis Joseph AU 20.00 50.00
ACO Chris Osgood AU 12.00 30.00
AJL John LeClair AU 10.00 25.00
AJR Jeremy Roenick AU 15.00 40.00
AMB Martin Brodeur AU 25.00 60.00
AMM Mark Messier AU 30.00 80.00
AMR Mike Richter AU 12.00 30.00
APB Pavel Bure AU 15.00 40.00
ARB Ray Bourque AU 15.00 40.00
ASS Sergei Samsonov AU 12.00 30.00
ASY Steve Yzerman AU 30.00 80.00
EBH Brett Hull Jersey 10.00 25.00
ECJ Curtis Joseph JSY 10.00 25.00
ECO Chris Osgood JSY 6.00 15.00
EJL John LeClair JSY 6.00 15.00
EJR Jeremy Roenick JSY 6.00 15.00
EMB Martin Brodeur JSY 10.00 25.00
EMR Mike Richter JSY 8.00 20.00
EPB Pavel Bure JSY 10.00 25.00
ERB Ray Bourque JSY 8.00 20.00
ESS Sergei Samsonov JSY 6.00 15.00
ESY Steve Yzerman JSY 15.00 40.00
SRB Ray Bourque GJ/AU 40.00 100.00
SEBH Brett Hull GJ/AU 40.00 100.00
SECJ Curtis oseph GJ/AU 20.00 50.00
SECO Chris Osgood GJ/AU 20.00 50.00
SEJL John LeClair GJ/AU 15.00 40.00
SEJR Jeremy Roenick GJ/AU 20.00 50.00
SEMB Martin Brodeur GJ/AU 50.00 120.00
SEMM Mark Messier GJ/AU 40.00 100.00
SEMR Mike Richter GJ/AU 20.00 50.00
SEPB P.Bure GJ/AU 20.00 50.00
SESS S.Samsonov GJ/AU 15.00 40.00
SESY S.Yzerman GJ/AU 60.00 150.00

2000-01 Upper Deck Fantastic Finishers

COMPLETE SET (11) 15.00 30.00
STATED ODDS 1:23 SERIES 1
FF1 Paul Kariya .75 2.00
FF2 Teemu Selanne .75 2.00
FF3 Peter Forsberg 2.00 5.00
FF4 Brett Hull 1.00 2.50
FF5 Steve Yzerman 4.00 10.00
FF6 Pavel Bure 1.00 2.50
FF7 John LeClair 1.00 2.50
FF8 Keith Tkachuk .75 2.00
FF9 Jaromir Jagr 1.25 3.00
FF10 Owen Nolan .60 1.50
FF11 Mats Sundin .75 2.00

2000-01 Upper Deck Frozen in Time

COMPLETE SET (8) 8.00 15.00
STATED ODDS 1:12 SER. 2
FT1 Doug Gilmour .60 1.50
FT2 Ray Bourque 1.25 3.00
FT3 Brett Hull .75 2.00
FT4 Steve Yzerman 3.00 8.00
FT5 Mark Messier .75 2.00
FT6 Jeremy Roenick .75 2.00
FT7 Jaromir Jagr 1.00 2.50
FT8 Curtis Joseph .60 1.50

2000-01 Upper Deck Fun-Damentals

COMPLETE SET (9) 10.00 20.00
STATED ODDS 1:10 SER.2
F1 Paul Kariya .60 1.50
F2 Dominik Hasek 1.25 3.00
F3 Peter Forsberg 1.50 4.00
F4 Mike Modano 1.00 2.50
F5 Sergei Fedorov 1.25 3.00
F6 Pavel Bure .75 2.00
F7 Marian Hossa .60 1.50
F8 Jaromir Jagr 1.00 2.50
F9 Curtis Joseph .60 1.50

2000-01 Upper Deck Game Jerseys

Randomly inserted in packs at the rate of 1:287, this 25-card set features full color player photography and a swatch of a game worn jersey.
BS Brendan Shanahan Ser.2 8.00 20.00
BS Brendan Shanahan Ser.1 8.00 20.00
CP Chris Pronger Ser.1 8.00 20.00
JJ Jaromir Jagr Ser.2 12.50 30.00
JJ Jaromir Jagr Ser.1 12.50 30.00
JL John LeClair Ser.1 8.00 20.00
JN Joe Nieuwendyk Ser.1 8.00 20.00
JS Joe Sakic Ser.2 12.50 30.00
JS Joe Sakic Ser.1 12.50 30.00
JT Joe Thornton Ser.1 8.00 20.00
KT Keith Tkachuk Ser.1 8.00 20.00
MB Martin Brodeur Ser.1 25.00 60.00
MS Mats Sundin Ser.1 8.00 20.00
MS Mats Sundin Ser.2 8.00 20.00
PB Pavel Bure Ser.2 8.00 20.00
PE Peter Bondra Ser.1 8.00 20.00
PF Peter Forsberg Ser.2 15.00 40.00
PK Paul Kariya Ser.1 8.00 20.00
PK Paul Kariya Ser.2 8.00 20.00
SF Sergei Fedorov Ser.2 10.00 25.00
SF Sergei Fedorov Ser.1 10.00 25.00
TS Teemu Selanne Ser.2 8.00 20.00
TS Teemu Selanne Ser.1 8.00 20.00
WG Wayne Gretzky Ser.1 25.00 60.00
WG Wayne Gretzky AS Ser.2 25.00 60.00

2000-01 Upper Deck Game Jersey Autographs

Randomly inserted in Hobby packs at the rate of 1:287, this 18-card set features color action photography coupled with both and authentic player signature and a swatch of a game worn jersey.
HBH Brett Hull Ser.1 40.00 80.00
HCO Chris Osgood Ser.2 10.00 25.00
HJH Jochen Hecht Ser.1 10.00 25.00
HJL John LeClair Ser.2 15.00 40.00
HJR Jeremy Roenick Ser.2 20.00 50.00
HJT Joe Thornton Ser.2 15.00 40.00
HKT Keith Tkachuk Ser.2 12.00 30.00
HMA Martin Biron Ser.1 10.00 25.00
HMR Mike Richter Ser.2 15.00 40.00
HMY Mike York Ser.1 10.00 25.00
HNL Nicklas Lidstrom Ser.1 15.00 40.00
HPB Pavel Bure Ser.1 15.00 40.00
HSG Scott Gomez Ser.1 10.00 25.00
HSS Sergei Samsonov Ser.2 10.00 25.00
HSS Sergei Samsonov Ser.1 10.00 25.00
HSY Steve Yzerman Ser.2 75.00 150.00
HSY Steve Yzerman Ser.1 75.00 150.00
HTC Tim Connolly Ser.1 10.00 25.00

2000-01 Upper Deck Game Jersey Autographs Canadian

Randomly inserted in Canadian Hobby packs at the rate of 1:287, this set features four of Canada's own bright stars. Each card contains both an authentic player signature and a swatch of a game worn jersey.
CCJ Curtis Joseph Ser.1 15.00 40.00
CJT Jose Theodore Ser.2 25.00 60.00
CMM Mark Messier Ser.2 100.00 250.00
CRL Roberto Luongo Ser.1 10.00 25.00

2000-01 Upper Deck Game Jersey Autographs Exclusives

Randomly inserted in packs, this 36-card set partially paralleled the basic jersey set in an autographed version that was hand numbered to 25. The Gretzky, Hecht, and Richter cards were issued as exchanges.
STATED PRINT RUN 25 SER.#'d SETS
EBH Brett Hull Ser.1 75.00 150.00
EBS Brendan Shanahan Ser.1
ECP Chris Pronger Ser.1
EJH Jochen Hecht Ser.1 20.00 50.00
EJJ Jaromir Jagr Ser.1
EJL John LeClair Ser.1 25.00 60.00
EJN Joe Nieuwendyk Ser.1 25.00 60.00
EJS Joe Sakic Ser.1 60.00 120.00
EJT Joe Thornton Ser.1 75.00 150.00
EKT Keith Tkachuk Ser.1 40.00 80.00
EMB Martin Biron Ser.1 25.00 60.00
EMB Martin Brodeur Ser.1 150.00 250.00
EMS Mats Sundin Ser.1
EMY Mike York Ser.1 20.00 50.00
ENL Nicklas Lidstrom Ser.1 60.00 120.00
EPB Pavel Bure Ser.1 60.00 120.00
EPE Peter Bondra Ser.1 25.00 60.00
EPK Paul Kariya Ser.1
ESF Sergei Fedorov Ser.1 100.00 200.00
ESG Scott Gomez Ser.1
ESY Steve Yzerman Ser.1 175.00 300.00
ETC Tim Connolly Ser.1 25.00 60.00
ETS Teemu Selanne Ser.1
EWG Wayne Gretzky Ser.1 250.00 400.00
ESCO Chris Osgood Ser.2 75.00 150.00
ESJL John LeClair Ser.2 25.00 60.00
ESJN Joe Nieuwendyk Ser.2
ESJR Jeremy Roenick Ser.2 60.00 120.00
ESJT Joe Thornton Ser.2 75.00 150.00
ESKT Keith Tkachuk Ser.2 40.00 80.00
ESMR Mike Richter Ser.2 60.00 120.00
ESPB Pavel Bure Ser.2 60.00 120.00
ESSF Sergei Fedorov Ser.2 100.00 200.00
ESSS Sergei Samsonov Ser.2 25.00 60.00
ESSY Steve Yzerman Ser.2 200.00 300.00
ESWG Wayne Gretzky AS Ser.2 250.00 400.00

2000-01 Upper Deck Game Jersey Combos

Randomly inserted in series one packs, this 15-card set features a dual player card design with two swatches of game worn jerseys. Each card is sequentially numbered to 50.
DBF R.Bourque/P.Forsberg 50.00 100.00
DBH E.Belfour/D.Hasek 60.00 120.00
DCL T.Connolly/R.Luongo 20.00 50.00
DFB S.Fedorov/P.Bure 20.00 50.00
DGB S.Gomez/M.Brodeur 75.00 150.00
DGH W.Gretzky/B.Hull 100.00 200.00
DGL W.Gretzky/M.Lemieux 125.00 250.00
DGM W.Gretzky/M.Messier 75.00 150.00
DJL J.Jagr/M.Lemieux 50.00 100.00
DLC J.LeClair/B.Clarke 20.00 50.00
DSJ M.Sundin/C.Joseph 20.00 50.00
DSK T.Selanne/P.Kariya 20.00 50.00
DTS J.Thornton/S.Samsonov 15.00 40.00
DYL M.York/B.Leetch 12.00 30.00
DYS S.Yzrmn/B.Shnahan 50.00 100.00

2000-01 Upper Deck Game Jersey Doubles

Randomly inserted in series two packs, this 10-card set features top NHL players in action coupled with two swatches of game worn jerseys. Each jersey swatch represents either more than one team played on, or a team and an all-star jersey. Each card is sequentially numbered to 100.
DBH Brett Hull 20.00 50.00
DBS Brendan Shanahan 15.00 40.00
DDH Dominik Hasek 25.00 60.00
DFP Felix Potvin 15.00 40.00
DJJ Jaromir Jagr 25.00 60.00
DJN Joe Nieuwendyk 12.50 30.00
DJS Joe Sakic 25.00 60.00
DPB Pavel Bure 12.50 30.00
DTS Teemu Selanne 12.50 30.00
DWG Wayne Gretzky AS 60.00 120.00

2000-01 Upper Deck Game Jersey Patches

Randomly inserted in series one packs at the rate of 1:2500 and series two packs at the rate of one in 5000, this 36-card set features premium swatches of game worn jersey emblems and patches.
BHP Brett Hull Ser.1 50.00 120.00
BSP Brendan Shanahan Ser.1 40.00 100.00
CJP Curtis Joseph Ser.1 40.00 100.00
DHP Dominik Hasek Ser.1 50.00 120.00
ELP Eric Lindros Ser.1 40.00 100.00
JHP Jochen Hecht Ser.1 25.00 60.00
JJP Jaromir Jagr Ser.1 50.00 120.00
JLP John LeClair Ser.1 30.00 80.00
JSP Joe Sakic Ser.1 75.00 150.00
JTP Joe Thornton Ser.1 50.00 120.00
KTP Keith Tkachuk Ser.1 25.00 60.00
MBP Martin Brodeur Ser.1 125.00 250.00
MMP Mark Messier Ser.1 40.00 100.00
MYP Mike York Ser.1 25.00 60.00
PBP Pavel Bure Ser.1 40.00 100.00
PBS Brendan Shanahan Ser.2 40.00 100.00
PCO Chris Osgood Ser.2 30.00 80.00
PFP Peter Forsberg Ser.1 30.00 80.00
PJJ Jaromir Jagr Ser.2 50.00 120.00
PJL John LeClair Ser.2 40.00 100.00
PKP Paul Kariya Ser.1 40.00 100.00
PKT Keith Tkachuk Ser.2 40.00 100.00
PPF Peter Forsberg Ser.2 40.00 100.00
PPK Paul Kariya Ser.2 40.00 100.00
PRP Patrick Roy Ser.1 125.00 250.00
PSF Sergei Fedorov Ser.2 50.00 120.00
PSY Steve Yzerman Ser.2 75.00 150.00
PTS Teemu Selanne Ser.2 30.00 80.00
PWG Wayne Gretzky AS Ser.2 200.00 400.00
SFP Sergei Fedorov Ser.1 50.00 120.00
SGP Scott Gomez Ser.1 30.00 80.00
SSP Sergei Samsonov Ser.1 25.00 60.00
SYP Steve Yzerman Ser.1 75.00 150.00
TCP Tim Connolly Ser.1 25.00 60.00
TSP Teemu Selanne Ser.1 30.00 80.00
WGP Wayne Gretzky Ser.1 200.00 350.00

2000-01 Upper Deck Game Jersey Patch Autographs Exclusives

Randomly inserted in packs, this 28-card set parallels the base Game Jersey Patches set enhanced with player autographs. Series 1 cards are numbered one of one, series 2 cards are numbered to the featured player's jersey number. Cards with print runs under 25 are not priced due to scarcity.
PSJL John LeClair/10
PSSY Steve Yzerman/19
PSWG W.Gretzky AS/99 400.00 800.00

2000-01 Upper Deck Gate Attractions

COMPLETE SET (11) 15.00 30.00
STATED ODDS 1:11 SER.1
GA1 Paul Kariya .75 2.00
GA2 Dominik Hasek 1.25 3.00
GA3 Ray Bourque 1.25 3.00
GA4 Patrick Roy 3.00 8.00
GA5 Mike Modano .75 2.00
GA6 Steve Yzerman 3.00 8.00
GA7 Pavel Bure .75 2.00
GA8 Martin Brodeur 1.50 4.00
GA9 John LeClair .75 2.00
GA10 Jaromir Jagr 1.00 2.50
GA11 Curtis Joseph .75 2.00

2000-01 Upper Deck Lord Stanley's Heroes

COMPLETE SET (9) 10.00 20.00
STATED ODDS 1:10 SERIES 2
L1 Patrick Roy 3.00 8.00
L2 Joe Sakic 1.25 3.00
L3 Brett Hull .75 2.00
L4 Steve Yzerman 2.50 6.00
L5 Brendan Shanahan 1.00 2.50
L6 Martin Brodeur 1.25 3.00
L7 Scott Gomez .75 2.00
L8 Mark Messier .75 2.00
L9 Jaromir Jagr 1.00 2.50

2000-01 Upper Deck Mario Lemieux Return to Excellence

Available in various Upper Deck products, this set features game-used jersey swatches from Mario Lemieux and each card was serial numbered out of 66. Cards ML1-ML3 were randomly available in Upper Deck Pros & Prospects, cards ML4-ML6 were randomly available in SP Authentic, and cards ML7-ML9were randomly available in Upper Deck Rookie Update.
COMMON CARD 40.00 100.00

2000-01 Upper Deck Number Crunchers

COMPLETE SET (10) 10.00 20.00
STATED ODDS 1:9 SERIES 1
NC1 Peter Forsberg 1.50 4.00
NC2 Brendan Shanahan 1.00 2.50
NC3 John LeClair .75 2.00
NC4 Eric Lindros 1.00 2.50
NC5 Keith Tkachuk .60 1.50
NC6 Jeremy Roenick .75 2.00
NC7 Jaromir Jagr 1.00 2.50
NC8 Owen Nolan .60 1.50
NC9 Chris Pronger .60 1.50
NC10 Mark Messier .75 2.00

2000-01 Upper Deck Profiles

COMPLETE SET (10) 12.00 25.00
STATED ODDS 1:23 SERIES 2
P1 Dominik Hasek 1.50 4.00
P2 Joe Sakic 1.50 4.00
P3 Mike Modano 1.25 3.00
P4 Brendan Shanahan 1.25 3.00
P5 Pavel Bure 1.00 2.50
P6 Martin Brodeur 2.00 5.00
P7 John LeClair 1.00 2.50
P8 Jaromir Jagr 1.25 3.00
P9 Mats Sundin .75 2.00
P10 Olaf Kolzig .60 1.50

2000-01 Upper Deck Prospects In Depth

COMPLETE SET (10) 10.00 20.00
STATED ODDS 1:11 SERIES 1
P1 Patrik Stefan 1.00 2.50
P2 Maxim Afinogenov 1.00 2.50
P3 Alex Tanguay 1.00 2.50
P4 Brenden Morrow 1.00 2.50
P5 Scott Gomez 1.00 2.50
P6 Tim Connolly 1.00 2.50
P7 Mike York 1.00 2.50
P8 Simon Gagne 1.25 3.00
P9 Brian Boucher 1.25 3.00
P10 Jochen Hecht 1.00 2.50

2000-01 Upper Deck Rise to Prominence

COMPLETE SET (8) 5.00 12.00
STATED ODDS 1:12 SER. 2
RP1 Paul Kariya .60 1.50
RP2 Pavel Bure .75 2.00
RP3 Jose Theodore .75 2.00
RP4 Scott Gomez .50 1.25
RP5 Marian Hossa .60 1.50
RP6 Brian Boucher .50 1.25
RP7 Roman Turek .50 1.25
RP8 Vincent Lecavalier .60 1.50

2000-01 Upper Deck Signs of Greatness

Randomly inserted in series two packs, this nine card set features an all white borderless card stock. The player'n name appears along the top of the card in gray tone, and full color action photography is centered on the card. Each card is autographed and numbered out of 250. The Amonte card has yet to be confirmed and it is believed that he never signed.
SBO Bobby Orr 75.00 150.00
SCJ Curtis Joseph 20.00 40.00
SKT Keith Tkachuk 20.00 40.00
SMB Martin Brodeur 30.00 80.00
SMY Mike York 12.50 30.00
SPB Pavel Brendl 12.50 30.00
SSS Sergei Samsonov 20.00 40.00
SWG Wayne Gretzky 100.00 250.00

2000-01 Upper Deck Skilled Stars

COMPLETE SET (20) 15.00 30.00
STATED ODDS 1:5 SERIES 1
SS1 Paul Kariya .50 1.25
SS2 Teemu Selanne .50 1.25
SS3 Dominik Hasek 1.00 2.50
SS4 Valeri Bure .40 1.00
SS5 Patrick Roy 2.50 6.00
SS6 Peter Forsberg 1.25 3.00
SS7 Ed Belfour .50 1.25
SS8 Mike Modano .75 2.00
SS9 Sergei Fedorov 1.00 2.50
SS10 Brendan Shanahan .75 2.00
SS11 Pavel Bure .60 1.50
SS12 Zigmund Palffy .40 1.00
SS13 Martin Brodeur 1.25 3.00
SS14 Tim Connolly .40 1.00
SS15 John LeClair .60 1.50
SS16 Jeremy Roenick .60 1.50
SS17 Jaromir Jagr .75 2.00
SS18 Vincent Lecavalier .50 1.25
SS19 Mats Sundin .50 1.25
SS20 Olaf Kolzig .40 1.00

2000-01 Upper Deck Triple Threat

Randomly inserted in series two pack at the rate of 1:72, this 10-card set pairs three players of the same position that dominate year after year. Base cards feature a doctored action shot where three players are present doing what they do best. Cards are all silver foil and are enhanced with light blue foil highlights.
COMPLETE SET (10) 30.00 80.00
TT1 Kariya/Gomez/Hejduk 4.00 10.00
TT2 Roy/Brodeur/Belfour 10.00 25.00
TT3 Forsberg/Sundin/Sedin 6.00 15.00
TT4 Hull/Roenick/LeClair 4.00 10.00
TT5 Yzerman/Sakic/Modano 10.00 25.00
TT6 Shanahan/Tkachuk/Messier 4.00 10.00
TT7 Bure/Samsonov/Fedorov 3.00 8.00
TT8 Bourque/Pronger/Blake 4.00 10.00
TT9 Jagr/Selanne/Kraft 4.00 10.00
TT10 Turek/Hasek/Kolzig 4.00 10.00

2000-01 Upper Deck UD Flashback

Randomly inserted in series two packs at the rate of 1:12, this eight card set features players in action on a holofoil version of the 1990-91 Upper Deck card design.
COMPLETE SET (8) 4.00 10.00
UD1 Teemu Selanne .60 1.50
UD2 Tony Amonte .40 1.00
UD3 Milan Hejduk .60 1.50
UD4 Scott Gomez .40 1.00
UD5 Tim Connolly .40 1.00
UD6 John LeClair .75 2.00
UD7 Keith Tkachuk .60 1.50
UD8 Olaf Kolzig .40 1.00

2001 Upper Deck EA Sports

This 9-card set was inserted one-card-per-game in EA Sports' NHL 2002 video game and was produced by Upper Deck. A Gold parallel was also produced and inserted randomly. An autographed Mario Lemieux card has also been rumored to exist, but no verification of that has been made.
COMPLETE SET (9)
*GOLD: 1.2X TO 3X BASIC CARD
1 Mario Lemieux 4.00 10.00
2 Mario Lemieux 4.00 10.00
3 Owen Nolan .40 1.00
4 Jere Lehtinen .40 1.00
5 Martin Rucinsky .40 1.00
6 Chris Pronger .50 1.25
7 Markus Naslund .40 2.00
8 Peter Forsberg 1.50 4.00
9 Steve Yzerman 4.00 10.00

2001 Upper Deck Pearson Awards

These three extremely rare cards were handed out only to attendees of the 2001 NHLPA Pearson Awards Banquet. It is commonly believed that most were either thrown out or stashed away, and that very few got into circulation within the hobby.
COMPLETE SET (3) 400.00 700.00
LPBJJ Jaromir Jagr 100.00 200.00
LPBML Mario Lemieux 200.00 400.00
LPBJS Joe Sakic 100.00 200.00

2001-02 Upper Deck

This 441-card set was released in two different series of 231 cards and 210 cards. Series I was released in late October 2001 and Series II was released in early February 2002. Both series carried an SRP of $2.99 for an 8-card pack. Series I consisted of 180 regular base cards and 51 Young Guns subset shortprints. Series II consisted of 180 regular base cards and 30 Young Guns shortprints. Series II Young Guns had two different versions of each card and shortprints for both series were inserted at 1:4. The Jared Aulin card (#220B) was printed in error and is known to have been inserted into some packs, though only a handful have been verified. The "B" suffix on the Aulin card is for checklisting purposes only.
COMPLETE SET (441) 300.00 600.00
COMP.SERIES 1 (231) 150.00 300.00
COMP.SER. 1 w/o SP's (180) 15.00 30.00
COMP.SERIES 2 (210) 150.00 300.00
COMP.SER. 2 w/o SP's (180) 15.00 30.00
1 Paul Kariya .30 .75
2 Jeff Friesen .15 .40
3 Mike Leclerc .15 .40
4 Andy McDonald .15 .40
5 Jean-Sebastien Giguere .20 .50
6 Steve Rucchin .15 .40
7 Ray Ferraro .15 .40
8 Milan Hnilicka .20 .50
9 Patrik Stefan .20 .50
10 Jiri Slegr .15 .40
11 Jeff Odgers .15 .40
12 Steve Guolla .15 .40
13 Joe Thornton .30 .75
14 Sergei Samsonov .20 .50
15 Kyle McLaren .15 .40
16 Jonathan Girard .15 .40
17 Brian Rolston .20 .50
18 Byron Dafoe .20 .50
19 Miroslav Satan .20 .50
20 Curtis Brown .15 .40
21 Stu Barnes .20 .50
22 Maxim Afinogenov .15 .40
23 Vaclav Varada .15 .40
24 Chris Gratton .15 .40
25 Jarome Iginla .25 .60
26 Dave Lowry .15 .40
27 Derek Morris .15 .40
28 Marc Savard .15 .40
29 Oleg Saprykin .15 .40
30 Craig Conroy .15 .40
31 Jeff O'Neill .15 .40
32 Arturs Irbe .20 .50
33 Shane Willis .15 .40
34 Dave Tanabe .15 .40
35 Josef Vasicek .15 .40
36 Sami Kapanen .15 .40
37 Steve Sullivan .15 .40
38 Tony Amonte .20 .50
39 Michael Nylander .15 .40
40 Eric Daze .20 .50
41 Jocelyn Thibault .20 .50
42 Boris Mironov .15 .40
43 Ville Nieminen .15 .40
44 Alex Tanguay .20 .50
45 Milan Hejduk .20 .50
46 Chris Drury .20 .50
47 Peter Forsberg .30 .75
48 Steven Reinprecht .15 .40
49 Ron Tugnutt .20 .50
50 Ray Whitney .15 .40
51 Geoff Sanderson .15 .40
52 Serge Aubin .15 .40
53 Espen Knutsen .15 .40
54 Rostislav Klesla .15 .40
55 Mike Modano .40 1.00
56 Ed Belfour .25 .60
57 Pierre Turgeon .25 .60
58 Jamie Langenbrunner .15 .40
59 Brenden Morrow .20 .50
60 Donald Audette .15 .40
61 Steve Yzerman .75 2.00
62 Brett Hull .30 .75
63 Nicklas Lidstrom .25 .60
64 Darren McCarty .15 .40
65 Luc Robitaille .25 .60
66 Dominik Hasek .40 1.00
67 Mike Comrie .20 .50
68 Tommy Salo .20 .50
69 Todd Marchant .15 .40
70 Mike Grier .15 .40
71 Ryan Smyth .20 .50
72 Tom Poti .15 .40
73 Pavel Bure .30 .75
74 Marcus Nilsson .15 .40
75 Roberto Luongo .40 1.00
76 Kevyn Adams .15 .40
77 Dan Boyle .20 .50
78 Robert Svehla .15 .40
79 Zigmund Palffy .25 .60
80 Eric Belanger .15 .40
81 Ian Laperriere .15 .40
82 Bryan Smolinski .15 .40
83 Jozef Stumpel .15 .40
84 Adam Deadmarsh .20 .50
85 Marian Gaborik .40 1.00
86 Lubomir Sekeras .15 .40
87 Manny Fernandez .20 .50
88 Darby Hendrickson .15 .40
89 Roman Simicek .15 .40
90 Saku Koivu .25 .60
91 Richard Zednik .20 .50
92 Oleg Petrov .15 .40
93 Patrice Brisebois .15 .40
94 Brian Savage .15 .40
95 Jan Bulis .15 .40
96 David Legwand .20 .50
97 Cliff Ronning .15 .40
98 Mike Dunham .20 .50
99 Greg Johnson .15 .40
100 Kimmo Timonen .15 .40
101 Denis Arkhipov .15 .40
102 Patrik Elias .25 .60
103 Jason Arnott .20 .50
104 Scott Niedermayer .25 .60
105 Scott Gomez .20 .50
106 Scott Stevens .25 .60
107 John Madden .20 .50
108 Rick DiPietro .20 .50
109 Mark Parrish .15 .40
110 Brad Isbister .15 .40
111 Michael Peca .20 .50
112 Kenny Jonsson .15 .40
113 Mariusz Czerkawski .15 .40
114 Mark Messier .40 1.00
115 Theo Fleury .30 .75
116 Radek Dvorak .20 .50
117 Brian Leetch .25 .60
118 Eric Lindros .40 1.00
119 Mike Mottau .15 .40
120 Radek Bonk .15 .40
121 Daniel Alfredsson .25 .60
122 Marian Hossa .20 .50
123 Magnus Arvedson .15 .40
124 Patrick Lalime .20 .50
125 Martin Havlat .20 .50
126 Eric Desjardins .20 .50
127 Keith Primeau .20 .50
128 Mark Recchi .30 .75
129 Justin Williams .15 .40
130 Roman Cechmanek .20 .50
131 Jeremy Roenick .25 .60
132 Sean Burke .15 .40
133 Shane Doan .20 .50
134 Paul Mara .15 .40
135 Michal Handzus .15 .40
136 Ladislav Nagy .15 .40
137 Mike Johnson .15 .40
138 Mario Lemieux .75 2.00
139 Alexei Kovalev .20 .50
140 Robert Lang .15 .40
141 Kevin Stevens .15 .40
142 Andrew Ference .15 .40
143 Johan Hedberg .20 .50
144 Owen Nolan .25 .60
145 Teemu Selanne .50 1.25
146 Scott Thornton .20 .50
147 Patrick Marleau .25 .60
148 Alexander Korolyuk .15 .40
149 Todd Harvey .15 .40
150 Keith Tkachuk .25 .60
151 Pavol Demitra .30 .75
152 Al MacInnis .25 .60
153 Scott Young .15 .40
154 Cory Stillman .15 .40
155 Doug Weight .25 .60
156 Brad Richards .25 .60
157 Nikolai Khabibulin .25 .60
158 Martin St. Louis .25 .60
159 Fredrik Modin .15 .40
160 Matthew Barnaby .15 .40
161 Gary Roberts .15 .40
162 Jonas Hoglund .15 .40
163 Curtis Joseph .25 .60
164 Mats Sundin .25 .60
165 Darcy Tucker .15 .40
166 Shayne Corson .15 .40
167 Markus Naslund .25 .60
168 Daniel Sedin .25 .60
169 Henrik Sedin .25 .60
170 Brendan Morrison .20 .50
171 Peter Schaefer .15 .40
172 Harold Druken .15 .40
173 Peter Bondra .25 .60
174 Olaf Kolzig .25 .60
175 Sergei Gonchar .15 .40
176 Jeff Halpern .15 .40
177 Andrei Nikolishin .15 .40
178 Jaromir Jagr .60 1.50
179 Steve Yzerman CL .50 1.25
180 Pavel Bure CL .20 .50
181 Dan Snyder YG RC 2.50 6.00
182 Zdenek Kutlak YG RC 2.00 5.00
183 Michel Larocque YG RC 2.00 5.00
184 Casey Hankinson YG RC 2.00 5.00
185 Jody Shelley YG RC 2.50 6.00
186 Martin Spanhel YG RC 2.00 5.00
187 Mathieu Darche YG RC 3.00 8.00
188 Matt Davidson YG RC 2.00 5.00
189 Sean Selmser YG RC 2.00 5.00
190 Jason Chimera YG RC 2.00 5.00

191 Andrej Podkonicky YG RC 2.00 5.00
192 Mike Matteucci YG RC 2.00 5.00
193 Pascal Dupuis YG RC 3.00 8.00
194 Francis Belanger YG RC 2.50 6.00
195 Bill Bowler YG RC 2.00 5.00
196 Mike Jefferson YG RC 2.00 5.00
197 Stanislav Gron YG RC 2.00 5.00
198 Mikael Samuelsson YG RC 2.50 6.00
199 Peter Smrek YG RC 2.00 5.00
200 Joel Kwiatkowski YG RC 2.00 5.00
201 Tomas Divisek YG RC 2.50 6.00
202 Kirby Law YG RC 2.00 5.00
203 David Cullen YG RC 2.00 5.00
204 Greg Crozier YG RC 2.00 5.00
205 Billy Tibbetts YG RC 2.00 5.00
206 Dale Clarke YG RC 2.00 5.00
207 Jaroslav Obsut YG RC 2.00 5.00
208 Thomas Ziegler YG RC 2.50 6.00
209 Pat Kavanagh YG RC 2.50 6.00
210 Mike Brown YG 2.50 6.00
211 Ilya Kovalchuk YG RC 20.00 50.00
212 Ray Bourque YGF 4.00 10.00
213 Brett Hull YGF 3.00 8.00
214 Dominik Hasek YGF 4.00 10.00
215 Vaclav Nedorost YG RC 2.50 6.00
216 Steve Yzerman YGF 12.00 30.00
217 Mark Messier YGF 6.00 15.00
218 Mike Modano YGF 6.00 15.00
219 Patrick Roy YGF 10.00 25.00
220A John LeClair YGF 4.00 10.00
220B Jared Aulin YG SP 12.50 30.00
221 Martin Brodeur YGF 8.00 20.00
222 Tony Amonte YGF 3.00 8.00
223 Zigmund Palffy YGF 4.00 10.00
224 Roman Cechmanek YG 2.00 5.00
225 Jeff Jillson YG RC 1.50 4.00
226 Jaromir Jagr YGF 10.00 25.00
227 Nikita Alexeev YG RC 2.50 6.00
228 Krystofer Kolanos YG RC 2.50 6.00
229 Peter Forsberg YGF 5.00 12.00
230 Pavel Bure YGF 5.00 12.00
231 Brian Sutherby YG RC 2.50 6.00
232 Oleg Tverdovsky .15 .40
233 Steve Shields .20 .50
234 Matt Cullen .15 .40
235 Jason York .15 .40
236 Vitali Vishnevsky .15 .40
237 Marty McInnis .20 .50
238 Yannick Tremblay .15 .40
239 Dany Heatley .25 .60
240 Lubos Bartecko .15 .40
241 Damian Rhodes .20 .50
242 Ilya Kovalchuk 5.00 12.00
243 Hnat Domenichelli .15 .40
244 Bill Guerin .25 .60
245 Martin Lapointe .15 .40
246 Scott Pellerin .15 .40
247 Rob Zamuner .15 .40
248 Jozef Stumpel .15 .40
249 Glen Murray .20 .50
250 Martin Biron .20 .50
251 Tim Connolly .15 .40
252 Slava Kozlov .20 .50
253 Jay McKee .15 .40
254 J-P Dumont .15 .40
255 Alexei Zhitnik .15 .40
256 Roman Turek .20 .50
257 Igor Kravchuk .15 .40
258 Clarke Wilm .15 .40
259 Robyn Regehr .15 .40
260 Rob Niedermayer .20 .50
261 Dean McAmmond .15 .40
262 Ron Francis .30 .75
263 Martin Gelinas .15 .40
264 Rod Brind'Amour .25 .60
265 Sandis Ozolinsh .15 .40
266 Bates Battaglia .15 .40
267 Chris Dingman .15 .40
268 Igor Korolev .15 .40
269 Jaroslav Spacek .15 .40
270 Alexei Zhamnov .20 .50
271 Steve Thomas .15 .40
272 Jon Klemm .15 .40
273 Adam Foote .20 .50
274 Joe Sakic .40 1.00
275 Rob Blake .25 .60
276 Patrick Roy .60 1.50
277 Greg deVries .15 .40
278 Dan Hinote .15 .40
279 Marc Denis .20 .50
280 David Vyborny .15 .40
281 Tyler Wright .15 .40
282 Mike Sillinger .15 .40
283 Bruce Gardiner .15 .40
284 Sergei Zubov .20 .50
285 Jere Lehtinen .20 .50
286 Joe Nieuwendyk .25 .60
287 Darryl Sydor .15 .40
288 Rob DiMaio .15 .40
289 Valeri Kamensky .15 .40
290 Brendan Shanahan .30 .75
291 Igor Larionov .25 .60
292 Tomas Holmstrom .15 .40
293 Mathieu Dandenault .15 .40
294 Sergei Fedorov .40 1.00
295 Fredrik Olausson .15 .40
296 Anson Carter .20 .50
297 Jochen Hecht .15 .40
298 Daniel Cleary .20 .50
299 Janne Niinimaa .15 .40
300 Rem Murray .20 .50
301 Eric Brewer .15 .40
302 Valeri Bure .15 .40
303 Viktor Kozlov .15 .40
304 Denis Shvidki .15 .40
305 Olli Jokinen .20 .50
306 Jason Wiemer .15 .40
307 Ryan Johnson .15 .40
308 Felix Potvin .40 1.00
309 Jason Allison .20 .50
310 Mathieu Schneider .15 .40
311 Lubomir Visnovsky .15 .40
312 Mattias Norstrom .15 .40
313 Steve Heinze .15 .40
314 Jim Dowd .15 .40
315 Wes Walz .15 .40
316 Filip Kuba .15 .40
317 Andrew Brunette .15 .40
318 Sergei Zholtok .15 .40
319 Stacy Roest .15 .40
320 Jose Theodore .25 .60
321 Yanic Perreault .15 .40
322 Doug Gilmour .30 .75
323 Andreas Dackell .15 .40
324 Martin Rucinsky .15 .40
325 Chad Kilger .15 .40
326 Scott Walker .15 .40
327 Andy Delmore .15 .40
328 Patric Kjellberg .15 .40
329 Tomas Vokoun .20 .50
330 Vitali Yachmenev .15 .40
331 Bill Houlder .15 .40
332 Martin Brodeur .50 1.25
333 Bobby Holik .15 .40
334 Petr Sykora .15 .40
335 Brian Rafalski .15 .40
336 Sergei Brylin .15 .40
337 Randy McKay .15 .40
338 Alexei Yashin .20 .50
339 Roman Hamrlik .15 .40
340 Michael Peca .20 .50
341 Dave Scatchard .15 .40
342 Claude Lapointe .15 .40
343 Chris Osgood .25 .60
344 Mike Richter .25 .60
345 Mike York .15 .40
346 Eric Lindros .40 1.00
347 Petr Nedved .20 .50
348 Barrett Heisten .15 .40
349 Zdeno Ciger .15 .40
350 Shawn McEachern .15 .40
351 Wade Redden .15 .40
352 Bill Muckalt .15 .40
353 Andre Roy .15 .40
354 Sami Salo .15 .40
355 Todd White .15 .40
356 John LeClair .25 .60
357 Brian Boucher .20 .50
358 Pavel Brendl .15 .40
359 Jan Hlavac .15 .40
360 Dan McGillis .15 .40
361 Simon Gagne .25 .60
362 Daymond Langkow .20 .50
363 Sergei Berezin .15 .40
364 Danny Markov .15 .40
365 Tyler Bouck .15 .40
366 Teppo Numminen .15 .40
367 Trevor Letowski .15 .40
368 Martin Straka .15 .40
369 Jan Hrdina .15 .40
370 Alexei Morozov .15 .40
371 Darius Kasparaitis .15 .40
372 Toby Petersen .15 .40
373 Kris Beech .15 .40
374 Evgeni Nabokov .20 .50
375 Mike Ricci .20 .50
376 Brad Stuart .15 .40
377 Adam Graves .20 .50
378 Vincent Damphousse .20 .50
379 Stephane Matteau .15 .40
380 Chris Pronger .20 .50
381 Brent Johnson .20 .50
382 Fred Brathwaite .20 .50
383 Dallas Drake .15 .40
384 Mike Eastwood .15 .40
385 Daniel Corso .15 .40
386 Brian Holzinger .15 .40
387 Vincent Lecavalier .20 .50
388 Jassen Cullimore .15 .40
389 Vaclav Prospal .15 .40
390 Dave Andreychuk .25 .60
391 Jimmie Olvestad .15 .40
392 Alexander Mogilny .20 .50
393 Tomas Kaberle .15 .40
394 Mikael Renberg .15 .40
395 Travis Green .15 .40
396 Robert Reichel .15 .40
397 Nikolai Antropov .15 .40
398 Andrew Cassels .15 .40
399 Dan Cloutier .20 .50
400 Ed Jovanovski .20 .50
401 Todd Bertuzzi .25 .60
402 Trent Klatt .15 .40
403 Donald Brashear .15 .40
404 Jaromir Jagr .60 1.50
405 Joe Sacco .15 .40
406 Steve Konowalchuk .15 .40
407 Adam Oates .25 .60
408 Dimitri Khristich .15 .40
409 Dainius Zubrus .15 .40
410 John LeClair .25 .60
411 Martin Brodeur .50 1.25
412A Timo Parssinen YG RC 2.50 6.00
(Dodge ad on boards)
412B Timo Parssinen YG RC 2.50 6.00
(Stick in right hand)
413A Ilja Bryzgalov YG RC 5.00 12.00
(facing his right)
413B Ilja Bryzgalov YG RC 5.00 12.00
(facing his left)
414A Kevin Sawyer YG RC 2.00 5.00
(facing his right)
414B Kevin Sawyer YG RC 2.00 5.00
(facing his left)
415A Kamil Piros YG RC 2.00 5.00
(facing forward)
415B Kamil Piros YG RC 2.00 5.00
(facing right)
416A Ivan Huml YG RC 2.00 5.00
(skating profile)
416B Ivan Huml YG RC 2.00 5.00
(facing forward)
417A Scott Nichol YG RC 2.00 5.00
(white jersey)
417B Scott Nichol YG RC 2.00 5.00
(black jersey)
418A Jukka Hentunen YG RC 2.00 5.00
(black jersey)
418B Jukka Hentunen YG RC 2.00 5.00
(white jersey)
419A Erik Cole YG RC 4.00 10.00
(skating left)
419B Erik Cole YG RC 4.00 10.00
(skating right)
420A Ben Simon YG RC 2.50 6.00
(skating left)
420B Ben Simon YG RC 2.50 6.00
(skating right)
421A Niko Kapanen YG RC 3.00 8.00
(facing forward)
421B Niko Kapanen YG RC 3.00 8.00
(Staples add on boards)
422A Pavel Datsyuk YG RC 50.00 120.00
(purple board in background)
422B Pavel Datsyuk YG RC 50.00 120.00
(opponent in background)
423A Ty Conklin YG RC 3.00 8.00
(facing left)
423B Ty Conklin YG RC 3.00 8.00
(facing right)
424A Wayne Gretzky YGF 12.00 30.00
(full body photo)
424B Wayne Gretzky YGF 15.00 40.00
(waist up photo)
425A Niklas Hagman YG RC 2.50 6.00
(skating right)
425B Niklas Hagman YG RC 2.50 6.00
(skating left)
426A Kristian Huselius YG RC 3.00 8.00
(facing forward)
426B Kristian Huselius YG RC 3.00 8.00
(Panthers logos on boards)
427A Jaroslav Bednar YG RC 2.00 5.00
(facing forward)
427B Jaroslav Bednar YG RC 2.00 5.00
(facing left)
428A Nick Schultz YG RC 2.00 5.00
(green jersey)
428B Nick Schultz YG RC 2.00 5.00
(white jersey)
429A Travis Roche YG RC 2.00 5.00
(bending)
429B Travis Roche YG RC 2.00 5.00
(standing)
430A Martin Erat YG RC 3.00 8.00
(white jersey)
430B Martin Erat YG RC 3.00 8.00
(blue jersey)
431A Andreas Salomonsson YG RC 2.00 5.00
(faceoff)
431B Andreas Salomonsson YG RC 2.00 5.00
(skating)
432A Josef Boumedienne YG RC 2.00 5.00
(stick at waist)
432B Josef Boumedienne YG RC 2.00 5.00
(stick on ice)
433A Scott Clemmensen YG RC 2.00 5.00
(mask on)
433B Scott Clemmensen YG RC 2.00 5.00
(mask off)
434A Dan Blackburn YG RC 2.50 6.00
(white jersey)
434B Dan Blackburn YG RC 2.50 6.00
(blue jersey)
435A Radek Martinek YG RC 2.00 5.00
(shooting)
435B Radek Martinek YG RC 2.00 5.00
436A Raffi Torres YG RC 3.00 8.00
(red logo on boards)
436B Raffi Torres YG RC 3.00 8.00
(left hand at knee)
437A Ivan Ciernik YG RC 2.00 5.00
(looking right)
437B Ivan Ciernik YG RC 2.00 5.00
438A Jiri Dopita YG RC 2.00 5.00
(skating)
438B Jiri Dopita YG RC 2.00 5.00
(face close up)
439A Mark Rycroft YG RC 2.50 6.00
(blue jersey)
439B Mark Rycroft YG RC 2.50 6.00
(white jersey)
440A Ryan Tobler YG RC 2.50 6.00
(standing)
440B Ryan Tobler YG RC 2.50 6.00
(skating)
441A Chris Corrinet YG RC 2.00 5.00
(facing forward)
441B Chris Corrinet YG RC 2.00 5.00
(shooting)

2001-02 Upper Deck Exclusives

This 440-card set paralleled the base set with serial-numbering added. Regular base cards were serial-numbered to 100 copies each and Young Guns subset cards were serial-numbered to 50 copies each.

*VETS/100: 10X TO 25X BASIC CARDS
*VET YGF/50: 1.2X TO 3X BASIC YGF
*YG ROOK/50: 2X TO 5X BASIC YG RC
114 Mark Messier 8.00 20.00
211 Ilya Kovalchuk YG 150.00 300.00
217 Mark Messier YGF 12.00 30.00
422 Pavel Datsyuk YG 75.00 150.00

2001-02 Upper Deck Crunch Timers

COMPLETE SET (15) 15.00 30.00
STATED ODDS 1:24 SERIES 2
CT1 Joe Sakic 1.25 3.00
CT2 Milan Hejduk .60 1.50
CT3 Chris Drury .50 1.25
CT4 Mike Modano 1.00 2.50
CT5 Brett Hull .75 2.00
CT6 Steve Yzerman 3.00 8.00
CT7 Zigmund Palffy .50 1.25
CT8 Alexei Yashin .50 1.25
CT9 Jeremy Roenick .75 2.00
CT10 Mark Recchi .50 1.25
CT11 Teemu Selanne .60 1.50
CT12 Keith Tkachuk .60 1.50
CT13 Markus Naslund .60 1.50
CT14 Jaromir Jagr 1.00 2.50
CT15 Peter Bondra .60 1.50

2001-02 Upper Deck Fantastic Finishers

COMPLETE SET (10) 10.00 20.00
STATED ODDS 1:36 SERIES 1
FF1 Pavel Bure .75 2.00
FF2 Pavol Demitra .50 1.25
FF3 Markus Naslund .60 1.50
FF4 Mario Lemieux 4.00 10.00
FF5 John LeClair .75 2.00
FF6 Keith Tkachuk .60 1.50
FF7 Marian Hossa .60 1.50
FF8 Teemu Selanne .60 1.50
FF9 Joe Sakic 1.25 3.00
FF10 Zigmund Palffy .50 1.25

2001-02 Upper Deck Franchise Cornerstones

COMPLETE SET (15) 25.00 50.00
STATED ODDS 1:24 SERIES 1
FC1 Paul Kariya .60 1.50
FC2 Pavel Bure .75 2.00
FC3 Mario Lemieux 4.00 10.00
FC4 Peter Forsberg 1.50 4.00
FC5 Vincent Lecavalier .50 1.25
FC6 Joe Sakic 1.25 3.00
FC7 Zigmund Palffy .50 1.25
FC8 Martin Brodeur 1.50 4.00
FC9 Patrick Roy 3.00 8.00
FC10 Steve Yzerman 3.00 8.00
FC11 Mike Modano 1.00 2.50
FC12 Tony Amonte .50 1.25
FC13 Teemu Selanne .60 1.50
FC14 John LeClair .75 2.00
FC15 Mats Sundin .60 1.50

2001-02 Upper Deck Game Jerseys

Inserted into random packs of Series I, this 38-card set featured swatches of game-worn jerseys and consisted of 4 subsets: All-Stars, Goalies, Next Generation, and Combos. All-Stars jerseys were denoted with an "A" prefix and inserted at 1:144. Goalie jerseys were denoted with a "GJ" prefix and inserted at 1:288. Next Generation jerseys were denoted with a "NG" prefix and inserted at 1:144. Combo jerseys were denoted with a "C" prefix fro dual jerseys or numbered using the first letter of the players' last names for triple jerseys. Combo jerseys were inserted at 1:144.

AAM Al MacInnis AS 4.00 10.00
ACC Chris Chelios AS 5.00 12.00
AGL Guy Lafleur AS 4.00 10.00
AJJ Jaromir Jagr AS 8.00 20.00
AJO Joe Sakic AS 10.00 25.00
AMM Mike Modano AS 10.00 20.00
AMS Mats Sundin AS 5.00 12.00
ATF Theo Fleury AS 4.00 10.00
ATS Teemu Selanne AS 5.00 12.00
GJBB Brian Boucher G 10.00 25.00
GJCJ Curtis Joseph G 10.00 25.00
GJDH Dominik Hasek G 12.50 30.00
GJEB Ed Belfour G 10.00 25.00
GJJH Jani Hurme G 10.00 25.00
GJJT Jocelyn Thibault G 10.00 25.00
GJMO Maxime Ouellet G 10.00 25.00
GJMR Mike Richter G 10.00 25.00
GJMT Marty Turco G 10.00 25.00
GJOK Olaf Kolzig G 10.00 25.00
GJPR Patrick Roy G 12.50 30.00
GJRC Roman Cechmanek G 10.00 25.00
GJSB Sean Burke G 10.00 25.00
GJVY Vitali Yeremeyev G 10.00 25.00
NGCB Curtis Brown NG 4.00 10.00
NGDS Daniel Sedin NG 4.00 10.00
NGED Eric Daze NG 4.00 10.00
NGHS Henrik Sedin NG 4.00 10.00
NGJH Jani Hurme NG 4.00 10.00
NGJI Jarome Iginla NG 10.00 25.00
NGJW Justin Williams NG 4.00 10.00
NGMH Marian Hossa NG 5.00 12.00
NGMM Manny Malhotra NG 3.00 8.00
NGMT Marty Turco NG 4.00 10.00
NGMY Mike York NG 4.00 10.00
NGPS Patrik Stefan NG 4.00 10.00
NGRF Ruslan Fedotenko NG 4.00 10.00
NGSD Shane Doan NG 4.00 10.00
NGVL Vincent Lecavalier NG 5.00 12.00
CFR P.Forsberg/P.Roy 15.00 40.00
CHH M.Hossa/J.Hurme 10.00 25.00
CKS P.Kariya/T.Selanne 12.50 30.00
CLJ M.Lemieux/J.Jagr 15.00 40.00
CMN M.Modano/J.Nieuwendyk 15.00 40.00
CPC K.Primeau/R.Cechmanek 12.50 30.00
CSS H.Sedin/D.Sedin 12.50 30.00
FSR Forsberg/Sakic/Roy 20.00 50.00
MNB Modano/Niedyk/Belfour 15.00 40.00
YSF Yzerman/Shanny/Fedorov 15.00 40.00

2001-02 Upper Deck Game Jerseys Series II

Randomly inserted into Series II packs, this 58-card set featured swatches of game-worn jersey swatches and consisted of 6 subsets: Finals Jerseys, Generation Next, Phenomenal Finishers, Superstar Sweaters, Dual Jerseys and Triple Jerseys. Single swatch jerseys were inserted at 1:144 odds, dual jerseys were inserted at 1:288. Triple swatch jerseys were serial-numbered to just 25.

FJBS Brendan Shanahan 6.00 15.00
FJCD Chris Drury 4.00 10.00
FJCL Claude Lemieux 4.00 10.00
FJCO Chris Osgood 6.00 15.00
FJEB Ed Belfour 6.00 15.00
FJJL John LeClair 4.00 10.00
FJJN Joe Nieuwendyk 4.00 10.00
FJJS Joe Sakic 10.00 25.00
FJMB Martin Brodeur 12.50 30.00
FJMH Milan Hejduk 6.00 15.00
FJMM Mike Modano 8.00 20.00
FJMS Miroslav Satan 4.00 10.00
FJPF Peter Forsberg 10.00 25.00
FJPR Patrick Roy 12.50 30.00
FJSF Sergei Fedorov 8.00 20.00
FJSS Scott Stevens 4.00 10.00
FJSY Steve Yzerman 12.50 30.00
GNJW Justin Williams 4.00 10.00
GNMB Martin Biron 4.00 10.00
GNMM Manny Malhotra 4.00 10.00
GNMO Maxime Ouellet 4.00 10.00
GNMY Mike York 4.00 10.00
GNPM Patrick Marleau 6.00 15.00
GNRB Radek Bonk 4.00 10.00
GNRF Rico Fata 4.00 10.00
GNSA Serge Aubin 4.00 10.00
GNSG Simon Gagne 6.00 15.00
PFAK Alexei Kovalev 4.00 10.00
PFBS Brendan Shanahan 6.00 15.00
PFJJ Jaromir Jagr 8.00 20.00
PFJL John LeClair 6.00 15.00
PFJS Joe Sakic 10.00 25.00
PFKP Keith Primeau 4.00 10.00
PFML Mario Lemieux 12.00 30.00
PFMN Markus Naslund 4.00 10.00
PFPK Paul Kariya 6.00 15.00
PFZP Zigmund Palffy 4.00 10.00
SSAM Al MacInnis 4.00 10.00
SSCD Chris Drury 6.00 15.00
SSMB Martin Brodeur 12.50 30.00
SSMM Mike Modano 8.00 20.00
SSPF Peter Forsberg 10.00 25.00
SSPK Paul Kariya 6.00 15.00
SSPR Patrick Roy 12.50 30.00
SSRB Ray Bourque 8.00 20.00
SSSY Steve Yzerman 12.50 30.00
SSWG Wayne Gretzky 25.00 60.00
DJBR R.Bourque/P.Roy 15.00 40.00
DJFS S.Fedorov/B.Shanahan 10.00 25.00
DJMN M.Modano/J.Nieuwendyk 10.00 25.00
DJSB S.Stevens/M.Brodeur 20.00 50.00
DJSF J.Sakic/P.Forsberg 25.00 60.00
DJSH M.Satan/D.Hasek 10.00 25.00
DJTD A.Tanguay/C.Drury 10.00 25.00
DJYL S.Yzerman/N.Lidstrom 15.00 40.00
TJNMB Nieuw/Modano/Belfour 15.00 40.00
TJRBH Roy/Sakic/Hejduk 60.00 150.00
TJYFS Yzerman/Fedorov/Shan 25.00 60.00

2001-02 Upper Deck Game Jersey Autographs

Inserted randomly into both Series I and Series II, this 16-card set featured game-worn jersey swatches and authentic player autographs. Series I cards were inserted randomly at 1:288 packs. Series II cards were serial-numbered to 150 copies each.

SDS Daniel Sedin Ser.1 10.00 25.00
SDW Doug Weight Ser.1 15.00 40.00
SHS Henrik Sedin Ser.1 15.00 40.00
SJL John LeClair Ser.1 10.00 25.00
SMM Mike Modano Ser.1 25.00 60.00
SRB Ray Bourque Ser.1 50.00 100.00
SSY Steve Yzerman Ser.1 100.00 200.00
SJBO Ray Bourque/150 40.00 80.00
SJCJ Curtis Joseph/150 15.00 40.00
SJEB Ed Belfour/150 20.00 50.00
SJJL John LeClair/150 10.00 25.00
SJMB Martin Brodeur/150 50.00 120.00
SJMO Maxime Ouellet/150 10.00 25.00
SJRB Ray Bourque/150 40.00 80.00
SJSG Simon Gagne/150 10.00 25.00
SJSY Steve Yzerman/150 60.00 120.00

2001-02 Upper Deck Gate Attractions

COMPLETE SET (15) 20.00 40.00
STATED ODDS 1:24 SERIES 1
GA1 Mark Messier .75 2.00
GA2 Theo Fleury .50 1.25
GA3 Keith Tkachuk .60 1.50
GA4 John LeClair .75 2.00
GA5 Mario Lemieux 4.00 10.00
GA6 Alexei Kovalev .50 1.25
GA7 Chris Drury .50 1.25
GA8 Joe Sakic 1.25 3.00
GA9 Peter Forsberg 1.50 4.00
GA10 Paul Kariya .60 1.50
GA11 Teemu Selanne .60 1.50
GA12 Steve Yzerman 3.00 8.00
GA13 Brendan Shanahan 1.00 2.50
GA14 Mike Modano 1.00 2.50
GA15 Chris Pronger .50 1.25

2001-02 Upper Deck Goalies in Action

COMPLETE SET (10) 12.50 25.00
STATED ODDS 1:36 SERIES 1
GL1 Curtis Joseph .75 2.00
GL2 Ed Belfour .75 2.00
GL3 Martin Brodeur 2.00 5.00
GL4 Evgeni Nabokov .60 1.50
GL5 Johan Hedberg .75 2.00
GL6 Patrick Roy 4.00 10.00
GL7 Tommy Salo .60 1.50
GL8 Patrick Lalime .60 1.50
GL9 Olaf Kolzig .60 1.50
GL10 Roberto Luongo 1.00 2.50

2001-02 Upper Deck Goaltender Threads

Randomly inserted at 1:240 Series II packs, this 10-card set featured swatches game-worn goalie jerseys.

TTBB Brian Boucher 8.00 20.00
TTCJ Curtis Joseph 8.00 20.00
TTCO Chris Osgood 8.00 20.00
TTJO Jose Theodore 10.00 25.00
TTJT Jocelyn Thibault 8.00 20.00
TTMB Martin Brodeur 12.50 30.00
TTMD Mike Dunham 8.00 20.00
TTMR Mike Richter 8.00 20.00
TTPR Patrick Roy 12.50 30.00
TTRC Roman Cechmanek 8.00 20.00

2001-02 Upper Deck Last Line of Defense

COMPLETE SET (10) 12.50 25.00
STATED ODDS 1:36 SERIES 2
LL1 Patrick Roy 4.00 10.00
LL2 Ed Belfour .75 2.00
LL3 Dominik Hasek 1.50 4.00
LL4 Felix Potvin .75 2.00
LL5 Martin Brodeur 2.00 5.00
LL6 Roman Cechmanek .60 1.50
LL7 Johan Hedberg .75 2.00
LL8 Evgeni Nabokov .60 1.50
LL9 Curtis Joseph .75 2.00
LL10 Olaf Kolzig .60 1.50

2001-02 Upper Deck Leaders of the Pack

COMPLETE SET (15) 15.00 30.00
STATED ODDS 1:24 SERIES 2
LP1 Paul Kariya .60 1.50
LP2 Tony Amonte .50 1.25
LP3 Joe Sakic 1.25 3.00
LP4 Mike Modano 1.00 2.50
LP5 Steve Yzerman 3.00 8.00
LP6 Pavel Bure .75 2.00
LP7 Scott Stevens .50 1.25
LP8 Mark Messier .75 2.00
LP9 Michael Peca .50 1.25
LP10 Daniel Alfredsson .50 1.25
LP11 Mario Lemieux 4.00 10.00
LP12 Owen Nolan .50 1.25
LP13 Doug Weight .50 1.25
LP14 Chris Pronger .50 1.25
LP15 Mats Sundin .60 1.50

2001-02 Upper Deck Patches

Inserted at 1:2500 Series I packs, this 19-card set featured swatches of game-used jersey patches.

PBS Brendan Shanahan 25.00 60.00
PDW Doug Weight 25.00 60.00
PEB Ed Belfour 30.00 80.00
PJJ Jaromir Jagr 30.00 80.00
PJL John LeClair 25.00 60.00
PJS Joe Sakic 30.00 80.00
PMH Marian Hossa 15.00 40.00
PML Mario Lemieux 60.00 150.00
PMM Mike Modano 25.00 60.00
PMO Mike Modano 25.00 60.00
PMS Mats Sundin 15.00 40.00
PPF Peter Forsberg 40.00 100.00
PPK Paul Kariya 25.00 60.00
PPR Patrick Roy 50.00 120.00
PRB Ray Bourque 40.00 100.00
PSA Joe Sakic 40.00 100.00
PSF Sergei Fedorov 30.00 80.00
PSY Steve Yzerman 50.00 125.00
PTS Teemu Selanne 20.00 50.00

2001-02 Upper Deck Patches Series II

Randomly inserted into Series II packs, this 24-card set partially paralleled the Series II jersey set but featured swatches of jersey logos, name plates or numbers. Number patches were denoted with a "PN" prefix and inserted at 1:2500. Logo patches were denoted with a "PL" prefix and inserted at 1:2500. Name Plate patches were denoted with a "NA" prefix and inserted at 1:7500. Please note that the Modano Name Plate card had a "PL" prefix according to Upper Deck.

PLJJ Jaromir Jagr 30.00 80.00
PLMB Martin Brodeur 40.00 100.00
PLML Mario Lemieux 40.00 100.00
PLPF Peter Forsberg 40.00 100.00
PLPK Paul Kariya 20.00 50.00
PLPR Patrick Roy 40.00 100.00
PLSF Sergei Fedorov 30.00 80.00
PLSY Steve Yzerman 40.00 100.00
PNBS Brendan Shanahan 20.00 50.00
PNJL John LeClair 20.00 50.00
PNJS Joe Sakic 30.00 80.00
PNML Mario Lemieux 40.00 100.00
PNMM Mike Modano 25.00 60.00
PNPK Paul Kariya 20.00 50.00
PNPR Patrick Roy 40.00 100.00
PNSY Steve Yzerman 40.00 100.00
NABS Brendan Shanahan 40.00 100.00
NAJL John LeClair 40.00 100.00
NAJS Joe Sakic 75.00 200.00
NAML Mario Lemieux 100.00 250.00
NAPF Peter Forsberg 75.00 200.00
NAPR Patrick Roy 100.00 250.00
NASY Steve Yzerman 100.00 250.00
PLMM Mike Modano 60.00 150.00

2001-02 Upper Deck Pride of a Nation

Inserted at a rate of 1:240 for single players and 1:576 for double players, this 30-card set highlighted the homelands of players of the NHL. Each card carried game-worn jersey piece(s) of the player(s) featured. Triple player cards were serial-numbered to just 20 copies.

PNBG Bill Guerin 6.00 15.00
PNDH Dominik Hasek 8.00 20.00
PNDW Doug Weight 6.00 15.00
PNJJ Jaromir Jagr 8.00 20.00
PNJS Joe Sakic 10.00 25.00
PNMB Martin Brodeur 12.00 30.00
PNML Mario Lemieux 15.00 40.00
PNPF Peter Forsberg 8.00 20.00
PNPR Patrick Roy 15.00 40.00
PNSF Sergei Fedorov 8.00 20.00
PNSK Saku Koivu 6.00 15.00
PNSY Steve Yzerman 12.00 30.00
PNTA Tony Amonte 6.00 15.00
PNTS Teemu Selanne 6.00 15.00
PNVK Viktor Kozlov 6.00 15.00
DPAG T.Amonte/B.Guerin 12.50 30.00
DPFK S.Fedorov/V.Kozlov 12.50 30.00
DPFS P.Forsberg/M.Sundin 15.00 40.00
DPHJ D.Hasek/J.Jagr 15.00 40.00
DPLK M.Lemieux/P.Kariya 15.00 40.00
DPLM J.LeClair/M.Modano 12.50 30.00
DPRS P.Roy/J.Sakic 30.00 80.00
DPSB S.Stevens/M.Brodeur 12.50 30.00
DPSK T.Selanne/S.Koivu 12.50 30.00
DPYS S.Yzerman/B.Shanahan 25.00 60.00
TPAWL Amonte/Weight/Leetch 20.00 50.00
TPFKK Fedorov/Kovalev/Kozlov 20.00 50.00
TPFSL Forsberg/Sundin/Lidstrom 30.00 80.00
TPHJL Hasek/Jagr/Lang 40.00 100.00
TPYRL Yzerman/Roy/Lemieux 60.00 150.00

2001-02 Upper Deck Pride of the Leafs

Serial-numbered to just 75 sets, this 9 card set featured past and present Toronto Maple Leafs with full color action photos alongside a swatch of game-worn jersey on the card fronts.

MLBJ Borje Salming 40.00 100.00
MLCJ Curtis Joseph 30.00 80.00
MLDG Doug Gilmour 30.00 80.00
MLFP Felix Potvin 40.00 100.00
MLMS Mats Sundin 30.00 80.00
MLNA Nikolai Antropov 25.00 60.00
MLSB Sergei Berezin 20.00 50.00
MLTD Tie Domi 30.00 80.00
MLWC Wendel Clark 50.00 125.00

2001-02 Upper Deck Shooting Stars

COMPLETE SET (20) 15.00 30.00
STATED ODDS 1:9 SERIES 2
SS1 Paul Kariya .40 1.00
SS2 Bill Guerin .30 .75
SS3 Joe Sakic .75 2.00
SS4 Milan Hejduk .40 1.00
SS5 Brett Hull .50 1.25
SS6 Brendan Shanahan .60 1.50
SS7 Luc Robitaille .30 .75
SS8 Pavel Bure .60 1.50
SS9 Zigmund Palffy .30 .75
SS10 Patrik Elias .30 .75
SS11 Alexei Yashin .30 .75
SS12 John LeClair .50 1.25
SS13 Alexei Kovalev .30 .75
SS14 Mario Lemieux 2.50 6.00
SS15 Owen Nolan .30 .75
SS16 Teemu Selanne .40 1.00
SS17 Alexander Mogilny .30 .75
SS18 Markus Naslund .40 1.00
SS19 Jaromir Jagr .60 1.50
SS20 Peter Bondra .30 .75

2001-02 Upper Deck Skilled Stars

COMPLETE SET (20) 15.00 30.00
STATED ODDS 1:9 SERIES 1
SS1 Paul Kariya .40 1.00
SS2 Mario Lemieux 2.50 6.00
SS3 Chris Pronger .30 .75
SS4 Teemu Selanne .40 1.00
SS5 Owen Nolan .30 .75
SS6 Pavel Bure .50 1.25
SS7 Keith Tkachuk .40 1.00
SS8 Mike Modano .60 1.50
SS9 Peter Forsberg 1.00 2.50
SS10 Zigmund Palffy .30 .75
SS11 Martin Brodeur 1.00 2.50
SS12 Patrick Roy 2.00 5.00
SS13 Joe Sakic .75 2.00
SS14 Ray Bourque .75 2.00
SS15 Steve Yzerman 2.00 5.00
SS16 Roman Cechmanek .30 .75
SS17 Mark Messier .50 1.25
SS18 Vincent Lecavalier .40 1.00
SS19 John LeClair .50 1.25
SS20 Tony Amonte .30 .75

2001-02 Upper Deck Tandems

COMPLETE SET (10) 20.00 40.00
STATED ODDS 1:36 SERIES 2
T1 S.Samsonov/J.Thornton 2.00 5.00
T2 J.Sakic/M.Hejduk 4.00 10.00
T3 B.Shanahan/S.Yzerman 5.00 12.00
T4 V.Bure/P.Bure 1.25 3.00
T5 P.Elias/J.Arnott 1.25 3.00
T6 M.Hossa/R.Bonk 1.25 3.00
T7 J.LeClair/J.Roenick 1.25 3.00
T8 T.Selanne/O.Nolan 1.25 3.00
T9 K.Tkachuk/P.Demitra 1.25 3.00
T10 B.Richards/V.Lecavalier 1.25 3.00

2002 Upper Deck Collectors Club

COMPLETE SET (20) 16.00 40.00
NHL1 Wayne Gretzky 2.00 5.00
NHL2 Gordie Howe 1.20 2.00
NHL3 Bobby Orr 2.00 5.00
NHL4 Ray Bourque .80 2.00
NHL5 Mario Lemieux 1.60 4.00
NHL6 Patrick Roy 1.60 4.00
NHL7 Steve Yzerman 1.60 4.00
NHL8 Jaromir Jagr .80 1.50
NHL9 Dominik Hasek .40 1.00
NHL10 Martin Brodeur .80 2.00
NHL11 Joe Sakic .80 2.00
NHL12 Paul Kariya .80 1.50
NHL13 Teemu Selanne .40 1.00
NHL14 Chris Pronger .20 .50
NHL15 Pavel Bure .40 1.00
NHL16 Peter Forsberg .80 1.50
NHL17 Nicklas Lidstrom .40 1.00
NHL18 Ilya Kovalchuk 2.00 3.00
NHL19 Kristian Huselius .40 .50
NHL20 Dan Blackburn .80 1.00

2002 Upper Deck Collectors Club Jerseys

One memorabilia card was included in each UD Collector's Club boxed set. The Yzerman features a swatch from a game jersey and appears to be slightly more scarce than the Bourque, which features a practice jersey swatch.

COMPLETE SET (2) 40.00 100.00
RBJ Ray Bourque 16.00 40.00
SYJ Steve Yzerman 30.00 75.00

2002 Upper Deck Pearson Awards

Like the set from the previous year, these three cards were available exclusively to attendees of the annual NHLPA Pearson Awards Banquet. Their relative scarcity makes them very unique and desirable.

COMPLETE SET (3) 250.00 500.00
1 Patrick Roy 200.00 400.00
2 Jarome Iginla 75.00 150.00
3 Sean Burke 30.00 75.00

2002 Upper Deck USHL Gordie Howe

This rare single was given away at the USHL All-Star Game in Sioux Falls. It commemorated Mr. Howe as the honorary spokesman for Upper Deck.

1 Gordie Howe AU 200.00 300.00

2002-03 Upper Deck

This 456-card set was issued in two different series. Series I consisted of 180 base cards; 15 Memorable Season subset cards (181-195) inserted at 1:6; 30 Young Guns subset cards (196-225) inserted at 1:4; 9 more Memorable Seasons subset cards and 12 more Young Guns subset cards (226-246) inserted one per box. Series 2 consisted of 180 base cards and 30 Young Guns subset cards (427-456) inserted at 1:4.

1 Vitali Vishnevsky .12 .30
2 Jean-Sebastien Giguere .20 .50
3 Steve Rucchin .12 .30
4 Paul Kariya .25 .60
5 Andy McDonald .20 .50
6 Lubos Bartecko .12 .30
7 Ilya Kovalchuk .25 .60
8 Tomi Kallio .12 .30
9 Milan Hnilicka .15 .40
10 Patrik Stefan .12 .30
11 Joe Thornton .25 .60
12 Brian Rolston .15 .40
13 Martin Lapointe .15 .40
14 Nick Boynton .12 .30
15 Andy Hilbert .12 .30
16 Glen Murray .15 .40
17 J-P Dumont .12 .30
18 Tim Connolly .12 .30
19 Miroslav Satan .20 .50
20 Maxim Afinogenov .12 .30
21 Taylor Pyatt .12 .30
22 Jay McKee .12 .30
23 Marc Savard .12 .30
24 Roman Turek .20 .50
25 Dean McAmmond .12 .30
26 Craig Conroy .12 .30
27 Derek Morris .12 .30
28 Rod Brind'Amour .20 .50
29 Josef Vasicek .12 .30
30 Niclas Wallin .12 .30
31 Jaroslav Svoboda .12 .30
32 Sami Kapanen .12 .30
33 Erik Cole .15 .40
34 Jeff O'Neill .12 .30
35 Michael Nylander .12 .30
36 Alexei Zhamnov .15 .40
37 Jon Klemm .12 .30
38 Kyle Calder .12 .30
39 Eric Daze .12 .30
40 Steve Sullivan .12 .30
41 Stephane Yelle .12 .30
42 Rob Blake .20 .50
43 Patrick Roy .50 1.25
44 Radim Vrbata .15 .40
45 Chris Drury .20 .50
46 Milan Hejduk .15 .40
47 Joe Sakic .30 .75
48 Peter Forsberg .25 .60
49 Rostislav Klesla .12 .30
50 Marc Denis .15 .40
51 Grant Marshall .12 .30
52 Ray Whitney .15 .40
53 Espen Knutsen .12 .30
54 Mike Sillinger .12 .30
55 Bill Guerin .20 .50
56 Mike Modano .30 .75
57 Sergei Zubov .15 .40
58 Marty Turco .20 .50
59 Jason Arnott .15 .40
60 Jere Lehtinen .20 .50
61 Steve Yzerman .40 1.00
62 Sergei Fedorov .30 .75
63 Nicklas Lidstrom .20 .50
64 Curtis Joseph .20 .50
65 Igor Larionov .20 .50
66 Luc Robitaille .20 .50
67 Tomas Holmstrom .12 .30
68 Brett Hull .25 .60
69 Mike Comrie .20 .50
70 Marty Reasoner .12 .30
71 Tommy Salo .15 .40
72 Ryan Smyth .15 .40
73 Anson Carter .15 .40
74 Janne Niinimaa .12 .30
75 Sandis Ozolinsh .15 .40
76 Roberto Luongo .30 .75

Card	Low	High
77 Kristian Huselius	.12	.30
78 Valeri Bure	.15	.40
79 Brad Ference	.12	.30
80 Ian Laperriere	.15	.40
81 Mattias Norstrom	.12	.30
82 Adam Deadmarsh	.15	.40
83 Jason Allison	.15	.40
84 Eric Belanger	.12	.30
85 Felix Potvin	.30	.75
86 Wes Walz	.12	.30
87 Darby Hendrickson	.12	.30
88 Dwayne Roloson	.12	.30
89 Marian Gaborik	.30	.75
90 Filip Kuba	.12	.30
91 Andrei Markov	.20	.50
92 Jose Theodore	.20	.50
93 Mike Ribeiro	.15	.40
94 Richard Zednik	.12	.30
95 Gino Odjick	.12	.30
96 Saku Koivu	.20	.50
97 Andy Delmore	.12	.30
98 Tomas Vokoun	.15	.40
99 Martin Erat	.12	.30
100 Denis Arkhipov	.12	.30
101 Scott Hartnell	.20	.50
102 Scott Stevens	.20	.50
103 Patrik Elias	.20	.50
104 Jamie Langenbrunner	.15	.40
105 Brian Gionta	.15	.40
106 Joe Nieuwendyk	.20	.50
107 Martin Brodeur	.40	1.00
108 Roman Hamrlik	.12	.30
109 Shawn Bates	.12	.30
110 Steve Webb	.12	.30
111 Alexei Yashin	.15	.40
112 Chris Osgood	.20	.50
113 Mark Parrish	.12	.30
114 Petr Nedved	.12	.30
115 Eric Lindros	.30	.75
116 Dan Blackburn	.15	.40
117 Radek Dvorak	.15	.40
118 Tom Poti	.12	.30
119 Pavel Bure	.25	.60
120 Todd White	.12	.30
121 Patrick Lalime	.15	.40
122 Marian Hossa	.15	.40
123 Daniel Alfredsson	.20	.50
124 Wade Redden	.12	.30
125 Mike Fisher	.12	.30
126 Keith Primeau	.20	.50
127 Jeremy Roenick	.20	.50
128 Eric Weinrich	.12	.30
129 Roman Cechmanek	.15	.40
130 Mark Recchi	.25	.60
131 Justin Williams	.15	.40
132 Brad May	.12	.30
133 Sean Burke	.12	.30
134 Paul Mara	.12	.30
135 Shane Doan	.15	.40
136 Tony Amonte	.15	.40
137 Daniel Briere	.15	.40
138 Kris Beech	.12	.30
139 Martin Straka	.15	.40
140 Alexei Kovalev	.20	.50
141 Mario Lemieux	.60	1.50
142 Andrew Ference	.12	.30
143 Johan Hedberg	.20	.50
144 Patrick Marleau	.20	.50
145 Owen Nolan	.20	.50
146 Mike Rathje	.12	.30
147 Evgeni Nabokov	.15	.40
148 Marco Sturm	.12	.30
149 Todd Harvey	.12	.30
150 Pavol Demitra	.25	.60
151 Doug Weight	.20	.50
152 Al MacInnis	.20	.50
153 Brent Johnson	.15	.40
154 Keith Tkachuk	.20	.50
155 Cory Stillman	.12	.30
156 Brad Richards	.20	.50
157 Pavel Kubina	.12	.30
158 Nikolai Khabibulin	.20	.50
159 Martin St. Louis	.20	.50
160 Vincent Lecavalier	.15	.40
161 Bryan McCabe	.12	.30
162 Gary Roberts	.12	.30
163 Ed Belfour	.20	.50
164 Mats Sundin	.20	.50
165 Tie Domi	.15	.40
166 Alexander Mogilny	.15	.40
167 Daniel Sedin	.20	.50
168 Todd Bertuzzi	.20	.50
169 Mattias Ohlund	.12	.30
170 Dan Cloutier	.15	.40
171 Markus Naslund	.15	.40
172 Jan Hlavac	.12	.30
173 Olaf Kolzig	.20	.50
174 Peter Bondra	.20	.50
175 Sergei Gonchar	.15	.40
176 Steve Konowalchuk	.12	.30
177 Chris Simon	.12	.30
178 Dainius Zubrus	.12	.30
179 Patrick Roy CL	.40	1.00
180 Steve Yzerman CL	.30	.75
181 Paul Kariya MS	.60	1.50
182 Bobby Orr MS	1.50	4.00
183 Jarome Iginla MS	.50	1.25
184 Joe Sakic MS	.75	2.00
185 Patrick Roy MS	1.25	3.00
186 Steve Yzerman MS	1.00	2.50
187 Gordie Howe MS	1.50	4.00
188 Wayne Gretzky MS	2.50	6.00
189 Wayne Gretzky MS	2.50	6.00
190 Martin Brodeur MS	1.00	2.50
191 Mario Lemieux MS	1.50	4.00
192 Brett Hull MS	.60	1.50
193 Jaromir Jagr MS	1.25	3.00
194 Pavel Bure MS	.60	1.50
195 Teemu Selanne MS	1.00	2.50
196 Mark Hartigan YG	1.25	3.00
197 Pasi Nurminen YG	1.25	3.00
198 Henrik Tallinder YG	1.25	3.00
199 Micki Dupont YG RC	1.25	3.00
200 Tyler Arnason YG	2.00	5.00
201 Jordan Krestanovich YG	1.25	3.00
202 Kelly Fairchild YG	1.25	3.00
203 Andrei Nedorost YG	1.25	3.00
204 Sean Avery YG	1.50	4.00
205 Stephen Weiss YG	2.00	5.00
206 Lukas Krajicek YG	1.50	4.00
207 Kyle Rossiter YG	1.25	3.00
208 Eric Beaudoin YG	1.25	3.00
209 Sylvain Blouin YG RC	1.25	3.00
210 Marcel Hossa YG	1.25	3.00
211 Adam Hall YG RC	1.25	3.00
212 Greg Koehler YG RC	1.25	3.00
213 Trent Hunter YG	1.25	3.00
214 Ray Schultz YG RC	1.25	3.00
215 Martin Prusek YG	1.25	3.00
216 Chris Bala YG	1.25	3.00
217 Josh Langfeld YG	1.25	3.00
218 Bruno St. Jacques YG	1.25	3.00
219 Branko Radivojevic YG	1.25	3.00
220 Martin Cibak YG	1.25	3.00
221 Evgeni Konstantinov YG	1.25	3.00
222 Karel Pilar YG	1.25	3.00
223 Sebastien Centomo YG	1.25	3.00
224 Sebastien Charpentier YG	1.25	3.00
225 J-F Fortin YG	1.25	3.00
226 Stanislav Chistov YG RC	5.00	12.00
227 Alexei Smirnov YG RC	6.00	15.00
228 Chuck Kobasew YG RC	6.00	15.00
229 Tony Amonte MS	15.00	40.00
230 Peter Forsberg MS	15.00	40.00
231 Chris Drury MS	20.00	50.00
232 Rick Nash YG RC	80.00	200.00
233 Brendan Shanahan MS	25.00	60.00
234 Henrik Zetterberg YG RC	150.00	250.00
235 Ales Hemsky YG RC	20.00	50.00
236 Jay Bouwmeester YG RC	15.00	40.00
237 Alexei Yashin MS	15.00	40.00
238 Alexander Frolov YG RC	12.00	30.00
239 P-M Bouchard YG RC	10.00	25.00
240 Ron Hainsey YG RC	5.00	12.00
241 Sean Burke MS	12.00	30.00
242 Owen Nolan MS	20.00	50.00
243 Chris Pronger MS	15.00	40.00
244 Mats Sundin MS	20.00	50.00
245 Alexander Svitov YG RC	5.00	12.00
246 Steve Eminger YG RC	5.00	12.00
247 Adam Oates	.20	.50
248 Petr Sykora	.15	.40
249 Fredrik Olausson	.12	.30
250 Matt Cullen	.12	.30
251 Ruslan Salei	.12	.30
252 Slava Kozlov	.12	.30
253 Dany Heatley	.20	.50
254 Frantisek Kaberle	.12	.30
255 Pasi Nurminen	.12	.30
256 Shawn McEachern	.12	.30
257 Sergei Samsonov	.15	.40
258 Steve Shields	.15	.40
259 Jonathan Girard	.12	.30
260 Jozef Stumpel	.12	.30
261 Bryan Berard	.12	.30
262 Marty McInnis	.12	.30
263 Stu Barnes	.12	.30
264 Curtis Brown	.12	.30
265 Chris Gratton	.12	.30
266 Rhett Warrener	.12	.30
267 Jochen Hecht	.12	.30
268 James Patrick	.12	.30
269 Jarome Iginla	.20	.50
270 Martin Gelinas	.12	.30
271 Chris Drury	.20	.50
272 Stephane Yelle	.12	.30
273 Jamie Wright	.12	.30
274 Kevin Weekes	.15	.40
275 Bret Hedican	.12	.30
276 Ron Francis	.25	.60
277 Kevyn Adams	.12	.30
278 Marek Malik	.12	.30
279 Bates Battaglia	.12	.30
280 Theo Fleury	.25	.60
281 Sergei Berezin	.12	.30
282 Mark Bell	.12	.30
283 Alexander Karpovtsev	.12	.30
284 Steve Passmore	.12	.30
285 Bob Probert	.20	.50
286 Alex Tanguay	.15	.40
287 Steven Reinprecht	.12	.30
288 Adam Foote	.12	.30
289 David Aebischer	.15	.40
290 Greg deVries	.12	.30
291 Dan Hinote	.12	.30
292 Derek Morris	.12	.30
293 Scott Parker	.12	.30
294 Geoff Sanderson	.15	.40
295 Andrew Cassels	.12	.30
296 Jean-Luc Grand-Pierre	.12	.30
297 Luke Richardson	.12	.30
298 Tyler Wright	.12	.30
299 Jody Shelley	.12	.30
300 Ron Tugnutt	.15	.40
301 Scott Young	.12	.30
302 Pierre Turgeon	.20	.50
303 Derian Hatcher	.15	.40
304 Richard Matvichuk	.12	.30
305 Kirk Muller	.12	.30
306 Brendan Shanahan	.25	.60
307 Chris Chelios	.20	.50
308 Mathieu Dandenault	.12	.30
309 Pavel Datsyuk	.25	.60
310 Kris Draper	.12	.30
311 Boyd Devereaux	.12	.30
312 Kirk Maltby	.12	.30
313 Manny Legace	.20	.50
314 Jani Rita	.12	.30
315 Todd Marchant	.12	.30
316 Daniel Cleary	.15	.40
317 Georges Laraque	.15	.40
318 Mike York	.12	.30
319 Jason Smith	.12	.30
320 Viktor Kozlov	.12	.30
321 Dimitri Yushkevich	.12	.30
322 Olli Jokinen	.20	.50
323 Marcus Nilsson	.12	.30
324 Ivan Novoseltsev	.12	.30
325 Aaron Miller	.12	.30
326 Zigmund Palffy	.20	.50
327 Jamie Storr	.15	.40
328 Bryan Smolinski	.15	.40
329 Mathieu Schneider	.12	.30
330 Erik Rasmussen	.12	.30
331 Andrew Brunette	.12	.30
332 Richard Park	.12	.30
333 Manny Fernandez	.15	.40
334 Matt Johnson	.12	.30
335 Ladislav Benysek	.12	.30
336 Mariusz Czerkawski	.12	.30
337 Sheldon Souray	.12	.30
338 Chad Kilger	.12	.30
339 Yanic Perreault	.12	.30
340 Mathieu Garon	.15	.40
341 Craig Rivet	.12	.30
342 Mike Dunham	.15	.40
343 David Legwand	.15	.40
344 Vladimir Orszagh	.12	.30
345 Kimmo Timonen	.12	.30
346 Cale Hulse	.12	.30
347 Oleg Tverdovsky	.12	.30
348 Jeff Friesen	.12	.30
349 Brian Rafalski	.12	.30
350 Sergei Brylin	.12	.30
351 John Madden	.12	.30
352 Colin White	.12	.30
353 Michael Peca	.15	.40
354 Eric Cairns	.12	.30
355 Dave Scatchard	.12	.30
356 Brad Isbister	.12	.30
357 Oleg Kvasha	.12	.30
358 Mattias Timander	.12	.30
359 Matthew Barnaby	.12	.30
360 Bobby Holik	.12	.30
361 Darius Kasparaitis	.12	.30
362 Vladimir Malakhov	.12	.30
363 Brian Leetch	.20	.50
364 Mark Messier	.30	.75
365 Mike Richter	.20	.50
366 Martin Havlat	.15	.40
367 Radek Bonk	.15	.40
368 Petr Schastlivy	.12	.30
369 Zdeno Chara	.20	.50
370 Chris Neil	.12	.30
371 Magnus Arvedson	.12	.30
372 Pavel Brendl	.12	.30
373 Donald Brashear	.12	.30
374 Michal Handzus	.15	.40
375 Kim Johnsson	.12	.30
376 John LeClair	.20	.50
377 Simon Gagne	.20	.50
378 Claude Lemieux	.15	.40
379 Brian Boucher	.15	.40
380 Teppo Numminen	.15	.40
381 Daymond Langkow	.15	.40
382 Ladislav Nagy	.12	.30
383 Brian Savage	.12	.30
384 Ville Nieminen	.12	.30
385 Randy Robitaille	.12	.30
386 Alexei Morozov	.12	.30
387 Jan Hrdina	.12	.30
388 Michal Rozsival	.15	.40
389 Alexandre Daigle	.12	.30
390 Mike Ricci	.15	.40
391 Vincent Damphousse	.15	.40
392 Teemu Selanne	.40	1.00
393 Adam Graves	.15	.40
394 Scott Thornton	.12	.30
395 Scott Hannan	.12	.30
396 Fred Brathwaite	.15	.40
397 Jamal Mayers	.12	.30
398 Reed Low	.12	.30
399 Chris Pronger	.15	.40
400 Scott Mellanby	.12	.30
401 Alexander Khavanov	.12	.30
402 Ruslan Fedotenko	.12	.30
403 Fredrik Modin	.12	.30
404 Nikita Alexeev	.12	.30
405 Shane Willis	.12	.30
406 Dave Andreychuk	.20	.50
407 Trevor Kidd	.12	.30
408 Robert Reichel	.12	.30
409 Robert Svehla	.12	.30
410 Alyn McCauley	.12	.30
411 Tomas Kaberle	.12	.30
412 Travis Green	.12	.30
413 Henrik Sedin	.20	.50
414 Brendan Morrison	.15	.40
415 Matt Cooke	.12	.30
416 Ed Jovanovski	.15	.40
417 Mattias Ohlund	.12	.30
418 Trevor Linden	.20	.50
419 Jaromir Jagr	.50	1.25
420 Robert Lang	.12	.30
421 Matt Pettinger	.12	.30
422 Ken Klee	.12	.30
423 Stephen Peat	.12	.30
424 Brian Sutherby	.12	.30
425 Joe Thornton	.25	.60
426 Wayne Gretzky	1.00	2.50
427 Martin Gerber YG RC	2.50	6.00
428 Kurt Sauer YG RC	1.50	4.00
429 Tim Thomas YG RC	8.00	20.00
430 Jordan Leopold YG RC	2.50	6.00
431 Levente Szuper YG RC	2.50	6.00
432 Shawn Thornton YG RC	2.00	5.00
433 Jeff Paul YG RC	1.50	4.00
434 Lasse Pirjeta YG RC	1.50	4.00
435 Dmitri Bykov YG RC	1.50	4.00
436 Ryan Miller YG RC	8.00	20.00
437 Kari Haakana YG RC	1.50	4.00
438 Ivan Majesky YG RC	1.50	4.00
439 Stephane Veilleux YG RC	1.50	4.00
440 Scottie Upshall YG RC	2.00	5.00
441 Shaone Morrisonn YG RC	1.50	4.00
442 Eric Godard YG RC	1.50	4.00
443 Jason Spezza YG RC	8.00	20.00
444 Anton Volchenkov YG RC	1.50	4.00
445 Dennis Seidenberg YG RC	3.00	8.00
446 Radovan Somik YG RC	1.50	4.00
447 Patrick Sharp YG RC	8.00	20.00
448 Jeff Taffe YG RC	1.50	4.00
449 Lynn Loyns YG RC	1.50	4.00
450 Mike Cammalleri YG RC	8.00	20.00
451 Tom Koivisto YG RC	1.50	4.00
452 Curtis Sanford YG RC	2.50	6.00
453 Cody Rudkowsky YG RC	1.50	4.00
454 Carlo Colaiacovo YG RC	2.50	6.00
455 Mikael Tellqvist YG RC	1.50	4.00
456 Vernon Fiddler YG RC	2.00	5.00

2002-03 Upper Deck Exclusives

Available only in Canadian hobby packs, this 456-card set paralleled the base set but was enhanced with gold foil maple leafs across the card front and serial-numbered to 75 copies each. Cards 1-180 were available in Series I and cards 181-456 were available in Series II.

*1-180/247-426 VETS/75: 4X TO 10X BASE
*181-195 MS/75: 2X TO 5X BASIC MS
*196-225 YG/75: 2X TO 5X BASIC YG
*226-246 MS/75: .5X TO 1.2X BASIC MS
*226-246 YG/75: .5X TO 1.2X BASIC YG
*427-456 YG/75: 1.5X TO 4X BASIC YG
STATED PRINT RUN 75 SER.#'d SETS

Card	Low	High
364 Mark Messier	3.00	8.00
429 Tim Thomas YG	30.00	80.00
436 Ryan Miller YG	30.00	80.00
443 Jason Spezza YG	30.00	80.00
450 Mike Cammalleri YG	20.00	50.00

2002-03 Upper Deck All-Star Jerseys

STATED ODDS 1:96 SERIES 1 HOBBY

Card	Low	High
ASCC Chris Chelios	3.00	8.00
ASEJ Ed Jovanovski	3.00	8.00
ASJS Joe Sakic	6.00	15.00
ASJT Jose Theodore	4.00	10.00
ASMN Markus Naslund	3.00	8.00
ASPK Paul Kariya	3.00	8.00
ASRB Rob Blake	3.00	8.00
ASSB Sean Burke	3.00	8.00
ASSF Sergei Fedorov	5.00	12.00
ASSK Sami Kapanen	3.00	8.00
ASSO Sandis Ozolinsh	3.00	8.00
ASTS Teemu Selanne	3.00	8.00
ASVD Vincent Damphousse	3.00	8.00
ASWG Wayne Gretzky	30.00	80.00

2002-03 Upper Deck All-Star Performers Jerseys

STATED ODDS 1:96 SERIES 2

Card	Low	High
ASEJ Ed Jovanovski	4.00	10.00
ASJT Jose Theodore	5.00	12.00
ASMM Mike Modano	8.00	20.00
ASMN Markus Naslund	3.00	8.00
ASPK Paul Kariya	3.00	8.00
ASPR Patrick Roy	12.00	30.00
ASRB Rob Blake	4.00	10.00
ASSB Sean Burke	4.00	10.00
ASSK Sami Kapanen	4.00	10.00
ASSO Sandis Ozolinsh	4.00	10.00
ASTS Teemu Selanne	3.00	8.00
ASVD Vincent Damphousse	4.00	10.00
ASWG Wayne Gretzky	30.00	80.00

2002-03 Upper Deck UD Promos

Inserted into issues of Beckett Hockey Collector #148, this 180-card set paralleled the basic Upper Deck Series II set but carried a "UD Promo" stamp in silver foil across the card fronts.
*UD PROMOS: .8X TO 2X BASIC CARDS

2002-03 Upper Deck Blow-Ups

Found in Canadian retail boxes only, this 42-card set was larger sized parallels of the base set. Cards were serial-numbered out of 299.

Card	Low	High
COMPLETE SET (42)	75.00	150.00
C1 Paul Kariya	4.00	10.00
C2 Ilya Kovalchuk	2.50	6.00
C3 Joe Thornton	2.50	6.00
C4 Roman Turek	.75	2.00
C5 Jeff O'Neill	.75	2.00
C6 Rob Blake	.75	2.00
C7 Patrick Roy	6.00	15.00
C8 Joe Sakic	4.00	10.00
C9 Peter Forsberg	4.00	10.00
C10 Marc Denis	1.25	3.00
C11 Mike Modano	2.50	6.00
C12 Marty Turco	1.50	4.00
C13 Steve Yzerman	6.00	15.00
C14 Curtis Joseph	2.50	6.00
C15 Nicklas Lidstrom	1.50	4.00
C16 Mike Comrie	1.50	4.00
C17 Tommy Salo	1.25	3.00
C18 Roberto Luongo	1.25	3.00
C19 Felix Potvin	1.50	4.00
C20 Marian Gaborik	2.50	6.00
C21 Jose Theodore	1.50	4.00
C22 Saku Koivu	1.50	4.00
C23 Scott Hartnell	1.25	3.00
C24 Scott Stevens	.75	2.00
C25 Martin Brodeur	4.00	10.00
C26 Eric Lindros	1.50	4.00
C27 Pavel Bure	2.50	6.00
C28 Marian Hossa	1.50	4.00
C29 Daniel Alfredsson	1.25	3.00
C30 Keith Primeau	.75	2.00
C31 Sean Burke	1.25	3.00
C32 Tony Amonte	1.50	4.00
C33 Mario Lemieux	8.00	20.00
C34 Owen Nolan	1.25	3.00
C35 Al MacInnis	1.25	3.00
C36 Brad Richards	1.25	3.00
C37 Vincent Lecavalier	1.25	3.00
C38 Mats Sundin	1.50	4.00
C39 Ed Belfour	1.50	4.00
C40 Todd Bertuzzi	1.25	3.00
C41 Markus Naslund	1.25	3.00
C42 Olaf Kolzig	1.25	3.00

2002-03 Upper Deck Bright Futures Jerseys

COMMON CARD 4.00 10.00
STATED ODDS 1:72 SERIES 2
ALL CARDS CARRY BF PREFIX

Card	Low	High
AM Alexei Morozov	4.00	10.00
BB Brian Boucher	4.00	10.00
DA Denis Arkhipov	4.00	10.00
DL David Legwand	4.00	10.00
IB Ilja Bryzgalov	5.00	12.00
JB Jaroslav Bednar	4.00	10.00
JG Jean-Sebastien Giguere	4.00	10.00
JL Jamie Lundmark	4.00	10.00
ME Martin Erat	4.00	10.00
MM Manny Malhotra	4.00	10.00
MP Matt Pettinger	4.00	10.00
MR Mike Ribeiro	4.00	10.00
MY Mike York	4.00	10.00
PA Timo Parssinen	4.00	10.00
PB Pavel Brendl	4.00	10.00
PS Patrik Stefan	4.00	10.00
RK Rostislav Klesla	4.00	10.00
SG Simon Gagne	5.00	12.00
TC Tim Connolly	4.00	10.00
TP Taylor Pyatt	4.00	10.00
VN Ville Nieminen	4.00	10.00

2002-03 Upper Deck CHL Graduates Jerseys

STATED ODDS 1:96 SERIES 1 HOBBY

Card	Low	High
CGAT Alex Tanguay	4.00	10.00
CGBL Dan Blackburn	4.00	10.00
CGDB Daniel Briere	4.00	10.00
CGDL David Legwand	4.00	10.00
CGED Eric Daze	4.00	10.00
CGEL Eric Lindros	8.00	20.00
CGGM Glen Murray	4.00	10.00
CGJA Jason Arnott	4.00	10.00
CGJF Jeff Friesen	4.00	10.00
CGJS Joe Sakic	6.00	15.00
CGJT Joe Thornton	8.00	20.00
CGKP Keith Primeau	4.00	10.00
CGMD Marc Denis	4.00	10.00
CGML Mario Lemieux	20.00	50.00
CGMM Mike Modano	8.00	20.00
CGMR Mark Recchi	4.00	10.00
CGRT Ron Tugnutt	4.00	10.00
CGSS Steve Sullivan	4.00	10.00
CGSY Steve Yzerman	12.50	30.00
CGTL Trevor Linden	5.00	12.00

2002-03 Upper Deck CHL Graduates Gold

*GOLD: 2X TO 5X BASIC JERSEY
STATED PRINT RUN 25 SER.#'d SETS

2002-03 Upper Deck Difference Makers Jerseys

STATED ODDS 1:72 SERIES 2

Card	Low	High
BL Brian Leetch	3.00	8.00
BS Brendan Shanahan	3.00	8.00
ED Eric Daze	3.00	8.00
IK Ilya Kovalchuk	5.00	12.00
JA Jason Allison	3.00	8.00
JI Jarome Iginla	4.00	10.00
JJ Jaromir Jagr	6.00	15.00
JT Joe Thornton	8.00	20.00
JT Jose Theodore	4.00	10.00
MD Mike Dunham	3.00	8.00
ML Mario Lemieux	12.50	30.00
MM Mike Modano	6.00	15.00
MS Mats Sundin	3.00	8.00
PK Paul Kariya	3.00	8.00
PR Patrick Roy	12.00	30.00
RB Rob Blake	3.00	8.00
RT Roman Turek	3.00	8.00
SA Miroslav Satan	3.00	8.00
SS Sergei Samsonov	3.00	8.00
SY Steve Yzerman	10.00	25.00
ZP Zigmund Palffy	3.00	8.00

2002-03 Upper Deck Fan Favorites Jerseys

STATED ODDS 1:96 SERIES 2 RETAIL
ALL CARDS CARRY FF PREFIX

Card	Low	High
AD Adam Deadmarsh	3.00	8.00
BL Brian Leetch	3.00	8.00
JI Jarome Iginla	4.00	10.00
JJ Jaromir Jagr	6.00	15.00
KP Keith Primeau	3.00	8.00
MB Martin Brodeur	10.00	25.00
MM Mike Modano	8.00	20.00
MN Markus Naslund	3.00	8.00
NL Nicklas Lidstrom	3.00	8.00
PF Peter Forsberg	10.00	25.00
PK Paul Kariya	3.00	8.00
SD Shane Doan	3.00	8.00
SK Saku Koivu	3.00	8.00
SS Sergei Samsonov	3.00	8.00

2002-03 Upper Deck First Class

STATED ODDS 1:288 SERIES 1
*GOLD/75: .8X TO 2X BASE JSY

Card	Low	High
UDJJ Jaromir Jagr	6.00	15.00
UDJS Joe Sakic	10.00	25.00
UDJT Jose Theodore	8.00	20.00
UDML Mario Lemieux	12.50	30.00
UDPK Paul Kariya	6.00	15.00
UDPR Patrick Roy	12.50	30.00
UDSY Steve Yzerman	10.00	25.00

2002-03 Upper Deck Game Jersey Autographs

*GJ AUTO: 3X TO 8X BASE JSY
RANDOM INSERTS IN SERIES 2 PACKS
PRINT RUN 50 SERIAL #'d SETS
ALL CARDS CARRY SGJ PREFIX

Card	Low	High
PR Patrick Roy	75.00	150.00
SY Steve Yzerman	75.00	150.00
WG Wayne Gretzky	200.00	350.00

2002-03 Upper Deck Game Jersey Series II

STATED ODDS 1:96 SERIES 2

Card	Low	High
GJEB Ed Belfour	4.00	10.00
GJHZ Henrik Zetterberg	10.00	25.00
GJIK Ilya Kovalchuk	6.00	15.00
GJJL John LeClair	2.50	6.00
GJJS Joe Sakic	6.00	15.00
GJJT Joe Thornton	6.00	15.00
GJMB Martin Brodeur	12.50	30.00
GJPB Pavel Bure	3.00	8.00
GJPR Patrick Roy	12.50	30.00
GJSG Simon Gagne	4.00	10.00
GJSH Scott Hartnell	4.00	10.00
GJSS Sergei Samsonov	2.50	6.00
GJSY Steve Yzerman	10.00	25.00
GJWG Wayne Gretzky	25.00	60.00

2002-03 Upper Deck Gifted Greats

Card	Low	High
COMPLETE SET (14)	15.00	30.00
STATED ODDS 1:12 SERIES 1		
GG1 Paul Kariya	.40	1.00
GG2 Bobby Orr	2.50	6.00
GG3 Joe Sakic	.60	1.50
GG4 Patrick Roy	1.50	4.00
GG5 Peter Forsberg	1.00	2.50
GG6 Mike Modano	.60	1.50
GG7 Dominik Hasek	.75	2.00
GG8 Steve Yzerman	1.50	4.00
GG9 Gordie Howe	1.50	4.00
GG10 Martin Brodeur	1.25	3.00
GG11 Wayne Gretzky	3.00	8.00
GG12 Pavel Bure	.40	1.00
GG13 Mario Lemieux	2.50	6.00
GG14 Jaromir Jagr	.60	1.50

2002-03 Upper Deck Goaltender Threads Jerseys

STATED ODDS 1:96 SERIES 2
ALL CARDS CARRY GT PREFIX
*GOLD: 2X TO 5X BASE HI
GOLD PRINT RUN 25 SER.#'d SETS

Card	Low	High
FP Felix Potvin	2.50	6.00
IB Ilja Bryzgalov	3.00	8.00
JG Jean-Sebastien Giguere	2.50	6.00
JT Jose Theodore	3.00	8.00
MB Martin Biron	2.50	6.00
MD Mike Dunham	2.50	6.00
MN Mika Noronen	2.50	6.00
MT Marty Turco	3.00	8.00
OK Olaf Kolzig	2.50	6.00
RC Roman Cechmanek	2.50	6.00
RL Roberto Luongo	4.00	10.00
RT Roman Turek	2.50	6.00
SS Steve Shields	2.50	6.00
TH Jocelyn Thibault	2.50	6.00

2002-03 Upper Deck Good Old Days Jerseys

This 14-card memorabilia set was inserted at a rate of 1:96 Series 1 packs.

Card	Low	High
GOAM Al MacInnis	2.00	5.00
GOBG Bill Guerin	2.00	5.00
GOBH Brett Hull	2.50	6.00
GOBS Brendan Shanahan	2.50	6.00
GOCJ Curtis Joseph	2.00	5.00
GODM Dominik Hasek	3.00	8.00
GOJN Joe Nieuwendyk	2.00	5.00
GOJS Joe Sakic	3.00	8.00
GOKP Keith Primeau	4.00	10.00
GOKT Keith Tkachuk	3.00	8.00
GOMS Mats Sundin	2.00	5.00
GOPB Pavel Bure	6.00	15.00
GOTF Theo Fleury	2.50	6.00
GOTS Teemu Selanne	4.00	10.00

2002-03 Upper Deck Hot Spots Jerseys

STATED ODDS 1:96 SERIES 1 HOBBY

Card	Low	High
HSCL Claude Lemieux	3.00	8.00
HSDA Denis Arkhipov	3.00	8.00
HSDB Daniel Briere	4.00	10.00
HSDL David Legwand	3.00	8.00
HSDU Mike Dunham	3.00	8.00
HSIK Ilya Kovalchuk	5.00	12.00
HSMD Marc Denis	3.00	8.00
HSME Martin Erat	3.00	8.00
HSRK Rostislav Klesla	3.00	8.00
HSRW Ray Whitney	3.00	8.00
HSSD Shane Doan	3.00	8.00
HSSH Scott Hartnell	4.00	10.00

2002-03 Upper Deck Last Line of Defense

Card	Low	High
COMPLETE SET (14)	10.00	20.00
STATED ODDS 1:12 SERIES 2		
LL1 Jean-Sebastien Giguere	.40	1.00
LL2 Martin Biron	.40	1.00
LL3 Patrick Roy	2.00	5.00
LL4 Curtis Joseph	.50	1.25
LL5 Tommy Salo	.40	1.00
LL6 Roberto Luongo	.75	2.00
LL7 Jose Theodore	.60	1.50
LL8 Martin Brodeur	1.50	4.00
LL9 Chris Osgood	.40	1.00
LL10 Sean Burke	.40	1.00
LL11 Evgeni Nabokov	.40	1.00
LL12 Nikolai Khabibulin	.50	1.25
LL13 Ed Belfour	.50	1.25
LL14 Olaf Kolzig	.40	1.00

2002-03 Upper Deck Letters of Note Jerseys

STATED ODDS 1:144 SERIES 1
*GOLD/50: .6X TO 1.5X BASIC JERSEY

Card	Low	High
LNCD Chris Drury	6.00	15.00
LNCP Chris Pronger	6.00	15.00
LNJI Jarome Iginla	5.00	12.00
LNJS Joe Sakic	10.00	25.00
LNML Mario Lemieux	20.00	50.00
LNMM Mike Modano	6.00	15.00
LNMN Markus Naslund	6.00	15.00
LNMS Mats Sundin	6.00	15.00
LNON Owen Nolan	6.00	15.00
LNPB Peter Bondra	6.00	15.00
LNPK Paul Kariya	6.00	15.00
LNSK Saku Koivu	6.00	15.00
LNSS Scott Stevens	8.00	20.00
LNSY Steve Yzerman	15.00	40.00

2002-03 Upper Deck Number Crunchers

Card	Low	High
COMPLETE SET (14)	10.00	20.00
STATED ODDS 1:12 SERIES 2		
NC1 Joe Thornton	.75	2.00
NC2 Theo Fleury	.30	.75
NC3 Brenden Morrow	.40	1.00
NC4 Gordie Howe	2.00	5.00
NC5 Brendan Shanahan	.50	1.25
NC6 Georges Laraque	.30	.75
NC7 Scott Hartnell	.40	1.00
NC8 Eric Lindros	.50	1.25
NC9 Donald Brashear	.30	.75
NC10 Keith Primeau	.30	.75
NC11 Jeremy Roenick	.60	1.50
NC12 Keith Tkachuk	.40	1.00
NC13 Ed Jovanovski	.40	1.00
NC14 Todd Bertuzzi	.40	1.00

2002-03 Upper Deck On the Rise Jerseys

STATED ODDS 1:96 SERIES 1 HOBBY

Card	Low	High
ORBM Brenden Morrow	3.00	8.00
ORDB Dan Blackburn	3.00	8.00
ORIK Ilya Kovalchuk	5.00	12.00
ORKK Krystofer Kolanos	3.00	8.00
ORMB Mark Bell	3.00	8.00
ORRK Rostislav Klesla	3.00	8.00
ORSR Steven Reinprecht	3.00	8.00

2002-03 Upper Deck Patch Card Name Plate

STATED ODDS 1:7500 SERIES 2

Card	Low	High
JJ Jaromir Jagr		
JR Jeremy Roenick		
MB Martin Brodeur		
ML Mario Lemieux	75.00	150.00
PF Peter Forsberg	30.00	80.00
PK Paul Kariya		
SF Sergei Fedorov		
SS Sergei Samsonov	30.00	60.00
VL Vincent Lecavalier		
WG Wayne Gretzky	200.00	300.00

2002-03 Upper Deck Patchwork

Inserted at a rate of 1:2500 Series 1 packs, this 30-card set featured swatches of game jersey patches. As of press time, not all cards have been verified.

Card	Low	High
PWAK Alexei Kovalev	25.00	60.00
PWBG Bill Guerin	25.00	60.00
PWBS Brendan Shanahan	30.00	80.00
PWCD Chris Drury	25.00	60.00
PWJJ Jaromir Jagr	60.00	150.00
PWJL John LeClair	25.00	60.00
PWJS Joe Sakic	40.00	100.00
PWJT Joe Thornton	30.00	80.00
PWKP Keith Primeau	25.00	60.00
PWMB Martin Brodeur	50.00	125.00
PWMD Mike Dunham	20.00	50.00
PWMH Milan Hejduk	20.00	50.00
PWML Mario Lemieux	80.00	200.00
PWMM Mike Modano	40.00	100.00
PWMN Markus Naslund	20.00	50.00
PWMS Mats Sundin	25.00	60.00
PWMT Marty Turco	25.00	60.00
PWNL Nicklas Lidstrom	25.00	60.00
PWPF Peter Forsberg	30.00	80.00
PWPK Paul Kariya	30.00	80.00
PWPR Patrick Roy	60.00	150.00
PWSB Sean Burke		
PWSF Sergei Fedorov	40.00	100.00
PWSG Simon Gagne	25.00	60.00
PWSK Saku Koivu	25.00	60.00
PWSS Sergei Samsonov	20.00	50.00
PWSY Steve Yzerman	50.00	125.00
PWTA Tony Amonte	20.00	50.00
PWTH Jose Theodore	25.00	60.00
PWZP Zigmund Palffy	25.00	60.00

2002-03 Upper Deck Pinpoint Accuracy Jerseys

STATED ODDS 1:96 SERIES 2

Card	Low	High
PAAT Alex Tanguay	3.00	8.00
PABS Brendan Shanahan	3.00	8.00
PACD Chris Drury	3.00	8.00
PAED Eric Daze	3.00	8.00
PAGS Geoff Sanderson	3.00	8.00
PAJI Jarome Iginla	5.00	12.00
PAJT Joe Thornton	6.00	15.00
PAMH Milan Hejduk	3.00	8.00
PAML Mario Lemieux	12.50	30.00
PAMM Mike Modano	8.00	20.00
PAMR Mark Recchi	3.00	8.00
PAPB Pavel Bure	3.00	8.00
PAPK Paul Kariya	3.00	8.00
PASF Sergei Fedorov	5.00	12.00

2002-03 Upper Deck Reaching Fifty Jerseys

STATED ODDS 1:96 SERIES 2

Card	Low	High
50BH Brett Hull	4.00	10.00
50BO Peter Bondra	3.00	8.00
50JI Jarome Iginla	4.00	10.00
50JJ Jaromir Jagr	5.00	12.00
50JL John LeClair	3.00	8.00
50JS Joe Sakic	6.00	15.00
50KT Keith Tkachuk	3.00	8.00
50ML Mario Lemieux	15.00	40.00
50MM Mike Modano	4.00	10.00
50PB Pavel Bure	3.00	8.00
50PK Paul Kariya	3.00	8.00
50SF Sergei Fedorov	6.00	15.00
50SY Steve Yzerman	10.00	25.00
50WG Wayne Gretzky	25.00	60.00

2002-03 Upper Deck Reaching Fifty Gold

*STARS: 2X TO 5X BASIC JERSEY
PRINT RUN 50 SERIAL #'d SETS

2002-03 Upper Deck Saviors Jerseys

Known print runs and short prints are listed below.
STATED ODDS 1:96 SERIES 1

Card	Low	High
SVBB Brian Boucher	3.00	8.00
SVBD Byron Dafoe	3.00	8.00
SVBJ Brent Johnson	3.00	8.00
SVJG Jean-Sebastien Giguere	3.00	8.00
SVJT Jose Theodore SP	5.00	12.00
SVMB Martin Biron	3.00	8.00
SVMD Mike Dunham	3.00	8.00
SVMT Marty Turco	4.00	10.00
SVOK Olaf Kolzig	3.00	8.00
SVPR Patrick Roy SP	25.00	60.00
SVRT Roman Turek	3.00	8.00
SVTH Jocelyn Thibault/100	12.50	30.00
SVTU Ron Tugnutt/100	8.00	20.00

2002-03 Upper Deck Shooting Stars

Card	Low	High
COMPLETE SET (14)	15.00	30.00
STATED ODDS 1:12 SERIES 2		
SS1 Paul Kariya	.40	1.00
SS2 Jarome Iginla	.60	1.50
SS3 Joe Thornton	.60	1.50
SS4 Joe Sakic	.75	2.00
SS5 Mike Modano	.60	1.50
SS6 Gordie Howe	2.00	5.00
SS7 Steve Yzerman	2.00	5.00
SS8 Mike Comrie	.30	.75
SS9 Wayne Gretzky	3.00	8.00
SS10 Pavel Bure	.40	1.00
SS11 Simon Gagne	.50	1.25
SS12 Mario Lemieux	2.50	6.00
SS13 Teemu Selanne	.40	1.00
SS14 Jaromir Jagr	.60	1.50

2002-03 Upper Deck Sizzling Scorers

Card	Low	High
COMPLETE SET (14)	8.00	15.00
STATED ODDS 1:12 SERIES 1		
SS1 Ilya Kovalchuk	.60	1.50
SS2 Joe Thornton	.60	1.50
SS3 Jarome Iginla	.60	1.50
SS4 Ron Francis	.40	1.00
SS5 Joe Sakic	.75	2.00
SS6 Mike Modano	.60	1.50
SS7 Brendan Shanahan	.40	1.00
SS8 Mike Comrie	.40	1.00
SS9 Marian Gaborik	.60	1.50
SS10 Patrik Elias	.40	1.00
SS11 Pavel Bure	.40	1.00
SS12 Jeremy Roenick	.50	1.25
SS13 Mats Sundin	.40	1.00
SS14 Todd Bertuzzi	.40	1.00

2002-03 Upper Deck Specialists Jerseys

STATED ODDS 1:96 SERIES 1 HOBBY

Card	Low	High
SAZ Alexei Zhamnov	3.00	8.00
SBL Brian Leetch	4.00	10.00
SCD Chris Drury	4.00	10.00
SEB Eric Belanger	3.00	8.00
SJL Jere Lehtinen	3.00	8.00
SMM Mike Modano	6.00	15.00
SMR Mark Recchi	4.00	10.00
SMS Miroslav Satan	3.00	8.00
SPB Peter Bondra	4.00	10.00
SRB Jarome Iginla	6.00	15.00
SRL Robert Lang	3.00	8.00
SSF Sergei Fedorov	5.00	12.00
SSS Sergei Samsonov	4.00	10.00
STM Todd Marchant	3.00	8.00

2002-03 Upper Deck Speed Demons Jerseys

STATED ODDS 1:96 SERIES 1 RETAIL

Card	Low	High
SDDB Daniel Briere	3.00	8.00
SDPB Pavel Bure	3.00	8.00
SDSF Sergei Fedorov	4.00	10.00
SDSG Simon Gagne	4.00	10.00
SDSS Steve Sullivan	3.00	8.00
SDTM Todd Marchant	3.00	8.00
SDZP Zigmund Palffy	3.00	8.00

2002-03 Upper Deck Super Saviors

Card	Low	High
COMPLETE SET (14)	12.50	25.00
STATED ODDS 1:12 SERIES 1		
SA1 Martin Biron	.40	1.00
SA2 Roman Turek	.40	1.00
SA3 Arturs Irbe	.40	1.00
SA4 Patrick Roy	2.00	5.00
SA5 Marty Turco	.40	1.00
SA6 Dominik Hasek	1.00	2.50
SA7 Jose Theodore	1.00	2.50
SA8 Martin Brodeur	1.50	4.00
SA9 Chris Osgood	.40	1.00
SA10 Patrick Lalime	.40	1.00
SA11 Sean Burke	.40	1.00
SA12 Evgeni Nabokov	.40	1.00
SA13 Brent Johnson	.40	1.00
SA14 Olaf Kolzig	.40	1.00

2003-04 Upper Deck

This 475-card set was issued in two different sets of 245 cards and 230 cards. The "Young Guns" rookie subset cards were inserted at odds of 1:4.

Card	Low	High
COMP.SERIES 1 (245)	200.00	400.00
COMP.SER.1 w/o SPs	20.00	40.00
COMP.SERIES 2 (230)	125.00	250.00
COMP.SER.2 w/o SPs	20.00	40.00
1 Petr Sykora	.20	.50
2 Steve Rucchin	.15	.40
3 Sandis Ozolinsh	.15	.40
4 Jason Krog	.15	.40
5 Sergei Fedorov	.40	1.00
6 Rob Niedermayer	.20	.50
7 Jean-Sebastien Giguere	.25	.60
8 Dany Heatley	.25	.60
9 Slava Kozlov	.20	.50
10 Patrik Stefan	.15	.40
11 Yannick Tremblay	.15	.40
12 Shawn McEachern	.15	.40
13 Byron Dafoe	.20	.50
14 Joe Thornton	.30	.75
15 Bryan Berard	.20	.50
16 P-J Axelsson	.15	.40
17 Hal Gill	.15	.40
18 P.J. Stock	.15	.40
19 Mike Knuble	.15	.40
20 Steve Shields	.20	.50
21 Daniel Briere	.25	.60
22 Ales Kotalik	.15	.40
23 Curtis Brown	.15	.40
24 JP Dumont	.15	.40
25 Alexei Zhitnik	.20	.50
26 Maxim Afinogenov	.15	.40
27 Martin Biron	.20	.50
28 Dean McAmmond	.15	.40
29 Jarome Iginla	.25	.60
30 Martin Gelinas	.15	.40
31 Jordan Leopold	.15	.40
32 Chuck Kobasew	.15	.40
33 Roman Turek	.20	.50
34 Jeff O'Neill	.15	.40
35 Ron Francis	.30	.75
36 Sean Hill	.15	.40
37 Erik Cole	.20	.50
38 Pavel Brendl	.15	.40
39 Kevin Weekes	.20	.50
40 Alexei Zhamnov	.20	.50
41 Kyle Calder	.15	.40
42 Tyler Arnason	.15	.40
43 Igor Radulov	.15	.40
44 Jocelyn Thibault	.20	.50
45 Peter Forsberg	.30	.75
46 Alex Tanguay	.20	.50
47 Derek Morris	.15	.40
48 Rob Blake	.25	.60
49 Paul Kariya	.30	.75
50 Teemu Selanne	.50	1.25
51 David Aebischer	.20	.50
52 Patrick Roy	.60	1.50
53 Pascal Leclaire	.15	.40
54 Geoff Sanderson	.15	.40
55 Rick Nash	.25	.60
56 Rostislav Klesla	.15	.40
57 Jody Shelley	.15	.40
58 Marc Denis	.20	.50
59 Mike Modano	.40	1.00
60 Sergei Zubov	.20	.50
61 Jere Lehtinen	.20	.50
62 Steve Ott	.20	.50
63 Niko Kapanen	.15	.40
64 Jason Bacashihua	.15	.40
65 Marty Turco	.25	.60
66 Brett Hull	.30	.75
67 Nicklas Lidstrom	.25	.60
68 Mathieu Schneider	.15	.40
69 Henrik Zetterberg	.30	.75
70 Pavel Datsyuk	.30	.75
71 Derian Hatcher	.15	.40
72 Steve Yzerman	.60	1.50
73 Manny Legace	.15	.40
74 Ryan Smyth	.20	.50
75 Mike York	.15	.40
76 Ales Hemsky	.25	.60
77 Eric Brewer	.15	.40
78 Fernando Pisani	.15	.40
79 Georges Laraque	.20	.50
80 Tommy Salo	.20	.50
81 Viktor Kozlov	.15	.40
82 Kristian Huselius	.15	.40
83 Stephen Weiss	.15	.40
84 Jay Bouwmeester	.25	.60
85 Roberto Luongo	.40	1.00
86 Zigmund Palffy	.25	.60
87 Alexander Frolov	.20	.50
88 Luc Robitaille	.25	.60
89 Ian Laperriere	.15	.40
90 Jared Aulin	.15	.40
91 Roman Cechmanek	.20	.50
92 Marian Gaborik	.40	1.00
93 Pascal Dupuis	.15	.40
94 Andrew Brunette	.15	.40
95 Wes Walz	.15	.40
96 Pierre-Marc Bouchard	.25	.60
97 Willie Mitchell	.15	.40
98 Manny Fernandez	.20	.50
99 Saku Koivu	.25	.60
100 Jan Bulis	.15	.40
101 Marcel Hossa	.15	.40
102 Michael Komisarek	.15	.40
103 Richard Zednik	.15	.40
104 Mathieu Garon	.15	.40
105 Ron Hainsey	.15	.40
106 David Legwand	.20	.50
107 Greg Johnson	.15	.40
108 Scott Hartnell	.25	.60
109 Scottie Upshall	.20	.50
110 Tomas Vokoun	.20	.50
111 Patrik Elias	.25	.60
112 Jeff Friesen	.15	.40
113 Joe Nieuwendyk	.25	.60
114 Scott Niedermayer	.25	.60
115 Grant Marshall	.15	.40
116 Scott Stevens	.25	.60
117 Martin Brodeur	.50	1.25
118 Jason Blake	.15	.40
119 Mark Parrish	.15	.40
120 Michael Peca	.20	.50
121 Adrian Aucoin	.15	.40
122 Rick DiPietro	.20	.50
123 Eric Godard	.15	.40
124 Alex Kovalev	.20	.50
125 Anson Carter	.20	.50
126 Mark Messier	.40	1.00
127 Petr Nedved	.15	.40
128 Tom Poti	.15	.40
129 Jamie Lundmark	.15	.40
130 Mike Dunham	.20	.50
131 Marian Hossa	.20	.50
132 Martin Havlat	.25	.60
133 Zdeno Chara	.25	.60
134 Peter Schaefer	.15	.40
135 Ray Emery	.20	.50
136 Jason Spezza	.25	.60
137 Patrick Lalime	.20	.50
138 Mark Recchi	.30	.75
139 Tony Amonte	.20	.50
140 Keith Primeau	.25	.60
141 Simon Gagne	.25	.60
142 Eric Weinrich	.15	.40
143 Jim Vandermeer	.15	.40
144 Robert Esche	.15	.40
145 Shane Doan	.20	.50
146 Chris Gratton	.15	.40
147 Jan Hrdina	.15	.40
148 Daymond Langkow	.15	.40
149 Tyson Nash	.15	.40
150 Brian Boucher	.20	.50
151 Mario Lemieux	.75	2.00
152 Aleksey Morozov	.15	.40
153 Ramzi Abid	.15	.40
154 Dick Tarnstrom	.15	.40
155 Rico Fata	.15	.40
156 Brooks Orpik	.20	.50
157 Vincent Damphousse	.20	.50
158 Marco Sturm	.15	.40
159 Mike Ricci	.20	.50
160 Jim Fahey	.15	.40
161 Niko Dimitrakos	.15	.40
162 Kyle McLaren	.15	.40
163 Evgeni Nabokov	.20	.50
164 Al MacInnis	.25	.60
165 Scott Mellanby	.15	.40
166 Keith Tkachuk	.25	.60
167 Barret Jackman	.15	.40
168 Reed Low	.15	.40
169 Chris Pronger	.20	.50
170 Chris Osgood	.25	.60
171 Vincent Lecavalier	.20	.50
172 Dave Andreychuk	.25	.60
173 Brad Richards	.25	.60
174 Pavel Kubina	.15	.40
175 Alexander Svitov	.15	.40
176 John Grahame	.15	.40
177 Alexander Mogilny	.20	.50
178 Owen Nolan	.20	.50
179 Darcy Tucker	.20	.50
180 Doug Gilmour	.30	.75
181 Tie Domi	.20	.50
182 Phil Housley	.15	.40
183 Gary Roberts	.15	.40
184 Ed Belfour	.25	.60
185 Markus Naslund	.25	.60
186 Brendan Morrison	.20	.50
187 Ed Jovanovski	.20	.50
188 Matt Cooke	.15	.40
189 Henrik Sedin	.25	.60
190 Brandon Reid	.15	.40
191 Marek Malik	.15	.40
192 Alexander Auld	.15	.40
193 Robert Lang	.15	.40
194 Sergei Gonchar	.15	.40
195 Michael Nylander	.15	.40
196 Mike Grier	.15	.40
197 Steve Konowalchuk	.15	.40
198 Olaf Kolzig	.25	.60
199 Joe Thornton CL	.25	.60
200 Martin Brodeur CL	.40	1.00
201 Garrett Burnett YG RC	1.50	4.00
202 Joffrey Lupul YG RC	4.00	10.00
203 Jiri Hudler YG RC	4.00	10.00
204 Patrice Bergeron YG RC	30.00	60.00
205 Matthew Lombardi YG RC	2.00	5.00
206 Eric Staal YG RC	15.00	30.00
207 Lasse Kukkonen YG RC	1.50	4.00
208 Pavel Vorobiev YG RC	2.00	5.00
209 Travis Moen YG RC	2.00	5.00
210 Tuomo Ruutu YG RC	4.00	10.00
211 Cody McCormick YG RC	2.00	5.00
212 John-Michael Liles YG RC	2.00	5.00
213 Marek Svatos YG RC	3.00	8.00
214 Dan Fritsche YG RC	1.50	4.00
215 Antti Miettinen YG RC	2.50	6.00
216 Nathan Horton YG RC	10.00	20.00
217 Dustin Brown YG RC	12.50	25.00
218 Esa Pirnes YG RC	1.50	4.00
219 Alexander Semin YG RC	12.50	25.00
220 Tim Gleason YG RC	2.00	5.00
221 Brent Burns YG RC	50.00	120.00
222 Christoph Brandner YG RC	2.00	5.00
223 Chris Higgins YG RC	3.00	8.00
224 Dan Hamhuis YG RC	2.00	5.00
225 Jordin Tootoo YG RC	6.00	15.00
226 Marek Zidlicky YG RC	1.50	4.00
227 Wade Brookbank YG RC	2.00	5.00
228 David Hale YG RC	1.50	4.00
229 Paul Martin YG RC	2.00	5.00
230 Sean Bergenheim YG RC	2.00	5.00
231 Antoine Vermette YG RC	3.00	8.00
232 Joni Pitkanen YG RC	2.50	6.00
233 Matthew Spiller YG RC	2.00	5.00
234 Marc-Andre Fleury YG RC	60.00	150.00
235 Matt Murley YG RC	2.00	5.00
236 Ryan Malone YG RC	3.00	8.00
237 Christian Ehrhoff YG RC	2.00	5.00
238 Milan Michalek YG RC	5.00	12.00
239 Andrew Peters YG RC	2.00	5.00
240 Tom Preissing YG RC	2.00	5.00
241 Peter Sejna YG RC	2.00	5.00
242 Matt Stajan YG RC	2.50	6.00
243 Maxim Kondratiev YG RC	1.50	4.00
244 Boyd Gordon YG RC	2.00	5.00
245 Fleury/Staal/Horton CL	2.00	5.00
246 Vaclav Prospal	.15	.40
247 Stanislav Chistov	.15	.40
248 Mike Leclerc	.15	.40
249 Keith Carney	.15	.40
250 Martin Gerber	.15	.40
251 Sammy Pahlsson	.15	.40
252 Ruslan Salei	.15	.40
253 Marc Savard	.20	.50
254 Ilya Kovalchuk	.25	.60
255 Kamil Piros	.15	.40
256 Frantisek Kaberle	.15	.40
257 Pasi Nurminen	.20	.50
258 Sergei Samsonov	.20	.50
259 Brian Rolston	.20	.50
260 Travis Green	.15	.40
261 Glen Murray	.20	.50
262 Nick Boynton	.15	.40
263 Jeff Jillson	.15	.40
264 Felix Potvin	.40	1.00
265 Andrew Raycroft	.20	.50
266 Jochen Hecht	.15	.40
267 Chris Drury	.20	.50
268 Miroslav Satan	.20	.50
269 Andy Delmore	.15	.40
270 Ryan Miller	.25	.60
271 Tim Connolly	.15	.40
272 Oleg Saprykin	.15	.40
273 Craig Conroy	.15	.40
274 Steve Reinprecht	.15	.40
275 Toni Lydman	.15	.40
276 Robyn Regehr	.15	.40
277 Jamie McLennan	.15	.40
278 Jaroslav Svoboda	.15	.40
279 Rod Brind'Amour	.25	.60
280 Radim Vrbata	.20	.50
281 Bret Hedican	.15	.40
282 Danny Markov	.15	.40
283 Jamie Storr	.20	.50
284 Eric Daze	.20	.50
285 Steve Sullivan	.15	.40
286 Jon Klemm	.15	.40
287 Alexander Karpovtsev	.15	.40
288 Michael Leighton	.15	.40
289 Joe Sakic	.40	1.00
290 Steve Konowalchuk	.15	.40
291 Milan Hejduk	.20	.50
292 Adam Foote	.15	.40
293 Dan Hinote	.15	.40
294 Philippe Sauve	.20	.50
295 Trevor Letowski	.15	.40
296 Andrew Cassels	.15	.40
297 Todd Marchant	.15	.40
298 David Vyborny	.15	.40
299 Darryl Sydor	.15	.40
300 Jaroslav Spacek	.15	.40
301 Espen Knutsen	.15	.40
302 Brenden Morrow	.20	.50
303 Jason Arnott	.20	.50
304 Pierre Turgeon	.25	.60
305 Bill Guerin	.25	.60
306 Teppo Numminen	.15	.40
307 Ron Tugnutt	.20	.50
308 Stu Barnes	.15	.40
309 Brendan Shanahan	.30	.75
310 Ray Whitney	.20	.50
311 Tomas Holmstrom	.20	.50
312 Chris Chelios	.25	.60
313 Jiri Fischer	.15	.40
314 Dominik Hasek	.40	1.00
315 Darren McCarty	.15	.40
316 Brad Isbister	.15	.40
317 Ethan Moreau	.15	.40
318 Raffi Torres	.15	.40
319 Mike Comrie	.20	.50
320 Radek Dvorak	.20	.50
321 Jason Smith	.15	.40
322 Ty Conklin	.20	.50
323 Adam Oates	.25	.60
324 Marcus Nilsson	.15	.40
325 Olli Jokinen	.25	.60
326 Valeri Bure	.15	.40
327 Eric Messier	.15	.40
328 Branislav Mezei	.15	.40
329 Steve Shields	.20	.50
330 Matt Cullen	.15	.40
331 Adam Deadmarsh	.20	.50
332 Jason Allison	.20	.50
333 Jozef Stumpel	.15	.40
334 Eric Belanger	.15	.40
335 Mattias Norstrom	.15	.40
336 Cristobal Huet	.20	.50
337 Martin Straka	.15	.40
338 Antti Laaksonen	.15	.40
339 Sergei Zholtok	.15	.40
340 Alexandre Daigle	.20	.50
341 Filip Kuba	.15	.40
342 Dwayne Roloson	.20	.50
343 Mike Ribeiro	.20	.50
344 Donald Audette	.15	.40
345 Michael Ryder	.20	.50
346 Andrei Markov	.25	.60
347 Jose Theodore	.25	.60
348 Yanic Perreault	.15	.40
349 Andreas Johansson	.15	.40
350 Denis Arkhipov	.15	.40
351 Rem Murray	.15	.40
352 Scott Walker	.15	.40
353 Adam Hall	.15	.40
354 Kimmo Timonen	.15	.40
355 Jason York	.15	.40
356 Sergei Brylin	.15	.40
357 John Madden	.15	.40
358 Scott Gomez	.20	.50
359 Jamie Langenbrunner	.20	.50
360 Brian Gionta	.20	.50
361 Brian Rafalski	.20	.50
362 Corey Schwab	.20	.50
363 Igor Larionov	.25	.60
364 Oleg Kvasha	.15	.40
365 Alexei Yashin	.20	.50
366 Mariusz Czerkawski	.15	.40
367 Roman Hamrlik	.20	.50
368 Janne Niinimaa	.15	.40
369 Arron Asham	.15	.40
370 Garth Snow	.20	.50
371 Jan Hlavac	.15	.40
372 Matthew Barnaby	.20	.50
373 Eric Lindros	.40	1.00
374 Brian Leetch	.25	.60
375 Jussi Markkanen	.15	.40
376 Mike Fisher	.15	.40
377 Radek Bonk	.20	.50
378 Bryan Smolinski	.15	.40
379 Daniel Alfredsson	.25	.60
380 Wade Redden	.15	.40
381 Chris Phillips	.15	.40
382 Todd White	.15	.40
383 Jeremy Roenick	.25	.60
384 Michal Handzus	.20	.50
385 Donald Brashear	.15	.40
386 John LeClair	.25	.60
387 Justin Williams	.20	.50
388 Kim Johnsson	.15	.40
389 Eric Desjardins	.20	.50
390 Jeff Hackett	.20	.50
391 Ladislav Nagy	.15	.40
392 Brian Savage	.15	.40
393 Mike Johnson	.15	.40
394 Branko Radivojevic	.15	.40
395 Paul Mara	.15	.40
396 David Tanabe	.15	.40
397 Sean Burke	.15	.40
398 Mike Sillinger	.15	.40
399 Drake Berehowsky	.15	.40
400 Steve McKenna	.15	.40
401 Konstantin Koltsov	.15	.40
402 Michal Rozsival	.15	.40
403 Sebastien Caron	.20	.50
404 Patrick Marleau	.25	.60
405 Wayne Primeau	.15	.40
406 Alexander Korolyuk	.15	.40
407 Jonathan Cheechoo	.20	.50
408 Mike Rathje	.15	.40
409 Brad Stuart	.15	.40
410 Scott Thornton	.15	.40
411 Pavol Demitra	.30	.75
412 Doug Weight	.25	.60
413 Eric Boguniecki	.15	.40
414 Petr Cajanek	.15	.40
415 Brent Johnson	.20	.50
416 Dallas Drake	.15	.40
417 Cory Stillman	.15	.40
418 Fredrik Modin	.15	.40
419 Martin St. Louis	.25	.60
420 Ruslan Fedotenko	.15	.40
421 Dan Boyle	.20	.50
422 Nikolai Khabibulin	.25	.60
423 Mats Sundin	.25	.60
424 Joe Nieuwendyk	.25	.60
425 Nik Antropov	.20	.50
426 Tomas Kaberle	.15	.40
427 Bryan McCabe	.15	.40
428 Mikael Tellqvist	.20	.50
429 Ken Klee	.15	.40
430 Daniel Sedin	.25	.60
431 Magnus Arvedson	.15	.40
432 Trevor Linden	.25	.60
433 Todd Bertuzzi	.25	.60
434 Mattias Ohlund	.15	.40
435 Dan Cloutier	.20	.50
436 Johan Hedberg	.20	.50
437 Jason King	.15	.40
438 Peter Bondra	.20	.50
439 Jeff Halpern	.15	.40
440 Jaromir Jagr	.60	1.50
441 Steve Eminger	.15	.40
442 Sebastien Charpentier	.15	.40
443 Dainius Zubrus	.15	.40
444 Mario Lemieux	.75	2.00
445 Jason Spezza	.25	.60
446 Brent Krahn YG RC	1.50	4.00
447 Boyd Kane YG RC	1.50	4.00
448 Greg Campbell YG RC	1.50	4.00
449 A.Hutchinson YG RC	1.50	4.00
450 Mike Stuart YG RC	1.50	4.00
451 Nikolai Zherdev YG RC	3.00	8.00
452 Sergei Zinovjev YG RC	1.50	4.00
453 Julien Vauclair YG RC	1.50	4.00
454 Ryan Kesler YG RC	12.50	30.00
455 Fredrik Sjostrom YG RC	2.50	6.00
456 Mikhail Yakubov YG RC	1.50	4.00
457 Nathan Smith YG RC	1.50	4.00
458 Grant McNeill YG RC	1.50	4.00
459 Seamus Kotyk YG RC	1.50	4.00
460 Alan Rourke YG RC	1.50	4.00
461 John Pohl YG RC	1.50	4.00
462 Dominic Moore YG RC	1.50	4.00
463 Tony Salmelainen YG RC	1.50	4.00
464 Rastislav Stana YG RC	2.50	6.00
465 Karl Stewart YG RC	1.50	4.00
466 Darryl Bootland YG RC	2.00	5.00
467 Trevor Daley YG RC	2.50	6.00
468 Peter Sarno YG RC	1.50	4.00
469 Jed Ortmeyer YG RC	1.50	4.00
470 N.Robinson YG RC	1.50	4.00
471 Pat Rissmiller YG RC	2.00	5.00
472 Grtzky/Laflr/Mssier CL	6.00	15.00
473 Jose Theodore HC	4.00	10.00
474 Don Cherry HC	4.00	10.00
475 Salmeln/Moore/Zinov	.75	2.00

2003-04 Upper Deck 500 Goal Club

This 8-card set featured the newest members to the exclusive 500 Goal Club. Cards were inserted at 1:237 for the non-autographed cards and the autographed versions were serial-numbered to 25.

Card	Low	High
500BS Brendan Shanahan	12.50	30.00
500JJ Jaromir Jagr	15.00	40.00
500JN Joe Nieuwendyk	12.50	30.00
500JS Joe Sakic	20.00	50.00
500RF Ron Francis	12.50	30.00
500JJA Jaromir Jagr AU	250.00	400.00
500JNA Joe Nieuwendyk AU	200.00	300.00
500RFA Ron Francis AU	150.00	300.00

2003-04 Upper Deck All-Star Class

Card	Low	High
COMPLETE SET (30)	10.00	20.00
STATED ODDS 1:1 RETAIL		
AS1 Jean-Sebastien Giguere	.20	.50
AS2 Ilya Kovalchuk	.40	1.00
AS3 Joe Thornton	.40	1.00
AS4 Paul Kariya	.20	.50
AS5 Peter Forsberg	.60	1.50
AS6 Teemu Selanne	.30	.75
AS7 Marty Turco	.20	.50
AS8 Mike Modano	.50	1.25
AS9 Steve Yzerman	1.25	3.00
AS10 Dominik Hasek	.60	1.50
AS11 Nicklas Lidstrom	.30	.75
AS12 Jay Bouwmeester	.20	.50
AS13 Zigmund Palffy	.20	.50
AS14 Marian Gaborik	.60	1.50
AS15 Saku Koivu	.20	.50
AS16 Martin Brodeur	.75	2.00
AS17 Alexei Yashin	.20	.50
AS18 Tom Poti	.20	.50
AS19 Jason Spezza	.30	.75
AS20 Marian Hossa	.30	.75
AS21 Jeremy Roenick	.40	1.00
AS22 Sean Burke	.20	.50
AS23 Mario Lemieux	1.50	4.00
AS24 Patrick Marleau	.20	.50
AS25 Chris Pronger	.20	.50
AS26 Vincent Lecavalier	.20	.50
AS27 Mats Sundin	.30	.75
AS28 Ed Belfour	.30	.75
AS29 Todd Bertuzzi	.30	.75
AS30 Jaromir Jagr	.50	1.25

2003-04 Upper Deck All-Star Lineup

Card	Low	High
COMPLETE SET (10)	40.00	80.00
STATED ODDS 1:40		
AS1 Marian Gaborik	3.00	8.00
AS2 Dany Heatley	3.00	8.00
AS3 Joe Thornton	3.00	8.00
AS4 Mario Lemieux	6.00	15.00
AS5 Martin Brodeur	5.00	12.00
AS6 Jason Spezza	2.50	6.00
AS7 Rick Nash	3.00	8.00
AS8 Henrik Zetterberg	2.50	6.00
AS9 Ales Hemsky	2.50	6.00
AS10 Ryan Miller	2.50	6.00

2003-04 Upper Deck Big Playmakers

Card	Low	High
STATED ODDS 1:905		
PRINT RUN 50 SERIAL #'d SETS		
BPDH Dany Heatley	15.00	40.00
BPIK Ilya Kovalchuk	12.00	30.00
BPJB Jason Blake	10.00	25.00
BPJJ Jaromir Jagr	12.00	30.00
BPJL Jamie Langenbrunner	10.00	25.00
BPJR Jeremy Roenick	20.00	50.00
BPJS Jean-Sebastien Giguere	15.00	40.00
BPJT Joe Thornton	20.00	50.00
BPMB Martin Brodeur	30.00	80.00
BPMG Marian Gaborik	20.00	50.00
BPMH Marian Hossa	12.50	30.00
BPML Mario Lemieux	30.00	80.00
BPMM Mike Modano	20.00	50.00
BPMN Markus Naslund	10.00	25.00
BPMS Mats Sundin	15.00	40.00
BPMT Marty Turco	10.00	25.00
BPON Owen Nolan	10.00	25.00
BPPB Pavel Bure	15.00	40.00
BPPF Peter Forsberg	20.00	50.00
BPPL Pavel Brendl	10.00	25.00
BPPR Patrick Roy	30.00	80.00
BPRL Roberto Luongo	20.00	50.00
BPRN Rick Nash	25.00	60.00
BPSF Sergei Fedorov	20.00	50.00
BPSK Saku Koivu	12.50	30.00
BPTB Todd Bertuzzi	10.00	25.00
BPTH Jocelyn Thibault	10.00	25.00
BPTS Teemu Selanne	15.00	40.00
BPWG Wayne Gretzky	100.00	250.00
BPZP Zigmund Palffy	10.00	25.00

2003-04 Upper Deck Buyback Autographs

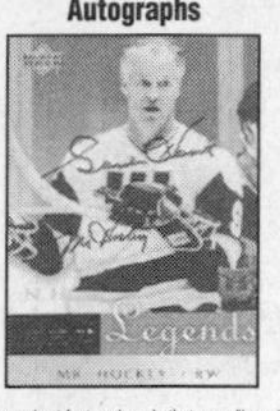

This 182-card set featured cards that were "bought back" by UD and then autographed by the player. Print runs and original set ids are listed below.

Card	Low	High
7 Joe Thornton 02UD/22	30.00	80.00
8 Markus Naslund 92UD/38	20.00	50.00
18 Markus Naslund 02UD/21	20.00	50.00
24 Todd Bertuzzi 02UD/48	25.00	60.00
25 J.Giguere 02UD/48	15.00	40.00
36 Gordie Howe 02UD/23	60.00	120.00
37 Zigmund Palffy 91UD/28	20.00	50.00
47 Zigmund Palffy 02UD/23	12.00	30.00
48 Jason Spezza 02UD/29	50.00	120.00
54 John LeClair 02UD/23	15.00	40.00
67 Pavel Bure 02UD/48	15.00	40.00
68 Pavel Bure MS 02UD/24		
70 Mike Comrie 02UD/30	12.50	30.00
84 Sergei Fedorov 02UD/39	30.00	80.00
96 Ron Francis 02UD/47	20.00	50.00
98 Marian Gaborik 02UD/48	20.00	50.00
104 Marian Hossa 02UD/48	15.00	40.00
109 Curtis Joseph 02UD/48	15.00	40.00
111 Jarome Iginla MS 02UD/47	15.00	40.00
112 Jarome Iginla 02UD/48	15.00	40.00
122 Saku Koivu 02UD/48	20.00	50.00
125 Ilya Kovalchuk 02UD/48	25.00	60.00
138 Joe Nieuwendyk 02UD/48	12.50	30.00
151 Jeremy Roenick 02UD/48	15.00	40.00
165 Patrick Roy 02UD/48	50.00	125.00
166 Patrick Roy MS 02UD/48	50.00	125.00
173 Sergei Samsonov 02UD/48	20.00	50.00
178 Jose Theodore 02UD/48	15.00	40.00
181 Stanislav Chistov 02UD/29	25.00	60.00

2003-04 Upper Deck Canadian Exclusives

Inserted exclusively in Canadian hobby boxes, this 475 card parallel set carried distinctive red foil serial-numbering and a red foil maple leaf on the card fronts. Cards 1-445 were numbered out of 50 while cards 446-475 were numbered to 25.

*1-200/246-445 VETS/50: 8X TO 20X BASIC CARDS
*201-245 YG/50: 1X TO 2.5X BASIC YG
*446-471 YG/25: 1.5X TO 4X BASIC YG
*472-475 CAN/25: 1.5X TO 4X BASIC CARDS

Card	Low	High
454 Ryan Kesler YG	50.00	100.00

2003-04 Upper Deck Fan Favorites

Card	Low	High
COMPLETE SET (10)	12.50	25.00
STATED ODDS 1:21		
FF1 Jeremy Roenick	1.25	3.00
FF2 Todd Bertuzzi	.75	2.00
FF3 Roberto Luongo	1.25	3.00
FF4 Georges Laraque	.75	2.00
FF5 Tie Domi	.75	2.00
FF6 Steve Yzerman	3.00	8.00
FF7 Mike Modano	1.50	4.00
FF8 P.J. Stock	.75	2.00
FF9 Mario Lemieux	3.00	8.00
FF10 Jean-Sebastien Giguere	.75	2.00

2003-04 Upper Deck Franchise Fabrics

Card	Low	High
STATED ODDS 1:24		
FFAY Alexei Yashin	3.00	8.00
FFBL Brian Leetch	3.00	8.00
FFCD Chris Drury	3.00	8.00
FFDH Dany Heatley	5.00	12.00
FFHZ Henrik Zetterberg	3.00	8.00
FFJI Jarome Iginla	6.00	15.00
FFJJ Jaromir Jagr	8.00	20.00
FFJT Joe Thornton	8.00	20.00
FFJT Jose Theodore	6.00	15.00
FFMB Martin Brodeur	10.00	25.00
FFMG Marian Gaborik	6.00	15.00
FFMH Marian Hossa	3.00	8.00
FFML Mario Lemieux	10.00	25.00
FFMN Markus Naslund	3.00	8.00
FFMS Mats Sundin	3.00	8.00
FFMT Marty Turco	3.00	8.00
FFNL Nicklas Lidstrom	4.00	10.00
FFPF Peter Forsberg	6.00	15.00
FFPK Paul Kariya	6.00	15.00
FFRL Roberto Luongo	6.00	15.00
FFRS Ryan Smyth	3.00	8.00
FFSF Sergei Fedorov	6.00	15.00
FFTB Todd Bertuzzi	5.00	12.00
FFVL Vincent Lecavalier	4.00	10.00
FFZP Zigmund Palffy	3.00	8.00

2003-04 Upper Deck Gifted Greats

Card	Low	High
COMPLETE SET (10)	25.00	60.00
STATED ODDS 1:40		
GG1 Wayne Gretzky	6.00	15.00
GG2 Jean-Sebastien Giguere	2.00	5.00
GG3 Joe Thornton	3.00	8.00
GG4 Mario Lemieux	6.00	15.00
GG5 Eric Lindros	2.00	5.00
GG6 Todd Bertuzzi	2.00	5.00
GG7 Marian Gaborik	4.00	10.00
GG8 Dany Heatley	3.00	8.00
GG9 Marian Hossa	2.00	5.00
GG10 Martin Brodeur	5.00	12.00

2003-04 Upper Deck High Gloss Parallel

This 475-card parallel set featured a "high-gloss" finish and the letters "HG" embossed on the card fronts. Cards 1-200 and 246-445 were serial-numbered out of 25. Cards 201-245 and 446-475 were serial-numbered out of 10.

*1-200/246-445 VETS/25: 10X TO 25X BASIC CARDS
UNPRICED YOUNG GUN PRINT RUN 10

2003-04 Upper Deck Highlight Heroes

Card	Low	High
COMPLETE SET (10)	15.00	30.00
STATED ODDS 1:40		
HHAM Alexander Mogilny	2.00	5.00
HHJJ Jaromir Jagr	3.00	8.00
HHJS Jason Spezza	2.00	5.00
HHJT Jocelyn Thibault	2.00	5.00
HHMG Marian Gaborik	3.00	8.00
HHPB Pavel Bure	2.00	5.00
HHRN Rick Nash	2.50	6.00
HHSS Sergei Samsonov	2.00	5.00
HHTA Tony Amonte	2.00	5.00
HHTS Teemu Selanne	2.50	6.00

2003-04 Upper Deck Highlight Heroes Jerseys

Card	Low	High
STATED ODDS 1:96		
HHAM Alexander Mogilny	5.00	12.00
HHJJ Jaromir Jagr	8.00	20.00
HHJS Jason Spezza	6.00	15.00
HHJT Jocelyn Thibault	5.00	12.00
HHMG Marian Gaborik	10.00	25.00
HHPB Pavel Bure	8.00	20.00
HHRN Rick Nash	8.00	20.00
HHSS Sergei Samsonov	5.00	12.00
HHTA Tony Amonte	5.00	12.00
HHTS Teemu Selanne	6.00	15.00

2003-04 Upper Deck Jerseys

This 27-card memorabilia set was inserted at a rate of 1:96 for Series I and 1:72 for Series 2. Notations are made below distinguishing which cards were available in which series.

Card	Low	High
GJAK Alex Kovalev Ser. 1	6.00	15.00
GJBG Bill Guerin Ser. 1	6.00	15.00
GJEL Eric Lindros Ser. 1	6.00	15.00
GJIK Ilya Kovalchuk Ser. 1	8.00	20.00
GJJB Owen Nolan Ser. 1	6.00	15.00
GJJG Jean-Sebastien Giguere Ser. 1	6.00	15.00
GJJI Jarome Iginla Ser. 1	8.00	20.00
GJMA Maxim Afinogenov Ser. 1	6.00	15.00
GJMB Martin Brodeur Ser. 1	15.00	40.00
GJMC Mike Comrie Ser. 1	6.00	15.00
GJML Mario Lemieux Ser. 1	15.00	40.00
GJMR Mark Recchi Ser. 1	6.00	15.00
GJMS Martin St. Louis Ser. 1	8.00	20.00
GJSK Saku Koivu Ser. 1	6.00	15.00
GJTB Todd Bertuzzi Ser. 1	6.00	15.00
UDAF Alexander Frolov Ser. 2	6.00	15.00
UDAH Ales Hemsky Ser. 2	6.00	15.00
UDBH Brett Hull Ser. 2	8.00	20.00
UDEJ Ed Jovanovski Ser. 2	6.00	15.00
UDIK Ilya Kovalchuk Ser. 2	8.00	20.00
UDJSG Jean-Sebastien Giguere Ser. 2	6.00	15.00
UDMC Mike Comrie Ser. 2	6.00	15.00
UDMH Marian Hossa Ser. 2	6.00	15.00
UDMK Mike Komisarek Ser. 2	6.00	15.00
UDMS Martin St. Louis Ser. 2	6.00	15.00
UDON Owen Nolan Ser. 2	6.00	15.00
UDRB Rob Blake Ser. 2	6.00	15.00

2003-04 Upper Deck Jersey Autographs

Card	Low	High
STATED ODDS 1:480 SER.2		
SJAH Ales Hemsky	12.00	30.00
SJCJ Curtis Joseph	15.00	40.00
SJDA David Aebischer	12.00	30.00
SJEL Eric Lindros	15.00	40.00
SJJA Jared Aulin	10.00	25.00
SJJI Jarome Iginla	30.00	80.00
SJJR Jeremy Roenick	15.00	40.00
SJJS Jason Spezza	40.00	100.00
SJJT Joe Thornton	20.00	50.00
SJJSG Jean-Sebastien Giguere	12.00	30.00
SJMH Marian Hossa	20.00	50.00
SJPR Patrick Roy	75.00	200.00
SJRN Rick Nash	40.00	100.00
SJSF Sergei Fedorov	20.00	50.00
SJSH Scott Hartnell	10.00	25.00
SJSK Saku Koivu	15.00	40.00
SJSS Sergei Samsonov	12.00	30.00
SJTB Todd Bertuzzi	12.00	30.00
SJWG Wayne Gretzky	200.00	300.00
SJZP Zigmund Palffy	12.00	30.00

2003-04 Upper Deck Magic Moments

Card	Low	High
COMPLETE SET (15)	30.00	60.00
STATED ODDS 1:14		
MM1 Jean-Sebastien Giguere	1.00	2.50
MM2 Scott Stevens	1.00	2.50
MM3 Jason Spezza	1.25	3.00
MM4 Steve Yzerman	3.00	8.00
MM5 Paul Kariya	1.00	2.50
MM6 Patrick Roy	3.00	8.00
MM7 Joe Thornton	1.25	3.00
MM8 Wayne Gretzky	4.00	10.00
MM9 Marc-Andre Fleury	3.00	8.00
MM10 Milan Hejduk	1.00	2.50
MM11 Dominik Hasek	1.50	4.00
MM12 Martin Brodeur	3.00	8.00
MM13 Peter Forsberg	2.00	5.00
MM14 Sergei Fedorov	1.25	3.00
MM15 Jordin Tootoo	2.00	5.00

2003-04 Upper Deck Memorable Matchups

Card	Low	High
STATED ODDS 1:144		
MMBG T.Bertuzzi M.Gaborik	5.00	12.00
MMFK S.Fedorov/P.Kariya	8.00	20.00
MMGB J.Giguere/M.Brodeur	12.50	30.00
MMHH B.Hull/D.Hasek	12.50	30.00
MMLS E.Lindros/S.Stevens	8.00	20.00
MMNN R.Niedermayer/S.Niedermayer	5.00	12.00
MMRR J.Roenick/P.Roy	20.00	50.00
MMTH J.Theodore/A.Hemsky	5.00	12.00
MMTT J.Thornton/J.Theodore	8.00	20.00

2003-04 Upper Deck Mr. Hockey

Card	Low	High
COMPLETE SET (30)	30.00	80.00
COMMON CARD (GH1-GH30)	2.00	5.00

2003-04 Upper Deck NHL's Best

Card	Low	High
MULT.COLOR SWATCH: .5X TO 1.25X		
STATED ODDS 1:48		
NBDH Dany Heatley	6.00	15.00
NBGM Glen Murray	5.00	12.00
NBIK Ilya Kovalchuk	6.00	15.00
NBJG Jean-Sebastien Giguere	5.00	12.00
NBJI Jarome Iginla	6.00	15.00
NBJR Jeremy Roenick	6.00	15.00
NBKT Keith Tkachuk	5.00	12.00
NBMB Martin Brodeur	12.50	30.00
NBML Mario Lemieux	12.50	30.00
NBMM Mike Modano	8.00	20.00
NBNL Nicklas Lidstrom	6.00	15.00
NBPR Patrick Roy	15.00	40.00
NBPS Sergei Fedorov	6.00	15.00
NBVL Vincent Lecavalier	5.00	12.00
NBZP Zigmund Palffy	5.00	12.00

2003-04 Upper Deck Patches

This 60-card memorabilia set was inserted at the rate of 1:7500 Series I and Series II packs. Notations are made below distinguishing cards available in each series.

Card	Low	High
LD1 Steve Yzerman Ser.2		
LD2 Mike Modano Ser.2		
LD3 Mario Lemieux Ser.2	100.00	250.00
LD4 Mats Sundin Ser.2	60.00	150.00
LD5 Joe Thornton Ser.2	75.00	200.00
LD6 Ron Francis Ser.2	60.00	125.00
LD7 Markus Naslund Ser.2	40.00	100.00
LD8 Brian Leetch Ser.2		
LD9 Jeremy Roenick Ser.2	60.00	150.00
LD10 Jaromir Jagr Ser.2		
SP1 Paul Kariya Ser.		
SP2 Marian Gaborik Ser.2		
SP3 Jeremy Roenick Ser.2	60.00	150.00
SP4 Brett Hull Ser.2	75.00	200.00
SP5 Dany Heatley Ser.2	75.00	200.00
SP6 Jarome Iginla Ser.2		
SP7 Chris Drury Ser.2		
SP8 Vincent Lecavalier Ser.2	50.00	125.00
SP9 Bill Guerin Ser.2	30.00	80.00
SP10 Glen Murray Ser.2	40.00	100.00
SV1 Martin Brodeur Ser.2	100.00	200.00
SV2 Roberto Luongo Ser.2	75.00	200.00
SV3 Roman Cechmanek Ser.2	40.00	100.00
SV4 Marty Turco Ser.2		
SV5 Tommy Salo Ser.2	40.00	100.00
SV6 Jocelyn Thibault Ser.2		
SV7 David Aebischer Ser.2	40.00	100.00
SV8 Patrick Lalime Ser.2	40.00	100.00
SV9 Dominik Hasek Ser.2	50.00	125.00
SV10 Ed Belfour Ser.2	50.00	125.00
PLGJG J-S Giguere Ser.1	40.00	100.00
PLGJS Jason Spezza Ser.1	40.00	100.00
PLGJT Joe Thornton Ser.1	60.00	150.00
PLGMB Martin Brodeur Ser.1	100.00	200.00
PLGMG Marian Gaborik Ser.1		
PLGMH Marian Hossa Ser.1	40.00	100.00
PLGML Mario Lemieux Ser.1	100.00	200.00
PLGMN Markus Naslund Ser.1	40.00	100.00
PLGPR Patrick Roy Ser.1	150.00	300.00
PLGRN Rick Nash Ser.1	75.00	200.00
PNMJG J-S Giguere Ser.1	40.00	100.00
PNMJS Jason Spezza Ser.1	75.00	200.00
PNMJT Joe Thornton Ser.1	75.00	200.00
PNMMB Martin Brodeur Ser.1	100.00	200.00
PNMMG Marian Gaborik Ser.1		
PNMMH Marian Hossa Ser.1	40.00	100.00
PNMML Mario Lemieux Ser.1	75.00	200.00
PNMMN Markus Naslund Ser.1	40.00	100.00
PNMPR Patrick Roy Ser.1	150.00	300.00
PNMRN Rick Nash Ser.1	75.00	150.00
PNRJG J-S Giguere Ser.1	75.00	150.00
PNRJS Jason Spezza Ser.1	75.00	200.00
PNRJT Joe Thornton Ser.1	75.00	200.00
PNRMB Martin Brodeur Ser.1	100.00	200.00
PNRMG Marian Gaborik Ser.1		
PNRMH Marian Hossa Ser.1	40.00	100.00
PNRML Mario Lemieux Ser.1	100.00	250.00
PNRMN Markus Naslund Ser.1	40.00	100.00
PNRPR Patrick Roy Ser.1	150.00	300.00
PNRRN Rick Nash Ser.1	75.00	150.00

2003-04 Upper Deck Performers

Card	Low	High
COMPLETE SET (15)	20.00	40.00
STATED ODDS 1:14		
PS1 Jean-Sebastien Giguere	.60	1.50
PS2 Scott Stevens	.60	1.50
PS3 Steve Yzerman	2.50	6.00
PS4 Jeremy Roenick	.75	2.00
PS5 Peter Forsberg	1.25	3.00
PS6 Jose Theodore	.75	2.00
PS7 Marian Gaborik	1.00	2.50
PS8 Martin Brodeur	1.50	4.00
PS9 Ed Belfour	.60	1.50
PS10 Mike Modano	.75	2.00
PS11 Joe Sakic	1.00	2.50
PS12 Bobby Orr	4.00	10.00
PS13 Mario Lemieux	3.00	8.00
PS14 Wayne Gretzky	4.00	10.00
PS15 Patrick Roy	2.50	6.00

2003-04 Upper Deck Power Zone

Card	Low	High
COMPLETE SET (10)	10.00	25.00
STATED ODDS 1:21		
PZ1 Joe Thornton	1.00	2.50
PZ2 Keith Tkachuk	.75	2.00
PZ3 Jeremy Roenick	1.25	3.00
PZ4 Brendan Shanahan	1.00	2.50
PZ5 Todd Bertuzzi	.75	2.00
PZ6 Rick Nash	1.25	3.00
PZ7 Peter Forsberg	1.50	4.00
PZ8 Owen Nolan	.75	2.00
PZ9 Mario Lemieux	4.00	10.00
PZ10 Eric Lindros	1.00	2.50

2003-04 Upper Deck Rookie Threads Autographs

Card	Low	High
STATED PRINT RUN 75 SER.#'d SETS		
RT1 Joffrey Lupul	15.00	40.00
RT2 Dustin Brown	15.00	40.00
RT3 Marc-Andre Fleury	30.00	80.00
RT4 Joni Pitkanen	12.50	30.00
RT5 Peter Sejna	12.50	30.00
RT6 Eric Staal	25.00	60.00
RT7 Tuomo Ruutu	15.00	40.00
RT8 Dan Hamhuis	12.50	30.00
RT9 Nathan Horton	20.00	50.00
RT10 Jordin Tootoo	20.00	50.00

2003-04 Upper Deck Shooting Stars

Card	Low	High
MULT.COLOR SWATCH: .5X TO 1.25X		
STATED ODDS 1:48		
STAH Ales Hemsky	4.00	10.00

TAS Alexander Svitov 4.00 10.00
TAV Anton Volchenkov 4.00 10.00
TJA Jared Aulin 4.00 10.00
TJB Jay Bouwmeester 5.00 12.00
TJL Jordan Leopold 4.00 10.00
TJS Jason Spezza 8.00 20.00
TJW Justin Williams 5.00 12.00
TMH Marcel Hossa 4.00 10.00
TPM Pierre-Marc Bouchard 5.00 12.00
TRD Rick DiPietro 5.00 12.00
TRM Ryan Miller 6.00 15.00
TRN Rick Nash 12.00 30.00
TSO Steve Ott 5.00 12.00
TSV Alexei Smirnov 4.00 10.00

2003-04 Upper Deck Super Saviors

ULT.COLOR SWATCH: .5X TO 1.25X
TATED ODDS 1:144
SJG Jean-Sebastien Giguere 6.00 15.00
SMB Martin Brodeur 12.00 30.00
SMT Marty Turco 8.00 20.00
SPL Patrick Lalime 6.00 15.00
SPR Patrick Roy 15.00 40.00
SRC Roman Cechmanek 6.00 15.00

2003-04 Upper Deck Superstar Spotlight

his 15-card set featured a holographic mirrored action nage on the majority of the card front with a smaller olor photo of the featured player along side. This set as inserted at odds of 1:144.

S1 Jean-Sebastien Giguere 4.00 10.00
S2 Joe Thornton 6.00 15.00
S3 Marian Gaborik 6.00 15.00
S4 Rick Nash 5.00 12.00
S5 Steve Yzerman 12.50 30.00
S6 Martin Brodeur 12.50 30.00
S7 Jason Spezza 5.00 12.00
S8 Mike Modano 6.00 15.00
S9 Mario Lemieux 15.00 40.00
S10 Jaromir Jagr 6.00 15.00
S11 Todd Bertuzzi 4.00 10.00
S12 Dany Heatley 5.00 12.00
S13 Patrick Roy 15.00 40.00
S14 Bobby Orr 20.00 50.00
S15 Gordie Howe 12.50 30.00

2003-04 Upper Deck Team Essentials

NLISTED STARS 6.00 15.00
L/TP STATED ODDS 1:96
S STATED ODDS 1:288
LJS Joe Sakic 10.00 25.00
LJT Joe Thornton 8.00 20.00
LML Mario Lemieux 15.00 40.00
LMN Markus Naslund 6.00 15.00
LMP Michael Peca 6.00 15.00
LMS Mats Sundin 6.00 15.00
LSS Scott Stevens 6.00 15.00
LSY Steve Yzerman 12.50 30.00
PAM Al MacInnis 6.00 15.00
PDA Daniel Alfredsson 6.00 15.00
PDH Dany Heatley 8.00 20.00
PJT Joe Thornton 8.00 20.00
PML Mario Lemieux 10.00 25.00
PMM Mike Modano 8.00 20.00
PMS Miroslav Satan 6.00 15.00
PPF Peter Forsberg 10.00 25.00
PPK Paul Kariya 6.00 15.00
PVL Vincent Lecavalier 6.00 15.00
SDH Dany Heatley 10.00 25.00
SJJ Jaromir Jagr 12.50 30.00
SMH Milan Hejduk 8.00 20.00
SMH Marian Hossa 8.00 20.00
SPB Pavel Bure 8.00 20.00
STB Todd Bertuzzi 6.00 15.00

2003-04 Upper Deck Three Stars

OMPLETE SET (15) 20.00 40.00
TATED ODDS 1:14
S1 Paul Kariya .60 1.50
S2 Marian Hossa .60 1.50
S3 Dany Heatley .75 2.00
S4 Alexei Yashin .60 1.50
S5 Jaromir Jagr .75 2.00
S6 Martin Brodeur 1.50 4.00
S7 Marian Gaborik 1.00 2.50
S8 Ziggy Palffy .60 1.50
S9 Marty Turco .60 1.50
S10 Mats Sundin .60 1.50
S11 Jean-Sebastien Giguere .60 1.50
S12 Mario Lemieux 3.00 8.00
S13 Jarome Iginla .75 2.00
S14 Markus Naslund .60 1.50
S15 Joe Thornton .75 2.00

2003-04 Upper Deck Tough Customers

OMPLETE SET (15) 12.00 25.00
OMMON CARD (TC1-TC15) .75 2.00
TATED ODDS 1:14
C1 Jody Shelley .75 2.00
C2 Andrei Nazarov .75 2.00
C3 Reed Low .75 2.00
C4 Andrew Peters .75 2.00
C5 Wade Belak .75 2.00
C6 Darren McCarty 1.00 2.50
C7 Krzysztof Oliwa .75 2.00
C8 P.J. Stock .75 2.00
C9 Matt Johnson .75 2.00
C10 Chris Neil .75 2.00
C11 Garrett Burnett .75 2.00
C12 Georges Laraque 1.00 2.50
C13 Tie Domi 1.00 2.50
C14 Jason Strudwick .75 2.00
C15 Donald Brashear .75 2.00

2003-04 Upper Deck Exclusives

This 230-card set paralleled cards 246-475 of the base set. Cards 246-445 were serial-numbered out of 50 and cards 446-475 were serial-numbered out of 10. Each card carried an "Exclusive" foil stamp.

*246-445 VETS/50: 6X TO 15X BASIC CARDS
446-475 UNPRICED PRINT RUN 10

2004 Upper Deck Pearson Awards

Like the sets from previous years, these three cards were available exclusively to attendees of the annual NHLPA Pearson Awards Banquet. Their relative scarcity makes them very unique and desirable.

COMPLETE SET (3) 250.00 400.00
JS Joe Sakic 100.00 200.00
MSL Martin St.Louis 30.00 75.00
RL Roberto Luongo 100.00 200.00

1999 Wayne Gretzky Living Legend

Released as a 99-card set, Wayne Gretzky Living Legend traces The Great One's course of life from beginning to New York. Base cards feature both portrait and action photography with enhanced gold foil stamping. Wayne Gretzky Living Legend was packaged in 24-pack boxes with packs containing six cards and carried a suggested retail price of $1.99. One Wayne Gretzky bonus pack was inserted in every box.

COMMON GRETZKY (1-99) .20 .50

2004-05 Upper Deck

This 210-card set was released in just one series for the 2004-05 season that was ultimately canceled due to the labor dispute. The set consisted of 180 veteran cards and 30 Young Gun subset cards inserted at 1:4. Due to a lack of a true rookie class, many of the Young Gun cards were labeled "Retro" or "Legend" and featured veteran players.

COMPLETE SET (210) 125.00 250.00
COMP.SET w/o SP's (180) 15.00 30.00
YOUNG GUN STATED ODDS 1:4
1 Petr Sykora .15 .40
2 Andy McDonald .15 .40
3 Sandis Ozolinsh .12 .30
4 Sergei Fedorov .30 .75
5 Joffrey Lupul .15 .40
6 Jean-Sebastien Giguere .20 .50
7 Dany Heatley .20 .50
8 Ilya Kovalchuk .20 .50
9 Patrik Stefan .12 .30
10 Jaroslav Modry .12 .30
11 Serge Aubin .12 .30
12 Kari Lehtonen .25 .60
13 Joe Thornton .25 .60
14 Sergei Gonchar .15 .40
15 Patrice Bergeron .25 .60
16 Nick Boynton .12 .30
17 Sergei Samsonov .15 .40
18 Andrew Raycroft .15 .40
19 Daniel Briere .20 .50
20 Miroslav Satan .15 .40
21 Mika Noronen .15 .40
22 J.P. Dumont .12 .30
23 Maxim Afinogenov .12 .30
24 Martin Biron .15 .40
25 Chris Simon .12 .30
26 Jarome Iginla .20 .50
27 Robyn Regehr .12 .30
28 Jordan Leopold .12 .30
29 Chuck Kobasew .12 .30
30 Miikka Kiprusoff .15 .40
31 Jeff O'Neill .12 .30
32 Ron Francis .25 .60
33 Aaron Ward .12 .30
34 Erik Cole .15 .40
35 Eric Staal .25 .60
36 Martin Gerber .15 .40
37 Matthew Barnaby .12 .30
38 Kyle Calder .12 .30
39 Tyler Arnason .12 .30
40 Eric Daze .15 .40
41 Jocelyn Thibault .15 .40
42 Peter Forsberg .25 .60
43 Alex Tanguay .15 .40
44 Milan Hejduk .15 .40
45 Rob Blake .20 .50
46 Paul Kariya .25 .60
47 Teemu Selanne .40 1.00
48 David Aebischer .15 .40
49 Luke Richardson .12 .30
50 Rick Nash .20 .50
51 Rostislav Klesla .12 .30
52 Nikolai Zherdev .15 .40
53 Marc Denis .15 .40
54 Mike Modano .30 .75
55 Sergei Zubov .15 .40
56 Bill Guerin .20 .50
57 Jason Arnott .15 .40
58 Niko Kapanen .12 .30
59 Marty Turco .20 .50
60 Kirk Maltby .12 .30
61 Nicklas Lidstrom .20 .50
62 Kris Draper .12 .30
63 Brendan Shanahan .25 .60
64 Pavel Datsyuk .25 .60
65 Robert Lang .12 .30
66 Steve Yzerman .60 1.50
67 Curtis Joseph .20 .50
68 Ryan Smyth .15 .40
69 Jason Smith .12 .30
70 Ales Hemsky .20 .50
71 Eric Brewer .12 .30
72 Raffi Torres .12 .30
73 Ty Conklin .15 .40
74 Mike Van Ryn .12 .30
75 Kristian Huselius .12 .30
76 Stephen Weiss .12 .30
77 Jay Bouwmeester .20 .50
78 Roberto Luongo .30 .75
79 Craig Conroy .12 .30
80 Aaron Miller .12 .30
81 Luc Robitaille .20 .50
82 Martin Straka .12 .30
83 Mattias Norstrom .12 .30
84 Roman Cechmanek .15 .40
85 Marian Gaborik .30 .75
86 Pascal Dupuis .12 .30
87 Alexander Daigle .12 .30
88 Pierre-Marc Bouchard .20 .50
89 Filip Kuba .12 .30
90 Manny Fernandez .15 .40
91 Saku Koivu .20 .50
92 Michael Ryder .15 .40
93 Marcel Hossa .12 .30
94 Mike Ribeiro .15 .40
95 Jose Theodore .20 .50
96 Sheldon Souray .12 .30
97 David Legwand .15 .40
98 Steve Sullivan .12 .30
99 Marek Zidlicky .12 .30
100 Martin Erat .12 .30
101 Tomas Vokoun .15 .40
102 Patrik Elias .20 .50
103 Jeff Friesen .12 .30
104 Brian Rafalski .15 .40
105 Scott Niedermayer .20 .50
106 Scott Stevens .20 .50
107 Martin Brodeur .40 1.00
108 Oleg Kvasha .12 .30
109 Mark Parrish .12 .30
110 Michael Peca .15 .40
111 Adrian Aucoin .12 .30
112 Rick DiPietro .15 .40
113 Trent Hunter .12 .30
114 Eric Lindros .30 .75
115 Tom Poti .12 .30
116 Mark Messier .50 1.25
117 Jaromir Jagr .50 1.25
118 Bobby Holik .12 .30
119 Mike Dunham .15 .40
120 Marian Hossa .15 .40
121 Martin Havlat .20 .50
122 Zdeno Chara .20 .50
123 Daniel Alfredsson .20 .50
124 Jason Spezza .20 .50
125 Dominik Hasek .30 .75
126 Jeremy Roenick .20 .50
127 Tony Amonte .15 .40
128 Keith Primeau .20 .50
129 Simon Gagne .20 .50
130 Danny Markov .12 .30
131 Robert Esche .15 .40
132 Shane Doan .15 .40
133 Mike Comrie .15 .40
134 Ladislav Nagy .12 .30
135 Brett Hull .25 .60
136 Derek Morris .12 .30
137 Brian Boucher .15 .40
138 Mario Lemieux .60 1.50
139 Mark Recchi .25 .60
140 Ryan Malone .12 .30
141 Dick Tarnstrom .12 .30
142 Rico Fata .12 .30
143 Marc-Andre Fleury .50 1.25
144 Alyn McCauley .12 .30
145 Marco Sturm .12 .30
146 Patrick Marleau .20 .50
147 Scott Hannan .12 .30
148 Kyle McLaren .12 .30
149 Evgeni Nabokov .15 .40
150 Al MacInnis .20 .50
151 Petr Cajanek .12 .30
152 Keith Tkachuk .20 .50
153 Barret Jackman .12 .30
154 Chris Pronger .15 .40
155 Patrick Lalime .15 .40
156 Vincent Lecavalier .15 .40
157 Dave Andreychuk .20 .50
158 Brad Richards .20 .50
159 Pavel Kubina .12 .30
160 Ruslan Fedotenko .12 .30
161 Nikolai Khabibulin .20 .50
162 Alexander Mogilny .15 .40
163 Owen Nolan .15 .40
164 Gary Roberts .12 .30
165 Bryan McCabe .12 .30
166 Ed Belfour .20 .50
167 Joe Nieuwendyk .20 .50
168 Markus Naslund .20 .50
169 Brendan Morrison .15 .40
170 Todd Bertuzzi .20 .50
171 Ed Jovanovski .15 .40
172 Trevor Linden .20 .50
173 Dan Cloutier .15 .40
174 Jeff Halpern .12 .30
175 Dainius Zubrus .12 .30
176 Jason Doig .12 .30
177 Brendan Witt .12 .30
178 Olaf Kolzig .20 .50
179 Wayne Gretzky CL 1.00 2.50
180 Gordie Howe CL .60 1.50
181 Brad Fast YG RC 2.00 5.00
182 Brennan Evans YG RC 2.00 5.00
183 Wayne Gretzky YGR 15.00 40.00
184 Mark Messier YGR 6.00 15.00
185 Peter Forsberg YGR 3.00 8.00
186 Steve Yzerman YGR 8.00 20.00
187 Ron Francis YGR 8.00 20.00
188 Patrick Roy YGR 12.00 30.00
189 Mario Lemieux YGR 15.00 40.00
190 Dave Andreychuk YGR 8.00 20.00
191 Luc Robitaille YGR 8.00 20.00
192 Gordie Howe YGR 8.00 20.00
193 Don Cherry YGR 5.00 12.00
194 Hobey Baker YGL 2.50 6.00
195 Mike Modano YGL 4.00 10.00
196 Denis Brodeur YGL 1.50 4.00
197 Keith Tkachuk YGL 2.00 5.00
198 Bob Goodenow YGL 1.50 4.00
199 Cammi Granato YG RC 2.50 6.00
200 Foster Hewitt YGL 1.50 4.00
201 Mike Keenan YGL 2.00 5.00
202 Dick Irvin Jr. YGL 1.50 4.00
203 Jeremy Roenick YGL 3.00 8.00
204 James Norris YGL 1.50 4.00
205 Alexander Ragulin YG RC 2.50 6.00
206 Brendan Shanahan YGL 2.50 6.00
207 Lord Stanley YGL 1.50 4.00
208 Gary Thorne YGL 1.50 4.00
209 Scott Stevens YGL 2.00 5.00
210 Joe Sakic YGL 3.00 8.00

1999 Wayne Gretzky Living Legend A Leader by Example

Randomly inserted in Wayne Gretzky bonus packs at the rate of 1:23, this 6-card set photos Gretzky in each of his NHL as well as some All-Star jerseys.

COMPLETE SET (6) 15.00 30.00
COMMON GRETZKY (L1-L6) 2.00 5.00

2004-05 Upper Deck 1997 Game Jerseys

This insert set recaptured the design of Upper Deck's first jersey cards from the 1997-98 season. Cards were inserted at a rate of 1:288 and carried a "97" prefix.

97BB Joe Thornton 15.00 40.00
97BS Brendan Shanahan/100* 25.00 60.00
97GH Gordie Howe/15*
97JI Jarome Iginla 15.00 40.00
97JS Jason Spezza 10.00 25.00
97MB Martin Brodeur 25.00 60.00
97MM Mike Modano 12.50 30.00
97MS Martin St. Louis 10.00 25.00
97PF Peter Forsberg/50* 25.00 60.00
97PR Patrick Roy/50* 30.00 80.00
97SF Sergei Fedorov 15.00 40.00
97SK Saku Koivu 10.00 25.00
97SU Mats Sundin 10.00 25.00
97WG2 Wayne Gretzky/25*

1999 Wayne Gretzky Living Legend Authentics

Randomly inserted in packs at the rate of 1:288 for pucks, 1:1196 for sticks, and jerseys autographed and sequentially numbered to 99, this 10-card set features swatches of authentic game used items.

COMMON WG PUCK (P1-P6) 15.00 40.00
COMMON WG STICK (S1-S2) 25.00 60.00
C1 W.Gretzky Collection/99 AU 150.00 300.00
GJ1 Wayne Gretzky Jersey/99 AU 150.00 300.00

2004-05 Upper Deck Big Playmakers

STATED PRINT RUN 50 SER.#'d SETS
BPAT Alex Tanguay 10.00 25.00
BPBH Brett Hull 12.00 30.00
BPEF Sergei Fedorov 12.00 30.00
BPGH Gordie Howe 100.00 200.00
BPHE Milan Hejduk 10.00 25.00
BPHO Marian Hossa 10.00 25.00
BPIK Ilya Kovalchuk 15.00 40.00
BPJI Jarome Iginla 15.00 40.00
BPJJ Jaromir Jagr 20.00 50.00
BPJR Jeremy Roenick 12.00 30.00
BPJS Joe Sakic 20.00 50.00
BPKP Keith Primeau 10.00 25.00
BPKT Keith Tkachuk 10.00 25.00
BPML Mario Lemieux 40.00 100.00
BPMM Mike Modano 12.00 30.00
BPMN Markus Naslund 10.00 25.00
BPMS Martin St. Louis 10.00 25.00
BPPB Pavel Bure 12.00 30.00
BPPD Pavel Datsyuk 12.00 30.00
BPSU Mats Sundin 12.00 30.00
BPTH Joe Thornton 15.00 40.00
BPWG Wayne Gretzky 100.00 200.00

1999 Wayne Gretzky Living Legend Goodwill Ambassador

Randomly inserted in packs at the rate of 1:11, this nine card set showcases Wayne Gretzky not just as a player of the game, but as a spokesman and ambassador of hockey. Cards are enhanced with holofoil borders and gold foil stamping.

COMMON GRETZKY (GW1-GW9) 1.50 4.00

2004-05 Upper Deck Canadian Exclusives

*1-180 EXCL/50: 8X TO 20X BASIC CARDS
1-180 STATED PRINT RUN 50.
*181-210 YG EXCL/25: 2X TO 5X BASIC YG
181-210 STATED PRINT RUN 25
183 Wayne Gretzky YG 75.00 150.00

1999 Wayne Gretzky Living Legend Great Accolades

Randomly seeded in packs at the rate of 1:6, this 45-card set highlights some of Wayne Gretzky's greatest achievements. Cards are enhanced with silver foil stamping.

COMMON GRETZKY (GA1-GA45) 2.50 6.00

2004-05 Upper Deck Clutch Performers

COMPLETE SET (7) 12.50 25.00
STATED ODDS 1:24
CP1 Jarome Iginla 1.50 4.00
CP2 Brad Richards .75 2.00
CP3 Joe Sakic 2.00 5.00
CP4 Joe Thornton 1.50 4.00
CP5 Keith Primeau .75 2.00
CP6 Nikolai Khabibulin 1.25 3.00
CP7 Mario Lemieux 4.00 10.00

1999 Wayne Gretzky Living Legend Great Stats

Randomly inserted in Wayne Gretzky bonus packs at the rate of 1:23, this six card set features Wayne in all of his professional Hockey and All-Star jerseys. Cards are enhanced with holofoil borders and gold foil highlights.

COMMON GRETZKY (GS1-GS6) 2.00 5.00

2004-05 Upper Deck Hardware Heroes

COMPLETE SET (14) 15.00 30.00
STATED ODDS 1:12
AW1 S.Niedermeyer .75 2.00
Norris
AW2 M.St.Louis/Art Ross .75 2.00
AW3 B.Richards/Conn Smythe .75 2.00
AW4 A.Raycroft/Calder .75 2.00
AW5 M.Brodeur/Vezina 2.50 6.00
AW6 Iginla/Nash/Kova/Richard 2.00 5.00
AW7 M.St.Louis/Hart .75 2.00
AW8 B.Richards/Lady Byng .75 2.00
AW9 K.Draper/Selke .75 2.00
AW10 B.Berard/Masterton .75 2.00
AW11 J.Iginla/Clancy 1.00 2.50
AW12 M.Brodeur/Jennings 2.50 6.00
AW13 Red Wings/President's 2.00 5.00
AW14 Lightning/Stanley Cup 2.50 6.00

1999 Wayne Gretzky Living Legend Magic Moments

Randomly inserted in Wayne Gretzky bonus packs at the rate of 1:23, this six card set highlights some of Wayne Gretzky's greatest NHL achievements. Cards are enhanced with holofoil borders and gold foil stamping.

COMMON GRETZKY (MM1-MM6) 2.00 5.00

2004-05 Upper Deck Heritage Classic

Inserted at 1:288, this 15-card set featured jersey swatches of players who played in the 2003-04 Heritage Classic.

CCAH Ales Hemsky 12.00 30.00
CCEB Eric Brewer 12.00 30.00
CCGF Grant Fuhr 20.00 50.00
CCJK Jari Kurri 25.00 60.00
CCJT Jose Theodore/75* 30.00 80.00
CCLU Guy Lafleur/82* 40.00 80.00
CCMM Mark Messier/25* 125.00 250.00
CCMR Mike Ribeiro 12.00 30.00
CCPC Paul Coffey/75* 30.00 80.00
CCRS Ryan Smyth 20.00 50.00
CCRT Raffi Torres 12.00 30.00
CCRY Michael Ryder 20.00 50.00
CCSK Saku Koivu 20.00 50.00
CCSS Steve Shutt 12.00 30.00
CCTC Ty Conklin 12.00 30.00

1999 Wayne Gretzky Living Legend More Than a Number

COMMON GRETZKY (1-99) 25.00 60.00

1999 Wayne Gretzky Living Legend Only One 99

NOT PRICED DUE TO SCARCITY

1999 Wayne Gretzky Living Legend The Great One

Randomly inserted in packs at the rate of 1:2, this 9-card set highlights Wayne Gretzkys impact on the sport of hockey. Cards are enhanced with holofoil borders and gold foil stamping.

COMMON GRETZKY (G01-G09) .75 2.00

2004-05 Upper Deck Jersey Autographs

STATED ODDS 1:288
SINGLE PRINT RUN 25 SER.#'d SETS
DUAL JSY PRINT RUN 10 SER.#'d SETS
DUAL NOT PRICED DUE TO SCARCITY
GJAAA Arron Asham 15.00 40.00
GJAAF Alexander Frolov 15.00 40.00
GJAAH Adam Hall 15.00 30.00
GJAAL Ales Hemsky 20.00 50.00
GJAAS Alexander Svitov 15.00 40.00
GJAAY Alexei Yashin 15.00 40.00
GJABO Brooks Orpik 15.00 40.00
GJABU Pavel Bure 30.00 80.00
GJACK Chuck Kobasew 15.00 40.00
GJADA David Aebischer 20.00 50.00
GJAGH Gordie Howe 125.00 250.00
GJAHO Marcel Hossa 15.00 30.00
GJAHS Marian Hossa 25.00 60.00
GJAIK Ilya Kovalchuk 60.00 125.00
GJAJG Jean-Sebastien Giguere 15.00 40.00
GJAJI Jarome Iginla 60.00 150.00
GJAJL John LeClair 15.00 40.00
GJAJR Jeremy Roenick 40.00 100.00
GJAJS Jason Spezza 60.00 150.00
GJAMC Mike Comrie
GJAMG Marian Gaborik 60.00 125.00
GJAMH Martin Havlat 20.00 50.00
GJAMK Markus Naslund 30.00 80.00
GJAMN Markus Naslund 25.00 60.00
GJAMP Mark Parrish 15.00 40.00
GJAMT Marty Turco 25.00 60.00
GJAPB Pavel Bure 40.00 100.00
GJAPE Michael Peca 15.00 30.00
GJAPH Phil Esposito 25.00 60.00
GJAPR Patrick Roy 150.00 300.00
GJARD Rick DiPietro 25.00 60.00
GJARF Ron Francis 25.00 60.00
GJARL Roberto Luongo 40.00 100.00
GJARN Rick Nash 40.00 100.00
GJASF Sergei Fedorov 30.00 80.00
GJATB Todd Bertuzzi 25.00 60.00
GJATH Joe Thornton 50.00 125.00
GJAWG Wayne Gretzky 200.00 400.00

1999 Wayne Gretzky Living Legend Wearing the Leaf

Randomly inserted in Wayne Gretzky bonus packs at the rate of 1:23, this six card holofoil set features Gretzky in his Team Canada jersey. Cards are enhanced with holofoil borders and gold foil stamping.

COMMON GRETZKY (WL1-WL6) 2.00 5.00

2004-05 Upper Deck NHL's Best

STATED ODDS 1:96
NBBL Brian Leetch 6.00 15.00
NBEB Ed Belfour 6.00 15.00
NBGH Gordie Howe/15*
NBJT Jose Theodore 8.00 20.00
NBMB Martin Brodeur 10.00 25.00
NBML Mario Lemieux/50* 30.00 80.00
NBNL Nicklas Lidstrom 6.00 15.00
NBPF Peter Forsberg/75* 15.00 40.00
NBPR Patrick Roy/50* 40.00 100.00
NBRB Rob Blake 6.00 15.00
NBRN Rick Nash 8.00 20.00
NBSG Sergei Gonchar 6.00 15.00
NBSN Scott Niedermayer 6.00 15.00
NBTB Todd Bertuzzi 8.00 15.00
NBWG Wayne Gretzky/25* 150.00 300.00

1999 Wayne Gretzky Living Legend Year of the Great One

COMMON GRETZKY (1-99) 1.50 4.00

2004-05 Upper Deck School of Hard Knocks

COMPLETE SET (7) 8.00 15.00
STATED ODDS 1:24
SHK1 Brendan Shanahan 1.00 2.50
SHK2 Scott Stevens 1.00 2.50
SHK3 Gary Roberts 1.00 2.50
SHK4 Jeremy Roenick 1.50 4.00
SHK5 Zdeno Chara 1.00 2.50
SHK6 Ed Jovanovski 1.00 2.50
SHK7 Todd Bertuzzi 1.00 2.50

2004-05 Upper Deck Swatch of Six

STATED ODDS 1:96
SSAR Andrew Raycroft 8.00 20.00
SSBS Brendan Shanahan 8.00 20.00
SSEB Ed Belfour 8.00 20.00
SSGH Gordie Howe/15
SSGR Gary Roberts 6.00 15.00
SSJJ Jaromir Jagr/50 15.00 40.00
SSJO Jocelyn Thibault 6.00 15.00
SSJT Jose Theodore 10.00 25.00
SSMM Mark Messier/25 100.00 200.00
SSPD Pavel Datsyuk 8.00 20.00
SSSK Saku Koivu 8.00 20.00
SSSY Steve Yzerman 15.00 40.00
SSTH Joe Thornton 12.50 30.00
SSTR Tuomo Ruutu 8.00 20.00
SSWG Wayne Gretzky/25 150.00 300.00

2004-05 Upper Deck Three Stars

COMPLETE SET (14) 15.00 30.00
STATED ODDS 1:12
AS1 Steve Yzerman 1.50 4.00
AS2 Joe Sakic 1.25 3.00
AS3 Mats Sundin .60 1.50
AS4 Mike Modano .75 2.00
AS5 Jarome Iginla .75 2.00
AS6 Jeremy Roenick .75 2.00
AS7 Martin Brodeur 1.50 4.00
AS8 Vincent Lecavalier .60 1.50
AS9 Markus Naslund .60 1.50
AS10 Jaromir Jagr .75 2.00
AS11 Mario Lemieux 3.00 8.00
AS12 Patrick Roy 1.50 4.00
AS13 Wayne Gretzky 3.00 8.00
AS14 Gordie Howe 1.50 4.00

2004-05 Upper Deck World's Best

This 30-card retail only set featured players who have represented their countries in international competition.

COMPLETE SET (30) 12.50 30.00
WB1 Joe Sakic .60 1.50
WB2 Jarome Iginla .40 1.00
WB3 Martin St. Louis .25 .60
WB4 Martin Brodeur 1.25 3.00
WB5 Mario Lemieux 1.50 4.00
WB6 Joe Thornton .50 1.25
WB7 Dany Heatley .40 1.00
WB8 Milan Hejduk .30 .75
WB9 Jaromir Jagr .50 1.25
WB10 Tomas Kaberle .25 .60
WB11 Tomas Vokoun .25 .60
WB12 Saku Koivu .30 .75
WB13 Kari Lehtonen .40 1.00
WB14 Teemu Selanne .30 .75
WB15 Olaf Kolzig .25 .60
WB16 Jochen Hecht .25 .60
WB17 Sergei Gonchar .25 .60
WB18 Ilya Kovalchuk .40 1.00
WB19 Pavel Datsyuk .40 1.00
WB20 Zdeno Chara .25 .60
WB21 Pavel Demitra .25 .60
WB22 Marian Hossa .30 .75
WB23 Marian Gaborik .60 1.50
WB24 Mats Sundin .30 .75
WB25 Peter Forsberg .75 2.00
WB26 Nicklas Lidstrom .30 .75
WB27 Robert Esche .25 .60
WB28 Chris Chelios .30 .75
WB29 Mike Modano .50 1.25
WB30 Keith Tkachuk .30 .75

2004-05 Upper Deck World Cup Tribute

SINGLE ODDS 1:48
DUAL JSY ODDS 1:72
TRIPLE JSY ODDS 1:700
TRIPLE JSY PRINT RUN 25 SER.#'d SETS
AK Alex Kovalev 4.00 10.00
BB Joe Thornton 10.00 25.00
BG Bill Guerin 3.00 8.00
BH Brett Hull SP 12.00 30.00
BL Brian Leetch 8.00 20.00
BR Brad Richards 3.00 8.00
CC Chris Chelios 4.00 10.00
CD Chris Drury 3.00 8.00
DH Dany Heatley SP 12.00 30.00
HE Milan Hejduk 4.00 10.00
IK Ilya Kovalchuk SP 15.00 40.00
JB Jay Bouwmeester 3.00 8.00
JH Jochen Hecht 3.00 8.00
JI Jarome Iginla 5.00 12.00
JJ Jaromir Jagr 12.00 30.00
JS Joe Sakic 15.00 40.00
MB Martin Brodeur 20.00 50.00
MH Marian Hossa 4.00 10.00
MK Miikka Kiprusoff 10.00 25.00
ML Martin St. Louis 4.00 10.00
MM Mike Modano 8.00 20.00
MS Mats Sundin 4.00 10.00
NL Nicklas Lidstrom 4.00 10.00
OK Olaf Kolzig 3.00 8.00
PD Pavel Datsyuk 5.00 10.00
PE Patrik Elias 3.00 8.00
PF Peter Forsberg SP 15.00 40.00
RD Rick DiPietro 3.00 8.00
RE Robert Esche 3.00 8.00
RL Roberto Luongo 8.00 20.00
SK Saku Koivu SP 10.00 25.00
VL Vincent Lecavalier 5.00 12.00
ZC Zdeno Chara 3.00 8.00
BLBR B.Leetch/B.Ralfalski 8.00 20.00
CCTA C.Chelios/T.Amonte 8.00 20.00
IKAK I.Kovalchuk/A.Kovalev SP 15.00 40.00
JBAF J.Bouwmeester/A.Foote 8.00 20.00
JHOK J.Hecht/O.Kolzig 8.00 20.00
KLMK K.Lehtonen/M.Kiprusoff 12.00 30.00
MBRL M.Brodeur/R.Luongo SP 15.00 40.00
NLMO N.Lidstrom/M.Ohlund 8.00 20.00
RCTV R.Cechmanek/T.Vokoun 8.00 20.00
SNEJ S.Niedermayer/E.Jovanovski 8.00 20.00
WREB W.Redden/E.Brewer 8.00 20.00
ZCMG Z.Chara/M.Gaborik 8.00 20.00
AKAYSS Kovalev/Yashin/Samsonov 20.00 50.00
CCRELDH Chelios/Esche/Leetch 30.00 80.00
DHPMSD Heatley/Marleau/Doan 30.00 80.00
DWMOCD Weight/Modano/Drury 40.00 80.00
EBEJWR Brewer/Jovanoski/Redden 20.00 50.00
HZTSNL Zetterberg/Salo/Lidstrom
JSMLJI Sakic/Lemieux/Iginla 125.00 250.00
KLJPTR Lehtonen/Pitkanen/Ruutu 25.00 60.00
KTDWBH Tkachuk/Weight/Hull 40.00 100.00
MBRLJT Brodeur/Luongo/Theo 125.00 250.00
MGHOMI Gaborik/Hossa/Satan 50.00 125.00
MHSKTV Havlat/Straka/Vokoun 20.00 50.00
MSVLBR St. Louis/Lecav/Richards 75.00 200.00
OJSKTS Jokinen/Koivu/Selanne 50.00 100.00
PBPDZC Bondra/Demitra/Chara 25.00 60.00
PDMAIK Datsyuk/Afinogen/Koval 50.00 100.00
PEJJHE Elias/Jagr/Hejduk 75.00 200.00
PFSUDA Forsberg/Sundin/Alfred 50.00 100.00
SGTHRS Gagne/Thornton/Smyth 60.00 125.00
TASGBG Amonte/Gomez/Guerin 40.00 80.00
TCRDRE Conklin/DiPietro/Esche 25.00 60.00

2004-05 Upper Deck YoungStars

STATED ODDS 1:72
YSAR Andrew Raycroft 8.00 20.00
YSES Eric Staal 8.00 20.00
YSJC Jonathan Cheechoo 15.00 40.00
YSJL Joffrey Lupul 4.00 10.00
YSMR Michael Ryder 6.00 15.00
YSMS Matt Stajan 5.00 12.00
YSNZ Nikolai Zherdev 6.00 15.00
YSPB Patrice Bergeron 12.50 30.00
YSPS Philippe Sauve 4.00 10.00
YSRT Raffi Torres 4.00 10.00
YSTH Trent Hunter 4.00 10.00
YSTR Tuomo Ruutu 8.00 20.00

2005 Upper Deck Holiday Card

NNO Sidney Crosby 2.50 6.00

2005-06 Upper Deck

This 487-card set was issued over two series. The set was released in eight-card packs, with an $2.99 SRP, which came 24 packs to a box and 12 boxes to a case. Both series had a Young Guns (Rookie Cards) subset which were inserted at a stated rate of one in four. Those cards comprise cards numbered 201-242 and 443-487.

COMPLETE SET (487) 400.00 750.00
COMP.SER 1 w/o SP's (200) 12.00 25.00
COMPLETE SERIES 1 (242) 250.00 500.00
COMP.SER 2 w/o SP's (200) 12.00 25.00
COMPLETE SERIES 2 (245) 200.00 400.00
YOUNG GUN STATED ODDS 1:4
1 Sergei Fedorov .40 1.00
2 Sandis Ozolinsh .15 .40
3 Rob Niedermayer .20 .50
4 Andy McDonald .20 .50
5 Joffrey Lupul .20 .50
6 Jean-Sebastien Giguere .25 .60
7 Ilya Kovalchuk .25 .60
8 Patrik Stefan .15 .40
9 Kari Lehtonen .20 .50
10 Marc Savard .15 .40
11 Andy Sutton .15 .40
12 Niclas Havelid .15 .40
13 Nick Boynton .15 .40
14 Joe Thornton .30 .75
15 Andrew Raycroft .20 .50
16 P.J. Axelsson .15 .40
17 Patrice Bergeron .30 .75
18 Sergei Samsonov .20 .50
19 Chris Drury .20 .50
20 Derek Roy .15 .40
21 Maxim Afinogenov .15 .40
22 Daniel Briere .25 .60
23 Mika Noronen .20 .50
24 J.P. Dumont .15 .40
25 Jarome Iginla .25 .60
26 Jordan Leopold .15 .40
27 Robyn Regehr .15 .40
28 Marcus Nilson .15 .40
29 Shean Donovan .15 .40
30 Miikka Kiprusoff .20 .50
31 Erik Cole .20 .50
32 Bret Hedican .15 .40
33 Josef Vasicek .15 .40
34 Radim Vrbata .20 .50
35 Niclas Wallin .15 .40
36 Justin Williams .20 .50
37 Mark Bell .15 .40
38 Tuomo Ruutu .25 .60
39 Eric Daze .20 .50
40 Kyle Calder .15 .40
41 Matthew Barnaby .15 .40
42 Tyler Arnason .15 .40
43 Joe Sakic .40 1.00
44 Rob Blake .25 .60
45 Alex Tanguay .25 .60
46 Dan Hinote .15 .40
47 J-M Liles .15 .40
48 Steve Konowalchuk .15 .40
49 David Aebischer .20 .50
50 Riku Hahl .15 .40
51 Rick Nash .25 .60
52 Marc Denis .20 .50
53 Jody Shelley .15 .40
54 David Vyborny .15 .40
55 Manny Malhotra .20 .50
56 Todd Marchant .15 .40
57 Geoff Sanderson .15 .40
58 Bill Guerin .25 .60
59 Brenden Morrow .20 .50
60 Sergei Zubov .20 .50
61 Jaroslav Svoboda .15 .40
62 Steve Ott .20 .50
63 Jason Arnott .20 .50
64 Niko Kapanen .15 .40
65 Stu Barnes .15 .40
66 Steve Yzerman .60 1.50
67 Nicklas Lidstrom .25 .60
68 Robert Lang .15 .40
69 Manny Legace .25 .60
70 Tomas Holmstrom .20 .50
71 Kris Draper .30 .75
72 Jiri Fischer .15 .40
73 Henrik Zetterberg .30 .75
74 Ty Conklin .20 .50
75 Raffi Torres .15 .40
76 Jason Smith .15 .40
77 Radek Dvorak .15 .40
78 Ales Hemsky .20 .50
79 Shawn Horcoff .15 .40
80 Roberto Luongo .40 1.00
81 Mike Van Ryn .15 .40
82 Olli Jokinen .25 .60
83 Jay Bouwmeester .25 .60
84 Nathan Horton .25 .60
85 Niklas Hagman .15 .40
86 Luc Robitaille .25 .60
87 Mathieu Garon .20 .50
88 Lubomir Visnovsky .15 .40
89 Trent Klatt .15 .40
90 Mattias Norstrom .15 .40
91 Dustin Brown .25 .60
92 Dwayne Roloson .20 .50
93 Marian Gaborik .40 1.00
94 Pascal Dupuis .15 .40
95 Filip Kuba .15 .40
96 Pierre-Marc Bouchard .25 .60
97 Alexandre Daigle .15 .40
98 Saku Koivu .25 .60
99 Richard Zednik .15 .40
100 Michael Ryder .20 .50
101 Sheldon Souray .15 .40
102 Craig Rivet .15 .40
103 Jan Bulis .15 .40
104 Pierre Dagenais .15 .40
105 Tomas Vokoun .20 .50
106 David Legwand .20 .50
107 Steve Sullivan .15 .40
108 Adam Hall .15 .40
109 Jordin Tootoo .25 .60
110 Denis Arkhipov .15 .40
111 Scott Gomez .20 .50
112 Patrik Elias .25 .60
113 Scott Stevens .25 .60
114 Sergei Brylin .15 .40
115 John Madden .15 .40
116 Jeff Friesen .15 .40
117 Paul Martin .15 .40
118 Alexei Yashin .20 .50
119 Trent Hunter .15 .40
120 Mark Parrish .15 .40
121 Garth Snow .20 .50
122 Jason Blake .15 .40
123 Janne Niinimaa .15 .40
124 Jamie Lundmark .15 .40
125 Tom Poti .15 .40
126 Jaromir Jagr .60 1.50
127 Darius Kasparaitis .15 .40
128 Michael Nylander .15 .40
129 Kevin Weekes .20 .50
130 Daniel Alfredsson .25 .60
131 Dominik Hasek .40 1.00
132 Wade Redden .15 .40
133 Jason Spezza .25 .60
134 Chris Phillips .15 .40
135 Vaclav Varada .15 .40
136 Zdeno Chara .25 .60
137 Simon Gagne .25 .60
138 Joni Pitkanen .15 .40
139 Keith Primeau .25 .60
140 Michal Handzus .20 .50
141 Kim Johnsson .15 .40
142 Sami Kapanen .15 .40
143 Donald Brashear .15 .40
144 Brett Hull .30 .75
145 Tyson Nash .15 .40
146 Shane Doan .20 .50
147 Derek Morris .15 .40
148 Mike Johnson .15 .40
149 Paul Mara .15 .40
150 Mario Lemieux .75 2.00
151 Mark Recchi .30 .75
152 Ryan Malone .15 .40
153 Rico Fata .15 .40
154 Lasse Pirjeta .15 .40
155 Dick Tarnstrom .15 .40
156 Jonathan Cheechoo .25 .60
157 Marco Sturm .15 .40
158 Evgeni Nabokov .20 .50
159 Alyn McCauley .15 .40
160 Kyle McLaren .15 .40
161 Brad Stuart .15 .40
162 Wayne Primeau .15 .40
163 Christian Ehrhoff .15 .40
164 Keith Tkachuk .25 .60
165 Barret Jackman .15 .40
166 Patrick Lalime .20 .50
167 Dallas Drake .15 .40
168 Mark Rycroft .15 .40
169 Christian Backman .15 .40

170 Brad Richards .25 .60
171 Fredrik Modin .15 .40
172 Martin St. Louis .25 .60
173 Ruslan Fedotenko .15 .40
174 Darryl Sydor .15 .40
175 Pavel Kubina .15 .40
176 Tim Taylor .15 .40
177 Mats Sundin .25 .60
178 Matt Stajan .20 .50
179 Bryan McCabe .15 .40
180 Darcy Tucker .20 .50
181 Tomas Kaberle .15 .40
182 Owen Nolan .20 .50
183 Nikolai Antropov .20 .50
184 Ken Klee .15 .40
185 Ed Jovanovski .20 .50
186 Dan Cloutier .20 .50
187 Trevor Linden .25 .60
188 Matt Cooke .15 .40
189 Todd Bertuzzi .25 .60
190 Alex Auld .15 .40
191 Sami Salo .15 .40
192 Mattias Ohlund .15 .40
193 Olaf Kolzig .25 .60
194 Brendan Witt .15 .40
195 Jeff Halpern .15 .40
196 Dainius Zubrus .15 .40
197 Alexander Semin .25 .60
198 Boyd Gordon .15 .40
199 Joe Thornton CL .30 .75
200 Jarome Iginla CL .25 .60
201 Sidney Crosby YG RC 550.00 850.00
202 Mike Richards YG RC 5.00 12.00
203 Dion Phaneuf YG RC 4.00 10.00
204 Corey Perry YG RC 8.00 20.00
205 Alexander Steen YG RC 5.00 12.00
206 Zach Parise YG RC 6.00 15.00
207 Rostislav Olesz YG RC 2.00 5.00
208 Matt Foy YG RC 1.50 4.00
209 Brent Seabrook YG RC 6.00 15.00
210 Jeff Hoggan YG RC 1.50 4.00
211 Petteri Nokelainen YG RC 1.50 4.00
212 Andrew Wozniewski YG RC 2.00 5.00
213 Peter Budaj YG RC 3.00 8.00
214 Chris Campoli YG RC 1.50 4.00
215 Jim Howard YG RC 6.00 15.00
216 Henrik Lundqvist YG RC 25.00 60.00
217 David Leneveu YG RC 2.00 5.00
218 George Parros YG RC 1.50 4.00
219 Kevin Dallman YG RC 2.00 5.00
220 Jeff Woywitka YG RC 1.50 4.00
221 Rene Bourque YG RC 2.50 6.00
222 Jim Slater YG RC 2.00 5.00
223 Niklas Nordgren YG RC 2.50 6.00
224 Jay McClement YG RC 1.50 4.00
225 Andrew Alberts YG RC 1.50 4.00
226 A.Perezhogin YG RC 2.00 5.00
227 Yann Danis YG RC 2.00 5.00
228 Andrej Meszaros YG RC 2.00 5.00
229 Cam Ward YG RC 6.00 15.00
230 Duncan Keith YG RC 15.00 40.00
231 Timo Helbling YG RC 1.50 4.00
232 Keith Ballard YG RC 2.00 5.00
233 Braydon Coburn YG RC 2.50 6.00
234 Ryane Clowe YG RC 3.00 8.00
235 Ryan Hollweg YG RC 1.50 4.00
236 Maxime Talbot YG RC 2.50 6.00
237 Brett Lebda YG RC 1.50 4.00
238 Brandon Bochenski YG RC 2.50 6.00
239 Jaroslav Balastik YG RC 1.50 4.00
240 Wojtek Wolski YG RC 2.00 5.00
241 Hannu Toivonen YG RC 2.50 6.00
242 S.Crosby/C.Perry YG CL 6.00 15.00
243 Teemu Selanne .50 1.25
244 Scott Niedermayer .25 .60
245 Ilya Bryzgalov .25 .60
246 Todd Fedoruk .15 .40
247 Chris Kunitz .25 .60
248 Petr Sykora .20 .50
249 Keith Carney .15 .40
250 Marian Hossa .20 .50
251 Peter Bondra .20 .50
252 Bobby Holik .15 .40
253 Mike Dunham .15 .40
254 Vyacheslav Kozlov .15 .40
255 Steve Shields .15 .40
256 Glen Murray .20 .50
257 Brian Leetch .25 .60
258 Brad Boyes .20 .50
259 Jiri Slegr .15 .40
260 Travis Green .15 .40
261 Hal Gill .15 .40
262 Marco Sturm .15 .40
263 Brad Stuart .15 .40
264 Ryan Miller .25 .60
265 Teppo Numminen .20 .50
266 Jochen Hecht .15 .40
267 Martin Biron .20 .50
268 Paul Gaustad .15 .40
269 Ales Kotalik .15 .40
270 Tim Connolly .15 .40
271 Mike Grier .15 .40
272 Tony Amonte .20 .50
273 Philippe Sauve .20 .50
274 Daymond Langkow .15 .40
275 Chuck Kobasew .15 .40
276 Chris Simon .15 .40
277 Matthew Lombardi .15 .40
278 Roman Hamrlik .20 .50
279 Stephane Yelle .15 .40
280 Eric Staal .30 .75
281 Rod Brind'Amour .25 .60
282 Cory Stillman .20 .50
283 Martin Gerber .20 .50
284 Glen Wesley .15 .40
285 Oleg Tverdovsky .15 .40
286 Nikolai Khabibulin .25 .60
287 Pavel Vorobiev .15 .40
288 Martin Lapointe .15 .40
289 Adrian Aucoin .15 .40
290 Matt Ellison .15 .40
291 Jaroslav Spacek .15 .40
292 Milan Hejduk .20 .50
293 Pierre Turgeon .25 .60
294 Ian Laperriere .15 .40
295 Marek Svatos .20 .50
296 Patrice Brisebois .15 .40
297 Antti Laaksonen .15 .40
298 Nikolai Zherdev .15 .40
299 Bryan Berard .15 .40
300 Pascal Leclaire .20 .50
301 Adam Foote .15 .40
302 Sergei Fedorov .40 1.00
303 Trevor Letowski .15 .40
304 Dan Fritsche .15 .40
305 Mike Modano .40 1.00
306 Marty Turco .25 .60
307 Jere Lehtinen .20 .50
308 Johan Hedberg .20 .50
309 Philippe Boucher .15 .40
310 Antti Miettinen .15 .40
311 Trevor Daley .15 .40
312 Brendan Shanahan .30 .75
313 Chris Osgood .25 .60
314 Pavel Datsyuk .30 .75
315 Chris Chelios .25 .60
316 Jason Williams .15 .40
317 Mikael Samuelsson .15 .40
318 Mathieu Schneider .15 .40
319 Ryan Smyth .20 .50
320 Chris Pronger .20 .50
321 Jussi Markkanen .15 .40
322 Georges Laraque .20 .50
323 Michael Peca .20 .50
324 Marc-Andre Bergeron .15 .40
325 Jarret Stoll .20 .50
326 Jani Rita .15 .40
327 Stephen Weiss .15 .40
328 Joe Nieuwendyk .25 .60
329 Gary Roberts .15 .40
330 Martin Gelinas .15 .40
331 Chris Gratton .15 .40
332 Juraj Kolnik .15 .40
333 Lukas Krajicek .15 .40
334 Jeremy Roenick .25 .60
335 Alexander Frolov .15 .40
336 Pavol Demitra .30 .75
337 Craig Conroy .15 .40
338 Jason LaBarbera .20 .50
339 Mike Cammalleri .25 .60
340 Tim Gleason .15 .40
341 Manny Fernandez .20 .50
342 Marc Chouinard .15 .40
343 Brian Rolston .20 .50
344 Todd White .15 .40
345 Nick Schultz .15 .40
346 Brent Burns .30 .75
347 Jose Theodore .25 .60
348 Mike Ribeiro .20 .50
349 Steve Begin .15 .40
350 Alex Kovalev .20 .50
351 Tomas Plekanec .25 .60
352 Andrei Markov .25 .60
353 Radek Bonk .15 .40
354 Chris Higgins .15 .40
355 Paul Kariya .30 .75
356 Yanic Perreault .15 .40
357 Scott Hartnell .25 .60
358 Kimmo Timonen .15 .40
359 Scott Walker .15 .40
360 Dan Hamhuis .20 .50
361 Martin Erat .15 .40
362 Martin Brodeur .50 1.25
363 David Hale .15 .40
364 Brian Gionta .20 .50
365 Viktor Kozlov .15 .40
366 Scott Clemmensen .15 .40
367 Jamie Langenbrunner .15 .40
368 Brian Rafalski .20 .50
369 Miroslav Satan .20 .50
370 Rick DiPietro .20 .50
371 Alexei Zhitnik .15 .40
372 Mike York .15 .40
373 Brent Sopel .15 .40
374 Martin Rucinsky .15 .40
375 Martin Straka .15 .40
376 Steve Rucchin .15 .40
377 Marcel Hossa .15 .40
378 Fedor Tyutin .15 .40
379 Dominic Moore .15 .40
380 Dany Heatley .25 .60
381 Martin Havlat .25 .60
382 Peter Schaefer .15 .40
383 Bryan Smolinski .15 .40
384 Antoine Vermette .20 .50
385 Anton Volchenkov .15 .40
386 Peter Forsberg .30 .75
387 Robert Esche .20 .50
388 Mike Rathje .15 .40
389 Eric Desjardins .20 .50
390 Patrick Sharp .25 .60
391 Mike Knuble .15 .40
392 Curtis Joseph .25 .60
393 Ladislav Nagy .15 .40
394 Geoff Sanderson .15 .40
395 Mike Comrie .20 .50
396 Oleg Saprykin .15 .40
397 Petr Nedved .15 .40
398 Zigmund Palffy .25 .60
399 John LeClair .25 .60
400 Marc-Andre Fleury .40 1.00
401 Sergei Gonchar .15 .40
402 Jocelyn Thibault .20 .50
403 Sebastien Caron .15 .40
404 Patrick Marleau .25 .60
405 Vesa Toskala .20 .50
406 Marcel Goc .20 .50
407 Joe Thornton .30 .75
408 Milan Michalek .15 .40
409 Niko Dimotrakos .15 .40
410 Doug Weight .25 .60
411 Petr Cajanek .15 .40
412 Reinhard Divis .15 .40
413 Jamal Mayers .15 .40
414 Scott Young .15 .40
415 Eric Brewer .15 .40
416 Vincent Lecavalier .20 .50
417 Sean Burke .15 .40
418 Vaclav Prospal .15 .40
419 Dave Andreychuk .25 .60
420 Cory Sarich .15 .40
421 John Grahame .15 .40
422 Ed Belfour .25 .60
423 Jason Allison .20 .50
424 Jeff O'Neill .15 .40
425 Eric Lindros .40 1.00
426 Tie Domi .20 .50
427 Kyle Wellwood .20 .50
428 Mikael Tellqvist .20 .50
429 Markus Naslund .25 .60
430 Henrik Sedin .25 .60
431 Daniel Sedin .25 .60
432 Ryan Kesler .30 .75
433 Brendan Morrison .15 .40
434 Anson Carter .20 .50
435 Jeff Friesen .15 .40
436 Steve Eminger .15 .40
437 Jamie Heward .15 .40
438 Mike Green RC 3.00 8.00
439 Andrew Cassels .15 .40
440 Shaone Morrisonn .15 .40
441 Peter Forsberg CL .30 .75
442 Dany Heatley CL .25 .60
443 Alexander Ovechkin YG RC 80.00 200.00
444 Jeff Carter YG RC 6.00 15.00
445 Cam Barker YG RC 2.00 5.00
446 Gilbert Brule YG RC 2.50 6.00
447 Brad Winchester YG RC 2.50 6.00
448 Eric Nystrom YG RC 2.00 5.00
449 R.J. Umberger YG RC 2.50 6.00
450 Mikko Koivu YG RC 3.00 8.00
451 Robert Nilsson YG RC 2.50 6.00
452 Ryan Getzlaf YG RC 8.00 20.00
453 Anthony Stewart YG RC 2.00 5.00
454 Ryan Suter YG RC 3.00 8.00
455 Al Montoya YG RC 2.50 6.00
456 Johan Franzen YG RC 4.00 10.00
457 Thomas Vanek YG RC 5.00 12.00
458 Patrick Eaves YG RC 2.50 6.00
459 Jussi Jokinen YG RC 2.50 6.00
460 Christoph Schubert YG RC 1.50 4.00
461 Ryan Whitney YG RC 2.50 6.00
462 Evgeny Artyukhin YG RC 2.00 5.00
463 Jordan Sigalet YG RC 1.50 4.00
464 Milan Jurcina YG RC 2.00 5.00
465 Dimitri Patzold YG RC 1.50 4.00
466 Staffan Kronwall YG RC 1.50 4.00
467 Erik Christensen YG RC 1.50 4.00
468 Kyle Brodziak YG RC 1.50 4.00
469 Ryan Craig YG RC 1.50 4.00
470 Steve Bernier YG RC 2.50 6.00
471 Matt Greene YG RC 1.50 4.00
472 Barry Tallackson YG RC 2.00 5.00
473 Jakub Klepis YG RC 1.50 4.00
474 Maxim Lapierre YG RC 2.50 6.00
475 Danny Richmond YG RC 1.50 4.00
476 Tomas Fleischmann YG RC 2.50 6.00
477 Adam Berkhoel YG RC 2.00 5.00
478 Kevin Bieksa YG RC 3.00 8.00
479 Greg Jacina YG RC 1.50 4.00
480 Gerald Coleman YG RC 1.50 4.00
481 Jeremy Colliton YG RC 1.50 4.00
482 Andrei Kostitsyn YG RC 3.00 8.00
483 Valtteri Filppula YG RC 3.00 8.00
484 Dennis Wideman YG RC 1.50 4.00
485 Brad Richardson YG RC 2.50 6.00
486 Jeff Tambellini YG RC 1.50 4.00
487 A.Ovechkin/J.Carter CL 5.00 12.00

2005-06 Upper Deck All-Time Greatest

COMPLETE SET (90) 20.00 50.00
1 Jean-Sebastien Giguere .40 1.00
2 Paul Kariya .50 1.25
3 Ilya Kovalchuk .40 1.00
4 Dany Heatley .40 1.00
5 Joe Thornton .50 1.25
6 Cam Neely .40 1.00
7 Dominik Hasek .60 1.50
8 Gilbert Perreault .40 1.00
9 Jarome Iginla .40 1.00
10 Lanny McDonald .40 1.00
11 Rod Brind'Amour .40 1.00
12 Gary Roberts .25 .60
13 Tony Esposito .40 1.00
14 Stan Mikita .50 1.25
15 Joe Sakic .60 1.50
16 Patrick Roy 1.00 2.50
17 Rick Nash .40 1.00
18 Marc Denis .30 .75
19 Mike Modano .60 1.50
20 Ed Belfour .40 1.00
21 Gordie Howe 1.25 3.00
22 Steve Yzerman 1.00 2.50
23 Wayne Gretzky 2.00 5.00
24 Jari Kurri .40 1.00
25 Roberto Luongo .60 1.50
26 Olli Jokinen .40 1.00
27 Wayne Gretzky 2.00 5.00
28 Luc Robitaille .40 1.00
29 Marian Gaborik .60 1.50
30 Dwayne Roloson .30 .75
31 Patrick Roy 1.00 2.50
32 Jose Theodore .40 1.00
33 Steve Sullivan .25 .60
34 Tomas Vokoun .30 .75
35 Martin Brodeur .75 2.00
36 Patrik Elias .40 1.00
37 Mike Bossy .40 1.00
38 Alexei Yashin .30 .75
39 Jaromir Jagr 1.00 2.50
40 Brian Leetch .40 1.00
41 Daniel Alfredsson .40 1.00
42 Jason Spezza .40 1.00
43 Keith Tkachuk .40 1.00
44 Shane Doan .30 .75
45 Bobby Clarke .40 1.00
46 Ron Hextall .60 1.50
47 Mario Lemieux 1.25 3.00
48 Jaromir Jagr 1.00 2.50
49 Doug Weight .40 1.00
50 Chris Pronger .30 .75
51 Patrick Marleau .40 1.00
52 Evgeni Nabokov .30 .75
53 Martin St. Louis .40 1.00
54 Vincent Lecavalier .30 .75
55 Mats Sundin .40 1.00
56 Darryl Sittler .30 .75
57 Markus Naslund .40 1.00
58 Trevor Linden .40 1.00
59 Olaf Kolzig .40 1.00
60 Peter Bondra .30 .75
61 Dany Heatley .40 1.00
62 Ray Bourque .60 1.50
63 Andrew Raycroft .30 .75
64 Gilbert Perreault .40 1.00
65 Jarome Iginla .40 1.00
66 Tony Esposito .40 1.00
67 Ed Belfour .40 1.00
68 Rick Nash .40 1.00
69 Paul Kariya .50 1.25
70 Gordie Howe 1.25 3.00
71 Steve Yzerman 1.00 2.50
72 Sergei Fedorov .60 1.50
73 Wayne Gretzky 2.00 5.00
74 Luc Robitaille .40 1.00
75 Mike Modano .60 1.50
76 Guy Lafleur .50 1.25
77 Patrick Roy 1.00 2.50
78 Martin Brodeur .75 2.00
79 Mike Bossy .40 1.00
80 Brian Leetch .40 1.00
81 Daniel Alfredsson .40 1.00
82 Ron Hextall .60 1.50
83 Eric Lindros .60 1.50
84 Sidney Crosby 2.00 5.00
85 Mario Lemieux 1.25 3.00
86 Joe Sakic .60 1.50
87 Peter Forsberg .50 1.25
88 Peter Stastny .40 1.00
89 Evgeni Nabokov .30 .75
90 Teemu Selanne .75 2.00

2005-06 Upper Deck Big Playmakers Jerseys

PRINT RUN 50 SER.#'d SETS
BBMO Bryan McCabe 10.00 25.00
BDAE David Aebischer 12.00 30.00
BDHA Dominik Hasek 25.00 60.00
BDHE Dany Heatley 15.00 40.00
BMBI Mike Bossy
BMME Mark Messier 25.00 60.00
BMRY Michael Ryder
BPBO Peter Bondra 12.00 30.00
BROB Rob Blake 15.00 40.00
BMRE Mark Recchi 20.00 50.00
BMRI Mike Ribeiro 12.00 30.00
BBMC Brendan Morrison 10.00 25.00
BDAR Denis Arkhipov 10.00 25.00
BJEL Jamie Lundmark 10.00 25.00
BJLU Jere Lehtinen 12.00 30.00
BJOL Jordan Leopold 10.00 25.00
BMBO Martin Biron 12.00 30.00
BMDU Mike Dunham 10.00 25.00
BRNI Rob Niedermayer 12.00 30.00
BSST Scott Stevens 15.00 40.00
BMST Martin St. Louis 15.00 40.00
BMAH Marcel Hossa 10.00 25.00
BSSA Sergei Samsonov 12.00 30.00
BMDE Marc Denis 12.00 30.00
BMHA Martin Havlat 15.00 40.00
BJBL Jay Bouwmeester 15.00 40.00
BJBO Jason Blake 10.00 25.00
BMPA Michael Peca 12.00 30.00
BMPE Mark Parrish 10.00 25.00
BMHO Marian Hossa 12.00 30.00
BMSU Mats Sundin 15.00 40.00
BAC Anson Carter 12.00 30.00
BAF Alexander Frolov 10.00 25.00
BAH Adam Hall 10.00 25.00
BAM Al MacInnis 15.00 40.00
BAT Alexander Mogilny 12.00 30.00
BAT Alex Tanguay 15.00 40.00
BAY Alexei Yashin 12.00 30.00
BBC Bobby Clarke 20.00 50.00
BBG Bill Guerin 15.00 40.00
BBH Brett Hull 20.00 50.00
BBJ Barret Jackman 10.00 25.00
BBS Brendan Shanahan 20.00 50.00
BCC Chris Chelios 15.00 40.00
BCD Chris Drury 12.00 30.00
BCJ Curtis Joseph 15.00 40.00
BCN Cam Neely 15.00 40.00
BCP Chris Pronger 12.00 30.00
BCS Chris Simon 10.00 25.00
BDB Daniel Briere 15.00 40.00
BDC Dan Cloutier 12.00 30.00
BDL David Legwand 12.00 30.00
BDW Doug Weight 15.00 40.00
BEB Ed Belfour 15.00 40.00
BED Eric Daze 12.00 30.00
BEJ Ed Jovanovski 12.00 30.00
BEL Eric Lindros 25.00 60.00
BES Eric Staal 20.00 50.00
BGM Glen Murray 12.00 30.00
BGO Scott Gomez 12.00 30.00
BGS Geoff Sanderson 10.00 25.00
BHJ Milan Hejduk 12.00 30.00
BIK Ilya Kovalchuk 25.00 60.00
BJA Jason Allison 12.00 30.00
BJC Jonathan Cheechoo 15.00 40.00
BJG Jean-Sebastien Giguere 15.00 40.00
BJI Jarome Iginla 25.00 60.00
BJJ Jaromir Jagr 25.00 60.00
BJK Jari Kurri 15.00 40.00
BJL John LeClair 15.00 40.00
BJN Joe Nieuwendyk
BJO Jose Theodore 20.00 50.00
BJP Joni Pitkanen 10.00 25.00
BJR Jeremy Roenick 15.00 40.00
BJS Jason Smith 10.00 25.00
BJT Joe Thornton 25.00 60.00
BJW Justin Williams 12.00 30.00
BKP Keith Primeau 15.00 40.00
BKT Keith Tkachuk 15.00 40.00
BLR Luc Robitaille 15.00 40.00
BMA Maxim Afinogenov 10.00 25.00
BMB Martin Brodeur 30.00 80.00
BMF Manny Fernandez 12.00 30.00
BMG Marian Gaborik 25.00 60.00
BML Mario Lemieux 50.00 125.00
BMM Mike Modano 20.00 50.00
BMN Markus Naslund 15.00 40.00
BMO Mattias Ohlund 10.00 25.00
BMS Martin Straka 10.00 25.00
BMT Marty Turco 15.00 40.00
BNA Nik Antropov 12.00 30.00
BNK Nikolai Khabibulin 15.00 40.00
BNL Nicklas Lidstrom 15.00 40.00
BOJ Olli Jokinen 15.00 40.00
BOK Olaf Kolzig 15.00 40.00
BON Owen Nolan 12.00 30.00
BPB Patrice Bergeron 20.00 50.00
BPD Pavel Datsyuk 20.00 50.00
BPE Patrik Elias 15.00 40.00
BPF Peter Forsberg 25.00 60.00
BPK Paul Kariya 20.00 50.00
BPL Patrick Lalime 12.00 30.00
BPM Patrick Marleau
BPR Patrick Roy 30.00 80.00
BRB Ray Bourque 20.00 50.00
BRF Ruslan Fedotenko 10.00 25.00
BRH Ron Hextall 20.00 50.00
BRK Rostislav Klesla 10.00 25.00
BRL Roberto Luongo 25.00 60.00
BRN Rick Nash 15.00 40.00
BRS Ryan Smyth 12.00 30.00
BSB Sean Burke 10.00 25.00
BSD Shane Doan 12.00 30.00
BSF Sergei Fedorov 25.00 60.00
BSG Simon Gagne 15.00 40.00
BSH Scott Hartnell 15.00 40.00
BSK Saku Koivu 15.00 40.00
BSO Sandis Ozolinsh 10.00 25.00
BSP Jason Spezza 15.00 40.00
BSY Steve Yzerman 30.00 80.00
BSZ Sergei Zubov 12.00 30.00
BTA Tony Amonte 12.00 30.00
BTB Todd Bertuzzi 15.00 40.00
BTC Ty Conklin 12.00 30.00
BTH Trent Hunter 10.00 25.00
BTP Tom Poti 10.00 25.00
BTR Tuomo Ruutu 15.00 40.00
BTV Tomas Vokoun 12.00 30.00
BVD Vincent Damphousse 12.00 30.00
BVL Vincent Lecavalier 15.00 40.00
BVN Ville Nieminen 10.00 25.00
BWG Wayne Gretzky 100.00 250.00
BZC Zdeno Chara 15.00 40.00

2005-06 Upper Deck Destined for the Hall

COMPLETE SET (7) 12.00 25.00
STATED ODDS 1:24
DH1 Steve Yzerman 4.00 10.00
DH2 Martin Brodeur 3.00 8.00
DH3 Joe Sakic 2.50 6.00
DH4 Dominik Hasek 2.50 6.00
DH5 Jaromir Jagr 4.00 10.00
DH6 Mario Lemieux 5.00 12.00
DH7 Brendan Shanahan 2.00 5.00

2005-06 Upper Deck Diary of a Phenom

COMPLETE SET (30) 15.00 40.00
COMMON CROSBY (DP1-DP30) .50 1.25
ONE PER RETAIL PACK

2005-06 Upper Deck Goal Celebrations

COMPLETE SET (7) 8.00 20.00
STATED ODDS 1:24
GC1 Ilya Kovalchuk 1.50 4.00
GC2 Dany Heatley 1.50 4.00
GC3 Jaromir Jagr 4.00 10.00
GC4 Jarome Iginla 1.50 4.00
GC5 Martin St. Louis 1.50 4.00
GC6 Rick Nash 1.50 4.00
GC7 Mats Sundin 1.50 4.00

2005-06 Upper Deck Goal Rush

COMPLETE SET (14) 10.00 20.00
STATED ODDS 1:12
GR1 Rick Nash .75 2.00
GR2 Martin St. Louis .75 2.00
GR3 Milan Hejduk .60 1.50
GR4 Steve Yzerman 2.00 5.00
GR5 Joe Sakic 1.25 3.00
GR6 Wayne Gretzky 4.00 10.00
GR7 Mario Lemieux 2.50 6.00
GR8 Ilya Kovalchuk .75 2.00
GR9 Patrice Bergeron 1.00 2.50
GR10 Markus Naslund .75 2.00
GR11 Marian Hossa .60 1.50
GR12 Mike Modano 1.25 3.00
GR13 Jarome Iginla .75 2.00
GR14 Dany Heatley .75 2.00

2005-06 Upper Deck Hometown Heroes

COMPLETE SET (28) 20.00 40.00
STATED ODDS 1:12
HH1 Joe Sakic 1.25 3.00
HH2 Martin Brodeur 1.50 4.00
HH3 Joe Thornton 1.00 2.50
HH4 Jarome Iginla .75 2.00
HH5 Mats Sundin .75 2.00
HH6 Steve Yzerman 2.00 5.00
HH7 Saku Koivu .75 2.00
HH8 Jaromir Jagr 2.00 5.00
HH9 Ilya Kovalchuk .75 2.00
HH10 Mike Modano 1.25 3.00
HH11 Martin St. Louis .75 2.00
HH12 Mark Messier 1.25 3.00
HH13 Mario Lemieux 2.50 6.00
HH14 Keith Tkachuk .75 2.00
HH15 Daniel Alfredsson .75 2.00
HH16 Evgeni Nabokov .60 1.50
HH17 Jaromir Jagr 2.00 5.00
HH18 Rick Nash .75 2.00
HH19 Peter Forsberg 1.00 2.50
HH20 Paul Kariya 1.00 2.50
HH21 Jean-Sebastien Giguere .75 2.00
HH22 Nikolai Khabibulin .75 2.00
HH23 Alexei Yashin .60 1.50
HH24 Shane Doan .60 1.50
HH25 Markus Naslund .75 2.00
HH26 Dany Heatley .75 2.00
HH27 Eric Lindros 1.25 3.00
HH28 Olaf Kolzig .75 2.00

2005-06 Upper Deck Jerseys

JBGE Bernie Geoffrion SP 50.00 120.00
JBHU Brett Hull 4.00 10.00
JDSA Denis Savard SP 15.00 40.00
JRHX Ron Hextall SP 15.00 40.00
JRLU Roberto Luongo 5.00 12.00
JGUL Georges Laraque 2.50 6.00
JHSE Henrik Sedin 3.00 8.00
JJAB Jay Bouwmeester 3.00 8.00
JJAR Jason Arnott 2.50 6.00
JJOL Joffrey Lupul 2.50 6.00
JMAH Marcel Hossa 2.00 5.00
JMCA Mike Cammalleri 3.00 8.00
JMGR Mike Grier 2.00 5.00
JMLO Matthew Lombardi 2.00 5.00
JMNI Marcus Nilson 2.00 5.00
JMPA Mark Parrish 2.00 5.00
JMPE Michael Peca 2.50 6.00
JMST Matt Stajan 2.50 6.00
JNIB Nick Boynton 2.00 5.00
JPAS Patrik Stefan 2.00 5.00
JPSY Petr Sykora 2.50 6.00
JMRY Michael Ryder 2.50 6.00
JTRU Tuomo Ruutu 3.00 8.00
JRBK Radek Bonk 2.00 5.00
JRIH Riku Hahl 2.00 5.00
JSGO Scott Gomez 2.50 6.00
JSKA Sami Kapanen 2.00 5.00
JSKO Steve Konowalchuk 2.00 5.00
JSOT Steve Ott 2.50 6.00
JSOZ Sandis Ozolinsh 2.00 5.00
JSTR Steven Reinprecht 2.00 5.00
JBHO Bobby Holik 2.00 5.00
JBMC Bryan McCabe 2.00 5.00
JDAR Denis Arkhipov 2.00 5.00
JDBR Donald Brashear 2.00 5.00
JDSE Daniel Sedin 3.00 8.00
JAHE Ales Hemsky 2.50 6.00
JDAE David Aebischer 2.50 6.00
JJLE Jere Lehtinen 2.50 6.00
JMAD Marc Denis 2.50 6.00
JMBI Martin Biron 2.50 6.00
JMCO Mike Comrie 2.50 6.00
JMGA Mathieu Garon 2.50 6.00
JPDE Pavol Demitra 4.00 10.00
JSSA Sergei Samsonov 2.50 6.00
JSST Scott Stevens 3.00 8.00
JTDO Tie Domi 2.50 6.00
JMHE Milan Hejduk 2.50 6.00
JSGA Simon Gagne 3.00 8.00
JTSE Teemu Selanne 6.00 15.00
JAA Adrian Aucoin 2.00 5.00
JAF Adam Foote 2.00 5.00
JAK Alexei Kovalev 2.50 6.00
JAM Alexander Mogilny 2.50 6.00
JAY Alexei Yashin 2.50 6.00
JBC Bobby Clarke SP 20.00 60.00
JBG Bill Guerin SP 8.00 20.00
JBL Rob Blake 3.00 8.00
JBM Brendan Morrison 2.00 5.00
JBR Dustin Brown 3.00 8.00
JBT Bryan Trottier 4.00 10.00
JBW Brendan Witt 2.00 5.00
JCC Chris Chelios SP 15.00 40.00
JCD Chris Drury 2.50 6.00
JCJ Curtis Joseph 3.00 8.00
JCK Chuck Kobasew 2.00 5.00
JCO Chris Osgood 3.00 8.00
JCP Chris Pronger 2.50 6.00
JDB Daniel Briere 3.00 8.00
JDH Dany Heatley 3.00 8.00
JDL David Legwand 2.50 6.00
JDO Dominik Hasek 5.00 12.00
JDW Doug Weight 3.00 8.00
JEB Ed Belfour 3.00 8.00
JEJ Ed Jovanovski 2.50 6.00
JEL Eric Lindros 5.00 12.00
JGF Grant Fuhr SP 15.00 40.00
JGL Guy Lafleur SP 30.00 80.00
JGM Glen Murray 2.50 6.00
JGR Gary Roberts 2.00 5.00
JHA Dan Hamhuis 2.50 6.00
JJF Jeff Friesen 2.00 5.00
JJG Jean-Sebastien Giguere 3.00 8.00
JJH Jani Hurme 2.50 6.00
JJI Jarome Iginla 3.00 8.00
JJO Jose Theodore 3.00 8.00
JJP Joni Pitkanen SP 2.00 5.00
JJR Jeremy Roenick 3.00 8.00
JJS Joe Sakic SP 10.00 25.00
JJS Jason Smith 2.00 5.00
JJT Joe Thornton 4.00 10.00
JJW Justin Williams 2.50 6.00
JKD Kris Draper 4.00 10.00
JKL Kari Lehtonen SP 8.00 20.00
JKP Keith Primeau 3.00 8.00
JKT Keith Tkachuk 3.00 8.00
JLR Luc Robitaille 3.00 8.00
JMA Maxim Afinogenov 2.00 5.00
JMB Martin Brodeur 6.00 15.00
JMD Mike Dunham 2.00 5.00
JMK Miikka Kiprusoff 2.50 6.00
JML Mario Lemieux SP 15.00 40.00
JMM Mike Modano 5.00 12.00
JMO Mattias Ohlund 2.00 5.00
JMR Mark Recchi 4.00 10.00
JMS Mats Sundin 3.00 8.00
JNA Nik Antropov 2.50 6.00
JNH Nathan Horton 3.00 8.00
JNK Nikolai Khabibulin 3.00 8.00
JNS Nathan Smith 2.00 5.00
JOJ Olli Jokinen 3.00 8.00
JOK Olaf Kolzig 3.00 8.00
JON Owen Nolan 2.50 6.00
JPD Pavel Datsyuk 4.00 10.00
JPF Peter Forsberg 4.00 10.00
JPK Paul Kariya SP 4.00 10.00
JPR Patrick Roy 8.00 20.00
JPT Pierre Turgeon 3.00 8.00
JRB Ray Bourque SP 8.00 20.00
JRE Robert Esche 2.50 6.00
JRM Ryan Miller 3.00 8.00
JRN Rob Niedermayer 2.50 6.00
JRT Raffi Torres 2.00 5.00
JSC Stanislav Chistov 2.00 5.00
JSF Sergei Fedorov 5.00 12.00
JSH Scott Hartnell 3.00 8.00
JSK Saku Koivu 3.00 8.00
JSM Scott Mellanby 2.00 5.00
JSP Jason Spezza 3.00 8.00
JSU Scottie Upshall 2.00 5.00
JSY Steve Yzerman 8.00 20.00
JSZ Sergei Zubov 2.50 6.00
JTA Tony Amonte 2.50 6.00
JTC Ty Conklin 2.50 6.00
JTO Jordin Tootoo 3.00 8.00
JTP Tom Poti 2.00 5.00
JVB Valeri Bure 2.00 5.00
JVK Viktor Kozlov 2.00 5.00
JVL Vincent Lecavalier 2.50 6.00
JVN Ville Nieminen 2.00 5.00
JWG Wayne Gretzky SP 30.00 80.00

2005-06 Upper Deck Jerseys Series II

STATED ODDS 1:12
J2AA Alex Auld 4.00 10.00
J2AC Anson Carter 5.00 12.00
J2AF Alexander Frolov 4.00 10.00
J2AK Alex Kovalev 5.00 12.00
J2AR Andrew Raycroft 5.00 12.00
J2AT Alex Tanguay 6.00 15.00
J2BG Bill Guerin 6.00 15.00
J2BI Martin Biron 5.00 12.00
J2BJ Barrett Jackman 4.00 10.00
J2BL Brian Leetch 6.00 15.00
J2BM Brendan Morrison 4.00 10.00
J2BR Brad Richards 6.00 15.00
J2BS Brendan Shanahan 8.00 20.00
J2CK Matt Cooke 4.00 10.00
J2CM Mike Comrie 5.00 12.00
J2CO Chris Osgood 6.00 15.00
J2CP Chris Pronger 5.00 12.00
J2CS Cory Stillman 5.00 12.00
J2CY Tim Connolly 4.00 10.00
J2DA Daniel Alfredsson 6.00 15.00
J2DC Dan Cloutier 5.00 12.00
J2DM Dominic Moore 4.00 10.00
J2DW Doug Weight 6.00 15.00
J2DY Trevor Daley 4.00 10.00
J2EB Ed Belfour 6.00 15.00
J2EJ Ed Jovanovski 5.00 12.00
J2EL Eric Lindros 10.00 25.00
J2ES Eric Staal 8.00 20.00
J2FT Fedor Tyutin 4.00 10.00
J2GA Simon Gagne 6.00 15.00
J2GE Martin Gerber 5.00 12.00
J2GI Brian Gionta 5.00 12.00
J2GM Glen Murray 5.00 12.00
J2GO Scott Gomez 5.00 12.00
J2HJ Milan Hejduk 5.00 12.00
J2HO Marcel Hossa 4.00 10.00
J2HZ Michal Handzus 5.00 12.00
J2HZ Henrik Zetterberg 8.00 20.00
J2IK Ilya Kovalchuk 6.00 15.00
J2JA Jason Allison 5.00 12.00
J2JB Jay Bouwmeester 6.00 15.00
J2JC Jonathan Cheechoo 8.00 20.00
J2JE Jere Lehtinen 5.00 12.00
J2JG Jean-Sebastien Giguere 6.00 15.00
J2JH Jeff Halpern 4.00 10.00
J2JI Jarome Iginla 6.00 15.00
J2JJ Jaromir Jagr 12.00 30.00
J2JO Jose Theodore 6.00 15.00
J2JP Joni Pitkanen 4.00 10.00
J2JR Jeremy Roenick 6.00 15.00
J2JS Joe Sakic 10.00 25.00
J2JU Justin Williams 5.00 12.00
J2JW Jason Williams 4.00 10.00
J2KC Kyle Calder 4.00 10.00
J2KD Kris Draper 8.00 20.00
J2KL Kari Lehtonen 5.00 12.00
J2KP Keith Primeau 6.00 15.00
J2LE Jordan Leopold 4.00 10.00
J2LO Matthew Lombardi 4.00 10.00
J2LR Luc Robitaille 6.00 15.00
J2LU Joffrey Lupul 5.00 12.00
J2LX Mario Lemieux SP 75.00 150.00
J2MA Maxim Afinogenov 4.00 10.00
J2MB Martin Brodeur 12.00 30.00
J2MC Bryan McCabe 4.00 10.00
J2MG Marian Gaborik 10.00 25.00
J2MH Martin Havlat 6.00 15.00
J2MK Miikka Kiprusoff 5.00 12.00
J2ML Manny Legace 6.00 15.00
J2MM Mike Modano 10.00 25.00
J2MN Markus Naslund 6.00 15.00
J2MO Mattias Ohlund 4.00 10.00
J2MP Michael Peca 5.00 12.00
J2MR Mike Ribeiro 5.00 12.00
J2MS Miroslav Satan 5.00 12.00
J2MT Marty Turco 6.00 15.00
J2MW Brenden Morrow 5.00 12.00
J2NA Nik Antropov 5.00 12.00
J2NB Nick Boynton 4.00 10.00
J2NI Rob Niedermayer 5.00 12.00
J2NK Nikolai Khabibulin SP 40.00 80.00
J2NL Nicklas Lidstrom 6.00 15.00
J2NO Mika Noronen 5.00 12.00
J2NZ Nikolai Zherdev 4.00 10.00
J2OK Olaf Kolzig 6.00 15.00
J2ON Jeff O'Neill 4.00 10.00
J2PA Mark Parrish 4.00 10.00
J2PB Peter Bondra 5.00 12.00
J2PE Patrik Elias 6.00 15.00
J2PF Peter Forsberg 10.00 25.00
J2PK Paul Kariya 8.00 20.00
J2PS Patrick Sharp 6.00 15.00
J2PT Pierre Turgeon 6.00 15.00
J2RD Rick DiPietro 5.00 12.00
J2RE Robert Esche 5.00 12.00
J2RF Ruslan Fedotenko 4.00 10.00
J2RK Brian Rafalski 5.00 12.00
J2RL Roberto Luongo 10.00 25.00
J2RN Rick Nash 6.00 15.00
J2RO Brian Rolston 5.00 12.00
J2RS Ryan Smyth 5.00 12.00
J2RT Raffi Torres 4.00 10.00
J2RY Ryan Miller 6.00 15.00
J2SA Philippe Sauve 5.00 12.00
J2SB Sean Burke 4.00 10.00
J2SD Shane Doan 5.00 12.00
J2SH Shawn Horcoff 4.00 10.00
J2SK Sami Kapanen 4.00 10.00
J2SL Martin St. Louis 6.00 15.00
J2SN Scott Niedermayer 6.00 15.00
J2SO Sandis Ozolinsh 4.00 10.00
J2SP Jason Spezza 6.00 15.00
J2SV Marc Savard 4.00 10.00
J2SS Steve Sullivan 4.00 10.00
J2SU Mats Sundin 6.00 15.00
J2SV Sergei Samsonov 5.00 12.00
J2SW Stephen Weiss 4.00 10.00
J2SY Steve Yzerman SP 50.00 125.00
J2TB Todd Bertuzzi 6.00 15.00
J2TC Ty Conklin 5.00 12.00
J2TD Tie Domi 5.00 12.00
J2TH Trent Hunter 4.00 10.00
J2TL Trevor Linden 6.00 15.00
J2TO Tony Amonte 5.00 12.00
J2TP Tom Poti 4.00 10.00
J2TS Teemu Selanne 12.00 30.00
J2TV Tomas Vokoun 5.00 12.00
J2VK Viktor Kozlov 4.00 10.00
J2VL Vincent Lecavalier 5.00 12.00
J2VP Vaclav Prospal 4.00 10.00
J2WR Wade Redden 4.00 10.00
J2ZC Zdeno Chara 6.00 15.00
J2ZP Zigmund Palffy 6.00 15.00

2005-06 Upper Deck Majestic Materials

PRINT RUN 50 SER.#'d SETS
MMAF Alexander Frolov 8.00 20.00
MMAO Alexander Ovechkin 75.00 175.00
MMAP Alexander Perezhogin 10.00 25.00
MMAR Andrew Raycroft 15.00 40.00
MMAS Alexander Steen 15.00 40.00
MMAT Alex Tanguay 12.00 30.00
MMAY Alexei Yashin 15.00 40.00
MMBG Bill Guerin 8.00 20.00
MMBR Brad Richards 20.00 50.00
MMBS Brendan Shanahan 15.00 40.00
MMCH Jonathan Cheechoo 15.00 40.00
MMCP Chris Pronger 12.00 30.00
MMDA Daniel Alfredsson 15.00 40.00
MMDP Dion Phaneuf 20.00 50.00
MMDW Doug Weight 8.00 20.00
MMEB Ed Belfour 15.00 40.00
MMEJ Ed Jovanovski 8.00 20.00
MMEL Eric Lindros 15.00 40.00
MMES Eric Staal 15.00 40.00
MMGB Gilbert Brule 10.00 25.00
MMGI Brian Gionta 15.00 40.00
MMHE Milan Hejduk 8.00 20.00
MMHK Dominik Hasek 20.00 50.00
MMHL Henrik Lundqvist 25.00 60.00
MMHT Hannu Toivonen 10.00 25.00
MMHV Martin Havlat 8.00 20.00
MMHZ Henrik Zetterberg 15.00 40.00
MMIK Ilya Kovalchuk 20.00 50.00
MMJA Jason Allison 12.00 30.00
MMJB Jay Bouwmeester 12.00 30.00
MMJC Jeff Carter 15.00 40.00
MMJG Jean-Sebastien Giguere 8.00 20.00
MMJI Jarome Iginla 30.00 60.00
MMJJ Jaromir Jagr 25.00 60.00
MMJL Joffrey Lupul 8.00 20.00
MMJO Jose Theodore 15.00 40.00
MMJR Jeremy Roenick 15.00 40.00
MMJS Joe Sakic/40 30.00 60.00
MMJT Joe Thornton 15.00 40.00
MMKL Kari Lehtonen 10.00 25.00
MMKP Keith Primeau 8.00 20.00
MMKT Keith Tkachuk 8.00 20.00
MMLE Manny Legace 12.00 30.00
MMLR Luc Robitaille 15.00 40.00
MMMB Martin Brodeur 30.00 80.00
MMMG Marian Gaborik 25.00 60.00
MMML Mario Lemieux 50.00 100.00
MMMM Mike Modano 30.00 60.00
MMMN Markus Naslund 8.00 20.00
MMMP Michael Peca 8.00 20.00
MMMR Michael Ryder 8.00 20.00
MMMS Martin St.Louis 12.00 30.00
MMMT Marty Turco 10.00 25.00
MMMW Brenden Morrow 8.00 20.00
MMNL Nicklas Lidstrom 8.00 20.00
MMNZ Nikolai Zherdev 15.00 40.00
MMOK Olaf Kolzig 12.00 30.00
MMPB Patrice Bergeron 15.00 40.00

PD Pavel Datsyuk 12.50 30.00
PE Patrik Elias 8.00 20.00
PF Peter Forsberg 25.00 60.00
PK Paul Kariya 20.00 50.00
RB Rob Blake 8.00 20.00
RD Rick DiPietro 12.00 30.00
RE Mark Recchi 8.00 20.00
RI Mike Richards 12.00 30.00
RL Roberto Luongo 12.00 30.00
RM Ryan Miller 12.00 30.00
RN Rick Nash 25.00 60.00
RO Mike Ribeiro 8.00 20.00
RS Ryan Smyth 15.00 40.00
SA Miroslav Satan 10.00 25.00
SC Sidney Crosby 125.00 225.00
SD Shane Doan 12.00 30.00
SG Simon Gagne 20.00 50.00
SH Shawn Horcoff 8.00 20.00
SK Saku Koivu 15.00 40.00
SN Scott Niedermayer 15.00 40.00
SP Jason Spezza 20.00 50.00
SS Steve Sullivan 8.00 20.00
ST Matt Stajan 15.00 40.00
SU Mats Sundin
SW Stephen Weiss 12.00 30.00
SY Steve Yzerman 30.00 80.00
TB Todd Bertuzzi 10.00 25.00
TC Ty Conklin 10.00 25.00
TS Teemu Selanne 12.00 30.00
TV Tomas Vokoun 15.00 40.00
VA Thomas Vanek 12.00 30.00
VL Vincent Lecavalier 12.00 30.00
ZC Zdeno Chara 8.00 20.00
ZP Zigmund Palffy 15.00 40.00

2005-06 Upper Deck NHL Generations

AL ODDS 1:144
PLE ODDS 1:288
R J. Arnott/M.Ryder 5.00 12.00
B R.Bourque/J.Bouwmeest 8.00 20.00
T M.Brodeur/J.Theodore 15.00 40.00
D S.Fedorov/P.Datsyuk 8.00 20.00
B B.Guerin/D.Brown 5.00 12.00
L W.Gretzky/M.Lemieux 100.00 200.00
R S.Gagne/M.Ribeiro 5.00 12.00
V D.Hasek/T.Vokoun 10.00 25.00
J.Iginla/R.Nash 12.00 30.00
H J.Jagr/M.Havlat 10.00 25.00
S J.Kurri/T.Selanne 15.00 40.00
Z I.Kovalchuk/N.Zherdev 6.00 15.00
H J.Lehtinen/R.Hahl 5.00 12.00
L M.Messier/V.Lecavalier 8.00 20.00
Z M.Naslund/H.Zetterberg 8.00 20.00
B W.Redden/N.Boynton 5.00 12.00
C S.Stevens/Z.Chara 5.00 12.00
T B.Shanahan/J.Thornton 12.50 30.00
C M.Turco/T.Conklin 6.00 15.00
S S.Yzerman/J.Spezza 15.00 40.00
L Brodeur/Luongo/Leht 20.00 50.00
N Bossy/Thornton/Nash
P Clarke/Gagne/Primeau 15.00 40.00
A Fedorov/Kovalchuk/Afinog 20.00 50.00
S Gretzky/Yzerman/Sakic 225.00 350.00
R LaFleur/Koivu/Ribeiro 15.00 40.00
ST Messier/Shanahan/Thor 20.00 50.00
SN Neely/Shanahan/Nash 20.00 50.00
L Roy/Brodeur/Luongo 60.00 150.00
Z Sundin/Forsberg/Zetter 15.00 40.00
T Sakic/Heiduk/Tanguay 12.00 30.00
R Sakic/Iginla/Ribeiro 20.00 50.00
J Selanne/Koivu/Jokinen 12.50 30.00
P Sakic/Thornton/Spezza 20.00 50.00

2005-06 Upper Deck Notable Numbers

TED ODDS 1:288
TED PRINT RUN 1-99
RA Brian Rafalski/28 15.00 40.00
CH Chris Chelios/24
CO Carlo Colaiacovo/45 15.00 40.00
RC Craig Conroy/22 12.00 30.00
UB Dustin Brown/23 20.00 50.00
L Jamie Lundmark/21 15.00 40.00
L Jason Allison/41
R Jason Arnott/44 15.00 40.00
R Jani Rita/22 15.00 40.00
O Jeff O'Neill/92 10.00 25.00
J John-Michael Liles/26 20.00 50.00
H Jocelyn Thibault/41 20.00 50.00
AS Marco Sturm/19 20.00 50.00
BA Matthew Barnaby/38 12.00 30.00
BR Martin Brodeur/30 75.00 200.00
BY Mike Bossy/22 30.00 60.00
CO Matt Cooke/24
DE Marc Denis/30
DI Marcel Dionne/16 40.00 100.00
GA Mathieu Garon/30
GE Martin Gerber/29 30.00 80.00
HA Michal Handzus/26
NY Michael Nylander/92 8.00 20.00
PH Mark Parrish/37 25.00 60.00
RI Mike Ricci/40
SA Miroslav Satan/81 10.00 25.00
K Niko Kapanen/39 8.00 20.00
LE Pascal Leclaire/31 20.00 50.00
SY Petr Sykora/39
BO Ray Bourque/77 40.00 80.00
GO Sergei Gonchar/55
GZ Scott Gomez/23
SA Tony Salmelainen/42 15.00 40.00
MB P-M Bouchard/96 10.00 25.00
ON Rob Niedermayer/44 15.00 40.00
HS Philippe Sauve/30 15.00 40.00
A Adrian Aucoin/33
F Marc-Andre Fleury/29 75.00 150.00
H Ales Hemsky/83 12.00 30.00
N Nikolai Antropov/80 12.00 30.00
T Alex Tanguay/18 30.00 80.00
Y Alexei Yashin/79 10.00 25.00
A Milan Bartovic/15
B Brad Boyes/26 20.00 50.00
C Bobby Clarke/16 30.00 80.00
Martin Biron/43 15.00 40.00
R Brad Richards/19 30.00 80.00
S Borje Salming/21
Y Bryan McCabe/24 30.00 80.00
B Christian Backman/55 6.00 15.00
D Chris Drury/23 15.00 40.00
E Christian Ehrhoff/44 12.00 30.00
O Chris Osgood/30 20.00 50.00
P Chris Pronger/44 20.00 50.00
S Cory Stillman/61 10.00 25.00
A Dave Andreychuk/25
B Daniel Briere/48 20.00 50.00
C Dan Cloutier/39 20.00 50.00
F Dan Fritsche/49 10.00 25.00
H Dominik Hasek/39 40.00 100.00
M Darren McCarty/25 10.00 25.00
R Dwayne Roloson/30 20.00 50.00
S Darryl Sittler/27

NDW Doug Weight/39 20.00 50.00
NEB Ed Belfour/20 25.00 60.00
NEC Erik Cole/26 25.00 60.00
NED Eric Daze/55 12.00 30.00
NEJ Ed Jovanovski/55 15.00 40.00
NEN Evgeni Nabokov/20 15.00 40.00
NFP Fernando Pisani/34
NFR Alexander Frolov/24 25.00 60.00
NFT Fedor Tyutin/51 10.00 25.00
NGC Gerry Cheevers/30 30.00 80.00
NGF Grant Fuhr/31 30.00 80.00
NGI Jean-Sebastien Giguere/35 15.00 40.00
NGL Georges Laraque/27 20.00 50.00
NGM Glen Murray/27 20.00 40.00
NHE Dany Heatley/15
NHJ Milan Hejduk/23 15.00 40.00
NHO Marcel Hossa/81 10.00 25.00
NHZ Henrik Zetterberg/40 25.00 60.00
NIK Ilya Kovalchuk/17 40.00 100.00
NIL Ian Laperriere/22 15.00 40.00
NJH Jochen Hecht/55 6.00 15.00
NJK Jari Kurri/17 40.00 100.00
NJL Joffrey Lupul/15 25.00 60.00
NJO Jose Theodore/60 20.00 50.00
NJP Joni Pitkanen/44 20.00 50.00
NJS Jason Spezza/19 50.00 120.00
NJT Joe Thornton/19 40.00 100.00
NJV Josef Vasicek/63 8.00 20.00
NKD Kris Draper/33 15.00 40.00
NKH Kristian Huselius/22 12.00 30.00
NKL Kari Lehtonen/32 25.00 60.00
NKP Keith Primeau/25 20.00 50.00
NKT Kimmo Timonen/44 8.00 20.00
NKW K.Weekes NOT MADE 8.00 20.00
NLM Larry Murphy/55 12.00 30.00
NLN Ladislav Nagy/17 25.00 60.00
NLR Luc Robitaille/20 25.00 60.00
NMA Maxim Afinogenov/61 15.00 40.00
NMC Mike Comrie/89 8.00 20.00
NMH Marian Hossa/18 30.00 80.00
NML Manny Legace/34 20.00 50.00
NMN Markus Naslund/19 20.00 50.00
NMO Olaf Kolzig/37 50.00 100.00
NMP Michael Peca/27 25.00 60.00
NMR Mike Ribeiro/71 12.00 30.00
NMS Martin St. Louis/26 20.00 50.00
NMT Marty Turco/35 20.00 50.00
NNB Nick Boynton/44 8.00 20.00
NND Niko Dimitrakos/23
NNH Nathan Horton/16 30.00 80.00
NNK Nikolai Khabibulin/53 20.00 50.00
NNO Mika Noronen/35 20.00 50.00
NPB Patrice Bergeron/37 20.00 50.00
NPD Pavol Demitra/38
NPO Mark Popovic/33 10.00 25.00
NPW Peter Worrell/28 15.00 40.00
NRE Robert Esche/42 15.00 40.00
NRF Ruslan Fedotenko/17 25.00 60.00
NRH Riku Hahl/32
NRM Ryan Miller/30 15.00 60.00
NRN Rick Nash/61 30.00 80.00
NRO Jeremy Roenick/97 20.00 50.00
NRS Ryan Smyth/94 20.00 50.00
NRV Rogie Vachon/30 30.00 60.00
NRY Michael Ryder/73 15.00 40.00
NRZ Richard Zednik/20
NSB Sean Burke/41 10.00 25.00
NSD Shane Doan/19 20.00 50.00
NSN Scott Niedermayer/27 20.00 50.00
NSS Sheldon Souray/44 10.00 25.00
NSZ Sergei Zubov/56 6.00 15.00
NTA Tyler Arnason/39 10.00 25.00
NTB Todd Bertuzzi/44 25.00 60.00
NTE Tony Esposito/35 25.00 60.00
NTG Tim Gleason/42 12.00 30.00
NTL Trevor Linden/16 40.00 100.00
NTN Tyson Nash/18
NTO Terry O'Reilly/24 30.00 60.00
NTR Tuomo Ruutu/15 25.00 60.00
NTV Steve Sullivan/26 10.00 25.00
NVP Vaclav Prospal/20 15.00 40.00
NVR Mike Van Ryn/26 10.00 25.00
NWG Wayne Gretzky/99 150.00 250.00

2005-06 Upper Deck Playoff Performers

COMPLETE SET (7) 12.00 25.00
STATED ODDS 1:24
PP1 Jarome Iginla 1.00 2.50
PP2 Martin St. Louis .75 2.00
PP3 Peter Forsberg 2.00 5.00
PP4 Wayne Gretzky 4.00 10.00
PP5 Jarome Iginla 1.00 2.50
PP6 Joe Sakic 1.50 4.00
PP7 Mario Lemieux 4.00 10.00

2005-06 Upper Deck Rookie Ink

RIAA Andrew Alberts/41 12.00 30.00
RIAM Andrej Meszaros/14 30.00 80.00
RIAP Alexander Perezhogin/42 12.00 30.00
RIAS Anthony Stewart/57 12.00 30.00
RIAW Andrew Wozniewski/55 12.00 30.00
RIBW Brad Winchester/26 20.00 50.00
RICB Cam Barker/25 12.00 30.00
RICC Chris Campoli/14 12.00 30.00
RICP Corey Perry/61 20.00 50.00
RICW Cam Ward/30 60.00 125.00
RIDL David Leneveu/30 20.00 50.00
RIEN Eric Nystrom/23 25.00 60.00
RIGB Gilbert Brule/17 15.00 40.00
RIGP George Parros/57 12.00 30.00
RIHL Henrik Lundqvist/30 50.00 100.00
RIHO Jeff Hoggan/22 15.00 40.00
RIHT Hannu Toivonen/33 25.00 60.00
RIJB Jaroslav Balastik/29 12.00 30.00
RIJC Jeff Carter/17 50.00 125.00
RIJF Johan Franzen/39 30.00 80.00
RIJH Jim Howard/35 25.00 60.00
RIJJ Jussi Jokinen/36 25.00 60.00
RIJS Jim Slater/23 12.00 30.00
RIJW Jeff Woywitka/29 15.00 40.00
RIKD Kevin Dallman/58 10.00 25.00
RIKN Kevin Nastiuk/35 15.00 40.00
RIMF Matt Foy/83 10.00 25.00
RIMJ Milan Jurcina/68 12.00 30.00
RIMK Mikko Koivu/21 60.00 100.00
RIMO Alvaro Montoya/29 25.00 60.00
RIMR Mike Richards/18 40.00 100.00
RIMT Maxime Talbot/25 25.00 60.00
RIPB Peter Budaj/31 30.00 80.00
RIPN Petteri Nokelainen/29 12.00 30.00
RIPP Petr Prucha/25 40.00 100.00
RIRB Rene Bourque/14 25.00 60.00
RIRC Ryane Clowe/29 15.00 40.00
RIRG Ryan Getzlaf/51 30.00 80.00
RIRH Ryan Hollweg/44 15.00 40.00
RIRN Robert Nilsson/21 25.00 60.00
RIRO Rostislav Olesz/85 12.00 30.00
RIRS Ryan Suter/20 30.00 80.00
RIRU R.J. Umberger/20 20.00 50.00
RIRW Ryan Whitney/19 25.00 60.00
RISC Sidney Crosby/87 225.00 400.00
RITV Thomas Vanek/26 75.00 150.00
RIYD Yann Danis/75 15.00 40.00

2005-06 Upper Deck Rookie Showcase

Available only via the Upper Deck website and one per customer, this 36-card set featured rookies making their debut in the 2005-06 season. Print run was limited to 1000 copies each.
ANNOUNCED PRINT RUN 1000
*BECKETT PROMO: .2X TO .5X
RS1 Corey Perry 20.00 50.00
RS2 Braydon Coburn 5.00 12.00
RS3 Hannu Toivonen 5.00 12.00
RS4 Thomas Vanek 10.00 25.00
RS5 Dion Phaneuf 8.00 20.00
RS6 Cam Ward 8.00 20.00
RS7 Brent Seabrook 10.00 25.00
RS8 Wojtek Wolski 4.00 10.00
RS9 Gilbert Brule 5.00 12.00
RS10 Jussi Jokinen 5.00 12.00
RS11 Jim Howard 12.00 30.00
RS12 Brad Winchester 5.00 12.00
RS13 Rostislav Olesz 4.00 10.00
RS14 George Parros 3.00 8.00
RS15 Matt Foy 3.00 8.00
RS16 Alexander Perezhogin 4.00 10.00
RS17 Ryan Suter 6.00 15.00
RS18 Zach Parise 12.00 30.00
RS19 Robert Nilsson 5.00 12.00
RS20 Henrik Lundqvist 20.00 50.00
RS21 Andrej Meszaros 4.00 10.00
RS22 Jeff Carter 8.00 20.00
RS23 David Leneveu 4.00 10.00
RS24 Sidney Crosby 25.00 60.00
RS25 Ryane Clowe 6.00 15.00
RS26 Jeff Woywitka 3.00 8.00
RS27 Evgeni Artyukhin 4.00 10.00
RS28 Alexander Steen 10.00 25.00
RS29 Rob McVicar 4.00 10.00
RS30 Alexander Ovechkin 25.00 60.00
RS31 Yann Danis 4.00 10.00
RS32 Eric Nystrom 4.00 10.00
RS33 Mike Richards 10.00 25.00
RS34 Ryan Getzlaf 12.00 30.00
RS35 Johan Franzen 8.00 20.00
RS36 Brandon Bochenski 5.00 12.00

2005-06 Upper Deck Rookie Threads

STATED ODDS 1:24
RTAA Andrew Alberts 2.00 5.00
RTAM Andrej Meszaros 2.50 6.00
RTAO Alexander Ovechkin 15.00 40.00
RTAP Alexander Perezhogin 2.50 6.00
RTAS Anthony Stewart 2.50 6.00
RTAW Andrew Wozniewski 2.50 6.00
RTBB Brandon Bochenski 3.00 8.00
RTBC Braydon Coburn 3.00 8.00
RTBL Brett Lebda 2.00 5.00
RTBS Brent Seabrook 6.00 15.00
RTBW Brad Winchester 3.00 8.00
RTCB Cam Barker 2.50 6.00
RTCP Corey Perry 12.00 30.00
RTCW Cam Ward 5.00 12.00
RTDK Duncan Keith 6.00 15.00
RTDL David Leneveu 2.50 6.00
RTDP Dion Phaneuf 5.00 12.00
RTEN Eric Nystrom 2.50 6.00
RTGB Gilbert Brule 3.00 8.00
RTGP George Parros 2.00 5.00
RTHL Henrik Lundqvist 12.00 30.00
RTHO Jim Howard 8.00 20.00
RTHT Hannu Toivonen 3.00 8.00
RTJB Jaroslav Balastik 2.00 5.00
RTJC Jeff Carter 5.00 12.00
RTJF Johan Franzen 5.00 12.00
RTJG Josh Gorges 2.50 6.00
RTJH Jeff Hoggan 2.00 5.00
RTJJ Jussi Jokinen 3.00 8.00
RTJM Jay McClement 2.00 5.00
RTJS Jim Slater 2.50 6.00
RTJW Jeff Woywitka 2.00 5.00
RTKB Keith Ballard 2.50 6.00
RTKD Kevin Dallman 2.50 6.00
RTKN Kevin Nastiuk 2.00 5.00
RTMF Matt Foy 2.00 5.00
RTMJ Milan Jurcina 2.50 6.00
RTMO Alvaro Montoya 3.00 8.00
RTMR Mike Richards 6.00 15.00
RTMT Maxime Talbot 3.00 8.00
RTNN Niklas Nordgren 3.00 8.00
RTPB Peter Budaj 4.00 10.00
RTPE Patrick Eaves 3.00 8.00
RTPN Petteri Nokelainen 2.00 5.00
RTPP Petr Prucha 3.00 8.00
RTRB Rene Bourque 3.00 8.00
RTRC Ryane Clowe 4.00 10.00
RTRG Ryan Getzlaf 8.00 20.00
RTRH Ryan Hollweg 2.00 5.00
RTRI Raitis Ivanans 2.00 5.00
RTRN Robert Nilsson 3.00 8.00
RTRO Rostislav Olesz 2.50 6.00
RTRS Ryan Suter 4.00 10.00
RTSC Sidney Crosby 30.00 80.00
RTST Alexander Steen 6.00 15.00
RTTH Timo Helbling 2.00 5.00
RTTV Thomas Vanek 6.00 15.00
RTWW Wojtek Wolski 2.50 6.00
RTYD Yann Danis 2.50 6.00
RTZP Zach Parise 8.00 20.00

2005-06 Upper Deck Rookie Threads Autographs

PRINT RUN 75 SER.#'d SETS
ARTAA Andrew Alberts 12.00 30.00
ARTAM Andrej Meszaros 15.00 40.00
ARTAS Anthony Stewart 15.00 40.00
ARTAW Andrew Wozniewski 15.00 40.00
ARTBB Brandon Bochenski 20.00 50.00
ARTBC Braydon Coburn 20.00 50.00
ARTBL Brett Lebda 12.00 30.00
ARTBS Brent Seabrook 40.00 100.00
ARTBW Brad Winchester 20.00 50.00
ARTCW Cam Ward 30.00 80.00
ARTDK Duncan Keith 40.00 100.00
ARTDL David Leneveu 15.00 40.00
ARTDP Dion Phaneuf 30.00 80.00
ARTEN Eric Nystrom 15.00 40.00
ARTGB Gilbert Brule 20.00 50.00
ARTGP George Parros 12.00 30.00
ARTHO Jim Howard 25.00 60.00
ARTHT Hannu Toivonen 20.00 50.00
ARTJB Jaroslav Balastik 12.00 30.00
ARTJF Johan Franzen 20.00 50.00
ARTJG Josh Gorges 15.00 40.00
ARTJH Jeff Hoggan 12.00 30.00
ARTJJ Jussi Jokinen 15.00 40.00
ARTJM Jay McClement 12.00 30.00
ARTJS Jim Slater 15.00 40.00
ARTJW Jeff Woywitka 12.00 30.00
ARTKB Keith Ballard 15.00 40.00
ARTKD Kevin Dallman 15.00 40.00
ARTKN Kevin Nastiuk 12.00 30.00
ARTMF Matt Foy 12.00 30.00
ARTMJ Milan Jurcina 15.00 40.00
ARTMO Alvaro Montoya 20.00 50.00
ARTMT Maxime Talbot 20.00 50.00
ARTNN Niklas Nordgren 20.00 50.00
ARTPB Peter Budaj 25.00 60.00
ARTPE Patrick Eaves 20.00 50.00
ARTPN Petteri Nokelainen 12.00 30.00
ARTPP Petr Prucha 15.00 40.00
ARTRB Rene Bourque 20.00 50.00
ARTRH Ryan Hollweg 12.00 30.00
ARTRI Raitis Ivanans 12.00 30.00
ARTRN Robert Nilsson 20.00 50.00
ARTRO Rostislav Olesz 15.00 40.00
ARTRS Ryan Suter 25.00 60.00
ARTTH Timo Helbling 12.00 30.00
ARTWW Wojtek Wolski 15.00 40.00
ARTYD Yann Danis 15.00 40.00
ARTZP Zach Parise 25.00 60.00

2005-06 Upper Deck School of Hard Knocks

COMPLETE SET (7) 5.00 10.00
STATED ODDS 1:24
HK1 Scott Stevens .75 2.00
HK2 Chris Pronger .60 1.50
HK3 Chris Simon .50 1.25
HK4 Jeremy Roenick .75 2.00
HK5 Tie Domi .60 1.50
HK6 Ed Jovanovski .60 1.50
HK7 Brendan Shanahan 1.00 2.50

2005-06 Upper Deck Scrapbooks

COMPLETE SET (30) 10.00 25.00
RANDOM INSERT IN RETAIL PACKS
HS1 Ilya Kovalchuk .30 .75
HS2 Wayne Gretzky 1.50 4.00
HS3 Joe Thornton .40 1.00
HS4 Kari Lehtonen .25 .60
HS5 Dominik Hasek .50 1.25
HS6 Mario Lemieux 1.00 2.50
HS7 Jose Theodore .30 .75
HS8 Paul Kariya .40 1.00
HS9 Mike Modano .50 1.25
HS10 Rick Nash .30 .75
HS11 Mark Messier .50 1.25
HS12 Jarome Iginla .30 .75
HS13 Peter Forsberg .40 1.00
HS14 Nikolai Khabibulin .30 .75
HS15 Dany Heatley .30 .75
HS16 Brett Hull .40 1.00
HS17 Marian Gaborik .50 1.25
HS18 Mats Sundin .30 .75
HS19 Steve Yzerman .75 2.00
HS20 Joe Sakic .50 1.25
HS21 Marian Hossa .25 .60
HS22 Markus Naslund .30 .75
HS23 Jaromir Jagr .75 2.00
HS24 Andrew Raycroft .25 .60
HS25 Ed Belfour .30 .75
HS26 Martin St. Louis .30 .75
HS27 Jeremy Roenick .30 .75
HS28 Brendan Shanahan .40 1.00
HS29 Sergei Fedorov .50 1.25
HS30 Martin Brodeur .60 1.50

2005-06 Upper Deck Shooting Stars Jerseys

STATED ODDS 1:32
SAM Alexander Mogilny 3.00 8.00
SBG Bill Guerin 4.00 10.00
SBH Brett Hull 5.00 12.00
SBR Brad Richards 4.00 10.00
SBS Brendan Shanahan 5.00 12.00
SCD Chris Drury 3.00 8.00
SDA Daniel Alfredsson 4.00 10.00
SDH Dany Heatley 6.00 15.00
SEL Eric Lindros 6.00 15.00
SGM Glen Murray 3.00 8.00
SHZ Henrik Zetterberg 5.00 12.00
SIK Ilya Kovalchuk 6.00 15.00
SJI Jarome Iginla 6.00 15.00
SJJ Jaromir Jagr SP 40.00 100.00
SJL John LeClair 4.00 10.00
SJR Jeremy Roenick 4.00 10.00
SJS Joe Sakic 8.00 20.00
SJT Joe Thornton 6.00 15.00
SKP Keith Primeau 4.00 10.00
SKT Keith Tkachuk 4.00 10.00
SLR Luc Robitaille 4.00 10.00
SMG Marian Gaborik 6.00 15.00
SMH Milan Hejduk 3.00 8.00
SMHA Martin Havlat 4.00 10.00
SMHO Marian Hossa 3.00 8.00
SML Mario Lemieux SP 25.00 60.00
SMME Mark Messier 10.00 25.00
SMMO Mike Modano 6.00 15.00
SMN Markus Naslund 4.00 10.00
SMP Michael Peca 3.00 8.00
SMP Mark Parrish 2.50 6.00
SMRI Mike Ribeiro 3.00 8.00
SMRY Michael Ryder 3.00 8.00
SMS Martin St. Louis 4.00 10.00
SMS Mats Sundin 4.00 10.00
SPB Peter Bondra 3.00 8.00
SPE Patrik Elias 4.00 10.00
SPK Paul Kariya 5.00 12.00
SRB Rob Blake 4.00 10.00
SRE Mark Recchi 5.00 12.00
SRN Rick Nash
SRS Ryan Smyth 3.00 8.00
SSF Sergei Fedorov 6.00 15.00
SSG Simon Gagne 4.00 10.00
SSS Sergei Samsonov 3.00 8.00
SSY Steve Yzerman 12.00 30.00
STA Tony Amonte 3.00 8.00
SVL Vincent Lecavalier 5.00 12.00
SZP Zigmund Palffy 4.00 10.00

2005-06 Upper Deck Sportsfest

NHL1 Sidney Crosby 10.00 25.00
NHL2 Wayne Gretzky 4.00 10.00
NHL3 Alexander Ovechkin 15.00
NHLAU Sidney Crosby AU/5

2005-06 Upper Deck Stars in the Making

SM1 Sidney Crosby 4.00 10.00
SM2 Alexander Ovechkin 4.00 10.00
SM3 Jeff Carter 1.25 3.00
SM4 Corey Perry 3.00 8.00
SM5 Thomas Vanek 1.50 4.00
SM6 Henrik Lundqvist 3.00 8.00
SM7 Alexander Perezhogin .60 1.50
SM8 Dion Phaneuf 1.25 3.00
SM9 Hannu Toivonen .75 2.00
SM10 Alexander Steen 1.50 4.00
SM11 Gilbert Brule .75 2.00
SM12 Mike Richards 1.50 4.00
SM13 Zach Parise 2.00 5.00
SM14 Wojtek Wolski .60 1.50

2005-06 Upper Deck Phenomenal Beginnings

COMPLETE SET (20) 15.00 30.00
COMMON CARD (1-20) .60 1.50
NNO Sidney Crosby AU

2006 Upper Deck Entry Draft

Set was issued as a wrapper redemption exclusively at the 2006 NHL Entry Draft in Vancouver.
COMPLETE SET (6) 15.00 30.00
DR1 Sidney Crosby 6.00 15.00
DR2 Alexander Ovechkin 4.00 10.00
DR3 Marc-Andre Fleury 1.25 3.00
DR4 Rick Nash 1.50 4.00
DR5 Ilya Kovalchuk 1.50 4.00
DR6 Joe Thornton 1.50 4.00

2006 Upper Deck Rookie Showdown

RSSCAO S.Crosby/A.Ovechkin 3.00 8.00

2006-07 Upper Deck

This 495-card set was issued in two series during the 2006-07 season. The first series of 245 cards was released in eight-card packs, with a $2.99 SRP which came 24 packs to a box and 12 boxes to a case. There are two Young Guns subsets in this product (201-250, 451-495) both of which were inserted into packs at a stated rate of one in four.
COMPLETE SET (495) 250.00 500.00
COMP.SER.1 w/o SPs (200) 12.00 30.00
COMP.SER.2 w/o SPs (200) 12.00 30.00
YOUNG GUN STATED ODDS 1:4
1 Corey Perry .25 .60
2 Ilya Bryzgalov .25 .60
3 Teemu Selanne .50 1.25
4 Andy McDonald .20 .50
5 Ryan Getzlaf .40 1.00
6 Francois Beauchemin .15 .40
7 Scott Niedermayer .25 .60
8 Kari Lehtonen .20 .50
9 Marian Hossa .20 .50
10 Slava Kozlov .15 .40
11 Jim Slater .15 .40
12 Garnet Exelby .15 .40
13 Bobby Holik .15 .40
14 Niclas Havelid .15 .40
15 Brad Boyes .15 .40
16 Brad Stuart .15 .40
17 Tim Thomas .30 .75
18 Marco Sturm .15 .40
19 Hannu Toivonen .20 .50
20 Glen Murray .20 .50
21 Ryan Miller .25 .60
22 Thomas Vanek .30 .75
23 Chris Drury .20 .50
24 Henrik Tallinder .15 .40
25 Jochen Hecht .15 .40
26 Brian Campbell .20 .50
27 Derek Roy .15 .40
28 Jarome Iginla .25 .60
29 Dion Phaneuf .25 .60
30 Robyn Regehr .15 .40
31 Jamie Lundmark .15 .40
32 Darren McCarty .15 .40
33 Kristian Huselius .15 .40
34 Chuck Kobasew .15 .40
35 Eric Staal .30 .75
36 Cam Ward .25 .60
37 Justin Williams .20 .50
38 Glen Wesley .15 .40
39 Mike Commodore .15 .40
40 Cory Stillman .15 .40
41 Ray Whitney .20 .50
42 Tuomo Ruutu .25 .60
43 Radim Vrbata .20 .50
44 Duncan Keith .30 .75
45 Nikolai Khabibulin .25 .60
46 Rene Bourque .15 .40
47 Patrick Sharp .25 .60
48 Jose Theodore .25 .60
49 Milan Hejduk .20 .50
50 Pierre Turgeon .25 .60
51 Andrew Brunette .15 .40
52 Wojtek Wolski .20 .50
53 John-Michael Liles .15 .40
54 Joe Sakic .40 1.00
55 Rick Nash .25 .60
56 Pascal Leclaire .20 .50
57 Adam Foote .15 .40
58 Alexandre Picard .15 .40
59 Bryan Berard .15 .40
60 Sergei Fedorov .40 1.00
61 Marty Turco .25 .60
62 Brenden Morrow .20 .50
63 Jussi Jokinen .20 .50
64 Sergei Zubov .20 .50
65 Jere Lehtinen .15 .40
66 Steve Ott .20 .50
67 Philippe Boucher .15 .40
68 Pavel Datsyuk .30 .75
69 Mikael Samuelsson .15 .40
70 Tomas Holmstrom .20 .50
71 Kris Draper .15 .40
72 Jason Williams .15 .40
73 Chris Osgood .25 .60
74 Robert Lang .15 .40
75 Ales Hemsky .20 .50
76 Fernando Pisani .15 .40
77 Jarret Stoll .20 .50
78 Marc-Andre Bergeron .15 .40
79 Dwayne Roloson .20 .50
80 Ethan Moreau .15 .40
81 Raffi Torres .15 .40
82 Joe Nieuwendyk .25 .60
83 Jay Bouwmeester .25 .60
84 Nathan Horton .25 .60
85 Rostislav Olesz .15 .40
86 Martin Gelinas .15 .40
87 Stephen Weiss .15 .40
88 Mathieu Garon .20 .50
89 Mike Cammalleri .15 .40
90 Alexander Frolov .15 .40
91 Lubomir Visnovsky .15 .40
92 George Parros .15 .40
93 Dustin Brown .25 .60
94 Marian Gaborik .30 .75
95 Wes Walz .15 .40
96 Pierre-Marc Bouchard .25 .60
97 Nick Schultz .15 .40
98 Derek Boogaard .15 .40
99 Todd White .15 .40
100 Saku Koivu .25 .60
101 Cristobal Huet .20 .50
102 Alex Kovalev .20 .50
103 Chris Higgins .15 .40
104 Andrei Markov .25 .60
105 Alexander Perezhogin .15 .40
106 Mathieu Dandenault .15 .40
107 Steve Sullivan .15 .40
108 Tomas Vokoun .20 .50
109 David Legwand .20 .50
110 Marek Zidlicky .15 .40
111 Kimmo Timonen .15 .40
112 Ryan Suter .20 .50
113 Jordin Tootoo .25 .60
114 Martin Brodeur .50 1.25
115 Brian Gionta .20 .50
116 Zach Parise .30 .75
117 Brian Rafalski .20 .50
118 Jamie Langenbrunner .15 .40
119 John Madden .15 .40
120 Jay Pandolfo .15 .40
121 Miroslav Satan .20 .50
122 Rick DiPietro .20 .50
123 Alexei Zhitnik .15 .40
124 Jeff Tambellini .15 .40
125 Chris Campoli .15 .40
126 Jason Blake .15 .40
127 Trent Hunter .15 .40
128 Jaromir Jagr .60 1.50
129 Petr Prucha .20 .50
130 Kevin Weekes .20 .50
131 Sandis Ozolinsh .15 .40
132 Ryan Hollweg .15 .40
133 Darius Kasparaitis .15 .40
134 Martin Straka .15 .40
135 Jason Spezza .25 .60
136 Ray Emery .20 .50
137 Andrej Meszaros .15 .40
138 Patrick Eaves .15 .40
139 Daniel Alfredsson .25 .60
140 Antoine Vermette .20 .50
141 Chris Phillips .15 .40
142 Peter Forsberg .30 .75
143 Robert Esche .20 .50
144 Mike Knuble .15 .40
145 Joni Pitkanen .15 .40
146 Mike Richards .25 .60
147 R.J. Umberger .15 .40
148 Sami Kapanen .15 .40
149 Shane Doan .20 .50
150 Keith Ballard .15 .40
151 Ladislav Nagy .15 .40
152 Mike Ricci .20 .50
153 Oleg Saprykin .15 .40
154 David Leneveu .20 .50
155 Sidney Crosby 1.00 2.50
156 Colby Armstrong .20 .50
157 John LeClair .25 .60
158 Sergei Gonchar .15 .40
159 Ryan Whitney .20 .50
160 Ryan Malone .15 .40
161 Joe Thornton .30 .75
162 Vesa Toskala .20 .50
163 Milan Michalek .15 .40
164 Marcel Goc .20 .50
165 Steve Bernier .15 .40
166 Jonathan Cheechoo .25 .60
167 Christian Ehrhoff .15 .40
168 Keith Tkachuk .25 .60
169 Barret Jackman .15 .40
170 Curtis Sanford .20 .50
171 Lee Stempniak .15 .40
172 Petr Cajanek .15 .40
173 Dallas Drake .15 .40
174 Martin St. Louis .25 .60
175 Vaclav Prospal .15 .40
176 Dan Boyle .20 .50
177 Ryan Craig .15 .40
178 Ruslan Fedotenko .15 .40
179 Paul Ranger .15 .40
180 Sean Burke .15 .40
181 Mats Sundin .25 .60
182 Darcy Tucker .20 .50
183 Alexander Steen .25 .60
184 Mikael Tellqvist .25 .60
185 Tomas Kaberle .15 .40
186 Nikolai Antropov .20 .50
187 Bryan McCabe .15 .40
188 Markus Naslund .20 .50
189 Henrik Sedin .25 .60
190 Mattias Ohlund .15 .40
191 Daniel Sedin .25 .60
192 Matt Cooke .15 .40
193 Sami Salo .15 .40
194 Ryan Kesler .30 .75
195 Brooks Laich .15 .40
196 Shaone Morrisonn .15 .40
197 Chris Clark .15 .40
198 Alexander Semin .25 .60
199 Sidney Crosby 1.00 2.50
200 Jaromir Jagr .60 1.50
201 Shane O'Brien YG RC 2.00 5.00
202 Ryan Shannon YG RC 2.00 5.00
203 Yan Stastny YG RC 2.00 5.00
204 Phil Kessel YG RC 25.00 60.00
205 Carsen Germyn YG RC 2.00 5.00
206 Dustin Byfuglien YG RC 12.00 30.00
207 Paul Stastny YG RC 8.00 20.00
208 Fredrik Norrena YG RC 2.00 5.00
209 Filip Novak YG RC 2.00 5.00
210 Loui Eriksson YG RC 6.00 15.00
211 Tomas Kopecky YG RC 2.50 6.00
212 M-A Pouliot YG RC 2.00 5.00
213 Ladislav Smid YG RC 2.00 5.00
214 Patrick Thoresen YG RC 2.00 5.00
215 Patrick O'Sullivan YG RC 3.00 8.00
216 Anze Kopitar YG RC 20.00 50.00
217 K.Pushkarev YG RC 2.50 6.00
218 Erik Reitz YG RC 2.00 5.00
219 Miroslav Kopriva YG RC 2.00 5.00
220 Niklas Backstrom YG RC 4.00 10.00
221 G.Latendresse YG RC 3.00 8.00
222 Shea Weber YG RC 15.00 40.00
223 Mikko Lehtonen YG RC 2.50 6.00
224 Frank Doyle YG RC 2.50 6.00
225 Travis Zajac YG RC 4.00 10.00
226 John Oduya YG RC 3.00 8.00
227 Ryan Caldwell YG RC 2.00 5.00
228 Masi Marjamaki YG RC 2.00 5.00
229 Matt Koalska YG RC 2.00 5.00
230 Jarkko Immonen YG RC 2.00 5.00
231 Nigel Dawes YG RC 2.00 5.00
232 Ryan Potulny YG RC 2.00 5.00
233 David Printz YG RC 2.00 5.00
234 Bill Thomas YG RC 2.00 5.00
235 Joel Perrault YG RC 2.00 5.00
236 Patrick Fischer YG RC 2.00 5.00
237 Noah Welch YG RC 2.00 5.00
238 Michel Ouellet YG RC 2.50 6.00
239 Jordan Staal YG RC 8.00 20.00
240 Kristopher Letang YG RC 15.00 40.00
241 Matt Carle YG RC 2.00 5.00
242 Marc-Edouard Vlasic YG RC 2.00 5.00
243 D.J. King YG RC 2.00 5.00
244 Ben Ondrus YG RC 2.00 5.00
245 Brendan Bell YG RC 2.00 5.00
246 Ian White YG RC 2.50 6.00
247 Jeremy Williams YG RC 2.00 5.00
248 Luc Bourdon YG RC 3.00 8.00
249 Eric Fehr YG RC 3.00 8.00
250 Phil Kessel YG CL 4.00 10.00
251 Chris Pronger .20 .50
252 Todd Fedoruk .15 .40
253 Chris Kunitz .25 .60
254 Jean-Sebastien Giguere .25 .60
255 Rob Niedermayer .20 .50
256 Todd Marchant .15 .40
257 Samuel Pahlsson .15 .40
258 Ilya Kovalchuk .25 .60
259 Steve Rucchin .15 .40
260 Niko Kapanen .15 .40
261 Greg de Vries .15 .40
262 Johan Hedberg .20 .50
263 Andy Sutton .15 .40
264 Scott Mellanby .15 .40
265 Patrice Bergeron .30 .75
266 Zdeno Chara .25 .60
267 Andrew Alberts .15 .40
268 P.J. Axelsson .15 .40
269 Marc Savard .15 .40
270 Paul Mara .15 .40
271 Wayne Primeau .15 .40
272 Daniel Briere .25 .60
273 Ales Kotalik .15 .40
274 Jiri Novotny .15 .40
275 Martin Biron .20 .50
276 Jason Pominville .25 .60
277 Maxim Afinogenov .15 .40
278 Jaroslav Spacek .15 .40
279 Alex Tanguay .15 .40
280 Daymond Langkow .15 .40
281 Roman Hamrlik .20 .50
282 Miikka Kiprusoff .20 .50
283 Jeff Friesen .15 .40
284 Andrew Ference .15 .40
285 Stephane Yelle .15 .40
286 Rod Brind`Amour .25 .60
287 Erik Cole .20 .50
288 Andrew Ladd .25 .60
289 John Grahame .15 .40
290 Tim Gleason .15 .40
291 Kevyn Adams .15 .40
292 Martin Havlat .15 .40
293 Brent Seabrook .25 .60
294 Adrian Aucoin .15 .40
295 Brian Boucher .20 .50
296 Bryan Smolinski .15 .40
297 Martin Lapointe .15 .40
298 Michal Handzus .20 .50
299 Marek Svatos .15 .40
300 Mark Rycroft .15 .40
301 Tyler Arnason .15 .40
302 Peter Budaj .20 .50
303 Patrice Brisebois .15 .40
304 Antti Laaksonen .15 .40
305 Ian Laperriere .15 .40
306 Fredrik Modin .15 .40
307 Rostislav Klesla .15 .40
308 Nikolai Zherdev .15 .40
309 Gilbert Brule .20 .50
310 David Vyborny .15 .40
311 Manny Malhotra .15 .40
312 Jody Shelley .15 .40
313 Mike Modano .40 1.00
314 Antti Miettinen .15 .40
315 Jeff Halpern .15 .40
316 Patrik Stefan .15 .40
317 Mike Ribeiro .20 .50
318 Eric Lindros .40 1.00
319 Dominik Hasek .30 .75
320 Chris Chelios .25 .60
321 Johan Franzen .25 .60
322 Mathieu Schneider .15 .40
323 Henrik Zetterberg .30 .75
324 Nicklas Lidstrom .25 .60
325 Ryan Smyth .20 .50
326 Steve Staios .15 .40
327 Jussi Markkanen .15 .40
328 Joffrey Lupul .20 .50
329 Jason Smith .15 .40
330 Shawn Horcoff .15 .40
331 Petr Sykora .20 .50
332 Olli Jokinen .25 .60
333 Ed Belfour .25 .60
334 Mike Van Ryn .15 .40
335 Jozef Stumpel .15 .40
336 Alexander Auld .15 .40
337 Todd Bertuzzi .25 .60
338 Gary Roberts .15 .40
339 Rob Blake .25 .60
340 Craig Conroy .15 .40
341 Dan Cloutier .20 .50
342 Mattias Norstrom .15 .40
343 Sean Avery .15 .40
344 Oleg Tverdovsky .15 .40
345 Manny Fernandez .20 .50
346 Brian Rolston .20 .50
347 Mikko Koivu .20 .50
348 Kim Johnsson .15 .40
349 Pavol Demitra .30 .75
350 Mark Parrish .15 .40
351 Kurtis Foster .15 .40
352 Michael Ryder .15 .40
353 David Aebischer .20 .50
354 Sergei Samsonov .20 .50
355 Sheldon Souray .15 .40
356 Mike Johnson .15 .40
357 Craig Rivet .15 .40
358 Radek Bonk .15 .40
359 Paul Kariya .30 .75
360 Scott Hartnell .25 .60
361 Martin Erat .15 .40
362 Jason Arnott .20 .50

363 Chris Mason .20 .50
364 J.P. Dumont .15 .40
365 Patrik Elias .25 .60
366 Scott Gomez .20 .50
367 Colin White .15 .40
368 Sergei Brylin .15 .40
369 Paul Martin .15 .40
370 Cam Janssen .15 .40
371 Alexei Yashin .20 .50
372 Mike Sillinger .15 .40
373 Arron Asham .15 .40
374 Mike York .15 .40
375 Mike Dunham .15 .40
376 Brendan Witt .15 .40
377 Henrik Lundqvist .50 1.25
378 Adam Hall .15 .40
379 Wayne Gretzky 1.25 3.00
380 Matt Cullen .15 .40
381 Michal Rozsival .15 .40
382 Michael Nylander .15 .40
383 Brendan Shanahan .30 .75
384 Dany Heatley .25 .60
385 Joe Corvo .15 .40
386 Peter Schaefer .15 .40
387 Chris Neil .15 .40
388 Wade Redden .15 .40
389 Martin Gerber .20 .50
390 Mike Fisher .15 .40
391 Simon Gagne .25 .60
392 Jeff Carter .25 .60
393 Antero Niittymaki .20 .50
394 Geoff Sanderson .15 .40
395 Fredrick Meyer .15 .40
396 Kyle Calder .15 .40
397 Curtis Joseph .25 .60
398 Ed Jovanovski .20 .50
399 Mike Comrie .20 .50
400 Nick Boynton .15 .40
401 Jeremy Roenick .25 .60
402 Georges Laraque .20 .50
403 Owen Nolan .20 .50
404 Marc-Andre Fleury .40 1.00
405 Nils Ekman .15 .40
406 Jarkko Ruutu .15 .40
407 Mark Eaton .15 .40
408 Dominic Moore .15 .40
409 Mark Recchi .30 .75
410 Patrick Marleau .25 .60
411 Scott Hannan .15 .40
412 Josh Gorges .15 .40
413 Mike Grier .15 .40
414 Mark Bell .15 .40
415 Evgeni Nabokov .20 .50
416 Doug Weight .25 .60
417 Dennis Wideman .15 .40
418 Jay McClement .15 .40
419 Manny Legace .20 .50
420 Bill Guerin .25 .60
421 Jay McKee .15 .40
422 Vincent Lecavalier .20 .50
423 Marc Denis .20 .50
424 Filip Kuba .15 .40
425 Tim Taylor .15 .40
426 Brad Richards .25 .60
427 Dimitry Afanasenkov .15 .40
428 Andrew Raycroft .20 .50
429 Kyle Wellwood .20 .50
430 Michael Peca .20 .50
431 Alexei Ponikarovsky .15 .40
432 Jeff O'Neill .15 .40
433 Jean-Sebastien Aubin .20 .50
434 Matt Stajan .20 .50
435 Dany Sabourin .15 .40
436 Roberto Luongo .40 1.00
437 Willie Mitchell .15 .40
438 Jan Bulis .15 .40
439 Brendan Morrison .15 .40
440 Trevor Linden .25 .60
441 Lukas Krajicek .15 .40
442 Alexander Ovechkin 1.00 2.50
443 Olaf Kolzig .25 .60
444 Richard Zednik .15 .40
445 Brian Pothier .15 .40
446 Donald Brashear .15 .40
447 Dainius Zubrus .15 .40
448 Ben Clymer .15 .40
449 Miikka Kiprusoff .20 .50
450 Wayne Gretzky 1.25 3.00
451 David McKee YG RC 2.00 5.00
452 Mark Stuart YG RC 2.00 5.00
453 Matt Lashoff YG RC 2.00 5.00
454 Mike Brown YG RC 2.00 5.00
455 Nate Thompson YG RC 2.00 5.00
456 Drew Stafford YG RC 3.00 8.00
457 Adam Dennis YG RC 2.00 5.00
458 Mike Card YG RC 2.00 5.00
459 Michael Funk YG RC 2.00 5.00
460 Michael Ryan YG RC 2.00 5.00
461 Dustin Boyd YG RC 2.00 5.00
462 Brandon Prust YG RC 2.00 5.00
463 Dave Bolland YG RC 4.00 10.00
464 Michael Blunden YG RC 2.00 5.00
465 Adam Burish YG RC 3.00 8.00
466 Stefan Liv YG RC 2.00 5.00
467 Alexei Mikhnov YG RC 2.00 5.00
468 Jeff Deslauriers YG RC 2.00 5.00
469 Jan Hejda YG RC 2.00 5.00
470 David Booth YG RC 2.50 6.00
471 Drew Larman YG RC 2.00 5.00
472 Peter Harrold YG RC 2.00 5.00
473 Barry Brust YG RC 2.50 6.00
474 Karri Ramo YG RC 2.00 5.00
475 Benoit Pouliot YG RC 2.50 6.00
476 Alex Radulov YG RC 10.00 25.00
477 Alex Brooks YG RC 2.00 5.00
478 Alexei Kaigorodov YG RC 2.00 5.00
479 Kelly Guard YG RC 2.50 6.00
480 Jussi Timonen YG RC 2.50 6.00
481 Martin Houle YG RC 2.50 6.00
482 Lars Jonsson YG RC 2.00 5.00
483 Triston Grant YG RC 2.00 5.00
484 Enver Lisin YG RC 2.00 5.00
485 Keith Yandle YG RC 4.00 10.00
486 Evgeni Malkin YG RC 100.00 200.00
487 Joe Pavelski YG RC 12.00 30.00
488 Roman Polak YG RC 2.50 6.00
489 Blair Jones YG RC 2.00 5.00
490 J-F Racine YG RC 2.50 6.00
491 Alexander Edler YG RC 3.00 8.00
492 Jesse Schultz YG RC 2.00 5.00
493 Nathan McIver YG RC 2.00 5.00
494 Patrick Coulombe YG RC 2.00 5.00
495 Evgeni Malkin YG CL 8.00 20.00

2006-07 Upper Deck Exclusives

*VETS/100: 10X TO 25X BASIC CARDS
*YOUNG GUNS/100: 1X TO 2.5X BASIC YG
486 Evgeni Malkin 150.00 300.00

2006-07 Upper Deck All-Time Greatest

COMPLETE SET (28) 15.00 40.00
STATED ODDS 1:12 SER. 2 PACKS
ATG1 Teemu Selanne 1.50 4.00
ATG2 Ilya Kovalchuk .75 2.00
ATG3 Bobby Orr 3.00 8.00
ATG4 Gilbert Perreault .75 2.00
ATG5 Joe Sakic 1.25 3.00
ATG6 Rick Nash .75 2.00
ATG7 Mike Modano 1.25 3.00
ATG8 Ted Lindsay .60 1.50
ATG9 Wayne Gretzky 3.00 8.00
ATG10 Marcel Dionne 1.00 2.50
ATG11 Marian Gaborik 1.00 2.50
ATG12 Tomas Vokoun .60 1.50
ATG13 Martin Brodeur 1.25 3.00
ATG14 Andy Bathgate .60 1.50
ATG15 Daniel Alfredsson .75 2.00
ATG16 Bobby Clarke .75 2.00
ATG17 Shane Doan .60 1.50
ATG18 Mario Lemieux 2.00 5.00
ATG19 Evgeni Nabokov .60 1.50
ATG20 Martin St. Louis .75 2.00
ATG21 Darryl Sittler .75 2.00
ATG22 Alexander Ovechkin 1.50 4.00
ATG23 Tony Esposito .75 2.00
ATG24 Mario Lemieux 2.00 5.00
ATG25 Guy Lafleur 1.00 2.50
ATG26 Gilbert Perreault .75 2.00
ATG27 Wayne Gretzky 3.00 8.00
ATG28 Johnny Bower 1.25 3.00

2006-07 Upper Deck All World

COMPLETE SET (30) 200.00 350.00
STATED ODDS 1:24 SER. 2 PACKS
AW1 Mike Modano 5.00 12.00
AW2 Nicklas Lidstrom 3.00 8.00
AW3 Joe Thornton 4.00 10.00
AW4 Teemu Selanne 6.00 15.00
AW5 Kari Lehtonen 2.50 6.00
AW6 Zdeno Chara 3.00 8.00
AW7 Jarome Iginla 3.00 8.00
AW8 Eric Staal 4.00 10.00
AW9 Martin Havlat 2.00 5.00
AW10 Milan Hejduk 2.50 6.00
AW11 Sergei Fedorov 5.00 12.00
AW12 Rick Nash 3.00 8.00
AW13 Henrik Zetterberg 4.00 10.00
AW14 Olli Jokinen 3.00 8.00
AW15 Marian Gaborik 4.00 10.00
AW16 Saku Koivu 3.00 8.00
AW17 Tomas Vokoun 2.50 6.00
AW18 Paul Kariya 4.00 10.00
AW19 Martin Gerber 2.50 6.00
AW20 Markus Naslund 2.50 6.00
AW21 Ilya Kovalchuk SP 12.50 30.00
AW22 Miikka Kiprusoff SP 12.50 30.00
AW23 Joe Sakic SP 25.00 60.00
AW24 Dominik Hasek SP 12.50 30.00
AW25 Martin Brodeur SP 15.00 40.00
AW26 Jaromir Jagr SP 15.00 40.00
AW27 Peter Forsberg SP 10.00 25.00
AW28 Sidney Crosby SP 15.00 40.00
AW29 Mats Sundin SP 10.00 25.00
AW30 Alexander Ovechkin SP 12.50 30.00

2006-07 Upper Deck Award Winners

COMPLETE SET (7) 8.00 20.00
COMMON CARDS .75 2.00
UNLISTED STARS 1.25 3.00
STATED ODDS 1:24
AW1 Joe Thornton 1.50 4.00
AW2 Miikka Kiprusoff 1.25 3.00
AW3 Nicklas Lidstrom .75 2.00
AW4 Alexander Ovechkin 2.00 5.00
AW5 Jaromir Jagr 1.50 4.00
AW6 Rod Brind'Amour .75 2.00
AW7 Cam Ward .75 2.00

2006-07 Upper Deck Biography of a Season

COMPLETE SET (15) 4.00 10.00
BOS1 Eric Staal .40 1.00
BOS2 Brendan Shanahan .40 1.00
BOS3 Mats Sundin .30 .75
BOS4 Evgeni Malkin 1.25 3.00
BOS5 Evgeni Malkin 1.25 3.00
BOS6 Ryan Miller .30 .75
BOS7 Patrick Roy .75 2.00
BOS8 Chris Pronger .25 .60
BOS9 Sidney Crosby 1.25 3.00
BOS10 Alexander Ovechkin 1.25 3.00
BOS11 Daniel Briere .30 .75
BOS12 Zach Parise .40 1.00
BOS13 Mark Recchi .40 1.00
BOS14 Joe Sakic .50 1.25
BOS15 Sidney Crosby 1.25 3.00

2006-07 Upper Deck Century Marks

COMPLETE SET (7) 10.00 25.00
STATED ODDS 1:24 SER. 2 PACKS
CM1 Joe Thornton 1.50 4.00
CM2 Alexander Ovechkin 5.00 12.00
CM3 Dany Heatley 1.25 3.00
CM4 Jaromir Jagr 3.00 8.00
CM5 Sidney Crosby 4.00 10.00
CM6 Eric Staal 1.50 4.00
CM7 Daniel Alfredsson 1.25 3.00

2006-07 Upper Deck Diary of a Phenom

COMPLETE SET (25) 15.00 40.00
COMMON MALKIN 1.00 2.50
ONE PER SER. 2 FAT PACK

2006-07 Upper Deck Game Dated Moments

STATED ODDS 1:288
GD1 Sidney Crosby 30.00 80.00
GD2 Alexander Ovechkin 20.00 50.00
GD3 Luc Robitaille 15.00 40.00
GD4 Dion Phaneuf 12.00 30.00
GD5 Miikka Kiprusoff 12.00 30.00
GD6 Jaromir Jagr 15.00 40.00
GD7 Jonathan Cheechoo 10.00 25.00
GD8 Martin Brodeur 20.00 50.00
GD9 Ilya Bryzgalov 6.00 15.00
GD10 Joffrey Lupul 6.00 15.00
GD11 Ryan Miller 10.00 25.00
GD12 Cam Ward 8.00 20.00
GD13 Teemu Selanne 12.00 30.00
GD14 Pierre Turgeon 6.00 15.00
GD15 Joe Thornton 15.00 40.00
GD16 Brian Leetch 12.00 30.00
GD17 Henrik Lundqvist 15.00 40.00
GD18 Alexander Ovechkin 20.00 50.00
GD19 Sidney Crosby 30.00 80.00
GD20 Ilya Kovalchuk 15.00 40.00
GD21 Sidney Crosby 30.00 80.00
GD22 Alexander Ovechkin 20.00 50.00
GD23 Joe Thornton 15.00 40.00
GD24 Fernando Pisani 6.00 15.00
GD25 Ryan Smyth 10.00 25.00
GD26 Rod Brind'Amour 10.00 25.00
GD27 Shawn Horcoff 6.00 15.00
GD28 Jose Theodore 10.00 25.00
GD29 Patrick Marleau 10.00 25.00
GD30 Daniel Briere 10.00 25.00
GD31 Chris Drury 10.00 25.00
GD32 Cam Ward 10.00 25.00
GD33 Martin Havlat 6.00 15.00
GD34 Michael Ryder 10.00 25.00
GD35 Martin Brodeur 15.00 40.00
GD36 R.J. Umberger 8.00 20.00
GD37 Jarome Iginla 12.00 30.00
GD38 Marian Gaborik 12.00 30.00
GD39 Marek Svatos 6.00 15.00
GD40 Joe Sakic 15.00 40.00
GD41 Cristobal Huet 15.00 40.00
GD42 Patrice Bergeron 10.00 25.00

2006-07 Upper Deck Game Jerseys

STATED ODDS 1:12
JAA Arron Asham 3.00 8.00
JAF Alexander Frolov 4.00 10.00
JAH Ales Hemsky 4.00 10.00
JAK Alex Kovalev 3.00 8.00
JAL Jason Allison 3.00 8.00
JAM Andrej Meszaros 3.00 8.00
JAO Alexander Ovechkin SP 20.00 50.00
JAT Alex Tanguay 6.00 15.00
JAY Alexei Yashin 3.00 8.00
JBA Barret Jackman 3.00 8.00
JBB Brad Boyes 3.00 8.00
JBE Patrice Bergeron 6.00 15.00
JBG Bill Guerin 4.00 10.00
JBI Martin Biron 5.00 12.00
JBL Rob Blake 5.00 12.00
JBM Mark Bell 3.00 8.00
JBR Brian Rolston 3.00 8.00
JBS Brad Stuart 3.00 8.00
JBT Barry Tallackson 3.00 8.00
JBU Peter Budaj 5.00 12.00
JCC Chris Chelios 5.00 12.00
JCD Chris Drury 4.00 10.00
JCJ Curtis Joseph 6.00 15.00
JCO Chris Osgood 5.00 12.00
JCP Corey Perry 5.00 12.00
JCS Curtis Sanford 5.00 12.00
JDA Daniel Alfredsson 5.00 12.00
JDE Pavol Demitra 3.00 8.00
JDK Duncan Keith 3.00 8.00
JDP Daniel Paille 3.00 8.00
JDW Doug Weight 4.00 10.00
JEB Ed Belfour 6.00 15.00
JEJ Ed Jovanovski 3.00 8.00
JEL Eric Lindros 6.00 15.00
JGA Simon Gagne 5.00 12.00
JGL Georges Laraque 3.00 8.00
JHA Martin Havlat 5.00 12.00
JHE Milan Hejduk 5.00 12.00
JHO Marcel Hossa 3.00 8.00
JIK Ilya Kovalchuk SP 20.00 50.00
JJA Jason Arnott 3.00 8.00
JJB Jay Bouwmeester 4.00 10.00
JJC Jonathan Cheechoo 5.00 12.00
JJF Jeff Friesen 3.00 8.00
JJG Jean-Sebastien Giguere 5.00 12.00
JJI Jarome Iginla 8.00 20.00
JJJ Jaromir Jagr 8.00 20.00
JJL Joffrey Lupul 3.00 8.00
JJN Joe Nieuwendyk 5.00 12.00
JJO Jordan Leopold 3.00 8.00
JJS Jason Spezza 6.00 15.00
JJT Joe Thornton 8.00 20.00
JJW Jason Williams 3.00 8.00
JKD Kris Draper 3.00 8.00
JKP Keith Primeau 3.00 8.00
JKS Andrei Kostitsyn 3.00 8.00
JKT Keith Tkachuk 5.00 12.00
JLA Andrew Ladd 3.00 8.00
JLE Jere Lehtinen 4.00 10.00
JLU Jamie Lundmark 3.00 8.00
JLX Mario Lemieux SP 20.00 50.00
JMB Martin Brodeur 10.00 25.00
JMC Mike Comrie 3.00 8.00
JME Martin Erat 3.00 8.00
JMG Marian Gaborik 8.00 20.00
JMH Marian Hossa 6.00 15.00
JMI Mike Komisarek 3.00 8.00
JMK Miikka Kiprusoff 8.00 20.00
JML Manny Legace 3.00 8.00
JMM Mike Modano 8.00 20.00
JMN Markus Naslund 6.00 15.00
JMO Brendan Morrison 3.00 8.00
JMP Michael Peca 4.00 10.00
JMR Mark Recchi 4.00 10.00
JMS Marc Savard 4.00 10.00
JNK Nikolai Khabibulin 5.00 12.00
JPB Peter Bondra 5.00 12.00
JPD Pavel Datsyuk 5.00 12.00
JPF Peter Forsberg 8.00 20.00
JPP Petr Prucha 3.00 8.00
JRB Rod Brind'Amour 5.00 12.00
JRF Ruslan Fedotenko 3.00 8.00
JRH Ryan Hollweg 3.00 8.00
JRI Brad Richards 6.00 15.00
JRM Ryan Miller 6.00 15.00
JRU R.J. Umberger 3.00 8.00
JSC Sidney Crosby SP 200.00 350.00
JSG Scott Gomez 4.00 10.00
JSH Brendan Shanahan 6.00 15.00
JSM Matt Stajan 3.00 8.00
JSN Scott Niedermayer 4.00 10.00
JSS Sergei Samsonov 5.00 12.00
JST Steve Sullivan 3.00 8.00
JSU Scottie Upshall 3.00 8.00
JSW Stephen Weiss 3.00 8.00
JTC Ty Conklin 5.00 12.00
JTL Trevor Linden 6.00 15.00
JTP Tom Poti 3.00 8.00
JVL Vincent Lecavalier SP 15.00 30.00
JWR Wade Redden 3.00 8.00
J2AP Alexander Perezhogin 4.00 10.00
J2AR Andrew Raycroft 6.00 15.00
J2AS Alexander Steen 4.00 10.00
J2BB Brandon Bochenski 3.00 8.00
J2BC Bobby Clarke 5.00 12.00
J2BG Brian Gionta 4.00 10.00
J2BM Brenden Morrow 4.00 10.00
J2BP Brad Park 4.00 10.00
J2BR Bryan McCabe 3.00 8.00
J2BW Brendan Witt 3.00 8.00
J2CA Mike Cammalleri 4.00 10.00
J2CH Cristobal Huet 5.00 12.00
J2CK Chuck Kobasew 3.00 8.00
J2CN Cam Neely 8.00 20.00
J2CP Chris Pronger 4.00 10.00
J2CW Cam Ward 4.00 10.00
J2DB Daniel Briere 4.00 10.00
J2DC Dan Cloutier 3.00 8.00
J2DH Dominik Hasek 8.00 20.00
J2DP Dion Phaneuf 6.00 15.00
J2DR Dwayne Roloson 5.00 12.00
J2DS Daniel Sedin 4.00 10.00
J2DT Darcy Tucker 3.00 8.00
J2DU Ron Duguay 4.00 10.00
J2DW Dave Williams 6.00 15.00
J2EC Erik Cole 3.00 8.00
J2ES Eric Staal 6.00 15.00
J2GM Glen Murray 4.00 10.00
J2GR Gary Roberts 4.00 10.00
J2HE Dany Heatley 5.00 12.00
J2HL Henrik Lundqvist 5.00 12.00
J2HS Henrik Sedin 4.00 10.00
J2HZ Henrik Zetterberg 6.00 15.00
J2JB Jason Bacashihua 4.00 10.00
J2JC Jeff Carter 6.00 15.00
J2JJ Jussi Jokinen 4.00 10.00
J2JK Jakub Klepis 3.00 8.00
J2JP Joni Pitkanen 3.00 8.00
J2JR Jeremy Roenick 6.00 15.00
J2JS Joe Sakic 10.00 25.00
J2JT Jose Theodore 6.00 15.00
J2JW Justin Williams 3.00 8.00
J2KB Kevin Bieksa 3.00 8.00
J2KC Kyle Calder 3.00 8.00
J2KL Kari Lehtonen 6.00 15.00
J2KM Kirk Muller 3.00 8.00
J2KO Saku Koivu 6.00 15.00
J2LA Lanny McDonald 5.00 12.00
J2LM Larry Murphy 3.00 8.00
J2LX Mario Lemieux 15.00 40.00
J2MA Martin St. Louis 5.00 12.00
J2MC Mike Commodore 3.00 8.00
J2MF Manny Fernandez 5.00 12.00
J2MG Mike Grier 3.00 8.00
J2MH Michal Handzus 3.00 8.00
J2MJ Milan Jurcina 3.00 8.00
J2MP Mark Parrish 3.00 8.00
J2MR Michael Ryder 5.00 12.00
J2MS Marek Svatos 3.00 8.00
J2MT Marty Turco 5.00 12.00
J2MY Mike York 3.00 8.00
J2NH Nathan Horton 3.00 8.00
J2NL Nicklas Lidstrom 5.00 12.00
J2OJ Olli Jokinen 3.00 8.00
J2OK Olaf Kolzig 8.00 20.00
J2PE Patrik Elias/ 8.00 20.00
J2PK Paul Kariya 5.00 12.00
J2PM Patrick Marleau 5.00 12.00
J2PR Bob Probert 5.00 12.00
J2PS Peter Stastny 4.00 10.00
J2RB Ray Bourque 6.00 15.00
J2RD Rick DiPietro 5.00 12.00
J2RE Ron Ellis 3.00 8.00
J2RI Mike Ribeiro 3.00 8.00
J2RK Ryan Kesler 4.00 10.00
J2RL Roberto Luongo 6.00 15.00
J2RN Rick Nash 8.00 20.00
J2RO Patrick Roy 15.00 40.00
J2RS Ryan Smyth 5.00 12.00
J2SA Miroslav Satan 4.00 10.00
J2SB Steve Bernier 4.00 10.00
J2SC Stanislav Chistov 3.00 8.00
J2SD Shane Doan 4.00 10.00
J2SF Sergei Federov 5.00 12.00
J2SH Jody Shelley 4.00 10.00
J2SK Steve Konowalchuk 3.00 8.00
J2SO Sandis Ozolinsh 3.00 8.00
J2SS Sergei Samsonov 3.00 8.00
J2ST Jarret Stoll 3.00 8.00
J2SU Mats Sundin 5.00 12.00
J2SZ Sergei Zubov 3.00 8.00
J2TF Tomas Fleischmann 3.00 8.00
J2TH Tomas Holmstrom 4.00 10.00
J2TS Teemu Selanne 6.00 15.00
J2TT Tim Thomas 5.00 12.00
J2TV Tomas Vokoun 5.00 12.00
J2WG Wayne Gretzky SP 75.00 175.00
J2ZC Zdeno Chara 4.00 10.00

2006-07 Upper Deck Generations Duals

G2BL Brodeur/Luongo 30.00 60.00
G2BP Blake/Phaneuf 12.00 30.00
G2BW Belfour/Ward 10.00 25.00
G2DH Doan/Horton 10.00 25.00
G2EG Elias/Gaborik 10.00 25.00
G2FD Datsyuk/Fedorov 12.00 30.00
G2FK Frolov/Kovalev 8.00 20.00
G2FS Forsberg/Steen 15.00 40.00
G2GB Guerin/Brown 8.00 20.00
G2GC Gretzky/Crosby 75.00 150.00
G2HH Hossa/Hemsky 8.00 20.00
G2HS Hejduk/Svatos 8.00 20.00
G2IL Iginla/Lupul 12.00 30.00
G2JK Jokinen/Koivu 8.00 20.00
G2JO Jagr/Ovechkin 20.00 50.00
G2KD Koivu/Datsyuk 12.00 30.00
G2KL Kipper/Lehtonen 15.00 40.00
G2LP Lidstrom/Pitkanen 12.00 30.00
G2NB S.Nieder/J.Bouw 8.00 20.00
G2NZ Naslund/Zetty 10.00 25.00
G2PG Primeau/Getzlaf 10.00 25.00
G2RM Redden/Meszaros 8.00 20.00
G2SN Shanahan/Nash 10.00 25.00
G2SS Sakic/Spezza 20.00 50.00
G2TS Thornton/Staal 12.50 30.00
G2VH Vokoun/Hasek 12.00 30.00
G2PJD Sakic/Heatley 20.00 50.00
G2PSH Satan/Havlat 10.00 25.00

2006-07 Upper Deck Goal Rush

COMPLETE SET (14) 10.00 25.00
COMMON CARDS .75 2.00
SEMISTARS .75 2.00
UNLISTED STARS 1.00 2.50
ODDS 1:24 SER. 2 PACKS
GR1 Jonathan Cheechoo 1.00 2.50
GR2 Jaromir Jagr 2.50 6.00
GR3 Dany Heatley 1.00 2.50
GR4 Ilya Kovalchuk 1.00 2.50
GR5 Rick Nash 1.00 2.50
GR6 Marian Gaborik 1.25 3.00
GR7 Markus Naslund .75 2.00
GR8 Jarome Iginla 1.00 2.50
GR9 Alexander Ovechkin 1.25 3.00
GR10 Simon Gagne 1.00 2.50
GR11 Eric Staal 1.25 3.00
GR12 Teemu Selanne 2.00 5.00
GR13 Brendan Shanahan 1.25 3.00
GR14 Sidney Crosby 2.00 5.00

2006-07 Upper Deck Hometown Heroes

COMPLETE SET (28) 20.00 50.00
COMMON CARD .75 2.00
SEMISTARS .75 2.00
UNLISTED STARS 1.00 2.50
STATED ODDS 1:12
HH29 Teemu Selanne 2.00 5.00
HH30 Patrice Bergeron 1.25 3.00
HH31 Ryan Miller 1.00 2.50
HH32 Miikka Kiprusoff .75 2.00
HH33 Eric Staal 1.25 3.00
HH34 Henrik Zetterberg 1.25 3.00
HH35 Michael Ryder .60 1.50
HH36 Henrik Lundqvist 2.00 5.00
HH37 Jason Spezza 1.00 2.50
HH38 Simon Gagne 1.00 2.50
HH39 Sidney Crosby 3.00 8.00
HH40 Jonathan Cheechoo 1.00 2.50
HH41 Darcy Tucker .75 2.00
HH42 Alexander Ovechkin 4.00 10.00
HH43 Milan Hejduk .75 2.00
HH44 Patrick Marleau 1.00 2.50
HH45 Cristobal Huet .75 2.00
HH46 Cam Ward 1.00 2.50
HH47 Vincent Lecavalier .75 2.00
HH48 Kari Lehtonen .75 2.00
HH49 Nicklas Lidstrom 1.00 2.50
HH50 Roberto Luongo 1.50 4.00
HH51 Rob Blake 1.00 2.50
HH52 Marian Gaborik 1.25 3.00
HH53 Alexander Steen 1.00 2.50
HH54 Doug Weight 1.00 2.50
HH55 Marc-Andre Fleury 1.50 4.00
HH56 Dion Phaneuf 1.00 2.50

2006-07 Upper Deck Oversized Wal-Mart Exclusives

251 Chris Pronger 1.50 4.00
254 Jean-Sebastien Giguere 2.00 5.00
258 Ilya Kovalchuk 2.00 5.00
265 Patrice Bergeron 2.50 6.00
279 Alex Tanguay 1.25 3.00
282 Miikka Kiprusoff 1.50 4.00
286 Rod Brind'Amour 2.00 5.00
292 Martin Havlat 1.25 3.00
299 Marek Svatos 1.25 3.00
309 Gilbert Brule 1.50 4.00
313 Mike Modano 3.00 8.00
318 Eric Lindros 3.00 8.00
319 Dominik Hasek 2.50 6.00
323 Henrik Zetterberg 2.50 6.00
324 Nicklas Lidstrom 2.00 5.00
325 Ryan Smyth
333 Ed Belfour 2.00 5.00
337 Todd Bertuzzi 2.00 5.00
339 Rob Blake 2.00 5.00
345 Manny Fernandez
352 Michael Ryder
359 Paul Kariya
365 Patrik Elias 2.00 5.00
377 Henrik Lundqvist 4.00 10.00
379 Wayne Gretzky 5.00 12.00
383 Brendan Shanahan 2.50 6.00
384 Dany Heatley 2.00 5.00
391 Simon Gagne 2.00 5.00
392 Jeff Carter 2.00 5.00
401 Jeremy Roenick 2.00 5.00
403 Owen Nolan 1.50 4.00
404 Marc-Andre Fleury 3.00 8.00
409 Mark Recchi 3.00 8.00
410 Patrick Marleau 2.00 5.00
415 Evgeni Nabokov 1.50 4.00
417 Doug Weight 2.00 5.00
422 Vincent Lecavalier 1.50 4.00
426 Brad Richards 2.00 5.00
428 Andrew Raycroft 1.50 4.00
430 Michael Peca 1.50 4.00
436 Roberto Luongo 3.00 8.00
442 Alexander Ovechkin 4.00 10.00

2006-07 Upper Deck Rookie Game Dated Moments

STATED ODDS 1:288
RGD1 Ryan Shannon 4.00 10.00
RGD2 Phil Kessel 10.00 25.00
RGD3 Mark Stuart 4.00 10.00
RGD4 Yan Stastny 4.00 10.00
RGD5 Paul Stastny 10.00 25.00
RGD6 Loui Eriksson 6.00 15.00
RGD7 Tomas Kopecky 5.00 12.00
RGD8 Patrick Thoresen 4.00 10.00
RGD9 Ladislav Smid 4.00 10.00
RGD10 Marc-Antoine Pouliot 4.00 10.00
RGD11 Patrick O'Sullivan 6.00 15.00
RGD12 Anze Kopitar 15.00 40.00
RGD13 Guillaume Latendresse 6.00 15.00
RGD14 Shea Weber 10.00 25.00
RGD15 Mikko Lehtonen 5.00 12.00
RGD16 Travis Zajac 8.00 20.00
RGD17 Nigel Dawes 4.00 10.00
RGD18 Alexei Kaigorodov 4.00 10.00
RGD19 Ryan Potulny 4.00 10.00
RGD20 Joel Perrault 4.00 10.00
RGD21 Evgeni Malkin 25.00 60.00
RGD22 Jordan Staal 10.00 25.00
RGD23 Kristopher Letang 12.00 30.00
RGD24 Noah Welch 4.00 10.00
RGD25 Marc-Edouard Vlasic 4.00 10.00
RGD26 Matt Carle 4.00 10.00
RGD27 Ian White 5.00 12.00
RGD28 Ben Ondrus 4.00 10.00
RGD29 Luc Bourdon 6.00 15.00
RGD30 Eric Fehr 6.00 15.00

2006-07 Upper Deck Rookie Headliners

COMPLETE SET (30) 40.00 100.00
ONE PER SER. 2 FAT PACK
RH1 Patrick O'Sullivan 1.50 4.00
RH2 Loui Eriksson 1.50 4.00
RH3 Enver Lisin 1.00 2.50
RH4 Luc Bourdon 1.50 4.00
RH5 Noah Welch 1.00 2.50
RH6 Travis Zajac 2.00 5.00
RH7 Ladislav Smid 1.00 2.50
RH8 Ryan Potulny 1.00 2.50
RH9 Marc-Antoine Pouliot 1.00 2.50
RH10 Dave Bolland 1.50 4.00
RH11 Nigel Dawes 1.00 2.50
RH12 Marc-Edouard Vlasic 1.00 2.50
RH13 Patrick Thoresen 1.00 2.50
RH14 Matt Lashoff 1.00 2.50
RH15 Ian White 1.25 3.00
RH16 Alexei Mikhnov 1.00 2.50
RH17 Tomas Kopecky 1.25 3.00
RH18 Kristopher Letang 3.00 8.00
RH19 Michael Blunden 1.00 2.50
RH20 Brandon Prust 1.00 2.50
RH21 Evgeni Malkin SP 15.00 40.00
RH22 Phil Kessel SP 6.00 15.00
RH23 Jordan Staal SP 6.00 15.00
RH24 G. Latendresse SP 4.00 10.00
RH25 Anze Kopitar SP 10.00 25.00
RH26 Matt Carle SP 2.50 6.00
RH27 Paul Stastny SP 6.00 15.00
RH28 Alexander Radulov SP 5.00 12.00
RH29 Dustin Boyd SP 2.50 6.00
RH30 Drew Stafford SP 4.00 10.00

2006-07 Upper Deck Rookie Materials

STATED ODDS 1:24
*PATCH/15: 1X TO 2.5X BASIC JSY
RMBB Brendan Bell 2.50 6.00
RMBO Ben Ondrus 2.50 6.00
RMBT Billy Thompson 2.50 6.00
RMCG Carsen Germyn 2.50 6.00
RMDB Dustin Byfuglien 6.00 15.00
RMDK D.J. King 2.50 6.00
RMEF Eric Fehr 4.00 10.00
RMEM Evgeni Malkin 15.00 40.00
RMFN Filip Novak 2.50 6.00
RMGL Guillaume Latendresse 4.00 10.00
RMIW Ian White 3.00 8.00
RMJI Jarkko Immonen 2.50 6.00
RMJS Jordan Staal 6.00 15.00
RMJW Jeremy Williams 2.50 6.00
RMKL Kristopher Letang 8.00 20.00
RMKO Anze Kopitar 10.00 25.00
RMKP Konstantin Pushkarev 3.00 8.00
RMKY Keith Yandle 5.00 12.00
RMLB Luc Bourdon 4.00 10.00
RMLE Loui Eriksson 4.00 10.00
RMLS Ladislav Smid 2.50 6.00
RMMC Matt Carle 2.50 6.00
RMMP Marc-Antoine Pouliot 2.50 6.00
RMMS Mark Stuart 2.50 6.00
RMMV Marc-Edouard Vlasic 2.50 6.00
RMNB Niklas Backstrom 5.00 12.00
RMND Nigel Dawes 2.50 6.00
RMNO Fredrik Norrena 2.50 6.00
RMNW Noah Welch 2.50 6.00
RMPK Phil Kessel 6.00 15.00
RMPO Patrick O'Sullivan 4.00 10.00
RMPS Paul Stastny 6.00 15.00
RMPT Patrick Thoresen 2.50 6.00
RMRO Roman Polak 3.00 8.00
RMRP Ryan Potulny 2.50 6.00
RMRS Ryan Shannon 2.50 6.00
RMSO Shane O'Brien 2.50 6.00
RMSW Shea Weber 6.00 15.00
RMTK Tomas Kopecky 3.00 8.00
RMTZ Travis Zajac 5.00 12.00
RMYS Yan Stastny 2.50 6.00

2006-07 Upper Deck Shootout Artists

COMPLETE SET (14) 10.00 25.00
STATED ODDS 1:12
SA1 Jussi Jokinen .60 1.50
SA2 Miroslav Satan .60 1.50
SA3 Brad Richards .75 2.00
SA4 Alexander Ovechkin 2.00 5.00
SA5 Paul Kariya 1.00 2.50
SA6 Ales Hemsky .75 2.00
SA7 Mikko Koivu .75 2.00
SA8 Alexander Frolov .60 1.50
SA9 Jason Williams .60 1.50
SA10 Slava Kozlov .60 1.50
SA11 Brian Gionta .60 1.50
SA12 Vincent Lecavalier 1.00 2.50
SA13 Jaroslav Balastik .30 .75
SA14 Sergei Zubov .60 1.50

2006-07 Upper Deck Signatures

PRINT RUN 25 COPIES EXCEPT FOR SPs
RANDOM INSERTS IN SER. 2 PACKS
SAO Alexander Ovechkin SP 400.00 600.00
SAP A. Perezhogin 10.00 25.00
SAR Andrew Raycroft 15.00 40.00
SAT Alex Tanguay 20.00 50.00
SBB Brad Boyes 10.00 25.00
SBC Braydon Coburn 10.00 25.00
SBL Brett Lebda 10.00 25.00
SBO J. Bouwmeester
SCP Corey Perry SP
SCS Cory Stillman 10.00 25.00
SCT Chris Thorburn 10.00 25.00
SDC Dan Cloutier 10.00 25.00
SDH Dany Heatley SP 60.00 100.00
SDL David Legwand SP
SDP Daniel Paille 10.00 25.00
SDW Doug Weight SP
SEC Erik Cole 10.00 25.00
SEL Enver Lisin 10.00 25.00
SEM Evgeni Malkin 40.00 100.00
SEN Eric Nystrom 10.00 25.00
SES Eric Staal SP
SFP Fernando Pisani 10.00 25.00
SGB Gilbert Brule 20.00 40.00
SGH Gordie Howe SP 75.00 125.00
SGL G. Latendresse 15.00 40.00
SGM Glen Murray 15.00 40.00
SHL Henrik Lundqvist 30.00 80.00
SHZ Henrik Zetterberg 40.00 80.00
SJI Jarome Iginla SP
SJR Jeremy Roenick 20.00 50.00
SJS Jordan Staal 60.00 125.00
SJT Jeff Tambellini SP 12.00 30.00
SJW Justin Williams 10.00 25.00
SMB Martin Brodeur SP 125.00 200.00
SMG Marian Gaborik SP 75.00 125.00
SMM Mike Modano SP 40.00 80.00
SMN Markus Naslund 20.00 50.00
SMP Michael Peca 10.00 25.00
SMR Mike Ribeiro 10.00 25.00
SMS Martin St. Louis 15.00 40.00
SNK Nikolai Khabibulin 12.00 30.00
SPB Patrice Bergeron 20.00 50.00
SPH Dion Phaneuf 15.00 40.00
SPK Phil Kessel 25.00 60.00
SRH Ryan Hollweg 10.00 25.00
SRK Ryan Kesler 15.00 40.00
SRL Roberto Luongo 50.00 125.00
SSB Steve Bernier 12.00 30.00
SSC Sidney Crosby 200.00 300.00
SSG Simon Gagne 20.00 50.00
SSS Sergei Samsonov 10.00 25.00
SST Matt Stajan 15.00 40.00
STA Tyler Arnason 10.00 25.00
STV Thomas Vanek 25.00 60.00
SVL Vincent Lecavalier SP 200.00 300.00
SWG Wayne Gretzky SP
SYD Yann Danis 10.00 25.00
SZP Zach Parise 25.00 60.00

2006-07 Upper Deck Signature Sensations

STATED ODDS 1:288
SSAA Aaron Asham 3.00 8.00
SSAF Alexander Frolov 8.00 20.00
SSAH Adam Hall 3.00 8.00
SSAR Andrew Raycroft 8.00 20.00
SSAS Alexander Steen 8.00 20.00
SSAT Alex Tanguay 12.00 30.00
SSBB Brad Boyes 6.00 15.00
SSBL Brian Leetch 25.00 50.00
SSBO Jay Bouwmeester 10.00 25.00
SSBR Brian Rafalski 3.00 8.00
SSBW Brad Winchester
SSCH Chris Higgins 12.00 30.00
SSCK Chris Kunitz 8.00 20.00
SSCP Chris Phillips 3.00 8.00
SSDW Doug Weight 6.00 15.00
SSEJ Ed Jovanovski 5.00 12.00
SSEN Evgeni Nabokov 12.00 30.00
SSFL Marc-Andre Fleury 25.00 60.00
SSFS Fredrik Sjostrom 3.00 8.00
SSGM Glen Murray 6.00 15.00
SSHA Michal Handzus
SSHE Milan Hejduk
SSHT Hannu Toivonen 10.00 25.00
SSJB Jason Blake 3.00 8.00
SSJP Joni Pitkanen 12.00 30.00
SSJR Jeremy Roenick 12.00 30.00
SSJT Jose Theodore 8.00 20.00
SSKB Keith Ballard 3.00 8.00
SSKL Kari Lehtonen 12.00 30.00
SSKP Keith Primeau 3.00 8.00
SSKT Kimmo Timonen
SSMC Mike Comrie 3.00 8.00
SSMG Marian Gaborik 20.00 50.00
SSMH Martin Havlat 10.00 25.00
SSMK Miikka Kiprusoff 25.00 50.00
SSML Mario Lemieux 100.00 150.00
SSMP Mark Parrish 3.00 8.00
SSMS Miroslav Satan 5.00 12.00
SSNK Nikolai Khabibulin 15.00 40.00
SSPB Pierre-Marc Bouchard 6.00 15.00
SSPM Patrick Marleau
SSPR Chris Pronger 12.00 30.00
SSRB Rene Bourque 3.00 8.00
SSRF Ruslan Fedotenko 3.00 8.00
SSRN Rick Nash 20.00 50.00
SSRS Ryan Smyth EXCH 12.00 30.00
SSRU R.J. Umberger 6.00 12.00
SSRW Ryan Whitney 8.00 20.00
SSSC Sidney Crosby 75.00 150.00
SSSD Shane Doan 6.00 12.00
SSSG Scott Gomez 8.00 20.00
SSSH Shawn Horcoff
SSSS Steve Sullivan 3.00 8.00
SSTA Tyler Arnason 3.00 8.00
SSTL Trevor Linden 20.00 50.00
SSVT Vesa Toskala 12.00 30.00
SSWG Wayne Gretzky SP
SSWR Wade Redden 3.00 8.00
SSWW Wojtek Wolski 6.00 15.00

2006-07 Upper Deck Statistical Leaders

COMPLETE SET (7) 10.00 25.00
STATED ODDS 1:24
SL1 Joe Thornton 2.00 5.00
SL2 Jonathan Cheechoo .75 2.00
SL3 Alexander Ovechkin 4.00 10.00
SL4 Wade Redden .75 2.00
SL5 Martin Brodeur 3.00 8.00
SL6 Miikka Kiprusoff 2.00 5.00
SL7 Sean Avery .40 1.00

2006-07 Upper Deck Zero Men

COMPLETE SET (7) 8.00 20.00
ODDS 1:24 SER. 2 PACKS
ZM1 Martin Brodeur 3.00 8.00
ZM2 Dominik Hasek 2.00 5.00
ZM3 Roberto Luongo 1.25 3.00
ZM4 Miikka Kiprusoff 1.25 3.00
ZM5 Marty Turco 1.00 2.50
ZM6 Cam Ward 1.00 2.50
ZM7 Ed Belfour 1.00 2.50

2007 Upper Deck BAP Draft Redemption Premium

TYSC Sidney Crosby 4.00 10.00

2007 Upper Deck Goudey Sport Royalty

ONE PER HOBBY BOX LOADER
GH Gordie Howe 12.50 30.00
SC Sidney Crosby 12.50 30.00

2007 Upper Deck Goudey Sport Royalty Autographs

STATED ODDS TWO PER CASE
FOUND IN HOBBY BOX LOADER PACKS
EXCH DEADLINE 8/8/2009
GH Gordie Howe 50.00 100.00
SC Sidney Crosby 175.00 300.00

2007-08 Upper Deck

This set, which was issued over two series, was released in November, 2007 and February, 2008. The set was issued into the hobby in eight-card packs, with a $2.99 SRP, which came 24 packs to a box and 12 boxes to a case. As in previous years, the primary subset is a Young Guns (Rookie Cards) subsets which are found in packs at a stated rate of one in four. The Young Guns subsets comprise cards 201-250 and 451-500.

COMP.SER.1 SET w/o SPs (200) 20.00 50.00
COMP.SER.2 SET w/o SPs (200) 20.00 50.00
YOUNG GUN STATED ODDS 1:4
1 Nicklas Lidstrom .25 .60
2 Dan Cleary .20 .50
3 Kris Draper .15 .40
4 Dominik Hasek .30 .75
5 Henrik Zetterberg .30 .75
6 Jiri Hudler .20 .50
7 Brett Lebda .15 .40
8 J.P. Dumont .15 .40
9 Steve Sullivan .15 .40
10 Shea Weber .20 .50
11 Martin Erat .15 .40

2 Alexander Radulov .25 .60
3 David Legwand .20 .50
4 Manny Legace .20 .50
5 Lee Stempniak .20 .50
6 Jay McClement .15 .40
7 Eric Brewer .15 .40
8 Brad Boyes .15 .40
9 Barret Jackman .15 .40
0 Rick Nash .25 .60
1 Fredrik Norrena .15 .40
2 Rostislav Klesla .15 .40
3 Gilbert Brule .20 .50
4 David Vyborny .15 .40
5 Manny Malhotra .15 .40
6 Martin Havlat .25 .60
7 Rene Bourque .15 .40
8 Patrick Lalime .20 .50
9 Jason Williams .15 .40
0 Cam Barker .15 .40
1 Patrick Sharp .25 .60
2 Duncan Keith .25 .60
3 Markus Naslund .25 .60
4 Ryan Kesler .30 .75
5 Matt Cooke .15 .40
6 Kevin Bieksa .20 .50
7 Henrik Sedin .25 .60
8 Brendan Morrison .15 .40
9 Mattias Ohlund .15 .40
0 Marian Gaborik .30 .75
1 Stephane Veilleux .15 .40
2 Kim Johnsson .15 .40
3 Niklas Backstrom .25 .60
4 Brian Rolston .20 .50
5 Mikko Koivu .20 .50
6 Derek Boogaard .15 .40
7 Miikka Kiprusoff .20 .50
8 Matthew Lombardi .15 .40
9 Dion Phaneuf .25 .60
0 Craig Conroy .15 .40
1 Alex Tanguay .15 .40
2 Wayne Primeau .15 .40
3 Robyn Regehr .15 .40
4 Joe Sakic .40 1.00
5 Brett Clark .15 .40
6 Ian Laperriere .15 .40
7 Marek Svatos .15 .40
3 Peter Budaj .20 .50
9 John-Michael Liles .15 .40
0 Paul Stastny .25 .60
1 Dwayne Roloson .15 .40
2 Jarret Stoll .15 .40
3 Ladislav Smid .15 .40
4 Raffi Torres .15 .40
5 Marc-Antoine Pouliot .15 .40
6 Ales Hemsky .20 .50
7 Fernando Pisani .15 .40
8 Ryan Getzlaf .40 1.00
9 Andy McDonald .20 .50
0 Chris Pronger .20 .50
1 Ilya Bryzgalov .25 .60
2 Chris Kunitz .25 .60
3 Francois Beauchemin .15 .40
4 Dustin Penner .20 .50
5 Joe Thornton .30 .75
6 Milan Michalek .15 .40
7 Matt Carle .15 .40
8 Evgeni Nabokov .20 .50
9 Steve Bernier .15 .40
0 Mike Grier .15 .40
1 Joe Pavelski .25 .60
2 Mike Modano .40 1.00
3 Sergei Zubov .20 .50
4 Mike Smith .25 .60
5 Mike Ribeiro .20 .50
6 Brenden Morrow .25 .60
7 Jussi Jokinen .15 .40
8 Jeff Halpern .15 .40
9 Anze Kopitar .40 1.00
0 Dan Cloutier .20 .50
1 Dustin Brown .25 .60
2 Mike Cammalleri .20 .50
3 Rob Blake .25 .60
4 Patrick O'Sullivan .20 .50
5 Shane Doan .20 .50
6 Mikael Tellqvist .20 .50
7 Zbynek Michalek .15 .40
8 Keith Ballard .15 .40
9 Kevyn Adams .15 .40
00 Ed Jovanovski .15 .40
01 Patrik Elias .25 .60
02 Travis Zajac .20 .50
03 Jay Pandolfo .15 .40
04 Paul Martin .15 .40
05 Brian Gionta .20 .50
06 John Madden .15 .40
07 Zach Parise .30 .75
08 Sidney Crosby 1.00 2.50
09 Jordan Staal .25 .60
10 Jocelyn Thibault .20 .50
11 Sergei Gonchar .25 .60
12 Gary Roberts .15 .40
13 Erik Christensen .15 .40
14 Evgeni Malkin .75 2.00
15 Jaromir Jagr .60 1.50
16 Petr Prucha .15 .40
17 Marek Malik .15 .40
18 Sean Avery .15 .40
19 Marcel Hossa .15 .40
20 Michal Rozsival .15 .40
21 Ryan Hollweg .15 .40
22 Miroslav Satan .20 .50
23 Trent Hunter .15 .40
24 Mike Sillinger .15 .40
25 Marc-Andre Bergeron .15 .40
26 Rick DiPietro .20 .50
27 Brendan Witt .15 .40
28 Martin Biron .20 .50
29 Jeff Carter .25 .60
30 Ben Eager .15 .40
31 Simon Gagne .25 .60
32 R.J. Umberger .15 .40
33 Scottie Upshall .15 .40
34 Ryan Miller .25 .60
35 Thomas Vanek .30 .75
36 Derek Roy .15 .40
37 Brian Campbell .20 .50
38 Drew Stafford .20 .50
39 Maxim Afinogenov .15 .40
40 Jason Pominville .25 .60
41 Dany Heatley .25 .60
42 Wade Redden .15 .40
43 Chris Kelly .20 .50
44 Ray Emery .20 .50
45 Chris Neil .15 .40
46 Mike Fisher .15 .40
47 Chris Phillips .15 .40
48 Darcy Tucker .20 .50
49 Ian White .15 .40
50 Alexei Ponikarovsky .15 .40
51 Alexander Steen .25 .60
52 Andrew Raycroft .20 .50
153 Bryan McCabe .15 .40
154 Matt Stajan .20 .50
155 Michael Ryder .15 .40
156 Guillaume Latendresse .20 .50
157 Cristobal Huet .20 .50
158 Alex Kovalev .15 .40
159 Mark Streit .15 .40
160 Chris Higgins .15 .40
161 Tomas Plekanec .25 .60
162 Patrice Bergeron .30 .75
163 Hannu Toivonen .20 .50
164 Zdeno Chara .25 .60
165 Phil Kessel .30 .75
166 Chuck Kobasew .15 .40
167 P.J. Axelsson .15 .40
168 Glen Murray .15 .40
169 Ilya Kovalchuk .25 .60
170 Jim Slater .15 .40
171 Johan Hedberg .20 .50
172 Marian Hossa .20 .50
173 Bobby Holik .15 .40
174 Alexei Zhitnik .15 .40
175 Vincent Lecavalier .20 .50
176 Dan Boyle .20 .50
177 Ryan Craig .15 .40
178 Vaclav Prospal .15 .40
179 Marc Denis .20 .50
180 Brad Richards .25 .60
181 Eric Staal .30 .75
182 Rod Brind'Amour .25 .60
183 Cory Stillman .15 .40
184 Mike Commodore .15 .40
185 Erik Cole .15 .40
186 John Grahame .15 .40
187 Olli Jokinen .20 .50
188 Nathan Horton .25 .60
189 Stephen Weiss .15 .40
190 Jay Bouwmeester .20 .50
191 Alex Auld .15 .40
192 Rostislav Olesz .15 .40
193 Alexander Semin .25 .60
194 Chris Clark .15 .40
195 Olaf Kolzig .25 .60
196 Mike Green .25 .60
197 Brian Pothier .15 .40
198 Milan Jurcina .15 .40
199 Nicklas Lidstrom CL .25 .60
200 Sidney Crosby CL 1.00 2.50
201 Drew Miller YG RC 2.50 6.00
202 Bobby Ryan YG RC 12.00 30.00
203 Ryan Carter YG RC 2.00 5.00
204 Jonas Hiller YG RC 4.00 10.00
205 Bryan Little YG RC 3.00 8.00
206 Tobias Enstrom YG RC 3.00 8.00
207 Milan Lucic YG RC 10.00 25.00
208 David Krejci YG RC 6.00 15.00
209 Curtis McElhinney YG RC 2.50 6.00
210 Patrick Kane YG RC 50.00 125.00
211 Magnus Johansson YG RC 2.00 5.00
212 Jaroslav Hlinka YG RC 2.50 6.00
213 Tyler Weiman YG RC 2.50 6.00
214 Kris Russell YG RC 2.50 6.00
215 Jared Boll YG RC 2.50 6.00
216 Matt Niskanen YG RC 3.00 8.00
217 Matt Ellis YG RC 2.50 6.00
218 Sam Gagner YG RC 4.00 10.00
219 Rob Schremp YG RC 2.00 5.00
220 Tom Gilbert YG RC 2.50 6.00
221 Cory Murphy YG RC 2.00 5.00
222 Jack Johnson YG RC 2.50 6.00
223 Jonathan Bernier YG RC 6.00 15.00
224 Lauri Tukonen YG RC 2.00 5.00
225 Brady Murray YG RC 2.00 5.00
226 Petr Kalus YG RC 2.00 5.00
227 Carey Price YG RC 80.00 200.00
228 Jaroslav Halak YG RC 5.00 12.00
229 Ville Koistinen YG RC 2.00 5.00
230 Nicklas Bergfors YG RC 2.00 5.00
231 Andy Greene YG RC 2.00 5.00
232 Frans Nielsen YG RC 3.00 8.00
233 Ryan Callahan YG RC 4.00 10.00
234 Marc Staal YG RC 3.00 8.00
235 Brandon Dubinsky YG RC 4.00 10.00
236 Daniel Girardi YG RC 2.50 6.00
237 Brian Elliott YG RC 4.00 10.00
238 Nick Foligno YG RC 4.00 10.00
239 Denis Tolpeko YG RC 2.00 5.00
240 Peter Mueller YG RC 2.50 6.00
241 Daniel Winnik YG RC 2.50 6.00
242 Torrey Mitchell YG RC 2.50 6.00
243 Erik Johnson YG RC 3.00 8.00
244 Steve Wagner YG RC 2.00 5.00
245 Matt Smaby YG RC 2.00 5.00
246 Mike Lundin YG RC 2.00 5.00
247 Mason Raymond YG RC 3.00 8.00
248 Jannik Hansen YG RC 2.00 5.00
249 Nicklas Backstrom YG RC 12.00 30.00
250 Kane/Price/Jnsn YG CL 10.00 25.00
251 Pavel Datsyuk .30 .75
252 Chris Osgood .25 .60
253 Brian Rafalski .15 .40
254 Henrik Zetterberg .30 .75
255 Tomas Holmstrom .20 .50
256 Chris Chelios .25 .60
257 Johan Franzen .20 .50
258 Chris Mason .20 .50
259 Dan Hamhuis .15 .40
260 Radek Bonk .15 .40
261 Jordin Tootoo .25 .60
262 Jason Arnott .20 .50
263 Ryan Suter .20 .50
264 Marek Zidlicky .15 .40
265 Paul Kariya .30 .75
266 Christian Backman .15 .40
267 Doug Weight .25 .60
268 Martin Rucinsky .15 .40
269 Jay McKee .15 .40
270 Keith Tkachuk .25 .60
271 Pascal Leclaire .20 .50
272 Nikolai Zherdev .15 .40
273 Jason Chimera .15 .40
274 Adam Foote .15 .40
275 Rick Nash .25 .60
276 Sergei Fedorov .40 1.00
277 Fredrik Modin .15 .40
278 Nikolai Khabibulin .25 .60
279 Yanic Perreault .15 .40
280 Tuomo Ruutu .25 .60
281 Robert Lang .15 .40
282 Brent Sopel .15 .40
283 Brent Seabrook .25 .60
284 Sergei Samsonov .20 .50
285 Roberto Luongo .30 .75
286 Willie Mitchell .15 .40
287 Taylor Pyatt .15 .40
288 Aaron Miller .15 .40
289 Markus Naslund .25 .60
290 Lukas Krajicek .15 .40
291 Daniel Sedin .25 .60
292 Pavol Demitra .30 .75
293 Kurtis Foster .15 .40
294 Marian Gaborik .30 .75
295 Pierre-Marc Bouchard .25 .60
296 Josh Harding .20 .50
297 Mark Parrish .20 .50
298 Jarome Iginla .25 .60
299 Adrian Aucoin .15 .40
300 Marcus Nilson .15 .40
301 Daymond Langkow .15 .40
302 Cory Sarich .15 .40
303 Kristian Huselius .15 .40
304 Owen Nolan .20 .50
305 Jose Theodore .25 .60
306 Milan Hejduk .15 .40
307 Joe Sakic .40 1.00
308 Scott Hannan .15 .40
309 Wojtek Wolski .20 .50
310 Tyler Arnason .15 .40
311 Ryan Smyth .20 .50
312 Joni Pitkanen .15 .40
313 Ethan Moreau .15 .40
314 Dustin Penner .20 .50
315 Ales Hemsky .20 .50
316 Shawn Horcoff .15 .40
317 Matt Greene .15 .40
318 Geoff Sanderson .15 .40
319 Jean-Sebastien Giguere .25 .60
320 Todd Bertuzzi .25 .60
321 Scott Niedermayer .25 .60
322 Corey Perry .25 .60
323 Travis Moen .15 .40
324 Mathieu Schneider .15 .40
325 Sean O'Donnell .15 .40
326 Jonathan Cheechoo .20 .50
327 Marc-Edouard Vlasic .15 .40
328 Ryane Clowe .20 .50
329 Craig Rivet .15 .40
330 Joe Thornton .30 .75
331 Patrick Marleau .25 .60
332 Joe Pavelski .25 .60
333 Marty Turco .25 .60
334 Philippe Boucher .15 .40
335 Loui Eriksson .25 .60
336 Mattias Norstrom .15 .40
337 Mike Modano .40 1.00
338 Jere Lehtinen .15 .40
339 Alexander Frolov .15 .40
340 Lubomir Visnovsky .15 .40
341 Michal Handzus .20 .50
342 Brad Stuart .15 .40
343 Tom Preissing .15 .40
344 Ladislav Nagy .15 .40
345 Niko Kapanen .15 .40
346 Shane Doan .20 .50
347 Nick Boynton .15 .40
348 Fredrik Sjostrom .15 .40
349 Derek Morris .15 .40
350 Steven Reinprecht .15 .40
351 Martin Brodeur .50 1.25
352 Johnny Oduya .20 .50
353 Arron Asham .15 .40
354 Sergei Brylin .15 .40
355 Kevin Weekes .20 .50
356 Dainius Zubrus .15 .40
357 Marc-Andre Fleury .40 1.00
358 Ryan Malone .15 .40
359 Darryl Sydor .15 .40
360 Petr Sykora .20 .50
361 Evgeni Malkin .75 2.00
362 Colby Armstrong .15 .40
363 Mark Recchi .30 .75
364 Henrik Lundqvist .30 .75
365 Chris Drury .20 .50
366 Colton Orr .15 .40
367 Scott Gomez .20 .50
368 Michal Rozsival .15 .40
369 Brendan Shanahan .30 .75
370 Martin Straka .15 .40
371 Bill Guerin .25 .60
372 Wade Dubielewicz .20 .50
373 Chris Campoli .15 .40
374 Ruslan Fedotenko .15 .40
375 Bruno Gervais .15 .40
376 Mike Comrie .20 .50
377 Daniel Briere .25 .60
378 Mike Richards .25 .60
379 Kimmo Timonen .15 .40
380 Antero Niittymaki .20 .50
381 Simon Gagne .25 .60
382 Joffrey Lupul .20 .50
383 Scott Hartnell .25 .60
384 Tim Connolly .15 .40
385 Daniel Paille .15 .40
386 Jochen Hecht .15 .40
387 Ales Kotalik .15 .40
388 Ryan Miller .25 .60
389 Andrew Peters .15 .40
390 Daniel Alfredsson .25 .60
391 Dany Heatley .25 .60
392 Patrick Eaves .15 .40
393 Antoine Vermette .15 .40
394 Martin Gerber .20 .50
395 Jason Spezza .25 .60
396 Anton Volchenkov .15 .40
397 Vesa Toskala .20 .50
398 Nikolai Antropov .15 .40
399 Tomas Kaberle .15 .40
400 Jason Blake .20 .50
401 Simon Gamache .15 .40
402 Mats Sundin .25 .60
403 Kris Newbury .15 .40
404 Roman Hamrlik .15 .40
405 Bryan Smolinski .15 .40
406 Mike Komisarek .15 .40
407 Saku Koivu .25 .60
408 Andrei Kostitsyn .20 .50
409 Maxim Lapierre .15 .40
410 Josh Gorges .15 .40
411 Manny Fernandez .20 .50
412 Brandon Bochenski .15 .40
413 Patrice Bergeron .30 .75
414 Marco Sturm .15 .40
415 Dennis Wideman .15 .40
416 Tim Thomas .30 .75
417 Marc Savard .15 .40
418 Kari Lehtonen .20 .50
419 Ken Klee .15 .40
420 Ilya Kovalchuk .25 .60
421 Garnet Exelby .15 .40
422 Todd White .15 .40
423 Slava Kozlov .15 .40
424 Johan Holmqvist .20 .50
425 Chris Gratton .15 .40
426 Filip Kuba .15 .40
427 Michel Ouellet .15 .40
428 Paul Ranger .15 .40
429 Martin St. Louis .25 .60
430 Cam Ward .25 .60
431 Ray Whitney .20 .50
432 Eric Staal .30 .75
433 Tim Gleason .15 .40
434 Andrew Ladd .25 .60
435 Glen Wesley .15 .40
436 Justin Williams .20 .50
437 Tomas Vokoun .20 .50
438 Brett McLean .15 .40
439 Noah Welch .15 .40
440 Jozef Stumpel .15 .40
441 Steve Montador .15 .40
442 Mike Van Ryn .15 .40
443 Richard Zednik .15 .40
444 Alexander Ovechkin 1.00 2.50
445 Tom Poti .15 .40
446 Viktor Kozlov .15 .40
447 Donald Brashear .15 .40
448 Michael Nylander .15 .40
449 Joe Thornton .30 .75
450 Evgeni Malkin .75 2.00
451 Petteri Wirtanen YG RC 2.00 5.00
452 Kent Huskins YG RC 2.00 5.00
453 Ondrej Pavelec YG RC 6.00 15.00
454 Brett Sterling YG RC 2.00 5.00
455 Jonathan Sigalet YG RC 2.00 5.00
456 Tuukka Rask YG RC 20.00 50.00
457 Matt Hunwick YG RC 2.50 6.00
458 Vladimir Sobotka YG RC 2.50 6.00
459 Mark Mancari YG RC 2.50 6.00
460 Mike Weber YG RC 2.50 6.00
461 Matt Keetley YG RC 2.00 5.00
462 Jonathan Toews YG RC 100.00 200.00
463 Petri Kontiola YG RC 2.00 5.00
464 Jake Dowell YG RC 2.00 5.00
465 T.J. Hensick YG RC 2.50 6.00
466 Tomas Popperle YG RC 2.50 6.00
467 Marc Methot YG RC 2.00 5.00
468 Tobias Stephan YG RC 2.50 6.00
469 Chris Conner YG RC 2.00 5.00
470 Andrew Cogliano YG RC 3.00 8.00
471 Bryan Young YG RC 2.00 5.00
472 Zach Stortini YG RC 2.00 5.00
473 Martin Lojek YG RC 2.00 5.00
474 Stefan Meyer YG RC 2.50 6.00
475 Tanner Glass YG RC 2.00 5.00
476 Matt Moulson YG RC 3.00 8.00
477 James Sheppard YG RC 2.00 5.00
478 Cal Clutterbuck YG RC 3.00 8.00
479 Kyle Chipchura YG RC 3.00 8.00
480 Rich Peverley YG RC 3.00 8.00
481 Mark Fraser YG RC 2.00 5.00
482 David Clarkson YG RC 3.00 8.00
483 Rod Pelley YG RC 2.00 5.00
484 Greg Moore YG RC 2.50 6.00
485 Ivan Baranka YG RC 2.50 6.00
486 Alexander Nikulin YG RC 2.50 6.00
487 Steve Downie RC 2.50 6.00
488 Riley Cote YG RC 2.50 6.00
489 Martin Hanzal YG RC 2.50 6.00
490 Craig Weller YG RC 2.00 5.00
491 Daniel Carcillo YG RC 2.50 6.00
492 Tyler Kennedy YG RC 3.00 8.00
493 Devin Setoguchi YG RC 3.00 8.00
494 Lukas Kaspar YG RC 2.00 5.00
495 Thomas Greiss YG RC 4.00 10.00
496 David Perron YG RC 3.00 8.00
497 Jiri Tlusty YG RC 3.00 8.00
498 Anton Stralman YG RC 2.00 5.00
499 Chris Bourque YG RC 2.00 5.00
500 Toews/Tlusty/Setog YG CL 6.00 15.00

2007-08 Upper Deck Exclusives

*VETS/100: 12X TO 30X BASIC CARDS
*YOUNG GUN/100: 1.5X TO 4X BASIC YG
STATED PRINT RUN 100 SERIAL #'d SETS
210 Patrick Kane 300.00 450.00
227 Carey Price 300.00 450.00
250 Price/Kane/Johnson 10.00 25.00
462 Jonathan Toews 400.00 600.00

2007-08 Upper Deck All-Star Highlights

COMPLETE SET (21) 12.00 30.00
ONE PER SER. 1 FAT PACK
AS1 Zach Parise .75 2.00
AS2 Andy McDonald .50 1.25
AS3 Zdeno Chara .60 1.50
AS4 Roberto Luongo .75 2.00
AS5 Daniel Briere .60 1.50
AS6 Sidney Crosby 2.50 6.00
AS7 Alexander Ovechkin 2.50 6.00
AS8 Joe Sakic 1.00 2.50
AS9 Rick Nash .60 1.50
AS10 Brian Rolston .50 1.25
AS11 Dany Heatley .60 1.50
AS12 Marian Hossa .50 1.25
AS13 Dion Phaneuf .60 1.50
AS14 Phil Kessel .75 2.00
AS15 Ryan Getzlaf 1.00 2.50
AS16 Anze Kopitar 1.00 2.50
AS17 Eric Staal .75 2.00
AS18 Martin Brodeur 1.25 3.00
AS19 Evgeni Malkin 2.00 5.00
AS20 Ryan Miller .60 1.50
AS21 Joe Thornton .75 2.00

2007-08 Upper Deck All-World Team

COMPLETE SET (35)
AW1 Jarome Iginla 2.00 5.00
AW2 Martin Brodeur 4.00 10.00
AW3 Joe Thornton 2.50 6.00
AW4 Dany Heatley 2.00 5.00
AW5 Tomas Vokoun 1.50 4.00
AW6 Dominik Hasek 2.50 6.00
AW7 Saku Koivu 2.00 5.00
AW8 Miikka Kiprusoff 1.50 4.00
AW9 Ilya Kovalchuk 2.00 5.00
AW10 Alexander Ovechkin 8.00 20.00
AW11 Marian Gaborik 2.00 5.00
AW12 Henrik Lundqvist 2.50 6.00
AW13 Nicklas Lidstrom 2.00 5.00
AW14 Doug Weight 2.00 5.00
AW15 Ryan Miller 2.00 5.00
AW16 Sidney Crosby SP 25.00 60.00
AW17 Vincent Lecavalier SP 5.00 12.00
AW18 Michael Ryder 1.50 4.00
AW19 Eric Staal SP 8.00 20.00
AW20 Rick Nash SP 6.00 15.00
AW21 Jonathan Cheechoo SP 6.00 15.00
AW22 Patrik Elias 2.00 5.00
AW23 Martin Havlat 2.00 5.00
AW24 Milan Hejduk 1.50 4.00
AW25 Ales Hemsky 1.50 4.00
AW26 Kari Lehtonen 1.50 4.00
AW27 Ilya Kovalchuk SP 6.00 15.00
AW28 Evgeni Malkin SP 20.00 50.00
AW29 Miroslav Satan 1.50 4.00
AW30 Anze Kopitar 3.00 8.00
AW31 Henrik Zetterberg SP 8.00 20.00
AW32 Tomas Holmstrom 1.50 4.00
AW33 Dwayne Roloson 1.50 4.00
AW34 Zach Parise SP 8.00 20.00
AW35 Mike Modano SP 10.00 25.00

2007-08 Upper Deck Big Playmakers

STATED PRINT RUN 50 SER.#'d SETS
BPAA Alex Auld 8.00 20.00
BPAF Alexander Frolov 8.00 20.00
BPAH Ales Hemsky 10.00 25.00
BPAK Alex Kovalev 10.00 25.00
BPAM Andrej Meszaros 8.00 20.00
BPAN Anze Kopitar 20.00 50.00
BPAO Alexander Ovechkin 50.00 125.00
BPAR Alexander Radulov 12.00 30.00
BPAS Alexander Steen 12.00 30.00
BPAT Alex Tanguay 8.00 20.00
BPAY Alexei Yashin 10.00 25.00
BPBG Bill Guerin 12.00 30.00
BPBI Martin Biron 10.00 25.00
BPBL Rob Blake 12.00 30.00
BPBM Brendan Morrison 8.00 20.00
BPBO Peter Bondra 8.00 20.00
BPBR Brad Richards 12.00 30.00
BPBS Brendan Shanahan 15.00 40.00
BPBU Peter Budaj 10.00 25.00
BPCA Matt Carle 8.00 20.00
BPCH Chris Higgins 8.00 20.00
BPCW Cam Ward 12.00 30.00
BPDA Daniel Alfredsson 12.00 30.00
BPDH Dany Heatley 12.00 30.00
BPDL David Legwand 10.00 25.00
BPDR Dwayne Roloson 10.00 25.00
BPDW Doug Weight 12.00 30.00
BPEJ Ed Jovanovski 10.00 25.00
BPEL Eric Lindros 20.00 50.00
BPEN Evgeni Nabokov 10.00 25.00
BPES Eric Staal 15.00 40.00
BPFL Marc-Andre Fleury 20.00 50.00
BPGA Simon Gagne 12.00 30.00
BPGM Glen Murray 10.00 25.00
BPHA Dominik Hasek 15.00 40.00
BPHL Henrik Lundqvist 15.00 40.00
BPHS Henrik Sedin 12.00 30.00
BPIK Ilya Kovalchuk 12.00 30.00
BPJA Jason Arnott 10.00 25.00
BPJB Jay Bouwmeester 12.00 30.00
BPJC Jeff Carter 12.00 30.00
BPJG Jean-Sebastien Giguere 12.00 30.00
BPJI Jarome Iginla 12.00 30.00
BPJJ Jaromir Jagr 30.00 80.00
BPJL Jere Lehtinen 8.00 20.00
BPJS Jason Spezza 12.00 30.00
BPJT Joe Thornton 15.00 40.00
BPJW Justin Williams 10.00 25.00
BPKC Kyle Calder 8.00 20.00
BPKL Kari Lehtonen 10.00 25.00
BPKO Andrei Kostitsyn 10.00 25.00
BPKT Keith Tkachuk 12.00 30.00
BPLE Mario Lemieux 30.00 80.00
BPLN Ladislav Nagy 8.00 20.00
BPMA Maxim Afinogenov 8.00 20.00
BPMB Martin Brodeur 25.00 60.00
BPMC Bryan McCabe 8.00 20.00
BPMF Manny Fernandez 10.00 25.00
BPMG Marian Gaborik 15.00 40.00
BPMH Marian Hossa 15.00 40.00
BPMI Mikko Koivu 8.00 20.00
BPMK Miikka Kiprusoff 10.00 25.00
BPML Manny Legace 10.00 25.00
BPMM Milan Michalek 8.00 20.00
BPMN Markus Naslund 12.00 30.00
BPMO Mike Modano 20.00 50.00
BPMR Mark Recchi 15.00 40.00
BPMS Marc Savard 8.00 20.00
BPMT Marty Turco 12.00 30.00
BPNL Nicklas Lidstrom 12.00 30.00
BPPB Patrice Bergeron 15.00 40.00
BPPD Pavol Demitra 12.00 30.00
BPPE Patrik Elias 12.00 30.00
BPPF Peter Forsberg 15.00 40.00
BPPK Paul Kariya 15.00 40.00
BPPM Patrick Marleau 12.00 30.00
BPPR Patrick Roy 30.00 80.00
BPRA Andrew Raycroft 10.00 25.00
BPRB Ray Bourque 20.00 50.00
BPRD Rick DiPietro 10.00 25.00
BPRI Mike Ribeiro 10.00 25.00
BPRL Roberto Luongo 15.00 40.00
BPRM Ryan Miller 12.00 30.00
BPRN Rick Nash 12.00 30.00
BPRO Rod Brind'Amour 12.00 30.00
BPRS Ryan Smyth 12.00 30.00
BPSA Joe Sakic 20.00 50.00
BPSC Sidney Crosby 50.00 125.00
BPSD Shane Doan 10.00 25.00
BPSF Sergei Fedorov 20.00 50.00
BPSG Simon Gagne 10.00 25.00
BPSK Saku Koivu 12.00 30.00
BPSM Miroslav Satan 10.00 25.00
BPSN Scott Niedermayer 12.00 30.00
BPSU Mats Sundin 12.00 30.00
BPSV Marek Svatos 8.00 20.00
BPSW Shea Weber 10.00 25.00
BPTB Todd Bertuzzi 10.00 25.00
BPTS Teemu Selanne 25.00 60.00
BPVL Vincent Lecavalier 10.00 25.00

2007-08 Upper Deck Clear Cut Winners

STATED PRINT RUN 100 SER.#'d SETS
CCW1 Jean-Sebastien Giguere 8.00 20.00
CCW2 Ryan Getzlaf 12.00 30.00
CCW3 Ilya Kovalchuk 8.00 20.00
CCW4 Marian Hossa 6.00 15.00
CCW5 Patrice Bergeron 10.00 25.00
CCW6 Bobby Orr 30.00 80.00
CCW7 Ryan Miller 8.00 20.00
CCW8 Thomas Vanek 10.00 25.00
CCW9 Jarome Iginla 8.00 20.00
CCW10 Miikka Kiprusoff 6.00 15.00
CCW11 Dion Phaneuf 8.00 20.00
CCW12 Eric Staal 10.00 25.00
CCW13 Patrick Roy 30.00 80.00
CCW14 Joe Sakic 12.00 30.00
CCW15 Rick Nash 8.00 20.00
CCW16 Mike Modano 12.00 30.00
CCW17 Nicklas Lidstrom 8.00 20.00
CCW18 Henrik Zetterberg 10.00 25.00
CCW19 Gordie Howe 20.00 50.00
CCW20 Ales Hemsky 6.00 15.00
CCW21 Wayne Gretzky 40.00 100.00
CCW22 Olli Jokinen 6.00 15.00
CCW23 Anze Kopitar 20.00 50.00
CCW24 Marian Gaborik 10.00 25.00
CCW25 Saku Koivu 8.00 20.00
CCW26 Martin Brodeur 15.00 40.00
CCW27 Miroslav Satan 6.00 15.00
CCW28 Jaromir Jagr 20.00 50.00
CCW29 Henrik Lundqvist 10.00 25.00
CCW30 Mark Messier 20.00 50.00
CCW31 Ray Emery 6.00 15.00
CCW32 Dany Heatley 8.00 20.00
CCW33 Simon Gagne 8.00 20.00
CCW34 Shane Doan 6.00 15.00
CCW35 Marc-Andre Fleury 12.00 30.00
CCW36 Sidney Crosby 30.00 80.00
CCW37 Mario Lemieux 25.00 60.00
CCW38 Joe Thornton 10.00 25.00
CCW39 Vincent Lecavalier 6.00 15.00
CCW40 Mats Sundin 8.00 20.00
CCW41 Roberto Luongo 10.00 25.00
CCW42 Alexander Ovechkin 15.00 40.00
CCW43 Chris Pronger 6.00 15.00
CCW44 Scott Niedermayer 8.00 20.00
CCW45 Kari Lehtonen 6.00 15.00
CCW46 Phil Kessel 10.00 25.00
CCW47 Ray Bourque 12.00 30.00
CCW48 Marc Savard 5.00 12.00
CCW49 Jason Pominville 8.00 20.00
CCW50 Gilbert Perreault 8.00 20.00
CCW51 Alex Tanguay 5.00 12.00
CCW52 Cam Ward 8.00 20.00
CCW53 Justin Williams 6.00 15.00
CCW54 Ryan Smyth 6.00 15.00
CCW55 Paul Stastny 8.00 20.00
CCW56 Sergei Fedorov 12.00 30.00
CCW57 Marty Turco 8.00 20.00
CCW58 Pavel Datsyuk 10.00 25.00
CCW59 Dominik Hasek 10.00 25.00
CCW60 Dwayne Roloson 6.00 15.00
CCW61 Tomas Vokoun 6.00 15.00
CCW62 Alexander Frolov 5.00 12.00
CCW63 Mikko Koivu 6.00 15.00
CCW64 Michael Ryder 5.00 12.00
CCW65 Guillaume Latendresse 6.00 15.00
CCW66 Patrik Elias 8.00 20.00
CCW67 Bill Guerin 8.00 20.00
CCW68 Rick DiPietro 6.00 15.00
CCW69 Brendan Shanahan 10.00 25.00
CCW70 Chris Drury 6.00 15.00
CCW71 Jason Spezza 8.00 20.00
CCW72 Daniel Alfredsson 8.00 20.00
CCW73 Daniel Briere 8.00 20.00
CCW74 Jeff Carter 8.00 20.00
CCW75 Ed Jovanovski 6.00 15.00
CCW76 Evgeni Malkin 12.00 30.00
CCW77 Jordan Staal 8.00 20.00
CCW78 Jonathan Cheechoo 8.00 20.00
CCW79 Patrick Marleau 8.00 20.00
CCW80 Vesa Toskala 6.00 15.00
CCW81 Darcy Tucker 6.00 15.00
CCW82 Markus Naslund 8.00 20.00
CCW83 Daniel Sedin 8.00 20.00
CCW84 Alexander Semin 8.00 20.00

2007-08 Upper Deck Clutch Performers

COMPLETE SET (7) 8.00 20.00
STATED ODDS 1:16
CP1 Martin Brodeur 2.00 5.00
CP2 Alexander Ovechkin 4.00 10.00
CP3 Mats Sundin 1.00 2.50
CP4 Dominik Hasek 1.25 3.00
CP5 Jean-Sebastien Giguere 1.00 2.50
CP6 Joe Sakic 1.50 4.00
CP7 Jaromir Jagr 2.50 6.00

2007-08 Upper Deck Fab Four Fabrics

STATED ODDS 1:288
STATED PRINT RUN 100 SER.#'d SETS
FFBEGP Brod/Elias/Gion/Par 20.00 50.00
FFBLCM Brod/Lid/Cros/Malk 50.00 125.00
FFBNFK Blake/Nag/Fro/Kop 20.00 50.00
FFBRSS Bell/Ray/Staj/Sten 12.00 30.00
FFCAMV Conn/Afino/Mil/Van 15.00 40.00
FFDGBK Dem/Gab/Bouch/Koi 15.00 40.00
FFFCBK Ferr/Chara/Berg/Kess 10.00 25.00
FFGBLC Gag/Briere/Lupul/Cart 12.00 30.00
FFGSWD Guer/Sat/Witt/DiPiet 12.00 30.00
FFHLDZ Hasek/Lid/Dats/Zett 15.00 40.00
FFHRKK Hav/Ruut/Keith/Khabi 12.00 30.00
FFITKP Iginla/Tang/Kipr/Phan 12.00 30.00
FFJHHE Jagr/Hasek/Hej/Elias 30.00 80.00
FFKGOK Kolz/Green/Ovech/Klep 50.00 125.00
FFKTHN Kar/Tang/Heat/Nash 15.00 40.00
FFKWTL Kar/Weight/Tkach/Leg 15.00 40.00
FFLCGM Lem/Cros/Gretz/Mess 60.00 150.00
FFLMKB Luon/Morr/Kes/Biek 15.00 40.00
FFLNZF Lecl/Nash/Zher/Fed 20.00 50.00
FFLRSD Lecav/Richs/St. L/Den 12.00 30.00
FFLSWR Legw/Sull/Web/Radu 12.00 30.00
FFMTMJ Mo/Turco/Morr/Jokin 20.00 50.00
FFMWTM Mo/Weight/Tkach/Mill 20.00 50.00
FFNKFO Nab/Koval/Fed/Ovech 20.00 50.00
FFNLSS Nasl/Luongo/Sedins 15.00 40.00
FFRBLG Roy/Brod/Luon/Gig 30.00 80.00
FFRFCM Recc/Fleur/Cros/Malk 50.00 125.00
FFRJDB Roen/Jova/Doan/Bell 12.00 30.00
FFSHRH Stoll/Horc/Rolo/Hems 10.00 25.00
FFSJSL Shan/Jagr/Straka/Lund 30.00 80.00
FFSLFA Sund/Lids/Fors/Alf 15.00 40.00
FFSLKJ Selan/Leht/Koivu/Jokin 25.00 60.00
FFSLLS Sakic/Lind/Lecav/Spez 20.00 50.00
FFSNGG Selan/Nied/Gig/Getz 10.00 25.00
FFSSJS Sakic/Shan/Jagr/Sund 30.00 80.00
FFSTMT Sund/Tuck/McCa/Tosk 12.00 30.00
FFTKNL Tosk/Kipr/Niitt/Leht 10.00 25.00
FFTNCM Thorn/Nab/Chee/Mich 15.00 40.00
FFVJBH Vok/Jok/Bouw/Hort 12.00 30.00
FFWBSW Witt/Brind/Staal/Ward 15.00 40.00

2007-08 Upper Deck Game Jerseys

STATED ODDS 1:12
JAA Arron Asham 3.00 8.00
JAH Ales Hemsky 4.00 10.00
JAK Alex Kovalev 4.00 10.00
JAM Al MacInnis 5.00 12.00
JAO Alexander Ovechkin 20.00 50.00
JAP Alexander Perezhogin 3.00 8.00
JAR Andrew Raycroft 4.00 10.00
JAS Alexander Steen 5.00 12.00
JAT Alex Tanguay 4.00 10.00
JAY Alexei Yashin 4.00 10.00
JBB Brad Boyes 3.00 8.00
JBF Bernie Federko 3.00 8.00
JBG Bill Guerin 5.00 12.00
JBJ Barret Jackman 3.00 8.00
JBM Brendan Morrison 3.00 8.00
JBO Ray Bourque 8.00 20.00
JBR Bill Ranford 6.00 15.00
JBS Billy Smith 5.00 12.00
JCH Chris Higgins 5.00 12.00
JCI Dino Ciccarelli 5.00 12.00
JCJ Jonathan Cheechoo 5.00 12.00
JCP Chris Pronger 5.00 12.00
JCS Curtis Sanford 4.00 10.00
JCW Cam Ward 5.00 12.00
JDA Daniel Alfredsson 5.00 12.00
JDB Dustin Brown 5.00 12.00
JDC Dan Cloutier 4.00 10.00
JDH Dale Hawerchuk 6.00 15.00
JDK Duncan Keith 5.00 12.00
JDL David Legwand 4.00 10.00
JDP Daniel Paille 3.00 8.00
JDR Dwayne Roloson 4.00 10.00
JDS Daniel Sedin 5.00 12.00
JDW Doug Weight 5.00 12.00
JEJ Ed Jovanovski 4.00 10.00
JEL Eric Lindros 8.00 20.00
JEM Evgeni Malkin 12.00 30.00
JEN Evgeni Nabokov 4.00 10.00
JES Eric Staal 6.00 15.00
JGI Brian Gionta 4.00 10.00
JGM Glen Murray 4.00 10.00
JHA Dominik Hasek 6.00 15.00
JHE Dany Heatley 5.00 12.00
JHL Henrik Lundqvist 6.00 15.00
JHT Hannu Toivonen 4.00 10.00
JIK Ilya Kovalchuk 5.00 12.00
JJA Jay Bouwmeester 5.00 12.00
JJB Jason Bacashihua 4.00 10.00
JJC Jeff Carter 5.00 12.00
JJD J.P. Dumont 3.00 8.00
JJG Jean-Sebastien Giguere 5.00 12.00
JJH Jeff Hoggan 3.00 8.00
JJI Jarome Iginla 5.00 12.00
JJJ Jaromir Jagr 12.00 30.00
JJL Jamie Lundmark 3.00 8.00
JJO Joe Sakic 8.00 20.00
JJS Jarret Stoll 4.00 10.00
JJT Joe Thornton 6.00 15.00
JJW Justin Williams 4.00 10.00
JKC Kyle Calder 3.00 8.00
JKL Kari Lehtonen 4.00 10.00
JKO Andrei Kostitsyn 4.00 10.00
JKT Keith Tkachuk 5.00 12.00
JLR Larry Robinson 5.00 12.00
JLU Joffrey Lupul 4.00 10.00
JMA Mark Stuart 3.00 8.00
JMB Martin Brodeur 10.00 25.00
JMC Bryan McCabe 3.00 8.00
JME Andrej Meszaros 3.00 8.00
JMF Manny Fernandez 4.00 10.00
JMG Marian Gaborik 6.00 15.00
JMH Marian Hossa 4.00 10.00
JMI Milan Michalek 3.00 8.00
JMJ Milan Jurcina 3.00 8.00
JML M. Lemieux waist up 12.00 30.00
JMM Mike Modano 8.00 20.00
JMN Markus Naslund 5.00 12.00
JMO Brenden Morrow 4.00 10.00
JMR Michael Ryder 3.00 8.00
JMS Marek Svatos 3.00 8.00
JMT Marty Turco 5.00 12.00
JNL Nicklas Lidstrom 5.00 12.00
JON Ben Ondrus 3.00 8.00
JPB Patrice Bergeron 6.00 15.00
JPE Corey Perry 5.00 12.00
JPF Peter Forsberg 6.00 15.00
JPK Paul Kariya 6.00 15.00
JPS Patrik Stefan 3.00 8.00
JRB Rod Brind'Amour 5.00 12.00
JRI Brad Richards 5.00 12.00
JRS Ryan Smyth 4.00 10.00
JSA Borje Salming 5.00 12.00
JSC S. Crosby bent waist 12.00 30.00
JSH Brendan Shanahan 6.00 15.00
JSI Darryl Sittler 4.00 10.00
JSK Saku Koivu 5.00 12.00
JSP Jason Spezza 5.00 12.00
JST Brad Stuart 3.00 8.00
JSU Mats Sundin 5.00 12.00
JTW Tiger Williams 4.00 10.00
GJ2AF Alexander Frolov 3.00 8.00
GJ2AK Alex Kovalev 3.00 8.00
GJ2AL Andrew Ladd 3.00 8.00
GJ2BR Brian Rafalski 4.00 10.00
GJ2CC Carlo Colaiacovo 3.00 8.00
GJ2CD Chris Drury 4.00 10.00
GJ2CH Chris Chelios 5.00 12.00
GJ2CJ Curtis Joseph 5.00 12.00
GJ2CO Chris Osgood 5.00 12.00
GJ2DB Daniel Briere 5.00 12.00
GJ2DP Dion Phaneuf 5.00 12.00
GJ2DT Darcy Tucker 4.00 10.00
GJ2GG Scott Gomez 3.00 8.00
GJ2GR Gary Roberts 3.00 8.00
GJ2HS Henrik Sedin 5.00 12.00
GJ2HZ Henrik Zetterberg 6.00 15.00
GJ2JA Jason Arnott 4.00 10.00
GJ2JJ Jaromir Jagr 12.00 30.00
GJ2JL Jere Lehtinen 3.00 8.00
GJ2JP Joni Pitkanen 3.00 8.00
GJ2JS Jordan Staal 5.00 12.00
GJ2KB Kevin Bieksa 4.00 10.00
GJ2KO Anze Kopitar 8.00 20.00
GJ2LN Ladislav Nagy 3.00 8.00
GJ2MA Martin Brodeur 10.00 25.00
GJ2MB Mark Bell 3.00 8.00
GJ2MF Marc-Andre Fleury 8.00 20.00
GJ2ML M. Lemieux knees up 12.00 30.00
GJ2MM Mark Messier 8.00 20.00
GJ2OJ Olli Jokinen 4.00 10.00
GJ2OK Olaf Kolzig 5.00 12.00
GJ2PB Pierre-Marc Bouchard 5.00 12.00
GJ2PD Pavel Datsyuk 6.00 15.00
GJ2PF Peter Forsberg 6.00 15.00
GJ2PK Phil Kessel 6.00 15.00
GJ2PP Petr Prucha 3.00 8.00
GJ2PR Patrick Roy 12.00 30.00
GJ2RB Rob Blake 5.00 12.00
GJ2RD Rick DiPietro 4.00 10.00
GJ2RG Ryan Getzlaf 8.00 20.00
GJ2RL Roberto Luongo 6.00 15.00
GJ2RM Ryan Miller 5.00 12.00
GJ2RN Rick Nash 5.00 12.00
GJ2RS Ryan Smyth 4.00 10.00
GJ2RT Raffi Torres 3.00 8.00
GJ2SC S. Crosby upright 20.00 50.00
GJ2SD Shane Doan 4.00 10.00
GJ2SF Sergei Fedorov 8.00 20.00
GJ2SG Simon Gagne 5.00 12.00
GJ2SN Scott Niedermayer 5.00 12.00
GJ2SS Steve Sullivan 3.00 8.00
GJ2SW Stephen Weiss 3.00 8.00
GJ2TB Todd Bertuzzi 5.00 12.00
GJ2TS Teemu Selanne 10.00 25.00
GJ2TV Tomas Vokoun 4.00 10.00
GJ2VL Vincent Lecavalier 4.00 10.00
GJ2VT Vesa Toskala 4.00 10.00
GJ2WE Shea Weber 4.00 10.00

2007-08 Upper Deck Generation Next

COMPLETE SET (30) 12.00 30.00
RANDOM INSERTS IN TARGET PACKS
GN1 Alexander Ovechkin 3.00 8.00
GN2 Cam Ward .75 2.00
GN3 Corey Perry .75 2.00
GN4 Dion Phaneuf .75 2.00
GN5 Evgeni Malkin 2.50 6.00
GN6 Gilbert Brule .60 1.50
GN7 Guillaume Latendresse .60 1.50
GN8 Jordan Staal .75 2.00

GN9 Thomas Vanek 1.00 2.50
GN10 Phil Kessel 1.00 2.50
GN11 Ryan Getzlaf 1.25 3.00
GN12 Kari Lehtonen .60 1.50
GN13 Sidney Crosby 3.00 8.00
GN14 Steve Bernier .50 1.25
GN15 Zach Parise 1.00 2.50
GN16 Alexander Radulov .75 2.00
GN17 Alexander Semin .75 2.00
GN18 Anze Kopitar 1.25 3.00
GN19 Jack Johnson .60 1.50
GN20 Jeff Carter .75 2.00
GN21 Josh Harding .75 2.00
GN22 Kevin Bieksa .60 1.50
GN23 Lee Stempniak .50 1.25
GN24 Matt Carle .50 1.25
GN25 Mikko Koivu .60 1.50
GN26 Milan Michalek .50 1.25
GN27 Patrick Eaves .50 1.25
GN28 Paul Stastny .75 2.00
GN29 Rob Schremp .60 1.50
GN30 Wojtek Wolski .60 1.50

2007-08 Upper Deck Hometown Heroes

COMPLETE SET (28) 20.00 50.00
STATED ODDS 1:24
HH57 Marian Hossa 1.25 3.00
HH58 Thomas Vanek 2.00 5.00
HH59 Rick DiPietro 1.25 3.00
HH60 Pavel Datsyuk 2.00 5.00
HH61 Evgeni Malkin 5.00 12.00
HH62 Ray Emery 1.25 3.00
HH63 Paul Stastny 1.50 4.00
HH64 Zach Parise 2.00 5.00
HH65 Ryan Getzlaf 2.50 6.00
HH66 Alexander Semin 1.50 4.00
HH67 Dwayne Roloson 1.25 3.00
HH68 Marty Turco 1.50 4.00
HH69 Guillaume Latendresse 1.25 3.00
HH70 Andrew Raycroft 1.25 3.00
HH71 Daniel Briere 1.50 4.00
HH72 Ryan Smyth 1.25 3.00
HH73 Paul Kariya 2.00 5.00
HH74 Tomas Vokoun 1.25 3.00
HH75 Alexander Radulov 1.50 4.00
HH76 Miroslav Satan 1.25 3.00
HH77 Mark Recchi 2.00 5.00
HH78 Phil Kessel 2.00 5.00
HH79 Chris Chelios 1.50 4.00
HH80 Anze Kopitar 2.50 6.00
HH81 Justin Williams 1.25 3.00
HH82 Joe Thornton 2.00 5.00
HH83 Mikko Koivu 1.25 3.00
HH84 Brad Richards 1.50 4.00

2007-08 Upper Deck Lord Stanley's Heroes

COMPLETE SET (7) 5.00 12.00
STATED ODDS 1:24
LSH1 Teemu Selanne 3.00 8.00
LSH2 Jean-Sebastien Giguere 1.50 4.00
LSH3 Chris Pronger 1.25 3.00
LSH4 Scott Niedermayer 1.50 4.00
LSH5 Andy McDonald 1.25 3.00
LSH6 Ryan Getzlaf 2.50 6.00
LSH7 Travis Moen 1.00 2.50

2007-08 Upper Deck NHL's Best

COMPLETE SET (14) 20.00 50.00
STATED ODDS 1:24
B1 Sidney Crosby 6.00 15.00
B2 Martin Brodeur 3.00 8.00
B3 Dany Heatley 1.50 4.00
B4 Alexander Ovechkin 6.00 15.00
B5 Joe Thornton 2.00 5.00
B6 Jarome Iginla 1.50 4.00
B7 Vincent Lecavalier 1.25 3.00
B8 Roberto Luongo 2.00 5.00
B9 Joe Sakic 2.50 6.00
B10 Jaromir Jagr 4.00 10.00
B11 Teemu Selanne 3.00 8.00
B12 Ilya Kovalchuk 1.50 4.00
B13 Ryan Miller 1.50 4.00
B14 Eric Staal 2.00 5.00

2007-08 Upper Deck NHL Award Winners

COMPLETE SET (7) 12.00 30.00
STATED ODDS 1:24
AW1 Sidney Crosby 6.00 15.00
AW2 Martin Brodeur 3.00 8.00
AW3 Nicklas Lidstrom 1.50 4.00
AW4 Evgeni Malkin 5.00 12.00
AW5 Rod Brind'Amour 1.50 4.00
AW6 Pavel Datsyuk 2.00 5.00
AW7 Phil Kessel 2.00 5.00

2007-08 Upper Deck Rookie Headliners

RH1 Jonathan Toews SP 12.00 30.00
RH2 Patrick Kane SP 12.00 30.00
RH3 Carey Price SP 20.00 50.00
RH4 Devin Setoguchi SP 3.00 8.00
RH5 Jiri Tlusty SP 3.00 8.00
RH6 Jack Johnson SP 2.50 6.00
RH7 Bobby Ryan SP 5.00 12.00
RH8 Peter Mueller SP 2.50 6.00
RH9 Bryan Little SP 2.50 6.00
RH10 Sam Gagner SP 4.00 10.00
RH11 Andrew Cogliano 1.25 3.00
RH12 Jonathan Bernier 2.00 5.00
RH13 Nicklas Backstrom 2.50 6.00
RH14 Marc Staal 1.25 3.00
RH15 Erik Johnson 1.25 3.00
RH16 Milan Lucic 4.00 10.00
RH17 James Sheppard .75 2.00
RH18 Nicklas Bergfors .75 2.00
RH19 Nick Foligno 1.50 4.00
RH20 Kyle Chipchura 1.25 3.00

2007-08 Upper Deck Rookie Materials

STATED ODDS 1:24
RMAC Andrew Cogliano 5.00 12.00
RMAG Andy Greene 4.00 10.00
RMAS Anton Stralman 3.00 8.00
RMBA Nicklas Backstrom 10.00 25.00
RMBL Bryan Little 4.00 10.00
RMBR Bobby Ryan 8.00 20.00
RMBS Brett Sterling 3.00 8.00
RMCM Curtis McElhinney 5.00 12.00
RMCP Carey Price 30.00 80.00
RMDK David Krejci 10.00 25.00
RMDM Drew Miller 4.00 10.00
RMDP David Perron 5.00 12.00
RMDS Devin Setoguchi 5.00 12.00
RMEJ Erik Johnson 5.00 12.00
RMFN Frans Nielsen 5.00 12.00
RMJB Jonathan Bernier 8.00 20.00
RMJH Jaroslav Halak 8.00 20.00
RMJJ Jack Johnson 6.00 15.00
RMJS James Sheppard 3.00 8.00
RMJT Jonathan Toews 20.00 50.00
RMKA Petr Kalus 3.00 8.00
RMKC Kyle Chipchura 5.00 12.00
RMMH Martin Hanzal 4.00 10.00
RMML Milan Lucic 15.00 40.00
RMMN Matt Niskanen 5.00 12.00
RMMR Mason Raymond 5.00 12.00
RMMS Marc Staal 5.00 12.00
RMNB Nicklas Bergfors 3.00 8.00
RMNF Nick Foligno 6.00 15.00
RMOP Ondrej Pavelec 6.00 15.00
RMPK Patrick Kane 20.00 50.00
RMPM Peter Mueller 4.00 10.00
RMRC Ryan Callahan 6.00 15.00
RMRP Ryan Parent 3.00 8.00
RMRS Rob Schremp 4.00 10.00
RMSG Sam Gagner 6.00 15.00
RMTL Jiri Tlusty 5.00 12.00
RMTM Torrey Mitchell 4.00 10.00
RMVK Ville Koistinen 3.00 8.00

2007-08 Upper Deck Signature Sensations

STATED ODDS 1:288
SSAK Andrei Kostitsyn 5.00 12.00
SSAO Alex Ovechkin SP 125.00 200.00
SSAR Andrew Raycroft 5.00 12.00
SSAT Alex Tanguay
SSBM Brenden Morrow 5.00 12.00
SSBO Bobby Orr SP
SSBP Benoit Pouliot 4.00 10.00
SSBR Brad Richardson 5.00 12.00
SSBW Ben Walter 4.00 10.00
SSCK Chuck Kobasew 4.00 10.00
SSCO Erik Cole
SSCT Chris Thorburn 4.00 10.00
SSDB Daniel Briere
SSDH Dany Heatley
SSDK Duncan Keith 6.00 15.00
SSDP Dion Phaneuf 6.00 15.00
SSDS Drew Stafford 5.00 12.00
SSEC Erik Christensen 4.00 10.00
SSEM Evgeni Malkin 20.00 50.00
SSEN Evgeni Nabokov 5.00 12.00
SSES Eric Staal 10.00 25.00
SSFN Filip Novak 4.00 10.00
SSFP Fernando Pisani 4.00 10.00
SSGE Martin Gerber 5.00 12.00
SSGL G. Latendresse 5.00 12.00
SSGM Glen Murray
SSGO Scott Gomez 5.00 12.00
SSHA Dominik Hasek 25.00 50.00
SSHZ Henrik Zetterberg 8.00 20.00
SSIK Ilya Kovalchuk 6.00 15.00
SSIM Jarkko Immonen
SSIW Ian White 4.00 10.00
SSJA Jay Bouwmeester 6.00 15.00
SSJC Jonathan Cheechoo 6.00 15.00
SSJF Johan Franzen 6.00 15.00
SSJG Jean-Sebastien Giguere 6.00 15.00
SSJI Jarome Iginla 6.00 15.00
SSJL John-Michael Liles 4.00 10.00
SSJM Jay McClement 4.00 10.00
SSJO Jeff O'Neill 4.00 10.00
SSJT Joe Thornton 8.00 20.00
SSJW Jeremy Williams 4.00 10.00
SSKC Kyle Calder 4.00 10.00
SSKE Ryan Kesler 8.00 20.00
SSKL Kari Lehtonen 5.00 12.00
SSKO Anze Kopitar SP 8.00 20.00
SSKU Chris Kunitz
SSLA Maxim Lapierre 4.00 10.00
SSLB Luc Bourdon
SSMA Maxim Afinogenov 4.00 10.00
SSME M-E Vlasic 4.00 10.00
SSMG Marian Gaborik 8.00 20.00
SSMH Marcel Hossa 4.00 10.00
SSMI Michal Handzus 5.00 12.00
SSMK Miikka Kiprusoff SP 40.00 80.00
SSML Mario Lemieux SP 60.00 120.00
SSMM Mark Messier SP
SSMP Michael Peca 5.00 12.00
SSMS Marek Svatos 4.00 10.00
SSMT Mikael Tellqvist 5.00 12.00
SSNA Nikolai Antropov 5.00 12.00
SSON Ben Ondrus 4.00 10.00
SSPB Pierre-Marc Bouchard
SSPE Patrick Eaves 4.00 10.00
SSPK Phil Kessel 8.00 20.00
SSPR Brandon Prust 4.00 10.00
SSPS Paul Stastny 6.00 15.00
SSRE Robert Esche 5.00 12.00
SSRK Rostislav Klesla 4.00 10.00
SSRM Ryan Malone 4.00 10.00
SSRN Rick Nash 6.00 15.00
SSRS Ryan Smyth 5.00 12.00
SSSC Sidney Crosby SP 100.00 200.00
SSSG Simon Gagne 6.00 15.00
SSSH Shawn Horcoff 4.00 10.00
SSSS Steve Sullivan
SSST Martin St. Louis
SSTM Travis Moen 4.00 10.00
SSTR Tuomo Ruutu 6.00 15.00
SSTV Thomas Vanek 8.00 20.00
SSVL Vincent Lecavalier 5.00 12.00
SSWG Wayne Gretzky SP
SSWR Wade Redden 4.00 10.00
SSYS Yan Stastny 4.00 10.00

2007-08 Upper Deck Stars In The Making

COMPLETE SET (14) 8.00 20.00
STATED ODDS 1:16
SM1 Zach Parise 1.25 3.00
SM2 Mikko Koivu .75 2.00
SM3 Jordan Staal 1.00 2.50
SM4 Thomas Vanek 1.25 3.00
SM5 Phil Kessel 1.25 3.00
SM6 Alexander Semin 1.00 2.50
SM7 Drew Stafford .75 2.00
SM8 Ryan Getzlaf 1.50 4.00
SM9 Alexander Radulov 1.00 2.50
SM10 Steve Bernier .60 1.50
SM11 Dion Phaneuf 1.00 2.50
SM12 Paul Stastny 1.00 2.50
SM13 Anze Kopitar 1.50 4.00
SM14 Brent Seabrook 1.00 2.50

2007-08 Upper Deck Super Snipers

COMPLETE SET (21) 20.00 50.00
SN1 Vincent Lecavalier 1.00 2.50
SN2 Dany Heatley 1.25 3.00
SN3 Jonathan Cheechoo 1.25 3.00
SN4 Martin St. Louis 1.25 3.00
SN5 Ilya Kovalchuk 1.25 3.00
SN6 Joe Sakic 2.00 5.00
SN7 Jaromir Jagr 3.00 8.00
SN8 Jarome Iginla 1.25 3.00
SN9 Marian Hossa 1.00 2.50
SN10 Martin Havlat 1.25 3.00
SN11 Teemu Selanne 2.50 6.00
SN12 Alexander Ovechkin 5.00 12.00
SN13 Jason Spezza 1.25 3.00
SN14 Thomas Vanek 1.50 4.00
SN15 Sidney Crosby 5.00 12.00
SN16 Mike Modano 2.00 5.00
SN17 Henrik Zetterberg 1.50 4.00
SN18 Markus Naslund 1.25 3.00
SN19 Marian Gaborik 1.50 4.00
SN20 Rick Nash 1.25 3.00
SN21 Mats Sundin 1.25 3.00

2007-08 Upper Deck The Men Behind The Mask

COMPLETE SET (15) 25.00 60.00
ONE PER SER. 2 FAT PACK
BM1 Cam Ward 2.50 6.00
BM2 Dominik Hasek 3.00 8.00
BM3 Dwayne Roloson 2.00 5.00
BM4 Henrik Lundqvist 3.00 8.00
BM5 Jean-Sebastien Giguere 2.50 6.00
BM6 Kari Lehtonen 2.00 5.00
BM7 Marc-Andre Fleury 4.00 10.00
BM8 Martin Brodeur 5.00 12.00
BM9 Marty Turco 2.50 6.00
BM10 Miikka Kiprusoff 2.00 5.00
BM11 Ray Emery 2.00 5.00
BM12 Roberto Luongo 3.00 8.00
BM13 Ryan Miller 2.50 6.00
BM14 Tomas Vokoun 2.00 5.00
BM15 Vesa Toskala 2.00 5.00

2007-08 Upper Deck Top Picks

COMPLETE SET (7) 8.00 20.00
STATED ODDS 1:16
TP1 Sidney Crosby 4.00 10.00
TP2 Alexander Ovechkin 4.00 10.00
TP3 Marc-Andre Fleury 1.50 4.00
TP4 Rick Nash 1.00 2.50
TP5 Ilya Kovalchuk 1.00 2.50
TP6 Vincent Lecavalier .75 2.00
TP7 Joe Thornton 1.25 3.00

2007-08 Upper Deck UD Signatures

STATED ODDS 1:288
UDSAK Andrei Kostitsyn 8.00 20.00
UDSAM Al Montoya 8.00 20.00
UDSAO Alexander Ovechkin SP 100.00 150.00
UDSBC Blake Comeau 6.00 15.00
UDSBO Bobby Orr SP 75.00 150.00
UDSBP Benoit Pouliot 6.00 15.00
UDSBR Mike Brown 6.00 15.00
UDSCC Chris Campoli 6.00 15.00
UDSCS Cory Stillman SP
UDSDB Daniel Briere 10.00 25.00
UDSDH Dominik Hasek SP 20.00 50.00
UDSDS Drew Stafford 8.00 20.00
UDSEM Evgeni Malkin SP 125.00 200.00
UDSGH Gordie Howe SP 50.00 100.00
UDSIK Ilya Kovalchuk SP 15.00 40.00
UDSJB Jaroslav Balastik 6.00 15.00
UDSJC Jeff Carter SP 20.00 50.00
UDSJF Johan Franzen 10.00 25.00
UDSJG Jean-Sebastien Giguere SP
UDSJJ Jack Johnson 8.00 20.00
UDSJK Jakub Klepis 6.00 15.00
UDSJM Jay McClement 6.00 15.00
UDSJS Jordan Staal SP 15.00 30.00
UDSJW Jeremy Williams 6.00 15.00
UDSKB Kevin Bieksa 8.00 20.00
UDSKO Anze Kopitar 15.00 40.00
UDSLA Maxim Lapierre 6.00 15.00
UDSLN Ladislav Nagy 6.00 15.00
UDSLT Lauri Tukonen 6.00 15.00
UDSML Mario Lemieux SP 100.00 200.00
UDSMM Mark Messier SP
UDSMR Mike Ribeiro SP 12.00 30.00
UDSNB Niklas Backstrom 10.00 25.00
UDSNK Nikolai Khabibulin SP
UDSPH Dion Phaneuf 10.00 25.00
UDSPK Phil Kessel SP
UDSPM Paul Mara 6.00 15.00
UDSPS Paul Stastny SP
UDSRI Mike Richards 10.00 25.00
UDSRK Rostislav Klesla 6.00 15.00
UDSRM Ryan Miller 10.00 25.00
UDSRN Rick Nash SP 30.00 60.00
UDSRO Rob Schremp 8.00 20.00
UDSRS Ryan Smyth SP
UDSSC Sidney Crosby SP 150.00 300.00
UDSSS Steve Sullivan SP
UDSSW Stephen Weiss 6.00 15.00
UDSTB Todd Bertuzzi SP 10.00 25.00
UDSTV Thomas Vanek 12.00 30.00
UDSWR Wade Redden SP
UDSZP Zach Parise 12.00 30.00

2007-08 Upper Deck Young Guns Retro Oversized

COMPLETE SET (14) 60.00 120.00
YG1 Patrick Kane 8.00 20.00
YG2 Carey Price 25.00 60.00
YG3 Erik Johnson 4.00 10.00
YG4 Bobby Ryan 6.00 15.00
YG5 Marc Staal 4.00 10.00
YG6 Nicklas Backstrom 8.00 20.00
YG7 Jonathan Bernier 6.00 15.00
YG8 Bryan Little 3.00 8.00
YG9 Sam Gagner 5.00 12.00
YG10 Nick Foligno 5.00 12.00
YG11 Peter Mueller 3.00 8.00
YG12 Jack Johnson 3.00 8.00
YG13 Nicklas Bergfors 2.50 6.00
YG14 Rob Schremp 3.00 8.00

2007-08 Upper Deck Lucky Shot Arena Giveaways

These cards were issued as arena giveaways over the second half of the 2007-08 season. Each team gave away a five-card set at a single home game. The sixth card for each team could be acquired with the purchase of a specified number of Upper Deck packs at the team's pro shop on the night of that game. As a result, the sixth card for each team tends to sell for a much higher rate.

LA1 Dustin Brown 2.50 6.00
LA2 Mike Cammalleri 2.00 5.00
LA3 Rob Blake 2.50 6.00
LA4 Alexander Frolov 1.50 4.00
LA5 Lubomir Visnovsky 1.50 4.00
LA6 Anze Kopitar 12.00 30.00
NJ1 Travis Zajac 2.00 5.00
NJ2 Jay Pandolfo 1.50 4.00
NJ3 Brian Gionta 2.00 5.00
NJ4 Sergei Brylin 1.50 4.00
NJ5 Dainius Zubrus 1.50 4.00
NJ6 Martin Brodeur 15.00 40.00
SJ1 Joe Pavelski 2.50 6.00
SJ2 Jonathan Cheechoo 2.50 6.00
SJ3 Marc-Edouard Vlasic 1.50 4.00
SJ4 Craig Rivet 1.50 4.00
SJ5 Patrick Marleau 2.50 6.00
SJ6 Joe Thornton 10.00 25.00
TB1 Dan Boyle 2.00 5.00
TB2 Ryan Craig 1.50 4.00
TB3 Vaclav Prospal 1.50 4.00
TB4 Marc Denis 2.00 5.00
TB5 Brad Richards 2.50 6.00
TB6 Vincent Lecavalier 6.00 15.00
ANA1 Andy McDonald 2.00 5.00
ANA2 Chris Pronger 2.00 5.00
ANA3 Chris Kunitz 2.50 6.00
ANA4 Jean-Sebastien Giguere 2.50 6.00
ANA5 Corey Perry 2.50 6.00
ANA6 Ryan Getzlaf 12.00 30.00
ATL1 Ilya Kovalchuk 2.50 6.00
ATL2 Marian Hossa 2.00 5.00
ATL3 Bobby Holik 1.50 4.00
ATL4 Kari Lehtonen 2.00 5.00
ATL5 Slava Kozlov 1.50 4.00
ATL6 Garnet Exelby 5.00 12.00
BOS1 Zdeno Chara 2.50 6.00
BOS2 Phil Kessel 3.00 8.00
BOS3 Glen Murray 2.00 5.00
BOS4 Marco Sturm 1.50 4.00
BOS5 Marc Savard 1.50 4.00
BOS6 Tim Thomas 10.00 25.00
BUF1 Thomas Vanek 3.00 8.00
BUF2 Derek Roy 1.50 4.00
BUF3 Brian Campbell 2.00 5.00
BUF4 Maxim Afinogenov 1.50 4.00
BUF5 Jason Pominville 2.50 6.00
BUF6 Ryan Miller 8.00 20.00
CAR1 Cory Stillman 1.50 4.00
CAR2 Ray Whitney 2.00 5.00
CAR3 Eric Staal 3.00 8.00
CAR4 Glen Wesley 1.50 4.00
CAR5 Justin Williams 2.00 5.00
CAR6 Cam Ward 8.00 20.00
CGY1 Miikka Kiprusoff 2.00 5.00
CGY2 Dion Phaneuf 2.50 6.00
CGY3 Alex Tanguay 1.50 4.00
CGY4 Daymond Langkow 1.50 4.00
CGY5 Kristian Huselius 1.50 4.00
CGY6 Jarome Iginla 8.00 20.00
CHI1 Patrick Kane 10.00 25.00
CHI2 Martin Havlat 2.50 6.00
CHI3 Patrick Sharp 2.50 6.00
CHI4 Nikolai Khabibulin 2.50 6.00
CHI5 Tuomo Ruutu 2.50 6.00
CHI6 Jonathan Toews 15.00 40.00
CLB1 Pascal Leclaire 2.00 5.00
CLB2 Nikolai Zherdev 1.50 4.00
CLB3 Adam Foote 1.50 4.00
CLB4 Sergei Fedorov 4.00 10.00
CLB5 Fredrik Modin 1.50 4.00
CLB6 Rick Nash 8.00 20.00
COL1 Joe Sakic 4.00 10.00
COL2 Ian Laperriere 1.50 4.00
COL3 Milan Hejduk 2.00 5.00
COL4 Scott Hannan 1.50 4.00
COL5 Ryan Smyth 2.00 5.00
COL6 Paul Stastny 8.00 20.00
DAL1 Sergei Zubov 2.00 5.00
DAL2 Mike Ribeiro 2.00 5.00
DAL3 Brenden Morrow 2.00 5.00
DAL4 Marty Turco 2.50 6.00
DAL5 Jere Lehtinen 1.50 4.00
DAL6 Mike Modano 12.00 30.00
DET1 Nicklas Lidstrom 2.50 6.00
DET2 Kris Draper 1.50 4.00
DET3 Pavel Datsyuk 3.00 8.00
DET4 Tomas Holmstrom 2.00 5.00
DET5 Chris Chelios 2.50 6.00
DET6 Henrik Zetterberg 10.00 25.00
EDM1 Dwayne Roloson 2.00 5.00
EDM2 Jarret Stoll 2.00 5.00
EDM3 Dustin Penner 2.00 5.00
EDM4 Shawn Horcoff 1.50 4.00
EDM5 Ethan Moreau 1.50 4.00
EDM6 Ales Hemsky 6.00 15.00
FLA1 Olli Jokinen 2.00 5.00
FLA2 Nathan Horton 2.50 6.00
FLA3 Stephen Weiss 1.50 4.00
FLA4 Jay Bouwmeester 2.50 6.00
FLA5 Tomas Vokoun 2.00 5.00
FLA6 Rostislav Olesz 5.00 12.00
MIN1 Pavol Demitra 3.00 8.00
MIN2 Kurtis Foster 1.50 4.00
MIN3 Pierre-Marc Bouchard 2.50 6.00
MIN4 Josh Harding 2.50 6.00
MIN5 Mark Parrish 1.50 4.00
MIN6 Marian Gaborik 10.00 25.00
MTL1 Guillaume Latendresse 2.00 5.00
MTL2 Cristobal Huet 2.00 5.00
MTL3 Mark Streit 1.50 4.00
MTL4 Chris Higgins 1.50 4.00
MTL5 Roman Hamrlik 2.00 5.00
MTL6 Saku Koivu 8.00 20.00
NAS1 J.P. Dumont 1.50 4.00
NAS2 Martin Erat 1.50 4.00
NAS3 David Legwand 2.00 5.00
NAS4 Chris Mason 2.00 5.00
NAS5 Jason Arnott 2.00 5.00
NAS6 Alexander Radulov 8.00 20.00
NYI1 Mike Sillinger 1.50 4.00
NYI2 Rick DiPietro 2.00 5.00
NYI3 Brendan Witt 1.50 4.00
NYI4 Bill Guerin 2.50 6.00
NYI5 Mike Comrie 2.00 5.00
NYI6 Miroslav Satan 6.00 15.00
NYR1 Jaromir Jagr 6.00 15.00
NYR2 Sean Avery 1.50 4.00
NYR3 Chris Drury 2.00 5.00
NYR4 Scott Gomez 2.00 5.00
NYR5 Brendan Shanahan 3.00 8.00
NYR6 Henrik Lundqvist 10.00 25.00
OTT1 Daniel Alfredsson 2.50 6.00
OTT2 Dany Heatley 2.50 6.00
OTT3 Antoine Vermette 1.50 4.00
OTT4 Jason Spezza 2.50 6.00
OTT5 Anton Volchenkov 1.50 4.00
OTT6 Martin Gerber 6.00 15.00
PHI1 Martin Biron 2.00 5.00
PHI2 Simon Gagne 2.50 6.00
PHI3 Daniel Briere 2.50 6.00
PHI4 Mike Richards 2.50 6.00
PHI5 Kimmo Timonen 1.50 4.00
PHI6 Scottie Upshall 5.00 12.00
PHX1 Zbynek Michalek 1.50 4.00
PHX2 Keith Ballard 1.50 4.00
PHX3 Ed Jovanovski 2.00 5.00
PHX4 Nick Boynton 1.50 4.00
PHX5 Derek Morris 1.50 4.00
PHX6 Shane Doan 6.00 15.00
PIT1 Sidney Crosby 10.00 25.00
PIT2 Sergei Gonchar 1.50 4.00
PIT3 Marc-Andre Fleury 4.00 10.00
PIT4 Petr Sykora 2.00 5.00
PIT5 Evgeni Malkin 8.00 20.00
PIT6 Jordan Staal 8.00 20.00
STL1 Manny Legace 2.00 5.00
STL2 Barret Jackman 1.50 4.00
STL3 Paul Kariya 3.00 8.00
STL4 Doug Weight 2.50 6.00
STL5 Keith Tkachuk 2.50 6.00
STL6 Brad Boyes 5.00 12.00
TOR1 Darcy Tucker 2.00 5.00
TOR2 Bryan McCabe 1.50 4.00
TOR3 Matt Stajan 2.00 5.00
TOR4 Jason Blake 1.50 4.00
TOR5 Mats Sundin 2.50 6.00
TOR6 Tomas Kaberle 5.00 12.00
VAN1 Markus Naslund 2.50 6.00
VAN2 Henrik Sedin 2.50 6.00
VAN3 Mattias Ohlund 1.50 4.00
VAN4 Willie Mitchell 1.50 4.00
VAN5 Daniel Sedin 2.50 6.00
VAN6 Roberto Luongo 10.00 25.00
WAS1 Alexander Semin 2.50 6.00
WAS2 Chris Clark 1.50 4.00
WAS3 Olaf Kolzig 2.50 6.00
WAS4 Alexander Ovechkin 10.00 25.00
WAS5 Michael Nylander 1.50 4.00
WAS6 Donald Brashear 5.00 12.00

2008-09 Upper Deck

This base set consists of 500 cards. Series 1 (cards 1-250) was released on November 11, 2008. Cards 1-200 feature veterans, and cards 201-250 are rookies. Series 2 (cards 251-500) was released on February 10, 2009. Cards 251-450 feature veterans, and cards 451-500 are rookies.

COMPLETE SET (500) 200.00 400.00
COMP.SER.1 SET (250) 200.00 350.00
COMP.SER.2 SET (250) 100.00 200.00
COMP.SET w/o SP's (400) 30.00 80.00
COMP.SER.1 SET w/o SPs (200) 15.00 40.00
COMP.SER.2 SET w/o SPs (200) 15.00 40.00
YG STATED ODDS 1:4
1 Nicklas Backstrom .50 1.25
2 Alexander Semin .30 .75
3 Mike Green .30 .75
4 Viktor Kozlov .20 .50
5 Jeff Schultz .20 .50
6 Boyd Gordon .20 .50
7 Mattias Ohlund .20 .50
8 Roberto Luongo .40 1.00
9 Alexander Edler .20 .50
10 Mason Raymond .30 .75
11 Daniel Sedin .30 .75
12 Henrik Sedin .30 .75
13 Curtis Sanford .25 .60
14 Ryan Kesler .40 1.00
15 Pavel Kubina .20 .50
16 Vesa Toskala .25 .60
17 Alexander Steen .30 .75
18 Tomas Kaberle .20 .50
19 Jiri Tlusty .25 .60
20 Nik Antropov .25 .60
21 Ian White .20 .50
22 Paul Ranger .20 .50
23 Martin St. Louis .30 .75
24 Jussi Jokinen .20 .50
25 Mike Smith .30 .75
26 Jeff Halpern .20 .50
27 Mike Lundin .20 .50
28 Lee Stempniak .20 .50
29 Paul Kariya .40 1.00
30 Erik Johnson .25 .60
31 Manny Legace .30 .75
32 Brad Boyes .20 .50
33 Andy McDonald .25 .60
34 David Perron .25 .60
35 Joe Thornton .40 1.00
36 Devin Setoguchi .25 .60
37 Evgeni Nabokov .25 .60
38 Jonathan Cheechoo .30 .75
39 Milan Michalek .20 .50
40 Torrey Mitchell .20 .50
41 Mike Grier .20 .50
42 Sidney Crosby 1.25 3.00
43 Marc-Andre Fleury .50 1.25
44 Kristopher Letang .30 .75
45 Tyler Kennedy .25 .60
46 Jordan Staal .30 .75
47 Sergei Gonchar .20 .50
48 Petr Sykora .25 .60
49 Peter Mueller .25 .60
50 Ilya Bryzgalov .25 .60
51 Zbynek Michalek .20 .50
52 Martin Hanzal .25 .60
53 Daniel Carcillo .20 .50
54 Ed Jovanovski .25 .60
55 Riley Cote .20 .50
56 Simon Gagne .30 .75
57 Mike Richards .30 .75
58 Martin Biron .25 .60
59 Kimmo Timonen .20 .50
60 Joffrey Lupul .25 .60
61 Mike Knuble .20 .50
62 Daniel Alfredsson .30 .75
63 Chris Phillips .20 .50
64 Mike Fisher .20 .50
65 Antoine Vermette .20 .50
66 Andrej Meszaros .20 .50
67 Jason Spezza .30 .75
68 Chris Neil .20 .50
69 Stephen Valiquette .25 .60
70 Nigel Dawes .20 .50
71 Marc Staal .30 .75
72 Brandon Dubinsky .25 .60
73 Scott Gomez .25 .60
74 Henrik Lundqvist .40 1.00
75 Bill Guerin .30 .75
76 Rick DiPietro .25 .60
77 Blake Comeau .20 .50
78 Trent Hunter .20 .50
79 Brendan Witt .20 .50
80 Mike Sillinger .20 .50
81 Martin Brodeur .60 1.50
82 Patrik Elias .30 .75
83 Johnny Oduya .25 .60
84 Brian Gionta .25 .60
85 Paul Martin .20 .50
86 John Madden .20 .50
87 Radek Bonk .20 .50
88 Martin Erat .20 .50
89 Shea Weber .25 .60
90 David Legwand .25 .60
91 Ryan Suter .25 .60
92 Francis Bouillon .25 .60
93 Saku Koivu .30 .75
94 Guillaume Latendresse .20 .50
95 Carey Price 1.25 3.00
96 Tomas Plekanec .30 .75
97 Mike Komisarek .20 .50
98 Sergei Kostitsyn .20 .50
99 Andrei Kostitsyn .25 .60
100 Josh Harding .30 .75
101 Marian Gaborik .40 1.00
102 Mikko Koivu .25 .60
103 James Sheppard .20 .50
104 Nick Schultz .20 .50
105 Pierre-Marc Bouchard .30 .75
106 Benoit Pouliot .20 .50
107 Anze Kopitar .50 1.25
108 Jack Johnson .20 .50
109 Jason LaBarbera .25 .60
110 Dustin Brown .30 .75
111 Patrick O'Sullivan .25 .60
112 Tomas Vokoun .25 .60
113 Stephen Weiss .20 .50
114 Nathan Horton .25 .60
115 Jay Bouwmeester .30 .75
116 David Booth .20 .50
117 Rostislav Olesz .20 .50
118 Fernando Pisani .20 .50
119 Andrew Cogliano .25 .60
120 Shawn Horcoff .20 .50
121 Sheldon Souray .20 .50
122 Ales Hemsky .25 .60
123 Mathieu Garon .25 .60
124 Robert Nilsson .20 .50
125 Dustin Penner .25 .60
126 Henrik Zetterberg .40 1.00
127 Chris Osgood .30 .75
128 Nicklas Lidstrom .30 .75
129 Kris Draper .20 .50
130 Jiri Hudler .25 .60
131 Niklas Kronwall .25 .60
132 Tomas Holmstrom .25 .60
133 Mike Modano .50 1.25
134 Sergei Zubov .25 .60
135 Brenden Morrow .25 .60
136 Brad Richards .30 .75
137 Trevor Daley .20 .50
138 Matt Niskanen .25 .60
139 Steve Ott .20 .50
140 Rick Nash .30 .75
141 Pascal Leclaire .25 .60
142 Jared Boll .20 .50
143 Rostislav Klesla .20 .50
144 Kris Russell .20 .50
145 Michael Peca .25 .60
146 Ole-Kristian Tollefsen .20 .50
147 Paul Stastny .30 .75
148 John-Michael Liles .20 .50
149 Marek Svatos .20 .50
150 Peter Budaj .25 .60
151 Ryan Smyth .25 .60
152 Milan Hejduk .25 .60
153 Jordan Leopold .20 .50
154 Wojtek Wolski .25 .60
155 Jonathan Toews .75 2.00
156 Patrick Sharp .30 .75
157 Adam Burish .25 .60
158 Cam Barker .20 .50
159 Martin Havlat .30 .75
160 Duncan Keith .30 .75
161 Robert Lang .20 .50
162 Eric Staal .40 1.00
163 Tuomo Ruutu .30 .75
164 Joe Corvo .20 .50
165 Rod Brind'Amour .30 .75
166 Matt Cullen .20 .50
167 Ray Whitney .25 .60
168 Daymond Langkow .20 .50
169 Jarome Iginla .30 .75
170 Dion Phaneuf .30 .75
171 Matthew Lombardi .20 .50
172 Cory Sarich .20 .50
173 Adrian Aucoin .20 .50
174 Maxim Afinogenov .20 .50
175 Ryan Miller .30 .75
176 Derek Roy .20 .50
177 Jason Pominville .30 .75
178 Jaroslav Spacek .20 .50
179 Drew Stafford .25 .60
180 Phil Kessel .40 1.00
181 Tim Thomas .30 .75
182 Zdeno Chara .30 .75
183 Manny Fernandez .25 .60
184 Milan Lucic .50 1.25
185 Mark Stuart .20 .50
186 Chuck Kobasew .20 .50
187 Kari Lehtonen .25 .60
188 Tobias Enstrom .20 .50
189 Ilya Kovalchuk .30 .75
190 Colby Armstrong .20 .50
191 Todd White .20 .50
192 Erik Christensen .20 .50
193 Ryan Getzlaf .50 1.25
194 Chris Kunitz .30 .75
195 Scott Niedermayer .30 .75
196 Bobby Ryan .30 .75
197 Francois Beauchemin .20 .50
198 Jean-Sebastien Giguere .30 .75
199 Martin Brodeur CL .60 1.50
200 Sidney Crosby CL 1.25 3.00
201 Zach Bogosian YG RC 3.00 8.00
202 Blake Wheeler YG RC 10.00 25.00
203 Adam Pardy YG RC 2.50 6.00
204 Brandon Sutter YG RC 3.00 8.00
205 Jakub Voracek YG RC 6.00 15.00
206 Adam Pineault YG RC 2.50 6.00
207 Derick Brassard YG RC 2.50 6.00
208 Steve Mason YG RC 5.00 12.00
209 James Neal YG RC 6.00 15.00
210 Mark Fistric YG RC 2.50 6.00
211 Justin Abdelkader YG RC 5.00 12.00
212 Jonathan Ericsson YG RC 3.00 8.00
213 Darren Helm YG RC 3.00 8.00
214 Mattias Ritola YG RC 2.50 6.00
215 Tom Sestito YG RC 3.00 8.00
216 Chris Porter YG RC 3.00 8.00
217 Michael Frolik YG RC 3.00 8.00
218 T.J. Oshie YG RC 10.00 25.00
219 Shawn Matthias YG RC 3.00 8.00
220 Drew Doughty YG RC 12.00 30.00
221 Wayne Simmonds YG RC 6.00 15.00
222 Oscar Moller YG RC 2.50 6.00
223 Erik Ersberg YG RC 2.50 6.00
224 Colton Gillies YG RC 2.50 6.00
225 Matt D'Agostini YG RC 2.50 6.00
226 Ryan Jones YG RC 3.00 8.00
227 Patric Hornqvist YG RC 3.00 8.00
228 Anssi Salmela YG RC 3.00 8.00
229 Kyle Okposo YG RC 5.00 12.00
230 Lauri Korpikoski YG RC 2.00 5.00
231 Brian Lee YG RC 2.50 6.00
232 Ilya Zubov YG RC 2.50 6.00
233 Jared Ross YG RC 3.00 8.00
234 Luca Sbisa YG RC 2.00 5.00
235 Claude Giroux YG RC 12.00 30.00
236 Kyle Turris YG RC 5.00 12.00
237 Mikkel Boedker YG RC 4.00 10.00
238 Alex Goligoski YG RC 4.00 10.00
239 Jon Filewich YG RC 2.50 6.00
240 Ryan Stone YG RC 2.00 5.00
241 Alex Pietrangelo YG RC 4.00 10.00
242 Patrik Berglund YG RC 2.50 6.00
243 Vladimir Mihalik YG RC 2.00 5.00
244 Janne Niskala YG RC 3.00 8.00
245 Steven Stamkos YG RC 30.00 80.00
246 John Mitchell YG RC 2.50 6.00
247 Robbie Earl YG RC 2.00 5.00
248 Luke Schenn YG RC 4.00 10.00
249 Mike Brown YG RC 4.00 10.00
250 Dougty/Stamk/Pietrnglo CL 6.00 15.00
251 Teemu Selanne .60 1.50
252 Chris Pronger .25 .60
253 Kent Huskins .20 .50
254 Jonas Hiller .25 .60
255 Corey Perry .30 .75
256 Mathieu Schneider .20 .50
257 Brett Sterling .25 .60
258 Johan Hedberg .25 .60
259 Niclas Havelid .20 .50
260 Slava Kozlov .20 .50
261 Bryan Little .25 .60
262 Jason Williams .20 .50
263 Ron Hainsey .20 .50
264 P.J. Axelsson .20 .50
265 Tuukka Rask .30 .75
266 Patrice Bergeron .40 1.00
267 Dennis Wideman .20 .50
268 Marc Savard .20 .50
269 David Krejci .30 .75
270 Marco Sturm .20 .50
271 Thomas Vanek .30 .75
272 Teppo Numminen .25 .60
273 Jochen Hecht .20 .50
274 Tim Connolly .20 .50
275 Toni Lydman .20 .50
276 Daniel Paille .20 .50
277 Paul Gaustad .20 .50
278 Patrick Lalime .25 .60
279 Craig Rivet .20 .50
280 Todd Bertuzzi .30 .75
281 Robyn Regehr .20 .50
282 Mike Cammalleri .25 .60
283 Miikka Kiprusoff .25 .60
284 Cam Ward .30 .75
285 Patrick Eaves .20 .50
286 Joni Pitkanen .20 .50
287 Sergei Samsonov .25 .60
288 Scott Walker .20 .50
289 Tim Gleason .20 .50
290 Patrick Kane .60 1.50
291 Nikolai Khabibulin .30 .75
292 Dustin Byfuglien .30 .75
293 Brent Seabrook .30 .75
294 Jack Skille .25 .60
295 Brian Campbell .25 .60
296 Cristobal Huet .25 .60
297 Joe Sakic .50 1.25
298 Peter Forsberg .40 1.00
299 Ian Laperriere .20 .50
300 Adam Foote .20 .50
301 Darcy Tucker .25 .60
302 Andrew Raycroft .25 .60
303 Kristian Huselius .20 .50
304 Fedor Tyutin .20 .50
305 R.J. Umberger .20 .50
306 Fredrik Norrena .20 .50
307 Jason Chimera .20 .50
308 Fredrik Modin .20 .50
309 Mike Commodore .20 .50
310 Jere Lehtinen .20 .50
311 Mike Ribeiro .25 .60
312 Philippe Boucher .20 .50
313 Marty Turco .30 .75
314 Stephane Robidas .20 .50
315 Toby Petersen .20 .50
316 Loui Eriksson .30 .75
317 Sean Avery .20 .50
318 Pavel Datsyuk .40 1.00
319 Chris Chelios .30 .75
320 Mikael Samuelsson .20 .50
321 Dan Cleary .25 .60
322 Johan Franzen .30 .75
323 Brian Rafalski .25 .60
324 Valtteri Filppula .30 .75
325 Marian Hossa .25 .60
326 Ty Conklin .25 .60
327 Dwayne Roloson .25 .60
328 Lubomir Visnovsky .20 .50
329 Tom Gilbert .20 .50
330 Sam Gagner .25 .60
331 Zach Stortini .20 .50
332 Erik Cole .25 .60
333 Craig Anderson .30 .75
334 Richard Zednik .30 .75
335 Keith Ballard .20 .50
336 Nick Boynton .20 .50
337 Brett McLean .20 .50
338 Cory Murphy .20 .50
339 Cory Stillman .20 .50
340 Jarret Stoll .25 .60
341 Jonathan Bernier .40 1.00
342 Alexander Frolov .20 .50
343 Kyle Calder .20 .50
344 Derek Armstrong .20 .50
345 Michal Handzus .25 .60
346 Tom Preissing .20 .50
347 Andrew Brunette .20 .50
348 Niklas Backstrom .30 .75
349 Owen Nolan .25 .60
350 Brent Burns .40 1.00
351 Eric Belanger .20 .50
352 Derek Boogaard .20 .50
353 Kim Johnsson .20 .50
354 Marek Zidlicky .20 .50
355 Andrei Markov .30 .75
356 Jaroslav Halak .30 .75
357 Chris Higgins .20 .50
358 Alex Kovalev .25 .60
359 Roman Hamrlik .25 .60
360 Alex Tanguay .20 .50
361 Marc Denis .25 .60
362 Jason Arnott .25 .60
363 J.P. Dumont .20 .50
364 Dan Ellis .20 .50
365 Jordin Tootoo .30 .75
366 Rich Peverley .25 .60
367 Bobby Holik .20 .50
368 Zach Parise .30 .75
369 Jamie Langenbrunner .20 .50
370 Dainius Zubrus .20 .50
371 David Clarkson .25 .60
372 Travis Zajac .25 .60

Brian Rolston	.25	.60
Doug Weight	.30	.75
Mark Streit	.20	.50
Jeff Tambellini	.20	.50
Mike Comrie	.25	.60
Chris Campoli	.20	.50
Sean Bergenheim	.20	.50
Richard Park	.20	.50
Chris Drury	.25	.60
Aaron Voros	.20	.50
Nikolai Zherdev	.20	.50
Michal Rozsival	.20	.50
Daniel Girardi	.20	.50
Wade Redden	.20	.50
Dany Heatley	.30	.75
Martin Gerber	.25	.60
Chris Kelly	.25	.60
Chris Phillips	.20	.50
Nick Foligno	.30	.75
Jeff Carter	.30	.75
Antero Niittymaki	.25	.60
Braydon Coburn	.20	.50
Riley Cote	.20	.50
Daniel Briere	.30	.75
Scott Hartnell	.30	.75
Randy Jones	.20	.50
Shane Doan	.25	.60
Olli Jokinen	.25	.60
Mikael Tellqvist	.25	.60
Steven Reinprecht	.20	.50
Derek Morris	.20	.50
Eric Godard	.20	.50
Miroslav Satan	.30	.75
Hal Gill	.20	.50
Evgeni Malkin	1.00	2.50
Maxime Talbot	.30	.75
Ryan Whitney	.30	.75
Patrick Marleau	.30	.75
Jeremy Roenick	.30	.75
Mike Grier	.20	.50
Rob Blake	.30	.75
Brad Winchester	.20	.50
Keith Tkachuk	.30	.75
Chris Mason	.25	.60
David Backes	.30	.75
Barret Jackman	.20	.50
Yan Stastny	.25	.60
Mark Recchi	.40	1.00
Radim Vrbata	.25	.60
Ryan Malone	.20	.50
Vaclav Prospal	.20	.50
Vincent Lecavalier	.25	.60
Andrej Meszaros	.20	.50
Evgeni Artyukhin	.20	.50
Gary Roberts	.20	.50
Olaf Kolzig	.30	.75
Jeff Finger	.20	.50
Curtis Joseph	.30	.75
Jason Blake	.20	.50
Niklas Hagman	.20	.50
Matt Stajan	.25	.60
Alexei Ponikarovsky	.20	.50
Pavol Demitra	.40	1.00
Curtis Sanford	.25	.60
Sami Salo	.20	.50
Kevin Bieksa	.25	.60
Steve Bernier	.20	.50
Taylor Pyatt	.20	.50
Alexandre Burrows	.30	.75
Willie Mitchell	.20	.50
Jose Theodore	.30	.75
Alexander Ovechkin	1.25	3.00
Sergei Fedorov	.50	1.25
Tom Poti	.20	.50
Michael Nylander	.20	.50
Brooks Laich	.20	.50
Evgeni Malkin CL	1.00	2.50
Alexander Ovechkin CL	1.25	3.00
Andrew Ebbett YG RC	2.00	5.00
Brett Festerling YG RC	2.50	6.00
Nathan Oystrick YG RC	3.00	8.00
Boris Valabik YG RC	3.00	8.00
Nathan Gerbe YG RC	3.00	8.00
Justin Peters YG RC	3.00	8.00
Zach Boychuk YG RC	3.00	8.00
Dwight Helminen YG RC	3.00	8.00
Patrick Dwyer YG RC	3.00	8.00
Simeon Varlamov YG RC	6.00	15.00
Joe Jensen YG RC	3.00	8.00
Chris Stewart YG RC	3.00	8.00
Dan LaCosta YG RC	3.00	8.00
Nikita Filatov YG RC	3.00	8.00
Derek Dorsett YG RC	4.00	10.00
Andrew Murray YG RC	2.50	6.00
Fabian Brunnstrom YG RC	2.50	6.00
Steve MacIntyre YG RC	3.00	8.00
Theo Peckham YG RC	3.00	8.00
Michal Repik YG RC	3.00	8.00
Jason Garrison YG RC	3.00	8.00
Brian Boyle YG RC	2.50	6.00
Teddy Purcell YG RC	4.00	10.00
Danny Taylor YG RC	2.50	6.00
Matthew Halischuk YG RC	2.00	5.00
Petr Vrana YG RC	2.00	5.00
Patrick Davis YG RC	2.50	6.00
Pierre-Luc	2.00	5.00
etourneau-Leblond YG RC		
Josh Bailey YG RC	8.00	20.00
Brett Skinner YG RC	2.50	6.00
Mitch Fritz YG RC	2.50	6.00
Jesse Winchester YG RC	2.00	5.00
Andreas Nodl YG RC	2.00	5.00
Kenndal McArdle YG RC	2.50	6.00
Darroll Powe YG RC	3.00	8.00
Viktor Tikhonov YG RC	2.50	6.00
Kevin Porter YG RC	2.50	6.00
Janne Pesonen YG RC	2.50	6.00
John Curry YG RC	3.00	8.00
Jamie McGinn YG RC	3.00	8.00
Brad Staubitz YG RC	2.50	6.00
Tom Cavanagh YG RC	2.50	6.00
Ben Bishop YG RC	10.00	20.00
Justin Pogge YG RC	3.00	8.00
Nikolai Kulemin YG RC	3.00	8.00
Jonas Frogren YG RC	2.00	5.00
Cory Schneider YG RC	8.00	20.00
Tyler Sloan YG RC	4.00	10.00
Karl Alzner YG RC	2.00	5.00
Brunns/Tikhnv/Filatv CL	4.00	10.00

008-09 Upper Deck Exclusives

TS/100: 2.5X TO 6X BASE
UNG GUNS/100: 1X TO 2.5X BASE
TED PRINT RUN 100 SERIAL #'d SETS

icklas Backstrom	5.00	12.00
Mike Smith	3.00	8.00
Kristopher Letang	3.00	8.00
Claude Giroux YG	40.00	100.00
Steven Stamkos YG	125.00	250.00

2008-09 Upper Deck All Star Game Montreal

COMPLETE SET (10)	15.00	40.00
MTL1 Alex Kovalev	.75	2.00
MTL2 Alexander Ovechkin	4.00	10.00
MTL3 Carey Price	4.00	10.00
MTL4 Guy Lafleur	1.25	3.00
MTL5 Larry Robinson	1.00	2.50
MTL6 Jarome Iginla	1.00	2.50
MTL7 Patrick Roy	2.50	6.00
MTL8 Sidney Crosby	4.00	10.00
MTL9 Saku Koivu	1.00	2.50
MTL10 Jean Beliveau	1.00	2.50

2008-09 Upper Deck All-Stars

COMPLETE SET (30)	40.00	100.00
SP STATED ODDS 1:		
AS1 Tomas Kaberle	.60	1.50
AS2 Daniel Alfredsson	1.00	2.50
AS3 Marian Hossa	.75	2.00
AS4 Eric Staal	1.25	3.00
AS5 Rick DiPietro	.75	2.00
AS6 Anze Kopitar	1.50	4.00
AS7 Zdeno Chara	1.00	2.50
AS8 Henrik Sedin	1.00	2.50
AS9 Jason Spezza	1.00	2.50
AS10 Shawn Horcoff	.60	1.50
AS11 Marian Gaborik	1.25	3.00
AS12 Andrei Markov	1.00	2.50
AS13 Martin St. Louis	1.00	2.50
AS14 Nicklas Lidstrom	1.00	2.50
AS15 Pavel Datsyuk	1.25	3.00
AS16 Rick Nash	1.00	2.50
AS17 Mike Ribeiro	.75	2.00
AS18 Ryan Getzlaf	1.50	4.00
AS19 Tomas Vokoun	.75	2.00
AS20 Vincent Lecavalier	.75	2.00
AS21 Joe Thornton SP	4.00	10.00
AS22 Evgeni Nabokov SP	2.50	6.00
AS23 Dion Phaneuf SP	3.00	8.00
AS24 Jarome Iginla SP	3.00	8.00
AS25 Chris Pronger SP	2.50	6.00
AS26 Mike Richards SP	3.00	8.00
AS27 Chris Osgood SP	3.00	8.00
AS28 Evgeni Malkin SP	10.00	25.00
AS29 Alexander Ovechkin SP	12.00	30.00
AS30 Ilya Kovalchuk SP	3.00	8.00

2008-09 Upper Deck All-World Team

COMPLETE SET (20)	50.00	100.00
SP STATED ODDS 1:		
AWT1 Sidney Crosby	5.00	12.00
AWT2 Alexander Ovechkin	5.00	12.00
AWT3 Evgeni Malkin	4.00	10.00
AWT4 Nicklas Lidstrom	1.25	3.00
AWT5 Martin Brodeur	2.50	6.00
AWT6 Henrik Zetterberg	1.50	4.00
AWT7 Jarome Iginla	1.25	3.00
AWT8 Mike Modano	2.00	5.00
AWT9 Ilya Kovalchuk	1.25	3.00
AWT10 Marian Gaborik	1.50	4.00
AWT11 Joe Thornton SP	6.00	15.00
AWT12 Anze Kopitar SP	8.00	20.00
AWT13 Miikka Kiprusoff SP	4.00	10.00
AWT14 Ales Hemsky SP	4.00	10.00
AWT15 Patrick Kane SP	10.00	25.00
AWT16 Michael Ryder SP	3.00	8.00
AWT17 Scott Gomez SP	4.00	10.00
AWT18 Saku Koivu SP	5.00	12.00
AWT19 Evgeni Nabokov SP	4.00	10.00
AWT20 Markus Naslund SP	4.00	10.00

2008-09 Upper Deck Big Game Hunters

COMPLETE SET (30)	125.00	250.00
BGHAK Alex Kovalev	3.00	8.00
BGHAO Alexander Ovechkin SP	15.00	40.00
BGHBR Brad Richards	4.00	10.00
BGHCO Chris Osgood	4.00	10.00
BGHCP Chris Pronger	3.00	8.00
BGHDB Daniel Briere	4.00	10.00
BGHDP Dion Phaneuf	4.00	10.00
BGHEM Evgeni Malkin SP	12.00	30.00
BGHES Eric Staal	5.00	12.00
BGHHZ Henrik Zetterberg SP	5.00	12.00
BGHJF Johan Franzen	4.00	10.00
BGHJG Jean-Sebastien Giguere	4.00	10.00
BGHJI Jarome Iginla SP	4.00	10.00
BGHJS Joe Sakic SP	6.00	15.00
BGHJT Joe Thornton SP	5.00	12.00
BGHMB Martin Brodeur SP	8.00	20.00
BGHMG Marian Gaborik	5.00	12.00
BGHMH Marian Hossa	3.00	8.00
BGHMM Mike Modano	6.00	15.00
BGHMT Marty Turco	4.00	10.00
BGHNL Nicklas Lidstrom	4.00	10.00
BGHPE Patrik Elias	4.00	10.00
BGHPR Carey Price	10.00	25.00
BGHSC Sidney Crosby SP	12.00	30.00
BGHSG Scott Gomez	3.00	8.00
BGHSN Scott Niedermayer	4.00	10.00
BGHST Martin St. Louis	4.00	10.00
BGHTO Jonathan Toews SP	10.00	25.00
BGHTS Teemu Selanne	8.00	20.00
BGHVL Vincent Lecavalier SP	3.00	8.00

2008-09 Upper Deck Biography of a Season

BS1 Alexander Ovechkin	1.25	3.00
BS2 Henrik Zetterberg	.40	1.00
BS3 Nicklas Lidstrom	.30	.75
BS4 Steven Stamkos	2.00	5.00
BS5 Fabian Brunstrom	1.25	3.00
BS6 H.Lundqvist/M.Staal	.40	1.00
BS7 Sidney Crosby	1.25	3.00
BS8 Carey Price	1.25	3.00
BS9 Jordan Staal	.30	.75
BS10 Roberto Luongo	.40	1.00
BS11 Patrick Marleau	.30	.75
BS12 Alexander Ovechkin	1.25	3.00
BS13 Sidney Crosby	1.25	3.00
BS14 Keith Tkachuk	.30	.75
BS15 Thomas Vanek	.30	.75
BS16 Scott Hartnell	.30	.75
BS17 Steve Mason	.50	1.25
BS18 Henrik Zetterberg	.40	1.00
BS19 Doug Weight	.30	.75
BS20 Carey Price	1.25	3.00
BS21 Mats Sundin	.30	.75
BS22 Dion Phaneuf	.30	.75
BS23 Blake Wheeler	.75	2.00
BS24 Alex Kovalev	.25	.60
BS25 Martin Brodeur	.60	1.50
BS26 Mike Green	.30	.75
BS27 Jarome Iginla	.30	.75
BS28 Steven Stamkos	2.00	5.00
BS29 Evgeni Malkin	1.00	2.50
BS30 Alexander Ovechkin	1.25	3.00

2008-09 Upper Deck Captains Calling

COMPLETE SET (7)	6.00	15.00
CPT1 Sidney Crosby	3.00	8.00
CPT2 Jarome Iginla	.75	2.00
CPT3 Joe Sakic	1.25	3.00
CPT4 Nicklas Lidstrom	.75	2.00
CPT5 Saku Koivu	.75	2.00
CPT6 Brenden Morrow	.60	1.50
CPT7 Rick Nash	.75	2.00

2008-09 Upper Deck Clear Cut Duos

STATED PRINT RUN 25 SERIAL #'d SETS		
CD1 M.Lemieux/S.Crosby	40.00	100.00
CD2 E.Malkin/J.Staal	30.00	80.00
CD3 W.Gretzky/M.Messier	50.00	125.00
CD4 B.Orr/P.Esposito	30.00	80.00
CD5 R.Getzlaf/J.Giguere	15.00	40.00
CD6 P.Roy/C.Price	40.00	100.00
CD7 T.Selanne/S.Niedermayer	20.00	50.00
CD8 I.Kovalchuk/K.Lehtonen	10.00	25.00
CD9 P.Bergeron/M.Savard	12.00	30.00
CD10 R.Miller/T.Vanek	10.00	25.00
CD11 J.Iginla/M.Kiprusoff	10.00	25.00
CD12 E.Staal/C.Ward	12.00	30.00
CD13 J.Sakic/P.Stastny	15.00	40.00
CD14 R.Nash/S.Mason	15.00	40.00
CD15 J.Toews/P.Kane	25.00	60.00
CD16 M.Modano/M.Turco	15.00	40.00
CD17 H.Zetterberg/P.Datsyuk	12.00	30.00
CD18 S.Gagner/A.Cogliano	8.00	20.00
CD19 T.Vokoun/N.Horton	8.00	20.00
CD20 A.Kopitar/J.Johnson	15.00	40.00
CD21 M.Gaborik/J.Harding	12.00	30.00
CD22 C.Price/S.Koivu	40.00	100.00
CD23 J.Arnott/J.Dumont	8.00	20.00
CD24 M.Brodeur/Z.Parise	20.00	50.00
CD25 G.Howe/H.Zetterberg	25.00	60.00
CD26 H.Lundqvist/C.Drury	12.00	30.00
CD27 M.Messier/B.Leetch	12.00	30.00
CD28 J.Spezza/D.Heatley	10.00	25.00
CD29 S.Gagne/D.Briere	10.00	25.00
CD30 S.Doan/P.Mueller	8.00	20.00
CD31 S.Crosby/E.Malkin	40.00	100.00
CD32 J.Thornton/E.Nabokov	12.00	30.00
CD33 P.Kariya/B.Boyes	12.00	30.00
CD34 V.Lecavalier/M.St. Louis	10.00	25.00
CD35 M.Sundin/A.Steen	10.00	25.00
CD36 R.Luongo/H.Sedin	12.00	30.00
CD37 A.Ovechkin/N.Backstrom	40.00	100.00
CD38 R.Getzlaf/C.Perry	15.00	40.00
CD39 C.Osgood/N.Lidstrom	10.00	25.00
CD40 M.Sundin/T.Kaberle	10.00	25.00
CD41 J.Thornton/P.Marleau	12.00	30.00
CD42 M.Modano/B.Richards	15.00	40.00

2008-09 Upper Deck Clear Cut Rookies

STATED ODDS 1:288		
STATED PRINT RUN 100 SERIAL #'d SETS		
CCR1 Ilya Zubov	5.00	12.00
CCR2 Blake Wheeler	25.00	60.00
CCR3 Petr Vrana	4.00	10.00
CCR4 Jakub Voracek	12.00	30.00
CCR5 Kyle Turris	10.00	25.00
CCR6 Viktor Tikhonov	5.00	12.00
CCR7 Brandon Sutter	6.00	15.00
CCR8 Steven Stamkos	40.00	100.00
CCR9 Luke Schenn	25.00	60.00
CCR10 Luca Sbisa	4.00	10.00
CCR11 Mattias Ritola	5.00	12.00
CCR12 Kevin Porter	5.00	12.00
CCR13 Matt D'Agostini	5.00	12.00
CCR14 Alex Pietrangelo	8.00	20.00
CCR15 Nathan Oystrick	6.00	15.00
CCR16 T.J. Oshie	15.00	40.00
CCR17 Kyle Okposo	6.00	15.00
CCR18 Andreas Nodl	4.00	10.00
CCR19 James Neal	12.00	30.00
CCR20 Oscar Moller	5.00	12.00
CCR21 Vladimir Mihalik	4.00	10.00
CCR22 Shawn Matthias	6.00	15.00
CCR23 Steve Mason	40.00	100.00
CCR24 Nikolai Kulemin	6.00	15.00
CCR25 Ryan Jones	6.00	15.00
CCR26 Patric Hornqvist	6.00	15.00
CCR27 Darren Helm	6.00	15.00
CCR28 Alex Goligoski	8.00	20.00
CCR29 Claude Giroux	12.00	30.00
CCR30 Colton Gillies	5.00	12.00
CCR31 Michael Frolik	6.00	15.00
CCR32 Nikita Filatov	6.00	15.00
CCR33 Erik Ersberg	5.00	12.00
CCR34 Robbie Earl	4.00	10.00
CCR35 Drew Doughty	15.00	40.00
CCR36 Fabian Brunnstrom	25.00	60.00
CCR37 Derick Brassard	5.00	12.00
CCR38 Zach Boychuk	6.00	15.00
CCR39 Zach Bogosian	6.00	15.00
CCR40 Mikkel Boedker	8.00	20.00
CCR41 Patrik Berglund	5.00	12.00
CCR42 Justin Abdelkader	10.00	25.00

2008-09 Upper Deck Clear Cut Winners

STATED PRINT RUN 100 SERIAL #'d SETS		
CC1 Alexander Ovechkin	20.00	50.00
CC2 Bobby Orr	15.00	40.00
CC3 Carey Price	20.00	50.00
CC4 Evgeni Malkin	15.00	40.00
CC5 Gordie Howe	12.00	30.00
CC6 Henrik Lundqvist	6.00	15.00
CC7 Henrik Zetterberg	6.00	15.00
CC8 Ilya Kovalchuk	5.00	12.00
CC9 Jarome Iginla	5.00	12.00
CC10 Jason Arnott	4.00	10.00
CC11 Jason Spezza	5.00	12.00
CC12 Joe Sakic	8.00	20.00
CC13 Joe Thornton	6.00	15.00
CC14 Jonathan Toews	12.00	30.00
CC15 Marian Gaborik	6.00	15.00
CC16 Mario Lemieux	15.00	40.00
CC17 Mark Messier	6.00	15.00
CC18 Martin Brodeur	10.00	25.00
CC19 Martin St. Louis	5.00	12.00
CC20 Mats Sundin	5.00	12.00
CC21 Miikka Kiprusoff	4.00	10.00
CC22 Mike Modano	8.00	20.00
CC23 Nicklas Backstrom	8.00	20.00
CC24 Patrick Kane	10.00	25.00
CC25 Patrick Roy	12.00	30.00
CC26 Paul Kariya	6.00	15.00
CC27 Pavel Datsyuk	6.00	15.00
CC28 Peter Mueller	4.00	10.00
CC29 Rick DiPietro	4.00	10.00
CC30 Rick Nash	5.00	12.00
CC31 Roberto Luongo	6.00	15.00
CC32 Ryan Getzlaf	8.00	20.00
CC33 Ryan Miller	5.00	12.00
CC34 Saku Koivu	5.00	12.00
CC35 Sam Gagner	4.00	10.00
CC36 Shane Doan	4.00	10.00
CC37 Sidney Crosby	20.00	50.00
CC38 Simon Gagne	5.00	12.00
CC39 Teemu Selanne	10.00	25.00
CC40 Tomas Vokoun	4.00	10.00
CC41 Vincent Lecavalier	4.00	10.00
CC42 Wayne Gretzky	25.00	60.00

2008-09 Upper Deck Fab Four Fabrics

STATED PRINT RUN 100 SERIAL #'d SETS		
FFANA Selane/GetzlGig/Nieder	15.00	40.00
FFASG Crsby/Sakc/Thrn/Lecv	25.00	60.00
FFATL Kovl/Leht/Armst/Enstrm	8.00	20.00
FFBOS Berg/Svrd/Kessl/Chara	10.00	25.00
FFBUF Vank/Millr/Stffrd/Conly	8.00	20.00
FFCAN Iginl/Ryd/Chch/Ribeiro	8.00	20.00
FFCAR Staal/Ward/Will/Brind	10.00	25.00
FFCEN Staal/Spez/Rich/Berg	10.00	25.00
FFCGY Igin/Phnf/Kiprsf/Caml	8.00	20.00
FFCHI Toews/Kne/Kth/Khab	20.00	50.00
FFCLB Nash/Lecl/Picrd/Peca	8.00	20.00
FFCOL Sakc/Frsb/Stst/Wlski	12.00	30.00
FFCZS Hssa/Hjdk/Elias/Mich	8.00	20.00
FFDAL Modn/Trco/Rich/Morr	12.00	30.00
FFDEF Phnf/Jhns/Jhns/Webr	8.00	20.00
FFDET Zettr/Dtsyk/Lids/Chel	10.00	25.00
FFEDM Ggnr/Hmsk/Brule/Rolo	6.00	15.00
FFFIN Selne/Koivu/Joki/Kvu	15.00	40.00
FFFLA Vokn/Hrtn/Bouw/Weis	8.00	20.00
FFLAK Kopit/Frlv/Jhns/Brwn	12.00	30.00
FFMIN Gabr/Kvu/Bouch/Nln	10.00	25.00
FFMTL Kovl/Tng/Ltnd/Koivu	8.00	20.00
FFNAS Arntt/Wbr/Dmnt/Lgwn	6.00	15.00
FFNET Trco/Lgce/Rlsn/Thms	8.00	20.00
FFNJD Brod/Prse/Gnta/Elias	15.00	40.00
FFNYI DiPtr/Wght/Grin/Cmrie	8.00	20.00
FFNYR Lund/Zhrdv/Gomz/Dru	10.00	25.00
FFOTT Htly/Spez/Alfrd/Phill	8.00	20.00
FFPHI Ggne/Rchr/Brie/Cartr	8.00	20.00
FFPHX Muellr/Doan/Jkin/Jov	6.00	15.00
FFPIT Crsby/Mlkn/Stal/Wht	30.00	80.00
FFQUE Brod/Lngo/Flry/Theod	15.00	40.00
FFRUS Ovch/Mlkn/Kovl/Fedr	30.00	80.00
FFSJS Thrnt/Chech/Marl/Mich	10.00	25.00
FFSTL Krya/Byes/Tkchk/Leg	10.00	25.00
FFSWE Snd/Nasl/Bckstr/Zett	12.00	30.00
FFTBL Lecav/St.L/Rnger/Joki	8.00	20.00
FFTOR Sund/Sten/Blke/Tosk	8.00	20.00
FFUSA Rnck/Mdno/Tkch/Chl	12.00	30.00
FFVAN Lngo/Sdin/Sdin/Bernr	10.00	25.00
FFWAS Ovch/Bck/Semn/Gren	30.00	80.00
FFWNG Nash/Htly/Ggne/St.L	8.00	20.00

2008-09 Upper Deck Favourite Sons

COMPLETE SET (14)	12.00	30.00
BASIC SER.2 INSERT ODDS 1:4		
FS1 Ryan Smyth	.60	1.50
FS2 Brad Richards	.75	2.00
FS3 Jonathan Cheechoo	.75	2.00
FS4 Sidney Crosby	3.00	8.00
FS5 Jason Spezza	.75	2.00
FS6 Shane Doan	.60	1.50
FS7 Devin Setoguchi	.60	1.50
FS8 Brenden Morrow	.60	1.50
FS9 Carey Price	3.00	8.00
FS10 Jonathan Toews	2.00	5.00
FS11 Michael Ryder	.50	1.25
FS12 Martin St. Louis	.75	2.00
FS13 Vincent Lecavalier	.60	1.50
FS14 Patrice Bergeron	1.00	2.50

2008-09 Upper Deck Game Jerseys

STATED ODDS 1:12		
GJAA Alex Auld	2.50	6.00
GJAE Alexander Edler	2.50	6.00
GJAH Ales Hemsky	3.00	8.00
GJAK Alex Kovalev	3.00	8.00
GJAL Alexander Steen	4.00	10.00
GJAM Andrej Meszaros	2.50	6.00
GJAN Antero Niittymaki	3.00	8.00
GJAO Alexander Ovechkin	8.00	20.00
GJAP Alexandre Picard	2.50	6.00
GJAS Alexander Semin	4.00	10.00
GJAT Alex Tanguay	2.50	6.00
GJBB Brad Boyes	2.50	6.00
GJBE Brendan Bell	2.50	6.00
GJBG Bill Guerin	4.00	10.00
GJBM Brenden Morrow	3.00	8.00
GJBR Brad Richards	4.00	10.00
GJCA Colby Armstrong	2.50	6.00
GJCC Chris Chelios	4.00	10.00
GJCD Chris Drury	3.00	8.00
GJCP Chris Phillips	2.50	6.00
GJCW Cam Ward	4.00	10.00
GJDA Daniel Alfredsson	4.00	10.00
GJDB Daniel Briere	4.00	10.00
GJDH Dany Heatley	4.00	10.00
GJDK Duncan Keith	4.00	10.00
GJDL David Legwand	3.00	8.00
GJDP Dion Phaneuf	4.00	10.00
GJDR Dwayne Roloson	3.00	8.00
GJDS Daniel Sedin	4.00	10.00
GJDT Darcy Tucker	3.00	8.00
GJDW Doug Weight	4.00	10.00
GJEC Erik Cole	3.00	8.00
GJEN Evgeni Nabokov	3.00	8.00
GJES Eric Staal	5.00	12.00
GJGA Marian Gaborik	5.00	12.00
GJGB Gilbert Brule	2.50	6.00
GJGI Brian Gionta	3.00	8.00
GJGM Glen Murray	3.00	8.00
GJGR Gary Roberts	2.50	6.00
GJHT Hannu Toivonen	3.00	8.00
GJHZ Henrik Zetterberg	5.00	12.00
GJIK Ilya Kovalchuk	4.00	10.00
GJIW Ian White	2.50	6.00
GJJA Jason Arnott	3.00	8.00
GJJB Jay Bouwmeester	4.00	10.00
GJJC Jonathan Cheechoo	4.00	10.00
GJJE Jeff Carter	4.00	10.00
GJJG Jean-Sebastien Giguere	4.00	10.00
GJJI Jarome Iginla	4.00	10.00
GJJO Jussi Jokinen	2.50	6.00
GJJP Joni Pitkanen	2.50	6.00
GJJR Jeremy Roenick	4.00	10.00
GJJS Jason Spezza	4.00	10.00
GJJT Joe Thornton	5.00	12.00
GJKA Patrick Kane	8.00	20.00
GJKL Kari Lehtonen	3.00	8.00
GJKO Anze Kopitar	6.00	15.00
GJKT Keith Tkachuk	4.00	10.00
GJLE Manny Legace	4.00	10.00
GJLS Lee Stempniak	2.50	6.00
GJMA Marc Savard	2.50	6.00
GJMB Martin Brodeur	8.00	20.00
GJMC Mike Cammalleri	3.00	8.00
GJMG Mike Green	4.00	10.00
GJMK Miikka Kiprusoff	3.00	8.00
GJML Mario Lemieux	12.00	30.00
GJMM Mark Messier	5.00	12.00
GJMN Markus Naslund	3.00	8.00
GJMO Mike Modano	6.00	15.00
GJMR Mark Recchi	5.00	12.00
GJMS Matt Stajan	3.00	8.00
GJMT Marty Turco	4.00	10.00
GJNZ Nikolai Zherdev	2.50	6.00
GJOJ Olli Jokinen	3.00	8.00
GJPA Patrice Bergeron	5.00	12.00
GJPB Pierre-Marc Bouchard	4.00	10.00
GJPF Peter Forsberg	5.00	12.00
GJPK Paul Kariya	5.00	12.00
GJPL Pascal Leclaire	3.00	8.00
GJPR Patrick Roy	12.50	30.00
GJPS Paul Stastny	4.00	10.00
GJRA Andrew Raycroft	3.00	8.00
GJRB Brian Rafalski	3.00	8.00
GJRI Mike Richards	4.00	10.00
GJRL Roberto Luongo	5.00	12.00
GJRN Rick Nash	4.00	10.00
GJRY Michael Ryder	2.50	6.00
GJSA Joe Sakic	6.00	15.00
GJSC Sidney Crosby	15.00	40.00
GJSM Ladislav Smid	2.50	6.00
GJST Martin St. Louis	4.00	10.00
GJSU Mats Sundin	4.00	10.00
GJTH Jose Theodore	4.00	10.00
GJTI Kimmo Timonen	2.50	6.00
GJTS Teemu Selanne	8.00	20.00
GJTV Thomas Vanek	4.00	10.00
GJWG Wayne Gretzky	20.00	50.00
GJ2AA Arron Asham	2.50	6.00
GJ2AF Maxim Afinogenov	2.50	6.00
GJ2AL Andrew Ladd	4.00	10.00
GJ2AO Alexander Ovechkin	15.00	40.00
GJ2AV Nik Antropov	3.00	8.00
GJ2AW Andrew Wozniewski	2.50	6.00
GJ2BB Brandon Bochenski	2.50	6.00
GJ2BD Martin Brodeur	8.00	20.00
GJ2BL Brian Leetch	4.00	10.00
GJ2BM Brendan Morrison	2.50	6.00
GJ2BS Brad Stuart	2.50	6.00
GJ2CA Matt Carle	2.50	6.00
GJ2CC Chris Campoli	2.50	6.00
GJ2CD Chris Drury	3.00	8.00
GJ2CJ Curtis Joseph	4.00	10.00
GJ2CP Carey Price	15.00	40.00
GJ2CS Curtis Sanford	3.00	8.00
GJ2DB Donald Brashear	2.50	6.00
GJ2DT Darcy Tucker	3.00	8.00
GJ2EC Erik Cole	3.00	8.00
GJ2EJ Ed Jovanovski	3.00	8.00
GJ2EM Evgeni Malkin	12.00	30.00
GJ2ES Eric Staal	5.00	12.00
GJ2FZ Manny Fernandez	3.00	8.00
GJ2HA Martin Havlat	4.00	10.00
GJ2HE Milan Hejduk	3.00	8.00
GJ2HL Henrik Lundqvist	5.00	12.00
GJ2HO Marian Hossa	3.00	8.00
GJ2IK Ilya Kovalchuk	4.00	10.00
GJ2JS Jarret Stoll	3.00	8.00
GJ2JT Jeff Tambellini	2.50	6.00
GJ2JW Justin Williams	3.00	8.00
GJ2KC Kyle Calder	2.50	6.00
GJ2KZ Viktor Kozlov	2.50	6.00
GJ2MA Mark Stuart	2.50	6.00
GJ2MC Bryan McCabe	2.50	6.00
GJ2MD Marc Denis	3.00	8.00
GJ2ME Martin Erat	2.50	6.00
GJ2MF Marc-Andre Fleury	8.00	20.00
GJ2MG Martin Gerber	3.00	8.00
GJ2MK Mikko Koivu	3.00	8.00
GJ2ML Milan Lucic	6.00	15.00
GJ2MM Mark Messier	5.00	12.00
GJ2MN Matt Niskanen	3.00	8.00
GJ2MO Mattias Ohlund	2.50	6.00
GJ2MP Marc-Antoine Pouliot	2.50	6.00
GJ2MR Mark Recchi	5.00	12.00
GJ2MS Marc Savard	2.50	6.00
GJ2MT Marty Turco	4.00	10.00
GJ2OJ Olli Jokinen	3.00	8.00
GJ2PE Michael Peca	3.00	8.00
GJ2PH Chris Phillips	2.50	6.00
GJ2PM Peter Mueller	3.00	8.00
GJ2PY Corey Perry	4.00	10.00
GJ2RB Mike Ribeiro	3.00	8.00
GJ2RO Patrick Roy	10.00	25.00
GJ2RU Tuomo Ruutu	4.00	10.00
GJ2SB Steve Bernier	2.50	6.00
GJ2SE Brent Seabrook	4.00	10.00
GJ2SG Simon Gagne	4.00	10.00
GJ2SH Brendan Shanahan	5.00	12.00
GJ2ST Jordan Staal	4.00	10.00
GJ2SU Mats Sundin	4.00	10.00
GJ2SV Marek Svatos	2.50	6.00
GJ2SW Shea Weber	3.00	8.00
GJ2TO Jonathan Toews	10.00	25.00
GJ2TW Tiger Williams	3.00	8.00
GJ2VL Vincent Lecavalier	3.00	8.00

2008-09 Upper Deck Hat Trick Heroes

COMPLETE SET (14)	6.00	15.00
HT1 Alexander Ovechkin	2.50	6.00
HT2 Teemu Selanne	1.25	3.00
HT3 Jarome Iginla	.60	1.50
HT4 Joe Sakic	1.00	2.50
HT5 Thomas Vanek	.60	1.50
HT6 Evgeni Malkin	2.00	5.00
HT7 Ilya Kovalchuk	.60	1.50
HT8 Vincent Lecavalier	.50	1.25
HT9 Henrik Zetterberg	.75	2.00
HT10 Dany Heatley	.60	1.50
HT11 Rick Nash	.60	1.50
HT12 Marian Gaborik	.75	2.00
HT13 Marian Hossa	.50	1.25
HT14 Eric Staal	.75	2.00

2008-09 Upper Deck Hockey Heroes Sidney Crosby

COMPLETE SET (10)	75.00	150.00
COMP.SET w/o SPs (8)	12.00	30.00
COMMON CROSBY (HH1-HH8)	3.00	8.00
HH9 Crosby Painting	10.00	25.00
HHSC Crosby Header Card	15.00	40.00
HHSCA Crosby AU/87	175.00	300.00

2008-09 Upper Deck Masked Men

COMPLETE SET (30)	25.00	60.00
SP STATED ODDS 1:		
MM1 Martin Brodeur	2.00	5.00
MM2 Miikka Kiprusoff	.75	2.00
MM3 Roberto Luongo	1.25	3.00
MM4 Chris Osgood	1.00	2.50
MM5 Carey Price	4.00	10.00
MM6 Henrik Lundqvist	1.25	3.00
MM7 Ryan Miller	1.00	2.50
MM8 Vesa Toskala	.75	2.00
MM9 Jean-Sebastien Giguere	1.00	2.50
MM10 Evgeni Nabokov	.75	2.00
MM11 Marty Turco	1.00	2.50
MM12 Manny Legace	1.00	2.50
MM13 Mathieu Garon	.75	2.00
MM14 Martin Gerber	.75	2.00
MM15 Josh Harding	1.00	2.50
MM16 Tomas Vokoun	.75	2.00
MM17 Rick DiPietro	.75	2.00
MM18 Kari Lehtonen	.75	2.00
MM19 Marc-Andre Fleury	1.50	4.00
MM20 Cam Ward	1.00	2.50
MM21 Pascal Leclaire SP	1.00	2.50
MM22 Peter Budaj SP	1.00	2.50
MM23 Martin Biron SP	1.00	2.50
MM24 Tim Thomas SP	1.25	3.00
MM25 Cristobal Huet SP	1.00	2.50
MM26 Mike Smith SP	1.25	3.00
MM27 Chris Mason SP	1.00	2.50
MM28 Nikolai Khabibulin SP	1.25	3.00
MM29 Ilya Bryzgalov SP	1.00	2.50
MM30 Jason LaBarbera SP	1.00	2.50

2008-09 Upper Deck Rookie Impressions

COMPLETE SET (30)	100.00	200.00
RI1 Michael Frolik	3.00	8.00
RI2 Claude Giroux	6.00	15.00
RI3 Oscar Moller	2.50	6.00
RI4 Viktor Tikhonov	2.50	6.00
RI5 Derick Brassard	8.00	20.00
RI6 Kyle Okposo	3.00	8.00
RI7 Zach Boychuk	3.00	8.00
RI8 Patric Hornqvist	3.00	8.00
RI9 Petr Vrana	2.00	5.00
RI10 Luca Sbisa	2.00	5.00
RI11 T.J. Oshie	10.00	25.00
RI12 Nikolai Kulemin	3.00	8.00
RI13 Nikita Filatov	8.00	20.00
RI14 Mikkel Boedker	6.00	15.00
RI15 James Neal	6.00	15.00
RI16 Brian Boyle	2.50	6.00
RI17 Jamie McGinn	3.00	8.00
RI18 Andreas Nodl	2.00	5.00
RI19 Jakub Voracek	6.00	15.00
RI20 Shawn Matthias	3.00	8.00
RI21 Steven Stamkos SP	12.00	30.00
RI22 Kyle Turris SP	5.00	12.00
RI23 Luke Schenn SP	10.00	25.00
RI24 Drew Doughty SP	8.00	20.00
RI25 Colton Gillies SP	2.50	6.00
RI26 Brandon Sutter SP	3.00	8.00
RI27 Blake Wheeler SP	10.00	25.00
RI28 Fabian Brunnstrom SP	10.00	25.00
RI29 Zach Bogosian SP	3.00	8.00
RI30 Alex Pietrangelo SP	4.00	10.00

2008-09 Upper Deck Rookie Materials

OVERALL SER.2 MEM ODDS 1:12		
*PATCH/15: 1X TO 2.5X BASIC JSY		
RMAP Alex Pietrangelo	4.00	10.00
RMBK Zach Boychuk	3.00	8.00
RMBS Brandon Sutter	3.00	8.00
RMBW Blake Wheeler	8.00	20.00
RMCG Claude Giroux	8.00	20.00
RMDB Derick Brassard	2.50	6.00
RMDD Drew Doughty	8.00	20.00
RMFB Fabian Brunnstrom	2.50	6.00
RMGI Colton Gillies	2.50	6.00
RMJA Justin Abdelkader	5.00	12.00
RMJN James Neal	6.00	15.00
RMJV Jakub Voracek	6.00	15.00
RMKO Kyle Okposo	3.00	8.00
RMKP Kevin Porter	2.50	6.00
RMKT Kyle Turris	5.00	12.00
RMLK Lauri Korpikoski	2.00	5.00
RMLS Luca Sbisa	2.00	5.00
RMMA Steve Mason	5.00	12.00
RMMB Mikkel Boedker	4.00	10.00
RMMF Michael Frolik	3.00	8.00
RMNF Nikita Filatov	3.00	8.00
RMNK Nikolai Kulemin	3.00	8.00
RMPB Patrik Berglund	2.50	6.00
RMPH Patric Hornqvist	3.00	8.00
RMSC Luke Schenn	8.00	20.00
RMSM Shawn Matthias	3.00	8.00
RMSS Steven Stamkos	10.00	25.00
RMTO T.J. Oshie	6.00	15.00
RMVT Viktor Tikhonov	2.50	6.00
RMZB Zach Bogosian	3.00	8.00

2008-09 Upper Deck Rookie Playmakers

STATED ODDS 1:288		
STATED PRINT RUN 100 SERIAL #'d SETS		
RPAG Alex Goligoski	8.00	20.00
RPAP Alex Pietrangelo	8.00	20.00
RPBB Brian Boyle	5.00	12.00
RPBG Zach Bogosian	6.00	15.00
RPBL Brian Lee	5.00	12.00
RPBS Brandon Sutter	6.00	15.00
RPBW Blake Wheeler	15.00	40.00
RPCG Colton Gillies	5.00	12.00
RPDB Derick Brassard	5.00	12.00
RPDD Drew Doughty	15.00	40.00
RPEE Erik Ersberg	5.00	12.00
RPFB Fabian Brunnstrom	5.00	12.00
RPFR Michael Frolik	6.00	15.00
RPGI Claude Giroux	10.00	25.00
RPIZ Ilya Zubov	5.00	12.00
RPJA Justin Abdelkader	10.00	25.00
RPJN James Neal	12.00	30.00
RPJV Jakub Voracek	12.00	30.00
RPKO Kyle Okposo	6.00	15.00
RPKP Kevin Porter	5.00	12.00
RPKT Kyle Turris	10.00	25.00
RPLK Lauri Korpikoski	4.00	10.00
RPLS Luca Sbisa	4.00	10.00
RPMA Shawn Matthias	6.00	15.00
RPMB Mikkel Boedker	8.00	20.00
RPMF Mark Fistric	5.00	12.00
RPNF Nikita Filatov	6.00	15.00
RPNK Nikolai Kulemin	6.00	15.00
RPOM Oscar Moller	5.00	12.00
RPPB Patrik Berglund	12.00	30.00
RPPH Patric Hornqvist	6.00	15.00
RPPV Petr Vrana	4.00	10.00
RPRE Robbie Earl	4.00	10.00
RPRS Ryan Stone	4.00	10.00
RPSC Luke Schenn	25.00	60.00
RPSM Steve Mason	25.00	60.00
RPSS Steven Stamkos	30.00	80.00
RPTO T.J. Oshie	12.00	30.00
RPTS Tom Sestito	6.00	15.00
RPVM Vladimir Mihalik	4.00	10.00
RPVT Viktor Tikhonov	5.00	12.00
RPZB Zach Boychuk	6.00	15.00

2008-09 Upper Deck Signature Sensations

STATED ODDS 1:288		
CARD NUMBERS SS2 ARE FROM SER.2		
SSAC Andrew Cogliano	6.00	15.00
SSAO Alexander Ovechkin		
SSBB Brendan Bell Coyotes	5.00	12.00
SSBC Blake Comeau		
SSBD Brandon Dubinsky road	10.00	25.00
SSBM Bryan McCabe	5.00	12.00
SSBO Johnny Boychuk	5.00	12.00
SSBR Bobby Ryan skating	8.00	20.00
SSCB Casey Borer	8.00	20.00
SSCH Chris Higgins		
SSCL Dan Cleary	15.00	40.00
SSCM Cory Murphy		
SSCP Chris Phillips	5.00	12.00
SSCS Cory Stillman home	5.00	12.00
SSDA Daniel Sedin	8.00	20.00
SSDB Dan Boyle	6.00	15.00
SSDC Daniel Carcillo road	5.00	12.00
SSDG Daniel Girardi	10.00	25.00
SSDI Dimitri Patzold	5.00	12.00
SSDJ David Jones	5.00	12.00
SSDL Drew Larman	5.00	12.00
SSDM Drew MacIntyre	8.00	20.00
SSDP Dustin Penner	6.00	15.00
SSDS Drew Stafford	6.00	15.00
SSGH Gordie Howe	60.00	120.00
SSGL Guillaume Latendresse	10.00	25.00
SSGM Greg Moore	5.00	12.00
SSHA Jaroslav Halak	8.00	20.00
SSHE T.J. Hensick	10.00	25.00
SSHI Jonas Hiller	6.00	15.00
SSHJ Jannik Hansen	8.00	20.00
SSHS Henrik Sedin	10.00	25.00
SSJA Jared Boll	5.00	12.00
SSJB Jonathan Bernier skating	10.00	25.00
SSJD Jeff Drouin-Deslauriers	8.00	20.00
SSJG Jean-Sebastien Giguere		
SSJH Josh Harding road	8.00	20.00
SSJL John-Michael Liles	5.00	12.00
SSJO Joe Thornton		
SSJP Jason Pominville	12.00	30.00
SSJS Jordan Staal	8.00	20.00
SSJT Jonathan Toews	20.00	50.00
SSKN Kevin Nastiuk	5.00	12.00
SSKQ Kyle Quincey		
SSKR Kris Russell		
SSLK Lukas Kaspar	5.00	12.00
SSLT Lauri Tukonen	5.00	12.00
SSLU Joffrey Lupul	6.00	15.00
SSMA Mark Mancari	5.00	12.00
SSME Matt Ellis Kings	5.00	12.00
SSMF Mark Fraser portrait	6.00	15.00
SSMH Michal Handzus	6.00	15.00
SSMI Milan Michalek	12.00	30.00
SSMK Mike Knuble	5.00	12.00
SSML Milan Lucic	8.00	20.00
SSMM Marc Methot	5.00	12.00
SSMN Matt Niskanen face front	6.00	15.00
SSMO Mike Modano		
SSMP Marc-Antoine Pouliot	5.00	12.00
SSMR Mason Raymond	8.00	20.00
SSMS Marek Schwarz profile	8.00	20.00
SSNA Markus Naslund		
SSNK Nikolai Khabibulin profile	12.00	30.00
SSNW Noah Welch		
SSPA Ryan Parent	10.00	25.00
SSPD Daniel Paille road	5.00	12.00
SSPE Rod Pelley	5.00	12.00
SSPK Patrick Kane	15.00	40.00
SSPM Peter Mueller	6.00	15.00
SSPS Paul Stastny		
SSRB Rene Bourque	5.00	12.00
SSRC Ryane Clowe	10.00	25.00
SSRI Rich Peverley	6.00	15.00
SSRK Rostislav Klesla	5.00	12.00
SSRP Ryan Potulny		
SSRS Ryan Smyth boards	6.00	15.00
SSSC Sidney Crosby road	75.00	150.00
SSSD Steve Downie	8.00	20.00
SSSE Devin Setoguchi	6.00	15.00
SSSJ Jack Skille		
SSSM Stefan Meyer	5.00	12.00
SSST Marco Sturm	5.00	12.00
SSSW Stephen Weiss	5.00	12.00
SSTG Tom Gilbert	10.00	25.00
SSTH Tomas Holmstrom		
SSTK Tyler Kennedy	6.00	15.00
SSTL Jiri Tlusty boards w/crowd	6.00	15.00
SSTP Tomas Plihal		
SSTS Tobias Stephan	15.00	40.00
SSTV Thomas Vanek		
SSTZ Travis Zajac road	6.00	15.00
SS2AB Adam Burish	10.00	25.00
SS2AG Andy Greene	5.00	12.00
SS2AR Andrew Raycroft	12.00	30.00
SS2BB Brad Boyes	5.00	12.00
SS2BD Brandon Dubinsky home	10.00	25.00
SS2BH Bobby Hull		
SS2BL Brendan Bell Senators	5.00	12.00
SS2BO Martin Brodeur		
SS2BQ Rene Bourque	5.00	12.00
SS2BR Bobby Ryan standing	8.00	20.00
SS2BS Brett Sterling	6.00	15.00
SS2CB Chris Bourque	6.00	15.00
SS2CD Chris Drury		
SS2CH Chuck Kobasew	5.00	12.00
SS2CK Chris Kunitz		
SS2CO Jiri Tlusty boards	6.00	15.00
SS2CS Cory Stillman road	5.00	12.00
SS2DA Daniel Sedin home	8.00	20.00
SS2DC Daniel Carcillo home	5.00	12.00
SS2DP Daniel Paille home	5.00	12.00
SS2DR Dwayne Roloson	6.00	15.00
SS2DS Derek Sanderson	12.00	30.00
SS2DS2 Drew Stafford road	6.00	15.00
SS2DT Darcy Tucker	6.00	15.00
SS2DV David Perron	6.00	15.00
SS2EM Evgeni Malkin		
SS2EN Evgeni Nabokov	6.00	15.00
SS2GH Gordie Howe		
SS2HG Josh Harding home	8.00	20.00
SS2IK Marc-Antoine Pouliot road	5.00	12.00
SS2JB Jonathan Bernier in-goal	10.00	25.00
SS2JG Jean-Sebastien Giguere	25.00	60.00
SS2JH Jannik Hansen	8.00	20.00
SS2JL John-Michael Liles	5.00	12.00
SS2JM Jay McClement	5.00	12.00
SS2JP Jason Pominville		
SS2JS Jordan Staal home	8.00	20.00
SS2KA Petr Kalus	6.00	15.00
SS2KB Nikolai Khabibulin face	12.00	30.00
SS2KC Kyle Chipchura	6.00	15.00

SS2ME Matt Ellis Sabres 5.00 12.00
SS2MH Milan Hejduk 15.00 40.00
SS2ML Mike Lundin 5.00 12.00
SS2MN Matt Niskanen profile 6.00 15.00
SS2MO Brendan Morrison 6.00 15.00
SS2MR Mike Richards
SS2MS Mark Fraser in-action 6.00 15.00
SS2MY Stefan Meyer 5.00 12.00
SS2NW Noah Welch 5.00 12.00
SS2NZ Nikolai Zherdev 10.00 25.00
SS2OR Bobby Orr 75.00 150.00
SS2PA Patrick Kane
SS2PK Phil Kessel 12.00 30.00
SS2PV Rich Peverley 6.00 15.00
SS2PY Ryan Potulny 5.00 12.00
SS2RA Mason Raymond 8.00 20.00
SS2RI Mike Ribeiro
SS2RK Rostislav Klesla 5.00 12.00
SS2RS Ryan Smyth boards w/crowd 6.00 15.00
SS2SC Sidney Crosby home 75.00 150.00
SS2SE Devin Setoguchi road 6.00 15.00
SS2SH James Sheppard 5.00 12.00
SS2SJ Jack Skille road 6.00 15.00
SS2SM Matt Smaby 6.00 15.00
SS2ST Marc Staal 8.00 20.00
SS2SW Marek Schwarz face 8.00 20.00
SS2TE Tobias Enstrom 5.00 12.00
SS2TJ T.J. Hensick 10.00 25.00
SS2TM Torrey Mitchell 5.00 12.00
SS2TP Tomas Popperle 6.00 15.00
SS2TR Tuukka Rask 20.00 50.00
SS2TZ Travis Zajac home 6.00 15.00
SS2WG Wayne Gretzky

2008-09 Upper Deck Sophomore Sensations

COMPLETE SET (7) 8.00 20.00
SS1 Patrick Kane 2.00 5.00
SS2 Jonathan Toews 2.50 6.00
SS3 Carey Price 4.00 10.00
SS4 Marc Staal 1.00 2.50
SS5 Sam Gagner .75 2.00
SS6 Peter Mueller .75 2.00
SS7 Nicklas Backstrom 1.50 4.00

2008-09 Upper Deck Spectacular Saves

COMPLETE SET (7) 8.00 20.00
BASIC SER.2 INSERTS 1:4
SAVE1 Chris Osgood 1.25 3.00
SAVE2 Evgeni Nabokov 1.00 2.50
SAVE3 Henrik Lundqvist 1.50 4.00
SAVE4 Jean-Sebastien Giguere 1.25 3.00
SAVE5 Martin Brodeur 2.50 6.00
SAVE6 Marty Turco 1.25 3.00
SAVE7 Roberto Luongo 1.50 4.00

2008-09 Upper Deck Super Skills

COMPLETE SET (20) 150.00 300.00
SP STATED ODDS 1:
SS1 Martin Brodeur 6.00 15.00
SS2 Sidney Crosby 12.00 30.00
SS3 Alexander Ovechkin 12.00 30.00
SS4 Joe Thornton 4.00 10.00
SS5 Jarome Iginla 3.00 8.00
SS6 Martin St. Louis 3.00 8.00
SS7 Ilya Kovalchuk 3.00 8.00
SS8 Jonathan Toews 8.00 20.00
SS9 Evgeni Malkin 10.00 25.00
SS10 Henrik Zetterberg 4.00 10.00
SS11 Rick Nash SP 6.00 15.00
SS12 Carey Price SP 12.00 30.00
SS13 Ryan Getzlaf SP 10.00 25.00
SS14 Mike Richards SP 6.00 15.00
SS15 Paul Stastny SP 6.00 15.00
SS16 Andrew Cogliano SP 5.00 12.00
SS17 Peter Mueller SP 5.00 12.00
SS18 Anze Kopitar SP 10.00 25.00
SS19 Nicklas Backstrom SP 10.00 25.00
SS20 Eric Staal SP 8.00 20.00

2008-09 Upper Deck Tales of the Cup

COMPLETE SET (7) 4.00 10.00
BASIC INSERTS SER.2 1:4
TC1 Peter Forsberg 1.00 2.50
TC2 Mark Messier 1.00 2.50
TC3 Doug Weight .75 2.00
TC4 Ted Lindsay .75 2.00
TC5 Clark Gillies .75 2.00
TC6 Montreal Canadiens .60 1.50
TC7 Ottawa Senators .60 1.50

2008-09 Upper Deck The New Guard

COMPLETE SET (14) 15.00 40.00
BASIC INSERTS SER.2 1:4
NE1 Anze Kopitar 1.50 4.00
NE2 Alexander Ovechkin 4.00 10.00
NE3 Marian Gaborik 1.25 3.00
NE4 Carey Price 4.00 10.00
NE5 Dion Phaneuf 1.00 2.50
NE6 Evgeni Malkin 3.00 8.00
NE7 Eric Staal 1.25 3.00
NE8 Henrik Lundqvist 1.25 3.00
NE9 Ilya Kovalchuk 1.00 2.50
NE10 Jonathan Toews 2.50 6.00
NE11 Nicklas Backstrom 1.50 4.00
NE12 Patrick Kane 2.00 5.00
NE13 Ryan Getzlaf 1.50 4.00
NE14 Sidney Crosby 4.00 10.00

2008-09 Upper Deck Winter Classic

COMPLETE SET (14) 15.00 40.00
WC1 Sidney Crosby 8.00 20.00
WC2 Ryan Miller 2.00 5.00
WC3 Colby Armstrong 1.25 3.00
WC4 Ales Kotalik 1.25 3.00
WC5 Kristopher Letang 2.00 5.00
WC6 Thomas Vanek 2.00 5.00
WC7 Evgeni Malkin 6.00 15.00
WC8 Brian Campbell 1.50 4.00
WC9 Ty Conklin 1.50 4.00
WC10 Jason Pominville 2.00 5.00
WC11 Ryan Malone 1.25 3.00
WC12 Maxim Afinogenov 1.25 3.00
WC13 Jordan Staal 2.00 5.00
WC14 Tim Connolly 1.25 3.00

2008-09 Upper Deck Winter Classic Highlights Oversized

COMPLETE SET (14) 10.00 25.00
STATED ODDS 1 PER BLASTER BOX
WAL1 Sidney Crosby 5.00 12.00
WAL2 Kristopher Letang 1.25 3.00
WAL3 Colby Armstrong .75 2.00
WAL4 Ryan Malone .75 2.00
WAL5 Jordan Staal 1.25 3.00
WAL6 Thomas Vanek 1.25 3.00
WAL7 Evgeni Malkin 4.00 10.00
WAL8 Brian Campbell 1.00 2.50
WAL9 Ty Conklin 1.00 2.50
WAL10 Ryan Miller 1.25 3.00
WAL11 Ales Kotalik .75 2.00
WAL12 Maxim Afinogenov .75 2.00
WAL13 Jason Pominville 1.25 3.00
WAL14 Tim Connolly .75 2.00

2008-09 Upper Deck Young Guns Oversized

COMPLETE SET (14) 25.00 60.00
STATED ODDS ONE PER BLASTER BOX
OYG1 Zach Bogosian 1.00 2.50
OYG2 Blake Wheeler 2.50 6.00
OYG3 Brandon Sutter 1.00 2.50
OYG4 Jakub Voracek 2.00 5.00
OYG5 James Neal 2.00 5.00
OYG6 Drew Doughty 2.50 6.00
OYG7 Colton Gillies .75 2.00
OYG8 Kyle Okposo 1.00 2.50
OYG9 Luca Sbisa .60 1.50
OYG10 Mikkel Boedker 1.25 3.00
OYG11 Kyle Turris 1.50 4.00
OYG12 Alex Pietrangelo 1.25 3.00
OYG13 Steven Stamkos 10.00 25.00
OYG14 Luke Schenn 1.25 3.00

2009-10 Upper Deck

COMPLETE SET (500) 300.00 600.00
COMP.SER.1 SET (250) 200.00 350.00
COMP.SER.1 SET w/o SPs (200) 12.00 30.00
COMP.SER.2 SET (250) 125.00 250.00
COMP.SER.2 SET w/o SPs (200) 12.00 30.00
YG STATED ODDS 1:4
1 Phil Kessel .40 1.00
2 David Krejci .30 .75
3 Mark Recchi .40 1.00
4 Zdeno Chara .30 .75
5 Tim Thomas .30 .75
6 Blake Wheeler .30 .75
7 Dennis Wideman .20 .50
8 Tim Connolly .20 .50
9 Ryan Miller .30 .75
10 Craig Rivet .20 .50
11 Derek Roy .25 .60
12 Nathan Gerbe .25 .60
13 Daniel Paille .25 .60
14 Chris Butler .30 .75
15 Andrei Markov .30 .75
16 Maxim Lapierre .20 .50
17 Andrei Kostitsyn .25 .60
18 Carey Price 1.25 3.00
19 Josh Gorges .20 .50
20 Tomas Plekanec .30 .75
21 Georges Laraque .25 .60
22 Jason Spezza .30 .75
23 Daniel Alfredsson .30 .75
24 Nick Foligno .25 .60
25 Chris Phillips .20 .50
26 Jarkko Ruutu .20 .50
27 Jesse Winchester .25 .60
28 Brian Lee .30 .75
29 Mikhail Grabovski .30 .75
30 Luke Schenn .25 .60
31 Vesa Toskala .30 .75
32 Matt Stajan .25 .60
33 Alexei Ponikarovsky .20 .50
34 Ian White .25 .60
35 Nikolai Kulemin .25 .60
36 Jeff Carter .30 .75
37 Claude Giroux .30 .75
38 Ryan Parent .25 .60
39 Simon Gagne .30 .75
40 Daniel Carcillo .20 .50
41 Matt Carle .25 .60
42 Scott Hartnell .30 .75
43 Sidney Crosby 1.25 3.00
44 Maxime Talbot .30 .75
45 Sergei Gonchar .20 .50
46 Ruslan Fedotenko .20 .50
47 Marc-Andre Fleury .50 1.25
48 Evgeni Malkin 1.00 2.50
49 Bill Guerin .30 .75
50 Martin Brodeur .60 1.50
51 Paul Martin .20 .50
52 Patrik Elias .30 .75
53 Johnny Oduya .25 .60
54 David Clarkson .25 .60
55 Jamie Langenbrunner .20 .50
56 Josh Bailey .25 .60
57 Rick DiPietro .25 .60
58 Mark Streit .20 .50
59 Kyle Okposo .30 .75
60 Bruno Gervais .20 .50
61 Doug Weight .30 .75
62 Henrik Lundqvist .50 1.25
63 Sean Avery .25 .60
64 Wade Redden .20 .50
65 Chris Drury .25 .60
66 Michal Rozsival .20 .50
67 Brandon Dubinsky .25 .60
68 Marc Staal .30 .75
69 Nathan Horton .30 .75
70 David Booth .20 .50
71 Bryan McCabe .25 .60
72 Stephen Weiss .20 .50
73 Keith Ballard .20 .50
74 Michael Frolik .25 .60
75 Bryan Little .30 .75
76 Zach Bogosian .25 .60
77 Kari Lehtonen .25 .60
78 Todd White .20 .50
79 Tobias Enstrom .30 .75
80 Colby Armstrong .20 .50
81 Rod Brind`Amour .30 .75
82 Eric Staal .40 1.00
83 Joe Corvo .20 .50
84 Chad LaRose .20 .50
85 Jussi Jokinen .20 .50
86 Joni Pitkanen .25 .60
87 Martin St. Louis .30 .75
88 Mike Smith .30 .75
89 Paul Ranger .20 .50
90 Steven Stamkos .60 1.50
91 Ryan Malone .20 .50
92 Noah Welch .20 .50
93 Nicklas Backstrom .50 1.25
94 Mike Green .30 .75
95 Simeon Varlamov .30 .75
96 Brooks Laich .30 .75
97 Tom Poti .20 .50
98 Alexander Semin .30 .75
99 Eric Fehr .20 .50
100 Paul Kariya .40 1.00
101 Chris Mason .25 .60
102 Jeff Woywitka .20 .50
103 David Perron .20 .50
104 Patrik Berglund .20 .50
105 T.J. Oshie .50 1.25
106 Keith Tkachuk .30 .75
107 Jonathan Toews .60 1.50
108 Brian Campbell .25 .60
109 Patrick Sharp .30 .75
110 Cristobal Huet .30 .75
111 Cam Barker .20 .50
112 Dustin Byfuglien .30 .75
113 Kris Versteeg .30 .75
114 Steve Mason .25 .60
115 R.J. Umberger .25 .60
116 Jakub Voracek .30 .75
117 Mike Commodore .20 .50
118 Derick Brassard .30 .75
119 Rick Nash .25 .60
120 Pavel Datsyuk .40 1.00
121 Brian Rafalski .20 .50
122 Johan Franzen .30 .75
123 Chris Osgood .30 .75
124 Darren Helm .25 .60
125 Niklas Kronwall .25 .60
126 Nicklas Lidstrom .30 .75
127 Jason Arnott .25 .60
128 J.P. Dumont .20 .50
129 Steve Sullivan .20 .50
130 Shea Weber .25 .60
131 Jordin Tootoo .30 .75
132 Pekka Rinne .40 1.00
133 Anze Kopitar .50 1.25
134 Jack Johnson .20 .50
135 Jonathan Quick .60 1.50
136 Dustin Brown .25 .60
137 Jarret Stoll .25 .60
138 Drew Doughty .40 1.00
139 Mike Modano .50 1.25
140 Stephane Robidas .20 .50
141 Brenden Morrow .25 .60
142 Mike Ribeiro .25 .60
143 Matt Niskanen .25 .60
144 Loui Eriksson .25 .60
145 Teemu Selanne .60 1.50
146 Jonas Hiller .25 .60
147 Bobby Ryan .30 .75
148 Ryan Getzlaf .50 1.25
149 Ryan Whitney .20 .50
150 George Parros .20 .50
151 Scott Niedermayer .30 .75
152 Joe Thornton .30 .75
153 Joe Pavelski .30 .75
154 Dan Boyle .25 .60
155 Rob Blake .30 .75
156 Torrey Mitchell .30 .75
157 Ryane Clowe .25 .60
158 Evgeni Nabokov .25 .60
159 Peter Mueller .25 .60
160 Keith Yandle .30 .75
161 Mikkel Boedker .20 .50
162 Matthew Lombardi .20 .50
163 Scottie Upshall .20 .50
164 Kyle Turris .30 .75
165 Roberto Luongo .40 1.00
166 Daniel Sedin .30 .75
167 Kevin Bieksa .25 .60
168 Mason Raymond .30 .75
169 Steve Bernier .20 .50
170 Ryan Kesler .30 .75
171 Alexander Edler .20 .50
172 Jarome Iginla .30 .75
173 Rene Bourque .20 .50
174 Craig Conroy .20 .50
175 Cory Sarich .20 .50
176 Olli Jokinen .25 .60
177 Daymond Langkow .20 .50
178 Robyn Regehr .25 .60
179 Paul Stastny .30 .75
180 John-Michael Liles .20 .50
181 Peter Budaj .25 .60
182 Cody McLeod .20 .50
183 Darcy Tucker .25 .60
184 Milan Hejduk .25 .60
185 Chris Stewart .25 .60
186 Niklas Backstrom .30 .75
187 Brent Burns .40 1.00
188 Owen Nolan .30 .75
189 Mikko Koivu .30 .75
190 Marek Zidlicky .20 .50
191 James Sheppard .20 .50
192 Sam Gagner .25 .60
193 Tom Gilbert .20 .50
194 Ethan Moreau .20 .50
195 Patrick O'Sullivan .25 .60
196 Sheldon Souray .20 .50
197 Shawn Horcoff .20 .50
198 Ales Hemsky .25 .60
199 Roberto Luongo CL .40 1.00
200 Sidney Crosby CL 1.25 3.00
201 John Tavares YG RC 80.00 150.00
202 Victor Hedman YG RC 12.00 30.00
203 Matt Duchene YG RC 8.00 20.00
204 Ville Leino YG RC 2.50 6.00
205 Evander Kane YG RC 8.00 20.00
206 Michael Del Zotto YG RC 3.00 8.00
207 James van Riemsdyk YG RC 8.00 20.00
208 Viktor Stalberg YG RC 3.00 8.00
209 Sergei Shirokov YG RC 2.00 5.00
210 Erik Karlsson YG RC 25.00 60.00
211 Dmitri Kulikov YG RC 3.00 8.00
212 Jamie Benn YG RC 12.00 30.00
213 Ryan O'Reilly YG RC 5.00 12.00
214 Tyler Myers YG RC 5.00 12.00
215 Jason Demers YG RC 5.00 12.00
216 Jay Rosehill YG RC 3.00 8.00
217 Brian Salcido YG RC 2.50 6.00
218 Luca Caputi YG RC 3.00 8.00
219 Spencer Machacek YG RC 3.00 8.00
220 Yannick Weber YG RC 3.00 8.00
221 Artem Anisimov YG RC 3.00 8.00
222 Ivan Vishnevskiy YG RC 2.50 6.00
223 Riku Helenius YG RC 3.00 8.00
224 Peter Regin YG RC 2.50 6.00
225 Antti Niemi YG RC 5.00 12.00
226 Byron Bitz YG RC 2.50 6.00
227 John Negrin YG RC 3.00 8.00
228 Ray Macias YG RC 2.50 6.00
229 Taylor Chorney YG RC 3.00 8.00
230 Mika Pyorala YG RC 2.50 6.00
231 Alec Martinez YG RC 4.00 10.00
232 Grant Lewis YG RC 2.50 6.00
233 Cal O'Reilly YG RC 2.50 6.00
234 Jesse Joensuu YG RC 2.50 6.00
235 Michal Neuvirth YG RC 5.00 12.00
236 John Scott YG RC 3.00 8.00
237 Benn Ferriero YG RC 3.00 8.00
238 Teemu Laakso YG RC 2.00 5.00
239 Jhonas Enroth YG RC 4.00 10.00
240 Matt Beleskey YG RC 2.50 6.00
241 T.J. Galiardi YG RC 3.00 8.00
242 Kris Chucko YG RC 2.50 6.00
243 James Wright YG RC 3.00 8.00
244 Joel Rechlicz YG RC 2.00 5.00
245 Matt Pelech YG RC 3.00 8.00
246 Christian Hanson YG RC 3.00 8.00
247 Matt Hendricks YG RC 2.50 6.00
248 Mike Santorelli YG RC 3.00 8.00
249 Frazer McLaren YG RC 2.50 6.00
250 Duchene/Hedman/Tavares CL 4.00 10.00
251 Milan Lucic .25 .60
252 Patrice Bergeron .40 1.00
253 Michael Ryder .20 .50
254 Andrew Ference .20 .50
255 Marco Sturm .20 .50
256 Marc Savard .20 .50
257 Daniel Paille .25 .60
258 Thomas Vanek .30 .75
259 Jason Pominville .30 .75
260 Mike Grier .20 .50
261 Jochen Hecht .20 .50
262 Henrik Tallinder .20 .50
263 Adam Mair .20 .50
264 Clarke MacArthur .20 .50
265 Scott Gomez .25 .60
266 Mike Cammalleri .25 .60
267 Roman Hamrlik .20 .50
268 Max Pacioretty .40 1.00
269 Sergei Kostitsyn .20 .50
270 Guillaume Latendresse .25 .60
271 Brian Gionta .25 .60
272 Alex Kovalev .30 .75
273 Chris Kelly .25 .60
274 Chris Neil .20 .50
275 Pascal Leclaire .30 .75
276 Mike Fisher .20 .50
277 Filip Kuba .20 .50
278 Jonathan Cheechoo .30 .75
279 Jason Blake .20 .50
280 Phil Kessel .40 1.00
281 Francois Beauchemin .20 .50
282 John Mitchell .20 .50
283 Tomas Kaberle .20 .50
284 Niklas Hagman .20 .50
285 Mike Komisarek .25 .60
286 Mike Richards .30 .75
287 Chris Pronger .25 .60
288 Ian Laperriere .20 .50
289 Braydon Coburn .20 .50
290 Kimmo Timonen .25 .60
291 Ray Emery .25 .60
292 Daniel Briere .30 .75
293 Evgeni Malkin 1.00 2.50
294 Pascal Dupuis .20 .50
295 Alex Goligoski .25 .60
296 Chris Kunitz .30 .75
297 Tyler Kennedy .25 .60
298 Brooks Orpik .25 .60
299 Jordan Staal .30 .75
300 Zach Parise .30 .75
301 Travis Zajac .25 .60
302 Andy Greene .20 .50
303 Jay Pandolfo .20 .50
304 Dainius Zubrus .20 .50
305 Rob Niedermayer .20 .50
306 Frederick Meyer .20 .50
307 Sean Bergenheim .20 .50
308 Dwayne Roloson .25 .60
309 Brendan Witt .20 .50
310 Trent Hunter .20 .50
311 Martin Biron .25 .60
312 Marian Gaborik .40 1.00
313 Vaclav Prospal .20 .50
314 Daniel Girardi .20 .50
315 Stephen Valiquette .20 .50
316 Donald Brashear .20 .50
317 Aaron Voros .20 .50
318 Chris Higgins .20 .50
319 Tomas Vokoun .25 .60
320 Jordan Leopold .20 .50
321 Rostislav Olesz .20 .50
322 Bryan Allen .20 .50
323 Nick Tarnasky .20 .50
324 Cory Stillman .20 .50
325 Nik Antropov .25 .60
326 Slava Kozlov .20 .50
327 Boris Valabik .30 .75
328 Johan Hedberg .25 .60
329 Jim Slater .20 .50
330 Ilya Kovalchuk .30 .75
331 Cam Ward .30 .75
332 Tuomo Ruutu .20 .50
333 Manny Legace .25 .60
334 Brandon Sutter .25 .60
335 Ray Whitney .25 .60
336 Erik Cole .25 .60
337 Vincent Lecavalier .25 .60
338 Mattias Ohlund .20 .50
339 Antero Niittymaki .30 .75
340 Lukas Krajicek .20 .50
341 Steve Downie .20 .50
342 Alex Tanguay .20 .50
343 Alexander Ovechkin 1.25 3.00
344 Karl Alzner .20 .50
345 Chris Clark .20 .50
346 Jose Theodore .30 .75
347 Michael Nylander .20 .50
348 Mike Knuble .20 .50
349 Brendan Morrison .25 .60
350 Brad Boyes .20 .50
351 Andy McDonald .25 .60
352 Eric Brewer .20 .50
353 Alexander Steen .30 .75
354 Ty Conklin .25 .60
355 Erik Johnson .25 .60
356 David Backes .30 .75
357 Patrick Kane .60 1.50
358 Andrew Ladd .30 .75
359 Dave Bolland .25 .60
360 Duncan Keith .30 .75
361 Marian Hossa .25 .60
362 John Madden .20 .50
363 Brent Seabrook .25 .60
364 Samuel Pahlsson .20 .50
365 Kristian Huselius .20 .50
366 Kris Russell .30 .75
367 Raffi Torres .20 .50
368 Rostislav Klesla .30 .75
369 Fredrik Modin .20 .50
370 Henrik Zetterberg .40 1.00
371 Todd Bertuzzi .30 .75
372 Valtteri Filppula .30 .75
373 Tomas Holmstrom .25 .60
374 Kirk Maltby .20 .50
375 Jason Williams .20 .50
376 Dan Cleary .30 .75
377 Dan Ellis .20 .50
378 David Legwand .25 .60
379 Ryan Suter .30 .75
380 Marcel Goc .25 .60
381 Dan Hamhuis .25 .60
382 Martin Erat .20 .50
383 Ryan Smyth .25 .60
384 Justin Williams .25 .60
385 Oscar Moller .20 .50
386 Wayne Simmonds .40 1.00
387 Raitis Ivanans .20 .50
388 Alexander Frolov .25 .60
389 Marty Turco .30 .75
390 James Neal .30 .75
391 Steve Ott .20 .50
392 Jere Lehtinen .25 .60
393 Fabian Brunnstrom .25 .60
394 Brad Richards .30 .75
395 Saku Koivu .30 .75
396 Luca Sbisa .30 .75
397 Mike Brown .20 .50
398 Joffrey Lupul .25 .60
399 Corey Perry .30 .75
400 Evgeni Artyukhin .20 .50
401 Jean-Sebastien Giguere .30 .75
402 Patrick Marleau .30 .75
403 Jed Ortmeyer .20 .50
404 Scott Nichol .20 .50
405 Devin Setoguchi .25 .60
406 Jody Shelley .20 .50
407 Marc-Edouard Vlasic .20 .50
408 Dany Heatley .30 .75
409 Shane Doan .25 .60
410 Ed Jovanovski .20 .50
411 Ilya Bryzgalov .25 .60
412 Martin Hanzal .25 .60
413 Vernon Fiddler .20 .50
414 Viktor Tikhonov .25 .60
415 Henrik Sedin .30 .75
416 Willie Mitchell .20 .50
417 Alexandre Burrows .30 .75
418 Christian Ehrhoff .20 .50
419 Kyle Wellwood .25 .60
420 Sami Salo .30 .75
421 Mathieu Schneider .20 .50
422 Miikka Kiprusoff .25 .60
423 Curtis Glencross .20 .50
424 David Moss .25 .60
425 Dion Phaneuf .40 1.00
426 Dustin Boyd .20 .50
427 Fredrik Sjostrom .20 .50
428 Jay Bouwmeester .30 .75
429 Wojtek Wolski .20 .50
430 Craig Anderson .30 .75
431 T.J. Hensick .20 .50
432 Kyle Quincey .20 .50
433 Marek Svatos .20 .50
434 Scott Hannan .20 .50
435 Adam Foote .20 .50
436 Pierre-Marc Bouchard .30 .75
437 Martin Havlat .25 .60
438 Josh Harding .30 .75
439 Antti Miettinen .20 .50
440 Eric Belanger .20 .50
441 Colton Gillies .30 .75
442 Andrew Cogliano .25 .60
443 Steve Staios .20 .50
444 Fernando Pisani .20 .50
445 Lubomir Visnovsky .20 .50
446 Dustin Penner .20 .50
447 Ladislav Smid .20 .50
448 Nikolai Khabibulin .30 .75
449 Evgeni Malkin CL 1.00 2.50
450 Alexander Ovechkin CL 1.25 3.00
451 MacGregor Sharp YG RC 3.00 8.00
452 Brad Marchand YG RC 25.00 60.00
453 Tyler Ennis YG RC 4.00 10.00
454 Mikael Backlund YG RC 3.00 8.00
455 Ryan Wilson YG RC 3.00 8.00
456 Ryan Stoa YG RC 2.50 6.00
457 Philippe Dupuis YG RC 3.00 8.00
458 Perttu Lindgren YG RC 2.50 6.00
459 Aaron Gagnon YG RC 2.00 5.00
460 Daniel Larsson YG RC 2.50 6.00
461 Ryan O'Marra YG RC 2.00 5.00
462 Devan Dubnyk YG RC 6.00 15.00
463 Colin McDonald YG RC 2.50 6.00
464 Alexander Salak YG RC 2.50 6.00
465 Jakub Kindl YG RC 3.00 8.00
466 Andrei Loktionov YG RC 4.00 10.00
467 Scott Parse YG RC 3.00 8.00
468 Danny Irmen YG RC 2.00 5.00
469 Anton Khudobin YG RC 3.00 8.00
470 David Desharnais YG RC 6.00 15.00
471 Tom Pyatt YG RC 3.00 8.00
472 Mathieu Carle YG RC 3.00 8.00
473 Ryan White YG RC 4.00 10.00
474 Colin Wilson YG RC 3.00 8.00
475 Cody Franson YG RC 3.00 8.00
476 Peter Olvecky YG RC 3.00 8.00
477 Andreas Thuresson YG RC 2.50 6.00
478 Matthew Corrente YG RC 2.50 6.00
479 Vladimir Zharkov YG RC 3.00 8.00
480 Tyler Eckford YG RC 2.50 6.00
481 Matt Gilroy YG RC 3.00 8.00
482 Bobby Sanguinetti YG RC 2.00 5.00
483 Ryan Keller YG RC 3.00 8.00
484 Oskars Bartulis YG RC 3.00 8.00
485 David Laliberte YG RC 2.50 6.00
486 Mark Letestu YG RC 3.00 8.00
487 Logan Couture YG RC 8.00 20.00
488 Steven Zalewski YG RC 2.50 6.00
489 Lars Eller YG RC 5.00 12.00
490 Jonas Gustavsson YG RC 4.00 10.00
491 Tyler Bozak YG RC 5.00 12.00
492 Carl Gunnarsson YG RC 2.50 6.00
493 James Reimer YG RC 8.00 20.00
494 Michael Grabner YG RC 4.00 10.00
495 Mario Bliznak YG RC 3.00 8.00
496 Guillaume Desbiens YG RC 3.00 8.00
497 John Carlson YG RC 12.00 30.00
498 Mathieu Perreault YG RC 5.00 12.00
499 Braden Holtby YG RC 15.00 40.00
500 Gustv/Wilsn/Cture YG CL 6.00 15.00

2009-10 Upper Deck Exclusives

*SINGLES: 3X TO 8X BASIC CARDS
*YG SINGLES: 1.5X TO 4X BASIC CARDS
STATED PRINT RUN 100 SER.#'d SETS
37 Claude Giroux 2.50 6.00
48 Kristopher Letang 2.50 6.00
88 Mike Smith 2.50 6.00
93 Nicklas Backstrom 4.00 10.00
201 John Tavares YG 150.00 250.00
203 Matt Duchene YG 40.00 80.00
210 Erik Karlsson YG 50.00 120.00
212 Jamie Benn YG 175.00 300.00
452 Brad Marchand YG 50.00 120.00
487 Logan Couture YG 40.00 80.00
499 Braden Holtby YG 60.00 100.00

2009-10 Upper Deck All World

COMPLETE SET (40) 75.00 150.00
COMP.SET w/o SPs (30) 12.00 30.00
STATED ODDS 1:12
AW1 Marian Hossa 1.25 3.00
AW2 Martin Brodeur 3.00 8.00
AW3 Marc-Andre Fleury 2.50 6.00
AW4 Alexander Semin 1.50 4.00
AW5 Mike Green 1.50 4.00
AW6 Johan Franzen 1.50 4.00
AW7 Mikko Koivu 1.50 4.00
AW8 Pavel Datsyuk 2.00 5.00
AW9 Jarome Iginla 1.50 4.00
AW10 Evgeni Nabokov 1.25 3.00
AW11 Zdeno Chara 1.50 4.00
AW12 Henrik Lundqvist 2.50 6.00
AW13 Niklas Backstrom 1.50 4.00
AW14 Jason Spezza 1.50 4.00
AW15 Patrick Kane 3.00 8.00
AW16 Carey Price 6.00 15.00
AW17 Eric Staal 2.00 5.00
AW18 Shea Weber 1.25 3.00
AW19 Anze Kopitar 2.50 6.00
AW20 Pekka Rinne 2.00 5.00
AW21 Jonas Hiller 1.25 3.00
AW22 Martin St. Louis 1.50 4.00
AW23 Ales Hemsky 1.25 3.00
AW24 Miikka Kiprusoff 1.25 3.00
AW25 Mike Richards 1.50 4.00
AW26 Joe Thornton 1.50 4.00
AW27 Jeff Carter 1.50 4.00
AW28 Daniel Sedin 1.50 4.00
AW29 Henrik Sedin 1.50 4.00
AW30 Daniel Alfredsson 1.50 4.00
AW31 Zach Parise SP 2.50 6.00
AW32 Sidney Crosby SP 10.00 25.00
AW33 Evgeni Malkin SP 8.00 20.00
AW34 Ilya Kovalchuk SP 2.50 6.00
AW35 Alexander Ovechkin SP 10.00 25.00
AW36 Tim Thomas SP 2.50 6.00
AW37 Henrik Zetterberg SP 3.00 8.00
AW38 Dany Heatley SP 2.50 6.00
AW39 Rick Nash SP 2.00 5.00
AW40 Jonathan Toews SP 5.00 12.00

2009-10 Upper Deck Ambassadors of the Game

COMPLETE SET (30) 50.00 100.00
COMP.SET w/o SPs (20) 12.00 30.00
STATED ODDS 1:4
AG1 Steve Sullivan 1.25 3.00
AG2 Jason Blake 1.25 3.00
AG3 Phil Kessel 2.50 6.00
AG4 Teemu Selanne 4.00 10.00
AG5 Saku Koivu 2.00 5.00
AG6 Bobby Clarke 2.00 5.00
AG7 Lanny McDonald 2.00 5.00
AG8 Patrice Bergeron 2.50 6.00
AG9 Rod Brind`Amour 2.00 5.00
AG10 Daniel Alfredsson 2.00 5.00
AG11 Shane Doan 1.50 4.00
AG12 Tim Thomas 2.00 5.00
AG13 Vincent Lecavalier 1.50 4.00
AG14 Eric Staal 2.50 6.00
AG15 Rick Nash 1.50 4.00
AG16 Dustin Brown 1.50 4.00
AG17 Marty Turco 2.00 5.00
AG18 Alex Kovalev 2.00 5.00
AG19 Luc Robitaille 2.00 5.00
AG20 Mike Modano 3.00 8.00
AG21 Steve Yzerman SP 6.00 15.00
AG22 Cam Neely SP 2.50 6.00
AG23 Mario Lemieux SP 8.00 20.00
AG24 Jarome Iginla SP 2.50 6.00
AG25 Ray Bourque SP 4.00 10.00
AG26 Alexander Ovechkin SP 10.00 25.00
AG27 Wayne Gretzky SP 8.00 20.00
AG28 Gordie Howe SP 6.00 15.00
AG29 Bobby Orr SP 8.00 20.00
AG30 Bobby Hull SP 3.00 8.00
AG31 Scott Niedermayer 2.00 5.00
AG32 Zdeno Chara 2.00 5.00
AG33 Ryan Miller 2.00 5.00
AG34 Dion Phaneuf 2.50 6.00
AG35 Cam Ward 2.00 5.00
AG36 Kris Versteeg 2.00 5.00
AG37 Kris Draper 1.25 3.00
AG38 Pavel Datsyuk 2.50 6.00
AG39 Sheldon Souray 1.25 3.00
AG40 Ryan Smyth 1.50 4.00
AG41 Georges Laraque 1.50 4.00
AG42 Chris Drury 1.50 4.00
AG43 Don Cherry 2.00 5.00
AG44 Barry Melrose 2.00 5.00
AG45 Jason Spezza 2.00 5.00
AG46 Daniel Alfredsson 2.00 5.00
AG47 Simon Gagne 2.00 5.00
AG48 Marc-Andre Fleury 3.00 8.00
AG49 Paul Kariya 2.50 6.00
AG50 Mike Green 2.00 5.00
AG51 Ilya Kovalchuk SP 2.50 6.00
AG52 Jonathan Toews SP 5.00 12.00
AG53 Tony Esposito SP 2.50 6.00
AG54 Patrick Roy SP 6.00 15.00
AG55 Martin Brodeur SP 5.00 12.00
AG56 John Tavares SP 12.00 30.00
AG57 Mark Messier SP 3.00 8.00
AG58 Mike Richards SP 2.50 6.00
AG59 Jordan Staal SP 2.50 6.00
AG60 Roberto Luongo SP 3.00 8.00

2009-10 Upper Deck Big Playmakers Jerseys

STATED PRINT RUN 12-100
BP96 Wayne Gretzky/25 125.00 200.00
BPAF Alexander Frolov/75 5.00 12.00
BPAK Alex Kovalev/75 6.00 15.00
BPAO Alexander Ovechkin/75 15.00 40.00
BPBC Brian Campbell/25 12.00 30.00
BPBD Brandon Dubinsky/75 5.00 12.00
BPBL Bryan Little/75 6.00 15.00
BPBR Derick Brassard/75 6.00 15.00
BPCH Cristobal Huet/75 6.00 15.00
BPCN Cam Neely/75 6.00 15.00
BPCP Carey Price/75 20.00 40.00
BPCW Cam Ward/75 6.00 15.00
BPDB Dave Bolland/75 5.00 12.00
BPDD Drew Doughty/75 8.00 20.00
BPDM J.P. Dumont/75 4.00 10.00
BPDP David Perron/75 4.00 10.00
BPDR Derek Roy/75 5.00 12.00
BPDU Dustin Brown/75 5.00 12.00
BPEM Evgeni Malkin/75 20.00 50.00
BPES Eric Staal/75 8.00 20.00
BPIK Ilya Kovalchuk/75 6.00 15.00
BPJB Jay Bouwmeester/75 6.00 15.00
BPJO Jordan Staal/75 6.00 15.00
BPJP Jason Pominville/75 6.00 15.00
BPJS Jason Spezza/75 6.00 15.00
BPJV Jakub Voracek/75 6.00 15.00
BPKL Kari Lehtonen/75 5.00 12.00
BPLU Milan Lucic/25 10.00 25.00
BPMB Martin Brodeur/12 100.00 175.00
BPMF Michael Frolik/75 5.00 12.00
BPMG Marian Gaborik/75 8.00 20.00
BPMH Marian Hossa/75 5.00 12.00
BPMI Mikkel Boedker/75 4.00 10.00
BPNB Nicklas Backstrom/75 10.00 25.00
BPNK Nikolai Khabibulin/75 6.00 15.00
BPNL Nicklas Lidstrom/75 6.00 15.00
BPOJ Olli Jokinen/75 5.00 12.00
BPPD Pavel Datsyuk/75 8.00 20.00
BPPE Pekka Rinne/75 8.00 20.00
BPPH Dion Phaneuf/27 12.00 30.00
BPPK Patrick Kane/75 12.00 30.00
BPPL Paul Stastny/100 6.00 15.00
BPPM Peter Mueller/75 5.00 12.00
BPPR Patrick Roy/75 15.00 40.00
BPRB Ray Bourque/75 10.00 25.00
BPRI Mike Richards/75 6.00 15.00
BPRM Ryan Miller/75 6.00 15.00
BPRN Rick Nash/75 5.00 12.00
BPSD Shane Doan/75 5.00 12.00
BPSG Sam Gagner/75 5.00 12.00
BPSP Patrick Sharp/75 6.00 15.00
BPST Drew Stafford/75 6.00 15.00
BPSW Stephen Weiss/75 4.00 10.00
BPTO Jonathan Toews/75 12.00 30.00
BPTP Tomas Plekanec/75 6.00 15.00
BPTV Thomas Vanek/75 6.00 15.00
BPVL Vincent Lecavalier/75 5.00 12.00
BPVO Tomas Vokoun/75 5.00 12.00
BPZP Zach Parise/75 6.00 15.00

2009-10 Upper Deck Biography of a Season

COMPLETE SET (30) 8.00 20.00
BOS1 Sidney Crosby 1.25 3.00
BOS2 Evgeni Malkin 1.00 2.50
BOS3 Alexander Ovechkin 1.25 3.00
BOS4 John Tavares 1.50 4.00
BOS5 Alexander Ovechkin 1.25 3.00
BOS6 Sidney Crosby 1.25 3.00
BOS7 Brent Seabrook .25 .60
BOS8 Nicklas Lidstrom .30 .75
BOS9 Roberto Luongo .40 1.00
BOS10 Michael Del Zotto .30 .75
BOS11 Phil Kessel .40 1.00
BOS12 Steve Yzerman .75 2.00
BOS13 Marian Hossa .25 .60
BOS14 Jarome Iginla .30 .75
BOS15 Carey Price 1.25 3.00
BOS16 Martin Brodeur .60 1.50
BOS17 Jonas Gustavsson .40 1.00
BOS18 Scott Niedermayer .30 .75
BOS19 B.Clarke/B.Orr 1.00 2.50
BOS20 Marco Sturm .20 .50
BOS21 Cam Ward .30 .75
BOS22 Alexander Ovechkin 1.25 3.00
BOS23 Ilya Kovalchuk .30 .75
BOS24 Jean-Sebastien Giguere .30 .75
BOS25 Martin Brodeur .60 1.50
BOS26 Ilya Bryzgalov .25 .60
BOS27 Paul Kariya .40 1.00
BOS28 Teemu Selanne .60 1.50
BOS29 Steven Stamkos .60 1.50
BOS30 Martin Brodeur .60 1.50

2009-10 Upper Deck Captain's Calling

COMPLETE SET (9) 10.00 25.00
STATED ODDS 1:4
CC1 Sidney Crosby 3.00 8.00
CC2 Jonathan Toews 1.50 4.00
CC3 Jarome Iginla .75 2.00
CC4 Roberto Luongo 1.00 2.50
CC5 Rick Nash .60 1.50
CC6 Nicklas Lidstrom .75 2.00
CC7 Vincent Lecavalier .60 1.50
CC8 Ilya Kovalchuk .75 2.00
CC9 Mike Richards .75 2.00

2009-10 Upper Deck Clearcut Trios

STATED PRINT RUN 25 SER.#'d SETS
CT1 Marleau/Thornton/Setoguchi 10.00 25.00
CT2 Perry/Ryan/Getzlaf 15.00 40.00
CT3 Jokinen/Iginla/Kiprusoff 10.00 25.00
CT4 Toews/Kane/Campbell 20.00 50.00
CT5 Datsyuk/Lidstrom/Zetterberg 12.00 30.00
CT6 Brodeur/Parise/Elias 20.00 50.00
CT7 Crosby/Malkin/Fleury 40.00 100.00
CT8 Anderson/Gretzky/Kurri 50.00 125.00
CT9 Lecavalier/St. Louis/Stamkos 20.00 50.00
CT10 Zetterberg/Howe/Yzerman 25.00 60.00
CT11 Yzerman/Messier/Lemieux 30.00 80.00
CT12 Kulemin/Stajan/Schenn 8.00 20.00
CT13 Luongo/D.Sedin/H.Sedin 12.00 30.00
CT14 Backstrom/Semin/Ovechkin 40.00 100.00
CT15 P.Esposito/Bucyk/Orr 30.00 80.00
CT16 Robinson/Lafleur/Shutt 12.00 30.00
CT17 Kane/Toews/Hull 20.00 50.00
CT18 Vachon/Mahovlich/Beliveau 12.00 30.00
CT19 Roy/Price/Brodeur 30.00 80.00
CT20 Miller/Lundqvist/DiPietro 15.00 40.00
CT21 Kiprusoff/Luongo/Backstrom 12.00 30.00

2009-10 Upper Deck Clearly Canadian

STATED PRINT RUN 100 SER.#'d SETS
CANAF Adam Foote 6.00 15.00
CANAM Al MacInnis 10.00 25.00
CANBC Bobby Clarke 10.00 25.00
CANBM Brenden Morrow 8.00 20.00
CANBO Bobby Orr 30.00 80.00
CANBR Brad Richards 10.00 25.00
CANCW Cam Ward 10.00 25.00
CANDH Dany Heatley 10.00 25.00
CANDP Denis Potvin 10.00 25.00
CANDR Derek Roy 8.00 20.00
CANES Eric Staal 12.00 30.00
CANFY Marc-Andre Fleury 15.00 40.00
CANGF Grant Fuhr 10.00 25.00
CANGL Guy Lafleur 12.00 30.00
CANGP Gilbert Perreault 10.00 25.00
CANJB Jay Bouwmeester 10.00 25.00
CANJI Jarome Iginla 10.00 25.00
CANJS Joe Sakic 15.00 40.00
CANJT Jonathan Toews 20.00 50.00
CANKD Kris Draper 6.00 15.00
CANLR Luc Robitaille 10.00 25.00
CANMB Martin Brodeur 20.00 50.00
CANMG Mike Green 10.00 25.00
CANML Mario Lemieux 30.00 80.00
CANMM Mark Messier 12.00 30.00
CANMR Mike Richards 10.00 25.00
CANMS Martin St. Louis 10.00 25.00
CANPR Patrick Roy 25.00 60.00
CANPS Patrick Sharp 10.00 25.00
CANRB Ray Bourque 15.00 40.00
CANRG Ryan Getzlaf 15.00 40.00
CANRL Roberto Luongo 12.00 30.00
CANRN Rick Nash 8.00 20.00
CANRR Robyn Regehr 8.00 20.00
CANRS Ryan Smyth 8.00 20.00
CANSC Sidney Crosby 40.00 100.00

ANSG Simon Gagne 10.00 25.00
ANSM Steve Mason 8.00 20.00
ANTH Joe Thornton 10.00 25.00
ANVL Vincent Lecavalier 8.00 20.00
ANWG Wayne Gretzky 40.00 100.00
ANYZ Steve Yzerman 25.00 60.00

2009-10 Upper Deck Draft Day Gems

OMPLETE SET (14) 8.00 20.00
TATED ODDS 1:4
EM1 Henrik Zetterberg 1.25 3.00
EM2 Pavel Datsyuk 1.25 3.00
EM3 Tomas Kaberle .60 1.50
EM4 Andrei Markov 1.00 2.50
EM5 Luc Robitaille 1.00 2.50
EM6 Theoren Fleury 1.50 4.00
EM7 Ron Hextall 1.50 4.00
EM8 Dominik Hasek 1.25 3.00
EM9 Evgeni Nabokov .75 2.00
EM10 Marty Turco 1.00 2.50
EM11 Henrik Lundqvist 1.50 4.00
EM12 Ryan Miller 1.00 2.50
EM13 Pekka Rinne 1.25 3.00
EM14 Mark Messier 1.25 3.00
EM15 Tim Thomas 1.00 2.50
EM16 Mark Recchi 1.25 3.00
EM17 Patrick Roy 2.50 6.00
EM18 Milan Hejduk .75 2.00
EM19 Cristobal Huet 1.00 2.50
EM20 Tomas Vokoun .75 2.00
EM21 Doug Gilmour 1.25 3.00
EM22 Nikolai Khabibulin 1.00 2.50
EM23 Michael Ryder .60 1.50
EM24 Miikka Kiprusoff .75 2.00
EM25 Nicklas Lidstrom 1.00 2.50
EM26 Jari Kurri 1.00 2.50
EM27 Brian Campbell .75 2.00
EM28 Daniel Alfredsson 1.00 2.50
EM29 Dustin Byfuglien 1.00 2.50
EM30 Mark Streit .60 1.50

2009-10 Upper Deck Fab Four Fabrics

TATED PRINT RUN 100 SER.#'d SETS
RUN Bergrn/Kssl/Lucic/Ryder 10.00 25.00
ANE Ward/Brind/Ruutu/Staal 10.00 25.00
APS Jrcina/Ovch/Morris/Theo 12.00 30.00
ATS Hrtn/Booth/Weiss/Vokn 8.00 20.00
NKS Bernr/Lngo/Sedin/Sedin 10.00 25.00
EVL Clarksn/Paris/Brodr/Elias 15.00 40.00
LAM Ignla/Jokn/Kiprsff/Phnef 10.00 25.00
LYR Cartr/Rchrds/Emry/Ggne 8.00 20.00
RTS Mess/Grtzky/Yzer/Crosby 60.00 120.00
WKS Kane/Toews/Shrp/Cmpb 15.00 40.00
LE Okps/Bley/DiPtro/Wght 8.00 20.00
NGS Brown/Frolv/Dghty/Kpitr 12.00 30.00
EAF Schn/Kmsk/Hllwg/Tskla 8.00 20.00
OILR Khab/Cogli/Ggnr/O'Sulli 8.00 20.00
NGR Gabrk/Drury/Lund/Staal 12.00 30.00
ABR Pomnv/Vank/Stffrd/Millr
C00 Gomz/Arntt/Brdeur/Elias 15.00 40.00
C01 Drury/Roy/Tngy/Brque 20.00 50.00
C06 Staal/Will/Stllman/Ward 10.00 25.00
C89 McDn/Mlln/Gilmr/Mclns 10.00 25.00
C90 Mess/Kurri/Fuhr/Andrsn 10.00 25.00
ENS Spez/Alfrdsn/Htley/Kovl 8.00 20.00
TAR Ribro/Mdno/Lhtin/Turco 12.00 30.00
ING Lidstrm/Zttr/Dtsyk/Hlms 10.00 25.00

2009-10 Upper Deck Face of the Franchise

OMPLETE SET (14) 10.00 25.00
TATED ODDS 1:4
F1 Sidney Crosby 3.00 8.00
F2 Alexander Ovechkin 3.00 8.00
F3 Carey Price 3.00 8.00
F4 Ales Hemsky .60 1.50
F5 Roberto Luongo 1.00 2.50
F6 Marc Savard .50 1.25
F7 Henrik Lundqvist 1.25 3.00
F8 Jarome Iginla .75 2.00
F9 Mike Richards .75 2.00
F10 Jonathan Toews 1.50 4.00
F11 Jason Spezza .75 2.00
F12 Luke Schenn .60 1.50
F13 Joe Thornton .75 2.00
F14 Martin Brodeur 1.50 4.00

2009-10 Upper Deck Game Jerseys

TATED ODDS 1:12
JAK Anze Kopitar 4.00 10.00
JAO Alexander Ovechkin 10.00 25.00
JBB Bob Bourne 2.00 5.00
JBC Brian Campbell 2.00 5.00
JBG Butch Goring 2.50 6.00
JBM Brendan Morrison 2.00 5.00
JBN Bernie Nicholls 1.50 4.00
JBO Brooks Orpik 2.00 5.00
JBP Bob Probert 2.00 5.00
JBR Brad Richards 2.50 6.00
JCC Carlo Colaiacovo 1.50 4.00
JCH Cristobal Huet 2.50 6.00
JCN Cam Neely 2.50 6.00
JCO Chris Osgood 2.50 6.00
JCP Carey Price 10.00 25.00
JDA David Booth 1.50 4.00
JDB Dave Bolland 2.00 5.00
JDC Dino Ciccarelli 2.50 6.00
JDD Drew Doughty 3.00 8.00
JDE Derick Brassard 2.50 6.00
JDH Dale Hawerchuk 3.00 8.00
JDO Donald Brashear 1.50 4.00
JDP Dion Phaneuf 3.00 8.00
JDR Derek Roy 2.00 5.00
JDS Daniel Sedin 2.50 6.00
JDU Dustin Brown 2.00 5.00
JEC Erik Cole 2.00 5.00
JEM Evgeni Malkin 8.00 20.00
JES Eric Staal 3.00 8.00
JFB Francis Bouillon 1.50 4.00
JFR Michael Frolik 2.00 5.00
JGA Glenn Anderson 2.50 6.00
JGC Guy Carbonneau 4.00 10.00
JGF Grant Fuhr 2.50 6.00
JGG Simon Gagne 2.50 6.00
JIK Ilya Kovalchuk 2.50 6.00
JJB Jay Bouwmeester 2.50 6.00
JJC Jonathan Cheechoo 2.50 6.00
JJH Jeff Halpern 1.50 4.00
JJL Joffrey Lupul 2.00 5.00
JJO Jordin Tootoo 2.50 6.00
JJP Jason Pominville 2.50 6.00
JJS Jason Spezza 2.50 6.00
JJT Jeff Tambellini 1.50 4.00
JJV Jakub Voracek 2.50 6.00
JKL Kari Lehtonen 2.00 5.00
JKT Kimmo Timonen 2.00 5.00
JLG Robert Lang 1.50 4.00
JLM Lanny McDonald 2.50 6.00
JLX Mario Lemieux 8.00 20.00
GJMA Matt Carle 2.00 5.00
GJMB Martin Brodeur 5.00 12.00
GJMC Bryan McCabe 2.00 5.00
GJMD Marc Denis 1.50 4.00
GJMF Manny Fernandez 2.00 5.00
GJMG Marian Gaborik 3.00 8.00
GJMH Marian Hossa 2.00 5.00
GJML Mike Lundin 1.50 4.00
GJMM Mark Messier 10.00 25.00
GJMP Marc-Antoine Pouliot 2.00 5.00
GJMR Mason Raymond 2.50 6.00
GJMS Marc Staal 2.50 6.00
GJMT Marty Turco 2.50 6.00
GJMU Larry Murphy 2.00 5.00
GJNB Nicklas Backstrom 4.00 10.00
GJNH Nathan Horton 2.50 6.00
GJPA Patrice Brisebois 1.50 4.00
GJPB Patrice Bergeron 3.00 8.00
GJPD Pavel Datsyuk 3.00 8.00
GJPE Peter Stastny 2.50 6.00
GJPK Patrick Kane 5.00 12.00
GJPO Patrick O'Sullivan 2.00 5.00
GJPR Patrick Roy 6.00 15.00
GJPS Patrick Sharp 2.50 6.00
GJRA Paul Ranger 1.50 4.00
GJRB Richard Brodeur 2.50 6.00
GJRI Mike Richards 2.50 6.00
GJRL Roberto Luongo 3.00 8.00
GJRM Ryan Miller 2.50 6.00
GJRN Rick Nash 2.00 5.00
GJSA Borje Salming 2.50 6.00
GJSC Sidney Crosby 10.00 25.00
GJSD Shane Doan 2.00 5.00
GJSG Sam Gagner 2.00 5.00
GJSI Darryl Sittler 3.00 8.00
GJSK Saku Koivu 2.50 6.00
GJSP Paul Stastny 2.50 6.00
GJSS Steve Shutt 2.50 6.00
GJST Drew Stafford 2.50 6.00
GJSU Steve Sullivan 1.50 4.00
GJSW Shea Weber 2.00 5.00
GJSY Steve Yzerman 12.00 30.00
GJTO Jonathan Toews 5.00 12.00
GJTV Thomas Vanek 2.50 6.00
GJTW Tiger Williams 2.00 5.00
GJVO Tomas Vokoun 2.00 5.00
GJVT Vesa Toskala 2.50 6.00
GJWE Stephen Weiss 1.50 4.00
GJWG Wayne Gretzky 75.00 150.00
GJWR Wade Redden 1.50 4.00
GJ2AC Andrew Cogliano 2.00 5.00
GJ2AF Alexander Frolov 2.00 5.00
GJ2AH Adam Hall 1.50 4.00
GJ2AK Anze Kopitar 4.00 10.00
GJ2BA Josh Bailey 2.00 5.00
GJ2BC Brian Campbell 2.00 5.00
GJ2BM Brendan Morrison 2.00 5.00
GJ2BS Borje Salming 2.50 6.00
GJ2CH Jonathan Cheechoo 2.50 6.00
GJ2DH Dale Hawerchuk 3.00 8.00
GJ2DS Devin Setoguchi 2.00 5.00
GJ2DT Dave Taylor 3.00 8.00
GJ2ES Eric Staal 3.00 8.00
GJ2GA Simon Gagne 2.50 6.00
GJ2GH Gordie Howe 80.00 150.00
GJ2HZ Henrik Zetterberg 3.00 8.00
GJ2IK Ilya Kovalchuk 2.50 6.00
GJ2JA Jason Arnott 2.00 5.00
GJ2JC Jeff Carter 2.50 6.00
GJ2JD J.P. Dumont 1.50 4.00
GJ2JI Jarome Iginla 2.50 6.00
GJ2JL Joffrey Lupul 2.00 5.00
GJ2JT Jonathan Toews 5.00 12.00
GJ2KE Phil Kessel 3.00 8.00
GJ2KO Kyle Okposo 2.50 6.00
GJ2LM Lanny McDonald 2.50 6.00
GJ2MC Bryan McCabe 2.00 5.00
GJ2MK Mike Komisarek 2.00 5.00
GJ2ML Milan Lucic 2.00 5.00
GJ2MM Mike Modano 4.00 10.00
GJ2MP Marc-Antoine Pouliot 2.00 5.00
GJ2MR Michael Ryder 1.50 4.00
GJ2MS Marc Staal 2.50 6.00
GJ2OJ Olli Jokinen 2.00 5.00
GJ2PK Paul Kariya 3.00 8.00
GJ2PM Peter Mueller 2.00 5.00
GJ2PS Paul Stastny 2.50 6.00
GJ2RB Rob Blake 2.50 6.00
GJ2RE Ray Emery 2.00 5.00
GJ2RG Ryan Getzlaf 4.00 10.00
GJ2RH Roman Hamrlik 1.50 4.00
GJ2RS Ryan Smyth 2.00 5.00
GJ2SD Shane Doan 2.00 5.00
GJ2SG Scott Gomez 2.00 5.00
GJ2SR Steven Reinprecht 1.50 4.00
GJ2ST Drew Stafford 2.50 6.00
GJ2SY Steve Yzerman 6.00 15.00
GJ2TF Tomas Fleischmann 1.50 4.00
GJ2TH Tomas Holmstrom 2.00 5.00
GJ2TR Tuomo Ruutu 1.50 4.00
GJ2TS Teemu Selanne 5.00 12.00
GJ2VP Vaclav Prospal 1.50 4.00
GJ2VT Vesa Toskala 2.50 6.00

2009-10 Upper Deck Hockey Heroes Mark Messier

HH27 Mark Messier Header 10.00 25.00
HH28 Mark Messier Painted 10.00 25.00
HHMM Mark Messier AU/30 150.00 250.00

2009-10 Upper Deck Hockey Heroes Martin Brodeur

COMPLETE SET (10) 20.00 50.00
COMP.SET w/o SPs (8) 8.00 20.00
COMMON BRODEUR 2.50 6.00
HH18 Martin Brodeur Painting 10.00 25.00
HHMB Martin Brodeur AU/30 150.00 250.00
HHMB Martin Brodeur Header 8.00 20.00

2009-10 Upper Deck Netminders

COMPLETE SET (30) 50.00 100.00
COMP.SET w/o SPs (20) 12.00 30.00
STATED ODDS 1:4
NET1 Marty Turco 1.50 4.00
NET2 Jean Sebastien Giguere 1.50 4.00
NET3 Nikolai Khabibulin 1.50 4.00
NET4 Chris Mason 1.25 3.00
NET5 Vesa Toskala 1.50 4.00
NET6 Pascal Leclaire 1.50 4.00
NET7 Tomas Vokoun 1.25 3.00
NET8 Mike Smith 1.50 4.00
NET9 Pekka Rinne 2.00 5.00
NET10 Kari Lehtonen 1.25 3.00
NET11 Jonathan Quick 3.00 8.00
NET12 Evgeni Nabokov 1.25 3.00
NET13 Rick DiPietro 1.25 3.00
NET14 Ilya Bryzgalov 1.25 3.00
NET15 Cristobal Huet 1.50 4.00
NET16 Simeon Varlamov 1.50 4.00
NET17 Ray Emery 1.25 3.00
NET18 Niklas Backstrom 1.50 4.00
NET19 Chris Osgood 1.50 4.00
NET20 Peter Budaj 1.25 3.00
NET21 Martin Brodeur SP 4.00 10.00
NET22 Miikka Kiprusoff SP 1.50 4.00
NET23 Roberto Luongo SP 2.50 6.00
NET24 Steve Mason SP 1.50 4.00
NET25 Carey Price SP 8.00 20.00
NET26 Henrik Lundqvist SP 3.00 8.00
NET27 Marc-Andre Fleury SP 3.00 8.00
NET28 Cam Ward SP 2.00 5.00
NET29 Tim Thomas SP 2.00 5.00
NET30 Ryan Miller SP 2.00 5.00

2009-10 Upper Deck Oversize Wal-Mart

COMPLETE SET (42) 15.00 40.00
OS1 Milan Lucic .40 1.00
OS2 Marc Savard .30 .75
OS3 Thomas Vanek .50 1.25
OS4 Jason Pominville .50 1.25
OS5 Scott Gomez .40 1.00
OS6 Mike Cammalleri .40 1.00
OS7 Alex Kovalev .50 1.25
OS8 Jonathan Cheechoo .50 1.25
OS9 Phil Kessel .60 1.50
OS10 Tomas Kaberle .30 .75
OS11 Mike Richards .50 1.25
OS12 Chris Pronger .40 1.00
OS13 Evgeni Malkin 1.50 4.00
OS14 Jordan Staal .50 1.25
OS15 Zach Parise .50 1.25
OS16 Marian Gaborik .60 1.50
OS17 Tomas Vokoun .40 1.00
OS18 Ilya Kovalchuk .50 1.25
OS19 Cam Ward .50 1.25
OS20 Vincent Lecavalier .40 1.00
OS21 Alexander Ovechkin 2.00 5.00
OS22 Patrick Kane 1.00 2.50
OS23 Marian Hossa .40 1.00
OS24 Brad Richards .50 1.25
OS25 Henrik Zetterberg .60 1.50
OS26 Jay Bouwmeester .50 1.25
OS27 Ryan Smyth .40 1.00
OS28 Marty Turco .50 1.25
OS29 James Neal .50 1.25
OS30 Saku Koivu .50 1.25
OS31 Corey Perry .50 1.25
OS32 Patrick Marleau .50 1.25
OS33 Dany Heatley .50 1.25
OS34 Shane Doan .40 1.00
OS35 Henrik Sedin .50 1.25
OS36 Miikka Kiprusoff .40 1.00
OS37 Dion Phaneuf .60 1.50
OS38 Wojtek Wolski .30 .75
OS39 Marek Svatos .30 .75
OS40 Martin Havlat .40 1.00
OS41 Andrew Cogliano .40 1.00
OS42 Dustin Penner .30 .75

2009-10 Upper Deck Playoff Performers

COMPLETE SET (16) 12.00 30.00
STATED ODDS 1:4
PP1 Alexander Ovechkin 3.00 8.00
PP2 Cam Ward .75 2.00
PP3 Evgeni Malkin 2.50 6.00
PP4 Henrik Zetterberg 1.00 2.50
PP5 Jarome Iginla .75 2.00
PP6 Johan Franzen .75 2.00
PP7 Jonas Hiller .60 1.50
PP8 Marc-Andre Fleury 1.25 3.00
PP9 Martin Brodeur 1.50 4.00
PP10 Patrick Kane 1.50 4.00
PP11 Roberto Luongo 1.00 2.50
PP12 Scott Niedermayer .75 2.00
PP13 Sidney Crosby 3.00 8.00
PP14 Tim Thomas .75 2.00
PP15 Chris Osgood .75 2.00
PP16 Eric Staal 1.00 2.50

2009-10 Upper Deck Rookie Breakouts

STATED PRINT RUN 100 SER.#'d SETS
RB1 John Tavares 25.00 60.00
RB2 Victor Hedman 10.00 25.00
RB3 Matt Duchene 10.00 25.00
RB4 James van Riemsdyk 10.00 25.00
RB5 Jonas Gustavsson 6.00 15.00
RB6 Evander Kane 10.00 25.00
RB7 Colin Wilson 5.00 12.00
RB8 Michael Grabner 5.00 12.00
RB9 Tyler Myers 8.00 20.00
RB10 Jamie Benn 15.00 40.00
RB11 Dmitry Kulikov 5.00 12.00
RB12 Mikael Backlund 5.00 12.00
RB13 Artem Anisimov 5.00 12.00
RB14 Antti Niemi 8.00 20.00
RB15 Michael Del Zotto 5.00 12.00
RB16 Tyler Bozak 8.00 20.00
RB17 Erik Karlsson 15.00 30.00
RB18 Ryan O'Reilly 8.00 20.00
RB19 Ville Leino 4.00 10.00
RB20 Yannick Weber 5.00 12.00
RB21 Christian Hanson 5.00 12.00
RB22 Cody Franson 5.00 12.00
RB23 Ivan Vishnevskiy 4.00 10.00
RB24 Luca Caputi 5.00 12.00
RB25 Jhonas Enroth 6.00 15.00
RB26 Matt Pelech 5.00 12.00
RB27 Matt Gilroy 5.00 12.00
RB28 Viktor Stalberg 5.00 12.00
RB29 James Wright 5.00 12.00
RB30 Sergei Shirokov 3.00 8.00
RB31 Alec Martinez 6.00 15.00
RB32 Spencer Machacek 5.00 12.00
RB33 T.J. Galiardi 5.00 12.00
RB34 Jason Demers 8.00 20.00

2009-10 Upper Deck Rookie Debuts

COMPLETE SET (9) 15.00 40.00
STATED ODDS 1:4
RD1 John Tavares 4.00 10.00
RD2 James van Riemsdyk 1.50 4.00
RD3 Victor Hedman 1.50 4.00
RD4 Matt Duchene 1.50 4.00
RD5 Jonas Gustavsson 1.00 2.50
RD6 Jamie Benn 2.50 6.00
RD7 Evander Kane 1.50 4.00
RD8 Colin Wilson .75 2.00
RD9 Michael Del Zotto .75 2.00

2009-10 Upper Deck Rookie Headliners

COMPLETE SET (30) 50.00 100.00
COMP.SET w/o SPs (20) 15.00 40.00
STATED ODDS 1:4
RH1 Matt Pelech 1.00 2.50
RH2 Kris Chucko .75 2.00
RH3 Antti Niemi 1.50 4.00
RH4 Ryan O'Reilly 1.50 4.00
RH5 T.J. Galiardi 1.00 2.50
RH6 Perttu Lindgren .75 2.00
RH7 Ivan Vishnevskiy .75 2.00
RH8 Ville Leino .75 2.00
RH9 Dmitry Kulikov 1.00 2.50
RH10 Yannick Weber 1.00 2.50
RH11 Cody Franson 1.00 2.50
RH12 Michael Del Zotto 1.00 2.50
RH13 Matt Gilroy 1.00 2.50
RH14 Artem Anisimov 1.00 2.50
RH15 Erik Karlsson 3.00 8.00
RH16 Tyler Bozak 1.50 4.00
RH17 Viktor Stalberg 1.00 2.50
RH18 Christian Hanson 1.00 2.50
RH19 Michael Grabner 1.00 2.50
RH20 Sergei Shirokov .60 1.50
RH21 Evander Kane SP 2.50 6.00
RH22 Tyler Myers SP 2.00 5.00
RH23 Mikael Backlund SP 1.25 3.00
RH24 Matt Duchene SP 2.50 6.00
RH25 Jamie Benn SP 4.00 10.00
RH26 Colin Wilson SP 1.25 3.00
RH27 John Tavares SP 6.00 15.00
RH28 James van Riemsdyk SP 2.50 6.00
RH29 Victor Hedman SP 2.50 6.00
RH30 Jonas Gustavsson SP 1.50 4.00

2009-10 Upper Deck Rookie Materials

STATED ODDS 1:12
*PATCH/25: 1.2X TO 3X BASIC JSY
RMAM Alec Martinez 5.00 12.00
RMAN Antti Niemi 6.00 15.00
RMBE Matt Beleskey 3.00 8.00
RMBF Benn Ferriero 4.00 10.00
RMBM Brad Marchand 10.00 25.00
RMBS Brian Salcido 3.00 8.00
RMCB Chris Butler 4.00 10.00
RMCF Cody Franson 4.00 10.00
RMCO Cal O'Reilly 3.00 8.00
RMCW Colin Wilson 4.00 10.00
RMDK Dmitry Kulikov 4.00 10.00
RMDU Matt Duchene 8.00 20.00
RMEK Erik Karlsson 12.00 30.00
RMIV Ivan Vishnevskiy 3.00 8.00
RMJB Jamie Benn 12.00 30.00
RMJD Jason Demers 6.00 15.00
RMJE Jhonas Enroth 5.00 12.00
RMJG Jonas Gustavsson 5.00 12.00
RMJJ Jesse Joensuu 3.00 8.00
RMJS John Scott 4.00 10.00
RMJT John Tavares 15.00 40.00
RMJV James van Riemsdyk 8.00 20.00
RMKA Evander Kane 8.00 20.00
RMKC Kris Chucko 3.00 8.00
RMLC Luca Caputi 4.00 10.00
RMLO Logan Couture 8.00 20.00
RMMA Andrew MacDonald 2.50 6.00
RMMB Mikael Backlund 4.00 10.00
RMMD Michael Del Zotto 4.00 10.00
RMMG Michael Grabner 4.00 10.00
RMMP Matt Pelech 4.00 10.00
RMMS Mike Santorelli 4.00 10.00
RMPL Perttu Lindgren 3.00 8.00
RMRE Joel Rechlicz 2.50 6.00
RMRH Riku Helenius 4.00 10.00
RMRM Ray Macias 3.00 8.00
RMRO Ryan O'Reilly 6.00 15.00
RMSA Michael Sauer 3.00 8.00
RMSM Spencer Machacek 4.00 10.00
RMSS Sergei Shirokov 2.50 6.00
RMTB Tyler Bozak 6.00 15.00
RMTG T.J. Galiardi 4.00 10.00
RMTM Tyler Myers 6.00 15.00
RMVH Victor Hedman 8.00 20.00
RMVL Ville Leino 3.00 8.00
RMYW Yannick Weber 4.00 10.00

2009-10 Upper Deck Season Highlights

COMPLETE SET (7) 6.00 15.00
STATED ODDS 1:4
SH1 Sidney Crosby 1.50 4.00
SH2 Martin Brodeur .75 2.00
SH3 Tim Thomas .40 1.00
SH4 Alexander Ovechkin 1.50 4.00
SH5 Henrik Lundqvist .60 1.50
SH6 Evgeni Malkin 1.25 3.00
SH7 Henrik Zetterberg .50 1.25

2009-10 Upper Deck Signatures

STATED ODDS 1:288
UDSAE Andrew Ebbett 5.00 12.00
UDSAM Andrei Markov 8.00 20.00
UDSAO Alexander Ovechkin
UDSAP Alex Pietrangelo 6.00 15.00
UDSBM Brendan Mikkelson 5.00 12.00
UDSBO Bobby Orr 150.00 250.00
UDSBR Bobby Ryan 8.00 20.00
UDSBV Boris Valabik 8.00 20.00
UDSBW Blake Wheeler 8.00 20.00
UDSBY Brad Boyes 5.00 12.00
UDSCD Chris Drury 6.00 15.00
UDSCG Claude Giroux 8.00 20.00
UDSCR Sidney Crosby 150.00 250.00
UDSDH Darren Helm 6.00 15.00
UDSDP Dion Phaneuf 10.00 25.00
UDSFB Fabian Brunnstrom 6.00 15.00
UDSFI Mark Fistric 5.00 12.00
UDSFO Nick Foligno 6.00 15.00
UDSGB Gilbert Brule 10.00 25.00
UDSGH Gordie Howe
UDSHZ Henrik Zetterberg
UDSJB Josh Bailey
UDSJE Jonathan Ericsson 6.00 15.00
UDSJG Jean-Sebastien Giguere 6.00 15.00
UDSJH Josh Harding 6.00 15.00
UDSJI Jarome Iginla
UDSJP Justin Pogge 8.00 20.00
UDSJT Joe Thornton
UDSKA Karl Alzner 5.00 12.00
UDSLS Luke Schenn 6.00 15.00
UDSMD Matt D'Agostini 6.00 15.00
UDSME Matt Ellis 5.00 12.00
UDSMF Marc-Andre Fleury 25.00 50.00
UDSMI Mike Iggulden 5.00 12.00
UDSMP Max Pacioretty 10.00 25.00
UDSMR Mattias Ritola 6.00 15.00
UDSNF Nikita Filatov 6.00 15.00
UDSNK Nikolai Kulemin 6.00 15.00
UDSOM Oscar Moller 5.00 12.00
UDSPD Pavel Datsyuk 50.00 100.00
UDSPE Michael Peca 25.00 50.00
UDSPK Phil Kessel 15.00 40.00
UDSPR Patrick Roy
UDSRO Rostislav Olesz 5.00 12.00
UDSRP Ryan Parent 6.00 15.00
UDSRS Ryan Smyth 25.00 50.00
UDSRY Ryan Potulny 5.00 12.00
UDSSC Cory Schneider 12.00 30.00
UDSSS Steven Stamkos 40.00 80.00
UDSSY Steve Yzerman 125.00 250.00
UDSTK Tim Kennedy 6.00 15.00
UDSTS Tom Sestito 5.00 12.00
UDSTV Thomas Vanek 8.00 20.00
UDSTW Ty Wishart 6.00 15.00
UDSWG Wayne Gretzky 125.00 200.00

2009-10 Upper Deck Signature Sensations

STATED ODDS 1:288
SSAB Adam Burish 10.00 25.00
SSAE Andrew Ebbett 5.00 12.00
SSAM Al MacInnis 30.00 60.00
SSAN Andreas Nodl 6.00 15.00
SSAO Adam Oates 8.00 20.00
SSAP Alexandre Picard 6.00 15.00
SSAT Alex Tanguay 5.00 12.00
SSBB Brian Boyle 5.00 12.00
SSBE Brendan Bell 5.00 12.00
SSBO Brad Boyes
SSCG Clark Gillies
SSCN Cam Neely 25.00 50.00
SSDC Don Cherry 20.00 40.00
SSDH Dominik Hasek 40.00 80.00
SSDL Dan LaCosta 6.00 15.00
SSDN Marcel Dionne 10.00 25.00
SSDP Dimitri Patzold 6.00 15.00
SSDS Darryl Sittler
SSEF Eric Fehr 5.00 12.00
SSEL Patrik Elias 8.00 20.00
SSEM Evgeni Malkin
SSES Phil Esposito 12.00 30.00
SSFL Marc-Andre Fleury
SSFN Fredrik Norrena 5.00 12.00
SSGB Gilbert Brule 10.00 25.00
SSGH Gordie Howe 100.00 200.00
SSHA Jannik Hansen 5.00 12.00
SSHE Dany Heatley
SSHZ Henrik Zetterberg 40.00 80.00
SSJB Jean Beliveau 40.00 80.00
SSJD Jeff Drouin-Deslauriers
SSJE Jonathan Ericsson 6.00 15.00
SSJG Jean-Sebastien Giguere 40.00 80.00
SSJH Josh Hennessy 5.00 12.00
SSJK Jari Kurri 8.00 20.00
SSJL John-Michael Liles 5.00 12.00
SSJS Jarret Stoll 6.00 15.00
SSJT Joe Thornton 8.00 20.00
SSKN Mike Knuble
SSKQ Kyle Quincey 5.00 12.00
SSKT Kyle Turris 8.00 20.00
SSLA Drew Larman 5.00 12.00
SSLR Larry Robinson 8.00 20.00
SSLT Lauri Tukonen 5.00 12.00
SSLU Joffrey Lupul 6.00 15.00
SSMD Matt D'Agostini 6.00 15.00
SSME Matt Ellis 5.00 12.00
SSMF Mark Fistric 5.00 12.00
SSMI Mike Iggulden 5.00 12.00
SSMK Matt Keetley 5.00 12.00
SSML Mike Lundin 5.00 12.00
SSMM Mark Mancari 5.00 12.00
SSMO Mike Modano 40.00 80.00
SSMP Michael Peca 6.00 15.00
SSMR Mattias Ritola 6.00 15.00
SSND Nigel Dawes 5.00 12.00
SSNK Nikolai Khabibulin 8.00 20.00
SSOP Ondrej Pavelec 10.00 25.00
SSOV Alexander Ovechkin 100.00 200.00
SSPA Daniel Paille 6.00 15.00
SSPE Rich Peverley 6.00 15.00
SSPI Adam Pineault 6.00 15.00
SSPR Patrick Roy 100.00 200.00
SSPY Ryan Potulny 5.00 12.00
SSRH Ron Hextall 12.00 30.00
SSRK Rostislav Klesla
SSRO Rostislav Olesz 5.00 12.00
SSRU R.J. Umberger 6.00 15.00
SSRY Michael Ryder 5.00 12.00
SSSB Scotty Bowman 30.00 60.00
SSSC Sidney Crosby 200.00 300.00
SSSM Stefan Meyer 6.00 15.00
SSST Martin St. Louis 8.00 20.00
SSSW Steve Wagner 5.00 12.00
SSTC Ty Conklin 6.00 15.00
SSTL Jiri Tlusty 6.00 15.00
SSTO Tobias Stephan 5.00 12.00
SSTS Tom Sestito 5.00 12.00
SSTV Thomas Vanek 8.00 20.00
SSTW Tyler Weiman 8.00 20.00
SSVF Valtteri Filppula 8.00 20.00
SSWG Wayne Gretzky
SSZC Zdeno Chara 20.00 50.00

2009-10 Upper Deck The Champions

COMPLETE SET (40) 40.00 80.00
STATED ODDS 1:12
CHAB Amanda Beard 2.00 5.00
CHAC Alissa Czisny 2.00 5.00
CHAG Alexe Gilles 2.00 5.00
CHAN Miki Ando 2.00 5.00
CHBA Ben Agosto 2.00 5.00
CHBM Bode Miller 2.00 5.00
CHBS Beckie Scott 2.00 5.00
CHBT Jennifer Botterill 2.00 5.00
CHCC Cassie Campbell 2.50 6.00
CHCG Cammie Granato 2.00 5.00
CHCO Sasha Cohen 2.00 5.00
CHDD Derrick Delmore 2.00 5.00
CHGB Gaetan Boucher 2.00 5.00
CHGI Todd Gilles 2.00 5.00
CHGZ Greg Zuerlein 2.00 5.00
CHHW Hayley Wickenheiser 2.00 5.00
CHJA Jeremy Abbott 2.00 5.00
CHJB Jean Luc Brassard 2.00 5.00
CHJC Julie Chu 2.50 6.00
CHJE Jeremy Bloom 2.00 5.00
CHJJ Jojo Starbuck 2.00 5.00
CHJM Julia Mancuso 2.00 5.00
CHKG Kerrin Lee Gartner 2.00 5.00
CHMC Madison Chock 2.00 5.00
CHME Melissa Gregory 2.00 5.00
CHMR Brandon Mroz 2.00 5.00
CHND Natalie Darwitz 2.00 5.00
CHNK Nancy Kerrigan 2.00 5.00
CHNO Nobunari Oda 2.00 5.00
CHPE Denis Petukhov 2.00 5.00
CHPG Piper Gilles 2.00 5.00
CHRF Rachael Flatt 2.00 5.00
CHSB Shae-Lynn Bourne 2.00 5.00
CHSP Kim St. Pierre 2.00 5.00
CHST Jane Summersett 2.00 5.00
CHTB Tanith Belbin 2.00 5.00
CHTG Timothy Goebel 2.00 5.00
CHWE Johnny Weir 2.00 5.00
CHYU Yuka Sato 2.00 5.00
CHZD Zach Donahue 2.00 5.00

2009-10 Upper Deck The Champions Autographs Gold

*SILVER: .4X TO 1X GOLD AUTO
CHAB Amanda Beard 12.00 30.00
CHAG Alexe Gilles 6.00 15.00
CHAN Miki Ando SP 60.00 120.00
CHBA Ben Agosto 4.00 10.00
CHBM Bode Miller 10.00 25.00
CHBS Beckie Scott SP 30.00 60.00
CHBT Jennifer Botterill 8.00 20.00
CHCC Cassie Campbell 15.00 40.00
CHCG Cammi Granato 8.00 20.00
CHDD Derrick Delmore 5.00 12.00
CHGB Gaetan Boucher 6.00 15.00
CHGI Todd Gilles 5.00 12.00
CHGZ Greg Zuerlein 5.00 12.00
CHHW Haley Wickenheiser 12.00 30.00
CHJA Jeremy Abbott SP 12.00 30.00
CHJB Jeremy Bloom 6.00 15.00
CHJC Julie Chu 6.00 15.00
CHJM Julia Mancuso 12.00 30.00
CHKG Kerrin Lee Gartner 5.00 12.00
CHMC Madison Chock 5.00 12.00
CHME Melissa Gregory 5.00 12.00
CHND Natalie Darwitz 5.00 12.00
CHNK Nancy Kerrigan 10.00 25.00
CHPE Denis Petukhov 6.00 15.00
CHPG Piper Gilles 5.00 12.00
CHRF Rachael Flatt 5.00 12.00
CHRR Ross Rebagliati 6.00 15.00
CHSP Kim St. Pierre 6.00 15.00
CHST Jane Summersett 5.00 12.00
CHTB Tanith Belbin 5.00 12.00
CHTG Timothy Goebel 4.00 10.00
CHWE Johnny Weir 4.00 10.00

2009-10 Upper Deck Top Guns

COMPLETE SET (7) 6.00 15.00
STATED ODDS 1:4
TG1 Alexander Semin .60 1.50
TG2 Zach Parise .60 1.50
TG3 Evgeni Malkin 2.00 5.00
TG4 Eric Staal .75 2.00
TG5 Jarome Iginla .60 1.50
TG6 Thomas Vanek .60 1.50
TG7 Alexander Ovechkin 2.50 6.00

2009-10 Upper Deck Winter Classic Oversized

COMPLETE SET (14) 10.00 25.00
WC1 Dustin Byfuglien 1.25 3.00
WC2 Patrick Kane 2.50 6.00
WC3 Brian Campbell 1.00 2.50
WC4 Patrick Sharp 1.25 3.00
WC5 Jonathan Toews 2.50 6.00
WC6 Kris Versteeg 1.25 3.00
WC7 Ben Eager 1.00 2.50
WC8 Marian Hossa 1.00 2.50
WC9 Nicklas Lidstrom 1.25 3.00
WC10 Brian Rafalski .75 2.00
WC11 Ty Conklin 1.00 2.50
WC12 Jiri Hudler 1.00 2.50
WC13 Pavel Datsyuk 1.50 4.00
WC14 Henrik Zetterberg 1.50 4.00

2009-10 Upper Deck Young Guns Oversized

COMPLETE SET (14) 60.00 120.00
XL1 Evander Kane 3.00 8.00
XL2 Tyler Myers 2.50 6.00
XL3 Matt Duchene 3.00 8.00
XL4 Jamie Benn 6.00 15.00
XL5 Ville Leino 1.25 3.00
XL6 Yannick Weber 1.50 4.00
XL7 John Tavares 15.00 40.00
XL8 Michael Del Zotto 1.50 4.00
XL9 Artem Anisimov 1.50 4.00
XL10 Erik Karlsson 5.00 12.00
XL11 James van Riemsdyk 3.00 8.00
XL12 Victor Hedman 3.00 8.00
XL13 Viktor Stalberg 1.50 4.00
XL14 Sergei Shirokov 1.00 2.50

2010-11 Upper Deck

COMPLETE SET (500) 250.00 500.00
COMP.SET w/o SPs (400) 20.00 50.00
COMP.SER.1 SET (250) 125.00 250.00
COMP.SER.1 w/o SPs (200) 10.00 25.00
COMP.SER.2 SET (250) 125.00 250.00
COMP.SER.2 w/o SPs (200) 10.00 25.00
201-250/451-500 YOUNG GUN ODDS 1:4
1 Nicklas Backstrom .50 1.25
2 Mike Green .30 .75
3 Tomas Fleischmann .20 .50
4 Brooks Laich .20 .50
5 Semyon Varlamov .30 .75
6 Tom Poti .20 .50
7 Henrik Sedin .30 .75
8 Ryan Kesler .30 .75
9 Alexandre Burrows .30 .75
10 Alexander Edler .20 .50
11 Mikael Samuelsson .20 .50
12 Mason Raymond .25 .60
13 Sami Salo .20 .50
14 Phil Kessel .40 1.00
15 Dion Phaneuf .30 .75
16 Jean-Sebastien Giguere .25 .60
17 Mikhail Grabovski .25 .60
18 Francois Beauchemin .20 .50
19 Colton Orr .20 .50
20 John Mitchell .20 .50
21 Steven Stamkos .60 1.50
22 Martin St. Louis .30 .75
23 Steve Downie .20 .50
24 Ryan Malone .20 .50
25 Mattias Ohlund .20 .50
26 Stephane Veilleux .20 .50
27 Mike Smith .30 .75
28 Brad Boyes .20 .50
29 David Backes .30 .75
30 Andy McDonald .25 .60
31 Erik Johnson .20 .50
32 Patrik Berglund .20 .50
33 Jay McClement .20 .50
34 Joe Thornton .30 .75
35 Dan Boyle .25 .60
36 Joe Pavelski .30 .75
37 Devin Setoguchi .25 .60
38 Ryane Clowe .20 .50
39 Logan Couture .30 .75
40 Marc Edouard Vlasic .20 .50
41 Sidney Crosby 1.25 3.00
42 Jordan Staal .30 .75
43 Maxime Talbot .30 .75
44 Pascal Dupuis .20 .50
45 Brooks Orpik .25 .60
46 Tyler Kennedy .20 .50
47 Alex Goligoski .25 .60
48 Ilya Bryzgalov .25 .60
49 Scottie Upshall .20 .50
50 Radim Vrbata .25 .60
51 Wojtek Wolski .20 .50
52 Martin Hanzal .20 .50
53 Vernon Fiddler .20 .50
54 Derek Morris .20 .50
55 Mike Richards .30 .75
56 Daniel Briere .30 .75
57 Claude Giroux .30 .75
58 Ville Leino .25 .60
59 Scott Hartnell .30 .75
60 Matt Carle .25 .60
61 Brian Boucher .25 .60
62 Jarkko Ruutu .20 .50
63 Daniel Alfredsson .30 .75
64 Mike Fisher .30 .75
65 Filip Kuba .20 .50
66 Erik Karlsson .60 1.50
67 Brian Elliott .25 .60
68 Milan Michalek .20 .50
69 Michal Rozsival .20 .50
70 Marian Gaborik .40 1.00
71 Brandon Dubinsky .25 .60
72 Ryan Callahan .30 .75
73 Artem Anisimov .25 .60
74 Marc Staal .30 .75
75 Daniel Girardi .20 .50
76 Trent Hunter .20 .50
77 John Tavares .60 1.50
78 Mark Streit .20 .50
79 Matt Moulson .25 .60
80 Blake Comeau .20 .50
81 Dwayne Roloson .25 .60
82 Dainius Zubrus .20 .50
83 Zach Parise .30 .75
84 Martin Brodeur .60 1.50
85 Jamie Langenbrunner .20 .50
86 Andy Greene .20 .50
87 David Clarkson .20 .50
88 Joel Ward .20 .50
89 Shea Weber .25 .60
90 Martin Erat .20 .50
91 J.P. Dumont .20 .50
92 Pekka Rinne .40 1.00
93 Steve Sullivan .20 .50
94 Jaroslav Spacek .20 .50
95 Mike Cammalleri .30 .75
96 Carey Price 1.25 3.00
97 Brian Gionta .25 .60
98 Josh Gorges .20 .50
99 Tom Pyatt .20 .50
100 Hal Gill .20 .50
101 Kyle Brodziak .20 .50
102 Niklas Backstrom .30 .75
103 Guillaume Latendresse .25 .60
104 Martin Havlat .25 .60
105 Andrew Brunette .20 .50
106 Cal Clutterbuck .30 .75
107 Brent Burns .40 1.00
108 Nick Schultz .20 .50
109 Brad Richardson .25 .60
110 Drew Doughty .30 .75
111 Dustin Brown .30 .75
112 Michal Handzus .25 .60
113 Jonathan Quick .50 1.25
114 Rob Scuderi .20 .50
115 Jarret Stoll .25 .60
116 Cory Stillman .20 .50
117 Tomas Vokoun .25 .60
118 Stephen Weiss .25 .60
119 Michael Frolik .20 .50
120 Bryan McCabe .20 .50
121 Jeff Deslauriers .20 .50
122 Dustin Penner .20 .50
123 Andrew Cogliano .20 .50
124 Shawn Horcoff .20 .50
125 Tom Gilbert .20 .50
126 Gilbert Brule .30 .75
127 Ryan Whitney .20 .50
128 Jonathan Ericsson .20 .50
129 Henrik Zetterberg .40 1.00
130 Johan Franzen .30 .75
131 Brian Rafalski .20 .50
132 Valtteri Filppula .30 .75
133 Brad Stuart .20 .50
134 Darren Helm .25 .60
135 Matt Niskanen .25 .60
136 Brad Richards .30 .75
137 Loui Eriksson .25 .60
138 Brenden Morrow .25 .60
139 Jamie Benn .40 1.00
140 Stephane Robidas .20 .50
141 R.J. Umberger .20 .50
142 Rick Nash .30 .75
143 Antoine Vermette .20 .50
144 Kristian Huselius .20 .50
145 Fedor Tyutin .20 .50
146 Kris Russell .20 .50
147 Cody McLeod .20 .50
148 Matt Duchene .30 .75
149 Craig Anderson .30 .75
150 Chris Stewart .25 .60
151 Ryan O'Reilly .30 .75
152 T.J. Galiardi .25 .60
153 Troy Brouwer .30 .75
154 Jonathan Toews .60 1.50
155 Duncan Keith .30 .75
156 Marian Hossa .25 .60
157 Brent Seabrook .30 .75
158 Dave Bolland .25 .60
159 Brian Campbell .20 .50
160 Sergei Samsonov .25 .60
161 Chad LaRose .20 .50
162 Cam Ward .30 .75
163 Jussi Jokinen .20 .50
164 Joni Pitkanen .25 .60
165 Tuomo Ruutu .25 .60
166 Erik Cole .25 .60
167 Curtis Glencross .20 .50
168 Niklas Hagman .20 .50
169 Jarome Iginla .30 .75
170 Jay Bouwmeester .40 1.00
171 Rene Bourque .20 .50
172 Mark Giordano .25 .60
173 Jochen Hecht .20 .50
174 Chris Butler .20 .50
175 Ryan Miller .30 .75
176 Derek Roy .30 .75
177 Tyler Myers .30 .75
178 Tim Connolly .20 .50
179 Daniel Paille .20 .50
180 Marco Sturm .20 .50
181 Patrice Bergeron .40 1.00
182 Milan Lucic .30 .75
183 Tuukka Rask .30 .75
184 David Krejci .30 .75

185 Michael Ryder .20 .50
186 Niclas Bergfors .25 .60
187 Ron Hainsey .20 .50
188 Nik Antropov .25 .60
189 Evander Kane .30 .75
190 Rich Peverley .30 .75
191 Tobias Enstrom .20 .50
192 Bryan Little .30 .75
193 George Parros .25 .60
194 Jason Blake .20 .50
195 Corey Perry .30 .75
196 Bobby Ryan .30 .75
197 Jonas Hiller .25 .60
198 Lubomir Visnovsky .20 .50
199 Toews/Keith/Kane CL .60 1.50
200 Richards/Pronger/Carter CL .30 .75
201 Cam Fowler YG RC 2.50 6.00
202 Nick Bonino YG RC 2.50 6.00
203 Alexander Burmistrov YG RC 2.00 5.00
204 Arturs Kulda YG RC 2.00 5.00
205 Jordan Caron YG RC 3.00 8.00
206 Zach Hamill YG RC 2.00 5.00
207 Jeff Penner YG RC 3.00 8.00
208 Andrew Bodnarchuk YG RC 2.00 5.00
209 Henrik Karlsson YG RC 2.00 5.00
210 T.J. Brodie YG RC 2.00 5.00
211 Jeff Skinner YG RC 5.00 12.00
212 Zac Dalpe YG RC 2.00 5.00
213 Jamie McBain YG RC 2.00 5.00
214 Nick Leddy YG RC 2.00 5.00
215 Brandon Pirri YG RC 2.00 5.00
216 Mark Olver YG RC 2.00 5.00
217 Brandon Yip YG RC 2.00 5.00
218 Philip Larsen YG RC 2.00 5.00
219 Taylor Hall YG RC 30.00 80.00
220 Jordan Eberle YG RC 8.00 20.00
221 Alex Plante YG RC 2.00 5.00
222 Evgeny Dadonov YG RC 2.50 6.00
223 Brayden Schenn YG RC 8.00 20.00
224 Kyle Clifford YG RC 2.00 5.00
225 Jake Muzzin YG RC 2.00 5.00
226 Cody Almond YG RC 2.00 5.00
227 Casey Wellman YG RC 2.00 5.00
228 Clayton Stoner YG RC 2.00 5.00
229 Justin Falk YG RC 1.50 4.00
230 Maxim Noreau YG RC 1.50 4.00
231 P.K. Subban YG RC 20.00 50.00
232 J.T. Wyman YG RC 2.00 5.00
233 Matt Martin YG RC 3.00 8.00
234 Anders Lindback YG RC 2.00 5.00
235 Matt Taormina YG RC 2.00 5.00
236 Alexander Urbom YG RC 2.00 5.00
237 Nick Palmieri YG RC 2.00 5.00
238 Derek Stepan YG RC 4.00 10.00
239 Jared Cowen YG RC 2.00 5.00
240 Sergei Bobrovsky YG RC 12.00 30.00
241 Eric Tangradi YG RC 2.00 5.00
242 Nick Johnson YG RC 1.50 4.00
243 Tommy Wingels YG RC 2.00 5.00
244 Dustin Kohn YG RC 2.00 5.00
245 Dana Tyrell YG RC 2.00 5.00
246 Dustin Tokarski YG RC 2.00 5.00
247 Nazem Kadri YG RC 12.00 30.00
248 Brayden Irwin YG RC 2.00 5.00
249 Marcus Johansson YG RC 3.00 8.00
250 Kadri/Subban/Hall YG CL 3.00 8.00
251 Teemu Selanne .60 1.50
252 Saku Koivu .30 .75
253 Ryan Getzlaf .50 1.25
254 Dan Sexton .25 .60
255 Matt Beleskey .25 .60
256 Toni Lydman .20 .50
257 Zach Bogosian .25 .60
258 Dustin Byfuglien .30 .75
259 Ben Eager .20 .50
260 Chris Mason .25 .60
261 Brent Sopel .20 .50
262 Andrew Ladd .30 .75
263 Marc Savard .20 .50
264 Zdeno Chara .25 .60
265 Tim Thomas .25 .60
266 Blake Wheeler .30 .75
267 Mark Recchi .40 1.00
268 Nathan Horton .25 .60
269 Shawn Thornton .20 .50
270 Jason Pominville .30 .75
271 Thomas Vanek .30 .75
272 Drew Stafford .30 .75
273 Craig Rivet .20 .50
274 Jordan Leopold .20 .50
275 Tyler Ennis .25 .60
276 Miikka Kiprusoff .25 .60
277 Brendan Morrison .25 .60
278 Matt Stajan .25 .60
279 Tom Kostopoulos .20 .50
280 Robyn Regehr .20 .50
281 Olli Jokinen .25 .60
282 Alex Tanguay .20 .50
283 Mikael Backlund .20 .50
284 Patrick Dwyer .20 .50
285 Eric Staal .40 1.00
286 Brandon Sutter .25 .60
287 Joe Corvo .20 .50
288 Ian White .25 .60
289 Tim Gleason .20 .50
290 Patrick Sharp .30 .75
291 Patrick Kane .60 1.50
292 Marty Turco .30 .75
293 Niklas Hjalmarsson .20 .50
294 Milan Hejduk .25 .60
295 Paul Stastny .30 .75
296 Peter Mueller .25 .60
297 John-Michael Liles .20 .50
298 Kyle Quincey .20 .50
299 David Jones .20 .50
300 Jakub Voracek .30 .75
301 Steve Mason .25 .60
302 Derick Brassard .30 .75
303 Anton Stralman .20 .50
304 Samuel Pahlsson .20 .50
305 Rostislav Klesla .20 .50
306 Ethan Moreau .20 .50
307 James Neal .30 .75
308 Mike Ribeiro .25 .60
309 Kari Lehtonen .25 .60
310 Steve Ott .25 .60
311 Trevor Daley .20 .50
312 Fabian Brunnstrom .20 .50
313 Mike Modano .50 1.25
314 Jim Howard .40 1.00
315 Nicklas Lidstrom .30 .75
316 Pavel Datsyuk .40 1.00
317 Dan Cleary .30 .75
318 Niklas Kronwall .20 .50
319 Tomas Holmstrom .20 .50
320 Ales Hemsky .25 .60
321 Sam Gagner .25 .60
322 Nikolai Khabibulin .25 .60
323 Kurtis Foster .20 .50
324 Ladislav Smid .20 .50
325 Zach Stortini .20 .50
326 Steve Bernier .20 .50
327 Dennis Wideman .20 .50
328 David Booth .20 .50
329 Radek Dvorak .20 .50
330 Dmitry Kulikov .25 .60
331 Rostislav Olesz .20 .50
332 Bryan Allen .20 .50
333 Steven Reinprecht .20 .50
334 Chris Higgins .20 .50
335 Justin Williams .25 .60
336 Ryan Smyth .25 .60
337 Jack Johnson .20 .50
338 Anze Kopitar .50 1.25
339 Wayne Simmonds .40 1.00
340 Alexei Ponikarovsky .20 .50
341 Matt Greene .20 .50
342 Mikko Koivu .30 .75
343 Antti Miettinen .20 .50
344 Marek Zidlicky .20 .50
345 Cam Barker .20 .50
346 Pierre-Marc Bouchard .30 .75
347 Matt Cullen .20 .50
348 John Madden .20 .50
349 Eric Nystrom .20 .50
350 Scott Gomez .25 .60
351 Tomas Plekanec .30 .75
352 Andrei Markov .30 .75
353 Maxim Lapierre .20 .50
354 Andrei Kostitsyn .25 .60
355 Travis Moen .20 .50
356 Roman Hamrlik .25 .60
357 Ryan Suter .20 .50
358 Patric Hornqvist .25 .60
359 David Legwand .25 .60
360 Cody Franson .20 .50
361 Colin Wilson .25 .60
362 Matthew Lombardi .20 .50
363 Cal O'Reilly .20 .50
364 Jason Arnott .25 .60
365 Brian Rolston .25 .60
366 Travis Zajac .25 .60
367 Patrik Elias .30 .75
368 Ilya Kovalchuk .30 .75
369 Johan Hedberg .25 .60
370 Henrik Tallinder .20 .50
371 Anton Volchenkov .20 .50
372 James Wisniewski .20 .50
373 Kyle Okposo .30 .75
374 Frans Nielsen .20 .50
375 Josh Bailey .25 .60
376 Rob Schremp .20 .50
377 Rick DiPietro .25 .60
378 Doug Weight .30 .75
379 Chris Drury .25 .60
380 Henrik Lundqvist .50 1.25
381 Vaclav Prospal .20 .50
382 Michael Del Zotto .25 .60
383 Sean Avery .25 .60
384 Todd White .20 .50
385 Alexander Frolov .20 .50
386 Jason Spezza .20 .50
387 Alex Kovalev .30 .75
388 Peter Regin .25 .60
389 Chris Kelly .25 .60
390 Chris Phillips .20 .50
391 Sergei Gonchar .20 .50
392 Pascal Leclaire .25 .60
393 James van Riemsdyk .50 1.25
394 Chris Pronger .25 .60
395 Jeff Carter .30 .75
396 Kimmo Timonen .20 .50
397 Daniel Carcillo .20 .50
398 Andrej Meszaros .20 .50
399 Michael Leighton .25 .60
400 Ray Whitney .25 .60
401 Eric Belanger .20 .50
402 Shane Doan .25 .60
403 Keith Yandle .30 .75
404 Ed Jovanovski .20 .50
405 Adrian Aucoin .20 .50
406 Lee Stempniak .20 .50
407 Paul Martin .20 .50
408 Chris Kunitz .30 .75
409 Marc-Andre Fleury .50 1.25
410 Evgeni Malkin 1.00 2.50
411 Kristopher Letang .30 .75
412 Patrick Marleau .30 .75
413 Dany Heatley .25 .60
414 Doug Murray .20 .50
415 Antero Niittymaki .25 .60
416 Antti Niemi .25 .60
417 T.J. Oshie .50 1.25
418 David Perron .20 .50
419 Alexander Steen .30 .75
420 B.J. Crombeen .20 .50
421 Carlo Colaiacovo .20 .50
422 Jaroslav Halak .30 .75
423 Dan Ellis .25 .60
424 Victor Hedman .40 1.00
425 Vincent Lecavalier .25 .60
426 Pavel Kubina .20 .50
427 Sean Bergenheim .20 .50
428 Dominic Moore .20 .50
429 Simon Gagne .30 .75
430 Nikolai Kulemin .25 .60
431 Tyler Bozak .30 .75
432 Mike Komisarek .20 .50
433 Jonas Gustavsson .40 1.00
434 Luca Caputi .25 .60
435 Colby Armstrong .20 .50
436 Kris Versteeg .25 .60
437 Luke Schenn .25 .60
438 Daniel Sedin .30 .75
439 Roberto Luongo .30 .75
440 Kevin Bieksa .25 .60
441 Dan Hamhuis .25 .60
442 Keith Ballard .20 .50
443 Alexander Semin .30 .75
444 Alexander Ovechkin 1.25 3.00
445 Eric Fehr .20 .50
446 John Carlson .40 1.00
447 Mike Knuble .20 .50
448 Jeff Schultz .20 .50
449 Fleury/Mlkin/Crsby CL 1.25 3.00
450 Bckstm/Ovch/Grn CL 1.25 3.00
451 Brandon McMillan YG RC 2.00 5.00
452 Nick Bonino YG RC 3.00 8.00
453 Kyle Palmieri YG RC 4.00 10.00
454 Jamie Arniel YG RC 2.00 5.00
455 Colby Cohen YG RC 2.00 5.00
456 Tyler Seguin YG RC 60.00 150.00
457 Luke Adam YG RC 2.00 5.00
458 Jon Matsumoto YG RC 2.00 5.00
459 Evan Brophey YG RC 2.00 5.00
460 Ben Smith YG RC 2.00 5.00
461 Jeremy Morin YG RC 2.00 5.00
462 Justin Mercier YG RC 2.00 5.00
463 Jonas Holos YG RC 2.00 5.00
464 Kevin Shattenkirk YG RC 6.00 15.00
465 Nick Holden YG RC 2.00 5.00
466 Magnus Paajarvi YG RC 8.00 20.00
467 Linus Omark YG RC 5.00 12.00
468 Dwight King YG RC 2.00 5.00
469 Nate Prosser YG RC 2.00 5.00
470 Matt Kassian YG RC 2.00 5.00
471 Olivier Magnan-Grenier YG RC 2.00 5.00
472 Jared Spurgeon YG RC 2.00 5.00
473 Linus Klasen YG RC 2.00 5.00
474 Mark Dekanich YG RC 2.00 5.00
475 Stephen Gionta YG RC 2.50 6.00
476 Brad Mills YG RC 2.00 5.00
477 Mark Fayne YG RC 2.00 5.00
478 Alexander Vasyunov YG RC 2.00 5.00
479 Jacob Josefson YG RC 2.00 5.00
480 Mattias Tedenby YG RC 1.50 4.00
481 Olivier Magnan-Grenier YG RC 2.00 5.00
482 Nino Niederreiter YG RC 5.00 12.00
483 Travis Hamonic YG RC 2.50 6.00
484 Matt Zaba YG RC 2.50 6.00
485 Evgeny Grachev YG RC 2.00 5.00
486 Robin Lehner YG RC 5.00 12.00
487 Eric Wellwood YG RC 2.50 6.00
488 Oliver Ekman-Larsson YG RC 10.00 25.00
489 Justin Braun YG RC 2.00 5.00
490 Mike Moore YG RC 2.00 5.00
491 Ian Cole YG RC 2.00 5.00
492 Nikita Nikitin YG RC 2.00 5.00
493 Ryan Reaves YG RC 2.50 6.00
494 Nicholas Drazenovic YG RC 2.50 6.00
495 Stefan Della Rovere YG RC 2.00 5.00
496 Johan Harju YG RC 2.00 5.00
497 Korbinian Holzer YG RC 2.00 5.00
498 Keith Aulie YG RC 2.00 5.00
499 Brian Fahey YG RC 2.00 5.00
500 Seguin/Paajarvi YG CL 4.00 10.00

2010-11 Upper Deck 20th Anniversary Parallel

*1-200/251-450 VETS: 3X TO 8X BASE
*201-250/451-500 YG: .6X TO 1.5X
OVERALL STATED ODDS 1:4
203 Alexander Burmistrov YG 3.00 8.00
219 Taylor Hall YG 30.00 80.00
220 Jordan Eberle YG 25.00 60.00
250 Eberle/Hall YG CL 20.00 50.00
456 Tyler Seguin YG 50.00 100.00
500 T.Seguin/M.Paajarvi YG CL 12.00 30.00
501 Wayne Gretzky 30.00 80.00
502 Mark Messier 10.00 25.00
503 Gordie Howe 15.00 40.00
504 Mario Lemieux 12.00 30.00
505 Steve Yzerman 15.00 40.00
506 Bobby Hull 10.00 25.00
507 Tony Esposito 6.00 15.00
508 Brian Leetch 6.00 15.00
509 Bobby Orr 15.00 40.00
510 Bobby Clarke 6.00 15.00
511 Guy Lafleur 12.00 30.00
512 Grant Fuhr 8.00 20.00
513 Patrick Roy 20.00 50.00
514 Ray Bourque 10.00 25.00
515 Cam Neely 6.00 15.00
516 Phil Esposito 8.00 20.00
517 Lanny McDonald 8.00 20.00
518 Marcel Dionne 8.00 20.00
519 Luc Robitaille 6.00 15.00
520 Alex Delvecchio 5.00 12.00
521 Jonathan Toews AW 12.00 30.00
522 Tyler Myers AW 6.00 15.00
523 Martin St. Louis AW 6.00 15.00
524 Duncan Keith AW 6.00 15.00
525 Henrik Sedin AW 6.00 15.00
526 Henrik Sedin AW 6.00 15.00
527 Ryan Miller AW 6.00 15.00
528 Pavel Datsyuk AW 8.00 20.00
529 Martin Brodeur AW 12.00 30.00
530 Jim Howard AW 10.00 25.00
531 Michael Del Zotto ART 10.00 25.00
532 Tyler Myers ART 6.00 15.00
533 Niclas Bergfors ART 5.00 12.00
534 Matt Duchene ART 6.00 15.00
535 John Tavares ART 12.00 30.00
536 Dana Tyrell CWJ 5.00 12.00
537 Keith Aulie CWJ 5.00 12.00
538 Brandon McMillan CWJ 5.00 12.00
539 Dustin Tokarski CWJ 5.00 12.00
540 Travis Hamonic CWJ 6.00 15.00
541 Marco Scandella CWJ 5.00 12.00
542 Stefan Della Rovere CWJ 5.00 12.00
543 Luke Adam CWJ 5.00 12.00
544 Brayden Schenn CWJ 12.00 30.00
545 Jared Cowen CWJ 12.00 30.00
546 Jordan Caron CWJ 8.00 20.00
547 Nazem Kadri CWJ 15.00 40.00
548 P.K. Subban CWJ 25.00 60.00
549 Jordan Eberle CWJ 50.00 100.00
550 Taylor Hall CWJ 50.00 100.00
551 Martin Brodeur YG SP 25.00 60.00
552 Eric Lindros YG SP 50.00 100.00
20ABO Bobby Orr AU/90 200.00 350.00
20ASC Sidney Crosby AU/90 150.00 300.00

2010-11 Upper Deck Exclusives

*1-450 VETS: 6X TO 15X BASE
*YOUNG GUNS: 1.2X TO 3X BASE
STATED PRINT RUN 100 SER.#'d SETS
211 Jeff Skinner YG 40.00 80.00
219 Taylor Hall YG 150.00 250.00
220 Jordan Eberle YG 75.00 150.00
231 P.K. Subban YG 75.00 135.00
456 Tyler Seguin YG 175.00 300.00

2010-11 Upper Deck French

COMPLETE SET (250) 250.00 400.00
COMP.SER.1 SET w/o SPs (200) 12.00 30.00
*FRENCH: .4X TO 1X BASE
*FRENCH YG: .4X TO 1X BASE
219 Taylor Hall YG RC 20.00 50.00
220 Jordan Eberle YG RC 20.00 50.00
223 Brayden Schenn YG RC 8.00 20.00
231 P.K. Subban YG RC 15.00 40.00
240 Sergei Bobrovsky YG RC 12.00 30.00
247 Nazem Kadri YG RC 12.00 30.00

2010-11 Upper Deck French Red

*FRENCH RED: 10X TO 25X BASE
*FRENCH RED YG: 2X TO 5X BASE
STATED PRINT RUN 25 SER.#'d SETS
211 Jeff Skinner YG 60.00 120.00
219 Taylor Hall YG 250.00 400.00
220 Jordan Eberle YG 100.00 200.00
224 Kyle Clifford YG 15.00 40.00
231 P.K. Subban YG 75.00 150.00
240 Sergei Bobrovsky YG 50.00 120.00
250 Kadri/Subban/Hall YG CL 50.00 100.00

2010-11 Upper Deck All World Team

COMP.SET w/o SPs (30) 12.00 30.00
AW1 Patrick Kane 2.50 6.00
AW2 Rick Nash 1.25 3.00
AW3 Patrick Marleau 1.25 3.00
AW4 Zach Parise 1.25 3.00
AW5 Roberto Luongo 1.25 3.00
AW6 Alexander Semin 1.25 3.00
AW7 Mike Richards 1.25 3.00
AW8 Nicklas Backstrom 2.00 5.00
AW9 Jarome Iginla 1.25 3.00
AW10 Anze Kopitar 2.00 5.00
AW11 Dany Heatley 1.00 2.50
AW12 Martin St. Louis 1.25 3.00
AW13 Ilya Bryzgalov 1.00 2.50
AW14 Mikko Koivu 1.25 3.00
AW15 Henrik Zetterberg 1.50 4.00
AW16 Joe Thornton 1.25 3.00
AW17 Jeff Carter 1.25 3.00
AW18 Tomas Vokoun 1.00 2.50
AW19 Ryan Miller 1.25 3.00
AW20 Zdeno Chara 1.00 2.50
AW21 Nicklas Lidstrom 1.25 3.00
AW22 Paul Stastny 1.25 3.00
AW23 Drew Doughty 1.25 3.00
AW24 Teemu Selanne 2.50 6.00
AW25 Phil Kessel 1.50 4.00
AW26 Ryan Getzlaf 2.00 5.00
AW27 Daniel Alfredsson 1.25 3.00
AW28 Eric Staal 1.50 4.00
AW29 Bobby Ryan 1.25 3.00
AW30 Marian Hossa 1.00 2.50
AW31 Jonathan Toews SP 5.00 12.00
AW32 Steven Stamkos SP 6.00 15.00
AW33 Henrik Sedin SP 2.50 6.00
AW34 Marian Gaborik SP 3.00 8.00
AW35 Martin Brodeur SP 5.00 12.00
AW36 Pavel Datsyuk SP 3.00 8.00
AW37 Henrik Lundqvist SP 4.00 10.00
AW38 Alexander Ovechkin SP 10.00 25.00
AW39 Ilya Kovalchuk SP 4.00 10.00
AW40 Sidney Crosby SP 10.00 25.00

2010-11 Upper Deck Ambassadors of the Game

COMP.SET w/o SPs (40) 20.00 50.00
COMP.SER.1 SET w/o SPs (20) 10.00 25.00
COMP.SER.2 SET w/o SPs (20) 12.00 30.00
AG1 Adam Foote .75 2.00
AG2 J.P. Dumont .75 2.00
AG3 Jonathan Toews 2.50 6.00
AG4 Ryan Miller 1.25 3.00
AG5 Jose Theodore 1.25 3.00
AG6 Steve Sullivan .75 2.00
AG7 Phil Kessel 1.50 4.00
AG8 Teemu Selanne 2.50 6.00
AG9 Martin St. Louis 1.25 3.00
AG10 Brad Richards 1.25 3.00
AG11 Marty Turco 1.25 3.00
AG12 Vincent Lecavalier 1.00 2.50
AG13 Dustin Brown 1.25 3.00
AG14 Mike Green 1.25 3.00
AG15 Roberto Luongo 1.25 3.00
AG16 Zdeno Chara 1.00 2.50
AG17 Shane Doan 1.00 2.50
AG18 Nicklas Lidstrom 1.25 3.00
AG19 Jamie Langenbrunner .75 2.00
AG20 Don Cherry 1.25 3.00
AG21 Pavel Datsyuk SP 4.00 10.00
AG22 Jarome Iginla SP 2.50 6.00
AG23 Alexander Ovechkin SP 10.00 25.00
AG24 Bobby Orr SP 8.00 20.00
AG25 Sidney Crosby SP 10.00 25.00
AG26 Bobby Clarke SP 4.00 10.00
AG27 Mario Lemieux SP 8.00 20.00
AG28 Steve Yzerman SP 6.00 15.00
AG29 Mark Messier SP 4.00 10.00
AG30 Wayne Gretzky SP 10.00 25.00
AG31 Corey Perry 1.25 3.00
AG32 Patrick Marleau 1.25 3.00
AG33 Bobby Ryan 1.25 3.00
AG34 Jeff Carter 1.25 3.00
AG35 Paul Stastny 1.25 3.00
AG36 Steven Stamkos 2.50 6.00
AG37 Daniel Sedin 1.25 3.00
AG38 Drew Doughty 1.25 3.00
AG39 Jean-Sebastien Giguere 1.00 2.50
AG40 Brian Gionta 1.00 2.50
AG41 Henrik Zetterberg 1.50 4.00
AG42 Joe Thornton 1.25 3.00
AG43 Eric Staal 1.50 4.00
AG44 Paul Kariya 1.50 4.00
AG45 Mike Richards 1.25 3.00
AG46 Nicklas Backstrom 2.00 5.00
AG47 Zach Parise 1.25 3.00
AG48 Brenden Morrow 1.00 2.50
AG49 Henrik Lundqvist 2.00 5.00
AG50 Daniel Alfredsson 1.25 3.00
AG51 Rick Nash SP 2.50 6.00
AG52 Jonathan Toews SP 5.00 12.00
AG53 Patrick Roy SP 6.00 15.00
AG54 Henrik Sedin SP 2.50 6.00
AG55 Lanny McDonald SP 2.50 6.00
AG56 Martin Brodeur SP 5.00 12.00
AG57 Ray Bourque SP 4.00 10.00
AG58 Cam Neely SP 2.50 6.00
AG59 Bobby Hull SP 2.50 6.00
AG60 Luc Robitaille SP 2.50 6.00

2010-11 Upper Deck Biography of A Season

COMPLETE SET (30) 8.00 20.00
BOS1 Alexander Ovechkin 1.00 2.50
BOS2 Sidney Crosby 1.00 2.50
BOS3 Henrik Sedin .25 .60
BOS4 Steven Stamkos .50 1.25
BOS5 Mike Cammalleri .25 .60
BOS6 Mike Richards .25 .60
BOS7 Patrick Kane .50 1.25
BOS8 Jonathan Toews .50 1.25
BOS9 Taylor Hall .75 2.00
BOS10 Jaroslav Halak .25 .60
BOS11 Carey Price 1.00 2.50
BOS12 Steven Stamkos .50 1.25
BOS13 Sergei Bobrovsky .50 1.25
BOS14 Daniel Alfredsson .25 .60
BOS15 Ondrej Pavelec .25 .60
BOS16 Tim Thomas .20 .50
BOS17 Milan Lucic .25 .60
BOS18 Sidney Crosby 1.00 2.50
BOS19 Evgeni Malkin .75 2.00
BOS20 Brandon Dubinsky .20 .50
BOS21 Semyon Varlamov .25 .60
BOS22 Zdeno Chara .20 .50
BOS23 Marian Gaborik .30 .75
BOS24 Patrick Sharp .25 .60
BOS25 Johan Franzen .25 .60
BOS26 Miikka Kiprusoff .20 .50
BOS27 Ryan Callahan .25 .60
BOS28 Jarome Iginla .25 .60
BOS29 P.K. Subban .60 1.50
BOS30 Corey Perry .25 .60

2010-11 Upper Deck Clear Cut Champions

STATED PRINT RUN 100 SER.#'d SETS
CCCAM Al MacInnis 12.00 30.00
CCCBC Bobby Clarke 8.00 20.00
CCCBH Bobby Hull 8.00 20.00
CCCBL Brian Leetch 8.00 20.00
CCCBO Bobby Orr 25.00 50.00
CCCBP Bernie Parent 8.00 20.00
CCCBR Brad Richards 8.00 20.00
CCCBU Johnny Bucyk 8.00 20.00
CCCCW Cam Ward 8.00 20.00
CCCDP Denis Potvin 8.00 20.00
CCCEM Evgeni Malkin 20.00 60.00
CCCES Eric Staal 8.00 20.00
CCCFM Frank Mahovlich 8.00 20.00
CCCGF Grant Fuhr 8.00 20.00
CCCGH Gordie Howe 12.00 30.00
CCCGL Guy Lafleur 10.00 25.00
CCCHZ Henrik Zetterberg 8.00 20.00
CCCJB Jean Beliveau 12.00 30.00
CCCJK Jari Kurri 8.00 20.00
CCCJM Joe Mullen 6.00 15.00
CCCJO Johnny Bower 8.00 20.00
CCCJT Jonathan Toews 15.00 40.00
CCCLM Lanny McDonald 8.00 20.00
CCCLR Larry Robinson 8.00 20.00
CCCMB Martin Brodeur 15.00 40.00
CCCMI Mike Bossy 8.00 20.00
CCCML Mario Lemieux 25.00 60.00
CCCMM Mark Messier 12.00 30.00
CCCMO Mike Modano 12.00 30.00
CCCNL Nicklas Lidstrom 8.00 20.00
CCCPE Phil Esposito 12.00 30.00
CCCPK Patrick Kane 15.00 40.00
CCCPR Patrick Roy 20.00 50.00
CCCRB Ray Bourque 12.00 30.00
CCCRG Ryan Getzlaf 12.00 30.00
CCCSC Sidney Crosby 30.00 80.00
CCCSM Stan Mikita 8.00 20.00
CCCSN Scott Niedermayer 8.00 20.00
CCCSY Steve Yzerman 15.00 40.00
CCCTL Ted Lindsay 8.00 20.00
CCCVL Vincent Lecavalier 6.00 15.00
CCCWG Wayne Gretzky 40.00 100.00

2010-11 Upper Deck Clear Cut Hall of Fame

STATED PRINT RUN 25 SER.#'d SETS
CCHBH J.Beliveau/G.Howe 40.00 100.00
CCHBM F.Mahovlich/J.Bucyk 15.00 40.00
CCHBP D.Potvin/M.Bossy 15.00 40.00
CCHDM M.Dionne/L.McDonald 20.00 50.00
CCHEL G.Lafleur/T.Esposito 20.00 50.00
CCHHM S.Mikita/B.Hull 20.00 50.00
CCHKH D.Hawerchuk/J.Kurri 20.00 50.00
CCHLT B.Trottier/M.Lemieux 30.00 80.00
CCHMM M.Messier/A.MacInnis 25.00 60.00
CCHRF G.Fuhr/P.Roy 40.00 100.00
CCHSG P.Stastny/W.Gretzky 100.00 200.00
CCHYR S.Yzerman/L.Robitaille 25.00 60.00

2010-11 Upper Deck Clear Cut Lineage

STATED PRINT RUN 25 SER.#'d SETS
CCLBOS Orr/Esposito/Bourque 40.00 100.00
CCLCGY Fleury/MacInnis/Iginla 20.00 50.00
CCLCHI Toews/Hull/Kane 25.00 60.00
CCLDET Yzerman/Howe/Zetter 30.00 80.00
CCLLAK Robitlle/Dionne/Gretzky 60.00 150.00
CCLMTL Cammall/Lafleur/Beliveau 15.00 40.00
CCLPHI Carter/Clarke/Richards 12.00 30.00
CCLPIT Crosby/Malkin/Lemieux 50.00 125.00
CCLTOR Mahov/Gilmour/Kessel 15.00 40.00

2010-11 Upper Deck EA Superstars

COMPLETE SET (15) 15.00 40.00
COMP.SET w/o SPs (10) 8.00 20.00
EA1 Jonathan Toews SP 5.00 12.00
EA2 Patrick Kane SP 5.00 12.00
EA3 Dion Phaneuf SP 2.50 6.00
EA4 Jarome Iginla SP 2.50 6.00
EA5 Chris Pronger SP 2.00 5.00
EA6 Milan Lucic 1.25 3.00
EA7 John Tavares 2.50 6.00
EA8 Eric Staal 1.50 4.00
EA9 Nicklas Backstrom 2.00 5.00
EA10 Mark Streit .75 2.00
EA11 Josh Harding 1.25 3.00
EA12 Mikko Koivu 1.25 3.00
EA13 Henrik Sedin 1.25 3.00
EA14 Daniel Sedin 1.25 3.00
EA15 Zach Stortini .75 2.00

2010-11 Upper Deck Game Jerseys

STATED ODDS 1:12
GJAF Alexander Frolov 2.50 6.00
GJAH Adam Hall 2.50 6.00
GJAK Alex Kovalev 4.00 10.00
GJAN Antero Niittymaki 3.00 8.00
GJAO Adam Oates 3.00 8.00
GJAW Andy Wozniewski 2.50 6.00
GJBG Brian Gionta 3.00 8.00
GJBO David Booth 2.50 6.00
GJBR Derick Brassard 4.00 10.00
GJCA Mike Cammalleri 4.00 10.00
GJCD Chris Drury 3.00 8.00
GJCH Jonathan Cheechoo 3.00 8.00
GJDA Daniel Alfredsson 4.00 10.00
GJDB Daniel Briere 4.00 10.00
GJDC Dino Ciccarelli 3.00 8.00
GJDG Doug Gilmour 4.00 10.00
GJDR Derek Roy 4.00 10.00
GJDS Devin Setoguchi 3.00 8.00
GJDT Darcy Tucker 3.00 8.00
GJDU Dustin Brown 4.00 10.00
GJDW Doug Wilson 2.50 6.00
GJEL Patrik Elias 4.00 10.00
GJEM Evgeni Malkin 12.00 30.00
GJFB Francis Bouillon 2.50 6.00
GJFL Marc-Andre Fleury 6.00 15.00
GJFR Michael Frolik 2.50 6.00
GJGB Gilbert Brule 4.00 10.00
GJGL Guillaume Latendresse 3.00 8.00
GJHL Henrik Lundqvist 6.00 15.00
GJHZ Henrik Zetterberg 5.00 12.00
GJIK Ilya Kovalchuk 4.00 10.00
GJJB Jay Bouwmeester 5.00 12.00
GJJC Jeff Carter 4.00 10.00
GJJG Jean-Sebastien Giguere 3.00 8.00
GJJI Jarome Iginla 4.00 10.00
GJJP Jason Pominville 4.00 10.00
GJJT Jeff Tambellini 2.50 6.00
GJJV Jakub Voracek 4.00 10.00
GJKA Anze Kopitar 6.00 15.00
GJKL Kristopher Letang 4.00 10.00
GJKO Andrei Kostitsyn 3.00 8.00
GJLR Luc Robitaille 3.00 8.00
GJLS Luke Schenn 3.00 8.00
GJMA Martin St. Louis 4.00 10.00
GJMC Matt Carle 3.00 8.00
GJMG Marian Gaborik 5.00 12.00
GJMH Marian Hossa 3.00 8.00
GJMJ Milan Jurcina 2.50 6.00
GJMK Miikka Kiprusoff 3.00 8.00
GJMO Mattias Ohlund 2.50 6.00
GJMP Marc-Antoine Pouliot 3.00 8.00
GJMR Mark Recchi 5.00 12.00
GJMS Marek Svatos 2.50 6.00
GJMT Marty Turco 4.00 10.00
GJNA Nik Antropov 3.00 8.00
GJNB Nicklas Backstrom 6.00 15.00
GJNH Nathan Horton 3.00 8.00
GJNI Rob Niedermayer 2.50 6.00
GJOK Kyle Okposo 4.00 10.00
GJOV Alexander Ovechkin 6.00 15.00
GJPE Patrick Eaves 2.50 6.00
GJPK Patrick Kane 8.00 20.00
GJPM Patrick Marleau 4.00 10.00
GJPS Paul Stastny 4.00 10.00
GJRE Ray Emery 3.00 8.00
GJRG Ryan Getzlaf 6.00 15.00
GJRI Mike Richards 4.00 10.00
GJRL Roberto Luongo 4.00 10.00
GJRM Ryan Miller 4.00 10.00
GJRN Rick Nash 4.00 10.00
GJSA Miroslav Satan 3.00 8.00
GJSC Sidney Crosby 8.00 20.00
GJSG Scott Gomez 3.00 8.00
GJSH Shaone Morrisonn 2.50 6.00
GJSM Steve Mason 3.00 8.00
GJSS Steven Stamkos 8.00 20.00
GJST Drew Stafford 4.00 10.00
GJSV Sergei Samsonov 3.00 8.00
GJSW Shea Weber 3.00 8.00
GJTA John Tavares 6.00 15.00
GJTB Todd Bertuzzi 3.00 8.00
GJTF Tomas Fleischmann 2.50 6.00
GJTH Joe Thornton 4.00 10.00
GJTO Jonathan Toews 8.00 20.00
GJTP Tomas Plekanec 4.00 10.00
GJTR Tuomo Ruutu 3.00 8.00
GJTT Tim Thomas 5.00 12.00
GJTV Thomas Vanek 4.00 10.00
GJVL Vincent Lecavalier 3.00 8.00
GJVO Tomas Vokoun 3.00 8.00
GJWE Stephen Weiss 3.00 8.00
GJWG Wayne Gretzky 20.00 50.00
GJZP Zach Parise 4.00 10.00
GJ2AM Andrei Markov 4.00 10.00
GJ2AO Alexander Ovechkin 8.00 20.00
GJ2BD Brandon Dubinsky 3.00 8.00
GJ2CG Claude Giroux 5.00 12.00
GJ2CO Colton Orr 2.50 6.00
GJ2CP Carey Price 6.00 15.00
GJ2CW Cam Ward 4.00 10.00
GJ2DD Drew Doughty 4.00 10.00
GJ2DH Dany Heatley 3.00 8.00
GJ2DP Dustin Penner 2.50 6.00
GJ2GL Georges Laraque 3.00 8.00
GJ2GP George Parros 3.00 8.00
GJ2HE Milan Hejduk 3.00 8.00
GJ2HL Henrik Lundqvist 5.00 12.00
GJ2JH Jonas Hiller 3.00 8.00
GJ2JL Jamie Langenbrunner 2.50 6.00
GJ2JT John Tavares 6.00 15.00
GJ2JV James van Riemsdyk 5.00 12.00
GJ2KV Kris Versteeg 3.00 8.00
GJ2LA Guillaume Latendresse 3.00 8.00
GJ2LE Loui Eriksson 3.00 8.00
GJ2MB Martin Brodeur 4.00 10.00
GJ2MC Matt Carkner 3.00 8.00
GJ2MD Matt Duchene 4.00 10.00
GJ2MG Marian Gaborik 5.00 12.00
GJ2MH Marian Hossa 3.00 8.00
GJ2MS Martin St. Louis 4.00 10.00
GJ2NB Nicklas Backstrom 6.00 15.00
GJ2NL Nicklas Lidstrom 4.00 10.00
GJ2NZ Nikolai Zherdev 2.50 6.00
GJ2PB Patrice Bergeron 5.00 12.00
GJ2PE Patrik Elias 4.00 10.00
GJ2PS Patrick Sharp 4.00 10.00
GJ2RG Ryan Getzlaf 6.00 15.00
GJ2RK Ryan Kesler 4.00 10.00
GJ2RL Roberto Luongo 4.00 10.00
GJ2SC Sidney Crosby 12.00 30.00
GJ2SD Shane Doan 3.00 8.00
GJ2ST Paul Stastny 4.00 10.00
GJ2SV Semyon Varlamov 4.00 10.00
GJ2TM Tyler Myers 4.00 10.00
GJ2TR Tuukka Rask 4.00 10.00
GJ2ZC Zdeno Chara 3.00 8.00

2010-11 Upper Deck Hockey Heroes Bobby Orr

COMPLETE SET (10) 40.00 80.00
COMP.SET w/o SPs (8) 8.00 20.00
COMMON ORR 2.50 6.00
HH18 Bobby Orr Header 15.00 40.00
HHBO Bobby Orr Art 20.00 50.00
HHBOA Bobby Orr Art AU
HHBOAU Bobby Orr AU 250.00 400.00

2010-11 Upper Deck Hockey Heroes Steve Yzerman

COMPLETE SET (10) 30.00 80.00
COMP.SET w/o SPs (8) 8.00 20.00
COMMON YZERMAN 2.50 6.00
HH9 Steve Yzerman Header 12.00 30.00
HHYZ Steve Yzerman 10.00 25.00
HHYZA Steve Yzerman AU/19

2010-11 Upper Deck Netminders

COMPLETE SET (30) 15.00 40.00
COMP.SET w/o SPs (20) 12.00 30.00
N1 Rick DiPietro 1.25 3.00
N2 Semyon Varlamov 1.50 4.00
N3 Marty Turco 1.50 4.00
N4 Kari Lehtonen 1.25 3.00
N5 Jonathan Quick 2.50 6.00
N6 Craig Anderson 1.50 4.00
N7 Jim Howard 2.00 5.00
N8 Pekka Rinne 2.00 5.00
N9 Jonas Hiller 1.25 3.00
N10 Niklas Backstrom 1.50 4.00
N11 Tomas Vokoun 1.25 3.0
N12 Tuukka Rask 1.50 4.0
N13 Mike Smith 1.50 4.
N14 Steve Mason 1.25 3.
N15 Michael Leighton 1.25 3.
N16 Carey Price 6.00 15.
N17 Jean-Sebastien Giguere 1.25 3.
N18 Brian Elliott 1.25 3.0
N19 Jeff Deslauriers 1.00 2.
N20 Chris Mason 1.25 3.0
N21 Ryan Miller SP 3.00 8.
N22 Miikka Kiprusoff SP 2.50 6.0
N23 Cam Ward SP 3.00 8.0
N24 Antti Niemi SP 2.50 6.0
N25 Roberto Luongo SP 3.00 8.0
N26 Henrik Lundqvist SP 5.00 12.0
N27 Ilya Bryzgalov SP 2.50 6.0
N28 Marc-Andre Fleury SP 5.00 12.0
N29 Jaroslav Halak SP 3.00 8.0
N30 Martin Brodeur SP 6.00 15.0

2010-11 Upper Deck Oversized

COMPLETE SET (42) 15.00 40.0
OS1 Bobby Ryan .50 1.2
OS2 Ryan Getzlaf .75 2.0
OS3 Zdeno Chara .40 1.0
OS4 Ryan Miller .50 1.2
OS5 Thomas Vanek .50 1.2
OS6 Jarome Iginla .50 1.2
OS7 Miikka Kiprusoff .40 1.0
OS8 Eric Staal .60 1.5
OS9 Jonathan Toews 1.00 2.5
OS10 Duncan Keith .50 1.2
OS11 Patrick Kane 1.00 2.5
OS12 Antti Niemi .40 1.0
OS13 Matt Duchene .50 1.2
OS14 Paul Stastny .50 1.2
OS15 Rick Nash .50 1.2
OS16 Brad Richards .50 1.2
OS17 Henrik Zetterberg .60 1.5
OS18 Nicklas Lidstrom .50 1.2
OS19 Pavel Datsyuk .60 1.5
OS20 Dustin Penner .30
OS21 Drew Doughty .50 1.2
OS22 Anze Kopitar .75 2.0
OS23 Brian Gionta .40 1.0
OS24 Zach Parise .50 1.2
OS25 Martin Brodeur 1.00 2.5
OS26 Ilya Kovalchuk .50 1.2
OS27 John Tavares 1.00 2.5
OS28 Marian Gaborik .60 1.5
OS29 Mike Richards .50 1.2
OS30 Jeff Carter .50 1.2
OS31 Shane Doan .40 1.0
OS32 Sidney Crosby 2.00 5.0
OS33 Evgeni Malkin 1.50 4.0
OS34 Joe Thornton .50 1.2
OS35 Dany Heatley .40 1.0
OS36 Steven Stamkos 1.00 2.5
OS37 Phil Kessel .60 1.5
OS38 Henrik Sedin .50 1.2
OS39 Roberto Luongo .50 1.2
OS40 Daniel Sedin .50 1.2
OS41 Nicklas Backstrom .75 2.0
OS42 Alexander Ovechkin 2.00 5.0

2010-11 Upper Deck Rookie Breakouts

STATED PRINT RUN 100 SER.#'d SETS
RB1 Cam Fowler 6.00 15.0
RB2 Alexander Burmistrov 5.00 12.0
RB3 Zach Hamill 5.00 12.0
RB4 Tyler Seguin 20.00 50.0
RB5 Jordan Caron 8.00 20.0
RB6 Henrik Karlsson 5.00 12.0
RB7 Zac Dalpe 5.00 12.0
RB8 Jeff Skinner 10.00 25.0
RB9 Jamie McBain 5.00 12.0
RB10 Nick Leddy 5.00 12.0
RB11 Kevin Shattenkirk 10.00 25.0
RB12 Brandon Yip 5.00 12.0
RB13 Taylor Hall 30.00 80.0
RB14 Magnus Paajarvi 6.00 15.0
RB15 Jordan Eberle 12.00 30.0
RB16 Brayden Schenn 8.00 20.0
RB17 Mattias Tedenby 4.00 10.0
RB18 P.K. Subban 25.00 60.0
RB19 Anders Lindback 5.00 12.0
RB20 Jacob Josefson 5.00 12.0
RB21 Nino Niederreiter 6.00 15.0
RB22 Derek Stepan 10.00 25.0
RB23 Jared Cowen 5.00 12.0
RB24 Sergei Bobrovsky 12.50 30.0
RB25 Oliver Ekman-Larsson 8.00 20.0
RB26 Eric Tangradi 5.00 12.0
RB27 Dustin Tokarski 5.00 12.0
RB28 Dana Tyrell 5.00 12.0
RB29 Nazem Kadri 15.00 40.0
RB30 Marcus Johansson 8.00 20.0

2010-11 Upper Deck Rookie Headliners

COMPLETE SET (30) 20.00 50.0
COMP.SET w/o SPs (20) 12.00 30.0
STATED ODDS 1:4
RH1 Dustin Tokarski .75 2.0
RH2 Kevin Shattenkirk 1.50 4.0
RH3 Nick Leddy .75 2.0
RH4 Dana Tyrell .75 2.0
RH5 Anders Lindback .75 2.0
RH6 Oliver Ekman-Larsson 1.25 3.0
RH7 Zac Dalpe .75 2.0
RH8 Jacob Josefson .75 2.0
RH9 Marcus Johansson 1.25 3.0
RH10 Zach Hamill .75 2.0
RH11 Jordan Caron 1.25 3.0
RH12 Cam Fowler 1.00 2.5
RH13 Sergei Bobrovsky 2.00 5.0
RH14 Henrik Karlsson .75 2.0
RH15 Jared Cowen .75 2.0
RH16 Jamie McBain .75 2.0
RH17 Eric Tangradi .75 2.0
RH18 Alexander Burmistrov .75 2.0
RH19 Brandon Yip .75 2.0
RH20 Justin Falk .60 1.5
RH21 Derek Stepan SP 2.00 5.0
RH22 Nino Niederreiter SP 1.25 3.0
RH23 Nazem Kadri SP 3.00 8.0
RH24 P.K. Subban SP 3.00 8.0
RH25 Magnus Paajarvi SP 1.25 3.0
RH26 Brayden Schenn SP 1.50 4.0
RH27 Jeff Skinner SP 2.00 5.0
RH28 Jordan Eberle SP 2.50 6.0
RH29 Tyler Seguin SP 4.00 10.0
RH30 Taylor Hall SP 4.00 10.0

2010-11 Upper Deck Rookie Materials

*PATCH/25: 1.2X TO 3X BASE MATERIALS
RMAB Andrew Bodnarchuk 3.00 8.0
RMAK Arturs Kulda 3.00 8.0
RMAL Anders Lindback 3.00 8.0

MBS Brayden Schenn 8.00 20.00
MBU Alexander Burmistrov 3.00 8.00
MBY Brandon Yip 3.00 8.00
MCA Cody Almond 3.00 8.00
MCF Cam Fowler 4.00 10.00
MCW Casey Wellman 3.00 8.00
MDS Derek Stepan 6.00 15.00
MDT Dustin Tokarski 3.00 8.00
MEG Evgeny Grachev 3.00 8.00
MET Eric Tangradi 3.00 8.00
MEW Eric Wellwood 4.00 10.00
MFA Justin Falk 2.50 6.00
MHK Henrik Karlsson 3.00 8.00
MIC Ian Cole 3.00 8.00
MJC Jared Cowen 3.00 8.00
MJE Jordan Eberle 6.00 15.00
MJJ Jacob Josefson 3.00 8.00
MJO Jordan Caron 5.00 12.00
MJS Jeff Skinner 12.00 30.00
MKC Kyle Clifford 3.00 8.00
MKP Kyle Palmieri 6.00 15.00
MKS Kevin Shattenkirk 6.00 15.00
MLA Luke Adam 3.00 8.00
MLS Philip Larsen 3.00 8.00
MMC Jamie McBain 3.00 8.00
MMJ Marcus Johansson 5.00 12.00
MMN Maxim Noreau 2.50 6.00
MMO Mark Olver 3.00 8.00
MMP Magnus Paajarvi 4.00 10.00
MMS Marco Scandella 3.00 8.00
MMT Mattias Tedenby 2.50 6.00
MNJ Nick Johnson 2.50 6.00
MNK Nazem Kadri 6.00 15.00
MNL Nick Leddy 3.00 8.00
MNN Nino Niederreiter 4.00 10.00
MNP Nick Palmieri 3.00 8.00
MOE Oliver Ekman-Larsson 5.00 12.00
MPL Alex Plante 3.00 8.00
MPS P.K. Subban 15.00 40.00
MSB Sergei Bobrovsky 8.00 20.00
MTB T.J. Brodie 3.00 8.00
MTH Taylor Hall 8.00 20.00
MTS Tyler Seguin 12.00 30.00
MTW Tommy Wingels 3.00 8.00
MTY Dana Tyrell 3.00 8.00
MZD Zac Dalpe 3.00 8.00
MZH Zach Hamill 3.00 8.00

2010-11 Upper Deck Signature Sensations

SAB Justin Abdelkader 5.00 12.00
SAM Andrew MacDonald 4.00 10.00
SAN Andreas Nodl 4.00 10.00
SAO Alexander Ovechkin
SBA David Backes 6.00 15.00
SBE Patrik Berglund 4.00 10.00
SBJ Jamie Benn 8.00 20.00
SBO Johnny Bower
SBR Brian Salcido 4.00 10.00
SBS Bobby Sanguinetti 4.00 10.00
SCG Claude Giroux 12.00 30.00
SCH Don Cherry 20.00 40.00
SCS Chris Stewart
SDB Derick Brassard 6.00 15.00
SDC David Clarkson
SDG Doug Gilmour 30.00 60.00
SDH Dany Heatley
SDP David Perron
SEK Evander Kane 6.00 15.00
SEL Patrik Elias 6.00 15.00
SFB Fabian Brunnstrom 4.00 10.00
SFM Frank Mahovlich
SFR Michael Frolik 8.00 20.00
SGA Marian Gaborik 8.00 20.00
SGC Guy Carbonneau 5.00 12.00
SGF Grant Fuhr
SGH Gordie Howe 50.00 100.00
SGO Scott Gomez 12.00 30.00
SHE Matt Hendricks 4.00 10.00
SHH Harry Howell
SHS Henrik Sedin
SIV Ivan Vishnevskiy 4.00 10.00
SJA Jason Arnott 5.00 12.00
SJC Jeff Carter 15.00 40.00
SJG Jean-Sebastien Giguere 10.00 25.00
SJI Jarome Iginla
SJK Jari Kurri 6.00 15.00
SJL John-Michael Liles 6.00 15.00
SJR Joel Rechlicz 4.00 10.00
SJS John Scott 4.00 10.00
SJT John Tavares 12.00 30.00
SJV James van Riemsdyk 10.00 25.00
SKC Kris Chucko
SKD Kris Draper 4.00 10.00
SKE Tim Kennedy
SKH Nikolai Khabibulin
SKL Kari Lehtonen 12.00 30.00
SLE Trevor Lewis 5.00 12.00
SLR Luc Robitaille
SMB Mike Brodeur 6.00 15.00
SMD Matt Duchene 6.00 15.00
SME Matt Ellis 4.00 10.00
SMF Mark Fraser 4.00 10.00
SMG Matt Gilroy 4.00 10.00
SMH Matthew Halischuk 5.00 12.00
SMI Stan Mikita 12.00 30.00
SML Mario Lemieux
SMM Mike Modano 10.00 25.00
SMN Markus Naslund
SMP Matt Pelech 4.00 10.00
SMR Michael Ryder
SMS Marek Svatos
SNE John Negrin 5.00 12.00
SNF Nick Foligno 5.00 12.00
SNG Nathan Gerbe 4.00 10.00
SNH Nathan Horton 5.00 12.00
SNK Nikolai Kulemin 5.00 12.00
SOR Bobby Orr
SPA Pascal Leclaire 5.00 12.00
SPB Patrice Bergeron 40.00 80.00
SPE Phil Esposito 6.00 15.00
SPH Patric Hornqvist 12.00 30.00
SPK Patrick Kane 12.00 30.00
SPL Perttu Lindgren 4.00 10.00
SPM Peter Mueller 5.00 12.00
SPR Peter Regin 8.00 20.00
SPS Peter Stastny 12.00 30.00
SRM Ray Macias 4.00 10.00
SSA Michael Sauer 4.00 10.00
SSC Sidney Crosby 100.00 200.00
SSG Simon Gagne
SSH James Sheppard 4.00 10.00
SSK Saku Koivu 25.00 50.00
SSM Spencer Machacek 4.00 10.00
SSS Steven Stamkos 40.00 100.00
SST Jarret Stoll
SSV Sergei Shirokov 5.00 12.00
SSW Stephen Weiss 5.00 12.00
SSY Steve Yzerman
STC Taylor Chorney 5.00 12.00
STE Tony Esposito 12.00 30.00
SSTH Joe Thornton 6.00 15.00
SSTK Tomas Kopecky 5.00 12.00
SSTL Jiri Tlusty 5.00 12.00
SSTO Jonathan Toews
SSWE Shea Weber 5.00 12.00
SSWG Wayne Gretzky 150.00 250.00
SSYW Yannick Weber 6.00 15.00
SSSC2 Sidney Crosby

2010-11 Upper Deck Signatures

UDSAL Andrew Ladd 6.00 15.00
UDSAN Antti Niemi 5.00 12.00
UDSAO Alexander Ovechkin 40.00 100.00
UDSBD Brandon Dubinsky 5.00 12.00
UDSBE Matt Beleskey 5.00 12.00
UDSBM Brendan Mikkelson 4.00 10.00
UDSBO Bobby Orr
UDSBR Brent Seabrook 6.00 15.00
UDSBS Brandon Sutter 5.00 12.00
UDSBV Boris Valabik 6.00 15.00
UDSBY Brandon Yip 10.00 25.00
UDSCA Colby Armstrong 8.00 20.00
UDSCF Cody Franson 4.00 10.00
UDSCH Chris Higgins 4.00 10.00
UDSCK Chuck Kobasew 4.00 10.00
UDSCS Chris Stewart 5.00 12.00
UDSDA Daniel Carcillo 4.00 10.00
UDSDB Dave Bolland 5.00 12.00
UDSDC Dan Cleary 6.00 15.00
UDSDE Derek Stepan 10.00 25.00
UDSDP David Perron 4.00 10.00
UDSDS Drew Stafford 6.00 15.00
UDSEM Evgeni Malkin 20.00 50.00
UDSET Eric Tangradi
UDSFR Michael Frolik 4.00 10.00
UDSGB Gilbert Brule
UDSGL Guillaume Latendresse 5.00 12.00
UDSHL Henrik Lundqvist 10.00 25.00
UDSHO Tomas Holmstrom 10.00 25.00
UDSIK Ilya Kovalchuk 15.00 40.00
UDSJA Jason Arnott 5.00 12.00
UDSJB Josh Bailey 5.00 12.00
UDSJE Jordan Eberle 12.00 30.00
UDSJG Jean-Sebastien Giguere 25.00 60.00
UDSJH Josh Harding 6.00 15.00
UDSJJ Jesse Joensuu
UDSJM Jay McClement 4.00 10.00
UDSJP Jason Pominville 6.00 15.00
UDSJS John Scott 4.00 10.00
UDSJT John Tavares 12.00 30.00
UDSJV Jakub Voracek 6.00 15.00
UDSKD Kris Draper
UDSLC Logan Couture 12.00 30.00
UDSLE Lars Eller 15.00 40.00
UDSLS Luke Schenn
UDSMB Mikael Backlund
UDSMD Michael Del Zotto 5.00 12.00
UDSMF Mark Fraser 4.00 10.00
UDSMG Matt Gilroy 4.00 10.00
UDSMI John Mitchell 4.00 10.00
UDSML Maxim Lapierre 4.00 10.00
UDSMN Michal Neuvirth 5.00 12.00
UDSMP Marc-Antoine Pouliot 6.00 15.00
UDSMR Michael Ryder
UDSMS Marc Savard 4.00 10.00
UDSND Nigel Dawes 4.00 10.00
UDSNH Nathan Horton
UDSNI Peter Mueller 8.00 20.00
UDSNK Nazem Kadri 15.00 40.00
UDSOP Ondrej Pavelec 6.00 15.00
UDSPA Max Pacioretty 6.00 15.00
UDSPL Matt Niskanen 6.00 15.00
UDSPO Patrick O'Sullivan 4.00 10.00
UDSPS P.K. Subban 15.00 40.00
UDSRI Mike Ribeiro 12.00 30.00
UDSSA Bobby Sanguinetti 4.00 10.00
UDSSC Sidney Crosby 100.00 200.00
UDSSH James Sheppard 4.00 10.00
UDSSM Steve Mason 10.00 25.00
UDSSS Steven Stamkos
UDSST Marc Staal 6.00 15.00
UDSSW Shea Weber 20.00 50.00
UDSTB Tyler Bozak
UDSTE Tyler Ennis 5.00 12.00
UDSTG T.J. Galiardi 5.00 12.00
UDSTH Taylor Hall 40.00 80.00
UDSTK Tomas Kopecky 8.00 20.00
UDSTL Jiri Tlusty 5.00 12.00
UDSTR Tuukka Rask 10.00 25.00
UDSTS Tom Sestito 4.00 10.00
UDSTW Ty Wishart 4.00 10.00
UDSVS Viktor Stalberg 5.00 12.00
UDSWG Wayne Gretzky 250.00 400.00

2010-11 Upper Deck Winter Classic Oversized

COMPLETE SET (14) 10.00 25.00
STATED ODDS 1 PER BLASTER BOX
WC1 B.Clarke/B.Orr 4.00 10.00
WC2 Zdeno Chara 1.00 2.50
WC3 Patrice Bergeron 1.50 4.00
WC4 Marco Sturm .75 2.00
WC5 Mark Recchi 1.50 4.00
WC6 Shawn Thornton .75 2.00
WC7 David Krejci 1.25 3.00
WC8 Tim Thomas 1.00 2.50
WC9 Danny Syvret .75 2.00
WC10 Jeff Carter 1.25 3.00
WC11 Scott Hartnell 1.25 3.00
WC12 Mike Richards 1.25 3.00
WC13 Daniel Carcillo .75 2.00
WC14 Michael Leighton 1.00 2.50

2010-11 Upper Deck Young Guns Oversized

ONE PER SPECIAL BLASTER BOX
OS1 Jordan Eberle 10.00 25.00
OS2 Brayden Schenn 2.00 5.00
OS3 Derek Stepan 2.50 6.00
OS4 Eric Tangradi 2.50 6.00
OS5 Jamie McBain 2.50 6.00
OS6 Jeff Skinner 8.00 20.00
OS7 Jordan Caron 4.00 10.00
OS8 Alexander Burmistrov 1.25 3.00
OS9 Marcus Johansson 2.00 5.00
OS10 Nazem Kadri 4.00 10.00
OS11 P.K. Subban 8.00 20.00
OS12 Sergei Bobrovsky 4.00 10.00
OS13 Zac Dalpe 2.50 6.00
OS14 Taylor Hall 15.00 40.00

2010-11 Upper Deck Stanley Cup Finals

COMPLETE SET (15) 8.00 20.00
ISSUED AT ARENAS DURING THE SERIES
SC1B Patrice Bergeron .50 1.25
SC2B Tim Thomas .30 .75
SC3B Zdeno Chara .30 .75
SC4B Brad Marchand .60 1.50
SC5B Milan Lucic .40 1.00
SC1V Ryan Kesler .40 1.00
SC2V Roberto Luongo .40 1.00
SC3V Daniel Sedin .40 1.00
SC4V Henrik Sedin .40 1.00
SC5V Alexandre Burrows .40 1.00
SC6 Ray Bourque MM .60 1.50
SC7 Wayne Gretzky MM 2.00 5.00
SC8 Patrick Kane MM .75 2.00
SC9 Bobby Orr MM 1.25 3.00
SC10 Alex Ovechkin MM 1.50 4.00

2011-12 Upper Deck

COMP.SERIES 1 (250) 150.00 300.00
COMP.SERIES 2 (250) 125.00 250.00
COMP.SER.1 w/o SPs (200) 10.00 25.00
COMP.SER.2 w/o SPs (200) 10.00 25.00
YOUNG GUN STATED ODDS 1:4
1 Dustin Byfuglien .30 .75
2 Patrice Cormier .20 .50
3 Tobias Enstrom .20 .50
4 Evander Kane .30 .75
5 Blake Wheeler .60 1.50
6 Ondrej Pavelec .30 .75
7 Alexander Semin .30 .75
8 Alexander Ovechkin 1.25 3.00
9 Mike Knuble .20 .50
10 Mike Green .30 .75
11 Michal Neuvirth .25 .60
12 John Carlson .40 1.00
13 Henrik Sedin .30 .75
14 Daniel Sedin .30 .75
15 Roberto Luongo .30 .75
16 Ryan Kesler .30 .75
17 Alexander Edler .20 .50
18 Cory Schneider .25 .60
19 Phil Kessel .40 1.00
20 Dion Phaneuf .30 .75
21 James Reimer .30 .75
22 Nazem Kadri .50 1.25
23 Clarke MacArthur .20 .50
24 Nikolai Kulemin .30 .75
25 Luke Schenn .25 .60
26 Steven Stamkos .60 1.50
27 Ryan Malone .20 .50
28 Martin St. Louis .30 .75
29 Dwayne Roloson .25 .60
30 Victor Hedman .40 1.00
31 Steve Downie .20 .50
32 Jaroslav Halak .30 .75
33 David Backes .30 .75
34 Patrik Berglund .25 .60
35 Kevin Shattenkirk .25 .60
36 Chris Stewart .25 .60
37 Alexander Steen .30 .75
38 David Perron .20 .50
39 Joe Thornton .30 .75
40 Patrick Marleau .30 .75
41 Joe Pavelski .30 .75
42 Antti Niemi .25 .60
43 Dan Boyle .25 .60
44 Logan Couture .30 .75
45 Ryane Clowe .20 .50
46 Pascal Dupuis .20 .50
47 Jordan Staal .30 .75
48 Kristopher Letang .30 .75
49 Chris Kunitz .30 .75
50 Marc-Andre Fleury .50 1.25
51 Matt Cooke .20 .50
52 James Neal .30 .75
53 Shane Doan .25 .60
54 Keith Yandle .30 .75
55 Lauri Korpikoski .20 .50
56 Brett MacLean .20 .50
57 Oliver Ekman-Larsson .30 .75
58 Radim Vrbata .25 .60
59 Claude Giroux .30 .75
60 Kimmo Timonen .20 .50
61 Daniel Briere .30 .75
62 Chris Pronger .25 .60
63 James van Riemsdyk .30 .75
64 Braydon Coburn .20 .50
65 Andreas Nodl .20 .50
66 Jason Spezza .30 .75
67 Daniel Alfredsson .30 .75
68 Erik Karlsson .60 1.50
69 Nick Foligno .25 .60
70 Sergei Gonchar .20 .50
71 Bobby Butler .25 .60
72 Peter Regin .20 .50
73 Henrik Lundqvist .40 1.00
74 Marc Staal .30 .75
75 Derek Stepan .30 .75
76 Ryan Callahan .30 .75
77 Brandon Dubinsky .25 .60
78 Mats Zuccarello-Aasen .30 .75
79 Brian Boyle .20 .50
80 John Tavares .60 1.50
81 Michael Grabner .25 .60
82 P.A. Parenteau .20 .50
83 Blake Comeau .20 .50
84 Kyle Okposo .30 .75
85 Josh Bailey .25 .60
86 Al Montoya .20 .50
87 Martin Brodeur .60 1.50
88 Zach Parise .30 .75
89 Travis Zajac .25 .60
90 Mattias Tedenby .20 .50
91 Anton Volchenkov .20 .50
92 David Clarkson .20 .50
93 Patric Hornqvist .25 .60
94 Ryan Suter .20 .50
95 Sergei Kostitsyn .20 .50
96 Pekka Rinne .40 1.00
97 Shea Weber .25 .60
98 Mike Fisher .30 .75
99 Carey Price 1.00 2.50
100 Andrei Kostitsyn .25 .60
101 Scott Gomez .25 .60
102 P.K. Subban .60 1.50
103 Brian Gionta .25 .60
104 Jaroslav Spacek .20 .50
105 Max Pacioretty .30 .75
106 Mikko Koivu .25 .60
107 Cal Clutterbuck .30 .75
108 Nick Schultz .20 .50
109 Pierre-Marc Bouchard .30 .75
110 Guillaume Latendresse .25 .60
111 Matt Cullen .20 .50
112 Marek Zidlicky .20 .50
113 Drew Doughty .30 .75
114 Dustin Penner .25 .60
115 Rob Scuderi .20 .50
116 Jarret Stoll .25 .60
117 Justin Williams .25 .60
118 Jonathan Quick .50 1.25
119 Jack Johnson .20 .50
120 David Booth .20 .50
121 Stephen Weiss .25 .60
122 Jacob Markstrom .30 .75
123 Mike Santorelli .20 .50
124 Dmitry Kulikov .20 .50
125 Evgeny Dadonov .25 .60
126 Taylor Hall .60 1.50
127 Devan Dubnyk .30 .75
128 Sam Gagner .25 .60
129 Magnus Paajarvi .25 .60
130 Linus Omark .30 .75
131 Ryan Whitney .20 .50
132 Theo Peckham .20 .50
133 Nicklas Lidstrom .30 .75
134 Johan Franzen .30 .75
135 Jim Howard .30 .75
136 Niklas Kronwall .25 .60
137 Justin Abdelkader .25 .60
138 Henrik Zetterberg .40 1.00
139 Darren Helm .25 .60
140 Brenden Morrow .25 .60
141 Kari Lehtonen .25 .60
142 Alex Goligoski .25 .60
143 Mike Ribeiro .25 .60
144 Jamie Benn .40 1.00
145 Steve Ott .25 .60
146 Rick Nash .30 .75
147 Kristian Huselius .20 .50
148 Derick Brassard .30 .75
149 Kris Russell .20 .50
150 Antoine Vermette .20 .50
151 R.J. Umberger .20 .50
152 Anton Stralman .20 .50
153 Erik Johnson .20 .50
154 Paul Stastny .30 .75
155 Jay McClement .20 .50
156 Ryan O'Byrne .20 .50
157 David Jones .20 .50
158 Ryan O'Reilly .30 .75
159 Kevin Porter .20 .50
160 Jonathan Toews .60 1.50
161 Patrick Sharp .30 .75
162 Marian Hossa .25 .60
163 Brent Seabrook .30 .75
164 Dave Bolland .25 .60
165 Corey Crawford .40 1.00
166 Duncan Keith .30 .75
167 Jeff Skinner .30 .75
168 Jamie McBain .20 .50
169 Eric Staal .40 1.00
170 Cam Ward .30 .75
171 Tuomo Ruutu .25 .60
172 Joni Pitkanen .25 .60
173 Jarome Iginla .30 .75
174 Miikka Kiprusoff .30 .75
175 Rene Bourque .20 .50
176 Matt Stajan .25 .60
177 Anton Babchuk .20 .50
178 Mark Giordano .25 .60
179 Jay Bouwmeester .30 .75
180 Ryan Miller .30 .75
181 Drew Stafford .30 .75
182 Derek Roy .25 .60
183 Tyler Myers .30 .75
184 Tyler Ennis .25 .60
185 Nathan Gerbe .20 .50
186 Jason Pominville .25 .60
187 Tim Thomas .30 .75
188 Zdeno Chara .30 .75
189 Brad Marchand .40 1.00
190 Nathan Horton .30 .75
191 David Krejci .30 .75
192 Dennis Seidenberg .25 .60
193 Milan Lucic .30 .75
194 Corey Perry .30 .75
195 Lubomir Visnovsky .20 .50
196 Jonas Hiller .25 .60
197 Ryan Getzlaf .50 1.25
198 Cam Fowler .25 .60
199 Sedin/Luongo/Kesler CL .25 .60
200 Lucic/Thomas/Chara CL .25 .60
201 Devante Smith-Pelly YG RC 3.00 8.00
202 Maxime Macenauer YG RC 2.00 5.00
203 Greg Nemisz YG RC 2.00 5.00
204 Roman Horak YG RC 2.00 5.00
205 Justin Faulk YG RC 3.00 8.00
206 Marcus Kruger YG RC 5.00 12.00
207 Brandon Saad YG RC 8.00 20.00
208 Gabriel Landeskog YG RC 8.00 20.00
209 Cameron Gaunce YG RC 1.50 4.00
210 John Moore YG RC 2.00 5.00
211 David Savard YG RC 2.00 5.00
212 Cam Atkinson YG RC 5.00 12.00
213 Tomas Vincour YG RC 2.00 5.00
214 R.Nugent-Hopkins YG RC 15.00 40.00
215 Anton Lander YG RC 2.00 5.00
216 Teemu Hartikainen YG RC 2.00 5.00
217 Erik Gudbranson YG RC 2.50 6.00
218 Brett Bulmer YG RC 2.00 5.00
219 Aaron Palushaj YG RC 2.00 5.00
220 Alexei Yemelin YG RC 2.00 5.00
221 Raphael Diaz YG RC 2.00 5.00
222 Brendon Nash YG RC 2.00 5.00
223 Jonathon Blum YG RC 2.00 5.00
224 Blake Geoffrion YG RC 2.00 5.00
225 Craig Smith YG RC 2.50 6.00
226 Adam Henrique YG RC 5.00 12.00
227 Adam Larsson YG RC 2.50 6.00
228 Tim Erixon YG RC 2.00 5.00
229 Mika Zibanejad YG RC 5.00 12.00
230 Colin Greening YG RC 2.00 5.00
231 Patrick Wiercioch YG RC 2.00 5.00
232 Erik Condra YG RC 2.00 5.00
233 Stephane Da Costa YG RC 2.00 5.00
234 Sean Couturier YG RC 10.00 25.00
235 Matt Read YG RC 4.00 10.00
236 Erik Gustafsson YG RC 2.50 6.00
237 Joe Vitale YG RC 2.00 5.00
238 Harri Sateri YG RC 2.00 5.00
239 Alex Stalock YG 2.00 5.00
240 Brett Connolly YG RC 2.00 5.00
241 Jake Gardiner YG RC 8.00 20.00
242 Joe Colborne YG RC 2.00 5.00
243 Matt Frattin YG RC 2.00 5.00
244 Ben Scrivens YG RC 3.00 8.00
245 Cody Hodgson YG RC 4.00 10.00
246 Yann Sauve YG RC 2.00 5.00
247 Carl Klingberg YG RC 2.00 5.00
248 Mark Scheifele YG RC 30.00 80.00
249 Paul Postma YG RC 2.00 5.00
250 Ngnt-Hpk/Land/Larsn CL 3.00 8.00
251 Alexander Burmistrov .25 .60
252 Nik Antropov .25 .60
253 Eric Fehr .20 .50
254 Chris Mason .25 .60
255 Jim Slater .20 .50
256 Bryan Little .30 .75
257 Andrew Ladd .30 .75
258 Zach Bogosian .25 .60
259 Tomas Vokoun .25 .60
260 Troy Brouwer .25 .60
261 Nicklas Backstrom .50 1.25
262 Brooks Laich .20 .50
263 Marcus Johansson .25 .60
264 Roman Hamrlik .25 .60
265 Joel Ward .20 .50
266 John Erskine .25 .60
267 Alexandre Burrows .30 .75
268 Mason Raymond .25 .60
269 Jannik Hansen .25 .60
270 Dan Hamhuis .25 .60
271 Kevin Bieksa .25 .60
272 David Booth .20 .50
273 Manny Malhotra .25 .60
274 Chris Higgins .20 .50
275 John-Michael Liles .20 .50
276 Mikhail Grabovski .25 .60
277 Jonas Gustavsson .30 .75
278 Joffrey Lupul .25 .60
279 Matthew Lombardi .20 .50
280 Tyler Bozak .30 .75
281 Colton Orr .20 .50
282 Vincent Lecavalier .25 .60
283 Teddy Purcell .30 .75
284 Nate Thompson .20 .50
285 Dominic Moore .20 .50
286 Eric Brewer .20 .50
287 Mathieu Garon .25 .60
288 Andy McDonald .25 .60
289 Brian Elliott .25 .60
290 T.J. Oshie .50 1.25
291 Jason Arnott .25 .60
292 Jamie Langenbrunner .20 .50
293 Alex Pietrangelo .25 .60
294 Barret Jackman .20 .50
295 Martin Havlat .25 .60
296 Torrey Mitchell .20 .50
297 Brent Burns .40 1.00
298 Benn Ferriero .20 .50
299 Michal Handzus .20 .50
300 Thomas Greiss .25 .60
301 Sidney Crosby 1.25 3.00
302 Evgeni Malkin 1.00 2.50
303 Tyler Kennedy .20 .50
304 Arron Asham .20 .50
305 Paul Martin .20 .50
306 Brent Johnson .25 .60
307 Steve Sullivan .20 .50
308 Mike Smith .30 .75
309 Jason LaBarbera .25 .60
310 Raffi Torres .20 .50
311 Daymond Langkow .20 .50
312 Ray Whitney .25 .60
313 Boyd Gordon .20 .50
314 Martin Hanzal .20 .50
315 Brayden Schenn .30 .75
316 Jaromir Jagr .75 2.00
317 Wayne Simmonds .40 1.00
318 Scott Hartnell .30 .75
319 Jakub Voracek .30 .75
320 Maxime Talbot .25 .60
321 Ilya Bryzgalov .30 .75
322 Milan Michalek .20 .50
323 Zenon Konopka .25 .60
324 Craig Anderson .30 .75
325 Jared Cowen .30 .75
326 Alex Auld .25 .60
327 Filip Kuba .20 .50
328 Brad Richards .30 .75
329 Wojtek Wolski .20 .50
330 Marian Gaborik .40 1.00
331 Ruslan Fedotenko .20 .50
332 Artem Anisimov .25 .60
333 Martin Biron .25 .60
334 Brandon Prust .20 .50
335 Andrew MacDonald .20 .50
336 Matt Moulson .25 .60
337 Frans Nielsen .20 .50
338 Nino Niederreiter .20 .50
339 Brian Rolston .25 .60
340 Evgeni Nabokov .25 .60
341 Matt Martin (NYI) .20 .50
342 Mark Streit .20 .50
343 Ilya Kovalchuk .30 .75
344 Dainius Zubrus .20 .50
345 Nick Palmieri .25 .60
346 Patrik Elias .30 .75
347 Johan Hedberg .25 .60
348 Andy Greene .20 .50
349 Martin Erat .20 .50
350 Nicklas Bergfors .25 .60
351 Matthew Halischuk .20 .50
352 Colin Wilson .25 .60
353 Nick Spaling .20 .50
354 David Legwand .25 .60
355 Michael Cammalleri .25 .60
356 Tomas Plekanec .30 .75
357 Erik Cole .25 .60
358 Peter Budaj .25 .60
359 Andrei Markov .30 .75
360 Lars Eller .25 .60
361 Travis Moen .20 .50
362 Devin Setoguchi .25 .60
363 Dany Heatley .25 .60
364 Niklas Backstrom .30 .75
365 Darroll Powe .20 .50
366 Nick Johnson .25 .60
367 Josh Harding .30 .75
368 Mike Richards .30 .75
369 Simon Gagne .30 .75
370 Anze Kopitar .50 1.25
371 Jonathan Bernier .30 .75
372 Dustin Brown .30 .75
373 Kyle Clifford .20 .50
374 Scottie Upshall .20 .50
375 Tomas Fleischmann .20 .50
376 Kris Versteeg .25 .60
377 Marcel Goc .25 .60
378 Jack Skille .25 .60
379 Brian Campbell .20 .50
380 Ed Jovanovski .20 .50
381 Jordan Eberle .30 .75
382 Ales Hemsky .25 .60
383 Ryan Smyth .25 .60
384 Nikolai Khabibulin .25 .60
385 Ben Eager .20 .50
386 Tom Gilbert .20 .50
387 Pavel Datsyuk .40 1.00
388 Dan Cleary .30 .75
389 Jonathan Ericsson .25 .60
390 Tomas Holmstrom .20 .50
391 Ty Conklin .25 .60
392 Valttori Filppula .30 .75
393 Jakub Kindl .20 .50
394 Loui Eriksson .25 .60
395 Sheldon Souray .20 .50
396 Michael Ryder .20 .50
397 Toby Petersen .20 .50
398 Stephane Robidas .20 .50
399 Andrew Raycroft .25 .60
400 Jeff Carter .30 .75
401 Steve Mason .25 .60
402 Fedor Tyutin .20 .50
403 Vaclav Prospal .20 .50
404 Matt Calvert .25 .60
405 James Wisniewski .20 .50
406 Matt Duchene .30 .75
407 Jean-Sebastien Giguere .25 .60
408 Semyon Varlamov .30 .75
409 Milan Hejduk .25 .60
410 Kyle Quincey .20 .50
411 Patrick Kane .60 1.50
412 Michael Frolik .20 .50
413 Andrew Brunette .20 .50
414 Niklas Hjalmarsson .20 .50
415 Ray Emery .25 .60
416 Anthony Stewart .20 .50
417 Jussi Jokinen .20 .50
418 Zach Boychuk .20 .50
419 Zac Dalpe .20 .50
420 Brandon Sutter .25 .60
421 Jiri Tlusty .25 .60
422 Olli Jokinen .25 .60
423 Mikael Backlund .30 .75
424 David Moss .20 .50
425 Lee Stempniak .20 .50
426 Curtis Glencross .20 .50
427 Henrik Karlsson .25 .60
428 Cory Sarich .20 .50
429 Brad Boyes .20 .50
430 Ville Leino .25 .60
431 Luke Adam .25 .60
432 Thomas Vanek .30 .75
433 Robyn Regehr .20 .50
434 Christian Ehrhoff .20 .50
435 Jordan Leopold .20 .50
436 Tuukka Rask .30 .75
437 Rich Peverley .30 .75
438 Patrice Bergeron .40 1.00
439 Daniel Paille .20 .50
440 Tyler Seguin .60 1.50
441 Shawn Thornton .25 .60
442 Chris Kelly .25 .60
443 Gregory Campbell .20 .50
444 Bobby Ryan .30 .75
445 Teemu Selanne .60 1.50
446 Andrew Cogliano .20 .50
447 George Parros .25 .60
448 Luca Sbisa .25 .60
449 Rinne/Quick/Backstrom CL .50 1.25
450 Miller/Lundqvist/Vokoun CL .40 1.00
451 Pat Maroon YG RC 2.50 6.00
452 Peter Holland YG RC 2.50 6.00
453 Corey Tropp YG RC 2.50 6.00
454 Brayden McNabb YG RC 2.50 6.00
455 Zack Kassian YG RC 5.00 12.00
456 Marcus Foligno YG RC 6.00 15.00
457 Joe Finley YG RC 2.50 6.00
458 T.J. Brennan YG RC 2.50 6.00
459 Leland Irving YG RC 2.50 6.00
460 Riley Nash YG RC 2.50 6.00
461 Mike Murphy YG RC 2.50 6.00
462 Jimmy Hayes YG RC 3.00 8.00
463 Brad Malone YG RC 2.50 6.00
464 Stefan Elliott YG RC 2.50 6.00
465 Ryan Johansen YG RC 8.00 20.00
466 Jordie Benn YG RC 2.50 6.00
467 Brendan Smith YG RC 2.50 6.00
468 Gustav Nyquist YG RC 6.00 15.00
469 Joakim Andersson YG RC 2.50 6.00
470 Colten Teubert YG RC 2.50 6.00
471 Viatcheslav Voynov YG RC 2.50 6.00
472 Jarod Palmer YG RC 2.50 6.00
473 David McIntyre YG RC 2.50 6.00
474 Kris Fredheim YG RC 2.50 6.00
475 Frederic St. Denis YG RC 2.50 6.00
476 Louis Leblanc YG RC 5.00 12.00
477 Gabriel Bourque YG RC 2.50 6.00
478 Roman Josi YG RC 4.00 10.00
479 Ryan Ellis YG RC 5.00 12.00
480 Mattias Ekholm YG RC 2.50 6.00
481 David Ullstrom YG RC 2.50 6.00
482 Anders Nilsson YG RC 2.50 6.00
483 Calvin de Haan YG RC 2.50 6.00
484 Carl Hagelin YG RC 5.00 12.00
485 Stu Bickel YG RC 2.50 6.00
486 Harry Zolnierczyk YG RC 2.50 6.00
487 Zac Rinaldo YG RC 2.50 6.00
488 Kevin Marshall YG RC 2.50 6.00
489 Marc-Andre Bourdon YG RC 2.50 6.00
490 David Rundblad YG RC 2.50 6.00
491 Andy Miele YG RC 2.50 6.00
492 Carl Sneep YG RC 2.50 6.00
493 Simon Despres YG RC 2.50 6.00
494 Robert Bortuzzo YG RC 2.50 6.00
495 Cade Fairchild YG RC 2.00 5.00
496 Bill Sweatt YG RC 2.50 6.00
497 Eddie Lack YG RC 2.50 6.00
498 Dmitry Orlov YG RC 3.00 8.00
499 Cody Eakin YG RC 5.00 12.00
500 Leblnc/Kass/Johan CL 2.50 6.00

2011-12 Upper Deck Exclusives

*VETS 1-200/251-400: 6X TO 15X BASE
*YG 201-250: 1.2X TO 3X BASE
*YG 401-450: 1X TO 2.5X BASE
STATED PRINT RUN 100 SER.#'d SETS
165 Corey Crawford 5.00 12.00
208 Gabriel Landeskog YG 50.00 100.00
214 Ryan Nugent-Hopkins YG 125.00 250.00
225 Craig Smith YG 15.00 40.00
226 Adam Henrique YG 20.00 50.00
227 Adam Larsson YG 20.00 50.00
229 Mika Zibanejad YG 15.00 40.00
234 Sean Couturier YG 30.00 80.00
235 Matt Read YG 20.00 50.00
240 Brett Connolly YG 10.00 25.00
245 Cody Hodgson YG 15.00 40.00
247 Carl Klingberg YG 6.00 15.00
248 Mark Scheifele YG 40.00 80.00
261 Nicklas Backstrom 6.00 15.00
453 Corey Tropp YG 6.00 15.00
459 Leland Irving YG 6.00 15.00
464 Stefan Elliott YG 6.00 15.00
468 Gustav Nyquist YG 40.00 80.00
476 Louis Leblanc YG 20.00 50.00
484 Carl Hagelin YG 20.00 50.00
485 Stu Bickel YG 6.00 15.00

2011-12 Upper Deck All World Team

COMP.SET w/o SPs (30) 12.00 30.00
STATED ODDS 1:12
SP STATED ODDS 1:120
AW1 Alexander Semin 1.25 3.00
AW2 Antti Niemi 1.00 2.50
AW3 Anze Kopitar 2.00 5.00
AW4 Carey Price 4.00 10.00
AW5 Corey Perry 1.25 3.00
AW6 Daniel Sedin 1.25 3.00
AW7 David Krejci 1.25 3.00
AW8 Drew Doughty 1.25 3.00
AW9 Duncan Keith 1.25 3.00
AW10 Dustin Byfuglien 1.25 3.00
AW11 Henrik Sedin 1.25 3.00
AW12 Henrik Zetterberg 1.50 4.00
AW13 Jaroslav Halak 1.25 3.00
AW14 John Tavares 2.50 6.00
AW15 Jonas Hiller 1.00 2.50
AW16 Jonathan Quick 2.00 5.00
AW17 Marian Gaborik 1.50 4.00
AW18 Marian Hossa 1.00 2.50
AW19 Martin Brodeur 2.50 6.00
AW20 Mats Zuccarello-Aasen 1.25 3.00
AW21 Mikko Koivu 1.00 2.50
AW22 Nicklas Backstrom 2.00 5.00
AW23 Patrick Kane 2.50 6.00
AW24 Patrick Marleau 1.25 3.00
AW25 Paul Stastny 1.25 3.00
AW26 Phil Kessel 1.50 4.00
AW27 Ryan Kesler 1.25 3.00
AW28 Ryan Miller 1.25 3.00
AW29 Shea Weber 1.00 2.50
AW30 Victor Hedman 1.50 4.00
AW31 Zdeno Chara SP 2.50 6.00
AW32 Tim Thomas SP 2.50 6.00
AW33 Steven Stamkos SP 5.00 12.00
AW34 Sidney Crosby SP 10.00 25.00
AW35 Roberto Luongo SP 2.50 6.00
AW36 Nicklas Lidstrom SP 2.50 6.00
AW37 Miikka Kiprusoff SP 2.50 6.00
AW38 Jonathan Toews SP 5.00 12.00
AW39 Henrik Lundqvist SP 3.00 8.00
AW40 Alexander Ovechkin SP 10.00 25.00

2011-12 Upper Deck Biography of A Season

COMPLETE SET (30) 6.00 15.00
BOS1 Tim Thomas .30 .75
BOS2 Ryan Nugent-Hopkins 1.00 2.50
BOS3 Bruins Champions/Z.Chara .30 .75
BOS4 Corey Perry .30 .75
BOS5 Nicklas Lidstrom .30 .75
BOS6 Jeff Skinner .30 .75
BOS7 Jaromir Jagr .75 2.00
BOS8 Mike Richards .30 .75
BOS9 Mike Modano .50 1.25
BOS10 Back In Winnipeg/N.Antropov .25 .60
BOS11 Phil Kessel .40 1.00
BOS12 Jonathan Quick .50 1.25
BOS13 Joffrey Lupul .25 .60
BOS14 Tyler Seguin .60 1.50
BOS15 Ryan Nugent-Hopkins 1.00 2.50
BOS16 Sidney Crosby 1.25 3.00
BOS17 Jonathan Toews .60 1.50
BOS18 Zdeno Chara .30 .75
BOS19 Jimmy Howard .30 .75
BOS30 Steven Stamkos .60 1.50
BOS29 Evgeni Malkin 1.00 2.50
BOS28 Ilya Bryzgalov .30 .75
BOS27 Ryan Miller .30 .75
BOS26 Henrik Zetterberg .40 1.00
BOS25 Sam Gagner .25 .60
BOS24 Marian Gaborik .40 1.00
BOS23 Shane Doan .25 .60
BOS22 Jarome Iginla .30 .75
BOS21 Henrik Lundqvist .40 1.00
BOS20 Claude Giroux .30 .75

2011-12 Upper Deck Buyback Autographs

STATED PRINT RUN 2-21
AO A.Ovechkin 05-06 PP/21 75.00 150.00

2011-12 Upper Deck Canvas

COMP.SER.1 w/o SPs (90) 100.00 200.00
C1-C90 VETERAN ODDS 1:6 SER.1
C121-C210 VET ODDS 1:6 SER.2
C91-C120 YG ODDS 1:48 SER.1
C211-C240 YG ODDS 1:48 SER.2
C241-C270 RET/POE ODDS 1:192 SER.2
C1 Ryan Getzlaf 1.50 4.00
C2 Bobby Ryan 1.00 2.50
C3 Jonas Hiller .75 2.00
C4 Cam Fowler .75 2.00
C5 Zdeno Chara 1.00 2.50
C6 Tuukka Rask 1.00 2.50
C7 Patrice Bergeron 1.25 3.00
C8 Dennis Seidenberg .75 2.00
C9 Brad Marchand 1.25 3.00
C10 Nathan Horton 1.00 2.50
C11 Thomas Vanek 1.00 2.50
C12 Ryan Miller 1.00 2.50
C13 Tyler Myers 1.00 2.50
C14 Drew Stafford 1.00 2.50
C15 Rene Bourque .60 1.50
C16 Jarome Iginla 1.00 2.50
C17 Jay Bouwmeester 1.00 2.50
C18 Miikka Kiprusoff 1.00 2.50
C19 Matt Stajan .75 2.00
C20 Eric Staal 1.25 3.00
C21 Cam Ward 1.00 2.50
C22 Jussi Jokinen .60 1.50
C23 Jonathan Toews 2.00 5.00
C24 Patrick Kane 2.00 5.00
C25 Marian Hossa .75 2.00
C26 Duncan Keith 1.00 2.50
C27 Matt Duchene 1.00 2.50
C28 Paul Stastny 1.00 2.50
C29 Rick Nash 1.00 2.50
C30 Steve Mason .75 2.00
C31 Kari Lehtonen .75 2.00
C32 Mike Ribeiro .75 2.00
C33 Brenden Morrow .75 2.00
C34 Jim Howard 1.00 2.50
C35 Henrik Zetterberg 1.25 3.00
C36 Pavel Datsyuk 1.25 3.00
C37 Nicklas Lidstrom 1.00 2.50
C38 Stephen Weiss .75 2.00
C39 Drew Doughty 1.00 2.50
C40 Jonathan Quick 1.50 4.00
C41 Anze Kopitar 1.50 4.00
C42 Mikko Koivu .75 2.00
C43 Niklas Backstrom 1.00 2.50
C44 Guillaume Latendresse .75 2.00
C45 Tomas Plekanec 1.00 2.50
C46 Carey Price 3.00 8.00
C47 Michael Cammalleri .75 2.00
C48 Pekka Rinne 1.25 3.00
C49 Patric Hornqvist .75 2.00
C50 Shea Weber .75 2.00
C51 Martin Brodeur 2.00 5.00
C52 Zach Parise 1.00 2.50
C53 Ilya Kovalchuk 1.00 2.50
C54 Kyle Okposo 1.00 2.50
C55 John Tavares 2.00 5.00
C56 Henrik Lundqvist 1.25 3.00
C57 Marian Gaborik 1.25 3.00

C58 Sean Avery .75 2.00
C59 Jason Spezza 1.00 2.50
C60 Chris Pronger .75 2.00
C61 Daniel Briere 1.00 2.50
C62 Scott Hartnell 1.00 2.50
C63 Claude Giroux 1.00 2.50
C64 Shane Doan .75 2.00
C65 Jordan Staal 1.00 2.50
C66 Evgeni Malkin 3.00 8.00
C67 Marc-Andre Fleury 1.50 4.00
C68 Joe Thornton 1.00 2.50
C69 Joe Pavelski 1.00 2.50
C70 Patrick Marleau 1.00 2.50
C71 Antti Niemi .75 2.00
C72 Jaroslav Halak 1.00 2.50
C73 Patrik Berglund .75 2.00
C74 David Backes 1.00 2.50
C75 Kevin Shattenkirk .75 2.00
C76 Steven Stamkos 2.00 5.00
C77 Vincent Lecavalier .75 2.00
C78 Dion Phaneuf 1.00 2.50
C79 Phil Kessel 1.25 3.00
C80 Roberto Luongo 1.00 2.50
C81 Daniel Sedin 1.00 2.50
C82 Henrik Sedin 1.00 2.50
C83 Alexandre Burrows 1.00 2.50
C84 Michal Neuvirth .75 2.00
C85 Alexander Ovechkin 4.00 10.00
C86 Nicklas Backstrom 1.50 4.00
C87 Mike Green 1.00 2.50
C88 Dustin Byfuglien 1.00 2.50
C89 Evander Kane 1.00 2.50
C90 Crosby/Ovechkin/Stamkos CL 3.00 8.00
C91 Devante Smith-Pelly YG 6.00 15.00
C92 Greg Nemisz YG 4.00 10.00
C93 Justin Faulk YG 6.00 15.00
C94 Marcus Kruger YG 6.00 15.00
C95 Brandon Saad YG 8.00 20.00
C96 John Moore YG 4.00 10.00
C97 Ryan Johansen YG 8.00 20.00
C98 Ryan Nugent-Hopkins YG 25.00 60.00
C99 Anton Lander YG 4.00 10.00
C100 Teemu Hartikainen YG 4.00 10.00
C101 Brett Bulmer YG 4.00 10.00
C102 Aaron Palushaj YG 4.00 10.00
C103 Raphael Diaz YG 4.00 10.00
C104 Jonathon Blum YG 4.00 10.00
C105 Blake Geoffrion YG 4.00 10.00
C106 Craig Smith YG 6.00 15.00
C107 Adam Henrique YG 10.00 25.00
C108 Mika Zibanejad YG 10.00 25.00
C109 Sean Couturier YG 10.00 25.00
C110 Matt Read YG 8.00 20.00
C111 Erik Gustafsson YG 5.00 12.00
C112 Harri Sateri YG 4.00 10.00
C113 Brett Connolly YG 4.00 10.00
C114 Jake Gardiner YG 6.00 15.00
C115 Joe Colborne YG 4.00 10.00
C116 Matt Frattin YG 4.00 10.00
C117 Cody Hodgson YG 15.00 40.00
C118 Carl Klingberg YG 4.00 10.00
C119 Mark Scheifele YG 20.00 50.00
C120 Ngnt-Hpk/Cnlly/Ctrier CL 10.00 25.00
C121 Corey Perry 1.00 2.50
C122 Teemu Selanne 2.00 5.00
C123 David Krejci 1.00 2.50
C124 Milan Lucic 1.00 2.50
C125 Tim Thomas 1.00 2.50
C126 Tyler Seguin 2.00 5.00
C127 Derek Roy .75 2.00
C128 Luke Adam .75 2.00
C129 Nathan Gerbe .60 1.50
C130 Tyler Ennis .75 2.00
C131 Mark Giordano .75 2.00
C132 Rene Bourque .60 1.50
C133 Jamie McBain .60 1.50
C134 Jeff Skinner 1.00 2.50
C135 Tomas Kaberle .60 1.50
C136 Brent Seabrook 1.00 2.50
C137 Corey Crawford 1.25 3.00
C138 Patrick Sharp 1.00 2.50
C139 Erik Johnson .60 1.50
C140 Antoine Vermette .60 1.50
C141 Derick Brassard 1.00 2.50
C142 Jeff Carter 1.00 2.50
C143 Jamie Benn 1.25 3.00
C144 Sheldon Souray .60 1.50
C145 Steve Ott .75 2.00
C146 Dan Cleary 1.00 2.50
C147 Johan Franzen 1.00 2.50
C148 Valtteri Filppula 1.00 2.50
C149 Jordan Eberle 1.00 2.50
C150 Magnus Paajarvi .75 2.00
C151 Taylor Hall 2.50 6.00
C152 Jose Theodore 1.00 2.50
C153 Jacob Markstrom 1.00 2.50
C154 Kris Versteeg .75 2.00
C155 Mike Richards 1.00 2.50
C156 Simon Gagne 1.00 2.50
C157 Cal Clutterbuck 1.00 2.50
C158 Dany Heatley .75 2.00
C159 Devin Setoguchi .75 2.00
C160 Brian Gionta .75 2.00
C161 P.K. Subban 2.00 5.00
C162 Mike Fisher 1.00 2.50
C163 Ryan Suter .60 1.50
C164 Sergei Kostitsyn .60 1.50
C165 Mattias Tedenby .60 1.50
C166 Jacob Josefson .60 1.50
C167 Travis Zajac .75 2.00
C168 Al Montoya .60 1.50
C169 Evgeni Nabokov .75 2.00
C170 Michael Grabner .75 2.00
C171 P.A. Parenteau .60 1.50
C172 Brad Richards 1.00 2.50
C173 Ryan Callahan 1.00 2.50
C174 Daniel Alfredsson 1.00 2.50
C175 Erik Karlsson 2.00 5.00
C176 Robin Lehner .75 2.00
C177 Brayden Schenn 1.00 2.50
C178 Ilya Bryzgalov 1.00 2.50
C179 Jaromir Jagr 2.50 6.00
C180 Maxime Talbot .75 2.00
C181 Lauri Korpikoski .60 1.50
C182 Oliver Ekman-Larsson 1.00 2.50
C183 James Neal 1.00 2.50
C184 Kristopher Letang 1.00 2.50
C185 Sidney Crosby 4.00 10.00
C186 Brent Burns 1.25 3.00
C187 Dan Boyle .75 2.00
C188 Logan Couture 1.00 2.50
C189 Martin Havlat .75 2.00
C190 Ryane Clowe .60 1.50
C191 Jason Arnott .75 2.00
C192 T.J. Oshie 1.50 4.00
C193 Martin St. Louis 1.00 2.50
C194 Steve Downie .60 1.50
C195 Victor Hedman 1.25 3.00
C196 Colton Orr .60 1.50
C197 James Reimer 1.00 2.50
C198 Nikolai Kulemin 1.00 2.50
C199 Cory Schneider .75 2.00
C200 David Booth .60 1.50
C201 Ryan Kesler 1.00 2.50
C202 Alexander Semin 1.00 2.50
C203 Marcus Johansson .75 2.00
C204 Michal Neuvirth .75 2.00
C205 Nicklas Backstrom 1.50 4.00
C206 Tomas Vokoun .75 2.00
C207 Alexander Burmistrov .75 2.00
C208 Tobias Enstrom .60 1.50
C209 Ondrej Pavelec 1.00 2.50
C210 Lngo/Thms/Prce CL 2.50 6.00
C211 Cody Eakin YG 6.00 15.00
C212 Dmitry Orlov YG 6.00 15.00
C213 Eddie Lack YG 5.00 12.00
C214 Ben Scrivens YG 8.00 20.00
C215 Simon Despres YG 5.00 12.00
C216 David Rundblad YG 5.00 12.00
C217 Andy Miele YG 5.00 12.00
C218 Colin Greening YG 5.00 12.00
C219 Calvin de Haan YG 5.00 12.00
C220 David Ullstrom YG 5.00 12.00
C221 Adam Larsson YG 6.00 15.00
C222 Ryan Ellis YG 10.00 25.00
C223 Louis Leblanc YG 12.00 30.00
C224 Viatcheslav Voynov YG 5.00 12.00
C225 Erik Gudbranson YG 6.00 15.00
C226 Colten Teubert YG 5.00 12.00
C227 Lennart Petrell YG 6.00 15.00
C228 Brendan Smith YG 8.00 20.00
C229 Gustav Nyquist YG 12.50 30.00
C230 Stefan Elliott YG 5.00 12.00
C231 Gabriel Landeskog YG 20.00 40.00
C232 Andrew Shaw YG 15.00 40.00
C233 Riley Nash YG 5.00 12.00
C234 Mike Murphy YG 5.00 12.00
C235 Leland Irving YG 5.00 12.00
C236 Zack Kassian YG 6.00 15.00
C237 Marcus Foligno YG 8.00 20.00
C238 Brayden McNabb YG 5.00 12.00
C239 Peter Holland YG 5.00 12.00
C240 Lnde/Kssn/Leblnc CL 10.00 25.00
C241 Wayne Gretzky RET 40.00 100.00
C242 Mario Lemieux RET 25.00 50.00
C243 Mark Messier RET 15.00 40.00
C244 Patrick Roy RET 25.00 50.00
C245 Paul Coffey RET 12.00 30.00
C246 Pelle Lindbergh RET 15.00 40.00
C247 Bobby Orr RET 25.00 60.00
C248 Eric Lindros RET 20.00 50.00
C249 Joe Sakic RET 10.00 25.00
C250 Jean Beliveau RET 15.00 30.00
C251 Dave Schultz RET 12.00 30.00
C252 Curtis Joseph RET 12.00 30.00
C253 Tony Twist RET 12.00 30.00
C254 Doug Gilmour RET 15.00 40.00
C255 Brett Hull RET 15.00 40.00
C256 Adam Henrique POE 15.00 40.00
C257 Brett Connolly POE 12.00 30.00
C258 Calvin de Haan POE 10.00 25.00
C259 Cody Eakin POE 12.00 30.00
C260 Cody Hodgson POE 12.00 30.00
C261 Colten Teubert POE 10.00 25.00
C262 Erik Gudbranson POE 12.00 30.00
C263 Ryan Ellis POE 20.00 50.00
C264 Louis Leblanc POE 12.00 30.00
C265 Mark Scheifele POE 60.00 120.00
C266 Ryan Johansen POE 12.00 30.00
C267 Ryan Nugent-Hopkins POE 30.00 80.00
C268 Sean Couturier POE 15.00 40.00
C269 Simon Despres POE 12.00 30.00
C270 Zack Kassian POE 12.00 30.00

2011-12 Upper Deck Canvas Autographs

STATED PRINT RUN 31-66
BO Bobby Orr/66 175.00 300.00
CP Carey Price/31 50.00 100.00

2011-12 Upper Deck Clear Cut Foundations

STATED PRINT RUN 25 SER.#'d SETS
CCF1 R.Getzlaf/C.Perry 30.00 80.00
CCF2 Z.Chara/T.Thomas 40.00 80.00
CCF3 D.Roy/R.Miller 20.00 50.00
CCF4 Kiprusoff/Iginla 25.00 60.00
CCF5 E.Staal/J.Skinner 25.00 60.00
CCF6 J.Toews/P.Kane 40.00 100.00
CCF7 Stastny/Duchene 30.00 80.00
CCF8 S.Mason/R.Nash 20.00 50.00
CCF9 Morrow/Goligoski 15.00 40.00
CCF10 Datsyuk/Zetterberg 25.00 60.00
CCF11 J.Eberle/T.Hall 40.00 100.00
CCF12 Markstrom/Weiss 30.00 80.00
CCF13 Doughty/Kopitar 30.00 80.00
CCF14 Backstrom/M.Koivu 40.00 100.00
CCF15 C.Price/P.Subban 60.00 150.00
CCF16 P.Rinne/S.Weber 25.00 60.00
CCF17 Z.Parise/M.Brodeur 25.00 60.00
CCF18 Tavares/Moulson 25.00 60.00
CCF19 Gaborik/Lundqvist 25.00 60.00
CCF20 J.Spezza/E.Karlsson 30.00 60.00
CCF21 D.Briere/C.Giroux 20.00 50.00
CCF22 Doan/Ekman-Lrssn 25.00 60.00
CCF23 S.Crosby/E.Malkin 80.00 200.00
CCF24 Marleau/Thornton 30.00 80.00
CCF25 J.Halak/D.Backes 20.00 50.00
CCF26 Stamkos/St. Louis 25.00 60.00
CCF27 D.Phaneuf/P.Kessel 25.00 60.00
CCF28 R.Kesler/R.Luongo 40.00 80.00
CCF29 Ovechkin/A.Semin 80.00 200.00
CCF30 D.Byfuglien/E.Kane 40.00 80.00

2011-12 Upper Deck Clear Cut Honoured Members

STATED PRINT RUN 100 SER.#'d SETS
HOF1 Bobby Orr 40.00 80.00
HOF2 Ray Bourque 12.00 30.00
HOF3 Phil Esposito 12.00 30.00
HOF4 Johnny Bucyk 8.00 20.00
HOF5 Milt Schmidt 6.00 15.00
HOF6 Gilbert Perreault 8.00 20.00
HOF7 Bobby Hull 8.00 20.00
HOF8 Stan Mikita 10.00 25.00
HOF9 Tony Esposito 8.00 20.00
HOF10 Alex Delvecchio 6.00 15.00
HOF11 Igor Larionov 8.00 20.00
HOF12 Gordie Howe 15.00 40.00
HOF13 Ted Lindsay 8.00 20.00
HOF14 Paul Coffey 8.00 20.00
HOF15 Wayne Gretzky 40.00 100.00
HOF16 Jari Kurri 8.00 20.00
HOF17 Grant Fuhr 8.00 20.00
HOF18 Glenn Anderson 8.00 20.00
HOF19 Ron Francis 10.00 25.00
HOF20 Marcel Dionne 10.00 25.00
HOF21 Luc Robitaille 8.00 20.00
HOF22 Dino Ciccarelli 8.00 20.00
HOF23 Patrick Roy 20.00 50.00
HOF24 Jean Beliveau 8.00 20.00
HOF25 Guy Lafleur 10.00 25.00
HOF26 Larry Robinson 8.00 20.00
HOF27 Steve Shutt 8.00 20.00
HOF28 Mike Bossy 8.00 20.00
HOF29 Denis Potvin 8.00 20.00
HOF30 Brian Leetch 8.00 20.00
HOF31 Mark Messier 10.00 25.00
HOF32 Andy Bathgate 8.00 20.00
HOF33 Bobby Clarke 8.00 20.00
HOF34 Bill Barber 8.00 20.00
HOF35 Mario Lemieux 25.00 50.00
HOF36 Brett Hull 10.00 25.00
HOF37 Doug Gilmour 10.00 25.00
HOF38 Darryl Sittler 8.00 20.00
HOF39 Borje Salming 8.00 20.00
HOF40 Johnny Bower 8.00 20.00
HOF41 Red Kelly 6.00 15.00
HOF42 Dale Hawerchuk 10.00 25.00

2011-12 Upper Deck Day With the Cup

DC1-DC14 INSERTS IN SERIES ONE
DC15-DC25 INSERTS IN SERIES TWO
DC1 Nathan Horton 50.00 100.00
DC2 Tomas Kaberle 50.00 100.00
DC3 David Krejci 60.00 120.00
DC4 Zdeno Chara 60.00 120.00
DC5 Tuukka Rask 60.00 120.00
DC6 Shawn Thornton 60.00 120.00
DC7 Daniel Paille 60.00 120.00
DC8 Rich Peverley 50.00 100.00
DC9 Gregory Campbell 50.00 100.00
DC10 Tyler Seguin 75.00 150.00
DC11 Marc Savard 50.00 100.00
DC12 Chris Kelly 40.00 80.00
DC13 Patrice Bergeron 150.00 300.00
DC14 Dennis Seidenberg 50.00 100.00
DC15 Cam Neely 50.00 120.00
DC16 Mark Recchi 50.00 100.00
DC17 Milan Lucic 40.00 100.00
DC18 Shane Hnidy 60.00 120.00
DC19 John Boychuk 50.00 100.00
DC20 Tim Thomas 50.00 120.00
DC21 Steve Kampfer 40.00 80.00
DC22 Adam McQuaid 50.00 100.00
DC23 Brad Marchand 50.00 100.00
DC24 Michael Ryder 50.00 100.00
DC25 Andrew Ference 50.00 100.00

2011-12 Upper Deck EA Ultimate Team

COMPLETE SET (15) 8.00 20.00
STATED ODDS 1:24
EA1 Steven Stamkos 3.00 8.00
EA2 Drew Doughty 1.25 3.00
EA3 Daniel Sedin 1.25 3.00
EA4 Henrik Sedin 1.25 3.00
EA5 Jonathan Toews 2.50 6.00
EA6 Patrick Kane 2.50 6.00
EA7 Duncan Keith 1.25 3.00
EA8 Milan Lucic 1.25 3.00
EA9 Corey Perry 1.25 3.00
EA10 Tyler Seguin 2.50 6.00
EA11 Taylor Hall 2.50 6.00
EA12 Dion Phaneuf 1.25 3.00
EA13 Mark Streit .75 2.00
EA14 Jarret Stoll 1.00 2.50
EA15 Jonathan Quick 2.00 5.00

2011-12 Upper Deck Game Jerseys

UD1 OVERALL ODDS 1:12 HOB, 1:24 RET
UD2 OVERALL ODDS 1:24 HOB
UD1 GROUP A ANNC'D ODDS 1:4276
UD1 GROUP B ANNC'D ODDS 1:604
UD1 GROUP C ANNC'D ODDS 1:366
UD1 GROUP D ANNC'D ODDS 1:74
UD1 GROUP E ANNC'D ODDS 1:37
UD1 GROUP F ANNC'D ODDS 1:26
UD2 GROUP A ANNC'D ODDS 1:4624
UD2 GROUP B ANNC'D ODDS 1:44
UD2 GROUP C ANNC'D ODDS 1:53
GJAB Alexandre Burrows E 4.00 10.00
GJAM Andrei Markov F 4.00 10.00
GJAO Alexander Ovechkin 1 B 12.00 30.00
GJAP Alex Pietrangelo F 3.00 8.00
GJAS Alexander Semin E 4.00 10.00
GJBJ Brent Johnson F 4.00 10.00
GJBM Brendan Morrison E 2.50 6.00
GJBO Jay Bouwmeester D 4.00 10.00
GJBR Bobby Ryan E 4.00 10.00
GJBY Dustin Byfuglien E 4.00 10.00
GJCA Craig Anderson F 4.00 10.00
GJCG Claude Giroux E 4.00 10.00
GJCM Clarke MacArthur E 2.50 6.00
GJCP Carey Price C 12.00 30.00
GJCS Chris Stewart 1 F 3.00 8.00
GJDB Daniel Briere E 4.00 10.00
GJDD Drew Doughty E 4.00 10.00
GJDH Dale Hawerchuk F 5.00 12.00
GJDP Dion Phaneuf E 4.00 10.00
GJDS Daniel Sedin F 5.00 12.00
GJDU Dustin Brown 1 C 4.00 10.00
GJEM Evgeni Malkin B 8.00 20.00
GJES Eric Staal D 5.00 12.00
GJHE Milan Hejduk A 50.00 100.00
GJHI Jonas Hiller F 3.00 8.00
GJHL Henrik Lundqvist D 5.00 12.00
GJHS Henrik Sedin B 12.00 30.00
GJIK Ilya Kovalchuk D 4.00 10.00
GJJB Jamie Benn D 5.00 12.00
GJJC Jeff Carter 1 C 4.00 10.00
GJJE Jordan Eberle B 8.00 20.00
GJJF Johan Franzen D 4.00 10.00
GJJG Jean-Sebastien Giguere 1 F 3.00 8.00
GJJH Jim Howard F 4.00 10.00
GJJI Jarome Iginla C 8.00 20.00
GJJO John Carlson D 5.00 12.00
GJJQ Jonathan Quick E 6.00 15.00
GJJS Jason Spezza 1 C 4.00 10.00
GJJT Jonathan Toews 1 B 12.00 30.00
GJVA James van Riemsdyk 1 D 4.00 10.00
GJKE Phil Kessel E 5.00 12.00
GJKL Kristopher Letang D 4.00 10.00
GJKO Anze Kopitar E 6.00 15.00
GJKS Kevin Shattenkirk D 3.00 8.00
GJLE Lars Eller E 3.00 8.00
GJLS Luke Schenn 1 C 3.00 8.00
GJMB Martin Brodeur D 8.00 20.00
GJMC Mike Commodore E 3.00 8.00
GJMD Matt Duchene 1 E 4.00 10.00
GJMF Marc-Andre Fleury C 5.00 12.00
GJMG Mike Green D 4.00 10.00
GJMH Marian Hossa E 3.00 8.00
GJMK Miikka Kiprusoff D 8.00 20.00
GJMR Mike Richards D 4.00 10.00
GJMS Martin St. Louis B 12.00 30.00
GJMW Mike Weber D 2.50 6.00
GJNG Nathan Gerbe 1 D 2.50 6.00
GJNH Nathan Horton E 4.00 10.00
GJNK Nikolai Kulemin E 4.00 10.00
GJNL Nicklas Lidstrom 1 C 8.00 20.00
GJOK Kyle Okposo F 4.00 10.00
GJOP Ondrej Pavelec D 4.00 10.00
GJPA Paul Stastny D 4.00 10.00
GJPB Patrik Berglund D 3.00 8.00
GJPD Dustin Penner B 4.00 10.00
GJPE Corey Perry B 5.00 12.00
GJPF Peter Forsberg F 4.00 10.00
GJPI Pierre-Marc Bouchard D 4.00 10.00
GJPK Patrick Kane D 8.00 20.00
GJPR Chris Pronger 1 F 3.00 8.00
GJPS P.K. Subban B 8.00 20.00
GJRB Rene Bourque F 2.50 6.00
GJRG Ryan Getzlaf D 6.00 15.00
GJRI Brad Richards E 4.00 10.00
GJRK Ryan Kesler D 4.00 10.00
GJRL Roberto Luongo 1 E 4.00 10.00
GJRM Ryan Miller 1 F 4.00 10.00
GJRS Ryan Smyth F 3.00 8.00
GJSB Sergei Bobrovsky E 4.00 10.00
GJSC Sidney Crosby 1 B 15.00 40.00
GJSE Tyler Seguin B 10.00 25.00
GJSG Simon Gagne F 4.00 10.00
GJSH Scott Hartnell 1 E 4.00 10.00
GJSJ Jordan Staal F 4.00 10.00
GJSM Steve Mason F 3.00 8.00
GJSS Steven Stamkos A 50.00 100.00
GJST Drew Stafford 1 F 4.00 10.00
GJSV Semyon Varlamov 1 F 4.00 10.00
GJSW Stephen Weiss E 3.00 8.00
GJTE Tyler Ennis F 3.00 8.00
GJTH Taylor Hall A 40.00 80.00
GJTP Tomas Plekanec E 4.00 10.00
GJTR Tuukka Rask F 4.00 10.00
GJTV Thomas Vanek 1 F 4.00 10.00
GJTZ Travis Zajac 1 E 3.00 8.00
GJVL Vincent Lecavalier F 3.00 8.00
GJVO Tomas Vokoun F 3.00 8.00
GJWG Wayne Gretzky A 125.00 250.00
GJZC Zdeno Chara 1 F 4.00 10.00
GJZP Zach Parise E 4.00 10.00
GJ2AE Alexander Edler C 2.50 6.00
GJ2AH Ales Hemsky B 5.00 12.00
GJ2AO Alexander Ovechkin 2 A 50.00 100.00
GJ2AT Alex Tanguay B 2.50 6.00
GJ2AV Antoine Vermette C 2.50 6.00
GJ2BB Brian Boyle B 4.00 10.00
GJ2BD Brandon Dubinsky B 3.00 8.00
GJ2BR Dustin Brown 2 B 5.00 12.00
GJ2CA Jeff Carter 2 B 4.00 10.00
GJ2CP Chris Pronger 2 B 3.00 8.00
GJ2CS Chris Stewart 2 B 3.00 8.00
GJ2DB Derick Brassard C 4.00 10.00
GJ2DK David Krejci B 4.00 10.00
GJ2DR Derek Roy C 3.00 8.00
GJ2ED Evgeny Dadonov C 3.00 8.00
GJ2GP George Parros C 3.00 8.00
GJ2JA Jason Arnott B 3.00 8.00
GJ2JB Josh Bailey B 3.00 8.00
GJ2JG Jean-Sebastien Giguere 2 C 3.00 8.00
GJ2JJ Jack Johnson B 2.50 6.00
GJ2JL John-Michael Liles C 3.00 8.00
GJ2JP Jason Pominville B 3.00 8.00
GJ2JS Jason Spezza 2 C 4.00 10.00
GJ2JT Jonathan Toews 2 A 75.00 150.00
GJ2JV Jakub Voracek B 4.00 10.00
GJ2KL Kari Lehtonen B 3.00 8.00
GJ2KV Kris Versteeg B 3.00 8.00
GJ2LE Loui Eriksson B 3.00 8.00
GJ2LS Luke Schenn 2 C 3.00 8.00
GJ2MC Matt Carkner B 3.00 8.00
GJ2MD Matt Duchene 2 C 4.00 10.00
GJ2MF Michael Frolik B 2.50 6.00
GJ2MS Marc Staal B 4.00 10.00
GJMT Marty Turco C 4.00 10.00
GJ2NB Nicklas Backstrom C 6.00 15.00
GJ2NF Nikita Filatov C 2.50 6.00
GJ2NG Nathan Gerbe 2 C 2.50 6.00
GJ2NL Nicklas Lidstrom 2 B 4.00 10.00
GJ2RL Roberto Luongo 2 A 75.00 150.00
GJ2RM Ryan Miller 2 B 4.00 10.00
GJ2SC Sidney Crosby 2 A 12.00 30.00
GJ2SE Devin Setoguchi B 3.00 8.00
GJ2SH Scott Hartnell 2 B 4.00 10.00
GJ2SO Steve Ott B 3.00 8.00
GJ2ST Drew Stafford 2 B 4.00 10.00
GJ2SV Semyon Varlamov 2 C 4.00 10.00
GJ2TV Thomas Vanek 2 B 4.00 10.00
GJ2TZ Travis Zajac 2 B 3.00 8.00
GJ2VA James van Riemsdyk 2 B 4.00 10.00
GJ2ZC Zdeno Chara 2 B 4.00 10.00

2011-12 Upper Deck Game Jerseys Patches

*PATCH/15: 1.2X TO 3X BASIC JSY
PATCH STATED PRINT RUN 15
GJHE Milan Hejduk 25.00 50.00
GJJE Jordan Eberle 25.00 60.00
GJJT Jonathan Toews 25.00 60.00
GJMK Miikka Kiprusoff 15.00 40.00
GJNL Nicklas Lidstrom 20.00 50.00
GJSC Sidney Crosby 40.00 80.00
GJSE Tyler Seguin 30.00 60.00
GJSS Steven Stamkos 25.00 60.00
GJTH Taylor Hall 60.00 100.00
GJWG Wayne Gretzky 175.00 300.00
GJ2JT Jonathan Toews 25.00 60.00
GJ2NB Nicklas Backstrom 20.00 50.00
GJ2SC Sidney Crosby 40.00 80.00

2011-12 Upper Deck Hockey Heroes

COMP.SER.1 w/o SPs (12) 8.00 20.00
STATED ODDS 1:12
ART CARD STATED ODDS 1:600
HEADER STATED ODDS 1:600
HH1 Johnny Bower 1.00 2.50
HH2 Gump Worsley 1.00 2.50
HH3 Andy Bathgate 1.00 2.50
HH4 Bobby Hull 1.00 2.50
HH5 Johnny Bucyk 1.00 2.50
HH6 Milt Schmidt .75 2.00
HH7 Alex Delvecchio .75 2.00
HH8 Terry Sawchuk 1.00 2.50
HH9 Gordie Howe 2.00 5.00
HH10 Red Kelly .75 2.00
HH11 Ted Lindsay 1.00 2.50
HH12 Jean Beliveau 1.00 2.50
HH13 Hull/Howe/Bathgt ART 15.00 40.00
HH14 Bobby Hull 1.00 2.50
HH15 Stan Mikita 1.25 3.00
HH16 Phil Esposito 1.50 4.00
HH17 Bobby Orr 3.00 8.00
HH18 Brad Park .75 2.00
HH19 Alex Delvecchio .75 2.00
HH20 Red Kelly .75 2.00
HH21 Terry Sawchuk 1.00 2.50
HH22 Johnny Bower 1.00 2.50
HH23 Rogie Vachon 1.25 3.00
HH24 Gump Worsley 1.00 2.50
HH25 Jean Beliveau 1.00 2.50
HH26 B.Hull/S.Mikita ART 15.00 30.00
HDR2 Hockey Heroes '60S Header 12.00 30.00
HDR1 Hockey Heroes '50S Header 12.00 30.00

2011-12 Upper Deck Hockey Heroes Autographs

H1-H13 ISSUED IN SERIES 1 UD
H14-H26 ISSUED IN SERIES 2 UD
STATED PRINT RUN 10-15
HH1 Johnny Bower 125.00 200.00
HH3 Andy Bathgate 60.00 120.00
HH4 Bobby Hull 75.00 135.00
HH5 Johnny Bucyk 75.00 150.00
HH6 Milt Schmidt 100.00 200.00
HH7 Alex Delvecchio 60.00 120.00
HH9 Gordie Howe 200.00 300.00
HH10 Red Kelly 50.00 100.00
HH11 Ted Lindsay 100.00 200.00
HH12 Jean Beliveau 100.00 200.00
HH13 Hull/Howe/Bthgte ART/10
HH14 Bobby Hull/15
HH15 Stan Mikita/15 50.00 100.00
HH16 Phil Esposito/15 50.00 100.00
HH17 Bobby Orr/15 250.00 400.00
HH19 Alex Delvecchio/15 60.00 100.00
HH20 Red Kelly/15 50.00 100.00
HH22 Johnny Bower/15 40.00 80.00
HH23 Rogie Vachon/15
HH25 Jean Beliveau/15
HH26 B.Hull/10/S.Mikita ART

2011-12 Upper Deck Oversized

ONE PER SPECIAL RETAIL BLASTER
OS1 Tim Thomas 1.50 4.00
OS2 Jonathan Toews 3.00 8.00
OS3 Rick Nash 1.50 4.00
OS4 Nicklas Lidstrom 1.50 4.00
OS5 Henrik Zetterberg 2.00 5.00
OS6 Taylor Hall 3.00 8.00
OS7 Carey Price 5.00 12.00
OS8 P.K. Subban 3.00 8.00
OS9 Zach Parise 1.50 4.00
OS10 John Tavares 3.00 8.00
OS11 Henrik Lundqvist 2.00 5.00
OS12 Steven Stamkos 3.00 8.00
OS13 Roberto Luongo 1.50 4.00
OS14 Alexander Ovechkin 6.00 15.00

2011-12 Upper Deck Rookie Breakouts

STATED PRINT RUN 100 SER.#'d SETS
RBAH Adam Henrique 12.00 30.00
RBAL Adam Larsson 8.00 20.00
RBAP Aaron Palushaj 6.00 15.00
RBBC Brett Connolly 6.00 15.00
RBBG Blake Geoffrion 6.00 15.00
RBCH Cody Hodgson 20.00 50.00
RBCK Carl Klingberg 20.00 50.00
RBCS Craig Smith 8.00 20.00
RBDR David Rundblad 6.00 15.00
RBDS Devante Smith-Pelly 10.00 25.00
RBEG Erik Gudbranson 8.00 20.00
RBGL Gabriel Landeskog 20.00 50.00
RBGN Greg Nemisz 6.00 15.00
RBJC Joe Colborne 6.00 15.00
RBJG Jake Gardiner 10.00 25.00
RBMF Matt Frattin 6.00 15.00
RBMK Marcus Kruger 10.00 25.00
RBMR Matt Read 12.00 30.00
RBMS Mark Scheifele 15.00 40.00
RBMZ Mika Zibanejad 15.00 40.00
RBRJ Ryan Johansen 12.00 30.00
RBRN Ryan Nugent-Hopkins 75.00 150.00
RBSC Sean Couturier 20.00 50.00
RBTH Teemu Hartikainen 6.00 15.00

2011-12 Upper Deck Rookie Materials

RANDOM INSERTS IN SERIES 2
*PATCH/25: 1.2X TO 3X BASIC JSY
RMAH Adam Henrique 6.00 15.00
RMAL Adam Larsson 4.00 10.00
RMAP Aaron Palushaj 3.00 8.00
RMBC Brett Connolly 3.00 8.00
RMBG Blake Geoffrion 3.00 8.00
RMBH Ben Holmstrom 3.00 8.00
RMBS Brandon Saad 6.00 15.00
RMCA Cam Atkinson 8.00 20.00
RMCE Cody Eakin 5.00 12.00
RMCG Colin Greening 3.00 8.00
RMCH Cody Hodgson 8.00 20.00
RMDP Simon Despres 3.00 8.00
RMDR David Rundblad 3.00 8.00
RMDS Devante Smith-Pelly 5.00 12.00
RMEG Erik Gudbranson 3.00 8.00
RMGL Gabriel Landeskog 6.00 15.00
RMGN Greg Nemisz 3.00 8.00
RMHS Harri Sateri 3.00 8.00
RMJB Jonathon Blum 3.00 8.00
RMJF Justin Faulk 5.00 12.00
RMJG Jake Gardiner 5.00 12.00
RMJM John Moore 3.00 8.00
RMLA Anton Lander 3.00 8.00
RMLL Louis Leblanc 3.00 8.00
RMLP Lennart Petrell 4.00 10.00
RMMK Marcus Kruger 5.00 12.00
RMMZ Mika Zibanejad 5.00 12.00
RMPW Patrick Wiercioch 3.00 8.00
RMRH Roman Horak 3.00 8.00
RMRJ Ryan Johansen 6.00 15.00
RMRN Ryan Nugent-Hopkins 8.00 20.00
RMSC Sean Couturier 6.00 15.00
RMTE Tim Erixon 3.00 8.00
RMVV Viatcheslav Voynov 3.00 8.00
RMZK Zack Kassian 5.00 12.00

2011-12 Upper Deck Signatures

STATED ODDS 1:480 UD SER.2
GROUP A ANNC'D ODDS 1:2970
GROUP B ANNC'D ODDS 1:2792
GROUP C ANNC'D ODDS 1:720
UDSAD Adam Larsson A
UDSAL Andrew Ladd C 10.00 25.00
UDSAO Alexander Ovechkin A
UDSAP Alex Pietrangelo A
UDSAS Alex Stalock B 5.00 12.00
UDSBA Josh Bailey B 4.00 10.00
UDSBL Brian Lee A
UDSBM Brett MacLean A 10.00 25.00
UDSBR Derick Brassard C
UDSCH Cody Hodgson A 30.00 60.00
UDSCL David Clarkson B
UDSCO Cal O'Reilly C 6.00 15.00
UDSDA David Backes A
UDSDB Drayson Bowman C
UDSDC Daniel Carcillo B
UDSDP Dion Phaneuf A 10.00 25.00
UDSER Jonathan Ericsson B
UDSGL Gabriel Landeskog A 25.00 50.00
UDSJB Jonathon Blum A
UDSJE Jordan Eberle B
UDSJH Josh Harding A
UDSJM Jacob Markstrom A 8.00 20.00
UDSJN James Neal B 12.00 30.00
UDSJO Johnny Oduya C 6.00 15.00
UDSJS James Sheppard C 5.00 12.00
UDSKA Keith Aulie C
UDSLC Logan Couture B
UDSLK Lauri Korpikoski C 5.00 12.00
UDSMD Michael Del Zotto B
UDSMF Michael Frolik B
UDSMI Brendan Mikkelson B
UDSML Maxim Lapierre C 10.00 25.00
UDSMR Mike Ribeiro A
UDSMS Marc Savard A
UDSMT Mattias Tedenby B
UDSNF Nick Foligno B
UDSNG Nicklas Grossman B
UDSNH Ryan Nugent-Hopkins A 200.00 300.00
UDSPA Daniel Paille A 15.00 40.00
UDSPK Patrick Kane A 20.00 40.00
UDSPL Pascal Leclaire A
UDSPM Philip McRae C
UDSPO Patrick O'Sullivan B 5.00 12.00
UDSRJ Ryan Jones A 10.00 25.00
UDSSC Sidney Crosby A
UDSSG Sam Gagner A
UDSSS Steven Stamkos A
UDSSW Shea Weber A
UDSTM Thomas McCollum B 5.00 12.00
UDSWG Wayne Gretzky A 150.00 250.00

2011-12 Upper Deck Signature Sensations

OVERALL STATED ODDS 1:288
GROUP A ANNC'D ODDS 1:3645
GROUP B ANNC'D ODDS 1:1007
SSAC Andrew Cogliano B 4.00 10.00
SSAH Ales Hemsky B
SSAK Arturs Kulda C 4.00 10.00
SSAM Al MacInnis A
SSAN Antti Niemi B 5.00 12.00
SSAO Alexander Ovechkin A 60.00 120.00
SSAS Alex Stalock C 5.00 12.00
SSAT Alex Tanguay A 4.00 10.00
SSBA Josh Bailey B
SSBB Butch Bouchard A 10.00 25.00
SSBE Jamie Benn B 8.00 20.00
SSBF Benn Ferriero C 4.00 10.00
SSBJ Johnny Bower B 6.00 15.00
SSBM Brett MacLean C 4.00 10.00
SSBN Brandon Sutter C 5.00 12.00
SSBO Brian Boyle C 4.00 10.00
SSBP Brad Park B
SSBR Brad Richards A
SSBS Brayden Schenn B
SSBW Blake Wheeler C 10.00 25.00
SSCH Cody Hodgson B 50.00 100.00
SSCS Chris Stewart B 5.00 12.00
SSDA David Backes B 6.00 15.00
SSDB Dustin Byfuglien B 12.00 30.00
SSDG Doug Gilmour A 60.00 120.00
SSDR Kris Draper B 4.00 10.00
SSEE Erik Ersberg B 4.00 10.00
SSEK Erik Karlsson B 30.00 60.00
SSEN Tyler Ennis B 8.00 20.00
SSFR Mark Fraser B 10.00 25.00
SSGE Martin Gerber B
SSGH Gordie Howe A 40.00 80.00
SSGL Guillaume Latendresse B
SSGR Michael Grabner B
SSGU Jonas Gustavsson B 8.00 20.00
SSHA Taylor Hall A 40.00 80.00
SSIL Igor Larionov A 6.00 15.00
SSJA Jason Arnott A
SSJB Jay Bouwmeester B 6.00 15.00
SSJC Jared Cowen B
SSJF Johan Franzen B 20.00 40.00
SSJG Jean-Sebastien Giguere A 10.00 25.00
SSJH Jonas Hiller B
SSJM John Moore B 5.00 12.00
SSJN John Negrin C 5.00 12.00
SSJO Jim O'Brien C 6.00 15.00
SSJP Jason Pominville B 5.00 12.00
SSJS Jordan Staal B 8.00 20.00
SSJT John Tavares A 12.00 30.00
SSKA Evander Kane B 6.00 15.00
SSKD Kaspars Daugavins C 4.00 10.00
SSKS Kevin Shattenkirk C 8.00 20.00
SSKT Kyle Turris B 4.00 10.00
SSLM Lanny McDonald A 12.00 30.00
SSLR Luc Robitaille A 40.00 80.00
SSLS Luke Schenn B 5.00 12.00
SSMA Jacob Markstrom C 12.00 30.00
SSMD Matt Duchene B 6.00 15.00
SSMF Michael Frolik B 4.00 10.00
SSMG Marc-Andre Gragnani B
SSMI Mike Iggulden C 4.00 10.00
SSMM Mark Messier A 60.00 120.00
SSMN Michal Neuvirth B 5.00 12.00
SSMR Mike Ribeiro B 5.00 12.00
SSMT Mattias Tedenby C 4.00 10.00
SSMZ Mats Zuccarello-Aasen B 6.00 15.00
SSNB Niclas Bergfors C 5.00 12.00
SSNH Nathan Horton B 6.00 15.00
SSNK Nazem Kadri B 12.50 30.00
SSPA Patrick Marleau A 10.00 25.00
SSPB Patrice Bergeron A 40.00 80.00
SSPK Patrick Kane A 12.50 30.00
SSPM Peter Mueller B 8.00 20.00
SSPO Justin Pogge B
SSPS Peter Stastny A 10.00 25.00
SSRB Richard Brodeur B 20.00 50.00
SSRI Rick MacLeish B 8.00 20.00
SSRK Ryan Kesler B 12.00 30.00
SSRM Ryan McDonagh C 6.00 15.00
SSRY Michael Ryder A 10.00 25.00
SSSB Steve Bernier B 4.00 10.00
SSSC Sidney Crosby A 100.00 200.00
SSSG Scott Gomez B 5.00 12.00
SSSH Steve Shutt A
SSSK Saku Koivu A
SSSN Scott Niedermayer A 10.00 25.00
SSSS Steven Stamkos A 20.00 40.00
SSSU Brent Sutter B 4.00 10.00
SSSW Shea Weber C 8.00 20.00
SSSY Steve Yzerman A 60.00 120.00
SSTA Maxime Talbot C 5.00 12.00
SSTE Tobias Enstrom C 4.00 10.00
SSTG T.J. Galiardi B 8.00 20.00
SSTH Joe Thornton A 8.00 20.00
SSTM Tyler Myers B 6.00 15.00
SSTP Teddy Purcell B 8.00 20.00
SSTT Tomas Tatar C 5.00 12.00
SSWC Wendel Clark A 40.00 100.00
SSWG Wayne Gretzky A 250.00 500.00

2011-12 Upper Deck Winter Classic Oversized

COMPLETE SET (14) 15.00 40.00
ONE PER SPECIAL RETAIL TIN
WC1 Sidney Crosby 5.00 12.00
WC2 Alexander Ovechkin 5.00 12.00
WC3 Evgeni Malkin 4.00 10.00
WC4 Alexander Semin 1.25 3.00
WC5 Jordan Staal 1.25 3.00
WC6 Nicklas Backstrom 2.00 5.00
WC7 Marc-Andre Fleury 2.00 5.00
WC8 Semyon Varlamov 1.25 3.00
WC9 Maxime Talbot 1.00 2.50
WC10 Mike Knuble .75 2.00
WC11 Kristopher Letang 1.25 3.00
WC12 John Erskine 1.00 2.50
WC13 Michael Rupp .75 2.00
WC14 Eric Fehr .75 2.00

2011-12 Upper Deck Young Guns Oversized

ONE PER SPECIAL RETAIL BLASTER
YG1 Devante Smith-Pelly 2.00 5.00
YG2 Greg Nemisz 1.25 3.00
YG3 Brandon Saad 2.50 6.00
YG4 Marcus Kruger 2.00 5.00
YG5 Gabriel Landeskog 8.00 20.00
YG6 Ryan Nugent-Hopkins 20.00 50.00
YG7 Erik Gudbranson 1.50 4.00
YG8 Adam Larsson 1.50 4.00
YG9 Adam Henrique 3.00 8.00
YG10 Mika Zibanejad 3.00 8.00
YG11 Sean Couturier 2.50 6.00
YG12 Brett Connolly 1.25 3.00
YG13 Cody Hodgson 2.50 6.00
YG14 Mark Scheifele 4.00 10.00

2012-13 Upper Deck

COMP.SET w/o RC's (200) 10.00 25.00
201-250 YG STATED ODDS 1:4 H/R
R1-R3 TRADE ODDS 1:517 H, 1:7232 R
251-300 UPDATE ODDS 1:6 SP AUTH
ROOKIE TRADE EXPIRATION: 11/15/2014
1 Saku Koivu .30 .75
2 Teemu Selanne .60 1.50
3 Francois Beauchemin .20 .50
4 Cam Fowler .25 .60
5 Ryan Getzlaf .50 1.25
6 Luca Sbisa .25 .60
7 Jonas Hiller .25 .60
8 Zdeno Chara .30 .75
9 David Krejci .30 .75
10 Shawn Thornton .25 .60
11 Tuukka Rask .30 .75
12 Brad Marchand .40 1.00
13 Tyler Seguin .50 1.25
14 Rich Peverley .30 .75
15 Christian Ehrhoff .20 .50
16 Ville Leino .25 .60
17 Drew Stafford .30 .75
18 Ryan Miller .30 .75
19 Luke Adam .25 .60
20 Tyler Myers .25 .60
21 Jason Pominville .25 .60
22 Miikka Kiprusoff .25 .60
23 Alex Tanguay .20 .50
24 Jay Bouwmeester .30 .75
25 Michael Cammalleri .25 .60
26 Curtis Glencross .20 .50
27 Jarome Iginla .30 .75
28 Eric Staal .40 1.00
29 Jeff Skinner .30 .75
30 Cam Ward .30 .75
31 Anthony Stewart .20 .50
32 Joni Pitkanen .25 .60
33 Tuomo Ruutu .25 .60
34 Dave Bolland .25 .60
35 Jonathan Toews .60 1.50
36 Brent Seabrook .30 .75
37 Marian Hossa .25 .60
38 Ray Emery .25 .60
39 Patrick Sharp .30 .75
40 Marcus Kruger .40 1.00
41 Ryan O'Reilly .30 .75
42 Milan Hejduk .25 .60
43 Gabriel Landeskog .30 .75
44 Paul Stastny .30 .75
45 Erik Johnson .20 .50
46 Semyon Varlamov .30 .75
47 R.J. Umberger .20 .50
48 James Wisniewski .20 .50
49 Jack Johnson .20 .50
50 Derek Dorsett .20 .50
51 Nikita Nikitin .20 .50
52 Ryan Johansen .40 1.00
53 Kari Lehtonen .25 .60
54 Stephane Robidas .20 .50
55 Alex Goligoski .20 .50
56 Brenden Morrow .25 .60
57 Jamie Benn .40 1.00
58 Michael Ryder .20 .50
59 Johan Franzen .30 .75
60 Nicklas Lidstrom .30 .75
61 Valtteri Filppula .30 .75
62 Dan Cleary .30 .75
63 Henrik Zetterberg .40 1.00
64 Niklas Kronwall .25 .60
65 Ian White .25 .60
66 Ryan Nugent-Hopkins .30 .75
67 Ryan Whitney .20 .50
68 Nikolai Khabibulin .30 .75
69 Shawn Horcoff .20 .50
70 Jordan Eberle .30 .75
71 Ales Hemsky .25 .60
72 Kris Versteeg .25 .60
73 Dmitry Kulikov .20 .50
74 Tomas Fleischmann .20 .50
75 Jose Theodore .30 .75
76 Brian Campbell .20 .50
77 Sean Bergenheim .20 .50
78 Mike Richards .30 .75
79 Jonathan Quick .50 1.25
80 Jeff Carter .30 .75
81 Simon Gagne .30 .75
82 Dwight King .20 .50
83 Drew Doughty .30 .75
84 Dustin Brown .30 .75
85 Niklas Backstrom .25 .60
86 Matt Cullen .20 .50
87 Mikko Koivu .25 .60
88 Pierre-Marc Bouchard .30 .75
89 Dany Heatley .25 .60
90 Cal Clutterbuck .30 .75
91 Max Pacioretty .30 .75
92 P.K. Subban .50 1.25
93 Lars Eller .25 .60
94 Brian Gionta .25 .60
95 Louis Leblanc .30 .75
96 Tomas Plekanec .30 .75
97 David Desharnais .30 .75
98 Shea Weber .25 .60
99 Patric Hornqvist .25 .60
100 Gabriel Bourque .25 .60
101 Mike Fisher .25 .60
102 Ryan Ellis .20 .50
103 Martin Erat .20 .50
104 Martin Brodeur .60 1.50
105 Ilya Kovalchuk .30 .75
106 Adam Larsson .30 .75
107 Adam Henrique .30 .75
108 Bryce Salvador .20 .50

Henrik Tallinder .20 .50
Patrik Elias .30 .75
Matt Moulson .25 .60
Kyle Okposo .30 .75
Nino Niederreiter .20 .50
Evgeni Nabokov .25 .60
Mark Streit .20 .50
John Tavares .60 1.50
Marian Gaborik .30 .75
Carl Hagelin .30 .75
Michael Del Zotto .20 .50
Ryan Callahan .30 .75
Marc Staal .25 .60
Henrik Lundqvist .40 1.00
Brian Boyle .20 .50
Derek Stepan .30 .75
Milan Michalek .20 .50
Craig Anderson .30 .75
Sergei Gonchar .20 .50
Daniel Alfredsson .30 .75
Kyle Turris .20 .50
Erik Karlsson .60 1.50
Chris Neil .20 .50
Sean Couturier .30 .75
Wayne Simmonds .40 1.00
Brayden Schenn .30 .75
Maxime Talbot .25 .60
Daniel Briere .30 .75
Claude Giroux .30 .75
Scott Hartnell .30 .75
Oliver Ekman-Larsson .30 .75
Mike Smith .30 .75
Antoine Vermette .20 .50
Mikkel Boedker .20 .50
Keith Yandle .30 .75
Martin Hanzal .20 .50
Radim Vrbata .25 .60
Kris Letang .30 .75
Marc-Andre Fleury .50 1.25
Paul Martin .20 .50
Chris Kunitz .30 .75
Matt Cooke .20 .50
Sidney Crosby 1.25 3.00
James Neal .30 .75
Patrick Marleau .30 .75
Ryane Clowe .20 .50
Dan Boyle .25 .60
Brent Burns .40 1.00
Michal Handzus .20 .50
Martin Havlat .25 .60
Joe Pavelski .30 .75
Patrik Berglund .20 .50
David Backes .30 .75
David Perron .20 .50
Kevin Shattenkirk .30 .75
Andy McDonald .25 .60
Alex Pietrangelo .25 .60
Brian Elliott .25 .60
Ryan Malone .20 .50
Steven Stamkos .60 1.50
Marc-Andre Bergeron .20 .50
Victor Hedman .40 1.00
Mathieu Garon .25 .60
Vincent Lecavalier .25 .60
Brett Connolly .25 .60
James Reimer .30 .75
Dion Phaneuf .30 .75
Mikhail Grabovski .25 .60
Mike Komisarek .25 .60
Jake Gardiner .30 .75
Phil Kessel .40 1.00
Alexandre Burrows .30 .75
Kevin Bieksa .25 .60
Ryan Kesler .30 .75
Cory Schneider .25 .60
Dan Hamhuis .25 .60
David Booth .20 .50
Daniel Sedin .30 .75
Karl Alzner .20 .50
Braden Holtby .50 1.25
John Carlson .40 1.00
Brooks Laich .20 .50
Mike Green .30 .75
Marcus Johansson .25 .60
Mark Stuart .20 .50
Andrew Ladd .30 .75
Tobias Enstrom .20 .50
Dustin Byfuglien .30 .75
Alexander Burmistrov .25 .60
Bryan Little .30 .75
Parise/Brodeur/Koval CL .60 1.50
Kopitar/Quick/Doughty CL .50 1.25
Mat Clark YG RC 2.00 5.00
Carter Camper YG RC 1.50 4.00
Maxime Sauve YG RC 2.00 5.00
Lane MacDermid YG RC 2.00 5.00
Torey Krug YG RC 8.00 20.00
Michael Hutchinson YG RC 4.00 10.00
Travis Turnbull YG RC 2.00 5.00
Sven Baertschi YG RC 4.00 10.00
Akim Aliu YG RC 2.00 5.00
Jeremy Welsh YG RC 2.00 5.00
Brandon Bollig YG RC 2.00 5.00
Tyson Barrie YG RC 4.00 10.00
Mike Connolly YG RC 2.00 5.00
Dalton Prout YG RC 2.00 5.00
Cody Goloubef YG RC 2.00 5.00
Shawn Hunwick YG RC 2.00 5.00
Andrew Joudrey YG RC 2.00 5.00
Ryan Garbutt YG RC 2.00 5.00
Reilly Smith YG RC 4.00 10.00
Brenden Dillon YG RC 2.00 5.00
Scott Glennie YG RC 2.00 5.00
Riley Sheahan YG RC 2.00 5.00
Philippe Cornet YG RC 2.00 5.00
Colby Robak YG RC 2.00 5.00
Jordan Nolan YG RC 2.00 5.00
Kristopher Foucault YG RC 2.00 5.00
Jason Zucker YG RC 5.00 12.00
Tyler Cuma YG RC 2.00 5.00
Chay Genoway YG RC 2.00 5.00
Warren Peters YG RC 2.00 5.00
Gabriel Dumont YG RC 2.00 5.00
Robert Mayer YG RC 2.50 6.00
Chet Pickard YG RC 2.00 5.00
Aaron Ness YG RC 2.00 5.00
Casey Cizikas YG RC 2.00 5.00
Matt Donovan YG RC 2.00 5.00
Chris Kreider YG RC 6.00 15.00
Jakob Silfverberg YG RC 4.00 10.00
Mark Stone YG RC 10.00 25.00
Brandon Manning YG RC 2.00 5.00
Michael Stone YG RC 2.00 5.00
Matt Watkins YG RC 2.00 5.00
Tyson Sexsmith YG RC 2.00 5.00
Jake Allen YG RC 10.00 25.00
Jaden Schwartz YG RC 10.00 25.00
J.T. Brown YG RC 2.00 5.00
Carter Ashton YG RC 1.50 4.00
Ryan Hamilton YG RC 2.00 5.00
Jussi Rynnas YG RC 2.00 5.00

250 Krder/Schwrtz/Brtsch YG CL 2.00 5.00
251 Olli Jokinen 1.25 3.00
252 Evander Kane 1.50 4.00
253 Ondrej Pavelec 1.50 4.00
254 Mike Ribeiro 1.25 3.00
255 Alexander Ovechkin 6.00 15.00
256 Jason Garrison 1.00 2.50
257 Zack Kassian 1.25 3.00
258 James van Riemsdyk 1.50 4.00
259 John-Michael Liles 1.00 2.50
260 Anders Lindback 1.00 2.50
261 Brad Stuart 1.00 2.50
262 Joe Thornton 1.50 4.00
263 Evgeni Malkin 5.00 12.00
264 Brandon Sutter 1.25 3.00
265 Tomas Vokoun 1.25 3.00
266 Jarome Iginla 1.50 4.00
267 Luke Schenn 1.00 2.50
268 Guillaume Latendresse 1.25 3.00
269 Jason Spezza 1.50 4.00
270 Rick Nash 1.50 4.00
271 David Clarkson 1.00 2.50
272 Pekka Rinne 2.00 5.00
273 Michael Ryder 1.00 2.50
274 Ryan Suter 1.00 2.50
275 Zach Parise 1.50 4.00
276 Torrey Mitchell 1.00 2.50
277 Anze Kopitar 2.50 6.00
278 George Parros 1.25 3.00
279 Taylor Hall 3.00 8.00
280 Sam Gagner 1.25 3.00
281 Pavel Datsyuk 2.00 5.00
282 Jordin Tootoo 1.25 3.00
283 Derek Roy 1.25 3.00
284 Jaromir Jagr 4.00 10.00
285 Ray Whitney 1.25 3.00
286 Brandon Dubinsky 1.25 3.00
287 Nick Foligno 1.25 3.00
288 P.A. Parenteau 1.00 2.50
289 Marian Gaborik 1.50 4.00
290 Patrick Kane 3.00 8.00
291 Alexander Semin 1.50 4.00
292 Jordan Staal 1.50 4.00
293 Jiri Hudler 1.25 3.00
294 Blake Comeau 1.00 2.50
295 Steve Ott 1.25 3.00
296 Cody Hodgson 1.50 4.00
297 Milan Lucic 1.50 4.00
298 Patrice Bergeron 2.00 5.00
299 Corey Perry 1.50 4.00
300 Crosby/Stamkos/Kane CL 5.00 12.00

2012-13 Upper Deck A Piece of History Game Jerseys

GROUP A ODDS 1:16,605 HOB
GROUP A ODDS 1:4754 HOB
GROUP A ODDS 1:3730 HOB
GROUP A ODDS 1:1616 HOB
OVERALL ODDS 1:864 HOB
300CJ Curtis Joseph C 10.00 25.00
300CO Chris Osgood C 10.00 25.00
300DH Dominik Hasek D 12.00 30.00
300EB Ed Belfour A 30.00 60.00
300EN Evgeni Nabokov B 15.00 40.00
300MB Martin Brodeur D 20.00 50.00
300MK Miikka Kiprusoff B 10.00 25.00
300NK Nikolai Khabibulin D 12.00 30.00

2012-13 Upper Deck Canvas

C1-C90 STATED ODDS 1:6 HOB/RET
C91-C120 YG ODDS 1:48 HOB/RET
C1 Ryan Getzlaf 2.00 5.00
C2 Corey Perry 1.25 3.00
C3 Jonas Hiller 1.00 2.50
C4 Teemu Selanne 2.50 6.00
C5 Shawn Thornton 1.00 2.50
C6 Tuukka Rask 1.25 3.00
C7 Patrice Bergeron 1.50 4.00
C8 Tyler Seguin 2.00 5.00
C9 Brad Marchand 1.50 4.00
C10 Nathan Horton 1.25 3.00
C11 Thomas Vanek 1.25 3.00
C12 Ryan Miller 1.25 3.00
C13 Jason Pominville 1.00 2.50
C14 Cody Hodgson 1.25 3.00
C15 Jarome Iginla 1.25 3.00
C16 Michael Cammalleri 1.00 2.50
C17 Miikka Kiprusoff 1.00 2.50
C18 Jeff Skinner 1.25 3.00
C19 Cam Ward 1.25 3.00
C20 Brent Seabrook 1.25 3.00
C21 Patrick Kane 2.50 6.00
C22 Corey Crawford 1.50 4.00
C23 Duncan Keith 1.25 3.00
C24 Matt Duchene 1.25 3.00
C25 Gabriel Landeskog 1.25 3.00
C26 Jack Johnson .75 2.00
C27 Kari Lehtonen 1.00 2.50
C28 Jamie Benn 1.50 4.00
C29 Jim Howard 1.25 3.00
C30 Henrik Zetterberg 1.50 4.00
C31 Pavel Datsyuk 1.50 4.00
C32 Johan Franzen 1.25 3.00
C33 Magnus Paajarvi 1.00 2.50
C34 Jordan Eberle 1.25 3.00
C35 Ryan Nugent-Hopkins 1.25 3.00
C36 Stephen Weiss 1.00 2.50
C37 Drew Doughty 1.25 3.00
C38 Jonathan Quick 2.00 5.00
C39 Mike Richards 1.25 3.00
C40 Jeff Carter 1.25 3.00
C41 Mikko Koivu 1.00 2.50
C42 Niklas Backstrom 1.00 2.50
C43 Rene Bourque .75 2.00
C44 Josh Gorges 1.00 2.50
C45 Carey Price 4.00 10.00
C46 P.K. Subban 2.00 5.00
C47 Pekka Rinne 1.50 4.00
C48 Craig Smith .75 2.00
C49 Shea Weber 1.00 2.50
C50 Martin Brodeur 2.50 6.00
C51 David Clarkson .75 2.00
C52 Ilya Kovalchuk 1.25 3.00
C53 Kyle Okposo 1.25 3.00
C54 John Tavares 2.50 6.00
C55 Henrik Lundqvist 1.50 4.00
C56 Marian Gaborik 1.25 3.00
C57 Brad Richards 1.00 2.50
C58 Daniel Alfredsson 1.25 3.00
C59 Jason Spezza 1.25 3.00
C60 Erik Karlsson 2.50 6.00
C61 Brayden Schenn 1.25 3.00
C62 Daniel Briere 1.25 3.00
C63 Scott Hartnell 1.25 3.00
C64 Claude Giroux 1.25 3.00
C65 Mike Smith 1.25 3.00
C66 Mikkel Boedker .75 2.00
C67 Sidney Crosby 5.00 12.00
C68 Evgeni Malkin 4.00 10.00
C69 Marc-Andre Fleury 2.00 5.00
C70 Joe Pavelski 1.25 3.00
C71 Antti Niemi 1.00 2.50
C72 Jaroslav Halak 1.25 3.00
C73 David Perron .75 2.00
C74 David Backes 1.25 3.00
C75 Kevin Shattenkirk 1.25 3.00
C76 Steven Stamkos 2.50 6.00
C77 Martin St. Louis 1.25 3.00
C78 Dion Phaneuf 1.25 3.00
C79 Phil Kessel 1.50 4.00
C80 Cory Schneider 1.00 2.50
C81 Daniel Sedin 1.25 3.00
C82 Ryan Kesler 1.25 3.00
C83 Alexandre Burrows 1.25 3.00
C84 Alexander Ovechkin 2.50 6.00
C85 Nicklas Backstrom 2.00 5.00
C86 Mike Green 1.25 3.00
C87 Andrew Ladd 1.25 3.00
C88 Ondrej Pavelec 1.25 3.00
C89 Evander Kane 1.25 3.00
C90 Crosby/Stamkos/Giroux CL 3.00 8.00
C91 Torey Krug YG 15.00 40.00
C92 Maxime Sauve YG 4.00 10.00
C93 Sven Baertschi YG 5.00 12.00
C94 Akim Aliu YG 4.00 10.00
C95 Brandon Bollig YG 4.00 10.00
C96 Tyson Barrie YG 8.00 20.00
C97 Cody Goloubef YG 4.00 10.00
C98 Brendon Dillon YG 4.00 10.00
C99 Reilly Smith YG 8.00 20.00
C100 Scott Glennie YG 4.00 10.00
C101 Riley Sheahan YG 4.00 10.00
C102 Colby Robak YG 4.00 10.00
C103 Jordan Nolan YG 4.00 10.00
C104 Jason Zucker YG 5.00 12.00
C105 Tyler Cuma YG 4.00 10.00
C106 Gabriel Dumont YG 4.00 10.00
C107 Chet Pickard YG 4.00 10.00
C108 Matt Donovan YG 4.00 10.00
C109 Casey Cizikas YG 4.00 10.00
C110 Chris Kreider YG 12.00 30.00
C111 Mark Stone YG 12.00 30.00
C112 Jakob Silfverberg YG 8.00 20.00
C113 Brandon Manning YG 4.00 10.00
C114 Michael Stone YG 4.00 10.00
C115 Jake Allen YG 12.00 30.00
C116 Jaden Schwartz YG 10.00 25.00
C117 J.T. Brown YG 4.00 10.00
C118 Jussi Rynnas YG 4.00 10.00
C119 Carter Ashton YG 3.00 8.00
C120 Kreider/Schwartz YG CL 12.00 30.00

2012-13 Upper Deck Canvas Autographs

CAJE Jordan Eberle/14
CAWG Wayne Gretzky/79 400.00 600.00

2012-13 Upper Deck Clear Cut Foundations

CCF1 J.Hiller/T.Selanne 30.00 60.00
CCF2 T.Rask/T.Seguin 30.00 80.00
CCF3 T.Myers/R.Miller 20.00 50.00
CCF4 Iginla/Cammalleri 20.00 50.00
CCF5 J.Skinner/C.Ward 25.00 60.00
CCF6 D.Keith/J.Toews 40.00 100.00
CCF7 Duchene/Landeskog 20.00 50.00
CCF8 J.Johnson/S.Mason 25.00 60.00
CCF9 J.Benn/K.Lehtonen 15.00 40.00
CCF10 Datsyuk/Zetterberg 40.00 80.00
CCF11 Hall/Nugent-Hopkins 40.00 80.00
CCF12 Markstrom/Gudbranson 20.00 50.00
CCF13 D.Doughty/A.Kopitar
CCF14 Backstrom/Harding
CCF15 J.Gorges/P.Subban 30.00 80.00
CCF16 P.Rinne/M.Fisher 25.00 60.00
CCF17 Brodeur/Kovalchuk 40.00 80.00
CCF18 Nabokov/Tavares 40.00 100.00
CCF19 Gaborik/Lundqvist 25.00 60.00
CCF20 E.Karlsson/J.Spezza 40.00 100.00
CCF21 B.Schenn/C.Giroux 20.00 50.00
CCF22 K.Yandle/M.Smith 20.00 50.00
CCF23 M.Fleury/E.Malkin 60.00 150.00
CCF24 A.Niemi/L.Couture 25.00 60.00
CCF25 J.Halak/B.Elliott 20.00 50.00
CCF26 St. Louis/Stamkos 40.00 100.00
CCF27 Kessel/Phaneuf 15.00 40.00
CCF28 Schneider/Burrows 25.00 60.00
CCF29 Ovechkin/Holtby 80.00 200.00
CCF30 E.Kane/O.Pavelec 25.00 60.00

2012-13 Upper Deck Clear Cut Honoured Members

STATED PRINT RUN 100 SER.#'d SETS
HOF43 Eddie Shore 10.00 25.00
HOF44 King Clancy 10.00 25.00
HOF45 Cam Neely 12.00 30.00
HOF46 Ed Belfour 12.00 30.00
HOF47 Terry Sawchuk 12.00 30.00
HOF48 Howie Morenz 10.00 25.00

2012-13 Upper Deck Clear Cut Pride of Canada

STATED PRINT RUN 100 SER.#'d SETS
PCA1 Sidney Crosby 30.00 80.00
PCA2 Jonathan Toews 15.00 40.00
PCA3 Steven Stamkos 15.00 40.00
PCA4 Jordan Eberle 8.00 20.00
PCA5 Carey Price 25.00 60.00
PCA6 Claude Giroux 12.00 30.00
PCR1 Wayne Gretzky 50.00 100.00
PCR2 Mario Lemieux 20.00 50.00
PCR3 Bobby Orr 30.00 60.00
PCR4 Mark Messier 12.00 30.00
PCR5 Eric Lindros 25.00 50.00
PCR6 Patrick Roy 20.00 50.00

2012-13 Upper Deck Clear Cut Pride of Finland

STATED PRINT RUN 100 SER.#'d SETS
FIN1 Pekka Rinne 12.00 30.00
FIN2 Miikka Kiprusoff 8.00 20.00
FIN3 Mikko Koivu 8.00 20.00
FIN4 Saku Koivu 10.00 25.00
FIN5 Teemu Selanne 20.00 50.00
FIN6 Jari Kurri 10.00 25.00

2012-13 Upper Deck Clear Cut Pride of Russia

STATED PRINT RUN 100 SER.#'d SETS
RUS1 Alexander Ovechkin 40.00 100.00
RUS2 Pavel Datsyuk 12.00 30.00
RUS3 Alexander Semin 10.00 25.00
RUS4 Ilya Kovalchuk 12.00 30.00
RUS5 Evgeni Nabokov 8.00 20.00
RUS6 Igor Larionov 10.00 25.00

2012-13 Upper Deck Clear Cut Pride of Sweden

STATED PRINT RUN 100 SER.#'d SETS
SWE1 Daniel Sedin 12.00 30.00
SWE2 Henrik Lundqvist 12.00 30.00
SWE3 Nicklas Lidstrom 12.00 30.00
SWE4 Henrik Zetterberg 15.00 40.00
SWE5 Daniel Alfredsson 12.00 30.00
SWE6 Pelle Lindbergh 30.00 60.00

2012-13 Upper Deck Clear Cut Pride of USA

STATED PRINT RUN 100 SER.#'d SETS
USA1 Jonathan Quick 15.00 40.00
USA2 Zach Parise 12.00 30.00
USA3 Tim Thomas 10.00 25.00
USA4 Ryan Miller 20.00 40.00
USA5 Phil Kessel 12.00 30.00
USA6 Brett Hull 10.00 25.00

2012-13 Upper Deck Day With the Cup

DC1 Viatcheslav Voynov 25.00 60.00
DC2 Andrei Loktionov 15.00 40.00
DC3 Anze Kopitar 50.00 100.00
DC4 Jonathan Bernier
DC5 Simon Gagne 40.00 100.00
DC6 Rob Scuderi 25.00 60.00
DC7 Colin Fraser 40.00 100.00
DC8 Darryl Sutter 60.00 120.00
DC9 Jonathan Quick 100.00 200.00
DC10 Dustin Brown 50.00 100.00
DC11 Justin Williams 25.00 60.00
DC12 Matt Greene 25.00 60.00
DC13 Willie Mitchell 60.00 120.00
DC14 Dwight King 30.00 60.00
DC15 Jarret Stoll 60.00 120.00
DC16 Dustin Penner 25.00 60.00
DC17 Mike Richards 75.00 150.00
DC18 Jordan Nolan 30.00 80.00
DC19 Kevin Westgarth 30.00 80.00
DC20 Kyle Clifford 20.00 50.00
DC21 Drew Doughty 40.00 80.00
DC22 Jeff Carter
DC23 Brad Richardson 25.00 60.00
DC24 Davis Drewiske 25.00 60.00
DC25 Trevor Lewis 30.00 80.00
DC26 Alec Martinez 30.00 80.00
DC27 Luc Robitaille 50.00 100.00
DC28 Phil Pritchard 30.00 80.00

2012-13 Upper Deck Distributor Promos

*GOLD: .8X TO 2X BASIC CARDS
P1 Alexander Ovechkin 2.50 6.00
P2 Adam Henrique .60 1.50
P3 Taylor Hall 1.25 3.00
P4 Bobby Orr 2.00 5.00
P5 Phil Kessel .75 2.00
P6 Eric Lindros 1.00 2.50
P7 Dion Phaneuf .60 1.50
P8 Evander Kane .60 1.50
P9 Ryan Nugent-Hopkins .60 1.50
P10 Steven Stamkos 1.25 3.00
P11 Nikolai Kulemin .50 1.25
P12 Jean Beliveau .60 1.50
P13 John Tavares 1.25 3.00
P14 Patrick Kane 1.25 3.00
P15 Thomas Vanek .60 1.50
P16 Chris Kreider .75 2.00
P17 Chet Pickard .40 1.00
P18 Jaden Schwartz .75 2.00
P19 Jake Allen 1.25 3.00
P20 Jakob Silfverberg .75 2.00
P21 Akim Aliu .40 1.00
P22 Tyson Barrie .75 2.00
P23 Jussi Rynnas .40 1.00
P24 Sven Baertschi .50 1.25
P25 Scott Glennie .40 1.00
P26 Jason Zucker .50 1.25
P27 Tyler Cuma .40 1.00
P28 Casey Cizikas .40 1.00
P29 Carter Ashton .30 .75
P30 Cody Goloubef .40 1.00

2012-13 Upper Deck Distributor Promos Autographs

UNPRICED GRP A ODDS 1:495
UNPRICED GRP B ODDS 1:310
UNPRICED GRP C ODDS 1:563
GROUP D ODDS 1:47
OVERALL AUTO ODDS 1:36
P1 Alexander Ovechkin A
P2 Adam Henrique C
P3 Taylor Hall B
P4 Bobby Orr A
P5 Phil Kessel B
P6 Eric Lindros A
P7 Dion Phaneuf B
P8 Evander Kane B
P9 Ryan Nugent-Hopkins A
P10 Steven Stamkos B
P11 Nikolai Kulemin A
P12 Jean Beliveau A
P13 John Tavares B
P14 Patrick Kane B
P15 Thomas Vanek C
P16 Chris Kreider D 6.00 15.00
P17 Chet Pickard D 3.00 8.00
P18 Jaden Schwartz D 6.00 15.00
P19 Jake Allen D 10.00 25.00
P21 Akim Aliu D 3.00 8.00
P22 Tyson Barrie D 6.00 15.00
P23 Jussi Rynnas D 3.00 8.00
P24 Sven Baertschi D 4.00 10.00
P25 Scott Glennie D 3.00 8.00
P28 Casey Cizikas D 3.00 8.00
P29 Carter Ashton D 2.50 6.00
P30 Cody Goloubef D 3.00 8.00

2012-13 Upper Deck Exclusives

*1-200 VETS/100: 6X TO 15X BASIC CARDS
*201-250 ROOKIE/100: 1X TO 2.5X BASIC RC
*251-300 UPD/100: 1X TO 2.5X BASIC CARDS
251-300 INSERTED IN SP AUTHENTIC
STATED PRINT RUN 100 SER.#'d SETS

2012-13 Upper Deck Game Jerseys

GROUP A ODDS 1:20,176 HOB
GROUP B ODDS 1:4112 HOB
GROUP C ODDS 1:1154 HOB
GROUP D ODDS 1:321 HOB
GROUP E ODDS 1:210 HOB
GROUP F ODDS 1:139 HOB
GROUP G ODDS 1:57 HOB
GROUP H ODDS 1:20 HOB
GJAK Andrei Kostitsyn G 3.00 8.00
GJAL Anders Lindback G 3.00 8.00
GJAM Andrei Markov G 4.00 10.00
GJAN Antti Niemi D 5.00 12.00
GJAO Alexander Ovechkin G 15.00 40.00
GJAP Alex Pietrangelo A 125.00 200.00
GJAV Antoine Vermette G 2.50 6.00
GJBJ Brent Johnson E 3.00 8.00
GJBQ Ray Bourque C 6.00 15.00
GJBR Martin Brodeur F 15.00 40.00
GJBS Brent Seabrook D 4.00 10.00
GJBT Bryan Trottier F 4.00 10.00
GJBY Josh Bailey E 3.00 8.00
GJCA Craig Anderson H 3.00 8.00
GJCF Cam Fowler H 3.00 8.00
GJCG Claude Giroux H 5.00 12.00
GJCP Carey Price F 8.00 20.00
GJDA Daniel Alfredsson G 4.00 10.00
GJDB Dustin Brown E 4.00 10.00
GJDD Drew Doughty C 20.00 40.00
GJDE Derick Brassard H 4.00 10.00
GJDR Derek Stepan H 4.00 10.00
GJDS Daniel Sedin F 4.00 10.00
GJDU Brandon Dubinsky F 3.00 8.00
GJDV David Booth F 2.50 6.00
GJEB Jordan Eberle C 8.00 20.00
GJED Evgeny Dadonov H 3.00 8.00
GJEJ Erik Johnson H 2.50 6.00
GJEL Lars Eller H 3.00 8.00
GJGB Michael Grabner H 3.00 8.00
GJGP Gilbert Perreault F 4.00 10.00
GJHK Henrik Karlsson H 3.00 8.00
GJHO Tomas Holmstrom G 2.50 6.00
GJHS Henrik Sedin D 4.00 10.00
GJHZ Henrik Zetterberg D 6.00 15.00
GJIB Ilya Bryzgalov G 4.00 10.00
GJIK Ilya Kovalchuk E 4.00 10.00
GJJA Justin Abdelkader H 3.00 8.00
GJJB Jonathan Bernier H 4.00 10.00
GJJC John Carlson E 5.00 12.00
GJJE Jonathan Ericsson H 3.00 8.00
GJJF Jeff Carter G 4.00 10.00
GJJG Jean-Sebastien Giguere H 3.00 8.00
GJJH Jonas Hiller H 3.00 8.00
GJJI Jarome Iginla G 4.00 10.00
GJJJ Jaromir Jagr F 6.00 15.00
GJJS Jordan Staal H 4.00 10.00
GJJT Jonathan Toews D 8.00 20.00
GJJV James van Riemsdyk H 4.00 10.00
GJKL Kris Letang H 5.00 12.00
GJKO Kyle Okposo H 4.00 10.00
GJKS Kevin Shattenkirk G 4.00 10.00
GJKV Kris Versteeg G 3.00 8.00
GJLE Loui Eriksson F 3.00 8.00
GJLI John-Michael Liles G 3.00 8.00
GJLX Mario Lemieux B 15.00 40.00
GJMA Marc Staal H 3.00 8.00
GJMB Mikkel Boedker D 2.50 6.00
GJMC Michael Cammalleri G 4.00 10.00
GJMD Matt Duchene F 4.00 10.00
GJME Mark Messier D 6.00 15.00
GJMF Marc-Andre Fleury H 6.00 15.00
GJMG Mike Green H 4.00 10.00
GJMI Ryan Miller G 4.00 10.00
GJMM Matt Moulson H 3.00 8.00
GJMP Magnus Paajarvi E 3.00 8.00
GJMR Mike Richards G 4.00 10.00
GJNL Nicklas Lidstrom H 5.00 12.00
GJPH Patric Hornqvist H 3.00 8.00
GJRG Ryan Getzlaf H 6.00 15.00
GJRO Derek Roy H 3.00 8.00
GJRS Ryan Suter H 3.00 8.00
GJRY Bobby Ryan H 4.00 10.00
GJSC Sidney Crosby D 10.00 25.00
GJSE Alexander Semin D 4.00 10.00
GJSF Drew Stafford H 4.00 10.00
GJSG Sam Gagner H 3.00 8.00
GJSH Luke Schenn G 2.50 6.00
GJSK Saku Koivu G 4.00 10.00
GJSM Steve Mason H 3.00 8.00
GJSS Steven Stamkos C 8.00 20.00
GJSV Semyon Varlamov G 4.00 10.00
GJTD Trevor Daley H 2.50 6.00
GJTE Tyler Ennis E 3.00 8.00
GJTH Taylor Hall E 8.00 20.00
GJTR Tuukka Rask H 4.00 10.00
GJTV Thomas Vanek E 4.00 10.00
GJTZ Travis Zajac H 3.00 8.00
GJVH Victor Hedman F 5.00 12.00
GJWE Shea Weber H 3.00 8.00
GJWG Wayne Gretzky AS B 75.00 150.00
GJWS Stephen Weiss H 3.00 8.00

2012-13 Upper Deck Game Jerseys Patches

*PATCH/15: 1.2X TO 3X BASIC INSERTS
STATED PRINT RUN 15 SER.#'d SETS
GJLX Mario Lemieux 40.00 80.00
GJSC Sidney Crosby
GJWG Wayne Gretzky AS

2012-13 Upper Deck Hockey Heroes

HH27-HH38 ODDS 1:12 HOB/RET
HH39/HDR ODDS 1:600 HOB/RET
HH27 Wayne Gretzky 3.00 8.00
HH28 Bobby Clarke 1.00 2.50
HH29 Bobby Orr 3.00 8.00
HH30 Bryan Trottier 1.25 3.00
HH31 Denis Potvin 1.00 2.50
HH32 Gilbert Perreault 1.00 2.50
HH33 Guy Lafleur 1.25 3.00
HH34 Larry Robinson 1.00 2.50
HH35 Marcel Dionne 1.25 3.00
HH36 Phil Esposito 1.50 4.00
HH37 Borje Salming 1.00 2.50
HH38 Tony Esposito 1.00 2.50
HH39 Laflr/Orr/Clrke ART 15.00 40.00
HDR Header Card 1970s 10.00 25.00

2012-13 Upper Deck Hockey Heroes Autographs

STATED PRINT RUN 10-15
HH27 Wayne Gretzky
HH28 Bobby Clarke 50.00 100.00
HH29 Bobby Orr 150.00 250.00
HH30 Bryan Trottier 15.00 30.00
HH31 Denis Potvin 50.00 100.00
HH32 Gilbert Perreault
HH33 Guy Lafleur
HH34 Larry Robinson
HH35 Marcel Dionne 75.00 135.00
HH36 Phil Esposito
HH37 Borje Salming 50.00 100.00
HH38 Tony Esposito

2012-13 Upper Deck Requisite Radiance

STATED ODDS 1:432 H, 1:3360 R
RR1 Corey Perry 10.00 25.00
RR2 Teemu Selanne 20.00 50.00
RR3 Tuukka Rask 10.00 25.00
RR4 Zdeno Chara 10.00 25.00
RR5 Patrice Bergeron 12.00 30.00
RR6 Thomas Vanek 10.00 25.00
RR7 Ryan Miller 10.00 25.00
RR8 Jarome Iginla 10.00 25.00
RR9 Miikka Kiprusoff 8.00 20.00
RR10 Jonathan Toews 20.00 50.00
RR11 Patrick Kane 20.00 50.00
RR12 Patrick Sharp 10.00 25.00
RR13 Matt Duchene 10.00 25.00
RR14 Gabriel Landeskog 10.00 25.00
RR15 Loui Eriksson 8.00 20.00
RR16 Nicklas Lidstrom 12.00 30.00
RR17 Pavel Datsyuk 12.00 30.00
RR18 Ryan Nugent-Hopkins 10.00 25.00
RR19 Taylor Hall 20.00 50.00
RR20 Jordan Eberle 10.00 25.00
RR21 Jacob Markstrom 10.00 25.00
RR22 Drew Doughty 10.00 25.00
RR23 Jonathan Quick 12.00 30.00
RR24 Anze Kopitar 15.00 40.00
RR25 Niklas Backstrom 12.00 30.00
RR26 Mikko Koivu 8.00 20.00
RR27 Josh Gorges 8.00 20.00
RR28 P.K. Subban 15.00 40.00
RR29 Carey Price 30.00 80.00
RR30 Louis Leblanc 10.00 25.00
RR31 Pekka Rinne 12.00 30.00
RR32 Ilya Kovalchuk 10.00 25.00
RR33 Martin Brodeur 20.00 50.00
RR34 John Tavares 20.00 50.00
RR35 Henrik Lundqvist 12.00 30.00
RR36 Marian Gaborik 10.00 25.00
RR37 Carl Hagelin 10.00 25.00
RR38 Ilya Bryzgalov 10.00 25.00
RR39 Claude Giroux 10.00 25.00
RR40 Scott Hartnell 10.00 25.00
RR41 Brayden Schenn 10.00 25.00
RR42 Daniel Briere 10.00 25.00
RR43 Keith Yandle 10.00 25.00
RR44 Sidney Crosby 40.00 80.00
RR45 James Neal 10.00 25.00
RR46 Evgeni Malkin 30.00 80.00
RR47 Marc-Andre Fleury 15.00 40.00
RR48 Logan Couture 10.00 25.00
RR49 Brian Elliott 8.00 20.00
RR50 Jaroslav Halak 10.00 25.00
RR51 David Backes 10.00 25.00
RR52 Steven Stamkos 20.00 50.00
RR53 Joffrey Lupul 8.00 20.00
RR54 Phil Kessel 12.00 30.00
RR55 Braden Holtby 15.00 40.00
RR56 Alexander Ovechkin 20.00 50.00
RR57 Nicklas Backstrom 15.00 40.00
RR58 Ondrej Pavelec 15.00 40.00
RR59 Evander Kane 10.00 25.00
RR60 Alexander Burmistrov 8.00 20.00

2012-13 Upper Deck Rookie Trade

R1 Rookie Trade 1/Yakupov 30.00 80.00
R2 Rookie Trade 2/Huberdeau 20.00 50.00
R3 Rookie Trade 3/Galchenyuk 25.00 60.00
TC1 Nail Yakupov 40.00 80.00
TC2 Jonathan Huberdeau 25.00 50.00
TC3 Alex Galchenyuk 30.00 60.00

2012-13 Upper Deck Signature Sensations

GROUP A ODDS 1:18,468 HOB
GROUP B ODDS 1:2301 HOB
GROUP C ODDS 1:735 HOB
GROUP D ODDS 1:591 HOB
OVERALL ODDS 1:288 HOB
SSAB Alexander Burmistrov C
SSAC Andrew Cogliano C 8.00 20.00
SSAH Adam Henrique C 12.00 30.00
SSAK Arturs Kulda C 8.00 20.00
SSAL Anders Lindback C 8.00 20.00
SSAM Andrei Markov C 12.00 30.00
SSAO Alexander Ovechkin B
SSBC Brett Connolly C
SSBE Jamie Benn C 15.00 40.00
SSBF Benn Ferriero D 8.00 20.00
SSBG Blake Geoffrion C 10.00 25.00
SSBH Bobby Hull B 25.00 50.00
SSBI Brayden Irwin D 8.00 20.00
SSBL Brian Lee C 8.00 20.00
SSBM Brett MacLean C
SSBO Bobby Orr B 75.00 150.00
SSBR Martin Brodeur B
SSBS Brendan Smith C 10.00 25.00
SSBT Bryan Trottier B 20.00 40.00
SSBU Adam Burish C 8.00 20.00
SSBY Mike Bossy B
SSCE Cody Eakin C 8.00 20.00
SSCF Cam Fowler C
SSCG Claude Giroux B
SSCK Carl Klingberg C
SSCS Chris Stewart C 10.00 25.00
SSCT Colten Teubert C 8.00 20.00
SSDC Daniel Carcillo C 8.00 20.00
SSDE Stefan Della Rovere D 8.00 20.00
SSDG Daniel Girardi C 8.00 20.00
SSDJ Dustin Jeffrey D 8.00 20.00
SSEB Ed Belfour A
SSEL Eric Lindros A
SSEN Evgeni Nabokov C 8.00 20.00
SSER Jonathan Ericsson C 10.00 25.00
SSFW Francis Wathier D 8.00 20.00
SSGL Gabriel Landeskog B 12.00 30.00
SSGP Gilbert Perreault B
SSGU Guillaume Latendresse C
SSHA Travis Hamonic C 10.00 25.00
SSHI Jonas Hiller B 10.00 25.00
SSHM Martin Hanzal D 8.00 20.00
SSHO Tomas Holmstrom C 8.00 20.00
SSHS Harri Sateri D 8.00 20.00
SSHU Brett Hull A 60.00 120.00
SSJA Jason Arnott C 10.00 25.00
SSJB Jonathan Bernier C
SSJC John Carlson C 15.00 40.00
SSJE Jordan Eberle B 25.00 60.00
SSJH Josh Harding B
SSJJ Jaromir Jagr A
SSJR Jay Rosehill D 8.00 20.00
SSJS Joe Sakic A 50.00 100.00
SSJT Jonathan Toews A
SSKA Keith Aulie C
SSKC Kyle Clifford B 8.00 20.00
SSKU Chris Kunitz B 12.00 30.00
SSLA Maxim Lapierre C 10.00 25.00
SSLS Luke Schenn B
SSMA Matt Martin C 8.00 20.00
SSMB Matt Beleskey D 8.00 20.00
SSMC Philip McRae C 8.00 20.00
SSMF Michael Frolik C 8.00 20.00
SSMH Matthew Halischuk D 8.00 20.00
SSMI Brendan Mikkelson D 8.00 20.00
SSML Mario Lemieux A
SSMM Mark Messier A 50.00 100.00
SSMN Michal Neuvirth B
SSMS Matt Stajan C 8.00 20.00
SSNA Markus Naslund B
SSNF Nick Foligno B 10.00 25.00
SSNG Nicklas Grossman C 8.00 20.00
SSPL Pascal Leclaire C
SSPM Peter Mueller C
SSPR Patrick Roy B
SSRA Tuukka Rask C 12.00 30.00
SSRE Ryan Ellis C
SSRJ Ryan Jones C 12.00 30.00
SSRN Ryan Nugent-Hopkins B 20.00 50.00
SSRS Ryan Smyth B 10.00 25.00
SSSC Sidney Crosby B
SSSD Simon Despres C 10.00 25.00
SSSG Sam Gagner C 10.00 25.00
SSSS Steven Stamkos B 25.00 60.00
SSST Steve Shutt B 10.00 25.00
SSSW Stephen Weiss B 10.00 25.00
SSTH Taylor Hall B
SSTL Jiri Tlusty C 8.00 20.00
SSTO T.J. Oshie C 8.00 20.00
SSTR Tuomo Ruutu B
SSTS Tim Stapleton C 8.00 20.00
SSTV Tomas Vokoun C 10.00 25.00
SSVA Thomas Vanek B
SSVF Valtteri Filppula B 30.00 60.00
SSVS Viktor Stalberg C 8.00 20.00
SSWG Wayne Gretzky B 150.00 250.00
SSWR Wade Redden D 8.00 20.00
SSZB Zach Boychuk D 8.00 20.00
SSZD Zac Dalpe B

2012-13 Upper Deck Silver Skates

SS1-SS30 ODDS 1:12 HOB/RET
SS31-SS40 SP ODDS 1:120 HOB/RET
*SS1-SS30 GOLD: 2.5X TO 6X BASIC INSERTS
*SS31-SS40 GOLD: 1.5X TO 3X BASIC INSERTS
SS1 Corey Perry 1.25 3.00
SS2 Teemu Selanne 2.50 6.00
SS3 Patrice Bergeron 1.50 4.00
SS4 Zdeno Chara 1.25 3.00
SS5 Milan Lucic 1.25 3.00
SS6 Tyler Seguin 2.00 5.00
SS7 Thomas Vanek 1.25 3.00
SS8 Sven Baertschi 1.25 3.00
SS9 Patrick Kane 2.50 6.00
SS10 Jonathan Toews 2.50 6.00
SS11 Riley Sheahan 1.00 2.50
SS12 Henrik Zetterberg 1.50 4.00
SS13 Ryan Nugent-Hopkins 3.00 8.00
SS14 Taylor Hall 3.00 8.00
SS15 Jordan Eberle 1.25 3.00
SS16 P.K. Subban 2.00 5.00
SS17 Adam Henrique 1.25 3.00
SS18 Ilya Kovalchuk 1.25 3.00
SS19 Marian Gaborik 1.25 3.00
SS20 Jakob Silfverberg 2.50 6.00
SS21 Daniel Briere 1.25 3.00
SS22 Claude Giroux 1.25 3.00
SS23 Evgeni Malkin 4.00 10.00
SS24 Jaden Schwartz 2.00 5.00
SS25 Steven Stamkos 2.50 6.00
SS26 Martin St. Louis 1.25 3.00
SS27 Phil Kessel 1.50 4.00
SS28 Henrik Sedin 1.25 3.00
SS29 Daniel Sedin 1.25 3.00
SS30 Nicklas Backstrom 2.00 5.00
SS31 Bobby Orr SP 6.00 15.00
SS32 Chris Kreider SP 4.00 10.00
SS33 Wayne Gretzky SP 15.00 40.00
SS34 Jean Beliveau SP 6.00 15.00
SS35 Mark Messier SP 6.00 15.00
SS36 Eric Lindros SP 8.00 20.00
SS37 Mario Lemieux SP 8.00 20.00
SS38 Sidney Crosby SP 10.00 25.00
SS39 Brett Hull SP 6.00 15.00
SS40 Alexander Ovechkin SP 6.00 15.00

2012-13 Upper Deck Winter Classic Oversized

STATED ODDS 1:12 TIN
WC1 Claude Giroux 1.25 3.00
WC2 Scott Hartnell 1.25 3.00
WC3 Brayden Schenn 1.25 3.00
WC4 Daniel Briere 1.25 3.00
WC5 Sergei Bobrovsky 1.25 3.00
WC6 Matt Carle 1.00 2.50
WC7 Maxime Talbot 1.00 2.50
WC8 Marian Gaborik 1.25 3.00
WC9 Henrik Lundqvist 1.50 4.00
WC10 Michael Rupp .75 2.00
WC11 Ryan Callahan 1.25 3.00
WC12 Brad Richards 1.25 3.00
WC13 Brandon Prust .75 2.00
WC14 Ryan McDonagh 1.25 3.00

2013-14 Upper Deck

COMPLETE SET (500) 350.00 600.00
COMP.SERIES 1 (250) 175.00 300.00
COMP.SERIES 2 (250) 175.00 300.00
COMP.SER.1 w/o RC's (200) 10.00 25.00
COMP.SER.2 w/o RC's (200) 10.00 25.00
201-250 YOUNG GUN ODDS 1:4 SER.1
451-500 YOUNG GUN ODDS 1:4 SER.2
1 David Krejci .30 .75
2 Johnny Boychuk .20 .50
3 Torey Krug .40 1.00
4 Milan Lucic .30 .75
5 Brad Marchand .40 1.00
6 Dennis Seidenberg .25 .60
7 Patrice Bergeron .40 1.00
8 Gregory Campbell .20 .50
9 Max Pacioretty .30 .75
10 David Desharnais .30 .75
11 Travis Moen .20 .50
12 Brandon Prust .20 .50
13 Andrei Markov .30 .75
14 P.K. Subban .50 1.25
15 Brian Gionta .25 .60
16 Frans Nielsen .20 .50
17 Lubomir Visnovsky .20 .50
18 Josh Bailey .25 .60
19 John Tavares .60 1.50
20 Andrew MacDonald .20 .50
21 Casey Cizikas .20 .50
22 Kyle Okposo .30 .75
23 Ryan McDonagh .30 .75
24 Derick Brassard .30 .75
25 Mats Zuccarello-Aasen .25 .60
26 Rick Nash .30 .75
27 Daniel Girardi .20 .50
28 Henrik Lundqvist .40 1.00
29 Derek Dorsett .20 .50
30 Andy Greene .20 .50
31 Ilya Kovalchuk .30 .75
32 Adam Henrique .30 .75
33 Ryan Carter .20 .50
34 Martin Brodeur .60 1.50
35 Adam Larsson .30 .75
36 Matt Read .20 .50
37 Wayne Simmonds .40 1.00
38 Luke Schenn .20 .50
39 Scott Hartnell .30 .75
40 Jakub Voracek .30 .75
41 Sean Couturier .30 .75
42 Erik Gustafsson .20 .50
43 Craig Anderson .30 .75
44 Mika Zibanejad .30 .75
45 Chris Neil .20 .50
46 Colin Greening .20 .50
47 Patrick Wiercioch .20 .50
48 Erik Karlsson .60 1.50

2013-14 Upper Deck

49 Karl Alzner .20 .50
50 Nicklas Backstrom .50 1.25
51 Braden Holtby .50 1.25
52 Martin Erat .20 .50
53 Troy Brouwer .25 .60
54 John Carlson .40 1.00
55 Justin Faulk .20 .50
56 Jiri Tlusty .25 .60
57 Jay Harrison .20 .50
58 Jordan Staal .30 .75
59 Jeff Skinner .25 .60
60 Alexander Semin .30 .75
61 Steve Ott .25 .60
62 Thomas Vanek .30 .75
63 Jhonas Enroth .30 .75
64 Marcus Foligno .20 .50
65 Tyler Myers .25 .60
66 Tyler Ennis .25 .60
67 Carl Gunnarsson .20 .50
68 Dion Phaneuf .30 .75
69 Ryan O'Byrne .20 .50
70 Joffrey Lupul .25 .60
71 James Reimer .30 .75
72 James van Riemsdyk .30 .75
73 Nikolai Kulemin .25 .60
74 Brooks Orpik .25 .60
75 James Neal .30 .75
76 Kris Letang .30 .75
77 Tomas Vokoun .25 .60
78 Chris Kunitz .30 .75
79 Matt Niskanen .25 .60
80 Sidney Crosby 1.25 3.00
81 Erik Gudbranson .30 .75
82 Tomas Kopecky .25 .60
83 Jacob Markstrom .25 .60
84 Marcel Goc .25 .60
85 Dmitry Kulikov .20 .50
86 Tomas Fleischmann .20 .50
87 Victor Hedman .40 1.00
88 Anders Lindback .20 .50
89 B.J. Crombeen .20 .50
90 Sami Salo .20 .50
91 Teddy Purcell .30 .75
92 Martin St. Louis .30 .75
93 Fedor Tyutin .20 .50
94 R.J. Umberger .20 .50
95 James Wisniewski .20 .50
96 Marian Gaborik .30 .75
97 Jared Boll .20 .50
98 Mark Letestu .25 .60
99 Sergei Bobrovsky .30 .75
100 Jonathan Ericsson .25 .60
101 Gustav Nyquist .25 .60
102 Justin Abdelkader .25 .60
103 Brendan Smith .25 .60
104 Pavel Datsyuk .40 1.00
105 Niklas Kronwall .25 .60
106 Jakub Kindl .20 .50
107 David Legwand .25 .60
108 Patric Hornqvist .25 .60
109 Shea Weber .25 .60
110 Craig Smith .20 .50
111 Roman Josi .30 .75
112 Gabriel Bourque .25 .60
113 Corey Crawford .40 1.00
114 Andrew Shaw .30 .75
115 Johnny Oduya .25 .60
116 Brandon Saad .30 .75
117 Jonathan Toews .60 1.50
118 Brent Seabrook .30 .75
119 Patrick Sharp .30 .75
120 Bryan Bickell .20 .50
121 Jay Bouwmeester .30 .75
122 T.J. Oshie .50 1.25
123 Alexander Steen .30 .75
124 Kevin Shattenkirk .30 .75
125 Jaroslav Halak .30 .75
126 David Backes .30 .75
127 Barret Jackman .20 .50
128 Jason Pominville .25 .60
129 Mikko Koivu .25 .60
130 Ryan Suter .20 .50
131 Kyle Brodziak .20 .50
132 Niklas Backstrom .25 .60
133 Jared Spurgeon .20 .50
134 Jason Zucker .25 .60
135 Jamie Benn .40 1.00
136 Alex Goligoski .20 .50
137 Ray Whitney .25 .60
138 Cody Eakin .20 .50
139 Brenden Dillon .25 .60
140 Kari Lehtonen .25 .60
141 Andrew Ladd .30 .75
142 Tobias Enstrom .20 .50
143 Evander Kane .30 .75
144 Zach Bogosian .25 .60
145 Ondrej Pavelec .30 .75
146 Olli Jokinen .25 .60
147 Matt Duchene .30 .75
148 Tyson Barrie .30 .75
149 Gabriel Landeskog .25 .60
150 Semyon Varlamov .30 .75
151 P.A. Parenteau .20 .50
152 Matt Hunwick .20 .50
153 Martin Hanzal .20 .50
154 Keith Yandle .30 .75
155 Lauri Korpikoski .20 .50
156 Mikkel Boedker .20 .50
157 Shane Doan .25 .60
158 Derek Morris .20 .50
159 Sam Gagner .25 .60
160 Ladislav Smid .20 .50
161 Taylor Hall .60 1.50
162 Jeff Petry .25 .60
163 Ryan Smyth .25 .60
164 Ryan Nugent-Hopkins .30 .75
165 Mikael Backlund .25 .60
166 Dennis Wideman .20 .50
167 Jiri Hudler .25 .60
168 Michael Cammalleri .25 .60
169 Joey MacDonald .20 .50
170 Sven Baertschi .25 .60
171 Ryan Getzlaf .50 1.25
172 Nick Bonino .20 .50
173 Matt Beleskey .20 .50
174 Francois Beauchemin .20 .50
175 Saku Koivu .30 .75
176 Andrew Cogliano .20 .50
177 Teemu Selanne .60 1.50
178 Jarret Stoll .25 .60
179 Matt Greene .20 .50
180 Jeff Carter .30 .75
181 Kyle Clifford .20 .50
182 Jonathan Quick .50 1.25
183 Slava Voynov .25 .60
184 Anze Kopitar .50 1.25
185 Marc-Edouard Vlasic .20 .50
186 Tommy Wingels .20 .50
187 Logan Couture .30 .75
188 Raffi Torres .20 .50
189 Scott Hannan .20 .50
190 Joe Thornton .30 .75
191 Dan Boyle .25 .60
192 Zack Kassian .25 .60
193 Dan Hamhuis .25 .60
194 Daniel Sedin .30 .75
195 Alexander Edler .20 .50
196 Alexandre Burrows .30 .75
197 Jannik Hansen .25 .60
198 Roberto Luongo .30 .75
199 Chara/Rask/Bergrn CL .40 1.00
200 Sbrk/Crwfrd/Kane CL .60 1.50
201 Carl Soderberg YG RC 2.50 6.00
202 Dougie Hamilton YG RC 5.00 12.00
203 Alex Galchenyuk YG RC 10.00 25.00
204 Brock Nelson YG RC 4.00 10.00
205 J.T. Miller YG RC 3.00 8.00
206 Jesper Fast YG RC 2.00 5.00
207 Nathan Beaulieu YG RC 2.00 5.00
208 Damien Brunner YG RC 2.00 5.00
209 Jean-Gabriel Pageau YG RC 2.00 5.00
210 Cory Conacher YG RC 1.50 4.00
211 Connor Carrick YG RC 2.00 5.00
212 Tom Wilson YG RC 4.00 10.00
213 Michael Latta YG RC 2.00 5.00
214 Ryan Murphy YG RC 2.50 6.00
215 Mikhail Grigorenko YG RC 3.00 8.00
216 Zemgus Girgensons YG RC 5.00 12.00
217 Rasmus Ristolainen YG RC 4.00 10.00
218 Morgan Rielly YG RC 8.00 20.00
219 Beau Bennett YG RC 3.00 8.00
220 Olli Maatta YG RC 4.00 10.00
221 Drew Shore YG RC 2.00 5.00
222 Jonathan Huberdeau YG RC 10.00 25.00
223 Alex Killorn YG RC 2.50 6.00
224 Richard Panik YG RC 2.50 6.00
225 Boone Jenner YG RC 2.50 6.00
226 Ryan Murray YG RC 4.00 10.00
227 Danny DeKeyser YG RC 3.00 8.00
228 Seth Jones YG RC 5.00 12.00
229 Joakim Nordstrom YG RC 2.00 5.00
230 Vladimir Tarasenko YG RC 30.00 80.00
231 Mathew Dumba YG RC 2.50 6.00
232 Justin Fontaine YG RC 2.50 6.00
233 Charlie Coyle YG RC 2.50 6.00
234 Jonas Brodin YG RC 2.00 5.00
235 Alex Chiasson YG RC 2.50 6.00
236 Valeri Nichushkin YG RC 2.50 6.00
237 Jacob Trouba YG RC 5.00 12.00
238 Nathan MacKinnon YG RC 40.00 100.00
239 Lucas Lessio YG RC 1.50 4.00
240 Justin Schultz YG RC 2.50 6.00
241 Nail Yakupov YG RC 8.00 20.00
242 Sean Monahan YG RC 12.00 30.00
243 Sami Vatanen YG RC 2.50 6.00
244 Viktor Fasth YG RC 2.50 6.00
245 Emerson Etem YG RC 2.50 6.00
246 Tyler Toffoli YG RC 6.00 15.00
247 Matt Nieto YG RC 2.00 5.00
248 Tomas Hertl YG RC 3.00 8.00
249 Nicklas Jensen YG RC 2.00 5.00
250 McKn/Jns/Glch YG CL 3.00 8.00
251 Henrik Sedin .30 .75
252 Jason Garrison .20 .50
253 Brad Richardson .20 .50
254 Mike Santorelli .25 .60
255 Kevin Bieksa .25 .60
256 Ryan Kesler .30 .75
257 Alex Stalock .25 .60
258 Joe Pavelski .30 .75
259 Brent Burns .40 1.00
260 Antti Niemi .25 .60
261 Tyler Kennedy .20 .50
262 Patrick Marleau .30 .75
263 Brad Stuart .20 .50
264 Justin Williams .25 .60
265 Trevor Lewis .20 .50
266 Willie Mitchell .20 .50
267 Mike Richards .30 .75
268 Ben Scrivens .25 .60
269 Drew Doughty .30 .75
270 Dustin Brown .30 .75
271 Jonas Hiller .25 .60
272 Dustin Penner .25 .60
273 Sheldon Souray .20 .50
274 Jakob Silfverberg .25 .60
275 Corey Perry .30 .75
276 Daniel Winnik .20 .50
277 Kyle Palmieri .25 .60
278 T.J. Brodie .20 .50
279 David Jones .20 .50
280 Mark Giordano .25 .60
281 Matt Stajan .25 .60
282 Lee Stempniak .20 .50
283 Curtis Glencross .20 .50
284 Devan Dubnyk .30 .75
285 Jordan Eberle .30 .75
286 Philip Larsen .20 .50
287 Andrew Ference .20 .50
288 David Perron .20 .50
289 Ales Hemsky .20 .50
290 Oliver Ekman-Larsson .25 .60
291 Mike Smith .30 .75
292 Kyle Chipchura .20 .50
293 Mike Ribeiro .25 .60
294 Radim Vrbata .25 .60
295 Antoine Vermette .20 .50
296 Ryan O'Reilly .30 .75
297 Alex Tanguay .20 .50
298 Maxime Talbot .25 .60
299 Jamie McGinn .20 .50
300 Erik Johnson .20 .50
301 Paul Stastny .30 .75
302 Dustin Byfuglien .30 .75
303 Blake Wheeler .30 .75
304 Michael Frolik .20 .50
305 Mark Scheifele .40 1.00
306 Grant Clitsome .20 .50
307 Bryan Little .30 .75
308 Devin Setoguchi .25 .60
309 Stephane Robidas .20 .50
310 Shawn Horcoff .20 .50
311 Erik Cole .25 .60
312 Tyler Seguin .50 1.25
313 Trevor Daley .20 .50
314 Rich Peverley .30 .75
315 Sergei Gonchar .20 .50
316 Zach Parise .30 .75
317 Marco Scandella .20 .50
318 Josh Harding .30 .75
319 Matt Cooke .20 .50
320 Dany Heatley .25 .60
321 Nino Niederreiter .20 .50
322 Patrik Berglund .20 .50
323 Alex Pietrangelo .25 .60
324 Chris Stewart .25 .60
325 Jaden Schwartz .40 1.00
326 Derek Roy .25 .60
327 Brian Elliott .25 .60
328 Magnus Paajarvi .30 .75
329 Nick Leddy .20 .50
330 Patrick Kane .60 1.50
331 Marian Hossa .25 .60
332 Niklas Hjalmarsson .20 .50
333 Michal Handzus .20 .50
334 Duncan Keith .30 .75
335 Kris Versteeg .25 .60
336 Colin Wilson .25 .60
337 Pekka Rinne .40 1.00
338 Matt Cullen .20 .50
339 Kevin Klein .20 .50
340 Viktor Stalberg .20 .50
341 Mike Fisher .25 .60
342 Matt Hendricks .20 .50
343 Johan Franzen .30 .75
344 Daniel Alfredsson .30 .75
345 Jim Howard .30 .75
346 Stephen Weiss .25 .60
347 Henrik Zetterberg .40 1.00
348 Joakim Andersson .25 .60
349 Jack Johnson .20 .50
350 Cam Atkinson .30 .75
351 Brandon Dubinsky .25 .60
352 Nick Foligno .25 .60
353 Ryan Johansen .40 1.00
354 Artem Anisimov .25 .60
355 Valtteri Filppula .30 .75
356 Ben Bishop .30 .75
357 Steven Stamkos .60 1.50
358 Eric Brewer .20 .50
359 Brett Connolly .20 .50
360 Matt Carle .25 .60
361 Shawn Matthias .20 .50
362 Brian Campbell .20 .50
363 Sean Bergenheim .20 .50
364 Scott Gomez .25 .60
365 Tim Thomas .30 .75
366 Scottie Upshall .20 .50
367 Paul Martin .20 .50
368 Pascal Dupuis .20 .50
369 Evgeni Malkin 1.00 2.50
370 Marc-Andre Fleury .50 1.25
371 Brandon Sutter .25 .60
372 Rob Scuderi .20 .50
373 Jussi Jokinen .20 .50
374 Tyler Bozak .25 .60
375 David Clarkson .20 .50
376 Cody Franson .20 .50
377 Dave Bolland .20 .50
378 Nazem Kadri .30 .75
379 Jonathan Bernier .30 .75
380 Phil Kessel .40 1.00
381 Jamie McBain .20 .50
382 Drew Stafford .30 .75
383 Ryan Miller .30 .75
384 Matt Moulson .25 .60
385 Cody Hodgson .30 .75
386 Christian Ehrhoff .20 .50
387 Tuomo Ruutu .25 .60
388 Eric Staal .40 1.00
389 Ron Hainsey .20 .50
390 Nathan Gerbe .20 .50
391 Cam Ward .30 .75
392 Andrej Sekera .20 .50
393 Joel Ward .20 .50
394 Jason Chimera .20 .50
395 Alexander Ovechkin 1.25 3.00
396 Mike Green .30 .75
397 Eric Fehr .20 .50
398 Mikhail Grabovski .25 .60
399 Marcus Johansson .25 .60
400 Jason Spezza .30 .75
401 Jared Cowen .20 .50
402 Bobby Ryan .30 .75
403 Kyle Turris .20 .50
404 Chris Phillips .20 .50
405 Milan Michalek .20 .50
406 Clarke MacArthur .20 .50
407 Kimmo Timonen .20 .50
408 Brayden Schenn .30 .75
409 Mark Streit .20 .50
410 Steve Downie .20 .50
411 Claude Giroux .30 .75
412 Braydon Coburn .20 .50
413 Vincent Lecavalier .25 .60
414 Patrik Elias .30 .75
415 Bryce Salvador .20 .50
416 Jaromir Jagr .75 2.00
417 Cory Schneider .25 .60
418 Travis Zajac .25 .60
419 Michael Ryder .20 .50
420 Ryane Clowe .20 .50
421 Carl Hagelin .30 .75
422 Marc Staal .25 .60
423 Brad Richards .30 .75
424 Ryan Callahan .30 .75
425 Michael Del Zotto .20 .50
426 Derek Stepan .30 .75
427 Benoit Pouliot .20 .50
428 Cal Clutterbuck .30 .75
429 Pierre-Marc Bouchard .30 .75
430 Travis Hamonic .20 .50
431 Michael Grabner .25 .60
432 Evgeni Nabokov .25 .60
433 Thomas Vanek .30 .75
434 Douglas Murray .20 .50
435 Lars Eller .25 .60
436 Alexei Emelin .25 .60
437 Tomas Plekanec .30 .75
438 Josh Gorges .25 .60
439 Rene Bourque .20 .50
440 Carey Price 1.00 2.50
441 Daniel Briere .30 .75
442 Adam McQuaid .20 .50
443 Reilly Smith .30 .75
444 Tuukka Rask .30 .75
445 Jarome Iginla .30 .75
446 Daniel Paille .20 .50
447 Loui Eriksson .25 .60
448 Zdeno Chara .30 .75
449 Ztrbg/Hwrd/Frnz CL .40 1.00
450 Ksl/Kdri/Frnsn CL .40 1.00
451 Filip Forsberg YG RC 15.00 40.00
452 Dylan McIlrath YG RC 1.50 4.00
453 Michael Bournival YG RC 2.50 6.00
454 Michael Sgarbossa YG RC 2.00 5.00
455 Martin Marincin YG RC 2.00 5.00
456 Ryan Spooner YG RC 2.50 6.00
457 Mark Pysyk YG RC 2.50 6.00
458 Freddie Hamilton YG RC 2.50 6.00
459 Joacim Eriksson YG RC 2.50 6.00
460 Christian Thomas YG RC 2.00 5.00
461 Reto Berra YG RC 2.50 6.00
462 Frederik Andersen YG RC 15.00 40.00
463 Mark Arcobello YG RC 2.50 6.00
464 Jon Merrill YG RC 2.50 6.00
465 Linden Vey YG RC 1.50 4.00
466 Petr Mrazek YG RC 8.00 20.00
467 Philipp Grubauer YG RC 2.50 6.00
468 Marek Mazanec YG RC 2.50 6.00
469 Elias Lindholm YG RC 4.00 10.00
470 Aleksander Barkov YG RC 12.00 30.00
471 Nikita Zadorov YG RC 2.50 6.00
472 Taylor Beck YG RC 2.00 5.00
473 Jack Campbell YG RC 2.00 5.00
474 Mikael Granlund YG RC 6.00 15.00
475 Cody Ceci YG RC 2.00 5.00
476 Tomas Jurco YG RC 4.00 10.00
477 Brendan Gallagher YG RC 12.00 30.00
478 Jarred Tinordi YG RC 2.50 6.00
479 Josh Leivo YG RC 2.50 6.00
480 Rickard Rakell YG RC 2.50 6.00
481 Ondrej Palat YG RC 3.00 8.00
482 Ryan Strome YG RC 3.00 8.00
483 Nikita Kucherov YG RC 40.00 100.00
484 Reid Boucher YG RC 2.50 6.00
485 Martin Jones YG RC 8.00 20.00
486 John Gibson YG RC 8.00 20.00
487 Antti Raanta YG RC 3.00 8.00
488 Nick Bjugstad YG RC 3.00 8.00
489 Scott Laughton YG RC 2.50 6.00
490 Antoine Roussel YG RC 2.50 6.00
491 Thomas Hickey YG RC 2.00 5.00
492 Tyler Johnson YG RC 8.00 20.00
493 Connor Murphy YG RC 2.00 5.00
494 Max Reinhart YG RC 2.50 6.00
495 Jordan Schroeder YG RC 2.50 6.00
496 Matt Irwin YG RC 2.00 5.00
497 Jerry D'Amigo YG RC 2.50 6.00
498 Tanner Pearson YG RC 2.50 6.00
499 Hampus Lindholm YG RC 4.00 10.00
500 Glgr/Mrz/Bkv YG CL 3.00 8.00
ST1 Sam Tageson YG 25.00 50.00

2013-14 Upper Deck Exclusives

*1-450 VETS/100: 6X TO 15X BASIC CARDS
*201-250/451-500 YG/100: 1.5X TO 4X BASIC RC
50 Nicklas Backstrom 6.00 15.00
113 Corey Crawford 5.00 12.00
203 Alex Galchenyuk YG 90.00 150.00
220 Olli Maatta YG 12.00 30.00
230 Vladimir Tarasenko YG 150.00 250.00
236 Valeri Nichushkin YG 25.00 60.00
238 Nathan MacKinnon YG 200.00 350.00
241 Nail Yakupov YG 50.00 120.00
248 Tomas Hertl YG 10.00 25.00
451 Filip Forsberg YG 80.00 150.00
481 Ondrej Palat YG 25.00 60.00
483 Nikita Kucherov YG 250.00 350.00
486 John Gibson YG 40.00 100.00
492 Tyler Johnson YG 50.00 120.00

2013-14 Upper Deck A Piece of History 300 Win Club Jerseys

GROUP A ODDS 1:2763 SER.1
GROUP B ODDS 1:1239 SER.1
OVERALL ODDS 1:864 SER.1 HOBBY
300GF Grant Fuhr B 12.00 30.00
300GW Gump Worsley A 12.00 30.00
300MR Mike Richter B 10.00 25.00
300OK Olaf Kolzig B 12.00 30.00
300PR Patrick Roy B 15.00 40.00
300RL Roberto Luongo A 12.00 30.00
300TE Tony Esposito A 15.00 40.00

2013-14 Upper Deck Buyback Autographs

SC Crosby '09-10 UD1/87 S1 60.00 120.00
535 Tavares '10-11 RtrA/24 S2 60.00 100.00

2013-14 Upper Deck Canvas

C1-C90 VETERAN ODDS 1:7 SER.1
C121-C210 VET ODDS 1:7 SER.2
C91-C120 YG ODDS 1:48 SER.1
C211-C240 YG ODDS 1:48 SER.2
C241-C270 RET/POE ODDS 1:192 SER.2
C1 Patrice Bergeron 1.50 4.00
C2 Tuukka Rask 1.25 3.00
C3 David Krejci 1.25 3.00
C4 Milan Lucic 1.25 3.00
C5 Max Pacioretty 1.25 3.00
C6 Tomas Plekanec 1.25 3.00
C7 Carey Price 4.00 10.00
C8 Matt Moulson 1.00 2.50
C9 Evgeni Nabokov 1.00 2.50
C10 Kyle Okposo 1.25 3.00
C11 Frans Nielsen .75 2.00
C12 Derek Stepan 1.25 3.00
C13 Ryan Callahan 1.25 3.00
C14 Derick Brassard 1.25 3.00
C15 Brad Richards 1.25 3.00
C16 Patrik Elias 1.25 3.00
C17 Martin Brodeur 2.50 6.00
C18 Adam Henrique 1.25 3.00
C19 Jakub Voracek 1.25 3.00
C20 Wayne Simmonds 1.50 4.00
C21 Brayden Schenn 1.25 3.00
C22 Craig Anderson 1.25 3.00
C23 Kyle Turris .75 2.00
C24 Colin Greening .75 2.00
C25 Alexander Ovechkin 5.00 12.00
C26 Braden Holtby 2.00 5.00
C27 Eric Staal 1.50 4.00
C28 Jiri Tlusty 1.00 2.50
C29 Thomas Vanek 1.25 3.00
C30 Tyler Ennis 1.00 2.50
C31 Ryan Miller 1.25 3.00
C32 Phil Kessel 1.50 4.00
C33 James van Riemsdyk 1.25 3.00
C34 Chris Kunitz 1.25 3.00
C35 Pascal Dupuis .75 2.00
C36 James Neal 1.25 3.00
C37 Evgeni Malkin 4.00 10.00
C38 Marc-Andre Fleury 2.00 5.00
C39 Tomas Fleischmann .75 2.00
C40 Tomas Kopecky 1.00 2.50
C41 Steven Stamkos 2.50 6.00
C42 Teddy Purcell 1.25 3.00
C43 Sergei Bobrovsky 1.25 3.00
C44 Mark Letestu 1.00 2.50
C45 Jim Howard 1.25 3.00
C46 Johan Franzen 1.25 3.00
C47 Pavel Datsyuk 1.50 4.00
C48 David Legwand 1.00 2.50
C49 Pekka Rinne 1.50 4.00
C50 Patrick Kane 2.50 6.00
C51 Duncan Keith 1.25 3.00
C52 Patrick Sharp 1.25 3.00
C53 Corey Crawford 1.50 4.00
C54 Chris Stewart 1.00 2.50
C55 Alexander Steen 1.25 3.00
C56 Brian Elliott 1.00 2.50
C57 Kevin Shattenkirk 1.25 3.00
C58 Dany Heatley 1.00 2.50
C59 Ryan Suter .75 2.00
C60 Niklas Backstrom 1.00 2.50
C61 Jamie Benn 1.50 4.00
C62 Kari Lehtonen 1.00 2.50
C63 Evander Kane 1.25 3.00
C64 Andrew Ladd 1.25 3.00
C65 Matt Duchene 1.25 3.00
C66 Paul Stastny 1.25 3.00
C67 Keith Yandle 1.25 3.00
C68 Shane Doan 1.00 2.50
C69 Mikkel Boedker .75 2.00
C70 Taylor Hall 2.50 6.00
C71 Jordan Eberle 1.25 3.00
C72 Devan Dubnyk 1.25 3.00
C73 Curtis Glencross .75 2.00
C74 Michael Cammalleri 1.00 2.50
C75 Lee Stempniak .75 2.00
C76 Ryan Getzlaf 2.00 5.00
C77 Jonas Hiller 1.00 2.50
C78 Saku Koivu 1.25 3.00
C79 Teemu Selanne 2.50 6.00
C80 Jonathan Quick 2.00 5.00
C81 Justin Williams 1.00 2.50
C82 Dustin Brown 1.25 3.00
C83 Slava Voynov 1.00 2.50
C84 Joe Thornton 1.25 3.00
C85 Dan Boyle 1.00 2.50
C86 Antti Niemi 1.00 2.50
C87 Tommy Wingels .75 2.00
C88 Alexandre Burrows 1.25 3.00
C89 Roberto Luongo 1.25 3.00
C90 Kane/Crwfrd/Keith CL 1.50 4.00
C91 Ryan Spooner YG 4.00 10.00
C92 Dougie Hamilton YG 10.00 25.00
C93 Brendan Gallagher YG 12.00 30.00
C94 Jarred Tinordi YG 4.00 10.00
C95 Michael Bournival YG 4.00 10.00
C96 J.T. Miller YG 4.00 10.00
C97 Damien Brunner YG 6.00 15.00
C98 Connor Carrick YG 3.00 8.00
C99 Elias Lindholm YG 6.00 15.00
C100 Rasmus Ristolainen YG 6.00 15.00
C101 Mikhail Grigorenko YG 5.00 12.00
C102 Olli Maatta YG 6.00 15.00
C103 Nick Bjugstad YG 5.00 12.00
C104 Aleksander Barkov YG 10.00 25.00
C105 Jonathan Huberdeau YG 8.00 20.00
C106 Boone Jenner YG 5.00 12.00
C107 Petr Mrazek YG 12.00 30.00
C108 Seth Jones YG 10.00 25.00
C109 Filip Forsberg YG 15.00 40.00
C110 Mikael Granlund YG 6.00 15.00
C111 Jack Campbell YG 3.00 8.00
C112 Valeri Nichushkin YG 4.00 10.00
C113 Jacob Trouba YG 6.00 15.00
C114 Nathan MacKinnon YG 40.00 80.00
C115 Justin Schultz YG 4.00 10.00
C116 Nail Yakupov YG 12.00 30.00
C117 Viktor Fasth YG 4.00 10.00
C118 Tanner Pearson YG 6.00 15.00
C119 Tomas Hertl YG 10.00 25.00
C120 Yakupv/MacKin YG CL 8.00 20.00
C121 Brad Marchand 1.50 4.00
C122 Loui Eriksson 1.00 2.50
C123 Zdeno Chara 1.25 3.00
C124 P.K. Subban 2.00 5.00
C125 Lars Eller 1.00 2.50
C126 David Desharnais 1.25 3.00
C127 Brian Gionta 1.00 2.50
C128 John Tavares 2.50 6.00
C129 Thomas Vanek 1.25 3.00
C130 Rick Nash 1.25 3.00
C131 Henrik Lundqvist 1.50 4.00
C132 Carl Hagelin 1.25 3.00
C133 Jaromir Jagr 3.00 8.00
C134 Cory Schneider 1.00 2.50
C135 Michael Ryder .75 2.00
C136 Travis Zajac 1.00 2.50
C137 Claude Giroux 1.25 3.00
C138 Vincent Lecavalier 1.00 2.50
C139 Sean Couturier 1.25 3.00
C140 Steve Mason 1.00 2.50
C141 Bobby Ryan 1.25 3.00
C142 Robin Lehner 1.00 2.50
C143 Jason Spezza 1.25 3.00
C144 Mike Green 1.25 3.00
C145 Nicklas Backstrom 2.00 5.00
C146 Jeff Skinner 1.00 2.50
C147 Alexander Semin 1.25 3.00
C148 Jordan Staal 1.25 3.00
C149 Cody Hodgson 1.25 3.00
C150 Matt Moulson 1.00 2.50
C151 Nazem Kadri 1.25 3.00
C152 Cody Franson .75 2.00
C153 Jonathan Bernier 1.25 3.00
C154 James Reimer 1.25 3.00
C155 David Clarkson .75 2.00
C156 Sidney Crosby 5.00 12.00
C157 Kris Letang 1.25 3.00
C158 Paul Martin .75 2.00
C159 Jacob Markstrom 1.00 2.50
C160 Brian Campbell .75 2.00
C161 Martin St. Louis 1.25 3.00
C162 Ben Bishop 1.25 3.00
C163 Marian Gaborik 1.25 3.00
C164 Ryan Johansen 1.50 4.00
C165 Jack Johnson .75 2.00
C166 Henrik Zetterberg 1.50 4.00
C167 Daniel Alfredsson 1.25 3.00
C168 Niklas Kronwall 1.00 2.50
C169 Shea Weber 1.00 2.50
C170 Matt Cullen .75 2.00
C171 Jonathan Toews 2.50 6.00
C172 Brent Seabrook 1.25 3.00
C173 Marian Hossa 1.00 2.50
C174 Andrew Shaw 1.25 3.00
C175 David Backes 1.25 3.00
C176 Alex Pietrangelo 1.00 2.50
C177 Jaroslav Halak 1.25 3.00
C178 Zach Parise 1.25 3.00
C179 Mikko Koivu 1.00 2.50
C180 Jason Pominville 1.00 2.50
C181 Tyler Seguin 2.00 5.00
C182 Ray Whitney 1.00 2.50
C183 Shawn Horcoff .75 2.00
C184 Blake Wheeler 1.25 3.00
C185 Dustin Byfuglien 1.25 3.00
C186 P.A. Parenteau .75 2.00
C187 Gabriel Landeskog 1.00 2.50
C188 Alex Tanguay .75 2.00
C189 Semyon Varlamov 1.25 3.00
C190 Mike Smith 1.25 3.00
C191 Oliver Ekman-Larsson 1.00 2.50
C192 Sam Gagner 1.00 2.50
C193 Ryan Nugent-Hopkins 1.25 3.00
C194 Ales Hemsky .75 2.00
C195 David Perron .75 2.00
C196 Jiri Hudler 1.00 2.50
C197 Matt Stajan 1.00 2.50
C198 Dennis Wideman .75 2.00
C199 Corey Perry 1.25 3.00
C200 Cam Fowler 1.00 2.50
C201 Jeff Carter 1.25 3.00
C202 Logan Couture 1.25 3.00
C203 Patrick Marleau 1.25 3.00
C204 Marc-Edouard Vlasic .75 2.00
C205 Brent Burns 1.50 4.00
C206 Henrik Sedin 1.25 3.00
C207 Daniel Sedin 1.25 3.00
C208 Ryan Kesler 1.25 3.00
C209 Alexander Edler .75 2.00
C210 Crsby/Tvrs/St.L CL 5.00 12.00
C211 Jordan Schroeder YG 4.00 10.00
C212 Freddie Hamilton YG 4.00 10.00
C213 Matt Nieto YG 3.00 8.00
C214 Martin Jones YG 8.00 20.00
C215 Linden Vey YG 2.50 6.00
C216 Tyler Toffoli YG 8.00 20.00
C217 Emerson Etem YG 4.00 10.00
C218 Sean Monahan YG 6.00 15.00
C219 Mark Arcobello YG 4.00 10.00
C220 Alex Chiasson YG 4.00 10.00
C221 Charlie Coyle YG 4.00 10.00
C222 Jonas Brodin YG 3.00 8.00
C223 Vladimir Tarasenko YG 25.00 60.00
C224 Antti Raanta YG 5.00 12.00
C225 Danny DeKeyser YG 5.00 12.00
C226 Tomas Jurco YG 8.00 20.00
C227 Tyler Johnson YG 10.00 25.00
C228 Alex Killorn YG 4.00 10.00
C229 Beau Bennett YG 6.00 15.00
C230 Morgan Rielly YG 10.00 25.00
C231 Josh Leivo YG 4.00 10.00
C232 Zemgus Girgensons YG 6.00 15.00
C233 Tom Wilson YG 6.00 15.00
C234 Cody Ceci YG 3.00 8.00
C235 Reid Boucher YG 4.00 10.00
C236 Jon Merrill YG 4.00 10.00
C237 Ryan Strome YG 5.00 12.00
C238 Brock Nelson YG 4.00 10.00
C239 Alex Galchenyuk YG 20.00 50.00
C240 Glcnyk/Mnhn YG CL 5.00 12.00
C241 Wayne Gretzky RET 20.00 50.00
C242 Bobby Orr RET 15.00 40.00
C243 Mario Lemieux RET 30.00 80.00
C244 Peter Forsberg RET 10.00 25.00
C245 Dominik Hasek RET 12.00 30.00
C246 Paul Coffey RET 10.00 25.00
C247 Felix Potvin RET 15.00 40.00
C248 Bobby Clarke RET 10.00 25.00
C249 Guy Lafleur RET 12.00 30.00
C250 Arturs Irbe RET 8.00 20.00
C251 Larry Robinson RET 10.00 25.00
C252 Jeremy Roenick RET 10.00 25.00
C253 Steve Yzerman RET 15.00 40.00
C254 Patrick Roy RET 25.00 60.00
C255 Eric Lindros RET 15.00 40.00
C256 Morgan Rielly POE 15.00 40.00
C257 Nathan MacKinnon POE 30.00 80.00
C258 Mathew Dumba POE 10.00 25.00
C259 Brendan Gallagher POE 20.00 50.00
C260 Jonathan Huberdeau POE 15.00 40.00
C261 Ryan Murphy POE 6.00 15.00
C262 Scott Laughton POE 10.00 25.00
C263 Michael Bournival POE 10.00 25.00
C264 Boone Jenner POE 8.00 20.00
C265 Tanner Pearson POE 10.00 25.00
C266 Sean Monahan POE 15.00 40.00
C267 Freddie Hamilton POE 8.00 20.00
C268 Nathan Beaulieu POE 10.00 25.00
C269 Xavier Ouellet POE 12.00 30.00
C270 Dougie Hamilton POE 12.00 30.00

2013-14 Upper Deck Canvas Autographs

CSJT John Tavares/91 2 75.00 125.00
CSTF Theo Fleury/14 1

2013-14 Upper Deck Clear Cut Foundations

CCF1 M.Brodeur/P.Elias 40.00 100.00
CCF2 J.Toews/P.Kane 40.00 100.00
CCF3 P.Subban/Pacioretty 30.00 80.00
CCF4 H.Lundqvist/R.Nash 25.00 60.00
CCF5 C.Anderson/K.Turris 20.00 50.00
CCF6 Zetterberg/J.Howard 15.00 40.00
CCF7 D.Byfuglien/A.Ladd 20.00 50.00
CCF8 E.Staal/A.Semin 25.00 60.00
CCF9 Markstrom/Fleischmann 15.00 40.00
CCF10 J.Quick/D.Doughty 30.00 80.00
CCF11 J.Tavares/K.Okposo 40.00 100.00
CCF12 N.Kadri/van Riemsdyk 20.00 50.00
CCF13 Marchand/Bergeron 25.00 60.00
CCF14 T.Hall/J.Eberle 40.00 100.00
CCF15 Gaborik/Bobrovsky 15.00 40.00
CCF16 Backstrom/Ovechkin 80.00 200.00
CCF17 P.Dupuis/C.Kunitz 20.00 50.00
CCF18 P.Hornqvist/S.Weber 15.00 40.00
CCF19 K.Lehtonen/R.Whitney 15.00 40.00
CCF20 R.Kesler/H.Sedin 20.00 50.00
CCF21 R.Suter/Z.Parise 20.00 50.00
CCF22 S.Doan/K.Yandle 20.00 50.00
CCF23 Cammalleri/Stempniak 15.00 40.00
CCF24 T.Vanek/R.Miller 20.00 50.00
CCF25 L.Couture/P.Marleau 20.00 50.00
CCF26 Duchene/Parenteau 15.00 40.00
CCF27 C.Perry/R.Getzlaf 15.00 40.00
CCF28 T.Purcell/S.Stamkos 40.00 100.00
CCF29 B.Elliott/D.Backes 12.00 30.00
CCF30 C.Giroux/J.Voracek 20.00 50.00

2013-14 Upper Deck Clear Cut Honoured Members

HOF49 Adam Oates 8.00 20.00
HOF50 Denis Savard 10.00 25.00
HOF51 Joe Sakic 12.00 30.00
HOF52 Pavel Bure 10.00 25.00
HOF53 Mike Gartner 8.00 20.00
HOF54 Mats Sundin 8.00 20.00

2013-14 Upper Deck Clear Cut Stoppers

CCS1 Dominik Hasek 10.00 25.00
CCS2 Grant Fuhr 10.00 25.00
CCS3 Tuukka Rask 10.00 25.00
CCS4 James Reimer 8.00 20.00
CCS5 Pekka Rinne 10.00 25.00
CCS6 Patrick Roy 20.00 50.00
CCS7 Carey Price 25.00 60.00
CCS8 Steve Mason 6.00 15.00
CCS9 Brian Elliott 6.00 15.00
CCS10 Semyon Varlamov 8.00 20.00
CCS11 Mike Smith 8.00 20.00
CCS12 Roberto Luongo 12.00 30.00
CCS13 Martin Brodeur 15.00 40.00
CCS14 Curtis Joseph 8.00 20.00
CCS15 Rogie Vachon 10.00 25.00
CCS16 Ryan Miller 8.00 20.00
CCS17 Viktor Fasth 5.00 12.00
CCS18 Ondrej Pavelec 8.00 20.00
CCS19 Craig Anderson 8.00 20.00
CCS20 Antti Niemi 6.00 15.00
CCS21 Ed Belfour 8.00 20.00
CCS22 Henrik Lundqvist 10.00 25.00
CCS23 Jim Howard 8.00 20.00
CCS24 Marc-Andre Fleury 12.00 30.00
CCS25 Evgeni Nabokov 6.00 15.00
CCS26 Kari Lehtonen 6.00 15.00
CCS27 Braden Holtby 12.00 30.00
CCS28 Corey Crawford 10.00 25.00
CCS29 Andy Moog 10.00 25.00
CCS30 Bill Ranford 8.00 20.00
CCS31 Jonas Hiller 6.00 15.00
CCS32 Jonathan Quick 12.00 30.00
CCS33 Jaroslav Halak 10.00 25
CCS34 Felix Potvin 12.00 30
CCS35 Niklas Backstrom 6.00 15
CCS36 Tomas Vokoun 6.00 15

2013-14 Upper Deck Day With The Cup

SER.1 ODDS 1:1000 H, 1:2500 R, 1:5000 BLST
SER.2 ODDS 1:1728 H, 1:4320 R, 1:8640 BLST
DC1 Nick Leddy 1 15.00 40
DC2 Ray Emery 2 20.00 50
DC3 Daniel Carcillo 1 15.00 40.
DC4 Ben Smith 2 20.00 50.
DC5 Andrew Shaw 1 25.00 60.
DC6 Jonathan Toews 1 50.00 100
DC7 Brandon Bollig 2 20.00 50
DC8 Dave Bolland 1 15.00 40.
DC9 Patrick Sharp 1 25.00 60
DC10 Michael Frolik 1 20.00 50
DC11 Michal Rozsival 2 15.00 40
DC12 Michal Handzus 1 15.00 40.
DC13 Marian Hossa 1 30.00 80.
DC14 Johnny Oduya 1 20.00 50.
DC15 Marcus Kruger 1 25.00 60.
DC16 Viktor Stalberg 1 15.00 40
DC17 Niklas Hjalmarsson 1 15.00 40
DC18 Jamal Mayers 2 15.00 40
DC19 Brandon Saad 1 20.00 50
DC20 Patrick Kane 1 60.00 100
DC21 Bryan Bickell 1 15.00 40
DC22 Ryan Stanton 2 20.00 50.
DC23 Sheldon Brookbank 2 15.00 40.
DC24 Brent Seabrook 1 25.00 60.
DC25 Duncan Keith 2 30.00 80.
DC26 Corey Crawford 1 30.00 80.

2013-14 Upper Deck Game Jerseys

GROUP 1A ODDS 1:3481 SER.1
GROUP 2A ODDS 1:1502 SER.2
GROUP 1B ODDS 1:2901 SER.1
GROUP 2B ODDS 1:126 SER.2
GROUP 1C ODDS 1:428 SER.1
GROUP 2C ODDS 1:65 SER.2
GROUP 1D ODDS 1:87 SER.1
GROUP 2D ODDS 1:57 SER.2
GROUP 1E ODDS 139 SER.1
GROUP 1F ODDS 1:23 SER.1
SER.1 OVERALL ODDS 1:12 HOB,1:24 RET
SER.2 OVERALL ODDS 1:24H,1:48R,1:480BL
GJAH Adam Henrique 1E 3.00 8.
GJAK Anze Kopitar 2C 5.00 12.
GJAL Adam Larsson 1D 3.00 8
GJAL Anders Lindback 2B 2.00 5.
GJAN Antti Niemi 2C 2.50 6
GJAO Alexander Ovechkin 1C 15.00 40
GJBD Brandon Dubinsky 1E 2.50 6
GJBH Brett Hull 2C 3.00 8
GJBL Brian Leetch 1F 3.00 8
GJBM Brad Marchand 1D 4.00 10
GJBN Bernie Nicholls 1F 2.50 6.
GJRB Ray Bourque 1E 5.00 12.
GJBR Bill Ranford 1F 3.00 8.
GJBS Borje Salming 1F 3.00 8.
GJBT Bryan Trottier 1F 4.00 10.
GJBY Dustin Byfuglien 1D 3.00 8
GJCA Craig Anderson 1D 3.00 8
GJCF Cam Fowler 2C 2.50 6.
GJCH Carl Hagelin 2D 3.00 8.
GJCJ Curtis Joseph 1F 3.00 8.
GJCL Claude Lemieux 1E 2.50 6.
GJCP Carey Price 1F 4.00 10.
GJCP Corey Perry 2B 3.00 8.
GJCS Chris Stewart 1F 2.50 6.
GJDC Dino Ciccarelli 1F 3.00 8.
GJDD Drew Doughty 2D 3.00 8.
GJDE David Desharnais 2B 3.00 8
GJDH Dale Hawerchuk 1F 4.00 10
GJDI Marcel Dionne 1F 5.00 12
GJDK Duncan Keith 1D 3.00 8
GJDP David Perron 2D 2.00 5
GJDS Derek Stepan 2B 3.00 8.
GJDU Dustin Brown 2C 3.00 8.
GJDW Doug Wilson 1F 2.50 6.
GJEB Ed Belfour 1F 3.00 8.
GJEK Evander Kane 1F 3.00 8.
GJEK Erik Karlsson 2C 6.00 15.
GJEL Eric Lindros 1A 30.00 60
GJES Eric Staal 1E 4.00 10
GJFA Justin Faulk 2D 2.00 5
GJGA Mathieu Garon 1E 2.50 6
GJGC Guy Carbonneau 1F 3.00 8
GJGF Grant Fuhr 2C 3.00 8
GJGL Gabriel Landeskog 2D 2.50 6.
GJGO Michel Goulet 1D 2.50 6.
GJGP Gilbert Perreault 1E 3.00 8.
GJGR Colin Greening 2B 2.50 6.
GJHA Dominik Hasek 1F 4.00 10
GJHE Ales Hemsky 1D 2.00 5
GJHL Henrik Lundqvist 2B 5.00 12
GJHS Scott Hartnell 1D 3.00 8.
GJHS Henrik Sedin 2A 40.00 80
GJIK Ilya Kovalchuk 1D 3.00 8
GJJB Jamie Benn 2C 4.00 10
GJJC Jeff Carter 1E 3.00 8.
GJJE Jordan Eberle 1E 3.00 8.
GJJF Johan Franzen 2C 3.00 8.
GJJG Jean-Sebastien Giguere 1D 2.50 6.
GJJH Jaroslav Halak 1D 3.00 8.
GJJH Jonas Hiller 2D 2.50 6
GJJJ Jaromir Jagr 1E 4.00 10
GJJK Jari Kurri 1E 4.00 10
GJJL Jacques Lemaire 1E 3.00 8
GJJM Joe Mullen 1F 2.50 6.
GJJQ Jonathan Quick 2C 5.00 12.
GJJS Joe Sakic 1C 8.00 20.
GJJS Jason Spezza 2B 3.00 8.
GJJT Joe Thornton D 3.00 8.
GJJV Jakub Voracek 1E 3.00 8.
GJKE Phil Kessel 2B 4.00 10
GJKY Keith Yandle 2C 3.00 8
GJLC Logan Couture 2D 3.00 8
GJLE Lars Eller 1E 2.50 6
GJLI Eric Lindros 1F 5.00 12.
GJLM Lanny McDonald 1F 3.00 8.
GJLR Larry Robinson 1D 3.00 8.
GJLR Luc Robitaille 2D 3.00 8.
GJLU Milan Lucic 1C 4.00 10.
GJMA Martin Brodeur AS 1C 8.00 20.
GJMB Martin Brodeur 1B 10.00 25
GJMD Matt Duchene 1E 3.00 8
GJMF Marc-Andre Fleury 1C 6.00 15
GJMH Michal Handzus 1E 2.00 5
GJML Mario Lemieux 1A 40.00 100
GJMM Mark Messier 1A 40.00 100
GJMN Michal Neuvirth 1D 2.50 6
GJMP Michael Peca 1F 2.50 6
GJMP Max Pacioretty 2C 3.00 8
GJMR1 Mike Richards 1F 3.00 8
GJMR2 Mike Richards 2B 3.00 8
GJMS Marc Staal 1D 2.50 6

JMS Matt Stajan 2A 12.00 30.00
JMW Mike Weber 1E 2.00 5.00
JNB Nicklas Backstrom 1E 5.00 12.00
JNF Nick Foligno 1E 2.50 6.00
JNL Nicklas Lidstrom 1F 3.00 8.00
JOE Oliver Ekman-Larsson 1E 2.50 6.00
JOP Ondrej Pavelec 1E 3.00 8.00
JPA Paul Coffey 2B 4.00 10.00
JPB Patrice Bergeron 1C 5.00 12.00
JPC Paul Coffey 1F 3.00 8.00
JPD Pavel Datsyuk 1D 4.00 10.00
JPF Peter Forsberg 1F 3.00 8.00
JPM Patrick Marleau 1B 6.00 15.00
JPR Patrick Roy 1A 50.00 100.00
JPS P.K. Subban 1C 6.00 15.00
JRF Ron Francis 1D 4.00 10.00
JRG Ryan Getzlaf 1F 5.00 12.00
JRI Pekka Rinne 1D 4.00 10.00
JRL Roberto Luongo 1F 3.00 8.00
JRO Robin Lehner 1D 3.00 8.00
JRY Ryan Miller 1F 3.00 8.00
JSC Brayden Schenn 1E 3.00 8.00
JSC Sidney Crosby 2A 20.00 50.00
JSD Shane Doan 2D 2.50 6.00
JSG Sam Gagner 1C 3.00 8.00
JSH Patrick Sharp 1C 4.00 10.00
JSL Martin St. Louis 2C 3.00 8.00
JST Jordan Staal 1F 3.00 8.00
JST Paul Stastny 2D 3.00 8.00
JSU Mats Sundin 2C 3.00 8.00
JSV Slava Voynov 2D 2.50 6.00
JSY Steve Yzerman 2C 6.00 15.00
JTA Taylor Hall 1E 6.00 15.00
JTE Tyler Ennis 2D 2.50 6.00
JTF Theoren Fleury 2B 4.00 10.00
JTH Jose Theodore 1F 3.00 8.00
JTM Tyler Myers 1E 2.50 6.00
JTO Jonathan Toews 1A 40.00 100.00
JTP Tomas Plekanec 2D 3.00 8.00
JTR Tuukka Rask 1D 3.00 8.00
JTV Thomas Vanek 1B 5.00 12.00
JVD Vincent Damphousse 2B 2.50 6.00
JWG Wayne Gretzky 1A 60.00 120.00
JWS Wayne Simmonds 2B 4.00 10.00
WJMS Mandi Schwartz 1F 50.00 100.00

2013-14 Upper Deck Hockey Heroes

OMP.SER 1 SET (14) 15.00 40.00
OMP. SER 1 w/o SPs (12) 6.00 15.00
H40-HH51 STATED ODDS 1:13 SER.1
H40-HH51 READ '12-13 UD SERIES 2 ON BACK
H53-HH64 STATED ODDS 1:12 SER.2
H65/HEADER2 ODDS 1:576 SER.2
H40 Wayne Gretzky 4.00 10.00
H41 Paul Coffey .75 2.00
H42 Mark Messier 1.00 2.50
H43 Grant Fuhr .75 2.00
H44 Jari Kurri .75 2.00
H45 Mike Bossy .75 2.00
H46 Mike Gartner .75 2.00
H47 Ray Bourque 1.25 3.00
H48 Patrick Roy 2.00 5.00
H49 Dale Hawerchuk 1.00 2.50
H50 Mario Lemieux 2.50 6.00
H51 Peter Stastny .60 1.50
H52 Bossy/Gretzky ART 8.00 20.00
H53 Wayne Gretzky 4.00 10.00
H54 Mats Sundin .75 2.00
H55 Joe Sakic 1.25 3.00
H56 Ed Belfour .75 2.00
H57 Steve Yzerman 1.50 4.00
H58 Dominik Hasek 1.00 2.50
H59 Patrick Roy 2.00 5.00
H60 Ron Francis 1.00 2.50
H61 Ray Bourque 1.25 3.00
H62 Mark Messier 1.00 2.50
H63 Mario Lemieux 2.50 6.00
H64 Jaromir Jagr 2.00 5.00
H65 M.Lemieux/P.Roy ART 10.00 25.00
EADER Header Card 1980s 8.00 20.00
EADER2 Header Card 1990s 10.00 25.00

2013-14 Upper Deck Hockey Heroes Autographs

H40 Wayne Gretzky/15 500.00 750.00
H41 Paul Coffey/15 75.00 150.00
H42 Mark Messier/15 100.00 200.00
H43 Grant Fuhr/15 60.00 120.00
H44 Jari Kurri/15 100.00 200.00
H45 Mike Bossy/15 60.00 120.00
H46 Mike Gartner/15 50.00 100.00
H47 Ray Bourque/15 60.00 120.00
H48 Patrick Roy/15 175.00 300.00
H49 Dale Hawerchuk/15 50.00 100.00
H50 Mario Lemieux/15 125.00 250.00
H53 Wayne Gretzky/15 300.00 500.00
H54 Mats Sundin/15
H55 Joe Sakic/15 100.00 200.00
H56 Ed Belfour/15
H57 Steve Yzerman/15 150.00 250.00
H58 Dominik Hasek/15
H59 Patrick Roy/15 150.00 250.00
H60 Ron Francis/15
H61 Ray Bourque/15
H62 Mark Messier /15
H63 Mario Lemieux /15
H64 Jaromir Jagr/15

2013-14 Upper Deck Lord Stanley's Futures

ATED ODDS 1:2880 SER.1 HOBBY
FAG Alex Galchenyuk 40.00 100.00
FBB Beau Bennett 15.00 40.00
FBG Brendan Gallagher 40.00 100.00
FCC Cory Conacher 8.00 20.00
FJH Jonathan Huberdeau 25.00 60.00
FJM J.T. Miller 12.00 30.00
FJS Justin Schultz 12.00 30.00
FJT Jarred Tinordi 12.00 30.00
FMG Mikael Granlund 20.00 50.00
FNB Nathan Beaulieu 10.00 25.00
FNY Nail Yakupov 40.00 100.00
FVT Vladimir Tarasenko 30.00 80.00

2013-14 Upper Deck Lord Stanley's Heroes

ATED ODDS 1:720 SER.1 HOBBY
H1 Alexander Ovechkin 20.00 50.00
H2 Pavel Bure 15.00 40.00
H3 Alexandre Burrows 12.00 30.00
H4 Roberto Luongo 12.00 30.00
H5 Daniel Sedin 12.00 30.00
H6 Henrik Sedin 12.00 30.00
H7 Mats Sundin 12.00 30.00
H8 Steven Stamkos 25.00 60.00
H9 Antti Niemi 10.00 25.00
H10 Mario Lemieux 30.00 80.00
H11 Evgeni Malkin 40.00 100.00
H12 Sidney Crosby 60.00 120.00
H13 Bobby Clarke 25.00 50.00
H14 Eric Lindros 20.00 50.00

LSH15 Mark Messier 15.00 40.00
LSH16 Ilya Kovalchuk 10.00 25.00
LSH17 Martin Brodeur 25.00 60.00
LSH18 Carey Price 40.00 100.00
LSH19 Patrick Roy 40.00 100.00
LSH20 Jeff Carter 12.00 30.00
LSH21 Drew Doughty 12.00 30.00
LSH22 Mike Richards 12.00 30.00
LSH23 Jonathan Quick 20.00 50.00
LSH24 Jari Kurri 12.00 30.00
LSH25 Jordan Eberle 12.00 30.00
LSH26 Ryan Nugent-Hopkins 12.00 30.00
LSH27 Wayne Gretzky 60.00 120.00
LSH28 Taylor Hall 25.00 60.00
LSH29 Nicklas Lidstrom 12.00 30.00
LSH30 Pavel Datsyuk 15.00 40.00
LSH31 Brett Hull 25.00 50.00
LSH32 Milan Hejduk 10.00 25.00
LSH33 Peter Forsberg 12.00 30.00
LSH34 Ray Bourque 20.00 50.00
LSH35 Joe Sakic 20.00 50.00
LSH36 Jonathan Toews 25.00 60.00
LSH37 Patrick Sharp 12.00 30.00
LSH38 Patrick Kane 25.00 60.00
LSH39 Theoren Fleury 15.00 40.00
LSH40 Patrice Bergeron 15.00 40.00
LSH41 Bobby Orr 40.00 100.00
LSH42 Milan Lucic 12.00 30.00
LSH43 Zdeno Chara 12.00 30.00
LSH44 Tyler Seguin 20.00 50.00
LSH45 Brad Marchand 15.00 40.00
LSH46 Jaromir Jagr 30.00 80.00
LSH47 Scott Niedermayer 12.00 30.00
LSH48 Teemu Selanne 25.00 60.00

2013-14 Upper Deck Oversized

ONE OVERSIZED CARD PER SER.2 TIN
7 Patrice Bergeron 1.50 4.00
19 John Tavares 2.50 6.00
43 Craig Anderson 1.25 3.00
62 Thomas Vanek 1.25 3.00
80 Sidney Crosby 5.00 12.00
92 Martin St. Louis 1.25 3.00
109 Shea Weber 1.00 2.50
113 Corey Crawford 1.50 4.00
117 Jonathan Toews 2.50 6.00
143 Evander Kane 1.25 3.00
147 Matt Duchene 1.25 3.00
161 Taylor Hall 2.50 6.00
182 Jonathan Quick 2.00 5.00
187 Logan Couture 1.25 3.00

2013-14 Upper Deck Rookie Breakouts

RANDOM INSERTS IN SER.2 PACKS
RB1 Hampus Lindholm 8.00 20.00
RB2 Dougie Hamilton 10.00 25.00
RB3 Ryan Murray 4.00 10.00
RB4 Aleksander Barkov 12.00 30.00
RB5 Olli Maatta 15.00 40.00
RB6 Elias Lindholm 8.00 20.00
RB7 Justin Fontaine 5.00 12.00
RB8 Alex Killorn 6.00 15.00
RB9 Morgan Rielly 12.00 30.00
RB10 Jonathan Huberdeau 12.00 30.00
RB11 Petr Mrazek 10.00 25.00
RB12 Rasmus Ristolainen 8.00 20.00
RB13 Alex Galchenyuk 25.00 60.00
RB14 Alex Chiasson 5.00 12.00
RB15 Danny DeKeyser 6.00 15.00
RB16 Sean Monahan 8.00 20.00
RB17 Nathan MacKinnon 50.00 100.00
RB18 Jacob Trouba 8.00 20.00
RB19 Michael Bournival 5.00 12.00
RB20 Boone Jenner 5.00 12.00
RB21 Seth Jones 5.00 12.00
RB22 Michael Latta 4.00 10.00
RB23 Mark Arcobello 5.00 12.00
RB24 Nail Yakupov 15.00 40.00
RB25 Matt Nieto 4.00 10.00
RB26 Valeri Nichushkin 12.00 30.00
RB27 Sami Vatanen 5.00 12.00
RB28 Tomas Hertl 6.00 15.00

2013-14 Upper Deck Rookie Materials

GROUP A ODDS 1:218
GROUP B ODDS 1:67
GROUP C ODDS 1:45
OVERALL ODDS 1:24H, 1:48R, 1:480 BL
*PATCH/25: 1X TO 2.5X BASIC JSY
RMAB Aleksander Barkov B 5.00 12.00
RMAC Alex Chiasson C 2.50 6.00
RMAG Alex Galchenyuk A 10.00 25.00
RMBB Beau Bennett C 4.00 10.00
RMBG Brendan Gallagher A 8.00 20.00
RMBJ Boone Jenner C 3.00 8.00
RMBN Brock Nelson C 2.50 6.00
RMCC Charlie Coyle B 2.50 6.00
RMCO Cory Conacher C 3.00 8.00
RMCT Christian Thomas C 2.00 5.00
RMDB Damien Brunner C 2.00 5.00
RMDH Dougie Hamilton A 5.00 12.00
RMEE Emerson Etem B 2.50 6.00
RMEL Elias Lindholm C 4.00 10.00
RMFF Filip Forsberg B 6.00 15.00
RMGR Mikhail Grigorenko A 3.00 8.00
RMHL Hampus Lindholm C 4.00 10.00
RMJF Jesper Fast C 2.00 5.00
RMJH Jonathan Huberdeau A 5.00 12.00
RMJS Justin Schultz B 2.50 6.00
RMJT Jacob Trouba C 4.00 10.00
RMLL Lucas Lessio C 1.50 4.00
RMMD Mathew Dumba C 2.50 6.00
RMMG Mikael Granlund B 4.00 10.00
RMMN Matt Nieto C 2.00 5.00
RMMR Morgan Rielly A 5.00 12.00
RMMU Ryan Murray A 4.00 10.00
RMNJ Nicklas Jensen B 3.00 8.00
RMNM Nathan MacKinnon B 8.00 20.00
RMNY Nail Yakupov A 8.00 20.00
RMOM Olli Maatta B 5.00 12.00
RMPM Petr Mrazek B 5.00 12.00
RMRM Ryan Murphy C 2.50 6.00
RMRR Rasmus Ristolainen C 4.00 10.00
RMSJ Seth Jones B 4.00 10.00
RMSM Sean Monahan B 6.00 15.00
RMTH Tomas Hertl B 8.00 20.00
RMJI Jarred Tinordi B 2.50 6.00
RMTP Tanner Pearson B 2.50 6.00
RMTT Tyler Toffoli B 5.00 12.00
RMTW Tom Wilson C 4.00 10.00
RMVF Viktor Fasth B 2.50 6.00
RMVN Valeri Nichushkin A 5.00 12.00
RMVT Vladimir Tarasenko A 6.00 15.00
RMZG Zemgus Girgensons C 4.00 10.00

2013-14 Upper Deck Shining Stars Centers

COMPLETE SET (10) 12.00 30.00
STATED ODDS 1:20 SERIES 1
*RAINBOW VET: 1.5X TO 4X BASIC INSERTS
*RAINBOW ROOK: 1.2X TO 3X BASIC INSERTS
C1 Pavel Datsyuk 1.50 4.00
C2 Jonathan Toews 2.50 6.00
C3 Ryan Nugent-Hopkins 1.25 3.00
C4 Alex Galchenyuk 2.50 6.00
C5 Jonathan Huberdeau 1.25 3.00
C6 John Tavares 2.50 6.00
C7 Evgeni Malkin 4.00 10.00
C8 Sidney Crosby 5.00 12.00
C9 Steven Stamkos 2.50 6.00
C10 Nazem Kadri 1.25 3.00

2013-14 Upper Deck Shining Stars Defense

STATED ODDS 1:24 BLASTER SER.1
D1 Ryan Suter 4.00 10.00
D2 Oliver Ekman-Larsson 5.00 12.00
D3 Erik Karlsson 12.00 30.00
D4 Shea Weber 5.00 12.00
D5 Duncan Keith 6.00 15.00
D6 Kris Letang 6.00 15.00
D7 Drew Doughty 6.00 15.00
D8 Niklas Kronwall 5.00 12.00
D9 Zdeno Chara 6.00 15.00
D10 P.K. Subban 10.00 25.00

2013-14 Upper Deck Shining Stars Goalies

SERIES 1 ODDS 1:6 FAT PACK, 1:12 TIN
*RAINBOW: 1X TO 2.5X BASIC INSERTS
G1 Jim Howard 2.50 6.00
G2 Henrik Lundqvist 3.00 8.00
G3 Jonathan Quick 4.00 10.00
G4 Carey Price 8.00 20.00
G5 Mike Smith 2.50 6.00
G6 Pekka Rinne 3.00 8.00
G7 Martin Brodeur 5.00 12.00
G8 Roberto Luongo 2.50 6.00
G9 Ondrej Pavelec 2.50 6.00
G10 Antti Niemi 2.00 5.00

2013-14 Upper Deck Shining Stars Left Wing

COMPLETE SET (10) 12.00 30.00
STATED ODDS 1:60 HOB/RET SERIES 1
*RAINBOW: 1X TO 2.5X BASIC INSERTS
LW1 Thomas Vanek 2.00 5.00
LW2 Evander Kane 2.00 5.00
LW3 James Neal 2.00 5.00
LW4 Daniel Sedin 2.00 5.00
LW5 Chris Kunitz 2.00 5.00
LW6 Rick Nash 2.00 5.00
LW7 Zach Parise 2.00 5.00
LW8 Taylor Hall 4.00 10.00
LW9 Brad Marchand 2.50 6.00
LW10 Milan Lucic 2.00 5.00

2013-14 Upper Deck Shining Stars Right Wing

COMPLETE SET (10) 12.00 30.00
STATED ODDS 1:60 HOB/RET SER.1
*RAINBOW: 1X TO 2.5X BASIC INSERTS
RW1 Ryan Callahan 2.00 5.00
RW2 Claude Giroux 2.00 5.00
RW3 Patrick Sharp 2.00 5.00
RW4 Patrick Kane 3.00 8.00
RW5 Corey Perry 2.00 5.00
RW6 Nail Yakupov 2.00 5.00
RW7 Jordan Eberle 2.00 5.00
RW8 Chris Stewart 1.50 4.00
RW9 Alexander Ovechkin 8.00 20.00
RW10 Alexandre Burrows 2.00 5.00

2013-14 Upper Deck Signatures

UNPRICED GRP A ODDS 1:12,501
UNPRICED GRP B ODDS 1:6,580
GROUP C ODDS 1:1,701
GROUP D ODDS 1:521
UDSAB Alexander Burmistrov C
UDSAH Adam Henrique C
UDSAS Andrew Shaw D 8.00 20.00
UDSBD Brandon Dubinsky C
UDSBO Bobby Orr B 90.00 150.00
UDSCA Cam Atkinson D 6.00 15.00
UDSCE Cody Eakin D 4.00 10.00
UDSCK Chris Kreider D 6.00 15.00
UDSCN Cam Neely A
UDSCO Cal O'Reilly D 4.00 10.00
UDSCS Cory Schneider D 5.00 12.00
UDSDR Derek Roy D 5.00 12.00
UDSFP Felix Potvin C 15.00 30.00
UDSGL Gabriel Landeskog B
UDSGM Glen Murray B 6.00 15.00
UDSJR James van Riemsdyk A 20.00 50.00
UDSLC Logan Couture C 8.00 20.00
UDSLR Luc Robitaille A
UDSMG Marian Gaborik A
UDSMR Mike Richards C 8.00 20.00
UDSPR Pekka Rinne D 8.00 20.00
UDSST Peter Stastny A 8.00 20.00
UDSSW Shea Weber A 15.00 40.00
UDSWG Wayne Gretzky B 75.00 150.00

2013-14 Upper Deck Signature Sensations

UNPRICED GRP A ODDS 1:13,562
UNPRICED GRP B ODDS 1:5738
GROUP C ODDS 1:1421
GROUP D ODDS 1:1194
GROUP E ODDS 1:563
OVERALL ODDS 1:288 SERIES 1
SSAE Alexei Emelin E 5.00 12.00
SSAK Arturs Kulda E 4.00 10.00
SSAL Anders Lindback E 4.00 10.00
SSAO Alexander Ovechkin A 30.00 60.00
SSAP Alex Pietrangelo A 15.00 40.00
SSAS Alex Stalock D 6.00 15.00
SSBO Bobby Orr A 100.00 175.00
SSBP Brandon Prust C 4.00 10.00
SSBS Brandon Sutter D 5.00 12.00
SSBU Alexander Burmistrov B
SSCF Cam Fowler C 5.00 12.00
SSCG Colin Greening E 5.00 12.00
SSCJ Joe Colborne D 4.00 10.00
SSDE Alex Delvecchio B
SSDP Daniel Paille E 6.00 15.00
SSEL Lars Eller C 6.00 15.00
SSGC Grant Clitsome E 4.00 10.00
SSGL Guillaume Latendresse A
SSHA Scott Hartnell B 8.00 20.00
SSJE Jonathan Ericsson A
SSJF Justin Faulk C 4.00 10.00
SSJH Jonas Hiller E 5.00 12.00
SSJI Jiri Tlusty B
SSJM Jacob Markstrom C 5.00 12.00
SSJR Jay Rosehill A
SSKP Kyle Palmieri E 5.00 12.00
SSLA Anton Lander C 4.00 10.00
SSLB Lance Bouma D 4.00 10.00
SSMD Michael Del Zotto B 6.00 15.00
SSMG Michael Grabner D 5.00 12.00
SSMH Martin Hanzal E 4.00 10.00
SSMK Marcus Kruger D 6.00 15.00
SSMM Mark Messier A
SSMO Jeremy Morin C 5.00 12.00
SSMR Matt Read E 4.00 10.00
SSMS Michael Sauer E 4.00 10.00
SSMT Maxime Talbot D 5.00 12.00
SSMZ Mats Zuccarello-Aasen D 6.00 15.00
SSNF Nick Foligno B
SSNL Nick Leddy C 6.00 15.00
SSPB Patrik Berglund C 4.00 10.00
SSPS Paul Stastny A
SSRD Raphael Diaz C 4.00 10.00
SSRT Raffi Torres D 6.00 15.00
SSSB Sergei Bobrovsky B 6.00 15.00
SSSC Sidney Crosby A
SSSH Andrew Shaw C 6.00 15.00
SSTA John Tavares A
SSTB Tyler Bozak C 5.00 12.00
SSTL Trevor Lewis C 4.00 10.00
SSTO T.J. Oshie C 10.00 25.00
SSTR Tuukka Rask B 12.50 25.00
SSTV Tomas Vokoun D 5.00 12.00
SSVA Thomas Vanek B 6.00 15.00
SSVV Slava Voynov E 5.00 12.00
SSWG Wayne Gretzky A 150.00 300.00
SSZD Zac Dalpe E 4.00 10.00
SSZK Zenon Konopka B 8.00 20.00

2013-14 Upper Deck Young Guns Acetate

RANDOM INSERTS IN SERIES 2
201 Carl Soderberg 20.00 50.00
202 Dougie Hamilton 50.00 100.00
203 Alex Galchenyuk 175.00 300.00
204 Brock Nelson 20.00 50.00
205 J.T. Miller 20.00 50.00
206 Jesper Fast 15.00 40.00
207 Nathan Beaulieu 15.00 40.00
208 Damien Brunner 15.00 40.00
209 Jean-Gabriel Pageau 15.00 40.00
210 Cory Conacher 12.00 30.00
211 Connor Carrick 15.00 40.00
212 Tom Wilson 30.00 80.00
213 Michael Latta 15.00 40.00
214 Ryan Murphy 25.00 60.00
215 Mikhail Grigorenko 25.00 60.00
216 Zemgus Girgensons 50.00 100.00
217 Rasmus Ristolainen 30.00 80.00
218 Morgan Rielly 60.00 120.00
219 Beau Bennett 40.00 80.00
220 Olli Maatta 75.00 150.00
221 Drew Shore 15.00 40.00
222 Jonathan Huberdeau 60.00 120.00
223 Alex Killorn 20.00 50.00
224 Richard Panik 20.00 50.00
225 Boone Jenner 20.00 50.00
226 Ryan Murray 30.00 80.00
227 Danny DeKeyser 25.00 60.00
228 Seth Jones 40.00 80.00
229 Joakim Nordstrom 15.00 40.00
230 Vladimir Tarasenko 175.00 300.00
231 Mathew Dumba 25.00 60.00
232 Justin Fontaine 20.00 50.00
233 Charlie Coyle 20.00 50.00
234 Jonas Brodin 15.00 40.00
235 Alex Chiasson 20.00 50.00
236 Valeri Nichushkin 75.00 150.00
237 Jacob Trouba 100.00 200.00
238 Nathan MacKinnon 300.00 500.00
239 Lucas Lessio 12.00 30.00
240 Justin Schultz 20.00 50.00
241 Nail Yakupov 100.00 175.00
242 Sean Monahan 75.00 150.00
243 Sami Vatanen 20.00 50.00
244 Viktor Fasth 20.00 50.00
245 Emerson Etem 20.00 50.00
246 Tyler Toffoli 40.00 80.00
247 Matt Nieto 15.00 40.00
248 Tomas Hertl 125.00 200.00
249 Nicklas Jensen 15.00 40.00
451 Filip Forsberg 50.00 125.00
452 Dylan McIlrath 12.00 30.00
453 Michael Bournival 20.00 50.00
454 Michael Sgarbossa 15.00 40.00
455 Martin Marincin 15.00 40.00
456 Ryan Spooner 20.00 50.00
457 Mark Pysyk 20.00 50.00
458 Freddie Hamilton 20.00 50.00
459 Joacim Eriksson 20.00 50.00
460 Christian Thomas 15.00 40.00
461 Reto Berra 20.00 50.00
462 Frederik Andersen 30.00 80.00
463 Mark Arcobello 20.00 50.00
464 Jon Merrill 20.00 50.00
465 Linden Vey 12.00 30.00
466 Petr Mrazek 40.00 100.00
467 Philipp Grubauer 20.00 50.00
468 Marek Mazanec 20.00 50.00
469 Elias Lindholm 30.00 80.00
470 Aleksander Barkov 50.00 125.00
471 Nikita Zadorov 20.00 50.00
472 Taylor Beck 15.00 40.00
473 Jack Campbell 15.00 40.00
474 Mikael Granlund 30.00 80.00
475 Cody Ceci 15.00 40.00
476 Tomas Jurco 30.00 80.00
477 Brendan Gallagher 125.00 200.00
478 Jarred Tinordi 20.00 50.00
479 Josh Leivo 20.00 50.00
480 Rickard Rakell 20.00 50.00
481 Ondrej Palat 25.00 60.00
482 Ryan Strome 75.00 150.00
483 Nikita Kucherov 125.00 200.00
484 Reid Boucher 20.00 50.00
485 Martin Jones 50.00 125.00
486 John Gibson 60.00 150.00
487 Antti Raanta 25.00 60.00
488 Nick Bjugstad 30.00 80.00
489 Scott Laughton 20.00 50.00
490 Antoine Roussel 20.00 50.00
491 Thomas Hickey 15.00 40.00
492 Tyler Johnson 50.00 125.00
493 Connor Murphy 15.00 40.00
494 Max Reinhart 20.00 50.00
495 Jordan Schroeder 20.00 50.00
496 Matthew Irwin 15.00 40.00
497 Jerry D'Amigo 20.00 50.00
498 Tanner Pearson 40.00 80.00
499 Hampus Lindholm 30.00 80.00

2013-14 Upper Deck Young Guns Oversized

ONE PER SPECIAL BLASTER BOX
202 Dougie Hamilton 3.00 8.00
203 Alex Galchenyuk 8.00 20.00
215 Mikhail Grigorenko 2.00 5.00
222 Jonathan Huberdeau 4.00 10.00
225 Boone Jenner 1.50 4.00
226 Ryan Murray 2.50 6.00
228 Seth Jones 1.50 4.00
230 Vladimir Tarasenko 6.00 15.00
233 Charlie Coyle 1.50 4.00
236 Valeri Nichushkin 1.50 4.00
237 Jacob Trouba 2.50 6.00
238 Nathan MacKinnon 12.00 30.00
240 Justin Schultz 1.50 4.00
242 Sean Monahan 2.50 6.00

2014-15 Upper Deck

COMPLETE SET (250) 175.00 300.00
COMP.SET w/o RC's (200) 12.00 30.00
201-250 YOUNG GUN ODDS 1:4 SER.1
451-500 YOUNG GUN ODDS 1:4 SER.2
501-530 INSERTED IN 2014-15 SP AUTHENTIC
1 Ryan Getzlaf .50 1.25
2 Cam Fowler .25 .60
3 Andrew Cogliano .20 .50
4 Kyle Palmieri .25 .60
5 Jakob Silfverberg .25 .60
6 Hampus Lindholm .25 .60
7 John Gibson .40 1.00
8 Lauri Korpikoski .20 .50
9 Shane Doan .25 .60
10 Antoine Vermette .20 .50
11 Martin Hanzal .20 .50
12 Rob Klinkhammer .20 .50
13 Mike Smith .30 .75
14 Milan Lucic .30 .75
15 Brad Marchand .40 1.00
16 Carl Soderberg .30 .75
17 Torey Krug .30 .75
18 Dougie Hamilton .30 .75
19 Dennis Seidenberg .25 .60
20 David Krejci .30 .75
21 Tyler Ennis .25 .60
22 Zemgus Girgensons .30 .75
23 Tyler Myers .25 .60
24 Marcus Foligno .20 .50
25 Jhonas Enroth .30 .75
26 Mark Giordano .25 .60
27 Jiri Hudler .25 .60
28 Sean Monahan .30 .75
29 T.J. Brodie .20 .50
30 Joe Colborne .20 .50
31 Curtis Glencross .20 .50
32 Jeff Skinner .30 .75
33 Alexander Semin .30 .75
34 Justin Faulk .20 .50
35 Jiri Tlusty .25 .60
36 Anton Khudobin .25 .60
37 Patrick Sharp .30 .75
38 Jonathan Toews .60 1.50
39 Marian Hossa .25 .60
40 Brent Seabrook .30 .75
41 Kris Versteeg .25 .60
42 Marcus Kruger .30 .75
43 Ben Smith .25 .60
44 Corey Crawford .40 1.00
45 Matt Duchene .30 .75
46 Ryan O'Reilly .30 .75
47 Nathan MacKinnon .60 1.50
48 Jamie McGinn .20 .50
49 Erik Johnson .20 .50
50 Nate Guenin .20 .50
51 Semyon Varlamov .30 .75
52 Ryan Johansen .40 1.00
53 Brandon Dubinsky .25 .60
54 Nick Foligno .25 .60
55 Mark Letestu .25 .60
56 Jack Johnson .20 .50
57 Sergei Bobrovsky .30 .75
58 Tyler Seguin .50 1.25
59 Alex Goligoski .20 .50
60 Cody Eakin .20 .50
61 Ryan Garbutt .20 .50
62 Rich Peverley .30 .75
63 Vernon Fiddler .20 .50
64 Erik Cole .25 .60
65 Shawn Horcoff .20 .50
66 Colton Sceviour .20 .50
67 Niklas Kronwall .25 .60
68 Henrik Zetterberg .40 1.00
69 Johan Franzen .30 .75
70 Pavel Datsyuk .40 1.00
71 Danny DeKeyser .25 .60
72 Jim Howard .30 .75
73 Ben Scrivens .25 .60
74 Jordan Eberle .30 .75
75 Ryan Nugent-Hopkins .30 .75
76 Justin Schultz .25 .60
77 Jeff Petry .20 .50
78 Andrew Ference .20 .50
79 Anton Belov .30 .75
80 Brian Campbell .20 .50
81 Brad Boyes .20 .50
82 Tomas Fleischmann .20 .50
83 Aleksander Barkov .30 .75
84 Nick Bjugstad .25 .60
85 Erik Gudbranson .30 .75
86 Mike Richards .30 .75
87 Slava Voynov .30 .75
88 Dwight King .20 .50
89 Jarret Stoll .25 .60
90 Jonathan Quick .50 1.25
91 Tanner Pearson .20 .50
92 Jeff Carter .30 .75
93 Ryan Suter .30 .75
94 Nino Niederreiter .20 .50
95 Matt Cooke .20 .50
96 Zach Parise .30 .75
97 Jonas Brodin .20 .50
98 Jared Spurgeon .20 .50
99 Darcy Kuemper .25 .60
100 Carey Price 1.00 2.50
101 Max Pacioretty .30 .75
102 David Desharnais .30 .75
103 Andrei Markov .30 .75
104 Brendan Gallagher .30 .75
105 Alex Galchenyuk .50 1.25
106 Michael Bournival .25 .60
107 Ryan Ellis .20 .50
108 Carter Hutton .30 .75
109 Mike Fisher .25 .60
110 Matt Cullen .20 .50
111 Roman Josi .30 .75
112 Seth Jones .25 .60
113 Pekka Rinne .40 1.00
114 Filip Forsberg .40 1.00
115 Cory Schneider .25 .60
116 Jaromir Jagr .75 2.00
117 Travis Zajac .25 .60
118 Marek Zidlicky .20 .50
119 Eric Gelinas .25 .60
120 Damien Brunner .20 .50
121 Travis Hamonic .20 .50
122 John Tavares .60 1.50
123 Josh Bailey .25 .60
124 Brock Nelson .25 .60
125 Cal Clutterbuck .30 .75
126 Thomas Hickey .20 .50
127 Martin St. Louis .30 .75
128 Derek Stepan .30 .75
129 Derick Brassard .30 .75
130 Rick Nash .30 .75
131 Ryan McDonagh .30 .75
132 Henrik Lundqvist .40 1.00
133 Erik Karlsson .60 1.50
134 Kyle Turris .30 .75
135 Bobby Ryan .30 .75
136 Milan Michalek .20 .50
137 Patrick Wiercioch .20 .50
138 Craig Anderson .30 .75
139 Claude Giroux .30 .75
140 Wayne Simmonds .40 1.00
141 Mark Streit .20 .50
142 Matt Read .20 .50
143 Vincent Lecavalier .25 .60
144 Andrew MacDonald .20 .50
145 Ray Emery .25 .60
146 Evgeni Malkin 1.00 2.50
147 Pascal Dupuis .20 .50
148 Chris Kunitz .30 .75
149 Olli Maatta .30 .75
150 Kris Letang .30 .75
151 Paul Martin .20 .50
152 Jeff Zatkoff .25 .60
153 Joe Pavelski .30 .75
154 Logan Couture .30 .75
155 Tommy Wingels .20 .50
156 Jason Demers .20 .50
157 Marc-Edouard Vlasic .20 .50
158 Matt Nieto .25 .60
159 Matt Irwin .20 .50
160 Alex Stalock .25 .60
161 T.J. Oshie .50 1.25
162 Jaden Schwartz .40 1.00
163 Kevin Shattenkirk .30 .75
164 Jay Bouwmeester .30 .75
165 Vladimir Sobotka .20 .50
166 Vladimir Tarasenko .50 1.25
167 Barret Jackman .20 .50
168 Brian Elliott .25 .60
169 Steven Stamkos .60 1.50
170 Valtteri Filppula .30 .75
171 Tyler Johnson .30 .75
172 Alex Killorn .25 .60
173 Matt Carle .20 .50
174 Radko Gudas .20 .50
175 Ondrej Palat .25 .60
176 James van Riemsdyk .30 .75
177 Tyler Bozak .25 .60
178 Joffrey Lupul .25 .60
179 Dion Phaneuf .30 .75
180 Morgan Rielly .30 .75
181 Jonathan Bernier .30 .75
182 David Clarkson .20 .50
183 Daniel Sedin .30 .75
184 Chris Higgins .20 .50
185 Zack Kassian .25 .60
186 Kevin Bieksa .25 .60
187 Alexander Edler .20 .50
188 Eddie Lack .25 .60
189 Alexander Ovechkin 1.25 3.00
190 Joel Ward .20 .50
191 Troy Brouwer .25 .60
192 Mike Green .30 .75
193 John Carlson .40 1.00
194 Blake Wheeler .30 .75
195 Dustin Byfuglien .30 .75
196 Mark Scheifele .40 1.00
197 Jacob Trouba .25 .60
198 Evander Kane .30 .75
199 Quick/Kopitar/Gaborik CL .50 1.25
200 Lundqvist/Nash/St. Louis CL .40 1.00
201 William Karlsson YG RC 10.00 25.00
202 Brandon Gormley YG RC 2.50 6.00
203 Mark Visentin YG RC 2.50 6.00
204 Alexander Khokhlachev YG RC 2.50 6.00
205 Bobby Robins YG RC 2.00 5.00
206 Sam Reinhart YG RC 8.00 20.00
207 Nicolas Deslauriers YG RC 2.50 6.00
208 Jake McCabe YG RC 2.50 6.00
209 Corban Knight YG RC 2.50 6.00
210 Tyler Wotherspoon YG RC 2.50 6.00
211 Johnny Gaudreau YG RC 25.00 60.00
212 Victor Rask YG RC 2.50 6.00
213 Patrick Brown YG RC 2.50 6.00
214 Teuvo Teravainen YG RC 6.00 15.00
215 Trevor van Riemsdyk YG RC 4.00 10.00
216 Joey Hishon YG RC 3.00 8.00
217 Dennis Everberg YG RC 2.50 6.00
218 Alexander Wennberg YG RC 5.00 12.00
219 Patrik Nemeth YG RC 2.50 6.00
220 Ryan Sproul YG RC 2.50 6.00
221 Teemu Pulkkinen YG RC 3.00 8.00
222 Andrej Nestrasil YG RC 2.50 6.00
223 Leon Draisaitl YG RC 25.00 60.00
224 Oscar Klefbom YG RC 8.00 20.00
225 Aaron Ekblad YG RC 8.00 20.00
226 Vincent Trocheck YG RC 5.00 12.00
227 Jonathan Racine YG RC 2.50 6.00
228 Christian Folin YG RC 2.50 6.00
229 Jiri Sekac YG RC 2.50 6.00
230 Calle Jarnkrok YG RC 2.50 6.00
231 Colton Sissons YG RC 2.50 6.00
232 Damon Severson YG RC 2.50 6.00
233 Griffin Reinhart YG RC 3.00 8.00
234 Scott Mayfield YG RC 2.00 5.00
235 Johan Sundstrom YG RC 2.50 6.00
236 Anthony Duclair YG RC 5.00 12.00
237 Curtis Lazar YG RC 3.00 8.00
238 Pierre-Edouard Bellemare YG RC 2.50 6.00
239 Adam Payerl YG RC 2.00 5.00
240 Chris Tierney YG RC 2.50 6.00
241 Jori Lehtera YG RC 3.00 8.00
242 Ty Rattie YG RC 3.00 8.00
243 Vladislav Namestnikov YG RC 4.00 10.00
244 Brandon Kozun YG RC 2.00 5.00
245 Stuart Percy YG RC 2.50 6.00
246 Greg McKegg YG RC 2.00 5.00
247 Michael Zalewski YG RC 2.00 5.00
248 Evgeny Kuznetsov YG RC 15.00 40.00
249 Adam Lowry YG RC 2.50 6.00
250 Ekblad/Reinhart/Draisaitl YG CL 4.00 10.00
251 Ryan Kesler .30 .75
252 Frederik Andersen .25 .60
253 Devante Smith-Pelly .25 .60
254 Corey Perry .30 .75
255 Emerson Etem .25 .60
256 Pat Maroon .20 .50
257 Sami Vatanen .20 .50
258 Mikkel Boedker .20 .50
259 Sam Gagner .25 .60
260 Martin Erat .20 .50
261 Keith Yandle .30 .75
262 Oliver Ekman-Larsson .25 .60
263 Michael Stone .20 .50
264 Loui Eriksson .25 .60
265 Patrice Bergeron .40 1.00
266 Daniel Paille .20 .50
267 Zdeno Chara .30 .75
268 Tuukka Rask .30 .75
269 Ryan Spooner .25 .60
270 Brian Gionta .25 .60
271 Drew Stafford .30 .75
272 Michal Neuvirth .25 .60
273 Chris Stewart .25 .60
274 Cody Hodgson .30 .75
275 Matt Moulson .25 .60
276 Jonas Hiller .25 .60
277 Dennis Wideman .20 .50
278 Matt Stajan .25 .60
279 Sven Baertschi .20 .50
280 Devin Setoguchi .25 .60
281 Mason Raymond .25 .60
282 Elias Lindholm .30 .75
283 Cam Ward .30 .75
284 Ryan Murphy .20 .50
285 Eric Staal .40 1.00
286 Jordan Staal .30 .75
287 Andrew Shaw .30 .75
288 Antti Raanta .30 .75
289 Patrick Kane .60 1.50
290 Brad Richards .30 .75
291 Bryan Bickell .20 .50
292 Duncan Keith .30 .75
293 Niklas Hjalmarsson .20 .50
294 John Mitchell .20 .50
295 Alex Tanguay .20 .50
296 Daniel Briere .25 .60
297 Jarome Iginla .30 .75
298 Reto Berra .25 .60
299 Gabriel Landeskog .25 .60
300 Tyson Barrie .30 .75
301 Cam Atkinson .30 .75
302 Scott Hartnell .30 .75
303 Curtis McElhinney .25 .60
304 David Savard .20 .50
305 James Wisniewski .20 .50
306 Jared Boll .20 .50
307 Antoine Roussel .20 .50
308 Jordie Benn .20 .50
309 Jason Spezza .30 .75
310 Trevor Daley .20 .50
311 Kari Lehtonen .25 .60
312 Jamie Benn .40 1.00
313 Valeri Nichushkin .25 .60
314 Ales Hemsky .20 .50
315 Tomas Jurco .30 .75
316 Justin Abdelkader .25 .60
317 Tomas Tatar .25 .60
318 Jonas Gustavsson .25 .60
319 Gustav Nyquist .25 .60
320 Riley Sheahan .30 .75
321 Darren Helm .25 .60
322 Benoit Pouliot .20 .50
323 Viktor Fasth .25 .60
324 Nail Yakupov .25 .60
325 Teddy Purcell .30 .75
326 Boyd Gordon .20 .50
327 David Perron .20 .50
328 Taylor Hall .60 1.50
329 Sean Bergenheim .20 .50
330 Jonathan Huberdeau .30 .75
331 Willie Mitchell .20 .50
332 Jussi Jokinen .20 .50
333 Roberto Luongo .30 .75
334 Dave Bolland .20 .50
335 Justin Williams .25 .60
336 Dustin Brown .25 .60
337 Tyler Toffoli .30 .75
338 Drew Doughty .30 .75
339 Alec Martinez .20 .50
340 Marian Gaborik .30 .75
341 Anze Kopitar .50 1.25
342 Charlie Coyle .25 .60
343 Niklas Backstrom .25 .60
344 Mikael Granlund .25 .60
345 Erik Haula .25 .60
346 Mikko Koivu .25 .60
347 Thomas Vanek .30 .75
348 Mathew Dumba .25 .60
349 Alexei Emelin .25 .60
350 Tomas Plekanec .30 .75
351 P.K. Subban .50 1.25
352 P.A. Parenteau .20 .50
353 Lars Eller .25 .60
354 Nathan Beaulieu .25 .60
355 Dustin Tokarski .20 .50
356 Shea Weber .25 .60
357 Derek Roy .25 .60
358 Mike Ribeiro .25 .60
359 Colin Wilson .20 .50
360 James Neal .30 .75
361 Craig Smith .20 .50
362 Bryce Salvador .20 .50
363 Stephen Gionta .20 .50
364 Martin Havlat .25 .60
365 Patrik Elias .30 .75
366 Michael Cammalleri .25 .60
367 Adam Henrique .30 .75
368 Andy Greene .20 .50
369 Nick Leddy .20 .50
370 Nikolai Kulemin .25 .60
371 Frans Nielsen .20 .50
372 Jaroslav Halak .25 .60
373 Kyle Okposo .30 .75
374 Ryan Strome .25 .60
375 Johnny Boychuk .20 .50
376 Mikhail Grabovski .25 .60
377 Daniel Girardi .20 .50
378 Chris Kreider .30 .75
379 Lee Stempniak .20 .50
380 Carl Hagelin .30 .75
381 Marc Staal .25 .60
382 Mats Zuccarello .30 .75
383 Alex Chiasson .25 .60
384 Clarke MacArthur .20 .50
385 Mika Zibanejad .30 .75
386 Robin Lehner .25 .60
387 Chris Neil .20 .50
388 David Legwand .25 .60
389 Brayden Schenn .30 .75
390 Michael Del Zotto .20 .50
391 Sean Couturier .30 .75
392 Luke Schenn .20 .50
393 Steve Mason .25 .60
394 R.J. Umberger .20 .50
395 Jakub Voracek .30 .75
396 Marc-Andre Fleury .50 1.25
397 Beau Bennett .20 .50
398 Sidney Crosby 1.25 3.00
399 Brandon Sutter .25 .60
400 Christian Ehrhoff .20 .50
401 Patric Hornqvist .25 .60
402 Thomas Greiss .25 .60
403 Brent Burns .40 1.00
404 Patrick Marleau .30 .75
405 Antti Niemi .25 .60
406 Tomas Hertl .30 .75
407 Joe Thornton .30 .75
408 Justin Braun .20 .50
409 Alexander Steen .30 .75
410 David Backes .30 .75
411 Patrik Berglund .20 .50

412 Dmitrij Jaskin .25 .60
413 Jake Allen .40 1.00
414 Alex Pietrangelo .25 .60
415 Paul Stastny .30 .75
416 Martin Brodeur .60 1.50
417 Ben Bishop .30 .75
418 J.T. Brown .20 .50
419 Brenden Morrow .25 .60
420 Evgeni Nabokov .25 .60
421 Victor Hedman .40 1.00
422 Ryan Callahan .30 .75
423 Anton Stralman .20 .50
424 Leo Komarov .30 .75
425 James Reimer .30 .75
426 Jake Gardiner .30 .75
427 Phil Kessel .40 1.00
428 Peter Holland .20 .50
429 Nazem Kadri .30 .75
430 Cody Franson .20 .50
431 Henrik Sedin .30 .75
432 Ryan Miller .30 .75
433 Radim Vrbata .25 .60
434 Luca Sbisa .25 .60
435 Nick Bonino .20 .50
436 Alexandre Burrows .30 .75
437 Matt Niskanen .25 .60
438 Braden Holtby .50 1.25
439 Brooks Orpik .25 .60
440 Marcus Johansson .25 .60
441 Nicklas Backstrom .50 1.25
442 Brooks Laich .20 .50
443 Andrew Ladd .30 .75
444 Bryan Little .30 .75
445 Ondrej Pavelec .30 .75
446 Tobias Enstrom .20 .50
447 Zach Bogosian .25 .60
448 Mathieu Perreault .20 .50
449 Price/Subban/Pacioretty CL 1.00 2.50
450 T.Hall/RNH/Eberle CL .60 1.50
451 Joe Morrow YG RC 3.00 8.00
452 Marko Dano YG RC 2.50 6.00
453 Markus Granlund YG RC 4.00 10.00
454 Rob Zepp YG RC 4.00 10.00
455 Tobias Rieder YG RC 2.50 6.00
456 Scott Harrington YG RC 2.50 6.00
457 Darnell Nurse YG RC 10.00 25.00
458 Laurent Brossoit YG RC 2.50 6.00
459 Colin Smith YG RC 2.50 6.00
460 Joel Armia YG RC 2.50 6.00
461 Jyrki Jokipakka YG RC 2.50 6.00
462 Phillip Danault YG RC 2.50 6.00
463 Cedric Paquette YG RC 2.50 6.00
464 Shayne Gostisbehere YG RC 12.00 30.00
465 Joni Ortio YG RC 3.00 8.00
466 Scott Wilson YG RC 2.00 5.00
467 Andre Burakovsky YG RC 4.00 10.00
468 Melker Karlsson YG RC 2.50 6.00
469 Jordan Binnington YG RC 2.50 6.00
470 Bogdan Yakimov YG RC 2.50 6.00
471 Seth Griffith YG RC 3.00 8.00
472 Seth Helgeson YG RC 2.00 5.00
473 Brendan Shinnimin YG RC 2.00 5.00
474 Borna Rendulic YG RC 2.50 6.00
475 Derrick Pouliot YG RC 3.00 8.00
476 John Klingberg YG RC 12.00 30.00
477 Jonathan Drouin YG RC 40.00 100.00
478 Andrei Vasilevskiy YG RC 25.00 60.00
479 Andrew Agozzino YG RC 2.00 5.00
480 Petteri Lindbohm YG RC 2.00 5.00
481 Adam Clendening YG RC 2.50 6.00
482 Curtis McKenzie YG RC 2.00 5.00
483 Christopher Gibson YG RC 4.00 10.00
484 Mirco Mueller YG RC 2.50 6.00
485 Barclay Goodrow YG RC 2.50 6.00
486 Anton Forsberg YG RC 2.50 6.00
487 Max Friberg YG RC 2.00 5.00
488 Josh Jooris YG RC 2.50 6.00
489 Tyler Graovac YG RC 2.00 5.00
490 Kevin Hayes YG RC 8.00 20.00
491 Chris Wagner YG RC 2.50 6.00
492 Andy Andreoff YG RC 2.50 6.00
493 Sven Andrighetto YG RC 3.00 8.00
494 Bo Horvat YG RC 30.00 80.00
495 David Pastrnak YG RC 40.00 100.00
496 Brett Ritchie YG RC 2.50 6.00
497 Dominik Uher YG RC 2.00 5.00
498 Scott Darling YG RC 8.00 20.00
499 Kerby Rychel YG RC 2.00 5.00
500 Drouin/Pouliot/Horvat YG CL 4.00 10.00
501 Brandon Saad .30 .75
502 Niklas Svedberg .30 .75
503 Mike Santorelli .20 .50
504 Steve Downie .20 .50
505 Michael Hutchinson .30 .75
506 Anders Lee .30 .75
507 Nikita Kucherov .50 1.25
508 Reilly Smith .30 .75
509 Jason Zucker .25 .60
510 Matt Beleskey .20 .50
511 Antoine Vermette .20 .50
512 Jaromir Jagr .75 2.00
513 Zach Bogosian .25 .60
514 David Perron .20 .50
515 Devan Dubnyk .30 .75
516 Derek Roy .25 .60
517 Tyler Myers .25 .60
518 Drew Stafford .30 .75
519 Devante Smith-Pelly .25 .60
520 Keith Yandle .30 .75
521 Jesse Blacker YG RC 3.00 8.00
522 Julien Brouillette YG RC 2.00 5.00
523 Miikka Salomaki YG RC 2.00 5.00
524 Adam Clendening YG 2.00 5.00
525 Nikita Nesterov YG RC 2.00 5.00
526 Jiri Sekac YG 2.00 5.00
527 Tyler Gaudet YG RC 1.50 4.00
528 Andrew Hammond YG RC 6.00 15.00
529 Rocco Grimaldi YG RC 2.00 5.00
530 Anthony Duclair YG 3.00 8.00
JB Jean Beliveau Tribute 25.00 60.00

2014-15 Upper Deck Exclusives

*1-200 VETS/100: 6X TO 15X BASIC CARDS
*201-250 YG/100: 1.5X TO 4X BASIC RC
501-530 INSERTED IN 2014-15 SP AUTHENTIC
201 William Karlsson YG 30.00 80.00
206 Sam Reinhart YG 40.00 100.00
211 Johnny Gaudreau YG 150.00 250.00
223 Leon Draisaitl YG 100.00 250.00
225 Aaron Ekblad YG 75.00 150.00
248 Evgeny Kuznetsov YG 90.00 150.00
464 Shayne Gostisbehere YG 60.00 100.00
476 John Klingberg YG 60.00 100.00
477 Jonathan Drouin YG 60.00 150.00
494 Bo Horvat YG 60.00 100.00
495 David Pastrnak YG 60.00 100.00
528 Andrew Hammond YG 50.00 100.00

2014-15 Upper Deck 25th Anniversary Buyback Autographs

32 Mike Richter 20.00 50.00
43 Pierre Turgeon 20.00 50.00
44 Mark Messier 60.00 120.00
46 Mike Modano 30.00 80.00
47 Theoren Fleury 25.00 60.00
52 Larry Robinson 20.00 50.00
54 Wayne Gretzky 300.00 500.00
55 Ed Belfour SR 125.00 300.00
56 Steve Yzerman
63 Jeremy Roenick 30.00 60.00
64 Ray Bourque 50.00 100.00
67 Ron Francis 25.00 60.00
73 Luc Robitaille 20.00 50.00
126 Brian Bellows 15.00 40.00
133 Michel Goulet 15.00 40.00
142 Rob Brown 15.00 40.00
143 Al MacInnis 30.00 60.00
144 Mario Lemieux
146 Jari Kurri 30.00 80.00
153 Patrick Roy
154 Brett Hull 50.00 100.00
156 Cam Neely 20.00 50.00
162 Guy Lafleur 25.00 60.00
164 Joe Sakic 75.00 150.00
173 Adam Oates 40.00 80.00
175 Curtis Joseph SR 75.00 150.00
188 Guy Carbonneau 20.00 50.00
190 Joe Murphy 20.00 50.00
201 Bill Ranford 20.00 50.00
Conn Smythe Trophy
223 Doug Wilson 15.00 40.00
224 Vincent Damphousse 15.00 40.00
227 Ron Hextall 30.00 60.00
232 Andy Moog 20.00 50.00
253 Brian Leetch 20.00 50.00
256 Trevor Linden 20.00 50.00
264 Grant Fuhr 20.00 50.00
271 Doug Gilmour 25.00 60.00
277 Mike Gartner 20.00 50.00
284 Glenn Anderson 20.00 50.00
356 Jaromir Jagr DP
365 Mats Sundin 20.00 50.00
422 Chris Chelios 30.00 60.00
426 Denis Savard 40.00 80.00
443 Dale Hawerchuk 25.00 60.00
447 Claude Lemieux
458 Felix Potvin WJC
483 Adam Oates AS 40.00 80.00
489 Ray Bourque AS
493 Cam Neely AS 40.00 80.00
504 Darryl Sittler NH 20.00 50.00
509 Bobby Clarke NH 30.00 60.00
510 Phil Esposito NH 30.00 80.00
526 Pavel Bure YG 150.00 250.00
545 Wayne Gretzky 2000th Pt.
546 Brett Hull 50/50 50.00 100.00

2014-15 Upper Deck A Piece of History 1000 Point Club Jerseys

GROUP A ODDS 1:14,815 SER.1
GROUP A ODDS 1:8720 SER.2
GROUP B ODDS 1:2528 SER.1
GROUP B ODDS 1:785 SER.2
GROUP C ODDS 1:2469 SER.1
OVERALL ODDS 1:1152 SER.1
OVERALL ODDS 1:720 SER.2
PCAO Adam Oates 1B 20.00 50.00
PCBB Brian Bellows 1C 15.00 40.00
PCBL Brian Leetch 1C 15.00 40.00
PCGP Gilbert Perreault 1B 20.00 50.00
PCJT Joe Thornton 2B 15.00 40.00
PCLR Luc Robitaille 1B 20.00 50.00
PCMB Mike Bossy 2B 15.00 40.00
PCMS Mats Sundin 2B 15.00 40.00
PCNL Nicklas Lidstrom 2A 50.00 100.00
PCPE Phil Esposito 2B 25.00 50.00
PCRB Rod Brind'Amour 2B 12.00 30.00
PCSY Steve Yzerman 1A 60.00 150.00

2014-15 Upper Deck A Piece of History 500 Goal Club Jerseys

GCJI Jarome Iginla 1 30.00 80.00
GCJR Jeremy Roenick 2 30.00 80.00
GCMM Mike Modano 2 50.00 120.00
GCMS Mats Sundin 1 30.00 80.00
GCTS Teemu Selanne 1 60.00 150.00

2014-15 Upper Deck A Piece of History 500 Goal Club Jerseys Autographs

GCJI Jarome Iginla 150.00 250.00

2014-15 Upper Deck Buyback Autographs

SERIES 1 STATED PRINT RUN 13-45
8 Ovechkin 11-12UD/13
26 S.Stamkos 11-12UD/40 20.00 40.00
80 J.Tavares 11-12UD/25 25.00 50.00
133 N.Lidstrom 11-12UD/45 25.00 50.00

2014-15 Upper Deck Canvas

C1-C90 ODDS 1:7H, 1:7R, 1:14B SER.1
C121-C210 ODDS 1:6H, 1:6R, 1:12B SER.2
C1-C90 YG ODDS 1:48H/R, 1:96B SER.1
C211-C240 YG ODDS 1:48H/R, 1:96B SER.2
C241-C270 RET/POE ODDS 1:192H/R, 1:384B SER.2
C1 Corey Perry 1.25 3.00
C2 John Gibson 1.50 4.00
C3 Cam Fowler 1.00 2.50
C4 Mike Smith 1.25 3.00
C5 Antoine Vermette .75 2.00
C6 Keith Yandle 1.25 3.00
C7 Patrice Bergeron 1.50 4.00
C8 Brad Marchand 1.50 4.00
C9 Reilly Smith 1.25 3.00
C10 Loui Eriksson 1.00 2.50
C11 Zemgus Girgensons 1.25 3.00
C12 Cody Hodgson 1.25 3.00
C13 Mark Giordano 1.00 2.50
C14 Matt Stajan 1.00 2.50
C15 Elias Lindholm 1.25 3.00
C16 Alexander Semin 1.25 3.00
C17 Jonathan Toews 2.50 6.00
C18 Duncan Keith 1.25 3.00
C19 Brandon Saad 1.25 3.00
C20 Brent Seabrook 1.25 3.00
C21 Semyon Varlamov 1.25 3.00
C22 Gabriel Landeskog 1.00 2.50
C23 Nathan MacKinnon 2.50 6.00
C24 Brandon Dubinsky 1.00 2.50
C25 Ryan Johansen 1.50 4.00
C26 Boone Jenner .75 2.00
C27 Valeri Nichushkin 1.00 2.50
C28 Tyler Seguin 2.00 5.00
C29 Antoine Roussel .75 2.00
C30 Henrik Zetterberg 1.50 4.00
C31 Pavel Datsyuk 1.50 4.00
C32 Gustav Nyquist 1.00 2.50
C33 Taylor Hall 2.50 6.00
C34 Nail Yakupov 1.00 2.50
C35 Jordan Eberle 1.25 3.00
C36 Roberto Luongo 1.25 3.00
C37 Aleksander Barkov 1.25 3.00
C38 Marian Gaborik 1.25 3.00
C39 Tanner Pearson .75 2.00
C40 Tyler Toffoli 1.25 3.00
C41 Anze Kopitar 2.00 5.00
C42 Jason Pominville 1.00 2.50
C43 Mikael Granlund 1.00 2.50
C44 Zach Parise 1.25 3.00
C45 Max Pacioretty 1.25 3.00
C46 P.K. Subban 2.00 5.00
C47 Brendan Gallagher 1.25 3.00
C48 Seth Jones 1.00 2.50
C49 Ryan Ellis .75 2.00
C50 Pekka Rinne 1.50 4.00
C51 Jaromir Jagr 3.00 8.00
C52 Eric Gelinas 1.00 2.50
C53 Cory Schneider 1.00 2.50
C54 Kyle Okposo 1.25 3.00
C55 Ryan Strome 1.00 2.50
C56 John Tavares 2.50 6.00
C57 Henrik Lundqvist 1.50 4.00
C58 Rick Nash 1.25 3.00
C59 Chris Kreider 1.25 3.00
C60 Mika Zibanejad 1.25 3.00
C61 Craig Anderson 1.25 3.00
C62 Jakub Voracek 1.25 3.00
C63 Brayden Schenn 1.25 3.00
C64 Steve Mason 1.00 2.50
C65 Olli Maatta 1.25 3.00
C66 Chris Kunitz 1.25 3.00
C67 Kris Letang 1.25 3.00
C68 Evgeni Malkin 4.00 10.00
C69 Logan Couture 1.25 3.00
C70 Tomas Hertl 1.25 3.00
C71 Antti Niemi 1.00 2.50
C72 Brian Elliott 1.00 2.50
C73 Alex Pietrangelo 1.00 2.50
C74 Vladimir Tarasenko 2.00 5.00
C75 T.J. Oshie 2.00 5.00
C76 Ryan Callahan 1.25 3.00
C77 Ben Bishop 1.25 3.00
C78 Ondrej Palat 1.00 2.50
C79 Nazem Kadri 1.25 3.00
C80 Morgan Rielly 1.25 3.00
C81 Phil Kessel 1.50 4.00
C82 Zack Kassian 1.00 2.50
C83 Henrik Sedin 1.25 3.00
C84 Alexandre Burrows 1.25 3.00
C85 Alexander Ovechkin 5.00 12.00
C86 Mike Green 1.25 3.00
C87 Philipp Grubauer 1.25 3.00
C88 Dustin Byfuglien 1.25 3.00
C89 Andrew Ladd 1.25 3.00
C90 Doughty/Brown/Williams CL .75 2.00
C91 William Karlsson YG 15.00 40.00
C92 Brandon Gormley YG 4.00 10.00
C93 Alexander Khokhlachev YG 4.00 10.00
C94 Sam Reinhart YG 12.00 30.00
C95 Jake McCabe YG 4.00 10.00
C96 Johnny Gaudreau YG 30.00 50.00
C97 Victor Rask YG 4.00 10.00
C98 Teuvo Teravainen YG 12.00 30.00
C99 Joey Hishon YG 5.00 12.00
C100 Alexander Wennberg YG 8.00 20.00
C101 Marko Dano YG 4.00 10.00
C102 Patrik Nemeth YG 4.00 10.00
C103 Andrej Nestrasil YG 4.00 10.00
C104 Leon Draisaitl YG 20.00 50.00
C105 Aaron Ekblad YG 12.00 30.00
C106 Jiri Sekac YG 4.00 10.00
C107 Calle Jarnkrok YG 4.00 10.00
C108 Damon Severson YG 4.00 10.00
C109 Griffin Reinhart YG 5.00 12.00
C110 Anthony Duclair YG 6.00 15.00
C111 Curtis Lazar YG 5.00 12.00
C112 Chris Tierney YG 4.00 10.00
C113 Mirco Mueller YG 4.00 10.00
C114 Ty Rattie YG 5.00 12.00
C115 Vladislav Namestnikov YG 6.00 15.00
C116 Stuart Percy YG 4.00 10.00
C117 Evgeny Kuznetsov YG 20.00 50.00
C118 Andre Burakovsky YG 6.00 15.00
C119 Adam Lowry YG 4.00 10.00
C120 A.Ekblad/S.Reinhart YG CL 10.00 25.00
C121 Ryan Kesler 1.25 3.00
C122 Ryan Getzlaf 2.00 5.00
C123 Frederik Andersen 1.00 2.50
C124 Shane Doan 1.00 2.50
C125 Sam Gagner 1.00 2.50
C126 Mikkel Boedker .75 2.00
C127 Zdeno Chara 1.25 3.00
C128 Tuukka Rask 1.25 3.00
C129 Milan Lucic 1.25 3.00
C130 Drew Stafford 1.25 3.00
C131 Matt Moulson 1.00 2.50
C132 Tyler Myers 1.00 2.50
C133 Jiri Hudler 1.00 2.50
C134 Sean Monahan 1.25 3.00
C135 Eric Staal 1.50 4.00
C136 Jeff Skinner 1.25 3.00
C137 Patrick Sharp 1.25 3.00
C138 Corey Crawford 1.50 4.00
C139 Patrick Kane 2.50 6.00
C140 Jarome Iginla 1.25 3.00
C141 Ryan O'Reilly 1.25 3.00
C142 Matt Duchene 1.25 3.00
C143 Sergei Bobrovsky 1.25 3.00
C144 Jack Johnson .75 2.00
C145 Scott Hartnell 1.25 3.00
C146 Kari Lehtonen 1.00 2.50
C147 Jamie Benn 1.50 4.00
C148 Jason Spezza 1.25 3.00
C149 Johan Franzen 1.25 3.00
C150 Niklas Kronwall 1.00 2.50
C151 Jim Howard 1.25 3.00
C152 Ben Scrivens 1.00 2.50
C153 Ryan Nugent-Hopkins 1.25 3.00
C154 David Perron .75 2.00
C155 Jonathan Huberdeau 1.25 3.00
C156 Nick Bjugstad 1.00 2.50
C157 Jonathan Quick 2.00 5.00
C158 Jeff Carter 1.25 3.00
C159 Dustin Brown 1.00 2.50
C160 Drew Doughty 1.25 3.00
C161 Ryan Suter 1.25 3.00
C162 Darcy Kuemper 1.00 2.50
C163 Thomas Vanek 1.25 3.00
C164 Alex Galchenyuk 2.00 5.00
C165 Carey Price 4.00 10.00
C166 Tomas Plekanec 1.25 3.00
C167 Shea Weber 1.00 2.50
C168 James Neal 1.25 3.00
C169 Mike Ribeiro 1.00 2.50
C170 Michael Cammalleri 1.00 2.50
C171 Patrik Elias 1.25 3.00
C172 Jaroslav Halak 1.00 2.50
C173 Brock Nelson 1.00 2.50
C174 Martin St. Louis 1.25 3.00
C175 Ryan McDonagh 1.25 3.00
C176 Mats Zuccarello 1.25 3.00
C177 Derek Stepan 1.25 3.00
C178 Marc Staal 1.00 2.50
C179 Kyle Turris 1.25 3.00
C180 Erik Karlsson 2.50 6.00
C181 Wayne Simmonds 1.50 4.00
C182 Claude Giroux 1.25 3.00
C183 Vincent Lecavalier 1.00 2.50
C184 Marc-Andre Fleury 2.00 5.00
C185 Sidney Crosby 5.00 12.00
C186 Patric Hornqvist 1.00 2.50
C187 Beau Bennett .75 2.00
C188 Patrick Marleau 1.25 3.00
C189 Joe Pavelski 1.25 3.00
C190 Joe Thornton 1.25 3.00
C191 Paul Stastny 1.25 3.00
C192 Patrik Berglund .75 2.00
C193 Alexander Steen 1.25 3.00
C194 David Backes 1.25 3.00
C195 Steven Stamkos 2.50 6.00
C196 Tyler Johnson 1.25 3.00
C197 Victor Hedman 1.50 4.00
C198 Jonathan Bernier 1.25 3.00
C199 Dion Phaneuf 1.25 3.00
C200 James van Riemsdyk 1.25 3.00
C201 Ryan Miller 1.25 3.00
C202 Daniel Sedin 1.25 3.00
C203 Nick Bonino .75 2.00
C204 Nicklas Backstrom 2.00 5.00
C205 Braden Holtby 2.00 5.00
C206 Brooks Orpik 1.00 2.50
C207 Matt Niskanen 1.00 2.50
C208 Evander Kane 1.25 3.00
C209 Blake Wheeler 1.25 3.00
C210 Kessel/Bernier/van Riem CL 1.00 2.50
C211 Phillip Danault YG 4.00 10.00
C212 Markus Granlund YG 6.00 15.00
C213 Colton Sissons YG 4.00 10.00
C214 Jonathan Drouin YG 30.00 80.00
C215 Teemu Pulkkinen YG 5.00 12.00
C216 Josh Jooris YG 4.00 10.00
C217 Sven Andrighetto YG 5.00 12.00
C218 Joe Morrow YG 5.00 12.00
C219 Andy Andreoff YG 4.00 10.00
C220 Tobias Rieder YG 4.00 10.00
C221 Derrick Pouliot YG 5.00 12.00
C222 Barclay Goodrow YG 4.00 10.00
C223 Curtis McKenzie YG 3.00 8.00
C224 Brett Ritchie YG 4.00 10.00
C225 David Pastrnak YG 20.00 40.00
C226 Rocco Grimaldi YG 4.00 10.00
C227 Darnell Nurse YG 10.00 25.00
C228 Jori Lehtera YG 5.00 12.00
C229 Seth Griffith YG 5.00 12.00
C230 Jordan Binnington YG 4.00 10.00
C231 Dennis Everberg YG 4.00 10.00
C232 Ryan Sproul YG 4.00 10.00
C233 Seth Helgeson YG 3.00 8.00
C234 Bo Horvat YG 12.00 30.00
C235 Christian Folin YG 4.00 10.00
C236 Andrei Vasilevskiy YG 12.00 30.00
C237 Trevor van Riemsdyk YG 6.00 15.00
C238 Kevin Hayes YG 12.00 30.00
C239 Shayne Gostisbehere YG 15.00 30.00
C240 Drouin/Horvat YG CL 6.00 15.00
C241 Arturs Irbe RET 8.00 20.00
C242 Chris Chelios RET 10.00 25.00
C243 Cam Neely RET 10.00 25.00
C244 Teemu Selanne RET 20.00 50.00
C245 Darryl Sittler RET 10.00 25.00
C246 Dominik Hasek RET 12.00 30.00
C247 Adam Oates RET 10.00 25.00
C248 John LeClair RET 10.00 25.00
C249 Doug Harvey RET 10.00 25.00
C250 Tony Esposito RET 10.00 25.00
C251 Bobby Orr RET 30.00 80.00
C252 Wendel Clark RET 10.00 25.00
C253 Terry Sawchuk RET 20.00 40.00
C254 Wayne Gretzky RET 30.00 60.00
C255 Mats Sundin RET 10.00 25.00
C256 Mark Visentin POE 8.00 20.00
C257 Brandon Kozun POE 6.00 15.00
C258 Brandon Gormley POE 8.00 20.00
C259 Curtis Lazar POE 10.00 25.00
C260 Ty Rattie POE 10.00 25.00
C261 Griffin Reinhart POE 8.00 20.00
C262 Jonathan Drouin POE 30.00 60.00
C263 Derrick Pouliot POE 12.00 30.00
C264 Anthony Duclair POE 10.00 25.00
C265 Sam Reinhart POE 12.00 30.00
C266 Bo Horvat POE 25.00 60.00
C267 Tyler Wotherspoon POE 8.00 20.00
C268 Aaron Ekblad POE 15.00 40.00
C269 Darnell Nurse POE 12.00 30.00
C270 Brett Ritchie POE 8.00 20.00

2014-15 Upper Deck Canvas Autographs

SERIES 2 AUTO PRINT RUN 19
CAJS Joe Sakic 150.00 250.00
CAJT Jonathan Toews 250.00 400.00

2014-15 Upper Deck Clear Cut Captains

CCCAF Andrew Ference 5.00 12.00
CCCAL Andrew Ladd 8.00 20.00
CCCAO Alexander Ovechkin 30.00 80.00
CCCBA David Backes 8.00 20.00
CCCBE Jean Beliveau 8.00 20.00
CCCBS Bryce Salvador 5.00 12.00
CCCCG Claude Giroux 8.00 20.00
CCCDB Dustin Brown 6.00 15.00
CCCDP Dion Phaneuf 8.00 20.00
CCCES Eric Staal 10.00 25.00
CCCGL Gabriel Landeskog 6.00 15.00
CCCGP Gilbert Perreault 8.00 20.00
CCCHS Henrik Sedin 8.00 20.00
CCCHZ Henrik Zetterberg 10.00 25.00
CCCJB Jamie Benn 10.00 25.00
CCCJT Jonathan Toews 15.00 40.00
CCCMG Mark Giordano 6.00 15.00
CCCMK Mikko Koivu 6.00 15.00
CCCML Mario Lemieux 25.00 60.00
CCCMM Mark Messier 8.00 20.00
CCCPB Pavel Bure 10.00 25.00
CCCRG Ryan Getzlaf 12.00 30.00
CCCSC Sidney Crosby 30.00 80.00
CCCSD Shane Doan 6.00 15.00
CCCSS Steven Stamkos 15.00 40.00
CCCSW Shea Weber 8.00 20.00
CCCTA John Tavares 15.00 40.00
CCCTH Joe Thornton 8.00 20.00
CCCWG Wayne Gretzky 40.00 80.00
CCCZC Zdeno Chara 8.00 20.00

2014-15 Upper Deck Clear Cut Foundations

CCFBM O.Maatta/B.Bennett 12.00 30.00
CCFBR J.Bernier/M.Rielly 12.00 30.00
CCFBS T.Seguin/J.Benn 20.00 50.00
CCFBT Byfuglien/J.Trouba 12.00 30.00
CCFCT J.Carter/T.Toffoli 12.00 30.00
CCFDE Doan/O.Ekman-Lars 10.00 25.00
CCFDJ B.Dubinsky/B.Jenner 10.00 25.00
CCFDM Duchene/MacKinnon 20.00 50.00
CCFDN P.Datsyuk/G.Nyquist 15.00 40.00
CCFGK Kuemper/M.Granlund 10.00 25.00
CCFGM E.Gelinas/J.Merrill 10.00 25.00
CCFGR Ristolainen/Girgensons
CCFHB A.Barkov/J.Huberdeau 12.00 30.00
CCFHG P.Grubauer/B.Holtby 20.00 50.00
CCFHM S.Monahan/J.Hudler 12.00 30.00
CCFJP T.Johnson/O.Palat 12.00 30.00
CCFKC E.Karlsson/C.Ceci
CCFKJ Z.Kassian/N.Jensen 10.00 25.00
CCFKS T.Krug/R.Smith 12.00 30.00
CCFLG R.Getzlaf/H.Lindholm 20.00 50.00
CCFML E.Lindholm/R.Murphy 12.00 30.00
CCFNY RNH/N.Yakupov 12.00 30.00
CCFPH J.Pavelski/T.Hertl 12.00 30.00
CCFPT C.Price/D.Tokarski 30.00 60.00
CCFSK D.Keith/B.Seabrook 12.00 30.00
CCFSO A.Steen/T.Oshie 20.00 50.00
CCFSR B.Schenn/M.Read 12.00 30.00
CCFTS J.Tavares/R.Strome 25.00 60.00
CCFWJ S.Weber/S.Jones 10.00 25.00
CCFZM McDonagh/Zuccarello 15.00 40.00

2014-15 Upper Deck Clear Cut Stoppers

CCSCC Corey Crawford 10.00 25.00
CCSCJ Curtis Joseph 12.00 30.00
CCSCP Carey Price 15.00 40.00
CCSDH Dominik Hasek 10.00 25.00
CCSEB Ed Belfour 8.00 20.00
CCSHL Henrik Lundqvist 10.00 25.00
CCSJG John Gibson 10.00 25.00
CCSJQ Jonathan Quick 12.00 30.00
CCSMB Martin Brodeur 15.00 40.00
CCSPR Patrick Roy 30.00 60.00
CCSSB Sergei Bobrovsky 8.00 20.00
CCSTR Tuukka Rask 8.00 20.00

2014-15 Upper Deck Day With The Cup

DC1-DC18 ODDS 1:1000H, 1:2500R, 1:5000B SER.1
DC19-DC22 ODDS 1:1728 H, 1:4320 R/B SER.2
DC1 Tyler Toffoli 30.00 80.00
DC2 Dustin Brown 25.00 60.00
DC3 Jonathan Quick 30.00 80.00
DC4 Marian Gaborik 30.00 80.00
DC5 Anze Kopitar 30.00 80.00
DC6 Slava Voynov 20.00 50.00
DC7 Justin Williams 25.00 60.00
DC8 Tanner Pearson 20.00 50.00
DC9 Drew Doughty 30.00 80.00
DC10 Jake Muzzin 20.00 50.00
DC11 Mike Richards 30.00 80.00
DC12 Jarret Stoll 25.00 60.00
DC13 Robyn Regehr 20.00 50.00
DC14 Jordan Nolan 30.00 80.00
DC15 Matt Greene 20.00 50.00
DC16 Colin Fraser 20.00 50.00
DC17 Willie Mitchell 20.00 50.00
DC18 Martin Jones 30.00 80.00
DC19 Bill Ranford 30.00 80.00
DC20 Alec Martinez 20.00 50.00
DC21 Trevor Lewis 20.00 50.00
DC22 P.Pritchard/C.Campbell 25.00 60.00

2014-15 Upper Deck Day With The Cup Flashback

DCF1 Mario Lemieux 125.00 200.00
DCF2 Ron Francis 40.00 80.00
DCF3 Jaromir Jagr 90.00 150.00
DCF4 Tom Barrasso 30.00 60.00

2014-15 Upper Deck Game Jerseys

GROUP A ODDS 1:1031 SER.1
GROUP B ODDS 1:552 SER.1
GROUP C ODDS 1:249 SER.1
GROUP D ODDS 1:88 SER.1
GROUP E ODDS 1:86 SER.1
GROUP F ODDS 1:19 SER.1
SER.1 OVERALL ODDS 1:12 HOB,1:24 RET
SER.2 ODDS 1:24 H,1:48 R, 1:480 B
GJAG Alex Galchenyuk 1F 5.00 12.00
GJAH Adam Henrique 1F 3.00 8.00
GJAM Andrei Markov 1E 3.00 8.00
GJAN Antti Niemi 1F 2.50 6.00
GJBB Brian Bellows 1E 2.50 6.00
GJBC Braydon Coburn 1F 2.00 5.00
GJBH Brett Hull 2 4.00 10.00
GJBI Bryan Bickell 1F 2.00 5.00
GJBL Rob Blake 2 4.00 10.00
GJBO Ray Bourque 2 6.00 15.00
GJBS Ben Scrivens 1E 2.50 6.00
GJBW Blake Wheeler 2 3.00 8.00
GJCA John Carlson 1F 4.00 10.00
GJCC Corey Crawford 1D 4.00 10.00
GJCC Chris Chelios 2 3.00 8.00
GJCH Cody Hodgson 1E 3.00 8.00
GJCJ Curtis Joseph 1A 10.00 25.00
GJCK Chris Kreider 1F 3.00 8.00
GJCO Sean Couturier 1F 3.00 8.00
GJCP Carey Price 1F 10.00 25.00
GJCS Cory Schneider 1D 2.50 6.00
GJDA Damien Brunner 1F 2.00 5.00
GJDB Dustin Brown 1F 2.50 6.00
GJDD Drew Doughty 1F 3.00 8.00
GJDD2 Drew Doughty TC 2 4.00 10.00
GJDG Doug Gilmour 2 5.00 12.00
GJDH2 Dale Hawerchuk 2 4.00 10.00
GJDH Dominik Hasek Wings 1A 12.00 30.00
GJDK Darcy Kuemper 2 2.50 6.00
GJDS Denis Savard 2 4.00 10.00
GJDS Drew Stafford 1F 3.00 8.00
GJEB Ed Belfour Panth 1B 5.00 12.00
GJEB Ed Belfour Stars 2 4.00 10.00
GJEJ Jhonas Enroth 2 3.00 8.00
GJEK Erik Karlsson 2 6.00 15.00
GJEL Eric Lindros Stars 1B 8.00 20.00
GJEM Evgeni Malkin TC 1D 12.00 30.00
GJER Eric Lindros Flyers 1F 5.00 12.00
GJES Eric Staal 1F 4.00 10.00
GJFO Peter Forsberg Pred 1C 4.00 10.00
GJGE Georges Laraque 1E 2.00 5.00
GJGF Grant Fuhr 1D 3.00 8.00
GJGL Gabriel Landeskog 1C 3.00 8.00
GJGL Guy Lafleur 2 5.00 12.00
GJGM Glen Murray 1F 2.50 6.00
GJGO Michel Goulet 1D 2.50 6.00
GJGR Mikael Granlund 2 2.50 6.00
GJHA Dominik Hasek Sen 2 4.00 10.00
GJHE Dany Heatley TC 1F 3.00 8.00
GJHO Jim Howard 1F 3.00 8.00
GJHZ Henrik Zetterberg 1D 4.00 10.00
GJJA Jake Allen 2 4.00 10.00
GJJC Jeff Carter 1F 3.00 8.00
GJJE Jordan Eberle 2 3.00 8.00
GJJF Johan Franzen 2 3.00 8.00
GJJI Jarome Iginla TC 2 4.00 10.00
GJJL John LeClair 1F 3.00 8.00
GJJO Jamie Oleksiak TC 2 3.00 8.00
GJJQ Jonathan Quick 1F 5.00 12.00
GJJR Jeremy Roenick TC 1D 4.00 10.00
GJJS Jeff Skinner TC 1B 5.00 12.00
GJJS Joe Sakic TC 2 6.00 15.00
GJJT Joe Thornton TC 2 4.00 10.00
GJJT Joe Thornton 1F 3.00 8.00
GJKL Kari Lehtonen 1F 2.50 6.00
GJKT Kyle Turris 1E 3.00 8.00
GJLC Logan Couture 2 3.00 8.00
GJLI Eric Lindros Rngrs 1F 5.00 12.00
GJLM Larry Murphy 1C 4.00 10.00
GJLR Luc Robitaille 1D 3.00 8.00
GJLR Larry Robinson TC 2 4.00 10.00
GJLU Milan Lucic 1C 4.00 10.00
GJMD Matt Duchene 1F 3.00 8.00
GJMF Marc-Andre Fleury TC 1F 6.00 15.00
GJMF Marc-Andre Fleury Pens 2 5.00 12.00
GJMG Mike Gartner 2 3.00 8.00
GJML Mario Lemieux 1A 30.00 80.00
GJMM Mark Messier 1A 10.00 25.00
GJMM Matt Moulson 2 2.50 6.00
GJMN Markus Naslund 1F 2.50 6.00
GJMS Mike Smith 2 3.00 8.00
GJNB Nicklas Backstrom 1D 5.00 12.00
GJNI Nicklas Lidstrom 1F 3.00 8.00
GJNK Niklas Kronwall 1F 2.50 6.00
GJNL Nick Leddy 1F 2.00 5.00
GJNY Nail Yakupov 1D 2.50 6.00
GJOK Olaf Kolzig 1E 3.00 8.00
GJOR Colton Orr 1E 2.00 5.00
GJPB Patrice Bergeron Bruin 1D 4.00 10.00
GJPB Patrice Bergeron TC 2 5.00 12.00
GJPC Paul Coffey TC 1F 4.00 10.00
GJPD Pavel Datsyuk 2 4.00 10.00
GJPF Peter Forsberg Flyers 1D 3.00 8.00
GJPM Patrick Marleau TC 1E 5.00 12.00
GJPR Pekka Rinne 1D 4.00 10.00
GJPS P.K. Subban 1E 5.00 12.00
GJQH Quinton Howden TC 2 2.50 6.00
GJRA Bill Ranford 1C 4.00 10.00
GJRB Richard Brodeur 1E 3.00 8.00
GJRB Rod Brind'Amour 2 2.50 6.00
GJRE Matt Read 1E 2.00 5.00
GJRF Ron Francis 2 4.00 10.00
GJRG Ryan Getzlaf 2 5.00 12.00
GJRH Ron Hextall 1F 3.00 8.00
GJRI Mike Richards 1F 3.00 8.00
GJRL Larry Robinson Kings 1C 4.00 10.00
GJRL Roberto Luongo 2 3.00 8.00
GJRN Rick Nash 1E 3.00 8.00
GJRO Rob Brown 1F 2.50 6.00
GJRS Ryan Strome TC 2 3.00 8.00
GJSA Joe Sakic 1D 5.00 12.00
GJSC Sidney Crosby 1A 40.00 100.00
GJSD Simon Despres 1F 3.00 8.00
GJSE Daniel Sedin 1F 3.00 8.00
GJSK Saku Koivu 1B 5.00 12.00
GJSM Steve Mason 1F 2.50 6.00
GJSV Semyon Varlamov 1F 3.00 8.00
GJTA John Tavares 2 6.00 15.00
GJTH Taylor Hall 1D 6.00 15.00
GJTL Trevor Linden 1F 3.00 8.00
GJTM Tyler Myers 1F 2.50 6.00
GJTS Tyler Seguin 1D 5.00 12.00
GJVD Vincent Damphousse 2 2.50 6.00
GJVO Slava Voynov 1F 3.00 8.00
GJZB Zach Bogosian 1A 10.00 25.00

2014-15 Upper Deck Hockey Heroes

HH66-HH78 ODDS 1:13 H/R, 1:25 B SER.1
HH79-HH91 ODDS 1:12 H/R, 1:24 SER.2
HH66 Steve Yzerman 1.50 4.00
HH67 Sidney Crosby 3.00 8.00
HH68 Jaromir Jagr 2.00 5.00
HH69 Peter Forsberg .75 2.00
HH70 Martin Brodeur 1.50 4.00
HH71 Vincent Lecavalier .60 1.50
HH72 Pavel Datsyuk 1.00 2.50
HH73 Nicklas Lidstrom .75 2.00
HH74 Alexander Ovechkin 3.00 8.00
HH75 Joe Sakic 1.25 3.00
HH76 Martin St. Louis .75 2.00
HH77 Jarome Iginla .75 2.00
HH78 M.Brodeur/N.Lidstrom ART 12.00 30.00
HH79 John Tavares 1.50 4.00
HH80 Alexander Ovechkin 3.00 8.00
HH81 Phil Kessel 1.00 2.50
HH82 Evgeni Malkin 2.50 6.00
HH83 Anze Kopitar 1.25 3.00
HH84 Carey Price 2.50 6.00
HH85 Claude Giroux .75 2.00
HH86 Shea Weber .60 1.50
HH87 Sidney Crosby 3.00 8.00
HH88 Patrick Kane 1.50 4.00
HH89 Ryan Getzlaf 1.25 3.00
HH90 Jonathan Toews 1.50 4.00
HH91 P.Kane/A.Ovechkin ART 12.00 30.00
HEADER Header Card 2000s 10.00 25.00
HEADER2 Header Card 2010s 10.00 25.00

2014-15 Upper Deck Hockey Heroes Autographs

HH66 Steve Yzerman/15
HH68 Jaromir Jagr/15 90.00 150.00
HH69 Peter Forsberg/15 ser.2 60.00 120.00
HH70 Martin Brodeur/15 50.00 100.00
HH71 Vincent Lecavalier/15
HH72 Pavel Datsyuk/15 ser.2 100.00 175.00
HH73 Nicklas Lidstrom/15
HH74 Alexander Ovechkin/15 75.00 125.00
HH75 Joe Sakic/15 90.00 150.00
HH76 Martin St. Louis/15
HH77 Jarome Iginla/15
HH79 John Tavares/15 ser.2 75.00 135.00
HH80 Alexander Ovechkin/15 ser.2
HH81 Phil Kessel/15 ser.2 40.00 100.00
HH83 Anze Kopitar/15 ser.2 50.00 100.00
HH84 Carey Price/15 ser.2 60.00 120.00
HH86 Shea Weber/15 ser.2 25.00 60.00
HH89 Ryan Getzlaf/15 ser.2
HH90 Jonathan Toews/15 ser.2 125.00 200.00

2014-15 Upper Deck NCAA Young Guns

NCAABG Bill Guerin 12.00 30.00
NCAABL Rob Blake 12.00 30.00
NCAABL Brian Leetch 12.00 30.00
NCAACJ Curtis Joseph 15.00 40.00
NCAAMR Mike Richter
NCAARB Rod Brind'Amour

2014-15 Upper Deck Oversized

ONE OVERSIZED CARD PER SER.2 TIN
1 Ryan Getzlaf 2.00 5.00
38 Jonathan Toews 2.50 6.00
58 Tyler Seguin 2.00 5.00
68 Henrik Zetterberg 1.50 4.00
70 Pavel Datsyuk 1.50 4.00
90 Jonathan Quick 2.00 5.00
100 Carey Price 4.00 10.00
116 Jaromir Jagr 3.00 8.00
122 John Tavares 2.50 6.00
132 Henrik Lundqvist 1.50 4.00
139 Claude Giroux 1.25 3.00
146 Evgeni Malkin 4.00 10.00
169 Steven Stamkos 2.50 6.00
189 Alexander Ovechkin 5.00 12.00

2014-15 Upper Deck Rookie Breakouts

RB1 Leon Draisaitl 12.00 30.00
RB2 William Karlsson 20.00 50.00
RB3 Anthony Duclair 8.00 20.00
RB4 Dennis Everberg 5.00 12.00
RB5 Johnny Gaudreau 40.00 80.00
RB6 Chris Tierney 5.00 12.00
RB7 Vladislav Namestnikov 8.00 20.00
RB8 Kerby Rychel 6.00 15.00
RB9 Jonathan Drouin 25.00 50.00
RB10 Seth Griffith 6.00 15.00
RB11 Stuart Percy 5.00 12.00
RB12 Trevor van Riemsdyk 8.00 20.00
RB13 Jori Lehtera 6.00 15.00
RB14 Evgeny Kuznetsov 20.00 50.00
RB15 Teuvo Teravainen 8.00 20.00
RB16 Aaron Ekblad 20.00 50.00
RB17 Marko Dano 5.00 12.00
RB18 Darnell Nurse 15.00 40.00
RB19 Curtis Lazar 6.00 15.00
RB20 Andre Burakovsky 8.00 20.00
RB21 David Pastrnak 30.00 60.00
RB22 Kevin Hayes 15.00 40.00
RB23 Griffin Reinhart 6.00 15.00
RB24 Sam Reinhart 15.00 40.00
RB25 Victor Rask 5.00 12.00
RB26 Damon Severson 5.00 12.00
RB27 Alexander Wennberg 10.00 25.00
RB28 Jiri Sekac 5.00 12.00

2014-15 Upper Deck Rookie Materials

SERIES 2 ODDS 1:24H, 1:48R, 1:480B
*PATCH/25: 1X TO 2.5X BASIC JSY
RM1 Damon Severson 2.50 6.00
RM2 Jonathan Drouin 6.00 15.00
RM3 Marko Dano 2.50 6.00
RM4 Aaron Ekblad 5.00 12.00
RM5 Greg McKegg 2.00 5.00
RM6 Alexander Wennberg 5.00 12.00
RM7 Darnell Nurse 8.00 20.00
RM8 Adam Lowry 2.50 6.00
RM9 Jake McCabe 2.50 6.00
RM10 Teuvo Teravainen 4.00 10.00
RM11 Mirco Mueller 2.50 6.00
RM12 Ty Rattie 3.00 8.00
RM14 Ryan Sproul 2.50 6.00
RM16 Leon Draisaitl 12.00 30.00
RM17 Patrik Nemeth 2.50 6.00
RM18 Jiri Sekac 2.50 6.00
RM20 Brandon Kozun 2.00 5.00
RM21 Laurent Brossoit 2.50 6.00
RM22 Sam Reinhart 5.00 12.00
RM23 Bo Horvat 8.00 20.00
RM24 Griffin Reinhart 3.00 8.00
RM25 Alexander Khokhlachev 2.50 6.00
RM26 Colton Sissons 2.50 6.00
RM27 Andre Burakovsky 5.00 12.00
RM28 Vincent Trocheck 3.00 8.00
RM29 Vladislav Namestnikov 4.00 10.00
RM31 Joey Hishon 3.00 8.00
RM32 Curtis McKenzie 2.00 5.00
RM33 Seth Griffith 3.00 8.00
RM34 Stuart Percy 2.50 6.00
RM35 Curtis Lazar 4.00 10.00
RM36 Evgeny Kuznetsov 5.00 12.00
RM37 Mark Visentin 2.50 6.00
RM38 Dennis Everberg 2.50 6.00
RM39 Johnny Gaudreau 10.00 25.00
RM40 William Karlsson 10.00 25.00
RM41 Chris Tierney 2.50 6.00
RM42 Andrej Nestrasil 2.50 6.00

2014-15 Upper Deck Shining Stars

SS1-SS10 ODDS 1:24 BLASTER SER.1
SS11-SS20 ODDS 1:12 TIN, 1:6 FAT SER.1
SS21-SS30 ODDS 1:16 H/R SER.1
SS31-SS40 ODDS 1:24 H/R SER.1
SS41-SS50 ODDS 1:48 H/R SER.1
*BLUE: .6X TO 1.5X BASIC INSERTS
SS1 Duncan Keith 2.00 5.00
SS2 Erik Karlsson 4.00 10.00
SS3 P.K. Subban 3.00 8.00
SS4 Alex Pietrangelo 1.50 4.00
SS5 Shea Weber 1.50 4.00
SS6 Ryan McDonagh 2.00 5.00
SS7 Drew Doughty 2.00 5.00
SS8 Jacob Trouba 1.50 4.00
SS9 Mark Giordano 1.50 4.00
SS10 Zdeno Chara 2.00 5.00
SS11 Tuukka Rask 2.00 5.00
SS12 Corey Crawford 2.50 6.00
SS13 Semyon Varlamov 2.00 5.00
SS14 Sergei Bobrovsky 2.00 5.00
SS15 Jonathan Quick 3.00 8.00
SS16 Carey Price 6.00 15.00
SS17 Cory Schneider 1.50 4.00
SS18 Henrik Lundqvist 2.50 6.00
SS19 Ben Bishop 2.00 5.00
SS20 Jonathan Bernier 2.00 5.00
SS21 Ryan Getzlaf 3.00 8.00
SS22 Patrice Bergeron 2.50 6.00
SS23 Jonathan Toews 4.00 10.00
SS24 Tyler Seguin 3.00 8.00
SS25 Anze Kopitar 3.00 8.00
SS26 John Tavares 4.00 10.00
SS27 Claude Giroux 2.00 5.00
SS28 Sidney Crosby 8.00 20.00
SS29 Evgeni Malkin 6.00 15.00
SS30 Steven Stamkos 4.00 10.00
SS31 Corey Perry 2.00 5.00
SS32 Patrick Kane 4.00 10.00
SS33 Alexander Ovechkin 8.00 20.00
SS34 Jamie Benn 2.50 6.00
SS35 Patrick Sharp 2.00 5.00
SS36 Taylor Hall 4.00 10.00
SS37 Max Pacioretty 2.00 5.00
SS38 Martin St. Louis 2.00 5.00
SS39 Alexander Steen 2.00 5.00
SS40 Phil Kessel 2.50 6.00
SS41 Phil Esposito 3.00 8.00
SS42 Steve Yzerman 4.00 10.00
SS43 Mike Bossy 2.00 5.00
SS44 Teemu Selanne 4.00 10.00
SS45 Wayne Gretzky 10.00 25.00
SS46 Mark Messier 2.00 5.00
SS47 Nicklas Lidstrom 2.00 5.00
SS48 Bobby Orr 6.00 15.00
SS49 Peter Forsberg 2.00 5.00
SS50 Mario Lemieux 6.00 15.00

2014-15 Upper Deck Signature Sensations

GROUP A ODDS 1:8939
GROUP B ODDS 1:6351

GROUP C ODDS 1:4554
GROUP D ODDS 1:3017
GROUP E ODDS 1:377
OVERALL ODDS 1:288 HOBBY
SSAP Alex Pietrangelo B 8.00 20.00
SSAW Austin Watson E 4.00 10.00
SSBO Bobby Orr A 150.00 250.00
SSBS Brayden Schenn B 10.00 25.00
SSBU Johnny Bucyk A
SSCC Charlie Coyle E 5.00 12.00
SSCK Chris Kreider B 10.00 25.00
SSCN Cristopher Nilstorp E 5.00 12.00
SSCT Christian Thomas D 5.00 12.00
SSDB Damien Brunner D 4.00 10.00
SSEL Elias Lindholm E 6.00 15.00
SSGI Jean-Sebastien Giguere A
SSJG John Gibson E 6.00 15.00
SSJJ Jaromir Jagr A 30.00 60.00
SSJM Jon Merrill E 4.00 10.00
SSJO Jamie Oleksiak E 5.00 12.00
SSJR Jussi Rynnas E 4.00 10.00
SSJS Jeff Skinner A
SSJT John Tavares A
SSKT Kyle Turris B 10.00 25.00
SSKU Chris Kunitz A
SSLE Lars Eller E 5.00 12.00
SSMB Mike Brown C 4.00 10.00
SSRE Ray Emery E 5.00 12.00
SSRF Ron Francis B 12.00 30.00
SSRM Ryan Murphy E 4.00 10.00
SSRP Richard Panik E 4.00 10.00
SSRR Rickard Rakell E 5.00 12.00
SSRS Riley Sheahan C 6.00 15.00
SSSB Scotty Bowman A
SSSH Shawn Horcoff B 6.00 15.00
SSSR Ryan Strome E 6.00 15.00
SSST Jared Staal E 6.00 15.00
SSTO T.J. Oshie C 10.00 25.00
SSTT Tomas Tatar D 5.00 12.00
SSTW Tom Wilson E 6.00 15.00
SSWG Wayne Gretzky A 150.00 300.00

2014-15 Upper Deck Signatures

GROUP A ODDS 1:63,420 SER.2 HOB
GROUP B ODDS 1:4230 SER.2 HOB
GROUP C ODDS 1:1410 SER.2 HOB
GROUP D ODDS 1:705 SER.2 HOB
OVERALL ODDS 1:420 SER.2 HOB
UDSAP Alex Pietrangelo B
UDSBM Brad Marchand C 10.00 25.00
UDSCC Charlie Coyle D 6.00 15.00
UDSCF Cody Franson C 5.00 12.00
UDSCP Chris Pronger B 8.00 20.00
UDSCS Cameron Schilling D 5.00 12.00
UDSEL Elias Lindholm C 8.00 20.00
UDSFP Felix Potvin B 25.00 50.00
UDSJB Jonathan Bernier B 15.00 40.00
UDSJM Jon Merrill D 5.00 12.00
UDSJT Jamie Tardif D 6.00 15.00
UDSLE Lars Eller D 6.00 15.00
UDSLK Lauri Korpikoski D 5.00 12.00
UDSLL Lucas Lessio D 5.00 12.00
UDSLS Luke Schenn C 5.00 12.00
UDSML Michael Latta D 8.00 20.00
UDSMT Marty Turco B 15.00 30.00
UDSNY Nail Yakupov C 6.00 15.00
UDSRM Ryan McDonagh C 8.00 20.00
UDSRS Ryan Strome D 6.00 15.00
UDSSH Scott Hartnell C 8.00 20.00
UDSSP Ryan Spooner D 6.00 15.00
UDSTA John Tavares A 30.00 60.00
UDSTR Tuukka Rask B 15.00 40.00
UDSTV Thomas Vanek C 8.00 20.00
UDSVN Valeri Nichushkin C 6.00 15.00
UDSZG Zemgus Girgensons D 8.00 20.00
UDSZR Zach Redmond D 5.00 12.00

2014-15 Upper Deck UD Portraits

P1-P40 SER.2 ODDS 1:9H, 1:12R, 1:24B
P41-P45 SER.2 ODDS 1:72H, 1:96R, 1:192B
P46-P60 SER.2 ODDS 1:24H, 1:32R, 1:64B
*P46-P60 BLUE/25: 1.5X TO 4X BASIC INSERTS
P1 Drew Doughty 1.50 4.00
P2 Pavel Datsyuk 2.00 5.00
P3 Alexander Ovechkin 6.00 15.00
P4 Martin St. Louis 1.50 4.00
P5 Evgeni Malkin 5.00 12.00
P6 Thomas Vanek 1.50 4.00
P7 Carey Price 5.00 12.00
P8 Claude Giroux 1.50 4.00
P9 T.J. Oshie 2.50 6.00
P10 Joe Thornton 1.50 4.00
P11 Erik Karlsson 3.00 8.00
P12 Duncan Keith 1.50 4.00
P13 Patrick Sharp 1.50 4.00
P14 Shea Weber 1.25 3.00
P15 Jarome Iginla 1.50 4.00
P16 Patrice Bergeron 2.00 5.00
P17 Eric Staal 1.50 4.00
P18 Max Pacioretty 1.50 4.00
P19 P.K. Subban 2.50 6.00
P20 Phil Kessel 2.00 5.00
P21 Joe Pavelski 1.50 4.00
P22 Steven Stamkos 3.00 8.00
P23 John Tavares 3.00 8.00
P24 Jonathan Quick 2.50 6.00
P25 Patrick Kane 3.00 8.00
P26 Zach Parise 1.50 4.00
P27 Matt Duchene 1.50 4.00
P28 Sidney Crosby 6.00 15.00
P29 Jonathan Toews 3.00 8.00
P30 Jamie Benn 2.00 5.00
P31 Jason Spezza 1.50 4.00
P32 Jaromir Jagr 4.00 10.00
P33 Tyler Seguin 2.50 6.00
P34 Taylor Hall 3.00 8.00
P35 Henrik Lundqvist 3.00 8.00
P36 Anze Kopitar 2.50 6.00
P37 Tuukka Rask 1.50 4.00
P38 Nathan MacKinnon 3.00 8.00
P39 Henrik Zetterberg 2.00 5.00
P40 Ryan Getzlaf 2.50 6.00
P41 Wayne Gretzky LEG 10.00 25.00
P42 Terry Sawchuk LEG 2.00 5.00
P43 Steve Yzerman LEG 4.00 10.00
P44 Patrick Roy LEG 5.00 12.00
P45 Joe Sakic LEG 3.00 8.00
P46 Anthony Duclair 2.00 5.00
P47 Griffin Reinhart 1.50 4.00
P48 Curtis Lazar 1.50 4.00
P49 Shayne Gostisbehere 5.00 12.00
P50 Alexander Wennberg 2.50 6.00
P51 Andre Burakovsky 2.00 5.00
P52 Sam Reinhart 4.00 10.00
P53 Johnny Gaudreau 5.00 12.00
P54 Teuvo Teravainen 2.00 5.00
P55 Bo Horvat 4.00 10.00
P56 Aaron Ekblad 3.00 8.00
P57 Jiri Sekac 1.25 3.00
P58 Evgeny Kuznetsov 5.00 12.00
P59 Jonathan Drouin 4.00 10.00
P60 Leon Draisaitl 3.00 8.00

2014-15 Upper Deck UD Portraits Gold

*P1-45 GOLD/25: 1.5X TO 4X BASIC INSERTS
*P46-P60 GOLD/99: 1X TO 2.5X BASIC INSERTS
P41 Wayne Gretzky LEG 40.00 80.00

2014-15 Upper Deck Winter Classic Jumbos

ONE JUMBO PER SERIES 1 TIN
WC1 Pavel Datsyuk 1.50 4.00
WC2 Phil Kessel 1.50 4.00
WC3 Brendan Smith 1.00 2.50
WC4 Justin Abdelkader 1.00 2.50
WC5 Dion Phaneuf 1.25 3.00
WC6 Henrik Zetterberg 1.50 4.00
WC7 Jay McClement .75 2.00
WC8 Jonathan Bernier 1.25 3.00
WC9 Daniel Alfredsson 1.25 3.00
WC10 Gustav Nyquist 1.00 2.50
WC11 Tyler Bozak 1.00 2.50
WC12 Jim Howard 1.25 3.00
WC13 Morgan Rielly 1.25 3.00
WC14 James van Riemsdyk 1.25 3.00

2014-15 Upper Deck Young Guns Acetate

201-249 INSERTED IN UD SERIES 2
451-499 INSERTED IN SP AUTHENTIC
201 William Karlsson 60.00 150.00
202 Brandon Gormley 15.00 40.00
203 Mark Visentin 15.00 40.00
204 Alexander Khokhlachev 15.00 40.00
205 Bobby Robins 12.00 30.00
206 Sam Reinhart 50.00 100.00
207 Nicolas Deslauriers 15.00 40.00
208 Jake McCabe 15.00 40.00
209 Corban Knight 15.00 40.00
210 Tyler Wotherspoon 15.00 40.00
211 Johnny Gaudreau 200.00 350.00
212 Victor Rask 15.00 40.00
213 Patrick Brown 15.00 40.00
214 Teuvo Teravainen 50.00 100.00
215 Trevor van Riemsdyk 20.00 50.00
216 Joey Hishon 20.00 50.00
217 Dennis Everberg 15.00 40.00
218 Alexander Wennberg 30.00 80.00
219 Patrik Nemeth 15.00 40.00
220 Ryan Sproul 15.00 40.00
221 Teemu Pulkkinen 40.00 80.00
222 Andrej Nestrasil 15.00 40.00
223 Leon Draisaitl 80.00 200.00
224 Oscar Klefbom 30.00 80.00
225 Aaron Ekblad 100.00 175.00
226 Vincent Trocheck 20.00 50.00
227 Jonathan Racine 15.00 40.00
228 Christian Folin 15.00 40.00
229 Jiri Sekac 15.00 40.00
230 Calle Jarnkrok 15.00 40.00
231 Colton Sissons 15.00 40.00
232 Damon Severson 15.00 40.00
233 Griffin Reinhart 20.00 50.00
234 Scott Mayfield 15.00 40.00
235 Johan Sundstrom 15.00 40.00
236 Anthony Duclair 25.00 60.00
237 Curtis Lazar 20.00 50.00
238 Pierre-Edouard Bellemare 15.00 40.00
239 Adam Payerl 12.00 30.00
240 Chris Tierney 15.00 40.00
241 Jori Lehtera 20.00 50.00
242 Ty Rattie 20.00 50.00
243 Vladislav Namestnikov 25.00 60.00
244 Brandon Kozun 12.00 30.00
245 Stuart Percy 15.00 40.00
246 Greg McKegg 12.00 30.00
247 Michael Zalewski 12.00 30.00
248 Evgeny Kuznetsov 50.00 100.00
249 Adam Lowry 25.00 50.00
451 Joe Morrow 20.00 50.00
452 Marko Dano 50.00 100.00
453 Markus Granlund 25.00 60.00
454 Rob Zepp 25.00 60.00
455 Tobias Rieder 15.00 40.00
456 Scott Harrington 15.00 40.00
457 Darnell Nurse 40.00 80.00
458 Laurent Brossoit 15.00 40.00
459 Colin Smith 15.00 40.00
460 Joel Armia 15.00 40.00
461 Jyrki Jokipakka 15.00 40.00
462 Phillip Danault 15.00 40.00
463 Cedric Paquette 15.00 40.00
464 Shayne Gostisbehere 60.00 150.00
465 Joni Ortio 20.00 50.00
466 Scott Wilson 12.00 30.00
467 Andre Burakovsky 60.00 120.00
468 Melker Karlsson 15.00 40.00
469 Jordan Binnington 15.00 40.00
470 Bogdan Yakimov 15.00 40.00
471 Seth Griffith 20.00 50.00
472 Seth Helgeson 12.00 30.00
473 Brendan Shinnimin 12.00 30.00
474 Borna Rendulic 15.00 40.00
475 Derrick Pouliot 20.00 50.00
476 John Klingberg 75.00 125.00
477 Jonathan Drouin 100.00 175.00
478 Andrei Vasilevskiy 60.00 120.00
479 Andrew Agozzino 12.00 30.00
480 Petteri Lindbohm 12.00 30.00
481 Adam Clendening 15.00 40.00
482 Curtis McKenzie 12.00 30.00
483 Christopher Gibson 25.00 60.00
484 Mirco Mueller 15.00 40.00
485 Barclay Goodrow 15.00 40.00
486 Anton Forsberg 15.00 40.00
487 Max Friberg 12.00 30.00
488 Josh Jooris 15.00 40.00
489 Tyler Graovac 12.00 30.00
490 Kevin Hayes 40.00 80.00
491 Chris Wagner 15.00 40.00
492 Andy Andreoff 15.00 40.00
493 Sven Andrighetto 20.00 50.00
494 Bo Horvat 125.00 200.00
495 David Pastrnak 150.00 250.00
496 Brett Ritchie 15.00 40.00
497 Dominik Uher 12.00 30.00
498 Scott Darling 40.00 80.00
499 Kerby Rychel 12.00 30.00
521 Jesse Blacker 15.00 40.00
522 Julien Brouillette 10.00 25.00
523 Miikka Salomaki 10.00 25.00
524 Adam Clendening 10.00 25.00
525 Nikita Nesterov 10.00 25.00
526 Jiri Sekac 10.00 25.00
527 Tyler Gaudet 8.00 20.00
528 Andrew Hammond 40.00 80.00
529 Rocco Grimaldi 10.00 25.00
530 Anthony Duclair 30.00 60.00

2015 Upper Deck Holiday Card

UDHC Connor McDavid 8.00 20.00

2015-16 Upper Deck

COMP.SERIES 1 (250) 300.00 450.00
COMP.SER. 1 w/o RC's (200) 8.00 20.00
COMP.SERIES 2 (250) 150.00 250.00
COMP.SER. 2 w/o RC's (200) 8.00 20.00
201-250 YOUNG GUN ODDS 1:4 SER.1
451-500 YOUNG GUN ODDS 1:4 SER.2
1 Cam Fowler .25 .60
2 Frederik Andersen .25 .60
3 Hampus Lindholm .25 .60
4 Sami Vatanen .25 .60
5 Pat Maroon .20 .50
6 Rickard Rakell .25 .60
7 Ryan Getzlaf .50 1.25
8 Martin Hanzal .20 .50
9 Michael Stone .20 .50
10 Mike Smith .30 .75
11 Oliver Ekman-Larsson .25 .60
12 Joe Vitale .20 .50
13 Shane Doan .20 .50
14 Brad Marchand .40 1.00
15 David Krejci .25 .60
16 David Pastrnak .50 1.25
17 Dennis Seidenberg .25 .60
18 Loui Eriksson .25 .60
19 Zdeno Chara .30 .75
20 Tuukka Rask .30 .75
21 Brian Gionta .25 .60
22 Nicolas Deslauriers .20 .50
23 Zemgus Girgensons .25 .60
24 Marcus Foligno .20 .50
25 Sam Reinhart .30 .75
26 Tyler Ennis .25 .60
27 Dennis Wideman .20 .50
28 Jiri Hudler .20 .50
29 Joe Colborne .20 .50
30 Johnny Gaudreau .50 1.25
31 Jonas Hiller .25 .60
32 Karri Ramo .25 .60
33 Cam Ward .30 .75
34 Elias Lindholm .25 .60
35 Jeff Skinner .25 .60
36 Justin Faulk .25 .60
37 Nathan Gerbe .20 .50
38 Andrew Shaw .30 .75
39 Bryan Bickell .20 .50
40 Corey Crawford .40 1.00
41 Duncan Keith .30 .75
42 Marian Hossa .25 .60
43 Niklas Hjalmarsson .20 .50
44 Jonathan Toews .60 1.50
45 Tyson Barrie .30 .75
46 Erik Johnson .20 .50
47 Gabriel Landeskog .30 .75
48 Matt Duchene .30 .75
49 Semyon Varlamov .30 .75
50 Brandon Dubinsky .25 .60
51 Cam Atkinson .30 .75
52 David Savard .20 .50
53 Jack Johnson .20 .50
54 Matt Calvert .20 .50
55 Scott Hartnell .30 .75
56 Nick Foligno .25 .60
57 Ales Hemsky .20 .50
58 Antoine Roussel .20 .50
59 Alex Goligoski .25 .60
60 John Klingberg .25 .60
61 Kari Lehtonen .25 .60
62 Tyler Seguin .50 1.25
63 Danny DeKeyser .25 .60
64 Darren Helm .20 .50
65 Riley Sheahan .20 .50
66 Jonathan Ericsson .20 .50
67 Niklas Kronwall .25 .60
68 Pavel Datsyuk .40 1.00
69 Tomas Tatar .25 .60
70 Ben Scrivens .25 .60
71 Benoit Pouliot .20 .50
72 Teddy Purcell .20 .50
73 Jordan Eberle .30 .75
74 Matt Hendricks .20 .50
75 Taylor Hall .60 1.50
76 Aaron Ekblad .30 .75
77 Brian Campbell .20 .50
78 Dave Bolland .20 .50
79 Erik Gudbranson .20 .50
80 Jussi Jokinen .20 .50
81 Roberto Luongo .50 1.25
82 Dustin Brown .25 .60
83 Jake Muzzin .25 .60
84 Jeff Carter .25 .60
85 Jonathan Quick .50 1.25
86 Marian Gaborik .30 .75
87 Tanner Pearson .20 .50
88 Trevor Lewis .20 .50
89 Jared Spurgeon .20 .50
90 Jason Zucker .25 .60
91 Devan Dubnyk .30 .75
92 Nino Niederreiter .25 .60
93 Ryan Suter .30 .75
94 Zach Parise .30 .75
95 Andrei Markov .25 .60
96 Tomas Plekanec .25 .60
97 David Desharnais .25 .60
98 Alexei Emelin .25 .60
99 Lars Eller .20 .50
100 Max Pacioretty .30 .75
101 Nathan Beaulieu .25 .60
102 P.K. Subban .50 1.25
103 Carter Hutton .20 .50
104 Eric Nystrom .20 .50
105 Filip Forsberg .40 1.00
106 James Neal .30 .75
107 Seth Jones .25 .60
108 Mike Fisher .25 .60
109 Pekka Rinne .40 1.00
110 Shea Weber .25 .60
111 Adam Henrique .25 .60
112 Andy Greene .20 .50
113 Cory Schneider .25 .60
114 Michael Cammalleri .25 .60
115 Patrik Elias .25 .60
116 Travis Zajac .25 .60
117 Frans Nielsen .20 .50
118 Jaroslav Halak .25 .60
119 John Tavares .60 1.50
120 Josh Bailey .20 .50
121 Nikolai Kulemin .25 .60
122 Ryan Strome .25 .60
123 Travis Hamonic .20 .50
124 Keith Yandle .25 .60
125 Derek Stepan .25 .60
126 Chris Kreider .25 .60
127 Daniel Girardi .20 .50
128 Derick Brassard .25 .60
129 Marc Staal .20 .50
130 Rick Nash .30 .75
131 Ryan McDonagh .25 .60
132 Clarke MacArthur .20 .50
133 Cody Ceci .20 .50
134 Andrew Hammond 1.00 2.50
135 Erik Karlsson .60 1.50
136 Kyle Turris .25 .60
137 Mika Zibanejad .30 .75
138 Brayden Schenn .30 .75
139 Claude Giroux .30 .75
140 Mark Streit .20 .50
141 Matt Read .20 .50
142 R.J. Umberger .20 .50
143 Michael Del Zotto .20 .50
144 Derrick Pouliot .25 .60
145 Chris Kunitz .30 .75
146 Marc-Andre Fleury .50 1.25
147 Evgeni Malkin 1.00 2.50
148 Kris Letang .30 .75
149 David Perron .20 .50
150 Patric Hornqvist .25 .60
151 Brent Burns .40 1.00
152 Joe Thornton .30 .75
153 Logan Couture .30 .75
154 Marc-Edouard Vlasic .20 .50
155 Patrick Marleau .30 .75
156 Tomas Hertl .30 .75
157 Alex Pietrangelo .25 .60
158 Alexander Steen .25 .60
159 David Backes .25 .60
160 Jake Allen .40 1.00
161 Kevin Shattenkirk .25 .60
162 Patrik Berglund .25 .60
163 Jori Lehtera .25 .60
164 Alex Killorn .25 .60
165 Brian Boyle .20 .50
166 Jonathan Drouin .40 1.00
167 Nikita Kucherov .50 1.25
168 Steven Stamkos .60 1.50
169 Tyler Johnson .25 .60
170 Victor Hedman .40 1.00
171 James Reimer .30 .75
172 James van Riemsdyk .30 .75
173 Joffrey Lupul .25 .60
174 Leo Komarov .25 .60
175 Morgan Rielly .25 .60
176 Nazem Kadri .25 .60
177 Tyler Bozak .25 .60
178 Christopher Tanev .20 .50
179 Bo Horvat .30 .75
180 Alexandre Burrows .25 .60
181 Henrik Sedin .30 .75
182 Jannik Hansen .20 .50
183 Derek Dorsett .25 .60
184 Ryan Miller .30 .75
185 Alexander Ovechkin 1.25 3.00
186 Brooks Orpik .20 .50
187 Evgeny Kuznetsov .50 1.25
188 John Carlson .40 1.00
189 Matt Niskanen .25 .60
190 Nicklas Backstrom .50 1.25
191 Jay Beagle .25 .60
192 Blake Wheeler .30 .75
193 Bryan Little .25 .60
194 Dustin Byfuglien .30 .75
195 Mathieu Perreault .20 .50
196 Ondrej Pavelec .30 .75
197 Tobias Enstrom .20 .50
198 Mark Scheifele .40 1.00
199 F.Forsberg/D.Keith CL .40 1.00
200 R.Nash/P.Subban CL .50 1.25
201 Connor McDavid YG RC 200.00 400.00
202 Jordan Weal YG RC 2.00 5.00
203 Sergei Plotnikov YG RC 1.50 4.00
204 Max Domi YG RC 8.00 20.00
205 Andrew Copp YG RC 2.00 5.00
206 Mikko Rantanen YG RC 8.00 20.00
207 Joel Edmundson YG RC 1.50 4.00
208 Kevin Fiala YG RC 2.00 5.00
209 Nick Cousins YG RC 2.00 5.00
210 Emile Poirier YG RC 2.00 5.00
211 Malcolm Subban YG RC 5.00 12.00
212 Jacob de la Rose YG RC 2.00 5.00
213 Henrik Samuelsson YG RC 1.50 4.00
214 Connor Hellebuyck YG RC 8.00 20.00
215 Matt Puempel YG RC 1.50 4.00
216 Nick Shore YG RC 2.00 5.00
217 Josh Anderson YG RC 2.00 5.00
218 Shane Prince YG RC 1.50 4.00
219 Jared McCann YG RC 2.00 5.00
220 Stanislav Galiev YG RC 2.00 5.00
221 Artemi Panarin YG RC 8.00 20.00
222 Viktor Arvidsson YG RC 8.00 20.00
223 Nikolaj Ehlers YG RC 6.00 15.00
224 Slater Koekkoek YG RC 1.50 4.00
225 Ronalds Kenins YG RC 2.00 5.00
226 Daniel Sprong YG RC 4.00 10.00
227 Nicolas Petan YG RC 2.50 6.00
228 Dylan Larkin YG RC 12.00 30.00
229 Robby Fabbri YG RC 4.00 10.00
230 Joonas Donskoi YG RC 4.00 10.00
231 Sam Bennett YG RC 5.00 12.00
232 Ben Hutton YG RC 2.00 5.00
233 Matt O'Connor YG RC 1.50 4.00
234 Oscar Lindberg YG RC 2.00 5.00
235 Colton Parayko YG RC 2.50 6.00
236 Stefan Noesen YG RC 1.50 4.00
237 Anton Slepyshev YG RC 1.50 4.00
238 Sergei Kalinin YG RC 1.50 4.00
239 Mike Condon YG RC 2.50 6.00
240 Antoine Bibeau YG RC 2.00 5.00
241 Kyle Baun YG RC 2.00 5.00
242 J-F Berube YG RC 1.50 4.00
243 Joonas Kemppainen YG RC 1.50 4.00
244 Mattias Janmark YG RC 2.00 5.00
245 Evgeny Medvedev YG RC 1.50 4.00
246 Keegan Lowe YG RC 2.00 5.00
247 Colin Miller YG RC 1.50 4.00
248 Brett Kulak YG RC 1.50 4.00
249 Connor Brickley YG RC 1.50 4.00
250 C.McDavid/S.Bennett CL 4.00 10.00
251 Andrew Cogliano .20 .50
252 Jiri Sekac .20 .50
253 Chris Stewart .20 .50
254 Corey Perry .30 .75
255 Jakob Silfverberg .25 .60
256 Ryan Kesler .25 .60
257 Carl Hagelin .25 .60
258 Antoine Vermette .20 .50
259 Mikkel Boedker .20 .50
260 Steve Downie .20 .50
261 Tobias Rieder .20 .50
262 Anthony Duclair .25 .60
263 Connor Murphy .20 .50
264 Matt Beleskey .20 .50
265 Ryan Spooner .25 .60
266 Torey Krug .25 .60
267 Patrice Bergeron .40 1.00
268 Brett Connolly .25 .60
269 Jimmy Hayes .20 .50
270 Matt Moulson .20 .50
271 David Legwand .20 .50
272 Ryan O'Reilly .30 .75
273 Chad Johnson .25 .60
274 Rasmus Ristolainen .25 .60
275 Evander Kane .30 .75
276 Mikael Backlund .25 .60
277 David Jones .20 .50
278 Mark Giordano .30 .75
279 T.J. Brodie .20 .50
280 Lance Bouma .20 .50
281 Dougie Hamilton .30 .75
282 Michael Frolik .20 .50
283 Sean Monahan .30 .75
284 Jordan Staal .25 .60
285 Riley Nash .20 .50
286 Eric Staal .40 1.00
287 Ron Hainsey .20 .50
288 Ryan Murphy .20 .50
289 Kris Versteeg .25 .60
290 Victor Rask .20 .50
291 Marko Dano .20 .50
292 Scott Darling .30 .75
293 Artem Anisimov .25 .60
294 Trevor Daley .20 .50
295 Teuvo Teravainen .30 .75
296 Brent Seabrook .30 .75
297 Patrick Kane .60 1.50
298 Mikhail Grigorenko .25 .60
299 Francois Beauchemin .20 .50
300 Blake Comeau .20 .50
301 Jarome Iginla .40 1.00
302 Nathan MacKinnon .60 1.50
303 Carl Soderberg .25 .60
304 Alex Tanguay .25 .60
305 Nikita Zadorov .25 .60
306 Boone Jenner .25 .60
307 Brandon Saad .30 .75
308 Sergei Bobrovsky .30 .75
309 Ryan Johansen .40 1.00
310 Ryan Murray .25 .60
311 Patrick Sharp .30 .75
312 Jason Spezza .25 .60
313 Johnny Oduya .20 .50
314 Jamie Benn .40 1.00
315 Antti Niemi .25 .60
316 Cody Eakin .25 .60
317 Henrik Zetterberg UER .40 1.00
Last name spelled
318 Justin Abdelkader .25 .60
319 Petr Mrazek .40 1.00
320 Mike Green .30 .75
321 Tomas Jurco .30 .75
322 Gustav Nyquist .30 .75
323 Brad Richards .30 .75
324 Jim Howard .30 .75
325 Andrej Sekera .20 .50
326 Justin Schultz .20 .50
327 Nail Yakupov .25 .60
328 Anton Lander .20 .50
329 Cam Talbot .40 1.00
330 Ryan Nugent-Hopkins .30 .75
331 Nick Bjugstad .25 .60
332 Vincent Trocheck .25 .60
333 Jaromir Jagr .75 2.00
334 Aleksander Barkov .30 .75
335 Brandon Pirri .30 .75
336 Reilly Smith .30 .75
337 Jonathan Huberdeau .30 .75
338 Tyler Toffoli .30 .75
339 Milan Lucic .30 .75
340 Alec Martinez .20 .50
341 Christian Ehrhoff .20 .50
342 Drew Doughty .30 .75
343 Brayden McNabb .20 .50
344 Anze Kopitar .50 1.25
345 Justin Fontaine .25 .60
346 Mathew Dumba .25 .60
347 Thomas Vanek .30 .75
348 Jason Pominville .25 .60
349 Mikko Koivu .25 .60
350 Charlie Coyle .25 .60
351 Marco Scandella .20 .50
352 Devante Smith-Pelly .20 .50
353 Dale Weise .20 .50
354 Tomas Fleischmann .20 .50
355 Jeff Petry .20 .50
356 Carey Price 1.00 2.50
357 Brendan Gallagher .40 1.00
358 Alex Galchenyuk .40 1.00
359 Craig Smith .25 .60
360 Roman Josi .30 .75
361 Calle Jarnkrok .25 .60
362 Mike Ribeiro .20 .50
363 Barret Jackman .20 .50
364 Colin Wilson .20 .50
365 Cody Hodgson .25 .60
366 Jacob Josefson .20 .50
367 Lee Stempniak .20 .50
368 Kyle Palmieri .25 .60
369 John Moore .20 .50
370 Adam Larsson .20 .50
371 Eric Gelinas .20 .50
372 Nick Leddy .20 .50
373 Kyle Okposo .30 .75
374 Marek Zidlicky .20 .50
375 Johnny Boychuk .25 .60
376 Anders Lee .25 .60
377 Brock Nelson .25 .60
378 Antti Raanta .25 .60
379 J.T. Miller .20 .50
380 Viktor Stalberg .20 .50
381 Kevin Hayes .25 .60
382 Henrik Lundqvist .40 1.00
383 Mats Zuccarello .25 .60
384 Milan Michalek .25 .60
385 Mark Stone .30 .75
386 Chris Neil .20 .50
387 Craig Anderson .25 .60
388 Bobby Ryan .25 .60
389 Mike Hoffman .25 .60
390 Curtis Lazar .25 .60
391 Jakub Voracek .30 .75
392 Scott Laughton .20 .50
393 Wayne Simmonds .40 1.00
394 Sam Gagner .20 .50
395 Steve Mason .20 .50
396 Sean Couturier .25 .60
397 Michael Raffl .25 .60
398 Sidney Crosby 1.25 3.00
399 Ian Cole .20 .50
400 Phil Kessel .50 1.25
401 Olli Maatta .25 .60
402 Nick Bonino .25 .60
403 Beau Bennett .20 .50
404 Martin Jones .30 .75
405 Matt Nieto .20 .50
406 Tommy Wingels .20 .50
407 Joel Ward .20 .50
408 Joe Pavelski .30 .75
409 Paul Martin .20 .50
410 Jay Bouwmeester .20 .50
411 Dmitrij Jaskin .20 .50
412 Vladimir Tarasenko .50 1.25
413 Paul Stastny .25 .60
414 Jaden Schwartz .40 1.00
415 Troy Brouwer .25 .60
416 Brian Elliott .25 .60
417 Valtteri Filppula .25 .60
418 Ben Bishop .30 .75
419 Anton Stralman .20 .50
420 Ryan Callahan .25 .60
421 Ondrej Palat .25 .60
422 Cedric Paquette .20 .50
423 Peter Holland .20 .50
424 Jake Gardiner .25 .60
425 P.A. Parenteau .20 .50
426 Jonathan Bernier .30 .75
427 Brad Boyes .20 .50
428 Nick Spaling .20 .50
429 Dion Phaneuf .30 .75
430 Daniel Sedin .30 .75
431 Brandon Sutter .25 .60
432 Radim Vrbata .25 .60
433 Alexander Edler .20 .50
434 Chris Higgins .20 .50
435 Brandon Prust .20 .50
436 Karl Alzner .20 .50
437 Marcus Johansson .25 .60
438 Braden Holtby .50 1.25
439 T.J. Oshie .50 1.25
440 Justin Williams .25 .60
441 Andre Burakovsky .25 .60
442 Michael Hutchinson .25 .60
443 Andrew Ladd .25 .60
444 Jacob Trouba .25 .60
445 Tyler Myers .25 .60
446 Drew Stafford .20 .50
447 Alexander Burmistrov .25 .60
448 Adam Lowry .20 .50
449 C.Price/H.Zetterberg CL 1.00 2.50
450 C.Perry/V.Tarasenko CL .50 1.25
451 Jack Eichel YG RC 30.00 80.00
452 Charles Hudon YG RC 2.00 5.00
453 Nikolay Goldobin YG RC 2.00 5.00
454 Logan Shaw YG RC 2.00 5.00
455 Frank Vatrano YG RC 4.00 10.00
456 Jujhar Khaira YG RC 1.50 4.00
457 Jake Virtanen YG RC 6.00 15.00
458 Andreas Athanasiou YG RC 6.00 15.00
459 Tanner Kero YG RC 2.00 5.00
460 Chris Wideman YG RC 2.00 5.00
461 Zachary Fucale YG RC 5.00 12.00
462 Hunter Shinkaruk YG RC 1.50 4.00
463 Brendan Ranford YG RC 1.50 4.00
464 Juuse Saros YG RC 2.50 6.00
465 Adam Pelech YG RC 1.50 4.00
466 Michael Keranen YG RC 1.50 4.00
467 Dylan DeMelo YG RC 1.50 4.00
468 Mark Alt YG RC 1.25 3.00
469 Jacob Slavin YG RC 1.50 4.00
470 Alexandre Grenier YG RC 1.50 4.00
471 Louis Domingue YG RC 2.50 6.00
472 Linus Ullmark YG RC 2.50 6.00
473 Derek Forbort YG RC 1.50 4.00
474 Brady Skjei YG RC 1.50 4.00
475 Ryan Hartman YG RC 2.50 6.00
476 Max McCormick YG RC 1.50 4.00
477 Vincent Hinostroza YG RC 1.25 3.00
478 Taylor Leier YG RC 2.00 5.00
479 Radek Faksa YG RC 2.00 5.00
480 Garret Sparks YG RC 3.00 8.00
481 Brendan Gaunce YG RC 2.00 5.00
482 Chris Driedger YG RC 1.50 4.00
483 Joel Vermin YG RC 1.50 4.00
484 Chandler Stephenson YG RC 2.00 5.00
485 David Musil YG RC 1.50 4.00
486 Gustav Olofsson YG RC 1.50 4.00
487 Brett Pesce YG RC 1.50 4.00
488 Anthony Stolarz YG RC 2.50 6.00
489 Devin Shore YG RC 1.50 4.00
490 Petr Straka YG RC 1.50 4.00
491 Mike McCarron YG RC 4.00 10.00
492 Raman Hrabarenka YG RC 1.50 4.00
493 Markus Hannikainen YG RC 1.50 4.00
494 Sam Brittain YG RC 2.00 5.00
495 Shea Theodore YG RC 2.50 6.00
496 Nick Ritchie YG RC 2.00 5.00
497 Brock McGinn YG RC 2.00 5.00
498 Tyler Randell YG RC 2.00 5.00
499 Noah Hanifin YG RC 2.50 6.00
500 J.Eichel/Z.Fucale YG CL 4.00 10.00
501 Ryan Johansen .40 1.00
502 Seth Jones .25 .60
503 Richard Panik .25 .60
504 Ben Scrivens .25 .60
505 Trevor Daley .25 .60
506 Zack Kassian .25 .60
507 Vincent Lecavalier .25 .60
508 Landon Ferraro
509 Mike Richards .30 .75
510 Mikael Granlund .25 .60
511 Vladislav Namestnikov .30 .75
512 Carl Hagelin .30 .75
513 Jarret Stoll .25 .60
514 Ryan Ellis .20 .50
515 Eric Staal .40 1.00
516 Luke Schenn .20 .50
517 Dion Phaneuf .30 .75
518 Andrew Ladd .30 .75
519 Mikkel Boedker .20 .50
520 David Perron .20 .50
521 Joonas Korpisalo YG RC 4.00 10.00
522 Laurent Dauphin YG RC 2.00 5.00
523 Michael Mersch YG RC 2.00 5.00
524 Daniel Carr YG RC 1.50 4.00
525 Joseph Blandisi YG RC 2.00 5.00
526 Matt Murray YG RC 40.00 100.00
527 Fredrik Claesson YG RC 2.00 5.00
528 Yanni Gourde YG RC 20.00 50.00
529 Phil Di Giuseppe YG RC 2.00 5.00
530 Jordan Weal YG RC 2.00 5.00
SP3 C.McDavid/W.Gretzky 60.00 150.00

2015-16 Upper Deck Exclusives

*1-450 VETS/100: 6X TO 15X BASIC CARDS
*201-250/451-500 YG/100: 2.5X TO 6X YG
40 Corey Crawford 5.00 12.00
166 Jonathan Drouin 5.00 12.00
187 Evgeny Kuznetsov 6.00 15.00
190 Nicklas Backstrom 6.00 15.00
201 Connor McDavid YG 1000.00 2000.00
204 Max Domi YG 80.00 150.00
221 Artemi Panarin YG 100.00 200.00
223 Nikolaj Ehlers YG 60.00 120.00
228 Dylan Larkin YG 100.00 200.00
231 Sam Bennett YG 50.00 100.00
239 Mike Condon YG 50.00 100.00
250 McDavid/S.Bennett CL 50.00 120.00
451 Jack Eichel YG 300.00 500.00
455 Frank Vatrano YG 30.00 80.00
475 Ryan Hartman YG 15.00 40.00
528 Yanni Gourde YG 25.00 60.00

2015-16 Upper Deck Foil

*VETERANS: 5X TO 12X BASIC CARDS
*YOUNG GUNS: .75X TO 2X BASIC YG
ISSUED VIA E-PACK OFFER
107 Evgeny Kuznetsov 5.00 12.00
190 Nicklas Backstrom 5.00 12.00
201 Connor McDavid YG 250.00 400.00
204 Max Domi YG 15.00 40.00
221 Artemi Panarin YG 20.00 50.00
228 Dylan Larkin YG 25.00 60.00
451 Jack Eichel YG 100.00 200.00

2015-16 Upper Deck A Piece of History 1000 Point Club

GRP A ODDS 1:47,952 SER.1
GRP B ODDS 1:24,218 SER.1
GRP C ODDS 1:9590 SER.1
GRP D ODDS 1:3996 SER.1
OVERALL ODDS 1:2400 SER.1
GRP A ODDS 1:8352 SER.2
GRP B ODDS 1:5011 SER.2
GRP C ODDS 1:1193 SER.2
OVERALL ODDS 1:864 SER.2
PCAO Adam Oates 2C 15.00 40.00
PCDG Doug Gilmour 2A 50.00 100.00
PCDH Dale Hawerchuk 2C 15.00 40.00
PCDS Denis Savard 2C 10.00 25.00
PCJI Jarome Iginla 1D 12.00 30.00
PCJJ Jaromir Jagr 2C 25.00 50.00
PCJK Jari Kurri 2C 15.00 40.00
PCJR Jeremy Roenick 2B 20.00 50.00
PCMD Marcel Dionne STK 1C 30.00 60.00
PCMG Mike Gartner 2B 20.00 50.00
PCMM Mike Modano STK 1A 150.00 300.00
PCMS Martin St. Louis 2A 50.00 100.00
PCRB Ray Bourque 2C 15.00 40.00
PCSL Steve Larmer STK 1C 30.00 60.00
PCTS Teemu Selanne 1B 30.00 60.00
PCVD Vincent Damphousse 1D 10.00 25.00

2015-16 Upper Deck A Piece of History 300 Win Club

GROUP A ODDS 1:8160
GROUP B ODDS 1:3400
OVERALL ODDS 1:2400
300HL Henrik Lundqvist B 25.00 50.00
300JV John Vanbiesbrouck STK A 60.00 100.00
300MF Marc-Andre Fleury B 20.00 50.00
300RM Ryan Miller B 12.00 30.00
300TB Tom Barrasso STK A 30.00 60.00
300TS Terry Sawchuk STK A 90.00 150.00

2015-16 Upper Deck Canvas

C1-C90 ODDS 1:7H, 1:7R, 1:14B SER.1
C121-C210 ODDS 1:6H, 1:6R, 1:12B SER.2
C1-C90 YG ODDS 1:48H/R, 1:96B SER.1
C211-C240 YG ODDS 1:48H/R, .75 2.00
1:96B SER.2
C241-C270 RET/POE ODDS 3.00 8.00
1:192H/R, 1:384B SER.2
C1 Corey Perry 1.00 2.50
C2 Cam Fowler .75 2.00
C3 Ryan Kesler .75 2.00
C4 Oliver Ekman-Larsson .75 2.00
C5 Mike Smith 1.00 2.50
C6 Tuukka Rask 1.00 2.50
C7 Brad Marchand 1.25 3.00
C8 Loui Eriksson .75 2.00
C9 David Pastrnak 1.50 4.00
C10 Zemgus Girgensons .75 2.00
C11 Tyler Ennis .75 2.00
C12 Jiri Hudler .75 2.00
C13 Sean Monahan 1.00 2.50
C14 Jonas Hiller .75 2.00
C15 Karri Ramo .75 2.00
C16 Cam Ward 1.00 2.50
C17 Elias Lindholm .60 1.50
C18 Justin Faulk .75 2.00
C19 Jonathan Toews 2.00 5.00
C20 Duncan Keith 1.00 2.50
C21 Marian Hossa .75 2.00
C22 Corey Crawford 1.25 3.00
C23 Matt Duchene 1.00 2.50
C24 Semyon Varlamov 1.00 2.50
C25 Scott Hartnell 1.00 2.50
C26 Brandon Dubinsky .75 2.00
C27 Jamie Benn 1.25 3.00
C28 Kari Lehtonen .75 2.00
C29 Henrik Zetterberg 1.25 3.00
C30 Niklas Kronwall .75 2.00
C31 Danny DeKeyser .75 2.00
C32 Tomas Tatar .75 2.00
C33 Ryan Nugent-Hopkins 1.00 2.50
C34 Jordan Eberle 1.00 2.50
C35 Ben Scrivens .75 2.00
C36 Aaron Ekblad 1.00 2.50
C37 Roberto Luongo 1.00 2.50
C38 Jussi Jokinen .60 1.50
C39 Jonathan Quick 1.50 4.00
C40 Marian Gaborik 1.00 2.50
C41 Jeff Carter 1.00 2.50
C42 Ryan Suter .60 1.50
C43 Zach Parise 1.00 2.50
C44 Carey Price 3.00 8.00
C45 Max Pacioretty 1.00 2.50
C46 Lars Eller .75 2.00
C47 Devante Smith-Pelly .75 2.00
C48 Filip Forsberg 1.25 3.00
C49 Pekka Rinne 1.25 3.00
C50 Shea Weber .75 2.00
C51 Mike Fisher .75 2.00
C52 Cory Schneider .75 2.00
C53 Michael Cammalleri .75 2.00
C54 Adam Henrique 1.00 2.50
C55 John Tavares 2.00 5.00
C56 Jaroslav Halak .75 2.00
C57 Ryan Strome .75 2.00
C58 Rick Nash 1.00 2.50
C59 Derick Brassard 1.00 2.50
C60 Keith Yandle 1.00 2.50
C61 Chris Kreider 1.00 2.50
C62 Clarke MacArthur .60 1.50
C63 Erik Karlsson 2.00 5.00
C64 Kyle Turris .75 2.00
C65 Claude Giroux 1.00 2.50
C66 Wayne Simmonds 1.25 3.00
C67 Matt Read .60 1.50
C68 Sidney Crosby 4.00 10.00
C69 David Perron .60 1.50
C70 Patric Hornqvist .75 2.00
C71 Kris Letang 1.00 2.50
C72 Logan Couture 1.00 2.50
C73 Patrick Marleau 1.00 2.50
C74 Brent Burns 1.25 3.00
C75 David Backes 1.00 2.50
C76 Alexander Steen 1.00 2.50
C77 Jake Allen 1.00 2.50
C78 Steven Stamkos 2.00 5.00
C79 Jonathan Drouin 1.25 3.00
C80 Victor Hedman 1.25 3.00
C81 James van Riemsdyk 1.00 2.50
C82 Nazem Kadri .75 2.00
C83 Morgan Rielly .75 2.00
C84 Ryan Miller 1.00 2.50
C85 Henrik Sedin 1.00 2.50
C86 Nicklas Backstrom 1.50 4.00
C87 Evgeny Kuznetsov 1.50 4.00
C88 Ondrej Pavelec 1.00 2.50
C89 Blake Wheeler 1.00 2.50

C90 J.Toews/S.Stamkos CL 1.25 3.00
C91 Jack Eichel YG 50.00 100.00
C92 Emile Poirier YG 4.00 10.00
C93 Colton Parayko YG 5.00 12.00
C94 Joonas Donskoi YG 4.00 10.00
C95 Andrew Copp YG 4.00 10.00
C96 Max Domi YG 8.00 20.00
C97 Kevin Fiala YG 4.00 10.00
C98 Mikko Rantanen YG 5.00 12.00
C99 Mattias Janmark YG 4.00 10.00
C100 Malcolm Subban YG 10.00 25.00
C101 Sam Bennett YG 10.00 25.00
C102 Jacob de la Rose YG 4.00 10.00
C103 Colin Miller YG 3.00 8.00
C104 Connor Hellebuyck YG 10.00 25.00
C105 Nick Shore YG 4.00 10.00
C106 Matt Puempel YG 3.00 8.00
C107 Stanislav Galiev YG 4.00 10.00
C108 Artemi Panarin YG 15.00 30.00
C109 Noah Hanifin YG 10.00 25.00
C110 Daniel Sprong YG 8.00 20.00
C111 Ronalds Kenins YG 4.00 10.00
C112 Dylan Larkin YG 25.00 50.00
C113 Antoine Bibeau YG 4.00 10.00
C114 Jared McCann YG 4.00 10.00
C115 Oscar Lindberg YG 4.00 10.00
C116 Nikolaj Ehlers YG 8.00 20.00
C117 Sergei Plotnikov YG 3.00 8.00
C118 Robby Fabbri YG 5.00 12.00
C119 Nicolas Petan YG 4.00 10.00
C120 J.Eichel/Larkin YG CL 10.00 25.00
C121 Ryan Getzlaf 1.50 4.00
C122 Frederik Andersen .75 2.00
C123 Sami Vatanen .60 1.50
C124 Shane Doan .75 2.00
C125 Mikkel Boedker .60 1.50
C126 Patrice Bergeron 1.25 3.00
C127 Zdeno Chara 1.00 2.50
C128 David Krejci .75 2.00
C129 Ryan O'Reilly 1.00 2.50
C130 Evander Kane 1.00 2.50
C131 Matt Moulson .75 2.00
C132 Mark Giordano 1.00 2.50
C133 Johnny Gaudreau 1.50 4.00
C134 Michael Frolik .60 1.50
C135 Eric Staal 1.25 3.00
C136 Victor Rask .60 1.50
C137 Teuvo Teravainen 1.00 2.50
C138 Patrick Kane 2.00 5.00
C139 Brent Seabrook 1.00 2.50
C140 Gabriel Landeskog 1.00 2.50
C141 Jarome Iginla 1.00 2.50
C142 Nathan MacKinnon 2.00 5.00
C143 Brandon Saad 1.00 2.50
C144 Ryan Johansen 1.25 3.00
C145 Sergei Bobrovsky 1.00 2.50
C146 Patrick Sharp 1.00 2.50
C147 John Klingberg .75 2.00
C148 Tyler Seguin 1.50 4.00
C149 Jason Spezza .75 2.00
C150 Pavel Datsyuk 1.25 3.00
C151 Jim Howard 1.00 2.50
C152 Justin Abdelkader .75 2.00
C153 Teddy Purcell 1.00 2.50
C154 Taylor Hall 2.00 5.00
C155 Nail Yakupov .75 2.00
C156 Nick Bjugstad .75 2.00
C157 Jaromir Jagr 2.50 6.00
C158 Jonathan Huberdeau 1.00 2.50
C159 Milan Lucic .75 2.00
C160 Drew Doughty 1.00 2.50
C161 Anze Kopitar 1.50 4.00
C162 Mikael Granlund .75 2.00
C163 Devan Dubnyk 1.00 2.50
C164 Mikko Koivu .75 2.00
C165 Jason Pominville .75 2.00
C166 P.K. Subban 1.50 4.00
C167 Brendan Gallagher 1.25 3.00
C168 Tomas Plekanec 1.00 2.50
C169 Roman Josi 1.00 2.50
C170 Mike Ribeiro .75 2.00
C171 James Neal 1.00 2.50
C172 Lee Stempniak .60 1.50
C173 Travis Zajac .75 2.00
C174 Nick Leddy .60 1.50
C175 Kyle Okposo 1.00 2.50
C176 Anders Lee 1.00 2.50
C177 Henrik Lundqvist 1.25 3.00
C178 Ryan McDonagh .75 2.00
C179 Derek Stepan 1.00 2.50
C180 Mike Hoffman .75 2.00
C181 Mark Stone .75 2.00
C182 Bobby Ryan .75 2.00
C183 Andrew Hammond 3.00 8.00
C184 Jakub Voracek 1.00 2.50
C185 Steve Mason .75 2.00
C186 Marc-Andre Fleury 1.50 4.00
C187 Evgeni Malkin 3.00 8.00
C188 Phil Kessel 1.50 4.00
C189 Joe Thornton 1.00 2.50
C190 Joe Pavelski 1.00 2.50
C191 Brian Elliott .75 2.00
C192 Vladimir Tarasenko 1.50 4.00
C193 Paul Stastny 1.00 2.50
C194 Ryan Callahan 1.00 2.50
C195 Ben Bishop 1.00 2.50
C196 Tyler Johnson .75 2.00
C197 Dion Phaneuf 1.00 2.50
C198 Tyler Bozak .75 2.00
C199 Jonathan Bernier 1.00 2.50
C200 Alexandre Burrows .75 2.00
C201 Radim Vrbata .75 2.00
C202 Daniel Sedin 1.00 2.50
C203 Alexander Ovechkin 4.00 10.00
C204 Andre Burakovsky .75 2.00
C205 T.J. Oshie 1.50 4.00
C206 Braden Holtby 1.50 4.00
C207 Andrew Ladd 1.00 2.50
C208 Bryan Little .75 2.00
C209 Dustin Byfuglien 1.00 2.50
C210 P.Subban/P.Kane CL 1.25 3.00
C211 Connor McDavid YG 175.00 250.00
C212 Andreas Athanasiou YG 6.00 15.00
C213 Adam Pelech YG 3.00 8.00
C214 Zachary Fucale YG 8.00 20.00
C215 Jake Virtanen YG 8.00 20.00
C216 Brady Skjei YG 3.00 8.00
C217 Linus Ullmark YG 5.00 12.00
C218 Viktor Arvidsson YG 5.00 12.00
C219 Juuse Saros YG 5.00 12.00
C220 Brendan Gaunce YG 5.00 12.00
C221 Brock McGinn YG 4.00 10.00
C222 Chris Wideman YG 4.00 10.00
C223 Connor Brickley YG 3.00 8.00
C224 Hunter Shinkaruk YG 4.00 10.00
C225 Nick Cousins YG 4.00 10.00
C226 Brett Pesce YG 3.00 8.00
C227 Shea Theodore YG 4.00 10.00
C228 Garret Sparks YG 6.00 15.00
C229 Devin Shore YG 4.00 10.00
C230 Mike McCarron YG 5.00 12.00
C231 Jaccob Slavin YG 3.00 8.00
C232 Shane Prince YG 3.00 8.00
C233 Ryan Hartman YG 5.00 12.00
C234 Nick Ritchie YG 4.00 10.00
C235 Gustav Olofsson YG 4.00 10.00
C236 Mike Condon YG 4.00 10.00
C237 Charles Hudon YG 4.00 10.00
C238 Nikolay Goldobin YG 4.00 10.00
C239 Ben Hutton YG 4.00 10.00
C240 C.McDavid/J.Virtanen YG CL 20.00 40.00
C241 Bobby Clarke RET 10.00 25.00
C242 Joe Sakic RET 15.00 40.00
C243 Bobby Hull RET 10.00 25.00
C244 Guy Lafleur RET 12.00 30.00
C245 Phil Esposito RET 15.00 40.00
C246 Patrick Roy RET 12.00 30.00
C247 Martin Brodeur RET 12.00 30.00
C248 Jeremy Roenick RET 10.00 25.00
C249 Wayne Gretzky RET 25.00 50.00
C250 Mark Messier RET 15.00 40.00
C251 Teemu Selanne RET 20.00 50.00
C252 Theoren Fleury RET 12.00 30.00
C253 Bobby Orr RET 30.00 80.00
C254 Doug Gilmour RET 12.00 30.00
C255 Jari Kurri RET 10.00 25.00
C256 Charles Hudon POE 8.00 20.00
C257 Sam Bennett POE 10.00 25.00
C258 Malcolm Subban POE 20.00 50.00
C259 Hunter Shinkaruk POE 8.00 20.00
C260 Max Domi POE 15.00 40.00
C261 Jake Virtanen POE 10.00 25.00
C262 Slater Koekkoek POE 6.00 15.00
C263 Nicolas Petan POE 8.00 20.00
C264 Josh Anderson POE 8.00 20.00
C265 Robby Fabbri POE 10.00 25.00
C266 Zachary Fucale POE 8.00 20.00
C267 Nick Ritchie POE 8.00 20.00
C268 Shea Theodore POE 8.00 20.00
C269 Brendan Gaunce POE 10.00 25.00
C270 Connor McDavid POE 150.00 300.00

2015-16 Upper Deck Canvas Autographs

CABH Brett Hull/16 125.00 200.00
CARN Rick Nash/61 40.00 80.00

2015-16 Upper Deck Clear Cut Foundations

STATED PRINT RUN 25 SER.#'d SETS
CCF1 C.Perry/J.Silfverberg 15.00 40.00
CCF2 M.Boedker/T.Rieder 10.00 25.00
CCF3 P.Bergeron/D.Pastrnak 40.00 80.00
CCF4 Z.Girgensons/T.Ennis 25.00 50.00
CCF5 J.Hudler/J.Gaudreau 20.00 50.00
CCF6 E.Staal/J.Faulk 20.00 50.00
CCF7 J.Toews/C.Crawford 30.00 80.00
CCF8 N.MacKinnon/T.Barrie 30.00 80.00
CCF9 R.Johansen/N.Foligno 20.00 50.00
CCF10 T.Seguin/C.Eakin 25.00 60.00
CCF11 H.Zetterberg/T.Tatar 20.00 50.00
CCF12 J.Eberle/L.Draisaitl 15.00 40.00
CCF13 J.Jagr/J.Huberdeau 20.00 50.00
CCF14 T.Pearson/T.Toffoli 15.00 40.00
CCF15 D.Dubnyk/M.Dumba 15.00 40.00
CCF16 M.Pacioretty/A.Galchenyuk 20.00 50.00
CCF17 R.Josi/F.Forsberg 20.00 50.00
CCF18 C.Schneider/A.Henrique 12.00 30.00
CCF19 J.Tavares/B.Nelson 30.00 80.00
CCF20 H.Lundqvist/C.Kreider 20.00 50.00
CCF21 E.Karlsson/M.Stone 30.00 80.00
CCF22 C.Giroux/W.Simmonds 20.00 50.00
CCF23 K.Letang/M.Fleury 25.00 60.00
CCF24 L.Couture/B.Burns 12.00 30.00
CCF25 J.Schwartz/V.Tarasenko 25.00 60.00
CCF26 S.Stamkos/T.Johnson 15.00 40.00
CCF27 M.Rielly/J.van Riemsdyk 15.00 40.00
CCF28 B.Horvat/D.Sedin 20.00 50.00
CCF29 A.Ovechkin/M.Johansson 60.00 150.00
CCF30 M.Scheifele/J.Trouba 20.00 50.00

2015-16 Upper Deck Clear Cut Honoured Members

HOF55 Rob Blake 12.00 30.00
HOF56 Chris Chelios 12.00 30.00
HOF57 Mike Modano 20.00 50.00
HOF58 Brad Park 15.00 40.00
HOF59 Steve Yzerman 20.00 50.00
HOF60 Lanny McDonald 12.00 30.00

2015-16 Upper Deck Clear Cut Superstars

CC33-CC62 ODDS 1:360 SERIES 1
CC33-CC62 ODDS 1:640 SERIES 2
CCS1 Patrick Kane 12.00 30.00
CCS2 John Tavares 12.00 30.00
CCS3 Jakub Voracek 8.00 20.00
CCS4 Patrice Bergeron 8.00 20.00
CCS5 Drew Doughty 6.00 15.00
CCS6 Oliver Ekman-Larsson 5.00 12.00
CCS7 Marc-Andre Fleury 10.00 25.00
CCS8 Bobby Orr 25.00 50.00
CCS9 Shea Weber 5.00 12.00
CCS10 Mark Messier 10.00 25.00
CCS11 Vladimir Tarasenko 10.00 25.00
CCS12 Rick Nash 6.00 15.00
CCS13 Jamie Benn 8.00 20.00
CCS14 Johnny Gaudreau 10.00 25.00
CCS15 Aaron Ekblad 6.00 15.00
CCS16 Henrik Zetterberg 8.00 20.00
CCS17 Martin Brodeur 12.00 30.00
CCS18 Henrik Lundqvist 8.00 20.00
CCS19 Erik Karlsson 12.00 30.00
CCS20 James van Riemsdyk 6.00 15.00
CCS21 Brett Hull 6.00 15.00
CCS22 Pavel Datsyuk 8.00 20.00
CCS23 Daniel Sedin 6.00 15.00
CCS24 Wayne Gretzky 25.00 50.00
CCS25 Filip Forsberg 8.00 20.00
CCS26 Duncan Keith 6.00 15.00
CCS27 Alexander Ovechkin 25.00 60.00
CCS28 Steven Stamkos 12.00 30.00
CCS29 Ryan Getzlaf 10.00 25.00
CCS30 Max Pacioretty 6.00 15.00
CCS31 Sidney Crosby 25.00 60.00
CCS32 Carey Price 20.00 40.00
CCS33 Brian Leetch 8.00 20.00
CCS34 Jiri Hudler 6.00 15.00
CCS35 Corey Perry 8.00 20.00
CCS36 Brandon Saad 8.00 20.00
CCS37 Zach Parise 8.00 20.00
CCS38 David Krejci 6.00 15.00
CCS39 Adam Henrique 8.00 20.00
CCS40 Doug Gilmour 10.00 25.00
CCS41 Ryan O'Reilly 8.00 20.00
CCS42 Anthony Duclair 6.00 15.00
CCS43 Alexander Steen 8.00 20.00
CCS44 Connor McDavid 175.00 300.00
CCS45 Nathan MacKinnon 15.00 40.00
CCS46 Tyler Seguin 12.00 30.00
CCS47 Claude Giroux 8.00 20.00
CCS48 Evgeny Kuznetsov 12.00 30.00
CCS49 Roberto Luongo 8.00 20.00
CCS50 Jonathan Toews 15.00 40.00
CCS51 Blake Wheeler 8.00 20.00
CCS52 Kris Versteeg 6.00 15.00
CCS53 Victor Hedman 10.00 25.00
CCS54 Steve Yzerman 12.00 30.00
CCS55 Joe Pavelski 8.00 20.00
CCS56 Ryan Miller 8.00 20.00
CCS57 Patrick Roy 20.00 50.00
CCS58 Mike Bossy 8.00 20.00
CCS59 Jonathan Quick 12.00 30.00
CCS60 Mark Stone 6.00 15.00
CCS61 Pekka Rinne 10.00 25.00
CCS62 Mario Lemieux 25.00 60.00

2015-16 Upper Deck Code to Greatness

ISSUED VIA E-PACK OFFER
CTG00 Connor McDavid 175.00 300.00
CTG0 Connor McDavid 15.00 40.00
CTG1 P.K. Subban 3.00 8.00
CTG2 Alexander Ovechkin 8.00 20.00
CTG3 Patrick Kane 4.00 10.00
CTG4 Jamie Benn 2.50 6.00
CTG5 Wayne Simmonds 2.50 6.00
CTG6 Jaromir Jagr 5.00 12.00
CTG7 Jonathan Bernier 2.00 5.00
CTG8 Tuukka Rask 2.00 5.00
CTG9 Jordan Eberle 2.00 5.00
CTG10 Ryan Johansen 2.50 6.00
CTG11 Pavel Datsyuk 2.50 6.00
CTG12 Evgeni Malkin 6.00 15.00
CTG13 Ryan Getzlaf 3.00 8.00
CTG14 Sidney Crosby 8.00 20.00
CTG15 Steven Stamkos 4.00 10.00
CTG16 Pekka Rinne 2.50 6.00
CTG17 Jonathan Quick 3.00 8.00
CTG18 Henrik Zetterberg 2.50 6.00
CTG19 John Tavares 4.00 10.00
CTG20 Carey Price 6.00 15.00
CTG21 Brett Hull 2.00 5.00
CTG22 Ray Bourque 3.00 8.00
CTG23 Steve Yzerman 3.00 8.00
CTG24 Mario Lemieux 6.00 15.00
CTG25 Wayne Gretzky 10.00 25.00

2015-16 Upper Deck Day With The Cup

1-15 RANDOM INSERTS IN SERIES 1
16-26 RANDOM INSERTS IN SERIES 2
DC1 Patrick Sharp 25.00 50.00
DC2 Niklas Hjalmarsson 15.00 40.00
DC3 Jonathan Toews 30.00 60.00
DC4 Brent Seabrook 15.00 40.00
DC5 Antti Raanta 15.00 40.00
DC6 Andrew Desjardins 10.00 25.00
DC7 Daniel Carcillo 12.00 30.00
DC8 Antoine Vermette 10.00 25.00
DC9 Brandon Saad 15.00 40.00
DC10 Brad Richards 15.00 40.00
DC11 Kimmo Timonen 12.00 30.00
DC12 Duncan Keith 15.00 40.00
DC13 Marian Hossa 12.00 30.00
DC14 Teuvo Teravainen 15.00 40.00
DC15 Trevor van Riemsdyk 12.00 30.00
DC16 Johnny Oduya 12.00 30.00
DC17 Marcus Kruger 15.00 40.00
DC18 Corey Crawford 20.00 50.00
DC19 Scott Darling 15.00 40.00
DC20 Patrick Kane 50.00 100.00
DC21 Bryan Bickell 10.00 25.00
DC22 Kris Versteeg 12.00 30.00
DC23 Andrew Shaw 15.00 40.00
DC24 David Rundblad 12.00 30.00
DC25 Kyle Cumiskey 10.00 25.00
DC26 Joakim Nordstrom 12.00 30.00

2015-16 Upper Deck Day With The Cup Flashback

RANDOM INSERTS IN SERIES 2
DCF1 Mike Bossy 15.00 40.00
DCF2 Denis Potvin 15.00 40.00
DCF3 Bob Nystrom 12.00 30.00

2015-16 Upper Deck Game Jerseys

COMPLETE SET (72)
GRP A ODDS 1:10,724 SER.1
GRP B ODDS 1:1071 SER.1
GRP C ODDS 1:266 SER.1
GRP D ODDS 1:209 SER.1
GRP E ODDS 1:104 SER.1
GRP F ODDS 1:90 SER.1
GRP G ODDS 1:89 SER.1
OVERALL STATED ODDS 1:24
UNPRICED GRP A ODDS 1:588,924 SER.2
GRP B ODDS 1:18,846 SER.2
GRP C ODDS 1:2,319 SER.2
GRP D ODDS 1:1,322 SER.2
GRP E ODDS 1:1,047 SER.2
GRP F ODDS 1:117 SER.2
GRP G ODDS 1:99 SER.2
OVERALL STATED ODDS 1:48
GJAB Aleksander Barkov 2G 3.00 8.00
GJAE Aaron Ekblad 1E 3.00 8.00
GJAG Alex Galchenyuk 1F 4.00 10.00
GJAK Anze Kopitar 2E 5.00 12.00
GJAO Alexander Ovechkin 1B 25.00 60.00
GJBB Brent Burns 1C 5.00 12.00
GJBE Jamie Benn 1E 4.00 10.00
GJBH Brett Hull 2C 10.00 25.00
GJBI Ben Bishop 1F 3.00 8.00
GJBR Bobby Ryan 1G 2.50 6.00
GJBW Blake Wheeler 1C 4.00 10.00
GJCC Charlie Coyle 1F 2.50 6.00
GJCG Claude Giroux 2D 4.00 10.00
GJCK1 Chris Kreider 1F 3.00 8.00
GJCK2 Chris Kreider 2G 3.00 8.00
GJCO Corey Crawford 1E 4.00 10.00
GJCP1 Corey Perry 2F 3.00 8.00
GJCP2 Carey Price 1B 20.00 50.00
GJCR Sidney Crosby 1B 25.00 60.00
GJCW Cam Ward 2G 3.00 8.00
GJDB Dustin Byfuglien 2F 3.00 8.00
GJDD1 Drew Doughty 1F 3.00 8.00
GJDD2 Drew Doughty 2D 4.00 10.00
GJDG Doug Gilmour 2A
GJDK David Krejci 1E 2.50 6.00
GJDP Dion Phaneuf 2D 4.00 10.00
GJDS Derek Stepan 2G 3.00 8.00
GJEK1 Erik Karlsson 2F 6.00 15.00
GJEK2 Evgeny Kuznetsov 1D 6.00 15.00
GJEL Elias Lindholm 1G 2.50 6.00
GJEM Evgeni Malkin 1C 4.00 10.00
GJES Eric Staal 2G 4.00 10.00
GJFA Frederik Andersen 2F 2.50 6.00
GJFF Filip Forsberg 2F 4.00 10.00
GJGF Grant Fuhr 2C 10.00 25.00
GJGL Gabriel Landeskog 2F 3.00 8.00
GJGN Gustav Nyquist 1D 4.00 10.00
GJHE Tomas Hertl 1G 3.00 8.00
GJHL1 Henrik Lundqvist 1C 4.00 10.00
GJHL2 Henrik Lundqvist 2F 4.00 10.00
GJHS Henrik Sedin 1E 3.00 8.00
GJHU Jonathan Huberdeau 1E 3.00 8.00
GJHZ Henrik Zetterberg 1C 5.00 12.00
GJJB Jonathan Bernier 1G 3.00 8.00
GJJC John Carlson 2G 2.50 6.00
GJJD Jonathan Drouin 1D 5.00 12.00
GJJE Jordan Eberle 1E 3.00 8.00
GJJG Johnny Gaudreau 1C 6.00 15.00
GJJH Jonas Hiller 1G 2.50 6.00
GJJI Jiri Hudler 1F 2.50 6.00
GJJN James Neal 1E 3.00 8.00
GJJO Roman Josi 2F 3.00 8.00
GJJP1 Joe Pavelski 2E 3.00 8.00
GJJP2 Jason Pominville 1E 2.50 6.00
GJJQ1 Jonathan Quick 1G 5.00 12.00
GJJQ2 Jonathan Quick 2G 5.00 12.00
GJJS Jeff Skinner 2G 2.50 6.00
GJJT1 Jacob Trouba 1F 2.50 6.00
GJJT2 Jacob Trouba 2F 2.50 6.00
GJJV1 James van Riemsdyk 1G 3.00 8.00
GJJV2 Jakub Voracek 2G 3.00 8.00
GJKA Erik Karlsson 1C 8.00 20.00
GJKE Duncan Keith 2F 3.00 8.00
GJKH Kevin Hayes 2F 3.00 8.00
GJKL Kari Lehtonen 2F 2.50 6.00
GJKO Kyle Okposo 1E 3.00 8.00
GJKR Niklas Kronwall 2G 2.50 6.00
GJLC Logan Couture 2F 3.00 8.00
GJLE Kris Letang 2G 3.00 8.00
GJMF Marc-Andre Fleury 2G 5.00 12.00
GJMG Mikael Granlund 2G 2.50 6.00
GJML Milan Lucic 1E 2.50 6.00
GJMP Max Pacioretty 1F 3.00 8.00
GJMS Mark Scheifele 2G 4.00 10.00
GJNB Nicklas Backstrom 1C 6.00 15.00
GJNK Nazem Kadri 1F 2.50 6.00
GJNM Nathan MacKinnon 1E 6.00 15.00
GJOE Oliver Ekman-Larsson 2F 2.50 6.00
GJOL Oliver Ekman-Larsson 1E 2.50 6.00
GJOP Ondrej Palat 1D 3.00 8.00
GJPA Ondrej Pavelec 1G 3.00 8.00
GJPK1 Phil Kessel 2F 5.00 12.00
GJPK2 P.K. Subban 1D 6.00 15.00
GJPM Patrick Marleau 2G 3.00 8.00
GJPR Patrick Roy 1A 50.00 100.00
GJPS1 Patrick Sharp 1E 3.00 8.00
GJPS2 P.K. Subban 2F 5.00 12.00
GJRG Ryan Getzlaf 1D 6.00 15.00
GJRI Pekka Rinne 1E 4.00 10.00
GJRJ Ryan Johansen 2F 4.00 10.00
GJRL Roberto Luongo 2F 3.00 8.00
GJRM Ryan Miller 1E 3.00 8.00
GJRN Rick Nash 1E 3.00 8.00
GJRS Ryan Strome 2F 2.50 6.00
GJSB Sergei Bobrovsky 1F 3.00 8.00
GJSC Sean Couturier 1F 3.00 8.00
GJSD Shane Doan 1G 2.50 6.00
GJSH Scott Hartnell 1F 3.00 8.00
GJSJ Seth Jones 1G 2.50 6.00
GJSM1 Steve Mason 1F 2.50 6.00
GJSM2 Steve Mason 2G 2.50 6.00
GJSP Jason Spezza 2G 2.50 6.00
GJSR Sam Reinhart 1F 3.00 8.00
GJSS Steven Stamkos 1C 4.00 10.00
GJSV Semyon Varlamov 1G 3.00 8.00
GJSY Steve Yzerman 2B 25.00 50.00
GJTA John Tavares 1C 8.00 20.00
GJTF Theoren Fleury 2C 15.00 30.00
GJTH Taylor Hall 1D 8.00 20.00
GJTJ Tomas Jurco 1F 3.00 8.00
GJTO Jonathan Toews 1B 12.00 30.00
GJTR Tuukka Rask 2F 3.00 8.00
GJTS1 Tyler Seguin 1D 6.00 15.00
GJTS2 Tyler Seguin 2E 5.00 12.00
GJTT Tyler Toffoli 1G 3.00 8.00
GJVH Victor Hedman 1D 5.00 12.00
GJVN Valeri Nichushkin 1F 2.50 6.00
GJVT Vladimir Tarasenko 1B 10.00 25.00
GJZC Zdeno Chara 1F 3.00 8.00
GJZG Zemgus Girgensons 1D 3.00 8.00

2015-16 Upper Deck Instant Impressions

ISSUED VIA E-PACK OFFER
II00 Jack Eichel 50.00 100.00
II0 Jack Eichel 5.00 12.00
II1 Malcolm Subban 3.00 8.00
II2 Johnny Gaudreau 2.00 5.00
II3 Mike Hoffman 1.00 2.50
II4 Vladimir Tarasenko 2.00 5.00
II5 Jonathan Drouin 1.50 4.00
II6 Nathan MacKinnon 2.50 6.00
II7 Seth Jones 1.00 2.50
II8 Sean Monahan 1.25 3.00
II9 Elias Lindholm .75 2.00
II10 Jonathan Huberdeau 1.25 3.00
II11 Ryan Strome 1.00 2.50
II12 Alex Galchenyuk 1.50 4.00
II13 Jacob Trouba 1.00 2.50
II14 Zemgus Girgensons 1.00 2.50
II15 Nick Bjugstad 1.00 2.50
II16 Kevin Hayes 1.25 3.00
II17 Mikael Granlund 1.00 2.50
II18 Riley Sheahan 1.00 2.50
II19 Morgan Rielly 1.00 2.50
II20 Aaron Ekblad 1.25 3.00
II21 Sam Bennett 1.50 4.00
II22 Ryan Hartman 1.50 4.00
II23 Filip Forsberg 1.50 4.00
II24 Nikita Kucherov 2.00 5.00
II25 Jacob de la Rose 1.25 3.00

2015-16 Upper Deck NHL Draft

SP1 Connor McDavid SP 150.00 300.00
SP2 Jack Eichel SP 100.00 200.00
SP1A Connor McDavid AU SP 1200.00 2000.00

2015-16 Upper Deck Oversized

VETS ONE PER SPECIAL SER.2 BLASTER
YG's ONE PER SPECIAL SER.1 BLASTER
20 Tuukka Rask 1.50 4.00
44 Jonathan Toews 3.00 8.00
62 Tyler Seguin 2.50 6.00
68 Pavel Datsyuk 2.00 5.00
85 Jonathan Quick 2.50 6.00
102 P.K. Subban 2.50 6.00
110 Shea Weber 1.25 3.00
119 John Tavares 3.00 8.00
130 Rick Nash 1.50 4.00
139 Claude Giroux 1.50 4.00
147 Evgeni Malkin 5.00 12.00
168 Steven Stamkos 3.00 8.00
172 James van Riemsdyk 1.50 4.00
185 Alexander Ovechkin 6.00 15.00
201 Connor McDavid YG 40.00 80.00
204 Max Domi YG 3.00 8.00
206 Mikko Rantanen YG 3.00 8.00
208 Kevin Fiala YG 1.50 4.00
210 Emile Poirier YG 1.50 4.00
211 Malcolm Subban YG 4.00 10.00
212 Jacob de la Rose YG 1.50 4.00
214 Connor Hellebuyck YG 4.00 10.00
219 Jared McCann YG 1.50 4.00
221 Artemi Panarin YG 6.00 15.00
223 Nikolaj Ehlers YG 3.00 8.00
228 Dylan Larkin YG 12.50 25.00
229 Robby Fabbri YG 2.00 5.00
231 Sam Bennett YG 2.00 5.00
451 Jack Eichel 6.00 15.00
452 Charles Hudon 1.50 4.00
453 Nikolay Goldobin 1.50 4.00
457 Jake Virtanen 2.00 5.00
458 Andreas Athanasiou 4.00 10.00
461 Zachary Fucale 1.50 4.00
462 Hunter Shinkaruk 1.50 4.00
464 Juuse Saros 2.00 5.00
471 Louis Domingue 1.50 4.00
472 Linus Ullmark 2.00 5.00
480 Garret Sparks 2.00 5.00
495 Shea Theodore 1.50 4.00
496 Nick Ritchie 1.50 4.00
499 Noah Hanifin 2.00 5.00

2015-16 Upper Deck Parkhurst Rookies

*BLUE: .8X TO 2X BASIC INSERTS
PR1 Connor McDavid 10.00 25.00
PR2 Jack Eichel 5.00 12.00
PR3 Sam Bennett 1.50 4.00
PR4 Dylan Larkin 4.00 10.00
PR5 Nikolaj Ehlers 2.50 6.00
PR6 Max Domi 2.50 6.00
PR7 Mikko Rantanen 2.50 6.00
PR8 Robby Fabbri 1.50 4.00
PR9 Jared McCann 1.25 3.00
PR10 Artemi Panarin 4.00 10.00

2015-16 Upper Deck Parkhurst Rookies Red

*RED: 1.5X TO 4X BASIC INSERTS
PR1 Connor McDavid 60.00 120.00

2015-16 Upper Deck Puck Wizards

COMPLETE SET (6)
ONE PER TOYS'R'US PACK
PW1 Patrick Kane 6.00 15.00
PW6 Sidney Crosby 12.00 30.00

2015-16 Upper Deck Rookie Breakouts

SER. 2 STATED PRINT RUN 100
RB1 Connor McDavid 350.00 500.00
RB2 Mikko Rantanen 15.00 40.00
RB3 Daniel Sprong 15.00 40.00
RB4 Kevin Fiala 8.00 20.00
RB5 Sam Bennett 10.00 25.00
RB6 Oscar Lindberg 8.00 20.00
RB7 Sergei Plotnikov 6.00 15.00
RB8 Nick Shore 8.00 20.00
RB9 Malcolm Subban 20.00 40.00
RB10 Max Domi 30.00 60.00
RB11 Robby Fabbri 20.00 40.00
RB12 Jared McCann 8.00 20.00
RB13 Matt Puempel 6.00 15.00
RB14 Viktor Arvidsson 10.00 25.00
RB15 Emile Poirier 8.00 20.00
RB16 Jordan Weal 8.00 20.00
RB17 Noah Hanifin 10.00 25.00
RB18 Nicolas Petan 8.00 20.00
RB19 Nikolaj Ehlers 20.00 40.00
RB20 Jake Virtanen 20.00 40.00
RB21 Nikolay Goldobin 8.00 20.00
RB22 Joonas Donskoi 8.00 20.00
RB23 Nick Ritchie 8.00 20.00
RB24 Andreas Athanasiou 25.00 50.00
RB25 Jacob de la Rose 8.00 20.00
RB26 Artemi Panarin 40.00 80.00
RB27 Dylan Larkin 60.00 120.00
RB28 Jack Eichel 125.00 200.00

2015-16 Upper Deck Rookie Breakouts Gold

COMPLETE SET (12)
STATED PRINT RUN 25 SER.#'d SETS

2015-16 Upper Deck Rookie Materials

COMPLETE SET (36)
GROUP A ODDS 1:2401
GROUP B ODDS 1:1554
GROUP C ODDS 1:271
GROUP D ODDS 1:62
OVERALL STATED ODDS 1:48
RMAA Andreas Athanasiou D 4.00 10.00
RMAB Antoine Bibeau D 1.50 4.00
RMAP Artemi Panarin D 5.00 12.00
RMAS Anthony Stolarz D 1.50 4.00
RMBR Brendan Ranford D 1.25 3.00
RMCH Connor Hellebuyck D 4.00 10.00
RMCM Connor McDavid B 12.00 30.00
RMDF Derek Forbort D 1.25 3.00
RMDL Dylan Larkin C 5.00 12.00
RMEP Emile Poirier D 1.50 4.00
RMHS Henrik Samuelsson D 1.25 3.00
RMJA Josh Anderson C 1.50 4.00
RMJD Jacob de la Rose D 1.50 4.00
RMJE Jack Eichel B 6.00 15.00
RMJM Jared McCann A 1.50 4.00
RMJV Jake Virtanen C 2.00 5.00
RMJW Jordan Weal D 1.50 4.00
RMKF Kevin Fiala D 1.50 4.00
RMMD Max Domi C 3.00 8.00
RMMP Matt Puempel D 1.25 3.00
RMMR Mikko Rantanen D 3.00 8.00
RMMS Mackenzie Skapski D 1.50 4.00
RMNC Nick Cousins D 1.50 4.00
RMNE Nikolaj Ehlers C 3.00 8.00
RMNH Noah Hanifin D 2.00 5.00
RMNP Nicolas Petan D 1.50 4.00
RMNS Nick Shore D 1.50 4.00
RMRF Robby Fabbri C 2.00 5.00
RMRH Ryan Hartman D 2.00 5.00
RMRK Ronalds Kenins C 1.50 4.00
RMSB Sam Bennett A 2.00 5.00
RMSK Slater Koekkoek D 1.25 3.00
RMSN Stefan Noesen D 1.25 3.00
RMSP Shane Prince D 1.25 3.00
RMSU Malcolm Subban D 4.00 10.00
RMDS1 Daniel Sprong D 3.00 8.00

2015-16 Upper Deck Shining Stars

SS1-SS10 DEFENSE ODDS 1:12 BL/STRT
SS11-SS20 GOALIE ODDS 1:12 TIN, 1:6 FAT PCK
SS21-SS30 CENTER ODDS 1:16 H/R
SS31-SS40 WINGERS ODDS 1:24 H/R
SS41-SS50 LEGENDS ODDS 1:48 H/R
*1-10 BLUE: 1.5X TO 4X BASIC INSERTS
*11-20 BLUE: 1.2X TO 3X BASIC INSERTS
*21-50 BLUE: .6X TO 1.5X BASIC INSERTS
SS1 Aaron Ekblad 1.00 2.50
SS2 Alex Pietrangelo .75 2.00
SS3 Drew Doughty 1.00 2.50
SS4 Duncan Keith 1.00 2.50
SS5 Erik Karlsson 2.00 5.00
SS6 Kris Letang 1.00 2.50
SS7 Mark Giordano 1.00 2.50
SS8 Oliver Ekman-Larsson .75 2.00
SS9 P.K. Subban 1.50 4.00
SS10 Shea Weber .75 2.00
SS11 Braden Holtby 2.00 5.00
SS12 Corey Crawford 1.50 4.00
SS13 Carey Price 4.00 10.00
SS14 Henrik Lundqvist 1.50 4.00
SS15 Devan Dubnyk 1.25 3.00
SS16 Jonathan Quick 2.00 5.00
SS17 Marc-Andre Fleury 2.00 5.00
SS18 Pekka Rinne 1.50 4.00
SS19 Roberto Luongo 1.25 3.00
SS20 Tuukka Rask 1.25 3.00
SS21 Evgeni Malkin 2.50 6.00
SS22 Filip Forsberg 1.00 2.50
SS23 Jonathan Toews 1.50 4.00
SS24 Patrice Bergeron 1.00 2.50
SS25 Pavel Datsyuk 1.00 2.50
SS26 Ryan Nugent-Hopkins .75 2.00
SS27 Sidney Crosby 3.00 8.00
SS28 Steven Stamkos 1.50 4.00
SS29 John Tavares 1.50 4.00
SS30 Tyler Seguin 1.25 3.00
SS31 Alexander Ovechkin 4.00 10.00
SS32 Corey Perry 1.00 2.50
SS33 Henrik Zetterberg 1.25 3.00
SS34 Johnny Gaudreau 1.50 4.00
SS35 Jakub Voracek 1.00 2.50
SS36 Marian Hossa .75 2.00
SS37 Max Pacioretty 1.00 2.50
SS38 Patrick Kane 2.00 5.00
SS39 Rick Nash 1.00 2.50
SS40 Vladimir Tarasenko 1.50 4.00
SS41 Bobby Hull 1.25 3.00
SS42 Joe Sakic 2.00 5.00
SS43 Grant Fuhr 1.25 3.00
SS44 Martin Brodeur 2.50 6.00
SS45 Mario Lemieux 4.00 10.00
SS46 Mark Messier 2.00 5.00
SS47 Mats Sundin 1.25 3.00
SS48 Patrick Roy 3.00 8.00
SS49 Teemu Selanne 2.50 6.00
SS50 Wayne Gretzky 6.00 15.00

2015-16 Upper Deck Signature Sensations

GROUP A ODDS 1:52,532
GROUP B ODDS 1:28,162
GROUP C ODDS 1:9585
GROUP D ODDS 1:8431
GROUP E ODDS 1:4268
GROUP F ODDS 1:1846
GROUP G ODDS 1:1271
GROUP H ODDS 1:613
OVERALL ODDS 1:
SSAG Alex Galchenyuk G 12.00 30.00
SSAH Andrew Hammond H 15.00 40.00
SSAK Alex Killorn F 4.00 10.00
SSBB Ben Bishop D 6.00 15.00
SSBD Brenden Dillon F 3.00 8.00
SSBH Bo Horvat H 6.00 15.00
SSBO Bobby Orr B 75.00 125.00
SSBR Brett Ritchie F 3.00 8.00
SSBS Brendan Smith A
SSCG Cody Goloubef F 3.00 8.00
SSDE Dennis Everberg H 3.00 8.00
SSDJ Dmitrij Jaskin E 6.00 15.00
SSDS Derek Stepan C 10.00 25.00
SSEL Elias Lindholm E 4.00 10.00
SSES Eric Staal G 6.00 15.00
SSFF Filip Forsberg B
SSJB Jordie Benn H 3.00 8.00
SSJC Jared Cowen E 4.00 10.00
SSJP Jason Pominville D 5.00 12.00
SSJS Jaden Schwartz F 6.00 15.00
SSLE Lars Eller G 4.00 10.00
SSLG Luke Glendening H 4.00 10.00
SSLS Luke Schenn F 3.00 8.00
SSNT Nate Thompson G 3.00 8.00
SSPS Paul Stastny F 5.00 12.00
SSRN Riley Nash C 6.00 15.00
SSRS Ryan Strome G 4.00 10.00
SSSB Sergei Bobrovsky E 6.00 15.00
SSSC Sean Couturier G 5.00 12.00
SSSG Seth Griffith G 4.00 10.00
SSSV Semyon Varlamov D 6.00 15.00
SSSW Shea Weber C 8.00 20.00
SSTK Torey Krug H 6.00 15.00
SSTM Tyler Myers C 8.00 20.00
SSTR Tuukka Rask H 6.00 15.00
SSTT Tomas Tatar H 4.00 10.00
SSTY Ty Rattie H 4.00 10.00
SSVN Valeri Nichushkin G 4.00 10.00
SSVR Victor Rask H 3.00 8.00
SSWG Wayne Gretzky A 200.00 300.00
SSZG Zemgus Girgensons H 4.00 10.00

2015-16 Upper Deck Signatures

COMPLETE SET (20)
UNPRICED GRP A ODDS 1:17,874 SER.2
GROUP B ODDS 1:14,879 SER.2
GROUP C ODDS 1:5322 SER.2
GROUP D ODDS 1:2988 SER.2
GROUP E ODDS 1:917 SER.2
OVERALL ODDS 1:576 SER.2
UDSAD Anthony Duclair E 4.00 10.00
UDSAL Anton Lander C 5.00 12.00
UDSBC Brett Connolly B 8.00 20.00
UDSBG Brandon Gormley C 5.00 12.00
UDSBH Bo Horvat E 8.00 20.00
UDSBO Bobby Orr A
UDSBS Brandon Sutter D 6.00 15.00
UDSCG Claude Giroux B 15.00 30.00
UDSCJ Calle Jarnkrok E 4.00 10.00
UDSCS Colton Sissons E 5.00 12.00
UDSES Eric Staal A
UDSJA Jake Allen D 10.00 25.00
UDSJH Joey Hishon D 5.00 12.00
UDSJJ Jaromir Jagr A
UDSKL Kari Lehtonen C 12.50 25.00
UDSPH Patric Hornqvist D 6.00 15.00
UDSRS Ryan Sproul C 6.00 15.00
UDSTT Tomas Tatar E 4.00 10.00
UDSVR Victor Rask E 3.00 8.00
UDSVT Vincent Trocheck E 4.00 10.00

2015-16 Upper Deck Super Snipers

ONE PER ALBUM STARTER KIT
SS1 Sidney Crosby 15.00 40.00
SS2 John Tavares 8.00 20.00
SS3 Steven Stamkos 8.00 20.00
SS4 Jonathan Toews 8.00 20.00
SS5 Rick Nash 4.00 10.00
SS6 Alexander Ovechkin 15.00 40.00

2015-16 Upper Deck UD Portraits

P1-P48 STATED ODDS 1:7.5 SER.1
P49-P54 LEGEND ODDS 1:60 SER.1
P55-P60 ROOKIE ODDS 1:60 SER.1
P61-P110 ROOKIE ODDS 1:6 SER.2
P1 Alexander Ovechkin 3.00 8.00
P2 Oliver Ekman-Larsson .60 1.50
P3 John Tavares 1.50 4.00
P4 Rick Nash .75 2.00
P5 Pavel Datsyuk 1.00 2.50
P6 Corey Crawford 1.00 2.50
P7 Henrik Lundqvist 1.00 2.50
P8 Jonathan Quick 1.25 3.00
P9 Ryan Miller .75 2.00
P10 Marian Hossa .60 1.50
P11 Tuukka Rask .75 2.00
P12 Eric Staal 1.00 2.50
P13 Claude Giroux .75 2.00
P14 Ryan Nugent-Hopkins .75 2.00
P15 Shea Weber .60 1.50
P16 Erik Karlsson 1.50 4.00
P17 Pekka Rinne 1.00 2.50
P18 Tyler Johnson .60 1.50
P19 Nicklas Backstrom 1.25 3.00
P20 Evgeni Malkin 2.50 6.00
P21 Ryan Johansen 1.00 2.50
P22 Jaromir Jagr 2.00 5.00
P23 Henrik Zetterberg 1.00 2.50
P24 Daniel Sedin .75 2.00
P25 Sidney Crosby 3.00 8.00
P26 Kyle Okposo .75 2.00
P27 Marc-Andre Fleury 1.25 3.00
P28 Jakub Voracek .75 2.00
P29 Ryan Getzlaf 1.25 3.00
P30 Jordan Eberle .75 2.00
P31 Vladimir Tarasenko 1.25 3.00
P32 Jiri Hudler .60 1.50
P33 James van Riemsdyk .75 2.00
P34 Max Pacioretty .75 2.00
P35 P.K. Subban 1.25 3.00
P36 Zach Parise .75 2.00
P37 Johnny Gaudreau 1.25 3.00
P38 Aaron Ekblad .75 2.00
P39 Anze Kopitar 1.25 3.00
P40 Adam Henrique .75 2.00
P41 Jonathan Toews 1.50 4.00
P42 Patrick Kane 1.50 4.00
P43 Corey Perry .75 2.00
P44 Tyler Seguin 1.25 3.00
P45 Joe Pavelski .75 2.00
P46 Patrice Bergeron 1.00 2.50
P47 Carey Price 2.50 6.00
P48 Steven Stamkos 1.50 4.00
P49 Guy Lafleur LEG 1.00 2.50
P50 Wayne Gretzky LEG 4.00 10.00
P51 Phil Esposito LEG 1.25 3.00
P52 Martin Brodeur LEG 1.50 4.00
P53 Mario Lemieux LEG 2.50 6.00
P54 Bobby Hull LEG .75 2.00
P55 Malcolm Subban 3.00 8.00
P56 Jacob de la Rose 1.25 3.00
P57 Sam Bennett 4.00 10.00
P58 Kevin Fiala 1.25 3.00
P59 Ryan Hartman 1.50 4.00
P60 Matt Puempel 1.00 2.50
P61 Jack Eichel 5.00 12.00
P62 Nick Cousins 1.25 3.00
P63 Antoine Bibeau 1.25 3.00
P64 Colin Miller 1.00 2.50
P65 Andreas Athanasiou 3.00 8.00
P66 Shane Prince 1.00 2.50
P67 Henrik Samuelsson 1.00 2.50
P68 Nick Shore 1.25 3.00
P69 Ronalds Kenins 1.25 3.00
P70 Nick Ritchie 1.25 3.00
P71 Emile Poirier 1.25 3.00
P72 Connor Hellebuyck 3.00 8.00
P73 Viktor Arvidsson 1.50 4.00
P74 Sergei Plotnikov 1.00 2.50
P75 Max Domi 2.50 6.00
P76 Stefan Noesen 1.00 2.50
P77 Connor Brickley 1.00 2.50
P78 Nikolay Goldobin 1.25 3.00
P79 Hunter Shinkaruk 1.25 3.00
P80 Derek Forbort 1.00 2.50
P81 Noah Hanifin 1.50 4.00
P82 Anton Slepyshev 1.00 2.50
P83 Jake Virtanen 1.50 4.00
P84 Oscar Lindberg 1.25 3.00
P85 Mike Condon 1.25 3.00
P86 Daniel Sprong 2.50 6.00
P87 Josh Anderson 1.25 3.00
P88 Joonas Donskoi 1.25 3.00
P89 Stanislav Galiev 1.25 3.00
P90 Mikko Rantanen 2.50 6.00
P91 Slater Koekkoek 1.00 2.50
P92 Kyle Baun 1.25 3.00
P93 Jordan Weal 1.25 3.00
P94 Andrew Copp 1.25 3.00
P95 Dylan Larkin 4.00 10.00
P96 Dylan DeMelo 1.00 2.50
P97 Mattias Janmark 1.25 3.00
P98 Jean-Francois Berube 1.00 2.50
P99 Colton Parayko 1.50 4.00
P100 Connor McDavid 10.00 25.00
P101 Chandler Stephenson 1.25 3.00
P102 Jared McCann 1.25 3.00
P103 Matt O'Connor 1.00 2.50
P104 Radek Faksa 1.25 3.00
P105 Robby Fabbri 1.50 4.00
P106 Nicolas Petan 1.25 3.00
P107 Nikolaj Ehlers 2.50 6.00
P108 Sam Brittain 1.25 3.00
P109 Brock McGinn 1.25 3.00
P110 Artemi Panarin 4.00 10.00

2015-16 Upper Deck UD Portraits Gold

*P1-P54 GOLD/25: 2.5X TO 6X BASIC INSERTS
*P55-P110 GLD RK/99: .8X TO 2X BASIC INSERTS
P6 Corey Crawford 6.00 15.00
P19 Nicklas Backstrom 8.00 20.00
P59 Ryan Hartman 3.00 8.00
P61 Jack Eichel 20.00 40.00
P100 Connor McDavid 175.00 325.00
P110 Artemi Panarin 20.00 40.00

2015-16 Upper Deck UD Portraits Platinum Blue

*P55-P110 BLU RK/25: 2X TO 5X BASIC INSERTS
P59 Ryan Hartman 8.00 20.00
P61 Jack Eichel 40.00 80.00
P100 Connor McDavid 325.00 400.00
P110 Artemi Panarin 40.00 80.00

2015-16 Upper Deck Winter Classic Jumbos

ONE PER RETAIL TIN
WC1 Troy Brouwer .75 2.00
WC2 Patrick Sharp 1.00 2.50
WC3 Alexander Ovechkin 4.00 10.00
WC4 Brandon Saad 1.00 2.50
WC5 Mike Green 1.00 2.50
WC6 Duncan Keith 1.00 2.50
WC7 Nicklas Backstrom 1.50 4.00

WC8 Marian Hossa .75 2.00
WC9 John Carlson 1.25 3.00
WC10 Patrick Kane 2.00 5.00
WC11 Eric Fehr .60 1.50
WC12 Jonathan Toews 2.00 5.00
WC13 Braden Holtby 1.50 4.00
WC14 Corey Crawford 1.25 3.00

2015-16 Upper Deck Young Guns Acetate

201 Connor McDavid 2500.00 3500.00
202 Jordan Weal 25.00 60.00
203 Sergei Plotnikov 20.00 50.00
204 Max Domi 150.00 250.00
205 Andrew Copp 30.00 80.00
206 Mikko Rantanen 60.00 150.00
207 Joel Edmundson 25.00 60.00
208 Kevin Fiala 30.00 80.00
209 Nick Cousins 30.00 80.00
210 Emile Poirier 30.00 80.00
211 Malcolm Subban 80.00 200.00
212 Jacob de la Rose 30.00 80.00
213 Henrik Samuelsson 25.00 60.00
214 Connor Hellebuyck 150.00 250.00
215 Matt Puempel 25.00 60.00
216 Nick Shore 30.00 80.00
217 Josh Anderson 30.00 80.00
218 Shane Prince 25.00 60.00
219 Jared McCann 60.00 150.00
220 Stanislav Galiev 30.00 80.00
221 Artemi Panarin 300.00 500.00
222 Viktor Arvidsson 40.00 100.00
223 Nikolaj Ehlers 200.00 400.00
224 Slater Koekkoek 25.00 60.00
225 Ronalds Kenins 30.00 80.00
226 Daniel Sprong 60.00 150.00
227 Nicolas Petan 80.00 200.00
228 Dylan Larkin 500.00 1000.00
229 Robby Fabbri 100.00 300.00
230 Joonas Donskoi 30.00 80.00
231 Ben Hutton 30.00 80.00
232 Sam Bennett 200.00 400.00
233 Matt O'Connor 25.00 60.00
234 Oscar Lindberg 30.00 80.00
235 Colton Parayko 40.00 100.00
236 Stefan Noesen 25.00 60.00
237 Anton Slepyshev 25.00 60.00
238 Sergei Kalinin 25.00 60.00
239 Mike Condon 30.00 80.00
240 Antoine Bibeau 30.00 80.00
241 Kyle Baun 30.00 80.00
242 Jean-Francois Berube 25.00 60.00
243 Joonas Kemppainen 25.00 60.00
244 Mattias Janmark 30.00 80.00
245 Evgeny Medvedev 25.00 60.00
246 Keegan Lowe 30.00 80.00
247 Colin Miller 25.00 60.00
248 Brett Kulak 25.00 60.00
249 Connor Brickley 25.00 60.00
451 Jack Eichel 500.00 1000.00
452 Charles Hudon 30.00 80.00
453 Nikolay Goldobin 30.00 80.00
454 Logan Shaw 30.00 80.00
455 Frank Vatrano 60.00 150.00
456 Jujhar Khaira 25.00 60.00
457 Jake Virtanen 200.00 400.00
458 Andreas Athanasiou 100.00 250.00
459 Tanner Kero 30.00 80.00
460 Chris Wideman 30.00 80.00
461 Zachary Fucale 60.00 150.00
462 Hunter Shinkaruk 30.00 80.00
463 Brendan Ranford 25.00 60.00
464 Juuse Saros 40.00 100.00
465 Adam Pelech 25.00 60.00
466 Michael Keranen 25.00 60.00
467 Dylan DeMelo 25.00 60.00
468 Mark Alt 20.00 50.00
469 Jaccob Slavin 25.00 60.00
470 Alexandre Grenier 25.00 60.00
471 Louis Domingue 60.00 150.00
472 Linus Ullmark 60.00 150.00
473 Derek Forbort 25.00 60.00
474 Brady Skjei 25.00 60.00
475 Ryan Hartman 40.00 100.00
476 Max McCormick 25.00 60.00
477 Vincent Hinostroza 20.00 50.00
478 Taylor Leier 30.00 80.00
479 Radek Faksa 30.00 80.00
480 Garret Sparks 40.00 100.00
481 Brendan Gaunce 40.00 100.00
482 Chris Driedger 25.00 60.00
483 Joel Vermin 25.00 60.00
484 Chandler Stephenson 30.00 80.00
485 David Musil 25.00 60.00
486 Gustav Olofsson 30.00 80.00
487 Brett Pesce 25.00 60.00
488 Anthony Stolarz 30.00 80.00
489 Devin Shore 30.00 80.00
490 Petr Straka 25.00 60.00
491 Mike McCarron 40.00 100.00
492 Raman Hrabarenka 25.00 60.00
493 Markus Hannikainen 25.00 60.00
494 Sam Brittain 30.00 80.00
495 Shea Theodore 60.00 150.00
496 Nick Ritchie 30.00 80.00
497 Brock McGinn 30.00 80.00
498 Tyler Randell 30.00 80.00
499 Noah Hanifin 60.00 150.00

2015-16 Upper Deck Biography of a Season

COMPLETE SET (12) 15.00 40.00
COMMON McDAVID 2.00 5.00
COMMON GRETZKY 1.00 2.50
ISSUED VIA INTERNET OFFER

2015-16 Upper Deck Rookie Showcase Moments Fall Expo

COMPLETE SET (6) 20.00 50.00
COMMON McDAVID 4.00 10.00
ISSUED AT 2015 TORONTO FALL EXPO

2016-17 Upper Deck

1 John Gibson .30 .75
2 Cam Fowler .25 .60
3 Jakob Silfverberg .30 .75
4 Andrew Cogliano .20 .50
5 Kevin Bieksa .20 .50
6 Ryan Getzlaf .50 1.25
7 Ryan Kesler .30 .75
8 Anthony Duclair .30 .75
9 Shane Doan .25 .60
10 Jordan Martinook .20 .50
11 Martin Hanzal .25 .60
12 Mike Smith .30 .75
13 Oliver Ekman-Larsson .25 .60
14 Brad Marchand .40 1.00
15 David Krejci .30 .75
16 David Pastrnak .50 1.25
17 Jimmy Hayes .20 .50
18 Matt Beleskey .25 .60
19 Ryan Spooner .25 .60
20 Zdeno Chara .30 .75
21 Josh Gorges .20 .50
22 Matt Moulson .25 .60
23 Robin Lehner .25 .60
24 Ryan O'Reilly .30 .75
25 Sam Reinhart .25 .60
26 Zach Bogosian .25 .60
27 Dougie Hamilton .30 .75
28 Mark Giordano .25 .60
29 Michael Frolik .25 .60
30 Mikael Backlund .25 .60
31 Sam Bennett .40 1.00
32 T.J. Brodie .25 .60
33 Andrej Nestrasil .25 .60
34 Cam Ward .30 .75
35 Elias Lindholm .30 .75
36 Jeff Skinner .30 .75
37 Justin Faulk .25 .60
38 Noah Hanifin .30 .75
39 Artem Anisimov .25 .60
40 Artemi Panarin .40 1.00
41 Brent Seabrook .25 .60
42 Marcus Kruger .30 .75
43 Marian Hossa .25 .60
44 Patrick Kane .60 1.50
45 Niklas Hjalmarsson .25 .60
46 Carl Soderberg .20 .50
47 Erik Johnson .20 .50
48 Francois Beauchemin .25 .60
49 Gabriel Landeskog .25 .60
50 Jarome Iginla .30 .75
51 Matt Duchene .30 .75
52 Alexander Wennberg .25 .60
53 Boone Jenner .30 .75
54 Brandon Dubinsky .30 .75
55 Cam Atkinson .30 .75
56 David Savard .20 .50
57 Nick Foligno .25 .60
58 Scott Hartnell .30 .75
59 Ales Hemsky .25 .60
60 Cody Eakin .25 .60
61 Jamie Benn .40 1.00
62 Jason Spezza .30 .75
63 John Klingberg .30 .75
64 Johnny Oduya .25 .60
65 Kari Lehtonen .25 .60
66 Dylan Larkin .50 1.25
67 Henrik Zetterberg .40 1.00
68 Mike Green .30 .75
69 Jonathan Ericsson .20 .50
70 Justin Abdelkader .25 .60
71 Tomas Tatar .25 .60
72 Andrej Sekera .20 .50
73 Benoit Pouliot .25 .60
74 Cam Talbot .40 1.00
75 Connor McDavid 1.50 4.00
76 Darnell Nurse .25 .60
77 Oscar Klefbom .50 1.25
78 Leon Draisaitl .40 1.00
79 Aaron Ekblad .30 .75
80 Aleksander Barkov .30 .75
81 Jaromir Jagr .75 2.00
82 Reilly Smith .30 .75
83 Roberto Luongo .30 .75
84 Vincent Trocheck .30 .75
85 Alec Martinez .20 .50
86 Jeff Carter .30 .75
87 Dwight King .25 .60
88 Jake Muzzin .25 .60
89 Jonathan Quick .50 1.25
90 Kyle Clifford .25 .60
91 Tanner Pearson .25 .60
92 Tyler Toffoli .30 .75
93 Devan Dubnyk .30 .75
94 Erik Haula .25 .60
95 Jason Pominville .25 .60
96 Mikko Koivu .25 .60
97 Nino Niederreiter .30 .75
98 Ryan Suter .25 .60
99 Alex Galchenyuk .40 1.00
100 Andrei Markov .30 .75
101 Brendan Gallagher .40 1.00
102 Nathan Beaulieu .20 .50
103 Max Pacioretty .30 .75
104 Tomas Plekanec .30 .75
105 Craig Smith .20 .50
106 James Neal .25 .60
107 Mattias Ekholm .20 .50
108 Mike Fisher .25 .60
109 Pekka Rinne .40 1.00
110 Ryan Johansen .40 1.00
111 Filip Forsberg .40 1.00
112 Adam Henrique .30 .75
113 Kyle Palmieri .25 .60
114 Andy Greene .20 .50
115 Damon Severson .25 .60
116 Michael Cammalleri .25 .60
117 Anders Lee .30 .75
118 Brock Nelson .25 .60
119 Calvin de Haan .20 .50
120 Jaroslav Halak .30 .75
121 John Tavares .60 1.50
122 Nick Leddy .20 .50
123 Daniel Girardi .20 .50
124 Derek Stepan .25 .60
125 Chris Kreider .30 .75
126 Marc Staal .20 .50
127 Mats Zuccarello .30 .75
128 Rick Nash .30 .75
129 Ryan McDonagh .25 .60
130 Andrew Hammond .25 .60
131 Bobby Ryan .25 .60
132 Curtis Lazar .20 .50
133 Erik Karlsson .60 1.50
134 Mark Stone .30 .75
135 Kyle Turris .25 .60
136 Claude Giroux .30 .75
137 Mark Streit .25 .60
138 Michael Del Zotto .25 .60
139 Sean Couturier .30 .75
140 Shayne Gostisbehere .40 1.00
141 Wayne Simmonds .40 1.00
142 Carl Hagelin .30 .75
143 Kris Letang .30 .75
144 Matt Murray .50 1.25
145 Phil Kessel .40 1.00
146 Sidney Crosby 1.25 3.00
147 Trevor Daley .25 .60
148 Brent Burns .40 1.00
149 Chris Tierney .20 .50
150 Joe Pavelski .30 .75
151 Joel Ward .25 .60
152 Logan Couture .30 .75
153 Martin Jones .30 .75
154 Paul Martin .25 .60
155 Alex Pietrangelo .25 .60
156 Alexander Steen .30 .75
157 Jake Allen .40 1.00
158 Jori Lehtera .25 .60
159 Patrik Berglund .20 .50
160 Paul Stastny .30 .75
161 Robby Fabbri .30 .75
162 Vladimir Tarasenko .50 1.25
163 Anton Stralman .25 .60
164 Ben Bishop .30 .75
165 Ondrej Palat .25 .60
166 Ryan Callahan .30 .75
167 Tyler Johnson .25 .60
168 Victor Hedman .40 1.00
169 Brooks Laich .20 .50
170 James van Riemsdyk .30 .75
171 Joffrey Lupul .25 .60
172 Jake Gardiner .30 .75
173 Leo Komarov .30 .75
174 Peter Holland .20 .50
175 Tyler Bozak .25 .60
176 Alexander Edler .20 .50
177 Bo Horvat .50 1.25
178 Brandon Sutter .25 .60
179 Daniel Sedin .30 .75
180 Derek Dorsett .20 .50
181 Jake Virtanen .40 1.00
182 Jannik Hansen .20 .50
183 Ryan Miller .30 .75
184 Alexander Ovechkin 1.25 3.00
185 Andre Burakovsky .25 .60
186 Brooks Orpik .25 .60
187 Evgeny Kuznetsov .50 1.25
188 Justin Williams .25 .60
189 Karl Alznor .20 .50
190 Matt Niskanen .25 .60
191 Nicklas Backstrom .50 1.25
192 Alexander Burmistrov .20 .50
193 Mark Scheifele .40 1.00
194 Drew Stafford .25 .60
195 Dustin Byfuglien .30 .75
196 Ondrej Pavelec .30 .75
197 Tobias Enstrom .20 .50
198 Tyler Myers .25 .60
199 S.Crosby/J.Pavelski CL 1.25 3.00
200 D.Krejci/A.Galchenyuk CL .40 1.00
201 Auston Matthews YG RC 150.00 250.00
202 Lawson Crouse YG RC 2.00 5.00
203 Nick Sorensen YG RC 2.50 6.00
204 Connor Brown YG RC 6.00 15.00
205 Brayden Point YG RC 10.00 25.00
206 Jakob Chychrun YG RC 2.50 6.00
207 Steven Santini YG RC 2.00 5.00
208 Alan Quine YG RC 2.50 6.00
209 Danton Heinen YG RC 6.00 15.00
210 Sebastian Aho YG RC 8.00 20.00
211 Pontus Aberg YG RC 3.00 8.00
212 Kyle Connor YG RC 8.00 20.00
213 Anthony Mantha YG RC 6.00 15.00
214 Ivan Provorov YG RC 5.00 12.00
215 Zach Sanford YG RC 2.50 6.00
216 Tyler Motte YG RC 2.50 6.00
217 Travis Konecny YG RC 5.00 12.00
218 Jimmy Vesey YG RC 6.00 15.00
219 Nick Paul YG RC 3.00 8.00
220 Anthony Beauvillier YG RC 2.50 6.00
221 Nikita Tryamkin YG RC 2.00 5.00
222 Zach Hyman YG RC 3.00 8.00
223 Tom Kuhnhackl YG RC 2.00 5.00
224 Zach Werenski YG RC 6.00 15.00
225 Jesse Puljujarvi YG RC 8.00 20.00
226 Josh Morrissey YG RC 3.00 8.00
227 Pavel Buchnevich YG RC 5.00 12.00
228 Sonny Milano YG RC 3.00 8.00
229 Nick Schmaltz YG RC 2.50 6.00
230 Trevor Carrick YG RC 2.50 6.00
231 Matthew Tkachuk YG RC 8.00 20.00
232 Artturi Lehkonen YG RC 5.00 12.00
233 Denis Malgin YG RC 2.50 6.00
234 Nikita Zaitsev YG RC 2.50 6.00
235 Christian Dvorak YG RC 2.50 6.00
236 Mikhail Sergachev YG RC 8.00 20.00
237 Esa Lindell YG RC 2.50 6.00
238 Noel Acciari YG RC 3.00 8.00
239 Mike Reilly YG RC 2.00 5.00
240 Gustav Forsling YG RC 2.50 6.00
241 Michael Matheson YG RC 2.50 6.00
242 Hudson Fasching YG RC 2.50 6.00
243 Oliver Bjorkstrand YG RC 2.00 5.00
244 Austin Czarnik YG RC 4.00 10.00
245 Chris Bigras YG RC 2.00 5.00
246 Justin Bailey YG RC 2.50 6.00
247 Nic Dowd YG RC 2.50 6.00
248 Pavel Zacha YG RC 3.00 8.00
249 William Nylander YG RC 15.00 40.00
250 A.Matthews YG RC 8.00 20.00
W.Nylander YG RC CL
251 Hampus Lindholm .20 .50
252 Rickard Rakell .30 .75
253 Sami Vatanen .25 .60
254 Corey Perry .30 .75
255 Antoine Vermette .25 .60
256 Jonathan Bernier .30 .75
257 Tobias Rieder .20 .50
258 Max Domi .40 1.00
259 Alex Goligoski .20 .50
260 Radim Vrbata .25 .60
261 Brad Richardson .25 .60
262 Louis Domingue .25 .60
263 Luke Schenn .20 .50
264 Patrice Bergeron .40 1.00
265 Tuukka Rask .30 .75
266 Torey Krug .30 .75
267 David Backes .30 .75
268 Dominic Moore .20 .50
269 Joe Morrow .25 .60
270 Rasmus Ristolainen .25 .60
271 Zemgus Girgensons .25 .60
272 Brian Gionta .25 .60
273 Evander Kane .30 .75
274 Jack Eichel .60 1.50
275 Tyler Ennis .25 .60
276 Dmitry Kulikov .25 .60
277 Kyle Okposo .30 .75
278 Johnny Gaudreau .50 1.25
279 Sean Monahan .30 .75
280 Dennis Wideman .20 .50
281 Troy Brouwer .25 .60
282 Brian Elliott .25 .60
283 Micheal Ferland .20 .50
284 Lee Stempniak .25 .60
285 Victor Rask .25 .60
286 Jordan Staal .30 .75
287 Ron Hainsey .25 .60
288 Teuvo Teravainen .30 .75
289 Joakim Nordstrom .20 .50
290 Corey Crawford .40 1.00
291 Duncan Keith .30 .75
292 Jonathan Toews .60 1.50
293 Richard Panik .25 .60
294 Trevor van Riemsdyk .25 .60
295 Ryan Hartman .30 .75
296 Joe Colborne .20 .50
297 Mikhail Grigorenko .20 .50
298 Nathan MacKinnon .60 1.50
299 Tyson Barrie .30 .75
300 Nikita Zadorov .25 .60
301 Semyon Varlamov .30 .75
302 Blake Comeau .20 .50
303 Seth Jones .25 .60
304 Brandon Saad .30 .75
305 Jack Johnson .20 .50
306 Ryan Murray .20 .50
307 Sergei Bobrovsky .30 .75
308 Matt Calvert .20 .50
309 Antti Niemi .25 .60
310 Patrick Sharp .25 .60
311 Tyler Seguin .50 1.25
312 Jiri Hudler .25 .60
313 Dan Hamhuis .25 .60
314 Antoine Roussel .20 .50
315 Petr Mrazek .30 .75
316 Riley Sheahan .25 .60
317 Darren Helm .20 .50
318 Gustav Nyquist .30 .75
319 Niklas Kronwall .20 .50
320 Thomas Vanek .25 .60
321 Frans Nielsen .25 .60
322 Andreas Athanasiou .30 .75
323 Kris Russell .25 .60
324 Jordan Eberle .30 .75
325 Patrick Maroon .20 .50
326 Ryan Nugent-Hopkins .30 .75
327 Milan Lucic .25 .60
328 Adam Larsson .30 .75
329 Zack Kassian .25 .60
330 Jason Demers .20 .50
331 Jonathan Marchessault .30 .75
332 Jussi Jokinen .30 .75
333 Nick Bjugstad .25 .60
334 James Reimer .30 .75
335 Keith Yandle .30 .75
336 Jared McCann .20 .50
337 Drew Doughty .30 .75
338 Anze Kopitar .50 1.25
339 Devin Setoguchi .20 .50
340 Dustin Brown .25 .60
341 Nick Shore .25 .60
342 Matt Dumba .25 .60
343 Charlie Coyle .25 .60
344 Mikael Granlund .25 .60
345 Zach Parise .30 .75
346 Eric Staal .40 1.00
347 Jared Spurgeon .20 .50
348 Andrew Shaw .30 .75
349 Carey Price 1.00 2.50
350 David Desharnais .25 .60
351 Shea Weber .25 .60
352 Alexei Emelin .20 .50
353 Alexander Radulov .30 .75
354 Kevin Fiala .25 .60
355 P.K. Subban .50 1.25
356 Mike Ribeiro .25 .60
357 Roman Josi .30 .75
358 Colin Wilson .30 .75
359 Ryan Ellis .25 .60
360 Taylor Hall .60 1.50
361 Cory Schneider .25 .60
362 Travis Zajac .25 .60
363 Devante Smith-Pelly .25 .60
364 John Moore .20 .50
365 P.A. Parenteau .20 .50
366 Andrew Ladd .30 .75
367 Ryan Strome .25 .60
368 Travis Hamonic .20 .50
369 Johnny Boychuk .30 .75
370 Thomas Greiss .25 .60
371 Jason Chimera .20 .50
372 Josh Bailey .25 .60
373 Cal Clutterbuck .20 .50
374 J.T. Miller .25 .60
375 Henrik Lundqvist .30 .75
376 Oscar Lindberg .20 .50
377 Kevin Hayes .25 .60
378 Mika Zibanejad .30 .75
379 Michael Grabner .25 .60
380 Jean-Gabriel Pageau .25 .60
381 Derick Brassard .30 .75
382 Cody Ceci .25 .60
383 Mike Hoffman .25 .60
384 Dion Phaneuf .30 .75
385 Craig Anderson .30 .75
386 Zack Smith .20 .50
387 Brayden Schenn .30 .75
388 Jakub Voracek .30 .75
389 Steve Mason .25 .60
390 Michael Raffl .20 .50
391 Scott Laughton .20 .50
392 Matt Read .25 .60
393 Chris Kunitz .30 .75
394 Marc-Andre Fleury .50 1.25
395 Evgeni Malkin 1.00 2.50
396 Patric Hornqvist .25 .60
397 Olli Maatta .30 .75
398 Nick Bonino .20 .50
399 Bryan Rust .30 .75
400 Mikkel Boedker .25 .60
401 David Schlemko .20 .50
402 Tomas Hertl .30 .75
403 Joe Thornton .30 .75
404 Joonas Donskoi .25 .60
405 Marc-Edouard Vlasic .20 .50
406 Patrick Marleau .30 .75
407 Matt Nieto .20 .50
408 David Perron .25 .60
409 Jaden Schwartz .40 1.00
410 Colton Parayko .30 .75
411 Jay Bouwmeester .30 .75
412 Kevin Shattenkirk .25 .60
413 Nail Yakupov .25 .60
414 Nikita Kucherov .50 1.25
415 Vladislav Namestnikov .20 .50
416 Steven Stamkos .60 1.50
417 Andrei Vasilevskiy .40 1.00
418 Valtteri Filppula .25 .60
419 Alex Killorn .20 .50
420 Jonathan Drouin .40 1.00
421 Frederik Andersen .25 .60
422 Morgan Rielly .25 .60
423 Nazem Kadri .25 .60
424 Jhonas Enroth .30 .75
425 Matt Hunwick .25 .60
426 Matt Martin .25 .60
427 Erik Gudbranson .30 .75
428 Loui Eriksson .30 .75
429 Sven Baertschi .20 .50
430 Alexandre Burrows .25 .60
431 Christopher Tanev .25 .60
432 Henrik Sedin .30 .75
433 Jacob Markstrom .25 .60
434 Lars Eller .25 .60
435 Dmitry Orlov .25 .60
436 Marcus Johansson .30 .75
437 Braden Holtby .50 1.25
438 John Carlson .40 1.00
439 T.J. Oshie .50 1.25
440 Tom Wilson .30 .75
441 Brett Connolly .25 .60
442 Shawn Matthias .20 .50
443 Jacob Trouba .25 .60
444 Blake Wheeler .30 .75
445 Bryan Little .25 .60
446 Mathieu Perreault .25 .60
447 Nikolaj Ehlers .30 .75
448 Connor Hellebuyck .50 1.25
449 C.Schneider/B.Holtby CL .50 1.25
450 P.Subban/S.Weber CL .50 1.25
451 Patrik Laine YG RC 40.00 100.00
452 Kasperi Kapanen YG RC 6.00 15.00
453 Miles Wood YG RC 2.00 5.00
454 William Carrier YG RC 2.50 6.00
455 Drake Caggiula YG RC 2.50 6.00
456 Yohann Auvitu YG RC 2.50 6.00
457 Markus Nutivaara YG RC 2.50 6.00
458 Mathew Barzal YG RC 30.00 80.00
459 Joel Eriksson Ek YG RC 2.50 6.00
460 Frederik Gauthier YG RC 2.00 5.00
461 Blake Speers YG RC 2.50 6.00
462 Casey Nelson YG RC 2.50 6.00
463 Anthony DeAngelo YG RC 2.50 6.00
464 Mark McNeill YG RC 2.50 6.00
465 Gemel Smith YG RC 2.50 6.00
466 Tristan Jarry YG RC 5.00 12.00
467 Brandon Tanev YG RC 2.50 6.00
468 Mitch Marner YG RC 30.00 80.00
469 Dominik Simon YG RC 2.50 6.00
470 Rob O'Gara YG RC 2.50 6.00
471 Tyler Bertuzzi YG RC 3.00 8.00
472 Thatcher Demko YG RC 8.00 20.00
473 Charlie Lindgren YG RC 5.00 12.00
474 Kevin Gravel YG RC 3.00 8.00
475 Troy Stecher YG RC 2.50 6.00
476 Brandon Montour YG RC 2.50 6.00
477 Nick Baptiste YG RC 2.50 6.00
478 Aaron Dell YG RC 3.00 8.00
479 Timo Meier YG RC 2.50 6.00
480 Michal Kempny YG RC 2.50 6.00
481 Stephen Johns YG RC 2.00 5.00
482 Brandon Carlo YG RC 2.50 6.00
483 Kyle Rau YG RC 3.00 8.00
484 Nikita Soshnikov YG RC 1.50 4.00
485 Chase De Leo YG RC 2.50 6.00
486 Kevin Labanc YG RC 2.50 6.00
487 Oskar Sundqvist YG RC 2.50 6.00
488 Thomas Chabot YG RC 6.00 15.00
489 Ondrej Kase YG RC 2.50 6.00
490 Ryan Pulock YG RC 2.50 6.00
491 Tobias Lindberg YG RC 4.00 10.00
492 Scott Wedgewood YG RC 4.00 10.00
493 Oliver Kylington YG RC 2.00 5.00
494 Shane Harper YG RC 4.00 10.00
495 Jacob Larsson YG RC 4.00 10.00
496 Zane Mcintyre YG RC 3.00 8.00
497 Jason Dickinson YG RC 2.00 5.00
498 Dylan Strome YG RC 5.00 12.00
499 Brendan Leipsic YG RC 2.50 6.00
500 M.Marner 4.00 10.00
P.Laine YG CL
501 Sam Gagner .25 .60
502 Brandon Pirri .20 .50
503 Markus Granlund .25 .60
504 Carter Hutton .30 .75
505 Jamie McGinn .25 .60
506 Lauri Korpikoski .20 .50
507 Tim Schaller .25 .60
508 Patrick Wiercioch .25 .60
509 Brian Campbell .25 .60
510 Viktor Stalberg .25 .60
511 Alex Chiasson .25 .60
512 Mike Condon .30 .75
513 Rene Bourque .20 .50
514 Dennis Seidenberg .20 .50
515 Colton Sceviour .25 .60
516 A.J. Greer YG RC 3.00 8.00
517 Cole Schneider YG RC 3.00 8.00
518 Joel Hanley YG RC 3.00 8.00
519 Joseph Cramarossa YG RC 3.00 8.00
520 Jakub Vrana YG RC 3.00 8.00
521 Lukas Sedlak YG RC 3.00 8.00
522 Matthew Benning YG RC 4.00 10.00
523 Nick Lappin YG RC 3.00 8.00
524 Roman Lyubimov YG RC 3.00 8.00
525 Jake Guentzel YG RC 20.00 50.00
526 Ryan Getzlaf SH 3.00 8.00
527 Mark Scheifele SH 2.50 6.00
528 Vladimir Tarasenko SH 3.00 8.00
529 Tuukka Rask SH 2.00 5.00
530 Patrik Laine SH 8.00 20.00

2016-17 Upper Deck Exclusives

*VETS: 6X TO 15X BASIC CARDS
*ROOKIES: 2.5X TO 6X BASIC CARDS
201 Auston Matthews YG 1000.00 2500.00
204 Connor Brown YG 40.00 100.00
206 Jakob Chychrun YG 30.00 80.00
210 Sebastian Aho YG 30.00 80.00
212 Kyle Connor YG 60.00 150.00
214 Ivan Provorov YG 40.00 100.00
225 Jesse Puljujarvi YG 60.00 150.00
250 Auston Matthews YG 60.00 150.00
William Nylander YG CL
451 Patrik Laine YG 550.00 700.00
468 Mitch Marner YG 300.00 450.00
500 Mitch Marner 40.00 100.00
Patrik Laine YG CL
525 Jake Guentzel YG 150.00 300.00

2016-17 Upper Deck A Piece of History 1000 Point Club

PCBC Bobby Clarke A
PCDT Dave Taylor C
PCJS Joe Sakic B 30.00 80.00
PCLM Larry Murphy B 30.00 80.00
PCMC Lanny McDonald B 10.00 25.00
PCMH Marian Hossa C
PCML Mario Lemieux A
PCMM Mark Messier A
PCPC Paul Coffey B 15.00 40.00
PCPE Patrik Elias C
PCPL Pat LaFontaine A
PCPM Patrick Marleau B 25.00 60.00
PCTF Theoren Fleury B

2016-17 Upper Deck A Piece of History 500 Goal Club

GCAO Alexander Ovechkin 30.00 80.00
GCMH Marian Hossa 30.00 80.00

2016-17 Upper Deck A Piece of History 300 Win Club

300BS Billy Smith A 30.00 80.00
300GH Glenn Hall A 30.00 80.00

2016-17 Upper Deck Canvas

C1 Ryan Getzlaf 1.50 4.00
C2 John Gibson 1.00 2.50
C3 Jakob Silfverberg 1.00 2.50
C4 Max Domi 1.25 3.00
C5 Anthony Duclair 1.00 2.50
C6 Shane Doan .75 2.00
C7 Patrice Bergeron 1.25 3.00
C8 Matt Beleskey .75 2.00
C9 Brad Marchand 1.25 3.00
C10 Jack Eichel 2.00 5.00
C11 Rasmus Ristolainen .75 2.00
C12 Ryan O'Reilly 1.00 2.50
C13 Johnny Gaudreau 1.50 4.00
C14 Dougie Hamilton 1.00 2.50
C15 Sam Bennett 1.25 3.00
C16 Noah Hanifin 1.00 2.50
C17 Jeff Skinner 1.00 2.50
C18 Jordan Staal 1.00 2.50
C19 Patrick Kane 2.00 5.00
C20 Brent Seabrook .75 2.00
C21 Artemi Panarin 1.25 3.00
C22 Corey Crawford 1.25 3.00
C23 Nathan MacKinnon 2.00 5.00
C24 Gabriel Landeskog .75 2.00
C25 Jarome Iginla 1.00 2.50
C26 Brandon Saad 1.00 2.50
C27 Seth Jones .75 2.00
C28 Boone Jenner 1.00 2.50
C29 Tyler Seguin 1.50 4.00
C30 John Klingberg 1.00 2.50
C31 Jason Spezza 1.00 2.50
C32 Dylan Larkin 1.50 4.00
C33 Tomas Tatar .75 2.00
C34 Mike Green 1.00 2.50
C35 Connor McDavid 5.00 12.00
C36 Leon Draisaitl 1.25 3.00
C37 Darnell Nurse .75 2.00
C38 Nick Bjugstad .75 2.00
C39 Aleksander Barkov 1.00 2.50
C40 Roberto Luongo 1.00 2.50
C41 Anze Kopitar 1.50 4.00
C42 Tyler Toffoli 1.00 2.50
C43 Drew Doughty 1.00 2.50
C44 Jonathan Quick 1.50 4.00
C45 Devan Dubnyk 1.00 2.50
C46 Charlie Coyle .75 2.00
C47 Nino Niederreiter 1.00 2.50
C48 Brendan Gallagher 1.25 3.00
C49 Carey Price 3.00 8.00
C50 Ryan Johansen 1.25 3.00
C51 James Neal .75 2.00
C52 Travis Zajac .75 2.00
C53 Kyle Palmieri .75 2.00
C54 Brock Nelson .75 2.00
C55 Anders Lee 1.00 2.50
C56 Henrik Lundqvist 1.00 2.50
C57 Derek Stepan .75 2.00
C58 Erik Karlsson 2.00 5.00
C59 Bobby Ryan .75 2.00
C60 Mark Stone 1.00 2.50
C61 Dion Phaneuf 1.00 2.50
C62 Jakub Voracek 1.00 2.50
C63 Shayne Gostisbehere 1.25 3.00
C64 Evgeni Malkin 3.00 8.00
C65 Matt Murray 1.50 4.00
C66 Phil Kessel 1.25 3.00
C67 Carl Hagelin 1.00 2.50
C68 Joe Pavelski 1.00 2.50
C69 Martin Jones 1.00 2.50
C70 Joe Thornton 1.00 2.50
C71 Vladimir Tarasenko 1.50 4.00
C72 Alex Pietrangelo .75 2.00
C73 Jake Allen 1.25 3.00
C74 Ben Bishop 1.00 2.50
C75 Nikita Kucherov 1.50 4.00
C76 Victor Hedman 1.25 3.00
C77 Leo Komarov 1.00 2.50
C78 Jake Gardiner 1.00 2.50
C79 Morgan Rielly .75 2.00
C80 Daniel Sedin 1.00 2.50
C81 Ryan Miller 1.00 2.50
C82 Jannik Hansen .60 1.50
C83 Braden Holtby 1.50 4.00
C84 John Carlson 1.25 3.00
C85 Alexander Ovechkin 4.00 10.00
C86 Evgeny Kuznetsov 1.50 4.00
C87 Dustin Byfuglien 1.00 2.50
C88 Bryan Little .75 2.00
C89 Mark Scheifele 1.25 3.00
C90 P.Kane/E.Karlsson CL 2.00 5.00
C91 Mitch Marner YG 40.00 100.00
C92 Anthony Mantha YG 10.00 25.00
C93 Esa Lindell YG 4.00 10.00
C94 Sonny Milano YG 5.00 12.00
C95 Connor Brown YG 6.00 15.00
C96 Sebastian Aho YG 8.00 20.00
C97 Brandon Carlo YG 4.00 10.00
C98 Jakob Chychrun YG 4.00 10.00
C99 Brendan Leipsic YG 4.00 10.00
C100 Mikhail Sergachev YG 12.00 30.00
C101 Danton Heinen YG 6.00 15.00
C102 Michael Matheson YG 4.00 10.00
C103 Chris Bigras YG 3.00 8.00
C104 Charlie Lindgren YG 12.00 30.00
C105 Jimmy Vesey YG 8.00 20.00
C106 Patrik Laine YG 60.00 150.00
C107 Mathew Barzal YG 30.00 80.00
C108 Hudson Fasching YG 4.00 10.00
C109 Justin Bailey YG 4.00 10.00
C110 Pavel Zacha YG 5.00 12.00
C111 Oliver Kylington YG 3.00 8.00
C112 Pavel Buchnevich YG 6.00 15.00
C113 Lawson Crouse YG 3.00 8.00
C114 Miles Wood YG 3.00 8.00
C115 Tyler Motte YG 4.00 10.00
C116 Oliver Bjorkstrand YG 3.00 8.00
C117 Anthony Beauvillier YG 4.00 10.00
C118 Gustav Forsling YG 4.00 10.00
C119 Nick Sorensen YG 4.00 10.00
C120 M.Marner YG/P.Laine YG CL 10.00 25.00
C121 Corey Perry 1.00 2.50
C122 Rickard Rakell 1.00 2.50
C123 Hampus Lindholm .60 1.50
C124 Oliver Ekman-Larsson .75 2.00
C125 Martin Hanzal .75 2.00
C126 Tuukka Rask 1.00 2.50
C127 David Krejci 1.00 2.50
C128 David Backes 1.00 2.50
C129 Sam Reinhart .75 2.00
C130 Kyle Okposo 1.00 2.50
C131 Sean Monahan 1.00 2.50
C132 Mark Giordano .75 2.00
C133 Brian Elliott .75 2.00
C134 Justin Faulk .75 2.00
C135 Victor Rask .75 2.00
C136 Teuvo Teravainen 1.00 2.50
C137 Duncan Keith 1.00 2.50
C138 Jonathan Toews 2.00 5.00
C139 Artem Anisimov .75 2.00
C140 Matt Duchene 1.00 2.50
C141 Carl Soderberg .60 1.50
C142 Cam Atkinson 1.00 2.50
C143 Alexander Wennberg .75 2.00
C144 Jamie Benn 1.25 3.00
C145 Patrick Sharp .75 2.00
C146 Andreas Athanasiou 1.00 2.50
C147 Henrik Zetterberg 1.25 3.00
C148 Jordan Eberle 1.00 2.50
C149 Milan Lucic .75 2.00
C150 Adam Larsson 1.00 2.50
C151 Jaromir Jagr 2.50 6.00
C152 Aaron Ekblad 1.00 2.50
C153 Vincent Trocheck 1.00 2.50
C154 Jake Muzzin .75 2.00
C155 Jeff Carter 1.00 2.50
C156 Tanner Pearson .75 2.00
C157 Ryan Suter .75 2.00
C158 Zach Parise 1.00 2.50
C159 Mikko Koivu .75 2.00
C160 Eric Staal 1.25 3.00
C161 Shea Weber .75 2.00
C162 Max Pacioretty 1.00 2.50
C163 Alex Galchenyuk 1.25 3.00
C164 Pekka Rinne 1.25 3.00
C165 Roman Josi 1.00 2.50
C166 Filip Forsberg 1.25 3.00
C167 P.K. Subban 1.50 4.00
C168 Adam Henrique 1.00 2.50
C169 Cory Schneider .75 2.00
C170 Taylor Hall 2.00 5.00
C171 John Tavares 2.00 5.00
C172 Andrew Ladd 1.00 2.50
C173 Jaroslav Halak 1.00 2.50
C174 Travis Hamonic .60 1.50
C175 Mats Zuccarello 1.00 2.50
C176 J.T. Miller .75 2.00
C177 Mika Zibanejad 1.00 2.50
C178 Derick Brassard 1.00 2.50
C179 Jean-Gabriel Pageau .75 2.00
C180 Mike Hoffman .75 2.00
C181 Claude Giroux 1.00 2.50
C182 Wayne Simmonds 1.25 3.00
C183 Brayden Schenn 1.00 2.50
C184 Kris Letang 1.00 2.50
C185 Patric Hornqvist .75 2.00
C186 Logan Couture 1.00 2.50
C187 Patrick Marleau 1.00 2.50
C188 Mikkel Boedker .75 2.00
C189 Robby Fabbri 1.00 2.50
C190 Jaden Schwartz 1.25 3.00
C191 David Perron .75 2.00
C192 Ondrej Palat .75 2.00
C193 Alex Killorn .60 1.50
C194 Vladislav Namestnikov .60 1.50
C195 Steven Stamkos 2.00 5.00
C196 Frederik Andersen .75 2.00
C197 James van Riemsdyk 1.00 2.50
C198 Nazem Kadri .75 2.00
C199 Loui Eriksson 1.00 2.50
C200 Henrik Sedin 1.00 2.50
C201 Bo Horvat 1.50 4.00
C202 Sven Baertschi .60 1.50
C203 Nicklas Backstrom 1.50 4.00
C204 Justin Williams .75 2.00
C205 Andre Burakovsky .75 2.00
C206 T.J. Oshie 1.50 4.00
C207 Blake Wheeler 1.00 2.50
C208 Mathieu Perreault .75 2.00
C209 Connor Hellebuyck 1.50 4.00
C210 S.Stamkos/J.Tavares CL 2.00 5.00
C211 Auston Matthews YG 200.00 300.00
C212 Jesse Puljujarvi YG 15.00 40.00
C213 Dylan Strome YG 8.00 20.00
C214 William Nylander YG 25.00 60.00
C215 Brandon Montour YG 4.00 10.00
C216 Kyle Connor YG 10.00 25.00
C217 Joel Eriksson Ek YG 4.00 10.00
C218 Matthew Tkachuk YG 12.00 30.00
C219 Drake Caggiula YG 4.00 10.00
C220 Jacob Larsson YG 6.00 15.00
C221 Nick Baptiste YG 4.00 10.00
C222 Thomas Chabot YG 8.00 20.00
C223 Nikita Zaitsev YG 4.00 10.00
C224 Mike Reilly YG 3.00 8.00
C225 Timo Meier YG 4.00 10.00
C226 Zach Werenski YG 8.00 20.00
C227 Adam Erne YG 6.00 15.00
C228 Kasperi Kapanen YG 12.00 30.00
C229 Nick Schmaltz YG 4.00 10.00
C230 Christian Dvorak YG 4.00 10.00
C231 Josh Morrissey YG 5.00 12.00
C232 Artturi Lehkonen YG 4.00 10.00
C233 Brayden Point YG 10.00 25.00
C234 Travis Konecny YG 8.00 20.00
C235 Jake Guentzel YG 50.00 120.00
C236 Thatcher Demko YG 8.00 20.00
C237 Zach Sanford YG 4.00 10.00
C238 Julius Honka YG 4.00 10.00
C239 Ivan Provorov YG 8.00 20.00
C240 A.Matthews/W.Nylander YG CL 15.00 40.00
C241 Bobby Orr RS 30.00 80.00
C242 Wayne Gretzky RS 50.00 125.00
C243 Mario Lemieux RS 30.00 80.00
C244 Dale Hawerchuk RS 12.00 30.00
C245 Brett Hull RS 10.00 25.00
C246 Norm Ullman RS 10.00 25.00
C247 Trevor Linden RS 12.00 30.00
C248 Mike Richter RS 10.00 25.00
C249 Dominik Hasek RS 10.00 25.00
C250 Mike Modano RS 15.00 40.00
C251 Pat LaFontaine RS 10.00 25.00
C252 Darryl Sittler RS 10.00 25.00
C253 Luc Robitaille RS 10.00 25.00
C254 Steve Yzerman RS 12.00 30.00
C255 Stan Mikita RS 12.00 30.00
C256 Jason Dickinson POE 5.00 12.00
C257 Josh Morrissey POE 8.00 20.00
C258 Ryan Pulock POE 6.00 15.00
C259 Alan Quine POE 6.00 15.00
C260 Anthony Mantha POE 15.00 40.00
C261 Thomas Chabot POE 12.00 30.00
C262 Michael Matheson POE 6.00 15.00
C263 Chris Bigras POE 5.00 12.00
C264 Travis Konecny POE 12.00 30.00
C265 Mitch Marner POE 60.00 150.00
C266 Lawson Crouse POE 5.00 12.00
C267 Brayden Point POE 15.00 40.00
C268 Dylan Strome POE 12.00 30.00
C269 Anthony Beauvillier POE 6.00 15.00
C270 Mathew Barzal POE 20.00 50.00

2016-17 Upper Deck Clear Cut

*VETS: 8X TO 20X BASIC CARDS
*ROOKIES: 2.5X TO 6X BASIC CARDS
STATED ODDS 1:72 HOBBY PACKS
187 Evgeny Kuznetsov 10.00 25.00
191 Nicklas Backstrom 10.00 25.00
201 Auston Matthews YG 600.00 1500.00
225 Jesse Puljujarvi YG 150.00 250.00
226 Josh Morrissey YG 30.00 80.00
227A Pavel Buchnevich YG 30.00 80.00
231A Matthew Tkachuk YG 60.00 150.00
244 Austin Czarnik YG 40.00 100.00
249A William Nylander YG 150.00 300.00

2016-17 Upper Deck Clear Cut Foundations

CCF1 R.Getzlaf/J.Gibson 20.00 50.00

CCF2 M.Domi/M.Hanzal 15.00 40.00
CCF3 D.Krejci/B.Marchand 15.00 40.00
CCF4 J.Eichel/R.O'Reilly 25.00 60.00
CCF5 S.Bennett/S.Monahan 15.00 40.00
CCF6 J.Skinner/N.Hanifin 12.00 30.00
CCF7 P.Kane/A.Panarin 25.00 60.00
CCF8 G.Landeskog/J.Iginla 12.00 30.00
CCF9 B.Saad/S.Jones 12.00 30.00
CCF10 J.Benn/J.Klingberg 15.00 40.00
CCF11 N.Kronwall/D.Larkin 20.00 50.00
CCF12 C.McDavid/O.Klefbom 60.00 150.00
CCF13 A.Ekblad/A.Barkov 12.00 30.00
CCF14 J.Carter/D.Doughty 12.00 30.00
CCF15 Z.Parise/N.Niederreiter 12.00 30.00
CCF16 C.Price/B.Gallagher 40.00 100.00
CCF17 R.Johansen/J.Neal 15.00 40.00
CCF18 K.Palmieri/T.Zajac 10.00 25.00
CCF19 J.Halak/C.de Haan 12.00 30.00
CCF20 R.Nash/R.McDonagh 12.00 30.00
CCF21 K.Turris/B.Ryan 10.00 25.00
CCF22 J.Voracek/S.Gostisbehere 15.00 40.00
CCF23 P.Kessel/M.Murray 20.00 50.00
CCF24 J.Pavelski/M.Jones 12.00 30.00
CCF25 R.Fabbri/A.Pietrangelo 12.00 30.00
CCF26 B.Bishop/N.Kucherov 20.00 50.00
CCF27 N.Kadri/L.Komarov 12.00 30.00
CCF28 H.Sedin/J.Virtanen 15.00 40.00
CCF29 E.Kuznetsov/N.Backstrom 20.00 50.00
CCF30 B.Wheeler/D.Byfuglien 12.00 30.00

2016-17 Upper Deck Clear Cut Honoured Members

HOF61 Nicklas Lidstrom 15.00 40.00
HOF62 Dominik Hasek 15.00 40.00
HOF63 Glenn Hall 15.00 40.00
HOF64 Billy Smith 15.00 40.00
HOF65 Gerry Cheevers 15.00 40.00
HOF66 Larry Murphy 15.00 40.00
HOF67 Norm Ullman 15.00 40.00

2016-17 Upper Deck Clear Cut Superstars

CCSAB Aleksander Barkov 10.00 25.00
CCSAK Anze Kopitar 15.00 40.00
CCSAO Alexander Ovechkin 40.00 100.00
CCSBB Brent Burns 12.00 30.00
CCSBH Braden Holtby 15.00 40.00
CCSBW Blake Wheeler 10.00 25.00
CCSCG Claude Giroux 10.00 25.00
CCSCM Connor McDavid 50.00 120.00
CCSCP Carey Price 30.00 80.00
CCSDD Drew Doughty 10.00 25.00
CCSDL Dylan Larkin 15.00 40.00
CCSEK Erik Karlsson 20.00 50.00
CCSEM Evgeni Malkin 30.00 80.00
CCSHL Henrik Lundqvist 10.00 25.00
CCSJB Jamie Benn 12.00 30.00
CCSJE Jack Eichel 20.00 50.00
CCSJG Johnny Gaudreau 15.00 40.00
CCSJI Jarome Iginla 10.00 25.00
CCSJJ Jaromir Jagr 25.00 60.00
CCSJT Jonathan Toews 20.00 50.00
CCSNM Nathan MacKinnon 20.00 50.00
CCSPB Patrice Bergeron 12.00 30.00
CCSPE Corey Perry 10.00 25.00
CCSPK Patrick Kane 20.00 50.00
CCSRG Ryan Getzlaf 15.00 40.00
CCSRS Ryan Suter 8.00 20.00
CCSSC Sidney Crosby 40.00 100.00
CCSSS Steven Stamkos 20.00 50.00
CCSTA John Tavares 20.00 50.00
CCSTH Joe Thornton 10.00 25.00
CCSTS Tyler Seguin 15.00 40.00
CCSVT Vladimir Tarasenko 15.00 40.00

2016-17 Upper Deck Day With The Cup

DC1 Sidney Crosby 100.00 200.00
DC2 Kris Letang 20.00 50.00
DC3 Justin Schultz 15.00 40.00
DC4 Matt Murray 30.00 80.00
DC5 Phil Kessel 30.00 80.00
DC6 Conor Sheary 25.00 60.00
DC7 Matt Cullen 20.00 50.00
DC8 Ian Cole 15.00 40.00
DC9 Eric Fehr 20.00 50.00
DC10 Beau Bennett 15.00 40.00
DC11 Derrick Pouliot 20.00 50.00
DC12 Jeff Zatkoff 20.00 50.00
DC13 Marc-Andre Fleury 30.00 80.00
DC14 Brian Dumoulin 15.00 40.00
DC15 Bryan Rust 20.00 50.00
DC16 Carl Hagelin 20.00 50.00
DC17 Olli Maatta 20.00 50.00
DC18 Trevor Daley 15.00 40.00
DC19 Chris Kunitz 20.00 50.00
DC20 Nick Bonino 12.00 30.00
DC21 Patric Hornqvist 15.00 40.00
DC22 Evgeni Malkin 60.00 150.00
DC23 Ben Lovejoy 12.00 30.00

2016-17 Upper Deck Game Jerseys

GJAD Anthony Duclair F 3.00 8.00
GJAH Andrew Hammond F 2.50 6.00
GJAH Adam Henrique F 3.00 8.00
GJAO Alexander Ovechkin C 12.00 30.00
GJAS Alexander Steen E 3.00 8.00
GJBB Brent Burns C 4.00 10.00
GJBE Matt Beleskey F 2.50 6.00
GJBG Brendan Gallagher G 4.00 10.00
GJBH Braden Holtby G 5.00 12.00
GJBR Brayden Schenn E 3.00 8.00
GJBS Brandon Saad E 3.00 8.00
GJCA Craig Anderson F 3.00 8.00
GJCA John Carlson D 4.00 10.00
GJCC Corey Crawford E 4.00 10.00
GJCG Claude Giroux D 3.00 8.00
GJCM Connor McDavid D 15.00 40.00
GJCP Carey Price C 10.00 25.00
GJCS Cory Schneider G 2.50 6.00
GJDB Dustin Byfuglien D 3.00 8.00
GJDD Drew Doughty E 3.00 8.00
GJDH Dale Hawerchuk B 20.00 50.00
GJDH Dougie Hamilton F 3.00 8.00
GJDK Duncan Keith C 3.00 8.00
GJDO Max Domi F 4.00 10.00
GJDS Daniel Sedin E 3.00 8.00
GJDU Devan Dubnyk F 3.00 8.00
GJEK Erik Karlsson B
GJEM Evgeni Malkin C 10.00 25.00
GJFF Filip Forsberg D 4.00 10.00
GJGL Gabriel Landeskog D 2.50 6.00
GJHL Henrik Lundqvist C 3.00 8.00
GJHS Henrik Sedin C 3.00 8.00
GJHU Jonathan Huberdeau E 3.00 8.00
GJHZ Henrik Zetterberg C 4.00 10.00
GJJA Jake Allen F 4.00 10.00
GJJB Jamie Benn C 4.00 10.00
GJJC Jeff Carter G 3.00 8.00
GJJE Jack Eichel E 6.00 15.00
GJJF Justin Faulk E 2.50 6.00
GJJG Johnny Gaudreau D 5.00 12.00
GJJH Jaroslav Halak F 3.00 8.00
GJJL John LeClair A 30.00 80.00
GJJP Joe Pavelski D 3.00 8.00
GJJQ Jonathan Quick D 5.00 12.00
GJJS Jordan Staal F 3.00 8.00
GJJS Jeff Skinner F 3.00 8.00
GJKA Nazem Kadri E 2.50 6.00
GJKL John Klingberg G 3.00 8.00
GJKT Kyle Turris F 2.50 6.00
GJKU Evgeny Kuznetsov D 5.00 12.00
GJLE Kris Letang D 3.00 8.00
GJMA Mark Stone E 3.00 8.00
GJMB Martin Brodeur A 50.00 120.00
GJMC Michael Cammalleri F 2.50 6.00
GJMD Matt Duchene G 3.00 8.00
GJMJ Martin Jones E 3.00 8.00
GJMR Morgan Rielly F 2.50 6.00
GJMS Mark Scheifele D 4.00 10.00
GJNA Nathan MacKinnon D 6.00 15.00
GJNB Nick Bjugstad E 2.50 6.00
GJNF Nick Foligno E 2.50 6.00
GJNK Nikita Kucherov C 5.00 12.00
GJNK Niklas Kronwall F 2.00 5.00
GJNL Nick Leddy F 2.00 5.00
GJNN Nino Niederreiter F 3.00 8.00
GJOE Oliver Ekman-Larsson A
GJOM Olli Maatta D 3.00 8.00
GJON Owen Nolan B 25.00 60.00
GJOP Ondrej Palat E 2.50 6.00
GJPB Patrice Bergeron E 4.00 10.00
GJPE Corey Perry B 10.00 25.00
GJPK Patrick Kane E 6.00 15.00
GJPM Petr Mrazek F 3.00 8.00
GJRG Ryan Getzlaf C 5.00 12.00
GJRJ Roman Josi C 3.00 8.00
GJRK Ryan Kesler E 3.00 8.00
GJRL Roberto Luongo G 3.00 8.00
GJRN Rick Nash G 3.00 8.00
GJRO Ryan O'Reilly E 3.00 8.00
GJSB Sam Bennett D 4.00 10.00
GJSC Sidney Crosby D 12.00 30.00
GJSI Jakob Silfverberg E 3.00 8.00
GJSM Sean Monahan D 3.00 8.00
GJSP Jason Spezza D 3.00 8.00
GJSR Sam Reinhart E 2.50 6.00
GJST Derek Stepan D 2.50 6.00
GJTA John Tavares C 6.00 15.00
GJTO Tomas Tatar F 2.50 6.00
GJTR Tuukka Rask G 3.00 8.00
GJTT Tyler Toffoli D 3.00 8.00
GJVH Victor Hedman D 4.00 10.00
GJZP Zach Parise E 3.00 8.00

2016-17 Upper Deck Goalie Nightmares

GN1 Corey Perry 1.00 2.50
GN2 Max Domi 1.25 3.00
GN3 Brad Marchand 1.25 3.00
GN4 Jack Eichel 2.00 5.00
GN5 Johnny Gaudreau 1.50 4.00
GN6 Jeff Skinner 1.00 2.50
GN7 Patrick Kane 2.00 5.00
GN8 Matt Duchene 1.00 2.50
GN9 Brandon Saad 1.00 2.50
GN10 Jamie Benn 1.25 3.00
GN11 Dylan Larkin 1.50 4.00
GN12 Connor McDavid 5.00 12.00
GN13 Aleksander Barkov 1.00 2.50
GN14 Tyler Toffoli 1.00 2.50
GN15 Zach Parise 1.00 2.50
GN16 Alex Galchenyuk 1.25 3.00
GN17 Filip Forsberg 1.25 3.00
GN18 Kyle Palmieri .75 2.00
GN19 John Tavares 2.00 5.00
GN20 Mats Zuccarello 1.00 2.50
GN21 Mark Stone 1.00 2.50
GN22 Claude Giroux 1.00 2.50
GN23 Sidney Crosby 4.00 10.00
GN24 Joe Pavelski 1.00 2.50
GN25 Vladimir Tarasenko 1.50 4.00
GN26 Nikita Kucherov 1.50 4.00
GN27 James van Riemsdyk 1.00 2.50
GN28 Daniel Sedin 1.00 2.50
GN29 Alexander Ovechkin 4.00 10.00
GN30 Mark Scheifele 1.25 3.00

2016-17 Upper Deck Oversized

44 Patrick Kane 4.00 10.00
61 Jamie Benn 2.50 6.00
75 Connor McDavid 10.00 25.00
86 Jeff Carter 2.00 5.00
101 Brendan Gallagher 2.50 6.00
133 Erik Karlsson 4.00 10.00
146 Sidney Crosby 8.00 20.00
150 Joe Pavelski 2.00 5.00
162 Vladimir Tarasenko 3.00 8.00
170 James van Riemsdyk 2.00 5.00
179 Daniel Sedin 2.00 5.00
184 Alexander Ovechkin 8.00 20.00
187 Evgeny Kuznetsov 3.00 8.00
195 Dustin Byfuglien 2.00 5.00
201 Auston Matthews YG 25.00 60.00
206 Jakob Chychrun YG 2.00 5.00
212 Kyle Connor YG 5.00 12.00
214 Ivan Provorov YG 4.00 10.00
218 Jimmy Vesey YG 4.00 10.00
224 Zach Werenski YG 4.00 10.00
225 Jesse Puljujarvi YG 5.00 12.00
227 Pavel Buchnevich YG 3.00 8.00
231 Matthew Tkachuk YG 6.00 15.00
235 Christian Dvorak YG 2.00 5.00
236 Mikhail Sergachev YG 4.00 10.00
242 Hudson Fasching YG 2.00 5.00
248 Pavel Zacha YG 2.50 6.00
249 William Nylander YG 8.00 20.00
451 Patrik Laine YG 25.00 60.00
452 Kasperi Kapanen YG 4.00 10.00
458 Mathew Barzal YG 6.00 15.00
459 Joel Eriksson Ek YG 2.00 5.00
463 Anthony DeAngelo YG 2.00 5.00
468 Mitch Marner YG 10.00 25.00
471 Tyler Bertuzzi YG 2.50 6.00
475 Troy Stecher YG 2.00 5.00
482 Brandon Carlo YG 2.00 5.00
484 Nikita Soshnikov YG 1.25 3.00
486 Kevin Labanc YG 2.00 5.00
488 Thomas Chabot YG 4.00 10.00
498 Dylan Strome YG 4.00 10.00
499 Brendan Leipsic YG 2.00 5.00

2016-17 Upper Deck Parkhurst Rookies

PR1 William Nylander 4.00 10.00
PR2 Matthew Tkachuk 3.00 8.00
PR3 Kyle Connor 2.50 6.00
PR4 Sebastian Aho 2.00 5.00
PR5 Ivan Provorov 2.00 5.00
PR6 Christian Dvorak 1.00 2.50
PR7 Mitch Marner 5.00 12.00
PR8 Jesse Puljujarvi 2.50 6.00
PR9 Patrik Laine 4.00 10.00
PR10 Auston Matthews 6.00 15.00

2016-17 Upper Deck Shining Stars

SS1 Brent Burns 1.25 3.00
SS2 Brent Seabrook .75 2.00
SS3 Drew Doughty 1.00 2.50
SS4 Dustin Byfuglien 1.00 2.50
SS5 Erik Karlsson 2.00 5.00
SS6 John Klingberg 1.00 2.50
SS7 Roman Josi 1.00 2.50
SS8 Ryan Suter .75 2.00
SS9 Shayne Gostisbehere 1.25 3.00
SS10 Victor Hedman 1.25 3.00
SS11 Blake Wheeler 1.00 2.50
SS12 Vladimir Tarasenko 1.50 4.00
SS13 James Neal .75 2.00
SS14 Jaromir Jagr 2.50 6.00
SS15 Kyle Palmieri .75 2.00
SS16 Mark Stone 1.00 2.50
SS17 Patrick Kane 2.00 5.00
SS18 Nikita Kucherov 1.50 4.00
SS19 Phil Kessel 1.25 3.00
SS20 Wayne Simmonds 1.25 3.00
SS21 Anze Kopitar 1.50 4.00
SS22 Claude Giroux 1.00 2.50
SS23 Evgeny Kuznetsov 1.50 4.00
SS24 Joe Pavelski 1.00 2.50
SS25 Joe Thornton 1.00 2.50
SS26 Mark Scheifele 1.25 3.00
SS27 Nicklas Backstrom 1.50 4.00
SS28 Ryan Getzlaf 1.50 4.00
SS29 Sean Monahan 1.00 2.50
SS30 Sidney Crosby 4.00 10.00
SS31 Alexander Ovechkin 8.00 20.00
SS32 Artemi Panarin 2.50 6.00
SS33 Brad Marchand 2.50 6.00
SS34 Brandon Saad 2.00 5.00
SS35 Daniel Sedin 2.00 5.00
SS36 Filip Forsberg 2.50 6.00
SS37 Jamie Benn 2.50 6.00
SS38 Jonathan Huberdeau 2.00 5.00
SS39 Johnny Gaudreau 3.00 8.00
SS40 Zach Parise 2.00 5.00
SS41 Ben Bishop 3.00 8.00
SS42 Braden Holtby 5.00 12.00
SS43 Corey Crawford 4.00 10.00
SS44 Cory Schneider 2.50 6.00
SS45 Jake Allen 4.00 10.00
SS46 John Gibson 3.00 8.00
SS47 Martin Jones 3.00 8.00
SS48 Matt Murray 5.00 12.00
SS49 Petr Mrazek 3.00 8.00
SS50 Thomas Greiss 2.50 6.00

2016-17 Upper Deck Sophomore Sensations

SS1 Jack Eichel 1.50 4.00
SS2 Artemi Panarin 1.00 2.50
SS4 Matt Murray 1.25 3.00
SS5 Dylan Larkin 1.25 3.00
SS6 Connor McDavid 4.00 10.00

2016-17 Upper Deck Super Colossal

SC1 Clayton Stoner 1.50 4.00
SC2 Cody McLeod 1.25 3.00
SC3 Derek Dorsett 1.25 3.00
SC4 Brian Boyle 1.25 3.00
SC5 Chris Neil 1.25 3.00
SC6 Dalton Prout 1.25 3.00
SC7 Matt Hendricks 1.25 3.00
SC8 Chris Thorburn 1.25 3.00
SC9 Brandon Bollig 1.50 4.00
SC10 Alex Petrovic 1.25 3.00
SC11 Antoine Roussel 1.25 3.00
SC12 Kyle Clifford 1.50 4.00
SC13 Shawn Thornton 1.50 4.00
SC14 Tom Wilson 2.00 5.00
SC15 Dustin Byfuglien 2.00 5.00
SC16 Radko Gudas 1.25 3.00
SC17 Wayne Simmonds 2.50 6.00
SC18 Zdeno Chara 2.00 5.00
SC19 Mark Borowiecki 1.50 4.00
SC20 Zac Rinaldo 1.50 4.00

2016-17 Upper Deck Team Triples

DTCA Laine/Matthews/Puljujarvi 20.00 50.00
TTC1 Kylington/Bennett/Shinkaruk 4.00 10.00
TTC2 Monahan/Gaudreau/Giordano 5.00 12.00
TTE1 Draisaitl/McDavid/Nurse 15.00 40.00
TTE2 Eberle/Nugent-Hopkins/Talbot 4.00 10.00
TTM1 Lindgren/Galchenyuk/McCarron 6.00 15.00
TTM2 Pacioretty/Price/Gallagher 10.00 25.00
TTO1 Lazar/Paul/Puempel 4.00 10.00
TTO2 Stone/Karlsson/Turris 6.00 15.00
TTT1 Nylander/Matthews/Leipsic 20.00 50.00
TTT2 Kadri/Rielly/van Riemsdyk 2.50 6.00
TTT3 Kapanen/Brown/Soshnikov 6.00 15.00
TTV1 Horvat/Virtanen/Hutton 5.00 12.00
TTV2 Sedin/Sedin/Edler 3.00 8.00
TTW1 Hellebuyck/Laine/Ehlers 12.00 30.00
TTW2 Wheeler/Scheifele/Byfuglien 4.00 10.00

2016-17 Upper Deck UD Portraits

P1 Seth Jones 1.25 3.00
P2 Mats Zuccarello 1.50 4.00
P3 Wayne Simmonds 2.00 5.00
P4 Joe Thornton 1.50 4.00
P5 Pekka Rinne 2.00 5.00
P6 Evgeny Kuznetsov 2.50 6.00
P7 Mark Scheifele 2.00 5.00
P8 Robby Fabbri 1.50 4.00
P9 Tyler Toffoli 1.50 4.00
P10 Noah Hanifin 1.50 4.00
P11 Matt Murray 2.50 6.00
P12 Braden Holtby 2.50 6.00
P13 Drew Doughty 1.50 4.00
P14 Justin Faulk 1.25 3.00
P15 Artemi Panarin 2.00 5.00
P16 Aleksander Barkov 1.50 4.00
P17 Jamie Benn 2.00 5.00
P18 Corey Crawford 2.00 5.00
P19 Dylan Larkin 2.50 6.00
P20 Roberto Luongo 1.50 4.00
P21 Shayne Gostisbehere 2.00 5.00
P22 Anthony Duclair 1.50 4.00
P23 Mark Stone 1.50 4.00
P24 Rickard Rakell 1.50 4.00
P25 Travis Hamonic 1.00 2.50
P26 Victor Hedman 2.00 5.00
P27 John Klingberg 1.50 4.00
P28 Cory Schneider 1.25 3.00
P29 Henrik Sedin 1.50 4.00
P30 Nathan MacKinnon 3.00 8.00
P31 Jack Eichel 3.00 8.00
P32 Nikita Kucherov 2.50 6.00
P33 Alex Galchenyuk 2.00 5.00
P34 Ryan Johansen 2.00 5.00
P35 Sean Monahan 1.50 4.00
P36 Leon Draisaitl 2.00 5.00
P37 Morgan Rielly 1.25 3.00
P38 Sam Bennett 2.00 5.00
P39 Martin Jones 1.50 4.00
P40 Max Domi 2.00 5.00
P41 Alex Pietrangelo 1.25 3.00
P42 Brent Burns 2.00 5.00
P43 Ryan Suter 1.25 3.00
P44 Blake Wheeler 1.50 4.00
P45 Brendan Gallagher 2.00 5.00
P46 Phil Kessel 2.00 5.00
P47 John Gibson 1.50 4.00
P48 Brad Marchand 2.00 5.00
P49 Sidney Crosby 10.00 25.00
P50 Patrick Kane 5.00 12.00
P51 Vladimir Tarasenko 4.00 10.00
P52 Erik Karlsson 5.00 12.00
P53 Connor McDavid 12.00 30.00
P54 Alexander Ovechkin 10.00 25.00
P55 Josh Morrissey 3.00 8.00
P56 Anthony Mantha 6.00 15.00
P57 William Nylander 10.00 25.00
P58 Sonny Milano 3.00 8.00
P59 Hudson Fasching 2.50 6.00
P60 Pavel Zacha 3.00 8.00
P61 Patrik Laine 6.00 15.00
P62 Pontus Aberg 2.00 5.00
P63 Mike Reilly 1.25 3.00
P64 Steven Santini 1.25 3.00
P65 Artturi Lehkonen 1.50 4.00
P66 Brandon Carlo 1.50 4.00
P67 Nick Schmaltz 1.50 4.00
P68 Christian Dvorak 1.50 4.00
P69 Kasperi Kapanen 3.00 8.00
P70 Justin Bailey 1.50 4.00
P71 Anthony Beauvillier 1.50 4.00
P72 Connor Brown 2.50 6.00
P73 Jakob Chychrun 1.50 4.00
P74 Brendan Leipsic 1.50 4.00
P75 Travis Konecny 3.00 8.00
P76 Zach Sanford 1.50 4.00
P77 Joel Eriksson Ek 1.50 4.00
P78 Drake Caggiula 1.50 4.00
P79 Brayden Point 4.00 10.00
P80 Jake Guentzel 6.00 15.00
P81 Mitch Marner 8.00 20.00
P82 Jacob Larsson 2.50 6.00
P83 Oliver Kylington 1.25 3.00
P84 Charlie Lindgren 3.00 8.00
P85 Troy Stecher 1.50 4.00
P86 Ivan Provorov 3.00 8.00
P87 Jesse Puljujarvi 4.00 10.00
P88 Michael Matheson 1.50 4.00
P89 Zach Werenski 3.00 8.00
P90 Tyler Motte 1.50 4.00
P91 Dylan Strome 3.00 8.00
P92 Jason Dickinson 1.25 3.00
P93 Thomas Chabot 3.00 8.00
P94 Kyle Connor 4.00 10.00
P95 Mikhail Sergachev 3.00 8.00
P96 Nikita Zaitsev 1.50 4.00
P97 Jimmy Vesey 3.00 8.00
P98 Oliver Bjorkstrand 1.25 3.00
P99 Blake Speers 1.50 4.00
P100 Kevin Labanc 1.50 4.00
P101 Sebastian Aho 3.00 8.00
P102 Tristan Jarry 3.00 8.00
P103 Miles Wood 1.25 3.00
P104 Pavel Buchnevich 2.50 6.00
P105 Julius Honka 1.50 4.00
P106 Mathew Barzal 5.00 12.00
P107 Nick Paul 2.00 5.00
P108 Chris Bigras 1.25 3.00
P109 Matthew Tkachuk 5.00 12.00
P110 Auston Matthews 10.00 25.00

2016-17 Upper Deck Winter Classic Jumbos

WC1 Brendan Gallagher 1.25 3.00
WC2 Matt Beleskey .75 2.00
WC3 Mike Condon 1.00 2.50
WC4 Zdeno Chara 1.00 2.50
WC5 Tomas Plekanec 1.00 2.50
WC6 Patrice Bergeron 1.25 3.00
WC7 Paul Byron .75 2.00
WC8 Torey Krug 1.00 2.50
WC9 Max Pacioretty 1.00 2.50
WC10 Loui Eriksson 1.00 2.50
WC11 P.K. Subban 1.50 4.00
WC12 Ryan Spooner .75 2.00
WC13 Nathan Beaulieu .60 1.50
WC14 Jimmy Hayes .60 1.50

2016-17 Upper Deck Ceremonial Puck Drop

CDP1 Mario Lemieux 50.00 120.00
CDP2 Rob Blake 15.00 40.00
CDP3 Steve Yzerman 20.00 50.00
CDP4 Brett Hull 15.00 40.00
CDP5 Luc Robitaille 15.00 40.00
CDP6 Nicklas Lidstrom 15.00 40.00
CDP7 Martin Brodeur 30.00 80.00
CDP8 Peter Forsberg 15.00 40.00
CDP9 Wayne Gretzky 80.00 200.00
CDP10 Mike Bossy 15.00 40.00
CDP11 Chris Chelios 15.00 40.00
CDP12 Tony Esposito 15.00 40.00

2016-17 Upper Deck Ceremonial Puck Drop Autograph

CDP4 Brett Hull 60.00 150.00
CDP5 Luc Robitaille 40.00 100.00
CDP6 Nicklas Lidstrom 30.00 80.00
CDP9 Wayne Gretzky
CDP10 Mike Bossy 30.00 80.00
CDP12 Tony Esposito 60.00 150.00

2016-17 Upper Deck Day With The Cup Flashbacks

DCF1 Steve Yzerman 90.00 150.00
DCF2 Igor Larionov 90.00 150.00
DCF3 Nicklas Lidstrom
DCF4 Larry Murphy 25.00 60.00
DCF5 Chris Osgood 25.00 60.00

2016-17 Upper Deck Rookie Breakouts

RB1 Artturi Lehkonen 8.00 20.00
RB2 William Nylander 30.00 80.00
RB3 Brandon Carlo 8.00 20.00
RB4 Dylan Strome 15.00 40.00
RB5 Travis Konecny 15.00 40.00
RB6 Sebastian Aho 15.00 40.00
RB7 Mathew Barzal 25.00 60.00
RB8 Jimmy Vesey 15.00 40.00
RB9 Hudson Fasching 8.00 20.00
RB10 Christian Dvorak 8.00 20.00
RB11 Mikhail Sergachev 15.00 40.00
RB12 Kyle Connor 20.00 50.00
RB13 Jakub Vrana 8.00 20.00
RB14 Joel Eriksson Ek 8.00 20.00
RB15 Jakob Chychrun 8.00 20.00
RB16 Matthew Tkachuk 25.00 60.00
RB17 Sonny Milano 10.00 25.00
RB18 Nick Schmaltz 8.00 20.00
RB19 Pavel Buchnevich 12.00 30.00
RB20 Ivan Provorov 15.00 40.00
RB21 Pavel Zacha 10.00 25.00
RB22 Zach Werenski 15.00 40.00
RB23 Anthony Beauvillier 8.00 20.00
RB24 Mitch Marner 40.00 100.00
RB25 Anthony Mantha 25.00 60.00
RB26 Jesse Puljujarvi 20.00 50.00
RB27 Patrik Laine
RB28 Auston Matthews

2016-17 Upper Deck Rookie Materials

RMAB Anthony Beauvillier C 3.00 8.00
RMAM Auston Matthews A 20.00 50.00
RMBL Brendan Leipsic D 3.00 8.00
RMBP Brayden Point E 8.00 20.00
RMBR Chris Bigras E 2.50 6.00
RMCB Connor Brown C 5.00 12.00
RMCD Christian Dvorak C 3.00 8.00
RMEL Esa Lindell E 3.00 8.00
RMHF Hudson Fasching C 3.00 8.00
RMIP Ivan Provorov B 6.00 15.00
RMJB Justin Bailey E 3.00 8.00
RMJC Jakob Chychrun B 3.00 8.00
RMJE Joel Eriksson Ek D 3.00 8.00
RMJP Jesse Puljujarvi A 8.00 20.00
RMJV Jimmy Vesey D 6.00 15.00
RMKC Kyle Connor A 8.00 20.00
RMKK Kasperi Kapanen C 6.00 15.00
RMLC Lawson Crouse C 2.50 6.00
RMMA Anthony Mantha C 8.00 20.00
RMMB Mathew Barzal B 10.00 25.00
RMMI Michael Matheson E 3.00 8.00
RMMM Mitch Marner A 15.00 40.00
RMMR Mike Reilly E 2.50 6.00
RMMS Mikhail Sergachev A 6.00 15.00
RMMT Matthew Tkachuk A 10.00 25.00
RMNS Nick Schmaltz B 3.00 8.00
RMOB Oliver Bjorkstrand C 2.50 6.00
RMOK Oliver Kylington E 2.50 6.00
RMOS Oskar Sundqvist E 3.00 8.00
RMPB Pavel Buchnevich B 5.00 12.00
RMPL Patrik Laine A 12.00 30.00
RMPZ Pavel Zacha B 4.00 10.00
RMRP Ryan Pulock E 3.00 8.00
RMSA Sebastian Aho C 6.00 15.00
RMSM Sonny Milano B 4.00 10.00
RMSO Nikita Soshnikov E 2.00 5.00
RMTC Thomas Chabot B 6.00 15.00
RMTK Travis Konecny B 6.00 15.00
RMTM Tyler Motte D 3.00 8.00
RMWN William Nylander A 12.00 30.00
RMZW Zach Werenski B 6.00 15.00

2016-17 Upper Deck Rookie Materials Patch

COMMON CARD 6.00 15.00
RMAM Auston Matthews 100.00 200.00
RMMT Matthew Tkachuk 90.00 150.00
RMPL Patrik Laine 60.00 150.00

2016-17 Upper Deck Silver Foil

*VETS: 5X TO 12X BASIC CARDS
*ROOKIES: .6X TO 1.5X BASIC CARDS
187 Evgeny Kuznetsov 5.00 12.00
191 Nicklas Backstrom 5.00 12.00
201 Auston Matthews YG 400.00 500.00
249 William Nylander YG 40.00 100.00
250 A.Matthews YG RC 20.00 50.00
W.Nylander YG RC CL
290 Corey Crawford 4.00 10.00
420 Jonathan Drouin 4.00 10.00

2017-18 Upper Deck

1 Hampus Lindholm .25 .60
2 Corey Perry .30 .75
3 Cam Fowler .25 .60
4 Kevin Bieksa .20 .50
5 Rickard Rakell .25 .60
6 Ryan Kesler .30 .75
7 Alex Goligoski .25 .60
8 Christian Dvorak .25 .60
9 Jakob Chychrun .25 .60
10 Max Domi .30 .75
11 Tobias Rieder .20 .50
12 Oliver Ekman-Larsson .30 .75
13 Brad Marchand .40 1.00
14 Brandon Carlo .25 .60
15 David Backes .25 .60
16 Torey Krug .30 .75
17 Tuukka Rask .30 .75
18 Zdeno Chara .30 .75
19 Jack Eichel .50 1.25
20 Jake McCabe .20 .50
21 Kyle Okposo .25 .60
22 Matt Moulson .20 .50
23 Rasmus Ristolainen .30 .75
24 Zach Bogosian .25 .60
25 Matt Stajan .20 .50
26 Matthew Tkachuk .30 .75
27 Michael Frolik .20 .50
28 Mikael Backlund .20 .50
29 Sean Monahan .30 .75
30 Troy Brouwer .25 .60
31 T.J. Brodie .25 .60
32 Brett Pesce .20 .50
33 Jaccob Slavin .20 .50
34 Jordan Staal .30 .75
35 Lee Stempniak .20 .50
36 Sebastian Aho .30 .75
37 Teuvo Teravainen .25 .60
38 Cam Ward .25 .60
39 Brent Seabrook .25 .60
40 Corey Crawford .40 1.00
41 Jonathan Toews .60 1.50
42 Nick Schmaltz .25 .60
43 Richard Panik .25 .60
44 Ryan Hartman .30 .75
45 Blake Comeau .20 .50
46 Semyon Varlamov .30 .75
47 Mikko Rantanen .30 .75
48 Nathan MacKinnon .60 1.50
49 Tyson Barrie .30 .75
50 Carl Soderberg .20 .50
51 Brandon Dubinsky .25 .60
52 David Savard .25 .60
53 Lukas Sedlak .20 .50
54 Sergei Bobrovsky .30 .75
55 Seth Jones .25 .60
56 Zach Werenski .30 .75
57 Boone Jenner .25 .60
58 Antoine Roussel .25 .60
59 Radek Faksa .25 .60
60 Dan Hamhuis .20 .50
61 Jason Spezza .30 .75
62 Kari Lehtonen .25 .60
63 Stephen Johns .25 .60
64 Tyler Seguin .50 1.25
65 Anthony Mantha .30 .75
66 Gustav Nyquist .30 .75
67 Henrik Zetterberg .30 .75
68 Luke Glendening .20 .50
69 Petr Mrazek .30 .75
70 Riley Sheahan .20 .50
71 Darren Helm .20 .50
72 Adam Larsson .30 .75
73 Andrej Sekera .20 .50
74 Drake Caggiula .25 .60
75 Leon Draisaitl .50 1.25
76 Mark Letestu .25 .60
77 Matthew Benning .20 .50
78 Patrick Maroon .25 .60
79 Colton Sceviour .20 .50
80 Derek MacKenzie .20 .50
81 Jason Demers .20 .50
82 Jonathan Huberdeau .25 .60
83 Michael Matheson .25 .60
84 Vincent Trocheck .25 .60
85 Roberto Luongo .30 .75
86 Alec Martinez .20 .50
87 Anze Kopitar .50 1.25
88 Derek Forbort .25 .60
89 Dustin Brown .25 .60
90 Jonathan Quick .50 1.25
91 Nic Dowd .25 .60
92 Trevor Lewis .25 .60
93 Charlie Coyle .25 .60
94 Eric Staal .40 1.00
95 Jared Spurgeon .20 .50
96 Jason Zucker .25 .60
97 Jonas Brodin .25 .60
98 Matt Dumba .25 .60
99 Zach Parise .30 .75
100 Andrew Shaw .25 .60
101 Artturi Lehkonen .25 .60
102 Carey Price 1.00 2.50
103 Jeff Petry .20 .50
104 Paul Byron .25 .60
105 Phillip Danault .20 .50
106 Shea Weber .25 .60
107 Viktor Arvidsson .25 .60
108 Calle Jarnkrok .25 .60
109 Filip Forsberg .40 1.00
110 Mattias Ekholm .20 .50
111 P.K. Subban .30 .75
112 Kevin Fiala .25 .60
113 Pekka Rinne .40 1.00
114 Adam Henrique .25 .60
115 Miles Wood .20 .50
116 Pavel Zacha .30 .75
117 Taylor Hall .60 1.50
118 Travis Zajac .20 .50
119 Andy Greene .20 .50
120 Anthony Beauvillier .30 .75
121 Calvin de Haan .25 .60
122 Casey Cizikas .20 .50
123 Josh Bailey .25 .60
124 Nikolay Kulemin .25 .60
125 Thomas Greiss .25 .60
126 Brady Skjei .25 .60
127 J.T. Miller .25 .60
128 Jimmy Vesey .30 .75
129 Michael Grabner .20 .50
130 Nick Holden .25 .60
131 Rick Nash .30 .75
132 Kevin Hayes .25 .60
133 Clarke MacArthur .20 .50
134 Derick Brassard .30 .75
135 Dion Phaneuf .25 .60
136 Kyle Turris .30 .75
137 Jean-Gabriel Pageau .20 .50
138 Mike Hoffman .25 .60
139 Wayne Simmonds .40 1.00
140 Dale Weise .20 .50
141 Ivan Provorov .30 .75
142 Jakub Voracek .30 .75
143 Travis Konecny .30 .75
144 Valtteri Filppula .20 .50
145 Carl Hagelin .30 .75
146 Evgeni Malkin 1.00 2.50
147 Ian Cole .25 .60
148 Matt Murray .50 1.25
149 Phil Kessel .40 1.00
150 Scott Wilson .20 .50
151 Jake Guentzel .40 1.00
152 Joe Thornton .30 .75
153 Joel Ward .25 .60
154 Justin Braun .25 .60
155 Marc-Edouard Vlasic .20 .50
156 Mikkel Boedker .25 .60
157 Paul Martin .20 .50
158 Alex Pietrangelo .25 .60
159 Jaden Schwartz .40 1.00
160 Jake Allen .40 1.00
161 Kyle Brodziak .20 .50
162 Patrik Berglund .20 .50
163 Paul Stastny .30 .75
164 Alex Killorn .25 .60
165 Andrei Vasilevskiy .40 1.00
166 Anton Stralman .25 .60
167 Brayden Point .30 .75
168 Nikita Kucherov .50 1.25
169 Ondrej Palat .30 .75
170 Auston Matthews 1.25 3.00
171 Frederik Andersen .25 .60
172 Leo Komarov .20 .50
173 Matt Martin .20 .50
174 Mitch Marner .50 1.25
175 Nazem Kadri .25 .60
176 William Nylander .50 1.25
177 Henrik Sedin .30 .75
178 Jacob Markstrom .20 .50
179 Brandon Sutter .25 .60
180 Markus Granlund .25 .60
181 Sven Baertschi .20 .50
182 Troy Stecher .25 .60
183 Marc-Andre Fleury .50 1.25
184 Jason Garrison .20 .50
185 Brayden McNabb .20 .50
186 Braden Holtby .50 1.25
187 Jay Beagle .25 .60
188 John Carlson .40 1.00
189 Lars Eller .25 .60
190 Evgeny Kuznetsov .50 1.25
191 Matt Niskanen .25 .60
192 Nicklas Backstrom .50 1.25
193 Adam Lowry .25 .60
194 Blake Wheeler .30 .75
195 Bryan Little .25 .60
196 Josh Morrissey .20 .50
197 Mathieu Perreault .25 .60
198 Patrik Laine .50 1.25
199 Pekka Rinne .50 1.25
Matt Murray CL
200 Marc-Andre Fleury .50 1.25
Brayden McNabb CL
201 Nico Hischier YG RC 20.00 50.00
202 Kailer Yamamoto YG RC 8.00 20.00
203 Anders Bjork YG RC 4.00 10.00
204 Pierre-Luc Dubois YG RC 8.00 20.00
205 Josh Ho-Sang YG RC 4.00 10.00
206 Jon Gillies YG RC 3.00 8.00
207 Lucas Wallmark YG RC 3.00 8.00
208 Denis Gurianov YG RC 3.00 8.00
209 Alex Kerfoot YG RC 3.00 8.00
210 Adrian Kempe YG RC 4.00 10.00
211 John Hayden YG RC 2.50 6.00
212 Jake DeBrusk YG RC 5.00 12.00
213 Janne Kuokkanen YG RC 3.00 8.00
214 Travis Sanheim YG RC 3.00 8.00
215 Gabriel Carlsson YG RC 2.50 6.00
216 Calle Rosen YG RC 3.00 8.00
217 Logan Brown YG RC 3.00 8.00
218 Rasmus Andersson YG RC 3.00 8.00
219 Alex Formenton YG RC 3.00 8.00
220 Ian McCoshen YG RC 3.00 8.00
221 Alex DeBrincat YG RC 12.00 30.00
222 Alexander Nylander YG RC 5.00 12.00
223 Nathan Walker YG RC 3.00 8.00
224 Evgeny Svechnikov YG RC 6.00 15.00
225 C.J. Smith YG RC 2.50 6.00
226 Samuel Morin YG RC 3.00 8.00
227 Filip Chytil YG RC 3.00 8.00
228 Tage Thompson YG RC 5.00 12.00
229 Andreas Borgman YG RC 3.00 8.00
230 Ivan Barbashev YG RC 5.00 12.00
231 Jonny Brodzinski YG RC 3.00 8.00
232 Robert Hagg YG RC 3.00 8.00
233 Riley Barber YG RC 2.50 6.00
234 Christian Fischer YG RC 4.00 10.00
235 Jakob Forsbacka-Karlsson YG RC 3.00 8.00
236 Haydn Fleury YG RC 3.00 8.00
237 Marcus Sorensen YG RC 2.50 6.00
238 Vladislav Kamenev YG RC 5.00 12.00
239 Jake Dotchin YG RC 2.50 6.00
240 Jack Roslovic YG RC 4.00 10.00
241 Nicolas Kerdiles YG RC 3.00 8.00
242 Charlie McAvoy YG RC 15.00 40.00
243 Carter Rowney YG RC 2.50 6.00
244 Vince Dunn YG RC 3.00 8.00
245 Victor Mete YG RC 3.00 8.00
246 Tyson Jost YG RC 6.00 15.00
247 Brock Boeser YG RC 30.00 80.00
248 Will Butcher YG RC 4.00 10.00
249 Alex Tuch YG RC 8.00 20.00
250 N.Hischier/B.Boeser YG CL 5.00 12.00
251 Ryan Getzlaf .30 .75
252 John Gibson .30 .75
253 Brandon Montour .25 .60
254 Andrew Cogliano .20 .50
255 Patrick Eaves .25 .60
256 Ryan Miller .25 .60
257 Antti Raanta .30 .75
258 Derek Stepan .25 .60
259 Niklas Hjalmarsson .20 .50
260 Brad Richardson .20 .50
261 Dylan Strome .30 .75
262 Anthony Duclair .20 .50
263 David Krejci .25 .60
264 Patrice Bergeron .40 1.00
265 David Pastrnak .50 1.25
266 Ryan Spooner .25 .60
267 Riley Nash .20 .50
268 Matt Beleskey .20 .50
269 Frank Vatrano .30 .75
270 Benoit Pouliot .20 .50
271 Ryan O'Reilly .30 .75
272 Sam Reinhart .25 .60
273 Robin Lehner .20 .50
274 Evander Kane .30 .75
275 Jason Pominville .25 .60
276 Jaromir Jagr .75 2.00
277 Dougie Hamilton .25 .60
278 Johnny Gaudreau .50 1.25
279 Mike Smith .30 .75
280 Mark Giordano .25 .60
281 Travis Hamonic .25 .60
282 Justin Williams .25 .60
283 Scott Darling .25 .60
284 Jeff Skinner .25 .60
285 Victor Rask .30 .75
286 Elias Lindholm .25 .60
287 Trevor van Riemsdyk .30 .75
288 Marcus Kruger .30 .75
289 Patrick Sharp .25 .60
290 Patrick Kane .60 1.50
291 Brandon Saad .30 .75
292 Duncan Keith .30 .75
293 Artem Anisimov .25 .60
294 Connor Murphy .20 .50
295 Nail Yakupov .25 .60
296 Gabriel Landeskog .25 .60
297 Erik Johnson .25 .60
298 Matt Nieto .20 .50
299 Colin Wilson .25 .60
300 Jonathan Bernier .25 .60
301 Cam Atkinson .30 .75
302 Artemi Panarin .30 .75
303 Alexander Wennberg .25 .60
304 Ryan Murray .30 .75
305 Nick Foligno .25 .60
306 Jack Johnson .20 .50
307 Marc Methot .20 .50
308 Jamie Benn .40 1.00
309 Martin Hanzal .25 .60
310 Ben Bishop .30 .75
311 Alexander Radulov .30 .75
312 Esa Lindell .25 .60
313 Trevor Daley .25 .60
314 Jim Howard .20 .50
315 Tomas Tatar .30 .75
316 Frans Nielsen .25 .60
317 Dylan Larkin .30 .75
318 Mike Green .25 .60
319 Michael Cammalleri .25 .60
320 Connor McDavid 1.25 3.00
321 Darnell Nurse .25 .60
322 Cam Talbot .30 .75
323 Oscar Klefbom .25 .60
324 Ryan Nugent-Hopkins .30 .75
325 Milan Lucic .30 .75
326 Jamie McGinn .20 .50
327 Aleksander Barkov .30 .75
328 Aaron Ekblad .30 .75
329 Nick Bjugstad .25 .60
330 Evgeny Dadonov .20 .50
331 James Reimer .30 .75
332 Radim Vrbata .20 .50
333 Jeff Carter .30 .75
334 Darcy Kuemper .25 .60
335 Tyler Toffoli .25 .60
336 Tanner Pearson .25 .60
337 Christian Folin .20 .50
338 Jussi Jokinen .25 .60
339 Ryan Suter .20 .50
340 Devan Dubnyk .30 .75
341 Nino Niederreiter .25 .60
342 Mikael Granlund .30 .75
343 Matt Cullen .25 .60

Mikko Koivu .25 .60
Tyler Ennis .30 .75
Max Pacioretty .30 .75
Brendan Gallagher .30 .75
Alex Galchenyuk .40 1.00
Jonathan Drouin .30 .75
Karl Alzner .20 .50
Ales Hemsky .25 .60
Phillip Danault .20 .50
Austin Watson .25 .60
Nick Bonino .25 .60
Roman Josi .30 .75
Ryan Johansen .30 .75
Craig Smith .20 .50
P.K. Subban .30 .75
Scott Hartnell .20 .50
John Moore .25 .60
Marcus Johansson .25 .60
Brian Boyle .20 .50
Cory Schneider .25 .60
Drew Stafford .20 .50
Kyle Palmieri .25 .60
John Tavares .60 1.50
Jordan Eberle .30 .75
Andrew Ladd .30 .75
Anders Lee .30 .75
Johnny Boychuk .25 .60
Brock Nelson .25 .60
Henrik Lundqvist .50 1.25
Mika Zibanejad .30 .75
Ryan McDonagh .25 .60
Brendan Smith .25 .60
Chris Kreider .30 .75
David Desharnais .25 .60
Kevin Shattenkirk .30 .75
Erik Karlsson .40 1.00
Craig Anderson .30 .75
Johnny Oduya .25 .60
Bobby Ryan .25 .60
Cody Ceci .20 .50
Mark Stone .30 .75
Brian Elliott .25 .60
Jori Lehtera .20 .50
Shayne Gostisbehere .30 .75
Claude Giroux .30 .75
Sean Couturier .25 .60
Andrew MacDonald .25 .60
Sidney Crosby 1.25 3.00
Matt Hunwick .20 .50
Kris Letang .30 .75
Chad Ruhwedel .20 .50
Bryan Rust .30 .75
Justin Schultz .30 .75
Brent Burns .40 1.00
Martin Jones .30 .75
Paul Martin .20 .50
Jannik Hansen .25 .60
Tomas Hertl .30 .75
Logan Couture .30 .75
Brayden Schenn .30 .75
Jaden Schwartz .40 1.00
Colton Parayko .30 .75
Vladimir Tarasenko .50 1.25
Alexander Steen .30 .75
Paul Stastny .30 .75
Vladimir Sobotka .20 .50
Steven Stamkos .60 1.50
Ondrej Palat .30 .75
Victor Hedman .40 1.00
Vladislav Namestnikov .25 .60
Tyler Johnson .25 .60
Chris Kunitz .30 .75
Patrick Marleau .30 .75
Morgan Rielly .30 .75
Tyler Bozak .25 .60
James van Riemsdyk .30 .75
Jake Gardiner .25 .60
Ron Hainsey .25 .60
Daniel Sedin .30 .75
Alexander Edler .20 .50
Bo Horvat .30 .75
Michael Del Zotto .20 .50
Erik Gudbranson .20 .50
Sam Gagner .25 .60
Alexander Burmistrov .20 .50
Deryk Engelland .20 .50
Nate Schmidt .25 .60
David Perron .30 .75
Reilly Smith .30 .75
William Karlsson .60 1.50
James Neal .25 .60
Jonathan Marchessault .30 .75
Oscar Lindberg .25 .60
Alexander Ovechkin 1.25 3.00
T.J. Oshie .50 1.25
Andre Burakovsky .25 .60
Tom Wilson .30 .75
Dmitry Orlov .25 .60
Brett Connolly .20 .50
Mark Scheifele .40 1.00
Dustin Byfuglien .30 .75
Jacob Trouba .25 .60
Kyle Connor .30 .75
Nikolaj Ehlers .30 .75
Connor Hellebuyck .50 1.25
B.Saad/A.Panarin CL .30 .75
A.Ovechkin/S.Stamkos CL 1.25 3.00
Christian Djoos YG RC 3.00 8.00
Jan Rutta YG RC 3.00 8.00
Samuel Blais YG RC 3.00 8.00
Adin Hill YG RC 3.00 8.00
Nolan Patrick YG RC 20.00 50.00
Anton Lindholm YG RC 3.00 8.00
Madison Bowey YG RC 2.50 6.00
Alex Iafallo YG RC 3.00 8.00
MacKenzie Weegar YG RC 3.00 8.00
Kalle Kossila YG RC 2.50 6.00
Alex Nedeljkovic YG RC 2.50 6.00
Christian Jaros YG RC 3.00 8.00
Remi Elie YG RC 2.50 6.00
Martin Necas YG RC 5.00 12.00
Samuel Girard YG RC 3.00 8.00
Jesper Bratt YG RC 5.00 12.00
Valentin Zykov YG RC 3.00 8.00
Kevin Roy YG RC 3.00 8.00
Owen Tippett YG RC 6.00 15.00
Jordan Schmaltz YG RC 4.00 10.00
Peter Cehlarik YG RC 3.00 8.00
Filip Chlapik YG RC 3.00 8.00
Robbie Russo YG RC 3.00 8.00
Paul LaDue YG RC 2.50 6.00
Roland McKeown YG RC 3.00 8.00
Eric Comrie YG RC 2.50 6.00
Clayton Keller YG RC 15.00 40.00
Ville Husso YG RC 3.00 8.00
Oscar Fantenberg YG RC 3.00 8.00
J.T. Compher YG RC 4.00 10.00
Mike Vecchione YG RC 2.50 6.00
Maxime Lagace YG RC 3.00 8.00
Andrew Poturalski YG RC 3.00 8.00
Tim Heed YG RC 3.00 8.00
485 Alexandre Carrier YG RC 2.50 6.00
486 Dryden Hunt YG RC 3.00 8.00
487 Brendan Lemieux YG RC 3.00 8.00
488 Dylan Ferguson YG RC 3.00 8.00
489 Jack Rodewald YG RC 3.00 8.00
490 Luke Kunin YG RC 3.00 8.00
491 Michael Amadio YG RC 3.00 8.00
492 Joakim Ryan YG RC 3.00 8.00
493 Colin White YG RC 3.00 8.00
494 Nikita Scherbak YG RC 6.00 15.00
495 Kyle Capobianco YG RC 3.00 8.00
496 Henrik Haapala YG RC 3.00 8.00
497 Andrew Mangiapane YG RC 3.00 8.00
498 Danick Martel YG RC 3.00 8.00
499 Nick Merkley YG RC 3.00 8.00
500 C.Keller/N.Patrick YG CL 2.50 6.00
501 Rick Nash .30 .75
502 Kyle Turris .30 .75
503 Matt Duchene .30 .75
504 Paul Stastny .30 .75
505 Adam Henrique .25 .60
506 Petr Mrazek .30 .75
507 Evander Kane .30 .75
508 Tomas Tatar .30 .75
509 Drew Doughty .30 .75
510 Kyle Criscuolo YG RC 2.50 6.00
511 Dominic Toninato YG RC 2.50 6.00
512 Casey DeSmith YG RC 2.50 6.00
513 Travis Boyd YG RC 2.50 6.00
514 Alexandar Georgiev YG RC 2.50 6.00
515 Andy Welinski YG RC 2.50 6.00
516 Colby Cave YG RC 2.50 6.00
517 David Kampf YG RC 2.50 6.00
518 Sebastian Aho YG RC 2.50 6.00
519 Vinni Lettieri YG RC 2.50 6.00
520 Tanner Fritz YG RC 2.50 6.00
521 Jeff Glass YG RC 5.00 12.00

2017-18 Upper Deck Exclusives

*VETS/100: 5X TO 12X BASIC CARDS
*YG/100: 2.5X TO 6X BASIC CARDS
201 Nico Hischier YG 250.00 350.00
202 Kailer Yamamoto YG 80.00 150.00
204 Pierre-Luc Dubois YG 60.00 150.00
205 Josh Ho-Sang YG 80.00 150.00
221 Alex DeBrincat YG 100.00 200.00
477 Clayton Keller YG 250.00 350.00

2017-18 Upper Deck Day With The Cup Flashbacks

DC1 Frank Mahovlich 10.00 25.00
DC2 Red Kelly 8.00 20.00
DC3 Mike Walton 8.00 20.00
DC4 Ron Ellis 8.00 20.00
DC5 Pete Stemkowski 8.00 20.00
DC6 Johnny Bower 10.00 25.00

2017-18 Upper Deck A Piece of History 1000 Point Club

PCAD Alex Delvecchio A 250.00 500.00
PCAO Alexander Ovechkin C 80.00 150.00
PCBP Brian Propp C
PCDP Denis Potvin B 50.00 125.00
PCDS Daniel Sedin C
PCFM Frank Mahovlich A
PCHS Henrik Sedin D 25.00 60.00
PCJB Jean Beliveau B 60.00 150.00
PCMR Mark Recchi B
PCPT Pierre Turgeon B
PCSC Sidney Crosby B 200.00 300.00
PCSM Stan Mikita A

2017-18 Upper Deck A Piece of History 500 Goal Club

GCPM Patrick Marleau 35.00 80.00

2017-18 Upper Deck Canvas

C1 Ryan Kesler 1.00 2.50
C2 Ryan Getzlaf 1.00 2.50
C3 Cam Fowler .75 2.00
C4 Alex Goligoski .75 2.00
C5 Tobias Rieder .60 1.50
C6 Oliver Ekman-Larsson 1.00 2.50
C7 Brad Marchand 1.25 3.00
C8 Ryan Spooner .75 2.00
C9 Torey Krug 1.00 2.50
C10 Jack Eichel 1.50 4.00
C11 Jake McCabe .60 1.50
C12 Evander Kane 1.00 2.50
C13 Mikael Backlund .60 1.50
C14 T.J. Brodie .75 2.00
C15 Matthew Tkachuk 1.00 2.50
C16 Elias Lindholm .75 2.00
C17 Jaccob Slavin .60 1.50
C18 Sebastian Aho 1.00 2.50
C19 Duncan Keith 1.00 2.50
C20 Ryan Hartman 1.00 2.50
C21 Jonathan Toews 2.00 5.00
C22 Mikko Rantanen 1.00 2.50
C23 Nathan MacKinnon 2.00 5.00
C24 Zach Werenski 1.00 2.50
C25 Sergei Bobrovsky 1.00 2.50
C26 Brandon Dubinsky .75 2.00
C27 John Klingberg .75 2.00
C28 Antoine Roussel .75 2.00
C29 Tyler Seguin 1.50 4.00
C30 Anthony Mantha 1.00 2.50
C31 Frans Nielsen .75 2.00
C32 Mike Green .75 2.00
C33 Connor McDavid 4.00 10.00
C34 Patrick Maroon .75 2.00
C35 Cam Talbot 1.00 2.50
C36 Vincent Trocheck .75 2.00
C37 Jason Demers .60 1.50
C38 Michael Matheson .75 2.00
C39 Jonathan Quick 1.50 4.00
C40 Jeff Carter 1.00 2.50
C41 Alec Martinez .60 1.50
C42 Jason Zucker .75 2.00
C43 Jared Spurgeon .60 1.50
C44 Mikko Koivu .75 2.00
C45 Paul Byron .75 2.00
C46 Shea Weber .75 2.00
C47 Carey Price 3.00 8.00
C48 Ryan Ellis .75 2.00
C49 Filip Forsberg 1.25 3.00
C50 Calle Jarnkrok .75 2.00
C51 Andy Greene .60 1.50
C52 Taylor Hall 2.00 5.00
C53 Pavel Zacha 1.00 2.50
C54 John Tavares 2.00 5.00
C55 Thomas Greiss .75 2.00
C56 Nick Leddy .60 1.50
C57 Kevin Hayes .75 2.00
C58 Rick Nash 1.00 2.50
C59 Jimmy Vesey 1.00 2.50
C60 Mike Hoffman .75 2.00
C61 Craig Anderson 1.00 2.50
C62 Alexandre Burrows .60 1.50
C63 Claude Giroux 1.00 2.50
C64 Ivan Provorov 1.00 2.50
C65 Sean Couturier .75 2.00
C66 Sidney Crosby 4.00 10.00
C67 Bryan Rust 1.00 2.50
C68 Kris Letang 1.00 2.50
C69 Brent Burns 1.25 3.00
C70 Marc-Edouard Vlasic .60 1.50
C71 Joel Ward .75 2.00
C72 Alex Pietrangelo .75 2.00
C73 Colton Parayko 1.00 2.50
C74 Paul Stastny 1.00 2.50
C75 Brayden Point 1.00 2.50
C76 Andrei Vasilevskiy 1.25 3.00
C77 Nikita Kucherov 1.50 4.00
C78 Tyler Bozak .75 2.00
C79 Auston Matthews 4.00 10.00
C80 Jake Gardiner .75 2.00
C81 Troy Stecher .75 2.00
C82 Jacob Markstrom .60 1.50
C83 Markus Granlund .75 2.00
C84 Tom Wilson 1.00 2.50
C85 Nicklas Backstrom 1.50 4.00
C86 Matt Niskanen .75 2.00
C87 Mathieu Perreault .75 2.00
C88 Nikolaj Ehlers 1.00 2.50
C89 Patrik Laine 1.50 4.00
C90 Carey Price 3.00 8.00
Sergei Bobrovsky CL
C91 Nolan Patrick YG 40.00 100.00
C92 Logan Brown YG 6.00 15.00
C93 Tyson Jost YG 12.00 30.00
C94 Adrian Kempe YG 8.00 20.00
C95 Filip Chytil YG 6.00 15.00
C96 Evgeny Svechnikov YG 12.00 30.00
C97 Haydn Fleury YG 6.00 15.00
C98 Pierre-Luc Dubois YG 12.00 30.00
C99 Denis Gurianov YG 6.00 15.00
C100 Tage Thompson YG 10.00 25.00
C101 Jon Gillies YG 6.00 15.00
C102 Kailer Yamamoto YG 12.00 30.00
C103 Christian Fischer YG 8.00 20.00
C104 Calle Rosen YG 6.00 15.00
C105 Charlie McAvoy YG 30.00 80.00
C106 Ivan Barbashev YG 6.00 15.00
C107 Nikita Scherbak YG 12.00 30.00
C108 Jack Roslovic YG 8.00 20.00
C109 Will Butcher YG 8.00 20.00
C110 Clayton Keller YG 30.00 80.00
C111 Alexander Nylander YG 10.00 25.00
C112 Jake DeBrusk YG 10.00 25.00
C113 Janne Kuokkanen YG 6.00 15.00
C114 Alex DeBrincat YG 15.00 40.00
C115 Victor Mete YG 6.00 15.00
C116 Alex Tuch YG 15.00 40.00
C117 Travis Sanheim YG 6.00 15.00
C118 Colin White YG 6.00 15.00
C119 J.T. Compher YG 8.00 20.00
C120 C.Keller/C.McAvoy YG CL 8.00 20.00
C121 Brandon Montour .75 2.00
C122 Corey Perry 1.00 2.50
C123 Patrick Eaves .75 2.00
C124 Christian Dvorak .75 2.00
C125 Derek Stepan .75 2.00
C126 Antti Raanta 1.00 2.50
C127 Niklas Hjalmarsson .60 1.50
C128 David Pastrnak 1.50 4.00
C129 Zdeno Chara 1.00 2.50
C130 Patrice Bergeron 1.25 3.00
C131 Mike Smith 1.00 2.50
C132 Travis Hamonic .75 2.00
C133 Kris Versteeg .60 1.50
C134 Justin Williams .75 2.00
C135 Trevor van Riemsdyk 1.00 2.50
C136 Marcus Kruger 1.00 2.50
C137 Corey Crawford 1.25 3.00
C138 Brandon Saad 1.00 2.50
C139 Patrick Sharp .75 2.00
C140 Semyon Varlamov 1.00 2.50
C141 Erik Johnson .75 2.00
C142 Tyson Barrie 1.00 2.50
C143 Artemi Panarin 1.00 2.50
C144 Jack Johnson .60 1.50
C145 Ryan Murray 1.00 2.50
C146 Alexander Radulov 1.00 2.50
C147 Martin Hanzal .75 2.00
C148 Ben Bishop 1.00 2.50
C149 Jim Howard .60 1.50
C150 Tomas Tatar 1.00 2.50
C151 Trevor Daley .75 2.00
C152 Drake Caggiula .75 2.00
C153 Ryan Nugent-Hopkins 1.00 2.50
C154 Oscar Klefbom .75 2.00
C155 Jonathan Huberdeau .75 2.00
C156 Evgeny Dadonov .60 1.50
C157 Derek MacKenzie .60 1.50
C158 Tyler Toffoli .75 2.00
C159 Anze Kopitar 1.50 4.00
C160 Dustin Brown .75 2.00
C161 Nino Niederreiter .75 2.00
C162 Eric Staal 1.25 3.00
C163 Tyler Ennis 1.00 2.50
C164 Jonathan Drouin 1.00 2.50
C165 Karl Alzner .60 1.50
C166 Alex Galchenyuk 1.25 3.00
C167 Austin Watson .75 2.00
C168 Viktor Arvidsson .75 2.00
C169 Marcus Johansson .75 2.00
C170 Brian Boyle .60 1.50
C171 Brian Gibbons .60 1.50
C172 Jordan Eberle 1.00 2.50
C173 Calvin de Haan .75 2.00
C174 Johnny Boychuk .75 2.00
C175 Kevin Shattenkirk 1.00 2.50
C176 Henrik Lundqvist 1.50 4.00
C177 Michael Grabner .60 1.50
C178 Johnny Oduya .75 2.00
C179 Erik Karlsson 1.25 3.00
C180 Derick Brassard 1.00 2.50
C181 Brian Elliott .75 2.00
C182 Jori Lehtera .60 1.50
C183 Valtteri Filppula .60 1.50
C184 Phil Kessel 1.25 3.00
C185 Conor Sheary 1.00 2.50
C186 Jake Guentzel 1.25 3.00
C187 Brayden Schenn 1.00 2.50
C188 Vladimir Tarasenko 1.50 4.00
C189 Vladimir Sobotka .60 1.50
C190 Victor Hedman 1.25 3.00
C191 Chris Kunitz 1.00 2.50
C192 Ryan Callahan .75 2.00
C193 Mitch Marner 1.50 4.00
C194 Leo Komarov .60 1.50
C195 Nikita Zaitsev .75 2.00
C196 Michael Del Zotto .60 1.50
C197 Alexander Edler .60 1.50
C198 Erik Gudbranson .60 1.50
C199 Marc-Andre Fleury 1.50 4.00
C200 James Neal .75 2.00
C201 Jonathan Marchessault 1.00 2.50
C202 David Perron 1.00 2.50
C203 Alexander Ovechkin 4.00 10.00
C204 Dmitry Orlov .75 2.00
C205 John Carlson 1.25 3.00
C206 Mark Scheifele 1.25 3.00
C207 Steve Mason .75 2.00
C208 Tyler Myers .75 2.00
C209 Shawn Matthias 1.00 2.50
C210 E.Karlsson/V.Hedman CL 1.25 3.00
C211 Nico Hischier YG 50.00 125.00
C212 Jakob Forsbacka-Karlsson YG 6.00 15.00
C213 Filip Chlapik YG 6.00 15.00
C214 Lucas Wallmark YG 6.00 15.00
C215 Robert Hagg YG 6.00 15.00
C216 Vadim Shipachyov YG 20.00 50.00
C217 Michael Amadio YG 6.00 15.00
C218 Eric Comrie YG 5.00 12.00
C219 Nick Merkley YG 6.00 15.00
C220 Alex Formenton YG 6.00 15.00
C221 Josh Ho-Sang YG 8.00 20.00
C222 Christian Jaros YG 6.00 15.00
C223 Brock Boeser YG 100.00 200.00
C224 Jesper Bratt YG 10.00 25.00
C225 Martin Necas YG 6.00 15.00
C226 Alex Iafallo YG 6.00 15.00
C227 Owen Tippett YG 12.00 30.00
C228 Vince Dunn YG 6.00 15.00
C229 Alex Kerfoot YG 6.00 15.00
C230 Luke Kunin YG 6.00 15.00
C231 Henrik Haapala YG 6.00 15.00
C232 Samuel Blais YG 6.00 15.00
C233 Christian Djoos YG 6.00 15.00
C234 Anders Bjork YG 8.00 20.00
C235 John Hayden YG 5.00 12.00
C236 Ville Husso YG 6.00 15.00
C237 Samuel Morin YG 6.00 15.00
C238 Madison Bowey YG 5.00 12.00
C239 Samuel Girard YG 6.00 15.00
C240 N.Hischier/B.Boeser YG CL 12.00 30.00
C241 Jean Beliveau RS 30.00 80.00
C242 Wayne Gretzky RS 50.00 120.00
C243 Pierre Pilote RS 10.00 25.00
C244 Frank Mahovlich RS 15.00 40.00
C245 Brian Propp RS 8.00 20.00
C246 Ed Olczyk RS 8.00 20.00
C247 Rogie Vachon RS 12.00 30.00
C248 Glenn Anderson RS 15.00 40.00
C249 Pavel Bure RS 10.00 25.00
C250 Marcel Dionne RS 12.00 30.00
C251 Tom Barrasso RS 8.00 20.00
C252 Rod Langway RS 10.00 25.00
C253 Alex Delvecchio RS 10.00 25.00
C254 Rod Brind'Amour RS 10.00 25.00
C255 Maurice Richard RS 25.00 60.00
C256 Tyson Jost POE 15.00 40.00
C257 Madison Bowey POE 6.00 15.00
C258 Victor Mete POE 8.00 20.00
C259 Alexandre Carrier POE 6.00 15.00
C260 Josh Ho-Sang POE 10.00 25.00
C261 Samuel Morin POE 8.00 20.00
C262 Chris DiDomenico POE 6.00 15.00
C263 Travis Sanheim POE 8.00 20.00
C264 Haydn Fleury POE 8.00 20.00
C265 Samuel Girard POE 8.00 20.00
C266 Roland McKeown POE 8.00 20.00
C267 Garrett Mitchell POE 8.00 20.00
C268 Pierre-Luc Dubois POE 15.00 40.00
C269 Owen Tippett POE 15.00 40.00
C270 Nolan Patrick POE 40.00 100.00

2017-18 Upper Deck Canvas Autographs

CHL Henrik Lundqvist/30 150.00 300.00
CSY Steve Yzerman/19

2017-18 Upper Deck Centennial Standouts

CS1 Wayne Gretzky 5.00 12.00
CS2 Duncan Keith 1.00 2.50
CS3 Patrick Roy 2.50 6.00
CS4 Bobby Orr 3.00 8.00
CS5 Nicklas Lidstrom .75 2.00
CS6 Joe Thornton 1.00 2.50
CS7 Paul Coffey 1.00 2.50
CS8 Alexander Ovechkin 4.00 10.00
CS9 Maurice Richard 1.00 2.50
CS10 Darryl Sittler 1.00 2.50
CS11 Mark Messier 1.50 4.00
CS12 Dickie Moore 1.00 2.50
CS13 Grant Fuhr 1.25 3.00
CS14 Jamie Benn 1.25 3.00
CS15 Ryan Getzlaf 1.00 2.50
CS16 Marcel Dionne 1.25 3.00
CS17 Jari Kurri 1.00 2.50
CS18 Phil Esposito 1.50 4.00
CS19 Steve Yzerman 1.25 3.00
CS20 Ed Belfour 1.25 3.00
CS21 Stan Mikita 1.25 3.00
CS22 Daniel Sedin 1.00 2.50
CS23 Henrik Lundqvist 1.50 4.00
CS24 Chris Chelios 1.00 2.50
CS25 Wayne Gretzky 5.00 12.00
CS26 Eddie Shore 1.00 2.50
CS27 Frank Mahovlich 1.00 2.50
CS28 Claude Giroux 1.00 2.50
CS29 Patrik Laine 1.50 4.00
CS30 Martin Brodeur 2.00 5.00
CS31 Carey Price 3.00 8.00
CS32 Jonathan Quick 1.50 4.00
CS33 Henrik Sedin 1.00 2.50
CS34 Auston Matthews 4.00 10.00
CS35 Rod Brind'Amour 1.00 2.50
CS36 Shea Weber .75 2.00
CS37 Syl Apps .75 2.00
CS38 Bobby Orr 3.00 8.00
CS39 Dominik Hasek 1.00 2.50
CS40 Ray Bourque 1.50 4.00
CS41 John Tavares 2.00 5.00
CS42 Syl Apps .75 2.00
CS43 P.K. Subban 1.00 2.50
CS44 Guy Lafleur 1.25 3.00
CS45 Connor McDavid 4.00 10.00
CS46 Patrice Bergeron 1.25 3.00
CS47 Roberto Luongo 1.00 2.50
CS48 Bobby Orr 3.00 8.00
CS49 Jonathan Toews 2.00 5.00
CS50 Maurice Richard 1.00 2.50
CS51 Bill Barilko .75 2.00
CS52 Jarome Iginla 1.00 2.50
CS53 Mark Recchi 1.25 3.00
CS54 Red Kelly .75 2.00
CS55 Charlie Conacher .75 2.00
CS56 Jean Beliveau 1.00 2.50
CS57 Drew Doughty 1.00 2.50
CS58 Pierre Pilote 1.00 2.50
CS59 Alex Delvecchio 1.00 2.50
CS60 Steven Stamkos 2.00 5.00
CS61 Corey Perry 1.00 2.50
CS62 Bobby Hull 1.00 2.50
CS63 Nicklas Backstrom 1.50 4.00
CS64 Jean Beliveau 1.00 2.50
CS65 Erik Karlsson 1.25 3.00
CS66 Mario Lemieux 3.00 8.00
CS67 Johnny Bower 1.00 2.50
CS68 Jaromir Jagr 2.50 6.00
CS69 Zdeno Chara 1.00 2.50
CS70 Braden Holtby 1.50 4.00
CS71 Evgeni Malkin 3.00 8.00
CS72 Bobby Clarke 1.00 2.50
CS73 Borje Salming .75 2.00
CS74 Denis Potvin 1.00 2.50
CS75 Mario Lemieux 3.00 8.00
CS76 Teemu Selanne 1.25 3.00
CS77 Ray Bourque 1.50 4.00
CS78 Larry Robinson 1.00 2.50
CS79 Guy Lafleur 1.25 3.00
CS80 Mike Gartner 1.00 2.50
CS81 Marian Hossa .75 2.00
CS82 Dale Hawerchuk 1.25 3.00
CS83 Mike Bossy 1.50 4.00
CS84 Pat LaFontaine 1.00 2.50
CS85 Brent Burns 1.25 3.00
CS86 Patrick Roy 2.50 6.00
CS87 Sidney Crosby 4.00 10.00
CS88 Patrick Kane 2.00 5.00
CS89 Mike Modano 1.50 4.00
CS90 Brett Hull 1.00 2.50
CS91 Vladimir Tarasenko 1.50 4.00
CS92 Pavel Bure 1.00 2.50
CS93 Doug Gilmour 1.25 3.00
CS94 Mark Messier 1.50 4.00
CS95 Peter Forsberg 1.50 4.00
CS96 Joe Sakic 1.25 3.00
CS97 Connor McDavid 4.00 10.00
CS98 Martin Brodeur 2.00 5.00
CS99 Wayne Gretzky 5.00 12.00
CS100 Mario Lemieux 3.00 8.00

2017-18 Upper Deck Ceremonial Puck Drop

CPD1 Phil Housley 20.00 50.00
CPD2 Ray Bourque 15.00 40.00
CPD3 Igor Larionov 8.00 20.00
CPD4 Mark Recchi 8.00 20.00
CPD5 Mark Messier 40.00 100.00
CPD6 Derek Sanderson 15.00 40.00
CPD7 Bob Probert 8.00 20.00
CPD8 John Vanbiesbrouck 8.00 20.00
CPD9 Maurice Richard 25.00 60.00
CPD10 Bobby Hull 40.00 100.00
Brett Hull
CPD11 M.Lemieux/S.Yzerman 40.00 100.00
CPD12 W.Gretzky/D.Hawerchuk 80.00 150.00

2017-18 Upper Deck Ceremonial Puck Drop Autographs

CPD1 Phil Housley 30.00 80.00
CPD2 Ray Bourque
CPD3 Igor Larionov 25.00 60.00
CPD5 Mark Messier
CPD6 Derek Sanderson 60.00 150.00

2017-18 Upper Deck Clear Cut

*VETS: 8X TO 20X BASIC CARDS
*YG: 1.5X TO 4X BASIC CARDS
201 Nico Hischier YG 250.00 400.00
202 Kailer Yamamoto YG 150.00 250.00
222 Alexander Nylander YG 80.00 150.00
242 Charlie McAvoy YG 200.00 350.00
246 Tyson Jost YG 50.00 125.00
247 Brock Boeser YG 200.00 300.00
250 Nico Hischier 40.00 100.00
Brock Boeser YG CL
469 Owen Tippett YG 50.00 125.00

2017-18 Upper Deck Clear Cut Foundations

CCF1 R.Rakell/H.Lindholm 10.00 25.00
CCF2 C.Dvorak/O.Ekman-Larsson 12.00 30.00
CCF3 D.Pastrnak/T.Krug 20.00 50.00
CCF4 J.Eichel/R.Ristolainen 20.00 50.00
CCF5 M.Tkachuk/D.Hamilton 12.00 30.00
CCF6 J.Staal/J.Slavin 12.00 30.00
CCF7 C.Crawford/D.Keith 15.00 40.00
CCF8 N.MacKinnon/M.Rantanen 25.00 60.00
CCF9 C.Atkinson/Z.Werenski 12.00 30.00
CCF10 T.Seguin/J.Spezza 20.00 50.00
CCF11 A.Athanasiou/M.Green 12.00 30.00
CCF12 A.Larsson/C.Talbot 12.00 30.00
CCF13 V.Trocheck/J.Huberdeau 10.00 25.00
CCF14 T.Pearson/J.Quick 20.00 50.00
CCF15 E.Staal/D.Dubnyk 15.00 40.00
CCF16 M.Pacioretty/S.Weber 12.00 30.00
CCF17 F.Forsberg/P.Subban 15.00 40.00
CCF18 T.Hall/A.Henrique 25.00 60.00
CCF19 J.Tavares/C.de Haan 25.00 60.00
CCF20 J.Miller/M.Zuccarello 12.00 30.00
CCF21 E.Karlsson/M.Hoffman 15.00 40.00
CCF22 W.Simmonds/I.Provorov 15.00 40.00
CCF23 E.Malkin/K.Letang 40.00 100.00
CCF24 B.Burns/M.Jones 15.00 40.00
CCF25 V.Tarasenko/C.Parayko 20.00 50.00
CCF26 O.Palat/A.Stralman 12.00 30.00
CCF27 A.Matthews/M.Marner 50.00 125.00
CCF28 B.Horvat/J.Markstrom 12.00 30.00
CCF29 T.Oshie/B.Holtby 20.00 50.00
CCF30 P.Laine/N.Ehlers 20.00 50.00

2017-18 Upper Deck Clear Cut Honoured Members

HOF68 Dickie Moore 8.00 20.00
HOF69 Syl Apps 6.00 15.00
HOF70 Phil Housley 15.00 40.00
HOF71 Ace Bailey 8.00 20.00
HOF72 Red Horner 6.00 15.00
HOF73 Pat LaFontaine 15.00 40.00
HOF74 Rogie Vachon 10.00 25.00

2017-18 Upper Deck Clear Cut Superstars

CCSAM Auston Matthews 30.00 80.00
CCSAO Alexander Ovechkin 30.00 80.00
CCSAW Alexander Wennberg 6.00 15.00
CCSBB Brent Burns 10.00 25.00
CCSBM Brad Marchand 10.00 25.00
CCSCM Connor McDavid 30.00 80.00
CCSCP Carey Price 25.00 60.00
CCSCT Cam Talbot 8.00 20.00
CCSDD Devan Dubnyk 8.00 20.00
CCSDK Duncan Keith 8.00 20.00
CCSDP David Pastrnak 12.00 30.00
CCSES Eric Staal 10.00 25.00
CCSHZ Henrik Zetterberg 8.00 20.00
CCSJC Jeff Carter 8.00 20.00
CCSJE Jack Eichel 12.00 30.00
CCSJP Joe Pavelski 8.00 20.00
CCSJV Jakub Voracek 8.00 20.00
CCSLD Leon Draisaitl 12.00 30.00
CCSMG Mikael Granlund 8.00 20.00
CCSMM Mitch Marner 12.00 30.00
CCSMS Mark Scheifele 10.00 25.00
CCSNE Nikolaj Ehlers 8.00 20.00
CCSNK Nikita Kucherov 12.00 30.00
CCSPK Phil Kessel 10.00 25.00
CCSPL Patrik Laine 12.00 30.00
CCSSB Sergei Bobrovsky 8.00 20.00
CCSSC Sidney Crosby 30.00 80.00
CCSSJ Seth Jones 6.00 15.00
CCSSM Sean Monahan 8.00 20.00
CCSTH Taylor Hall 15.00 40.00
CCSTR Tuukka Rask 8.00 20.00
CCSVH Victor Hedman 10.00 25.00

2017-18 Upper Deck Fluorescence

F1 Josh Ho-Sang 6.00 15.00
F2 Tyson Jost 10.00 25.00
F3 Calle Rosen 5.00 12.00
F4 Will Butcher 6.00 15.00
F5 J.T. Compher 6.00 15.00
F6 Colin White 5.00 12.00
F7 Jon Gillies 5.00 12.00
F8 Alex Kerfoot 5.00 12.00
F9 Logan Brown 5.00 12.00
F10 Travis Sanheim 5.00 12.00
F11 Alex Formenton 5.00 12.00
F12 Jake Dotchin 4.00 10.00
F13 Victor Mete 5.00 12.00
F14 Alex Iafallo 5.00 12.00
F15 Nolan Patrick 10.00 25.00
F16 Filip Chytil 5.00 12.00
F17 Luke Kunin 5.00 12.00
F18 Michael Amadio 5.00 12.00
F19 Brock Boeser 30.00 80.00
F20 Vince Dunn 5.00 12.00
F21 Evgeny Svechnikov 10.00 25.00
F22 Kailer Yamamoto 12.00 30.00
F23 Samuel Girard 5.00 12.00
F24 Christian Fischer 6.00 15.00
F25 Haydn Fleury 5.00 12.00
F26 Alex DeBrincat 12.00 30.00
F27 Jakob Forsbacka-Karlsson 5.00 12.00
F28 Martin Necas 5.00 12.00
F29 Samuel Morin 5.00 12.00
F30 Anders Bjork 6.00 15.00
F31 Jack Roslovic 6.00 15.00
F32 Rasmus Andersson 5.00 12.00
F33 Alex Tuch 12.00 30.00
F34 Robert Hagg 5.00 12.00
F35 Janne Kuokkanen 5.00 12.00
F36 Ivan Barbashev 5.00 12.00
F37 Nico Hischier 15.00 40.00
F38 Charlie McAvoy 15.00 40.00
F39 Owen Tippett 10.00 25.00
F40 Christian Djoos 5.00 12.00
F41 Nikita Scherbak 10.00 25.00
F42 Jesper Bratt 8.00 20.00
F43 Tage Thompson 8.00 20.00
F44 Clayton Keller 12.00 30.00
F45 Jake DeBrusk 8.00 20.00
F46 Pierre-Luc Dubois 10.00 25.00
F47 Eric Comrie 4.00 10.00
F48 Madison Bowey 4.00 10.00
F49 Adrian Kempe 6.00 15.00
F50 Alexander Nylander 8.00 20.00

2017-18 Upper Deck Day with The Cup

DC1 Patric Hornqvist 15.00 40.00
DC2 Marc-Andre Fleury 30.00 80.00
DC3 Chad Ruhwedel 12.00 30.00
DC4 Justin Schultz 20.00 50.00
DC5 Jake Guentzel 25.00 60.00
DC6 Trevor Daley 15.00 40.00
DC7 Tom Kuhnhackl 12.00 30.00
DC8 Carter Rowney 15.00 40.00
DC9 Carl Hagelin 20.00 50.00
DC10 Scott Wilson 12.00 30.00
DC11 Olli Maatta 12.00 30.00
DC12 Mark Streit 15.00 40.00
DC13 Kris Letang 20.00 50.00
DC14 Chris Kunitz 20.00 50.00
DC15 Evgeni Malkin 60.00 150.00
DC16 Josh Archibald 20.00 50.00
DC17 Conor Sheary 20.00 50.00
DC18 Bryan Rust 20.00 50.00
DC19 Brian Dumoulin 15.00 40.00
DC20 Matt Murray 30.00 80.00
DC21 Phil Kessel 25.00 60.00
DC22 Ron Hainsey 15.00 40.00
DC23 Matt Cullen 15.00 40.00
DC24 Ian Cole 15.00 40.00
DC25 Nick Bonino 15.00 40.00
DC26 Sidney Crosby 80.00 200.00
DC27 Mario Lemieux 60.00 150.00

2017-18 Upper Deck Game Jerseys

GJAA Artem Anisimov D 2.50 6.00
GJAB Aleksander Barkov E 3.00 8.00
GJAE Aaron Ekblad D 3.00 8.00
GJAG Alex Galchenyuk E 4.00 10.00
GJAH Adam Henrique D 2.50 6.00
GJAK Anze Kopitar D 5.00 12.00
GJAL Andrew Ladd E 3.00 8.00
GJAP Alex Pietrangelo D 2.50 6.00
GJAS Andrew Shaw F 2.50 6.00
GJAT Andreas Athanasiou D 3.00 8.00
GJAV Andrei Vasilevskiy E 4.00 10.00
GJAW Alexander Wennberg F 2.50 6.00
GJBA David Backes F 2.50 6.00
GJBB Brent Burns A 4.00 10.00
GJBH Bo Horvat E 3.00 8.00
GJBJ Boone Jenner F 2.50 6.00
GJBN Brock Nelson E 2.50 6.00
GJBR Derick Brassard E 3.00 8.00
GJBS Brent Seabrook E 2.50 6.00
GJBU Andre Burakovsky F 2.50 6.00
GJBW Blake Wheeler B 3.00 8.00
GJCA Craig Anderson E 3.00 8.00
GJCC Corey Crawford A 4.00 10.00
GJCD Christian Dvorak E 2.50 6.00
GJCP Colton Parayko E 3.00 8.00
GJCS Cory Schneider F 2.50 6.00
GJCT Cam Talbot E 3.00 8.00
GJCW Cam Ward F 2.50 6.00
GJDB Dustin Byfuglien A 3.00 8.00
GJDH Dougie Hamilton C 2.50 6.00
GJDO Louis Domingue E 2.00 5.00
GJDP David Pastrnak D 5.00 12.00
GJEK Evgeny Kuznetsov B 5.00 12.00
GJEL Elias Lindholm F 2.50 6.00
GJES Eric Staal F 4.00 10.00
GJFA Frederik Andersen E 2.50 6.00
GJFN Frans Nielsen E 2.50 6.00
GJGL Gabriel Landeskog E 2.50 6.00
GJIP Ivan Provorov E 3.00 8.00
GJJA Justin Abdelkader E 2.50 6.00
GJJG John Gibson C 3.00 8.00
GJJK John Klingberg D 2.50 6.00
GJJM Jake Muzzin F 2.50 6.00
GJJO Roman Josi E 3.00 8.00
GJJQ Jonathan Quick E 5.00 12.00
GJKL Kris Letang A 20.00 50.00
GJKO Kyle Okposo F 2.50 6.00
GJKP Kyle Palmieri F 2.50 6.00
GJLA Adam Larsson F 3.00 8.00
GJLC Logan Couture F 3.00 8.00
GJLD Leon Draisaitl D 5.00 12.00
GJLE Loui Eriksson B 8.00 20.00
GJMA Max Domi A 25.00 60.00
GJMD Matt Duchene B 8.00 20.00
GJMG Mark Giordano F 2.50 6.00
GJMH Mike Hoffman E 2.50 6.00
GJMJ Martin Jones E 3.00 8.00
GJMK Mikko Koivu E 2.50 6.00
GJML Milan Lucic A 12.00 30.00
GJMM Matt Murray A 12.00 30.00
GJMR Morgan Rielly C 3.00 8.00
GJMS Mark Scheifele D 4.00 10.00
GJMZ Mats Zuccarello B 3.00 8.00
GJNB Nicklas Backstrom B 5.00 12.00
GJNK Nikita Kucherov B 5.00 12.00
GJNL Nick Leddy F 2.00 5.00
GJPK Phil Kessel C 4.00 10.00
GJPR Carey Price B 12.00 30.00
GJRF Robby Fabbri F 3.00 8.00
GJRI Rasmus Ristolainen F 3.00 8.00
GJRJ Ryan Johansen B 3.00 8.00
GJRK Ryan Kesler C 3.00 8.00
GJRR Rickard Rakell D 2.50 6.00
GJRS Ryan Suter E 2.00 5.00
GJSB Sam Bennett F 2.50 6.00
GJSG Shayne Gostisbehere E 3.00 8.00
GJSJ Seth Jones E 2.50 6.00
GJSP Ryan Spooner E 2.50 6.00
GJSR Sam Reinhart E 2.50 6.00
GJSW Shea Weber A 12.00 30.00
GJTA Vladimir Tarasenko D 5.00 12.00
GJTB Tyson Barrie D 3.00 8.00
GJTH Taylor Hall D 6.00 15.00
GJTS Tyler Seguin B 5.00 12.00
GJTT Tyler Toffoli D 2.50 6.00
GJVH Victor Hedman A 12.00 30.00
GJVR Victor Rask F 3.00 8.00
GJVT Vincent Trocheck D 2.50 6.00
GJWS Wayne Simmonds D 4.00 10.00
GJZI Mika Zibanejad F 3.00 8.00

2017-18 Upper Deck NHL Draft

SP1 Nico Hischier 125.00 250.00
SP1V Nico Hischier VAR

2017-18 Upper Deck Oversized

13 Brad Marchand 2.50 6.00
41 Jonathan Toews 4.00 10.00
48 Nathan MacKinnon 4.00 10.00
54 Sergei Bobrovsky 2.00 5.00
75 Leon Draisaitl 3.00 8.00
102 Carey Price 6.00 15.00
146 Evgeni Malkin 6.00 15.00
148 Matt Murray 3.00 8.00
152 Joe Thornton 2.00 5.00
168 Nikita Kucherov 3.00 8.00
170 Auston Matthews 8.00 20.00
183 Marc-Andre Fleury 3.00 8.00
186 Braden Holtby 3.00 8.00
198 Patrik Laine 3.00 8.00
201 Nico Hischier 6.00 15.00
202 Kailer Yamamoto 5.00 12.00
203 Anders Bjork 2.50 6.00
204 Pierre-Luc Dubois 4.00 10.00
205 Josh Ho-Sang 2.50 6.00
206 Jon Gillies 2.00 5.00
207 Lucas Wallmark 2.00 5.00
208 Denis Gurianov 2.00 5.00
210 Adrian Kempe 2.50 6.00
211 John Hayden 1.50 4.00
212 Jake DeBrusk 3.00 8.00
214 Travis Sanheim 2.00 5.00
216 Calle Rosen 2.00 5.00
217 Logan Brown 2.00 5.00
218 Rasmus Andersson 2.00 5.00
221 Alex DeBrincat 5.00 12.00
222 Alexander Nylander 3.00 8.00
224 Evgeny Svechnikov 4.00 10.00
227 Filip Chytil 2.00 5.00
228 Tage Thompson 3.00 8.00
234 Christian Fischer 2.50 6.00
235 Jakob Forsbacka-Karlsson 2.00 5.00
236 Haydn Fleury 2.00 5.00
240 Jack Roslovic 2.50 6.00
245 Victor Mete 2.00 5.00
246 Tyson Jost 4.00 10.00
247 Brock Boeser 15.00 40.00
249 Alex Tuch 5.00 12.00

2017-18 Upper Deck Parkhurst Rookies

PR1 Clayton Keller 2.50 6.00
PR2 Tyson Jost 2.00 5.00
PR3 Nolan Patrick 2.00 5.00
PR4 Charlie McAvoy 3.00 8.00
PR5 Kailer Yamamoto 2.50 6.00
PR6 Nico Hischier 3.00 8.00
PR7 Pierre-Luc Dubois 2.00 5.00
PR8 Filip Chytil 1.00 2.50
PR9 Alex DeBrincat 2.50 6.00
PR10 Josh Ho-Sang 1.25 3.00

2017-18 Upper Deck Rookie Materials

RMAB Anders Bjork E 4.00 10.00
RMAD Alex DeBrincat C 8.00 20.00
RMAK Adrian Kempe F 4.00 10.00
RMAN Alexander Nylander E 5.00 12.00
RMAT Alex Tuch D 8.00 20.00
RMBB Brock Boeser C 15.00 40.00
RMBR Jesper Bratt D 5.00 12.00
RMCF Christian Fischer D 4.00 10.00
RMCK Clayton Keller C 8.00 20.00
RMCM Charlie McAvoy C 10.00 25.00
RMCW Colin White B 3.00 8.00
RMDG Denis Gurianov D 3.00 8.00
RMES Evgeny Svechnikov E 6.00 15.00
RMGC Gabriel Carlsson F 2.50 6.00
RMHF Haydn Fleury B 3.00 8.00
RMIB Ivan Barbashev D 3.00 8.00
RMJB Jonny Brodzinski F 3.00 8.00
RMJC J.T. Compher D 4.00 10.00
RMJD Jake DeBrusk C 5.00 12.00
RMJF Jakob Forsbacka-Karlsson D 3.00 8.00
RMJG Jon Gillies D 3.00 8.00
RMJH Josh Ho-Sang E 4.00 10.00
RMJK Janne Kuokkanen B 3.00 8.00
RMJR Jack Roslovic B 4.00 10.00
RMJS Jordan Schmaltz F 4.00 10.00
RMKY Kailer Yamamoto A 8.00 20.00
RMLB Logan Brown B 3.00 8.00
RMLW Lucas Wallmark F 3.00 8.00
RMMB Madison Bowey D 2.50 6.00
RMNH Nico Hischier A 10.00 25.00
RMNP Nolan Patrick A 6.00 15.00
RMNS Nikita Scherbak F 6.00 15.00
RMOT Owen Tippett E 6.00 15.00
RMPC Peter Cehlarik F 3.00 8.00
RMPD Pierre-Luc Dubois A 6.00 15.00
RMRB Riley Barber F 2.50 6.00
RMRH Robert Hagg F 3.00 8.00
RMSM Samuel Morin F 3.00 8.00
RMTJ Tyson Jost E 6.00 15.00
RMTS Travis Sanheim F 3.00 8.00

RMTT Tage Thompson E 5.00 12.00
RMVZ Valentin Zykov F 3.00 8.00

2017-18 Upper Deck Shining Stars Centers

SSC1 Auston Matthews 4.00 10.00
SSC2 Alexander Wennberg .75 2.00
SSC3 Connor McDavid 4.00 10.00
SSC4 Jeff Carter 1.00 2.50
SSC5 Mikael Granlund 1.00 2.50
SSC6 Mark Scheifele 1.25 3.00
SSC7 Nicklas Backstrom 1.50 4.00
SSC8 Ryan Johansen 1.00 2.50
SSC9 Sidney Crosby 4.00 10.00
SSC10 Tyler Seguin 1.50 4.00

2017-18 Upper Deck Shining Stars Defensemen

SSD1 Brent Burns 1.25 3.00
SSD2 Dougie Hamilton .75 2.00
SSD3 Duncan Keith 1.00 2.50
SSD4 Erik Karlsson 1.25 3.00
SSD5 Hampus Lindholm .75 2.00
SSD6 P.K. Subban 1.00 2.50
SSD7 Seth Jones .75 2.00
SSD8 Shea Weber .75 2.00
SSD9 Torey Krug 1.00 2.50
SSD10 Zach Werenski 1.00 2.50

2017-18 Upper Deck Shining Stars Left Wingers

SSL1 Alexander Ovechkin 5.00 12.00
SSL2 Taylor Hall 2.50 6.00
SSL3 Brad Marchand 1.50 4.00
SSL4 Henrik Zetterberg 1.25 3.00
SSL5 James van Riemsdyk 1.25 3.00
SSL6 Johnny Gaudreau 2.00 5.00
SSL7 Jeff Skinner 1.00 2.50
SSL8 Max Pacioretty 1.25 3.00
SSL9 Nikolaj Ehlers 1.25 3.00
SSL10 Viktor Arvidsson 1.00 2.50

2017-18 Upper Deck Shining Stars Right Wingers

SSR1 Blake Wheeler 1.00 2.50
SSR2 Cam Atkinson 1.00 2.50
SSR3 David Pastrnak 1.50 4.00
SSR4 Jakub Voracek 1.00 2.50
SSR5 Mats Zuccarello 1.00 2.50
SSR6 Nikita Kucherov 1.50 4.00
SSR7 Nino Niederreiter .75 2.00
SSR8 Patrick Kane 2.00 5.00
SSR9 Patrik Laine 1.50 4.00
SSR10 Vladimir Tarasenko 1.50 4.00

2017-18 Upper Deck Signature Sensations

SSAB Aleksander Barkov B 8.00 20.00
SSAM Anthony Mantha C 15.00 40.00
SSAV Andrei Vasilevskiy A
SSBJ Boone Jenner C 6.00 15.00
SSBP Brendan Perlini E 6.00 15.00
SSCA Cam Atkinson B 8.00 20.00
SSCB Connor Brown E 8.00 20.00
SSCD Christian Dvorak E 6.00 15.00
SSCS Conor Sheary E 20.00 50.00
SSEK Evander Kane D 8.00 20.00
SSEL Esa Lindell E 6.00 15.00
SSFV Frank Vatrano E 8.00 20.00
SSGU Jake Guentzel D 30.00 80.00
SSJG John Gibson D 8.00 20.00
SSJM Josh Morrissey D 5.00 12.00
SSMA Michael Matheson D 6.00 15.00
SSMH Mike Hoffman C 6.00 15.00
SSMJ Martin Jones B 12.00 30.00
SSMM Matt Murray A
SSMS Mark Scheifele C 15.00 40.00
SSMT Matthew Tkachuk C 30.00 80.00
SSNE Nikolaj Ehlers C 8.00 20.00
SSNN Nino Niederreiter C 6.00 15.00
SSPA Jean-Gabriel Pageau D 5.00 12.00
SSPZ Pavel Zacha E 8.00 20.00
SSRF Radek Faksa E 6.00 15.00
SSRH Ryan Hartman E 8.00 20.00
SSRK Ryan Kesler B 12.00 30.00
SSRP Richard Panik D 6.00 15.00
SSSA Sebastian Aho E 8.00 20.00
SSTH Taylor Hall B 15.00 40.00
SSTS Troy Stecher E 6.00 15.00
SSVA Viktor Arvidsson D 6.00 15.00
SSWS Wayne Simmonds B 10.00 25.00

2017-18 Upper Deck Sophomore Sensations

SOAM Auston Matthews 3.00 8.00
SOJG Jake Guentzel 1.00 2.50
SOMM Mitch Marner 1.25 3.00
SOMT Matthew Tkachuk .75 2.00
SOPL Patrik Laine 1.25 3.00
SOWN William Nylander 1.25 3.00

2017-18 Upper Deck Team Triples

TTARI Strome/Keller/Fischer 8.00 20.00
TTAVS Rantanen/Jost/Compher 6.00 15.00
TTBOS Forsbacka-Karlsson 10.00 25.00
McAvoy/Cehlarik
TTCGY Andersson/Tkachuk/Gillies 3.00 8.00
TTDET Mantha/Svechnikov/Larkin 6.00 15.00
TTEDM Caggiula/Puljujarvi/Benning 4.00 10.00
TTMTL Lindgren/Scherbak/Lehkonen 6.00 15.00
TTNJD Zacha/Hischier/Wood 10.00 25.00
TTNYI Barzal/Ho-Sang/Beauvillier 5.00 12.00
TTOTT Chabot/White/Englund 5.00 12.00
TTPHI Provorov/Patrick/Konecny 6.00 15.00
TTTOR Marner/Matthews/Nylander 12.00 30.00
TTVAN Stecher/Boeser/Horvat 15.00 40.00
TTJETS Comrie/Laine/Roslovic 5.00 12.00
TTPENS Rowney/Guentzel/Dea 4.00 10.00

2017-18 Upper Deck The Second Six

S61 Bob Baun 6.00 15.00
S62 Charlie Simmer 8.00 20.00
S63 Marcel Dionne 10.00 25.00
S64 Dave Taylor 6.00 15.00
S65 Wayne Gretzky 40.00 100.00
S66 Bob Rouse 6.00 15.00
S67 Larry Murphy 6.00 15.00
S68 Mike Modano 12.00 30.00
S69 Bobby Clarke 8.00 20.00
S610 Rod Brind'Amour 8.00 20.00
S611 Claude Giroux 8.00 20.00
S612 Mario Lemieux 25.00 60.00
S613 Jaromir Jagr 20.00 50.00
S614 Sidney Crosby 30.00 80.00
S615 Evgeni Malkin 25.00 60.00
S616 Brett Hull 8.00 20.00
S617 Alex Pietrangelo 6.00 15.00
S618 Vladimir Tarasenko 12.00 30.00

2017-18 Upper Deck UD Portraits

P1 Nicklas Backstrom 1.00 2.50
P2 Shea Weber .50 1.25
P3 Daniel Sedin .60 1.50
P4 Max Domi .60 1.50
P5 Artem Anisimov .50 1.25
P6 Rasmus Ristolainen .60 1.50
P7 Gustav Nyquist .60 1.50
P8 Dougie Hamilton .50 1.25
P9 Jack Eichel 1.00 2.50
P10 Marc-Edouard Vlasic .40 1.00
P11 Taylor Hall 1.25 3.00
P12 Jakub Voracek .60 1.50
P13 Mitch Marner 1.00 2.50
P14 Mike Hoffman .50 1.25
P15 Jaden Schwartz .75 2.00
P16 Patrick Kane 1.25 3.00
P17 Sergei Bobrovsky .60 1.50
P18 Jonathan Huberdeau .50 1.25
P19 Jaccob Slavin .40 1.00
P20 Vladimir Tarasenko 1.00 2.50
P21 Leon Draisaitl 1.00 2.50
P22 Filip Forsberg .75 2.00
P23 Eric Staal .75 2.00
P24 Ryan McDonagh .50 1.25
P25 John Tavares 1.25 3.00
P26 P.K. Subban .60 1.50
P27 Vincent Trocheck .50 1.25
P28 Max Pacioretty .60 1.50
P29 Mikko Rantanen .60 1.50
P30 J.T. Miller .50 1.25
P31 Patrik Laine 1.00 2.50
P32 Zach Werenski .60 1.50
P33 David Krejci .50 1.25
P34 Hampus Lindholm .50 1.25
P35 Sebastian Aho .60 1.50
P36 Josh Bailey .50 1.25
P37 Devan Dubnyk .60 1.50
P38 Erik Karlsson .75 2.00
P39 Ryan Getzlaf .60 1.50
P40 Sean Couturier .50 1.25
P41 Tyler Seguin 1.00 2.50
P42 Patrick Maroon .50 1.25
P43 Brad Marchand .75 2.00
P44 Jonathan Toews 1.25 3.00
P45 Nazem Kadri .50 1.25
P46 Carey Price 2.00 5.00
P47 Jeff Carter .60 1.50
P48 Matthew Tkachuk .60 1.50
P49 Brent Burns .75 2.00
P50 Auston Matthews 2.50 6.00
P51 Evgeni Malkin 2.00 5.00
P52 Alexander Ovechkin 2.50 6.00
P53 Connor McDavid 2.50 6.00
P54 Sidney Crosby 2.50 6.00
P55 Tyson Jost 3.00 8.00
P56 Josh Ho-Sang 2.00 5.00
P57 Alexander Nylander 2.50 6.00
P58 Brock Boeser 8.00 20.00
P59 Charlie McAvoy 5.00 12.00
P60 Clayton Keller 4.00 10.00
P61 Nolan Patrick 3.00 8.00
P62 Nikita Scherbak 3.00 8.00
P63 Jon Gillies 1.50 4.00
P64 Denis Gurianov 1.50 4.00
P65 Logan Brown 1.50 4.00
P66 Alex Tuch 4.00 10.00
P67 Ivan Barbashev 1.50 4.00
P68 Riley Barber 1.25 3.00
P69 Will Butcher 2.00 5.00
P70 Pierre-Luc Dubois 3.00 8.00
P71 Tucker Poolman 1.50 4.00
P72 Jake Dotchin 1.25 3.00
P73 Jesper Bratt 2.50 6.00
P74 Jake DeBrusk 2.50 6.00
P75 Samuel Morin 1.50 4.00
P76 Alex Kerfoot 1.50 4.00
P77 Marcus Sorensen 1.25 3.00
P78 Alex Formenton 1.50 4.00
P79 Rasmus Andersson 1.50 4.00
P80 Carter Rowney 1.25 3.00
P81 Nathan Walker 1.50 4.00
P82 Victor Mete 1.50 4.00
P83 Vladislav Kamenev 2.50 6.00
P84 C.J. Smith 1.25 3.00
P85 Colin White 1.50 4.00
P86 Luke Kunin 1.50 4.00
P87 Alex DeBrincat 4.00 10.00
P88 Christian Fischer 2.00 5.00
P89 Giovanni Fiore 1.50 4.00
P90 Haydn Fleury 1.50 4.00
P91 J.T. Compher 2.00 5.00
P92 Tage Thompson 2.50 6.00
P93 Owen Tippett 3.00 8.00
P94 Evgeny Svechnikov 3.00 8.00
P95 Kailer Yamamoto 4.00 10.00
P96 Travis Sanheim 1.50 4.00
P97 Vince Dunn 1.50 4.00
P98 Jack Roslovic 2.00 5.00
P99 Valentin Zykov 1.50 4.00
P100 Adrian Kempe 2.00 5.00
P101 Anders Bjork 2.00 5.00
P102 Calle Rosen 1.50 4.00
P103 Andreas Borgman 1.50 4.00
P104 Eric Comrie 1.25 3.00
P105 Filip Chytil 1.50 4.00
P106 Janne Kuokkanen 1.50 4.00
P107 Martin Necas 1.50 4.00
P108 Robert Hagg 1.50 4.00
P109 Jakob Forsbacka-Karlsson 1.50 4.00
P110 Nico Hischier 5.00 12.00

2017-18 Upper Deck Winter Classic Jumbo

WC1 Vladimir Tarasenko 3.00 8.00
WC2 Artemi Panarin 2.00 5.00
WC3 Robby Fabbri 2.00 5.00
WC4 Duncan Keith 2.00 5.00
WC5 Jake Allen 2.50 6.00
WC6 Patrick Kane 4.00 10.00
WC7 Alex Pietrangelo 1.50 4.00
WC8 Michal Kempny 1.50 4.00
WC9 Jay Bouwmeester 2.00 5.00
WC10 Corey Crawford 2.50 6.00
WC11 Paul Stastny 2.00 5.00
WC12 Jonathan Toews 4.00 10.00
WC13 Colton Parayko 2.00 5.00
WC14 Artem Anisimov 1.50 4.00

2003 Upper Deck All-Star Promos

Handed out in packs at the Upper Deck booth during the 2003 NHL All-Star Block Party, this 21-card set resembled the base UD set but card fronts carried a special All-Star logo and each card (except the checklists) was serial-numbered out of 500. Each pack contained 5-cards including the checklist card. Cards S1-S6 were randomly inserted into packs and carried authentic player autographs and were rumored to be limited to just 30 copies each..

COMP.SET w/o AUs (15) 12.00 30.00
AS1 Joe Thornton CL .50 1.25
AS2 Rick Nash 4.00 10.00
AS3 Stanislav Chistov 2.00 5.00
AS4 Chuck Kobasew 1.25 3.00
AS5 Stephen Weiss .75 2.00
AS6 Martin Brodeur CL .75 2.00
AS7 Jason Spezza 3.00 8.00
AS8 Alexander Frolov 1.25 3.00
AS9 Carlo Colaiacovo .75 2.00
AS10 Alexander Svitov .75 2.00
AS11 Nikolai Khabibulin CL .40 1.00
AS12 Henrik Zetterberg 4.00 10.00
AS13 Jordan Leopold .75 2.00
AS14 Jay Bouwmeester 2.00 5.00
AS15 P-M Bouchard 2.00 5.00
S1 Rick Nash AU 75.00 150.00
S2 Stanislav Chistov AU 15.00 40.00
S3 Jason Spezza AU 30.00 60.00
S4 Alexander Frolov AU 8.00 20.00
S5 Jay Bouwmeester AU 15.00 40.00
S6 Jordan Leopold AU 8.00 20.00

2004 Upper Deck All-Star Promos

Available only via wrapper redemption at the Upper Deck booth during the 2004 NHL All-Star Fanfest, this 15-card set featured perennial all-stars as well as popular prospects. Each card was serial-numbered out of 750.

COMPLETE SET (15)
BB Brent Burns 4.00 15.00
CB Christoph Brandner 4.00 10.00
ES Eric Staal 6.00 15.00
FS Fredrik Sjostrom 4.00 10.00
GH Gordie Howe 5.00 15.00
JP Joni Pitkanen 4.00 10.00
JS Jason Spezza 5.00 15.00
JT Joe Thornton 6.00 15.00
MF Marc-Andre Fleury 12.50 30.00
MG Marian Gaborik 6.00 15.00
NH Nathan Horton 6.00 12.00
NZ Nikolai Zherdev 8.00 20.00
PB Patrice Bergeron 10.00 30.00
PR Patrick Roy 8.00 30.00
TO Jordin Tootoo 6.00 15.00

2007 Upper Deck All Star Game Redemptions

Single cards were available as wrapper redemptions over the course of the three-day card show held in conjunction with the 2007 NHL All-Star Game in Dallas.

AS1 Martin Brodeur 4.00 10.00
AS2 Phil Kessel 2.00 5.00
AS3 Eric Lindros 1.50 4.00
AS4 Joe Sakic 3.00 8.00
AS5 Jordan Staal 4.00 10.00
AS6 Marty Turco 1.25 3.00
AS7 Sidney Crosby 8.00 20.00
AS8 Alexander Radulov 2.00 5.00
AS9 Brenden Morrow 1.25 3.00
AS10 Alexander Ovechkin 4.00 10.00
AS11 Evgeni Malkin 6.00 15.00
AS12 Mike Modano 2.00 5.00

2010-11 Upper Deck All Star Game

COMPLETE SET (10) 15.00 40.00
ASG1 Sidney Crosby 4.00 10.00
ASG2 Alexander Ovechkin 4.00 10.00
ASG3 Steven Stamkos 2.00 5.00
ASG4 Wayne Gretzky 5.00 12.00
ASG5 Gordie Howe 2.50 6.00
ASG6 Bobby Orr 3.00 8.00
ASG7 Jeff Skinner 1.50 4.00
ASG8 Eric Staal 1.25 3.00
ASG9 Cam Ward 1.00 2.50
ASG10 Eric Staal 1.25 3.00
Ron Francis
Cam Ward

2015-16 Upper Deck All Star Game

COMPLETE SET (7) 8.00 20.00
FG1 Roman Josi 1.50 4.00
FG2 Pekka Rinne 2.00 5.00
FG3 Shea Weber 1.25 3.00
FG4 P.K. Subban 2.50 6.00
FG5 Alex Ovechkin 6.00 15.00
FG6 Ryan McDonagh 1.25 3.00
NNO Checklist Card .75 2.00

2001 Upper Deck Avalanche NHL All-Star Game

This 15-card set was produced by Upper Deck as a wrapper redemption for the 2001 All-Star Fan Fest and feature members of the host Avalanche. The cards were distributed in three-card packs, with each card serial numbered out of 500. A Wayne Gretzky e-card was given away also, these cards carried an interactive number that could be entered at the Upper Deck website to see if it "evolved" into a memorabilia card winner. The e-card is listed, but not considered part of the complete set.

COMPLETE SET (15) 50.00 125.00
CA1 Ray Bourque 6.00 15.00
CA2 Adam Foote .80 2.00
CA3 Adam Deadmarsh .80 2.00
CA4 Alex Tanguay 4.00 10.00
CA5 Aaron Miller .40 1.00
CA6 Stephane Yelle .40 1.00
HH1 D.Aebischer 8.00 20.00
P.Roy
HH2 M.Hejduk 6.00 15.00
P.Forsberg
HH3 J.Sakic 6.00 15.00
R.Bourque
PP1 Patrick Roy 8.00 20.00
PP2 Joe Sakic 4.80 12.00
PP3 Peter Forsberg 6.00 15.00
PP4 Chris Drury 4.00 10.00
PP5 Milan Hejduk 4.00 10.00
PP6 David Aebischer 4.00 10.00
WG Wayne Gretzky e-Card 2.00 5.00

2001-02 Upper Deck Gretzky Expo e-Card

Available at the Upper Deck booth during the Toronto Fall Expo, these cards featured Wayne Gretzky on the card front and a scratch-off code that could be entered into the Upper Deck web site to win prizes. A Gretzky jersey card serial-numbered out of 200 was one of the prizes and was created especially for this promotion.

WG Wayne Gretzky Jsy/200 75.00 150.00
NNO Wayne Gretzky .40 1.00

2002 Upper Deck Gretzky All-Star Game

This three-card set was available via wrapper redemption from the Upper Deck booth at the NHL All-Star Fantasy in Los Angeles. The cards were individually serial numbered out of 2002 and featured highlights of Wayne Gretzky's career.

COMPLETE SET (3) 10.00 25.00
AS1 Wayne Gretzky 4.00 10.00
All-Time Leading Scorer
AS2 Wayne Gretzky 4.00 10.00
All-Time Leading Goal Scorer
AS3 Wayne Gretzky 4.00 10.00
All-Star Game Goals in a Period Record

2000-01 Upper Deck Jason Spezza Giveaways

These cards were given away at the Upper Deck booth at the 2000 and 2001 Toronto Expos. The version numbered to 300 was given away at the Fall Expo while the version numbered to 600 was given away at the Spring Expo. In order to receive a card, one had to open a box of Upper Deck product at the booth. Differently numbered and unnumberd varitions have also surfaced fueling speculation that some cards were distributed differently.

1 Jason Spezza AU/300 25.00 60.00
2 Jason Spezza AU/600 15.00 40.00

2008 Upper Deck 20th Anniversary

Upper Deck produced this 80-card set featuring past and present athletes from baseball, football, basketball and hockey and issued them through their Certified Diamond Dealers program. Eight cards were released every month from March through December 2008. By entering in all 80 unique codes from the back of the cards on the company's website by December 31, 2008, collectors had a chance to win a trip to four major sporting events.

UD31 Sidney Crosby 1.00 2.50
UD32 Wayne Gretzky .75 2.00
UD33 Mario Lemieux .50 1.25
UD34 Gordie Howe .60 1.50
UD35 Bobby Orr .60 1.50
UD36 Mark Messier .50 1.25
UD37 Joe Thornton .20 .50
UD38 Patrick Roy .50 1.25
UD39 Jarome Iginla .25 .60
UD40 Sergei Fedorov .50 1.25
UD41 Vincent Lecavalier .30 .75
UD42 Evgeni Malkin .50 1.25
UD43 Alexander Ovechkin 1.50 3.00
UD44 Rick Nash .25 .60
UD45 Jason Spezza .20 .50
UD71 Ilya Kovalchuk .20 .50
UD72 Pavel Datsyuk .30 .75
UD73 Carey Price .50 1.25
UD74 Patrick Kane .40 1.00
UD75 Henrik Zetterberg .30 .75

2009 Upper Deck 20th Anniversary

CARDS ISSUED IN FIVE CARD RUNS
EACH PRICED EQUALLY WITHIN RUNS

86 Wayne Gretzky 2.00 5.00
87 Wayne Gretzky 2.00 5.00
88 Wayne Gretzky 2.00 5.00
89 Wayne Gretzky 2.00 5.00
90 Wayne Gretzky 2.00 5.00
111 Wayne Gretzky 2.00 5.00
112 Wayne Gretzky 2.00 5.00
113 Wayne Gretzky 2.00 5.00
114 Wayne Gretzky 2.00 5.00
115 Wayne Gretzky 2.00 5.00
121 Calgary Flames .20 .50
122 Calgary Flames .20 .50
123 Calgary Flames .20 .50
124 Calgary Flames .20 .50
125 Calgary Flames .20 .50
191 Edmonton Oilers .20 .50
192 Edmonton Oilers/Messier .20 .50
193 Edmonton Oilers .20 .50
194 Edmonton Oilers .20 .50
195 Edmonton Oilers .20 .50
196 Wayne Gretzky 2.00 5.00
197 Wayne Gretzky 2.00 5.00
198 Wayne Gretzky 2.00 5.00
199 Wayne Gretzky 2.00 5.00
200 Wayne Gretzky 2.00 5.00
296 Pittsburgh Penguins/Lemieux .40 1.00
297 Pittsburgh Penguins .20 .50
298 Pittsburgh Penguins .20 .50
299 Pittsburgh Penguins .20 .50
300 Pittsburgh Penguins .20 .50
316 San Jose Sharks .20 .50
317 San Jose Sharks/Wilson .20 .50
318 San Jose Sharks .20 .50
319 San Jose Sharks .20 .50
320 San Jose Sharks .20 .50
351 Montreal Canadiens .20 .50
352 Montreal Canadiens .20 .50
353 Montreal Canadiens .20 .50
354 Montreal Canadiens .20 .50
355 Montreal Canadiens .20 .50
361 Wayne Gretzky 2.00 5.00
362 Wayne Gretzky 2.00 5.00
363 Wayne Gretzky 2.00 5.00
364 Wayne Gretzky 2.00 5.00
365 Wayne Gretzky 2.00 5.00
386 Mike Bossy .40 1.00
387 Mike Bossy .40 1.00
388 Mike Bossy .40 1.00
389 Mike Bossy .40 1.00
390 Mike Bossy .40 1.00
401 Martin Brodeur 1.25 3.00
402 Martin Brodeur 1.25 3.00
403 Martin Brodeur 1.25 3.00
404 Martin Brodeur 1.25 3.00
405 Martin Brodeur 1.25 3.00
411 Tampa Bay Lightning .20 .50
412 Tampa Bay Lightning .20 .50
413 Tampa Bay Lightning .20 .50
414 Tampa Bay Lightning .20 .50
415 Tampa Bay Lightning .20 .50
441 Pittsburgh Penguins .20 .50
442 Pittsburgh Penguins .20 .50
443 Pittsburgh Penguins .20 .50
444 Pittsburgh Penguins .20 .50
445 Pittsburgh Penguins .20 .50
446 Mark Messier .60 1.50
447 Mark Messier .60 1.50
448 Mark Messier .60 1.50
449 Mark Messier .60 1.50
450 Mark Messier .60 1.50
526 Montreal Canadiens .20 .50
527 Montreal Canadiens .20 .50
528 Montreal Canadiens .20 .50
529 Montreal Canadiens .20 .50
530 Montreal Canadiens .20 .50
581 Anaheim Ducks .20 .50
582 Anaheim Ducks .20 .50
583 Anaheim Ducks .20 .50
584 Anaheim Ducks .20 .50
585 Anaheim Ducks .20 .50
601 Mario Lemieux 1.50 4.00
602 Mario Lemieux 1.50 4.00
603 Mario Lemieux 1.50 4.00
604 Mario Lemieux 1.50 4.00
605 Mario Lemieux 1.50 4.00
646 Wayne Gretzky 2.00 5.00
647 Wayne Gretzky 2.00 5.00
648 Wayne Gretzky 2.00 5.00
649 Wayne Gretzky 2.00 5.00
650 Wayne Gretzky 2.00 5.00
651 New York Rangers .20 .50
652 New York Rangers .20 .50
653 New York Rangers .20 .50
654 New York Rangers .20 .50
655 New York Rangers .20 .50
706 Wayne Gretzky 2.00 5.00
707 Wayne Gretzky 2.00 5.00
708 Wayne Gretzky 2.00 5.00
709 Wayne Gretzky 2.00 5.00
710 Wayne Gretzky 2.00 5.00
731 Sergei Fedorov .40 1.00
732 Sergei Fedorov .40 1.00
733 Sergei Fedorov .40 1.00
734 Sergei Fedorov .40 1.00
735 Sergei Fedorov .40 1.00
736 Ray Bourque .60 1.50
737 Ray Bourque .60 1.50
738 Ray Bourque .60 1.50
739 Ray Bourque .60 1.50
740 Ray Bourque .60 1.50
791 New Jersey Devils/Brodeur .40 1.00
792 New Jersey Devils .20 .50
793 New Jersey Devils .20 .50
794 New Jersey Devils .20 .50
795 New Jersey Devils .20 .50
826 Colorado Avalanche .20 .50
827 Colorado Avalanche .20 .50
828 Colorado Avalanche .20 .50
829 Colorado Avalanche .20 .50
830 Colorado Avalanche .20 .50
896 Phoenix Coyotes .20 .50
897 Phoenix Coyotes .20 .50
898 Phoenix Coyotes .20 .50
899 Phoenix Coyotes .20 .50
900 Phoenix Coyotes .20 .50
926 Joe Sakic .40 1.00
927 Joe Sakic .40 1.00
928 Joe Sakic .40 1.00
929 Joe Sakic .40 1.00
930 Joe Sakic .40 1.00
971 Mario Lemieux 1.50 4.00
972 Mario Lemieux 1.50 4.00
973 Mario Lemieux 1.50 4.00
974 Mario Lemieux 1.50 4.00
975 Mario Lemieux 1.50 4.00
1026 Carolina Hurricanes .20 .50
1027 Carolina Hurricanes .20 .50
1028 Carolina Hurricanes .20 .50
1029 Carolina Hurricanes .20 .50
1030 Carolina Hurricanes .20 .50
1036 Detroit Red Wings .30 .75
1037 Detroit Red Wings .30 .75
1038 Detroit Red Wings .30 .75
1039 Detroit Red Wings .30 .75
1040 Detroit Red Wings .30 .75
1056 Historic NHL Game in Japan .20 .50
1057 Historic NHL Game in Japan .20 .50
1058 Historic NHL Game in Japan .20 .50
1059 Historic NHL Game in Japan .20 .50
1060 Historic NHL Game in Japan .20 .50
1071 Mario Lemieux 1.50 4.00
1072 Mario Lemieux 1.50 4.00
1073 Mario Lemieux 1.50 4.00
1074 Mario Lemieux 1.50 4.00
1075 Mario Lemieux 1.50 4.00
1151 Detroit Red Wings .30 .75
1152 Detroit Red Wings .30 .75
1153 Detroit Red Wings .30 .75
1154 Detroit Red Wings .30 .75
1155 Detroit Red Wings .30 .75
1231 Nashville Predators .20 .50
1232 Nashville Predators .20 .50
1233 Nashville Predators .20 .50
1234 Nashville Predators .20 .50
1235 Nashville Predators .20 .50
1266 Dallas Stars .20 .50
1267 Dallas Stars .20 .50
1268 Dallas Stars .20 .50
1269 Dallas Stars .20 .50
1270 Dallas Stars .20 .50
1401 New Jersey Devils .20 .50
1402 New Jersey Devils .20 .50
1403 New Jersey Devils .20 .50
1404 New Jersey Devils .20 .50
1405 New Jersey Devils .20 .50
1486 Columbus Blue Jackets .20 .50
1487 Columbus Blue Jackets .20 .50
1488 Columbus Blue Jackets .20 .50
1489 Columbus Blue Jackets .20 .50
1490 Columbus Blue Jackets .20 .50
1491 Minnesota Wild .20 .50
1492 Minnesota Wild .20 .50
1493 Minnesota Wild .20 .50
1494 Minnesota Wild .20 .50
1495 Minnesota Wild .20 .50
1521 Colorado Avalanche .20 .50
1522 Colorado Avalanche .20 .50
1523 Colorado Avalanche .20 .50
1524 Colorado Avalanche .20 .50
1525 Colorado Avalanche .20 .50
1591 Joe Sakic .40 1.00
1592 Joe Sakic .40 1.00
1593 Joe Sakic .40 1.00
1594 Joe Sakic .40 1.00
1595 Joe Sakic .40 1.00
1601 Patrick Roy .75 2.00
1602 Patrick Roy .75 2.00
1603 Patrick Roy .75 2.00
1604 Patrick Roy .75 2.00
1605 Patrick Roy .75 2.00
1636 Detroit Red Wings .30 .75
1637 Detroit Red Wings .30 .75
1638 Detroit Red Wings .30 .75
1639 Detroit Red Wings .30 .75
1640 Detroit Red Wings .30 .75
1671 Rick Nash .40 1.00
1672 Rick Nash .40 1.00
1673 Rick Nash .40 1.00
1674 Rick Nash .40 1.00
1675 Rick Nash .40 1.00
1791 New Jersey Devils .20 .50
1792 New Jersey Devils .20 .50
1793 New Jersey Devils .20 .50
1794 New Jersey Devils .20 .50
1795 New Jersey Devils .20 .50
1811 Eric Staal .75 2.00
1812 Eric Staal .75 2.00
1813 Eric Staal .75 2.00
1814 Eric Staal .75 2.00
1815 Eric Staal .75 2.00
1831 Marc-Andre Fleury .40 1.00
1832 Marc-Andre Fleury .40 1.00
1833 Marc-Andre Fleury .40 1.00
1834 Marc-Andre Fleury .40 1.00
1835 Marc-Andre Fleury .40 1.00
1921 Tampa Bay Lightning .20 .50
1922 Tampa Bay Lightning .20 .50
1923 Tampa Bay Lightning .20 .50
1924 Tampa Bay Lightning .20 .50
1925 Tampa Bay Lightning .20 .50
2001 Alexander Ovechkin 1.25 3.00
2002 Alexander Ovechkin 1.25 3.00
2003 Alexander Ovechkin 1.25 3.00
2004 Alexander Ovechkin 1.25 3.00
2005 Alexander Ovechkin 1.25 3.00
2061 Sidney Crosby 2.00 5.00
2062 Sidney Crosby 2.00 5.00
2063 Sidney Crosby 2.00 5.00
2064 Sidney Crosby 2.00 5.00
2065 Sidney Crosby 2.00 5.00
2141 Carolina Hurricanes .20 .50
2142 Carolina Hurricanes .20 .50
2143 Carolina Hurricanes .20 .50
2144 Carolina Hurricanes .20 .50
2145 Carolina Hurricanes .20 .50
2181 Evgeni Malkin 1.00 2.50
2182 Evgeni Malkin 1.00 2.50
2183 Evgeni Malkin 1.00 2.50
2184 Evgeni Malkin 1.00 2.50
2185 Evgeni Malkin 1.00 2.50
2216 Patrick Roy .75 2.00
2217 Patrick Roy .75 2.00
2218 Patrick Roy .75 2.00
2219 Patrick Roy .75 2.00
2220 Patrick Roy .75 2.00
2326 Carey Price 1.25 3.00
2327 Carey Price 1.25 3.00
2328 Carey Price 1.25 3.00
2329 Carey Price 1.25 3.00
2330 Carey Price 1.25 3.00
2346 Anaheim Mighty Ducks .20 .50
2347 Anaheim Mighty Ducks .20 .50
2348 Anaheim Mighty Ducks .20 .50
2349 Anaheim Mighty Ducks .20 .50
2350 Anaheim Mighty Ducks .20 .50
2351 Patrick Kane 1.00 2.50
2352 Patrick Kane 1.00 2.50
2353 Patrick Kane 1.00 2.50
2354 Patrick Kane 1.00 2.50
2355 Patrick Kane 1.00 2.50
2371 Mark Messier .60 1.50
2372 Mark Messier .60 1.50
2373 Mark Messier .60 1.50
2374 Mark Messier .60 1.50
2375 Mark Messier .60 1.50
2411 Detroit Red Wings .30 .75
2412 Detroit Red Wings .30 .75
2413 Detroit Red Wings .30 .75
2414 Detroit Red Wings .30 .75
2415 Detroit Red Wings .30 .75

2009 Upper Deck 20th Anniversary Memorabilia

NHLAO Alexander Ovechkin 12.50 30.00
NHLEM Evgeni Malkin 10.00 25.00
NHLIK Ilya Kovalchuk 10.00 25.00
NHLMB Martin Brodeur 30.00 60.00
NHLML Mario Lemieux 40.00 80.00
NHLMM Mark Messier 10.00 25.00
NHLPR Patrick Roy 10.00 25.00
NHLRB Ray Bourque 6.00 15.00
NHLRN Rick Nash 5.00 12.00
NHLSC Sidney Crosby 30.00 60.00
NHLVL Vincent Lecavalier 12.50 30.00
NHLWG Wayne Gretzky 75.00 150.00

2014 Upper Deck 25th Anniversary

3 Dion Phaneuf .50 1.25
4 Bobby Orr .60 1.50
10 Guy Lafleur .50 1.25
12 Joe Sakic .60 1.50
14 Hayley Wickenheiser .75 2.00
20 Claude Giroux .50 1.25
26 Martin St. Louis .50 1.25
29 Patrick Roy .75 2.00
31 Jonathan Toews .75 2.00
38 Adam Oates .40 1.00
51 Ryan Getzlaf .50 1.25
55 Patrick Marleau .40 1.00
62 Teemu Selanne .60 1.50
71 Matt Duchene .50 1.25
74 Mark Scheifele .50 1.25
75 Chris Kunitz .40 1.00
76 P.K. Subban .60 1.50
79 Marian Gaborik .50 1.25
81 Phil Kessel .50 1.25
85 Bobby Hull .50 1.25
87 Julie Chu .75 2.00
93 Doug Gilmour .50 1.25
96 Ryan Nugent-Hopkins .60 1.50
97 Grant Fuhr .50 1.25
99 Wayne Gretzky 1.50 4.00
102 Dominik Hasek .60 1.50
103 Jari Kurri .40 1.00
105 Nicklas Lidstrom .50 1.25
108 Sidney Crosby 1.00 2.50
124 Sean Monahan 1.00 2.50
129 Nathan MacKinnon 2.00 5.00
134 Alex Galchenyuk 1.00 2.50
139 Mikhail Grigorenko .60 1.50
146 Seth Jones .60 1.50
150 Morgan Rielly .50 1.25

2014 Upper Deck 25th Anniversary Silver

*SILVER/250: 1.2X TO 3X BASIC CARDS

2014 Upper Deck 25th Anniversary Autographs

3 Dion Phaneuf/25
4 Bobby Orr/25
14 Hayley Wickenheiser/125 8.00 20.00
38 Adam Oates/25
71 Matt Duchene/25
74 Mark Scheifele/25
75 Chris Kunitz/25
79 Marian Gaborik/25
81 Phil Kessel/25
96 Ryan Nugent-Hopkins/25
99 Wayne Gretzky/25
103 Jari Kurri/25
124 Sean Monahan/25
134 Alex Galchenyuk/25
139 Mikhail Grigorenko/125 10.00 25
146 Seth Jones/25
150 Morgan Rielly/25

2014 Upper Deck 25th Anniversary Promos

UD25WG Wayne Gretzky 4.00 10

2014-15 Upper Deck 25th Anniversary Young Guns

NCDC ISSUED IN NATL CARD DAY CANADA PAC
NCDU ISSUED IN NATL CARD DAY USA PACKS
TFE ISSUED AT 2014 TORONTO FALL EXPO
TSE ISSUED AT 2015 TORONTO SPRING EXPO

UD25AO Adam Oates TSE .75 2
UD25BL Brian Leetch NCDU .75 2
UD25BP Brad Park TSE .60 1
UD25BR Brad Richards TSE .75 2
UD25CC Corey Crawford NCDU 1.00 2
UD25CJ Curtis Joseph TFE .75 2
UD25CO1 Chris Osgood NCDU ERR red.75 2
(photo is Tim Cheveldae)
UD25CO2 Chris Osgood .75 2
NCDU COR white
(wearing white jersey)
UD25DA Daniel Alfredsson TFE .75 2
UD25DG Doug Gilmour TFE 1.00 2
UD25DH Doug Harvey NCDC .75 2
UD25DH Dominik Hasek TFE 1.00 2
UD25GC Guy Carbonneau TFE .75 2
UD25JB Johnny Boychuk NCDU .50 1
UD25JQ Jonathan Quick TFE 1.25 3
UD25JW Joel Ward TSE .50 1
UD25KV Kris Versteeg TFE .60 1
UD25MB Martin Brodeur TFE 1.50 4
UD25MG Mike Gartner TSE .75 2
UD25MS Martin St. Louis TFE .75 2
UD25PF Peter Forsberg NCDU .75 2
UD25PT Pierre Turgeon NCDC .75 2
UD25RF Ron Francis NCDC 1.00 2
UD25TF Theoren Fleury NCDC 1.00 2
UD25TL Trevor Linden TFE .75 2
UD25VD Vincent Damphousse NCDC .60 1

2014-15 Upper Deck 25th Anniversary Young Guns Autographs

FALL ISSUED AT 2014 TORONTO FALL EXPO
SPRING ISSUED AT 2015 TORONTO SPRING EXPO

PSAE Aaron Ekblad/15 Fall
PSAG Alex Galchenyuk/15 Fall
PSAH Adam Henrique/15 Spring
PSAK Alexander Khokhlachev/50 Fall
PSAL Adam Lowry/20 Spring
PSAM Andy Moog/20 Spring
PSAO Adam Oates/20 Fall
PSAP Alex Pietrangelo/20 Spring
PSBB Brent Burns/25 Spring
PSBC Brett Connolly/25 Spring
PSBG Brandon Gormley/50 Fall
PSBK Brandon Kozun/40 Spring
PSBM Brad Marchand/15 Spring
PSBP Brad Park/15 Spring
PSBR1 Bill Ranford/20 Fall
PSBS Brayden Schenn/20 Spring
PSCC Cory Conacher/35 Fall
PSCH Cody Hodgson/20 Fall
PSCK Corban Knight/50 Fall
PSCL Claude Lemieux/20 Fall
PSDC David Clarkson/25 Spring
PSDP1 David Perron/35 Fall
PSDS1 Dave Schultz/15 Fall
PSDS2 Derek Stepan/15 Spring
PSEK1 Erik Karlsson/25 Spring
PSEK2 Evgeny Kuznetsov/35 Fall
PSFF Filip Forsberg/25 Spring
PSGC Guy Carbonneau/20 Fall
PSGL Gabriel Landeskog/15 Spring
PSGM Greg McKegg/50 Fall
PSHE Ales Hemsky/15 Spring
PSJB Jonathan Bernier/35 Fall
PSJC Jared Cowen/25 Fall
PSJG Johnny Gaudreau/50 Fall
PSJH Jonathan Huberdeau/20 Fall
PSJL John LeClair/15 Spring
PSJS1 Justin Schultz/35 Fall
PSJT2 Jacob Trouba/50 Fall
PSKO Kyle Okposo/20 Spring
PSKR Kerby Rychel/30 Spring
PSKY Keith Yandle/25 Spring
PSLE Loui Eriksson/15 Spring
PSLL Louis Leblanc/35 Fall
PSLS Luke Schenn/20 Fall
PSMD1 Marko Dano/40 Spring 15.00 30
PSMG2 Markus Granlund/35 Fall
PSMV Mark Visentin/40 Spring
PSNB Nathan Beaulieu/22 Fall
PSNF Nick Foligno/30 Spring
PSOK Oscar Klefbom/50 Fall
PSPS Paul Stastny/15 Spring
PSRN Ryan Nugent-Hopkins/15 Spring
PSRS Ryan Strome/20 Fall
PSSA Sven Andrighetto/30 Spring
PSSE Jiri Sekac/40 Spring
PSSG1 Sam Gagner/50 Fall
PSSG2 Shayne Gostisbehere/40 Spring 30.00 60
PSSM Sean Monahan/20 Fall
PSTG T.J. Galiardi/25 Fall
PSTM Tyler Myers/20 Fall
PSTR Ty Rattie/50 Fall
PSTT Teuvo Teravainen/35 Fall
PSVR Victor Rask/40 Spring

1993 Upper Deck Adventures Toon World

IT'S WAY COOLER! This new Upper Deck produced definitely builds the success of the 'Comic Ball' ser on. Indeed, nothing creates funnier stories than pai Looney Tune characters with respected professiona athletes. The base set is divided into 9-card subsets 'Act 1' (A1S1-A1S9) through 'Act 10' (A10S1-A10S each of 18 scenes and with each card being double-sided with two different scenes.

COMPLETE SET (91) 10.00 25
COMMON CARD (1-90) .20

1993 Upper Deck Adventures Toon World Bugs Bunny Hare-

BBH2 Wayne Gretzky with Bugs
(comic art)
BBH5 Michael Jordan
Wayne Gretzky
Joe Montana
Reggie Jackson with Bugs
(comic art)

1993 Upper Deck Adventures Toon World Holograms

1 Wayne Gretzky
with Wiley Coyote

ichael Jordan
ayne Gretzky
oe Montana
eggie Jackson
with Bugs and Toonimator

2012 Upper Deck All-Time Greats

ATED PRINT RUN 99 SER. #'d SETS
Bobby Orr 8.00 20.00
Bobby Orr 8.00 20.00
Bobby Orr 8.00 20.00
Bobby Orr 8.00 20.00
Joe Sakic 5.00 12.00
Joe Sakic 5.00 12.00
Joe Sakic 5.00 12.00
Joe Sakic 5.00 12.00
Joe Sakic 5.00 12.00
Wayne Gretzky 12.00 30.00
Wayne Gretzky 12.00 30.00
Wayne Gretzky 12.00 30.00
Wayne Gretzky 12.00 30.00
Wayne Gretzky 12.00 30.00
Mario Lemieux 6.00 15.00
Mario Lemieux 6.00 15.00
Mario Lemieux 6.00 15.00
Mario Lemieux 6.00 15.00
Mario Lemieux 6.00 15.00

2012 Upper Deck All-Time Greats Bronze

RONZE/65: .5X TO 1.2X BASIC CARDS

2012 Upper Deck All-Time Greats Silver

ILVER/35: .6X TO 1.5X BASIC CARDS

2012 Upper Deck All-Time Greats Athletes of the Century Booklet Autographs

ATED PRINT RUN 5-35
BO Bobby Orr/35 75.00 150.00
JS Joe Sakic/25 40.00 80.00
ML Mario Lemieux/20

2012 Upper Deck All-Time Greats Letterman Autographs

INT RUN 7-140
O Bobby Orr/75 75.00 150.00
S Joe Sakic/50 40.00 80.00
L Mario Lemieux/70 50.00 100.00
/G Wayne Gretzky/7

2012 Upper Deck All-Time Greats Shining Moments Autographs

INT RUN 2-30
BO1 Bobby Orr/30 75.00 150.00
BO2 Bobby Orr/30 75.00 150.00
BO3 Bobby Orr/30 75.00 150.00
JS1 Joe Sakic/10
JS2 Joe Sakic/10
JS3 Joe Sakic/10
JS4 Joe Sakic/10
JS5 Joe Sakic/10
ML1 Mario Lemieux/10
ML2 Mario Lemieux/10
ML3 Mario Lemieux/10
ML4 Mario Lemieux/10
ML5 Mario Lemieux/10
WG1 Wayne Gretzky/2
WG2 Wayne Gretzky/2
WG3 Wayne Gretzky/2
WG4 Wayne Gretzky/2

2012 Upper Deck All-Time Greats Signatures

INT RUN 3-70
BO1 Bobby Orr/45 100.00 175.00
BO2 Bobby Orr/45 100.00 175.00
BO3 Bobby Orr/45 100.00 175.00
JS1 Joe Sakic/10 60.00 120.00
JS2 Joe Sakic/10 60.00 120.00
JS3 Joe Sakic/10 60.00 120.00
JS4 Joe Sakic/10 60.00 120.00
JS5 Joe Sakic/10 60.00 120.00
JS6 Joe Sakic/10 60.00 120.00
ML1 Mario Lemieux/15 50.00 100.00
ML2 Mario Lemieux/15 50.00 100.00
ML3 Mario Lemieux/15 50.00 100.00
ML4 Mario Lemieux/15 50.00 100.00
ML5 Mario Lemieux/15 50.00 100.00
WG1 Wayne Gretzky/3
WG2 Wayne Gretzky/3
WG3 Wayne Gretzky/3

2012 Upper Deck All-Time Greats Signatures Silver

ILVER: X TO X BASIC CARDS
INT RUN 2-25

2012 Upper Deck All-Time reats SPx All-Time Dual Forces Autographs

INT RUN 1-25
F2GS Wayne Gretzky
oe Sakic/1
F2JG Michael Jordan
Vayne Gretzky/1
F2LG Mario Lemieux
Vayne Gretzky/1
F2LO M.Lemieux/B.Orr/15
F2OG Bobby Orr
Vayne Gretzky/1
F2SL Joe Sakic
Mario Lemieux/10

2012 Upper Deck All-Time Greats SPx All-Time Forces Autographs

INT RUN 1-30
FBO Bobby Orr/35
FJS Joe Sakic/15
FML Mario Lemieux/15
FWG Wayne Gretzky/1

1999-00 Upper Deck Arena Giveaways

ese promo cards were issued in various NHL cities d included 6 cards per team. Manufacturers Topps, per Deck, and Pacific were all represented with two ds per team set. The cards have the word's morrow's Stars across the top, and are numbered h a team-coded prefix. They can be extremely ficult to find in the secondary market. Only the Upper ck cards are listed below as the other cards can be nd with the manufacturer's listings.
MPLETE SET (56) 15.00 40.00
1 Ladislav Kohn .20 .50
2 Mike Leclerc .20 .50
1 Patrik Stefan .40 1.00
2 Shean Donovan .20 .50
1 Jonathan Girard .40 1.00
BB2 Sergei Samsonov 1.25 3.00
BS1 Maxim Afinogenov .75 2.00
BS2 Cory Sarich .20 .50
CA1 Alex Tanguay 1.25 3.00
CA2 Chris Drury 1.25 3.00
CB1 J-P Dumont .40 1.00
CB2 Bryan McCabe .20 .50
CF1 Robyn Regehr .20 .50
CF2 Derek Morris .40 1.00
CH1 Dave Tanabe .20 .50
CH2 Jeff O'Neill .40 1.00
DR1 Jiri Fischer .40 1.00
DR2 Darryl Laplante .20 .50
DS1 Brenden Morrow .75 2.00
DS2 Jamie Langenbrunner .40 1.00
EO1 Paul Comrie .20 .50
EO2 Boyd Devereaux .20 .50
FP1 Ivan Novoseltsev .40 1.00
FP2 Mark Parrish .40 1.00
LK1 Frantisek Kaberle .20 .50
LK2 Aki Berg .20 .50
MC1 Mike Ribeiro .20 .50
MC2 Arron Asham .20 .50
ND1 Scott Gomez .75 2.00
ND2 Sheldon Souray .20 .50
NI1 Roberto Luongo 2.50 6.00
NI2 Tim Connolly .75 2.00
NP1 David Legwand .40 1.00
NP2 Randy Robitaille .20 .50
NR1 Michael York .40 1.00
NR2 Manny Malhotra .20 .50
OS1 Mike Fisher .40 1.00
OS2 Chris Phillips .20 .50
PC1 Trevor Letowski .75 2.00
PC2 Shane Doan .75 2.00
PF1 Simon Gagne 1.25 3.00
PF2 Daymond Langkow .40 1.00
PP1 Andrew Ference .20 .50
PP2 Michal Rozsival .20 .50
SB1 Jochen Hecht .40 1.00
SB2 Michal Handzus .75 2.00
SS1 Brad Stuart .40 1.00
SS2 Jeff Friesen .40 1.00
TL1 Paul Mara .20 .50
TL2 Andrei Zyuzin .20 .50
TM1 Nikolai Antropov .75 2.00
TM2 Danny Markov .20 .50
VC1 Steve Kariya .75 2.00
VC2 Peter Schaefer .20 .50
WC1 Jeff Halpern .40 1.00
WC2 Alexei Tezikov .20 .50

2006-07 Upper Deck Arena Giveaways

ANA1 Corey Perry 2.50 6.00
ANA2 Teemu Selanne 5.00 12.00
ANA3 Andy McDonald 2.00 5.00
ANA4 Scott Niedermayer 2.50 6.00
ANA5 Jean-Sebastien Giguere 2.50 6.00
ANA6 Chris Pronger 2.00 5.00
ATL1 Marian Hossa 2.00 5.00
ATL2 Slava Kozlov 1.50 4.00
ATL3 Bobby Holik 1.50 4.00
ATL4 Ilya Kovalchuk 2.50 6.00
ATL5 Steve Rucchin 1.50 4.00
ATL6 Kari Lehtonen 2.00 5.00
BOS1 Brad Boyes 1.50 4.00
BOS2 Hannu Toivonen 2.00 5.00
BOS3 Patrice Bergeron 3.00 8.00
BOS4 Zdeno Chara 2.50 6.00
BOS5 Marc Savard 1.50 4.00
BOS6 Glen Murray 2.00 5.00
BUF1 Ryan Miller 2.50 6.00
BUF2 Thomas Vanek 3.00 8.00
BUF3 Daniel Briere 2.50 6.00
BUF4 Jason Pominville 2.50 6.00
BUF5 Maxim Afinogenov 1.50 4.00
BUF6 Chris Drury 2.00 5.00
CAR1 Eric Staal 3.00 8.00
CAR2 Cam Ward 2.50 6.00
CAR3 Justin Williams 2.00 5.00
CAR4 Erik Cole 2.00 5.00
CAR5 Andrew Ladd 2.50 6.00
CAR6 Rod Brind'Amour 2.50 6.00
CGY1 Jarome Iginla 2.50 6.00
CGY2 Dion Phaneuf 2.50 6.00
CGY3 Chuck Kobasew 1.50 4.00
CGY4 Alex Tanguay 1.50 4.00
CGY5 Daymond Langkow 1.50 4.00
CGY6 Miikka Kiprusoff 2.00 5.00
CHI1 Tuomo Ruutu 2.50 6.00
CHI2 Martin Havlat 1.50 4.00
CHI3 Brent Seabrook 2.50 6.00
CHI4 Adrian Aucoin 1.50 4.00
CHI5 Bryan Smolinski 1.50 4.00
CHI6 Nikolai Khabibulin 2.50 6.00
CLB1 Rick Nash 2.50 6.00
CLB2 Pascal LeClaire 2.00 5.00
CLB3 Adam Foote 1.50 4.00
CLB4 Fredrik Modin 1.50 4.00
CLB5 Gilbert Brule 2.00 5.00
CLB6 Sergei Fedorov 4.00 10.00
COL1 Jose Theodore 2.50 6.00
COL2 Wojtek Wolski 2.00 5.00
COL3 John-Michael Liles 1.50 4.00
COL4 Joe Sakic 4.00 10.00
COL5 Marek Svatos 1.50 4.00
COL6 Milan Hejduk 2.00 5.00
DAL1 Brenden Morrow 2.00 5.00
DAL1 Brenden Morrow 2.00 5.00
DAL2 Jussi Jokinen 2.00 5.00
DAL2 Jussi Jokinen 2.00 5.00
DAL3 Sergei Zubov 2.00 5.00
DAL3 Sergei Zubov 2.00 5.00
DAL4 Mike Modano 4.00 10.00
DAL4 Mike Modano 4.00 10.00
DAL5 Eric Lindros 4.00 10.00
DAL5 Eric Lindros 4.00 10.00
DAL6 Marty Turco 2.50 6.00
DET1 Kris Draper 1.50 4.00
DET2 Dominik Hasek 3.00 8.00
DET3 Chris Chelios 2.50 6.00
DET4 Henrik Zetterberg 3.00 8.00
DET5 Nicklas Lidstrom 2.50 6.00
DET6 Pavel Datsyuk 3.00 8.00
EDM1 Ales Hemsky 2.00 5.00
FDM2 Fernando Pisani 1.50 4.00
EDM3 Jarret Stoll 2.00 5.00
EDM4 Ryan Smyth 2.00 5.00
EDM5 Joffrey Lupul 2.00 5.00
EDM6 Dwayne Roloson 2.00 5.00
FLA1 Jay Bouwmeester 2.50 6.00
FLA2 Nathan Horton 2.50 6.00
FLA3 Stephen Weiss 1.50 4.00
FLA4 Olli Jokinen 2.50 6.00
FLA5 Ed Belfour 2.50 6.00
FLA6 Todd Bertuzzi 2.50 6.00
LAK1 Alexander Frolov 1.50 4.00
LAK2 Lubomir Visnovsky 1.50 4.00
LAK3 Dustin Brown 2.50 6.00
LAK4 Rob Blake 2.50 6.00
LAK5 Craig Conroy 1.50 4.00
LAK6 Mike Cammalleri 1.50 4.00
MIN1 Marian Gaborik 3.00 8.00
MIN2 Pierre-Marc Bouchard 2.50 6.00
MIN3 Brian Rolston 2.00 5.00
MIN4 Pavol Demitra 3.00 8.00
MIN5 Mark Parrish 1.50 4.00
MIN6 Manny Fernandez 2.00 5.00
NJD1 Martin Brodeur 5.00 12.00
NJD2 Brian Gionta 2.00 5.00
NJD3 Zach Parise 3.00 8.00
NJD4 Brian Rafalski 2.00 5.00
NJD5 Scott Gomez 2.00 5.00
NJD6 Patrik Elias 2.50 6.00
NSH1 Tomas Vokoun 2.00 5.00
NSH2 David Legwand 2.00 5.00
NSH3 Kimmo Timonen 1.50 4.00
NSH4 Paul Kariya 3.00 8.00
NSH5 Jason Arnott 2.00 5.00
NSH6 Steve Sullivan 1.50 4.00
NYI1 Rick DiPietro 2.00 5.00
NYI2 Jeff Tambellini 1.50 4.00
NYI3 Jason Blake 1.50 4.00
NYI4 Trent Hunter 1.50 4.00
NYI5 Alexei Yashin 2.00 5.00
NYI6 Miroslav Satan 2.00 5.00
NYR1 Jaromir Jagr 6.00 15.00
NYR2 Petr Prucha 2.00 5.00
NYR3 Martin Straka 1.50 4.00
NYR4 Henrik Lundqvist 5.00 12.00
NYR5 Michael Nylander 1.50 4.00
NYR6 Brendan Shanahan 3.00 8.00
OTT1 Jason Spezza 2.50 6.00
OTT2 Chris Phillips 1.50 4.00
OTT3 Dany Heatley 2.50 6.00
OTT4 Wade Redden 1.50 4.00
OTT5 Martin Gerber 2.00 5.00
OTT6 Daniel Alfredsson 2.50 6.00
PHI1 Peter Forsberg 3.00 8.00
PHI2 Robert Esche 2.00 5.00
PHI3 Joni Pitkanen 1.50 4.00
PHI4 Simon Gagne 2.50 6.00
PHI5 Antero Niittymaki 2.00 5.00
PHI6 Jeff Carter 2.50 6.00
PHX1 Shane Doan 2.00 5.00
PHX2 Ladislav Nagy 1.50 4.00
PHX3 Ed Jovanovski 2.00 5.00
PHX4 Jeremy Roenick 2.50 6.00
PHX5 Owen Nolan 2.00 5.00
PHX6 Curtis Joseph 2.50 6.00
PIT1 Sidney Crosby 10.00 25.00
PIT2 Colby Armstrong 2.00 5.00
PIT3 Sergei Gonchar 1.50 4.00
PIT4 Ryan Malone 1.50 4.00
PIT5 Mark Recchi 3.00 8.00
PIT6 Marc-Andre Fleury 4.00 10.00
SJS1 Joe Thornton 3.00 8.00
SJS2 Vesa Toskala 2.00 5.00
SJS3 Steve Bernier 1.50 4.00
SJS4 Patrick Marleau 2.50 6.00
SJS5 Evgeni Nabokov 2.00 5.00
SJS6 Jonathan Cheechoo 2.50 6.00
STL1 Keith Tkachuk 2.50 6.00
STL2 Barret Jackman 1.50 4.00
STL3 Lee Stempniak 1.50 4.00
STL4 Manny Legace 2.00 5.00
STL5 Bill Guerin 2.50 6.00
STL6 Doug Weight 2.50 6.00
TBL1 Martin St. Louis 2.50 6.00
TBL2 Vaclav Prospal 1.50 4.00
TBL3 Ruslan Fedotenko 1.50 4.00
TBL4 Vincent Lecavalier 2.00 5.00
TBL5 Marc Denis 2.00 5.00
TBL6 Brad Richards 2.50 6.00
TOR1 Mats Sundin 2.50 6.00
TOR2 Darcy Tucker 2.00 5.00
TOR3 Alexander Steen 2.50 6.00
TOR4 Andrew Raycroft 2.00 5.00
TOR5 Michael Peca 2.00 5.00
TOR6 Bryan McCabe 1.50 4.00
VAN1 Markus Naslund 2.00 5.00
VAN2 Henrik Sedin 2.50 6.00
VAN3 Roberto Luongo 4.00 10.00
VAN4 Brendan Morrison 1.50 4.00
VAN5 Trevor Linden 2.50 6.00
VAN6 Daniel Sedin 2.50 6.00
WSH1 Shaone Morrisonn 1.50 4.00
WSH2 Alexander Semin 2.50 6.00
WSH3 Alexander Ovechkin 10.00 25.00
WSH4 Richard Zednik 1.50 4.00
WSH5 Dainius Zubrus 1.50 4.00
WSH6 Olaf Kolzig 2.50 6.00

2017-18 Upper Deck Arena Giveaway Buffalo Sabres

BUF1 Jason Pominville 1.25 3.00
BUF2 Ryan O'Reilly 1.25 3.00
BUF3 Rasmus RistolainenÂ• 1.25 3.00
BUF4 Justin Bailey 1.25 3.00
BUF5 Sam Reinhart 1.25 3.00
BUF6 Jack Eichel 1.25 3.00

2010-11 Upper Deck Arena Giveaway Pittsburgh Penguins

COMPLETE SET (7) 3.00 8.00
PIT1 Sidney Crosby 2.00 5.00
PIT2 Jordan Staal .50 1.25
PIT3 Maxime Talbot .50 1.25
PIT4 Brooks Orpik .40 1.00
PIT5 Marc-Andre Fleury .75 2.00
PIT6 Kristopher Letang .50 1.25
PIT7 Evgeni Malkin 1.50 4.00

2015-16 Upper Deck Buybacks

*GOLD/24: .6X TO 1.5X BASIC CARD/49
1 Sidney Crosby 12.00 30.00
2 Alexander Ovechkin 12.00 30.00
3 Ryan Miller 3.00 8.00
4 Blake Wheeler 3.00 8.00
5 Nazem Kadri 2.50 6.00
6 Steven Stamkos 6.00 15.00
7 Tuukka Rask 3.00 8.00
8 Ryan Getzlaf 5.00 12.00
9 Jonathan Toews 6.00 15.00
10 Henrik Lundqvist 4.00 10.00
11 Jonathan Drouin 4.00 10.00
12 Taylor Hall 6.00 15.00
13 Jaromir Jagr 8.00 20.00
14 Shea Weber 2.50 6.00
15 Carey Price 8.00 20.00
16 Jonathan Quick 5.00 12.00
17 Evgeni Malkin 10.00 25.00
18 Sam Reinhart 3.00 8.00
19 Henrik Zetterberg 4.00 10.00
20 Zach Parise 3.00 8.00
21 Brock Nelson 2.50 6.00
22 Aaron Ekblad 3.00 8.00
23 Claude Giroux 3.00 8.00
24 Marc-Andre Fleury 5.00 12.00
25 Corey Perry 3.00 8.00
26 Nicklas Backstrom 5.00 12.00
27 Wayne Simmonds 4.00 10.00
28 Nathan MacKinnon 6.00 15.00
29 Tyler Seguin 5.00 12.00
30 Sam Gagner 2.50 6.00
31 Vladimir Tarasenko 5.00 12.00
32 Logan Couture 3.00 8.00
33 Erik Karlsson 6.00 15.00
34 Kyle Turris 2.50 6.00
35 Eric Staal 4.00 10.00
36 Anze Kopitar 5.00 12.00
37 P.K. Subban 4.00 10.00
38 Rick Nash 3.00 8.00
39 Daniel Sedin 3.00 8.00
40 James van Riemsdyk 3.00 8.00
41 Johnny Gaudreau 5.00 12.00
42 Joe Pavelski 3.00 8.00
43 Ryan Nugent-Hopkins 3.00 8.00
44 Max Pacioretty 3.00 8.00
45 Sergei Bobrovsky 3.00 8.00
46 Craig Anderson 3.00 8.00
47 Kevin Fiala RC 3.00 8.00
48 Cory Schneider 2.50 6.00
49 Patrick Kane 5.00 12.00
50 Marian Hossa 2.50 6.00
51 Gustav Nyquist 5.00 12.00
52 Jonathan Bernier 3.00 8.00
53 Mark Giordano 3.00 8.00
54 Patrice Bergeron 4.00 10.00
55 Roberto Luongo 3.00 8.00
56 David Pastrnak 5.00 12.00
57 Ryan Strome 2.50 6.00
58 Alex Galchenyuk 4.00 10.00
59 Filip Forsberg 4.00 10.00
60 Pekka Rinne 4.00 10.00
61 Henrik Sedin 3.00 8.00
62 Nail Yakupov 2.50 6.00
63 Devan Dubnyk 3.00 8.00
64 Evgeny Kuznetsov 4.00 10.00
65 Jake Allen 4.00 10.00
66 Cam Ward 3.00 8.00
67 Frederik Andersen 2.50 6.00
68 Jonathan Huberdeau 3.00 8.00
69 Malcolm Subban RC 8.00 20.00
70 Chris Kreider 3.00 8.00
71 John Tavares 6.00 15.00
72 Tyler Johnson 2.50 6.00
73 Jamie Benn 4.00 10.00
74 Ryan Johansen 4.00 10.00
75 Petr Mrazek 6.00 15.00
76 Sean Monahan 3.00 8.00
77 Corey Crawford 4.00 10.00
78 Patrik Elias 3.00 8.00
79 Zemgus Girgensons 2.50 6.00
80 Duncan Keith 3.00 8.00
81 Jaroslav Halak 2.50 6.00
82 Brian Elliott 2.50 6.00
83 Jacob de la Rose RC 3.00 8.00
84 Radim Vrbata 2.50 6.00
85 Jakub Voracek 3.00 8.00
86 Ondrej Pavelec 3.00 8.00
87 Sam Bennett RC 4.00 10.00
88 Oliver Ekman-Larsson 2.50 6.00
89 Gabriel Landeskog 3.00 8.00
90 Tomas Tatar 2.50 6.00
91 Bobby Clarke 4.00 10.00
92 Wayne Gretzky 20.00 40.00
93 Bobby Orr 8.00 20.00
94 Patrick Roy 8.00 20.00
95 Mario Lemieux 12.00 30.00
96 Doug Gilmour 5.00 12.00
97 Grant Fuhr 4.00 10.00
98 Brett Hull 4.00 10.00
99 Steve Yzerman 8.00 20.00
100 Peter Forsberg 4.00 10.00

2015-16 Upper Deck Buybacks Gold

*GOLD/24: .6X TO 1.5X BASIC CARD/49
11 Jonathan Drouin 6.00 15.00
26 Nicklas Backstrom 8.00 20.00
77 Corey Crawford 6.00 15.00

2015-16 Upper Deck Buybacks Autographs '05-06

RUAO Ovechkin ULT RUJ/17 75.00 150.00
SM2 A.Ovechkin UD SM/25 75.00 150.00

2015-16 Upper Deck Buybacks Autographs '09-10

201 J.Tavares YG UD/91 100.00 175.00

2015-16 Upper Deck Buybacks Autographs '10-11

211B J.Skinner YG UD Gld/25 20.00 40.00
253 R.Getzlaf UD 20th/25 20.00 40.00

2015-16 Upper Deck Buybacks Autographs '11-12

208 Landeskog YG UD Gld/25 30.00 60.00
438 J.Tavares OPC/20 40.00 80.00
465 R.Johansen YG UD/24 60.00 100.00
468 G.Nyquist YG UD Gld/25 30.00 60.00

2015-16 Upper Deck Buybacks Autographs '12-13

60 N.Lidstrom UD/36 15.00 40.00
68 N.Lidstrom ART/18 30.00 60.00
69 N.Lidstrom SPGU/20 15.00 30.00
237 C.Kreider YG UD/20 30.00 60.00
585A C.Kreider OPC/20 20.00 40.00
585B C.Kreider OPC R/20 20.00 40.00
C110 C.Kreider YG UD C/20 30.00 60.00

2015-16 Upper Deck Buybacks Autographs '13-14

35D J.Tavares SPx R/15
202B D.Hamilton YG UD/27 30.00 60.00
202C Hamilton YG UD Gld/25 30.00 60.00
203B A.Galchenyuk YG UD/27 100.00 200.00
203C Galchnyk YG UD Gld/25 100.00 200.00
216A Girgensons YG UD/28 25.00 50.00
216B Girgnsns YG UD Gld/25 25.00 50.00
218A M.Rielly YG UD/44 30.00 60.00
218B M. Rielly YG UD/25 30.00 60.00
222B Hubrdeau YG UD Gld/25 40.00 80.00
228B S.Jones YG UD Gld/25 25.00 50.00
237C J.Trouba YG UD Gld/25 15.00 40.00
242A S.Monahan YG UD/23 75.00 135.00
242B Monahan YG UD Gld/25 75.00 135.00
246A T.Toffoli YG UD/73 40.00 80.00
246B T.Toffoli YG UD Gld/25 50.00 100.00
248A T.Hertl YG UD/35 25.00 50.00
240D T.Hertl YG UD Gld/25 25.00 50.00
451B F.Forsbrg YG UD Gld/25 60.00 120.00
462A F.Andersen YG UD/31 25.00 50.00
462B F.Andersn YG UD Gld/25 25.00 50.00
466A P.Mrazek YG UD/34 40.00 80.00
466B P.Mrazek YG UD Gld/25 50.00 100.00
474A M.Granlund YG UD/64 15.00 40.00
474B Granlund YG UD Gld/25 25.00 50.00
476A T.Jurco YG UD/26 15.00 40.00
476B T.Jurco YG UD Gld/25 15.00 40.00
477B Gallagher YG UD Gld/25 75.00 125.00
482B R.Strome YG UD/18 40.00 80.00
482C R.Strome YG UD Gld/25 25.00 50.00
483A N.Kucherov YG UD/86 40.00 80.00
483B Kucherov YG UD Gld/25 40.00 80.00
485A M.Jones YG UD/31 25.00 50.00
485B M.Jones YG UD Gld/25 25.00 50.00
486A J.Gibson YG UD/36 30.00 60.00
486B J.Gibson YG UD Gld/25 30.00 60.00
498A T.Pearson YG UD/70 15.00 40.00
498B Pearson YG UD Gld/25 25.00 50.00

2015-16 Upper Deck Buybacks Autographs '14-15

206 S.Reinhart YG UD/23 40.00 80.00
206G S. Reinhart YG UD Gld/25 30.00 60.00
211G Gaudreau YG UD Gld/25 125.00 200.00
214 Teravainen YG UD/86 50.00 100.00
214G Teravainen YG UD Gld/25 60.00 120.00
223 L.Draisaitl YG UD/29 30.00 60.00
223G Draisaitl YG UD Gld/25 30.00 60.00
229 J.Sekac YG UD/26 20.00 40.00
229G J. Sekac YG UD Gld/25 20.00 40.00
236A A.Duclair YG UD/63 25.00 50.00
236B A. Duclair YG UD Gld/25 30.00 60.00
241G J. Lehtera YG UD Gld/25 20.00 40.00
457 D. Nurse YG UD/25 30.00 60.00
457G D. Nurse YG UD Gld/25 30.00 60.00
464 Gostisbehere YG UD/53 40.00 80.00
464G Gostisbehere YG UD Gld/25 40.00 80.00
467 Burakovsky YG UD/65 20.00 40.00
467G Burakovsky YG UD Gld/25 20.00 40.00
475 D. Poulliot YG UD/51 20.00 40.00
475G D. Poulliot YG UD Gld/25 25.00 50.00
478 Vasilevskiy YG UD/88 25.00 50.00
478G Vasilevskiy YG UD Gld/25 25.00 50.00
490G K. Hayes YG UD Gld/25 20.00 40.00
494 B. Horvat YG UD/53 60.00 100.00
494G B. Horvat YG UD Gld/25 60.00 100.00
498 S. Darling YG UD/33 30.00 60.00
498G S. Darling YG UD Gld/25 30.00 60.00
NHCD16 W.Gretzky NHCD/22 125.00 200.00

2017-18 Upper Deck Buyback Autographs

201 Connor McDavid/97 2750.00 3500.00
('15-16 UD YG)

2008-09 Upper Deck Champ's

This set was released on March 26, 2009. The base set consists of 200 cards.
COMPLETE SET (200) 75.00 150.00
COMP.SET w/o SPs 12.00 30.00
1 Ales Hemsky .25 .60
2 Alex Kovalev .25 .60
3 Alex Tanguay .20 .50
4 Alexander Frolov .20 .50
5 Alexander Ovechkin 1.25 3.00
6 Anze Kopitar .50 1.25
7 Bobby Hull .50 1.25
8 Bobby Orr 1.00 2.50
9 Brad Boyes .20 .50
10 Brad Richards .30 .75
11 Brenden Morrow .25 .60
12 Brian Campbell .25 .60
13 Brian Leetch .30 .75
14 Cam Ward .30 .75
15 Carey Price 1.25 3.00
16 Chris Drury .25 .60
17 Chris Osgood .30 .75
18 Chris Pronger .25 .60
19 Corey Perry .30 .75
20 Cristobal Huet .25 .60
21 Dan Ellis .20 .50
22 Daniel Alfredsson .30 .75
23 Daniel Briere .30 .75
24 Daniel Sedin .30 .75
25 Dany Heatley .30 .75
26 Derek Roy .20 .50
27 Dion Phaneuf .30 .75
28 Eric Staal .40 1.00
29 Evgeni Malkin 1.00 2.50
30 Evgeni Nabokov .25 .60
31 Gordie Howe .75 2.00
32 Guy Lafleur .40 1.00
33 Henrik Lundqvist .40 1.00
34 Henrik Sedin .30 .75
35 Henrik Zetterberg .40 1.00
36 Ilya Kovalchuk .30 .75
37 Jari Kurri .30 .75
38 Jarome Iginla .30 .75
39 Jason Arnott .25 .60
40 Jason Pominville .30 .75
41 Jason Spezza .30 .75
42 Jean-Sebastien Giguere .30 .75
43 Joe Sakic .50 1.25
44 Joe Thornton .40 1.00
45 Johan Franzen .30 .75
46 Jonathan Toews .75 2.00
47 Jordan Staal .30 .75
48 Kari Lehtonen .25 .60
49 Marc Savard .20 .50
50 Marc-Andre Fleury .50 1.25
51 Marian Gaborik .40 1.00
52 Marian Hossa .25 .60
53 Mario Lemieux 1.00 2.50
54 Mark Messier .40 1.00
55 Martin Brodeur .60 1.50
56 Martin St. Louis .30 .75
57 Marty Turco .30 .75
58 Mats Sundin .30 .75
59 Miikka Kiprusoff .25 .60
60 Mike Bossy .30 .75
61 Mike Modano .50 1.25
62 Mike Ribeiro .25 .60
63 Mike Richards .30 .75
64 Nathan Horton .25 .60
65 Nicklas Backstrom .50 1.25
66 Nicklas Lidstrom .30 .75
67 Niklas Backstrom .30 .75
68 Olli Jokinen .25 .60
69 Pascal Leclaire .25 .60
70 Patrick Kane .60 1.50
71 Patrick Roy .75 2.00
72 Patrick Sharp .30 .75
73 Patrik Elias .30 .75
74 Paul Kariya .40 1.00
75 Paul Stastny .30 .75
76 Pavel Datsyuk .40 1.00
77 Ryan Smyth .25 .60
78 Peter Mueller .25 .60
79 Phil Esposito .50 1.25
80 Rick DiPietro .25 .60
81 Rick Nash .30 .75
82 Roberto Luongo .40 1.00
83 Rod Brind'Amour .30 .75
84 Ron Hextall .50 1.25
85 Ryan Getzlaf .50 1.25
86 Ryan Miller .30 .75
87 Saku Koivu .30 .75
88 Scott Niedermayer .30 .75
89 Shane Doan .25 .60
90 Shawn Horcoff .20 .50
91 Sidney Crosby 1.25 3.00
92 Simon Gagne .30 .75
93 Thomas Vanek .30 .75
94 Tomas Kaberle .20 .50
95 Tomas Vokoun .25 .60
96 Tony Esposito .30 .75
97 Vesa Toskala .25 .60
98 Vincent Lecavalier .25 .60
99 Wayne Gretzky 1.50 4.00
100 Zach Parise .30 .75
101 Ilya Zubov RC 1.50 4.00
102 Ty Wishart RC 1.50 4.00
103 John Mitchell RC 1.50 4.00
104 Boris Valabik RC 2.00 5.00
105 Kyle Turris RC 3.00 8.00
106 Danny Taylor RC 1.50 4.00
107 Brendan Mikkelson RC 1.25 3.00
108 Justin Pogge RC 2.00 5.00
109 Janne Pesonen RC 1.50 4.00
110 Tom Sestito RC 2.00 5.00
111 Mattias Ritola RC 1.50 4.00
112 Kenndal McArdle RC 1.50 4.00
113 Teddy Purcell RC 2.50 6.00
114 Cory Schneider RC 5.00 12.00
115 Adam Pineault RC 1.50 4.00
116 Pascal Pelletier RC 1.25 3.00
117 Theo Peckham RC 2.00 5.00
118 Kyle Okposo RC 2.00 5.00
119 Michal Repik RC 2.00 5.00
120 Andrew Murray RC 1.50 4.00
121 Trevor Smith RC 1.50 4.00
122 Brett Skinner RC 1.50 4.00
123 Patrick Davis RC 1.50 4.00
124 Adam Pardy RC 1.50 4.00
125 Shawn Matthias RC 2.00 5.00
126 Steve Mason RC 3.00 8.00
127 Paul Bissonnette RC 2.50 6.00
128 Sami Lepisto RC 1.50 4.00
129 Brian Lee RC 1.50 4.00
130 Tim Kennedy RC 2.00 5.00
131 Dan LaCosta RC 2.00 5.00
132 Joe Jensen RC 2.00 5.00
133 Anssi Salmela RC 2.00 5.00
134 Niklas Hjalmarsson RC 3.00 8.00
135 Brad Staubitz RC 1.50 4.00
136 Max Pacioretty RC 8.00 20.00
137 Darren Helm RC 2.00 5.00
138 Brett Sutter RC 2.00 5.00
139 Jonas Frogren RC 1.25 3.00
140 Alex Goligoski RC 2.50 6.00
141 Claude Giroux RC 4.00 10.00
142 Simeon Varlamov RC 4.00 10.00
143 Derek Joslin RC 1.50 4.00
144 Mark Fistric RC 1.50 4.00
145 Karl Alzner RC 1.25 3.00
146 Erik Ersberg RC 1.50 4.00
147 Jonathan Ericsson RC 2.00 5.00
148 Andrew Ebbett RC 1.25 3.00
149 Robbie Earl RC 1.25 3.00
150 Tyler Sloan RC 2.50 6.00
151 Matt D'Agostini RC 1.50 4.00
152 Ben Maxwell RC 2.00 5.00
153 Trevor Lewis RC 2.00 5.00
154 Tom Cavanagh RC 1.50 4.00
155 Mike Brown RC 2.50 6.00
156 David Brine RC 1.25 3.00
157 Derick Brassard RC 1.50 4.00
158 Brian Boyle RC 1.50 4.00
159 Darryl Boyce RC 1.50 4.00
160 Justin Abdelkader RC 3.00 8.00
161 Wayne Simmonds RC 3.00 8.00
162 Zach Bogosian RC 2.00 5.00
163 Nathan Oystrick RC 2.00 5.00
164 Blake Wheeler RC 5.00 12.00
165 Zach Boychuk RC 2.00 5.00
166 Brandon Sutter RC 2.00 5.00
167 Nikita Filatov RC 2.00 5.00
168 Jakub Voracek RC 4.00 10.00
169 James Neal RC 4.00 10.00
170 Michael Frolik RC 2.00 5.00
171 Oscar Moller RC 1.50 4.00
172 Colton Gillies RC 1.50 4.00
173 Patric Hornqvist RC 2.00 5.00
174 Ryan Jones RC 2.00 5.00
175 Matthew Halischuk RC 1.25 3.00
176 Petr Vrana RC 1.25 3.00
177 Andreas Nodl RC 1.25 3.00
178 Luca Sbisa RC 1.25 3.00
179 Ben Bishop RC 3.00 8.00
180 T.J. Oshie RC 4.00 10.00
181 Patrik Berglund RC 1.50 4.00
182 Chris Porter RC 2.00 5.00
183 Jamie McGinn RC 2.00 5.00
184 Vladimir Mihalik RC 1.25 3.00
185 Luke Schenn RC 2.50 6.00
186 Nikolai Kulemin RC 2.00 5.00
187 Dwight Helminen RC 2.00 5.00
188 Patrick Dwyer RC 2.00 5.00
189 Alex Pietrangelo RC 2.50 6.00
190 Derek Dorsett RC 2.50 6.00
191 Steve MacIntyre RC 2.00 5.00
192 Darroll Powe RC 2.00 5.00
193 Chris Stewart RC 2.00 5.00
194 Dustin Jeffrey RC 2.00 5.00
195 Drew Doughty RC 5.00 12.00
196 Kevin Porter RC 1.50 4.00
197 Viktor Tikhonov RC 1.50 4.00
198 Mikkel Boedker RC 2.50 6.00
199 Fabian Brunnstrom RC 1.50 4.00
200 Steven Stamkos RC 10.00 25.00

2008-09 Upper Deck Champ's Fossils and Artifacts

FAAT Aterian Scraper 75.00 150.00
FAAU Auroch Femur 25.00 60.00
FANE Neolithic Stone Tools 200.00 300.00
FANM Neanderthal Mousterian Flint Knife
FAPT Pterosaur Tooth
FAST Spinosaurus Teeth
FATT Tyrannosaurus Rex Tooth
FAWM Woolly Mammoth Femur 25.00 60.00
FAWR Woolly Rhino Humerus 50.00 100.00

2008-09 Upper Deck Champ's Hall of Legends Sports Memorabilia

HOLAN Glenn Anderson 10.00 25.00
HOLBT Bryan Trottier 12.00 30.00
HOLCN Cam Neely 10.00 25.00
HOLDH Dale Hawerchuk 12.00 30.00
HOLDS Darryl Sittler 12.00 30.00
HOLFM Frank Mahovlich 10.00 25.00
HOLGF Grant Fuhr 15.00 40.00
HOLGH Gordie Howe 25.00 60.00
HOLGP Gilbert Perreault 10.00 25.00
HOLHK Dominik Hasek 12.00 30.00
HOLJB Johnny Bucyk 10.00 25.00
HOLJI Jarome Iginla 10.00 25.00
HOLJK Jari Kurri 10.00 25.00
HOLLY Larry Robinson 10.00 25.00
HOLML Mario Lemieux 30.00 80.00
HOLMM Mark Messier 12.00 30.00
HOLMW Mike Weir 15.00 40.00
HOLPE Phil Esposito 15.00 40.00
HOLPR Patrick Roy 25.00 60.00
HOLRB Ray Bourque 15.00 40.00
HOLTE Tony Esposito 10.00 25.00
HOLTW Tiger Woods 150.00 300.00
HOLWG Wayne Gretzky 50.00 125.00

2008-09 Upper Deck Champ's Mini

COMP.BASE w/o SPs (200) 15.00 40.00
NATURAL HISTORY STATED ODDS 1:3
*BLUE BACK: 3X TO 8X BASIC CARDS
*BROWN BACK: 1X TO 2.5X BASIC CARDS
*PURPLE BACK: 5X TO 12X BASIC CARDS
*RED BACK: 3X TO 8X BASIC CARDS
C1 Ales Hemsky .50 1.25
C2 Alex Kovalev .50 1.25
C3 Alex Tanguay .40 1.00
C4 Alexander Frolov .40 1.00
C5 Alexander Ovechkin 2.50 6.00
C6 Alexander Semin .60 1.50
C7 Andrei Kostitsyn .50 1.25
C8 Andrew Cogliano .50 1.25
C9 Anze Kopitar 1.00 2.50
C10 Bill Guerin .60 1.50
C11 Brad Boyes .40 1.00
C12 Brad Richards .60 1.50
C13 Brendan Morrison .40 1.00
C14 Aaron Voros .40 1.00
C15 Brenden Morrow .50 1.25
C16 Brian Campbell .50 1.25
C17 Brian Gionta .50 1.25
C18 Brian Rolston .50 1.25
C19 Cam Ward .60 1.50
C20 Carey Price 2.50 6.00
C21 Chris Drury .50 1.25
C22 Chris Higgins .40 1.00
C23 Chris Kunitz .60 1.50
C24 Chris Osgood .60 1.50
C25 Chris Pronger .50 1.25
C26 Colby Armstrong .40 1.00
C27 Corey Perry .60 1.50
C28 Cristobal Huet .50 1.25
C29 Dan Boyle .50 1.25
C30 Dan Cleary .50 1.25
C31 Dan Ellis .40 1.00
C32 Daniel Alfredsson .60 1.50
C33 Daniel Briere .60 1.50
C34 Daniel Carcillo .40 1.00
C35 Daniel Sedin .60 1.50
C36 Dany Heatley .60 1.50
C37 Darcy Tucker .50 1.25
C38 David Legwand .50 1.25
C39 Daymond Langkow .40 1.00
C40 Derek Roy .40 1.00
C41 Dion Phaneuf .60 1.50
C42 Doug Weight .60 1.50
C43 Drew Stafford .50 1.25
C44 Duncan Keith .60 1.50
C45 Dustin Brown .60 1.50
C46 Dustin Penner .50 1.25
C47 Dwayne Roloson .50 1.25
C48 Ed Jovanovski .50 1.25
C49 Eric Staal .75 2.00
C50 Erik Cole .50 1.25
C51 Erik Johnson .50 1.25
C52 Evgeni Malkin 2.00 5.00
C53 Evgeni Nabokov .50 1.25
C54 George Parros .40 1.00
C55 Sheldon Souray .40 1.00
C56 David Krejci .60 1.50
C57 Guillaume Latendresse .40 1.00
C58 Henrik Lundqvist .75 2.00
C59 Henrik Sedin .60 1.50
C60 Henrik Zetterberg .75 2.00
C61 Ilya Bryzgalov .50 1.25
C62 Ilya Kovalchuk .60 1.50
C63 J.P. Dumont .40 1.00
C64 Jack Johnson .40 1.00
C65 Jarome Iginla .60 1.50
C66 Jarret Stoll .50 1.25
C67 Jason Arnott .50 1.25
C68 Jason LaBarbera .50 1.25
C69 Jason Pominville .60 1.50
C70 Jason Spezza .60 1.50
C71 Jay Bouwmeester .60 1.50
C72 Jean-Sebastien Giguere .60 1.50
C73 Jeff Carter .60 1.50
C74 Jere Lehtinen .40 1.00
C75 Joe Sakic 1.00 2.50
C76 Joe Thornton .75 2.00
C77 Johan Franzen .60 1.50
C78 Johan Hedberg .50 1.25
C79 Loui Eriksson .60 1.50
C80 Jonathan Cheechoo .60 1.50
C81 Jonathan Toews 1.50 4.00
C82 Jordan Staal .60 1.50
C83 Josh Harding .60 1.50
C84 Jussi Jokinen .40 1.00
C85 Justin Williams .50 1.25
C86 Kari Lehtonen .50 1.25
C87 Keith Tkachuk .60 1.50
C88 Kristian Huselius .40 1.00
C89 Lee Stempniak .40 1.00
C90 Manny Legace .60 1.50
C91 Marc Savard .40 1.00
C92 Marc Staal .60 1.50
C93 Marc-Andre Fleury 1.00 2.50
C94 Marek Zidlicky .40 1.00
C95 Marian Gaborik .75 2.00
C96 Marian Hossa .50 1.25
C97 Markus Naslund .50 1.25
C98 Martin Biron .50 1.25
C99 Martin Brodeur 1.25 3.00
C100 Martin Erat .40 1.00
C101 Martin Gerber .50 1.25
C102 Martin Hanzal .50 1.25
C103 Martin Havlat .60 1.50
C104 Martin St. Louis .60 1.50
C105 Marty Turco .60 1.50
C106 Mats Sundin .60 1.50
C107 Matt Stajan .50 1.25
C108 Matthew Lombardi .40 1.00
C109 Michael Peca .50 1.25
C110 Michael Ryder .40 1.00
C111 Michal Rozsival .40 1.00
C112 Miikka Kiprusoff .50 1.25
C113 Mike Cammalleri .50 1.25
C114 Mike Comrie .50 1.25
C115 Mike Knuble .40 1.00
C116 Mike Modano 1.00 2.50
C117 Mike Ribeiro .50 1.25
C118 Mike Richards .60 1.50
C119 Mike Smith .60 1.50
C120 Mikko Koivu .50 1.25
C121 Milan Hejduk .50 1.25
C122 Milan Lucic 1.00 2.50
C123 Milan Michalek .40 1.00
C124 Miroslav Satan .60 1.50
C125 Nathan Horton .50 1.25

C126 Nicklas Backstrom 1.00 2.50
C127 Nicklas Lidstrom .60 1.50
C128 Niklas Backstrom .60 1.50
C129 Nik Antropov .50 1.25
C130 Nikolai Khabibulin .60 1.50
C131 Nikolai Zherdev .40 1.00
C132 Olli Jokinen .50 1.25
C133 Pascal Leclaire .50 1.25
C134 Patrice Bergeron .75 2.00
C135 Patrick Kane 1.25 3.00
C136 Patrick Marleau .60 1.50
C137 Patrick O'Sullivan .50 1.25
C138 Patrick Sharp .60 1.50
C139 Patrik Elias .60 1.50
C140 Paul Kariya .75 2.00
C141 Paul Stastny .60 1.50
C142 Pavel Datsyuk .75 2.00
C143 Peter Budaj .50 1.25
C144 John-Michael Liles .40 1.00
C145 Peter Mueller .50 1.25
C146 Phil Kessel .75 2.00
C147 Pierre-Marc Bouchard .60 1.50
C148 R.J. Umberger .40 1.00
C149 Mark Recchi .75 2.00
C150 Ray Whitney .50 1.25
C151 Rick DiPietro .50 1.25
C152 Rick Nash .60 1.50
C153 Robert Lang .40 1.00
C154 Roberto Luongo .75 2.00
C155 Rod Brind`Amour .60 1.50
C156 Ryan Getzlaf 1.00 2.50
C157 Ryan Kesler .75 2.00
C158 Ryan Malone .40 1.00
C159 Ryan Miller .60 1.50
C160 Ryan Smyth .50 1.25
C161 Ryan Suter .50 1.25
C162 Saku Koivu .60 1.50
C163 Sam Gagner .50 1.25
C164 Scott Gomez .50 1.25
C165 Scott Niedermayer .60 1.50
C166 Sergei Fedorov 1.00 2.50
C167 Sergei Zubov .50 1.25
C168 Shane Doan .50 1.25
C169 Shawn Horcoff .40 1.00
C170 Shea Weber .50 1.25
C171 Sidney Crosby 2.50 6.00
C172 Simon Gagne .60 1.50
C173 Slava Kozlov .40 1.00
C174 Steve Bernier .40 1.00
C175 Teemu Selanne 1.25 3.00
C176 Thomas Vanek .60 1.50
C177 Tim Thomas .60 1.50
C178 Tobias Enstrom .40 1.00
C179 Todd White .40 1.00
C180 Tomas Holmstrom .50 1.25
C181 Tomas Kaberle .40 1.00
C182 Tomas Vokoun .50 1.25
C183 Trent Hunter .40 1.00
C184 Ty Conklin .50 1.25
C185 Vaclav Prospal .40 1.00
C186 Valtteri Filppula .60 1.50
C187 Vesa Toskala .50 1.25
C188 Vincent Lecavalier .50 1.25
C189 Wade Redden .40 1.00
C190 Wojtek Wolski .50 1.25
C191 Zach Parise .60 1.50
C192 Zdeno Chara .60 1.50
C193 Adam Pardy .50 1.25
C194 Adam Pineault .50 1.25
C195 Simeon Varlamov 1.25 3.00
C196 Alex Goligoski .75 2.00
C197 Alex Pietrangelo .75 2.00
C198 Andreas Nodl .40 1.00
C199 Andrew Ebbett .40 1.00
C200 Andrew Murray .50 1.25
C201 Anssi Salmela 2.50 6.00
C202 Max Pacioretty 10.00 25.00
C203 Ben Bishop 4.00 10.00
C204 Blake Wheeler 6.00 15.00
C205 Boris Valabik 2.50 6.00
C206 Brad Staubitz 2.00 5.00
C207 Tim Kennedy 2.50 6.00
C208 Brandon Sutter 2.50 6.00
C209 Brett Skinner 2.00 5.00
C210 Brian Boyle 2.00 5.00
C211 Brian Lee 2.00 5.00
C212 Chris Porter 2.50 6.00
C213 Claude Giroux 5.00 12.00
C214 Colton Gillies 2.00 5.00
C215 Kenndal McArdle 2.00 5.00
C216 Darren Helm 2.50 6.00
C217 Cory Schneider 6.00 15.00
C218 David Brine 1.50 4.00
C219 Derek Dorsett 3.00 8.00
C220 Derick Brassard 2.00 5.00
C221 Drew Doughty 6.00 15.00
C222 Dwight Helminen 2.50 6.00
C223 Erik Ersberg 2.00 5.00
C224 Fabian Brunnstrom 2.00 5.00
C225 Ilya Zubov 2.00 5.00
C226 Jakub Voracek 5.00 12.00
C227 James Neal 5.00 12.00
C228 Jamie McGinn 2.50 6.00
C229 Janne Pesonen 2.00 5.00
C230 Ty Wishart 2.00 5.00
C231 Joe Jensen 2.50 6.00
C232 John Mitchell 2.00 5.00
C233 Justin Pogge 2.50 6.00
C234 Jonas Frogren 1.50 4.00
C235 Jonathan Ericsson 2.50 6.00
C236 Trevor Lewis 2.50 6.00
C237 Brendan Mikkelson 1.50 4.00
C238 Justin Abdelkader 4.00 10.00
C239 Kevin Porter 2.00 5.00
C240 Brett Sutter 2.50 6.00
C241 Kyle Okposo 2.50 6.00
C242 Kyle Turris 4.00 10.00
C243 Luca Sbisa 1.50 4.00
C244 Luke Schenn 3.00 8.00
C245 Mark Fistric 2.00 5.00
C246 Matt D'Agostini 2.00 5.00
C247 Matthew Halischuk 1.50 4.00
C248 Mattias Ritola 2.00 5.00
C249 Michael Frolik 2.50 6.00
C250 Mike Brown 3.00 8.00
C251 Mikkel Boedker 3.00 8.00
C252 Trevor Smith 2.00 5.00
C253 Josh Bailey 3.00 8.00
C254 Nathan Oystrick 2.50 6.00
C255 Nikita Filatov 2.50 6.00
C256 Niklas Hjalmarsson 4.00 10.00
C257 Nikolai Kulemin 2.50 6.00
C258 Oscar Moller 2.00 5.00
C259 Pascal Pelletier 1.50 4.00
C260 Patric Hornqvist 2.50 6.00
C261 Patrick Davis 2.00 5.00
C262 Patrick Dwyer 2.50 6.00
C263 Patrik Berglund 2.00 5.00
C264 Chris Stewart 2.50 6.00
C265 Petr Vrana 1.50 4.00
C266 Dustin Jeffrey 2.50 6.00
C267 Robbie Earl 1.50 4.00
C268 Ryan Jones 2.50 6.00
C269 Karl Alzner 1.50 4.00
C270 Sami Lepisto 2.00 5.00
C271 Shawn Matthias 2.50 6.00
C272 Steve MacIntyre 2.50 6.00
C273 Steve Mason 4.00 10.00
C274 Steven Stamkos 15.00 40.00
C275 T.J. Oshie 5.00 12.00
C276 Teddy Purcell 3.00 8.00
C277 Theo Peckham 2.50 6.00
C278 Michal Repik 2.50 6.00
C279 Ben Maxwell 2.50 6.00
C280 Tom Sestito 2.50 6.00
C281 Tyler Plante 2.00 5.00
C282 Tyler Sloan 3.00 8.00
C283 Viktor Tikhonov 2.00 5.00
C284 Vladimir Mihalik 1.50 4.00
C285 Wayne Simmonds 4.00 10.00
C286 Zach Bogosian 2.50 6.00
C287 Zach Boychuk 2.50 6.00
C288 Derek Joslin 2.00 5.00
C289 Great White Shark 1.25 3.00
C290 Tiger Shark 1.25 3.00
C291 Acrocanthosaurus 1.25 3.00
C292 African Elephant 1.25 3.00
C293 African Leopard 1.25 3.00
C294 African Lion 1.25 3.00
C295 African Wild Dog 1.25 3.00
C296 Hammerhead Shark 1.25 3.00
C297 Albertosaurus 1.25 3.00
C298 Alectrosaurus 1.25 3.00
C299 Allosaurus 1.25 3.00
C300 Amargasaurus 1.25 3.00
C301 American Alligator 1.25 3.00
C302 American Lion 1.25 3.00
C303 Bull Shark 1.25 3.00
C304 Shortfin Mako Shark 1.25 3.00
C305 Anchiceratops 1.25 3.00
C306 Ankylosaur 1.25 3.00
C307 Sand Tiger Shark 1.25 3.00
C308 Apatosaurus 1.25 3.00
C309 Archelon 1.25 3.00
C310 Archaeopteryx 1.25 3.00
C311 Arctic fox 1.25 3.00
C312 Auroch 1.25 3.00
C313 Baiji Dolphin 1.25 3.00
C314 Bald Eagle 1.25 3.00
C315 Baryonyx 1.25 3.00
C316 Oceanic Whitetip Shark 1.25 3.00
C317 Bird of Paradise 1.25 3.00
C318 Black Rhino 1.25 3.00
C319 Blue Whale 1.25 3.00
C320 Bowhead Whale 1.25 3.00
C321 Brachiosaurus 1.25 3.00
C322 Brontops 1.25 3.00
C323 Brontosaurus 1.25 3.00
C324 Brown Bear 1.25 3.00
C325 Brown Pelican 1.25 3.00
C326 Burgess Shale 1.25 3.00
C327 California Condor 1.25 3.00
C328 Cambropallas Trilobite 1.25 3.00
C329 Cape Buffalo 1.25 3.00
C330 Carcharodontosaurus 1.25 3.00
C331 Carrier Pigeon 1.25 3.00
C332 Cave Bear 1.25 3.00
C333 Cheetah 1.25 3.00
C334 Chimpanzee 1.25 3.00
C335 Chinese Alligator 1.25 3.00
C336 Chinook Salmon 1.25 3.00
C337 Blue Shark 1.25 3.00
C338 Clouded Leopard 1.25 3.00
C339 Piranha 1.25 3.00
C340 Compsognathus 1.25 3.00
C341 Corythosaurus 1.25 3.00
C342 Barracuda 1.25 3.00
C343 Cro-Magnon Man 1.25 3.00
C344 Moray Eel 1.25 3.00
C345 Electric Eel 1.25 3.00
C346 Deinonychus 1.25 3.00
C347 Diatryma 1.25 3.00
C348 Dilong 1.25 3.00
C349 Dimetrodon 1.25 3.00
C350 Dimorphodon 1.25 3.00
C351 Australopithecus robustus 1.25 3.00
C352 Diplodocus 1.25 3.00
C353 Dire Wolf 1.25 3.00
C354 Dodo 1.25 3.00
C355 Dromaeosaurus 1.25 3.00
C356 Dunkleostreus 1.25 3.00
C357 Edmontosaurus 1.25 3.00
C358 Einiosaurus 1.25 3.00
C359 Elasmosaurus 1.25 3.00
C360 Emperor Penguin 1.25 3.00
C361 Euoplocephalus 1.25 3.00
C362 Fin Whale 1.25 3.00
C363 Fox 1.25 3.00
C364 Galapagos Hawk 1.25 3.00
C365 Galapagos Penguin 1.25 3.00
C366 Galapagos Tortoise 1.25 3.00
C367 Black Widow 1.25 3.00
C368 Giant Panda 1.25 3.00
C369 Giganotosaurus 1.25 3.00
C370 Portuguese Man O'War 1.25 3.00
C371 Glyptodon 1.25 3.00
C372 Gorgosaurus 1.25 3.00
C373 Gray Wolf 1.25 3.00
C374 Ground Sloth 1.25 3.00
C375 Hesperornis 1.25 3.00
C376 Hippopotamus 1.25 3.00
C377 Hominids 1.25 3.00
C378 Hoplophoncus 1.25 3.00
C379 Humpback Whale 1.25 3.00
C380 Hyaenodon 1.25 3.00
C381 Ichthyosaurus 1.25 3.00
C382 Coelacanth 1.25 3.00
C383 Iguanodon 1.25 3.00
C384 Jaguar 1.25 3.00
C385 Jobaria 1.25 3.00
C386 Kakapo 1.25 3.00
C387 Killer Whale 1.25 3.00
C388 Golden-Mantled Tree Kangaroo 1.25 3.00
C389 Komodo Dragon 1.25 3.00
C390 Lambeosaurus 1.25 3.00
C391 Lannacus Trilobite 1.25 3.00
C392 Box Jellyfish 1.25 3.00
C393 Leopard Seal 1.25 3.00
C394 Leptoceratops 1.25 3.00
C395 Lesothosaurus 1.25 3.00
C396 Maiasaura 1.25 3.00
C397 Mastodon 1.25 3.00
C398 Marbled Cone Snail 1.25 3.00
C399 Megalodon 1.25 3.00
C400 Megalosaurus 1.25 3.00
C401 Megatherium 1.25 3.00
C402 Australopithecus africanus 1.25 3.00
C403 Blue Ringed Octopus 1.25 3.00
C404 Microraptor 1.25 3.00
C405 Death Stalker Scorpion 1.25 3.00
C406 Moa 1.25 3.00
C407 Stonefish 1.25 3.00
C408 Moose 1.25 3.00
C409 Mountain Lion 1.25 3.00
C410 Muttaburrasaurus 1.25 3.00
C411 Sydney Funnel Web Spider 1.25 3.00
C412 Neanderthal Man 1.25 3.00
C413 Inland Taipan 1.25 3.00
C414 Ocelot 1.25 3.00
C415 Orangutan 1.25 3.00
C416 King Cobra 1.25 3.00
C417 Ornithomimus 1.25 3.00
C418 Ouranosaurus 1.25 3.00
C419 Oviraptor 1.25 3.00
C420 Brazilian Wandering Spider 1.25 3.00
C421 Panther 1.25 3.00
C422 Paradoxides trilobite 1.25 3.00
C423 Parasaurolophus 1.25 3.00
C424 Puffer Fish 1.25 3.00
C425 Homo habilis 1.25 3.00
C426 Plateosaurus 1.25 3.00
C427 Plesiosaurus 1.25 3.00
C428 Polacanthus 1.25 3.00
C429 Polar Bear 1.25 3.00
C430 Prairie Dog 1.25 3.00
C431 Pterodactyl 1.25 3.00
C432 Pterosaur 1.25 3.00
C433 Quetzalcoatlus 1.25 3.00
C434 Red Deer 1.25 3.00
C435 Red Wolf 1.25 3.00
C436 Rhoetosaurus 1.25 3.00
C437 Right Whale 1.25 3.00
C438 Royal Bengal Tiger 1.25 3.00
C439 Australopithecus afarensis 1.25 3.00
C440 Saber-Toothed Cat 1.25 3.00
C441 Salt Water Crocodile 1.25 3.00
C442 Saltasaurus 1.25 3.00
C443 Sarcosuchus 1.25 3.00
C444 Sea Otter 1.25 3.00
C445 Sea Turtle 1.25 3.00
C446 Seismosaurus 1.25 3.00
C447 Homo ergaster 1.25 3.00
C448 Poison Dart Frog 1.25 3.00
C449 Sinornithosaurus 1.25 3.00
C450 Sinosauropteryx 1.25 3.00
C451 Snow Leopard 1.25 3.00
C452 Sperm Whale 1.25 3.00
C453 Spider Monkey 1.25 3.00
C454 Spinosaurus 1.25 3.00
C455 Spotted Hyena 1.25 3.00
C456 Homo heidelbergensis 1.25 3.00
C457 Steelhead 1.25 3.00
C458 Stegosaurus 1.25 3.00
C459 Sturgeon 1.25 3.00
C460 Styracosaurus 1.25 3.00
C461 Sun Bear 1.25 3.00
C462 Tasmanian Devil 1.25 3.00
C463 Tasmanian Tiger 1.25 3.00
C464 Homo erectus 1.25 3.00
C465 Torosaurus 1.25 3.00
C466 Toxodon 1.25 3.00
C467 Triceratops 1.25 3.00
C468 Troodon 1.25 3.00
C469 Tropeognathus 1.25 3.00
C470 Tylosaurus 1.25 3.00
C471 Tyrannosaurus Rex 1.25 3.00
C472 Velociraptor 1.25 3.00
C473 Western Gorilla 1.25 3.00
C474 Whooping Crane 1.25 3.00
C475 Wolverine 1.25 3.00
C476 Woodpecker 1.25 3.00
C477 Woolly Mammoth 1.25 3.00
C478 Woolly Rhino 1.25 3.00
C479 Zebra 1.25 3.00
C480 Sahelanthropus tchadensis 1.25 3.00

2008-09 Upper Deck Champ's Mini Signatures

STATED ODDS 1:12
CSAG Alex Goligoski 8.00 20.00
CSBK Mikkel Boedker 8.00 20.00
CSBY Brad Boyes 4.00 10.00
CSCM Cory Murphy 4.00 10.00
CSDC Dan Cleary 5.00 12.00
CSDD Drew Doughty 15.00 40.00
CSDH Dany Heatley 6.00 15.00
CSDN Daniel Negreanu 60.00 100.00
CSEE Erik Ersberg 5.00 12.00
CSEM Evgeni Malkin 30.00 60.00
CSES Eric Staal 8.00 20.00
CSFB Fabian Brunnstrom 12.00 30.00
CSFW Jon Filewich 5.00 12.00
CSGH Gordie Howe 75.00 150.00
CSGU Guillaume Latendresse 4.00 10.00
CSHI Jonas Hiller 5.00 12.00
CSIZ Ilya Zubov 5.00 12.00
CSJD Jordan Staal 6.00 15.00
CSJG Jean-Sebastien Giguere 12.00 30.00
CSJI Jarome Iginla 6.00 15.00
CSJP J.P. Dumont 4.00 10.00
CSJT Jonathan Toews 15.00 40.00
CSKO Kyle Okposo 6.00 15.00
CSKT Kyle Turris 10.00 25.00
CSKU Nikolai Kulemin 6.00 15.00
CSKY Tyler Kennedy 5.00 12.00
CSLS Les Stroud 30.00 60.00
CSLU Luke Schenn 15.00 40.00
CSMB Martin Brodeur 50.00 100.00
CSMF Mark Fistric 5.00 12.00
CSMG Marc-Andre Gragnani 5.00 12.00
CSMI Mike Iggulden 5.00 12.00
CSML Mario Lemieux 40.00 100.00
CSMM Mark Messier 30.00 80.00
CSNK Niklas Kronwall 5.00 12.00
CSOR Bobby Orr 100.00 200.00
CSPK Patrick Kane 12.00 30.00
CSPM Peter Mueller 5.00 12.00
CSRE Robbie Earl 4.00 10.00
CSRK Red Kelly 8.00 20.00
CSRN Rick Nash 6.00 15.00
CSSC Sidney Crosby 100.00 200.00
CSSE Shannon Elizabeth 50.00 100.00
CSSF Drew Stafford 5.00 12.00
CSSM Steve Mason 10.00 25.00
CSSS Steven Stamkos 40.00 100.00
CSTB Tobias Stephan 5.00 12.00
CSTH Tomas Holmstrom 5.00 12.00
CSTI Jennifer Tilly
CSTW Tiger Woods SP
CSVL Vincent Lecavalier 20.00 50.00
CSVN Thomas Vanek 6.00 15.00
CSWG Wayne Gretzky 150.00 250.00
CSWO Willie O'Ree 6.00 15.00
CSWT Walt Tkaczuk 4.00 10.00

2008-09 Upper Deck Champ's Mini Signatures Blue Backs

*BLUE BACK: .6X TO 1.5X BASIC AU
STATED ODDS 1:576
CSGH Gordie Howe 150.00 300.00
CSOR Bobby Orr 200.00 350.00
CSSC Sidney Crosby 200.00 350.00
CSVL Vincent Lecavalier 60.00 120.00
CSWG Wayne Gretzky 350.00 600.00

2008-09 Upper Deck Champ's Mini Signatures Red Backs

*RED BACK: .5X TO 1.2X BASIC AU
STATED ODDS 1:288
CSGH Gordie Howe 125.00 250.00
CSVL Vincent Lecavalier 40.00 80.00
CSWG Wayne Gretzky 200.00 400.00

2008-09 Upper Deck Champ's Mini Threads

STATED ODDS 1:24
CTAN Antero Niittymaki 4.00 10.00
CTAO Alexander Ovechkin 20.00 50.00
CTAP Alex Pietrangelo 6.00 15.00
CTBB Bob Bourne 3.00 8.00
CTBD Brandon Sutter 5.00 12.00
CTBG Brian Gionta 4.00 10.00
CTBK Mikkel Boedker 6.00 15.00
CTBN Bernie Nicholls 4.00 10.00
CTBO Ray Bourque 8.00 20.00
CTBS Billy Smith 5.00 12.00
CTBT Bryan Trottier 6.00 15.00
CTBW Blake Wheeler 12.00 30.00
CTCG Colton Gillies 4.00 10.00
CTCJ Curtis Joseph 5.00 12.00
CTDB Derick Brassard 4.00 10.00
CTDC Dino Ciccarelli 5.00 12.00
CTDD Drew Doughty 12.00 30.00
CTDG Doug Gilmour 6.00 15.00
CTDP Dion Phaneuf 5.00 12.00
CTEC Erik Cole 4.00 10.00
CTES Eric Staal 6.00 15.00
CTFB Fabian Brunnstrom 4.00 10.00
CTGA Glenn Anderson 5.00 12.00
CTHA Dale Hawerchuk 6.00 15.00
CTIK Ilya Kovalchuk 5.00 12.00
CTJL Jere Lehtinen 3.00 8.00
CTJS Joe Sakic 8.00 20.00
CTJV Jakub Voracek 10.00 25.00
CTKL Kari Lehtonen 4.00 10.00
CTLM Lanny McDonald 5.00 12.00
CTLR Luc Robitaille 5.00 12.00
CTMB Martin Brodeur 10.00 25.00
CTMF Manny Fernandez 4.00 10.00
CTMG Marian Gaborik 6.00 15.00
CTMH Marian Hossa 4.00 10.00
CTMK Mikko Koivu 4.00 10.00
CTML Mario Lemieux 15.00 40.00
CTMR Mike Ribeiro 4.00 10.00
CTMS Mats Sundin 5.00 12.00
CTMT Marty Turco 5.00 12.00
CTNZ Nikolai Zherdev 3.00 8.00
CTOA Adam Oates 5.00 12.00
CTOJ Olli Jokinen 4.00 10.00
CTOK Olaf Kolzig 5.00 12.00
CTPB Pierre-Marc Bouchard 5.00 12.00
CTPF Peter Forsberg 6.00 15.00
CTPS Peter Stastny 5.00 12.00
CTRB Rod Brind`Amour 5.00 12.00
CTRL Roberto Luongo 6.00 15.00
CTRM Ryan Malone 3.00 8.00
CTRN Rick Nash 5.00 12.00
CTRT Raffi Torres 3.00 8.00
CTRU Tuomo Ruutu 5.00 12.00
CTRY Michael Ryder 3.00 8.00
CTSB Steve Bernier 3.00 8.00
CTSC Sidney Crosby 15.00 40.00
CTSF Sergei Fedorov 8.00 20.00
CTSG Simon Gagne 5.00 12.00
CTSK Saku Koivu 5.00 12.00
CTSS Steve Shutt 5.00 12.00
CTST Steven Stamkos 15.00 40.00
CTSW Shea Weber 4.00 10.00
CTTF Theoren Fleury 6.00 15.00
CTTR Tuukka Rask 5.00 12.00
CTTW Tiger Williams 4.00 10.00
CTUM R.J. Umberger 3.00 8.00
CTVT Vesa Toskala 4.00 10.00
CTWR Wade Redden 3.00 8.00
CTWW Wojtek Wolski 4.00 10.00
CTZP Zach Parise 5.00 12.00

2009-10 Upper Deck Champ's

COMP.SET w/o SPs (100) 15.00 40.00
ROOKIE STATED ODDS 1:4
MINI STATED ODDS 1:2
W/H STATED ODDS 1:2
HF STATED ODDS 1:2
1 Ryan Getzlaf .50 1.25
2 Bobby Ryan .30 .75
3 Scott Niedermayer .30 .75
4 Ilya Kovalchuk .30 .75
5 Bryan Little .30 .75
6 Milan Lucic .25 .60
7 Terry O'Reilly .25 .60
8 Blake Wheeler .30 .75
9 Ray Bourque .50 1.25
10 Bobby Orr 1.00 2.50
11 Gilbert Perreault .30 .75
12 Derek Roy .25 .60
13 Thomas Vanek .30 .75
14 Ryan Miller .30 .75
15 Miikka Kiprusoff .25 .60
16 Al MacInnis .30 .75
17 Dion Phaneuf .40 1.00
18 Jarome Iginla .30 .75
19 Eric Staal .40 1.00
20 Cam Ward .30 .75
21 Jonathan Toews .60 1.50
22 Tony Esposito .30 .75
23 Denis Savard .40 1.00
24 Patrick Kane .60 1.50
25 Bobby Hull .40 1.00
26 Paul Stastny .30 .75
27 Craig Anderson .30 .75
28 Milan Hejduk .25 .60
29 Steve Mason .25 .60
30 Rick Nash .25 .60
31 Derick Brassard .30 .75
32 Mike Modano .50 1.25
33 Brad Richards .30 .75
34 James Neal .30 .75
35 Marty Turco .30 .75
36 Henrik Zetterberg .40 1.00
37 Nicklas Lidstrom .30 .75
38 Red Kelly .30 .75
39 Steve Yzerman .75 2.00
40 Gordie Howe .75 2.00
41 Alex Delvecchio .40 1.00
42 Ted Lindsay .25 .60
43 Jari Kurri .30 .75
44 Sam Gagner .25 .60
45 Nikolai Khabibulin .30 .75
46 Ales Hemsky .25 .60
47 Sheldon Souray .20 .50
48 Michael Frolik .25 .60
49 Drew Doughty .40 1.00
50 Anze Kopitar .50 1.25
51 Ryan Smyth .25 .60
52 Mikko Koivu .30 .75
53 Martin Havlat .25 .60
54 Niklas Backstrom .30 .75
55 Carey Price 1.25 3.00
56 Scotty Bowman .30 .75
57 Patrick Roy .75 2.00
58 Mike Cammalleri .25 .60
59 Pekka Rinne .40 1.00
60 Jason Arnott .25 .60
61 Martin Brodeur .60 1.50
62 Zach Parise .30 .75
63 Mike Bossy .30 .75
64 Clark Gillies .30 .75
65 Kyle Okposo .30 .75
66 Mark Messier .40 1.00
67 Marian Gaborik .40 1.00
68 Brandon Dubinsky .25 .60
69 Henrik Lundqvist .50 1.25
70 Wayne Gretzky 1.50 4.00
71 Brian Leetch .30 .75
72 Jason Spezza .30 .75
73 Daniel Alfredsson .30 .75
74 Mike Richards .30 .75
75 Bobby Clarke .30 .75
76 Jeff Carter .30 .75
77 Simon Gagne .30 .75
78 Daniel Carcillo .20 .50
79 Shane Doan .25 .60
80 Mario Lemieux 1.00 2.50
81 Marc-Andre Fleury .50 1.25
82 Evgeni Malkin 1.00 2.50
83 Sidney Crosby 1.25 3.00
84 Joe Thornton .30 .75
85 Dany Heatley .30 .75
86 Patrik Berglund .20 .50
87 Vincent Lecavalier .25 .60
88 Martin St. Louis .30 .75
89 Steven Stamkos .60 1.50
90 Phil Kessel .40 1.00
91 Lanny McDonald .30 .75
92 Doug Gilmour .40 1.00
93 Roberto Luongo .40 1.00
94 Markus Naslund .25 .60
95 Ryan Kesler .30 .75
96 Alexander Ovechkin 1.25 3.00
97 Mike Green .30 .75
98 Alexander Semin .30 .75
99 Simeon Varlamov .30 .75
100 Dale Hawerchuk .40 1.00
101 Jakub Kindl RC 2.00 5.00
102 Alec Martinez RC 2.50 6.00
103 John Carlson RC 3.00 8.00
104 Andrew MacDonald RC 1.25 3.00
105 Antti Niemi RC 3.00 8.00
106 Artem Anisimov RC 2.00 5.00
107 Ben Lovejoy RC 2.00 5.00
108 Benn Ferriero RC 2.00 5.00
109 Brandon Segal RC 1.50 4.00
110 Brian Salcido RC 1.50 4.00
111 Bryan Rodney RC 1.50 4.00
112 Byron Bitz RC 1.50 4.00
113 Cal O'Reilly RC 1.50 4.00
114 Chris Durno RC 1.50 4.00
115 Christian Hanson RC 2.00 5.00
116 Dan Turple RC 2.00 5.00
117 David Schlemko RC 1.50 4.00
118 David Sloane RC 2.00 5.00
119 David Van Der Gulik RC 1.50 4.00
120 Davis Drewiske RC 2.00 5.00
121 Derek Peltier RC 1.25 3.00
122 Dmitry Kulikov RC 2.00 5.00
123 Erik Karlsson RC 6.00 15.00
124 Evander Kane RC 4.00 10.00
125 Frazer McLaren RC 1.50 4.00
126 Geoff Kinrade RC 2.00 5.00
127 Lars Eller RC 2.00 5.00
128 Ivan Vishnevskiy RC 1.50 4.00
129 Matthew Corrente RC 1.50 4.00
130 Jakub Petruzalek RC 2.00 5.00
131 James van Riemsdyk RC 4.00 10.00
132 Jamie Benn RC 6.00 15.00
133 Jamie Fraser RC 1.50 4.00
134 Jamie Fritsch RC 2.00 5.00
135 Jason Demers RC 3.00 8.00
136 Jay Beagle RC 2.50 6.00
137 Jay Rosehill RC 2.00 5.00
138 Jesse Joensuu RC 1.50 4.00
139 Jhonas Enroth RC 2.50 6.00
140 Joel Rechlicz RC 1.25 3.00
141 Johan Backlund RC 2.00 5.00
142 John Negrin RC 2.00 5.00
143 John Scott RC 2.00 5.00
144 John Tavares RC 15.00 40.00
145 Jonas Gustavsson RC 2.50 6.00
146 Kevin Quick RC 1.25 3.00
147 Devan Dubnyk RC 4.00 10.00
148 Kris Chucko RC 1.50 4.00
149 Kurtis McLean RC 1.50 4.00
150 Luca Caputi RC 2.00 5.00
151 Matt Beleskey RC 1.50 4.00
152 Matt Climie RC 1.50 4.00
153 Matt Duchene RC 4.00 10.00
154 Matt Gilroy RC 2.00 5.00
155 Matt Hendricks RC 1.50 4.00
156 Matt Pelech RC 2.00 5.00
157 Michael Del Zotto RC 2.00 5.00
158 Michael Sauer RC 1.50 4.00
159 Michael Vernace RC 1.50 4.00
160 Michal Neuvirth RC 3.00 8.00
161 Mika Pyorala RC 1.50 4.00
162 Mikael Backlund RC 2.00 5.00
163 Ryan O'Marra RC 1.25 3.00
164 Mike Santorelli RC 2.00 5.00
165 Per Ledin RC 2.00 5.00
166 Peter Regin RC 1.50 4.00
167 Phil Oreskovic RC 2.00 5.00
168 Ray Macias RC 1.50 4.00
169 Riku Helenius RC 2.00 5.00
170 Bobby Sanguinetti RC 1.25 3.00
171 Ryan O'Reilly RC 3.00 8.00
172 Ryan Vesce RC 1.50 4.00
173 Scott Lehman RC 1.25 3.00
174 Sean Bentivoglio RC 1.50 4.00
175 Sean Collins RC 1.50 4.00
176 Sergei Shirokov RC 1.25 3.00
177 Spencer Machacek RC 2.00 5.00
178 T.J. Galiardi RC 2.00 5.00
179 Taylor Chorney RC 2.00 5.00
180 Teemu Laakso RC 1.25 3.00
181 Tim Stapleton RC 2.00 5.00
182 Tim Wallace RC 1.25 3.00
183 Tom Wandell RC 2.00 5.00
184 Tyler Bozak RC 3.00 8.00
185 Tyler Myers RC 3.00 8.00
186 Tyson Strachan RC 1.25 3.00
187 Victor Hedman RC 4.00 10.00
188 Viktor Stalberg RC 2.00 5.00
189 Ville Leino RC 1.50 4.00
190 Wes O'Neill RC 2.00 5.00
191 Yannick Weber RC 2.00 5.00
192 Logan Couture RC 4.00 10.00
193 Michael Grabner RC 2.00 5.00
194 Brad Marchand RC 5.00 12.00
195 Cody Franson RC 2.00 5.00
196 Colin Wilson RC 2.00 5.00
197 Ryan Getzlaf 1.00 2.50
198 Bobby Ryan .60 1.50
199 Scott Niedermayer .60 1.50
200 Ilya Kovalchuk .60 1.50
201 Bryan Little .60 1.50
202 Milan Lucic .50 1.25
203 Terry O'Reilly .50 1.25
204 Blake Wheeler .60 1.50
205 Ray Bourque 1.00 2.50
206 Bobby Orr 2.00 5.00
207 Gilbert Perreault .60 1.50
208 Derek Roy .50 1.25
209 Thomas Vanek .60 1.50
210 Ryan Miller .60 1.50
211 Miikka Kiprusoff .50 1.25
212 Al MacInnis .60 1.50
213 Dion Phaneuf .75 2.00
214 Jarome Iginla .60 1.50
215 Eric Staal .75 2.00
216 Cam Ward .60 1.50
217 Jonathan Toews 1.25 3.00
218 Tony Esposito .60 1.50
219 Denis Savard .75 2.00
220 Patrick Kane 1.25 3.00
221 Bobby Hull .75 2.00
222 Paul Stastny .60 1.50
223 Craig Anderson .60 1.50
224 Milan Hejduk .50 1.25
225 Steve Mason .50 1.25
226 Rick Nash .50 1.25
227 Derick Brassard .60 1.50
228 Mike Modano 1.00 2.50
229 Brad Richards .60 1.50
230 James Neal .60 1.50
231 Marty Turco .60 1.50
232 Henrik Zetterberg .75 2.00
233 Nicklas Lidstrom .60 1.50
234 Red Kelly .60 1.50
235 Steve Yzerman 1.50 4.00
236 Gordie Howe 1.50 4.00
237 Alex Delvecchio .75 2.00
238 Ted Lindsay .50 1.25
239 Jari Kurri .60 1.50
240 Sam Gagner .50 1.25
241 Nikolai Khabibulin .60 1.50
242 Ales Hemsky .50 1.25
243 Sheldon Souray .40 1.00
244 Michael Frolik .50 1.25
245 Drew Doughty .75 2.00
246 Anze Kopitar 1.00 2.50
247 Ryan Smyth .50 1.25
248 Mikko Koivu .60 1.50
249 Martin Havlat .50 1.25
250 Niklas Backstrom .60 1.50
251 Carey Price 2.50 6.00
252 Scotty Bowman .60 1.50
253 Patrick Roy 1.50 4.00
254 Brian Gionta .50 1.25
255 Pekka Rinne .75 2.00
256 Jason Arnott .50 1.25
257 Martin Brodeur 1.25 3.00
258 Zach Parise .60 1.50
259 Mike Bossy .60 1.50
260 Clark Gillies .60 1.50
261 Kyle Okposo .60 1.50
262 Mark Messier .75 2.00
263 Marian Gaborik .75 2.00
264 Brandon Dubinsky .50 1.25
265 Henrik Lundqvist 1.00 2.50
266 Wayne Gretzky 3.00 8.00
267 Brian Leetch .60 1.50
268 Jason Spezza .60 1.50
269 Daniel Alfredsson .60 1.50
270 Mike Richards .60 1.50
271 Bobby Clarke .60 1.50
272 Jeff Carter .60 1.50
273 Simon Gagne .60 1.50
274 Daniel Carcillo .40 1.00
275 Shane Doan .50 1.25
276 Mario Lemieux 2.00 5.00
277 Marc-Andre Fleury 1.00 2.50
278 Evgeni Malkin 2.00 5.00
279 Sidney Crosby 2.50 6.00
280 Joe Thornton .60 1.50
281 Dany Heatley .60 1.50
282 Patrik Berglund .40 1.00
283 Vincent Lecavalier .50 1.25
284 Martin St. Louis .60 1.50
285 Steven Stamkos 1.25 3.00
286 Phil Kessel .75 2.00
287 Lanny McDonald .60 1.50
288 Doug Gilmour .75 2.00
289 Roberto Luongo .75 2.00
290 Markus Naslund .50 1.25
291 Ryan Kesler .60 1.50
292 Alexander Ovechkin 2.50 6.00
293 Mike Green .60 1.50
294 Alexander Semin .60 1.50
295 Simeon Varlamov .60 1.50
296 Dale Hawerchuk .75 2.00
297 Jay Bouwmeester .60 1.50
298 Olli Jokinen .50 1.25
299 Robyn Regehr .50 1.25
300 Tuomo Ruutu .40 1.00
301 Marian Hossa .50 1.25
302 Dustin Byfuglien .60 1.50
303 Marek Svatos .40 1.00
304 Loui Eriksson .50 1.25
305 Brenden Morrow .50 1.25
306 Fabian Brunnstrom .50 1.25
307 Zdeno Chara .60 1.50
308 Mike Cammalleri .50 1.25
309 Ryan Malone .40 1.00
310 Mike Smith .60 1.50
311 Mike Knuble .40 1.00
312 Jussi Jokinen .40 1.00
313 Brent Burns .75 2.00
314 Don Cherry .60 1.50
315 Dino Ciccarelli .60 1.50
316 J.P. Dumont .40 1.00
317 Ryan Suter .60 1.50
318 Chris Pronger .50 1.25
319 Scott Hartnell .60 1.
320 Daniel Briere .60 1.
321 Ray Emery .50 1.
322 Kris Versteeg .60 1.
323 Nik Antropov .50 1.2
324 Ilya Bryzgalov .50 1.2
325 Peter Mueller .50 1.2
326 Devin Setoguchi .50 1.2
327 Evgeni Nabokov .50 1.2
328 Jordan Staal .60 1.5
329 Bill Guerin .60 1.5
330 Patrick Marleau .60 1.5
331 Rob Blake .60 1.5
332 Dan Boyle .50 1.2
333 Alex Kovalev .60 1.5
334 Frank Mahovlich .75 2.0
335 Darryl Sittler .75 2.0
336 Matt Stajan .50 1.2
337 Tomas Kaberle .40 1.0
338 Alexei Ponikarovsky .40 1.0
339 Luke Schenn .50 1.2
340 Paul Kariya .75 2.0
341 T.J. Oshie 1.00 2.5
342 Chris Mason .50 1.2
343 Andy McDonald .50 1.2
344 Shea Weber .50 1.2
345 Nikita Filatov .50 1.2
346 Fedor Tyutin .40 1.0
347 Jack Johnson .40 1.0
348 Bernie Federko .50 1.2
349 Joe Mullen .50 1.2
350 Jakub Voracek .60 1.5
351 Marc Staal .60 1.5
352 Patrik Elias .60 1.5
353 David Clarkson .50 1.2
354 Paul Martin .40 1.0
355 Chris Drury .50 1.2
356 Ales Kotalik .40 1.0
357 Doug Weight .60 1.5
358 Willie Mitchell .40 1.0
359 Daniel Sedin .60 1.5
360 Tomas Vokoun .50 1.2
361 Nathan Horton .60 1.5
362 David Booth .40 1.0
363 Jonathan Quick 1.25 3.0
364 Dustin Brown .50 1.2
365 Rod Brind`Amour .60 1.5
366 Henrik Sedin .60 1.5
367 Ryan Kesler .60 1.5
368 Alexandre Burrows .60 1.5
369 Ryane Clowe .50 1.2
370 Joe Pavelski .60 1.5
371 Chris Neil .40 1.0
372 Ed Jovanovski .40 1.0
373 Jody Shelley .40 1.0
374 Donald Brashear .40 1.0
375 George Parros .40 1.0
376 Georges Laraque .50 1.2
377 Eric Godard .40 1.0
378 Grant Fuhr .60 1.5
379 Glenn Anderson .60 1.5
380 Drew Stafford .60 1.5
381 Jason Pominville .60 1.5
382 Dennis Wideman .40 1.0
383 Tim Thomas .60 1.5
384 Zach Bogosian .50 1.2
385 Kari Lehtonen .50 1.2
386 Jonas Hiller .50 1.2
387 Saku Koivu .60 1.5
388 Teemu Selanne 1.25 3.0
389 Great Pyramid of Giza 1.25 3.0
390 Hanging Gardens of Babylon 1.25 3.0
391 Statue of Zeus at Olympia 1.25 3.0
392 Temple of Artemis at Ephesus 1.25 3.0
393 Mausoleum at Halicarnassus 1.25 3.0
394 Colossus of Rhodes 1.25 3.0
395 Lighthouse of Alexandria 1.25 3.0
396 Chichen Itza 1.25 3.0
397 Christ the Redeemer 1.25 3.0
398 Colosseum 1.25 3.0
399 Great Wall of China 1.25 3.0
400 Machu Picchu 1.25 3.0
401 Petra 1.25 3.0
402 Taj Mahal 1.25 3.0
403 Grand Canyon 1.25 3.0
404 Great Barrier Reef 1.25 3.0
405 Harbour of Rio de Janeiro 1.25 3.0
406 Mount Everest 1.25 3.0
407 Aurora 1.25 3.0
408 Parcutin Volcano 1.25 3.0
409 Victoria Falls 1.25 3.0
410 Palau 1.25 3.0
411 Belize Barrier Reef 1.25 3.0
412 Great Barrier Reef 1.25 3.0
413 Deep-Sea Vents 1.25 3.0
414 Galpagos Islands 1.25 3.0
415 Lake Baikal 1.25 3.0
416 Northern Red Sea 1.25 3.0
417 Niagara Falls 1.25 3.0
418 Bay of Fundy, the Maritimes 1.25 3.0
419 Rocky Mountains 1.25 3.0
(British Columbia Alberta
420 Nahanni National Park Reserve 1.25 3.0
421 Gros Morne National Park 1.25 3.0
422 Dinosaur Provincial Park 1.25 3.0
423 Richer- Perce 1.25 3.0
424 Nichollsia borealis 1.25 3.0
425 Torosaurus 1.25 3.0
426 Sauronitholestes 1.25 3.0
427 Troodon 1.25 3.0
428 Dromaeosaurus 1.25 3.0
429 Tyrannosaurus rex 1.25 3.0
430 Pachyhinosausrus canadensis 1.25 3.0
431 Arrhinoceratops brachyops 1.25 3.0
432 Anchiceratops ornatus 1.25 3.0
433 Panoplosaurus 1.25 3.0
434 Euoplocephalus tutus 1.25 3.0
435 Edmontonia longiceps 1.25 3.0
436 Saurolophus osborni 1.25 3.0
437 Hypacrosaurus altispinus 1.25 3.0
438 Triceratops 1.25 3.0
439 Stegoceras edmontonense 1.25 3.0
440 Parksosaurus warreni 1.25 3.0
441 Velocirapterinae 1.25 3.0
442 Struthiomimus altus 1.25 3.0
443 Ornithomimus edmontonticus 1.25 3.0
444 Pachycephalosauridae 1.25 3.0
445 Daspletosaurus 1.25 3.0
446 Chirostenotes pergracilis 1.25 3.0
447 Aublysodon 1.25 3.0
448 Albertosaurus 1.25 3.0
449 Styracosaurus albertensis 1.25 3.0
450 Leptoceratops 1.25 3.0
451 Chasmosaurus 1.25 3.0
452 Ankylosauria 1.25 3.0
453 Richardoestesia 1.25 3.0
454 Gorgosaurus 1.25 3.0
455 Edmontosaurus saskatchewanensis 1.25 3.0
456 Orodromeus 1.25 3.0
457 Ornithomimidae 1.25 3.0
458 Montanoceratops cerorhynchus 1.25 3.0

59 Dawson's Caribou 1.25 3.00
60 Sea Mink 1.25 3.00
61 Great Auk 1.25 3.00
62 Labrador Duck 1.25 3.00
63 Passenger Pigeon 1.25 3.00
64 Deepwater Cisco 1.25 3.00
65 Longjaw Cisco 1.25 3.00
66 Banff Longnose Dace 1.25 3.00
67 Blue Walleye 1.25 3.00
68 Grizzly Bear 1.25 3.00
69 Black-Footed Ferret 1.25 3.00
70 Swift Fox 1.25 3.00
71 Walrus 1.25 3.00
72 Gray Whale 1.25 3.00
73 Pygmy Short-horned Lizard 1.25 3.00
74 Gravel Chub 1.25 3.00
75 Paddlefish 1.25 3.00
76 Eastern Cougar 1.25 3.00
77 Vancouver Island Marmot 1.25 3.00
78 Bowhead Whale 1.25 3.00
79 Right Whale 1.25 3.00
80 Beluga Whale 1.25 3.00
81 Wolverine 1.25 3.00
82 Whooping Crane 1.25 3.00
83 Eskimo Curlew 1.25 3.00
84 Aurora Trout 1.25 3.00
85 Anatum Peregrine Falcon 1.25 3.00
86 Blanchard's Cricket Frog 1.25 3.00
87 Leatherback Turtle 1.25 3.00
88 Lake Erie Water Snake 1.25 3.00
89 White Trillium 1.25 3.00
90 Common Loon 1.25 3.00
91 Blue Flag Iris 1.25 3.00
92 Snowy Owl 1.25 3.00
93 Mayflower 1.25 3.00
94 Osprey 1.25 3.00
95 Purple Violet 1.25 3.00
96 Black Capped Chickadee 1.25 3.00
97 Prairie Crocus 1.25 3.00
98 Great Grey Owl 1.25 3.00
99 Pacific Dogwood 1.25 3.00
00 Steller's Jay 1.25 3.00
01 Pink Lady's Slipper 1.25 3.00
02 Blue Jay 1.25 3.00
03 Western Red Lily 1.25 3.00
04 Sharp Tailed Grouse 1.25 3.00
05 Wild Rose 1.25 3.00
06 Great Horned Owl 1.25 3.00
07 Pitcher Plant 1.25 3.00
08 Atlantic Puffin 1.25 3.00
09 Mountain Avens 1.25 3.00
10 Gyrfalcon 1.25 3.00
11 Fireweed 1.25 3.00
12 Common Raven 1.25 3.00
13 Purple Saxifrage 1.25 3.00
14 Rock Ptarmigan 1.25 3.00
15 Sir John A. Macdonald 1.50 4.00
16 Alexander Mackenzie 1.50 4.00
17 Sir John Abbott 1.50 4.00
18 Sir John Thompson 1.50 4.00
19 Sir Mackenzie Bowell 1.50 4.00
20 Sir Charles Tupper 1.50 4.00
21 Sir Wilfrid Laurier 1.50 4.00
22 Sir Robert Borden 1.50 4.00
23 Arthur Meighen 1.50 4.00
24 William Lyon Mackenzie King 1.50 4.00
25 Richard Bedford Bennett 1.50 4.00
26 Louis St. Laurent 1.50 4.00
27 John Diefenbaker 1.50 4.00
28 Lester B. Pearson 1.50 4.00
29 Pierre Trudeau 1.50 4.00
30 Joe Clark 1.50 4.00
31 John Turner 1.50 4.00
32 Brian Mulroney 1.50 4.00
33 Kim Campbell 1.50 4.00
34 Jean Chretien 1.50 4.00
35 Paul Martin 1.50 4.00
36 Stephen Harper 1.50 4.00
37 George Washington 2.00 5.00
38 John Adams 1.50 4.00
39 Thomas Jefferson 2.00 5.00
40 James Madison 1.50 4.00
41 James Monroe 1.50 4.00
42 John Quincy Adams 1.50 4.00
43 Andrew Jackson 1.50 4.00
44 Martin Van Buren 1.50 4.00
45 William Henry Harrison 1.50 4.00
46 John Tyler 1.50 4.00
47 James K. Polk 1.50 4.00
48 Zachary Taylor 1.50 4.00
49 Millard Fillmore 1.50 4.00
50 Franklin Pierce 1.50 4.00
51 James Buchanon 1.50 4.00
52 Abraham Lincoln 2.00 5.00
53 Andrew Johnson 1.50 4.00
54 Ulysses S. Grant 1.50 4.00
55 Rutherford B. Hayes 1.50 4.00
56 James A. Garfield 1.50 4.00
57 Chester Arthur 1.50 4.00
58 Grover Cleveland 1.50 4.00
59 Benjamin Harrison 1.50 4.00
60 Grover Cleveland 1.50 4.00
61 William McKinley 1.50 4.00
62 Theodore Roosevelt 1.50 4.00
63 William Howard Taft 1.50 4.00
64 Woodrow Wilson 1.50 4.00
65 Warren G. Harding 1.50 4.00
66 Calvin Coolidge 1.50 4.00
67 Herbert Hoover 1.50 4.00
68 Franklin Delano Roosevelt 1.50 4.00
69 Harry Truman 1.50 4.00
70 Dwight D. Eisenhower 1.50 4.00
71 John F. Kennedy 3.00 8.00
72 Lyndon B. Johnson 1.50 4.00
73 Richard Nixon 1.50 4.00
74 Gerald Ford 1.50 4.00
75 Jimmy Carter 1.50 4.00
76 Ronald Reagan 2.00 5.00
77 George H.W. Bush 2.00 5.00
78 Bill Clinton 2.00 5.00
79 George W. Bush 2.00 5.00
80 Barack Obama 3.00 8.00

2009-10 Upper Deck Champ's Green

COMPLETE SET (100) 40.00 100.00
SINGLES: 1.5X TO 4X BASIC CARDS
STATED ODDS 1:4

2009-10 Upper Deck Champ's Red

COMPLETE SET (100) 125.00 250.00
SINGLES: 2.5X TO 6X BASIC CARDS
STATED ODDS 1:10

2009-10 Upper Deck Champ's Yellow

COMPLETE SET (100) 200.00 400.00
SINGLES: 4X TO 10X BASIC CARDS
STATED ODDS 1:20

2009-10 Upper Deck Champ's Yellow Animal Icon

COMPLETE SET (100) 500.00 1000.00
*SINGLES: 8X TO 20X BASIC CARDS
STATED ODDS 1:80

2009-10 Upper Deck Champ's Hall of Legends Memorabilia

STATED ODDS 1:160
HLAO Alexander Ovechkin 25.00 60.00
HLBO Bo Jackson 20.00 50.00
HLBS Borje Salming 8.00 20.00
HLCB Chris Bosh 8.00 20.00
HLCN Cam Neely 8.00 20.00
HLCR Cal Ripken Jr.
HLDH Dale Hawerchuk 10.00 25.00
HLDM Dan Marino 25.00 60.00
HLEW John Elway 25.00 50.00
HLFH Franco Harris 12.00 30.00
HLGA Glenn Anderson 8.00 20.00
HLGH Gordie Howe 20.00 50.00
HLJA Bo Jackson 20.00 50.00
HLJE Julius Erving 12.00 30.00
HLJR Jerry Rice 15.00 40.00
HLKB Kobe Bryant 25.00 60.00
HLLB Larry Bird 20.00 50.00
HLLJ LeBron James 40.00 80.00
HLLM Lanny McDonald 8.00 20.00
HLMB Martin Brodeur 15.00 40.00
HLMG Magic Johnson 15.00 40.00
HLMJ Michael Jordan 50.00 100.00
HLMS Mike Schmidt 20.00 50.00
HLNR Nolan Ryan 25.00 60.00
HLPR Patrick Roy 20.00 50.00
HLRL Rod Langway 6.00 15.00
HLSB Scotty Bowman 8.00 20.00
HLSC Sidney Crosby 30.00 80.00
HLSN Steve Nash 8.00 20.00
HLSS Steve Shutt 8.00 20.00
HLSY Steve Yzerman 20.00 50.00
HLTW Tiger Woods 100.00 200.00
HLWG Wayne Gretzky 30.00 80.00
HLWM Warren Moon 10.00 25.00

2009-10 Upper Deck Champ's Mini Blue Backs

*ROOKIES: .8X TO 2X BASIC
ROOKIES STATED ODDS 1:360
*VETERANS: 4X TO 10X BASIC
VETERAN STATED ODDS 1:80

2009-10 Upper Deck Champ's Mini Green Backs

*ROOKIES: 1.2X TO 3X BASIC
ROOKIES STATED ODDS 1:640
*VETERANS: 5X TO 12X BASIC
VETERAN STATED ODDS 1:160

2009-10 Upper Deck Champ's Mini Parkhurst Backs

ROOKIES STATED ODDS 1:5000
*VETERANS: 6X TO 15X BASIC
VETERAN STATED ODDS 1:320

2009-10 Upper Deck Champ's Mini Red Backs

*ROOKIES: .5X TO 1.2X BASIC
ROOKIES STATED ODDS 1:240
*VETERANS: 2X TO 5X BASIC
VETERAN STATED ODDS 1:20

2009-10 Upper Deck Champ's Signatures

STATED ODDS 1:15
CSAA Artem Anisimov 6.00 15.00
CSAC Andrew Cogliano 4.00 10.00
CSAE Andrew Ebbett 4.00 10.00
CSAM Andrei Markov 6.00 15.00
CSAO Alexander Ovechkin 40.00 100.00
CSAP Alex Pietrangelo 5.00 12.00
CSBA Mikael Backlund 6.00 15.00
CSBF Bob Feller 25.00 60.00
CSBL Brian Leetch 6.00 15.00
CSBO Bobby Orr 60.00 120.00
CSBR Martin Brodeur EXCH 20.00 50.00
CSBS Brandon Sutter 5.00 12.00
CSBW Blake Wheeler 15.00 40.00
CSCB Cam Barker 4.00 10.00
CSCH Christian Hanson 6.00 15.00
CSCP Carey Price 25.00 60.00
CSCR Cal Ripken Jr. 125.00 200.00
CSCS Chris Stewart 5.00 12.00
CSDB David Backes 6.00 15.00
CSDC Daniel Carcillo 4.00 10.00
CSDF Doug Flutie 25.00 60.00
CSDR Derrick Rose 50.00 125.00
CSEK Evander Kane 12.00 30.00
CSEM Evgeni Malkin 20.00 50.00
CSEN Jhonas Enroth 8.00 20.00
CSER Jonathan Ericsson 5.00 12.00
CSES Emmitt Smith
CSFA Fabian Brunnstrom 5.00 12.00
CSFO Nick Foligno 5.00 12.00
CSGA Marian Gaborik 8.00 20.00
CSGH Gordie Howe 60.00 120.00
CSHZ Henrik Zetterberg 8.00 20.00
CSJA Jason Arnott 5.00 12.00
CSJB Josh Bailey 5.00 12.00
CSJD J.P. Dumont 4.00 10.00
CSJE Julius Erving SP 200.00 350.00
CSJG Jonas Gustavsson 6.00 15.00
CSJH Josh Harding 6.00 15.00
CSJI Jarome Iginla 10.00 25.00
CSJN John Tavares 25.00 60.00
CSJR Jerry Rice 75.00 150.00
CSJS James Sheppard 4.00 10.00
CSJT Jonathan Toews 12.00 30.00
CSLB Larry Bird 60.00 120.00
CSLS Luke Schenn 5.00 12.00
CSMA Mark Streit 4.00 10.00
CSMB Mikkel Boedker 4.00 10.00
CSMD Matt Duchene 15.00 40.00
CSMJ Michael Jordan 400.00 700.00
CSMP Max Pacioretty 8.00 20.00
CSMR Mike Richards 6.00 15.00
CSMS Mike Schmidt 20.00 40.00
CSMT Maxime Talbot 6.00 15.00
CSNB Nicklas Backstrom 10.00 25.00
CSNG Nathan Gerbe 5.00 12.00
CSNL Nicklas Lidstrom 20.00 50.00
CSNR Nolan Ryan 125.00 200.00
CSOA Adam Oates 6.00 15.00
CSOM Oscar Moller 4.00 10.00
CSPK Phil Kessel 8.00 20.00
CSPL Pascal Leclaire 6.00 15.00
CSPM Peter Mueller 5.00 12.00
CSRN Rick Nash
CSRY Bobby Ryan 6.00 15.00
CSSA Barry Sanders
CSSC Sidney Crosby 60.00 120.00
CSSH Sergei Shirokov 6.00 15.00
CSSS Steven Stamkos 12.00 30.00
CSST Matt Stajan 5.00 12.00
CSSW Shea Weber 5.00 12.00
CSSY Steve Yzerman
CSTH Joe Thornton 6.00 15.00
CSTK Tim Kennedy 5.00 12.00
CSTM Tracy McGrady 10.00 25.00
CSTV Thomas Vanek 5.00 12.00
CSVH Victor Hedman 10.00 25.00
CSVL Ville Leino 5.00 12.00
CSVR James van Riemsdyk 12.00 30.00
CSWG Wayne Gretzky 100.00 200.00
CSWM Warren Moon 60.00 120.00
CSYM Yao Ming 40.00 80.00

2009-10 Upper Deck Champ's Threads

STATED ODDS 1:9
MTAO Alexander Ovechkin 12.00 30.00
MTAS Alexander Semin 3.00 8.00
MTBL Brian Leetch 3.00 8.00
MTCG Andrew Cogliano 2.50 6.00
MTCN Cam Neely 3.00 8.00
MTCO Chris Osgood 3.00 8.00
MTCP Carey Price 12.00 30.00
MTCW Cam Ward 3.00 8.00
MTDA Daniel Alfredsson 3.00 8.00
MTDB Derick Brassard 3.00 8.00
MTDG Doug Gilmour 4.00 10.00
MTDP Dion Phaneuf 4.00 10.00
MTEM Evgeni Malkin 10.00 25.00
MTGA Glenn Anderson 3.00 8.00
MTGB Marian Gaborik 4.00 10.00
MTGF Grant Fuhr 3.00 8.00
MTGH Gordie Howe 8.00 20.00
MTGP Gilbert Perreault 3.00 8.00
MTGR Sergei Gonchar 2.00 5.00
MTHL Henrik Lundqvist 5.00 12.00
MTHZ Henrik Zetterberg 4.00 10.00
MTIK Ilya Kovalchuk 3.00 8.00
MTJB Josh Bailey 2.50 6.00
MTJC Jeff Carter 3.00 8.00
MTJF Johan Franzen 3.00 8.00
MTJI Jarome Iginla 3.00 8.00
MTJM Joe Mullen 2.50 6.00
MTKI Miikka Kiprusoff 2.50 6.00
MTKL Kristopher Letang 3.00 8.00
MTLR Larry Robinson 3.00 8.00
MTMB Martin Brodeur 6.00 15.00
MTMF Marc-Andre Fleury 5.00 12.00
MTML Milan Lucic 2.50 6.00
MTMM Mike Modano 5.00 12.00
MTMR Mike Richards 3.00 8.00
MTMT Marty Turco 3.00 8.00
MTNA Nik Antropov 4.00 10.00
MTNH Nathan Horton 3.00 8.00
MTNL Nicklas Lidstrom 3.00 8.00
MTPD Pavel Datsyuk 4.00 10.00
MTPK Phil Kessel 4.00 10.00
MTPR Patrick Roy 8.00 20.00
MTPS Paul Stastny 3.00 8.00
MTRK Ryan Kesler 3.00 8.00
MTRL Roberto Luongo 4.00 10.00
MTRN Rick Nash 2.50 6.00
MTSB Steve Bernier 2.00 5.00
MTSC Sidney Crosby 8.00 20.00
MTSG Simon Gagne
MTSH Steve Shutt 3.00 8.00
MTSP Patrick Sharp 3.00 8.00
MTSS Steven Stamkos 6.00 15.00
MTST Jordan Staal 3.00 8.00
MTSW Shea Weber
MTTK Tomas Kaberle 2.00 5.00
MTVO Tomas Vokoun 2.50 6.00
MTWW Wojtek Wolski 2.00 5.00

2015-16 Upper Deck Champ's

1 Dustin Brown .30 .75
2 Nino Niederreiter .25 .60
3 Ryan Nugent-Hopkins .40 1.00
4 James Neal .40 1.00
5 Vernon Fiddler .25 .60
6 Mats Zuccarello .30 .75
7 Antti Niemi .30 .75
8 Brad Marchand .50 1.25
9 Artem Anisimov .30 .75
10 Andrew Cogliano .25 .60
11 Victor Rask .25 .60
12 Joel Ward .25 .60
13 Dion Phaneuf .40 1.00
14 Mark Scheifele .50 1.25
15 Paul Stastny .40 1.00
16 Brent Burns .50 1.25
17 Semyon Varlamov .40 1.00
18 Bo Horvat .60 1.50
19 Michael Cammalleri .30 .75
20 Cam Ward .40 1.00
21 P.A. Parenteau .25 .60
22 Ryan Kesler .40 1.00
23 Jonathan Huberdeau .40 1.00
24 Roman Josi .40 1.00
25 Kyle Okposo .40 1.00
26 Justin Abdelkader .30 .75
27 Leon Draisaitl .40 1.00
28 Mika Zibanejad .40 1.00
29 Ryan Suter .25 .60
30 Tyler Bozak .30 .75
31 Michael Frolik .25 .60
32 Ondrej Palat .30 .75
33 Patrik Elias .40 1.00
34 Lars Eller .30 .75
35 Brian Elliott .30 .75
36 Tomas Plekanec .40 1.00
37 Teuvo Teravainen .40 1.00
38 Troy Brouwer .30 .75
39 Nikita Kucherov .60 1.50
40 John Carlson .50 1.25
41 Jonas Hiller .30 .75
42 Steve Mason .30 .75
43 Justin Williams .30 .75
44 James Reimer .40 1.00
45 Chris Kunitz .40 1.00
46 Tyler Myers .30 .75
47 Chris Kreider .40 1.00
48 Evander Kane .40 1.00
49 Teddy Purcell .40 1.00
50 Joe Thornton .40 1.00
51 Kevin Hayes .40 1.00
52 Mikko Koivu .30 .75
53 Aleksander Barkov .40 1.00
54 Mike Hoffman .30 .75
55 Andrew Ladd .40 1.00
56 Dougie Hamilton .40 1.00
57 Chris Stewart .25 .60
58 Brandon Dubinsky .30 .75
59 Shane Doan .30 .75
60 Zdeno Chara .40 1.00
61 Carl Soderberg .30 .75
62 Jaden Schwartz .50 1.25
63 Blake Comeau .25 .60
64 Jason Zucker .30 .75
65 Niklas Kronwall .30 .75
66 Kyle Turris .30 .75
67 Kris Letang .40 1.00
68 Nazem Kadri .30 .75
69 Milan Lucic .30 .75
70 Kyle Palmieri .25 .60
71 Jeff Skinner .30 .75
72 Alex Galchenyuk .50 1.25
73 Patrick Sharp .40 1.00
74 Evgeny Kuznetsov .60 1.50
75 Lee Stempniak .25 .60
76 Nathan MacKinnon .75 2.00
77 Justin Faulk .40 1.00
78 Torey Krug .40 1.00
79 Vincent Trocheck .30 .75
80 Derek Stepan .40 1.00
81 David Jones .25 .60
82 Jim Howard .40 1.00
83 Victor Hedman .50 1.25
84 Matt Beleskey .25 .60
85 Brent Seabrook .40 1.00
86 Seth Jones .30 .75
87 Blake Wheeler .40 1.00
88 Marcus Johansson .30 .75
89 Andrew Shaw .40 1.00
90 Brayden Schenn .40 1.00
91 David Pastrnak .60 1.50
92 Marian Gaborik .40 1.00
93 Kris Versteeg .30 .75
94 Mike Green .40 1.00
95 John Klingberg .30 .75
96 Colin Wilson .25 .60
97 Nick Leddy .25 .60
98 Martin Hanzal .25 .60
99 Jack Johnson .25 .60
100 Ryan O'Reilly .40 1.00
101 Radim Vrbata .30 .75
102 Jussi Jokinen .25 .60
103 Corey Crawford .50 1.25
104 Chris Neil .25 .60
105 Thomas Vanek .40 1.00
106 Bryan Little .30 .75
107 Brad Richards .40 1.00
108 Mark Giordano .40 1.00
109 Jake Allen .50 1.25
110 Ryan McDonagh .30 .75
111 Ales Hemsky .25 .60
112 Mike Smith .40 1.00
113 Chad Johnson .30 .75
114 David Krejci .30 .75
115 Anders Lee .40 1.00
116 Derick Brassard .40 1.00
117 Brandon Saad .40 1.00
118 Ryan Callahan .40 1.00
119 Martin Jones .40 1.00
120 Wayne Simmonds .50 1.25
121 Morgan Rielly .30 .75
122 Alexander Steen .40 1.00
123 Patric Hornqvist .30 .75
124 Jiri Sekac .30 .75
125 Loui Eriksson .30 .75
126 Scott Hartnell .40 1.00
127 Riley Sheahan .30 .75
128 Cody Eakin .25 .60
129 Mikkel Boedker .25 .60
130 Tyler Toffoli .40 1.00
131 David Desharnais .30 .75
132 Mark Stone .30 .75
133 Jaroslav Halak .30 .75
134 Alex Pietrangelo .30 .75
135 Cam Talbot .50 1.25
136 David Perron .25 .60
137 Alexandre Burrows .30 .75
138 Frans Nielsen .25 .60
139 Marc-Edouard Vlasic .25 .60
140 Valtteri Filppula .30 .75
141 T.J. Oshie .60 1.50
142 Tyler Ennis .30 .75
143 Brendan Gallagher .50 1.25
144 Nail Yakupov .30 .75
145 Jeff Carter .40 1.00
146 Mark Streit .25 .60
147 Jonathan Bernier .40 1.00
148 Gustav Nyquist .40 1.00
149 Jakob Silfverberg .30 .75
150 Curtis Lazar .30 .75
151 Frederik Andersen .30 .75
152 Sam Gagner .30 .75
153 Keith Yandle .40 1.00
154 Anthony Duclair .30 .75
155 Jonathan Drouin .50 1.25
156 Ryan Hartman RC 2.00 5.00
157 Emile Poirier RC 1.50 4.00
158 Jacob de la Rose RC 1.50 4.00
159 Andreas Athanasiou RC 4.00 10.00
160 Andrew Copp RC 1.50 4.00
161 Chandler Stephenson RC 1.50 4.00
162 Mattias Janmark RC 1.50 4.00
163 Brendan Gaunce RC 2.00 5.00
164 Derek Forbort RC 1.25 3.00
165 Mike McCarron RC 2.00 5.00
166 Viktor Arvidsson RC 2.00 5.00
167 Brady Skjei RC 1.25 3.00
168 Devin Shore RC 1.50 4.00
169 Brock McGinn RC 1.50 4.00
170 Antoine Bibeau RC 1.50 4.00
171 Matt Puempel RC 1.25 3.00
172 Stanislav Galiev RC 1.50 4.00
173 Colton Parayko RC 2.00 5.00
174 Brett Pesce RC 1.25 3.00
175 Hunter Shinkaruk RC 1.50 4.00
176 Henrik Samuelsson RC 1.25 3.00
177 Radek Faksa RC 1.50 4.00
178 Linus Ullmark RC 2.00 5.00
179 Nick Ritchie RC 1.50 4.00
180 Shane Prince RC 1.25 3.00
181 Aaron Ekblad SP .60 1.50
182 Dustin Byfuglien SP .60 1.50
183 Daniel Sedin SP .60 1.50
184 Jiri Hudler SP .50 1.25
185 Jonathan Quick SP 1.00 2.50
186 Jakub Voracek SP .60 1.50
187 Cory Schneider SP .50 1.25
188 Logan Couture SP .60 1.50
189 Gabriel Landeskog SP .60 1.50
190 Matt Moulson SP .50 1.25
191 David Backes SP .60 1.50
192 Eric Staal SP .75 2.00
193 Ben Bishop SP .60 1.50
194 Sean Monahan SP .60 1.50
195 Nicklas Backstrom SP 1.00 2.50
196 Corey Perry SP .60 1.50
197 Oliver Ekman-Larsson SP .50 1.25
198 Zemgus Girgensons SP .50 1.25
199 Shea Weber SP .50 1.25
200 James van Riemsdyk SP .60 1.50
201 Ryan Strome SP .50 1.25
202 Tyler Seguin SP 1.00 2.50
203 Jason Pominville SP .50 1.25
204 Braden Holtby SP 1.00 2.50
205 Adam Henrique SP .60 1.50
206 Devan Dubnyk SP .60 1.50
207 Henrik Sedin SP .60 1.50
208 Jason Spezza SP .50 1.25
209 Matt Duchene SP .60 1.50
210 Roberto Luongo SP .60 1.50
211 Tyler Johnson SP .50 1.25
212 Jarome Iginla SP .60 1.50
213 Marc-Andre Fleury SP 1.00 2.50
214 Erik Karlsson SP 1.25 3.00
215 Ryan Johansen SP .75 2.00
216 Pavel Datsyuk SP .75 2.00
217 Tuukka Rask SP .60 1.50
218 Max Pacioretty SP .60 1.50
219 Andrew Hammond SP 2.00 5.00
220 Filip Forsberg SP .75 2.00
221 Joe Pavelski SP .60 1.50
222 Jordan Eberle SP .60 1.50
223 Duncan Keith SP .60 1.50
224 Marian Hossa SP .50 1.25
225 Patrick Marleau SP .60 1.50
226 Rick Nash SP .60 1.50
227 Taylor Hall SP 1.25 3.00
228 Ondrej Pavelec SP .60 1.50
229 Phil Kessel SP 1.00 2.50
230 Tomas Tatar SP .50 1.25
231 Bobby Ryan SP .50 1.25
232 Drew Doughty SP .60 1.50
233 Nick Foligno SP .50 1.25
234 Patrice Bergeron SP .75 2.00
235 Sergei Bobrovsky SP .60 1.50
236 Bobby Orr SP 2.00 5.00
237 Jari Kurri SP .60 1.50
238 Borje Salming SP .60 1.50
239 Guy Carbonneau SP .50 1.25
240 Lanny McDonald SP .60 1.50
241 Gilbert Perreault SP .60 1.50
242 Mike Richter SP .60 1.50
243 Steve Yzerman SP 1.00 2.50
244 Dominik Hasek SP .75 2.00
245 Doug Gilmour SP .75 2.00
246 Skookum Jim Mason SP .60 1.50
247 Pitikwahanapiwiyin SP .60 1.50
248 Kaylyn Kyle SP .60 1.50
249 Samuel de Champlain SP .60 1.50
250 Damian Warner SP .60 1.50
251 Louis Jolliet SP .60 1.50
252 Sir. Frederick Banting SP .60 1.50
253 John Moonlight SP .60 1.50
254 George Vancouver SP .60 1.50
255 Phil Mack SP .60 1.50
256 Malcolm Subban SP RC 5.00 12.00
257 Shea Theodore SP RC 2.00 5.00
258 Oscar Lindberg SP RC 2.00 5.00
259 Nicolas Petan SP RC 2.00 5.00
260 Kevin Fiala SP RC 2.00 5.00
261 Jared McCann SP RC 2.00 5.00
262 Noah Hanifin SP RC 2.50 6.00
263 Charles Hudon SP RC 2.00 5.00
264 Connor Hellebuyck SP RC 5.00 12.00
265 Daniel Sprong SP RC 4.00 10.00
266 Robby Fabbri SP RC 2.50 6.00
267 Mikko Rantanen SP RC 4.00 10.00
268 Jake Virtanen SP RC 2.50 6.00
269 Artemi Panarin SP RC 6.00 15.00
270 Sam Bennett SP RC 2.50 6.00
271 Evgeni Malkin SP 5.00 12.00
272 Jonathan Toews SP 3.00 8.00
273 P.K. Subban SP 2.50 6.00
274 Vladimir Tarasenko SP 2.50 6.00
275 Patrick Kane SP 3.00 8.00
276 Carey Price SP 5.00 12.00
277 Ryan Miller SP 1.50 4.00
278 Alexander Ovechkin SP 6.00 15.00
279 Zach Parise SP 1.50 4.00
280 Ryan Getzlaf SP 2.50 6.00
281 Johnny Gaudreau SP 2.50 6.00
282 Claude Giroux SP 1.50 4.00
283 John Tavares SP 3.00 8.00
284 Anze Kopitar SP 2.50 6.00
285 Steven Stamkos SP 3.00 8.00
286 Jamie Benn SP 2.00 5.00
287 Henrik Zetterberg SP 2.00 5.00
288 Jaromir Jagr SP 4.00 10.00
289 Sidney Crosby SP 6.00 15.00
290 Pekka Rinne SP 2.00 5.00
291 Henrik Lundqvist SP 2.00 5.00
292 Sir John A. Macdonald SP 1.50 4.00
293 Henry Hudson SP 1.50 4.00
294 Camille Leblanc-Bazinet SP 1.50 4.00
295 Jacques Cartier SP 1.50 4.00
296 Louis Riel SP 1.50 4.00
297 Sir Alexander MacKenzie SP 1.50 4.00
298 Alex McDonald SP 1.50 4.00
299 Jerry Potts SP 1.50 4.00
300 Jason Priestley SP 1.50 4.00
301 Bret Hart SP 1.50 4.00
302 Theoren Fleury SP 2.00 5.00
303 Denis Savard SP 2.00 5.00
304 Bob Bourne SP 1.25 3.00
305 Phil Esposito SP 2.50 6.00
306 Teemu Selanne SP 3.00 8.00
307 Peter Forsberg SP 1.50 4.00
308 Mark Messier SP 2.50 6.00
309 Patrick Roy SP 4.00 10.00
310 Wayne Gretzky SP 8.00 20.00
311 Nikolaj Ehlers SP RC 5.00 12.00
312 Max Domi SP RC 5.00 12.00
313 Dylan Larkin SP RC 8.00 20.00
314 Jack Eichel SP RC 10.00 25.00
315 Connor McDavid SP RC 20.00 40.00
316 Sam Bennett RR 10.00 25.00
317 Nikolaj Ehlers RR 15.00 40.00
318 Dylan Larkin RR 25.00 60.00
319 Max Domi RR 15.00 40.00
320 Jack Eichel RR 30.00 80.00
321 Connor McDavid RR 200.00 400.00
322 Carey Price RS 90.00 150.00
323 Alexander Ovechkin RS
324 Sidney Crosby RS
325 Patrick Roy RS 90.00 150.00
326 Mario Lemieux RS
327 Wayne Gretzky RS 40.00 100.00

2015-16 Upper Deck Champ's #1 Picks

1AE Aaron Ekblad 10.00 25.00
1AO Alexander Ovechkin 40.00 100.00
1CM Connor McDavid 80.00 200.00
1DH Dale Hawerchuk 12.00 30.00
1JT John Tavares 20.00 50.00
1ML Mario Lemieux 30.00 80.00
1MM Mike Modano 15.00 40.00
1RN Rick Nash 10.00 25.00
1SC Sidney Crosby 40.00 100.00
1TH Taylor Hall 20.00 50.00

2015-16 Upper Deck Champ's Autographs

7 Antti Niemi D 4.00 10.00
14 Mark Scheifele C 10.00 25.00
16 Brent Burns B 10.00 25.00
17 Semyon Varlamov B 8.00 20.00
18 Bo Horvat B 12.00 30.00
20 Cam Ward D 5.00 12.00
23 Jonathan Huberdeau E 5.00 12.00
39 Nikita Kucherov A 15.00 40.00
40 John Carlson D 6.00 15.00
42 Steve Mason C 6.00 15.00
51 Kevin Hayes B 8.00 20.00
54 Mike Hoffman D 4.00 10.00
64 Jason Zucker E 4.00 10.00
66 Kyle Turris C 6.00 15.00
77 Justin Faulk D 5.00 12.00
84 Matt Beleskey E 3.00 8.00
109 Jake Allen E 6.00 15.00
110 Ryan McDonagh C 6.00 15.00
117 Brandon Saad B 8.00 20.00
126 Scott Hartnell B 8.00 20.00
127 Riley Sheahan E 4.00 10.00
128 Cody Eakin D 3.00 8.00
130 Tyler Toffoli E 5.00 12.00
132 Mark Stone B 6.00 15.00
134 Alex Pietrangelo C 6.00 15.00
136 David Perron D 3.00 8.00
143 Brendan Gallagher C 10.00 25.00
148 Gustav Nyquist B 8.00 20.00
151 Frederik Andersen D 4.00 10.00
158 Jacob de la Rose D 5.00 12.00
159 Andreas Athanasiou E 12.00 30.00
160 Andrew Copp E 5.00 12.00
161 Chandler Stephenson E 5.00 12.00
162 Mattias Janmark D 5.00 12.00
163 Brendan Gaunce E 6.00 15.00
164 Derek Forbort E 4.00 10.00
165 Mike McCarron E 6.00 15.00
166 Viktor Arvidsson E 6.00 15.00
167 Brady Skjei D 4.00 10.00
168 Devin Shore E 5.00 12.00
169 Brock McGinn E 5.00 12.00
170 Antoine Bibeau E 5.00 12.00
171 Matt Puempel D 4.00 10.00
173 Colton Parayko A 12.00 30.00
174 Brett Pesce B 6.00 15.00
176 Henrik Samuelsson E 4.00 10.00
177 Radek Faksa E 5.00 12.00
178 Linus Ullmark E 6.00 15.00
180 Shane Prince D 4.00 10.00
181 Aaron Ekblad SP D 8.00 20.00
184 Jiri Hudler SP E 6.00 15.00
186 Jakub Voracek SP D 8.00 20.00
187 Cory Schneider SP C 8.00 20.00
189 Gabriel Landeskog SP D 8.00 20.00
190 Matt Moulson SP D 6.00 15.00
192 Eric Staal SP D 10.00 25.00
194 Sean Monahan SP D 8.00 20.00
201 Ryan Strome SP C 8.00 20.00
202 Tyler Seguin SP B 15.00 40.00
203 Jason Pominville SP D 6.00 15.00
205 Adam Henrique SP D 8.00 20.00
208 Jason Spezza SP D 6.00 15.00
212 Jarome Iginla SP B 10.00 25.00
213 Marc-Andre Fleury SP D 12.00 30.00
216 Pavel Datsyuk SP B 12.00 30.00
221 Joe Pavelski SP D 8.00 20.00
226 Rick Nash SP D 8.00 20.00
227 Taylor Hall SP C 20.00 50.00
230 Tomas Tatar SP D 6.00 15.00
231 Bobby Ryan SP D 6.00 15.00
233 Nick Foligno SP E 6.00 15.00
235 Sergei Bobrovsky SP C 10.00 25.00
236 Bobby Orr SP B 75.00 150.00
237 Jari Kurri SP D 8.00 20.00
240 Lanny McDonald SP D 15.00 40.00
241 Gilbert Perreault SP D 8.00 20.00
242 Mike Richter SP D 8.00 20.00
243 Steve Yzerman SP A 50.00 120.00
244 Dominik Hasek SP B 40.00 100.00
245 Doug Gilmour SP B 40.00 100.00
250 Damian Warner SP E 6.00 15.00
253 John Moonlight SP E 6.00 15.00
255 Phil Mack SP E 6.00 15.00
256 Malcolm Subban SP E 20.00 50.00
258 Oscar Lindberg SP E 8.00 20.00
263 Charles Hudon SP E 8.00 20.00
266 Robby Fabbri SP E 10.00 25.00
270 Sam Bennett SP E 10.00 25.00
271 Evgeni Malkin SP C 30.00 80.00
272 Jonathan Toews SP B 200.00 350.00
276 Carey Price SP B 60.00 150.00
278 Alexander Ovechkin SP B 40.00 100.00
279 Zach Parise SP B 15.00 40.00
283 John Tavares SP C 15.00 40.00
284 Anze Kopitar SP C 40.00 100.00
50 Jamie Benn SP C 20.00 50.00
288 Jaromir Jagr SP B 40.00 100.00
289 Sidney Crosby SP A 200.00 400.00
290 Pekka Rinne SP C 8.00 20.00
302 Theoren Fleury SP C 150.00 300.00
303 Denis Savard SP C 8.00 20.00
304 Bob Bourne SP D 6.00 15.00
306 Teemu Selanne SP B 40.00 100.00
307 Peter Forsberg SP A 30.00 80.00
308 Mark Messier SP B 40.00 100.00
309 Patrick Roy SP A 200.00 350.00
310 Wayne Gretzky SP A 200.00 350.00
313 Dylan Larkin SP D 40.00 100.00
315 Connor McDavid SP D 200.00 400.00

2015-16 Upper Deck Champ's Canadiana Relics

CRCPC 1906 Canadian Pacific Coast Map D 20.00 50.00
CRLWC 1856 Lower Canada Map C 25.00 60.00
CRMON 1895 City of Montreal Map B 30.00 80.00
CROTT 1906 City of Ottawa Map A
CRTOR 1914 City of Toronto Map B 30.00 80.00
CRUPC 1862 Upper Canada Map C 25.00 60.00
CRWCG 1907 Western Canada and Gold Fields Map D 20.00 50.00
CRWIN 1906 City of Winnipeg Map C 25.00 60.00

2015-16 Upper Deck Champ's Canadiana Relics Oversized

RED Redemption Card 90.00 150.00
CRBG Bluegill B 90.00 150.00
CRBR Brook Trout C 90.00 150.00
CRBT Brown Trout A 90.00 150.00
CRCC Channel Catfish B 90.00 150.00
CRCO Coho Salmon B 90.00 150.00
CRLS Lake Sturgeon C 90.00 150.00
CRMU Muskellunge C 90.00 150.00
CRNP Northern Pike C 90.00 150.00
CRRT Rainbow Trout B 90.00 150.00
CRSM Smallmouth Bass C 90.00 150.00
CRSP Striper B 90.00 150.00
CRST Steelhead B 90.00 150.00
CRTM Tiger Musky B 90.00 150.00
CRWA Walleye C 90.00 150.00
CRACC Antique Crow Call A 90.00 150.00
CRACM Antique Casting Medal D 90.00 150.00
CRACW Antique N.A.A.C.C. Casting Weight C 90.00 150.00
CRADU Antique Duck Call D 90.00 150.00
CRAFF Antique Fishing Float D 90.00 150.00
CRAFR Antique Fly Reel D 90.00 150.00
CRAFS Antique Fish Scale A 90.00 150.00
CRAFW Antique Fishing Weight B 90.00 150.00
CRAGC Antique Goose Call A 90.00 150.00
CRAPC Antique Predator Call C 90.00 150.00
CRFDT Fly Line Dressing Tin C 90.00 150.00
CRFFS Antique Fishing Float Small A 90.00 150.00

2015-16 Upper Deck Champ's Conn Smythe Trophies

CSAM Al MacInnis 6.00 15.00
CSEM Evgeni Malkin 20.00 50.00
CSJT Jonathan Toews 12.00 30.00
CSLR Larry Robinson 6.00 15.00
CSNL Nicklas Lidstrom 6.00 15.00
CSPR Patrick Roy 15.00 40.00
CSSY Steve Yzerman 10.00 25.00
CSWG Wayne Gretzky 30.00 80.00

2015-16 Upper Deck Champ's Famous Foods

FF1 Coney Dog - Detroit 2.00 5.00
FF2 Smoked Meat Sandwich - Montreal 2.00 5.00
FF3 Peameal Bacon Sandwich - Toronto 2.00 5.00
FF4 Cheesesteak - Philadelphia 2.00 5.00
FF5 Pierogi - Pittsburgh 2.00 5.00
FF6 Deep-Dish Pizza - Chicago 2.00 5.00
FF7 Lobster Rolls - Boston 2.00 5.00
FF8 Reuben - New York 2.00 5.00
FF9 Poutine - Ottawa 2.00 5.00
FF10 Chicken Wings - Buffalo 2.00 5.00

2015-16 Upper Deck Champ's Fish

F1 Longnose Gar .75 2.00
F2 Black Crappie .75 2.00
F3 Steelhead .75 2.00
F4 Bowfin .75 2.00
F5 Brown Trout .75 2.00
F6 Flathead Catfish .75 2.00
F7 Chinook Salmon .75 2.00
F8 Coho Salmon .75 2.00
F9 Bull Trout .75 2.00
F10 Bluegill .75 2.00
F11 Cisco .75 2.00
F12 Brook Trout .75 2.00
F13 Common Carp .75 2.00
F14 Lake Trout .75 2.00
F15 Burbot .75 2.00
F16 Muskie .75 2.00
F17 Northern Pike .75 2.00
F18 Pink Salmon .75 2.00
F19 Pumpkinseed .75 2.00
F20 Rainbow Trout .75 2.00
F21 Rock Bass .75 2.00
F22 Green Sunfish .75 2.00
F23 Largemouth Bass .75 2.00
F24 Smallmouth Bass .75 2.00
F25 Sockeye Salmon .75 2.00
F26 Brook Stickleback .75 2.00
F27 Golden Shiner .75 2.00
F28 Walleye .75 2.00
F29 Yellow Perch .75 2.00
F30 Yellow Bullhead .75 2.00

2015-16 Upper Deck Champ's Framed Mini Autographs

MAHU Charles Hudon D
MAJI Jarome Iginla B
MAMG Markus Granlund D 20.00 50.00
MATT Tomas Tatar C 10.00 25.00
MAWG Wayne Gretzky A

2015-16 Upper Deck Champ's Framed Mini Jerseys

MJAO Alexander Ovechkin C 30.00 80.00
MJCM Connor McDavid C 75.00 150.00
MJCP Carey Price C 20.00 50.00
MJDG Doug Gilmour A 30.00 80.00
MJDL Dylan Larkin C 25.00 60.00
MJJE Jack Eichel C 30.00 80.00
MJJI Jarome Iginla C 8.00 20.00
MJJT Jonathan Toews C 15.00 40.00
MJMD Max Domi C 15.00 40.00
MJNE Nikolaj Ehlers C 15.00 40.00
MJPR Patrick Roy A 20.00 50.00
MJRF Robby Fabbri C 10.00 25.00
MJSC Sidney Crosby B 30.00 80.00
MJSS Steven Stamkos B 15.00 40.00
MJZP Zach Parise C 8.00 20.00

2015-16 Upper Deck Champ's Framed Tobacco Cards

NA Automobiles 20.00 50.00
NA Animals 20.00 50.00
NA Air Balloons 20.00 50.00
NA Fish 20.00 50.00
NA Canadian Scenes 20.00 50.00

2015-16 Upper Deck Champ's Jerseys

JAE Aaron Ekblad C 5.00 12.00
JAK Anze Kopitar C 8.00 20.00
JAO Alexander Ovechkin B 20.00 50.00
JBE Jonathan Bernier C 5.00 12.00
JCG Claude Giroux C 5.00 12.00
JCP Corey Perry C 5.00 12.00
JCW Cam Ward C 5.00 12.00
JDD Drew Doughty C 5.00 12.00
JDK Duncan Keith C 5.00 12.00
JDS Daniel Sedin C 5.00 12.00
JEK Erik Karlsson B 10.00 25.00
JHL Henrik Lundqvist B 6.00 15.00
JJI Jarome Iginla C 5.00 12.00
JJP Joe Pavelski C 5.00 12.00
JJS Jason Spezza C 4.00 10.00
JJT Jonathan Toews B 10.00 25.00
JKT Kyle Turris C 4.00 10.00
JMH Marian Hossa C 4.00 10.00
JMS Mark Scheifele C 6.00 15.00
JPE Carey Price B 15.00 40.00
JPK P.K. Subban B 8.00 20.00
JRL Roberto Luongo C 5.00 12.00
JRN Ryan Nugent-Hopkins C 5.00 12.00
JRO Patrick Roy A 12.00 30.00
JSC Sidney Crosby A 20.00 50.00
JSW Shea Weber C 4.00 10.00
JTH Taylor Hall C 10.00 25.00
JTR Tuukka Rask C 5.00 12.00
JTS Tyler Seguin B 8.00 20.00
JZP Zach Parise C 5.00 12.00

2015-16 Upper Deck Champ's Northern Wonders

NW1 Banff National Park 1.00 2.50
NW2 Gros Morne National Park 1.00 2.50
NW3 Haida Gwaii 1.00 2.50
NW4 Jasper National Park 1.00 2.50
NW5 Kootenay National Park 1.00 2.50
NW6 Nahanni National Park 1.00 2.50
NW7 Yoho National Park 1.00 2.50
NW8 Mingan Archipelago National Park 1.00 2.50

NW9 Cape Breton Highlands 1.00 2.50
NW10 Sleeping Giant 1.00 2.50
NW11 Bay of Fundy 1.00 2.50
NW12 Niagara Falls 1.00 2.50
NW13 Northern Lights 1.00 2.50
NW14 Perce Rock 1.00 2.50
NW15 Pacific Rim National Park 1.00 2.50

2015-16 Upper Deck Champ's Rookie Jerseys

JAP Artemi Panarin B 10.00 25.00
JBM Brock McGinn C 3.00 8.00
JCH Connor Hellebuyck C 8.00 20.00
JCM Connor McDavid A 25.00 50.00
JDF Derek Forbort C 2.50 6.00
JDL Dylan Larkin A 10.00 25.00
JEP Emile Poirier C 3.00 8.00
JHS Henrik Samuelsson C 2.50 6.00
JHU Charles Hudon C 3.00 8.00
JJD Jacob de la Rose B 3.00 8.00
JJE Jack Eichel A 12.00 30.00
JJM Jared McCann C 3.00 8.00
JKF Kevin Fiala B 3.00 8.00
JMD Max Domi A 6.00 15.00
JMP Matt Puempel C 2.50 6.00
JMR Mikko Rantanen B 6.00 15.00
JNE Nikolaj Ehlers A 6.00 15.00
JNG Nikolay Goldobin B 3.00 8.00
JNH Noah Hanifin B 4.00 10.00
JNP Nicolas Petan C 3.00 8.00
JNR Nick Ritchie B 3.00 8.00
JOL Oscar Lindberg B 3.00 8.00
JPR Shane Prince C 2.50 6.00
JRF Robby Fabbri A 4.00 10.00
JRH Ryan Hartman C 4.00 10.00
JSB Sam Bennett A 4.00 10.00
JSK Hunter Shinkaruk B 3.00 8.00
JSP Daniel Sprong C 6.00 15.00
JST Shea Theodore B 3.00 8.00
JVI Jake Virtanen B 4.00 10.00

2015-16 Upper Deck Champ's Traditions

T1 Don't Touch the Cup 1.00 2.50
T2 Playoff Beard 1.00 2.50
T3 Tapping the Goalie Pads 1.00 2.50
T4 Hat Trick Toss 1.00 2.50
T5 Playoff Handshake 1.00 2.50
T6 From Failing Hands 1.00 2.50
T7 Octopus Toss 1.00 2.50
T8 Fireman's Hat 1.00 2.50
T9 Victory Rats 1.00 2.50
T10 Winnipeg White Out 1.00 2.50
T11 Patrick Roy Talks to Goal Posts 1.00 2.50
T12 Chris Chelios Last to Put on Jersey 1.00 2.50
T13 Bill Ranford Puck Flip 1.00 2.50
T14 Ray Bourque Shoelaces 1.00 2.50
T15 Wayne Gretzky Drinks 1.00 2.50

1999-00 Upper Deck Century Legends

Released as an 89-card base set, Upper Deck Century Legends commemorates the NHL's timeless players spanning to the beginning of the century. Base cards feature action photography, a right side silver foil border and gold foil highlights. Card number 23 was not released. Century Legends was packaged in 24-pack boxes with 12 cards per pack and carried a suggested retail price of $4.99.

COMPLETE SET (89) 30.00 60.00
1 Wayne Gretzky 1.25 3.00
2 Bobby Orr 1.00 2.50
3 Gordie Howe .75 2.00
4 Mario Lemieux 1.00 2.50
5 Maurice Richard .50 1.25
6 Jean Beliveau .30 .75
7 Doug Harvey .20 .50
8 Bobby Hull .40 1.00
9 Jacques Plante .40 1.00
10 Eddie Shore .20 .50
11 Guy Lafleur .30 .75
12 Mark Messier .20 .50
13 Terry Sawchuk .40 1.00
14 Howie Morenz .15 .40
15 Denis Potvin .15 .40
16 Ray Bourque .30 .75
17 Glenn Hall .25 .60
18 Stan Mikita .30 .75
19 Phil Esposito .40 1.00
20 Mike Bossy .25 .60
21 Ted Lindsay .20 .50
22 Red Kelly .15 .40
24 Bobby Clarke .25 .60
25 Larry Robinson .20 .50
26 Milt Schmidt .15 .40
27 Frank Mahovlich .20 .50
28 Henri Richard .15 .40
29 Paul Coffey .20 .50
30 Bryan Trottier .15 .40
31 Dickie Moore .15 .40
32 Newsy Lalonde .15 .40
33 Syl Apps .15 .40
34 Bill Durnan .15 .40
35 Patrick Roy 1.00 2.50
36 Peter Stastny .20 .50
37 Jaromir Jagr .30 .75
38 Charlie Conacher .15 .40
39 Marcel Dionne .20 .50
40 Tim Horton .20 .50
41 Joe Malone .15 .40
42 Chris Chelios .20 .50
43 Bernie Geoffrion .30 .75
44 Dit Clapper .15 .40
45 Bill Cook .15 .40
46 Johnny Bucyk .15 .40
47 Serge Savard .20 .50
48 Jari Kurri .20 .50
49 Max Bentley .15 .40
50 Gilbert Perreault .15 .40
51 Dominik Hasek .40 1.00
52 Jaromir Jagr .30 .75
53 Peter Forsberg .50 1.25
54 Paul Kariya .20 .50
55 Patrick Roy 1.00 2.50
56 Steve Yzerman 1.00 2.50
57 Ray Bourque .30 .75
58 Pavel Bure .20 .50
59 Teemu Selanne .20 .50
60 Mike Modano .30 .75
61 Eric Lindros .20 .50
62 Brett Hull .25 .60
63 Martin Brodeur .60 1.50
64 Keith Tkachuk .20 .50
65 Joe Sakic .40 1.00
66 Mats Sundin .20 .50
67 John LeClair .20 .50
68 Alexei Yashin .02 .10
69 Peter Bondra .15 .40
70 Brendan Shanahan .20 .50
71 Sergei Samsonov .15 .40
72 Vincent Lecavalier .20 .50
73 Marian Hossa .20 .50
74 Chris Drury .15 .40
75 Milan Hejduk .20 .50
76 Paul Mara .02 .10
77 David Legwand .15 .40
78 Joe Thornton .30 .75
79 Pavel Rosa .02 .10
80 Patrik Elias .15 .40
81 Wayne Gretzky .75 2.00
82 Wayne Gretzky .75 2.00
83 Wayne Gretzky .75 2.00
84 Wayne Gretzky .75 2.00
85 Wayne Gretzky .75 2.00
86 Wayne Gretzky .75 2.00
87 Wayne Gretzky .75 2.00
88 Wayne Gretzky .75 2.00
89 Wayne Gretzky .75 2.00
90 Wayne Gretzky .75 2.00

1999-00 Upper Deck Century Legends All Century Team

Randomly inserted in packs at the rate of 1:11, this 12-card set picks an All-Century first and second team.

COMPLETE SET (12) 40.00 80.00
AC1 Wayne Gretzky 6.00 15.00
AC2 Gordie Howe 4.00 10.00
AC3 Bobby Hull 2.50 6.00
AC4 Bobby Orr 5.00 12.00
AC5 Doug Harvey 2.00 5.00
AC6 Jacques Plante 2.00 5.00
AC7 Mario Lemieux 5.00 12.00
AC8 Maurice Richard 3.00 8.00
AC9 Ted Lindsay 2.00 5.00
AC10 Eddie Shore 2.00 5.00
AC11 Ray Bourque 4.00 10.00
AC12 Terry Sawchuk 2.50 6.00

1999-00 Upper Deck Century Legends Century Collection

Randomly inserted in packs, this 90-card die cut and holographic foil enhanced set parallels the base Century Legends set. Each card is sequentially numbered to 100.

*CENTURY COLL: 15X TO 40X BASIC CARDS

1999-00 Upper Deck Century Legends Epic Signatures

Randomly inserted in packs at the rate of 1:23, this 23-card set features authentic autographs of hockey's all time greats. The Gretzky card originally checklisted was never issued.

BC Bobby Clarke 10.00 25.00
BH Bobby Hull 20.00 50.00
BO Bobby Orr 75.00 150.00
BP Brad Park 6.00 15.00
FM Frank Mahovlich 12.00 30.00
GC Gerry Cheevers 8.00 20.00
GH Gordie Howe 75.00 150.00
JB John Bucyk 8.00 20.00
LR Larry Robinson 15.00 40.00
MB Mike Bossy 8.00 20.00
MD Marcel Dionne 10.00 25.00
ML Mario Lemieux 75.00 150.00
MR Maurice Richard 125.00 200.00
PB Pavel Bure 25.00 50.00
PE Phil Esposito 15.00 40.00
RB Ray Bourque 40.00 80.00
SM Stan Mikita 12.00 30.00
SS Sergei Samsonov 8.00 20.00
TE Tony Esposito 8.00 20.00
TL Ted Lindsay 10.00 25.00
BRH Brett Hull 12.00 30.00
JEB Jean Beliveau 25.00 50.00

1999-00 Upper Deck Century Legends Epic Signatures Gold 100

Randomly seeded in packs, this 23-card set parallels the regular Epic Signature set. Each card is sequentially numbered out of 100.

*GOLD/100: .8X TO 2X SILVER AU

BO Bobby Orr 100.00 250.00
GH Gordie Howe 125.00 250.00
ML Mario Lemieux 150.00 300.00
MR Maurice Richard 125.00 250.00
WG Wayne Gretzky 250.00 500.00

1999-00 Upper Deck Century Legends Essence of the Game

Randomly inserted in packs at the rate of 1:11, this 8-card set couples a player of the past with a present player. The "past" side of the card is in black and white, and the "present" side of the card is in color.

COMPLETE SET (8) 25.00 50.00
E1 W.Gretzky/P.Kariya 5.00 12.00
E2 B.Orr/R.Bourque 5.00 12.00
E3 M.Lemieux/J.Jagr 4.00 10.00
E4 G.Howe/E.Lindros 2.50 6.00
E5 J. Plante/P. Roy 5.00 12.00
E6 M.Richard/P.Bure 2.50 6.00
E7 B.Hull/B.Hull 3.00 8.00
E8 T.Lindsay/K.Tkachuk 2.50 6.00

1999-00 Upper Deck Century Legends Greatest Moments

Randomly inserted in packs at the rate of 1:23, this 10-card set pays tribute to the career of Wayne Gretzky.

COMPLETE SET (10) 60.00 125.00
COMMON GRETZKY (GM1-GM10) 6.00 15.00

1999-00 Upper Deck Century Legends Jerseys of the Century

Randomly inserted in packs at the rate of 1:475, this 6-card set features swatches of game used jersey coupled with a player photo. Bobby Clark and Mario Lemieux cards are signed and numbered out of 25. Note: set price does not include JCA1 and JCA2.

JC1 Bobby Clarke 12.00 30.00
JC2 Mike Bossy 15.00 40.00
JC3 Larry Robinson 12.00 30.00
JC4 Ray Bourque 15.00 40.00
JC5 Mario Lemieux 30.00 80.00
JC6 Wayne Gretzky 40.00 100.00
JCA1 Bobby Clarke AU/25 150.00 300.00
JCA2 Mario Lemieux AU/25 400.00 800.00

2002-03 Upper Deck Classic Portraits

Released in February, this 138-card set consisted of 100 veteran base cards (#1-100), and 38 shortprinted rookie cards (#101-138). Cards 131-138 were only available in UD Rookie Update packs. Rookies were serial-numbered to 1500 copies each.

COMPLETE SET (138) 125.00 250.00
COMP.SET w/o SP's (100) 25.00 50.00
1 Jean-Sebastien Giguere .40 1.00
2 Paul Kariya .50 1.25
3 Mike LeClerc .25 .60
4 Dany Heatley .40 1.00
5 Ilya Kovalchuk .50 1.25
6 Milan Hnilicka .30 .75
7 Joe Thornton .50 1.25
8 Brian Rolston .30 .75
9 Sergei Samsonov .30 .75
10 Miroslav Satan .40 1.00
11 Martin Biron .30 .75
12 Tim Connolly .25 .60
13 Roman Turek .40 1.00
14 Jarome Iginla .40 1.00
15 Craig Conroy .25 .60
16 Arturs Irbe .30 .75
17 Ron Francis .50 1.25
18 Rod Brind'Amour .40 1.00
19 Jeff O'Neill .25 .60
20 Alexei Zhamnov .30 .75
21 Eric Daze .25 .60
22 Jocelyn Thibault .30 .75
23 Rob Blake .40 1.00
24 Patrick Roy 1.00 2.50
25 Joe Sakic .60 1.50
26 Peter Forsberg .50 1.25
27 Chris Drury .40 1.00
28 Marc Denis .30 .75
29 Espen Knutsen .25 .60
30 Rostislav Klesla .25 .60
31 Marty Turco .40 1.00
32 Brenden Morrow .30 .75
33 Mike Modano .60 1.50
34 Steve Yzerman .75 2.00
35 Nicklas Lidstrom .40 1.00
36 Sergei Fedorov .60 1.50
37 Brendan Shanahan .50 1.25
38 Curtis Joseph .40 1.00
39 Mike Comrie .40 1.00
40 Tommy Salo .30 .75
41 Ryan Smyth .30 .75
42 Roberto Luongo .60 1.50
43 Viktor Kozlov .25 .60
44 Kristian Huselius .25 .60
45 Zigmund Palffy .40 1.00
46 Felix Potvin .60 1.50
47 Jason Allison .30 .75
48 Manny Fernandez .30 .75
49 Andrew Brunette .25 .60
50 Marian Gaborik .60 1.50
51 Saku Koivu .40 1.00
52 Yanic Perreault .25 .60
53 Jose Theodore .40 1.00
54 Denis Arkhipov .25 .60
55 Scott Hartnell .40 1.00
56 Mike Dunham .30 .75
57 Martin Brodeur .75 2.00
58 Patrik Elias .40 1.00
59 Joe Nieuwendyk .40 1.00
60 Scott Niedermayer .40 1.00
61 Alexei Yashin .30 .75
62 Michael Peca .30 .75
63 Chris Osgood .40 1.00
64 Eric Lindros .60 1.50
65 Pavel Bure .50 1.25
66 Brian Leetch .40 1.00
67 Dan Blackburn .30 .75
68 Martin Havlat .30 .75
69 Marian Hossa .30 .75
70 Daniel Alfredsson .40 1.00
71 John LeClair .40 1.00
72 Jeremy Roenick .40 1.00
73 Keith Primeau .40 1.00
74 Simon Gagne .40 1.00
75 Tony Amonte .30 .75
76 Sean Burke .25 .60
77 Daniel Briere .30 .75
78 Alexei Kovalev .40 1.00
79 Johan Hedberg .40 1.00
80 Mario Lemieux 1.25 3.00
81 Patrick Marleau .40 1.00
82 Teemu Selanne .75 2.00
83 Evgeni Nabokov .30 .75
84 Owen Nolan .40 1.00
85 Chris Pronger .30 .75
86 Doug Weight .40 1.00
87 Keith Tkachuk .40 1.00
88 Brad Richards .40 1.00
89 Nikolai Khabibulin .40 1.00
90 Vincent Lecavalier .30 .75
91 Mats Sundin .40 1.00
92 Gary Roberts .25 .60
93 Ed Belfour .40 1.00
94 Alexander Mogilny .30 .75
95 Todd Bertuzzi .40 1.00
96 Brendan Morrison .30 .75
97 Markus Naslund .30 .75
98 Jaromir Jagr 1.00 2.50
99 Peter Bondra .40 1.00
100 Olaf Kolzig .40 1.00
101 Alexei Smirnov RC 1.50 4.00
102 Stanislav Chistov RC 1.25 3.00
103 Martin Gerber RC 2.00 5.00
104 Kurt Sauer RC 1.25 3.00
105 Chuck Kobasew RC 1.50 4.00
106 Micki Dupont RC 1.25 3.00
107 Shawn Thornton RC 1.50 4.00
108 Jeff Paul RC 1.25 3.00
109 Rick Nash RC 6.00 15.00
110 Lasse Pirjeta RC 1.25 3.00
111 Henrik Zetterberg RC 6.00 15.00
112 Dmitri Bykov RC 1.25 3.00
113 Ales Hemsky RC 4.00 10.00
114 Mike Cammalleri RC 3.00 8.00
115 Ivan Majesky RC 1.25 3.00
116 Jay Bouwmeester RC 4.00 10.00
117 Alexander Frolov RC 4.00 10.00
118 P-M Bouchard RC 4.00 10.00
119 Ron Hainsey RC 1.25 3.00
120 Adam Hall RC 1.25 3.00
121 Scottie Upshall RC 1.50 4.00
122 Anton Volchenkov RC 1.25 3.00
123 Dennis Seidenberg RC 2.00 5.00
124 Patrick Sharp RC 3.00 8.00
125 Jeff Taffe RC 1.25 3.00
126 Jason Spezza RC 6.00 15.00
127 Tom Koivisto RC 1.25 3.00
128 Alexander Svitov RC 1.25 3.00
129 Carlo Colaiacovo RC 2.00 5.00
130 Steve Eminger RC 1.25 3.00
131 Jared Aulin RC 1.25 3.00
132 Pascal LeClaire RC 1.50 4.00
133 Steve Ott RC 2.50 6.00
134 Brooks Orpik RC 2.00 5.00
135 Ari Ahonen RC 1.25 3.00
136 Mike Komisarek RC 2.00 5.00
137 Ryan Miller RC 5.00 12.00
138 Ray Emery RC 4.00 10.00

2002-03 Upper Deck Classic Portraits Etched in Time

COMPLETE SET (15) 15.00 30.00
STATED ODDS 1:12
ET1 Paul Kariya .50 1.25
ET2 Joe Sakic 1.00 2.50
ET3 Patrick Roy 2.00 5.00
ET4 Mike Modano .75 2.00
ET5 Steve Yzerman 2.50 6.00
ET6 Brendan Shanahan .75 2.00
ET7 Brett Hull .60 1.50
ET8 Mike Comrie .40 1.00
ET9 Jose Theodore .60 1.50
ET10 Martin Brodeur 1.50 4.00
ET11 Pavel Bure .60 1.50
ET12 Simon Gagne .60 1.50
ET13 Mario Lemieux 3.00 8.00
ET14 Teemu Selanne .50 1.25
ET15 Mats Sundin .50 1.25

2002-03 Upper Deck Classic Portraits Genuine Greatness

COMPLETE SET (7) 20.00 40.00
STATED ODDS 1:24
GG1 Paul Kariya 1.00 2.50
GG2 Peter Forsberg 1.50 4.00
GG3 Patrick Roy 3.00 8.00
GG4 Steve Yzerman 3.00 8.00
GG5 Wayne Gretzky 4.00 10.00
GG6 Pavel Bure 1.00 2.50
GG7 Jaromir Jagr 1.00 2.50

2002-03 Upper Deck Classic Portraits Headliners

This 12-card set featured dual jersey swatches. Cards were inserted at a rate of 1:48. A limited parallel was also created and serial-numbered out of 25.

*LTD: 1X TO 2.5X BASE HI

DZ E.Daze/A.Zhamnov 4.00 10.00
FS P.Forsberg/J.Sakic 12.50 30.00
JB J.Jagr/P.Bondra 4.00 10.00
KF P.Kariya/J.Friesen 4.00 10.00
LF N.Lidstrom/S.Fedorov 6.00 15.00
LK C.Lemieux/K.Kolanos 4.00 10.00
LM M.Lemieux/A.Morozov 12.50 30.00
RA P.Roy/D.Aebischer 8.00 20.00
RG J.Roenick/S.Gagne 6.00 15.00
ST S.Samsonov/J.Thornton 6.00 15.00
TK J.Theodore/S.Koivu 10.00 25.00
YH S.Yzerman/D.Hasek 12.50 30.00

2002-03 Upper Deck Classic Portraits Hockey Royalty

This 30-card set featured three jersey swatches per card. Each card was serial-numbered to just 90 copies. A limited parallel was also created and serial-numbered out of 25.

*LIMITED/25: .8X TO 2X BASIC JSY/90

BLB Burke/C.Lemieux/Briere 12.50 30.00
BPT Brodeur/Potvin/Thibault 25.00 60.00
DLH Dunham/Legwand/Hartnell 12.50 30.00
DPP Deadmarsh/Potvin/Palffy 15.00 40.00
DZT Daze/Zhamnov/Thibault 12.50 30.00
GLS Gretzky/M.Lemieux/Sakic 60.00 150.00
GTD Gagne/Tanguay/Daze 12.50 30.00
GTM Guerin/Thornton/Murray 20.00 50.00
GWA Weight/Amonte/Guerin 12.50 30.00
HBK Halpern/Bondra/Kolzig 12.50 30.00
JHL Jagr/Hejduk/Lang 12.50 30.00
KFB Fedorov/Bure/Kovalchuk 20.00 50.00
KFG Kariya/Friesen/Giguere 12.50 30.00
KGJ Konowalchuk/Gonchar/Jagr 12.50 30.00
KSI Kariya/Sakic/Iginla 30.00 80.00
KTK Knutsen/Tugnutt/Klesla 12.50 30.00
LBL Lindros/Bure/Leetch 12.50 30.00
LLN M.Lemieux/Lang/Nieminen 15.00 40.00
LLT M.Lemieux/Lindros/Thornton 30.00 80.00
LRR LeClair/Roenick/Recchi 20.00 50.00
MML Modano/Morrow/Lehtinen 20.00 50.00
PGF Primeau/Gagne/Fedotenko 12.50 30.00
RBT Brodeur/Roy/Theodore 40.00 100.00
RDF Reinprecht/Drury/Forsberg 15.00 40.00
SCA Satan/Connolly/Afinogenov 12.50 30.00
SIT Savard/Iginla/Turek 12.50 30.00
SLN Selanne/Lehtinen/Nieminen 12.50 30.00
SNL Naslund/Lidstrom/Sundin 15.00 40.00
SYL Shanahan/Yzerman/Lidstrom 30.00 80.00
TSH Tanguay/Sakic/Hinote 12.50 30.00

2002-03 Upper Deck Classic Portraits Mini-Busts

Inserted one per box, these mini-busts stood approximately 12 in. high and carried a player likeness on top of a column base. Each player had several variations including; home, away, glass and marble. Several players also had autographed versions and alternate jersey versions. Individual print runs for autographs are listed below, print runs of less than 25 are not priced due to scarcity.

1 Brendan Shanahan A 8.00 20.00
2 Brendan Shanahan G 8.00 20.00
3 Brendan Shanahan H 6.00 15.00
4 Brendan Shanahan M 6.00 15.00
5 Curtis Joseph A 8.00 20.00
6 Curtis Joseph A AU/31 40.00 100.00
7 Curtis Joseph G 8.00 20.00
8 Curtis Joseph G AU/10
9 Curtis Joseph H 6.00 15.00
10 Curtis Joseph H AU 30.00 80.00
11 Curtis Joseph M 6.00 15.00
12 Curtis Joseph M AU/25 40.00 100.00
13 Dany Heatley A 8.00 20.00
14 Dany Heatley A AU/15
15 Dany Heatley G 8.00 20.00
16 Dany Heatley G AU/10
17 Dany Heatley H 6.00 15.00
18 Dany Heatley H AU 20.00 50.00
19 Dany Heatley M 6.00 15.00
20 Dany Heatley M AU/25 30.00 80.00
21 Dominik Hasek A 8.00 20.00
22 Dominik Hasek G 8.00 20.00
23 Dominik Hasek H 6.00 15.00
24 Dominik Hasek M 6.00 15.00
25 Dominik Hasek Third 6.00 15.00
26 Gordie Howe A 20.00 50.00
27 Gordie Howe A AU/9
28 Gordie Howe G 20.00 50.00
29 Gordie Howe G AU/10
30 Gordie Howe H 15.00 40.00
31 Gordie Howe H AU SP 50.00 125.00
32 Gordie Howe M 15.00 40.00
33 Gordie Howe M AU/25 100.00 250.00
34 Gordie Howe Third 15.00 40.00
35 Gordie Howe Third AU/50 60.00 150.00
36 Ilya Kovalchuk A 8.00 20.00
37 Ilya Kovalchuk A AU/17
38 Ilya Kovalchuk G 8.00 20.00
39 Ilya Kovalchuk G AU/10
40 Ilya Kovalchuk H 6.00 15.00
41 Ilya Kovalchuk H AU 20.00 50.00
42 Ilya Kovalchuk M 6.00 15.00
43 Ilya Kovalchuk M AU/25 30.00 80.00
44 Jarome Iginla A 8.00 20.00
45 Jarome Iginla A AU/12
46 Jarome Iginla G 8.00 20.00
47 Jarome Iginla G AU/10
48 Jarome Iginla H 6.00 15.00
49 Jarome Iginla H AU 12.50 30.00
50 Jarome Iginla M 6.00 15.00
51 Jarome Iginla M AU/25 20.00 50.00
52 Jaromir Jagr A 8.00 20.00
53 Jaromir Jagr G 8.00 20.00
54 Jaromir Jagr H 6.00 15.00
55 Jaromir Jagr M 12.50 30.00
56 Jason Spezza A 8.00 20.00
57 Jason Spezza A AU/39 50.00 125.00
58 Jason Spezza G 8.00 20.00
59 Jason Spezza G AU/10
60 Jason Spezza H 6.00 15.00
61 Jason Spezza H AU 25.00 60.00
62 Jason Spezza M 10.00 25.00
63 Jason Spezza M AU/25 40.00 100.00
64 Jason Spezza Third 6.00 15.00
65 Jason Spezza Third AU/50 30.00 80.00
66 Joe Sakic A 20.00 50.00
67 Joe Sakic G 20.00 50.00
68 Joe Sakic H 12.50 30.00
69 Joe Sakic M 15.00 40.00
70 Joe Sakic Third 15.00 40.00
71 Joe Thornton A 8.00 20.00
72 Joe Thornton A AU/19
73 Joe Thornton G 8.00 20.00
74 Joe Thornton G AU/10
75 Joe Thornton H 6.00 15.00
76 Joe Thornton H AU 30.00 80.00
77 Joe Thornton M 6.00 15.00
78 Joe Thornton M AU/25 50.00 125.00
79 Joe Thornton Third 6.00 15.00
80 Joe Thornton Third AU/50 40.00 100.00
81 Mario Lemieux H 50.00 125.00
82 Mario Lemieux G 60.00 150.00
83 Martin Brodeur A 25.00 60.00
84 Martin Brodeur A AU/30 50.00 125.00
85 Martin Brodeur G 25.00 60.00
86 Martin Brodeur G AU/10
87 Martin Brodeur H 12.50 30.00
88 Martin Brodeur H AU 50.00 125.00
89 Martin Brodeur M 15.00 40.00
90 Martin Brodeur M AU/25 75.00 200.00
91 Patrick Roy A 30.00 80.00
92 Patrick Roy A AU/33 125.00 300.00
93 Patrick Roy G 30.00 80.00
94 Patrick Roy G AU/10
95 Patrick Roy H 20.00 50.00
96 Patrick Roy H AU SP 75.00 150.00
97 Patrick Roy M 25.00 60.00
98 Patrick Roy M AU/25 125.00 300.00
99 Patrick Roy Third 25.00 60.00
100 Patrick Roy Third AU/50 100.00 250.00
101 Paul Kariya A 8.00 20.00
102 Paul Kariya G 8.00 20.00
103 Paul Kariya H 6.00 15.00
104 Paul Kariya M 6.00 15.00
105 Pavel Bure A 8.00 20.00
106 Pavel Bure A AU/9
107 Pavel Bure G 8.00 20.00
108 Pavel Bure G AU/10
109 Pavel Bure H 6.00 15.00
110 Pavel Bure H AU SP 30.00 80.00
111 Pavel Bure M 6.00 15.00
112 Pavel Bure M AU/25 60.00 150.00
113 Pavel Bure Third 6.00 15.00
114 Pavel Bure Third AU/50 40.00 100.00
115 Ray Bourque Bos.A 20.00 50.00
116 Ray Bourque Bos.A AU/77 50.00 125.00
117 Ray Bourque G 20.00 50.00
118 Ray Bourque G AU/10
119 Ray Bourque Bos.H 12.50 30.00
120 Ray Bourque Bos.H AU SP 40.00 100.00
121 Ray Bourque M 15.00 40.00
122 Ray Bourque M AU/25 60.00 150.00
123 Ray Bourque Col.Third 15.00 40.00
124 Ray Bourque Col.Third AU/50 50.00 125.00

2002-03 Upper Deck Classic Portraits Pillars of Strength

COMPLETE SET (10) 10.00 20.00
STATED ODDS 1:18
PS1 Ilya Kovalchuk .75 2.00
PS2 Jarome Iginla .50 1.25
PS3 Joe Sakic 1.00 2.50
PS4 Mike Modano .75 2.00
PS5 Brendan Shanahan .75 2.00
PS6 Martin Brodeur 1.25 3.00
PS7 Eric Lindros .40 1.00
PS8 Mario Lemieux 3.00 8.00
PS9 Teemu Selanne .40 1.00
PS10 Olaf Kolzig .40 1.00

2002-03 Upper Deck Classic Portraits Portrait of a Legend

This 10-card set was dedicated to the career of Bobby Orr. Cards were inserted at 1:18.

COMPLETE SET (10) 20.00 40.00
COMMON ORR (PL1-PL10) 2.00 5.00

2002-03 Upper Deck Classic Portraits Starring Cast

This 15-card memorabilia set was inserted at 1:48. A limited parallel was also created and serial-numbered out of 50.

*LTD: .6X TO 1.5X BASE HI

CAT Alex Tanguay 4.00 10.00
CBG Bill Guerin 4.00 10.00
CBS Brendan Shanahan 5.00 12.00
CFP Felix Potvin 6.00 15.00
CJR Jeremy Roenick 5.00 12.00
CKT Keith Tkachuk 5.00 12.00
CMM Mike Modano 4.00 10.00
CMN Markus Naslund 4.00 10.00
CMS Mats Sundin 5.00 12.00
CPK Paul Kariya 5.00 12.00
CSA Miroslav Satan 4.00 10.00
CSB Sean Burke 4.00 10.00
CSG Simon Gagne 5.00 12.00
CSY Steve Yzerman 12.50 30.00
CZP Zigmund Palffy 4.00 10.00

2002-03 Upper Deck Classic Portraits Stitches

This 15-card memorabilia set was inserted at 1:24. A limited parallel was also created and serial-numbered out of 75.

*LTD: .5X TO 1.25X BASE HI

CAD Adam Deadmarsh 3.00 8.00
CBO Peter Bondra 3.00 8.00
CCD Chris Drury 3.00 8.00
CJF Jeff Friesen 3.00 8.00
CJI Jarome Iginla 5.00 12.00
CJT Joe Thornton 6.00 15.00
CKK Krys Kolanos 3.00 8.00
CMD Mike Dunham 3.00 8.00
CPB Pavel Bure 4.00 10.00
CRS Rostislav Klesla 3.00 8.00
CSF Sergei Fedorov 5.00 12.00
CSG Simon Gagne 4.00 10.00
CSR Steven Reinprecht 3.00 8.00
CSS Sergei Samsonov 3.00 8.00
CTH Jose Theodore 5.00 12.00

2003-04 Upper Deck Classic Portraits

Released in late-October, this 188-card set consisted of 100 veteran cards, 15 "Etched in Time" subset cards (101-115) serial-numbered to 1100, 18 Patrick Roy "Portrait of a Legend" cards (116-135) serial-numbered to 800, 25 "Pillars of Strength" subset cards (136-160) serial-numbered to 650, 6 pack issued rookies (161-166); 20 shortprinted rookies available via exchange cards (167-188) and 8 shortprinted rookies (189-196) available in packs of UD Rookie Update. Cards 161-196 were serial-numbered out of 1150.

COMP.SET w/o SP's (100) 15.00 30.00
1 Sergei Fedorov .50 1.25
2 Stanislav Chistov .20 .50
3 Jean-Sebastien Giguere .30 .75
4 Dany Heatley .30 .75
5 Ilya Kovalchuk .30 .75
6 Joe Thornton .40 1.00
7 Glen Murray .25 .60
8 Sergei Samsonov .25 .60
9 Miroslav Satan .25 .60
10 Maxim Afinogenov .20 .50
11 Chris Drury .25 .60
12 Jarome Iginla .30 .75
13 Steve Reinprecht .20 .50
14 Roman Turek .25 .60
15 Ron Francis .40 1.00
16 Jeff O'Neill .20 .50
17 Alexei Zhamnov .25 .60
18 Kyle Calder .20 .50
19 Jocelyn Thibault .25 .60
20 Teemu Selanne .60 1.50
21 Peter Forsberg .40 1.00
22 Paul Kariya .40 1.00
23 Joe Sakic .50 1.25
24 David Aebischer .25 .60
25 Rick Nash .30 .75
26 Marc Denis .25 .60
27 Todd Marchant .20 .50
28 Mike Modano .50 1.25
29 Bill Guerin .30 .75
30 Marty Turco .30 .75
31 Brendan Shanahan .40 1.00
32 Henrik Zetterberg .40 1.00
33 Steve Yzerman .75 2.00
34 Dominik Hasek .50 1.25
35 Ryan Smyth .25 .60
36 Mike Comrie .25 .60
37 Ales Hemsky .30 .75
38 Tommy Salo .25 .60
39 Olli Jokinen .30 .75
40 Stephen Weiss .20 .50
41 Jay Bouwmeester .30 .75
42 Roberto Luongo .50 1.25
43 Zigmund Palffy .30 .75
44 Alexander Frolov .25 .60
45 Roman Cechmanek .25 .60
46 Marian Gaborik .50 1.25
47 P-M Bouchard .30 .75
48 Manny Fernandez .25 .60
49 Dwayne Roloson .25 .60
50 Saku Koivu .30 .75
51 Marcel Hossa .20 .50
52 Jose Theodore .30 .75
53 Michael Komisarek .20 .50
54 David Legwand .25 .60
55 Tomas Vokoun .25 .60
56 Patrik Elias .30 .75
57 Jamie Langenbrunner .25 .60
58 Scott Stevens .30 .75
59 Martin Brodeur .60 1.50
60 Alexei Yashin .25 .60
61 Rick DiPietro .25 .60
62 Alex Kovalev .25 .60
63 Eric Lindros .50 1.25
64 Pavel Bure .40 1.00
65 Mike Dunham .25 .60
66 Marian Hossa .25 .60
67 Daniel Alfredsson .30 .75
68 Jason Spezza .30 .75
69 Patrick Lalime .25 .60
70 Jeremy Roenick .30 .75
71 Tony Amonte .25 .60
72 John LeClair .30 .75
73 Simon Gagne .30 .75
74 Mike Johnson .20 .50
75 Chris Gratton .20 .50
76 Sean Burke .20 .50
77 Mario Lemieux 1.00 2.50
78 Martin Straka .20 .50
79 Sebastien Caron .25 .60
80 Mike Ricci .25 .60
81 Nicholas Dimitrakos .20 .50
82 Evgeni Nabokov .25 .60
83 Al MacInnis .30 .75
84 Keith Tkachuk .30 .75
85 Chris Pronger .25 .60
86 Chris Osgood .30 .75
87 Vincent Lecavalier .25 .60
88 Martin St. Louis .30 .75
89 Nikolai Khabibulin .30 .75
90 Alexander Mogilny .25 .60
91 Mats Sundin .30 .75
92 Owen Nolan .25 .60
93 Ed Belfour .30 .75
94 Alexander Auld .20 .50
95 Markus Naslund .25 .60
96 Todd Bertuzzi .30 .75
97 Ed Jovanovski .25 .60
98 Jaromir Jagr .75 2.00
99 Peter Bondra .25 .60
100 Olaf Kolzig .30 .75
101 Jean-Sebastien Giguere ET 1.00 2.50
102 Joe Thornton ET 1.25 3.00
103 Mario Lemieux ET 3.00 8.00
104 Peter Forsberg ET 1.25 3.00
105 Steve Yzerman ET 2.50 6.00
106 Eric Lindros ET 1.50 4.00
107 Marian Gaborik ET 1.50 4.00
108 Paul Kariya ET 1.25 3.00
109 Joe Sakic ET 1.50 4.00
110 Martin Brodeur ET 2.00 5.00
111 Ed Belfour ET 1.00 2.50
112 Marian Hossa ET .75 2.00
113 Gordie Howe ET 3.00 8.00
114 Wayne Gretzky ET 5.00 12.00
115 Bobby Orr ET 3.00 8.00
116 Patrick Roy PL 4.00 10.00
117 Patrick Roy PL 4.00 10.00
118 Patrick Roy PL 4.00 10.00
119 Patrick Roy PL 4.00 10.00
120 Patrick Roy PL 4.00 10.00
121 Patrick Roy PL 4.00 10.00
122 Patrick Roy PL 4.00 10.00
123 Patrick Roy PL 4.00 10.00
124 Patrick Roy PL 4.00 10.00
125 Patrick Roy PL 4.00 10.00
126 Patrick Roy PL 4.00 10.00
127 Patrick Roy PL 4.00 10.00
128 Patrick Roy PL 4.00 10.00
129 Patrick Roy PL 4.00 10.00
130 Patrick Roy PL 4.00 10.00
131 Patrick Roy PL 4.00 10.00
132 Patrick Roy PL 4.00 10.00
133 Patrick Roy PL 4.00 10.00
134 Patrick Roy Martin Brodeur PL 4.00 10.00
135 Patrick Roy/J-S Giguere PL 4.00 10.00
136 Mario Lemieux PS 5.00 12.00
137 Gordie Howe PS 5.00 12.00
138 Keith Tkachuk PS 1.50 4.00
139 Peter Forsberg PS 2.00 5.00
140 Jeremy Roenick PS 1.50 4.00
141 Eric Lindros PS 2.50 6.00
142 Jaromir Jagr PS 4.00 10.00
143 Zdeno Chara PS 1.50 4.00
144 Owen Nolan PS 1.25 3.00
145 Martin Brodeur PS 3.00 8.00
146 Ed Belfour PS 1.50 4.00
147 Marian Hossa PS 1.25 3.00
148 Jarome Iginla PS 1.50 4.00
149 Jocelyn Thibault PS 1.25 3.00
150 Marian Gaborik PS 2.50 6.00
151 Vincent Lecavalier PS 1.25 3.00
152 Joe Thornton PS 2.00 5.00
153 Rick Nash PS 1.50 4.00
154 Joe Sakic PS 2.50 6.00
155 Mike Modano PS 2.50 6.00
156 Jean-Sebastien Giguere PS 1.50 4.00
157 Olli Jokinen PS 1.50 4.00
158 Steve Yzerman PS 4.00 10.00
159 Jason Spezza PS 1.50 4.00
160 Chris Pronger PS 1.25 3.00
161 Joe DiPenta RC 1.50 4.00
162 Milan Bartovic RC 1.50 4.00
163 Rick Mrozik RC 1.25 3.00
164 Kent McDonell RC 1.50 4.00
165 Peter Sejna RC 1.50 4.00
166 Matt Stajan RC 2.00 5.00
167 Marc-Andre Fleury RC 8.00 20.00
168 Nathan Horton RC 3.00 8.00
169 Eric Staal RC 6.00 15.00
170 Joffrey Lupul RC 3.00 8.00
171 Dustin Brown RC 2.50 6.00
172 Jordin Tootoo RC 2.50 6.00
173 Joni Pitkanen RC 2.00 5.00
174 Milan Michalek RC 2.50 6.00
175 Pavel Vorobiev RC 1.50 4.00
176 Tuomo Ruutu RC 2.00 5.00
177 Patrice Bergeron RC 6.00 15.00
178 Antoine Vermette RC 4.00 10.00
179 Antti Miettinen RC 2.00 5.00
180 Dan Hamhuis RC 1.50 4.00
181 Sean Bergenheim RC 1.50 4.00
182 Maxim Kondratiev RC 1.25 3.00
183 Chris Higgins RC 2.50 6.00
184 John-Michael Liles RC 1.50 4.00
185 Brent Burns RC 3.00 8.00
186 Marek Svatos RC 2.50 6.00
187 Boyd Gordon RC 1.50 4.00
188 Cody McCormick RC 1.50 4.00
189 Alexander Semin RC 4.00 10.00
190 Timofei Shishkanov RC 1.25 3.00
191 Mikhail Yakubov RC 1.25 3.00
192 Ryan Kesler RC 6.00 15.00
193 Fredrik Sjostrom RC 2.00 5.00
194 Nikolai Zherdev RC 2.50 6.00
195 Derek Roy RC 2.00 5.00
196 Tomas Plekanec RC 4.00 10.00

2003-04 Upper Deck Classic Portraits Classic Colors

PRINT RUN 50 SERIAL #'d SETS

CCAM Al MacInnis 8.00 20.00
CCBH Brett Hull 20.00 50.00
CCBS Brendan Shanahan 12.50 30.00
CCCD Chris Drury 8.00 20.00
CCCJ Curtis Joseph 12.50 30.00
CCCO Chris Osgood 8.00 20.00
CCDW Doug Weight 8.00 20.00
CCEL Eric Lindros 12.50 30.00
CCJA Jason Allison 8.00 20.00
CCJB Jay Bouwmeester 8.00 20.00
CCJJ Jaromir Jagr 20.00 50.00
CCJS Jason Spezza 20.00 50.00
CCJS Joe Sakic 30.00 80.00
CCMD Mike Dunham 8.00 20.00
CCON Ed Belfour 12.50 30.00
CCPK Paul Kariya 12.50 30.00
CCRN Rick Nash 20.00 50.00
CCTA Tony Amonte 8.00 20.00
CCTS Teemu Selanne 12.50 30.00
CCWG Wayne Gretzky 75.00 150.00

2003-04 Upper Deck Classic Portraits Classic Stitches

STATED ODDS 1:18
CSAD Adam Deadmarsh 3.00 8.00
CSBB Brian Boucher 3.00 8.00
CSCP Chris Pronger 3.00 8.00
CSEB Ed Belfour 4.00 10.00
CSGM Glen Murray 3.00 8.00
CSJT Joe Thornton 6.00 15.00
CSMA Maxim Afinogenov 3.00 8.00
CSSK Saku Koivu 4.00 10.00
CSSY Steve Yzerman 10.00 25.00
CSTH Jocelyn Thibault 3.00 8.00

2003-04 Upper Deck Classic Portraits Genuine Greatness

PRINT RUN 75 SERIAL #'d SETS
GGDH Dany Heatley 10.00 25.00
GGGR Wayne Gretzky 50.00 125.00
GGJR Jeremy Roenick 10.00 25.00
GGJS Jason Spezza 12.50 30.00
GGJT Joe Thornton 12.50 30.00
GGMB Martin Brodeur 15.00 40.00
GGML Mario Lemieux 20.00 50.00
GGPR Patrick Roy 20.00 50.00
GGRN Rick Nash 12.50 30.00
GGSY Steve Yzerman 20.00 50.00
GGWG Wayne Gretzky 50.00 125.00

2003-04 Upper DeckClassic Portraits Headliners

STATED ODDS 1:36
HHEL Eric Lindros 8.00 20.00
HHHA Marcel Hossa 4.00 10.00
HHJJ Jaromir Jagr 10.00 25.00
HHJT Joe Thornton 8.00 20.00
HHMG Marian Gaborik 8.00 20.00
HHML Mario Lemieux 12.50 30.00
HHMN Markus Naslund 6.00 15.00
HHPK Paul Kariya 5.00 12.00
HHVB Valeri Bure 4.00 10.00

2003-04 Upper Deck Classic Portraits Hockey Royalty

PRINT RUN 99 SERIAL #'d SETS
BLC Bure/Lindros/Kovalev 10.00 25.00
BNM Bertuzzi/Naslund/Morrison 10.00 25.00
BSM Belfour/Sundin/Mogilny 15.00 40.00
DSB Domi/Stock/Brashear 15.00 40.00
FSK Forsberg/Sakic/Kariya 25.00 60.00
KTH Koivu/Theodore/Hossa 15.00 40.00
LYG Lemieux/Yzerman/Gilmour 30.00 80.00
PLB Pronger/Lidstrom/Bowmster 12.00 30.00
RLA Roenick/LeClair/Amonte 10.00 25.00
YHS Yzerman/Hull/Shanahan 30.00 80.00

2003-04 Upper Deck Classic Portraits Mini-Busts

Inserted one per box, these ceramic busts carried two themes; Stanley Cup Winners and 500 Goal scorers. A bronze version was also created and limited to 25 copies each.
*BRONZE: 1X TO 2.5X
1 Patrick Roy COL 15.00 40.00
2 Patrick Roy MON/50 25.00 60.00
3 Gordie Howe SC 15.00 40.00
4 Martin Brodeur SC 15.00 40.00
5 Mike Modano SC 15.00 40.00
6 Joe Sakic SC 15.00 40.00
7 Peter Forsberg SC 15.00 40.00
8 Brett Hull DET 15.00 40.00
9 Brett Hull DAL/50 20.00 50.00
10 Ray Bourque SC 15.00 40.00
11 Jaromir Jagr PITT 15.00 40.00
12 Mario Lemieux SC 25.00 60.00
13 Steve Yzerman SC 20.00 50.00
14 Mark Messier NYR SC 15.00 40.00
15 Mark Messier EDM SC/50 20.00 50.00
16 Phil Esposito SC 15.00 40.00
17 Terry Sawchuk DET 15.00 40.00
18 Terry Sawchuk TOR/50 20.00 50.00
19 Bryan Trottier NYI SC 15.00 40.00
20 Bryan Trottier PITT SC/50 15.00 40.00
21 Bobby Clarke SC 15.00 40.00
22 Guy Lafleur SC 15.00 40.00
23 Scotty Bowman DET 20.00 50.00
24 Scotty Bowman MON/50 20.00 50.00
25 Scotty Bowman PITT/50 20.00 50.00
26 Phil Esposito 500 15.00 40.00
27 Steve Yzerman 500 20.00 50.00
28 Guy Lafleur 500 25.00 60.00
29 Mario Lemieux 500 25.00 60.00
30 Brett Hull 500 20.00 50.00
31 Jaromir Jagr 500 15.00 40.00
32 Gordie Howe 500 15.00 40.00
33 Mark Messier 500 15.00 40.00
34 Bryan Trottier 500 15.00 40.00
35 Joe Sakic 500 15.00 40.00

2003-04 Upper Deck Classic Portraits Mini-Busts Signed

This 21-card set partially parallels the regular bust but carried authentic player autographs. The busts in the 500 Goal Scorers subset were limited to 50 copies each and the Sawchuk busts were 1 of 1's. A bronze version was also created and limited to 10 copies or less each. Those busts are not priced due to scarcity.
BRONZE PRINT RUN 10 OR LESS
Patrick Roy COL 100.00 250.00
2 Patrick Roy MON/25 250.00 500.00
3 Gordie Howe SC 60.00 150.00
4 Martin Brodeur SC 60.00 150.00
10 Ray Bourque SC 40.00 100.00
11 Jaromir Jagr PITT 40.00 100.00
16 Phil Esposito SC 40.00 100.00
17 Terry Sawchuk DET/1
18 Terry Sawchuk TOR/1
19 Bryan Trottier NYI SC 40.00 100.00
20 Bryan Trottier PITT SC/25 60.00 150.00
21 Bobby Clarke SC 25.00 60.00
22 Guy Lafleur SC 50.00 125.00
23 Scotty Bowman DET 40.00 100.00
24 Scotty Bowman MON
25 Scotty Bowman PITT/25 50.00 125.00
26 Phil Esposito 500 30.00 80.00
28 Guy Lafleur 500 50.00 125.00
31 Jaromir Jagr 500 75.00 200.00
32 Gordie Howe 500 150.00 300.00
34 Bryan Trottier 500 75.00 200.00

2003-04 Upper Deck Classic Portraits Premium Portraits

PRINT RUN 25 SERIAL #'d SETS
PPJT Joe Thornton 25.00 60.00
PPMB Martin Brodeur 30.00 80.00
PPMH Gordie Howe 40.00 100.00
PPML Mario Lemieux 40.00 100.00
PPPF Peter Forsberg 25.00 60.00
PPPR Patrick Roy 40.00 100.00
PPSY Steve Yzerman 40.00 100.00
PPWG Wayne Gretzky 60.00 150.00

2003-04 Upper Deck Classic Portraits Starring Cast

STATED ODDS 1:36
SCCD Chris Drury 4.00 10.00
SCJG Jean-Sebastien Giguere 4.00 10.00
SCJH Johan Hedberg 4.00 10.00
SCMB Martin Brodeur 12.50 30.00
SCMM Mike Modano 8.00 20.00
SCPR Patrick Roy 12.50 30.00
SCRN Rick Nash 8.00 20.00
SCTA Tony Amonte 4.00 10.00
SCTB Todd Bertuzzi 4.00 10.00

2015-16 Upper Deck Connor McDavid Collection

COMP.FACT.SET (26) 15.00 30.00
COMPLETE SET (25) 8.00 20.00
COMMON McDAVID .50 1.25

2015-16 Upper Deck Connor McDavid Collection Jumbos

C1 Connor McDavid AU/17
C1 Connor McDavid 4.00 10.00

2015-16 Upper Deck Contours

1 Jonathan Toews 2.00 5.00
2 Steven Stamkos 2.00 5.00
3 Carey Price 3.00 8.00
4 Adam Henrique 1.00 2.50
5 Jarome Iginla 1.00 2.50
6 Phil Kessel 1.50 4.00
7 Anze Kopitar 1.50 4.00
8 Jamie Benn 1.25 3.00
9 Radim Vrbata .75 2.00
10 Corey Perry 1.00 2.50
11 Andrew Ladd 1.00 2.50
12 James van Riemsdyk 1.00 2.50
13 Alexander Ovechkin 4.00 10.00
14 Alexandre Burrows .75 2.00
15 Pekka Rinne 1.25 3.00
16 Zach Parise 1.00 2.50
17 Ryan Getzlaf 1.50 4.00
18 Jaden Schwartz 1.25 3.00
19 Kyle Turris .75 2.00
20 Pavel Datsyuk 1.25 3.00
21 John Tavares 2.00 5.00
22 Logan Couture 1.00 2.50
23 Eric Staal 1.25 3.00
24 Rick Nash 1.00 2.50
25 Patrice Bergeron 1.25 3.00
26 Evgeni Malkin 3.00 8.00
27 Oliver Ekman-Larsson .75 2.00
28 Jonathan Quick 1.50 4.00
29 Tyler Johnson .75 2.00
30 Patrick Kane 2.00 5.00
31 Jonathan Huberdeau 1.00 2.50
32 Ryan Johansen 1.25 3.00
33 Mark Stone .75 2.00
34 Jiri Hudler .75 2.00
35 P.K. Subban 1.50 4.00
36 T.J. Oshie 1.50 4.00
37 Blake Wheeler 1.00 2.50
38 Tyler Bozak .75 2.00
39 Thomas Vanek 1.00 2.50
40 Tyler Seguin 1.50 4.00
41 Henrik Zetterberg 1.25 3.00
42 Filip Forsberg 1.25 3.00
43 Henrik Lundqvist 1.25 3.00
44 Jordan Staal 1.00 2.50
45 Max Pacioretty 1.00 2.50
46 Michael Cammalleri .75 2.00
47 Taylor Hall 2.00 5.00
48 Nicklas Backstrom 1.50 4.00
49 Derick Brassard 1.00 2.50
50 Gabriel Landeskog 1.00 2.50
51 David Backes 1.00 2.50
52 Ben Bishop 1.00 2.50
53 Kyle Okposo 1.00 2.50
54 Jakub Voracek 1.00 2.50
55 Ryan Kesler 1.00 2.50
56 Nick Bjugstad .75 2.00
57 Daniel Sedin 1.00 2.50
58 Milan Lucic .75 2.00
59 Claude Giroux 1.00 2.50
60 Sean Monahan 1.00 2.50
61 Sergei Bobrovsky 1.00 2.50
62 Elias Lindholm .60 1.50
63 Loui Eriksson .75 2.00
64 Shea Weber .75 2.00
65 Joe Pavelski 1.00 2.50
66 Nikita Kucherov 1.50 4.00
67 John Gibson .75 2.00
68 Sam Gagner .75 2.00
69 Jason Spezza .75 2.00
70 Nazem Kadri .75 2.00
71 Johnny Gaudreau 1.50 4.00
72 Mikko Koivu .75 2.00
73 Colin Wilson .60 1.50
74 Erik Karlsson 2.00 5.00
75 Cory Schneider .75 2.00
76 Aaron Ekblad 1.00 2.50
77 Marcus Johansson .75 2.00
78 Chris Kreider 1.00 2.50
79 Brad Marchand 1.25 3.00
80 Marian Hossa .75 2.00
81 Shane Doan .75 2.00
82 Henrik Sedin 1.00 2.50
83 Anders Lee 1.00 2.50
84 Mark Scheifele 1.25 3.00
85 Jordan Eberle 1.00 2.50
86 Joe Thornton 1.00 2.50
87 Sidney Crosby 4.00 10.00
88 Nick Foligno .75 2.00
89 Vladimir Tarasenko 1.50 4.00
90 Corey Crawford 1.25 3.00
91 Curtis Joseph 1.00 2.50
92 Steve Yzerman 1.50 4.00
93 Jeremy Roenick 1.00 2.50
94 Glenn Hall .75 2.00
95 Paul Coffey 1.00 2.50
96 Doug Gilmour 1.25 3.00
97 Mark Messier 1.50 4.00
98 Borje Salming 1.00 2.50
99 Wayne Gretzky 5.00 12.00
100 Owen Nolan .75 2.00
101 Nick Ritchie AU RC 4.00 10.00
102 Zachary Fucale AU RC 4.00 10.00
103 Brady Skjei AU RC 3.00 8.00
104 Malcolm Subban AU RC 10.00 25.00
105 Andreas Athanasiou AU RC 10.00 25.00
106 Daniel Sprong AU RC 8.00 20.00
107 Hunter Shinkaruk AU RC 4.00 10.00
108 Dylan DeMelo AU RC 3.00 8.00
109 Sergei Plotnikov AU RC 3.00 8.00
110 Vincent Hinostroza AU RC 2.50 6.00
111 Charles Hudon AU RC 4.00 10.00
112 Andrew Copp AU RC 4.00 10.00
113 Colton Parayko AU RC 5.00 12.00
114 Chandler Stephenson AU RC 4.00 10.00
115 Anthony Stolarz AU RC 4.00 10.00
116 Brendan Ranford AU RC 3.00 8.00
117 Joel Edmundson AU RC 3.00 8.00
118 Tyler Randell AU RC 4.00 10.00
119 Mattias Janmark AU RC 4.00 10.00
120 Mike Condon AU RC 4.00 10.00
121 Anton Slepyshev AU RC 3.00 8.00
122 Ben Hutton AU RC 4.00 10.00
123 Joonas Donskoi AU RC 4.00 10.00
124 Radek Faksa AU RC 4.00 10.00
125 Nick Shore AU RC 4.00 10.00
126 Oscar Lindberg AU RC 4.00 10.00
127 Matt O'Connor AU RC 3.00 8.00
128 Jared McCann AU RC 4.00 10.00
129 Viktor Arvidsson AU RC 5.00 12.00
130 Shea Theodore AU RC 4.00 10.00
131 Connor McDavid JSY AU RC 200.00 300.00
132 Henrik Samuelsson JSY AU RC 3.00 8.00
133 Emile Poirier JSY AU RC 4.00 10.00
134 Slater Koekkoek JSY AU RC 3.00 8.00
135 Dylan Larkin JSY AU RC 60.00 120.00
136 Kyle Baun JSY AU RC 4.00 10.00
137 Antoine Bibeau JSY AU RC 4.00 10.00
138 Noah Hanifin JSY AU RC 5.00 12.00
139 Derek Forbort JSY AU RC 3.00 8.00
140 Matt Puempel JSY AU RC 3.00 8.00
141 Stefan Noesen JSY AU RC 3.00 8.00
142 Connor Hellebuyck JSY AU RC 10.00 25.00
143 Brock McGinn JSY AU RC 4.00 10.00
144 Sam Bennett JSY AU RC 5.00 12.00
145 Nikolaj Ehlers JSY AU RC 8.00 20.00
146 Jake Virtanen JSY AU RC 5.00 12.00
147 Shane Prince JSY AU RC 3.00 8.00
148 Mackenzie Skapski JSY AU RC 4.00 10.00
149 Robby Fabbri JSY AU RC 5.00 12.00
150 Kevin Fiala JSY AU RC 4.00 10.00
151 Nick Cousins JSY AU RC 4.00 10.00
152 Nikolay Goldobin JSY AU RC 4.00 10.00
153 Ryan Hartman JSY AU RC 5.00 12.00
154 Jacob de la Rose JSY AU RC 4.00 10.00
155 Nicolas Petan JSY AU RC 4.00 10.00
156 Max Domi JSY AU RC 20.00 50.00
157 Josh Anderson JSY AU RC 4.00 10.00
158 Artemi Panarin JSY AU RC 60.00 120.00
159 Mikko Rantanen JSY AU RC 8.00 20.00
160 Jack Eichel JSY RC 15.00 40.00

2015-16 Upper Deck Contours Blue

48 Nicklas Backstrom 2.00 5.00
90 Corey Crawford 1.50 4.00

2015-16 Upper Deck Contours Red

48 Nicklas Backstrom 3.00 8.00
90 Corey Crawford 2.50 6.00

2015-16 Upper Deck Contours Club Crest Jerseys

GRP A STATED ODDS 1:151
GRP B STATED ODDS 1:60
GRP C STATED ODDS 1:8
OVERALL STATED ODDS 1:7
*PATCH/75 .6X TO 1.5X JSY
STATED PRINT RUN 75
CC1 Jack Eichel A 12.00 30.00
CC2 Artemi Panarin B 10.00 25.00
CC3 Malcolm Subban C 8.00 20.00
CC4 Antoine Bibeau C 3.00 8.00
CC5 Sam Bennett B 4.00 10.00
CC6 Kevin Fiala C 3.00 8.00
CC7 Connor Hellebuyck C 8.00 20.00
CC8 Henrik Samuelsson C 2.50 6.00
CC9 Zachary Fucale B 3.00 8.00
CC10 Matt Puempel C 2.50 6.00
CC11 Nick Cousins C 3.00 8.00
CC12 Jake Virtanen C 4.00 10.00
CC13 Mackenzie Skapski C 3.00 8.00
CC14 Robby Fabbri C 4.00 10.00
CC15 Connor McDavid A 25.00 60.00
CC16 Nicolas Petan C 3.00 8.00
CC17 Dylan Larkin A 10.00 25.00
CC18 Noah Hanifin C 4.00 10.00
CC19 Nikolay Goldobin C 3.00 8.00
CC20 Daniel Sprong C 6.00 15.00
CC21 Slater Koekkoek C 2.50 6.00
CC22 Shea Theodore C 3.00 8.00
CC23 Shane Prince C 2.50 6.00
CC24 Mikko Rantanen B 6.00 15.00
CC25 Stefan Noesen C 2.50 6.00
CC26 Max Domi B 6.00 15.00
CC27 Jacob de la Rose C 3.00 8.00
CC28 Josh Anderson C 3.00 8.00
CC29 Nikolaj Ehlers C 6.00 15.00
CC30 Ryan Hartman C 4.00 10.00
CC31 Emile Poirier C 3.00 8.00
CC32 Brock McGinn C 3.00 8.00

2015-16 Upper Deck Contours High Profile Fans Jersey Autographs

OVERALL STATED ODDS 1:41
PRINT RUNS B/WN 149-199 COPIES PER
*PATCH/25 X TO X JSY/149-199
RANDOM INSERTS IN PACKS
HPAJBH
HPAJCM
HPAJJP Jason Priestley 5.00 12.00
HPAJKH Kevin Harvick 12.00 30.00
HPAJKS Kevin Smith 30.00 80.00
HPAJLK Larry King 20.00 50.00
HPAJRN Rachel Nichols 50.00 120.00

2015-16 Upper Deck Contours High Profile Fans Jerseys

GRP A STATED ODDS 1:646
GRP B STATED ODDS 1:44
OVERALL STATED ODDS 1:41
RANDOM INSERTS IN PACKS
*PATCHES: .75X TO 2X BASIC
HPJBH Bret Hart B 4.00 10.00
HPJCM CM Punk B 8.00 20.00
HPJJP Jason Priestley B 3.00 8.00
HPJKH Kevin Harvick B 2.50 6.00
HPJKS Kevin Smith B 5.00 12.00
HPJLK Larry King B 4.00 10.00
HPJRN Rachel Nichols A 12.00 30.00

2015-16 Upper Deck Contours Jumbo Fabrics

GRP A STATED ODDS 1:58
GRP B STATED ODDS 1:19
OVERALL STATED ODDS 1:15
JJAB Aleksander Barkov B 2.50 6.00
JJCG Claude Giroux B 2.50 6.00
JJEK Erik Karlsson B 5.00 12.00
JJHZ Henrik Zetterberg A 3.00 8.00
JJJC Jeff Carter B 2.50 6.00
JJJP Joe Pavelski B 2.50 6.00
JJMH Marian Hossa A 2.00 5.00
JJMP Max Pacioretty B 2.50 6.00
JJNB Nicklas Backstrom A 4.00 10.00
JJNM Nathan MacKinnon B 5.00 12.00
JJOL Oliver Ekman-Larsson B 2.00 5.00
JJPB Patrice Bergeron A 3.00 8.00
JJRK Ryan Kesler B 2.50 6.00
JJTH Taylor Hall A 5.00 12.00
JJTS Tyler Seguin A 4.00 10.00
JJVH Victor Hedman B 3.00 8.00
JJVT Vladimir Tarasenko B 4.00 10.00
JJZP Zach Parise B 2.50 6.00

2015-16 Upper Deck Contours Rookie Jumbo Fabrics

GRP A STATED ODDS 1:225
GRP B STATED ODDS 1:72
GRP C STATED ODDS 1:9
OVERALL STATED ODDS 1:8
RJJAB Antoine Bibeau C 3.00 8.00
RJJAP Artemi Panarin B 10.00 25.00
RJJBM Brock McGinn C 3.00 8.00
RJJCH Connor Hellebuyck C 8.00 20.00
RJJCM Connor McDavid A 25.00 60.00
RJJDF Derek Forbort C 2.50 6.00
RJJDL Dylan Larkin A 10.00 25.00
RJJEP Emile Poirier C 3.00 8.00
RJJHS Henrik Samuelsson C 2.50 6.00
RJJJA Josh Anderson C 3.00 8.00
RJJJD Jacob de la Rose C 3.00 8.00
RJJJE Jack Eichel B 12.00 30.00
RJJJV Jake Virtanen C 4.00 10.00
RJJKB Kyle Baun C 3.00 8.00
RJJKF Kevin Fiala C 3.00 8.00
RJJMD Max Domi B 6.00 15.00
RJJMP Matt Puempel C 2.50 6.00
RJJMR Mikko Rantanen C 6.00 15.00
RJJMS Mackenzie Skapski C 3.00 8.00
RJJNC Nick Cousins C 3.00 8.00
RJJNE Nikolaj Ehlers C 6.00 15.00
RJJNG Nikolay Goldobin C 3.00 8.00
RJJNH Noah Hanifin C 4.00 10.00
RJJNP Nicolas Petan C 3.00 8.00
RJJRF Robby Fabbri C 4.00 10.00
RJJRH Ryan Hartman C 4.00 10.00
RJJSB Sam Bennett B 4.00 10.00
RJJSK Slater Koekkoek C 2.50 6.00
RJJSN Stefan Noesen C 2.50 6.00
RJJSP Shane Prince C 2.50 6.00

2015-16 Upper Deck Contours Rookie Resume

STATED PRINT RUN 399 SER.#'d SETS
RR1 Jack Eichel 8.00 20.00
RR2 Oscar Lindberg 2.00 5.00
RR3 Matt Puempel 1.50 4.00
RR4 Emile Poirier 2.00 5.00
RR5 Dylan Larkin 6.00 15.00
RR6 Nikolaj Ehlers 4.00 10.00
RR7 Shane Prince 1.50 4.00
RR8 Colin Miller 1.50 4.00
RR9 Daniel Sprong 4.00 10.00
RR10 Antoine Bibeau 2.00 5.00
RR11 Phil Di Giuseppe 2.00 5.00
RR12 Vincent Hinostroza 1.25 3.00
RR13 Jake Virtanen 2.50 6.00
RR14 Ronalds Kenins 2.00 5.00
RR15 Connor McDavid 25.00 60.00
RR16 Stefan Noesen 1.50 4.00
RR17 Joseph Blandisi 2.00 5.00
RR18 Max Domi 4.00 10.00
RR19 Shea Theodore 2.00 5.00
RR20 Artemi Panarin 6.00 15.00
RR21 Viktor Arvidsson 2.50 6.00
RR22 Nick Ritchie 2.00 5.00
RR23 Colton Parayko 2.50 6.00
RR24 Connor Hellebuyck 5.00 12.00
RR25 Hunter Shinkaruk 2.00 5.00
RR26 Noah Hanifin 2.50 6.00
RR27 Garret Sparks 2.50 6.00
RR28 Andrew Copp 2.00 5.00
RR29 Juuse Saros 2.50 6.00
RR30 Mike McCarron 2.50 6.00
RR31 Andreas Athanasiou 5.00 12.00
RR32 Sergei Plotnikov 1.50 4.00
RR33 Mike Condon 2.00 5.00
RR34 Stanislav Galiev 2.00 5.00
RR35 Jared McCann 2.00 5.00
RR36 Malcolm Subban 5.00 12.00
RR37 Brock McGinn 2.00 5.00
RR38 Nikolay Goldobin 2.00 5.00
RR39 Nicolas Petan 2.00 5.00
RR40 Ryan Hartman 2.50 6.00
RR41 Jacob de la Rose 2.00 5.00
RR42 Mikko Rantanen 4.00 10.00
RR43 Kevin Fiala 2.00 5.00
RR44 Zachary Fucale 2.00 5.00
RR45 Mattias Janmark 2.00 5.00
RR46 Robby Fabbri 2.50 6.00
RR47 Chandler Stephenson 2.00 5.00
RR48 Nick Shore 2.00 5.00
RR49 Joonas Donskoi 2.00 5.00
RR50 Sam Bennett 2.50 6.00

2015-16 Upper Deck Contours Rookie Resume Gold Rainbow

*SINGLES: .6X TO 1.5X BASIC INSERTS
STATED PRINT RUN 99 SER.#'d SETS
RR15 Connor McDavid 100.00 200.00
RR40 Ryan Hartman 4.00 10.00

2015-16 Upper Deck Contours Rookie Resume Gold Rainbow Autographs

GRP A STATED ODDS 1:1,736
GRP B STATED ODDS 1:174
GRP C STATED ODDS 1:42
GRP D STATED ODDS 1:10
OVERALL STATED ODDS 1:7.5
RR2 Oscar Lindberg D 3.00 8.00
RR3 Matt Puempel C 2.50 6.00
RR4 Emile Poirier D 3.00 8.00
RR5 Dylan Larkin B 60.00 120.00
RR6 Nikolaj Ehlers C 6.00 15.00
RR7 Shane Prince D 2.50 6.00
RR8 Colin Miller D 2.50 6.00
RR9 Daniel Sprong C 8.00 20.00
RR10 Antoine Bibeau D 3.00 8.00
RR11 Phil Di Giuseppe D 3.00 8.00
RR12 Vincent Hinostroza D 2.00 5.00
RR13 Jake Virtanen B 4.00 10.00
RR14 Ronalds Kenins D 3.00 8.00
RR15 Connor McDavid A 150.00 300.00
RR16 Stefan Noesen D 2.50 6.00
RR19 Shea Theodore D 3.00 8.00
RR21 Viktor Arvidsson B 4.00 10.00
RR22 Nick Ritchie C 3.00 8.00
RR23 Colton Parayko C 4.00 10.00
RR25 Hunter Shinkaruk D 3.00 8.00
RR26 Noah Hanifin C 4.00 10.00
RR27 Garret Sparks D 4.00 10.00
RR28 Andrew Copp D 3.00 8.00
RR29 Juuse Saros D 4.00 10.00
RR30 Mike McCarron D 4.00 10.00
RR31 Andreas Athanasiou D 8.00 20.00
RR32 Sergei Plotnikov D 2.50 6.00
RR33 Mike Condon C 3.00 8.00
RR35 Jared McCann C 3.00 8.00
RR36 Malcolm Subban C 8.00 20.00
RR38 Nikolay Goldobin D 3.00 8.00
RR39 Nicolas Petan D 3.00 8.00
RR40 Ryan Hartman D 4.00 10.00
RR41 Jacob de la Rose D 3.00 8.00
RR43 Kevin Fiala D 3.00 8.00
RR44 Zachary Fucale C 3.00 8.00
RR45 Mattias Janmark D 3.00 8.00
RR46 Robby Fabbri B 4.00 10.00
RR47 Chandler Stephenson D 3.00 8.00
RR48 Nick Shore D 3.00 8.00
RR49 Joonas Donskoi D 3.00 8.00
RR50 Sam Bennett B 4.00 10.00

2015-16 Upper Deck Contours Rookie Resume Gold Rainbow Proofs

RR15 Connor McDavid 100.00 200.00
RR40 Ryan Hartman 5.00 12.00

2015-16 Upper Deck Contours Show Me Some Glove Jerseys

GRP A STATED ODDS 1:199
GRP B STATED ODDS 1:51
OVERALL STATED ODDS 1:11
STATED PRINT RUN X SER.#'d SETS
*PATCH/20: 1.5X TO 4X JSY
STATED PRINT RUN 20
S1 Frederik Andersen C 2.50 6.00
S2 Tuukka Rask B 3.00 8.00
S4 Jonas Hiller C 2.50 6.00
S5 Cam Ward C 3.00 8.00
S6 Corey Crawford B 4.00 10.00
S7 Patrick Roy A 8.00 20.00
S8 Sergei Bobrovsky C 3.00 8.00
S9 Kari Lehtonen C 2.50 6.00
S11 Grant Fuhr A 3.00 8.00
S12 Roberto Luongo C 3.00 8.00
S13 Jonathan Quick C 5.00 12.00
S14 Devan Dubnyk C 3.00 8.00
S15 Carey Price B 10.00 25.00
S16 Pekka Rinne B 4.00 10.00
S17 Martin Brodeur A 8.00 20.00
S18 Jaroslav Halak C 2.50 6.00
S19 Henrik Lundqvist B 4.00 10.00
S20 Craig Anderson C 3.00 8.00
S21 Steve Mason C 2.50 6.00
S22 Mike Smith C 3.00 8.00
S23 Marc-Andre Fleury B 6.00 15.00
S24 Martin Jones C 3.00 8.00
S25 Jake Allen C 4.00 10.00
S27 Jonathan Bernier C 3.00 8.00
S28 Ryan Miller C 3.00 8.00
S29 Braden Holtby B 5.00 12.00
S30 Ondrej Pavelec C 3.00 8.00

2015-16 Upper Deck Contours Team Fanatics Jersey Autographs

STATED PRINT RUN 50 SER.#'d SETS
RANDOM INSERTS IN PACKS
TFAJLV Lindsey Vonn 30.00 80.00
TFAJTG Tom Glavine 8.00 20.00

2015-16 Upper Deck Contours Team Fanatics Jerseys

OVERALL STATED ODDS 1:144
TFJLV Lindsey Vonn 8.00 20.00
TFJTG Tom Glavine 5.00 12.00

2015-16 Upper Deck Contours Youth Movement Autographs

STATED PRINT RUN B/WN 49-399 SER.#'d SETS
RANDOM INSERTS IN PACKS
YM1 Leon Draisaitl/399 5.00 12.00
YM3 Alexander Wennberg/399 4.00 10.00
YM4 Mark Scheifele/399 6.00 15.00
YM5 John Klingberg/399 4.00 10.00
YM6 Charlie Coyle/399 4.00 10.00
YM7 Nail Yakupov/399 4.00 10.00
YM8 Calle Jarnkrok/399 4.00 10.00
YM9 Curtis Lazar/399 4.00 10.00
YM10 Justin Faulk/399 5.00 12.00
YM11 Jake Allen/399 6.00 15.00
YM12 Morgan Rielly/399 4.00 10.00
YM13 Tomas Hertl/399 5.00 12.00
YM14 Dougie Hamilton/399 5.00 12.00
YM15 Kevin Hayes/399 5.00 12.00
YM16 Griffin Reinhart/399 4.00 10.00
YM17 Nikita Kucherov/399 8.00 20.00
YM18 Markus Granlund/399 4.00 10.00
YM19 Sean Couturier/399 5.00 12.00
YM20 Mike Hoffman/399 4.00 10.00
YM21 Aaron Ekblad/249 5.00 12.00
YM22 Sean Monahan/249 5.00 12.00
YM23 Taylor Hall/249 10.00 25.00
YM24 Johnny Gaudreau/249 8.00 20.00
YM25 Jonathan Drouin/249 6.00 15.00
YM26 Gabriel Landeskog/249 5.00 12.00
YM27 Alex Galchenyuk/249 6.00 15.00
YM28 Nathan MacKinnon/249 10.00 25.00
YM29 Ryan Johansen/249 6.00 15.00
YM30 Connor McDavid/49 175.00 300.00

1997-98 Upper Deck Diamond Vision

This 25-card set was distributed in one-card packs with a suggested retail price of $7.99. The cards feature actual NHL game footage of the named player on each card combined with the latest technology to create fluid action sequences. Inserted one in every 500 packs is a Wayne Gretzky REEL Time card which displays his greatest moments in frame-by-frame action Imagery.
COMPLETE SET (25) 40.00 100.00
1 Wayne Gretzky 10.00 25.00
2 Patrick Roy 8.00 20.00
3 Jaromir Jagr 3.00 8.00
4 Steve Yzerman 6.00 15.00
5 Martin Brodeur 5.00 12.00
6 Paul Kariya 2.00 5.00
7 John Vanbiesbrouck 1.25 3.00
8 Ray Bourque 2.00 5.00
9 Theo Fleury 1.25 3.00
10 Pavel Bure 1.50 4.00
11 Brendan Shanahan 2.00 5.00
12 Brian Leetch 1.25 3.00
13 Owen Nolan 1.25 3.00
14 Peter Forsberg 3.00 8.00
15 Doug Weight 1.25 3.00
16 Teemu Selanne 2.00 5.00
17 Mats Sundin 2.00 5.00
18 Keith Tkachuk 1.25 3.00
19 Tony Amonte 1.25 3.00
20 Joe Sakic 4.00 10.00
21 Zigmund Palffy 1.25 3.00
22 Eric Lindros 1.50 4.00
23 Sergei Fedorov 2.00 5.00
24 Dominik Hasek 4.00 10.00
25 Brett Hull 2.00 5.00
RT1 W.Gretzky REEL TIME 60.00 150.00

1997-98 Upper Deck Diamond Vision Defining Moments

Randomly inserted in packs at the rate of 1:40, this six-card set features incredible action technology to show the memorable highlights of the pictured player's career.
DM1 Wayne Gretzky 20.00 50.00
DM2 Patrick Roy 15.00 40.00
DM3 Steve Yzerman 15.00 40.00
DM4 Jaromir Jagr 12.50 30.00
DM5 Joe Sakic 12.00 30.00
DM6 Brendan Shanahan 8.00 20.00

1997-98 Upper Deck Diamond Vision Signature Moves

Randomly inserted in packs at the rate of 1:5, this 25-card set is parallel to the regular Diamond Vision set only with a facsimile signature of the player pictured on the card.
*SIGN.MOVES: .8X TO 1.5X BASIC CARDS

2013-14 Upper Deck Edmonton Oilers

COMPLETE SET (90) 25.00 50.00
1 Wayne Gretzky 4.00 10.00
2 Al Hamilton .40 1.00
3 Dave Hunter .40 1.00
4 Mark Messier .75 2.00
5 Ronald Low .50 1.25
6 Eddie Mio .40 1.00
7 David Lumley .40 1.00
8 Dave Semenko .40 1.00
9 Lee Fogolin .40 1.00
10 Paul Coffey .60 1.50
11 Charlie Huddy .40 1.00
12 Matti Hagman .40 1.00
13 Andy Moog .60 1.50
14 Jari Kurri .60 1.50
15 Glenn Anderson .60 1.50
16 Don Jackson .40 1.00
17 Randy Gregg .40 1.00
18 Kevin McClelland .40 1.00
19 Grant Fuhr .60 1.50
20 Steve Smith .40 1.00
21 Mike Krushelnyski .40 1.00
22 Jeff Beukeboom .40 1.00
23 Craig MacTavish .50 1.25
24 Marty McSorley .50 1.25
25 Kent Nilsson .40 1.00
26 Craig Muni .40 1.00
27 Kelly Buchberger .40 1.00
28 Craig Simpson .40 1.00
29 Mark Lamb .40 1.00
30 Bill Ranford .60 1.50
31 Ken Linseman .40 1.00
32 Jimmy Carson .40 1.00
33 Joe Murphy .40 1.00
34 Bernie Nicholls .50 1.25
35 Vincent Damphousse .50 1.25
36 Louie Debrusk .40 1.00
37 Dave Manson .40 1.00
38 Doug Weight .60 1.50
39 Todd Marchant .40 1.00
40 Jason Arnott .50 1.25
41 Martin Gelinas .40 1.00
42 Curtis Joseph .60 1.50
43 Bob Essensa .60 1.50
44 Mike Grier .40 1.00
45 Janne Niinimaa .40 1.00
46 Georges Laraque .40 1.00
47 Sheldon Souray .40 1.00
48 Tommy Salo .50 1.25
49 Ethan Moreau .40 1.00
50 Jason Smith .40 1.00
51 Dan Cleary .60 1.50
52 Mike Comrie .40 1.00
53 Jason Chimera .40 1.00
54 Shawn Horcoff .40 1.00
55 Anson Carter .50 1.25
56 Marty Reasoner .40 1.00
57 Ty Conklin .50 1.25
58 Jussi Markkanen .40 1.00
59 Marc-Andre Bergeron .40 1.00
60 Bill Guerin .60 1.50
61 Scott Thornton .40 1.00
62 Jarret Stoll .50 1.25
63 Adam Oates .60 1.50
64 Raffi Torres .40 1.00
65 Matt Greene .40 1.00
66 Fernando Pisani .40 1.00
67 Chris Pronger .50 1.25
68 Dwayne Roloson .40 1.00
69 Robert Nilsson .40 1.00
70 Ladislav Smid .40 1.00
71 Dustin Penner .50 1.25
72 Sam Gagner .50 1.25
73 Andrew Cogliano .40 1.00
74 Mathieu Garon .50 1.25
75 Ryan Smyth .50 1.25
76 Ryan Jones .50 1.25
77 Devan Dubnyk .60 1.50
78 Nikolai Khabibulin .60 1.50
79 Ales Hemsky .40 1.00
80 Jordan Eberle .60 1.50
81 Taylor Hall 1.25 3.00
82 Magnus Paajarvi .60 1.50
83 Ryan Nugent-Hopkins .60 1.50
84 Darcy Hordichuk .40 1.00
85 Nick Schultz .40 1.00
86 Justin Schultz .60 1.50
87 Nail Yakupov 2.00 5.00
88 Boyd Gordon .40 1.00
89 David Perron .40 1.00
90 Andrew Ference .40 1.00

2013-14 Upper Deck Edmonton Oilers Rainbow

*RAINBOW: 1X TO 2.5X BASIC CARDS
STATED ODDS 1:2

2013-14 Upper Deck Edmonton Oilers Championship Banners

CBAM Andy Moog/99 15.00 40.00
CBAM Andy Moog/25 30.00 80.00
CBBR Bill Ranford/99 10.00 25.00
CBCH Charlie Huddy/99 10.00 25.00
CBCH Charlie Huddy/15 20.00 50.00
CBCH Charlie Huddy/25 20.00 50.00
CBCH Charlie Huddy/25 20.00 50.00
CBCM Craig MacTavish/99 8.00 20.00
CBCM Craig MacTavish/25 15.00 40.00
CBCS Craig Simpson/99 6.00 15.00
CBCS Craig Simpson/25 12.00 30.00
CBDH Dave Hunter/99 6.00 15.00
CBDH Dave Hunter/25 12.00 30.00
CBDJ Don Jackson/25 12.00 30.00
CBDL David Lumley/99 6.00 15.00
CBDS Dave Semenko/25 40.00 80.00
CBDS Dave Semenko/99 20.00 40.00
CBGA Glenn Anderson/15 20.00 50.00
CBGA Glenn Anderson/25 20.00 50.00
CBGA Glenn Anderson/99 10.00 25.00
CBGA Glenn Anderson/25 20.00 50.00
CBGA Glenn Anderson/99 10.00 25.00
CBGF Grant Fuhr/99 12.00 30.00
CBGF Grant Fuhr/25 25.00 60.00
CBGF Grant Fuhr/25 25.00 60.00
CBGF Grant Fuhr/99 15.00 40.00
CBJB Jeff Beukeboom/25 12.00 30.00
CBJB Jeff Beukeboom/99 6.00 15.00
CBJK Jari Kurri/25 20.00 50.00
CBJK Jari Kurri/99 10.00 25.00
CBJK Jari Kurri/25 20.00 50.00
CBJK Jari Kurri/99 10.00 25.00
CBJM Joe Murphy/99 6.00 15.00
CBKB Kelly Buchberger/99 6.00 15.00
CBKL Ken Linseman/25 12.00 30.00
CBKM Kevin McClelland/99 8.00 20.00
CBKM Kevin McClelland/25 15.00 40.00
CBKM Kevin McClelland/25 15.00 40.00
CBKN Kent Nilsson/99 6.00 15.00
CBLF Lee Fogolin/25 12.00 30.00
CBLF Lee Fogolin/99 6.00 15.00
CBMC Marty McSorley/25 15.00 40.00
CBMC Marty McSorley/99 8.00 20.00
CBMG Martin Gelinas/99 8.00 20.00
CBMK Mike Krushelnyski/99 6.00 15.00
CBMK Mike Krushelnyski/25 12.00 30.00
CBML Mark Lamb/25 12.00 30.00
CBMM Mark Messier/25 40.00 80.00
CBMM Mark Messier/25 40.00 80.00
CBMM Mark Messier/25 40.00 80.00
CBMM Mark Messier/25 40.00 80.00
CBMM Mark Messier/99 15.00 40.00
CBMU Craig Muni/25 15.00 40.00
CBMU Craig Muni/99 8.00 20.00
CBPC Paul Coffey/25 25.00 60.00
CBPC Paul Coffey/25 25.00 60.00
CBPC Paul Coffey/99 12.00 30.00
CBRG Randy Gregg/25 15.00 40.00
CBRG Randy Gregg/99 8.00 20.00
CBRG Randy Gregg/99 8.00 20.00
CBRG Randy Gregg/25 15.00 40.00
CBSS Steve Smith/99 6.00 15.00
CBSS Steve Smith/25 12.00 30.00
CBWG Wayne Gretzky/99 75.00 150.00
CBWG Wayne Gretzky/25 175.00 300.00
CBWG Wayne Gretzky/99 75.00 150.00

2013-14 Upper Deck Edmonton Oilers Franchise Ink

GROUP A ODDS 1:3041
GROUP B ODDS 1:882
GROUP C ODDS 1:208
GROUP D ODDS 1:64
GROUP E ODDS 1:46
GROUP F ODDS 1:17
GROUP G ODDS 1:6
OVERALL STATED ODDS 1:4
FIAC Anson Carter F 6.00 15.00
FIAH Al Hamilton G 4.00 10.00
FIAM Andy Moog D 20.00 40.00
FIAN Andrew Cogliano F 4.00 10.00
FIAO Adam Oates E 8.00 20.00
FIBE Bob Essensa G 6.00 15.00
FIBG Bill Guerin D 6.00 15.00
FIBN Bernie Nicholls E 8.00 20.00
FIBR Bill Ranford D 20.00 40.00
FICA Jimmy Carson G 4.00 10.00
FICH Charlie Huddy G 4.00 10.00
FICJ Curtis Joseph C 20.00 40.00
FICM Craig MacTavish D 25.00 50.00
FICP Chris Pronger B 40.00 80.00
FICS Craig Simpson F 4.00 10.00
FIDC Dan Cleary F 6.00 15.00
FIDD Devan Dubnyk G 6.00 15.00
FIDL David Lumley G 4.00 10.00
FIDM Dave Manson G 4.00 10.00
FIDP Dustin Penner D 6.00 15.00
FIDR Dwayne Roloson G 4.00 10.00
FIDW Doug Weight D 12.50 25.00
FIEM Eddie Mio G 4.00 10.00
FIFL Francois Leroux G 4.00 10.00
FIFP Fernando Pisani G 4.00 10.00
FIGA Glenn Anderson C 30.00 60.00
FIGF Grant Fuhr C 20.00 40.00
FIGL Georges Laraque G 4.00 10.00
FIGM Mathieu Garon F 5.00 12.00
FIGR Mike Grier G 4.00 10.00
FIHE Ales Hemsky D 12.50 25.00
FIHO Darcy Hordichuk F 4.00 10.00
FIJA Jason Arnott D 15.00 30.00
FIJB Jeff Beukeboom G 4.00 10.00
FIJC Jason Chimera G 4.00 10.00
FIJD Jeff Deslauriers G 4.00 10.00
FIJE Jordan Eberle C 20.00 40.00
FIJK Jari Kurri B 30.00 60.00
FIJM Joe Murphy G 4.00 10.00
FIJN Janne Niinimaa G 6.00 15.00
FIJS Jason Smith F 5.00 12.00
FIKB Kelly Buchberger F 4.00 10.00
FIKM Kevin McClelland G 4.00 10.00
FIKN Kent Nilsson F 4.00 10.00
FILD Louie Debrusk G 4.00 10.00
FILF Lee Fogolin G 4.00 10.00
FILI Ken Linseman G 6.00 15.00
FILS Ladislav Smid F 4.00 10.00
FIMA Marty McSorley D 15.00 30.00
FIMB Marc-Andre Bergeron F 5.00 12.00
FIMG Martin Gelinas G 5.00 12.00
FIMH Matti Hagman G 4.00 10.00
FIMK Mike Krushelnyski G 4.00 10.00
FIML Mark Lamb G 4.00 10.00
FIMM Mark Messier A
FIMO Ethan Moreau E 5.00 12.00
FIMP Magnus Paajarvi E 8.00 20.00
FIMR Marty Reasoner G 4.00 10.00
FIMU Craig Muni G 4.00 10.00
FINU Ryan Nugent-Hopkins C
FINY Nail Yakupov C 30.00 60.00
FIPC Paul Coffey A
FIPO Patrick O'Sullivan G 4.00 10.00
FIRG Randy Gregg G 4.00 10.00
FIRL Ronald Low G 5.00 12.00
FIRN Robert Nilsson F 4.00 10.00
FIRT Raffi Torres E 6.00 15.00

FISG Sam Gagner E 6.00 15.00
FISH Shawn Horcoff E 6.00 15.00
FISM Ryan Smyth C 20.00 40.00
FISO Sheldon Souray F 6.00 15.00
FISS Steve Smith F 4.00 10.00
FIST Jarret Stoll D 6.00 15.00
FISZ Justin Schultz E 8.00 20.00
FITC Ty Conklin F 5.00 12.00
FITH Taylor Hall C 30.00 60.00
FITM Todd Marchant G 4.00 10.00
FITN Scott Thornton F 4.00 10.00
FITS Tommy Salo F 8.00 20.00
FIVD Vincent Damphousse E 12.50 25.00
FIWG Wayne Gretzky B

2013-14 Upper Deck Edmonton Oilers Franchise Ink Duos

UNPRICED GROUP A ODDS 1:17,640
GROUP B ODDS 1:1729
GROUP C ODDS 1:353
GROUP D ODDS 1:294
GROUP E ODDS 1:160
OVERALL DUAL AU ODDS 1:80
FI2CH P.Coffey/C.Huddy B 40.00 80.00
FI2CS T.Salo/T.Conklin E 20.00 50.00
FI2DS D.Dubnyk/J.Schultz D 15.00 40.00
FI2EH T.Hall/J.Eberle B
FI2FM G.Fuhr/A.Moog B
FI2GB Buchberger/B.Guerin C 20.00 50.00
FI2GM W.Gretzky/M.Messier A
FI2GR D.Roloson/M.Garon E 15.00 40.00
FI2HH A.Hemsky/S.Horcoff C
FI2KM McSorley/Krushlnyski D 12.00 30.00
FI2KS J.Kurri/C.Simpson D 12.00 30.00
FI2LM D.Manson/G.Laraque E 12.00 30.00
FI2LS K.Linseman/S.Smith C 10.00 25.00
FI2MC Messier/MacTavish B
FI2MM McSorley/D.Manson D 15.00 40.00
FI2NY RNH/N.Yakupov B
FI2PC D.Penner/A.Cogliano C 12.00 30.00
FI2SB S.Smith/K.Buchberger E 10.00 25.00
FI2SG L.Smid/T.Gilbert E 10.00 25.00
FI2WA D.Weight/J.Arnott C 40.00 80.00

2013-14 Upper Deck Edmonton Oilers Franchise Ink Quads

GROUP A ODDS 1:5880
GROUP B ODDS 1:4009
GROUP C ODDS 1:4410
OVERALL QUAD AU ODDS 1:900
FI4AKCS Andrsn/Kurri/Cffy/Smth
FI4CGHS Cffy/Gregg/Hddy/Smth
FI4GCKF Grtzky/Cffy/Krri/Fuhr
FI4GMSF Grtzky/Mssr/Smspn/Fuhr
FI4MFAK Mssr/Fuhr/Andrsn/Kurri
FI4MKWM Mssr/Krslnski/Wght/MacTvsh

2013-14 Upper Deck Edmonton Oilers Franchise Ink Trios

UNPRICED GROUP A ODDS 1:9800
GROUP A ODDS 1:1604
GROUP A ODDS 1:653
GROUP A ODDS 1:1470
OVERALL TRIO ODDS 1:300
FI3AMS Smpsn/Mssr/Andrsn B 60.00 120.00
FI3EHN Hall/RNH/Eberle A 15.00 40.00
FI3FRM Fuhr/Moog/Rnfrd B
FI3GCK Cffey/Grtzky/Krri A
FI3GFH Grgg/Fglin/Huddy C 25.00 50.00
FI3HPG Pnner/Ggner/Hmsky C 30.00 60.00
FI3LMM McSrly/McCln/Lrque D 25.00 50.00
FI3MRS Mreau/Rsner/Stoll C 15.00 40.00
FI3PSR Smyth/Prnger/Rlson B
FI3SHG Smyth/Ggner/Hmsky C 60.00 120.00
FI3SHO Oates/Stll/Hrcff B 12.00 30.00
FI3WSG Smyth/Wght/Grier C

2013-14 Upper Deck Edmonton Oilers Monumental Emblems

STATED ODDS 1:18
MEAH Ales Hemsky 8.00 20.00
MEAM Andy Moog 15.00 40.00
MEBR Bill Ranford 15.00 40.00
MECH Charlie Huddy 10.00 25.00
MECM Craig MacTavish 12.00 30.00
MECS Craig Simpson 12.00 30.00
MEDH Dave Hunter 8.00 20.00
MEDW Doug Weight 12.00 30.00
MEGA Glenn Anderson 12.00 30.00
MEGF Grant Fuhr 15.00 40.00
MEJE Jordan Eberle 12.00 30.00
MEJK Jari Kurri 15.00 40.00
MEJS Justin Schultz 12.00 30.00
MEMC Marty McSorley 10.00 25.00
MEMM Mark Messier 15.00 40.00
MENK Nikolai Khabibulin 12.00 30.00
MENY Nail Yakupov 25.00 50.00
MEPC Paul Coffey 12.00 30.00
MERN Ryan Nugent-Hopkins 15.00 40.00
MERS Ryan Smyth 15.00 40.00
MESG Sam Gagner 10.00 25.00
MESH Shawn Horcoff 8.00 20.00
METH Taylor Hall 25.00 60.00
MEWG Wayne Gretzky 100.00 175.00

2013-14 Upper Deck Edmonton Oilers Monumental Emblems Autographs

ANNOUNCED PRINT RUN 24
MEAM Andy Moog
MEBR Bill Ranford 75.00 150.00
MECH Charlie Huddy
MECS Craig Simpson 40.00 80.00
MEDW Doug Weight
MEGA Glenn Anderson 25.00 50.00
MEGF Grant Fuhr
MEJE Jordan Eberle 30.00 60.00
MEJK Jari Kurri
MEJS Justin Schultz
MEMC Marty McSorley
MEMM Mark Messier 100.00 200.00
MENY Nail Yakupov
MEPC Paul Coffey
MERN Ryan Nugent-Hopkins 60.00 120.00
MERS Ryan Smyth 40.00 80.00
MESH Shawn Horcoff
METH Taylor Hall
MEWG Wayne Gretzky

2013-14 Upper Deck Edmonton Oilers Retired Numbers

RNAH Al Hamilton 12.00 30.00
RNGA Glenn Anderson 20.00 50.00
RNGF Grant Fuhr 20.00 50.00
RNJK Jari Kurri 30.00 60.00
RNMM Mark Messier 30.00 60.00
RNPC Paul Coffey 25.00 50.00
RNWG Wayne Gretzky 100.00 175.00

2013-14 Upper Deck Edmonton Oilers Retired Numbers Autographs

RNAH Al Hamilton/25 30.00 60.00
RNGA Glenn Anderson/15
RNGF Grant Fuhr/15
RNJK Jari Kurri/25 40.00 80.00

2013-14 Upper Deck Edmonton Oilers Team Logo Patches

TL1-TL35 STATED ODDS 1:15
TL36-TL60 STATED ODDS 1:48
TL61-TL75 STATED ODDS 1:135
UNPRICED TL76-TL90 ODDS 1:270
UNPRICED TL91-TL100 ODDS 1:676
TL1 Dave Hunter 4.00 10.00
TL2 David Lumley 4.00 10.00
TL3 Jari Kurri 8.00 20.00
TL4 Glenn Anderson 6.00 15.00
TL5 Louie DeBrusk 4.00 10.00
TL6 Erik Cole 5.00 12.00
TL7 Curtis Glencross 4.00 10.00
TL8 Radek Dvorak 4.00 10.00
TL9 Scott Thornton 4.00 10.00
TL10 Craig Simpson 4.00 10.00
TL11 Martin Gelinas 5.00 12.00
TL12 Joe Murphy 4.00 10.00
TL13 Ryan Jones 6.00 15.00
TL14 Joffrey Lupul 5.00 12.00
TL15 Kent Nilsson 4.00 10.00
TL16 Todd Marchant 4.00 10.00
TL17 Ben Eager 5.00 12.00
TL18 Ryan Smyth 6.00 15.00
TL19 Fernando Pisani 4.00 10.00
TL20 Mike Grier 4.00 10.00
TL21 Ray Whitney 5.00 12.00
TL22 Ethan Moreau 4.00 10.00
TL23 Dan Cleary 6.00 15.00
TL24 Jason Chimera 4.00 10.00
TL25 Kevin McClelland 4.00 10.00
TL26 Anson Carter 5.00 12.00
TL27 David Perron 4.00 10.00
TL28 Ales Hemsky 4.00 10.00
TL29 Dean McAmmond 4.00 10.00
TL30 Raffi Torres 4.00 10.00
TL31 Dustin Penner 5.00 12.00
TL32 Jordan Eberle 6.00 15.00
TL33 Taylor Hall 12.00 30.00
TL34 Magnus Paajarvi 6.00 15.00
TL35 Nail Yakupov 12.00 30.00
TL36 Wayne Gretzky 30.00 60.00
TL37 Mark Messier 15.00 40.00
TL38 Boyd Gordon 5.00 12.00
TL39 Eric Belanger 5.00 12.00
TL40 Matti Hagman 5.00 12.00
TL41 Shawn Horcoff 5.00 12.00
TL42 Mike Krushelnyski 5.00 12.00
TL43 Kyle Brodziak 5.00 12.00
TL44 Craig MacTavish 6.00 15.00
TL45 Mark Lamb 5.00 12.00
TL46 Jimmy Carson 5.00 12.00
TL47 Vincent Damphousse 6.00 15.00
TL48 Bernie Nicholls 6.00 15.00
TL49 Doug Weight 8.00 20.00
TL50 Jason Arnott 6.00 15.00
TL51 Patrick O'Sullivan 5.00 12.00
TL52 Anton Lander 6.00 15.00
TL53 Mike Comrie 5.00 12.00
TL54 Marty Reasoner 5.00 12.00
TL55 Jarret Stoll 6.00 15.00
TL56 Adam Oates 8.00 20.00
TL57 Robert Nilsson 5.00 12.00
TL58 Sam Gagner 6.00 15.00
TL59 Andrew Cogliano 6.00 15.00
TL60 Ryan Nugent-Hopkins 10.00 25.00
TL61 Al Hamilton 8.00 20.00
TL62 Justin Schultz 12.00 30.00
TL63 Lee Fogolin 8.00 20.00
TL64 Charlie Huddy 8.00 20.00
TL65 Paul Coffey 12.00 30.00
TL66 Randy Gregg 8.00 20.00
TL67 Matt Greene 8.00 20.00
TL68 Steve Smith 8.00 20.00
TL69 Craig Muni 8.00 20.00
TL70 Janne Niinimaa 8.00 20.00
TL71 Sheldon Souray 8.00 20.00
TL72 Jason Smith 8.00 20.00
TL73 Marc-Andre Bergeron 8.00 20.00
TL74 Chris Pronger 15.00 40.00
TL75 Ladislav Smid 25.00 60.00
TL76 Eddie Mio
TL77 Ronald Low 12.00 30.00
TL78 Andy Moog
TL79 Grant Fuhr
TL80 Bill Ranford
TL81 Curtis Joseph
TL82 Bob Essensa
TL83 Tommy Salo
TL84 Ty Conklin
TL85 Jussi Markkanen 20.00 50.00
TL86 Dwayne Roloson
TL87 Mathieu Garon
TL88 Jeff Deslauriers
TL89 Devan Dubnyk
TL90 Nikolai Khabibulin
TL91 Dave Semenko
TL92 Theo Peckham
TL93 Marty McSorley
TL94 Jeff Beukeboom
TL95 Kelly Buchberger
TL96 Don Jackson
TL97 Mike Brown
TL98 Dave Manson
TL99 Georges Laraque
TL100 Darcy Hordichuk

2002-03 Upper Deck Foundations

Released in November 2002, this 167-card set consited of 100 veteran base cards (#1-100), 20 "Speceial Efforts" subset cards (101-121), and 46 "New Foundations" prospect cards (#122-167). All subset cards were serial-numbered out of 1250. Cards 164-167 were available only in packs of UD Rookie Update.

1 Andy Moog .20 .50
2 Bill Ranford .15 .40
3 Cam Neely .20 .50
4 Bobby Orr .60 1.50
5 Terry O'Reilly .20 .50
6 Ray Bourque .30 .75
7 Phil Esposito .30 .75
8 Clark Gillies .20 .50
9 Grant Fuhr .20 .50
10 Dale Hawerchuk .25 .60
11 Kent Nilsson .12 .30
12 Willi Plett .12 .30
13 Al Secord .12 .30
14 Denis Savard .25 .60
15 Bob Probert .20 .50
16 Steve Larmer .15 .40
17 Patrick Roy .50 1.25
18 Ray Bourque .30 .75
19 Andy Moog .20 .50
20 Alex Delvecchio .20 .50
21 Borje Salming .15 .40
22 Dino Ciccarelli .20 .50
23 Gordie Howe .60 1.50
24 John Ogrodnick .12 .30
25 Marcel Dionne .25 .60
26 Mark Howe .20 .50
27 Ron Duguay .15 .40
28 Steve Yzerman .40 1.00
29 Andy Moog .20 .50
30 Bill Ranford .15 .40
31 Grant Fuhr .20 .50
32 Mark Messier .30 .75
33 Marty McSorley .15 .40
34 Wayne Gretzky 1.00 2.50
35 Glenn Anderson .20 .50
36 Gordie Howe .60 1.50
37 Mark Howe .20 .50
38 Gordie Howe .60 1.50
39 Butch Goring .12 .30
40 Charlie Simmer .15 .40
41 Ron Duguay .15 .40
42 Marcel Dionne .25 .60
43 Marty McSorley .15 .40
44 Wayne Gretzky 1.00 2.50
45 Wayne Gretzky 1.00 2.50
46 Brian Bellows .15 .40
47 Dino Ciccarelli .20 .50
48 Mike Modano .30 .75
49 Brian Bellows .15 .40
50 Denis Savard .25 .60
51 Guy Lafleur .25 .60
52 Mats Naslund .15 .40
53 Doug Gilmour .25 .60
54 Patrick Roy .50 1.25
55 Rod Langway .15 .40
56 Ryan Walter .12 .30
57 Yvan Cournoyer .20 .50
58 Martin Brodeur .40 1.00
59 Bob Nystrom .15 .40
60 Butch Goring .12 .30
61 Clark Gillies .20 .50
62 Mike Bossy .20 .50
63 Glenn Anderson .20 .50
64 Guy Lafleur .25 .60
65 Mark Messier .30 .75
66 Marcel Dionne .25 .60
67 Phil Esposito .30 .75
68 Ron Duguay .15 .40
69 Steve Larmer .15 .40
70 Wayne Gretzky 1.00 2.50
71 Brian Propp .12 .30
72 Jeremy Roenick .20 .50
73 Mark Howe .20 .50
74 Ron Hextall .20 .50
75 Tim Kerr .15 .40
76 Anton Stastny .12 .30
77 Dale Hunter .15 .40
78 Guy Lafleur .25 .60
79 Ron Hextall .20 .50
80 Wendel Clark .20 .50
81 Wilf Paiement .12 .30
82 Brett Hull .25 .60
83 Bernie Federko .15 .40
84 Dale Hawerchuk .25 .60
85 Grant Fuhr .20 .50
86 Tony Twist .15 .40
87 Wayne Gretzky 1.00 2.50
88 Borje Salming .15 .40
89 Mats Sundin .20 .50
90 Glenn Anderson .20 .50
91 Grant Fuhr .20 .50
92 Wendel Clark .20 .50
93 Wilf Paiement .12 .30
94 Harold Snepsts .12 .30
95 Pavel Bure .25 .60
96 Tony Tanti .12 .30
97 Dale Hunter .15 .40
98 Dino Ciccarelli .20 .50
99 Rod Langway .15 .40
100 Dale Hawerchuk .25 .60
101 Wayne Gretzky SE 4.00 10.00
102 Gordie Howe SE 2.50 6.00
103 Bobby Orr SE 2.50 6.00
104 Gordie Howe SE 2.50 6.00
105 Wayne Gretzky SE 4.00 10.00
106 Wayne Gretzky SE 4.00 10.00
107 Cam Neely SE .75 2.00
108 Ray Bourque SE 1.25 3.00
109 Phil Esposito SE 1.25 3.00
110 Grant Fuhr SE .75 2.00
111 Denis Savard SE 1.00 2.50
112 Patrick Roy SE 2.00 5.00
113 Steve Yzerman SE 1.50 4.00
114 Marcel Dionne SE 1.00 2.50
115 Guy Lafleur SE 1.00 2.50
116 Bernie Federko SE .60 1.50
117 Wayne Gretzky SE 4.00 10.00
118 Ray Bourque SE 1.25 3.00
Phil Esposito
119 Mike Bossy SE .75 2.00
120 Patrick Roy SE 2.00 5.00
121 Bob Nystrom SE .60 1.50
122 Pasi Nurminen NF .50 1.25
123 Mark Hartigan NF .50 1.25
124 Henrik Tallinder NF .50 1.25
125 Micki Dupont NF RC .50 1.25
126 Riku Hahl NF .50 1.25
127 Andrej Nedorost NF .50 1.25
128 Ales Pisa NF .50 1.25
129 Jani Rita NF .50 1.25
130 Stephen Weiss NF .75 2.00
131 Lukas Krajicek NF .60 1.50
132 Sylvain Blouin NF RC .50 1.25
133 Marcel Hossa NF .50 1.25
134 Adam Hall NF RC .50 1.25
135 Jan Lasak NF .60 1.50
136 Ray Schultz NF RC .50 1.25
137 Trent Hunter NF .50 1.25
138 Martin Prusek NF .50 1.25
139 Branko Radivojevic NF .50 1.25
140 Sebastien Centomo NF .50 1.25
141 Karel Pilar NF .50 1.25
142 Sebastien Charpentier NF .50 1.25
143 Stanislav Chistov NF RC .50 1.25
144 Alexei Smirnov NF RC .60 1.50
145 Joe Thornton SE 1.00 2.50
146 Chuck Kobasew NF RC .60 1.50
147 Patrick Roy SE 2.00 5.00
148 Mike Modano SE 1.25 3.00
149 Rick Nash NF RC 4.00 10.00
150 Mike Comrie SE .75 2.00
151 Henrik Zetterberg NF RC 5.00 12.00
152 Ales Hemsky NF RC 2.00 5.00
153 Jay Bouwmeester NF RC 1.50 4.00
154 Pavel Bure SE 1.00 2.50
155 Alexander Frolov NF RC 1.00 2.50
156 P-M Bouchard NF RC .75 2.00
157 Ron Hainsey NF RC .50 1.25
158 Sean Burke SE .50 1.25
159 Mario Lemieux SE 2.50 6.00
160 Anton Volchenkov NF RC .50 1.25
161 Mats Sundin SE .75 2.00
162 Alexander Svitov NF RC .50 1.25
163 Steve Eminger NF RC .50 1.25
164 Jason Spezza NF RC 3.00 8.00
165 Pascal LeClaire NF RC .60 1.50
166 Ari Ahonen NF RC .50 1.25
167 Steve Ott NF RC 1.00 2.50

2002-03 Upper Deck Foundations 1000 Point Club

This 39-card memorabilia set featured swatches of game jerseys or sticks. Jersey cards were serial-numbered to 110 and stick cards were serial-numbered to 150. Gold jersey parallels numbered to 15 and silver jersey parallels numbered to 85 were also created.

*SILVER JSY/85: .5X TO 1.2X BRONZE/110
*GOLD JSY/15: 1.2X TO 3X BRONZE/110
BT Bryan Trottier JSY 5.00 12.00
DC Dino Ciccarelli JSY 4.00 10.00
DE Denis Savard JSY 4.00 10.00
DP Denis Potvin JSY 4.00 10.00
GL Guy Lafleur JSY 6.00 15.00
JB Johnny Bucyk JSY 5.00 12.00
LA Guy Lafleur JSY 6.00 15.00
MB Mike Bossy JSY 6.00 15.00
MG Michel Goulet JSY 4.00 10.00
SY Steve Yzerman JSY 10.00 25.00
WG Wayne Gretzky JSY 20.00 50.00
YZ Steve Yzerman STK 10.00 25.00
AN Glenn Anderson STK 4.00 10.00
AN2 Glenn Anderson STK 4.00 10.00
BE Jean Beliveau STK 8.00 20.00
BO Mike Bossy STK 6.00 15.00
BO1 Ray Bourque STK 8.00 20.00
BO2 Ray Bourque STK 8.00 20.00
BU Johnny Bucyk STK 5.00 12.00
CI Dino Ciccarelli STK 4.00 10.00
DI Marcel Dionne STK 4.00 10.00
DI2 Marcel Dionne STK 4.00 10.00
ES Phil Esposito STK 6.00 15.00
ES2 Phil Esposito STK 6.00 15.00
GA Mike Gartner STK 5.00 12.00
GR Wayne Gretzky STK 20.00 50.00
HA Dale Hawerchuk STK 6.00 15.00
HA2 Dale Hawerchuk STK 6.00 15.00
HO Gordie Howe STK 15.00 40.00
KU Jari Kurri STK 6.00 15.00
KU2 Jari Kurri STK 6.00 15.00
LA1 Guy Lafleur STK 5.00 12.00
LA2 Guy Lafleur STK 5.00 12.00
LA3 Guy Lafleur STK 5.00 12.00
MC Lanny McDonald STK 4.00 10.00
MI Stan Mikita STK 6.00 15.00
PO Denis Potvin STK 5.00 12.00
SA Denis Savard STK 4.00 10.00
TR Bryan Trottier STK 5.00 12.00

2002-03 Upper Deck Foundations Calder Winners

Gold parallels of this memorabilia set numbered to 15 and silver parallels numbered to 85 were also created. Silver prices can be found by using the multipliers below; gold cards are not priced due to scarcity.

*SILVER/85: .5X TO 1.2X BASIC JERSEY
*GOLD/15: 1.2X TO 3X BASIC JERSEY
TBT Bryan Trottier 6.00 15.00
TMB Mike Bossy 6.00 15.00
TPB Pavel Bure 6.00 15.00
TRB Ray Bourque 8.00 20.00
TWP Willi Plett 4.00 10.00

2002-03 Upper Deck Foundations Canadian Heroes

Singles in this 22-card set were serial-numbered to 150. Gold parallels numbered to 50 and silver parallels numbered to 95 were also created. Prices for those parallels can be found by using the multipliers below.

*SILVER/95: .5X TO 1.2X BASE JSY
*GOLD/50: .8X TO 2X BASE JSY
CBO Ray Bourque 6.00 15.00
CBT Bryan Trottier 6.00 15.00
CCN Cam Neely 6.00 15.00
CDC Dino Ciccarelli 5.00 12.00
CGF Grant Fuhr 8.00 20.00
CGL Guy Lafleur 5.00 12.00
CHS Harold Snepsts 5.00 12.00
CJB Johnny Bucyk 5.00 12.00
CMB Mike Bossy 5.00 12.00
CMG Michel Goulet 5.00 12.00
CMH Mark Howe 6.00 15.00
CMM Marty McSorley 5.00 12.00
CPR Patrick Roy 10.00 25.00
CRD Ron Duguay 5.00 12.00
CRO Patrick Roy 10.00 25.00
CRV Rick Vaive 4.00 10.00
CSA Denis Savard 5.00 12.00
CSY Steve Yzerman 8.00 20.00
CTT Tony Twist 5.00 12.00
CWC Wendel Clark 5.00 12.00
CWG Wayne Gretzky 20.00 50.00
CWP Willi Plett 4.00 10.00

2002-03 Upper Deck Foundations Classic Greats

Singles in this 17-card memorabilia set were serial-numbered to 150. Gold parallels numbered to 50 and silver parallels numbered to 95 were also created. Prices for those parallels can be found by using the multipliers below.

*SILVER/95: .5X TO 1.2X BASE JSY
*GOLD/50: .8X TO 2X BASE JSY
GBN Bob Nystrom 5.00 12.00
GBO Ray Bourque 8.00 20.00
GBR Bill Ranford 5.00 12.00
GBS Borje Salming 6.00 15.00
GCN Cam Neely 6.00 15.00
GDC Dino Ciccarelli 5.00 12.00
GDP Denis Potvin 5.00 12.00
GDS Denis Savard 5.00 12.00
GGF Grant Fuhr 10.00 25.00
GGL Guy Lafleur 5.00 12.00
GMB Mike Bossy 5.00 12.00
GMG Michel Goulet 4.00 10.00
GMH Mark Howe 6.00 15.00
GRB Ray Bourque 8.00 20.00
GRD Ron Duguay 4.00 10.00
GWC Wendel Clark 6.00 15.00
GWG Wayne Gretzky 20.00 50.00

2002-03 Upper Deck Foundations Defense First

Singles in this 8-card memorabilia set were serial-numbered to 110. Gold parallels numbered to 15 and silver parallels numbered to 85 were also created.

*SILVER/85: .5X TO 1.2X BASE JSY
*GOLD/15: 1.2X TO 3X BASE JSY
DBO Ray Bourque 8.00 20.00
DBS Borje Salming 6.00 15.00
DDP Denis Potvin 5.00 12.00
DGF Grant Fuhr 10.00 25.00
DHS Harold Snepsts 5.00 12.00
DMH Mark Howe 6.00 15.00
DMM Marty McSorley 5.00 12.00
DRB Ray Bourque 8.00 20.00

2002-03 Upper Deck Foundations Lasting Impressions Sticks

STAT.PRINT RUN 150 SER.#'d SETS
LBN Bob Nystrom 6.00 15.00
LBO Bobby Orr 40.00 100.00
LBR Bill Ranford 6.00 15.00
LCN Cam Neely 6.00 15.00
LJP Jacques Plante 12.50 30.00
LMN Mats Naslund 8.00 20.00
LWC Wendel Clark 8.00 20.00
LYC Yvan Cournoyer 6.00 15.00

2002-03 Upper Deck Foundations Milestones

Gold parallels of this memorabilia set numbered to 50 and silver parallels numbered to 95 were also created. Prices for those parallels can be found by using the multipliers below.

STATED PRINT RUN 150 SER.#'d SETS
*SILVER/95: .5X TO 1.25X BASE JSY
*GOLD/50: .8X TO 2X BASE JSY
NBO Ray Bourque 8.00 20.00
NBT Bryan Trottier 5.00 12.00
NCN Cam Neely 10.00 25.00
NDP Denis Potvin 5.00 12.00
NGF Grant Fuhr 10.00 25.00
NMB Mike Bossy 5.00 12.00
NPR Patrick Roy 12.50 30.00
NSY Steve Yzerman 12.50 30.00
NWG Wayne Gretzky 25.00 60.00

2002-03 Upper Deck Foundations Playoff Performers

Gold parallels of this memorabilia set numbered to 50 and silver parallels numbered to 95 were also created. Prices for those parallels can be found by using the multipliers below.

PRINT RUN 150 SER.#'d SETS
*SILVER/95: .5X TO 1.2X BASE JSY
*GOLD/50: .8X TO 2X BASE JSY
PBN Bob Nystrom 5.00 12.00
PBS Borje Salming 6.00 15.00
PBT Bryan Trottier 5.00 12.00
PCN Cam Neely 6.00 15.00
PDC Dino Ciccarelli 5.00 12.00
PGF Grant Fuhr 8.00 20.00
PJB Johnny Bucyk 5.00 12.00
PMB Mike Bossy 5.00 12.00
PMG Michel Goulet 5.00 12.00
PMM Marty McSorley 5.00 12.00
PPB Pavel Bure 6.00 15.00
PPR Patrick Roy 12.50 30.00
PRB Ray Bourque 8.00 20.00
PRO Patrick Roy 12.50 30.00
PSY Steve Yzerman 12.50 30.00
PWG Wayne Gretzky 25.00 60.00

2002-03 Upper Deck Foundations Power Stations

Singles in this 11-card set were serial-numbered to 110 with Gold parallels numbered to 15 and silver parallels numbered to 85.

*SILVER/85: .5X TO 1.2X BASE JSY
*GOLD/15: 1.2X TO 3X BASE JSY
SBN Bob Nystrom 5.00 12.00
SCN Cam Neely 6.00 15.00
SDC Dino Ciccarelli 5.00 12.00
SHS Harold Snepsts 5.00 12.00
SMB Mike Bossy 5.00 12.00
SMH Mark Howe 6.00 15.00
SMM Marty McSorley 5.00 12.00
SRV Rick Vaive 4.00 10.00
STT Tony Twist 5.00 12.00
SWC Wendel Clark 5.00 12.00
SWP Willi Plett 4.00 10.00

2002-03 Upper Deck Foundations Signs of Greatness

Inserted at 1:53, this 36-card set featured certified player autographs. Known shortprints are listed below.

SGAS Al Secord/26* 40.00 80.00
SGBB Brian Bellows/26* 20.00 50.00
SGBC Bobby Clarke SP 10.00 25.00
SGBO Bobby Orr/48* 200.00 350.00
SGBP Brian Propp/87* 12.00 30.00
SGBS Billy Smith 10.00 25.00
SGCG Clark Gillies/26* 20.00 50.00
SGCN Cam Neely SP 15.00 40.00
SGCS Charlie Simmer/26* 30.00 80.00
SGDC Dino Ciccarelli SP 10.00 25.00
SGDH Dale Hawerchuk 10.00 25.00
SGDP Denis Potvin 10.00 25.00
SGDS Denis Savard SP 20.00 50.00
SGFM Frank Mahovlich SP 10.00 25.00
SGGA Glenn Anderson 10.00 25.00
SGGF Grant Fuhr SP 15.00 40.00
SGGH Gordie Howe/43* 75.00 150.00
SGGL Guy Lafleur SP 15.00 40.00
SGGP Gilbert Perreault SP 12.00 30.00
SGJB Jean Beliveau SP 25.00 50.00
SGJBU Johnny Bucyk 10.00 25.00
SGJK Jari Kurri 12.50 30.00
SGLM Lanny McDonald 10.00 25.00
SGMB Mike Bossy 10.00 25.00
SGMD Marcel Dionne SP 10.00 25.00
SGMG Mike Gartner 12.50 30.00
SGMGU Michel Goulet SP 12.00 30.00
SGMN Mats Naslund/87* 25.00 60.00
SGPS Peter Stastny 10.00 25.00
SGRA Ray Bourque/23* 40.00 100.00
SGRB Ray Bourque/23* 40.00 100.00
SGRH Ron Hextall/51* 20.00 50.00
SGSL Steve Larmer/26* 20.00 50.00
SGSM Stan Mikita SP 10.00 25.00
SGTL Ted Lindsay SP 10.00 25.00
SGWG Wayne Gretzky/46* 150.00 350.00

2015-16 Upper Deck Full Force

COMP.SET w/o RC's (100) 10.00 25.00
101-123 ROOKIE ODDS 1:18 H, 1:32 R/BL
1 Drew Doughty .40 1.00
2 John Tavares .75 2.00
3 Anders Lee .40 1.00
4 Sean Monahan .40 1.00
5 Jakub Voracek .40 1.00
6 John Carlson .50 1.25
7 Tyler Bozak .30 .75
8 Nazem Kadri .30 .75
9 Nail Yakupov .30 .75
10 Tyler Johnson .30 .75
11 Loui Eriksson .30 .75
12 Jason Pominville .30 .75
13 Oliver Ekman-Larsson .30 .75
14 Jiri Hudler .30 .75
15 Kyle Turris .30 .75
16 Henrik Zetterberg .50 1.25
17 Semyon Varlamov .40 1.00
18 Sergei Bobrovsky .40 1.00
19 Patrick Kane .75 2.00
20 Logan Couture .40 1.00
21 Jonathan Quick .60 1.50
22 David Backes .40 1.00
23 Steve Mason .30 .75
24 Nicklas Backstrom .60 1.50
25 Ryan Strome .30 .75
26 Andrew Hammond 1.25 3.00
27 Ryan Johansen .50 1.25
28 Justin Faulk .40 1.00
29 Nathan MacKinnon .75 2.00
30 Tuukka Rask .40 1.00
31 Vladimir Tarasenko .60 1.50
32 Henrik Lundqvist .50 1.25
33 Derek Stepan .40 1.00
34 P.K. Subban .60 1.50
35 Jonas Hiller .30 .75
36 Corey Crawford .50 1.25
37 Tomas Plekanec .40 1.00
38 Niklas Kronwall .30 .75
39 Cory Schneider .30 .75
40 Mikkel Boedker .25 .60
41 Devan Dubnyk .40 1.00
42 Corey Perry .40 1.00
43 Elias Lindholm .25 .60
44 Jamie Benn .50 1.25
45 Shea Weber .30 .75
46 Daniel Sedin .40 1.00
47 Tobias Rieder .25 .60
48 Brad Marchand .50 1.25
49 Patrik Elias .40 1.00
50 John Klingberg .30 .75
51 Taylor Hall .75 2.00
52 Sidney Crosby 1.50 4.00
53 Rick Nash .40 1.00
54 Carey Price 1.25 3.00
55 Roberto Luongo .40 1.00
56 Marc-Andre Fleury .60 1.50
57 Pavel Datsyuk .50 1.25
58 Brian Elliott .30 .75
59 Jonathan Toews .75 2.00
60 Nikita Kucherov .60 1.50
61 Ryan Miller .40 1.00
62 Joe Pavelski .40 1.00
63 Andrew Ladd .40 1.00
64 Aaron Ekblad .40 1.00
65 Gabriel Landeskog .40 1.00
66 Steven Stamkos .75 2.00
67 Jonathan Huberdeau .40 1.00
68 Matt Moulson .30 .75
69 Ryan Getzlaf .60 1.50
70 Max Pacioretty .40 1.00
71 Jordan Eberle .40 1.00
72 Derick Brassard .40 1.00
73 Blake Wheeler .40 1.00
74 Cam Ward .40 1.00
75 Tyler Seguin .60 1.50
76 Alex Pietrangelo .30 .75
77 Evgeni Malkin 1.25 3.00
78 Claude Giroux .40 1.00
79 Frederik Andersen .30 .75
80 Erik Karlsson .75 2.00
81 Ryan Nugent-Hopkins .40 1.00
82 Joe Thornton .40 1.00
83 Henrik Sedin .40 1.00
84 Zemgus Girgensons .30 .75
85 Patric Hornqvist .30 .75
86 Patrice Bergeron .50 1.25
87 Anze Kopitar .60 1.50
88 Ondrej Pavelec .40 1.00
89 Alexander Ovechkin 1.50 4.00
90 Jonathan Bernier .40 1.00
91 Pekka Rinne .50 1.25
92 Evgeny Kuznetsov .60 1.50
93 James van Riemsdyk .40 1.00
94 Marian Hossa .30 .75
95 Filip Forsberg .50 1.25
96 Zach Parise .40 1.00
97 Adam Henrique .40 1.00
98 Nick Foligno .30 .75
99 Tomas Tatar .30 .75
100 Tyler Ennis .30 .75
101 Connor McDavid RC 40.00 80.00
102 Jacob de la Rose RC 3.00 8.00
103 Sam Bennett RC 4.00 10.00
104 Malcolm Subban RC 8.00 20.00
105 Matt Puempel RC 2.50 6.00
106 Emile Poirier RC 3.00 8.00
107 Ryan Hartman RC 4.00 10.00
108 Nick Cousins RC 3.00 8.00
109 Antoine Bibeau RC 3.00 8.00
110 Josh Anderson RC 3.00 8.00
111 Kevin Fiala RC 3.00 8.00
112 Jack Eichel RC 20.00 40.00
113 Max Domi RC 6.00 15.00
114 Noah Hanifin RC 4.00 10.00
115 Mikko Rantanen RC 6.00 15.00
116 Nikolaj Ehlers RC 6.00 15.00
117 Robby Fabbri RC 4.00 10.00
118 Jared McCann RC 3.00 8.00
119 Artemi Panarin RC 10.00 25.00
120 Dylan Larkin RC 20.00 40.00
121 Shane Prince RC 2.50 6.00
122 Connor Hellebuyck RC 8.00 20.00
123 Jake Virtanen RC 4.00 10.00

2015-16 Upper Deck Full Force Die Cuts

*1-100 VETS/25: 5X TO 12X BASIC CARDS
*ROOKIES: .8X TO 2X BASIC CARDS
101-123 ROOKIE ODDS 1:120 HOB
24 Nicklas Backstrom 8.00 20.00
36 Corey Crawford 6.00 15.00
92 Evgeny Kuznetsov 8.00 20.00
107 Ryan Hartman 8.00 20.00

2015-16 Upper Deck Full Force Blueprint

VETERAN ODDS 1:2 H, 1:8 R/BL
ROOKIE SP ODDS 1:45 H, 1:120 R/BL
BPAO Alexander Ovechkin 5.00 12.00
BPAS Andrew Shaw 1.25 3.00
BPBE Jonathan Bernier 1.25 3.00
BPBO Bobby Orr 4.00 10.00
BPBS Brayden Schenn 1.25 3.00
BPCM Connor McDavid SP 15.00 30.00
BPCP Carey Price 4.00 10.00
BPCS Cory Schneider 1.00 2.50
BPDD Devan Dubnyk 1.25 3.00
BPDL Dylan Larkin SP 5.00 12.00
BPDO Max Domi SP 3.00 8.00
BPDP Denis Potvin 1.25 3.00
BPDW Doug Weight 1.25 3.00
BPEM Evgeni Malkin 4.00 10.00
BPEP Emile Poirier 1.25 3.00
BPFA Frederik Andersen 1.00 2.50
BPHU Jonathan Huberdeau 1.25 3.00
BPJB Jamie Benn 1.50 4.00
BPJE Jack Eichel SP 6.00 15.00
BPJG Johnny Gaudreau 2.00 5.00
BPJH Jim Howard 1.25 3.00
BPJQ Jonathan Quick 2.00 5.00
BPJT John Tavares 2.50 6.00
BPJV Jakub Voracek 1.25 3.00
BPKF Kevin Fiala 1.25 3.00
BPMB Mike Bossy 1.25 3.00
BPMD Marcel Dionne 1.50 4.00
BPML Mario Lemieux 4.00 10.00
BPMM Mark Messier 2.00 5.00
BPMS Malcolm Subban 3.00 8.00
BPNE Nikolaj Ehlers SP 3.00 8.00
BPNH Noah Hanifin SP 2.00 5.00
BPNK Niklas Kronwall 1.00 2.50
BPNP Nicolas Petan SP 1.50 4.00
BPPE Phil Esposito 2.00 5.00
BPPR Pekka Rinne 1.50 4.00
BPRF Robby Fabbri SP 2.00 5.00
BPRH Ryan Hartman 1.50 4.00
BPRJ Ryan Johansen 1.50 4.00
BPRN Ryan Nugent-Hopkins 1.25 3.00
BPRO Patrick Roy 3.00 8.00
BPSB Sam Bennett 1.50 4.00
BPSC Sidney Crosby 5.00 12.00
BPSR Sean Couturier 1.25 3.00
BPSS Steven Stamkos 2.50 6.00
BPSW Shea Weber 1.00 2.50
BPTB Tyson Barrie 1.25 3.00
BPTH Taylor Hall 2.50 6.00
BPTO Jonathan Toews 2.50 6.00
BPTR Tuukka Rask 1.25 3.00
BPTT Tomas Tatar 1.00 2.50
BPVT Vladimir Tarasenko 2.00 5.00
BPWG Wayne Gretzky 6.00 15.00

2015-16 Upper Deck Full Force Blueprint Autographs

GROUP A ODDS 1:18,136
GROUP B ODDS 1:2028
GROUP C ODDS 1:1979
GROUP D ODDS 1:1632
GROUP E ODDS 1:1518
GROUP F ODDS 1:1040
GROUP G ODDS 1:396
ROOKIE GRP A ODDS 1:12,960
ROOKIE GRP B ODDS 1:926
BPAO Alexander Ovechkin B
BPAS Andrew Shaw D 5.00 12.00
BPBE Jonathan Bernier C 5.00 12.00
BPBO Bobby Orr B 90.00 150.00
BPBS Brayden Schenn D 5.00 12.00
BPCH Connor Hellebuyck B 15.00 40.00
BPCM Connor McDavid A 175.00 300.00
BPCP Carey Price C 15.00 40.00
BPCS Cory Schneider F 4.00 10.00
BPDD Devan Dubnyk C 5.00 12.00
BPDL Dylan Larkin B 90.00 150.00
BPDO Max Domi B 20.00 40.00
BPDP Denis Potvin B
BPDW Doug Weight B 10.00 25.00
BPEM Evgeni Malkin B 20.00 40.00
BPEP Emile Poirier G 5.00 12.00
BPFA Frederik Andersen G 4.00 10.00
BPHU Jonathan Huberdeau B 6.00 15.00
BPJB Jamie Benn C 6.00 15.00
BPJG Johnny Gaudreau E 8.00 20.00
BPJH Jim Howard C 5.00 12.00
BPJQ Jonathan Quick B 25.00 50.00
BPJT John Tavares D 10.00 25.00
BPKF Kevin Fiala E 5.00 12.00
BPMB Mike Bossy B 10.00 25.00
BPMD Marcel Dionne B
BPML Mario Lemieux A
BPMM Mark Messier A
BPMS Malcolm Subban G 12.00 30.00
BPNE Nikolaj Ehlers B 6.00 15.00
BPNH Noah Hanifin B 12.00 30.00
BPNK Niklas Kronwall E 4.00 10.00
BPNP Nicolas Petan B 10.00 25.00
BPPE Phil Esposito B
BPRF Robby Fabbri B 5.00 12.00
BPRH Ryan Hartman G 6.00 15.00
BPRJ Ryan Johansen C 6.00 15.00
BPRN Ryan Nugent-Hopkins C 5.00 12.00
BPRO Patrick Roy B 25.00 50.00
BPSB Sam Bennett F 6.00 15.00
BPSC Sidney Crosby A 75.00 135.00
BPSR Sean Couturier G 5.00 12.00
BPSW Shea Weber B
BPTB Tyson Barrie F 5.00 12.00
BPTO Jonathan Toews B
BPTT Tomas Tatar D 4.00 10.00
BPWG Wayne Gretzky B

2015-16 Upper Deck Full Force Calder Competitors

STATED ODDS 1:90 H, 1:240 R/BL
CCCM Connor McDavid 15.00 40.00
CCDL Dylan Larkin 8.00 20.00
CCJE Jack Eichel 10.00 25.00
CCJV Jake Virtanen 3.00 8.00
CCKF Kevin Fiala 2.50 6.00
CCMD Max Domi 5.00 12.00
CCNE Nikolaj Ehlers 5.00 12.00
CCSB Sam Bennett 3.00 8.00

2015-16 Upper Deck Full Force Draft Board

VETERAN ODDS 1:11 H, 1:31 R/BL
ROOKIE SP ODDS 1:54 H, 1:144 R/BL
DBAE Aaron Ekblad 1.50 4.00
DBAO Alexander Ovechkin 6.00 15.00
DBCH Connor Hellebuyck SP 5.00 12.00
DBCM Connor McDavid SP 15.00 40.00
DBCP Carey Price 5.00 12.00
DBDD Drew Doughty 1.50 4.00
DBEI Jack Eichel SP 8.00 20.00
DBEM Evgeni Malkin 5.00 12.00
DBEP Emile Poirier SP 2.00 5.00
DBFF Filip Forsberg 2.00 5.00
DBHS Henrik Samuelsson SP 1.50 4.00
DBJD Jacob de la Rose 1.50 4.00
DBJE Jordan Eberle 1.50 4.00
DBJI Jarome Iginla 1.50 4.00
DBJJ Jaromir Jagr 4.00 10.00
DBJT Jonathan Toews 3.00 8.00

BKF Kevin Fiala SP 2.00 5.00
BMB Martin Brodeur 3.00 8.00
BML Mario Lemieux 5.00 12.00
BMS Mats Sundin 1.50 4.00
BPF Peter Forsberg 1.50 4.00
BPK Patrick Kane 3.00 8.00
BRF Robby Fabbri SP 2.50 6.00
BRG Ryan Getzlaf 2.50 6.00
BRH Ryan Hartman SP 2.50 6.00
BRN Rick Nash 1.50 4.00
BSB Sam Bennett SP 2.50 6.00
BSC Sidney Crosby 6.00 15.00
BSS Steven Stamkos 3.00 8.00
BSU Malcolm Subban SP 5.00 12.00
BSY Steve Yzerman 2.50 6.00
BTA John Tavares 3.00 8.00
BVT Vladimir Tarasenko 2.50 6.00

2015-16 Upper Deck Full Force Dual Force

ATED PRINT RUN 649 SER.#'d SETS
OLD/49: .8X TO 2X BASIC INSERT/649
F1 W.Gretzky/M.Messier 15.00 40.00
F2 J.Toews/P.Kane 6.00 15.00
F3 B.Orr/P.Esposito 10.00 25.00
F4 E.Malkin/P.Hornqvist 10.00 25.00
F5 S.Yzerman/N.Lidstrom 5.00 12.00
F6 P.Datsyuk/H.Zetterberg 4.00 10.00
F7 A.Oates/B.Hull 3.00 8.00
F8 C.Price/P.Subban 10.00 25.00
F9 J.Jagr/M.Lemieux 10.00 25.00
F10 J.Gaudreau/S.Monahan 5.00 12.00
F11 G.Anderson/G.Fuhr 3.00 8.00
F12 C.Giroux/J.Voracek 3.00 8.00

2015-16 Upper Deck Full Force Goooal

ETERAN ODDS 1:7 H, 1:15 R/BL
OOKIE SP ODDS 1:108 H, 1:216 R/BL
AE Aaron Ekblad 1.25 3.00
AN Andrej Nestrasil .75 2.00
AO Alexander Ovechkin 5.00 12.00
BB Brent Burns 1.50 4.00
CM Connor McDavid SP 12.00 30.00
EK Evgeny Kuznetsov 2.00 5.00
JD Jacob de la Rose 1.25 3.00
JG Johnny Gaudreau 2.00 5.00
JJ Josh Jooris .75 2.00
JT John Tavares 2.50 6.00
JV James van Riemsdyk 1.25 3.00
NE Nikolaj Ehlers SP 3.00 8.00
NY Nail Yakupov 1.00 2.50
PK Patrick Kane 2.50 6.00
PS P.K. Subban 2.00 5.00
RJ Ryan Johansen 1.50 4.00
RK Ronalds Kenins 1.25 3.00
SB Jack Eichel SP 6.00 15.00
SC Sidney Crosby 5.00 12.00
TF Theoren Fleury 1.50 4.00
TJ Tyler Johnson 1.00 2.50
TS Teemu Selanne 2.50 6.00
WG Wayne Gretzky 6.00 15.00

2015-16 Upper Deck Full Force Goooal Autographs

NPRICED VET GRP A ODDS 1:12,252
ET GROUP B ODDS 1:4288
ET GROUP C ODDS 1:762
ET GROUP D ODDS 1:381
ET GROUP E ODDS 1:158
VERALL VET ODDS 1:94H, 1:315R/BL
AM BENNETT ODDS 1:2871
IKOLAJ EHLERS ODDS 1:2110
ONNOR McDAVID ODDS 1:4220
XCH EXPIRATION: 11/11/2017
AN Andrej Nestrasil E 4.00 10.00
AO Alexander Ovechkin A
BB Brent Burns E 8.00 20.00
CM Connor McDavid A 250.00 400.00
EK Evgeny Kuznetsov E 8.00 20.00
JD Jacob de la Rose E 6.00 15.00
JG Johnny Gaudreau C 15.00 40.00
JJ Josh Jooris E 4.00 10.00
JT John Tavares D 12.00 30.00
JV James van Riemsdyk D 6.00 15.00
NE Nikolaj Ehlers C 10.00 25.00
NY Nail Yakupov D 5.00 12.00
PS P.K. Subban A 30.00 60.00
RJ Ryan Johansen C 8.00 20.00
RK Ronalds Kenins D EXCH 8.00 20.00
SB Sam Bennett B 8.00 20.00
SC Sidney Crosby A
TF Theoren Fleury C 12.00 30.00
TS Teemu Selanne B 40.00 80.00
WG Wayne Gretzky B

2015-16 Upper Deck Full Force Ice Encounters

TATED ODDS 1:54 HOB, 1:144 R/BL
EAR Antoine Roussel 1.50 4.00
ECM Cody McLeod 1.50 4.00
ECN Chris Neil 1.50 4.00
EDB Dustin Byfuglien 2.50 6.00
EDD Derek Dorsett 1.50 4.00
EDP Dion Phaneuf 2.50 6.00
EJT Jordin Tootoo 2.00 5.00
EML Wayne Simmonds 3.00 8.00
ERR Ryan Reaves 1.50 4.00
ETW Tom Wilson 2.50 6.00

2015-16 Upper Deck Full Force Immediate Impacts

TATED ODDS 1:18 H, 1:37 R/BL
OIL SP ODDS 1:108H, 1:216R/BL
AB Antoine Bibeau 1.25 3.00
BR Brendan Ranford 1.00 2.50
CM Connor McDavid SP 8.00 20.00
EP Emile Poirier 1.25 3.00
HS Henrik Samuelsson 1.00 2.50
JD Jacob de la Rose 1.25 3.00
JE Jack Eichel SP 5.00 12.00
KF Kevin Fiala 1.25 3.00
MD Max Domi SP 3.00 8.00
MP Matt Puempel 1.00 2.50
MS Malcolm Subban 3.00 8.00
NE Nikolaj Ehlers SP 3.00 8.00
NS Nick Shore 1.25 3.00
RH Ryan Hartman 1.50 4.00
SB Sam Bennett 1.50 4.00
SP Shane Prince 1.00 2.50

2015-16 Upper Deck Full Force Immediate Impacts Autographs

ROUP A ODDS 1:1652
ROUP B ODDS 1:620
ROUP C ODDS 1:496
ET ODDS 1:236 H, 1:787 R/BL
OOKIE GRP A ODDS 1:8024 H
OOKIE GRP B ODDS 1:1070 H
AB Antoine Bibeau B 6.00 15.00
CM Connor McDavid A
EP Emile Poirier B 6.00 15.00

IIHS Henrik Samuelsson C 5.00 12.00
IIJD Jacob de la Rose C 6.00 15.00
IIKF Kevin Fiala A 6.00 15.00
IIMD Max Domi B 12.00 30.00
IIMP Matt Puempel B 5.00 12.00
IIMS Malcolm Subban B 15.00 40.00
IINE Nikolaj Ehlers B 12.00 30.00
IINP Nicolas Petan B 6.00 15.00
IIRH Ryan Hartman C 8.00 20.00
IISB Sam Bennett A 8.00 20.00
IISP Shane Prince C 5.00 12.00

2015-16 Upper Deck Full Force Rising Force

STATED PRINT RUN 999 SER.#'d SETS
RFAB Aleksander Barkov 2.50 6.00
RFAE Aaron Ekblad 2.50 6.00
RFCM Connor McDavid 30.00 60.00
RFDE Jacob de la Rose 2.50 6.00
RFEK Evgeny Kuznetsov 4.00 10.00
RFEL Elias Lindholm 1.50 4.00
RFEP Emile Poirier 2.50 6.00
RFGI John Gibson 2.50 6.00
RFJD Jonathan Drouin 3.00 8.00
RFJE Jack Eichel 10.00 25.00
RFJG Johnny Gaudreau 4.00 10.00
RFJK John Klingberg 2.00 5.00
RFJV Jako Virtanon 3.00 8.00
RFKF Kevin Fiala 2.50 6.00
RFKH Kevin Hayes 2.50 6.00
RFMD Max Domi 5.00 12.00
RFMR Morgan Rielly 2.00 5.00
RFMS Mark Stone 2.00 5.00
RFNE Nikolaj Ehlers 5.00 12.00
RFNK Nikita Kucherov 4.00 10.00
RFNM Nathan MacKinnon 5.00 12.00
RFRH Ryan Hartman 3.00 8.00
RFRR Rasmus Ristolainen 2.00 5.00
RFRS Ryan Strome 2.00 5.00
RFSB Sam Bennett 3.00 8.00
RFSJ Seth Jones 2.00 5.00
RFSM Sean Monahan 2.50 6.00
RFTT Teuvo Teravainen 2.50 6.00
RFVT Vladimir Tarasenko 4.00 10.00
RFZG Zemgus Girgensons 2.00 5.00

2015-16 Upper Deck Full Force Rising Force Gold

*GOLD/99: .8X TO 2X BASIC INSERT/999
RFCM Connor McDavid 200.00 350.00
RFEK Evgeny Kuznetsov 8.00 20.00
RFJD Jonathan Drouin 6.00 15.00
RFJE Jack Eichel 75.00 150.00
RFRH Ryan Hartman 6.00 15.00

2015-16 Upper Deck Full Force Thermal Threats

VETERAN ODDS 1:15 HOB, 1:42 R/BL
ROOKIE SP ODDS 1:67 HOB, 1:180 R/BL
TTAH Andrew Hammond 4.00 10.00
TTAO Alexander Ovechkin 5.00 12.00
TTCM Connor McDavid SP 12.00 30.00
TTGI Claude Giroux 1.25 3.00
TTHL Henrik Lundqvist 1.50 4.00
TTHZ Henrik Zetterberg 1.50 4.00
TTJB Jamie Benn 1.50 4.00
TTJE Jack Eichel SP 6.00 15.00
TTJV James van Riemsdyk 1.25 3.00
TTKF Kevin Fiala 1.25 3.00
TTMD Max Domi SP 3.00 8.00
TTMP Max Pacioretty 1.25 3.00
TTNE Nikolaj Ehlers SP 3.00 8.00
TTNK Nikita Kucherov 2.00 5.00
TTPD Pavel Datsyuk 1.50 4.00
TTPE Phil Esposito 2.00 5.00
TTPK P.K. Subban 2.00 5.00
TTPR Pekka Rinne 1.50 4.00
TTRG Ryan Getzlaf 2.00 5.00
TTSB Sam Bennett SP 2.00 5.00
TTSC Sidney Crosby 5.00 12.00
TTWG Wayne Gretzky 6.00 15.00

2015-16 Upper Deck Full Force Valuable Assets

VETERAN ODDS 1:28 H, 1:56 R/BL
ROOKIE SP ODDS 1:108 H, 1:216 R/BL
VAB Andre Burakovsky 1.00 2.50
VAE Aaron Ekblad 1.25 3.00
VCM Connor McDavid SP 8.00 20.00
VJD Jonathan Drouin 1.50 4.00
VJE Jack Eichel SP 5.00 12.00
VJG Johnny Gaudreau 2.00 5.00
VJH Jonathan Huberdeau 1.25 3.00
VMD Max Domi SP 3.00 8.00
VPM Petr Mrazek 1.50 4.00
VSM Sean Monahan 1.25 3.00
VTB Tyson Barrie 1.25 3.00

2015-16 Upper Deck Full Force Valuable Assets Autographs

UNPRICED GRP A ODDS 1:21,757
GROUP B ODDS 1:8081
GROUP C ODDS 1:1003
GROUP D ODDS 1:603
OVERALL VET ODDS 1:354H, 178R/BL
SAM BENNETT ODDS 1:3021
MAX DOMI ODDS 1:1888
CONNOR McDAVID ODDS 1:5035
VAB Andre Burakovsky D 6.00 15.00
VCM Connor McDavid A 150.00 250.00
VJD Jonathan Drouin C 10.00 25.00
VJE Sam Bennett B 10.00 25.00
VJG Johnny Gaudreau B 12.50 25.00
VJH Jonathan Huberdeau A
VMD Max Domi C 25.00 50.00
VPM Petr Mrazek D 10.00 25.00
VTB Tyson Barrie C 8.00 20.00

1998-99 Upper Deck Gold Reserve

Distributed as a predominately retail product, this brand mirrored the regular Upper Deck brand in look and checklist, the only difference being that this set carried gold foil where Upper Deck was silver.
COMPLETE SET (420) 100.00 200.00
COMP.SER.1 SET (210) 60.00 120.00
COMP.SER.2 SET (210) 40.00 80.00
*1-30 GOLD SR/RR: .6X TO 1.5X BASIC CARDS
*31-390 GOLD VETS: 1.2X TO 3X BASIC CARDS
*391-412 GOLD PE: .6X TO 1.5X UPPER DECK
*413-420 GOLD CC: .6X TO 1.5X UPPER DECK
SY S.Yzerman Stick/200 75.00 200.00
SYA S.Yzerman Stick AU/19
WG W.Gretzky Stick/200 60.00 150.00
WGA W.Gretzky Stick AU/99 250.00 500.00
NNO1 W.Gretzky AU/200 200.00 500.00
NNO2 S.Yzerman AU/200 60.00 150.00

1999-00 Upper Deck Gold Reserve

1999-00 Upper Deck Gold Reserve was packaged as a two-series release. Series one contained 170 cards and series two contained 180 cards. Base cards use the same design as the basic 1999-00 Upper Deck release but are enhanced with an all-foil card stock and gold foil highlights. Prospect cards in both series were short printed and the series two cards were numbered out of 2500. This release was packaged in 24-pack boxes where packs contained 10 cards and carried a suggested retail price of $2.99. Cards #164 and 199 were intended to be Brendl and Jillson but were replaced by two other players prior to the packout. However a very small number of both cards were unofficially released and are considered very scarce.
COMPLETE SET (350) 200.00 400.00
COMP.SERIES 1 (170) 75.00 150.00
COMP.SER.1. w/o SP's (135) 20.00 40.00
COMP.SERIES 2 (180) 100.00 250.00
COMP.SER.2. w/o SP's (150) 15.00 30.00
*GOLD RES VETS: .8X TO 2X BASIC UD
*GOLD RES SP: .8X TO 2X BASIC UD SP
*GOLD RES/2500: 1.5X TO 4X BASIC UD SP

1999-00 Upper Deck Gold Reserve Game-Used Souvenirs

Randomly inserted in Gold Reserve Update packs at the rate of 1:480, this 7-card set features NHL players coupled with a swatch of a game-used puck.
GRBH Brett Hull 12.00 30.00
GREL Eric Lindros 12.00 30.00
GRPB Pavel Bure 10.00 25.00
GRPK Paul Kariya 10.00 25.00
GRPR Patrick Roy 15.00 40.00
GRSY Steve Yzerman 15.00 40.00
GRWG Wayne Gretzky 30.00 80.00

1999-00 Upper Deck Gold Reserve UD Authentics

Randomly seeded in packs at the rate of 1:480, this 6-card set features authentic player autographs on the card front. Cards that carry the "UPD" suffix are found in Gold Reserve Update packs.
BH Brett Hull 15.00 40.00
BL Brian Leetch UPD 8.00 20.00
BM Bill Muckalt 6.00 15.00
CD Chris Drury 8.00 20.00
CJ Curtis Joseph 8.00 20.00
DL David Legwand 8.00 20.00
PB Pavel Bure 8.00 20.00
PS Patrik Stefan UPD 6.00 15.00
SS Sergei Samsonov UPD 8.00 20.00
SY Steve Yzerman UPD 30.00 80.00

2009 Upper Deck Goodwin Champions

COMMON CARD (1-150) .15 .40
COMMON NIGHT 5.00 12.00
COMMON SP (151-190) 1.25 3.00
151-190 STATED ODDS 1:2 HOBBY
COMMON SUPER SP (191-210) 1.50 4.00
SUPER SP MINORS 1.50 4.00
SUPER SP SEMIS 1.50 4.00
SUPER SP UNLISTED 1.50 4.00
191-210 STATED ODDS 1:10 HOBBY
PLATES RANDOMLY INSERTED
PLATE PRINT RUN 1 SET PER COLOR
BLACK-CYAN-MAGENTA-YELLOW ISSUED
NO PLATE PRICING DUE TO SCARCITY
34 Alexander Ovechkin 1.25 3.00
38 Carey Price 1.00 2.50
81 Wayne Gretzky 1.50 4.00
90 Jonathan Toews .60 1.50
140a G.Howe Day 1.25 3.00
140b G.Howe Night SP 5.00 12.00
141 Bobby Orr 1.00 2.50

2009 Upper Deck Goodwin Champions Mini

COMPLETE SET (192) 75.00 150.00
*MINI 1-150: 1X TO 2.5X BASIC
APPX.MINI ODDS ONE PER PACK
PLATES RANDOMLY INSERTED
PLATE PRINT RUN 1 SET PER COLOR
BLACK-CYAN-MAGENTA-YELLOW ISSUED
NO PLATE PRICING DUE TO SCARCITY

2009 Upper Deck Goodwin Champions Mini Black Border

*MINI BLK 1-150: 1.5X TO 4X BASE
*MINI BLK 211-252: .75X TO 2X MINI
RANDOM INSERTS IN PACKS

2009 Upper Deck Goodwin Champions Mini Foil

*MINI FOIL 1-150: 3X TO 8X BASE
*MINI FOIL 211-252: 1.5X TO 4X MINI
RANDOM INSERTS IN PACKS
ANNCD PRINT RUN OF 88 TOTAL SETS

2009 Upper Deck Goodwin Champions Autographs

STATED ODDS 1:20 HOBBY
EXCHANGE DEADLINE 8/31/2011
BO Bobby Orr/25 * 90.00 150.00

2009 Upper Deck Goodwin Champions Preview

RANDOM INSERTS IN PACKS
GCP5 Gordie Howe 6.00 15.00

2011 Upper Deck Goodwin Champions

COMP.SET w/o VAR (210) 40.00 80.00
COMP.SET w/o SP's (150) 10.00 25.00
COMMON SP (151-190) 1.00 2.50
151-190 SP ODDS 1:3 HOBBY
COMMON SP (191-210) 1.50 4.00
191-210 SP ODDS 1:12 HOBBY
COMMON VARIATION SP 4.00 10.00
4 Bobby Orr .60 1.50
5 Cam Neely .30 .75
9 Gordie Howe .75 2.00
17 King Clancy .15 .40
30 Evgeni Malkin .50 1.25
32 Eric Lindros .25 .60
49 Cammi Granato .20 .50
59 Steve Yzerman .60 1.50
70 Ray Bourque .50 1.25
72 Joe Sakic .40 1.00
73 Steven Stamkos .50 1.25
75 Hayley Wickenheiser .15 .40
77 John Tavares .50 1.25
79 Howie Morenz .20 .50
87 Sidney Crosby .75 2.00
89 Alexander Ovechkin .60 1.50
99 Wayne Gretzky 1.25 3.00
130 Mario Lemieux .60 1.50
134 Patrick Roy .75 2.00
136 Igor Larionov .25 .60
148 Mark Messier .50 1.25
155 Terry Sawchuk SP 1.00 2.50
177 Eddie Shore SP 1.00 2.50
203 Lord Stanley SP 1.50 4.00
208 James Creighton SP 1.50 4.00

2011 Upper Deck Goodwin Champions Mini

*1-150 MINI: 1X TO 2.5X BASIC
1-150 MINI ODDS 1:4 HOBBY
COMMON CARD (211-231) .60 1.50
211-231 MINI ODDS 1:13 HOBBY
PRINTING PLATES RANDOMLY INSERTED
PLATE PRINT RUN 1 SET PER COLOR
BLACK-CYAN-MAGENTA-YELLOW ISSUED
NO PLATE PRICING DUE TO SCARCITY

2011 Upper Deck Goodwin Champions Mini Black

*1-150 MINI BLACK: 1.2X TO 3X BASIC
1-150 MINI BLACK ODDS 1:13 HOBBY
*211-231 MINI BLK: .6X TO 1.5X BASIC MINI
211-231 MINI BLACK ODDS 1:46 HOBBY

2011 Upper Deck Goodwin Champions Mini Foil

*1-150 MINI FOIL: 2.5X TO 6X BASIC
1-150 ANNCD PRINT RUN OF 89
*211-231 MINI FOIL : 1X TO 2.5X BASIC MINI
211-231 ANNCD PRINT RUN OF 178
PRINT RUNS PROVIDED BY UD
99 Wayne Gretzky 10.00 25.00

2011 Upper Deck Goodwin Champions Autographs

Please note that the Dwayne De Rosario card in this set was issued in the 2014 Upper Deck Goodwin Champions product.
GROUP A ODDS 1:1577 HOBBY
GROUP B ODDS 1:729 HOBBY
GROUP C ODDS 1:339 HOBBY
GROUP D ODDS 1:246 HOBBY
GROUP E ODDS 1:72 HOBBY
GROUP F ODDS 1:35 HOBBY
OVERALL AUTO ODDS 1:20 HOBBY
EXCHANGE DEADLINE 6/7/2013
AO Alexander Ovechkin A
CG Cammi Granato F 5.00 12.00
CN Cam Neely C 15.00 40.00
HO Gordie Howe C 50.00 100.00
HW Hayley Wickenheiser E 4.00 10.00
IL Igor Larionov B 30.00 60.00
JT John Tavares B 12.00 30.00
OR Bobby Orr D 60.00 120.00
SC Sidney Crosby C 90.00 150.00
SS Steven Stamkos 2012 30.00 60.00
WG Wayne Gretzky B 150.00 250.00

2011 Upper Deck Goodwin Champions Figures of Sport

COMP.SET. w/o SP's (14) 10.00 25.00
COMMON CARD (1-14) .60 1.50
1-14 STATED ODDS 1:21 HOBBY
15-18 SP ODDS 1:300 HOBBY
FS7 Bobby Orr 2.50 6.00
FS10 Sidney Crosby 2.00 5.00
FS18 Wayne Gretzky SP 8.00 20.00

2011 Upper Deck Goodwin Champions Memorabilia

GROUP A ODDS 1:14,613 HOBBY
GROUP B ODDS 1:179 HOBBY
GROUP C ODDS 1:31 HOBBY
GROUP D ODDS 1:22 HOBBY
AO Alexander Ovechkin C 5.00 12.00
CN Cam Neely D 3.00 8.00
EL Eric Lindros D 3.00 8.00
IL Igor Larionov D 3.00 8.00
ME Mark Messier C 3.00 8.00
ML Mario Lemieux C 6.00 15.00
RB Ray Bourque D 3.00 8.00
RY Patrick Roy C 5.00 12.00
SC Sidney Crosby B 10.00 25.00
SY Steve Yzerman B 4.00 10.00
TA John Tavares D 3.00 8.00
WG Wayne Gretzky B 15.00 40.00

2011 Upper Deck Goodwin Champions Memorabilia Dual

GROUP A ODDS 1:87,680 HOBBY
GROUP B ODDS 1:8768 HOBBY
GROUP C ODDS 1:2923 HOBBY
GROUP D ODDS 1:877 HOBBY
GROUP E ODDS 1:585 HOBBY
NO GROUP A PRICING AVAILABLE
AO Alexander Ovechkin C 6.00 15.00
SC Sidney Crosby D 6.00 15.00
SY Steve Yzerman C 6.00 15.00

2012 Upper Deck Goodwin Champions

COMP.SET w/o VAR (210) 25.00 50.00
COMP.SET w/o SP's (150) 10.00 25.00
151-190 SP ODDS 1:3 HOBBY, BLASTER
191-210 SP ODDS 1:12 HOBBY, BLASTER
1 Bobby Orr .60 1.50
12 Dale Hawerchuk .20 .50
28 Ron Francis .25 .60
32 Wayne Gretzky 1.25 3.00
36 Eric Lindros .25 .60
49 Sidney Crosby .75 2.00
74 Brett Hull .30 .75
78 Brian Leetch .20 .50
82 Wendel Clark .20 .50
85 Luc Robitaille .25 .60
89 Paul Coffey .30 .75
91 Jonathan Huberdeau .40 1.00
105 Mike Bossy .25 .60
119 Mario Lemieux .60 1.50
124 Brendan Shanahan .20 .50
129 Larry Robinson .20 .50
154 Ryan Strome SP 1.00 2.50
181 Ray Bourque SP 1.00 2.50
191 Sid Abel SP 1.50 4.00

2012 Upper Deck Goodwin Champions Mini

*1-150 MINI: 1X TO 2.5X BASIC CARDS
1-150 MINI STATED ODDS 1:2 HOBBY, BLASTER
211-231 MINI ODDS 1:2 HOBBY, BLASTER

2012 Upper Deck Goodwin Champions Mini Foil

*1-150 MINI FOIL: 2.5X TO 6X BASIC
1-150 MINI FOIL ANNCD. PRINT RUN 99
*211-231 MINI FOIL: 1X TO 2.5X BASIC MINI
211-231 MINI FOIL ANNCD. PRINT RUN 199

2012 Upper Deck Goodwin Champions Mini Green

*1-150 MINI GREEN: 1.25X TO 3X BASIC
*211-231 MINI GREEN: .6X TO 1.5X BASIC MINI
TWO MINI GREEN PER HOBBY BOX
ONE MINI GREEN PER BLASTER

2012 Upper Deck Goodwin Champions Mini Green Blank Back

UNPRICED DUE TO SCARCITY

2012 Upper Deck Goodwin Champions Autographs

GROUP A ODDS 1:1,977
GROUP B ODDS 1:353
GROUP C ODDS 1:264
GROUP D ODDS 1:185
GROUP E ODDS 1:82
GROUP F ODDS 1:36
OVERALL AUTO ODDS 1:20
EXCHANGE DEADLINE 7/12/2014
ABO Bobby Orr D 50.00 100.00
ACR Sidney Crosby A 150.00 250.00
AHK Dale Hawerchuk C 4.00 10.00
AHL Brett Hull B 20.00 40.00
AHU Jonathan Huberdeau C 15.00 40.00
ALR Luc Robitaille C 5.00 12.00
ARB Ray Bourque B 15.00 40.00
AWG Wayne Gretzky A 125.00 250.00

2012 Upper Deck Goodwin Champions Memorabilia

GROUP A ODDS 1:10,631
GROUP B ODDS 1:4,784
GROUP C ODDS 1:302
GROUP D ODDS 1:118
GROUP E ODDS 1:36
GROUP F ODDS 1:23
MBH Brett Hull D 4.00 10.00
MBL Brian Leetch F 3.00 8.00
MBS Brendan Shanahan F 3.00 8.00
MDH Dale Hawerchuk F 3.00 8.00
MEL Eric Lindros F 3.00 8.00
MHU Jonathan Huberdeau F 3.00 8.00
MLR Luc Robitaille E 3.00 8.00
MMB Mike Bossy C 3.00 8.00
MML Mario Lemieux E 5.00 12.00
MPC Paul Coffey F 3.00 8.00
MRB Ray Bourque F 4.00 10.00
MRF Ron Francis F 3.00 8.00
MRO Larry Robinson F 3.00 8.00
MRS Ryan Strome F 3.00 8.00
MSC Sidney Crosby C 6.00 15.00
MWC Wendel Clark E 4.00 10.00
MWG Wayne Gretzky C 15.00 40.00

2012 Upper Deck Goodwin Champions Memorabilia Dual

GROUP A ODDS 1:95,680
GROUP B ODDS 1:31,893
GROUP C ODDS 1:2,514
GROUP D ODDS 1:1,306
GROUP E ODDS 1:520
NO PRICING ON GROUP A
M2SC Sidney Crosby C 20.00 40.00

2013 Upper Deck Goodwin Champions

COMP. SET w/o VAR (210) 25.00 60.00
COMP. SET w/o SPs (150) 8.00 20.00
151-190 SP ODDS 1:3 HOBBY,BLASTER
191-210 SP ODDS 1:12 HOBBY,BLASTER
OVERALL VARIATION ODDS 1:320 H, 1:1,200 B
GROUP A ODDS 1:4,800
GROUP B ODDS 1:2,400
GROUP C ODDS 1:1,400
1 Wayne Gretzky 1.25 3.00
12 Mike Bossy .25 .60
20A Mario Lemieux .60 1.50
20B M.Lemieux/J.Jagr SP 12.00 30.00
28A Joe Sakic .30 .75
28B Joe Sakic Horizontal SP B 20.00 50.00
29 Dave Schultz .20 .50
32 Ray Bourque .30 .75
42 Mats Sundin .25 .60
45 Nicklas Lidstrom .25 .60
47A Sidney Crosby .60 1.50
47B Sidney Crosby Horizontal SP B 20.00 50.00
70A Luc Robitaille .25 .60
70B L.Robitaille/B.Hull SP 6.00 15.00
73 Dominik Hasek .25 .60
76 Bryan Trottier .15 .40
83 Ed Belfour .20 .50
132 Theoren Fleury .25 .60
137 Bobby Orr .60 1.50
138 Mark Messier .40 1.00
148 Pavel Bure .25 .60
185 Larry Robinson SP 1.00 2.50
194A Doug Gilmour SP 1.50 4.00
194B D.Gilmour/E.Belfour SP 12.00 30.00
196 Hobey Baker SP 1.50 4.00
204 Frank Calder SP 1.50 4.00

2013 Upper Deck Goodwin Champions Mini

*1-150 MINI: 1X TO 2.5X BASIC CARDS
7 MINIS PER HOBBY BOX, 4 MINIS PER BLASTER

2013 Upper Deck Goodwin Champions Mini Canvas

*1-150 MINI CANVAS: 2.5X TO 6X BASIC CARDS
1-150 MINI CANVAS ANNCD. PRINT RUN 99
*211-225 MINI CANVAS: 1X TO 2.5 BASIC MINI
211-225 MINI CANVAS ANNCD. PRINT RUN 198

2013 Upper Deck Goodwin Champions Mini Green

STATED ODDS 1:12 HOBBY, 1:15 BLASTER
STATED SP ODDS 1:60 HOBBY, 1:72 BLASTER

2013 Upper Deck Goodwin Champions Autographs

OVERALL ODDS 1:20
GROUP A ODDS 1:7,517
GROUP B ODDS 1:1,224
GROUP C ODDS 1:489
GROUP D ODDS 1:142
GROUP E ODDS 1:206
GROUP F ODDS 1:28
ABT Bryan Trottier C 6.00 15.00
ADS Dave Schultz C 8.00 20.00
AMM Mark Messier C 15.00 40.00
AMS Mats Sundin C 20.00 50.00
ANL Nicklas Lidstrom D 10.00 25.00

2013 Upper Deck Goodwin Champions Memorabilia

OVERALL ODDS 1:12
GROUP A ODDS 1:23,082
GROUP B ODDS 1:5,970
GROUP C ODDS 1:104
GROUP D ODDS 1:22
GROUP E ODDS 1:37
MBT Bryan Trottier D 3.00 8.00
MDH Dominik Hasek D 3.00 8.00
MEB Ed Belfour D 3.00 8.00
MJS Joe Sakic C 3.00 8.00
MLR Larry Robinson C 3.00 8.00
MMB Mike Bossy D 3.00 8.00
MNL Nicklas Lidstrom D 3.00 8.00
MPB Pavel Bure C 4.00 10.00
MRB Ray Bourque D 4.00 10.00
MRO Luc Robitaille D 3.00 8.00
MTF Theoren Fleury D 3.00 8.00
MWG Wayne Gretzky B 20.00 50.00

2013 Upper Deck Goodwin Champions Sport Royalty Autographs

OVERALL ODDS 1:1,161
GROUP A ODDS 1:7,473
GROUP B ODDS 1:4,171
GROUP C ODDS 1:2,050
SRABO Bobby Orr C 50.00 100.00
SRAML Mario Lemieux B 60.00 120.00
SRASC S.Crosby B EXCH 75.00 135.00

2013 Upper Deck Goodwin Champions Sport Royalty Memorabilia

OVERALL ODDS 1:350
GROUP A ODDS 1:2,391
GROUP B ODDS 1:957
GROUP C ODDS 1:717
SRMML Mario Lemieux C 12.00 30.00
SRMSC Sidney Crosby C 8.00 20.00

2014 Upper Deck Goodwin Champions

COMPLETE SET w/o AU's(180) 40.00 100.00
COMPLETE SET w/o SP's(155) 12.00 30.00
131-155 SP ODDS 1:3 HOBBY,BLAST
156-180 SP ODDS 1:12 HOB/1:12 BLAST
AU ODDS 1:60 HOB/1:720 BLAST
NOLA AU ODDS 1:860 '15 PACKS
NOLA AU ISSUED IN '15 GOODWIN
7 Chris Osgood .25 .60
12 Bobby Hull .25 .60
19 Hayley Wickenheiser .15 .40
20 Mike Richter .25 .60
26 Bill Guerin .15 .40
27 Guy Carbonneau .25 .60
31 Patrick Roy .50 1.25
34 Guy Lafleur .25 .60
35 Peter Forsberg .25 .60
36 Adam Oates .25 .60
41 Jean Beliveau .25 .60
43 Jeremy Roenick .25 .60
48 Bill Barber .25 .60
54 Paul Coffey .20 .50
55 Mark Messier .25 .60
58 Rogie Vachon .25 .60
62 Bobby Orr .60 1.50
72 Glenn Anderson .20 .50
73 Grant Fuhr .25 .60
75 Julie Chu .15 .40
77 Marcel Dionne .25 .60
88 Gilbert Perreault .30 .75
99 Wayne Gretzky 1.00 2.50
101 Claude Lemieux .25 .60
102 Jari Kurri .25 .60
104 Mike Gartner .20 .50
110 Scotty Bowman .25 .60
111 Bobby Clarke .25 .60
114A Mario Lemieux .50 1.25
114B Lemieux/Bettis SP 12.00 30.00
130A Stan Mikita .25 .60
130B Mikita/Hull SP 4.00 10.00

2014 Upper Deck Goodwin Champions Mini

*1-130 MINI: .75X TO 2X BASIC
COMMON CARD (131-180) .50 1.25
7 MINIS PER HOBBY 4 PER BLASTER

2014 Upper Deck Goodwin Champions Mini Canvas

*1-130 MINI CANVAS: 2X TO 5X BASIC
COMMON CARD (131-180) 1.25 3.00
RANDOM INSERTS IN PACKS

2014 Upper Deck Goodwin Champions Mini Green

*1-130 MINI GREEN: 1X TO 2.5X BASIC
COMMON CARD (131-180) .60 1.50
STATED ODDS 1:10 HOB/1:12 BLAST

2014 Upper Deck Goodwin Champions Autographs

GROUP A ODDS 1:54,400 HOBBY
GROUP B ODDS 1:6590 HOBBY
GROUP C ODDS 1:17,525 HOBBY
GROUP D ODDS 1:1280 HOBBY
GROUP E ODDS 1:410 HOBBY
GROUP F ODDS 1:135 HOBBY
GROUP G ODDS 1:42 HOBBY
'16 STATED ODDS 1:4352 HOBBY
ACL Claude Lemieux F 2.50 6.00
ACO Chris Osgood E 2.50 6.00
AGL Guy Lafleur C
AHW Hayley Wickenheiser G 3.00 8.00
APR Patrick Roy 30.00 80.00
AWG Wayne Gretzky C

2014 Upper Deck Goodwin Champions Goudey

COMPLETE SET (52) 25.00 60.00
BB ODDS 1:13 HOB/1:32 BLAST
BK ODDS 1:25 HOB/1:60 BLAST
FB ODDS 1:25 HOB/1:60 BLAST
HK ODDS 1:33 HOB/1:80 BLAST
GOLF ODDS 1:33 HOB/1:80 BLAST
MISC SPORT ODDS 1:100 HOB/1:240 BLAST
HISTORY ODDS 1:40 HOB/1:96 BLAST
27 Bill Guerin .40 1.00
28 Wayne Gretzky 2.50 6.00
29 Bobby Orr 1.50 4.00
30 Theoren Fleury .60 1.50
31 Mario Lemieux 1.25 3.00
32 Patrick Roy 1.25 3.00

2014 Upper Deck Goodwin Champions Goudey Autographs

GROUP A ODDS 1:7200 HOBBY
GROUP B ODDS 1:4800 HOBBY
GROUP C ODDS 1:1650 HOBBY
GROUP D ODDS 1:1200 HOBBY
'16 GROUP A ODDS 1:21,760 HOBBY
'16 GROUP B ODDS 1:8369 HOBBY
28 Wayne Gretzky A
30 Theoren Fleury C 12.00 30.00
31 Mario Lemieux A
32 Patrick Roy A 30.00 80.00

2014 Upper Deck Goodwin Champions Memorabilia

GROUP A ODDS 1:5140
GROUP B ODDS 1:685
GROUP C ODDS 1:80
GROUP D ODDS 1:18
MBG Bill Guerin D 2.50 6.00
MGF Grant Fuhr C 3.00 8.00
MGL Guy Lafleur B 4.00 10.00
MHW Hayley Wickenheiser D 3.00 8.00
MJK Jari Kurri C 2.50 6.00
MJR Jeremy Roenick C 2.50 6.00
MMD Marcel Dionne C 2.50 6.00
MMM Mark Messier B 2.50 6.00
MPC Paul Coffey C 3.00 8.00
MPF Peter Forsberg C 2.50 6.00
MPR Patrick Roy C 4.00 10.00

2014 Upper Deck Goodwin Champions Memorabilia Dual

GROUP A ODDS 1:2055 HOBBY
GROUP B ODDS 1:1285 HOBBY
GROUP C ODDS 1:860 HOBBY
GROUP D ODDS 1:1285 HOBBY
M2BG Bill Guerin B 3.00 8.00
M2GF Grant Fuhr B 4.00 10.00
M2GL Guy Lafleur A 5.00 12.00
M2JK Jari Kurri B 3.00 8.00
M2JR Jeremy Roenick C 3.00 8.00
M2MM Mark Messier A 5.00 12.00
M2PF Peter Forsberg A 5.00 12.00
M2PR Patrick Roy A 10.00 25.00

2014 Upper Deck Goodwin Champions Memorabilia Premium

*PREMIUM: .75X TO 2X BASIC
RANDOM INSERTS IN PACKS
PRINT RUNS B/WN 10-50 COPIES PER
NO PRICING ON QTY 15 OR LESS
MBG Bill Guerin/50
MGF Grant Fuhr/25
MJR Jeremy Roenick/35
MMM Mark Messier/50
MRV Rogie Vachon/25

2014 Upper Deck Goodwin Champions Sport Royalty Autographs

GROUP A ODDS 1:17,130 HOBBY
GROUP B ODDS 1:4670 HOBBY
GROUP C ODDS 1:2855 HOBBY
GROUP D ODDS 1:1070 HOBBY
'16 GROUP A ODDS 1:21,760 HOBBY
'16 GROUP B ODDS 1:5440 HOBBY
SRAGL Guy Lafleur B 30.00 60.00
SRAWG Wayne Gretzky B 150.00 250.00

2014 Upper Deck Goodwin Champions Sport Royalty Memorabilia

GROUP A ODDS 1:3425 HOBBY
GROUP B ODDS 1:5140 HOBBY
GROUP C ODDS 1:495 HOBBY
GROUP D ODDS 1:285 HOBBY
SRMML Mario Lemieux C 5.00 12.00
SRMWG Wayne Gretzky A 40.00 100.00

2015 Upper Deck Goodwin Champions

COMPLETE SET w/o AU's(150) 25.00 60.00
COMPLETE SET w/o SP's(100) 6.00 15.00
131-155 SP ODDS APPX. 1:3 PACKS
156-180 SP ODDS 1:8 PACKS
GROUP A AU ODDS 1:755 PACKS
GROUP B AU ODDS 1:65 PACKS
PRINTING PLATES RANDOMLY INSERTED
PLATE PRINT RUN 1 SET PER COLOR
BLACK-CYAN-MAGENTA-YELLOW ISSUED
NO PLATE PRICING DUE TO SCARCITY
EXCHNAGE DEADLINE 6/10/2017
16 Brett Hull .25 .60
31 Ray Bourque .30 .75
38 John Vanbiesbrouck .25 .60
59 Marty Turco .20 .50
61 Mark Messier .25 .60
66 Mario Lemieux .50 1.25
68 Marty McSorley .25 .60
78 Mike Bossy .25 .60
80 Chris Chelios .25 .60
83 Teemu Selanne .25 .60
97 Pierre Turgeon .20 .50
98 Terry Sawchuk .25 .60
99 Wayne Gretzky .75 2.00
100 Marcel Dionne .25 .60
110 Brett Hull SP .75 2.00
121 Teemu Selanne SP .75 2.00
125 Terry Sawchuk SP .75 2.00
128 Mario Lemieux SP 2.00 5.00
131 Patrick Roy SP 2.00 5.00
134 Adam Oates SP 1.00 2.50
136 Jean Beliveau SP 1.00 2.50
147 Wayne Gretzky SP 3.00 8.00
149 Phil Esposito SP 1.00 2.50
150 Mark Messier SP 1.00 2.50

2015 Upper Deck Goodwin Champions Mini

*MINI 1-100: 1X TO 2.5X BASIC
*MINI 101-125: .3X TO .75X BASIC
*MINI 126-150: .25X TO .6X BASIC
STATED ODDS THREE PER BOX

2015 Upper Deck Goodwin Champions Mini Canvas

*CANVAS 1-100: 2X TO 5X BASIC
*CANVAS 101-125: .6X TO 1.5X BASIC
*CANVAS 126-150: .5X TO 1.2X BASIC
RANDOM INSERTS IN PACKS
ANNCD PRINT RUN OF 99 COPIES PER

2015 Upper Deck Goodwin Champions Mini Cloth Lady Luck

*LUCK 1-100: 2.5X TO 6X BASIC
*LUCK 101-125: .75X TO 2X BASIC
*LUCK 126-150: .6X TO 1.5X BASIC
RANDOM INSERTS IN PACKS
STATED PRINT RUN 50 SER.#'d SETS
99 Wayne Gretzky 10.00 25.00
147 Wayne Gretzky 10.00 25.00

2015 Upper Deck Goodwin Champions Mini Leather Magician

*MAGICIAN 1-100: 6X TO 15X BASIC
*MAGICIAN 101-125: 2X TO 5X BASIC
*MAGICIAN 126-150: 1.5X TO 4X BASIC
RANDOM INSERTS IN PACKS
STATED PRINT RUN 15 SER.#'d SETS
99 Wayne Gretzky 25.00 60.00
147 Wayne Gretzky 25.00 60.00

2015 Upper Deck Goodwin Champions Autographs
GROUP A ODDS 1:6830 PACKS
GROUP B ODDS 1:780 PACKS
GROUP C ODDS 1:685 PACKS
GROUP D ODDS 1:350 PACKS
GROUP E ODDS 1:150 PACKS
GROUP F ODDS 1:65 PACKS
'16 GROUP A ODDS 1:14,836 PACKS
'16 GROUP B ODDS 1:1106 PACKS
EXCHANGE DEADLINE 6/10/2017
ACC Chris Chelios D 4.00 10.00
AMM Mark Messier B 12.00 30.00
APT Pierre Turgeon D 2.50 6.00
ATS Teemu Selanne B 12.00 30.00
AWG Wayne Gretzky B 100.00 200.00

2015 Upper Deck Goodwin Champions Autographs Black and White
GROUP A ODDS 1:24,800 PACKS
GROUP B ODDS 1:7630 PACKS
GROUP C ODDS 1:5670 PACKS
GROUP D ODDS 1:6615 PACKS
OVERALL B/W ODDS 1:2000 PACKS
EXCHANGE DEADLINE 6/10/2017
110 Brett Hull B 12.00 30.00
135 Wayne Gretzky C 150.00 300.00

2015 Upper Deck Goodwin Champions Autographs Inscribed
RANDOM INSERTS IN PACKS
PRINT RUNS B/WN 2-298 COPIES PER
NO PRICING ON QTY 16 OR LESS
EXCHANGE DEADLINE 6/10/2017

2015 Upper Deck Goodwin Champions Goudey
COMPLETE SET (60) 15.00 40.00
1-40 STATED ODDS 1:5 PACKS
41-60 STATED ODDS 1:20 PACKS
4 Wayne Gretzky 2.00 5.00
12 Teemu Selanne .60 1.50
30 Jean Beliveau .75 2.00
32 Mario Lemieux 1.25 3.00
33 Brett Hull .60 1.50
34 Patrick Roy 1.25 3.00
35 Doug Harvey .40 1.00

2015 Upper Deck Goodwin Champions Goudey Autographs
GROUP A ODDS 1:1:16,535 PACKS
GROUP B ODDS 1:15,260 PACKS
GROUP C ODDS 1:1585 PACKS
GROUP D ODDS 1:1340 PACKS
OVERALL GOUDEY ODDS 1:660 PACKS
EXCHANGE DEADLINE 6/10/2017
GATS Teemu Selanne C 8.00 20.00
GAWG Wayne Gretzky C

2015 Upper Deck Goodwin Champions Goudey Memorabilia Premium Series
*PREMIUM: .6X TO 1.5X BASIC
RANDOM INSERTS IN PACKS
PRINT RUNS B/WN 10-50 COPIES PER
NO PRICING ON QTY 10
EXCHANGE DEADLINE 6/10/2017
GMTS Teemu Selanne Stick/20 6.00 15.00

2015 Upper Deck Goodwin Champions Goudey Sport Royalty Autographs
GROUP A ODDS 1:1:24,960 PACKS
GROUP B ODDS 1:9985 PACKS
GROUP C ODDS 1:3995 PACKS
OVERALL GOUDEY ODDS 1:2560 PACKS
'16 STATED ODDS 1:32,640 HOBBY
EXCHANGE DEADLINE 6/10/2017
SRAML Mario Lemieux B 40.00 100.00
SRAWG Wayne Gretzky B

2015 Upper Deck Goodwin Champions Goudey Sport Royalty Dual Memorabilia
GROUP A ODDS 1:16,215 PACKS
GROUP B ODDS 1:3040 PACKS
OVERAL SR DUAL 1:2560 PACKS
SRM2LG Gretzky/Lemieux B 25.00 60.00

2015 Upper Deck Goodwin Champions Goudey Sport Royalty Memorabilia
OVERAL SR MEM ODDS 1:320 PACKS
SRMPR Patrick Roy Jsy 4.00 10.00
SRMWG Wayne Gretzky Practice Jsy 12.00 30.00

2015 Upper Deck Goodwin Champions Goudey Sport Royalty Memorabilia Premium Series
*PREMIUM: .6X TO 1.5X BASIC
RANDOM INSERTS IN PACKS
PRINT RUNS B/WN 5-25 COPIES PER
NO PRICING ON QTY 10 OR LESS

2015 Upper Deck Goodwin Champions Memorabilia
GROUP A ODDS 1:420 PACKS
GROUP B ODDS 1:175 PACKS
GROUP C ODDS 1:28 PACKS
MMM Mark Messier Jsy B 2.50 6.00
MRB Ray Bourque Jsy C 2.50 6.00

2015 Upper Deck Goodwin Champions Memorabilia Black and White
GROUP A ODDS 1:3970 PACKS
GROUP B ODDS 1:400 PACKS
OVERAL B/W MEM ODDS 1:360 PACKS
BWMBH Brett Hull Jsy A
BWMMM Mark Messier Jsy B 4.00 10.00
BWMWG Wayne Gretzky Practice Jsy A 12.00 30.00

2015 Upper Deck Goodwin Champions Memorabilia Black and White Premium Series
*PREMIUM: .6X TO 1.5X BASIC
RANDOM INSERTS IN PACKS
PRINT RUNS B/WN 5-25 COPIES PER
NO PRICING ON QTY 10 OR LESS
BWMTS Terry Sawchuk Stick/25 10.00 25.00

2015 Upper Deck Goodwin Champions Memorabilia Premium Series
*PREMIUM: .6X TO 1.5X BASIC
RANDOM INSERTS IN PACKS
PRINT RUNS B/WN 10-75 COPIES PER
NO PRICING ON QTY 15 OR LESS
MCC Chris Chelios Stick/50 4.00 10.00
MPT Pierre Turgeon Stick/50 6.00 15.00

2016 Upper Deck Goodwin Champions
COMPLETE SET w/o SP's(100) 6.00 15.00
101-150 SP ODDS 1:4 HOBBY
SP1 STATED ODDS 1:1280 HOBBY
PRINTING PLATES RANDOMLY INSERTED
PLATE PRINT RUN 1 SET PER COLOR
BLACK-CYAN-MAGENTA-YELLOW ISSUED
NO PLATE PRICING DUE TO SCARCITY
2 Wayne Gretzky .60 1.50
5 Mario Lemieux .50 1.25
7 Patrick Roy .40 1.00
9 Martin Brodeur .40 1.00
30 Aito Iguchi .25 .60
52 Wayne Gretzky .60 1.50
55 Mario Lemieux .50 1.25
57 Patrick Roy .40 1.00
59 Martin Brodeur .40 1.00
80 Aito Iguchi .25 .60
103 Wayne Gretzky BW SP 1.50 4.00
105 Patrick Roy BW SP 1.00 2.50
106 Mario Lemieux BW SP 1.25 3.00
108 Martin Brodeur BW SP 1.00 2.50
135 Aito Iguchi BW SP .60 1.50

2016 Upper Deck Goodwin Champions Autographs
GROUP A STATED ODDS 1:5584 PACKS
GROUP B STATED ODDS 1:871 PACKS
GROUP C STATED ODDS 1:576 PACKS
GROUP D STATED ODDS 1:29 PACKS
EXCHANGE DEADLINE 6/21/2018
AFP Felix Potvin B 10.00 25.00
AIA Aito Iguchi D 5.00 12.00
AJB Johnny Bucyk B 5.00 12.00
AJL John LeClair B 5.00 12.00
AMS Martin St. Louis C 4.00 10.00

2016 Upper Deck Goodwin Champions Autographs Inscription
RANDOM INSERTS IN PACKS
PRINT RUNS B/WN 10-500 COPIES PER
NO PRICING ON QTY 10
EXCHANGE DEADLINE 6/21/2018
AFP Felix Potvin/25 20.00 50.00
AIA Aito Iguchi/50 25.00 60.00
AJB Johnny Bucyk/25 8.00 20.00
AJL John LeClair/25 10.00 25.00

2016 Upper Deck Goodwin Champions Black and White Autographs
GROUP A STATED ODDS 1:24,235 PACKS
GROUP B STATED ODDS 1:17,310 PACKS
GROUP C STATED ODDS 1:9694 PACKS
GROUP D STATED ODDS 1:1727 PACKS
EXCHANGE DEADLINE 6/21/2018
BAWG Wayne Gretzky A

2016 Upper Deck Goodwin Champions Goudey
COMPLETE SET (50) 12.00 30.00
STATED ODDS 1:4 PACKS
PRINTING PLATES RANDOMLY INSERTED
PLATE PRINT RUN 1 SET PER COLOR
BLACK-CYAN-MAGENTA-YELLOW ISSUED
NO PLATE PRICING DUE TO SCARCITY
15 Martin St. Louis .40 1.00
16 Mark Messier .50 1.25
24 Dominik Hasek .60 1.50
30 Wayne Gretzky 1.25 3.00
31 Jeremy Roenick .50 1.25

2016 Upper Deck Goodwin Champions Goudey Autographs
GROUP A STATED ODDS 1:119,716 PACKS
GROUP B STATED ODDS 1:30,784 PACKS
GROUP C STATED ODDS 1:7280 PACKS
GROUP D STATED ODDS 1:1796 PACKS
GROUP E STATED ODDS 1:1247 PACKS
GROUP F STATED ODDS 1:630 PACKS
EXCHANGE DEADLINE 6/21/2018
GADH Dominik Hasek C 15.00 40.00
GAJR Jeremy Roenick D 6.00 15.00
GAMM Mark Messier C 20.00 50.00
GAWG Wayne Gretzky B 75.00 200.00

2016 Upper Deck Goodwin Champions Goudey Sport Royalty Autographs
GROUP A STATED ODDS 1:200,192 PACKS
GROUP B STATED ODDS 1:52,682 PACKS
GROUP C STATED ODDS 1:19,627 PACKS
GROUP D STATED ODDS 1:3168 PACKS
EXCHANGE DEADLINE 6/21/2018
SRML Mario Lemieux C
SRWG Wayne Gretzky B

2016 Upper Deck Goodwin Champions Goudey Sport Royalty Memorabilia
GROUP A STATED ODDS 1:7200 PACKS
GROUP B STATED ODDS 1:4800 PACKS
GROUP C STATED ODDS 1:3600 PACKS
GROUP D STATED ODDS 1:2400 PACKS
SRMWG Wayne Gretzky B 12.00 30.00

2016 Upper Deck Goodwin Champions Goudey Sport Royalty Memorabilia Dual Swatch
GROUP A STATED ODDS 1:8320 PACKS
GROUP B STATED ODDS 1:2496 PACKS
SR2MWG Wayne Gretzky A 20.00 50.00

2016 Upper Deck Goodwin Champions Goudey Sport Royalty Memorabilia Premium
RANDOM INSERTS IN PACKS
STATED PRINT RUN 15 SER.#'d SETS
SRMWG Wayne Gretzky 25.00 60.00

2016 Upper Deck Goodwin Champions Memorabilia
GROUP A STATED ODDS 1:12,634 PACKS
GROUP B STATED ODDS 1:4512 PACKS
GROUP C STATED ODDS 1:1263 PACKS
GROUP D STATED ODDS 1:275 PACKS
GROUP E STATED ODDS 1:111 PACKS
GROUP F STATED ODDS 1:51 PACKS
MAI Aito Iguchi F 2.50 6.00

2016 Upper Deck Goodwin Champions Memorabilia Premium
GROUP A STATED ODDS 1:129,280 PACKS
GROUP B STATED ODDS 1:5621 PACKS
GROUP C STATED ODDS 1:6804 PACKS
GROUP D STATED ODDS 1:6529 PACKS
GROUP E STATED ODDS 1:260 PACKS
MAI Aito Iguchi E 10.00 25.00

2016 Upper Deck Goodwin Champions Mini
*MINI 1-100: 1X TO 2.5X BASIC
*MINI BW 101-150: .4X TO 1X BASIC BW
STATED ODDS 1:4 HOBBY

2016 Upper Deck Goodwin Champions Mini Canvas
*CANVAS 1-100: 1.2X TO 3X BASIC
*CANVAS BW 101-150: .5X TO 1.2X BASIC BW
STATED ODDS 1:12 HOBBY

2016 Upper Deck Goodwin Champions Mini Cloth Lady Luck
*CLOTH 1-100: 5X TO 12X BASIC
*CLOTH BW 101-150: 2X TO 5X BASIC BW
RANDOM INSERTS IN PACKS
STATED PRINT RUN 25 SER.#'d SETS

2016 Upper Deck Goodwin Champions Variations
STATED ODDS 1:1080 HOBBY
SP3 Wayne Gretzky 20.00 50.00

2017 Upper Deck Goodwin Champions
COMPLETE SET w/o SP's(100) 6.00 15.00
101-150 SP ODDS 1:4 HOBBY
SP1 STATED ODDS 1:1280 HOBBY
PRINTING PLATES RANDOMLY INSERTED
PLATE PRINT RUN 1 SET PER COLOR
BLACK-CYAN-MAGENTA-YELLOW ISSUED
NO PLATE PRICING DUE TO SCARCITY
29 Rudi Ying .25 .60
30 Wayne Gretzky 1.00 2.50
44 Ed Olczyk .20 .50
79 Rudi Ying .25 .60
80 Wayne Gretzky 1.00 2.50
94 Ed Olczyk .20 .50
129 Rudi Ying BW SP .40 1.00
130 Wayne Gretzky BW SP 1.50 4.00
144 Ed Olczyk BW SP .30 .75

2017 Upper Deck Goodwin Champions Autographs
GROUP A 1:25,933 HOBBY
GROUP B 1:4914 HOBBY
GROUP C 1:3154 HOBBY
GROUP D 1:546 HOBBY
GROUP E 1:280 HOBBY
GROUP F 1:99 HOBBY
AEO Ed Olczyk D 5.00 12.00
AWG Wayne Gretzky A 75.00 200.00

2017 Upper Deck Goodwin Champions Goudey
COMPLETE SET (25) 10.00 25.00
STATED ODDS 1:8 PACKS
PRINTING PLATES RANDOMLY INSERTED
PLATE PRINT RUN 1 SET PER COLOR
BLACK-CYAN-MAGENTA-YELLOW ISSUED
NO PLATE PRICING DUE TO SCARCITY
G4 Rudi Ying .50 1.25
G5 Wayne Gretzky 2.00 5.00
G19 Ed Olczyk .40 1.00

2017 Upper Deck Goodwin Champions Goudey Autographs
GROUP A 1:113,664 HOBBY
GROUP B 1:56,832 HOBBY
GROUP C 1:22,733 HOBBY
GROUP D 1:5683 HOBBY
GROUP E 1:760 HOBBY
G5 Wayne Gretzky B 75.00 200.00

2017 Upper Deck Goodwin Champions Goudey Memorabilia
STATED GROUP A ODDS 1:2,288 HOBBY
STATED GROUP B ODDS 1:161 HOBBY
*PREMIUM/35-65: .5X TO 1.2X BASIC
*PREMIUM/25: 1X TO 2.5X BASIC
GMRY Rudi Ying B 2.50 6.00

2017 Upper Deck Goodwin Champions Goudey Sport Royalty Autographs
GROUP A 1:155,520 HOBBY
GROUP B 1:55,543 HOBBY
GROUP C 1:31,104 HOBBY
GROUP D 1:3908 HOBBY
SRAWG Wayne Gretzky B

2017 Upper Deck Goodwin Champions Memorabilia
STATED GROUP A ODDS 1:1,285 HOBBY
STATED GROUP B ODDS 1:1,573 HOBBY
STATED GROUP C ODDS 1:541 HOBBY
STATED GROUP D ODDS 1:198 HOBBY
STATED GROUP E ODDS 1:51 HOBBY
*PREMIUM/35-65: .5X TO 1.2X BASIC
*PREMIUM/25: 1X TO 2.5X BASIC
MRY Rudi Ying E 2.50 6.00

2017 Upper Deck Goodwin Champions Memorabilia Dual Swatch
STATED GROUP A ODDS 1:4061 HOBBY
STATED GROUP B ODDS 1:1218 HOBBY
STATED GROUP C ODDS 1:1248 HOBBY
STATED GROUP D ODDS 1:435 HOBBY
*PREMIUM/25: 1X TO 2.5X BASIC
M2RY Rudi Ying D 2.50 6.00

2017 Upper Deck Goodwin Champions Mini
*MINI 1-100: .6X TO 1.5X BASIC
*MINI BW 101-150: .4X TO 1X BASIC BW
STATED ODDS 1:4 HOBBY

2017 Upper Deck Goodwin Champions Mini Canvas
*CANVAS 1-100: 1.2X TO 3X BASIC
*CANVAS BW 101-150: .75X TO 2X BASIC BW
RANDOM INSERTS IN PACKS

2017 Upper Deck Goodwin Champions Mini Cloth Lady Luck
*CLOTH 1-100: 5X TO 12X BASIC
*CLOTH BW 101-150: 3X TO 8X BASIC BW
RANDOM INSERTS IN PACKS
STATED PRINT RUN 25 SER.#'d SETS

2008 Upper Deck Goudey
COMP.SET w/o HIGH #s (200) 20.00 50.00
COMMON CARD (1-200) .20 .50
COMMON ROOKIE (1-200) .30 .75
COMMON SP (201-230) 2.00 5.00
COMMON SP (231-250) 1.50 4.00
COMMON SP (251-270) 2.00 5.00
COMMON CARD (271-300) 2.00 5.00
COMMON CARD (301-330) 3.00 8.00
293 Gordie Howe SR SP 3.00 8.00
315 Mark Messier SP 4.00 10.00
325 Sidney Crosby SR SP 10.00 25.00

2008 Upper Deck Goudey Mini Black Backs
*BLACK 1-200: .75X TO 2X GRN 1-200
*BLACK RC 1-200: .75X TO 2X GRN RC 1-200
*BLACK SP 201-250: .75X TO 2X GRN 201-250
*BLACK SP 251-270: .5X TO 1.2X GRN 251-270
*BLACK SR 271-330: .5X TO 1.2X GRN 271-330
RANDOM INSERTS IN PACKS
STATED PRINT RUN 34 SER.#'d SETS

2008 Upper Deck Goudey Mini Blue Backs
*BLUE 1-200: 1.5X TO 4X BASIC 1-200
*BLUE RC 1-200: 1X TO 2.5X BASIC RC 1-200
*BLUE 201-270: .6X TO 1.5X BASIC SP 201-270
*BLUE 271-330: .6X TO 1.5X BASIC SR 201-270
RANDOM INSERTS IN PACKS

2008 Upper Deck Goudey Mini Green Backs
RANDOM INSERTS IN PACKS
STATED PRINT RUN 88 SER.#'d SETS
293 Gordie Howe SR 4.00 10.00
315 Mark Messier 3.00 8.00
325 Sidney Crosby 8.00 20.00

2008 Upper Deck Goudey Mini Red Backs
*RED 1-200: 1X TO 2.5X BASIC 1-200
*RED RC 1-200: .75X TO 2X BASIC RC 1-200
*RED 201-270: .5X TO 1.2X BASIC SP 201-270
*RED 271-330: .5X to 1.2X BASIC SR 271-330
RANDOM INSERTS IN PACKS

2008 Upper Deck Goudey Hit Parade of Champions
RANDOM INSERTS IN PACKS
5 Bobby Orr 2.50 6.00
10 Gordie Howe 1.50 4.00
19 Mario Lemieux 2.50 6.00
23 Patrick Roy 1.50 4.00
30 Wayne Gretzky 3.00 8.00

2008 Upper Deck Goudey Sport Royalty Autographs
OVERALL AUTO ODDS 1:18 HOBBY
ASTERISK EQUALS PARTIAL EXCHANGE
EXCHANGE DEADLINE 7/17/2010

2009 Upper Deck Goudey
COMPLETE SET (300) 200.00 300.00
COMP.SET w/o SP's (200) 20.00 50.00
COMMON CARD (1-200) .20 .50
COMMON RC (1-200) .40 1.00
COMMON SP (201-300) 2.00 5.00
APPX.SP ODDS 201-220 1:9 HOBBY
APPX.SP ODDS 221-260 1:6 HOBBY
APPX.SP ODDS 261-300 1:6 HOBBY
246 Guy Lafleur SR SP 2.50 6.00
247 Nicklas Lidstrom SR SP 2.00 5.00
248 Mike Bossy SR SP 2.50 6.00
249 Bobby Orr SR SP 4.00 10.00
250 Patrick Roy SR SP 5.00 12.00

2009 Upper Deck Goudey Mini Green Back
*GREEN 1-200: 1.2X TO 3X BASIC
*GREEN RC 1-200: .6X TO 1.5X BASIC
COMMON CARD (201-300) .75 2.00
APPROX.ODDS 1:6 HOBBY
246 Guy Lafleur SR 4.00 10.00
247 Nicklas Lidstrom SR 2.00 5.00
248 Mike Bossy SR 2.00 5.00
249 Bobby Orr SR 6.00 15.00
250 Patrick Roy SR 6.00 15.00

2009 Upper Deck Goudey Mini Navy Blue Back
*BLUE 1-200: 1.5X TO 4X BASIC
*BLUE RC 1-200: .75X TO 2X BASIC
*BLUE: 201-300: .6X TO 1.5X MINI GREEN
APPROX.ODDS 1:9 HOBBY

2009 Upper Deck Goudey Sport Royalty Autographs
OVERALL AUTO ODDS 1:18 HOBBY
EXCHANGE DEADLINE 4/1/2011
MI Mike Bossy 12.50 30.00
NL Nicklas Lidstrom 30.00 60.00
OR Bobby Orr 100.00 200.00

1999-00 Upper Deck Gretzky Exclusives
Inserted one pack per box of Upper Deck, these cards featured special tributes to Wayne Gretzky's career. Gold and platinum parallels to the set were also created and inserted randomly. Gold parallels were numbered to just 99.
COMPLETE SET (99) 100.00 250.00
COMMON GRETZKY (1-99) 1.00 3.00
*GOLD/99: 6X TO 15X BASIC INSERTS
NNO Gretzky Blues AU/99 150.00 300.00
NNO Gretzky Kings AU/99 150.00 300.00
NNO Gretzky Oilers AU/50 300.00 600.00
NNO Gretzky Rangers AU/25 400.00 800.00

1999-00 Upper Deck Gretzky Game Jersey Autographs
These cards were randomly inserted in packs of Upper Deck Century Legend , Upper Deck Retro, and Upper Deck MVP. Each product had one version of the card numbered to 40 sets. The cards contain an actual piece of a game worn Wayne Gretzy jersey embedded in the cards and an authentic autograph.
WGJ W.Gretzky GJ AU/40 300.00 800.00
WGJ W.Gretzky GJ AU/40 300.00 800.00
WGJ W.Gretzky GJ AU/40 300.00 800.00

2000 Upper Deck Hawaii
These cards were issued by Upper Deck and given away at the Kit Young annual conference in Hawaii in 2000. These cards feature autographs of four athletes Upper Deck brought over to the conference. Each player signed a card serial numbered to 500. The card featuring all four players signed was not included in the factory set, but 100 cards featuring all four players were also signed and distributed. Two Kit Young cards were also included with the factory sets.
COMPLETE SET (6) 160.00 400.00
GH Gordie Howe AU 40.00 100.00
GAJ Julius Erving AU/100 200.00 400.00
Gordie Howe AU
Joe Namath AU
Tom Seaver AU

2007 Upper Deck Hawaii Trade Conference
COMPLETE SET (13) 15.00 40.00
11 Sidney Crosby 1.50 4.00

2000-01 Upper Deck Heroes
The 2000-01 Upper Deck Heroes set consisted of 180 cards. There were 30 rookies and 2 checklist cards. The set design for the card fronts had a photo of the featured player in action and a gold-foil UD Heroes stamp on the bottom of the card by the player name. The card backs used a small photo cut from the card front photo and included the player's vitals and his stats.
1 Steve Rucchin .12 .30
2 Marty McInnis .15 .40
3 Oleg Tverdovsky .12 .30
4 Guy Hebert .15 .40
5 Patrik Stefan .15 .40
6 Donald Audette .15 .40
7 Andrew Brunette .12 .30
8 Jason Allison .15 .40
9 Sergei Samsonov .15 .40
10 Joe Thornton .30 .75
11 Byron Dafoe .15 .40
12 Dominik Hasek .30 .75
13 Miroslav Satan .12 .30
14 Doug Gilmour .25 .60
15 J-P Dumont .12 .30
16 Fred Brathwaite .15 .40
17 Valeri Bure .15 .40
18 Marc Savard .15 .40
19 Cory Stillman .12 .30
20 Ron Francis .25 .60
21 Arturs Irbe .15 .40
22 Jeff O'Neill .15 .40
23 Sandis Ozolinsh .15 .40
24 Tony Amonte .15 .40
25 Jocelyn Thibault .15 .40
26 Alexei Zhamnov .15 .40
27 Steve Sullivan .12 .30
28 Chris Drury .15 .40
29 Milan Hejduk .15 .40
30 Alex Tanguay .15 .40
31 Peter Forsberg .25 .60
32 Adam Deadmarsh .15 .40
33 Marc Denis .15 .40
34 Ron Tugnutt .15 .40
35 Tyler Wright .12 .30
36 David Vyborny .12 .30
37 Brett Hull .30 .75
38 Ed Belfour .20 .50
39 Joe Nieuwendyk .15 .40
40 Sergei Zubov .15 .40
41 Jere Lehtinen .15 .40
42 Sergei Fedorov .30 .75
43 Martin Lapointe .15 .40
44 Chris Osgood .20 .50
45 Pat Verbeek .15 .40
46 Nicklas Lidstrom .20 .50
47 Doug Weight .15 .40
48 Tommy Salo .15 .40
49 Ryan Smyth .15 .40
50 Sean Brown .12 .30
51 Ray Whitney .15 .40
52 Trevor Kidd .15 .40
53 Viktor Kozlov .15 .40
54 Denis Shvidki .12 .30
55 Rob Blake .15 .40
56 Zigmund Palffy .15 .40
57 Luc Robitaille .15 .40
58 Glen Murray .12 .30
59 Manny Fernandez .15 .40
60 Scott Pellerin .12 .30
61 Maxim Sushinski .12 .30
62 Saku Koivu .20 .50
63 Jose Theodore .25 .60
64 Martin Rucinsky .12 .30
65 Darryl Shannon .12 .30
66 Cliff Ronning .12 .30
67 Randy Robitaille .12 .30
68 David Legwand .20 .50
69 Mike Dunham .15 .40
70 Alexander Mogilny .15 .40
71 Patrik Elias .20 .50
72 Bobby Holik .12 .30
73 Scott Stevens .20 .50
74 Mariusz Czerkawski .12 .30
75 Tim Connolly .12 .30
76 Aris Brimanis .12 .30
77 John Vanbiesbrouck .15 .40
78 Brian Leetch .20 .50
79 Mike York .12 .30
80 Theo Fleury .25 .60
81 Mike Richter .20 .50
82 Alexei Yashin .15 .40
83 Ricard Persson .12 .30
84 Radek Bonk .12 .30
85 Patrick Lalime .15 .40
86 Simon Gagne .20 .50
87 Brian Boucher .15 .40
88 Keith Primeau .15 .40
89 Mark Greig .12 .30
90 Teppo Numminen .12 .30
91 Shane Doan .12 .30
92 Keith Tkachuk .20 .50
93 Sean Burke .12 .30
94 Milan Kraft .12 .30
95 Alexei Kovalev .15 .40
96 Jean-Sebastien Aubin .15 .40
97 Martin Straka .12 .30
98 Vincent Damphousse .15 .40
99 Steve Shields .12 .30
100 Brad Stuart .15 .40
101 Owen Nolan .20 .50
102 Chris Pronger .20 .50
103 Pavol Demitra .25 .60
104 Roman Turek .15 .40
105 Pierre Turgeon .15 .40
106 Dan Cloutier .15 .40
107 Brad Richards .20 .50
108 Paul Mara .12 .30
109 Gary Roberts .12 .30
110 Sergei Berezin .12 .30
111 Mats Sundin .20 .50
112 Bryan McCabe .12 .30
113 Henrik Sedin .20 .50
114 Daniel Sedin .30 .75
115 Greg Hawgood .40 1.00
116 Adam Oates .12 .30
117 Olaf Kolzig .20 .50
118 Sergei Gonchar .20 .50
119 Bobby Orr .60 1.50
120 Cam Neely .30 .75
121 Gilbert Perreault .20 .50
122 Bobby Hull .30 .75
123 Stan Mikita .25 .60
124 Tony Esposito .20 .50
125 Gordie Howe .60 1.50
126 Wayne Gretzky 1.00 2.50
127 Marcel Dionne .25 .60
128 Maurice Richard .40 1.00
129 Guy Lafleur .25 .60
130 Jean Beliveau .25 .60
131 Bryan Trottier .20 .50
132 Denis Potvin .20 .50
133 Mike Bossy .20 .50
134 Bobby Clarke .20 .50
135 Bernie Parent .20 .50
136 Mario Lemieux .60 1.50
137 Michel Goulet .15 .40
138 Frank Mahovlich .20 .50
139 Paul Kariya .25 .60
140 Teemu Selanne .40 1.00
141 Patrick Roy .50 1.25
142 Joe Sakic .30 .75
143 Peter Forsberg .25 .60
144 Ray Bourque .30 .75
145 Mike Modano .30 .75
146 Steve Yzerman .60 1.50
147 Brendan Shanahan .25 .60
148 Pavel Bure .25 .60
149 Martin Brodeur .40 1.00
150 Scott Gomez .15 .40
151 Mark Messier .30 .75
152 Marian Hossa .15 .40
153 John LeClair .20 .50
154 Jeremy Roenick .20 .50
155 Jaromir Jagr .50 1.25
156 Jeff Friesen .12 .30
157 Vincent Lecavalier .15 .40
158 Curtis Joseph .25 .60
159 Jonas Ronnqvist RC .20 .50
160 Jeff Cowan RC .20 .50
161 David Aebischer RC .40 1.00
162 Rostislav Klesla RC .50 1.25
163 Tyler Bouck RC .20 .50
164 Michel Riesen RC .25 .60
165 Steven Reinprecht RC .25 .60
166 Marian Gaborik RC 2.50 6.00
167 David Gosselin RC .20 .50
168 Scott Hartnell RC .50 1.25
169 Colin White RC .20 .50
170 Rick DiPietro RC .75 2.00
171 Johan Holmqvist RC .20 .50
172 Jani Hurme RC .20 .50
173 Martin Havlat RC 1.25 3.00
174 Justin Williams RC .50 1.25
175 Roman Cechmanek RC .25 .60
176 Roman Simicek RC .20 .50
177 Zdenek Blatny RC .20 .50
178 Jordan Krestanovich RC .20 .50
179 Mark Messier CL .25 .60
180 Wayne Gretzky CL .60 1.50

2000-01 Upper Deck Heroes Game Used Twigs
In 2000-01 UD Heroes inserted the Game-Used Twigs cards in packs at a rate of 1:63. The 20-card set featured a piece of a game-used hockey stick on the card. The card numbering had a 'T' prefix.
TBH Bobby Hull 12.00 30.00
TBO Bobby Orr 50.00 125.00
TBO Mike Bossy 5.00 12.00
TCJ Curtis Joseph 6.00 15.00
TDH Dominik Hasek 6.00 15.00
TGH Gordie Howe 20.00 50.00
TGP Gilbert Perreault 8.00 20.00
TJJ Jaromir Jagr 6.00 15.00
TJL John LeClair 5.00 12.00
TMB Martin Brodeur 10.00 25.00
TML Mario Lemieux 12.00 30.00
TMM Mark Messier 5.00 12.00
TMS Mats Sundin 5.00 12.00
TPK Paul Kariya 6.00 15.00
TPR Patrick Roy 8.00 20.00
TRB Ray Bourque 6.00 15.00
TSY Steve Yzerman 15.00 40.00
TTF Theo Fleury 8.00 20.00
TTS Teemu Selanne 5.00 12.00
TWG Wayne Gretzky 40.00 100.00

2000-01 Upper Deck Heroes Game Used Twigs Gold
In 2000-01 UD Heroes inserted the Game-Used Twigs Gold cards in packs. The 10-card combo set featured a piece of a game-used hockey stick from both players on the card. The card numbering had a 'C' prefix. The cards were serial numbered to 50.
CBO R.Bourque/B.Orr 150.00 400.00
CFL T.Fleury/J.LeClair 30.00 80.00
CGM W.Gretzky/M.Messier 100.00 200.00
CHB Bo.Hull/M.Bossy 60.00 150.00
CHP D.Hasek/G.Perreault 30.00 80.00
CHY G.Howe/S.Yzerman 150.00 350.00
CJS C.Joseph/M.Sundin 25.00 60.00
CKS P.Kariya/T.Selanne 30.00 80.00
CLJ M.Lemieux/J.Jagr 75.00 200.00
CRB P.Roy/M.Brodeur 60.00 150.00

2000-01 Upper Deck Heroes NHL Leaders
COMPLETE SET (10) 10.00 20.00
STATED ODDS 1:13
L1 Paul Kariya .50 1.25
L2 Ray Bourque 1.25 3.00
L3 Joe Sakic 1.25 3.00
L4 Steve Yzerman 3.00 8.00
L5 Mark Messier .75 2.00
L6 Alexei Yashin .50 1.25
L7 John LeClair .75 2.00
L8 Keith Tkachuk .60 1.50
L9 Jaromir Jagr 1.00 2.50
L10 Al MacInnis .50 1.25

2000-01 Upper Deck Heroes Player Idols
Inserted into packs at a rate of 1:23, This 6-card set featured young stars and their idols.
COMPLETE SET (6) 12.00 25.00
PI1 B.Shanahan/M.Messier 1.00 2.50
PI2 M.Brodeur/P.Roy 3.00 8.00
PI3 M.Afinogenov/P.Bure 1.00 2.50
PI4 P.Kariya/W.Gretzky 3.00 8.00
PI5 V.Lecavalier/M.Lemieux 4.00 10.00
PI6 R.Turek/D.Hasek 1.50 4.00

2000-01 Upper Deck Heroes Second Season Heroes
COMPLETE SET (10) 20.00 40.00
STATED ODDS 1:13
SS1 Patrick Roy 4.00 10.00
SS2 Peter Forsberg 2.00 5.00
SS3 Mike Modano 1.00 2.50
SS4 Ed Belfour 1.00 2.50
SS5 Steve Yzerman 4.00 10.00
SS6 Wayne Gretzky 5.00 12.00
SS7 Martin Brodeur 2.00 5.00
SS8 Mark Messier 1.00 2.50
SS9 John LeClair 1.00 2.50
SS10 Jaromir Jagr 1.25 3.00

2000-01 Upper Deck Heroes Signs of Greatness
Randomly inserted in 2000-01 UD Heroes packs at a rate of 1:71, this 33-card set featured autograph cards from the top current and former player from the NHL. Please note that at time of release the Orr and Yzerman cards were inserted into packs as redemption cards, also note there are some short prints specified below.
BC Bobby Clarke 10.00 25.00
BH Bobby Hull SP 20.00 50.00
BO Bobby Orr SP 60.00 120.00
BP Bernie Parent 10.00 25.0
BT Bryan Trottier 10.00 25.0
CN Cam Neely 10.00 25.0
DP Denis Potvin 8.00 20.0
FM Frank Mahovlich 10.00 25.0
FP Felix Potvin 15.00 40.0
GH Gordie Howe SP 50.00 100.0
GL Guy Lafleur 15.00 40.0
GP Gilbert Perreault 6.00 15.0
JB Jean Beliveau 25.00 50.0
JL John LeClair 6.00 15.0
JR Jeremy Roenick SP 20.00 50.0
KJ Kenny Jonsson 4.00 10.0
MA Marc Denis 4.00 10.0
MD Marcel Dionne 10.00 25.0
MG Michel Goulet 10.00 25.0
ML Mario Lemieux SP 75.00 150.0
MM Mark Messier SP 50.00 100.0
MS Miroslav Satan 4.00 10.0
MY Mike York 4.00 10.0
PA Pavel Brendl 4.00 10.0
PB Pavel Bure SP 10.00 25.0
PB Peter Bondra 4.00 10.0
RL Roberto Luongo 8.00 20.0
RT Roman Turek 4.00 10.0
SG Scott Gomez 6.00 15.0
SM Stan Mikita 10.00 25.0
SY Steve Yzerman 30.00 80.0
TS Tommy Salo 4.00 10.0
WG Wayne Gretzky SP 100.00 200.0

2000-01 Upper Deck Heroes Timeless Moments
COMPLETE SET (10) 10.00 20.00
STATED ODDS 1:13
TM1 Teemu Selanne .60 1.5
TM2 Dominik Hasek 1.25 3.0
TM3 Patrick Roy 3.00 8.0
TM4 Brett Hull .75 2.0
TM5 Pavel Bure .75 2.0
TM6 Martin Brodeur 1.50 4.0
TM7 Mike York .50 1.2
TM8 Brian Boucher .60 1.5
TM9 Jaromir Jagr 1.00 2.5
TM10 Curtis Joseph .60 1.5

2000-01 Upper Deck Heroes Today's Snipers
COMPLETE SET (6) 5.00 10.0
STATED ODDS 1:23
TS1 Paul Kariya .60 1.5
TS2 Brendan Shanahan .75 2.0
TS3 Pavel Bure .75 2.0
TS4 John LeClair .75 2.0
TS5 Jaromir Jagr 1.00 2.5
TS6 Mats Sundin .60 1.5

2009 Upper Deck Heroes
This set was released on June 16, 2009 and was issued in 8-card packs with 24-packs per box at an SRP of $1.59 per pack. The base set consists of 416 skip-numbered cards and each subject in the set has between 2-4 different cards. Cards #1-100 feature veterans, cards 101-198 are rookies, 201-300 are NFL legends, 301-340 feature miscellaneous subjects from track and field, tennis, volleyball and ice skating, 341-360 feature famous historical figures, 361-384 are famous guitarists, 401-470 are artist's renderings of various subjects in the set, and 471-489 feature dual player cards including some hockey players. Finally, cards #301-489 were short printed.
481 B.Sanders/G.Howe HH 1.50 4.0
483 R.Bourque/T.Brady HH 3.00 8.0
484 E.Manning/M.Messier HH 1.00 2.5
485 Roethlis/E.Malkin HH 1.00 2.5
486 Lemieux/Bradshaw HH 1.25 3.0
488 M.Modano/T.Romo HH .75 2.0
489 B.Hull/M.Ditka HH 1.00 2.5

2009 Upper Deck Heroes Blue
*1-100 VETS: 2.5X TO 6X BASIC INSERTS
*101-198 ROOKIES: 1X TO 2.5X
*201-300 LEGENDS: 1.5X TO 4X
*301-384 MISC: 1.5X TO 4X
*401-440 ART NFL: 1.2X TO 3X
*441-470 ART MISC: 1.2X TO 3X
*471-489 ART DUAL: 1X TO 2.5X
BLUE PRINT RUN 99 SER.#'d SETS

2009 Upper Deck Heroes Orange
*1-100 VETS: 4X TO 10X BASIC INSERTS
*101-198 ROOKIES: 1.5X TO 4X
*201-300 LEGENDS: 2.5X TO 6X
*301-384 MISC: 2.5X TO 6X
*401-440 ART NFL: 2X TO 5X
*441-470 ART MISC: 2X TO 5X
*471-489 ART DUAL: 1.5X TO 4X
STATED PRINT RUN 35 SER.#'d SETS

2009 Upper Deck Heroes Purple
*1-100 VETS: 8X TO 20X BASIC INSERTS
*101-198 ROOKIES: 4X TO 10X
*201-300 LEGENDS: 5X TO 12X
*301-384 MISC: 5X TO 12X
*401-440 ART NFL: 4X TO 10X
*441-470 ART MISC: 4X TO 10X
*471-489 ART DUAL: 3X TO 8X
STATED PRINT RUN 10 SER.#'d SETS

2009 Upper Deck Heroes Autographs Gold
*101-198 ROOK/25: .6X TO 1.5X SILVER/199
*101-198 ROOK/25: .5X TO 1.2X SILVER/99
101-198 ROOKIE PRINT RUN 10-25
402-440 ART NFL PRINT RUN 9-50
441-450 ART MISC PRINT RUN 25
472-488 ART DUAL PRINT RUN 40
481 Sndrs/Howe HH/40 EXCH 150.00 250.00

2009 Upper Deck Heroes Jerseys Purple
1-100 PURPLE VET PRINT RUN 50
402-420 UNPRICED VET ART PRINT RUN 15
421-440 UNPRICED LEG ART PRINT RUN 5
472-480 DUAL ART PRINT RUN 25
481-488 DUAL ART PRINT RUN 150
*7-98 GREEN VET/150: .3X TO .8X PURPLE/50
7-98 GREEN VET PRINT RUN 150
3-100 UNPRICED SILVER VET PRINT RUN 10
201-292 UNPRICED SILVER LEG PRINT RUN 15
PLAYERS HAVE MULTIPLE CARDS OF EQUAL VALUE
481 B.Sanders/G.Howe/150 12.00 30.00
483 R.Bourque/T.Brady/150 10.00 25.00
484 E.Manning/M.Messier/150 10.00 25.00
485 Roethlis/E.Malkin/150 12.00 30.00
486 Bradshaw/M.Lemieux/150 15.00 40.00
488 T.Romo/M.Modano/150 8.00 20.00

2014-15 Upper Deck Heroic Inspirations Autographs
HEROJH Josh Harding/25 30.00 60.00

2005-06 Upper Deck Hockey Showcase

Cards were issued via a special online redemption offer through Upper Deck over an eight-week period. The stated print run was 1,000 copies of each card.

*BECKETT PROMOS: .4X TO 1X BASIC CARDS
HS1 Peter Forsberg 5.00 12.00
HS2 Chris Pronger 3.00 8.00
HS3 Adam Foote 2.50 6.00
HS4 Gary Roberts 2.50 6.00
HS5 Sergei Gonchar 2.50 6.00
HS6 Brian Leetch 4.00 10.00
HS7 Darren McCarty 2.50 6.00
HS8 Michael Peca 3.00 8.00
HS9 Bobby Holik 2.50 6.00
HS10 Eric Brewer 2.50 6.00
HS11 Paul Kariya 5.00 12.00
HS12 Jason Allison 3.00 8.00
HS13 Derian Hatcher 2.50 6.00
HS14 Sean Burke 2.50 6.00
HS15 Adrian Aucoin 2.50 6.00
HS16 Jeremy Roenick 4.00 10.00
HS17 Jocelyn Thibault 3.00 8.00
HS18 Alexander Mogilny 3.00 8.00
HS19 Pierre Turgeon 4.00 10.00
HS20 Anson Carter 3.00 8.00
HS21 Tony Amonte 3.00 8.00
HS22 Curtis Joseph 4.00 10.00
HS23 Miroslav Satan 3.00 8.00
HS24 Teemu Selanne 8.00 20.00
HS25 Mike York 2.50 6.00
HS26 Dany Heatley 4.00 10.00
HS27 Zigmund Palffy 4.00 10.00
HS28 Scott Niedermayer 4.00 10.00
HS29 Jeff O'Neill 2.50 6.00
HS30 Joe Nieuwendyk 4.00 10.00
HS31 Marian Hossa 3.00 8.00
HS32 Eric Lindros 6.00 15.00
HS33 Nikolai Khabibulin 4.00 10.00
HS34 Martin Straka 2.50 6.00
HS35 Chris Osgood 4.00 10.00
HS36 Pavol Demitra 5.00 12.00
HS37 Peter Bondra 3.00 8.00
HS38 John LeClair 4.00 10.00
HS39 Cory Stillman 3.00 8.00
HS40 Alexei Zhamnov 2.50 6.00

1999-00 Upper Deck HoloGrFx

The 1999-00 Upper Deck HoloGrFx set was released as a 60-card one series set. The cards themselves feature NHL players on a silver rainbow foil holographic card with background color to match each player's team colors. This set was packaged as a 36-pack box with packs containing three cards at a suggested retail price of $1.99.

COMPLETE SET (60) 15.00 30.00
1 Teemu Selanne .25 .60
2 Paul Kariya .25 .60
3 Patrik Stefan RC 1.50 4.00
4 Sergei Samsonov .20 .50
5 Ray Bourque .40 1.00
6 Dominik Hasek .50 1.25
7 Brian Campbell RC .07 .20
8 Marc Savard .07 .20
9 Oleg Saprykin RC 1.50 4.00
10 Sami Kapanen .07 .20
11 Keith Primeau .07 .20
12 Tony Amonte .20 .50
13 J-P Dumont .20 .50
14 Peter Forsberg .60 1.50
15 Joe Sakic .50 1.25
16 Chris Drury .20 .50
17 Patrick Roy 1.25 3.00
18 Brett Hull .30 .75
19 Mike Modano .40 1.00
20 Ed Belfour .25 .60
21 Steve Yzerman 1.25 3.00
22 Brendan Shanahan .25 .60
23 Sergei Fedorov .40 1.00
24 Doug Weight .20 .50
25 Bill Guerin .07 .20
26 Pavel Bure .25 .60
27 Mark Parrish .07 .20
28 Luc Robitaille .20 .50
29 Zigmund Palffy .20 .50
30 Mike Ribeiro .20 .50
31 David Legwand .20 .50
32 Scott Gomez .07 .20
33 Martin Brodeur .60 1.50
34 Vadim Sharifijanov .07 .20
35 Jorgen Jonsson RC .07 .20
36 Eric Brewer .20 .50
37 Tim Connolly .07 .20
38 Theo Fleury .07 .20
39 Brian Leetch .25 .60
40 Mike Richter .25 .60
41 Marian Hossa .25 .60
42 Simon Gagne .25 .60
43 Eric Lindros .25 .60
44 John LeClair .25 .60
45 Keith Tkachuk .25 .60
46 Jeremy Roenick .30 .75
47 Jaromir Jagr .40 1.00
48 Niklas Sundstrom .07 .20
49 Jeff Friesen .07 .20
50 Brad Stuart .20 .50
51 Pavol Demitra .20 .50
52 Al MacInnis .20 .50
53 Paul Mara .20 .50
54 Vincent Lecavalier .25 .60
55 Mats Sundin .25 .60
56 Sergei Berezin .20 .50
57 Curtis Joseph .25 .60
58 Steve Kariya RC 1.00 2.50
59 Peter Bondra .20 .50
60 Olaf Kolzig .20 .50

1999-00 Upper Deck HoloGrFx Ausome

Randomly inserted in packs at 1:17, this gold parallel set features the base card enhanced with a gold foil background. Card backs carry an "AU" prefix.

*AUSOME: 5X TO 12X BASIC CARDS

1999-00 Upper Deck HoloGrFx Gretzky GrFx

Randomly inserted in packs at 1:3, this 15-card set pays tribute to The Great One by following his career from Edmonton to New York on the base HoloGrFx card stock. An AU-SOME parallel was also released for this set that featured a gold foil background. Parallels were inserted randomly at 1:105.

COMPLETE SET (15) 15.00 30.00
COMMON GRETZKY (GG1-GG15) 1.25 3.00
*AUSOME: 3X TO 8X BASIC INSERTS

1999-00 Upper Deck HoloGrFx Impact Zone

Randomly inserted in packs at 1:34, this 6-card set showcases some of the NHL's top players. The right 1/3 of the card front is black with the HoloGrFx logo and the players name, and the rest of the card features the player set against a silver rainbow foil background that has a laser etching effect. Card backs carry an "IZ" prefix. An AU-SOME gold foil parallel of this set was also released and inserted at 1:431.

COMPLETE SET (6) 15.00 30.00
*AUSOME: 2.5X TO 6X BASIC INSERTS
IZ1 Dominik Hasek 2.50 6.00
IZ2 Jaromir Jagr 2.00 5.00
IZ3 Eric Lindros 2.50 6.00
IZ4 Patrick Roy 4.00 10.00
IZ5 Paul Kariya 2.50 6.00
IZ6 Peter Forsberg 3.00 8.00

1999-00 Upper Deck HoloGrFx Pure Skill

Randomly inserted in packs at 1:17, this 9-card set pictures some of the NHL's most dominating offensive threats and goalies on a silver holographic foil card. Card backs carry a "PS" prefix. A gold foil AU-SOME parallel of this set was also seeded in packs at 1:210.

COMPLETE SET (9) 12.00 25.00
*AUSOME: 2.5X TO 6X BASIC INSERTS
PS1 Paul Kariya .75 2.00
PS2 Peter Forsberg 2.00 5.00
PS3 Dominik Hasek 1.50 4.00
PS4 Sergei Samsonov .75 2.00
PS5 Teemu Selanne .75 2.00
PS6 Patrick Roy 4.00 10.00
PS7 Brett Hull 1.00 2.50
PS8 Eric Lindros .75 2.00
PS9 Jaromir Jagr 1.25 3.00

1999-00 Upper Deck HoloGrFx UD Authentics

Randomly inserted in packs, this set features autographed cards of some of the NHL's top veterans and up and coming youngsters.

BH Brett Hull 15.00 40.00
BM Bill Muckalt 6.00 15.00
CD Chris Drury 10.00 25.00
DL David Legwand 6.00 15.00
PB Pavel Bure 15.00 40.00
PS Patrik Stefan 6.00 15.00
RB Ray Bourque 40.00 80.00
WG Wayne Gretzky 150.00 300.00
WG2 Wayne Gretzky Kings 150.00 300.00

2001-02 Upper Deck Honor Roll

Released in mid-March 2002, this 100-card set carried an SRP of $2.99 for a 5-card pack. The set consisted of 60 regular cards, 30 shortprinted rookies serial-numbered to 1499 and 10 dual jersey cards serial-numbered to 1000. Dual jersey cards featured one rookie and one veteran player.

COMP.SET w/o SP's (60) 10.00 25.00
1 Bobby Hull .30 .75
2 Wayne Gretzky 1.00 2.50
3 Gordie Howe .60 1.50
4 Bobby Orr .60 1.50
5 Ray Bourque .30 .75
6 Patrick Roy .50 1.25
7 Luc Robitaille .20 .50
8 Mario Lemieux .60 1.50
9 Jaromir Jagr .50 1.25
10 Chris Pronger .15 .40
11 Rob Blake .20 .50
12 Martin Brodeur .40 1.00
13 Paul Kariya .25 .60
14 Joe Sakic .30 .75
15 Pavel Bure .25 .60
16 Nicklas Lidstrom .20 .50
17 Brian Leetch .20 .50
18 Dominik Hasek .30 .75
19 Brendan Shanahan .25 .60
20 Steve Yzerman .60 1.50
21 Teemu Selanne .40 1.00
22 Al MacInnis .20 .50
23 Scott Stevens .20 .50
24 Curtis Joseph .20 .50
25 Dany Heatley .20 .50
26 Joe Thornton .25 .60
27 Mark Parrish .12 .30
28 Rostislav Klesla .12 .30
29 Brad Stuart .12 .30
30 Rick DiPietro .15 .40
31 Bobby Hull .30 .75
32 Wayne Gretzky 1.00 2.50
33 Gordie Howe .60 1.50
34 Bobby Orr .60 1.50
35 Ray Bourque .30 .75
36 Patrick Roy .50 1.25
37 Luc Robitaille .20 .50
38 Mario Lemieux .60 1.50
39 Jaromir Jagr .50 1.25
40 Chris Pronger .15 .40
41 Rob Blake .20 .50
42 Martin Brodeur .40 1.00
43 Paul Kariya .25 .60
44 Joe Sakic .30 .75
45 Pavel Bure .25 .60
46 Nicklas Lidstrom .20 .50
47 Brian Leetch .20 .50
48 Dominik Hasek .30 .75
49 Brendan Shanahan .25 .60
50 Steve Yzerman .60 1.50
51 Teemu Selanne .40 1.00
52 Al MacInnis .20 .50
53 Scott Stevens .20 .50
54 Curtis Joseph .20 .50
55 Dany Heatley .20 .50
56 Joe Thornton .25 .60
57 Mark Parrish .12 .30
58 Rostislav Klesla .12 .30
59 Brad Stuart .12 .30
60 Rick DiPietro .15 .40
61 Ilja Bryzgalov RC 3.00 8.00
62 Mike Weaver RC 1.25 3.00
63 Kamil Piros RC 1.25 3.00
64 Ben Simon RC 1.50 4.00
65 Ivan Huml RC 1.25 3.00
66 Ales Kotalik RC 2.50 6.00
67 Scott Nichol RC 1.25 3.00
68 Kelly Fairchild RC 1.25 3.00
69 Vaclav Nedorost RC 1.25 3.00
70 Niko Kapanen RC 2.00 5.00
71 Pavel Datsyuk RC 10.00 20.00
72 Sean Avery RC 1.25 3.00
73 Kristian Huselius RC 2.00 5.00
74 Nick Smith RC 1.25 3.00
75 Nick Schultz RC 1.25 3.00
76 Marcel Hossa RC 2.00 5.00
77 Olivier Michaud RC 2.00 5.00
78 Martin Erat RC 2.00 5.00
79 Christian Berglund RC 1.50 4.00
80 Andreas Salomonsson RC 1.25 3.00
81 Radek Martinek RC 1.25 3.00
82 Richard Scott RC 1.25 3.00
83 Ivan Ciernik RC 1.25 3.00
84 Bruno St. Jacques RC 1.25 3.00
85 Dan Focht RC 1.25 3.00
86 Jeff Jillson RC 1.25 3.00
87 Mark Rycroft RC 1.50 4.00
88 Nikita Alexeev RC 1.25 3.00
89 Justin Kurtz RC 2.00 5.00
90 Chris Corrinet RC 1.25 3.00
91 M.Spanhel RC/Amonte JSY 5.00 12.00
92 M.Davidson RC/C.Drury JSY 6.00 15.00
93 J.Bednar RC/Z.Palffy JSY 5.00 12.00
94 R.Torres RC/Shanahan JSY 8.00 20.00
95 Samuelsson RC/Fedorov JSY 6.00 15.00
96 Blackburn RC/Richter JSY 6.00 15.00
97 T.Divisek RC/J.LeClair JSY 6.00 15.00
98 J.Dopita RC/P.Demitra JSY 4.00 10.00
99 K.Kolanos RC/Modano JSY 6.00 15.00
100 I.Kovalchuk RC/J.Jagr JSY 12.50 30.00

2001-02 Upper Deck Honor Roll Defense First

Inserted at 1:40, this 6-card set highlights the league's most defensive minded forwards.

COMPLETE SET (6) 10.00 20.00
DF1 Mike Modano 1.25 3.00
DF2 Jere Lehtinen .75 2.00
DF3 Steve Yzerman 4.00 10.00
DF4 Sergei Fedorov 1.25 3.00
DF5 John Madden .75 2.00
DF6 Michael Peca .75 2.00

2001-02 Upper Deck Honor Roll Honor Society

Serial-numbered to just 100 copies each, this 4-card set featured dual game-worn jersey swatches of the featured players. A gold parallel of this set was also created and serial-numbered to just 25 copies each. As of press time, not all cards have been verified.

*GOLD/25: .8X TO 2X BASIC DUAL/100
HSBB P.Bure/V.Bure 20.00 50.00
HSCH R.Cechmanek/D.Hasek 20.00 50.00
HSHK M.Hejduk/P.Kariya 20.00 50.00
HSRB P.Roy/M.Brodeur 30.00 80.00

2001-02 Upper Deck Honor Roll Jerseys

Serial-numbered to 225 copies each, this 31-card set featured game-worn jersey swatches of the featured players. A gold parallel was also created and serial-numbered to just 50 copies each.

*GOLD/50: 1.2X TO 3X BASIC JSY/225
BB Brian Boucher 4.00 10.00
BH Brett Hull 6.00 15.00
BL Brian Leetch 5.00 12.00
BS Brendan Shanahan 5.00 12.00
CD Chris Drury 4.00 10.00
DL David Legwand 4.00 10.00
DW Doug Weight 4.00 10.00
EB Ed Belfour 5.00 12.00
EL Eric Lindros 5.00 12.00
JH Jochen Hecht 4.00 10.00
JL John LeClair 4.00 10.00
JN Joe Nieuwendyk 4.00 10.00
JS Joe Sakic 8.00 20.00
JT Joe Thornton 6.00 15.00
LI Eric Lindros 5.00 12.00
LR Luc Robitaille 5.00 12.00
MB Martin Brodeur 8.00 20.00
ML Mario Lemieux 12.50 30.00
MM Mike Modano 6.00 15.00
MN Markus Naslund 4.00 10.00
MO Maxime Ouellet 4.00 10.00
MS Miroslav Satan 4.00 10.00
NL Nicklas Lidstrom 4.00 10.00
PB Peter Bondra 4.00 10.00
PD Pavol Demitra 4.00 10.00
PK Paul Kariya 5.00 12.00
RB Ray Bourque 8.00 20.00
RL Roberto Luongo 6.00 15.00
SF Sergei Fedorov 6.00 15.00
SS Sergei Samsonov 5.00 12.00
SU Mats Sundin 5.00 12.00
TC Tim Connolly 4.00 10.00

2001-02 Upper Deck Honor Roll Original Six

This 6-card set was inserted at 1:40 packs.

COMPLETE SET (6) 20.00 40.00
OS1 Bobby Orr 4.00 10.00
OS2 Bobby Hull 2.50 6.00
OS3 Gordie Howe 4.00 10.00
OS4 Patrick Roy 4.00 10.00
OS5 Wayne Gretzky 5.00 12.00
OS6 Curtis Joseph .75 2.00

2001-02 Upper Deck Honor Roll Playoff Matchups

Serial-numbered to 200 copies each, this 6-card set featured dual game-worn jersey swatches of the featured players. A gold parallel was also created and serial-numbered to 25.

*GOLD/25: .8X TO 2X BASIC DUAL/200
HSHT B.Hull/K.Tkachuk 12.50 30.00
HSLH M.Lemieux/D.Hasek 20.00 50.00
HSRB P.Roy/M.Brodeur 30.00 80.00
HSSR J.Sakic/L.Robitaille 20.00 50.00
HSSS M.Sundin/S.Stevens 12.50 30.00
HSTM A.Tanguay/A.MacInnis 12.50 30.00

2001-02 Upper Deck Honor Roll Pucks

Serial-numbered to 225 copies each, this 12-card set featured a piece of game-used puck on each card. A gold parallel was also created and serial-numbered to 100 each.

GOLD/100: .8X TO 2X BASIC INSERT
PAK Alexei Kovalev 8.00 20.00
PBL Brian Leetch 8.00 20.00
PJI Jarome Iginla 15.00 40.00
PMH Marian Hossa 10.00 25.00
PMM Mark Messier 10.00 25.00
PMS Mats Sundin 10.00 25.00
PPB Pavel Bure 10.00 25.00
PPE Patrik Elias 8.00 20.00
PPO Peter Bondra 10.00 25.00
PSK Saku Koivu 10.00 25.00
PSS Scott Stevens 8.00 20.00
PVL Vincent Lecavalier 10.00 25.00

2001-02 Upper Deck Honor Roll Sharp Skaters

This 6-card set was inserted at 1:40 packs.

COMPLETE SET (6) 10.00 20.00
SS1 Paul Kariya .75 2.00
SS2 Mike Modano 1.25 3.00
SS3 Sergei Fedorov 1.50 4.00
SS4 Pavel Bure 1.00 2.50
SS5 Marian Hossa .75 2.00
SS6 Simon Gagne .75 2.00

2001-02 Upper Deck Honor Roll Student of the Game

This 6-card set was inserted at 1:40 packs.

COMPLETE SET (6) 10.00 20.00
SG1 Paul Kariya .75 2.00
SG2 Joe Sakic 1.50 4.00
SG3 Mike Modano 1.25 3.00
SG4 Steve Yzerman 4.00 10.00
SG5 Patrik Elias .75 2.00
SG6 Mats Sundin .75 2.00

2001-02 Upper Deck Honor Roll Tough Customers

This 6-card set was inserted at 1:40 packs.

COMPLETE SET (6) 4.00 8.00
TC1 Martin Lapointe .60 1.50
TC2 Rob Blake .60 1.50
TC3 Scott Stevens .60 1.50
TC4 Jeremy Roenick .75 2.00
TC5 Owen Nolan .60 1.50
TC6 Chris Pronger .60 1.50

2001-02 Upper Deck Honor Roll Tribute to 500

This 2-card set featured swatches of game-used jerseys from Patrick Roy. Each card was serial-numbered to 500 copies each.

1 Patrick Roy Mon. 20.00 50.00
2 Patrick Roy Col. 20.00 50.00

2002-03 Upper Deck Honor Roll

This 166-card set consisted of 100 veteran cards, 45 shortprinted rookie cards and 21 Dean's List jersey card rookies. Rookies #101-145 were serial-numbered to 1499 each and the jersey cards #146-166 were inserted at 1:48.

1 Paul Kariya .20 .50
2 Jean-Sebastien Giguere .15 .40
3 Ilya Kovalchuk .20 .50
4 Dany Heatley .15 .40
5 Joe Thornton .20 .50
6 Sergei Samsonov .12 .30
7 Miroslav Satan .15 .40
8 Martin Biron .12 .30
9 Chris Drury .15 .40
10 Jarome Iginla .15 .40
11 Ron Francis .20 .50
12 Arturs Irbe .12 .30
13 Tyler Arnason .15 .40
14 Jocelyn Thibault .12 .30
15 Patrick Roy .40 1.00
16 Joe Sakic .25 .60
17 Peter Forsberg .20 .50
18 Rob Blake .15 .40
19 Ray Whitney .12 .30
20 Marc Denis .12 .30
21 Mike Modano .25 .60
22 Marty Turco .15 .40
23 Bill Guerin .15 .40
24 Steve Yzerman .30 .75
25 Sergei Fedorov .25 .60
26 Nicklas Lidstrom .15 .40
27 Brett Hull .20 .50
28 Curtis Joseph .15 .40
29 Brendan Shanahan .20 .50
30 Mike Comrie .15 .40
31 Tommy Salo .12 .30
32 Roberto Luongo .25 .60
33 Kristian Huselius .10 .25
34 Felix Potvin .25 .60
35 Zigmund Palffy .15 .40
36 Marian Gaborik .25 .60
37 Manny Fernandez .12 .30
38 Jose Theodore .15 .40
39 Saku Koivu .15 .40
40 Patrik Elias .15 .40
41 Martin Brodeur .30 .75
42 David Legwand .12 .30
43 Tomas Vokoun .12 .30
44 Alexei Yashin .12 .30
45 Chris Osgood .15 .40
46 Michael Peca .12 .30
47 Eric Lindros .25 .60
48 Mike Richter .15 .40
49 Pavel Bure .20 .50
50 Marian Hossa .12 .30
51 Daniel Alfredsson .15 .40
52 Jeremy Roenick .15 .40
53 John LeClair .15 .40
54 Roman Cechmanek .12 .30
55 Sean Burke .10 .25
56 Tony Amonte .12 .30
57 Alex Kovalev .15 .40
58 Mario Lemieux .50 1.25
59 Owen Nolan .15 .40
60 Evgeni Nabokov .12 .30
61 Keith Tkachuk .15 .40
62 Brent Johnson .12 .30
63 Nikolai Khabibulin .15 .40
64 Vincent Lecavalier .12 .30
65 Mats Sundin .15 .40
66 Ed Belfour .15 .40
67 Todd Bertuzzi .15 .40
68 Markus Naslund .12 .30
69 Olaf Kolzig .15 .40
70 Jaromir Jagr .40 1.00
71 Paul Kariya .20 .50
72 Shawn McEachern .10 .25
73 Joe Thornton .20 .50
74 Stu Barnes .10 .25
75 Craig Conroy .10 .25
76 Ron Francis .20 .50
77 Alexei Zhamnov .12 .30
78 Joe Sakic .25 .60
79 Ray Whitney .12 .30
80 Derian Hatcher .12 .30
81 Steve Yzerman .30 .75
82 Jason Smith .10 .25
83 Valeri Bure .12 .30
84 Mattias Norstrom .10 .25
85 Andrew Brunette .10 .25
86 Saku Koivu .15 .40
87 Greg Johnson .10 .25
88 Scott Stevens .15 .40
89 Michael Peca .12 .30
90 Brian Leetch .15 .40
91 Daniel Alfredsson .15 .40
92 Keith Primeau .15 .40
93 Teppo Numminen .12 .30
94 Mario Lemieux .50 1.25
95 Owen Nolan .15 .40
96 Chris Pronger .12 .30
97 Vincent Lecavalier .12 .30
98 Mats Sundin .15 .40
99 Markus Naslund .12 .30
100 Steve Konowalchuk .10 .25
101 Alexei Smirnov RC 2.00 5.00
102 Martin Gerber RC 2.50 6.00
103 Kurt Sauer RC 1.50 4.00
104 Tim Thomas RC 6.00 15.00
105 Jordan Leopold RC 2.50 6.00
106 Dany Sabourin RC 1.50 4.00
107 Levente Szuper RC 2.50 6.00
108 Shawn Thornton RC 2.00 5.00
109 Matt Henderson RC 1.50 4.00
110 Lasse Pirjeta RC 1.50 4.00
111 Pascal LeClaire RC 2.00 5.00
112 Dmitri Bykov RC 1.50 4.00
113 Kari Haakana RC 1.50 4.00
114 Craig Andersson RC 5.00 12.00
115 Mike Cammalleri RC 5.00 12.00
116 Stephane Veilleux RC 1.50 4.00
117 Adam Hall RC 1.50 4.00
118 Greg Koehler RC 1.50 4.00
119 Vernon Fiddler RC 2.00 5.00
120 Ray Emery RC 5.00 12.00
121 Eric Godard RC 1.50 4.00
122 Dennis Seidenberg RC 2.50 6.00
123 Jeff Taffe RC 1.50 4.00
124 Dick Tarnstrom RC 1.50 4.00
125 Tom Koivisto RC 1.50 4.00
126 Curtis Sanford RC 2.50 6.00
127 Cody Rudkowsky RC 1.50 4.00
128 Carlo Colaiacovo RC 2.50 6.00
129 Paul Manning RC 1.50 4.00
130 Shaone Morrisonn RC 1.50 4.00
131 Ryan Miller RC 10.00 25.00
132 Jerred Smithson RC 1.50 4.00
133 Alexei Semenov RC 1.50 4.00
134 Michael Leighton RC 2.50 6.00
135 Ian MacNeil RC 1.50 4.00
136 Jared Aulin RC 1.50 4.00
137 Curtis Murphy RC 1.50 4.00
138 Jim Vandermeer RC 1.50 4.00
139 Steve Ott RC 3.00 8.00
140 Brooks Orpik RC 2.50 6.00
141 Jim Fahey RC 1.50 4.00
142 Matt Walker RC 1.50 4.00
143 Rickard Wallin RC 1.50 4.00
144 Tomas Malec RC 1.50 4.00
145 Jonathan Hedstrom RC 1.50 4.00
146 Stanislav Chistov JSY RC 2.00 5.00
147 Chuck Kobasew JSY RC 2.50 6.00
148 Micki Dupont JSY RC 2.00 5.00
149 Jeff Paul JSY RC 2.00 5.00
150 Rick Nash JSY RC 12.00 30.00
151 Henrik Zetterberg JSY RC 12.00 30.00
152 Ales Hemsky JSY RC 8.00 20.00
153 Jay Bouwmeester JSY RC 6.00 15.00
154 Alexander Frolov JSY RC 4.00 10.00
155 P-M Bouchard JSY RC 3.00 8.00
156 Sylvain Blouin JSY RC 2.00 5.00
157 Ron Hainsey JSY RC 2.00 5.00
158 Scottie Upshall JSY RC 2.50 6.00
159 Tomi Pettinen JSY RC 2.00 5.00
160 Jason Spezza JSY RC 15.00 40.00
161 Anton Volchenkov JSY RC 2.00 5.00
162 Radovan Somik JSY RC 2.00 5.00
163 Lynn Loyns JSY RC 2.00 5.00
164 Alexander Svitov JSY RC 2.00 5.00
165 Mikael Tellqvist JSY RC 2.00 5.00
166 Steve Eminger JSY RC 2.00 5.00

2002-03 Upper Deck Honor Roll Grade A Jerseys

SINGLE JSY.ODDS 1:26
TRIPLE JSY.ODDS 1:480
GAED Eric Daze 3.00 8.00
GAJJ Jaromir Jagr 5.00 12.00
GAMB Martin Brodeur 8.00 20.00
GAMD Mike Dunham 3.00 8.00
GAMM Mike Modano 4.00 10.00
GAMS Mats Sundin 3.00 8.00
GAOK Olaf Kolzig 3.00 8.00
GAPF Peter Forsberg 5.00 12.00
GAPK Paul Kariya 3.00 8.00
GAPR Patrick Roy 10.00 25.00
GARB Ray Bourque 5.00 12.00
GASA Miroslav Satan 3.00 8.00
GASG Simon Gagne 4.00 10.00
GASK Saku Koivu 3.00 8.00
TJKB Jagr/Kolzig/Bondra 12.50 30.00
TPRG Primeau/Roenick/Gagne 25.00 60.00
TRFS Roy/Forsberg/Sakic 40.00 100.00
TSTM Sams/Thornton/Murray 15.00 40.00
TYFS Yzerman/Fedorov/Shanny 30.00 80.00

2002-03 Upper Deck Honor Roll Signature Class

STATED ODDS 1:480
AS Alexander Svitov 10.00 25.00
BO Bobby Orr/10*
BR Pavel Brendl 6.00 15.00
DH Dany Heatley 10.00 25.00
GH Gordie Howe/9*
HZ Henrik Zetterberg 50.00 100.00
JB Jay Bouwmeester 8.00 20.00
JL John LeClair 8.00 20.00
JS Jason Spezza 200.00 350.00
MA Maxim Afinogenov 6.00 15.00
MB Martin Brodeur SP 150.00 300.00
MF Manny Fernandez 6.00 15.00
NK Nikolai Khabibulin SP
PB Pavel Bure 6.00 15.00
PR Patrick Roy 75.00 150.00
SC Stanislav Chistov 6.00 15.00
SY Steve Yzerman 40.00 100.00
TS Teemu Selanne SP 90.00 150.00
WG0 Wayne Gretzky/9*

2002-03 Upper Deck Honor Roll Students of the Game

COMPLETE SET (30) 20.00 40.00
STATED ODDS 1:6
SG1 Paul Kariya .60 1.50
SG2 Dany Heatley .50 1.25
SG3 Joe Thornton .60 1.50
SG4 Jarome Iginla .50 1.25
SG5 Chris Drury .50 1.25
SG6 Joe Sakic .75 2.00
SG7 Patrick Roy 1.25 3.00
SG8 Peter Forsberg .60 1.50
SG9 Rick Nash 2.50 6.00
SG10 Mike Modano .75 2.00
SG11 Bill Guerin .50 1.25
SG12 Curtis Joseph .50 1.25
SG13 Steve Yzerman 1.00 2.50
SG14 Sergei Fedorov .75 2.00
SG15 Mike Comrie .50 1.25
SG16 Marian Gaborik .75 2.00
SG17 Saku Koivu .50 1.25
SG18 Martin Brodeur 1.00 2.50
SG19 Alexei Yashin .40 1.00
SG20 Pavel Bure .60 1.50
SG21 Eric Lindros .75 2.00
SG22 Jason Spezza 2.00 5.00
SG23 Jeremy Roenick .50 1.25
SG24 Tony Amonte .40 1.00
SG25 Mario Lemieux 1.50 4.00
SG26 Teemu Selanne 1.00 2.50
SG27 Keith Tkachuk .50 1.25
SG28 Vincent Lecavalier .40 1.00
SG29 Mats Sundin .50 1.25
SG30 Jaromir Jagr 1.25 3.00

2002-03 Upper Deck Honor Roll Team Warriors

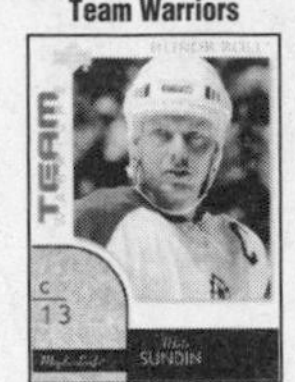

COMPLETE SET (15) 10.00 20.00
STATED ODDS 1:12
TW1 Joe Thornton .60 1.50
TW2 Jarome Iginla .50 1.25
TW3 Jeff O'Neill .30 .75
TW4 Peter Forsberg 1.00 2.50
TW5 Mike Modano .60 1.50
TW6 Brendan Shanahan .60 1.50
TW7 Adam Deadmarsh .30 .75
TW8 Saku Koivu .40 1.00
TW9 Michael Peca .30 .75
TW10 Eric Lindros .40 1.00
TW11 John LeClair .40 1.00
TW12 Mario Lemieux 2.50 6.00
TW13 Owen Nolan .30 .75
TW14 Mats Sundin .40 1.00
TW15 Todd Bertuzzi .40 1.00

2003-04 Upper Deck Honor Roll

This 191-card set consisted of several subsets: cards 1-90 were base veteran cards; cards 91-110 made up the "Students of the Game" subset and were serial-numbered out of 999; cards 111-125 made up the "Class Reunion" subset and were serial-numbered out of 500; cards 126-132 made up the "Head of the Class" subset and were serial-numbered to 250; cards 133-167 were rookie cards serial-numbered to 800 and cards 133-167 were rookie jersey cards that made up the "Dean's List" subset . The "Dean's List" jerseys were inserted at 1:24. Please note that there is no card #63 and there are two cards numbered #48.

COMPLETE SET (191)
COMP. SET w/o SP's (90) 6.00 15.00
1 Jean-Sebastien Giguere .15 .40
2 Sergei Fedorov .25 .60
3 Dany Heatley .15 .40
4 Ilya Kovalchuk .15 .40
5 Felix Potvin .25 .60
6 Joe Thornton .20 .50
7 Sergei Samsonov .12 .30
8 Chris Drury .12 .30
9 Daniel Briere .15 .40
10 Jarome Iginla .15 .40
11 Roman Turek .12 .30
12 Jamie Storr .12 .30
13 Ron Francis .20 .50
14 Kyle Calder .10 .25
15 Jocelyn Thibault .12 .30
16 Tyler Arnason .10 .25
17 David Aebischer .12 .30
18 Joe Sakic .25 .60
19 Paul Kariya .20 .50
20 Peter Forsberg .20 .50
21 Marc Denis .12 .30
22 Rick Nash .15 .40
23 Todd Marchant .10 .25
24 Bill Guerin .15 .40
25 Marty Turco .15 .40
26 Mike Modano .25 .60
27 Dominik Hasek .25 .60
28 Henrik Zetterberg .20 .50
29 Steve Yzerman .40 1.00
30 Ales Hemsky .15 .40
31 Mike Comrie .12 .30
32 Tommy Salo .12 .30
33 Jay Bouwmeester .15 .40
34 Olli Jokinen .15 .40
35 Roberto Luongo .25 .60
36 Alexander Frolov .12 .30
37 Jason Allison .12 .30
38 Roman Cechmanek .12 .30
39 Zigmund Palffy .15 .40
40 Manny Fernandez .12 .30
41 Marian Gaborik .25 .60
42 Pierre-Marc Bouchard .15 .40
43 Jose Theodore .15 .40
44 Marcel Hossa .10 .25
45 Saku Koivu .15 .40
46 David Legwand .12 .30
47 Tomas Vokoun .12 .30
48 Martin Brodeur .30 .75
48 Jeff Hackett .12 .30
49 Scott Gomez .12 .30
50 Scott Stevens .15 .40
51 Alexei Yashin .12 .30
52 Michael Peca .12 .30
53 Rick DiPietro .12 .30
54 Alex Kovalev .12 .30
55 Eric Lindros .25 .60
56 Mark Messier .25 .60
57 Mike Dunham .12 .30
58 Daniel Alfredsson .15 .40
59 Jason Spezza .15 .40
60 Marian Hossa .12 .30
61 Patrick Lalime .12 .30
62 John LeClair .15 .40
64 Jeremy Roenick .15 .40
65 Simon Gagne .15 .40
66 Mike Johnson .10 .25
67 Sean Burke .10 .25
68 Mario Lemieux .50 1.25
69 Martin Straka .10 .25
70 Evgeni Nabokov .12 .30
71 Patrick Marleau .15 .40
72 Vincent Damphousse .12 .30
73 Chris Pronger .12 .30
74 Chris Osgood .15 .40
75 Doug Weight .15 .40
76 Keith Tkachuk .15 .40
77 Pavol Demitra .20 .50
78 Nikolai Khabibulin .15 .40
79 Vincent Lecavalier .12 .30
80 Alexander Mogilny .12 .30
81 Ed Belfour .15 .40
82 Mats Sundin .15 .40
83 Owen Nolan .12 .30
84 Ed Jovanovski .12 .30
85 Johan Hedberg .12 .30
86 Markus Naslund .15 .40
87 Todd Bertuzzi .15 .40
88 Jaromir Jagr .40 1.00
89 Olaf Kolzig .15 .40
90 Peter Bondra .12 .30
91 Marian Gaborik SOG 1.50 4.00
92 Joe Thornton SOG 1.25 3.00
93 Jean-Sebastien Giguere SOG 1.00 2.50
94 Ilya Kovalchuk SOG 1.00 2.50
95 Ales Hemsky SOG 1.00 2.50
96 Mike Komisarek SOG .60 1.50
97 Rick Nash SOG 1.00 2.50
98 Marty Turco SOG 1.00 2.50
99 Alexander Frolov SOG .75 2.00
100 Jay Bouwmeester SOG 1.00 2.50
101 Henrik Zetterberg SOG 1.25 3.00
102 Marian Hossa SOG .75 2.00
103 Ales Kotalik SOG .60 1.50
104 Vincent Lecavalier SOG .75 2.00
105 Pavel Datsyuk SOG 1.25 3.00
106 Andrew Raycroft SOG .75 2.00
107 Philippe Sauve SOG .75 2.00
108 Marcel Hossa SOG .60 1.50
109 Rick DiPietro SOG .75 2.00
110 Jason Spezza SOG 1.00 2.50
111 Brendan Shanahan CR 2.00 5.00
112 Joe Sakic CR 2.50 6.00
113 Mike Modano CR 2.50 6.00
114 Jeremy Roenick CR 1.50 4.00
115 Teemu Selanne CR 3.00 8.00
116 Mats Sundin CR 1.50 4.00
117 Sergei Fedorov CR 2.50 6.00
118 Owen Nolan CR 1.25 3.00
119 Jaromir Jagr CR 4.00 10.00
120 Peter Forsberg CR 2.00 5.00
121 Markus Naslund CR 1.50 4.00
122 Alexei Yashin CR 1.25 3.00
123 Manny Fernandez CR 1.25 3.00
124 Paul Kariya CR 2.00 5.00
125 Saku Koivu CR 1.50 4.00
126 Peter Forsberg HOC 3.00 8.00
127 Steve Yzerman HOC 6.00 15.00
128 Joe Thornton HOC 3.00 8.00
129 Martin Brodeur HOC 5.00 12.00
130 Mario Lemieux HOC 8.00 20.00
131 Ed Belfour HOC 2.50 6.00
132 Mike Modano HOC 4.00 10.00
133 Darryl Bootland RC 1.50 4.00
134 Trevor Daley RC 2.00 5.00
135 John-Michael Liles RC 1.50 4.00
136 Paul Martin RC 1.50 4.00
137 Esa Pirnes RC 1.25 3.00
138 Seamus Kotyk RC 1.25 3.00
139 Pat Rissmiller RC 1.50 4.00
140 Marek Svatos RC 2.50 6.00
141 Maxim Kondratiev RC 1.25 3.00
142 Marek Zidlicky RC 1.25 3.00
143 Matthew Spiller RC 1.50 4.00
144 Nathan Smith RC 1.25 3.00
145 Brent Burns RC 3.00 8.00
146 Boyd Gordon RC 1.50 4.00
147 Andrew Hutchinson RC 1.25 3.00
148 Peter Sarno RC 1.25 3.00
149 Jed Ortmeyer RC 1.25 3.00
150 Cody McCormick RC 1.50 4.00
151 Christoph Brandner RC 1.50 4.00
152 Grant McNeill RC 1.25 3.00
153 Greg Campbell RC 1.25 3.00
154 Tony Salmelainen RC 1.25 3.00
155 Kent McDonell RC 1.50 4.00
156 Martin Strbak RC 1.50 4.00
157 Matt Murley RC 1.50 4.00
158 Rastislav Stana RC 2.00 5.00
159 Karl Stewart RC 1.25 3.00
160 Ryan Malone RC 2.50 6.00
161 Wade Brookbank RC 1.50 4.00
162 Mike Stuart RC 1.25 3.00
163 Sergei Zinovjev RC 1.25 3.00
164 Julien Vauclair RC 1.25 3.00
165 Alan Rourke RC 1.25 3.00
166 John Pohl RC 1.25 3.00
167 Dominic Moore RC 1.25 3.00
168 Peter Sejna JSY RC 2.50 6.00
169 Matt Stajan JSY RC 3.00 8.00
170 Milan Michalek JSY RC 4.00 10.00
171 Pavel Vorobiev JSY RC 2.50 6.00
172 Dan Hamhuis JSY RC 2.50 6.00
173 Chris Higgins JSY RC 4.00 10.00
174 Antti Miettinen JSY RC 3.00 8.00
175 Christian Ehrhoff JSY RC 2.50 6.00
176 Alexander Semin JSY RC 6.00 15.00
177 Antoine Vermette JSY RC 4.00 10.00
178 Travis Moen JSY RC 2.50 6.00
179 Joni Pitkanen JSY RC 3.00 8.00
180 Patrice Bergeron JSY RC 10.00 25.00
181 Jiri Hudler JSY RC 5.00 12.00
182 Marc-Andre Fleury JSY RC 15.00 40.00
183 Dustin Brown JSY RC 4.00 10.00
184 Joffrey Lupul JSY RC 5.00 12.00
185 Tuomo Ruutu JSY RC 3.00 8.00
186 Jordin Tootoo JSY RC 4.00 10.00
187 Eric Staal JSY RC 10.00 25.00
188 Nathan Horton JSY RC 5.00 12.00
189 Tim Gleason JSY RC 2.50 6.00
190 Sean Bergenheim JSY RC 2.50 6.00
191 Matthew Lombardi JSY RC 2.50 6.00

2003-04 Upper Deck Honor Roll Grade A Jerseys

STATED ODDS 1:24
TRIPLE JSY ODDS 1:480
GAAY Alexei Yashin 3.00 8.00
GAJI Jarome Iginla 4.00 10.00
GAJT Joe Thornton 4.00 10.00
GAMB Martin Brodeur 8.00 20.00
GAML Mario Lemieux 10.00 25.00
GAMM Mark Messier 6.00 15.00
GAMS Miroslav Satan 3.00 8.00
GASG Simon Gagne 4.00 10.00
GATM Marty Turco 3.00 8.00
GAVL Vincent Lecavalier 3.00 8.00
TBOS Thrntn/Smsnv/Mrray 12.00 30.00
TCOL Kariya/Sakic/Forsberg 20.00 50.00
TDET Hasek/Yzrmn/Zetter 25.00 60.00
TNYR Lindros/Bure/Kovalev 15.00 40.00
TTOR Sundin/Nolan/Belfour 12.00 30.00
TVAN Naslnd/Brtuzzi/Linden 15.00 40.00

2003-04 Upper Deck Honor Roll Signature Class

STATED ODDS 1:480
SC1 David Aebischer/10*
SC2 Todd Bertuzzi/24*
SC3 Martin Brodeur/10*
SC4 Pavel Bure/24*
SC5 Sergei Fedorov/10*
SC6 Marian Gaborik/24* 10.00 25.00
SC7 Jean-Sebastien Giguere/24* 15.00 40.00
SC8 Wayne Gretzky/10*
SC9 Scott Hartnell/24*
SC10 Martin Havlat/24*
SC11 Marian Hossa/24*

SC12 Gordie Howe/10*
SC13 Jarome Iginla/24*
SC14 Curtis Joseph/49* 20.00 50.00
SC15 Saku Koivu/10*
SC16 Ilya Kovalchuk/10*
SC17 John LeClair/49* 10.00 25.00
SC18 Eric Lindros/24*
SC19 Joe Nieuwendyk/24*
SC20 Bobby Orr/10*
SC21 Ziggy Palffy/24* 15.00 40.00
SC22 Jeremy Roenick/24* 20.00 40.00
SC23 Patrick Roy/10*
SC24 Sergei Samsonov/49* 10.00 25.00
SC25 Jose Theodore/49* 15.00 40.00
SC26 Joe Thornton/24* 15.00 40.00
SC27 Marty Turco/24*
SC28 Adam Hall/24*
SC29 Chuck Kobasew/24*
SC30 Jason Spezza/10*
SC31 Jason Blake/10*
SC32 Mark Parrish/24*

1996-97 Upper Deck Ice

This retail-only set was issued in one series totaling 150 cards. Each pack contained three see-through cel cards and carried a suggested retail price of $3.99. The set is broken down into four subsets: Ice Performers (1-75), Ice Phenoms (76-105), Ice Legends (106-115), and World Juniors (116-150).

COMPLETE SET (150) 25.00 60.00
1 Kevin Todd .40 1.00
2 Adam Oates .60 1.50
3 Bill Ranford .50 1.25
4 Rick Tocchet .50 1.25
5 Dominik Hasek 1.00 2.50
6 Richard Smehlik .40 1.00
7 Derek Plante .40 1.00
8 Joel Bouchard .40 1.00
9 Theo Fleury 1.25 3.00
10 Chris Chelios .60 1.50
11 Ed Belfour .60 1.50
12 Eric Weinrich .40 1.00
13 Tony Amonte .50 1.25
14 Greg Adams .40 1.00
15 Jamie Langenbrunner .40 1.00
16 Sergei Zubov .40 1.00
17 Pat Verbeek .40 1.00
18 Chris Osgood .60 1.50
19 Rem Murray RC .60 1.50
20 Jason Arnott .50 1.25
21 Curtis Joseph .60 1.50
22 Bill Lindsay .40 1.00
23 Ray Sheppard .50 1.25
24 Martin Straka .40 1.00
25 Jean-Sebastien Giguere RC 4.00 10.00
26 Sean Burke .40 1.00
27 Keith Primeau .40 1.00
28 Geoff Sanderson .50 1.25
29 Rob Blake .60 1.50
30 Ian Laperriere .60 1.50
31 Byron Dafoe .40 1.00
32 Vincent Damphousse .50 1.25
33 Darcy Tucker .40 1.00
34 Brian Savage .40 1.00
35 Bill Guerin .60 1.50
36 Scott Niedermayer .60 1.50
37 Steve Thomas .40 1.00
38 Valeri Zelepukin .50 1.25
39 Bryan Smolinski .40 1.00
40 Derek King .40 1.00
41 Mike Richter .60 1.50
42 Daniel Goneau RC .60 1.50
43 Brian Leetch .60 1.50
44 Adam Graves .40 1.00
45 Damian Rhodes .50 1.25
46 Mikael Renberg .50 1.25
47 Eric Desjardins .50 1.25
48 Rod Brind'Amour .60 1.50
49 Janne Niinimaa .60 1.50
50 Dale Hawerchuk .75 2.00
51 Jeremy Roenick 1.00 2.50
52 Mike Gartner .60 1.50
53 Cliff Ronning .40 1.00
54 Patrick Lalime RC 2.00 5.00
55 Ron Francis .75 2.00
56 Petr Nedved .50 1.25
57 Bernie Nicholls .40 1.00
58 Jeff Friesen .40 1.00
59 Owen Nolan .60 1.50
60 Marty McSorley .40 1.00
61 Pierre Turgeon .60 1.50
62 Grant Fuhr .60 1.50
63 Chris Pronger .50 1.25
64 Jim Campbell .40 1.00
65 Chris Gratton .50 1.25
66 Dino Ciccarelli .60 1.50
67 Felix Potvin .60 1.50
68 Tie Domi .50 1.25
69 Doug Gilmour .75 2.00
70 Trevor Linden .50 1.25
71 Corey Hirsch .50 1.25
72 Jim Carey .60 1.50
73 Chris Simon .40 1.00
74 Mark Tinordi .40 1.00
75 Sergei Gonchar .40 1.00
76 Paul Kariya .75 2.00
77 Teemu Selanne 1.25 3.00
78 Jarome Iginla .75 2.00
79 Eric Daze .50 1.25
80 Sandis Ozolinsh .40 1.00
81 Peter Forsberg 1.00 2.50
82 Mike Modano 1.00 2.50
83 Anders Eriksson .40 1.00
84 Sergei Fedorov 1.00 2.50
85 Brendan Shanahan .75 2.00
86 Mike Grier RC .75 2.00
87 Doug Weight .60 1.50
88 Ed Jovanovski .50 1.25
89 Saku Koivu .60 1.50
90 Jose Theodore .75 2.00
91 Jocelyn Thibault .60 1.50
92 Martin Brodeur 1.25 3.00
93 Bryan Berard .60 1.50
94 Zigmund Palffy .60 1.50
95 Daniel Alfredsson .60 1.50
96 Alexei Yashin .50 1.25
97 Wade Redden .40 1.00
98 John LeClair .60 1.50
99 Oleg Tverdovsky .50 1.25
100 Keith Tkachuk .60 1.50
101 Jaromir Jagr 1.50 4.00
102 Roman Hamrlik .50 1.25
103 Sergei Berezin RC 1.00 2.50
104 Alexander Mogilny .50 1.25
105 Pavel Bure .75 2.00
106 Ray Bourque 1.00 2.50
107 Patrick Roy 1.50 4.00
108 Joe Sakic 1.00 2.50
109 Steve Yzerman 1.50 4.00
110 John Vanbiesbrouck .60 1.50
111 Mark Messier 1.00 2.50
112 Wayne Gretzky 3.00 8.00
113 Eric Lindros 1.00 2.50
114 Mario Lemieux 2.00 5.00
115 Brett Hull 3.00 8.00
116 Joe Thornton RC 4.00 10.00
117 Marc Denis .60 1.50
118 Martin Biron RC .75 2.00
119 Jason Doig .40 1.00
120 Daniel Briere RC 4.00 10.00
121 Trevor Letowski RC .50 1.25
122 Boyd Devereaux RC .60 1.50
123 Dwayne Hay RC .50 1.25
124 Hugh Hamilton RC .50 1.25
125 Brad Isbister RC .50 1.25
126 Shane Willis RC .60 1.50
127 Trent Whitfield RC .50 1.25
128 Jesse Wallin RC .50 1.25
129 Alyn McCauley .60 1.50
130 Cameron Mann RC .50 1.25
131 Jeff Ware .50 1.25
132 Corey Sarich .50 1.25
133 Richard Jackman RC .50 1.25
134 Brad Larsen .50 1.25
135 Peter Schaefer RC .50 1.25
136 Christian Dube .40 1.00
137 Chris Phillips .60 1.50
138 Sergei Samsonov .50 1.25
139 Alexei Morozov .50 1.25
140 Sergei Fedotov RC .50 1.25
141 Denis Khlopotnov RC .50 1.25
142 Andrei Markov RC 4.00 10.00
143 Andrei Petrunin .50 1.25
144 Roman Liachenko RC .50 1.25
145 Joe Corvo RC .50 1.25
146 Erik Rasmussen .50 1.25
147 Mike York RC .50 1.25
148 Brian Boucher .50 1.25
149 Paul Mara RC .50 1.25
150 Marty Reasoner .50 1.25

1996-97 Upper Deck Ice Acetate Parallel

This 115-card set is a partial parallel version of the regular Upper Deck Ice set and features a special Light F/X acetate card design. The set contains three subsets: Ice Performers (1-75) inserted at the rate of 1:9 with a bronze design, Ice Phenoms (76-105) inserted at the rate of 1:47 with a silver design, and Ice Legends (106-115) inserted at the rate of 1:325 with a gold design. The World Juniors subset, present in the regular issue, is not included in the parallel version, leaving the set complete at 115 cards.

*PERF.VETS: 3X TO 8X BASIC CARDS
*PERF.ROOKIES: 1.5X TO 4X
*PHENOM VETS: 6X TO 15X BASIC CARDS
*PHENOM ROOKIES: 2.5X TO 6X
*LEGENDS: 10X TO 25X BASIC CARDS

1996-97 Upper Deck Ice Stanley Cup Foundation

Randomly inserted in packs at a rate of 1:96, this 10-card set features color player photos of winning teammate pairs in colored borders on an acetate card. Dynasty parallels were also inserted randomly at 1:960.

COMPLETE SET (10) 125.00 250.00
*DYNASTY: 1.5X TO 4X BASIC INSERTS
S1 W.Gretzky/M.Messier 12.00 30.00
S2 B.Shanahan/S.Yzerman 10.00 25.00
S3 J.Vanbies./E.Jovan. 6.00 15.00
S4 J.Thibault/S.Koivu 6.00 15.00
S5 J.Sakic/P.Roy 8.00 20.00
S6 P.Kariya/T.Selanne 5.00 12.00
S7 M.Lemieux/J.Jagr 12.50 30.00
S8 J.Roenick/K.Tkachuk 6.00 15.00
S9 D.Weight/J.Arnott 3.00 8.00
S10 J.LeClair/E.Lindros 10.00 25.00

1997-98 Upper Deck Ice

The 1997-98 Upper Deck Ice set was issued in one series totaling 90 cards and was distributed in three-card packs with a suggested retail price of $4.99. The fronts feature color action player photos printed on acetate card stock. The backs carry player information.

COMPLETE SET (90) 30.00 80.00
1 Nelson Emerson .30 .75
2 Derian Hatcher .30 .75
3 Mike Richter .40 1.00
4 Sergei Berezin .30 .75
5 Nicklas Lidstrom .40 1.00
6 Ryan Smyth .30 .75
7 Martin Brodeur .75 2.00
8 Geoff Sanderson .30 .75
9 Doug Weight .40 1.00
10 Owen Nolan .40 1.00
11 Daniel Alfredsson .40 1.00
12 Peter Bondra .30 .75
13 Jim Campbell .25 .60
14 Rob Niedermayer .25 .60
15 Daymond Langkow .25 .60
16 Zigmund Palffy .40 1.00
17 Adam Oates .40 1.00
18 Adam Deadmarsh .25 .60
19 Brian Holzinger .30 .75
20 Jarome Iginla .40 1.00
21 Janne Niinimaa .30 .75
22 Dino Ciccarelli .40 1.00
23 Mark Recchi .50 1.25
24 Sandis Ozolinsh .30 .75
25 Keith Primeau .30 .75
26 Ed Jovanovski .25 .60
27 Jeremy Roenick .50 1.25
28 Alexei Yashin .30 .75
29 Felix Potvin .40 1.00
30 Chris Osgood .40 1.00
31 Marc Denis .40 1.00
32 Tyler Moss RC .30 .75
33 Kevin Hodson .30 .75
34 Jamie Storr .30 .75
35 Roman Turek .30 .75
36 Jose Theodore .40 1.00
37 Magnus Arvedson .40 1.00
38 Daniel Cleary .30 .75
39 Mike Knuble .40 1.00
40 Jaroslav Svejkovsky .30 .75
41 Patrick Marleau .50 1.25
42 Mattias Ohlund .30 .75
43 Sergei Samsonov .25 .60
44 Espen Knutsen RC 1.00 2.50
45 Vaclav Prospal RC .30 .75
46 Joe Thornton .40 1.00
47 Chris Phillips .30 .75
48 Mike Johnson RC .30 .75
49 Dainius Zubrus .30 .75
50 Wade Redden .25 .60
51 Derek Morris RC .40 1.00
52 Marco Sturm RC .40 1.00
53 Don MacLean .40 1.00
54 Bryan Berard .25 .60
55 Richard Zednik .30 .75
56 Alexei Morozov .30 .75
57 Erik Rasmussen .30 .75
58 Olli Jokinen RC 1.00 2.50
59 Jan Bulis RC .40 1.00
60 Patrik Elias RC 3.00 8.00
61 Peter Forsberg .50 1.25
62 Mike Modano .60 1.50
63 Tony Amonte .30 .75
64 Theo Fleury .50 1.25
65 Ron Francis .50 1.25
66 Brett Hull .50 1.25
67 Chris Chelios .40 1.00
68 Jaromir Jagr 1.00 2.50
69 Sergei Fedorov .60 1.50
70 Keith Tkachuk .40 1.00
71 Mark Messier .60 1.50
72 Pat LaFontaine .40 1.00
73 Mats Sundin .40 1.00
74 John Vanbiesbrouck .40 1.00
75 John LeClair .40 1.00
76 Brian Leetch .40 1.00
77 Ray Bourque .60 1.50
78 Saku Koivu .40 1.00
79 Joe Sakic .60 1.50
80 Teemu Selanne .75 2.00
81 Curtis Joseph .40 1.00
82 Doug Gilmour .50 1.25
83 Patrick Roy 1.00 2.50
84 Brendan Shanahan .50 1.25
85 Paul Kariya .50 1.25
86 Pavel Bure .50 1.25
87 Dominik Hasek .60 1.50
88 Eric Lindros .60 1.50
89 Steve Yzerman .75 2.00
90 Wayne Gretzky 2.00 5.00

1997-98 Upper Deck Ice Parallel

This 90-card set is a parallel version of the base set and is divided into three partial parallel sets. Ice Performers consists of cards 1-30 with an insertion rate of 1:2; Ice Phenoms consists of cards 31-60 with an insertion rate of 1:5; Ice Legends consists of the top 30 NHL players whose cards are 61-90 and have an insertion rate of 1:11.

*VETS: .6X TO 1.5X BASIC CARDS
*PHENOMS: .8X TO 2X BASIC CARDS
*LEGENDS: 2X TO 5X BASIC CARDS

1997-98 Upper Deck Ice Champions

Randomly inserted in packs at the rate of 1:47 and numbered out of 100, this 20-card set features color player head photos and action images printed with a Light FX/litho/acetate combination. An Ice Champions 2 Die Cuts parallel was also produced and limited to 100 copies each.

COMPLETE SET (20) 150.00 300.00
*DIE CUT/100: 2.5X TO 6X BASIC INSERTS
IC1 Wayne Gretzky 40.00 100.00
IC2 Patrick Roy 15.00 40.00
IC3 Eric Lindros 5.00 12.00
IC4 Saku Koivu 5.00 12.00
IC5 Dominik Hasek 10.00 25.00
IC6 Joe Thornton 8.00 20.00
IC7 Martin Brodeur 12.50 30.00
IC8 Teemu Selanne 5.00 12.00
IC9 Paul Kariya 5.00 12.00
IC10 Joe Sakic 10.00 25.00
IC11 Mark Messier 5.00 12.00
IC12 Peter Forsberg 12.50 30.00
IC13 Mats Sundin 5.00 12.00
IC14 Brendan Shanahan 5.00 12.00
IC15 Keith Tkachuk 5.00 12.00
IC16 Brett Hull 6.00 15.00
IC17 John Vanbiesbrouck 5.00 12.00
IC18 Jaromir Jagr 8.00 20.00
IC19 Steve Yzerman 12.00 30.00
IC20 Sergei Samsonov 5.00 12.00

1997-98 Upper Deck Ice Lethal Lines

Randomly inserted in packs at the rate of 1:11, this 30-card set features ten sets of three cards each displaying an action player photo which create an interlocking complete die-cut "lethal line" card when placed side-by-side in the correct order. A lethal line 2 parallel was also created and inserted at 1:120.

COMPLETE SET (30) 60.00 150.00
*LETHAL LINES 2: 2X TO 5X BASIC INSERTS
LETHAL LINES 2 STATED ODDS 1:120
L1A Paul Kariya 2.00 5.00
L1B Wayne Gretzky 10.00 25.00
L1C Joe Thornton 4.00 10.00
L2A Brendan Shanahan 2.00 5.00
L2B Eric Lindros 2.50 6.00
L2C Jaromir Jagr 3.00 8.00
L3A Keith Tkachuk 1.50 4.00
L3B Mark Messier 2.00 5.00
L3C Owen Nolan 1.50 4.00
L4A Daniel Alfredsson 1.50 4.00
L4B Peter Forsberg 3.00 8.00
L4C Mats Sundin 2.00 5.00
L5A Ryan Smyth 1.50 4.00
L5B Steve Yzerman 6.00 15.00
L5C Jarome Iginla 2.00 5.00
L6A Sergei Samsonov 1.50 4.00
L6B Igor Larionov 1.25 3.00
L6C Sergei Fedorov 3.00 8.00
L7A Patrik Elias 2.00 5.00
L7B Alexei Morozov 1.25 3.00
L7C Vaclav Prospal 1.25 3.00
L8A John LeClair 2.00 5.00
L8B Mike Modano 2.50 6.00
L8C Brett Hull 2.50 6.00
L9A Olli Jokinen 1.50 4.00
L9B Saku Koivu 2.00 5.00
L9C Teemu Selanne 2.50 6.00
L10A Brian Leetch 1.50 4.00
L10B Patrick Roy 8.00 20.00
L10C Nicklas Lidstrom 2.00 5.00

1997-98 Upper Deck Ice Power Shift

Randomly inserted in packs at the rate of 1:23, this 90-card set is a gold foil parallel version of the base set.

*VETS: 5X TO 12X BASIC CARDS
*ROOKIES: 2.5X TO 6X BASIC CARDS

2000-01 Upper Deck Ice

Released in mid-September, Upper Deck Ice featured a 60-card set comprised of 40 Veterans, 14 Fresh Faces cards die cut and sequentially numbered to 1500, and six Prime Performers cards die cut and sequentially numbered to 1500. Base cards were printed on clear acetate plastic card stock. Ice was released in 18-pack boxes with each pack containing four cards and carried a suggested retail price of $3.99. There was an update set that included an additional 63 cards, which was packaged along with other Upper Deck product updates.

COMPLETE SET (123) 200.00 400.00
COMP.SER.1 w/o SP's (40) 6.00 15.00
1 Paul Kariya .40 1.00
2 Teemu Selanne .60 1.50
3 Patrik Stefan .25 .60
4 Joe Thornton .50 1.25
5 Dominik Hasek .50 1.25
6 Michael Peca .25 .60
7 Valeri Bure .25 .60
8 Ron Francis .40 1.00
9 Tony Amonte .25 .60
10 Patrick Roy .75 2.00
11 Ray Bourque .50 1.25
12 Milan Hejduk .25 .60
13 Peter Forsberg .40 1.00
14 Brett Hull .50 1.25
15 Mike Modano .50 1.25
16 Brendan Shanahan .40 1.00
17 Chris Osgood .30 .75
18 Steve Yzerman 1.00 2.50
19 Doug Weight .30 .75
20 Pavel Bure .40 1.00
21 Luc Robitaille .30 .75
22 Jose Theodore .40 1.00
23 David Legwand .30 .75
24 Martin Brodeur .60 1.50
25 Scott Gomez .25 .60
26 Tim Connolly .20 .50
27 Mike York .20 .50
28 Marian Hossa .25 .60
29 Brian Boucher .25 .60
30 John LeClair .30 .75
31 Jeremy Roenick .30 .75
32 Jaromir Jagr .75 2.00
33 Steve Shields .20 .50
34 Chris Pronger .25 .60
35 Roman Turek .25 .60
36 Vincent Lecavalier .25 .60
37 Curtis Joseph .40 1.00
38 Mats Sundin .30 .75
39 Mark Messier .50 1.25
40 Olaf Kolzig .30 .75
41 Matt Pettinger RC 1.50 4.00
42 Chris Nielsen RC 1.50 4.00
43 Dany Heatley RC 6.00 15.00
44 Matt Zultek RC 1.50 4.00
45 Dmitri Afanasenkov RC 1.50 4.00
46 Tyler Bouck RC 1.50 4.00
47 Jonas Andersson RC 1.50 4.00
48 Marc-Andre Thinel RC 1.50 4.00
49 Jaroslav Svoboda RC 1.50 4.00
50 Josef Vasicek RC 4.00 10.00
51 Andrew Raycroft RC 4.00 10.00
52 Juraj Kolnik RC 1.50 4.00
53 Zdenek Blatny RC 1.50 4.00
54 Sebastien Caron RC 2.00 5.00
55 Eric Nickulas RC 1.50 4.00
56 Serge Aubin RC 2.00 5.00
57 Steven Reinprecht RC 2.50 6.00
58 David Gosselin RC 2.00 5.00
59 Colin White RC 1.50 4.00
60 Steve Valiquette RC 2.00 5.00
61 Jeff Friesen .20 .50
62 Bill Guerin .30 .75
63 J-P Dumont .20 .50
64 Oleg Saprykin .20 .50
65 Shane Willis .20 .50
66 Josef Vasicek .50 1.25
67 Steve Reinprecht .30 .75
68 Marc Denis .25 .60
69 Marty Turco RC 3.00 8.00
70 Sergei Fedorov .50 1.25
71 Adam Deadmarsh .25 .60
72 Keith Tkachuk .30 .75
73 Mark Messier .50 1.25
74 Alexei Yashin .25 .60
75 Mario Lemieux 1.00 2.50
76 Evgeni Nabakov .25 .60
77 Brad Richards .30 .75
78 Henrik Sedin .50 1.25
79 Daniel Sedin .60 1.50
80 Matt Pettinger .20 .50
81 Marc Chouinard RC 1.50 4.00
82 Bryan Adams RC 1.50 4.00
83 Martin Brochu RC 1.50 4.00
84 Craig Adams RC 1.50 4.00
85 David Aebischer RC 3.00 8.00
86 Rostislav Klesla RC 4.00 10.00
87 Shawn Horcoff RC 3.00 8.00
88 Mike Comrie RC 4.00 10.00
89 Eric Belanger RC 2.00 5.00
90 Marian Gaborik RC 5.00 12.00
91 Eric Landry RC 1.50 4.00
92 Scott Hartnell RC 5.00 12.00
93 Chris Mason RC 3.00 8.00
94 Rick DiPietro RC 6.00 15.00
95 Martin Havlat RC 5.00 12.00
96 Roman Cechmanek RC 2.00 5.00
97 Justin Williams RC 4.00 10.00
98 Ruslan Fedotenko RC 1.50 4.00
99 Jean-Guy Trudel RC 1.50 4.00
100 Reed Low RC 1.50 4.00
101 Alexei Ponikarovsky RC 2.50 6.00
102 Rob Blake .30 .75
103 Andy McDonald RC 3.00 8.00
104 Petr Tenkrat RC 1.50 4.00
105 Brad Tapper RC 1.50 4.00
106 Darcy Hordichuk RC 1.50 4.00
107 J.P. Vigier RC 1.50 4.00
108 Pavel Kolarik RC 1.50 4.00
109 Jarno Kultanen RC 1.50 4.00
110 Eric Manlow RC 1.50 4.00
111 Eric Boulton RC 1.50 4.00
112 Brian Swanson RC 1.50 4.00
113 Lubomir Sekeras RC 1.50 4.00
114 Greg Classen RC 1.50 4.00
115 Jiri Bicek RC 1.50 4.00
116 Jeff Ulmer RC 1.50 4.00
117 Johan Holmqvist RC 1.50 4.00
118 Shane Hnidy RC 1.50 4.00
119 Ossi Vaananen RC 2.00 5.00
120 Johan Hedberg RC 2.00 5.00
121 Mark Smith RC 1.50 4.00
122 Alexander Khavanov RC 1.50 4.00
123 Bryce Salvador RC 2.00 5.00

2000-01 Upper Deck Ice Champions

COMPLETE SET (6) 15.00 30.00
STATED ODDS 1:18
IC1 Patrick Roy 5.00 12.00
IC2 Mike Modano 2.00 5.00
IC3 Steve Yzerman 5.00 12.00
IC4 Martin Brodeur 2.50 6.00
IC5 John LeClair 1.50 4.00
IC6 Jaromir Jagr 1.50 4.00

2000-01 Upper Deck Ice Clear Cut Autographs

Randomly inserted in packs at the rate of 1:108, this 10-card set features authentic player autographs on the right side of the card on a gray background, and full color player action shots on the right.

BH Brett Hull 15.00 40.00
BL Brian Leetch 8.00 20.00
CJ Curtis Joseph 10.00 25.00
MY Mike York 4.00 10.00
PB Pavel Bure 10.00 25.00
PS Patrik Stefan 4.00 10.00
RT Roman Turek 4.00 10.00
SG Scott Gomez 4.00 10.00
SY Steve Yzerman 30.00 80.00
TC Tim Connolly 4.00 10.00

2000-01 Upper Deck Ice Cool Competitors

Randomly inserted in packs at the rate of 1:53, this six card set features player action shots on clear acetate plastic card stock with gold foil highlights.

CC1 Paul Kariya 3.00 8.00
CC2 Peter Forsberg 3.00 8.00
CC3 Pavel Bure 3.00 8.00
CC4 Scott Gomez 2.00 5.00
CC5 Jaromir Jagr 6.00 15.00
CC6 Curtis Joseph 3.00 8.00

2000-01 Upper Deck Ice Gallery

COMPLETE SET (9) 15.00 30.00
STATED ODDS 1:6
IG1 Teemu Selanne .75 2.00
IG2 Patrick Roy 4.00 10.00
IG3 Brendan Shanahan 1.25 3.00
IG4 Pavel Bure 1.00 2.50
IG5 Scott Gomez .75 2.00
IG6 John LeClair 1.00 2.50
IG7 Jaromir Jagr 1.25 3.00
IG8 Vincent Lecavalier .75 2.00
IG9 Curtis Joseph .75 2.00

2000-01 Upper Deck Ice Game Jerseys

Randomly inserted in UD Ice packs at the rate of 1:45 and 1:60 in UD Update packs this 20-card set features swatches of authentic game jerseys on acetate plastic card stock. The backs of these cards are clear as well, so the jersey swatch can be viewed from both sides of the card. Update cards are marked below.

JCAC Anson Carter 4.00 10.00
JCBH Brett Hull 5.00 12.00
JCBS Brendan Shanahan 5.00 12.00
JCCO Chris Osgood 5.00 12.00
JCDL David Legwand 4.00 10.00
JCJJ Jaromir Jagr 6.00 15.00
JCJL John LeClair 5.00 12.00
JCJN Joe Nieuwendyk 5.00 12.00
JCMB Martin Brodeur 12.50 30.00
JCMH Michal Handzus 4.00 10.00
JCMM Mike Modano 6.00 15.00
JCMS Miroslav Satan 4.00 10.00
JCPB Pavel Bure 5.00 12.00
JCPD Pavol Demitra 4.00 10.00
JCPK Paul Kariya 4.00 10.00
JCRB Ray Bourque 8.00 20.00
JCSF Sergei Fedorov 5.00 12.00
JCSS Sergei Samsonov 4.00 10.00
JCTC Tim Connolly 4.00 10.00
JCTS Teemu Selanne 5.00 12.00
IFO Peter Forsberg Upd 10.00 25.00
IJT Joe Thornton Upd 5.00 12.00
ILE John LeClair Upd 5.00 12.00
IMO Mike Modano Upd 6.00 15.00
IRO Patrick Roy Upd 15.00 40.00
ISA Joe Sakic Upd 10.00 25.00
ISH Brendan Shanahan Upd 5.00 12.00
ITH Jocelyn Thibault Upd 4.00 10.00
ITK Keith Tkachuk Upd 4.00 10.00

2000-01 Upper Deck Ice Immortals

Randomly inserted in packs, this 60-card set parallels the Series I set sequentially numbered to 25.

*1-40 VETS: 20X TO 50X BASIC CARDS
*41-60 ROOKIES: 1.2X TO 3X SP/1500

2000-01 Upper Deck Ice Legends

Randomly inserted in packs, this 60-card set parallels the Series I set and is sequentially numbered to 150.

*1-40 VETS: 3X TO 8X BASIC CARDS
*41-60 ROOKIES: .6X TO 1.5X SP/1500

2000-01 Upper Deck Ice Rink Favorites

COMPLETE SET (9) 15.00 30.00
STATED ODDS 1:9
FP1 Paul Kariya 1.00 2.50
FP2 Peter Forsberg 2.00 5.00
FP3 Ray Bourque 1.50 4.00
FP4 Mike Modano 1.25 3.00
FP5 Steve Yzerman 4.00 10.00
FP6 Pavel Bure 1.00 2.50
FP7 Martin Brodeur 2.00 5.00
FP8 John LeClair 1.00 2.50
FP9 Jaromir Jagr 1.25 3.00

2000-01 Upper Deck Ice Stars

Randomly inserted in packs, this 60-card set parallels the Series I set enhanced with gold foil stamping and is sequentially numbered to 500.

*1-40 VETS/500: 2X TO 5X BASIC CARDS
*41-60 ROOK/500: .5X TO 1.2X RC/1500

2001-02 Upper Deck Ice

Released in early September 2001, this 151-card set featured all acetate card stock and carried an SRP of $3.99 for a 4-card pack. Ice was originally released as a 84-card set of 42 regular base cards and 42 Fresh Faces redemption cards which entitled the holder to a first year card of a rookie who made his debut during the 2001-02 season. Cards 85-151 were available in random packs of UD Rookie Update. Cards 43-84 were serial-numbered to 1500 and cards 127-151 were serial-numbered to 1000 copies each.

COMP.SET w/o RC's (84) 20.00 50.00
1 Paul Kariya .60 1.50
2 Joe Thornton .60 1.50
3 Sergei Samsonov .40 1.00
4 Martin Biron .40 1.00
5 Jarome Iginla .50 1.25
6 Arturs Irbe .40 1.00
7 Tony Amonte .40 1.00
8 Patrick Roy 1.25 3.00
9 Peter Forsberg .60 1.50
10 Ray Bourque .75 2.00
11 Ron Tugnutt .40 1.00
12 Mike Modano .75 2.00
13 Ed Belfour .50 1.25
14 Brett Hull .60 1.50
15 Steve Yzerman 1.50 4.00
16 Dominik Hasek .75 2.00
17 Sergei Fedorov .75 2.00
18 Tommy Salo .40 1.00
19 Mike Comrie .40 1.00
20 Pavel Bure .60 1.50
21 Adam Deadmarsh .40 1.00
22 Zigmund Palffy .50 1.25
23 Marian Gaborik .75 2.00
24 Manny Fernandez .40 1.00
25 Jose Theodore .50 1.25
26 Mike Dunham .40 1.00
27 Martin Brodeur 1.00 2.50
28 Patrik Elias .50 1.25
29 Rick DiPietro .40 1.00
30 Mark Messier .75 2.00
31 Martin Havlat .40 1.00
32 Marian Hossa .40 1.00
33 Jeremy Roenick .50 1.25
34 Sean Burke .30 .75
35 Johan Hedberg .40 1.00
36 Mario Lemieux 1.50 4.00
37 Evgeni Nabokov .40 1.00
38 Keith Tkachuk .50 1.25
39 Vincent Lecavalier .40 1.00
40 Curtis Joseph .50 1.25
41 Markus Naslund .50 1.25
42 Jaromir Jagr 1.25 3.00
43 Ilja Bryzgalov RC 4.00 10.00
44 Ilya Kovalchuk RC 12.00 30.00
45 Zdenek Kutlak RC 1.50 4.00
46 Ales Kotalik RC 3.00 8.00
47 Scott Nichol RC 1.50 4.00
48 Erik Cole RC 3.00 8.00
49 Casey Hankinson RC 1.50 4.00
50 Vaclav Nedorost RC 1.50 4.00
51 Martin Spanhel RC 1.50 4.00
52 Niko Kapanen RC 2.50 6.00
53 Pavel Datsyuk RC 15.00 30.00
54 Ty Conklin RC 2.50 6.00
55 Kristian Huselius RC 2.50 6.00
56 Jaroslav Bednar RC 1.50 4.00
57 Nick Schultz RC 1.50 4.00
58 Martti Jarventie 1.50 4.00
59 Martin Erat RC 2.50 6.00
60 Andreas Salomonsson RC 1.50 4.00
61 Radek Martinek RC 1.50 4.00
62 Dan Blackburn RC 2.00 5.00
63 Ivan Ciernik RC 1.50 4.00
64 Jiri Dopita RC 1.50 4.00
65 Krys Kolanos RC 1.50 4.00
66 Bill Tibbetts RC 1.50 4.00
67 Jeff Jillson RC 1.50 4.00
68 Mark Rycroft RC 2.00 5.00
69 Nikita Alexeev RC 1.50 4.00
70 Bob Wren RC 1.50 4.00
71 Pat Kavanagh RC 2.00 5.00
72 Brian Sutherby RC 1.50 4.00
73 Timo Parssinen RC 2.00 5.00
74 Kamil Piros RC 1.50 4.00
75 Jukka Hentunen RC 1.50 4.00
76 Niklas Hagman RC 2.00 5.00
77 Travis Roche RC 1.50 4.00
78 Pavel Skrbek RC 1.50 4.00
79 Scott Clemmensen RC 1.50 4.00
80 Chris Neil RC RC 2.00 5.00
81 Vaclav Pletka RC 1.50 4.00
82 Josef Boumedienne RC 1.50 4.00
83 Ryan Tobler RC 2.00 5.00
84 Chris Corrinet RC 1.50 4.00
85 Dany Heatley .50 1.25
86 Glen Murray .40 1.00
87 Jozef Stumpel .30 .75
88 Tim Connolly .30 .75
89 Roman Turek .40 1.00
90 Joe Sakic .75 2.00
91 Radim Vrbata .30 .75
92 Milan Hejduk .40 1.00
93 Brenden Morrow .40 1.00
94 Pierre Turgeon .50 1.25
95 Brett Hull .60 1.50
96 Luc Robitaille .50 1.25
97 Brendan Shanahan .60 1.50
98 Nicklas Lidstrom .50 1.25
99 Sandis Ozolinsh .30 .75
100 Jason Allison .40 1.00
101 Felix Potvin .75 2.00
102 Donald Audette .30 .75
103 Chris Osgood .50 1.25
104 Alexei Yashin .40 1.00
105 Mark Parrish .30 .75
106 Eric Lindros .75 2.00
107 Theo Fleury .60 1.50
108 Barrett Heisten .30 .75
109 Daniel Alfredsson .50 1.25
110 Donald Brashear .30 .75
111 Luke Richardson .30 .75
112 John LeClair .50 1.25
113 Brian Boucher .40 1.00
114 Alexei Kovalev .40 1.00
115 Teemu Selanne 1.00 2.50
116 Owen Nolan .50 1.25
117 Pavol Demitra .60 1.50
118 Chris Pronger .40 1.00
119 Doug Weight .50 1.25
120 Sheldon Keefe .30 .75
121 Nikolai Khabibulin .50 1.25
122 Mats Sundin .50 1.25
123 Jan Hlavac .30 .75
124 Trevor Linden .50 1.25
125 Peter Bondra .50 1.25
126 Olaf Kolzig .50 1.25
127 Pasi Nurminen RC 2.00 5.00
128 Ivan Huml RC 2.00 5.00
129 Tony Tuzzolino RC 2.00 5.00
130 Steve Montador RC 2.00 5.00
131 Mike Peluso RC 2.00 5.00
132 Steve Poapst RC 2.00 5.00
133 Riku Hahl RC 2.00 5.00
134 Blake Bellefeuille RC 2.00 5.00
135 David Ling RC 2.00 5.00
136 John Erskine RC 2.00 5.00
137 Brad Norton RC 2.00 5.00
138 Nick Smith RC 2.00 5.00
139 Ryan Flinn RC 2.00 5.00
140 Pascal Dupuis RC 3.00 8.00
141 Olivier Michaud RC 3.00 8.00
142 Marcel Hossa RC 3.00 8.00
143 Raffi Torres RC 3.00 8.00
144 Mikael Samuelsson RC 2.50 6.00
145 Christian Berglund RC 2.50 6.00
146 Shane Endicott RC 2.00 5.00
147 Eric Meloche RC 2.00 5.00
148 Steve Bancroft RC 3.00 8.00
149 Martin Cibak RC 2.00 5.00
150 Dean Melanson RC 2.00 5.00
151 Mike Farrell RC 2.00 5.00

2001-02 Upper Deck Ice Autographs

Inserted at 1:179 in UD Ice and 1:180 in UD Update, this 22-card set featured authentic player autographs on acetate card stock. Update cards are marked below.

AI Arturs Irbe Upd 6.00 15.00
CJ Curtis Joseph Upd/31 20.00 50.00
DH Dany Heatley Upd 10.00 25.00
DS Daniel Sedin 8.00 20.00
HS Henrik Sedin 10.00 25.00
IK Ilya Kovalchuk Upd/10
JI Jarome Iginla Upd 15.00 40.00
KH Kristian Huselius Upd 6.00 15.00
KK Krys Kolanos Upd 6.00 15.00
MB Martin Brodeur 30.00 80.00
MC Mike Comrie 8.00 20.00
MCU Mike Comrie Upd 8.00 20.00
MG Marian Gaborik Upd/20
MH Milan Hejduk Upd 8.00 20.00
MK Milan Kraft 6.00 15.00
MM Mike Modano 15.00 40.00
PB Peter Bondra Upd 8.00 20.00
PS Petr Sykora 6.00 15.00
RK Rostislav Klesla Upd 6.00 15.00
RL Roberto Luongo 10.00 25.00
SY Steve Yzerman 40.00 100.00
WG Wayne Gretzky 125.00 250.00

2001-02 Upper Deck Ice Jersey Combos

Inserted at 1:179, this 10-card set featured swatches of game-used jerseys coupled with a piece of game-used stick from the featured player. Cards were produced on all acetate stock. A gold parallel was also produced and serial-numbered to just 25 copies each.

*GOLD/25: .8X TO 2X BASIC DUAL
JJ Jaromir Jagr 12.50 30.00
JL John LeClair 8.00 20.00
JR Jeremy Roenick 15.00 40.00
JS Joe Sakic 12.50 30.00
ML Mario Lemieux 30.00 80.00
MM Mike Modano 12.50 30.00
PK Paul Kariya 8.00 20.00
PR Patrick Roy 20.00 50.00
SF Sergei Fedorov 12.50 30.00
SY Steve Yzerman 20.00 50.00

2001-02 Upper Deck Ice First Rounders Jerseys

Inserted at 1:36, this 7-card set featured swatches of game-used jersey of former first round draft picks.

FJJ Jaromir Jagr 8.00 20.00
FJR Jeremy Roenick 5.00 12.00
FJS Joe Sakic 8.00 20.00
FMM Mike Modano 6.00 15.00
FPK Paul Kariya 5.00 12.00
FPS Patrik Stefan 5.00 12.00
FSY Steve Yzerman 6.00 15.00

2001-02 Upper Deck Ice Jerseys

Inserted at 1:32, this 8-card set featured swatches of game-worn jersey on all acetate card stock.

JBH Brett Hull 5.00 12.00
JDW Doug Weight 6.00 15.00
JED Eric Daze 6.00 15.00
JJL John LeClair 4.00 10.00
JMS Marc Savard 4.00 10.00
JPR Patrick Roy 6.00 15.00
JSA Serge Aubin 4.00 10.00
JSF Sergei Fedorov 6.00 15.00

2003-04 Upper Deck Ice

Upper Deck Ice was re-introduced in 2003-04 as a 130-card set featuring 90 veteran base cards (1-90); 30 Tier 1 rookie cards (91-120) serial-numbered to 999 and 10 Tier 2 Rookie cards serial-numbered to 99.

COMP.SET w/o SP's (90) 12.50 25.00
1 Sergei Fedorov .40 1.00
2 Vaclav Prospal .15 .40
3 Jean-Sebastien Giguere .25 .60
4 Dany Heatley .25 .60
5 Ilya Kovalchuk .25 .60
6 Andrew Raycroft .20 .50
7 Joe Thornton .30 .75
8 Sergei Samsonov .20 .50
9 Mika Noronen .15 .40
10 Chris Drury .20 .50
11 Daniel Briere .25 .60
12 Roman Turek .20 .50
13 Jarome Iginla .25 .60
14 Justin Williams .20 .50
15 Ron Francis .30 .75
16 Bryan Berard .20 .50
17 Alexei Zhamnov .20 .50
18 Jocelyn Thibault .20 .50
19 Joe Sakic .40 1.00
20 Paul Kariya .30 .75
21 Peter Forsberg .30 .75
22 David Aebischer .20 .50
23 Todd Marchant .15 .40
24 Rick Nash .25 .60
25 Marc Denis .20 .50
26 Mike Modano .40 1.00
27 Marty Turco .25 .60
28 Bill Guerin .25 .60
29 Brett Hull .30 .75
30 Pavel Datsyuk .30 .75
31 Henrik Zetterberg .30 .75
32 Steve Yzerman .60 1.50
33 Adam Oates .25 .60
34 Tommy Salo .20 .50
35 Raffi Torres .15 .40
36 Ales Hemsky .25 .60
37 Olli Jokinen .25 .60
38 Roberto Luongo .40 1.00
39 Jay Bouwmeester .25 .60
40 Martin Straka .15 .40
41 Roman Cechmanek .20 .50
42 Zigmund Palffy .25 .60
43 Marian Gaborik .40 1.00
44 Alexandre Daigle .20 .50
45 Manny Fernandez .20 .50
46 Mike Ribeiro .20 .50
47 Saku Koivu .25 .60

1996-97 Upper Deck Ice

48 Jose Theodore .25 .60
49 David Legwand .20 .50
50 Tomas Vokoun .20 .50
51 Patrik Elias .25 .60
52 Martin Brodeur .50 1.25
53 Scott Stevens .25 .60
54 Scott Gomez .20 .50
55 Rick DiPietro .20 .50
56 Alexei Yashin .20 .50
57 Trent Hunter .15 .40
58 Mark Messier .40 1.00
59 Eric Lindros .40 1.00
60 Jaromir Jagr .60 1.50
61 Patrick Lalime .20 .50
62 Jason Spezza .25 .60
63 Marian Hossa .20 .50
64 Sean Burke .15 .40
65 Jeremy Roenick .25 .60
66 Tony Amonte .20 .50
67 Ladislav Nagy .15 .40
68 Mike Comrie .20 .50
69 Mario Lemieux .75 2.00
70 Rico Fata .15 .40
71 Vincent Damphousse .20 .50
72 Patrick Marleau .25 .60
73 Evgeni Nabokov .20 .50
74 Keith Tkachuk .25 .60
75 Chris Osgood .25 .60
76 Doug Weight .25 .60
77 Pavol Demitra .30 .75
78 Vincent Lecavalier .20 .50
79 Nikolai Khabibulin .25 .60
80 Ed Belfour .25 .60
81 Mats Sundin .25 .60
82 Alexander Mogilny .20 .50
83 Owen Nolan .20 .50
84 Todd Bertuzzi .25 .60
85 Ed Jovanovski .20 .50
86 Jason King .15 .40
87 Markus Naslund .25 .60
88 Peter Bondra .20 .50
89 Anson Carter .20 .50
90 Olaf Kolzig .25 .60
91 Pavel Vorobiev RC 2.00 5.00
92 Antti Miettinen RC 2.50 6.00
93 Chris Higgins RC 4.00 10.00
94 Dan Hamhuis RC 2.00 5.00
95 Marek Zidlicky RC 1.50 4.00
96 Mikhail Yakubov RC 1.50 4.00
97 Antoine Vermette RC 3.00 8.00
98 Jiri Hudler RC 4.00 10.00
99 Milan Michalek RC 3.00 8.00
100 Peter Sejna RC 2.00 5.00
101 Matt Stajan RC 2.50 6.00
102 Maxim Kondratiev RC 1.50 4.00
103 Alexander Semin RC 8.00 20.00
104 Sergei Zinovjev RC 1.50 4.00
105 Julien Vauclair RC 1.50 4.00
106 Dominic Moore RC 1.50 4.00
107 Tony Salmelainen RC 1.50 4.00
108 Rastislav Stana RC 2.50 6.00
109 Peter Sarno RC 1.50 4.00
110 Jed Ortmeyer RC 1.50 4.00
111 Nathan Smith RC 1.50 4.00
112 Matthew Lombardi RC 2.00 5.00
113 Dustin Brown RC 6.00 15.00
114 John-Michael Liles RC 2.00 5.00
115 Tim Gleason RC 2.00 5.00
116 Boyd Gordon RC 2.00 5.00
117 Greg Campbell RC 1.50 4.00
118 Ryan Kesler RC 8.00 20.00
119 Trevor Daley RC 2.50 6.00
120 John Pohl RC 1.50 4.00
121 Joffrey Lupul RC 40.00 80.00
122 Patrice Bergeron RC 60.00 120.00
123 Eric Staal RC 75.00 150.00
124 Tuomo Ruutu RC 30.00 60.00
125 Nikolai Zherdev RC 25.00 50.00
126 Nathan Horton RC 40.00 100.00
127 Fredrik Sjostrom RC 12.00 30.00
128 Jordin Tootoo RC 15.00 40.00
129 Joni Pitkanen RC 15.00 40.00
130 Marc-Andre Fleury RC 100.00 200.00
90P Marc-Andre Fleury PROMO .75 2.00

2003-04 Upper Deck Ice Glass

This 40-card set paralleled the rookie cards in the base set on clear acetate stock cards. Each card was serial-numbered out of 25.
*91-120 ROOK/25: 1.5X TO 4X RC/999
*121-130 ROOK/25: .4X TO 1X RC/99

2003-04 Upper Deck Ice Gold

This 90-card set paralleled the first 90 cards in the base set. Each card was serial-numbered out of 40.
*1-90 VETS/40: 5X TO 12X BASIC CARDS

2003-04 Upper Deck Ice Authentics

This 26-card memorabilia set featured certified autographs and jersey swatches. They were inserted at 1:80.
IAAC Anson Carter 8.00 20.00
IAAH Ales Hemsky 10.00 25.00
IACK Chuck Kobasew 6.00 15.00
IADA David Aebischer 10.00 25.00
IAHA Marcel Hossa 6.00 15.00
IAHZ Henrik Zetterberg 12.00 30.00
IAIK Ilya Kovalchuk 25.00 60.00
IAJI Jarome Iginla 25.00 60.00
IAJR Jeremy Roenick 15.00 40.00
IAJS Jason Spezza 15.00 40.00
IAJT Joe Thornton 25.00 60.00
IAMB Martin Brodeur 75.00 150.00
IAMH Marian Hossa 12.00 30.00
IAMH Gordie Howe 75.00 150.00
IAMN Markus Naslund 15.00 40.00
IAMT Marty Turco SP 40.00 100.00
IAON Owen Nolan 8.00 20.00
IAPR Patrick Roy SP 75.00 200.00
IARD Rick DiPietro 10.00 25.00
IARL Roberto Luongo 15.00 40.00
IARN Rick Nash 15.00 40.00
IASK Saku Koivu 10.00 25.00
IATB Todd Bertuzzi 10.00 25.00
IATH Jose Theodore 15.00 40.00
IAWG Wayne Gretzky 150.00 300.00
IAZP Zigmund Palffy 8.00 20.00

2003-04 Upper Deck Ice Breakers

This 42-card set featured swatches of jersey on acetate card stock. Each card was serial-numbered out of 75. A patch parallel was also created and serial-numbered out of 25
*PATCH/25: 1.5X TO 4X BASIC JSY/75
IBAH Ales Hemsky 6.00 15.00
IBBG Bill Guerin 6.00 15.00
IBBH Brett Hull 8.00 20.00
IBBL Brian Leetch 6.00 15.00
IBBS Brendan Shanahan 6.00 15.00
IBDA David Aebischer 6.00 15.00
IBDH Dominik Hasek 10.00 25.00
IBEB Ed Belfour 10.00 25.00
IBHK Milan Hejduk 4.00 10.00
IBIK Ilya Kovalchuk 8.00 20.00
IBJJ Jaromir Jagr 10.00 25.00
IBJK Jason King 4.00 10.00
IBJR Jeremy Roenick 8.00 20.00
IBJS Joe Sakic 12.50 30.00
IBJT Joe Thornton 8.00 20.00
IBJSG Jean-Sebastien Giguere 6.00 15.00
IBKT Keith Tkachuk 6.00 15.00
IBMB Martin Brodeur 15.00 40.00
IBMH Marian Hossa 6.00 15.00
IBML Mario Lemieux 20.00 50.00
IBMM Mike Modano 8.00 20.00
IBMN Markus Naslund 6.00 15.00
IBMR Mark Messier 8.00 20.00
IBMS Mats Sundin 6.00 15.00
IBMT Marty Turco 6.00 15.00
IBNL Nicklas Lidstrom 4.00 10.00
IBPF Peter Forsberg 10.00 25.00
IBPK Paul Kariya 6.00 15.00
IBPR Patrick Roy 20.00 50.00
IBRB Rob Blake 4.00 10.00
IBRF Ron Francis 6.00 15.00
IBRN Rick Nash 10.00 25.00
IBRT Raffi Torres 4.00 10.00
IBSG Scott Gomez 4.00 10.00
IBSP Jason Spezza 8.00 20.00
IBSS Sergei Samsonov 6.00 15.00
IBST Scott Stevens 4.00 10.00
IBSY Steve Yzerman 15.00 40.00
IBTB Todd Bertuzzi 6.00 15.00
IBTH Jose Theodore 8.00 20.00
IBVL Vincent Lecavalier 6.00 15.00
IBZP Zigmund Palffy 6.00 15.00

2003-04 Upper Deck Ice Clear Cut Winners

This 20-card set featured jersey swatches on acetate card stock. Cards from this set were inserted at 1:10. A patch parallel was also created and serial-numbered to 25.
*PATCH/25: 1.5X TO 4X BASIC JSY
CCBH Brett Hull 4.00 10.00
CCBL Brian Leetch 3.00 8.00
CCBS Brendan Shanahan 6.00 15.00
CCDH Dominik Hasek 6.00 15.00
CCEB Ed Belfour 6.00 15.00
CCJJ Jaromir Jagr 6.00 15.00
CCJS Joe Sakic 8.00 20.00
CCMB Martin Brodeur 8.00 20.00
CCMH Milan Hejduk 6.00 15.00
CCML Mario Lemieux 15.00 40.00
CCMM Mike Modano 6.00 15.00
CCMR Mark Messier 6.00 15.00
CCNL Nicklas Lidstrom 6.00 15.00
CCPF Peter Forsberg 8.00 20.00
CCPR Patrick Roy 12.50 30.00
CCRB Rob Blake 3.00 8.00
CCRF Ron Francis 3.00 8.00
CCSG Scott Gomez 3.00 8.00
CCSS Scott Stevens 3.00 8.00
CCSY Steve Yzerman 12.50 30.00

2003-04 Upper Deck Ice Frozen Fabrics

This 20-card set featured swatches of jersey on acetate card stock. A patch parallel was also created and serial-numbered to 25.
COMPLETE SET (20)
*PATCHES: 2X TO 5X
FFAH Ales Hemsky 4.00 10.00
FFBG Bill Guerin 4.00 10.00
FFDA David Aebischer 4.00 10.00
FFJK Jason King 4.00 10.00
FFJR Jeremy Roenick 5.00 12.00
FFJS Jason Spezza 5.00 12.00
FFJT Joe Thornton 6.00 15.00
FFJSG Jean-Sebastien Giguere 4.00 10.00
FFKT Keith Tkachuk 4.00 10.00
FFMH Marian Hossa 4.00 10.00
FFMN Markus Naslund 4.00 10.00
FFMS Mats Sundin 4.00 10.00
FFMT Marty Turco 4.00 10.00
FFPK Paul Kariya 4.00 10.00
FFRN Rick Nash 6.00 15.00
FFRT Raffi Torres 4.00 10.00
FFSS Sergei Samsonov 4.00 10.00
FFTB Todd Bertuzzi 4.00 10.00
FFTH Jose Theodore 5.00 12.00
FFZP Zigmund Palffy 4.00 10.00

2003-04 Upper Deck Ice Icons

COMPLETE SET (10) 20.00 50.00
STATED ODDS 1:40
IAM Al MacInnis 2.00 5.00
IBL Brian Leetch 2.00 5.00
IEB Ed Belfour 2.00 5.00
IJR Jeremy Roenick 2.50 6.00
IJS Joe Sakic 3.00 8.00
IMB Martin Brodeur 4.00 10.00
IML Mario Lemieux 5.00 12.00
IMM Mike Modano 2.50 6.00
ISY Steve Yzerman 5.00 12.00
ITD Tie Domi 2.00 5.00

2003-04 Upper Deck Ice Icons Jerseys

STATED ODDS 1:40
IAM Al MacInnis 4.00 10.00
IBL Brian Leetch 4.00 10.00
IEB Ed Belfour 6.00 15.00
IJR Jeremy Roenick 5.00 12.00
IMB Martin Brodeur 10.00 25.00
IML Mario Lemieux 12.50 30.00
IMM Mike Modano 5.00 12.00
ISY Steve Yzerman 12.50 30.00
ITD Tie Domi 4.00 10.00

2003-04 Upper Deck Ice Under Glass Autographs

This 20-card set featured certified player autographs on thick acetate card stock. Cards in this set were inserted at 1:160.
UGAH Ales Hemsky 12.00 30.00
UGBO Bobby Orr 75.00 150.00
UGDC Don Cherry 25.00 60.00
UGEL Eric Lindros SP 50.00 100.00
UGHA Marian Hossa 12.00 30.00
UGHZ Henrik Zetterberg 20.00 50.00
UGIK Ilya Kovalchuk 15.00 40.00
UGJR Jeremy Roenick 20.00 50.00
UGJS Jason Spezza 40.00 100.00
UGJT Joe Thornton 15.00 40.00
UGMB Martin Brodeur 80.00 200.00
UGMG Marian Gaborik 25.00 60.00
UGMH Gordie Howe 75.00 150.00
UGON Owen Nolan 12.00 30.00
UGPR Patrick Roy SP 200.00 350.00
UGRD Rick DiPietro 20.00 50.00
UGRL Roberto Luongo 25.00 60.00
UGRN Rick Nash 15.00 40.00
UGTB Todd Bertuzzi 12.00 30.00
UGWG Wayne Gretzky 250.00 400.00

2005-06 Upper Deck Ice

COMP. SET w/o SPs (1-100) 10.00 25.00
101-106 ROOKIE PRINT RUN 99
107-118 ROOKIE PRINT RUN 999
119-142 ROOKIE PRINT RUN 1999
143-268 ROOKIE PRINT RUN 2999
1 Joffrey Lupul .30 .75
2 Scott Niedermayer .40 1.00
3 Jean-Sebastien Giguere .40 1.00
4 Teemu Selanne .75 2.00
5 Ilya Kovalchuk .40 1.00
6 Kari Lehtonen .30 .75
7 Marian Hossa .30 .75
8 Andrew Raycroft .30 .75
9 Patrice Bergeron .50 1.25
10 Brian Leetch .40 1.00
11 Glen Murray .30 .75
12 Ryan Miller .40 1.00
13 Chris Drury .30 .75
14 Jarome Iginla .40 1.00
15 Miikka Kiprusoff .30 .75
16 Jordan Leopold .25 .60
17 Tony Amonte .30 .75
18 Erik Cole .30 .75
19 Eric Staal .50 1.25
20 Nikolai Khabibulin .40 1.00
21 Tuomo Ruutu .40 1.00
22 Joe Sakic .60 1.50
23 Milan Hejduk .30 .75
24 Alex Tanguay .40 1.00
25 David Aebischer .30 .75
26 Rick Nash .40 1.00
27 Sergei Fedorov .60 1.50
28 Mike Modano .60 1.50
29 Marty Turco .40 1.00
30 Bill Guerin .40 1.00
31 Steve Yzerman 1.00 2.50
32 Pavel Datsyuk .50 1.25
33 Brendan Shanahan .50 1.25
34 Nicklas Lidstrom .40 1.00
35 Henrik Zetterberg .50 1.25
36 Chris Pronger .30 .75
37 Ty Conklin .30 .75
38 Ryan Smyth .30 .75
39 Michael Peca .30 .75
40 Roberto Luongo .60 1.50
41 Joe Nieuwendyk .40 1.00
42 Jay Bouwmeester .40 1.00
43 Stephen Weiss .25 .60
44 Jeremy Roenick .40 1.00
45 Luc Robitaille .40 1.00
46 Alexander Frolov .25 .60
47 Marian Gaborik .60 1.50
48 Dwayne Roloson .30 .75
49 Jose Theodore .40 1.00
50 Saku Koivu .40 1.00
51 Michael Ryder .30 .75
52 Mike Ribeiro .30 .75
53 Steve Sullivan .25 .60
54 Paul Kariya .50 1.25
55 Tomas Vokoun .30 .75
56 Martin Brodeur .75 2.00
57 Patrik Elias .40 1.00
58 Brian Gionta .30 .75
59 Alexei Yashin .30 .75
60 Miroslav Satan .30 .75
61 Rick DiPietro .30 .75
62 Jaromir Jagr 1.00 2.50
63 Kevin Weekes .30 .75
64 Tom Poti .25 .60
65 Dany Heatley .40 1.00
66 Dominik Hasek .60 1.50
67 Martin Havlat .40 1.00
68 Jason Spezza .40 1.00
69 Daniel Alfredsson .40 1.00
70 Robert Esche .30 .75
71 Peter Forsberg .50 1.25
72 Keith Primeau .40 1.00
73 Simon Gagne .40 1.00
74 Shane Doan .30 .75
75 Curtis Joseph .40 1.00
76 Mario Lemieux 1.25 3.00
77 Zigmund Palffy .40 1.00
78 Mark Recchi .50 1.25
79 Marc-Andre Fleury .60 1.50
80 Joe Thornton .50 1.25
81 Jonathan Cheechoo .40 1.00
82 Evgeni Nabokov .30 .75
83 Patrick Marleau .40 1.00
84 Keith Tkachuk .40 1.00
85 Doug Weight .40 1.00
86 Martin St. Louis .40 1.00
87 Brad Richards .40 1.00
88 Sean Burke .25 .60
89 Vincent Lecavalier .30 .75
90 Mats Sundin .40 1.00
91 Nik Antropov .30 .75
92 Eric Lindros .60 1.50
93 Ed Belfour .40 1.00
94 Jason Allison .30 .75
95 Markus Naslund .40 1.00
96 Todd Bertuzzi .40 1.00
97 Brendan Morrison .25 .60
98 Ed Jovanovski .30 .75
99 Jeff Friesen .25 .60
100 Olaf Kolzig .40 1.00
101 Gilbert Brule RC 60.00 120.00
102 Thomas Vanek RC 150.00 300.00
103 Alexander Ovechkin RC 750.00 1000.00
104 Jeff Carter RC 200.00 400.00
105 Corey Perry RC 150.00 300.00
106 Sidney Crosby RC 2000.00 3500.00
107 Ryan Getzlaf RC 8.00 20.00
108 Hannu Toivonen RC 4.00 10.00
109 Dion Phaneuf RC 8.00 20.00
110 Cam Ward RC 6.00 15.00
111 Wojtek Wolski RC 3.00 8.00
112 Jim Howard RC 10.00 25.00
113 Rostislav Olesz RC 3.00 8.00
114 Alexander Perezhogin RC 3.00 8.00
115 Zach Parise RC 12.00 30.00
116 Mikko Koivu RC 5.00 12.00
117 Mike Richards RC 10.00 25.00
118 Alexander Steen RC 8.00 20.00
119 Braydon Coburn RC 3.00 8.00
120 Andrew Alberts RC 2.00 5.00
121 Eric Nystrom RC 2.50 6.00
122 Kevin Nastiuk RC 2.00 5.00
123 Brent Seabrook RC 6.00 15.00
124 R.J. Umberger RC 3.00 8.00
125 Cam Barker RC 2.50 6.00
126 Peter Budaj RC 4.00 10.00
127 Jussi Jokinen RC 3.00 8.00
128 Johan Franzen RC 6.00 15.00
129 Brad Winchester RC 3.00 8.00
130 Anthony Stewart RC 2.50 6.00
131 Matt Foy RC 2.00 5.00
132 Yann Danis RC 2.50 6.00
133 Ryan Suter RC 4.00 10.00
134 Petteri Nokelainen RC 2.00 5.00
135 Chris Campoli RC 2.00 5.00
136 Al Montoya RC 3.00 8.00
137 Henrik Lundqvist RC 15.00 40.00
138 Ryan Whitney RC 3.00 8.00
139 Andrej Meszaros RC 2.50 6.00
140 Keith Ballard RC 2.50 6.00
141 David Leneveu RC 2.50 6.00
142 Jeff Woywitka RC 2.00 5.00
143 Jim Slater RC 2.00 5.00
144 Adam Berkhoel RC 2.00 5.00
145 Kevin Dallman RC 2.00 5.00
146 Milan Jurcina RC 2.00 5.00
147 Niklas Nordgren RC 2.50 6.00
148 Duncan Keith RC 7.50 15.00
149 Jaroslav Balastik RC 1.50 4.00
150 Brett Lebda RC 1.50 4.00
151 Kyle Brodziak RC 1.50 4.00
152 George Parros RC 1.50 4.00
153 Derek Boogaard RC 3.00 8.00
154 Mark Streit RC 1.50 4.00
155 Raitis Ivanans RC 1.50 4.00
156 Ryan Hollweg RC 1.50 4.00
157 Chris Holt RC 1.50 4.00
158 Petr Prucha RC 2.50 6.00
159 Brian McGrattan RC 1.50 4.00
160 Patrick Eaves RC 2.50 6.00
161 Wade Skolney RC 1.50 4.00
162 Maxime Talbot RC 2.50 6.00
163 Ryane Clowe RC 3.00 8.00
164 Josh Gorges RC 2.00 5.00
165 Andy Roach RC 1.50 4.00
166 Jay McClement RC 1.50 4.00
167 Jeff Hoggan RC 1.50 4.00
168 Lee Stempniak RC 2.50 6.00
169 Colin Hemingway RC 1.50 4.00
170 Timo Helbling RC 1.50 4.00
171 Paul Ranger RC 1.50 4.00
172 Andrew Wozniewski RC 2.00 5.00
173 Robert Nilsson RC 2.50 6.00
174 Rene Bourque RC 2.50 6.00
175 Brandon Bochenski RC 2.50 6.00
176 Steve Bernier RC 2.50 6.00
177 Evgeny Artyukhin RC 2.00 5.00
178 Christoph Schubert RC 1.50 4.00
179 Jakub Klepis RC 1.50 4.00
180 Dimitri Patzold RC 1.50 4.00
181 Vojtech Polak RC 1.50 4.00
182 Rob McVicar RC 2.00 5.00
183 Staffan Kronwall RC 1.50 4.00
184 Jordan Sigalet RC 1.50 4.00
185 Dustin Penner RC 2.50 6.00
186 Michael Wall RC 2.00 5.00
187 Zenon Konopka RC 1.50 4.00
188 Jay Leach RC 2.00 5.00
189 Danny Richmond RC 1.50 4.00
190 Martin St. Pierre RC 1.50 4.00
191 Andrew Penner RC 2.00 5.00
192 Steve Goertzen RC 1.50 4.00
193 Ole-Kristian Tollefsen RC 2.00 5.00
194 Junior Lessard RC 1.50 4.00
195 Danny Syvret RC 1.50 4.00
196 Greg Jacina RC 1.50 4.00
197 Jeff Giuliano RC 2.00 5.00
198 Adam Hauser RC 2.00 5.00
199 Maxim Lapierre RC 2.50 6.00
200 Barry Tallackson RC 2.00 5.00
201 Cam Janssen RC 2.00 5.00
202 Kevin Colley RC 2.00 5.00
203 Jeremy Colliton RC 1.50 4.00
204 Yanick Lehoux RC 2.50 6.00
205 Erik Christensen RC 1.50 4.00
206 Dennis Wideman RC 1.50 4.00
207 Nick Tarnasky RC 1.50 4.00
208 Brian Eklund RC 2.00 5.00
209 Gerald Coleman RC 1.50 4.00
210 Tomas Fleischmann RC 2.50 6.00
211 Brad Richardson RC 2.50 6.00
212 Mark Cullen RC 2.00 5.00
213 Jean-Philippe Cote RC 1.50 4.00
214 Andrei Kostitsyn RC 4.00 10.00
215 Matt Jones RC 1.50 4.00
216 Ben Eager RC 2.00 5.00
217 Andrew Ladd RC 3.00 8.00
218 Bruno Gervais RC 1.50 4.00
219 Jeff Tambellini RC 1.50 4.00
220 Kevin Klein RC 1.50 4.00
221 Kyle Quincey RC 2.00 5.00
222 Chris Thorburn RC 2.00 5.00
223 Doug Murray RC 1.50 4.00
224 Eric Healey RC 2.00 5.00
225 Grant Stevenson RC 1.50 4.00
226 Ryan Ready RC 2.00 5.00
227 Vitaly Kolesnik RC 2.00 5.00
228 Geoff Platt RC 2.00 5.00
229 Chris Beckford-Tseu RC 2.00 5.00
230 Jon DiSalvatore RC 2.00 5.00
231 Ben Walter RC 1.50 4.00
232 Jonathan Ferland RC 2.00 5.00
233 Kevin Bieksa RC 3.00 8.00
234 Rick Rypien RC 3.00 8.00
235 Alexandre Burrows RC 3.00 8.00
236 David Steckel RC 2.00 5.00
237 Mike Green RC 4.00 10.00
238 Richie Regehr RC 1.50 4.00
239 Josh Gratton RC 2.00 5.00
240 Chad Larose RC 1.50 4.00
241 Petr Kanko RC 2.00 5.00
242 Matt Ryan RC 2.00 5.00
243 Connor James RC 2.00 5.00
244 Richard Petiot RC 2.00 5.00
245 Darren Reid RC 1.50 4.00
246 Ryan Craig RC 1.50 4.00
247 Matt Greene RC 1.50 4.00
248 Rob Globke RC 1.50 4.00
249 Colby Armstrong RC 2.50 6.00
250 Greg Zanon RC 2.00 5.00
251 Pekka Rinne RC 8.00 20.00
252 Valtteri Filppula RC 3.00 8.00
253 Daniel Paille RC 2.50 6.00
254 Nathan Paetsch RC 2.00 5.00
255 Jiri Novotny RC 2.00 5.00
256 Petr Taticek RC 2.00 5.00
257 Alexandre Picard RC 1.50 4.00
258 Keith Aucoin RC 1.50 4.00
259 Alexandre Picard RC 1.50 4.00
260 Corey Crawford RC 8.00 20.00
261 Jason Ryznar RC 1.50 4.00
262 Doug O'Brien RC 1.50 4.00
263 Mike Glumac RC 2.00 5.00
264 Jay Harrison RC 2.00 5.00
265 Ben Guite RC 2.00 5.00
266 Mark Giordano RC 2.50 6.00
267 David Gove RC 2.00 5.00
268 J-F Jacques RC 1.50 4.00

2005-06 Upper Deck Ice Rainbow

*RAINBOW/100: 6X TO 15X BASIC CARDS
STATED PRINT RUN 100 SER.#'d SETS

2005-06 Upper Deck Ice Cool Threads

STATED ODDS 1:36
*GLASS/100: .5X TO 2X BASIC JSY
*PATCH/50: 1.5X TO 4X BASIC JSY
CTAO Alexander Ovechkin 10.00 25.00
CTAP Alexander Perezhogin 2.00 5.00
CTAR Andrew Raycroft 2.50 6.00
CTAS Alexander Steen 5.00 12.00
CTBS Brent Seabrook 5.00 12.00
CTCP Corey Perry 10.00 25.00
CTCW Cam Ward 4.00 10.00
CTDP Dion Phaneuf 4.00 10.00
CTGB Gilbert Brule 2.50 6.00
CTHL Henrik Lundqvist 10.00 25.00
CTHT Hannu Toivonen 2.50 6.00
CTJB Jay Bouwmeester 3.00 8.00
CTJC Jeff Carter 5.00 12.00
CTJJ Jaromir Jagr 8.00 20.00
CTJK Jussi Jokinen 2.50 6.00
CTJO Jose Theodore 3.00 8.00
CTJT Joe Thornton 4.00 10.00
CTMB Martin Brodeur 6.00 15.00
CTMH Milan Hejduk 2.50 6.00
CTML Matthew Lombardi 2.00 5.00
CTMM Mike Modano 5.00 12.00
CTMN Markus Naslund 3.00 8.00
CTMP Michael Peca 2.50 6.00
CTMR Mike Richards 5.00 12.00
CTMV Martin Havlat 3.00 8.00
CTNH Nathan Horton 3.00 8.00
CTNI Robert Nilsson 2.50 6.00
CTPB Patrice Bergeron 4.00 10.00
CTPE Patrik Elias 3.00 8.00
CTRG Ryan Getzlaf 6.00 15.00
CTRL Roberto Luongo 5.00 12.00
CTRN Rick Nash 3.00 8.00
CTRS Ryan Suter 3.00 8.00
CTSC Sidney Crosby 15.00 40.00
CTSG Simon Gagne 3.00 8.00
CTTR Tuomo Ruutu 3.00 8.00
CTTV Thomas Vanek 5.00 12.00
CTVO Tomas Vokoun 2.50 6.00
CTZC Zdeno Chara 3.00 8.00
CTZP Zach Parise 6.00 15.00

2005-06 Upper Deck Ice Cool Threads Autographs

STATED PRINT RUN 35 SER.#'d SETS
ACTAO Alexander Ovechkin 125.00 250.00
ACTAP Alexander Perezhogin 8.00 20.00
ACTAR Andrew Raycroft 20.00 50.00
ACTAS Alexander Steen 40.00 80.00
ACTBS Brent Seabrook 20.00 50.00
ACTCP Corey Perry 30.00 60.00
ACTCW Cam Ward 25.00 60.00
ACTDP Dion Phaneuf 50.00 100.00
ACTGB Gilbert Brule 15.00 40.00
ACTHL Henrik Lundqvist 50.00 100.00
ACTHT Hannu Toivonen 10.00 25.00
ACTJB Jay Bouwmeester 10.00 25.00
ACTJC Jeff Carter 25.00 60.00
ACTJK Jussi Jokinen 10.00 25.00
ACTJO Jose Theodore 25.00 60.00
ACTJT Joe Thornton 30.00 60.00
ACTMB Martin Brodeur 40.00 100.00
ACTMH Milan Hejduk 8.00 20.00
ACTMM Mike Modano 20.00 40.00
ACTMN Markus Naslund 20.00 50.00
ACTMP Michael Peca 10.00 25.00
ACTMR Mike Richards 20.00 40.00
ACTMV Martin Havlat 20.00 40.00
ACTNH Nathan Horton
ACTNI Robert Nilsson 10.00 25.00
ACTPB Patrice Bergeron 30.00 60.00
ACTRG Ryan Getzlaf 20.00 50.00
ACTRL Roberto Luongo 15.00 40.00
ACTRN Rick Nash 25.00 50.00
ACTRS Ryan Suter 12.00 30.00
ACTSC Sidney Crosby 350.00 500.00
ACTSD Shane Doan 8.00 20.00
ACTSG Simon Gagne 10.00 25.00
ACTTR Tuomo Ruutu 15.00 40.00
ACTTV Thomas Vanek 20.00 50.00
ACTZC Zdeno Chara 10.00 25.00
ACTZP Zach Parise 25.00 60.00

2005-06 Upper Deck Ice Fresh Ice

*GLASS: .8X TO 2X BASIC JSY
*GLSS PTCH/35-50: 1.5X TO 4X BASIC JSY
FIAF Alexander Frolov 2.00 5.00
FIAH Adam Hall 2.00 5.00
FIAS Anthony Stewart 2.50 6.00
FIBB Brandon Bochenski 3.00 8.00
FIBC Braydon Coburn 3.00 8.00
FIBS Brent Seabrook 6.00 15.00
FIBU Peter Budaj 4.00 10.00
FIBW Brad Winchester 3.00 8.00
FIDB Dustin Brown 3.00 8.00
FIEN Eric Nystrom 2.50 6.00
FIGP George Parros 2.00 5.00
FIHE Ales Hemsky 2.50 6.00
FIHV Martin Havlat 3.00 8.00
FIHZ Henrik Zetterberg 4.00 10.00
FIJB Jay Bouwmeester 3.00 8.00
FIJF Johan Franzen 5.00 12.00
FIJJ Jussi Jokinen 3.00 8.00
FIJL Jordan Leopold 2.00 5.00
FIJP Joni Pitkanen 2.00 5.00
FIKL Kari Lehtonen 2.50 6.00
FILU Joffrey Lupul 2.50 6.00
FIMC Jay McClement 2.00 5.00
FIMH Marcel Hossa 2.00 5.00
FIMJ Milan Jurcina 2.50 6.00
FIMM Milan Michalek 2.00 5.00
FIMR Mike Richards 6.00 15.00
FIMT Maxime Talbot 3.00 8.00
FIPB Patrice Bergeron 4.00 10.00
FIPN Petteri Nokelainen 2.00 5.00
FIPP Petr Prucha 3.00 8.00
FIPS Philippe Sauve 2.50 6.00
FIRC Ryane Clowe 4.00 10.00
FIRG Ryan Getzlaf 8.00 20.00
FIRI Mike Ribeiro 2.50 6.00
FIRK Ryan Kesler 4.00 10.00
FIRM Ryan Miller 3.00 8.00
FIRS Ryan Suter 4.00 10.00
FIRT Raffi Torres 2.00 5.00
FIYD Yann Danis 2.50 6.00
FIZP Zach Parise 8.00 20.00

2005-06 Upper Deck Ice Frozen Fabrics

*GLASS/100: .6X TO 1.5X BASIC JSY
*PATCH/50: 1X TO 2.5X BASIC JSY
FFAT Alex Tanguay 5.00 12.00
FFAY Alexei Yashin 4.00 10.00
FFBS Brendan Shanahan 6.00 15.00
FFCO Chris Osgood 5.00 12.00
FFCP Chris Pronger 4.00 10.00
FFDA Daniel Alfredsson 5.00 12.00
FFDH Dany Heatley 5.00 12.00
FFDW Doug Weight 5.00 12.00
FFEB Ed Belfour 5.00 12.00
FFGM Glen Murray 4.00 10.00
FFIK Ilya Kovalchuk 5.00 12.00
FFJI Jarome Iginla 5.00 12.00
FFJP Joni Pitkanen 3.00 8.00
FFJR Jeremy Roenick 5.00 12.00
FFJS Joe Sakic 6.00 15.00
FFJT Jocelyn Thibault 4.00 10.00
FFKP Keith Primeau 5.00 12.00
FFKT Keith Tkachuk 5.00 12.00
FFMB Martin Brodeur 8.00 20.00
FFMK Miikka Kiprusoff 4.00 10.00
FFML Mario Lemieux 8.00 20.00
FFMM Milan Michalek 3.00 8.00
FFMS Mats Sundin 5.00 12.00
FFMT Marty Turco 5.00 12.00
FFNK Nikolai Khabibulin 5.00 12.00
FFPD Pavel Datsyuk 6.00 15.00
FFPF Peter Forsberg 8.00 20.00
FFPK Paul Kariya 6.00 15.00
FFPM Patrick Marleau 5.00 12.00
FFPR Patrick Roy 8.00 20.00
FFRB Ray Bourque 6.00 15.00
FFRS Ryan Smyth 4.00 10.00
FFSC Sidney Crosby 15.00 40.00
FFSK Saku Koivu 5.00 12.00
FFSL Martin St. Louis 5.00 12.00
FFSP Jason Spezza 5.00 12.00
FFSY Steve Yzerman 8.00 20.00
FFSZ Sergei Zubov 4.00 10.00
FFTB Todd Bertuzzi 5.00 12.00
FFVL Vincent Lecavalier 4.00 10.00
FFZP Zigmund Palffy 5.00 12.00

2005-06 Upper Deck Ice Frozen Fabrics Autographs

STATED PRINT RUN 35 SER.#'d SETS
AFFAT Alex Tanguay 15.00 40.00
AFFAY Alexei Yashin 12.00 30.00
AFFCO Chris Osgood 15.00 40.00
AFFCP Chris Pronger 15.00 40.00
AFFDA Daniel Alfredsson
AFFDH Dany Heatley 15.00 40.00
AFFDW Doug Weight 12.00 30.00
AFFEB Ed Belfour 30.00 80.00
AFFGM Glen Murray 15.00 40.00
AFFIK Ilya Kovalchuk 20.00 50.00
AFFJI Jarome Iginla 20.00 50.00
AFFJP Joni Pitkanen 12.00 30.00
AFFJR Jeremy Roenick 20.00 50.00
AFFJT Jocelyn Thibault 12.00 30.00
AFFKP Keith Primeau 15.00 40.00
AFFMB Martin Brodeur 60.00 125.00
AFFMM Milan Michalek 30.00 60.00
AFFMS Mats Sundin
AFFMT Marty Turco
AFFPR Patrick Roy 100.00 200.00
AFFRB Ray Bourque 40.00 75.00
AFFRS Ryan Smyth 25.00 60.00
AFFSC Sidney Crosby 300.00 500.00
AFFSK Saku Koivu 20.00 50.00
AFFSL Martin St. Louis 12.50 30.00
AFFSP Jason Spezza 15.00 40.00
AFFSZ Sergei Zubov
AFFTB Todd Bertuzzi 15.00 40.00
AFFVL Vincent Lecavalier 40.00 80.00
AFFZP Zigmund Palffy 12.00 30.00

2005-06 Upper Deck Ice Glacial Graphs

GGAF Alexander Frolov 4.00 10.00
GGAO Alexander Ovechkin 50.00 120.00
GGAP Alex Perezhogin 6.00 15.00
GGAR Andrew Raycroft 5.00 12.00
GGCB Cam Barker 5.00 12.00
GGCP Corey Perry 10.00 25.00
GGCW Cam Ward 12.00 30.00
GGDP Dion Phaneuf 15.00 40.00
GGEN Eric Nystrom 4.00 10.00
GGGB Gilbert Brule 6.00 15.00
GGGH Gordie Howe SP 75.00 150.00
GGHO Marian Hossa 6.00 15.00
GGHT Hannu Toivonen 4.00 10.00
GGHV Martin Havlat 6.00 15.00
GGIK Ilya Kovalchuk 15.00 40.00
GGJB Jay Bouwmeester 4.00 10.00
GGJC Jeff Carter 12.00 30.00
GGJI Jarome Iginla 15.00 30.00
GGKB Keith Ballard 4.00 10.00
GGMB Martin Brodeur 40.00 80.00
GGMM Mike Modano SP 20.00 50.00
GGMP Michael Peca 6.00 15.00
GGMR Mike Ribeiro 4.00 10.00
GGMS Matt Stajan 4.00 10.00
GGMT Marty Turco 8.00 20.00
GGNA Rick Nash 12.00 30.00
GGRB Rob Blake SP 12.00 30.00
GGRI Mike Richards 10.00 25.00
GGRK Ryan Kesler 8.00 20.00
GGRL Roberto Luongo 15.00 40.00
GGRM Ryan Miller 15.00 30.00
GGRN Robert Nilsson 4.00 10.00
GGSC Sidney Crosby 175.00 350.00
GGSD Shane Doan 4.00 10.00
GGST Alexander Steen 8.00 20.00
GGTA Tyler Arnason 4.00 10.00
GGTH Trent Hunter 4.00 10.00
GGTL Trevor Linden 10.00 25.00
GGTV Thomas Vanek 10.00 25.00
GGWG Wayne Gretzky SP 750.00 1500.00
GGWW Wojtek Wolski 8.00 20.00
GGZP Zach Parise 8.00 20.00

2005-06 Upper Deck Ice Glacial Graphs Labels

GGCB Cam Barker 8.00 20.00
GGCW Cam Ward 20.00 50.00
GGEN Eric Nystrom 8.00 20.00
GGHT Hannu Toivonen 12.50 30.00
GGJB Jay Bouwmeester 8.00 20.00
GGKB Keith Ballard 8.00 20.00
GGMS Matt Stajan 8.00 20.00
GGRK Ryan Kesler 8.00 20.00
GGRN Robert Nilsson 8.00 20.00
GGTA Tyler Arnason 8.00 20.00
GGTH Trent Hunter 8.00 20.00
GGTV Thomas Vanek 20.00 50.00
GGWW Wojtek Wolski 20.00 50.00
GGZP Zach Parise 12.50 30.00

2005-06 Upper Deck Ice Signature Swatches

SSAO Alexander Ovechkin 100.00 175.00
SSAS Alexander Steen 15.00 40.00
SSAT Alex Tanguay 15.00 40.00
SSBL Brian Leetch 15.00 40.00
SSBO Mike Bossy SP 30.00 80.00
SSCP Chris Pronger 12.00 30.00
SSCW Cam Ward 15.00 40.00
SSDH Dominik Hasek SP 75.00 125.00
SSDW Doug Weight 15.00 40.00
SSEB Ed Belfour SP 20.00 50.00
SSGB Gilbert Brule 15.00 40.00
SSHE Dany Heatley SP 25.00 60.00
SSHZ Henrik Zetterberg 20.00 50.00
SSIK Ilya Kovalchuk/50 SP 30.00 80.00
SSJC Jeff Carter 15.00 40.00
SSJI Jarome Iginla 25.00 60.00
SSJK Jari Kurri/100 SP 25.00 60.00
SSJR Jeremy Roenick SP 15.00 40.00
SSJS Jason Spezza/25 SP 100.00 200.00
SSJT Joe Thornton SP 30.00 80.00
SSLC Luc Robitaille 10.00 25.00
SSMB Martin Brodeur SP 250.00 400.00
SSMH Milan Hejduk 15.00 40.00
SSMM Mike Modano/50 SP 25.00 60.00
SSMN Markus Naslund 15.00 40.00
SSMS Martin St. Louis SP 25.00 60.00
SSNZ Nikolai Zherdev 15.00 40.00
SSPB Patrice Bergeron 15.00 40.00
SSPR Patrick Roy/10 SP
SSRB Ray Bourque SP 60.00 125.00
SSRN Rick Nash/25 SP 100.00 200.00
SSSC S.Crosby/100 SP 250.00 400.00
SSSG Simon Gagne 10.00 25.00
SSSK Saku Koivu SP 25.00 60.00
SSSU Mats Sundin/15 SP
SSTB Todd Bertuzzi 15.00 40.00
SSTH Jose Theodore 12.00 30.00
SSVL Vincent Lecavalier SP 30.00 80.00
SSZP Z.Palffy/55 SP 25.00 60.00

2007-08 Upper Deck Ice

This set was released on March 14, 2008. The base set consists of 226 cards. Cards 1-100 feature veterans, cards 101-142 are rookies serial numbered of 1999, cards 143-184 are rookies serial numbered of 999, cards 185-210 are rookies serial numbered of 499, and cards 211-226 are rookies serial numbered of 99.
COMP.SET w/o SPs (100) 15.00 40.00
101-142 ROOKIE PRINT RUN 1999
143-184 ROOKIE PRINT RUN 999
185-210 ROOKIE PRINT RUN 499
211-226 ROOKIE PRINT RUN 99
1 Martin Brodeur 1.00 2.50
2 Zach Parise .60 1.50
3 Patrik Elias .50 1.25
4 Rick DiPietro .40 1.00
5 Bill Guerin .50 1.25
6 Miroslav Satan .40 1.00
7 Jaromir Jagr 1.25 3.00
8 Henrik Lundqvist .60 1.50
9 Chris Drury .40 1.00
10 Brendan Shanahan .60 1.50
11 Simon Gagne .50 1.25
12 Daniel Briere .50 1.25
13 Jeff Carter .50 1.25
14 Sidney Crosby 2.00 5.00
15 Marc-Andre Fleury .75 2.00
16 Evgeni Malkin 1.50 4.00
17 Jordan Staal .50 1.25
18 Patrice Bergeron .60 1.50
19 Phil Kessel .60 1.50
20 Marc Savard .30 .75
21 Thomas Vanek .60 1.50
22 Ryan Miller .50 1.25
23 Jason Pominville .50 1.25
24 Saku Koivu .50 1.25
25 Michael Ryder .30 .75
26 Guillaume Latendresse .40 1.00
27 Cristobal Huet .40 1.00
28 Jason Spezza .50 1.25
29 Daniel Alfredsson .50 1.25
30 Ray Emery .40 1.00
31 Dany Heatley .50 1.25
32 Mats Sundin .50 1.25
33 Darcy Tucker .40 1.00
34 Alexander Steen .50 1.25
35 Vesa Toskala .40 1.00
36 Kari Lehtonen .40 1.00
37 Ilya Kovalchuk .50 1.25
38 Marian Hossa .40 1.00
39 Eric Staal .60 1.50
40 Cam Ward .50 1.25
41 Justin Williams .40 1.00
42 Tomas Vokoun .40 1.00
43 Nathan Horton .50 1.25
44 Olli Jokinen .40 1.00
45 Vincent Lecavalier .40 1.00
46 Martin St. Louis .50 1.25
47 Brad Richards .50 1.25
48 Alexander Ovechkin 2.00 5.00
49 Olaf Kolzig .50 1.25
50 Alexander Semin .50 1.25
51 Martin Havlat .50 1.25
52 Nikolai Khabibulin .50 1.25
53 Sergei Samsonov .40 1.00
54 Rick Nash .50 1.25
55 Sergei Fedorov .75 2.00
56 David Vyborny .30 .75
57 Gilbert Brule .40 1.00
58 Henrik Zetterberg .60 1.50
59 Nicklas Lidstrom .50 1.25
60 Dominik Hasek .60 1.50
61 Pavel Datsyuk .60 1.50
62 Alexander Radulov .50 1.25
63 Chris Mason .40 1.00
64 Jason Arnott .40 1.00
65 Paul Kariya .60 1.50
66 Doug Weight .50 1.25
67 Keith Tkachuk .50 1.25

68 Jerome Iginla .50 1.25
69 Miikka Kiprusoff .40 1.00
70 Alex Tanguay .30 .75
71 Dion Phaneuf .50 1.25
72 Joe Sakic .75 2.00
73 Milan Hejduk .40 1.00
74 Paul Stastny .50 1.25
75 Ryan Smyth .40 1.00
76 Ales Hemsky .40 1.00
77 Dwayne Roloson .40 1.00
78 Joni Pitkanen .30 .75
79 Jarret Stoll .40 1.00
80 Marian Gaborik .60 1.50
81 Pavol Demitra .60 1.50
82 Mikko Koivu .40 1.00
83 Roberto Luongo .60 1.50
84 Markus Naslund .50 1.25
85 Daniel Sedin .50 1.25
86 Henrik Sedin .50 1.25
87 Ryan Getzlaf .75 2.00
88 Jean-Sebastien Giguere .50 1.25
89 Corey Perry .50 1.25
90 Mike Ribeiro .40 1.00
91 Mike Modano .75 2.00
92 Marty Turco .50 1.25
93 Rob Blake .50 1.25
94 Anze Kopitar .75 2.00
95 Alexander Frolov .30 .75
96 David Aebischer .40 1.00
97 Shane Doan .40 1.00
98 Patrick Marleau .50 1.25
99 Jonathan Cheechoo .50 1.25
100 Joe Thornton .60 1.50
101 Tomi Maki/1999 RC 3.00 8.00
102 Tomas Plihal/1999 RC 4.00 10.00
103 Sheldon Brookbank/1999 RC 3.00 8.00
104 Shay Stephenson/1999 RC 3.00 8.00
105 Sebastien Bisaillon/1999 RC 3.00 8.00
106 Scott Munroe/1999 RC 3.00 8.00
107 Riley Cote/1999 RC 4.00 10.00
108 Rich Peverley/1999 RC 5.00 12.00
109 Pierre Parenteau/1999 RC 4.00 10.00
110 Olli Malmivaara/1999 RC 3.00 8.00
111 Nathan Guenin/1999 RC 4.00 10.00
112 Matt Ellis/1999 RC 4.00 10.00
113 Martin Lojek/1999 RC 3.00 8.00
114 Mark Mancari/1999 RC 4.00 10.00
115 Magnus Johansson/1999 RC 3.00 8.00
116 Krys Barch/1999 RC 4.00 10.00
117 Kent Huskins/1999 RC 3.00 8.00
118 Jonas Nordqvist/1999 RC 3.00 8.00
119 Joel Ward/1999 RC 5.00 12.00
120 Joel Lundqvist/1999 RC 3.00 8.00
121 Joe Piskula/1999 RC 3.00 8.00
122 Jamie Hunt/1999 RC 3.00 8.00
123 Gabe Gauthier/1999 RC 3.00 8.00
124 Duncan Milroy/1999 RC 3.00 8.00
125 Drew Fata/1999 RC 3.00 8.00
126 David Koci/1999 RC 3.00 8.00
127 Darcy Campbell/1999 RC 3.00 8.00
128 Danny Bois/1999 RC 3.00 8.00
129 Curtis Glencross/1999 RC 5.00 12.00
130 Colin Fraser/1999 RC 3.00 8.00
131 Bryan Young/1999 RC 3.00 8.00
132 Bryan Bickell/1999 RC 6.00 15.00
133 Bjorn Melin/1999 RC 3.00 8.00
134 Aaron Rome/1999 RC 4.00 10.00
135 Chris Bourque/1999 RC 4.00 10.00
136 Matt Hunwick/1999 RC 4.00 10.00
137 Tanner Glass/1999 RC 3.00 8.00
138 Aaron Voros/1999 RC 3.00 8.00
139 Alexander Nikulin/1999 RC 4.00 10.00
140 Vladimir Sobotka/1999 RC 4.00 10.00
141 Thomas Greiss/1999 RC 6.00 15.00
142 Ivan Baranka/1999 RC 4.00 10.00
143 Jonathan Sigalet/999 RC 4.00 10.00
144 Tom Gilbert/999 RC 5.00 12.00
145 Jeff Schultz/999 RC 5.00 12.00
146 Mark Fraser/999 RC 4.00 10.00
147 David Krejci/999 RC 12.00 30.00
148 David Moss/999 RC 6.00 15.00
149 Petteri Wirtanen/999 RC 4.00 10.00
150 Tomas Popperle/999 RC 5.00 12.00
151 Daniel Girardi/999 RC 5.00 12.00
152 Ryan Parent/999 RC 4.00 10.00
153 Tobias Stephan/999 RC 5.00 12.00
154 Marc Methot/999 RC 4.00 10.00
155 David Clarkson/999 RC 6.00 15.00
156 Tyler Weiman/999 RC 5.00 12.00
157 Mike Lundin/999 RC 4.00 10.00
158 Ryan Carter/999 RC 4.00 10.00
159 Mike Weber/999 RC 4.00 10.00
160 Daniel Winnik/999 RC 5.00 12.00
161 Tobias Enstrom/999 RC 6.00 15.00
162 Jared Boll/999 RC 5.00 12.00
163 Matt Keetley/999 RC 5.00 12.00
164 Stefan Meyer/999 RC 5.00 12.00
165 Patrick Kaleta/999 RC 4.00 10.00
166 Rod Pelley/999 RC 4.00 10.00
167 Jonas Hiller/999 RC 8.00 20.00
168 Brandon Dubinsky/999 RC 8.00 20.00
169 Jaroslav Hlinka/999 RC 5.00 12.00
170 Cory Murphy/999 RC 4.00 10.00
171 Denis Tolpeko/999 RC 4.00 10.00
172 Craig Weller/999 RC 4.00 10.00
173 Steve Wagner/999 RC 4.00 10.00
174 Jeff Finger/999 RC 4.00 10.00
175 Chris Conner/999 RC 4.00 10.00
176 Lukas Kaspar/999 RC 4.00 10.00
177 Ville Koistinen/999 RC 4.00 10.00
178 Zach Stortini/999 RC 4.00 10.00
179 Brady Murray/999 RC 4.00 10.00
180 Tyler Kennedy/999 RC 6.00 15.00
181 Matt Moulson/999 RC 6.00 15.00
182 John Zeiler/999 RC 4.00 10.00
183 Cal Clutterbuck/999 RC 8.00 20.00
184 Daniel Carcillo/999 RC 5.00 12.00
185 Kris Russell/499 RC 6.00 15.00
186 Matt Niskanen/499 RC 8.00 20.00
187 Nicklas Bergfors/499 RC 5.00 12.00
188 Brett Sterling/499 RC 5.00 12.00
189 Martin Hanzal/499 RC 6.00 15.00
190 Matt Smaby/499 RC 5.00 12.00
191 Petr Kalus/499 RC 5.00 12.00
192 Andy Greene/499 RC 6.00 15.00
193 Frans Nielsen/499 RC 8.00 20.00
194 Rob Schremp/499 RC 6.00 15.00
195 Kyle Chipchura/499 RC 8.00 20.00
196 Jonathan Bernier/499 RC 25.00 40.00
197 Tuukka Rask/499 RC 20.00 50.00
198 Lauri Tukonen/499 RC 5.00 12.00
199 Ondrej Pavelec/499 RC 10.00 25.00
200 Mason Raymond/499 RC 8.00 20.00
201 Ryan Callahan/499 RC 10.00 25.00
202 Curtis McElhinney/499 RC 8.00 20.00
203 Brian Elliott/499 RC 10.00 25.00
204 Drew Miller/499 RC 6.00 15.00
205 David Perron/499 RC 8.00 20.00
206 Anton Stralman/499 RC 5.00 12.00
207 Torrey Mitchell/499 RC 6.00 15.00
208 Jaroslav Halak/499 RC 12.00 30.00
209 Jannik Hansen/499 RC 6.00 15.00
210 Milan Lucic/499 RC 25.00 60.00
211 Bobby Ryan/99 RC 60.00 150.00
212 Jonathan Toews/99 RC 400.00 800.00
213 Sam Gagner/99 RC 125.00 200.00
214 Carey Price/99 RC 500.00 800.00
215 Jiri Tlusty/99 RC 40.00 100.00
216 Erik Johnson/99 RC 30.00 80.00
217 Nicklas Backstrom/99 RC 75.00 150.00
218 Jack Johnson/99 RC 25.00 60.00
219 Devin Setoguchi/99 RC 40.00 100.00
220 Bryan Little/99 RC 40.00 80.00
221 Patrick Kane/99 RC 400.00 800.00
222 Andrew Cogliano/99 RC 40.00 100.00
223 Marc Staal/99 RC 40.00 100.00
224 Nick Foligno/99 RC 25.00 60.00
225 Peter Mueller/99 RC 30.00 80.00
226 James Sheppard/99 RC 25.00 60.00

2007-08 Upper Deck Ice Black Ice Jerseys

BIAO Alexander Ovechkin 15.00 40.00
BIAT Alex Tanguay 3.00 8.00
BIBC Bobby Clarke 6.00 15.00
BIBR Martin Brodeur 10.00 25.00
BIBS Borje Salming 5.00 12.00
BIDH Dany Heatley 5.00 12.00
BIEM Evgeni Malkin 15.00 40.00
BIES Eric Staal 6.00 15.00
BIGF Grant Fuhr 6.00 15.00
BIGP Gilbert Perreault 6.00 15.00
BIHA Dominik Hasek 6.00 15.00
BIIK Ilya Kovalchuk 5.00 12.00
BIJG Jean-Sebastien Giguere 5.00 12.00
BIJI Jarome Iginla 5.00 12.00
BIJS Jordan Staal 5.00 12.00
BIJT Joe Thornton 6.00 15.00
BILR Larry Robinson 6.00 15.00
BIMB Mike Bossy 5.00 12.00
BIMD Marcel Dionne 8.00 20.00
BIMG Marian Gaborik 6.00 15.00
BIML Mario Lemieux SP 15.00 40.00
BIMM Mark Messier SP 30.00 60.00
BIMN Markus Naslund 5.00 12.00
BIMO Mike Modano 8.00 20.00
BIMR Michael Ryder 3.00 8.00
BIMS Martin St. Louis 5.00 12.00
BINL Nicklas Lidstrom 5.00 12.00
BIPB Patrice Bergeron 6.00 15.00
BIPR Patrick Roy SP 25.00 60.00
BIRB Ray Bourque 10.00 25.00
BIRG Ryan Getzlaf 8.00 20.00
BIRM Ryan Miller 5.00 12.00
BIRN Rick Nash 5.00 12.00
BISC Sidney Crosby 20.00 50.00
BISD Shane Doan 4.00 10.00
BISG Simon Gagne 5.00 12.00
BISM Stan Mikita 8.00 20.00
BITV Thomas Vanek 6.00 15.00
BIVL Vincent Lecavalier 4.00 10.00
BIVO Tomas Vokoun 4.00 10.00
BIWG Wayne Gretzky SP 40.00 100.00
BIZP Zach Parise 6.00 15.00

2007-08 Upper Deck Ice Black Ice Jerseys Autographs

BIAO A. Ovechkin EXCH 300.00 450.00
BIEM Evgeni Malkin 60.00 120.00
BIES Eric Staal 25.00 60.00
BIHA D. Hasek EXCH 40.00 80.00
BIIK Ilya Kovalchuk 40.00 80.00
BIJI Jarome Iginla 40.00 80.00
BIJT Joe Thornton 30.00 80.00
BILR Larry Robinson 20.00 50.00
BIMG Marian Gaborik 20.00 50.00
BIML Mario Lemieux SP 250.00 350.00
BIMO Mike Modano 40.00 80.00
BIMS Martin St. Louis 20.00 50.00
BIPB Patrice Bergeron 25.00 60.00
BIPR P. Roy SP EXCH 300.00 450.00
BIRB R. Bourque EXCH 30.00 80.00
BIRG Ryan Getzlaf 20.00 50.00
BIRN Rick Nash 40.00 80.00
BISC S. Crosby EXCH 350.00 500.00
BISD Shane Doan 15.00 40.00
BISM Stan Mikita 20.00 50.00
BIVL Vincent Lecavalier 15.00 40.00
BIVO Tomas Vokoun 15.00 40.00
BIWG Wayne Gretzky SP 500.00 800.00

2007-08 Upper Deck Ice Fresh Threads

*BLACK/25: 1X TO 2.5X BASIC JSY
*PARALLEL/100: .5X TO 1.2X BASIC JSY
*PATCH/25: 1.2X TO 3X BASIC JSY
FTAC Andrew Cogliano 3.00 8.00
FTAG Andy Greene 2.50 6.00
FTBA Nicklas Backstrom 6.00 15.00
FTBD Brandon Dubinsky 4.00 10.00
FTBE Brian Elliott 4.00 10.00
FTBL Bryan Little 2.50 6.00
FTBR Bobby Ryan 6.00 15.00
FTBS Brett Sterling 2.00 5.00
FTCA Ryan Callahan 4.00 10.00
FTCM Curtis McElhinney 3.00 8.00
FTCP Carey Price 12.00 30.00
FTDK David Krejci 6.00 15.00
FTDM Drew Miller 2.50 6.00
FTDP David Perron 3.00 8.00
FTEJ Erik Johnson 3.00 8.00
FTFN Frans Nielsen 3.00 8.00
FTHA Jaroslav Halak 5.00 12.00
FTJA Jannik Hansen 2.50 6.00
FTJB Jonathan Bernier 5.00 12.00
FTJH Jaroslav Hlinka 2.50 6.00
FTJJ Jack Johnson 2.50 6.00
FTJS James Sheppard 2.00 5.00
FTJT Jonathan Toews 12.00 30.00
FTKA Petr Kalus 2.00 5.00
FTKC Kyle Chipchura 3.00 8.00
FTKR Kris Russell 2.50 6.00
FTLT Lauri Tukonen 2.00 5.00
FTMH Martin Hanzal 2.50 6.00
FTML Milan Lucic 10.00 25.00
FTMN Matt Niskanen 3.00 8.00
FTMR Mason Raymond 3.00 8.00
FTMS Matt Smaby 2.00 5.00
FTNB Nicklas Bergfors 2.00 5.00
FTNF Nick Foligno 4.00 10.00
FTPK Patrick Kane 6.00 15.00
FTPM Peter Mueller 2.50 6.00
FTRC Ryan Carter 2.00 5.00
FTRP Ryan Parent 2.00 5.00
FTRS Rob Schremp 2.50 6.00
FTSG Sam Gagner 4.00 10.00
FTTG Tom Gilbert 2.50 6.00
FTTM Torrey Mitchell 2.50 6.00

2007-08 Upper Deck Ice Frozen Fabrics

*BLACK/25: .8X TO 2X BASIC JSY
*PATCH/25: 1X TO 2.5X BASIC JSY
FFAE David Aebischer 3.00 8.00
FFAH Ales Hemsky 3.00 8.00
FFAO Alexander Ovechkin 15.00 40.00
FFAT Alex Tanguay 2.50 6.00
FFBB Brad Boyes 2.50 6.00
FFBR Brad Richards 4.00 10.00
FFBS Brendan Shanahan 5.00 12.00
FFCD Chris Drury 3.00 8.00
FFDA Daniel Alfredsson 4.00 10.00
FFDB Daniel Briere 4.00 10.00
FFDH Dany Heatley 4.00 10.00
FFDR Dwayne Roloson 3.00 8.00
FFDW Doug Weight 4.00 10.00
FFES Eric Staal 5.00 12.00
FFHE Milan Hejduk 3.00 8.00
FFHZ Henrik Zetterberg 5.00 12.00
FFIK Ilya Kovalchuk 4.00 10.00
FFJB Jay Bouwmeester 4.00 10.00
FFJG Jean-Sebastien Giguere 4.00 10.00
FFJI Jarome Iginla 4.00 10.00
FFJJ Jaromir Jagr 10.00 25.00
FFJS Jason Spezza 4.00 10.00
FFJT Joe Thornton 5.00 12.00
FFKL Kari Lehtonen 3.00 8.00
FFKT Keith Tkachuk 4.00 10.00
FFMB Martin Brodeur 8.00 20.00
FFMG Marian Gaborik 5.00 12.00
FFMH Marian Hossa 3.00 8.00
FFMK Miikka Kiprusoff 3.00 8.00
FFMN Markus Naslund 4.00 10.00
FFMS Mats Sundin 4.00 10.00
FFPB Patrice Bergeron 5.00 12.00
FFPD Pavel Datsyuk 5.00 12.00
FFPF Peter Forsberg 5.00 12.00
FFPK Paul Kariya 5.00 12.00
FFPM Patrick Marleau 4.00 10.00
FFRL Roberto Luongo 5.00 12.00
FFRS Ryan Smyth 3.00 8.00
FFSA Joe Sakic 6.00 15.00
FFSC Sidney Crosby 15.00 40.00
FFSF Sergei Fedorov 6.00 15.00
FFZP Zach Parise 5.00 12.00

2007-08 Upper Deck Ice Glacial Graphs

GGAK Anze Kopitar 12.00 30.00
GGAO Adam Oates 8.00 20.00
GGAR Alexander Radulov 8.00 20.00
GGAT Alex Tanguay 5.00 12.00
GGBC Blake Comeau 5.00 12.00
GGBD Brandon Dubinsky 10.00 25.00
GGBH Bobby Hull SP 12.00 30.00
GGBO Dustin Boyd 5.00 12.00
GGCA Mike Cammalleri 6.00 15.00
GGCH Cristobal Huet 6.00 15.00
GGCM Clarke MacArthur 5.00 12.00
GGCP Chris Phillips 5.00 12.00
GGCW Cam Ward 8.00 20.00
GGDB Dustin Brown 8.00 20.00
GGDH Dany Heatley 8.00 20.00
GGDS Drew Stafford 6.00 15.00
GGDT Darcy Tucker 6.00 15.00
GGEM Evgeni Malkin 30.00 60.00
GGES Eric Staal 10.00 25.00
GGGA Simon Gagne 8.00 20.00
GGGH Gordie Howe SP 100.00 200.00
GGHA Dominik Hasek SP 30.00 80.00
GGHL Henrik Lundqvist 10.00 25.00
GGIK Ilya Kovalchuk 10.00 25.00
GGIW Ian White 5.00 12.00
GGJC Jonathan Cheechoo 8.00 20.00
GGJG Jean-Sebastien Giguere 8.00 20.00
GGJI Jarome Iginla
GGJJ Jack Johnson 6.00 15.00
GGJL John-Michael Liles 5.00 12.00
GGJS Jarret Stoll 6.00 15.00
GGJT Joe Thornton SP 30.00 80.00
GGJW Jeremy Williams 5.00 12.00
GGKB Kevin Bieksa 6.00 15.00
GGKD Kris Draper 5.00 12.00
GGKE Phil Kessel 10.00 25.00
GGLT Lauri Tukonen 5.00 12.00
GGMA Martin St. Louis 8.00 20.00
GGMB Martin Brodeur SP 50.00 100.00
GGMC Matt Carle 5.00 12.00
GGMF Marc-Andre Fleury 10.00 25.00
GGMG Marian Gaborik
GGMI Miroslav Satan 6.00 15.00
GGML Mario Lemieux SP 150.00 250.00
GGMM Mark Messier SP 250.00 400.00
GGMN Markus Naslund 8.00 20.00
GGMO Mike Modano 10.00 25.00
GGMP Marc-Antoine Pouliot 5.00 12.00
GGMR Michael Ryder 5.00 12.00
GGMS Marek Schwarz 8.00 20.00
GGMT Marty Turco 8.00 20.00
GGNL Nicklas Lidstrom 15.00 30.00
GGNW Noah Welch 5.00 12.00
GGOV Alexander Ovechkin SP 50.00 120.00
GGPB Patrice Bergeron 10.00 25.00
GGPE Corey Perry 8.00 20.00
GGPI Pierre-Marc Bouchard 8.00 20.00
GGPK Petr Kalus 5.00 12.00
GGPO Patrick O'Sullivan 6.00 15.00
GGPR Patrick Roy SP 75.00 150.00
GGRA Andrew Raycroft 6.00 15.00
GGRI Mike Richards 8.00 20.00
GGRM Ryan Miller 8.00 20.00
GGRN Rick Nash 8.00 20.00
GGRP Ryan Parent 5.00 12.00
GGRS Rob Schremp 6.00 15.00
GGRY Ryan Potulny 5.00 12.00
GGSA Marc Savard 5.00 12.00
GGSB Steve Bernier 5.00 12.00
GGSC Sidney Crosby SP 150.00 250.00
GGSD Shane Doan 6.00 15.00
GGSG Scott Gomez 6.00 15.00
GGSK Saku Koivu SP
GGST Jordan Staal 8.00 20.00
GGSW Shea Weber 6.00 15.00
GGTH Jose Theodore 8.00 20.00
GGTV Tomas Vokoun 6.00 15.00
GGVF Valtteri Filppula 8.00 20.00
GGVL Vincent Lecavalier 10.00 25.00
GGWG Wayne Gretzky SP 300.00 600.00
GGWI Justin Williams 6.00 15.00
GGWW Wojtek Wolski 6.00 15.00

2007-08 Upper Deck Ice Signature Swatches

STATED ODDS 1:320
SSAO Alexander Ovechkin 60.00 120.00
SSBB Brad Boyes 8.00 20.00
SSCW Cam Ward 12.00 30.00
SSDH Dany Heatley 12.00 30.00
SSDS Drew Stafford 10.00 25.00
SSES Eric Staal 15.00 40.00
SSGA Simon Gagne 12.00 30.00
SSIK Ilya Kovalchuk 12.00 30.00
SSJC Jonathan Cheechoo 12.00 30.00
SSJI Jarome Iginla
SSJL Joffrey Lupul 10.00 25.00
SSJP Joni Pitkanen 8.00 20.00
SSJT Joe Thornton
SSJW Justin Williams 10.00 25.00
SSMB Martin Brodeur 50.00 100.00
SSMC Mike Cammalleri 12.00 30.00
SSMG Marian Gaborik 15.00 40.00
SSML M. Lemieux EXCH 100.00 175.00
SSMM Mike Modano 20.00 40.00
SSMN Markus Naslund 12.00 30.00
SSMS Martin St. Louis 12.00 30.00
SSMT Marty Turco 12.00 30.00
SSNL Nicklas Lidstrom
SSPB Patrice Bergeron 15.00 40.00
SSPK Phil Kessel 15.00 40.00
SSPR Patrick Roy 100.00 175.00
SSRM Ryan Miller 12.00 30.00
SSRN Rick Nash 12.00 30.00
SSSC Sidney Crosby 200.00 400.00
SSSG Scott Gomez 10.00 25.00
SSTH Tomas Holmstrom 10.00 25.00
SSTV Tomas Vokoun 10.00 25.00
SSVL Vincent Lecavalier 10.00 25.00
SSWG Wayne Gretzky 300.00 500.00

2008-09 Upper Deck Ice

This set was released on March 10, 2009. The base set consists of 226 cards.

COMP.SET w/o SPs (100) 12.00 30.00
(101-121) PRINT RUN 1999 SERIAL #'d SETS
(122-142) PRINT RUN 999 SERIAL #'d SETS
(143-168) PRINT RUN 499 SERIAL #'d SETS
(169-184) PRINT RUN 99 SERIAL #'d SETS
1 Ales Hemsky .40 1.00
2 Alex Kovalev .40 1.00
3 Alex Tanguay .30 .75
4 Alexander Frolov .30 .75
5 Alexander Ovechkin 2.00 5.00
6 Anze Kopitar .75 2.00
7 Brad Boyes .30 .75
8 Brad Richards .50 1.25
9 Alexander Semin .50 1.25
10 Brenden Morrow .40 1.00
11 Cam Ward .50 1.25
12 Carey Price 2.00 5.00
13 Chris Drury .40 1.00
14 Chris Osgood .50 1.25
15 Chris Pronger .40 1.00
16 Corey Perry .50 1.25
17 Cristobal Huet .40 1.00
18 Dan Ellis .30 .75
19 Daniel Alfredsson .50 1.25
20 Daniel Briere .50 1.25
21 Daniel Carcillo .30 .75
22 Daniel Sedin .50 1.25
23 Dany Heatley .50 1.25
24 Derek Roy .30 .75
25 Dion Phaneuf .50 1.25
26 Eric Staal .60 1.50
27 Evgeni Malkin 1.50 4.00
28 Evgeni Nabokov .40 1.00
29 Henrik Lundqvist .60 1.50
30 Henrik Zetterberg .60 1.50
31 Ilya Kovalchuk .50 1.25
32 J.P. Dumont .30 .75
33 Jarome Iginla .50 1.25
34 Jason Arnott .40 1.00
35 Jason Pominville .50 1.25
36 Jason Spezza .50 1.25
37 Jean-Sebastien Giguere .50 1.25
38 Joe Sakic .75 2.00
39 Joe Thornton .60 1.50
40 Jonathan Cheechoo .50 1.25
41 Jonathan Toews 1.25 3.00
42 Joni Pitkanen .30 .75
43 Jordan Staal .50 1.25
44 Kari Lehtonen .40 1.00
45 Manny Legace .50 1.25
46 Marc Savard .30 .75
47 Marc-Andre Fleury .75 2.00
48 Marek Svatos .30 .75
49 Marian Gaborik .60 1.50
50 Markus Naslund .40 1.00
51 Martin Biron .40 1.00
52 Martin Brodeur 1.00 2.50
53 Martin St. Louis .50 1.25
54 Marty Turco .50 1.25
55 Mikhail Grabovski .50 1.25
56 Miikka Kiprusoff .40 1.00
57 Mike Comrie .40 1.00
58 Mike Green .50 1.25
59 Mike Modano .75 2.00
60 Mike Ribeiro .40 1.00
61 Mike Richards .50 1.25
62 Milan Hejduk .40 1.00
63 Nathan Horton .40 1.00
64 Nicklas Backstrom .75 2.00
65 Nicklas Lidstrom .50 1.25
66 Nikolai Zherdev .30 .75
67 Olli Jokinen .40 1.00
68 Patrice Bergeron .60 1.50
69 Patrick Kane 1.00 2.50
70 Patrick Sharp .50 1.25
71 Patrik Elias .50 1.25
72 Paul Kariya .60 1.50
73 Paul Martin .30 .75
74 Paul Stastny .50 1.25
75 Pavel Datsyuk .60 1.50
76 Peter Mueller .40 1.00
77 Phil Kessel .60 1.50
78 Pierre-Marc Bouchard .50 1.25
79 Rick DiPietro .40 1.00
80 Rick Nash .50 1.25
81 Roberto Luongo .60 1.50
82 Ryan Getzlaf .75 2.00
83 Ryan Miller .50 1.25
84 Saku Koivu .50 1.25
85 Sam Gagner .40 1.00
86 Sean Avery .30 .75
87 Shane Doan .40 1.00
88 Shawn Horcoff .30 .75
89 Sidney Crosby 2.00 5.00
90 Simon Gagne .50 1.25
91 Thomas Vanek .50 1.25
92 Tim Thomas .50 1.25
93 Tobias Enstrom .30 .75
94 Tomas Kaberle .30 .75
95 Tomas Vokoun .40 1.00
96 Vesa Toskala .40 1.00
97 Vincent Lecavalier .40 1.00
98 Wade Redden .30 .75
99 Zach Parise .50 1.25
100 Zdeno Chara .50 1.25
101 Jack Hillen RC 2.00 5.00
102 Mark Fistric RC 2.00 5.00
103 Tom Cavanagh RC 2.00 5.00
104 Dane Byers RC 2.00 5.00
105 Dwight Helminen RC 2.50 6.00
106 Jason Garrison RC 2.50 6.00
107 Pierre-Luc Letourneau-Leblond RC 1.50 4.00
108 Tyler Sloan RC 3.00 8.00
109 Simeon Varlamov RC 6.00 15.00
110 Janne Pesonen RC 2.00 5.00
111 Brad Staubitz RC 2.00 5.00
112 Patrick Davis RC 2.00 5.00
113 Cam Paddock RC 1.50 4.00
114 Karl Alzner RC 1.50 4.00
115 John Curry RC 2.50 6.00
116 Zack Smith RC 2.00 5.00
117 Jonathon Kalinski RC 2.50 6.00
118 Tim Sestito RC 2.00 5.00
119 Joey Crabb RC 2.00 5.00
120 Andre Deveaux RC 2.50 6.00
121 Alexandre Bolduc RC 2.00 5.00
122 Brian Boyle RC 2.50 6.00
123 Mike Brown RC 4.00 10.00
124 Ben Maxwell RC 3.00 8.00
125 Matt D'Agostini RC 2.50 6.00
126 Robbie Earl RC 2.00 5.00
127 Jonathan Ericsson RC 3.00 8.00
128 Erik Ersberg RC 2.50 6.00
129 Justin Pogge RC 3.00 8.00
130 Cory Schneider RC 8.00 20.00
131 Jonas Frogren RC 2.00 5.00
132 Alex Goligoski RC 4.00 10.00
133 Shawn Matthias RC 3.00 8.00
134 John Mitchell RC 2.50 6.00
135 Brian Lee RC 2.50 6.00
136 Adam Pardy RC 2.50 6.00
137 Theo Peckham RC 3.00 8.00
138 Teddy Purcell RC 4.00 10.00
139 Mattias Ritola RC 2.50 6.00
140 Tom Sestito RC 3.00 8.00
141 Ryan Stone RC 2.00 5.00
142 Ilya Zubov RC 2.50 6.00
143 T.J. Oshie RC 8.00 20.00
144 Andreas Nodl RC 2.50 6.00
145 Kyle Okposo RC 4.00 10.00
146 Vladimir Mihalik RC 2.50 6.00
147 Darroll Powe RC 4.00 10.00
148 Alex Pietrangelo RC 5.00 12.00
149 Patrik Berglund RC 3.00 8.00
150 Steve Mason RC 6.00 15.00
151 Wayne Simmonds RC 6.00 15.00
152 Drew Doughty RC 10.00 25.00
153 Kevin Porter RC 3.00 8.00
154 Ryan Jones RC 4.00 10.00
155 Matthew Halischuk RC 2.50 6.00
156 Luca Sbisa RC 2.50 6.00
157 Oscar Moller RC 3.00 8.00
158 Patric Hornqvist RC 4.00 10.00
159 Jamie McGinn RC 4.00 10.00
160 Petr Vrana RC 2.50 6.00
161 Claude Giroux RC 15.00 40.00
162 Derek Dorsett RC 5.00 12.00
163 Lauri Korpikoski RC 2.50 6.00
164 Steve MacIntyre RC 4.00 10.00
165 Nikolai Kulemin RC 4.00 10.00
166 Viktor Tikhonov RC 3.00 8.00
167 Justin Abdelkader RC 6.00 15.00
168 Ben Bishop RC 6.00 15.00
169 Jakub Voracek RC 50.00 100.00
170 Josh Bailey RC 25.00 60.00
171 Mikkel Boedker RC 25.00 60.00
172 James Neal RC 30.00 80.00
173 Derick Brassard RC 25.00 60.00
174 Zach Boychuk RC 15.00 40.00
175 Nikita Filatov RC 25.00 60.00
176 Colton Gillies RC 15.00 40.00
177 Luke Schenn RC 40.00 100.00
178 Blake Wheeler RC 40.00 100.00
179 Brandon Sutter RC 25.00 60.00
180 Kyle Turris RC 40.00 80.00
181 Michael Frolik RC 20.00 50.00
182 Fabian Brunnstrom RC 15.00 40.00
183 Zach Bogosian RC 20.00 50.00
184 Steven Stamkos RC 950.00 1400.00

2008-09 Upper Deck Ice Fresh Threads

FTAG Alex Goligoski 4.00 10.00
FTAN Andreas Nodl 2.00 5.00
FTAP Alex Pietrangelo 4.00 10.00
FTBB Brian Boyle 2.50 6.00
FTBL Brian Lee 2.50 6.00
FTBO Zach Bogosian 3.00 8.00
FTBS Brandon Sutter 3.00 8.00
FTBW Blake Wheeler 8.00 20.00
FTCG Colton Gillies 2.50 6.00
FTDB Derick Brassard 2.50 6.00
FTDD Drew Doughty 8.00 20.00
FTFB Fabian Brunnstrom 2.50 6.00
FTFI Mark Fistric 2.50 6.00
FTGI Claude Giroux 6.00 15.00
FTIZ Ilya Zubov 2.50 6.00
FTJA Justin Abdelkader 5.00 12.00
FTJE Jonathan Ericsson 3.00 8.00
FTJF Jon Filewich 2.50 6.00
FTJN James Neal 6.00 15.00
FTJV Jakub Voracek 6.00 15.00
FTKO Kyle Okposo 3.00 8.00
FTKP Kevin Porter 2.50 6.00
FTKT Kyle Turris 5.00 12.00
FTLK Lauri Korpikoski 2.00 5.00
FTLS Luke Schenn 4.00 10.00
FTMA Steve Mason 5.00 12.00
FTMB Mikkel Boedker 4.00 10.00
FTMF Michael Frolik 3.00 8.00
FTMH Matthew Halischuk 2.00 5.00
FTNF Nikita Filatov 3.00 8.00
FTNK Nikolai Kulemin 3.00 8.00
FTOM Oscar Moller 2.50 6.00
FTPB Patrik Berglund 2.50 6.00
FTPH Patric Hornqvist 3.00 8.00
FTPV Petr Vrana 2.00 5.00
FTSB Luca Sbisa 2.00 5.00
FTSM Shawn Matthias 3.00 8.00
FTSS Steven Stamkos 20.00 50.00
FTTO T.J. Oshie 6.00 15.00
FTVM Vladimir Mihalik 2.00 5.00
FTVT Viktor Tikhonov 2.50 6.00
FTZB Zach Boychuk 3.00 8.00

2008-09 Upper Deck Ice Fresh Threads Black Parallel

*BLACK: .6X TO 1.5X BASE
STATED PRINT RUN 25 SERIAL #'d SETS

2008-09 Upper Deck Ice Fresh Threads Parallel

*PARALLEL: .5X TO 1.2X BASE
STATED PRINT RUN 100 SERIAL #'d SETS

2008-09 Upper Deck Ice Fresh Threads Patches

*PATCHES: .8X TO 2X BASE
STATED PRINT RUN 25 SERIAL #'d SETS

2008-09 Upper Deck Ice Frozen Fabrics

FFAK Alex Kovalev 4.00 10.00
FFBD Brendan Shanahan 6.00 15.00
FFDG Doug Gilmour 6.00 15.00
FFDP Dion Phaneuf 5.00 12.00
FFEM Evgeni Malkin 8.00 20.00
FFES Eric Staal 6.00 15.00
FFFV Sergei Fedorov 8.00 20.00
FFGZ Scott Gomez 4.00 10.00
FFHW Dale Hawerchuk 6.00 15.00
FFIK Ilya Kovalchuk 5.00 12.00
FFJC Jonathan Cheechoo 5.00 12.00
FFJJ Joe Sakic 8.00 20.00
FFKL Kari Lehtonen 4.00 10.00
FFLR Larry Robinson 5.00 12.00
FFLW Rod Langway 4.00 10.00
FFMB Martin Brodeur 10.00 25.00
FFMH Marian Hossa 4.00 10.00
FFMK Mikko Koivu 4.00 10.00
FFMS Mats Sundin 5.00 12.00
FFNL Nicklas Lidstrom 5.00 12.00
FFOK Olaf Kolzig 5.00 12.00
FFOV Alexander Ovechkin 20.00 50.00
FFPE Patrik Elias 5.00 12.00
FFPF Peter Forsberg 6.00 15.00
FFPK Paul Kariya 6.00 15.00
FFPL Pascal Leclaire 4.00 10.00
FFPS Peter Stastny 5.00 12.00
FFRD Rod Brind`Amour 5.00 12.00
FFRN Rick Nash 5.00 12.00
FFSC Sidney Crosby 20.00 50.00
FFSD Shane Doan 4.00 10.00
FFSG Simon Gagne 5.00 12.00
FFSS Steve Shutt 5.00 12.00
FFST Jordan Staal 5.00 12.00
FFTB Todd Bertuzzi 5.00 12.00
FFTR Tuomo Ruutu 5.00 12.00
FFTS Teemu Selanne 10.00 25.00
FFVT Vesa Toskala 4.00 10.00
FFWB Shea Weber 4.00 10.00
FFWR Wade Redden 3.00 8.00
FFWW Wojtek Wolski 4.00 10.00
FFZP Zach Parise 5.00 12.00

2008-09 Upper Deck Ice Frozen Fabrics Black Parallel

*BLACK: .6X TO 1.5X BASE
STATED PRINT RUN 25 SERIAL #'d SETS

2008-09 Upper Deck Ice Frozen Fabrics Parallel

*PARALLEL: .5X TO 1.2X BASE
STATED PRINT RUN 100 SERIAL #'d SETS

2008-09 Upper Deck Ice Frozen Fabrics Patches

*PATCHES: 1X TO 2.5X BASE
STATED PRINT RUN 25 SERIAL #'d SETS

2008-09 Upper Deck Ice Glacial Graphs

GGAE Alexander Edler 5.00 12.00
GGAP Alex Pietrangelo 10.00 25.00
GGAR Andrew Raycroft 6.00 15.00
GGCA Jeff Carter 8.00 20.00
GGCD Daniel Carcillo
GGCM Cory Murphy 5.00 12.00
GGDA Daniel Paille 5.00 12.00
GGDC Dan Cleary 6.00 15.00
GGDD Drew Doughty 20.00 50.00
GGDH Eddie Shack 8.00 20.00
GGDJ David Jones 5.00 12.00
GGDS Devin Setoguchi 6.00 15.00
GGEM Evgeni Malkin 25.00 60.00
GGES Eric Staal 10.00 25.00
GGHS Henrik Sedin 8.00 20.00
GGJH Jonas Hiller 6.00 15.00
GGJL Joffrey Lupul 6.00 15.00
GGJP Jason Pominville 8.00 20.00
GGJS Jordan Staal 8.00 20.00
GGJT Joe Thornton 10.00 25.00
GGJV Jakub Voracek 12.00 30.00
GGKC Kyle Chipchura 6.00 15.00
GGLS Luke Schenn 25.00 60.00
GGMB Mikkel Boedker 15.00 40.00
GGMC Marty McSorley 6.00 15.00
GGMF Marc-Andre Fleury 10.00 25.00
GGMH Milan Hejduk 6.00 15.00
GGMN Matt Niskanen 6.00 15.00
GGMT Maxime Talbot 8.00 20.00
GGND Nigel Dawes 5.00 12.00
GGNH Nathan Horton 6.00 15.00
GGNZ Nikolai Zherdev 5.00 12.00
GGOR Bobby Orr 75.00 135.00
GGPA Patrick Kane 15.00 40.00
GGPM Peter Mueller 6.00 15.00
GGPN Dustin Penner 6.00 15.00
GGPR Carey Price 20.00 50.00
GGRG Ryan Getzlaf 12.00 30.00
GGRL Rod Langway 6.00 15.00
GGRO Rob Schremp 6.00 15.00
GGRP Rod Pelley 5.00 12.00
GGSB Steve Bernier 5.00 12.00
GGSC Sidney Crosby 100.00 175.00
GGSE Daniel Sedin 6.00 15.00
GGSS Steven Stamkos 40.00 100.00
GGTH Tomas Holmstrom 6.00 15.00
GGTK Tyler Kennedy 6.00 15.00
GGTL Jiri Tlusty 6.00 15.00
GGTV Tomas Vokoun 6.00 15.00
GGTW Jonathan Toews 20.00 50.00
GGWG Wayne Gretzky 125.00 250.00
GGZB Zach Bogosian 8.00 20.00
GGZB2 Henrik Zetterberg 10.00 25.00

2008-09 Upper Deck Ice Pride of Canada

GOLD1 Bobby Clarke 8.00 20.00
GOLD2 Bobby Hull 12.00 30.00
GOLD3 Bobby Orr 25.00 60.00
GOLD4 Bryan Trottier 10.00 25.00
GOLD5 Darryl Sittler 8.00 20.00
GOLD6 Denis Potvin 8.00 20.00
GOLD7 Gilbert Perreault 8.00 20.00
GOLD8 Guy Lafleur 10.00 25.00
GOLD9 Jarome Iginla 8.00 20.00
GOLD10 Joe Sakic 12.00 30.00
GOLD11 Jonathan Toews 20.00 50.00
GOLD12 Marcel Dionne 10.00 25.00
GOLD13 Mario Lemieux 25.00 60.00
GOLD14 Martin Brodeur 15.00 40.00
GOLD15 Mike Bossy 8.00 20.00
GOLD16 Dany Heatley 8.00 20.00
GOLD17 Paul Coffey 10.00 25.00
GOLD18 Phil Esposito 12.00 30.00
GOLD19 Sidney Crosby 40.00 100.00
GOLD20 Steve Yzerman 25.00 60.00
GOLD21 Wayne Gretzky 75.00 150.00

2008-09 Upper Deck Ice Signature Swatches

SSJBN Bernie Nicholls 10.00 25.00
SSJCP Carey Price 50.00 125.00
SSJEM Evgeni Malkin 40.00 100.00
SSJGC Guy Carbonneau 12.00 30.00
SSJGH Gordie Howe 75.00 150.00
SSJGO Scott Gomez 10.00 25.00
SSJJF Jon Filewich 10.00 25.00
SSJJT Jonathan Toews 25.00 60.00
SSJKT Kyle Turris 20.00 50.00
SSJLR Luc Robitaille 12.00 30.00
SSJLX Mario Lemieux 60.00 120.00
SSJMA Shawn Matthias 12.00 30.00
SSJNZ Nikolai Zherdev 8.00 20.00
SSJPR Patrick Roy 30.00 80.00
SSJRE Robbie Earl 8.00 20.00
SSJRH Ron Hextall 20.00 50.00
SSJRL Rod Langway 10.00 25.00
SSJRS Ryan Stone 8.00 20.00
SSJSC Sidney Crosby 100.00 200.00
SSJSM Steve Mason 15.00 40.00
SSJTK Tuukka Rask 15.00 40.00
SSJZB Ilya Zubov 10.00 25.00

2008-09 Upper Deck Ice Stanley Cup Foundations

SCFAM Al MacInnis 8.00 20.00
SCFBH Bobby Hull 12.00 30.00
SCFBO Bobby Orr 25.00 60.00
SCFGH Gordie Howe 20.00 50.00
SCFGL Guy Lafleur 10.00 25.00
SCFHZ Henrik Zetterberg 10.00 25.00
SCFJB Jean Beliveau 8.00 20.00
SCFJK Jari Kurri 8.00 20.00
SCFJS Joe Sakic 12.00 30.00
SCFLM Lanny McDonald 8.00 20.00
SCFLR Larry Robinson 8.00 20.00
SCFMB Martin Brodeur 15.00 40.00
SCFMI Mike Bossy 8.00 20.00
SCFML Mario Lemieux 25.00 60.00
SCFMM Mark Messier 10.00 25.00
SCFMO Mike Modano 12.00 30.00
SCFNL Nicklas Lidstrom 8.00 20.00
SCFPF Peter Forsberg 10.00 25.00
SCFPR Patrick Roy 20.00 50.00
SCFSN Scott Niedermayer 6.00 15.00
SCFWG Wayne Gretzky 40.00 100.00

2009-10 Upper Deck Ice

COMP.SET w/o SPS (100) 15.00 40.00
(101-121) PRINT RUN 1999 SER.#'d SETS
(122-142) PRINT RUN 999 SER.#'d SETS
(143-168) PRINT RUN 499 SER.#'d SETS
(169-184) PRINT RUN 99 SER.#'d SETS
1 Zdeno Chara .50 1.25
2 Patrice Bergeron .60 1.50
3 Tim Thomas .50 1.25
4 Marc Savard .30 .75
5 Alexander Ovechkin 2.00 5.00
6 Alexander Semin .50 1.25
7 Mike Green .50 1.25
8 Nicklas Backstrom .75 2.00
9 Martin Brodeur 1.00 2.50
10 Zach Parise .50 1.25
11 Patrik Elias .50 1.25
12 Sidney Crosby 2.00 5.00
13 Evgeni Malkin 1.50 4.00
14 Jordan Staal .50 1.25
15 Marc-Andre Fleury .75 2.00
16 Simon Gagne .50 1.25
17 Mike Richards .50 1.25
18 Jeff Carter .50 1.25
19 Daniel Briere .50 1.25
20 Eric Staal .60 1.50
21 Cam Ward .50 1.25
22 Jussi Jokinen .30 .75
23 Henrik Lundqvist .75 2.00
24 Marian Gaborik .60 1.50
25 Chris Drury .40 1.00
26 Sean Avery .40 1.00
27 Carey Price 2.00 5.00
28 Scott Gomez .40 1.00
29 Andrei Markov .50 1.25
30 Nathan Horton .50 1.25
31 Tomas Vokoun .40 1.00
32 David Booth .30 .75
33 Thomas Vanek .60 1.50
34 Ryan Miller .50 1.25
35 Jason Pominville .50 1.25
36 Derek Roy .40 1.00
37 Jason Spezza .50 1.25
38 Jonathan Cheechoo .50 1.25
39 Daniel Alfredsson .50 1.25
40 Luke Schenn .40 1.00
41 Mikhail Grabovski .50 1.25
42 Vesa Toskala .50 1.25
43 Phil Kessel .60 1.50
44 Ilya Kovalchuk .50 1.25
45 Kari Lehtonen .40 1.00
46 Bryan Little .50 1.25
47 Vincent Lecavalier .40 1.00
48 Martin St. Louis .50 1.25
49 Steven Stamkos 1.00 2.50
50 Doug Weight .50 1.25
51 Rick DiPietro .40 1.00
52 Kyle Okposo .50 1.25
53 Joe Thornton .50 1.25
54 Patrick Marleau .50 1.25
55 Evgeni Nabokov .40 1.00
56 Dany Heatley .50 1.25
57 Henrik Zetterberg .60 1.50
58 Nicklas Lidstrom .50 1.25
59 Pavel Datsyuk .60 1.50
60 Chris Osgood .50 1.25
61 Roberto Luongo .60 1.50
62 Ryan Kesler .50 1.25
63 Daniel Sedin .50 1.25
64 Henrik Sedin .50 1.25
65 Patrick Kane 1.00 2.50
66 Jonathan Toews 1.00 2.50
67 Brian Campbell .40 1.00
68 Marian Hossa .40 1.00
69 Jarome Iginla .50 1.25
70 Dion Phaneuf .60 1.50
71 Olli Jokinen .40 1.00
72 Miikka Kiprusoff .40 1.00
73 David Perron .30 .75
74 Paul Kariya .60 1.50
75 Patrik Berglund .30 .75
76 Rick Nash .40 1.00
77 Steve Mason .40 1.00
78 Derick Brassard .50 1.25
79 Ryan Getzlaf .75 2.00
80 Bobby Ryan .50 1.25

81 Saku Koivu .50 1.25
82 Mikko Koivu .50 1.25
83 Niklas Backstrom .50 1.25
84 Owen Nolan .50 1.25
85 Jason Arnott .40 1.00
86 Pekka Rinne .60 1.50
87 Shea Weber .40 1.00
88 Sam Gagner .40 1.00
89 Andrew Cogliano .40 1.00
90 Nikolai Khabibulin .50 1.25
91 James Neal .50 1.25
92 Mike Ribeiro .40 1.00
93 Marty Turco .50 1.25
94 Shane Doan .40 1.00
95 Peter Mueller .40 1.00
96 Drew Doughty .60 1.50
97 Anze Kopitar .75 2.00
98 Paul Stastny .50 1.25
99 Wojtek Wolski .30 .75
100 Milan Hejduk .40 1.00
101 Scott Parse RC 2.50 6.00
102 Phil Oreskovic RC 2.50 6.00
103 Andreas Thuresson RC 2.00 5.00
104 Philippe Dupuis RC 2.50 6.00
105 Jaime Sifers RC 2.00 5.00
106 Matt Hendricks RC 2.00 5.00
107 Teemu Laakso RC 1.50 4.00
108 Ilkka Pikkarainen RC 2.50 6.00
109 Grant Lewis RC 2.00 5.00
110 Peter Olvecky RC 2.50 6.00
111 Byron Bitz RC 2.00 5.00
112 John Scott RC 2.50 6.00
113 Francis Wathier RC 2.00 5.00
114 James Reimer RC 10.00 25.00
115 Peter Regin RC 2.00 5.00
116 Matt Climie RC 2.00 5.00
117 Taylor Chorney RC 2.50 6.00
118 Davis Drewiske RC 2.50 6.00
119 Mika Pyorala RC 2.00 5.00
120 Victor Oreskovich RC 2.00 5.00
121 Tom Wandell RC 2.50 6.00
122 Michal Neuvirth RC 5.00 12.00
123 Mathieu Carle RC 3.00 8.00
124 Lars Eller RC 3.00 8.00
125 Alexander Salak RC 2.50 6.00
126 John Negrin RC 3.00 8.00
127 Aaron Gagnon RC 2.00 5.00
128 Mario Bliznak RC 3.00 8.00
129 Anton Khudobin RC 3.00 8.00
130 Jakub Kindl RC 3.00 8.00
131 Matthew Corrente RC 2.50 6.00
132 Steven Zalewski RC 2.50 6.00
133 David Laliberte RC 2.50 6.00
134 Bobby Sanguinetti RC 2.00 5.00
135 Devan Dubnyk RC 6.00 15.00
136 Matt Pelech RC 3.00 8.00
137 Alexander Sulzer RC 2.00 5.00
138 Frazer McLaren RC 2.50 6.00
139 Michael Sauer RC 2.50 6.00
140 Ryan Wilson RC 3.00 8.00
141 Danny Irmen RC 2.00 5.00
142 Braden Holtby RC 15.00 25.00
143 Brian Salcido RC 3.00 8.00
144 Luca Caputi RC 4.00 10.00
145 Spencer Machacek RC 4.00 10.00
146 T.J. Galiardi RC 4.00 10.00
147 Yannick Weber RC 4.00 10.00
148 Christian Hanson RC 4.00 10.00
149 Jhonas Enroth RC 5.00 12.00
150 Ivan Vishnevskiy RC 3.00 8.00
151 Riku Helenius RC 4.00 10.00
152 Kris Chucko RC 3.00 8.00
153 Perttu Lindgren RC 3.00 8.00
154 Ryan O'Reilly RC 6.00 15.00
155 Dmitry Kulikov RC 4.00 10.00
156 Matt Gilroy RC 4.00 10.00
157 Sergei Shirokov RC 2.50 6.00
158 Benn Ferriero RC 4.00 10.00
159 Alec Martinez RC 5.00 12.00
160 Erik Karlsson RC 25.00 50.00
161 Cal O'Reilly RC 3.00 8.00
162 Matt Beleskey RC 3.00 8.00
163 Ville Leino RC 3.00 8.00
164 Artem Anisimov RC 4.00 10.00
165 Antti Niemi RC 12.50 25.00
166 Jason Demers RC 6.00 15.00
167 Cody Franson RC 4.00 10.00
168 Ray Macias RC 3.00 8.00
169 Tyler Myers RC 30.00 80.00
170 Jamie Benn RC 150.00 225.00
171 Michael Del Zotto RC 25.00 60.00
172 Brad Marchand RC 40.00 80.00
173 Mikael Backlund RC 30.00 60.00
174 Tyler Bozak RC 30.00 60.00
175 Logan Couture RC 60.00 100.00
176 Michael Grabner RC 30.00 60.00
177 Viktor Stalberg RC 20.00 50.00
178 Jonas Gustavsson RC 25.00 50.00
179 Colin Wilson RC 20.00 50.00
180 James van Riemsdyk RC 125.00 200.00
181 Evander Kane RC 50.00 100.00
182 Victor Hedman RC 40.00 100.00
183 Matt Duchene RC 100.00 200.00
184 John Tavares RC 350.00 600.00

2009-10 Upper Deck Ice Fresh Threads

OVERALL AU/MEM ODDS 1:7
FTAA Artem Anisimov 5.00 12.00
FTAC Andrew Cogliano 4.00 10.00
FTAN Antti Niemi 8.00 20.00
FTBA Mikael Backlund 5.00 12.00
FTBF Benn Ferriero 5.00 12.00
FTBW Blake Wheeler 5.00 12.00
FTCB Chris Butler 5.00 12.00
FTCF Cody Franson 5.00 12.00
FTCG Claude Giroux 5.00 12.00
FTCW Colin Wilson 5.00 12.00
FTDD Drew Doughty 6.00 15.00
FTDK Dmitry Kulikov 5.00 12.00
FTDS Drew Stafford 5.00 12.00
FTDU Matt Duchene 12.00 30.00
FTEK Erik Karlsson 10.00 25.00
FTIV Ivan Vishnevskiy 4.00 10.00
FTJB Jamie Benn 15.00 40.00
FTJE Jhonas Enroth 6.00 15.00
FTJG Jonas Gustavsson 8.00 20.00
FTJT John Tavares 15.00 40.00
FTJV Jakub Voracek 5.00 12.00
FTKA Evander Kane 8.00 20.00
FTKC Kris Chucko 4.00 10.00
FTLC Luca Caputi 5.00 12.00
FTMD Michael Del Zotto 5.00 12.00
FTMG Michael Grabner 5.00 12.00
FTPL Perttu Lindgren 4.00 10.00
FTPO Patrick O'Sullivan 4.00 10.00
FTRH Riku Helenius 5.00 12.00
FTRO Ryan O'Reilly 8.00 20.00
FTSM Spencer Machacek 5.00 12.00
FTSS Sergei Shirokov 3.00 8.00
FTTB Tyler Bozak 8.00 20.00
FTTG T.J. Galiardi 5.00 12.00
FTTM Tyler Myers 12.00 30.00
FTVA James van Riemsdyk 10.00 25.00
FTVH Victor Hedman 8.00 20.00
FTVL Ville Leino 4.00 10.00
FTVS Viktor Stalberg 5.00 12.00
FTYW Yannick Weber 5.00 12.00

2009-10 Upper Deck Ice Fresh Threads Autographs

STATED PRINT RUN 35 SER.#'d SETS
FTAC Andrew Cogliano 8.00 20.00
FTAN Antti Niemi 15.00 40.00
FTBA Mikael Backlund 10.00 25.00
FTBF Benn Ferriero 10.00 25.00
FTBW Blake Wheeler 10.00 25.00
FTCF Cody Franson 10.00 25.00
FTCG Claude Giroux 20.00 40.00
FTCW Colin Wilson
FTDB Derick Brassard 10.00 25.00
FTDD Drew Doughty 12.00 30.00
FTDS Drew Stafford 10.00 25.00
FTDU Matt Duchene 50.00 100.00
FTEK Erik Karlsson 40.00 80.00
FTIV Ivan Vishnevskiy 8.00 20.00
FTJB Jamie Benn 25.00 50.00
FTJE Jhonas Enroth 20.00 40.00
FTJG Jonas Gustavsson 12.00 30.00
FTJT John Tavares 50.00 125.00
FTJV Jakub Voracek 10.00 25.00
FTKA Evander Kane
FTKC Kris Chucko 8.00 20.00
FTLC Luca Caputi 10.00 25.00
FTMD Michael Del Zotto
FTMG Michael Grabner
FTMR Mason Raymond 10.00 25.00
FTPK Patrick Kane 30.00 60.00
FTPL Perttu Lindgren
FTPO Patrick O'Sullivan 8.00 20.00
FTRH Riku Helenius 10.00 25.00
FTRO Ryan O'Reilly 15.00 40.00
FTSM Spencer Machacek 10.00 25.00
FTSS Sergei Shirokov 6.00 15.00
FTTB Tyler Bozak 15.00 40.00
FTTC Taylor Chorney
FTTG T.J. Galiardi 10.00 25.00
FTTM Tyler Myers 50.00 100.00
FTTO Jonathan Toews 30.00 60.00
FTVA James van Riemsdyk 20.00 50.00
FTVH Victor Hedman 20.00 50.00
FTVL Ville Leino 8.00 20.00
FTVS Viktor Stalberg
FTYW Yannick Weber 10.00 25.00

2009-10 Upper Deck Ice Frozen Fabrics

*PATCH/15: 1.5X TO 4X BASIC JSY
OVERALL STATED AU/MEM ODDS 1:7
FRAF Alexander Frolov 3.00 8.00
FRAK Anze Kopitar 6.00 15.00
FRBB Bob Bourne 3.00 8.00
FRBC Brian Campbell 3.00 8.00
FRBS Borje Salming 4.00 10.00
FRCH Cristobal Huet 4.00 10.00
FRCN Cam Neely 4.00 10.00
FRCP Carey Price 15.00 40.00
FRCW Cam Ward 4.00 10.00
FRDB Dustin Brown 3.00 8.00
FRDG Doug Gilmour 5.00 12.00
FRDH Dale Hawerchuk 5.00 12.00
FRDP Dion Phaneuf 5.00 12.00
FRDR Derek Roy 3.00 8.00
FRGA Glenn Anderson 4.00 10.00
FRHZ Henrik Zetterberg 5.00 12.00
FRIK Ilya Kovalchuk 4.00 10.00
FRJB Jay Bouwmeester 4.00 10.00
FRJC Jeff Carter 4.00 10.00
FRJI Jarome Iginla 4.00 10.00
FRJL Jordan Leopold 2.50 6.00
FRJP Jason Pominville 4.00 10.00
FRJT Joe Thornton 4.00 10.00
FRKT Kimmo Timonen 3.00 8.00
FRLM Lanny McDonald 4.00 10.00
FRMB Martin Brodeur 8.00 20.00
FRMR Mike Richards 4.00 10.00
FRNH Nathan Horton 4.00 10.00
FRPD Pavel Datsyuk 5.00 12.00
FRRD Rick DiPietro 3.00 8.00
FRRG Ryan Getzlaf 6.00 15.00
FRRM Ryan Miller 4.00 10.00
FRRN Rick Nash 3.00 8.00
FRSC Sidney Crosby 12.00 30.00
FRSK Saku Koivu 4.00 10.00
FRSP Jason Spezza 4.00 10.00
FRSS Steve Shutt 4.00 10.00
FRST Peter Stastny 4.00 10.00
FRSY Steve Yzerman 10.00 25.00
FRTV Thomas Vanek 4.00 10.00
FRVL Vincent Lecavalier 3.00 8.00
FRVO Tomas Vokoun 3.00 8.00

2009-10 Upper Deck Ice Frozen Fabrics Autographs

STATED PRINT RUN 35 SER.#'d SETS
FRAK Anze Kopitar 20.00 50.00
FRBB Bob Bourne 10.00 25.00
FRBS Borje Salming 15.00 40.00
FRCN Cam Neely 12.00 30.00
FRCP Carey Price 50.00 125.00
FRCW Cam Ward 12.00 30.00
FRDG Doug Gilmour 15.00 40.00
FRDH Dale Hawerchuk 15.00 40.00
FRDP Dion Phaneuf 15.00 40.00
FREM Evgeni Malkin 25.00 60.00
FRHZ Henrik Zetterberg 15.00 40.00
FRIK Ilya Kovalchuk 12.00 30.00
FRJC Jeff Carter 12.00 30.00
FRJI Jarome Iginla 12.00 30.00
FRJP Jason Pominville 12.00 30.00
FRJT Joe Thornton 12.00 30.00
FRLM Lanny McDonald 12.00 30.00
FRMB Martin Brodeur 25.00 60.00
FRNH Nathan Horton 12.00 30.00
FRPB Patrice Bergeron 15.00 40.00
FRPD Pavel Datsyuk 15.00 40.00
FRRM Ryan Miller 12.00 30.00
FRRN Rick Nash 10.00 25.00
FRSC Sidney Crosby 125.00 200.00
FRSD Shane Doan 10.00 25.00
FRSS Steve Shutt 12.00 30.00
FRST Peter Stastny 15.00 40.00
FRSY Steve Yzerman 30.00 80.00
FRTV Thomas Vanek 10.00 25.00
FRVL Vincent Lecavalier 12.00 30.00
FRVO Tomas Vokoun 10.00 25.00

2009-10 Upper Deck Ice Glacial Graphs

OVERALL AU/MEM ODDS 1:7
GGAC Andrew Cogliano 5.00 12.00
GGAE Andrew Ebbett 4.00 10.00
GGBA Josh Bailey 5.00 12.00
GGBE Jamie Benn 20.00 50.00
GGBL Brian Lee 6.00 15.00
GGBO Bobby Orr 75.00 150.00
GGBR Bobby Ryan 6.00 15.00
GGBS Brian Sutter 6.00 15.00
GGBW Blake Wheeler
GGCB Cam Barker
GGCG Colton Gillies 6.00 15.00
GGCH Chris Stewart 5.00 12.00
GGCS Cory Schneider 8.00 20.00
GGDO Drew Doughty
GGDP Dustin Penner 4.00 10.00
GGDS Darryl Sutter 5.00 12.00
GGDU Matt Duchene 12.00 30.00
GGDZ Michael Del Zotto 6.00 15.00
GGEK Evander Kane 12.00 30.00
GGER Erik Karlsson 30.00 60.00
GGFB Fabian Brunnstrom 5.00 12.00
GGGC Guy Carbonneau 10.00 25.00
GGGH Gordie Howe 75.00 150.00
GGGI Claude Giroux 15.00 30.00
GGJA Justin Abdelkader 5.00 12.00
GGJC Jeff Carter 12.00 30.00
GGJE Jonathan Ericsson 5.00 12.00
GGJG Jonas Gustavsson 12.00 30.00
GGJJ Jack Johnson 4.00 10.00
GGJN James Neal
GGJS Jordan Staal 6.00 15.00
GGJV Jakub Voracek 6.00 15.00
GGKA Karl Alzner 4.00 10.00
GGKM Kenndal McArdle 5.00 12.00
GGKR Niklas Kronwall 5.00 12.00
GGLM Lanny McDonald
GGLS Luke Schenn 6.00 15.00
GGMF Mike Foligno 4.00 10.00
GGMG Mike Green
GGMK Mikael Backlund 6.00 15.00
GGML Mario Lemieux 50.00 100.00
GGMP Max Pacioretty 8.00 20.00
GGMR Mike Ribeiro 5.00 12.00
GGMT Maxime Talbot 6.00 15.00
GGMY Tyler Myers 15.00 40.00
GGNB Nicklas Backstrom 10.00 25.00
GGNG Nathan Gerbe 5.00 12.00
GGNK Nikolai Kulemin 5.00 12.00
GGPB Patrice Bergeron
GGPD Pavel Datsyuk 15.00 40.00
GGPE Phil Esposito 20.00 50.00
GGPR Patrick Roy 75.00 150.00
GGPS Peter Stastny 12.00 30.00
GGRI Mike Richards 6.00 15.00
GGRS Ron Sutter 8.00 20.00
GGRV Rogie Vachon
GGSB Scotty Bowman 15.00 40.00
GGSC Sidney Crosby 75.00 150.00
GGSK Steven Stamkos 40.00 80.00
GGSM Steve Mason 8.00 20.00
GGSS Steve Shutt 6.00 15.00
GGST Paul Stastny 6.00 15.00
GGSU Brandon Sutter 5.00 12.00
GGSY Steve Yzerman 50.00 100.00
GGTA John Tavares 75.00 150.00
GGTJ T.J. Galiardi 6.00 15.00
GGTK Tim Kennedy 5.00 12.00
GGTL Ted Lindsay 12.00 30.00
GGTO T.J. Oshie 10.00 25.00
GGTV Thomas Vanek 6.00 15.00
GGVH Victor Hedman 12.00 30.00
GGVL Ville Leino 5.00 12.00
GGVR James van Riemsdyk 12.00 30.00
GGWG Wayne Gretzky
GGZA Zach Boychuk 5.00 12.00

2009-10 Upper Deck Ice Rinkside Signings

OVERALL AU/MEM ODDS 1:7
RSAK Anze Kopitar 15.00 40.00
RSDC Don Cherry 25.00 50.00
RSHL Henrik Lundqvist 30.00 60.00
RSHZ Henrik Zetterberg 15.00 40.00
RSMG Marian Gaborik 25.00 50.00
RSMM Mike Modano 25.00 50.00
RSNB Nicklas Backstrom 12.00 30.00
RSNL Nicklas Lidstrom 25.00 50.00
RSPK Patrick Kane 40.00 80.00
RSRM Ryan Miller 12.00 30.00
RSSD Shane Doan 10.00 25.00
RSTV Tomas Vokoun 12.00 30.00

2009-10 Upper Deck Ice Rinkside Signings Canadian

OVERALL AU/MEM ODDS 1:7
RSBO Bobby Orr 200.00 300.00
RSBR Bobby Ryan 12.00 30.00
RSCP Carey Price 25.00 60.00
RSCW Cam Ward 12.00 30.00
RSDD Drew Doughty EXCH 40.00 80.00
RSDH Dany Heatley 20.00 50.00
RSGH Gordie Howe 60.00 120.00
RSJC Jeff Carter 15.00 40.00
RSJI Jarome Iginla 20.00 50.00
RSJS Jordan Staal 15.00 40.00
RSJT Jonathan Toews 40.00 80.00
RSLS Luke Schenn 15.00 40.00
RSMB Martin Brodeur
RSME Mark Messier
RSML Mario Lemieux 75.00 150.00
RSMS Martin St. Louis
RSPS Paul Stastny 25.00 50.00
RSRB Ray Bourque
RSRN Rick Nash EXCH 25.00 50.00
RSSC Sidney Crosby 100.00 200.00
RSSD Shane Doan
RSSG Simon Gagne
RSSM Steve Mason 15.00 40.00
RSSS Steven Stamkos 40.00 80.00
RSSY Steve Yzerman 200.00 300.00
RSTE Tony Esposito 30.00 80.00
RSTH Joe Thornton 25.00 50.00
RSVL Vincent Lecavalier EXCH 25.00 50.00
RSWG Wayne Gretzky 175.00 350.00

2009-10 Upper Deck Ice Signature Swatches

OVERALL AU/MEM ODDS 1:7
SSBL Brian Leetch 12.00 30.00
SSCN Cam Neely 12.00 30.00
SSCP Carey Price 50.00 125.00
SSDD Drew Doughty EXCH
SSDP Dion Phaneuf EXCH
SSEM Evgeni Malkin 40.00 100.00
SSGF Grant Fuhr 12.00 30.00
SSHZ Henrik Zetterberg 15.00 40.00
SSIK Ilya Kovalchuk 12.00 30.00
SSJC Jeff Carter EXCH
SSJI Jarome Iginla 12.00 30.00
SSJK Jari Kurri 12.00 30.00
SSJT Joe Thornton 12.00 30.00
SSKE Phil Kessel EXCH
SSLS Luke Schenn 10.00 25.00
SSMB Martin Brodeur 50.00 100.00
SSMF Marc-Andre Fleury 20.00 50.00
SSML Mario Lemieux 60.00 120.00
SSMR Mike Richards 12.00 30.00
SSMT Marty Turco 12.00 30.00
SSNB Nicklas Backstrom 20.00 50.00
SSPD Pavel Datsyuk 25.00 50.00
SSPK Patrick Kane 50.00 100.00
SSPR Patrick Roy 100.00 200.00
SSRM Ryan Miller 25.00 50.00
SSRN Rick Nash 10.00 25.00
SSSC Sidney Crosby 175.00 350.00
SSSS Steven Stamkos 25.00 60.00
SSSY Steve Yzerman EXCH
SSTO Jonathan Toews 50.00 100.00
SSTV Thomas Vanek 12.00 30.00
SSVL Vincent Lecavalier 10.00 25.00
SSWG Wayne Gretzky EXCH

2010-11 Upper Deck Ice

This 110-card set was released as box topper, bonus packs in 2010-11 Black Diamond and 2010-11 SPx hobby boxes. Each card was limited to one specific product, and the Rookies are identified as to which product they were available inside, by the "B" or "S" notation in the card description. The RCs were numbered to either 1999, 999, 499 or 99. Tyler Seguin was numbered to 99, except for several copies which were misnumbered to 499. Upper Deck has confirmed that only 99 copies of these exist.

COMP.SET w/o SPs (60) 20.00 50.00
1-30 AVAILABLE IN 10-11 BLACK DIAMOND
31-60 AVAILABLE IN 10-11 SPx
61-70 PRINT RUN 1999 SER.#'d SETS
71-84 PRINT RUN 999 SER.#'d SETS
85-100 PRINT RUN 499 SER.#'d SETS
101-110 PRINT RUN 99 SER.#'d SETS
CARDS WITH B ONLY IN 10-11 BLACK DIAM.
CARDS WITH S ONLY IN 10-11 SPx
1 Ilya Bryzgalov .40 1.00
2 Dustin Penner .30 .75
3 Henrik Lundqvist .75 2.00
4 Cam Ward .50 1.25
5 Andy McDonald .40 1.00
6 Tomas Plekanec .50 1.25
7 Patrick Kane 1.00 2.50
8 Drew Doughty .50 1.25
9 Evgeni Malkin 1.50 4.00
10 Bobby Ryan .50 1.25
11 Patrick Marleau .50 1.25
12 Pavel Datsyuk .60 1.50
13 Mikko Koivu .50 1.25
14 Brad Richards .50 1.25
15 Steven Stamkos 1.00 2.50
16 John Tavares 1.00 2.50
17 Mike Richards .50 1.25
18 Nik Antropov .40 1.00
19 Zdeno Chara .40 1.00
20 Zach Parise .50 1.25
21 Henrik Sedin .50 1.25
22 Jarome Iginla .50 1.25
23 Ryan Miller .50 1.25
24 Phil Kessel .60 1.50
25 Daniel Alfredsson .50 1.25
26 Tomas Vokoun .40 1.00
27 Shea Weber .40 1.00
28 Alexander Ovechkin 2.00 5.00
29 Paul Stastny .50 1.25
30 Steve Mason .40 1.00
31 Ryan Getzlaf .75 2.00
32 Dustin Byfuglien .50 1.25
33 Patrice Bergeron .60 1.50
34 Thomas Vanek .50 1.25
35 Rene Bourque .30 .75
36 Eric Staal .60 1.50
37 Jonathan Toews 1.00 2.50
38 Matt Duchene .50 1.25
39 Rick Nash .50 1.25
40 Nicklas Lidstrom .50 1.25
41 Henrik Zetterberg .60 1.50
42 Ales Hemsky .40 1.00
43 Anze Kopitar .75 2.00
44 Guillaume Latendresse .40 1.00
45 Carey Price 2.00 5.00
46 Pekka Rinne .60 1.50
47 Ilya Kovalchuk .50 1.25
48 Martin Brodeur 1.00 2.50
49 Marian Gaborik .60 1.50
50 Jason Spezza .30 .75
51 Jeff Carter .50 1.25
52 Shane Doan .40 1.00
53 Sidney Crosby 2.00 5.00
54 Dany Heatley .40 1.00
55 Jaroslav Halak .50 1.25
56 Martin St. Louis .50 1.25
57 Simon Gagne .50 1.25
58 Dion Phaneuf .50 1.25
59 Roberto Luongo .50 1.25
60 Nicklas Backstrom .75 2.00
61 Jake Muzzin/1999 B RC 2.00 5.00
62 Kyle Clifford/1999 B RC 2.00 5.00
63 Alexander Urbom/1999 B RC 2.00 5.00
64 Matt Taormina/1999 B RC 2.00 5.00
65 T.J. Brodie/1999 B RC 2.00 5.00
66 Jeremy Morin/1999 S RC 2.00 5.00
67 Evan Brophey/1999 S RC 2.00 5.00
68 Marco Scandella/1999 S RC 2.00 5.00
69 Jonas Holos/1999 S RC 2.00 5.00
70 Brandon Pirri/1999 S RC 2.00 5.00
71 Anders Lindback/999 B RC 2.50 6.00
72 Mark Olver/999 B RC 2.50 6.00
73 Nick Leddy/999 B RC 2.50 6.00
74 Justin Falk/999 B RC 2.00 5.00
75 Alex Plante/999 B RC 2.50 6.00
76 Brandon Yip/999 B RC 2.50 6.00
77 Dana Tyrell/999 B RC 2.50 6.00
78 Ian Cole/999 S RC 2.50 6.00
79 Philip Larsen/999 S RC 2.50 6.00
80 Eric Wellwood/999 S RC 3.00 8.00
81 Matt Kassian/999 S RC 2.50 6.00
82 Linus Klasen/999 S RC 2.50 6.00
83 Kyle Palmieri/999 S RC 5.00 12.00
84 Jared Cowen/999 S RC 2.50 6.00
85 Sergei Bobrovsky/499 B RC 8.00 20.00
86 Henrik Karlsson/499 B RC 3.00 8.00
87 Zach Hamill/499 B RC 3.00 8.00
88 Nino Niederreiter/499 B RC 6.00 15.00
89 Cam Fowler/499 B RC 4.00 10.00
90 Alexander Burmistrov/499 B RC 3.00 8.00
91 Oliver Ekman-Larsson/499 B RC 5.00 12.00
92 Jordan Caron/499 B RC 5.00 12.00
93 Luke Adam/499 S RC 3.00 8.00
94 Eric Tangradi/499 S RC 3.00 8.00
95 Jamie McBain/499 S RC 3.00 8.00
96 Evgeny Grachev/499 S RC 3.00 8.00
97 Zac Dalpe/499 S RC 3.00 8.00
98 Jacob Josefson/499 S RC 3.00 8.00
99 Marcus Johansson/499 S RC 5.00 12.00
100 Kevin Shattenkirk/499 S RC 6.00 15.00
101 Nazem Kadri/99 B RC 150.00 300.00
102 Derek Stepan/99 B RC 60.00 120.00
103 P.K. Subban/99 B RC 250.00 400.00
104A Tyler Seguin/99 B RC 250.00 450.00
104B Tyler Seguin/499
Mis-numbered to 499; only 99 total exist
105 Taylor Hall/99 B RC 400.00 700.00
106 Mattias Tedenby/99 S RC 12.00 30.00
107 Brayden Schenn/99 S RC 40.00 100.00
108 Jeff Skinner/99 S RC 200.00 400.00
109 Magnus Paajarvi/99 S RC 100.00 200.00
110 Jordan Eberle/99 S RC 300.00 450.00

2011-12 Upper Deck Ice

Cards from this set were sealed in specially marked bonus packs and inserted one per hobby box into 2011-12 Upper Deck series two and 2011-12 SPx hobby boxes. UD Series 2 boxes included base cards 1-25 and rookies 51-54, 58-65, 74-82, and 96-100 and SPx boxes included packs featuring the remainder of the card numbers.

51-57 ROOKIE PRINT RUN 1999
58-73 ROOKIE PRINT RUN 999
74-95 ROOKIE PRINT RUN 499
96-104 ROOKIE PRINT RUN 99
1 Corey Perry .60 1.50
2 Ryan Miller .60 1.50
3 Jarome Iginla .60 1.50
4 Eric Staal .75 2.00
5 Jonathan Toews 1.25 3.00
6 Matt Duchene .60 1.50
7 Rick Nash .60 1.50
8 Taylor Hall 1.25 3.00
9 Drew Doughty .60 1.50
10 Mikko Koivu .50 1.25
11 P.K. Subban 1.25 3.00
12 Shea Weber .50 1.25
13 Martin Brodeur 1.25 3.00
14 Michael Grabner .50 1.25
15 Henrik Lundqvist .75 2.00
16 Jason Spezza .60 1.50
17 Claude Giroux .60 1.50
18 Shane Doan .50 1.25
19 Sidney Crosby 2.50 6.00
20 Patrick Marleau .60 1.50
21 Steven Stamkos 1.25 3.00
22 Phil Kessel .75 2.00
23 Roberto Luongo .60 1.50
24 Nicklas Backstrom 1.00 2.50
25 Dustin Byfuglien .60 1.50
26 Ryan Getzlaf 1.00 2.50
27 Tim Thomas .60 1.50
28 Drew Stafford .60 1.50
29 Miikka Kiprusoff .60 1.50
30 Jeff Skinner .60 1.50
31 Patrick Kane 1.25 3.00
32 Paul Stastny .60 1.50
33 Steve Mason .50 1.25
34 Brenden Morrow .50 1.25
35 Henrik Zetterberg .75 2.00
36 Jordan Eberle .60 1.50
37 Anze Kopitar 1.00 2.50
38 Niklas Backstrom .60 1.50
39 Carey Price 2.00 5.00
40 Pekka Rinne .75 2.00
41 Ilya Kovalchuk .60 1.50
42 John Tavares 1.25 3.00
43 Daniel Alfredsson .60 1.50
44 Daniel Briere .60 1.50
45 Marc-Andre Fleury 1.00 2.50
46 Logan Couture .60 1.50
47 Dion Phaneuf .60 1.50
48 Ryan Kesler .60 1.50
49 Alexander Ovechkin 2.50 6.00
50 Evander Kane .60 1.50
51 Ben Scrivens RC 3.00 8.00
52 Joe Vitale RC 2.00 5.00
53 Erik Condra RC 2.00 5.00
54 Patrick Wiercioch RC 2.00 5.00
55 Ryan Ellis RC 2.00 5.00
56 Dmitry Orlov RC 2.50 6.00
57 Gustav Nyquist RC 8.00 12.00
58 Colin Greening RC 2.50 6.00
59 Alex Stalock 2.50 6.00
60 Jonathon Blum RC 2.50 6.00
61 Cam Atkinson RC 6.00 15.00
62 Brett Bulmer RC 2.50 6.00
63 Craig Smith RC 3.00 8.00
64 Erik Gustafsson RC 3.00 8.00
65 Raphael Diaz RC 2.50 6.00
66 Alexei Emelin RC 2.50 6.00
67 Colten Teubert RC 2.50 6.00
68 John Moore RC 2.50 6.00
69 Viatcheslav Voynov RC 2.50 6.00
70 Roman Horak RC 3.00 8.00
71 Stephane Da Costa RC 2.50 6.00
72 Keith Kinkaid RC 2.50 6.00
73 Peter Holland RC 2.50 6.00
74 Devante Smith-Pelly RC 5.00 12.00
75 Erik Gudbranson RC 4.00 10.00
76 Matt Frattin RC 3.00 8.00
77 Jake Gardiner RC 6.00 15.00
78 Aaron Palushaj RC 3.00 8.00
79 Adam Henrique RC 15.00 40.00
80 Marcus Kruger RC 5.00 12.00
81 Blake Geoffrion RC 8.00 20.00
82 Adam Larsson RC 12.50 25.00
83 Cody Eakin RC 5.00 12.00
84 David Rundblad RC 3.00 8.00
85 Teemu Hartikainen RC 3.00 8.00
86 Anton Lander RC 3.00 8.00
87 Brett Connolly RC 5.00 12.00
88 Joe Colborne RC 3.00 8.00
89 Justin Faulk RC 5.00 12.00
90 Brendan Smith RC 3.00 8.00
91 Andy Miele RC 3.00 8.00
92 Lennart Petrell RC 4.00 10.00
93 Andrew Shaw RC 10.00 25.00
94 Carl Klingberg RC 3.00 8.00
95 Zack Kassian RC 4.00 10.00
96 Mika Zibanejad RC 60.00 120.00
97 Ryan Johansen RC 90.00 150.00
98 Gabriel Landeskog RC 100.00 175.00
99 Cody Hodgson RC 75.00 150.00
100 Ryan Nugent-Hopkins RC 300.00 500.00
101 Matt Read/99 RC 50.00 120.00
102 Louis Leblanc/99 RC 30.00 80.00
103 Mark Scheifele/99 RC 50.00 120.00
104 Sean Couturier/99 RC 75.00 150.00

2012-13 Upper Deck Ice

INSERTED IN BLACK DIAMOND
1 Ryan Getzlaf 1.25 3.00
2 Patrice Bergeron 1.00 2.50
3 Ryan Miller .75 2.00
4 Jarome Iginla .75 2.00
5 Jonathan Toews 1.50 4.00
6 Jamie Benn 1.00 2.50
7 Taylor Hall 1.50 4.00
8 Kris Versteeg .60 1.50
9 Jonathan Quick 1.25 3.00
10 Dany Heatley .60 1.50
11 Carey Price 2.50 6.00
12 Shea Weber .60 1.50
13 Martin Brodeur 1.50 4.00
14 John Tavares 1.50 4.00
15 Ryan Callahan .75 2.00
16 Jason Spezza .75 2.00
17 Claude Giroux .75 2.00
18 Mike Smith .75 2.00
19 Evgeni Malkin 2.50 6.00
20 Antti Niemi .60 1.50
21 Steven Stamkos 1.50 4.00
22 Dion Phaneuf .75 2.00
23 Daniel Sedin .75 2.00
24 Alexander Ovechkin 3.00 8.00
25 Ondrej Pavelec .75 2.00
26 Reilly Smith/999 RC 5.00 12.00
27 Cody Goloubef/999 RC 2.50 6.00
28 Gabriel Dumont/999 RC 2.50 6.00
29 Tyler Cuma/999 RC 2.50 6.00
30 J.T. Brown/999 RC 2.50 6.00
31 Maxime Sauve/999 RC 2.50 6.00
32 Tyson Barrie/999 RC 5.00 12.00
33 Jason Zucker/999 RC 3.00 8.00
34 Jordan Nolan/999 RC 2.50 6.00
35 Mark Stone/999 RC 10.00 20.00
36 Scott Glennie/999 RC 2.50 6.00
37 Chet Pickard/499 RC 2.50 6.00
38 Riley Sheahan/499 RC 5.00 12.00
39 Jussi Rynnas/499 RC 10.00 25.00
40 Casey Cizikas/499 RC 5.00 12.00
41 Jakob Silfverberg/499 RC 10.00 25.00
42 Jake Allen/499 RC 8.00 20.00
43 Carter Ashton/499 RC 4.00 10.00
44 Jaden Schwartz/99 RC 80.00 200.00
45 Sven Baertschi/99 RC 40.00 80.00
46 Chris Kreider/99 RC 75.00 150.00

2013-14 Upper Deck Ice

COMP.SET w/o SP's (50) 10.00 25.00
1-25/51-62/87-98/105-114/121-128 IN BLACK DIA.
26-50/63-86/99-104/115-120/129-134 IN SPx
1 Corey Perry .75 2.00
2 Brad Marchand 1.00 2.50
3 Tyler Ennis .60 1.50
4 Patrick Kane 1.50 4.00
5 Matt Duchene .75 2.00
6 Sergei Bobrovsky .75 2.00
7 Pavel Datsyuk 1.00 2.50
8 Jordan Eberle .75 2.00
9 Anze Kopitar 1.25 3.00
10 Ryan Suter .50 1.25
11 P.K. Subban 1.25 3.00
12 Pekka Rinne 1.00 2.50
13 Martin Brodeur 1.50 4.00
14 John Tavares 1.50 4.00
15 Derek Stepan .75 2.00
16 Erik Karlsson 1.50 4.00
17 Jakub Voracek .75 2.00
18 Shane Doan .60 1.50
19 Evgeni Malkin 2.50 6.00
20 Logan Couture .75 2.00
21 Alexander Steen .75 2.00
22 Martin St. Louis .75 2.00
23 Alexandre Burrows .75 2.00
24 Mike Green .75 2.00
25 Evander Kane .75 2.00
26 Ryan Getzlaf 1.25 3.00
27 Patrice Bergeron 1.00 2.50
28 Lee Stempniak .50 1.25
29 Eric Staal 1.00 2.50
30 Jonathan Toews 1.50 4.00
31 Marian Gaborik .75 2.00
32 Jamie Benn 1.00 2.50
33 Henrik Zetterberg 1.00 2.50
34 Taylor Hall 1.50 4.00
35 Tomas Fleischmann .50 1.25
36 Jonathan Quick 1.25 3.00
37 Zach Parise .75 2.00
38 Carey Price 2.50 6.00
39 Shea Weber .60 1.50
40 Patrik Elias .75 2.00
41 Ryan Callahan .75 2.00
42 Craig Anderson .75 2.00
43 Claude Giroux .75 2.00
44 Sidney Crosby 3.00 8.00
45 Joe Thornton .75 2.00
46 Steven Stamkos 1.50 4.00
47 Phil Kessel 1.00 2.50
48 Henrik Sedin .75 2.00
49 Alexander Ovechkin 3.00 8.00
50 Andrew Ladd .75 2.00
51 Chris Brown/999 RC 2.00 5.00
52 Danny DeKeyser/999 RC 4.00 10.00
53 Johan Larsson/999 RC 2.50 6.00
54 Connor Carrick/999 RC 2.50 6.00
55 Austin Watson/999 RC 2.50 6.00
56 Zach Redmond/999 RC 2.50 6.00
57 Anton Belov/999 RC 3.00 8.00
58 Justin Fontaine/999 RC 3.00 8.00
59 Jean-Gabriel Pageau/999 RC 2.50 6.00
60 Brock Nelson/999 RC 3.00 8.00
61 Joakim Nordstrom/999 RC 2.50 6.00
62 Drew LeBlanc/999 RC 2.00 5.00
63 Alex Petrovic/999 RC 2.50 6.00
64 Max Reinhart/999 RC 3.00 8.00
65 Jesper Fast/999 RC 2.50 6.00
66 Jason Akeson/999 RC 2.50 6.00
67 Eric Gryba/999 RC 2.50 6.00
68 Matthew Irwin/999 RC 2.50 6.00
69 Jeff Zatkoff/999 RC 3.00 8.00
70 Will Acton/999 RC 2.50 6.00
71 Ryan Stanton/999 RC 3.00 8.00
72 Spencer Abbott/999 RC 2.50 6.00
73 Carl Soderberg/499 RC 4.00 10.00
74 Matt Nieto/499 RC 3.00 8.00
75 Michael Latta/499 RC 3.00 8.00
76 Alex Chiasson/499 RC 4.00 10.00
77 Darcy Kuemper/499 RC 4.00 10.00
78 Tyler Johnson/499 RC 25.00 50.00
79 Anders Lee/499 RC 6.00 15.00
80 Nick Bjugstad/499 RC 5.00 12.00
81 Taylor Beck/499 RC 3.00 8.00
82 Edward Pasquale/499 RC 2.50 6.00
83 Mark Pysyk/499 RC 4.00 10.00
84 Radko Gudas/499 RC 4.00 10.00
85 Philipp Grubauer/499 RC 4.00 10.00
86 Sami Vatanen/499 RC 4.00 10.00
87 Damien Brunner/499 RC 3.00 8.00
88 Ryan Murphy/499 RC 4.00 10.00
89 Rickard Rakell/499 RC 4.00 10.00
90 Lucas Lessio/499 RC 2.50 6.00
91 Mathew Dumba/499 RC 4.00 10.00
92 Olli Maatta/499 RC 15.00 40.00
93 Tom Wilson/499 RC 6.00 15.00
94 Jarred Tinordi/499 RC 4.00 10.00
95 Viktor Fasth/499 RC 4.00 10.00
96 Zemgus Girgensons/499 RC 8.00 20.00
97 Jonas Brodin/499 RC 3.00 8.00
98 Nathan Beaulieu/499 RC 3.00 8.00
99 Charlie Coyle/249 RC 5.00 12.00
100 Jack Campbell/249 RC 8.00 20.00
101 Hampus Lindholm/249 RC 8.00 20.00
102 Ryan Spooner/249 RC 5.00 12.00
103 Scott Laughton/249 RC 5.00 12.00
104 Tanner Pearson/249 RC 10.00 25.00
105 J.T. Miller/249 RC 8.00 20.00
106 Petr Mrazek/249 RC 10.00 25.00
107 Morgan Rielly/249 RC 15.00 40.00
108 Emerson Etem/249 RC 5.00 12.00
109 Boone Jenner/249 RC 5.00 12.00
110 Mikael Granlund/249 RC 8.00 20.00
111 Tyler Toffoli/249 RC 12.00 30.00
112 Rasmus Ristolainen/249 RC 8.00 20.00
113 Cory Conacher/249 RC 3.00 8.00
114 Jacob Trouba/249 RC 12.00 30.00
115 Michael Bournival/249 RC 5.00 12.00
116 Nicklas Jensen/249 RC 4.00 10.00
117 Ryan Murray/249 RC 8.00 20.00
118 Beau Bennett/99 RC 40.00 100.00
119 Filip Forsberg/99 RC 125.00 250.00
120 Elias Lindholm/99 RC 60.00 120.00
121 Mikhail Grigorenko/99 RC 50.00 100.00
122 Justin Schultz/99 RC 40.00 100.00
123 Nathan MacKinnon/99 RC 300.00 700.00
124 Vladimir Tarasenko/99 RC 250.00 400.00
125 Sean Monahan/99 RC 150.00 250.00
126 Jonathan Huberdeau/99 RC 125.00 250.00
127 Brendan Gallagher/99 RC 150.00 300.00
128 Nail Yakupov/99 RC 150.00 300.00
129 Alex Galchenyuk/99 RC 350.00 500.00
130 Aleksander Barkov/99 RC 100.00 200.00
131 Tomas Hertl/99 RC 100.00 200.00
132 Dougie Hamilton/99 RC 75.00 150.00
133 Seth Jones/99 RC 75.00 150.00
134 Valeri Nichushkin/99 RC 100.00 200.00

2014-15 Upper Deck Ice

43-72 GOALIE STATED ODDS 1:3
73-84 LEGEND STATED ODDS 1:7
1 Claude Giroux .75 2.00
2 Shea Weber .60 1.50
3 Rick Nash .75 2.00
4 Phil Kessel 1.00 2.50
5 Duncan Keith .75 2.00
6 Jamie Benn 1.00 2.50
7 Anze Kopitar 1.25 3.00
8 Sean Monahan .75 2.00
9 Alexander Ovechkin 3.00 8.00
10 Jordan Eberle .75 2.00
11 Blake Wheeler .75 2.00
12 Ryan Getzlaf 1.25 3.00
13 Zdeno Chara .75 2.00
14 Jonathan Toews 1.50 4.00
15 Martin St. Louis .75 2.00
16 Henrik Zetterberg 1.00 2.50
17 John Tavares 1.50 4.00
18 Drew Doughty .75 2.00
19 Jonathan Huberdeau .75 2.00
20 Max Pacioretty .75 2.00
21 Steven Stamkos 1.50 4.00
22 P.K. Subban 1.25 3.00
23 Cody Hodgson .75 2.00
24 Nathan MacKinnon 1.50 4.00
25 T.J. Oshie 1.25 3.00
26 Henrik Sedin .75 2.00
27 Matt Duchene .75 2.00
28 Zach Parise .75 2.00
29 Joe Pavelski .75 2.00
30 Patrice Bergeron 1.00 2.50
31 Pavel Datsyuk 1.00 2.50
32 Erik Karlsson 1.50 4.00
33 Eric Staal 1.00 2.50
34 Ryan Johansen 1.00 2.50
35 Patrick Kane 1.50 4.00
36 Marian Gaborik .75 2.00
37 Jaromir Jagr 2.00 5.00
38 Evgeni Malkin 2.50 6.00
39 Shane Doan .60 1.50
40 Sidney Crosby 3.00 8.00
41 Taylor Hall 1.50 4.00
42 Tyler Seguin 1.25 3.00
43 Ben Bishop 2.00 5.00
44 Corey Crawford 2.50 6.00
45 Jonathan Bernier 2.00 5.00
46 Cam Ward 2.00 5.00
47 Antti Niemi 1.50 4.00
48 Cory Schneider 1.50 4.00
49 Craig Anderson 2.00 5.00
50 Martin Brodeur 4.00 10.00
52 Roberto Luongo 2.00 5.00
53 Karri Ramo 1.50 4.00
54 Tuukka Rask 2.00 5.00
55 Steve Mason 1.50 4.00
56 Carey Price 6.00 15.00
57 Ben Scrivens 1.50 4.00
58 Ryan Miller 2.00 5.00
59 Jhonas Enroth 2.00 5.00
60 Mike Smith 2.00 5.00
61 Ondrej Pavelec 2.00 5.00
62 Kari Lehtonen 1.50 4.00
63 Marc-Andre Fleury 3.00 8.00
64 Henrik Lundqvist 2.50 6.00
65 Jaroslav Halak 1.50 4.00
66 Darcy Kuemper 1.50 4.00
67 Jonathan Quick 3.00 8.00
68 Pekka Rinne 2.50 6.00
69 Semyon Varlamov 2.00 5.00
70 John Gibson 2.50 6.00
71 Jim Howard 2.00 5.00
72 Sergei Bobrovsky 2.00 5.00
73 Patrick Roy 5.00 12.00
74 Ray Bourque 3.00 8.00
75 Steve Yzerman 4.00 10.00
76 Wayne Gretzky 10.00 25.00
77 Peter Forsberg 2.00 5.00
78 Guy Lafleur 2.50 6.00
79 Bobby Hull 2.00 5.00
80 Mario Lemieux 6.00 15.00
81 Bobby Orr 6.00 15.00
82 Jean Beliveau 2.00 5.00
83 Joe Sakic 3.00 8.00
84 Mike Bossy 2.00 5.00
85 Brandon Defazio/999 RC 2.50 6.00
86 Micheel Ferland/999 RC 3.00 8.00
87 Mike Halmo/999 RC 2.00 5.00
88 Joe Morrow/999 RC 4.00 10.00
89 Joonas Nattinen/999 RC 3.00 8.00
90 Liam O'Brien/999 RC 3.00 8.00
91 Justin Hodgman/999 RC 2.50 6.00
92 Trevor van Riemsdyk/999 RC 5.00 12.00

93 Dennis Everberg/999 RC 3.00 8.00
94 Andrej Nestrasil/999 RC 3.00 8.00
95 Laurent Brossoit/999 RC 3.00 8.00
96 Andy Andreoff/999 RC 3.00 8.00
97 Christian Folin/999 RC 3.00 8.00
98 Nicolas Deslauriers/999 RC 3.00 8.00
99 Mark Visentin/999 RC 3.00 8.00
100 Patrik Nemeth/999 RC 3.00 8.00
101 Corban Knight/999 RC 3.00 8.00
102 Scott Mayfield/999 RC 2.50 6.00
103 Michael Zalewski/999 RC 2.50 6.00
104 Bogdan Yakimov/999 RC 3.00 8.00
105 P-E Bellemare/999 RC 3.00 8.00
106 Brandon Kozun/999 RC 2.50 6.00
107 Jake McCabe/999 RC 3.00 8.00
108 Scott Wilson/999 RC 2.50 6.00
109 Petter Granberg/999 RC 2.50 6.00
110 Andrew Agozzino/999 RC 2.50 6.00
111 Greg McKegg/999 RC 2.50 6.00
112 Curtis McKenzie/999 RC 2.50 6.00
113 Colton Sissons/999 RC 3.00 8.00
114 Oscar Klefbom/999 RC 6.00 15.00
115 Markus Granlund/799 RC 5.00 12.00
116 Scott Darling/799 RC 12.50 25.00
117 Rocco Grimaldi/799 RC 3.00 8.00
118 William Karlsson/799 RC 12.00 30.00
119 Barclay Goodrow/799 RC 3.00 8.00
120 Scott Harrington/799 RC 3.00 8.00
121 Jori Lehtera/799 RC 4.00 10.00
122 Brett Ritchie/799 RC 3.00 8.00
123 Jordan Binnington/799 RC 3.00 8.00
124 Teemu Pulkkinen/799 RC 4.00 10.00
125 Colin Smith/799 RC 3.00 8.00
126 Phillip Danault/799 RC 3.00 8.00
127 Ryan Sproul/499 RC 4.00 10.00
128 Mirco Mueller/499 RC 4.00 10.00
129 Adam Lowry/499 RC 4.00 10.00
130 Seth Helgeson/499 RC 3.00 8.00
131 John Klingberg/499 RC 12.00 30.00
132 Ty Rattie/499 RC 5.00 12.00
133 Brandon Gormley/499 RC 4.00 10.00
134 Marko Dano/499 RC 4.00 10.00
135 Vincent Trocheck/499 RC 5.00 12.00
136 Calle Jarnkrok/499 RC 4.00 10.00
137 Kerby Rychel/499 RC 3.00 8.00
138 Joey Hishon/499 RC 5.00 12.00
139 Josh Jooris/499 RC 4.00 10.00
140 Adam Clendening/499 RC 4.00 10.00
141 A.Khokhlachev/499 RC 4.00 10.00
142 V.Namestnikov/499 RC 6.00 15.00
143 Victor Rask/499 RC 4.00 10.00
144 Chris Tierney/499 RC 4.00 10.00
145 Damon Severson/499 RC 4.00 10.00
146 Stuart Percy/499 RC 4.00 10.00
147 Kevin Hayes/249 RC 15.00 40.00
148 Andrei Vasilevskiy/249 RC 15.00 30.00
149 Sven Andrighetto/249 RC 6.00 15.00
150 Jiri Sekac/249 RC 5.00 12.00
151 Derrick Pouliot/249 RC 6.00 15.00
152 Seth Griffith/249 RC 6.00 15.00
153 Darnell Nurse/249 RC 15.00 30.00
154 Griffin Reinhart/249 RC 6.00 15.00
155 Shayne Gostisbehere/249 RC 60.00 100.00
156 Alexander Wennberg/249 RC 10.00 25.00
157 Anthony Duclair/249 RC 8.00 20.00
158 Evgeny Kuznetsov/249 RC 25.00 50.00
159 David Pastrnak/99 RC 125.00 250.00
160 Sam Reinhart/99 RC 125.00 250.00
161 Leon Draisaitl/99 RC 100.00 200.00
162 Aaron Ekblad/99 RC 100.00 200.00
163 Curtis Lazar/99 RC 50.00 100.00
164 Bo Horvat/99 RC 75.00 150.00
165 Teuvo Teravainen/99 RC 100.00 200.00
166 Jonathan Drouin/99 RC 100.00 200.00
167 Johnny Gaudreau/99 RC 250.00 400.00
168 Andre Burakovsky/99 RC 60.00 120.00
51 Philipp Grubauer 2.00 5.00

2014-15 Upper Deck Ice Fresh Threads

STATED ODDS 1:21 HOBBY
*GOLD/30: 1.2X TO 3X BASIC JSY
*GOLD/20: 1.5X TO 4X BASIC JSY
FTAB Andre Burakovsky 3.00 8.00
FTAE Aaron Ekblad 8.00 20.00
FTAL Adam Lowry 2.00 5.00
FTAW Alexander Wennberg 4.00 10.00
FTCL Curtis Lazar 2.50 6.00
FTCT Chris Tierney 2.00 5.00
FTDN Darnell Nurse 6.00 15.00
FTDS Damon Severson 3.00 8.00
FTEK Evgeny Kuznetsov 8.00 20.00
FTGR Griffin Reinhart 2.50 6.00
FTJD Jonathan Drouin 5.00 12.00
FTJG Johnny Gaudreau 6.00 15.00
FTJS Jiri Sekac 2.00 5.00
FTKR Kerby Rychel 1.50 4.00
FTLD Leon Draisaitl 10.00 25.00
FTMD Marko Dano 2.00 5.00
FTSG Shayne Gostisbehere 4.00 10.00
FTSP Stuart Percy 2.00 5.00
FTSR Sam Reinhart 6.00 15.00
FTVR Victor Rask 2.00 5.00

2014-15 Upper Deck Ice Frozen Fabrics

GROUP A ODDS 1:260
GROUP B ODDS 1:160
GROUP C ODDS 1:27
OVERALL ODDS 1:21
*GOLD/30: .8X TO 2X BASIC JSY
*GOLD/20: 1X TO 2.5X BASIC JSY
FZFAO Alexander Ovechkin B 15.00 40.00
FZFAP Alex Pietrangelo C 3.00 8.00
FZFBD Brandon Dubinsky C 3.00 8.00
FZFBS Ben Scrivens C 3.00 8.00
FZFCP Corey Perry C 4.00 10.00
FZFGF Grant Fuhr A 6.00 15.00
FZFGL Gabriel Landeskog C 3.00 8.00
FZFHZ Henrik Zetterberg C 5.00 12.00
FZFLR Larry Robinson A 6.00 15.00
FZFMM Mark Messier A 6.00 15.00
FZFMO Sean Monahan C 4.00 10.00
FZFMR Morgan Rielly C 4.00 10.00
FZFPR Pekka Rinne C 5.00 12.00
FZFPS Patrick Sharp B 4.00 10.00
FZFRN Rick Nash C 4.00 10.00
FZFRO Patrick Roy A 10.00 25.00
FZFRS Ryan Strome C 3.00 8.00
FZFSB Sergei Bobrovsky C 4.00 10.00
FZFSM Steve Mason C 3.00 8.00
FZFSU P.K. Subban B 6.00 15.00

2014-15 Upper Deck Ice Frozen Foursomes

GROUP A STATED ODDS 1:1600
GROUP B STATED ODDS 1:265
GROUP C STATED ODDS 1:41
OVERALL STATED ODDS 1:35
*GOLD/30: .8X TO 2X BASIC QUAD
*GOLD/20: .6X TO 1.5X BASIC QUAD GRP A
*GOLD/15-25: 1X TO 2.5X BASIC QUAD
FFRC Ekbld/Lzr/Rnhrt/Drstl C 12.00 30.00
FFTC Stl/Ptrnglo/Bnn/Ctrr 6.00 15.00
FFAVS Ry/Frsbrg/Skc/Blke B 12.00 30.00
FFBEES Ots/Mrry/Brqe/Ptrs C 8.00 20.00
FFBOS Rsk/Khlchv/Chra/Lcc A 8.00 20.00
FFCAN1 Hmltn/Gllghr/Hbrdu/Hcky C 6.00 15.00
FFCAN2 Jnnr/Mrry/Strme/Hmltn C 4.00 10.00
FFCAPS Ovkn/Hlby/Kznsv/Brksky C 8.00 20.00
FFDAL Blfr/Hll/Lhtnn/Bnn C 6.00 15.00
FFKINGS Qck/Dghty/Vyny/Tffli C 8.00 20.00
FFLAK Kptr/Crtr/Tffli/Vynv B 8.00 20.00
FFMTL Prce/Sbbn/Glchn/Gllghr C 10.00 25.00
FFNJD Schndr/Hnrqe/Brnnr/Jgr B 12.00 30.00
FFNYR Krdr/Zcrllo/Stpn/McDng C 5.00 12.00
FFRC2 Kzntsv/Trvnn/Gdru/Nmst C 10.00 25.00

2014-15 Upper Deck Ice Glacial Graphs

GROUP A STATED ODDS 1:660
GROUP B STATED ODDS 1:265
GROUP C STATED ODDS 1:110
GROUP D STATED ODDS 1:74
OVERALL STATED ODDS 1:36
GGAB Aleksander Barkov D 6.00 15.00
GGAO Adam Oates C 6.00 15.00
GGBR Dustin Brown A 6.00 15.00
GGCH Carl Hagelin D 6.00 15.00
GGCO Colton Orr C 4.00 10.00
GGCP Carey Price B 20.00 40.00
GGDD Danny DeKeyser D 5.00 12.00
GGDK Darcy Kuemper D 5.00 12.00
GGJB Jonathan Bernier C 6.00 15.00
GGJL John LeClair C 6.00 15.00
GGJP Joe Pavelski C 6.00 15.00
GGJT John Tavares A
GGKT Kyle Turris C 6.00 15.00
GGMK Mike Krushelnyski D 5.00 12.00
GGML Mike Liut C 6.00 15.00
GGMP Max Pacioretty D 6.00 15.00
GGNL Nicklas Lidstrom B 10.00 25.00
GGOM Olli Maatta D 6.00 15.00
GGPE Corey Perry B 8.00 20.00
GGPK Patrik Kane 30.00 80.00
GGPS Patrick Sharp B 10.00 25.00
GGRB Bobby Ryan A 8.00 20.00
GGSA Brandon Saad D 6.00 15.00
GGTE Tony Esposito B 12.00 30.00
GGTH Tomas Hertl D 6.00 15.00
GGTL Trevor Linden A 10.00 25.00
GGTT Tomas Tatar C 5.00 12.00

2014-15 Upper Deck Ice Glacial Graphs Gold

UNPRICED GROUP A ODDS 1:3925
UNPRICED GROUP B ODDS 1:1050
UNPRICED GROUP C ODDS 1:850
GROUP D STATED ODDS 1:185
OVERALL STATED ODDS 1:121
GGAO Adam Oates 12.00 30.00
Go Bees D
GGCH Carl Hagelin 12.00 30.00
Go Rangers D
GGCO Colton Orr 8.00 20.00
Go Leafs D
GGDD Danny DeKeyser 10.00 25.00
Go Wings D
GGDK Darcy Kuemper 10.00 25.00
Go Wild D
GGJB Jonathan Bernier D 12.00 30.00
GGJP Joe Pavelski 12.00 30.00
Go Sharks D
GGJT John Tavares D 25.00 60.00
GGMK Mike Krushelnyski 10.00 25.00
Go Oilers D
GGML Mike Liut 10.00 25.00
Go Whalers D
GGOM Olli Maatta 12.00 30.00
Go Pens D
GGPK Patrik Kane 80.00 150.00
Go Hawks
GGTH Tomas Hertl 12.00 30.00
Go Sharks D
GGTT Tomas Tatar D 10.00 25.00

2014-15 Upper Deck Ice Ice Premieres Autographs

GROUP A STATED ODDS 1:140
GROUP B STATED ODDS 1:39
GROUP C STATED ODDS 1:33
OVERALL STATED ODDS 1:16
IPAAB Andre Burakovsky A 8.00 20.00
IPAAD Anthony Duclair B 5.00 12.00
IPAAE Aaron Ekblad B 15.00 30.00
IPAAK Alexander Khokhlachev B 3.00 8.00
IPAAL Adam Lowry A 5.00 12.00
IPAAW Alexander Wennberg B 6.00 15.00
IPABG Brandon Gormley C 3.00 8.00
IPACJ Calle Jarnkrok B 3.00 8.00
IPACL Curtis Lazar B 4.00 10.00
IPADN Darnell Nurse B 10.00 25.00
IPAEK Evgeny Kuznetsov C 15.00 30.00
IPAGO Shayne Gostisbehere C 40.00 80.00
IPAGR Griffin Reinhart B 4.00 10.00
IPAJD Jonathan Drouin B 12.00 30.00
IPAJG Johnny Gaudreau A 30.00 60.00
IPAJH Joey Hishon C 4.00 10.00
IPAJL Jori Lehtera A 6.00 15.00
IPAJM Jake McCabe A 5.00 12.00
IPAJS Jiri Sekac C 3.00 8.00
IPAKH Kevin Hayes C 10.00 25.00
IPALB Laurent Brossoit A 5.00 12.00
IPALD Leon Draisaitl B 12.00 30.00
IPAMD Marko Dano B 3.00 8.00
IPAMM Mirco Mueller C 3.00 8.00
IPAPN Patrik Nemeth B 3.00 8.00
IPASG Seth Griffith C 4.00 10.00
IPASP Stuart Percy C 3.00 8.00
IPASR Sam Reinhart B 10.00 25.00
IPATP Teemu Pulkkinen B 5.00 12.00
IPATR Ty Rattie B 4.00 10.00
IPATT Teuvo Teravainen C 15.00 30.00
IPAVR Victor Rask C 3.00 8.00
IPAVT Vincent Trocheck A 6.00 15.00

2014-15 Upper Deck Ice Rinkside Signings

GROUP A STATED ODDS 1:1119
GROUP B STATED ODDS 1:320
GROUP C STATED ODDS 1:232
GROUP D STATED ODDS 1:137
OVERALL STATED ODDS 1:64
RSAC Andrew Cogliano D 5.00 12.00
RSAG Alex Galchenyuk C 15.00 40.00
RSAI Arturs Irbe C 8.00 20.00
RSBD Brandon Dubinsky D 6.00 15.00
RSBH Brett Hull A
RSBS Brandon Saad D 8.00 20.00
RSCP Corey Perry B 8.00 20.00
RSDP Dion Phaneuf C 8.00 20.00
RSES Eric Staal B 10.00 25.00
RSFA Frederik Andersen D 6.00 15.00
RSFP Felix Potvin C 12.00 30.00
RSGN Gustav Nyquist D 6.00 15.00
RSJF Johan Franzen C 8.00 20.00
RSJR Jeremy Roenick B 8.00 20.00
RSJS Joe Sakic B
RSJT Jonathan Toews B 60.00 100.00
RSJV John Vanbiesbrouck B 30.00 60.00
RSLC Logan Couture B 8.00 20.00
RSMF Marc-Andre Fleury A
RSMR Morgan Rielly D 8.00 20.00
RSNY Nail Yakupov B
RSPD Pavel Datsyuk A
RSPG Philipp Grubauer D 8.00 20.00
RSPM Petr Mrazek C 8.00 20.00
RSRM Ryan McDonagh D 8.00 20.00
RSRO Ryan O'Reilly D 8.00 20.00
RSSH Andrew Shaw C 8.00 20.00
RSSW Shea Weber B 6.00 15.00
RSTB Tom Barrasso C 8.00 20.00
RSTH Taylor Hall B 15.00 40.00
RSTK Torey Krug D 8.00 20.00
RSTR Jacob Trouba D 6.00 15.00
RSVA James van Riemsdyk C 8.00 20.00
RSZP Zach Parise A

2014-15 Upper Deck Ice Signature Swatches

GROUP A STATED ODDS 1:4180
GROUP B STATED ODDS 1:3165
GROUP C STATED ODDS 1:1395
GROUP D STATED ODDS 1:152
OVERALL STATED ODDS 1:128
SSAK Anze Kopitar D 12.00 30.00
SSDH Dale Hawerchuk D 10.00 25.00
SSDS Denis Savard D 10.00 25.00
SSJP Joe Pavelski D 8.00 20.00
SSJR Jeremy Roenick D 10.00 25.00
SSMF Marc-Andre Fleury C
SSMG Mike Gartner D 8.00 20.00
SSPR Pekka Rinne D 10.00 25.00
SSSC Sidney Crosby A
SSWG Wayne Gretzky B 150.00 250.00

2015-16 Upper Deck Ice

1 Alexander Ovechkin 4.00 10.00
2 Tyler Seguin 1.50 4.00
3 Mats Zuccarello .75 2.00
4 Tyler Toffoli 1.00 2.50
5 Erik Karlsson 2.00 5.00
6 Alexander Steen 1.00 2.50
7 Max Pacioretty 1.00 2.50
8 Pekka Rinne 1.25 3.00
9 Steven Stamkos 2.00 5.00
10 Joe Pavelski 1.00 2.50
11 Sidney Crosby 4.00 10.00
12 Ryan Suter .60 1.50
13 Henrik Zetterberg 1.25 3.00
14 Mikkel Boedker .60 1.50
15 Tuukka Rask 1.00 2.50
16 Jonathan Toews 2.00 5.00
17 Kyle Okposo 1.00 2.50
18 Daniel Sedin 1.00 2.50
19 Reilly Smith 1.00 2.50
20 Blake Wheeler 1.00 2.50
21 Adam Henrique 1.00 2.50
22 Ryan Getzlaf 1.50 4.00
23 Ryan O'Reilly 1.00 2.50
24 Nathan MacKinnon 2.00 5.00
25 Tyler Bozak .75 2.00
26 Johnny Gaudreau 1.50 4.00
27 Eric Staal 1.25 3.00
28 Taylor Hall 2.00 5.00
29 Brandon Saad 1.00 2.50
30 Claude Giroux 1.00 2.50
31 Frederik Andersen .75 2.00
32 John Klingberg .75 2.00
33 Brendan Gallagher 1.25 3.00
34 Loui Eriksson .75 2.00
35 Tomas Plekanec 1.00 2.50
36 Braden Holtby 1.50 4.00
37 Tyler Johnson .75 2.00
38 Patrick Sharp 1.00 2.50
39 Sergei Bobrovsky 1.00 2.50
40 Nicklas Backstrom 1.50 4.00
41 Marc-Andre Fleury 1.50 4.00
42 Henrik Lundqvist 1.25 3.00
43 Jarome Iginla 1.00 2.50
44 Oliver Ekman-Larsson .75 2.00
45 Brandon Sutter .75 2.00
46 Anze Kopitar 1.50 4.00
47 Patrick Kane 2.00 5.00
48 David Krejci .75 2.00
49 Corey Perry 1.00 2.50
50 P.K. Subban 1.50 4.00
51 Sean Monahan 1.00 2.50
52 Evgeni Malkin 3.00 8.00
53 T.J. Oshie 1.50 4.00
54 Jakub Voracek 1.00 2.50
55 Vladimir Tarasenko 1.50 4.00
56 Scott Hartnell 1.00 2.50
57 Corey Crawford 1.25 3.00
58 Ryan Nugent-Hopkins 1.00 2.50
59 Jim Howard 1.00 2.50
60 Gabriel Landeskog 1.00 2.50
61 John Tavares 2.00 5.00
62 Milan Lucic .75 2.00
63 Justin Faulk 1.00 2.50
64 Mikko Koivu .75 2.00
65 Martin Hanzal .60 1.50
66 Evgeny Kuznetsov 1.50 4.00
67 Dion Phaneuf 1.00 2.50
68 Jannik Hansen .60 1.50
69 James Neal 1.00 2.50
70 Michael Cammalleri .75 2.00
71 Carey Price 3.00 8.00
72 Bryan Little .75 2.00
73 Brent Burns 1.25 3.00
74 Phil Kessel 1.50 4.00
75 Derick Brassard 1.00 2.50
76 Patrice Bergeron 1.25 3.00
77 Bobby Ryan .75 2.00
78 Jaromir Jagr 2.50 6.00
79 Jamie Benn 1.25 3.00
80 Brent Seabrook 1.00 2.50
81 Nikita Kucherov 1.50 4.00
82 Tyler Ennis .75 2.00
83 Jonathan Quick 1.50 4.00
84 Gustav Nyquist 1.00 2.50
85 Jiri Hudler .75 2.00
86 Pavel Bure 1.50 4.00
87 Borje Salming 1.00 2.50
88 Phil Esposito 1.50 4.00
89 Marcel Dionne 1.25 3.00
90 Bobby Orr 3.00 8.00
91 Martin Brodeur 2.00 5.00
92 Teemu Selanne 2.00 5.00
93 Luc Robitaille 1.25 3.00
94 Jari Kurri 1.00 2.50
95 Mark Messier 1.50 4.00
96 Larry Robinson 1.00 2.50
97 Paul Coffey 1.00 2.50
98 Doug Gilmour 1.25 3.00
99 Wayne Gretzky 5.00 12.00
100 Terry Sawchuk 1.00 2.50
101 Dylan DeMelo/1999 RC 2.50 6.00
102 Slater Koekkoek/1999 RC 2.50 6.00
103 Joel Edmundson/1999 RC 2.50 6.00
104 Ronalds Kenins/1999 RC 3.00 8.00
105 Joel Vermin/1999 RC 2.50 6.00
106 Duncan Siemens/1999 RC 4.00 10.00
107 Chris Driedger/1999 RC 2.50 6.00
108 Tyler Randell/1999 RC 3.00 8.00
109 Jean-Francois Berube/1999 RC 2.50 6.00
110 Taylor Leier/1999 RC 3.00 8.00
111 Michael Keranen/1999 RC 2.50 6.00
112 Derek Forbort/1999 RC 2.50 6.00
113 Sam Brittain/1999 RC 3.00 8.00
114 Josh Anderson/1999 RC 3.00 8.00
115 Brendan Ranford/1999 RC 2.50 6.00
116 Laurent Dauphin/1999 RC 3.00 8.00
117 Markus Hannikainen/1999 RC 2.50 6.00
118 Keegan Lowe/1999 RC 3.00 8.00
119 Brett Kulak/1999 RC 2.50 6.00
120 Nick Shore/1999 RC 3.00 8.00
121 Stefan Noesen/1999 RC 2.50 6.00
122 Joonas Kemppainen/1999 RC 2.50 6.00
123 Frank Vatrano/1999 RC 6.00 15.00
124 Petr Straka/1999 RC 2.50 6.00
125 Ryan Hartman/1999 RC 4.00 10.00
126 Matt O'Connor/1999 RC 2.50 6.00
127 Mark Alt/1999 RC 2.00 5.00
128 Radek Faksa/1999 RC 3.00 8.00
129 Alexandre Grenier/1999 RC 2.50 6.00
130 Mackenzie Skapski/1999 RC 3.00 8.00
131 Jujhar Khaira/1999 RC 2.50 6.00
132 David Musil/1999 RC 2.50 6.00
133 Erik Gustafsson/1999 RC 4.00 10.00
134 Jaccob Slavin/1999 RC 2.50 6.00
135 Chris Wideman/1999 RC 3.00 8.00
136 Kyle Baun/1999 RC 3.00 8.00
137 Antoine Bibeau/1499 RC 4.00 10.00
138 Vincent Hinostroza/1499 RC 2.50 6.00
139 Brendan Gaunce/1499 RC 5.00 12.00
140 Andrew Copp/1499 RC 4.00 10.00
141 Henrik Samuelsson/1499 RC 3.00 8.00
142 Adam Pelech/1499 RC 3.00 8.00
143 Jacob de la Rose/1499 RC 4.00 10.00
144 Nick Cousins/1499 RC 4.00 10.00
145 Anton Slepyshev/1499 RC 3.00 8.00
146 Devin Shore/1499 RC 4.00 10.00
147 Christoph Bertschy/1499 RC 3.00 8.00
148 Matt Puempel/1499 RC 3.00 8.00
149 Connor Brickley/1499 RC 3.00 8.00
150 Stanislav Galiev/1499 RC 4.00 10.00
151 Jordan Weal/1499 RC 4.00 10.00
152 Brady Skjei/1499 RC 3.00 8.00
153 Viktor Arvidsson/1499 RC 5.00 12.00
154 Sergei Kalinin/1499 RC 3.00 8.00
155 Chandler Stephenson/1499 RC 4.00 10.00
156 Anthony Stolarz/1499 RC 4.00 10.00
157 Sergei Plotnikov/1499 RC 3.00 8.00
158 Daniel Carr/1499 RC 3.00 8.00
159 Brett Pesce/1499 RC 3.00 8.00
160 Shane Prince/1499 RC 3.00 8.00
161 Brock McGinn/999 RC 4.00 10.00
162 Andreas Athanasiou/999 RC 10.00 25.00
163 Gustav Olofsson/999 RC 4.00 10.00
164 Mattias Janmark/999 RC 4.00 10.00
165 Linus Ullmark/999 RC 5.00 12.00
166 Charles Hudon/999 RC 4.00 10.00
167 Mike McCarron/999 RC 4.00 10.00
168 Colton Parayko/999 RC 5.00 12.00
169 Daniel Sprong/999 RC 8.00 20.00
170 Matt Murray/999 RC 30.00 80.00
171 Hunter Shinkaruk/999 RC 4.00 10.00
172 Emile Poirier/999 RC 4.00 10.00
173 Colin Miller/999 RC 3.00 8.00
174 Joonas Donskoi/999 RC 4.00 10.00
175 Ben Hutton/999 RC 4.00 10.00
176 Juuse Saros/999 RC 5.00 12.00
177 Shea Theodore/999 RC 4.00 10.00
178 Louis Domingue/999 RC 4.00 10.00
179 Noah Hanifin/499 RC 8.00 20.00
180 Kevin Fiala/499 RC 6.00 15.00
181 Jared McCann/499 RC 6.00 15.00
182 Garret Sparks/499 RC 8.00 20.00
183 Nikolay Goldobin/499 RC 6.00 15.00
184 Zachary Fucale/499 RC 6.00 15.00
185 Nick Ritchie/499 RC 6.00 15.00
186 Mikko Rantanen/499 RC 12.00 30.00
187 Malcolm Subban/499 RC 15.00 40.00
188 Nicolas Petan/499 RC 6.00 15.00
189 Mike Condon/499 RC 6.00 15.00
190 Oscar Lindberg/499 RC 6.00 15.00
191 Robby Fabbri/99 RC 150.00 250.00
192 Nikolaj Ehlers/99 RC 100.00 200.00
193 Jake Virtanen/99 RC 75.00 150.00
194 Sam Bennett/99 RC 200.00 300.00
195 Connor Hellebuyck/99 RC 100.00 200.00
196 Max Domi/99 RC 150.00 250.00
197 Artemi Panarin/99 RC 300.00 400.00
198 Dylan Larkin/99 RC 350.00 450.00
199 Jack Eichel/99 RC 700.00 1000.00
200 Connor McDavid/99 RC 2500.00 3000.00

2015-16 Upper Deck Ice Frozen Fabrics

GRP A STATED ODDS 1:1,040
GRP B STATED ODDS 1:108
GRP C STATED ODDS 1:32
FFAO Alexander Ovechkin B 20.00 50.00
FFBR Bill Ranford B 5.00 12.00
FFBW Blake Wheeler C 4.00 10.00
FFDH Dominik Hasek B 6.00 15.00
FFDS Daniel Sedin C 4.00 10.00
FFHL Henrik Lundqvist C 5.00 12.00
FFJA Jake Allen C 5.00 12.00
FFJF Justin Faulk C 4.00 10.00
FFJI Jarome Iginla C 4.00 10.00
FFJR Jeremy Roenick B 5.00 12.00
FFKE Phil Kessel C 6.00 15.00
FFML Mario Lemieux A 20.00 50.00
FFMZ Mats Zuccarello C 3.00 8.00
FFPB Pavel Bure A 10.00 25.00
FFPK Patrick Kane B 10.00 25.00
FFPR Pekka Rinne C 5.00 12.00
FFPS P.K. Subban C 6.00 15.00
FFSC Sidney Crosby B 20.00 50.00
FFSS Steven Stamkos C 8.00 20.00
FFST Tyler Seguin C 6.00 15.00
FFTH Taylor Hall C 8.00 20.00
FFVT Vladimir Tarasenko C 6.00 15.00
FFWG Wayne Gretzky A 30.00 80.00

2015-16 Upper Deck Ice Glacial Graphs

COMMON CARD 4.00 10.00
SEMISTARS 5.00 12.00
UNLISTED STARS 6.00 15.00
GRP A STATED ODDS 1:1,092
GRP B STATED ODDS 1:300
GRP C STATED ODDS 1:76
GRP D STATED ODDS 1:72
GGAB Aleksander Barkov C 6.00 15.00
GGAH Andrew Hammond D 20.00 50.00
GGAL Anders Lee D 6.00 15.00
GGAM Andy Moog C 6.00 15.00
GGAN Antti Niemi C 5.00 12.00
GGAO Alexander Ovechkin A 40.00 80.00
GGAV Andrei Vasilevskiy 8.00 20.00
GGBC Bobby Clarke B 6.00 15.00
GGBR Bobby Ryan B 5.00 12.00
GGCC Charlie Coyle D 5.00 12.00
GGCH Carl Hagelin B 5.00 12.00
GGCM Connor McDavid A 300.00 400.00
GGCW Cam Ward B 6.00 15.00
GGDL Dylan Larkin D 20.00 50.00
GGDS Daniel Sprong C 12.00 30.00
GGEM Evgeni Malkin A 20.00 50.00
GGGA Glenn Anderson A 10.00 25.00
GGGL Guy Lafleur A 15.00 40.00
GGJC John Carlson C 8.00 20.00
GGJK John Klingberg D 5.00 12.00
GGJP Joe Pavelski B 6.00 15.00
GGJS Jason Spezza B 5.00 12.00
GGKY Keith Yandle 6.00 15.00
GGLA Andrew Ladd C 6.00 15.00
GGLC Logan Couture B 6.00 15.00
GGLE John LeClair C 6.00 15.00
GGMD Matt Duchene B 6.00 15.00
GGMF Marc-Andre Fleury A 15.00 40.00
GGMM Mike Modano A 15.00 40.00
GGMR Mike Richter B 6.00 15.00
GGMS Mark Stone C 5.00 12.00
GGNH Noah Hanifin 8.00 20.00
GGNK Nikita Kucherov C 10.00 25.00
GGOP Ondrej Palat D 5.00 12.00
GGPF Peter Forsberg A 30.00 60.00
GGPR Pekka Rinne 8.00 20.00
GGRF Robby Fabbri D 8.00 20.00
GGRM Ryan McDonagh C 5.00 12.00
GGSC Ben Scrivens C 5.00 12.00
GGSG Shayne Gostisbehere D 6.00 15.00
GGSP Stuart Percy D 6.00 15.00
GGSV Semyon Varlamov C 6.00 15.00
GGTB Tom Barrasso C 6.00 15.00
GGTH Taylor Hall B 12.00 30.00
GGTP Teemu Pulkkinen D 6.00 15.00
GGZP Zach Parise B 6.00 15.00

2015-16 Upper Deck Ice Glacial Graphs Black

*BLACK/75: .6X TO 1.5X BASIC INSERTS
*BLACK/49: .75X TO 2X BASIC INSERTS
STATED PRINT RUN 5-75 SER.#'d SETS
NO PRICING #'d 5-15 DUE TO SCARCITY
GGAP Artemi Panarin/75 50.00 100.00
Go Hawks
GGDL Dylan Larkin/75 40.00 100.00
GGSG Shayne Gostisbehere/75 30.00 80.00
Flyer Hockey

2015-16 Upper Deck Ice Global Impact

STATED ODDS 1:8 PACKS
GIAP Artemi Panarin 5.00 12.00
GICM Connor McDavid 12.00 30.00
GIDL Dylan Larkin 5.00 12.00
GIDS Daniel Sprong 3.00 8.00
GIEP Emile Poirier 1.50 4.00
GIJE Jack Eichel 6.00 15.00
GIJM Jared McCann 1.50 4.00
GIJS Juuse Saros 2.00 5.00
GIJV Jake Virtanen 2.00 5.00
GIKF Kevin Fiala 1.50 4.00
GIMC Mike Condon 1.50 4.00
GIMD Max Domi 3.00 8.00
GIMJ Mattias Janmark 1.50 4.00
GIMR Mikko Rantanen 3.00 8.00
GINE Nikolaj Ehlers 3.00 8.00
GING Nikolay Goldobin 1.50 4.00
GINH Noah Hanifin 2.00 5.00
GINP Nicolas Petan 1.50 4.00
GINR Nick Ritchie 1.50 4.00
GIOL Oscar Lindberg 1.50 4.00
GIRF Robby Fabbri 2.00 5.00
GISB Sam Bennett 2.00 5.00
GISG Stanislav Galiev 1.50 4.00
GIVA Viktor Arvidsson 2.00 5.00
GIZF Zachary Fucale 1.50 4.00

2015-16 Upper Deck Ice Ice Premieres Autographs

IPAAB Antoine Bibeau AU/499 5.00 12.00
IPAAS Anton Slepyshev AU/499 4.00 10.00
IPABG Brendan Gaunce AU/499 6.00 15.00
IPABH Ben Hutton AU/499 5.00 12.00
IPABR Brendan Ranford AU/499 4.00 10.00
IPACH Connor Hellebuyck AU/499 12.00 30.00
IPACM Connor McDavid AU/125 400.00 500.00
IPACP Colton Parayko AU/499 6.00 15.00
IPACS Chandler Stephenson AU/499 5.00 12.00
IPADF Derek Forbort AU/499 4.00 10.00
IPADL Dylan Larkin AU/199 60.00 120.00
IPADO Joonas Donskoi AU/499 5.00 12.00
IPADS Daniel Sprong AU/499 10.00 25.00
IPAEP Emile Poirier AU/499 5.00 12.00
IPAFA Robby Fabbri AU/199 12.00 30.00
IPAHS Henrik Samuelsson AU/499 4.00 10.00
IPAHU Hunter Shinkaruk AU/499 5.00 12.00
IPAJD Jacob de la Rose AU/499 5.00 12.00
IPAJM Jared McCann AU/499 5.00 12.00
IPAJV Jake Virtanen AU/199 12.00 30.00
IPAJW Jordan Weal AU/499 5.00 12.00
IPAKF Kevin Fiala AU/499 5.00 12.00
IPALU Linus Ullmark AU/499 6.00 15.00
IPAMD Max Domi AU/199 20.00 50.00
IPAMI Colin Miller AU/499 4.00 10.00
IPAMJ Mattias Janmark AU/499 5.00 12.00
IPAMR Mikko Rantanen AU/499 10.00 25.00
IPANC Nick Cousins AU/499 5.00 12.00
IPANE Nikolaj Ehlers AU/199 20.00 50.00
IPANG Nikolay Goldobin AU/199 10.00 25.00
IPANH Noah Hanifin AU/499 6.00 15.00
IPANP Nicolas Petan AU/499 5.00 12.00
IPANR Nick Ritchie AU/499 5.00 12.00
IPAOL Oscar Lindberg AU/499 5.00 12.00
IPAPS Shane Prince AU/499 4.00 10.00
IPARF Radek Faksa AU/499 5.00 12.00
IPARH Ryan Hartman AU/499 6.00 15.00
IPARK Ronalds Kenins AU/499 5.00 12.00
IPASB Sam Bennett AU/199 12.00 30.00
IPASP Sergei Plotnikov AU/499 4.00 10.00
IPAST Shea Theodore AU/499 5.00 12.00
IPAVA Viktor Arvidsson AU/499 6.00 15.00
IPAVH Vincent Hinostroza AU/199 6.00 15.00

2015-16 Upper Deck Ice '05-06 Retro Ice Premieres

STATED PRINT RUN 799 SER.#'d SETS
STATED PRINT RUN 149 SER.#'d SETS
R1 Zachary Fucale/799 4.00 10.00
R2 Nick Ritchie/799 4.00 10.00
R3 Malcolm Subban/799 10.00 25.00
R4 Jake Virtanen/799 5.00 12.00
R5 Oscar Lindberg/799 4.00 10.00
R6 Shane Prince/799 3.00 8.00
R7 Jared McCann/799 4.00 10.00
R8 Stanislav Galiev/799 4.00 10.00
R9 Mattias Janmark/799 4.00 10.00
R10 Garret Sparks/799 5.00 12.00
R11 Nicolas Petan/799 4.00 10.00
R12 Juuse Saros/799 5.00 12.00
R13 Kevin Fiala/799 4.00 10.00
R14 Linus Ullmark/799 5.00 12.00
R15 Robby Fabbri/799 5.00 12.00
R16 Andreas Athanasiou/799 10.00 25.00
R17 Noah Hanifin/799 5.00 12.00
R18 Nikolay Goldobin/799 4.00 10.00
R19 Mikko Rantanen/799 8.00 20.00
R20 Mike Condon/799 4.00 10.00
R21 Colton Parayko/799 5.00 12.00
R22 Gustav Olofsson/799 4.00 10.00
R23 Daniel Sprong/799 8.00 20.00
R24 Sam Bennett/149 20.00 50.00
R25 Artemi Panarin/149 100.00 200.00
R26 Dylan Larkin/149 100.00 200.00
R27 Nikolaj Ehlers/149 30.00 80.00
R28 Max Domi/149 30.00 80.00
R29 Jack Eichel/149 150.00 250.00
R30 Connor McDavid/149 500.00 900.00

2015-16 Upper Deck Ice Rinkside Signings

GRP A STATED ODDS 1:3,298
GRP B STATED ODDS 1:636
GRP C STATED ODDS 1:510
GRP D STATED ODDS 1:85
RSAB Andre Burakovsky D 6.00 15.00
RSAI Arturs Irbe D 6.00 15.00
RSAK Anze Kopitar A
RSBE Jonathan Bernier B 8.00 20.00
RSBG Bill Guerin B 8.00 20.00
RSCM Connor McDavid A 300.00 500.00
RSCO Chris Osgood 8.00 20.00
RSCP Carey Price A
RSDS Daniel Sprong D 15.00 40.00
RSES Eric Staal B 10.00 25.00
RSGL Gabriel Landeskog 8.00 20.00
RSJA Jake Allen D 10.00 25.00
RSJB Jamie Benn B 10.00 25.00
RSJH Jiri Hudler D 6.00 15.00
RSJP Joe Pavelski B 8.00 20.00
RSJS Jason Spezza B 6.00 15.00
RSJT Jonathan Toews A 50.00 120.00
RSJV Jakub Voracek 8.00 20.00
RSKY Keith Yandle 8.00 20.00
RSMB Martin Brodeur A
RSMK Mike Keane D 6.00 15.00
RSMM Mark Messier A 25.00 60.00
RSMO Matt Moulson C 6.00 15.00
RSMR Mikko Rantanen D 15.00 40.00
RSNL Nicklas Lidstrom A 8.00 20.00
RSON Owen Nolan B 6.00 15.00
RSRB Rod Brind'Amour D 6.00 15.00
RSSB Sergei Bobrovsky B 8.00 20.00
RSSD Scott Darling D 8.00 20.00
RSSG Shayne Gostisbehere D 8.00 20.00
RSSJ Seth Jones C 6.00 15.00
RSSM Sean Monahan 8.00 20.00
RSSR Sam Reinhart C 8.00 20.00
RSTH Tomas Hertl D 8.00 20.00
RSTO Tyler Toffoli C 8.00 20.00
RSTT Tomas Tatar C 6.00 15.00
RSZP Zach Parise A 20.00 50.00

2015-16 Upper Deck Ice Rookie Relic Jumbos

RANDOM INSERTS IN PACKS
RRJAB Antoine Bibeau 2.00 5.00
RRJAP Artemi Panarin 6.00 15.00
RRJBH Ben Hutton 2.00 5.00
RRJBM Brock McGinn 2.00 5.00
RRJCH Connor Hellebuyck 5.00 12.00
RRJCM Connor McDavid 20.00 50.00
RRJDL Dylan Larkin 6.00 15.00
RRJEP Emile Poirier 2.00 5.00
RRJHS Henrik Samuelsson 1.50 4.00
RRJJD Jacob de la Rose 2.00 5.00
RRJJE Jack Eichel 15.00 40.00
RRJJM Jared McCann 2.00 5.00
RRJJV Jake Virtanen 2.50 6.00
RRJKF Kevin Fiala 2.00 5.00
RRJMC Mike Condon 2.00 5.00
RRJMD Max Domi 4.00 10.00
RRJMP Matt Puempel 1.50 4.00
RRJMR Mikko Rantanen 4.00 10.00
RRJMS Malcolm Subban 5.00 12.00
RRJNE Nikolaj Ehlers 4.00 10.00
RRJNG Nikolay Goldobin 2.00 5.00
RRJNH Noah Hanifin 2.50 6.00
RRJNP Nicolas Petan 2.00 5.00
RRJNR Nick Ritchie 2.00 5.00
RRJRF Robby Fabbri 2.50 6.00
RRJRH Ryan Hartman 2.50 6.00
RRJSB Sam Bennett 2.50 6.00
RRJSH Hunter Shinkaruk 2.00 5.00
RRJSP Shane Prince 1.50 4.00
RRJST Shea Theodore 2.00 5.00

2015-16 Upper Deck Ice Signature Swatches

GRP A STATED ODDS 1:3,193
GRP B STATED ODDS 1:3,560
GRP C STATED ODDS 1:496
GRP D STATED ODDS 1:433
GRP E STATED ODDS 1:93
SSAL Andrew Ladd E 6.00 15.00
SSAO Alexander Ovechkin A 40.00 80.00
SSCM Connor McDavid A 300.00 400.00
SSCP Corey Perry D 6.00 15.00
SSDG Doug Gilmour B 10.00 25.00
SSDL Dylan Larkin D 60.00 120.00
SSEM Evgeni Malkin B 15.00 40.00
SSEP Emile Poirier E 6.00 15.00
SSGF Grant Fuhr C 12.00 30.00
SSJB Jonathan Bernier E 6.00 15.00
SSJC John Carlson E 8.00 20.00
SSJH Jiri Hudler E 5.00 12.00
SSKT Kyle Turris E 5.00 12.00
SSLR Luc Robitaille A 12.00 30.00
SSMA Mark Scheifele E 8.00 20.00
SSMF Marc-Andre Fleury D 12.00 30.00
SSMG Mike Gartner C 8.00 20.00
SSMS Martin St. Louis C 12.00 30.00
SSNE Nikolaj Ehlers E 12.00 30.00
SSNG Nikolay Goldobin E 6.00 15.00
SSOP Ondrej Palat C 5.00 12.00
SSRB Rod Brind'Amour C 5.00 12.00
SSSB Sam Bennett D 8.00 20.00
SSSC Sidney Crosby A 75.00 150.00
SSSJ Seth Jones E 5.00 12.00
SSTH Tomas Hertl C 6.00 15.00

2015-16 Upper Deck Ice Superb Script

SSAB Antoine Bibeau 8.00 20.00
SSCH Connor Hellebuyck 20.00 50.00
SSCM Connor McDavid 300.00 600.00
SSDL Dylan Larkin 75.00 150.00
SSDS Daniel Sprong 15.00 40.00
SSFA Robby Fabbri 10.00 25.00
SSJD Jacob de la Rose 8.00 20.00
SSJM Jared McCann 8.00 20.00
SSJV Jake Virtanen 10.00 25.00
SSKF Kevin Fiala 8.00 20.00
SSMD Max Domi 15.00 40.00
SSMP Matt Puempel 6.00 15.00
SSMR Mikko Rantanen 15.00 40.00
SSMS Malcolm Subban 20.00 50.00
SSNE Nikolaj Ehlers 15.00 40.00
SSNG Nikolay Goldobin 8.00 20.00
SSNH Noah Hanifin 10.00 25.00
SSNP Nicolas Petan 8.00 20.00
SSOL Oscar Lindberg 8.00 20.00
SSRF Radek Faksa 8.00 20.00
SSSB Sam Bennett 10.00 25.00
SSSP Sergei Plotnikov 6.00 15.00
SSVA Viktor Arvidsson 10.00 25.00

2015-16 Upper Deck Ice World Juniors Championship

STATED PRINT RUN 699 - 1299 SER.#'d SETS
WJCM Connor McDavid/699 30.00 80.00
WJHS Hunter Shinkaruk/1299 3.00 8.00
WJJV Jake Virtanen/1299 4.00 10.00
WJMD Max Domi/699 6.00 15.00
WJMS Malcolm Subban/1299 8.00 20.00
WJNP Nicolas Petan/1299 3.00 8.00
WJNR Nick Ritchie/1299 3.00 8.00
WJRF Robby Fabbri/1299 4.00 10.00
WJSB Sam Bennett/1299 4.00 10.00
WJST Shea Theodore/1299 3.00 8.00
WJZF Zachary Fucale/1299 3.00 8.00

2016-17 Upper Deck Ice

1 Sidney Crosby 4.00 10.00
2 John Tavares 2.00 5.00
3 Jamie Benn 1.25 3.00
4 Vladimir Tarasenko 1.50 4.00
5 Johnny Gaudreau 1.50 4.00
6 Oliver Ekman-Larsson .75 2.00
7 Aaron Ekblad 1.00 2.50
8 Drew Doughty 1.00 2.50
9 Taylor Hall 2.00 5.00
10 Carey Price 3.00 8.00
11 Milan Lucic .75 2.00
12 Teuvo Teravainen 1.00 2.50
13 Frans Nielsen .75 2.00
14 Seth Jones .75 2.00
15 Eric Staal 1.25 3.00
16 Brad Marchand 1.25 3.00
17 Matt Duchene 1.00 2.50
18 P.K. Subban 1.50 4.00
19 Jonathan Toews 2.00 5.00
20 Mike Hoffman .75 2.00
21 Nikita Kucherov 1.50 4.00
22 Mats Zuccarello 1.00 2.50
23 John Gibson 1.00 2.50
24 Kyle Okposo 1.00 2.50
25 Alexander Ovechkin 4.00 10.00
26 Shayne Gostisbehere 1.25 3.00
27 Joe Thornton 1.00 2.50
28 Morgan Rielly .75 2.00
29 Matt Murray 1.50 4.00
30 Ryan Miller 1.00 2.50
31 Jonathan Drouin 1.25 3.00
32 Tuukka Rask 1.00 2.50
33 Robby Fabbri 1.00 2.50
34 Blake Wheeler 1.00 2.50
35 Torey Krug 1.00 2.50
36 Jonathan Quick 1.50 4.00
37 Jaden Schwartz 1.25 3.00
38 Cory Schneider .75 2.00
39 Andrew Ladd 1.00 2.50
40 Devan Dubnyk 1.00 2.50
41 Ryan Johansen 1.25 3.00
42 John Klingberg 1.00 2.50
43 Max Pacioretty 1.00 2.50
44 Steven Stamkos 2.00 5.00
45 Evgeny Kuznetsov 1.50 4.00
46 Mika Zibanejad 1.00 2.50
47 Sam Reinhart .75 2.00
48 Ryan Nugent-Hopkins 1.00 2.50
49 Frederik Andersen .75 2.00
50 Evgeni Malkin 3.00 8.00
51 Brayden Schenn 1.00 2.50
52 Bobby Ryan .75 2.00
53 Brock Nelson .75 2.00
54 Logan Couture 1.00 2.50
55 Brandon Dubinsky 1.00 2.50
56 Jeff Skinner 1.00 2.50
57 Patrick Kane 2.00 5.00
58 Vincent Trocheck 1.00 2.50
59 Petr Mrazek 1.00 2.50
60 Jarome Iginla 1.00 2.50
61 David Backes 1.00 2.50
62 Mark Scheifele 1.25 3.00
63 Jason Spezza 1.00 2.50
64 Jeff Carter 1.00 2.50
65 Mikko Koivu .75 2.00
66 James Neal .75 2.00
67 John Carlson 1.25 3.00
68 Derek Stepan .75 2.00
69 Brendan Gallagher 1.25 3.00
70 Brian Elliott .75 2.00
71 Dylan Larkin 1.50 4.00
72 Loui Eriksson 1.00 2.50
73 Patrick Sharp .75 2.00
74 Nikolaj Ehlers 1.00 2.50
75 Claude Giroux 1.00 2.50
76 Ryan O'Reilly 1.00 2.50
77 Tyler Johnson .75 2.00
78 Artemi Panarin 1.25 3.00
79 Tyson Barrie 1.00 2.50
80 Ryan McDonagh .75 2.00
81 Victor Rask .75 2.00
82 Kevin Shattenkirk .75 2.00
83 Leon Draisaitl 1.25 3.00
84 Boone Jenner 1.00 2.50
85 Thomas Greiss .75 2.00
86 Michael Cammalleri .75 2.00
87 Ryan Getzlaf 1.50 4.00
88 Brent Burns 1.25 3.00
89 Anthony Duclair 1.00 2.50
90 Alex Galchenyuk 1.25 3.00
91 Mark Giordano .75 2.00
92 Pekka Rinne 1.25 3.00
93 Kris Letang 1.00 2.50
94 Corey Crawford 1.25 3.00
95 Nicklas Backstrom 1.50 4.00
96 Mark Stone 1.00 2.50
97 Ryan Kesler 1.00 2.50
98 Keith Yandle 1.00 2.50
99 Bo Horvat 1.50 4.00

100 Connor McDavid 5.00 12.00
101 Anthony DeAngelo RC 4.00 10.00
102 Frederik Gauthier RC 3.00 8.00
103 Stephen Johns RC 3.00 8.00
104 Chase De Leo RC 4.00 10.00
105 Miles Wood RC 3.00 8.00
106 Joseph Cramarossa RC 4.00 10.00
107 Michal Kempny RC 4.00 10.00
108 Hudson Fasching RC 4.00 10.00
109 Markus Nutivaara RC 4.00 10.00
110 Jacob Larsson RC 6.00 15.00
111 Julius Honka RC 4.00 10.00
112 Mike Reilly RC 3.00 8.00
113 Denis Malgin RC 4.00 10.00
114 Alan Quine RC 4.00 10.00
115 Nikita Zaitsev RC 4.00 10.00
116 Yohann Auvitu RC 4.00 10.00
117 Jake Guentzel RC 15.00 40.00
118 Zane Mcintyre RC 5.00 12.00
119 Charlie Lindgren RC 8.00 20.00
120 Justin Bailey RC 4.00 10.00
121 Tom Kuhnhackl RC 3.00 8.00
122 Rob O'Gara RC 4.00 10.00
123 Chris Bigras RC 3.00 8.00
124 Roman Lyubimov RC 4.00 10.00
125 Nick Lappin RC 4.00 10.00
126 Cristoval Nieves RC 5.00 12.00
127 Nikita Tryamkin RC 3.00 8.00
128 John Quenneville RC 4.00 10.00
129 Aaron Dell RC 5.00 12.00
130 Gustav Forsling RC 4.00 10.00
131 Zack Mitchell RC 4.00 10.00
132 Gemel Smith RC 4.00 10.00
133 Lukas Sedlak RC 4.00 10.00
134 Kevin Gravel RC 5.00 12.00
135 Mark Jankowski RC 3.00 8.00
136 Kyle Rau RC 5.00 12.00
137 Drake Caggiula RC 4.00 10.00
138 Tristan Jarry RC 8.00 20.00
139 Thatcher Demko RC 8.00 20.00
140 Zach Hyman RC 5.00 12.00
141 Nikita Soshnikov RC 2.50 6.00
142 Trevor Carrick RC 4.00 10.00
143 Austin Czarnik RC 6.00 15.00
144 Jason Dickinson RC 3.00 8.00
145 Kevin Labanc RC 4.00 10.00
146 Nic Dowd RC 4.00 10.00
147 Zach Sanford RC 4.00 10.00
148 Jakob Chychrun RC 4.00 10.00
149 Dominik Simon RC 4.00 10.00
150 Ryan Pulock RC 4.00 10.00
151 Blake Speers RC 4.00 10.00
152 Pontus Aberg RC 5.00 12.00
153 Steven Santini RC 3.00 8.00
154 A.J. Greer RC 4.00 10.00
155 Michael Matheson RC 4.00 10.00
156 Matthew Benning RC 5.00 12.00
157 Oliver Kylington RC 3.00 8.00
158 Thomas Chabot RC 8.00 20.00
159 Brandon Tanev RC 4.00 10.00
160 Esa Lindell RC 4.00 10.00
161 Oliver Bjorkstrand RC 3.00 8.00
162 Nick Sorensen RC 4.00 10.00
163 Tyler Bertuzzi RC 5.00 12.00
164 Nick Baptiste RC 4.00 10.00
165 Nick Schmaltz RC 6.00 15.00
166 Brandon Carlo RC 5.00 12.00
167 Lawson Crouse RC 4.00 10.00
168 Timo Meier RC 5.00 12.00
169 Jakub Vrana RC 5.00 12.00
170 Tyler Motte RC 5.00 12.00
171 Sonny Milano RC 6.00 15.00
172 Danton Heinen RC 8.00 20.00
173 Josh Morrissey RC 6.00 15.00
174 Anthony Beauvillier RC 5.00 12.00
175 Mathew Barzal RC 15.00 40.00
176 Artturi Lehkonen RC 5.00 12.00
177 Brandon Leipsic RC 5.00 12.00
178 Troy Stecher RC 5.00 12.00
179 Kasperi Kapanen RC 10.00 25.00
180 Connor Brown RC 8.00 20.00
181 Ivan Provorov RC 15.00 40.00
182 Travis Konecny RC 15.00 40.00
183 Pavel Zacha RC 10.00 25.00
184 Brayden Point RC 20.00 50.00
185 Sebastian Aho RC 15.00 40.00
186 Kyle Connor RC 20.00 50.00
187 Joel Eriksson Ek RC 8.00 20.00
188 Christian Dvorak RC 8.00 20.00
189 Anthony Mantha RC 20.00 50.00
190 Pavel Buchnevich RC 12.00 30.00
191 William Nylander RC 200.00 500.00
192 Patrik Laine RC 600.00 1000.00
193 Jimmy Vesey RC 60.00 150.00
194 Matthew Tkachuk RC 150.00 300.00
195 Mitch Marner RC 300.00 600.00
196 Jesse Puljujarvi RC 100.00 250.00
197 Dylan Strome RC 60.00 150.00
198 Mikhail Sergachev RC 100.00 250.00
199 Zach Werenski RC 60.00 150.00
200 Auston Matthews RC 1500.00 2500.00

2016-17 Upper Deck Ice Fresh Threads

FTAB Anthony Beauvillier 2.00 5.00
FTAM Auston Matthews 25.00 60.00
FTBP Brayden Point 5.00 12.00
FTCD Christian Dvorak 2.00 5.00
FTCL Charlie Lindgren 4.00 10.00
FTDS Dylan Strome 4.00 10.00
FTIP Ivan Provorov 4.00 10.00
FTJC Jakob Chychrun 2.00 5.00
FTJE Joel Eriksson Ek 2.00 5.00
FTJP Jesse Puljujarvi 5.00 12.00
FTJV Jimmy Vesey 4.00 10.00
FTKC Kyle Connor 5.00 12.00
FTKK Kasperi Kapanen 4.00 10.00
FTMA Anthony Mantha 5.00 12.00
FTMB Mathew Barzal 6.00 15.00
FTMM Mitch Marner 10.00 25.00
FTMS Mikhail Sergachev 4.00 10.00
FTMT Matthew Tkachuk 6.00 15.00
FTNS Nick Schmaltz 2.00 5.00
FTPB Pavel Buchnevich 3.00 8.00
FTPL Patrik Laine 10.00 25.00
FTPZ Pavel Zacha 2.50 6.00
FTSA Sebastian Aho 4.00 10.00
FTSM Sonny Milano 2.50 6.00
FTSO Nikita Soshnikov 1.25 3.00
FTTC Thomas Chabot 2.00 5.00
FTTK Travis Konecny 4.00 10.00
FTTM Tyler Motte 2.00 5.00
FTWN William Nylander 8.00 20.00
FTZW Zach Werenski 4.00 10.00

2016-17 Upper Deck Ice Fresh Threads Red

*RED/25: 1X TO 2.5X BASIC INSERTS
FTAM Auston Matthews 50.00 125.00
FTPL Patrik Laine 40.00 100.00

2016-17 Upper Deck Ice Frozen Fabrics

FFAE Aaron Ekblad 3.00 8.00
FFCM Connor McDavid 25.00 60.00
FFCP Corey Perry 3.00 8.00
FFEK Erik Karlsson 6.00 15.00
FFEM Evgeni Malkin 10.00 25.00
FFFP Felix Potvin 5.00 12.00
FFHS Henrik Sedin 3.00 8.00
FFHZ Henrik Zetterberg 6.00 15.00
FFJB Jamie Benn 4.00 10.00
FFJG Johnny Gaudreau 5.00 12.00
FFJQ Jonathan Quick 5.00 12.00
FFJS Joe Sakic 8.00 20.00
FFJT John Tavares 6.00 15.00
FFMB Martin Brodeur 6.00 15.00
FFML Milan Lucic 2.50 6.00
FFMM Mark Messier 6.00 15.00
FFMP Max Pacioretty 3.00 8.00
FFMZ Mika Zibanejad 3.00 8.00
FFNH Noah Hanifin 3.00 8.00
FFPS P.K. Subban 5.00 12.00
FFSC Sidney Crosby 20.00 50.00
FFTO Jonathan Toews 15.00 40.00

2016-17 Upper Deck Ice Frozen Foursome

F4FW FW 20.00 50.00
F4DEF DEF 10.00 25.00
F4RC1 RC1 25.00 60.00
F4RC2 RC2 20.00 50.00
F4RC3 RC3 30.00 80.00
F4RC4 RC4 10.00 25.00
F4HABS HABS 15.00 40.00
F4NASH NASH 8.00 20.00
F4BLUES Blues 8.00 20.00
F4HAWKS HAWKS 10.00 25.00
F4WINGS WINGS 8.00 20.00
F4SHARKS SHARKS 6.00 15.00

2016-17 Upper Deck Ice Glacial Graphs

GGAA Andreas Athanasiou D 8.00 20.00
GGAE Aaron Ekblad 8.00 20.00
GGAM Al MacInnis 8.00 20.00
GGBB Bob Baun 8.00 20.00
GGBH Bo Horvat 12.00 30.00
GGBJ Boone Jenner 8.00 20.00
GGBS Borje Salming 8.00 20.00
GGBU Brent Burns 10.00 25.00
GGCH Carl Hagelin 8.00 20.00
GGCS Cory Schneider 6.00 15.00
GGDK David Krejci 8.00 20.00
GGDL Leon Draisaitl 10.00 25.00
GGDT Dave Taylor 8.00 20.00
GGGC Guy Carbonneau 8.00 20.00
GGHZ Henrik Zetterberg 10.00 25.00
GGJG John Gibson D 8.00 20.00
GGJO Ryan Johansen B 10.00 25.00
GGJZ Jason Zucker 6.00 15.00
GGKM Kirk McLean 8.00 20.00
GGKP Kyle Palmieri C 6.00 15.00
GGLD Louis Domingue 6.00 15.00
GGLM Larry Murphy A 8.00 20.00
GGMB Matt Beleskey 6.00 15.00
GGMM Matt Murray 12.00 30.00
GGMR Morgan Rielly 6.00 15.00
GGMS Mark Scheifele 10.00 25.00
GGNK Nikita Kucherov 12.00 30.00
GGNN Nino Niederreiter 8.00 20.00
GGRJ Roman Josi 8.00 20.00
GGRM Ryan Miller 8.00 20.00
GGRS Ryan Spooner 6.00 15.00
GGTB Tyson Barrie 8.00 20.00
GGTL Trevor Linden 10.00 25.00
GGTT Tyler Toffoli 8.00 20.00
GGTW Tom Wilson 8.00 20.00
GGVR Victor Rask 6.00 15.00

2016-17 Upper Deck Ice Champions

IC1 Sidney Crosby 15.00 40.00
IC2 Jonathan Quick 6.00 15.00
IC3 Zdeno Chara 4.00 10.00
IC4 Corey Perry 4.00 10.00
IC5 Patrick Kane 8.00 20.00
IC6 Cam Ward 4.00 10.00
IC7 Evgeni Malkin 12.00 30.00
IC8 Duncan Keith 4.00 10.00
IC9 Drew Doughty 4.00 10.00
IC10 Henrik Zetterberg 5.00 12.00
IC11 Matt Murray 6.00 15.00
IC12 Doug Harvey 4.00 10.00
IC13 Teemu Selanne 8.00 20.00
IC14 Bobby Orr 25.00 60.00
IC15 Ray Bourque 6.00 15.00
IC16 Red Kelly 4.00 10.00
IC17 Mark Messier 5.00 12.00
IC18 Al MacInnis 4.00 10.00
IC19 Mario Lemieux 15.00 40.00
IC20 Martin St. Louis 4.00 10.00
IC21 Steve Yzerman 12.00 30.00
IC22 Brian Leetch 4.00 10.00
IC23 Martin Brodeur 8.00 20.00
IC24 Wayne Gretzky 25.00 60.00

2016-17 Upper Deck Ice Rookie Relic Jumbos

RRJAB Anthony Beauvillier 5.00 12.00
RRJAD Anthony DeAngelo 5.00 12.00
RRJAM Auston Matthews 30.00 80.00
RRJBL Brendan Leipsic 5.00 12.00
RRJBP Brayden Point 5.00 12.00
RRJCB Connor Brown 8.00 20.00
RRJCD Christian Dvorak 5.00 12.00
RRJDS Dylan Strome 10.00 25.00
RRJHF Hudson Fasching 10.00 25.00
RRJIP Ivan Provorov 10.00 25.00
RRJJE Joel Eriksson Ek 5.00 12.00
RRJJM Josh Morrissey 6.00 15.00
RRJJP Jesse Puljujarvi 12.00 30.00
RRJJV Jimmy Vesey 10.00 25.00
RRJKC Kyle Connor 12.00 30.00
RRJKK Kasperi Kapanen 10.00 25.00
RRJKL Kevin Labanc 5.00 12.00
RRJMA Anthony Mantha 12.00 30.00
RRJMB Mathew Barzal 15.00 40.00
RRJMM Mitch Marner 25.00 60.00
RRJMS Mikhail Sergachev 12.00 30.00
RRJMT Matthew Tkachuk 15.00 40.00
RRJPB Pavel Buchnevich 8.00 20.00
RRJPL Patrik Laine 20.00 50.00
RRJPZ Pavel Zacha 6.00 15.00
RRJSA Sebastian Aho 10.00 25.00
RRJTK Travis Konecny 10.00 25.00
RRJTM Tyler Motte 5.00 12.00
RRJWN William Nylander 20.00 50.00
RRJZW Zach Werenski 10.00 25.00

2016-17 Upper Deck Ice Signature Swatches

SSAE Aaron Ekblad C 8.00 20.00
SSAG Alex Galchenyuk C 10.00 25.00
SSAH Adam Henrique C 8.00 20.00
SSAM Auston Matthews A 250.00 400.00
SSAO Alexander Ovechkin A
SSCP Carey Price A 40.00 100.00
SSHZ Henrik Zetterberg A 12.00 30.00
SSJG John Gibson B
SSJJ Jaromir Jagr B 40.00 100.00
SSJP Joe Pavelski B 8.00 20.00
SSJT Jonathan Toews A 60.00 150.00
SSMA Anthony Mantha C 20.00 50.00
SSMB Matt Beleskey C 6.00 15.00
SSMG Marian Gaborik C
SSON Owen Nolan C 8.00 20.00
SSPC Paul Coffey A
SSPL Patrik Laine B 50.00 120.00
SSRB Ray Bourque A 25.00 60.00
SSRJ Roman Josi C 8.00 20.00
SSRK Ryan Kesler C 8.00 20.00
SSRL Roberto Luongo B 8.00 20.00
SSTT Tyler Toffoli C 8.00 20.00
SSWN William Nylander C 30.00 80.00
SSZP Zach Parise C 8.00 20.00

2016-17 Upper Deck Ice Sub Zero

SZ1 Connor McDavid 5.00 12.00
SZ2 Henrik Zetterberg 1.25 3.00
SZ3 Braden Holtby 1.50 4.00
SZ4 Evgeni Malkin 3.00 8.00
SZ5 Jaromir Jagr 2.50 6.00
SZ6 Erik Karlsson 2.00 5.00
SZ7 Tyler Seguin 1.50 4.00
SZ8 Jordan Eberle 1.00 2.50
SZ9 Gustav Nyquist 1.00 2.50
SZ10 Patrick Kane 2.00 5.00
SZ11 Roberto Luongo 1.00 2.50
SZ12 Tyler Toffoli 1.00 2.50
SZ13 Joe Pavelski 1.00 2.50
SZ14 Filip Forsberg 1.25 3.00
SZ15 Daniel Sedin 1.00 2.50
SZ16 Dustin Byfuglien 1.00 2.50
SZ17 Jaroslav Halak 1.00 2.50
SZ18 Zach Parise 1.00 2.50
SZ19 Anze Kopitar 1.50 4.00
SZ20 Alexander Ovechkin 4.00 10.00
SZ21 Shea Weber .75 2.00
SZ22 Sam Bennett 1.25 3.00
SZ23 Ben Bishop 1.00 2.50
SZ24 Alexander Steen 1.00 2.50
SZ25 Jonathan Toews 2.00 5.00
SZ26 Alexander Wennberg .75 2.00
SZ27 Max Domi 1.25 3.00
SZ28 Henrik Lundqvist 1.50 4.00
SZ29 Adam Henrique 1.00 2.50
SZ30 John Tavares 2.00 5.00
SZ31 P.K. Subban 1.50 4.00
SZ32 Nino Niederreiter 1.00 2.50
SZ33 Mark Scheifele 1.25 3.00
SZ34 Nathan MacKinnon 2.00 5.00
SZ35 Sidney Crosby 4.00 10.00
SZ36 Jordan Staal 1.00 2.50
SZ37 James van Riemsdyk 1.00 2.50
SZ38 Sean Monahan 1.00 2.50
SZ39 Jack Eichel 2.00 5.00
SZ40 Carey Price 3.00 8.00
SZ41 David Krejci 1.00 2.50
SZ42 Kevin Hayes .75 2.00
SZ43 Corey Perry 1.00 2.50
SZ44 Jake Allen 1.00 2.50
SZ45 Jamie Benn 1.25 3.00
SZ46 Patrice Bergeron 1.25 3.00
SZ47 Henrik Sedin 1.00 2.50
SZ48 Martin Jones 1.00 2.50
SZ49 Gabriel Landeskog .75 2.00
SZ50 Steven Stamkos 2.00 5.00
SZ51 Jakub Voracek 1.00 2.50
SZ52 Brandon Saad 1.00 2.50
SZ53 Mario Lemieux 3.00 8.00
SZ54 Pat LaFontaine 1.00 2.50
SZ55 Mark Messier 1.25 3.00
SZ56 Stan Mikita 1.25 3.00
SZ57 Steve Yzerman 2.50 6.00
SZ58 Bobby Orr 3.00 8.00
SZ59 Patrick Roy 2.50 6.00
SZ60 Wayne Gretzky 5.00 12.00
SZ61 Auston Matthews 12.00 30.00
SZ62 Zach Werenski 2.00 5.00
SZ63 Patrik Laine 10.00 25.00
SZ64 Matthew Tkachuk 3.00 8.00
SZ65 William Nylander 4.00 10.00
SZ66 Jesse Puljujarvi 2.50 6.00
SZ67 Jimmy Vesey 2.00 5.00
SZ68 Anthony Mantha 2.50 6.00
SZ69 Tyler Motte 1.00 2.50
SZ70 Travis Konecny 2.00 5.00
SZ71 Pavel Zacha 1.25 3.00
SZ72 Pavel Buchnevich 1.50 4.00
SZ73 Dylan Strome 2.00 5.00
SZ74 Sebastian Aho 2.00 5.00
SZ75 Mitch Marner 5.00 12.00
SZ76 Brayden Point 2.50 6.00
SZ77 Connor Brown 1.50 4.00
SZ78 Mikhail Sergachev 2.00 5.00
SZ79 Anthony Beauvillier 1.00 2.50
SZ80 Kasperi Kapanen 2.00 5.00
SZ81 Ivan Provorov 2.00 5.00
SZ82 Christian Dvorak 1.00 2.50
SZ83 Kyle Connor 2.50 6.00
SZ84 Mathew Barzal 3.00 8.00
SZ85 Brandon Carlo 1.00 2.50
SZ86 Gustav Forsling 1.00 2.50
SZ87 Joel Eriksson Ek 1.00 2.50
SZ88 Frederik Gauthier .75 2.00
SZ89 Troy Stecher 1.00 2.50
SZ90 A.J. Greer 1.00 2.50
SZ91 Artturi Lehkonen 1.00 2.50
SZ92 Anthony DeAngelo 1.00 2.50
SZ93 Josh Morrissey 1.25 3.00
SZ94 Tyler Bertuzzi 1.50 4.00
SZ95 Nick Baptiste 1.00 2.50
SZ96 Mitch Marner 20.00 50.00
SZ97 Patrik Laine 60.00 150.00
SZ98 William Nylander 20.00 50.00
SZ99 Jesse Puljujarvi 20.00 50.00
SZ100 Auston Matthews 60.00 150.00

2016-17 Upper Deck Ice Superb Script

SSAM Auston Matthews 250.00 400.00
SSCB Connor Brown 15.00 40.00
SSCD Christian Dvorak 10.00 25.00
SSDH Danton Heinen 15.00 40.00
SSDS Dylan Strome 30.00 80.00
SSIP Ivan Provorov 40.00 100.00
SSJE Joel Eriksson Ek 20.00 50.00
SSJP Jesse Puljujarvi 25.00 60.00
SSJV Jimmy Vesey 20.00 50.00
SSKC Kyle Connor 25.00 60.00
SSKK Kasperi Kapanen 20.00 50.00
SSMA Anthony Mantha 25.00 60.00
SSMB Mathew Barzal 30.00 80.00
SSMM Mitch Marner 50.00 125.00
SSMS Mikhail Sergachev 40.00 100.00
SSMT Matthew Tkachuk 60.00 150.00
SSPL Patrik Laine 250.00 350.00
SSPZ Pavel Zacha/25
SSSA Sebastian Aho/49
SSSM Sonny Milano/49
SSTC Thomas Chabot 20.00 50.00
SSWN William Nylander 40.00 100.00
SSZW Zach Werenski 20.00 50.00

2016-17 Upper Deck Ice World Juniors

WJBP Brayden Point 5.00 12.00
WJBS Blake Speers 2.00 5.00
WJDS Dylan Strome 4.00 10.00
WJJQ John Quenneville 2.00 5.00
WJLC Lawson Crouse 1.50 4.00
WJMB Mathew Barzal 6.00 15.00
WJMM Mitch Marner 10.00 25.00
WJTC Thomas Chabot 4.00 10.00
WJTK Travis Konecny 10.00 25.00

2017-18 Upper Deck Ice

1 Cory Schneider .75 2.00
2 Scott Hartnell .60 1.50
3 Justin Williams .75 2.00
4 Leon Draisaitl 1.50 4.00
5 Nathan MacKinnon 2.00 5.00
6 Niklas Hjalmarsson .60 1.50
7 Patrick Kane 2.00 5.00
8 Tuukka Rask 1.00 2.50
9 Artemi Panarin 1.00 2.50
10 Mark Giordano .75 2.00
11 Drew Doughty 1.00 2.50
12 Patrik Laine 1.50 4.00
13 Daniel Sedin 1.00 2.50
14 Calvin de Haan .75 2.00
15 Filip Forsberg 1.25 3.00
16 Erik Karlsson 1.25 3.00
17 Alexander Ovechkin 4.00 10.00
18 Aleksander Barkov 1.00 2.50
19 John Tavares 2.00 5.00
20 Brayden Schenn 1.00 2.50
21 David Krejci .75 2.00
22 Nail Yakupov .75 2.00
23 Kevin Labanc .60 1.50
24 Brayden Point 1.00 2.50
25 Wayne Simmonds 1.25 3.00
26 Shea Weber .75 2.00
27 Chris Kreider 1.00 2.50
28 Cam Talbot 1.00 2.50
29 Dustin Byfuglien 1.00 2.50
30 Patrick Marleau 1.00 2.50
31 Christopher Tanev .60 1.50
32 Darnell Nurse .75 2.00
33 Henrik Zetterberg 1.00 2.50
34 Josh Bailey .75 2.00
35 Brandon Saad 1.00 2.50
36 Steven Stamkos 2.00 5.00
37 Matt Duchene 1.00 2.50
38 Travis Hamonic .75 2.00
39 Kris Letang 1.00 2.50
40 Mark Scheifele 1.25 3.00
41 Nate Schmidt .75 2.00
42 Alex Pietrangelo .75 2.00
43 Brett Pesce .60 1.50
44 Andrew Cogliano .60 1.50
45 Mike Green .75 2.00
46 Nikita Kucherov 1.50 4.00
47 Matt Murray 1.50 4.00
48 Jordan Staal 1.00 2.50
49 Reilly Smith .75 2.00
50 Jake Gardiner .75 2.00
51 Marcus Johansson .75 2.00
52 Jonathan Marchessault 1.00 2.50
53 Mikael Backlund .60 1.50
54 Erik Johnson .75 2.00
55 Jonathan Toews 2.00 5.00
56 Mika Zibanejad 1.00 2.50
57 Oscar Klefbom .75 2.00
58 Ben Bishop 1.00 2.50
59 Nicklas Backstrom 1.50 4.00
60 Derick Brassard 1.00 2.50
61 Jakub Voracek 1.00 2.50
62 Evander Kane 1.00 2.50
63 Nick Bjugstad .75 2.00
64 Max Domi 1.00 2.50
65 Josh Manson .60 1.50
66 Anze Kopitar 1.50 4.00
67 Viktor Arvidsson 1.00 2.50
68 Jason Zucker .75 2.00
69 Patrice Bergeron 1.25 3.00
70 Jonathan Drouin 1.00 2.50
71 Corey Perry 1.00 2.50
72 Carey Price 3.00 8.00
73 Jared Spurgeon .60 1.50
74 Roberto Luongo 1.00 2.50
75 Thomas Vanek .75 2.00
76 Anthony Mantha 1.00 2.50
77 Brad Marchand 1.25 3.00
78 Henrik Lundqvist 1.50 4.00
79 Cam Atkinson 1.00 2.50
80 Sean Couturier .75 2.00
81 Ryan O'Reilly 1.00 2.50
82 Ryan Getzlaf 1.00 2.50
83 Mitch Marner 2.00 5.00
84 Kyle Okposo .75 2.00
85 Colton Parayko 1.00 2.50
86 Bryan Rust 1.00 2.50
87 Martin Jones 1.00 2.50
88 Jack Eichel 1.50 4.00
89 Tyler Seguin 1.50 4.00
90 Braden Holtby 1.50 4.00
91 Sami Vatanen .60 1.50
92 Alexander Radulov 1.00 2.50
93 Nino Niederreiter .75 2.00
94 Evgeni Malkin 3.00 8.00
95 Evgeny Kuznetsov 1.50 4.00
96 Joe Pavelski 1.00 2.50
97 Nick Foligno .75 2.00
98 William Nylander 1.50 4.00
99 Dustin Brown .75 2.00
100 Marc-Edouard Vlasic .60 1.50
101 Giovanni Fiore/1299 RC 8.00 20.00
102 David Rittich/1299 RC 8.00 20.00
103 Robbie Russo/1299 RC 4.00 10.00
104 Jaycob Megna/1299 RC 4.00 10.00
105 Joakim Ryan/1299 RC 4.00 10.00
106 Oscar Fantenberg/1299 RC 4.00 10.00
107 Griffen Molino/1299 RC 3.00 8.00
108 Vladislav Kamenev/1299 RC 6.00 15.00
109 Kalle Kossila/1299 RC 3.00 8.00
110 Tim Heed/1299 RC 4.00 10.00
111 Jan Rutta/1299 RC 4.00 10.00
112 Vadim Shipachyov/1299 RC 12.00 30.00
113 Michael Kapla/1299 RC 4.00 10.00
114 Alex Iafallo/1299 RC 4.00 10.00
115 Viktor Antipin/1299 RC 4.00 10.00
116 Andrew Poturalski/1299 RC 4.00 10.00
117 Marcus Sorensen/1299 RC 3.00 8.00
118 Michael Amadio/1299 RC 4.00 10.00
119 Ville Husso/1299 RC 4.00 10.00
120 Jonny Brodzinski/499 RC 5.00 12.00
121 Jake Dotchin/1299 RC 3.00 8.00
122 Jean-Sebastien Dea/1299 RC 4.00 10.00
123 Brendan Lemieux/1299 RC 4.00 10.00
124 Valentin Zykov/1299 RC 4.00 10.00
125 Carter Rowney/1299 RC 3.00 8.00
126 Tucker Poolman/999 RC 3.00 8.00
127 Kyle Capobianco/999 RC 4.00 10.00
128 Alex Nedeljkovic/999 RC 3.00 8.00
129 MacKenzie Weegar/999 RC 4.00 10.00
130 Lucas Wallmark/999 RC 4.00 10.00
131 Anton Lindholm/999 RC 4.00 10.00
132 Riley Barber/999 RC 3.00 8.00
133 Alexandre Carrier/999 RC 3.00 8.00
134 Ian McCoshen/999 RC 4.00 10.00
135 Mike Vecchione/999 RC 3.00 8.00
136 Remi Elie/999 RC 3.00 8.00
137 Henrik Haapala/999 RC 3.00 8.00
138 Jordan Schmaltz/999 RC 5.00 12.00
139 Maxime Lagace/999 RC 4.00 10.00
140 Rasmus Andersson/999 RC 4.00 10.00
141 Adin Hill/999 RC 4.00 10.00
142 Andreas Borgman/999 RC 4.00 10.00
143 Roland McKeown/999 RC 4.00 10.00
144 C.J. Smith/999 RC 3.00 8.00
145 Nicolas Kerdiles/999 RC 4.00 10.00
146 Peter Cehlarik/999 RC 4.00 10.00
147 Blake Coleman/999 RC 3.00 8.00
148 Gabriel Carlsson/999 RC 3.00 8.00
149 Robert Hagg/999 RC 4.00 10.00
150 John Hayden/999 RC 3.00 8.00
151 Samuel Blais/499 RC 5.00 12.00
152 Nick Merkley/1299 RC 4.00 10.00
153 Christian Jaros/499 RC 5.00 12.00
154 Samuel Morin/499 RC 4.00 10.00
155 Jesper Bratt/499 RC 8.00 20.00
156 Vince Dunn/499 RC 5.00 12.00
157 Alex Formenton/499 RC 5.00 12.00
158 Martin Necas/499 RC 5.00 12.00
159 Madison Bowey/499 RC 4.00 10.00
160 J.T. Compher/499 RC 6.00 15.00
161 Evgeny Svechnikov/499 RC 10.00 25.00
162 Jon Gillies/499 RC 5.00 12.00
163 Samuel Girard/499 RC 5.00 12.00
164 Nikita Scherbak/499 RC 10.00 25.00
165 Janne Kuokkanen/499 RC 5.00 12.00
166 Jakob Forsbacka-Karlsson/499 RC 5.00 12.00
167 Ivan Barbashev/499 RC 5.00 12.00
168 Filip Chlapik/499 RC 5.00 12.00
169 Eric Comrie/499 RC 4.00 10.00
170 Denis Gurianov/499 RC 5.00 12.00
171 Christian Fischer/499 RC 6.00 15.00
172 Christian Djoos/499 RC 5.00 12.00
173 Calle Rosen/499 RC 5.00 12.00
174 Haydn Fleury/499 RC 5.00 12.00
175 Jack Roslovic/499 RC 6.00 15.00
176 Will Butcher/249 RC 10.00 25.00
177 Alex Kerfoot/249 RC 8.00 20.00
178 Luke Kunin/249 RC 8.00 20.00
179 Tage Thompson/249 RC 12.00 30.00
180 Adrian Kempe/249 RC 10.00 25.00
181 Anders Bjork/249 RC 10.00 25.00
182 Colin White/249 RC 8.00 20.00
183 Victor Mete/249 RC 8.00 20.00
184 Jake DeBrusk/249 RC 12.00 30.00
185 Kailer Yamamoto/249 RC 20.00 50.00
186 Logan Brown/249 RC 8.00 20.00
187 Travis Sanheim/249 RC 8.00 20.00
188 Filip Chytil/249 RC 8.00 20.00
189 Alex Tuch/249 RC 20.00 50.00
190 Owen Tippett/249 RC 15.00 40.00
191 Charlie McAvoy/99 RC 350.00 700.00
192 Clayton Keller/99 RC 200.00 300.00
193 Brock Boeser/99 RC 350.00 600.00
194 Josh Ho-Sang/99 RC 250.00 350.00
195 Tyson Jost/99 RC 200.00 300.00
196 Pierre-Luc Dubois/99 RC 200.00 300.00
197 Alex DeBrincat/99 RC 200.00 300.00
198 Alexander Nylander/99 RC
199 Nolan Patrick/99 RC 350.00 450.00
200 Nico Hischier/99 RC 350.00 450.00

2017-18 Upper Deck Ice '07-08 Retro Ice Premieres

1 Nico Hischier 60.00 150.00
2 Clayton Keller 50.00 125.00
3 Brock Boeser 100.00 250.00
4 Charlie McAvoy 60.00 150.00
5 Pierre-Luc Dubois 40.00 100.00
6 Tyson Jost 40.00 100.00
7 Josh Ho-Sang 25.00 60.00
8 Alex DeBrincat 50.00 125.00
9 Filip Chytil 20.00 50.00
10 Nolan Patrick 40.00 100.00

2017-18 Upper Deck Ice Frozen Foursomes

F4BUF Eichel/O'Reilly 8.00 20.00
Pominville/Ristolainen C
F4DIV Pacioretty/Toews 20.00 50.00
Ovechkin/Getzlaf A
F4NOR Burns/Doughty/Karlsson/Keith B 6.00 15.00
F4OIL McDavid/Lucic/Larsson/Talbot A 20.00 50.00
F4RC1 McAvoy/Boeser/Keller/Ho-Sang D 25.00 60.00
F4RC2 Hischier/Patrick 15.00 40.00
DeBrincat/Dubois D
F4CBUS Wennberg/Jones 5.00 12.00
Werenski/Bobrovsky D
F4JETS Wheeler/Scheifele/Laine/Ehlers B 8.00 20.00
F4PENS Letang/Malkin/Kessel/Murray A 15.00 40.00
F4SENS Hoffman/Stone 5.00 12.00
Brassard/Anderson C
F4WILD Granlund/Niederreiter 6.00 15.00
Staal/Dubnyk C
F4BOLTS Stamkos/Kucherov 10.00 25.00
Hedman/Vasilevskiy B
F4BRUIN Marchand/Spooner 8.00 20.00
Pastrnak/Krug B
F4CANES Williams 5.00 12.00
Slavin/Rask/Teravainen D
F4HAWKS Toews/Saad/Sharp/Crawford B 10.00 25.00
F4KINGS Carter/Toffoli/Pearson/Quick C 8.00 20.00
F4LEAFS Marner/Nylander 8.00 20.00
Rielly/Andersen C
F4SELKE Bergeron/Kopitar 10.00 25.00
Toews/Kesler A
F4YOTES Ekman-Larsson
Domi/Dvorak/Duclair D

2017-18 Upper Deck Ice Ice Caps Autographs

ICAK Anze Kopitar/30 25.00 60.00
ICCM Connor McDavid/15
ICEK Erik Karlsson/30
ICMM Mark Messier/30 25.00 60.00
ICMP Max Pacioretty/65
ICRB Rod Brind'Amour/65
ICRL Rod Langway/65 6.00 15.00
ICSY Steve Yzerman/15
ICWG Wayne Gretzky/15

2017-18 Upper Deck Ice Ice Premieres Autographs

IPAAD Alex DeBrincat/299 25.00 60.00
IPAAF Alex Formenton/299 4.00 10.00
IPAAK Adrian Kempe/299 5.00 12.00
IPAAN Alexander Nylander/199 20.00 50.00
IPAAT Alex Tuch/299 15.00 40.00
IPABB Brock Boeser/199 100.00 200.00
IPACF Christian Fischer/299 5.00 12.00
IPACH Filip Chlapik/299 4.00 10.00
IPACK Clayton Keller/99 80.00 150.00
IPACM Charlie McAvoy/199 12.00 30.00
IPACW Colin White/299 4.00 10.00
IPADG Denis Gurianov/299 4.00 10.00
IPAES Evgeny Svechnikov/299 8.00 20.00
IPAFC Filip Chytil/299 4.00 10.00
IPAFK Jakob Forsbacka-Karlsson/299 4.00 10.00
IPAIB Ivan Barbashev/299 4.00 10.00
IPAJD Jake DeBrusk/299 6.00 15.00
IPAJG Jon Gillies/299 4.00 10.00
IPAJH Josh Ho-Sang/199 5.00 12.00
IPAJR Jack Roslovic/299 5.00 12.00
IPAJT J.T. Compher/299 5.00 12.00
IPAKY Kailer Yamamoto/299 20.00 50.00
IPALK Luke Kunin/299 4.00 10.00
IPAMB Madison Bowey/299 3.00 8.00
IPANS Nikita Scherbak/299 8.00 20.00
IPAOT Owen Tippett/199 8.00 20.00
IPAPL Pierre-Luc Dubois/199 8.00 20.00
IPARH Robert Hagg/299 4.00 10.00
IPATJ Tyson Jost/199 8.00 20.00
IPATT Tage Thompson/299 6.00 15.00
IPAVD Vince Dunn/299 4.00 10.00
IPAVH Ville Husso/299 4.00 10.00
IPAVK Vladislav Kamenev/299 6.00 15.00
IPAVM Victor Mete/299 4.00 10.00
IPAVZ Valentin Zykov/299 4.00 10.00

2017-18 Upper Deck Ice Premieres Jerseys

IPJAB Anders Bjork B 4.00 10.00
IPJAD Alex DeBrincat B 8.00 20.00
IPJAF Alex Formenton D 3.00 8.00
IPJAK Adrian Kempe C 4.00 10.00
IPJAN Alexander Nylander B 5.00 12.00
IPJAT Alex Tuch B 8.00 20.00
IPJBB Brock Boeser A 15.00 40.00
IPJCF Christian Fischer C 4.00 10.00
IPJCH Filip Chlapik C 3.00 8.00
IPJCK Clayton Keller A 8.00 20.00
IPJCM Charlie McAvoy A 10.00 25.00
IPJCW Colin White C 3.00 8.00
IPJDG Denis Gurianov D 3.00 8.00
IPJES Evgeny Svechnikov D 6.00 15.00
IPJFC Filip Chytil C 3.00 8.00
IPJFK Jakob Forsbacka-Karlsson D 3.00 8.00
IPJIB Ivan Barbashev D 3.00 8.00
IPJJD Jake DeBrusk B 5.00 12.00
IPJJG Jon Gillies D 3.00 8.00
IPJJH Josh Ho-Sang B 4.00 10.00
IPJJK Janne Kuokkanen D 3.00 8.00
IPJJR Jack Roslovic C 4.00 10.00
IPJJT J.T. Compher C 4.00 10.00
IPJKY Kailer Yamamoto C 8.00 20.00
IPJLB Logan Brown C 3.00 8.00
IPJLK Luke Kunin B 3.00 8.00
IPJMB Madison Bowey D 2.50 6.00
IPJNH Nico Hischier A 10.00 25.00
IPJNP Nolan Patrick A 6.00 15.00
IPJNS Nikita Scherbak C 6.00 15.00
IPJOT Owen Tippett B 6.00 15.00
IPJPL Pierre-Luc Dubois A 6.00 15.00
IPJRH Robert Hagg D 3.00 8.00
IPJTJ Tyson Jost B 6.00 15.00
IPJTT Tage Thompson C 5.00 12.00
IPJVD Vince Dunn D 3.00 8.00
IPJVK Vladislav Kamenev D 5.00 12.00
IPJVS Vadim Shipachyov B 10.00 25.00
IPJVZ Valentin Zykov D 3.00 8.00

2017-18 Upper Deck Ice Rinkside Signings

RSAA Artem Anisimov C 6.00 15.00
RSAD Alex DeBrincat C 20.00 50.00
RSBB Brock Boeser C 40.00 100.00
RSBP Brian Propp C 8.00 20.00
RSCK Clayton Keller C 20.00 50.00
RSDG Denis Gurianov C 6.00 15.00
RSDK David Krejci C 6.00 15.00
RSFC Filip Chytil C 6.00 15.00
RSFP Felix Potvin B 30.00 80.00
RSJH Josh Ho-Sang C 10.00 25.00
RSJR Jack Roslovic C 10.00 25.00
RSLC Logan Couture A 8.00 20.00
RSMD Marcel Dionne A 10.00 25.00
RSMS Mark Scheifele B 10.00 25.00
RSNK Nikita Kucherov B 12.00 30.00
RSNS Nikita Scherbak C 15.00 40.00
RSPL Patrik Laine A 80.00 150.00
RSRL Roberto Luongo A 10.00 25.00
RSTJ Tyson Jost C 15.00 40.00
RSVH Victor Hedman B 10.00 25.00

2017-18 Upper Deck Ice Rookie Relic Jumbos

RRJAB Anders Bjork 2.00 5.00
RRJAD Alex DeBrincat 4.00 10.00
RRJAN Alexander Nylander 2.50 6.00
RRJBB Brock Boeser 8.00 20.00
RRJCK Clayton Keller 4.00 10.00
RRJCM Charlie McAvoy 5.00 12.00
RRJCW Colin White 1.50 4.00
RRJES Evgeny Svechnikov 3.00 8.00
RRJHF Haydn Fleury 1.50 4.00
RRJHS Josh Ho-Sang 2.00 5.00
RRJIB Ivan Barbashev 1.50 4.00
RRJJG Jon Gillies 1.50 4.00
RRJNH Nico Hischier 5.00 12.00
RRJNP Nolan Patrick 3.00 8.00
RRJNS Nikita Scherbak 3.00 8.00
RRJPD Pierre-Luc Dubois 3.00 8.00
RRJSM Samuel Morin 1.50 4.00
RRJTJ Tyson Jost 3.00 8.00
RRJTS Travis Sanheim 1.50 4.00
RRJVS Vadim Shipachyov 5.00 12.00

2017-18 Upper Deck Ice Signature Swatches

SSCD Christian Dvorak/150 5.00 12.00
SSCP Carey Price/25 60.00 150.00
SSCW Colin White/150 6.00 15.00
SSDD Devan Dubnyk/150 6.00 15.00
SSEK Erik Karlsson/25 25.00 60.00
SSHL Henrik Lundqvist/75 25.00 60.00
SSHZ Henrik Zetterberg/75 15.00 40.00
SSIP Ivan Provorov/150 6.00 15.00
SSJP Joe Pavelski/75 15.00 40.00
SSJT Jonathan Toews/25 40.00 100.00
SSNH Noah Hanifin/150 6.00 15.00
SSNN Nino Niederreiter/150 5.00 12.00
SSSS Steven Stamkos/25 40.00 100.00
SSTA John Tavares/75 30.00 80.00
SSTF Theoren Fleury/75 15.00 40.00
SSTH Taylor Hall/75 30.00 80.00
SSTN Tage Thompson/150 10.00 25.00
SSTT Teuvo Teravainen/150 5.00 12.00

2017-18 Upper Deck Ice Sub Zero

SZ1 Wendel Clark 4.00 10.00
SZ2 Maurice Richard 3.00 8.00
SZ3 Ray Bourque 5.00 12.00
SZ4 Wayne Gretzky 15.00 40.00
SZ5 Pierre Pilote 3.00 8.00
SZ6 Alex Delvecchio 3.00 8.00
SZ7 Jarome Iginla 3.00 8.00
SZ8 Pelle Lindbergh 3.00 8.00
SZ9 Martin Brodeur 6.00 15.00
SZ10 Brett Hull 3.00 8.00
SZ11 Sergei Bobrovsky 3.00 8.00
SZ12 Marc-Andre Fleury 2.50 6.00
SZ13 Sidney Crosby 6.00 15.00
SZ14 Claude Giroux 1.50 4.00
SZ15 Henrik Lundqvist 2.50 6.00
SZ16 Derek Stepan 1.25 3.00
SZ17 William Nylander 2.50 6.00
SZ18 Taylor Hall 3.00 8.00
SZ19 Nikita Kucherov 2.50 6.00
SZ20 Corey Crawford 2.00 5.00
SZ21 James Neal 1.25 3.00
SZ22 Joe Thornton 1.50 4.00
SZ23 Erik Karlsson 2.00 5.00
SZ24 Evgeni Malkin 5.00 12.00
SZ25 Nathan MacKinnon 3.00 8.00
SZ26 Patrik Laine 2.50 6.00
SZ27 Ryan Getzlaf 1.50 4.00
SZ28 Alexander Ovechkin 6.00 15.00
SZ29 Jonathan Drouin 1.50 4.00
SZ30 Vincent Trocheck 1.25 3.00
SZ31 John Tavares 3.00 8.00
SZ32 Brent Burns 2.00 5.00
SZ33 Filip Forsberg 2.00 5.00
SZ34 Jeff Carter 1.50 4.00
SZ35 Jaromir Jagr 4.00 10.00
SZ36 Jack Eichel 2.50 6.00
SZ37 Connor McDavid 6.00 15.00
SZ38 Bo Horvat 1.50 4.00
SZ39 Johnny Gaudreau 2.50 6.00
SZ40 Auston Matthews 6.00 15.00
SZ41 Jeff Skinner 1.25 3.00
SZ42 Vladimir Tarasenko 2.50 6.00
SZ43 David Pastrnak 2.50 6.00
SZ44 Pekka Rinne 2.00 5.00
SZ45 Jamie Benn 2.00 5.00
SZ46 Patrick Kane 3.00 8.00
SZ47 Devan Dubnyk 1.50 4.00
SZ48 Matt Murray 2.50 6.00
SZ49 Steven Stamkos 3.00 8.00
SZ50 Dylan Larkin 1.50 4.00
SZ51 Christian Fischer 2.00 5.00
SZ52 Travis Sanheim 1.50 4.00
SZ53 Pierre-Luc Dubois 3.00 8.00
SZ54 Alex DeBrincat 4.00 10.00
SZ55 Adrian Kempe 2.00 5.00
SZ56 Alex Tuch 4.00 10.00
SZ57 Tyson Jost 3.00 8.00
SZ58 Colin White 1.50 4.00
SZ59 Jake DeBrusk 2.50 6.00
SZ60 Brock Boeser 5.00 12.00
SZ61 Owen Tippett 3.00 8.00
SZ62 Charlie McAvoy 5.00 12.00
SZ63 Nico Hischier 5.00 12.00
SZ64 Anders Bjork 2.00 5.00
SZ65 Clayton Keller 4.00 10.00
SZ66 Kailer Yamamoto 4.00 10.00
SZ67 Ivan Barbashev 1.50 4.00
SZ68 Alexander Nylander 2.50 6.00
SZ69 Evgeny Svechnikov 2.50 6.00
SZ70 Martin Necas 1.50 4.00
SZ71 Filip Chytil 1.50 4.00
SZ72 Luke Kunin 1.50 4.00
SZ73 Nolan Patrick 3.00 8.00
SZ74 Logan Brown 1.50 4.00
SZ75 Alex Kerfoot 1.50 4.00
SZ76 Haydn Fleury 1.50 4.00
SZ77 Victor Mete 1.00 2.50
SZ78 Tage Thompson 2.50 6.00
SZ79 Josh Ho-Sang 2.00 5.00
SZ80 Will Butcher 2.00 5.00

2017-18 Upper Deck Ice Sub Zero Rookie Variations

V1 Brock Boeser 25.00 60.00
V2 Charlie McAvoy 15.00 40.00
V3 Clayton Keller 12.00 30.00
V4 Nico Hischier 15.00 40.00
V5 Nolan Patrick 10.00 25.00
V6 Alex DeBrincat 12.00 30.00
V7 Josh Ho-Sang 6.00 15.00
V8 Pierre-Luc Dubois 10.00 25.00
V9 Tyson Jost 10.00 25.00
V10 Will Butcher 6.00 15.00

2012 Upper Deck Industry Summit Signature Icons Autographs

LAS VEGAS INDUSTRY SUMMIT EXCLUSIVE

2001-02 Upper Deck Legends

Issued in early-December 2001, this 100-card set carried an SRP of $4.99 for a 5-card pack. The set focused on legendary NHL players of the past.

COMPLETE SET (100) 25.00 50.00
1 Bobby Orr 1.25 3.00
2 Eddie Shore .40 1.00
3 Phil Esposito .60 1.50
4 Johnny Bucyk .30 .75
5 Cam Neely .40 1.00
6 Gerry Cheevers .40 1.00
7 Gilbert Perreault .30 .75
8 Rene Robert .10 .25
9 Lanny McDonald .30 .75
10 Al Secord .10 .25
11 Bobby Hull .75 2.00
12 Glenn Hall .40 1.00
13 Stan Mikita .40 1.00

14 Tony Esposito .40 1.00
15 Gordie Howe 1.25 3.00
16 Terry Sawchuk .60 1.50
17 Ted Lindsay .40 1.00
18 Sid Abel .10 .25
19 Red Kelly .40 1.00
20 Alex Delvecchio .40 1.00
21 Glenn Anderson .10 .25
22 Wayne Gretzky 1.50 4.00
23 Jari Kurri .30 .75
24 Grant Fuhr .30 .75
25 Bill Ranford .30 .75
26 Gordie Howe 1.25 3.00
27 Marcel Dionne .30 .75
28 Butch Goring .10 .25
29 Rogie Vachon .15 .40
30 Maurice Richard .75 2.00
31 Jean Beliveau .40 1.00
32 Serge Savard .40 1.00
33 Jacques Plante .60 1.50
34 Guy Lafleur .40 1.00
35 Yvan Cournoyer .40 1.00
36 Steve Shutt .10 .25
37 Rick Green .10 .25
38 Henri Richard .40 1.00
39 Bernie Geoffrion .40 1.00
40 Guy Lapointe .10 .25
41 Denis Potvin .30 .75
42 Mike Bossy .30 .75
43 Bryan Trottier .30 .75
44 Clark Gillies .10 .25
45 Billy Smith .30 .75
46 Ed Giacomin .40 1.00
47 Jean Ratelle .10 .25
48 Lester Patrick .10 .25
49 William Jennings .10 .25
50 Ray Bourque .75 2.00
51 Frank Calder .10 .25
52 Andy van Hellemond .10 .25
53 Bobby Clarke .30 .75
54 Bernie Parent .40 1.00
55 Bill Barber .10 .25
56 Syl Apps .10 .25
57 Bernie Federko .10 .25
58 Frank Mahovlich .40 1.00
59 Darryl Sittler .40 1.00
60 Tim Horton .40 1.00
61 Rick Vaive .10 .25
62 Frank Selke .10 .25
63 Conn Smythe .10 .25
64 King Clancy .10 .25
65 Tony Tanti .10 .25
66 Mike Ridley .10 .25
67 Rod Langway .10 .25
68 Mike Gartner .30 .75
69 Kent Nilsson .10 .25
70 Reggie Leach .10 .25
71 Dennis Maruk .10 .25
72 Wilf Paiement .10 .25
73 Barry Beck .10 .25
74 Simon Nolet .10 .25
75 Don Beaupre .10 .25
76 Peter Stastny .30 .75
77 Michel Goulet .30 .75
78 Dale Hawerchuk .30 .75
79 Gerry Cheevers .40 1.00
80 Glenn Hall .40 1.00
81 Terry Sawchuk .60 1.50
82 Grant Fuhr .30 .75
83 Bernie Parent .40 1.00
84 Jacques Plante .60 1.50
85 Ed Giacomin .40 1.00
86 Bill Ranford .30 .75
87 Billy Smith .30 .75
88 Tony Esposito .40 1.00
89 Bobby Orr 1.25 3.00
90 Bobby Hull .75 2.00
91 Gordie Howe 1.25 3.00
92 Wayne Gretzky 1.50 4.00
93 Marcel Dionne .30 .75
94 Maurice Richard .75 2.00
95 Guy Lafleur .50 1.25
96 Mike Bossy .30 .75
97 Jari Kurri .40 1.00
98 Mike Gartner .40 1.00
99 Gordie Howe CL .60 1.50
100 Wayne Gretzky CL .75 2.00

2001-02 Upper Deck Legends Epic Signatures

Randomly inserted at 1:54 packs, this 18-card set featured authentic autographs of NHL alums.

AD Alex Delvecchio 12.50 30.00
BC Bobby Clarke 12.50 30.00
BH Bobby Hull 20.00 50.00
BO Bobby Orr 100.00 200.00
BT Bryan Trottier 10.00 25.00
CN Cam Neely 12.00 30.00
FM Frank Mahovlich 12.50 30.00
GH Gordie Howe 60.00 150.00
GL Guy Lafleur 15.00 40.00
GP Gilbert Perreault 12.50 30.00
JB Jean Beliveau 25.00 50.00
MB Mike Bossy 12.50 30.00
MD Marcel Dionne 10.00 25.00
PE Phil Esposito 12.50 30.00
SM Stan Mikita 15.00 40.00
TE Tony Esposito 15.00 40.00
TL Ted Lindsay 12.50 30.00
WG Wayne Gretzky 125.00 250.00

2001-02 Upper Deck Legends Fiorentino Collection

Randomly inserted at 1:18, this 15-card set featured reproductions of photographs taken by renowned sports photographer James Fiorentino.

COMPLETE SET (15) 40.00 80.00
FCBC Bobby Clarke 1.50 4.00
FCBH Bobby Hull 2.50 6.00
FCBO Bobby Orr 6.00 15.00
FCBT Bryan Trottier 1.50 4.00
FCGH Gordie Howe 3.00 8.00
FCGL Guy Lafleur 1.50 4.00
FCJP Jacques Plante 1.50 4.00
FCMB Mike Bossy 1.50 4.00
FCMD Marcel Dionne 1.50 4.00
FCMR Maurice Richard 3.00 8.00
FCPE Phil Esposito 1.50 4.00
FCSM Stan Mikita 1.50 4.00
FCTE Tony Esposito 1.50 4.00
FCTS Terry Sawchuk 1.50 4.00
FCWG Wayne Gretzky 6.00 15.00

2001-02 Upper Deck Legends Timeless Tributes Jerseys

Randomly inserted at 1:18 packs, this 27-card set featured game-worn jersey swatches form the player(s) featured on the card fronts. A platinum parallel was also created and serial-numbered to 100 copies each.

*PLATINUM/100: .5X TO 1.2X BASIC JSY
TTBB Bill Barber 5.00 12.00
TTBH Bobby Hull 10.00 25.00
TTBR Bill Ranford 5.00 12.00
TTBS Billy Smith 5.00 12.00
TTBT Bryan Trottier 5.00 12.00
TTCG Clark Gillies 5.00 12.00
TTCN Cam Neely 12.50 30.00
TTDP Denis Potvin 5.00 12.00
TTFL Guy Lafleur Que. 5.00 12.00
TTGC Gerry Cheevers 5.00 12.00
TTGH Gordie Howe 12.50 30.00
TTGL Guy Lafleur AS 5.00 12.00
TTGP Gilbert Perreault 5.00 12.00
TTGU Guy Lafleur Mon/Que 10.00 25.00
TTGY Guy Lafleur NY/AS 12.50 30.00
TTHM B.Hull/S.Mikita 12.50 30.00
TTLA Guy Lafleur Mon. 5.00 12.00
TTLF Guy Lafleur NY 5.00 12.00
TTMG Mike Gartner 5.00 12.00
TTPE Phil Esposito 6.00 15.00
TTSL S.Shutt/G.Lafleur 10.00 25.00
TTSM Stan Mikita 5.00 12.00
TTSS Steve Shutt 5.00 12.00
TTST B.Smith/B.Trottier 12.50 30.00
TTVH Andy van Hellemond 5.00 12.00
TTWG Wayne Gretzky 15.00 40.00

2001-02 Upper Deck Legends Milestones Jerseys

Randomly inserted at 1:18, this 16-card set honored past players and the different career milestones they achieved. Each card carried a swatch of game-used jersey from the featured player. A platinum parallel was also created and serial-numbered to just 25 copies each.

MBB Bill Barber 8.00 20.00
MBC Bobby Clarke 10.00 25.00
MBS Brent Sutter 8.00 20.00
MBT Bryan Trottier 8.00 20.00
MCN Cam Neely 8.00 20.00
MDP Denis Potvin 8.00 20.00
MGP Gilbert Perreault 8.00 20.00
MLM Lanny McDonald 8.00 20.00
MMB Mike Bossy 8.00 20.00
MMG Mike Gartner 8.00 20.00
MNB Neal Broten 8.00 20.00
MSS Steve Shutt 8.00 20.00
MSY Steve Yzerman 6.00 15.00
MWG Wayne Gretzky 20.00 40.00

2001-02 Upper Deck Legends Pieces of History Sticks

Randomly inserted at 1:18, this 29-card set featured a piece of game-used stick from the pictured player.

PHBC Bobby Clarke 12.50 30.00
PHBH Bobby Hull 12.50 30.00
PHBO Bobby Orr 25.00 60.00
PHBS Billy Smith 8.00 20.00
PHBT Bryan Trottier 10.00 25.00
PHDP Denis Potvin 8.00 20.00
PHDS Darryl Sittler 8.00 20.00
PHES Phil Esposito 10.00 25.00
PHFM Frank Mahovlich 8.00 20.00
PHGC Gerry Cheevers 10.00 25.00
PHGH Gordie Howe Det. 15.00 40.00
PHGL Guy Lafleur 8.00 20.00
PHGR Wayne Gretzky LA 40.00 100.00
PHHU Bobby Hull 10.00 25.00
PHJB Jean Beliveau 15.00 40.00
PHJK Jari Kurri 15.00 40.00
PHJP Jacques Plante 15.00 40.00
PHJR Jean Ratelle 8.00 20.00
PHMB Mike Bossy 10.00 25.00
PHMD Marcel Dionne 8.00 20.00
PHMG Mike Gartner 8.00 20.00
PHMH Gordie Howe NE 15.00 40.00
PHMR Maurice Richard 30.00 80.00
PHPE Phil Esposito 10.00 25.00
PHRA Ray Bourque Col. 15.00 40.00
PHRB Ray Bourque Bos. 12.50 30.00
PHSM Stan Mikita 10.00 25.00
PHTE Tony Esposito 10.00 25.00
PHWG Wayne Gretzky Edm. 50.00 100.00

2000-01 Upper Deck Legends

Released in mid November 2000, Upper Deck Legends features a 135-card set where base design features both color and black and white photos of the greats of hockey. Base cards are enhanced with blue foil highlights and a white border that fades to each respective player's team color along the bottom. Legends was packaged in 24-pack boxes with each pack containing five cards and carried a suggested retail price of $4.99.

1 Paul Kariya .25 .60
2 Teemu Selanne .40 1.00
3 P.Kariya/T.Selanne .40 1.00
4 Patrik Stefan .15 .40
5 P.Stefan/D.Rhodes .15 .40
6 Bobby Orr .60 1.50
7 Phil Esposito .30 .75
8 Johnny Bucyk .15 .40
9 Cam Neely .20 .50
10 Eddie Shore .20 .50
11 Joe Thornton .30 .75
12 Sergei Samsonov .15 .40
13 C.Neely/J.Thornton .30 .75
14 Gilbert Perreault .20 .50
15 Pat LaFontaine .20 .50
16 Dominik Hasek .30 .75
17 Doug Gilmour .25 .60
18 G.Perreault/D.Hasek .30 .75
19 Lanny McDonald .15 .40
20 Valeri Bure .15 .40
21 T.Fleury/V.Bure .25 .60
22 Ron Francis .25 .60
23 Arturs Irbe .15 .40
24 R.Francis/A.Irbe .25 .60
25 Bobby Hull .30 .75
26 Stan Mikita .25 .60
27 Tony Esposito .20 .50
28 Glenn Hall .20 .50
29 Tony Amonte .15 .40
30 B.Hull/T.Amonte .30 .75
31 Patrick Roy .50 1.25
32 Ray Bourque .30 .75
33 Chris Drury .15 .40
34 Peter Forsberg .25 .60
35 Milan Hejduk .15 .40
36 P.Roy/P.Forsberg .50 1.25
37 Brett Hull .30 .75
38 Ed Belfour .20 .50
39 Mike Modano .30 .75
40 M.Modano/E.Belfour .30 .75
41 Gordie Howe .60 1.50
42 Ted Lindsay .20 .50
43 Terry Sawchuk .30 .75
44 Brendan Shanahan .25 .60
45 Chris Osgood .20 .50
46 Steve Yzerman .60 1.50
47 G.Howe/S.Yzerman .60 1.50
48 Grant Fuhr .20 .50
49 Wayne Gretzky 1.00 2.50
50 Jari Kurri .20 .50
51 Mark Messier .30 .75
52 Paul Coffey .20 .50
53 Doug Weight .20 .50
54 W.Gretzky/D.Weight 1.00 2.50
55 Pavel Bure .25 .60
56 Viktor Kozlov .15 .40
57 Vanbiesbrouck/Bure .25 .60
58 Marcel Dionne .25 .60
59 Zigmund Palffy .20 .50
60 Luc Robitaille .20 .50
61 Gretzky/L.Robitaille 1.00 2.50
62 Dino Ciccarelli .20 .50
63 Saku Koivu .20 .50
64 Jean Beliveau .25 .60
65 Doug Harvey .20 .50
66 Jacques Plante .20 .50
67 Guy Lafleur .25 .60
68 Serge Savard .20 .50
69 Larry Robinson .20 .50
70 Eric Weinrich .12 .30
71 Bernie Geoffrion .20 .50
72 Jose Theodore .25 .60
73 G.Lafleur/P.Roy .50 1.25
74 David Legwand .20 .50
75 D.Legwand/M.Dunham .20 .50
76 Martin Brodeur .40 1.00
77 Scott Gomez .15 .40
78 Scott Stevens .20 .50
79 S.Stevens/M.Brodeur .40 1.00
80 Denis Potvin .20 .50
81 Mike Bossy .20 .50
82 Bryan Trottier .25 .60
83 Butch Goring .12 .30
84 Bob Nystrom .15 .40
85 Chico Resch .12 .30
86 Clark Gilles .20 .50
87 Tim Connolly .12 .30
88 B.Trottier/T.Connolly .25 .60
89 Ed Giacomin .15 .40
90 Rod Gilbert .20 .50
91 Theo Fleury .25 .60
92 M.Messier/B.Leetch .30 .75
93 Marian Hossa .15 .40
94 Radek Bonk .15 .40
95 R.Bonk/M.Hossa .15 .40
96 Bobby Clarke .20 .50
97 Bernie Parent .20 .50
98 Eric Lindros .30 .75
99 Brian Boucher .15 .40
100 John LeClair .20 .50
101 B.Clarke/J.LeClair .20 .50
102 Jeremy Roenick .20 .50
103 Keith Tkachuk .20 .50
104 J.Roenick/K.Tkachuk .20 .50
105 Mario Lemieux .60 1.50
106 Joe Mullen .15 .40
107 Jaromir Jagr .50 1.25
108 M.Lemieux/J.Jagr .60 1.50
109 Peter Stastny .15 .40
110 Michel Goulet .15 .40
111 Steve Shields .12 .30
112 Jeff Friesen .12 .30
113 O.Nolan/J.Friesen .20 .50
114 Bernie Federko .15 .40
115 Chris Pronger .15 .40
116 Roman Turek .15 .40
117 B.Hull/P.Demitra .30 .75
118 Vincent Lecavalier .15 .40
119 V.Lecavalier/P.Mara .15 .40
120 Frank Mahovlich .20 .50
121 Syl Apps .15 .40
122 Tim Horton .20 .50
123 Eddie Shack .20 .50
124 Curtis Joseph .25 .60
125 Mats Sundin .20 .50
126 F.Mahovlich/C.Joseph .25 .60
127 Richard Brodeur .15 .40
128 R.Brodeur/M.Naslund .15 .40
129 Mike Gartner .20 .50
130 Adam Oates .20 .50
131 Olaf Kolzig .20 .50
132 M.Gartner/O.Kolzig .20 .50
133 Dale Hawerchuk .25 .60
134 Wayne Gretzky CL 1.00 2.50
135 Steve Yzerman CL .60 1.50

2000-01 Upper Deck Legends Enshrined Stars

Randomly inserted in packs at the rate of 1:12, this 15-card set features Hall of Famers on a foil bordered card with silver foil highlights.

COMPLETE SET (15) 30.00 60.00
ES1 Wayne Gretzky 6.00 15.00
ES2 Gordie Howe 4.00 10.00
ES3 Mario Lemieux 5.00 12.00
ES4 Bobby Hull 2.50 6.00
ES5 Marcel Dionne 1.50 4.00
ES6 Denis Potvin 1.50 4.00
ES7 Guy Lafleur 2.00 5.00
ES8 Mike Bossy 1.50 4.00
ES9 Bobby Clarke 1.50 4.00
ES10 Frank Mahovlich 1.50 4.00
ES11 Gilbert Perreault 1.50 4.00
ES12 Phil Esposito 2.50 6.00
ES13 Tony Esposito 2.00 5.00
ES14 Stan Mikita 2.00 5.00
ES15 Ted Lindsay 1.50 4.00

2000-01 Upper Deck Legends Epic Signatures

Randomly inserted in packs at the rate of 1:23, this 43-card set features player photography and authentic player autographs.

BC Bobby Clarke 10.00 25.00
BG Bernie Geoffrion 20.00 50.00
BH Brett Hull 15.00 40.00
BO Bobby Orr 60.00 150.00
BT Bryan Trottier 10.00 25.00
CJ Curtis Joseph 8.00 20.00
CN Cam Neely 12.00 30.00
DH Dale Hawerchuk 8.00 20.00
DP Denis Potvin 6.00 15.00
FM Frank Mahovlich 12.00 30.00
GH Gordie Howe 80.00 200.00
GL Guy Lafleur 15.00 40.00
GP Gilbert Perreault 8.00 20.00
JB John Bucyk 6.00 15.00
JK Jari Kurri 8.00 20.00
JL John LeClair 5.00 12.00
JM Joe Mullen 8.00 20.00
JN Joe Nieuwendyk 12.00 30.00
JT Joe Thornton 8.00 20.00
KT Keith Tkachuk 6.00 15.00
LM Lanny McDonald 8.00 20.00
LR Larry Robinson 6.00 15.00
MB Mike Bossy 8.00 20.00
MD Marcel Dionne 6.00 15.00
MG Mike Gartner 8.00 20.00
ML Mario Lemieux 50.00 120.00
MM Mark Messier 30.00 80.00
PB Pavel Bure 15.00 40.00
PE Phil Esposito 15.00 40.00
PL Pat LaFontaine 8.00 20.00
PS Patrik Stefan 6.00 15.00
PV Pat Verbeek 8.00 20.00
SF Sergei Fedorov 40.00 100.00
SM Stan Mikita 15.00 40.00
SS Sergei Samsonov 5.00 12.00
SY Steve Yzerman 40.00 100.00
TE Tony Esposito 8.00 20.00
TL Ted Lindsay 8.00 20.00
WG Wayne Gretzky 100.00 200.00
BHU Bobby Hull 20.00 50.00
JBE Jean Beliveau 20.00 50.00
MBR Martin Brodeur 25.00 60.00
MGO Michel Goulet 6.00 15.00
PBO Peter Bondra 8.00 20.00

2000-01 Upper Deck Legends Essence of the Game

Randomly inserted in packs at the rate of 1:23, this 8-card set combines a star from yesterday with a star from today on this all foil insert card with silver foil highlights.

COMPLETE SET (8) 30.00 60.00
EG1 G.Lafleur/P.Kariya 1.50 4.00
EG2 J.Jagr/W.Gretzky 4.00 10.00
EG3 P.Bure/M.Bossy 1.50 4.00
EG4 P.Roy/T.Sawchuk 5.00 12.00
EG5 M.Brodeur/B.Parent 2.50 6.00
EG6 C.Neely/B.Shanahan 1.50 4.00
EG7 R.Bourque/B.Orr 5.00 12.00
EG8 S.Yzerman/G.Howe 5.00 12.00

2000-01 Upper Deck Legends Legendary Collection Bronze

Randomly inserted in packs, this 135-card set parallels the base Legends set enhanced with bronze foil highlights and cards are sequentially numbered to 25.

*BRONZE/25: 20X TO 50X BASIC CARDS

2000-01 Upper Deck Legends Legendary Collection Gold

Randomly inserted in packs, this 135-card set parallels the base Legends set enhanced with gold foil highlights and cards are sequentially numbered to 375.

*GOLD/375: 4X TO 10X BASIC CARDS

2000-01 Upper Deck Legends Legendary Collection Silver

Randomly inserted in packs, this 135-card set parallels the base Legends set enhanced with silver foil highlights and cards are sequentially numbered to 100.

*SILVER/100: 6X TO 15X BASIC CARDS

2000-01 Upper Deck Legends Legendary Game Jerseys

Randomly inserted in packs at the rate of 1:23, this 36-card set features both color and black and white player photos, silver foil highlights, and a swatch of an authentic game jersey in the lower right hand corner of the card front.

JAM Al Macinnis 4.00 10.00
JBG Butch Goring 2.50 6.00
JBH Brett Hull 6.00 15.00
JBN Bob Nystrom 3.00 8.00
JBO Bobby Orr SP 25.00 60.00
JBT Bryan Trottier 5.00 12.00
JCG Clark Gillies 4.00 10.00
JCR Chico Resch 2.50 6.00
JDG Doug Gilmour 5.00 12.00
JDH Dominik Hasek 6.00 15.00
JDP Denis Potvin 4.00 10.00
JGF Grant Fuhr SP 4.00 10.00
JGH Gordie Howe 12.00 30.00
JJJ Jaromir Jagr 10.00 25.00
JJK Jari Kurri SP 4.00 10.00
JJL John LeClair 4.00 10.00
JJS Joe Sakic 6.00 15.00
JKT Keith Tkachuk 4.00 10.00
JLR Larry Robinson SP 4.00 10.00
JMB Mike Bossy 4.00 10.00
JMD Marcel Dionne SP 5.00 12.00
JMG Mike Gartner 4.00 10.00
JML Mario Lemieux 12.00 30.00
JMM Mike Modano 6.00 15.00
JMS Mats Sundin 4.00 10.00
JPB Pavel Bure 5.00 12.00
JPF Peter Forsberg 5.00 12.00
JPK Paul Kariya 5.00 12.00
JPL Pat LaFontaine 4.00 10.00
JPR Patrick Roy 10.00 25.00
JRB Ray Bourque 6.00 15.00
JSF Sergei Fedorov 6.00 15.00
JSY Steve Yzerman 12.00 30.00
JTS Teemu Selanne 8.00 20.00
JWG Wayne Gretzky 20.00 50.00
JMBR Martin Brodeur 8.00 20.00

2000-01 Upper Deck Legends of the Cage

Randomly inserted in packs at the rate of 1:18, this 10-card set showcases the greatest goalies to grace the game of hockey. Base cards feature and all-foil backdrop with player action photography and silver foil highlights.

COMPLETE SET (10) 20.00 40.00
LC1 Patrick Roy 5.00 12.00
LC2 Martin Brodeur 3.00 8.00
LC3 Dominik Hasek 2.50 6.00
LC4 Curtis Joseph 1.25 3.00
LC5 Ed Belfour 1.50 4.00
LC6 Grant Fuhr 1.25 3.00
LC7 Mike Richter 1.25 3.00
LC8 Jacques Plante 1.50 4.00
LC9 Terry Sawchuk 2.50 6.00
LC10 Tony Esposito 2.00 5.00

2000-01 Upper Deck Legends Playoff Heroes

Randomly inserted in packs at the rate of 1:15, this 12-card set showcases NHL players who year after year stepped it up in the playoffs. Cards feature 3 action panels along the center of the card set against an all foil backdrop with a close up photo of the featured player. Cards have silver foil highlights.

COMPLETE SET (12) 30.00 60.00
PH1 Patrick Roy 5.00 12.00
PH2 Steve Yzerman 5.00 12.00
PH3 Jaromir Jagr 1.50 4.00
PH4 Mike Modano 2.00 5.00
PH5 Peter Forsberg 2.50 6.00
PH6 Mark Messier 1.50 4.00
PH7 Wayne Gretzky 6.00 15.00
PH8 Brett Hull 1.50 4.00
PH9 Gordie Howe 4.00 10.00
PH10 Bobby Hull 2.50 6.00
PH11 Bryan Trottier 1.50 4.00
PH12 Phil Esposito 2.50 6.00

2000-01 Upper Deck Legends Supreme Milestones

Randomly inserted in packs at the rate of 1:4, this 15-card set spotlights NHL legends and highlights some of their most significant career achievements on an all holo-foil card with silver foil highlights. Player photos are set against a larger "faded" player photo in the background.

COMPLETE SET (15) 25.00 50.00
SM1 Wayne Gretzky 4.00 10.00
SM2 Gordie Howe 2.50 6.00
SM3 Bobby Hull 1.50 4.00
SM4 Wayne Gretzky 4.00 10.00
SM5 Steve Yzerman 2.00 5.00
SM6 Brett Hull .75 2.00
SM7 Joe Sakic 1.25 3.00
SM8 Mark Messier .75 2.00
SM9 Patrick Roy 3.00 8.00
SM10 Luc Robitaille .75 2.00
SM11 Mario Lemieux 3.00 8.00
SM12 Mike Bossy 1.00 2.50
SM13 Phil Esposito 1.50 4.00
SM14 Tony Esposito 1.25 3.00
SM15 Ray Bourque 1.00 2.50

2003 Upper Deck Magazine

As a bonus to buyers of the Upper Deck magazine produced by Krause Publications late in 2003, a nine-card perforated sheet featuring players basically signed to Upper Deck exclusives was included. When the cards were perforated, these cards measured the standard size. Please note that all of these cards have a "UD" prefix.

COMPLETE SET (9) 8.00 20.00
UD9 Wayne Gretzky 1.25 3.00

2014-15 Upper Deck Memorable Moments Spring Expo

MMAH1 Andrew Hammond
MMCM1 Connor McDavid 15.00 25.00

2008-09 Upper Deck Montreal Canadiens Centennial

COMPLETE SET (300) 125.00 250.00
COMP.SET w/o SPs (200) 30.00 80.00
(201-300) STATED ODDS 1 PER PACK
1 Toe Blake .20 .50
2 Jean Beliveau .30 .75
3 Donnie Marshall .20 .50
4 Bill Nyrop .20 .50
5 Mickey Redmond .20 .50
6 Yvan Cournoyer .30 .75
7 Dick Duff .25 .60
8 Ken Dryden .60 1.50
9 Bill Durnan .30 .75
10 Bob Gainey .30 .75
11 Herb Gardiner .20 .50
12 Bernard Geoffrion .20 .50
13 George Hainsworth .40 1.00
14 Doug Harvey .30 .75
15 Tom Johnson .25 .60
16 Aurele Joliat .30 .75
17 Elmer Lach .50 1.25
18 Guy Lafleur .40 1.00
19 Newsy Lalonde .25 .60
20 Rod Langway .25 .60
21 Jacques Laperriere .40 1.00
22 Guy Lapointe .25 .60
23 Jack Laviolette .25 .60
24 Jacques Lemaire .25 .60
25 Frank Mahovlich .30 .75
26 Joe Malone .25 .60
27 Sylvio Mantha .25 .60
28 Dickie Moore .25 .60
29 Howie Morenz .20 .50
30 Buddy O'Connor .20 .50
31 Bert Olmstead .25 .60
32 Didier Pitre .20 .50
33 Jacques Plante .50 1.25
34 Ken Reardon .20 .50
35 Henri Richard .40 1.00
36 Larry Robinson .30 .75
37 Maurice Richard .75 2.00
38 Mark Recchi .40 1.00
39 Patrick Roy .75 2.00
40 Denis Savard .40 1.00
41 Serge Savard .50 1.25
42 Albert Siebert .25 .60
43 Steve Shutt .30 .75
44 Georges Vezina .50 1.25
45 Butch Bouchard .40 1.00
46 Chris Nilan .20 .50
47 Doug Jarvis .20 .50
48 Pete Mahovlich .40 1.00
49 Mats Naslund .25 .60
50 Claude Provost .20 .50
51 Pierre Mondou .20 .50
52 Craig Ludwig .20 .50
53 Karl Dykhuis .20 .50
54 Ken Mosdell .20 .50
55 Georges Mantha .20 .50
56 Mark Napier .30 .75
57 Peter Popovic .20 .50
58 Vladimir Malakhov .20 .50
59 Cliff Goupille .20 .50
60 Lyle Odelein .20 .50
61 Ted Harris .20 .50
62 Gerry McNeil .20 .50
63 Murph Chamberlain .20 .50
64 Mike McPhee .20 .50
65 Andre Pronovost .20 .50
66 Kirk Muller .25 .60
67 Scott Thornton .20 .50
68 Keith Acton .20 .50
69 Brian Engblom .20 .50
70 Ralph Backstrom .20 .50
71 John Ambrose O'Brien .25 .60
72 Marcel Bonin .30 .75
73 Pierre Bouchard .30 .75
74 Armand Mondou .20 .50
75 Benoit Brunet .20 .50
76 Valeri Bure .20 .50
77 Walter Buswell .20 .50
78 Guy Carbonneau .30 .75
79 Albert LeDuc .25 .60
80 Chris Chelios .30 .75
81 Sprague Cleghorn .50 1.25
82 Bob Fillion .20 .50
83 Shayne Corson .20 .50
84 Russ Courtnall .20 .50
85 Billy Coutu .25 .60
86 Wilf Cude .40 1.00
87 Floyd Curry .20 .50
88 Leo Lamoureux .20 .50
89 Jean-Jacques Daigneault .25 .60
90 Vincent Damphousse .25 .60
91 Lorne Worsley .25 .60
92 Dave Balon .20 .50
93 Eric Desjardins .25 .60
94 Patrick Poulin .20 .50
95 John Ferguson .20 .50
96 Johnny Gagnon .20 .50
97 James Gardner .20 .50
98 Ray Getliffe .20 .50
99 Brent Gilchrist .25 .60
100 Gaston Gingras .20 .50
101 Phil Goyette .20 .50
102 Rick Green .20 .50
103 Howard McNamara .20 .50
104 Glen Harmon .20 .50
105 Terry Harper .20 .50
106 Bill Hicke .20 .50
107 Charlie Hodge .25 .60
108 Rejean Houle .30 .75
109 Marty Burke .20 .50
110 Joe Juneau .20 .50
111 Mike Keane .25 .60
112 Ab McDonald .25 .60
113 Patrice Brisebois .20 .50
114 Marc Tardif .25 .60
115 Yvon Lambert .30 .75
116 Wildor Larochelle .20 .50
117 Michel Larocque .25 .60
118 Claude Larose .20 .50
119 Pierre Larouche .25 .60
120 Stephan Lebeau .20 .50
121 John LeClair .30 .75
122 Roman Hamrlik .25 .60
123 Claude Lemieux .25 .60
124 Pit Lepine .40 1.00
125 Francis Bouillon .25 .60
126 Billy Reay .20 .50
127 Stephane Richer .25 .60
128 Doug Risebrough .25 .60
129 Craig Rivet .20 .50
130 Jim Roberts .20 .50
131 Bud MacPherson .20 .50
132 Bobby Rousseau .25 .60
133 Martin Rucinsky .20 .50
134 Brian Savage .20 .50
135 Mathieu Schneider .20 .50
136 Brian Skrudland .20 .50
137 Bobby Smith .20 .50
138 Turner Stevenson .20 .50
139 Petr Svoboda .20 .50
140 Jean-Guy Talbot .25 .60
141 Jose Theodore .30 .75
142 Gilles Tremblay .50 1.25
143 Jean-Claude Tremblay .20 .50
144 Mario Tremblay .40 1.00
145 Pierre Turgeon .30 .75
146 Rogie Vachon .40 1.00
147 Ryan Walter .20 .50
148 Paul Meger .20 .50
149 Dick Irvin .20 .50
150 Murray Wilson .30 .75
151 Joe Hall .20 .50
152 William Northey .20 .50
153 Senator Donat Raymond .20 .50
154 Leo Dandurand .20 .50
Jos Cattarinich
Louis Letourneau
155 Hartland De Montarville Molson .20 .50
156 Sam Pollock .20 .50
157 Frank J. Selke .20 .50
158 Tom P. Gorman .20 .50
159 Bob Turner .20 .50
160 Scotty Bowman .30 .75
161 Calum MacKay .20 .50
162 Paul Haynes .20 .50
163 Youppi MASCOT .20 .50
164 Toe Blake .20 .50
165 Oleg Petrov .20 .50
166 Stephane Quintal .20 .50
167 Saku Koivu .30 .75
168 Carey Price 1.25 3.00
169 Alex Kovalev .25 .60
170 Tomas Plekanec .30 .75
171 Andrei Markov .30 .75
172 Andrei Kostitsyn .25 .60
173 Christopher Higgins .20 .50
174 Rick Chartraw .20 .50
175 Dollard St. Laurent .20 .50
176 Mike Komisarek .20 .50
177 Coupe Stanley Cup .20 .50
178 Coupe Stanley Cup .20 .50
179 Coupe Stanley Cup .20 .50
180 Coupe Stanley Cup .20 .50
181 Coupe Stanley Cup .20 .50
182 Coupe Stanley Cup .20 .50
183 Coupe Stanley Cup .20 .50
184 Coupe Stanley Cup .20 .50
185 Coupe Stanley Cup .20 .50
186 Coupe Stanley Cup .20 .50
187 Coupe Stanley Cup .20 .50
188 Coupe Stanley Cup .20 .50
189 Coupe Stanley Cup .20 .50
190 Coupe Stanley Cup .20 .50
191 Coupe Stanley Cup .20 .50
192 Coupe Stanley Cup .20 .50
193 Coupe Stanley Cup .20 .50
194 Coupe Stanley Cup .20 .50
195 Coupe Stanley Cup .20 .50
196 Coupe Stanley Cup .20 .50
197 Coupe Stanley Cup .20 .50
198 Coupe Stanley Cup .20 .50
199 Coupe Stanley Cup .20 .50
200 Coupe Stanley Cup .20 .50
201 Jack Laviolette 1.50 4.00
202 Newsy Lalonde 1.50 4.00
203 James Gardner 1.25 3.00
204 Howard McNamara 1.25 3.00
205 Sprague Cleghorn 3.00 8.00
206 Billy Coutu 1.50 4.00
207 Sylvio Mantha 1.50 4.00
208 George Hainsworth 2.50 6.00
209 Albert Siebert 1.50 4.00
210 Walter Buswell 1.25 3.00
211 Toe Blake 1.25 3.00
212 Bill Durnan 2.00 5.00
213 Butch Bouchard 2.50 6.00
214 Maurice Richard 5.00 12.00
215 Doug Harvey 2.00 5.00
216 Jean Beliveau 2.00 5.00
217 Henri Richard 2.50 6.00
218 Yvan Cournoyer 2.00 5.00
219 Serge Savard 3.00 8.00
220 Bob Gainey 2.00 5.00
221 Chris Chelios 2.00 5.00
222 Guy Carbonneau 2.00 5.00
223 Kirk Muller 1.50 4.00
224 Mike Keane 1.50 4.00
225 Pierre Turgeon 2.00 5.00
226 Vincent Damphousse 1.50 4.00
227 Saku Koivu 2.00 5.00
228 Arena Jubilee Arena 1.25 3.00
229 Arena Westmount Arena 1.25 3.00
230 Arena Mont-Royal Arena 1.25 3.00
231 Forum - 1924 1.25 3.00
232 Forum - 1949 1.25 3.00
233 Forum - 1949 1.25 3.00
234 Centre Bell Centre 1.25 3.00
235 Henri Richard 2.50 6.00
236 Maurice Richard 5.00 12.00
237 Guy Lafleur 2.50 6.00
238 Guy Lafleur 2.50 6.00
239 Chris Nilan 1.25 3.00
240 Maurice Richard 5.00 12.00
241 Jacques Plante 3.00 8.00
242 George Hainsworth 2.50 6.00
243 Larry Robinson 2.00 5.00
244 Henri Richard 2.50 6.00
245 Jean Beliveau 2.00 5.00
246 Jacques Plante 3.00 8.00
247 George Hainsworth 2.50 6.00
248 Henri Richard 2.50 6.00
249 Maurice Richard 5.00 12.00
250 Guy Lafleur 2.50 6.00
251 Newsy Lalonde 1.50 4.00
252 Howie Morenz 1.25 3.00
253 Toe Blake 1.25 3.00
254 Elmer Lach 3.00 8.00
255 Bernard Geoffrion 1.25 3.00
256 Guy Lafleur 2.50 6.00
257 Ken Dryden 4.00 10.00
258 Doug Harvey 2.00 5.00
259 Guy Carbonneau 2.00 5.00
260 Jacques Plante 3.00 8.00
261 Jean Beliveau 2.00 5.00
262 Bob Gainey 2.00 5.00
263 Bill Durnan 2.00 5.00
264 George Hainsworth 2.50 6.00
265 Dickie Moore 1.50 4.00
266 Jacques Laperriere 2.50 6.00
267 Michel Larocque 1.50 4.00
268 Serge Savard 3.00 8.00
269 Charlie Hodge 1.50 4.00
270 Lorne Worsley 1.50 4.00
271 Patrick Roy 5.00 12.00
272 Larry Robinson 2.00 5.00
273 Jacques Plante 3.00 8.00
274 Doug Harvey 2.00 5.00
275 Jean Beliveau 2.00 5.00
276 Bernard Geoffrion 1.25 3.00
277 Howie Morenz 1.25 3.00
278 Maurice Richard 5.00 12.00
279 Guy Lafleur 2.50 6.00
280 Dickie Moore 1.50 4.00
281 Yvan Cournoyer 2.00 5.00
282 Henri Richard 2.50 6.00
283 Serge Savard 3.00 8.00
284 Larry Robinson 2.00 5.00
285 Ken Dryden 4.00 10.00
286 Bob Gainey 2.00 5.00
287 Georges Vezina 3.00 8.00
288 Howie Morenz 1.25 3.00
289 Jean Beliveau 2.00 5.00
290 Maurice Richard 5.00 12.00
291 Elmer Lach 3.00 8.00
292 Jacques Plante 3.00 8.00
293 Bernard Geoffrion 1.25 3.00
294 Henri Richard 2.50 6.00
295 Guy Lafleur 2.50 6.00
296 Bob Gainey 2.00 5.00
297 Patrick Roy 5.00 12.00
298 Guy Carbonneau 2.00 5.00
299 Maurice Richard 5.00 12.00
300 Saku Koivu 2.00 5.00

2008-09 Upper Deck Montreal Canadiens Centennial Parallel 100

*PARALLEL (1-200): 10X TO 25X BASIC CARDS
*PARALLEL (201-300): .8X TO 2X BASIC CARDS
STATED PRINT RUN 100 SERIAL #'d SETS

2008-09 Upper Deck Montreal Canadiens Centennial AKA Signings

STATED PRINT RUN 25 SER.#'d SETS
AKAAK Alex Kovalev 100.00 175.00
AKABG Bob Gainey 100.00 175.00
AKACN Chris Nilan 200.00 350.00
AKADD Dick Duff 125.00 200.00
AKADM Dickie Moore 100.00 175.00
AKAGC Guy Carbonneau 175.00 300.00
AKAGL Guy Lafleur 125.00 250.00
AKAHR Henri Richard 150.00 250.00
AKAJB Jean Beliveau 175.00 300.00
AKAJL Jacques Laperriere 150.00 250.00
AKALA Guy Lapointe 150.00 250.00
AKALE Jacques Lemaire 350.00 500.00
AKALR Larry Robinson 125.00 400.00
AKAMT Mario Tremblay 150.00 400.00
AKAPB Patrice Brisebois 175.00 300.00
AKAPR Patrick Roy 350.00 600.00
AKARH Rejean Houle 175.00 400.00
AKASS Serge Savard 350.00 500.00
AKAYC Yvan Cournoyer 150.00 250.00

2008-09 Upper Deck Montreal Canadiens Centennial Habs INKS

STATED ODDS 1:12
HABSAK Alex Kovalev 10.00 25.00
HABSAM Andrei Markov 12.00 30.00
HABSBB Benoit Brunet 15.00 40.00
HABSBG Bob Gainey 40.00 100.00
HABSCH Chris Chelios SP 150.00 300.00
HABSCL Claude Larose 60.00 120.00
HABSCN Chris Nilan SP 100.00 200.00
HABSCP Carey Price 50.00 100.00
HABSDD Dick Duff 75.00 125.00
HABSDJ Doug Jarvis 12.00 30.00
HABSDM Dickie Moore 125.00 200.00
HABSDR Doug Risebrough 25.00 50.00
HABSDS Denis Savard SP 150.00 250.00

HABSED Eric Desjardins 25.00 50.00
HABSFB Francis Bouillon 10.00 25.00
HABSGC Guy Carbonneau 15.00 40.00
HABSGG Gaston Gingras 10.00 25.00
HABSGL Guy Lafleur 60.00 100.00
HABSGT Gilles Tremblay SP 60.00 120.00
HABSHA Roman Hamrlik 10.00 25.00
HABSHI Christopher Higgins 10.00 25.00
HABSHR Henri Richard 40.00 80.00
HABSJA Jacques Lemaire
HABSJB Jean Beliveau SP 200.00 350.00
HABSJD Jean-Jacques Daigneault 20.00 50.00
HABSJL Jacques Laperriere 60.00 120.00
HABSJO John LeClair 25.00 50.00
HABSJT Jean-Guy Talbot SP 50.00 100.00
HABSKA Keith Acton 20.00 40.00
HABSKM Kirk Muller 10.00 25.00
HABSKO Andrei Kostitsyn 10.00 25.00
HABSKS Saku Koivu 12.00 30.00
HABSLA Guy Lapointe SP 100.00 200.00
HABSLE Claude Lemieux 25.00 60.00
HABSLO Lyle Odelein 60.00 120.00
HABSLR Larry Robinson SP 200.00 350.00
HABSMB Marcel Bonin 30.00 60.00
HABSMI Mike Komisarek 8.00 20.00
HABSMN Mark Napier 15.00 40.00
HABSMO Pierre Mondou 15.00 40.00
HABSMT Mario Tremblay 30.00 80.00
HABSMW Murray Wilson 15.00 40.00
HABSPB Patrice Brisebois 10.00 25.00
HABSPG Phil Goyette 50.00 100.00
HABSPI Pierre Bouchard 30.00 60.00
HABSPL Pierre Larouche SP 60.00 120.00
HABSPM Pete Mahovlich 20.00 50.00
HABSPR Patrick Roy 150.00 250.00
HABSPT Pierre Turgeon SP 75.00 150.00
HABSRH Rejean Houle 12.00 30.00
HABSRL Rod Langway SP 250.00 400.00
HABSRV Rogie Vachon 40.00 100.00
HABSSA Brian Savage 12.00 30.00
HABSSB Scotty Bowman SP 400.00 600.00
HABSSH Steve Shutt 12.00 30.00
HABSSK Brian Skrudland 15.00 40.00
HABSSQ Stephane Quintal 8.00 20.00
HABSSR Stephane Richer 25.00 60.00
HABSSS Serge Savard SP 100.00 175.00
HABSTP Tomas Plekanec 10.00 25.00
HABSVD Vincent Damphousse 15.00 40.00
HABSY Youppi MASCOT 12.00 30.00
HABSYC Yvan Cournoyer 25.00 60.00
HABSYI Youppi MASCOT 12.00 30.00
HABSYL Yvon Lambert 15.00 40.00

2008-09 Upper Deck Montreal Canadiens Centennial HOF Induction INKS

STATED PRINT RUN 66-106
HOFBB Butch Bouchard/66 125.00 200.00
HOFBG Bob Gainey/92 90.00 150.00
HOFBO Bert Olmstead/85 90.00 150.00
HOFDD Dick Duff/106 90.00 150.00
HOFDS Denis Savard/100 90.00 150.00
HOFEL Elmer Lach/66 150.00 250.00
HOFGL Guy Lapointe/93 125.00 225.00
HOFGU Guy Lafleur/88 150.00 250.00
HOFHR Henri Richard/79 125.00 250.00
HOFJB Jean Beliveau/72 250.00 450.00
HOFJL Jacques Lemaire/84 100.00 175.00
HOFLA Jacques Laperriere/87 100.00 175.00
HOFLR Larry Robinson/95 100.00 175.00
HOFPR Patrick Roy/106 200.00 350.00
HOFRL Rod Langway/102 100.00 175.00
HOFSA Serge Savard/86 90.00 150.00
HOFSB Scotty Bowman/91 125.00 200.00
HOFSS Steve Shutt/93 100.00 175.00
HOFYC Yvan Cournoyer/82 125.00 200.00

2008-09 Upper Deck Montreal Canadiens Centennial Le Bleu Blanc Rouge Jerseys

LBBRAK Alex Kovalev 6.00 15.00
LBBRAL Alex Kovalev 6.00 15.00
LBBRAM Andrei Markov 8.00 20.00
LBBRBO Francis Bouillon 6.00 15.00
LBBRCH Christopher Higgins 6.00 15.00
LBBRCP Carey Price 30.00 80.00
LBBRFB Francis Bouillon 6.00 15.00
LBBRFR Francis Bouillon 6.00 15.00
LBBRGL Guy Lapointe 8.00 20.00
LBBRHA Roman Hamrlik 6.00 15.00
LBBRJB Jean Beliveau
LBBRKO Andrei Kostitsyn 6.00 15.00
LBBRKV Saku Koivu 8.00 20.00
LBBRMA Andrei Markov 8.00 20.00
LBBRMI Mike Komisarek 8.00 20.00
LBBRMK Mike Komisarek 5.00 12.00
LBBRPB Patrice Brisebois 5.00 12.00
LBBRPL Tomas Plekanec 8.00 20.00
LBBRRH Roman Hamrlik 6.00 15.00
LBBRSK Saku Koivu 8.00 20.00
LBBRTP Tomas Plekanec 8.00 20.00

2008-09 Upper Deck Montreal Canadiens Centennial Mini Banners

COMPLETE SET (24) 350.00 500.00
1 Stanley Cup 1915-16 10.00 25.00
2 Stanley Cup 1923-24 10.00 25.00
3 Stanley Cup 1929-30 10.00 25.00
4 Stanley Cup 1930-31 10.00 25.00
5 Stanley Cup 1943-44 10.00 25.00
6 Stanley Cup 1945-46 10.00 25.00
7 Stanley Cup 1952-53 10.00 25.00
8 Stanley Cup 1955-56 10.00 25.00
9 Stanley Cup 1956-57 10.00 25.00
10 Stanley Cup 1957-58 10.00 25.00
11 Stanley Cup 1958-59 10.00 25.00
12 Stanley Cup 1959-60 10.00 25.00
13 Stanley Cup 1964-65 10.00 25.00
14 Stanley Cup 1965-66 10.00 25.00
15 Stanley Cup 1967-68 10.00 25.00
16 Stanley Cup 1968-69 10.00 25.00
17 Stanley Cup 1970-71 10.00 25.00
18 Stanley Cup 1972-73 10.00 25.00
19 Stanley Cup 1975-76 10.00 25.00
20 Stanley Cup 1976-77 10.00 25.00
21 Stanley Cup 1977-78 10.00 25.00
22 Stanley Cup 1978-79 10.00 25.00
23 Stanley Cup 1985-86 10.00 25.00
24 Stanley Cup 1992-93 10.00 25.00

2008-09 Upper Deck Montreal Canadiens Centennial Signatures Dual

STATED PRINT RUN 50 SERIAL #'d SETS
CARD NUMBERS HAVE PREFIX: DUAL
AA A.Kostitsyn/A.Kovalev 75.00 150.00
BB B.Bouchard/P.Bouchard 100.00 200.00
BH F.Bouillon/R.Hamrlik 100.00 200.00
BL J.Laperriere/P.Brisebois 60.00 120.00
BS S.Bowman/S.Savard 75.00 150.00
CC Carbonneau/C.Chelios 90.00 150.00
CG B.Gainey/Carbonneau 100.00 175.00
CN C.Lemieux/C.Nilan 60.00 120.00
DL D.Duff/J.Lemaire 15.00 40.00
GA G.Lapointe/A.Markov 25.00 60.00
HL R.Houle/Y.Lambert 75.00 150.00
HM K.Muller/C.Higgins 15.00 40.00
HR R.Houle/D.Risebrough 20.00 50.00
JG B.Gainey/D.Jarvis 75.00 150.00
JR D.Jarvis/D.Risebrough 60.00 120.00
KB J.Beliveau/S.Koivu 40.00 80.00
KD Damphousse/S.Koivu 20.00 50.00
KP M.Komisarek/C.Price 100.00 175.00
KS S.Savard/M.Komisarek 30.00 80.00
LK G.Lafleur/A.Kovalev 75.00 150.00
LN P.Larouche/M.Napier 20.00 50.00
LR G.Lafleur/S.Richer 25.00 60.00
MC Y.Cournoyer/D.Moore 20.00 50.00
MD K.Muller/Damphousse 150.00 250.00
MH D.Moore/C.Higgins 20.00 50.00
MP A.Markov/C.Price 125.00 250.00
MT P.Mondou/M.Tremblay 100.00 200.00
ON C.Nilan/L.Odelein 50.00 100.00
PC Cournoyer/Piekanec 150.00 250.00
QB S.Quintal/P.Brisebois 12.00 30.00
RB J.Beliveau/H.Richard 200.00 350.00
RH L.Robinson/R.Hamrlik 20.00 50.00
RL H.Richard/E.Lach 50.00 100.00
TL M.Tremblay/J.Lemaire 40.00 80.00

1998-99 Upper Deck MVP

The 1998-99 new Upper Deck MVP set was issued in one series totaling 220 cards and distributed in ten-card packs with a suggested retail price of $1.59. The fronts feature color action player photos printed on internally die-cut, double laminated cards with player information on the backs.

COMPLETE SET (220) 15.00 30.00
1 Paul Kariya .20 .50
2 Teemu Selanne .30 .75
3 Tomas Sandstrom .10 .25
4 Johan Davidsson .10 .25
5 Mike Crowley RC .12 .30
6 Guy Hebert .12 .30
7 Marty McInnis .10 .25
8 Steve Rucchin .10 .25
9 Ray Bourque .25 .60
10 Sergei Samsonov .12 .30
11 Cameron Mann .10 .25
12 Joe Thornton .30 .75
13 Jason Allison .12 .30
14 Byron Dafoe .12 .30
15 Kyle McLaren .10 .25
16 Dimitri Khristich .10 .25
17 Hal Gill .10 .25
18 Anson Carter .12 .30
19 Miroslav Satan .12 .30
20 Brian Holzinger .10 .25
21 Dominik Hasek .30 .75
22 Matthew Barnaby .10 .25
23 Erik Rasmussen .10 .25
24 Geoff Sanderson .10 .25
25 Michal Grosek .10 .25
26 Michael Peca .10 .25
27 Rico Fata .12 .30
28 Derek Morris .10 .25
29 Phil Housley .12 .30
30 Valeri Bure .10 .25
31 Ed Ward .10 .25
32 Jean-Sebastien Giguere .12 .30
33 Jeff Shantz .10 .25
34 Jarome Iginla .30 .75
35 Ron Francis .20 .50
36 Trevor Kidd .10 .25
37 Keith Primeau .10 .25
38 Sami Kapanen .10 .25
39 Martin Gelinas .10 .25
40 Jeff O'Neill .10 .25
41 Gary Roberts .10 .25
42 Jocelyn Thibault .12 .30
43 Doug Gilmour .20 .50
44 Chris Chelios .15 .40
45 Tony Amonte .12 .30
46 Bob Probert .10 .25
47 Daniel Cleary .10 .25
48 Eric Daze .12 .30
49 Mike Maneluk RC .10 .25
50 Remi Royer RC .10 .25
51 Peter Forsberg .25 .60
52 Patrick Roy .40 1.00
53 Joe Sakic .25 .60
54 Chris Drury .12 .30
55 Milan Hejduk RC .25 .60
56 Greg DeVries .10 .25
57 Theo Fleury .20 .50
58 Adam Deadmarsh .10 .25
59 Brett Hull .25 .60
60 Ed Belfour .15 .40
61 Mike Modano .25 .60
62 Darryl Sydor .10 .25
63 Joe Nieuwendyk .15 .40
64 Grant Marshall .10 .25
65 Sergei Zubov .10 .25
66 Derian Hatcher .10 .25
67 Jere Lehtinen .12 .30
68 Sergei Fedorov .25 .60
69 Steve Yzerman .50 1.25
70 Nicklas Lidstrom .20 .50
71 Chris Osgood .15 .40
72 Brendan Shanahan .20 .50
73 Darren McCarty .10 .25
74 Tomas Holmstrom .10 .25
75 Norm Maracle RC .10 .25
76 Doug Brown .10 .25
77 Doug Weight .15 .40
78 Janne Niinimaa .10 .25
79 Tom Poti .10 .25
80 Bill Guerin .15 .40
81 Mike Grier .10 .25
82 Ryan Smyth .12 .30
83 Roman Hamrlik .10 .25
84 Kevin Brown .10 .25
85 Pavel Bure .20 .50
86 Jaroslav Spacek .10 .25
87 Rob Niedermayer .10 .25
88 Robert Svehla .10 .25
89 Ray Whitney .10 .25
90 Peter Worrell RC .12 .30
91 Mark Parrish RC .25 .60
92 Oleg Kvasha RC .15 .40
93 Steve Duchesne .12 .30
94 Rob Blake .15 .40
95 Olli Jokinen .12 .30
96 Donald Audette .10 .25
97 Luc Robitaille .15 .40
98 Josh Green .15 .40
99 Philippe Boucher .10 .25
100 Matt Johnson .10 .25
101 Vincent Damphousse .12 .30
102 Dainius Zubrus .10 .25
103 Terry Ryan .10 .25
104 Saku Koivu .15 .40
105 Brett Clark RC .10 .25
106 Dave Morissette RC .12 .30
107 Eric Weinrich .10 .25
108 Brian Savage .10 .25
109 Shayne Corson .12 .30
110 Mike Dunham .12 .30
111 Greg Johnson .10 .25
112 Cliff Ronning .10 .25
113 Andrew Brunette .12 .30
114 Sergei Krivokrasov .10 .25
115 Sebastien Bordeleau .10 .25
116 Scott Stevens .15 .40
117 Martin Brodeur .30 .75
118 Brendan Morrison .10 .25
119 Patrik Elias .15 .40
120 Scott Niedermayer .15 .40
121 Bobby Holik .10 .25
122 Jason Arnott .12 .30
123 Jay Pandolfo .10 .25
124 Eric Brewer .15 .40
125 Zigmund Palffy .15 .40
126 Felix Potvin .15 .40
127 Robert Reichel .10 .25
128 Mike Watt .10 .25
129 Tommy Salo .12 .30
130 Kenny Jonsson .10 .25
131 Trevor Linden .12 .30
132 Wayne Gretzky .75 2.00
133 Brian Leetch .15 .40
134 Manny Malhotra .15 .40
135 Mike Richter .15 .40
136 Mike Knuble .10 .25
137 Niklas Sundstrom .10 .25
138 Todd Harvey .10 .25
139 Alexei Yashin .12 .30
140 Damian Rhodes .15 .40
141 Daniel Alfredsson .15 .40
142 Magnus Arvedson .10 .25
143 Shawn McEachern .10 .25
144 Chris Phillips .10 .25
145 Vaclav Prospal .10 .25
146 Wade Redden .10 .25
147 Eric Lindros .25 .60
148 John LeClair .15 .40
149 John Vanbiesbrouck .12 .30
150 Keith Jones .10 .25
151 Colin Forbes .10 .25
152 Mark Recchi .20 .50
153 Dan McGillis .10 .25
154 Eric Desjardins .12 .30
155 Rod Brind'Amour .15 .40
156 Keith Tkachuk .15 .40
157 Daniel Briere .12 .30
158 Nikolai Khabibulin .15 .40
159 Brad Isbister .10 .25
160 Jeremy Roenick .25 .60
161 Oleg Tverdovsky .15 .40
162 Rick Tocchet .12 .30
163 Jaromir Jagr .40 1.00
164 Tom Barrasso .12 .30
165 Alexei Morozov .10 .25
166 Robert Dome .10 .25
167 Stu Barnes .10 .25
168 Martin Straka .10 .25
169 German Titov .10 .25
170 Patrick Marleau .15 .40
171 Andrei Zyuzin .10 .25
172 Marco Sturm .10 .25
173 Owen Nolan .15 .40
174 Jeff Friesen .10 .25
175 Bob Rouse .10 .25
176 Mike Vernon .12 .30
177 Mike Ricci .10 .25
178 Marty Reasoner .15 .40
179 Al MacInnis .15 .40
180 Chris Pronger .12 .30
181 Pierre Turgeon .15 .40
182 Michal Handzus RC .20 .50
183 Jim Campbell .10 .25
184 Tony Twist .10 .25
185 Pavol Demitra .20 .50
186 Daren Puppa .12 .30
187 Vincent Lecavalier .30 .75
188 Bill Ranford .12 .30
189 Alexandre Daigle .10 .25
190 Wendel Clark .12 .30
191 Rob Zamuner .10 .25
192 Chris Gratton .12 .30
193 Fredrik Modin .10 .25
194 Curtis Joseph .15 .40
195 Mats Sundin .15 .40
196 Steve Thomas .10 .25
197 Tomas Kaberle RC .20 .50
198 Alyn McCauley .10 .25
199 Mike Johnson .10 .25
200 Bryan Berard .12 .30
201 Mark Messier .25 .60
202 Jason Strudwick RC .15 .40
203 Mattias Ohlund .10 .25
204 Alexander Mogilny .12 .30
205 Bill Muckalt RC .10 .25
206 Ed Jovanovski .12 .30
207 Josh Holden .10 .25
208 Peter Schaefer .10 .25
209 Peter Bondra .12 .30
210 Olaf Kolzig .15 .40
211 Sergei Gonchar .10 .25
212 Adam Oates .15 .40
213 Brian Bellows .12 .30
214 Matt Herr RC .10 .25
215 Richard Zednik .10 .25
216 Joe Juneau .12 .30
217 Jaroslav Svejkovski .10 .25
218 Wayne Gretzky CL .75 2.00
219 Wayne Gretzky CL .75 2.00
220 Wayne Gretzky CL .75 2.00
NNO Wayne Gretzky Retire/99 100.00 200.00

1998-99 Upper Deck MVP Gold Script

Randomly inserted in hobby packs only, this 220-card set is a gold foil hobby parallel version of the base set. Only 100 sequentially numbered sets were produced.
*VETS: 20X TO 50X BASIC CARDS
*ROOKIES: 10X TO 25X BASIC CARDS

1998-99 Upper Deck MVP Silver Script

Randomly inserted into packs at the rate of 1:2, this 220-card set is a silver foil parallel version of the base set.
COMPLETE SET (220) 75.00 150.00
*VETS: .8X TO 2X BASIC CARDS
*ROOKIES: .5X TO 1.2X BASIC CARDS

1998-99 Upper Deck MVP Super Script

Randomly inserted into hobby packs only, this 220-card set is a hobby limited edition, holographic foil parallel version of the base set. Only 25 sequentially numbered sets were produced.
*VETS: 40X TO 100X BASIC CARDS
*ROOKIES: 12X TO 30X BASIC CARDS

1998-99 Upper Deck MVP Dynamics

Randomly inserted into packs at a ratio of 1:28, this set commemorates the brilliant career of Wayne Gretzky.
COMPLETE SET (15) 75.00 150.00
COMMON GRETZKY (D1-D15) 5.00 12.00

1998-99 Upper Deck MVP Game Souvenirs

Randomly inserted in hobby packs only at the rate of 1:144, this 10-card set features color action player photos with actual pieces of game used memorabilia right on the cards.
BH Brett Hull 12.50 30.00
BS Brendan Shanahan 8.00 20.00
EL Eric Lindros 8.00 20.00
JL John LeClair 8.00 20.00
MM Mike Modano 15.00 40.00
PR Patrick Roy 20.00 50.00
RB Ray Bourque 15.00 40.00
SF Sergei Fedorov 15.00 40.00
SS Sergei Samsonov 8.00 20.00
SY Steve Yzerman 15.00 40.00
VL Vincent Lecavalier 12.50 30.00
WG Wayne Gretzky 40.00 100.00
SYA S.Yzerman AU/19 500.00 1000.00
VLA V.Lecavalier AU/14 250.00 500.00

1998-99 Upper Deck MVP OT Heroes

COMPLETE SET (15) 20.00 40.00
STATED ODDS 1:9
OT1 Steve Yzerman 4.00 10.00
OT2 Patrick Roy 4.00 10.00
OT3 Jaromir Jagr 1.25 3.00
OT4 Ray Bourque 1.25 3.00
OT5 Wayne Gretzky 5.00 12.00
OT6 Sergei Samsonov .60 1.50
OT7 Dominik Hasek 1.50 4.00
OT8 Peter Forsberg 2.00 5.00
OT9 Paul Kariya .75 2.00
OT10 Eric Lindros .75 2.00
OT11 Pavel Bure .75 2.00
OT12 Keith Tkachuk .75 2.00
OT13 Brendan Shanahan .75 2.00
OT14 John LeClair .75 2.00
OT15 Joe Sakic 1.50 4.00

1998-99 Upper Deck MVP Power Game

COMPLETE SET (15) 12.00 25.00
STATED ODDS 1:9
PG1 Brendan Shanahan .75 2.00
PG2 Keith Tkachuk .75 2.00
PG3 Eric Lindros .75 2.00
PG4 Mike Modano 1.25 3.00
PG5 Vincent Lecavalier 2.00 5.00
PG6 John LeClair .75 2.00
PG7 Mark Messier .75 2.00
PG8 Mats Sundin .75 2.00
PG9 Peter Forsberg 2.00 5.00
PG10 Jaromir Jagr 1.25 3.00
PG11 Keith Primeau .40 1.00
PG12 Mark Parrish .60 1.50
PG13 Patrick Marleau .40 1.00
PG14 Bill Guerin .60 1.50
PG15 Jeremy Roenick 1.00 2.50

1998-99 Upper Deck MVP ProSign

Randomly inserted in retail packs only at the rate of 1:216, this 23-card set features color action photos of the NHL's superstars with the player's autograph in the wide bottom margin. These cards were among this years toughest autograph pulls.
AM Alyn McCauley 4.00 10.00
BB Brian Bellows 4.00 10.00
BM Brendan Morrison 4.00 10.00
CD Chris Drury 5.00 12.00
DN Dmitri Nabokov 4.00 10.00
DW Doug Weight 5.00 12.00
EB Eric Brewer 4.00 10.00
ER Erik Rasmussen 4.00 10.00
JA Jason Allison 4.00 10.00
JI Jarome Iginla 12.50 30.00
JT Jose Theodore 12.50 30.00
MD Mike Dunham 4.00 10.00
MJ Mike Johnson 4.00 10.00
MM Manny Malhotra 4.00 10.00
MP Mark Parrish 4.00 10.00
OT Oleg Tverdovsky 4.00 10.00
RF Rico Fata 4.00 10.00
RN Rob Niedermayer 4.00 10.00
SY Steve Yzerman 40.00 100.00
VL Vincent Lecavalier 10.00 25.00
WG Wayne Gretzky 125.00 300.00
WR Wade Redden 4.00 10.00
JAR Jason Arnott 4.00 10.00

1998-99 Upper Deck MVP Snipers

COMPLETE SET (12) 10.00 20.00
STATED ODDS 1:6
S1 Vincent Lecavalier 1.00 2.50
S2 Wayne Gretzky 2.50 6.00
S3 Sergei Samsonov .30 .75
S4 Teemu Selanne .40 1.00
S5 Peter Forsberg 1.00 2.50
S6 Paul Kariya .40 1.00
S7 Eric Lindros .40 1.00
S8 Pavel Bure .40 1.00
S9 Peter Bondra .30 .75
S10 Joe Sakic .75 2.00
S11 Steve Yzerman 2.00 5.00
S12 Sergei Fedorov .60 1.50

1998-99 Upper Deck MVP Special Forces

COMPLETE SET (15) 30.00 60.00
STATED ODDS 1:14
F1 Brett Hull 1.25 3.00
F2 Sergei Samsonov .75 2.00
F3 Vincent Lecavalier 2.50 6.00
F4 Dominik Hasek 2.00 5.00
F5 Eric Lindros 1.00 2.50
F6 Paul Kariya 1.00 2.50
F7 Steve Yzerman 5.00 12.00
F8 Brendan Shanahan 1.00 2.50
F9 Martin Brodeur 2.50 6.00
F10 Teemu Selanne 1.00 2.50
F11 Jaromir Jagr 1.50 4.00
F12 Wayne Gretzky 6.00 15.00
F13 Patrick Roy 5.00 12.00
F14 Peter Forsberg 2.50 6.00
F15 Joe Sakic 2.00 5.00

1999-00 Upper Deck MVP

Released as a 220-card set, Upper Deck MVP featured white bordered cards with enhanced bronze foil stamping. The base set is composed of 218 regular cards and two Wayne Gretzky checklist cards. Also released with this set is a special Wayne Gretzky autographed Game Jersey card limited to just 40. MVP was packaged in 28-pack boxes of 10 card packs and carried a suggested retail price of $1.59.

COMPLETE SET (220) 15.00 30.00
1 Wayne Gretzky .75 2.00
2 Damian Rhodes .08 .25
3 Jody Hull .02 .10
4 Paul Kariya .10 .30
5 Teemu Selanne .10 .30
6 Guy Hebert .08 .25
7 Matt Cullen .02 .10
8 Steve Rucchin .08 .25
9 Oleg Tverdovsky .02 .10
10 Johan Davidsson .02 .10
11 Ray Bourque .20 .50
12 Sergei Samsonov .08 .25
13 Joe Thornton .20 .50
14 Anson Carter .08 .25
15 Jason Allison .02 .10
16 Kyle McLaren .02 .10
17 Byron Dafoe .08 .25
18 Shawn Bates .08 .25
19 Jonathan Girard .02 .10
20 Hal Gill .02 .10
21 Dominik Hasek .25 .60
22 Joe Juneau .08 .25
23 Michael Peca .08 .25
24 Cory Sarich .02 .10
25 Martin Biron .08 .25
26 Miroslav Satan .08 .25
27 Dixon Ward .02 .10
28 Michal Grosek .02 .10
29 Valeri Bure .02 .10
30 Phil Housley .08 .25
31 Derek Morris .02 .10
32 Jarome Iginla .15 .40
33 Wade Belak .02 .10
34 Rico Fata .02 .10
35 Jean-Sebastien Giguere .08 .25
36 Rene Corbet .02 .10
37 Arturs Irbe .08 .25
38 Keith Primeau .02 .10
39 Sami Kapanen .02 .10
40 Ron Francis .08 .25
41 Shane Willis .08 .25
42 Gary Roberts .02 .10
43 Bates Battaglia .08 .25
44 J-P Dumont .08 .25
45 Ty Jones .02 .10
46 Tony Amonte .08 .25
47 Jocelyn Thibault .08 .25
48 Doug Gilmour .08 .25
49 Remi Royer .02 .10
50 Alexei Zhamnov .02 .10
51 Joe Sakic .30 .75
52 Peter Forsberg .30 .75
53 Theo Fleury .02 .10
54 Chris Drury .08 .25
55 Patrick Roy .60 1.50
56 Sandis Ozolinsh .02 .10
57 Adam Deadmarsh .02 .10
58 Milan Hejduk .10 .30
59 Mike Modano .20 .50
60 Brett Hull .15 .40
61 Darryl Sydor .02 .10
62 Ed Belfour .10 .30
63 Jere Lehtinen .08 .25
64 Jamie Langenbrunner .02 .10
65 Derian Hatcher .02 .10
66 Jon Sim RC .08 .25
67 Joe Nieuwendyk .08 .25
68 Sergei Fedorov .20 .50
69 Steve Yzerman .60 1.50
70 Brendan Shanahan .10 .30
71 Chris Osgood .08 .25
72 Nicklas Lidstrom .10 .30
73 Chris Chelios .10 .30
74 Igor Larionov .02 .10
75 Tomas Holmstrom .02 .10
76 Vyacheslav Kozlov .08 .25
77 Josef Beranek .02 .10
78 Bill Guerin .02 .10
79 Doug Weight .08 .25
80 Tommy Salo .08 .25
81 Mike Grier .08 .25
82 Tom Poti .02 .10
83 Fredrik Lindquist .02 .10
84 Mark Parrish .02 .10
85 Pavel Bure .10 .30
86 Viktor Kozlov .02 .10
87 Ray Whitney .08 .25
88 Rob Niedermayer .08 .25
89 Oleg Kvasha .08 .25
90 Scott Mellanby .02 .10
91 Chris Allen RC .08 .25
92 Rob Blake .08 .25
93 Pavel Rosa .02 .10
94 Jamie Storr .08 .25
95 Donald Audette .02 .10
96 Luc Robitaille .08 .25
97 Jozef Stumpel .08 .25
98 Vladimir Tsyplakov .02 .10
99 Manny Legace .15 .40
100 Saku Koivu .10 .30
101 Martin Rucinsky .02 .10
102 Vladimir Malakhov .02 .10
103 Eric Weinrich .02 .10
104 Jeff Hackett .08 .25
105 Arron Asham .02 .10
106 Trevor Linden .08 .25
107 Brian Savage .02 .10
108 Cliff Ronning .08 .25
109 Sergei Krivokrasov .02 .10
110 David Legwand .08 .25
111 Kimmo Timonen .02 .10
112 Mark Mowers RC .02 .10
113 Mike Dunham .08 .25
114 Scott Stevens .08 .25
115 Martin Brodeur .30 .75
116 Patrik Elias .08 .25
117 Brendan Morrison .08 .25
118 Scott Niedermayer .02 .10
119 Petr Sykora .02 .10
120 Jason Arnott .02 .10
121 Vadim Sharifijanov .02 .10
122 John Madden RC .25 .60
123 Mariusz Czerkawski .02 .10
124 Felix Potvin .10 .30
125 Mike Watt .02 .10
126 Eric Brewer .08 .25
127 Dmitri Nabokov .02 .10
128 Claude Lapointe .02 .10
129 Kenny Jonsson .02 .10
130 Zdeno Chara .10 .25
131 Wayne Gretzky .75 2.00
132 Brian Leetch .10 .30
133 Mike Richter .10 .30
134 Petr Nedved .08 .25
135 Adam Graves .02 .10
136 Manny Malhotra .08 .25
137 John MacLean .02 .10
138 Alexei Yashin .02 .10
139 Magnus Arvedson .02 .10
140 Daniel Alfredsson .08 .25
141 Wade Redden .02 .10
142 Ron Tugnutt .08 .25
143 Sami Salo .08 .25
144 Marian Hossa .10 .30
145 Shawn McEachern .02 .10
146 Eric Lindros .10 .30
147 Jean-Marc Pelletier .08 .25
148 John LeClair .10 .30
149 Rod Brind'Amour .08 .25
150 Mark Recchi .08 .25
151 Keith Jones .02 .10
152 Eric Desjardins .08 .25
153 Ryan Bast RC .02 .10
154 Brian Wesenberg RC .02 .10
155 John Vanbiesbrouck .08 .25
156 Jeremy Roenick .15 .40
157 Robert Reichel .02 .10
158 Keith Tkachuk .10 .30
159 Rick Tocchet .08 .25
160 Robert Esche RC .10 .30
161 Nikolai Khabibulin .08 .25
162 Daniel Briere .02 .10
163 Greg Adams .02 .10
164 Trevor Letowski .02 .10
165 Jaromir Jagr .20 .50
166 Martin Straka .02 .10
167 German Titov .02 .10
168 Tom Barrasso .08 .25
169 Jan Hrdina .02 .10
170 Alexei Kovalev .02 .10
171 Matthew Barnaby .08 .25
172 Jean-Sebastien Aubin .08 .25
173 Vincent Damphousse .02 .10
174 Owen Nolan .08 .25
175 Jeff Friesen .02 .10
176 Patrick Marleau .08 .25
177 Marco Sturm .08 .25
178 Mike Ricci .08 .25
179 Gary Suter .02 .10
180 Scott Hannan .02 .10
181 Andy Sutton .02 .10
182 Pavol Demitra .08 .25
183 Al MacInnis .08 .25
184 Pierre Turgeon .08 .25
185 Grant Fuhr .08 .25
186 Chris Pronger .08 .25
187 Lubos Bartecko .02 .10
188 Jochen Hecht RC .30 .75
189 Michal Handzus .08 .25
190 Vincent Lecavalier .10 .30
191 Paul Mara .08 .25
192 Darcy Tucker .02 .10
193 Chris Gratton .02 .10
194 Pavel Kubina .02 .10
195 Kevin Hodson .08 .25
196 Mats Sundin .10 .30
197 Daniil Markov .02 .10
198 Curtis Joseph .10 .30
199 Sergei Berezin .08 .25
200 Steve Thomas .02 .10
201 Bryan Berard .08 .25
202 Mike Johnson .08 .25
203 Tomas Kaberle .02 .10
204 Mark Messier .10 .30
205 Bill Muckalt .08 .25
206 Markus Naslund .10 .30
207 Mattias Ohlund .08 .25
208 Kevin Weekes .08 .25
209 Ed Jovanovski .02 .10
210 Alexander Mogilny .08 .25
211 Josh Holden .08 .25
212 Richard Zednik .02 .10
213 Jaroslav Svejkovsky .02 .10
214 Adam Oates .08 .25
215 Peter Bondra .08 .25
216 Sergei Gonchar .02 .10
217 Olaf Kolzig .08 .25
218 Jan Bulis .02 .10
219 Wayne Gretzky CL .40 1.00
220 Wayne Gretzky CL .40 1.00

1999-00 Upper Deck MVP Gold Script

Randomly inserted in packs, this 220-card set parallels the base MVP set on cards enhanced with gold foil highlights and feature a foil facsimile signature of the respective player. For several players, signatures were not available, therefore these cards appear with just the gold foil highlights.
*GOLD SCRIPT: 30X TO 80X BASIC CARDS
1 Wayne Gretzky 30.00 80.00
55 Patrick Roy 25.00 60.00
69 Steve Yzerman 25.00 60.00
131 Wayne Gretzky 30.00 80.00
219 Wayne Gretzky CL 30.00 80.00
220 Wayne Gretzky CL 30.00 80.00

1999-00 Upper Deck MVP Silver Script

Randomly inserted in packs, this 220-card set parallels the base MVP set on cards enhanced with silver foil highlights and feature a foil facsimile signature of the respective player. For several players, signatures were not available, therefore these cards appear with just the silver foil highlights.
COMPLETE SET (220) 75.00 150.00
*SILVER SCRIPT: 1.2X TO 3X BASIC CARDS

1999-00 Upper Deck MVP Super Script

Randomly inserted in packs, this 220-card set parallels the base MVP set on cards enhanced with holographic foil highlights and feature a holographic foil facsimile signature of the respective player. For several players, signatures were not available, therefore these cards appear with just the holographic foil highlights. Each Super Script card is sequentially numbered to 25.
*SUPER SCRIPT: 50X TO 120X BASIC CARDS

1999-00 Upper Deck MVP 21st Century NHL

COMPLETE SET (10) 5.00 10.00
STATED ODDS 1:13
1 David Legwand .30 .75
2 Sergei Samsonov .30 .75
3 Paul Kariya .40 1.00
4 Peter Forsberg 1.00 2.50
5 Vincent Lecavalier .40 1.00
6 Jaromir Jagr .60 1.50
7 Paul Mara .30 .75
8 Marian Hossa .40 1.00
9 Pavel Bure .50 1.25
10 Chris Drury .30 .75

1999-00 Upper Deck MVP 90's Snapshots

Randomly inserted in packs at the rate of 1:27, this 10-card set features multiple snapshots on the card front that highlight each player's accomplishments during the '90's.
COMPLETE SET (10) 15.00 40.00
S1 Wayne Gretzky 6.00 15.00
S2 Jaromir Jagr 1.50 4.00
S3 Patrick Roy 4.00 10.00
S4 Eric Lindros 1.50 4.00
S5 Brendan Shanahan 1.50 4.00
S6 Peter Forsberg 2.00 5.00
S7 Steve Yzerman 3.00 8.00
S8 Teemu Selanne 1.50 4.00
S9 Dominik Hasek 2.00 5.00
S10 Pavel Bure 1.25 3.00

1999-00 Upper Deck MVP Draft Report

Randomly inserted in packs at the rate of 1:6, this 10-card set was designed to showcase some of the new stars from the 1999 amateur draft by way of a current veteran. Each card features an unidentified veteran player on the card front and a brief report about three draftees for the same team on the card back along with the team's first draft pick named at the top of the card on the back.
COMPLETE SET (10) 2.50 6.00
DR1 Damian Rhodes .20 .50
(Patrick Stefan named on back)
DR2 Bill Muckalt .20 .50
(Daniel Sedin named on back)
DR3 Wayne Gretzky 1.50 4.00
(Pavel Brendl named on back)
DR4 Eric Brewer .20 .50
(Tim Connolly named on back)
DR5 David Legwand .20 .50
(Brian Finley named on back)
DR6 Peter Bondra .25 .60
(Kris Beech named on back)
DR7 Rico Fata .20 .50
(Oleg Saprykin named on back)
DR8 Mark Parrish .20 .50
(Denis Shvidki named on back)
DR9 Tom Poti .20 .50
(Jani Rita named on back)
DR10 Jeff Friesen .25 .60
(Jeff Jillison named on back)

1999-00 Upper Deck MVP Draw Your Own Trading Card

Randomly inserted in packs, this 30-card set features the winning artwork from Upper Deck's Draw Your Own Trading Card contest.
COMPLETE SET (45) 15.00 30.00
W1 Joey Kocur .08 .25
W2 Mike Richter .10 .30
W3 Wayne Gretzky 1.25 3.00
W4 Dominik Hasek .40 1.00
W5 Steve Yzerman 1.00 2.50
W6 Ray Bourque .30 .75
W7 Arturs Irbe .08 .25
W8 Wayne Gretzky 1.25 3.00
W9 Martin Brodeur .50 1.25
W10 Patrick Roy 1.00 2.50
W11 Wayne Gretzky 1.25 3.00
W12 Paul Kariya .20 .50
W13 Wayne Gretzky 1.25 3.00
W14 Jaromir Jagr .30 .75
W15 Wayne Gretzky 1.25 3.00
W16 Felix Potvin .10 .30
W17 Marc Denis .08 .25
W18 Dominik Hasek .40 1.00
W19 Patrick Roy .75 2.00
W20 Robert Svehla .08 .25
W21 Joe Juneau .08 .25
W22 Mattias Ohlund .08 .25
W23 Kirk Muller .08 .25
W24 Peter Forsberg .50 1.25
W25 Stu Barnes .08 .25
W26 Nikolai Khabibulin .08 .25
W27 Sergei Samsonov .08 .25
W28 Jeremy Roenick .15 .40
W29 Wayne Gretzky 1.25 3.00
W30 Sergei Fedorov .40 1.00
W31 Wayne Gretzky .75 2.00
W32 Wayne Gretzky .75 2.00
W33 Wayne Gretzky .75 2.00
W34 Wayne Gretzky .75 2.00
W35 Wayne Gretzky .75 2.00
W36 Wayne Gretzky .75 2.00
W37 Wayne Gretzky .75 2.00
W38 Wayne Gretzky .75 2.00
W39 Wayne Gretzky .75 2.00
W40 Wayne Gretzky .75 2.00
W41 Wayne Gretzky .75 2.00
W42 Wayne Gretzky .75 2.00

W43 Wayne Gretzky .75 2.00
W44 Wayne Gretzky .75 2.00
W45 Wayne Gretzky .75 2.00

1999-00 Upper Deck MVP Game-Used Souvenirs

Randomly inserted in packs at the rate of 1:130, this 30-card set features swatches from game used pucks or game used sticks coupled with an image of the featured player. Autographed cards of Wayne Gretzky and Pavel Bure were limited to a print run of 25.

GU1 Paul Kariya P 6.00 15.00
GU2 Teemu Selanne P 6.00 15.00
GU3 Brett Hull P 8.00 20.00
GU4 Pavel Bure P 6.00 15.00
GU5 Marian Hossa P 6.00 15.00
GU6 Wayne Gretzky P 15.00 40.00
GU7 Brendan Shanahan P 6.00 15.00
GU8 Sergei Samsonov P 6.00 15.00
GU9 Eric Lindros P 6.00 15.00
GU10 Keith Tkachuk P 6.00 15.00
GU11 Steve Yzerman P 20.00 50.00
GU12 Jaromir Jagr P 10.00 25.00
GU13 Alexei Yashin P 6.00 15.00
GU14 Curtis Joseph P 6.00 15.00
GU15 Paul Kariya S 8.00 20.00
GU16 Teemu Selanne S 8.00 20.00
GU17 Dominik Hasek S 15.00 40.00
GU18 Pavel Bure S 10.00 25.00
GU19 Peter Forsberg S 12.50 30.00
GU20 Wayne Gretzky S 30.00 80.00
GU21 Brendan Shanahan S 8.00 20.00
GU22 Joe Sakic S 15.00 40.00
GU23 Eric Lindros S 8.00 20.00
GU24 Keith Tkachuk S 8.00 20.00
GU25 Jeremy Roenick S 10.00 25.00
GU26 Alexei Yashin S 8.00 20.00
GU27 Curtis Joseph S 8.00 20.00
GU28 Steve Yzerman S 15.00 40.00
GUS1 W.Gretzky AU/25 250.00 550.00
GUS2 P.Bure AU/25 125.00 250.00

1999-00 Upper Deck MVP Hands of Gold

COMPLETE SET (10) 12.00 25.00
STATED ODDS 1:9
H1 Wayne Gretzky 2.50 6.00
H2 Brett Hull .50 1.25
H3 Pavel Bure .60 1.50
H4 Teemu Selanne .60 1.50
H5 Sergei Samsonov .30 .75
H6 Peter Forsberg 1.00 2.50
H7 Eric Lindros .60 1.50
H8 Paul Kariya .60 1.50
H9 Jaromir Jagr .60 1.50
H10 Steve Yzerman 2.00 5.00
H11 Mike Modano .60 1.50

1999-00 Upper Deck MVP Last Line

COMPLETE SET (10) 5.00 10.00
STATED ODDS 1:9
LL1 Dominik Hasek .75 2.00
LL2 Martin Brodeur 1.00 2.50
LL3 Patrick Roy 2.00 5.00
LL4 Byron Dafoe .30 .75
LL5 Ed Belfour .40 1.00
LL6 Curtis Joseph .30 .75
LL7 John Vanbiesbrouck .30 .75
LL8 Tom Barrasso .30 .75
LL9 Chris Osgood .30 .75
LL10 Nikolai Khabibulin .30 .75

1999-00 Upper Deck MVP Legendary One

Randomly inserted in packs at the rate of 1:27, this 10-card set pays tribute to Wayne Gretzky and highlights some of the greatest moments of his career. Card backs carry an "LO" prefix.

COMPLETE SET (10) 25.00 60.00
COMMON GRETZKY (LO1-LO10) 3.00 8.00

1999-00 Upper Deck MVP ProSign

Randomly inserted in retail packs at the rate of 1:144, this 30-card set features authentic player autographs coupled with an action photo.

BH Brett Hull 12.00 30.00
BM Bill Muckalt 2.00 5.00
CD Chris Drury 5.00 12.00
DA Donald Audette 2.00 5.00
DM Derek Morris 2.00 5.00
GM Glen Murray 4.00 10.00
IL Igor Larionov 4.00 10.00
JF Jeff Friesen 4.00 10.00
JH Jeff Hackett 5.00 12.00
JR Jeremy Roenick 12.00 30.00
JT Joe Thornton 12.00 30.00
LR Luc Robitaille 8.00 20.00
MC Matt Cullen 2.00 5.00
PB Pavel Bure 8.00 20.00
PD Pavol Demitra 6.00 15.00
RB Ray Bourque 30.00 80.00
RT Ron Tugnutt 5.00 12.00
SG Sergei Gonchar 2.00 5.00
SK Sami Kapanen 2.00 5.00
SY Steve Yzerman 40.00 80.00
TF Theo Fleury 4.00 10.00
TK Tomas Kaberle 2.00 5.00
TL Trevor Linden 4.00 10.00
TP Tom Poti 2.00 5.00
WC Wendel Clark 4.00 10.00
WG Wayne Gretzky 125.00 250.00
JHR Jan Hrdina 2.00 5.00
RBR Rod Brind'Amour 5.00 12.00

1999-00 Upper Deck MVP Talent

Randomly inserted in packs at the rate of 1:13, this 10-card set identifies some of the most likely candidates for the 1999-00 Hart Trophy.

COMPLETE SET (10) 10.00 20.00
MVP1 Wayne Gretzky 2.50 6.00
MVP2 Paul Kariya .75 2.00
MVP3 Dominik Hasek .75 2.00
MVP4 Eric Lindros .60 1.50
MVP5 Ray Bourque .60 1.50
MVP6 Steve Yzerman 2.00 5.00
MVP7 Patrick Roy 2.00 5.00
MVP8 Jaromir Jagr .75 2.00
MVP9 Martin Brodeur 1.25 3.00
MVP10 Mike Modano .60 1.50

1999-00 Upper Deck MVP SC Edition

Released late in the 1999-00 hockey season, the 1999-00 Upper Deck MVP Stanley Cup Edition set features 193 regular cards, 25 CHL Prospects cards, and 2 Checklists to comprise the 220-card set. MVP Stanley Cup Edition was packaged in boxes containing 28-packs with 10-cards per pack, and carried a suggested retail price of $1.59.

COMPLETE SET (220) 20.00 40.00
1 Teemu Selanne .10 .30
2 Paul Kariya .10 .30
3 Guy Hebert .08 .25
4 Oleg Tverdovsky .05 .15
5 Tony Hrkac .05 .15
6 Mike Leclerc .05 .15
7 Ladislav Kohn .05 .15
8 Ray Ferraro .05 .15
9 Ed Ward .05 .15
10 Norm Maracle .08 .25
11 Dean Sylvester RC .08 .25
12 Yannick Tremblay .05 .15
13 Patrik Stefan RC .40 1.00
14 Johan Garpenlov .05 .15
15 Per-Johan Axelsson .05 .15
16 Joe Thornton .20 .50
17 Sergei Samsonov .08 .25
18 Jay Henderson RC .05 .15
19 Byron Dafoe .08 .25
20 Steve Heinze .05 .15
21 Marty McSorley .05 .15
22 Dominik Hasek .25 .60
23 Miroslav Satan .08 .25
24 Curtis Brown .05 .15
25 Martin Biron .08 .25
26 Jason Woolley .05 .15
27 Michael Peca .08 .25
28 Wayne Primeau .05 .15
29 Valeri Bure .05 .15
30 Derek Morris .08 .25
31 Cory Stillman .05 .15
32 Fred Brathwaite .08 .25
33 Jarome Iginla .15 .40
34 Andre Nazarov .05 .15
35 Jeff Shantz .05 .15
36 Ron Francis .05 .15
37 Jeff O'Neill .05 .15
38 Arturs Irbe .08 .25
39 Sami Kapanen .05 .15
40 Sean Hill .05 .15
41 Byron Ritchie RC .08 .25
42 Tommy Westlund RC .05 .15
43 Tony Amonte .08 .25
44 Doug Gilmour .08 .25
45 Blair Atcheynum .05 .15
46 Alexei Zhamnov .05 .15
47 Dean Mcammond .05 .15
48 Michael Nylander .05 .15
49 Aaron Miller .05 .15
50 Milan Hejduk .10 .30
51 Patrick Roy .60 1.50
52 Joe Sakic .30 .75
53 Chris Drury .08 .25
54 Peter Forsberg .30 .75
55 Ray Bourque .20 .50
56 Marc Denis .08 .25
57 Brett Hull .15 .40
58 Mike Modano .20 .50
59 Ed Belfour .10 .30
60 Kirk Muller .05 .15
61 Brenden Morrow .10 .30
62 Mike Keane .05 .15
63 Brad Lukowich RC .05 .15
64 Sergei Fedorov .20 .50
65 Steve Yzerman .60 1.50
66 Chris Osgood .08 .25
67 Brendan Shanahan .10 .30
68 Martin Lapointe .08 .25
69 Pat Verbeek .05 .15
70 Stacy Roest .05 .15
71 Tommy Salo .08 .25
72 Doug Weight .08 .25
73 Alexander Selivanov .05 .15
74 Ryan Smyth .05 .15
75 Boyd Devereaux .05 .15
76 Ethan Moreau .05 .15
77 Pavel Bure .10 .30
78 Viktor Kozlov .05 .15
79 Mike Vernon .08 .25
80 Ivan Novoseltsev RC .25 .60
81 Ray Whitney .08 .25
82 Filip Kuba RC .05 .15
83 Ray Sheppard .05 .15
84 Zigmund Palffy .08 .25
85 Luc Robitaille .08 .25
86 Bryan Smolinski .08 .25
87 Rob Blake .08 .25
88 Jere Karalahti RC .05 .15
89 Marko Tuomainen .05 .15
90 Garry Galley .05 .15
91 Saku Koivu .10 .30
92 Dainius Zubrus .05 .15
93 Jose Theodore .15 .40
94 Karl Dykhuis .05 .15
95 Sergei Zholtok .05 .15
96 Francis Bouillon RC .05 .15
97 David Legwand .08 .25
98 Mike Dunham .08 .25
99 Rob Valicevic RC .05 .15
100 Cliff Ronning .08 .25
101 Drake Berehowsky .05 .15
102 Greg Johnson .05 .15
103 Patric Kjellberg .05 .15
104 Martin Brodeur .30 .75
105 Scott Stevens .08 .25
106 Claude Lemieux .05 .15
107 Scott Gomez .05 .15
108 Partik Elias .08 .25
109 Randy McKay .05 .15
110 Sergei Brylin .05 .15
111 Tim Connolly .05 .15
112 Roberto Luongo .15 .40
113 Dave Scatchard .05 .15
114 Kenny Jonsson .05 .15
115 Vladimir Orszagh RC .05 .15
116 Ted Drury .05 .15
117 Theo Fleury .05 .15
118 Mike Richter .10 .30
119 Mike York .05 .15
120 Brian Leetch .10 .30
121 Petr Nedved .05 .15
122 Radek Dvorak .05 .15
123 Jan Hlavac .05 .15
124 Marian Hossa .10 .30
125 Radek Bonk .05 .15
126 Daniel Alfredsson .08 .25
127 Ron Tugnutt .08 .25
128 Rob Zamuner .05 .15
129 Jason York .05 .15
130 Shaun Van Allen .05 .15
131 Eric Lindros .10 .30
132 John LeClair .10 .30
133 Simon Gagne .10 .30
134 Mark Recchi .08 .25
135 Keith Primeau .05 .15
136 Daymond Langkow .08 .25
137 Brian Boucher .10 .30
138 Luke Richardson .05 .15
139 Keith Tkachuk .10 .30
140 Jeremy Roenick .15 .40
141 Travis Green .05 .15
142 Dallas Drake .05 .15
143 Jyrki Lumme .05 .15
144 Shane Doan .05 .15
145 Sean Burke .08 .25
146 Jaromir Jagr .20 .50
147 Alexei Kovalev .05 .15
148 Tom Barrasso .08 .25
149 Martin Sonnenberg RC .05 .15
150 Robert Lang .05 .15
151 Robert Dome .05 .15
152 Darius Kasparaitis .05 .15
153 Owen Nolan .08 .25
154 Jeff Friesen .05 .15
155 Steve Shields .08 .25
156 Vincent Damphousse .05 .15
157 Mike Rathje .05 .15
158 Alexander Korolyuk .05 .15
159 Todd Harvey .08 .25
160 Pavol Demitra .08 .25
161 Pierre Turgeon .08 .25
162 Roman Turek .08 .25
163 Chris Pronger .08 .25
164 Jochen Hecht RC .50 1.25
165 Todd Reirden RC .05 .15
166 Scott Young .05 .15
167 Vincent Lecavalier .10 .30
168 Dan Cloutier .05 .15
169 Chris Gratton .05 .15
170 Todd Warriner .05 .15
171 Mike Sillinger .05 .15
172 Petr Svoboda .05 .15
173 Mats Sundin .10 .30
174 Curtis Joseph .10 .30
175 Jonas Hoglund .05 .15
176 Sergei Berezin .05 .15
177 Nathan Dempsey RC .05 .15
178 Nikolai Antropov RC .50 1.25
179 Alyn McCauley .05 .15
180 Alexander Karpovtsev .05 .15
181 Steve Kariya RC .30 .75
182 Mark Messier .10 .30
183 Markus Naslund .10 .30
184 Adrian Aucoin .05 .15
185 Andrew Cassels .05 .15
186 Artem Chubarov .05 .15
187 Brad May .08 .25
188 Peter Bondra .10 .30
189 Olaf Kolzig .08 .25
190 Dmitri Mironov .05 .15
191 Jeff Halpern RC .30 .75
192 Andrei Nikolishin .05 .15
193 Terry Yake .08 .25
194 Pavel Brendl RC .50 1.25
195 Sheldon Keefe RC .40 1.00
196 Branislav Mezei RC .08 .25
197 Milan Kraft RC .50 1.25
198 Ryan Jardine RC .30 .75
199 Kristian Kudroc RC .08 .25
200 Alexander Buturlin RC .15 .40
201 Jaroslav Kristek RC .10 .30
202 Andrei Shefer RC .10 .30
203 Brad Moran RC .15 .40
204 Brett Lysak RC .08 .25
205 Michal Sivek RC .15 .40
206 Luke Sellars RC .08 .25
207 Brad Ralph RC .08 .25
208 Bryan Kazarian RC .08 .25
209 Barret Jackman .08 .25
210 Brian Finley .08 .25
211 Jamie Lundmark .08 .25
212 Denis Shvidki .08 .25
213 Taylor Pyatt .08 .25
214 Kris Beech .05 .15
215 Michael Zigomanis .08 .25
216 Justin Papineau .08 .25
217 Daniel Sedin .05 .15
218 Henrik Sedin .05 .15
219 Checklist .05 .15
220 Checklist .05 .15

1999-00 Upper Deck MVP SC Edition Gold Script

Randomly seeded in packs, this 220-card set parallels the base set and is enhanced with gold foil instead of bronze, and on the regular cards, a gold-foil signature. Cards are serial numbered out of 100.

*GOLD SCRIPT: 30X TO 80X BASIC CARDS

1999-00 Upper Deck MVP SC Edition Silver Script

Randomly seeded in packs at 1:2, this 220-card set parallels the base set and is enhanced with silver foil instead of bronze, and on the regular cards, a silver-foil signature.

*SILVER SCRIPT: 1.2X TO 3X BASIC CARDS

1999-00 Upper Deck MVP SC Edition Super Script

Randomly inserted in packs, this 220-card set parallels the base set and features a printed signature on the front of the regular cards. Each card is serial numbered out of 25.

*SUPER SCRIPT: 50X TO 120X BASIC CARDS

1999-00 Upper Deck MVP SC Edition Clutch Performers

Randomly inserted in packs at 1:28, this 10-card set showcases some of the NHL's key clutch players.

COMPLETE SET (10) 15.00 30.00
CP1 Paul Kariya 1.00 2.50
CP2 Ray Bourque 1.50 4.00
CP3 Joe Sakic 2.00 5.00
CP4 Steve Yzerman 5.00 12.00
CP5 Luc Robitaille .75 2.00
CP6 Martin Brodeur 2.50 6.00
CP7 Theo Fleury .75 2.00
CP8 John LeClair 1.25 3.00
CP9 Jaromir Jagr 1.50 4.00
CP10 Curtis Joseph 1.00 2.50

1999-00 Upper Deck MVP SC Edition Cup Contenders

Randomly inserted in packs at 1:9, this 10-card set features emerging NHL superstars.

COMPLETE SET (10) 5.00 10.00
CC1 Patrik Stefan .75 2.00
CC2 Sergei Samsonov .60 1.50
CC3 Milan Hejduk .75 2.00
CC4 Chris Drury .60 1.50
CC5 David Legwand .40 1.00
CC6 Scott Gomez .50 1.25
CC7 Marian Hossa .60 1.50
CC8 Jeff Friesen .50 1.25
CC9 Vincent Lecavalier .50 1.25
CC10 Steve Kariya .50 1.25

1999-00 Upper Deck MVP SC Edition Game-Used Souvenirs

Randomly inserted in packs at the rate of 1:130, this 18-card set features players with swatches of game-used sticks. Super Game Used Souvenirs came inserted into Canadian packs at the rate of 1:130, and feature two swatches of material instead of one.

GUBH Brett Hull 6.00 15.00
GUBJ Barret Jackman 3.00 8.00
GUCJ Curtis Joseph 5.00 12.00
GUDS Denis Shvidki 3.00 8.00
GUEL Eric Lindros 6.00 15.00
GUJC John LeClair 5.00 12.00
GUJS Joe Sakic 10.00 25.00
GUKB Kris Beech 3.00 8.00
GUMK Milan Kraft 3.00 8.00
GUMO Maxime Ouellet 3.00 8.00
GUPB Pavel Brendl 3.00 8.00
GUPF Peter Forsberg 10.00 25.00
GUPV Pavel Bure 6.00 15.00
GURB Ray Bourque 10.00 25.00
GUSK Scott Kelman 3.00 8.00
GUSY Steve Yzerman 10.00 25.00
GUTP Taylor Pyatt 3.00 8.00
GUTS Teemu Selanne 5.00 12.00
SGDS Denis Shvidki Super 4.00 10.00
SGKB Kris Beech Super 4.00 10.00
SGMK Milan Kraft Super 4.00 10.00
SGPB Pavel Brendl Super 4.00 10.00

1999-00 Upper Deck MVP SC Edition Golden Memories

Randomly inserted in packs at 1:14, this 10-card set spotlights outstanding moments in NHL post-season play.

COMPLETE SET (10) 12.00 25.00
GM1 Paul Kariya .50 1.25
GM2 Patrick Roy 2.50 6.00
GM3 Peter Forsberg 1.25 3.00
GM4 Mike Modano .75 2.00
GM5 Steve Yzerman 2.50 6.00
GM6 Martin Brodeur 1.25 3.00
GM7 Theo Fleury .50 1.25
GM8 Eric Lindros .75 2.00
GM9 Jaromir Jagr .75 2.00
GM10 Curtis Joseph .50 1.25

1999-00 Upper Deck MVP SC Edition Great Combinations

Randomly inserted in packs at the rate of 1:196, this 16-card set showcases some of the NHL's most dominating teammates. Parallels numbered to just 25 were also randomly inserted in packs.

*GOLD/25: 1.2X TO 3X SILVER
GCBK P.Bure/V.Kozlov 10.00 25.00
GCGL W.Gretzky/B.Leetch 15.00 40.00
GCGR W.Gretzky/M.Richter 15.00 40.00
GCHM B.Hull/M.Modano 12.50 30.00
GCHP D.Hasek/M.Peca 8.00 20.00
GCJS J.Jagr/M.Straka 10.00 25.00
GCKS P.Kariya/T.Selanne 10.00 25.00
GCLL E.Lindros/J.LeClair 10.00 25.00
GCLS V.Lecavalier/P.Svoboda 8.00 20.00
GCRF P.Roy/P.Forsberg 15.00 40.00
GCSF B.Shanahan/S.Fedorov 10.00 25.00
GCSJ M.Sundin/C.Joseph 8.00 20.00
GCSR P.Stefan/D.Rhodes 8.00 20.00
GCTR K.Tkachuk/J.Roenick 8.00 20.00
GCTS J.Thornton/S.Samsonov 10.00 25.00
GCYO S.Yzerman/C.Osgood 12.50 30.00

1999-00 Upper Deck MVP SC Edition Great Combinations Gold

*GOLD/25: 1.2X TO 3X SILVER
GOLD/25 ODDS 1:196 HOBBY
GOLD PRINT RUN 25 SER.#'d SETS

1999-00 Upper Deck MVP SC Edition Playoff Heroes

Randomly seeded in packs at the rate of 1:72, this 10-card set pays tribute to the rare superstars who have performed exceptionally in the post season.

COMPLETE SET (10) 40.00 80.00
PH1 Paul Kariya 3.00 8.00
PH2 Dominik Hasek 5.00 12.00
PH3 Patrick Roy 12.50 30.00
PH4 Mike Modano 4.00 10.00
PH5 Sergei Fedorov 5.00 12.00
PH6 Pavel Bure 3.00 8.00
PH7 Martin Brodeur 6.00 15.00
PH8 Eric Lindros 4.00 10.00
PH9 Jaromir Jagr 4.00 10.00
PH10 Mark Messier 3.00 8.00

1999-00 Upper Deck MVP SC Edition ProSign

Randomly inserted in reatil packs at the rate of 1:144, this 24-card set featured an authentic autograph.

AM Al MacInnis 6.00 15.00
AT Alex Tanguay 6.00 15.00
BF Brian Finley 4.00 10.00
BH Brett Hull 15.00 40.00
BJ Barret Jackman 6.00 15.00
BL Brian Leetch 8.00 20.00
CJ Curtis Joseph 20.00 50.00
DA Dave Andreychuk 4.00 10.00
DL David Legwand 4.00 10.00
DS Denis Shvidki 2.00 5.00
JH Jochen Hecht 4.00 10.00
JS Jozef Stumpel 2.00 5.00
KB Kris Beech 2.00 5.00
MB Martin Biron 4.00 10.00
MK Milan Kraft 2.00 5.00
MO Maxime Ouellet 4.00 10.00
PB Pavel Bure 6.00 15.00
PS Patrik Stefan 2.00 5.00
SG Simon Gagne 6.00 15.00
SK Scott Kelman 2.00 5.00
SS Sergei Samsonov 6.00 15.00
SY Steve Yzerman 100.00 175.00
TP Taylor Pyatt 6.00 15.00
PBR Pavel Brendl 4.00 10.00

1999-00 Upper Deck MVP SC Edition Second Season Snipers

Randomly inserted in packs at 1:28, this 12-card set spotlights players that have a knack for scoring clutch goals.

COMPLETE SET (12) 12.00 25.00
SS1 Teemu Selanne 1.00 2.50
SS2 Joe Thornton 1.00 2.50
SS3 Peter Forsberg 2.50 6.00
SS4 Brendan Shanahan 1.00 2.50
SS5 Pavel Bure 1.00 2.50
SS6 Claude Lemieux .75 2.00
SS7 Eric Lindros 1.00 2.50
SS8 John LeClair 1.00 2.50
SS9 Keith Tkachuk 1.00 2.50
SS10 Jaromir Jagr 1.50 4.00
SS11 Mats Sundin 1.00 2.50
SS12 Mark Messier 1.00 2.50

1999-00 Upper Deck MVP SC Edition Stanley Cup Talent

Inserted at a rate of 1:5 packs, this 20-card set features elite players of top teams in full color action photos on the card fronts, and a breakdown of individual stats on card backs.

COMPLETE SET (20) 8.00 15.00
SC1 Paul Kariya .30 .75
SC2 Teemu Selanne .30 .75
SC3 Ray Bourque .50 1.25
SC4 Joe Sakic .60 1.50
SC5 Patrick Roy 1.50 4.00
SC6 Brett Hull .40 1.00
SC7 Sergei Fedorov .50 1.25
SC8 Pave Bure .30 .75
SC9 Zigmund Palffy .25 .60
SC10 Martin Brodeur .75 2.00
SC11 Theo Fleury .20 .50
SC12 Eric Lindros .30 .75
SC13 John LeClair .30 .75
SC14 Jaromir Jagr .50 1.25
SC15 Jeremy Roenick .40 1.00
SC16 Keith Tkachuk .30 .75
SC17 Steve Shields .20 .50
SC18 Mats Sundin .30 .75
SC19 Mark Messier .30 .75
SC20 Peter Bondra .20 .50

2000-01 Upper Deck MVP

Released in late September 2000, Upper Deck MVP features a 220-card base set comprised of 183 veteran player cards and 35 NHL Prospect cards. Base cards are white bordered and have copper foil highlights. MVP was packaged in 28-pack boxes with each pack containing 10 cards and carried a suggested retail price of $1.59.

COMPLETE SET (220) 12.00 30.00
1 Antti Aalto .12 .30
2 Matt Cullen .12 .30
3 Oleg Tverdovsky .12 .30
4 Paul Kariya .25 .60
5 Steve Rucchin .12 .30
6 Teemu Selanne .40 1.00
7 Maxim Balmochnyk .12 .30
8 Andrew Brunette .12 .30
9 Damian Rhodes .12 .30
10 Dean Sylvester .12 .30
11 Donald Audette .15 .40
12 Patrik Stefan .15 .40
13 Ray Ferraro .12 .30
14 Brian Rolston .15 .40
15 Sergei Samsonov .15 .40
16 Jason Allison .15 .40
17 Joe Thornton .30 .75
18 Kyle McLaren .12 .30
19 Byron Dafoe .15 .40
20 Hal Gill .12 .30
21 Curtis Brown .12 .30
22 Stu Barnes .15 .40
23 Dominik Hasek .30 .75
24 Doug Gilmour .25 .60
25 Maxim Afinogenov .12 .30
26 Michael Peca .15 .40
27 Miroslav Satan .12 .30
28 Chris Gratton .12 .30
29 Derek Morris .12 .30
30 Fred Brathwaite .15 .40
31 Jarome Iginla .20 .50
32 Marc Savard .15 .40
33 Phil Housley .15 .40
34 Valeri Bure .15 .40
35 Arturs Irbe .15 .40
36 Dave Tanabe .12 .30
37 Jeff O'Neill .15 .40
38 Rod Brind'Amour .20 .50
39 Ron Francis .25 .60
40 Sami Kapanen .12 .30
41 Alexei Zhamnov .15 .40
42 Eric Daze .15 .40
43 Jocelyn Thibault .15 .40
44 Michael Nylander .12 .30
45 Steve Sullivan .12 .30
46 Tony Amonte .15 .40
47 Chris Drury .15 .40
48 Joe Sakic .30 .75
49 Milan Hejduk .15 .40
50 Patrick Roy .50 1.25
51 Peter Forsberg .25 .60
52 Ray Bourque .30 .75
53 Adam Deadmarsh .15 .40
54 Alex Tanguay .15 .40
55 Marc Denis .15 .40
56 Brenden Morrow .15 .40
57 Brett Hull .30 .75
58 Derian Hatcher .15 .40
59 Ed Belfour .20 .50
60 Jamie Langenbrunner .15 .40
61 Mike Modano .30 .75
62 Sergei Zubov .15 .40
63 Joe Nieuwendyk .20 .50
64 Brendan Shanahan .25 .60
65 Chris Chelios .20 .50
66 Chris Osgood .20 .50
67 Nicklas Lidstrom .20 .50
68 Pat Verbeek .15 .40
69 Sergei Fedorov .30 .75
70 Steve Yzerman .60 1.50
71 Darren McCarty .12 .30
72 Tom Poti .12 .30
73 Bill Guerin .20 .50
74 Doug Weight .20 .50
75 Mike Grier .12 .30
76 Ryan Smyth .15 .40
77 Tommy Salo .15 .40
78 Bret Hedican .12 .30
79 Pavel Bure .25 .60
80 Ray Whitney .15 .40
81 Scott Mellanby .12 .30
82 Trevor Kidd .12 .30
83 Viktor Kozlov .15 .40
84 Bryan Smolinski .15 .40
85 Stephane Fiset .12 .30
86 Jozef Stumpel .12 .30
87 Luc Robitaille .20 .50
88 Rob Blake .20 .50
89 Zigmund Palffy .20 .50
90 Brian Savage .12 .30
91 Dainius Zubrus .12 .30
92 Jose Theodore .25 .60
93 Martin Rucinsky .12 .30
94 Saku Koivu .20 .50
95 Sergei Zholtok .12 .30
96 Manny Fernandez .15 .40
97 Cliff Ronning .12 .30
98 David Legwand .20 .50
99 Drake Berehowsky .12 .30
100 Vitali Yachmenev .12 .30
101 Mike Dunham .12 .30
102 Patric Kjellberg .12 .30
103 Alexander Mogilny .15 .40
104 Claude Lemieux .15 .40
105 John Madden .15 .40
106 Martin Brodeur .40 1.00
107 Patrik Elias .20 .50
108 Scott Gomez .15 .40
109 Scott Stevens .20 .50
110 Dave Scatchard .12 .30
111 Kenny Jonsson .12 .30
112 Mariusz Czerkawski .12 .30
113 Mathieu Biron .12 .30
114 Tim Connolly .12 .30
115 Claude Lapointe .12 .30
116 Adam Graves .15 .40
117 Brian Leetch .20 .50
118 Mike York .12 .30
119 Mike Richter .20 .50
120 Petr Nedved .15 .40
121 Theo Fleury .25 .60
122 Daniel Alfredsson .20 .50
123 Patrick Lalime .15 .40
124 John LeClair .20 .50
125 Marian Hossa .15 .40
126 Keith Primeau .15 .40
127 Radek Bonk .15 .40
128 Shawn McEachern .12 .30
129 Andreas Dackell .12 .30
130 Brian Boucher .15 .40
131 Mark Recchi .25 .60
132 Simon Gagne .20 .50
133 Eric Desjardins .15 .40
134 Jeremy Roenick .20 .50
135 Keith Tkachuk .20 .50
136 Teppo Numminen .12 .30
137 Eric Lindros .30 .75
138 Shane Doan .15 .40
139 Travis Green .12 .30
140 Trevor Letowski .12 .30
141 Alexei Kovalev .15 .40
142 Jan Hrdina .12 .30
143 Jaromir Jagr .50 1.25
144 Jean-Sebastien Aubin .15 .40
145 Martin Straka .15 .40
146 Matthew Barnaby .15 .40
147 Brad Stuart .15 .40
148 Jeff Friesen .12 .30
149 Mike Ricci .15 .40
150 Owen Nolan .20 .50
151 Steve Shields .12 .30
152 Vincent Damphousse .15 .40
153 Al MacInnis .20 .50
154 Chris Pronger .15 .40
155 Jochen Hecht .12 .30
156 Pavol Demitra .25 .60
157 Pierre Turgeon .20 .50
158 Roman Turek .15 .40
159 Dan Cloutier .15 .40
160 Fredrik Modin .12 .30
161 Mike Johnson .12 .30
162 Paul Mara .12 .30
163 Vincent Lecavalier .15 .40
164 Petr Svoboda .12 .30
165 Curtis Joseph .25 .60
166 Darcy Tucker .12 .30
167 Mats Sundin .20 .50
168 Nikolai Antropov .15 .40
169 Sergei Berezin .12 .30
170 Steve Thomas .12 .30
171 Dimitri Yushkevich .12 .30
172 Brendan Morrison .20 .50
173 Ed Jovanovski .15 .40
174 Felix Potvin .30 .75
175 Harold Druken .12 .30
176 Todd Bertuzzi .15 .40
177 Markus Naslund .15 .40
178 Adam Oates .20 .50
179 Chris Simon .12 .30
180 Jeff Halpern .12 .30
181 Olaf Kolzig .20 .50
182 Peter Bondra .15 .40
183 Sergei Gonchar .12 .30
184 Vitali Vishnevsky .12 .30
185 Andreas Karlsson .12 .30
186 Eric Nickulas RC .20 .50
187 Brandon Smith RC .20 .50
188 Dimitri Kalinin .20 .50
189 Chris Herperger .20 .50
190 Serge Aubin RC .25 .60
191 Alan Letang .20 .50
192 Keith Aldridge RC .20 .50
193 Steven Reinprecht RC .30 .75
194 Brad Chartrand .20 .50
195 David Gosselin RC .25 .60
196 Colin White RC .20 .50
197 Willie Mitchell RC .30 .75
198 Jason Krog .20 .50
199 Steve Valiquette RC .25 .60
200 Petr Schastlivy .20 .50
201 Andy Delmore .20 .50
202 Mark Eaton .20 .50
203 Evgeni Nabokov .25 .60
204 Ladislav Nagy .20 .50
205 Kyle Freadrich RC .20 .50
206 Greg Andrusak RC .25 .60
207 Alfie Michaud .30 .75
208 Brent Sopel RC .30 .75
209 Matt Pettinger RC .20 .50
210 Chris Nielsen RC .20 .50
211 Dany Heatley RC 2.00 5.00
212 Josef Vasicek RC .50 1.25
213 Matt Zultek RC .20 .50
214 Dmitri Afanasenkov RC .20 .50
215 Tyler Bouck RC .20 .50
216 Jonas Andersson RC .20 .50
217 Juraj Kolnik RC .20 .50
218 Andrew Raycroft RC 1.00 2.50
219 Pavel Bure CL .25 .60
220 Steve Yzerman CL .60 1.50

2000-01 Upper Deck MVP Excellence

Randomly inserted in packs at the rate of 1:18, this 10-card set pairs up top NHL players on an all foil card with holographic foil highlights. Full color action shots are set side to side on the card front.

COMPLETE SET (10) 15.00 30.00
ME1 C.Joseph/R.Luongo 1.25 3.00
ME2 P.Bure/P.Brendl 1.25 3.00
ME3 S.Samsonov/O.Saprykin 1.25 3.00
ME4 M.Hejduk/I.Novoseltsev 1.25 3.00
ME5 S.Yzerman/P.Verbeek 4.00 10.00
ME6 R.Turek/M.Biron 1.25 3.00
ME7 H.Sedin/D.Sedin 2.00 5.00
ME8 P.Stefan/L.Nagy 1.25 3.00
ME9 M.Malhotra/M.York 1.25 3.00
ME10 W.Gretzky/R.Bourque 6.00 15.00

2000-01 Upper Deck MVP First Stars

Randomly inserted in Hobby packs, this 218-card set parallels the base MVP set on cards enhanced with a single star along the right side. Each card is sequentially numbered to 25.

*VETS/25: 20X TO 50X BASIC CARDS
*ROOKIES/25: 12X TO 30X BASIC RC

2000-01 Upper Deck MVP Game-Used Souvenirs

Randomly inserted in packs at the rate of 1:83, this 29-card set features cards with swatches of game used sticks. Cards with a "C" prefix were found in Canadian hobby packs only.

CGCJ Curtis Joseph 6.00 15.00
CGCO Chris Osgood 6.00 15.00
CGEB Ed Belfour 6.00 15.00
CGFP Felix Potvin 10.00 25.00
CGMB Martin Brodeur 10.00 25.00
CGMS Mats Sundin 6.00 15.00
CGWG Wayne Gretzky 25.00 60.00
GSAI Arturs Irbe 6.00 15.00
GSBS Brendan Shanahan 6.00 15.00
GSCC Chris Chelios 6.00 15.00
GSDH Dominik Hasek 10.00 25.00
GSEL Eric Lindros 6.00 15.00
GSJA Jason Allison 6.00 15.00
GSJJ Jaromir Jagr 10.00 25.00
GSJL John LeClair 6.00 15.00
GSKT Keith Tkachuk 6.00 15.00
GSMM Mark Messier 6.00 15.00
GSMR Mike Richter 10.00 25.00
GSPB Pavel Bure 6.00 15.00
GSPF Peter Forsberg 12.50 30.00
GSPK Paul Kariya 6.00 15.00
GSPR Patrick Roy 15.00 40.00
GSRB Ray Bourque 8.00 20.00
GSRL Roberto Luongo 10.00 25.00
GSSF Sergei Fedorov 10.00 25.00
GSSY Steve Yzerman 15.00 40.00
GSTS Teemu Selanne 6.00 15.00
GSWG Wayne Gretzky 25.00 60.00
GSZP Zigmund Palffy 6.00 15.00

2000-01 Upper Deck MVP Mark of Excellence

Randomly inserted in packs, this 10-card set parallels the base Excellence insert set. Each card is autographed by both players and is sequentially numbered to 50. The original checklist included a Gretzky/Bourque card which does not exist.

SGBB P.Bure/P.Brendl 20.00 50.00
SGHN M.Hejduk/I.Novoseltsev 15.00 40.00
SGJL C.Joseph/R.Luongo 40.00 100.00
SGMY M.Malhotra/M.York 12.00 30.00
SGSE H.Sedin/D.Sedin 125.00 300.00
SGSL P.Stefan/L.Nagy 15.00 40.00
SGSS S.Samsonov/O.Saprykin 15.00 40.00
SGTB R.Turek/M.Biron 15.00 40.00
SGYV S.Yzerman/P.Verbeek 75.00 150.00

2000-01 Upper Deck MVP Masked Men

COMPLETE SET (10) 15.00 30.00
STATED ODDS 1:18
MM1 Dominik Hasek 2.00 5.00
MM2 Patrick Roy 5.00 12.00
MM3 Ed Belfour 1.00 2.50
MM4 Chris Osgood .75 2.00
MM5 Martin Brodeur 2.50 6.00
MM6 Brian Boucher 1.00 2.50
MM7 Steve Shields .75 2.00
MM8 Roman Turek .75 2.00
MM9 Curtis Joseph 1.00 2.50
MM10 Olaf Kolzig .75 2.00

2000-01 Upper Deck MVP ProSign

Randomly inserted in retail packs, this 18-card set features a small portrait player photo centered that fades into a white-out background and authentic player autographs. The Boucher card has never been confirmed and probably does not exist.

AM Al MacInnis 8.00 20.00
BM Brenden Morrow 8.00 20.00
CB Curtis Brown 6.00 15.00
CJ Curtis Joseph 12.50 30.00
DL David Legwand 8.00 20.00
IV Ivan Novoseltsev 6.00 15.00
LN Ladislav Nagy 6.00 15.00
MJ Mike Johnson 6.00 15.00
MM Manny Malhotra 6.00 15.00
MR Mike Ribeiro 6.00 15.00
MY Mike York 6.00 15.00
OS Oleg Saprykin 6.00 15.00
PB Pavel Bure 10.00 25.00
PS Patrik Stefan 6.00 15.00
RL Roberto Luongo 12.50 30.00
RT Roman Turek 6.00 15.00
SM Steven McCarthy 6.00 15.00
SS Sergei Samsonov 8.00 20.00

2000-01 Upper Deck MVP Second Stars

Randomly inserted in Hobby packs, this 218-card set parallels the base MVP set on cards enhanced with two stars along the right side. Each card is sequentially numbered to 100.

*VETS/100: 12X TO 30X BASIC CARDS
*ROOKIES/100: 6X TO 15X BASIC RC

2000-01 Upper Deck MVP Talent

COMPLETE SET (15) 10.00 20.00
STATED ODDS 1:6
M1 Paul Kariya .30 .75
M2 Teemu Selanne .30 .75
M3 Ray Bourque .60 1.50
M4 Joe Sakic .60 1.50
M5 Patrick Roy 1.50 4.00
M6 Brett Hull .40 1.00
M7 Sergei Fedorov .60 1.50
M8 Pavel Bure .40 1.00
M9 Zigmund Palffy .30 .75
M10 Martin Brodeur .75 2.00
M11 Theo Fleury .30 .75
M12 Eric Lindros .50 1.25
M13 John LeClair .40 1.00
M14 Jaromir Jagr .50 1.25
M15 Jeremy Roenick .40 1.00

2000-01 Upper Deck MVP Third Stars

Randomly inserted in packs at the rate of 1:2, this 218-card set parallels the base MVP set on cards enhanced with a silver border, silver foil stamping, and three white stars along the right edge.

COMPLETE SET (218) 75.00 150.00
*VETS: 1.5X TO 4X BASIC CARDS
*ROOKIES: .8X TO 2X BASIC CARDS

2000-01 Upper Deck MVP Top Draws

COMPLETE SET (10) 5.00 10.00
STATED ODDS 1:9
TD1 Teemu Selanne .30 .75
TD2 Dominik Hasek .60 1.50
TD3 Peter Forsberg .75 2.00
TD4 Brendan Shanahan .50 1.25
TD5 Pavel Bure .40 1.00
TD6 Scott Gomez .30 .75
TD7 Eric Lindros .50 1.25
TD8 John LeClair .40 1.00
TD9 Keith Tkachuk .30 .75
TD10 Jaromir Jagr .50 1.25

2000-01 Upper Deck MVP Top Playmakers

COMPLETE SET (10) 15.00 30.00
STATED ODDS 1:18
TP1 Paul Kariya .75 2.00
TP2 Dominik Hasek 1.50 4.00
TP3 Peter Forsberg 2.00 5.00
TP4 Mike Modano 1.25 3.00
TP5 Steve Yzerman 4.00 10.00
TP6 Pavel Bure 1.00 2.50
TP7 Scott Gomez .75 2.00
TP8 Eric Lindros 1.25 3.00
TP9 Jaromir Jagr 1.25 3.00
TP10 Jeremy Roenick 1.00 2.50

2000-01 Upper Deck MVP Valuable Commodities

COMPLETE SET (10) 20.00 40.00
STATED ODDS 1:18
VC1 Paul Kariya .75 2.00
VC2 Patrick Roy 4.00 10.00
VC3 Peter Forsberg 2.00 5.00
VC4 Mike Modano 1.25 3.00
VC5 Steve Yzerman 4.00 10.00
VC6 Martin Brodeur 2.00 5.00
VC7 Theo Fleury .75 2.00
VC8 Eric Lindros 1.25 3.00
VC9 Jaromir Jagr 1.25 3.00
VC10 Curtis Joseph .75 2.00

2001-02 Upper Deck MVP

Released in late September, this 233-card set was originally released as a smaller 220-card set. Cards 221-233 were randomly available in UD Rookie Update packs.

COMPLETE SET (233) 40.00 80.00
COMP.SERIES I (220) 15.00 30.00
1 Jean-Sebastien Giguere .12 .30
2 Paul Kariya .20 .50
3 Jeff Friesen .10 .25
4 Oleg Tverdovsky .10 .25
5 Mike Leclerc .10 .25
6 Milan Hnilicka .12 .30
7 Patrik Stefan .12 .30
8 Ray Ferraro .10 .25
9 Jiri Slegr .10 .25
10 Hnat Domenichelli .10 .25
11 Jason Allison .12 .30
12 Joe Thornton .20 .50
13 Bill Guerin .15 .40
14 Sergei Samsonov .12 .30
15 Kyle McLaren .10 .25
16 Jonathan Girard .10 .25
17 Maxim Afinogenov .10 .25
18 Stu Barnes .12 .30
19 Doug Gilmour .20 .50
20 Chris Gratton .10 .25
21 Martin Biron .12 .30
22 J-P Dumont .10 .25
23 Miroslav Satan .12 .30
24 Craig Conroy .10 .25
25 Jarome Iginla .15 .40
26 Rico Fata .10 .25
27 Derek Morris .10 .25
28 Marc Savard .10 .25
29 Oleg Saprykin .10 .25
30 Arturs Irbe .12 .30
31 Shane Willis .10 .25
32 Rod Brind'Amour .15 .40
33 Jeff O'Neill .10 .25
34 Sami Kapanen .10 .25
35 Ron Francis .20 .50
36 Dave Tanabe .10 .25
37 Steve Sullivan .10 .25
38 Tony Amonte .12 .30
39 Jaroslav Spacek .10 .25
40 Eric Daze .12 .30
41 Michael Nylander .10 .25
42 Alexei Zhamnov .12 .30
43 Joe Sakic .25 .60
44 Peter Forsberg .20 .50
45 Milan Hejduk .12 .30
46 Chris Drury .12 .30
47 Rob Blake .15 .40
48 Ray Bourque .25 .60
49 Patrick Roy .40 1.00
50 Alex Tanguay .12 .30
51 Geoff Sanderson .10 .25
52 Espen Knutsen .10 .25
53 Ray Whitney .10 .25
54 Rostislav Klesla .10 .25
55 Ron Tugnutt .12 .30
56 Tyler Wright .10 .25
57 Mike Modano .25 .60
58 Jere Lehtinen .12 .30
59 Sergei Zubov .12 .30
60 Brenden Morrow .12 .30
61 Ed Belfour .15 .40
62 Joe Nieuwendyk .15 .40
63 Pierre Turgeon .15 .40
64 Steve Yzerman .50 1.25
65 Brendan Shanahan .20 .50
66 Brett Hull .20 .50
67 Luc Robitaille .15 .40
68 Sergei Fedorov .25 .60
69 Dominik Hasek .25 .60
70 Darren McCarty .10 .25
71 Mike Grier .10 .25
72 Ryan Smyth .12 .30
73 Anson Carter .12 .30
74 Tom Poti .10 .25
75 Tommy Salo .12 .30
76 Mike Comrie .12 .30
77 Todd Marchant .10 .25
78 Pavel Bure .20 .50
79 Viktor Kozlov .10 .25
80 Marcus Nilson .10 .25
81 Kevyn Adams .10 .25
82 Roberto Luongo .25 .60
83 Denis Shvidki .10 .25
84 Zigmund Palffy .15 .40
85 Jozef Stumpel .10 .25
86 Adam Deadmarsh .12 .30
87 Mathieu Schneider .10 .25
88 Bryan Smolinski .10 .25
89 Eric Belanger .10 .25
90 Lubomir Visnovsky .10 .25
91 Marian Gaborik .25 .60
92 Lubomir Sekeras .10 .25
93 Wes Walz .10 .25
94 Manny Fernandez .12 .30
95 Roman Simicek .10 .25
96 Stacy Roest .10 .25
97 Saku Koivu .15 .40
98 Oleg Petrov .10 .25
99 Patrice Brisebois .10 .25
100 Jose Theodore .15 .40
101 Richard Zednik .12 .30
102 Martin Rucinsky .10 .25
103 Andrei Markov .15 .40
104 David Legwand .12 .30
105 Cliff Ronning .10 .25
106 Mike Dunham .12 .30
107 Kimmo Timonen .10 .25
108 Scott Walker .10 .25
109 Patric Kjellberg .10 .25
110 Martin Brodeur .30 .75
111 Scott Stevens .15 .40
112 Patrik Elias .15 .40
113 Scott Niedermayer .15 .40
114 Petr Sykora .10 .25
115 Jason Arnott .12 .30
116 Scott Gomez .12 .30
117 Rick DiPietro .12 .30
118 Mark Parrish .10 .25
119 Roman Hamrlik .10 .25
120 Mariusz Czerkawski .10 .25
121 Kenny Jonsson .10 .25
122 Dave Scatchard .10 .25
123 Mark Messier .25 .60
124 Brian Leetch .15 .40
125 Jan Hlavac .10 .25
126 Theo Fleury .20 .50
127 Eric Lindros .25 .60
128 Petr Nedved .12 .30
129 Daniel Alfredsson .15 .40
130 Radek Bonk .10 .25
131 Marian Hossa .12 .30
132 Shawn McEachern .10 .25
133 Patrick Lalime .12 .30
134 Wade Redden .10 .25
135 Magnus Arvedson .10 .25
136 Martin Havlat .12 .30
137 Simon Gagne .15 .40
138 Roman Cechmanek .12 .30
139 Justin Williams .10 .25
140 John LeClair .15 .40
141 Mark Recchi .20 .50
142 Eric Desjardins .12 .30
143 Jeremy Roenick .15 .40
144 Paul Mara .10 .25
145 Shane Doan .12 .30
146 Landon Wilson .10 .25
147 Sean Burke .10 .25
148 Michal Handzus .10 .25
149 Ladislav Nagy .10 .25
150 Mario Lemieux .50 1.25
151 Jan Hrdina .10 .25
152 Johan Hedberg .12 .30
153 Robert Lang .10 .25
154 Alexei Kovalev .12 .30
155 Martin Straka .10 .25
156 Owen Nolan .15 .40
157 Vincent Damphousse .12 .30
158 Brad Stuart .10 .25
159 Teemu Selanne .30 .75
160 Evgeni Nabokov .12 .30
161 Mike Ricci .12 .30
162 Chris Pronger .12 .30
163 Keith Tkachuk .15 .40
164 Scott Young .10 .25
165 Pavol Demitra .20 .50
166 Doug Weight .15 .40
167 Al MacInnis .15 .40
168 Cory Stillman .10 .25
169 Vincent Lecavalier .12 .30
170 Brad Richards .15 .40
171 Nikolai Khabibulin .15 .40
172 Fredrik Modin .10 .25
173 Mats Sundin .15 .40
174 Gary Roberts .10 .25
175 Curtis Joseph .15 .40
176 Nikolai Antropov .10 .25
177 Darcy Tucker .10 .25
178 Jonas Hoglund .10 .25
179 Markus Naslund .15 .40
180 Brendan Morrison .12 .30
181 Todd Bertuzzi .15 .40
182 Daniel Sedin .15 .40
183 Ed Jovanovski .12 .30
184 Peter Bondra .15 .40
185 Sergei Gonchar .10 .25
186 Jeff Halpern .10 .25
187 Olaf Kolzig .15 .40
188 Jaromir Jagr .40 1.00
189 Gregg Naumenko .30 .75
190 Dan Snyder RC .40 1.00
191 Zdenek Kutlak RC .30 .75
192 Niclas Wallin .30 .75
193 Michel Larocque RC .30 .75
194 Casey Hankinson RC .30 .75
195 Chris Nielsen .30 .75
196 Martin Spanhel RC .30 .75
197 Mathieu Darche RC .50 1.25
198 Matt Davidson RC .30 .75
199 Brad Larsen .30 .75
200 Steve Gainey .30 .75
201 Jason Chimera RC .30 .75
202 Andrej Podkonicky RC .30 .75
203 Mike Matteucci RC .30 .75
204 Pascal Dupuis RC .50 1.25
205 Francis Belanger RC .40 1.00
206 Mike Jefferson RC .30 .75
207 Stanislav Gron RC .30 .75
208 Peter Smrek RC .30 .75
209 Joel Kwiatkowski RC .30 .75
210 Kirby Law RC .30 .75
211 Tomas Divisek RC .40 1.00
212 David Cullen RC .30 .75
213 Billy Tibbets RC .30 .75
214 Dan Lacouture .30 .75
215 Jaroslav Obsut RC .30 .75
216 Dale Clarke RC .30 .75
217 Thomas Ziegler RC .40 1.00
218 Mike Brown .40 1.00
219 Steve Yzerman CL .30 .75
220 Curtis Joseph CL .10 .25
221 Ilya Kovalchuk RC 5.00 12.00
222 Erik Cole RC 2.00 5.00
223 Pavel Datsyuk RC 5.00 12.00
224 Kristian Huselius RC 1.50 4.00
225 Marcel Hossa RC 1.50 4.00
226 Martin Erat RC 1.50 4.00
227 Christian Berglund RC 1.25 3.00
228 Raffi Torres RC 1.50 4.00
229 Dan Blackburn RC 1.25 3.00
230 Jiri Dopita RC 1.00 2.50
231 Krys Kolanos RC 1.00 2.50
232 Brian Sutherby RC 1.00 2.50
233 Olivier Michaud RC 1.50 4.00

2001-02 Upper Deck MVP Goalie Sticks

Randomly inserted in 1:288 hobby and 1:240 retail packs, this 15-card set featured pieces of game-used sticks from the goalie pictured.

GAI Arturs Irbe 12.50 30.00
GBD Byron Dafoe 12.50 30.00
GCJ Curtis Joseph 20.00 50.00
GCO Chris Osgood 12.50 30.00
GDH Dominik Hasek 25.00 60.00
GEB Ed Belfour 20.00 50.00
GJT Jose Theodore 25.00 60.00
GMB Martin Brodeur 30.00 80.00
GMR Mike Richter 15.00 40.00
GNK Nikolai Khabibulin 20.00 50.00
GOK Olaf Kolzig 12.50 30.00
GPR Patrick Roy 40.00 100.00
GRC Roman Cechmanek 12.50 30.00
GRD Rick DiPietro 12.50 30.00
GTS Tommy Salo 12.50 30.00

2001-02 Upper Deck MVP Masked Men

This 14-card set was randomly inserted at 1:12 packs.

COMPLETE SET (14) 10.00 20.00
MM1 Martin Brodeur 1.50 4.00
MM2 Ed Belfour .60 1.50
MM3 Patrick Roy 3.00 8.00
MM4 Jocelyn Thibault .50 1.25
MM5 Tommy Salo .50 1.25
MM6 Olaf Kolzig .50 1.25
MM7 Johan Hedberg .50 1.25
MM8 Evgeni Nabokov .50 1.25
MM9 Patrick Lalime .50 1.25
MM10 Sean Burke .50 1.25
MM11 Curtis Joseph .60 1.50
MM12 Arturs Irbe .50 1.25
MM13 Roman Cechmanek .50 1.25
MM14 Felix Potvin .60 1.50

2001-02 Upper Deck MVP Morning Skate Jersey Autographs

Serial-numbered to 100 copies each, this 10-card set partially paralleled the base morning skate jersey set but included authentic player autographs.

SJBB Brian Boucher 12.00 30.00
SJJA Jarome Iginla 25.00 60.00
SJJI Jarome Iginla 25.00 60.00
SJJL John LeClair 15.00 40.00
SJKP Keith Primeau 15.00 40.00
SJMH Milan Hejduk 10.00 25.00
SJMM Mike Modano 20.00 50.00
SJMR Mark Recchi 15.00 40.00
SJRB Rod Brind'Amour 15.00 40.00
SJSG Simon Gagne 15.00 40.00

2001-02 Upper Deck MVP Morning Skate Jerseys

Randomly inserted in 1:96 hobby and 1:120 retail packs, this 15-card set featured swatches of player worn practice jerseys.

JBB Brian Boucher 4.00 10.00
JEL Eric Lindros 4.00 10.00
JJA Jarome Iginla 6.00 15.00
JJI Jarome Iginla 6.00 15.00
JJJ Jaromir Jagr 8.00 20.00
JJL John LeClair 4.00 10.00
JJO John LeClair 4.00 10.00
JJS Joe Sakic 8.00 20.00
JKP Keith Primeau 4.00 10.00
JMH Milan Hejduk 4.00 10.00
JMM Mike Modano 6.00 15.00
JMR Mark Recchi 4.00 10.00
JPF Peter Forsberg 8.00 20.00
JRB Rod Brind'Amour 4.00 10.00
JSG Simon Gagne 4.00 10.00

2001-02 Upper Deck MVP Souvenirs

Randomly inserted into hobby packs only, this 30-card set featured game-used swatches of equipment. Cards with a "C" prefix carried two pieces of memorabilia and cards with a "S" prefix carried one. Dual souvenir cards were inserted at 1:288 and single souvenir cards were inserted at 1:96. A gold parallel serial-numbered to 50 copies each was also created.
*GOLD/50: 1X TO 2.5X BASIC INSERT

CAM Al MacInnis 10.00 25.00
CDA Daniel Alfredsson 10.00 25.00
CJR Jeremy Roenick 12.50 30.00
CJS Joe Sakic 15.00 40.00
CMM Mike Modano 15.00 40.00
CPB Pavel Bure 10.00 25.00
CSS Sergei Samsonov 10.00 25.00
CVL Vincent Lecavalier 10.00 25.00
CWG Wayne Gretzky 50.00 100.00
CZP Zigmund Palffy 10.00 25.00
SAM Alexander Mogilny 6.00 15.00
SBH Brett Hull 12.50 30.00
SBS Brendan Shanahan 8.00 20.00
SJA Jason Allison 6.00 15.00
SJJ Jaromir Jagr 12.50 30.00
SJL John LeClair 8.00 20.00
SKT Keith Tkachuk 8.00 20.00
SLR Luc Robitaille 6.00 15.00
SML Mario Lemieux 30.00 60.00
SMM Mark Messier 8.00 20.00
SMR Mark Recchi 6.00 15.00
SMS Mats Sundin 8.00 20.00
SPB Peter Bondra 8.00 20.00
SPF Peter Forsberg 6.00 15.00
SPS Patrik Stefan 6.00 15.00
SRB Ray Bourque 12.50 30.00
SSH Scott Hartnell 6.00 15.00
SSY Steve Yzerman 20.00 40.00
STA Tony Amonte 6.00 15.00
STS Teemu Selanne 8.00 20.00

2001-02 Upper Deck MVP Talent

This 14-card set was randomly inserted at 1:12 packs.

COMPLETE SET (14) 12.00 30.00
MT1 Peter Forsberg 1.25 3.00
MT2 Joe Sakic 1.00 2.50
MT3 Mike Modano .75 2.00
MT4 Mario Lemieux 3.00 8.00
MT5 Sergei Fedorov 1.00 2.50
MT6 Steve Yzerman 2.50 6.00
MT7 Pavel Bure .60 1.50
MT8 Paul Kariya .40 1.00
MT9 Teemu Selanne .40 1.00
MT10 Patrik Elias .30 .75
MT11 Zigmund Palffy .30 .75
MT12 John LeClair .60 1.50
MT13 Chris Pronger .30 .75
MT14 Martin Brodeur 1.25 3.00

2001-02 Upper Deck MVP Valuable Commodities

This 7-card set was randomly inserted at 1:24 packs.

COMPLETE SET (7) 10.00 25.00
VC1 Steve Yzerman 3.00 8.00
VC2 Pavel Bure .75 2.00
VC3 Joe Sakic 1.25 3.00
VC4 Martin Brodeur 1.50 4.00
VC5 Mario Lemieux 4.00 10.00
VC6 Peter Forsberg 1.50 4.00
VC7 Mike Modano 1.00 2.50

2001-02 Upper Deck MVP Watch

This 7-card set was randomly inserted at 1:24 packs.

COMPLETE SET (7) 10.00 20.00
MW1 Mario Lemieux 4.00 10.00
MW2 Joe Sakic 1.25 3.00
MW3 Jaromir Jagr 1.00 2.50
MW4 Brett Hull .75 2.00
MW5 Sergei Fedorov 1.25 3.00
MW6 Mark Messier .75 2.00
MW7 Chris Pronger .40 1.00

2002-03 Upper Deck MVP

Released in September, this 220-card set carried an SRP of $1.99 for an 8-card pack, and had 24 packs per box.

COMPLETE SET (220) 15.00 40.00
1 Mike LeClerc .10 .25
2 Jean-Sebastien Giguere .15 .40
3 Matt Cullen .10 .25
4 Andy McDonald .15 .40
5 Jason York .10 .25
6 Paul Kariya .20 .50
7 Frantisek Kaberle .10 .25
8 Dany Heatley .15 .40
9 Pasi Nurminen .10 .25
10 Ilya Kovalchuk .20 .50
11 Patrik Stefan .12 .30
12 Pascal Rheaume .10 .25
13 Sergei Samsonov .12 .30
14 Joe Thornton .20 .50
15 Brian Rolston .12 .30
16 Martin Lapointe .12 .30
17 Nick Boynton .10 .25
18 Jozef Stumpel .10 .25
19 Stu Barnes .10 .25
20 J-P Dumont .10 .25
21 Miroslav Satan .15 .40
22 Tim Connolly .10 .25
23 Maxim Afinogenov .10 .25
24 Martin Biron .12 .30
25 Craig Conroy .10 .25
26 Roman Turek .15 .40
27 Derek Morris .10 .25
28 Marc Savard .10 .25
29 Jarome Iginla .15 .40
30 Igor Kravchuk .10 .25
31 Sami Kapanen .10 .25
32 Bates Battaglia .10 .25
33 Ron Francis .20 .50
34 Erik Cole .12 .30
35 Jeff O'Neill .10 .25
36 Arturs Irbe .12 .30
37 Rod Brind'Amour .15 .40
38 Alexei Zhamnov .12 .30
39 Michael Nylander .10 .25
40 Steve Sullivan .10 .25
41 Jocelyn Thibault .12 .30
42 Kyle Calder .10 .25
43 Eric Daze .10 .25
44 Patrick Roy .40 1.00
45 Milan Hejduk .12 .30
46 Peter Forsberg .20 .50
47 Rob Blake .15 .40
48 Chris Drury .15 .40
49 Joe Sakic .25 .60
50 Steven Reinprecht .10 .25
51 Brad Moran .10 .25
52 Jaroslav Spacek .10 .25
53 Marc Denis .12 .30
54 Ray Whitney .12 .30
55 Rostislav Klesla .10 .25
56 Espen Knutsen .10 .25
57 Marty Turco .15 .40
58 Jere Lehtinen .15 .40
59 Mike Modano .25 .60
60 Derian Hatcher .12 .30
61 Brenden Morrow .12 .30
62 Jason Arnott .12 .30
63 Dominik Hasek .25 .60
64 Brendan Shanahan .20 .50
65 Curtis Joseph .15 .40
66 Brett Hull .20 .50
67 Steve Yzerman .30 .75
68 Nicklas Lidstrom .15 .40
69 Pavel Datsyuk .20 .50
70 Ryan Smyth .12 .30
71 Anson Carter .12 .30
72 Mike Comrie .15 .40
73 Tommy Salo .12 .30
74 Eric Brewer .10 .25
75 Todd Marchant .10 .25
76 Roberto Luongo .25 .60
77 Kristian Huselius .10 .25
78 Marcus Nilsson .10 .25
79 Viktor Kozlov .10 .25
80 Sandis Ozolinsh .12 .30
81 Valeri Bure .12 .30
82 Jason Allison .12 .30
83 Zigmund Palffy .15 .40
84 Adam Deadmarsh .12 .30
85 Felix Potvin .25 .60
86 Mathieu Schneider .10 .25
87 Bryan Smolinski .12 .30
88 Jim Dowd .10 .25
89 Marian Gaborik .25 .60
90 Manny Fernandez .12 .30
91 Andrew Brunette .10 .25
92 Wes Walz .10 .25
93 Antti Laaksonen .10 .25
94 Yanic Perreault .10 .25
95 Richard Zednik .10 .25
96 Jose Theodore .15 .40
97 Oleg Petrov .10 .25
98 Donald Audette .10 .25
99 Saku Koivu .15 .40
100 Kimmo Timonen .10 .25
101 Stu Grimson .10 .25
102 Denis Arkhipov .10 .25
103 Scott Hartnell .15 .40
104 Mike Dunham .12 .30
105 Andy Delmore .10 .25
106 Brian Rafalski .10 .25
107 John Madden .10 .25
108 Martin Brodeur .30 .75
109 Scott Stevens .15 .40
110 Patrik Elias .15 .40
111 Scott Niedermayer .15 .40
112 Joe Nieuwendyk .15 .40
113 Mark Parrish .10 .25
114 Michael Peca .12 .30
115 Alexei Yashin .12 .30
116 Adrian Aucoin .10 .25
117 Chris Osgood .15 .40
118 Stephen Webb .10 .25
119 Eric Lindros .25 .60
120 Brian Leetch .15 .40
121 Tom Poti .10 .25
122 Pavel Bure .20 .50
123 Petr Nedved .10 .25
124 Dan Blackburn .12 .30
125 Daniel Alfredsson .15 .40
126 Patrick Lalime .12 .30
127 Marian Hossa .12 .30
128 Martin Havlat .12 .30
129 Zdeno Chara .15 .40
130 Radek Bonk .12 .30
131 Wade Redden .10 .25
132 Keith Primeau .15 .40
133 John LeClair .15 .40
134 Mark Recchi .20 .50
135 Eric Desjardins .10 .25
136 Jeremy Roenick .15 .40
137 Justin Williams .12 .30
138 Simon Gagne .15 .40
139 Tony Amonte .12 .30
140 Daniel Briere .12 .30
141 Sean Burke .10 .25
142 Ladislav Nagy .10 .25
143 Shane Doan .12 .30
144 Teppo Numminen .12 .30
145 Alexei Kovalev .15 .40
146 Johan Hedberg .15 .40
147 Jan Hrdina .10 .25
148 Mario Lemieux .50 1.25
149 Martin Straka .12 .30
150 Hans Jonsson .10 .25
151 Vincent Damphousse .12 .30
152 Owen Nolan .15 .40
153 Adam Graves .12 .30
154 Evgeni Nabokov .12 .30
155 Mike Ricci .12 .30
156 Patrick Marleau .15 .40
157 Teemu Selanne .30 .75
158 Brent Johnson .12 .30
159 Doug Weight .15 .40
160 Keith Tkachuk .15 .40
161 Al MacInnis .15 .40
162 Chris Pronger .12 .30
163 Pavol Demitra .20 .50
164 Tyson Nash .10 .25
165 Nikolai Khabibulin .15 .40
166 Vincent Lecavalier .12 .30
167 Martin St. Louis .15 .40
168 Fredrik Modin .10 .25
169 Brad Richards .15 .40
170 Shane Willis .10 .25
171 Alyn McCauley .10 .25
172 Gary Roberts .10 .25
173 Darcy Tucker .10 .25
174 Ed Belfour .15 .40
175 Mats Sundin .15 .40
176 Alexander Mogilny .12 .30
177 Todd Bertuzzi .15 .40
178 Brendan Morrison .12 .30
179 Markus Naslund .12 .30
180 Dan Cloutier .12 .30
181 Daniel Sedin .15 .40
182 Henrik Sedin .15 .40
183 Sergei Gonchar .12 .30
184 Jaromir Jagr .40 1.00
185 Peter Bondra .15 .40
186 Olaf Kolzig .15 .40
187 Robert Lang .10 .25
188 Steve Konowalchuk .10 .25
189 Patrick Roy .40 1.00
190 Steve Yzerman .30 .75
191 Mark Hartigan .10 .25
192 Mike Weaver .10 .25
193 Frederic Cassivi .10 .25
194 Andy Hilbert .10 .25
195 Chris Kelleher .10 .25
196 Henrik Tallinder .10 .25
197 Micki Dupont RC .10 .25
198 Tyler Arnason .15 .40
199 Riku Hahl .10 .25
200 Andrej Nedorost .10 .25
201 Sean Avery .12 .30
202 Stephen Weiss .15 .40
203 Lukas Krajicek .12 .30
204 Kyle Rossiter .10 .25
205 Eric Beaudoin .10 .25
206 Tony Virta .10 .25
207 Marcel Hossa .10 .25
208 Jan Lasak .12 .30
209 Trent Hunter .10 .25
210 Ray Schultz RC .10 .25
211 Martin Prusek .10 .25
212 Chris Bala .10 .25
213 Neil Little .10 .25
214 Guillaume Lefebvre .10 .25
215 Hannes Hyvonen .10 .25
216 Gaetan Royer .10 .25
217 Martin Cibak .10 .25
218 Sebastien Centomo .10 .25
219 Karel Pilar .10 .25
220 Sebastien Charpentier .10 .25

2002-03 Upper Deck MVP Classics

This 220-card set paralleled the base set with silver borders and was inserted at odds of 1:2.
*CLASSICS: .75X TO 1.5X BASE HI

2002-03 Upper Deck MVP Gold

This 220-card hobby only set directly paralleled the base set but was serial-numbered to 100 copies each.
*GOLD: 6X TO 15X BASIC CARDS

2002-03 Upper Deck MVP Golden Classics

This 220-card hobby only set paralleled the base set with gold borders and was serial-numbered to 50 copies each.
*GLDN CLASSICS: 12.5X TO 30X BASE HI

2002-03 Upper Deck MVP Highlight Nights

COMPLETE SET (7) 8.00 15.00
STATED ODDS 1:18
HN1 Ilya Kovalchuk .75 2.00
HN2 Joe Thornton 1.00 2.50
HN3 Jarome Iginla .50 1.25
HN4 Brendan Shanahan .60 1.50
HN5 Eric Lindros .40 1.00
HN6 Mario Lemieux 3.00 8.00
HN7 Markus Naslund .40 1.00

2002-03 Upper Deck MVP Masked Men

COMPLETE SET (7) 10.00 20.00
STATED ODDS 1:18
MM1 Patrick Roy 2.50 6.00
MM2 Dominik Hasek 1.50 4.00
MM3 Jose Theodore .75 2.00
MM4 Martin Brodeur 2.00 5.00
MM5 Mike Richter .50 1.25
MM6 Sean Burke .50 1.25
MM7 Olaf Kolzig .50 1.25

2002-03 Upper Deck MVP Overdrive

COMPLETE SET (14) 6.00 12.00
STATED ODDS 1:9
SO1 Paul Kariya .50 1.25
SO2 Ilya Kovalchuk .60 1.50
SO3 Jarome Iginla .60 1.50
SO4 Sami Kapanen .40 1.00
SO5 Chris Drury .40 1.00
SO6 Peter Forsberg 1.00 2.50
SO7 Mike Modano .60 1.50
SO8 Sergei Fedorov .60 1.50
SO9 Sandis Ozolinsh .40 1.00
SO10 Marian Hossa .50 1.25
SO11 Simon Gagne .50 1.25
SO12 Alexei Kovalev .40 1.00
SO13 Markus Naslund .50 1.25
SO14 Peter Bondra .50 1.25

2002-03 Upper Deck MVP Prosign

Inserted at 1:144, this 15-card set featured authentic player autographs. The Henrik Sedin card was originally issued as an exchange card. Known print runs were provided by UD.

BO Bobby Orr 125.00 250.00
CJ Curtis Joseph 15.00 40.00
DH Dany Heatley 10.00 25.00
DS Daniel Sedin 8.00 20.00
GH Gordie Howe 75.00 150.00
HS Henrik Sedin/33 10.00 25.00
KH Kristian Huselius 6.00 15.00
MF Manny Fernandez 6.00 15.00
MO Maxime Ouellet 6.00 15.00
PB Pavel Bure/145 10.00 25.00
PR Patrick Roy/48 100.00 200.00
RB Ray Bourque 30.00 80.00
SE Teemu Selanne 12.00 30.00
TS Tommy Salo 10.00 25.00
WG Wayne Gretzky 100.00 200.00

2002-03 Upper Deck MVP Skate Around Jerseys

This 57-card set featured swatches of practice-worn jerseys from the players featured alongside color action photos. Single jersey cards were inserted at 1:72, dual jersey cards were inserted at 1:288 and triple jersey cards were serial-numbered out of 100. Dual jersey cards were hobby exclusives.

SAAD Adam Deadmarsh 4.00 10.00
SACD Chris Drury 4.00 10.00
SAEK Espen Knutsen 4.00 10.00
SAEL Eric Lindros 5.00 12.00
SAFP Felix Potvin 5.00 12.00
SAJI Jarome Iginla 6.00 15.00
SAJL John LeClair 4.00 10.00
SAJS Joe Sakic 10.00 25.00
SAJT Joe Thornton 8.00 20.00
SAKP Keith Primeau 4.00 10.00
SAMM Mike Modano 8.00 20.00
SAOK Olaf Kolzig 5.00 12.00
SAPF Peter Forsberg 10.00 25.00
SAPK Paul Kariya 5.00 12.00
SAPR Patrick Roy 12.50 30.00
SDBK R.Blake/R.Klesla 8.00 20.00
SDBN R.Brind'Amour/J.Nieuwendyk 8.00 20.00
SDBP E.Belfour/F.Potvin 10.00 25.00
SDCB R.Cechmanek/B.Boucher 8.00 20.00
SDDB J.Dumont/M.Biron 8.00 20.00
SDDG C.Drury/S.Gagne 10.00 25.00
SDDH C.Drury/M.Hejduk 10.00 25.00
SDDL A.Deadmarsh/J.LeClair 8.00 20.00
SDFL P.Forsberg/E.Lindros 15.00 40.00
SDHP M.Hejduk/Z.Palffy 10.00 25.00
SDHR D.Hinote/S.Reinprecht 8.00 20.00
SDJM J.Jagr/M.Messier 12.00 30.00
SDKC O.Kolzig/R.Cechmanek 10.00 25.00
SDKR A.Kovalev/M.Recchi 8.00 20.00
SDLC J.LeClair/R.Cechmanek 8.00 20.00
SDLF E.Lindros/T.Fleury 10.00 25.00
SDLP J.LeClair/K.Primeau 8.00 20.00
SDMS M.Modano/T.Selanne 10.00 25.00
SDMT M.Modano/M.Turco 10.00 25.00
SDNL J.Nieuwendyk/E.Lindros 8.00 20.00
SDPO F.Potvin/C.Osgood 15.00 40.00
SDPP Z.Palffy/F.Potvin 12.00 30.00
SDRA P.Roy/D.Aebischer 40.00 100.00
SDRG M.Recchi/S.Gagne 8.00 20.00
SDSD J.Sakic/C.Drury 20.00 50.00
SDTBE M.Turco/E.Belfour 10.00 25.00
SDTBL A.Tanguay/R.Blake 8.00 20.00
SDTD R.Tugnutt/M.Denis 8.00 20.00
SDWF J.Williams/R.Fedotenko 8.00 20.00
SDWG J.Williams/S.Gagne 8.00 20.00
STDAP Deadmarsh/Allison/Palffy 8.00 20.00
STDSB Dumont/Satan/Biron 10.00 25.00
STKFS Kovalev/Fleury/Satan 12.50 30.00
STLNT Lindros/Nieuwdyk/Thrnton 15.00 40.00
STLPR LeClair/Primeau/Recchi 12.50 30.00
STMMT Mess./Mdno/Thornton 25.00 60.00
STSFR Sakic/Forsberg/Roy 25.00 60.00
STSHP Selanne/Hejduk/Palffy 12.50 30.00
STSMJ Selanne/Modano/Jagr 20.00 50.00
STTDG Thornton/Drury/Gagne 12.50 30.00
STTDH Tanguay/Drury/Hejduk 12.50 30.00
STWKT Whitney/Klesla/Tugnutt 10.00 25.00

2002-03 Upper Deck MVP Souvenirs Jerseys

Inserted at 1:48, this 27-card set featured swatches of practice-worn jerseys alongside color action photos of the feaured player.

SAK Alexei Kovalev 3.00 8.00
SAT Alex Tanguay 4.00 10.00
SBB Brian Boucher 3.00 8.00
SBR Rod Brind'Amour 3.00 8.00
SCO Chris Osgood 6.00 15.00
SDH Dan Hinote 3.00 8.00
SDU Mike Dunham 3.00 8.00
SEB Ed Belfour 4.00 10.00
SJJ Jaromir Jagr 8.00 20.00
SJN Joe Nieuwendyk 3.00 8.00
SJW Justin Williams 3.00 8.00
SMB Martin Biron 3.00 8.00
SMD Marc Denis 3.00 8.00
SMM Mark Messier 8.00 20.00
SMO Mike Modano 8.00 20.00
SMR Mark Recchi 3.00 8.00
SMS Miroslav Satan 3.00 8.00
SMT Marty Turco 4.00 10.00
SRB Rob Blake 3.00 8.00
SRC Roman Cechmanek 3.00 8.00
SRK Rostislav Klesla 3.00 8.00
SRT Ron Tugnutt 3.00 8.00
SSG Simon Gagne 6.00 15.00
STF0 Theo Fleury 3.00 8.00
STS Teemu Selanne 6.00 15.00
SVN Ville Nieminen 3.00 8.00
SZP Zigmund Palffy 3.00 8.00

2002-03 Upper Deck MVP Vital Forces

COMPLETE SET (14) 15.00 30.00
STATED ODDS 1:9
VF1 Paul Kariya .40 1.00
VF2 Ilya Kovalchuk .60 1.50
VF3 Joe Thornton .60 1.50
VF4 Jarome Iginla .60 1.50
VF5 Patrick Roy 2.00 5.00
VF6 Joe Sakic .75 2.00
VF7 Mike Modano .60 1.50
VF8 Dominik Hasek .75 2.00
VF9 Steve Yzerman 2.00 5.00
VF10 Eric Lindros .40 1.00
VF11 Jeremy Roenick .50 1.25
VF12 Mario Lemieux 2.50 6.00
VF13 Teemu Selanne .40 1.00
VF14 Jaromir Jagr .60 1.50

2003-04 Upper Deck MVP

This 470-card set consisted of 440 base cards and 30 rookie cards that were avaialble only via redemption cards found in packs. Three different redemption cards represented groups of 10 rookies. Groups "A" and "B" were inserted at 1:35 while Group "C" was inserted at 1:72 hobby packs.

COMPLETE SET (470) 30.00 60.00
COMP.SET w/o SP's (440) 20.00 40.00
1 Jason Krog .12 .30
2 Petr Sykora .15 .40
3 Steve Rucchin .12 .30
4 Cam Severson .12 .30
5 Sandis Ozolinsh .12 .30
6 Steve Thomas .12 .30
7 Stanislav Chistov .12 .30
8 Sergei Fedorov .30 .75
9 Rob Niedermayer .15 .40
10 Keith Carney .12 .30
11 Alexei Smirnov .12 .30
12 Kurt Sauer .12 .30
13 Martin Gerber .12 .30
14 Jean-Sebastien Giguere .20 .50
15 Dany Heatley .20 .50
16 Slava Kozlov .12 .30
17 Ilya Kovalchuk .20 .50
18 Marc Savard .15 .40
19 Patrik Stefan .12 .30
20 Yannick Tremblay .12 .30
21 Shawn McEachern .12 .30
22 Frantisek Kaberle .12 .30
23 Andy Sutton .12 .30
24 Lubos Bartecko .12 .30
25 Jeff Odgers .12 .30
26 Pasi Nurminen .15 .40
27 Simon Gamache .12 .30
28 Byron Dafoe .15 .40
29 Garnet Exelby .12 .30
30 Joe DiPenta RC .15 .40
31 Joe Thornton .25 .60
32 Glen Murray .15 .40
33 Mike Knuble .12 .30
34 Brian Rolston .15 .40
35 Ivan Huml .12 .30
36 Bryan Berard .15 .40
37 P-J Axelsson .12 .30
38 Nick Boynton .12 .30
39 Jonathan Girard .12 .30
40 Dan McGillis .12 .30
41 Michal Grosek .12 .30
42 Hal Gill .12 .30
43 Sergei Samsonov .15 .40
44 P.J. Stock .12 .30
45 Martin Lapointe .15 .40
46 Jeff Jillson .12 .30
47 Andrew Raycroft .15 .40
48 Martin Samuelsson .15 .40
49 Krzysztof Oliwa .12 .30
50 Steve Shields .15 .40
51 Miroslav Satan .15 .40
52 Daniel Briere .20 .50
53 Ales Kotalik .12 .30
54 J-P Dumont .12 .30
55 Curtis Brown .12 .30
56 Taylor Pyatt .12 .30
57 Jochen Hecht .12 .30
58 Chris Drury .15 .40
59 Alexei Zhitnik .15 .40
60 Maxim Afinogenov .12 .30
61 Martin Biron .15 .40
62 Mika Noronen .12 .30
63 Ryan Miller .20 .50
64 Milan Bartovic RC .15 .40
65 Jarome Iginla .20 .50
66 Craig Conroy .12 .30
67 Steve Reinprecht .12 .30
68 Martin Gelinas .12 .30
69 Oleg Saprykin .12 .30
70 Dave Lowry .12 .30
71 Dean McAmmond .12 .30
72 Jordan Leopold .12 .30
73 Chuck Kobasew .12 .30
74 Roman Turek .15 .40
75 Jamie McLennan .12 .30
76 Rick Mrozik RC .12 .30
77 Jeff O'Neill .12 .30
78 Ron Francis .25 .60
79 Rod Brind'Amour .20 .50
80 Radim Vrbata .15 .40
81 Sean Hill .12 .30
82 Erik Cole .15 .40

83 Jan Hlavac .12 .30
84 Ryan Bayda .12 .30
85 Jaroslav Svoboda .12 .30
86 Pavel Brendl .12 .30
87 Aaron Ward .12 .30
88 Patrick DesRochers .12 .30
89 Kevin Weekes .15 .40
90 Steve Sullivan .12 .30
91 Alexei Zhamnov .15 .40
92 Eric Daze .15 .40
93 Kyle Calder .12 .30
94 Tyler Arnason .12 .30
95 Mark Bell .12 .30
96 Chris Simon .12 .30
97 Alexander Karpovtsev .12 .30
98 Igor Radulov .12 .30
99 Michael Leighton .12 .30
100 Jocelyn Thibault .15 .40
101 Peter Forsberg .25 .60
102 Milan Hejduk .15 .40
103 Alex Tanguay .15 .40
104 Joe Sakic .30 .75
105 Paul Kariya .25 .60
106 Derek Morris .12 .30
107 Rob Blake .20 .50
108 Adam Foote .12 .30
109 Eric Messier .12 .30
110 Teemu Selanne .40 1.00
111 Dan Hinote .12 .30
112 David Aebischer .15 .40
113 Patrick Roy .50 1.25
114 Ray Whitney .15 .40
115 Andrew Cassels .12 .30
116 Geoff Sanderson .12 .30
117 David Vyborny .12 .30
118 Jaroslav Spacek .12 .30
119 Mike Sillinger .12 .30
120 Rick Nash .20 .50
121 Tyler Wright .12 .30
122 Todd Marchant .12 .30
123 Rostislav Klesla .12 .30
124 Jody Shelley .12 .30
125 Marc Denis .15 .40
126 Kent McDonell RC .15 .40
127 Mike Modano .30 .75
128 Sergei Zubov .15 .40
129 Bill Guerin .20 .50
130 Jere Lehtinen .15 .40
131 Jason Arnott .15 .40
132 Brenden Morrow .15 .40
133 Scott Young .12 .30
134 Darryl Sydor .12 .30
135 Niko Kapanen .12 .30
136 Don Sweeney .12 .30
137 Steve Ott .15 .40
138 Jason Bacashihua .12 .30
139 Marty Turco .20 .50
140 Stephane Robidas .15 .40
141 Ron Tugnutt .15 .40
142 Sergei Fedorov .30 .75
143 Brett Hull .25 .60
144 Brendan Shanahan .25 .60
145 Nicklas Lidstrom .20 .50
146 Pavel Datsyuk .25 .60
147 Mathieu Schneider .12 .30
148 Henrik Zetterberg .25 .60
149 Igor Larionov .20 .50
150 Tomas Holmstrom .15 .40
151 Jason Woolley .12 .30
152 Darren McCarty .12 .30
153 Derian Hatcher .12 .30
154 Chris Chelios .20 .50
155 Dominik Hasek .30 .75
156 Steve Yzerman .50 1.25
157 Jiri Fischer .12 .30
158 Manny Legace .12 .30
159 Curtis Joseph .20 .50
160 Ryan Smyth .15 .40
161 Marty Reasoner .12 .30
162 Mike York .12 .30
163 Mike Comrie .15 .40
164 Radek Dvorak .15 .40
165 Ales Hemsky .20 .50
166 Eric Brewer .12 .30
167 Brad Isbister .12 .30
168 Fernando Pisani .12 .30
169 Georges Laraque .15 .40
170 Alexei Semenov .12 .30
171 Raffi Torres .12 .30
172 Jani Rita .12 .30
173 Jarret Stoll .12 .30
174 Cory Cross .12 .30
175 Jason Chimera .12 .30
176 Tommy Salo .15 .40
177 Olli Jokinen .20 .50
178 Viktor Kozlov .12 .30
179 Kristian Huselius .12 .30
180 Marcus Nilson .12 .30
181 Ivan Novoseltsev .12 .30
182 Stephen Weiss .12 .30
183 Jay Bouwmeester .20 .50
184 Valeri Bure .12 .30
185 Denis Shvidki .12 .30
186 Jaroslav Bednar .12 .30
187 Peter Worrell .12 .30
188 Roberto Luongo .30 .75
189 Jani Hurme .12 .30
190 Zigmund Palffy .20 .50
191 Jaroslav Modry .12 .30
192 Eric Belanger .12 .30
193 Alexander Frolov .15 .40
194 Jason Allison .15 .40
195 Lubomir Visnovsky .12 .30
196 Ian Laperriere .12 .30
197 Adam Deadmarsh .15 .40
198 Maxim Kuznetsov .12 .30
199 Joe Corvo .12 .30
200 Mike Cammalleri .20 .50
201 Aaron Miller .12 .30
202 Mattias Norstrom .12 .30
203 Jared Aulin .12 .30
204 Jozef Stumpel .12 .30
205 Roman Cechmanek .15 .40
206 Cristobal Huet .15 .40
207 Marian Gaborik .30 .75
208 Pascal Dupuis .12 .30
209 Cliff Ronning .12 .30
210 Andrew Brunette .12 .30
211 Sergei Zholtok .12 .30
212 Wes Walz .12 .30
213 Filip Kuba .12 .30
214 P-M Bouchard .20 .50
215 Willie Mitchell .12 .30
216 Matt Johnson .12 .30
217 Darby Hendrickson .12 .30
218 Andrei Zyuzin .12 .30
219 Manny Fernandez .15 .40
220 Dwayne Roloson .15 .40
221 Saku Koivu .20 .50
222 Richard Zednik .12 .30
223 Yanic Perreault .12 .30
224 Jan Bulis .12 .30
225 Andrei Markov .20 .50
226 Niklas Sundstrom .12 .30
227 Joe Juneau .15 .40
228 Mike Ribeiro .15 .40
229 Marcel Hossa .12 .30
230 Stephane Quintal .12 .30
231 Jose Theodore .20 .50
232 Michael Komisarek .12 .30
233 Mathieu Garon .12 .30
234 Ron Hainsey .12 .30
235 David Legwand .15 .40
236 Kimmo Timonen .12 .30
237 Andreas Johansson .12 .30
238 Denis Arkhipov .12 .30
239 Darren Haydar .12 .30
240 Scott Hartnell .20 .50
241 Scott Walker .12 .30
242 Adam Hall .12 .30
243 Greg Johnson .12 .30
244 Scottie Upshall .15 .40
245 Tomas Vokoun .15 .40
246 Brian Finley .12 .30
247 Patrik Elias .20 .50
248 Jamie Langenbrunner .15 .40
249 Scott Gomez .15 .40
250 Jeff Friesen .12 .30
251 Joe Nieuwendyk .20 .50
252 John Madden .12 .30
253 Brian Rafalski .15 .40
254 Scott Niedermayer .20 .50
255 Grant Marshall .12 .30
256 Brian Gionta .15 .40
257 Scott Stevens .20 .50
258 Colin White .12 .30
259 Michael Rupp .12 .30
260 Martin Brodeur .40 1.00
261 Corey Schwab .15 .40
262 Ken Daneyko .12 .30
263 Alexei Yashin .15 .40
264 Jason Blake .12 .30
265 Mark Parrish .12 .30
266 Dave Scatchard .12 .30
267 Michael Peca .15 .40
268 Roman Hamrlik .15 .40
269 Adrian Aucoin .12 .30
270 Arron Asham .12 .30
271 Janne Niinimaa .12 .30
272 Mattias Weinhandl .12 .30
273 Rick DiPietro .15 .40
274 Garth Snow .15 .40
275 Eric Godard .12 .30
276 Alex Kovalev .15 .40
277 Anson Carter .15 .40
278 Petr Nedved .12 .30
279 Eric Lindros .30 .75
280 Tom Poti .12 .30
281 Bobby Holik .12 .30
282 Matthew Barnaby .15 .40
283 Pavel Bure .25 .60
284 Vladimir Malakhov .12 .30
285 Jamie Lundmark .12 .30
286 Mike Dunham .15 .40
287 Dan Blackburn .15 .40
288 Marian Hossa .15 .40
289 Daniel Alfredsson .20 .50
290 Todd White .12 .30
291 Martin Havlat .20 .50
292 Radek Bonk .15 .40
293 Wade Redden .12 .30
294 Zdeno Chara .20 .50
295 Magnus Arvedson .12 .30
296 Shaun Van Allen .12 .30
297 Karel Rachunek .12 .30
298 Peter Schaefer .12 .30
299 Jason Spezza .20 .50
300 Vaclav Varada .12 .30
301 Anton Volchenkov .12 .30
302 Patrick Lalime .15 .40
303 Ray Emery .15 .40
304 Jody Hull .12 .30
305 Jeremy Roenick .20 .50
306 Mark Recchi .25 .60
307 Tony Amonte .15 .40
308 Keith Primeau .20 .50
309 Michal Handzus .15 .40
310 Kim Johnsson .12 .30
311 Eric Desjardins .15 .40
312 Sami Kapanen .12 .30
313 John LeClair .20 .50
314 Simon Gagne .20 .50
315 Donald Brashear .12 .30
316 Justin Williams .15 .40
317 Eric Weinrich .12 .30
318 Jeff Hackett .15 .40
319 Robert Esche .12 .30
320 Mike Johnson .12 .30
321 Shane Doan .15 .40
322 Ladislav Nagy .12 .30
323 Daymond Langkow .12 .30
324 Chris Gratton .12 .30
325 Jan Hrdina .12 .30
326 Teppo Numminen .12 .30
327 Branko Radivojevic .12 .30
328 Paul Mara .12 .30
329 Tyson Nash .12 .30
330 Jeff Taffe .12 .30
331 Brian Boucher .15 .40
332 Sean Burke .12 .30
333 Mario Lemieux .60 1.50
334 Martin Straka .12 .30
335 Dick Tarnstrom .12 .30
336 Aleksey Morozov .12 .30
337 Mikael Samuelsson .12 .30
338 Ville Nieminen .12 .30
339 Rico Fata .12 .30
340 Dan Focht .12 .30
341 Johan Hedberg .15 .40
342 Sebastien Caron .15 .40
343 Brooks Orpik .15 .40
344 Vincent Damphousse .15 .40
345 Patrick Marleau .20 .50
346 Marco Sturm .12 .30
347 Mike Ricci .15 .40
348 Scott Hannan .12 .30
349 Jim Fahey .12 .30
350 Todd Harvey .12 .30
351 Adam Graves .15 .40
352 Jonathan Cheechoo .15 .40
353 Brad Stuart .12 .30
354 Niko Dimitrakos .12 .30
355 Kyle McLaren .12 .30
356 Miikka Kiprusoff .15 .40
357 Evgeni Nabokov .15 .40
358 Pavol Demitra .25 .60
359 Al MacInnis .20 .50
360 Eric Boguniecki .12 .30
361 Doug Weight .20 .50
362 Scott Mellanby .12 .30
363 Keith Tkachuk .20 .50
364 Petr Cajanek .12 .30
365 Alexander Khavanov .12 .30
366 Barret Jackman .12 .30
367 Steve Martins .12 .30
368 Bryce Salvador .12 .30
369 Dallas Drake .12 .30
370 Ryan Johnson .12 .30
371 Reed Low .12 .30
372 Chris Pronger .15 .40
373 Brent Johnson .15 .40
374 Chris Osgood .20 .50
375 Peter Sejna RC .15 .40
376 Vaclav Prospal .12 .30
377 Vincent Lecavalier .15 .40
378 Brad Richards .20 .50
379 Martin St. Louis .20 .50
380 Dan Boyle .15 .40
381 Fredrik Modin .12 .30
382 Dave Andreychuk .20 .50
383 Pavel Kubina .12 .30
384 Alexander Svitov .12 .30
385 Nikita Alexeev .12 .30
386 Nikolai Khabibulin .20 .50
387 John Grahame .12 .30
388 Chris Dingman .12 .30
389 Tim Taylor .12 .30
390 Alexander Mogilny .15 .40
391 Mats Sundin .20 .50
392 Owen Nolan .15 .40
393 Tomas Kaberle .12 .30
394 Nik Antropov .15 .40
395 Ed Belfour .20 .50
396 Darcy Tucker .15 .40
397 Doug Gilmour .25 .60
398 Tie Domi .15 .40
399 Phil Housley .12 .30
400 Aki Berg .12 .30
401 Bryan McCabe .12 .30
402 Gary Roberts .12 .30
403 Carlo Colaiacovo .12 .30
404 Jyrki Lumme .12 .30
405 Mikael Tellqvist .15 .40
406 Trevor Kidd .12 .30
407 Matt Stajan RC .20 .50
408 Markus Naslund .20 .50
409 Todd Bertuzzi .20 .50
410 Brendan Morrison .15 .40
411 Ed Jovanovski .15 .40
412 Matt Cooke .12 .30
413 Trevor Linden .20 .50
414 Henrik Sedin .20 .50
415 Brent Sopel .12 .30
416 Daniel Sedin .20 .50
417 Mattias Ohlund .12 .30
418 Brandon Reid .12 .30
419 Marek Malik .12 .30
420 Bryan Allen .12 .30
421 Jarkko Ruutu .12 .30
422 Alexander Auld .12 .30
423 Dan Cloutier .15 .40
424 Jaromir Jagr .50 1.25
425 Robert Lang .12 .30
426 Sergei Gonchar .12 .30
427 Michael Nylander .12 .30
428 Peter Bondra .15 .40
429 Sergei Berezin .12 .30
430 Jeff Halpern .12 .30
431 Mike Grier .12 .30
432 Steve Konowalchuk .12 .30
433 Ivan Ciernik .12 .30
434 Steve Eminger .12 .30
435 Olaf Kolzig .20 .50
436 Sebastien Charpentier .12 .30
437 Joe Thornton CL .25 .60
438 Martin Brodeur CL .40 1.00
439 Dany Heatley CL .20 .50
440 Jean-Sebastien Giguere CL .20 .50
441 Eric Staal RC 5.00 12.00
442 Boyd Gordon RC .75 2.00
443 Joni Pitkanen RC 1.00 2.50
444 Christopher Brandner RC .75 2.00
445 Joffrey Lupul RC 1.50 4.00
446 Matthew Lombardi RC .75 2.00
447 Cody McCormick RC .75 2.00
448 Tim Gleason RC .75 2.00
449 Jiri Hudler RC 1.50 4.00
450 Antoine Vermette RC 1.25 3.00
451 Alexander Semin RC 2.00 5.00
452 Tuomo Ruutu RC 1.00 2.50
453 Dan Hamhuis RC .75 2.00
454 Sean Bergenheim RC .75 2.00
455 Brent Burns RC 1.50 4.00
456 Dan Fritsche RC .60 1.50
457 Antti Miettinen RC 1.00 2.50
458 Nathan Horton RC 1.50 4.00
459 Maxim Kondratiev RC .60 1.50
460 Matthew Spiller RC .75 2.00
461 Marc-Andre Fleury RC 8.00 20.00
462 David Hale RC .60 1.50
463 Marek Svatos RC 1.25 3.00
464 Milan Michalek RC 1.25 3.00
465 John-Michael Liles RC .75 2.00
466 Dustin Brown RC 1.25 3.00
467 Chris Higgins RC 1.25 3.00
468 Patrice Bergeron RC 6.00 15.00
469 Pavel Vorobiev RC .75 2.00
470 Jordin Tootoo RC 3.00 8.00
188J Roberto Luongo JUM/299 1.50 4.00

2003-04 Upper Deck MVP Gold Script

*1-440 VETS/25: 15X TO 40X BASIC CARDS
*1-440 ROOKIES/25: 10X TO 25X RC

2003-04 Upper Deck MVP Silver Script

*1-440 VETS/150: 5X TO 12X BASIC CARDS
*1-440 ROOKIE/150: 3X TO 8X RC

2003-04 Upper Deck MVP Canadian Exclusives

1-440 VETS/25: 15X TO 40X BASIC CARDS
*1-440 ROOKIES/25: 10X TO 25X RC

2003-04 Upper Deck MVP Clutch Performers

COMPLETE SET (7) 8.00 15.00
STATED ODDS 1:24
CP1 Patrick Roy 2.50 6.00
CP2 Markus Naslund .60 1.50
CP3 Martin Brodeur 2.00 5.00
CP4 Joe Thornton .75 2.00
CP5 Jean-Sebastien Giguere .60 1.50
CP6 Marian Gaborik .75 2.00
CP7 Steve Yzerman 2.00 5.00

2003-04 Upper Deck MVP Lethal Lineups

STAT.PRINT RUN 50 SER.#'d SETS
LL1 Hejduk/Sakic/Forsberg 60.00 150.00
LL2 Amonte/Roenick/LeClair 20.00 50.00
LL3 Thornton/Samsonov/Murray 30.00 80.00
LL4 Naslund/Bertuzzi/Linden 30.00 80.00
LL5 Gilmour/Sundin/Nolan 30.00 80.00
LL6 Shanahan/Hull/Yzerman 60.00 150.00

2003-04 Upper Deck MVP Masked Men

STATED ODDS 1:18
MM1 Martin Brodeur 2.00 5.00
MM2 Patrick Roy 2.50 6.00
MM3 Nikolai Khabibulin .50 1.25
MM4 Jocelyn Thibault .50 1.25
MM5 Jean-Sebastien Giguere .50 1.25
MM6 Patrick Lalime .50 1.25
MM7 Roberto Luongo .60 1.50
MM8 Ed Belfour .50 1.25
MM9 David Aebischer .50 1.25
MM10 Marty Turco .50 1.25

2003-04 Upper Deck MVP ProSign

This 19-card set featured certified player autographs on diamond-mirrored stickers affixed to the card fronts. Cards from this set were inserted at a rate of 1:480. Please note that the Gretzky card has been confirmed to exist though there is not significant market information to price it currently; the Joseph card has yet to be confirmed.
PSBO Bobby Orr 100.00 200.00
PSDH Dany Heatley 15.00 40.00
PSEC Erik Cole 6.00 15.00
PSGH Gordie Howe 100.00 200.00
PSHZ Henrik Zetterberg 15.00 40.00
PSJT Joe Thornton 30.00 80.00
PSMA Maxim Afinogenov 6.00 15.00
PSMB Martin Brodeur 100.00 200.00
PSMC Mike Comrie 10.00 25.00
PSMH Martin Havlat 10.00 25.00
PSMN Markus Naslund 15.00 40.00
PSRB Ray Bourque 30.00 80.00
PSRD Rick DiPietro 10.00 25.00
PSRM Adam Hall 6.00 15.00
PSSC Stanislav Chistov 6.00 15.00
PSSG Simon Gagne 12.50 30.00
PSSH Scott Hartnell 10.00 25.00
PSWG Wayne Gretzky 200.00 400.00

2003-04 Upper Deck MVP Souvenirs

This 26-card set featured swatches of practice-worn jerseys. Cards were randomly inserted at 1:24.
S1 Chris Drury 5.00 12.00
S2 Joe Sakic 10.00 25.00
S3 Patrick Roy 12.00 30.00
S4 Rob Blake 5.00 12.00
S5 Ray Whitney 5.00 12.00
S6 Jaromir Jagr 8.00 20.00
S7 Olaf Kolzig 5.00 12.00
S8 Peter Bondra 5.00 12.00
S9 Paul Kariya 5.00 12.00
S10 John LeClair 5.00 12.00
S11 Keith Primeau 5.00 12.00
S12 Mark Recchi 5.00 12.00
S13 Roman Cechmanek 5.00 12.00
S14 Felix Potvin 5.00 12.00
S15 Jason Allison 5.00 12.00
S16 Zigmund Palffy 5.00 12.00
S17 Peter Forsberg 8.00 20.00
S18 Alex Kovalev 5.00 12.00
S19 J-P Dumont 5.00 12.00
S20 Maxim Afinogenov 5.00 12.00
S21 Brett Hull 6.00 15.00
S22 Simon Gagne 5.00 12.00
S23 Brian Boucher 5.00 12.00
S24 Ville Nieminen 5.00 12.00
S25 Eric Lindros 5.00 12.00
S26 Jarome Iginla 6.00 15.00

2003-04 Upper Deck MVP SportsNut

This 91-card set featured a scratch off area that revealed a game code. Collectors could enter the code on the cards at the UD website to accumulate points redeemable for UD merchandise.
SN1 Jean-Sebastien Giguere .40 1.00
SN2 Paul Kariya .40 1.00
SN3 Petr Sykora .40 1.00
SN4 Pasi Nurminen .40 1.00
SN5 Ilya Kovalchuk 1.00 2.50
SN6 Dany Heatley 1.00 2.50
SN7 Jeff Hackett .40 1.00
SN8 Joe Thornton 1.25 3.00
SN9 Glen Murray .20 .50
SN10 Sergei Samsonov .40 1.00
SN11 Martin Biron .40 1.00
SN12 Miroslav Satan .40 1.00
SN13 Maxim Afinogenov .20 .50
SN14 Roman Turek .40 1.00
SN15 Jarome Iginla .75 2.00
SN16 Chris Drury .40 1.00
SN17 Pavel Brendl .20 .50
SN18 Jeff O'Neill .20 .50
SN19 Jocelyn Thibault .40 1.00
SN20 Eric Daze .20 .50
SN21 David Aebischer .40 1.00
SN22 Peter Forsberg 1.50 4.00
SN23 Joe Sakic 2.00 5.00
SN24 Milan Hejduk .40 1.00
SN25 Marc Denis .40 1.00
SN26 Rick Nash .75 2.00
SN27 Marty Turco .40 1.00
SN28 Mike Modano 1.25 3.00
SN29 Bill Guerin .40 1.00
SN30 Dominik Hasek 2.00 5.00
SN31 Steve Yzerman 4.00 10.00
SN32 Sergei Fedorov 1.00 2.50
SN33 Brett Hull 1.00 2.50
SN34 Tommy Salo .40 1.00
SN35 Mike Comrie .40 1.00
SN36 Ryan Smyth .20 .50
SN37 Ales Hemsky .40 1.00
SN38 Roberto Luongo .75 2.00
SN39 Olli Jokinen .40 1.00
SN40 Stephen Weiss .20 .50
SN41 Roman Cechmanek .40 1.00
SN42 Zigmund Palffy .40 1.00
SN43 Dwayne Roloson .40 1.00
SN44 Manny Fernandez .40 1.00
SN45 Marian Gaborik 1.25 3.00
SN46 Jose Theodore .75 2.00
SN47 Saku Koivu .40 1.00
SN48 Marcel Hossa .20 .50
SN49 Tomas Vokoun .40 1.00
SN50 Martin Brodeur 2.00 5.00
SN51 Jamie Langenbrunner .20 .50
SN52 Patrik Elias .40 1.00
SN53 Garth Snow .40 1.00
SN54 Alexei Yashin .20 .50
SN55 Mike Dunham .40 1.00
SN56 Dan Blackburn .40 1.00
SN57 Eric Lindros .50 1.25
SN58 Pavel Bure .50 1.25
SN59 Alex Kovalev .40 1.00
SN60 Patrick Lalime .40 1.00
SN61 Marian Hossa .50 1.25
SN62 Daniel Alfredsson .40 1.00
SN63 Jason Spezza .60 1.50
SN64 Robert Esche .40 1.00
SN65 Jeremy Roenick 1.00 2.50
SN66 John LeClair .40 1.00
SN67 Tony Amonte .40 1.00
SN68 Sean Burke .40 1.00
SN69 Mike Johnson .20 .50
SN70 Johan Hedberg .40 1.00
SN71 Mario Lemieux 4.00 10.00
SN72 Martin Straka .20 .50
SN73 Evgeni Nabokov .40 1.00
SN74 Vincent Damphousse .20 .50
SN75 Chris Osgood .40 1.00
SN76 Keith Tkachuk .40 1.00
SN77 Al MacInnis .40 1.00
SN78 Nikolai Khabibulin .40 1.00
SN79 Vincent Lecavalier .50 1.25
SN80 Martin St. Louis .40 1.00
SN81 Ed Belfour .50 1.25
SN82 Mats Sundin .40 1.00
SN83 Owen Nolan .40 1.00
SN84 Alexander Mogilny .40 1.00
SN85 Alexander Auld .20 .50
SN86 Todd Bertuzzi .40 1.00
SN87 Markus Naslund .40 1.00
SN88 Ed Jovanovski .40 1.00
SN89 Olaf Kolzig .40 1.00
SN90 Jaromir Jagr 1.25 3.00
SN91 Peter Bondra .40 1.00

2003-04 Upper Deck MVP Talent

COMPLETE SET (15) 15.00 30.00
STATED ODDS 1:12
MT1 Mario Lemieux 3.00 8.00
MT2 Martin Brodeur 2.00 5.00
MT3 Markus Naslund .40 1.00
MT4 Marian Gaborik 1.50 4.00
MT5 Dany Heatley 1.00 2.50
MT6 Joe Thornton 1.25 3.00
MT7 Steve Yzerman 2.50 6.00
MT8 Marian Hossa .40 1.00
MT9 Ed Belfour .40 1.00
MT10 Pavel Bure .40 1.00
MT11 Peter Forsberg 1.50 4.00
MT12 Ilya Kovalchuk 1.00 2.50
MT13 Jaromir Jagr 1.25 3.00
MT14 Zigmund Palffy .40 1.00
MT15 Mike Modano 1.25 3.00

2003-04 Upper Deck MVP Threads

STAT.PRINT RUN 100 SER.#'d SETS
TC1 Al MacInnis 12.50 30.00
TC2 Bill Guerin 12.50 30.00
TC3 Brendan Shanahan 15.00 40.00
TC4 Brett Hull 20.00 50.00
TC5 Chris Osgood 12.50 30.00
TC6 Ed Belfour 15.00 40.00
TC7 Jaromir Jagr 20.00 50.00
TC8 Keith Primeau 12.50 30.00
TC9 Patrick Roy 30.00 80.00
TC10 Ray Bourque 25.00 60.00

2003-04 Upper Deck MVP Wal-Mart Jumbos

*VETS: 3X TO 8X BASIC CARDS
*ROOKIES: .6X TO 1.5X BASIC CARDS
STATED PRINT RUN 299 SER.#'d SETS

2003-04 Upper Deck MVP Winning Formula

COMPLETE SET (10) 10.00 20.00
STATED ODDS 1:18
WF1 Rick Nash .75 2.00
WF2 Todd Bertuzzi .75 2.00
WF3 Jeremy Roenick .75 2.00
WF4 Steve Yzerman 2.00 5.00
WF5 Jason Spezza .75 2.00
WF6 Brett Hull 1.00 2.50
WF7 Jean-Sebastien Giguere .75 2.00
WF8 Mike Modano 1.25 3.00
WF9 Paul Kariya 1.00 2.50
WF10 Henrik Zetterberg 1.00 2.50

2005-06 Upper Deck MVP

This 445-card set was issued into the hobby in eight-card packs, with a $1.99 SRP, which came 24 to a box. Cards numbered 1-392 feature veterans in alphabetical team order while cards 393-437 are Rookie Cards and the set concludes with Checklist cards from 438-445.
COMPLETE SET (445) 75.00 150.00
1 Sergei Fedorov .30 .75
2 Sandis Ozolinsh .12 .30
3 Scott Niedermayer .20 .50
4 Rob Niedermayer .15 .40
5 Teemu Selanne .40 1.00
6 Jean-Sebastien Giguere .20 .50
7 Ruslan Salei .12 .30
8 Joffrey Lupul .15 .40
9 Andy McDonald .15 .40
10 Keith Carney .12 .30
11 Vitali Vishnevsky .12 .30
12 Petr Sykora .15 .40
13 Marian Hossa .15 .40
14 Patrik Stefan .12 .30
15 Kari Lehtonen .15 .40
16 Bobby Holik .12 .30
17 Andy Sutton .12 .30
18 Serge Aubin .12 .30
19 Marc Savard .12 .30
20 Peter Bondra .15 .40
21 Jaroslav Modry .12 .30
22 Niclas Havelid .12 .30
23 Mike Dunham .12 .30
24 Slava Kozlov .12 .30
25 Scott Mellanby .12 .30
26 Ilya Kovalchuk .20 .50
27 Glen Murray .15 .40
28 Joe Thornton .25 .60
29 Andrew Raycroft .15 .40
30 Patrice Bergeron .25 .60
31 Hal Gill .12 .30
32 P.J. Axelsson .12 .30
33 Shawn McEachern .12 .30
34 Brian Leetch .20 .50
35 Alexei Zhamnov .12 .30
36 Nick Boynton .12 .30
37 Brad Isbister .12 .30
38 Jiri Slegr .12 .30
39 Brad Boyes .15 .40
40 Travis Green .12 .30
41 Tom Fitzgerald .12 .30
42 Dave Scatchard .12 .30
43 Chris Drury .15 .40
44 Martin Biron .15 .40
45 Maxim Afinogenov .12 .30
46 Daniel Briere .20 .50
47 Mika Noronen .15 .40
48 Jean-Pierre Dumont .12 .30
49 Derek Roy .12 .30
50 Mike Grier .12 .30
51 Jochen Hecht .12 .30
52 Jeff Jillson .12 .30
53 Teppo Numminen .15 .40
54 Ryan Miller .20 .50
55 Tim Connolly .12 .30
56 Jarome Iginla .20 .50
57 Jordan Leopold .12 .30
58 Tony Amonte .15 .40
59 Chris Simon .12 .30
60 Shean Donovan .12 .30
61 Roman Hamrlik .15 .40
62 Chuck Kobasew .12 .30
63 Darren McCarty .12 .30
64 Robyn Regehr .12 .30
65 Phillippe Sauve .15 .40
66 Stephane Yelle .12 .30
67 Daymond Langkow .12 .30
68 Matthew Lombardi .12 .30
69 Marcus Nilson .12 .30
70 Jason Wiemer .12 .30
71 Erik Cole .15 .40
72 Glen Wesley .12 .30
73 Josef Vasicek .12 .30
74 Radim Vrbata .15 .40
75 Niclas Wallin .12 .30
76 Martin Gerber .15 .40
77 Rod Brind'Amour .20 .50
78 Eric Staal .25 .60
79 Justin Williams .15 .40
80 Ray Whitney .15 .40
81 Oleg Tverdovsky .12 .30
82 Bret Hedican .12 .30
83 Jesse Boulerice .12 .30
84 Cory Stillman .15 .40
85 Nikolai Khabibulin .20 .50
86 Tuomo Ruutu .20 .50
87 Eric Daze .15 .40
88 Kyle Calder .12 .30
89 Matthew Barnaby .12 .30
90 Adrian Aucoin .12 .30
91 Tyler Arnason .12 .30
92 Martin Lapointe .12 .30
93 Jaroslav Spacek .12 .30
94 Curtis Brown .12 .30
95 Mark Bell .12 .30
96 Pavel Vorobiev .12 .30
97 Joe Sakic .30 .75
98 Rob Blake .20 .50
99 Alex Tanguay .20 .50
100 Milan Hejduk .15 .40
101 John-Michael Liles .12 .30
102 Steve Konowalchuk .12 .30
103 David Aebischer .15 .40
104 Brad May .12 .30
105 Patrice Brisebois .12 .30
106 Pierre Turgeon .20 .50
107 Andrew Brunette .12 .30
108 Antti Laaksonen .12 .30
109 Riku Hahl .12 .30
110 Dan Hinote .12 .30
111 Karlis Skrastins .12 .30
112 Rick Nash .20 .50
113 Marc Denis .15 .40
114 Todd Marchant .12 .30
115 David Vyborny .12 .30
116 Manny Malhotra .15 .40
117 Tyler Wright .12 .30
118 Jan Hrdina .12 .30
119 Nikolai Zherdev .12 .30
120 Bryan Berard .12 .30
121 Adam Foote .12 .30
122 Luke Richardson .12 .30
123 Trevor Letowski .12 .30
124 Jody Shelley .12 .30
125 Mike Modano .30 .75
126 Brenden Morrow .15 .40
127 Sergei Zubov .15 .40
128 Marty Turco .20 .50
129 Steve Ott .15 .40
130 Jason Arnott .15 .40
131 Bill Guerin .20 .50
132 Stu Barnes .12 .30
133 Jere Lehtinen .15 .40
134 Jaroslav Svoboda .12 .30
135 Phillippe Boucher .12 .30
136 Johan Hedberg .15 .40
137 Trevor Daley .12 .30
138 Martin Skoula .12 .30
139 Steve Yzerman .50 1.25
140 Chris Chelios .20 .50
141 Robert Lang .12 .30
142 Chris Osgood .20 .50
143 Tomas Holmstrom .15 .40
144 Kris Draper .25 .60
145 Jiri Fischer .12 .30
146 Brendan Shanahan .25 .60
147 Nicklas Lidstrom .20 .50
148 Manny Legace .20 .50
149 Henrik Zetterberg .25 .60
150 Mathieu Schneider .12 .30
151 Pavel Datsyuk .25 .60
152 Ty Conklin .15 .40
153 Ryan Smyth .15 .40
154 Jason Smith .12 .30
155 Ales Hemsky .15 .40
156 Michael Peca .15 .40
157 Chris Pronger .15 .40
158 Radek Dvorak .12 .30
159 Georges Laraque .15 .40
160 Raffi Torres .12 .30
161 Alexei Semenov .12 .30
162 Todd Harvey .12 .30
163 Igor Ulanov .12 .30
164 Jani Rita .12 .30
165 Roberto Luongo .30 .75
166 Jay Bouwmeester .20 .50
167 Olli Jokinen .20 .50
168 Sean Hill .12 .30
169 Nathan Horton .20 .50
170 Stephen Weiss .12 .30
171 Chris Gratton .12 .30
172 Joe Nieuwendyk .20 .50
173 Gary Roberts .12 .30
174 Jamie McLennan .12 .30
175 Mike Van Ryn .12 .30
176 Martin Gelinas .12 .30
177 Jozef Stumpel .12 .30
178 Luc Robitaille .20 .50
179 Mathieu Garon .15 .40
180 Lubomir Visnovsky .12 .30
181 Jeremy Roenick .20 .50
182 Mattias Norstrom .12 .30
183 Dustin Brown .20 .50
184 Alexander Frolov .12 .30
185 Valeri Bure .12 .30
186 Pavol Demitra .25 .60
187 Mike Cammalleri .20 .50
188 Aaron Miller .12 .30
189 Manny Fernandez .15 .40
190 Marian Gaborik .30 .75
191 Brian Rolston .15 .40
192 Filip Kuba .12 .30
193 P-M Bouchard .20 .50
194 Andrei Zyuzin .12 .30
195 Pascal Dupuis .12 .30
196 Alexandre Daigle .12 .30
197 Dwayne Roloson .15 .40
198 Marc Chouinard .12 .30
199 Nick Schultz .12 .30
200 Saku Koivu .20 .50
201 Richard Zednik .12 .30
202 Michael Ryder .15 .40
203 Radek Bonk .12 .30
204 Alexei Kovalev .15 .40
205 Jan Bulis .12 .30
206 Pierre Dagenais .12 .30
207 Mike Ribeiro .15 .40
208 Jose Theodore .20 .50
209 Mike Komisarek .12 .30
210 Sheldon Souray .12 .30
211 Niklas Sundstrom .12 .30
212 Mathieu Dandenault .12 .30
213 Andrei Markov .20 .50
214 Craig Rivet .12 .30
215 Tomas Vokoun .15 .40
216 David Legwand .15 .40
217 Steve Sullivan .12 .30
218 Adam Hall .12 .30
219 Scott Walker .12 .30
220 Martin Erat .12 .30
221 Paul Kariya .25 .60
222 Scott Hartnell .20 .50
223 Scott Nichol .12 .30
224 Randy Robitaille .12 .30
225 Kimmo Timonen .12 .30
226 Danny Markov .12 .30
227 Jordin Tootoo .20 .50
228 Scott Gomez .15 .40
229 Patrik Elias .20 .50
230 Martin Brodeur .30 .75
231 Sergei Brylin .12 .30
232 John Madden .12 .30
233 Dan McGillis .12 .30
234 Paul Martin .12 .30
235 Alexander Mogilny .15 .40
236 Brian Rafalski .15 .40
237 Brian Gionta .15 .40
238 Viktor Kozlov .12 .30
239 Jamie Langenbrunner .12 .30
240 Jay Pandolfo .12 .30
241 Erik Rasmussen .12 .30
242 Alexei Yashin .15 .40
243 Rick DiPietro .15 .40
244 Alexei Zhitnik .12 .30
245 Brent Sopel .12 .30
246 Jason Blake .12 .30
247 Janne Niinimaa .12 .30
248 Mark Parrish .12 .30
249 Miroslav Satan .15 .40
250 Trent Hunter .12 .30
251 Garth Snow .15 .40
252 Mike York .12 .30
253 Shawn Bates .12 .30
254 Tom Poti .12 .30
255 Martin Straka .12 .30
256 Jaromir Jagr .50 1.25
257 Darius Kasparaitis .12 .30
258 Michael Nylander .12 .30
259 Kevin Weekes .15 .40
260 Steve Rucchin .12 .30
261 Fedor Tyutin .12 .30
262 Martin Rucinsky .12 .30
263 Ville Nieminen .12 .30
264 Jason Ward .12 .30
265 Marcel Hossa .12 .30
266 Dany Heatley .20 .50
267 Dominik Hasek .30 .75
268 Wade Redden .12 .30
269 Jason Spezza .20 .50
270 Chris Phillips .12 .30
271 Bryan Smolinski .12 .30
272 Zdeno Chara .20 .50
273 Daniel Alfredsson .20 .50
274 Martin Havlat .20 .50
275 Vaclav Varada .12 .30
276 Peter Schaefer .12 .30
277 Antoine Vermette .15 .40
278 Mike Fisher .12 .30
279 Simon Gagne .20 .50
280 Peter Forsberg .25 .60
281 Keith Primeau .20 .50
282 Derian Hatcher .12 .30
283 Kim Johnsson .12 .30
284 Sami Kapanen .12 .30
285 Mike Knuble .12 .30
286 Eric Desjardins .15 .40
287 Robert Esche .15 .40
288 Donald Brashear .12 .30
289 Joni Pitkanen .12 .30
290 Mike Rathje .12 .30
291 Chris Therien .12 .30
292 Michal Handzus .15 .40
293 Geoff Sanderson .12 .30
294 Curtis Joseph .20 .50
295 Mike Ricci .15 .40
296 Derek Morris .12 .30
297 Mike Johnson .12 .30
298 Petr Nedved .12 .30
299 Oleg Saprykin .12 .30
300 Shane Doan .15 .40
301 Ladislav Nagy .12 .30
302 Tyson Nash .12 .30
303 Mike Comrie .15 .40
304 Brad Ference .12 .30
305 Paul Mara .12 .30
306 Mario Lemieux .60 1.50
307 Zigmund Palffy .20 .50
308 Ryan Malone .12 .30
309 Rico Fata .12 .30
310 John LeClair .20 .50
311 Lasse Pirjeta .12 .30
312 Konstantin Koltsov .12 .30
313 Mark Recchi .25 .60
314 Jocelyn Thibault .15 .40
315 Sergei Gonchar .12 .30
316 Lyle Odelein .12 .30
317 Dick Tarnstrom .12 .30
318 Jonathan Cheechoo .20 .50

19 Marco Sturm .12 .30
20 Evgeni Nabokov .15 .40
21 Alyn McCauley .12 .30
22 Milan Michalek .12 .30
23 Brad Stuart .12 .30
24 Wayne Primeau .12 .30
25 Patrick Marleau .20 .50
26 Scott Thornton .12 .30
27 Vesa Toskala .15 .40
28 Marcel Goc .15 .40
29 Kyle McLaren .12 .30
30 Christian Ehrhoff .12 .30
31 Keith Tkachuk .20 .50
32 Barret Jackman .12 .30
33 Patrick Lalime .15 .40
34 Doug Weight .20 .50
35 Mark Rycroft .12 .30
36 Christian Backman .12 .30
37 Dallas Drake .12 .30
38 Mike Sillinger .12 .30
39 Jamal Mayers .12 .30
40 Eric Brewer .12 .30
41 Scott Young .12 .30
42 Dean McAmmond .12 .30
43 Brad Richards .20 .50
44 Fredrik Modin .12 .30
45 Martin St. Louis .20 .50
46 Ruslan Fedotenko .12 .30
47 Dave Andreychuk .20 .50
48 Pavel Kubina .12 .30
49 Tim Taylor .12 .30
350 Vincent Lecavalier .15 .40
351 Sean Burke .12 .30
352 Darryl Sydor .12 .30
353 Vaclav Prospal .12 .30
354 Mats Sundin .20 .50
355 Tie Domi .15 .40
356 Bryan McCabe .12 .30
357 Darcy Tucker .15 .40
358 Tomas Kaberle .12 .30
359 Kyle Wellwood .15 .40
360 Nikolai Antropov .15 .40
361 Ken Klee .12 .30
362 Ed Belfour .20 .50
363 Matt Stajan .15 .40
364 Eric Lindros .30 .75
365 Jason Allison .15 .40
366 Jeff O'Neill .12 .30
367 Mariusz Czerkawski .12 .30
368 J-S Aubin .12 .30
369 Markus Naslund .20 .50
370 Dan Cloutier .15 .40
371 Trevor Linden .20 .50
372 Anson Carter .15 .40
373 Todd Bertuzzi .20 .50
374 Daniel Sedin .20 .50
375 Sami Salo .12 .30
376 Mattias Ohlund .12 .30
377 Henrik Sedin .20 .50
378 Jarkko Ruutu .12 .30
379 Brendan Morrison .12 .30
380 Ed Jovanovski .15 .40
381 Jason King .12 .30
382 Alex Auld .12 .30
383 Matt Cooke .12 .30
384 Olaf Kolzig .20 .50
385 Brendan Witt .12 .30
386 Jeff Halpern .12 .30
387 Dainius Zubrus .12 .30
388 Alexander Semin .20 .50
389 Jeff Friesen .12 .30
390 Andrew Cassels .12 .30
391 Brian Willsie .12 .30
392 Boyd Gordon .12 .30
393 Sidney Crosby RC 12.00 30.00
394 Alexander Ovechkin RC 8.00 20.00
395 Gilbert Brule RC 2.50 6.00
396 Wojtek Wolski RC 2.00 5.00
397 Rene Bourque RC 2.50 6.00
398 Jeff Woywitka RC 1.50 4.00
399 Hannu Toivonen RC 2.50 6.00
400 Yann Danis RC 2.00 5.00
401 Alexander Perezhogin RC 2.00 5.00
402 David Leneveu RC 2.00 5.00
403 Zach Parise RC 6.00 15.00
404 Dion Phaneuf RC 4.00 10.00
405 Eric Nystrom RC 2.00 5.00
406 Mike Richards RC 5.00 12.00
407 Jeff Carter RC 4.00 10.00
408 Cam Ward RC 4.00 10.00
409 Kevin Nastiuk RC 1.50 4.00
410 Petteri Nokelainen RC 1.50 4.00
411 Robert Nilsson RC 2.50 6.00
412 Andy Wozniewski RC 2.00 5.00
413 Alexander Steen RC 4.00 10.00
414 Ryan Getzlaf RC 6.00 15.00
415 Corey Perry RC 10.00 25.00
416 Rostislav Olesz RC 2.00 5.00
417 Ryan Suter RC 3.00 8.00
418 Henrik Lundqvist RC 6.00 15.00
419 Petr Prucha RC 2.50 6.00
420 Jimmy Howard RC 6.00 15.00
421 Johan Franzen RC 4.00 10.00
422 Thomas Vanek RC 5.00 12.00
423 Brandon Bochenski RC 2.50 6.00
424 Andrej Meszaros RC 2.00 5.00
425 Ryane Clowe RC 3.00 8.00
426 Jussi Jokinen RC 2.50 6.00
427 Braydon Coburn RC 2.50 6.00
428 Jim Slater RC 2.00 5.00
429 Matthew Foy RC 1.50 4.00
430 Peter Budaj RC 3.00 8.00
431 Brent Seabrook RC 5.00 12.00
432 Lee Stempniak RC 2.50 6.00
433 Andrew Alberts RC 1.50 4.00
434 Keith Ballard RC 2.00 5.00
435 Duncan Keith RC 5.00 12.00
436 Milan Jurcina RC 2.00 5.00
437 Chris Campoli RC 1.50 4.00
438 Joe Sakic CL .25 .60
439 Joe Thornton CL .20 .50
440 Jarome Iginla CL .15 .40
441 Steve Yzerman CL .40 1.00
442 Martin Brodeur CL .40 1.00
443 Peter Forsberg CL .20 .50
444 Mario Lemieux CL .50 1.25
445 Martin St. Louis CL .15 .40

2005-06 Upper Deck MVP Gold

*VETS/100: 10X TO 25X BASIC CARDS
*ROOKIES/100: 1.2X TO 3X BASE RC
STATED PRINT RUN 100 SER.#'d SETS
393 Sidney Crosby 150.00 250.00
394 Alexander Ovechkin 100.00 200.00

2005-06 Upper Deck MVP Materials

STATED ODDS 1:24
MAA Aaron Asham 3.00 8.00
MAF Adam Foote 3.00 8.00
MAH Adam Hall 3.00 8.00
MBB Brian Boucher 3.00 8.00
MBO Brooks Orpik 3.00 8.00
MCO Chris Osgood 3.00 8.00
MCS Chris Simon 3.00 8.00
MDC Dan Cloutier 3.00 8.00
MDH Derian Hatcher 3.00 8.00
MDR Derek Roy 3.00 8.00
MED Eric Daze 3.00 8.00
MGM Glen Murray 3.00 8.00
MJA Jason Arnott 3.00 8.00
MJB Jason Blake 3.00 8.00
MJJ Jaromir Jagr 5.00 12.00
MJL John LeClair 3.00 8.00
MJR Jarkko Ruutu 3.00 8.00
MKJ Kenny Jonsson 3.00 8.00
MLO Lyle Odelein 3.00 8.00
MMD Marc Denis 3.00 8.00
MMF Manny Fernandez 3.00 8.00
MMP Mark Parrish 3.00 8.00
MMR Mark Recchi 3.00 8.00
MMS Martin Straka 3.00 8.00
MPD Pavol Demitra 3.00 8.00
MPE Patrik Elias 3.00 8.00
MPL Patrick Lalime 3.00 8.00
MRB Rob Blake 3.00 8.00
MRF Ruslan Fedotenko 3.00 8.00
MRK Ryan Kesler 3.00 8.00
MRL Robert Lang 3.00 8.00
MSK Steve Konowalchuk 3.00 8.00
MSN Scott Niedermayer 3.00 8.00
MSS Scott Stevens 3.00 8.00
MSW Stephen Weiss 3.00 8.00
MSY Steve Yzerman SP 30.00 80.00
MTA Tony Amonte 3.00 8.00
MTB Todd Bertuzzi 3.00 8.00
MTP Tom Poti 3.00 8.00
MVD Vincent Damphousse 3.00 8.00
MVK Viktor Kozlov 3.00 8.00
MZC Zdeno Chara 3.00 8.00

2005-06 Upper Deck MVP Materials Duals

STATED PRINT RUN 100 SER.#'d SETS
DCO Z.Chara/L.Odelein 8.00 20.00
DDR P.Demitra/M.Recchi 8.00 20.00
DHH M.Havlat/M.Hejduk 12.00 30.00
DJF E.Jovanovski/A.Foote 8.00 20.00
DLC T.Linden/D.Cloutier 20.00 50.00
DLJ M.Lemieux/J.Jagr 30.00 80.00
DPB M.Peca/R.Blake 8.00 20.00
DPD K.Primeau/E.Daze 8.00 20.00
DRN W.Redden/S.Niedermayer 8.00 20.00
DSH J.Sakic/D.Hinote 20.00 50.00

2005-06 Upper Deck MVP Materials Triples

STATED PRINT RUN 25 SER.#'d SETS
TTFD Theo/Fernan/Denis 40.00 100.00
TGST Gretzky/Sakic/Thorn 100.00 250.00
TVAN Naslund/Linden/Jovo 40.00 100.00
TGPD Gaborik/Palffy/Demitra 40.00 100.00
TSKF Sakic/Kariya/Forsberg 50.00 125.00
TLKF St. Louis/Khabi/Fedot 30.00 80.00

2005-06 Upper Deck MVP Monumental Moments

COMPLETE SET (7) 8.00 20.00
STATED ODDS 1:24
MM1 Wayne Gretzky 4.00 10.00
MM2 Gordie Howe 2.50 6.00
MM3 Brett Hull 1.00 2.50
MM4 Steve Yzerman 2.00 5.00
MM5 Mario Lemieux 2.50 6.00
MM6 Jaromir Jagr 2.00 5.00
MM7 Dominik Hasek 1.25 3.00

2005-06 Upper Deck MVP Platinum

*VETS/25: 30X TO 80X BASIC CARDS
*ROOKIES/25: 3X TO 8X BASIC RC
STATED PRINT RUN 25 SER.#'d SETS
393 Sidney Crosby 250.00 400.00
394 Alexander Ovechkin 175.00 300.00

2005-06 Upper Deck MVP ProSign

STATED ODDS 1:480
PAL Daniel Alfredsson SP 20.00 50.00
PBG Boyd Gordon 6.00 15.00
PBM Bryan McCabe 10.00 25.00
PDA David Aebischer 15.00 40.00
PDH Dany Heatley SP 15.00 40.00
PDM Darren McCarty 15.00 40.00
PDW Doug Weight 10.00 25.00
PEC Erik Cole 10.00 25.00
PED Eric Daze 6.00 15.00
PJI Jarome Iginla SP 12.00 30.00
PJL John-Michael Liles 10.00 25.00
PJR Jeremy Roenick 20.00 50.00
PJT Joe Thornton SP 30.00 80.00
PMA Maxim Afinogenov
PMB Martin Biron 10.00 25.00
PMC Mike Cammalleri 10.00 25.00
PMH Milan Hejduk SP 15.00 40.00
PMO Brendan Morrison 12.00 30.00
PMP Michael Peca 10.00 25.00
PMW Brenden Morrow 10.00 25.00
PNA Nikolai Antropov 6.00 15.00
POK Olaf Kolzig 10.00 25.00
PON Owen Nolan 20.00 50.00
PPO Mark Popovic 6.00 15.00
PRB Rob Blake 15.00 40.00
PRE Robert Esche 10.00 25.00
PRK Ryan Kesler 6.00 15.00
PRN Rick Nash SP 40.00 80.00
PRS Ryan Smyth 10.00 25.00
PSD Shane Doan 10.00 25.00
PSG Simon Gagne 15.00 40.00
PSL Martin St. Louis 20.00 50.00
PSS Sheldon Souray 6.00 15.00
PSU Steve Sullivan 6.00 15.00
PTA Tyler Arnason 6.00 15.00
PTH Trent Hunter 6.00 15.00
PTL Trevor Linden 20.00 50.00
PTP Tom Poti 6.00 15.00
PTS Tony Salmelainen 6.00 15.00
PWG Wayne Gretzky SP
PZC Zdeno Chara 10.00 25.00
1MR Mike Ribeiro 6.00 15.00

2005-06 Upper Deck MVP Rising to the Occasion

COMPLETE SET (14) 8.00 20.00
STATED ODDS 1:12
RO1 Joe Sakic 1.00 2.50
RO2 Mario Lemieux 2.00 5.00
RO3 Martin St. Louis .60 1.50
RO4 Jarome Iginla .60 1.50
RO5 Martin Brodeur 1.25 3.00
RO6 Steve Yzerman 1.50 4.00
RO7 Dominik Hasek 1.00 2.50
RO8 Peter Forsberg .75 2.00
RO9 Mike Modano 1.00 2.50
RO10 Jose Theodore .60 1.50
RO11 Jaromir Jagr 1.50 4.00
RO12 Ed Belfour .60 1.50
RO13 Wayne Gretzky 3.00 8.00
RO14 Ilya Kovalchuk .60 1.50

2005-06 Upper Deck MVP Rookie Breakthrough

COMPLETE SET (14) 25.00 60.00
STATED ODDS 1:12
RB1 Sidney Crosby 5.00 12.00
RB2 Alexander Ovechkin 5.00 12.00
RB3 Jeff Carter 1.50 4.00
RB4 Gilbert Brule 1.00 2.50
RB5 Wojtek Wolski .75 2.00
RB6 Alexander Perezhogin .75 2.00
RB7 Zach Parise 2.50 6.00
RB8 Dion Phaneuf 1.50 4.00
RB9 Corey Perry 4.00 10.00
RB10 Alexander Steen 2.00 5.00
RB11 Thomas Vanek 2.00 5.00
RB12 Hannu Toivonen 1.00 2.50
RB13 Mike Richards 2.00 5.00
RB14 Robert Nilsson 1.00 2.50

2005-06 Upper Deck MVP Tribute to Greatness

COMPLETE SET (7) 10.00 25.00
COMMON GRETZKY (TG1-TG7) 2.00 5.00
STATED ODDS 1:24
TG1 Wayne Gretzky 2.00 5.00
TG2 Wayne Gretzky 2.00 5.00
TG3 Wayne Gretzky 2.00 5.00
TG4 Wayne Gretzky 2.00 5.00
TG5 Wayne Gretzky 2.00 5.00
TG6 Wayne Gretzky 2.00 5.00
TG7 Wayne Gretzky 2.00 5.00

2006-07 Upper Deck MVP

This 360-card set was issued into the hobby in 10-card packs, with an $1.99 SRP, which came 24 packs to a box. Cards numbered 1-297 are veterans sequenced in team alphabetical order while cards numbered from 298-356 are Rookie Cards. The set concludes with a checklist subset from cards 397-400.

COMPLETE SET (360) 75.00 150.00
1 Chris Pronger .15 .40
2 Ilya Bryzgalov .20 .50
3 Andy McDonald .15 .40
4 Teemu Selanne .40 1.00
5 Francois Beauchemin .12 .30
6 Chris Kunitz .20 .50
7 Corey Perry .20 .50
8 Scott Niedermayer .20 .50
9 Ryan Getzlaf .30 .75
10 Jean-Sebastien Giguere .20 .50
11 Ilya Kovalchuk .20 .50
12 Jim Slater .12 .30
13 Slava Kozlov .12 .30
14 Kari Lehtonen .15 .40
15 Bobby Holik .12 .30
16 Marian Hossa .15 .40
17 Niko Kapanen .12 .30
18 Steve Rucchin .12 .30
19 Johan Hedberg .15 .40
20 Brad Boyes .12 .30
21 Hannu Toivonen .15 .40
22 Zdeno Chara .20 .50
23 Tim Thomas .25 .60
24 Marco Sturm .12 .30
25 Patrice Bergeron .25 .60
26 Brad Stuart .12 .30
27 Marc Savard .12 .30
28 Glen Murray .15 .40
29 Paul Mara .12 .30
30 Daniel Briere .20 .50
31 Chris Drury .15 .40
32 Ryan Miller .20 .50
33 Ales Kotalik .12 .30
34 Thomas Vanek .25 .60
35 Jaroslav Spacek .12 .30
36 Maxim Afinogenov .12 .30
37 Jason Pominville .20 .50
38 Derek Roy .12 .30
39 Jochen Hecht .12 .30
40 Martin Biron .15 .40
41 Miikka Kiprusoff .15 .40
42 Alex Tanguay .12 .30
43 Jamie Lundmark .12 .30
44 Jeff Friesen .12 .30
45 Jarome Iginla .20 .50
46 Dion Phaneuf .20 .50
47 Tony Amonte .15 .40
48 Chuck Kobasew .12 .30
49 Kristian Huselius .20 .50
50 Daymond Langkow .12 .30
51 Cam Ward .20 .50
52 Rod Brind'Amour .20 .50
53 Erik Cole .15 .40
54 Mike Commodore .12 .30
55 Andrew Ladd .20 .50
56 Eric Staal .25 .60
57 Cory Stillman .12 .30
58 Justin Williams .15 .40
59 Ray Whitney .15 .40
60 Frantisek Kaberle .12 .30
61 Nikolai Khabibulin .20 .50
62 Michal Handzus .15 .40
63 Pavel Vorobiev .12 .30
64 Rene Bourque .12 .30
65 Martin Havlat .12 .30
66 Duncan Keith .25 .60
67 Bryan Smolinski .12 .30
68 Tuomo Ruutu .20 .50
69 Brandon Bochenski .12 .30
70 Joe Sakic .30 .75
71 Jose Theodore .20 .50
72 John-Michael Liles .12 .30
73 Marek Svatos .12 .30
74 Brad Richardson .15 .40
75 Wojtek Wolski .15 .40
76 Milan Hejduk .15 .40
77 Pierre Turgeon .20 .50
78 Andrew Brunette .12 .30
79 Peter Budaj .15 .40
80 Patrice Brisebois .12 .30
81 Rick Nash .20 .50
82 Rostislav Klesla .12 .30
83 Gilbert Brule .15 .40
84 Pascal Leclaire .15 .40
85 Bryan Berard .12 .30
86 Fredrik Modin .12 .30
87 David Vyborny .12 .30
88 Sergei Fedorov .30 .75
89 Nikolai Zherdev .12 .30
90 Adam Foote .12 .30
91 Jody Shelley .12 .30
92 Marty Turco .20 .50
93 Brenden Morrow .15 .40
94 Sergei Zubov .15 .40
95 Eric Lindros .30 .75
96 Jussi Jokinen .15 .40
97 Mike Modano .30 .75
98 Jere Lehtinen .12 .30
99 Steve Ott .15 .40
100 Jeff Halpern .12 .30
101 Pavel Datsyuk .25 .60
102 Tomas Holmstrom .15 .40
103 Kris Draper .12 .30
104 Dominik Hasek .25 .60
105 Nicklas Lidstrom .20 .50
106 Henrik Zetterberg .25 .60
107 Robert Lang .12 .30
108 Mikael Samuelsson .12 .30
109 Chris Chelios .20 .50
110 Mathieu Schneider .12 .30
111 Jason Williams .12 .30
112 Dwayne Roloson .15 .40
113 Ales Hemsky .15 .40
114 Fernando Pisani .12 .30
115 Shawn Horcoff .12 .30
116 Jarret Stoll .15 .40
117 Jason Smith .12 .30
118 Ryan Smyth .15 .40
119 Raffi Torres .12 .30
120 Jussi Markkanen .12 .30
121 Joffrey Lupul .15 .40
122 Marc-Andre Bergeron .12 .30
123 Nathan Horton .20 .50
124 Stephen Weiss .12 .30
125 Alex Auld .12 .30
126 Olli Jokinen .20 .50
127 Todd Bertuzzi .20 .50
128 Joe Nieuwendyk .20 .50
129 Ed Belfour .20 .50
130 Jay Bouwmeester .20 .50
131 Rostislav Olesz .12 .30
132 Alexander Frolov .12 .30
133 Dan Cloutier .15 .40
134 Mike Cammalleri .12 .30
135 Rob Blake .20 .50
136 Craig Conroy .12 .30
137 Lubomir Visnovsky .12 .30
138 Mathieu Garon .15 .40
139 Sean Avery .12 .30
140 Dustin Brown .20 .50
141 Marian Gaborik .25 .60
142 Mark Parrish .12 .30
143 Pierre-Marc Bouchard .20 .50
144 Mikko Koivu .15 .40
145 Wes Walz .12 .30
146 Brian Rolston .15 .40
147 Manny Fernandez .15 .40
148 Pavol Demitra .25 .60
149 Kim Johnsson .12 .30
150 Todd White .12 .30
151 Cristobal Huet .15 .40
152 Saku Koivu .20 .50
153 Chris Higgins .12 .30
154 Andrei Markov .20 .50
155 Mike Ribeiro .15 .40
156 David Aebischer .15 .40
157 Alex Kovalev .15 .40
158 Sergei Samsonov .15 .40
159 Michael Ryder .12 .30
160 Sheldon Souray .12 .30
161 Alexander Perezhogin .12 .30
162 Paul Kariya .25 .60
163 Jason Arnott .15 .40
164 Jordin Tootoo .20 .50
165 J.P. Dumont .12 .30
166 Steve Sullivan .12 .30
167 Tomas Vokoun .15 .40
168 Marek Zidlicky .12 .30
169 Martin Erat .12 .30
170 Scott Hartnell .20 .50
171 Martin Brodeur .40 1.00
172 Brian Gionta .15 .40
173 John Madden .12 .30
174 Zach Parise .25 .60
175 Brian Rafalski .15 .40
176 Patrik Elias .20 .50
177 Sergei Brylin .12 .30
178 Scott Gomez .15 .40
179 Jamie Langenbrunner .12 .30
180 Paul Martin .12 .30
181 Miroslav Satan .15 .40
182 Mike Sillinger .12 .30
183 Tom Poti .12 .30
184 Jason Blake .12 .30
185 Trent Hunter .12 .30
186 Alexei Yashin .15 .40
187 Rick DiPietro .15 .40
188 Alexei Zhitnik .12 .30
189 Shawn Bates .12 .30
190 Jeff Tambellini .12 .30
191 Jaromir Jagr .50 1.25
192 Brendan Shanahan .25 .60
193 Martin Straka .12 .30
194 Marek Malik .12 .30
195 Petr Prucha .15 .40
196 Henrik Lundqvist .40 1.00
197 Sandis Ozolinsh .12 .30
198 Matt Cullen .12 .30
199 Michael Nylander .12 .30
200 Fedor Tyutin .12 .30
201 Jason Spezza .20 .50
202 Ray Emery .15 .40
203 Wade Redden .12 .30
204 Patrick Eaves .12 .30
205 Daniel Alfredsson .20 .50
206 Martin Gerber .15 .40
207 Dany Heatley .20 .50
208 Andrej Meszaros .12 .30
209 Mike Fisher .12 .30
210 Peter Schaefer .12 .30
211 Simon Gagne .20 .50
212 Joni Pitkanen .12 .30
213 Jeff Carter .20 .50
214 R.J. Umberger .12 .30
215 Peter Forsberg .25 .60
216 Antero Niittymaki .15 .40
217 Mike Richards .20 .50
218 Mike Knuble .12 .30
219 Robert Esche .15 .40
220 Kyle Calder .12 .30
221 Geoff Sanderson .12 .30
222 Shane Doan .15 .40
223 Ed Jovanovski .15 .40
224 Ladislav Nagy .12 .30
225 Curtis Joseph .20 .50
226 Jeremy Roenick .20 .50
227 Keith Ballard .12 .30
228 Mike Comrie .15 .40
229 David Leneveu .15 .40
230 Owen Nolan .15 .40
231 Sidney Crosby .75 2.00
232 Mark Recchi .25 .60
233 Nils Ekman .12 .30
234 Ryan Whitney .15 .40
235 Colby Armstrong .15 .40
236 John LeClair .20 .50
237 Marc-Andre Fleury .30 .75
238 Sergei Gonchar .12 .30
239 Ryan Malone .12 .30
240 Joe Thornton .25 .60
241 Vesa Toskala .15 .40
242 Mark Bell .12 .30
243 Steve Bernier .12 .30
244 Christian Ehrhoff .12 .30
245 Jonathan Cheechoo .20 .50
246 Patrick Marleau .20 .50
247 Mike Grier .12 .30
248 Milan Michalek .12 .30
249 Evgeni Nabokov .15 .40
250 Keith Tkachuk .20 .50
251 Manny Legace .15 .40
252 Martin Rucinsky .12 .30
253 Bill Guerin .20 .50
254 Lee Stempniak .12 .30
255 Petr Cajanek .12 .30
256 Doug Weight .20 .50
257 Jay McKee .12 .30
258 Martin St. Louis .20 .50
259 Marc Denis .15 .40
260 Vaclav Prospal .12 .30
261 Brad Richards .20 .50
262 Paul Ranger .12 .30
263 Ruslan Fedotenko .12 .30
264 Vincent Lecavalier .15 .40
265 Filip Kuba .12 .30
266 Ryan Craig .12 .30
267 Dan Boyle .15 .40
268 Mats Sundin .20 .50
269 Michael Peca .15 .40
270 Alexander Steen .20 .50
271 Bryan McCabe .12 .30
272 Tomas Kaberle .12 .30
273 Andrew Raycroft .15 .40
274 Nikolai Antropov .15 .40
275 Kyle Wellwood .15 .40
276 Mikael Tellqvist .20 .50
277 Darcy Tucker .15 .40
278 Matt Stajan .15 .40
279 Jeff O'Neill .12 .30
280 Matt Cooke .12 .30
281 Sami Salo .12 .30
282 Roberto Luongo .30 .75
283 Markus Naslund .15 .40
284 Daniel Sedin .20 .50
285 Mattias Ohlund .12 .30
286 Ryan Kesler .25 .60
287 Henrik Sedin .20 .50
288 Brendan Morrison .12 .30
289 Mika Noronen .15 .40
290 Brian Sutherby .12 .30
291 Steve Eminger .12 .30
292 Alexander Ovechkin .75 2.00
293 Olaf Kolzig .20 .50
294 Richard Zednik .12 .30
295 Dainius Zubrus .12 .30
296 Brent Johnson .15 .40
297 Chris Clark .12 .30
298 Patrick O'Sullivan RC 2.00 5.00
299 Phil Kessel RC 6.00 15.00
300 G. Latendresse RC 2.00 5.00
301 Jordan Staal RC 3.00 8.00
302 Paul Stastny RC 3.00 8.00
303 Evgeni Malkin RC 8.00 20.00
304 Luc Bourdon RC 2.00 5.00
305 Alexei Kaigorodov RC 1.25 3.00
306 Anze Kopitar RC 5.00 12.00
307 Travis Zajac RC 2.50 6.00
308 Nigel Dawes RC 1.25 3.00
309 Kristopher Letang RC 4.00 10.00
310 Marc-Edouard Vlasic RC 1.25 3.00
311 Patrick Thoresen RC 1.25 3.00
312 Ladislav Smid RC 1.25 3.00
313 Loui Eriksson RC 2.00 5.00
314 Shane O'Brien RC 1.25 3.00
315 Ryan Shannon RC 1.25 3.00
316 John Oduya RC 2.00 5.00
317 Fredrik Norrena RC 1.25 3.00
318 Niklas Backstrom RC 2.50 6.00
319 D.J. King RC 1.25 3.00
320 Patrick Fischer RC 1.25 3.00
321 Mikko Lehtonen RC 1.50 4.00
322 Roman Polak RC 1.50 4.00
323 Ben Ondrus RC 1.25 3.00
324 Bill Thomas RC 1.25 3.00
325 Billy Thompson RC 1.25 3.00
326 Brendan Bell RC 1.25 3.00
327 Carsen Germyn RC 1.25 3.00
328 Keith Yandle RC 2.50 6.00
329 Dan Jancevski RC 1.25 3.00
330 David Liffiton RC 1.25 3.00
331 David Printz RC 1.25 3.00
332 Dustin Byfuglien RC 3.00 8.00
333 Eric Fehr RC 2.50 6.00
334 Erik Reitz RC 1.25 3.00
335 Filip Novak RC 1.25 3.00
336 Frank Doyle RC 1.50 4.00
337 Ian White RC 1.50 4.00
338 Jarkko Immonen RC 1.25 3.00
339 Jeremy Williams RC 1.25 3.00
340 Joel Perrault RC 1.25 3.00
341 Jonas Johansson RC 1.25 3.00
342 Konstantin Pushkarev RC 1.50 4.00
343 Marc-Antoine Pouliot RC 1.25 3.00
344 Mark Stuart RC 1.25 3.00
345 Masi Marjamaki RC 1.25 3.00
346 Matt Carle RC 1.25 3.00
347 Matt Koalska RC 1.25 3.00
348 Michel Ouellet RC 1.50 4.00
349 Miroslav Kopriva RC 1.25 3.00
350 Noah Welch RC 1.25 3.00
351 Rob Collins RC 1.25 3.00
352 Ryan Caldwell RC 1.25 3.00
353 Ryan Potulny RC 1.25 3.00
354 Shea Weber RC 3.00 8.00
355 Enver Lisin RC 1.25 3.00
356 Tomas Kopecky RC 1.50 4.00
357 Yan Stastny RC 1.25 3.00
358 Joe Thornton CL .20 .50
359 Martin St. Louis CL .15 .40
360 Peter Forsberg CL .20 .50

2006-07 Upper Deck MVP Gold Script

*VETS/100: 10X TO 25X BASIC CARDS
*ROOKIES/100 1.2X TO 3X BASIC RC
STATED PRINT RUN 100 SETS

2006-07 Upper Deck MVP Super Script

*VETS/25: 25X TO 60X BASIC CARDS
*ROOKIES: 2.5X TO 6X BASE HI
STATED PRINT RUN 25 #'d SETS
231 Sidney Crosby 125.00 250.00
303 Evgeni Malkin 100.00 200.00

2006-07 Upper Deck MVP Autographs

STATED ODDS 1:240
OAAT Antropov/Tellqvist 12.00 30.00
OABK Bourque/Keith 8.00 20.00
OABM Bernier/Michalek 12.00 30.00
OABP Bouchard/Parrish 12.00 30.00
OABS Boyes/Stastny EXCH 12.00 30.00
OACL Cole/Ladd 8.00 20.00
OACR Carter/Richards 30.00 80.00
OACS Chara/Stuart 12.00 30.00
OADA Drury/Afinogenov 12.00 30.00
OADO Draper/Osgood 15.00 40.00
OAEE Esche/Eager 8.00 20.00
OAEG Elias/Gionta 12.00 30.00
OAFC Frolov/Cammalleri 12.00 30.00
OAFQ Filppula/Quincey 12.00 30.00
OAGA Gerber/Aebischer SP 25.00 60.00
OAGL Gretzky/Lemieux SP
OAHC Heatley/Cheechoo SP 25.00 60.00
OAHH Havlat/Handzus 12.00 30.00
OAHT Hejduk/Theodore 15.00 40.00
OAKL Kipper/Luongo SP 40.00 80.00
OALH Lupul/Horcoff 8.00 20.00
OALS Leneveu/Sauve 8.00 20.00
OALW Legace/Woywitka 8.00 20.00
OALZ Lidstrom/Zetterbg SP
OAMC Malone/Christensen 12.00 30.00
OAMK McDonald/Kunitz 8.00 20.00
OANI Nash/Iginla SP 60.00 100.00
OANM Naslund/Morrison 12.00 30.00
OAPK Phaneuf/Kobasew SP 12.00 30.00
OAPT Peca/Tucker SP 20.00 50.00
OARK Ribeiro/Kostitsyn SP 15.00 40.00
OARL Richardson/Liles 8.00 20.00
OARS Ryder/Samsonov SP 12.00 30.00
OASC Satan/Colliton 8.00 20.00
OATM Thornton/Marleau 25.00 60.00
OAVV Vokoun/Vasicek SP 15.00 40.00

2006-07 Upper Deck MVP Clutch Performers

COMPLETE SET (25) 10.00 25.00
STATED ODDS 1:8
CP1 Cam Ward .60 1.50
CP2 Peter Forsberg .75 2.00
CP3 Joe Sakic 1.00 2.50
CP4 Martin Brodeur 1.25 3.00
CP5 Jarome Iginla .60 1.50
CP6 Jaromir Jagr 1.50 4.00
CP7 Mats Sundin .60 1.50
CP8 Dany Heatley .60 1.50
CP9 Ryan Miller .60 1.50
CP10 Alexander Ovechkin 1.50 4.00
CP11 Eric Staal .75 2.00
CP12 Mike Modano 1.00 2.50
CP13 Martin St. Louis .60 1.50
CP14 Ryan Smyth .50 1.25
CP15 Chris Pronger .50 1.25
CP16 Henrik Zetterberg .75 2.00
CP17 Jonathan Cheechoo .60 1.50
CP18 Ilya Kovalchuk .60 1.50
CP19 Marian Gaborik .75 2.00
CP20 Shane Doan .75 2.00
CP21 Rick Nash .60 1.50
CP22 Sidney Crosby 2.50 6.00
CP23 Markus Naslund .50 1.25
CP24 Dominik Hasek .75 2.00
CP25 Mario Lemieux 2.00 5.00

2006-07 Upper Deck MVP Gotta Have Hart

COMPLETE SET (25) 10.00 25.00
STATED ODDS 1:8
HH1 Joe Thornton .75 2.00
HH2 Peter Forsberg .75 2.00
HH3 Martin St. Louis .60 1.50
HH4 Jose Theodore .60 1.50
HH5 Joe Sakic 1.00 2.50
HH6 Chris Pronger .50 1.25
HH7 Jaromir Jagr 1.50 4.00
HH8 Mario Lemieux 2.00 5.00
HH9 Wayne Gretzky 3.00 8.00
HH10 Eric Lindros 1.00 2.50
HH11 Sergei Fedorov 1.00 2.50
HH12 Alexander Ovechkin 1.50 4.00
HH13 Sidney Crosby 2.50 6.00
HH14 Jarome Iginla .60 1.50
HH15 Eric Staal .75 2.00
HH16 Martin Brodeur 1.25 3.00
HH17 Miikka Kiprusoff .50 1.25
HH18 Rick Nash .60 1.50
HH19 Ilya Kovalchuk .60 1.50
HH20 Dominik Hasek .75 2.00
HH21 Marian Gaborik .75 2.00
HH22 Patrice Bergeron .75 2.00
HH23 Mats Sundin .60 1.50
HH24 Markus Naslund .50 1.25
HH25 Dany Heatley .60 1.50

2006-07 Upper Deck MVP International Icons

COMPLETE SET (25) 15.00 40.00
STATED ODDS 1:8
II1 Teemu Selanne 1.25 3.00
II2 Ilya Kovalchuk .60 1.50
II3 Marian Hossa .50 1.25
II4 Marco Sturm .40 1.00
II5 Milan Hejduk .50 1.25
II6 Sergei Fedorov 1.00 2.50
II7 Mike Modano 1.00 2.50
II8 Nicklas Lidstrom .60 1.50
II9 Dominik Hasek .75 2.00
II10 Olli Jokinen .60 1.50
II11 Marian Gaborik .75 2.00
II12 Saku Koivu .60 1.50
II13 Tomas Vokoun .50 1.25
II14 Martin Brodeur 1.25 3.00
II15 Miroslav Satan .50 1.25
II16 Rick DiPietro .50 1.25
II17 Jaromir Jagr 1.50 4.00
II18 Martin Gerber .50 1.25
II19 Peter Forsberg .75 2.00
II20 Sidney Crosby 2.50 6.00
II21 Vincent Lecavalier .50 1.25
II22 Mats Sundin .60 1.50
II23 Nikolai Antropov .50 1.25
II24 Alexander Ovechkin 2.50 6.00
II25 Olaf Kolzig .60 1.50

2006-07 Upper Deck MVP Jerseys

STATED ODDS 1:24
OJAB A.Picard/B.Bochenski 4.00 10.00
OJAR Aebischer/Raycroft 6.00 15.00
OJBJ J.Bouwmeester/O.Jokinen 4.00 10.00
OJBK P.Bouchard/R.Kesler 4.00 10.00
OJBL M.Brodeur/H.Lundqvist 15.00 40.00
OJBN Brodeur/Niittymaki 12.00 30.00
OJBR P.Bergeron/M.Ryder 6.00 15.00
OJCF Crosby/Forsberg SP 40.00 80.00
OJCG J.Carter/S.Gomez 6.00 15.00
OJCJ C.Kobasew/J.Stoll 4.00 10.00
OJCO Crosby/Ovechkin SP 75.00 150.00
OJCR Z.Chara/W.Redden 4.00 10.00
OJCS J.Cheechoo/T.Selanne 8.00 20.00
OJDH P.Demitra/A.Hemsky 4.00 10.00
OJDK C.Drury/A.Kovalev 4.00 10.00
OJDM S.Doan/B.Morrow 6.00 15.00
OJDP K.Draper/M.Peca 4.00 10.00
OJDR Brodeur/Jagr 15.00 40.00
OJEP P.Elias/P.Prucha 4.00 10.00
OJER E.Staal/R.Smyth 6.00 15.00
OJES P.Elias/M.Satan 4.00 10.00
OJEV Staal/Lecavalier 8.00 20.00
OJFA S.Fedorov/J.Arnott 6.00 15.00
OJFD Fedorov/Datsyuk 8.00 20.00
OJFM F.Pisani/M.Lombardi 4.00 10.00
OJFN A.Frolov/L.Nagy 6.00 15.00
OJFR M.Fernandez/D.Roloson 6.00 15.00
OJGC R.Getzlaf/M.Cammalleri 5.00 12.00
OJGH Gaborik/Havlat 10.00 25.00
OJGL Gretzky/Lemieux SP 150.00 300.00
OJHB Heatley/Briere SP 15.00 40.00
OJHF M.Hossa/R.Fedotenko 4.00 10.00
OJHH M.Hejduk/A.Hemsky 4.00 10.00
OJHL N.Horton/A.Ladd 4.00 10.00
OJHM T.Hunter/R.Malone 4.00 10.00
OJHS Heatley/Steen 8.00 20.00
OJHV Hasek/Vokoun 10.00 25.00
OJIS Iginla/Smyth 8.00 20.00
OJJC C.Joseph/D.Cloutier 6.00 15.00
OJJF Jagr/Forsberg 10.00 25.00
OJJJ J.Stoll/J.Friesen 4.00 10.00
OJJL E.Jovanovski/J.Leopold 4.00 10.00
OJJM J.Stoll/M.Svatos 4.00 10.00
OJJS Jagr/Satan 10.00 25.00
OJKD O.Kolzig/M.Denis 6.00 15.00
OJKL Kiprusoff/Luongo 15.00 40.00
OJKR M.Koivu/T.Ruutu 6.00 15.00
OJKS J.Spezza/S.Koivu 6.00 15.00
OJKW P.Kariya/D.Weight 6.00 15.00
OJKZ Kariya/Zetterberg 8.00 20.00
OJLD Lundqvist/DiPietro 10.00 25.00
OJLF A.Ladd/T.Fleischmann 4.00 10.00
OJLJ V.Lecavalier/O.Jokinen 6.00 15.00
OJLK K.Lehtonen/O.Kolzig 6.00 15.00
OJLM Lidstrom/McCabe 10.00 25.00
OJLS R.Lang/S.Sullivan 4.00 10.00
OJLZ N.Lidstrom/S.Zubov 6.00 15.00
OJMJ A.Meszaros/M.Jurcina 4.00 10.00
OJMS M.St.Louis/S.Gagne 6.00 15.00
OJMT M.Modano/P.Turgeon 6.00 15.00
OJNJ S.Niedermayer/E.Jovanovski 4.00 10.00
OJNT R.Nash/K.Tkachuk 6.00 15.00
OJOC C.Osgood/T.Conklin 6.00 15.00
OJOK Ovechkin/Kovalchuk 20.00 50.00
OJOT Spezza/Sundin 10.00 25.00
OJPB C.Pronger/R.Blake 6.00 15.00
OJPJ C.Perry/J.Jokinen 4.00 10.00
OJPL D.Phaneuf/J.Liles 10.00 25.00
OJPN D.Phaneuf/S.Niedermayer 6.00 15.00
OJPO J.Pitkanen/S.Ozolinsh 4.00 10.00
OJPR J.Pitkanen/B.Rafalski 4.00 10.00
OJRB B.Richards/R.Brind'Amour 6.00 15.00
OJRL J.Roenick/E.Lindros 8.00 20.00
OJRM R.Luongo/M.Fernandez 6.00 15.00
OJRW B.Rafalski/B.Witt 4.00 10.00
OJSA S.Samsonov/M.Afinogenov 4.00 10.00
OJSC S.Sullivan/K.Calder 4.00 10.00
OJSD M.Savard/C.Drury 4.00 10.00
OJSF T.Selanne/A.Frolov 6.00 15.00
OJSG Shanahan/Gagne 8.00 20.00
OJSH M.St.Louis/N.Horton 6.00 15.00
OJSK M.Sundin/S.Koivu 6.00 15.00
OJSL Shanahan/LeClair SP 15.00 40.00
OJSM Sakic/Modano 10.00 25.00
OJSN S.Samsonov/N.Antropov 4.00 10.00
OJSS M.Satan/M.Straka 4.00 10.00
OJST Sakic/Thornton 12.00 30.00
OJSV M.Svatos/J.Lupul 4.00 10.00
OJTG Turco/Giguere 8.00 20.00
OJTH K.Tkachuk/M.Havlat 4.00 10.00
OJTN A.Tanguay/M.Naslund 6.00 15.00
OJWA D.Weight/J.Arnott 4.00 10.00
OJWC D.Weight/K.Calder 4.00 10.00
OJWD Ward/Denis 8.00 20.00
OJWL Ward/Lehtonen 8.00 20.00
OJWW J.Williams/S.Weiss 4.00 10.00
OJZN Zetterberg/Nash 8.00 20.00

2006-07 Upper Deck MVP Last Line of Defense

COMPLETE SET (25) 10.00 25.00
STATED ODDS 1:8
LL1 Martin Brodeur 1.50 4.00
LL2 Miikka Kiprusoff .75 2.00
LL3 Henrik Lundqvist 2.00 5.00
LL4 Marty Turco 1.00 2.50
LL5 Cristobal Huet .75 2.00
LL6 Marc-Andre Fleury 1.50 4.00
LL7 Roberto Luongo 1.50 4.00
LL8 Cam Ward 1.00 2.50
LL9 Ryan Miller 1.00 2.50
LL10 Nikolai Khabibulin 1.00 2.50
LL11 Kari Lehtonen .75 2.00
LL12 Tomas Vokoun .75 2.00
LL13 Dwayne Roloson .75 2.00
LL14 Olaf Kolzig 1.00 2.50
LL15 Ed Belfour 1.00 2.50
LL16 Vesa Toskala .75 2.00
LL17 Jose Theodore 1.00 2.50
LL18 Curtis Joseph 1.00 2.50
LL19 Manny Fernandez .75 2.00
LL20 Dominik Hasek 1.25 3.00
LL21 Martin Gerber .75 2.00
LL22 Andrew Raycroft .75 2.00
LL23 Rick DiPietro .75 2.00
LL24 Hannu Toivonen .75 2.00
LL25 Manny Legace .75 2.00

2007-08 Upper Deck MVP

This 350-card set was released in October, 2007. The set was issued into the hobby in eight-card packs, with a $1.99 SRP, which came 24-packs to a box. Cards numbered 1-300 feature veterans while cards 301-350 are Rookie Cards which were inserted into packs at a stated rate of onein two. In addition, Cards numbered 351-380 were issued as three-card packs as redemptions from packs which were inserted at a stated rate of one in 24. By February 2008, all the MVP

redeemed rookies were live and we have notated that information in our checklist.
COMPLETE SET (380) 75.00 150.00
COMP.SET w/o RCs (300) 15.00 40.00
351-380 ISSUED IN 3-CARD RED.PACKS
1 Joe Sakic .30 .75
2 Brett Clark .12 .30
3 Peter Budaj .15 .40
4 Marek Svatos .12 .30
5 Andrew Brunette .12 .30
6 Paul Stastny .20 .50
7 Milan Hejduk .15 .40
8 Wojtek Wolski .15 .40
9 John-Michael Liles .12 .30
10 Tyler Arnason .12 .30
11 Jose Theodore .20 .50
12 Martin Havlat .20 .50
13 Patrick Sharp .20 .50
14 Nikolai Khabibulin .20 .50
15 Duncan Keith .20 .50
16 Jason Williams .12 .30
17 Radim Vrbata .15 .40
18 Brent Seabrook .20 .50
19 Patrick Lalime .15 .40
20 Jeff Hamilton .12 .30
21 Tuomo Ruutu .20 .50
22 Rick Nash .20 .50
23 Fredrik Norrena .12 .30
24 Fredrik Modin .12 .30
25 Gilbert Brule .15 .40
26 Jody Shelley .12 .30
27 David Vyborny .12 .30
28 Pascal Leclaire .15 .40
29 Sergei Fedorov .30 .75
30 Nikolai Zherdev .12 .30
31 Rostislav Klesla .12 .30
32 Doug Weight .20 .50
33 Jay McClement .12 .30
34 Manny Legace .15 .40
35 Barret Jackman .12 .30
36 David Backes .20 .50
37 Lee Stempniak .12 .30
38 Brad Boyes .12 .30
39 Eric Brewer .12 .30
40 Jason Bacashihua .15 .40
41 Patrice Bergeron .25 .60
42 Zdeno Chara .20 .50
43 Tim Thomas .25 .60
44 Marco Sturm .12 .30
45 Chuck Kobasew .12 .30
46 Glen Murray .15 .40
47 Phil Kessel .25 .60
48 Hannu Toivonen .15 .40
49 Marc Savard .12 .30
50 Dennis Wideman .12 .30
51 Saku Koivu .20 .50
52 Chris Higgins .12 .30
53 Andrei Markov .20 .50
54 Cristobal Huet .15 .40
55 Guillaume Latendresse .15 .40
56 Sheldon Souray .12 .30
57 Tomas Plekanec .20 .50
58 Alex Kovalev .15 .40
59 Michael Ryder .12 .30
60 Maxim Lapierre .12 .30
61 Andrei Kostitsyn .15 .40
62 Roberto Luongo .25 .60
63 Markus Naslund .20 .50
64 Sami Salo .12 .30
65 Taylor Pyatt .12 .30
66 Daniel Sedin .20 .50
67 Henrik Sedin .20 .50
68 Kevin Bieksa .15 .40
69 Brendan Morrison .12 .30
70 Ryan Kesler .25 .60
71 Mattias Ohlund .12 .30
72 Trevor Linden .20 .50
73 Alexander Ovechkin .75 2.00
74 Mike Green .20 .50
75 Brent Johnson .15 .40
76 Jiri Novotny .12 .30
77 Chris Clark .12 .30
78 Matt Pettinger .12 .30
79 Brian Pothier .12 .30
80 Alexander Semin .20 .50
81 Olaf Kolzig .20 .50
82 Shane Doan .15 .40
83 Mikael Tellqvist .15 .40
84 Zbynek Michalek .12 .30
85 Keith Ballard .12 .30
86 Owen Nolan .15 .40
87 Steven Reinprecht .12 .30
88 Derek Morris .12 .30
89 Ed Jovanovski .15 .40
90 Curtis Joseph .20 .50
91 Martin Brodeur .40 1.00
92 Scott Gomez .15 .40
93 Travis Zajac .15 .40
94 Brian Rafalski .15 .40
95 Patrik Elias .20 .50
96 Jamie Langenbrunner .12 .30
97 Brian Gionta .15 .40
98 Johnny Oduya .15 .40
99 Jay Pandolfo .12 .30
100 John Madden .12 .30
101 Teemu Selanne .40 1.00
102 Chris Pronger .15 .40
103 Ilya Bryzgalov .20 .50
104 Dustin Penner .15 .40
105 Ryan Getzlaf .30 .75
106 Scott Niedermayer .20 .50
107 Chris Kunitz .20 .50
108 Corey Perry .20 .50
109 Andy McDonald .15 .40
110 Jean-Sebastien Giguere .20 .50
111 Jarome Iginla .20 .50
112 Matthew Lombardi .12 .30
113 Daymond Langkow .12 .30
114 Miikka Kiprusoff .15 .40
115 Robyn Regehr .12 .30
116 Dion Phaneuf .20 .50
117 Kristian Huselius .12 .30
118 Stephane Yelle .12 .30
119 Alex Tanguay .12 .30
120 Roman Hamrlik .15 .40
121 Tony Amonte .15 .40
122 Simon Gagne .20 .50
123 Martin Biron .15 .40
124 Joni Pitkanen .12 .30
125 R.J. Umberger .12 .30
126 Jeff Carter .20 .50
127 Mike Knuble .12 .30
128 Ben Eager .12 .30
129 Mike Richards .20 .50
130 Antero Niittymaki .15 .40
131 Eric Staal .25 .60
132 Ray Whitney .15 .40
133 Mike Commodore .12 .30
134 Cory Stillman .12 .30
135 John Grahame .12 .30
136 Rod Brind'Amour .20 .50
137 Erik Cole .15 .40
138 Cam Ward .20 .50
139 Glen Wesley .12 .30
140 Justin Williams .15 .40
141 Alexei Yashin .15 .40
142 Rick DiPietro .15 .40
143 Ryan Smyth .15 .40
144 Brendan Witt .12 .30
145 Jason Blake .12 .30
146 Chris Simon .12 .30
147 Viktor Kozlov .12 .30
148 Mike Sillinger .12 .30
149 Miroslav Satan .15 .40
150 Alexander Frolov .12 .30
151 Dan Cloutier .15 .40
152 Rob Blake .20 .50
153 Dustin Brown .20 .50
154 Patrick O'Sullivan .15 .40
155 Lubomir Visnovsky .12 .30
156 Anze Kopitar .30 .75
157 Mike Cammalleri .15 .40
158 Derek Armstrong .12 .30
159 Vincent Lecavalier .15 .40
160 Marc Denis .15 .40
161 Dan Boyle .15 .40
162 Eric Perrin .12 .30
163 Filip Kuba .12 .30
164 Brad Richards .20 .50
165 Ruslan Fedotenko .12 .30
166 Vaclav Prospal .12 .30
167 Martin St. Louis .20 .50
168 Johan Holmqvist .15 .40
169 Mats Sundin .20 .50
170 Ian White .12 .30
171 Matt Stajan .15 .40
172 Darcy Tucker .15 .40
173 Bryan McCabe .12 .30
174 Andrew Raycroft .15 .40
175 Kyle Wellwood .15 .40
176 Alexei Ponikarovsky .12 .30
177 Alexander Steen .20 .50
178 Tomas Kaberle .12 .30
179 Vesa Toskala .15 .40
180 Dwayne Roloson .15 .40
181 Petr Sykora .15 .40
182 Marc-Antoine Pouliot .12 .30
183 Raffi Torres .12 .30
184 Joffrey Lupul .15 .40
185 Steve Staios .12 .30
186 Jussi Markkanen .15 .40
187 Shawn Horcoff .12 .30
188 Jarret Stoll .15 .40
189 Ladislav Smid .12 .30
190 Ales Hemsky .15 .40
191 Olli Jokinen .15 .40
192 Rostislav Olesz .12 .30
193 Jay Bouwmeester .20 .50
194 Alex Auld .12 .30
195 Nathan Horton .20 .50
196 Mike Van Ryn .12 .30
197 Jozef Stumpel .12 .30
198 Stephen Weiss .12 .30
199 Tomas Vokoun .15 .40
200 Sidney Crosby .75 2.00
201 Evgeni Malkin .60 1.50
202 Ryan Whitney .15 .40
203 Mark Recchi .25 .60
204 Marc-Andre Fleury .30 .75
205 Sergei Gonchar .12 .30
206 Michel Ouellet .12 .30
207 Jordan Staal .20 .50
208 Colby Armstrong .12 .30
209 Erik Christensen .12 .30
210 Peter Forsberg .25 .60
211 Paul Kariya .25 .60
212 Chris Mason .15 .40
213 Shea Weber .15 .40
214 Jason Arnott .15 .40
215 Alexander Radulov .20 .50
216 J.P. Dumont .12 .30
217 Steve Sullivan .12 .30
218 Kimmo Timonen .12 .30
219 David Legwand .15 .40
220 Jaromir Jagr .50 1.25
221 Sean Avery .12 .30
222 Petr Prucha .12 .30
223 Henrik Lundqvist .25 .60
224 Martin Straka .12 .30
225 Michael Nylander .12 .30
226 Michal Rozsival .12 .30
227 Marek Malik .12 .30
228 Matt Cullen .12 .30
229 Brendan Shanahan .25 .60
230 Dominik Hasek .25 .60
231 Pavel Datsyuk .25 .60
232 Robert Lang .12 .30
233 Dan Cleary .15 .40
234 Nicklas Lidstrom .20 .50
235 Johan Franzen .20 .50
236 Tomas Holmstrom .15 .40
237 Kris Draper .12 .30
238 Mathieu Schneider .12 .30
239 Jiri Hudler .15 .40
240 Henrik Zetterberg .25 .60
241 Daniel Briere .20 .50
242 Thomas Vanek .25 .60
243 Ryan Miller .20 .50
244 Brian Campbell .15 .40
245 Chris Drury .15 .40
246 Andrew Peters .12 .30
247 Maxim Afinogenov .12 .30
248 Derek Roy .12 .30
249 Jason Pominville .20 .50
250 Drew Stafford .15 .40
251 Dany Heatley .20 .50
252 Ray Emery .15 .40
253 Wade Redden .12 .30
254 Chris Neil .12 .30
255 Mike Fisher .12 .30
256 Patrick Eaves .12 .30
257 Jason Spezza .20 .50
258 Daniel Alfredsson .20 .50
259 Martin Gerber .15 .40
260 Antoine Vermette .12 .30
261 Chris Phillips .12 .30
262 Joe Thornton .25 .60
263 Evgeni Nabokov .15 .40
264 Patrick Marleau .20 .50
265 Bill Guerin .20 .50
266 Milan Michalek .12 .30
267 Steve Bernier .12 .30
268 Matt Carle .12 .30
269 Jonathan Cheechoo .20 .50
270 Marc-Edouard Vlasic .12 .30
271 Joe Pavelski .20 .50
272 Mike Modano .30 .75
273 Jere Lehtinen .12 .30
274 Marty Turco .20 .50
275 Mike Ribeiro .15 .40
276 Sergei Zubov .15 .40
277 Brenden Morrow .15 .40
278 Jussi Jokinen .12 .30
279 Philippe Boucher .12 .30
280 Eric Lindros .30 .75
281 Kari Lehtonen .15 .40
282 Marian Hossa .15 .40
283 Keith Tkachuk .20 .50
284 Alexei Zhitnik .12 .30
285 Bobby Holik .12 .30
286 Slava Kozlov .12 .30
287 Ilya Kovalchuk .20 .50
288 Eric Belanger .12 .30
289 Mark Parrish .12 .30
290 Marian Gaborik .25 .60
291 Pavol Demitra .25 .60
292 Manny Fernandez .15 .40
293 Brian Rolston .15 .40
294 Mikko Koivu .15 .40
295 Pierre-Marc Bouchard .20 .50
296 Derek Boogaard .12 .30
297 Niklas Backstrom .20 .50
298 Roberto Luongo CL .25 .60
299 Vincent Lecavalier CL .15 .40
300 Sidney Crosby CL .75 2.00
301 Jeff Finger RC .75 2.00
302 Colin Fraser RC .75 2.00
303 Pierre Parenteau RC 1.00 2.50
304 Bryan Bickell RC 1.50 4.00
305 Tomas Popperle RC 1.00 2.50
306 Curtis Glencross RC 1.25 3.00
307 Marc Methot RC .75 2.00
308 David Krejci RC 2.50 6.00
309 Jonathan Sigalet RC .75 2.00
310 Petr Kalus RC .75 2.00
311 Jaroslav Halak RC 2.00 5.00
312 Duncan Milroy RC .75 2.00
313 Jannik Hansen RC 1.00 2.50
314 Jeff Schultz RC 1.00 2.50
315 Jamie Hunt RC .75 2.00
316 Daniel Carcillo RC 1.00 2.50
317 Andy Greene RC 1.00 2.50
318 Mark Fraser RC .75 2.00
319 Rod Pelley RC .75 2.00
320 David Clarkson RC 1.25 3.00
321 Aaron Rome RC 1.00 2.50
322 Drew Miller RC 1.00 2.50
323 David Moss RC 1.25 3.00
324 Tomi Maki RC .75 2.00
325 Scott Munroe RC .75 2.00
326 Ryan Parent RC .75 2.00
327 Frans Nielsen RC 1.25 3.00
328 Lauri Tukonen RC .75 2.00
329 Yutaka Fukufuji RC 1.00 2.50
330 John Zeiler RC .75 2.00
331 Joe Piskula RC .75 2.00
332 Jack Johnson RC 1.00 2.50
333 Tom Gilbert RC 1.00 2.50
334 Mathieu Roy RC .75 2.00
335 Zack Stortini RC .75 2.00
336 Bryan Young RC .75 2.00
337 Sebastien Bisaillon RC .75 2.00
338 Rob Schremp RC 1.00 2.50
339 Martin Lojek RC .75 2.00
340 Rich Peverley RC 1.25 3.00
341 Ryan Callahan RC 1.50 4.00
342 Daniel Girardi RC 1.00 2.50
343 Brandon Dubinsky RC 1.50 4.00
344 Matt Ellis RC 1.00 2.50
345 Patrick Kaleta RC .75 2.00
346 Mark Mancari RC 1.00 2.50
347 Danny Bois RC .75 2.00
348 Thomas Plihal RC 1.00 2.50
349 Tobias Stephan RC 1.00 2.50
350 Krys Barch RC 1.00 2.50
351 Jonathan Toews RC 8.00 20.00
352 Carey Price RC 10.00 25.00
353 Bobby Ryan RC 2.50 6.00
354 Sam Gagner RC 2.00 5.00
355 Patrick Kane RC 6.00 15.00
356 Nicklas Bergfors RC 1.00 2.50
357 Erik Johnson RC 1.50 4.00
358 Nicklas Backstrom RC 3.00 8.00
359 Anton Stralman RC 1.00 2.50
360 Jonathan Bernier RC 2.50 6.00
361 Bryan Little RC 1.50 4.00
362 Kris Russell RC 1.25 3.00
363 Andrew Cogliano RC 1.50 4.00
364 Marc Staal RC 1.50 4.00
365 Nick Foligno RC 2.00 5.00
366 Peter Mueller RC 1.25 3.00
367 Ondrej Pavelec RC 2.00 5.00
368 Martin Hanzal RC 1.25 3.00
369 Matt Smaby RC 1.00 2.50
370 Brian Elliott RC 2.00 5.00
371 Brett Sterling RC 1.00 2.50
372 Matt Niskanen RC 1.50 4.00
373 Devin Setoguchi RC 1.50 4.00
374 James Sheppard RC 1.00 2.50
375 Kyle Chipchura RC 1.50 4.00
376 Tyler Kennedy RC 1.50 4.00
377 Jiri Tlusty RC 1.50 4.00
378 Mason Raymond RC 1.50 4.00
379 David Perron RC 1.50 4.00
380 Milan Lucic RC 5.00 12.00

2007-08 Upper Deck MVP Gold Script

*VETS/100: 10X TO 25X BASIC CARDS
*301-350 ROOK/100: 1.2X TO 3X RC
*351-380 ROOK/25: 1.2X TO 3X RC
STATED PRINT RUN 100 SER.#'d SETS

2007-08 Upper Deck MVP Super Script

*VETS/25: 20X TO 50X BASIC CARDS
*301-350 ROOK/25: 4X TO 10X RC
*351-380 ROOK/25: 4X TO 10X RC
STATED PRINT RUN 25 SER.#'d SETS

2007-08 Upper Deck MVP Game Faces

COMPLETE SET (7) 6.00 15.00
STATED ODDS 1:8
GF1 Sidney Crosby 2.00 5.00
GF2 Jaromir Jagr 1.25 3.00
GF3 Jarome Iginla .50 1.25
GF4 Ilya Kovalchuk .50 1.25
GF5 Peter Forsberg .60 1.50
GF6 Joe Thornton .60 1.50
GF7 Alexander Ovechkin 2.00 5.00

2007-08 Upper Deck MVP Hart Candidates

COMPLETE SET (7) 6.00 15.00
STATED ODDS 1:8
HC1 Roberto Luongo .60 1.50
HC2 Sidney Crosby 2.00 5.00
HC3 Martin Brodeur 1.00 2.50
HC4 Joe Thornton .60 1.50
HC5 Vincent Lecavalier .40 1.00
HC6 Miikka Kiprusoff .40 1.00
HC7 Dany Heatley .50 1.25

2007-08 Upper Deck MVP Monumental Moments

COMPLETE SET (14) 8.00 20.00
STATED ODDS 1:8
MM1 Joe Sakic .75 2.00
MM2 Mats Sundin .50 1.25
MM3 Sidney Crosby 2.00 5.00
MM4 Martin Brodeur 1.00 2.50
MM5 Evgeni Malkin 1.50 4.00
MM6 Mark Recchi .60 1.50
MM7 Mike Modano .75 2.00
MM8 Joe Thornton .60 1.50
MM9 Brendan Shanahan .60 1.50
MM10 Daniel Briere .50 1.25
MM11 Roberto Luongo .60 1.50
MM12 Vincent Lecavalier .40 1.00
MM13 Daniel Alfredsson .50 1.25
MM14 Scott Niedermayer .50 1.25

2007-08 Upper Deck MVP New World Order

COMPLETE SET (14) 8.00 20.00
STATED ODDS 1:8
NW1 Sidney Crosby 2.00 5.00
NW2 Alexander Ovechkin 2.00 5.00
NW3 Milan Michalek .30 .75
NW4 Ryan Miller .50 1.25
NW5 Marian Gaborik .60 1.50
NW6 Anze Kopitar .75 2.00
NW7 Mikko Koivu .40 1.00
NW8 Henrik Zetterberg .60 1.50
NW9 Evgeni Malkin 1.50 4.00
NW10 Thomas Vanek .60 1.50
NW11 Marc-Andre Fleury .75 2.00
NW12 Henrik Lundqvist .60 1.50
NW13 Kari Lehtonen .40 1.00
NW14 Zach Parise .60 1.50

2007-08 Upper Deck MVP One on One Autographs

STATED ODDS 1:288
OABF Bouchard/Foy SP
OABR Morrison/Kesler
OABS Briere/Stafford 12.00 30.00
OABV Bernier/Vlasic
OABW Budaj/Wolski SP 40.00 80.00
OACA Higgins/Kostitsyn 10.00 25.00
OACK Kessel/Chara 15.00 40.00
OACS Cole/Staal 10.00 25.00
OADB Drury/Briere SP
OADM Drury/Miller SP
OAEM Edler/McIver 8.00 20.00
OAFK Frolov/Kopitar 20.00 50.00
OAGP Gomez/Parise SP 40.00 80.00
OAHH Hemsky/Horcoff 10.00 25.00
OAHK Kovalchuk/Hossa SP 40.00 80.00
OAHL Hejduk/Liles 10.00 25.00
OAHS Hejduk/Stastny 12.00 30.00
OAHZ Hasek/Zetterberg 40.00 80.00
OAIK Kovalchuk/Lehtonen 12.00 30.00
OAIP Iginla/Phaneuf SP 25.00 60.00
OAJF Stoll/Pisani 10.00 25.00
OAJS Jurcina/Stuart 8.00 20.00
OAJW Jokinen/Weiss 10.00 25.00
OAKK Khabibulin/Keith 12.00 30.00
OALB Boogaard/Laraque SP
OALM Lemieux/Malkin SP 100.00 200.00
OALP Prucha/Lundqvist 15.00 40.00
OAMK McDonald/Kunitz
OAMR McCabe/Raycroft 10.00 25.00
OAMV Michalek/Vlasic 8.00 20.00
OANZ Nash/Zherdev
OAOB Orr/Bourque
OAOM Ovechkin/Malkin SP 150.00 250.00
OAPB Bouchard/Parrish 12.00 30.00
OAPD Dawes/Prucha 8.00 20.00
OAPG Perry/Getzlaf 20.00 50.00
OAPK Kostitsyn/Perezhogin SP
OARG Redden/Gerber 10.00 25.00
OARL Latendresse/Ryder 40.00 80.00
OARS Raycroft/Steen 12.00 30.00
OASS Stastny/Stastny SP
OAST Schremp/Thoresen 10.00 25.00
OASZ Sullivan/Zidlicky 8.00 20.00
OATC Thornton/Cheechoo SP 40.00 100.00
OATK Tanguay/Kiprusoff 10.00 25.00
OATM Morrow/Turco
OATW Tucker/Williams 10.00 25.00
OAVM Vanek/MacArthur 15.00 40.00
OAZB Brule/Zherdev 10.00 25.00

2007-08 Upper Deck MVP One on One Jerseys

STATED ODDS 1:24
OOAJ Tanguay/Lupul 4.00 10.00
OOAK Antropov/Kostitsyn 4.00 10.00
OOBL Brodeur/Lundqvist 10.00 25.00
OOBP Boyes/Picard 3.00 8.00
OOBS Briere/Savard 5.00 12.00
OOBW Belfour/Ward 5.00 12.00
OOCB Crosby/Brodeur SP 40.00 100.00
OOCK Cola/Komisarek 3.00 8.00
OOCM Chara/Meszaros 5.00 12.00
OOCP Carter/Parise 6.00 15.00
OOCV Lombardi/Kesler 6.00 15.00
OODE DiPietro/Esche 4.00 10.00
OODI Rafalski/Witt 4.00 10.00
OODL Datsyuk/Lehtinen 6.00 15.00
OODM Doan/Morrow 4.00 10.00
OOFL Forsberg/Lidstrom 6.00 15.00
OOFT Fernan/Theodore 5.00 12.00
OOGC Giguere/Cloutier 5.00 12.00
OOGG Gagne/Gionta 5.00 12.00
OOGH Gaborik/Hejduk 6.00 15.00
OOHG Huet/Gerber 4.00 10.00
OOHK Heatley/Kovalchuk 5.00 12.00
OOHM Horcoff/Morrison 3.00 8.00
OOHR Heatley/Ryder 5.00 12.00
OOHT Heatley/Tanguay 5.00 12.00
OOHV Hasek/Vokoun 6.00 15.00
OOIN Iginla/Naslund 5.00 12.00
OOJD Bouw/Hamhuis 5.00 12.00
OOJE Jagr/Elias 12.00 30.00
OOJT Joseph/Turco 5.00 12.00
OOKD Kolzig/Denis 5.00 12.00
OOKN Kariya/Nash 6.00 15.00
OOLC Ladd/Craig 5.00 12.00
OOLJ Lecavalier/Jokinen 4.00 10.00
OOLK Luongo/Kiprusoff 6.00 15.00
OOLL Leclaire/Legace 4.00 10.00
OOLN Lehtonen/Niittymaki 4.00 10.00
OOLR Luongo/Roloson 6.00 15.00
OOLW Lang/Williams 3.00 8.00
OOMH Morrison/Hall 3.00 8.00
OOMK Murray/Kovalev 4.00 10.00
OOMM Marleau/Modano 8.00 20.00
OOMR McCabe/Redden 3.00 8.00
OONM Nagy/Michalek 3.00 8.00
OONY Straka/Satan 4.00 10.00
OOOH Ondrus/Hoggan 3.00 8.00
OOOL Osgood/Lalime 5.00 12.00
OOOM Ovechkin/Malkin 20.00 50.00
OOPJ Pronger/Jovo 4.00 10.00
OORH Havlat/Rolston 5.00 12.00
OORS Brind/Weiss 5.00 12.00
OORT Raycroft/Thomas 6.00 15.00
OOSA Sundin/Alfredsson 5.00 12.00
OOSC Selanne/Cheech 10.00 25.00
OOSF Sakic/Forsberg 8.00 20.00
OOSS Shanahan/Smyth 6.00 15.00
OOTL Thornton/Lindros 8.00 20.00
OOTM Torres/McCarty 3.00 8.00
OOVS Vanek/Steen 6.00 15.00
OOWH Weight/Handzus 5.00 12.00

2008-09 Upper Deck MVP

This set was released on December 2, 2008. The base set consists of 392 cards. Cards 1-300 feature veterans, and cards 301-392 are rookies.
COMPLETE SET (392) 150.00 300.00
COMP.SET w/o RCs (300) 15.00 40.00
1 Ryan Getzlaf .50 1.25
2 Corey Perry .30 .75
3 Teemu Selanne .60 1.50
4 Jean-Sebastien Giguere .30 .75
5 Chris Pronger .25 .60
6 Mathieu Schneider .20 .50
7 George Parros .20 .50
8 Scott Niedermayer .30 .75
9 Chris Kunitz .30 .75
10 Brendan Morrison .20 .50
11 Ilya Kovalchuk .30 .75
12 Eric Perrin .20 .50
13 Tobias Enstrom .20 .50
14 Eric Boulton .20 .50
15 Colby Armstrong .20 .50
16 Bryan Little .25 .60
17 Erik Christensen .20 .50
18 Kari Lehtonen .25 .60
19 Johan Hedberg .25 .60
20 Jason Williams .20 .50
21 Patrice Bergeron .40 1.00
22 Marc Savard .20 .50
23 Zdeno Chara .30 .75
24 Chuck Kobasew .20 .50
25 Phil Kessel .40 1.00
26 Tim Thomas .30 .75
27 Marco Sturm .20 .50
28 Milan Lucic .50 1.25
29 Tuukka Rask .30 .75
30 Derek Roy .20 .50
31 Jason Pominville .30 .75
32 Thomas Vanek .30 .75
33 Maxim Afinogenov .20 .50
34 Jochen Hecht .20 .50
35 Ales Kotalik .20 .50
36 Ryan Miller .30 .75
37 Drew Stafford .25 .60
38 Andrew Peters .20 .50
39 Daniel Paille .20 .50
40 Craig Rivet .20 .50
41 Patrick Lalime .25 .60
42 Todd Bertuzzi .30 .75
43 Robyn Regehr .20 .50
44 Jarome Iginla .30 .75
45 Dion Phaneuf .30 .75
46 Daymond Langkow .20 .50
47 Miikka Kiprusoff .25 .60
48 Matthew Lombardi .20 .50
49 Adrian Aucoin .20 .50
50 Mike Cammalleri .25 .60
51 Eric Staal .40 1.00
52 Ray Whitney .25 .60
53 Rod Brind'Amour .30 .75
54 Matt Cullen .20 .50
55 Justin Williams .25 .60
56 Cam Ward .30 .75
57 Scott Walker .20 .50
58 Sergei Samsonov .25 .60
59 Joni Pitkanen .20 .50
60 Patrick Kane .60 1.50
61 Jonathan Toews .75 2.00
62 Patrick Sharp .30 .75
63 Dustin Byfuglien .30 .75
64 Adam Burish .25 .60
65 Nikolai Khabibulin .30 .75
66 Duncan Keith .30 .75
67 Martin Havlat .30 .75
68 James Wisniewski .20 .50
69 Brian Campbell .25 .60
70 Cristobal Huet .25 .60
71 Paul Stastny .30 .75
72 Joe Sakic .50 1.25
73 Peter Forsberg .40 1.00
74 Ryan Smyth .25 .60
75 Wojtek Wolski .25 .60
76 Milan Hejduk .25 .60
77 Marek Svatos .20 .50
78 Ian Laperriere .20 .50
79 Peter Budaj .25 .60
80 T.J. Hensick .25 .60
81 Darcy Tucker .25 .60
82 Kristian Huselius .20 .50
83 Rick Nash .30 .75
84 Michael Peca .25 .60
85 Pascal Leclaire .25 .60
86 Fredrik Norrena .20 .50
87 Jared Boll .20 .50
88 Kris Russell .20 .50
89 R.J. Umberger .20 .50
90 Mike Ribeiro .25 .60
91 Mike Modano .50 1.25
92 Brad Richards .30 .75
93 Marty Turco .30 .75
94 Sergei Zubov .25 .60
95 Jere Lehtinen .20 .50
96 Steve Ott .20 .50
97 Brenden Morrow .25 .60
98 Sean Avery .20 .50
99 Philippe Boucher .20 .50
100 Ty Conklin .25 .60
101 Niklas Kronwall .25 .60
102 Jiri Hudler .25 .60
103 Valtteri Filppula .30 .75
104 Mikael Samuelsson .20 .50
105 Chris Osgood .30 .75
106 Henrik Zetterberg .40 1.00
107 Pavel Datsyuk .40 1.00
108 Nicklas Lidstrom .30 .75
109 Brian Rafalski .25 .60
110 Dan Cleary .25 .60
111 Tomas Holmstrom .25 .60
112 Johan Franzen .30 .75
113 Marian Hossa .25 .60
114 Erik Cole .25 .60
115 Gilbert Brule .20 .50
116 Ales Hemsky .25 .60
117 Shawn Horcoff .20 .50
118 Sam Gagner .25 .60
119 Dustin Penner .25 .60
120 Andrew Cogliano .25 .60
121 Zach Stortini .20 .50
122 Robert Nilsson .20 .50
123 Mathieu Garon .25 .60
124 Dwayne Roloson .25 .60
125 Lubomir Visnovsky .20 .50
126 Nathan Horton .25 .60
127 Stephen Weiss .20 .50
128 Jay Bouwmeester .30 .75
129 Tomas Vokoun .25 .60
130 David Booth .20 .50
131 Brett McLean .20 .50
132 Rostislav Olesz .20 .50
133 Cory Stillman .20 .50
134 Jarret Stoll .25 .60
135 Anze Kopitar .50 1.25
136 Alexander Frolov .20 .50
137 Dustin Brown .30 .75
138 Patrick O'Sullivan .25 .60
139 Jason LaBarbera .25 .60
140 Jack Johnson .20 .50
141 Andrew Brunette .20 .50
142 Marian Gaborik .40 1.00
143 Pierre-Marc Bouchard .30 .75
144 Brent Burns .40 1.00
145 James Sheppard .20 .50
146 Mikko Koivu .25 .60
147 Niklas Backstrom .30 .75
148 Josh Harding .30 .75
149 Derek Boogaard .20 .50
150 Marek Zidlicky .20 .50
151 Alex Tanguay .20 .50
152 Alex Kovalev .25 .60
153 Tomas Plekanec .30 .75
154 Andrei Markov .30 .75
155 Saku Koivu .30 .75
156 Andrei Kostitsyn .25 .60
157 Sergei Kostitsyn .20 .50
158 Chris Higgins .20 .50
159 Carey Price 1.25 3.00
160 Kyle Chipchura .25 .60
161 Guillaume Latendresse .20 .50
162 Georges Laraque .25 .60
163 Jason Arnott .25 .60
164 J.P. Dumont .20 .50
165 Shea Weber .25 .60
166 Martin Erat .20 .50
167 David Legwand .25 .60
168 Dan Ellis .20 .50
169 Jordin Tootoo .30 .75
170 Ryan Suter .25 .60
171 Brian Rolston .25 .60
172 Zach Parise .30 .75
173 Patrik Elias .30 .75
174 Brian Gionta .25 .60
175 Martin Brodeur .60 1.50
176 David Clarkson .25 .60
177 John Madden .20 .50
178 Jamie Langenbrunner .20 .50
179 Dainius Zubrus .20 .50
180 Travis Zajac .25 .60
181 Mark Streit .20 .50
182 Mike Comrie .25 .60
183 Bill Guerin .30 .75
184 Trent Hunter .20 .50
185 Rick DiPietro .25 .60
186 Chris Campoli .20 .50
187 Sean Bergenheim .20 .50
188 Jeff Tambellini .20 .50
189 Blake Comeau .20 .50
190 Doug Weight .30 .75
191 Nikolai Zherdev .20 .50
192 Scott Gomez .25 .60
193 Brendan Shanahan .40 1.00
194 Chris Drury .25 .60
195 Brandon Dubinsky .25 .60
196 Henrik Lundqvist .40 1.00
197 Colton Orr .20 .50
198 Stephen Valiquette .25 .60
199 Marc Staal .30 .75
200 Wade Redden .20 .50
201 Markus Naslund .25 .60
202 Jason Spezza .30 .75
203 Daniel Alfredsson .30 .75
204 Dany Heatley .30 .75
205 Antoine Vermette .20 .50
206 Mike Fisher .20 .50
207 Filip Kuba .20 .50
208 Chris Neil .20 .50
209 Chris Phillips .20 .50
210 Martin Gerber .25 .60
211 Mike Richards .30 .75
212 Daniel Briere .30 .75
213 Mike Knuble .20 .50
214 Jeff Carter .30 .75
215 Martin Biron .25 .60
216 Joffrey Lupul .25 .60
217 Kimmo Timonen .20 .50
218 Riley Cote .20 .50
219 Scott Hartnell .30 .75
220 Olli Jokinen .25 .60
221 Ilya Bryzgalov .25 .60
222 Shane Doan .25 .60
223 Peter Mueller .25 .60
224 Ed Jovanovski .25 .60
225 Martin Hanzal .25 .60
226 Daniel Winnik .20 .50
227 Daniel Carcillo .20 .50
228 Mikael Tellqvist .25 .60
229 Eric Godard .20 .50
230 Miroslav Satan .30 .75
231 Sidney Crosby 1.25 3.00
232 Evgeni Malkin 1.00 2.50
233 Jordan Staal .30 .75
234 Sergei Gonchar .20 .50
235 Ryan Whitney .30 .75
236 Petr Sykora .25 .60
237 Marc-Andre Fleury .50 1.25
238 Tyler Kennedy .25 .60
239 Rob Blake .30 .75
240 Doug Murray .20 .50
241 Joe Thornton .40 1.00
242 Milan Michalek .25 .60
243 Patrick Marleau .30 .75
244 Joe Pavelski .30 .75
245 Jonathan Cheechoo .30 .75
246 Jeremy Roenick .30 .75
247 Evgeni Nabokov .40 1.00
248 Devin Setoguchi .25 .60
249 Dan Boyle .25 .60
250 Chris Mason .25 .60
251 Brad Boyes .20 .50
252 Paul Kariya .40 1.00
253 Manny Legace .30 .75
254 David Backes .30 .75
255 Erik Johnson .25 .60
256 David Perron .25 .60
257 Keith Tkachuk .30 .75
258 Andy McDonald .25 .60
259 Lee Stempniak .20 .50
260 Radim Vrbata .25 .60
261 Ryan Malone .20 .50
262 Vincent Lecavalier .25 .60
263 Martin St. Louis .30 .75
264 Mike Smith .30 .75
265 Michel Ouellet .20 .50
266 Paul Ranger .20 .50
267 Shane O'Brien .20 .50
268 Jussi Jokinen .20 .50
269 Andrej Meszaros .20 .50
270 Mats Sundin .30 .75
271 Nikolai Antropov .25 .60
272 Tomas Kaberle .20 .50
273 Pavel Kubina .20 .50
274 Jason Blake .20 .50
275 Alexander Steen .30 .75
276 Jiri Tlusty .25 .60
277 Vesa Toskala .25 .60
278 Matt Stajan .25 .60
279 Steve Bernier .20 .50
280 Pavol Demitra .40 1.00
281 Daniel Sedin .30 .75
282 Henrik Sedin .30 .75
283 Ryan Kesler .40 1.00
284 Alexander Edler .20 .50
285 Kevin Bieksa .25 .60
286 Roberto Luongo .40 1.00
287 Taylor Pyatt .20 .50
288 Alexandre Burrows .30 .75
289 Jason Blake .20 .50
290 Jose Theodore .30 .75
291 Alexander Ovechkin 1.25 3.00
292 Nicklas Backstrom .50 1.25
293 Mike Green .30 .75
294 Viktor Kozlov .20 .50
295 Alexander Semin .30 .75
296 Donald Brashear .20 .50
297 Sergei Fedorov .50 1.25
298 Jarome Iginla CL .30 .75
299 Evgeni Malkin CL 1.00 2.50
300 Alexander Ovechkin CL 1.25 3.00
301 Tyler Plante RC 1.00 2.50
302 Tom Sestito RC 1.25 3.00
303 Tom Cavanagh RC 1.00 2.50
304 Tim Ramholt RC 1.00 2.50
305 Tim Conboy RC 1.00 2.50
306 Theo Peckham RC 1.25 3.00
307 Teddy Purcell RC 1.50 4.00
308 Steve Mason RC 2.00 5.00
309 Shawn Matthias RC 1.25 3.00
310 Sami Lepisto RC 1.00 2.50
311 Ryan Stone RC .75 2.00
312 Robbie Earl RC .75 2.00
313 Zach Bogosian RC 1.25 3.00
314 Pascal Pelletier RC .75 2.00
315 Niklas Hjalmarsson RC 2.00 5.00
316 Mike Mole RC 1.00 2.50
317 Mike Iggulden RC 1.00 2.50
318 Mike Brown RC 1.50 4.00
319 Mattias Ritola RC 1.00 2.50
320 Matt D'Agostini RC 1.00 2.50
321 Mark Fistric RC 1.00 2.50
322 Marc-Andre Gragnani RC 1.00 2.50
323 Lauri Korpikoski RC .75 2.00
324 Kyle Turris RC 2.00 5.00
325 Kyle Okposo RC 1.25 3.00
326 Kyle Greentree RC 1.25 3.00
327 Blake Wheeler RC 3.00 8.00
328 Justin Abdelkader RC 2.00 5.00
329 Jordan LaVallee RC 1.25 3.00
330 Jordan Hendry RC 1.00 2.50
331 Jonathan Ericsson RC 1.25 3.00
332 Jon Filewich RC 1.00 2.50
333 Joey Mormina RC 1.00 2.50
334 Joe Jensen RC 1.25 3.00
335 Jesse Winchester RC .75 2.00
336 Jack Hillen RC 1.00 2.50
337 Ilya Zubov RC 1.00 2.50
338 Garrett Stafford RC 1.25 3.00
339 Erik Ersberg RC 1.00 2.50
340 Derick Brassard RC 1.00 2.50
341 David Brine RC .75 2.00
342 Darryl Boyce RC 1.00 2.50
343 Darren Helm RC 1.25 3.00
344 Danny Taylor RC 1.00 2.50
345 Dan LaCosta RC 1.25 3.00
346 Corey Locke RC 1.00 2.50
347 Colin Stuart RC 1.00 2.50
348 Cody McLeod RC 1.00 2.50
349 Clay Wilson RC .75 2.00
350 Claude Giroux RC 2.50 6.00
351 Chris Minard RC 1.25 3.00
352 Brian Lee RC 1.00 2.50
353 Brian Boyle RC 1.00 2.50
354 Brandon Nolan RC 1.00 2.50
355 Boris Valabik RC 1.25 3.00
356 B.J. Crombeen RC .75 2.00
357 Andrew Murray RC 1.00 2.50
358 Andrew Ebbett RC .75 2.00
359 Alex Goligoski RC 1.50 4.00
360 Alex Foster RC 1.00 2.50
361 Adam Pineault RC 1.00 2.50
362 Adam Pardy RC 1.00 2.50
363 Brandon Sutter RC 1.25 3.00
364 Jakub Voracek RC 2.50 6.00
365 Michael Frolik RC 1.25 3.00
366 James Neal RC 2.50 6.00
367 Drew Doughty RC 3.00 8.00
368 Wayne Simmonds RC 2.00 5.00
369 Oscar Moller RC 1.00 2.50
370 Colton Gillies RC 1.00 2.50
371 Ryan Jones RC 1.25 3.00
372 Patric Hornqvist RC 1.25 3.00
373 Anssi Salmela RC 1.25 3.00
374 Luca Sbisa RC .75 2.00
375 Jared Ross RC 1.25 3.00
376 Mikkel Boedker RC 1.50 4.00
377 Patrik Berglund RC 1.00 2.50
378 Chris Porter RC 1.25 3.00
379 T.J. Oshie RC 2.50 6.00
380 Alex Pietrangelo RC 1.50 4.00
381 Steven Stamkos RC 6.00 15.00
382 Vladimir Mihalik RC .75 2.00
383 Janne Niskala RC 1.25 3.00
384 Nikolai Kulemin RC 1.25 3.00
385 Luke Schenn RC 1.50 4.00
386 John Mitchell RC 1.00 2.50
387 Jonas Frogren RC .75 2.00
388 Derek Dorsett RC 1.50 4.00
389 Viktor Tikhonov RC 1.00 2.50

390 Kevin Porter RC 1.00 2.50
391 Paul Bissonnette RC 1.50 4.00
392 Zach Fitzgerald RC 1.25 3.00

2008-09 Upper Deck MVP Gold Script

*1-300 VETS: 2.5X TO 6X BASIC CARDS
*301-392 ROOKIES: .8X TO 2X BASIC RC
STATED PRINT RUN 100 SERIAL #'d SETS
292 Nicklas Backstrom 3.00 8.00
381 Steven Stamkos 15.00 40.00

2008-09 Upper Deck MVP Super Script

*1-300 VETS: 6X TO 15X BASIC CARDS
*301-392 ROOKIES: 2X TO 5X BASIC RC
STATED PRINT RUN 25 SER.#'d SETS
292 Nicklas Backstrom 8.00 20.00
381 Steven Stamkos 30.00 80.00

2008-09 Upper Deck MVP Alexander the Gr8

COMPLETE SET (8) 6.00 15.00
COMMON OVECHKIN (A01-A08) 1.25 3.00

2008-09 Upper Deck MVP First Line Phenoms

COMPLETE SET (15) 8.00 20.00
FL1 Alexander Ovechkin 2.00 5.00
FL2 Marian Gaborik .60 1.50
FL3 Andrei Kostitsyn .40 1.00
FL4 Evgeni Malkin 1.50 4.00
FL5 Jonathan Toews 1.25 3.00
FL6 Mike Richards .50 1.25
FL7 Nicklas Backstrom .75 2.00
FL8 Patrick Kane 1.00 2.50
FL9 Paul Stastny .50 1.25
FL10 Peter Mueller .40 1.00
FL11 Ryan Getzlaf .75 2.00
FL12 Sam Gagner .40 1.00
FL13 Sidney Crosby 2.00 5.00
FL14 Thomas Vanek .50 1.25
FL15 Zach Parise .50 1.25

2008-09 Upper Deck MVP Magnificent Sevens

COMPLETE SET (7) 8.00 20.00
M7CP Carey Price 3.00 8.00
M7CW Cam Ward .75 2.00
M7GL Guy Lafleur 1.00 2.50
M7MB Martin Brodeur 1.50 4.00
M7PL Pat LaFontaine .75 2.00
M7TB Turk Broda .75 2.00
M7WG Wayne Gretzky 4.00 10.00

2008-09 Upper Deck MVP Marked by Valor

COMPLETE SET (15) 10.00 25.00

2008-09 Upper Deck MVP One on One Autographs

ABC D.Cleary/B.Boyes 12.00 30.00
ABD Dubinsky/Clarkson 15.00 40.00
ABF M.Brodeur/M.Fleury
ABJ J.Johnson/B.Bell
ABN R.Nash/B.Boyes
ABW D.Boyle/N.Welch 6.00 15.00
ACB N.Backstrom/J.Carter 25.00 60.00
ACF N.Foligno/K.Chipchura 10.00 25.00
ACS A.Cogliano/J.Sheppard
ADC J.Carter/C.Drury 15.00 40.00
ADD S.Downie/B.Dubinsky 15.00 40.00
ADH Harding/Drouin-Deslauriers 8.00 20.00
ADJ D.Setoguchi/J.Pavelski 12.00 30.00
ADK C.Drury/P.Kessel
AED E.Johnson/D.Byfuglien 8.00 20.00
AES P.Elias/M.Satan 15.00 40.00
AFG D.Girardi/M.Fraser 10.00 25.00
AFM E.Malkin/M.Fleury 60.00 100.00
AFT J.Tlusty/N.Foligno 15.00 40.00
AGP J.Pominville/S.Gomez
AGR G.Moore/R.Pelley 15.00 40.00
AHB P.Budaj/M.Hejduk 15.00 40.00
AHM R.Malone/N.Horton 12.00 30.00
AHR M.Raymond/J.Hansen 15.00 40.00
AHS J.Sheppard/T.Hensick 12.00 30.00
AHV D.Heatley/T.Vanek
AIG J.Iginla/S.Gagner
AJB J.Bernier/J.Johnson 12.00 30.00
AKK A.Kostitsyn/S.Kostitsyn 20.00 50.00
AKL G.Latendresse/P.Kessel 15.00 40.00
AKP P.Kane/D.Perron 20.00 50.00
AKS E.Staal/I.Kovalchuk
AKT D.Krejci/J.Tlusty 15.00 40.00
ALK N.Lidstrom/T.Kaberle
ALS E.Staal/V.Lecavalier
AMG R.Getzlaf/B.Morrow 15.00 40.00
AMK M.Michalek/L.Kaspar 8.00 20.00
ANY M.Staal/R.Callahan 10.00 25.00
AOM A.Ovechkin/E.Malkin
APA P.Mueller/A.Kopitar 25.00 60.00
APK C.Perry/A.Kopitar 15.00 40.00
APM C.Phillips/B.McCabe 8.00 20.00
APP D.Penner/M.Pouliot 10.00 25.00
APR C.Price/T.Rask 25.00 60.00
APS P.Stastny/D.Penner
APT C.Price/J.Tlusty 25.00 60.00
ARG S.Gagner/M.Raymond
ARM M.Ribeiro/B.Morrow 10.00 25.00
ARP K.Russell/A.Picard
ART R.Smyth/T.Hensick
ASD D.Sedin/H.Sedin 12.00 30.00
ASH M.Stajan/C.Higgins 10.00 25.00
ASS M.Staal/J.Staal 12.00 30.00
ATG J.Thornton/R.Getzlaf
ATK P.Kane/J.Toews 50.00 100.00
AVL K.Lehtonen/T.Vokoun
AWH N.Horton/S.Weiss
AZC T.Zajac/D.Clarkson 12.00 30.00
AZT J.Toews/H.Zetterberg

2008-09 Upper Deck MVP Two on Two Jerseys

J2AWLS Arnt/Webr/Lgwnd/Sullvn 6.00 15.00
J2BDLP Brod/Prise/Lndqvst/Drury 15.00 40.00
J2BECP Brod/Parise/Elias/Gnta 15.00 40.00
J2BGRC Gagne/Rchrds/Crtr/Biron 8.00 20.00
J2BNLE Enstrm/Niska/Bksa/Lund 6.00 15.00
J2BTTL Tosk/Blake/Thms/Lucic 12.50 30.00
J2CHSN Crsby/Htly/Spza/Nash 12.00 30.00
J2DCKM Doan/Miler/Kopitr/Clder 12.00 30.00
J2DSTC Drury/Shan/Tamb/Cmrie 10.00 25.00
J2DZSK Zettr/Datsyk/Kane/Shrp 10.00 25.00
J2FCMS Crsby/Malkin/Flry/Staal 30.00 80.00
J2FGOB Ovech/Back/Grn/Fedor 30.00 80.00
J2GBSC Crsby/Satn/Bre/Ggne 30.00 80.00
J2GBSO Ggne/Brie/Ovch/Flsch 12.00 30.00
J2GCDA Gmez/Drury/Conly/Afing 6.00 15.00
J2GCOM Crsby/Mlkin/Ovch/Gren 60.00 120.00
J2HDSK Hasek/Drapr/Shrp/Khab 10.00 25.00
J2HHSB Osgd/Hlmst/Svtos/Budaj 8.00 20.00
J2HLDZ Zett/Lids/Hasek/Dtsyk 10.00 25.00
J2JSDL Lndq/Zhrdv/DiPiet/Hntr 10.00 25.00
J2KGBK Gabrik/Koiv/Brnr/Ksler 10.00 25.00
J2KKSJ Koivu/Kovl/Snd/Jseph 8.00 20.00
J2KPKL Koivu/Plkn/Latnd/Kov 8.00 20.00
J2KSLW Staal/Ward/Kvlck/Leht 10.00 25.00
J2KTAW Kriya/Tkch/Arnt/Webr 10.00 25.00
J2KTBP Kriya/Boyes/Tkch/Pron 10.00 25.00
J2LBSD Lngo/Bern/Sdin/Demit 10.00 25.00
J2LJLT Lngo/Josph/Lclre/Thms 10.00 25.00
J2LNCP Phnf/Ldstrm/Niedr/Chra 8.00 20.00
J2LOHG Lngo/Ohlnd/Ggnr/Hrcf 10.00 25.00
J2LSBS Staal/Brnd/Lecv/St.Lu 10.00 25.00
J2MMNT Nabv/Mrlu/Trco/Mdno 12.00 30.00
J2MTNC Thrn/Chch/Marlu/Nabkv 10.00 25.00
J2MZLT Mdno/Trco/Leht/Zbov 12.00 30.00
J2NGKJ Getz/Niedr/Kpitr/Jhnsn 12.00 30.00
J2PDGB Gabrk/Bch/Brnr/Dmtra 10.00 25.00
J2PRRC Phanf/Rghr/Rolsn/Cole 8.00 20.00
J2RDTG Brod/DiPiet/Tosk/Grbr 12.00 30.00
J2SBHR St.L/Rngr/Hortn/Bouw 8.00 20.00
J2SCBK Brgrn/Kessl/Svrd/Chara 10.00 25.00
J2SDRC Rchrds/Crtr/Drury/Shan 10.00 25.00
J2SHSW Skic/Hjdk/Wlski/Smyth 12.00 30.00
J2SHVS Spez/Htley/Vanek/Staf 8.00 20.00
J2SHZS Zett/Hlms/Sund/Steen 10.00 25.00
J2SJGL Prise/Rlstn/Shan/Gomz 10.00 25.00
J2SKHG Gabrik/Kvu/Skic/Hjduk 10.00 25.00
J2SMRG Getz/Sene/Mdno/Ribro 15.00 40.00
J2SNGG Selne/Gtz/Nieder/Gig 15.00 40.00
J2SSHA Sndin/Antv/Htley/Spez 8.00 20.00
J2SSTS Sund/Steen/Tsk/Stjan 8.00 20.00
J2STMA Sund/Tskla/Millr/Afing 8.00 20.00
J2TCKJ Chch/Thrnt/Kpitr/Jhnsn
J2TCPG Thrnt/Chch/Getz/Perry 12.00 30.00
J2THGS Htley/Grbr/Stn/Tosk 8.00 20.00
J2TLLN Tkch/Lgce/Nsh/Leclre 8.00 20.00
J2TRBK Berg/Kssl/Thms/Ryder 10.00 25.00
J2VWKL Kovl/Leht/Vokn/Weiss 8.00 20.00
J2WBSW Staal/Brind/Wrd/Willi 10.00 25.00

2008-09 Upper Deck MVP Winter Classic

COMPLETE SET (20) 8.00 20.00
INSERTS IN SPECIAL RETAIL
WC1 Sidney Crosby 2.00 5.00
WC2 Chris Chelios .50 1.25
WC3 Pavel Datsyuk .60 1.50
WC4 Johan Franzen .50 1.25
WC5 Tomas Holmstrom .40 1.00
WC6 Marian Hossa .40 1.00
WC7 Nicklas Lidstrom .50 1.25
WC8 Chris Osgood .50 1.25
WC9 Brian Rafalski .40 1.00
WC10 Henrik Zetterberg .60 1.50
WC11 Brian Campbell .40 1.00
WC12 Martin Havlat .50 1.25
WC13 Cristobal Huet .40 1.00
WC14 Duncan Keith .50 1.25
WC15 Patrick Kane 1.00 2.50
WC16 Dustin Byfuglien .50 1.25
WC17 Brent Seabrook .50 1.25
WC18 Patrick Sharp .50 1.25
WC19 Jonathan Toews 1.25 3.00
WC20 Wrigley Field .30 .75

2009-10 Upper Deck MVP

COMPLETE SET (394) 250.00 400.00
COMP.SET w/o SPS (300) 12.00 30.00
ROOKIE STATED ODDS 1:2
1 Alexander Ovechkin 1.25 3.00
2 Nicklas Backstrom .50 1.25
3 Alexander Semin .30 .75
4 Mike Green .30 .75
5 Brooks Laich .30 .75
6 Tomas Fleischmann .20 .50
7 Jose Theodore .30 .75
8 Michael Nylander .20 .50
9 Eric Fehr .20 .50
10 Karl Alzner .20 .50
11 Roberto Luongo .40 1.00
12 Ryan Kesler .30 .75
13 Pavol Demitra .40 1.00
14 Henrik Sedin .30 .75
15 Kevin Bieksa .25 .60
16 Alexander Edler .20 .50
17 Steve Bernier .20 .50
18 Daniel Sedin .30 .75
19 Willie Mitchell .20 .50
20 Mason Raymond .30 .75
21 Jason Blake .20 .50
22 Alexei Ponikarovsky .20 .50
23 Francois Beauchemin .20 .50
24 Mikhail Grabovski .30 .75
25 Lee Stempniak .20 .50
26 Tomas Kaberle .20 .50
27 Nikolai Kulemin .25 .60
28 Luke Schenn .25 .60
29 Vesa Toskala .30 .75
30 Mike Komisarek .25 .60
31 Martin St. Louis .30 .75
32 Vincent Lecavalier .25 .60
33 Steven Stamkos .60 1.50
34 Steve Downie .20 .50
35 Ryan Malone .20 .50
36 Mike Smith .30 .75
37 Alex Tanguay .20 .50
38 Lukas Krajicek .20 .50
39 Paul Ranger .20 .50
40 Brad Boyes .20 .50
41 David Backes .30 .75
42 David Perron .20 .50
43 Patrik Berglund .20 .50
44 T.J. Oshie .50 1.25
45 Paul Kariya .40 1.00
46 Chris Mason .25 .60
47 Andy McDonald .25 .60
48 Keith Tkachuk .30 .75
49 Ty Conklin .25 .60
50 Joe Thornton .30 .75
51 Patrick Marleau .30 .75
52 Devin Setoguchi .25 .60
53 Joe Pavelski .30 .75
54 Rob Blake .30 .75
55 Evgeni Nabokov .25 .60
56 Dan Boyle .25 .60
57 Ryane Clowe .25 .60
58 Jonathan Cheechoo .30 .75
59 Marc-Edouard Vlasic .20 .50
60 Evgeni Malkin 1.00 2.50
61 Sidney Crosby 1.25 3.00
62 Chris Kunitz .30 .75
63 Jordan Staal .30 .75
64 Tyler Kennedy .25 .60
65 Marc-Andre Fleury .50 1.25
66 Maxime Talbot .30 .75
67 Pascal Dupuis .20 .50
68 Kristopher Letang .30 .75
69 Brooks Orpik .25 .60
70 Shane Doan .25 .60
71 Matthew Lombardi .20 .50
72 Ed Jovanovski .20 .50
73 Peter Mueller .25 .60
74 Scottie Upshall .20 .50
75 Martin Hanzal .25 .60
76 Mikkel Boedker .20 .50
77 Kyle Turris .30 .75
78 Ilya Bryzgalov .25 .60
79 Viktor Tikhonov .25 .60
80 Jeff Carter .30 .75
81 Mike Richards .30 .75
82 Simon Gagne .30 .75
83 Scott Hartnell .30 .75
84 Chris Pronger .25 .60
85 Claude Giroux .30 .75
86 Daniel Briere .30 .75
87 Kimmo Timonen .25 .60
88 Braydon Coburn .20 .50
89 Daniel Carcillo .20 .50
90 Daniel Alfredsson .30 .75
91 Jason Spozza .30 .75
92 Dany Heatley .30 .75
93 Nick Foligno .25 .60
94 Brian Elliott .25 .60
95 Pascal Leclaire .30 .75
96 Jarkko Ruutu .20 .50
97 Filip Kuba .20 .50
98 Mike Fisher .20 .50
99 Alex Kovalev .30 .75
100 Marian Gaborik .40 1.00
101 Sean Avery .25 .60
102 Chris Drury .25 .60
103 Chris Higgins .20 .50
104 Brandon Dubinsky .25 .60
105 Ryan Callahan .30 .75
106 Michal Rozsival .20 .50
107 Henrik Lundqvist .50 1.25
108 Wade Redden .20 .50
109 Marc Staal .30 .75
110 Mark Streit .20 .50
111 Kyle Okposo .30 .75
112 Doug Weight .30 .75
113 Frans Nielsen .20 .50
114 Trent Hunter .20 .50
115 Josh Bailey .25 .60
116 Rick DiPietro .25 .60
117 Blake Comeau .20 .50
118 Richard Park .20 .50
119 Martin Brodeur .60 1.50
120 Zach Parise .30 .75
121 Patrik Elias .30 .75
122 Jamie Langenbrunner .20 .50
123 Travis Zajac .25 .60
124 Dainius Zubrus .20 .50
125 David Clarkson .25 .60
126 Paul Martin .20 .50
127 Brian Rolston .25 .60
128 Colin White .20 .50
129 Pekka Rinne .40 1.00
130 J.P. Dumont .20 .50
131 Jason Arnott .25 .60
132 Shea Weber .25 .60
133 Martin Erat .20 .50
134 Ryan Suter .30 .75
135 David Legwand .25 .60
136 Jordin Tootoo .30 .75
137 Dan Hamhuis .25 .60
138 Dan Ellis .20 .50
139 Andrei Markov .30 .75
140 Andrei Kostitsyn .25 .60
141 Carey Price 1.25 3.00
142 Tomas Plekanec .30 .75
143 Maxim Lapierre .20 .50
144 Guillaume Latendresse .25 .60
145 Scott Gomez .25 .60
146 Max Pacioretty .40 1.00
147 Roman Hamrlik .20 .50
148 Brian Gionta .25 .60
149 Mikko Koivu .30 .75
150 Andrew Brunette .20 .50
151 Pierre-Marc Bouchard .30 .75
152 Niklas Backstrom .30 .75
153 Colton Gillies .30 .75
154 Owen Nolan .30 .75
155 James Sheppard .20 .50
156 Marek Zidlicky .20 .50
157 Antti Miettinen .20 .50
158 Cal Clutterbuck .20 .50
159 Anze Kopitar .50 1.25
160 Alexander Frolov .25 .60
161 Dustin Brown .25 .60
162 Jarret Stoll .25 .60
163 Drew Doughty .40 1.00
164 Jack Johnson .20 .50
165 Jonathan Quick .60 1.50
166 Erik Ersberg .25 .60
167 Justin Williams .25 .60
168 Ryan Smyth .25 .60
169 Tomas Vokoun .25 .60
170 Stephen Weiss .20 .50
171 David Booth .20 .50
172 Cory Stillman .20 .50
173 Nathan Horton .30 .75
174 Michael Frolik .25 .60
175 Bryan McCabe .25 .60
176 Keith Ballard .20 .50
177 Gregory Campbell .20 .50
178 Brett McLean .20 .50
179 Ales Hemsky .25 .60
180 Sheldon Souray .20 .50
181 Shawn Horcoff .20 .50
182 Tom Gilbert .20 .50
183 Patrick O'Sullivan .25 .60
184 Sam Gagner .25 .60
185 Andrew Cogliano .25 .60
186 Ethan Moreau .20 .50
187 Lubomir Visnovsky .20 .50
188 Nikolai Khabibulin .30 .75
189 Pavel Datsyuk .40 1.00
190 Henrik Zetterberg .40 1.00
191 Nicklas Lidstrom .30 .75
192 Brian Rafalski .20 .50
193 Valtteri Filppula .30 .75
194 Tomas Holmstrom .25 .60
195 Kris Draper .20 .50
196 Chris Osgood .30 .75
197 Niklas Kronwall .25 .60
198 Johan Franzen .30 .75
199 Mike Ribeiro .25 .60
200 Loui Eriksson .25 .60
201 Brad Richards .30 .75
202 Mike Modano .50 1.25
203 Steve Ott .20 .50
204 James Neal .30 .75
205 Matt Niskanen .25 .60
206 Krys Barch .20 .50
207 Brenden Morrow .25 .60
208 Marty Turco .30 .75
209 Steve Mason .25 .60
210 Rick Nash .25 .60
211 Kristian Huselius .20 .50
212 R.J. Umberger .25 .60
213 Jakub Voracek .30 .75
214 Antoine Vermette .20 .50
215 Derick Brassard .30 .75
216 Mike Commodore .20 .50
217 Marc Methot .20 .50
218 Fedor Tyutin .20 .50
219 David Jones .20 .50
220 Milan Hejduk .25 .60
221 Wojtek Wolski .20 .50
222 Paul Stastny .30 .75
223 John-Michael Liles .20 .50
224 Chris Stewart .25 .60
225 T.J. Hensick .20 .50
226 Cody McLeod .20 .50
227 Peter Budaj .25 .60
228 Patrick Kane .60 1.50
229 Jonathan Toews .60 1.50
230 Kris Versteeg .30 .75
231 Cristobal Huet .30 .75
232 Brian Campbell .25 .60
233 Patrick Sharp .30 .75
234 Duncan Keith .30 .75
235 Dustin Byfuglien .30 .75
236 Marian Hossa .25 .60
237 Cam Barker .20 .50
238 Ray Whitney .25 .60
239 Eric Staal .40 1.00
240 Tuomo Ruutu .20 .50
241 Rod Brind'Amour .30 .75
242 Sergei Samsonov .20 .50
243 Jussi Jokinen .20 .50
244 Cam Ward .30 .75
245 Joe Corvo .20 .50
246 Brandon Sutter .25 .60
247 Anton Babchuk .25 .60
248 Jarome Iginla .30 .75
249 Olli Jokinen .25 .60
250 Daymond Langkow .20 .50
251 Miikka Kiprusoff .25 .60
252 Craig Conroy .20 .50
253 Dion Phaneuf .40 1.00
254 Rene Bourque .20 .50
255 Dustin Boyd .20 .50
256 Jay Bouwmeester .30 .75
257 Cory Sarich .20 .50
258 Derek Roy .25 .60
259 Jason Pominville .30 .75
260 Thomas Vanek .30 .75
261 Tim Connolly .20 .50
262 Ryan Miller .30 .75
263 Drew Stafford .30 .75
264 Clarke MacArthur .20 .50
265 Daniel Paille .25 .60
266 Paul Gaustad .25 .60
267 Jochen Hecht .20 .50
268 Marc Savard .20 .50
269 Tim Thomas .30 .75
270 David Krejci .30 .75
271 Phil Kessel .40 1.00
272 Michael Ryder .20 .50
273 Zdeno Chara .30 .75
274 Blake Wheeler .30 .75
275 Patrice Bergeron .40 1.00
276 Milan Lucic .25 .60
277 Dennis Wideman .20 .50
278 Ilya Kovalchuk .30 .75
279 Slava Kozlov .20 .50
280 Todd White .20 .50
281 Bryan Little .30 .75
282 Rich Peverley .25 .60
283 Colby Armstrong .20 .50
284 Kari Lehtonen .25 .60
285 Zach Bogosian .25 .60
286 Nik Antropov .25 .60
287 Tobias Enstrom .30 .75
288 Ryan Getzlaf .50 1.25
289 Corey Perry .30 .75
290 Bobby Ryan .30 .75
291 Teemu Selanne .60 1.50
292 Saku Koivu .30 .75
293 George Parros .20 .50
294 Jonas Hiller .25 .60
295 Jean-Sebastien Giguere .30 .75
296 Andrew Ebbett .20 .50
297 Scott Niedermayer .30 .75
298 Alexander Ovechkin CL .75 2.00
299 Carey Price CL .75 2.00
300 Sidney Crosby CL .75 2.00
301 Brian Salcido RC 1.00 2.50
302 Luca Caputi RC 1.25 3.00
303 Spencer Machacek RC 1.25 3.00
304 Matt Beleskey RC 1.00 2.50
305 T.J. Galiardi RC 1.25 3.00
306 Michael Sauer RC 1.00 2.50
307 Yannick Weber RC 1.25 3.00
308 Jesse Joensuu RC 1.00 2.50
309 Cal O'Reilly RC 1.00 2.50
310 Grant Lewis RC 1.00 2.50
311 Tim Stapleton RC 1.25 3.00
312 Christian Hanson RC 1.25 3.00
313 Mikael Backlund RC 1.25 3.00
314 Artem Anisimov RC 1.25 3.00
315 Jhonas Enroth RC 1.50 4.00
316 Ivan Vishnevskiy RC 1.00 2.50
317 Riku Helenius RC 1.25 3.00
318 Kris Chucko RC 1.00 2.50
319 Matt Pelech RC 1.25 3.00
320 Michal Neuvirth RC 2.00 5.00
321 Ray Macias RC 1.00 2.50
322 Ville Leino RC 1.00 2.50
323 Taylor Chorney RC 1.25 3.00
324 John Negrin RC 1.25 3.00
325 Alexander Sulzer RC .75 2.00
326 Mike Santorelli RC 1.25 3.00
327 Tom Wandell RC 1.25 3.00
328 Andrew MacDonald RC .75 2.00
329 Kevin Quick RC .75 2.00
330 David Van Der Gulik RC 1.00 2.50
331 Jakub Petruzalek RC 1.25 3.00
332 Chris Durno RC 1.00 2.50
333 Peter Regin RC 1.00 2.50
334 Kurtis McLean RC 1.00 2.50
335 John Scott RC 1.25 3.00
336 Bryan Rodney RC 1.00 2.50
337 Riley Armstrong RC 1.00 2.50
338 Ryan Vesce RC 1.00 2.50
339 Brandon Segal RC 1.00 2.50
340 Antti Niemi RC 2.00 5.00
341 Derek Peltier RC .75 2.00
342 Matt Hendricks RC 1.00 2.50
343 Mike McKenna RC 1.00 2.50
344 Aaron MacKenzie RC 1.25 3.00
345 David Sloane RC 1.25 3.00
346 Jamie Fritsch RC 1.25 3.00
347 Geoff Kinrade RC 1.25 3.00
348 Tyson Strachan RC .75 2.00
349 Troy Bodie RC 1.00 2.50
350 Kevin Westgarth RC 1.00 2.50
351 Byron Bitz RC 1.00 2.50
352 Tim Wallace RC .75 2.00
353 Ben Lovejoy RC 1.25 3.00
354 Jaime Sifers RC 1.00 2.50
355 Sean Collins RC 1.00 2.50
356 Davis Drewiske RC 1.25 3.00
357 David Schlemko RC 1.00 2.50
358 Jay Beagle RC 1.50 4.00
359 Phil Oreskovic RC 1.25 3.00
360 Joel Rechlicz RC .75 2.00
361 Michael Vernace RC 1.00 2.50
362 Scott Lehman RC .75 2.00
363 Dan Turple RC 1.25 3.00
364 Matt Climie RC 1.00 2.50
365 Jamie Fraser RC 1.00 2.50
366 Per Ledin RC 1.25 3.00
367 Wes O'Neill RC 1.25 3.00
368 Sean Bentivoglio RC 1.00 2.50
369 Evander Kane RC 2.50 6.00
370 Tyler Myers RC 2.00 5.00
371 Matt Duchene RC 2.50 6.00
372 Ryan O'Reilly RC 2.00 5.00
373 Jamie Benn RC 4.00 10.00
374 Dmitri Kulikov RC 1.25 3.00
375 Alec Martinez RC 1.50 4.00
376 Teemu Laakso RC .75 2.00
377 John Tavares RC 10.00 25.00
378 Matt Gilroy RC 1.25 3.00
379 Michael Del Zotto RC 1.25 3.00
380 Erik Karlsson RC 3.00 8.00
381 James van Riemsdyk RC 2.50 6.00
382 Johan Backlund RC 1.25 3.00
383 Mika Pyorala RC 1.00 2.50
384 Jason Demers RC 2.00 5.00
385 Benn Ferriero RC 1.25 3.00
386 Frazer McLaren RC 1.00 2.50
387 Victor Hedman RC 2.50 6.00
388 Viktor Stalberg RC 1.25 3.00
389 Jay Rosehill RC 1.25 3.00
390 Jonas Gustavsson RC 3.00 8.00
391 Sergei Shirokov RC .75 2.00
392 Ilkka Pikkarainen RC 1.25 3.00
393 Colin Wilson RC 1.25 3.00
394 Tyler Bozak RC 2.00 5.00

2009-10 Upper Deck MVP Gold Script

*1-300 VETS/100: 3X TO 8X BASIC CARDS
*301-394 ROOKIES: 1.2X TO 3X BASIC CARDS
STATED PRINT RUN 100 SER.#'d SETS
302 Luca Caputi 4.00 10.00
377 John Tavares 30.00 80.00
390 Jonas Gustavsson 5.00 12.00

2009-10 Upper Deck MVP Super Script

*VETS: 6X TO 15X BASIC CARDS
*ROOKIES: 2.5X TO 6X BASIC CARDS
STATED PRINT RUN 25 SER.#'d SETS
2 Nicklas Backstrom 8.00 20.00
36 Mike Smith 5.00 12.00
68 Kristopher Letang 5.00 12.00
85 Claude Giroux 5.00 12.00
120 Zach Parise 5.00 12.00
302 Luca Caputi 8.00 20.00
307 Yannick Weber 8.00 20.00
377 John Tavares 100.00 200.00
390 Jonas Gustavsson 40.00 100.00

2009-10 Upper Deck MVP Hart Candidates

COMPLETE SET (30) 12.00 30.00
STATED ODDS 1:4
HC1 Tim Thomas .75 2.00
HC2 Nicklas Backstrom 1.25 3.00
HC3 Zach Parise .75 2.00
HC4 Evgeni Malkin 2.50 6.00
HC5 Jeff Carter .75 2.00
HC6 Eric Staal 1.00 2.50
HC7 Henrik Lundqvist 1.25 3.00
HC8 Carey Price 3.00 8.00
HC9 Tomas Vokoun .60 1.50
HC10 Thomas Vanek .75 2.00
HC11 Jason Spezza .75 2.00
HC12 Luke Schenn .60 1.50
HC13 Ilya Kovalchuk .75 2.00
HC14 Steven Stamkos 1.50 4.00
HC15 Rick DiPietro .60 1.50
HC16 Evgeni Nabokov .60 1.50
HC17 Henrik Zetterberg 1.00 2.50
HC18 Roberto Luongo 1.00 2.50
HC19 Jonathan Toews 1.50 4.00
HC20 Jarome Iginla .75 2.00
HC21 David Perron .50 1.25
HC22 Rick Nash .60 1.50
HC23 Ryan Getzlaf 1.25 3.00
HC24 Niklas Backstrom .75 2.00
HC25 Pekka Rinne 1.00 2.50
HC26 Sam Gagner .60 1.50
HC27 Mike Ribeiro .60 1.50
HC28 Peter Mueller .60 1.50
HC29 Anze Kopitar 1.25 3.00
HC30 Paul Stastny .75 2.00

2009-10 Upper Deck MVP Hart Winners

COMPLETE SET (10) 20.00 50.00
STATED ODDS 1:4
HW1 Alexander Ovechkin 4.00 10.00
HW2 Sidney Crosby 4.00 10.00
HW3 Joe Thornton 1.00 2.50
HW4 Martin St. Louis 1.00 2.50
HW5 Mark Messier 1.25 3.00
HW6 Bobby Hull 1.25 3.00
HW7 Gordie Howe 2.50 6.00
HW8 Mario Lemieux 3.00 8.00
HW9 Bobby Orr 3.00 8.00
HW10 Wayne Gretzky 5.00 12.00

2009-10 Upper Deck MVP One on One Autographs

STATED ODDS 1:240
AAB Bogosian/Alzner 8.00 20.00
ABB Brunnstrom/Boedker 8.00 20.00
ACH Conklin/Huet 10.00 25.00
ACR Cleary/Ryder 10.00 25.00
AES Ebbett/Simmonds 12.00 30.00
AFD Doughty/Fistric 12.00 30.00
AFS Frolik/Stamkos 20.00 50.00
AGR Gomez/Ryder 8.00 20.00
AGS Gillies/Stewart 10.00 25.00
AGV Vanek/Gaborik 12.00 30.00
AHB Hornqvist/Berglund 15.00 40.00
AHE Ersberg/Hiller 8.00 20.00
AKG Kunitz/Giroux 10.00 25.00
AKO Kane/Oshie 30.00 60.00
ALP Price/Lundqvist 30.00 80.00
ALS Schenn/Lee 15.00 30.00
AMD Mikkelson/Doughty 12.00 30.00
AOM Malkin/Ovechkin 60.00 120.00
APA Hemsky/Stastny 10.00 25.00
APC Clowe/Perry 12.00 30.00
APL Price/Leclaire 25.00 60.00
APW Wheeler/Pominville 10.00 25.00
ARG Redden/Green 10.00 25.00
ARP Parise/Richards 30.00 60.00
ARS Setoguchi/Ryan 10.00 25.00
ASO Ovechkin/Staal 40.00 100.00
AST Setoguchi/Turris 15.00 30.00
AVM Vokoun/Mason 8.00 20.00
AWB Bogosian/Weber 8.00 20.00
AWP Wheeler/Pacioretty 12.00 30.00

2009-10 Upper Deck MVP Two on Two Jerseys

STATED ODDS 1:24
JBDLP Lundq/Drury/Parse/Brod 8.00 20.00
JBFCP Parse/Brodr/Sid/Fleur 15.00 40.00
JBKMB Bodkr/Muellr/Kopitr/Brwn 10.00 25.00
JBOCR Bernir/Rymd/O'Sull/Coglino 6.00 15.00
JBSHS Spez/Heatly/Blak/Stmpnk 6.00 15.00
JBSOF Fleisch/Ovie/Stal/Brind 12.00 30.00
JCHRW Weber/Rin/Cmpbll/Huet 8.00 20.00
JCMZH Zettr/Holms/Sid/Malkn 20.00 50.00
JCOMB Malk/Sid/Ovie/Backs 20.00 50.00
JCTHS Schen/Tskla/Campb/Huet 6.00 15.00
JDGCM Dubn/Gabrik/Sid/Malkn 15.00 40.00
JDLSB Svats/Budaj/Lngo/Dmtr 8.00 20.00
JDZTK Datsk/Zettr/Toews/Kan 12.00 30.00
JEGAC Asham/Gagn/Eli/Clrksn 6.00 15.00
JGDGR Ggne/Richr/Dubin/Gabrik
JGDPP Gabrik/Drury/Pomin/Paille
JHBKS Koiv/Bchrd/Hejdk/Ststny 6.00 15.00
JHDSB Holms/Drapr/Bollnd/Sharp 6.00 15.00
JIKBS Ststny/Budaj/Kiprsf/Igin
JJICG Igin/Jokn/Cogln/Gagnr 6.00 15.00
JKCVB Brglnd/Clco/Ksla/Vorck 6.00 15.00
JKLHV Horton/Vokn/Koval/Lehtn 6.00 15.00
JLDHS Sharp/Huet/Lngo/Dmtra 8.00 20.00
JLJKD Demt/Lngo/Kiprsf/Jokn 8.00 20.00
JMCFB Brwn/Frol/Chch/Marlu 6.00 15.00
JMDTS Setog/Thrntn/Doan/Muelr 6.00 15.00
JMFBS Frolk/Booth/Stamk/Malon 12.00 30.00
JMSKS Markv/Kostit/Stajn/Schen 6.00 15.00
JNDLW Dubin/Naslnd/Lucic/Wheel 6.00 15.00
JNHBO O'Sulli/Horcf/Bouchrd/Noln
JNJIB Noln/Bouchrd/Jokn/Igin
JNMKB Bouchrd/Koiv/Neal/Mdno 10.00 25.00
JNSPK Sharp/Kane/Peca/Nash 12.00 30.00
JPLWE Pitknn/Ward/Leht/Enstrm 6.00 15.00
JRCMS Rich/Cartr/Malkn/Staal 20.00 50.00
JRRDM Richrds/Ribir/Doan/Muelr 6.00 15.00
JRTCS Carle/Timon/Staal/Redden 6.00 15.00
JSBHJ Stillmn/Hortn/Jokin/Brind 6.00 15.00
JSDGB Getzlf/Selan/Boedkr/Doan 12.00 30.00
JSKLS Little/Koval/St.L/Stamk 12.00 30.00
JSORW Osgd/Webr/Rinne/Sturt 8.00 20.00
JSRBV Savard/Bergern/Roy/Vank 10.00 25.00
JTCRM Richs/Mod/Chch/Thrntn 10.00 25.00
JTJLS Jurcn/Theo/Lund/Staal 10.00 25.00
JTMSH Tskla/Hollwg/Staffrd/Millr 6.00 15.00
JTPGS Getzlf/Perry/Thrntn/Seto
JTWCG Wolski/Tuckr/Gagnr/Cogl 5.00 12.00
JWNDL Wght/DiPit/Naslnd/Lund 8.00 20.00
JWNJD Dgty/Jhsn/Whtny/Nied 8.00 20.00

2009-10 Upper Deck MVP Winter Classic

WC1 Jeff Carter 1.00 2.50
WC2 Daniel Briere 1.00 2.50
WC3 Chris Pronger .75 2.00
WC4 Ray Emery .75 2.00
WC5 Mike Richards 1.00 2.50
WC6 Simon Gagne 1.00 2.50
WC7 Claude Giroux 1.00 2.50
WC8 Daniel Carcillo .60 1.50
WC9 Scott Hartnell 1.00 2.50
WC10 Michael Ryder .60 1.50
WC11 Tim Thomas 1.00 2.50
WC12 Blake Wheeler 1.00 2.50
WC13 Zdeno Chara 1.00 2.50
WC14 Milan Lucic .75 2.00
WC15 Marc Savard .60 1.50
WC16 David Krejci 1.00 2.50
WC17 Mark Recchi 1.25 3.00
WC18 Patrice Bergeron 1.25 3.00
WC19 City of Boston .60 1.50
WC20 Wrigley Field .60 1.50

2011-12 Upper Deck MVP

COMPLETE SET (100) 40.00 100.00
COMP.SET w/o SPs (88) 12.00 30.00
MVP INSERTED IN VICTORY PACKS
1 Ryan Getzlaf .60 1.50
2 Corey Perry .40 1.00
3 Bobby Ryan .40 1.00
4 Evander Kane .40 1.00
5 Dustin Byfuglien .40 1.00
6 Ondrej Pavelec .40 1.00
7 Zdeno Chara .40 1.00
8 Nathan Horton .40 1.00
9 Tim Thomas .40 1.00
10 Milan Lucic .40 1.00
11 Derek Roy .30 .75
12 Ryan Miller .40 1.00
13 Jarome Iginla .40 1.00
14 Miikka Kiprusoff .40 1.00
15 Cam Ward .40 1.00
16 Eric Staal .50 1.25
17 Jeff Skinner .40 1.00
18 Duncan Keith .40 1.00
19 Patrick Kane .75 2.00
20 Patrick Sharp .40 1.00
21 Jonathan Toews .75 2.00
22 Matt Duchene .40 1.00
23 Paul Stastny .40 1.00
24 Erik Johnson .25 .60
25 Derick Brassard .40 1.00
26 Rick Nash .40 1.00
27 Loui Eriksson .30 .75
28 Mike Ribeiro .30 .75
29 Brad Richards .40 1.00
30 Henrik Zetterberg .50 1.25
31 Nicklas Lidstrom .40 1.00
32 Pavel Datsyuk .50 1.25
33 Taylor Hall .75 2.00
34 Jordan Eberle .40 1.00
35 Stephen Weiss .30 .75
36 Jacob Markstrom .40 1.00
37 Drew Doughty .40 1.00
38 Jonathan Quick .60 1.50
39 Anze Kopitar .60 1.50
40 Martin Havlat .30 .75
41 Niklas Backstrom .40 1.00
42 Mikko Koivu .30 .75
43 Tomas Plekanec .40 1.00
44 Michael Cammalleri .30 .75
45 Carey Price 1.25 3.00
46 P.K. Subban .75 2.00
47 Patric Hornqvist .30 .75
48 Shea Weber .30 .75
49 Ilya Kovalchuk .40 1.00
50 Martin Brodeur .75 2.00
51 Zach Parise .40 1.00
52 Matt Moulson .30 .75
53 John Tavares .75 2.00
54 Brandon Dubinsky .30 .75
55 Henrik Lundqvist .50 1.25
56 Marian Gaborik .50 1.25
57 Daniel Alfredsson .40 1.00
58 Jason Spezza .40 1.00
59 Jeff Carter .40 1.00
60 Claude Giroux .40 1.00
61 Sergei Bobrovsky .40 1.00
62 Mike Richards .40 1.00
63 Ilya Bryzgalov .40 1.00
64 Shane Doan .30 .75
65 Evgeni Malkin 1.25 3.00
66 Kristopher Letang .40 1.00
67 Marc-Andre Fleury .60 1.50
68 Sidney Crosby 1.50 4.00
69 Joe Thornton .40 1.00
70 Patrick Marleau .40 1.00
71 Dany Heatley .30 .75
72 Chris Stewart .30 .75
73 David Backes .40 1.00
74 Jaroslav Halak .40 1.00
75 Steven Stamkos .75 2.00
76 Martin St. Louis .40 1.00
77 Vincent Lecavalier .30 .75
78 Phil Kessel .50 1.25
79 Nikolai Kulemin .40 1.00
80 Dion Phaneuf .40 1.00
81 Daniel Sedin .40 1.00
82 Henrik Sedin .40 1.00
83 Ryan Kesler .40 1.00
84 Roberto Luongo .40 1.00
85 Alexander Ovechkin 1.50 4.00
86 Alexander Semin .40 1.00
87 Nicklas Backstrom .60 1.50
88 Mike Green .40 1.00
89 Carl Klingberg RC 1.00 2.50
90 Greg Nemisz RC 1.00 2.50
91 Marcus Kruger RC 1.50 4.00
92 John Moore RC 1.00 2.50
93 Aaron Palushaj RC 1.00 2.50
94 Jonathon Blum RC 1.00 2.50
95 Blake Geoffrion RC 1.00 2.50
96 Adam Henrique RC 2.50 6.00
97 Alex Stalock 1.00 2.50
98 Joe Colborne RC 1.00 2.50
99 Matt Frattin RC 1.00 2.50
100 Cody Hodgson RC 6.00 15.00
101 Ville Leino .30 .75
102 Christian Ehrhoff .25 .60
103 Semyon Varlamov .40 1.00
104 Jean-Sebastien Giguere .30 .75
105 Jeff Carter .40 1.00
106 Tomas Fleischmann .25 .60
107 Kris Versteeg .30 .75
108 Jose Theodore .40 1.00
109 Mike Richards .40 1.00
110 Dany Heatley .30 .75
111 Devin Setoguchi .30 .75
112 Evgeni Nabokov .30 .75
113 Brad Richards .40 1.00
114 Ilya Bryzgalov .40 1.00
115 Jaromir Jagr 1.00 2.50
116 Maxime Talbot .30 .75
117 Brent Burns .50 1.25
118 Martin Havlat .30 .75
119 John-Michael Liles .25 .60
120 David Booth .25 .60
121 Tomas Vokoun .30 .75
122 Ondrej Pavelec .40 1.00
123 Evander Kane .40 1.00
124 Alexander Burmistrov .30 .75
125 Gabriel Landeskog RC 2.00 5.00
126 Ryan Johansen RC 2.00 5.00
127 Ryan Nugent-Hopkins RC 8.00 20.00
128 Zack Kassian RC 1.25 3.00
129 Craig Smith RC 1.25 3.00
130 Adam Larsson RC 1.25 3.00
131 Mika Zibanejad RC 2.50 6.00
132 Sean Couturier RC 2.00 5.00
133 Matt Read RC 2.00 5.00
134 Brett Connolly RC 1.00 2.50
135 Louis Leblanc RC 2.50 6.00
136 Mark Scheifele RC 2.50 6.00

2011-12 Upper Deck MVP One on One Autographs

GROUP A ANNC'D ODDS 1:34,380 UD2
GROUP B ANNC'D ODDS 1:9419 UD2
GROUP C ANNC'D ODDS 1:7016 UD2
MVP12 N-Hopkins/Landeskog B 125.00 250.00
MVPCH J.Colborne/C.Hodgson C 25.00 60.00
MVPDT P.Datsyuk/J.Toews A 40.00 80.00
MVPHO B.Hull/A.Oates A 60.00 120.00
MVPOS A.Ovechkin/S.Stamkos B 100.00 200.00
MVPPE M.Paajarvi/J.Eberle C 30.00 60.00
MVPLBBR C.Price/L.Eller B

2012-13 Upper Deck MVP

1-50 ODDS 1:6 UD HOB/RET
51-70 ODDS 1:15 SP AUTHENTIC
1 Corey Perry .60 1.50
2 Teemu Selanne 1.25 3.00
3 Zdeno Chara .60 1.50
4 Patrice Bergeron .75 2.00
5 Brad Marchand .75 2.00
6 Thomas Vanek .60 1.50
7 Ryan Miller .60 1.50
8 Jarome Iginla .60 1.50
9 Miikka Kiprusoff .50 1.25
10 Jonathan Toews 1.25 3.00
11 Patrick Kane 1.25 3.00
12 Patrick Sharp .60 1.50
13 Matt Duchene .60 1.50
14 Jack Johnson .40 1.00
15 Ryan Nugent-Hopkins .60 1.50

16 Taylor Hall 1.25 3.00
17 Jordan Eberle .60 1.50
18 Tomas Fleischmann .40 1.00
19 Mike Richards .60 1.50
20 Jonathan Quick 1.00 2.50
21 Dany Heatley .50 1.25
22 Mikko Koivu .50 1.25
23 Josh Gorges .50 1.25
24 P.K. Subban 1.00 2.50
25 Carey Price 2.00 5.00
26 Pekka Rinne .75 2.00
27 Ilya Kovalchuk .60 1.50
28 Martin Brodeur 1.25 3.00
29 John Tavares 1.25 3.00
30 Brad Richards .60 1.50
31 Marian Gaborik .60 1.50
32 Henrik Lundqvist .75 2.00
33 Claude Giroux .60 1.50
34 Scott Hartnell .60 1.50
35 Brayden Schenn .60 1.50
36 Keith Yandle .60 1.50
37 Sidney Crosby 2.50 6.00
38 James Neal .60 1.50
39 Evgeni Malkin 2.00 5.00
40 Logan Couture .60 1.50
41 Joe Pavelski .60 1.50
42 Brian Elliott .50 1.25
43 Steven Stamkos 1.25 3.00
44 Joffrey Lupul .50 1.25
45 Phil Kessel .75 2.00
46 Braden Holtby 1.00 2.50
47 Alexander Ovechkin 2.50 6.00
48 Ondrej Pavelec .60 1.50
49 Evander Kane .60 1.50
50 Alexander Burmistrov .50 1.25
51 Sven Baertschi RC 1.25 3.00
52 Brandon Bollig RC 1.00 2.50
53 Tyson Barrie RC 2.00 5.00
54 Reilly Smith RC 2.00 5.00
55 Scott Glennie RC 1.00 2.50
56 Riley Sheahan RC 1.00 2.50
57 Jordan Nolan RC 1.00 2.50
58 Jason Zucker RC 1.25 3.00
59 Gabriel Dumont RC 1.00 2.50
60 Chet Pickard RC 1.00 2.50
61 Casey Cizikas RC 1.00 2.50
62 Chris Kreider RC 2.00 5.00
63 Jakob Silfverberg RC 2.00 5.00
64 Mark Stone RC 2.00 5.00
65 Michael Stone RC 1.00 2.50
66 Jake Allen RC 3.00 8.00
67 Jaden Schwartz RC 2.00 5.00
68 J.T. Brown RC 1.00 2.50
69 Carter Ashton RC .75 2.00
70 Jussi Rynnas RC 1.00 2.50

2013-14 Upper Deck MVP

COMP.SERIES 1 w/o SP's (30) 10.00 25.00
COMP.SERIES 1 (70) 40.00 80.00
1-30 VETERAN ODDS 1:8 UD
31-50 RETIRED ODDS 1:24 UD
51-70 ROOKIE ODDS 1:24 UD
COMMON CARD (71-75) .75 2.00
UNLISTED STARS 71-75 1.00 2.50
71-75 SER.2 ODDS 1:72H, 1:72R, 1:144BL
76-90 SER.2 ODDS 1:24H, 1:24R, 1:48BL
1 Tomas Fleischmann .40 1.00
2 Adam Henrique .60 1.50
3 Logan Couture .60 1.50
4 Taylor Hall 1.25 3.00
5 John Tavares 1.25 3.00
6 Jim Howard .60 1.50
7 Steven Stamkos 1.25 3.00
8 Jack Johnson .40 1.00
9 Alexander Ovechkin 2.50 6.00
10 Thomas Vanek .60 1.50
11 Jonathan Toews 1.25 3.00
12 Jason Spezza .60 1.50
13 Zdeno Chara .60 1.50
14 Matt Duchene .60 1.50
15 Nazem Kadri .60 1.50
16 Ondrej Pavelec .60 1.50
17 Kari Lehtonen .50 1.25
18 Mikko Koivu .50 1.25
19 Sidney Crosby 2.50 6.00
20 Mike Smith .60 1.50
21 Jeff Skinner .50 1.25
22 Pekka Rinne .75 2.00
23 P.K. Subban 1.00 2.50
24 Corey Perry .60 1.50
25 Alex Pietrangelo .50 1.25
26 Jakub Voracek .60 1.50
27 Matt Stajan .50 1.25
28 Roberto Luongo .60 1.50
29 Henrik Lundqvist .75 2.00
30 Jonathan Quick 1.00 2.50
31 Bobby Orr 5.00 12.00
32 Ray Bourque 2.50 6.00
33 Chris Pronger 1.25 3.00
34 Paul Coffey 1.50 4.00
35 Mario Lemieux 5.00 12.00
36 Patrick Roy 4.00 10.00
37 Dominik Hasek 2.00 5.00
38 Ed Belfour 1.50 4.00
39 Andy Moog 1.50 4.00
40 Mats Sundin 1.50 4.00
41 Bobby Hull 1.50 4.00
42 Wayne Gretzky 4.00 10.00
43 Brett Hull 1.50 4.00
44 Theoren Fleury 2.00 5.00
45 Mark Messier 2.00 5.00
46 Curtis Joseph 1.50 4.00
47 Pavel Bure 2.00 5.00
48 Joe Sakic 2.50 6.00
49 Ron Francis 2.00 5.00
50 Luc Robitaille 1.50 4.00
51 Justin Schultz RC .60 1.50
52 Nail Yakupov RC 2.00 5.00
53 J.T. Miller RC .75 2.00
54 Alex Galchenyuk RC 3.00 8.00
55 Mikael Granlund RC 1.00 2.50
56 Emerson Etem RC 1.00 2.50
57 Jonathan Huberdeau RC 1.50 4.00
58 Cory Conacher RC .40 1.00
59 Beau Bennett RC .75 2.00
60 Vladimir Tarasenko RC 2.50 6.00
61 Jonas Brodin RC .50 1.25
62 Charlie Coyle RC .60 1.50
63 Tyler Toffoli RC 1.25 3.00
64 Petr Mrazek RC 1.25 3.00
65 Nathan Beaulieu RC .50 1.25
66 Filip Forsberg RC 1.50 4.00
67 Dougie Hamilton RC 1.25 3.00
68 Brendan Gallagher RC 2.00 5.00
69 Mikhail Grigorenko RC .75 2.00
70 Damien Brunner RC .50 1.25
71 Ryan Getzlaf 1.50 4.00
72 Phil Kessel 1.25 3.00
73 Martin St. Louis 1.00 2.50
74 Tuukka Rask 1.00 2.50
75 Evgeni Malkin 2.00 5.00
76 Morgan Rielly RC 2.00 5.00
77 Martin Jones RC 2.00 5.00
78 Rasmus Ristolainen RC 1.25 3.00
79 Valeri Nichushkin RC .75 2.00
80 Nathan MacKinnon RC 6.00 15.00
81 Tomas Hertl RC 1.00 2.50
82 Elias Lindholm RC 1.00 2.50
83 Antti Raanta RC 1.00 2.50
84 Jacob Trouba RC 1.25 3.00
85 Tomas Jurco RC 1.25 3.00
86 Seth Jones RC .75 2.00
87 Sean Monahan RC 1.25 3.00
88 Mark Arcobello RC .75 2.00
89 Ryan Strome RC 1.00 2.50
90 Aleksander Barkov RC 2.00 5.00

2013-14 Upper Deck MVP Gold Script

*1-30 VETS/100: 2X TO 5X BASIC CARDS
*31-50 RET/100: 1.2X TO 3X BASIC CARD
*51-70 ROOK/100: 2X TO 5X BASIC RC
*71-75 VETS/100: 1.2X TO 3X BASIC CARDS
*75-90 ROOK/100: 1.2X TO 3X BASIC RC
42 Wayne Gretzky 25.00 60.00
80 Nathan MacKinnon 25.00 50.00

2013-14 Upper Deck MVP Oversized

ONE PER UD SER.1 RETAIL TIN
4 Taylor Hall 2.50 6.00
5 John Tavares 2.50 6.00
7 Steven Stamkos 2.50 6.00
9 Alexander Ovechkin 5.00 12.00
11 Jonathan Toews 2.50 6.00
19 Sidney Crosby 5.00 12.00
23 P.K. Subban 2.00 5.00
29 Henrik Lundqvist 1.50 4.00
30 Jonathan Quick 2.00 5.00
31 Bobby Orr 4.00 10.00
35 Mario Lemieux 4.00 10.00
36 Patrick Roy 3.00 8.00
42 Wayne Gretzky 6.00 15.00
47 Pavel Bure 1.50 4.00

2013-14 Upper Deck MVP Rookie Jumbos

*ROOKIE JUMBO: .4X TO 1X MVP RC
ONE PER SERIES 1 RETAIL TIN

2013-14 Upper Deck MVP Super Script

*1-30 VETS/25: 4X TO 10X BASIC CARDS
*31-50 RET/25: 2.5X TO 6X BASIC CARD
*51-70 ROOKIE/25: 3X TO 8X BASIC RC
*71-75 VETS/25: 2.5X TO 6X BASIC CARDS
*75-90 ROOK/25: 2.5X TO 6X BASIC RC
42 Wayne Gretzky 50.00 100.00
80 Nathan MacKinnon 150.00 250.00

2014-15 Upper Deck MVP

COMP.SET w/o SP's (200) 12.00 30.00
SP STATED ODDS 1:1 HOB, 1:2 RET
301-336 ISSUED VIA MAIL REDEMPTION
1 Ben Scrivens .20 .50
2 Ondrej Palat .20 .50
3 John Carlson .30 .75
4 Dion Phaneuf .25 .60
5 Seth Jones .20 .50
6 Colton Orr .15 .40
7 Tyler Myers .20 .50
8 Tanner Pearson .15 .40
9 David Clarkson .15 .40
10 Brayden Schenn .20 .50
11 Calle Jarnkrok RC .50 1.25
12 Paul Stastny .20 .50
13 Wayne Simmonds .30 .75
14 Brent Burns .30 .75
15 Oliver Ekman-Larsson .20 .50
16 Nathan MacKinnon .50 1.25
17 Mika Zibanejad .25 .60
18 Nick Bjugstad .25 .60
19 Cody Hodgson .20 .50
20 Brendan Gallagher .25 .60
21 Joe Pavelski .25 .60
22 Cody Eakin .15 .40
23 Braden Holtby .40 1.00
24 T.J. Oshie .40 1.00
25 Aleksander Semin .20 .50
26 Jaden Schwartz .30 .75
27 Michael Grabner .20 .50
28 Cam Ward .25 .60
29 Niklas Hjalmarsson .20 .50
30 Olli Jokinen .20 .50
31 Reilly Smith .20 .50
32 Antti Raanta .25 .60
33 Jussi Jokinen .15 .40
34 Thomas Vanek .25 .60
35 Mike Fisher .20 .50
36 Brian Campbell .15 .40
37 Dustin Penner .15 .40
38 Valtteri Filppula .20 .50
39 Saku Koivu .20 .50
40 Jay Bouwmeester .25 .60
41 Morgan Rielly .25 .60
42 Justin Williams .20 .50
43 Scottie Upshall .15 .40
44 Tomas Hertl .25 .60
45 David Desharnais .25 .60
46 Kyle Turris .20 .50
47 Justin Abdelkader .20 .50
48 Andrej Sekera .15 .40
49 Tom Wilson .25 .60
50 Jason Chimera .15 .40
51 Vladislav Namestnikov RC .75 2.00
52 Mike Richards .25 .60
53 Brandon Bollig .20 .50
54 Olli Maatta .25 .60
55 Matt Stajan .15 .40
56 Justin Faulk .20 .50
57 Brian Elliott .20 .50
58 Matt Cooke .15 .40
59 Nail Yakupov .25 .60
60 Blake Wheeler .25 .60
61 Alex Chiasson .20 .50
62 Dougie Hamilton .25 .60
63 Hampus Lindholm .20 .50
64 Erik Johnson .15 .40
65 Josh Bailey .15 .40
66 Semyon Varlamov .25 .60
67 Marcus Foligno .15 .40
68 Robin Lehner .20 .50
69 Patrik Berglund .15 .40
70 Bryan Little .20 .50
71 Daniel Paille .15 .40
72 Brandon Saad .25 .60
73 Alex Goligoski .15 .40
74 Jacob Markstrom .20 .50
75 Cam Fowler .20 .50
76 Ryan O'Reilly .25 .60
77 Joel Ward .15 .40
78 Mark Giordano .20 .50
79 Darcy Kuemper .20 .50
80 Jhonas Enroth .25 .60
81 Mike Ribeiro .20 .50
82 Jakub Voracek .25 .60
83 Tomas Fleischmann .15 .40
84 Lars Eller .20 .50
85 Ben Bishop .25 .60
86 Mike Smith .25 .60
87 Chris Kreider .25 .60
88 Mikael Granlund .20 .50
89 Kyle Okposo .25 .60
90 Alexander Edler .15 .40
91 Mikkel Boedker .15 .40
92 Ondrej Pavelec .25 .60
93 Alex Galchenyuk .40 1.00
94 Dan Boyle .20 .50
95 Frans Nielsen .15 .40
96 Carl Soderberg .20 .50
97 Victor Hedman .30 .75
98 Joffrey Lupul .20 .50
99 Brian Gionta .20 .50
100 Jean-Sebastien Giguere .25 .60
101 Keith Yandle .25 .60
102 Slava Voynov .20 .50
103 Steve Mason .25 .60
104 Cory Schneider .25 .60
105 David Krejci .25 .60
106 Paul Martin .15 .40
107 Martin Hanzal .15 .40
108 Sean Monahan .25 .60
109 Ryan Murray .20 .50
110 Ilya Bryzgalov .25 .60
111 Brent Seabrook .25 .60
112 Radim Vrbata .20 .50
113 Derek Roy .20 .50
114 Pascal Dupuis .20 .50
115 James Reimer .25 .60
116 Brad Boyes .15 .40
117 Zac Rinaldo .20 .50
118 Dennis Wideman .15 .40
119 Petr Mrazek .25 .60
120 Marc-Edouard Vlasic .20 .50
121 Andrew Ference .20 .50
122 Brandon Gormley RC .50 1.25
123 Tyler Bozak .25 .60
124 Kevin Shattenkirk .25 .60
125 Tyler Johnson .25 .60
126 Patrick Marleau .25 .60
127 Brock Nelson .25 .60
128 Vladimir Tarasenko .40 1.00
129 Zack Kassian .20 .50
130 Andy Greene .15 .40
131 Greg McKegg RC .40 1.00
132 Vladimir Sobotka .15 .40
133 Travis Zajac .20 .50
134 Kari Lehtonen .20 .50
135 Brandon Dubinsky .20 .50
136 Andrew Shaw .25 .60
137 David Perron .20 .50
138 Gustav Nyquist .25 .60
139 Jonathan Ericsson .20 .50
140 Ryan Johansen .30 .75
141 Ales Hemsky .30 .75
142 Clarke MacArthur .15 .40
143 Nick Bonino .15 .40
144 Nathan Gerbe .15 .40
145 Michael Ryder .15 .40
146 P.A. Parenteau .15 .40
147 Ryan McDonagh .25 .60
148 Loui Eriksson .20 .50
149 Marcus Johansson .20 .50
150 Valeri Nichushkin .25 .60
151 Dustin Brown .20 .50
152 Rich Peverley .25 .60
153 Matt Niskanen .20 .50
154 Marek Zidlicky .15 .40
155 Danny DeKeyser .20 .50
156 Zdeno Chara .25 .60
157 Nick Foligno .20 .50
158 Chris Higgins .15 .40
159 Lee Stempniak .15 .40
160 Jake Gardiner .25 .60
161 Patric Hornqvist .25 .60
162 Tomas Plekanec .25 .60
163 Jack Johnson .15 .40
164 Jacob Trouba .20 .50
165 Aleksander Barkov .25 .60
166 Daniel Girardi .15 .40
167 Antoine Vermette .15 .40
168 Scott Hartnell .25 .60
169 Marc Staal .20 .50
170 Brad Marchand .30 .75
171 Carl Hagelin .20 .50
172 Tommy Wingels .20 .50
173 Jiri Hudler .20 .50
174 Torey Krug .20 .50
175 Tyler Toffoli .25 .60
176 Dave Bolland .15 .40
177 Jonas Hiller .20 .50
178 Michael Cammalleri .20 .50
179 Mason Raymond .20 .50
180 Alexandre Burrows .25 .60
181 Jeff Skinner .30 .75
182 Mats Zuccarello-Aasen .25 .60
183 Tomas Tatar .20 .50
184 Sam Gagner .20 .50
185 Teddy Purcell .20 .50
186 Mark Scheifele .30 .75
187 Andrei Markov .25 .60
188 Jason Garrison .15 .40
189 Milan Lucic .25 .60
190 Evander Kane .25 .60
191 Oscar Klefbom RC 1.00 2.50
192 Derek Stepan .25 .60
193 Eddie Lack .25 .60
194 Andrew Cogliano .15 .40
195 Sean Couturier .20 .50
196 Matt Moulson .15 .40
197 Ryan Smyth .20 .50
198 Jonathan Huberdeau .25 .60
199 Alexander Ovechkin CL .60 1.50
200 Sidney Crosby CL .60 1.50
201 Patrick Kane SP 2.00 5.00
202 Jim Howard SP 1.00 2.50
203 Jaromir Jagr SP 2.50 6.00
204 Sergei Bobrovsky SP 1.00 2.50
205 Eric Staal SP 1.25 3.00
206 Rick Nash SP 1.25 3.00
207 Evgeni Malkin SP 3.00 8.00
208 Ryan Getzlaf SP 2.00 5.00
209 Henrik Lundqvist SP 1.25 3.00
210 Patrice Bergeron SP 1.25 3.00
211 Bobby Ryan SP 1.00 2.50
212 Alexander Steen SP 1.00 2.50
213 Taylor Hall SP 2.00 5.00
214 Brad Richards SP 1.00 2.50
215 James van Riemsdyk SP 1.00 2.50
216 Marian Gaborik SP 1.00 2.50
217 Joe Thornton SP 1.00 2.50
218 Jason Pominville SP .75 2.00
219 Chris Kunitz SP 1.00 2.50
220 Daniel Sedin SP 1.00 2.50
221 Martin St. Louis SP 1.00 2.50
222 Niklas Kronwall SP .75 2.00
223 Jonathan Quick SP 1.50 4.00
224 Mike Green SP 1.00 2.50
225 Patrik Elias SP 1.00 2.50
226 Evgeny Kuznetsov SP RC 8.00 20.00
227 Corey Perry SP 1.00 2.50
228 Jordan Eberle SP 1.00 2.50
229 Claude Giroux SP 1.00 2.50
230 Nazem Kadri SP 1.00 2.50
231 Drew Doughty SP 1.00 2.50
232 Henrik Sedin SP 1.00 2.50
233 P.K. Subban SP 1.50 4.00
234 Jarome Iginla SP 1.00 2.50
235 Nicklas Backstrom SP 1.50 4.00
236 Zach Parise SP 1.00 2.50
237 Logan Couture SP 1.00 2.50
238 Duncan Keith SP 1.00 2.50
239 John Tavares SP 2.00 5.00
240 Jason Spezza SP 1.00 2.50
241 Henrik Zetterberg SP 1.25 3.00
242 Shea Weber SP .75 2.00
243 Marc-Andre Fleury SP 1.50 4.00
244 Steven Stamkos SP 2.00 5.00
245 Craig Anderson SP 1.00 2.50
246 Matt Duchene SP 1.00 2.50
247 Carey Price SP 3.00 8.00
248 Phil Kessel SP 1.25 3.00
249 Mikko Koivu SP .75 2.00
250 Ryan Kesler SP 1.00 2.50
251 Tyler Seguin SP 1.50 4.00
252 Adam Henrique SP 1.00 2.50
253 Vincent Lecavalier SP .75 2.00
254 Antti Niemi SP .75 2.00
255 Anze Kopitar SP 1.50 4.00
256 Erik Karlsson SP 2.00 5.00
257 Marian Hossa SP .75 2.00
258 Tuukka Rask SP 1.25 3.00
259 Corey Crawford SP 1.25 3.00
260 Teemu Selanne SP 2.00 5.00
261 David Backes SP 1.00 2.50
262 Teuvo Teravainen SP RC 3.00 8.00
263 James Neal SP 1.00 2.50
264 Andrew Ladd SP 1.00 2.50
265 Ryan Suter SP 1.00 2.50
266 Ryan Nugent-Hopkins SP 1.00 2.50
267 Jamie Benn SP 1.25 3.00
268 Pekka Rinne SP 1.25 3.00
269 Patrick Sharp SP 1.00 2.50
270 Jonathan Bernier SP 1.00 2.50
271 Martin Brodeur SP 2.00 5.00
272 Johan Franzen SP 1.00 2.50
273 Alexander Ovechkin SP 4.00 10.00
274 Max Pacioretty SP 1.00 2.50
275 Kris Letang SP 1.00 2.50
276 Dustin Byfuglien SP 1.00 2.50
277 Daniel Alfredsson SP 1.00 2.50
278 Shane Doan SP .75 2.00
279 Ryan Callahan SP 1.00 2.50
280 Alex Pietrangelo SP .75 2.00
281 Roberto Luongo SP 1.00 2.50
282 Dany Heatley SP .75 2.00
283 Jonathan Toews SP 2.00 5.00
284 Tyler Ennis SP .75 2.00
285 Ryan Miller SP 1.00 2.50
286 Jeff Carter SP 1.00 2.50
287 Sidney Crosby SP 4.00 10.00
288 Gabriel Landeskog SP 1.25 3.00
289 Pavel Datsyuk SP 1.25 3.00
290 Theoren Fleury SP 1.25 3.00
291 Joe Sakic SP 1.50 4.00
292 Peter Forsberg SP 1.25 3.00
293 Steve Yzerman SP 2.50 6.00
294 Mario Lemieux SP 3.00 8.00
295 Felix Potvin SP 1.50 4.00
296 Bobby Orr SP 3.00 8.00
297 Mark Messier SP 1.00 2.50
298 Patrick Roy SP 2.50 6.00
299 Wayne Gretzky SP 5.00 12.00
300 Wayne Gretzky CL SP 3.00 8.00
301 Seth Griffith RC 2.50 6.00
302 Sam Reinhart RC 6.00 15.00
303 Teemu Pulkkinen RC 2.50 6.00
304 Aaron Ekblad RC 8.00 20.00
305 Jiri Sekac RC 2.00 5.00
306 Curtis Lazar RC 2.50 6.00
307 Jonathan Drouin RC 5.00 12.00
308 Stuart Percy RC 2.00 5.00
309 David Pastrnak RC 8.00 20.00
310 Victor Rask RC 2.00 5.00
311 Alexander Wennberg RC 4.00 10.00
312 Marko Dano RC 2.00 5.00
313 Damon Severson RC 2.00 5.00
314 Griffin Reinhart RC 2.00 5.00
315 Anthony Duclair RC 3.00 8.00
316 Shayne Gostisbehere RC 8.00 20.00
317 Adam Payerl RC 1.50 4.00
318 Andre Burakovsky RC 3.00 8.00
319 Dennis Everberg RC 2.00 5.00
320 Adam Clendening RC 2.00 5.00
321 Phillip Danault RC 3.00 8.00
322 Curtis McKenzie RC 1.50 4.00
323 Christian Folin RC 2.00 5.00
324 Colton Sissons RC 2.00 5.00
325 Ty Rattie RC 2.00 5.00
326 Jori Lehtera RC 2.50 6.00
327 Adam Lowry RC 2.00 5.00
328 Johnny Gaudreau RC 6.00 15.00
329 Leon Draisaitl RC 10.00 25.00
330 Darnell Nurse RC 6.00 15.00
331 Chris Tierney RC 2.00 5.00
332 Mirco Mueller RC 2.00 5.00
333 Tobias Rieder RC 2.50 6.00
334 William Karlsson RC 8.00 20.00
335 Bo Horvat RC 6.00 15.00
336 Andy Andreoff RC 2.00 5.00

2014-15 Upper Deck MVP Colors and Contours

*1-200 T3 VET: 3X TO 8X BASIC CARDS
*1-200 T3 ROOK: 1.5X TO 4X BASIC RC
*201-300 T3: .8X TO 2X BASIC SP
T3 STATED ODDS 1:8
*1-200 G2/T1 VET: 4X TO 10X BASIC CARDS
*201-300 G2/T1: 1X TO 2.5X BASIC SP
G2 STATED ODDS 1:24
T1 STATED ODDS 1:96
*1-200 G1/P1/T2 VET: 5X TO 12X BASIC CARDS
*201-300 G1/P1/T2: 1.2X TO 3X BASIC SP
G1 STATED ODDS 1:36
P1 STATED ODDS 1:60
T2 STATED ODDS 1:72
*1-200 G3/P2: 6X TO 15X BASIC CARDS
*201-300 G3/P2: 1.5X TO 4X BASIC SP
G3 STATED ODDS 1:172
P2 STATED ODDS 1:144
*1-200 P3: 10X TO 25X BASIC CARDS
*201-300 P3: 2.5X TO 6X BASIC SP
P3 STATED ODDS 1:520
235 Nicklas Backstrom T2 5.00 12.00
259 Corey Crawford P3 8.00 20.00

2014-15 Upper Deck MVP Gold Script

*1-200 VETS/100: 5X TO 12X BASIC CARDS
*1-200 ROOKIES/100: 2.5X TO 6X BASIC RC
*201-300 VETS/100: 1.2X TO 3X BASIC SP
*201-300 ROOK/100: .8X TO 2X BASIC SP RC
INSERTED IN BLASTER PACKS
STATED PRINT RUN 100 SER.#'d SETS
235 Nicklas Backstrom 5.00 12.00
259 Corey Crawford 4.00 10.00

2014-15 Upper Deck MVP Silver Script

*1-200 VETS: 1.5X TO 4X BASIC CARDS
*1-200 ROOKIES: .8X TO 2X BASIC RC
*201-300 VETS: .5X TO 1.2X BASIC SP
*201-300 ROOKIES: .5X TO 1.2X BASIC SP RC
STATED ODDS 1:3 HOB, 1:6 RET/BLST
235 Nicklas Backstrom 2.00 5.00
259 Corey Crawford 1.50 4.00

2014-15 Upper Deck MVP NHL Three Stars Player of the Month

STATED ODDS 1:48 HOB, 1:96 RET/BLST
3SM0114 Khdbrn/Kssl/Pvlski 1.50 4.00
3SM0314 Ignla/Nyqst/Grx 1.25 3.00
3SM1013 Strn/Crey Prce/Nmi 5.00 12.00
3SM1113 Kne/Mlkn/Hrdng 4.00 10.00
3SM1213 Kne/Crsby/Hllr 5.00 12.00

2014-15 Upper Deck MVP NHL Three Stars Player of the Week

STATED ODDS 1:6 HOB, 1:12 RET/BLST
3SW010614 Sknnr/Elltt/Ster 1.00 2.50
3SW011314 Tvrs/Hllr/Lndqvst 2.00 5.00
3SW012014 St.Ls/Qck/Crwfrd 1.50 4.00
3SW012714 Lhtnn/Nyqst/Skra .75 2.00
3SW020314 Prse/Kssl/Bcklnd 1.25 3.00
3SW021014 Prce/Lhtnn/Ignla 3.00 8.00
3SW030314 Frmn/Hnrqe/Kmpr 1.00 2.50
3SW031014 Sgn/Ansmv/Hnrqe 1.50 4.00
3SW031714 Bbrvsky/Okpso/Nmi 1.00 2.50
3SW032414 Nyqst/Lndqvst/Ignla 1.25 3.00
3SW033114 Trrs/Brgrn/Oshie 1.50 4.00
3SW040714 Hll/Vrlmv/Prtty 2.00 5.00
3SW041414 Lndbck/Gbrn/Jhnsn 1.25 3.00
3SW100713 Ovchkn/Ellr/Flry 4.00 10.00
3SW101413 Hrtl/Vrlmv/Ggre/Crsby 4.00 10.00
3SW102113 Gstvsn/Crsby/Mrlau 4.00 10.00
3SW102813 Stmks/Kssl/Kslr 2.00 5.00
3SW110413 Prmvlle/Flry/Chmra 1.50 4.00
3SW111113 Lhnr/Andrsn/Shrp 1.00 2.50
3SW111813 Scrvns/Sgn/Hrdng 1.50 4.00
3SW112513 Mlkn/Prtty/Dbnyk 3.00 8.00
3SW120213 Mlkn/Krwll/Kth 3.00 8.00
3SW120913 Sknnr/Hll/Lngo 2.00 5.00
3SW121613 Ovchkn/Jnes/Httn 4.00 10.00
3SW122313 Stwrt/Crsby/Dchne 4.00 10.00
3SW123013 Shrp/Mllr/Neal 1.00 2.50

2014-15 Upper Deck MVP One on One Autographs

STATED ODDS 1:2612
1ON1DM M.Duchene/N.MacKinnon 125.00 200.00
1ON1KR P.Kessel/J.Riemsdyk
1ON1SP R.Suter/Z.Parise 20.00 40.00
1ON1TK J.Toews/P.Kane 90.00 150.00
1ON1WJ S.Weber/S.Jones

2014-15 Upper Deck MVP Pro Sign

GROUP A ODDS 1:4060
GROUP B ODDS 1:891
GROUP C ODDS 1:161
OVERALL ODDS 1:132 HOB, 1:1320 RET
PROAL Adam Larsson B 5.00 12.00
PROBB Bill Barber B 6.00 15.00
PROBO Bobby Orr A
PROBR Bobby Ryan C 5.00 12.00
PROBY Dustin Byfuglien C 5.00 12.00
PROCC Casey Cizikas A
PROCK Chris Kreider A
PRODB David Backes C 5.00 12.00
PRODM Dylan McIlrath C 4.00 10.00
PRODR Derek Roy C 4.00 10.00
PRODW Doug Wilson B 6.00 15.00
PROJK Jari Kurri B 5.00 12.00
PROJT John Tavares B
PROKU Chris Kunitz C 5.00 12.00
PROMB Mike Brown C 5.00 12.00
PROMS Mike Smith C 5.00 12.00
PRONK Niklas Kronwall C 4.00 10.00
PROPH Peter Holland C 4.00 10.00
PROPU Teddy Purcell C 4.00 10.00
PRORF Ron Francis A 15.00 40.00
PRORS Ryan Strome C 4.00 10.00
PROSB Sergei Bobrovsky C 5.00 12.00
PROTM Todd Marchant B 6.00 15.00
PROTP Tanner Pearson C 4.00 10.00
PROTT Tomas Tatar C 6.00 15.00
PROTW Tom Wilson C 5.00 12.00
PROWG Wayne Gretzky A 200.00 350.00
PROZR Zach Redmond C 3.00 8.00

2014-15 Upper Deck MVP Rookie MVP Redemptions

STATED ODDS 1:384 HOBBY
RR1 Atlantic Conference 25.00 50.00
RR2 Metropolitan Conference 12.00 30.00
RR3 Central Conference 12.00 30.00
RR4 Pacific Conference 15.00 40.00

2014-15 Upper Deck MVP Rookie of the Month

STATED ODDS 1:40 HOB, 1:80 RET/BLST
ROM0114 Ondrej Palat 1.50 4.00
ROM0314 Ondrej Palat 1.50 4.00
ROM1013 Tomas Hertl 2.00 5.00
ROM1113 Marek Mazanec 1.50 4.00
ROM1213A Martin Jones 2.00 5.00
ROM1213B Antti Raanta 2.00 5.00

2014-15 Upper Deck MVP Souvenirs

UNPRICED GRP A ODDS 1:11,136
GROUP B ODDS 1:130
SJAH Adam Henrique B 3.00 8.00
SJAK Anze Kopitar B 5.00 12.00
SJAN Antti Niemi B 2.50 6.00
SJBE Brian Elliott B 2.50 6.00
SJCP Carey Price B 10.00 25.00
SJCS Cory Schneider B 2.50 6.00
SJDB Dustin Brown B 2.50 6.00
SJDK Duncan Keith B 3.00 8.00
SJDS Drew Stafford B 3.00 8.00
SJEM Evgeni Malkin B 10.00 25.00
SJGL Gabriel Landeskog B 2.50 6.00
SJMG Mike Green B 2.50 6.00
SJMR Matt Read B 2.00 5.00
SJPB Patrice Bergeron B 4.00 10.00
SJPK Phil Kessel B 4.00 10.00
SJRN Rick Nash B 3.00 8.00
SJSC Sean Couturier B 3.00 8.00
SJSE Tyler Seguin B 5.00 12.00
SJTR Tuukka Rask B 3.00 8.00
SJTS Teemu Selanne B 6.00 15.00
SJWG Wayne Gretzky Prct Bib A

2014-15 Upper Deck MVP Souvenirs Combos

STATED ODDS 1:320 HOBBY
SJSAO Alexander Ovechkin 15.00 40.00
SJSBR Brad Richards 4.00 10.00
SJSHZ Henrik Zetterberg 3.00 8.00
SJSJC Jeff Carter 4.00 10.00
SJSJV Jakub Voracek 3.00 8.00
SJSML Mario Lemieux 12.00 30.00
SJSMM Mark Messier 4.00 10.00
SJSPE Phil Esposito 6.00 15.00
SJSPK Phil Kessel 5.00 12.00
SJSPS P.K. Subban 6.00 15.00
SJSRN Rick Nash 4.00 10.00
SJSSC Sidney Crosby 15.00 40.00
SJSSE Tyler Seguin 3.00 8.00
SJSSV Semyon Varlamov 4.00 10.00
SJSTS Teemu Selanne 8.00 20.00

2014-15 Upper Deck MVP Super Script

*1-200 VETS/25: 10X TO 25X BASIC CARDS
*1-200 ROOKIES/25: 5X TO 12X BASIC RC
*201-300 VETS/25: 2.5X TO 6X BASIC SP
*201-300 ROOK/25: 1.2X TO 3X BASIC SP RC
235 Nicklas Backstrom 10.00 25.00
259 Corey Crawford 8.00 20.00
299 Wayne Gretzky 30.00 80.00
300 Wayne Gretzky CL 25.00 60.00

2014-15 Upper Deck MVP Two on Two Jerseys

STATED ODDS 1:480
2JANALAK Glzlf/Prry/Kptr/Crtr 8.00 20.00
2JBOSMON Mrchnd/Lcc/Sbbn/Pcrtty 10.00 25.00
2JBOSNYR Brgrn/Krjci/Nsh/Krder 8.00 20.00
2JCHIDRW Stzk/Saad/Zttrbrg/Hwrd 8.00 20.00
2JCHISTL Crwfrd/Kth/Elltt/Brglnd 8.00 20.00
2JCOLCHI Dchne/Lndskg/Kth/Crwfrd 8.00 20.00
2JEDMVAN Ebrle/Hll/Kslr/Edlr
2JLAKSJS Quck/Dghty/Nmi/Thrntn
2JNJDNYI Brdr/Hnrque/Tvrs/Okpso 12.00 30.00
2JNYINYR Tvrs/Nlsn/Nsh/Stpn
2JOTTTOR Krlssn/Trrs/Kdri/Frnsn 12.00 30.00
2JPHIPIT Hrtnll/Read/Mlkn/Orpk 8.00 20.00
2JTORDET Brnr/Kssl/Hwrd/Zttrbrg 8.00 20.00
2JWASPHI Bckstrm/Grn/Hrtnll/Smmnds

2015-16 Upper Deck MVP

COMP.SET w/o SP's (100) 12.00 30.00
101-200 SP ODDS 1:1 HOB, 1:2 RET
NT ODDS 1:8 HOB, 1:16 RET
251-282 ISSUED VIA REDEMPTION
1 Sean Monahan .25 .60
2 Milan Lucic .20 .50
3 Zemgus Girgensons .20 .50
4 Carl Soderberg .20 .50
5 Jonas Hiller .20 .50
6 Sergei Bobrovsky .25 .60
7 Drew Doughty .25 .60
8 Jason Pominville .20 .50
9 P.A. Parenteau .15 .40
10 Shea Weber .20 .50
11 Cory Schneider .25 .60
12 Ryan Strome .20 .50
13 Derick Brassard .25 .60
14 Brendan Gallagher .30 .75
15 Bobby Ryan .20 .50
16 Frederik Andersen .25 .60
17 Justin Faulk .20 .50
18 Curtis Lazar .25 .60
19 Roberto Luongo .25 .60
20 Brayden Schenn .20 .50
21 Keith Yandle .20 .50
22 Marian Hossa .20 .50
23 Bryan Little .20 .50
24 Chris Kunitz .25 .60
25 Zdeno Chara .25 .60
26 Braden Holtby .40 1.00
27 Tomas Hertl .25 .60
28 Joe Thornton .25 .60
29 Clarke MacArthur .15 .40
30 Cam Ward .25 .60
31 Kyle Turris .20 .50
32 David Desharnais .25 .60
33 Mark Scheifele .30 .75
34 Nazem Kadri .25 .60
35 Jeff Carter .25 .60
36 Mikkel Boedker .15 .40
37 Jason Spezza .25 .60
38 Brandon Sutter .20 .50
39 Peter Holland .15 .40
40 Jori Lehtera .20 .50
41 Ryan Callahan .20 .50
42 Joffrey Lupul .20 .50
43 Matt Moulson .15 .40
44 Patrick Marleau .25 .60
45 Radim Vrbata .20 .50
46 Bo Horvat .40 1.00
47 Ben Scrivens .20 .50
48 Marcus Johansson .20 .50
49 T.J. Oshie .40 1.00
50 Mike Green .25 .60
51 Matt Nieto .15 .40
52 Dustin Byfuglien .25 .60
53 T.J. Brodie .15 .40
54 Justin Abdelkader .20 .50
55 Blake Wheeler .25 .60
56 Kris Letang .25 .60
57 Henrik Sedin .25 .60
58 Nail Yakupov .25 .60
59 James Neal .25 .60
60 Mats Zuccarello .25 .60
61 Jonathan Drouin .30 .75
62 Alexander Steen .20 .50
63 Blake Comeau .15 .40
64 Alex Tanguay .15 .40
65 Steve Mason .20 .50
66 Andrew Shaw .20 .50
67 Johnny Boychuk .15 .40
68 Matt Duchene .25 .60
69 Vincent Lecavalier .25 .60
70 Sami Vatanen .15 .40
71 Marian Gaborik .25 .60
72 Jordan Eberle .25 .60
73 Sean Couturier .20 .50
74 Nathan MacKinnon .50 1.25
75 Loui Eriksson .20 .50
76 Duncan Keith .25 .60
77 Jarome Iginla .30 .75
78 Brock Nelson .20 .50
79 Gustav Nyquist .25 .60
80 Wayne Simmonds .30 .75
81 Kevin Hayes .20 .50
82 Mikko Koivu .20 .50
83 Jonathan Huberdeau .25 .60
84 Chris Kreider .25 .60
85 Ben Bishop .25 .60
86 Nick Foligno .20 .50
87 Derek Stepan .25 .60
88 Jaroslav Halak .20 .50
89 Patrik Elias .25 .60
90 Seth Jones .20 .50
91 Tomas Tatar .20 .50
92 Roman Josi .25 .60
93 Tomas Plekanec .25 .60
94 Ryan Suter .15 .40
95 Tyler Toffoli .25 .60
96 Andrew Cogliano .15 .40
97 Nick Bjugstad .20 .50
98 Jim Howard .25 .60
99 Jamie Benn .30 .75
100 Jonathan Drouin CL .25 .60
101 Ryan Getzlaf SP 1.00 2.50
102 Brandon Saad SP .60 1.50
103 Evgeni Malkin SP 2.00 5.00
104 Tuukka Rask SP .60 1.50
105 Tyler Ennis SP .50 1.25
106 Eric Staal SP .75 2.00
107 Jonathan Quick SP 1.00 2.50
108 Carey Price SP 2.00 5.00
109 Filip Forsberg SP .75 2.00
110 Tyler Seguin SP 1.00 2.50
111 Jaromir Jagr SP 1.50 4.00
112 John Tavares SP 1.25 3.00
113 Corey Perry SP .60 1.50
114 Rick Nash SP .60 1.50
115 Henrik Zetterberg SP .75 2.00
116 Erik Karlsson SP 1.25 3.00
117 Claude Giroux SP .60 1.50
118 Johnny Gaudreau SP 1.00 2.50
119 Marc-Andre Fleury SP 1.00 2.50
120 Vladimir Tarasenko SP 1.00 2.50
121 Steven Stamkos SP 1.25 3.00
122 Aaron Ekblad SP .60 1.50
123 Antti Niemi SP .50 1.25
124 Brian Elliott SP .50 1.25
125 Phil Kessel SP 1.00 2.50
126 Ryan Miller SP .60 1.50
127 Ryan Kesler SP .60 1.50
128 Jonathan Toews SP 1.25 3.00
129 Jaden Schwartz SP .50 1.25
130 Alexander Ovechkin SP 2.50 6.00
131 Patric Hornqvist SP .50 1.25
132 John Carlson SP .60 1.50
133 Daniel Sedin SP .60 1.50
134 Andrew Ladd SP .60 1.50
135 Pekka Rinne SP .75 2.00
136 Alex Galchenyuk SP .75 2.00
137 James van Riemsdyk SP .60 1.50
138 Tyler Bozak SP .50 1.25
139 Henrik Lundqvist SP .75 2.00
140 Max Pacioretty SP .60 1.50
141 Jiri Hudler SP .60 1.50
142 Michael Hutchinson SP .60 1.50
143 Patrick Kane SP 1.25 3.00
144 Evgeny Kuznetsov SP 1.00 2.50
145 Joe Pavelski SP .60 1.50
146 Tyler Johnson SP .60 1.50
147 Jonathan Bernier SP .60 1.50
148 Ryan Nugent-Hopkins SP .60 1.50
149 David Backes SP .60 1.50
150 Patrice Bergeron SP .75 2.00
151 Logan Couture SP .60 1.50
152 Niklas Backstrom SP .60 1.50
153 Sidney Crosby SP 2.50 6.00
154 Jakub Voracek SP .60 1.50
155 Andrew Hammond SP 2.00 5.00
156 Martin St. Louis SP .60 1.50
157 Kyle Okposo SP .60 1.50
158 Adam Henrique SP .60 1.50
159 P.K. Subban SP 1.00 2.50
160 Zach Parise SP .60 1.50
161 Corey Crawford SP .75 2.00
162 Anze Kopitar SP 1.00 2.50
163 Taylor Hall SP 1.25 3.00
164 Pavel Datsyuk SP .75 2.00
165 Ryan Johansen SP .75 2.00
166 Pelle Lindbergh SP .60 1.50
167 Wayne Gretzky SP 3.00 8.00
168 Arturs Irbe SP .50 1.25
169 Grant Fuhr SP .60 1.50
170 Bobby Orr SP 2.00 5.00
171 Mark Messier SP .60 1.50
172 Mario Lemieux SP 2.00 5.00
173 Mike Bossy SP .60 1.50
174 Terry Sawchuk SP .60 1.50
175 Brett Hull SP .60 1.50
176 Slater Koekkoek SP RC .75 2.00
177 Luke Witkowski SP RC .75 2.00
178 David Wolf SP RC 1.00 2.50
179 Antoine Bibeau SP RC 1.00 2.50
180 Malcolm Subban SP RC 2.50 6.00
181 Ronalds Kenins SP RC 1.00 2.50
182 Ryan Hartman SP RC 1.00 2.50
183 Josh Anderson SP RC 1.25 3.00
184 Shane Prince SP RC .75 2.00
185 Brendan Ranford SP RC .75 2.00
186 Viktor Arvidsson SP RC 1.25 3.00
187 Andrew Copp SP RC 1.00 2.50
188 Sam Bennett SP RC 1.25 3.00
189 Kevin Fiala SP RC 1.00 2.50
190 Nick Shore SP RC .60 1.50
191 Jacob de la Rose SP RC .60 1.50
192 Nick Cousins SP RC .60 1.50
193 Oscar Dansk SP RC .75 2.00
194 Petr Straka SP RC .75 2.00
195 Stefan Noesen SP RC .75 2.00
196 Matt Puempel SP RC .75 2.00
197 Kyle Baun SP RC 1.00 2.50
198 Mackenzie Skapski SP RC 1.00 2.50
199 Emile Poirier SP RC 1.00 2.50
200 Alexander Ovechkin CL SP 1.50 4.00
201 Sidney Crosby NT 5.00 12.00
202 Evgeni Malkin NT 4.00 10.00
203 Tyler Toffoli NT 1.25 3.00
204 Wayne Gretzky NT 6.00 15.00
205 Bobby Orr NT 4.00 10.00
206 Jamie Benn NT 1.50 4.00
207 Tomas Hertl NT 1.25 3.00
208 Ryan Kesler NT 1.25 3.00
209 Torey Krug NT 1.25 3.00
210 Jonathan Toews NT 2.50 6.00
211 Brett Hull NT 1.25 3.00
212 Gustav Nyquist NT 1.25 3.00
213 Taylor Hall NT 2.50 6.00
214 Patrick Roy NT 3.00 8.00
215 Charlie Coyle NT 1.00 2.50
216 Johnny Gaudreau NT 2.00 5.00
217 Max Pacioretty NT 1.25 3.00
218 Seth Jones NT 1.00 2.50
219 Cory Schneider NT 1.00 2.50
220 Kyle Okposo NT 1.25 3.00
221 David Backes NT 1.25 3.00
222 Ben Bishop NT 1.25 3.00
223 Jonathan Bernier NT 1.25 3.00
224 Daniel Sedin NT 1.25 3.00

225 Matt Moulson NT 1.00 2.50
226 Linden Vey NT .75 2.00
227 Tobias Rieder NT .75 2.00
228 Evgeny Kuznetsov NT 2.00 5.00
229 Eric Staal NT 1.50 4.00
230 Aaron Ekblad NT 1.25 3.00
231 Alexander Ovechkin NT 5.00 12.00
232 Matt Duchene NT 1.25 3.00
233 Grant Fuhr NT 1.25 3.00
234 Mats Zuccarello NT 1.00 2.50
235 Brandon Dubinsky NT 1.00 2.50
236 Claude Giroux NT 1.25 3.00
237 Blake Wheeler NT 1.25 3.00
238 Markus Granlund NT 1.00 2.50
239 Shea Weber NT 1.00 2.50
240 Vincent Damphousse NT 1.00 2.50
241 Arturs Irbe NT 1.00 2.50
242 Carey Price NT 4.00 10.00
243 Jakub Voracek NT 1.25 3.00
244 Ondrej Palat NT 1.00 2.50
245 Leon Draisaitl NT 1.25 3.00
246 Carl Hagelin NT 1.00 2.50
247 Kyle Quincey NT .75 2.00
248 Marc-Andre Fleury NT 2.00 5.00
249 Kyle Turris NT 1.00 2.50
250 Mats Sundin NT 1.25 3.00
251 Colin Miller RC 3.00 8.00
252 Jack Eichel RC 15.00 40.00
253 Dylan Larkin RC 12.00 30.00
254 Connor Brickley RC 3.00 8.00
255 Charles Hudon RC 4.00 10.00
256 Matt Oâ€™Connor RC 3.00 8.00
257 Joel Vermin RC 3.00 8.00
258 Garret Sparks RC 5.00 12.00
259 Artemi Panarin RC 12.00 30.00
260 Mikko Rantanen RC 8.00 20.00
261 Mattias Janmark RC 4.00 10.00
262 Gustav Olofsson RC 4.00 10.00
263 Anthony Bitetto RC 2.50 6.00
264 Robby Fabbri RC 5.00 12.00
265 Nicolas Petan RC 4.00 10.00
266 Nikolaj Ehlers RC 8.00 20.00
267 Noah Hanifin RC 5.00 12.00
268 Markus Hannikainen RC 3.00 8.00
269 Sergei Kalinin RC 3.00 8.00
270 Adam Pelech RC 3.00 8.00
271 Oscar Lindberg RC 4.00 10.00
272 Taylor Leier RC 4.00 10.00
273 Daniel Sprong RC 8.00 20.00
274 Chandler Stephenson RC 4.00 10.00
275 Nick Ritchie RC 4.00 10.00
276 Max Domi RC 8.00 20.00
277 Brett Kulak RC 3.00 8.00
278 Connor McDavid RC 80.00 200.00
279 Jordan Weal RC 4.00 10.00
280 Nikolay Goldobin RC 4.00 10.00
281 Jake Virtanen RC 5.00 12.00
282 Jared McCann RC 4.00 10.00
DP1 Draft Pick McDavid EXCH 150.00 250.00
DP1A Draft Pick McDavid AU EXCH 500.00 900.00
DP1AG DP Gold McDavid AU EXCH

2015-16 Upper Deck MVP Colors and Contours

*1-100 L1T/L2G/L3T: 2.5X TO 6X BASIC CARDS
*101-200 L1T/L2G/L3T: 1X TO 2.5X BASIC SP
*176-199 L1T/L2G/L3T: .6X TO 1.5X BASIC RC
L3T STATED ODDS 1:8 HOB
L2G STATED ODDS 1:24 HOB
L1T STATED ODDS 1:96 HOB
*1-100 L1G/L1P/L2T: 3X TO 8X BASIC CARDS
*101-200 L1G/L1P/L2T: 1.2X TO 3X BASIC SP
*176-199 L1G/L1P/L2T: .8X TO 2X BASIC RC
L1G STATED ODDS 1:32 HOB
L1P STATED ODDS 1:60 HOB
L2T STATED ODDS 1:72 HOB
*101-200 L3G: 1.5X TO 4X BASIC SP
L3G STATED ODDS 1:172 HOB
*101-200 L2P: 2X TO 5X BASIC SP
L2P STATED ODDS 1:136 HOB
*101-200 L3P: 3X TO 8X BASIC SP
L3P STATED ODDS 1:520 HOB
OVERALL STATED ODDS 1:4 HOB
61 Jonathan Drouin L1P 2.50 6.00
100 Jonathan Drouin CL L1T 1.25 3.00
144 Evgeny Kuznetsov L2P 5.00 12.00
161 Corey Crawford L3G 3.00 8.00
167 Wayne Gretzky L3P 40.00 80.00
170 Bobby Orr L3P 25.00 50.00
182 Ryan Hartman L3T 2.00 5.00

2015-16 Upper Deck MVP Gold Script

*1-100 VETS/100: 5X TO 12X BASIC CARDS
*101-200 VETS/100: 2X TO 5X BASIC SP
*176-199 ROOKIE/100: 1.2X TO 3X BASIC RC
RANDOM INSERTS IN BLASTER PACKS
61 Jonathan Drouin 4.00 10.00
100 Jonathan Drouin CL 3.00 8.00
144 Evgeny Kuznetsov 5.00 12.00
161 Corey Crawford 4.00 10.00
182 Ryan Hartman 4.00 10.00

2015-16 Upper Deck MVP Silver Script

*1-100 VETS: 1.5X TO 4X BASIC CARDS
*101-200 VETS: .8X TO 2X BASIC SP
*176-199 ROOKIES: .6X TO 1.5X BASIC RC
STATED ODDS 1:3 HOB, 1:6 RET
61 Jonathan Drouin 1.25 3.00
100 Jonathan Drouin CL 1.00 2.50
144 Evgeny Kuznetsov 2.00 5.00
161 Corey Crawford 1.50 4.00
182 Ryan Hartman 2.00 5.00

2015-16 Upper Deck MVP NHL Territory Autographs

UNPRICED GRP A ODDS 1:16,697 HOB
GROUP B ODDS 1:2135 HOB
GROUP C ODDS 1:2292 HOB
GROUP D ODDS 1:1461 HOB
GROUP E ODDS 1:678 HOB
OVERALL ODDS 1:320 HOB
NTAE Aaron Ekblad E 8.00 20.00
NTAI Arturs Irbe C 25.00 60.00
NTAO Alexander Ovechkin A 30.00 80.00
NTBB Ben Bishop B 10.00 25.00
NTBD Brandon Dubinsky C 6.00 15.00
NTBE Jonathan Bernier B 10.00 25.00
NTBO Bobby Orr A 150.00 300.00
NTCC Charlie Coyle E 6.00 15.00
NTCG Claude Giroux B 10.00 25.00
NTCH Carl Hagelin B 8.00 20.00
NTCP Carey Price B 30.00 80.00
NTCS Cory Schneider B 8.00 20.00
NTDB David Backes B 10.00 25.00
NTEK Evgeny Kuznetsov D 8.00 20.00
NTES Eric Staal B 12.00 30.00
NTGN Gustav Nyquist C 8.00 20.00
NTHE Tomas Hertl E 8.00 20.00
NTJB Jamie Benn B 12.00 30.00
NTJG Johnny Gaudreau D 15.00 30.00
NTJT Jonathan Toews A 20.00 50.00
NTKO Kyle Okposo B 10.00 25.00
NTKQ Kyle Quincey E 4.00 10.00
NTKT Kyle Turris C 6.00 15.00
NTLD Leon Draisaitl B 10.00 25.00
NTLV Linden Vey E 4.00 10.00
NTMD Matt Duchene B 10.00 25.00
NTMF Marc-Andre Fleury B 15.00 40.00
NTMG Markus Granlund D 5.00 12.00
NTMM Matt Moulson B 8.00 20.00
NTMP Max Pacioretty A 10.00 25.00
NTMS Mats Sundin B 10.00 25.00
NTMZ Mats Zuccarello A 8.00 20.00
NTOP Ondrej Palat B 8.00 20.00
NTPR Patrick Roy A 25.00 60.00
NTRK Ryan Kesler C 12.00 30.00
NTSJ Seth Jones C 6.00 15.00
NTSW Shea Weber B 8.00 20.00
NTTH Taylor Hall B 20.00 50.00
NTTK Torey Krug D 6.00 15.00
NTTR Tobias Rieder E 4.00 10.00
NTTT Tyler Toffoli C 10.00 25.00
NTVD Vincent Damphousse B 8.00 20.00

2015-16 Upper Deck MVP NHL Territory Jerseys

GROUP A ODDS 1:7500 HOB
GROUP B ODDS 1:77 HOB
OVERALL ODDS 1:75 HOB, 1:750 RET
TMAE Aaron Ekblad B 5.00 12.00
TMAO Alexander Ovechkin B 20.00 50.00
TMBB Ben Bishop B 5.00 12.00
TMBD Brandon Dubinsky B 4.00 10.00
TMBE Jonathan Bernier B 5.00 12.00
TMBH Brett Hull B 5.00 12.00
TMBW Blake Wheeler B 5.00 12.00
TMCC Charlie Coyle B 4.00 10.00
TMCG Claude Giroux B 5.00 12.00
TMCP Carey Price B 15.00 40.00
TMDB David Backes B 5.00 12.00
TMDS Daniel Sedin B 5.00 12.00
TMEK Evgeny Kuznetsov B 8.00 20.00
TMEM Evgeni Malkin B 6.00 15.00
TMES Eric Staal B 6.00 15.00
TMGF Grant Fuhr B 5.00 12.00
TMGN Gustav Nyquist B 5.00 12.00
TMHA Taylor Hall B 10.00 25.00
TMJB Jamie Benn B 6.00 15.00
TMJG Johnny Gaudreau B 8.00 20.00
TMJT Jonathan Toews B 10.00 25.00
TMJV Jakub Voracek B 5.00 12.00
TMKO Kyle Okposo B 5.00 12.00
TMKT Kyle Turris B 4.00 10.00
TMLD Leon Draisaitl B 5.00 12.00
TMMD Matt Duchene B 5.00 12.00
TMMF Marc-Andre Fleury B 8.00 20.00
TMMM Matt Moulson B 4.00 10.00
TMMP Max Pacioretty B 5.00 12.00
TMMZ Mats Zuccarello B 4.00 10.00
TMOP Ondrej Palat B 4.00 10.00
TMPR Patrick Roy A 20.00 50.00
TMRK Ryan Kesler B 5.00 12.00
TMSC Sidney Crosby A 20.00 50.00
TMSJ Seth Jones B 4.00 10.00
TMSW Shea Weber B 4.00 10.00
TMTH Tomas Hertl B 5.00 12.00
TMTK Torey Krug B 5.00 12.00
TMTT Tyler Toffoli B 5.00 12.00
TMVD Vincent Damphousse A 20.00 50.00
TMWG Wayne Gretzky A 40.00 100.00

2015-16 Upper Deck MVP One on One Autographs

UNPRICED GROUP A ODDS 1:46,080 HOB
UNPRICED GROUP B ODDS 1:30,720 HOB
GROUP C ODDS 1:10,716 HOB
GROUP D ODDS 1:7680 HOB
OVERALL ODDS 1:3600 HOB
1ON1BL J.Boychuk/Leddy D
1ON1JH Johansen/Hartnell C 15.00 40.00
1ON1NA Nyquist/Abdelkader C 12.00 30.00
1ON1NH R.N-Hopkins/T.Hall A 30.00 60.00
1ON1NL R.Nash/E.Lindholm D
1ON1TK T.Toffoli/A.Kopitar B

2015-16 Upper Deck MVP Post Season

STATED ODDS 1:384 HOBBY
PS1 Duncan Keith 6.00 15.00
PS2 Tyler Johnson 5.00 12.00
PS3 Jonathan Toews 12.00 30.00
PS4 Nikita Kucherov 10.00 25.00
PS5 Patrick Kane 12.00 30.00
PS6 Steven Stamkos 12.00 30.00
PS7 Brandon Saad 6.00 15.00
PS8 Ben Bishop 6.00 15.00
PS9 Antoine Vermette 4.00 10.00
PS10 Victor Hedman 8.00 20.00
PS11 Teuvo Teravainen 6.00 15.00
PS12 Anton Stralman 4.00 10.00
PS13 Corey Crawford 8.00 20.00
PS14 Ondrej Palat 5.00 12.00
PS15 Marian Hossa 5.00 12.00
PS16 Alex Killorn 5.00 12.00
PS17 Niklas Hjalmarsson 4.00 10.00
PS18 Andrei Vasilevskiy 8.00 20.00

2015-16 Upper Deck MVP Pro Sign

UNPRICED GRP A ODDS 1:13,661 HOB
UNPRICED GRP B ODDS 1:10,474 HOB
GROUP C ODDS 1:2732 HOB
GROUP D ODDS 1:2464 HOB
GROUP E ODDS 1:1591 HOB
GROUP F ODDS 1:1089 HOB
GROUP G ODDS 1:511 HOB
OVERALL ODDS 1:225 HOB
PSAH Andrew Hammond A 20.00 50.00
PSAI Arturs Irbe C 15.00 40.00
PSAO Adam Oates D 6.00 15.00
PSAV Andrei Vasilevskiy G 8.00 20.00
PSBB Ben Bishop C 6.00 15.00
PSBM Brad Marchand D 8.00 20.00
PSBO Bobby Orr B 100.00 250.00
PSBR Brett Ritchie G 4.00 10.00
PSCS Cory Schneider D 5.00 12.00
PSDC David Clarkson F 4.00 10.00
PSDD Danny DeKeyser C 5.00 12.00
PSDP Derrick Pouliot G 5.00 12.00
PSFA Frederik Andersen E 5.00 12.00
PSJG Johnny Gaudreau E 12.00 30.00
PSJT Jacob Trouba E 5.00 12.00
PSLS Luke Schenn D 4.00 10.00
PSMJ Martin Jones F 6.00 15.00
PSMS Michael Stone F 4.00 10.00
PSNM Nathan MacKinnon A 12.00 30.00
PSNY Nail Yakupov B 5.00 12.00
PSOP Ondrej Palat E 5.00 12.00
PSPS P.K. Subban A 10.00 25.00
PSRJ Ryan Johansen C 8.00 20.00
PSRM Ryan McDonagh C 5.00 12.00
PSRR Rasmus Ristolainen G 5.00 12.00
PSSC Sean Couturier C 6.00 15.00
PSTR Tuukka Rask D 6.00 15.00
PSTR Tobias Rieder F 4.00 10.00
PSVN Valeri Nichushkin B 5.00 12.00
PSWG Wayne Gretzky A 150.00 300.00

2015-16 Upper Deck MVP Rookie MVP Redemptions

STATED ODDS 1:384 HOB, 1:3840 RET
EXCH EXPIRATION: 8/1/2017
RR1 Atlantic Div/Eichel/Larkin 50.00 80.00
RR2 Metropolitan Division 25.00 50.00
RR3 Central Division/Panarin 25.00 50.00
RR4 Pacific Division/McDavid 100.00 175.00

2015-16 Upper Deck MVP Super Script

*1-100 VETS/25: X TO X BASIC CARDS
*101-200 VETS/25: X TO X BASIC SP
*176-199 ROOKIE/25: 3X TO 8X BASIC RC
61 Jonathan Drouin 8.00 20.00
100 Jonathan Drouin CL 5.00 12.00
144 Evgeny Kuznetsov 10.00 25.00
161 Corey Crawford 8.00 20.00
167 Wayne Gretzky 30.00 80.00
182 Ryan Hartman 10.00 25.00

2016-17 Upper Deck MVP

1 Patrick Sharp .20 .50
2 Roman Josi .25 .60
3 Ben Bishop .25 .60
4 Cam Fowler .20 .50
5 Cody Eakin .20 .50
6 Bo Horvat .40 1.00
7 Jussi Jokinen .25 .60
8 Ryan Strome .20 .50
9 Mark Streit .20 .50
10 John Klingberg .25 .60
11 Sam Reinhart .20 .50
12 Jiri Hudler .20 .50
13 Anton Stralman .20 .50
14 David Desharnais .20 .50
15 Patrik Elias .25 .60
16 Martin Jones .25 .60
17 Marian Hossa .20 .50
18 Jason Spezza .25 .60
19 Nazem Kadri .20 .50
20 Cody Ceci .20 .50
21 Tomas Tatar .20 .50
22 Noah Hanifin .25 .60
23 Niklas Hjalmarsson .20 .50
24 Tyler Bozak .20 .50
25 Jaroslav Halak .25 .60
26 Evgeny Kuznetsov .40 1.00
27 David Pastrnak .40 1.00
28 Torey Krug .25 .60
29 Jake Muzzin .20 .50
30 Teuvo Teravainen .25 .60
31 Shayne Gostisbehere .30 .75
32 Riley Sheahan .20 .50
33 Mike Green .25 .60
34 Vincent Trocheck .25 .60
35 Jason Pominville .20 .50
36 Gustav Nyquist .25 .60
37 Elias Lindholm .25 .60
38 Mike Smith .25 .60
39 Mark Stone .25 .60
40 Ryan McDonagh .20 .50
41 Bryan Little .20 .50
42 Kyle Palmieri .20 .50
43 Antti Niemi .20 .50
44 Hampus Lindholm .15 .40
45 Phil Kessel .30 .75
46 Sean Monahan .25 .60
47 Antoine Vermette .20 .50
48 Mike Hoffman .20 .50
49 Aaron Ekblad .25 .60
50 Charlie Coyle .20 .50
51 Jakob Silfverberg .25 .60
52 Zdeno Chara .25 .60
53 Darnell Nurse .20 .50
54 Jake Allen .30 .75
55 James Neal .20 .50
56 Max Domi .30 .75
57 Mats Zuccarello .25 .60
58 Alex Pietrangelo .20 .50
59 David Krejci .25 .60
60 Nathan MacKinnon .50 1.25
61 Nikita Kucherov .40 1.00
62 Thomas Vanek .20 .50
63 Frans Nielsen .20 .50
64 Brent Seabrook .20 .50
65 Aleksander Barkov .25 .60
66 Victor Rask .20 .50
67 Michael Cammalleri .20 .50
68 Braden Holtby .40 1.00
69 Mikko Rantanen .25 .60
70 Ryan Miller .25 .60
71 David Perron .20 .50
72 Nail Yakupov .20 .50
73 Jaden Schwartz .30 .75
74 Michael Frolik .20 .50
75 Tyson Barrie .25 .60
76 Dion Phaneuf .25 .60
77 Colton Parayko .25 .60
78 Brandon Saad .25 .60
79 T.J. Brodie .20 .50
80 Justin Schultz .20 .50
81 Nicklas Backstrom .40 1.00
82 Shane Doan .20 .50
83 Jack Johnson .15 .40
84 Leon Draisaitl .30 .75
85 Lee Stempniak .20 .50
86 Travis Zajac .20 .50
87 Olli Maatta .25 .60
88 Anthony Duclair .25 .60
89 Martin Hanzal .20 .50
90 Jonathan Quick .40 1.00
91 Marcus Johansson .25 .60
92 Scott Hartnell .25 .60
93 Jori Lehtera .20 .50
94 Colin Wilson .25 .60
95 Tyler Myers .20 .50
96 Andrew Ladd .25 .60
97 Anders Lee .25 .60
98 Mikael Backlund .20 .50
99 Carl Hagelin .25 .60
100 Alexander Ovechkin CL 1.00 2.50
101 Cam Talbot .30 .75
102 Alex Galchenyuk .30 .75
103 Craig Anderson .25 .60
104 Mikko Koivu .20 .50
105 Ryan Callahan .25 .60
106 Johnny Oduya .20 .50
107 Adam Larsson .25 .60
108 Robby Fabbri .25 .60
109 Jeff Skinner .25 .60
110 Cam Ward .25 .60
111 Steve Mason .20 .50
112 Alexander Steen .25 .60
113 J.T. Miller .20 .50
114 Mikael Granlund .20 .50
115 Milan Lucic .20 .50
116 Bobby Ryan .20 .50
117 Evander Kane .25 .60
118 Nino Niederreiter .25 .60
119 Brad Marchand .30 .75
120 Valeri Nichushkin .20 .50
121 Tanner Pearson .20 .50
122 Johnny Boychuk .25 .60
123 Zemgus Girgensons .20 .50
124 Jake Virtanen .30 .75
125 Dylan Larkin .40 1.00
126 Tyler Johnson .20 .50
127 Patrick Marleau .25 .60
128 Reilly Smith .25 .60
129 Rasmus Ristolainen .20 .50
130 Dan Hamhuis .20 .50
131 Brendan Gallagher .30 .75
132 Michael Del Zotto .20 .50
133 Ondrej Palat .20 .50
134 Corey Crawford .30 .75
135 Keith Yandle .25 .60
136 Valtteri Filppula .20 .50
137 Matt Beleskey .20 .50
138 Derick Brassard .25 .60
139 John Gibson .25 .60
140 Joel Ward .20 .50
141 Brayden Schenn .25 .60
142 Nick Bjugstad .20 .50
143 Mike Fisher .20 .50
144 Jeff Carter .25 .60
145 Ondrej Pavelec .25 .60
146 Sean Couturier .25 .60
147 Sami Vatanen .20 .50
148 Jim Howard .20 .50
149 Patric Hornqvist .20 .50
150 Justin Abdelkader .20 .50
151 Mathieu Perreault .20 .50
152 Boone Jenner .25 .60
153 Jonas Hiller .20 .50
154 Radim Vrbata .20 .50
155 Brian Gionta .20 .50
156 Cam Atkinson .25 .60
157 Peter Holland .15 .40
158 Brian Elliott .20 .50
159 Marian Gaborik .25 .60
160 Brent Burns .30 .75
161 Andrei Markov .25 .60
162 T.J. Oshie .40 1.00
163 Wayne Simmonds .30 .75
164 Andrew Hammond .20 .50
165 Brandon Dubinsky .25 .60
166 Devan Dubnyk .25 .60
167 Artemi Panarin .30 .75
168 Tyler Toffoli .25 .60
169 Nick Foligno .20 .50
170 Ryan Kesler .25 .60
171 Lars Eller .20 .50
172 Benoit Pouliot .20 .50
173 Jordan Staal .25 .60
174 Dougie Hamilton .25 .60
175 Brock Nelson .20 .50
176 Mike Ribeiro .20 .50
177 Jonathan Huberdeau .25 .60
178 Chris Kunitz .25 .60
179 Tomas Hertl .25 .60
180 Derek Stepan .20 .50
181 Mark Scheifele .30 .75
182 Robin Lehner .20 .50
183 Mika Zibanejad .25 .60
184 Seth Jones .20 .50
185 Joe Pavelski .25 .60
186 Brett Connolly .20 .50
187 Justin Williams .20 .50
188 Jonathan Bernier .25 .60
189 Mikkel Boedker .20 .50
190 Alex Tanguay .15 .40
191 Tyler Ennis .20 .50
192 Nikolaj Ehlers .25 .60
193 Marc-Andre Fleury .40 1.00
194 Tomas Plekanec .25 .60
195 Semyon Varlamov .25 .60
196 Chris Kreider .25 .60
197 Jarome Iginla .25 .60
198 Tuukka Rask .25 .60
199 Alexander Edler .15 .40
200 Patrick Kane CL .50 1.25
201 Steven Stamkos 1.25 3.00
202 Erik Karlsson 1.25 3.00
203 Anze Kopitar 1.00 2.50
204 Carey Price 2.00 5.00
205 Cory Schneider .50 1.25
206 Logan Couture .60 1.50
207 John Tavares 1.25 3.00
208 Jordan Eberle .60 1.50
209 Ryan Suter .50 1.25
210 Rick Nash .60 1.50
211 Henrik Lundqvist .60 1.50
212 Dustin Byfuglien .60 1.50
213 Henrik Zetterberg .75 2.00
214 Joe Thornton .60 1.50
215 Jack Eichel 1.25 3.00
216 Eric Staal .75 2.00
217 Duncan Keith .60 1.50
218 Jonathan Toews 1.25 3.00
219 Oliver Ekman-Larsson .50 1.25
220 Claude Giroux .60 1.50
221 Henrik Sedin .60 1.50
222 Jamie Benn .75 2.00
223 Ryan Nugent-Hopkins .60 1.50
224 Gabriel Landeskog .50 1.25
225 Matt Duchene .60 1.50
226 Ryan Getzlaf 1.00 2.50
227 Roberto Luongo .60 1.50
228 Ryan Johansen .75 2.00
229 Blake Wheeler .60 1.50
230 Pavel Datsyuk .75 2.00
231 Pekka Rinne .75 2.00
232 Adam Henrique .60 1.50
233 Tyler Seguin 1.00 2.50
234 Max Pacioretty .60 1.50
235 Evgeni Malkin 2.00 5.00
236 Sam Bennett .75 2.00
237 Jaromir Jagr 1.50 4.00
238 James van Riemsdyk .60 1.50
239 Alexander Ovechkin 2.50 6.00
240 Jakub Voracek .60 1.50
241 Kyle Turris .50 1.25
242 Connor McDavid 3.00 8.00
243 Kevin Shattenkirk .50 1.25
244 Kyle Okposo .60 1.50
245 Victor Hedman .75 2.00
246 Ryan O'Reilly .60 1.50
247 Patrice Bergeron .75 2.00
248 Kris Letang .60 1.50
249 Sergei Bobrovsky .60 1.50
250 Filip Forsberg .75 2.00
251 Taylor Hall 1.25 3.00
252 Vladimir Tarasenko 1.00 2.50
253 Morgan Rielly .50 1.25
254 Drew Doughty .60 1.50
255 Sidney Crosby 2.50 6.00
256 Daniel Sedin .60 1.50
257 Mark Giordano .50 1.25
258 Shea Weber .50 1.25
259 Johnny Gaudreau 1.00 2.50
260 Zach Parise .60 1.50
261 John Carlson .75 2.00
262 P.K. Subban 1.00 2.50
263 Corey Perry .60 1.50
264 Justin Faulk .50 1.25
265 Patrick Kane 1.25 3.00
266 Guy Lafleur .75 2.00
267 Peter Forsberg .60 1.50
268 Bobby Hull 1.00 2.50
269 Al MacInnis .60 1.50
270 Borje Salming .60 1.50
271 Mark Messier .75 2.00
272 Gerry Cheevers .60 1.50
273 Glenn Anderson .60 1.50
274 Larry Robinson .60 1.50
275 Wayne Gretzky 3.00 8.00
276 Mike Reilly RC .75 2.00
277 Kevin Gravel RC 1.25 3.00
278 Tom Kuhnhackl RC .75 2.00
279 Ryan Pulock RC 1.00 2.50
280 Mark McNeill RC 1.00 2.50
281 Charlie Lindgren RC 2.00 5.00
282 Josh Morrissey RC 1.25 3.00
283 Hudson Fasching RC 1.00 2.50
284 William Nylander RC 4.00 10.00
285 Oskar Sundqvist RC 1.00 2.50
286 Michael Matheson RC 1.00 2.50
287 Brendan Leipsic RC 1.00 2.50
288 Steven Santini RC .75 2.00
289 Justin Bailey RC 1.00 2.50
290 Kasperi Kapanen RC 2.00 5.00
291 Chris Bigras RC .75 2.00
292 Esa Lindell RC 1.00 2.50
293 Oliver Kylington RC .75 2.00
294 Connor Brown RC 1.50 4.00
295 Pavel Zacha RC 1.25 3.00
296 Anthony Mantha RC 2.50 6.00
297 Jason Dickinson RC .75 2.00
298 Sonny Milano RC 1.25 3.00
299 Nick Paul RC 1.25 3.00
300 Connor McDavid CL 3.00 8.00
301 John Gibson NHLT 1.25 3.00
302 Oliver Ekman-Larsson NHLT 1.00 2.50
303 Patrice Bergeron NHLT 1.50 4.00
304 Jack Eichel NHLT 2.50 6.00
305 Sean Monahan NHLT 1.25 3.00
306 Justin Faulk NHLT 1.00 2.50
307 Patrick Kane NHLT 2.50 6.00
308 Gabriel Landeskog NHLT 1.00 2.50
309 Nick Foligno NHLT 1.00 2.50
310 Tyler Seguin NHLT 2.00 5.00
311 Tomas Tatar NHLT 1.00 2.50
312 Connor McDavid NHLT 6.00 15.00
313 Aleksander Barkov NHLT 1.25 3.00
314 Anze Kopitar NHLT 2.00 5.00
315 Jason Zucker NHLT 1.00 2.50
316 P.K. Subban NHLT 2.00 5.00
317 Ryan Johansen NHLT 1.50 4.00
318 Adam Henrique NHLT 1.25 3.00
319 Ryan Strome NHLT 1.00 2.50
320 Derek Stepan NHLT 1.00 2.50
321 Mika Zibanejad NHLT 1.25 3.00
322 Shayne Gostisbehere NHLT 1.50 4.00
323 Marc-Andre Fleury NHLT 2.00 5.00
324 Joe Pavelski NHLT 1.25 3.00
325 Vladimir Tarasenko NHLT 2.00 5.00
326 Steven Stamkos NHLT 2.50 6.00
327 James van Riemsdyk NHLT 1.25 3.00
328 Bo Horvat NHLT 2.00 5.00
329 Braden Holtby NHLT 2.00 5.00
330 Jacob Trouba NHLT 1.00 2.50
331 Corey Perry LL 2.00 5.00
332 Tobias Rieder LL 1.25 3.00
333 David Krejci LL 2.00 5.00
334 Ryan O'Reilly LL 2.00 5.00
335 Johnny Gaudreau LL 3.00 8.00
336 Noah Hanifin LL 2.00 5.00
337 Jonathan Toews LL 4.00 10.00
338 Joe Sakic LL 3.00 8.00
339 Jack Johnson LL 1.25 3.00
340 John Klingberg LL 2.00 5.00
341 Dylan Larkin LL 3.00 8.00
342 Leon Draisaitl LL 2.50 6.00
343 Jonathan Huberdeau LL 2.00 5.00
344 Jeff Carter LL 2.00 5.00
345 Mikael Granlund LL 1.50 4.00
346 Carey Price LL 6.00 15.00
347 Shea Weber LL 1.50 4.00
348 Cory Schneider LL 1.50 4.00
349 John Tavares LL 4.00 10.00
350 Ryan McDonagh LL 1.50 4.00
351 Kyle Turris LL 1.50 4.00
352 Jakub Voracek LL 2.00 5.00
353 Evgeni Malkin LL 6.00 15.00
354 Owen Nolan LL 2.00 5.00
355 Jake Allen LL 2.50 6.00
356 Victor Hedman LL 2.50 6.00
357 Morgan Rielly LL 1.50 4.00
358 Daniel Sedin LL 2.00 5.00
359 John Carlson LL 2.50 6.00
360 Mark Scheifele LL 2.50 6.00
361 Brandon Carlo RC 2.00 5.00
362 Nick Baptiste RC 2.00 5.00
363 Tyler Bertuzzi RC 2.50 6.00
364 Mitch Marner RC 12.00 30.00
365 Mikhail Sergachev RC 4.00 10.00
366 Thomas Chabot RC 4.00 10.00
366 Brayden Point RC 5.00 12.00
368 Auston Matthews RC 30.00 80.00
369 Sebastian Aho RC 4.00 10.00
370 Zach Werenski RC 4.00 10.00
371 Nick Lappin RC 2.00 5.00
372 Anthony Beauvillier RC 2.00 5.00
373 Jimmy Vesey RC 4.00 10.00
374 Travis Konecny RC 4.00 10.00
375 Jake Guentzel RC 20.00 50.00
376 Jakub Vrana RC 2.00 5.00
377 Nick Schmaltz RC 2.00 5.00
378 A.J. Greer RC 2.00 5.00
379 Julius Honka RC 2.00 5.00
380 Joel Eriksson Ek RC 2.00 5.00
381 Pontus Aberg RC 2.50 6.00
382 Tyler Motte RC 2.00 5.00
383 Patrik Laine RC 15.00 40.00
384 Kyle Connor RC 5.00 12.00
385 Jacob Larsson RC 3.00 8.00
386 Dylan Strome RC 4.00 10.00
387 Matthew Tkachuk RC 6.00 15.00
388 Jesse Puljujarvi RC 5.00 12.00
389 Nic Dowd RC 2.00 5.00
390 Timo Meier RC 2.00 5.00
391 Thatcher Demko RC 4.00 10.00
392 Christian Dvorak RC 2.00 5.00

2016-17 Upper Deck MVP '16 NHL Draft Pick #1

DP1 Draft Pick Redemption SP 80.00 150.00
Exchanged for Auston Matthews

2016-17 Upper Deck MVP All Star Variations

AS1 Drew Doughty 6.00 15.00
AS2 John Tavares 12.00 30.00
AS3 Patrick Kane 12.00 30.00
AS4 John Gibson 6.00 15.00
AS5 Steven Stamkos 12.00 30.00
AS6 Dylan Larkin 10.00 25.00
AS7 Erik Karlsson 12.00 30.00
AS8 Braden Holtby 10.00 25.00
AS9 Vladimir Tarasenko 10.00 25.00
AS10 Shea Weber 5.00 12.00

2016-17 Upper Deck MVP Leading Lights Autographs Gold

331 Corey Perry A
335 Johnny Gaudreau C
340 John Klingberg A
343 Jonathan Huberdeau C
347 Shea Weber B
348 Cory Schneider C
350 Ryan McDonagh B
351 Kyle Turris D 8.00 20.00
357 Morgan Rielly E 8.00 20.00
360 Mark Scheifele D 8.00 20.00

2016-17 Upper Deck MVP Leading Lights Jerseys Gold

334 Ryan O'Reilly B 8.00 20.00
336 Noah Hanifin C 8.00 20.00
337 Jonathan Toews A 15.00 40.00
339 Jack Johnson C 5.00 12.00
342 Leon Draisaitl B 10.00 25.00
344 Jeff Carter B 8.00 20.00
346 Carey Price A 25.00 60.00
349 John Tavares A 15.00 40.00
352 Jakub Voracek C 8.00 20.00
353 Evgeni Malkin A 25.00 60.00
354 Owen Nolan A 8.00 20.00
355 Jake Allen C 10.00 25.00
356 Victor Hedman B 10.00 25.00
358 Daniel Sedin B 8.00 20.00
359 John Carlson C 10.00 25.00

2016-17 Upper Deck MVP NHL Territory Autographs

NTAB Aleksander Barkov B
NTAH Adam Henrique E
NTCM Connor McDavid D 100.00 250.00
NTGL Gabriel Landeskog C
NTJF Justin Faulk E 5.00 12.00
NTJP Joe Pavelski C
NTJZ Jason Zucker E 5.00 12.00
NTMF Marc-Andre Fleury A
NTNF Nick Foligno D 8.00 20.00
NTPS P.K. Subban A
NTRS Ryan Strome E 5.00 12.00
NTSM Sean Monahan B 5.00 12.00
NTTA Tomas Tatar E 6.00 15.00

2016-17 Upper Deck MVP NHL Territory Materials

TMAB Aleksander Barkov B 5.00 12.00
TMAH Adam Henrique B 5.00 12.00
TMAK Anze Kopitar B 8.00 20.00
TMBH Braden Holtby B 8.00 20.00
TMBO Bo Horvat C 6.00 15.00
TMCM Connor McDavid A 40.00 100.00
TMDS Derek Stepan C 3.00 8.00
TMGL Gabriel Landeskog C 3.00 8.00
TMJE Jack Eichel A 8.00 20.00
TMJF Justin Faulk C 3.00 8.00
TMJG John Gibson C 4.00 10.00
TMJP Joe Pavelski B 5.00 12.00
TMJT Jacob Trouba C 3.00 8.00
TMJV James van Riemsdyk C 4.00 10.00
TMJZ Jason Zucker C 3.00 8.00
TMMF Marc-Andre Fleury B 8.00 20.00
TMMZ Mika Zibanejad C 4.00 10.00
TMNF Nick Foligno C 3.00 8.00
TMOE Oliver Ekman-Larsson B 4.00 10.00
TMPB Patrice Bergeron B 6.00 15.00
TMPK Patrick Kane A 10.00 25.00
TMPS P.K. Subban A 5.00 12.00
TMRS Ryan Strome C 3.00 8.00
TMSM Sean Monahan B 5.00 12.00
TMSS Steven Stamkos A 6.00 15.00
TMTA Tomas Tatar C 3.00 8.00
TMTS Tyler Seguin B 8.00 20.00
TMVT Vladimir Tarasenko B 8.00 20.00

2016-17 Upper Deck MVP Pro Sign

PROAA Andy Andreoff E 5.00 12.00
PROAB Aleksander Barkov C 8.00 20.00
PROAS Andrew Shaw D 12.00 30.00
PROBD Brandon Dubinsky B 8.00 20.00
PROBH Bo Horvat D 12.00 30.00
PROCC Charlie Coyle C 15.00 30.00
PROCF Cody Franson C 5.00 12.00
PROCM Connor McDavid A
PROCT Chris Tierney E 5.00 12.00
PROJC John Carlson D 10.00 25.00
PROKT Kyle Turris D 10.00 25.00
PROMB Matt Beleskey D 10.00 25.00
PROOK Oscar Klefbom E 6.00 15.00
PRORS Reilly Smith D 5.00 12.00
PROTH Thomas Hickey E 6.00 15.00
PROTV Trevor van Riemsdyk C 8.00 20.00
PROVR Victor Rask E 5.00 12.00
PROWG Wayne Gretzky A

2016-17 Upper Deck MVP Rookie Redemption Cards

RR1 Atlantic Division 60.00 150.00
RR2 Central Division 40.00 100.00
RR3 Metropolitan Division 25.00 60.00
RR4 Pacific Division 30.00 80.00

2017-18 Upper Deck MVP

1 Evgeni Malkin .75 2.00
2 Patrice Bergeron .30 .75
3 Max Domi .25 .60
4 Corey Perry .25 .60
5 Sean Monahan .25 .60
6 Alexander Wennberg .20 .50
7 Milan Lucic .25 .60
8 Mikku Koivu .20 .50
9 Filip Forsberg .30 .75
10 Jonathan Toews .50 1.25
11 Mike Hoffman .20 .50
12 Jack Eichel .40 1.00
13 Bo Horvat .25 .60
14 Mark Scheifele .30 .75
15 Joe Thornton .25 .60
16 Jaden Schwartz .30 .75
17 Victor Hedman .30 .75
18 Rick Nash .25 .60
19 Nazem Kadri .20 .50
20 Evgeny Kuznetsov .40 1.00
21 Anders Lee .25 .60
22 Cory Schneider .20 .50
23 Alex Galchenyuk .30 .75
24 Aleksander Barkov .25 .60
25 Dylan Larkin .25 .60
26 Jeff Carter .25 .60
27 Tyler Seguin .40 1.00
28 Matt Duchene .25 .60
29 Jordan Staal .25 .60
30 Wayne Simmonds .30 .75
31 Ryan Getzlaf .25 .60
32 Leon Draisaitl .40 1.00
33 Martin Hanzal .20 .50
34 Martin Jones .25 .60
35 Phil Kessel .30 .75
36 Ryan Spooner .20 .50
37 Nick Foligno .20 .50
38 Kevin Shattenkirk .25 .60
39 Calle Jarnkrok .20 .50
40 Corey Crawford .30 .75
41 Nikolaj Ehlers .25 .60
42 Patrik Berglund .15 .40
43 Travis Konecny .25 .60
44 Loui Eriksson .20 .50
45 Max Pacioretty .25 .60
46 Matthew Tkachuk .25 .60
47 Patrick Marleau .25 .60
48 Kris Versteeg .15 .40
49 Mika Zibanejad .25 .60
50 William Nylander .40 1.00
51 Damon Severson .20 .50
52 Bobby Ryan .20 .50
53 Justin Abdelkader .20 .50
54 Rickard Rakell .20 .50
55 Mitch Marner .40 1.00
56 Drew Doughty .25 .60
57 Jordan Eberle .25 .60
58 Kris Letang .25 .60
59 David Backes .20 .50
60 Nicklas Backstrom .40 1.00
61 Alex Killorn .20 .50
62 Sam Gagner .20 .50
63 Richard Panik .20 .50
64 Mikko Rantanen .25 .60
65 Shea Weber .20 .50
66 Brandon Sutter .20 .50
67 Teuvo Teravainen .20 .50
68 Matt Moulson .15 .40
69 Vincent Trocheck .20 .50
70 Mikkel Boedker .20 .50
71 Alexander Steen .25 .60
72 James van Riemsdyk .25 .60
73 Jason Spezza .25 .60
74 Ryan Nugent-Hopkins .25 .60
75 Tuukka Rask .25 .60
76 Mark Giordano .20 .50
77 Anthony Mantha .25 .60
78 J.T. Miller .20 .50
79 Zack Smith .15 .40
80 Zach Werenski .25 .60
81 Devan Dubnyk .25 .60
82 Tanner Pearson .20 .50
83 Adam Henrique .20 .50
84 Jakub Voracek .25 .60
85 James Neal .20 .50
86 Blake Wheeler .25 .60
87 Andrei Vasilevskiy .30 .75
88 T.J. Oshie .40 1.00
89 Ryan Strome .20 .50
90 Markus Granlund .20 .50
91 Andrew Cogliano .15 .40
92 Marc-Edouard Vlasic .15 .40
93 Sebastian Aho .25 .60
94 Rasmus Ristolainen .25 .60
95 Matt Murray .40 1.00
96 Mike Smith .25 .60
97 Alexander Radulov .25 .60
98 Jonathan Marchessault .25 .60
99 Duncan Keith .25 .60
100 Connor McDavid 1.00 2.50
101 Tyson Barrie .25 .60
102 Patrick Eaves .20 .50
103 Pekka Rinne .30 .75
104 Michael Cammalleri .20 .50
105 Tyler Johnson .20 .50
106 Chris Kreider .25 .60
107 Paul Stastny .25 .60
108 Tomas Tatar .25 .60
109 Alec Martinez .15 .40
110 Dustin Byfuglien .25 .60
111 Andrew Ladd .25 .60
112 Cam Talbot .25 .60
113 Ryan O'Reilly .25 .60
114 Victor Rask .25 .60
115 Brayden Schenn .25 .60
116 Derick Brassard .25 .60
117 Artem Anisimov .20 .50
118 Thomas Vanek .20 .50
119 Andrew Shaw .20 .50
120 Morgan Rielly .25 .60
121 Patric Hornqvist .20 .50
122 Nino Niederreiter .20 .50
123 Radim Vrbata .15 .40
124 Gabriel Landeskog .20 .50
125 Brock Nelson .20 .50
126 Marcus Johansson .20 .50
127 Alex Pietrangelo .20 .50
128 Ryan Hartman .25 .60
129 Roberto Luongo .25 .60
130 Seth Jones .20 .50
131 Logan Couture .25 .60
132 Sam Bennett .20 .50
133 John Klingberg .20 .50
134 Tyler Toffoli .20 .50
135 Kevin Hayes .20 .50
136 Jonathan Drouin .25 .60
137 Roman Josi .25 .60
138 Mike Green .20 .50
139 Derek Stepan .20 .50
140 Phillip Danault .15 .40
141 Tobias Rieder .15 .40
142 Torey Krug .25 .60
143 Carl Soderberg .15 .40
144 Travis Zajac .15 .40
145 Kyle Turris .25 .60
146 Bryan Little .20 .50
147 John Gibson .25 .60
148 Charlie Coyle .20 .50
149 Sam Reinhart .20 .50
150 Adam Larsson .25 .60
151 Brett Ritchie .15 .40
152 Viktor Arvidsson .20 .50
153 Sergei Bobrovsky .25 .60
154 Shayne Gostisbehere .25 .60
155 Tyler Bozak .20 .50
156 Daniel Sedin .25 .60
157 Ben Bishop .25 .60
158 Aaron Ekblad .25 .60
159 Tomas Plekanec .20 .50

160 Nick Leddy .15 .40
161 Bryan Rust .25 .60
162 Conor Sheary .25 .60
163 Dougie Hamilton .20 .50
164 Marian Hossa .20 .50
165 Justin Faulk .20 .50
166 Gustav Nyquist .25 .60
167 Cam Fowler .20 .50
168 Shane Doan .20 .50
169 Braden Holtby .40 1.00
170 David Krejci .20 .50
171 Kyle Palmieri .20 .50
172 Adam Lowry .20 .50
173 Mark Stone .25 .60
174 Brent Burns .30 .75
175 Sean Couturier .20 .50
176 Jarome Iginla .25 .60
177 Evander Kane .25 .60
178 Ryan Johansen .25 .60
179 Cam Ward .20 .50
180 Reilly Smith .25 .60
181 Calvin Pickard .15 .40
182 Josh Bailey .20 .50
183 Kari Lehtonen .20 .50
184 Artemi Panarin .25 .60
185 Nikita Kucherov .40 1.00
186 Frederik Andersen .20 .50
187 Jake Guentzel .30 .75
188 Mats Zuccarello .25 .60
189 Frans Nielsen .20 .50
190 David Pastrnak .40 1.00
191 John Carlson .30 .75
192 Mikael Backlund .15 .40
193 Jakob Silfverberg .20 .50
194 Brandon Saad .25 .60
195 Jimmy Vesey .25 .60
196 Brendan Gallagher .25 .60
197 Christian Dvorak .20 .50
198 Mikael Granlund .25 .60
199 Jake Allen .30 .75
200 Sidney Crosby 1.00 2.50
201 Connor McDavid 2.50 6.00
202 Taylor Hall 1.25 3.00
203 Claude Giroux .60 1.50
204 Joe Pavelski .60 1.50
205 Carey Price 2.00 5.00
206 Jeff Skinner .50 1.25
207 Alexander Ovechkin 2.50 6.00
208 Anze Kopitar 1.00 2.50
209 Jaromir Jagr 1.50 4.00
210 Auston Matthews 2.50 6.00
211 Jamie Benn .75 2.00
212 Johnny Gaudreau 1.00 2.50
213 Nathan MacKinnon 1.25 3.00
214 Oliver Ekman-Larsson .60 1.50
215 Patrick Kane 1.25 3.00
216 Cam Atkinson .60 1.50
217 Henrik Zetterberg .60 1.50
218 Brad Marchand .75 2.00
219 Henrik Lundqvist 1.00 2.50
220 Sidney Crosby 2.50 6.00
221 Eric Staal .75 2.00
222 Vladimir Tarasenko 1.00 2.50
223 Patrik Laine 1.00 2.50
224 John Tavares 1.25 3.00
225 P.K. Subban .60 1.50
226 Ryan Kesler .60 1.50
227 Henrik Sedin .60 1.50
228 Erik Karlsson .75 2.00
229 Steven Stamkos 1.25 3.00
230 Alexander Ovechkin 2.50 6.00
231 Ivan Barbashev RC 2.00 5.00
232 Charlie McAvoy RC 6.00 15.00
233 Nikita Scherbak RC 4.00 10.00
234 Evgeny Svechnikov RC 4.00 10.00
235 Riley Barber RC 1.50 4.00
236 Nicolas Kerdiles RC 2.00 5.00
237 Vladislav Kamenev RC 3.00 8.00
238 Denis Gurianov RC 2.00 5.00
239 Christian Fischer RC 2.50 6.00
240 Adrian Kempe RC 2.50 6.00
241 Brock Boeser RC 10.00 25.00
242 Jack Roslovic RC 2.50 6.00
243 J.T. Compher RC 2.50 6.00
244 Jordan Schmaltz RC 2.50 6.00
245 Josh Ho-Sang RC 2.50 6.00
246 Colin White RC 2.00 5.00
247 Alex Tuch RC 5.00 12.00
248 Clayton Keller RC 5.00 12.00
249 Alexander Nylander RC 3.00 8.00
250 Tyson Jost RC 4.00 10.00

2017-18 Upper Deck MVP Super Script

*SUPER/25: 5X TO 12X BASIC CARDS
*SUPER.SP/25: 2X TO 5X BASIC CARDS
*SUPER.RC/25: 2X TO 5X BASIC CARDS
40 Corey Crawford 2.50 6.00
60 Nicklas Backstrom 3.00 8.00
141 Tobias Rieder 10.00 25.00
200 Sidney Crosby 12.00 30.00
201 Connor McDavid 25.00 60.00
210 Auston Matthews 80.00 200.00
215 Patrick Kane 15.00 40.00
223 Patrik Laine 12.00 30.00
246 Colin White 25.00 60.00
249 Alexander Nylander 15.00 40.00

2017-18 Upper Deck MVP Colors and Contours

*G1,G2,B1,B2: 2.5X TO 6X BASIC CARDS
*G3,B3: 3X TO 8X BASIC CARDS
*VETS P1,P2: 2X TO 5X BASIC CARDS
*RC P1,P2: .6X TO 1.5X BASIC CARDS
*P3: 3X TO 8X BASIC CARDS

2017-18 Upper Deck MVP NHL Player Credentials Level 1 Access

NHLAG Alex Galchenyuk 1.50 4.00
NHLAL Anders Lee 1.25 3.00
NHLAS Andrew Shaw 1.00 2.50
NHLAW Alexander Wennberg 1.00 2.50
NHLBB Brent Burns 1.50 4.00
NHLBH Braden Holtby 2.00 5.00
NHLCC Corey Crawford 1.50 4.00
NHLDD Jonathan Quick 2.00 5.00
NHLDP David Pastrnak 2.00 5.00
NHLHS Henrik Sedin 1.25 3.00
NHLHZ Henrik Zetterberg 1.25 3.00
NHLJE Jack Eichel 2.00 5.00
NHLJP Jason Pominville 1.00 2.50
NHLJS Jaden Schwartz 1.50 4.00
NHLMD Matt Duchene 1.25 3.00
NHLMH Mike Hoffman 1.00 2.50
NHLMM Matt Murray 2.00 5.00
NHLMS Mark Scheifele 1.50 4.00
NHLNB Nicklas Backstrom 2.00 5.00
NHLNK Nikita Kucherov 2.00 5.00
NHLOE Oliver Ekman-Larsson 1.25 3.00
NHLPS P.K. Subban 1.25 3.00
NHLRK Ryan Kesler 1.25 3.00
NHLSE Tyler Seguin 2.00 5.00
NHLSM Sean Monahan 1.25 3.00
NHLST Derek Stepan 1.00 2.50
NHLTH Taylor Hall 2.50 6.00
NHLTR Tuukka Rask 1.25 3.00
NHLTT Teuvo Teravainen 1.00 2.50
NHLWS Wayne Simmonds 1.50 4.00

2017-18 Upper Deck MVP NHL Player Credentials Level 1 VIP Access

NHLAM Auston Matthews 6.00 15.00
NHLCM Connor McDavid 6.00 15.00
NHLDS Darryl Sittler 1.50 4.00
NHLJJ Jaromir Jagr 4.00 10.00
NHLMB Martin Brodeur 3.00 8.00
NHLPK Patrick Kane 3.00 8.00
NHLSC Sidney Crosby 6.00 15.00
NHLSY Steve Yzerman 2.00 5.00
NHLTS Teemu Selanne 2.00 5.00
NHLWG Wayne Gretzky 8.00 20.00

2017-18 Upper Deck MVP NHL Player Credentials Level 4 Access

NHLAL Anders Lee AU C 8.00 20.00
NHLAW Alexander Wennberg AU C 8.00 20.00
NHLMM Matt Murray AU B 40.00 100.00
NHLMS Mark Scheifele AU B 25.00 60.00
NHLTT Teuvo Teravainen AU C 8.00 20.00

2018-19 Upper Deck MVP

1 John Tavares .30 .75
2 Ryan Getzlaf .25 .60
3 Brad Marchand .25 .60
4 Sean Monahan .20 .50
5 Jonathan Quick .25 .60
6 Sean Couturier .20 .50
7 Duncan Keith .20 .50
8 Mitch Marner .25 .60
9 Evgeny Kuznetsov .30 .75
10 Oliver Ekman-Larsson .20 .50
11 James Neal .20 .50
12 Ryan O'Reilly .20 .50
13 Teuvo Teravainen .20 .50
14 Seth Jones .20 .50
15 Jamie Benn .30 .75
16 Dylan Larkin .25 .60
17 Aleksander Barkov .20 .50
18 Mikael Granlund .20 .50
19 Max Pacioretty .20 .50
20 P.K. Subban .25 .60
21 Gabriel Landeskog .25 .60
22 Nico Hischier .25 .60
23 Mark Stone .20 .50
24 Joe Pavelski .25 .60
25 Evgeni Malkin .75 2.00
26 Leon Draisaitl .50 1.25
27 Brayden Schenn .25 .60
28 Mats Zuccarello .25 .60
29 Brayden Point .25 .60
30 Daniel Sedin .25 .60
31 Patrik Laine .25 .60
32 Evander Kane .20 .50
33 John Klingberg .20 .50
34 Mike Smith .20 .50
35 Artemi Panarin .25 .60
36 John Carlson .25 .60
37 Clayton Keller .25 .60
38 Nick Schmaltz .20 .50
39 Jonathan Huberdeau .20 .50
40 Henrik Zetterberg .40 1.00
41 Shayne Gostisbehere .25 .60
42 Jonathan Marchessault .25 .60
43 David Pastrnak .25 .60
44 Sebastian Aho .20 .50
45 William Nylander .25 .60
46 Jason Zucker .20 .50
47 Dustin Brown .20 .50
48 Filip Forsberg .25 .60
49 Mikko Rantanen .20 .50
50 Taylor Hall .50 1.25
51 Mike Hoffman .20 .50
52 Milan Lucic .20 .50
53 Logan Couture .20 .50
54 Jakob Silfverberg .20 .50
55 Alex Galchenyuk .20 .50
56 Josh Bailey .20 .50
57 Kris Letang .20 .50
58 Kyle Okposo .20 .50
59 Jaden Schwartz .20 .50
60 Kevin Shattenkirk .20 .50
61 Dougie Hamilton .20 .50
62 Max Domi .20 .50
63 T.J. Oshie .25 .60
64 Oliver Bjorkstrand .20 .50
65 Blake Wheeler .25 .60
66 Thomas Vanek .20 .50
67 Brandon Saad .20 .50
68 Alexander Radulov .20 .50
69 Vincent Trocheck .20 .50
70 Henrik Sedin .25 .60
71 Nazem Kadri .20 .50
72 Mika Zibanejad .20 .50
73 Alex Tuch .25 .60
74 Rickard Rakell .20 .50
75 Mark Scheifele .25 .60
76 Victor Hedman .20 .50
77 Viktor Arvidsson .25 .60
78 Justin Williams .20 .50
79 Rick Nash .25 .60
80 Eric Staal .25 .60
81 Tyson Barrie .20 .50
82 Nick Foligno .20 .50
83 Dion Phaneuf .20 .50
84 David Perron .20 .50
85 Ryan Nugent-Hopkins .20 .50
86 Derick Brassard .20 .50
87 Justin Abdelkader .20 .50
88 Jakub Voracek .20 .50
89 Cory Schneider .20 .50
90 Ben Bishop .20 .50
91 Anders Lee .20 .50
92 Micheal Ferland .20 .50
93 Sam Reinhart .20 .50
94 Tomas Hertl .20 .50
95 Roberto Luongo .25 .60
96 Alex DeBrincat .25 .60
97 Jake Gardiner .20 .50
98 Tom Wilson .20 .50
99 Jonathan Drouin .20 .50
100 Auston Matthews CL 1.00 2.50
101 Steven Stamkos .50 1.25
102 Alex Pietrangelo .20 .50
103 Ryan Suter .20 .50
104 Reilly Smith .20 .50
105 Joe Thornton .20 .50
106 Kevin Hayes .20 .50
107 Jordan Staal .20 .50
108 Alexander Wennberg .20 .50
109 Drew Doughty .25 .60
110 Patrick Marleau .20 .50
111 Phil Kessel .20 .50
112 Ryan McDonagh .20 .50
113 Wayne Simmonds .25 .60
114 Ryan Johansen .25 .60
115 Matt Duchene .25 .60
116 Tomas Tatar .20 .50
117 Ondrej Kase .20 .50
118 Alex Kerfoot .20 .50
119 Tyler Johnson .20 .50
120 Kyle Palmieri .20 .50
121 Rasmus Ristolainen .20 .50
122 Bo Horvat .20 .50
123 T.J. Brodie .20 .50
124 Oscar Klefbom .20 .50
125 Aaron Ekblad .20 .50
126 Andrew Shaw .20 .50
127 Nikolaj Ehlers .20 .50
128 Jake Muzzin .20 .50
129 Roman Josi .20 .50
130 Patrick Kane .40 1.00
131 Tuukka Rask .20 .50
132 Cody Eakin .20 .50
133 Ryan Spooner .20 .50
134 Christian Dvorak .20 .50
135 Jake Guentzel .25 .60
136 Cam Atkinson .25 .60
137 Andrei Vasilevskiy .40 1.00
138 Jordan Eberle .20 .50
139 Claude Giroux .25 .60
140 Chris Kreider .25 .60
141 Justin Faulk AS .20 .50
142 Alexander Steen .20 .50
143 Zach Hyman .20 .50
144 Anze Kopitar .40 1.00
145 Braden Holtby .40 1.00
146 Anthony Mantha .25 .60
147 Jason Spezza .20 .50
148 Corey Perry .25 .60
149 Carl Soderberg .20 .50
150 Matt Murray .25 .60
151 David Krejci .20 .50
152 Dustin Byfuglien .25 .60
153 William Karlsson .40 1.00
154 Ryan Strome .20 .50
155 Conor Sheary .20 .50
156 Martin Jones .20 .50
157 Andrew Ladd .20 .50
158 Colton Parayko .20 .50
159 Anthony Duclair .20 .50
160 Tomas Plekanec .20 .50
161 Pekka Rinne .20 .50
162 Connor Hellebuyck .25 .60
163 Alex Killorn .20 .50
164 Olli Maatta .20 .50
165 J.T. Miller .20 .50
166 Tyler Toffoli .25 .60
167 Jake Allen .25 .60
168 Connor Brown .20 .50
169 Ondrej Palat .20 .50
170 Loui Eriksson .20 .50
171 Shea Weber .25 .60
172 Nick Leddy .20 .50
173 Gustav Nyquist .20 .50
174 Jake DeBrusk .25 .60
175 Jesper Bratt .20 .50
176 Carl Hagelin .20 .50
177 Mikkel Boedker .20 .50
178 Kyle Turris .20 .50
179 Bobby Ryan .20 .50
180 Cam Talbot .20 .50
181 Keith Yandle .25 .60
182 Jason Pominville .20 .50
183 Danton Heinen .20 .50
184 Pierre-Luc Dubois .25 .60
185 Jim Howard .20 .50
186 Nicklas Backstrom .20 .50
187 Brendan Gallagher .20 .50
188 Erik Johnson .20 .50
189 Adam Henrique .25 .60
190 Victor Rask .20 .50
191 Radek Faksa .20 .50
192 Derek Stepan .20 .50
193 Matthew Tkachuk .20 .50
194 Jeff Skinner .20 .50
195 Ryan Hartman .20 .50
196 Nolan Patrick .25 .60
197 Frederik Andersen .25 .60
198 Erik Haula .20 .50
199 Devan Dubnyk .25 .60
200 Connor McDavid CL 1.00 2.50
201 Sidney Crosby 2.00 5.00
202 Marc-Andre Fleury 1.00 2.50
203 Tyler Seguin .60 1.50
204 Vladimir Tarasenko .75 2.00
205 Auston Matthews 2.00 5.00
206 Carey Price 1.50 4.00
207 Mathew Barzal 1.00 2.50
208 Johnny Gaudreau 1.00 2.50
209 Patrice Bergeron .60 1.50
210 Alexander Ovechkin 1.50 4.00
211 Brock Boeser 1.00 2.50
212 Erik Karlsson 1.00 2.50
213 Nathan MacKinnon 1.00 2.50
214 Jack Eichel .75 2.00
215 Jonathan Toews .75 2.00
216 Nikita Kucherov .75 2.00
217 Brent Burns .75 2.00
218 Henrik Lundqvist 1.00 2.50
219 Connor McDavid 2.00 5.00
220 Alexander Ovechkin CL 1.50 4.00
221 Michael Dal Colle RC 1.50 4.00
222 Dillon Heatherington RC 1.50 4.00
223 Dominic Turgeon RC 1.50 4.00
224 Daniel Brickley RC 1.50 4.00
225 Morgan Klimchuk RC 1.50 4.00
226 Justin Holl RC 1.50 4.00
227 Neal Pionk RC 1.50 4.00
228 Dylan Sikura RC 2.50 6.00
229 Ethan Bear RC 4.00 10.00
230 Oskar Lindblom RC 2.50 6.00
231 Maxim Mamin RC 1.50 4.00
232 Ryan Donato RC 2.50 6.00
233 Casey Mittelstadt RC 3.00 8.00
234 Adam Gaudette RC 2.50 6.00
235 Travis Dermott RC 1.50 4.00
236 Zach Aston-Reese RC 1.50 4.00
237 Jordan Greenway RC 2.50 6.00
238 Marcus Pettersson RC 1.50 4.00
239 Anthony Cirelli RC 1.50 4.00
240 Joe Hicketts RC 1.50 4.00
241 Eeli Tolvanen RC 3.00 8.00
242 Matthew Highmore RC 1.50 4.00
243 Henrik Borgstrom RC 3.00 8.00
244 Samuel Montembeault RC 1.50 4.00
245 Tomas Hyka RC 1.50 4.00
246 Lias Andersson RC 3.00 8.00
247 Warren Foegele RC 1.50 4.00
248 Ryan Lomberg RC 1.50 4.00
249 Andreas Johnsson RC 1.50 4.00
250 Noah Juulsen RC 1.50 4.00

2018-19 Upper Deck MVP 20th Anniversary Colors and Contours

1 Sidney Crosby 8.00 20.00
2 Ryan Getzlaf 2.00 5.00
3 Steven Stamkos 4.00 10.00
4 Evgeny Kuznetsov 2.50 6.00
5 Connor McDavid 8.00 20.00
6 Ryan O'Reilly 1.50 4.00
7 Dylan Larkin 2.00 5.00
8 Mikael Granlund 1.50 4.00
9 Nico Hischier 2.00 5.00
10 Auston Matthews 8.00 20.00
11 Leon Draisaitl 4.00 10.00
12 Brayden Schenn 2.00 5.00
13 Patrik Laine 2.00 5.00
14 Roberto Luongo 2.00 5.00
15 Brock Boeser 4.00 10.00
16 William Nylander 2.00 5.00
17 Taylor Hall 4.00 10.00
18 Alex Galchenyuk 1.50 4.00
19 Erik Karlsson 4.00 10.00
20 Johnny Gaudreau 4.00 10.00
21 Mark Scheifele 2.00 5.00
22 Eric Staal 2.00 5.00
23 Clayton Keller 2.00 5.00
24 Drew Doughty 2.00 5.00
25 Patrick Kane 3.00 8.00
26 Wayne Simmonds 2.00 5.00
27 Matt Duchene 2.00 5.00
28 Tomas Tatar 1.50 4.00
29 Aaron Ekblad 1.50 4.00
30 Carey Price 6.00 15.00
31 Blake Wheeler 2.00 5.00
32 Roman Josi 1.50 4.00
33 Matt Murray 2.00 5.00
34 Pierre-Luc Dubois 2.00 5.00
35 Vladimir Tarasenko 3.00 8.00
36 Nolan Patrick 2.00 5.00
37 Mathew Barzal 4.00 10.00
38 Tuukka Rask 1.50 4.00
39 Nikita Kucherov 3.00 8.00
40 Tyler Seguin 2.50 6.00
41 Jeff Skinner 1.50 4.00
42 Jonathan Quick 2.00 5.00
43 James Neal 1.50 4.00
44 Teuvo Teravainen 1.50 4.00
45 Marc-Andre Fleury 4.00 10.00
46 Joe Pavelski 2.00 5.00
47 Mats Zuccarello 2.00 5.00
48 Petr Mrazek 2.00 5.00
49 Mikko Rantanen 1.50 4.00
50 Alexander Ovechkin 6.00 15.00
51 Jaden Schwartz 1.50 4.00
52 Henrik Sedin 2.00 5.00
53 Joe Thornton 1.50 4.00
54 Jake Guentzel 2.00 5.00
55 John Tavares 2.50 6.00
56 Andrei Vasilevskiy 3.00 8.00
57 Corey Perry 2.00 5.00
58 William Karlsson 3.00 8.00
59 Pekka Rinne 1.50 4.00
60 Brad Marchand 2.00 5.00
61 Cam Talbot 1.50 4.00
62 Jack Eichel 3.00 8.00
63 Brent Burns 3.00 8.00
64 Mark Stone 1.50 4.00
65 Mitch Marner 2.00 5.00
66 Sean Couturier 1.50 4.00
67 Jonathan Marchessault 2.00 5.00
68 Anze Kopitar 3.00 8.00
69 Patrice Bergeron 2.50 6.00
70 Jamie Benn 2.50 6.00
71 Duncan Keith 1.50 4.00
72 Max Pacioretty 1.50 4.00
73 Artemi Panarin 2.00 5.00
74 Logan Couture 1.50 4.00
75 Henrik Lundqvist 4.00 10.00
76 Oliver Ekman-Larsson 1.50 4.00
77 Phil Kessel 1.50 4.00
78 Jonathan Drouin 1.50 4.00
79 Connor Hellebuyck 2.00 5.00
80 Jonathan Toews 3.00 8.00
81 David Pastrnak 2.00 5.00
82 Braden Holtby 3.00 8.00
83 Sean Monahan 1.50 4.00
84 Patrick Marleau 1.50 4.00
85 P.K. Subban 2.00 5.00
86 Nikolaj Ehlers 1.50 4.00
87 Frederik Andersen 2.00 5.00
88 Henrik Zetterberg 3.00 8.00
89 Daniel Sedin 2.00 5.00
90 Nathan MacKinnon 4.00 10.00
91 Evgeni Malkin 6.00 15.00
92 Lias Andersson 4.00 10.00
93 Oskar Lindblom 3.00 8.00
94 Travis Dermott 2.00 5.00
95 Eeli Tolvanen 4.00 10.00
96 Noah Juulsen 2.00 5.00
97 Zach Aston-Reese 2.00 5.00
98 Adam Gaudette 3.00 8.00
99 Ryan Donato 3.00 8.00
100 Casey Mittelstadt 4.00 10.00

2018-19 Upper Deck MVP 20th Anniversary Tribute Silver Script

1 Sidney Crosby 4.00 10.00
2 Ryan Getzlaf 1.00 2.50
3 Steven Stamkos 2.00 5.00
4 Evgeny Kuznetsov 1.25 3.00
5 Connor McDavid 4.00 10.00
6 Ryan O'Reilly .75 2.00
7 Dylan Larkin 1.00 2.50
8 Mikael Granlund .75 2.00
9 Nico Hischier 1.00 2.50
10 Auston Matthews 4.00 10.00
11 Leon Draisaitl 2.00 5.00
12 Brayden Schenn 1.00 2.50
13 Patrik Laine 1.00 2.50
14 Roberto Luongo 1.00 2.50
15 Brock Boeser 2.00 5.00
16 William Nylander 1.00 2.50
17 Taylor Hall 2.00 5.00
18 Alex Galchenyuk .75 2.00
19 Erik Karlsson 2.00 5.00
20 Johnny Gaudreau 2.00 5.00
21 Mark Scheifele 1.00 2.50
22 Eric Staal 1.00 2.50
23 Clayton Keller 1.00 2.50
24 Drew Doughty 1.00 2.50
25 Patrick Kane 1.50 4.00
26 Wayne Simmonds 1.00 2.50
27 Matt Duchene 1.00 2.50
28 Tomas Tatar .75 2.00
29 Aaron Ekblad .75 2.00
30 Carey Price 3.00 8.00
31 Blake Wheeler 1.00 2.50
32 Roman Josi .75 2.00
33 Matt Murray 1.00 2.50
34 Pierre-Luc Dubois 1.00 2.50
35 Vladimir Tarasenko 1.50 4.00
36 Nolan Patrick 1.00 2.50
37 Mathew Barzal 2.00 5.00
38 Tuukka Rask .75 2.00
39 Nikita Kucherov 1.50 4.00
40 Tyler Seguin 1.25 3.00
41 Jeff Skinner .75 2.00
42 Jonathan Quick 1.00 2.50
43 James Neal .75 2.00
44 Teuvo Teravainen .75 2.00
45 Marc-Andre Fleury 2.00 5.00
46 Joe Pavelski 1.00 2.50
47 Mats Zuccarello 1.00 2.50
48 Petr Mrazek 1.00 2.50
49 Mikko Rantanen .75 2.00
50 Alexander Ovechkin 3.00 8.00
51 Jaden Schwartz .75 2.00
52 Henrik Sedin 1.00 2.50
53 Joe Thornton .75 2.00
54 Jake Guentzel 1.00 2.50
55 John Tavares 1.25 3.00
56 Andrei Vasilevskiy 1.50 4.00
57 Corey Perry 1.00 2.50
58 William Karlsson 1.50 4.00
59 Pekka Rinne .75 2.00
60 Brad Marchand 1.00 2.50
61 Cam Talbot .75 2.00
62 Jack Eichel 1.50 4.00
63 Brent Burns 1.50 4.00
64 Mark Stone .75 2.00
65 Mitch Marner 1.00 2.50
66 Sean Couturier .75 2.00
67 Jonathan Marchessault 1.00 2.50
68 Anze Kopitar 1.50 4.00
69 Patrice Bergeron 1.25 3.00
70 Jamie Benn 1.25 3.00
71 Duncan Keith .75 2.00
72 Max Pacioretty .75 2.00
73 Artemi Panarin 1.00 2.50
74 Logan Couture .75 2.00
75 Henrik Lundqvist 2.00 5.00
76 Oliver Ekman-Larsson .75 2.00
77 Phil Kessel .75 2.00
78 Jonathan Drouin .75 2.00
79 Connor Hellebuyck 1.00 2.50
80 Jonathan Toews 1.50 4.00
81 David Pastrnak 1.00 2.50
82 Braden Holtby 1.50 4.00
83 Sean Monahan .75 2.00
84 Patrick Marleau .75 2.00
85 P.K. Subban 1.00 2.50
86 Nikolaj Ehlers .75 2.00
87 Frederik Andersen 1.00 2.50
88 Henrik Zetterberg 1.50 4.00
89 Daniel Sedin 1.00 2.50
90 Nathan MacKinnon 2.00 5.00
91 Evgeni Malkin 3.00 8.00
92 Lias Andersson 2.00 5.00
93 Oskar Lindblom 1.50 4.00
94 Travis Dermott 1.00 2.50
95 Eeli Tolvanen 2.00 5.00
96 Noah Juulsen 1.00 2.50
97 Zach Aston-Reese 1.00 2.50
98 Adam Gaudette 1.50 4.00
99 Ryan Donato 1.50 4.00
100 Casey Mittelstadt 2.00 5.00

2018-19 Upper Deck MVP NHL Player Credentials Entry Level Access

NHLET Eeli Tolvanen 2.50 6.00
NHLHB Henrik Borgstrom 2.50 6.00
NHLLA Lias Andersson 2.50 6.00
NHLMD Michael Dal Colle 1.25 3.00
NHLMI Casey Mittelstadt 2.50 6.00
NHLNJ Noah Juulsen 1.25 3.00
NHLOL Oskar Lindblom 2.00 5.00
NHLRD Ryan Donato 2.00 5.00
NHLTD Travis Dermott 1.25 3.00
NHLZA Zach Aston-Reese 1.25 3.00

2018-19 Upper Deck MVP NHL Player Credentials Level 1 Access

NHLAM Anthony Mantha 1.00 2.50
NHLAV Andrei Vasilevskiy 1.50 4.00
NHLBG Brendan Gallagher .75 2.00
NHLBM Brad Marchand 1.00 2.50
NHLDK Duncan Keith .75 2.00
NHLEM Evgeni Malkin 3.00 8.00
NHLGU Jake Guentzel 1.00 2.50
NHLJB Jamie Benn 1.25 3.00
NHLJC Jeff Carter 1.00 2.50
NHLJG Johnny Gaudreau 2.00 5.00
NHLJN James Neal .75 2.00
NHLJP Joe Pavelski 1.00 2.50
NHLKS Kevin Shattenkirk .75 2.00
NHLKU Evgeny Kuznetsov 1.25 3.00
NHLMB Mathew Barzal 2.00 5.00
NHLMM Mitch Marner 1.00 2.50
NHLMR Mikko Rantanen .75 2.00
NHLPL Patrik Laine 1.00 2.50
NHLRI Pekka Rinne .75 2.00
NHLTR Vincent Trocheck .75 2.00

2018-19 Upper Deck MVP NHL Player Credentials Level 1 Access Autographs

NHLAV Andrei Vasilevskiy C 15.00 40.00
NHLBG Brendan Gallagher B 8.00 20.00
NHLGU Jake Guentzel C 10.00 25.00
NHLJB Jamie Benn B 12.00 30.00
NHLJC Jeff Carter B 10.00 25.00
NHLJG Johnny Gaudreau B 20.00 50.00
NHLJP Joe Pavelski B 10.00 25.00
NHLKS Kevin Shattenkirk C 8.00 20.00
NHLKU Evgeny Kuznetsov A 12.00 30.00
NHLMB Mathew Barzal C 20.00 50.00
NHLMM Mitch Marner B 10.00 25.00
NHLMR Mikko Rantanen C 8.00 20.00
NHLPL Patrik Laine C 10.00 25.00
NHLRI Pekka Rinne C 8.00 20.00
NHLTR Vincent Trocheck C 8.00 20.00

2018-19 Upper Deck MVP NHL Player Credentials VIP Access

NHLAO Alexander Ovechkin 4.00 10.00
NHLBB Brock Boeser 2.50 6.00
NHLBO Bobby Orr 3.00 8.00
NHLCM Connor McDavid 5.00 12.00
NHLEK Erik Karlsson 2.50 6.00
NHLHL Henrik Lundqvist 2.50 6.00
NHLJT Jonathan Toews 2.00 5.00
NHLPD Pavel Datsyuk 2.00 5.00
NHLPR Patrick Roy 2.50 6.00
NHLVT Vladimir Tarasenko 2.00 5.00

2018-19 Upper Deck MVP NHL Player Credentials VIP Access Autographs

NHLAO Alexander Ovechkin A 30.00 80.00
NHLBB Brock Boeser B 20.00 50.00
NHLBO Bobby Orr B 25.00 60.00
NHLCM Connor McDavid A 40.00 100.00
NHLEK Erik Karlsson A 20.00 50.00
NHLHL Henrik Lundqvist B 20.00 50.00
NHLJT Jonathan Toews A 15.00 40.00
NHLPD Pavel Datsyuk B 15.00 40.00
NHLPR Patrick Roy A 20.00 50.00
NHLVT Vladimir Tarasenko A 15.00 40.00

2002 Upper Deck National Convention

N8 Wayne Gretzky 1.50 4.00
N9 Bobby Orr 1.00 2.50
N10 Gordie Howe 1.00 2.50

2004 Upper Deck National Convention

STATED PRINT RUN 500 SER.#'d SETS
TN13 Wayne Gretzky 3.00 8.00
TN14 Gordie Howe 1.00 2.50
TN15 Joe Thornton .60 1.50
TN17 Jason Spezza .60 1.50

2004 Upper Deck National Convention VIP

VIP5 Wayne Gretzky 4.00 10.00

2005 Upper Deck National Convention VIP

Upper Deck produced this set and distributed it to special VIP package members attending the 2005 National Sport Collectors Convention in Chicago. The set includes famous athletes from a variety of sports with the title "The National" printed on the cardfronts along with a "VIP" stamp.
VIP4 Wayne Gretzky 4.00 10.00

2006 Upper Deck National NHL

COMPLETE SET (3) 25.00 50.00
NHL1 Sidney Crosby 15.00 40.00
NHL2 Wayne Gretzky 6.00 15.00
NHL3 Alexander Ovechkin 6.00 15.00

2006 Upper Deck National NHL Autographs

Randomly inserted in VIP packages at the National Convention. Limited print runs preclude us from giving pricing.
COMPLETE SET (2)
NHL1 Sidney Crosby
NHL2 Wayne Gretzky

2006 Upper Deck National NHL VIP

COMPLETE SET (6) 30.00 60.00
1 Alexander Ovechkin 6.00 15.00
2 Wayne Gretzky 6.00 15.00
3 Sidney Crosby 15.00 40.00
4 Martin Brodeur 4.00 10.00
5 Steve Yzerman 4.00 10.00
6 Jean-Sebastien Giguere .75 2.00

2006 Upper Deck National Southern California

COMPLETE SET (6) 5.00 12.00
SoCal2 Wayne Gretzky 2.00 5.00

2007 Upper Deck National Convention

NTL12 Wayne Gretzky 1.25 3.00
NTL13 Rick Nash .75 2.00
NTL14 Sidney Crosby 1.25 3.00
NTL15 Evgeni Malkin 1.00 2.50

2007 Upper Deck National Convention VIP

VIP12 Wayne Gretzky 2.00 5.00
VIP13 Rick Nash 1.25 3.00
VIP14 Sidney Crosby 2.00 5.00
VIP15 Evgeni Malkin 1.50 4.00

2008 Upper Deck National Convention

NAT2 Patrick Kane 1.50 4.00
NAT8 Bobby Orr 1.00 2.50
NAT10 Jonathan Toews 1.25 3.00
NAT13 Carey Price 1.00 2.50
NAT14 Gordie Howe 1.00 2.50
NAT21 Sidney Crosby 1.00 2.50
NAT24 Alexander Ovechkin .60 1.50

2008 Upper Deck National Convention VIP

CARDS FEATURE VIP LOGO ON FRONT
NAT2 Patrick Kane 3.00 8.00
NAT8 Bobby Orr 2.00 5.00
NAT10 Jonathan Toews 2.50 6.00
NAT13 Carey Price 2.00 5.00
NAT14 Gordie Howe 2.00 5.00
NAT21 Sidney Crosby 2.00 5.00
NAT24 Alexander Ovechkin 1.50 4.00

2009 Upper Deck National Convention

NC10 Alexander Ovechkin 1.00 2.50
NC14 Evgeni Malkin 1.25 3.00
NC15 Gordie Howe 1.00 2.50
NC24 Sidney Crosby 1.25 3.00

2009 Upper Deck National Convention VIP

VIP5 Gordie Howe 1.25 4.00
VIP10 Sidney Crosby 2.00 5.00

2010 Upper Deck National Convention

COMPLETE SET (20) 15.00 40.00
NSC3 Alexander Ovechkin 1.50 4.00
NSC7 Gordie Howe 2.00 5.00
NSC10 Mike Green 1.25 3.00
NSC11 Sidney Crosby 3.00 8.00
NSC13 Nicklas Backstrom 1.25 3.00
NSC17 Wayne Gretzky 3.00 8.00
NSC20 Rod Langway 1.25 3.00

2010 Upper Deck National Convention Autographs

STATED PRINT RUN 9-90
NAGH Gordie Howe/9
NANB Nicklas Backstrom/75 15.00 40.00

2010 Upper Deck National Convention VIP

COMPLETE SET (6) 6.00 15.00
VIP1 Alexander Ovechkin 1.25 3.00
VIP2 Sidney Crosby 3.00 8.00
VIP6 Wayne Gretzky 2.00 5.00

2011 Upper Deck National Convention

NSCC5 Sidney Crosby 1.25 3.00
NSCC6 Jonathan Toews .75 2.00
NSCC7 Jeff Skinner .75 2.00
NSCC8 Tony Esposito .75 2.00
NSCC12 Bobby Orr 1.25 3.00
NSCC13 Wayne Gretzky 2.00 5.00
NSCC14 Gordie Howe 2.00 5.00

2011 Upper Deck National Convention Autographs

NSCCBO Bobby Orr/25
NSCCJS Jeff Skinner/35
NSCCJT Jonathan Toews/19
NSCCSC Sidney Crosby/25

2011 Upper Deck National Convention VIP

2 Wayne Gretzky 1.50 4.00
3 Sidney Crosby 1.00 2.50
5 Bobby Orr 1.00 2.50

2012 Upper Deck National Convention

NSCC6 Wayne Gretzky 3.00 8.00
NSCC13 Sidney Crosby 2.50 6.00
NSCC17 Bobby Orr 1.00 2.50
NSCC20 Alex Ovechkin 1.00 2.50

2012 Upper Deck National Convention Autographs

STATED PRINT RUN 1-35
NSCCBO Bobby Orr/30 90.00 150.00
NSCCSC Sidney Crosby/15 60.00 120.00

2012 Upper Deck National Convention VIP

4 Sidney Crosby 2.00 5.00
6 Wayne Gretzky 2.50 6.00

2013 Upper Deck National Convention

COMPLETE SET (20) 15.00 40.00
4 Jonathan Toews .40 1.00
8 Wayne Gretzky .75 2.00
10 Brandon Saad .30 .75
12 Bobby Hull .50 1.25
18 Patrick Kane .30 .75

2013 Upper Deck National Convention Autographs

3 Patrick Kane 50.00 100.00

2013 Upper Deck National Convention VIP

COMPLETE SET (6) 3.00 8.00
2 Wayne Gretzky 1.00 2.50
4 Jonathan Toews .50 1.25

2015 Upper Deck National Convention

NSCC1 Marian Hossa .30 .75
NSCC4 Brad Richards .30 .75
NSCC6 Patrick Sharp .30 .75
NSCC7 Patrick Kane .50 1.25
NSCC8 Denis Savard .25 .60
NSCC11 Corey Crawford .30 .75

2015 Upper Deck National Convention Autographs

NSCC1 Bobby Hull/20
NSCC2 Teuvo Teravainen/70
NSCC4 Denis Savard/15
NSCC6 Andrew Shaw/80
NSCC7 Johnny Oduya/43
NSCC10 Daniel Carcillo/70
NSCC11 Trevor van Riemsdyk/70

2015 Upper Deck National Convention VIP

VIP1 Jonathan Toews 1.25 3.00
VIP3 Wayne Gretzky 2.50 6.00

2008-09 Upper Deck National Hockey Card Day

COMPLETE SET (15) 8.00 20.00
HCD1 Steven Stamkos 4.00 10.00
HCD2 Kyle Turris 1.00 2.50
HCD3 Josh Bailey .75 2.00
HCD4 Colton Gillies .50 1.25
HCD5 Derick Brassard .50 1.25
HCD6 Sidney Crosby 2.50 6.00
HCD7 Vincent Lecavalier .50 1.25
HCD8 Jarome Iginla .60 1.50
HCD9 Joe Sakic 1.00 2.50
HCD10 Martin Brodeur 1.25 3.00
HCD11 Wayne Gretzky 3.00 8.00
HCD12 Mario Lemieux 2.00 5.00
HCD13 Gordie Howe 1.50 4.00
HCD14 Bobby Orr 2.00 5.00
HCD15 Don Cherry 1.50 4.00

2009-10 Upper Deck National Hockey Card Day

COMPLETE SET (15) 10.00 25.00
HCD1 John Tavares 2.00 5.00
HCD2 Matt Duchene .75 2.00
HCD3 Jamie Benn 1.25 3.00
HCD4 Evander Kane .75 2.00
HCD5 Logan Couture .75 2.00
HCD6 Sidney Crosby 1.50 4.00
HCD7 Vincent Lecavalier .30 .75
HCD8 Martin Brodeur .75 2.00
HCD9 Mike Richards .40 1.00
HCD10 Rick Nash .30 .75
HCD11 Jarome Iginla .40 1.00
HCD12 Jonathan Toews .75 2.00
HCD13 Roberto Luongo .50 1.25
HCD14 Wayne Gretzky 2.00 5.00
HCD15 Steve Yzerman 1.00 2.50

2010-11 Upper Deck National Hockey Card Day

NHCD1 Taylor Hall 1.00 2.50
NHCD2 Tyler Seguin 1.00 2.50
NHCD3 Jeff Skinner .50 1.25
NHCD4 Jordan Eberle .60 1.50
NHCD5 P.K. Subban .75 2.00
NHCD6 Jason Spezza .30 .75
NHCD7 Dion Phaneuf .50 1.25
NHCD8 Jarome Iginla .50 1.25
NHCD9 Roberto Luongo .50 1.25
NHCD10 Sidney Crosby 2.00 5.00
NHCD11 Patrick Roy 1.25 3.00
NHCD12 Mario Lemieux 1.50 4.00
NHCD13 Gordie Howe 1.25 3.00
NHCD14 Bobby Orr 1.50 4.00
NHCD15 Wayne Gretzky 2.50 6.00
NNO Cover Card CL .30 .75
PROMO Jonathan Toews Promo 1.00 2.50
HCDSC Sidney Crosby AU/87 60.00 120.00

2011-12 Upper Deck National Hockey Card Day Canada

MPLETE SET (17) 6.00 15.00
Cody Hodgson .50 1.25
Ryan Nugent-Hopkins 3.00 8.00
Brett Connolly .25 .60
Mark Scheifele .60 1.50
Sean Couturier .50 1.25
Taylor Hall .60 1.50
P.K. Subban .60 1.50
Roberto Luongo .30 .75
Steven Stamkos .60 1.50
Jonathan Toews .60 1.50
Wayne Gretzky 1.50 4.00
Bobby Orr 1.00 2.50
Mario Lemieux 1.00 2.50
Mark Messier .40 1.00
Martin Brodeur .60 1.50
Sidney Crosby SP 2.50 6.00
NO Checklist .20 .50

2011-12 Upper Deck National Hockey Card Day Canada Jumbos

OMPLETE SET (5)
1 Ryan Nugent-Hopkins 2.00 5.00
2 Roberto Luongo .60 1.50
3 Jonathan Toews 1.25 3.00
4 Mario Lemieux 2.00 5.00
5 Wayne Gretzky 3.00 8.00

2011-12 Upper Deck National Hockey Card Day USA

OMPLETE SET (17) 5.00 12.00
Gabriel Landeskog .50 1.25
Alexander Ovechkin 1.25 3.00
Henrik Lundqvist .40 1.00
Pekka Rinne .40 1.00
Jaromir Jagr .75 2.00
Zdeno Chara .30 .75
Ryan Kesler .30 .75
Patrick Kane .60 1.50
Ryan Miller .30 .75
Zach Parise .30 .75
Andy Miele .25 .60
Willie O'Ree .25 .60
Mike Modano .50 1.25
Brett Hull .40 1.00
Brian Leetch .30 .75
Tim Thomas SP .60 1.50
NO Checklist .20 .50

2012-13 Upper Deck National Hockey Card Day Canada

OMPLETE SET (17) 5.00 12.00
HCD1 Jaden Schwartz CR .40 1.00
HCD2 Tyson Barrie CR .40 1.00
HCD3 Carter Ashton CR .15 .40
HCD4 Mark Stone CR .40 1.00
HCD5 Casey Cizikas CR .20 .50
HCD6 Sidney Crosby PC 1.00 2.50
HCD7 Jarome Iginla PC .25 .60
HCD8 Jordan Eberle PC .25 .60
HCD9 John Tavares PC .50 1.25
HCD10 Martin Brodeur PC .50 1.25
HCD11 Bobby Orr HH .75 2.00
HCD12 Joe Sakic HH .40 1.00
HCD13 Eric Lindros HH .40 1.00
HCD14 Mario Lemieux HH .75 2.00
HCD15 Wayne Gretzky HH 1.25 3.00
HCD16 Gretzky/Lemieux MM SP 2.00 5.00
NO Checklist .15 .40

2012-13 Upper Deck National Hockey Card Day USA

OMPLETE SET (17) 5.00 12.00
HCD1 Evgeni Malkin AF 1.00 2.50
HCD2 Alexander Ovechkin AF 1.25 3.00
HCD3 Ilya Kovalchuk AF .30 .75
HCD4 Henrik Lundqvist AF .40 1.00
HCD5 Anze Kopitar AF .50 1.25
HCD6 Zach Parise SS .30 .75
HCD7 Jonathan Quick SS .50 1.25
HCD8 Patrick Kane SS .60 1.50
HCD9 Dustin Brown SS .30 .75
HCD10 Ryan Miller SS .30 .75
HCD11 Mike Modano AI .50 1.25
HCD12 Brett Hull AI .30 .75
HCD13 Brian Leetch AI .30 .75
HCD14 Tim Thomas AI .30 .75
HCD15 Neal Broten AI .25 .60
HCD16 Jonathan Quick MM SP 1.00 2.50
NO Checklist .20 .50

2013-14 Upper Deck National Hockey Card Day Canada

OMPLETE SET (22) 5.00 12.00
HCD1 Nathan MacKinnon CR .50 1.25
HCD2 Jonathan Huberdeau CR .30 .75
HCD3 Alex Galchenyuk CR .60 1.50
HCD4 Dougie Hamilton CR .25 .60
HCD5 Morgan Rielly CR .30 .75
HCD6 Nail Yakupov CR .40 1.00
HCD7 Justin Schultz CR .12 .30
HCD8 Sean Monahan CR .20 .50
HCD9 Brendan Gallagher CR .40 1.00
HCD10 Cory Conacher CR .20 .50
HCD11 Steven Stamkos PC .40 1.00
HCD12 Sidney Crosby PC .75 2.00
HCD13 Martin St. Louis PC .20 .50
HCD14 Taylor Hall PC .40 1.00
HCD15 Claude Giroux PC .20 .50
HCD16 Mario Lemieux 1.00 2.50
Wayne Gretzky HH
HCD17 Mario Lemieux HH .60 1.50
HCD18 Bobby Orr HH .60 1.50
HCD19 Steve Yzerman HH .40 1.00
HCD20 Dale Hawerchuk HH .25 .60
HCD21 Jonathan Huberdeau .50 1.25
Nathan MacKinnon MM SP

2013-14 Upper Deck National Hockey Card Day USA

OMPLETE SET (22)
HCD1 Aleksander Barkov AM .30 .75
HCD2 Alex Galchenyuk AM .60 1.50
HCD3 Beau Bennett AM .15 .40
HCD4 Charlie Coyle AM .20 .50
HCD5 Brock Nelson AM .20 .50
HCD6 Filip Forsberg AM .20 .50
HCD7 Petr Mrazek AM .25 .60
HCD8 Seth Jones AM .12 .30
HCD9 Tomas Hertl AM .15 .40
HCD10 Valeri Nichushkin AM .12 .30
HCD11 David Backes SS .20 .50
HCD12 Jonathan Quick SS .30 .75
HCD13 Patrick Kane SS .40 1.00
HCD14 Phil Kessel SS .25 .60
HCD15 Zach Parise SS .20 .50
HCD16 Bill Guerin AI .20 .50
HCD17 Brett Hull AI .20 .50
HCD18 Doug Weight AI .20 .50
NHCD19 Mike Modano AI .30 .75
NHCD20 Tony Esposito AI .20 .50
NHCD21 Alex Galchenyuk 1.00 2.50
Seth Jones MM
NNO Checklist .10 .25

2014-15 Upper Deck National Hockey Card Day Canada

COMPLETE SET (17) 4.00 10.00
NHCD1 Sidney Crosby .75 2.00
NHCD2 Steven Stamkos .40 1.00
NHCD3 Ryan Getzlaf .30 .75
NHCD4 Evander Kane .20 .50
NHCD5 P.K. Subban .30 .75
NHCD6 Bo Horvat .40 1.00
NHCD7 Sam Reinhart .40 1.00
NHCD8 Aaron Ekblad .50 1.25
NHCD9 Jonathan Drouin .30 .75
NHCD10 Curtis Lazar .15 .40
NHCD11 Joe Sakic .30 .75
NHCD12 Patrick Roy .50 1.25
NHCD13 Terry Sawchuk .20 .50
NHCD14 Bobby Orr .60 1.50
NHCD15 Wayne Gretzky 1.00 2.50
NHCD16 Jonathan Toews .40 1.00
NNO Checklist .10 .25

2014-15 Upper Deck National Hockey Card Day USA

COMPLETE SET (17) 4.00 10.00
NHCD1 Ryan Miller .20 .50
NHCD2 Joe Pavelski .20 .50
NHCD3 Bobby Ryan .20 .50
NHCD4 Phil Kessel .25 .60
NHCD5 Patrick Kane .40 1.00
NHCD6 Johnny Gaudreau .40 1.00
NHCD7 Kevin Hayes .40 1.00
NHCD8 Rocco Grimaldi .12 .30
NHCD9 Jori Lehtera .15 .40
NHCD10 Andre Burakovsky .20 .50
NHCD11 Mike Richter .20 .50
NHCD12 John Leclair .20 .50
NHCD13 Brian Leetch .20 .50
NHCD14 Chris Chelios .20 .50
NHCD15 Jeremy Roenick .20 .50
NHCD16 Wayne Gretzky 1.00 2.50
NNO Checklist .10 .25

2015-16 Upper Deck National Hockey Card Day Canada

COMPLETE SET (17)
NNO Checklist
CAN1 John Tavares .60 1.50
CAN2 Carey Price 1.00 2.50
CAN3 Taylor Hall .60 1.50
CAN4 Andrew Ladd .30 .75
CAN5 Sean Monahan .30 .75
CAN6 Connor McDavid 2.50 6.00
CAN7 Sam Bennett .40 1.00
CAN8 Robby Fabbri .40 1.00
CAN9 Max Domi .60 1.50
CAN10 Nicolas Petan .30 .75
CAN11 Wayne Gretzky 1.50 4.00
CAN12 Bobby Orr 1.00 2.50
CAN13 Lanny McDonald .30 .75
CAN14 Glenn Anderson .30 .75
CAN15 Doug Gilmour .40 1.00
CAN16 Connor McDavid MM 2.50 6.00

2015-16 Upper Deck National Hockey Card Day USA

COMPLETE SET (17)
USA1 John Carlson 1.00 2.50
USA2 Phil Kessel 1.25 3.00
USA3 Zach Parise .75 2.00
USA4 Kevin Shattenkirk .60 1.50
USA5 Cory Schneider .60 1.50
USA6 Jack Eichel 3.00 8.00
USA7 Dylan Larkin 2.50 6.00
USA8 Noah Hanifin 1.00 2.50
USA9 Artemi Panarin 2.50 6.00
USA10 Oscar Lindberg .75 2.00
USA11 John Vanbiesbrouck .75 2.00
USA12 Doug Weight .75 2.00
USA13 Chris Chelios .75 2.00
USA14 Brett Hull .75 2.00
USA15 John LeClair .75 2.00
USA16 Jack Eichel MM 3.00 8.00
NNO Checklist

2016-17 Upper Deck National Hockey Card Day Canada

CAN1 Auston Matthews 1.25 3.00
CAN2 Patrik Laine .75 2.00
CAN3 Matthew Tkachuk .60 1.50
CAN4 Mikhail Sergachev .40 1.00
CAN5 Mitch Marner 1.00 2.50
CAN6 Jonathan Toews .40 1.00
CAN7 Steven Stamkos .40 1.00
CAN8 John Tavares .40 1.00
CAN9 Connor McDavid 1.00 2.50
CAN10 Sidney Crosby .75 2.00
CAN11 Bobby Orr .60 1.50
CAN12 Patrick Roy .50 1.25
CAN13 Mike Bossy .20 .50
CAN14 Joe Sakic .30 .75
CAN15 Wayne Gretzky 1.00 2.50
CAN16 Auston Matthews 1.25 3.00

2016-17 Upper Deck National Hockey Card Day USA

USA1 Auston Matthews 1.25 3.00
USA2 Tyler Motte .20 .50
USA3 Zach Werenski .40 1.00
USA4 Ivan Provorov .40 1.00
USA5 Jimmy Vesey .40 1.00
USA6 Dylan Larkin .30 .75
USA7 Jack Eichel .40 1.00
USA8 Joe Pavelski .20 .50
USA9 Jonathan Quick .30 .75
USA10 Patrick Kane .40 1.00
USA11 Jeremy Roenick .20 .50
USA12 Bill Guerin .20 .50
USA13 Brian Leetch .20 .50
USA14 Ed Olczyk .15 .40
USA15 Mike Modano .30 .75
USA16 Auston Matthews 1.25 3.00

2012-13 Upper Deck NHL Draft

COMPLETE SET (6) 5.00 12.00
D1 Sidney Crosby 1.50 4.00
D2 Evgeni Malkin .75 2.00
D3 Marc-Andre Fleury .60 1.50
D4 Alex Ovechkin 1.00 2.50
D5 Steven Stamkos .75 2.00
D6 Jaromir Jagr .75 2.00

2013-14 Upper Deck NHL Draft

COMPLETE SET (6) 5.00 10.00
D1 Martin Brodeur 1.25 3.00
D2 Ilya Kovalchuk .60 1.50
D3 Patrik Elias .60 1.50
D4 Sidney Crosby 2.50 6.00
D5 Steven Stamkos 1.25 3.00
D6 Ryan Nugent-Hopkins .60 1.50

2014-15 Upper Deck NHL Draft

COMPLETE SET (6) 5.00 10.00
D1 Claude Giroux .60 1.50
D2 Sean Couturier .60 1.50
D3 Scott Laughton .40 1.00
D4 Alexander Ovechkin 2.50 6.00
D5 Sidney Crosby 2.50 6.00
D6 Nathan MacKinnon 1.25 3.00

1999-00 Upper Deck Ovation

Released as a 90-card set, Ovation was comprised of 60 regular issue base cards and 30 short prints. The short prints were divided up into Premier Prospects seeded at one in three and Superstar Spotlights seeded at one in six packs. Base cards featured an embossed border molded to look like a used ice rink and silver foil stamping.

COMPLETE SET (90) 30.00 80.00
1 Paul Kariya .30 .75
2 Teemu Selanne .30 .75
3 Patrik Stefan RC .75 2.00
4 Sergei Samsonov .25 .60
5 Ray Bourque .50 1.25
6 Dominik Hasek .60 1.50
7 Michael Peca .25 .60
8 Miroslav Satan .25 .60
9 Oleg Saprykin RC .60 1.50
10 Valeri Bure .20 .50
11 Ron Francis .25 .60
12 Dave Tanabe .20 .50
13 Tony Amonte .25 .60
14 J-P Dumont .25 .60
15 Patrick Roy 1.50 4.00
16 Alex Tanguay .25 .60
17 Joe Sakic .60 1.50
18 Peter Forsberg .60 1.50
19 Mike Modano .50 1.25
20 Ed Belfour .30 .75
21 Brett Hull .40 1.00
22 Sergei Fedorov .50 1.25
23 Chris Osgood .25 .60
24 Steve Yzerman 1.50 4.00
25 Doug Weight .25 .60
26 Tom Poti .20 .50
27 Pavel Bure .30 .75
28 Ivan Novoseltsev RC .50 1.25
29 Luc Robitaille .25 .60
30 Zigmund Palffy .25 .60
31 Mike Ribeiro .25 .60
32 David Legwand .20 .50
33 Martin Brodeur .75 2.00
34 Scott Gomez .25 .60
35 Tim Connolly .20 .50
36 Theo Fleury .30 .75
37 Mike Richter .30 .75
38 Brian Leetch .30 .75
39 Marian Hossa .30 .75
40 Daniel Alfredsson .25 .60
41 Eric Lindros .30 .75
42 John LeClair .30 .75
43 Simon Gagne .30 .75
44 Keith Tkachuk .40 1.00
45 Jeremy Roenick .40 1.00
46 Jaromir Jagr .50 1.25
47 Alexei Kovalev .25 .60
48 Pavol Demitra .25 .60
49 Al MacInnis .25 .60
50 Owen Nolan .25 .60
51 Brad Stuart .25 .60
52 Steve Shields .20 .50
53 Vincent Lecavalier .30 .75
54 Paul Mara .20 .50
55 Curtis Joseph .30 .75
56 Mats Sundin .30 .75
57 Steve Kariya RC .60 1.50
58 Mark Messier .30 .75
59 Peter Bondra .25 .60
60 Olaf Kolzig .25 .60
61 Pavel Brendl PP SP RC 1.25 3.00
62 Daniel Sedin PP SP 1.25 3.00
63 Henrik Sedin PP SP 1.25 3.00
64 Sheldon Keefe PP SP RC 1.25 3.00
65 Jeff Heerema PP SP .75 2.00
66 Norm Milley PP SP .75 2.00
67 Branislav Mezei PP SP RC .75 2.00
68 Denis Shvidki PP SP .75 2.00
69 Brian Finley PP SP .75 2.00
70 Taylor Pyatt PP SP .75 2.00
71 Jamie Lundmark PP SP .75 2.00
72 Milan Kraft PP SP RC 1.25 3.00
73 Kris Beech PP SP .75 2.00
74 Alexei Volkov PP SP 1.00 2.50
75 Mathieu Chouinard PP SP .75 2.00
76 Justin Papineau PP SP .75 2.00
77 Brad Moran PP SP RC .75 2.00
78 Jonathan Cheechoo PP SP 1.25 3.00
79 Mark Bell PP SP .75 2.00
80 Mattias Weinhandl PP SP .75 2.00
81 Jaromir Jagr SS SP 1.50 4.00
82 Steve Kariya SS SP 1.00 2.50
83 Dominik Hasek SS SP 2.00 5.00
84 Paul Kariya SS SP 1.25 3.00
85 Eric Lindros SS SP 1.00 2.50
86 Patrick Roy SS SP 5.00 12.00
87 Steve Yzerman SS SP 5.00 12.00
88 Pavel Bure SS SP 1.00 2.50
89 Theo Fleury SS SP 1.00 2.50
90 Patrik Stefan SS SP 1.25 3.00

1999-00 Upper Deck Ovation A Piece Of History

Randomly seeded in packs at the rate of 1:118, and autographs numbered to 25, this 16-card set features swatches of game used memorabilia.

BH Brett Hull 12.50 30.00
CJ Curtis Joseph 8.00 20.00
JJ Jaromir Jagr 12.50 30.00
MB Martin Brodeur 15.00 40.00
MR Mike Ribeiro 8.00 20.00
PB Pavel Bure 8.00 20.00
PK Paul Kariya 8.00 20.00
PR Patrick Roy 12.00 30.00
PS Patrik Stefan 8.00 20.00
SK Steve Kariya 8.00 20.00
SS Sergei Samsonov 8.00 20.00
TC Tim Connolly 8.00 20.00
WG Wayne Gretzky 15.00 40.00
BHS Brett Hull AU/25 150.00 300.00
CJS Curtis Joseph AU/25 125.00 250.00
PBS Pavel Bure AU/25 200.00 400.00
PSS Patrik Stefan AU/25 30.00 75.00

1999-00 Upper Deck Ovation Center Stage

Randomly inserted in packs as a tiered insert set, card numbers 1-10 are seeded at one in nine and feature silver foil highlights, card numbers 11-20 are seeded at one in 39 and feature gold foil highlights, and card numbers 21-30 are seeded at one in 99 and feature rainbow holofoil highlights.

COMMON GRETZKY (CS1-CS5) 2.00 5.00
COMMON HOWE (CS6-CS10) 1.25 3.00
COMMON GRETZY (CS11-CS20) 6.00 15.00
COMMON HOWE (CS16-CS19) 4.00 10.00
COMMON GRETZKY (CS22-CS25) 20.00 50.00
COMMON HOWE (CS26-CS27) 12.50 30.00
COMMON DUAL (CS21/CS28-CS30) 25.00 60.00

1999-00 Upper Deck Ovation Lead Performers

COMPLETE SET (20) 15.00 30.00
STATED ODDS 1:4
LP1 Mike Modano .75 2.00
LP2 Theo Fleury .25 .60
LP3 Paul Kariya .50 1.25
LP4 Peter Forsberg 1.25 3.00
LP5 Pavel Bure .60 1.50
LP6 John LeClair .60 1.50
LP7 Keith Tkachuk .50 1.25
LP8 Jaromir Jagr .75 2.00
LP9 Patrik Stefan .25 .60
LP10 Steve Kariya .25 .60
LP11 Ray Bourque .75 2.00
LP12 Teemu Selanne .50 1.25
LP13 Zigmund Palffy .50 1.25
LP14 Steve Yzerman 2.50 6.00
LP15 Eric Lindros .75 2.00
LP16 Dominik Hasek 1.00 2.50
LP17 Martin Brodeur 1.25 3.00
LP18 Brendan Shanahan .75 2.00
LP19 Ed Belfour .50 1.25
LP20 Patrick Roy 2.50 6.00

1999-00 Upper Deck Ovation Standing Ovation

Randomly inserted in packs, this 90-card set parallels the base Ovation set. Each card is enhanced with gold foil highlights and is sequentially numbered to 50.

*1-60 VET: 15X TO 40X BASIC CARDS
*1-60 ROOKIE/50: 5X TO 12X BASIC RC
*61-80 PP/50: 3X TO 8X BASIC SP
*81-90 SS/50: 4X TO 10X BASIC SP

1999-00 Upper Deck Ovation Super Signatures

Randomly inserted in packs, this set features Wayne Gretzky and Gordie Howe autographs. Base versions are sequentially numbered to 99, Gold versions are sequentially numbered to 50, Rainbow versions are numbered to 25, and the Rainbow Combination card is numbered to nine. Wayne Gretzky SS1 was issued as a redemption. The Gretzky/Howe card is not priced due to scarcity.

SS1 Wayne Gretzky/99 125.00 250.00
SS2 Gordie Howe/99 60.00 150.00
SSG1 Wayne Gretzky GOLD/50 200.00 400.00
SSG2 Gordie Howe GOLD/50 125.00 250.00
SSR1 W.Gretzky RNBW/25 500.00 800.00
SSR2 G.Howe RNBW/25 300.00 500.00
SSRC W.Gretzky
G.Howe/9

1999-00 Upper Deck Ovation Superstar Theater

COMPLETE SET (10) 10.00 20.00
STATED ODDS 1:9
ST1 Paul Kariya .60 1.50
ST2 Sergei Fedorov 1.00 2.50
ST3 Brett Hull .60 1.50
ST4 Patrick Roy 2.50 6.00
ST5 Dominik Hasek 1.00 2.50
ST6 Eric Lindros .75 2.00
ST7 Jaromir Jagr .75 2.00
ST8 Martin Brodeur 1.25 3.00
ST9 Pavel Bure .60 1.50
ST10 Teemu Selanne .60 1.50

2006-07 Upper Deck Ovation

COMPLETE SET (200) 75.00 125.00
1 Jean-Sebastien Giguere .30 .75
2 Teemu Selanne .60 1.50
3 Slava Kozlov .20 .50
4 Brad Boyes .20 .50
5 Hannu Toivonen .25 .60
6 Thomas Vanek .40 1.00
7 Ales Kotalik .20 .50
8 Miikka Kiprusoff .25 .60
9 Erik Cole .25 .60
10 Nikolai Khabibulin .30 .75
11 Tuomo Ruutu .30 .75
12 Alex Tanguay .20 .50
13 Jose Theodore .30 .75
14 David Vyborny .20 .50
15 Jason Arnott .25 .60
16 Brendan Shanahan .40 1.00
17 Pavel Datsyuk .40 1.00
18 Nicklas Lidstrom .30 .75
19 Chris Pronger .25 .60
20 Jarret Stoll .25 .60
21 M-A Pouliot RC .75 2.00
22 Joe Nieuwendyk .30 .75
23 Lubomir Visnovsky .20 .50
24 Manny Fernandez .25 .60
25 Erik Reitz RC .75 2.00
26 Mike Ribeiro .25 .60
27 Chris Higgins .20 .50
28 Martin Brodeur .60 1.50
29 Brian Gionta .25 .60
30 Miroslav Satan .25 .60
31 Jason Blake .20 .50
32 Petr Prucha .25 .60
33 Jason Spezza .30 .75
34 Filip Novak RC .75 2.00
35 Simon Gagne .30 .75
36 Robert Esche .25 .60
37 Ryan Potulny RC .75 2.00
38 Mike Comrie .25 .60
39 Bill Thomas RC .75 2.00
40 Marc-Andre Fleury .50 1.25
41 Sergei Gonchar .20 .50
42 Evgeni Nabokov .25 .60
43 Keith Tkachuk .30 .75
44 Martin St. Louis .30 .75
45 Mike Commodore .20 .50
46 Bryan McCabe .20 .50
47 Alexander Steen .30 .75
48 Markus Naslund .25 .60
49 Ed Jovanovski .25 .60
50 Dainius Zubrus .20 .50
51 Scott Niedermayer .30 .75
52 Joffrey Lupul .25 .60
53 Ilya Kovalchuk .30 .75
54 Brian Leetch .30 .75
55 Marco Sturm .20 .50
56 Martin Biron .25 .60
57 Dion Phaneuf .30 .75
58 Daymond Langkow .20 .50
59 Cam Ward .30 .75
60 Kyle Calder .20 .50
61 Dustin Byfuglien RC 2.00 5.00
62 Milan Hejduk .25 .60
63 Rick Nash .30 .75
64 Sergei Fedorov .50 1.25
65 Nikolai Zherdev .20 .50
66 Sergei Zubov .25 .60
67 Henrik Zetterberg .40 1.00
68 Kris Draper .20 .50
69 Tomas Kopecky RC 1.00 2.50
70 Dwayne Roloson .25 .60
71 Roberto Luongo .50 1.25
72 Jay Bouwmeester .30 .75
73 Nathan Horton .30 .75
74 Mathieu Garon .25 .60
75 Pierre-Marc Bouchard .30 .75
76 Cristobal Huet .25 .60
77 Steve Sullivan .20 .50
78 Scott Gomez .25 .60
79 Alexei Yashin .25 .60
80 Mike York .20 .50
81 Ryan Caldwell RC .75 2.00
82 Jaromir Jagr .75 2.00
83 Jason Spezza .30 .75
84 Ray Emery .25 .60
85 Jeff Carter .30 .75
86 Mike Knuble .20 .50
87 Keith Ballard .20 .50
88 Joel Perrault RC .75 2.00
89 John LeClair .30 .75
90 Joe Thornton .40 1.00
91 Matt Carle RC .75 2.00
92 Scott Young .20 .50
93 Vincent Lecavalier .25 .60
94 Brad Richards .30 .75
95 Vaclav Prospal .20 .50
96 Darcy Tucker .25 .60
97 Ian White RC 1.00 2.50
98 Brendan Morrison .20 .50
99 Alexander Ovechkin 1.50 4.00
100 Jeff Halpern .20 .50
101 Corey Perry .30 .75
102 Ryan Getzlaf .50 1.25
103 Kari Lehtonen .25 .60
104 Marian Hossa .25 .60
105 Tim Thomas .40 1.00
106 Mark Stuart RC .75 2.00
107 Ryan Miller .30 .75
108 Maxim Afinogenov .20 .50
109 Chuck Kobasew .20 .50
110 Carsen Germyn RC .75 2.00
111 Eric Staal .40 1.00
112 Rod Brind`Amour .30 .75
113 Mark Bell .20 .50
114 Rob Blake .30 .75
115 Pascal Leclaire .25 .60
116 Mike Modano .50 1.25
117 Brenden Morrow .25 .60
118 Jussi Jokinen .25 .60
119 Tomas Holmstrom .25 .60
120 Ryan Smyth .25 .60
121 Raffi Torres .20 .50
122 Alexander Frolov .20 .50
123 Mike Cammalleri .20 .50
124 Konstantin Pushkarev RC 1.00 2.50
125 Marian Gaborik .40 1.00
126 Brian Rolston .25 .60
127 Alex Kovalev .25 .60
128 Tomas Vokoun .25 .60
129 Scott Hartnell .30 .75
130 Brian Rafalski .25 .60
131 Henrik Lundqvist .60 1.50
132 Michael Nylander .20 .50
133 David Liffiton RC .75 2.00
134 Daniel Alfredsson .30 .75
135 Wade Redden .20 .50
136 Billy Thompson RC .75 2.00
137 Peter Forsberg .40 1.00
138 Keith Primeau .30 .75
139 Ladislav Nagy .20 .50
140 Sidney Crosby 1.25 3.00
141 Jonathan Cheechoo .30 .75
142 Vesa Toskala .25 .60
143 Petr Cajanek .20 .50
144 Fredrik Modin .20 .50
145 Mats Sundin .30 .75
146 Kyle Wellwood .25 .60
147 Alexander Steen .30 .75
148 Brendan Bell .20 .50
149 Daniel Sedin .30 .75
150 Eric Fehr RC 1.25 3.00
151 Marc Savard .20 .50
152 Patrice Bergeron .40 1.00
153 Glen Murray .25 .60
154 Phil Kessel RC 2.00 5.00
155 Chris Drury .25 .60
156 Daniel Briere .30 .75
157 Jarome Iginla .30 .75
158 Doug Weight .30 .75
159 Justin Williams .25 .60
160 Brent Seabrook .30 .75
161 Joe Sakic .50 1.25
162 Marek Svatos .25 .60
163 Paul Stastny RC 2.00 5.00
164 Marty Turco .30 .75
165 Jere Lehtinen .20 .50
166 Fernando Pisani .20 .50
167 Ales Hemsky .25 .60
168 Shawn Horcoff .20 .50
169 Olli Jokinen .30 .75
170 Pavol Demitra .40 1.00
171 Mikko Koivu .25 .60
172 Guillaume Latendresse RC 1.25 3.00
173 Saku Koivu .30 .75
174 Michael Ryder .20 .50
175 David Aebischer .25 .60
176 Paul Kariya .40 1.00
177 Mike Sillinger .20 .50
178 Shea Weber RC 2.00 5.00
179 Patrik Elias .30 .75
180 Rick DiPietro .25 .60
181 Steve Regier RC .75 2.00
182 Masi Marjamaki RC .75 2.00
183 Martin Straka .20 .50
184 Jarkko Immonen XRC .75 2.00
185 Patrick O'Sullivan RC 1.25 3.00
186 Martin Havlat .20 .50
187 Antero Niittymaki .25 .60
188 Shane Doan .25 .60
189 Curtis Joseph .30 .75
190 Colby Armstrong .25 .60
191 Jordan Staal RC 2.00 5.00
192 Evgeni Malkin RC 6.00 15.00
193 Patrick Marleau .30 .75
194 Steve Bernier .20 .50
195 Curtis Sanford .25 .60
196 Ruslan Fedotenko .20 .50
197 Andrew Raycroft .25 .60
198 Henrik Sedin .30 .75
199 Luc Bourdon RC 1.25 3.00
200 Alexander Ovechkin 1.25 3.00

2007-08 Upper Deck Ovation

COMPLETE SET (225) 60.00 120.00
1 Olaf Kolzig .40 1.00
2 Daniel Sedin .40 1.00
3 Henrik Sedin .40 1.00
4 Alexander Steen .40 1.00
5 Bryan McCabe .25 .60
6 Brad Richards .40 1.00
7 Manny Legace .30 .75
8 Jonathan Cheechoo .40 1.00
9 Joe Pavelski .40 1.00
10 Mark Recchi .50 1.25
11 Sidney Crosby 1.50 4.00
12 Shane Doan .30 .75
13 Jeff Carter .40 1.00
14 Jason Spezza .40 1.00
15 Martin Straka .25 .60
16 Brendan Shanahan .50 1.25
17 Rick DiPietro .30 .75
18 Martin Brodeur .75 2.00
19 Travis Zajac .30 .75
20 Kimmo Timonen .25 .60
21 Peter Forsberg .50 1.25
22 Cristobal Huet .30 .75
23 Guillaume Latendresse .30 .75
24 Manny Fernandez .30 .75
25 Pavol Demitra .50 1.25
26 Anze Kopitar .60 1.50
27 Jay Bouwmeester .40 1.00
28 Ales Hemsky .30 .75
29 Rob Schremp RC .50 1.25
30 Tomas Holmstrom .30 .75
31 Nicklas Lidstrom .40 1.00
32 Mike Ribeiro .30 .75
33 Brenden Morrow .30 .75
34 David Vyborny .25 .60
35 Pascal Leclaire .30 .75
36 Paul Stastny .40 1.00
37 Marek Svatos .25 .60
38 Tuomo Ruutu .40 1.00
39 Duncan Keith .40 1.00
40 Justin Williams .30 .75
41 Erik Cole .30 .75
42 Daymond Langkow .25 .60
43 Jarome Iginla .40 1.00
44 Thomas Vanek .50 1.25
45 Daniel Briere .40 1.00
46 Marc Savard .25 .60
47 Petr Kalus RC .40 1.00
48 Marian Hossa .30 .75
49 Andy McDonald .30 .75
50 Ryan Getzlaf .60 1.50
51 Alexander Ovechkin 1.50 4.00
52 Brendan Morrison .25 .60
53 Trevor Linden .40 1.00
54 Owen Nolan .30 .75
55 Andrew Raycroft .30 .75
56 Yanic Perreault .25 .60
57 Vincent Lecavalier .30 .75
58 Brad Boyes .25 .60
59 Barret Jackman .25 .60
60 Vesa Toskala .30 .75
61 Bill Guerin .40 1.00
62 Marc-Andre Fleury .60 1.50
63 Jordan Staal .40 1.00
64 Zbynek Michalek .25 .60
65 Simon Gagne .40 1.00
66 Daniel Alfredsson .40 1.00
67 Ray Emery .30 .75
68 Michael Nylander .25 .60
69 Michal Rozsival .25 .60
70 Jason Blake .25 .60
71 Alexei Yashin .30 .75
72 Zach Parise .50 1.25
73 Scott Gomez .30 .75
74 Paul Kariya .50 1.25
75 Jason Arnott .30 .75
76 Alex Kovalev .30 .75
77 Jaroslav Halak RC 1.00 2.50
78 Mikko Koivu .30 .75
79 Mike Cammalleri .30 .75
80 Jack Johnson RC .50 1.25
81 Nathan Horton .40 1.00
82 Olli Jokinen .30 .75
83 Shawn Horcoff .25 .60
84 Joffrey Lupul .30 .75
85 Dominik Hasek .50 1.25
86 Kris Draper .25 .60
87 Mike Modano .60 1.50
88 Rick Nash .40 1.00
89 Peter Budaj .30 .75
90 Wojtek Wolski .30 .75
91 Nikolai Khabibulin .40 1.00
92 Eric Staal .50 1.25
93 Dion Phaneuf .40 1.00
94 Matthew Lombardi .25 .60
95 Ryan Miller .40 1.00
96 Jason Pominville .40 1.00
97 Patrice Bergeron .50 1.25
98 Kari Lehtonen .30 .75
99 Scott Niedermayer .40 1.00
100 Corey Perry .40 1.00
101 Chris Clark .25 .60
102 Eric Fehr .25 .60
103 Markus Naslund .40 1.00
104 Tomas Kaberle .25 .60
105 Jeff O'Neill .25 .60
106 Johan Holmqvist .30 .75
107 Vaclav Prospal .25 .60
108 Lee Stempniak .25 .60
109 Jay McClement .25 .60
110 Patrick Marleau .40 1.00
111 Evgeni Nabokov .30 .75
112 Evgeni Malkin 1.25 3.00
113 Sergei Gonchar .25 .60
114 Curtis Joseph .40 1.00
115 Ryan Parent .25 .60
116 Mike Richards .40 1.00
117 Mike Fisher .25 .60
118 Wade Redden .25 .60
119 Henrik Lundqvist .50 1.25
120 Ryan Smyth .30 .75
121 Brian Rafalski .30 .75
122 Brian Gionta .30 .75
123 Steve Sullivan .25 .60
124 Chris Mason .30 .75
125 Saku Koivu .40 1.00
126 Brian Rolston .30 .75
127 P-M Bouchard .40 1.00
128 Lauri Tukonen RC .40 1.00
129 Alexander Frolov .25 .60
130 Stephen Weiss .25 .60
131 Jozef Stumpel .25 .60
132 Jarret Stoll .30 .75
133 Pavel Datsyuk .50 1.25
134 Philippe Boucher .25 .60
135 Eric Lindros .60 1.50
136 Gilbert Brule .30 .75
137 Fredrik Modin .25 .60
138 Andrew Brunette .25 .60
139 Joe Sakic .60 1.50
140 Martin Havlat .40 1.00
141 Cam Ward .40 1.00
142 Miikka Kiprusoff .30 .75
143 Maxim Afinogenov .25 .60
144 Brian Campbell .30 .75
145 Glen Murray .30 .75
146 Phil Kessel .50 1.25
147 Slava Kozlov .25 .60
148 Ilya Kovalchuk .40 1.00
149 Jean-Sebastien Giguere .40 1.00
150 Chris Pronger .30 .75
151 Alexander Semin .40 1.00
152 Nicklas Backstrom RC 1.25 3.00
153 Roberto Luongo .50 1.25
154 Darcy Tucker .30 .75
155 Mats Sundin .40 1.00
156 Martin St. Louis .40 1.00
157 Doug Weight .40 1.00
158 Erik Johnson RC .60 1.50
159 Joe Thornton .50 1.25
160 Ryan Whitney .30 .75
161 Peter Mueller RC .50 1.25
162 Martin Biron .30 .75
163 Dany Heatley .40 1.00
164 Nick Foligno RC .75 2.00
165 Jaromir Jagr 1.00 2.50
166 Marc Staal RC .60 1.50
167 Miroslav Satan .30 .75
168 Patrik Elias .40 1.00
169 Nicklas Bergfors RC .40 1.00
170 Carey Price RC 4.00 10.00
171 Chris Higgins .25 .60
172 Michael Ryder .25 .60
173 Mark Parrish .25 .60
174 Marian Gaborik .50 1.25
175 Jack Johnson RC .50 1.25
176 Jonathan Bernier RC 1.00 2.50
177 Rob Blake .40 1.00
178 Sam Gagner RC .75 2.00
179 Dwayne Roloson .30 .75
180 Andrew Cogliano RC .60 1.50
181 Henrik Zetterberg .50 1.25
182 Marty Turco .40 1.00
183 Sergei Fedorov .60 1.50
184 Fredrik Norrena .25 .60
185 Milan Hejduk .30 .75
186 John-Michael Liles .25 .60
187 Patrick Kane RC 2.50 6.00
188 Jason Williams .25 .60
189 Ray Whitney .30 .75
190 Rod Brind'Amour .40 1.00
191 Kristian Huselius .25 .60
192 Alex Tanguay .25 .60
193 Derek Roy .25 .60
194 Zdeno Chara .40 1.00
195 Tim Thomas .50 1.25
196 Bryan Little RC .60 1.50
197 Bobby Holik .25 .60
198 Brett Sterling RC .40 1.00
199 Bobby Ryan RC 1.50 4.00
200 Chris Kunitz .40 1.00
201 Vincent Lecavalier .30 .75
202 Daniel Alfredsson .40 1.00
203 Evgeni Malkin 1.25 3.00
204 Ilya Kovalchuk .40 1.00
205 Alexander Ovechkin 1.50 4.00
206 Eric Staal .50 1.25
207 Jason Spezza .40 1.00
208 Martin St. Louis .40 1.00
209 Andrei Markov .40 1.00
210 Tomas Kaberle .25 .60
211 Dion Phaneuf .40 1.00
212 Nicklas Lidstrom .40 1.00
213 Scott Niedermayer .40 1.00
214 Jarome Iginla .40 1.00
215 Joe Thornton .50 1.25
216 Rick Nash .40 1.00
217 Tuukka Rask RC 1.50 4.00
218 T.J. Hensick RC .50 1.25
219 Jonathan Toews RC 3.00 8.00
220 Steve Downie RC .50 1.25
221 Devin Setoguchi RC .60 1.50
222 David Perron RC .60 1.50
223 Jiri Tlusty RC .60 1.50
224 James Sheppard RC .40 1.00
225 Sergei Kostitsyn .30 .75

2007-08 Upper Deck Ovation 3x5s

XL1 Alexander Ovechkin 8.00 20.00
XL4 Andrew Raycroft 1.50 4.00
XL6 Vincent Lecavalier 1.50 4.00
XL7 Patrick Marleau 2.00 5.00
XL8 Sidney Crosby 8.00 20.00
XL10 Jason Spezza 2.00 5.00
XL11 Dany Heatley 2.00 5.00
XL12 Martin Brodeur 4.00 10.00
XL13 Guillaume Latendresse 1.50 4.00
XL18 Rick Nash 2.00 5.00
XL20 Eric Staal 2.50 6.00
XL21 Jarome Iginla 2.00 5.00
XL22 Dion Phaneuf 2.00 5.00
XL24 Thomas Vanek 2.50 6.00

2008-09 Upper Deck Ovation

COMPLETE SET (200) 75.00 150.00
COMP.FACT.SER.1 (50) 15.00 40.00
COMP.FACT.SER.2 (50) 15.00 40.00
COMP.FACT.SER.3 (50) 15.00 40.00
COMP.FACT.SER.4 (50) 20.00 50.00
1 Teemu Selanne .75 2.00
2 Jean-Sebastien Giguere .40 1.00
3 Tobias Enstrom .25 .60
4 Phil Kessel .50 1.25
5 Zdeno Chara .40 1.00
6 Marc-Andre Gragnani .30 .75
7 Jason Pominville .40 1.00
8 Alex Tanguay .25 .60
9 Kristian Huselius .25 .60
10 Erik Cole .30 .75
11 Patrick Kane .75 2.00
12 Duncan Keith .40 1.00
13 Ryan Smyth .30 .75
14 Wojtek Wolski .30 .75
15 Steve Mason RC 3.00 8.00
16 Rick Nash .40 1.00
17 Mike Modano .60 1.50
18 Brenden Morrow .30 .75
19 Dominik Hasek .50 1.25

20 Valtteri Filppula .40 1.00
21 Dwayne Roloson .30 .75
22 Shawn Matthias RC .40 1.00
23 Tomas Vokoun .30 .75
24 Jay Bouwmeester .40 1.00
25 Pierre-Marc Bouchard .40 1.00
26 Carey Price 1.50 4.00
27 Saku Koivu .40 1.00
28 Alex Kovalev .30 .75
29 Andrei Markov .40 1.00
30 Martin Erat .25 .60
31 Martin Brodeur .75 2.00
32 Travis Zajac .30 .75
33 Bill Guerin .40 1.00
34 Henrik Lundqvist .50 1.25
35 Chris Drury .30 .75
36 Ray Emery .30 .75
37 Simon Gagne .40 1.00
38 Daniel Briere .40 1.00
39 Ilya Bryzgalov .30 .75
40 Jon Filewich RC .30 .75
41 Evgeni Malkin 1.25 3.00
42 Jordan Staal .40 1.00
43 Evgeni Nabokov .30 .75
44 Lee Stempniak .25 .60
45 Martin St. Louis .40 1.00
46 Johan Holmqvist .30 .75
47 Robbie Earl RC .25 .60
48 Nikolai Antropov .30 .75
49 Darcy Tucker .30 .75
50 Alexander Edler .25 .60
51 Corey Perry .40 1.00
52 Bryan Little .30 .75
53 Ilya Kovalchuk .40 1.00
54 Derek Roy .25 .60
55 Thomas Vanek .40 1.00
56 Dion Phaneuf .40 1.00
57 Justin Williams .30 .75
58 Martin Havlat .40 1.00
59 Joe Sakic .60 1.50
60 Paul Stastny .40 1.00
61 Nikolai Zherdev .25 .60
62 Mark Fistric RC .30 .75
63 Marty Turco .40 1.00
64 Sergei Zubov .30 .75
65 Henrik Zetterberg .50 1.25
66 Ales Hemsky .30 .75
67 Dustin Penner .30 .75
68 Nathan Horton .30 .75
69 Anze Kopitar .60 1.50
70 Brian Boyle RC .30 .75
71 Mikko Koivu .30 .75
72 Andrei Kostitsyn .30 .75
73 Michael Ryder .25 .60
74 David Legwand .30 .75
75 Jason Arnott .30 .75
76 John Madden .25 .60
77 Mike Comrie .30 .75
78 Miroslav Satan .40 1.00
79 Jaromir Jagr 1.00 2.50
80 Scott Gomez .30 .75
81 Daniel Alfredsson .40 1.00
82 Ilya Zubov RC .30 .75
83 Nick Foligno .40 1.00
84 Claude Giroux RC .75 2.00
85 Mike Knuble .25 .60
86 R.J. Umberger .25 .60
87 Ed Jovanovski .30 .75
88 Shane Doan .30 .75
89 Marian Hossa .30 .75
90 Ryan Stone RC .25 .60
91 Joe Thornton .50 1.25
92 Jonathan Cheechoo .40 1.00
93 Milan Michalek .25 .60
94 Erik Johnson .30 .75
95 Dan Boyle .30 .75
96 Tomas Kaberle .25 .60
97 Daniel Sedin .40 1.00
98 Markus Naslund .30 .75
99 Alexander Ovechkin 1.50 4.00
100 Mike Green .40 1.00
101 Chris Pronger .30 .75
102 Ryan Getzlaf .60 1.50
103 Kari Lehtonen .30 .75
104 Johan Hedberg .30 .75
105 Marco Sturm .25 .60
106 Ryan Miller .40 1.00
107 Jarome Iginla .40 1.00
108 Daymond Langkow .25 .60
109 Eric Staal .50 1.25
110 Rod Brind`Amour .40 1.00
111 Jonathan Toews 1.00 2.50
112 Nikolai Khabibulin .40 1.00
113 Milan Hejduk .30 .75
114 Peter Budaj .30 .75
115 Derick Brassard RC .30 .75
116 Pascal Leclaire .30 .75
117 Jonathan Ericsson RC .40 1.00
118 Nicklas Lidstrom .40 1.00
119 Dan Cleary .30 .75
120 Sam Gagner .30 .75
121 Shawn Horcoff .25 .60
122 Olli Jokinen .30 .75
123 Teddy Purcell RC .50 1.25
124 Alexander Frolov .25 .60
125 Jack Johnson .25 .60
126 Marian Gaborik .50 1.25
127 Brian Rolston .30 .75
128 Chris Higgins .25 .60
129 Alexander Radulov .40 1.00
130 J.P. Dumont .25 .60
131 Patrik Elias .40 1.00
132 Trent Hunter .25 .60
133 Brendan Shanahan .50 1.25
134 Brandon Dubinsky .30 .75
135 Dany Heatley .40 1.00
136 Patrick Sharp .40 1.00
137 Jeff Carter .40 1.00
138 Peter Mueller .30 .75
139 Kyle Turris RC .60 1.50
140 Alex Goligoski RC .50 1.25
141 Mike Iggulden .30 .75
142 Brad Boyes .25 .60
143 David Perron .30 .75
144 Vincent Lecavalier .30 .75
145 Paul Ranger .25 .60
146 Vesa Toskala .30 .75
147 Henrik Sedin .40 1.00
148 Nicklas Backstrom .60 1.50
149 Alexander Semin .40 1.00
150 Viktor Kozlov .25 .60
151 Scott Niedermayer .40 1.00
152 Zach Bogosian RC .40 1.00
153 Tim Thomas .40 1.00
154 Patrice Bergeron .50 1.25
155 Marc Savard .25 .60
156 Chuck Kobasew .25 .60
157 Drew Stafford .30 .75
158 Miikka Kiprusoff .30 .75
159 Matthew Lombardi .25 .60
160 Cam Ward .40 1.00
161 Brandon Sutter RC .40 1.00
162 Robert Lang .25 .60
163 Peter Forsberg .50 1.25
164 Marek Svatos .25 .60
165 James Neal RC .75 2.00
166 Brad Richards .40 1.00
167 Pavel Datsyuk .50 1.25
168 Tomas Holmstrom .30 .75
169 Andrew Cogliano .30 .75
170 Michael Frolik RC .40 1.00
171 Stephen Weiss .25 .60
172 Dustin Brown .40 1.00
173 Drew Doughty RC 1.00 2.50
174 Josh Harding .40 1.00
175 Colton Gillies RC .30 .75
176 Guillaume Latendresse .25 .60
177 Chris Mason .30 .75
178 Zach Parise .40 1.00
179 Brian Gionta .30 .75
180 Rick DiPietro .30 .75
181 Ruslan Fedotenko .25 .60
182 Michal Rozsival .25 .60
183 Martin Gerber .30 .75
184 Jason Spezza .40 1.00
185 Mike Richards .40 1.00
186 Mikkel Boedker RC .50 1.25
187 Sidney Crosby 1.50 4.00
188 Marc-Andre Fleury .60 1.50
189 Ryan Whitney .40 1.00
190 Patrick Marleau .40 1.00
191 T.J. Oshie RC .75 2.00
192 Alex Pietrangelo RC .50 1.25
193 Steven Stamkos RC 4.00 10.00
194 Nikolai Kulemin RC .40 1.00
195 Matt Stajan .30 .75
196 Luke Schenn RC 4.00 10.00
197 Roberto Luongo .50 1.25
198 Brendan Morrison .25 .60
199 Sergei Fedorov .60 1.50
200 Cristobal Huet .30 .75

2008-09 Upper Deck Ovation Jumbo

STATED ODDS 1 PER TIN
XL1 Teemu Selanne 2.00 5.00
XL2 Patrick Kane 2.00 5.00
XL3 Dominik Hasek 1.25 3.00
XL4 Carey Price 4.00 10.00
XL5 Martin Brodeur 2.00 5.00
XL6 Evgeni Malkin 3.00 8.00
XL7 Joe Sakic 1.50 4.00
XL8 Henrik Zetterberg 1.25 3.00
XL9 Jaromir Jagr 2.50 6.00
XL10 Daniel Alfredsson 1.00 2.50
XL11 Joe Thornton 1.25 3.00
XL12 Alexander Ovechkin 4.00 10.00
XL13 Jarome Iginla 1.00 2.50
XL14 Eric Staal 1.25 3.00
XL15 Sam Gagner .75 2.00
XL16 Marian Gaborik 1.25 3.00
XL17 Dany Heatley 1.00 2.50
XL18 Vincent Lecavalier .75 2.00
XL19 Patrice Bergeron 1.25 3.00
XL20 Miikka Kiprusoff .75 2.00
XL21 Peter Forsberg 1.25 3.00
XL22 Sidney Crosby 4.00 10.00
XL23 Steven Stamkos 6.00 15.00
XL24 Roberto Luongo 1.25 3.00

2008-09 Upper Deck Ovation Jumbo Autographs

XLANB Nicklas Backstrom 15.00 40.00

2009-10 Upper Deck Ovation

COMPLETE SET (150) 25.00 60.00
1 Corey Perry .30 .75
2 Ryan Getzlaf .50 1.25
3 Brian Salcido RC .25 .60
4 Matt Beleskey RC .25 .60
5 Ilya Kovalchuk .30 .75
6 Bryan Little .30 .75
7 Spencer Machacek RC .30 .75
8 Tim Thomas .30 .75
9 Phil Kessel .40 1.00
10 Zdeno Chara .30 .75
11 Marc Savard .20 .50
12 David Krejci .30 .75
13 Byron Bitz RC .25 .60
14 Blake Wheeler .30 .75
15 Thomas Vanek .30 .75
16 Ryan Miller .30 .75
17 Jason Pominville .30 .75
18 Jhonas Enroth RC .40 1.00
19 Derek Roy .25 .60
20 Dion Phaneuf .40 1.00
21 Jarome Iginla .30 .75
22 Miikka Kiprusoff .25 .60
23 Olli Jokinen .25 .60
24 Daymond Langkow .20 .50
25 Kris Chucko RC .25 .60
26 Mikael Backlund RC .30 .75
27 Eric Staal .40 1.00
28 Cam Ward .30 .75
29 Erik Cole .25 .60
30 Jonathan Toews .60 1.50
31 Patrick Sharp .30 .75
32 Patrick Kane .60 1.50
33 Dustin Byfuglien .30 .75
34 Brian Campbell .25 .60
35 Kris Versteeg .30 .75
36 Paul Stastny .30 .75
37 Milan Hejduk .25 .60
38 T.J. Galiardi RC .30 .75
39 Steve Mason .25 .60
40 Rick Nash .25 .60
41 Derick Brassard .30 .75
42 Brenden Morrow .25 .60
43 Evander Kane RC .60 1.50
44 Marty Turco .30 .75
45 Henrik Zetterberg .40 1.00
46 Pavel Datsyuk .40 1.00
47 Johan Franzen .30 .75
48 Nicklas Lidstrom .30 .75
49 Tomas Holmstrom .25 .60
50 Chris Osgood .30 .75
51 Ville Leino RC .25 .60
52 Sheldon Souray .20 .50
53 Ales Hemsky .25 .60
54 Sam Gagner .25 .60
55 Andrew Cogliano .25 .60
56 Dustin Penner .20 .50
57 Dwayne Roloson .25 .60
58 Shawn Horcoff .20 .50
59 Tomas Vokoun .25 .60
60 Nathan Horton .30 .75
61 David Booth .20 .50
62 Anze Kopitar .50 1.25
63 Drew Doughty .40 1.00
64 Alexander Frolov .25 .60
65 Brent Burns .40 1.00
66 Niklas Backstrom .30 .75
67 Mikko Koivu .30 .75
68 Andrei Markov .30 .75
69 Carey Price 1.25 3.00
70 John Tavares RC 4.00 10.00
71 Saku Koivu .30 .75
72 Tomas Plekanec .30 .75
73 James van Riemsdyk RC .60 1.50
74 Yannick Weber RC .30 .75
75 J.P. Dumont .20 .50
76 Pekka Rinne .40 1.00
77 Jason Arnott .25 .60
78 Cal O'Reilly RC .25 .60
79 Mike Santorelli RC .30 .75
80 Martin Brodeur .60 1.50
81 Zach Parise .30 .75
82 Brian Gionta .25 .60
83 Jamie Langenbrunner .20 .50
84 Travis Zajac .25 .60
85 Kyle Okposo .30 .75
86 Rick DiPietro .25 .60
87 Jesse Joensuu RC .25 .60
88 Henrik Lundqvist .50 1.25
89 Nik Antropov .25 .60
90 Matt Duchene RC .60 1.50
91 Scott Gomez .25 .60
92 Artem Anisimov RC .30 .75
93 Victor Hedman RC .60 1.50
94 Ryan Stoa .25 .60
95 Dany Heatley .30 .75
96 Jason Spezza .30 .75
97 Brian Elliott .25 .60
98 Filip Kuba .20 .50
99 Daniel Alfredsson .30 .75
100 Mike Fisher .20 .50
101 Ryan Shannon .25 .60
102 Mike Richards .30 .75
103 Jeff Carter .30 .75
104 Martin Biron .25 .60
105 Daniel Briere .30 .75
106 Scott Hartnell .30 .75
107 Daniel Carcillo .20 .50
108 Sergei Shirokov RC .20 .50
109 Peter Mueller .25 .60
110 Shane Doan .25 .60
111 Jonas Gustavsson RC .40 1.00
112 Ilya Bryzgalov .25 .60
113 Sidney Crosby 1.25 3.00
114 Evgeni Malkin 1.00 2.50
115 Jordan Staal .30 .75
116 Marc-Andre Fleury .50 1.25
117 Chris Kunitz .30 .75
118 Luca Caputi RC .30 .75
119 Joe Thornton .30 .75
120 Evgeni Nabokov .25 .60
121 Patrick Marleau .30 .75
122 Rob Blake .30 .75
123 Dan Boyle .25 .60
124 Devin Setoguchi .25 .60
125 Joe Pavelski .30 .75
126 Brad Boyes .20 .50
127 Patrik Berglund .20 .50
128 David Backes .30 .75
129 Chris Mason .25 .60
130 Riku Helenius RC .30 .75
131 Steven Stamkos .60 1.50
132 Martin St. Louis .30 .75
133 Vincent Lecavalier .25 .60
134 Luke Schenn .25 .60
135 Matt Stajan .25 .60
136 Alexei Ponikarovsky .20 .50
137 Tomas Kaberle .20 .50
138 Nikolai Kulemin .25 .60
139 Niklas Hagman .20 .50
140 Matt Corrente .25 .60
141 Willie Mitchell .20 .50
142 Ryan Kesler .30 .75
143 Alexandre Burrows .30 .75
144 Kyle Wellwood .25 .60
145 Roberto Luongo .40 1.00
146 Michal Neuvirth RC .50 1.25
147 Alexander Ovechkin 1.25 3.00
148 Alexander Semin .30 .75
149 Nicklas Backstrom .50 1.25
150 Mike Green .30 .75

2009-10 Upper Deck Ovation Spotlight

COMPLETE SET (30) 15.00 40.00
OS1 Saku Koivu 1.00 2.50
OS2 Alexander Ovechkin 4.00 10.00
OS3 Marc-Andre Fleury 1.50 4.00
OS4 Steven Stamkos 2.00 5.00
OS5 Thomas Vanek 1.00 2.50
OS6 Carey Price 4.00 10.00
OS7 Jeff Carter 1.00 2.50
OS8 Jason Spezza 1.00 2.50
OS9 Evgeni Malkin 3.00 8.00
OS10 Miikka Kiprusoff .75 2.00
OS11 Martin Brodeur 2.00 5.00
OS12 Jonathan Toews 2.00 5.00
OS13 Dany Heatley 1.00 2.50
OS14 Henrik Lundqvist 1.50 4.00
OS15 Jarome Iginla 1.00 2.50
OS16 Mike Green 1.00 2.50
OS17 Joe Thornton 1.00 2.50
OS18 Henrik Zetterberg 1.25 3.00
OS19 Dion Phaneuf 1.25 3.00
OS20 Sidney Crosby 4.00 10.00
OS21 Ales Hemsky .75 2.00
OS22 Alexandre Burrows 1.00 2.50
OS23 Pavel Datsyuk 1.25 3.00
OS24 Luke Schenn .75 2.00
OS25 Patrick Kane 2.00 5.00
OS26 Mike Richards 1.00 2.50
OS27 Justin Pogge 1.00 2.50
OS28 Ilya Kovalchuk 1.00 2.50
OS29 Roberto Luongo 1.25 3.00
OS30 Rick Nash .75 2.00

2013-14 Upper Deck Overtime

COMPLETE SET (92) 30.00 80.00
COMP.SERIES 1 (50) 12.00 30.00
COMP.SERIES 2 (42) 20.00 50.00
ISSUED AS DISTRIBUTOR INCENTIVE
*GOLD/99: 2X TO 5X BASIC CARDS
1 Alex Chiasson .50 1.25
2 Alex Galchenyuk 2.50 6.00
3 Austin Watson .40 1.00
4 Beau Bennett .60 1.50
5 Brendan Gallagher 1.50 4.00
6 Calvin Pickard .50 1.25
7 Charlie Coyle .50 1.25
8 Chris Brown .30 .75
9 Christian Thomas .40 1.00
10 Cory Conacher .30 .75
11 Cristopher Nilstorp .40 1.00
12 Damien Brunner .40 1.00
13 Dougie Hamilton 1.00 2.50
14 Drew Shore .40 1.00
15 Emerson Etem .50 1.25
16 Filip Forsberg 1.25 3.00
17 Jack Campbell .40 1.00
18 Jamie Oleksiak .40 1.00
19 Jared Staal .50 1.25
20 Jarred Tinordi .50 1.25
21 Johan Larsson .40 1.00
22 Jonas Brodin .40 1.00
23 Jonathan Huberdeau 1.25 3.00
24 Jordan Schroeder .50 1.25
25 Justin Schultz .50 1.25
26 Leo Komarov .50 1.25
27 Mark Pysyk .50 1.25
28 Max Reinhart .50 1.25
29 Mikael Granlund .75 2.00
30 Mikhail Grigorenko .60 1.50
31 Nail Yakupov 1.50 4.00
32 Nathan Beaulieu .40 1.00
33 Nick Bjugstad .60 1.50
34 Nick Petrecki .30 .75
35 Nicklas Jensen .40 1.00
36 Petr Mrazek 1.00 2.50
37 Quinton Howden .40 1.00
38 Richard Panik .50 1.25
39 Rickard Rakell .50 1.25
40 Roman Cervenka .40 1.00
41 Ryan Murphy .50 1.25
42 Ryan Spooner .50 1.25
43 Scott Laughton .50 1.25
44 Stefan Matteau .40 1.00
45 Thomas Hickey .40 1.00
46 Tye McGinn .50 1.25
47 Tyler Toffoli 1.00 2.50
48 Viktor Fasth .50 1.25
49 Vladimir Tarasenko 2.00 5.00
50 Zach Redmond .40 1.00
51 Aleksander Barkov 1.25 3.00
52 Alex Killorn .50 1.25
53 Antoine Roussel .50 1.25
54 Anton Belov .50 1.25
55 Boone Jenner .50 1.25
56 Brock Nelson .50 1.25
57 Cameron Schilling .30 .75
58 Connor Carrick .40 1.00
59 Danny DeKeyser .60 1.50
60 Elias Lindholm .75 2.00
61 Hampus Lindholm .75 2.00
62 Jacob Trouba .75 2.00
63 Jamie Devane .40 1.00
64 Jean-Gabriel Pageau .40 1.00
65 Jeff Zatkoff .50 1.25
66 Jesper Fast .40 1.00
67 Joakim Nordstrom .40 1.00
68 Justin Fontaine .50 1.25
69 Lucas Lessio .30 .75
70 Luke Gazdic .40 1.00
71 Mark Barberio .30 .75
72 Mathew Dumba .50 1.25
73 Matthew Irwin .40 1.00
74 Matt Nieto .40 1.00
75 Michael Bournival .50 1.25
76 Michael Latta .40 1.00
77 Mike Kostka .40 1.00
78 Morgan Rielly 1.25 3.00
79 Nathan MacKinnon 4.00 10.00
80 Olli Maatta 2.00 5.00
81 Radko Gudas .50 1.25
82 Rasmus Ristolainen .75 2.00
83 Ryan Murray .75 2.00
84 Sami Vatanen .50 1.25
85 Sean Monahan .75 2.00
86 Seth Jones .50 1.25
87 Spencer Abbott .40 1.00
88 Tomas Hertl .60 1.50
89 Tyler Johnson 1.25 3.00
90 Valeri Nichushkin .60 1.50
91 Will Acton .40 1.00
92 Zemgus Girgensons 1.00 2.50

2013-14 Upper Deck Overtime Autographs

STATED ODDS 1:36
2 Alex Galchenyuk
3 Austin Watson 4.00 10.00
4 Beau Bennett 8.00 20.00
5 Brendan Gallagher 15.00 40.00
6 Calvin Pickard 5.00 12.00
7 Charlie Coyle 5.00 12.00
8 Chris Brown 3.00 8.00
9 Christian Thomas 4.00 10.00
10 Cory Conacher 3.00 8.00
13 Dougie Hamilton 10.00 25.00
15 Emerson Etem 6.00 15.00
17 Jack Campbell 8.00 20.00
18 Jamie Oleksiak
19 Jared Staal 5.00 12.00
20 Jarred Tinordi 5.00 12.00
23 Jonathan Huberdeau 12.00 30.00
25 Justin Schultz 5.00 12.00
27 Mark Pysyk 5.00 12.00
30 Mikhail Grigorenko 6.00 15.00
31 Nail Yakupov 20.00 40.00
32 Nathan Beaulieu 4.00 10.00
37 Quinton Howden 4.00 10.00
39 Rickard Rakell
41 Ryan Murphy 5.00 12.00
42 Ryan Spooner 8.00 20.00
43 Scott Laughton 10.00 25.00
45 Thomas Hickey 4.00 10.00
47 Tyler Toffoli 10.00 25.00
48 Viktor Fasth
50 Zach Redmond
51 Aleksander Barkov 12.00 30.00
56 Brock Nelson 5.00 12.00
57 Cameron Schilling 5.00 12.00
59 Danny DeKeyser 6.00 15.00
60 Elias Lindholm 8.00 20.00
61 Hampus Lindholm 6.00 15.00
62 Jacob Trouba 8.00 20.00
63 Jamie Devane 4.00 10.00
64 Jean-Gabriel Pageau 4.00 10.00
66 Jesper Fast 4.00 10.00
67 Joakim Nordstrom 6.00 15.00
69 Lucas Lessio 3.00 8.00
72 Mathew Dumba 5.00 12.00
77 Mike Kostka 4.00 10.00
78 Morgan Rielly 15.00 40.00
79 Nathan MacKinnon 30.00 80.00
85 Sean Monahan 15.00 40.00
86 Seth Jones 5.00 12.00
88 Tomas Hertl 12.00 30.00
91 Will Acton 4.00 10.00

2013-14 Upper Deck Overtime Rookie Profiles

COMPLETE SET (51) 40.00 80.00
COMP.SERIES 1 (30) 20.00 40.00
COMP.SERIES 2 (21) 20.00 40.00
ONE PER PRE-ORDER PACK
RP1 Nail Yakupov 2.50 6.00
RP2 Jonathan Huberdeau 2.00 5.00
RP3 Alex Galchenyuk 4.00 10.00
RP4 Brendan Gallagher 2.50 6.00
RP5 Vladimir Tarasenko 3.00 8.00
RP6 Mikhail Grigorenko 1.00 2.50
RP7 Mikael Granlund 1.25 3.00
RP8 Nathan Beaulieu .60 1.50
RP9 Justin Schultz .75 2.00
RP10 Charlie Coyle 1.00 2.50
RP11 Cory Conacher .50 1.25
RP12 Damien Brunner .60 1.50
RP13 Dougie Hamilton 1.50 4.00
RP14 Emerson Etem .75 2.00
RP15 Jonas Brodin .60 1.50
RP16 Jordan Schroeder .75 2.00
RP17 Petr Mrazek 1.50 4.00
RP18 Quinton Howden .60 1.50
RP19 Ryan Spooner .75 2.00
RP20 Scott Laughton .75 2.00
RP21 Stefan Matteau .60 1.50
RP22 Viktor Fasth .75 2.00
RP23 Jarred Tinordi .75 2.00
RP24 Tyler Toffoli 1.50 4.00
RP25 Beau Bennett 1.00 2.50
RP26 Jack Campbell .60 1.50
RP27 Ryan Murphy .75 2.00
RP28 Rickard Rakell .75 2.00
RP29 Thomas Hickey .60 1.50
RP30 Jamie Oleksiak .60 1.50
RP31 Nathan MacKinnon 3.00 8.00
RP32 Seth Jones .75 2.00
RP33 Morgan Rielly 2.00 5.00
RP34 Sean Monahan 1.25 3.00
RP35 Boone Jenner .75 2.00
RP36 Elias Lindholm 1.25 3.00
RP37 Hampus Lindholm 1.25 3.00
RP38 Rasmus Ristolainen 1.25 3.00
RP39 Ryan Murray 1.25 3.00
RP40 Jacob Trouba 1.25 3.00
RP41 Olli Maatta 3.00 8.00
RP42 Lucas Lessio .50 1.25
RP43 Valeri Nichushkin .75 2.00
RP44 Mathew Dumba .75 2.00
RP45 Jesper Fast .60 1.50
RP46 Tomas Hertl 1.00 2.50
RP47 Michael Latta .60 1.50
RP48 Zemgus Girgensons 1.50 4.00
RP49 Joakim Nordstrom .60 1.50
RP50 Sami Vatanen .75 2.00
RP51 Justin Fontaine .75 2.00

2014-15 Upper Deck Overtime

*BLUE VETS: .8X TO 2X BASIC CARDS
*BLUE LEG: .6X TO 1.5X BASIC CARDS
*BLUE ROOKIE: .5X TO 1.2X BASIC CARDS
*GREEN VETS/99: 3X TO 8X BASIC CARDS
*GREEN LEG/99: 2.5X TO 6X BASIC CARDS
*GREEN ROOKIE/99: 1X TO 2.5X BASIC CARDS
1 Jim Howard .40 1.00
2 Tuukka Rask .40 1.00
3 Steve Mason .30 .75
4 Carey Price 1.25 3.00
5 Joe Pavelski .40 1.00
6 James van Riemsdyk .40 1.00
7 Gabriel Landeskog .30 .75
8 Jonathan Quick .60 1.50
9 Patrick Kane .75 2.00
10 Sidney Crosby 1.50 4.00
11 Claude Giroux .40 1.00
12 Ryan Getzlaf .60 1.50
13 Patrice Bergeron .50 1.25
14 Cody Hodgson .40 1.00
15 Sean Monahan .40 1.00
16 Eric Staal .50 1.25
17 Jonathan Toews .75 2.00
18 Matt Duchene .40 1.00
19 Sergei Bobrovsky .40 1.00
20 Tyler Seguin .60 1.50
21 Pavel Datsyuk .50 1.25
22 Taylor Hall .75 2.00
23 Roberto Luongo .40 1.00
24 Anze Kopitar .60 1.50
25 Zach Parise .40 1.00
26 P.K. Subban .60 1.50
27 Shea Weber .30 .75
28 Adam Henrique .40 1.00
29 John Tavares .75 2.00
30 Martin St. Louis .40 1.00
31 Bobby Ryan .40 1.00
32 Keith Yandle .40 1.00
33 Logan Couture .40 1.00
34 T.J. Oshie .60 1.50
35 Steven Stamkos .75 2.00
36 Phil Kessel .50 1.25
37 Jonathan Bernier .40 1.00
38 Alexander Ovechkin 1.50 4.00
39 Blake Wheeler .40 1.00
40 Corey Perry .40 1.00
41 Theoren Fleury LEG 1.25 3.00
42 Mike Modano LEG 1.50 4.00
43 Dominik Hasek LEG 1.25 3.00
44 Stan Mikita LEG 1.25 3.00
45 Larry Robinson LEG 1.00 2.50
46 Guy Lafleur LEG 1.25 3.00
47 Mats Sundin LEG 1.00 2.50
48 Teemu Selanne LEG 2.00 5.00
49 Bobby Orr LEG 3.00 8.00
50 Wayne Gretzky LEG 5.00 12.00
51 Brandon Gormley RC 1.00 2.50
52 Mark Visentin RC 1.00 2.50
53 Teuvo Teravainen RC 1.50 4.00
54 Joey Hishon RC 1.25 3.00
55 Greg McKegg RC .75 2.00
56 Calle Jarnkrok RC 1.00 2.50
57 Ty Rattie RC 1.25 3.00
58 Vladislav Namestnikov RC 1.50 4.00
59 Evgeny Kuznetsov RC 4.00 10.00
60 Oscar Klefbom RC 2.00 5.00
61 Erik Karlsson .75 2.00
62 Duncan Keith .40 1.00
63 Patrick Marleau .40 1.00
64 Dany Heatley .30 .75
65 Drew Doughty .40 1.00
66 Chris Kunitz .40 1.00
67 Sam Gagner .30 .75
68 James Neal .40 1.00
69 Brandon Dubinsky .30 .75
70 Vincent Lecavalier .30 .75
71 John Gibson .50 1.25
72 Gustav Nyquist .30 .75
73 Jason Pominville .30 .75
74 Shane Doan .30 .75
75 Alex Galchenyuk .60 1.50
76 Jarome Iginla .40 1.00
77 Zdeno Chara .40 1.00
78 Ben Bishop .40 1.00
79 Dustin Byfuglien .40 1.00
80 Marc-Andre Fleury .60 1.50
81 Nail Yakupov .30 .75
82 Ryan Miller .40 1.00
83 Jonas Hiller .30 .75
84 Craig Anderson .40 1.00
85 Nicklas Backstrom .60 1.50
86 Valeri Nichushkin .30 .75
87 Matt Moulson .30 .75
88 Kyle Okposo .40 1.00
89 Alexandre Burrows .40 1.00
90 Dion Phaneuf .40 1.00
91 Jonathan Huberdeau .40 1.00
92 Patrick Sharp .40 1.00
93 Henrik Lundqvist .50 1.25
94 Kari Lehtonen .30 .75
95 Alexander Steen .40 1.00
96 Jaromir Jagr 1.00 2.50
97 Viktor Fasth .30 .75
98 Tomas Plekanec .40 1.00
99 Patrik Berglund .25 .60
100 Joe Thornton .40 1.00
101 Leon Draisaitl RC 5.00 12.00
102 Dennis Everberg RC 1.00 2.50
103 Johnny Gaudreau RC 3.00 8.00
104 Andre Burakovsky RC 1.50 4.00
105 Colton Sissons RC 1.00 2.50
106 Alexander Khokhlachev RC 1.00 2.50
107 Teemu Pulkkinen RC 1.25 3.00
108 Curtis Lazar RC 1.25 3.00
109 Patrik Nemeth RC 1.00 2.50
110 Sam Reinhart RC 3.00 8.00
111 Anthony Duclair RC 1.50 4.00
112 Christian Folin RC 1.00 2.50
113 Alexander Wennberg RC 2.00 5.00
114 Damon Severson RC 1.00 2.50
115 Pierre-Edouard Bellemare RC 1.00 2.50
116 Corban Knight RC 1.00 2.50
117 Stuart Percy RC 1.00 2.50
118 Markus Granlund RC 1.50 4.00
119 Chris Tierney RC 1.00 2.50
120 Aaron Ekblad RC 4.00 10.00
121 Antti Niemi .30 .75
122 Marian Gaborik .40 1.00
123 Nathan MacKinnon .75 2.00
124 Rick Nash .40 1.00
125 Evander Kane .40 1.00
126 Niklas Kronwall .30 .75
127 Ryan Kesler .40 1.00
128 Mark Giordano .30 .75
129 Seth Jones .30 .75
130 Jakub Voracek .40 1.00
131 Mike Smith .40 1.00
132 Niklas Backstrom .30 .75
133 Kris Letang .40 1.00
134 Scott Hartnell .40 1.00
135 Milan Lucic .40 1.00
136 Ryan McDonagh .40 1.00
137 Braden Holtby .60 1.50
138 Aleksander Barkov .40 1.00
139 Jiri Hudler .30 .75
140 Henrik Sedin .40 1.00
141 Ryan Nugent-Hopkins .40 1.00
142 Brad Marchand .50 1.25
143 Tyler Ennis .30 .75
144 Valtteri Filppula .40 1.00
145 Mikko Koivu .30 .75
146 Daniel Sedin .40 1.00
147 Marian Hossa .30 .75
148 Corey Crawford .50 1.25
149 Evgeni Malkin 1.25 3.00
150 Henrik Zetterberg .50 1.25
151 Kyle Turris .40 1.00
152 David Backes .40 1.00
153 Jamie Benn .50 1.25
154 Wayne Simmonds .50 1.25
155 Max Pacioretty .40 1.00
156 David Perron .25 .60
157 Jaroslav Halak .30 .75
158 Pekka Rinne .50 1.25
159 Jeff Carter .40 1.00
160 Cory Schneider .30 .75
161 Jonathan Drouin RC 2.50 6.00
162 Jiri Sekac RC 1.00 2.50
163 Tobias Rieder RC 1.00 2.50
164 Adam Clendening RC 1.00 2.50
165 Darnell Nurse RC 3.00 8.00
166 Trevor van Riemsdyk RC 1.50 4.00
167 Sven Andrighetto RC 1.25 3.00
168 Victor Rask RC 1.00 2.50
169 Bo Horvat RC 3.00 8.00
170 Jori Lehtera RC 1.25 3.00
171 Kerby Rychel RC .75 2.00
172 Griffin Reinhart RC 1.25 3.00
173 Mirco Mueller RC 1.00 2.50
174 William Karlsson RC 4.00 10.00
175 Adam Lowry RC 1.00 2.50
176 Andy Andreoff RC 1.00 2.50
177 Seth Helgeson RC .75 2.00
178 Kevin Hayes RC 3.00 8.00
179 David Pastrnak RC 4.00 10.00
180 Marko Dano RC 1.00 2.50

2014-15 Upper Deck Overtime Autographs

1 Jim Howard 5.00 12.00
2 Tuukka Rask 5.00 12.00
3 Steve Mason 8.00 20.00
4 Carey Price
5 Joe Pavelski 5.00 12.00
6 James van Riemsdyk 5.00 12.00
7 Gabriel Landeskog 4.00 10.00
8 Jonathan Quick 8.00 20.00
9 Patrick Kane 25.00 50.00
10 Sidney Crosby
11 Claude Giroux 20.00 40.00
12 Ryan Getzlaf 8.00 20.00
13 Patrice Bergeron 15.00 40.00
14 Cody Hodgson 8.00 20.00
15 Sean Monahan 5.00 12.00
16 Eric Staal 6.00 15.00
17 Jonathan Toews
18 Matt Duchene 5.00 12.00
19 Sergei Bobrovsky 5.00 12.00
20 Tyler Seguin 20.00 40.00
21 Pavel Datsyuk 6.00 15.00
22 Taylor Hall 15.00 40.00
23 Roberto Luongo
24 Anze Kopitar 8.00 20.00
25 Zach Parise 5.00 12.00
26 P.K. Subban
27 Shea Weber 4.00 10.00
28 Adam Henrique 5.00 12.00
29 John Tavares 8.00 20.00
30 Martin St. Louis 60.00
31 Bobby Ryan 8.00 20.00
32 Keith Yandle 5.00 12.00
33 Logan Couture 8.00 20.00
34 T.J. Oshie 10.00 25.00
35 Steven Stamkos
36 Phil Kessel 8.00 20.00
37 Jonathan Bernier 8.00 20.00
38 Alexander Ovechkin 30.00 80.00
39 Blake Wheeler 5.00 12.00
40 Corey Perry 12.00 30.00
41 Theoren Fleury 15.00 40.00
42 Mike Modano
43 Dominik Hasek
44 Stan Mikita
45 Larry Robinson 5.00 12.00
46 Guy Lafleur 20.00 50.00
47 Mats Sundin 5.00 12.00
48 Teemu Selanne 10.00 25.00
49 Bobby Orr 90.00 150.00
50 Wayne Gretzky 125.00 200.00
51 Brandon Gormley 5.00 12.00
52 Mark Visentin 10.00 25.00
53 Teuvo Teravainen 25.00 50.00
54 Joey Hishon 6.00 15.00
55 Greg McKegg 8.00 20.00
56 Calle Jarnkrok 5.00 12.00
57 Ty Rattie 6.00 15.00
58 Vladislav Namestnikov 8.00 20.00
59 Evgeny Kuznetsov 20.00 50.00
60 Oscar Klefbom 8.00 20.00
61 Erik Karlsson 10.00 25.00
62 Duncan Keith
63 Patrick Marleau 5.00 12.00
64 Dany Heatley 4.00 10.00
65 Drew Doughty 5.00 12.00
66 Chris Kunitz 5.00 12.00
67 Sam Gagner 4.00 10.00
68 James Neal 5.00 12.00
69 Brandon Dubinsky 4.00 10.00
70 Vincent Lecavalier
71 John Gibson
72 Gustav Nyquist 4.00 10.00
73 Jason Pominville 4.00 10.00
74 Shane Doan 4.00 10.00
75 Alex Galchenyuk
76 Jarome Iginla 8.00 20.00
77 Zdeno Chara
78 Ben Bishop
79 Dustin Byfuglien 5.00 12.00
80 Marc-Andre Fleury 8.00 20.00
81 Nail Yakupov 4.00 10.00
82 Ryan Miller 5.00 12.00
83 Jonas Hiller 4.00 10.00
84 Craig Anderson 5.00 12.00
85 Nicklas Backstrom 8.00 20.00
86 Valeri Nichushkin 4.00 10.00
87 Matt Moulson 4.00 10.00
88 Kyle Okposo 8.00 20.00
89 Alexandre Burrows 5.00 12.00
90 Dion Phaneuf 5.00 12.00
91 Jonathan Huberdeau 5.00 12.00
92 Patrick Sharp 5.00 12.00
93 Henrik Lundqvist 6.00 15.00
94 Kari Lehtonen 8.00 20.00
95 Alexander Steen 5.00 12.00
96 Jaromir Jagr
97 Viktor Fasth 4.00 10.00
98 Tomas Plekanec 5.00 12.00
99 Patrik Berglund 3.00 8.00
100 Joe Thornton
101 Leon Draisaitl
102 Dennis Everberg 5.00 12.00
103 Johnny Gaudreau 25.00 50.00
104 Andre Burakovsky 8.00 20.00
105 Colton Sissons 5.00 12.00
106 Alexander Khokhlachev 5.00 12.00
107 Teemu Pulkkinen 6.00 15.00
108 Curtis Lazar
109 Patrik Nemeth 5.00 12.00
110 Sam Reinhart 15.00 40.00
111 Anthony Duclair 8.00 20.00
112 Christian Folin 5.00 12.00
113 Alexander Wennberg 10.00 25.00
114 Damon Severson 5.00 12.00
115 Pierre-Edouard Bellemare 5.00 12.00
116 Corban Knight 5.00 12.00
117 Stuart Percy 5.00 12.00
118 Markus Granlund 8.00 20.00
119 Chris Tierney 5.00 12.00
120 Aaron Ekblad 25.00 50.00
121 Antti Niemi 4.00 10.00
122 Marian Gaborik 5.00 12.00
123 Nathan MacKinnon
124 Rick Nash 5.00 12.00
125 Evander Kane 5.00 12.00
126 Niklas Kronwall 4.00 10.00
127 Ryan Kesler 5.00 12.00
128 Mark Giordano 4.00 10.00
129 Seth Jones
130 Jakub Voracek 5.00 12.00
131 Mike Smith 5.00 12.00
132 Niklas Backstrom 4.00 10.00
133 Kris Letang 5.00 12.00
134 Scott Hartnell 5.00 12.00
135 Milan Lucic 5.00 12.00
136 Ryan McDonagh 10.00 25.00
137 Braden Holtby 8.00 20.00
138 Aleksander Barkov 8.00 20.00
139 Jiri Hudler 4.00 10.00
140 Henrik Sedin 5.00 12.00
141 Ryan Nugent-Hopkins 5.00 12.00
142 Brad Marchand 6.00 15.00
143 Tyler Ennis 4.00 10.00
144 Valtteri Filppula
145 Mikko Koivu 8.00 20.00
146 Daniel Sedin 5.00 12.00
147 Marian Hossa 4.00 10.00
148 Corey Crawford
149 Evgeni Malkin 10.00 25.00
150 Henrik Zetterberg 6.00 15.00
151 Kyle Turris 5.00 12.00
152 David Backes 5.00 12.00
153 Jamie Benn
154 Wayne Simmonds 6.00 15.00
155 Max Pacioretty 5.00 12.00
156 David Perron 3.00 8.00
157 Jaroslav Halak 25.00 60.00
158 Pekka Rinne 6.00 15.00
159 Jeff Carter 5.00 12.00
160 Cory Schneider 4.00 10.00
161 Jonathan Drouin 12.00 30.00
162 Jiri Sekac 5.00 12.00
163 Tobias Rieder 5.00 12.00
164 Adam Clendening 5.00 12.00
165 Darnell Nurse
166 Trevor van Riemsdyk 8.00 20.00
167 Sven Andrighetto 12.00 30.00
168 Victor Rask 5.00 12.00
169 Bo Horvat
170 Jori Lehtera
171 Kerby Rychel 4.00 10.00
172 Griffin Reinhart
173 Mirco Mueller 5.00 12.00
174 William Karlsson 20.00 50.00
175 Adam Lowry 5.00 12.00
176 Andy Andreoff 5.00 12.00
177 Seth Helgeson 4.00 10.00
178 Kevin Hayes
179 David Pastrnak
180 Marko Dano 5.00 12.00

2014-15 Upper Deck Overtime Flash of Excellence

COMPLETE SET (30) 15.00 40.00
*ORANGE/25: 4X TO 10X BASIC INSERTS
FOE1 Pavel Datsyuk .75 2.00

E2 Matt Duchene .60 1.50
E3 Dion Phaneuf .60 1.50
E4 Alex Galchenyuk 1.00 2.50
E5 Pekka Rinne .75 2.00
E6 Nail Yakupov .50 1.25
E7 Ryan Johansen .75 2.00
E8 Evander Kane .60 1.50
E9 Jonathan Toews 1.25 3.00
E10 Anze Kopitar 1.00 2.50
E11 Bobby Ryan .60 1.50
E12 Ryan Nugent-Hopkins .60 1.50
E13 David Backes .60 1.50
E14 Joe Thornton .60 1.50
E15 Tuukka Rask .60 1.50
E16 Dustin Byfuglien .60 1.50
E17 Jaromir Jagr 1.50 4.00
E18 Patrick Kane 1.25 3.00
E19 John Tavares 1.25 3.00
E20 Zach Parise .60 1.50
E21 Lars Eller .50 1.25
E22 Evgeni Malkin 2.00 5.00
E23 Martin St. Louis .60 1.50
E24 Steve Mason .50 1.25
E25 Doug Gilmour 1.00 2.50
E26 Wayne Gretzky 4.00 10.00
E27 Jean Beliveau .75 2.00
E28 Teuvo Teravainen .75 2.00
E29 Ty Rattie .60 1.50
E30 Evgeny Kuznetsov 2.00 5.00

2014-15 Upper Deck Overtime Lords of the Rink

LUE/25: 1.2X TO 3X BASIC INSERTS
1 Wayne Gretzky 12.00 30.00
2 Bobby Clarke 2.50 6.00
3 Jarome Iginla 2.00 5.00
4 Matt Duchene 2.00 5.00
5 Adam Oates 2.00 5.00
6 Tuukka Rask 2.00 5.00
7 Zach Parise 2.00 5.00
8 Dominik Hasek 2.50 6.00
9 Alexander Ovechkin 8.00 20.00
10 Joe Pavelski 2.00 5.00
11 Teemu Selanne 4.00 10.00
12 Ryan McDonagh 2.00 5.00
13 Anze Kopitar 3.00 8.00
14 David Backes 2.00 5.00
15 John Tavares 4.00 10.00
16 Corey Perry 2.00 5.00
17 Steve Mason 1.50 4.00
18 Jonathan Bernier 2.00 5.00
19 Mats Sundin 2.00 5.00
20 Jamie Benn 2.50 6.00
21 Doug Gilmour 3.00 8.00
22 Pavel Datsyuk 2.50 6.00
23 Evgeni Malkin 6.00 15.00
24 Nicklas Lidstrom 2.00 5.00
25 Nail Yakupov 1.50 4.00
26 Carey Price 6.00 15.00
27 Ryan Miller 2.00 5.00
28 Martin St. Louis 2.00 5.00
29 Phil Kessel 2.50 6.00
30 Nathan MacKinnon 4.00 10.00

2014-15 Upper Deck Overtime Rookie Review

LUE/25: 1.5X TO 4X BASIC INSERTS
C1 Aaron Ekblad 5.00 12.00
C2 Griffin Reinhart 1.50 4.00
C3 Johnny Gaudreau 4.00 10.00
C4 Adam Lowry 1.25 3.00
C5 Anthony Duclair 2.00 5.00
C6 Ty Rattie 1.50 4.00
C7 Brandon Gormley 1.25 3.00
C8 Jiri Sekac 1.25 3.00
C9 Vladislav Namestnikov 2.00 5.00
C10 Bo Horvat 4.00 10.00
C11 Joey Hishon 1.50 4.00
C12 Evgeny Kuznetsov 5.00 12.00
C13 Alexander Khokhlachev 1.25 3.00
C14 Jonathan Drouin 3.00 8.00
C15 Andre Burakovsky 2.00 5.00
C16 Teemu Pulkkinen 1.50 4.00
C17 Teuvo Teravainen 2.00 5.00
C18 Marko Dano 1.25 3.00
C19 Jori Lehtera 1.50 4.00
C20 Sam Reinhart 4.00 10.00
C21 Curtis Lazar 1.50 4.00
C22 Mirco Mueller 1.25 3.00
C23 Markus Granlund 2.00 5.00
C24 Alexander Wennberg 2.50 6.00
C25 Damon Severson 1.25 3.00
C26 Chris Tierney 1.25 3.00
C27 Leon Draisaitl 6.00 15.00
C28 Calle Jarnkrok 1.25 3.00
C29 Oscar Klefbom 2.50 6.00
C30 Vincent Trocheck 1.50 4.00

2015-16 Upper Deck Overtime

MP.SERIES 1 (60) 25.00 50.00
MP.SERIES 2 (60) 25.00 50.00
1-120 ROOKIE ODDS 1:2 WAVE 2
LUE VETS: 1X TO 2.5X BASIC CARDS
LUE LEG: .6X TO 1.5X BASIC CARDS
LUE ROOKIE: .5X TO 1.2X BASIC CARDS
ED VETS/99: 3X TO 8X BASIC CARDS
ED LEG/99: 2X TO 5X BASIC CARDS
ED ROOKIE/99: 1.5X TO 4X BASIC RC
Steven Stamkos .75 2.00
Pekka Rinne .50 1.25
Jamie Benn .50 1.25
Brad Marchand .50 1.25
Max Pacioretty .40 1.00
Mikko Koivu .30 .75
Drew Doughty .40 1.00
Kyle Okposo .40 1.00
Joe Pavelski .40 1.00
Matt Duchene .40 1.00
David Backes .40 1.00
Tyler Ennis .30 .75
Alexander Ovechkin 1.50 4.00
Oliver Ekman-Larsson .30 .75
Jonas Hiller .30 .75
Henrik Lundqvist .50 1.25
Erik Karlsson .75 2.00
Steve Mason .30 .75
Marc-Andre Fleury .60 1.50
James van Riemsdyk .40 1.00
Patrick Kane .75 2.00
Vladimir Tarasenko .60 1.50
Ryan Johansen .50 1.25
Andrew Ladd .40 1.00
Daniel Sedin .40 1.00
Jordan Eberle .40 1.00
Nathan MacKinnon .75 2.00
Patrice Bergeron .50 1.25
Carey Price 1.25 3.00
Adam Henrique .40 1.00
Rick Nash .40 1.00
Kris Letang .40 1.00
Ben Bishop .40 1.00
Pavel Datsyuk .50 1.25
35 Marian Hossa .30 .75
36 Logan Couture .40 1.00
37 Ryan Kesler .40 1.00
38 Roberto Luongo .40 1.00
39 Marian Gaborik .40 1.00
40 Eric Staal .50 1.25
41 Wayne Gretzky LEG 3.00 8.00
42 Patrick Roy LEG 1.50 4.00
43 Phil Esposito LEG 1.00 2.50
44 Mario Lemieux LEG 2.00 5.00
45 Mark Messier LEG 1.00 2.50
46 Glenn Anderson LEG .60 1.50
47 Ray Bourque LEG 1.00 2.50
48 Bobby Clarke LEG .60 1.50
49 Mike Bossy LEG .60 1.50
50 Guy Lafleur LEG .75 2.00
51 Malcolm Subban RC 2.00 5.00
52 Sam Bennett RC 1.00 2.50
53 Kevin Fiala RC .75 2.00
54 Ryan Hartman RC 1.00 2.50
55 Henrik Samuelsson RC .60 1.50
56 Nick Cousins RC .75 2.00
57 Josh Anderson RC .75 2.00
58 Jacob de la Rose RC .75 2.00
59 Emile Poirier RC .75 2.00
60 Matt Puempel RC .60 1.50
61 Sidney Crosby 1.50 4.00
62 Bobby Ryan .30 .75
63 Patrick Marleau .40 1.00
64 Filip Forsberg .50 1.25
65 P.K. Subban .60 1.50
66 Ryan Miller .40 1.00
67 Ryan Suter .25 .60
68 Derick Brassard .40 1.00
69 Dustin Brown .30 .75
70 John Tavares .75 2.00
71 Claude Giroux .40 1.00
72 Jonathan Toews .75 2.00
73 Gabriel Landeskog .40 1.00
74 Jeff Skinner .30 .75
75 Nikita Kucherov .60 1.50
76 John Carlson .50 1.25
77 Keith Yandle .40 1.00
78 Ryan Getzlaf .60 1.50
79 Ryan Nugent-Hopkins .40 1.00
80 Nick Foligno .30 .75
81 Jake Allen .50 1.25
82 David Perron .25 .60
83 Darcy Kuemper .30 .75
84 Michael Hutchinson .40 1.00
85 Gustav Nyquist .40 1.00
86 Kari Lehtonen .30 .75
87 Shane Doan .30 .75
88 Tomas Plekanec .40 1.00
89 Jonathan Bernier .40 1.00
90 Sean Monahan .40 1.00
91 Zemgus Girgensons .30 .75
92 Anze Kopitar .60 1.50
93 Corey Crawford .50 1.25
94 Ondrej Palat .30 .75
95 Jiri Hudler .30 .75
96 Cory Schneider .30 .75
97 Jaromir Jagr 1.00 2.50
98 Joe Thornton .40 1.00
99 Jaroslav Halak .30 .75
100 Sergei Bobrovsky .40 1.00
101 Artemi Panarin RC 2.50 6.00
102 Brian O'Neill RC .60 1.50
103 Connor Hellebuyck RC 2.00 5.00
104 Raman Hrabarenka RC .60 1.50
105 Shane Prince RC .60 1.50
106 Joel Edmundson RC .60 1.50
107 Nicolas Petan RC .75 2.00
108 Andrew Copp RC .75 2.00
109 Jared McCann RC .75 2.00
110 Anton Slepyshev RC .60 1.50
111 Noah Hanifin RC 1.00 2.50
112 Colin Miller RC .60 1.50
113 Sergei Plotnikov RC .60 1.50
114 Mike Condon RC .75 2.00
115 Robby Fabbri RC 1.00 2.50
116 Stefan Noesen RC .60 1.50
117 Sergei Kalinin RC .60 1.50
118 Slater Koekkoek RC .60 1.50
119 Joonas Donskoi RC .75 2.00
120 Jack Eichel RC 4.00 10.00
121 Taylor Hall 1.50 4.00
122 Jarome Iginla .75 2.00
123 Evgeni Malkin 2.50 6.00
124 Shea Weber .60 1.50
125 Tyler Seguin 1.25 3.00
126 Cody Franson .50 1.25
127 Dustin Byfuglien .75 2.00
128 Justin Abdelkader .60 1.50
129 Brendan Gallagher 1.00 2.50
130 Alex Pietrangelo .60 1.50
131 Jonathan Quick 1.25 3.00
132 Johnny Gaudreau 1.25 3.00
133 Patrik Elias .75 2.00
134 Matt Moulson .60 1.50
135 Corey Perry .75 2.00
136 Mike Hoffman .60 1.50
137 Tuukka Rask .75 2.00
138 Jonathan Huberdeau .75 2.00
139 Cam Atkinson .75 2.00
140 Zach Parise .75 2.00
141 Mike Ribeiro .60 1.50
142 Jakub Voracek .75 2.00
143 Henrik Zetterberg 1.00 2.50
144 Justin Faulk .75 2.00
145 Jeff Carter .75 2.00
146 Ondrej Pavelec .75 2.00
147 Mark Giordano .75 2.00
148 Henrik Sedin .75 2.00
149 Ryan Callahan .75 2.00
150 Kyle Turris .60 1.50
151 Patrick Sharp .75 2.00
152 Patric Hornqvist .60 1.50
153 Craig Anderson .75 2.00
154 Mikkel Boedker .50 1.25
155 Tyler Johnson .60 1.50
156 John Carlson 1.00 2.50
157 Brent Burns 1.00 2.50
158 Anders Lee .75 2.00
159 Nazem Kadri .60 1.50
160 Devan Dubnyk .75 2.00
161 Charles Hudon RC .75 2.00
162 Max Domi RC 1.50 4.00
163 Stanislav Galiev RC .75 2.00
164 Antoine Bibeau RC .75 2.00
165 Ben Hutton RC .75 2.00
166 Andreas Athanasiou RC 2.00 5.00
167 Colton Parayko RC 1.00 2.50
168 Mattias Janmark RC .75 2.00
169 Jordan Weal RC .75 2.00
170 Devin Shore RC .75 2.00
171 Mikko Rantanen RC 1.50 4.00
172 Daniel Sprong RC 1.50 4.00
173 Nikolay Goldobin RC .75 2.00
174 Dylan Larkin RC 2.50 6.00
175 Connor Brickley RC .60 1.50
176 Jake Virtanen RC 1.00 2.50
177 Viktor Svedberg RC .60 1.50
178 Matt O'Connor RC .60 1.50
179 Zachary Fucale RC .75 2.00
180 Connor McDavid RC 8.00 20.00

2015-16 Upper Deck Overtime Autographs

61-100 VETERAN ODDS 1:90 WAVE 2
101-118 ROOKIE ODDS 1:60 WAVE 2
1 Steven Stamkos 15.00 40.00
2 Pekka Rinne 10.00 25.00
3 Jamie Benn 10.00 25.00
4 Brad Marchand 10.00 25.00
5 Max Pacioretty 8.00 20.00
6 Mikko Koivu 6.00 15.00
7 Drew Doughty 8.00 20.00
8 Kyle Okposo 8.00 20.00
9 Joe Pavelski 8.00 20.00
10 Matt Duchene 8.00 20.00
11 David Backes 8.00 20.00
12 Tyler Ennis 6.00 15.00
13 Alexander Ovechkin 75.00 125.00
14 Oliver Ekman-Larsson 6.00 15.00
15 Jonas Hiller 6.00 15.00
16 Henrik Lundqvist 10.00 25.00
17 Erik Karlsson 15.00 40.00
18 Steve Mason 6.00 15.00
19 Marc-Andre Fleury 12.00 30.00
20 James van Riemsdyk 8.00 20.00
21 Patrick Kane 15.00 40.00
22 Vladimir Tarasenko 12.00 30.00
23 Ryan Johansen 10.00 25.00
24 Andrew Ladd 8.00 20.00
25 Daniel Sedin 8.00 20.00
26 Jordan Eberle 8.00 20.00
27 Nathan MacKinnon 15.00 40.00
28 Patrice Bergeron 10.00 25.00
29 Carey Price 25.00 60.00
30 Adam Henrique 8.00 20.00
31 Rick Nash 8.00 20.00
32 Kris Letang 8.00 20.00
33 Ben Bishop 8.00 20.00
34 Pavel Datsyuk 10.00 25.00
35 Marian Hossa 6.00 15.00
36 Logan Couture 8.00 20.00
37 Ryan Kesler 8.00 20.00
38 Roberto Luongo 8.00 20.00
39 Marian Gaborik 8.00 20.00
40 Eric Staal 10.00 25.00
41 Wayne Gretzky LEG 200.00 300.00
42 Patrick Roy LEG 40.00 80.00
43 Phil Esposito LEG 12.50 25.00
44 Mario Lemieux LEG 30.00 80.00
45 Mark Messier LEG 15.00 40.00
46 Glenn Anderson LEG 10.00 25.00
47 Ray Bourque LEG 15.00 40.00
48 Bobby Clarke LEG 10.00 25.00
49 Mike Bossy LEG 15.00 30.00
50 Guy Lafleur LEG 12.00 30.00
51 Malcolm Subban 15.00 30.00
52 Sam Bennett 6.00 15.00
53 Kevin Fiala 5.00 12.00
54 Ryan Hartman 6.00 15.00
55 Henrik Samuelsson 4.00 10.00
56 Nick Cousins 5.00 12.00
57 Josh Anderson 5.00 12.00
58 Jacob de la Rose 5.00 12.00
59 Emile Poirier 5.00 12.00
60 Matt Puempel 4.00 10.00
62 Bobby Ryan 6.00 15.00
63 Patrick Marleau 8.00 20.00
64 Filip Forsberg 10.00 25.00
65 P.K. Subban 12.00 30.00
67 Ryan Suter 5.00 12.00
69 Dustin Brown 6.00 15.00
70 John Tavares 15.00 40.00
71 Claude Giroux 8.00 20.00
72 Jonathan Toews 15.00 40.00
73 Gabriel Landeskog 8.00 20.00
74 Jeff Skinner 6.00 15.00
75 Nikita Kucherov 12.50 25.00
76 John Carlson 10.00 25.00
77 Keith Yandle 8.00 20.00
78 Ryan Getzlaf 12.00 30.00
79 Ryan Nugent-Hopkins 8.00 20.00
80 Nick Foligno 6.00 15.00
81 Jake Allen 10.00 25.00
82 David Perron 5.00 12.00
83 Darcy Kuemper 6.00 15.00
84 Michael Hutchinson 8.00 20.00
85 Gustav Nyquist 8.00 20.00
86 Kari Lehtonen 6.00 15.00
88 Tomas Plekanec 8.00 20.00
89 Jonathan Bernier 8.00 20.00
91 Zemgus Girgensons 6.00 15.00
92 Anze Kopitar 12.00 30.00
94 Ondrej Palat 6.00 15.00
96 Cory Schneider 6.00 15.00
97 Jaromir Jagr 20.00 50.00
98 Joe Thornton 8.00 20.00
99 Jaroslav Halak 6.00 15.00
100 Sergei Bobrovsky 8.00 20.00
103 Connor Hellebuyck 20.00 50.00
105 Shane Prince 6.00 15.00
107 Nicolas Petan 8.00 20.00
111 Noah Hanifin 10.00 25.00
115 Robby Fabbri 10.00 25.00
116 Stefan Noesen 6.00 15.00
118 Slater Koekkoek 6.00 15.00
122 Jarome Iginla 8.00 20.00
123 Evgeni Malkin 25.00 60.00
124 Shea Weber 6.00 15.00
125 Tyler Seguin 12.00 30.00
126 Cody Franson 5.00 12.00
128 Justin Abdelkader 6.00 15.00
129 Brendan Gallagher 10.00 25.00
130 Alex Pietrangelo 6.00 15.00
131 Jonathan Quick 12.00 30.00
133 Patrik Elias 8.00 20.00
134 Matt Moulson 6.00 15.00
135 Corey Perry 8.00 20.00
137 Tuukka Rask 8.00 20.00
138 Jonathan Huberdeau 8.00 20.00
139 Cam Atkinson 8.00 20.00
140 Zach Parise 8.00 20.00
141 Mike Ribeiro 6.00 15.00
142 Jakub Voracek 8.00 20.00
144 Justin Faulk 8.00 20.00
145 Jeff Carter 8.00 20.00
149 Ryan Callahan 8.00 20.00
150 Kyle Turris 6.00 15.00
151 Patrick Sharp 8.00 20.00
155 Tyler Johnson 6.00 15.00
156 John Carlson 10.00 25.00
157 Brent Burns 10.00 25.00
158 Anders Lee 8.00 20.00
161 Charles Hudon 8.00 20.00
164 Antoine Bibeau 8.00 20.00
166 Andreas Athanasiou 20.00 50.00
167 Colton Parayko 10.00 25.00
168 Mattias Janmark 8.00 20.00
169 Jordan Weal 8.00 20.00
170 Devin Shore 8.00 20.00
173 Nikolay Goldobin 8.00 20.00
174 Dylan Larkin 60.00 100.00
177 Viktor Svedberg 6.00 15.00
178 Matt O'Connor 6.00 15.00
179 Zachary Fucale 8.00 20.00
180 Connor McDavid 100.00 200.00

2015-16 Upper Deck Overtime Flash of Excellence

*BLUE/25: 3X TO 8X BASIC INSERTS
FOE1 Alexander Ovechkin 2.50 6.00
FOE2 Rick Nash .60 1.50
FOE3 Steven Stamkos 1.25 3.00
FOE4 Joe Pavelski .60 1.50
FOE5 Max Pacioretty .60 1.50
FOE6 Patrick Kane 1.25 3.00
FOE7 Patrice Bergeron .75 2.00
FOE8 Jamie Benn .75 2.00
FOE9 Pavel Datsyuk .75 2.00
FOE10 Andrew Ladd .60 1.50
FOE11 Carey Price 2.00 5.00
FOE12 Pekka Rinne .75 2.00
FOE13 Henrik Lundqvist .75 2.00
FOE14 Wayne Gretzky 3.00 8.00
FOE15 Bobby Clarke .60 1.50
FOE16 Bobby Hull .60 1.50
FOE17 Mario Lemieux 2.00 5.00
FOE18 Mark Messier 1.00 2.50
FOE19 Malcolm Subban 1.50 4.00
FOE20 Sam Bennett .75 2.00

2015-16 Upper Deck Overtime Luminary Legends

LL1 Sidney Crosby 6.00 15.00
LL2 Joe Pavelski 1.50 4.00
LL3 Jamie Benn 2.00 5.00
LL4 Nathan MacKinnon 3.00 8.00
LL5 Alexander Ovechkin 6.00 15.00
LL6 Pekka Rinne 2.00 5.00
LL7 Anze Kopitar 2.50 6.00
LL8 P.K. Subban 2.50 6.00
LL9 Henrik Zetterberg 2.00 5.00
LL10 Steven Stamkos 3.00 8.00
LL11 Evgeni Malkin 5.00 12.00
LL12 Tyler Seguin 2.50 6.00
LL13 Claude Giroux 1.50 4.00
LL14 Taylor Hall 3.00 8.00
LL15 Rick Nash 1.50 4.00
LL16 Corey Perry 1.50 4.00
LL17 John Tavares 3.00 8.00
LL18 Jonathan Toews 3.00 8.00
LL19 Vladimir Tarasenko 2.50 6.00
LL20 Carey Price 5.00 12.00
LL21 Wayne Gretzky 8.00 20.00
LL22 Mark Messier 2.50 6.00
LL23 Glenn Anderson 1.50 4.00
LL24 Mike Bossy 1.50 4.00
LL25 Curtis Joseph 1.50 4.00
LL26 Cam Neely 1.50 4.00
LL27 Mike Modano 2.50 6.00
LL28 Teemu Selanne 3.00 8.00
LL29 Bobby Clarke 1.50 4.00
LL30 Jeremy Roenick 1.50 4.00

2015-16 Upper Deck Overtime Next in Line

COMPLETE SET (30) 50.00 100.00
ONE PER WAVE 2 PACK
NL1 Jack Eichel 6.00 15.00
NL2 Joonas Donskoi 1.00 2.50
NL3 Artemi Panarin 3.00 8.00
NL4 Nikolaj Ehlers 2.00 5.00
NL5 Mattias Janmark 1.00 2.50
NL6 Connor Hellebuyck 2.50 6.00
NL7 Dylan Larkin 6.00 15.00
NL8 Anton Slepyshev .75 2.00
NL9 Jared McCann 1.00 2.50
NL10 Max Domi 2.00 5.00
NL11 Daniel Sprong 2.00 5.00
NL12 Oscar Lindberg 1.00 2.50
NL13 Jake Virtanen 1.25 3.00
NL14 Nikolay Goldobin 1.00 2.50
NL15 Viktor Arvidsson 1.25 3.00
NL16 Nick Shore 1.00 2.50
NL17 Stanislav Galiev 1.00 2.50
NL18 Malcolm Subban 2.50 6.00
NL19 Stefan Noesen .75 2.00
NL20 Slater Koekkoek .75 2.00
NL21 Colton Parayko 1.25 3.00
NL22 Mikko Rantanen 2.00 5.00
NL23 Sergei Plotnikov .75 2.00
NL24 Sam Bennett 1.25 3.00
NL25 Robby Fabbri 1.25 3.00
NL26 Matt O'Connor .75 2.00
NL27 Nicolas Petan 1.00 2.50
NL28 Brock McGinn 1.00 2.50
NL29 Noah Hanifin 1.25 3.00
NL30 Connor McDavid 12.00 30.00

2015-16 Upper Deck Overtime Next in Line Blue Rainbow

*BLUE/25: 2.5X TO 6X BASIC INSERTS
NL30 Connor McDavid 200.00 400.00

2016-17 Upper Deck Overtime

1 Connor McDavid 5.00 12.00
2 Aaron Ekblad 1.00 2.50
3 Ryan McDonagh .75 2.00
4 Ondrej Palat .75 2.00
5 John Gibson 1.00 2.50
6 Brayden Schenn 1.00 2.50
7 Claude Giroux 1.00 2.50
8 James van Riemsdyk 1.00 2.50
9 Ryan Nugent-Hopkins 1.00 2.50
10 Semyon Varlamov 1.00 2.50
11 Sam Reinhart .75 2.00
12 Dion Phaneuf 1.00 2.50
13 Michal Neuvirth .75 2.00
14 Rick Nash 1.00 2.50
15 Artemi Panarin 1.25 3.00
16 Ryan Miller 1.00 2.50
17 Brian Boyle .60 1.50
18 Riley Sheahan .75 2.00
19 Oscar Klefbom 1.50 4.00
20 Gabriel Landeskog .75 2.00
21 Alex Galchenyuk 1.25 3.00
22 Aleksander Barkov 1.00 2.50
23 Jamie Benn 1.25 3.00
24 Noah Hanifin 1.00 2.50
25 Jesper Fast .60 1.50
26 Dylan Larkin 1.50 4.00
27 Jacob Trouba .75 2.00
28 Robby Fabbri 1.00 2.50
29 Kevin Shattenkirk .75 2.00
30 Matt Beleskey .75 2.00
31 Seth Jones .75 2.00
32 Mark Giordano .75 2.00
33 John Tavares 2.00 5.00
34 Cory Schneider .75 2.00
35 Jonathan Quick 1.50 4.00
36 Joe Pavelski 1.00 2.50
37 Marian Gaborik 1.00 2.50
38 Olli Maatta 1.00 2.50
39 Sidney Crosby 4.00 10.00
40 Jaromir Jagr 2.50 6.00
41 Luc Robitaille LEG 2.00 5.00
42 Teemu Selanne LEG 4.00 10.00
43 Steve Yzerman LEG 2.50 6.00
44 Larry Robinson LEG 2.00 5.00
45 Rob Blake LEG 2.00 5.00
46 Glenn Hall LEG 2.00 5.00
47 Trevor Linden LEG 2.50 6.00
48 Wendel Clark LEG 2.00 5.00
49 Ron Hextall LEG 2.00 5.00
50 Wayne Gretzky LEG 10.00 25.00
51 Pavel Zacha RC 2.50 6.00
52 Jason Dickinson RC 1.50 4.00
53 Trevor Carrick RC 2.00 5.00
54 Chase De Leo RC 2.00 5.00
55 Connor Brown RC 3.00 8.00
56 Josh Morrissey RC 2.50 6.00
57 Sonny Milano RC 2.50 6.00
58 Kasperi Kapanen RC 4.00 10.00
59 Anthony Mantha RC 5.00 12.00
60 William Nylander RC 8.00 20.00
61 Braden Holtby 1.50 4.00
62 Evander Kane 1.00 2.50
63 Aaron Ekblad 1.00 2.50
64 Brock Nelson .75 2.00
65 Morgan Rielly .75 2.00
66 Martin Jones 1.00 2.50
67 Corey Crawford 1.25 3.00
68 Carl Hagelin 1.00 2.50
69 Matt Duchene 1.00 2.50
70 Nick Bjugstad .75 2.00
71 Ryan Johansen 1.25 3.00
72 Tyler Toffoli 1.00 2.50
73 Elias Lindholm 1.00 2.50
74 Jason Pominville .75 2.00
75 Richard Panik .75 2.00
76 Tyler Seguin 1.50 4.00
77 Patrick Marleau 1.00 2.50
78A Henrik Zetterberg 1.25 3.00
78B Henrik Zetterberg VAR 2.00 5.00
79 Brent Seabrook .75 2.00
80 Sam Reinhart .75 2.00
81 Ryan Spooner .75 2.00
82 Robby Fabbri 1.00 2.50
83 Jakub Voracek 1.00 2.50
84A Ryan Getzlaf 1.50 4.00
84B Ryan Getzlaf VAR 2.50 6.00
85 Leon Draisaitl 1.25 3.00
86 Sean Couturier 1.00 2.50
87 Tyler Johnson .75 2.00
88 Bobby Ryan .75 2.00
89 Andy Greene .60 1.50
90 Brad Marchand 1.25 3.00
91 Boone Jenner 1.00 2.50
92 Ondrej Pavelec 1.00 2.50
93 Kyle Palmieri .75 2.00
94 Johnny Boychuk 1.00 2.50
95 Alexander Wennberg .75 2.00
96 Kyle Turris .75 2.00
97 Derek Stepan .75 2.00
98A Carey Price 3.00 8.00
98B Carey Price VAR 5.00 12.00
99 Bo Horvat 1.50 4.00
100 Ben Bishop 1.00 2.50
101 Michael Matheson RC 2.00 5.00
102A Brendan Leipsic RC 2.00 5.00
102B Brendan Leipsic VAR 2.50 6.00
103 Nikita Soshnikov RC 1.25 3.00
104 Justin Bailey RC 2.00 5.00
105 Esa Lindell RC 2.00 5.00
106 Dominik Simon RC 2.00 5.00
107 Pontus Aberg RC 2.50 6.00
108 Chris Bigras RC 1.50 4.00
109 Oliver Kylington RC 1.50 4.00
110 Mike Reilly RC 1.50 4.00
111 JC Lipon RC 2.00 5.00
112 Daniel Altshuller RC 1.50 4.00
113 Miles Wood RC 1.50 4.00
114 Ryan Pulock RC 2.00 5.00
115 Oliver Bjorkstrand RC 1.50 4.00
116 Sergey Tolchinsky RC 1.50 4.00
117 Oskar Sundqvist RC 2.00 5.00
118 Pavel Zacha RC 2.50 6.00
119A Hudson Fasching RC 2.00 5.00
119B Hudson Fasching VAR 2.50 6.00
120A Charlie Lindgren RC 4.00 10.00
120B Charlie Lindgren VAR 2.50 6.00
121 Keith Yandle 1.00 2.50
122 Oscar Lindberg .60 1.50
123 Jason Zucker .75 2.00
124A Taylor Hall 2.00 5.00
124B Taylor Hall VAR 2.00 5.00
125 Jason Demers .60 1.50
126 Thomas Vanek .75 2.00
127 Vladislav Namestnikov .60 1.50
128 Radko Gudas .60 1.50
129 Tomas Tatar .75 2.00
130 Jiri Hudler .75 2.00
131A P.K. Subban 1.50 4.00
131B P.K. Subban VAR 1.50 4.00
132 Zemgus Girgensons .75 2.00
133 Alexander Radulov 1.00 2.50
134 Anders Lee 1.00 2.50
135 Adam Henrique 1.00 2.50
136 Nino Niederreiter 1.00 2.50
137 Nikita Kucherov 1.50 4.00
138 Cam Ward 1.00 2.50
139 Andrei Vasilevskiy 1.25 3.00
140 Andrew Ladd 1.00 2.50
141 Shayne Gostisbehere 1.25 3.00
142 Nick Ritchie .75 2.00
143 Kyle Okposo 1.00 2.50
144 Anthony Duclair 1.00 2.50
145 Mats Zuccarello 1.00 2.50
146 Viktor Arvidsson 1.25 3.00
147 Jean-Gabriel Pageau .75 2.00
148 Frank Vatrano 1.00 2.50
149 Eric Staal 1.25 3.00
150 Victor Rask .75 2.00
151 Marc-Andre Fleury 1.50 4.00
152 Casey Cizikas .60 1.50
153 Jake Allen 1.25 3.00
154 Zach Parise 1.00 2.50
155 Connor Hellebuyck 1.50 4.00
156 Loui Eriksson 1.00 2.50
157 Jake Muzzin .75 2.00
158 Teuvo Teravainen 1.00 2.50
159 Artem Anisimov .75 2.00
160A Brent Burns 1.25 3.00
160B Brent Burns VAR 3.00 8.00
161A Patrik Laine RC 8.00 20.00
161B Patrik Laine VAR 10.00 25.00
162 Jakob Chychrun RC 2.00 5.00
163 Christian Dvorak RC 2.00 5.00
164 Thomas Chabot RC 4.00 10.00
165 Tyler Motte RC 2.00 5.00
166 Ivan Provorov RC 4.00 10.00
167 Zach Werenski RC 4.00 10.00
168 Kyle Connor RC 5.00 12.00
169 Jimmy Vesey RC 4.00 10.00
170 Mathew Barzal RC 6.00 15.00
171 Pavel Buchnevich RC 3.00 8.00
172 Lawson Crouse RC 1.50 4.00
173 Dylan Strome RC 4.00 10.00
174 Matthew Tkachuk RC 6.00 15.00
175A Mitch Marner RC 10.00 25.00
175B Mitch Marner VAR 12.00 30.00
176 Mikhail Sergachev RC 4.00 10.00
177 Julius Honka RC 2.00 5.00
178 Jesse Puljujarvi RC 5.00 12.00
179 Nick Schmaltz RC 2.00 5.00
180A Auston Matthews RC 12.00 30.00
180B Auston Matthews VAR 15.00 40.00

2016-17 Upper Deck Overtime Autographs

1 Connor McDavid A 50.00 120.00
2 Aaron Ekblad C 6.00 15.00
3 Ryan McDonagh A 8.00 20.00
4 Ondrej Palat C 5.00 12.00
5 John Gibson C 6.00 15.00
6 Brayden Schenn B 8.00 20.00
7 Claude Giroux A 10.00 25.00
8 James van Riemsdyk C 6.00 15.00
9 Ryan Nugent-Hopkins B 8.00 20.00
10 Semyon Varlamov C 6.00 15.00
11 Sam Reinhart C 5.00 12.00
12 Dion Phaneuf B 8.00 20.00
13 Michal Neuvirth B 6.00 15.00
14 Rick Nash B 8.00 20.00
16 Ryan Miller C 6.00 15.00
17 Brian Boyle C 4.00 10.00
18 Riley Sheahan C 5.00 12.00
19 Oscar Klefbom C 10.00 25.00
20 Gabriel Landeskog B 6.00 15.00
21 Alex Galchenyuk B 10.00 25.00
22 Aleksander Barkov B 8.00 20.00
23 Jamie Benn A 12.00 30.00
24 Noah Hanifin C 6.00 15.00
25 Jesper Fast C 4.00 10.00
26 Dylan Larkin C 10.00 25.00
27 Jacob Trouba A 8.00 20.00
28 Robby Fabbri C 6.00 15.00
29 Kevin Shattenkirk C 5.00 12.00
30 Matt Beleskey C 5.00 12.00
31 Seth Jones C 5.00 12.00
33 John Tavares B 15.00 40.00
34 Cory Schneider C 5.00 12.00
35 Jonathan Quick B 12.00 30.00
36 Joe Pavelski B 8.00 20.00
37 Marian Gaborik A 10.00 25.00
41 Luc Robitaille LEG A 15.00 40.00
42 Teemu Selanne LEG B 30.00 80.00
43 Steve Yzerman LEG A 20.00 50.00
44 Larry Robinson LEG C 10.00 25.00
45 Rob Blake LEG B 15.00 40.00
46 Glenn Hall LEG C 10.00 25.00
47 Trevor Linden LEG C 12.00 30.00
48 Wendel Clark LEG C 10.00 25.00
50 Wayne Gretzky LEG A 80.00 200.00
51 Pavel Zacha A 10.00 25.00
52 Jason Dickinson A 6.00 15.00
53 Trevor Carrick B 8.00 20.00
54 Chase De Leo B 8.00 20.00
55 Connor Brown B 12.00 30.00
56 Josh Morrissey B 10.00 25.00
57 Sonny Milano A 10.00 25.00
58 Kasperi Kapanen B 15.00 40.00
59 Anthony Mantha A 20.00 50.00
60 William Nylander A 30.00 80.00
62 Evander Kane 5.00 12.00
63 Aaron Ekblad 5.00 12.00
64 Brock Nelson 4.00 10.00
65 Morgan Rielly 4.00 10.00
68 Carl Hagelin 5.00 12.00
69 Matt Duchene 5.00 12.00
70 Nick Bjugstad 4.00 10.00
72 Tyler Toffoli 5.00 12.00
74 Jason Pominville 4.00 10.00
75 Richard Panik 4.00 10.00
76 Tyler Seguin 8.00 20.00
77 Patrick Marleau 5.00 12.00
78 Henrik Zetterberg 6.00 15.00
80 Sam Reinhart 4.00 10.00
81 Ryan Spooner 4.00 10.00
82 Robby Fabbri 5.00 12.00
83 Jakub Voracek 5.00 12.00
85 Leon Draisaitl 6.00 15.00
86 Sean Couturier 5.00 12.00
87 Tyler Johnson 4.00 10.00
88 Bobby Ryan 4.00 10.00
90 Brad Marchand 6.00 15.00
91 Boone Jenner 5.00 12.00
93 Kyle Palmieri 4.00 10.00
94 Johnny Boychuk 5.00 12.00
95 Alexander Wennberg 4.00 10.00
96 Kyle Turris 4.00 10.00
97 Derek Stepan 4.00 10.00
98 Carey Price 15.00 40.00
99 Bo Horvat 8.00 20.00
100 Ben Bishop 5.00 12.00
101 Michael Matheson 5.00 12.00
102 Brendan Leipsic 5.00 12.00
103 Nikita Soshnikov 3.00 8.00
104 Justin Bailey 5.00 12.00
105 Esa Lindell 5.00 12.00
106 Dominik Simon 5.00 12.00
107 Pontus Aberg 6.00 15.00
108 Chris Bigras 4.00 10.00
110 Mike Reilly 4.00 10.00
111 JC Lipon 5.00 12.00
112 Daniel Altshuller 4.00 10.00
113 Miles Wood 4.00 10.00
114 Ryan Pulock 5.00 12.00
115 Oliver Bjorkstrand 4.00 10.00
116 Sergey Tolchinsky 4.00 10.00
117 Oskar Sundqvist 5.00 12.00
118 Pavel Zacha 6.00 15.00
119 Hudson Fasching 5.00 12.00
120 Charlie Lindgren 10.00 25.00
121 Keith Yandle 5.00 12.00
122 Oscar Lindberg 3.00 8.00
123 Jason Zucker 4.00 10.00
124 Taylor Hall 10.00 25.00
125 Jason Demers 3.00 8.00
126 Thomas Vanek 4.00 10.00
127 Vladislav Namestnikov 3.00 8.00
128 Radko Gudas 3.00 8.00
129 Tomas Tatar 4.00 10.00
130 Jiri Hudler 4.00 10.00
131 P.K. Subban 8.00 20.00
132 Zemgus Girgensons 4.00 10.00
133 Alexander Radulov 5.00 12.00
134 Anders Lee 5.00 12.00
135 Adam Henrique 5.00 12.00
138 Cam Ward 5.00 12.00
139 Andrei Vasilevskiy 6.00 15.00
140 Andrew Ladd 5.00 12.00
142 Nick Ritchie 4.00 10.00
144 Anthony Duclair 5.00 12.00
145 Mats Zuccarello 5.00 12.00
146 Viktor Arvidsson 6.00 15.00
147 Jean-Gabriel Pageau 4.00 10.00
148 Frank Vatrano 5.00 12.00
149 Eric Staal 6.00 15.00
150 Victor Rask 4.00 10.00
151 Marc-Andre Fleury 8.00 20.00
152 Casey Cizikas 3.00 8.00
153 Jake Allen 6.00 15.00
154 Zach Parise 5.00 12.00
155 Connor Hellebuyck 8.00 20.00
156 Loui Eriksson 5.00 12.00
157 Jake Muzzin 4.00 10.00
158 Teuvo Teravainen 5.00 12.00
159 Artem Anisimov 4.00 10.00
160 Brent Burns 6.00 15.00
161 Patrik Laine 80.00 150.00
162 Jakob Chychrun 8.00 20.00
163 Christian Dvorak 8.00 20.00
164 Thomas Chabot 15.00 40.00
166 Ivan Provorov 15.00 40.00
167 Zach Werenski 15.00 40.00
168 Kyle Connor 20.00 50.00
169 Jimmy Vesey 15.00 40.00
170 Mathew Barzal 25.00 60.00
171 Pavel Buchnevich 12.00 30.00
172 Lawson Crouse 6.00 15.00
173 Dylan Strome 15.00 40.00
174 Matthew Tkachuk 25.00 60.00
176 Mikhail Sergachev 15.00 40.00
177 Julius Honka 8.00 20.00
178 Jesse Puljujarvi 20.00 50.00
179 Nick Schmaltz 8.00 20.00
180 Auston Matthews 200.00 300.00

2016-17 Upper Deck Overtime Next in Line

NL1 Auston Matthews 8.00 20.00
NL2 Mikhail Sergachev 2.50 6.00
NL3 Dylan Strome 2.50 6.00
NL4 Jimmy Vesey 2.50 6.00
NL5 Kasperi Kapanen 2.50 6.00
NL6 Sebastian Aho 2.50 6.00
NL7 Ivan Provorov 2.50 6.00
NL8 Christian Dvorak 1.25 3.00
NL9 Sonny Milano 1.50 4.00
NL10 Kyle Connor 3.00 8.00
NL11 Nick Schmaltz 1.25 3.00
NL12 Zach Werenski 2.50 6.00
NL13 Anthony Mantha 3.00 8.00
NL14 Mathew Barzal 4.00 10.00
NL15 Pavel Buchnevich 2.00 5.00
NL16 Brayden Point 3.00 8.00
NL17 Thomas Chabot 2.50 6.00
NL18 William Nylander 5.00 12.00
NL19 Jakob Chychrun 1.25 3.00
NL20 Travis Konecny 2.50 6.00
NL21 Josh Morrissey 1.50 4.00
NL22 Jesse Puljujarvi 3.00 8.00
NL23 Danton Heinen 2.00 5.00
NL24 Anthony Beauvillier 1.25 3.00
NL25 Lawson Crouse 1.00 2.50
NL26 Artturi Lehkonen 1.25 3.00
NL27 Tyler Motte 1.25 3.00
NL28 Matthew Tkachuk 4.00 10.00
NL29 Mitch Marner 6.00 15.00
NL30 Patrik Laine 5.00 12.00

2016-17 Upper Deck Overtime Optimum Performance

OP1 Jonathan Toews 2.50 6.00
OP2 Henrik Lundqvist 1.25 3.00
OP3 Connor McDavid 6.00 15.00
OP4 Anthony Mantha 3.00 8.00
OP5 Jamie Benn 1.50 4.00
OP6 Pavel Zacha 1.50 4.00
OP7 Aaron Ekblad 1.25 3.00
OP8 Carey Price 4.00 10.00
OP9 Brent Burns 1.50 4.00
OP10 Bobby Hull 2.00 5.00
OP11 John Tavares 2.50 6.00
OP12 Oliver Ekman-Larsson 1.00 2.50
OP13 Steven Stamkos 2.50 6.00
OP14 Kyle Palmieri 1.00 2.50
OP15 Mark Messier 1.50 4.00
OP16 Kyle Okposo 1.25 3.00
OP17 Teemu Selanne 2.50 6.00
OP18 P.K. Subban 2.00 5.00
OP19 Steve Yzerman 1.50 4.00
OP20 Wayne Gretzky 6.00 15.00

2016-17 Upper Deck Overtime Top Rated

TR1 Connor McDavid 8.00 20.00
TR2 Marc-Andre Fleury 2.50 6.00
TR3 Luc Robitaille 1.50 4.00
TR4 Anze Kopitar 2.50 6.00
TR5 Pekka Rinne 2.00 5.00
TR6 Joe Pavelski 1.50 4.00
TR7 Rick Nash 1.50 4.00
TR8 William Nylander 6.00 15.00
TR9 Anthony Mantha 4.00 10.00
TR10 Corey Perry 1.50 4.00
TR11 Max Pacioretty 1.50 4.00
TR12 Rob Blake 2.00 5.00
TR13 John Tavares 3.00 8.00
TR14 Sean Monahan 1.50 4.00
TR15 Kyle Turris 1.25 3.00
TR16 Mark Scheifele 2.00 5.00
TR17 Ryan Strome 1.25 3.00
TR18 Pavel Zacha 2.00 5.00
TR19 James van Riemsdyk 1.50 4.00
TR20 Wayne Gretzky 8.00 20.00

2017-18 Upper Deck Overtime

1 Mats Zuccarello 1.00 2.50
2 Bobby Ryan .75 2.00
3 Radek Faksa .75 2.00
4 Brady Skjei .75 2.00
5A Max Pacioretty 1.00 2.50
5B Max Pacioretty VAR 1.50 4.00
6 Evander Kane 1.00 2.50
7 Keith Yandle .60 1.50
8 Martin Jones 1.00 2.50
9 Mikael Granlund 1.00 2.50
10 Sebastian Aho 1.00 2.50
11 David Krejci .75 2.00
12 Seth Jones .75 2.00
13 Tyler Johnson .75 2.00
14 Zach Parise 1.00 2.50
15 Henrik Zetterberg 1.00 2.50
16 Brendan Gallagher 1.00 2.50
17 Aleksander Barkov 1.00 2.50
18 Jakub Voracek 1.00 2.50
19 Rick Nash 1.00 2.50
20 Marian Gaborik 1.00 2.50
21 Max Domi 1.00 2.50
22 Ryan Nugent-Hopkins 1.00 2.50
23 David Backes .75 2.00

24 John Tavares 2.00 5.00
25 Kyle Turris 1.00 2.50
26 Jonathan Quick 1.50 4.00
27 Nikolaj Ehlers 1.00 2.50
28 Viktor Arvidsson .75 2.00
29 Jake Muzzin .75 2.00
30 Timo Meier .75 2.00
31 Carl Hagelin 1.00 2.50
32 Jason Spezza 1.00 2.50
33 Joe Pavelski 1.00 2.50
34 Loui Eriksson .75 2.00
35 Anthony Mantha 1.00 2.50
36A Mitch Marner 1.50 4.00
36B Mitch Marner VAR 2.50 6.00
37 Pavel Buchnevich .75 2.00
38 Jonathan Huberdeau .75 2.00
39 Dion Phaneuf .75 2.00
40 Nathan MacKinnon 2.00 5.00
41 Bobby Orr 3.00 8.00
42 Mike Bossy 1.50 4.00
43 Larry Murphy .75 2.00
44 Pavel Bure 1.00 2.50
45A Steve Yzerman 1.25 3.00
45B Steve Yzerman VAR 2.00 5.00
46 Vladislav Kamenev RC 3.00 8.00
47A Alexander Nylander RC 3.00 8.00
47B Alexander Nylander VAR 4.00 10.00
48 Jack Roslovic RC 2.50 6.00
49 Jon Gillies RC 2.00 5.00
50 Evgeny Svechnikov RC 4.00 10.00
51 Ivan Barbashev RC 2.00 5.00
52A Adrian Kempe RC 2.50 6.00
52B Adrian Kempe VAR 3.00 8.00
53 Riley Barber RC 1.50 4.00
54 Samuel Morin RC 2.00 5.00
55 Nikita Scherbak RC 4.00 10.00
56 Christian Fischer RC 2.50 6.00
57 Gabriel Carlsson RC 1.50 4.00
58 J.T. Compher RC 2.50 6.00
59 Jonny Brodzinski RC 2.00 5.00
60A Brock Boeser RC 10.00 25.00
60B Brock Boeser VAR 12.00 30.00
61 Nikita Kucherov 1.50 4.00
62 Antti Raanta 1.00 2.50
63 Jason Zucker .75 2.00
64 Anders Lee 1.00 2.50
65 Brayden Point 1.00 2.50
66 Oscar Lindberg .75 2.00
67 Brandon Carlo .75 2.00
68 Evgeny Dadonov .60 1.50
69 Ryan Spooner .75 2.00
70 Cam Atkinson 1.00 2.50
71 Mark Stone 1.00 2.50
72 Alex Galchenyuk 1.25 3.00
73 Ivan Provorov 1.00 2.50
74 Sam Gagner .75 2.00
75 Luke Glendening .60 1.50
76 Anthony DeAngelo .75 2.00
77 Vladislav Namestnikov .75 2.00
78 Brandon Montour .75 2.00
79 Mark Scheifele 1.25 3.00
80 John Carlson 1.25 3.00
81 Victor Hedman 1.25 3.00
82 Artem Anisimov .75 2.00
83 Mark Giordano .75 2.00
84 Jonathan Drouin 1.00 2.50
85 Leon Draisaitl 1.50 4.00
86 Teuvo Teravainen .75 2.00
87 Reilly Smith 1.00 2.50
88 Brian Boyle .60 1.50
89 Sam Bennett .75 2.00
90 David Desharnais .75 2.00
91 Josh Anderson .60 1.50
92 Jim Howard .60 1.50
93 Joe Colborne .75 2.00
94 Connor Brown 1.00 2.50
95 Colin Miller .60 1.50
96 Phillip Danault .60 1.50
97 Matt Moulson .60 1.50
98 Devan Dubnyk 1.00 2.50
99 Tanner Pearson .75 2.00
100 Jake Guentzel 1.25 3.00
101 Jakob Forsbacka-Karlsson RC 2.00 5.00
102 Alex Tuch RC 5.00 12.00
103 Jordan Schmaltz RC 2.50 6.00
104 Mike Vecchione RC 1.50 4.00
105 Tyson Jost RC 4.00 10.00
106 Remi Elie RC 1.50 4.00
107 Valentin Zykov RC 2.00 5.00
108 Alex Nedeljkovic RC 1.50 4.00
109 Denis Gurianov RC 2.00 5.00
110 Charlie McAvoy RC 6.00 15.00
111 Peter Cehlarik RC 2.00 5.00
112 Colin White RC 2.00 5.00
113 Lucas Wallmark RC 2.00 5.00
114 John Hayden RC 1.50 4.00
115 Josh Ho-Sang RC 2.50 6.00
116 Nicolas Kerdiles RC 2.00 5.00
117 Robbie Russo RC 2.00 5.00
118 Andrew Poturalski RC 2.00 5.00
119 Eric Comrie RC 1.50 4.00
120 Clayton Keller RC 5.00 12.00
121 Ben Bishop 1.00 2.50
122 Andrew Shaw .75 2.00
123 Alexander Wennberg .75 2.00
124 Andreas Athanasiou 1.00 2.50
125 Matthew Tkachuk 1.00 2.50
126 Jason Pominville .75 2.00
127 Marc-Andre Fleury 1.50 4.00
128 Chris Kreider 1.00 2.50
129 Charlie Coyle .75 2.00
130 Adam Henrique .75 2.00
131 Alexander Radulov 1.00 2.50
132 Petr Mrazek 1.00 2.50
133 Kevin Fiala .75 2.00
134 Bo Horvat 1.00 2.50
135 Joel Eriksson Ek 1.00 2.50
136 Matt Murray 1.50 4.00
137 Cam Ward .75 2.00
138 Brayden Schenn 1.00 2.50
139 Mikhail Sergachev 1.00 2.50
140 Ryan Miller .75 2.00
141 Slater Koekkoek .75 2.00
142 Miles Wood .60 1.50
143 Aaron Ekblad 1.00 2.50
144 Frederik Andersen .75 2.00
145 Andrei Vasilevskiy 1.25 3.00
146 Jonathan Bernier .75 2.00
147 Riley Sheahan .60 1.50
148 Nick Foligno .75 2.00
149 Michael Grabner .60 1.50
150 Nick Schmaltz .75 2.00
151 Jacob de la Rose .75 2.00
152 Ryan Pulock .75 2.00
153 Casey Cizikas .60 1.50
154 Ryan Hartman 1.00 2.50
155 Olli Maatta .60 1.50
156 Robin Lehner .60 1.50
157 Tobias Rieder .60 1.50
158 Nail Yakupov .75 2.00
159 Sonny Milano .75 2.00
160 Matt Duchene 1.00 2.50
161 Nolan Patrick RC 5.00 12.00
162 Alex DeBrincat RC 6.00 15.00
163 Filip Chytil RC 2.50 6.00
164 Jake DeBrusk RC 4.00 10.00
165 Logan Brown RC 2.50 6.00
166 Owen Tippett RC 5.00 12.00
167 Jesper Bratt RC 4.00 10.00
168 Luke Kunin RC 2.50 6.00
169 Anders Bjork RC 3.00 8.00
170 Martin Necas RC 2.50 6.00
171 Pierre-Luc Dubois RC 5.00 12.00
172 Alex Kerfoot RC 2.50 6.00
173 Kailer Yamamoto RC 6.00 15.00
174 Calle Rosen RC 2.50 6.00
175 Will Butcher RC 3.00 8.00
176 Chris DiDomenico RC 2.00 5.00
177 Victor Mete RC 2.50 6.00
178 Tage Thompson RC 4.00 10.00
179 Haydn Fleury RC 2.50 6.00
180 Nico Hischier RC 8.00 20.00

2017-18 Upper Deck Overtime Red

36 Mitch Marner 12.00 30.00
45 Steve Yzerman 25.00 60.00
47 Alexander Nylander 12.00 30.00
60 Brock Boeser 12.00 30.00

2017-18 Upper Deck Overtime A-1

A11 Mark Messier .75 2.00
A12 Henrik Lundqvist .75 2.00
A13 Leon Draisaitl .75 2.00
A14 Luc Robitaille .50 1.25
A15 Nicklas Lidstrom .40 1.00
A16 Mark Stone .50 1.25
A17 Jonathan Quick .75 2.00
A18 Alexander Ovechkin 2.00 5.00
A19 Brock Boeser 2.50 6.00
A110 Nikita Kucherov .75 2.00
A111 Carey Price 1.50 4.00
A112 Pat LaFontaine .50 1.25
A113 Tyler Seguin .75 2.00
A114 Vladimir Tarasenko .75 2.00
A115 Bobby Orr 1.50 4.00
A116 John Tavares 1.00 2.50
A117 Steven Stamkos 1.00 2.50
A118 Martin Brodeur 1.00 2.50
A119 Joe Thornton .50 1.25
A120 Clayton Keller 1.25 3.00

2017-18 Upper Deck Overtime A-1 Red

*RED/25: 1.5X TO 4X BASIC INSERTS
A111 Carey Price 12.00 30.00

2017-18 Upper Deck Overtime Ice Cold

IC1 Connor McDavid 6.00 15.00
IC2 Anze Kopitar 2.50 6.00
IC3 Ryan McDonagh 1.25 3.00
IC4 Jamie Benn 2.00 5.00
IC5 Jonathan Quick 2.50 6.00
IC6 Max Pacioretty 1.50 4.00
IC7 Frank Mahovlich 1.50 4.00
IC8 Zach Parise 1.50 4.00
IC9 Mitch Marner 2.50 6.00
IC10 Pat LaFontaine 1.50 4.00
IC11 Henrik Zetterberg 1.50 4.00
IC12 Roman Josi 1.50 4.00
IC13 Taylor Hall 3.00 8.00
IC14 Nikita Kucherov 2.50 6.00
IC15 Guy Lafleur 2.00 5.00
IC16 Patrick Kane 3.00 8.00
IC17 Ryan Kesler 1.50 4.00
IC18 Vladimir Tarasenko 2.50 6.00
IC19 John Tavares 3.00 8.00
IC20 Joe Pavelski 1.50 4.00

2017-18 Upper Deck Overtime Next In Line

NL1 Nico Hischier 1.50 4.00
NL2 Vadim Shipachyov 1.50 4.00
NL3 Brock Boeser 2.50 6.00
NL4 Pierre-Luc Dubois 1.00 2.50
NL5 Alex DeBrincat 1.25 3.00
NL6 Owen Tippett 1.00 2.50
NL7 Kailer Yamamoto 1.25 3.00
NL8 Logan Brown .50 1.25
NL9 Victor Mete .50 1.25
NL10 Filip Chytil .50 1.25
NL11 Josh Ho-Sang .60 1.50
NL12 Anders Bjork .60 1.50
NL13 Tucker Poolman .50 1.25
NL14 Tyson Jost 1.00 2.50
NL15 Jake DeBrusk .75 2.00
NL16 Martin Necas .50 1.25
NL17 Tage Thompson .75 2.00
NL18 Charlie McAvoy 1.50 4.00
NL19 Clayton Keller 1.25 3.00
NL20 Nolan Patrick 1.00 2.50

2017-18 Upper Deck Overtime Next In Line Red

NL1 Nico Hischier 10.00 25.00
NL3 Brock Boeser 30.00 80.00
NL7 Kailer Yamamoto 8.00 20.00

2015-16 Upper Deck Portfolio

1 Jeff Carter .40 1.00
2 Brent Seabrook .40 1.00
3 Leo Komarov .30 .75
4 David Krejci .30 .75
5 Tyler Ennis .30 .75
6 Tuukka Rask .40 1.00
7 Victor Hedman .50 1.25
8 Justin Faulk .40 1.00
9 Bobby Ryan .30 .75
10 Ryan Strome .30 .75
11 Dustin Byfuglien .40 1.00
12 Antti Niemi .30 .75
13 Nick Foligno .30 .75
14 Tomas Hertl .40 1.00
15 Aaron Ekblad .40 1.00
16 Ryan Nugent-Hopkins .40 1.00
17 Marc-Andre Fleury .60 1.50
18 Kris Versteeg .30 .75
19 Mikko Koivu .30 .75
20 Jonathan Huberdeau .40 1.00
21 Boone Jenner .25 .60
22 Mark Scheifele .50 1.25
23 Jack Johnson .25 .60
24 Duncan Keith .40 1.00
25 Mike Smith .40 1.00
26 Tyler Bozak .30 .75
27 James Neal .40 1.00
28 Jake Allen .50 1.25
29 Bo Horvat .60 1.50
30 Bryan Little .30 .75
31 Mathieu Perreault .25 .60
32 Alexander Ovechkin 1.50 4.00
33 Dougie Hamilton .40 1.00
34 Anthony Duclair .30 .75
35 Matt Duchene .40 1.00
36 Ben Bishop .40 1.00
37 Pavel Datsyuk .50 1.25
38 Nathan MacKinnon .75 2.00
39 Sergei Bobrovsky .40 1.00
40 Patrice Bergeron .50 1.25
41 Mats Zuccarello .30 .75
42 Nick Bjugstad .30 .75
43 Brent Burns .50 1.25
44 Kyle Palmieri .25 .60
45 Patrick Sharp .40 1.00
46 Jamie Benn .50 1.25
47 Tobias Rieder .25 .60
48 Filip Forsberg .50 1.25
49 Claude Giroux .40 1.00
50 Wayne Simmonds .50 1.25
51 Ryan Getzlaf .60 1.50
52 Brayden Schenn .40 1.00
53 P.K. Subban .60 1.50
54 Kyle Okposo .40 1.00
55 Dion Phaneuf .40 1.00
56 Kris Letang .40 1.00
57 Shayne Gostisbehere .40 1.00
58 Corey Perry .40 1.00
59 Mike Green .40 1.00
60 Mark Giordano .40 1.00
61 Johnny Gaudreau .60 1.50
62 Jarome Iginla .40 1.00
63 Jussi Jokinen .25 .60
64 John Klingberg .30 .75
65 Shea Weber .30 .75
66 Anze Kopitar .60 1.50
67 Brandon Saad .40 1.00
68 Brendan Gallagher .50 1.25
69 Mikkel Boedker .25 .60
70 Devan Dubnyk .40 1.00
71 Phil Kessel .60 1.50
72 Jaden Schwartz .50 1.25
73 Cory Schneider .30 .75
74 Carey Price 1.25 3.00
75 Tomas Plekanec .40 1.00
76 Pekka Rinne .50 1.25
77 Tyler Seguin .60 1.50
78 Victor Rask .25 .60
79 Jakub Voracek .40 1.00
80 Brock Nelson .30 .75
81 Martin Hanzal .25 .60
82 Evgeny Kuznetsov .60 1.50
83 T.J. Brodie .25 .60
84 Blake Wheeler .40 1.00
85 Gabriel Landeskog .40 1.00
86 Nikita Kucherov .60 1.50
87 Matt Moulson .30 .75
88 Mark Stone .30 .75
89 Steven Stamkos .75 2.00
90 John Tavares .75 2.00
91 Erik Johnson .25 .60
92 Kari Lehtonen .30 .75
93 Scott Hartnell .40 1.00
94 Mike Hoffman .30 .75
95 Joe Thornton .40 1.00
96 Henrik Lundqvist .50 1.25
97 Andrew Ladd .40 1.00
98 Martin Jones .40 1.00
99 Corey Crawford .50 1.25
100 Vladimir Tarasenko .60 1.50
101 Cam Fowler .30 .75
102 David Pastrnak .60 1.50
103 Mike Ribeiro .30 .75
104 Nino Niederreiter .25 .60
105 Henrik Zetterberg .50 1.25
106 Patrick Marleau .40 1.00
107 T.J. Oshie .60 1.50
108 Nicklas Backstrom .60 1.50
109 Teuvo Teravainen .40 1.00
110 Torey Krug .40 1.00
111 Petr Mrazek .50 1.25
112 Johnny Boychuk .25 .60
113 Zach Parise .40 1.00
114 Ryan Oâ•™Reilly .40 1.00
115 Loui Eriksson .30 .75
116 Kevin Shattenkirk .30 .75
117 Jason Spezza .30 .75
118 Jordan Staal .40 1.00
119 Drew Doughty .40 1.00
120 Taylor Hall .75 2.00
121 Jonathan Quick .60 1.50
122 Joe Pavelski .40 1.00
123 Patrick Kane .75 2.00
124 Rasmus Ristolainen .30 .75
125 Charlie Coyle .30 .75
126 John Carlson .50 1.25
127 Sidney Crosby 1.50 4.00
128 Semyon Varlamov .40 1.00
129 Alexander Steen .40 1.00
130 Ryan Kesler .40 1.00
131 Ryan Johansen .50 1.25
132 Adam Henrique .40 1.00
133 Michael Cammalleri .30 .75
134 Evgeni Malkin 1.25 3.00
135 Jiri Hudler .30 .75
136 Roman Josi .40 1.00
137 Marian Gaborik .40 1.00
138 Jordan Eberle .40 1.00
139 Eric Staal .50 1.25
140 Erik Karlsson .75 2.00
141 Sami Vatanen .25 .60
142 Kevin Hayes .40 1.00
143 Kyle Turris .30 .75
144 Tomas Tatar .30 .75
145 Morgan Rielly .30 .75
146 Oscar Klefbom .60 1.50
147 Rick Nash .40 1.00
148 Oliver Ekman-Larsson .30 .75
149 Evander Kane .40 1.00
150 Jonathan Toews .75 2.00
151 Craig Anderson .40 1.00
152 Mika Zibanejad .40 1.00
153 Ryan Miller .40 1.00
154 Justin Williams .30 .75
155 Alex Pietrangelo .30 .75
156 Jeff Skinner .30 .75
157 Nail Yakupov .30 .75
158 Tyler Johnson .30 .75
159 Gustav Nyquist .40 1.00
160 James van Riemsdyk .40 1.00
161 Sam Reinhart .40 1.00
162 Alex Galchenyuk .50 1.25
163 John Gibson .40 1.00
164 Leon Draisaitl .40 1.00
165 Jaromir Jagr 1.00 2.50
166 Tyler Toffoli .40 1.00
167 Henrik Sedin .40 1.00
168 Travis Hamonic .25 .60
169 James Reimer .40 1.00
170 Nazem Kadri .30 .75
171 Max Pacioretty .40 1.00
172 Derick Brassard .40 1.00
173 Braden Holtby .60 1.50
174 Radim Vrbata .30 .75
175 Roberto Luongo .40 1.00
176 Sean Monahan .40 1.00
177 Thomas Vanek .40 1.00
178 Daniel Sedin .40 1.00
179 Ryan Suter .25 .60
180 Aleksander Barkov .40 1.00
181 Brian Leetch .40 1.00
182 Lanny McDonald .40 1.00
183 Clark Gillies .40 1.00
184 Rod Brind`Amour .30 .75
185 Doug Gilmour .50 1.25
186 Pavel Bure .60 1.50
187 Bobby Orr 1.25 3.00
188 Glenn Hall .30 .75
189 Joe Sakic .60 1.50
190 Doug Harvey .40 1.00
191 Nicklas Lidstrom .40 1.00
192 Jari Kurri .40 1.00
193 Guy Lafleur .50 1.25
194 Martin Brodeur .75 2.00
195 Mark Messier .60 1.50
196 Bobby Clarke .40 1.00
197 Mario Lemieux 1.25 3.00
198 Al MacInnis .40 1.00
199 Borje Salming .40 1.00
200 Wayne Gretzky 2.00 5.00
201 Jack Eichel RC 3.00 8.00
202 Jake Virtanen RC 1.00 2.50
203 Brett Pesce RC .60 1.50
204 Jujhar Khaira RC .60 1.50
205 Brady Skjei RC .60 1.50
206 Nikolaj Ehlers RC 1.50 4.00
207 Shane Prince RC .60 1.50
208 Joonas Donskoi RC .75 2.00
209 Nick Ritchie RC .75 2.00
210 Andreas Athanasiou RC 2.00 5.00
211 Colton Parayko RC 1.00 2.50
212 Christoph Bertschy RC .60 1.50
213 Garret Sparks RC 1.00 2.50
214 Joonas Korpisalo RC 1.00 2.50
215 Artemi Panarin RC 2.50 6.00
216 Mikko Rantanen RC 1.50 4.00
217 Robby Fabbri RC 1.00 2.50
218 Joseph Blandisi RC .75 2.00
219 Nikolay Goldobin RC .75 2.00
220 Oscar Lindberg RC .75 2.00
221 Taylor Leier RC .75 2.00
222 Viktor Arvidsson RC 1.00 2.50
223 Matt Murray RC 4.00 10.00
224 Mike McCarron RC 1.00 2.50
225 Brock McGinn RC .75 2.00
226 Dylan Larkin RC 2.50 6.00
227 Ben Hutton RC .75 2.00
228 Charles Hudon RC .75 2.00
229 Sergei Plotnikov RC .60 1.50
230 Malcolm Subban RC 2.00 5.00
231 Juuse Saros RC 1.00 2.50
232 Linus Ullmark RC 1.00 2.50
233 Nicolas Petan RC .75 2.00
234 Sam Bennett RC 1.00 2.50
235 Jean-Francois Berube RC .60 1.50
236 Louis Domingue RC .75 2.00
237 Laurent Dauphin RC .75 2.00
238 Connor Hellebuyck RC 2.00 5.00
239 Hunter Shinkaruk RC .75 2.00
240 Mike Condon RC .75 2.00
241 Jared McCann RC .75 2.00
242 Colin Miller RC .60 1.50
243 Antoine Bibeau RC .75 2.00
244 Shea Theodore RC .75 2.00
245 Zachary Fucale RC .75 2.00
246 Daniel Carr RC .60 1.50
247 Frank Vatrano RC 1.50 4.00
248 Max Domi RC 1.50 4.00
249 Noah Hanifin RC 1.00 2.50
250 Connor McDavid RC 6.00 15.00
251 Alexander Ovechkin 5.00 12.00
252 Borje Salming 1.25 3.00
253 Jamie Benn 1.50 4.00
254 Bobby Clarke 1.25 3.00
255 Brian Leetch 1.25 3.00
256 Filip Forsberg 1.50 4.00
257 Jari Kurri 1.25 3.00
258 Vladimir Tarasenko 2.00 5.00
259 Cory Schneider 1.00 2.50
260 Clark Gillies 1.25 3.00
261 Max Pacioretty 1.25 3.00
262 Mario Lemieux 4.00 10.00
263 Guy Lafleur 1.50 4.00
264 Aaron Ekblad 1.25 3.00
265 Rod Brind`Amour 1.00 2.50
266 John Tavares 2.50 6.00
267 Taylor Hall 2.50 6.00
268 Shayne Gostisbehere 1.25 3.00
269 Lanny McDonald 1.25 3.00
270 Wayne Gretzky 6.00 15.00
271 Carey Price 5.00 12.00
272 Nicklas Lidstrom 1.50 4.00
273 Tyler Seguin 2.50 6.00
274 Bobby Ryan 1.25 3.00
275 Joe Pavelski 1.50 4.00
276 Henrik Lundqvist 2.00 5.00
277 Guy Lafleur 2.00 5.00
278 Jonathan Toews 3.00 8.00
279 Mark Scheifele 2.00 5.00
280 Nicklas Backstrom 2.50 6.00
281 Ryan Oâ•™Reilly 1.50 4.00
282 Morgan Rielly 1.25 3.00
283 Johnny Gaudreau 2.50 6.00
284 Vladimir Tarasenko 2.50 6.00
285 Wayne Gretzky 8.00 20.00
286 Vladimir Tarasenko 5.00 12.00
287 Taylor Hall 6.00 15.00
288 Alexander Ovechkin 12.00 30.00
289 Wayne Gretzky 15.00 40.00
290 John Tavares 6.00 15.00
291 Mario Lemieux 10.00 25.00
292 Bobby Clarke 3.00 8.00
293 Carey Price 12.00 30.00
294 Jari Kurri 3.00 8.00
295 Bobby Orr 10.00 25.00
296 Max Domi 2.50 6.00
297 Robby Fabbri 1.50 4.00
298 Shea Theodore 1.25 3.00
299 Nikolaj Ehlers 2.50 6.00
300 Charles Hudon 1.25 3.00
301 Mike McCarron 1.50 4.00
302 Noah Hanifin 1.50 4.00
303 Dylan Larkin 4.00 10.00
304 Oscar Lindberg 1.25 3.00
305 Matt Murray 6.00 15.00
306 Andreas Athanasiou 3.00 8.00
307 Jake Virtanen 1.50 4.00
308 Jack Eichel 5.00 12.00
309 Jared McCann 1.25 3.00
310 Mattias Janmark 1.25 3.00
311 Artemi Panarin 4.00 10.00
312 Colton Parayko 1.50 4.00
313 Nick Shore 1.25 3.00
314 Sam Bennett 1.50 4.00
315 Connor McDavid 10.00 25.00
316 Colton Parayko 2.50 6.00
317 Max Domi 4.00 10.00
318 Noah Hanifin 2.50 6.00
319 Jake Virtanen 2.50 6.00
320 Oscar Lindberg 2.00 5.00
321 Artemi Panarin 6.00 15.00
322 Nikolaj Ehlers 4.00 10.00
323 Jack Eichel 8.00 20.00
324 Robby Fabbri 2.50 6.00
325 Mike McCarron 2.50 6.00
326 Sam Bennett 2.50 6.00
327 Mattias Janmark 2.00 5.00
328 Dylan Larkin 6.00 15.00
329 Charles Hudon 2.00 5.00
330 Connor McDavid 15.00 40.00
331 Sam Bennett 4.00 10.00
332 Noah Hanifin 4.00 10.00
333 Zachary Fucale 3.00 8.00
334 Robby Fabbri 4.00 10.00
335 Jack Eichel 12.00 30.00
336 Dylan Larkin 10.00 25.00
337 Nikolaj Ehlers 6.00 15.00
338 Artemi Panarin 10.00 25.00
339 Max Domi 6.00 15.00
340 Connor McDavid 25.00 60.00

2015-16 Upper Deck Portfolio Autographs

3 Leo Komarov G 5.00 12.00
8 Justin Faulk F 8.00 20.00
9 Bobby Ryan E 8.00 20.00
10 Ryan Strome G 5.00 12.00
12 Antti Niemi E 8.00 20.00
13 Nick Foligno G 5.00 12.00
15 Aaron Ekblad E 10.00 25.00
17 Marc-Andre Fleury D 25.00 60.00
22 Mark Scheifele G 8.00 20.00
28 Jake Allen G 8.00 20.00
32 Alexander Ovechkin B 50.00 125.00
35 Matt Duchene E 10.00 25.00
37 Pavel Datsyuk D 20.00 50.00
39 Sergei Bobrovsky F 8.00 20.00
41 Mats Zuccarello A 25.00 60.00
42 Nick Bjugstad G 5.00 12.00
45 Patrick Sharp C 15.00 40.00
46 Jamie Benn D 20.00 50.00
48 Filip Forsberg C 20.00 50.00
49 Claude Giroux C 15.00 40.00
53 P.K. Subban C 25.00 60.00
57 Shayne Gostisbehere F 8.00 20.00
58 Corey Perry E 10.00 25.00
62 Jarome Iginla D 15.00 40.00
66 Anze Kopitar E 15.00 40.00
68 Brendan Gallagher D 20.00 50.00
73 Cory Schneider E 8.00 20.00
74 Carey Price D 50.00 125.00
76 Pekka Rinne F 10.00 25.00
77 Tyler Seguin A 50.00 120.00
79 Jakub Voracek F 8.00 20.00
82 Evgeny Kuznetsov F 12.00 30.00
85 Gabriel Landeskog E 10.00 25.00
86 Nikita Kucherov E 15.00 40.00
87 Matt Moulson G 5.00 12.00
88 Mark Stone G 5.00 12.00
90 John Tavares E 20.00 50.00
93 Scott Hartnell E 10.00 25.00
94 Mike Hoffman G 5.00 12.00
101 Cam Fowler E 8.00 20.00
114 Ryan Oâ•™Reilly G 6.00 15.00
120 Taylor Hall E 20.00 50.00
121 Jonathan Quick C 25.00 60.00
122 Joe Pavelski E 10.00 25.00
125 Charlie Coyle G 5.00 12.00
126 John Carlson E 12.00 30.00
128 Semyon Varlamov F 8.00 20.00
130 Ryan Kesler E 10.00 25.00
132 Adam Henrique F 8.00 20.00
134 Evgeni Malkin A 100.00 250.00
143 Kyle Turris G 5.00 12.00
144 Tomas Tatar F 6.00 15.00
145 Morgan Rielly E 8.00 20.00
146 Oscar Klefbom G 10.00 25.00
150 Jonathan Toews D 30.00 80.00
153 Ryan Miller D 15.00 40.00
157 Nail Yakupov E 8.00 20.00
158 Tyler Johnson F 6.00 15.00
161 Sam Reinhart F 8.00 20.00
162 Alex Galchenyuk B 25.00 60.00
164 Leon Draisaitl D 15.00 40.00
165 Jaromir Jagr B 30.00 80.00
166 Tyler Toffoli G 6.00 15.00
171 Max Pacioretty E 10.00 25.00
173 Braden Holtby A 50.00 125.00
180 Aleksander Barkov F 8.00 20.00
181 Brian Leetch D 15.00 40.00
182 Lanny McDonald D 15.00 40.00
183 Clark Gillies D 15.00 40.00
184 Rod Brind`Amour G 5.00 12.00
185 Doug Gilmour D 20.00 50.00
186 Pavel Bure B 20.00 50.00
187 Bobby Orr A 100.00 250.00
188 Glenn Hall E 8.00 20.00
189 Joe Sakic B 20.00 50.00
191 Nicklas Lidstrom D 15.00 40.00
192 Jari Kurri F 8.00 20.00
193 Guy Lafleur A 40.00 100.00
194 Martin Brodeur B 25.00 60.00
195 Mark Messier B 20.00 50.00
196 Bobby Clarke F 8.00 20.00
197 Mario Lemieux A 100.00 250.00
198 Al MacInnis D 15.00 40.00
200 Wayne Gretzky A 150.00 400.00
202 Jake Virtanen C 20.00 50.00
203 Brett Pesce E 8.00 20.00
204 Jujhar Khaira E 8.00 20.00
205 Brady Skjei E 8.00 20.00
206 Nikolaj Ehlers C 30.00 80.00
207 Shane Prince E 8.00 20.00
208 Joonas Donskoi D 12.00 30.00
209 Nick Ritchie D 12.00 30.00
210 Andreas Athanasiou B 30.00 80.00
211 Colton Parayko B 15.00 40.00
212 Christoph Bertschy E 8.00 20.00
213 Garret Sparks E 12.00 30.00
214 Joonas Korpisalo D 15.00 40.00
215 Artemi Panarin A 100.00 250.00
216 Mikko Rantanen B 25.00 60.00
217 Robby Fabbri C 20.00 50.00
219 Nikolay Goldobin D 12.00 30.00
220 Oscar Lindberg B 12.00 30.00
221 Taylor Leier D 12.00 30.00
222 Viktor Arvidsson E 12.00 30.00
223 Matt Murray D 60.00 150.00
224 Mike McCarron E 12.00 30.00
226 Dylan Larkin C 50.00 120.00
227 Ben Hutton D 12.00 30.00
228 Charles Hudon D 12.00 30.00
229 Sergei Plotnikov E 8.00 20.00
230 Malcolm Subban C 40.00 100.00
231 Juuse Saros E 12.00 30.00
232 Linus Ullmark E 12.00 30.00
233 Nicolas Petan E 10.00 25.00
234 Sam Bennett C 20.00 50.00
235 Jean-Francois Berube E 8.00 20.00
236 Louis Domingue E 10.00 25.00
238 Connor Hellebuyck C 40.00 100.00
240 Mike Condon D 12.00 30.00
241 Jared McCann D 12.00 30.00
242 Colin Miller E 8.00 20.00
243 Antoine Bibeau D 12.00 30.00
244 Shea Theodore E 10.00 25.00
245 Zachary Fucale D 12.00 30.00
246 Daniel Carr D 10.00 25.00
247 Frank Vatrano E 20.00 50.00
249 Noah Hanifin C 20.00 50.00
250 Connor McDavid C 250.00 350.00
251 Alexander Ovechkin B 30.00 80.00
253 Jamie Benn B 40.00 100.00
254 Bobby Clarke C 15.00 40.00
255 Brian Leetch B 12.00 30.00
256 Filip Forsberg A 40.00 100.00
257 Jari Kurri E 10.00 25.00
259 Cory Schneider E 8.00 20.00
260 Clark Gillies C 15.00 40.00
261 Max Pacioretty D 12.00 30.00
262 Mario Lemieux A 100.00 250.00
264 Aaron Ekblad D 12.00 30.00
265 Rod Brind`Amour E 8.00 20.00
266 John Tavares C 30.00 80.00
267 Taylor Hall D 25.00 60.00
268 Shayne Gostisbehere D 12.00 30.00
269 Lanny McDonald B 12.00 30.00
270 Wayne Gretzky A 150.00 400.00
271 Carey Price A 100.00 250.00
272 Nicklas Lidstrom A 30.00 80.00
273 Tyler Seguin A 50.00 120.00
274 Bobby Ryan B 10.00 25.00
275 Joe Pavelski B 12.00 30.00
278 Jonathan Toews A 60.00 150.00
279 Mark Scheifele C 20.00 50.00
280 Nicklas Backstrom A 50.00 125.00
281 Ryan O'Reilly C 15.00 40.00
282 Morgan Rielly B 10.00 25.00
285 Wayne Gretzky A 150.00 400.00
287 Taylor Hall C 30.00 80.00
288 Alexander Ovechkin A 125.00 300.00
289 Wayne Gretzky A 150.00 400.00
290 John Tavares B 25.00 60.00
291 Mario Lemieux A 100.00 250.00
293 Carey Price B 100.00 200.00
294 Jari Kurri C 15.00 40.00
297 Robby Fabbri C 20.00 50.00
298 Shea Theodore D 15.00 40.00
299 Nikolaj Ehlers D 20.00 50.00
300 Charles Hudon D 12.00 30.00
301 Mike McCarron D 15.00 40.00
302 Noah Hanifin C 20.00 50.00
303 Dylan Larkin B 60.00 150.00
304 Oscar Lindberg C 15.00 40.00
305 Matt Murray B 200.00 300.00
306 Andreas Athanasiou D 30.00 80.00
307 Jake Virtanen D 15.00 40.00
309 Jared McCann D 12.00 30.00
310 Mattias Janmark D 12.00 30.00
312 Colton Parayko B 15.00 40.00
313 Nick Shore D 12.00 30.00
314 Sam Bennett B 15.00 40.00
315 Connor McDavid A 250.00 600.00
316 Colton Parayko A 40.00 100.00
318 Noah Hanifin B 15.00 40.00
319 Jake Virtanen C 20.00 50.00
320 Oscar Lindberg A 30.00 80.00
322 Nikolaj Ehlers C 30.00 80.00
324 Robby Fabbri B 15.00 40.00
325 Mike McCarron C 20.00 50.00
326 Sam Bennett B 15.00 40.00
327 Mattias Janmark C 15.00 40.00
328 Dylan Larkin A 100.00 250.00
329 Charles Hudon C 15.00 40.00
330 Connor McDavid A 250.00 600.00
331 Sam Bennett B 15.00 40.00
333 Zachary Fucale C 15.00 40.00
334 Robby Fabbri C 20.00 50.00
336 Dylan Larkin B
337 Nikolaj Ehlers C 30.00 80.00
340 Connor McDavid A 250.00 600.00

2015-16 Upper Deck Portfolio Profiles Material

PMAK Anze Kopitar D 5.00 12.00
PMAO Alexander Ovechkin B 12.00 30.00
PMAP Artemi Panarin B 10.00 25.00
PMBH Brett Hull A 8.00 20.00
PMCG Claude Giroux D 3.00 8.00
PMCM Connor McDavid B 25.00 60.00
PMCP Carey Price B 10.00 25.00
PMDH Dale Hawerchuk C 4.00 10.00
PMDL Dylan Larkin B 10.00 25.00
PMEK Erik Karlsson C 6.00 15.00
PMGL Gabriel Landeskog D 3.00 8.00
PMHL Henrik Lundqvist C 4.00 10.00
PMHO Braden Holtby C 5.00 12.00
PMJC Jeff Carter D 3.00 8.00
PMJE Jack Eichel B 12.00 30.00
PMJI Jarome Iginla C 3.00 8.00
PMJK Jari Kurri A 3.00 8.00
PMJL John LeClair C 3.00 8.00
PMJO Joe Thornton C 3.00 8.00
PMJQ Jonathan Quick C 5.00 12.00
PMJR Jeremy Roenick B 3.00 8.00
PMJS Joe Sakic A 8.00 20.00
PMJT Jonathan Toews B 6.00 15.00
PMLR Larry Robinson A 3.00 8.00
PMMD Max Domi B 6.00 15.00
PMMR Morgan Rielly D 2.50 6.00
PMMS Mark Scheifele D 4.00 10.00
PMMZ Mats Zuccarello D 2.50 6.00
PMNE Nikolaj Ehlers D 6.00 15.00
PMNH Noah Hanifin D 4.00 10.00
PMNK Nazem Kadri D 2.50 6.00
PMOE Oliver Ekman-Larsson C 2.50 6.00
PMRB Ray Bourque A 6.00 15.00
PMRF Robby Fabbri C 4.00 10.00
PMRK Ryan Kesler D 3.00 8.00
PMRL Roberto Luongo D 3.00 8.00
PMRN Ryan Nugent-Hopkins D 3.00 8.00
PMSC Sidney Crosby B 12.00 30.00
PMSP Jason Spezza D 2.50 6.00
PMTH Taylor Hall D 6.00 15.00

1999 Upper Deck PowerDeck Athletes of the Century

These CD-Rom cards featuring four of the most prominent athletes of the 20th century were issued by Upper Deck in one boxed set. The cards are inserted into a computer and display various highlights of the player's career and his stats and other information.
COMPLETE SET (4) 8.00 20.00
4 Wayne Gretzky 2.00 5.00

1999-00 Upper Deck PowerDeck

The 1999-00 Upper Deck PowerDeck set was released as a 20-card base set featuring digital CD cards. Packaged at four cards per pack and 24-packs per bo PowerDeck carried a suggested retail price of $4.99. Auxiliary parallels were released as a paper parallel the CD base cards, this 20-card set is randomly inserted in packs. The card backs carry an "AUX" prefix.
COMPLETE SET (20) 25.00 60.00
1 Paul Kariya 1.25 3.00
2 Teemu Selanne 1.25 3.00
3 Patrik Stefan 1.00 2.50
4 Ray Bourque 2.00 5.00
5 Sergei Samsonov 1.25 3.00
6 Dominik Hasek 2.00 5.00
7 Peter Forsberg 2.00 5.00
8 Patrick Roy 5.00 12.00
9 Brett Hull 1.50 4.00
10 Mike Modano 2.00 5.00
11 Steve Yzerman 4.00 10.00
12 Pavel Bure 1.25 3.00
13 David Legwand 1.00 2.50
14 Martin Brodeur 2.50 6.00
15 Theo Fleury 1.25 3.00
16 Eric Lindros 1.25 3.00
17 Jaromir Jagr 1.50 4.00
18 Bobby Orr 6.00 15.00
19 Gordie Howe 4.00 10.00
20 Wayne Gretzky 6.00 15.00

1999-00 Upper Deck PowerDeck Auxiliary

Released as a paper parallel to the CD base cards, thi 20-card set is randomly inserted in packs. The card backs carry an "AUX" prefix.
COMPLETE SET (20) 30.00 60.00
*AUXILARY: .2X TO .5X BASIC CARDS

1999-00 Upper Deck PowerDeck Powerful Moments

Randomly inserted in packs at 1:23, this 4-card CD s features great moments from Wayne Gretzky's career. The card backs carry a "PM" prefix.
COMPLETE SET (4) 20.00 40.00
COMMON GRETZKY (PM1-PM4) 6.00 15.00
*AUXILIARY: .4X TO 1X BASIC INSERTS

1999-00 Upper Deck PowerDeck Time Capsule

Randomly inserted in packs at 1:7, this 8-card CD se features a digital flashback of current players as well a some of yesterday's greats. Card backs carry a "T" prefix. Auxiliary parallels were released as a paper parallels to the CD base cards, and inserted at 1:7.
COMPLETE SET (8) 20.00 50.00
*AUXILARY: .4X TO 1X
T1 Jaromir Jagr 2.00 5.00
T2 Paul Kariya 2.00 5.00
T3 Patrick Roy 6.00 15.00
T4 Bobby Orr 8.00 20.00
T5 Dominik Hasek 3.00 8.00
T6 Gordie Howe 4.00 10.00
T7 Brett Hull 2.00 5.00
T8 Steve Yzerman 5.00 12.00

2005-06 Upper Deck Power Play

This 172-card set issued into the hobby in six-card packs, with a $2.99 SRP, which came 24 packs to a box, Cards numbered 1-90 feature veterans in team alphabetical order while cards numbered 91-104 is ar Impact Photos subset; cards numbered 105-118 are I Action, Cards numbered 119-125 are Cup Celebration and Cards numbered 126-132 are Goal Robbers. Card numbered 133-172 are all Rookie Cards. Stated odds for cards 91-118 are one in 12 and 119-132 are one i 24. In addition, four rookie redemptions appear at the end of this checklist and those cards were inserted at stated rate of one in 12. The letters A, B, C and D refe respectively to cards 133-142, 143-152, 153-162 and 163-172.
COMP.SET w/o SP's (90) 8.00 15.00
91-118 IP/IA ODDS 1:12
119-132 GR/CC ODDS 1:24
1 Jean-Sebastien Giguere .20 .50
2 Joffrey Lupul .15 .40
3 Sergei Fedorov .30 .75
4 Dany Heatley .20 .50
5 Ilya Kovalchuk .20 .50
6 Kari Lehtonen .15 .40
7 Sergei Samsonov .15 .40
8 Joe Thornton .25 .60
9 Andrew Raycroft .15 .40
10 Glen Murray .15 .40
11 Ryan Miller .20 .50
12 Daniel Briere .20 .50
13 Miroslav Satan .15 .40
14 Jarome Iginla .20 .50
15 Jordan Leopold .12 .30
16 Miikka Kiprusoff .15 .40
17 Eric Staal .25 .60
18 Josef Vasicek .12 .30
19 Eric Daze .15 .40
20 Tuomo Ruutu .20 .50
21 Jocelyn Thibault .15 .40
22 Joe Sakic .30 .75
23 Alex Tanguay .20 .50
24 Milan Hejduk .15 .40
25 Peter Forsberg .25 .60
26 Rick Nash .20 .50
27 Nikolai Zherdev .12 .30
28 Marc Denis .15 .40
29 Mike Modano .30 .75
30 Bill Guerin .20 .50
31 Marty Turco .20 .50
32 Pavel Datsyuk .25 .60
33 Brendan Shanahan .25 .60
34 Steve Yzerman .50 1.25
35 Nicklas Lidstrom .20 .50
36 Ales Hemsky .15 .40
37 Ryan Smyth .15 .40
38 Patrice Bergeron .25 .60
39 Roberto Luongo .30 .75
40 Olli Jokinen .20 .50
41 Luc Robitaille .20 .50
42 Zigmund Palffy .20 .50
43 Lubomir Visnovsky .12 .30
44 Marian Gaborik .30 .75
45 Dwayne Roloson .15 .40
46 Michael Ryder .15 .40
47 Jose Theodore .20 .50
48 Mike Ribeiro .15 .40
49 Steve Sullivan .12 .30
50 Nathan Horton .20 .50
51 Tomas Vokoun .15 .40
52 Martin Brodeur .40 1.00
53 Patrik Elias .20 .50
54 Scott Niedermayer .20 .50
55 Michael Peca .15 .40
56 Mark Messier .30 .75
57 Jaromir Jagr .50 1.25
58 Mark Parrish .12 .30
59 Rick DiPietro .15 .40
60 Daniel Alfredsson .20 .50
61 Marian Hossa .15 .40

62 Jason Spezza .20 .50
63 Dominik Hasek .30 .75
64 Jeremy Roenick .20 .50
65 Keith Primeau .20 .50
66 John LeClair .20 .50
67 Brett Hull .25 .60
68 Ladislav Nagy .12 .30
69 Shane Doan .15 .40
70 Marc-Andre Fleury .30 .75
71 Mario Lemieux .60 1.50
72 Mark Recchi .25 .60
73 Jonathan Cheechoo .20 .50
74 Evgeni Nabokov .15 .40
75 Patrick Marleau .20 .50
76 Chris Pronger .15 .40
77 Doug Weight .20 .50
78 Keith Tkachuk .20 .50
79 Brad Richards .20 .50
80 Nikolai Khabibulin .20 .50
81 Martin St. Louis .20 .50
82 Dave Andreychuk .20 .50
83 Joe Nieuwendyk .20 .50
84 Ed Belfour .20 .50
85 Mats Sundin .20 .50
86 Brian Leetch .20 .50
87 Brendan Morrison .12 .30
88 Markus Naslund .20 .50
89 Todd Bertuzzi .20 .50
90 Olaf Kolzig .20 .50
91 Sergei Fedorov IP .60 1.50
92 Dany Heatley IP .40 1.00
93 Joe Thornton IP .50 1.25
94 Daniel Briere IP .40 1.00
95 Jarome Iginla IP .40 1.00
96 Joe Sakic IP .60 1.50
97 Steve Yzerman IP 1.00 2.50
98 Martin Havlat IP .40 1.00
99 Jeremy Roenick IP .40 1.00
100 Mario Lemieux IP 1.25 3.00
101 Chris Pronger IP .30 .75
102 Dave Andreychuk IP .40 1.00
103 Martin St. Louis IP .40 1.00
104 Mats Sundin IP .40 1.00
105 Ilya Kovalchuk IA .40 1.00
106 Andrew Raycroft IA .30 .75
107 Peter Forsberg IA .50 1.25
108 Rick Nash IA .40 1.00
109 Jose Theodore IA .40 1.00
110 Tomas Vokoun IA .30 .75
111 Jaromir Jagr IA 1.00 2.50
112 Mark Messier IA .60 1.50
113 Jason Spezza IA .40 1.00
114 Marc-Andre Fleury IA .60 1.50
115 Jonathan Cheechoo IA .40 1.00
116 Patrick Marleau IA .40 1.00
117 Nikolai Khabibulin IA .40 1.00
118 Markus Naslund IA .40 1.00
119 Dave Andreychuk CC .60 1.50
120 Martin Brodeur CC 4.00 10.00
121 Joe Sakic CC 3.00 8.00
122 Patrick Roy CC 5.00 12.00
123 Wayne Gretzky CC 10.00 25.00
124 Mark Messier CC 3.00 8.00
125 Steve Yzerman CC 5.00 12.00
126 Andrew Raycroft GR 1.00 2.50
127 Martin Brodeur GR 2.50 6.00
128 Patrick Roy GR 3.00 8.00
129 Jose Theodore GR 1.25 3.00
130 Marc-Andre Fleury GR 2.00 5.00
131 Marty Turco GR 1.25 3.00
132 Nikolai Khabibulin GR 1.25 3.00
131 Sidney Crosby RC
132 Wojtek Wolski RC
133 Hannu Toivonen RC
133 Sidney Crosby RC 10.00 25.00
134 Wojtek Wolski RC 1.00 2.50
134 Alexander Steen RC
135 Jeff Woywitka RC
135 Hannu Toivonen RC 1.25 3.00
136 Alexander Steen RC 2.50 6.00
136 Jussi Jokinen RC
137 Kevin Nastiuk RC
137 Jeff Woywitka RC .75 2.00
138 Jussi Jokinen RC 1.25 3.00
138 Brent Seabrook RC
139 Brad Winchester RC
139 Kevin Nastiuk RC .75 2.00
140 Brent Seabrook RC 2.50 6.00
140 Brandon Bochenski RC
141 Alexander Ovechkin RC
141 Brad Winchester RC 1.25 3.00
142 Brandon Bochenski RC 1.25 3.00
142 Thomas Vanek RC
143 Yann Danis RC
143 Alexander Ovechkin RC 12.00 30.00
144 Thomas Vanek RC 2.50 6.00
144 Ryan Getzlaf RC
145 Ryan Suter RC
145 Yann Danis RC 1.00 2.50
146 Ryan Getzlaf RC 3.00 8.00
146 Henrik Lundqvist RC
147 Johan Franzen RC
147 Ryan Suter RC 1.50 4.00
148 Henrik Lundqvist RC 5.00 12.00
148 Rene Bourque RC
149 Eric Nystrom RC
149 Johan Franzen RC 2.00 5.00
150 Rene Bourque RC 1.25 3.00
150 Patrick Eaves RC
151 Corey Perry RC
151 Eric Nystrom RC 1.00 2.50
152 Patrick Eaves RC 1.25 3.00
152 Alexander Perezhogin RC
153 Zach Parise RC
153 Corey Perry RC 5.00 12.00
154 Alexander Perezhogin RC 1.00 2.50
154 Mike Richards RC
155 Braydon Coburn RC
155 Zach Parise RC 3.00 8.00
156 Mike Richards RC 2.50 6.00
156 Cam Ward RC
157 David Leneveu RC
157 Braydon Coburn RC 1.25 3.00
158 Cam Ward RC 2.00 5.00
158 Andrew Alberts RC
159 Petteri Nokelainen RC
159 David Leneveu RC 1.00 2.50
160 Andrew Alberts RC .75 2.00
160 Lee Stempniak RC
161 Jeff Carter RC
161 Petteri Nokelainen RC .75 2.00
162 Lee Stempniak RC 1.25 3.00
162 Gilbert Brule RC
163 Dion Phaneuf RC
163 Jeff Carter RC 2.00 5.00
164 Gilbert Brule RC 1.25 3.00
164 Jim Howard RC
165 Rostislav Olesz RC
165 Dion Phaneuf RC 2.00 5.00
166 Jim Howard RC 3.00 8.00
166 Robert Nilsson RC
167 Peter Budaj RC
167 Rostislav Olesz RC 1.00 2.50
168 Robert Nilsson RC 1.25 3.00
168 Andrej Meszaros RC
169 Petr Prucha RC
169 Peter Budaj RC 1.50 4.00
170 Andrej Meszaros RC 1.00 2.50
170 Matt Foy RC
171 Petr Prucha RC 1.25 3.00
172 Matt Foy RC .75 2.00

2008-09 Upper Deck Power Play

This box set (cards 1-300) was released on November 18, 2008. The update set (cards 301-400) was released on March 23, 2009.

COMPLETE SET (400) 30.00 80.00
COMP.FACT.SET (300) 25.00 50.00
COMP.FACT.UPDATE (100) 12.00 30.00
1 Francois Beauchemin .10 .25
2 George Parros .10 .25
3 Bobby Ryan .15 .40
4 Ryan Getzlaf .25 .60
5 Jean-Sebastien Giguere .15 .40
6 Corey Perry .15 .40
7 Teemu Selanne .30 .75
8 Chris Pronger .12 .30
9 Chris Kunitz .15 .40
10 Scott Niedermayer .15 .40
11 Brendan Morrison .10 .25
12 Slava Kozlov .10 .25
13 Todd White .10 .25
14 Ilya Kovalchuk .15 .40
15 Eric Perrin .10 .25
16 Colby Armstrong .10 .25
17 Kari Lehtonen .12 .30
18 Bryan Little .12 .30
19 Tobias Enstrom .10 .25
20 Jason Williams .10 .25
21 David Krejci .15 .40
22 Milan Lucic .25 .60
23 Peter Schaefer .10 .25
24 Patrice Bergeron .20 .50
25 Marc Savard .10 .25
26 Tim Thomas .15 .40
27 Zdeno Chara .15 .40
28 Marco Sturm .10 .25
29 Phil Kessel .20 .50
30 Aaron Ward .10 .25
31 Michael Ryder .10 .25
32 Jochen Hecht .10 .25
33 Ales Kotalik .10 .25
34 Tim Connolly .10 .25
35 Thomas Vanek .15 .40
36 Ryan Miller .15 .40
37 Derek Roy .10 .25
38 Jason Pominville .15 .40
39 Drew Stafford .12 .30
40 Eric Nystrom .10 .25
41 Cory Sarich .10 .25
42 Adrian Aucoin .10 .25
43 Todd Bertuzzi .15 .40
44 Miikka Kiprusoff .12 .30
45 Jarome Iginla .15 .40
46 Daymond Langkow .10 .25
47 Dion Phaneuf .15 .40
48 Matthew Lombardi .10 .25
49 Robyn Regehr .10 .25
50 Mike Cammalleri .12 .30
51 Sergei Samsonov .12 .30
52 Matt Cullen .10 .25
53 Eric Staal .20 .50
54 Rod Brind'Amour .15 .40
55 Cam Ward .15 .40
56 Justin Williams .12 .30
57 Ray Whitney .12 .30
58 Joni Pitkanen .10 .25
59 Adam Burish .12 .30
60 Dustin Byfuglien .15 .40
61 Patrick Kane .30 .75
62 Nikolai Khabibulin .15 .40
63 Patrick Sharp .15 .40
64 Brent Seabrook .15 .40
65 Jonathan Toews .40 1.00
66 Martin Havlat .15 .40
67 Duncan Keith .15 .40
68 Brian Campbell .12 .30
69 Cristobal Huet .12 .30
70 John-Michael Liles .10 .25
71 T.J. Hensick .12 .30
72 David Jones .10 .25
73 Joe Sakic .25 .60
74 Ryan Smyth .12 .30
75 Milan Hejduk .12 .30
76 Marek Svatos .10 .25
77 Paul Stastny .15 .40
78 Wojtek Wolski .12 .30
79 Andrew Raycroft .12 .30
80 Darcy Tucker .12 .30
81 Kristian Huselius .10 .25
82 Derick Brassard RC .12 .30
83 Steve Mason RC 3.00 8.00
84 Jason Chimera .10 .25
85 Fredrik Norrena .10 .25
86 Rick Nash .15 .40
87 Kris Russell .10 .25
88 Pascal Leclaire .12 .30
89 Rostislav Klesla .10 .25
90 Jared Boll .10 .25
91 R.J. Umberger .10 .25
92 Loui Eriksson .15 .40
93 Sergei Zubov .12 .30
94 Stephane Robidas .10 .25
95 Mike Modano .25 .60
96 Brad Richards .15 .40
97 Marty Turco .15 .40
98 Mike Ribeiro .12 .30
99 Brenden Morrow .12 .30
100 Jere Lehtinen .10 .25
101 Sean Avery .10 .25
102 Johan Franzen .15 .40
103 Jiri Hudler .12 .30
104 Mikael Samuelsson .10 .25
105 Kris Draper .10 .25
106 Andreas Lilja .10 .25
107 Nicklas Lidstrom .15 .40
108 Pavel Datsyuk .20 .50
109 Chris Osgood .15 .40
110 Henrik Zetterberg .20 .50
111 Dan Cleary .12 .30
112 Tomas Holmstrom .12 .30
113 Valtteri Filppula .15 .40
114 Ty Conklin .12 .30
115 Marian Hossa .12 .30
116 Erik Cole .12 .30
117 Sheldon Souray .10 .25
118 Sam Gagner .12 .30
119 Ales Hemsky .12 .30
120 Mathieu Garon .12 .30
121 Shawn Horcoff .10 .25
122 Dustin Penner .12 .30
123 Andrew Cogliano .12 .30
124 Dwayne Roloson .12 .30
125 Shawn Matthias RC .15 .40
126 Craig Anderson .15 .40
127 Brett McLean .10 .25
128 Rostislav Olesz .10 .25
129 Tomas Vokoun .12 .30
130 Nathan Horton .12 .30
131 David Booth .10 .25
132 Stephen Weiss .10 .25
133 Jay Bouwmeester .15 .40
134 Jarret Stoll .12 .30
135 Jack Johnson .10 .25
136 Jason LaBarbera .12 .30
137 Anze Kopitar .25 .60
138 Alexander Frolov .10 .25
139 Dustin Brown .15 .40
140 Patrick O'Sullivan .12 .30
141 Andrew Brunette .10 .25
142 Brent Burns .20 .50
143 James Sheppard .10 .25
144 Derek Boogaard .10 .25
145 Marian Gaborik .20 .50
146 Niklas Backstrom .15 .40
147 Pierre-Marc Bouchard .15 .40
148 Josh Harding .15 .40
149 Mikko Koivu .12 .30
150 Marek Zidlicky .10 .25
151 Alex Tanguay .10 .25
152 Andrei Kostitsyn .12 .30
153 Sergei Kostitsyn .10 .25
154 Maxim Lapierre .10 .25
155 Saku Koivu .15 .40
156 Carey Price .60 1.50
157 Tomas Plekanec .15 .40
158 Alex Kovalev .12 .30
159 Chris Higgins .10 .25
160 Andrei Markov .15 .40
161 Guillaume Latendresse .10 .25
162 Dan Ellis .10 .25
163 Shea Weber .12 .30
164 Ryan Suter .12 .30
165 Jason Arnott .12 .30
166 Martin Erat .10 .25
167 J.P. Dumont .10 .25
168 David Legwand .12 .30
169 Bobby Holik .10 .25
170 Brian Rolston .12 .30
171 Paul Martin .10 .25
172 Jamie Langenbrunner .10 .25
173 Johnny Oduya .12 .30
174 Martin Brodeur .30 .75
175 Zach Parise .15 .40
176 Patrik Elias .15 .40
177 Brian Gionta .12 .30
178 John Madden .10 .25
179 Travis Zajac .12 .30
180 Kyle Okposo RC .15 .40
181 Mike Sillinger .10 .25
182 Blake Comeau .10 .25
183 Rick DiPietro .12 .30
184 Mike Comrie .12 .30
185 Bill Guerin .15 .40
186 Trent Hunter .10 .25
187 Nikolai Zherdev .10 .25
188 Stephen Valiquette .12 .30
189 Nigel Dawes .10 .25
190 Lauri Korpikoski RC .10 .25
191 Henrik Lundqvist .20 .50
192 Chris Drury .12 .30
193 Scott Gomez .12 .30
194 Brendan Shanahan .20 .50
195 Marc Staal .15 .40
196 Brandon Dubinsky .12 .30
197 Wade Redden .10 .25
198 Markus Naslund .12 .30
199 Chris Phillips .10 .25
200 Chris Neil .10 .25
201 Filip Kuba .10 .25
202 Anton Volchenkov .10 .25
203 Jason Spezza .15 .40
204 Dany Heatley .15 .40
205 Nick Foligno .15 .40
206 Antoine Vermette .10 .25
207 Mike Fisher .10 .25
208 Daniel Alfredsson .15 .40
209 Martin Gerber .12 .30
210 Kimmo Timonen .10 .25
211 Scottie Upshall .10 .25
212 Claude Giroux RC .30 .75
213 Mike Richards .15 .40
214 Martin Biron .12 .30
215 Daniel Briere .15 .40
216 Simon Gagne .15 .40
217 Mike Knuble .10 .25
218 Jeff Carter .15 .40
219 Olli Jokinen .12 .30
220 Kyle Turris RC .25 .60
221 Steven Reinprecht .10 .25
222 Daniel Carcillo .10 .25
223 Daniel Winnik .10 .25
224 Peter Mueller .12 .30
225 Shane Doan .12 .30
226 Ilya Bryzgalov .12 .30
227 Ed Jovanovski .12 .30
228 Martin Hanzal .12 .30
229 Miroslav Satan .15 .40
230 Ruslan Fedotenko .10 .25
231 Tyler Kennedy .12 .30
232 Brooks Orpik .12 .30
233 Maxime Talbot .15 .40
234 Sidney Crosby .60 1.50
235 Marc-Andre Fleury .25 .60
236 Evgeni Malkin .50 1.25
237 Sergei Gonchar .10 .25
238 Jordan Staal .15 .40
239 Ryan Whitney .15 .40
240 Rob Blake .15 .40
241 Ryane Clowe .12 .30
242 Joe Pavelski .15 .40
243 Torrey Mitchell .10 .25
244 Joe Thornton .20 .50
245 Evgeni Nabokov .12 .30
246 Jonathan Cheechoo .15 .40
247 Milan Michalek .10 .25
248 Patrick Marleau .15 .40
249 Dan Boyle .12 .30
250 Chris Mason .12 .30
251 Andy McDonald .12 .30
252 David Backes .15 .40
253 David Perron .12 .30
254 Paul Kariya .20 .50
255 Manny Legace .15 .40
256 Erik Johnson .12 .30
257 Brad Boyes .10 .25
258 Lee Stempniak .10 .25
259 Keith Tkachuk .15 .40
260 Radim Vrbata .12 .30
261 Ryan Malone .10 .25
262 Mark Recchi .20 .50
263 Vaclav Prospal .10 .25
264 Jussi Jokinen .10 .25
265 Michel Ouellet .10 .25
266 Vincent Lecavalier .12 .30
267 Mike Smith .15 .40
268 Matt Carle .10 .25
269 Martin St. Louis .15 .40
270 Paul Ranger .10 .25
271 Andrej Meszaros .10 .25
272 Olaf Kolzig .15 .40
273 Ian White .10 .25
274 Pavel Kubina .10 .25
275 Jason Blake .10 .25
276 Robbie Earl RC .10 .25
277 Mats Sundin .15 .40
278 Vesa Toskala .12 .30
279 Alexander Steen .15 .40
280 Tomas Kaberle .10 .25
281 Nikolai Antropov .12 .30
282 Matt Stajan .12 .30
283 Jiri Tlusty .12 .30
284 Steve Bernier .10 .25
285 Pavol Demitra .20 .50
286 Taylor Pyatt .10 .25
287 Kevin Bieksa .12 .30
288 Roberto Luongo .20 .50
289 Daniel Sedin .15 .40
290 Ryan Kesler .20 .50
291 Alexander Edler .10 .25
292 Henrik Sedin .15 .40
293 Jose Theodore .15 .40
294 Brooks Laich .10 .25
295 Tomas Fleischmann .10 .25
296 Alexander Ovechkin .60 1.50
297 Nicklas Backstrom .25 .60
298 Sergei Fedorov .25 .60
299 Mike Green .15 .40
300 Alexander Semin .15 .40
301 Brett Festerling RC .20 .50
302 Andrew Ebbett RC .15 .40
303 Zach Bogosian RC .25 .60
304 Boris Valabik RC .25 .60
305 Nathan Oystrick RC .25 .60
306 Blake Wheeler RC .60 1.50
307 Nathan Gerbe RC .25 .60
308 Adam Pardy RC .20 .50
309 Brandon Sutter RC .25 .60
310 Zach Boychuk RC .25 .60
311 Cristobal Huet .20 .50
312 Kris Versteeg .30 .75
313 Brian Campbell .20 .50
314 Chris Stewart RC .25 .60
315 Nikita Filatov RC .25 .60
316 Jakub Voracek RC .50 1.25
317 Adam Pineault RC .20 .50
318 Dan LaCosta RC .25 .60
319 Tom Sestito RC .25 .60
320 Derek Dorsett RC .30 .75
321 Mike Commodore .15 .40
322 Fabian Brunnstrom RC .20 .50
323 Mark Fistric RC .20 .50
324 James Neal RC .50 1.25
325 Mark Parrish .15 .40
326 Marian Hossa .20 .50
327 Justin Abdelkader RC .40 1.00
328 Jonathan Ericsson RC .25 .60
329 Darren Helm RC .25 .60
330 Jeff Drouin-Deslauriers .15 .40
331 Steve MacIntyre RC .25 .60
332 Theo Peckham RC .25 .60
333 Michael Frolik RC .25 .60
334 Kenndal McArdle RC .20 .50
335 Michal Repik RC .25 .60
336 Drew Doughty RC .60 1.50
337 Brian Boyle RC .20 .50
338 Oscar Moller RC .20 .50
339 Trevor Lewis RC .25 .60
340 Erik Ersberg RC .20 .50
341 Wayne Simmonds RC .40 1.00
342 Colton Gillies RC .20 .50
343 Antti Miettinen .15 .40
344 Alex Tanguay .15 .40
345 Matt D'Agostini RC .20 .50
346 Ben Maxwell RC .25 .60
347 Patric Hornqvist RC .25 .60
348 Ryan Jones RC .25 .60
349 Petr Vrana RC .15 .40
350 Scott Clemmensen .15 .40
351 Matthew Halischuk RC .15 .40
352 Patrick Davis RC .20 .50
353 Josh Bailey RC .30 .75
354 Mark Streit .15 .40
355 Peter Mannino RC .15 .40
356 Mitch Fritz RC .20 .50
357 Markus Naslund .20 .50
358 Brian Lee RC .20 .50
359 Ilya Zubov RC .20 .50
360 Alex Auld .15 .40
361 Jared Ross RC .25 .60
362 Luca Sbisa RC .15 .40
363 Nate Raduns RC .15 .40
364 Andreas Nodl RC .15 .40
365 Jonathon Kalinski RC .25 .60
366 Olli Jokinen .20 .50
367 Mikkel Boedker RC .30 .75
368 Viktor Tikhonov RC .20 .50
369 Kevin Porter RC .20 .50
370 Janne Pesonen RC .20 .50
371 Paul Bissonnette RC .30 .75
372 Alex Goligoski RC .30 .75
373 Jon Filewich RC .20 .50
374 Ryan Stone RC .15 .40
375 Miroslav Satan .25 .60
376 Brad Staubitz RC .20 .50
377 Rob Blake .25 .60
378 Devin Setoguchi .20 .50
379 Jamie McGinn RC .25 .60
380 Alex Pietrangelo RC .30 .75
381 Patrik Berglund RC .20 .50
382 T.J. Oshie RC .50 1.25
383 Ben Bishop RC .40 1.00
384 Chris Porter RC .25 .60
385 Cam Paddock RC .15 .40
386 Radek Smolenak RC .30 .75
387 Steven Stamkos RC 3.00 8.00
388 Vladimir Mihalik RC .15 .40
389 Luke Schenn RC .30 .75
390 Nikolai Kulemin RC .25 .60
391 Niklas Hagman .15 .40
392 Mikhail Grabovski .25 .60
393 Andre Deveaux RC .25 .60
394 Jonas Frogren RC .15 .40
395 John Mitchell RC .20 .50
396 Justin Pogge RC .25 .60
397 Cory Schneider RC .60 1.50
398 Mats Sundin .25 .60
399 Tyler Sloan RC .30 .75
400 Karl Alzner RC .15 .40

2008-09 Upper Deck Power Play Jerseys

ONE PER FACTORY SET
PPAO Alexander Ovechkin 20.00 50.00
PPEM Evgeni Malkin 15.00 40.00
PPHL Henrik Lundqvist 6.00 15.00
PPHZ Henrik Zetterberg 6.00 15.00
PPIK Ilya Kovalchuk 5.00 12.00
PPJC Jonathan Cheechoo 5.00 12.00
PPJG Jean-Sebastien Giguere 5.00 12.00
PPJI Jarome Iginla 5.00 12.00
PPJS Jason Spezza 5.00 12.00
PPJT Joe Thornton 6.00 15.00
PPKL Kari Lehtonen 4.00 10.00
PPKT Keith Tkachuk 5.00 12.00
PPMA Marc-Andre Fleury 8.00 20.00
PPMB Martin Brodeur 10.00 25.00
PPMG Marian Gaborik 6.00 15.00
PPMM Mike Modano 8.00 20.00
PPMN Markus Naslund 4.00 10.00
PPMR Mike Richards 5.00 12.00
PPMS Mats Sundin 5.00 12.00
PPMT Marty Turco 5.00 12.00
PPNL Nicklas Lidstrom 5.00 12.00
PPPB Patrice Bergeron 6.00 15.00
PPPD Pavel Datsyuk 6.00 15.00
PPPK Paul Kariya 6.00 15.00
PPRL Roberto Luongo 6.00 15.00
PPRM Ryan Miller 5.00 12.00
PPRN Rick Nash 5.00 12.00
PPSC Sidney Crosby 20.00 50.00
PPSK Saku Koivu 5.00 12.00
PPVL Vincent Lecavalier 4.00 10.00

2005-06 Upper Deck Power Play Power Marks

STATED ODDS 1:200
PMAC Anson Carter 10.00 25.00
PMBB Brad Boyes 8.00 20.00
PMCK Chuck Kobasew 6.00 15.00
PMDA Daniel Alfredsson SP 20.00 50.00
PMDB Dustin Brown 4.00 10.00
PMEJ Ed Jovanovski 6.00 15.00
PMEN Evgeni Nabokov SP 12.00 30.00
PMFS Fredrik Sjostrom 4.00 10.00
PMGH Gordie Howe SP 125.00 250.00
PMHA Martin Havlat 10.00 25.00
PMHE Milan Hejduk 12.00 30.00
PMHZ Henrik Zetterberg SP 20.00 50.00
PMIK Ilya Kovalchuk SP 50.00 100.00
PMJC Jonathan Cheechoo 12.00 30.00
PMJI Jarome Iginla SP 30.00 60.00
PMJP Joni Pitkanen 4.00 10.00
PMJT Joe Thornton 25.00 60.00
PMJW Justin Williams 10.00 25.00
PMKD Kris Draper 8.00 20.00
PMKP Keith Primeau 4.00 10.00
PMLR Luc Robitaille 30.00 80.00
PMMB Milan Bartovic 4.00 10.00
PMMC Mike Comrie SP 30.00 60.00
PMMG Marian Gaborik SP 20.00 50.00
PMMH Marian Hossa 20.00 50.00
PMMN Markus Naslund 10.00 25.00
PMMP Mark Popovic 4.00 10.00
PMMR Mike Ribeiro 8.00 20.00
PMMS Martin St. Louis SP 25.00 60.00
PMNK Nikolai Khabibulin SP 40.00 80.00
PMNO Mika Noronen 4.00 10.00
PMNS Nathan Smith 4.00 10.00
PMPS Peter Sejna 4.00 10.00
PMRK Ryan Kesler 12.00 30.00
PMRN Rick Nash 20.00 50.00
PMRY Michael Ryder 15.00 40.00
PMSS Sheldon Souray SP 15.00 40.00
PMWG Wayne Gretzky SP 350.00 500.00
PMZP Zigmund Palffy 10.00 25.00
PMZP Roman Turek 6.00 15.00

2005-06 Upper Deck Power Play Specialists Jerseys

*MULT.COLOR: 1.25X TO 3X HI
STATED ODDS 1:12
TSAB David Aebischer 3.00 8.00
TSAH Ales Hemsky 3.00 8.00
TSAKO Alex Kovalev 3.00 8.00
TSAS Alexei Semenov 2.50 6.00
TSAY Alexei Yashin 3.00 8.00
TSBH Brett Hull 5.00 12.00
TSBK Radek Bonk 2.50 6.00
TSBO Peter Bondra 3.00 8.00
TSBS Brendan Shanahan 5.00 12.00
TSCC Chris Chelios 4.00 10.00
TSCD Chris Drury 3.00 8.00
TSCE Christian Ehrhoff 2.50 6.00
TSDA Daniel Alfredsson 4.00 10.00
TSDH Dany Heatley 4.00 10.00
TSDO Dominik Hasek 6.00 15.00
TSDW Doug Weight 4.00 10.00
TSEB Eric Brewer 2.50 6.00
TSEJ Ed Jovanovski 3.00 8.00
TSGM Glen Murray 3.00 8.00
TSHA Derian Hatcher 2.50 6.00
TSJD J-P Dumont 2.50 6.00
TSJI Jarome Iginla 4.00 10.00
TSJJ Jaromir Jagr 10.00 25.00
TSJL Joffrey Lupul 3.00 8.00
TSJL John LeClair 4.00 10.00
TSJN Joe Nieuwendyk 4.00 10.00
TSJS Jean-Sebastien Giguere 4.00 10.00
TSJT Joe Thornton 5.00 12.00
TSKP Keith Primeau 4.00 10.00
TSLC Pascal Leclaire 3.00 8.00
TSLE Jordan Leopold 2.50 6.00
TSMB Martin Brodeur 10.00 25.00
TSMC Mike Comrie 3.00 8.00
TSMH Milan Hejduk 3.00 8.00
TSML Mario Lemieux 12.00 30.00
TSMM Mike Modano 6.00 15.00
TSMR Mark Recchi 5.00 12.00
TSMT Marty Turco SP 5.00 12.00
TSNA Nikolai Antropov 3.00 8.00
TSOJ Olli Jokinen 4.00 10.00
TSOK Olaf Kolzig 4.00 10.00
TSPB P-M Bouchard 4.00 10.00
TSPB Pavel Bure 5.00 12.00
TSPD Pavol Demitra 5.00 12.00
TSPK Paul Kariya SP 25.00 60.00
TSPL Patrick Lalime 3.00 8.00
TSRB Rob Blake 4.00 10.00
TSRE Robert Esche 3.00 8.00
TSRL Robert Lang 2.50 6.00
TSRT Roman Turek 3.00 8.00
TSSB Sean Burke 2.50 6.00
TSSG Scott Gomez 3.00 8.00
TSSP Jason Spezza 4.00 10.00
TSTA Tony Amonte SP 4.00 10.00
TSTH Jocelyn Thibault 3.00 8.00
TSTL Trevor Linden 8.00 20.00
TSTS Teemu Selanne 8.00 20.00
TSVL Vincent Lecavalier SP 25.00 60.00
TSVN Ville Nieminen 2.50 6.00
TSWG Wayne Gretzky SP 40.00 100.00

2014-15 Upper Deck Premier

1 Jaromir Jagr 5.00 12.00
2 Alexander Ovechkin 8.00 20.00
3 Kyle Okposo 2.00 5.00
4 Craig Anderson 2.00 5.00
5 Patrick Sharp 2.00 5.00
6 Steven Stamkos 4.00 10.00
7 Jonathan Quick 3.00 8.00
8 Dustin Brown 1.50 4.00
9 Marc-Andre Fleury 3.00 8.00
10 Tyler Seguin 3.00 8.00
11 Daniel Sedin 2.00 5.00
12 Ryan Suter 2.00 5.00
13 Tomas Hertl 2.00 5.00
14 Aleksander Barkov 2.00 5.00
15 P.K. Subban 3.00 8.00
16 Steve Mason 1.50 4.00
17 James van Riemsdyk 2.00 5.00
18 Ryan Getzlaf 3.00 8.00
19 Pekka Rinne 2.50 6.00
20 David Backes 2.00 5.00
21 Jonathan Bernier 2.00 5.00
22 Dustin Byfuglien 2.00 5.00
23 Claude Giroux 2.00 5.00
24 Eric Staal 2.50 6.00
25 Carey Price 6.00 15.00
26 Sean Monahan 2.00 5.00
27 Henrik Lundqvist 2.50 6.00
28 Chris Kunitz 2.00 5.00
29 Paul Stastny 2.00 5.00
30 Max Pacioretty 2.00 5.00
31 Jason Spezza 2.00 5.00
32 Phil Kessel 2.50 6.00
33 Rick Nash 2.00 5.00
34 Zdeno Chara 2.00 5.00
35 Jonathan Toews 4.00 10.00
36 Joe Pavelski 2.00 5.00
37 Antti Niemi 1.50 4.00
38 Taylor Hall 4.00 10.00
39 Anze Kopitar 3.00 8.00
40 Sergei Bobrovsky 2.00 5.00
41 Cory Schneider 1.50 4.00
42 Victor Hedman 2.50 6.00
43 Ryan Kesler 2.00 5.00
44 Alex Galchenyuk 3.00 8.00
45 Erik Karlsson 4.00 10.00
46 Sidney Crosby 8.00 20.00
47 Patrice Bergeron 2.50 6.00
48 Evgeni Malkin 6.00 15.00
49 John Tavares 4.00 10.00
50 Zach Parise 2.00 5.00
51 Ryan Miller 2.00 5.00
52 Chris Chelios 2.00 5.00
53 Doug Gilmour 2.50 6.00
54 Zemgus Girgensons 2.00 5.00
55 Brett Hull 2.00 5.00
56 Gabriel Landeskog 1.50 4.00
57 Ed Belfour 2.00 5.00
58 Pavel Datsyuk 2.50 6.00
59 Corey Perry 2.00 5.00
60 Jordan Eberle 2.00 5.00
61 Andy Andreoff AU/299 RC 5.00 12.00
62 Patrick Brown AU/299 RC 5.00 12.00
63 Greg McKegg AU/299 RC 4.00 10.00
64 P.E. Bellemare AU/299 RC 5.00 12.00
65 Nicolas Deslauriers AU/299 RC 5.00 12.00
66 Josh Jooris AU/299 RC 5.00 12.00
67 John Klingberg AU/299 RC 20.00 40.00
68 Brandon Kozun AU/299 RC 4.00 10.00
69 Joni Ortio AU/299 RC 6.00 15.00
70 Andrej Nestrasil AU/299 RC 5.00 12.00
71 Justin Hodgman AU/299 RC 4.00 10.00
72 Mark Visentin AU/299 RC 5.00 12.00
73 Teemu Pulkkinen AU/299 RC 6.00 15.00
74 Christian Folin AU/299 RC 5.00 12.00
75 Seth Helgeson AU/299 RC 4.00 10.00
76 Patrik Nemeth AU/299 RC 5.00 12.00
77 Liam O'Brien AU/299 RC 5.00 12.00
78 A.Hammond AU/299 RC EXCH 15.00 40.00
79 Barclay Goodrow AU/299 RC 5.00 12.00
80 Joonas Nattinen AU/299 RC 5.00 12.00
81 A.Vasilevskiy JSY AU/299 RC 30.00 80.00
82 C.McKenzie JSY AU/299 RC 8.00 20.00
83 Derrick Pouliot JSY AU/299 RC 12.00 30.00
84 Griffin Reinhart JSY AU/299 RC 12.00 30.00
85 A.Clendening JSY AU/299 RC 10.00 25.00
86 Gaudreau JSY AU/199 RC EXCH 80.00 200.00
87 Stuart Percy JSY AU/299 RC 10.00 25.00
88 V.Trocheck JSY AU/299 RC 15.00 30.00
89 Pastrnak JSY AU/199 RC EXCH 60.00 150.00
90 Mirco Mueller JSY AU/299 RC 10.00 25.00
91 Adam Lowry JSY AU/299 RC 10.00 25.00
92 C.Jarnkrok JSY AU/299 RC 15.00 30.00
93 A.Khokhlachev JSY AU/299 RC 10.00 25.00
94 Phillip Danault JSY AU/299 RC 10.00 25.00
95 D.Severson JSY AU/299 RC 10.00 25.00
96 Tobias Rieder JSY AU/299 RC 10.00 25.00
97 Marko Dano JSY AU/299 RC 10.00 25.00
98 Victor Rask JSY AU/299 RC 20.00 40.00
99 D.Nurse JSY AU/299 RC 30.00 80.00
100 Jori Lehtera JSY AU/299 RC 12.00 30.00
101 Kevin Hayes JSY AU/299 RC 30.00 80.00
102 Bo Horvat JSY AU/199 RC 60.00 150.00
103 Namestnikov JSY AU/299 RC 15.00 40.00
104 Gostisbehere JSY AU/299 RC 75.00 150.00
105 R.Sproul JSY AU/299 RC 10.00 25.00
106 Seth Griffith JSY AU/299 RC 12.00 30.00
107 E.Kuznetsov JSY AU/299 RC 50.00 80.00
108 K.Rychel JSY AU/299 RC 12.00 30.00
109 Chris Tierney JSY AU/299 RC 10.00 25.00
110 R.Grimaldi JSY AU/299 RC 12.00 30.00
111 Jiri Sekac JSY AU/299 RC 10.00 25.00
112 T.Teravainen JSY AU/299 RC 30.00 80.00
113 L.Brossoit JSY AU/299 RC 10.00 25.00
114 Burakovsky JSY AU/299 RC 15.00 40.00
115 W.Karlsson JSY AU/299 RC 40.00 100.00
116 Curtis Lazar JSY AU/299 RC 12.00 30.00
117 A.Duclair JSY AU/299 RC EX 15.00 40.00
118 A.Wennberg JSY AU/299 RC 20.00 50.00
119 L.Draisaitl JSY AU/299 RC 80.00 200.00
120 S.Reinhart JSY AU/199 RC 30.00 80.00
121 A.Ekblad JSY AU/199 RC 30.00 80.00
122 J.Drouin JSY AU/199 RC 60.00 150.00
123 Theoren Fleury JSY AU/49 25.00 60.00
124 Cory Schneider JSY AU/49 15.00 40.00
125 Chris Chelios JSY AU/49 20.00 50.00
126 Max Pacioretty JSY AU/49 40.00 80.00
127 Patrick Sharp JSY AU/49 30.00 60.00
128 Teemu Selanne JSY AU/49 40.00 80.00
129 Joe Sakic JSY AU/49 30.00 80.00
130 Taylor Hall JSY AU/49 40.00 80.00
131 Jamie Benn JSY AU/49 40.00 80.00
132 van Riemsdyk JSY AU/49 15.00 40.00
133 Carey Price JSY AU/49 75.00 150.00
134 Sergei Bobrovsky JSY AU/49 20.00 50.00
135 Tyler Seguin JSY AU/49 40.00 100.00
136 Evgeni Malkin JSY AU/49 40.00 100.00
137 Torey Krug JSY AU/49 20.00 50.00
139 Brett Hull JSY AU/25
140 Wayne Gretzky JSY AU/25 300.00 500.00
141 Sidney Crosby JSY AU/25
142 Mats Sundin JSY AU/25 30.00 80.00
143 Mark Messier JSY AU/25 30.00 80.00

2014-15 Upper Deck Premier Gold Spectrum

*GOLD JSY/25: 1.2X TO 3X SILVER JSY/125
25 Carey Price JSY 20.00 50.00

2006-07 Upper Deck Power Play

This 130-card set was issued into the hobby in six-card packs, with an $2.99 SRP, which came 24 packs to a box and 20 boxes to a case. Cards numbered 1-100 feature veterans in team alphabetical order while cards 101-130 feature Rookie Cards also in team alphabetical order.

COMPLETE SET (130) 30.00 60.00
1 Jean-Sebastien Giguere .20 .50
2 Teemu Selanne .40 1.00
3 Chris Pronger .15 .40
4 Ilya Kovalchuk .20 .50
5 Marian Hossa .15 .40
6 Kari Lehtonen .15 .40
7 Patrice Bergeron .25 .60
8 Brad Boyes .12 .30
9 Hannu Toivonen .15 .40
10 Zdeno Chara .20 .50
11 Chris Drury .15 .40
12 Ryan Miller .20 .50
13 Maxim Afinogenov .12 .30
14 Miikka Kiprusoff .15 .40
15 Jarome Iginla .20 .50
16 Dion Phaneuf .20 .50
17 Alex Tanguay .12 .30
18 Eric Staal .25 .60
19 Cam Ward .20 .50
20 Rod Brind'Amour .20 .50
21 Erik Cole .15 .40
22 Tuomo Ruutu .20 .50
23 Nikolai Khabibulin .20 .50
24 Michal Handzus .15 .40
25 Martin Havlat .12 .30
26 Marek Svatos .12 .30
27 Milan Hejduk .15 .40
28 Joe Sakic .30 .75
29 Rick Nash .20 .50
30 Sergei Fedorov .30 .75
31 Pascal Leclaire .15 .40
32 Mike Modano .30 .75
33 Brenden Morrow .15 .40
34 Marty Turco .20 .50
35 Eric Lindros .30 .75
36 Henrik Zetterberg .25 .60
37 Nicklas Lidstrom .20 .50
38 Pavel Datsyuk .25 .60
39 Dominik Hasek .25 .60
40 Joffrey Lupul .15 .40
41 Ales Hemsky .15 .40
42 Ryan Smyth .15 .40
43 Olli Jokinen .20 .50
44 Todd Bertuzzi .20 .50
45 Jay Bouwmeester .20 .50
46 Alexander Frolov .12 .30
47 Rob Blake .20 .50
48 Mike Cammalleri .12 .30
49 Marian Gaborik .25 .60
50 Manny Fernandez .15 .40
51 Pavol Demitra .25 .60
52 Saku Koivu .20 .50
53 Cristobal Huet .15 .40
54 Alex Kovalev .15 .40
55 Michael Ryder .12 .30
56 Steve Sullivan .12 .30
57 Paul Kariya .25 .60
58 Tomas Vokoun .15 .40
59 Martin Brodeur .40 1.00
60 Patrik Elias .20 .50
61 Brian Gionta .15 .40
62 Miroslav Satan .15 .40
63 Alexei Yashin .15 .40
64 Rick DiPietro .15 .40
65 Jaromir Jagr .50 1.25
66 Henrik Lundqvist .40 1.00
67 Brendan Shanahan .25 .60
68 Martin Gerber .15 .40
69 Jason Spezza .20 .50
70 Dany Heatley .20 .50
71 Daniel Alfredsson .20 .50
72 Peter Forsberg .25 .60
73 Simon Gagne .20 .50
74 Robert Esche .15 .40
75 Jeff Carter .20 .50
76 Shane Doan .15 .40
77 Curtis Joseph .20 .50
78 Jeremy Roenick .20 .50
79 Sergei Gonchar .12 .30
80 Sidney Crosby .75 2.00
81 Marc-Andre Fleury .30 .75
82 Joe Thornton .25 .60
83 Jonathan Cheechoo .20 .50
84 Patrick Marleau .20 .50
85 Doug Weight .20 .50
86 Keith Tkachuk .20 .50
87 Manny Legace .15 .40
88 Brad Richards .20 .50
89 Martin St. Louis .20 .50
90 Vincent Lecavalier .15 .40
91 Mats Sundin .20 .50
92 Alexander Steen .20 .50
93 Bryan McCabe .12 .30
94 Andrew Raycroft .15 .40
95 Markus Naslund .15 .40
96 Roberto Luongo .30 .75
97 Brendan Morrison .12 .30
98 Henrik Sedin .20 .50
99 Alexander Ovechkin .75 2.00
100 Olaf Kolzig .20 .50
101 Yan Stastny RC .75 2.00
102 Mark Stuart RC .75 2.00
103 Carsen Germyn RC .75 2.00
104 Dustin Byfuglien RC 2.00 5.00
105 Tomas Kopecky RC 1.00 2.50
106 Marc-Antoine Pouliot RC .75 2.00
107 Konstantin Pushkarev RC 1.00 2.50
108 Erik Reitz RC .75 2.00
109 Miroslav Kopriva RC .75 2.00
110 Shea Weber RC 2.00 5.00
111 David Printz RC .75 2.00
112 Steve Regier RC .75 2.00
113 Ryan Caldwell RC .75 2.00
114 Masi Marjamaki RC .75 2.00

115 Matt Koalska RC .75 2.00
116 Jarkko Immonen RC .75 2.00
117 Cole Jarrett RC .75 2.00
118 Rob Collins RC .75 2.00
119 Filip Novak RC .75 2.00
120 Ryan Potulny RC .75 2.00
121 Bill Thomas RC .75 2.00
122 Joel Perrault RC .75 2.00
123 Noah Welch RC .75 2.00
124 Michel Ouellet RC 1.00 2.50
125 Matt Carle RC .75 2.00
126 Ben Ondrus RC .75 2.00
127 Brendan Bell RC .75 2.00
128 Ian White RC 1.00 2.50
129 Jeremy Williams RC .75 2.00
130 Eric Fehr RC 1.25 3.00

2014-15 Upper Deck Premier Silver Spectrum

*SILVER AU/49: .6X TO 1.5X BASIC AU/299
*SLVR JSY AU/25: .6X TO 1.5X JSY AU/299
*SLVR JSY AU/25: .5X TO 1.2X JSY AU/199
1 Jaromir Jagr JSY 6.00 15.00
2 Alexander Ovechkin JSY 12.00 30.00
3 Kyle Okposo JSY 3.00 8.00
4 Craig Anderson JSY 3.00 8.00
5 Patrick Sharp JSY 3.00 8.00
6 Steven Stamkos JSY 6.00 15.00
7 Jonathan Quick JSY 5.00 12.00
8 Dustin Brown JSY 2.50 6.00
9 Marc-Andre Fleury JSY 5.00 12.00
10 Tyler Seguin JSY 5.00 12.00
11 Daniel Sedin JSY 3.00 8.00
13 Tomas Hertl JSY 3.00 8.00
14 Aleksander Barkov JSY 3.00 8.00
15 P.K. Subban JSY 5.00 12.00
16 Steve Mason JSY 2.50 6.00
17 James van Riemsdyk JSY 4.00 10.00
18 Ryan Getzlaf JSY 5.00 12.00
19 Pekka Rinne JSY 4.00 10.00
20 David Backes JSY 3.00 8.00
21 Jonathan Bernier JSY 3.00 8.00
22 Dustin Byfuglien JSY 3.00 8.00
23 Claude Giroux JSY 6.00 15.00
24 Eric Staal JSY 4.00 10.00
25 Carey Price JSY 6.00 15.00
26 Sean Monahan JSY 3.00 8.00
27 Henrik Lundqvist JSY 4.00 10.00
28 Chris Kunitz JSY 3.00 8.00
29 Paul Stastny JSY 3.00 8.00
30 Max Pacioretty JSY 3.00 8.00
31 Jason Spezza JSY 3.00 8.00
32 Phil Kessel JSY 4.00 10.00
33 Rick Nash JSY 3.00 8.00
34 Zdeno Chara JSY 3.00 8.00
35 Jonathan Toews JSY 6.00 15.00
36 Joe Pavelski JSY 3.00 8.00
37 Antti Niemi JSY 2.50 6.00
38 Taylor Hall JSY 6.00 15.00
39 Anze Kopitar JSY 5.00 12.00
40 Sergei Bobrovsky JSY 3.00 8.00
41 Cory Schneider JSY 2.50 6.00
42 Victor Hedman JSY 4.00 10.00
43 Ryan Kesler JSY 3.00 8.00
44 Alex Galchenyuk JSY 5.00 12.00
45 Erik Karlsson JSY 6.00 15.00
46 Sidney Crosby JSY 8.00 20.00
47 Patrice Bergeron JSY 4.00 10.00
48 Evgeni Malkin JSY 10.00 25.00
49 John Tavares JSY 6.00 15.00
50 Zach Parise JSY 3.00 8.00
51 Ryan Miller JSY 3.00 8.00
53 Doug Gilmour JSY 4.00 10.00
54 Zemgus Girgensons JSY 3.00 8.00
55 Brett Hull JSY 3.00 8.00
56 Gabriel Landeskog JSY 2.50 6.00
57 Ed Belfour JSY 3.00 8.00
58 Pavel Datsyuk JSY 4.00 10.00
59 Corey Perry JSY 3.00 8.00
60 Jordan Eberle JSY 3.00 8.00
86 Johnny Gaudreau JSY AU 200.00 400.00
89 David Pastrnak JSY AU 100.00 200.00
112 Teuvo Teravainen JSY AU 100.00 200.00
119 Leon Draisaitl JSY AU 75.00 150.00
120 Sam Reinhart JSY AU 75.00 150.00
121 Aaron Ekblad JSY AU 100.00 200.00
122 Jonathan Drouin JSY AU 100.00 200.00

2006-07 Upper Deck Power Play Impact Rainbow

*VETS/25: 20X TO 50X BASIC CARDS
*ROOKIES/25: 3X TO 8X BASIC RC
STATED PRINT RUN 25 SER.#'d SETS

2006-07 Upper Deck Power Play Cup Celebrations

COMPLETE SET (7) 10.00 25.00
STATED ODDS 1:24
CC1 Eric Staal 1.25 3.00
CC2 Cam Ward 1.25 3.00
CC3 Dominik Hasek 1.50 4.00
CC4 Mike Modano 1.25 3.00
CC5 Martin St. Louis 1.00 2.50
CC6 Mario Lemieux 4.00 10.00
CC7 Patrick Roy 3.00 8.00

2014-15 Upper Deck Premier 02-03 Tribute Rookies Autographs Patches

SRRAB Andre Burakovsky 20.00 50.00
SRRAE Aaron Ekblad 60.00 120.00
SRRAW Alexander Wennberg 25.00 60.00
SRRBH Bo Horvat 50.00 100.00
SRRCL Curtis Lazar 15.00 40.00
SRRDN Darnell Nurse 40.00 100.00
SRRDP David Pastrnak 100.00 200.00
SRRDS Damon Severson 12.00 30.00
SRREK Evgeny Kuznetsov 60.00 120.00
SRRGR Griffin Reinhart 15.00 40.00
SRRJD Jonathan Drouin 60.00 120.00
SRRJG Johnny Gaudreau 100.00 200.00
SRRJS Jiri Sekac 12.00 30.00
SRRLD Leon Draisaitl 50.00 100.00
SRRMD Marko Dano 40.00 80.00
SRRPD Phillip Danault 12.00 30.00
SRRRS Ryan Sproul 12.00 30.00
SRRSG Seth Griffith 15.00 40.00
SRRSH Shayne Gostisbehere 60.00 120.00
SRRSP Stuart Percy 12.00 30.00
SRRSR Sam Reinhart 50.00 100.00
SRRTT Teuvo Teravainen 60.00 120.00
SRRVN Vladislav Namestnikov 20.00 50.00

2006-07 Upper Deck Power Play Goal Robbers

COMPLETE SET (14) 12.00 30.00
STATED ODDS 1:12
GR1 Jean-Sebastien Giguere 1.25 3.00
GR2 Kari Lehtonen 1.00 2.50
GR3 Ryan Miller 1.25 3.00
GR4 Miikka Kiprusoff 1.00 2.50
GR5 Cam Ward 1.25 3.00
GR6 Jose Theodore 1.25 3.00
GR7 Marty Turco 1.25 3.00
GR8 Marc-Andre Fleury 2.00 5.00
GR9 Roberto Luongo 2.00 5.00
GR10 Manny Fernandez 1.00 2.50
GR11 Tomas Vokoun 1.00 2.50
GR12 Martin Brodeur 2.50 6.00
GR13 Henrik Lundqvist 2.50 6.00
GR14 Cristobal Huet 1.00 2.50

2006-07 Upper Deck Power Play In Action

COMPLETE SET (14) 10.00 25.00
STATED ODDS 1:12
IA1 Jarome Iginla .75 2.00
IA2 Joe Sakic 1.25 3.00
IA3 Rick Nash .75 2.00
IA4 Henrik Zetterberg 1.00 2.50
IA5 Saku Koivu .75 2.00
IA6 Martin Brodeur 1.50 4.00
IA7 Jaromir Jagr 2.00 5.00
IA8 Dany Heatley .75 2.00
IA9 Peter Forsberg 1.00 2.50
IA10 Sidney Crosby 3.00 8.00
IA11 Joe Thornton 1.00 2.50
IA12 Mats Sundin .75 2.00
IA13 Markus Naslund .60 1.50
IA14 Alexander Ovechkin 2.00 5.00

2014-15 Upper Deck Premier 02-03 Tribute Stars Autographs Patches

SRVAG Alex Galchenyuk 40.00 80.00
SRVCC Chris Chelios 25.00 60.00
SRVCK Chris Kunitz 25.00 60.00
SRVES Eric Staal 30.00 80.00
SRVJB Jonathan Bernier 25.00 60.00
SRVJR Jeremy Roenick EXCH 25.00 60.00
SRVJT Jonathan Toews EXCH 150.00 250.00
SRVKL Kari Lehtonen 20.00 50.00
SRVMF Marc-Andre Fleury 40.00 100.00
SRVMG Mike Gartner 25.00 60.00
SRVMO Sean Monahan 25.00 60.00
SRVMP Max Pacioretty 25.00 60.00
SRVPR Patrick Roy EXCH 60.00 120.00
SRVRM Ryan McDonagh 100.00 200.00
SRVSB Sergei Bobrovsky 25.00 60.00
SRVSC Sidney Crosby EXCH 150.00 250.00
SRVSE Teemu Selanne 50.00 100.00
SRVSJ Seth Jones 20.00 50.00
SRVSM Steve Mason 20.00 50.00
SRVSW Shea Weber 20.00 50.00
SRVTA John Tavares EXCH 50.00 125.00
SRVTH Taylor Hall EXCH 50.00 125.00
SRVVD Vincent Damphousse 20.00 50.00

2006-07 Upper Deck Power Play Last Man Standing

COMPLETE SET (7) 6.00 15.00
STATED ODDS 1:24
LM1 Jody Shelley 1.25 3.00
LM2 Derek Boogaard 1.25 3.00
LM3 George Parros 1.25 3.00
LM4 Donald Brashear 1.25 3.00
LM5 Georges Laraque 1.50 4.00
LM6 Chris Simon 1.25 3.00
LM7 Todd Fedoruk 1.25 3.00

2006-07 Upper Deck Power Play Power Marks Autographs

STATED ODDS 1:400
PMAA Andrew Alberts 8.00 20.00
PMAM Andrej Meszaros 12.00 30.00
PMAO Alexander Ovechkin SP
PMAS Anthony Stewart 8.00 20.00
PMAY Alexei Yashin 8.00 20.00
PMBB Brad Boyes 8.00 20.00
PMBE Ben Eager 8.00 20.00
PMCD Chris Drury SP 8.00 20.00
PMCK Chris Kunitz 8.00 20.00
PMCP Corey Perry
PMDW Doug Weight 8.00 20.00
PMFP Fernando Pisani SP
PMHZ Henrik Zetterberg 20.00 40.00
PMJH Jeff Hoggan 8.00 20.00
PMJI Jarome Iginla SP 40.00 80.00
PMJT Joe Thornton SP
PMMH Marian Hossa SP 25.00 50.00
PMMT Maxime Talbot 10.00 25.00
PMMV Mike Van Ryn 8.00 20.00
PMPM Patrick Marleau SP
PMPR Paul Ranger 8.00 20.00
PMRN Rick Nash SP
PMRS Ryan Smyth 12.00 30.00
PMSC Sidney Crosby 100.00 200.00
PMSG Scott Gomez 8.00 20.00
PMSH Scott Hartnell 10.00 25.00
PMSK Saku Koivu SP
PMTH Jose Theodore SP 30.00 60.00
PMWG Wayne Gretzky SP
PMZP Zach Parise 12.00 30.00

2014-15 Upper Deck Premier Duals

PQ2BC D.Brown/J.Carter 4.00 10.00
PQ2BH E.Belfour/B.Hull 4.00 10.00
PQ2BS J.Spezza/J.Benn 5.00 12.00
PQ2DJ B.Dubinsky/R.Johansen 5.00 12.00
PQ2DL M.Duchene/G.Landeskog 4.00 10.00
PQ2EH T.Hall/J.Eberle 8.00 20.00
PQ2EK E.Malkin/C.Kunitz 12.00 30.00
PQ2ES E.Staal/A.Semin 5.00 12.00
PQ2GA J.Gibson/F.Andersen 5.00 12.00
PQ2GK A.Kopitar/M.Gaborik 6.00 15.00
PQ2GP J.Pominville/M.Granlund 3.00 8.00
PQ2HB A.Barkov/J.Huberdeau 4.00 10.00
PQ2HN R.Nugent-Hopkins/T.Hall 8.00 20.00
PQ2HO D.Hasek/C.Osgood 5.00 12.00
PQ2KK T.Rask/P.Rinne 5.00 12.00
PQ2KS D.Keith/B.Seabrook 4.00 10.00
PQ2KT E.Kane/J.Trouba 4.00 10.00
PQ2LM B.Marchand/M.Lucic 5.00 12.00
PQ2LR L.Robinson/G.Lafleur 5.00 12.00
PQ2LW B.Wheeler/A.Ladd 4.00 10.00
PQ2MA M.Pacioretty/A.Galchenyuk 6.00 15.00
PQ2MB M.Pacioretty/B.Gallagher 4.00 10.00
PQ2ML R.Miller/E.Lack 4.00 10.00
PQ2NS T.Seguin/V.Nichushkin 6.00 15.00
PQ2OB A.Ovechkin/N.Backstrom 15.00 40.00
PQ2OC K.Okposo/C.Conacher 4.00 10.00
PQ2PC Z.Parise/C.Coyle 4.00 10.00
PQ2PG R.Getzlaf/C.Perry 6.00 15.00
PQ2PH J.Pavelski/T.Hertl 4.00 10.00
PQ2PR D.Phaneuf/M.Rielly 4.00 10.00
PQ2PS C.Price/P.Subban 12.00 30.00
PQ2RD P.Roy/V.Damphousse 10.00 25.00
PQ2RL J.Roenick/J.LeClair 4.00 10.00
PQ2RR R.Getzlaf/R.Kesler 6.00 15.00
PQ2SE D.Sedin/H.Sedin 4.00 10.00
PQ2SN R.Nash/M.St. Louis 4.00 10.00
PQ2SS S.Stamkos/M.St. Louis 5.00 12.00
PQ2TK P.Kane/J.Toews 8.00 20.00
PQ2TP T.Toffoli/T.Pearson 4.00 10.00
PQ2TR K.Turris/B.Ryan 4.00 10.00
PQ2TS J.Tavares/R.Strome 8.00 20.00
PQ2VB V.Hedman/B.Bishop 5.00 12.00
PQ2VK J.van Riemsdyk/N.Kadri 4.00 10.00
PQ2WJ S.Weber/S.Jones 3.00 8.00
PQ2ZL H.Lundqvist/H.Zetterberg 5.00 12.00

2006-07 Upper Deck Power Play Specialists Jerseys

STATED ODDS 1:24
SAF Alexander Frolov 3.00 8.00
SAH Ales Hemsky 3.00 8.00
SAK Alex Kovalev 3.00 8.00
SAL Jason Allison 3.00 8.00
SAO Alexander Ovechkin 20.00 50.00
SAT Alex Tanguay 4.00 10.00
SBG Bill Guerin 3.00 8.00
SBL Brian Leetch 5.00 12.00
SBM Bryan McCabe 3.00 8.00
SBR Brian Rolston 3.00 8.00
SBS Brendan Shanahan 5.00 12.00
SCP Chris Pronger 4.00 10.00
SDB Donald Brashear 3.00 8.00
SDH Dominik Hasek 8.00 20.00
SDP Dion Phaneuf 8.00 20.00
SDW Doug Weight 3.00 8.00
SEB Ed Belfour 5.00 12.00
SEJ Ed Jovanovski 3.00 8.00
SES Eric Staal 5.00 12.00
SGA Simon Gagne 5.00 12.00
SGM Glen Murray 3.00 8.00
SIK Ilya Kovalchuk 8.00 20.00
SJA Jason Arnott 3.00 8.00
SJG Jean-Sebastien Giguere 4.00 10.00
SJI Jarome Iginla 8.00 20.00
SJJ Jaromir Jagr 8.00 20.00
SJL Jere Lehtinen 3.00 8.00
SJS Joe Sakic SP 15.00 40.00
SJT Joe Thornton 8.00 20.00
SKL Kari Lehtonen 5.00 12.00
SKP Keith Primeau 3.00 8.00
SMB Martin Brodeur 8.00 20.00
SMF Manny Fernandez 4.00 10.00
SMG Marian Gaborik 8.00 20.00
SMH Marian Hossa 4.00 10.00
SMK Miikka Kiprusoff 5.00 12.00
SMM Mike Modano 8.00 20.00
SMN Markus Naslund 5.00 12.00
SMO Brendan Morrison 3.00 8.00
SMP Michael Peca 3.00 8.00
SMS Marc Savard 3.00 8.00
SMT Marty Turco 4.00 10.00
SOK Olaf Kolzig 10.00 25.00
SPB Patrice Bergeron 5.00 12.00
SPD Pavel Datsyuk 4.00 10.00
SPF Peter Forsberg 8.00 20.00
SPK Paul Kariya 5.00 12.00
SPM Patrick Marleau 4.00 10.00
SRB Rob Blake 4.00 10.00
SRE Robert Esche 4.00 10.00
SRI Brad Richards 4.00 10.00
SRM Ryan Miller 5.00 12.00
SSC Sidney Crosby SP 30.00 80.00
SSF Sergei Fedorov 5.00 12.00
SSG Scott Gomez 3.00 8.00
SSN Scott Niedermayer 3.00 8.00
SSP Jason Spezza 5.00 12.00
STR Tuomo Ruutu 3.00 8.00
STS Teemu Selanne 5.00 12.00
SZC Zdeno Chara 3.00 8.00

2014-15 Upper Deck Premier Emblems

PEAB Alexandre Burrows 12.00 30.00
PEAG Alex Galchenyuk 20.00 50.00
PEBG Bill Guerin 12.00 30.00
PEBH Brett Hull 12.00 30.00
PECC Chris Chelios 12.00 30.00
PECJ Curtis Joseph 12.00 30.00
PECR Corey Crawford 15.00 40.00
PECW Cam Ward 12.00 30.00
PEDB Dustin Brown 10.00 25.00
PEDE Derek Stepan 12.00 30.00
PEDS Daniel Sedin 12.00 30.00
PEEB Ed Belfour 12.00 30.00
PEEL Eddie Lack 10.00 25.00
PEES Eric Staal 15.00 40.00
PEGA Marian Gaborik 12.00 30.00
PEGM Glen Murray 10.00 25.00
PEHL Henrik Lundqvist 15.00 40.00
PEHZ Henrik Zetterberg 15.00 40.00
PEJB Jamie Benn 15.00 40.00
PEJE Jordan Eberle 12.00 30.00
PEJL John LeClair 12.00 30.00
PEJQ Jonathan Quick 15.00 40.00
PEJR Jeremy Roenick 12.00 30.00
PEJT Joe Thornton 12.00 30.00
PEMB Martin Biron 10.00 25.00
PEMD Marcel Dionne 15.00 40.00
PEMF Marc-Andre Fleury 25.00 50.00
PEMG Mike Green 12.00 30.00
PEMI Mike Gartner 12.00 30.00
PEMM Matt Moulson 10.00 25.00
PEMS Mats Sundin 12.00 30.00
PEPB Patrice Bergeron 15.00 40.00
PEPS P.K. Subban 15.00 40.00
PERG Ryan Getzlaf 20.00 50.00
PESC Sidney Crosby 50.00 125.00
PESS Steven Stamkos 15.00 40.00
PEST Drew Stafford 12.00 30.00
PETR Tuukka Rask 12.00 30.00

2014-15 Upper Deck Premier Inked Inscriptions

IIAE Aaron Ekblad/99 25.00 60.00
IIAI Arturs Irbe/50 8.00 20.00
IIAO Alexander Ovechkin/25 40.00 80.00
IIBH Bo Horvat/99 20.00 50.00
IICL Curtis Lazar/99 8.00 20.00
IICP Carey Price/25 30.00 60.00
IIES Eric Staal/50 10.00 25.00
IIJB Jonathan Bernier/25 10.00 25.00
IIJD Jonathan Drouin/99 15.00 40.00
IIJI Jarome Iginla/50 15.00 40.00
IIJT John Tavares/50 20.00 50.00
IILD Leon Draisaitl/99 30.00 80.00
IILI Mike Liut/99 5.00 12.00
IIMG Mikael Granlund/50 6.00 15.00
IIML Mario Lemieux/25 50.00 80.00
IIMM Mark Messier/25 40.00 80.00
IIMP Max Pacioretty/25 10.00 25.00
IIPF Peter Forsberg/25 30.00 60.00
IIRS Ryan Suter/50
(inserted in 2015-16 Premier)
IISM Sean Monahan/99 6.00 15.00
IISR Sam Reinhart/99 20.00 50.00
IISW Shea Weber/50 12.00 30.00
IITH Tomas Hertl/50 15.00 40.00
IITK Torey Krug/99 6.00 15.00
IITS Teemu Selanne/50 40.00 80.00

2014-15 Upper Deck Premier Legendary Premier Signatures

LPSBH Bobby Hull B 15.00 40.00
LPSBP Brad Park C 12.00 30.00
LPSCN Cam Neely C 15.00 40.00
LPSJS Joe Sakic B
LPSMB Mike Bossy B 12.00 30.00
LPSML Mario Lemieux A 50.00 100.00
LPSMS Mats Sundin B 15.00 40.00
LPSPR Patrick Roy A
LPSRB Ray Bourque B 20.00 50.00
LPSWG Wayne Gretzky A 150.00 250.00

2014-15 Upper Deck Premier Mega Patch Chest Logos

PMPAB Aleksander Barkov/28 40.00 80.00
PMPAE Aaron Ekblad/27 150.00 300.00
PMPAN Antti Niemi/24 15.00 40.00
PMPAS Alexander Semin/20 20.00 50.00
PMPBB Ben Bishop/20 20.00 50.00
PMPBS Brayden Schenn/19 20.00 50.00
PMPBU Alexandre Burrows/20 20.00 50.00
PMPBW Blake Wheeler/24 20.00 50.00
PMPCA Craig Anderson/24 40.00 80.00
PMPCC Charlie Coyle/20 30.00 60.00
PMPCH Cody Hodgson/20 20.00 50.00
PMPCJ Calle Jarnkrok/21 20.00 50.00
PMPDD Drew Doughty/18 75.00 150.00
PMPDK Darcy Kuemper/20 30.00 60.00
PMPDS Daniel Sedin/20 40.00 80.00
PMPEK Evgeny Kuznetsov/22 75.00 135.00
PMPGA Johnny Gaudreau/28 200.00 400.00
PMPHL Henrik Lundqvist/21 30.00 60.00
PMPHO Braden Holtby/20 50.00 100.00
PMPHS Henrik Sedin/20 60.00 120.00
PMPHZ Henrik Zetterberg/22 40.00 80.00
PMPJA Jack Johnson/24 30.00 60.00
PMPJB Jamie Benn/20 125.00 250.00
PMPJC Jeff Carter/18 60.00 120.00
PMPJD Jonathan Drouin/19 175.00 300.00
PMPJE Jordan Eberle/24 25.00 60.00
PMPJN James Neal/21 75.00 150.00
PMPJO John Carlson/19 60.00 120.00
PMPJQ Jonathan Quick/18 40.00 100.00
PMPJR Jeremy Roenick/25 100.00 200.00
PMPJS Jason Spezza/20 20.00 50.00
PMPJT John Tavares/22 40.00 80.00
PMPJU Tomas Jurco/21 40.00 80.00
PMPJV James van Riemsdyk/18 20.00 50.00
PMPKA Erik Karlsson/25 40.00 100.00
PMPKE Duncan Keith/24 50.00 100.00
PMPKT Kyle Turris/23 20.00 50.00
PMPLC Logan Couture/23 20.00 50.00
PMPLD Leon Draisaitl/24 40.00 100.00
PMPLL Morgan Rielly/16 75.00 135.00
PMPMG Mike Gartner/18 75.00 150.00
PMPML Milan Lucic/24 20.00 50.00
PMPMO Sean Monahan/28 30.00 80.00
PMPMR Mike Richards/18 30.00 60.00
PMPMS Mike Smith/26 50.00 100.00
PMPMZ Mats Zuccarello/17 40.00 80.00
PMPNB Nicklas Backstrom/23 40.00 80.00
PMPNK Nazem Kadri/18 50.00 100.00
PMPNM Nathan MacKinnon/16 40.00 100.00
PMPNU Ryan Nugent-Hopkins/24 20.00 50.00
PMPOM Olli Maatta/31 25.00 60.00
PMPOP Ondrej Palat/19 25.00 60.00
PMPPB Patrice Bergeron/24 40.00 80.00
PMPPC Carey Price/19 100.00 200.00
PMPPK Phil Kessel/18 25.00 60.00
PMPPM Patrick Marleau/23 50.00 100.00
PMPPR Patrick Roy/30 100.00 200.00
PMPRF Ron Francis/29 25.00 60.00
PMPRG Ryan Getzlaf/21 30.00 80.00
PMPRI Pekka Rinne/22 25.00 60.00
PMPRJ Ryan Johansen/24 25.00 60.00
PMPRK Ryan Kesler/20 30.00 60.00
PMPRL Roberto Luongo/27 40.00 80.00
PMPRY Ryan Strome/23 20.00 50.00
PMPSJ Seth Jones/21 15.00 40.00
PMPSK Jeff Skinner/20 20.00 50.00
PMPSM Steve Mason/19 40.00 80.00
PMPSR Sam Reinhart/18 100.00 200.00
PMPSU P.K. Subban/21 30.00 80.00
PMPTF Theoren Fleury/18 40.00 80.00
PMPTH Tomas Hertl/24 40.00 80.00
PMPTJ Jacob Trouba/24 40.00 80.00
PMPTL Trevor Linden/27 40.00 80.00
PMPTR Tuukka Rask/24 20.00 40.00
PMPVA Semyon Varlamov/30 20.00 50.00
PMPVO Jakub Voracek/19 50.00 100.00
PMPVT Vladimir Tarasenko/19 75.00 120.00
PMPZC Zdeno Chara/24 20.00 50.00
PMPZG Zemgus Girgensons/20 30.00 80.00
PMPZK Zack Kassian/20 15.00 40.00

2014-15 Upper Deck Premier Quads

PQ4ANALAK Gtzlf/Kslr/Kptr/Gbrk 8.00 20.00
PQ4BOSMON Rsk/Chra/Prce/Sbbn 15.00 40.00
PQ4BUFF Hdgsn/Mlsn/Grg/Enr 8.00 20.00
PQ4CAL Mnhn/Rmo/Hllr/Hdlr 5.00 12.00
PQ4CAR Stl/Sknr/Smn/Lndh 6.00 15.00
PQ4DETCBH Dtsyk/Zttr/Kne/Tws 15.00 40.00
PQ4FIN Rnne/Rsk/Nmi/Lht 6.00 15.00
PQ4FLO Bjgs/Lng/Brkv/Hbr 5.00 12.00
PQ4LAKANA Prry/Gbsn/Qck/Crtr 8.00 20.00
PQ4MON Sbbn/Pcrt/Glg/Glch 8.00 20.00
PQ4NET Gbsn/Grbr/Kmp/Jns 6.00 15.00
PQ4NYINYR Tvrs/Okps/Nsh/Stpn 10.00 25.00
PQ4NYR Zcrllo/St.L/Nsh/Krdr 8.00 20.00
PQ4OFFENSE McKn/Hrtl/Brk/Mnh 10.00 25.00
PQ4OTT Trrs/Krlsn/Ryn/Zbn 10.00 25.00
PQ4PHI Grx/Ctrr/Vrck/Msn 5.00 12.00
PQ4PREDS Wbr/Nl/Jns/Rnne 6.00 15.00
PQ4SJS Thrntn/Ctre/Pvl/Mrl 5.00 12.00
PQ4TBL Stmks/Plt/Hdm/Bsh 10.00 25.00
PQ4USA Kssl/Kne/Qck/Oshe 15.00 40.00
PQ4VAN Sdn/Mllr/Kssn/Brrws 5.00 12.00
PQ4WAS Ovch/Bckm/Crlsn/Hlt 10.00 25.00
PQ4WIN Whlr/Trba/Kne/Sch 6.00 15.00

2014-15 Upper Deck Premier Rinks of Honor Autographs Booklet

GROUP A STATED ODDS 1:720
GROUP B STATED ODDS 1:127
GROUP C STATED ODDS 1:53
GROUP D STATED ODDS 1:47
GROUP E STATED ODDS 1:13
GROUP F STATED ODDS 1:8
OVERALL STATED ODDS 1:4
RHAO Alexander Ovechkin B 50.00 100.00
RHBH Bobby Hull B 30.00 80.00
RHBO Bo Horvat F 20.00 50.00
RHCC Charlie Coyle E 8.00 20.00
RHCJ Curtis Joseph E 20.00 40.00
RHCN Cam Neely D 20.00 50.00
RHDH Dominik Hasek C 40.00 80.00
RHEM Evgeni Malkin C 60.00 150.00
RHES Eric Staal E 10.00 25.00
RHFP Felix Potvin E 20.00 40.00
RHGF Grant Fuhr C 20.00 50.00
RHHU Brett Hull C 30.00 60.00
RHJB Jonathan Bernier D 20.00 50.00
RHJD Jonathan Drouin F 15.00 40.00
RHJG Johnny Gaudreau F 40.00 80.00
RHJP Joe Pavelski E 15.00 40.00
RHJR James van Riemsdyk D 20.00 50.00
RHJT John Tavares E 40.00 80.00
RHJV John Vanbiesbrouck F 20.00 50.00
RHLA Gabriel Landeskog A
(inserted in 2015-16 Premier)
RHLI Mike Liut F 10.00 25.00
RHMI Mike Modano A 100.00 200.00
RHML Mario Lemieux C 100.00 200.00
RHMM Marty McSorley E 8.00 20.00
RHMP Max Pacioretty E 12.00 30.00
RHPD Pavel Datsyuk D 30.00 60.00
RHPR Patrick Roy C 60.00 120.00
RHRK Ryan Kesler E 8.00 20.00
RHRN Rick Nash D 20.00 50.00
RHSB Sergei Bobrovsky C
(inserted in 2015-16 Premier)
RHSJ Seth Jones F 5.00 12.00
RHSL Steve Larmer F 10.00 25.00
RHSR Sam Reinhart F 30.00 60.00
RHTB Tom Barrasso F 20.00 40.00
RHVO Jakub Voracek B
(inserted in 2015-16 Premier)
RHZP Zach Parise B 25.00 60.00

2014-15 Upper Deck Premier Rookie Premier Signatures

RPSAB Andre Burakovsky A 8.00 20.00
RPSAE Aaron Ekblad A 20.00 50.00
RPSBH Bo Horvat C 12.00 30.00
RPSCL Curtis Lazar B 6.00 15.00
RPSDN Darnell Nurse B 15.00 40.00
RPSDP Derrick Pouliot C 5.00 12.00
RPSDS Damon Severson C 4.00 10.00
RPSEK Evgeny Kuznetsov B 8.00 20.00
RPSJD Jonathan Drouin A
RPSJG Johnny Gaudreau B 15.00 40.00
RPSKR Kerby Rychel C 3.00 8.00
RPSLD Leon Draisaitl A 25.00 60.00
RPSSG Shayne Gostisbehere C 25.00 60.00
RPSSR Sam Reinhart A 15.00 40.00
RPSTT Teuvo Teravainen B EXCH 8.00 20.00

2014-15 Upper Deck Premier Rookies

R1 Victor Rask 2.00 5.00
R2 Leon Draisaitl 10.00 25.00
R3 Mirco Mueller 2.00 5.00
R4 Oscar Klefbom 4.00 10.00
R5 Joey Hishon 2.50 6.00
R6 Tobias Rieder 2.00 5.00
R7 Curtis Lazar 2.50 6.00
R8 Rocco Grimaldi 2.00 5.00
R9 Teemu Pulkkinen 2.50 6.00
R10 Ryan Sproul 2.00 5.00
R11 Andy Andreoff 2.00 5.00
R12 Damon Severson 2.00 5.00
R13 Seth Griffith 2.50 6.00
R14 Bogdan Yakimov 2.00 5.00
R15 Curtis McKenzie 1.50 4.00
R16 Adam Lowry 2.00 5.00
R17 Kevin Hayes 6.00 15.00
R18 Barclay Goodrow 2.00 5.00
R19 Griffin Reinhart 2.50 6.00
R20 Teuvo Teravainen 3.00 8.00
R21 Seth Helgeson 1.50 4.00
R22 Sam Reinhart 6.00 15.00
R23 Colton Sissons 2.00 5.00
R24 Mark Visentin 2.00 5.00
R25 Darnell Nurse 6.00 15.00
R26 Calle Jarnkrok 2.00 5.00
R27 Marko Dano 2.00 5.00
R28 Corban Knight 2.00 5.00
R29 Dennis Everberg 2.00 5.00
R30 Adam Clendening 2.00 5.00
R31 Jori Lehtera 2.50 6.00
R32 Vincent Trocheck 2.50 6.00
R33 John Klingberg 6.00 15.00
R34 Bo Horvat 6.00 15.00
R35 Evgeny Kuznetsov 8.00 20.00
R36 Vladislav Namestnikov 3.00 8.00
R37 David Pastrnak 6.00 15.00
R38 Greg McKegg 1.50 4.00
R39 Josh Jooris 2.00 5.00
R40 Ty Rattie 2.50 6.00
R41 William Karlsson 8.00 20.00
R42 Laurent Brossoit 2.00 5.00
R43 Jiri Sekac 2.00 5.00
R44 Shayne Gostisbehere 8.00 20.00
R45 P.E. Bellemare 2.00 5.00
R46 Chris Tierney 2.00 5.00
R47 Kerby Rychel 1.50 4.00
R48 Aaron Ekblad 5.00 12.00
R49 Alexander Wennberg 4.00 10.00
R50 Brandon Gormley 2.00 5.00
R51 Markus Granlund 3.00 8.00
R52 Anthony Duclair 3.00 8.00
R53 Johnny Gaudreau 6.00 15.00
R54 Alexander Khokhlachev 2.00 5.00
R55 Stuart Percy 2.00 5.00
R56 Joonas Nattinen 2.00 5.00
R57 Phillip Danault 2.00 5.00
R58 Trevor van Riemsdyk 3.00 8.00
R59 Andre Burakovsky 3.00 8.00
R60 Jonathan Drouin 5.00 12.00

2014-15 Upper Deck Premier Rookies Jerseys Silver Spectrum

*GOLD JSY/25: 1.2X TO 3X SILVER JSY/125
R1 Victor Rask 3.00 8.00
R2 Leon Draisaitl 15.00 40.00
R3 Mirco Mueller 3.00 8.00
R4 Oscar Klefbom 6.00 15.00
R5 Joey Hishon 4.00 10.00
R6 Tobias Rieder 3.00 8.00
R7 Curtis Lazar 4.00 10.00
R8 Rocco Grimaldi 3.00 8.00
R9 Teemu Pulkkinen 4.00 10.00
R10 Ryan Sproul 3.00 8.00
R11 Andy Andreoff 3.00 8.00
R12 Damon Severson 3.00 8.00
R13 Seth Griffith 4.00 10.00
R14 Bogdan Yakimov 3.00 8.00
R15 Curtis McKenzie 2.50 6.00
R16 Adam Lowry 3.00 8.00
R18 Barclay Goodrow 3.00 8.00
R19 Griffin Reinhart 4.00 10.00
R20 Teuvo Teravainen 6.00 15.00
R21 Seth Helgeson 2.50 6.00
R22 Sam Reinhart 6.00 15.00
R23 Colton Sissons 3.00 8.00
R24 Mark Visentin 3.00 8.00
R25 Darnell Nurse 10.00 25.00
R27 Marko Dano 3.00 8.00
R28 Corban Knight 3.00 8.00
R29 Dennis Everberg 3.00 8.00
R30 Adam Clendening 3.00 8.00
R31 Jori Lehtera 4.00 10.00
R32 Vincent Trocheck 4.00 10.00
R33 John Klingberg 10.00 25.00
R34 Bo Horvat 10.00 25.00
R35 Evgeny Kuznetsov 12.00 30.00
R36 Vladislav Namestnikov 5.00 12.00
R37 David Pastrnak 8.00 20.00
R38 Greg McKegg 2.50 6.00
R39 Josh Jooris 3.00 8.00
R40 Ty Rattie 4.00 10.00
R41 William Karlsson 12.00 30.00
R42 Laurent Brossoit 3.00 8.00
R43 Jiri Sekac 3.00 8.00
R44 Shayne Gostisbehere 12.00 30.00
R45 P.E. Bellemare 3.00 8.00
R46 Chris Tierney 3.00 8.00
R47 Kerby Rychel 2.50 6.00
R48 Aaron Ekblad 6.00 15.00
R49 Alexander Wennberg 6.00 15.00
R50 Brandon Gormley 3.00 8.00
R53 Johnny Gaudreau 10.00 25.00
R54 Alexander Khokhlachev 3.00 8.00
R55 Stuart Percy 3.00 8.00
R56 Joonas Nattinen 3.00 8.00
R57 Phillip Danault 3.00 8.00
R58 Trevor van Riemsdyk 5.00 12.00
R59 Andre Burakovsky 6.00 15.00
R60 Jonathan Drouin 6.00 15.00

2014-15 Upper Deck Premier Signature Champions

SCAK Anze Kopitar/50 25.00 60.00
SCCC Chris Chelios/99 12.00 30.00
SCCP Corey Perry/50
(inserted in 2015-16 Premier)
SCDB Dustin Brown/50 12.00 30.00
SCEM Evgeni Malkin/25
SCES Eric Staal/99 15.00 40.00
SCGF Grant Fuhr/50 15.00 40.00
SCGL Guy Lafleur/99 15.00 40.00
SCHU Brett Hull/25 20.00 50.00
SCJJ Jaromir Jagr/25 50.00 100.00
SCJS Joe Sakic/25 30.00 80.00
SCJT Jonathan Toews/50 100.00 200.00
SCMB Martin Brodeur/99 40.00 80.00
SCMF Marc-Andre Fleury/99 20.00 50.00
SCMK Mike Krushelnyski/99 10.00 25.00
SCMM Mark Messier/25 50.00 100.00
SCMS Martin St. Louis/99 12.00 30.00
SCPD Pavel Datsyuk/50 30.00 60.00
SCRB Rob Blake/99 12.00 30.00
SCTB Tom Barrasso/99 12.00 30.00

2014-15 Upper Deck Premier Signatures

PSAG Alex Galchenyuk 12.00 30.00
PSGL Gabriel Landeskog 6.00 15.00
(inserted in 2015-16 Premier)
PSGN Gustav Nyquist C 6.00 15.00
PSJT Jonathan Toews A 40.00 100.00
PSNM Nathan MacKinnon C 15.00 40.00
PSPD Pavel Datsyuk A 20.00 50.00
PSPK Patrick Kane
(inserted in 2016-17 Premier)
PSRN Rick Nash B 8.00 20.00
PSSC Sidney Crosby A
PSVN Valeri Nichushkin 6.00 15.00
(inserted in 2015-16 Premier)
PSZP Zach Parise A

2014-15 Upper Deck Premier Sixes

PQ6ANASJS Gz/Py/Ks/Pv/Ct/Mr
PQ6AVS Dch/Ld/Mc/Ig/Vr/Hs 15.00 40.00
PQ6BOSMON Lc/Mn/Rk/Pcy/Gk/Pr
PQ6CALVAN Mn/Hd/Rm/Mlr/Sn/Sd 12.00 30.00
PQ6CAPS Ov/Bck/Gr/Kz/Grn/Brk
PQ6DAL Sg/Bn/Spz/Lt/Nch/Rt
PQ6HAWKS Tw/Kn/Shp/Cr/Sb/Kh
PQ6KINGS Qk/Kp/Dgh/Cr/Tf/Bw
PQ6MON Pr/Sb/Pc/Glg/Gln/Plk
PQ6NYR Ns/St.L/Lnd/St/Zc/Kr
PQ6RC1 Dr/Dst/Rn/Lz/Wnb/Hr 40.00 80.00
PQ6RC2 Ek/Nr/Sv/Rn/Gb/Mlr
PQ6SJS Hrt/Pv/Ctr/Nm/Thr/Mlr
PQ6TOR Ksl/Kd/Rms/Brn/Rly/Or

2015-16 Upper Deck Premier

1 Ryan Kesler 2.50 6.00
2 Vladimir Tarasenko 4.00 10.00
3 Jonathan Toews 5.00 12.00
4 Alex Galchenyuk 3.00 8.00
5 Alexander Ovechkin 10.00 25.00
6 Oliver Ekman-Larsson 2.00 5.00
7 Henrik Lundqvist 3.00 8.00
8 Jiri Hudler 2.00 5.00
9 Scott Hartnell 2.50 6.00
10 Jamie Benn 3.00 8.00
11 Johnny Gaudreau 4.00 10.00
12 Claude Giroux 2.50 6.00
13 Adam Henrique 2.50 6.00
14 Carey Price 8.00 20.00
15 Steven Stamkos 5.00 12.00
16 Pavel Datsyuk 3.00 8.00
17 James van Riemsdyk 2.50 6.00
18 Anze Kopitar 4.00 10.00
19 David Krejci 2.00 5.00
20 Sidney Crosby 10.00 25.00
21 Nathan MacKinnon 5.00 12.00
22 Blake Wheeler 2.50 6.00
23 Joe Pavelski 2.50 6.00
24 Mike Hoffman 2.00 5.00
25 John Tavares 5.00 12.00
26 Mikael Granlund 2.00 5.00
27 Aaron Ekblad 2.50 6.00
28 Henrik Sedin 2.50 6.00
29 Pekka Rinne 3.00 8.00
30 Jakub Voracek 2.50 6.00
31 Drew Doughty 2.50 6.00
32 Shea Weber 2.00 5.00
33 Taylor Hall 5.00 12.00
34 Jake Allen 3.00 8.00
35 P.K. Subban 4.00 10.00
36 Jeff Skinner 2.00 5.00
37 Ryan Miller 2.50 6.00
38 Marc-Andre Fleury 4.00 10.00
39 Jason Spezza 2.00 5.00
40 Jonathan Quick 4.00 10.00
41 Ryan O'Reilly 2.50 6.00
42 Erik Karlsson 5.00 12.00
43 Evgeny Kuznetsov 4.00 10.00
44 Mario Lemieux 15.00 40.00
45 Joe Sakic 8.00 20.00
46 Mark Messier 8.00 20.00
47 Steve Yzerman 8.00 20.00
48 Patrick Roy 12.00 30.00
49 Pavel Bure 8.00 20.00
50 Wayne Gretzky 25.00 60.00
51 Frank Vatrano AU RC 15.00 40.00
52 Josh Anderson AU RC 8.00 20.00
53 Jaccob Slavin AU RC 6.00 15.00
54 Devin Shore AU RC 8.00 20.00
55 Juuse Saros AU RC 10.00 25.00
56 Anton Slepyshev AU RC 6.00 15.00
57 Garret Sparks AU RC 10.00 25.00
58 Connor Brickley AU RC 6.00 15.00
59 Matt Murray AU RC 40.00 100.00
60 Christoph Bertschy AU RC 6.00 15.00
61 Stanislav Galiev AU RC 8.00 20.00
62 Matt O'Connor AU RC 6.00 15.00
63 Louis Domingue AU RC 8.00 20.00
64 Anthony Stolarz AU RC 8.00 20.00
65 Tyler Randell AU RC 8.00 20.00
66 Viktor Svedberg AU RC 6.00 15.00
67 Daniel Carr AU RC 6.00 15.00
68 Brendan Ranford AU RC 6.00 15.00
69 Kyle Baun AU RC 8.00 20.00
70 Sam Brittain AU RC 8.00 20.00
71 Jake Virtanen JSY AU/375 RC 12.00 30.00
72 Kevin Fiala JSY AU/375 RC 10.00 25.00
73 Shane Prince JSY AU/375 RC 8.00 20.00
74 Derek Forbort JSY AU/375 RC 8.00 20.00
75 Ryan Hartman JSY AU/375 RC 12.00 30.00
76 Stefan Noesen JSY AU/375 RC 8.00 20.00
77 Nicolas Petan JSY AU/375 RC 10.00 25.00
78 Brock McGinn JSY AU/375 RC 10.00 25.00
79 Jacob de la Rose JSY AU/375 RC 10.00 25.00
80 Emile Poirier JSY AU/375 RC 10.00 25.00
81 Jared McCann JSY AU/375 RC 10.00 25.00
82 Zachary Fucale JSY AU/375 RC 10.00 25.00
83 Ronalds Kenins JSY AU/375 RC 10.00 25.00
84 Matt Puempel JSY AU/375 RC 8.00 20.00
85 Daniel Sprong JSY AU/375 RC 20.00 50.00
86 Nikolay Goldobin JSY AU/375 RC 10.00 25.00
87 Mike McCarron JSY AU/375 RC 12.00 30.00
88 Chandler Stephenson JSY AU/375 RC 10.00 25.00
89 Vincent Hinostroza JSY AU/375 RC 6.00 15.00
90 Shea Theodore JSY AU/375 RC 10.00 25.00
91 Joonas Donskoi JSY AU/375 RC 10.00 25.00
92 Slater Koekkoek JSY AU/375 RC 8.00 20.00
93 Nick Ritchie JSY AU/375 RC 10.00 25.00
94 Charles Hudon JSY AU/375 RC 10.00 25.00
95 Henrik Samuelsson JSY AU/375 RC 8.00 20.00
96 Radek Faksa JSY AU/375 RC 10.00 25.00
97 Nick Cousins JSY AU/375 RC 10.00 25.00
98 Mackenzie Skapski JSY AU/375 RC 10.00 25.00
99 Hunter Shinkaruk JSY AU/375 RC 10.00 25.00
100 Noah Hanifin JSY AU/375 RC 12.00 30.00
101 Mikko Rantanen JSY AU/375 RC 20.00 50.00
102 Oscar Lindberg JSY AU/375 RC 10.00 25.00
103 Brendan Gaunce JSY AU/375 RC 12.00 30.00
104 Antoine Bibeau JSY AU/375 RC 10.00 25.00
105 Andreas Athanasiou JSY AU/375 RC 25.00 60.00
106 Connor Hellebuyck JSY AU/375 RC 25.00 60.00
107 Brady Skjei JSY AU/375 RC 8.00 20.00
108 Colton Parayko JSY AU/375 RC 12.00 30.00
109 Mike Condon JSY AU/375 RC 10.00 25.00
110 Nikolaj Ehlers JSY AU/375 RC 20.00 50.00
111 Gustav Olofsson JSY AU/375 RC 10.00 25.00
112 Robby Fabbri JSY AU/375 RC 12.00 30.00
113 Artemi Panarin JSY AU/375 RC 60.00 150.00
114 Max Domi JSY AU/199 RC 40.00 100.00
115 Connor McDavid JSY AU/199 RC 900.00 1500.00
116 Sam Bennett JSY AU/199 RC 25.00 60.00
117 Dylan Larkin JSY AU/199 RC 60.00 150.00
118 Jack Eichel JSY RC 80.00 200.00

2015-16 Upper Deck Premier '03-04 Tribute Rookies Autograph Patches

SRRAP Artemi Panarin/49 100.00 250.00
SRRBG Brendan Gaunce/99 25.00 60.00
SRRBH Ben Hutton/99 20.00 50.00
SRRCM Connor McDavid/49 600.00 900.00
SRRCP Colton Parayko/99 25.00 60.00
SRRDL Dylan Larkin/49 100.00 250.00
SRRDS Daniel Sprong/99 40.00 100.00
SRRHS Hunter Shinkaruk/99 20.00 50.00
SRRJD Joonas Donskoi/99 20.00 50.00
SRRJE Jack Eichel/49 (No Auto) 125.00 300.00
SRRJM Jared McCann/99 20.00 50.00
SRRJV Jake Virtanen/49 40.00 100.00
SRRLU Linus Ullmark/99 25.00 60.00
SRRMC Mike Condon/99 20.00 50.00
SRRMD Max Domi/49 60.00 150.00
SRRMI Colin Miller/99 15.00 40.00
SRRMJ Mattias Janmark/99 20.00 50.00
SRRNE Nikolaj Ehlers/49 60.00 150.00
SRRNG Nikolay Goldobin/99 20.00 50.00
SRRNH Noah Hanifin/49 40.00 100.00
SRRNR Nick Ritchie/99 20.00 50.00
SRROL Oscar Lindberg/99 20.00 50.00
SRRRF Robby Fabbri/99 25.00 60.00
SRRSB Sam Bennett/49 40.00 100.00
SRRSP Shane Prince/99 15.00 40.00
SRRST Shea Theodore/99 20.00 50.00
SRRZF Zachary Fucale/49 30.00 80.00

2015-16 Upper Deck Premier Inked Script

INAH Anze Kopitar 80.00 200.00
INAO Alexander Ovechkin 200.00 500.00
INBO Bobby Hull 90.00 150.00
INBR Brett Hull 50.00 125.00
INBS Borje Salming
((inserted in 2016-17 Premier)
INCJ Curtis Joseph 50.00 125.00
INDH Dominik Hasek 60.00 150.00
INGH Glenn Hall 40.00 100.00
INJS Joe Sakic 80.00 200.00
INMM Mark Messier 90.00 150.00
INMP Max Pacioretty 50.00 125.00
INPB Pavel Bure 80.00 200.00
INSC Sidney Crosby 200.00 500.00
INTS Teemu Selanne 100.00 250.00
INWG Wayne Gretzky 250.00 600.00

2015-16 Upper Deck Premier Jerseys

1 Ryan Kesler 5.00 12.00
2 Vladimir Tarasenko 8.00 20.00
3 Jonathan Toews 10.00 25.00
4 Alex Galchenyuk 6.00 15.00
5 Alexander Ovechkin 20.00 50.00
6 Oliver Ekman-Larsson 4.00 10.00
7 Henrik Lundqvist 6.00 15.00
8 Jiri Hudler 4.00 10.00
10 Jamie Benn 6.00 15.00
11 Johnny Gaudreau 8.00 20.00

Claude Giroux 5.00 12.00
Adam Henrique 5.00 12.00
Carey Price 15.00 40.00
Steven Stamkos 10.00 25.00
Pavel Datsyuk 6.00 15.00
James van Riemsdyk 5.00 12.00
Anze Kopitar 8.00 20.00
David Krejci 4.00 10.00
Sidney Crosby 20.00 50.00
Blake Wheeler 5.00 12.00
Joe Pavelski 5.00 12.00
Mike Hoffman 4.00 10.00
John Tavares 10.00 25.00
Mikael Granlund 4.00 10.00
Aaron Ekblad 5.00 12.00
Henrik Sedin 5.00 12.00
Pekka Rinne 6.00 15.00
Jakub Voracek 5.00 12.00
Drew Doughty 5.00 12.00
Shea Weber 4.00 10.00
Taylor Hall 10.00 25.00
Jake Allen 6.00 15.00
P.K. Subban 8.00 20.00
Jeff Skinner 4.00 10.00
Ryan Miller 5.00 12.00
Marc-Andre Fleury 8.00 20.00
Jason Spezza 4.00 10.00
Jonathan Quick 8.00 20.00
Ryan O'Reilly 5.00 12.00
Evgeny Kuznetsov 8.00 20.00
Mario Lemieux 25.00 60.00
Joe Sakic 12.00 30.00
Patrick Roy 20.00 50.00
Pavel Bure 12.00 30.00

2015-16 Upper Deck Premier Mega Patch Chest Logos

PAB Aleksander Barkov/31 40.00 100.00
PAD Anthony Duclair/25 40.00 100.00
PAE Aaron Ekblad/25 50.00 125.00
PAG Alex Galchenyuk/20 60.00 150.00
PAH Adam Henrique/26 40.00 100.00
PAL Anders Lee/20 50.00 125.00
PAN Andrew Hammond/23 150.00 400.00
PAS Alexander Steen/18 50.00 125.00
PBB Bob Bourne/20 40.00 100.00
PBB Brent Burns/22 60.00 150.00
PBG Brendan Gallagher/19 60.00 150.00
PBO Sergei Bobrovsky/21 50.00 125.00
PBS Brandon Saad/21 50.00 125.00
PBW Blake Wheeler/24 50.00 125.00
PCC Corey Crawford/24 60.00 150.00
PCG Claude Giroux/18 50.00 125.00
PCK Chris Kreider/18 50.00 125.00
PCM Connor McDavid/20 600.00 900.00
PCP Corey Perry/22 50.00 125.00
PCS Cory Schneider/25 40.00 100.00
PCW Cam Ward/18 50.00 125.00
PDB Dustin Byfuglien/24 50.00 125.00
PDD Drew Doughty/18 50.00 125.00
PDD David Desharnais/20 40.00 100.00
PDE Devan Dubnyk/20 50.00 125.00
PDH Dougie Hamilton/20 50.00 125.00
PDK Duncan Keith/22 50.00 125.00
PDP David Pastrnak/24 80.00 200.00
PDS Derek Stepan/17 50.00 125.00
PDS Daniel Sedin/20 50.00 125.00
PDU Matt Duchene/26 40.00 100.00
PEB Jordan Eberle/22 50.00 125.00
PEK Evander Kane/24 50.00 125.00
PEM Evgeni Malkin/30 125.00 300.00
PES Eric Staal/20 60.00 150.00
PFA Frederik Andersen/21 40.00 100.00
PFF Filip Forsberg/20 60.00 150.00
PGL Gabriel Landeskog/27 40.00 100.00
PGN Gustav Nyquist/16 50.00 125.00
PGR Mikael Granlund/18 40.00 100.00
PHA Jaroslav Halak/22 40.00 100.00
PHL Henrik Lundqvist/18 60.00 150.00
PHO Marian Hossa/23 40.00 100.00
PHO Braden Holtby/18 80.00 200.00
PHS Henrik Sedin/20 50.00 125.00
PHU Jonathan Huberdeau/24 50.00 125.00
PHZ Henrik Zetterberg/17 60.00 150.00
PJA Jake Allen/19 60.00 150.00
PJB Jonathan Bernier/14
PJC John Carlson/21 60.00 150.00
PJE Jack Eichel/22 80.00 200.00
PJF Justin Faulk/19 50.00 125.00
PJG Johnny Gaudreau/20 80.00 200.00
PJH Jiri Hudler/20 40.00 100.00
PJI Jarome Iginla/24 50.00 125.00
PJJ Jaromir Jagr/22 120.00 300.00
PJK John Klingberg/19 40.00 100.00
PJO Jack Johnson/21 30.00 80.00
PJP Joe Pavelski/25 50.00 125.00
PJQ Jonathan Quick/16 80.00 200.00
PJR James van Riemsdyk/16 50.00 125.00
PJS Jakob Silfverberg/21 40.00 100.00
PJT Jacob Trouba/19 40.00 100.00
PJV Jakub Voracek/19 50.00 125.00
PJZ Jason Zucker/18 40.00 100.00
PKA Erik Karlsson/22 100.00 250.00
PKA Nazem Kadri/16 40.00 100.00
PKE Phil Kessel/29 60.00 150.00
PKH Kevin Hayes/19 50.00 125.00
PKL Kris Letang/30 40.00 100.00
PKS Kevin Shattenkirk/20 40.00 100.00
PKT Kyle Turris/23 40.00 100.00
PKU Evgeny Kuznetsov/20 80.00 200.00
PLE Loui Eriksson/24 40.00 100.00
PMB Matt Beleskey/20 30.00 80.00
PMC Michael Cammalleri/26 30.00 80.00
PMC Mike Condon/20 50.00 125.00
PMD Max Domi/26 80.00 200.00
PMF Marc-Andre Fleury/30 60.00 150.00
PMG Marian Gaborik/16 50.00 125.00
PMH Martin Hanzal/24 30.00 80.00
PMI Mike Hoffman/23 40.00 100.00
PMJ Martin Jones/21 50.00 125.00
PMP Max Pacioretty/19 50.00 125.00
PMR Michael Raffl/18 30.00 80.00
PMS Mike Smith/24 50.00 125.00
PMS Mark Scheifele/22 60.00 150.00
PNA Rick Nash/14
PNE Nikolaj Ehlers/20 100.00 250.00
PNF Nick Foligno/20 40.00 100.00
PNH Noah Hanifin/20 60.00 150.00
PNK Nikita Kucherov/20 80.00 200.00
PNL Nick Leddy/22 30.00 80.00
PNN Nino Niederreiter/18 30.00 80.00
POE Oliver Ekman-Larsson/22 40.00 100.00
PON Owen Nolan/27 30.00 80.00
POP Ondrej Palat/20 40.00 100.00
PPB Patrice Bergeron/20 60.00 150.00
PPE Patrik Elias/23 50.00 125.00
PPK Patrick Kane/24 100.00 250.00
PPM Petr Mrazek/17 60.00 150.00
PPM Patrick Marleau/22 50.00 125.00
PPR Pekka Rinne/19 60.00 150.00
PPS Patrick Sharp/18 50.00 125.00

PMPPT Pierre Turgeon/24 50.00 125.00
PMPRG Ryan Getzlaf/21 80.00 200.00
PMPRJ Roman Josi/20 50.00 125.00
PMPRK Ryan Kesler/26 40.00 100.00
PMPRL Roberto Luongo/29 40.00 100.00
PMPRM Ryan Miller/19 50.00 125.00
PMPRN Ryan Nugent-Hopkins/24 50.00 125.00
PMPRO Ryan O'Reilly/24 50.00 125.00
PMPRR Rasmus Ristolainen/24 40.00 100.00
PMPRS Ryan Strome/24 40.00 100.00
PMPSB Sam Bennett/18 60.00 150.00
PMPSK Jeff Skinner/20 40.00 100.00
PMPSM Steve Mason/18 40.00 100.00
PMPSM Sean Monahan/22 50.00 125.00
PMPSP Jason Spezza/21 40.00 100.00
PMPSR Sam Reinhart/22 50.00 125.00
PMPSS Steven Stamkos/22 100.00 250.00
PMPST Mark Stone/22 40.00 100.00
PMPSU P.K. Subban/18 80.00 200.00
PMPSV Semyon Varlamov/26 40.00 100.00
PMPSW Shea Weber/20 40.00 100.00
PMPTH Taylor Hall/22 100.00 250.00
PMPTJ Tyler Johnson/22 40.00 100.00
PMPTO Tyler Toffoli/18 50.00 125.00
PMPTO T.J. Oshie/20 80.00 200.00
PMPTR Tuukka Rask/24 50.00 125.00
PMPTR Tuukka Rask/22 50.00 125.00
PMPTS Tyler Seguin/18 80.00 200.00
PMPTT Tomas Tatar/19 40.00 100.00
PMPVH Victor Hedman/21 60.00 150.00
PMPVI Jake Virtanen/19 60.00 150.00
PMPVT Vladimir Tarasenko/19 80.00 200.00
PMPWS Wayne Simmonds/18 60.00 150.00
PMPZP Zach Parise/20 50.00 125.00

2015-16 Upper Deck Premier Mega Patch Duos

PMP2BE P.Bergeron/L.Eriksson 25.00 60.00
PMP2BJ P.Bure/J.Jagr 50.00 120.00
PMP2BS B.Saad/S.Hartnell 20.00 50.00
PMP2BT B.Bourne/J.Tavares 40.00 100.00
PMP2CM E.Malkin/P.Coffey 60.00 150.00
PMP2DZ H.Zetterberg/P.Datsyuk 25.00 60.00
PMP2GS C.Giroux/W.Simmonds 25.00 60.00
PMP2HB J.Huberdeau/A.Barkov 20.00 50.00
PMP2HC M.Cammalleri/A.Henrique 20.00 50.00
PMP2HD T.Hall/L.Draisaitl 40.00 100.00
PMP2ID M.Duchene/J.Iginla 20.00 50.00
PMP2KH E.Karlsson/M.Hoffman 40.00 100.00
PMP2KP C.Perry/R.Kesler 20.00 50.00
PMP2KT A.Kopitar/T.Toffoli 30.00 80.00
PMP2LD A.Duclair/O.Ekman-Larsson 15.00 40.00
PMP2LS B.Wheeler/M.Scheifele 25.00 60.00
PMP2MG J.Gaudreau/S.Monahan 30.00 80.00
PMP2MK E.Malkin/P.Kessel 60.00 150.00
PMP2MP J.Pavelski/P.Marleau 20.00 50.00
PMP2NT O.Nolan/J.Thornton 20.00 50.00
PMP2NZ M.Zuccarello/R.Nash 20.00 50.00
PMP2OB A.Ovechkin/N.Backstrom 80.00 200.00
PMP2OR R.O'Reilly/S.Reinhart 20.00 50.00
PMP2PS M.Pacioretty/P.Subban 30.00 80.00
PMP2SB J.Benn/P.Sharp 25.00 60.00
PMP2SK N.Kucherov/S.Stamkos 40.00 100.00
PMP2SS D.Sedin/H.Sedin 20.00 50.00
PMP2ST V.Tarasenko/A.Steen 30.00 80.00
PMP2TK P.Kane/J.Toews 40.00 100.00
PMP2TL J.Tavares/A.Lee 40.00 100.00
PMP2VK J.van Riemsdyk/N.Kadri 15.00 40.00
PMP2WJ R.Josi/S.Weber 20.00 50.00

2015-16 Upper Deck Premier Mega Patch Trios

PMP3BRE Bergeron/Rask/Eriksson/25 30.00 80.00
PMP3DML Duchene MacKinnon/Landeskog/25 50.00 125.00
PMP3HGM Hamilton/Gaudreau Monahan/25 40.00 100.00
PMP3KLS Karlsson/Ekman-Larsson Subban/25 50.00 125.00
PMP3KQT Kopitar/Quick/Toffoli/25 40.00 100.00
PMP3MZT Mrazek/Zetterberg/Tatar/25 30.00 80.00
PMP3NLK Nash/Lundqvist/Kreider/25 30.00 80.00
PMP3PGK Perry/Getzlaf/Kesler/25 40.00 100.00
PMP3PTM Pavelski/Thornton/Marleau/25 25.0060.00
PMP3SSB Sharp/Seguin/Benn/25 40.00 100.00
PMP3ZYD Zetterberg/Yzerman Datsyuk/25 40.00 100.00

2015-16 Upper Deck Premier Mega Stick Duos

PMS2BB R.Bourque/P.Bergeron 40.00 100.00
PMS2CH B.Clarke/R.Hextall 25.00 60.00
PMS2CS G.Carbonneau/D.Savard 30.00 80.00
PMS2DZ P.Datsyuk/H.Zetterberg 30.00 80.00
PMS2EH T.Esposito/B.Hull 25.00 60.00
PMS2GM W.Gretzky/M.Messier 120.00 300.00
PMS2HH D.Hawerchuk/D.Hasek 30.00 80.00
PMS2MG L.McDonald/D.Gilmour 30.00 80.00
PMS2OC A.Ovechkin/J.Carlson 100.00 250.00
PMS2RB L.Robinson/R.Blake 25.00 60.00
PMS2RH L.Robitaille/B.Hull 30.00 80.00
PMS2SF J.Sakic/P.Forsberg 40.00 100.00
PMS2YC S.Yzerman/C.Chelios 40.00 100.00

2015-16 Upper Deck Premier Mega Stick Trios

PMS3GOC Gartner/Ovechkin Carlson/30 100.00 250.00

2015-16 Upper Deck Premier Premier Duals Jerseys

PD2BE P.Bergeron/L.Eriksson/149 10.00 25.00
PD2BS P.Bure/H.Sedin/49 15.00 40.00
PD2CH B.Holtby/C.Crawford/149 12.00 30.00
PD2DB M.Domi/S.Bennett/149 15.00 40.00
PD2DL M.Duchene/G.Landeskog/149 8.00 20.00
PD2EP J.Eichel/A.Panarin/149 30.00 80.00
PD2GH J.Gaudreau/D.Hamilton/149 12.00 30.00
PD2GL W.Gretzky/M.Lemieux/49 50.00 120.00
PD2HB B.Hull/D.Backes/149 8.00 20.00
PD2HC C.Hellebuyck/M.Condon/149 20.00 50.00
PD2HJ J.Huberdeau/J.Jagr/149 20.00 50.00
PD2KK P.Kane/D.Keith/149 15.00 40.00
PD2MK E.Malkin/P.Kessel/149 25.00 60.00
PD2ML C.McDavid/D.Larkin/49 80.00 200.00
PD2NM O.Nolan/P.Marleau/49 10.00 25.00
PD2OK A.Ovechkin/E.Kuznetsov/149 30.00 80.00
PD2PK C.Perry/R.Kesler/149 8.00 20.00
PD2PR C.Price/T.Rask/149 25.00 60.00
PD2PS M.Pacioretty/P.Subban/149 12.00 30.00
PD2RE N.Ritchie/N.Ehlers/149 15.00 40.00
PD2RK J.van Riemsdyk/N.Kadri/149 6.00 15.00
PD2SB T.Seguin/J.Benn/149 12.00 30.00
PD2SK S.Stamkos/N.Kucherov/149 15.00 40.00
PD2SM D.Sedin/R.Miller/149 8.00 20.00
PD2TS V.Tarasenko/A.Steen/149 12.00 30.00
PD2ZD H.Zetterberg/P.Datsyuk/149 10.00 25.00

2015-16 Upper Deck Premier Premier Quads Jerseys

PQ4BCLR Bure/Coffey/LeClair/Robinson/15
PQ4BSKS Benn/Seguin/Klingberg Sharp/65 20.00 50.00
PQ4GMBH Gaudreau/Monahan Bennett/Hamilton/65 20.00 50.00
PQ4JHBL Jagr/Huberdeau Barkov/Luongo/65 30.00 80.00
PQ4KTCD Kopitar/Toffoli Carter/Doughty/65 20.00 50.00
PQ4MELD McDavid/Eichel/Larkin/Domi/15
PQ4MHHD McDavid/Hall/Nugent-Hopkins/Draisaitl/15
PQ4MKLF Malkin/Kessel Letang/Fleury/65 40.00 100.00
PQ4MRRZ McCann/Rantanen Ritchie/Fucale/65 25.00 60.00
PQ4OBKH Ovechkin/Backstrom Kuznetsov/Holtby/65 50.00 125.00
PQ4PBVE Panarin/Bennett Virtanen/Ehlers/65 40.00 100.00
PQ4PSGG Pacioretty/Subban Galchenyuk/Gallagher/65 20.00 50.00
PQ4TKSK Toews/Kane/Seabrook/Keith/65 25.0060.00
PQ4TSLH Tavares/Strome/Lee/Halak/65 25.00 60.00
PQ4TSSB Tarasenko/Steen Shattenkirk/Backes/65 20.00 50.00
PQ4ZDTN Zetterberg/Datsyuk Tatar/Nyquist/65 15.00 40.00

2015-16 Upper Deck Premier Premier Rookie Materials

PRMAA Andreas Athanasiou 40.00 100.00
PRMAP Artemi Panarin 50.00 120.00
PRMBG Brendan Gaunce 20.00 50.00
PRMBH Ben Hutton 15.00 40.00
PRMBM Brock McGinn 15.00 40.00
PRMCH Connor Hellebuyck 40.00 100.00
PRMCM Connor McDavid 120.00 300.00
PRMCP Colton Parayko 20.00 50.00
PRMDL Dylan Larkin 50.00 120.00
PRMDS Daniel Sprong 30.00 80.00
PRMHS Hunter Shinkaruk 15.00 40.00
PRMJE Jack Eichel 60.00 150.00
PRMJM Jared McCann 15.00 40.00
PRMJV Jake Virtanen 20.00 50.00
PRMLU Linus Ullmark 20.00 50.00
PRMMD Max Domi 30.00 80.00
PRMMI Colin Miller 12.00 30.00
PRMMJ Mattias Janmark 15.00 40.00
PRMMR Mikko Rantanen 30.00 80.00
PRMNE Nikolaj Ehlers 30.00 80.00
PRMNG Nikolay Goldobin 15.00 40.00
PRMNH Noah Hanifin 20.00 50.00
PRMNP Nicolas Petan 15.00 40.00
PRMNR Nick Ritchie 15.00 40.00
PRMNS Nick Shore 15.00 40.00
PRMOL Oscar Lindberg 15.00 40.00
PRMRF Robby Fabbri 20.00 50.00
PRMSB Sam Bennett 20.00 50.00
PRMST Shea Theodore 15.00 40.00
PRMZF Zachary Fucale 15.00 40.00

2015-16 Upper Deck Premier Premier Signatures

PSAE Aaron Ekblad A 15.00 40.00
PSEM Evgeni Malkin A 50.00 125.00
PSJA Jake Allen B 12.00 30.00
PSJD Jonathan Drouin B 12.00 30.00
PSJG Johnny Gaudreau B 15.00 40.00
PSJP Joe Pavelski B 10.00 25.00
PSJT Jonathan Toews A 30.00 80.00
PSKH Kevin Hayes B 10.00 25.00
PSMS Mark Stone B 8.00 20.00
PSPD Pavel Datsyuk A 20.00 50.00
PSTT Tyler Toffoli B 10.00 25.00
PSZP Zach Parise A 15.00 40.00

2015-16 Upper Deck Premier Premier Signatures Legends

LPSBO Bobby Orr C 80.00 150.00
LPSBS Borje Salming
(inserted in 2016-17 Premier)
LPSGH Glenn Hall C 12.00 30.00
LPSGL Guy Lafleur A 25.00 60.00
LPSJK Jari Kurri C 15.00 40.00
LPSJS Joe Sakic A 30.00 80.00
LPSLR Larry Robinson C 15.00 40.00
LPSMB Mike Bossy B 15.00 40.00
LPSMM Mike Modano B 25.00 60.00
LPSNL Nicklas Lidstrom B 15.00 40.00
LPSPC Paul Coffey B 15.00 40.00
LPSPE Phil Esposito A 30.00 80.00
LPSRO Luc Robitaille B 20.00 50.00
LPSTL Mario Lemieux A 60.00 150.00
LPSWG Wayne Gretzky C 150.00 300.00

2015-16 Upper Deck Premier Premier Signatures Rookies

RPSCM Connor McDavid A 150.00 400.00
RPSCP Colton Parayko C 10.00 25.00
RPSDL Dylan Larkin
(inserted in 2016-17 Premier)
RPSJM Jared McCann C 8.00 20.00
RPSJV Jake Virtanen B 12.00 30.00
RPSLU Linus Ullmark C 10.00 25.00
RPSMC Mike Condon C 8.00 20.00
RPSNE Nikolaj Ehlers C 15.00 40.00
RPSNR Nick Ritchie C 8.00 20.00
RPSOL Oscar Lindberg C 8.00 20.00
RPSRF Robby Fabbri C 10.00 25.00
RPSSB Sam Bennett B 12.00 30.00
RPSZF Zachary Fucale C 8.00 20.00

2015-16 Upper Deck Premier Premier Swatches

PSAS Alexander Steen 6.00 15.00
PSBB Brent Burns 8.00 20.00
PSBH Braden Holtby 10.00 25.00
PSBS Brandon Saad 6.00 15.00
PSCC Corey Crawford 8.00 20.00
PSCH Chris Chelios 6.00 15.00
PSCP Corey Perry 6.00 15.00
PSDH Dougie Hamilton 6.00 15.00
PSDS Daniel Sedin 6.00 15.00
PSEM Evgeni Malkin 20.00 50.00
PSJF Justin Faulk 6.00 15.00
PSJJ Jaromir Jagr 15.00 40.00
PSKU Nikita Kucherov 10.00 25.00
PSMC Michael Cammalleri 5.00 12.00
PSMD Matt Duchene 6.00 15.00
PSMP Max Pacioretty 6.00 15.00
PSMS Mark Scheifele 8.00 20.00
PSMZ Mats Zuccarello 5.00 12.00
PSNB Nicklas Backstrom 10.00 25.00
PSNK Nazem Kadri 5.00 12.00
PSON Owen Nolan 5.00 12.00
PSPB Patrice Bergeron 8.00 20.00
PSPC Paul Coffey 6.00 15.00
PSPK Patrick Kane 12.00 30.00
PSPS Patrick Sharp 6.00 15.00
PSRJ Roman Josi 6.00 15.00
PSRN Ryan Nugent-Hopkins 6.00 15.00
PSTS Tyler Seguin 10.00 25.00
PSTT Tyler Toffoli 6.00 15.00
PSZP Zach Parise 6.00 15.00

2015-16 Upper Deck Premier Premier Teammates Jerseys

PT3BJE Barkov/Jagr/Ekblad/25 25.00 60.00
PT3BRE Bergeron/Rask/Eriksson/99 8.00 20.00
PT3BSS Benn/Seguin/Spezza/25 15.00 40.00
PT3BWS Byfuglien/Wheeler/Scheifele/99 8.00 20.00
PT3CHS Cammalleri/Henrique Schneider/99 6.00 15.00
PT3HSF Hartnell/Saad/Foligno/99 6.00 15.00
PT3JFW Josi/Forsberg/Weber/99 8.00 20.00
PT3KHT Karlsson/Hoffman/Turris/99 12.00 30.00
PT3KQG Kopitar/Quick/Gaborik/25 15.00 40.00
PT3KSH Kucherov/Stamkos/Hedman/99 12.00 30.00
PT3NLK Nash/Lundqvist/Kreider/99 8.00 20.00
PT3OOC Oshie/Ovechkin/Carlson/25 40.00 100.00
PT3ORR O'Reilly/Ristolainen/Reinhart/99 6.00 15.00
PT3PGK Perry/Getzlaf/Kesler/99 10.00 25.00
PT3PMB Pavelski/Marleau/Burns/99 8.00 20.00
PT3SFS Staal/Faulk/Skinner/99 8.00 20.00
PT3SLH Smith/Ekman-Larsson/Hanzal/99 6.00 15.00
PT3TCH Toews/Crawford/Hossa/25 20.00 50.00
PT3VGS Voracek/Giroux/Simmonds/99 8.00 20.00

2015-16 Upper Deck Premier Rookies

R1 Nick Ritchie 5.00 12.00
R2 Andreas Athanasiou 12.00 30.00
R3 Jared McCann 5.00 12.00
R4 Andrew Copp 5.00 12.00
R5 Kevin Fiala 5.00 12.00
R6 Matt Puempel 4.00 10.00
R7 Colin Miller 4.00 10.00
R8 Daniel Sprong 10.00 25.00
R9 Nikolay Goldobin 5.00 12.00
R10 Mikko Rantanen 10.00 25.00
R11 Antoine Bibeau 5.00 12.00
R12 Mike McCarron 6.00 15.00
R13 Chandler Stephenson 5.00 12.00
R14 Connor Hellebuyck 12.00 30.00
R15 Oscar Lindberg 5.00 12.00
R16 Vincent Hinostroza 3.00 8.00
R17 Linus Ullmark 6.00 15.00
R18 Shea Theodore 5.00 12.00
R19 Charles Hudon 5.00 12.00
R20 Malcolm Subban 12.00 30.00
R21 Slater Koekkoek 4.00 10.00
R22 Emile Poirier 5.00 12.00
R23 Brendan Gaunce 6.00 15.00
R24 Henrik Samuelsson 4.00 10.00
R25 Colton Parayko 6.00 15.00
R26 Brady Skjei 4.00 10.00
R27 Nick Cousins 5.00 12.00
R28 Mackenzie Skapski 5.00 12.00
R29 Shane Prince 4.00 10.00
R30 Noah Hanifin 6.00 15.00
R31 Nicolas Petan 5.00 12.00
R32 Brock McGinn 5.00 12.00
R33 Jacob de la Rose 5.00 12.00
R34 Ronalds Kenins 5.00 12.00
R35 Hunter Shinkaruk 5.00 12.00
R36 Derek Forbort 4.00 10.00
R37 Ryan Hartman 6.00 15.00
R38 Gustav Olofsson 5.00 12.00
R39 Stefan Noesen 4.00 10.00
R40 Mike Condon 5.00 12.00
R41 Jack Eichel 25.00 60.00
R42 Artemi Panarin 20.00 50.00
R43 Jake Virtanen 8.00 20.00
R44 Max Domi 12.00 30.00
R45 Sam Bennett 8.00 20.00
R46 Robby Fabbri 8.00 20.00
R47 Connor McDavid 50.00 120.00
R48 Nikolaj Ehlers 12.00 30.00
R49 Zachary Fucale 6.00 15.00
R50 Dylan Larkin 20.00 50.00

2015-16 Upper Deck Premier Rookies Silver Spectrum

*SINGLES: 1.25X TO 3X BASIC INSERTS
R37 Ryan Hartman AU 20.00 50.00
R47 Connor McDavid AU 200.00 500.00

2015-16 Upper Deck Premier Signature Award Winners

SAAE Aaron Ekblad 15.00 40.00
SAAO Alexander Ovechkin 60.00 150.00
SABL Brian Leetch 15.00 40.00
SABO Bobby Orr 60.00 150.00
SACP Carey Price 50.00 125.00
SAJB Jamie Benn 20.00 50.00
SAJH Jiri Hudler
(inserted in 2016-17 Premier)
SAJI Jarome Iginla 15.00 40.00
SAJJ Jaromir Jagr 40.00 100.00
SAMB Martin Brodeur 30.00 80.00
SAMS Martin St. Louis 15.00 40.00
SANM Nathan MacKinnon 30.00 80.00
SAPE Corey Perry 15.00 40.00
SARB Rod Brind'Amour 12.00 30.00
SARO Ryan O'Reilly
(inserted in 2016-17 Premier)
SASC Sidney Crosby 60.00 150.00
SASY Steve Yzerman 25.00 60.00
SAWG Wayne Gretzky 200.00 350.00

2015-16 Upper Deck Premier Signature Champions

SCAK Anze Kopitar 25.00 60.00
SCBL Brian Leetch 15.00 40.00
SCBO Bobby Orr 60.00 150.00
SCCP Corey Perry 15.00 40.00
SCEM Evgeni Malkin 50.00 125.00
SCES Eric Staal 20.00 50.00
SCGL Guy Lafleur 20.00 50.00
SCJS Joe Sakic 25.00 60.00
SCJT Jonathan Toews 30.00 80.00
SCLM Lanny McDonald 15.00 40.00
SCMB Martin Brodeur 30.00 80.00
SCML Mario Lemieux 50.00 120.00
SCMM Mike Modano 25.00 60.00
SCPD Pavel Datsyuk 20.00 50.00
SCPK Patrick Kane
(inserted in 2016-17 Premier)
SCSC Sidney Crosby 60.00 150.00
SCSY Steve Yzerman 25.00 60.00
SCTS Teemu Selanne 30.00 80.00
SCWG Wayne Gretzky 200.00 400.00

2015-16 Upper Deck Premier Stars Autograph Patches

SAG Alex Galchenyuk/99 50.00 120.00
SAK Anze Kopitar/49 80.00 200.00
SAO Alexander Ovechkin/25
SBH Brett Hull/49 50.00 125.00
SCP Carey Price/49 150.00 400.00
SEM Evgeni Malkin/49 150.00 400.00
SJG Johnny Gaudreau/99 60.00 150.00
SJR Jeremy Roenick/99 40.00 100.00
SJS Joe Sakic/49 80.00 200.00
SJT Jonathan Toews/49 100.00 250.00
SNM Nathan MacKinnon/99 80.00 200.00
SPO Patrick Roy/25
SSC Sidney Crosby/25
SSY Steve Yzerman/25
STS Tyler Seguin/99 60.00 150.00
SWG Wayne Gretzky/25

2016-17 Upper Deck Premier

1 Sidney Crosby 5.00 12.00
2 Carey Price 4.00 10.00
3 Mika Zibanejad 1.25 3.00
4 Steven Stamkos 2.50 6.00
5 John Tavares 2.50 6.00
6 P.K. Subban 2.00 5.00
7 Mark Stone 1.25 3.00
8 Jamie Benn 1.50 4.00
9 Anze Kopitar 2.00 5.00
10 Jonathan Toews 2.50 6.00
11 Connor McDavid 6.00 15.00
12 Zach Parise 1.25 3.00
13 Loui Eriksson 1.25 3.00
14 Max Domi 1.50 4.00
15 Alexander Ovechkin 5.00 12.00
16 Joe Thornton 1.25 3.00
17 David Backes 1.25 3.00
18 Rasmus Ristolainen 1.00 2.50
19 Henrik Zetterberg 1.50 4.00
20 Roberto Luongo 1.25 3.00
21 Johnny Gaudreau 2.00 5.00
22 Corey Perry 1.25 3.00
23 Matt Duchene 1.25 3.00
24 Patrick Kane 2.50 6.00
25 Teuvo Teravainen 1.25 3.00
26 Andrew Shaw 1.25 3.00
27 Evgeni Malkin 4.00 10.00
28 Vladimir Tarasenko 2.00 5.00
29 Mark Scheifele 1.50 4.00
30 Henrik Lundqvist 1.25 3.00
31 Jakub Voracek 1.25 3.00
32 Boone Jenner 1.25 3.00
33 Roman Josi 1.25 3.00
34 Taylor Hall 2.50 6.00
35 Marcus Johansson 1.25 3.00
36 Frederik Andersen 1.00 2.50
37 Alex Galchenyuk 1.50 4.00
38 Jaromir Jagr 3.00 8.00
39 Jonathan Drouin 1.50 4.00
40 Matt Murray 2.00 5.00
41 Bobby Orr 4.00 10.00
42 Pat LaFontaine 1.25 3.00
43 Paul Coffey 1.25 3.00
44 Igor Larionov 1.25 3.00
45 Mario Lemieux 4.00 10.00
46 Darryl Sittler 1.25 3.00
47 Trevor Linden 1.50 4.00
48 Steve Yzerman 1.50 4.00
49 Martin Brodeur 2.50 6.00
50 Wayne Gretzky 6.00 15.00
52 Sergey Tolchinsky AU/399 RC 6.00 15.00
54 Daniel Altshuller AU/399 RC 6.00 15.00
55 Danton Heinen AU/399 RC 12.00 30.00
57 Brandon Montour AU/399 RC 8.00 20.00
58 Mark Jankowski AU/399 RC 6.00 15.00
59 Timo Meier AU/399 RC 8.00 20.00
60 Jake Guentzel AU/399 RC 30.00 80.00
61 J.C. Lipon AU/399 RC 8.00 20.00
62 Justin Bailey AU/399 RC 8.00 20.00
63 Brandon Carlo AU/399 RC 8.00 20.00
64 Mike Reilly AU/399 RC 6.00 15.00
66 Sebastian Aho JSY AU/299 RC 25.00 60.00
67 Christian Dvorak JSY AU/299 RC 12.00 30.00
68 Oskar Sundqvist JSY AU/299 RC 12.00 30.00
69 Brayden Point JSY AU/299 RC 30.00 80.00
70 Matthew Tkachuk JSY AU/299 RC 40.00 100.00
73 Thomas Chabot JSY AU/299 RC 25.00 60.00
74 Brendan Leipsic JSY AU/299 RC 12.00 30.00
75 Kyle Connor JSY AU/299 RC 30.00 80.00
76 Hudson Fasching JSY AU/299 RC 12.00 30.00
77 Jakob Chychrun JSY AU/299 RC 12.00 30.00
78 Anthony DeAngelo JSY AU/299 RC 12.00 30.00
79 Oliver Bjorkstrand JSY AU/299 RC 10.00 25.00
80 Dylan Strome JSY AU/299 RC 25.00 60.00
81 Sonny Milano JSY AU/299 RC 15.00 40.00
82 Kasperi Kapanen JSY AU/299 RC 25.00 60.00
83 Tyler Motte JSY AU/299 RC 12.00 30.00
84 Oliver Kylington JSY AU/299 RC 10.00 25.00
85 Pavel Zacha JSY AU/299 RC 15.00 40.00
87 Lawson Crouse JSY AU/299 RC 10.00 25.00
88 Zach Werenski JSY AU/299 RC 25.00 60.00
89 Michael Matheson JSY AU/299 RC 12.00 30.00
90 Anthony Beauvillier JSY AU/299 RC 12.00 30.00
91 Mikhail Sergachev JSY AU/299 RC 25.00 60.00
92 Travis Konecny JSY AU/299 RC 25.00 60.00
93 Nikita Soshnikov JSY AU/299 RC 8.00 20.00
95 Anthony Mantha JSY AU/299 RC 30.00 80.00
96 Ryan Pulock JSY AU/299 RC 12.00 30.00
97 Nick Schmaltz JSY AU/299 RC 12.00 30.00
99 Mathew Barzal JSY AU/299 RC 60.00 150.00
100 Josh Morrissey JSY AU/299 RC 15.00 40.00
102 Connor Brown JSY AU/299 RC 20.00 50.00
103 Jesse Puljujarvi JSY AU/299 RC 30.00 80.00
104 Mitch Marner JSY AU/199 RC 150.00 300.00
105 Jimmy Vesey JSY AU/199 RC 25.00 60.00
106 William Nylander JSY AU/199 RC 50.00 125.00
107 Patrik Laine JSY AU/199 RC 150.00 300.00
108 Auston Matthews JSY AU/199 RC 500.00 900.00
NNO1 TBD Rookie AU/399
NNO2 TBD Rookie JSY AU/299

2016-17 Upper Deck Premier '02-03 Tribute Rookies Autograph Patches

SRVAE Aaron Ekblad/25 20.00 50.00
SRVAK Anze Kopitar/25 80.00 150.00
SRVAO Alexander Ovechkin/15 150.00 250.00
SRVCM Connor McDavid/15
SRVEM Evgeni Malkin/25 40.00 100.00
SRVHZ Henrik Zetterberg/25 60.00 150.00
SRVJT Joe Thornton/25 30.00 80.00
SRVLD Leon Draisaitl/25 80.00 150.00
SRVML Mario Lemieux/15 300.00 400.00
SRVMM Matt Murray/25 300.00 400.00
SRVPK Patrick Kane/15 100.00 200.00
SRVRB Ray Bourque/25 40.00 100.00
SRVSM Sean Monahan/25 30.00 80.00
SRVSY Steve Yzerman/15 150.00 250.00

2016-17 Upper Deck Premier '03-04 Tribute Rookies Autograph Patches

SSRAD Anthony DeAngelo 20.00 50.00
SSRAM Auston Matthews 500.00 1000.00
SSRCB Connor Brown 30.00 80.00
SSRCD Christian Dvorak 20.00 50.00
SSRDS Dylan Strome 40.00 100.00
SSRIP Ivan Provorov 40.00 100.00
SSRJC Jakob Chychrun 20.00 50.00
SSRJP Jesse Puljujarvi 50.00 125.00
SSRJR Jakub Vrana 20.00 50.00
SSRJV Jimmy Vesey 40.00 100.00
SSRKC Kyle Connor 50.00 120.00
SSRKK Kasperi Kapanen 30.00 80.00
SSRLC Lawson Crouse 15.00 40.00
SSRMA Anthony Mantha 50.00 120.00
SSRMB Mathew Barzal 60.00 150.00
SSRME Timo Meier 20.00 50.00
SSRMM Mitch Marner 100.00 250.00
SSRMS Mikhail Sergachev 40.00 100.00
SSRMT Matthew Tkachuk 60.00 150.00
SSRPB Pavel Buchnevich 30.00 80.00
SSRPL Patrik Laine 200.00 400.00
SSRPZ Pavel Zacha 25.00 60.00
SSRSA Sebastian Aho 40.00 100.00
SSRTC Thomas Chabot 40.00 100.00
SSRTK Travis Konecny 40.00 100.00
SSRTM Tyler Motte 20.00 50.00
SSRWN William Nylander 80.00 200.00
SSRZW Zach Werenski 40.00 100.00

2016-17 Upper Deck Premier Acetate Stars Autograph Patches

ASCM Connor McDavid/25 400.00 600.00
ASGL Guy Lafleur/49 80.00 150.00
ASHL Henrik Lundqvist/49 50.00 125.00
ASHZ Henrik Zetterberg/49 30.00 80.00
ASJJ Jaromir Jagr/49 150.00 250.00
ASPK Patrick Kane/49 80.00 200.00
ASSC Sidney Crosby/25 300.00 400.00
ASSY Steve Yzerman/25 250.00 350.00
ASWG Wayne Gretzky/25 400.00 600.00

2016-17 Upper Deck Premier Inked Script

INFP Felix Potvin/99 25.00 60.00
INGL Guy Lafleur/25 40.00 100.00
INHL Henrik Lundqvist/25 30.00 80.00
INIL Igor Larionov/99 20.00 50.00
INJP Jesse Puljujarvi/99 25.00 60.00
INJT Joe Thornton/25 30.00 80.00
INLD Leon Draisaitl/99 40.00 100.00
INLM Lanny McDonald/25 25.00 60.00
INMD Marcel Dionne/25 30.00 80.00
INPA Joe Pavelski/99 15.00 40.00
INPK Patrick Kane/25 50.00 120.00
INPL Patrik Laine/25 150.00 250.00
INTL Trevor Linden/25 30.00 80.00
INWC Wendel Clark/25 20.00 50.00

2016-17 Upper Deck Premier Jerseys

1 Sidney Crosby/199 10.00 25.00
2 Carey Price/199 8.00 20.00
3 Mika Zibanejad/199 2.50 6.00
4 Steven Stamkos/199 5.00 12.00
5 John Tavares/199 5.00 12.00
6 P.K. Subban/199 4.00 10.00
7 Mark Stone/199 2.50 6.00
8 Jamie Benn/199 3.00 8.00
9 Anze Kopitar/199 4.00 10.00
10 Jonathan Toews/199 5.00 12.00
11 Connor McDavid/199 25.00 60.00
12 Zach Parise/199 2.50 6.00
13 Loui Eriksson/199 2.50 6.00
14 Max Domi/199 3.00 8.00
15 Alexander Ovechkin/199 10.00 25.00
16 Joe Thornton/199 2.50 6.00
17 David Backes/199 2.50 6.00
18 Rasmus Ristolainen/199 2.00 5.00
19 Henrik Zetterberg/199 3.00 8.00
20 Roberto Luongo/199 2.50 6.00
21 Johnny Gaudreau/199 4.00 10.00
22 Corey Perry/199 2.50 6.00
23 Matt Duchene/199 2.50 6.00
24 Patrick Kane/199 5.00 12.00
25 Teuvo Teravainen/199 2.50 6.00
26 Andrew Shaw/199 2.50 6.00
27 Evgeni Malkin/199 8.00 20.00
28 Vladimir Tarasenko/199 4.00 10.00
29 Mark Scheifele/199 3.00 8.00
30 Henrik Lundqvist/199 2.50 6.00
31 Jakub Voracek/199 2.50 6.00
32 Boone Jenner/199 2.50 6.00
33 Roman Josi/199 2.50 6.00
34 Taylor Hall/199 5.00 12.00
36 Frederik Andersen/199 2.00 5.00
37 Alex Galchenyuk/199 3.00 8.00
38 Jaromir Jagr/199 6.00 15.00
39 Jonathan Drouin/199 3.00 8.00
40 Matt Murray/199 4.00 10.00
44 Igor Larionov/99 2.50 6.00
45 Mario Lemieux/25 15.00 40.00
48 Steve Yzerman/25 15.00 40.00
49 Martin Brodeur/49
50 Wayne Gretzky/25 30.00 80.00

2016-17 Upper Deck Premier Mega Patch Chest Logos

PMPAB Justin Abdelkader/18 30.00 80.00
PMPAE Aaron Ekblad/22 25.00 60.00
PMPAG Alex Galchenyuk/19 30.00 80.00
PMPAH Adam Henrique/26 25.00 60.00
PMPAK Anze Kopitar/18 40.00 100.00
PMPAL Andrew Ladd/24 25.00 60.00
PMPAM Auston Matthews/25 250.00 600.00
PMPAP Artemi Panarin/23 30.00 80.00
PMPAS Andrew Shaw/19 25.00 60.00
PMPAW Alexander Wennberg/21 20.00 50.00
PMPBB Brent Burns/23 30.00 80.00
PMPBE Brian Elliott/28 20.00 50.00
PMPBH Bo Horvat/32 40.00 100.00
PMPBI Ben Bishop/24 25.00 60.00
PMPBJ Boone Jenner/21 25.00 60.00
PMPBM Brad Marchand/24 30.00 80.00
PMPBN Brock Nelson/23 20.00 50.00
PMPBR Derick Brassard/18 25.00 60.00
PMPBU Andre Burakovsky/21 20.00 50.00
PMPCA Craig Anderson/18 25.00 60.00
PMPCG Claude Giroux/24 25.00 60.00
PMPCP Corey Perry/21 25.00 60.00
PMPDB David Backes/24 25.00 60.00
PMPDD Drew Doughty/18 25.00 60.00
PMPDL Dylan Larkin/18 40.00 100.00
PMPDP David Pastrnak/24 40.00 100.00
PMPDS Derek Stepan/19 20.00 50.00
PMPDU Matt Duchene/24 25.00 60.00
PMPEK Evgeny Kuznetsov/22 40.00 100.00
PMPES Eric Staal/19 30.00 80.00
PMPFN Frans Nielsen/19 20.00 50.00
PMPGA Brendan Gallagher/20 30.00 80.00
PMPHS Henrik Sedin/20 25.00 60.00
PMPHZ Henrik Zetterberg/18 30.00 80.00
PMPJA Jake Allen/20 30.00 80.00
PMPJB Jamie Benn/19 30.00 80.00
PMPJD Jonathan Drouin/25 30.00 80.00
PMPJG Johnny Gaudreau/26 40.00 100.00
PMPJJ Jaromir Jagr/22 60.00 150.00
PMPJN James Neal/21 20.00 50.00
PMPJP Jesse Puljujarvi/24 60.00 150.00
PMPJS Jason Spezza/19 25.00 60.00
PMPJT Jonathan Toews/23 50.00 125.00
PMPJV Jimmy Vesey/20 50.00 125.00
PMPKE Phil Kessel/28 30.00 80.00
PMPKL Kris Letang/28 25.00 60.00
PMPKO Kyle Okposo/24 25.00 60.00
PMPKP Kyle Palmieri/26 20.00 50.00
PMPLD Leon Draisaitl/24 30.00 80.00
PMPLE Loui Eriksson/31 25.00 60.00
PMPMD Max Domi/22 30.00 80.00
PMPMJ Martin Jones/23 25.00 60.00
PMPMK Mikko Koivu/21 20.00 50.00
PMPML Milan Lucic/24 20.00 50.00
PMPMM Mitch Marner/19 125.00 300.00
PMPMS Mark Stone/16 25.00 60.00
PMPMU Matt Murray/28 40.00 100.00
PMPMZ Mats Zuccarello/20 25.00 60.00
PMPNB Nicklas Backstrom/21 40.00 100.00
PMPNK Nikita Kucherov/24 40.00 100.00
PMPNM Nathan MacKinnon/27 50.00 125.00
PMPNN Nino Niederreiter/20 25.00 60.00
PMPOE Oliver Ekman-Larsson/23 20.00 50.00
PMPPA Joe Pavelski/23 25.00 60.00
PMPPE Tanner Pearson/18 20.00 50.00
PMPPK Patrick Kane/23 50.00 125.00
PMPPL Patrik Laine/24 100.00 250.00
PMPPS P.K. Subban/19 40.00 100.00
PMPRF Robby Fabbri/20 25.00 60.00
PMPRJ Ryan Johansen/19 30.00 80.00
PMPRK Ryan Kesler/21 25.00 60.00
PMPRO Ryan O'Reilly/20 25.00 60.00
PMPRR Rickard Rakell/21 25.00 60.00
PMPSC Mark Scheifele/24 30.00 80.00
PMPSG Shayne Gostisbehere/21 30.00 80.00
PMPSM Sean Monahan/26 25.00 60.00
PMPSR Sam Reinhart/24 20.00 50.00
PMPSS Steven Stamkos/24 50.00 125.00
PMPST Jordan Staal/21 25.00 60.00
PMPSW Shea Weber/19 20.00 50.00
PMPTA John Tavares/23 50.00 125.00
PMPTB Tyson Barrie/26 25.00 60.00
PMPTH Taylor Hall/26 50.00 125.00
PMPTK Torey Krug/28 25.00 60.00
PMPTR Vincent Trocheck/20 25.00 60.00
PMPTS Tyler Seguin/21 40.00 100.00
PMPTT Teuvo Teravainen/19 25.00 60.00
PMPVH Victor Hedman/23 30.00 80.00
PMPVR Victor Rask/19 20.00 50.00
PMPVT Vladimir Tarasenko/23 40.00 100.00
PMPWN William Nylander/20 100.00 250.00
PMPWS Wayne Simmonds/21 30.00 80.00
PMPZW Zach Werenski/21 50.00 125.00

2016-17 Upper Deck Premier Mega Patch Duos

PMP2BS P.Bure/H.Sedin 40.00 100.00
PMP2CD J.Carter/D.Doughty 20.00 50.00
PMP2DE M.Domi/O.Ekman-Larsson 25.00 60.00
PMP2EO J.Eichel/K.Okposo 40.00 100.00
PMP2ES L.Eriksson/D.Sedin 20.00 50.00
PMP2GB J.Gaudreau/S.Bennett 30.00 80.00
PMP2HP T.Hall/K.Palmieri 40.00 100.00
PMP2JT J.Benn/T.Seguin 30.00 80.00
PMP2KG R.Kesler/R.Getzlaf 30.00 80.00
PMP2KP P.Kane/A.Panarin 40.00 100.00
PMP2KT P.Kane/V.Tarasenko 40.00 100.00
PMP2LL H.Lundqvist/R.Luongo 20.00 50.00
PMP2MB B.Marchand/D.Backes 25.00 60.00
PMP2MD C.McDavid/L.Draisaitl 200.00 500.00
PMP2MK E.Malkin/P.Kessel 60.00 150.00
PMP2ML N.MacKinnon/G.Landeskog 40.00 100.00
PMP2NL F.Nielsen/D.Larkin 30.00 80.00
PMP2OM A.Ovechkin/E.Malkin 80.00 200.00
PMP2PC J.Pavelski/L.Couture 20.00 50.00
PMP2RK M.Rielly/N.Kadri 15.00 40.00
PMP2RS P.Roy/J.Sakic 50.00 125.00
PMP2SB P.Subban/B.Burns 30.00 80.00
PMP2SE M.Scheifele/N.Ehlers 25.00 60.00
PMP2SH S.Stamkos/V.Hedman 40.00 100.00
PMP2SJ P.Subban/R.Johansen 30.00 80.00
PMP2TF V.Tarasenko/R.Fabbri 30.00 80.00
PMP2TT J.Tavares/J.Toews 40.00 100.00
PMP2VS J.Voracek/W.Simmonds 25.00 60.00
PMP2WB A.Wennberg/S.Bobrovsky 50.00 125.00
PMP2WP M.Pacioretty/S.Weber 20.00 50.00

2016-17 Upper Deck Premier Mega Stick Duos

PMS2BH J.Benn/T.Hall 60.00 150.00
PMS2BL J.Beliveau/G.Lafleur 40.00 100.00
PMS2BQ M.Brodeur/J.Quick 60.00 150.00
PMS2DK B.Dubinsky/W.Karlsson 60.00 150.00
PMS2GJ W.Gretzky/J.Jagr 150.00 400.00
PMS2JT J.Spezza/T.Seguin 50.00 120.00
PMS2KC A.Kopitar/J.Carter 50.00 125.00
PMS2KH P.Kessel/C.Hagelin 40.00 100.00
PMS2LN M.Lucic/R.Nugent-Hopkins 30.00 80.00
PMS2SB J.Sakic/R.Bourque 50.00 125.00
PMS2SH T.Selanne/D.Hawerchuk 60.00 150.00
PMS2SZ M.Zuccarello/M.Staal 30.00 80.00
PMS2TD J.Thornton/V.Damphousse 30.00 80.00
PMS2WH C.Ward/N.Hanifin 30.00 80.00
PMS2YP S.Yzerman/B.Probert 40.00 100.00

2016-17 Upper Deck Premier Premier Duals Jersey

PD2BD B.Burns/D.Doughty 5.00 12.00
PD2BM P.Bure/K.McLean 4.00 10.00
PD2BS J.Benn/J.Spezza 5.00 12.00
PD2BT A.Barkov/V.Trocheck 4.00 10.00
PD2DL L.Draisaitl/M.Lucic 5.00 12.00
PD2ED O.Ekman-Larsson/M.Domi 5.00 12.00
PD2GM J.Gaudreau/S.Monahan 6.00 15.00
PD2KH E.Karlsson/M.Hoffman 8.00 20.00
PD2LC P.Laine/K.Connor 15.00 40.00
PD2LD I.Larionov/P.Datsyuk 5.00 12.00
PD2LG K.Letang/S.Gostisbehere 5.00 12.00
PD2LY M.Lemieux/S.Yzerman 12.00 30.00
PD2MM A.Matthews/M.Marner 25.00 60.00
PD2MO C.McDavid/A.Ovechkin 20.00 50.00
PD2NB W.Nylander/C.Brown 15.00 40.00
PD2OE R.O'Reilly/J.Eichel 8.00 20.00
PD2PK I.Provorov/T.Konecny 8.00 20.00
PD2PR C.Perry/R.Rakell 4.00 10.00
PD2RK N.Kadri/M.Rielly 3.00 8.00
PD2SD E.Staal/D.Dubnyk 5.00 12.00
PD2SF P.Subban/F.Forsberg 6.00 15.00
PD2SR J.Skinner/V.Rask 4.00 10.00
PD2SW M.Scheifele/B.Wheeler 5.00 12.00
PD2TL J.Tavares/A.Ladd 8.00 20.00
PD2TP V.Tarasenko/A.Panarin 6.00 15.00
PD2TS J.Tavares/D.Stepan 8.00 20.00
PD2VB J.Vesey/P.Buchnevich 8.00 20.00
PD2VS J.Voracek/W.Simmonds 5.00 12.00
PD2WP Z.Werenski/J.Puljujarvi 10.00 25.00

2016-17 Upper Deck Premier Premier Quads Jersey

PQ4CBJ Wennberg/Saad Foligno/Bobrovsky/49 10.00 25.00
PQ4DRW Yzerman/Larionov Chelios/Datsyuk/25 12.00 30.00
PQ4NYR Stepan/Hayes Kreider/Zuccarello/49 10.00 25.00
PQ4BEES Pastrnak/Marchand Backes/Rask/49 15.00 40.00
PQ4CAPS Backstrom/Kuznetsov Carlson/Oshie/49x 15.00 40.00
PQ4DMEN Burns/Subban Hedman/Karlsson/49 20.00 50.00
PQ4GLTR Price/Lundqvist Holtby/Crawford/49 30.00 80.00
PQ4HABS Pacioretty/Weber Galchenyuk/Gallagher/49 12.00 30.00
PQ4HAWK Kane/Panarin/Toews/Hossa/49 20.0050.00
PQ4LMWP Laine/Marner Werenski/Puljujarvi/49 40.00 100.00
PQ4NYNY Tavares/Ladd/Stepan/Nash/49 20.00 50.00
PQ4PCKT Point/Connor Konecny/Tkachuk/49 30.00 80.00
PQ4PENS Malkin/Kessel Letang/Murray/49 30.00 80.00
PQ4RUSS Ovechkin/Malkin Tarasenko/Panarin/49 40.00 100.00
PQ4VNSM Vesey/Nylander Sergachev/Mantha/49 40.00 100.00
PQ4STARS Tavares/Ovechkin Kane/Malkin/25 40.00 100.00

2016-17 Upper Deck Premier Premier Signature Booklets

PSAB Anthony Beauvillier 12.00 30.00
PSBO Mike Bossy 12.00 30.00
PSCM Connor McDavid
PSDA Daniel Altshuller 10.00 25.00
PSDI Marcel Dionne 15.00 40.00
PSDS Dylan Strome 25.00 60.00
PSHL Henrik Lundqvist 12.00 30.00
PSIL Igor Larionov 12.00 30.00
PSIP Ivan Provorov 25.00 60.00
PSJG John Gibson 12.00 30.00
PSJS Joe Sakic 20.00 50.00
PSJT Joe Thornton 12.00 30.00
PSKM Kirk McLean 12.00 30.00
PSMB Martin Brodeur 25.00 60.00
PSMM Matt Murray 20.00 50.00
PSMS Mark Stone 12.00 30.00
PSPK Patrick Kane 25.00 60.00
PSPL Patrik Laine 50.00 120.00
PSRJ Roman Josi 12.00 30.00
PSRK Red Kelly 12.00 30.00
PSRL Roberto Luongo 12.00 30.00
PSRS Ryan Spooner 10.00 25.00
PSSE Tyler Seguin 20.00 50.00
PSTL Trevor Linden 15.00 40.00
PSWG Wayne Gretzky
PSZW Zach Werenski 25.00 60.00

2016-17 Upper Deck Premier Premier Signatures

PSAL Andrew Ladd 8.00 20.00
PSBE Brian Elliott 6.00 15.00
PSCM Connor McDavid 200.00 300.00
PSCS Cory Schneider 6.00 15.00
PSDB David Backes 8.00 20.00
PSEM Evgeni Malkin 40.00 100.00
PSGN Gustav Nyquist 8.00 20.00
PSHL Henrik Lundqvist 40.00 100.00
PSHZ Henrik Zetterberg 10.00 25.00
PSJJ Jaromir Jagr 50.00 125.00
PSJO Roman Josi 8.00 20.00
PSJT Joe Thornton 8.00 20.00
PSLD Leon Draisaitl 20.00 50.00
PSLE Loui Eriksson 8.00 20.00
PSMG Marian Gaborik 8.00 20.00
PSPK Patrick Kane 25.00 60.00
PSPR Carey Price 80.00 150.00
PSRJ Ryan Johansen 10.00 25.00
PSRL Roberto Luongo 8.00 20.00
PSRO Ryan O'Reilly 8.00 20.00

2016-17 Upper Deck Premier Premier Signatures Legends

LPSBO Bobby Orr 60.00 150.00
LPSCN Cam Neely 15.00 40.00
LPSGL Guy Lafleur 25.00 60.00
LPSML Mario Lemieux 50.00 125.00
LPSPH Phil Housley 20.00 50.00
LPSPL Pat LaFontaine 20.00 50.00
LPSPR Patrick Roy
LPSSY Steve Yzerman 60.00 150.00
LPSWG Wayne Gretzky

2016-17 Upper Deck Premier Premier Swatches

PSAB Aleksander Barkov/99 5.00 12.00
PSAK Anze Kopitar/49 8.00 20.00
PSBN Brock Nelson/99 4.00 10.00
PSCM Connor McDavid/25 60.00 150.00
PSDD Devan Dubnyk/99 5.00 12.00
PSDG Doug Gilmour/49 6.00 15.00
PSDP David Pastrnak/99 8.00 20.00
PSDS Derek Stepan/99 4.00 10.00
PSEK Erik Karlsson/49 10.00 25.00
PSGL Gabriel Landeskog/99 4.00 10.00
PSHS Henrik Sedin/49 5.00 12.00
PSHZ Henrik Zetterberg/49 6.00 15.00
PSJG Johnny Gaudreau/99 8.00 20.00
PSJP Joe Pavelski/99 5.00 12.00
PSJS Joe Sakic/25 8.00 20.00
PSJT Jonathan Toews/25 15.00 40.00
PSKO Kyle Okposo/99 5.00 12.00
PSKU Evgeny Kuznetsov/99 8.00 20.00
PSMD Max Domi/99 6.00 15.00
PSPK Phil Kessel/49 6.00 15.00
PSPS P.K. Subban/49 8.00 20.00
PSRR Rickard Rakell/99 5.00 12.00
PSSB Sergei Bobrovsky/99 5.00 12.00
PSSP Jason Spezza/99 5.00 12.00
PSSW Shea Weber/99 4.00 10.00
PSTH Taylor Hall/49 10.00 25.00
PSVH Victor Hedman/99 6.00 15.00
PSVT Vladimir Tarasenko/49 8.00 20.00
PSWS Wayne Simmonds/99 6.00 15.00

2016-17 Upper Deck Premier Premier Trios Jersey

PT3ARZ Strome/Dvorak/Crouse 8.00 20.00
PT3AVS MacKinnon/Duchene/Landeskog 8.00 20.00
PT3CGY Jankowski/Tkachuk/Kylington 12.00 30.00
PT3DEF Keith/Ekman-Larsson/Weber 4.00 10.00
PT3DET Zetterberg/Larkin/Nielsen 6.00 15.00
PT3GYR Dubnyk/Bobrovsky/Rask 4.00 10.00
PT3LAK Kopitar/Carter/Toffoli 6.00 15.00
PT3NJD Hall/Henrique/Schneider 8.00 20.00
PT3PTS Gretzky/Jagr/Messier 20.00 50.00
PT3STL Tarasenko/Fabbri/Schwartz 6.00 15.00
PT3TBL Stamkos/Hedman/Kucherov 8.00 20.00
PT3TOR Matthews/Marner/Nylander 30.00 80.00
PT3VAN Sedin/Horvat/Sedin 6.00 15.00
PT3MTLR Sergachev/Lehkonen/Lindgren 8.00 20.00
PT3SJCPT Nolan/Thornton/Marleau 4.00 10.00

2016-17 Upper Deck Premier Rookies

R1 Mikhail Sergachev/299 5.00 12.00
R2 Christian Dvorak/299 2.50 6.00
R3 Kevin Labanc/299 2.50 6.00
R4 Nick Baptiste/299 2.50 6.00
R5 Joel Eriksson Ek/299 2.50 6.00
R6 Oskar Sundqvist/299 2.50 6.00
R7 Tyler Motte/299 2.50 6.00
R8 Kasperi Kapanen/299 5.00 12.00
R9 Anthony Beauvillier/299 2.50 6.00
R10 Pavel Zacha/299 3.00 8.00
R11 Timo Meier/299 2.50 6.00
R12 Thomas Chabot/299 5.00 12.00
R13 Chris Bigras/299 2.00 5.00
R14 Anthony DeAngelo/299 2.50 6.00
R15 Anthony Mantha/299 6.00 15.00
R16 Jacob Larsson/299 4.00 10.00
R17 Nikita Soshnikov/299 1.50 4.00
R18 Mathew Barzal/299 8.00 20.00
R19 Oliver Kylington/299 2.00 5.00
R20 A.J. Greer/299 2.50 6.00
R21 Artturi Lehkonen/299 2.50 6.00
R22 John Quenneville/299 2.50 6.00
R23 Zach Werenski/299 5.00 12.00
R24 Julius Honka/299 2.50 6.00
R25 Jakob Chychrun/299 2.50 6.00
R26 Drake Caggiula/299 2.50 6.00
R27 Pavel Buchnevich/299 4.00 10.00
R28 Mark Jankowski/299 2.00 5.00
R29 Brayden Point/299 6.00 15.00
R30 Connor Brown/299 4.00 10.00
R31 Troy Stecher/299 2.50 6.00
R32 Nic Dowd/299 2.50 6.00
R33 Sebastian Aho/299 5.00 12.00
R34 Tyler Bertuzzi/299 3.00 8.00
R35 Nick Schmaltz/299 2.50 6.00
R36 Jakub Vrana/299 2.50 6.00
R37 Brandon Carlo/299 2.50 6.00
R38 Travis Konecny/299 5.00 12.00
R39 Oliver Bjorkstrand/299 2.00 5.00
R40 Lawson Crouse/299 2.00 5.00
R41 Jesse Puljujarvi/199 10.00 25.00
R42 Matthew Tkachuk/199 8.00 20.00
R43 Mitch Marner/199 20.00 50.00
R44 Dylan Strome/199 5.00 12.00
R45 Kyle Connor/199 6.00 15.00
R46 William Nylander/199 15.00 40.00
R47 Patrik Laine/199 20.00 50.00
R48 Ivan Provorov/199 5.00 12.00
R49 Jimmy Vesey/199 5.00 12.00
R50 Auston Matthews/199 60.00 150.00

2016-17 Upper Deck Premier Rookies Jerseys

R1 Mikhail Sergachev 6.00 15.00
R2 Christian Dvorak 3.00 8.00
R3 Kevin Labanc 3.00 8.00
R4 Nick Baptiste 3.00 8.00
R5 Joel Eriksson Ek 3.00 8.00
R6 Oskar Sundqvist 3.00 8.00
R7 Tyler Motte 3.00 8.00
R8 Kasperi Kapanen 6.00 15.00
R9 Anthony Beauvillier 3.00 8.00
R10 Pavel Zacha 4.00 10.00
R11 Timo Meier 3.00 8.00
R12 Thomas Chabot 6.00 15.00
R13 Chris Bigras 2.50 6.00
R14 Anthony DeAngelo 3.00 8.00
R15 Anthony Mantha 8.00 20.00
R17 Nikita Soshnikov 2.00 5.00
R18 Mathew Barzal 10.00 25.00
R19 Oliver Kylington 2.50 6.00
R20 A.J. Greer 3.00 8.00
R21 Artturi Lehkonen 3.00 8.00
R22 John Quenneville 3.00 8.00
R23 Zach Werenski 6.00 15.00
R24 Julius Honka 3.00 8.00
R25 Jakob Chychrun 3.00 8.00
R27 Pavel Buchnevich 5.00 12.00
R28 Mark Jankowski 2.50 6.00
R29 Brayden Point 8.00 20.00
R30 Connor Brown 5.00 12.00
R32 Nic Dowd 3.00 8.00
R33 Sebastian Aho 6.00 15.00
R34 Tyler Bertuzzi 4.00 10.00
R35 Nick Schmaltz 3.00 8.00
R36 Jakub Vrana 3.00 8.00
R37 Brandon Carlo 3.00 8.00
R38 Travis Konecny 6.00 15.00
R39 Oliver Bjorkstrand 2.50 6.00
R40 Lawson Crouse 2.50 6.00
R41 Jesse Puljujarvi 8.00 20.00
R42 Matthew Tkachuk 10.00 25.00
R43 Mitch Marner 15.00 40.00
R44 Dylan Strome 6.00 15.00
R45 Kyle Connor 8.00 20.00
R46 William Nylander 12.00 30.00
R47 Patrik Laine 12.00 30.00
R48 Ivan Provorov 6.00 15.00
R49 Jimmy Vesey 6.00 15.00
R50 Auston Matthews 30.00 80.00

2016-17 Upper Deck Premier Rookies Jerseys Patch

*PATCH/25: 1X TO 2.5X BASIC INSERTS
R47 Patrik Laine 80.00 150.00
R50 Auston Matthews 100.00 250.00

2016-17 Upper Deck Premier Signature Award Winners

SAAK Anze Kopitar/25 40.00 100.00
SAAM Al MacInnis/99 8.00 20.00
SACN Cam Neely/49 15.00 40.00
SADG Doug Gilmour/49 25.00 60.00
SADT Dave Taylor/99 6.00 15.00
SAHL Henrik Lundqvist/25 40.00 100.00
SAJJ Jaromir Jagr/25 80.00 150.00
SAJT Jonathan Toews/25 30.00 80.00
SAMG Mark Giordano/99 8.00 20.00
SAPK Patrick Kane/25 30.00 80.00
SARB Ray Bourque/25 12.00 30.00
SARK Ryan Kesler/99 6.00 15.00

2016-17 Upper Deck Premier Signature Champions

SCBG Bill Guerin/99 10.00 25.00
SCCW Cam Ward/99 5.00 12.00
SCEM Evgeni Malkin/25 40.00 100.00
SCGC Guy Carbonneau/99 6.00 15.00
SCHZ Henrik Zetterberg/25 15.00 40.00
SCJK Jari Kurri/25 15.00 40.00
SCJT Jonathan Toews/25 40.00 100.00
SCMO Mike Modano/99 20.00 50.00
SCMU Matt Murray/99 60.00 150.00
SCPK Patrick Kane/25 40.00 100.00
SCRB Ray Bourque/25 30.00 80.00

2017-18 Upper Deck Premier

1 Patrice Bergeron 2.00 5.00
2 Alexander Ovechkin 6.00 15.00
3 Filip Forsberg 2.00 5.00
4 Nikita Kucherov 2.50 6.00
5 Mikael Granlund 1.50 4.00
6 Auston Matthews 6.00 15.00
7 Vincent Trocheck 1.25 3.00
8 Patrik Laine 2.50 6.00
9 Jack Eichel 2.50 6.00
10 Claude Giroux 1.50 4.00
11 James Neal 1.25 3.00
12 Artemi Panarin 1.50 4.00
13 Jeff Skinner 1.25 3.00
14 Blake Wheeler 1.50 4.00
15 Bo Horvat 1.50 4.00
16 Jordan Eberle 1.50 4.00
17 Devan Dubnyk 1.50 4.00
18 Steven Stamkos 3.00 8.00
19 John Tavares 3.00 8.00
20 John Gibson 1.50 4.00
21 Nathan MacKinnon 3.00 8.00
22 Sidney Crosby 6.00 15.00
23 Vladimir Tarasenko 2.50 6.00
24 Taylor Hall 3.00 8.00
25 Jonathan Huberdeau 1.25 3.00
26 Kevin Shattenkirk 1.50 4.00
27 Anthony Mantha 1.50 4.00
28 Jonathan Quick 2.50 6.00
29 Mark Giordano 1.25 3.00
30 Erik Karlsson 2.00 5.00
31 Connor McDavid 6.00 15.00
32 Carey Price 5.00 12.00
33 Duncan Keith 1.50 4.00
34 Marc-Andre Fleury 2.50 6.00
35 Tyler Seguin 2.50 6.00
36 Logan Couture 1.50 4.00
37 Kris Letang 1.50 4.00
38 Jonathan Drouin 1.50 4.00
39 Derek Stepan 1.25 3.00
40 Nazem Kadri 1.25 3.00
41 Wayne Gretzky 8.00 20.00
42 Bobby Orr 5.00 12.00
43 Brett Hull 1.50 4.00
44 Dale Hawerchuk 2.00 5.00
45 Pavel Bure 1.50 4.00
46 Patrick Roy 4.00 10.00
47 Joe Sakic 2.00 5.00
48 Rod Langway 1.50 4.00
49 Ray Bourque 2.50 6.00
50 Mario Lemieux 5.00 12.00
51 Janne Kuokkanen RC 2.50 6.00
52 Filip Chlapik RC 2.50 6.00
53 Calle Rosen RC 2.50 6.00
54 Alex Kerfoot RC 2.50 6.00
55 Jesper Bratt RC 4.00 10.00
56 Victor Mete RC 2.50 6.00
57 Tage Thompson RC 4.00 10.00
58 Lucas Wallmark RC 2.50 6.00
59 Nick Merkley RC 2.50 6.00
60 Ville Husso RC 2.50 6.00
61 Martin Necas RC 2.50 6.00
62 Adrian Kempe RC 3.00 8.00
63 Logan Brown RC 2.50 6.00
64 Madison Bowey RC 2.00 5.00
65 Jake DeBrusk RC 4.00 10.00
66 Ivan Barbashev RC 2.50 6.00
67 Denis Gurianov RC 2.50 6.00
68 Alex Nedeljkovic RC 2.00 5.00
69 Samuel Morin RC 2.50 6.00
70 Alex Formenton RC 2.50 6.00
71 Evgeny Svechnikov RC 5.00 12.00
72 Jon Gillies RC 2.50 6.00
73 Filip Chytil RC 2.50 6.00
74 Vladislav Kamenev RC 4.00 10.00
75 Will Butcher RC 3.00 8.00
76 Travis Sanheim RC 2.50 6.00
77 Haydn Fleury RC 2.50 6.00
78 Nikita Scherbak RC 5.00 12.00
79 Vince Dunn RC 2.50 6.00
80 Christian Fischer RC 3.00 8.00
81 Colin White RC 2.50 6.00
82 Jack Roslovic RC 3.00 8.00
83 J.T. Compher RC 3.00 8.00
84 Luke Kunin RC 2.50 6.00
85 Jakob Forsbacka-Karlsson RC 2.50 6.00
86 Alex Tuch RC 6.00 15.00
87 Robert Hagg RC 2.50 6.00
88 Anders Bjork RC 3.00 8.00
89 Kailer Yamamoto RC 6.00 15.00
90 Owen Tippett RC 5.00 12.00
91 Brock Boeser RC 15.00 40.00
92 Clayton Keller RC 6.00 15.00
93 Charlie McAvoy RC 8.00 20.00
94 Tyson Jost RC 5.00 12.00
95 Alexander Nylander RC 4.00 10.00
96 Josh Ho-Sang RC 3.00 8.00
97 Alex DeBrincat RC 6.00 15.00
98 Pierre-Luc Dubois RC 5.00 12.00
99 Nolan Patrick RC 12.00 30.00
100 Nico Hischier RC 12.00 30.00

2017-18 Upper Deck Premier Silver Spectrum

*VETS/10-49: 2.5X TO 6X BASIC CARDS
*ROOKIES: 1.5X TO 4X BASIC CARDS
91 Brock Boeser AU 100.00 200.00

2017-18 Upper Deck Premier Inked Script

ISAD Alex Delvecchio/49
ISBH Brett Hull/99 25.00 60.00
ISBP Brian Propp/99 8.00 20.00
ISCN Cam Neely/99 15.00 40.00
ISJV John Vanbiesbrouck/99 12.00 30.00
ISNE Nikolaj Ehlers/49
ISRL Rod Langway/25
ISTF Theoren Fleury/49 25.00 60.00

2017-18 Upper Deck Premier Jerseys

1 Patrice Bergeron 3.00 8.00
2 Alexander Ovechkin 10.00 25.00
3 Filip Forsberg 3.00 8.00
4 Nikita Kucherov 4.00 10.00
5 Mikael Granlund 2.50 6.00
6 Auston Matthews 10.00 25.00
7 Vincent Trocheck 2.00 5.00
8 Patrik Laine 4.00 10.00
9 Jack Eichel 4.00 10.00
10 Claude Giroux 2.50 6.00
11 James Neal 2.00 5.00
12 Artemi Panarin 2.50 6.00
13 Jeff Skinner 2.00 5.00
14 Blake Wheeler 2.50 6.00
15 Bo Horvat 2.50 6.00
16 Jordan Eberle 2.50 6.00
17 Devan Dubnyk 2.50 6.00
18 Steven Stamkos 5.00 12.00
19 John Tavares 5.00 12.00
20 John Gibson 2.50 6.00
21 Nathan MacKinnon 5.00 12.00
22 Sidney Crosby 10.00 25.00
23 Vladimir Tarasenko 4.00 10.00
24 Taylor Hall 5.00 12.00
25 Jonathan Huberdeau 2.00 5.00
26 Kevin Shattenkirk 2.50 6.00
27 Anthony Mantha 2.50 6.00
28 Jonathan Quick 4.00 10.00
29 Mark Giordano 2.00 5.00
30 Erik Karlsson 3.00 8.00
31 Connor McDavid 10.00 25.00
32 Carey Price 8.00 20.00
33 Duncan Keith 2.50 6.00
34 Marc-Andre Fleury 4.00 10.00
35 Tyler Seguin 4.00 10.00
36 Logan Couture 2.50 6.00
37 Kris Letang 2.50 6.00
38 Jonathan Drouin 2.50 6.00
39 Derek Stepan 2.00 5.00
40 Nazem Kadri 2.00 5.00
41 Wayne Gretzky 12.00 30.00
43 Brett Hull 2.50 6.00
44 Dale Hawerchuk 3.00 8.00
45 Pavel Bure 2.50 6.00
46 Patrick Roy 6.00 15.00
47 Joe Sakic 3.00 8.00
48 Rod Langway 2.50 6.00
49 Ray Bourque 4.00 10.00
50 Mario Lemieux 8.00 20.00
51 Janne Kuokkanen 2.50 6.00
52 Filip Chlapik 2.50 6.00
55 Jesper Bratt 4.00 10.00
56 Victor Mete 2.50 6.00
57 Tage Thompson 4.00 10.00
58 Lucas Wallmark 2.50 6.00
59 Nick Merkley 2.50 6.00
60 Ville Husso 2.50 6.00
61 Martin Necas 2.50 6.00
62 Adrian Kempe 3.00 8.00
63 Logan Brown 2.50 6.00
64 Madison Bowey 2.00 5.00
66 Ivan Barbashev 2.50 6.00
67 Denis Gurianov 2.50 6.00
68 Alex Nedeljkovic 2.00 5.00
69 Samuel Morin 2.50 6.00
70 Alex Formenton 2.50 6.00
71 Evgeny Svechnikov 5.00 12.00
72 Jon Gillies 2.50 6.00
74 Vladislav Kamenev 4.00 10.00
75 Will Butcher 3.00 8.00
76 Travis Sanheim 2.50 6.00
77 Haydn Fleury 2.50 6.00
78 Nikita Scherbak 5.00 12.00
79 Vince Dunn 2.50 6.00
80 Christian Fischer 3.00 8.00
81 Colin White 2.50 6.00
82 Jack Roslovic 3.00 8.00
83 J.T. Compher 3.00 8.00
84 Luke Kunin 2.50 6.00
85 Jakob Forsbacka-Karlsson 2.50 6.00
86 Alex Tuch 6.00 15.00
87 Robert Hagg 2.50 6.00
88 Anders Bjork 3.00 8.00
89 Kailer Yamamoto 6.00 15.00
90 Owen Tippett 5.00 12.00
91 Brock Boeser 12.00 30.00
92 Clayton Keller 6.00 15.00
93 Charlie McAvoy 8.00 20.00
94 Tyson Jost 5.00 12.00
95 Alexander Nylander 4.00 10.00
96 Josh Ho-Sang 3.00 8.00
97 Alex DeBrincat 6.00 15.00
98 Pierre-Luc Dubois 5.00 12.00
99 Nolan Patrick 5.00 12.00
100 Nico Hischier 8.00 20.00

2017-18 Upper Deck Premier Jerseys Premium Materials

*PATCH/25-36: 1X TO 2.5X BASIC INSERTS
86 Alex Tuch/36 25.00 60.00
91 Brock Boeser/36 50.00 120.00

2017-18 Upper Deck Premier Magnificent Marks

MMAB Aleksander Barkov 10.00 25.00
MMAE Aaron Ekblad 10.00 25.00
MMAW Alexander Wennberg 8.00 20.00
MMBB Brock Boeser 50.00 125.00
MMBE Brian Elliott 8.00 20.00
MMBO Bobby Orr 100.00 200.00
MMBS Borje Salming 8.00 20.00
MMCA Cam Atkinson 10.00 25.00
MMCK Clayton Keller 25.00 60.00
MMCM Connor McDavid 150.00 300.00
MMCP Carey Price 30.00 80.00
MMCS Charlie Simmer 10.00 25.00
MMDT Dave Taylor 8.00 20.00
MMFC Filip Chlapik 10.00 25.00
MMHF Haydn Fleury 10.00 25.00
MMJC John Carlson 12.00 30.00
MMJD Jonathan Drouin 10.00 25.00
MMJI Jarome Iginla 10.00 25.00
MMKM Kirk Muller 8.00 20.00
MMKS Kevin Shattenkirk 10.00 25.00
MMLC Logan Couture 10.00 25.00
MMLD Leon Draisaitl 15.00 40.00
MMMG Mark Giordano 8.00 20.00
MMMH Mike Hoffman 8.00 20.00
MMMK Mike Krushelnyski 8.00 20.00
MMMM Mark Messier 15.00 40.00
MMMS Mark Scheifele 12.00 30.00
MMNK Nikita Kucherov 15.00 40.00
MMON Owen Nolan 10.00 25.00
MMPT Pierre Turgeon 10.00 25.00
MMPZ Pavel Zacha 10.00 25.00
MMRE Ryan Ellis 8.00 20.00
MMSH Conor Sheary 10.00 25.00
MMSS Steven Stamkos 20.00 50.00
MMTA Tony Amonte 10.00 25.00
MMTH Taylor Hall 20.00 50.00
MMTR Tobias Rieder 6.00 15.00
MMVH Ville Husso 10.00 25.00
MMVL Vladimir Tarasenko 15.00 40.00
MMVT Vincent Trocheck 8.00 20.00
MMWG Wayne Gretzky 150.00 300.00
MMWO Willie O'Ree 10.00 25.00

2017-18 Upper Deck Premier Mega Patch Chest Logos

PMPAA Artem Anisimov 15.00 40.00
PMPAE Aaron Ekblad 20.00 50.00
PMPAK Anze Kopitar 30.00 80.00
PMPAL Anders Lee 20.00 50.00
PMPAM Auston Matthews 80.00 200.00
PMPAO Alexander Ovechkin 80.00 200.00
PMPAP Artemi Panarin 20.00 50.00
PMPAV Andrei Vasilevskiy 25.00 60.00
PMPBB Ben Bishop 20.00 50.00
PMPBH Bo Horvat 20.00 50.00
PMPBM Brandon Montour 15.00 40.00
PMPBO Brock Boeser 100.00 250.00
PMPBR Brayden Schenn 20.00 50.00
PMPBS Brandon Saad 20.00 50.00
PMPBU Brent Burns 25.00 60.00
PMPCG Claude Giroux 20.00 50.00
PMPCK Clayton Keller 50.00 125.00
PMPCM Connor McDavid 80.00 200.00
PMPCP Carey Price 60.00 150.00
PMPCT Cam Talbot 20.00 50.00
PMPDE Derek Stepan 15.00 40.00
PMPDK David Krejci 15.00 40.00
PMPDL Dylan Larkin 20.00 50.00
PMPDS Daniel Sedin 20.00 50.00
PMPEB Jordan Eberle 20.00 50.00
PMPEE Joel Eriksson Ek 20.00 50.00
PMPEK Erik Karlsson 25.00 60.00
PMPEM Evgeni Malkin 60.00 150.00
PMPGL Gabriel Landeskog 15.00 40.00
PMPGU Jake Guentzel 25.00 60.00
PMPHL Henrik Lundqvist 30.00 80.00
PMPHZ Henrik Zetterberg 20.00 50.00
PMPJA Jake Allen 25.00 60.00
PMPJB Jamie Benn 25.00 60.00
PMPJD Jonathan Drouin 20.00 50.00
PMPJE Jack Eichel 30.00 80.00
PMPJG Johnny Gaudreau 30.00 80.00
PMPJH Jonathan Huberdeau 15.00 40.00
PMPJM Jonathan Marchessault 20.00 50.00
PMPJN James Neal 15.00 40.00
PMPJO Marcus Johansson 15.00 40.00
PMPJP Joe Pavelski 20.00 50.00
PMPJQ Jonathan Quick 30.00 80.00
PMPJS Jaden Schwartz 25.00 60.00
PMPJT John Tavares 40.00 100.00
PMPKA Nazem Kadri 15.00 40.00
PMPKP Kyle Palmieri 15.00 40.00
PMPKS Kevin Shattenkirk 20.00 50.00
PMPKU Evgeny Kuznetsov 30.00 80.00
PMPLD Leon Draisaitl 30.00 80.00
PMPMA Anthony Mantha 20.00 50.00
PMPMC Charlie McAvoy 60.00 150.00
PMPMD Max Domi 20.00 50.00
PMPMF Marc-Andre Fleury 30.00 80.00
PMPMG Mikael Granlund 20.00 50.00
PMPMI J.T. Miller 15.00 40.00
PMPMJ Martin Jones 20.00 50.00
PMPMM Matt Murray 30.00 80.00
PMPMO Sean Monahan 20.00 50.00
PMPMR Mikko Rantanen 20.00 50.00
PMPMS Mark Scheifele 25.00 60.00
PMPMT Matthew Tkachuk 20.00 50.00
PMPMZ Alec Martinez 12.00 30.00
PMPNB Nicklas Backstrom 30.00 80.00
PMPNE Nikolaj Ehlers 20.00 50.00
PMPNK Nikita Kucherov 30.00 80.00
PMPPB Patrice Bergeron 25.00 60.00
PMPPD Pierre-Luc Dubois 40.00 100.00
PMPPE Corey Perry 20.00 50.00
PMPPK Patrick Kane 40.00 100.00
PMPPL Patrik Laine 30.00 80.00
PMPPM Patrick Marleau 20.00 50.00
PMPPO Jason Pominville 15.00 40.00
PMPPR Pekka Rinne 25.00 60.00
PMPPS P.K. Subban 20.00 50.00
PMPRG Ryan Getzlaf 20.00 50.00
PMPRJ Roman Josi 20.00 50.00
PMPRO Ryan O'Reilly 20.00 50.00
PMPRY Ryan Johansen 20.00 50.00
PMPSA Sebastian Aho 20.00 50.00
PMPSB Sergei Bobrovsky 20.00 50.00
PMPSC Sidney Crosby 80.00 200.00
PMPSG Shayne Gostisbehere 20.00 50.00
PMPSK Jeff Skinner 15.00 40.00
PMPSM Mike Smith 20.00 50.00
PMPSS Steven Stamkos 40.00 100.00
PMPST Mark Stone 20.00 50.00
PMPSW Shea Weber 15.00 40.00
PMPTH Taylor Hall 40.00 100.00
PMPTJ Tyson Jost 40.00 100.00
PMPTO Jonathan Toews 40.00 100.00
PMPTR Vincent Trocheck 15.00 40.00
PMPTS Tyler Seguin 30.00 80.00
PMPVH Victor Hedman 25.00 60.00
PMPVT Vladimir Tarasenko 30.00 80.00
PMPWN William Nylander 30.00 80.00
PMPZU Mats Zuccarello 20.00 50.00
PMPZW Zach Werenski 20.00 50.00

2017-18 Upper Deck Premier Mega Patch Duos

PMP2BH A.Barkov/J.Huberdeau/25 20.00 50.00
PMP2BT B.Burns/J.Thornton/25 25.00 60.00
PMP2DL L.Draisaitl/M.Lucic/25 30.00 80.00
PMP2EO J.Eichel/R.O'Reilly/25 30.00 80.00
PMP2FN M.Fleury/J.Neal/25 30.00 80.00
PMP2GF R.Getzlaf/C.Fowler/25 20.00 50.00
PMP2GK C.Giroux/T.Konecny/25 20.00 50.00
PMP2GM J.Guentzel/M.Murray/25 30.00 80.00
PMP2GN M.Granlund/N.Niederreiter/25 20.00 50.00
PMP2GT J.Gaudreau/M.Tkachuk/25 30.00 80.00
PMP2HJ T.Hall/M.Johansson/25 40.00 100.00
PMP2HV V.Hedman/A.Vasilevskiy/25 25.00 60.00
PMP2KB A.Kopitar/D.Brown/25 30.00 80.00
PMP2KH E.Karlsson/M.Hoffman/25 25.00 60.00
PMP2KS C.Kreider/K.Shattenkirk/25 20.00 50.00
PMP2LE P.Laine/N.Ehlers/25 30.00 80.00
PMP2MB B.Marchand/P.Bergeron/25 25.00 60.00
PMP2MK P.Marleau/N.Kadri/25 20.00 50.00
PMP2ML A.Mantha/D.Larkin/25 20.00 50.00
PMP2MN A.Matthews/W.Nylander/25 80.00 200.00
PMP2MR N.MacKinnon/M.Rantanen/25 40.00 100.00
PMP2OK A.Ovechkin/E.Kuznetsov/25 80.00 200.00
PMP2PB A.Panarin/S.Bobrovsky/25 20.00 50.00
PMP2PD C.Price/J.Drouin/25 60.00 150.00
PMP2SA J.Skinner/S.Aho/25 20.00 50.00
PMP2SE D.Stepan/O.Ekman-Larsson/25 20.00 50.00
PMP2SJ P.Subban/R.Josi/25 20.00 50.00
PMP2SK S.Stamkos/N.Kucherov/25 40.00 100.00
PMP2ST B.Saad/J.Toews/25 40.00 100.00
PMP2SW M.Scheifele/B.Wheeler/25 25.00 60.00
PMP2TL J.Tavares/A.Lee/25 40.00 100.00
PMP2TS V.Tarasenko/J.Schwartz/25 30.00 80.00

2017-18 Upper Deck Premier Mega Stick Duos

PMS2AO A.Larsson/O.Klefbom/25 20.00 50.00
PMS2BS J.Benn/T.Seguin/25 30.00 80.00
PMS2DJ B.Dubinsky/J.Johnson/25 15.00 40.00
PMS2DK D.Doughty/E.Karlsson/25 25.00 60.00
PMS2DS D.Dubnyk/R.Suter/25 20.00 50.00
PMS2KB A.Kopitar/D.Brown/25 30.00 80.00
PMS2LK A.Ladd/N.Kulemin/25 20.00 50.00
PMS2NP J.Neal/D.Perron/25 20.00 50.00
PMS2SG D.Sedin/S.Gagner/25 20.00 50.00
PMS2SH J.Staal/N.Hanifin/25 20.00 50.00
PMS2TP T.Toffoli/T.Pearson/25 15.00 40.00

2017-18 Upper Deck Premier NHL Legendary Sticks

LSDH Doug Harvey 25.00 60.00
LSEB Ed Belfour 30.00 80.00
LSFM Frank Mahovlich 25.00 60.00
LSGF Grant Fuhr 30.00 80.00
LSJB Johnny Bower 25.00 60.00
LSJS Joe Sakic 30.00 80.00
LSMM Mark Messier 40.00 100.00
LSMR Maurice Richard 25.00 60.00
LSRB Ray Bourque 40.00 100.00
LSSM Stan Mikita 30.00 80.00

2017-18 Upper Deck Premier Premier Duals Jerseys

PD2AP J.Allen/A.Pietrangelo/99 6.00 15.00
PD2BB W.Butcher/J.Bratt/99 8.00 20.00
PD2BV B.Burns/M.Vlasic/99 6.00 15.00
PD2DC P.Dubois/G.Carlsson/99 10.00 25.00
PD2EL N.Ehlers/P.Laine/99 8.00 20.00
PD2EO J.Eichel/R.O'Reilly/99 8.00 20.00
PD2GB W.Gretzky/R.Blake/25 25.00 60.00
PD2HB B.Horvat/B.Boeser/99 25.00 60.00
PD2HP N.Hischier/N.Patrick/99 15.00 40.00
PD2HV V.Hedman/A.Vasilevskiy/99 6.00 15.00
PD2JC T.Jost/J.Compher/99 10.00 25.00
PD2JF R.Johansen/F.Forsberg/99 6.00 15.00
PD2JW S.Jones/Z.Werenski/99 5.00 12.00
PD2KB A.Kempe/J.Brodzinski/99 6.00 15.00
PD2KF C.Keller/C.Fischer/99 12.00 30.00
PD2LN M.Lucic/R.Nugent-Hopkins/99 5.00 12.00
PD2MA A.Mantha/A.Athanasiou/99 5.00 12.00
PD2MD C.McDavid/L.Draisaitl/99 20.00 50.00
PD2MF J.Marchessault/M.Fleury/99 8.00 20.00
PD2MG B.Montour/J.Gibson/99 5.00 12.00
PD2ML E.Malkin/K.Letang/99 15.00 40.00
PD2MN A.Matthews/W.Nylander/99 20.00 50.00
PD2MS V.Mete/N.Scherbak/99 10.00 25.00
PD2ND N.Niederreiter/D.Dubnyk/99 5.00 12.00
PD2PG I.Provorov/S.Gostisbehere/99 5.00 12.00
PD2RB A.Radulov/B.Bishop/99 5.00 12.00
PD2RP P.Roy/C.Price/99 15.00 40.00
PD2SF J.Staal/J.Faulk/99 5.00 12.00
PD2SJ P.Subban/R.Josi/99 5.00 12.00
PD2TA J.Toews/A.Anisimov/99 10.00 25.00

2017-18 Upper Deck Premier Premier Quads Jerseys

PQ4ANA Getzlaf/Perry/Kesler/49 6.00 15.00
PQ4AST Lafleur/Yzerman/Jagr/25 8.00 20.00
PQ4BUF Eichel/Pominville/O'Reilly/49 10.00 25.00
PQ4CAL Gaudreau/Monahan/Tkachuk/49 10.00 25.00
PQ4CAR Fleury/Necas/Kuokkanen/49 6.00 15.00
PQ4CHI Toews/Saad/Kane/49 12.00 30.00
PQ4COL Panarin/Werenski/Atkinson/49 6.00 15.00
PQ4FLO Barkov/Ekblad/Huberdeau/49 6.00 15.00
PQ4LAK Kopitar/Brown/Doughty/25 10.00 25.00
PQ4MIN Staal/Spurgeon/Zucker/49 8.00 20.00
PQ4OTT Karlsson/Brassard/Stone/49 8.00 20.00
PQ4PHI Giroux/Konecny/Couturier/49 6.00 15.00
PQ4RC4 Boeser/DeBrincat/Keller/49 30.00 80.00
PQ4SJS Thornton/Burns/Pavelski/49 6.00 15.00
PQ4TBL Stamkos/Hedman/Kucherov/25 12.00 30.00
PQ4TML Marleau/Kadri/van/49 6.00 15.00
PQ4VAN Bure/Larionov/Sedin/25 6.00 15.00
PQ4VEZ Bobrovsky/Holtby/Price/49 6.00 15.00
PQ4WAS Ovechkin/Kuznetsov Backstrom/49 25.00 60.00
PQ4WIN Scheifele/Ehlers/Laine/25 8.00 20.00

2017-18 Upper Deck Premier Premier Signature Booklets

PSBAE Aaron Ekblad 10.00 25.00
PSBAK Anze Kopitar 15.00 40.00
PSBAN Alexander Nylander 15.00 40.00
PSBBB Brock Boeser 50.00 125.00
PSBBO Bobby Orr 30.00 80.00
PSBCK Clayton Keller 25.00 60.00
PSBCM Connor McDavid 200.00 300.00
PSBDK Duncan Keith 10.00 25.00
PSBJT Jonathan Toews 20.00 50.00
PSBLD Leon Draisaitl 15.00 40.00
PSBLK Luke Kunin 10.00 25.00
PSBMP Max Pacioretty 10.00 25.00
PSBMS Mark Scheifele 12.00 30.00
PSBNK Nikita Kucherov 15.00 40.00
PSBOT Owen Tippett 20.00 50.00
PSBPC Paul Coffey 10.00 25.00
PSBPE Phil Esposito 15.00 40.00
PSBPH Phil Housley 8.00 20.00
PSBTS Tyler Seguin 15.00 40.00
PSBWG Wayne Gretzky 50.00 125.00

2017-18 Upper Deck Premier Premier Signature Booklets Dual

DSBBP M.Bossy/D.Potvin/40 80.00 150.00
DSBDY A.Delvecchio/S.Yzerman/40 80.00 150.00
DSBOE B.Orr/P.Esposito/20 150.00 250.00

2017-18 Upper Deck Premier Premier Swatches

PSAA Artem Anisimov/99 4.00 10.00
PSAL Anders Lee/99 5.00 12.00
PSAM Auston Matthews/25 20.00 50.00
PSBB Ben Bishop/50 5.00 12.00
PSBH Bo Horvat/99 5.00 12.00
PSBM Brandon Montour/99 4.00 10.00
PSBS Brayden Schenn/50 5.00 12.00
PSBW Blake Wheeler/50 5.00 12.00
PSCK Chris Kreider/99 5.00 12.00
PSCS Conor Sheary/99 5.00 12.00
PSDS Derek Stepan/99 4.00 10.00
PSJD Jonathan Drouin/50 5.00 12.00
PSJE Jack Eichel/50 8.00 20.00
PSJH Jonathan Huberdeau/99 4.00 10.00
PSJN James Neal/50 4.00 10.00
PSLD Leon Draisaitl/25 8.00 20.00
PSMA Anthony Mantha/99 5.00 12.00
PSMF Marc-Andre Fleury/25 8.00 20.00
PSMG Mikael Granlund/99 5.00 12.00
PSMH Mike Hoffman/50 4.00 10.00
PSMJ Martin Jones/50 5.00 12.00
PSMR Mikko Rantanen/99 5.00 12.00
PSMS Mark Scheifele/50 6.00 15.00
PSNB Nicklas Backstrom/50 8.00 20.00
PSNK Nikita Kucherov/25 8.00 20.00
PSPB Patrice Bergeron/25 6.00 15.00
PSRJ Roman Josi/99 5.00 12.00
PSSA Sebastian Aho/99 5.00 12.00
PSTK Travis Konecny/99 5.00 12.00
PSZW Zach Werenski/99 5.00 12.00

2017-18 Upper Deck Premier Premier Trios Jerseys

PT3BBR Bjork/McAvoy/DeBrusk 15.00 40.00
PT3BOS Marchand/Bergeron/Pastrnak 8.00 20.00
PT3CAL Tkachuk/Gaudreau/Monahan 8.00 20.00
PT3COL Landeskog/MacKinnon/Rantanen 10.0025.00
PT3DAL Benn/Seguin/Radulov 8.00 20.00
PT3DET Mantha/Larkin/Athanasiou 5.00 12.00
PT3FLO Huberdeau/Barkov/Bjugstad 5.00 12.00
PT3ISL Ladd/Barzal/Eberle 8.00 20.00
PT3NJD Johansson/Hall/Palmieri 10.00 25.00
PT3NJR Bratt/Hischier/Butcher 15.00 40.00
PT3NYI Lee/Tavares/Bailey 10.00 25.00
PT3NYR Zibanejad/Kreider/Zuccarello 5.00 12.00
PT3OTT Brown/White/Chlapik 5.00 12.00
PT3PEN Guentzel/Malkin/Kessel 15.00 40.00
PT3PHI Giroux/Couturier/Simmonds 6.00 15.00
PT3STL Schwartz/Schenn/Tarasenko 8.00 20.0
PT3TCL Simmer/Dionne/Taylor 6.00 15.0
PT3WAS Carlson/Ovechkin/Holtby 20.00 50.0
PT3WIN Ehlers/Scheifele/Wheeler 6.00 15.0

2017-18 Upper Deck Premier Signature Award Winners

SABB Bruce Boudreau/99 8.00 20.0
SACA Craig Anderson/49 10.00 25.0
SADH Dale Hawerchuk/99 12.00 30.0
SAJB Jason Blake/99 6.00 15.0
SAJV John Vanbiesbrouck/99 10.00 25.0
SAPC Paul Coffey/49 10.00 25.0
SARB Rod Brind'Amour/99 10.00 25.0
SARL Rod Langway/99 10.00 25.0
SASS Steven Stamkos/49 20.00 50.0

2017-18 Upper Deck Premier Signature Champions

SCBC Bobby Clarke/49 15.00 40.0
SCDK Duncan Keith/49 15.00 40.0
SCDP Denis Potvin/49 15.00 40.0
SCGF Grant Fuhr/49 20.00 50.0
SCJC Jeff Carter/99 15.00 40.0
SCKM Kirk Muller/99 12.00 30.0
SCSB Scotty Bowman/49 20.00 50.0
SCTB Tom Barrasso/99 12.00 30.0

2000-01 Upper Deck Pros and Prospects

Upper Deck Pros and Prospects were released as a 132-card set with 42 short-printed rookie cards. The set design featured a white bordered card with copper foil lettering, highlights, and logo. The card backs are white and blue with a small photo of the player on the top right corner. SP's are numbered to 1000 sets.

1 Paul Kariya .30 .7
2 Teemu Selanne .50 1.2
3 Guy Hebert .20 .5
4 Donald Audette .20 .5
5 Adam Burt .15 .4
6 Patrik Stefan .20 .5
7 Joe Thornton .40 1.0
8 Jason Allison .20 .5
9 Sergei Samsonov .20 .5
10 Dominik Hasek .40 1.0
11 Doug Gilmour .30 .7
12 Maxim Afinogenov .15 .4
13 Oleg Saprykin .15 .4
14 Valeri Bure .20 .5
15 Mike Vernon .20 .5
16 Ron Francis .30 .7
17 Jeff O'Neill .20 .5
18 Arturs Irbe .20 .5
19 Steve Sullivan .15 .4
20 Alexei Zhamnov .20 .5
21 Tony Amonte .20 .5
22 Ray Bourque .40 1.0
23 Patrick Roy .60 1.5
24 Peter Forsberg .30 .7
25 Marc Denis .20 .5
26 Tyler Wright .15 .4
27 Mike Modano .40 1.0
28 Brett Hull .40 1.0
29 Ed Belfour .25 .6
30 Brendan Shanahan .30 .7
31 Sergei Fedorov .40 1.0
32 Steve Yzerman .75 2.0
33 Ryan Smyth .20 .5
34 Tommy Salo .20 .5
35 Doug Weight .25 .6
36 Pavel Bure .30 .7
37 Ray Whitney .20 .5
38 Viktor Kozlov .20 .5
39 Luc Robitaille .25 .6
40 Rob Blake .25 .6
41 Zigmund Palffy .25 .6
42 Manny Fernandez .20 .5
43 Scott Pellerin .15 .4
44 Jose Theodore .30 .7
45 Brian Savage .15 .4
46 Martin Rucinsky .15 .4
47 David Legwand .25 .6
48 Mike Dunham .15 .4
49 Cliff Ronning .15 .4
50 Scott Gomez .20 .5
51 Scott Stevens .25 .6
52 Martin Brodeur .50 1.2
53 Tim Connolly .15 .4
54 Brad Isbister .15 .4
55 Roman Hamrlik .20 .5
56 Theo Fleury .30 .7
57 Mike Richter .25 .6
58 Mark Messier .40 1.0
59 Marian Hossa .20 .5
60 Alexei Yashin .20 .5
61 Radek Bonk .20 .5
62 John LeClair .25 .6
63 Mark Recchi .30 .7
64 Simon Gagne .25 .6
65 Jeremy Roenick .25 .6
66 Shane Doan .20 .5
67 Keith Tkachuk .25 .6
68 Jaromir Jagr .60 1.5
69 Mario Lemieux .75 2.0
70 Alexei Kovalev .20 .5
71 Owen Nolan .25 .6
72 Jeff Friesen .15 .4
73 Patrick Marleau .25 .6
74 Chris Pronger .20 .5
75 Roman Turek .20 .5
76 Pierre Turgeon .25 .6
77 Kevin Weekes .15 .4
78 Fredrik Modin .15 .4
79 Vincent Lecavalier .20 .5
80 Curtis Joseph .30 .7
81 Mats Sundin .25 .6
82 Gary Roberts .15 .4
83 Markus Naslund .20 .5
84 Daniel Sedin .50 1.2
85 Henrik Sedin .40 1.0
86 Adam Oates .25 .6
87 Peter Bondra .20 .5
88 Olaf Kolzig .25 .6
89 Mark Messier .40 1.0
90 Steve Yzerman .75 2.0
91 Jonas Ronnqvist RC 1.50 4.0
92 Andy McDonald RC 3.00 8.0

Eric Nickulas RC 1.50 4.00
Andrew Raycroft RC 4.00 10.00
Jarno Kultanen RC 1.50 4.00
Jeff Cowan RC 1.50 4.00
Josef Vasicek RC 4.00 10.00
Reto Von Arx RC 2.00 5.00
David Aebischer RC 3.00 8.00
0 Serge Aubin RC 2.00 5.00
1 Rostislav Klesla RC 4.00 10.00
2 Marty Turco RC 3.00 8.00
3 Tyler Bouck RC 1.50 4.00
4 Brian Swanson RC 1.50 4.00
5 Michel Riesen RC 2.00 5.00
6 Eric Belanger RC 2.00 5.00
7 Steven Reinprecht RC 2.50 6.00
8 Marian Gaborik RC 5.00 12.00
9 Scott Hartnell RC 4.00 10.00
0 Greg Classen RC 1.50 4.00
1 Willie Mitchell RC 2.50 6.00
2 Colin White RC 1.50 4.00
3 Petr Mika RC 1.50 4.00
4 Rick DiPietro RC 6.00 15.00
5 Jason Labarbera RC 2.00 5.00
6 Martin Havlat RC 5.00 12.00
7 Jani Hurme RC 1.50 4.00
8 Petr Hubacek RC 1.50 4.00
9 Justin Williams RC 4.00 10.00
0 Roman Cechmanek RC 2.00 5.00
1 Roman Simicek RC 1.50 4.00
2 Mark Smith RC 1.50 4.00
3 Alexander Kharitonov RC 1.50 4.00
4 Matt Elich RC 2.00 5.00
5 Jakub Cutta RC 1.50 4.00
6 Fedor Fedorov RC 2.00 5.00
7 Marc-Andre Thinel RC 1.50 4.00
8 Zdenek Blatny RC 1.50 4.00
9 Jeff Bateman RC 1.50 4.00
0 Jason Jaspers RC 1.50 4.00
1 Jordan Krestanovich RC 1.50 4.00
2 Damian Surma RC 1.50 4.00

2000-01 Upper Deck Pros and Prospects Championship Rings

MPLETE SET (8) 12.00 25.00
ATED ODDS 1:12
1 Patrick Roy 3.00 8.00
2 Brendan Shanahan 1.00 2.50
3 Steve Yzerman 3.00 8.00
4 Wayne Gretzky 4.00 10.00
5 Scott Stevens .60 1.50
6 Martin Brodeur 1.50 4.00
7 Mark Messier .75 2.00
8 Jaromir Jagr 1.00 2.50

2000-01 Upper Deck Pros and Prospects Game Jerseys

ndomly inserted in Upper Deck Pros and Prospects cks at a rate of 1:30, this 10-card set featured a atch of game jersey. An exclusives parallel serial-mbered to 50 was also created.
XCLUSIVE/50: .8X TO 2X BASIC JSY
Brendan Shanahan 3.00 8.00
Chris Pronger 3.00 8.00
Jaromir Jagr 5.00 12.00
M Mike Modano 4.00 10.00
Peter Forsberg 6.00 15.00
Paul Kariya 3.00 8.00
Patrick Roy 8.00 20.00
Ray Bourque 8.00 20.00
Sergei Fedorov 4.00 10.00
Teemu Selanne 3.00 8.00

2000-01 Upper Deck Pros and Prospects Game Jersey Autographs

ndomly inserted in Upper Deck Pros and Prospects cks at a rate of 1:96, this 10-card set featured a atch of game jersey, and an autograph. An clusives parallel was also created and serial-mbered to 50. Please note at the time of release the ott Gomez and Wayne Gretzky cards were issued as change/redemption cards.
XCLUSIVE/50: .8X TO 2X BASIC JSY AU
L John LeClair 10.00 25.00
R Jeremy Roenick 15.00 40.00
T Keith Tkachuk 12.50 30.00
B Lubos Bartecko 10.00 25.00
MM Mark Messier 40.00 80.00
B Pavel Bure 12.50 30.00
G Scott Gomez 10.00 25.00
S Sergei Samsonov 12.50 30.00
Y Steve Yzerman 40.00 100.00
G Wayne Gretzky 175.00 300.00

2000-01 Upper Deck Pros and Prospects Great Skates

MPLETE SET (8) 10.00 20.00
ATED ODDS 1:12
1 Paul Kariya .60 1.50
2 Mario Lemieux 4.00 10.00
3 Patrick Roy 3.00 8.00
4 Brendan Shanahan 1.00 2.50
5 Pavel Bure .75 2.00
6 Alexei Yashin .60 1.50
7 John LeClair .75 2.00
8 Jaromir Jagr 1.00 2.50

2000-01 Upper Deck Pros and Prospects NHL Passion

MPLETE SET (9) 10.00 20.00
ATED ODDS 1:10
1 Ray Bourque 1.00 3.00
2 Brett Hull .75 2.00
3 Steve Yzerman 3.00 8.00
4 Mark Messier .75 2.00
5 John LeClair .75 2.00
6 Jeremy Roenick .75 2.00
7 Jaromir Jagr 1.00 2.50
8 Mario Lemieux 4.00 10.00
9 Curtis Joseph .60 1.50

2000-01 Upper Deck Pros and Prospects Now Appearing

MPLETE SET (8) 10.00 20.00
ATED ODDS 1:12
1 Maxim Afinogenov .60 1.50
2 Marian Gaborik 3.00 8.00
3 Scott Hartnell 1.00 2.50
4 Scott Gomez .60 1.50
5 Rick DiPietro 3.00 8.00
6 Justin Williams 1.25 3.00
7 Daniel Sedin .60 1.50
8 Henrik Sedin .60 1.50

2000-01 Upper Deck Pros and Prospects ProMotion

MPLETE SET (9) 10.00 20.00
ATED ODDS 1:10
1 Teemu Selanne .75 2.00
2 Dominik Hasek 1.50 4.00
3 Peter Forsberg 1.50 4.00
4 Sergei Fedorov 1.25 3.00
PM5 Mike Modano 1.00 2.50
PM6 Pavel Bure 1.00 2.50
PM7 Martin Brodeur 1.50 4.00
PM8 John LeClair .75 2.00
PM9 Jaromir Jagr 1.00 2.50

1999-00 Upper Deck Retro

Released as a 109-card set, Upper Deck Retro features players from both today and yesterday on a "throwback" style base card enhanced with bronze foil stamping. Each Retro box was packaged in an actual Wayne Gretzky lunchbox, contained 24-packs per box with six cards per pack and carried a suggested retail price of $4.99. Card number 82 was supposed to be Gordie Howe, but a licensing agreement was never reached. A few of the Howe cards are known to exist with a crimp of Jeff Gordon over Howe's head.
COMPLETE SET (109) 20.00 40.00
1 Paul Kariya .20 .50
2 Teemu Selanne .20 .50
3 Jim McKenzie .02 .10
4 Ray Bourque .20 .50
5 Sergei Samsonov .15 .40
6 Joe Thornton .20 .50
7 Dominik Hasek .40 1.00
8 Miroslav Satan .15 .40
9 Michael Peca .15 .40
10 Todd Simpson .02 .10
11 Valeri Bure .02 .10
12 Jarome Iginla .25 .60
13 Kent Manderville .25 .60
14 Keith Primeau .02 .10
15 Sami Kapanen .02 .10
16 Mark Janssens .02 .10
17 Tony Amonte .15 .40
18 Doug Gilmour .15 .40
19 Peter Forsberg .50 1.25
20 Patrick Roy .50 1.25
21 Joe Sakic .40 1.00
22 Theo Fleury .15 .40
23 Chris Drury .15 .40
24 Mike Modano .20 .50
25 Brett Hull .20 .50
26 Ed Belfour .20 .50
27 Steve Yzerman 1.00 2.50
28 Sergei Fedorov .30 .75
29 Brendan Shanahan .20 .50
30 Chris Chelios .20 .50
31 Doug Weight .15 .40
32 Bill Guerin .15 .40
33 Tom Poti .02 .10
34 Gord Murphy .02 .10
35 Pavel Bure .20 .50
36 Mark Parrish .02 .10
37 Rob Blake .15 .40
38 Pavel Rosa .02 .10
39 Luc Robitaille .15 .40
40 Stephane Quintal .02 .10
41 Saku Koivu .20 .50
42 Bob Boughner .02 .10
43 David Legwand .15 .40
44 Mike Dunham .15 .40
45 Martin Brodeur .60 1.50
46 Scott Stevens .15 .40
47 John Madden RC .20 .50
48 Vadim Sharifijanov .02 .10
49 Wayne Gretzky 1.25 3.00
50 Manny Malhotra .02 .10
51 Brian Leetch .15 .40
52 Mike Richter .20 .50
53 Eric Brewer .02 .10
54 Alexei Yashin .02 .10
55 Marian Hossa .20 .50
56 Chris Phillips .02 .10
57 Eric Lindros .20 .50
58 John LeClair .20 .50
59 Mark Recchi .15 .40
60 Jeremy Roenick .30 .75
61 Keith Tkachuk .20 .50
62 Nikolia Khabibulin .15 .40
63 Robert Esche RC .15 .40
64 Jaromir Jagr .30 .75
65 Martin Straka .02 .10
66 Jeff Friesen .02 .10
67 Vincent Damphousse .02 .10
68 Chris Pronger .15 .40
69 Pavol Demitra .15 .40
70 Al MacInnis .15 .40
71 Paul Mara .02 .10
72 Vincent Lecavalier .20 .50
73 Sergei Berezin .02 .10
74 Mats Sundin .20 .50
75 Curtis Joseph .20 .50
76 Markus Naslund .20 .50
77 Mark Messier .20 .50
78 Bill Muckalt .02 .10
79 Peter Bondra .20 .50
80 Adam Oates .15 .40
81 Bobby Orr 1.00 2.50
82 Gordie Howe SP
(embossed with Gordon profile)
83 Mario Lemieux 1.00 2.50
84 Maurice Richard .50 1.25
85 Jean Beliveau .20 .50
86 Bobby Hull .40 1.00
87 Terry Sawchuk .40 1.00
88 Eddie Shore .25 .60
89 Alex Delvecchio .25 .60
90 Jacques Plante .25 .60
91 Stan Mikita .20 .50
92 Gerry Cheevers .40 1.00
93 Glenn Hall .25 .60
94 Phil Esposito .40 1.00
95 Lanny McDonald .25 .60
96 Mike Bossy .25 .60
97 Ted Lindsay .25 .60
98 Red Kelly .25 .60
99 Bobby Clarke .25 .60
100 Larry Robinson .25 .60
101 Ken Dryden 1.00 2.50
102 Vladislav Tretiak RC .50 1.25
103 Marcel Dionne .25 .60
104 Bernie Geoffrion .20 .50
105 Johnny Bucyk .25 .60
106 Brad Park .25 .60
107 Tony Esposito .20 .50
108 Jari Kurri .25 .60
109 Henri Richard .25 .60
110 Mike Gartner .25 .60

1999-00 Upper Deck Retro Distant Replay

Randomly inserted in packs at the rate on 1:11, this 14-card set features black and white photography on a card enhanced with gold foil highlights. Card number DR11 was not released. Level 2 parallels were also released and inserted randomly, these cards were numbered out of 100.
COMPLETE SET (14) 30.00 60.00
*LEVEL 2/100: 6X TO 15X BASIC INSERTS
DR1 Ray Bourque 1.50 4.00
DR2 Martin Brodeur 2.50 6.00
DR3 Jaromir Jagr 1.50 4.00
DR4 Paul Kariya 1.00 2.50
DR5 Steve Yzerman 5.00 12.00
DR6 Mark Messier 1.00 2.50
DR7 Patrick Roy 5.00 12.00
DR8 Dominik Hasek 2.50 5.00
DR9 Wayne Gretzky 6.00 15.00
DR10 Bobby Orr 5.00 12.00
DR12 Mario Lemieux 5.00 12.00
DR13 Lanny McDonald 1.00 2.50
DR14 Maurice Richard 3.00 8.00
DR15 Vladislav Tretiak 2.00 5.00

1999-00 Upper Deck Retro Epic Gretzky

Randomly inserted in packs at the rate of 1:23, this 10-card set spotlights Wayne Gretzky. Base cards feature action photography set against a blue background with gold foil highlights. Level 2 parallels were also released and inserted randomly, these cards were numbered out of 50.
COMPLETE SET (10) 75.00 150.00
COMMON GRETZKY (EG1-EG10) 6.00 15.00
*LEVEL 2/50: 3X TO 8X BASIC INSERTS

1999-00 Upper Deck Retro Generation

Randomly inserted in packs at the rate of 1:3, this 29-card set features tow players of the past on separate cards paired with another card featuring a player of today who has assumed a modern day role of a legend. Card number G2A was not released. Level 2 parallels were also released and inserted randomly, these cards were numbered out of 500.
COMPLETE SET (29) 20.00 40.00
*LEVEL 2/500: 1.5X TO 4X BASIC INSERTS
G1A Bobby Orr 2.50 6.00
G1B Brian Leetch .40 1.00
G1C Bryan Berard .40 1.00
G2B Bobby Clarke .75 2.00
G2C Keith Tkachuk .75 2.00
G3A Glenn Hall .75 2.00
G3B Patrick Roy 2.50 6.00
G3C Jean-Marc Pelletier .40 1.00
G4A Eddie Shore .75 2.00
G4B Bobby Orr 2.50 6.00
G4C Ray Bourque .75 2.00
G5A Jean Beliveau 1.00 2.50
G5B Mario Lemieux 2.50 6.00
G5C Vincent Lecavalier .75 2.00
G6A Maurice Richard 1.50 4.00
G6B Pavel Bure .75 2.00
G6C Sergei Samsonov .40 1.00
G7A Stan Mikita 1.00 2.50
G7B Theo Fleury .40 1.00
G7C Paul Kariya .75 2.00
G8A Jari Kurri .75 2.00
G8B Teemu Selanne .75 2.00
G8C Olli Jokinen .40 1.00
G9A Phil Esposito 1.25 3.00
G9B Brendan Shanahan .75 2.00
G9C Mark Parrish .40 1.00
G10A Terry Sawchuk 1.25 3.00
G10B Dominik Hasek 1.00 2.50
G10C Jean-Sebastien Giguere .40 1.00

1999-00 Upper Deck Retro Gold

Randomly inserted in packs, this 109-card set parallels the base Retro set and is enhanced with gold foil highlights. Each card is sequentially numbered to 150.
*GOLD: 12X TO 30X BASIC CARDS

1999-00 Upper Deck Retro Inkredible

Randomly inserted in packs at the rate of 1:23, this 29-card set features authentic player autographs.
AD Alex Delvecchio 12.00 30.00
BC Bobby Clarke 10.00 25.00
BG Bernie Geoffrion 25.00 60.00
BO Bobby Orr 250.00 400.00
BOH Bobby Hull 15.00 40.00
BP Brad Park 10.00 25.00
BRH Brett Hull 15.00 40.00
DW Doug Weight 6.00 15.00
GC Gerry Cheevers 10.00 25.00
JEB Jean Beliveau 30.00 80.00
JOB John Bucyk 8.00 20.00
KP Keith Primeau 6.00 15.00
LM Lanny McDonald 10.00 25.00
MAR Maurice Richard 100.00 200.00
MB Mike Bossy 12.00 30.00
MD Marcel Dionne 10.00 25.00
ML Mario Lemieux 100.00 200.00
PAB Pavel Bure 15.00 40.00
PE Phil Esposito 20.00 50.00
RB Ray Bourque 25.00 60.00
SM Stan Mikita 15.00 40.00
SS Sergei Samsonov 6.00 15.00
SY Steve Yzerman 30.00 80.00
TA Tony Amonte 10.00 25.00
TE Tony Esposito 15.00 40.00
TL Ted Lindsay 8.00 20.00
VL Vincent Lecavalier 15.00 40.00
VT Vladislav Tretiak 25.00 60.00
WG Wayne Gretzky 200.00 400.00

1999-00 Upper Deck Retro Inkredible Level 2

Parallel to the regular Inkredible set, these cards are randomly inserted into packs, and feature a serial number out of 25.
*LEVEL 2/25: 1.2X TO 3X BASIC INSERTS

1999-00 Upper Deck Retro Lunchboxes

Each box of Retro was packaged in a Wayne Gretzky lunchbox showcasing the great one in his Kings, Oilers, Ranger jerseys, as well as a special tribute lunchbox.
COMPLETE SET (4) 35.00 70.00
1 Wayne Gretzky Kings 7.50 15.00
2 Wayne Gretzky Oilers 7.50 15.00
3 Wayne Gretzky Rangers 7.50 15.00
4 Wayne Gretzky Tribute 15.00 40.00

1999-00 Upper Deck Retro Memento

Randomly inserted in packs, this 5-card set features hockey's greats coupled with a swatch of game used memorabilia.
RM1 Wayne Gretzky 75.00 150.00
RM2 Marcel Dionne 12.00 30.00
RM3 Mario Lemieux 40.00 100.00
RM4 Phil Esposito 20.00 50.00
RM5 Ken Dryden 75.00 150.00
RM6 Gordie Howe

1999-00 Upper Deck Retro Turn of the Century

Randomly inserted in packs at the rate of 1:23, this 14-card set features Light F/X holofoil technology and players from the past and present.
COMPLETE SET (14) 40.00 80.00
TC1 Vincent Lecavalier 1.50 4.00
TC2 Martin Brodeur 4.00 10.00
TC3 Jaromir Jagr 5.00 12.00
TC4 Paul Kariya 2.50 6.00
TC5 Steve Yzerman 6.00 15.00
TC6 Ray Bourque 3.00 8.00
TC7 Patrick Roy 8.00 20.00
TC8 Dominik Hasek 3.00 8.00
TC9 Wayne Gretzky 10.00 25.00
TC10 Bobby Clarke 2.00 5.00
TC11 Larry Robinson 2.00 5.00
TC13 Mario Lemieux 5.00 12.00
TC14 Maurice Richard 2.00 5.00
TC15 Bobby Orr 6.00 15.00

2006-07 Upper Deck Rookie Class

COMPLETE SET (50) 8.00 20.00
1 Shea Weber .60 1.50
2 Matt Carle .25 .60
3 Patrick O'Sullivan .40 1.00
4 Phil Kessel .60 1.50
5 Guillaume Latendresse .40 1.00
6 Loui Eriksson .40 1.00
7 Luc Bourdon .40 1.00
8 Enver Lisin .25 .60
9 Evgeni Malkin 1.50 4.00
10 Dustin Boyd .25 .60
11 Mark Stuart .25 .60
12 Eric Fehr .40 1.00
13 Noah Welch .25 .60
14 Anze Kopitar 1.00 2.50
15 Travis Zajac .50 1.25
16 Jordan Staal .60 1.50
17 Ladislav Smid .25 .60
18 Alexander Radulov .50 1.25
19 Ryan Potulny .25 .60
20 Marc-Antoine Pouliot .25 .60
21 Jarkko Immonen .25 .60
22 Paul Stastny .60 1.50
23 Alexei Kaigorodov .25 .60
24 Dave Bolland .40 1.00
25 Nigel Dawes .25 .60
26 Jeremy Williams .25 .60
27 Marc-Edouard Vlasic .25 .60
28 Keith Yandle .50 1.25
29 Matt Lashoff .25 .60
30 Ian White .30 .75
31 Alexei Mikhnov .25 .60
32 Tomas Kopecky .30 .75
33 Konstantin Pushkarev .30 .75
34 Kristopher Letang .75 2.00
35 Michael Blunden .25 .60
36 Brandon Prust .25 .60
37 Dustin Byfuglien .60 1.50
38 Ben Ondrus .25 .60
39 Brendan Bell .25 .60
40 Janis Sprukts .25 .60
41 Ryan Shannon .25 .60
42 Shane O'Brien .25 .60
43 Patrick Thoresen .25 .60
44 Nathan McIver .25 .60
45 Drew Stafford .40 1.00
46 Alexander Edler .40 1.00
47 Yan Stastny .25 .60
48 Kelly Guard .30 .75
49 Nate Thompson .25 .60
50 Adam Burish .40 1.00

2007-08 Upper Deck Rookie Class

COMPLETE SET (50) 8.00 20.00
COMP.FACT.SET (51) 10.00 25.00
1 Bobby Ryan .40 1.00
2 Ondrej Pavelec .30 .75
3 Patrick Kane 1.00 2.50
4 Kris Russell .20 .50
5 Matt Niskanen .25 .60
6 Andrew Cogliano .25 .60
7 Jonathan Bernier .40 1.00
8 Marc Staal .25 .60
9 Nick Foligno .30 .75
10 Peter Mueller .20 .50
11 Jiri Tlusty .25 .60
12 Brett Sterling .15 .40
13 Petr Kalus .15 .40
14 Rob Schremp .20 .50
15 Andy Greene .20 .50
16 Frans Nielsen .25 .60
17 Martin Hanzal .20 .50
18 Devin Setoguchi .25 .60
19 Matt Smaby .15 .40
20 James Sheppard .15 .40
21 Kyle Chipchura .25 .60
22 Ryan Parent .15 .40
23 David Krejci .50 1.25
24 Lauri Tukonen .15 .40
25 Anton Stralman .15 .40
26 Tobias Enstrom .25 .60
27 Tyler Kennedy .25 .60
28 Mason Raymond .25 .60
29 Thomas Greiss .30 .75
30 Drew Miller .20 .50
31 Curtis McElhinney .25 .60
32 Ryan Callahan .30 .75
33 Brian Elliott .30 .75
34 Vladimir Sobotka .20 .50
35 Jonathan Sigalet .15 .40
36 Ville Koistinen .15 .40
37 Torrey Mitchell .20 .50
38 David Perron .25 .60
39 Jannik Hansen .20 .50
40 Chris Bourque .20 .50
41 Milan Lucic .75 2.00
42 Tuukka Rask .60 1.50
43 Jonathan Toews 1.00 2.50
44 Sam Gagner .30 .75
45 Jack Johnson .20 .50
46 Carey Price 1.50 4.00
47 Nicklas Bergfors .15 .40
48 Erik Johnson .25 .60
49 Bryan Little .20 .50
50 Nicklas Backstrom .50 1.25

2007-08 Upper Deck Rookie Class C-Card Insert

STATED ODDS 1 PER BOX SET
CC1 Jonathan Toews 2.50 6.00
CC2 Patrick Kane 2.50 6.00
CC3 Carey Price 4.00 10.00
CC4 Jack Johnson .50 1.25
CC5 Nicklas Backstrom 1.25 3.00
CC6 Sam Gagner .75 2.00

2008-09 Upper Deck Rookie Class

This set was released on February 13, 2009. The base set consists of 50 cards.
COMP.FACT.SET (51) 10.00 25.00
COMPLETE SET (50) 8.00 20.00
1 Steven Stamkos 1.50 4.00
2 Michael Frolik .25 .60
3 Drew Doughty .60 1.50
4 Claude Giroux .50 1.25
5 Zach Bogosian .25 .60
6 Mark Fistric .20 .50
7 Alex Pietrangelo .30 .75
8 Vladimir Mihalik .15 .40
9 Luke Schenn .30 .75
10 Nikita Filatov .25 .60
11 Patrik Berglund .20 .50
12 Karl Alzner .15 .40
13 Mikkel Boedker .30 .75
14 Justin Abdelkader .40 1.00
15 Brian Boyle .20 .50
16 Adam Pineault .20 .50
17 Jonathan Ericsson .25 .60
18 Shawn Matthias .25 .60
19 Zach Boychuk .25 .60
20 Cory Schneider .60 1.50
21 Josh Bailey .30 .75
22 Oscar Moller .20 .50
23 Colton Gillies .20 .50
24 Matt D'Agostini .20 .50
25 Luca Sbisa .15 .40
26 Lauri Korpikoski .15 .40
27 Robbie Earl .15 .40
28 Andreas Nodl .15 .40
29 Blake Wheeler .60 1.50
30 Dan LaCosta .25 .60
31 Steve Mason .40 1.00
32 Viktor Tikhonov .20 .50
33 Tom Sestito .25 .60
34 Fabian Brunnstrom .20 .50
35 Teddy Purcell .30 .75
36 Kyle Okposo .25 .60
37 Brian Lee .20 .50
38 Kyle Turris .40 1.00
39 Alex Goligoski .30 .75
40 Patric Hornqvist .25 .60
41 Petr Vrana .15 .40
42 T.J. Oshie .50 1.25
43 Nikolai Kulemin .25 .60
44 Boris Valabik .25 .60
45 Brandon Sutter .25 .60
46 Derick Brassard .20 .50
47 Jakub Voracek .50 1.25
48 James Neal .50 1.25
49 Darren Helm .25 .60
50 Ilya Zubov .20 .50

2008-09 Upper Deck Rookie Class Autographs

OVERALL AUTO ODDS 1:20 FACT.SET
1 Steven Stamkos 60.00 120.00
2 Michael Frolik
3 Drew Doughty 50.00 100.00
5 Zach Bogosian
6 Mark Fistric
7 Alex Pietrangelo
8 Vladimir Mihalik
9 Luke Schenn
10 Nikita Filatov
11 Patrik Berglund 8.00 20.00
13 Mikkel Boedker
14 Justin Abdelkader
15 Brian Boyle
16 Adam Pineault
17 Jonathan Ericsson
18 Shawn Matthias
19 Zach Boychuk
22 Oscar Moller
23 Colton Gillies 8.00 20.00
25 Luca Sbisa
26 Lauri Korpikoski
27 Robbie Earl
29 Blake Wheeler
30 Dan LaCosta
31 Steve Mason 15.00 40.00
32 Viktor Tikhonov 8.00 20.00
33 Tom Sestito
34 Fabian Brunnstrom
37 Brian Lee
38 Kyle Turris
40 Patric Hornqvist
41 Petr Vrana
42 T.J. Oshie
43 Nikolai Kulemin 10.00 25.00
44 Boris Valabik
45 Brandon Sutter
46 Derick Brassard
47 Jakub Voracek
48 James Neal
49 Darren Helm 10.00 25.00
50 Ilya Zubov

2008-09 Upper Deck Rookie Class C-Card Insert

ONE PER FACTORY SET
C1 Steven Stamkos 4.00 10.00
C2 Kyle Turris 1.00 2.50
C3 Drew Doughty 1.50 4.00
C4 Luke Schenn .75 2.00
C5 Blake Wheeler 1.50 4.00
C6 Derick Brassard .50 1.25
C7 Cory Schneider 1.50 4.00
C8 Colton Gillies .50 1.25
C9 Fabian Brunnstrom .50 1.25
C10 Kyle Okposo .60 1.50
C11 Nikita Filatov .60 1.50
C12 Nikolai Kulemin .60 1.50
C13 Jakub Voracek 1.25 3.00
C14 Brandon Sutter .60 1.50

2001-02 Upper Deck Rookie Update Signs of History

This limited autograph card was randomly inserted into packs of UD Rookie Update and the card is serial-numbered out of 33.
STATED PRINT RUN 33
1 Patrick Roy AU

2002-03 Upper Deck Rookie Update

Released in May 2003, Rookie Update consisted of a 176-card base set, a jersey card insert set, an autograph insert set and update cards for SP Authentic, SPx, UD Foundations and UD Classic Portraits. In the base set, cards 101-116 were serial-numbered to 999, cards 117-148 and 173-176 were serial-numbered to 1500, and cards 163-171 were serial-numbered to 199. Cards 163-171 carried dual autographs. Cards 149-162 had three different versions, A, B and C. Each version was serial-numbered with the 'A' cards being serial-numbered from 1 to 400; the 'B' cards being serial-numbered 401-800 and the 'C' versions serial-numbered 801-1200 for a total of 1200 cards. Cards 149-162 carried jersey swatches of each player pictured.
1 Paul Kariya .30 .75
2 Adam Oates .25 .60
3 Jean-Sebastien Giguere .25 .60
4 Sandis Ozolinsh .20 .50
5 Dany Heatley .25 .60
6 Ilya Kovalchuk .30 .75
7 Patrik Stefan .20 .50
8 Dan McGillis .15 .40
9 Joe Thornton .30 .75
10 Sergei Samsonov .20 .50
11 Jeff Hackett .20 .50
12 Glen Murray .20 .50
13 Miroslav Satan .25 .60
14 Martin Biron .20 .50
15 Daniel Briere .20 .50
16 Chris Drury .25 .60
17 Jarome Iginla .25 .60
18 Roman Turek .25 .60
19 Pavel Brendl .15 .40
20 Rod Brind'Amour .25 .60
21 Ron Francis .30 .75
22 Tyler Arnason .25 .60
23 Jocelyn Thibault .20 .50
24 Bryan Marchment .20 .50
25 Joe Sakic .40 1.00
26 Peter Forsberg .30 .75
27 Patrick Roy .60 1.50
28 Rob Blake .25 .60
29 Geoff Sanderson .20 .50
30 Marc Denis .20 .50
31 Mike Modano .40 1.00
32 Bill Guerin .25 .60
33 Marty Turco .25 .60
34 Steve Yzerman .50 1.25
35 Brendan Shanahan .30 .75
36 Brett Hull .30 .75
37 Curtis Joseph .25 .60
38 Nicklas Lidstrom .25 .60
39 Sergei Fedorov .40 1.00
40 Mathieu Schneider .15 .40
41 Mike Comrie .25 .60
42 Tommy Salo .20 .50
43 Olli Jokinen .25 .60
44 Kristian Huselius .15 .40
45 Roberto Luongo .40 1.00
46 Adam Deadmarsh .20 .50
47 Zigmund Palffy .25 .60
48 Felix Potvin .40 1.00
49 Marian Gaborik .40 1.00
50 Gordie Howe .75 2.00
51 Pascal Dupuis .15 .40
52 Saku Koivu .25 .60
53 Marcel Hossa .15 .40
54 Jose Theodore .25 .60
55 David Legwand .20 .50
56 Scott Hartnell .25 .60
57 Tomas Vokoun .20 .50
58 John Madden .15 .40
59 Scott Gomez .20 .50
60 Martin Brodeur .50 1.25
61 Alexei Yashin .20 .50
62 Mark Parrish .15 .40
63 Janne Niinimaa .15 .40
64 Alex Kovalev .25 .60
65 Pavel Bure .30 .75
66 Mike Dunham .20 .50
67 Mark Messier .40 1.00
68 Brian Leetch .25 .60
69 Daniel Alfredsson .25 .60
70 Marian Hossa .20 .50
71 Patrick Lalime .20 .50
72 Jeremy Roenick .25 .60
73 John LeClair .25 .60
74 Tony Amonte .20 .50
75 Gordie Howe .75 2.00
76 Roman Cechmanek .20 .50
77 Brian Boucher .20 .50
78 Shane Doan .20 .50
79 Mario Lemieux .75 2.00
80 Martin Straka .20 .50
81 Sebastien Caron .20 .50
82 Alexei Morozov .15 .40
83 Doug Weight .25 .60
84 Keith Tkachuk .25 .60
85 Chris Osgood .25 .60
86 Teemu Selanne .50 1.25
87 Kyle McLaren .15 .40
88 Evgeni Nabokov .20 .50
89 Martin St. Louis .25 .60
90 Nikolai Khabibulin .25 .60
91 Doug Gilmour .30 .75
92 Mats Sundin .25 .60
93 Owen Nolan .25 .60
94 Ed Belfour .25 .60
95 Todd Bertuzzi .25 .60
96 Markus Naslund .20 .50
97 Dan Cloutier .20 .50
98 Jaromir Jagr .60 1.50
99 Olaf Kolzig .25 .60
100 Michael Nylander .15 .40
101 Gordie Howe RRM 2.50 6.00
102 Wayne Gretzky RRM 4.00 10.00
103 Bobby Orr RRM 2.50 6.00
104 Patrick Roy RRM 2.00 5.00
105 Mario Lemieux RRM 2.50 6.00
106 Joe Thornton RRM 1.00 2.50
107 Martin Brodeur RRM 1.50 4.00
108 Steve Yzerman RRM 1.50 4.00
109 Jaromir Jagr RRM 2.00 5.00
110 Paul Kariya RRM 1.00 2.50
111 Jarome Iginla RRM .75 2.00
112 Joe Sakic RRM 1.25 3.00
113 Mats Sundin RRM .75 2.00
114 Ilya Kovalchuk RRM 1.00 2.50
115 Marian Gaborik RRM 1.25 3.00
116 Mike Modano RRM 1.25 3.00
117 Carlo Colaiacovo RC 2.00 5.00
118 Jay Bouwmeester RC 4.00 10.00
119 Ari Ahonen RC 1.25 3.00
120 Patrick Boileau RC 1.25 3.00
121 Mike Komisarek RC 2.00 5.00
122 Cristobal Huet RC 2.50 6.00
123 Josh Harding RC 5.00 12.00
124 Chris Schmidt RC 1.25 3.00
125 Niko Dimitrakos RC 1.25 3.00
126 Ryan Bayda RC 1.25 3.00
127 Radoslav Hecl RC 1.25 3.00
128 Burke Henry RC 1.25 3.00
129 Frederic Cloutier RC 1.25 3.00
130 Tomas Kurka RC 1.25 3.00
131 John Tripp RC 1.25 3.00
132 Francois Beauchemin RC 2.00 5.00
133 Brandon Reid RC 1.25 3.00
134 Tomas Surovy RC 1.25 3.00
135 Chad Wiseman RC 1.25 3.00
136 Jason Bacashihua RC 1.50 4.00
137 Jesse Fibiger RC 1.25 3.00
138 Marc-Andre Bergeron RC 1.50 4.00
139 Ryan Miller RC 8.00 20.00
140 Ryan Kraft RC 1.25 3.00
141 Simon Gamache RC 1.25 3.00
142 Rob Davison RC 1.25 3.00
143 Jason King RC 2.00 5.00
144 Brad Defauw RC 1.25 3.00
145 Miroslav Zalesak RC 1.25 3.00
146 Sean McMorrow RC 1.25 3.00
147 Mike Siklenka RC 3.00 8.00
148 Doug Janik RC 1.25 3.00
149A A.Svitov RC/Shanahan 5.00 12.00
149B A.Svitov RC/T.Bertuzzi 4.00 10.00
149C A.Svitov RC/J.LeClair 4.00 10.00
150A A.Smirnov RC/A.Yashin 3.00 8.00
150B A.Smirnov RC/T.Bertuzzi 4.00 10.00
150C A.Smirnov RC/J.LeClair 4.00 10.00
151A B.Orpik RC/R.Blake 4.00 10.00
151B B.Orpik RC/E.Jovanoski 4.00 10.00
151C B.Orpik RC/S.Stevens 4.00 10.00
152A A.Hall RC/J.LeClair 4.00 10.00
152B A.Hall RC/A.Deadmarsh 3.00 8.00
152C A.Hall RC/J.Iginla 4.00 10.00
153A J.Taffe RC/C.Drury 4.00 10.00
153B J.Taffe RC/M.York 2.50 6.00
153C J.Taffe RC/J.Roenick 4.00 10.00
154A S.Eminger RC/N.Lidstrom 4.00 10.00
154B S.Eminger RC/S.Gonchar 3.00 8.00
154C S.Eminger RC/B.Leetch 4.00 10.00
155A J.Leopold RC/A.MacInnis 4.00 10.00
155B J.Leopold RC/B.Leetch 4.00 10.00
155C Leopold RC/S.Niedermayer 4.00 10.00
156A P.Sharp RC/S.Reinprecht 6.00 15.00
156B P.Sharp RC/M.Peca 6.00 15.00
156C P.Sharp RC/J.Roenick 6.00 15.00
157A S.Ott RC/P.Kariya 5.00 12.00
157B S.Ott RC/S.Samsonov 5.00 12.00
157C S.Ott RC/T.Fleury 5.00 12.00
158A A.Hemsky RC/J.Jagr 10.00 25.00
158B A.Hemsky RC/M.Hejduk 8.00 20.00
158C A.Hemsky RC/P.Elias 6.00 15.00
159A A.Frolov RC/J.LeClair 5.00 12.00
159B A.Frolov RC/A.Yashin 5.00 12.00
159C A.Frolov RC/J.Jagr 10.00 25.00
160A J.Stoll RC/J.LeClair 8.00 20.00
160B J.Stoll RC/K.Tkachuk 8.00 20.00
160C J.Stoll RC/B.Guerin 8.00 20.00
161A Volchenkov RC/R.Blake 4.00 10.00
161B Volchenkov RC/S.Stevens 4.00 10.00
161C Volchenkov RC/Jovanoski 3.00 8.00
162A D.Bykov RC/B.Leetch 4.00 10.00
162B D.Bykov RC/N.Lidstrom 4.00 10.00
162C D.Bykov RC/S.Gonchar 3.00 8.00
163 J.Spezza RC/W.Gretzky 175.00 300.00
164 P.Bouchard RC/S.Samsonov 15.00 40.00
165 R.Hainsey RC/R.Bourque 20.00 50.00
166 S.Chistov RC/P.Bure 12.00 30.00
167 C.Kobasew RC/J.Iginla 15.00 40.00
168 H.Zetterberg RC/G.Howe 75.00 150.00
169 S.Upshall RC/M.Comrie 12.00 30.00
170 P.LeClaire RC/P.Roy 30.00 80.00
171 M.Tellqvist RC/E.Belfour 20.00 50.00
172 R.Nash RC/J.Thornton 30.00 80.00
173 Igor Radulov RC 1.25 3.00
174 Paul Gaustad RC 1.25 3.00
175 Christian Backman RC 1.25 3.00
176 Cam Severson RC 1.25 3.00

2002-03 Upper Deck Rookie Update Autographs

Inserted in packs at 1:144, this 29-card set featured authentic player autographs inset vertically on the card fronts. The print run totals below were announced by Upper Deck but the cards are not serial numbered.
STATED ODDS 1:144
BO Bobby Orr/9*
BR Pavel Brendl 10.00 25.00
CJ Curtis Joseph 15.00 40.00
CK Chuck Kobasew/24* 10.00 25.00
DH Dany Heatley 15.00 40.00
EC Erik Cole 10.00 25.00
GH Gordie Howe/24* 100.00 175.00
HZ Henrik Zetterberg/24* 50.00 100.00
IK Ilya Kovalchuk 15.00 40.00
JA Jason Spezza/24* 30.00 80.00
JB Jay Bouwmeester/24* 15.00 40.00
JI Jarome Iginla 15.00 40.00
JL John LeClair 10.00 25.00
MA Maxim Afinogenov 10.00 25.00
MC Mike Comrie 10.00 25.00
MH Martin Havlat 12.50 30.00
MN Markus Naslund 10.00 25.00
MT Mikael Tellqvist/24* 25.00 60.00
PB Pavel Bure 10.00 25.00
PM P-M Bouchard/24* 12.50 30.00
PR Patrick Roy/24* 100.00 150.00
RB Ray Bourque/24* 30.00 80.00
RH Ron Hainsey/24* 20.00 40.00
SC Stanislav Chistov/24* 10.00 25.00
SG Simon Gagne 10.00 25.00
SO Steve Ott 10.00 25.00
SS Sergei Samsonov 10.00 25.00
SY Steve Yzerman 30.00 80.00
WG Wayne Gretzky 150.00 250.00

2002-03 Upper Deck Rookie Update Jerseys

Randomly insrted in packs, this 42-card set consisted of 36 single jersey cards and 6 dual jersey cards. Single jersey cards were serial-numbered out of 299 and dual cards were serial-numbered out of 99.
DAY Alexei Yashin 4.00 10.00
DBG Bill Guerin 4.00 10.00
DBS Brendan Shanahan 5.00 12.00
DCO Chris Osgood 4.00 10.00
DDH Dany Heatley 5.00 12.00
DEL Eric Lindros 6.00 15.00
DFP Felix Potvin 6.00 15.00

DHO Marian Hossa 4.00 10.00
DIK Ilya Kovalchuk 5.00 12.00
DJG Jean-Sebastien Giguere 10.00 25.00
DJI Jarome Iginla 6.00 15.00
DJJ Jaromir Jagr 8.00 20.00
DJR Jeremy Roenick 6.00 15.00
DJS Joe Sakic 8.00 20.00
DJT Joe Thornton 5.00 12.00
DKP Keith Primeau 4.00 10.00
DMD Mike Dunham 3.00 8.00
DMH Milan Hejduk 4.00 10.00
DML Mario Lemieux 12.50 30.00
DMM Mike Modano 6.00 15.00
DMS Mats Sundin 5.00 12.00
DOK Olaf Kolzig 4.00 10.00
DPB Pavel Bure 5.00 12.00
DPD Pavol Demitra 4.00 10.00
DPK Paul Kariya 5.00 12.00
DPR Patrick Roy 12.50 30.00
DRC Roman Cechmanek 4.00 10.00
DRL Roberto Luongo 6.00 15.00
DRT Roman Turek 4.00 10.00
DSK Saku Koivu 4.00 10.00
DSS Sergei Samsonov 4.00 10.00
DSY Steve Yzerman 12.50 30.00
DTB Todd Bertuzzi 4.00 10.00
DTH Jose Theodore 5.00 12.00
DTS Tommy Salo 4.00 10.00
DZP Zigmund Palffy 4.00 10.00
SJK J.Jagr/O.Kolzig 12.50 30.00
SKH I.Kovalchuk/D.Heatley 12.50 20.00
SLB E.Lindros/P.Bure 12.50 30.00
SRS P.Roy/J.Sakic 15.00 40.00
STS J.Thornton/S.Samsonov 12.50 30.00
SYS S.Yzerman/B.Shanahan 20.00 50.00

2003-04 Upper Deck Rookie Update

This 217-card set consisted of 90-veteran base cards, 65 base rookies (91-150 and 166-172) numbered to 999, 10 dual-jersey cards (151-158 and 173-174) numbered to 999 that featured both a rookie and a veteran, 8 dual-autograph cards (159-165 and 175) numbered to 199 that featured a rookie and a veteran and an additional 43 rookie cards (176-217) serial-numbered to 199 that were available only via a redemption card good for all 43 cards.

COMP.SET w/o SP's (90) 25.00 50.00
1 Petr Sykora .25 .60
2 Jean-Sebastien Giguere .30 .75
3 Sergei Fedorov .50 1.25
4 Dany Heatley .30 .75
5 Ilya Kovalchuk .30 .75
6 Sergei Samsonov .25 .60
7 Joe Thornton .40 1.00
8 Andrew Raycroft .25 .60
9 Chris Drury .25 .60
10 Daniel Briere .30 .75
11 Mika Noronen .20 .50
12 Jarome Iginla .30 .75
13 Miikka Kiprusoff .25 .60
14 Justin Williams .25 .60
15 Ron Francis .40 1.00
16 Jocelyn Thibault .25 .60
17 Bryan Berard .25 .60
18 Mark Bell .20 .50
19 Joe Sakic .50 1.25
20 Paul Kariya .40 1.00
21 Peter Forsberg .40 1.00
22 David Aebischer .25 .60
23 Todd Marchant .20 .50
24 Rick Nash .30 .75
25 Marc Denis .25 .60
26 Bill Guerin .30 .75
27 Marty Turco .30 .75
28 Mike Modano .50 1.25
29 Pavel Datsyuk .40 1.00
30 Henrik Zetterberg .40 1.00
31 Brett Hull .40 1.00
32 Steve Yzerman .75 2.00
33 Adam Oates .30 .75
34 Tommy Salo .25 .60
35 Raffi Torres .20 .50
36 Ales Hemsky .30 .75
37 Roberto Luongo .50 1.25
38 Jay Bouwmeester .30 .75
39 Olli Jokinen .30 .75
40 Martin Straka .20 .50
41 Roman Cechmanek .25 .60
42 Zigmund Palffy .30 .75
43 Marian Gaborik .50 1.25
44 Alexandre Daigle .25 .60
45 Manny Fernandez .25 .60
46 Jose Theodore .30 .75
47 Saku Koivu .30 .75
48 Mike Ribeiro .25 .60
49 Steve Sullivan .20 .50
50 Tomas Vokoun .25 .60
51 Patrik Elias .30 .75
52 Scott Gomez .25 .60
53 Martin Brodeur .60 1.50
54 Scott Stevens .30 .75
55 Alexei Yashin .25 .60
56 Trent Hunter .20 .50
57 Rick DiPietro .25 .60
58 Jaromir Jagr .75 2.00
59 Mark Messier .50 1.25
60 Peter Bondra .25 .60
61 Jason Spezza .30 .75
62 Marian Hossa .25 .60
63 Patrick Lalime .25 .60
64 Sean Burke .20 .50
65 Jeremy Roenick .30 .75
66 Alexei Zhamnov .25 .60
67 Brian Boucher .25 .60
68 Mike Comrie .25 .60
69 Mario Lemieux 1.00 2.50
70 Sebastien Caron .25 .60
71 Vincent Damphousse .25 .60
72 Evgeni Nabokov .25 .60
73 Patrick Marleau .30 .75
74 Chris Osgood .30 .75
75 Doug Weight .30 .75
76 Pavol Demitra .40 1.00
77 Keith Tkachuk .30 .75
78 Nikolai Khabibulin .30 .75
79 Vincent Lecavalier .25 .60
80 Mats Sundin .30 .75
81 Alexander Mogilny .25 .60
82 Owen Nolan .25 .60
83 Ed Belfour .30 .75
84 Todd Bertuzzi .30 .75
85 Ed Jovanovski .25 .60
86 Markus Naslund .30 .75
87 Jason King .20 .50
88 Dan Cloutier .25 .60
89 Anson Carter .25 .60
90 Olaf Kolzig .30 .75
91 Niklas Kronwall RC 4.00 10.00
92 Doug Doull RC 1.50 4.00
93 Fedor Tyutin RC 1.50 4.00
94 Dwayne Zinger RC 1.50 4.00
95 Jason MacDonald RC 1.50 4.00
96 Ryan Malone RC 3.00 8.00
97 Rob Skrlac RC 1.50 4.00
98 Jame Pollock RC 1.50 4.00
99 Grant McNeill RC 1.50 4.00
100 Noah Clarke RC 1.50 4.00
101 Joey MacDonald RC 3.00 8.00
102 John Pohl RC 1.50 4.00
103 Tony Martensson RC 1.50 4.00
104 Antti Miettinen RC 2.50 6.00
105 Ryan Barnes RC 1.50 4.00
106 Graham Mink RC 1.50 4.00
107 Patrick Leahy RC 2.00 5.00
108 Sergei Zinovjev RC 1.50 4.00
109 Steve McLaren RC 1.50 4.00
110 Seamus Kotyk RC 1.50 4.00
111 Tim Jackman RC 2.00 5.00
112 Andrew Hutchinson RC 1.50 4.00
113 Andy Chiodo RC 1.50 4.00
114 Timofei Shishkanov RC 1.50 4.00
115 Milan Michalek RC 3.00 8.00
116 Trevor Daley RC 2.50 6.00
117 Jeff MacMillan RC 2.00 5.00
118 Jason Pominville RC 4.00 10.00
119 Mikko Luoma RC 1.50 4.00
120 Brad Boyes RC 2.50 6.00
121 Michael Morrison RC 2.00 5.00
122 Tomas Plekanec RC 5.00 12.00
123 Mike Stuart RC 1.50 4.00
124 Tuomas Pihlman RC 2.00 5.00
125 Darcy Verot RC 1.50 4.00
126 Mark Popovic RC 2.00 5.00
127 Erik Westrum RC 1.50 4.00
128 Aaron Johnson RC 1.50 4.00
129 Doug Lynch RC 1.50 4.00
130 Randy Jones RC 1.50 4.00
131 Nathan Smith RC 1.50 4.00
132 Aleksander Suglobov RC 1.50 4.00
133 Kyle Wellwood RC 2.50 6.00
134 Chris Kunitz RC 3.00 8.00
135 Jeff Hamilton RC 1.50 4.00
136 Garth Murray RC 2.00 5.00
137 Peter Sejna RC 2.00 5.00
138 Mike Smith RC 5.00 12.00
139 Antero Niittymaki RC 4.00 10.00
140 Carl Corazzini RC 1.50 4.00
141 Anton Babchuk RC 1.50 4.00
142 Julien Vauclair RC 1.50 4.00
143 Nathan Robinson RC 1.50 4.00
144 Dan Ellis RC 2.00 5.00
145 Colton Orr RC 2.00 5.00
146 Rastislav Stana RC 2.50 6.00
147 Gavin Morgan RC 2.00 5.00
148 Dan Hamhuis RC 2.00 5.00
149 Nolan Schaefer RC 1.50 4.00
150 Pat Rissmiller RC 2.00 5.00
151 Bergeron J RC/Thornton J 8.00 20.00
152 Hudler J RC/Yzerman J 10.00 25.00
153 R.Kesler J RC/T.Bertuzzi J 6.00 15.00
154 Semin J RC/Bure J 8.00 20.00
155 Higgins J RC/Koivu J 6.00 15.00
156 J.Lupul J RC/S.Fedorov J 6.00 15.00
157 D.Brown J RC/Z.Palffy J 6.00 15.00
158 J.Pitkanen J RC/J. Roenick J 5.00 12.00
159 Fleury AU RC/Roy AU 75.00 150.00
160 Ruutu AU RC/Koivu AU 20.00 50.00
161 Staal AU RC/Gretzky AU 175.00 250.00
162 Horton AU RC/Howe AU 40.00 100.00
163 Zherdev AU RC/Nash AU 25.00 60.00
164 Sjostrom AU RC/Naslund AU 15.00 40.00
165 Tootoo AU RC/Nolan AU 20.00 50.00
166 Zbynek Michalek RC 1.50 4.00
167 Lawrence Nycholat RC 2.00 5.00
168 Fred Meyer RC 1.50 4.00
169 Mike Bishai RC 1.50 4.00
170 Mike Green RC 2.00 5.00
171 Matt Ellison RC 1.50 4.00
172 Joe Motzko RC 1.50 4.00
173 D.Roy J RC/C. Drury J 4.00 10.00
174 D.Fritsche J RC/Nash J 5.00 12.00
175 Stajan AU RC/Nolan AU 20.00 50.00
176 Kari Lehtonen RC 20.00 50.00
177 Goran Bezina RC 4.00 10.00
178 Owen Fussey RC 4.00 10.00
179 Josh Olson RC 4.00 10.00
180 Michal Barinka RC 4.00 10.00
181 Bryce Lampman RC 5.00 12.00
182 Matt Hussey RC 4.00 10.00
183 Mike Stutzel RC 4.00 10.00
184 Roman Tvrdon RC 4.00 10.00
185 Matthew Yeats RC 4.00 10.00
186 Thomas Pock RC 5.00 12.00
187 Wade Dubielewicz RC 4.00 10.00
188 Greg Mauldin RC 5.00 12.00
189 Mike Pandolfo RC 4.00 10.00
190 Eric Perrin RC 4.00 10.00
191 Christoph Brandner RC 5.00 12.00
192 Matthew Lombardi RC 5.00 12.00
193 John-Michael Liles RC 5.00 12.00
194 Marek Svatos RC 8.00 20.00
195 Tony Salmelainen RC 4.00 10.00
196 Dominic Moore RC 4.00 10.00
197 Brooks Laich RC 6.00 15.00
198 Cory Larose RC 4.00 10.00
199 Adam Munro RC 4.00 10.00
200 Mikhail Kuleshov RC 4.00 10.00
201 Matt Keith RC 4.00 10.00
202 Denis Grebeshkov RC 4.00 10.00
203 Quintin Laing RC 4.00 10.00
204 Benoit Dusablon RC 4.00 10.00
205 Matt Underhill RC 4.00 10.00
206 Jozef Balej RC 4.00 10.00
207 Robert Scuderi RC 5.00 12.00
208 Libor Pivko RC 4.00 10.00
209 Mikhail Yakubov RC 4.00 10.00
210 Tom Preissing RC 5.00 12.00
211 Cody McCormick RC 5.00 12.00
212 Pavel Vorobiev RC 5.00 12.00
213 Matt Murley RC 5.00 12.00
214 Matthew Spiller RC 5.00 12.00
215 Marek Zidlicky RC 4.00 10.00
216 Christian Ehrhoff RC 5.00 12.00
217 Brent Burns RC 10.00 25.00
RR1 Rookie EXCH expired .20 .50

2003-04 Upper Deck Rookie Update All-Star Lineup

This 12-card set featured swatches of game-used jersey and each card was serial-numbered out of 25. As of press time, all cards have not been verified.

AS1 Martin Brodeur 20.00 50.00
AS2 Ilya Kovalchuk 15.00 40.00
AS3 Joe Thornton 20.00 50.00
AS4 Marian Hossa 10.00 25.00
AS5 Scott Niedermayer 8.00 20.00
AS6 Zdeno Chara
AS7 Marty Turco 8.00 20.00
AS8 Markus Naslund 8.00 20.00
AS9 Joe Sakic 12.50 30.00
AS10 Brett Hull 20.00 50.00
AS11 Rob Blake 12.50 30.00
AS12 Nicklas Lidstrom 10.00 25.00

2003-04 Upper Deck Rookie Update Skills

PRINT RUN 75 SER.#'d SETS
SKJSG Jean-Sebastien Giguere 3.00 8.00
SKAH Ales Hemsky 3.00 8.00
SKAY Alexei Yashin 3.00 8.00
SKBG Bill Guerin 3.00 8.00
SKBH Brett Hull 5.00 12.00
SKCD Chris Drury 3.00 8.00
SKDA David Aebischer 3.00 8.00
SKDH Dany Heatley 5.00 12.00
SKDW Doug Weight 3.00 8.00
SKEB Ed Belfour 4.00 10.00
SKEL Eric Lindros 4.00 10.00
SKGM Glen Murray 3.00 8.00
SKJJ Jaromir Jagr 6.00 15.00
SKJR Jeremy Roenick 5.00 12.00
SKJS Jason Spezza 5.00 12.00
SKJT Jose Theodore 5.00 12.00
SKMB Martin Brodeur 12.50 30.00
SKMF Manny Fernandez 3.00 8.00
SKMG Marian Gaborik 6.00 15.00
SKMH Marian Hossa 4.00 10.00
SKMK Mark Messier 5.00 12.00
SKML Mario Lemieux 12.50 30.00
SKMM Mike Modano 6.00 15.00
SKMN Markus Naslund 4.00 10.00
SKMS Mats Sundin 4.00 10.00
SKMT Marty Turco 3.00 8.00
SKNK Nikolai Khabibulin 4.00 10.00
SKON Owen Nolan 3.00 8.00
SKPF Peter Forsberg 8.00 20.00
SKPK Paul Kariya 4.00 10.00
SKPL Patrick Lalime 3.00 8.00
SKRN Rick Nash 5.00 12.00
SKSA Joe Sakic 8.00 20.00
SKSB Sean Burke 3.00 8.00
SKSF Sergei Fedorov 6.00 15.00
SKSK Saku Koivu 4.00 10.00
SKSY Steve Yzerman 12.50 30.00
SKTA Tony Amonte 4.00 10.00
SKTB Todd Bertuzzi 4.00 10.00
SKTH Joe Thornton 6.00 15.00
SKVL Vincent Lecavalier 4.00 10.00
SKZP Zigmund Palffy 3.00 8.00

2003-04 Upper Deck Rookie Update Super Stars

PRINT RUN 75 SER.#'d SETS
SSMSL Martin St. Louis 3.00 8.00
SSHJK Milan Hejduk 4.00 10.00
SSAF Alexander Frolov 3.00 8.00
SSAM Alexander Mogilny 3.00 8.00
SSBH Brett Hull 5.00 12.00
SSBM Brendan Morrison 3.00 8.00
SSDA David Aebischer 3.00 8.00
SSDH Dany Heatley 5.00 12.00
SSDW Doug Weight 3.00 8.00
SSEB Ed Belfour 4.00 10.00
SSGM Glen Murray 3.00 8.00
SSHZ Henrik Zetterberg 5.00 12.00
SSJB Jay Bouwmeester 4.00 10.00
SSJI Jarome Iginla 5.00 12.00
SSJL John LeClair 4.00 10.00
SSJO Joe Sakic 8.00 20.00
SSJR Jeremy Roenick 6.00 15.00
SSJS Jason Spezza 5.00 12.00
SSJT Joe Thornton 6.00 15.00
SSKT Keith Tkachuk 4.00 10.00
SSLR Luc Robitaille 3.00 8.00
SSMB Martin Brodeur 12.50 30.00
SSMF Manny Fernandez 3.00 8.00
SSMG Marian Gaborik 8.00 20.00
SSMH Marian Hossa 4.00 10.00
SSMK Mark Messier 4.00 10.00
SSML Mario Lemieux 12.50 30.00
SSMM Mike Modano 6.00 15.00
SSMS Mats Sundin 4.00 10.00
SSMT Marty Turco 3.00 8.00
SSON Owen Nolan 3.00 8.00
SSPD Pavol Demitra 3.00 8.00
SSPF Peter Forsberg 8.00 20.00
SSPL Patrick Lalime 3.00 8.00
SSRC Roman Cechmanek 3.00 8.00
SSSD Shane Doan 3.00 8.00
SSSF Sergei Fedorov 6.00 15.00
SSSK Saku Koivu 4.00 10.00
SSSS Sergei Samsonov 3.00 8.00
SSSY Steve Yzerman 12.50 30.00
SSVL Vincent Lecavalier 4.00 10.00
SSZP Zigmund Palffy 3.00 8.00

2003-04 Upper Deck Rookie Update Top Draws

This 20-card autograph set featured "cut" autographs of current stars. Cards in this set were inserted at odds of 1:72.

TD1 Evgeni Nabokov 6.00 15.00
TD2 Teemu Selanne 8.00 20.00
TD3 Todd Bertuzzi SP 20.00 50.00
TD4 Wayne Gretzky/14
TD5 Gordie Howe/14
TD6 Jason Spezza SP 75.00 150.00
TD7 Rick DiPietro 6.00 15.00
TD8 Jean-Sebastien Giguere 50.00 100.00
TD9 Nikolai Zherdev 6.00 15.00
TD10 Ales Hemsky 6.00 15.00
TD11 Ilya Kovalchuk SP 12.50 30.00
TD12 Pascal Leclaire 6.00 15.00
TD13 Rick Nash 8.00 20.00
TD14 Nikolai Khabibulin SP 25.00 60.00
TD15 Steve Yzerman 25.00 60.00
TD16 John LeClair 8.00 15.00
TD17 Patrick Roy 60.00 150.00
TD18 Jay Bouwmeester 6.00 15.00
TD19 Alexander Svitov 6.00 15.00
TD20 Fredrik Sjostrom 6.00 15.00

2003-04 Upper Deck Rookie Update YoungStars

PRINT RUN 99 SER.#'d SETS
YS1 Michael Ryder 8.00 20.00
YS2 Eric Staal 12.00 30.00
YS2A Eric Staal 12.00 30.00
YS3 Patrice Bergeron 10.00 25.00
YS3A Patrice Bergeron 12.00 30.00
YS4 Trent Hunter 4.00 10.00
YS5 Ryan Malone 5.00 12.00
YS6 Derek Roy 4.00 10.00
YS6A Derek Roy 4.00 10.00
YS7 Matt Stajan 4.00 10.00
YS7A Matt Stajan 4.00 10.00
YS8 Joni Pitkanen 4.00 10.00
YS8A Joni Pitkanen 4.00 10.00
YS9 Paul Martin 4.00 10.00
YS10 Brooks Orpik 4.00 10.00
YS11 Andrew Raycroft 8.00 20.00
YS11A Andrew Raycroft 8.00 20.00
YS12 Pierre-Marc Bouchard 4.00 10.00
YS13 Joffrey Lupul 6.00 15.00
YS14 Matthew Lombardi 4.00 10.00
YS15 Tuomo Ruutu 8.00 20.00
YS15A Tuomo Ruutu 8.00 20.00
YS16 Raffi Torres 4.00 10.00
YS17 Nikolai Zherdev 8.00 20.00
YS17A Nikolai Zherdev 8.00 20.00
YS18 Jonathan Cheechoo 12.00 30.00
YS19 Christian Ehrhoff 4.00 10.00
YS20 Dan Hamhuis 5.00 12.00
YS21 Alexei Semenov 4.00 10.00
YS22 Philippe Sauve 4.00 10.00

2005-06 Upper Deck Rookie Update

This 277-card set was issued into the hobby in five-card packs which came 24 packs to a box and 12 boxes to a case. Cards numbered 1-100 feature veteran players in team alphabetical order while cards 101-277 feature single player Rookie Cards (101-195) and multi-player Rookie Cards (196-275) which feature both a rookie and a veteran player and has two game-worn jersey swatches. The set concludes with a Sidney Crosby Rookie Card which is issued to a stated print run of 199 serial numbered copies. All cards 101-275 are serial numbered with cards 101-195 being issued to a stated print run of 1999 serial numbered sets, cards 196-254 issued to a stated print run of 999 serial numbered sets; cards numbered 255-273 issued to a stated print run of 499 serial numbered sets and cards 274, 275 and 276 were also issued to a stated print run of 199 serial numbered sets. In addition, Rookie Cards not already issued in five products were also inserted into this set. The products which had updated Rookie Cards inserted were: SP Game Used, Trilogy, Black Diamond, SPx and Artifacts. There are two versions of card number 276 with the more common version serial numbered to 199 and a second version serial numbered to 23.

COMPLETE SET w/o SPs (100) 8.00 20.00
101-195 ROOKIE PRINT RUN 1999
196-254 DUAL JSY PRINT RUN 999
255-273 DUAL AU PRINT RUN 499
1 Jean-Sebastien Giguere .40 1.00
2 Teemu Selanne .75 2.00
3 Joffrey Lupul .30 .75
4 Ilya Kovalchuk .40 1.00
5 Marian Hossa .30 .75
6 Kari Lehtonen .30 .75
7 Andrew Raycroft .30 .75
8 Brian Leetch .40 1.00
9 Patrice Bergeron .50 1.25
10 Glen Murray .30 .75
11 Chris Drury .30 .75
12 Ryan Miller .40 1.00
13 Jarome Iginla .40 1.00
14 Miikka Kiprusoff .30 .75
15 Daymond Langkow .25 .60
16 Eric Staal .50 1.25
17 Martin Gerber .30 .75
18 Doug Weight .40 1.00
19 Erik Cole .30 .75
20 Nikolai Khabibulin .40 1.00
21 Tuomo Ruutu .40 1.00
22 Jose Theodore .40 1.00
23 Alex Tanguay .40 1.00
24 Joe Sakic .60 1.50
25 Marek Svatos .30 .75
26 Milan Hejduk .30 .75
27 Rob Blake .40 1.00
28 Rick Nash .40 1.00
29 Sergei Fedorov .60 1.50
30 Mike Modano .60 1.50
31 Brenden Morrow .30 .75
32 Marty Turco .40 1.00
33 Steve Yzerman 1.00 2.50
34 Pavel Datsyuk .50 1.25
35 Henrik Zetterberg .50 1.25
36 Brendan Shanahan .50 1.25
37 Nicklas Lidstrom .40 1.00
38 Ryan Smyth .30 .75
39 Chris Pronger .30 .75
40 Ales Hemsky .30 .75
41 Roberto Luongo .60 1.50
42 Nathan Horton .40 1.00
43 Olli Jokinen .40 1.00
44 Alexander Frolov .25 .60
45 Jeremy Roenick .40 1.00
46 Pavol Demitra .50 1.25
47 Luc Robitaille .40 1.00
48 Marian Gaborik .60 1.50
49 Manny Fernandez .30 .75
50 Saku Koivu .40 1.00
51 David Aebischer .30 .75
52 Michael Ryder .30 .75
53 Mike Ribeiro .30 .75
54 Paul Kariya .50 1.25
55 Tomas Vokoun .30 .75
56 Martin Brodeur .75 2.00
57 Patrik Elias .40 1.00
58 Brian Gionta .30 .75
59 Scott Gomez .30 .75
60 Alexei Yashin .30 .75
61 Miroslav Satan .30 .75
62 Rick DiPietro .30 .75
63 Jaromir Jagr 1.00 2.50
64 Martin Straka .25 .60
65 Dominik Hasek .60 1.50
66 Dany Heatley .40 1.00
67 Daniel Alfredsson .40 1.00
68 Jason Spezza .40 1.00
69 Wade Redden .25 .60
70 Peter Forsberg .50 1.25
71 Simon Gagne .40 1.00
72 Antero Niittymaki .30 .75
73 Keith Primeau .40 1.00
74 Joni Pitkanen .25 .60
75 Curtis Joseph .40 1.00
76 Shane Doan .30 .75
77 Ladislav Nagy .25 .60
78 Mario Lemieux 1.25 3.00
79 Ryan Malone .25 .60
80 Marc-Andre Fleury .60 1.50
81 Joe Thornton .50 1.25
82 Patrick Marleau .40 1.00
83 Evgeni Nabokov .30 .75
84 Jonathan Cheechoo .40 1.00
85 Keith Tkachuk .40 1.00
86 Barret Jackman .25 .60
87 Vincent Lecavalier .30 .75
88 Martin St. Louis .40 1.00
89 Brad Richards .40 1.00
90 Vaclav Prospal .25 .60
91 Mats Sundin .40 1.00
92 Ed Belfour .40 1.00
93 Jason Allison .30 .75
94 Bryan McCabe .25 .60
95 Eric Lindros .60 1.50
96 Markus Naslund .40 1.00
97 Alex Auld .25 .60
98 Todd Bertuzzi .40 1.00
99 Brendan Morrison .25 .60
100 Olaf Kolzig .40 1.00
101 Dustin Penner RC 3.00 8.00
102 Michael Wall RC 2.50 6.00
103 Zenon Konopka RC 2.00 5.00
104 Adam Berkhoel RC 2.50 6.00
105 Jay Leach RC 2.50 6.00
106 Eric Healey RC 2.50 6.00
107 Ben Guite RC 2.50 6.00
108 Ben Walter RC 2.00 5.00
109 Brian Eklund RC 2.50 6.00
110 Nathan Paetsch RC 2.50 6.00
111 Jiri Novotny RC 2.50 6.00
112 Mark Giordano RC 3.00 8.00
113 Richie Regehr RC 2.00 5.00
114 Chad Larose RC 2.00 5.00
115 Keith Aucoin RC 2.00 5.00
116 David Gove RC 2.50 6.00
117 Mark Cullen RC 2.50 6.00
118 Rene Bourque RC 3.00 8.00
119 Martin St. Pierre RC 2.00 5.00
120 Corey Crawford RC 12.00 30.00
121 James Wisniewski RC 2.50 6.00
122 Vitaly Kolesnik RC 2.50 6.00
123 Andrew Penner RC 2.50 6.00
124 Steven Goertzen RC 2.00 5.00
125 Geoff Platt RC 2.50 6.00
126 Joakim Lindstrom RC 2.00 5.00
127 Junior Lessard RC 2.00 5.00
128 Vojtech Polak RC 2.00 5.00
129 Brett Lebda RC 2.00 5.00
130 Kyle Brodziak RC 2.00 5.00
131 Danny Syvret RC 2.00 5.00
132 Matt Greene RC 2.00 5.00
133 J-F Jacques RC 2.00 5.00
134 Mathieu Roy RC 3.00 8.00
135 Greg Jacina RC 2.00 5.00
136 Rob Globke RC 2.00 5.00
137 Petr Taticek RC 2.50 6.00
138 Adam Hauser RC 2.50 6.00
139 George Parros RC 2.00 5.00
140 Yanick Lehoux RC 3.00 8.00
141 Petr Kanko RC 2.50 6.00
142 Jeff Giuliano RC 2.50 6.00
143 Matt Ryan RC 2.50 6.00
144 Connor James RC 2.50 6.00
145 Richard Petiot RC 2.50 6.00
146 Derek Boogaard RC 4.00 10.00
147 Matt Foy RC 2.00 5.00
148 Raitis Ivanans RC 2.00 5.00
149 Mark Streit RC 2.00 5.00
150 Jonathan Ferland RC 2.50 6.00
151 J-P Cote RC 2.00 5.00
152 Kevin Klein RC 2.00 5.00
153 Pekka Rinne RC 5.00 12.00
154 Greg Zanon RC 2.50 6.00
155 Cam Janssen RC 2.50 6.00
156 Jason Ryznar RC 2.00 5.00
157 Bruno Gervais RC 2.00 5.00
158 Kevin Colley RC 2.50 6.00
159 Ryan Hollweg RC 2.00 5.00
160 Chris Holt RC 2.00 5.00
161 Brian McGrattan RC 2.00 5.00
162 Wade Skolney RC 2.00 5.00
163 Josh Gratton RC 2.50 6.00
164 Ryan Ready RC 2.50 6.00
165 Alexandre Picard RC 2.00 5.00
166 Stefan Ruzicka RC 2.00 5.00
167 Matt Jones RC 2.00 5.00
168 Colby Armstrong RC 3.00 8.00
169 Doug Murray RC 2.00 5.00
170 Grant Stevenson RC 2.00 5.00
171 Kevin Dallman RC 2.50 6.00
172 Andy Roach RC 2.00 5.00
173 Jon DiSalvatore RC 2.50 6.00
174 Dennis Wideman RC 2.00 5.00
175 Jeff Hoggan RC 2.00 5.00
176 Colin Hemingway RC 2.00 5.00
177 Chris Beckford-Tseu RC 2.50 6.00
178 Mike Glumac RC 2.50 6.00
179 Timo Helbling RC 2.00 5.00
180 Nick Tarnasky RC 2.00 5.00
181 Gerald Coleman RC 2.00 5.00
182 Paul Ranger RC 2.00 5.00
183 Darren Reid RC 2.00 5.00
184 Doug O'Brien RC 2.00 5.00
185 Staffan Kronwall RC 2.00 5.00
186 Jay Harrison RC 2.50 6.00
187 Rick Rypien RC 4.00 10.00
188 Rob McVicar RC 2.50 6.00
189 Alexandre Burrows RC 4.00 10.00
190 Tomas Mojzis RC 2.00 5.00
191 Prestin Ryan RC 1.50 4.00
192 David Steckel RC 2.50 6.00
193 Mike Green RC 4.00 10.00
194 Joey Tenute RC 2.50 6.00
195 Louis Robitaille RC 2.00 5.00
196 Coburn JSY RC/Bouwmeester JSY 5.00 12.00
197 Slater JSY RC/Draper JSY 6.00 15.00
198 Jurcina JSY RC/Chara JSY 5.00 12.00
199 Sigalet JSY RC/Raycroft JSY 4.00 10.00
200 Nystrom JSY RC/Amonte JSY 4.00 10.00
201 Nastiuk JSY RC/Biron JSY 4.00 10.00
202 Richmond JSY RC/Rafalski JSY 4.00 10.00
203 Seabrook JSY RC/Jovn JSY 10.00 25.00
204 Barker JSY RC/Blake JSY 5.00 12.00
205 Budaj JSY RC/Vokoun JSY 6.00 15.00
206 Richrdsn JSY RC/Sakic JSY 8.00 20.00
207 Jokinen JSY RC/Lehtinen JSY 5.00 12.00
208 Howard JSY RC/Conklin JSY 8.00 20.00
209 Franzen JSY RC/Zetter JSY 8.00 20.00
210 Winchester JSY RC/Tkachuk JSY 5.00 12.00
211 Stewart JSY RC/Doan JSY 4.00 10.00
212 Tambellini JSY RC/St.Louis JSY 5.00 12.00
213 Danis JSY RC/Theodore JSY 5.00 12.00
214 Lapierre JSY RC/Turgeon JSY 5.00 12.00
215 Suter JSY RC/Chelios JSY 6.00 15.00
216 Parise JSY RC/Rnick JSY 8.00 20.00
217 Tallackson JSY RC/Guerin JSY 5.00 12.00
218 Nokelainen JSY RC/Jokinen JSY 5.00 12.00
219 Nilsson JSY RC/Naslund JSY 5.00 12.00
220 Campoli JSY RC/McCabe JSY 3.00 8.00
221 Montoya JSY RC/Esche JSY 5.00 12.00
222 Schubert JSY RC/Pitkanen JSY 3.00 8.00
223 Bochenski JSY RC/Parrish JSY 5.00 12.00
224 Eaves JSY RC/Peca JSY 5.00 12.00
225 Umberger JSY RC/Primeau JSY 5.00 12.00
226 Ballard JSY RC/Niedermayer JSY 5.00 12.00
227 Leneveu JSY RC/Joseph JSY 5.00 12.00
228 Talbot JSY RC/Morrison JSY 5.00 12.00
229 Whitney JSY RC/Leetch JSY 5.00 12.00
230 Bernier JSY RC/Heatley JSY 5.00 12.00
231 Clowe JSY RC/Cheech JSY 6.00 15.00
232 Woywitka JSY RC/Foote JSY 3.00 8.00
233 Stemp JSY RC/Bergeron JSY 6.00 15.00
234 Artyukin JSY RC/Jagr JSY 12.00 30.00
235 Woznw JSY RC/Hatcher JSY 4.00 10.00
236 Klepis JSY RC/Hemsky JSY 4.00 10.00
237 Fleischm JSY RC/Hejduk JSY 5.00 12.00
238 Alberts JSY RC/Boynton JSY 3.00 8.00
239 Eager JSY RC/Daze JSY 4.00 10.00
240 Picard JSY RC/Robitaille JSY 8.00 20.00
241 Tollefsen JSY RC/Klesla JSY 4.00 10.00
242 Paille JSY RC/Stillman JSY 5.00 12.00
243 Christensen JSY RC/Staal JSY 6.00 15.00
244 Patzold JSY RC/Nabokov JSY 4.00 10.00
245 Craig JSY RC/Lecavalier JSY 4.00 10.00
246 Bieksa JSY RC/Jackman JSY 5.00 12.00
247 Colliton JSY RC/Hunter JSY 3.00 8.00
248 McClement JSY RC/Arnott JSY 4.00 10.00
249 Gorges JSY RC/Hamhuis JSY 4.00 10.00
250 Quincey JSY RC/Regehr JSY 4.00 10.00
251 Thorburn JSY RC/Brind'A JSY 5.00 12.00
252 Nordgren JSY RC/Holms JSY 5.00 12.00
253 Keith JSY RC/Stuart JSY 6.00 15.00
254 Balastik JSY RC/Prospal JSY 3.00 8.00
255 Prucha JSY RC/Straka JSY 5.00 12.00
256 Getzlaf AU RC/Spezza AU 20.00 50.00
257 Perry AU RC/Tanguay AU 15.00 30.00
258 Toivonen AU RC/Lehtn AU 15.00 40.00
259 Vanek AU RC/Iginla AU 20.00 50.00
260 Steen AU RC/Gilmour AU 15.00 40.00
261 Ladd AU RC/Bertuzzi AU 12.00 30.00
262 Ward AU RC/Turco AU 8.00 20.00
263 Wolski AU RC/Smyth AU 10.00 25.00
264 Brule AU RC/Gagne AU 10.00 25.00
265 Filppula AU RC/Rtu AU 12.00 30.00
266 Olesz AU RC/Havlat AU 10.00 25.00
267 Koivu AU RC/Koivu AU 10.00 25.00
268 Perezhogin AU RC/Yashin AU 10.00 25.00
269 Kostitsyn AU RC/Frolov AU 15.00 40.00
270 Lundqvist AU RC/Hask AU 25.00 60.00
271 Meszaros AU RC/Redden AU 12.00 30.00
272 Carter AU RC/Thrntn AU 15.00 40.00
273 Richards AU RC/Mdno AU 12.00 30.00
274 Phanf AU RC/Prngr AU/199 30.00 80.00
275 Ovch AU RC/Kovl AU/199 150.00 300.00
276 Sidney Crosby/199 RC 800.00 1200.00
276B Sidney Crosby SP/23 1400.00 1800.00

2005-06 Upper Deck Rookie Update Inspirations Patch Rookies

*PATCH/25: 1X TO 2.5X BASIC DUAL JSY

2011 Upper Deck Signature Icons Las Vegas Summit Promos

UNPRICED AUTO PRINT RUN 4-15
LVAO Alexander Ovechkin/15
LVGH Gordie Howe/10
LVLG M.Lemieux/W.Gretzky/4
LVWG Wayne Gretzky/10

2004 Upper Deck Sportsfest

These cards were issued in groups of five over the course of three days at the 2004 Sportsfest card show in Chicago. Collectors would receive a group of 5 each day in exchange for 10 Upper Deck card wrappers that carried and SRP valued of $2.99 or higher. A 16th card was issued as an exchange card good for the first pick in the 2004 NBA draft.

STATED PRINT RUN 500 SER.#'d SETS
SF13 Wayne Gretzky 4.00 10.00
SF14 Gordie Howe 2.00 5.00
SF15 Joe Thornton 1.00 2.50

2007 Upper Deck Sportsfest

UNPRICED AUTO PRINT RUN 3 TO 5 SETS
SF10 Evgeni Malkin 2.00 5.00
SF11 Alex Ovechkin 2.00 5.00
SF12 Sidney Crosby 3.00 6.00

2008 Upper Deck Sportsfest

COMPLETE SET (12) 15.00 40.00
UNPRICED AUTO PRINT RUN 5 SETS
SF4 Patrick Kane 1.50 4.00
SF7 Jonathan Toews 1.50 4.00
SF12 Sidney Crosby 3.00 8.00

2015-16 Upper Deck Star Rookies

COMPLETE SET (25) 10.00 20.00
1 Connor McDavid 3.00 8.00
2 Mike Condon .40 1.00
3 Sam Bennett .50 1.25
4 Colton Parayko .50 1.25
5 Artemi Panarin 1.25 3.00
6 Joonas Donskoi .40 1.00
7 Max Domi .75 2.00
8 Nikolaj Ehlers .75 2.00
9 Colin Miller .30 .75
10 Noah Hanifin .50 1.25
11 Robby Fabbri .50 1.25
12 Dylan Larkin 1.25 3.00
13 Nicolas Petan .40 1.00
14 Mikko Rantanen .75 2.00
15 Daniel Sprong .75 2.00
16 Devin Shore .40 1.00
17 Jake Virtanen .50 1.25
18 Mattias Janmark .40 1.00
19 Matt O'Connor .30 .75
20 Andreas Athanasiou 1.00 2.50
21 Jared McCann .40 1.00
22 Vicktor Svedberg .30 .75
23 Tyler Randell .40 1.00
24 Jordan Weal .40 1.00
25 Jack Eichel 1.50 4.00

2015-16 Upper Deck Star Rookies Autographs

COMPLETE SET (24)
STATED ODDS 1:20 FACTORY SETS
1 Connor McDavid
2 Mike Condon
3 Sam Bennett
4 Colton Parayko
5 Artemi Panarin
6 Joonas Donskoi
7 Max Domi
8 Nikolaj Ehlers
9 Colin Miller
10 Noah Hanifin
11 Robby Fabbri
12 Dylan Larkin
13 Nicolas Petan
14 Mikko Rantanen
15 Daniel Sprong
16 Devin Shore
17 Jake Virtanen
18 Mattias Janmark
19 Matt O'Connor
20 Andreas Athanasiou
21 Jared McCann
22 Vicktor Svedberg
23 Tyler Randell
24 Jordan Weal

2005-06 Upper Deck Sunkist

COMPLETE SET (6) 6.00 15.00
1 Richard Brodeur 1.00 2.50
2 Wendel Clark 1.00 2.50
3 Yvan Cournoyer 1.00 2.50
4 Doug Gilmour 1.25 3.00
5 Dale Hawerchuk 1.00 2.
6 Lanny McDonald 1.25 3.

2006-07 Upper Deck Sunkist

COMPLETE SET (10) 10.00 20.
1 Alex Kovalev .40 1.
2 Jason Spezza .75 2.
3 Mats Sundin 1.25 3.
4 Jarome Iginla 1.25 3.
5 Ryan Smyth .75 2.
6 Markus Naslund .75 2.
7 Alexander Ovechkin 2.00 5.
8 Vincent Lecavalier 1.25 3.
9 Joe Thornton 1.50 4.
10 Miikka Kiprusoff 1.25 3.

2007-08 Upper Deck Sunkist

COMPLET SET (10) 10.00 25.
1 Saku Koivu 1.25 3.
2 Mats Sundin 1.25 3.
3 Dany Heatley 1.25 3.
4 Alex Hemsky 1.25 3.
5 Jarome Iginla 1.25 3.
6 Roberto Luongo 1.50 4.
7 Joe Thornton 1.50 4.
8 Vincent LeCavalier 1.25 3.
9 Chris Pronger 1.25 3.
10 Eric Staal 1.25 3.

2008-09 Upper Deck Sunkist

COMPLETE SET (10) 10.00 20.
1 Sidney Crosby 3.00 8.
2 Alexander Ovechkin 2.00 5.
3 Carey Price 1.50 4.
4 Mike Cammalleri .75 2.
5 Matt Stajan 1.00 2.
6 Dany Heatley 1.25 3.
7 Jarome Iginla 1.25 3.
8 Daniel Sedin 1.00 2.
9 Sam Gagner .75 2.
10 Sergei Kostitsyn .75 2.

2008-09 Upper Deck Sunkist Autographs

1 Sidney Crosby 60.00 100.
2 Alexander Ovechkin 40.00 80.
3 Carey Price
4 Mike Cammalleri
5 Matt Stajan 8.00 20.
6 Dany Heatley
7 Jarome Iginla
8 Daniel Sedin
9 Sam Gagner
10 Sergei Kostitsyn 8.00 20.

2009-10 Upper Deck Sunkist

COMPLETE SET (10) 10.00 20.
1 Sidney Crosby 3.00 8.
2 Martin Brodeur 1.50 4.
3 Jarome Iginla 1.25 3.
4 Rick Nash 1.25 3.
5 Mike Richards 1.00 2.
6 Vincent LeCavalier 1.25 3.
7 Roberto Luongo 1.50 4.
8 Ryan Getzlaf 1.00 2.
9 Scott Niedermayer 1.00 2.
10 Jay Bouwmeester 1.00 2.

2013-14 Upper Deck Team Canada

COMP.SET w/o SP's (100) 8.00 20.
101-200 ODDS 1:1
201-230 ODDS 1:6
1 Cam Ward .40 1.
2 Adam Henrique .40 1.
3 Milan Lucic .40 1.
4 Alex Pietrangelo .30 .7
5 Alex Tanguay .25 .6
6 Andrew Cogliano .25 .6
7 Andrew Ladd .40 1.
8 Bill Ranford .50 1.2
9 Blake Comeau .25 .6
10 Bobby Orr .75 2.
11 Brad Boyes .25 .6
12 Brad Marchand .50 1.2
13 Jason Spezza .40 1.
14 Braden Holtby .60 1.5
15 Brandon McMillan .25 .6
16 Brayden McNabb .25 .6
17 Brayden Schenn .40 1.
18 Brendan Mikkelson .25 .6
19 Brenden Morrow .30 .7
20 Brent Seabrook .40 1.
21 Brett Connolly .25 .6
22 Bryan Little .40 1.
23 Calvin de Haan .25 .6
24 Steve Yzerman .75 2.
25 Carter Ashton .25 .6
26 Chet Pickard .25 .6
27 Chris Phillips .25 .6
28 Chris Stewart .30 .7
29 Ryan Spooner .40 1.
30 Clarke MacArthur .25 .6
31 Cody Eakin .25 .6
32 Cody Hodgson .40 1.
33 Colby Armstrong .25 .6
34 Colten Teubert .25 .6
35 Dana Tyrell .25 .6
36 Daniel Carcillo .25 .6
37 Derek Roy .30 .7
38 Devante Smith-Pelly .30 .7
39 Dustin Tokarski .40 1.
40 Dylan Olsen .25 .6
41 Shane Doan .30 .7
42 Erik Gudbranson .40 1.
43 Glen Murray .30 .7
44 Greg Nemisz .25 .6
45 Jaden Schwartz .50 1.2
46 Jake Allen .50 1.2
47 James Neal .40 1.
48 Jamie Benn .50 1.
49 Jamie Oleksiak .30 .7
50 Chris Pronger .30 .7
51 Jay Bouwmeester .40 1.
52 Jay McClement .25 .6
53 Jeremy Colliton .25 .6
54 John Negrin .25 .6
55 Jordan Eberle .40 1.
56 Justin Pogge .25 .6
57 Karl Alzner .25 .6
58 Keaton Ellerby .25 .6
59 Keith Aulie .25 .6
60 Kyle Clifford .25 .6
61 Luke Adam .30 .7
62 Luke Schenn .25 .6
63 Devan Dubnyk .40 1.
64 Marc-Andre Gragnani .25 .6
65 Marco Scandella .25 .6
66 Mark Stone .30 .7
67 Matt Beleskey .25 .6
68 Matthew Halischuk .25 .6
69 Michael Cammalleri .30 .7
70 Justin Schultz .75 2.

1 Michael Ryder .25 .60
2 Patrice Cormier .25 .60
3 Pierre-Marc Bouchard .40 1.00
4 Quinton Howden .30 .75
5 Ryan Ellis .25 .60
6 Ryan Getzlaf .60 1.50
7 Ryan Johansen .50 1.25
8 Ryan Smyth .30 .75
9 Sam Gagner .30 .75
0 Scott Laughton .60 1.50
1 Sean Couturier .40 1.00
2 Sheldon Souray .25 .60
3 Simon Despres .30 .75
4 Simon Gagne .40 1.00
5 Stefan Della Rovere .25 .60
6 Stefan Elliott .30 .75
7 Stephen Weiss .30 .75
8 Steve Bernier .25 .60
9 Steve Sullivan .25 .60
0 Thomas Hickey .30 .75
1 Tim Brent .25 .60
2 Travis Hamonic .25 .60
3 Tyler Ennis .30 .75
4 Tyler Myers .30 .75
5 Zach Boychuk .25 .60
6 Tyson Barrie .40 1.00
7 Wade Redden .25 .60
8 Yann Sauve .25 .60
9 Wayne Gretzky 2.00 5.00
00 Zack Kassian .30 .75
01 Alexandre Burrows .75 2.00
02 Bill Barber .75 2.00
03 Mike Green .75 2.00
04 Bobby Clarke .75 2.00
05 Bobby Hull .75 2.00
06 Bobby Orr 2.50 6.00
07 Paul Coffey .75 2.00
08 Jared Cowen .50 1.25
09 Casey Cizikas .50 1.25
10 Corey Perry .75 2.00
11 Curtis Joseph .75 2.00
12 Dale Hawerchuk 1.00 2.50
13 Dan Boyle .60 1.50
14 Dany Heatley .60 1.50
15 Darryl Sittler .75 2.00
16 Dion Phaneuf .75 2.00
17 Dougie Hamilton 1.25 3.00
18 Drew Doughty .75 2.00
19 Ed Belfour .75 2.00
20 Brayden Schenn .75 2.00
21 Eric Lindros 1.25 3.00
22 Eric Staal 1.00 2.50
23 Evander Kane .75 2.00
24 Vincent Damphousse .60 1.50
25 Felix Potvin 1.25 3.00
26 Tanner Pearson .75 2.00
27 Gilbert Perreault .75 2.00
28 Guillaume Latendresse .60 1.50
29 Guy Lafleur 1.00 2.50
30 Jarome Iginla .75 2.00
31 Jean-Sebastien Giguere .60 1.50
32 Jeff Skinner .60 1.50
33 Joe Sakic 1.25 3.00
34 Joe Thornton .75 2.00
35 John Tavares 1.50 4.00
36 Jonathan Bernier .75 2.00
37 Carey Price 1.50 4.00
38 Jonathan Huberdeau 1.50 4.00
39 Jonathan Toews 1.50 4.00
40 Jordan Eberle .75 2.00
41 Theoren Fleury 1.00 2.50
42 Jordan Staal .75 2.00
43 Jose Theodore .75 2.00
44 Josh Gorges .60 1.50
45 Kris Draper .60 1.50
46 Kyle Turris .50 1.25
47 Nathan Beaulieu .60 1.50
48 Larry Robinson .75 2.00
49 Logan Couture .75 2.00
50 Louis Leblanc .75 2.00
51 Luc Robitaille .75 2.00
52 Marc-Andre Fleury 1.25 3.00
53 Marcel Dionne 1.00 2.50
54 Shea Weber .60 1.50
55 Mario Lemieux 2.50 6.00
56 Mark Messier 1.00 2.50
57 Mark Scheifele 1.00 2.50
58 Martin Brodeur 1.50 4.00
59 Roberto Luongo .75 2.00
60 Martin St. Louis .75 2.00
61 Marty Turco .75 2.00
62 Matt Duchene .75 2.00
63 Maxime Talbot .60 1.50
64 Mike Bossy .75 2.00
65 Mike Ribeiro .60 1.50
66 Mike Richards .75 2.00
67 Marc Staal .60 1.50
68 P.K. Subban 1.25 3.00
69 Patrice Bergeron 1.00 2.50
70 Patrick Marleau .75 2.00
71 Patrick Roy 2.00 5.00
72 Phil Esposito 1.25 3.00
73 Ray Bourque 1.25 3.00
74 Claude Giroux .75 2.00
75 Rick Nash 1.00 2.50
76 Kris Letang .75 2.00
77 Rogie Vachon 1.00 2.50
78 Ron Francis 1.00 2.50
79 Ron Hextall .75 2.00
80 Ryan Nugent-Hopkins .75 2.00
81 Nazem Kadri .75 2.00
82 Patrick Sharp .75 2.00
83 Scott Hartnell .75 2.00
84 Steve Mason .60 1.50
85 Steve Shutt .60 1.50
86 Sidney Crosby 3.00 8.00
87 Steven Stamkos 1.50 4.00
88 Taylor Hall 1.50 4.00
89 Michael Del Zotto .50 1.25
90 Tyler Seguin 1.25 3.00
91 Vincent Lecavalier .60 1.50
92 Wayne Gretzky 4.00 10.00
93 Wayne Simmonds 1.00 2.50
94 Wendel Clark .75 2.00
95 Josh Harding .75 2.00
96 Brendan Gallagher 1.50 4.00
97 Jamie Tardif .50 1.25
98 Michael Sgarbossa 1.00 2.50
99 Jaden Schwartz 1.00 2.50
00 Ryan Murphy .75 2.00
01 Stefan Elliott PEA 1.00 2.50
02 Cody Hodgson PEA 1.25 3.00
03 Jamie Oleksiak PEA 1.00 2.50
04 Scott Glennie PEA 1.25 3.00
05 Dougie Hamilton PEA 2.50 6.00
06 Jaden Schwartz PEA 1.50 4.00
07 Mark Scheifele PEA 1.50 4.00
08 Scott Laughton PEA 1.25 3.00
09 Thomas Hickey PEA 1.00 2.50
10 Ryan Murphy PEA 1.25 3.00
11 Quinton Howden PEA 1.00 2.50
212 Erik Gudbranson PEA 1.25 3.00
213 Dylan Olsen PEA .75 2.00
214 Carter Ashton PEA .75 2.00
215 Brendan Gallagher PEA 2.00 5.00
216 Jamie Tardif PEA .75 2.00
217 Michael Sgarbossa PEA 1.25 3.00
218 Ryan Spooner PEA 1.25 3.00
219 Jake Allen PEA 1.50 4.00
220 Casey Cizikas PEA .75 2.00
221 Tyson Barrie PEA 1.25 3.00
222 Cody Goloubef PEA 1.50 4.00
223 Mark Stone PEA 1.00 2.50
224 Chet Pickard PEA 1.50 4.00
225 Jeff Skinner PEA 1.00 2.50
226 Taylor Hall PEA 2.50 6.00
227 Jordan Eberle PEA 2.00 5.00
228 Ryan Nugent-Hopkins PEA 1.25 3.00
229 John Tavares PEA 2.00 5.00
230 Jonathan Huberdeau PEA 1.50 4.00
SP1 Nathan MacKinnon PEA 10.00 25.00
SP2 Sean Monahan PEA 6.00 15.00

2013-14 Upper Deck Team Canada Special Edition

STATED ODDS 1:6
SE1 Wayne Gretzky 8.00 20.00
SE2 Tyson Barrie 2.00 5.00
SE3 Thomas Hickey 1.25 3.00
SE4 Theoren Fleury 2.00 5.00
SE5 Taylor Hall 3.00 8.00
SE6 Steve Mason 1.25 3.00
SE7 Stefan Elliott 1.25 3.00
SE8 Sidney Crosby 5.00 12.00
SE9 Shea Weber 1.25 3.00
SE10 Scott Laughton 1.50 4.00
SE11 Scott Hartnell 1.50 4.00
SE12 Scott Glennie 1.25 3.00
SE13 Ryan Spooner .75 2.00
SE14 Ryan Smyth 1.50 4.00
SE15 Ryan Nugent-Hopkins 1.50 4.00
SE16 Ryan Murphy 1.50 4.00
SE17 Ryan Getzlaf 2.00 5.00
SE18 Roberto Luongo 1.50 4.00
SE19 Rick Nash 1.50 4.00
SE20 Quinton Howden 1.50 4.00
SE21 Patrice Bergeron 2.00 5.00
SE22 P.K. Subban 2.50 6.00
SE23 Mike Richards 1.50 4.00
SE24 Michael Sgarbossa 1.25 3.00
SE25 Martin Brodeur 3.00 8.00
SE26 Mark Stone 1.25 3.00
SE27 Mark Scheifele 2.00 5.00
SE28 Mark Messier 2.00 5.00
SE29 Mario Lemieux 5.00 12.00
SE30 Marc-Andre Fleury 2.50 6.00
SE31 Kris Letang 2.00 5.00
SE32 Jordan Eberle 1.50 4.00
SE33 Jonathan Toews 3.00 8.00
SE34 Jonathan Huberdeau 2.00 5.00
SE35 John Tavares 3.00 8.00
SE36 Joe Sakic 2.50 6.00
SE37 Jeff Skinner 1.25 3.00
SE38 Jeff Carter 1.50 4.00
SE39 Jarome Iginla 1.50 4.00
SE40 Jamie Oleksiak 1.25 3.00
SE41 Jake Allen 2.00 5.00
SE42 Jaden Schwartz 2.00 5.00
SE43 Erik Gudbranson 1.50 4.00
SE44 Eric Lindros 2.50 6.00
SE45 Ed Belfour 2.00 5.00
SE46 Drew Doughty 1.50 4.00
SE47 Dougie Hamilton 1.50 4.00
SE48 Curtis Joseph 2.00 5.00
SE49 Corey Perry 1.50 4.00
SE50 Cody Hodgson 1.50 4.00
SE51 Cody Goloubef 1.00 2.50
SE52 Claude Giroux 1.50 4.00
SE53 Chet Pickard 1.00 2.50
SE54 Casey Cizikas 1.25 3.00
SE55 Carey Price 5.00 12.00
SE56 Brendan Gallagher 2.50 6.00
SE57 Brayden Schenn 1.50 4.00
SE58 Brad Marchand 2.50 6.00
SE59 Bobby Orr 3.00 8.00
SE60 Adam Henrique 1.50 4.00

2013-14 Upper Deck Team Canada Special Edition Gold Die Cut

SE1 Wayne Gretzky 40.00 80.00

2013-14 Upper Deck Team Canada Red

*1-100 VETS/100: 4X TO 10X BASIC CARDS
*101-200 VETS/100: 2X TO 5X BASIC CARDS
*201-230 PEA/100: 1.2X TO 3X BASIC PEA
RED/100 STATED ODDS 1:22

2013-14 Upper Deck Team Canada Autographs

UNPRICED GROUP A ODDS 1:3630
UNPRICED GROUP B ODDS 1:1312
GROUP C STATED ODDS 1:572
GROUP D STATED ODDS 1:359
GROUP E STATED ODDS 1:156
GROUP F STATED ODDS 1:142
GROUP G STATED ODDS 1:67
GROUP H STATED ODDS 1:51
GROUP I STATED ODDS 1:35
OVERALL ODDS 1:12 HOB, 1:120 BLSTR
1 Cam Ward C 20.00 40.00
2 Adam Henrique G 6.00 15.00
4 Alex Pietrangelo G 6.00 15.00
5 Alex Tanguay C 8.00 20.00
6 Andrew Cogliano I 2.50 6.00
7 Andrew Ladd G 5.00 12.00
8 Bill Ranford E 10.00 25.00
9 Blake Comeau C 8.00 20.00
10 Bobby Orr E 100.00 175.00
11 Brad Boyes D 8.00 20.00
12 Brad Marchand E 8.00 20.00
14 Braden Holtby E 8.00 20.00
15 Brandon McMillan D 6.00 15.00
16 Brayden McNabb H 2.50 6.00
17 Brayden Schenn F 6.00 15.00
18 Brendan Mikkelson H 2.50 6.00
19 Brenden Morrow A
20 Brent Seabrook E 12.00 30.00
21 Brett Connolly H 4.00 10.00
22 Bryan Little C 12.00 30.00
23 Calvin de Haan D 15.00 40.00
24 Steve Yzerman A
25 Carter Ashton D 5.00 12.00
26 Chet Pickard D 20.00 50.00
27 Chris Phillips I 3.00 8.00
28 Chris Stewart C
29 Ryan Spooner H 4.00 10.00
30 Clarke MacArthur F 6.00 15.00
31 Cody Eakin G 2.50 6.00
32 Cody Hodgson E 8.00 20.00
33 Colby Armstrong C 15.00 30.00
34 Colten Teubert H 2.50 6.00
35 Dana Tyrell C
36 Daniel Carcillo H 2.50 6.00
37 Derek Roy G 3.00 8.00
38 Devante Smith-Pelly C 8.00 20.00
39 Dustin Tokarski E 8.00 20.00
40 Dylan Olsen E 6.00 15.00
41 Shane Doan C 10.00 25.00
42 Erik Gudbranson F 5.00 12.00
43 Glen Murray E 4.00 10.00
45 Jaden Schwartz B
46 Jake Allen E 6.00 15.00
47 James Neal A
48 Jamie Benn E 10.00 25.00
49 Jamie Oleksiak E 4.00 10.00
50 Chris Pronger C 25.00 60.00
52 Jay McClement D 6.00 15.00
53 Jeremy Colliton G 2.50 6.00
54 John Negrin F 3.00 8.00
56 Justin Pogge E 8.00 20.00
57 Karl Alzner F 8.00 20.00
58 Keaton Ellerby I 2.50 6.00
59 Keith Aulie F 3.00 8.00
60 Kyle Clifford F 4.00 10.00
61 Luke Adam C 10.00 25.00
62 Luke Schenn H 2.50 6.00
63 Devan Dubnyk E 12.00 30.00
64 Marc-Andre Gragnani B
65 Marco Scandella G 3.00 8.00
66 Mark Stone I 3.00 8.00
67 Matt Beleskey G 2.50 6.00
68 Matthew Halischuk G 3.00 8.00
69 Michael Cammalleri A
70 Justin Schultz E 5.00 12.00
71 Michael Ryder E 15.00 40.00
72 Patrice Cormier A
73 Pierre-Marc Bouchard B
74 Quinton Howden I 3.00 8.00
75 Ryan Ellis H 2.50 6.00
77 Ryan Johansen G 6.00 15.00
78 Ryan Smyth D 10.00 25.00
79 Sam Gagner F 6.00 15.00
80 Scott Laughton F 5.00 12.00
83 Simon Despres D 15.00 30.00
84 Simon Gagne C 20.00 40.00
85 Stefan Della Rovere H 2.50 6.00
87 Stephen Weiss H 3.00 8.00
88 Steve Bernier C 15.00 30.00
89 Steve Sullivan D 20.00 40.00
90 Thomas Hickey I 3.00 8.00
91 Tim Brent H 2.50 6.00
92 Travis Hamonic G 2.50 6.00
93 Tyler Ennis F 4.00 10.00
94 Tyler Myers D 6.00 15.00
95 Zach Boychuk G 2.50 6.00
96 Tyson Barrie G 5.00 12.00
97 Wade Redden F 5.00 12.00
98 Yann Sauve H 2.50 6.00
99 Wayne Gretzky E 200.00 400.00
100 Zack Kassian F 4.00 10.00
101 Alexandre Burrows H 4.00 10.00
102 Bill Barber F 8.00 20.00
104 Bobby Clarke E 15.00 30.00
105 Bobby Hull B
106 Bobby Orr F 75.00 150.00
107 Paul Coffey C 20.00 40.00
108 Jared Cowen F 3.00 8.00
109 Casey Cizikas I 2.50 6.00
110 Corey Perry F 12.00 30.00
111 Curtis Joseph C 25.00 50.00
113 Dan Boyle E 8.00 20.00
114 Dany Heatley B
115 Darryl Sittler B
116 Dion Phaneuf E 10.00 25.00
117 Dougie Hamilton G 6.00 15.00
119 Ed Belfour B
120 Brayden Schenn D 6.00 15.00
121 Eric Lindros A
122 Eric Staal E 8.00 20.00
123 Evander Kane D 10.00 25.00
124 Vincent Damphousse E 12.00 30.00
125 Felix Potvin E 30.00 60.00
126 Tanner Pearson G 4.00 10.00
127 Gilbert Perreault C
128 Guillaume Latendresse I 3.00 8.00
129 Guy Lafleur B 50.00 100.00
130 Jarome Iginla B
131 Jean-Sebastien Giguere E 15.00 30.00
132 Jeff Skinner D 15.00 40.00
133 Joe Sakic A 75.00 150.00
134 Joe Thornton B
135 John Tavares E 25.00 50.00
136 Jonathan Bernier G 8.00 20.00
137 Carey Price B 75.00 135.00
138 Jonathan Huberdeau D
139 Jonathan Toews B 50.00 100.00
141 Theoren Fleury A
142 Jordan Staal D
143 Jose Theodore A
144 Josh Gorges D 8.00 20.00
145 Kris Draper F 8.00 20.00
146 Kyle Turris G 4.00 10.00
147 Nathan Beaulieu I 3.00 8.00
148 Larry Robinson E 10.00 25.00
149 Logan Couture B
150 Louis Leblanc I 4.00 10.00
151 Luc Robitaille C 25.00 50.00
152 Marc-Andre Fleury C 25.00 50.00
153 Marcel Dionne E 25.00 50.00
155 Mario Lemieux A
156 Mark Messier B
157 Mark Scheifele H 5.00 12.00
158 Martin Brodeur B
160 Martin St. Louis C 25.00 50.00
161 Marty Turco E 25.00 50.00
162 Matt Duchene C 25.00 50.00
163 Maxime Talbot G 3.00 8.00
164 Mike Bossy C 50.00 120.00
165 Mike Ribeiro E 6.00 15.00
166 Mike Richards B
167 Marc Staal D 6.00 15.00
168 P.K. Subban C 40.00 80.00
170 Patrick Marleau C 30.00 60.00
171 Patrick Roy A
172 Phil Esposito A
173 Ray Bourque B
174 Claude Giroux B 75.00 125.00
175 Rick Nash C 60.00 120.00
177 Rogie Vachon B
178 Ron Francis C 20.00 40.00
179 Ron Hextall D 25.00 50.00
183 Scott Hartnell E 10.00 25.00
184 Steve Mason F 5.00 12.00
185 Steve Shutt C 30.00 60.00
186 Sidney Crosby D 150.00 250.00
187 Steven Stamkos E 30.00 80.00
188 Taylor Hall D 75.00 135.00
189 Michael Del Zotto F 5.00 12.00
190 Tyler Seguin B
191 Vincent Lecavalier A
192 Wayne Gretzky D 300.00 450.00
193 Wayne Simmonds C 50.00 100.00
194 Wendel Clark E 30.00 60.00
195 Josh Harding D 20.00 40.00
196 Brendan Gallagher H 12.00 30.00
198 Michael Sgarbossa I 3.00 8.00
199 Jaden Schwartz A
200 Ryan Murphy I 4.00 10.00
201S Stefan Elliott PEA 6.00 15.00
202S Cody Hodgson PEA 8.00 20.00
203S Jamie Oleksiak PEA 6.00 15.00
204S Scott Glennie PEA 5.00 12.00
205S Dougie Hamilton PEA 10.00 25.00
206S Jaden Schwartz PEA 10.00 25.00
207S Mark Scheifele PEA 10.00 25.00
208S Scott Laughton PEA 8.00 20.00
209S Thomas Hickey PEA 5.00 12.00
210S Ryan Murphy PEA 5.00 12.00
211S Quinton Howden PEA 5.00 12.00
212S Erik Gudbranson PEA 8.00 20.00
213S Dylan Olsen PEA 5.00 12.00
214S Carter Ashton PEA 5.00 12.00
215S Brendan Gallagher PEA 20.00 50.00
217S Michael Sgarbossa PEA 5.00 12.00
218S Ryan Spooner PEA 6.00 15.00
219S Jake Allen PEA 6.00 15.00
220S Casey Cizikas PEA 5.00 12.00
221S Tyson Barrie PEA 8.00 20.00
222S Cody Goloubef PEA 5.00 12.00
223S Mark Stone PEA 6.00 15.00
224S Chet Pickard PEA 6.00 15.00
225S Jeff Skinner PEA 12.00 30.00
226S Taylor Hall PEA 30.00 60.00
228S Ryan Nugent-Hopkins PEA 40.00 80.00
229S John Tavares PEA 25.00 50.00
230S Jonathan Huberdeau PEA 25.00 50.00
SP1 Nathan MacKinnon/99 75.00 150.00
SP2 Sean Monahan/99 30.00 60.00

2013-14 Upper Deck Team Canada Captains

C1-C10 STATED ODDS 1:54
C11-C22 SP STATED ODDS 1:144
C23-C32 AU GROUP A ODDS 1:17,664
C23-C32 AU GROUP B ODDS 1:4817
C23-C32 AU GROUP C ODDS 1:1755
C23-C32 AU OVERALL ODDS 1:1152
C1 Phil Esposito 2.50 6.00
C2 Marcel Dionne 2.00 5.00
C3 Bobby Clarke 1.50 4.00
C4 Darryl Sittler 1.50 4.00
C5 Theoren Fleury 2.00 5.00
C6 Paul Coffey 2.00 5.00
C7 Eric Lindros 2.50 6.00
C8 Luc Robitaille 1.50 4.00
C9 Mario Lemieux 5.00 12.00
C10 Jarret Stoll 2.00 5.00
C11 Ryan Smyth SP 6.00 15.00
C12 Joe Sakic SP 12.00 30.00
C13 Shane Doan SP 5.00 12.00
C14 Kris Letang SP 10.00 25.00
C15 Karl Alzner SP 5.00 12.00
C16 Thomas Hickey SP 6.00 15.00
C17 Patrice Cormier SP 8.00 20.00
C18 Rick Nash SP 8.00 20.00
C19 Ryan Ellis SP 5.00 12.00
C20 Ryan Getzlaf SP 12.00 30.00
C21 Jaden Schwartz SP 15.00 40.00
C22 Ryan Nugent-Hopkins SP 25.00 50.00
C23 Thomas Hickey AU C 30.00 60.00
C24 Steve Yzerman AU A 200.00 350.00
C25 Ryan Nugent-Hopkins AU A 150.00 250.00
C26 Mario Lemieux AU A
C28 Jaden Schwartz AU C 30.00 60.00
C29 Joe Sakic AU B 100.00 175.00
C30 Theoren Fleury AU B 60.00 120.00
C31 Phil Esposito AU B 90.00 150.00
C32 Ryan Ellis AU C 25.00 60.00

2013-14 Upper Deck Team Canada Clear Cut Program of Excellence

CLEAR CUT/99 ODDS 1:96
CCPOE1 Wayne Gretzky 30.00 60.00
CCPOE2 Theoren Fleury 12.00 30.00
CCPOE3 Taylor Hall 20.00 50.00
CCPOE4 Sidney Crosby 25.00 50.00
CCPOE5 Scott Laughton 8.00 20.00
CCPOE6 Ryan Spooner 8.00 20.00
CCPOE7 Ryan Smyth 10.00 25.00
CCPOE8 Ryan Nugent-Hopkins 15.00 30.00
CCPOE9 Ryan Murphy 10.00 25.00
CCPOE10 Ryan Getzlaf 15.00 40.00
CCPOE11 Roberto Luongo 10.00 25.00
CCPOE12 Rick Nash 10.00 25.00
CCPOE13 Quinton Howden 8.00 20.00
CCPOE14 Patrice Bergeron 12.00 30.00
CCPOE15 P.K. Subban 15.00 40.00
CCPOE16 Mike Richards 10.00 25.00
CCPOE17 Martin Brodeur 20.00 50.00
CCPOE18 Mark Messier 12.00 30.00
CCPOE19 Mario Lemieux 30.00 80.00
CCPOE20 Marc-Andre Fleury 15.00 40.00
CCPOE21 Kris Letang 10.00 25.00
CCPOE22 Jordan Eberle 10.00 25.00
CCPOE23 Jonathan Toews 20.00 50.00
CCPOE24 Jonathan Huberdeau 8.00 20.00
CCPOE25 John Tavares 20.00 50.00
CCPOE26 Joe Sakic 15.00 40.00
CCPOE27 Jarome Iginla 10.00 25.00
CCPOE28 Jamie Oleksiak 8.00 20.00
CCPOE29 Jake Allen 8.00 20.00
CCPOE30 Jaden Schwartz 12.00 30.00
CCPOE31 Eric Lindros 10.00 25.00
CCPOE32 Ed Belfour 12.00 30.00
CCPOE33 Drew Doughty 10.00 25.00
CCPOE34 Dougie Hamilton 6.00 15.00
CCPOE35 Curtis Joseph 10.00 25.00
CCPOE36 Corey Perry 10.00 25.00
CCPOE37 Cody Hodgson 10.00 25.00
CCPOE38 Carey Price 25.00 50.00
CCPOE39 Brendan Gallagher 10.00 25.00
CCPOE40 Brayden Schenn 10.00 25.00
CCPOE41 Brad Marchand 12.00 30.00
CCPOE42 Bobby Orr 40.00 80.00

2017-18 Upper Deck Team Canada

*SILVER/100: 1.25X TO 3X BASE
*SP/100: .6X TO 1.5X SP
*HEIR/100: .6X TO 1.5X HEIR
STATED PRINT RUN 100 SER.#'d SETS
1 Connor McDavid 1.25 3.00
2 Robby Fabbri .30 .75
3 Brendan Gallagher .30 .75
4 Matt Beleskey .20 .50
5 Matt Murray .50 1.25
6 Tyler Ennis .30 .75
7 Jeff Carter .30 .75
8 Sean Monahan .30 .75
9 Sean Couturier .25 .60
10 Jonathan Toews .60 1.50
11 Tyler Toffoli .25 .60
12 Andrew Ladd .30 .75
13 Jason Spezza .30 .75
14 Martin Jones .30 .75
15 Bo Horvat .30 .75
16 Ryan Ellis .25 .60
17 Josh Morrissey .20 .50
18 Derick Brassard .30 .75
19 Ryan Nugent-Hopkins .30 .75
20 Sidney Crosby 1.25 3.00
21 Mark Giordano .25 .60
22 Jaden Schwartz .40 1.00
23 Brett Ritchie .20 .50
24 Claude Giroux .30 .75
25 Cam Talbot .30 .75
26 Morgan Rielly .30 .75
27 Jarome Iginla .30 .75
28 David Savard .25 .60
29 Ryan Murray .30 .75
30 Marc-Andre Fleury .50 1.25
31 Eric Staal .40 1.00
32 Calvin Pickard .20 .50
33 Jordan Staal .30 .75
34 Brayden Schenn .30 .75
35 Matt Dumba .25 .60
36 Chris Kunitz .30 .75
37 Braden Holtby .50 1.25
38 Justin Williams .25 .60
39 Logan Couture .30 .75
40 Evander Kane .30 .75
41 Mark Stone .30 .75
42 Jeff Skinner .25 .60
43 Jake Muzzin .25 .60
44 Sam Reinhart .25 .60
45 Brent Seabrook .25 .60
46 Ryan O'Reilly .30 .75
47 Dan Hamhuis .20 .50
48 Ryan Spooner .25 .60
49 Marc Staal .25 .60
50 Mitch Marner .50 1.25
51 Jonathan Huberdeau .25 .60
52 Boone Jenner .25 .60
53 Jay Bouwmeester .30 .75
54 Ryan Johansen .30 .75
55 Griffin Reinhart .25 .60
56 Duncan Keith .30 .75
57 Devan Dubnyk .30 .75
58 Shane Doan .25 .60
59 Mike Smith .30 .75
60 Adam Henrique .25 .60
61 Patrick Sharp .25 .60
62 Kris Letang .30 .75
63 Tyson Barrie .30 .75
64 Nazem Kadri .25 .60
65 James Neal .25 .60
66 Alexandre Burrows .20 .50
67 Meaghan Mikkelson .25 .60
68 Marie-Philip Poulin .25 .60
69 Haily Wickenheiser .25 .60
70 Kirk Muller .25 .60
71 Ed Belfour .40 1.00
72 Lanny McDonald .30 .75
73 Dale Hawerchuk .40 1.00
74 Felix Potvin .30 .75
75 Larry Robinson .30 .75
76 Shayne Corson .25 .60
77 Larry Murphy .25 .60
78 Ray Bourque .50 1.25
79 Theoren Fleury .30 .75
80 Marcel Dionne .40 1.00
81 Charlie Simmer .30 .75
82 Mike Gartner .30 .75
83 Owen Nolan .30 .75
84 Bobby Clarke .30 .75
85 Grant Fuhr .40 1.00
86 Joe Sakic .40 1.00
87 Darryl Sittler .30 .75
88 Denis Potvin .30 .75
89 Mark Recchi .40 1.00
90 Doug Gilmour .40 1.00
91 Rod Brind'Amour .30 .75
92 Rogie Vachon .40 1.00
93 Bobby Orr 1.00 2.50
94 Wendel Clark .40 1.00
95 Phil Esposito .50 1.25
96 Bobby Hull .30 .75
97 Vincent Damphousse .25 .60
98 Glenn Anderson .30 .75
99 Trevor Linden .30 .75
100 Paul Coffey .30 .75
101 Sidney Crosby SP 5.00 12.00
102 Brad Marchand SP 1.50 4.00
103 P.K. Subban SP 1.25 3.00
104 Jonathan Toews SP 2.50 6.00
105 Jordan Eberle SP 1.25 3.00
106 Jamie Benn SP 1.50 4.00
107 Tyler Seguin SP 2.00 5.00
108 Aaron Ekblad SP 1.25 3.00
109 Taylor Hall SP 2.50 6.00
110 Nathan MacKinnon SP 2.50 6.00
111 Alex Pietrangelo SP 1.00 2.50
112 Shea Weber SP 1.00 2.50
113 Mark Scheifele SP 1.50 4.00
114 Wayne Simmonds SP 1.50 4.00
115 Carey Price SP 4.00 10.00
116 Jonathan Drouin SP 1.25 3.00
117 Brent Burns SP 1.50 4.00
118 Rick Nash SP 1.25 3.00
119 Matt Duchene SP 1.25 3.00
120 Steven Stamkos SP 2.50 6.00
121 Patrick Marleau SP 1.25 3.00
122 Drew Doughty SP 1.25 3.00
123 Roberto Luongo SP 1.25 3.00
124 Patrice Bergeron SP 1.50 4.00
125 John Tavares SP 2.50 6.00
126 Corey Perry SP 1.25 3.00
127 Joe Thornton SP 1.25 3.00
128 Connor McDavid SP 5.00 12.00
129 Ryan Getzlaf SP 1.25 3.00
130 Mitch Marner SP 2.00 5.00
131 Steve Yzerman SP 1.50 4.00
132 Mike Bossy SP 2.00 5.00
133 Mario Lemieux SP 4.00 10.00
134 Patrick Roy SP 3.00 8.00
135 Mark Messier SP 2.00 5.00
136 Guy Lafleur SP 1.50 4.00
137 Frank Mahovlich SP 1.25 3.00
138 Bobby Orr SP 4.00 10.00
139 Martin Brodeur SP 2.50 6.00
140 Wayne Gretzky SP 6.00 15.00
141 Connor McDavid HEIR 8.00 20.00
142 Brayden Point HEIR 2.00 5.00
143 Anthony Mantha HEIR 2.00 5.00
144 Dylan Strome HEIR 2.00 5.00
145 Alexandre Carrier HEIR 1.50 4.00
146 Matt Murray HEIR 3.00 8.00
147 Lawson Crouse HEIR 1.50 4.00
148 Mathew Barzal HEIR 3.00 8.00
149 Max Domi HEIR 2.00 5.00
150 Samuel Morin HEIR 2.00 5.00
151 Mitch Marner HEIR 3.00 8.00
152 Eric Comrie HEIR 1.50 4.00
153 Tyson Jost HEIR 4.00 10.00
154 Travis Konecny HEIR 2.00 5.00
155 Thomas Chabot HEIR 3.00 8.00
156 Anthony Beauvillier HEIR 2.00 5.00
157 Blake Speers HEIR 2.00 5.00
158 John Quenneville HEIR 1.50 4.00
159 Shea Theodore HEIR 1.50 4.00
160 Sam Bennett HEIR 1.50 4.00
SP1 Nolan Patrick 50.00 120.00

2017-18 Upper Deck Team Canada Canvas

TCC1 Sidney Crosby 8.00 20.00
TCC2 Brent Burns 2.50 6.00
TCC3 Jamie Benn 2.50 6.00
TCC4 Taylor Hall 4.00 10.00
TCC5 Connor McDavid 8.00 20.00
TCC6 Nathan MacKinnon 4.00 10.00
TCC7 Jeff Carter 2.00 5.00
TCC8 Ryan O'Reilly 2.00 5.00
TCC9 Mitch Marner 3.00 8.00
TCC10 Joe Thornton 2.00 5.00
TCC11 Corey Perry 2.00 5.00
TCC12 Matt Duchene 2.00 5.00
TCC13 Jonathan Toews 4.00 10.00
TCC14 Shea Weber 1.50 4.00
TCC15 P.K. Subban 2.00 5.00
TCC16 Patrice Bergeron 2.50 6.00
TCC17 Carey Price 6.00 15.00
TCC18 Duncan Keith 2.00 5.00
TCC19 Morgan Rielly 2.00 5.00
TCC20 Rick Nash 2.00 5.00
TCC21 Matt Murray 3.00 8.00
TCC22 Tyler Seguin 3.00 8.00
TCC23 Steven Stamkos 4.00 10.00
TCC24 Brad Marchand 2.50 6.00
TCC25 John Tavares 4.00 10.00
TCC26 Drew Doughty 2.00 5.00
TCC27 Jeff Skinner 1.50 4.00
TCC28 Ryan Getzlaf 2.00 5.00
TCC29 Claude Giroux 2.00 5.00
TCC30 Darryl Sittler 2.00 5.00
TCC31 Guy Lafleur 2.50 6.00
TCC32 Mike Bossy 3.00 8.00
TCC33 Bobby Hull 2.00 5.00
TCC34 Bobby Clarke 2.00 5.00
TCC35 Ed Belfour 2.50 6.00
TCC36 Bobby Orr 6.00 15.00
TCC37 Lanny McDonald 2.00 5.00
TCC38 Steve Yzerman 2.50 6.00
TCC39 Denis Potvin 2.00 5.00
TCC40 Theoren Fleury 2.00 5.00
TCC41 Phil Esposito 3.00 8.00
TCC42 Shayne Corson 1.50 4.00
TCC43 Larry Robinson 2.00 5.00
TCC44 Mike Gartner 2.00 5.00
TCC45 Marcel Dionne 2.50 6.00
TCC46 Mario Lemieux SP 12.00 30.00
TCC47 Ray Bourque SP 6.00 15.00
TCC48 Grant Fuhr SP 5.00 12.00
TCC49 Larry Murphy SP 3.00 8.00
TCC50 Doug Gilmour SP 5.00 12.00
TCC51 Mark Messier SP 6.00 15.00
TCC52 Paul Coffey SP 4.00 10.00
TCC53 Glenn Anderson SP 4.00 10.00
TCC54 Dale Hawerchuk SP 5.00 12.00
TCC55 Wayne Gretzky SP 20.00 50.00

2017-18 Upper Deck Team Canada Clear Cut Program of Excellence

POE1 Carey Price 30.00 80.00
POE2 Mitch Marner 15.00 40.00
POE3 Jonathan Toews 20.00 50.00
POE4 Taylor Hall 20.00 50.00
POE5 Sidney Crosby 40.00 100.00
POE6 Brent Burns 12.00 30.00
POE7 Ryan Getzlaf 10.00 25.00
POE8 Nathan MacKinnon 20.00 50.00
POE9 Shea Weber 8.00 20.00
POE10 Matt Murray 15.00 40.00
POE11 Brad Marchand 12.00 30.00
POE12 Corey Perry 10.00 25.00
POE13 Steven Stamkos 20.00 50.00
POE14 P.K. Subban 10.00 25.00
POE15 John Tavares 20.00 50.00
POE16 Claude Giroux 10.00 25.00
POE17 Mark Scheifele 12.00 30.00
POE18 Jamie Benn 12.00 30.00
POE19 Matt Duchene 10.00 25.00
POE20 Connor McDavid 40.00 100.00
POE21 Mario Lemieux 30.00 80.00
POE22 Martin Brodeur 20.00 50.00
POE23 Bobby Orr 30.00 80.00
POE24 Joe Sakic 12.00 30.00
POE25 Mark Messier 15.00 40.00
POE26 Steve Yzerman 12.00 30.00
POE27 Paul Coffey 10.00 25.00
POE28 Mike Bossy 15.00 40.00
POE29 Frank Mahovlich 10.00 25.00
POE30 Wayne Gretzky 50.00 120.00

2017-18 Upper Deck Team Canada Clear Cut World Juniors

WJC1 Connor McDavid 50.00 125.00
WJC2 Matt Murray 20.00 50.00
WJC3 Mitch Marner 20.00 50.00
WJC4 Anthony Mantha 12.00 30.00
WJC5 Dylan Strome 12.00 30.00
WJC6 Mathew Barzal 20.00 50.00
WJC7 Brayden Point 12.00 30.00
WJC8 Thomas Chabot 20.00 50.00
WJC9 Travis Konecny 12.00 30.00
WJC10 Tyson Jost 25.00 60.00
WJCSPNP Nolan Patrick

2017-18 Upper Deck Team Canada Retro

R1 Connor McDavid 8.00 20.00
R2 Mitch Marner 3.00 8.00
R3 Jonathan Toews 4.00 10.00
R4 John Tavares 4.00 10.00
R5 Sidney Crosby 8.00 20.00
R6 P.K. Subban 2.00 5.00
R7 Carey Price 6.00 15.00
R8 Steven Stamkos 4.00 10.00
R9 Patrick Roy 5.00 12.00
R10 Mario Lemieux 6.00 15.00
R11 Mark Messier 3.00 8.00
R12 Wayne Gretzky 10.00 25.00

2017-18 Upper Deck Team Canada VS

VS1 Auston Matthews 5.00 12.00
VS2 Alexander Ovechkin 5.00 12.00
VS3 Artemi Panarin 1.25 3.00
VS4 Anze Kopitar 2.00 5.00
VS5 Patrik Laine 2.00 5.00
VS6 Johnny Gaudreau 2.00 5.00
VS7 Jaromir Jagr 3.00 8.00
VS8 William Nylander 2.00 5.00
VS9 Evgeni Malkin 4.00 10.00
VS10 Patrick Kane 2.50 6.00
VS11 Roman Josi 1.25 3.00
VS12 Henrik Zetterberg 1.25 3.00
VS13 Leon Draisaitl 2.00 5.00
VS14 Vladimir Tarasenko 2.00 5.00
VS15 Erik Karlsson 1.50 4.00
VS16 Max Pacioretty 1.25 3.00
VS17 Henrik Sedin 1.25 3.00
VS18 Joe Pavelski 1.25 3.00
VS19 Marian Hossa 1.00 2.50
VS20 Mats Zuccarello 1.25 3.00
VS21 Gabriel Landeskog 1.00 2.50
VS22 Pavel Bure 1.25 3.00
VS23 Brett Hull 1.25 3.00
VS24 Teemu Selanne 1.50 4.00

2017-18 Upper Deck Team Canada VS Black

VSBAM Auston Matthews 6.00 15.00
VSBHL Henrik Lundqvist 4.00 10.00
VSBLD Leon Draisaitl 3.00 8.00
VSBNH Nico Hischier 30.00 80.00
VSBWN William Nylander 4.00 10.00

2014-15 Upper Deck Team Canada Juniors

COMP.SET w/o SP's (100) 15.00 40.00
101-150 ONE PER PACK
151-186 JSY STATED ODDS 1:8
187-207 JSY STATED ODDS 1:24
1 Rourke Chartier .25 .60
2 Michael Dal Colle .50 1.25
3 Robby Fabbri .30 .75
4 Brendan Lemieux .40 1.00
5 Carl Neill .25 .60
6 Alexis Pepin .30 .75
7 Spencer Watson .40 1.00
8 Nick Baptiste .25 .60
9 Sam Bennett .60 1.50
10 Madison Bowey .30 .75
11 Philippe Desrosiers .30 .75
12 Jason Dickinson .40 1.00
13 Hunter Garlent .25 .60
14 Dillon Heatherington .25 .60
15 Austin Lotz .30 .75
16 Spencer Martin .50 1.25
17 Samuel Morin .30 .75
18 Nick Ritchie .40 1.00
19 Shea Theodore .40 1.00
20 Carter Verhaeghe .25 .60
21 Kerby Rychel .30 .75
22 Daniel Audette .40 1.00
23 Mathew Barzal .75 2.00
24 Julio Billia .30 .75
25 Clark Bishop .25 .60
26 Conner Bleackley .40 1.00
27 Alexandre Carrier .30 .75
28 Lawson Crouse .40 1.00
29 Haydn Fleury .40 1.00
30 Ryan Gropp .40 1.00
31 Jayce Hawryluk .25 .60
32 Joe Hicketts .30 .75
33 Travis Konecny .60 1.50
34 Jared McCann .40 1.00
35 Mason McDonald .40 1.00
36 Roland McKeown .40 1.00
37 Brent Moran .30 .75
38 Brendan Perlini .60 1.50
39 Ryan Pilon .25 .60
40 Brayden Point .40 1.00
41 John Quenneville .30 .75
42 Travis Sanheim .50 1.25
43 Ben Thomas .40 1.00
44 Jake Virtanen .50 1.25
45 Josh Anderson .30 .75
46 Chris Bigras .30 .75
47 Jonathan Drouin 1.00 2.50
48 Aaron Ekblad .75 2.00
49 Zach Fucale .50 1.25
50 Frederik Gauthier .40 1.00
51 Bo Horvat 1.25 3.00
52 Charles Hudon .40 1.00
53 Curtis Lazar .50 1.25
54 Taylor Leier .40 1.00
55 Anthony Mantha .60 1.50
56 Connor McDavid 2.00 5.00
57 Jake Paterson .30 .75
58 Adam Pelech .30 .75
59 Nic Petan .40 1.00
60 Derrick Pouliot .50 1.25
61 Griffin Reinhart .50 1.25
62 Sam Reinhart 1.25 3.00
63 Hayley Wickenheiser .75 2.00
64 Courtney Birchard .40 1.00
65 Tessa Bonhomme .50 1.25
66 Bailey Bram .40 1.00
67 Sarah Vaillancourt .50 1.25
68 Meghan Agosta-Marciano .60 1.50
69 Gillian Apps .60 1.50
70 Melodie Daoust .60 1.50
71 Laura Fortino .40 1.00
72 Jayna Hefford .60 1.50
73 Haley Irwin .40 1.00
74 Brianne Jenner .50 1.25
75 Rebecca Johnston .40 1.00
76 Charline Labonte .60 1.50
77 Genevieve Lacasse .50 1.25
78 Jocelyne Larocque .50 1.25
79 Meaghan Mikkelson .60 1.50
80 Caroline Ouellette .60 1.50
81 Marie-Philip Poulin .60 1.50
82 Lauriane Rougeau .40 1.00
83 Natalie Spooner .60 1.50
84 Shannon Szabados .75 2.00
85 Jennifer Wakefield .40 1.00
86 Catherine Ward .50 1.25
87 Tara Watchorn .40 1.00
88 Kerby Rychel .30 .75
89 Nick Ritchie .40 1.00
90 Curtis Lazar .50 1.25
91 Anthony Mantha .60 1.50
92 Bo Horvat 1.25 3.00
93 Samuel Morin .30 .75
94 Griffin Reinhart .50 1.25
95 Michael Dal Colle .50 1.25
96 Sam Bennett .60 1.50
97 Sam Reinhart 1.25 3.00
98 Aaron Ekblad .75 2.00
99 Connor McDavid 2.00 5.00
100 Jonathan Drouin 1.00 2.50
101 Aaron Ekblad SP 1.50 4.00
102 Adam Pelech SP .60 1.50
103 Samuel Morin SP .60 1.50
104 Anthony Mantha SP 1.25 3.00
105 Bo Horvat SP 2.50 6.00
106 Brayden Point SP .75 2.00
107 Mason McDonald SP .75 2.00
108 Charles Hudon SP .75 2.00
109 Chris Bigras SP .60 1.50
110 Connor McDavid SP 4.00 10.00
111 Curtis Lazar SP 1.00 2.50

112 Derrick Pouliot SP 1.00 2.50
113 Frederik Gauthier SP .75 2.00
114 Griffin Reinhart SP 1.00 2.50
115 Haydn Fleury SP .75 2.00
116 Jake Paterson SP .60 1.50
117 Jake Virtanen SP 1.00 2.50
118 Jared McCann SP .75 2.00
119 Daniel Audette SP .75 2.00
120 Jonathan Drouin SP 2.00 5.00
121 Mathew Barzal SP 1.50 4.00
122 Josh Anderson SP .60 1.50
123 Nick Baptiste SP .50 1.25
124 Kerby Rychel SP .60 1.50
125 Nick Ritchie SP .75 2.00
126 Travis Sanheim SP 1.00 2.50
127 Michael Dal Colle SP 1.00 2.50
128 Julio Billia SP .60 1.50
129 Nic Petan SP .75 2.00
130 Travis Konecny SP 1.25 3.00
131 Conner Bleackley SP .75 2.00
132 Brendan Perlini SP 1.25 3.00
133 Robby Fabbri SP .60 1.50
134 Roland McKeown SP .75 2.00
135 Sam Bennett SP 1.25 3.00
136 Sam Reinhart SP 2.50 6.00
137 Lawson Crouse SP .75 2.00
138 Spencer Watson SP .75 2.00
139 Zach Fucale SP 1.00 2.50
140 Brianne Jenner SP 1.00 2.50
141 Charline Labonte SP 1.25 3.00
142 Caroline Ouellette SP 1.25 3.00
143 Catherine Ward SP 1.00 2.50
144 Hayley Wickenheiser SP 1.50 4.00
145 Jayna Hefford SP 1.25 3.00
146 Gillian Apps SP 1.25 3.00
147 Meghan Agosta-Marciano SP 1.25 3.00
148 Natalie Spooner SP 1.25 3.00
149 Rebecca Johnston SP .75 2.00
150 Shannon Szabados SP 1.50 4.00
151 Adam Pelech JSY 2.50 6.00
152 Alexandre Carrier JSY 2.50 6.00
153 Brayden Point JSY 3.00 8.00
154 Taylor Leier JSY 3.00 8.00
155 Chris Bigras JSY 2.50 6.00
156 Curtis Lazar JSY 4.00 10.00
157 Derrick Pouliot JSY 4.00 10.00
158 Frederik Gauthier JSY 3.00 8.00
159 Griffin Reinhart JSY 4.00 10.00
160 Haydn Fleury JSY 3.00 8.00
161 Jake Paterson JSY 2.50 6.00
162 Mason McDonald JSY 3.00 8.00
163 Lawson Crouse JSY 3.00 8.00
164 Josh Anderson JSY 2.50 6.00
165 Travis Konecny JSY 5.00 12.00
166 Julio Billia JSY 2.50 6.00
167 Kerby Rychel JSY 2.50 6.00
168 Mathew Barzal JSY 6.00 15.00
169 Travis Sanheim JSY 4.00 10.00
170 Brendan Perlini JSY 5.00 12.00
171 Nic Petan JSY 3.00 8.00
172 Jayce Hawryluk JSY 2.00 5.00
173 Clark Bishop JSY 2.00 5.00
174 Ryan Gropp JSY 3.00 8.00
175 Conner Bleackley JSY 3.00 8.00
176 Roland McKeown JSY 3.00 8.00
177 Daniel Audette JSY 3.00 8.00
178 John Quenneville JSY 2.50 6.00
179 Jared McCann JSY 3.00 8.00
180 Zach Fucale JSY 4.00 10.00
181 Aaron Ekblad JSY 5.00 12.00
182 Bo Horvat JSY 4.00 10.00
183 Connor McDavid JSY 25.00 50.00
184 Jonathan Drouin JSY 8.00 20.00
185 Anthony Mantha JSY 5.00 12.00
186 Sam Reinhart JSY 5.00 12.00
187 Brianne Jenner JSY 5.00 12.00
188 Caroline Ouellette JSY 6.00 15.00
189 Catherine Ward JSY 5.00 12.00
190 Charline Labonte JSY 6.00 15.00
191 Genevieve Lacasse JSY 5.00 12.00
192 Gillian Apps JSY 6.00 15.00
193 Haley Irwin JSY 4.00 10.00
194 Hayley Wickenheiser JSY 8.00 20.00
195 Jayna Hefford JSY 6.00 15.00
196 Jennifer Wakefield JSY 4.00 10.00
197 Jocelyne Larocque JSY 5.00 12.00
198 Laura Fortino JSY 4.00 10.00
199 Laurlane Rougeau JSY 4.00 10.00
200 Marie-Philip Poulin JSY 6.00 15.00
201 Meaghan Mikkelson JSY 6.00 15.00
202 Meghan Agosta-Marciano JSY 6.00 15.00
203 Melodie Daoust JSY 6.00 15.00
204 Natalie Spooner JSY 6.00 15.00
205 Rebecca Johnston JSY 4.00 10.00
206 Shannon Szabados JSY 8.00 20.00
207 Tara Watchorn JSY 4.00 10.00

2014-15 Upper Deck Team Canada Juniors Gold

*1-100 GOLD: .8X TO 2X BASIC CARDS
1-100 STATED ODDS 1:6
*101-150 GOLD: .6X TO 1.5X BASIC CARDS
101-150 SP STATED ODDS 1:12
*151-186 JSY/20-31: 1X TO 2.5X BASIC JSY
*151-186 JSY/14-19: 1.2X TO 3X BASIC JSY

2014-15 Upper Deck Team Canada Juniors Glossy

*1-100 GLOSSY/25: 3X TO 8X BASIC CARDS
*101-150 GLOSS/10: 2X TO 5X BASIC SP
56 Connor McDavid 60.00 120.00
99 Connor McDavid 60.00 120.00
110 Connor McDavid 125.00 200.00

2014-15 Upper Deck Team Canada Juniors Autographs Gold

UNPRICED GROUP A ODDS 1:5270
GROUP B ODDS 1:659
GROUP C ODDS 1:82
GROUP D ODDS 1:229
GROUP E ODDS 1:176
OVERALL STATED ODDS 1:42
21 Kerby Rychel A
22 Daniel Audette C 4.00 10.00
23 Mathew Barzal C 6.00 15.00
24 Julio Billia C 6.00 15.00
25 Clark Bishop C 8.00 20.00
26 Conner Bleackley C 6.00 15.00
27 Alexandre Carrier C 3.00 8.00
28 Lawson Crouse C 4.00 10.00
29 Haydn Fleury C 4.00 10.00
30 Ryan Gropp C 4.00 10.00
31 Jayce Hawryluk C 8.00 20.00
32 Joe Hicketts E 3.00 8.00
33 Travis Konecny C
34 Jared McCann C 6.00 15.00
35 Mason McDonald C 4.00 10.00
36 Roland McKeown C 5.00 12.00
37 Brent Moran E 4.00 10.00
38 Brendan Perlini C 6.00 15.00
39 Ryan Pilon E 4.00 10.00
40 Brayden Point C 4.00 10.00
41 John Quenneville C 15.00 30.00
42 Travis Sanheim C 10.00 25.00
43 Ben Thomas E 5.00 12.00
44 Jake Virtanen E 10.00 25.00
45 Josh Anderson C 3.00 8.00
46 Chris Bigras C 3.00 8.00
47 Jonathan Drouin D 60.00 120.00
48 Aaron Ekblad D 15.00 40.00
49 Zach Fucale C 6.00 15.00
51 Bo Horvat D 12.00 30.00
52 Charles Hudon E 8.00 20.00
53 Curtis Lazar D 10.00 25.00
54 Taylor Leier C 4.00 10.00
55 Anthony Mantha D 20.00 40.00
56 Connor McDavid D 200.00 350.00
57 Jake Paterson C 3.00 8.00
58 Adam Pelech C 4.00 10.00
59 Nic Petan C 6.00 15.00
60 Derrick Pouliot C 5.00 12.00
61 Griffin Reinhart D 10.00 25.00
62 Sam Reinhart D 15.00 40.00
63 Hayley Wickenheiser C 12.00 30.00
68 Meghan Agosta-Marciano C 10.00 25.00
69 Gillian Apps C 6.00 15.00
70 Melodie Daoust C 4.00 10.00
71 Laura Fortino C 8.00 20.00
72 Jayna Hefford C 12.00 30.00
74 Brianne Jenner C 5.00 12.00
75 Rebecca Johnston C 4.00 10.00
76 Charline Labonte C 6.00 15.00
77 Genevieve Lacasse C 6.00 15.00
78 Jocelyne Larocque C 5.00 12.00
79 Meaghan Mikkelson C 10.00 25.00
80 Caroline Ouellette C 6.00 15.00
81 Marie-Philip Poulin C 10.00 25.00
82 Lauriane Rougeau C 4.00 10.00
83 Natalie Spooner C 12.00 30.00
84 Shannon Szabados C 8.00 20.00
85 Jennifer Wakefield C 4.00 10.00
86 Catherine Ward C 5.00 12.00
87 Tara Watchorn C 4.00 10.00
88 Kerby Rychel A
90 Curtis Lazar B 8.00 20.00
91 Anthony Mantha B 25.00 50.00
93 Samuel Morin B
94 Griffin Reinhart B 12.00 30.00
97 Sam Reinhart B 20.00 40.00
98 Aaron Ekblad B 25.00 50.00
99 Connor McDavid B 250.00 450.00
100 Jonathan Drouin B 60.00 120.00

2014-15 Upper Deck Team Canada Juniors Clear Cut Playing for a Nation Combos

STATED PRINT RUN 25 SER.#'d SETS
PFNC1 A.Pelech/A.Ekblad 10.00 25.00
PFNC2 J.Drouin/A.Mantha 12.00 30.00
PFNC3 S.Reinhart/C.McDavid 40.00 80.00
PFNC4 S.Bennett/M.DalColle 10.00 25.00
PFNC5 J.Paterson/M.McDonald 6.00 15.00
PFNC6 B.Horvat/K.Rychel 20.00 50.00

2014-15 Upper Deck Team Canada Juniors Clear Cut Playing for a Nation

STATED PRINT RUN 75 SER.#'d SETS
PFN1 Aaron Ekblad 8.00 20.00
PFN2 Adam Pelech 4.00 10.00
PFN3 Anthony Mantha 8.00 20.00
PFN4 Bo Horvat 10.00 25.00
PFN5 Brayden Point 5.00 12.00
PFN6 Josh Anderson 4.00 10.00
PFN7 Chris Bigras 4.00 10.00
PFN8 Connor McDavid 40.00 80.00
PFN9 Curtis Lazar 8.00 20.00
PFN10 Derrick Pouliot 6.00 15.00
PFN11 Frederik Gauthier 5.00 12.00
PFN12 Griffin Reinhart 6.00 15.00
PFN13 Haydn Fleury 5.00 12.00
PFN14 Jake Paterson 4.00 10.00
PFN15 Jake Virtanen 6.00 15.00
PFN16 Jared McCann 5.00 12.00
PFN17 Brendan Perlini 8.00 20.00
PFN18 Jonathan Drouin 10.00 25.00
PFN19 Taylor Leier 5.00 12.00
PFN20 Michael Dal Colle 6.00 15.00
PFN21 Kerby Rychel 4.00 10.00
PFN22 Nick Ritchie 5.00 12.00
PFN23 Travis Sanheim 6.00 15.00
PFN24 Mathew Barzal 10.00 25.00
PFN25 Travis Konecny 8.00 20.00
PFN26 Nic Petan 4.00 10.00
PFN27 Julio Billia 4.00 10.00
PFN28 Sam Bennett 8.00 20.00
PFN29 Jayce Hawryluk 3.00 8.00
PFN30 Roland McKeown 5.00 12.00
PFN31 Lawson Crouse 5.00 12.00
PFN32 Sam Reinhart 8.00 20.00
PFN33 Daniel Audette 5.00 12.00
PFN34 Nick Baptiste 3.00 8.00
PFN35 Mason McDonald 5.00 12.00
PFN36 Samuel Morin 6.00 15.00

2014-15 Upper Deck Team Canada Juniors Dual Jerseys

STATED ODDS 1:48
*GOLD/99: .5X TO 1.2X BASIC DUAL
TCDBA C.Bishop/D.Audette 3.00 8.00
TCDBG B.Horvat/G.Reinhart 4.00 10.00
TCDBM M.McDonald/J.Billia 3.00 8.00
TCDDM J.Drouin/A.Mantha 8.00 20.00
TCDER S.Reinhart/A.Ekblad 6.00 15.00
TCDHR B.Horvat/K.Rychel 10.00 25.00
TCDLP N.Petan/C.Lazar 5.00 12.00
TCDMD C.McDavid/J.Drouin 15.00 40.00
TCDMR C.McDavid/S.Reinhart 15.00 40.00
TCDRG K.Rychel/F.Gauthier 3.00 8.00
TCDSP J.Paterson/Z.Fucale 4.00 10.00
TCDVP J.Virtanen/B.Perlini 5.00 12.00

2014-15 Upper Deck Team Canada Juniors Jumbo Swatch

JS1 Aaron Ekblad 6.00 15.00
JS2 Anthony Mantha 8.00 20.00
JS3 Bo Horvat 15.00 40.00
JS4 Connor McDavid 30.00 60.00
JS5 Curtis Lazar 6.00 15.00
JS6 Frederik Gauthier 5.00 12.00
JS7 Jake Virtanen 6.00 15.00
JS8 Jonathan Drouin 8.00 20.00
JS9 Kerby Rychel 4.00 10.00
JS10 Mathew Barzal 10.00 25.00
JS11 Jake Paterson 4.00 10.00
JS12 Travis Konecny 6.00 15.00
JS13 Brendan Perlini 6.00 15.00
JS14 Mason McDonald 5.00 12.00
JS15 Sam Reinhart 8.00 20.00

2014-15 Upper Deck Team Canada Juniors Patch Autographs

151 Adam Pelech 6.00 15.00
152 Alexandre Carrier 6.00 15.00
153 Brayden Point 8.00 20.00
154 Taylor Leier 8.00 20.00
155 Chris Bigras 6.00 15.00
156 Curtis Lazar 20.00 50.00
157 Derrick Pouliot 10.00 25.00
158 Frederik Gauthier
159 Griffin Reinhart 10.00 25.00
160 Haydn Fleury 8.00 20.00
161 Jake Paterson 6.00 15.00
162 Mason McDonald 8.00 20.00
163 Lawson Crouse 15.00 30.00
164 Josh Anderson 6.00 15.00
165 Travis Konecny 12.00 30.00
166 Julio Billia 6.00 15.00
167 Kerby Rychel 6.00 15.00
168 Mathew Barzal 8.00 20.00
169 Travis Sanheim 8.00 20.00
170 Brendan Perlini 12.00 30.00
171 Nic Petan 12.00 30.00
172 Jayce Hawryluk 5.00 12.00
173 Clark Bishop 5.00 12.00
174 Ryan Gropp
175 Conner Bleackley 8.00 20.00
176 Roland McKeown 6.00 15.00
177 Daniel Audette 8.00 20.00
178 John Quenneville 6.00 15.00
179 Jared McCann 8.00 20.00
180 Zach Fucale 25.00 50.00
181 Aaron Ekblad/125 20.00 40.00
182 Bo Horvat/125 25.00 50.00
183 Connor McDavid/125 250.00 500.00
184 Jonathan Drouin/125 30.00 80.00
185 Anthony Mantha/125 25.00 50.00
186 Sam Reinhart/125 40.00 80.00
187 Brianne Jenner 6.00 15.00
188 Caroline Ouellette 8.00 20.00
189 Catherine Ward 6.00 15.00
190 Charline Labonte 8.00 20.00
191 Genevieve Lacasse 6.00 15.00
192 Gillian Apps 8.00 20.00
194 Hayley Wickenheiser 10.00 25.00
195 Jayna Hefford 8.00 20.00
196 Jennifer Wakefield 5.00 12.00
197 Jocelyne Larocque 6.00 15.00
198 Laura Fortino 5.00 12.00
199 Lauriane Rougeau 5.00 12.00
200 Marie-Philip Poulin 8.00 20.00
201 Meaghan Mikkelson 8.00 20.00
202 Meghan Agosta-Marciano 8.00 20.00
203 Melodie Daoust 8.00 20.00
204 Natalie Spooner 8.00 20.00
205 Rebecca Johnston 5.00 12.00
206 Shannon Szabados 10.00 25.00
207 Tara Watchorn 5.00 12.00

2014-15 Upper Deck Team Canada Juniors Quad Jerseys

STATED ODDS 1:384
*GOLD/25: .6X TO 1.5X BASIC QUAD
EMDM Mnt/McD/Drn/Ekb 25.00 60.00
MDHR McD/Drn/Hrv/Rnh 25.00 60.00
PFMB Fcle/Ptr/McD/Bla 6.00 15.00
PKVB Prl/Kncy/Blcy/Vrt 6.00 15.00
PPLG Rnh/Gthr/Ryc/Lzr 8.00 20.00

2014-15 Upper Deck Team Canada Juniors Special Edition

STATED ODDS 1:3
*GOLD: .8X TO 2X BASIC INSERTS
SE1 Aaron Ekblad 5.00 12.00
SE2 Adam Pelech 1.00 2.50
SE3 Jayce Hawryluk .75 2.00
SE4 Lawson Crouse 1.25 3.00
SE5 Anthony Mantha 2.00 5.00
SE6 Bo Horvat 4.00 10.00
SE7 Brayden Point 1.25 3.00
SE8 Ryan Gropp 1.25 3.00
SE9 Charles Hudon 1.25 3.00
SE10 Chris Bigras 1.00 2.50
SE11 Connor McDavid 6.00 15.00
SE12 Curtis Lazar 1.50 4.00
SE13 Daniel Audette 1.25 3.00
SE14 Derrick Pouliot 1.50 4.00
SE15 Frederik Gauthier 1.25 3.00
SE16 Griffin Reinhart 1.50 4.00
SE17 Haydn Fleury 1.25 3.00
SE18 Travis Sanheim 1.50 4.00
SE19 Jake Paterson 1.00 2.50
SE20 Jake Virtanen 1.50 4.00
SE21 Jared McCann 1.25 3.00
SE22 Brendan Perlini 2.00 5.00
SE23 Jonathan Drouin 2.50 6.00
SE24 Alexandre Carrier 1.00 2.50
SE25 Josh Anderson 1.00 2.50
SE26 Spencer Martin 1.50 4.00
SE27 Julio Billia 1.00 2.50
SE28 Kerby Rychel 1.00 2.50
SE29 Conner Bleackley 1.25 3.00
SE30 Ben Thomas 1.25 3.00
SE31 Carter Verhaeghe .75 2.00
SE32 Sam Reinhart 4.00 10.00
SE33 Clark Bishop .75 2.00
SE34 Nic Petan 1.25 3.00
SE35 Mason McDonald 1.25 3.00
SE36 Joe Hicketts 1.00 2.50
SE37 John Quenneville 1.00 2.50
SE38 Mathew Barzal 2.50 6.00
SE39 Ryan Pilon .75 2.00
SE40 Roland McKeown 1.25 3.00
SE41 Travis Konecny 2.00 5.00
SE42 Zach Fucale 1.50 4.00
SE43 Taylor Leier 1.25 3.00
SE44 Michael Dal Colle 1.50 4.00
SE45 Nick Baptiste .75 2.00
SE46 Nick Ritchie 1.25 3.00
SE47 Robby Fabbri 1.00 2.50
SE48 Sam Bennett 2.00 5.00
SE49 Samuel Morin 1.00 2.50
SE50 Catherine Ward 1.25 3.00
SE51 Haley Irwin 1.00 2.50
SE52 Caroline Ouellette 1.50 4.00
SE53 Gillian Apps 1.50 4.00
SE54 Jayna Hefford 1.50 4.00
SE55 Meaghan Mikkelson 1.50 4.00
SE56 Meghan Agosta-Marciano 1.50 4.00
SE57 Hayley Wickenheiser 2.00 5.00
SE58 Natalie Spooner 1.50 4.00
SE59 Rebecca Johnston 1.00 2.50
SE60 Shannon Szabados 2.00 5.00

2014-15 Upper Deck Team Canada Juniors Triple Jerseys

STATED ODDS 1:192
*GOLD/49: .6X TO 1.5X BASIC TRIPLE
TCTDLP Petan/Lazr/Drouin 8.00 20.00
TCTEPR Plch/Ekbld/Rnhrt 12.00 30.00
TCTKPA Kncny/Adtte/Prlni 5.00 12.00
TCTMDR Drn/McDvd/Rnhrt 15.00 40.00
TCTMGR Rychl/Gthr/Mntha 5.00 12.00
TCTMHR Rnhrt/McDvd/Hrvt 15.00 40.00
TCTPMF Fcle/Ptrsn/McDnld 6.00 15.00

2015-16 Upper Deck Team Canada Juniors

COMP.SET w/o SPs (100) 10.00 25.00
101-140 JSY STATED ODDS 1:20
141-160 JSY STATED ODDS 1:30
1 Callum Booth .25 .60
2 Mitchell Vande Sompel .25 .60
3 Mitch Marner 1.25 3.00
4 Adam Musil .30 .75
5 Nick Merkley .50 1.25
6 Nicolas Meloche .30 .75
7 Dylan Strome .75 2.00
8 Connor Hobbs .30 .75
9 Tyler Soy .40 1.00
10 Travis Konecny .60 1.50
11 Graham Knott .25 .60
12 Nicolas Roy .30 .75
13 Jeremy Roy .40 1.00
14 Jansen Harkins .40 1.00
15 Ethan Bear .25 .60
16 Anthony Beauvillier .40 1.00
17 Matthew Spencer .30 .75
18 Zachary Sawchenko .25 .60
19 Mitchell Stephens .30 .75
20 Mathew Barzal 1.25 3.00
21 Guillaume Brisebois .30 .75
22 Evan Cormier .30 .75
23 Kyle Capobianco .25 .60
24 Thomas Chabot .40 1.00
25 Parker Wotherspoon .30 .75
26 Glenn Gawdin .25 .60
27 Nathan Noel .30 .75
28 Deven Sideroff .25 .60
29 Brett Howden .30 .75
30 Tyler Benson .50 1.25
31 Pierre-Luc Dubois .60 1.50
32 Joe Hicketts .30 .75
33 Max Domi .60 1.50
34 Nicolas Petan .40 1.00
35 Shea Theodore .40 1.00
36 Madison Bowey .30 .75
37 Nick Paul .30 .75
38 Lawson Crouse .40 1.00
39 Zach Fucale .40 1.00
40 Josh Morrissey .40 1.00
41 Brayden Point .40 1.00
42 Frederik Gauthier .40 1.00
43 Samuel Morin .30 .75
44 Robby Fabbri .50 1.25
45 Nick Ritchie .40 1.00
46 Dillon Heatherington .25 .60
47 Eric Comrie .40 1.00
48 Jake Virtanen .50 1.25
49 Connor McDavid 3.00 8.00
50 Jennifer Wakefield .30 .75
51 Tara Watchorn .30 .75
52 Brianne Jenner .30 .75
53 Bailey Bram .25 .60
54 Jessica Campbell .40 1.00
55 Laura Fortino .25 .60
56 Caroline Ouellette .40 1.00
57 Sarah Davis .25 .60
58 Halli Krzyzaniak .30 .75
59 Brigette Lacquette .25 .60
60 Jamie Lee Rattray .30 .75
61 Jillian Saulnier .25 .60
62 Emily Clark .40 1.00
63 Marie-Philip Poulin .40 1.00
64 Ann-Renee Desbiens .30 .75
65 Jocelyne Larocque .30 .75
66 Emerance Maschmeyer .30 .75
67 Kelly Terry .25 .60
68 Natalie Spooner .40 1.00
69 Rebecca Johnston .30 .75
70 Lauriane Rougeau .25 .60
71 Genevieve Lacasse .30 .75
72 Courtney Birchard .25 .60
73 Thomas Chabot .40 1.00
74 Anthony Beauvillier .40 1.00
75 Jansen Harkins .40 1.00
76 Mitch Marner 1.25 3.00
77 Dylan Strome .75 2.00
78 Travis Konecny .60 1.50
79 Nick Merkley .50 1.25
80 Mathew Barzal 1.25 3.00
81 Lawson Crouse .40 1.00
82 Josh Morrissey .40 1.00
83 Zach Fucale .40 1.00
84 Jake Virtanen .50 1.25
85 Frederik Gauthier .40 1.00
86 Nick Ritchie .40 1.00
87 Nicolas Petan .40 1.00
88 Robby Fabbri .50 1.25
89 Max Domi .60 1.50
90 Connor McDavid 3.00 8.00
91 Dylan Strome .75 2.00
92 Mitch Marner 1.25 3.00
93 Mathew Barzal 1.25 3.00
94 Mitchell Stephens .30 .75
95 Zach Fucale .40 1.00
96 Max Domi .60 1.50
97 Nicolas Petan .40 1.00
98 Connor McDavid 3.00 8.00
99 Ann-Renee Desbiens .30 .75
100 Natalie Spooner .40 1.00
101 Connor McDavid JSY 20.00 40.00
102 Zach Fucale JSY 4.00 10.00
103 Max Domi JSY 6.00 15.00
104 Jake Virtanen JSY 5.00 12.00
105 Nick Ritchie JSY 4.00 10.00
106 Lawson Crouse JSY 4.00 10.00
107 Nicolas Petan JSY 4.00 10.00
108 Eric Comrie JSY 4.00 10.00
109 Samuel Morin JSY 3.00 8.00
110 Nick Paul JSY 3.00 8.00
111 Brayden Point JSY 4.00 10.00
112 Dillon Heatherington JSY 2.50 6.00
113 Josh Morrissey JSY 4.00 10.00
114 Robby Fabbri JSY 5.00 12.00
115 Frederik Gauthier JSY 4.00 10.00
116 Shea Theodore JSY 4.00 10.00
117 Joe Hicketts JSY 3.00 8.00
118 Madison Bowey JSY 3.00 8.00
119 Evan Cormier JSY 3.00 8.00
120 Mitchell Stephens JSY 3.00 8.00
121 Ethan Bear JSY 2.50 6.00
122 Mathew Barzal JSY 12.00 30.00
123 Kyle Capobianco JSY 2.50 6.00
124 Parker Wotherspoon JSY 3.00 8.00
125 Anthony Beauvillier JSY 4.00 10.00
126 Jansen Harkins JSY 4.00 10.00
127 Nathan Noel JSY 3.00 8.00
128 Thomas Chabot JSY 4.00 10.00
129 Jeremy Roy JSY 4.00 10.00
130 Deven Sideroff JSY 2.50 6.00
131 Zachary Sawchenko JSY 2.50 6.00
132 Guillaume Brisebois JSY 3.00 8.00
133 Glenn Gawdin JSY 2.50 6.00
134 Matthew Spencer JSY 3.00 8.00
135 Nicolas Roy JSY 3.00 8.00
136 Tyler Benson JSY 5.00 12.00
137 Brett Howden JSY 3.00 8.00
138 Tyler Soy JSY 4.00 10.00
139 Graham Knott JSY 2.50 6.00
140 Pierre-Luc Dubois JSY 6.00 15.00
141 Sarah Davis JSY 2.50 6.00
142 Bailey Bram JSY 2.50 6.00
143 Jessica Campbell JSY 4.00 10.00
144 Halli Krzyzaniak JSY 3.00 8.00
145 Genevieve Lacasse JSY 3.00 8.00
146 Ann-Renee Desbiens JSY 3.00 8.00
147 Rebecca Johnston JSY 3.00 8.00
148 Marie-Philip Poulin JSY 4.00 10.00
149 Jillian Saulnier JSY 2.50 6.00
150 Natalie Spooner JSY 4.00 10.00
151 Caroline Ouellette JSY 4.00 10.00
152 Lauriane Rougeau JSY 2.50 6.00
153 Courtney Birchard JSY 2.50 6.00
154 Brigette Lacquette JSY 2.50 6.00
155 Laura Fortino JSY 2.50 6.00
156 Jennifer Wakefield JSY 3.00 8.00
157 Jamie Lee Rattray JSY 3.00 8.00
158 Tara Watchorn JSY 3.00 8.00
159 Emily Clark JSY 4.00 10.00
160 Brianne Jenner JSY 3.00 8.00

2015-16 Upper Deck Team Canada Juniors Exclusives Red

*EXCLUSIVE/199: 1.5X TO 4X BASIC CARDS

2015-16 Upper Deck Team Canada Juniors Glossy

*GLOSSY/25: 3X TO 8X BASIC CARDS
49 Connor McDavid 40.00 80.00
90 Connor McDavid 40.00 80.00
98 Connor McDavid 40.00 80.00

2015-16 Upper Deck Team Canada Juniors Gold

*1-100 GOLD: .8X TO 2X BASIC CARDS
1-100 STATED ODDS 1:3
*101-140 JSY/20-31: .8X TO 2X BASIC JSY
*101-140 JSY/14-19: 1X TO 2.5X BASIC JSY
*101-140 JSY/24-38: .8X TO 2X BASIC JSY
*101-140 JSY/14-19: 1X TO 2.5X BASIC JSY
101 Connor McDavid JSY/17 60.00 120.00

2015-16 Upper Deck Team Canada Juniors Patch Autographs

101 Connor McDavid JSY AU/125 200.00 350.00
102 Zach Fucale JSY AU/125 10.00 25.00
103 Max Domi JSY AU/125 40.00 80.00
104 Jake Virtanen JSY AU/125 20.00 40.00
105 Nick Ritchie JSY AU/125 10.00 25.00
106 Lawson Crouse JSY AU/125 10.00 25.00
107 Nicolas Petan JSY AU/199 8.00 20.00
109 Samuel Morin JSY AU/199 6.00 15.00
110 Nick Paul JSY AU/199 6.00 15.00
111 Brayden Point JSY AU/199 8.00 20.00
112 Dillon Heatherington JSY AU/199 5.00 12.00
113 Josh Morrissey JSY AU/199 8.00 20.00
114 Robby Fabbri JSY AU/199 10.00 25.00
115 Frederik Gauthier JSY AU/199 8.00 20.00
116 Shea Theodore JSY AU/199 8.00 20.00
117 Joe Hicketts JSY AU/199 6.00 15.00
118 Madison Bowey JSY AU/199 6.00 15.00
119 Evan Cormier JSY AU/199 6.00 15.00
120 Mitchell Stephens JSY AU/199 6.00 15.00
121 Ethan Bear JSY AU/199 5.00 12.00
122 Mathew Barzal JSY AU/199 25.00 60.00
123 Kyle Capobianco JSY AU/199 5.00 12.00
124 Parker Wotherspoon JSY AU/199 6.00 15.00
125 Anthony Beauvillier JSY AU/199 8.00 20.00
127 Nathan Noel JSY AU/199 6.00 15.00
128 Thomas Chabot JSY AU/199 8.00 20.00
129 Jeremy Roy JSY AU/199 8.00 20.00
130 Deven Sideroff JSY AU/199 5.00 12.00
131 Zachary Sawchenko JSY AU/199 5.00 12.00
132 Guillaume Brisebois JSY AU/199 6.00 15.00
133 Glenn Gawdin JSY AU/199 5.00 12.00
134 Matthew Spencer JSY AU/199 6.00 15.00
135 Nicolas Roy JSY AU/199 6.00 15.00
136 Tyler Benson JSY AU/199 10.00 25.00
137 Brett Howden JSY AU/199 6.00 15.00
138 Tyler Soy JSY AU/199 8.00 20.00
140 Pierre Luc Dubois JSY AU/199 12.00 30.00
141 Sarah Davis JSY AU/199 5.00 12.00
142 Bailey Bram JSY AU/199 5.00 12.00
144 Halli Krzyzaniak JSY AU/199 6.00 15.00
146 Ann-Renee Desbiens JSY AU/199 6.00 15.00
147 Rebecca Johnston JSY AU/199 6.00 15.00
148 Marie-Philip Poulin JSY AU/199 8.00 20.00
149 Jillian Saulnier JSY AU/199 5.00 12.00
150 Natalie Spooner JSY AU/199 8.00 20.00
151 Caroline Ouellette JSY AU/199 8.00 20.00
152 Lauriane Rougeau JSY AU/199 5.00 12.00
154 Brigette Lacquette JSY AU/199 5.00 12.00
155 Laura Fortino JSY AU/199 5.00 12.00
157 Jamie Lee Rattray JSY AU/199 6.00 15.00
159 Emily Clark JSY AU/199 8.00 20.00
160 Brianne Jenner JSY AU/199 6.00 15.00

2015-16 Upper Deck Team Canada Juniors '90-91 Retros U20

STATED ODDS 1:86
R201 Nick Ritchie 6.00 15.00
R202 Zach Fucale 6.00 15.00
R203 Max Domi 10.00 25.00
R204 Connor McDavid 75.00 150.00
R205 Samuel Morin 5.00 12.00
R206 Lawson Crouse 6.00 15.00
R207 Robby Fabbri 8.00 20.00
R208 Frederik Gauthier 6.00 15.00
R209 Madison Bowey 5.00 12.00
R2010 Nick Paul 5.00 12.00
R2011 Brayden Point 6.00 15.00
R2012 Eric Comrie 6.00 15.00
R2013 Jake Virtanen 10.00 25.00
R2014 Nicolas Petan 6.00 15.00
R2015 Josh Morrissey 6.00 15.00

2015-16 Upper Deck Team Canada Juniors '91-92 Retros U18

STATED ODDS 1:86
R181 Dylan Strome 10.00 25.00
R182 Mitch Marner 15.00 40.00
R183 Travis Konecny 8.00 20.00
R184 Nick Merkley 6.00 15.00
R185 Jeremy Roy 5.00 12.00
R186 Nicolas Roy 4.00 10.00
R187 Zachary Sawchenko 3.00 8.00
R188 Mathew Barzal 15.00 40.00
R189 Jansen Harkins 5.00 12.00
R1810 Mitchell Stephens 4.00 10.00
R1811 Thomas Chabot 5.00 12.00
R1812 Ethan Bear 3.00 8.00
R1813 Evan Cormier 4.00 10.00
R1814 Anthony Beauvillier 5.00 12.00
R1815 Matthew Spencer 4.00 10.00

2015-16 Upper Deck Team Canada Juniors '97-98 Retros Women

STATED ODDS 1:216
RW1 Jennifer Wakefield 4.00 10.00
RW2 Genevieve Lacasse 4.00 10.00
RW3 Marie-Philip Poulin 5.00 12.00
RW4 Natalie Spooner 5.00 12.00
RW5 Laura Fortino 3.00 8.00
RW6 Caroline Ouellette 5.00 12.00

2015-16 Upper Deck Team Canada Juniors Dual Jerseys

STATED ODDS 1:48
TCDBB M.Barzal/A.Beauvillier 12.00 30.00
TCDDF R.Fabbri/M.Domi 5.00 12.00
TCDFC Z.Fucale/E.Comrie 5.00 12.00
TCDGP F.Gauthier/N.Petan 4.00 10.00
TCDJL B.Jenner/G.Lacasse 5.00 12.00
TCDMC C.McDavid/L.Crouse 12.00 30.00
TCDMD C.McDavid/M.Domi 12.00 30.00
TCDRV J.Virtanen/N.Ritchie 5.00 12.00
TCDSC Z.Sawchenko/E.Cormier 2.50 6.00
TCDSP N.Spooner/M.Poulin 4.00 10.00

2015-16 Upper Deck Team Canada Juniors Hydro

STATED ODDS 1:3
*RED: .8X TO 2X BASIC INSERTS
H1 Nick Merkley 2.50 6.00
H2 Dylan Strome 2.50 6.00
H3 Travis Konecny 2.50 6.00
H4 Mitch Marner 6.00 15.00
H5 Adam Musil 1.50 4.00
H6 Jansen Harkins 2.00 5.00
H7 Anthony Beauvillier 2.00 5.00
H8 Tyler Soy 2.00 5.00
H9 Brett Howden 1.50 4.00
H10 Tyler Benson 2.50 6.00
H11 Kyle Capobianco 1.25 3.00
H12 Matthew Spencer 1.50 4.00
H13 Graham Knott 1.25 3.00
H14 Deven Sideroff 1.25 3.00
H15 Thomas Chabot 2.00 5.00
H16 Parker Wotherspoon 1.50 4.00
H17 Glenn Gawdin 1.25 3.00
H18 Nathan Noel 1.50 4.00
H19 Zachary Sawchenko 1.25 3.00
H20 Guillaume Brisebois 1.50 4.00
H21 Nicolas Roy 1.50 4.00
H22 Mitchell Stephens 1.50 4.00
H23 Jeremy Roy 2.00 5.00
H24 Pierre-Luc Dubois 3.00 8.00
H25 Mathew Barzal 6.00 15.00
H26 Ethan Bear 1.25 3.00
H27 Evan Cormier 1.50 4.00
H28 Josh Morrissey 2.00 5.00
H29 Brayden Point 2.00 5.00
H30 Nicolas Petan 2.00 5.00
H31 Samuel Morin 1.50 4.00
H32 Lawson Crouse 2.00 5.00
H33 Madison Bowey 1.50 4.00
H34 Max Domi 6.00 15.00
H35 Shea Theodore 2.00 5.00
H36 Robby Fabbri 2.50 6.00
H37 Connor McDavid 6.00 15.00
H38 Zach Fucale 2.00 5.00
H39 Jake Virtanen 2.50 6.00
H40 Frederik Gauthier 2.00 5.00
H41 Dillon Heatherington 1.25 3.00
H42 Nick Paul 1.50 4.00
H43 Joe Hicketts 1.50 4.00
H44 Nick Ritchie 2.00 5.00
H45 Eric Comrie 2.00 5.00
H46 Caroline Ouellette 2.00 5.00
H47 Ann-Renee Desbiens 1.50 4.00
H48 Brigette Lacquette 1.25 3.00
H49 Genevieve Lacasse 1.50 4.00
H50 Jennifer Wakefield 1.50 4.00
H51 Laura Fortino 1.25 3.00
H52 Rebecca Johnston 1.50 4.00
H53 Halli Krzyzaniak 1.50 4.00
H54 Jamie Lee Rattray 1.50 4.00
H55 Jessica Campbell 2.00 5.00
H56 Courtney Birchard 1.25 3.00
H57 Marie-Philip Poulin 2.00 5.00
H58 Brianne Jenner 1.50 4.00
H59 Emily Clark 2.00 5.00
H60 Natalie Spooner 2.00 5.00

2015-16 Upper Deck Team Canada Juniors Jumbo Jerseys

STATED PRINT RUN 199 SER.#'d SETS
JSAB Anthony Beauvillier 4.00 10.00
JSCM Connor McDavid 20.00 40.00
JSFG Frederik Gauthier 4.00 10.00
JSJH Jansen Harkins 4.00 10.00
JSJV Jake Virtanen 5.00 12.00
JSLC Lawson Crouse 4.00 10.00
JSMB Mathew Barzal 12.00 30.00
JSMD Max Domi 12.00 30.00
JSMS Mitchell Stephens 3.00 8.00
JSNP Nicolas Petan 4.00 10.00
JSNR Nick Ritchie 4.00 10.00
JSPA Nick Paul 3.00 8.00
JSRF Robby Fabbri 5.00 12.00
JSSM Samuel Morin 3.00 8.00
JSZF Zach Fucale 4.00 10.00
JSZS Zachary Sawchenko 2.50 6.00

2015-16 Upper Deck Team Canada Juniors Local Legends Jerseys

STATED ODDS 1:36
*GOLD/25: .6X TO 1.5X BASIC JSY
LLBJ Brianne Jenner 3.00 8.00
LLBP Brayden Point 4.00 10.00
LLCM Connor McDavid 20.00 40.00
LLEC Emily Clark 4.00 10.00
LLGL Genevieve Lacasse 3.00 8.00
LLJV Jake Virtanen 5.00 12.00
LLLC Lawson Crouse 4.00 10.00
LLMB Madison Bowey 3.00 8.00
LLMD Max Domi 12.00 30.00
LLNP Nicolas Petan 4.00 10.00
LLNR Nick Ritchie 4.00 10.00
LLRF Robby Fabbri 5.00 12.00
LLSM Samuel Morin 3.00 8.00
LLTB Tyler Benson 5.00 12.00
LLZF Zach Fucale 4.00 10.00

2015-16 Upper Deck Team Canada Juniors Maple Leaf Forever Autographs

MEN'S AU TIER 1 ODDS 1:216
MEN'S AU TIER 2 ODDS 1:108
WOMEN'S AU ODDS 1:180
MLAB Anthony Beauvillier M2 6.00 15.00
MLAD Ann-Renee Desbiens W 10.00 25.00
MLBB Bailey Bram W 6.00 15.00
MLBH Brett Howden M2 5.00 12.00
MLBJ Brianne Jenner W 10.00 25.00
MLBL Brigette Lacquette W 6.00 15.00
MLBP Brayden Point M2 6.00 15.00
MLCL Emily Clark W 10.00 25.00
MLCM Connor McDavid M1 125.00 200.00
MLDH Dillon Heatherington M2 4.00 10.00
MLDS Deven Sideroff M2 4.00 10.00
MLEB Ethan Bear M2 4.00 10.00
MLEC Evan Cormier M2 5.00 12.00
MLEM Emerance Maschmeyer W 10.00 25.00
MLFG Frederik Gauthier M2 6.00 15.00
MLGB Guillaume Brisebois M2 5.00 12.00
MLGG Glenn Gawdin M2 4.00 10.00
MLHI Joe Hicketts M2 5.00 12.00
MLHK Halli Krzyzaniak W 10.00 25.00
MLJM Josh Morrissey M2 6.00 15.00
MLJR Jeremy Roy M2 6.00 15.00
MLJS Jillian Saulnier W 6.00 15.00
MLJV Jake Virtanen M1 15.00 30.00
MLKC Kyle Capobianco M2 4.00 10.00
MLLC Lawson Crouse M1 6.00 15.00
MLLF Laura Fortino W 6.00 15.00
MLLR Lauriane Rougeau W 6.00 15.00
MLMB Mathew Barzal M2 20.00 50.00
MLMD Max Domi M1 25.00 50.00
MLMP Marie-Philip Poulin W 10.00 25.00
MLMS Matthew Spencer M2 5.00 12.00
MLNN Nathan Noel M2 5.00 12.00
MLNP Nick Paul M2 5.00 12.00
MLNS Natalie Spooner W 10.00 25.00
MLOU Caroline Ouellette W 10.00 25.00
MLPD Pierre-Luc Dubois M2 10.00 25.00
MLPE Nicolas Petan M2 6.00 15.00
MLPW Parker Wotherspoon M2 5.00 12.00
MLRA Jamie Lee Rattray W 8.00 20.00
MLRF Robby Fabbri M2 8.00 20.00
MLRJ Rebecca Johnston W 10.00 25.00
MLRO Nicolas Roy M2 5.00 12.00
MLSM Samuel Morin M2 5.00 12.00
MLST Mitchell Stephens M2 5.00 12.00
MLTB Tyler Benson M2 15.00 30.00
MLTC Thomas Chabot M2 6.00 15.00
MLTH Shea Theodore M2 6.00 15.00
MLTS Tyler Soy M2 6.00 15.00
MLTW Tara Watchorn W
MLZF Zach Fucale M1
MLZS Zachary Sawchenko M2

2015-16 Upper Deck Team Canada Juniors Quad Jerseys

STATED ODDS 1:384
TCQBBHC Brzl/Bvlr/Hrkns/Crse 10.00 25.00
TCQMPGF McDav/Fbr/Ghr/Pnt 25.00 50.00
TCQMRVP Mrn/Rtch/Vrtn/Ptan 10.00 25.00
TCQPJLS Jnr/Plin/Spnr/Lacse 8.00 20.00

2015-16 Upper Deck Team Canada Juniors Triple Jerseys

STATED ODDS 1:192
TCTBHB Barzal/Harkins/Beauv 8.00 20.00
TCTMFD McDavid/Fabbri/Domi 20.00 40.00
TCTMPC Morin/Petan/Crouse 6.00 15.00
TCTVGR Virtanen/Gauth/Ritchie 8.00 20.00
TCTWPS Wakefd/Poulin/Spooner 8.00 20.00

2015-16 Upper Deck Team Canada Juniors True North Jerseys

STATED ODDS 1:24
*GOLD/49: .5X TO 1.2X BASIC JSY
TNAB Anthony Beauvillier 4.00 10.00
TNBH Brett Howden 3.00 8.00
TNCM Connor McDavid 20.00 40.00
TNEC Evan Cormier 3.00 8.00
TNFG Frederik Gauthier 4.00 10.00
TNGL Genevieve Lacasse 3.00 8.00
TNJH Jansen Harkins 4.00 10.00
TNJM Josh Morrissey 4.00 10.00
TNJV Jake Virtanen 5.00 12.00
TNJW Jennifer Wakefield 3.00 8.00
TNLF Laura Fortino 2.50 6.00
TNMB Mathew Barzal 12.00 30.00
TNMD Max Domi 12.00 30.00
TNMP Marie-Philip Poulin 4.00 10.00
TNMS Mitchell Stephens 3.00 8.00
TNNN Nathan Noel 3.00 8.00
TNNP Nicolas Petan 4.00 10.00
TNNR Nick Ritchie 4.00 10.00
TNNS Natalie Spooner 4.00 10.00
TNRF Robby Fabbri 5.00 12.00
TNSM Samuel Morin 3.00 8.00
TNTB Tyler Benson 5.00 12.00
TNTC Thomas Chabot 4.00 10.00
TNZF Zach Fucale 4.00 10.00
TNZS Zachary Sawchenko 2.50 6.00

2015-16 Upper Deck Team Canada Master Collection

1 Wayne Gretzky 15.00 40.00
2 Corey Perry 2.50 6.00
3 Glenn Anderson 2.50 6.00
4 Ed Belfour 2.50 6.00
5 Paul Coffey 2.50 6.00
6 Mark Messier 4.00 10.00
7 Eric Lindros 3.00 8.00
8 Bill Ranford 3.00 8.00
9 Rick Nash 2.50 6.00
10 Jarome Iginla 2.50 6.00
11 Steven Stamkos 5.00 12.00
12 Luc Robitaille 3.00 8.00
13 Joe Sakic 4.00 10.00
14 Felix Potvin 4.00 10.00
15 Bobby Clarke 2.50 6.00
16 Vincent Lecavalier 2.00 5.00
17 Doug Gilmour 3.00 8.00
18 John Tavares 5.00 12.00
19 Theoren Fleury 3.00 8.00
20 Bobby Orr 8.00 20.00
21 Dale Hawerchuk 3.00 8.00
22 Marcel Dionne 3.00 8.00
23 Jordan Eberle 2.50 6.00
24 Sidney Crosby 6.00 15.00
25 Ryan Smyth 2.00 5.00
26 Bobby Hull 2.50 6.00
27 Marc-Andre Fleury 4.00 10.00
28 Larry Robinson 2.50 6.00
29 Grant Fuhr 2.50 6.00
30 Dany Heatley 2.00 5.00
31 Ryan Nugent-Hopkins 2.50 6.00
32 Shea Weber 2.00 5.00
33 Patrick Roy 6.00 15.00
34 Ron Hextall 2.50 6.00
35 Taylor Hall 3.00 8.00
36 Eric Staal 3.00 8.00
37 P.K. Subban 3.00 8.00
38 Mike Gartner 2.50 6.00
39 Jonathan Toews 5.00 12.00
40 Jeff Skinner 2.00 5.00
41 Mario Lemieux 8.00 20.00
42 Martin St. Louis 2.50 6.00
43 Mike Bossy 2.50 6.00
44 Chris Pronger 2.00 5.00

Ray Bourque 4.00 10.00
James Neal 2.50 6.00
Ryan Getzlaf 4.00 10.00
Martin Brodeur 5.00 12.00
Steve Yzerman 4.00 10.00
Carey Price 8.00 20.00

2015-16 Upper Deck Team Canada Master Collection Inscriptions

ATED PRINT RUN 10-25
Bobby Clarke/25
Bobby Orr/25
Cody Hodgson/25
Darryl Sittler/25
Dany Heatley/25
3 Mike Bossy/25 15.00 40.00
Mario Lemieux/10
Rick Nash/25 30.00 60.00
John Tavares/25
Vincent Lecavalier/25
3 Wayne Gretzky/25

2015-16 Upper Deck Team Canada Master Collection Luminaries Autographs

ATED PRINT RUN 10-99
3C Bobby Clarke/25 40.00 80.00
3O Bobby Orr/99 100.00 200.00
S Joe Sakic/25
MB Mike Bossy/25
MG Mike Gartner/25 15.00 40.00
MM Mark Messier/25
SC Sidney Crosby/25
SY Steve Yzerman/10
F Theoren Fleury/25
VG Wayne Gretzky/99 175.00 300.00

2015-16 Upper Deck Team Canada Master Collection Program of Excellence Dual Autographs

ATED PRINT RUN 15 SER.#'d SETS
ES2GP Ryan Getzlaf
orey Perry
ES2IS J.Iginla/R.Smyth
ES2KH Evander Kane 20.00 50.00
ody Hodgson
ES2NH Ryan Nugent-Hopkins
onathan Huberdeau
ES2PM Carey Price
teve Mason
ES2SS Jaden Schwartz 25.00 60.00
evante Smith-Pelly
ES2TD John Tavares
att Duchene

2015-16 Upper Deck Team Canada Master Collection Program of Excellence Quad Jersey Autographs

TCH/25: .6X TO 1.5X BASIC JSY AU/99
EBG Brendan Gallagher
EDH Dougie Hamilton 12.00 30.00
EJH Jonathan Huberdeau
EJS Jaden Schwartz
ENB Nathan Beaulieu
EQH Quinton Howden 8.00 20.00

2015-16 Upper Deck Team Canada Master Collection Signature Moments Booklets

TED PRINT RUN 25 SER.#'d SETS
BO Bobby Orr
BR Bill Ranford 30.00 60.00
CH Cody Hodgson
CP Carey Price
CR Sidney Crosby
GR Wayne Gretzky
JS Jeff Skinner 15.00 40.00
JT John Tavares 40.00 80.00
PB Patrice Bergeron
PS P.K. Subban
RN Rick Nash
RNH Ryan Nugent-Hopkins 20.00 50.00
RS Ryan Smyth
SA Joe Sakic
SM Steve Mason
TF Theoren Fleury 40.00 80.00
TH Taylor Hall
WA Wayne Gretzky
WG Wayne Gretzky

2015-16 Upper Deck Team Canada Master Collection Silver Spectrum Autographs

TED PRINT RUN 5-25
ayne Gretzky/25
ck Nash/15
arome Iginla/15
uc Robitaille/15 25.00 60.00
elix Potvin/25
Bobby Clarke/15
Vincent Lecavalier/25
Doug Gilmour/15
ohn Tavares/25 30.00 60.00
Bobby Orr/25
Dale Hawerchuk/15
Marcel Dionne/25
yan Smyth/25
Marc-Andre Fleury/20
Dany Heatley/15
yan Nugent-Hopkins/25
hea Weber/20
aylor Hall/15
ric Staal/15
P.K. Subban/15
Mike Gartner/25
Martin St. Louis/20
ames Neal/25 15.00 40.00
yan Getzlaf/20 25.00 60.00

2015-16 Upper Deck Team Canada Master Collection Team Canada Autographs

TED PRINT RUN 10-25
AB Alexandre Burrows/25 20.00 40.00
AP Alex Pietrangelo/25
BC Bobby Clarke/15
BO Bobby Orr/25 125.00 200.00
BR Brett Connolly/25 10.00 25.00
BS Brayden Schenn/25
CC Casey Cizikas/25
CH Cody Hodgson/25
CT Colten Teubert/25
CW Cam Ward/15 15.00 40.00
DH Dale Hawerchuk/15
DR Derek Roy/25
ES Eric Staal/15
GR Wayne Gretzky/25
GW Wayne Gretzky/25
TCSGZ Wayne Gretzky/25
TCSHA Taylor Hall/15
TCSHD Dougie Hamilton/25 25.00 50.00
TCSJA Jake Allen/25
TCSJB Jamie Benn/25
TCSJH Jonathan Huberdeau/15
TCSJN James Neal/25 25.00 50.00
TCSJT John Tavares/15 40.00 80.00
TCSKL Kris Letang/15
TCSMD Matt Duchene/25 15.00 40.00
TCSMG Mike Gartner/15
TCSOB Bobby Orr/25 125.00 200.00
TCSRG Ryan Getzlaf/15
TCSRS Ryan Smyth/15
TCSRW Ray Whitney/25 10.00 25.00
TCSSC Sidney Crosby/15
TCSSH Scott Hartnell/15
TCSSJ Jaden Schwartz/25 20.00 50.00
TCSSK Jeff Skinner/15 12.00 30.00
TCSSM Steve Mason/15
TCSSS Sheldon Souray/25 10.00 25.00
TCSSW Shea Weber/20
TCSSZ Justin Schultz/25
TCSTS Tyler Seguin/15 20.00 40.00
TCSWG Wayne Gretzky/25
TCSORR Bobby Orr/25 125.00 200.00
TCSRNH Ryan Nugent-Hopkins/15

2015-16 Upper Deck Team Canada Master Collection Team Canada Autographs Dual

STATED PRINT RUN 10-25
TCS2CS B.Clarke/S.Shutt
TCS2FH G.Fuhr/R.Hextall
TCS2GM W.Gretzky/M.Messier
TCS2GO W.Gretzky/B.Orr
TCS2HH Huberdeau/Hamilton
TCS2LG W.Gretzky/M.Lemieux
TCS2PM C.Price/S.Mason
TCS2PT Pietrangelo/C.Teubert
TCS2RH L.Robinson/Bobby Hull
TCS2SC J.Schwartz/B.Connolly 20.00 50.00
TCS2TN J.Tavares/J.Neal

2015-16 Upper Deck Team Canada Master Collection Team Canada Autographs Triple

STATED PRINT RUN 15 SER.#'d SETS
TCS3BPG Bssy/Prrlt/Grtnr
TCS3CAF Cffy/Andrsn/Fhr
TCS3DLR Rbnsn/Dnne/Shtt
TCS3FMA Flry/Msn/Alln
TCS3FVH Vchn/Fhr/Hxtll
TCS3GAH Glmr/Hwrchk/Andrsn
TCS3GCA Grtzky/Cffy/Andrsn
TCS3HTH Cnnlly/Czks/Schnn
TCS3MTH Thrntn/Mrlu/Htly
TCS3OVR Orr/Rbnsn/Vchn
TCS3SSC Schnn/Schwrtz/Czks
TCS3STG Stl/Thrntn/Gtzlf 40.00 80.00

2015-16 Upper Deck Team Canada Master Collection Winning Standard Autographed Jumbo Jersey

STATED PRINT RUN 25 SER.#'d SETS
WSSJCP Corey Perry
WSSJDH Dany Heatley
WSSJES Eric Staal
WSSJJI Jarome Iginla
WSSJJT Joe Thornton
WSSJMF Marc-Andre Fleury
WSSJPB Patrice Bergeron
WSSJPM Patrick Marleau
WSSJPR Chris Pronger
WSSJRG Ryan Getzlaf
WSSJRN Rick Nash
WSSJSC Sidney Crosby 200.00 350.00
WSSJSW Shea Weber 40.00 80.00
WSSJTO Jonathan Toews

2015-16 Upper Deck Team Canada Master Collection Winning Standard Autographs

STATED PRINT RUN 25 SER.#'d SETS
WSSCP Corey Perry
WSSDH Dany Heatley 12.00 30.00
WSSES Eric Staal
WSSJI Jarome Iginla 40.00 80.00
WSSJT Jonathan Toews
WSSMF Marc-Andre Fleury
WSSPB Patrice Bergeron 25.00 50.00
WSSPM Patrick Marleau
WSSPR Chris Pronger
WSSRG Ryan Getzlaf
WSSRN Rick Nash 15.00 40.00
WSSSC Sidney Crosby
WSSSW Shea Weber 12.00 30.00
WSSTH Joe Thornton

2015-16 Upper Deck Team Canada Master Collection Winning Standard Autographs Dual

STATED PRINT RUN 15 SER.#'d SETS
WSS2BF P.Bergeron/M.Fleury
WSS2NI R.Nash/J.Iginla
WSS2PG R.Getzlaf/C.Perry 30.00 80.00
WSS2ST E.Staal/J.Toews
WSS2WP S.Weber/C.Pronger

2015-16 Upper Deck Team Canada Master Collection Winning Standard Crosby Jersey Autographs

WSSC Sidney Crosby

2015-16 Upper Deck Team Canada Master Collection Winning Standard Jerseys

ONE SET PER FACTORY MASTER SET
*JUM.PATCH/10: 1X TO 2.5X BASIC JSY
*PATCH/35: .6X TO 1.5X BASIC JSY
WSBM Brenden Morrow 5.00 12.00
WSDS Brent Seabrook 6.00 15.00
WSCP Chris Pronger 5.00 12.00
WSDB Dan Boyle 5.00 12.00
WSDD Drew Doughty 6.00 15.00
WSDH Dany Heatley 5.00 12.00
WSDK Duncan Keith 6.00 15.00
WSES Eric Staal 8.00 20.00
WSJI Jarome Iginla 6.00 15.00
WSJT Joe Thornton 6.00 15.00
WSMB Martin Brodeur 12.00 30.00
WSMF Marc-Andre Fleury 10.00 25.00
WSMR Mike Richards 6.00 15.00
WSPB Patrice Bergeron 8.00 20.00
WSPE Corey Perry 6.00 15.00
WSPM Patrick Marleau 6.00 15.00
WSRG Ryan Getzlaf 10.00 25.00
WSRL Roberto Luongo 10.00 25.00
WSRN Rick Nash 6.00 15.00
WSSC Sidney Crosby 15.00 40.00
WSSW Shea Weber 5.00 12.00
WSTO Jonathan Toews 12.00 30.00

2015-16 Upper Deck Team Canada Master Collection Winning Standard Jerseys and Patch Dual

STATED PRINT RUN 25 SER.#'d SETS
*DUAL JSY/15: .4X TO 1X PATCH/25
WS2BD Dan Boyle 10.00 25.00
Drew Doughty
WS2BI Patrice Bergeron 12.00 30.00
Jarome Iginla
WS2BL Martin Brodeur
Roberto Luongo
WS2BP Dan Boyle 8.00 20.00
Chris Pronger
WS2GP Ryan Getzlaf
Corey Perry
WS2IN Jarome Iginla 15.00 40.00
Rick Nash
WS2KS Duncan Keith
Brent Seabrook
WS2MM Patrick Marleau 10.00 25.00
Brenden Morrow
WS2SR Eric Staal
Mike Richards
WS2TB Jonathan Toews 20.00 50.00
Patrice Bergeron
WS2TH Joe Thornton
Dany Heatley

2015-16 Upper Deck Team Canada Master Collection Winning Standard Jerseys and Patch Triple

STATED PRINT RUN 15 SER.#'d SETS
WS3BLF Martin Brodeur
Roberto Luongo
Marc-Andre Fleury
WS3BSR Eric Staal
Mike Richards
Patrice Bergeron
WS3KSW Duncan Keith
Brent Seabrook
Shea Weber
WS3MTH Joe Thornton
Patrick Marleau
Dany Heatley
WS3PBD Chris Pronger
Dan Boyle
Drew Doughty
WS3PGT Jonathan Toews
Ryan Getzlaf
Corey Perry
WS3SIN Eric Staal
Jarome Iginla
Rick Nash
WS3SKT Jonathan Toews
Duncan Keith
Brent Seabrook

2016-17 Upper Deck Team Canada Juniors

1 Hayley Wickenheiser .40 1.00
2 Tara Watchorn .40 1.00
3 Meghan Agosta-Marciano .40 1.00
4 Brigette Lacquette .40 1.00
5 Jamie Lee Rattray .30 .75
6 Jillian Saulnier .40 1.00
7 Jennifer Wakefield .30 .75
8 Marie-Philip Poulin .40 1.00
9 Halli Krzyzaniak .40 1.00
10 Lauriane Rougeau .30 .75
11 Natalie Spooner .30 .75
12 Brianne Jenner .40 1.00
13 Charline Labonte .40 1.00
14 Sarah Davis .30 .75
15 Blayre Turnbull .40 1.00
16 Meaghan Mikkelson .30 .75
17 Emerance Maschmeyer .30 .75
18 Rebecca Johnston .30 .75
19 Emily Clark .40 1.00
20 Jocelyne Larocque .40 1.00
21 Bailey Bram .30 .75
22 Laura Fortino .40 1.00
23 Dylan Strome .75 2.00
24 Mitch Marner 2.00 5.00
25 Brandon Hickey .30 .75
26 Mackenzie Blackwood .30 .75
27 Mason McDonald .40 1.00
28 Samuel Montembeault .40 1.00
29 Thomas Chabot .75 2.00
30 Travis Dermott .30 .75
31 Joe Hicketts .30 .75
32 Roland McKeown .30 .75
33 Mathew Barzal 1.25 3.00
34 Anthony Beauvillier .40 1.00
35 Rourke Chartier .40 1.00
36 Lawson Crouse .30 .75
37 Julien Gauthier .40 1.00
38 Travis Konecny .75 2.00
39 Brayden Point 1.00 2.50
40 Mitchell Stephens .40 1.00
41 Haydn Fleury .40 1.00
42 Travis Sanheim .30 .75
43 Brendan Perlini .40 1.00
44 John Quenneville .40 1.00
45 Sam Steel .40 1.00
46 Carter Hart .60 1.50
47 Dylan Wells .40 1.00
48 Jake Bean .30 .75
49 Kale Clague .40 1.00
50 Dante Fabbro .30 .75
51 Josh Mahura .30 .75
52 Samuel Girard .30 .75
53 Victor Mete .30 .75
54 David Quenneville .40 1.00
55 Tyler Benson .30 .75
56 William Bitten .30 .75
57 Dilon Dube .30 .75
58 Pierre-Luc Dubois .30 .75
59 Brett Howden .40 1.00
60 Tyson Jost .40 1.00
61 Tanner Kaspick .40 1.00
62 Jordan Kyrou .30 .75
63 Beck Malenstyn .40 1.00
64 Michael McLeod .40 1.00
65 Nolan Patrick 2.50 6.00
66 Zach Poirier .30 .75
67 Pascal Laberge .30 .75
68 Evan Fitzpatrick .40 1.00
69 Connor Hall .30 .75
70 Maxime Comtois .40 1.00
71 Stuart Skinner .40 1.00
72 Jakob Chychrun .40 1.00
73 Cameron Morrison .30 .75
74 Nicolas Hague .30 .75
75 Markus Phillips .30 .75
76 Logan Stanley .40 1.00
77 Boris Katchouk .75 2.00
78 Mason Shaw .40 1.00
79 Noah Gregor .40 1.00
80 Owen Tippett .40 1.00
81 Mitch Marner 2.00 5.00
82 Lawson Crouse .30 .75
83 Dylan Strome .75 2.00
84 Haydn Fleury .40 1.00
85 John Quenneville .40 1.00
86 Pierre-Luc Dubois .30 .75
87 Tyson Jost .40 1.00
88 Jakob Chychrun .40 1.00
89 Nolan Patrick 2.50 6.00
90 Michael McLeod .40 1.00
91 Doug Gilmour .50 1.25
92 Martin Brodeur .75 2.00
93 Grant Fuhr .40 1.00
94 Mark Messier .50 1.25
95 Rod Brind'Amour .40 1.00
96 Martin St. Louis .40 1.00
97 Joe Sakic .60 1.50
98 Steve Yzerman .50 1.25
99 Mario Lemieux 1.25 3.00
100 Wayne Gretzky 2.00 5.00
101 Mitch Marner JSY 20.00 50.00
102 Dylan Strome JSY 8.00 20.00
103 Lawson Crouse JSY 3.00 8.00
104 Mason McDonald JSY 4.00 10.00
105 Anthony Beauvillier JSY 4.00 10.00
106 Brayden Point JSY 10.00 25.00
107 Travis Dermott JSY 3.00 8.00
108 Joe Hicketts JSY 3.00 8.00
109 Roland McKeown JSY 3.00 8.00
110 Mathew Barzal JSY 12.00 30.00
111 Brandon Hickey JSY 3.00 8.00
112 Rourke Chartier JSY 4.00 10.00
113 Thomas Chabot JSY 8.00 20.00
114 Julien Gauthier JSY 4.00 10.00
115 Travis Konecny JSY 8.00 20.00
116 Samuel Montembeault JSY 4.00 10.00
117 Mitchell Stephens JSY 4.00 10.00
118 Haydn Fleury JSY 4.00 10.00
119 Travis Sanheim JSY 3.00 8.00
120 Brendan Perlini JSY 4.00 10.00
121 John Quenneville JSY 4.00 10.00
122 Mackenzie Blackwood JSY 3.00 8.00
123 Evan Fitzpatrick JSY 4.00 10.00
124 Dante Fabbro JSY 3.00 8.00
125 Jakob Chychrun JSY 4.00 10.00
126 David Quenneville JSY 4.00 10.00
127 Logan Stanley JSY 4.00 10.00
128 William Bitten JSY 3.00 8.00
129 Pascal Laberge JSY 3.00 8.00
130 Michael McLeod JSY 4.00 10.00
131 Tyson Jost JSY 4.00 10.00
132 Connor Hall JSY 3.00 8.00
133 Maxime Comtois JSY 4.00 10.00
134 Jordan Kyrou JSY 3.00 8.00
135 Cameron Morrison JSY 3.00 8.00
136 Boris Katchouk JSY 8.00 20.00
137 Mason Shaw JSY 4.00 10.00
138 Brett Howden JSY 4.00 10.00
139 Stuart Skinner JSY 4.00 10.00
140 Nicolas Hague JSY 3.00 8.00
141 Owen Tippett JSY 4.00 10.00
142 Noah Gregor JSY 4.00 10.00
143 Meaghan Mikkelson JSY 3.00 8.00
144 Meghan Agosta-Marciano JSY 4.00 10.00
145 Halli Krzyzaniak JSY 4.00 10.00
146 Jillian Saulnier JSY 4.00 10.00
147 Sarah Davis JSY 3.00 8.00
148 Jamie Lee Rattray JSY 3.00 8.00
149 Emerance Maschmeyer JSY 3.00 8.00
150 Tara Watchorn JSY 4.00 10.00
151 Emily Clark JSY 4.00 10.00
152 Bailey Bram JSY 3.00 8.00
153 Brianne Jenner JSY 4.00 10.00
154 Charline Labonte JSY 4.00 10.00
155 Rebecca Johnston JSY 3.00 8.00
156 Lauriane Rougeau JSY 3.00 8.00
157 Laura Fortino JSY 4.00 10.00
158 Jennifer Wakefield JSY 3.00 8.00
159 Jocelyne Larocque JSY 4.00 10.00
160 Natalie Spooner JSY 3.00 8.00
161 Hayley Wickenheiser JSY 4.00 10.00
162 Marie-Philip Poulin JSY 4.00 10.00

2016-17 Upper Deck Team Canada Juniors Jumbo Material Autographs

JSAB Anthony Beauvillier 6.00 15.00
JSBL Mackenzie Blackwood 5.00 12.00
JSBP Brayden Point 15.00 40.00
JSDS Dylan Strome 12.00 30.00
JSHF Haydn Fleury 6.00 15.00
JSJG Julien Gauthier 6.00 15.00
JSJH Joe Hicketts 5.00 12.00
JSJQ John Quenneville 6.00 15.00
JSLC Lawson Crouse 5.00 12.00
JSMB Mathew Barzal 20.00 50.00
JSMC Mason McDonald 6.00 15.00
JSMM Mitch Marner 30.00 80.00
JSMS Mitchell Stephens 6.00 15.00
JSRC Rourke Chartier 6.00 15.00
JSTC Thomas Chabot 12.00 30.00
JSTD Travis Dermott 5.00 12.00
JSTK Travis Konecny 12.00 30.00
JSTS Travis Sanheim 5.00 12.00

2016-17 Upper Deck Team Canada Juniors Jumbo Materials

JSAB Anthony Beauvillier 4.00 10.00
JSBL Mackenzie Blackwood 3.00 8.00
JSBP Brayden Point 10.00 25.00
JSDS Dylan Strome 8.00 20.00
JSHF Haydn Fleury 4.00 10.00
JSJG Julien Gauthier 4.00 10.00
JSJH Joe Hicketts 3.00 8.00
JSJQ John Quenneville 4.00 10.00
JSLC Lawson Crouse 3.00 8.00
JSMB Mathew Barzal 12.00 30.00
JSMC Mason McDonald 4.00 10.00
JSMM Mitch Marner 20.00 50.00
JSMS Mitchell Stephens 4.00 10.00
JSRC Rourke Chartier 4.00 10.00
JSTC Thomas Chabot 8.00 20.00
JSTD Travis Dermott 3.00 8.00
JSTK Travis Konecny 8.00 20.00
JSTS Travis Sanheim 3.00 8.00

2016-17 Upper Deck Team Canada Juniors Local Legends Relics

LLBA Mathew Barzal 10.00 25.00
LLBP Brendan Perlini 3.00 8.00
LLDS Dylan Strome 6.00 15.00
LLHW Hayley Wickenheiser 3.00 8.00
LLJH Joe Hicketts 2.50 6.00
LLJQ John Quenneville 3.00 8.00
LLLF Laura Fortino 3.00 8.00
LLMB Mackenzie Blackwood 2.50 6.00
LLMC Mason McDonald 3.00 8.00
LLMM Mitch Marner 15.00 40.00
LLMS Mitchell Stephens 3.00 8.00
LLNS Natalie Spooner 2.50 6.00
LLRC Rourke Chartier 3.00 8.00
LLTJ Tyson Jost 3.00 8.00
LLTK Travis Konecny 6.00 15.00

2016-17 Upper Deck Team Canada Juniors Manufactured Logo Patches 100 Years

LP-AB Anthony Beauvillier 8.00 20.00
LP-BP Brayden Point 20.00 50.00
LP-BR Martin Brodeur 15.00 40.00
LP-DG Doug Gilmour 10.00 25.00
LP-DS Dylan Strome 15.00 40.00
LP-EF Evan Fitzpatrick 8.00 20.00
LP-GL Guy Lafleur 10.00 25.00
LP-HF Haydn Fleury 8.00 20.00
LP-JC Jakob Chychrun 8.00 20.00
LP-JG Julien Gauthier 8.00 20.00
LP-JQ John Quenneville 8.00 20.00
LP-JS Joe Sakic 12.00 30.00
LP-LC Lawson Crouse 6.00 15.00
LP-MB Mathew Barzal 25.00 60.00
LP-MC Mason McDonald 8.00 20.00
LP-ME Mark Messier 10.00 25.00
LP-MI Michael McLeod 8.00 20.00
LP-ML Mario Lemieux 25.00 60.00
LP-MM Mitch Marner 30.00 80.00
LP-MS Mitchell Stephens 8.00 20.00
LP-RB Rod Brind'Amour 8.00 20.00
LP-RC Rourke Chartier 8.00 20.00
LP-ST Martin St. Louis 8.00 20.00
LP-SY Steve Yzerman 10.00 25.00
LP-TD Travis Dermott 6.00 15.00
LP-TK Travis Konecny 15.00 40.00
LP-TS Travis Sanheim 6.00 15.00
LP-WG Wayne Gretzky 90.00 150.00

2017-18 Upper Deck Team Canada Juniors

1 Connor Ingram .40 1.00
2 Jake Bean .30 .75
3 Noah Juulsen .40 1.00
4 Mitchell Stephens .40 1.00
5 Michael McLeod 1.25 3.00
6 Taylor Raddysh .40 1.00
7 Carter Hart .40 1.00
8 Pierre-Luc Dubois 2.50 6.00
9 Dillon Dube .30 .75
10 Kale Clague .30 .75
11 Mathieu Joseph .30 .75
12 Julien Gauthier .40 1.00
13 Nicolas Roy .30 .75
14 Anthony Cirelli .30 .75
15 Jeremy Lauzon .30 .75
16 Philippe Myers .30 .75
17 Dante Fabbro .40 1.00
18 Jennifer Wakefield .30 .75
19 Jocelyne Larocque .30 .75
20 Lauriane Rougeau .25 .60
21 Sarah Potomak .30 .75
22 Laura Stacey .30 .75
23 Erin Ambrose .30 .75
24 Natalie Spooner .30 .75
25 Brianne Jenner .40 1.00
26 Emily Clark .40 1.00
27 Halli Krzyzaniak .40 1.00
28 Rebecca Johnston .40 1.00
29 Marie-Philip Poulin .30 .75
30 Emerance Maschmeyer .30 .75
31 Genevieve Lacasse .30 .75
32 Meaghan Mikkelson .30 .75
33 Meghan Agosta .30 .75
34 Shannon Szabados .30 .75
35 Bailey Bram .30 .75
36 Renata Fast .30 .75
37 Sarah Davis .30 .75
38 Haley Irwin .30 .75
39 Laura Fortino .30 .75
40 Blayre Turnbull .30 .75
41 Jaret Anderson-Dolan .40 1.00
42 Jett Woo .30 .75
43 Isaac Ratcliffe .30 .75
44 Nate Schnarr .30 .75
45 Kyle Olson .30 .75
46 Josh Brook .30 .75
47 Jared McIsaac .30 .75
48 Ian Mitchell .30 .75
49 Cody Glass .40 1.00
50 Maxime Comtois .40 1.00
51 Ty Smith .30 .75
52 MacKenzie Entwistle .30 .75
53 Akil Thomas .30 .75
54 Alexis Gravel .30 .75
55 Matthew Strome .30 .75
56 Ty Dellandrea .30 .75
57 Jocktan Chainey .30 .75
58 Ian Scott .30 .75
59 Jacob McGrath .30 .75
60 Stelio Mattheos .30 .75
61 David Noel .30 .75
62 Liam Hawel .30 .75
63 Jack Studnicka .25 .60
64 Owen Tippett .75 2.00
65 Michael Rasmussen .25 .60
66 Michael DiPietro .25 .60
67 Markus Phillips .25 .60
68 Shane Bowers .25 .60
69 Evan Bouchard .40 1.00
70 Joseph Veleno .30 .75
71 Greg Meireles .30 .75
72 Jonathan Smart .30 .75
73 Ryan McLeod .30 .75
74 Antoine Crete-Belzile .30 .75
75 Nick Suzuki .30 .75
76 Jordy Bellerive .30 .75
77 Elijah Roberts .30 .75
78 Sam Steel .30 .75
79 Matthew Spencer .30 .75
80 Nolan Patrick .75 2.00
81 Jordan Kyrou .30 .75
82 Guillaume Brisebois .40 1.00
83 Mitchell Vande Sompel .30 .75
84 Brett Howden .30 .75
85 Nicholas Merkley .30 .75
86 Bobby Orr 1.25 3.00
87 Theoren Fleury .40 1.00
88 Mike Gartner .40 1.00
89 Glenn Anderson .40 1.00
90 Darryl Sittler .40 1.00
91 Doug Gilmour .50 1.25
92 Marcel Dionne .50 1.25
93 Grant Fuhr .50 1.25
94 Larry Murphy .30 .75
95 Joe Sakic .50 1.25
96 Steve Yzerman .50 1.25
97 Mike Bossy .60 1.50
98 Martin Brodeur .75 2.00
99 Mario Lemieux 1.25 3.00
100 Wayne Gretzky 2.00 5.00

2017-18 Upper Deck Team Canada Juniors Jerseys

1 Connor Ingram 1.50 4.00
2 Jake Bean 1.25 3.00
3 Noah Juulsen 1.50 4.00
4 Mitchell Stephens 1.50 4.00
5 Michael McLeod 5.00 12.00
6 Taylor Raddysh 1.50 4.00
7 Carter Hart 1.50 4.00
8 Pierre-Luc Dubois 3.00 8.00
9 Dillon Dube 1.25 3.00
10 Kale Clague 1.25 3.00
11 Mathieu Joseph 1.25 3.00
12 Julien Gauthier 1.50 4.00
13 Nicolas Roy 1.25 3.00
14 Anthony Cirelli 1.25 3.00
15 Jeremy Lauzon 1.25 3.00
16 Philippe Myers 1.25 3.00
17 Dante Fabbro 1.50 4.00
18 Jennifer Wakefield 1.25 3.00
19 Jocelyne Larocque 1.25 3.00
21 Sarah Potomak 1.25 3.00
23 Erin Ambrose 1.25 3.00
24 Natalie Spooner 1.25 3.00
25 Brianne Jenner 1.50 4.00
26 Emily Clark 1.50 4.00
28 Rebecca Johnston 1.50 4.00
29 Marie-Philip Poulin 1.25 3.00
33 Meghan Agosta 1.25 3.00
34 Shannon Szabados 1.25 3.00
38 Haley Irwin 1.25 3.00
40 Blayre Turnbull 1.25 3.00
41 Jaret Anderson-Dolan 1.50 4.00
42 Jett Woo 1.25 3.00
43 Isaac Ratcliffe 1.25 3.00
44 Nate Schnarr 1.25 3.00
45 Kyle Olson 1.25 3.00
46 Josh Brook 1.25 3.00
47 Jared McIsaac 1.25 3.00
48 Ian Mitchell 1.25 3.00
49 Cody Glass 1.50 4.00
50 Maxime Comtois 1.50 4.00
51 Ty Smith 1.25 3.00
52 MacKenzie Entwistle 1.25 3.00
53 Akil Thomas 1.25 3.00
54 Alexis Gravel 1.25 3.00
55 Matthew Strome 1.25 3.00
56 Ty Dellandrea 1.25 3.00
57 Jocktan Chainey 1.25 3.00
58 Ian Scott 1.25 3.00
59 Jacob McGrath 1.25 3.00
60 Stelio Mattheos 1.25 3.00

2017-18 Upper Deck Team Canada Juniors Local Legends

LLCH Carter Hart 1.00 2.50
LLDF Dante Fabbro 1.00 2.50
LLJA Jaret Anderson-Dolan 1.00 2.50
LLJG Julien Gauthier 1.00 2.50
LLJV Joseph Veleno .75 2.00
LLNP Nolan Patrick 2.00 5.00
LLNS Nick Suzuki .75 2.00
LLPD Pierre-Luc Dubois 2.00 5.00
LLSS Shannon Szabados .75 2.00
LLTR Taylor Raddysh 1.00 2.50

2017-18 Upper Deck Team Canada Juniors Local Legends Retired

LLRJS Joe Sakic 2.00 5.00
LLRMB Martin Brodeur 3.00 8.00
LLRMD Marcel Dionne 2.00 5.00
LLRSY Steve Yzerman 2.00 5.00
LLRWG Wayne Gretzky 8.00 20.00

2017-18 Upper Deck Team Canada Juniors Premium Material Autographs

1 Connor Ingram/199 8.00 20.00
2 Jake Bean/199 6.00 15.00
3 Noah Juulsen/199 8.00 20.00
4 Mitchell Stephens/199 8.00 20.00
5 Michael McLeod/125 25.00 60.00
6 Taylor Raddysh/125 10.00 25.00
7 Carter Hart/125 12.00 30.00
8 Pierre-Luc Dubois/125 40.00 100.00
9 Dillon Dube/199 6.00 15.00
10 Kale Clague/199 6.00 15.00
11 Mathieu Joseph/199 6.00 15.00
12 Julien Gauthier/199 8.00 20.00
13 Nicolas Roy/199 6.00 15.00
14 Anthony Cirelli/199 6.00 15.00
15 Jeremy Lauzon/199 6.00 15.00
16 Philippe Myers/199 6.00 15.00
17 Dante Fabbro/125 8.00 20.00
18 Jennifer Wakefield/199 6.00 15.00
19 Jocelyne Larocque/199 6.00 15.00
21 Sarah Potomak/199 6.00 15.00
23 Erin Ambrose/199 6.00 15.00
24 Natalie Spooner/199 6.00 15.00
25 Brianne Jenner/199 8.00 20.00
26 Emily Clark/199 8.00 20.00
28 Rebecca Johnston/199 8.00 20.00
29 Marie-Philip Poulin/199 6.00 15.00
33 Meghan Agosta/199 6.00 15.00
34 Shannon Szabados/199 6.00 15.00
38 Haley Irwin/199 6.00 15.00
40 Blayre Turnbull/199 6.00 15.00
41 Jaret Anderson-Dolan/125 12.00 30.00
42 Jett Woo/199 6.00 15.00
43 Isaac Ratcliffe/199 6.00 15.00
44 Nate Schnarr/199 6.00 15.00
45 Kyle Olson/199 6.00 15.00
46 Josh Brook/199 6.00 15.00
47 Jared McIsaac/199 6.00 15.00
48 Ian Mitchell/199 6.00 15.00
49 Cody Glass/125 12.00 30.00
50 Maxime Comtois/125 8.00 20.00
51 Ty Smith/199 6.00 15.00
52 MacKenzie Entwistle/199 6.00 15.00
53 Akil Thomas/199 6.00 15.00
54 Alexis Gravel/199 6.00 15.00
55 Matthew Strome/199 6.00 15.00
56 Ty Dellandrea/199 6.00 15.00
57 Jocktan Chainey/199 6.00 15.00
58 Ian Scott/199 6.00 15.00
59 Jacob McGrath/199 6.00 15.00
60 Stelio Mattheos/199 6.00 15.00

2017-18 Upper Deck Team Canada Juniors Program of Excellence

POE1 Pierre-Luc Dubois 1.50 4.00
POE2 Michael McLeod 2.50 6.00
POE3 Jake Bean .60 1.50
POE4 Mitchell Stephens .75 2.00
POE5 Taylor Raddysh .75 2.00
POE6 Noah Juulsen .75 2.00
POE7 Julien Gauthier .75 2.00
POE8 Kale Clague .60 1.50
POE9 Carter Hart .75 2.00
POE10 Dante Fabbro .75 2.00
POE11 Philippe Myers .60 1.50
POE12 Maxime Comtois .75 2.00
POE13 Ty Dellandrea .60 1.50
POE14 Jared McIsaac .60 1.50
POE15 Akil Thomas .60 1.50
POE16 Jaret Anderson-Dolan .75 2.00
POE17 MacKenzie Entwistle .60 1.50
POE18 Cody Glass .75 2.00
POE19 Stelio Mattheos .60 1.50
POE20 Matthew Strome .60 1.50
POE21 Sam Steel .60 1.50
POE22 Michael Rasmussen .50 1.25
POE23 Owen Tippett 1.50 4.00
POE24 Joseph Veleno .60 1.50
POE25 Wayne Gretzky 4.00 10.00
POE26 Nick Suzuki .60 1.50
POE27 Mario Lemieux 2.50 6.00
POE28 Martin Brodeur 1.50 4.00
POE29 Mike Bossy 1.25 3.00
POE30 Nolan Patrick 1.50 4.00

2017-18 Upper Deck Team Canada Juniors Program of Excellence Retro

POE971 Pierre-Luc Dubois 3.00 8.00
POE972 Taylor Raddysh 1.50 4.00
POE973 Noah Juulsen 1.50 4.00
POE974 Carter Hart 1.50 4.00
POE975 Joseph Veleno 1.25 3.00
POE976 Wayne Gretzky 10.00 25.00
POE977 Nick Suzuki 1.25 3.00
POE978 Mario Lemieux 8.00 20.00
POE979 Martin Brodeur 6.00 15.00
POE9710 Nolan Patrick 3.00 8.00

2017-18 Upper Deck Team Canada Juniors Team Canada Manufactured Patches

LPCH Carter Hart 3.00 8.00
LPDF Dante Fabbro 3.00 8.00
LPJG Julien Gauthier 3.00 8.00
LPML Mario Lemieux 20.00 50.00
LPMM Michael McLeod 10.00 25.00
LPNJ Noah Juulsen 3.00 8.00
LPPD Pierre-Luc Dubois 6.00 15.00
LPSY Steve Yzerman 15.00 40.00
LPTR Taylor Raddysh 3.00 8.00
LPWG Wayne Gretzky 30.00 80.00

2015-16 Upper Deck Tim Hortons

COMPLETE SET (100) 30.00 60.00
DRAFT EXCH ODDS 1:16,470
1 Tim Horton .50 1.25
2 Eric Staal .60 1.50
3 Andrew Hammond 1.50 4.00
4 Shea Weber .40 1.00
5 Mark Giordano .50 1.25
6 Bobby Ryan .40 1.00
7 Kyle Turris .40 1.00
8 Alexander Ovechkin 2.00 5.00
9 Tyler Johnson .40 1.00
10 Corey Perry .50 1.25
11 Zach Parise .50 1.25
12 Jarome Iginla .50 1.25
13 Pavel Datsyuk .60 1.50
14 Jamie Benn .60 1.50
15 Ryan Getzlaf .75 2.00
16 Andrew Ladd .50 1.25
17 Radim Vrbata .40 1.00
18 Ryan Strome .40 1.00
19 Jonathan Toews 1.00 2.50
20 Alexander Steen .30 .75
21 James van Riemsdyk .50 1.25
22 Daniel Sedin .50 1.25
23 Sean Monahan .50 1.25
24 Jiri Hudler .25 .60
25 Oliver Ekman-Larsson .40 1.00
26 Blake Wheeler .50 1.25
27 Matt Moulson .40 1.00
28 Claude Giroux .50 1.25
29 Jason Pominville .40 1.00
30 Henrik Lundqvist .60 1.50
31 Carey Price 1.50 4.00
32 Jonathan Quick .75 2.00
33 Henrik Sedin .50 1.25
34 Filip Forsberg .60 1.50
35 Pekka Rinne .60 1.50
36 Tuukka Rask .50 1.25
37 Patrice Bergeron .60 1.50
38 Bryan Little .40 1.00
39 Logan Couture .50 1.25
40 Henrik Zetterberg .60 1.50
41 Jaroslav Halak .40 1.00
42 Tyler Bozak .40 1.00
43 Adam Henrique .50 1.25
44 Marian Hossa .40 1.00
45 Jonathan Bernier .50 1.25
46 Shane Doan .40 1.00
47 Taylor Hall 1.00 2.50
48 Brian Elliott .40 1.00
49 Vladimir Tarasenko .75 2.00
50 Corey Crawford .60 1.50
51 Teddy Purcell .50 1.25
52 Aaron Ekblad .50 1.25
53 Jeff Skinner .40 1.00
54 Nicklas Backstrom .75 2.00
55 Roberto Luongo .50 1.25
56 Milan Lucic .40 1.00
57 Drew Doughty .50 1.25
58 Kris Letang .50 1.25
59 Gustav Nyquist .50 1.25
60 Frederik Andersen .40 1.00
61 Rick Nash .50 1.25
62 Johnny Gaudreau .75 2.00
63 Tyler Ennis .40 1.00
64 Marc-Andre Fleury .75 2.00
65 Erik Karlsson 1.00 2.50
66 Brian Gionta .40 1.00
67 Max Pacioretty .50 1.25
68 Jaden Schwartz .60 1.50
69 Kyle Okposo .50 1.25
70 Braden Holtby .75 2.00
71 Evgeni Malkin 1.50 4.00
72 Sergei Bobrovsky .50 1.25
73 Nick Foligno .40 1.00
74 Derick Brassard .50 1.25
75 Nathan MacKinnon 1.00 2.50
76 P.K. Subban .75 2.00
77 Jeff Carter .50 1.25
78 Jordan Eberle .50 1.25
79 Kari Lehtonen .40 1.00
80 Ryan Johansen .60 1.50
81 Phil Kessel .75 2.00
82 Tomas Plekanec .50 1.25
83 Anze Kopitar .75 2.00
84 Ryan Nugent-Hopkins .50 1.25
85 Steve Mason .40 1.00
86 Joe Pavelski .50 1.25

87 Sidney Crosby 2.00 5.00
88 Patrick Kane 1.00 2.50
89 Tyler Seguin .75 2.00
90 Steven Stamkos 1.00 2.50
91 John Tavares 1.00 2.50
92 Gabriel Landeskog .50 1.25
93 Jakub Voracek .50 1.25
94 Cory Schneider .40 1.00
95 Tomas Tatar .40 1.00
96 Ryan Miller .50 1.25
97 Derek Stepan .50 1.25
98 Devan Dubnyk .50 1.25
99 Dustin Byfuglien .50 1.25
100 Michael Cammalleri .40 1.00
SP1 Connor McDavid Draft 400.00 700.00
NNO Draft Pick/McDvd EXCH 400.00 700.00
SC S.Crosby AU/87 EXCH 1250.00 1750.00

2015-16 Upper Deck Tim Hortons Above the Ice

STATED ODDS 1:12
AIAO Alexander Ovechkin 10.00 25.00
AICG Claude Giroux 2.50 6.00
AICP Carey Price 8.00 20.00
AIDD Drew Doughty 2.50 6.00
AIEK Erik Karlsson 5.00 12.00
AIHL Henrik Lundqvist 3.00 8.00
AIHZ Henrik Zetterberg 3.00 8.00
AIJT John Tavares 5.00 12.00
AIPK Patrick Kane 5.00 12.00
AIRM Ryan Miller 2.50 6.00
AIRNH Ryan Nugent-Hopkins 2.50 6.00
AISC Sidney Crosby 10.00 25.00
AISS Steven Stamkos 5.00 12.00
AITS Tyler Seguin 4.00 10.00

2015-16 Upper Deck Tim Hortons Autographs

AAH Andrew Hammond EXCH 125.00 200.00
AAO Alexander Ovechkin EXCH 175.00 300.00
ABS Brayden Schenn EXCH 90.00 150.00
ACP Carey Price EXCH 250.00 400.00
ADP Dion Phaneuf EXCH 125.00 200.00
ADU Matt Duchene EXCH
AJI Jarome Iginla EXCH
AKH Kevin Hayes EXCH 75.00 125.00
ALB Lance Bouma EXCH
AMD Mathew Dumba EXCH 90.00 150.00
AMP Max Pacioretty EXCH 175.00 300.00
AMS Mark Scheifele EXCH 90.00 150.00
APH Patric Hornqvist EXCH 75.00 125.00
ARN Ryan Nugent-Hopkins EXCH 150.00 250.00
ASW Shea Weber EXCH

2015-16 Upper Deck Tim Hortons Die Cuts

COMPLETE SET (15) 8.00 20.00
STATED ODDS 1:3
TH1 Carey Price 2.00 5.00
TH2 Andrew Ladd .60 1.50
TH3 Jonathan Bernier .60 1.50
TH4 Erik Karlsson 1.25 3.00
TH5 Jordan Eberle .60 1.50
TH6 Jiri Hudler .50 1.25
TH7 Alexander Ovechkin 2.50 6.00
TH8 Henrik Lundqvist .75 2.00
TH9 John Tavares 1.25 3.00
TH10 Jonathan Toews 1.25 3.00
TH11 Sidney Crosby 2.50 6.00
TH12 Steven Stamkos 1.25 3.00
TH13 Zach Parise .60 1.50
TH14 Vladimir Tarasenko 1.00 2.50
TH15 Jamie Benn .75 2.00

2015-16 Upper Deck Tim Hortons Franchise Force

COMPLETE SET (12) 90.00 150.00
STATED ODDS 1:24
FF1 Mark Messier 8.00 20.00
FF2 Mario Lemieux 20.00 50.00
FF3 Patrick Roy 15.00 40.00
FF4 Johnny Gaudreau 10.00 25.00
FF5 Taylor Hall 12.00 30.00
FF6 Carey Price 20.00 50.00
FF7 Bobby Ryan 6.00 15.00
FF8 Phil Kessel 10.00 25.00
FF9 Ryan Miller 8.00 20.00
FF10 Blake Wheeler 6.00 15.00
FF11 Sidney Crosby 25.00 60.00
FF12 Alexander Ovechkin 25.00 60.00

2015-16 Upper Deck Tim Hortons Jerseys

JRAB Alexandre Burrows EXCH 75.00 125.00
JRAO Alexander Ovechkin EXCH 175.00 300.00
JRBW Blake Wheeler EXCH 75.00 125.00
JREK Erik Karlsson 75.00 125.00
JRHZ Henrik Zetterberg EXCH 100.00 175.00
JRJE Jordan Eberle EXCH 75.00 125.00
JRJG Johnny Gaudreau 75.00 125.00
JRJI Jarome Iginla EXCH 75.00 150.00
JRJP Jason Pominville 75.00 125.00
JRJT John Tavares 90.00 150.00
JRMM Matt Moulson 75.00 125.00
JRPK Phil Kessel EXCH 90.00 150.00
JRPS P.K. Subban 100.00 175.00
JRRJ Ryan Johansen EXCH 75.00 150.00
JRRN Rick Nash EXCH 75.00 150.00
JRSC Sidney Crosby EXCH 175.00 300.00
JRSS Steven Stamkos 90.00 150.00

2015-16 Upper Deck Tim Hortons Platinum Profiles

STATED ODDS 1:18
SS1 Mark Messier 6.00 15.00
SS2 Darryl Sittler 5.00 12.00
SS3 Peter Forsberg 4.00 10.00
SS4 Guy Lafleur 5.00 12.00
SS5 Theoren Fleury 5.00 12.00
SS6 Patrick Roy 10.00 25.00
SS7 Henrik Zetterberg 5.00 12.00
SS8 Alexander Ovechkin 15.00 40.00
SS9 John Tavares 8.00 20.00
SS10 Steven Stamkos 8.00 20.00
SS11 Henrik Lundqvist 5.00 12.00
SS12 Sidney Crosby 15.00 40.00

2015-16 Upper Deck Tim Hortons Season Highlights

COMPLETE SET (7) 2.00 5.00
STATED ODDS 1:12
SH1 Johnny Gaudreau .50 1.25
SH2 Jordan Eberle .30 .75
SH3 Carey Price 1.00 2.50
SH4 Erik Karlsson .60 1.50
SH5 James van Riemsdyk .30 .75
SH6 Bo Horvat .50 1.25
SH7 Ondrej Pavelec .30 .75

2015-16 Upper Deck Tim Hortons Shining Futures

COMPLETE SET (12) 10.00 25.00
STATED ODDS 1:5
SF1 Malcolm Subban 2.50 6.00
SF2 Kevin Fiala 1.00 2.50
SF3 Johnny Gaudreau 1.50 4.00
SF4 Vladimir Tarasenko 1.50 4.00
SF5 Nathan MacKinnon 2.00 5.00
SF6 Evgeny Kuznetsov 1.50 4.00
SF7 Ryan Johansen 1.25 3.00
SF8 Filip Forsberg 1.25 3.00
SF9 Aaron Ekblad 1.00 2.50
SF10 Mark Stone .75 2.00
SF11 Sean Monahan 1.00 2.50
SF12 Jacob de la Rose 1.00 2.50

2016-17 Upper Deck Tim Hortons

1 Tim Horton 1.00 2.50
2 Duncan Keith .50 1.25
3 Roberto Luongo .50 1.25
4 Taylor Hall 1.00 2.50
5 Aaron Ekblad .50 1.25
6 Joe Pavelski .50 1.25
7 Drew Doughty .50 1.25
8 Alex Ovechkin 2.00 5.00
9 Matt Duchene .50 1.25
10 Corey Perry .50 1.25
11 Anze Kopitar .75 2.00
12 Jarome Iginla .50 1.25
13 Pavel Datsyuk .60 1.50
14 Jamie Benn .60 1.50
15 Ryan Getzlaf .75 2.00
16 Max Domi .60 1.50
17 Wayne Simmonds .60 1.50
18 Bryan Little .40 1.00
19 Jonathan Toews 1.00 2.50
20 Brandon Saad .50 1.25
21 James van Riemsdyk .50 1.25
22 Daniel Sedin .50 1.25
23 Oliver Ekman-Larsson .40 1.00
24 Filip Forsberg .60 1.50
25 Mikko Koivu .40 1.00
26 Blake Wheeler .50 1.25
27 Alex Galchenyuk .60 1.50
28 Claude Giroux .50 1.25
29 Nathan MacKinnon 1.00 2.50
30 Henrik Lundqvist .50 1.25
31 Carey Price 1.50 4.00
32 Jonathan Quick .75 2.00
33 Henrik Sedin .50 1.25
34 Dustin Byfuglien .50 1.25
35 Pekka Rinne .60 1.50
36 Cory Schneider .40 1.00
37 Patrice Bergeron .60 1.50
38 Boone Jenner .50 1.25
39 Tuukka Rask .50 1.25
40 Henrik Zetterberg .60 1.50
41 Jaroslav Halak .50 1.25
42 Devan Dubnyk .50 1.25
43 Nazem Kadri .40 1.00
44 Craig Anderson .50 1.25
45 Jonathan Bernier .50 1.25
46 David Krejci .50 1.25
47 Brayden Schenn .50 1.25
48 Zach Parise .50 1.25
49 Eric Staal .60 1.50
50 Johnny Gaudreau .75 2.00
51 Frans Nielsen .40 1.00
52 Jeff Skinner .50 1.25
53 Bo Horvat .75 2.00
54 Adam Henrique .50 1.25
55 Justin Faulk .40 1.00
56 Robby Fabbri .50 1.25
57 Rasmus Ristolainen .40 1.00
58 P.A. Parenteau .30 .75
59 Roman Josi .50 1.25
60 Joe Thornton .50 1.25
61 Rick Nash .50 1.25
62 Mark Stone .50 1.25
63 Brad Marchand .60 1.50
64 Nicklas Backstrom .75 2.00
65 Erik Karlsson 1.00 2.50
66 Marc-Andre Fleury .75 2.00
67 Max Pacioretty .50 1.25
68 Jaromir Jagr 1.25 3.00
69 Mike Hoffman .40 1.00
70 Braden Holtby .75 2.00
71 Evgeni Malkin 1.50 4.00
72 Artemi Panarin .60 1.50
73 Dylan Larkin .75 2.00
74 Sergei Bobrovsky .50 1.25
75 Alexander Steen .50 1.25
76 P.K. Subban .75 2.00
77 Victor Hedman .60 1.50
78 Tomas Tatar .40 1.00
79 Sean Monahan .50 1.25
80 Sam Reinhart .40 1.00
81 Phil Kessel .60 1.50
82 Connor Hellebuyck .75 2.00
83 Ben Bishop .50 1.25
84 Ryan Miller .50 1.25
85 Karri Ramo .40 1.00
86 Cam Talbot .60 1.50
87 Sidney Crosby 2.00 5.00
88 Patrick Kane 1.00 2.50
89 Brent Burns .60 1.50
90 Evander Kane .50 1.25
91 Steven Stamkos 1.00 2.50
92 Evgeny Kuznetsov .75 2.00
93 Sam Bennett .60 1.50
94 Jason Spezza .50 1.25
95 Jordan Eberle .50 1.25
96 Jack Eichel 1.00 2.50
97 Connor McDavid 2.50 6.00
98 Tyler Seguin
99 John Tavares
100 Vladimir Tarasenko
DP1 Auston Matthews Draft 250.00 400.00

2016-17 Upper Deck Tim Hortons Clear Cut Phenoms

CC1 Max Domi 3.00 8.00
CC2 Jack Eichel 5.00 12.00
CC3 Sam Bennett 3.00 8.00
CC4 Artemi Panarin 3.00 8.00
CC5 Dylan Larkin 4.00 10.00
CC6 Connor McDavid 12.00 30.00
CC7 Alex Galchenyuk 3.00 8.00
CC8 Filip Forsberg 3.00 8.00
CC9 Mark Stone 2.50 6.00
CC10 Robby Fabbri 2.50 6.00
CC11 Nikita Kucherov 4.00 10.00
CC12 Shayne Gostisbehere 3.00 8.00
CC13 Bo Horvat 4.00 10.00
CC14 Nikolaj Ehlers 2.50 6.00

2016-17 Upper Deck Tim Hortons Franchise Force

FF1 Johnny Gaudreau 10.00 25.00
FF2 Jonathan Toews 12.00 30.00
FF3 Henrik Zetterberg 8.00 20.00
FF4 Connor McDavid 30.00 80.00
FF5 Carey Price 20.00 50.00
FF6 Henrik Lundqvist 6.00 15.00
FF7 Erik Karlsson 12.00 30.00
FF8 Sidney Crosby 25.00 60.00
FF9 Nazem Kadri 5.00 12.00
FF10 Ryan Miller 6.00 15.00
FF11 Alex Ovechkin 25.00 60.00
FF12 Dustin Byfuglien 6.00 15.00

2016-17 Upper Deck Tim Hortons Game Day Action

GDA1 Tuukka Rask 1.00 2.50
GDA2 Jack Eichel 2.00 5.00
GDA3 Johnny Gaudreau 1.50 4.00
GDA4 Jonathan Toews 2.00 5.00
GDA5 Jamie Benn 1.25 3.00
GDA6 Henrik Zetterberg 1.25 3.00
GDA7 Connor McDavid 5.00 12.00
GDA8 Carey Price 3.00 8.00
GDA9 Erik Karlsson 2.00 5.00
GDA10 Sidney Crosby 4.00 10.00
GDA11 Steven Stamkos 2.00 5.00
GDA12 Nazem Kadri .75 2.00
GDA13 Ryan Miller 1.00 2.50
GDA14 Alex Ovechkin 4.00 10.00
GDA15 Dustin Byfuglien 1.00 2.50

2016-17 Upper Deck Tim Hortons Local Leaders

LL1 Mark Giordano .75 2.00
LL2 Taylor Hall 2.00 5.00
LL3 Max Pacioretty 1.00 2.50
LL4 Erik Karlsson 2.00 5.00
LL5 Tyler Bozak .75 2.00
LL6 Henrik Sedin 1.00 2.50
LL7 Blake Wheeler 1.00 2.50

2016-17 Upper Deck Tim Hortons Platinum Profiles

PP1 Johnny Gaudreau 3.00 8.00
PP2 Jonathan Toews 4.00 10.00
PP3 Jarome Iginla 2.00 5.00
PP4 Pavel Datsyuk 2.50 6.00
PP5 Connor McDavid 10.00 25.00
PP6 Jaromir Jagr 5.00 12.00
PP7 Carey Price 6.00 15.00
PP8 Henrik Lundqvist 2.00 5.00
PP9 Erik Karlsson 4.00 10.00
PP10 James van Riemsdyk 2.00 5.00
PP11 Ryan Miller 2.00 5.00
PP12 Blake Wheeler 2.00 5.00

2016-17 Upper Deck Tim Hortons Pure Gold

PG1 Ryan Getzlaf 1.50 4.00
PG2 Patrice Bergeron 1.25 3.00
PG3 Sean Monahan 1.00 2.50
PG4 Patrick Kane 2.00 5.00
PG5 Tyler Seguin 1.50 4.00
PG6 Dylan Larkin 1.50 4.00
PG7 Jordan Eberle 1.00 2.50
PG8 Anze Kopitar 1.50 4.00
PG9 Zach Parise 1.00 2.50
PG10 Max Pacioretty 1.00 2.50
PG11 John Tavares 2.00 5.00
PG12 Rick Nash 1.00 2.50
PG13 Mike Hoffman .75 2.00
PG14 Daniel Sedin 1.00 2.50
PG15 Bryan Little .75 2.00

2016-17 Upper Deck Tim Hortons Timbits Autograps

2000 Nathan MacKinnon 500.00 800.00

2017-18 Upper Deck Tim Hortons

COMMON CARD .30 .75
SEMISTARS .40 1.00
UNLISTED STARS .50 1.25
1 Tim Horton .50 1.25
2 Duncan Keith .50 1.25
3 Charlie Coyle .40 1.00
4 Dougie Hamilton .40 1.00
5 Aaron Ekblad .50 1.25
6 Shea Weber .40 1.00
7 Joe Pavelski .50 1.25
8 Alexander Ovechkin 2.00 5.00
9 Taylor Hall 1.00 2.50
10 Corey Perry .50 1.25
11 Anze Kopitar .75 2.00
12 Cam Atkinson .50 1.25
13 Johnny Gaudreau .75 2.00
14 Jamie Benn .60 1.50
15 Jack Eichel .75 2.00
16 Mitch Marner .75 2.00
17 Ryan Kesler .50 1.25
18 Filip Forsberg .60 1.50
19 Jonathan Toews 1.00 2.50
20 Sebastian Aho .50 1.25
21 Kyle Okposo .40 1.00
22 Daniel Sedin .50 1.25
23 Oliver Ekman-Larsson .50 1.25
24 Aleksander Barkov .50 1.25
25 William Nylander .75 2.00
26 Kyle Palmieri .40 1.00
27 Patrik Laine .75 2.00
28 Claude Giroux .50 1.25
29 Nathan MacKinnon 1.00 2.50
30 Henrik Lundqvist .75 2.00
31 Carey Price 1.50 4.00
32 Leon Draisaitl .75 2.00
33 Henrik Sedin .50 1.25
34 Auston Matthews 2.00 5.00
35 Josh Bailey .40 1.00
36 Matthew Tkachuk .50 1.25
37 Matt Duchene .50 1.25
38 Nikolaj Ehlers .50 1.25
39 Frederik Andersen .40 1.00
40 Henrik Zetterberg .50 1.25
41 Craig Anderson .50 1.25
42 Vincent Trocheck .40 1.00
43 Blake Wheeler .50 1.25
44 Mike Smith .50 1.25
45 Morgan Reilly .75 2.00
46 Devan Dubnyk .50 1.25
47 Sergei Bobrovsky .50 1.25
48 Matt Murray .75 2.00
49 Bo Horvat .50 1.25
50 Zach Werenski .50 1.25
51 Evgeny Kuznetsov .75 2.00
52 Eric Staal .60 1.50
53 Jeff Skinner .40 1.00
54 Patrice Bergeron .60 1.50
55 Mark Scheifele .60 1.50
56 Wayne Simmonds .60 1.50
57 Alex Galchenyuk .60 1.50
58 Chris Kreider .50 1.25
59 Loui Eriksson .40 1.00
60 Thomas Greiss .40 1.00
61 Mark Stone .50 1.25
62 Mike Hoffman .40 1.00
63 Brad Marchand .60 1.50
64 Mikael Granlund .50 1.25
65 Erik Karlsson .60 1.50
66 Andreas Athanasiou .50 1.25
67 Max Pacioretty .50 1.25
68 Jaden Schwartz .60 1.50
69 Milan Lucic .50 1.25
70 Braden Holtby .75 2.00
71 Evgeni Malkin 1.50 4.00
72 Artemi Panarin .50 1.25
73 Dylan Larkin .50 1.25
74 Nicklas Backstrom .75 2.00
75 Phil Kessel .60 1.50
76 P.K. Subban .50 1.25
77 Jeff Carter .50 1.25
78 Drew Doughty .50 1.25
79 Dustin Byfuglien .50 1.25
80 Victor Hedman .60 1.50
81 Martin Jones .50 1.25
82 J.T. Miller .40 1.00
83 Tuukka Rask .50 1.25
84 Steven Stamkos 1.00 2.50
85 Colton Parayko .50 1.25
86 Nikita Kucherov .75 2.00
87 Sidney Crosby 2.00 5.00
88 Patrick Kane 1.00 2.50
89 Frans Nielsen .40 1.00
90 Ryan O'Reilly .50 1.25
91 John Tavares 1.00 2.50
92 Ryan Johnson .40 1.00
93 Jakub Voracek .50 1.25
94 Sam Reinhart .40 1.00
95 Tyler Seguin .75 2.00
96 Sean Monahan .50 1.25
97 Connor McDavid 2.00 5.00
98 David Pastrnak .75 2.00
99 Vladimir Tarasenko .75 2.00
100 Brent Burns .60 1.50

2017-18 Upper Deck Tim Hortons '17 NHL Draft NO.1 Draft Pick

DP1 Nico Hischier 150.00 250.00

2017-18 Upper Deck Tim Hortons Aaron Ekblad Timbits Autograph

1 Aaron Ekblad 500.00 600.00

2017-18 Upper Deck Tim Hortons Clear Cut Phenoms

COMMON CARD 3.00 8.00
SEMISTARS 4.00 10.00
UNLISTED STARS 5.00 12.00
CCP1 Connor McDavid 15.00 40.00
CCP2 Dylan Larkin 5.00 12.00
CCP3 Patrik Laine 8.00 20.00
CCP4 Jack Eichel 8.00 20.00
CCP5 Matthew Tkachuk 5.00 12.00
CCP6 Zach Werenski 5.00 12.00
CCP7 Mitch Marner 8.00 20.00
CCP8 William Nylander 8.00 20.00
CCP9 Thomas Chabot 8.00 20.00
CCP10 Nikolaj Ehlers 5.00 12.00
CCP11 Travis Konecny 5.00 12.00
CCP12 Matt Murray 8.00 20.00
CCP13 Colton Parayko 5.00 12.00
CCP14 Auston Matthews 20.00 50.00

2017-18 Upper Deck Tim Hortons Game Day Action

COMMON CARD .75 2.00
SEMISTARS 1.00 2.50
UNLISTED STARS 1.25 3.00
GDA1 Sidney Crosby 5.00 12.00
GDA2 Erik Karlsson 1.50 4.00
GDA3 Johnny Gaudreau 2.00 5.00
GDA4 Auston Matthews 5.00 12.00
GDA5 Tyler Seguin 2.00 5.00
GDA6 Bo Horvat 1.25 3.00
GDA7 Connor McDavid 5.00 12.00
GDA8 Max Pacioretty 1.25 3.00
GDA9 Brent Burns 1.50 4.00
GDA10 Mark Scheifele 1.50 4.00
GDA11 Aaron Ekblad 1.25 3.00
GDA12 Vladimir Tarasenko 2.00 5.00
GDA13 Mitch Marner 2.00 5.00
GDA14 Braden Holtby 2.00 5.00
GDA15 Alex Ovechkin 5.00 12.00

2017-18 Upper Deck Tim Hortons NHL Autograph Jersey

1 Brendan Gallagher
2 Bo Horvat 90.00 150.00
3 Mike Hoffman 90.00 150.00
4 Morgan Rielly
5 Mats Zuccarello 350.00 450.00
6 Nikolaj Ehlers

2017-18 Upper Deck Tim Hortons NHL Jersey

1 Alex Ovechkin 80.00 200.00
2 Brent Burns 80.00 150.00
3 Bo Horvat 80.00 150.00
4 Brad Marchand 80.00 150.00
5 Connor McDavid 300.00 400.00
6 Devan Dubnyk 80.00 150.00
7 Evgeni Malkin 80.00 150.00
8 Frederik Andersen 80.00 150.00
9 John Tavares 80.00 150.00
10 Mike Hoffman 80.00 150.00
11 Max Pacioretty 100.00 200.00
12 Mark Scheifele 80.00 150.00
13 Sidney Crosby 200.00 350.00
14 Sean Monahan 80.00 150.00
15 Jonathan Toews 80.00 150.00
16 Tyler Seguin 80.00 150.00
17 Vladimir Tarasenko 80.00 150.00
18 Wayne Simmonds 80.00 150.00

2017-18 Upper Deck Tim Hortons NHL Signatures

1 Artem Anisimov 100.00 200.00
2 Anthony Mantha 100.00 200.00
3 Andrew Shaw 100.00 200.00
4 Bo Horvat 100.00 200.00
5 Jakub Voracek 50.00 125.00
6 Leon Draisaitl 200.00 300.00
7 Mark Giordano 100.00 200.00
8 Morgan Rielly 150.00 250.00
9 Mark Stone 150.00 250.00
10 Mats Zuccarello 100.00 200.00
11 Nikolaj Ehlers 150.00 250.00
12 Nikita Kucherov
13 Nathan MacKinnon
14 Ryan Kesler 150.00 250.00
15 Taylor Hall 150.00 250.00

2017-18 Upper Deck Tim Hortons Platinum Profiles

PP1 Alex Ovechkin 6.00 15.00
PP2 Carey Price 5.00 12.00
PP3 Johnny Gaudreau 2.50 6.00
PP4 Brad Marchand 2.00 5.00
PP5 Henrik Lundqvist 2.50 6.00
PP6 Jonathan Toews 3.00 8.00
PP7 Auston Matthews 6.00 15.00
PP8 Nathan MacKinnon 3.00 8.00
PP9 Connor McDavid 6.00 15.00
PP10 Vladimir Tarasenko 2.50 6.00
PP11 Henrik Zetterberg 1.50 4.00
PP12 Sidney Crosby 6.00 15.00

2017-18 Upper Deck Tim Hortons Stat Makers

SM1 Connor McDavid 6.00 15.00
SM2 Auston Matthews 6.00 15.00
SM3 Mark Scheifele 2.00 5.00
SM4 Vladimir Tarasenko 2.50 6.00
SM5 Evgeni Malkin 5.00 12.00
SM6 Sean Monahan 1.50 4.00
SM7 Erik Karlsson 2.00 5.00
SM8 Alex Ovechkin 6.00 15.00
SM9 Henrik Sedin 1.50 4.00
SM10 Max Pacioretty 1.50 4.00
SM11 Patrick Kane 3.00 8.00
SM12 Nicklas Backstrom 2.50 6.00
SM13 Jeff Carter 1.50 4.00
SM14 Brent Burns 2.00 5.00
SM15 Sidney Crosby 6.00 15.00

2017-18 Upper Deck Tim Hortons Top 100

TOP1 Sidney Crosby 5.00 12.00
TOP2 Jonathan Toews 2.50 6.00
TOP3 Alex Ovechkin 5.00 12.00
TOP4 Patrick Kane 2.50 6.00
TOP5 Jaromir Jagr 3.00 8.00
TOP6 Duncan Keith 1.25 3.00
TOP7 Tim Horton 1.25 3.00

2017-18 Upper Deck Tim Hortons Triple Exposure

TE1 Sidney Crosby 25.00 60.00
TE2 Johnny Gaudreau 10.00 25.00
TE3 Max Pacioretty 6.00 15.00
TE4 Jamie Benn 8.00 20.00
TE5 Auston Matthews 25.00 60.00
TE6 Patrik Laine 10.00 25.00
TE7 Brad Marchand 8.00 20.00
TE8 Alex Ovechkin 25.00 60.00
TE9 Vladimir Tarasenko 10.00 25.00
TE10 Patrick Kane 12.00 30.00
TE11 Jeff Carter 6.00 15.00
TE12 Connor McDavid 25.00 60.00

2003-04 Upper Deck Toronto Fall Expo Priority Signings

This 11-card set was part of a wrapper redemption at the Upper Deck booth during the 2003 Fall Expo. Each card was hand serial-numbered and individual print runs were listed below.

CJ Curtis Joseph/41 20.00 50.00
DH Dany Heatley/25 30.00 80.00
GH Gordie Howe/40 60.00 150.00
IK Ilya Kovalchuk/78 20.00 50.00
JI Jarome Iginla/57 20.00 50.00
JS Jason Spezza/110 15.00 40.00
JT Joe Thornton/107 15.00 40.00
MB Martin Brodeur/70 50.00 125.00
PB Pavel Bure/29 25.00 60.00
PR Patrick Roy/44 75.00 200.00
RB Ray Bourque/75 25.00 60.00

2004 UD Toronto Fall Expo Pride of Canada

This 26-card set was available only at the Upper Deck booth during the 2004 Toronto Fall Expo. Each card was serial-numbered out of 75.

COMPLETE SET (26) 125.00 250.00
1 Martin Brodeur 15.00 40.00
2 Roberto Luongo 6.00 15.00
3 Jose Theodore 8.00 20.00
4 Jay Bouwmeester 4.00 10.00
5 Eric Brewer 4.00 10.00
6 Adam Foote 4.00 10.00
7 Scott Hannan 4.00 10.00
8 Ed Jovanovski 4.00 10.00
9 Scott Niedermayer 4.00 10.00
10 Wade Redden 4.00 10.00
11 Robyn Regehr 4.00 10.00
12 Shane Doan 4.00 10.00
13 Kris Draper 4.00 10.00
14 Simon Gagne 5.00 12.00
15 Dany Heatley 6.00 15.00
16 Jarome Iginla 8.00 20.00
17 Vincent Lecavalier 8.00 20.00
18 Mario Lemieux 15.00 40.00
19 Kirk Maltby 4.00 10.00
20 Patrick Marleau 4.00 10.00
21 Brenden Morrow 4.00 10.00
22 Brad Richards 4.00 10.00
23 Joe Sakic 10.00 25.00
24 Martin St. Louis 4.00 10.00
25 Ryan Smyth 4.00 10.00
26 Joe Thornton 6.00 15.00

2004-05 Upper Deck Toronto Fall Expo Priority Signings

Available only via wrapper redemption during the 2004 Toronto Fall Expo, this 28-card set featured authentic player autographs. Print runs are listed below. Please note, due to a production error, the Tootoo card was pulled from the redemption program though a few copies are known to have been released.

PRINT RUNS UNDER 25
NOT PRICED DUE TO SCARCITY
AH Ales Hemsky/50 10.00 25.00
AY Alexei Yashin/50 10.00 25.00
BU Pavel Bure/10
CK Chuck Kobasew/49 10.00 25.00
GR Wayne Gretzky/25 200.00 300.00
HO Marian Hossa/52 12.50 30.00
JI Jarome Iginla/7
JL John LeClair/50 10.00 25.00
JR Jeremy Roenick/31 40.00 80.00
JS Jason Spezza/39 25.00 60.00
JT Jordin Tootoo ERR
MB Martin Brodeur/14
MG Marian Gaborik/26
MH Martin Havlat/50 12.50 30.00
MN Markus Naslund/50 12.50 30.00
MP Mark Parrish/50 8.00 20.00
MT Marty Turco/35 20.00 50.00
PB Pavel Bure/60 12.50 30.00
PE Mike Peca/27 20.00 50.00
PR Patrick Roy/33 75.00 150.00
RD Rick DiPietro/20
RL Roberto Luongo/50 12.50 30.00
RN Rick Nash/61 30.00 80.00
RO Patrick Roy/10
SF Sergei Fedorov/3
SH Scott Hartnell/78 8.00 20.00
TB Todd Bertuzzi/44 20.00 50.00
WG Wayne Gretzky/9

2005-06 Upper Deck Toronto Fall Expo Priority Signings

PRINT RUNS UNDER 25 NOT
PRICED DUE TO SCARCITY
PSDA David Aebischer/2
PSTB Todd Bertuzzi/10
PSBU Pavel Bure/10
PSTE Tony Esposito/5
PSAF Alexander Frolov/40 20.00 50.00
PSWG Wayne Gretzky/5
PSGR Wayne Gretzky/25 250.00 400.00
PSMH Martin Havlat/24
PSAH Ales Hemsky/22
PSHO Marian Hossa/9
PSHS Marcel Hossa/16
PSGH Gordie Howe/15
PSJL John LeClair/20
PSRL Roberto Luongo/20
PSSM Stan Mikita/1
PSRN Rick Nash/20
PSMN Markus Naslund/10
PSBO Brooks Orpik/40 6.00 15.00
PSMP Mark Parrish/20
PSPE Michael Peca/20
PSPR Patrick Roy/3
PSRO Patrick Roy/10
PSJS Jason Spezza/10
PSJT Joe Thornton/5
PSMT Marty Turco/20
PSAY Alexei Yashin/20
PSSY Steve Yzerman/2
PSAR Andrew Raycroft/63 10.00 25.00
PSES Eric Staal/62 25.00 60.00
PSLU Joffrey Lupul/64 10.00 25.00
PSJC Jonathan Cheechoo/61 12.00 30.00
PSST Matt Stajan/70 10.00 25.00
PSML Matthew Lombardi/61 6.00 15.00
PSRY Michael Ryder/60 20.00 50.00
PSNZ Nikolai Zherdev/61 10.00 25.00
PSBE Patrice Bergeron/62 12.00 30.00
PSPS Philippe Sauve/63 6.00 15.00
PSRT Raffi Torres/60 10.00 25.00
PSRM Ryan Malone/62 10.00 25.00
PSTH Trent Hunter/61 10.00 25.00
PSTR Tuomo Ruutu/62 10.00 25.00
PSJI Jarome Iginla/10
PSMM Mike Modano/10
PSMG Marian Gaborik/10
PSMB Martin Brodeur/5
PSDH Dominik Hasek/5
PSSL Martin St. Louis/10
PSJG Jean-Sebastien Giguere/5
PSPB P-M Bouchard/61 8.00 20.00

2006-07 Upper Deck Toronto Spring Expo Priority Signings

PSAM Andrej Meszaros/40 8.00 20.00
PSAS Alexander Steen/40 15.00 30.00
PSPK Phil Kessel/40 10.00 25.00
PSTV Thomas Vanek/40 8.00 20.00
PSZP Zach Parise/40 10.00 25.00

2006-07 Upper Deck Toronto Fall Expo Priority Signings

AVAIL. AS REDEMPTION ONLY AT EXPO
PRINT RUNS UNDER 25 NOT PRICED DUE TO SCARCITY
PSAA Aaron Asham/75 4.00 10.00
PSAK Andrei Kostitsyn/10
PSAL Andrew Ladd/10
PSAP Alexandre Picard/10
PSAS Alexander Steen/50 12.00 30.00
PSBB Brad Boyes/50 10.00 25.00
PSBO Jay Bouwmeester/26 12.00 30.00
PSBR Brad Richardson/41 8.00 20.00
PSBS Brent Seabrook/53
PSCH Chris Higgins/82 12.00 30.00
PSDP Dion Phaneuf/15 50.00 80.00
PSFS Fredrik Sjostrom/94 4.00 10.00
PSGB Gilbert Brule/21 20.00 50.00
PSGH Gordie Howe/11
PSHL Henrik Lundqvist/26 30.00 60.00
PSJB Jason Blake/75 6.00 15.00
PSJC Jeff Carter/3
PSJS Jason Spezza/11
PSJT Jeff Tambellini/52 4.00 10.00
PSMB Martin Brodeur/11
PSMG Marian Gaborik/10
PSMP Michael Peca/20
PSMR Mike Richards/4
PSPB Pierre-Marc Bouchard/6
PSRN Robert Nilsson/57 4.00 10.00
PSRU R.J. Umberger/10
PSRW Ryan Whitney/65 8.00 20.00
PSSB Steve Bernier/12
PSSC Sidney Crosby/35 175.00 250.00
PSTV Thomas Vanek/42 20.00 40.00
PSWC Wendel Clark/6
PSWG1 Wayne Gretzky/9
PSWG2 Wayne Gretzky/4
PSZP Zach Parise/12

2007-08 Upper Deck Toronto Spring Expo Priority Signings

STATED PRINT RUN 25-75
PSBB Brad Boyes/75 5.00 12.00
PSBO Bobby Orr/25 150.00 250.00
PSCP Corey Perry/15 30.00 60.00
PSFM Frank Mahovlich/42 25.00 50.00

2008-09 Upper Deck Toronto Fall Expo Priority Signings

STATED PRINT RUN 5-75
PSAO Adam Oates/75 6.00 15.00
PSBB Brad Boyes/75 6.00 15.00
PSBE Brendan Bell/75
PSBL Bryan Little/75
PSCP Corey Perry/50 6.00 15.00
PSPA Daniel Paille/75 6.00 15.00
PSEM Evgeni Malkin/25 40.00 80.00
PSJT Joe Thornton/5
PSME Matt Ellis/75 6.00 15.00
PSMF Mark Fraser/75 6.00 15.00
PSMP Michael Peca/75 6.00 15.00
PSMR Mason Raymond/75 6.00 15.00
PSPS Paul Stastny/50
PSRC Ryane Clowe/75 6.00 15.00
PSRE Ron Ellis/40 6.00 15.00
PSRS Ryan Smyth/15
PSRV Rogie Vachon/15 20.00 40.00
PSSC Sidney Crosby/25
PSSM Stan Mikita/5
PSST Stefan Meyer/75 6.00 15.00
PSNH Nathan Horton/75

2010-11 Upper Deck Toronto Fall Expo Priority Signings

STATED PRINT RUN 2-75
PSAA Artem Anisimov/75
PSAO Alexander Ovechkin/15
PSBO Bobby Orr/15
PSCR Sidney Crosby/25
PSEK Evander Kane/25
PSET Eric Tangradi/25
PSGH Gordie Howe/9 DET
PSJB Jamie Benn/50 8.00 20.00
PSJG Jonas Gustavsson/25
PSJT John Tavares/25 25.00 60.00
PSJV James van Riemsdyk/25
PSMD Matt Duchene/25
PSMG Matt Gilroy/75
PSMP Matt Pelech/75
PSMS Matt Stajan/35
PSNG Nathan Gerbe/75
PSNK Nikolai Kulemin/75
PSNZ Nazem Kadri/25 20.00 50.
PSOV Alexander Ovechkin/3
PSPE Phil Esposito/10
PSPK P.K. Subban/25
PSSC Sidney Crosby/5
PSSM Stan Mikita/15 20.00 40.
PSTH Taylor Hall/25
PSTK Tim Kennedy/70
PSTS Tyler Seguin/25 25.00 50.
PSWA Wayne Gretzky/6
PSWG Wayne Gretzky/6
PSYW Yannick Weber/75
PSYZ Steve Yzerman/15 40.00 80.
PSZH Zach Hamill/75
PSCUP Antti Niemi/25
PSGR8 Wayne Gretzky/2
PSMRH Gordie Howe/3 HW
PSORR Bobby Orr/4

2011-12 Upper Deck Toronto Fa Expo Priority Signings

PSAH Adam Henrique/75
PSAS Anthony Stewart/75
PSBS Brayden Schenn/75
PSCH Cody Hodgson/75
PSCM Clarke MacArthur/16
PSEM Evgeni Malkin/71
PSGH Gordie Howe/9 DET
PSHO Gordie Howe/5 CAN
PSGH Gordie Howe/9 HW
PSGL Gabriel Landeskog/25
PSJC Joe Colborne/32
PSKA Keith Aulie/59
PSMG Michael Grabner/40
PSNK Nazem Kadri/43
PSRN Ryan Nugent-Hopkins/25
PSTH Travis Hamonic/75

2011-12 Upper Deck Toronto Spring Expo Priority Signings

AB Alexander Burmistrov/25
CD Calvin de Haan TC/75
CE Cody Eakin TC/75
CP Carey Price/5
DP Dion Phaneuf/10
EK Evander Kane/25
EL Eric Lindros TC/5
JB Jean Beliveau/5
JC Joe Colborne/75
JE Jordan Eberle/10
JG Jake Gardiner/75
JH Josh Harding TC/75
JN James Neal/25
KA Keith Aulie TC/75
PK Phil Kessel/10
SD Simon Despres TC/75
SG Sam Gagner/10
SW Stephen Weiss TC/25
TB Tyler Bozak/25
AO1 Alexander Ovechkin/5
AO2 Alexander Ovechkin AS/3
CS1 Cory Schneider/25
CS2 Chris Stewart TC/25
RN1 Ryan Nugent-Hopkins TC/5
RN2 Ryan Nugent-Hopkins/10
SC1 Sidney Crosby AS/5
SC2 Sidney Crosby TC/2
SC3 Sidney Crosby/10
SS1 Steven Stamkos AS/5
SS2 Steven Stamkos TC/2
SS3 Steven Stamkos/10
WG1 Wayne Gretzky/6
WG2 Wayne Gretzky/5
WG3 Wayne Gretzky/4
WG4 Wayne Gretzky AS/3
WG5 Wayne Gretzky TC/2
PSGH Gordie Howe/25
PSGH Gordie Howe/15

2012-13 Upper Deck Toronto Fa Expo Priority Signings

STATED PRINT RUN 1-75
PSAH Adam Henrique/75 8.00 20.
PSBG Blake Geoffrion/75 12.00 30.
PSBO Bobby Orr/75 60.00 125.
PSBS Brayden Schenn/25 15.00 40.
PSCA Carter Ashton/75 4.00 10.
PSCC Casey Cizikas/75 4.00 10.
PSCE Cody Eakin/30
PSCT Colten Teubert/75 10.00 25.
PSJB Jamie Benn/75 10.00 25.
PSJN Jonathan Bernier/75 5.00 12.
PSMF Marcus Foligno/70 15.00 40.
PSMS Mark Scheifele/75 10.00 25.
PSNK Nikolai Kulemin/75 4.00 10.
PSRE Ryan Ellis/30 15.00 40.
PSTB Tyson Barrie/75 4.00 10.

2013-14 Upper Deck Toronto Spring Expo Priority Signings

COMPLETE SET (36)
UNPRICED PRINT RUN 2-10
SAB Aleksander Barkov/15
SBN Brock Nelson/50 5.00 12.
SEL Elias Lindholm/15
SEP Edward Pasquale/50 4.00 10.
SFA Frederick Andersen/30 12.00 30.
SJF Justin Fontaine/50 5.00 12.
SJG John Gibson/25 12.00 30.
SMB Michael Bournival/50 3.00 8.
SMD Mathew Dumba/15 12.00 30.
SMG Mikael Granlund/25 10.00 25.
SMK Mike Kostka/25
SMR Morgan Rielly/25
SNB Nathan Beaulieu/15 8.00 20.
SNY Nail Yakupov/25 30.00 60.
SRE Max Reinhart/30 8.00 20.
SRS Ryan Strome/25 12.00 30.
SSM Sean Monahan/25
STH Tomas Hertl/25 25.00 50.
STJ Tomas Jurco/15 15.00 40.
STJ Tyler Johnson/30 8.00 20.
STP Tanner Pearson/40 8.00 20.

2013-14 Upper Deck Toronto Fa Expo Priority Signings

FAW Austin Watson/75
FBB Beau Bennett/75 12.00 30.
FBG Brendan Gallagher/25
FCC Cory Conacher/25
FCT Christian Thomas/75 6.00 15.
FDH Dougie Hamilton/15 10.00 25.
FJB Boone Jenner/75 5.00 12.
FJS Justin Schultz/15
FJT John Tavares/25
FMP Mark Pysyk/75

IR Morgan Rielly/25
B Nathan Beaulieu/25 10.00 25.00
M Nathan MacKinnon/25 100.00 200.00
H Quinton Howden/45
M Ryan Murray/25
S Ryan Spooner/45 6.00 15.00
C Jordan Schroeder/75 4.00 10.00
L Scott Laughton/45
M Sean Monahan/25
H Thomas Hickey/75
T Tyler Toffoli/75 8.00 20.00
W Tom Wilson/75 6.00 15.00
TI Jarred Tinordi/45 5.00 12.00

2003-04 Upper Deck Trilogy

leased in early December 2003, this 181-card set nsisted of 100 veteran base cards; two different kie subsets and the Crest of Honor subset. Crest ds carried miniature felt emblems on the card fronts. rds 142-171 were serial-numbered to 999 sets and ds 172-181 were serial-numbered to 499 each. rds 182-189 were only available in packs of UD okie Update and were serial numbered to 999. ase note that two cards carry the number 17 on the dbacks.

MP.SET w/o SP's 50.00 100.00
ergei Fedorov 1.25 3.00
tanislav Chistov .50 1.25
ean-Sebastien Giguere .75 2.00
any Heatley .75 2.00
ya Kovalchuk .75 2.00
oe Thornton 1.00 2.50
len Murray .60 1.50
obby Orr 6.00 15.00
iroslav Satan .60 1.50
Maxim Afinogenov .50 1.25
Chris Drury .60 1.50
Jarome Iginla .75 2.00
Lanny McDonald .60 1.50
Roman Turek .60 1.50
Ron Francis 1.00 2.50
Jeff O'Neill .50 1.25
Kyle Calder .50 1.25
Alexei Zhamnov .60 1.50
Jocelyn Thibault .60 1.50
Teemu Selanne 1.50 4.00
Peter Forsberg 1.00 2.50
Paul Kariya 1.00 2.50
Joe Sakic 1.25 3.00
Patrick Roy 2.00 5.00
Rick Nash .75 2.00
Marc Denis .60 1.50
Todd Marchant .50 1.25
Mike Modano 1.25 3.00
Bill Guerin .75 2.00
Marty Turco .75 2.00
Brendan Shanahan 1.00 2.50
Gordie Howe 3.00 8.00
Steve Yzerman 2.00 5.00
Dominik Hasek 1.25 3.00
Ryan Smyth .60 1.50
Mike Comrie .60 1.50
Ales Hemsky .75 2.00
Wayne Gretzky 5.00 12.00
Olli Jokinen .75 2.00
Stephen Weiss .50 1.25
Jay Bouwmeester .75 2.00
Roberto Luongo 1.25 3.00
Zigmund Palffy .75 2.00
Alexander Frolov .60 1.50
Roman Cechmanek .60 1.50
Marian Gaborik 1.25 3.00
Pierre-Marc Bouchard .75 2.00
Manny Fernandez .60 1.50
Dwayne Roloson .60 1.50
Saku Koivu .75 2.00
Marcel Hossa .50 1.25
Jose Theodore .75 2.00
Guy Lafleur 1.00 2.50
David Legwand .60 1.50
Tomas Vokoun .60 1.50
Patrik Elias .75 2.00
Jamie Langenbrunner .60 1.50
Scott Stevens .75 2.00
Martin Brodeur 1.50 4.00
Alexei Yashin .60 1.50
Rick DiPietro .60 1.50
Alex Kovalev .60 1.50
Eric Lindros 1.25 3.00
Pavel Bure 1.00 2.50
Mike Dunham .60 1.50
Marian Hossa .60 1.50
Daniel Alfredsson .75 2.00
Jason Spezza .75 2.00
Patrick Lalime .60 1.50
Jeremy Roenick .75 2.00
Tony Amonte .60 1.50
John LeClair .75 2.00
Bobby Clarke .75 2.00
Mike Johnson .50 1.25
Chris Gratton .50 1.25
Sean Burke .50 1.25
Mario Lemieux 3.00 8.00
Martin Straka .50 1.25
Sebastien Caron .60 1.50
Mike Ricci .60 1.50
Niko Dimitrakos .50 1.25
Evgeni Nabokov .60 1.50
Al MacInnis .75 2.00
Keith Tkachuk .75 2.00
Chris Pronger .60 1.50
Chris Osgood .75 2.00
Vincent Lecavalier .60 1.50
Martin St. Louis .75 2.00
Nikolai Khabibulin .75 2.00
Alexander Mogilny .60 1.50
Mats Sundin .75 2.00
Owen Nolan .60 1.50
Ed Belfour .75 2.00
Alexander Auld .50 1.25
Markus Naslund .75 2.00
Todd Bertuzzi .75 2.00
Ed Jovanovski .60 1.50
Jaromir Jagr 2.00 5.00
Peter Bondra .60 1.50
Olaf Kolzig .75 2.00
Joe Thornton COH 6.00 15.00
102 Sergei Fedorov COH 8.00 20.00
103 Dany Heatley COH 5.00 12.00
104 Steve Yzerman COH 12.00 30.00
105 Henrik Zetterberg COH 6.00 15.00
106 Patrick Roy COH 12.00 30.00
107 Peter Forsberg COH 6.00 15.00
108 Jean-Sebastien Giguere COH 5.00 12.00
109 Marian Gaborik COH 8.00 20.00
110 Markus Naslund COH 5.00 12.00
111 Jeremy Roenick COH 5.00 12.00
112 Mario Lemieux COH 12.00 30.00
113 Mats Sundin COH 5.00 12.00
114 Ed Belfour COH 5.00 12.00
115 Ilya Kovalchuk COH 5.00 12.00
116 Marian Hossa COH 4.00 10.00
117 Eric Lindros COH 8.00 20.00
118 Jocelyn Thibault COH 4.00 10.00
119 Jose Theodore COH 5.00 12.00
120 Mike Modano COH 8.00 20.00
121 Jason Spezza COH 5.00 12.00
122 Rick Nash COH 5.00 12.00
123 Jean Beliveau COH 6.00 15.00
124 Mike Bossy COH 5.00 12.00
125 Johnny Bucyk COH 5.00 12.00
126 Marcel Dionne COH 6.00 15.00
127 Grant Fuhr COH 5.00 12.00
128 Michel Goulet COH 4.00 10.00
129 Jari Kurri COH 5.00 12.00
130 Guy Lafleur COH 6.00 15.00
131 Ted Lindsay COH 5.00 12.00
132 Scotty Bowman COH 5.00 12.00
133 Lanny McDonald COH 4.00 10.00
134 Stan Mikita COH 6.00 15.00
135 Denis Potvin COH 5.00 12.00
136 Ray Bourque COH 8.00 20.00
137 Don Cherry COH 10.00 25.00
138 Bobby Orr COH 15.00 40.00
139 Gordie Howe COH 15.00 40.00
140 Bobby Clarke COH 5.00 12.00
141 Phil Esposito COH 8.00 20.00
142 Jiri Hudler RC 4.00 10.00
143 Patrice Bergeron RC 8.00 20.00
144 Matthew Lombardi RC 2.00 5.00
145 Lasse Kukkonen RC 1.50 4.00
146 John-Michael Liles RC 2.00 5.00
147 Marek Svatos RC 3.00 8.00
148 Cody McCormick RC 2.00 5.00
149 Dan Fritsche RC 1.50 4.00
150 Antti Miettinen RC 2.50 6.00
151 Esa Pirnes RC 1.50 4.00
152 Tim Gleason RC 2.00 5.00
153 Brent Burns RC 4.00 10.00
154 Christoph Brandner RC 2.00 5.00
155 Chris Higgins RC 3.00 8.00
156 Dan Hamhuis RC 2.00 5.00
157 Marek Zidlicky RC 1.50 4.00
158 Wade Brookbank RC 2.00 5.00
159 David Hale RC 1.50 4.00
160 Paul Martin RC 2.00 5.00
161 Sean Bergenheim RC 2.00 5.00
162 Antoine Vermette RC 3.00 8.00
163 Matthew Spiller RC 2.00 5.00
164 Ryan Malone RC 3.00 8.00
165 Christian Ehrhoff RC 2.00 5.00
166 Alexander Semin RC 5.00 12.00
167 Tom Preissing RC 2.00 5.00
168 Peter Sejna RC 2.00 5.00
169 Maxim Kondratiev RC 1.50 4.00
170 Matt Stajan RC 2.50 6.00
171 Boyd Gordon RC 2.00 5.00
172 Joffrey Lupul RC 5.00 12.00
173 Eric Staal RC 10.00 25.00
174 Tuomo Ruutu RC 3.00 8.00
175 Pavel Vorobiev RC 2.50 6.00
176 Nathan Horton RC 5.00 12.00
177 Dustin Brown RC 4.00 10.00
178 Jordin Tootoo RC 4.00 10.00
179 Joni Pitkanen RC 3.00 8.00
180 Marc-Andre Fleury RC 12.00 30.00
181 Milan Michalek RC 4.00 10.00
182 Mikhail Yakubov RC 1.50 4.00
183 Trevor Daley RC 2.50 6.00
184 Ryan Kesler RC 8.00 20.00
185 Fredrik Sjostrom RC 2.50 6.00
186 Nikolai Zherdev RC 3.00 8.00
187 Timofei Shishkanov RC 1.50 4.00
188 Niklas Kronwall RC 3.00 8.00
189 Fedor Tyutin RC 1.50 4.00

2003-04 Upper Deck Trilogy Limited

*1-100 VETS/30: 4X TO 10X BASIC CARDS
*101-141 CREST/30: 1X TO 2.5X BASIC COH
*ROOKIE/30: 1.2X TO 3X RC/999
*ROOKIE/30: 1X TO 2.5X RC/499

2003-04 Upper Deck Trilogy Limited Threads

This 30-card set featured a replica felt team logo on one side of the card front and a swatch of game-used jersey on the other. Cards were serial-numbered out of 50.

STATED PRINT RUN 50 SER.#'d SETS
LT1 Jaromir Jagr 30.00 80.00
LT2 Scott Stevens 15.00 40.00
LT3 Mario Lemieux 75.00 150.00
LT4 Jarome Iginla 40.00 100.00
LT5 Roman Turek 15.00 40.00
LT6 Patrick Roy 60.00 120.00
LT7 Steve Yzerman 60.00 120.00
LT8 Mats Sundin 15.00 40.00
LT9 Mike Modano 25.00 60.00
LT10 Zigmund Palffy 15.00 40.00
LT11 Peter Forsberg 25.00 60.00
LT12 Pavel Bure 20.00 50.00
LT13 Todd Bertuzzi 20.00 50.00
LT14 Jason Spezza 25.00 60.00
LT15 Scott Stevens 15.00 40.00
LT16 Jocelyn Thibault 15.00 40.00
LT17 Joe Sakic 30.00 80.00
LT18 Henrik Zetterberg 25.00 60.00
LT19 Joe Thornton 25.00 60.00
LT20 Patrick Lalime 15.00 40.00
LT21 Adam Deadmarsh 20.00 50.00
LT22 Markus Naslund 15.00 40.00
LT23 Ed Belfour 25.00 60.00
LT24 Scott Gomez 15.00 40.00
LT25 Marian Hossa 15.00 40.00
LT26 Alexei Yashin 15.00 40.00
LT27 Sergei Samsonov 15.00 40.00
LT28 Martin Brodeur 30.00 80.00
LT29 Martin Brodeur 30.00 80.00
LT30 Marian Gaborik

2003-04 Upper Deck Trilogy Authentic Patches

These jersey patch cards were inserted at 1:27.

AP1 Wayne Gretzky 100.00 200.00
AP2 Jean-Sebastien Giguere 8.00 20.00
AP3 Mike Modano 20.00 50.00
AP4 Jaromir Jagr 12.00 30.00
AP5 Steve Yzerman 20.00 50.00
AP6 Jose Theodore 20.00 50.00
AP7 Joe Sakic 20.00 50.00
AP8 Mario Lemieux 25.00 60.00
AP9 Marian Hossa 12.50 30.00
AP10 Martin Brodeur 25.00 60.00
AP11 Dominik Hasek 15.00 40.00
AP12 Mats Sundin 12.50 30.00
AP13 Milan Hejduk 12.50 30.00
AP14 Jeremy Roenick 12.50 30.00
AP15 Ray Bourque 25.00 60.00
AP16 Markus Naslund 12.50 30.00
AP17 Pavol Demitra 12.00 30.00
AP18 Doug Gilmour 12.50 30.00
AP19 Joe Thornton 20.00 50.00
AP20 Peter Forsberg 15.00 40.00
AP21 Scott Gomez 12.50 30.00
AP22 Sergei Fedorov 20.00 50.00
AP23 Pavel Bure 12.50 30.00
AP24 Dany Heatley 15.00 40.00
AP25 Teemu Selanne 12.50 30.00
AP26 John LeClair 12.50 30.00
AP27 Zigmund Palffy 12.50 30.00
AP28 Guy Lafleur 20.00 50.00
AP29 Ed Belfour 12.50 30.00
AP30 Jari Kurri 25.00 60.00
AP31 Marcel Dionne 10.00 25.00
AP32 Tony Amonte 12.50 30.00
AP33 Patrick Roy 40.00 100.00
AP34 Eric Lindros 15.00 40.00
AP35 Sergei Samsonov 12.50 30.00
AP36 Keith Tkachuk 12.50 30.00
AP37 Grant Fuhr 15.00 40.00
AP38 Guy Lafleur 15.00 40.00
AP39 Wayne Gretzky 100.00 200.00
AP40 Nicklas Lidstrom 15.00 40.00
AP41 Ray Bourque 25.00 60.00
AP42 Patrick Roy 25.00 60.00

2003-04 Upper Deck Trilogy Crest Variations

This parallel to the "Crest of Honor" subset carried different emblems on the card fronts. Cards 101-122 carried the player's jersey number and were limited to that number of copies. Cards 123-141 carried an image of the Stanley Cup, print runs were based on the last year the player won the Cup and are listed below. The cards of Marcel Dionne and Michel Goulet carried alternate team emblems since neither won a Cup during their career. The Don Cherry card carried a cherries emblem.

101 Joe Thornton JSY#/19* 15.00 40.00
102 Sergei Fedorov JSY#/91* 15.00 40.00
103 Dany Heatley JSY#/15*
104 Steve Yzerman JSY#/19* 50.00 120.00
105 H.Zetterberg JSY#/40* 20.00 50.00
106 Patrick Roy JSY#/33* 50.00 120.00
107 Peter Forsberg JSY#/21* 20.00 50.00
108 J.Giguere JSY#/35* 30.00 60.00
109 Marian Gaborik JSY#/10*
110 Markus Naslund JSY#/19* 20.00 50.00
111 Jeremy Roenick JSY#/97* 12.50 30.00
112 Mario Lemieux JSY#/66* 30.00 80.00
113 Mats Sundin JSY#/13*
114 Ed Belfour JSY#/20* 25.00 60.00
115 Ilya Kovalchuk JSY#/17*
116 Marian Hossa JSY#/18* 20.00 40.00
117 Eric Lindros JSY#/88* 12.50 30.00
118 Jocelyn Thibault JSY#/41* 15.00 40.00
119 Jose Theodore JSY#/60* 15.00 40.00
120 Mike Modano JSY#/9*
121 Jason Spezza JSY#/39* 30.00 60.00
122 Rick Nash JSY#/61* 15.00 40.00
123 Jean Beliveau SC/72* 12.50 30.00
124 Mike Bossy SC/91* 10.00 25.00
125 Johnny Bucyk SC/81* 12.50 30.00
126 Marcel Dionne DET/92* 12.50 30.00
127 Grant Fuhr SC/3*
128 Michel Goulet QUE/98* 12.50 30.00
129 Jari Kurri SC/1*
130 Guy Lafleur SC/88* 15.00 40.00
131 Ted Lindsay SC/66* 12.50 30.00
132 Scotty Bowman SC/91* 15.00 40.00
133 L.McDonald SC/92* 12.50 30.00
134 Stan Mikita SC/83* 12.50 30.00
135 Denis Potvin SC/91* 12.50 30.00
136 Ray Bourque SC/77* 20.00 50.00
137 D.Cherry Cherries/99* 20.00 50.00
138 Bobby Orr SC/79* 15.00 40.00
139 Gordie Howe SC/72* 25.00 60.00
140 Bobby Clarke SC/87* 12.50 30.00
141 Wayne Gretzky SC/99* 150.00 250.00
141 Phil Esposito SC/84* 12.50 30.00

2003-04 Upper Deck Trilogy Scripts

This autographed insert set consisted of 4 distinct subsets. Script 1 cards were rookies and prospects, Script 2 cards were current stars, Script 3 cards were retired greats. The Custom Scripts subset included special "customized" autographs of the featured player. Please note that several of the "Custom" cards on this checklist have yet to be confirmed while different, un-catalogued version appear frequently.

TIER 1-3 STATED ODDS 1:4
CUSTOM STATED ODDS 1:45
S1AH Ales Hemsky 6.00 15.00
S1BO Brooks Orpik 6.00 15.00
S1HL Adam Hall 3.00 8.00
S1HZ Henrik Zetterberg 12.50 30.00
S1JA Jared Aulin 3.00 8.00
S1JB Jay Bouwmeester 6.00 15.00
S1JL Jordan Leopold 3.00 8.00
S1JS Jason Spezza 12.50 30.00
S1PB P-M Bouchard 5.00 12.00
S1PL Pascal Leclaire 3.00 8.00
S1RH Ron Hainsey 3.00 8.00
S1SO Steve Ott 5.00 12.00
S2CJ Curtis Joseph 10.00 25.00
S2EC Erik Cole 3.00 8.00
S2JG Jean-Sebastien Giguere 5.00 12.00
S2JL John LeClair 6.00 15.00
S2JT Joe Thornton 25.00 60.00
S2JT Jose Theodore 10.00 25.00
S2JW Justin Williams 5.00 12.00
S2MA Maxim Afinogenov 5.00 12.00
S2MB Martin Brodeur 60.00 150.00
S2MH Martin Havlat 6.00 15.00
S2MH Marian Hossa 8.00 20.00
S2MN Markus Naslund 6.00 15.00
S2MT Marty Turco 8.00 20.00
S2PR Patrick Roy 75.00 200.00
S2SS Sergei Samsonov 5.00 12.00
S2TB Todd Bertuzzi 10.00 25.00
S3BC Bobby Clarke 12.50 30.00
S3BK Johnny Bucyk AS 8.00 20.00
S3BO Bobby Orr 100.00 200.00
S3BY Mike Bossy AS 10.00 25.00
S3DC Don Cherry 15.00 40.00
S3DP Denis Potvin NYI 6.00 15.00
S3G1 Wayne Gretzky AS 100.00 200.00
S3GF Grant Fuhr 8.00 20.00
S3GH Gordie Howe HAR 30.00 80.00
S3GL Guy Lafleur 12.50 30.00
S3GR Wayne Gretzky AS 100.00 200.00
S3GT Michel Goulet AS 5.00 12.00
S3GY Wayne Gretzky NYR 100.00 200.00
S3JB Jean Beliveau 30.00 60.00
S3JK Jari Kurri 10.00 25.00
S3JK Johnny Bucyk BOS 8.00 20.00
S3LM Lanny McDonald 6.00 15.00
S3MB Mike Bossy NYI 10.00 25.00
S3MD Marcel Dionne 5.00 12.00
S3MG Michel Goulet CHI 5.00 12.00
S3MH Gordie Howe DET 50.00 125.00
S3PE Phil Esposito 15.00 40.00
S3PN Denis Potvin AS 6.00 15.00
S3RB Ray Bourque 15.00 40.00
S3SB Scotty Bowman 15.00 40.00
S3SM Stan Mikita 12.00 30.00
S3TL Ted Lindsay 10.00 25.00
S3WA Wayne Gretzky LA 100.00 200.00
S3WG Wayne Gretzky EDM 100.00 200.00
S399 Wayne Gretzky HOF 100.00 200.00
CSBC Bobby Clarke HOF 20.00 50.00
CSBC2 B.Clarke Broad St. 30.00 80.00
CSBU J.Beliveau LeGros Bill 25.00 60.00
CSBU2 J.Beliveau HOF 25.00 60.00
CSBU3 J.Beliveau SC
CSBY M.Bossy HOF 10.00 25.00
CSBY2 M.Bossy SC 25.00 60.00
CSDC D.Cherry Grapes 20.00 50.00
CSGH Gordie Howe 50.00 100.00
CSGL Guy Lafleur HOF 20.00 50.00
CSGL2 G.Lafleur SC
CSJB J.Bucyk Chief 15.00 40.00
CSJG J.Giguere Jiggy 12.50 30.00
CSMC Mike Comrie 6.00 15.00
CSMH G.Howe HOF 50.00 125.00
CSMH2 G.Howe Mr.Elbows 50.00 125.00
CSMH3 G.Howe SC 50.00 125.00
CSMH4 G.Howe Prod.Line 50.00 125.00
CSRN R.Nash #1 Pick 20.00 50.00
CSSB S.Bowman HOF 30.00 80.00
CSSO S.Ott Otter 6.00 15.00
CSTB T.Bertuzzi Bert 20.00 50.00
CSTL T.Lindsay Prod.Line 15.00 40.00
CSTL2 T.Lindsay Art Ross 15.00 40.00
CSTL3 T.Lindsay HOF 15.00 40.00
CSTL4 T.Lindsay SC Winner 15.00 40.00
CSZP Z.Palffy Ziggy 15.00 40.00

2003-04 Upper Deck Trilogy Scripts Limited

This partial-parallel to the basic Sripts set carried a gold foil "Limited" stamp on the card fronts and serial-numbering out of 30.

S1AH Ales Hemsky 12.00 30.00
S1BO Brooks Orpik 10.00 25.00
S1HL Adam Hall 10.00 25.00
S1HZ Henrik Zetterberg 25.00 60.00
S1JA Jared Aulin 8.00 20.00
S1JB Jay Bouwmeester 12.00 30.00
S1JL Jordan Leopold 10.00 25.00
S1JS Jason Spezza 25.00 60.00
S1PB P-M Bouchard 10.00 25.00
S1PL Pascal Leclaire 10.00 25.00
S1RH Ron Hainsey 8.00 20.00
S1SO Steve Ott 12.00 30.00
S2CJ Curtis Joseph 20.00 50.00
S2EC Erik Cole 10.00 25.00
S2IK Ilya Kovalchuk
S2JG Jean-Sebastien Giguere 12.00 30.00
S2JL John LeClair 12.00 30.00
S2JT Joe Thornton 20.00 50.00
S2JT Jose Theodore 15.00 40.00
S2JW Justin Williams 10.00 25.00
S2MA Maxim Afinogenov 10.00 25.00
S2MB Martin Brodeur 100.00 200.00
S2MH Martin Havlat 12.00 30.00
S2MH Marian Hossa 20.00 40.00
S2MN Markus Naslund 12.00 30.00
S2MT Marty Turco 12.00 30.00
S2PR Patrick Roy 100.00 200.00
S2SS Sergei Samsonov 10.00 25.00
S2TB Todd Bertuzzi 12.00 30.00
S3BC Bobby Clarke 20.00 50.00
S3BK Johnny Bucyk AS 12.00 30.00
S3BO Bobby Orr 125.00 250.00
S3BY Mike Bossy AS 20.00 50.00
S3DC Don Cherry 30.00 80.00
S3DP Denis Potvin NYI 12.00 30.00
S3G1 Wayne Gretzky AS 100.00 200.00
S3GF Grant Fuhr 12.00 30.00
S3GH Gordie Howe HAR 75.00 150.00
S3GL Guy Lafleur 15.00 40.00
S3GR Wayne Gretzky AS 100.00 200.00
S3GT Michel Goulet AS 10.00 25.00
S3GY Wayne Gretzky NYR 125.00 250.00
S3JB Jean Beliveau 30.00 80.00
S3JK Jari Kurri 15.00 40.00
S3JK Johnny Bucyk BOS 12.00 30.00
S3LM Lanny McDonald 12.00 30.00
S3MB Mike Bossy NYI 20.00 50.00
S3MD Marcel Dionne 12.00 30.00
S3MG Michel Goulet CHI 12.00 30.00
S3MH Gordie Howe DET 100.00 200.00
S3PE Phil Esposito 30.00 60.00
S3PN Denis Potvin AS 12.00 30.00
S3RB Ray Bourque 30.00 60.00
S3SB Scotty Bowman 30.00 80.00
S3SM Stan Mikita 15.00 40.00
S3TL Ted Lindsay 20.00 50.00
S3WA Wayne Gretzky LA 100.00 250.00
S3WG Wayne Gretzky EDM 125.00 250.00
S399 Wayne Gretzky HOF 100.00 250.00

2003-04 Upper Deck Trilogy Scripts Red

This unannounced partial-parallel set to the basic Scripts set carried red ink signatures and hand written serial-numbering (listed below). Please note that the Gretzky cards were signed in blue ink, not red and that Gordie Howe signed all of his cards in this product with red ink.

S1HL Adam Hall/31 10.00 25.00
S1JB Jay Bouwmeester/31 12.00 30.00
S1PL Pascal Leclaire/31 10.00 25.00
S2CJ Curtis Joseph/30 20.00 50.00
S2IK Ilya Kovalchuk/30 30.00 80.00
S2MN Markus Naslund/30 15.00 40.00
S2PR Patrick Roy/27 150.00 250.00
S2TB Todd Bertuzzi/22 15.00 40.00
S3BC Bobby Clarke/30 20.00 50.00
S3BO Bobby Orr/30 125.00 250.00
S3DC Don Cherry/30 20.00 50.00
S3DP Denis Potvin/30 12.00 30.00
S3GF Grant Fuhr/30 12.00 30.00
S3GL Guy Lafleur/30 15.00 40.00
S3JB Jean Beliveau/30 30.00 80.00
S3JB Johnny Bucyk/30 12.00 30.00
S3JK Jari Kurri/30 15.00 40.00
S3LM Lanny McDonald/30 12.00 30.00
S3MB Mike Bossy/30 20.00 50.00
S3MD Marcel Dionne/30 12.00 30.00
S3MG Michel Goulet/30 12.00 30.00
S3MH Gordie Howe/30 60.00 125.00
S3RB Ray Bourque/30 30.00 60.00
S3SB Scotty Bowman/30 30.00 80.00
S3SM Stan Mikita/30 25.00 50.00
S3TL Ted Lindsay/30 25.00 50.00
S3WG W.Gretzky EDM Blu/30 200.00 400.00

2005-06 Upper Deck Trilogy

This 320-card was issued through both product specific unopened and inserts in the Rookie Update product. Cards numbered 1-220 were in the unopened product while cards 221-320 were in the Rookie Update product. The unopened product were five-cards packs which came nine packs to a box. Cards numbered 1-90 feature veterans in alphabetical team order while cards 91-170 is a veteran Frozen in Time subset. The pack issued set concludes with Rookie cards from 171-220. All cards numbered 90 and up were serial numbered: Cards 91-170 were issued to a stated print run of 599 serial numbered sets while cards 221-320 were issued to a stated print run of 999 serial numbered sets.

COMP.SET w/o SP's (90) 20.00 40.00
FIT PRINT RUN 599 SER.#'d SETS
RC PRINT RUN 999 SER.#'d SETS
1 Jean-Sebastien Giguere .60 1.50
2 Joffrey Lupul .50 1.25
3 Sergei Fedorov 1.00 2.50
4 Marian Hossa .50 1.25
5 Ilya Kovalchuk .60 1.50
6 Kari Lehtonen .50 1.25
7 Andrew Raycroft .50 1.25
8 Joe Thornton .75 2.00
9 Patrice Bergeron .75 2.00
10 Glen Murray .50 1.25
11 Brian Leetch .60 1.50
12 Daniel Briere .60 1.50
13 Chris Drury .50 1.25
14 Maxim Afinogenov .40 1.00
15 Jarome Iginla .60 1.50
16 Jordan Leopold .40 1.00
17 Miikka Kiprusoff .50 1.25
18 Eric Staal .75 2.00
19 Erik Cole .50 1.25
20 Nikolai Khabibulin .60 1.50
21 Tuomo Ruutu .60 1.50
22 David Aebischer .50 1.25
23 Joe Sakic 1.00 2.50
24 Rob Blake .60 1.50
25 Milan Hejduk .50 1.25
26 Alex Tanguay .60 1.50
27 Rick Nash .60 1.50
28 Nikolai Zherdev .40 1.00
29 Mike Modano 1.00 2.50
30 Bill Guerin .60 1.50
31 Marty Turco .60 1.50
32 Manny Legace .60 1.50
33 Pavel Datsyuk .75 2.00
34 Brendan Shanahan .75 2.00
35 Steve Yzerman 1.50 4.00
36 Henrik Zetterberg .75 2.00
37 Ty Conklin .50 1.25
38 Ryan Smyth .50 1.25
39 Chris Pronger .50 1.25
40 Roberto Luongo 1.00 2.50
41 Stephen Weiss .40 1.00
42 Luc Robitaille .60 1.50
43 Jeremy Roenick .60 1.50
44 Marian Gaborik 1.00 2.50
45 Mike Ribeiro .50 1.25
46 Michael Ryder .50 1.25
47 Jose Theodore .60 1.50
48 Saku Koivu .60 1.50
49 Paul Kariya .75 2.00
50 Steve Sullivan .40 1.00
51 Tomas Vokoun .50 1.25
52 Martin Brodeur 1.25 3.00
53 Scott Gomez .50 1.25
54 Patrik Elias .60 1.50
55 Jaromir Jagr 1.50 4.00
56 Kevin Weekes .50 1.25
57 Alexei Yashin .50 1.25
58 Miroslav Satan .50 1.25
59 Rick DiPietro .50 1.25
60 Daniel Alfredsson .60 1.50
61 Dany Heatley .60 1.50
62 Jason Spezza .60 1.50
63 Martin Havlat .60 1.50
64 Peter Forsberg .75 2.00
65 Keith Primeau .60 1.50
66 Simon Gagne .60 1.50
67 Robert Esche .50 1.25
68 Ladislav Nagy .40 1.00
69 Curtis Joseph .60 1.50
70 Shane Doan .50 1.25
71 Zigmund Palffy .60 1.50
72 Mario Lemieux 2.00 5.00
73 Mark Recchi .75 2.00
74 Evgeni Nabokov .50 1.25
75 Patrick Marleau .60 1.50
76 Jonathan Cheechoo .60 1.50
77 Patrick Lalime .50 1.25
78 Doug Weight .60 1.50
79 Keith Tkachuk .60 1.50
80 Brad Richards .60 1.50
81 Sean Burke .40 1.00
82 Martin St. Louis .60 1.50
83 Vincent Lecavalier .50 1.25
84 Ed Belfour .60 1.50
85 Mats Sundin .60 1.50
86 Eric Lindros 1.00 2.50
87 Kyle Wellwood .50 1.25
88 Markus Naslund .60 1.50
89 Ed Jovanovski .50 1.25
90 Olaf Kolzig .60 1.50
91 Jean-Sebastien Giguere FIT 4.00 10.00
92 Sergei Fedorov FIT 6.00 15.00
93 Sergei Fedorov FIT 4.00 10.00
94 Ilya Kovalchuk FIT 4.00 10.00
95 Joe Thornton FIT 4.00 10.00
96 Ray Bourque FIT 6.00 15.00
97 Chris Drury FIT 3.00 8.00
98 Jarome Iginla FIT 4.00 10.00
99 Miikka Kiprusoff FIT 3.00 8.00
100 Eric Staal FIT 5.00 12.00
101 Tuomo Ruutu FIT 4.00 10.00
102 Joe Sakic FIT 6.00 15.00
103 Patrick Roy FIT 10.00 25.00
104 Paul Kariya FIT 5.00 12.00
105 Peter Forsberg FIT 5.00 12.00
106 Nikolai Zherdev FIT 2.50 6.00
107 Rick Nash FIT 4.00 10.00
108 Mike Modano FIT 6.00 15.00
109 Gordie Howe FIT 12.00 30.00
110 Pavel Datsyuk FIT 5.00 12.00
111 Steve Yzerman FIT 10.00 25.00
112 Henrik Zetterberg FIT 5.00 12.00
113 Wayne Gretzky FIT 20.00 50.00
114 Marian Gaborik FIT 6.00 15.00
115 Jose Theodore FIT 4.00 10.00
116 Saku Koivu FIT 4.00 10.00
117 Martin Brodeur FIT 8.00 20.00
118 Jaromir Jagr FIT 10.00 25.00
119 Mark Messier FIT 6.00 15.00
120 Jason Spezza FIT 4.00 10.00
121 Jeremy Roenick FIT 4.00 10.00
122 Marc-Andre Fleury FIT 6.00 15.00
123 Mario Lemieux FIT 12.00 30.00
124 Chris Pronger FIT 3.00 8.00
125 Brad Richards FIT 4.00 10.00
126 Martin St. Louis FIT 4.00 10.00
127 Vincent Lecavalier FIT 3.00 8.00
128 Ed Belfour FIT 4.00 10.00
129 Mats Sundin FIT 4.00 10.00
130 Markus Naslund FIT 4.00 10.00
131 Kari Lehtonen FIT 3.00 8.00
132 Andrew Raycroft FIT 3.00 8.00
133 Patrice Bergeron FIT 5.00 12.00
134 Alex Tanguay FIT 4.00 10.00
135 Milan Hejduk FIT 3.00 8.00
136 Marty Turco FIT 4.00 10.00
137 Bill Guerin FIT 4.00 10.00
138 Brendan Shanahan FIT 3.00 8.00
139 Ryan Smyth FIT 3.00 8.00
140 Roberto Luongo FIT 6.00 15.00
141 Luc Robitaille FIT 4.00 10.00
142 Michael Ryder FIT 3.00 8.00
143 Tomas Vokoun FIT 3.00 8.00
144 Patrik Elias FIT 4.00 10.00
145 Rick DiPietro FIT 3.00 8.00
146 Daniel Alfredsson FIT 4.00 10.00
147 Marian Hossa FIT 3.00 8.00
148 Keith Primeau FIT 4.00 10.00
149 Brett Hull FIT 5.00 12.00
150 Evgeni Nabokov FIT 3.00 8.00
151 Patrick Marleau FIT 4.00 10.00
152 Doug Weight FIT 4.00 10.00
153 Keith Tkachuk FIT 4.00 10.00
154 Todd Bertuzzi FIT 4.00 10.00
155 Olaf Kolzig FIT 4.00 10.00
156 Cam Neely FIT 4.00 10.00
157 Gilbert Perreault FIT 4.00 10.00
158 Denis Savard FIT 5.00 12.00
159 Tony Esposito FIT 4.00 10.00
160 Jari Kurri FIT 4.00 10.00
161 Grant Fuhr FIT 4.00 10.00
162 Mike Ribeiro FIT 3.00 8.00
163 Guy LaFleur FIT 5.00 12.00
164 Mike Bossy FIT 4.00 10.00
165 Alexei Yashin FIT 3.00 8.00
166 Phil Esposito FIT 6.00 15.00
167 Dominik Hasek FIT 6.00 15.00
168 Martin Havlat FIT 4.00 10.00
169 Simon Gagne FIT 4.00 10.00
170 Ed Jovanovski FIT 3.00 8.00
171 Corey Perry RC 15.00 40.00
172 Ryan Getzlaf RC 8.00 20.00
173 Braydon Coburn RC 4.00 10.00
174 Jim Slater RC 3.00 8.00
175 Hannu Toivonen RC 4.00 10.00
176 Milan Jurcina RC 3.00 8.00
177 Andrew Alberts RC 2.50 6.00
178 Thomas Vanek RC 8.00 20.00
179 Dion Phaneuf RC 12.00 30.00
180 Eric Nystrom RC 3.00 8.00
181 Cam Ward RC 6.00 15.00
182 Brent Seabrook RC 8.00 20.00
183 Rene Bourque RC 4.00 10.00
184 Cam Barker RC 3.00 8.00
185 Wojtek Wolski RC 3.00 8.00
186 Peter Budaj RC 5.00 12.00
187 Gilbert Brule RC 4.00 10.00
188 Jussi Jokinen RC 4.00 10.00
189 Jim Howard RC 6.00 15.00
190 Johan Franzen RC 8.00 20.00
191 Brett Lebda RC 2.50 6.00
192 Rostislav Olesz RC 3.00 8.00
193 Anthony Stewart RC 3.00 8.00
194 Alexander Perezhogin RC 3.00 8.00
195 Yann Danis RC 3.00 8.00
196 Mark Streit RC 2.50 6.00
197 Ryan Suter RC 5.00 12.00
198 Zach Parise RC 6.00 15.00
199 Robert Nilsson RC 4.00 10.00
200 Petteri Nokelainen RC 2.50 6.00
201 Chris Campoli RC 2.50 6.00
202 Henrik Lundqvist RC 12.00 30.00
203 Petr Prucha RC 4.00 10.00
204 Al Montoya RC 4.00 10.00
205 Andrej Meszaros RC 3.00 8.00
206 Brandon Bochenski RC 4.00 10.00
207 Jeff Carter RC 8.00 20.00
208 Mike Richards RC 8.00 20.00
209 David Leneveu RC 3.00 8.00
210 Keith Ballard RC 3.00 8.00
211 Sidney Crosby RC 90.00 150.00
212 Maxime Talbot RC 4.00 10.00
213 Ryane Clowe RC 5.00 12.00
214 Jeff Woywitka RC 2.50 6.00
215 Jay McClement RC 2.50 6.00
216 Lee Stempniak RC 4.00 10.00
217 Jeff Hoggan RC 2.50 6.00
218 Alexander Steen RC 8.00 20.00
219 Andrew Wozniewski RC 3.00 8.00
220 Alexander Ovechkin RC 25.00 60.00
221 Dustin Penner RC 4.00 10.00
222 Zenon Konopka RC 2.50 6.00
223 Michael Wall RC 3.00 8.00
224 Adam Berkhoel RC 3.00 8.00
225 Jordan Sigalet RC 2.50 6.00
226 Ben Walter RC 2.50 6.00
227 Chris Thorburn RC 3.00 8.00
228 Daniel Paille RC 4.00 10.00
229 Nathan Paetsch RC 3.00 8.00
230 Jiri Novotny RC 3.00 8.00
231 Richie Regehr RC 2.50 6.00
232 Mark Giordano RC 4.00 10.00
233 Andrew Ladd RC 5.00 12.00
234 Chad Larose RC 2.50 6.00
235 Niklas Nordgren RC 4.00 10.00
236 Danny Richmond RC 2.50 6.00
237 Martin St. Pierre RC 2.50 6.00
238 Corey Crawford RC 12.00 30.00
239 James Wisniewski RC 3.00 8.00
240 Duncan Keith RC 8.00 20.00
241 Brad Richardson RC 4.00 10.00
242 Vitaly Kolesnik RC 3.00 8.00
243 Andrew Penner RC 3.00 8.00
244 Ole-Kristian Tollefsen RC 3.00 8.00
245 Alexandre Picard RC 2.50 6.00
246 Joakim Lindstrom RC 2.50 6.00
247 Steven Goertzen RC 2.50 6.00
248 Geoff Platt RC 3.00 8.00
249 Jaroslav Balastik RC 2.50 6.00
250 Junior Lessard RC 2.50 6.00
251 Vojtech Polak RC 2.50 6.00
252 Kyle Quincey RC 3.00 8.00
253 Valtteri Filppula RC 5.00 12.00
254 Brad Winchester RC 4.00 10.00
255 Matt Greene RC 2.50 6.00
256 Kyle Brodziak RC 2.50 6.00
257 J-F Jacques RC 2.50 6.00
258 Mathieu Roy RC 4.00 10.00
259 Danny Syvret RC 2.50 6.00
260 Greg Jacina RC 2.50 6.00
261 Rob Globke RC 2.50 6.00
262 Petr Taticek RC 3.00 8.00
263 Jeff Tambellini RC 2.50 6.00
264 Petr Kanko RC 3.00 8.00
265 Yanick Lehoux RC 4.00 10.00
266 Richard Petiot RC 3.00 8.00
267 Matt Ryan RC 3.00 8.00
268 Connor James RC 3.00 8.00
269 Mikko Koivu RC 5.00 12.00
270 Derek Boogaard RC 5.00 12.00
271 Maxim Lapierre RC 4.00 10.00
272 Andrei Kostitsyn RC 5.00 12.00
273 J-P Cote RC 2.50 6.00
274 Jonathan Ferland RC 3.00 8.00
275 Kevin Klein RC 2.50 6.00
276 Pekka Rinne RC 6.00 15.00
277 Barry Tallackson RC 3.00 8.00
278 Cam Janssen RC 3.00 8.00
279 Jason Ryznar RC 2.50 6.00
280 Jeremy Colliton RC 2.50 6.00
281 Bruno Gervais RC 2.50 6.00
282 Ryan Hollweg RC 2.50 6.00
283 Chris Holt RC 2.50 6.00
284 Patrick Eaves RC 4.00 10.00
285 Christoph Schubert RC 2.50 6.00
286 Brian McGrattan RC 2.50 6.00
287 R.J. Umberger RC 4.00 10.00
288 Ben Eager RC 3.00 8.00
289 Alexandre Picard RC 2.50 6.00
290 Stefan Ruzicka RC 2.50 6.00
291 Matt Jones RC 2.50 6.00
292 Ryan Whitney RC 4.00 10.00
293 Erik Christensen RC 2.50 6.00
294 Colby Armstrong RC 4.00 10.00
295 Steve Bernier RC 4.00 10.00
296 Dimitri Patzold RC 2.50 6.00
297 Grant Stevenson RC 2.50 6.00
298 Doug Murray RC 2.50 6.00
299 Josh Gorges RC 3.00 8.00
300 Dennis Wideman RC 2.50 6.00
301 Chris Beckford-Tseu RC 3.00 8.00
302 Colin Hemingway RC 2.50 6.00
303 Jon DiSalvatore RC 3.00 8.00
304 Evgeny Artyukhin RC 3.00 8.00
305 Gerald Coleman RC 2.50 6.00
306 Ryan Craig RC 2.50 6.00
307 Nick Tarnasky RC 2.50 6.00
308 Paul Ranger RC 2.50 6.00
309 Darren Reid RC 2.50 6.00
310 Doug O'Brien RC 2.50 6.00
311 Staffan Kronwall RC 2.50 6.00
312 Jay Harrison RC 3.00 8.00
313 Kevin Bieksa RC 5.00 12.00
314 Rob McVicar RC 3.00 8.00
315 Tomas Mojzis RC 2.50 6.00
316 Tomas Fleischmann RC 4.00 10.00
317 Jakub Klepis RC 2.50 6.00
318 Mike Green RC 5.00 12.00
319 David Steckel RC 3.00 8.00
320 Joey Tenute RC 3.00 8.00

2005-06 Upper Deck Trilogy Crystal

*FIT/25: 2X TO 5X BASIC CARDS
PRINT RUN 25 SER.#'d SETS
119 Mark Messier FIT 25.00 60.00

2005-06 Upper Deck Trilogy Honorary Swatches

STATED ODDS 1:3
HSIK Ilya Kovalchuk 6.00 15.00
HSKL Kari Lehtonen 5.00 12.00
HSAR Andrew Raycroft 5.00 12.00
HSJT Joe Thornton 8.00 20.00
HSDB Daniel Briere 6.00 15.00
HSJI Jarome Iginla 6.00 15.00
HSTR Tuomo Ruutu 6.00 15.00
HSJS Joe Sakic 10.00 25.00
HSMH Milan Hejduk 5.00 12.00
HSPF Peter Forsberg 6.00 15.00
HSNZ Nikolai Zherdev 4.00 10.00
HSRN Rick Nash 6.00 15.00
HSMT Marty Turco 6.00 15.00
HSSY Steve Yzerman 10.00 25.00
HSAH Ales Hemsky 5.00 12.00
HSRS Ryan Smyth 5.00 12.00
HSRL Roberto Luongo 10.00 25.00
HSAF Alexander Frolov 4.00 10.00
HSMG Marian Gaborik 10.00 25.00
HSJO Jose Theodore 6.00 15.00
HSSK Saku Koivu 6.00 15.00
HSMB Martin Brodeur 10.00 25.00
HSPE Patrik Elias 6.00 15.00
HSJJ Jaromir Jagr 15.00 40.00
HSMM Mark Messier 10.00 25.00
HSSP Jason Spezza 6.00 15.00
HSHO Marian Hossa 5.00 12.00
HSHA Martin Havlat 6.00 15.00
HSJR Jeremy Roenick 6.00 15.00
HSSG Simon Gagne 6.00 15.00
HSML Mario Lemieux 15.00 40.00
HSJC Jonathan Cheechoo 4.00 10.00
HSCP Chris Pronger 5.00 12.00
HSVL Vincent Lecavalier 5.00 12.00
HSMS Mats Sundin 6.00 15.00
HSEJ Ed Jovanovski 5.00 12.00
HSMN Markus Naslund 6.00 15.00
HSLU Joffrey Lupul 5.00 12.00
HSSF Sergei Fedorov 10.00 25.00
HSGM Glen Murray 5.00 12.00
HSSV Sergei Samsonov 5.00 12.00
HSED Eric Daze 5.00 12.00
HSJW Justin Williams 5.00 12.00

HSNK Nikolai Khabibulin 6.00 15.00
HSDA David Aebischer 5.00 12.00
HSMD Marc Denis 5.00 12.00
HSBG Bill Guerin 6.00 15.00
HSMO Mike Modano 10.00 25.00
HSCC Chris Chelios 6.00 15.00
HSNL Nicklas Lidstrom 6.00 15.00
HSKD Kris Draper 8.00 20.00
HSWG Wayne Gretzky 30.00 80.00
HSTC Ty Conklin 5.00 12.00
HSMP Michael Peca 5.00 12.00
HSJB Jay Bouwmeester 6.00 15.00
HSNH Nathan Horton 6.00 15.00
HSRE Robert Esche 5.00 12.00
HSRY Michael Ryder 5.00 12.00
HSRI Mike Ribeiro 5.00 12.00
HSDL David Legwand 5.00 12.00
HSPK Paul Kariya 8.00 20.00
HSOK Olaf Kolzig 6.00 15.00
HSSS Scott Stevens 6.00 15.00
HSAL Daniel Alfredsson 6.00 15.00
HSHK Dominik Hasek 8.00 20.00
HSKP Keith Primeau 6.00 15.00
HSCJ Curtis Joseph 6.00 15.00
HSBL Brian Leetch 6.00 15.00
HSJL John LeClair 6.00 15.00
HSZP Zigmund Palffy 6.00 15.00
HSTK Keith Tkachuk 6.00 15.00
HSAM Al MacInnis 6.00 15.00
HSAT Alex Tanguay 6.00 15.00
HSEL Eric Lindros 10.00 25.00
HSDW Doug Weight 6.00 15.00
HSDC Dan Cloutier 5.00 12.00
HSTB Todd Bertuzzi 6.00 15.00
HSJG Jean-Sebastien Giguere 6.00 15.00
HSMK Miikka Kiprusoff 4.00 10.00
HSBR Brad Richards SP 6.00 15.00

2005-06 Upper Deck Trilogy Ice Scripts

STATED ODDS 1:9
ISAH Ales Hemsky 8.00 20.00
ISAT Alex Tanguay 8.00 20.00
ISAR Andrew Raycroft 8.00 20.00
ISBC Bobby Clarke 25.00 60.00
ISCN Cam Neely 12.00 30.00
ISAL Daniel Alfredsson 75.00 150.00
ISDB Daniel Briere 10.00 25.00
ISDH Dany Heatley 12.50 30.00
ISDA David Aebischer 6.00 15.00
ISDC Don Cherry 20.00 50.00
ISGC Gerry Cheevers 12.00 30.00
ISGP Gilbert Perreault 10.00 25.00
ISHL Glenn Hall 20.00 50.00
ISGH Gordie Howe 60.00 125.00
ISIK Ilya Kovalchuk 30.00 60.00
ISJI Jarome Iginla 10.00 25.00
ISJT Joe Thornton 12.50 30.00
ISJO Jose Theodore 12.00 30.00
ISJG Jean-Sebastien Giguere 8.00 20.00
ISLR Luc Robitaille 10.00 25.00
ISMF Marc-Andre Fleury 12.00 30.00
ISHS Marcel Hossa 6.00 15.00
ISMG Marian Gaborik 15.00 40.00
ISHO Marian Hossa 10.00 25.00
ISMN Markus Naslund 10.00 25.00
ISMB Martin Brodeur 100.00 200.00
ISHA Martin Havlat 8.00 20.00
ISSL Martin St. Louis 12.00 30.00
ISMT Marty Turco 8.00 20.00
ISMS Mats Sundin SP 150.00 250.00
ISBO Mike Bossy 15.00 40.00
ISMM Mike Modano 12.00 30.00
ISMH Milan Hejduk 8.00 20.00
ISRB Ray Bourque SP 25.00 60.00
ISRN Rick Nash 15.00 40.00
ISRS Ryan Smyth 10.00 25.00
ISSK Saku Koivu SP 150.00 250.00
ISSW Stephen Weiss 6.00 15.00
ISVL Vincent Lecavalier SP 40.00 100.00
ISWG Wayne Gretzky 150.00 300.00

2005-06 Upper Deck Trilogy Legendary Scripts

STATED ODDS 1:45
LEGBC Bobby Clarke 12.00 30.00
LEGBH Bobby Hull SP 30.00 80.00
LEGCG Clark Gillies 6.00 15.00
LEGCN Cam Neely 10.00 25.00
LEGDC Don Cherry 15.00 40.00
LEGDS Denis Savard 6.00 15.00
LEGGA Glenn Anderson 6.00 15.00
LEGGC Gerry Cheevers 12.00 30.00
LEGGH Gordie Howe SP 60.00 125.00
LEGGL Guy Lafleur SP 60.00 125.00
LEGGP Gilbert Perreault 12.00 30.00
LEGJK Jari Kurri 12.00 30.00
LEGLM Lanny McDonald 6.00 15.00
LEGMD Marcel Dionne 10.00 25.00
LEGPE Phil Esposito SP 30.00 80.00
LEGRB Ray Bourque SP 60.00 125.00
LEGRR Rene Robert 6.00 15.00
LEGSM Stan Mikita SP 12.00 30.00
LEGTE Tony Esposito SP 20.00 50.00
LEGTL Ted Lindsay 12.00 30.00
LEGWG Wayne Gretzky SP 350.00 500.00

2005-06 Upper Deck Trilogy Personal Scripts

STATED ODDS 1:90
PERBC Bobby Clarke SP 20.00 50.00
PERBH Bobby Hull SP 25.00 60.00
PERCN Cam Neely SP 20.00 50.00
PERDS Denis Savard SP 10.00 25.00
PERGF Grant Fuhr 15.00 40.00
PERGH Gordie Howe 75.00 200.00
PERGL Guy Lafleur SP 50.00 100.00
PERGP Gilbert Perreault SP 25.00 50.00
PERLM Lanny McDonald 10.00 25.00
PERMB Martin Brodeur SP 200.00 300.00
PERMD Marcel Dionne 12.00 30.00
PERMF Marc-Andre Fleury 15.00 40.00
PERPE Phil Esposito SP 40.00 80.00
PERRB Ray Bourque SP 75.00 200.00
PERRH Ron Hextall 20.00 50.00
PERRN Rick Nash 15.00 40.00
PERRR Rene Robert SP 10.00 25.00
PERSM Stan Mikita SP 25.00 60.00
PERSP Jason Spezza 10.00 25.00
PERTE Tony Esposito SP 30.00 60.00
PERGC1 G.Cheevers No Inscrip. 12.50 30.00
PERGC2 G.Cheevers Cheesy 20.00 50.00

2005-06 Upper Deck Trilogy Scripts

FS1 ODDS 1:9
SS3 PRINT RUN 50 SER.#'d SETS
SCSAY Alexei Yashin 5.00 12.00
SCSCD Chris Drury 5.00 12.00
SCSJG Jean-Sebastien Giguere 8.00 20.00
SCSJL John LeClair 5.00 12.00
SCSJS Jason Spezza 10.00 25.00
SCSMN Markus Naslund 6.00 15.00
SCSMP Mark Parrish 5.00 12.00
SCSMT Marty Turco 4.00 10.00
SCSPB Pavel Bure 6.00 15.00
SCSPE Michael Peca 5.00 12.00
SCSRL Roberto Luongo 6.00 15.00
SCSRN Rick Nash 12.00 30.00
SCSRS Ryan Smyth 8.00 20.00
SCSTB Todd Bertuzzi 8.00 20.00
SCSTR Tuomo Ruutu 5.00 12.00
SFSAF Alexander Frolov 4.00 10.00
SFSAH Ales Hemsky 3.00 8.00
SFSAM Antti Miettinen 3.00 8.00
SFSAR Andrew Raycroft 4.00 10.00
SFSBB Brad Boyes 3.00 8.00
SFSBG Boyd Gordon 3.00 8.00
SFSBM Brenden Morrow 4.00 10.00
SFSCK Chuck Kobasew 3.00 8.00
SFSDA David Aebischer 4.00 10.00
SFSDB Dustin Brown 3.00 8.00
SFSFS Fredrik Sjostrom 3.00 8.00
SFSJB Jay Bouwmeester 3.00 8.00
SFSJL Joffrey Lupul 5.00 12.00
SFSJP Joni Pitkanen 3.00 8.00
SFSKL Kari Lehtonen 5.00 12.00
SFSLN Ladislav Nagy 3.00 8.00
SFSMA Maxim Afinogenov 3.00 8.00
SFSMC Mike Cammalleri 3.00 8.00
SFSMF Marc-Andre Fleury 12.00 30.00
SFSMH Martin Havlat 4.00 10.00
SFSMR Mike Ribeiro 3.00 8.00
SFSMS Matt Stajan 3.00 8.00
SFSNA Nik Antropov 3.00 8.00
SFSNH Nathan Horton 3.00 8.00
SFSNS Nathan Smith 3.00 8.00
SFSNZ Nikolai Zherdev 4.00 10.00
SFSPS Philippe Sauve 4.00 10.00
SFSRF Ruslan Fedotenko 3.00 8.00
SFSRK Ryan Kesler 10.00 25.00
SFSRM Ryan Miller 6.00 15.00
SFSSB Sean Bergenheim 3.00 8.00
SFSTC Ty Conklin 4.00 10.00
SFSTH Trent Hunter 3.00 8.00
SFSTM Travis Moen 3.00 8.00
SFSTP Tom Poti 3.00 8.00
SSSDH Dominik Hasek 25.00 60.00
SSSGL Guy Lafleur 20.00 50.00
SSSIK Ilya Kovalchuk 20.00 50.00
SSSJI Jarome Iginla 20.00 50.00
SSSJO Jose Theodore 12.50 30.00
SSSJT Joe Thornton 15.00 40.00
SSSMB Martin Brodeur 75.00 150.00
SSSMG Marian Gaborik 15.00 40.00
SSSRB Ray Bourque 30.00 80.00
SSSWG Wayne Gretzky 150.00 250.00

2006-07 Upper Deck Trilogy

This 160-card set was issued into the hobby in five-card packs, with an $19.99 SRP which came nine packs to a box. Cards numbered 1-100 feature veterans in team alphabetical order while cards 101-160 feature Rookie Cards also in team alphabetical order. The Rookie Cards were issued to a stated print run of 999 serial numbered sets.
ROOKIE STATED PRINT RUN 999
1 Chris Pronger .60 1.50
2 Teemu Selanne 1.50 4.00
3 Jean-Sebastien Giguere .75 2.00
4 Ilya Kovalchuk .75 2.00
5 Kari Lehtonen .60 1.50
6 Marian Hossa .60 1.50
7 Hannu Toivonen .60 1.50
8 Zdeno Chara .75 2.00
9 Patrice Bergeron 1.00 2.50
10 Brad Boyes .50 1.25
11 Ryan Miller .75 2.00
12 Chris Drury .60 1.50
13 Daniel Briere .75 2.00
14 Miikka Kiprusoff .60 1.50
15 Jarome Iginla .75 2.00
16 Alex Tanguay .50 1.25
17 Dion Phaneuf .75 2.00
18 Eric Staal 1.00 2.50
19 Cam Ward .75 2.00
20 Rod Brind'Amour .75 2.00
21 Martin Havlat .50 1.25
22 Nikolai Khabibulin .75 2.00
23 Tuomo Ruutu .75 2.00
24 Joe Sakic 1.25 3.00
25 Jose Theodore .75 2.00
26 Milan Hejduk .60 1.50
27 Marek Svatos .50 1.25
28 Pascal Leclaire .60 1.50
29 Rick Nash .75 2.00
30 Fredrik Modin .50 1.25
31 Sergei Fedorov 1.25 3.00
32 Mike Modano 1.25 3.00
33 Marty Turco .75 2.00
34 Eric Lindros 1.25 3.00
35 Pavel Datsyuk 1.00 2.50
36 Henrik Zetterberg 1.00 2.50
37 Nicklas Lidstrom .75 2.00
38 Dominik Hasek 1.00 2.50
39 Ryan Smyth .60 1.50
40 Joffrey Lupul .60 1.50
41 Ales Hemsky .60 1.50
42 Dwayne Roloson .60 1.50
43 Todd Bertuzzi .75 2.00
44 Olli Jokinen .75 2.00
45 Ed Belfour .75 2.00
46 Rob Blake .75 2.00
47 Alexander Frolov .50 1.25
48 Marian Gaborik 1.00 2.50
49 Pavol Demitra 1.00 2.50
50 Manny Fernandez .60 1.50
51 Saku Koivu .75 2.00
52 Cristobal Huet .60 1.50
53 Michael Ryder .50 1.25
54 Alex Kovalev .60 1.50
55 Tomas Vokoun .60 1.50
56 Paul Kariya 1.00 2.50
57 Jason Arnott .60 1.50
58 Martin Brodeur 1.50 4.00
59 Patrik Elias .75 2.00
60 Brian Gionta .60 1.50
61 Miroslav Satan .60 1.50
62 Rick DiPietro .60 1.50
63 Alexei Yashin .60 1.50
64 Jaromir Jagr 2.00 5.00
65 Henrik Lundqvist 1.50 4.00
66 Brendan Shanahan 1.00 2.50
67 Daniel Alfredsson .75 2.00
68 Jason Spezza .75 2.00
69 Dany Heatley .75 2.00
70 Martin Gerber .60 1.50
71 Peter Forsberg 1.00 2.50
72 Jeff Carter .75 2.00
73 Simon Gagne .75 2.00
74 Mike Richards .75 2.00
75 Shane Doan .60 1.50
76 Curtis Joseph .75 2.00
77 Jeremy Roenick .75 2.00
78 Mark Recchi 1.00 2.50
79 Sidney Crosby 3.00 8.00
80 Marc-Andre Fleury 1.25 3.00
81 Joe Thornton 1.00 2.50
82 Vesa Toskala .60 1.50
83 Patrick Marleau .75 2.00
84 Jonathan Cheechoo .75 2.00
85 Keith Tkachuk .75 2.00
86 Doug Weight .75 2.00
87 Manny Legace .60 1.50
88 Brad Richards .75 2.00
89 Vincent Lecavalier .60 1.50
90 Martin St. Louis .75 2.00
91 Mats Sundin .75 2.00
92 Andrew Raycroft .60 1.50
93 Michael Peca .60 1.50
94 Alexander Steen .75 2.00
95 Roberto Luongo 1.25 3.00
96 Markus Naslund .60 1.50
97 Henrik Sedin .75 2.00
98 Daniel Sedin .75 2.00
99 Alexander Ovechkin 3.00 8.00
100 Olaf Kolzig .75 2.00
101 Shane O'Brien RC 2.00 5.00
102 Ryan Shannon RC 2.00 5.00
103 Yan Stastny RC 2.00 5.00
104 Mark Stuart RC 2.00 5.00
105 Phil Kessel RC 5.00 12.00
106 Carsen Germyn RC 2.00 5.00
107 Dustin Byfuglien RC 5.00 12.00
108 Paul Stastny RC 10.00 25.00
109 Filip Novak RC 2.00 5.00
110 Fredrik Norrena RC 2.00 5.00
111 Loui Eriksson RC 3.00 8.00
112 Tomas Kopecky RC 2.50 6.00
113 M-A Pouliot RC 2.00 5.00
114 Patrick Thoresen RC 2.00 5.00
115 Ladislav Smid RC 2.00 5.00
116 K. Pushkarev RC 2.50 6.00
117 Patrick O'Sullivan RC 3.00 8.00
118 Anze Kopitar RC 8.00 20.00
119 Erik Reitz RC 2.00 5.00
120 Miroslav Kopriva RC 2.00 5.00
121 Niklas Backstrom RC 4.00 10.00
122 Dan Jancevski RC 2.00 5.00
123 G. Latendresse RC 3.00 8.00
124 Shea Weber RC 5.00 12.00
125 Mikko Lehtonen RC 2.50 6.00
126 Frank Doyle RC 2.50 6.00
127 John Oduya RC 3.00 8.00
128 Travis Zajac RC 4.00 10.00
129 Rob Collins RC 2.00 5.00
130 Steve Regier RC 2.00 5.00
131 Matt Koalska RC 2.00 5.00
132 Ryan Caldwell RC 2.00 5.00
133 Masi Marjamaki RC 2.00 5.00
134 Keith Yandle RC 4.00 10.00
135 Enver Lisin RC 2.00 5.00
136 Jarkko Immonen RC 2.00 5.00
137 David Liffiton RC 2.00 5.00
138 Nigel Dawes RC 2.00 5.00
139 Alexei Kaigorodov RC 2.00 5.00
140 Ryan Potulny RC 2.00 5.00
141 David Printz RC 2.00 5.00
142 Bill Thomas RC 2.00 5.00
143 Joel Perrault RC 2.00 5.00
144 Patrick Fischer RC 2.00 5.00
145 Noah Welch RC 2.00 5.00
146 Michel Ouellet RC 2.50 6.00
147 Jordan Staal RC 8.00 20.00
148 Kristopher Letang RC 10.00 25.00
149 Evgeni Malkin RC 20.00 50.00
150 Matt Carle RC 2.00 5.00
151 M-E Vlasic RC 2.00 5.00
152 D.J. King RC 2.00 5.00
153 Roman Polak RC 2.50 6.00
154 Ben Ondrus RC 2.00 5.00
155 Brendan Bell RC 2.00 5.00
156 Ian White RC 2.50 6.00
157 Jeremy Williams RC 2.00 5.00
158 Luc Bourdon RC 3.00 8.00
159 Eric Fehr RC 3.00 8.00
160 Jonas Johansson RC 2.00 5.00

2006-07 Upper Deck Trilogy Combo Clearcut Autographs

DOUBLE AU PRINT RUN 100 #'d SETS
TRIPLE AU PRINT RUN 25 SER.#'d SETS
C2AR Smyth/Hemsky 12.00 30.00
C2BB Boyes/Bergeron 12.00 30.00
C2CK Calder/Khabibulin 12.00 30.00
C2EE P.Espo/T.Espo 30.00 80.00
C2GP Gomez/Parise EXCH 15.00 40.00
C2HS Hejduk/Svatos 12.00 30.00
C2KK S.Koivu/M.Koivu 15.00 40.00
C2KN Kiprusoff/Niittymaki 20.00 50.00
C2LJ Luongo/Jokin EXCH 10.00 25.00
C2LS Lecav/St. Lou EXCH 20.00 50.00
C2LZ Legace/Zetter EXCH 25.00 50.00
C2MM Lanny/Mullen 12.00 30.00
C2MV Miller/Vanek 15.00 40.00
C2NM Naslund/Morrison 12.00 30.00
C2PG Perry/Getzlaf 20.00 50.00
C2PM Marleau/Michalek 15.00 40.00
C2RC Redden/Chara 15.00 40.00
C2SH Smith/Hextall EXCH 25.00 60.00
C2VS Vokoun/Sully EXCH 20.00 50.00
C3BLS Beliv/Lat/Shutt EXCH 90.00 150.00
C3BPS Bossy/Potvin/Smith 50.00 100.00
C3CGS Cole/Gerb/Staal EXCH 25.00 60.00
C3CLP Clarke/Leach/Parent
C3FCB Frolov/Cam/Brown 50.00 100.00
C3FEC Fuhr/Espo/Cheev EXCH 60.00 125.00
C3HTT Hejd/Theo/Tang EXCH 60.00 120.00
C3IKP Iggy/Kipper/Dion 40.00 100.00
C3LDZ Leg/Draper/Zett EXCH 100.00 200.00
C3MSS McDonald/Sittler/Salming 40.00 80.00
C3MTC Marleau/Thorn/Cheech
C3MTM Mo/Turco/Morrow 40.00 80.00
C3NOB Cam/Terry/Ray EXCH 75.00 150.00
C3NZB Nash/Zherdev/Brule
C3PGC Primeau/Gagne/Carter 30.00 60.00
C3RBH Roy/Brod/Hasek 125.00 250.00
C3RHH Red/Hav/Heat 40.00 80.00

2006-07 Upper Deck Trilogy Frozen In Time

COMPLETE SET (20) 150.00 250.00
STATED PRINT RUN 999 SER.#'d SETS
FT1 Alexander Ovechkin 15.00 40.00
FT2 Bobby Clarke 4.00 10.00
FT3 Brendan Shanahan 5.00 12.00
FT4 Cam Neely 4.00 10.00
FT5 Dominik Hasek 5.00 12.00
FT6 Gordie Howe 8.00 20.00
FT7 Guy Lafleur 5.00 12.00
FT8 Jaromir Jagr 10.00 25.00
FT9 Jean Beliveau 4.00 10.00
FT10 Joe Sakic 6.00 15.00
FT11 Martin Brodeur 8.00 20.00
FT12 Mats Sundin 4.00 10.00
FT13 Mike Bossy 4.00 10.00
FT14 Mike Modano 6.00 15.00
FT15 Patrick Roy 8.00 20.00
FT16 Ray Bourque 6.00 15.00
FT17 Sidney Crosby 15.00 40.00
FT18 Steve Yzerman 10.00 25.00
FT19 Tony Esposito 4.00 10.00
FT20 Wayne Gretzky 15.00 40.00

2006-07 Upper Deck Trilogy Honorary Scripted Swatches

STATED PRINT RUN 25 SER.#'d SETS
HSAH Ales Hemsky 15.00 40.00
HSSAF Alexander Frolov 12.00 30.00
HSSAO Alexander Ovechkin 50.00 100.00
HSSAR Andrew Raycroft 15.00 40.00
HSSAT Alex Tanguay 12.00 30.00
HSSBB Brad Boyes 12.00 30.00
HSSBG Brian Gionta 15.00 40.00
HSSBL Rob Blake 20.00 50.00
HSSBM Brenden Morrow 15.00 40.00
HSSBO Borje Salming 20.00 50.00
HSSBR Bill Ranford 20.00 50.00
HSSBS Billy Smith 20.00 50.00
HSSCA Jeff Carter 20.00 50.00
HSSCD Chris Drury 15.00 40.00
HSSCK Chuck Kobasew 12.00 30.00
HSSCN Cam Neely 20.00 50.00
HSSCO Corey Perry 20.00 50.00
HSSDA David Aebischer 15.00 40.00
HSSDB Dustin Brown 20.00 50.00
HSSDC Dan Cloutier 15.00 40.00
HSSDG Doug Gilmour 25.00 60.00
HSSDH Dany Heatley 20.00 50.00
HSSDR Dwayne Roloson 15.00 40.00
HSSDS Darryl Sittler 20.00 50.00
HSSDW Doug Weight 20.00 50.00
HSSEB Ed Belfour 20.00 50.00
HSSES Eric Staal 25.00 60.00
HSSGA Simon Gagne 20.00 50.00
HSSGH Gordie Howe 75.00 150.00
HSSGL Guy Lafleur 25.00 60.00
HSSHA Dominik Hasek 30.00 80.00
HSSHE Milan Hejduk 12.00 30.00
HSSHV Martin Havlat 12.00 30.00
HSSHZ Henrik Zetterberg 25.00 60.00
HSSIK Ilya Kovalchuk 20.00 50.00
HSSJA Jarret Stoll 15.00 40.00
HSSJB Jay Bouwmeester 20.00 50.00
HSSJI Jarome Iginla 12.00 30.00
HSSJL Joffrey Lupul 15.00 40.00
HSSJP Joni Pitkanen 12.00 30.00
HSSJR Jeremy Roenick 25.00 60.00
HSSJS Jason Spezza 20.00 50.00
HSSJT Joe Thornton 30.00 80.00
HSSJW Justin Williams 15.00 40.00
HSSKC Kyle Calder 12.00 30.00
HSSKD Kris Draper 12.00 30.00
HSSKL Kari Lehtonen 15.00 40.00
HSSKP Keith Primeau 20.00 50.00
HSSLE Mario Lemieux 75.00 200.00
HSSLM Lanny McDonald 20.00 50.00
HSSMB Martin Brodeur 60.00 125.00
HSSMC Mike Cammalleri 12.00 30.00
HSSMG Martin Gerber 15.00 40.00
HSSMH Marian Hossa 15.00 40.00
HSSMK Miikka Kiprusoff 15.00 40.00
HSSML Manny Legace 15.00 40.00
HSSMN Markus Naslund 15.00 40.00
HSSMP Michael Peca 15.00 40.00
HSSMR Michael Ryder 12.00 30.00
HSSMS Marek Svatos 12.00 30.00
HSSMT Marty Turco 20.00 50.00
HSSNH Nathan Horton 20.00 50.00
HSSNK Nikolai Khabibulin 20.00 50.00
HSSNL Nicklas Lidstrom 20.00 50.00
HSSON Owen Nolan 15.00 40.00
HSSPB Patrice Bergeron 25.00 60.00
HSSPE Patrik Elias 20.00 50.00
HSSPI Pierre-Marc Bouchard 20.00 50.00
HSSPM Patrick Marleau 20.00 50.00
HSSPR Patrick Roy 50.00 120.00
HSSRB Ray Bourque 40.00 100.00
HSSRE Robert Esche 15.00 40.00
HSSRL Roberto Luongo 50.00 100.00
HSSRM Ryan Miller 20.00 50.00
HSSRN Rick Nash 20.00 50.00
HSSRS Ryan Smyth 20.00 50.00
HSSSA Miroslav Satan 15.00 40.00
HSSSC Sidney Crosby 150.00 300.00
HSSSD Shane Doan 15.00 40.00
HSSSG Scott Gomez 15.00 40.00
HSSSK Saku Koivu 20.00 50.00
HSSSN Scott Niedermayer 20.00 50.00
HSSSS Sergei Samsonov 15.00 40.00
HSSST Martin St. Louis 20.00 50.00
HSSSU Steve Sullivan 12.00 30.00
HSSTB Todd Bertuzzi 20.00 50.00
HSSTV Tomas Vokoun 15.00 40.00
HSSVL Vincent Lecavalier 50.00 100.00
HSSWG Wayne Gretzky 150.00 300.00
HSSWI Doug Wilson 15.00 40.00

2006-07 Upper Deck Trilogy Honorary Swatches

STATED ODDS 1:3
HSAH Ales Hemsky 4.00 10.00
HSAO Alexander Ovechkin SP 10.00 25.00
HSBM Brenden Morrow 4.00 10.00
HSBO Ray Bourque 8.00 20.00
HSBR Bill Ranford 5.00 12.00
HSBS Borje Salming 5.00 12.00
HSCD Chris Drury 4.00 10.00
HSCN Cam Neely 5.00 12.00
HSCW Cam Ward 5.00 12.00
HSDG Doug Gilmour 6.00 15.00
HSDH Dany Heatley 5.00 12.00
HSDS Darryl Sittler 5.00 12.00
HSEB Ed Belfour 5.00 12.00
HSES Eric Staal 6.00 15.00
HSGH Gordie Howe SP 12.00 30.00
HSGL Guy Lafleur SP 6.00 15.00
HSGO Scott Gomez 4.00 10.00
HSHA Dominik Hasek SP 6.00 15.00
HSHO Marian Hossa 4.00 10.00
HSHZ Henrik Zetterberg 6.00 15.00
HSIK Ilya Kovalchuk 5.00 12.00
HSIM Jarkko Immonen 3.00 8.00
HSIW Ian White 4.00 10.00
HSJG Jean-Sebastien Giguere 5.00 12.00
HSJI Jarome Iginla 5.00 12.00
HSJS Jason Spezza 5.00 12.00
HSJT Joe Thornton 6.00 15.00
HSJW Justin Williams 4.00 10.00
HSKD Kris Draper 3.00 8.00
HSKL Kari Lehtonen SP 4.00 10.00
HSKP Keith Primeau 5.00 12.00
HSLE Manny Legace 4.00 10.00
HSLM Lanny McDonald 5.00 12.00
HSMA Marc-Antoine Pouliot 3.00 8.00
HSMB Martin Brodeur SP 10.00 25.00
HSMH Milan Hejduk 4.00 10.00
HSMK Miikka Kiprusoff 4.00 10.00
HSML Mario Lemieux SP 12.00 30.00
HSMN Markus Naslund 4.00 10.00
HSMR Michael Ryder 3.00 8.00
HSMS Marek Svatos 3.00 8.00
HSMT Marty Turco 5.00 12.00
HSOK Olaf Kolzig 5.00 12.00
HSPB Patrice Bergeron 6.00 15.00
HSPR Patrick Roy 10.00 30.00
HSRB Rob Blake 5.00 12.00
HSRL Roberto Luongo 8.00 20.00
HSRM Ryan Miller 5.00 12.00
HSRN Rick Nash 5.00 12.00
HSRS Ryan Smyth 4.00 10.00
HSSA Miroslav Satan 4.00 10.00
HSSC Sidney Crosby SP 20.00 50.00
HSSG Simon Gagne 5.00 12.00
HSSK Saku Koivu 5.00 12.00
HSSM Billy Smith 5.00 12.00
HSSN Scott Niedermayer 5.00 12.00
HSST Martin St. Louis 5.00 12.00
HSVL Vincent Lecavalier 4.00 10.00
HSWG Wayne Gretzky SP 40.00 80.00

2006-07 Upper Deck Trilogy Ice Scripts

STATED ODDS 1:9
ISAH Ales Hemsky 6.00 15.00
ISAK Andrei Kostitsyn 5.00 12.00
ISAL Andrew Ladd 8.00 20.00
ISAN Antero Niittymaki 6.00 15.00
ISAO Alexander Ovechkin 40.00 100.00
ISBB Brad Boyes 5.00 12.00
ISBH Bobby Hull EXCH 60.00 120.00
ISBR Dustin Brown 8.00 20.00
ISCD Chris Drury 6.00 15.00
ISCK Chuck Kobasew 5.00 12.00
ISCP Chris Pronger 8.00 20.00
ISDA David Aebischer 8.00 20.00
ISDB Daniel Briere 12.00 30.00
ISDC Don Cherry 20.00 50.00
ISDH Dominik Hasek 30.00 60.00
ISDR Dwayne Roloson 6.00 15.00
ISGF Grant Fuhr 25.00 50.00
ISGH Gordie Howe 50.00 100.00
ISGL Guy Lafleur SP 50.00 100.00
ISHE Dany Heatley 15.00 40.00
ISJB Johnny Bucyk 12.00 30.00
ISJC Jonathan Cheechoo 8.00 20.00
ISJI Jarome Iginla 30.00 60.00
ISJL Joffrey Lupul 6.00 15.00
ISJO Joe Thornton 20.00 40.00
ISJT Jose Theodore 8.00 20.00
ISKD Kris Draper 5.00 12.00
ISMA Martin Brodeur SP 75.00 150.00
ISMB Mike Bossy 12.00 30.00
ISMC Mike Cammalleri 5.00 12.00
ISMF Marc-Andre Fleury 20.00 40.00
ISMG Marian Gaborik 10.00 25.00
ISMH Milan Hejduk 6.00 15.00
ISMI Miikka Kiprusoff 12.00 30.00
ISMK Mikko Koivu 6.00 15.00
ISMM Milan Michalek 5.00 12.00
ISMN Markus Naslund 6.00 15.00
ISMR Mike Ribeiro 6.00 15.00
ISMS Marek Svatos 5.00 12.00
ISOJ Olli Jokinen 8.00 20.00
ISPB Patrice Bergeron 12.00 30.00
ISPE Phil Esposito 20.00 50.00
ISPR Patrick Roy EXCH 60.00 150.00
ISRB Ray Bourque 25.00 60.00
ISRM Ryan Malone 5.00 12.00
ISRY Ryan Miller 12.00 30.00
ISSB Scotty Bowman SP 50.00 100.00
ISSC Sidney Crosby SP 100.00 200.00
ISSH Shawn Horcoff 5.00 12.00
ISSK Saku Koivu 20.00 50.00
ISTV Thomas Vanek 10.00 25.00
ISVL Vincent Lecavalier 25.00 60.00
ISVO Tomas Vokoun 6.00 15.00
ISWG Wayne Gretzky SP 125.00 250.00

2006-07 Upper Deck Trilogy Legendary Scripts

PRINT RUN 50 UNLESS OTHERWISE NOTED
LSBC Bobby Clarke 25.00 60.00
LSBR Richard Brodeur 20.00 50.00
LSBS Billy Smith 15.00 40.00
LSCN Cam Neely 25.00 60.00
LSDC Don Cherry 25.00 60.00
LSDS Denis Savard 10.00 25.00
LSGA Glenn Anderson 6.00 15.00
LSGC Gerry Cheevers 15.00 40.00
LSGF Grant Fuhr 15.00 40.00
LSGH Gordie Howe/25 75.00 150.00
LSGL Guy Lafleur/25 30.00 80.00
LSJB Jean Beliveau 30.00 80.00
LSJM Joe Mullen 6.00 15.00
LSMB Mike Bossy 20.00 50.00
LSML Mario Lemieux/25 75.00 200.00
LSPE Phil Esposito 20.00 50.00
LSRB Ray Bourque/25 40.00 80.00
LSRH Ron Hextall 25.00 60.00
LSRL Reggie Leach 20.00 50.00
LSSB Scotty Bowman 25.00 50.00
LSTE Tony Esposito 15.00 40.00
LSTL Ted Lindsay 10.00 25.00
LSWG Wayne Gretzky/25 175.00 350.00

2006-07 Upper Deck Trilogy Scripts

S1AO Alexander Ovechkin/1
S1BC Bobby Clarke/15
S1BR Martin Brodeur/13
S1DH Dany Heatley/4
S1DP Dion Phaneuf/1
S1GC Gerry Cheevers/12
S1GH Gordie Howe/26 75.00 150.00
S1GL Guy Lafleur/17 100.00 200.00
S1HA Dominik Hasek/14
S1IK Ilya Kovalchuk/4
S1JB Jean Beliveau/19
S1KL Kari Lehtonen/2
S1MB Mike Bossy/10
S1MF Marc-Andre Fleury/2
S1MG Marian Gaborik/5
S1ML Mario Lemieux/17 100.00 200.00
S1PB Patrice Bergeron/2
S1PR Patrick Roy/19 100.00 200.00
S1RB Ray Bourque/23 40.00 80.00
S1RL Roberto Luongo/6
S1RN Rick Nash/3
S1SC Sidney Crosby/1
S1VL Vincent Lecavalier/7
S1WG Wayne Gretzky/20 200.00 400.00
S2CH Cristobal Huet/7
S2CN Cam Neely/3
S2DH Dominik Hasek/6
S2DS Darryl Sittler/10
S2ES Eric Staal/28 20.00 50.00
S2GH Gordie Howe/6
S2GL Guy Lafleur/3
S2HZ Henrik Zetterberg/39 20.00 50.00
S2IK Ilya Kovalchuk/27 20.00 50.00
S2JB Jean Beliveau/10
S2JC Jonathan Cheechoo/5
S2JI Jarome Iginla/2
S2JT Jose Theodore/1
S2MB Martin Brodeur/5
S2MK Miikka Kiprusoff/10
S2ML Mario Lemieux/6
S2MS Marek Svatos/9
S2PE Phil Esposito/5
S2PM Patrick Marleau/7
S2PR Patrick Roy/3
S2RB Ray Bourque/5
S2SC Sidney Crosby/3
S2TH Joe Thornton/1
S2WG Wayne Gretzky/9
S3AR Andrew Raycroft/25 20.00 40.00
S3DH Dany Heatley/25 25.00 60.00
S3ES Eric Staal/25 20.00 50.00
S3HA Dominik Hasek/25 40.00 80.00
S3HZ Henrik Zetterberg/25 30.00 60.00
S3IK Ilya Kovalchuk/25 25.00 60.00
S3JC Jonathan Cheechoo/25 20.00 50.00
S3JI Jarome Iginla/25 15.00 40.00
S3JR Jeremy Roenick/25 25.00 60.00
S3JT Joe Thornton/25 25.00 60.00
S3MB Martin Brodeur/25 50.00 100.00
S3MG Marian Gaborik/25 20.00 50.00
S3MK Miikka Kiprusoff/25 25.00 50.00
S3MN Markus Naslund/25 25.00 50.00
S3MT Marty Turco/25
S3NL Nicklas Lidstrom/25 25.00 60.00
S3PB Patrice Bergeron/25 15.00 40.00
S3RB Rob Blake/25 20.00 50.00
S3RL Roberto Luongo/25 25.00 60.00
S3RN Rick Nash/25 20.00 50.00
S3SC Sidney Crosby/25 250.00 400.00
S3SK Saku Koivu/25 20.00 50.00
S3TH Jose Theodore/25 20.00 40.00
S3TV Tomas Vokoun/25 20.00 50.00
S3VL Vincent Lecavalier/25 40.00 80.00
TSAA Adrian Aucoin 3.00 8.00
TSAF Alexander Frolov 5.00 12.00
TSAH Ales Hemsky 5.00 12.00
TSAL Andrew Ladd 3.00 8.00
TSAN Antero Niittymaki 6.00 15.00
TSAP Alexandre Picard 6.00 15.00
TSBB Brad Boyes 8.00 20.00
TSBR Dustin Brown 12.00 30.00
TSBS Billy Smith SP 15.00 40.00
TSCD Chris Drury 10.00 25.00
TSCK Chuck Kobasew 6.00 15.00
TSCN Cam Neely SP 15.00 40.00
TSDA David Aebischer 12.00 30.00
TSDB Daniel Briere SP 30.00 80.00
TSDC Dan Cloutier 8.00 20.00
TSDL David Leneveu 8.00 20.00
TSDO Doug Wilson 6.00 15.00
TSDP Dion Phaneuf SP 25.00 60.00
TSDR Danny Richmond 3.00 8.00
TSDS Derek Sanderson 8.00 20.00
TSDT Dave Taylor 4.00 10.00
TSDW Doug Weight 10.00 25.00
TSED Eric Daze 3.00 8.00
TSGH Gordie Howe SP 30.00 60.00
TSHO Shawn Horcoff 8.00 20.00
TSHZ Henrik Zetterberg 12.00 30.00
TSJB Johnny Bucyk 6.00 15.00
TSJC Jonathan Cheechoo 12.00 30.00
TSJH Jeff Halpern 6.00 15.00
TSJI Jarome Iginla SP 20.00 50.00
TSJL Jason Labarbera 4.00 10.00
TSJM Joe Mullen SP 8.00 20.00
TSJP Joni Pitkanen 8.00 20.00
TSJT Jose Theodore SP 15.00 40.00
TSKC Kyle Calder 6.00 15.00
TSKD Kris Draper 8.00 20.00
TSKL Kari Lehtonen SP 20.00 50.00
TSKM Kirk Muller SP 8.00 20.00
TSKU Chris Kunitz 8.00 20.00
TSLI John-Michael Liles 6.00 15.00
TSLN Ladislav Nagy 6.00 15.00
TSLS Lee Stempniak 6.00 15.00
TSLU Joffrey Lupul SP 15.00 40.00
TSMB Martin Biron 8.00 20.00
TSMC Mike Cammalleri 10.00 25.00
TSMF Marc-Andre Fleury SP 25.00 50.00
TSMG Marian Gaborik SP 25.00 60.00
TSMH Marcel Hossa 6.00 15.00
TSMI Ryan Miller 15.00 40.00
TSMK Miikka Kiprusoff SP
TSML Manny Legace 8.00 20.00
TSMM Milan Michalek 8.00 20.00
TSMN Markus Naslund SP 15.00 40.00
TSMP Mark Parrish 6.00 15.00
TSMR Mike Ribeiro 8.00 20.00
TSMS Marc Savard 8.00 20.00
TSMT Mikael Tellqvist 10.00 25.00
TSNA Nikolai Antropov 8.00 20.00
TSPM Patrick Marleau SP 30.00 80.00
TSPO Denis Potvin SP 30.00 80.00
TSPS Philippe Sauve 4.00 10.00
TSRB Richard Brodeur SP 12.00 30.00
TSRF Ruslan Fedotenko 6.00 15.00
TSRG Ryan Getzlaf 15.00 40.00
TSRH Ron Hextall 10.00 25.00
TSRL Reggie Leach SP 15.00 40.00
TSRM Ryan Malone 12.00 30.00
TSRV Rogie Vachon 15.00 40.00
TSRY Michael Ryder 6.00 15.00
TSSA Denis Savard 5.00 12.00
TSSC Sidney Crosby SP 125.00 250.00
TSSG Scott Gomez 8.00 20.00
TSSH Scott Hartnell 10.00 25.00
TSSS Steve Shutt 15.00 40.00
TSSW Stephen Weiss 6.00 15.00
TSTA Jeff Tambellini 6.00 15.00
TSTC Ty Conklin 8.00 20.00
TSTE Tony Esposito SP
TSTL Ted Lindsay SP 15.00 40.00
TSTV Tomas Vokoun 10.00 25.00
TSVA Rick Vaive 8.00 20.00
TSWC Wayne Cashman 10.00 25.00
TSWG Wayne Gretzky SP 125.00 225.00
TSWI Dave Williams 8.00 20.
TSWR Wade Redden 8.00 20.
TSZC Zdeno Chara 12.00 30.

2007-08 Upper Deck Trilogy

This 180-card set was released in January, 2008. Th set was issued into the hobby in five-card packs, wit $19.99 SRP, which came nine packs to a box and 1(boxes to a case. Cards numbered 1-100 feature veterans while cards numbered 101-120 are a Frozen in Time subset which was issued to a stated print ru of 799 serial numbered sets and cards 121-180 are Rookie Cards which were issued to a stated print ru 999 serial numbered sets.
COMP.SET w/o SPs (100) 20.00 50.
FIT PRINT RUN 799 SER.#'d SETS
ROOKIE PRINT RUN 999 SER.#'d SETS
1 Ryan Getzlaf 1.00 2.
2 Jean-Sebastien Giguere .60 1.
3 Chris Pronger .50 1.
4 Teemu Selanne 1.25 3.
5 Ilya Kovalchuk .60 1.
6 Kari Lehtonen .50 1.
7 Marian Hossa .50 1.
8 Phil Kessel .75 2.
9 Manny Fernandez .50 1.
10 Patrice Bergeron .75 2.
11 Ryan Miller .60 1.
12 Thomas Vanek .75 2.
13 Jason Pominville .60 1.
14 Drew Stafford .50 1.
15 Miikka Kiprusoff .50 1.
16 Dion Phaneuf .60 1.
17 Jarome Iginla .60 1.
18 Alex Tanguay .40 1.
19 Cam Ward .60 1.
20 Eric Staal .75 2.
21 Justin Williams .50 1.
22 Nikolai Khabibulin .60 1.
23 Martin Havlat .60 1.
24 Tuomo Ruutu .60 1.
25 Joe Sakic 1.00 2.
26 Ryan Smyth .50 1.
27 Paul Stastny .60 1.
28 Milan Hejduk .50 1.
29 Rick Nash .60 1.
30 David Vyborny .40 1.
31 Sergei Fedorov 1.00 2.
32 Mike Modano 1.00 2.
33 Marty Turco .60 1.
34 Mike Ribeiro .50 1.
35 Henrik Zetterberg .75 2.
36 Kris Draper .40 1.
37 Pavel Datsyuk .75 2.
38 Nicklas Lidstrom .60 1.
39 Dwayne Roloson .50 1.
40 Joni Pitkanen .40 1.
41 Shawn Horcoff .40 1.
42 Ales Hemsky .50 1.
43 Tomas Vokoun .50 1.
44 Olli Jokinen .50 1.
45 Nathan Horton .60 1.
46 Alexander Frolov .40 1.
47 Anze Kopitar 1.00 2.
48 Rob Blake .60 1.
49 Marian Gaborik .75 2.
50 Niklas Backstrom .75 1.
51 Mikko Koivu .60 1.
52 Saku Koivu .60 1.
53 Cristobal Huet .50 1.
54 Michael Ryder .40 1.
55 Guillaume Latendresse .50 1.
56 Alexander Radulov .60 1.
57 Chris Mason .50 1.
58 Steve Sullivan .40 1.
59 Martin Brodeur 1.25 3.
60 Zach Parise .75 2.
61 Patrik Elias .60 1.
62 Rick DiPietro .60 1.
63 Miroslav Satan .50 1.
64 Trent Hunter .40 1.
65 Jaromir Jagr 1.50 4.
66 Chris Drury .50 1.
67 Henrik Lundqvist .75 2.
68 Dany Heatley .60 1.
69 Ray Emery .50 1.
70 Daniel Alfredsson .60 1.
71 Jason Spezza .60 1.
72 Daniel Briere .60 1.
73 Simon Gagne .60 1.
74 Jeff Carter .60 1.
75 Shane Doan .50 1.
76 Ed Jovanovski .50 1.
77 Sidney Crosby 2.50 6.
78 Evgeni Malkin 2.00 5.
79 Marc-Andre Fleury 1.00 2.
80 Jordan Staal .60 1.
81 Joe Thornton .75 2.
82 Patrick Marleau .60 1.
83 Jonathan Cheechoo .60 1.
84 Paul Kariya .75 2.
85 Doug Weight .60 1.
86 Keith Tkachuk .60 1.
87 Martin St. Louis .60 1.
88 Vincent Lecavalier .50 1.
89 Brad Richards .60 1.
90 Mats Sundin .60 1.
91 Darcy Tucker .50 1.
92 Vesa Toskala .50 1.
93 Jason Blake .40 1.
94 Henrik Sedin .60 1.
95 Daniel Sedin .60 1.
96 Roberto Luongo .75 2.
97 Markus Naslund .60 1.
98 Alexander Semin .60 1.
99 Olaf Kolzig .60 1.
100 Alexander Ovechkin 2.50 6.
101 Alex Ovechkin/799 10.00 25.
102 Bobby Hull/799 4.00 10.
103 Bobby Orr/799 8.00 20.
104 Evgeni Malkin/799 8.00 20
105 Gordie Howe/799 6.00 15
106 Jarome Iginla/799 2.50 6
107 Jaromir Jagr/799 6.00 15
108 Joe Sakic/799 4.00 10
109 Joe Thornton/799 3.00 8
110 Larry Robinson/799 2.50 6
111 Mario Lemieux/799 8.00 20
112 Martin Brodeur/799 5.00 12
113 Mats Sundin/799 2.50 6
114 Nicklas Lidstrom/799 2.50 6
115 Patrick Roy/799 6.00 15
116 Phil Esposito/799 4.00 10
117 Roberto Luongo/799 3.00 8
118 Sidney Crosby/799 10.00 25
119 Vincent Lecavalier/799 2.00 5
120 Wayne Gretzky/799 12.00 30
121 Bobby Ryan RC 6.00 15
122 Drew Miller RC 3.00 8
123 Ryan Carter RC 2.50 6
124 Jonas Hiller RC 5.00 12

25 Bryan Little RC 4.00 10.00
26 Brett Sterling RC 2.50 6.00
27 Tobias Enstrom RC 4.00 10.00
28 David Krejci RC 8.00 20.00
29 Milan Lucic RC 12.00 30.00
0 Jonathan Sigalet RC 2.50 6.00
1 Curtis McElhinney RC 4.00 10.00
2 Jonathan Toews RC 20.00 40.00
3 Patrick Kane RC 12.00 30.00
4 Magnus Johansson RC 2.50 6.00
5 Tyler Weiman RC 3.00 8.00
6 Jaroslav Hlinka RC 3.00 8.00
7 Kris Russell RC 3.00 8.00
8 Jared Boll RC 3.00 8.00
9 Marc Methot RC 2.50 6.00
0 Matt Niskanen RC 4.00 10.00
1 Tobias Stephan RC 3.00 8.00
2 Matt Ellis RC 3.00 8.00
3 Sam Gagner RC 5.00 12.00
4 Andrew Cogliano RC 4.00 10.00
5 Rob Schremp RC 3.00 8.00
6 Tom Gilbert RC 3.00 8.00
7 Cory Murphy RC 2.50 6.00
8 Jack Johnson RC 3.00 8.00
9 Jonathan Bernier RC 6.00 15.00
0 Lauri Tukonen RC 2.50 6.00
1 Brady Murray RC 2.50 6.00
2 Petr Kalus RC 2.50 6.00
3 James Sheppard RC 2.50 6.00
4 Carey Price RC 25.00 60.00
5 Kyle Chipchura RC 4.00 10.00
6 Jaroslav Halak RC 6.00 15.00
7 Ville Koistinen RC 2.50 6.00
8 Nicklas Bergfors RC 2.50 6.00
9 Andy Greene RC 3.00 8.00
0 Frans Nielsen RC 4.00 10.00
1 Marc Staal RC 4.00 10.00
2 Brandon Dubinsky RC 5.00 12.00
3 Ryan Callahan RC 5.00 12.00
4 Daniel Girardi RC 3.00 8.00
5 Nick Foligno RC 5.00 12.00
6 Brian Elliott RC 5.00 12.00
7 Ryan Parent RC 2.50 6.00
8 Denis Tolpeko RC 2.50 6.00
9 Peter Mueller RC 3.00 8.00
0 Martin Hanzal RC 3.00 8.00
1 Craig Weller RC 2.50 6.00
2 Daniel Winnik RC 3.00 8.00
3 Torrey Mitchell RC 3.00 8.00
4 Erik Johnson RC 4.00 10.00
5 Steve Wagner RC 2.50 6.00
6 Matt Smaby RC 2.50 6.00
7 Mike Lundin RC 2.50 6.00
8 Mason Raymond RC 4.00 10.00
9 Jannik Hansen RC 3.00 8.00
0 Nicklas Backstrom RC 8.00 20.00

2007-08 Upper Deck Trilogy Combo Clearcut Autographs

ATED PRINT RUN 25-100
2BH Brodeur/Huet/25 40.00 100.00
2GL Mario/Gretz/25 EXCH 350.00 600.00
2HE T.Esposito/B.Hull/25 30.00 80.00
2HL Lindsay/Howe/100 60.00 150.00
2HN Heatley/Nash/25
2IC Iginla/Cheechoo/25 20.00 50.00
2MS Miller/Stafford/100 12.00 30.00
2MT Modano/Turco/25 30.00 80.00
2OC Orr/Cherry/100 100.00 200.00
2OM Ovechkin/Malkin/25 100.00 200.00
2RF Roy/Fuhr/25 75.00 150.00
2RP Potvin/Robinson/100 12.00 30.00
2SD Stastny/Dionne/100 15.00 40.00
2SR Shutt/Ryder/100 12.00 30.00
2SS Staal/Staal/100 15.00 40.00
2TL Lecav/Thornton/25
2ZL Zettrbrg/Lidstrom/100 15.00 40.00

2007-08 Upper Deck Trilogy Honorary Scripted Swatches

ATED PRINT RUN 50 #'d SETS
AH Ales Hemsky 15.00 40.00
AM Al MacInnis 20.00 50.00
AO Alexander Ovechkin 80.00 200.00
AR Andrew Raycroft 15.00 40.00
BE Patrice Bergeron 25.00 60.00
BG Brian Gionta 15.00 40.00
CN Cam Neely 15.00 40.00
DH Dale Hawerchuk 25.00 60.00
GF Grant Fuhr 25.00 60.00
GH Gordie Howe/10
HA Dominik Hasek 25.00 60.00
HE Dany Heatley 20.00 50.00
HL Henrik Lundqvist 25.00 60.00
IK Ilya Kovalchuk 20.00 50.00
JC Jonathan Cheechoo 20.00 50.00
JI Jarome Iginla 20.00 50.00
JT Joe Thornton 25.00 60.00
KL Kari Lehtonen 15.00 40.00
MB Martin Brodeur 40.00 100.00
MF Marc-Andre Fleury 30.00 80.00
MG Marian Gaborik 25.00 60.00
ML Mario Lemieux/10
MR Michael Ryder 12.00 30.00
MT Marty Turco 20.00 50.00
NL Nicklas Lidstrom 20.00 50.00
PB Pierre-Marc Bouchard 20.00 50.00
PM Patrick Marleau 20.00 50.00
PR Patrick Roy/10
PS Peter Stastny 15.00 40.00
RB Ray Bourque 30.00 80.00
RM Ryan Miller 20.00 50.00
RN Rick Nash 20.00 50.00
SC Sidney Crosby 100.00 200.00
SG Simon Gagne 12.00 30.00
TV Tomas Vokoun 15.00 40.00
VL Vincent Lecavalier 15.00 40.00
WG Wayne Gretzky/10

2007-08 Upper Deck Trilogy Honorary Swatches

ATED ODDS 1:3
AH Ales Hemsky 4.00 10.00
AM Al MacInnis 5.00 12.00
AO Alexander Ovechkin 20.00 50.00
AR Andrew Raycroft 4.00 10.00
AY Alexei Yashin 4.00 10.00
BC Bobby Clarke 5.00 12.00
BF Bernie Federko 3.00 8.00
BG Bill Guerin 5.00 12.00
BL Rob Blake 5.00 12.00
BO Pierre-Marc Bouchard 5.00 12.00
BR Brad Richards 5.00 12.00
BS Billy Smith 5.00 12.00
CH Jonathan Cheechoo 5.00 12.00
CJ Curtis Joseph 5.00 12.00
CN Cam Neely 5.00 12.00
CP Chris Pronger 4.00 10.00
CW Cam Ward 5.00 12.00
DA Daniel Alfredsson 5.00 12.00
DB Daniel Briere 5.00 12.00
DC Dino Ciccarelli 5.00 12.00

HSDE Denis Savard 6.00 15.00
HSDG Doug Gilmour 6.00 15.00
HSDH Dale Hawerchuk 6.00 15.00
HSDS Darryl Sittler 4.00 10.00
HSDW Doug Weight 5.00 12.00
HSEB Ed Belfour 5.00 12.00
HSEL Eric Lindros 8.00 20.00
HSES Eric Staal 6.00 15.00
HSFL Marc-Andre Fleury 8.00 20.00
HSGF Grant Fuhr 5.00 12.00
HSGH Gordie Howe 12.00 30.00
HSGI Brian Gionta 4.00 10.00
HSGL Guy Lafleur 6.00 15.00
HSHA Dominik Hasek 6.00 15.00
HSHE Dany Heatley 5.00 12.00
HSHL Henrik Lundqvist 6.00 15.00
HSIK Ilya Kovalchuk 5.00 12.00
HSJC Jeff Carter 5.00 12.00
HSJG Jean-Sebastien Giguere 5.00 12.00
HSJI Jarome Iginla 5.00 12.00
HSJJ Jaromir Jagr 12.00 30.00
HSJO Joe Sakic 8.00 20.00
HSJS Jason Spezza 5.00 12.00
HSJT Joe Thornton 6.00 15.00
HSKL Kari Lehtonen 4.00 10.00
HSKO Mikko Koivu 4.00 10.00
HSKT Keith Tkachuk 5.00 12.00
HSLM Lanny McDonald 5.00 12.00
HSLR Larry Robinson 5.00 12.00
HSMB Martin Brodeur 10.00 25.00
HSMF Manny Fernandez 4.00 10.00
HSMG Marian Gaborik 6.00 15.00
HSMH Marian Hossa 4.00 10.00
HSMK Miikka Kiprusoff 4.00 10.00
HSML Mario Lemieux 15.00 40.00
HSMM Mike Modano 8.00 20.00
HSMN Markus Naslund 5.00 12.00
HSMR Mark Recchi 6.00 15.00
HSMS Marek Svatos 3.00 8.00
HSMT Marty Turco 5.00 12.00
HSNH Nathan Horton 5.00 12.00
HSNK Nikolai Khabibulin 5.00 12.00
HSNL Nicklas Lidstrom 5.00 12.00
HSOK Olaf Kolzig 5.00 12.00
HSPB Patrice Bergeron 6.00 15.00
HSPD Pavel Datsyuk 6.00 15.00
HSPE Patrik Elias 5.00 12.00
HSPF Peter Forsberg 6.00 15.00
HSPK Paul Kariya 6.00 15.00
HSPM Patrick Marleau 5.00 12.00
HSPR Patrick Roy 12.00 30.00
HSPS Peter Stastny 4.00 10.00
HSRB Ray Bourque 8.00 20.00
HSRD Rick DiPietro 4.00 10.00
HSRH Ron Hextall 8.00 20.00
HSRL Roberto Luongo 6.00 15.00
HSRM Ryan Miller 5.00 12.00
HSRN Rick Nash 5.00 12.00
HSRS Ryan Smyth 4.00 10.00
HSRY Michael Ryder 3.00 8.00
HSSA Borje Salming 5.00 12.00
HSSC Sidney Crosby 20.00 50.00
HSSD Shane Doan 4.00 10.00
HSSF Sergei Fedorov 8.00 20.00
HSSG Simon Gagne 5.00 12.00
HSSH Brendan Shanahan 6.00 15.00
HSSK Saku Koivu 5.00 12.00
HSSN Scott Niedermayer 5.00 12.00
HSSS Steve Shutt 5.00 12.00
HSST Jordan Staal 5.00 12.00
HSSU Mats Sundin 5.00 12.00
HSSZ Sergei Zubov 4.00 10.00
HSTB Todd Bertuzzi 5.00 12.00
HSTS Teemu Selanne 10.00 25.00
HSTV Thomas Vanek 6.00 15.00
HSVL Vincent Lecavalier 4.00 10.00
HSVO Tomas Vokoun 4.00 10.00
HSWG Wayne Gretzky 25.00 60.00
HSWI Doug Wilson 4.00 10.00
HSZC Zdeno Chara 5.00 12.00

2007-08 Upper Deck Trilogy Ice Scripts

STATED ODDS 1:9
ISAH Ales Hemsky 10.00 25.00
ISAK Anze Kopitar 15.00 40.00
ISAM Al MacInnis 12.00 30.00
ISAO Alexander Ovechkin 40.00 100.00
ISAR Andrew Raycroft 10.00 25.00
ISBH Bobby Hull 20.00 50.00
ISBO Bobby Orr 75.00 150.00
ISBP Benoit Pouliot 8.00 20.00
ISCH Cristobal Huet 10.00 25.00
ISCI Dino Ciccarelli 12.00 30.00
ISCP Corey Perry EXCH 12.00 30.00
ISDH Dany Heatley 12.00 30.00
ISDP Denis Potvin 12.00 30.00
ISDS Drew Stafford 10.00 25.00
ISEM Evgeni Malkin 40.00 80.00
ISES Eric Staal 15.00 40.00
ISGF Grant Fuhr 12.00 30.00
ISGH Gordie Howe 50.00 100.00
ISGP Gilbert Perreault 12.00 30.00
ISJB Johnny Bower 15.00 40.00
ISJC Jonathan Cheechoo 12.00 30.00
ISJG Jean-Sebastien Giguere 12.00 30.00
ISJH Jaroslav Halak 12.00 30.00
ISJI Jarome Iginla 12.00 30.00
ISJK Jari Kurri 12.00 30.00
ISJS Jordan Staal 12.00 30.00
ISJT Joe Thornton
ISLR Larry Robinson 12.00 30.00
ISLT Lauri Tukonen 8.00 20.00
ISMB Martin Brodeur 75.00 150.00
ISMD Marcel Dionne 15.00 40.00
ISMF Marc-Andre Fleury 20.00 50.00
ISMG Marian Gaborik EXCH 15.00 40.00
ISML Mario Lemieux 75.00 150.00
ISMR Michael Ryder 8.00 20.00
ISMT Marty Turco 12.00 30.00
ISND Nigel Dawes 8.00 20.00
ISNL Nicklas Lidstrom 12.00 30.00
ISPK Phil Kessel 15.00 40.00
ISPR Patrick Roy 60.00 150.00
ISRH Ron Hextall 15.00 40.00
ISRM Ryan Miller 12.00 30.00
ISRN Rick Nash 12.00 30.00
ISSC Sidney Crosby 75.00 150.00
ISSG Simon Gagne 10.00 25.00
ISSS Steve Shutt 12.00 30.00
ISSV Marek Svatos 8.00 20.00
ISTE Tony Esposito 25.00 50.00
ISTL Ted Lindsay 12.00 30.00
ISTV Tomas Vokoun 10.00 25.00
ISVL Vincent Lecavalier 10.00 25.00
ISWG Wayne Gretzky 150.00 300.00
ISWW Wojtek Wolski 10.00 25.00

2007-08 Upper Deck Trilogy Personal Scripts

STATED PRINT RUN 10-25
PSAH Ales Hemsky 25.00 50.00
PSAK Anze Kopitar 50.00 100.00
PSAM Al MacInnis
PSAT Alex Tanguay 12.00 30.00
PSBC Bobby Clarke 30.00 60.00
PSBF Bernie Federko 12.00 30.00
PSBH Bobby Hull 30.00 80.00
PSBN Bob Nystrom 12.00 30.00
PSBO Bobby Orr 300.00 500.00
PSCP Corey Perry 30.00 60.00
PSCW Cam Ward 20.00 50.00
PSDH Dany Heatley 20.00 50.00
PSEM Evgeni Malkin 75.00 125.00
PSGF Grant Fuhr 20.00 50.00
PSGH Gordie Howe 75.00 150.00
PSGP Gilbert Perreault 20.00 50.00
PSHA Dominik Hasek 25.00 60.00
PSHO Gordie Howe 75.00 150.00
PSJC Jonathan Cheechoo 20.00 50.00
PSJG Jean-Sebastien Giguere 15.00 40.00
PSJI Jarome Iginla 40.00 80.00
PSJK Jari Kurri 30.00 60.00
PSJS Jordan Staal 15.00 40.00
PSJT Joe Thornton 25.00 60.00
PSLM Lanny McDonald 20.00 50.00
PSLR Larry Robinson 20.00 50.00
PSMB Martin Brodeur 75.00 150.00
PSME Mark Messier/10 150.00 300.00
PSMF Marc-Andre Fleury 30.00 80.00
PSML Mario Lemieux 125.00 200.00
PSMM Mark Messier/25 150.00 300.00
PSMR Michael Ryder 12.00 30.00
PSMS Martin St. Louis 20.00 50.00
PSMT Marty Turco 20.00 50.00
PSNL Nicklas Lidstrom 75.00 150.00
PSPE Phil Esposito 40.00 80.00
PSPK Phil Kessel 30.00 60.00
PSPR Patrick Roy 75.00 150.00
PSRB Ray Bourque 30.00 80.00
PSRH Ron Hextall 30.00 80.00
PSRM Ryan Miller 20.00 50.00
PSSC Sidney Crosby 250.00 400.00
PSSG Simon Gagne 20.00 50.00
PSTE Tony Esposito 40.00 80.00
PSVL Vincent Lecavalier 15.00 40.00

2007-08 Upper Deck Trilogy Scripts

S1AB Alex Brooks 4.00 10.00
S1AD Adam Dennis SP
S1AK Anze Kopitar 8.00 20.00
S1BC Blake Comeau 4.00 10.00
S1BE Benoit Pouliot 4.00 10.00
S1BJ Blair Jones 4.00 10.00
S1BO Dave Bolland 5.00 12.00
S1BP Brandon Prust 4.00 10.00
S1BR Brad Boyes 4.00 10.00
S1CH Chris Higgins 4.00 10.00
S1CK Chris Kunitz 6.00 15.00
S1CP Corey Perry 6.00 15.00
S1CW Cam Ward 6.00 15.00
S1DB Dustin Boyd 4.00 10.00
S1DS Drew Stafford 5.00 12.00
S1EC Erik Christensen 4.00 10.00
S1EF Eric Fehr 4.00 10.00
S1EM Evgeni Malkin SP 30.00 60.00
S1HL Henrik Lundqvist SP 15.00 30.00
S1HT Hannu Toivonen 5.00 12.00
S1IW Ian White 4.00 10.00
S1JC Jeff Carter 6.00 15.00
S1JG Josh Gorges 4.00 10.00
S1JH Josh Hennessy 4.00 10.00
S1JO Johnny Oduya 5.00 12.00
S1JP Joe Pavelski 6.00 15.00
S1JS Jordan Staal 6.00 15.00
S1MC Matt Carle 4.00 10.00
S1MJ Milan Jurcina 4.00 10.00
S1MP Marc-Antoine Pouliot SP
S1MR Mike Richards 6.00 15.00
S1MS Marek Svatos 4.00 10.00
S1NW Noah Welch SP
S1PK Phil Kessel SP
S1PN Petteri Nokelainen 4.00 10.00
S1PO Patrick O'Sullivan 5.00 12.00
S1PP Petr Prucha 4.00 10.00
S1PR Paul Ranger 4.00 10.00
S1PS Paul Stastny 6.00 15.00
S1RG Ryan Getzlaf 10.00 25.00
S1RK Ryan Kesler 8.00 20.00
S1RM Ryan Miller
S1RO Roman Polak 4.00 10.00
S1RP Ryan Potulny SP 6.00 15.00
S1RS Ryan Shannon 4.00 10.00
S1SB Steve Bernier 4.00 10.00
S1SO Shane O'Brien 4.00 10.00
S1TK Tomas Kopecky 5.00 12.00
S1TZ Travis Zajac SP
S1VF Valtteri Filppula 6.00 15.00
S1WW Wojtek Wolski 5.00 12.00
S1YS Yan Stastny 4.00 10.00
S2AF Alexander Frolov 4.00 10.00
S2AO Alex Ovechkin SP 75.00 150.00
S2AT Alex Tanguay 4.00 10.00
S2DH Dominik Hasek SP 40.00 100.00
S2DR Dwayne Roloson 5.00 12.00
S2ES Eric Staal 8.00 20.00
S2GO Scott Gomez 5.00 12.00
S2HE Dany Heatley 6.00 15.00
S2IK Ilya Kovalchuk 6.00 15.00
S2JC Jonathan Cheechoo 6.00 15.00
S2JG Jean-Sebastien Giguere SP 12.00 30.00
S2JI Jarome Iginla 12.00 30.00
S2JT Joe Thornton SP 30.00 60.00
S2MB Martin Brodeur SP 40.00 80.00
S2MF Marc-Andre Fleury 10.00 25.00
S2MG Marian Gaborik EXCH 8.00 20.00
S2MR Michael Ryder 4.00 10.00
S2NL Nicklas Lidstrom 15.00 30.00
S2PB Patrice Bergeron 10.00 25.00
S2RN Rick Nash 6.00 15.00
S2SC Sidney Crosby 75.00 150.00
S2SD Shane Doan SP
S2SG Simon Gagne 6.00 15.00
S2ST Martin St. Louis 6.00 15.00
S2TV Tomas Vokoun 5.00 12.00
S2VL Vincent Lecavalier 5.00 12.00
S2VT Vesa Toskala 5.00 12.00
S3AM Al MacInnis 6.00 15.00
S3BC Bobby Clarke 8.00 20.00
S3CN Cam Neely 6.00 15.00
S3GC Gerry Cheevers 12.00 30.00
S3GF Grant Fuhr 6.00 15.00
S3GH Gordie Howe SP 100.00 175.00
S3JK Jari Kurri 6.00 15.00
S3LM Lanny McDonald 6.00 15.00
S3LR Larry Robinson 6.00 15.00

2008-09 Upper Deck Trilogy

This set was released on December 30, 2008. The base set consists of 175 cards. Cards 1-100 feature veterans, and cards 101-175 are rookies.

COMP.SET w/o SPs (100) 15.00 40.00
STATED PRINT RUN 999 SERIAL #'d SETS
STATED PRINT RUN 499 SERIAL #'d SETS
OVERALL RC STATED ODDS 1:3
1 Ales Hemsky .75 2.00
2 Alex Kovalev .75 2.00
3 Alexander Frolov .60 1.50
4 Alexander Ovechkin 4.00 10.00
5 Andrew Cogliano .75 2.00
6 Anze Kopitar 1.50 4.00
7 Brad Boyes .60 1.50
8 Brad Richards 1.00 2.50
9 Brenden Morrow .75 2.00
10 Brian Campbell .75 2.00
11 Cam Ward 1.00 2.50
12 Carey Price 4.00 10.00
13 Chris Drury .75 2.00
14 Chris Osgood 1.00 2.50
15 Chris Pronger .75 2.00
16 Corey Perry 1.00 2.50
17 Cristobal Huet .75 2.00
18 Daniel Alfredsson 1.00 2.50
19 Daniel Briere 1.00 2.50
20 Daniel Sedin 1.00 2.50
21 Dany Heatley 1.00 2.50
22 Derek Roy .60 1.50
23 Dion Phaneuf 1.00 2.50
24 Eric Staal 1.25 3.00
25 Evgeni Malkin 3.00 8.00
26 Evgeni Nabokov .75 2.00
27 Henrik Lundqvist 1.25 3.00
28 Henrik Sedin 1.00 2.50
29 Henrik Zetterberg 1.25 3.00
30 Ilya Kovalchuk 1.00 2.50
31 J.P. Dumont .60 1.50
32 Jarome Iginla 1.00 2.50
33 Jason Arnott .75 2.00
34 Jason Pominville 1.00 2.50
35 Jason Spezza 1.00 2.50
36 Jean-Sebastien Giguere 1.00 2.50
37 Joe Sakic 1.50 4.00
38 Joe Thornton 1.25 3.00
39 Jonathan Cheechoo 1.00 2.50
40 Jonathan Toews 2.50 6.00
41 Jordan Staal 1.00 2.50
42 Jose Theodore 1.00 2.50
43 Justin Williams .75 2.00
44 Kari Lehtonen .75 2.00
45 Manny Legace 1.00 2.50
46 Marc-Andre Fleury 1.50 4.00
47 Marian Gaborik 1.25 3.00
48 Marian Hossa .75 2.00
49 Mark Streit .60 1.50
50 Markus Naslund .75 2.00
51 Martin Brodeur 2.00 5.00
52 Martin St. Louis 1.00 2.50
53 Marty Turco 1.00 2.50
54 Mats Sundin 1.00 2.50
55 Miikka Kiprusoff .75 2.00
56 Mike Comrie .75 2.00
57 Mike Green 1.00 2.50
58 Mike Modano 1.50 4.00
59 Mike Ribeiro .75 2.00
60 Mike Richards 1.00 2.50
61 Mikko Koivu .75 2.00
62 Nathan Horton .75 2.00
63 Nicklas Backstrom 1.50 4.00
64 Nicklas Lidstrom 1.00 2.50
65 Nik Antropov .75 2.00
66 Niklas Backstrom 1.00 2.50
67 Nikolai Zherdev .60 1.50
68 Olli Jokinen .75 2.00
69 Pascal Leclaire .75 2.00
70 Patrice Bergeron 1.25 3.00
71 Patrick Kane 2.00 5.00
72 Patrick Sharp 1.00 2.50
73 Patrik Elias 1.00 2.50
74 Paul Kariya 1.25 3.00
75 Paul Stastny 1.00 2.50
76 Pavel Datsyuk 1.25 3.00
77 Peter Mueller .75 2.00
78 Phil Kessel 1.25 3.00
79 Rick DiPietro .75 2.00
80 Rick Nash 1.00 2.50
81 Roberto Luongo 1.25 3.00
82 Ryan Getzlaf 1.50 4.00
83 Ryan Malone .60 1.50
84 Ryan Miller 1.00 2.50
85 Ryan Smyth .75 2.00
86 Saku Koivu 1.00 2.50
87 Sam Gagner .75 2.00
88 Scott Gomez .75 2.00
89 Shane Doan .75 2.00
90 Shawn Horcoff .60 1.50
91 Sidney Crosby 4.00 10.00
92 Simon Gagne 1.00 2.50
93 Thomas Vanek 1.00 2.50
94 Tim Thomas 1.00 2.50
95 Tobias Enstrom .60 1.50
96 Tomas Kaberle .60 1.50
97 Tomas Vokoun .75 2.00
98 Vesa Toskala .75 2.00
99 Vincent Lecavalier .75 2.00
100 Zach Parise 1.00 2.50
101 Sami Lepisto RC 3.00 8.00
102 Mike Brown RC 5.00 12.00
103 Zach Fitzgerald RC 4.00 10.00
104 Alex Foster RC 3.00 8.00
105 Darryl Boyce RC 3.00 8.00
106 John Mitchell RC 3.00 8.00
107 Robbie Earl RC 2.50 6.00
108 Jonas Frogren RC 2.50 6.00
109 Vladimir Mihalik RC 2.50 6.00
110 Janne Niskala RC 4.00 10.00
111 Tom Cavanagh RC 3.00 8.00
112 Alex Goligoski RC 5.00 12.00
113 Jon Filewich RC 3.00 8.00
114 Ryan Stone RC 2.50 6.00
115 Kevin Porter RC 3.00 8.00
116 Kyle Turris RC 6.00 15.00
117 Claude Giroux RC 8.00 20.00
118 Tim Ramholt RC 3.00 8.00
119 Brian Lee RC 3.00 8.00
120 Ilya Zubov RC 3.00 8.00
121 Jesse Winchester RC 2.50 6.00
122 Kyle Okposo RC 4.00 10.00
123 Mike Iggulden RC 3.00 8.00
124 Anssi Salmela RC 4.00 10.00
125 Ryan Jones RC 4.00 10.00
126 Matt D'Agostini RC 3.00 8.00
127 James Neal RC 8.00 20.00
128 Brian Boyle RC 3.00 8.00
129 Oscar Moller RC 3.00 8.00
130 Danny Taylor RC 3.00 8.00
131 Erik Ersberg RC 3.00 8.00
132 Wayne Simmonds RC 6.00 15.00
133 Michael Frolik RC 4.00 10.00
134 Shawn Matthias RC 4.00 10.00
135 Viktor Tikhonov RC 3.00 8.00
136 Patrik Berglund RC 3.00 8.00
137 Darren Helm RC 4.00 10.00
138 Jonathan Ericsson RC 4.00 10.00
139 Justin Abdelkader RC 6.00 15.00
140 Mattias Ritola RC 3.00 8.00
141 B.J. Crombeen RC 2.50 6.00
142 Garrett Stafford RC 4.00 10.00
143 Mark Fistric RC 3.00 8.00
144 Adam Pineault RC 3.00 8.00
145 Andrew Murray RC 3.00 8.00
146 Dan LaCosta RC 4.00 10.00
147 Derick Brassard RC 3.00 8.00
148 Derek Dorsett RC 5.00 12.00
149 Steve Mason RC 6.00 15.00
150 Tom Sestito RC 4.00 10.00
151 Cody McLeod RC 3.00 8.00
152 Jordan Hendry RC 3.00 8.00
153 Brandon Nolan RC 3.00 8.00
154 Joe Jensen RC 4.00 10.00
155 Tim Conboy RC 3.00 8.00
156 Kyle Greentree RC 4.00 10.00
157 Luca Sbisa RC 2.50 6.00
158 Pascal Pelletier RC 2.50 6.00
159 Boris Valabik RC 4.00 10.00
160 Andrew Ebbett RC 2.50 6.00
161 Luke Schenn RC 6.00 15.00
162 Nikolai Kulemin RC 5.00 12.00
163 Steven Stamkos RC 20.00 50.00
164 Alex Pietrangelo RC 6.00 15.00
165 T.J. Oshie RC 12.00 30.00
166 Zach Boychuk RC 5.00 12.00
167 Mikkel Boedker RC 6.00 15.00
168 Nikita Filatov RC 5.00 12.00
169 Fabian Brunnstrom RC 4.00 10.00
170 Drew Doughty RC 12.00 30.00
171 Colton Gillies RC 4.00 10.00
172 Jakub Voracek RC 10.00 25.00
173 Brandon Sutter RC 5.00 12.00
174 Blake Wheeler RC 12.00 30.00
175 Zach Bogosian RC 5.00 12.00

2008-09 Upper Deck Trilogy Combo Clearcut Autographs

STATED PRINT RUN 100 SERIAL #'d SETS
CC2BG Bossy/Gillies/25 15.00 40.00
CC2BO Orr/Bucyk/25 75.00 150.00
CC2BT Tkaczuk/Bathgate 15.00 40.00
CC2HD H.Sedin/D.Sedin 15.00 40.00
CC2HH Gordie/Mark Howe/25
CC2HN Heatley/Nash/25 15.00 40.00
CC2JJ E.Johnson/J.Johnson 10.00 25.00
CC2KP Price/Koivu/25 60.00 150.00
CC2LM Messier/Leetch/25 30.00 80.00
CC2LS Lidstrom/Salming/25 15.00 40.00
CC2OB Ovech/Backstrm/25 60.00 150.00
CC2PG Getzlaf/Perry 25.00 60.00
CC2SB St. Louis/Boyle 15.00 40.00
CC2SS Stastny/Stastny 15.00 40.00
CC2TK Kane/Toews 60.00 120.00
CC2TN Thornton/Nabokov/25 20.00 50.00
CC2VH Vokoun/Horton 12.00 30.00

2008-09 Upper Deck Trilogy Frozen in Time

COMPLETE SET (20) 150.00 300.00
STATED ODDS 1:12
STATED PRINT RUN 799 SERIAL #'d SETS
101 Bobby Orr 10.00 25.00
102 Alexander Ovechkin 12.00 30.00
103 Patrick Roy 8.00 20.00
104 Henrik Zetterberg 4.00 10.00
105 Ilya Kovalchuk 3.00 8.00
106 Mark Messier 4.00 10.00
107 Evgeni Malkin 10.00 25.00
108 Mats Sundin 3.00 8.00
109 Vincent Lecavalier 2.50 6.00
110 Carey Price 12.00 30.00
111 Gordie Howe 8.00 20.00
112 Jarome Iginla 3.00 8.00
113 Mike Richards 3.00 8.00
114 Marian Gaborik 4.00 10.00
115 Mario Lemieux 10.00 25.00
116 Joe Thornton 4.00 10.00
117 Jonathan Toews 8.00 20.00
118 Joe Sakic 5.00 12.00
119 Sidney Crosby 12.00 30.00
120 Wayne Gretzky 15.00 40.00

2008-09 Upper Deck Trilogy Honorary Swatches

OVERALL G-U STATED ODDS 1:3
HSBD Rod Brind'Amour 4.00 10.00
HSBS Brendan Shanahan 5.00 12.00
HSCP Carey Price 15.00 40.00
HSEM Evgeni Malkin 12.00 30.00
HSES Eric Staal 5.00 12.00
HSHL Henrik Lundqvist 5.00 12.00
HSIK Ilya Kovalchuk 4.00 10.00
HSJS Jason Spezza 4.00 10.00
HSJT Joe Thornton 5.00 12.00
HSKN Patrick Kane 8.00 20.00
HSMB Martin Brodeur 8.00 20.00
HSMG Marian Gaborik 5.00 12.00
HSMH Marian Hossa 3.00 8.00
HSMM Mike Modano 6.00 15.00
HSMS Martin St. Louis 4.00 10.00
HSNB Nicklas Backstrom 6.00 15.00
HSNZ Nikolai Zherdev 2.50 6.00
HSPK Phil Kessel 5.00 12.00
HSPM Pierre-Marc Bouchard 4.00 10.00
HSPS Paul Stastny 4.00 10.00
HSRB Rob Blake 4.00 10.00
HSRD Rick DiPietro 3.00 8.00
HSRL Roberto Luongo 5.00 12.00
HSRM Ryan Miller 4.00 10.00
HSRN Rick Nash 4.00 10.00
HSSC Sidney Crosby 15.00 40.00
HSSK Saku Koivu 4.00 10.00
HSSU Mats Sundin 4.00 10.00
HSSW Shea Weber 3.00 8.00
HSTO Jonathan Toews 10.00 25.00

2008-09 Upper Deck Trilogy Ice Scripts

STATED ODDS 1:9
OVERALL AU STAED ODDS 1:3
ISGI Clark Gillies 10.00 25.00
ISAC Andrew Cogliano 8.00 20.00
ISAD Alex Delvecchio 12.00 30.00
ISAO Alexander Ovechkin 40.00 80.00
ISBB Brad Boyes 6.00 15.00
ISBO Bobby Orr 75.00 150.00
ISCD Chris Drury 8.00 20.00
ISCG Claude Giroux 15.00 40.00
ISCP Carey Price 20.00 50.00
ISDB Derick Brassard 6.00 15.00
ISDC Don Cherry 60.00 150.00
ISDP David Perron 8.00 20.00
ISDS Daniel Sedin 10.00 25.00
ISEJ Erik Johnson 8.00 20.00
ISEM Evgeni Malkin 40.00 100.00
ISGH Gordie Howe
ISGP Gilbert Perreault 10.00 25.00
ISHS Henrik Sedin 10.00 25.00
ISHZ Henrik Zetterberg 12.00 30.00
ISJB Johnny Bucyk 10.00 25.00
ISJC Jeff Carter 10.00 25.00
ISJH Josh Harding 10.00 25.00
ISJJ Jack Johnson 6.00 15.00
ISJO Joe Thornton 12.00 30.00
ISJS Jordan Staal 8.00 20.00
ISJT Jonathan Toews 25.00 50.00
ISKE Phil Kessel 12.00 30.00
ISLI Ted Lindsay 10.00 25.00
ISMB Martin Brodeur 60.00 120.00
ISML Mario Lemieux 100.00 200.00
ISMM Mark Messier 60.00 120.00
ISMO Mike Modano 15.00 40.00
ISMR Mike Ribeiro 8.00 20.00
ISMS Marc Staal
ISMT Marty Turco 10.00 25.00
ISNB Nicklas Backstrom 15.00 40.00
ISNF Nick Foligno 10.00 25.00
ISNH Nathan Horton 8.00 20.00
ISPK Patrick Kane 30.00 60.00
ISPM Peter Mueller 8.00 20.00
ISPO Denis Potvin 10.00 25.00
ISPR Patrick Roy 40.00 100.00
ISPS Paul Stastny 10.00 25.00
ISRB Ray Bourque 40.00 100.00
ISRE Robbie Earl 6.00 15.00
ISRG Ryan Getzlaf 15.00 40.00
ISRL Rod Langway 8.00 20.00
ISSB Scotty Bowman 40.00 100.00
ISSC Sidney Crosby 125.00 250.00
ISSG Sam Gagner 8.00 20.00
ISSM Steve Mason 12.00 30.00
ISSS Steve Shutt 10.00 25.00
ISST Peter Stastny 10.00 25.00
ISTE Tony Esposito 20.00 50.00
ISTL Jiri Tlusty 8.00 20.00
ISTR Tuukka Rask 15.00 30.00
ISTV Tomas Vokoun 8.00 20.00
ISWG Wayne Gretzky
ISWT Walt Tkaczuk 6.00 15.00

2008-09 Upper Deck Trilogy Rivals

STATED ODDS 1:90
ANACOL Ducks/Avalanche 25.00 60.00
ANASJS Ducks/Sharks 20.00 50.00
BOSNYR Bruins/Rangers 15.00 40.00
CARTBY Hurricanes/Lightning 15.00 40.00
CGYEDM Flames/Oilers 12.00 30.00
CGYVAN Flames/Canucks 15.00 40.00
DETCHI Red Wings/Blackhawks
EDMCGY Oilers/Flames legends 30.00 60.00
EDMVAN Oilers/Canucks 15.00 40.00
LAKANA Kings/Ducks
MONBOS Canadiens/Bruins 50.00 120.00
NJDNYR Devils/Rangers 25.00 60.00
NYRNYI Rangers/Islanders
NYRPIT Rangers/Penguins 20.00 50.00
OTTMON Senators/Canadiens 20.00 50.00
PITPHI Penguins/Flyers 50.00 120.00
SJSDAL Sharks/Stars 15.00 40.00
TORBUF Leafs/Sabers 12.00 30.00
TORMON Leafs/Canadiens 50.00 125.00

2008-09 Upper Deck Trilogy Scripted Swatches Second Star

*SECOND STAR: .6X TO 1.5X THIRD STAR
STATED PRINT RUN 25 SERIAL #'d SETS

2008-09 Upper Deck Trilogy Scripted Swatches Third Star

STATED PRINT RUN 100 SERIAL #'d SETS
3RDAM Al MacInnis 10.00 25.00
3RDAO Alexander Ovechkin 40.00 100.00
3RDCP Carey Price 40.00 100.00
3RDCW Cam Ward 10.00 25.00
3RDDC Dino Ciccarelli 10.00 25.00
3RDEM Evgeni Malkin 30.00 80.00
3RDES Eric Staal 12.00 30.00
3RDGP Gilbert Perreault 10.00 25.00
3RDHA Dominik Hasek 12.00 30.00
3RDHE Milan Hejduk 8.00 20.00
3RDHZ Henrik Zetterberg 15.00 40.00
3RDIK Ilya Kovalchuk 10.00 25.00
3RDJC Jonathan Cheechoo 10.00 25.00
3RDJG Jean-Sebastien Giguere 10.00 25.00
3RDJL Joffrey Lupul 8.00 20.00
3RDJT Joe Thornton 12.00 30.00
3RDKL Kari Lehtonen 8.00 20.00
3RDLR Luc Robitaille 10.00 25.00
3RDMB Martin Brodeur 20.00 50.00
3RDMF Marc-Andre Fleury 15.00 40.00
3RDMH Marian Hossa 8.00 20.00
3RDMM Mike Modano 15.00 40.00
3RDMN Markus Naslund 8.00 20.00
3RDMT Marty Turco 10.00 25.00
3RDNH Nathan Horton 8.00 20.00
3RDNL Nicklas Lidstrom 10.00 25.00
3RDNZ Nikolai Zherdev 6.00 15.00
3RDPK Patrick Kane 40.00 80.00
3RDPS Paul Stastny 10.00 25.00
3RDRG Ryan Getzlaf 15.00 40.00
3RDRM Ryan Miller 10.00 25.00
3RDRN Rick Nash 10.00 25.00
3RDSC Sidney Crosby 40.00 100.00
3RDSG Simon Gagne 10.00 25.00
3RDSK Saku Koivu 10.00 25.00
3RDSM Sam Gagner 8.00 20.00
3RDTO Jonathan Toews 25.00 60.00
3RDVO Tomas Vokoun 8.00 20.00

2008-09 Upper Deck Trilogy Superstar Scripts

STATED ODDS 1:9
SSAO Alexander Ovechkin 30.00 80.00
SSAT Alex Tanguay 5.00 12.00
SSBB Brad Boyes 5.00 12.00
SSBM Brenden Morrow 6.00 15.00
SSCD Chris Drury 6.00 15.00
SSCN Cam Neely 8.00 20.00
SSCP Corey Perry 8.00 20.00
SSCW Cam Ward 8.00 20.00
SSDB Dan Boyle 6.00 15.00
SSDC Dan Cleary 6.00 15.00
SSDS Daniel Sedin 8.00 20.00
SSDT Darcy Tucker 6.00 15.00
SSEM Evgeni Malkin 25.00 60.00
SSES Eric Staal 10.00 25.00
SSGO Scott Gomez 6.00 15.00
SSHE Dany Heatley
SSHL Henrik Lundqvist 10.00 25.00
SSHO Marian Hossa
SSHS Henrik Sedin 8.00 20.00
SSHZ Henrik Zetterberg 10.00 25.00
SSJA Jason Arnott 6.00 15.00
SSJC Jonathan Cheechoo 8.00 20.00
SSJG Jean-Sebastien Giguere 8.00 20.00
SSJI Jarome Iginla 8.00 20.00
SSJT Joe Thornton 10.00 25.00
SSLR Luc Robitaille 8.00 20.00
SSMH Milan Hejduk 6.00 15.00
SSMK Mike Knuble 5.00 12.00
SSMM Milan Michalek 5.00 12.00
SSMN Markus Naslund 6.00 15.00
SSMO Mike Modano 10.00 25.00
SSMR Mike Ribeiro 6.00 15.00
SSMT Marty Turco 8.00 20.00
SSNL Nicklas Lidstrom 10.00 25.00
SSOA Adam Oates 8.00 20.00
SSPE Patrik Elias 8.00 20.00
SSPM Pierre-Marc Bouchard 8.00 20.00
SSPS Paul Stastny 8.00 20.00
SSRG Ryan Getzlaf 12.00 30.00
SSRM Ryan Miller 8.00 20.00
SSRS Ryan Smyth 6.00 15.00
SSSC Sidney Crosby 50.00 100.00
SSSG Simon Gagne
SSTV Tomas Vokoun 6.00 15.00
SSVA Thomas Vanek 8.00 20.00

2008-09 Upper Deck Trilogy Three Star Spotlights

OVERALL G-U STATED ODDS 1:3
3SADW Arnott/Dumont/Weber 5.00 12.00
3SBPP Bourque/Phaneuf/Pronger 10.00 25.00
3SCNT Crosby/Nash/Thornton 15.00 40.00
3SCOM Crosby/Ovechkin/Malkin 25.00 60.00
3SDMF Fleury/DiPietro/Miller 10.00 25.00
3SDSL Luongo/Sedin/Demitra 8.00 20.00
3SFMM Fleury/MacIns/McDonald 8.00 20.00
3SFSS Fleury/Staal/Sykora 10.00 25.00
3SGHL Gretzky/Howe/Lemieux
3SGNB Gaborik/Nolan/Bouchard 8.00 20.00
3SGSP Getzlaf/Selanne/Perry 12.00 30.00
3SHGP Hossa/Gaborik/Parise 8.00 20.00
3SHSG Heatley/Spezza/Gerber 6.00 15.00
3SKAA Koval/Afinogv/Antropov 6.00 15.00
3SKMF Messier/Kurri/Fuhr 8.00 20.00
3SKPM Kane/Parise/Mueller 12.00 30.00
3SKSK Koivu/Shutt/Kovalev 6.00 15.00
3SLBN Luongo/Brodeur/Nabokov 12.00 30.00
3SLLN St. Louis/Lecavalier/Nash 6.00 15.00
3SLMP Lundqvist/Miller/DiPietro 8.00 20.00
3SLNK Luongo/Nabokov/Kiprus 8.00 20.00
3SLPP Lidstrom/Phaneuf/Pronger 6.00 15.00
3SMKA Messier/Kurri/Anderson 8.00 20.00
3SMKG Malkin/Kovalev/Gonchar 20.00 50.00
3SMRL Modano/Ribeiro/Leht 10.00 25.00
3SNGS Naslnd/Gomez/Shanahn 8.00 20.00
3SNPL Nash/Peca/Leclaire 6.00 15.00
3SOMK Ovech/Malkin/Koval 25.00 60.00
3SPBC Phaneuf/Bertuz/Cammalri 6.00 15.00
3SRBG Richards/Briere/Gagne 6.00 15.00
3SRBP Roy/Price/Brodeur 25.00 60.00
3SSFS Stastny/Sakic/Forsberg 10.00 25.00
3SSGS Salming/Gilmour/Sundin 8.00 20.00
3SSSF Sundin/Sakic/Forsberg 10.00 25.00
3SSSG Staal/Getzlaf/St. Louis 10.00 25.00
3SSTA Sundin/Toskala/Antropov 6.00 15.00
3SSTC Savard/Thomas/Chara 6.00 15.00
3STKB Toews/Kane/Backstrom 12.00 30.00
3STTN Toews/Thornton/Nash 15.00 40.00
3SZHL Zetter/Holmstrm/Lidstrm 8.00 20.00

2008-09 Upper Deck Trilogy Tri-Color Tandems

STATED ODDS 1:45
TCTBF M.Brodeur/M.Fleury 25.00 60.00
TCTCH E.Cole/S.Horcoff
TCTCM S.Crosby/E.Malkin 50.00 125.00
TCTCO S.Crosby/A.Ovechkin 50.00 125.00
TCTDM S.Doan/P.Mueller 10.00 25.00
TCTEJ E.Staal/J.Staal
TCTEP Z.Parise/P.Elias 12.00 30.00
TCTGB M.Gaborik/P.Bouchard 15.00 40.00
TCTHG D.Heatley/M.Gerber 12.00 30.00
TCTJM E.Malkin/J.Staal 25.00 60.00
TCTJP D.Perron/E.Johnson 8.00 20.00
TCTJS J.Sakic/P.Stastny 20.00 50.00
TCTKJ A.Kopitar/J.Johnson 20.00 50.00
TCTKK S.Koivu/A.Kovalev 12.00 30.00
TCTKL I.Kovalchuk/K.Lehtonen 12.00 30.00
TCTKM E.Malkin/I.Kovalchuk 20.00 50.00
TCTKS P.Kariya/T.Selanne 25.00 60.00
TCTLD R.Luongo/P.Demitra 15.00 40.00
TCTLL K.Lehtonen/J.Lehtinen
TCTLP N.Lidstrom/D.Phaneuf 12.00 30.00
TCTLS V.Lecavalier/M.St. Louis
TCTLW C.Ward/P.Leclaire
TCTMD R.Miller/R.DiPietro 12.00 30.00
TCTNC E.Nabokov/J.Cheechoo 12.00 30.00
TCTOB A.Ovechkin/N.Backstrom 50.00 125.00
TCTPG R.Getzlaf/D.Phaneuf 40.00 100.00
TCTPL C.Price/H.Lundqvist 25.00 60.00
TCTPN C.Pronger/S.Niedermayer 12.00 30.00
TCTPR P.Forsberg/R.Blake 15.00 40.00
TCTRB M.Richards/D.Briere 12.00 30.00
TCTSD D.Sedin/P.Demitra 15.00 40.00
TCTSF M.Sundin/P.Forsberg 15.00 40.00
TCTSK M.Savard/P.Kessel 15.00 40.00
TCTSN R.Nash/J.Spezza 20.00 40.00
TCTTD J.Thornton/S.Doan 15.00 40.00
TCTTK P.Kane/J.Toews 20.00 50.00
TCTVH N.Horton/T.Vokoun 10.00 25.00
TCTWA S.Weber/J.Arnott 10.00 25.00
TCTZD H.Zetterberg/P.Datsyuk 15.00 40.00

2008-09 Upper Deck Trilogy Two-Way Threads

OVERALL G-U STATED ODDS 1:3
2WAO Alexander Ovechkin 8.00 20.00
2WAR Jason Arnott 5.00 12.00
2WDM Drendan Morrison 4.00 10.00
2WCP Chris Pronger 5.00 12.00
2WDP Dion Phaneuf 6.00 15.00
2WDW Doug Weight 6.00 15.00
2WEC Erik Cole 5.00 12.00
2WHZ Henrik Zetterberg 8.00 20.00
2WJL Jere Lehtinen 4.00 10.00
2WJS Jordan Staal 6.00 15.00
2WJT Joe Thornton 8.00 20.00
2WKD Kris Draper 4.00 10.00
2WMA Maxim Afinogenov
2WMP Michael Peca 5.00 12.00
2WNH Nathan Horton 5.00 12.00

2WNL Nicklas Lidstrom 6.00 15.00
2WOJ Olli Jokinen 5.00 12.00
2WPE Patrik Elias 6.00 15.00
2WPF Peter Forsberg 8.00 20.00
2WPM Patrick Marleau 6.00 15.00
2WPS Patrick Sharp 6.00 15.00
2WRB Rod Brind'Amour 6.00 15.00
2WRG Ryan Getzlaf 10.00 25.00
2WSD Shane Doan 5.00 12.00
2WSF Sergei Fedorov 10.00 25.00
2WSK Joe Sakic 10.00 25.00
2WTH Tomas Holmstrom 5.00 12.00
2WVL Vincent Lecavalier 5.00 12.00
2WZC Zdeno Chara 6.00 15.00
2WZP Zach Parise 6.00 15.00

2008-09 Upper Deck Trilogy Young Star Scripts

STATED ODDS 1:9
YSAB Adam Burish 6.00 15.00
YSAC Andrew Cogliano 6.00 15.00
YSBC Blake Comeau 5.00 12.00
YSBD Brandon Dubinsky 6.00 15.00
YSBE Jonathan Bernier 10.00 25.00
YSCB Cam Barker 5.00 12.00
YSCK Chris Kunitz 8.00 20.00
YSCL David Clarkson 6.00 15.00
YSCP Carey Price 30.00 80.00
YSDC Daniel Carcillo 5.00 12.00
YSDP Dustin Penner 6.00 15.00
YSDS Devin Setoguchi 6.00 15.00
YSEC Erik Christensen 5.00 12.00
YSEJ Erik Johnson 6.00 15.00
YSJB Jared Boll 5.00 12.00
YSJC Jeff Carter 8.00 20.00
YSJH Josh Harding 8.00 20.00
YSJJ Jack Johnson 5.00 12.00
YSJP Jason Pominville 8.00 20.00
YSJS Jordan Staal 8.00 20.00
YSJT Jiri Tlusty 6.00 15.00
YSKC Kyle Chipchura 6.00 15.00
YSKL Kari Lehtonen 5.00 12.00
YSKO Kyle Okposo 8.00 20.00
YSKT Kyle Turris 12.00 30.00
YSMF Marc-Andre Fleury 12.00 30.00
YSML Milan Lucic 12.00 30.00
YSMR Mike Richards 8.00 20.00
YSNB Nicklas Backstrom 12.00 30.00
YSND Nigel Dawes 5.00 12.00
YSNZ Nikolai Zherdev 5.00 12.00
YSPK Patrick Kane 15.00 40.00
YSPM Peter Mueller 6.00 15.00
YSPN David Perron 6.00 15.00
YSPS Paul Stastny 8.00 20.00
YSRS Rob Schremp 6.00 15.00
YSSB Steve Bernier 5.00 12.00
YSSG Sam Gagner 6.00 15.00
YSSM Steve Mason 12.00 30.00
YSST Drew Stafford 6.00 15.00
YSSW Shea Weber 6.00 15.00
YSTE Tobias Enstrom 5.00 12.00
YSTH T.J. Hensick 6.00 15.00
YSTK Tyler Kennedy 6.00 15.00
YSTO Jonathan Toews 20.00 50.00
YSVF Valtteri Filppula 8.00 20.00

2009-10 Upper Deck Trilogy

COMP.SET w/o SPS (100)
FIT PRINT RUN 599 SER.#'d SETS
121-155 PRINT RUN 799 SER.#'d SETS
156-170 PRINT RUN 499 SER.#'d SETS
OVERALL RC ODDS 1:3
FROZEN IN TIME ODDS 1:12
1 Roberto Luongo 1.25 3.00
2 Luke Schenn .75 2.00
3 Dion Phaneuf 1.25 3.00
4 Bobby Orr 3.00 8.00
5 Nicklas Lidstrom 1.00 2.50
6 Shea Weber .75 2.00
7 Phil Esposito 1.50 4.00
8 Alexander Ovechkin 4.00 10.00
9 Zach Parise 1.00 2.50
10 Corey Perry 1.00 2.50
11 Jordan Staal 1.00 2.50
12 Jarome Iginla 1.00 2.50
13 Pavel Datsyuk 1.25 3.00
14 Jonathan Cheechoo 1.00 2.50
15 Ryan Getzlaf 1.50 4.00
16 Devin Setoguchi .75 2.00
17 Jeff Carter 1.00 2.50
18 Mike Richards 1.00 2.50
19 Jonathan Toews 2.00 5.00
20 Evgeni Nabokov .75 2.00
21 Olli Jokinen .75 2.00
22 Dan Boyle .75 2.00
23 Chris Drury .75 2.00
24 Nathan Horton 1.00 2.50
25 Chris Pronger .75 2.00
26 Paul Stastny 1.00 2.50
27 Ilya Kovalchuk 1.00 2.50
28 Alexander Semin 1.00 2.50
29 Marc-Andre Fleury 1.50 4.00
30 Martin Brodeur 2.00 5.00
31 Carey Price 4.00 10.00
32 Niklas Backstrom 1.00 2.50
33 Patrick Roy 2.50 6.00
34 Miikka Kiprusoff .75 2.00
35 Marty Turco 1.00 2.50
36 Jussi Jokinen .60 1.50
37 J.P. Dumont .60 1.50
38 Daniel Sedin 1.00 2.50
39 Rick DiPietro .75 2.00
40 Henrik Zetterberg 1.25 3.00
41 Nikolai Kulemin .75 2.00
42 Josh Bailey .75 2.00
43 Mikko Koivu 1.00 2.50
44 Sheldon Souray .60 1.50
45 Marian Hossa .75 2.00
46 Daniel Alfredsson 1.00 2.50
47 Marian Gaborik 1.25 3.00
48 Daniel Briere 1.00 2.50
49 Thomas Vanek 1.00 2.50
50 Chris Mason .75 2.00
51 Brian Campbell .75 2.00
52 Mike Green 1.00 2.50
53 Bobby Ryan 1.00 2.50
54 Eric Staal 1.25 3.00
55 Jason Blake .60 1.50
56 Shane Doan .75 2.00
57 David Perron .60 1.50
58 James Neal 1.00 2.50
59 Joe Thornton 1.00 2.50
60 Henrik Sedin 1.00 2.50
61 Rick Nash .75 2.00
62 Martin St. Louis 1.00 2.50
63 Kris Versteeg 1.00 2.50
64 Mike Modano 1.50 4.00
65 Andrew Cogliano .75 2.00
66 Mario Lemieux 3.00 8.00
67 Michael Frolik .75 2.00
68 Bryan Little 1.00 2.50
69 Henrik Lundqvist 1.50 4.00
70 Derek Roy .75 2.00
71 Evgeni Malkin 3.00 8.00
72 Patrik Elias 1.00 2.50
73 Michael Ryder .60 1.50
74 T.J. Oshie 1.50 4.00
75 Tomas Vokoun .75 2.00
76 Kyle Okposo 1.00 2.50
77 Ray Bourque 1.50 4.00
78 Cam Ward 1.00 2.50
79 Andrei Markov 1.00 2.50
80 Jason Arnott .75 2.00
81 Phil Kessel 1.25 3.00
82 Mike Cammalleri .75 2.00
83 Ales Hemsky .75 2.00
84 Mikhail Grabovski 1.00 2.50
85 Dany Heatley 1.00 2.50
86 Scott Gomez .75 2.00
87 Sidney Crosby 4.00 10.00
88 Patrick Kane 2.00 5.00
89 Sam Gagner .75 2.00
90 Ryan Miller 1.00 2.50
91 Steven Stamkos 2.00 5.00
92 Simeon Varlamov 1.00 2.50
93 Jakub Voracek 1.00 2.50
94 Ryan Smyth .75 2.00
95 Patrik Berglund .60 1.50
96 Pierre-Marc Bouchard 1.00 2.50
97 Steve Mason .75 2.00
98 Peter Mueller .75 2.00
99 Wayne Gretzky 5.00 12.00
100 Jason Spezza 1.00 2.50
101 Alexander Ovechkin FIT 12.00 30.00
102 Bobby Orr FIT 10.00 25.00
103 Carey Price FIT 12.00 30.00
104 Evgeni Malkin FIT 10.00 25.00
105 Gordie Howe FIT 8.00 20.00
106 Ilya Kovalchuk FIT 3.00 8.00
107 Joe Thornton FIT 3.00 8.00
108 Jonathan Toews FIT 6.00 15.00
109 Mario Lemieux FIT 10.00 25.00
110 Mark Messier FIT 4.00 10.00
111 Martin Brodeur FIT 6.00 15.00
112 Mike Richards FIT 3.00 8.00
113 Nicklas Backstrom FIT 5.00 12.00
114 Patrick Kane FIT 6.00 15.00
115 Patrick Roy FIT 8.00 20.00
116 Roberto Luongo FIT 4.00 10.00
117 Ron Hextall FIT 5.00 12.00
118 Sidney Crosby FIT 12.00 30.00
119 Vincent Lecavalier FIT 2.50 6.00
120 Wayne Gretzky FIT 12.50 30.00
121 Michael Sauer RC 3.00 8.00
122 Tyler Bozak RC 6.00 15.00
123 Spencer Machacek RC 4.00 10.00
124 Jhonas Enroth RC 5.00 12.00
125 Benn Ferriero RC 4.00 10.00
126 Matt Hendricks RC 3.00 8.00
127 Cal O'Reilly RC 3.00 8.00
128 Michael Grabner RC 4.00 10.00
129 Mike Santorelli RC 4.00 10.00
130 Tom Wandell RC 4.00 10.00
131 Jay Rosehill RC 4.00 10.00
132 Luca Caputi RC 4.00 10.00
133 T.J. Galiardi RC 4.00 10.00
134 Frazer McLaren RC 3.00 8.00
135 Riku Helenius RC 4.00 10.00
136 Joel Rechlicz RC 2.50 6.00
137 Alec Martinez RC 5.00 12.00
138 Dmitry Kulikov RC 4.00 10.00
139 Matt Beleskey RC 3.00 8.00
140 Ivan Vishnevskiy RC 3.00 8.00
141 Antti Niemi RC 6.00 15.00
142 James Wright RC 4.00 10.00
143 Mikael Backlund RC 4.00 10.00
144 Teemu Laakso RC 2.50 6.00
145 Erik Karlsson RC 12.00 30.00
146 Michal Neuvirth RC 6.00 15.00
147 Mika Pyorala RC 3.00 8.00
148 Jason Demers RC 6.00 15.00
149 Taylor Chorney RC 4.00 10.00
150 John Negrin RC 4.00 10.00
151 Matt Gilroy RC 4.00 10.00
152 Yannick Weber RC 4.00 10.00
153 Christian Hanson RC 4.00 10.00
154 Artem Anisimov RC 4.00 10.00
155 Sergei Shirokov RC 2.50 6.00
156 Colin Wilson RC 5.00 12.00
157 Ryan O'Reilly RC 8.00 20.00
158 Brad Marchand RC 8.00 20.00
159 Ville Leino RC 4.00 10.00
160 Michael Del Zotto RC 5.00 12.00
161 Victor Hedman RC 10.00 25.00
162 Evander Kane RC 10.00 25.00
163 Matt Duchene RC 12.00 30.00
164 James van Riemsdyk RC 10.00 25.00
165 Jonas Gustavsson RC 6.00 15.00
166 Jamie Benn RC 15.00 40.00
167 Viktor Stalberg RC 5.00 12.00
168 Tyler Myers RC 10.00 25.00
169 Logan Couture RC 10.00 25.00
170 John Tavares RC 15.00 40.00

2009-10 Upper Deck Trilogy Classic Confrontations

STATED ODDS 1:45
CCBOBU Boston/Buffalo 12.00 30.00
CCCANJ Carolina/New Jersey 25.00 60.00
CCCGMT Calgary/Montreal
CCCHSL Chicago/St. Louis 20.00 50.00
CCCODA Colorado/Dallas 20.00 50.00
CCCONJ Colorado/New Jersey 30.00 80.00
CCDECH Detroit/Chicago 25.00 60.00
CCDECO Detroit/Colorado 25.00 60.00
CCDEPH Detroit/Philadelphia 20.00 50.00
CCDEPI Detroit/Pittsburgh 30.00 80.00
CCDESL Detroit/St. Louis 20.00 50.00
CCDETO Detroit/Toronto 20.00 50.00
CCEDCG Edmonton/Calgary 15.00 40.00
CCEDDA Edmonton/Dallas 20.00 50.00
CCEDNY Edmonton/NYI 12.00 30.00
CCHABO Hartford/Boston 12.00 30.00
CCLAED LA/Edmonton 40.00 100.00
CCLATO LA/Toronto 40.00 100.00
CCMTBO Montreal/Boston 20.00 50.00
CCMTCG Montreal/Calgary 15.00 40.00
CCNJPH New Jersey/Philly 25.00 60.00
CCNYNJ NYR/New Jersey 30.00 80.00
CCNYPH NYI/Philly 20.00 50.00
CCPHNY Philly/Rangers 20.00 50.00
CCPIPH Pittsburgh/Philly 40.00 100.00
CCPIWA Pittsburgh/Wash 20.00 50.00
CCTOMT Toronto/Montreal 25.00 60.00
CCWANY Washington/NYR 30.00 80.00

2009-10 Upper Deck Trilogy Combo Clearcut Autographs

OVERALL AUTO ODDS 1:3
PRINT RUN 100 SER.#'d SETS UNLESS NOTED
CC2BP Potvin/Bossy/25 EXCH 15.00 40.00
CC2CG Gagner/Cogliano/100 10.00 25.00
CC2EB Bourque/Esposito/25 25.00 60.00
CC2GB Backstrom/Green/100 20.00 50.00
CC2GG C.Gillies/C.Gillies/100 12.00 30.00
CC2GR Getzlaf/Ryan/100 20.00 50.00
CC2IP Iginla/Phaneuf/25 20.00 50.00
CC2JD Johnson/Doughty/100 15.00 40.00
CC2LD Delvecchio/Lindsay/100 15.00 40.00
CC2MS McDonald/Salming/25 15.00 40.00
CC2NK Kessel/Neely/25 EXCH 20.00 50.00
CC2NL Lundqvist/Naslund/25 EXCH 20.00 50.00
CC2NM Nash/Mason/25 12.00 30.00
CC2OB K.Okposo/J.Bailey/100 12.00 30.00
CC2PS Pogge/Schenn/100 15.00 40.00
CC2RC Richards/Carter/25 15.00 40.00
CC2SW Wishart/Stamkos/100 20.00 50.00
CC2TK Kane/Toews/25 EXCH 50.00 100.00
CC2TS Thornton/Setoguchi/25 15.00 40.00

2009-10 Upper Deck Trilogy Hat Trick Heroes

OVERALL MEM ODDS 1:3
HTHAK Andrei Kostitsyn 5.00 12.00
HTHAO Alexander Ovechkin 25.00 60.00
HTHBL Bryan Little 6.00 15.00
HTHBW Blake Wheeler 6.00 15.00
HTHCD Chris Drury 5.00 12.00
HTHDB David Booth 4.00 10.00
HTHDU Dustin Brown 5.00 12.00
HTHEM Evgeni Malkin 20.00 50.00
HTHES Eric Staal 8.00 20.00
HTHIK Ilya Kovalchuk 6.00 15.00
HTHJC Jeff Carter 6.00 15.00
HTHJN James Neal 6.00 15.00
HTHJS Jason Spezza 6.00 15.00
HTHKE Phil Kessel 8.00 20.00
HTHMC Mike Cammalleri 5.00 12.00
HTHML Milan Lucic 5.00 12.00
HTHMM Mark Messier 8.00 20.00
HTHOJ Olli Jokinen 5.00 12.00
HTHPK Patrick Kane 12.00 30.00
HTHPS Petr Sykora 5.00 12.00
HTHRN Rick Nash 5.00 12.00
HTHSC Sidney Crosby 15.00 40.00
HTHSG Sam Gagner 5.00 12.00
HTHST Jordan Staal 6.00 15.00
HTHTS Teemu Selanne 12.00 30.00
HTHTV Thomas Vanek 6.00 15.00
HTHWG Wayne Gretzky 30.00 80.00

2009-10 Upper Deck Trilogy Hat Trick Heroes Gold

*SINGLES: .5X TO 1.2X BASIC INSERTS
STATED PRINT RUN 50 SER.#'d SETS

2009-10 Upper Deck Trilogy Honorary Swatches

OVERALL MEM ODDS 1:3
HSAO Alexander Ovechkin 10.00 25.00
HSBL Brian Leetch 5.00 12.00
HSBS Borje Salming 5.00 12.00
HSCN Cam Neely 5.00 12.00
HSCP Carey Price 20.00 50.00
HSDC Dino Ciccarelli 5.00 12.00
HSDG Doug Gilmour 6.00 15.00
HSDH Dale Hawerchuk 6.00 15.00
HSDS Denis Savard 6.00 15.00
HSEM Evgeni Malkin 15.00 40.00
HSES Eric Staal 6.00 15.00
HSFM Frank Mahovlich 6.00 15.00
HSGA Glenn Anderson 5.00 12.00
HSGF Grant Fuhr 5.00 12.00
HSGH Gordie Howe 12.00 30.00
HSGP Gilbert Perreault 5.00 12.00
HSIK Ilya Kovalchuk 5.00 12.00
HSJB Johnny Bucyk 8.00 20.00
HSJK Jari Kurri 5.00 12.00
HSJT Jonathan Toews 8.00 20.00
HSLM Lanny McDonald 5.00 12.00
HSLR Larry Robinson 5.00 12.00
HSMB Martin Brodeur 10.00 25.00
HSMK Miikka Kiprusoff 4.00 10.00
HSML Mario Lemieux 15.00 40.00
HSMM Mark Messier 6.00 15.00
HSMO Mike Modano 8.00 20.00
HSMT Marty Turco 5.00 12.00
HSNL Nicklas Lidstrom 5.00 12.00
HSPE Phil Esposito 8.00 20.00
HSPK Patrick Kane 10.00 25.00
HSPR Patrick Roy 12.00 30.00
HSRB Ray Bourque 8.00 20.00
HSRH Ron Hextall 8.00 20.00
HSRL Roberto Luongo 6.00 15.00
HSRN Rick Nash 4.00 10.00
HSRO Luc Robitaille 5.00 12.00
HSSC Sidney Crosby 12.00 30.00
HSTE Tony Esposito 10.00 25.00
HSWG Wayne Gretzky 15.00 40.00

2009-10 Upper Deck Trilogy Honorary Swatches Gold

*SINGLES: .5X TO 1.2X BASIC INSERTS
STATED PRINT RUN 50 SER.#'d SETS

2009-10 Upper Deck Trilogy Ice Scripts

STATED ODDS 1:10
ISAC Andrew Cogliano 6.00 15.00
ISBA Josh Bailey 6.00 15.00
ISBH Bobby Hull SP 12.00 30.00
ISBL Brian Leetch 8.00 20.00
ISBO Bobby Orr SP 150.00 250.00
ISBR Bobby Ryan 8.00 20.00
ISBS Brandon Sutter 6.00 15.00
ISCN Cam Neely SP 25.00 60.00
ISDD Drew Doughty 15.00 40.00
ISDH Dany Heatley 8.00 20.00
ISDP Dion Phaneuf 10.00 25.00
ISES Eric Staal 8.00 20.00
ISGH Gordie Howe SP 75.00 150.00
ISHL Henrik Lundqvist 12.00 30.00
ISHZ Henrik Zetterberg SP 12.00 30.00
ISIK Ilya Kovalchuk SP 10.00 25.00
ISJB Jean Beliveau SP 75.00 150.00
ISJI Jarome Iginla SP 10.00 25.00
ISJK Jari Kurri 8.00 20.00
ISJN James Neal 6.00 15.00
ISJP Justin Pogge 8.00 20.00
ISJT Joe Thornton SP 10.00 25.00
ISKA Karl Alzner 5.00 12.00
ISKM Kenndal McArdle 6.00 15.00
ISLS Luke Schenn 8.00 20.00
ISMB Martin Brodeur SP 50.00 100.00
ISMF Marc-Andre Fleury 12.00 30.00
ISML Mario Lemieux SP 60.00 120.00
ISMP Max Pacioretty 8.00 20.00
ISMR Mike Richards 8.00 20.00
ISNB Nicklas Backstrom 12.00 30.00
ISNL Nicklas Lidstrom 12.00 30.00
ISPB Patrice Bergeron 12.00 30.00
ISPD Pavel Datsyuk SP 25.00 50.00
ISPE Phil Esposito SP 25.00 60.00
ISPH Chris Phillips 5.00 12.00
ISPK Patrick Kane 15.00 40.00
ISPR Patrick Roy SP 125.00 250.00
ISPS Paul Stastny 8.00 20.00
ISRB Ray Bourque SP 25.00 60.00
ISRM Ryan Miller 20.00 40.00
ISRN Rick Nash 6.00 15.00
ISSB Scotty Bowman SP 50.00 100.00
ISSC Sidney Crosby 60.00 120.00
ISSK Saku Koivu 15.00 40.00
ISSM Steve Mason 6.00 15.00
ISSS Steven Stamkos 25.00 50.00
ISTE Tony Esposito SP 25.00 60.00
ISTO Jonathan Toews 25.00 50.00
ISWG Wayne Gretzky SP EXCH 300.00 400.00
ISZB Zach Bogosian 6.00 15.00

2009-10 Upper Deck Trilogy Line Mates

OVERALL MEM ODDS 1:3
*GOLD/50: .5X TO 1.2X BASIC INSERTS
LMAD J.Dumont/J.Arnott 5.00 12.00
LMAM M.Messier/G.Anderson 8.00 20.00
LMBK A.Kopitar/D.Brown 10.00 25.00
LMCG S.Gagner/A.Cogliano 5.00 12.00
LMHD P.Datsyuk/T.Holmstrom 8.00 20.00
LMHS M.Hejduk/P.Stastny 6.00 15.00
LMJI O.Jokinen/J.Iginla 6.00 15.00
LMKL I.Kovalchuk/B.Little 6.00 15.00
LMLL V.Lecavalier/M.St. Louis 6.00 15.00
LMLS S.Shutt/G.Lafleur 8.00 20.00
LMMN M.Modano/J.Neal 10.00 25.00
LMMS L.McDonald/D.Sittler 8.00 20.00
LMMT J.Thornton/P.Marleau 6.00 15.00
LMNO A.Oates/C.Neely 6.00 15.00
LMOB A.Ovechkin/N.Backstrom 15.00 40.00
LMRG M.Richards/S.Gagne 6.00 15.00
LMRL B.Rafalski/N.Lidstrom 6.00 15.00
LMRS T.Ruutu/E.Staal 8.00 20.00
LMRV T.Vanek/D.Roy 6.00 15.00
LMRW B.Wheeler/M.Ryder 6.00 15.00
LMSC J.Spezza/J.Cheechoo 6.00 15.00
LMSH D.Heatley/J.Spezza
LMSM M.Satan/S.Crosby 12.00 30.00
LMSS P.Stastny/M.Svatos 6.00 15.00
LMTK P.Kane/J.Toews 12.00 30.00
LMWF M.Frolik/S.Weiss 5.00 12.00
LMWL L.Robitaille/W.Gretzky 15.00 40.00

2009-10 Upper Deck Trilogy Superstar Scripts

STATED ODDS 1:10
SSAC Andrew Cogliano 6.00 15.00
SSAM Al MacInnis 8.00 20.00
SSAO Alexander Ovechkin 30.00 80.00
SSCB Cam Barker 5.00 12.00
SSCC Cal Clutterbuck 6.00 15.00
SSCK Chris Kunitz 8.00 20.00
SSCL David Clarkson 6.00 15.00
SSCW Cam Ward 8.00 20.00
SSDC Dan Cleary 6.00 15.00
SSDP David Perron 5.00 12.00
SSEL Patrik Elias 8.00 20.00
SSEM Evgeni Malkin 25.00 60.00
SSHZ Henrik Zetterberg 10.00 25.00
SSJA Jason Arnott 6.00 15.00
SSJC Jeff Carter 8.00 20.00
SSJD J.P. Dumont 5.00 12.00
SSJH Josh Harding 8.00 20.00
SSJI Jarome Iginla 8.00 20.00
SSJJ Jack Johnson 5.00 12.00
SSJP Jason Pominville 8.00 20.00
SSMF Marc-Andre Fleury 12.00 30.00
SSMG Mike Green 8.00 20.00
SSMR Mike Richards 8.00 20.00
SSMS Matt Stajan 6.00 15.00
SSMT Maxime Talbot 8.00 20.00
SSNB Nicklas Backstrom 12.00 30.00
SSPB Peter Budaj 6.00 15.00
SSPD Pavel Datsyuk 20.00 40.00
SSPE Dustin Penner 5.00 12.00
SSPH Dion Phaneuf 10.00 25.00
SSPK Phil Kessel 10.00 25.00
SSPO Denis Potvin 8.00 20.00
SSRS Ryan Smyth 6.00 15.00
SSSB Steve Bernier 5.00 12.00
SSSC Sidney Crosby 75.00 150.00
SSSG Simon Gagne 8.00 20.00
SSSS Steve Shutt 8.00 20.00
SSSW Stephen Weiss 5.00 12.00
SSTH Tomas Holmstrom 6.00 15.00
SSTV Thomas Vanek 8.00 20.00

2009-10 Upper Deck Trilogy Young Star Scripts

STATED ODDS 1:10
YSAE Andrew Ebbett 4.00 10.00
YSAN Andreas Nodl 5.00 12.00
YSBB Ben Bishop 6.00 15.00
YSBL Brian Lee 6.00 15.00
YSBM Brendan Mikkelson 4.00 10.00
YSBO Brian Boyle 4.00 10.00
YSBS Brandon Sutter 5.00 12.00
YSBV Boris Valabik 6.00 15.00
YSBW Blake Wheeler 6.00 15.00
YSCG Colton Gillies 6.00 15.00
YSCS Chris Stewart 5.00 12.00
YSDD Drew Doughty 15.00 40.00
YSDL Dan LaCosta 5.00 12.00
YSDO Derek Dorsett 5.00 12.00
YSDT Danny Taylor 5.00 12.00
YSEE Erik Ersberg 5.00 12.00
YSFB Fabian Brunnstrom 5.00 12.00
YSGI Claude Giroux 20.00 40.00
YSJB Josh Bailey 5.00 12.00
YSJE Jonathan Ericsson 5.00 12.00
YSJF Jonas Frogren 5.00 12.00
YSJM John Mitchell 4.00 10.00
YSJP Justin Pogge 6.00 15.00
YSJT John Tavares 30.00 80.00
YSJV Jakub Voracek 6.00 15.00
YSKA Karl Alzner 4.00 10.00
YSKM Kenndal McArdle 5.00 12.00
YSKO Kyle Okposo 6.00 15.00
YSKP Kevin Porter 4.00 10.00
YSLS Luke Schenn 5.00 12.00
YSMA Ben Maxwell 5.00 12.00
YSMB Mikkel Boedker 4.00 10.00
YSMC Jamie McGinn 5.00 12.00
YSMD Matt D'Agostini 5.00 12.00
YSMH Matthew Halischuk 5.00 12.00
YSMP Max Pacioretty 8.00 20.00
YSMR Michal Repik 5.00 12.00
YSNF Nikita Filatov 5.00 12.00
YSNO Nathan Oystrick 4.00 10.00
YSOM Oscar Moller 4.00 10.00
YSPI Alex Pietrangelo 5.00 12.00
YSPV Petr Vrana 8.00 20.00
YSRJ Ryan Jones 5.00 12.00
YSRY Bobby Ryan 6.00 15.00
YSSC Cory Schneider 8.00 20.00
YSSM Shawn Matthias 6.00 15.00
YSSS Steven Stamkos 12.00 30.00
YSST Steve Mason 5.00 12.00
YSTK Tim Kennedy 5.00 12.00
YSTL Trevor Lewis 5.00 12.00
YSTO T.J. Oshie 10.00 25.00
YSTP Tyler Plante 5.00 12.00
YSTS Tom Sestito 4.00 10.00
YSTW Ty Wishart 5.00 12.00
YSVT Viktor Tikhonov 5.00 12.00
YSWS Wayne Simmonds 8.00 20.00
YSZA Zach Boychuk 5.00 12.00
YSZB Zach Bogosian 5.00 12.00

2013-14 Upper Deck Trilogy

COMP.SET w/o RC's (100) 20.00 40.00
EXCH EXPIRATION: 6/20/2015
201-218 ROOKIES INSERTED IN SPx
1 Bobby Ryan .75 2.00
2 Ryan Getzlaf 1.25 3.00
3 Jonas Hiller .60 1.50
4 Teemu Selanne 1.50 4.00
5 Bobby Orr 2.50 6.00
6 Cam Neely .75 2.00
7 Brad Marchand 1.00 2.50
8 Tuukka Rask .75 2.00
9 Patrice Bergeron 1.00 2.50
10 Ray Bourque 1.25 3.00
11 Terry O'Reilly .60 1.50
12 Tyler Seguin 1.25 3.00
13 Zdeno Chara .75 2.00
14 Ryan Miller .75 2.00
15 Dominik Hasek 1.00 2.50
16 Doug Gilmour 1.00 2.50
17 Jarome Iginla .75 2.00
18 Jeff Skinner .60 1.50
19 Eric Staal 1.00 2.50
20 Jordan Staal .75 2.00
21 Denis Savard 1.00 2.50
22 Doug Wilson .60 1.50
23 Ed Belfour .75 2.00
24 Jonathan Toews 1.50 4.00
25 Marian Hossa .60 1.50
26 Patrick Kane 1.50 4.00
27 Joe Sakic 1.25 3.00
28 Matt Duchene .75 2.00
29 Gabriel Landeskog .60 1.50
30 Derek Roy .60 1.50
31 Jamie Benn 1.00 2.50
32 Jaromir Jagr 2.00 5.00
33 Johan Franzen .75 2.00
34 Nicklas Lidstrom .75 2.00
35 Pavel Datsyuk 1.00 2.50
36 Grant Fuhr .75 2.00
37 Bill Ranford .75 2.00
38 Jordan Eberle .75 2.00
39 Jari Kurri .75 2.00
40 Paul Coffey .75 2.00
41 Ryan Nugent-Hopkins .75 2.00
42 Taylor Hall 1.50 4.00
43 Wayne Gretzky 4.00 10.00
44 Stephen Weiss .60 1.50
45 Ron Francis 1.00 2.50
46 Anze Kopitar 1.25 3.00
47 Drew Doughty .75 2.00
48 Mike Richards .75 2.00
49 Luc Robitaille .75 2.00
50 Jonathan Quick 1.25 3.00
51 Dino Ciccarelli .75 2.00
52 Mike Modano 1.25 3.00
53 Jean Beliveau .75 2.00
54 Larry Robinson .75 2.00
55 P.K. Subban 1.25 3.00
56 Carey Price 2.50 6.00
57 Pekka Rinne 1.00 2.50
58 Ilya Kovalchuk .75 2.00
59 Martin Brodeur 1.50 4.00
60 Mike Bossy .75 2.00
61 John Tavares 1.50 4.00
62 Bryan Trottier 1.00 2.50
63 Rick Nash .75 2.00
64 Brad Richards .75 2.00
65 Theoren Fleury 1.00 2.50
66 Marian Gaborik .75 2.00
67 Mark Messier 1.00 2.50
68 Henrik Lundqvist 1.00 2.50
69 Erik Karlsson 1.50 4.00
70 Jason Spezza .75 2.00
71 Claude Giroux .75 2.00
72 Eric Lindros 1.25 3.00
73 Bernie Parent .75 2.00
74 Brayden Schenn .75 2.00
75 Dave Schultz .75 2.00
76 Shane Doan .60 1.50
77 Evgeni Malkin 2.50 6.00
78 Marc-Andre Fleury 1.25 3.00
79 Mario Lemieux 2.50 6.00
80 Sidney Crosby 3.00 8.00
81 Patrick Marleau .75 2.00
82 Joe Pavelski .75 2.00
83 Antti Niemi .60 1.50
84 Logan Couture .75 2.00
85 Curtis Joseph .75 2.00
86 Brett Hull .75 2.00
87 David Backes .75 2.00
88 Jaroslav Halak .75 2.00
89 Steven Stamkos 1.50 4.00
90 Vincent Lecavalier .60 1.50
91 Dion Phaneuf .75 2.00
92 Phil Kessel 1.00 2.50
93 Markus Naslund .60 1.50
94 Ryan Kesler .75 2.00
95 Trevor Linden .75 2.00
96 Alexander Ovechkin 3.00 8.00
97 Braden Holtby 1.25 3.00
98 Nicklas Backstrom 1.25 3.00
99 Dale Hawerchuk 1.00 2.50
100 Evander Kane .75 2.00
101 Nail Yakupov AU/699 RC 12.00 30.00
102 Nail Yakupov AU/399 20.00 50.00
103 Nail Yakupov AU/49 150.00 300.00
104 Tarasenko AU/699 RC EXCH 25.00 60.00
105 Vladimir Tarasenko AU/399 30.00 80.00
106 Vladimir Tarasenko AU/49 150.00 250.00
107 A.Galchenyuk AU/699 RC 15.00 40.00
108 Alex Galchenyuk AU/399 20.00 50.00
109 Alex Galchenyuk AU/49 150.00 300.00
110 Justin Schultz AU/699 RC 4.00 10.00
111 Justin Schultz AU/399 5.00 12.00
112 Justin Schultz AU/49 150.00 250.00
113 Mikael Granlund AU/699 RC 6.00 15.00
114 Mikael Granlund AU/399 8.00 20.00
115 Mikael Granlund AU/49 40.00 100.00
116 M.Grigorenko AU/699 RC 5.00 12.00
117 Mikhail Grigorenko AU/399 6.00 15.00
118 Mikhail Grigorenko AU/49 75.00 150.00
119 J.Huberdeau AU/699 RC 10.00 25.00
120 Jonathan Huberdeau AU/399 10.00 25.00
121 Jonathan Huberdeau AU/49 100.00 200.00
122 Nathan Beaulieu AU/699 RC 3.00 8.00
123 Nathan Beaulieu AU/399 4.00 10.00
124 Nathan Beaulieu AU/49 15.00 40.00
125 B.Gallagher AU/699 RC 12.00 30.00
126 Brendan Gallagher AU/399 20.00 50.00
127 Brendan Gallagher AU/49 125.00 250.00
128 Charlie Coyle AU/699 RC 4.00 10.00
129 Charlie Coyle AU/399 5.00 12.00
130 Charlie Coyle AU/49 20.00 50.00
131 Cory Conacher AU/699 RC 2.50 6.00
132 Cory Conacher AU/399 3.00 8.00
133 Cory Conacher AU/49 15.00 40.00
134 D.Brunner AU/699 RC EXCH 3.00 8.00
135 D.Brunner AU/399 EXCH 4.00 10.00
136 D.Brunner AU/49 EXCH 15.00 40.00
137 Dougie Hamilton AU/699 RC 8.00 20.00
138 Dougie Hamilton AU/399 10.00 25.00
139 Dougie Hamilton AU/49 50.00 100.00
140 Emerson Etem AU/699 RC 4.00 10.00
141 Emerson Etem AU/399 5.00 12.00
142 Emerson Etem AU/49 20.00 50.00
143 Jonas Brodin AU/699 RC 3.00 8.00
144 Jonas Brodin AU/399 4.00 10.00
145 Jonas Brodin AU/49 15.00 40.00
146 J.Schroeder AU/699 RC 4.00 10.00
147 Jordan Schroeder AU/399 5.00 12.00
148 Jordan Schroeder AU/49 15.00 40.00
149 Petr Mrazek AU/699 RC 6.00 15.00
150 Petr Mrazek AU/399 8.00 20.00
151 Petr Mrazek AU/49 40.00 100.00
152 Quinton Howden AU/699 RC 3.00 8.00
153 Quinton Howden AU/399 4.00 10.00
154 Quinton Howden AU/49 15.00 40.00
155 Ryan Spooner AU/699 RC 4.00 10.00
156 Ryan Spooner AU/399 5.00 12.00
157 Ryan Spooner AU/49 25.00 60.00
158 Scott Laughton AU/699 RC 4.00 10.00
159 Scott Laughton AU/399 5.00 12.00
160 Scott Laughton AU/49 20.00 50.00
161 Stefan Matteau AU/699 RC 3.00 8.00
162 Stefan Matteau AU/399 4.00 10.00
163 Stefan Matteau AU/49 15.00 40.00
164 Viktor Fasth AU/699 RC 4.00 10.00
165 Viktor Fasth AU/399 5.00 12.00
166 Viktor Fasth AU/49 20.00 50.00
167 Jarred Tinordi AU/699 RC 4.00 10.00
168 Jarred Tinordi AU/399 5.00 12.00
169 Jarred Tinordi AU/49 30.00 80.00
170 R.Cervenka AU/699 RC 3.00 8.00
171 Roman Cervenka AU/399 4.00 10.00
172 Roman Cervenka AU/49 15.00 40.00
173 Jamie Oleksiak AU/699 RC 3.00 8.00
174 Jamie Oleksiak AU/399 4.00 10.00
175 Jamie Oleksiak AU/49 15.00 40.00
176 Beau Bennett AU/699 RC 5.00 12.00
177 Beau Bennett AU/399 6.00 15.00
178 Beau Bennett AU/49 30.00 80.00
179 Jack Campbell AU/699 RC 3.00 8.00
180 Jack Campbell AU/399 4.00 10.00
181 Jack Campbell AU/49 15.00 40.00
182 Leo Komarov AU/699 RC 4.00 10.00
183 Leo Komarov AU/399 5.00 12.00
184 Leo Komarov AU/49 20.00 50.00
185 Ryan Murphy AU/699 RC 4.00 10.00
186 Ryan Murphy AU/399 5.00 12.00
187 Ryan Murphy AU/49 20.00 50.00
188 Nick Petrecki AU/699 RC 2.50 6.00
189 Nick Petrecki AU/399 3.00 8.00
190 Nick Petrecki AU/49 12.00 30.00
191 Rickard Rakell AU/699 RC 4.00 10.00
192 Rickard Rakell AU/399 5.00 12.00
193 Rickard Rakell AU/49 15.00 40.00
194 T.Hickey AU/699 RC 3.00 8.00
195 Thomas Hickey AU/399 4.00 10.00
196 Thomas Hickey AU/49 15.00 40.00
197 Tyler Toffoli AU/699 RC 8.00 20.00
198 Tyler Toffoli AU/399 10.00 25.00
199 Tyler Toffoli AU/49 50.00 100.00
200 Ykp/Trsk/Glch AU/25 EX 300.00 500.00
201 Nathan MacKinnon AU/149 RC 100.00 200.00
202 Nathan MacKinnon AU/49 150.00 300.00
203 Nathan MacKinnon AU/25 250.00 500.00
204 Seth Jones AU/149 RC 8.00 20.00
205 Seth Jones AU/49 30.00 80.00
206 Seth Jones AU/25 75.00 150.00
207 Tomas Hertl AU/149 RC 30.00 60.00
208 Tomas Hertl AU/49 75.00 150.00
209 Tomas Hertl AU/25 125.00 250.00
210 Aleksander Barkov AU/149 RC 15.00 40.00
211 Aleksander Barkov AU/49 40.00 80.00
212 Aleksander Barkov AU/25 40.00 100.00
213 Morgan Rielly AU/149 RC 20.00 50.00
214 Morgan Rielly AU/49 40.00 100.00
215 Morgan Rielly AU/25 75.00 150.00
216 Sean Monahan AU/149 RC 12.00 30.00
217 Sean Monahan AU/49 60.00 120.00
218 Sean Monahan AU/25 100.00 200.00

2013-14 Upper Deck Trilogy Autographs

GROUP A ODDS 1:1859
GROUP B ODDS 1:159
GROUP C ODDS 1:56
GROUP D ODDS 1:76
OVERALL ODDS 1:30
1 Bobby Ryan C 6.00 15.00
2 Ryan Getzlaf B 6.00 15.00
3 Jonas Hiller C 8.00 20.00
5 Bobby Orr D 50.00 100.00
6 Cam Neely B 10.00 25.00
7 Brad Marchand B 12.00 30.00
8 Tuukka Rask C 10.00 25.00
10 Ray Bourque B 20.00 40.00
11 Terry O'Reilly C 8.00 20.00
12 Tyler Seguin C 10.00 25.00
14 Ryan Miller C 10.00 25.00
15 Dominik Hasek B 12.00 30.00
16 Doug Gilmour B
17 Jarome Iginla B 20.00 40.00
18 Jeff Skinner C
19 Eric Staal D 6.00 15.00
20 Jordan Staal C 10.00 25.00
21 Denis Savard D 10.00 25.00
22 Doug Wilson C 8.00 20.00
23 Ed Belfour C 15.00 30.00
24 Jonathan Toews B 30.00 60.00
26 Patrick Kane C 20.00 50.00
27 Joe Sakic A 25.00 60.00
28 Matt Duchene C 10.00 25.00
29 Gabriel Landeskog C 12.00 30.00
30 Derek Roy D 6.00 15.00
31 Jamie Benn C 6.00 15.00
32 Jaromir Jagr B 40.00 80.0
33 Johan Franzen C 10.00 25.0
34 Nicklas Lidstrom D 20.00 40.0
35 Pavel Datsyuk B 15.00 30.0
36 Grant Fuhr C 10.00 25.0
37 Bill Ranford C 15.00 30.0
39 Jari Kurri C 15.00 40.0
40 Paul Coffey B 10.00 25.0
41 Ryan Nugent-Hopkins C 10.00 25.0
42 Taylor Hall B 20.00 40.0
43 Wayne Gretzky C 150.00 250.0
44 Stephen Weiss C 4.00 10.0
45 Ron Francis B
46 Anze Kopitar C 8.00 20.0
48 Mike Richards B 25.00 50.0
49 Luc Robitaille B 10.00 25.0
50 Jonathan Quick C 10.00 25.0
52 Mike Modano B 15.00 30.0
53 Jean Beliveau B 30.00 60.0
54 Larry Robinson D 8.00 20.0
55 P.K. Subban C 15.00 40.0
56 Carey Price C 30.00 80.0
57 Pekka Rinne C 6.00 15.0
58 Ilya Kovalchuk A 10.00 25.0
59 Martin Brodeur B
60 Mike Bossy D 10.00 25.0
61 John Tavares D 15.00 30.0
62 Bryan Trottier C 10.00 25.0
63 Rick Nash B 10.00 25.0
65 Theoren Fleury D 10.00 25.0
67 Mark Messier B 25.00 50.0
69 Erik Karlsson C 8.00 20.0
72 Eric Lindros A 30.00 60.0
74 Brayden Schenn D 8.00 20.0
75 Dave Schultz C 10.00 25.0
77 Evgeni Malkin C 25.00 50.0
78 Marc-Andre Fleury C 15.00 40.0
79 Mario Lemieux A 75.00 125.0
80 Sidney Crosby A
81 Patrick Marleau C 6.00 15.0
82 Joe Pavelski C 10.00 25.0
84 Logan Couture C 8.00 20.0
85 Curtis Joseph C 10.00 25.0
86 Brett Hull B 25.00 50.0
87 David Backes C 10.00 25.0
88 Jaroslav Halak C 10.00 25.0
89 Steven Stamkos C 20.00 40.0
91 Dion Phaneuf B 6.00 15.0
92 Phil Kessel C
93 Markus Naslund D 6.00 15.0
94 Ryan Kesler C 8.00 20.0
95 Trevor Linden C 10.00 25.0
96 Alexander Ovechkin B 25.00 50.0
97 Braden Holtby C 15.00 30.0
98 Nicklas Backstrom C 15.00 40.0
99 Dale Hawerchuk C 12.00 30.0
100 Evander Kane C 10.00 25.0

2013-14 Upper Deck Trilogy Clear Cut Combo Autographs

GROUP A ODDS 1:2286
GROUP B ODDS 1:610
GROUP C ODDS 1:183
OVERALL ODDS 1:132
CC2RW P.Rinne/S.Weber 10.00 25.0
CCCBH J.Halak/D.Backes C 15.00 40.0
CCCBS T.Seguin/Bergeron C 25.00 50.0
CCCBT M.Bossy/J.Tavares B 25.00 50.0
CCCCG B.Clarke/C.Giroux B 40.00 80.0
CCCGO W.Gretzky/B.Orr A
CCCHE T.Hall/J.Eberle B
CCCLB R.Leach/B.Barber C 15.00 40.0
CCCLJ M.Lemieux/J.Jagr A 100.00 175.0
CCCML M.Messier/E.Lindros A 50.00 100.0
CCCMR B.Marchand/T.Rask C 25.00 50.0
CCCNS Nugent-Hpkns/Smyth C 30.00 60.0
CCCRP P.Roy/C.Price A 90.00 150.0
CCCSC B.Schenn/Couturier C 15.00 40.0
CCCSK C.Schneider/Kassian C 12.00 30.0
CCCSL Subban/L.Leblanc C 15.00 40.0
CCCSO D.Schultz/T.O'Reilly C 15.00 40.0
CCCTK J.Toews/P.Kane B 50.00 100.0

2013-14 Upper Deck Trilogy Crystal

C1-C10 STATED ODDS 1:33
C11-C15 STATED ODDS 1:90
C16-C20 STATED ODDS 1:145
C21-C25 STATED ODDS 1:66
C26-C35 STATED ODDS 1:45
C36-C40 STATED ODDS 1:145
C1 Patrick Kane 8.00 20.0
C2 Tyler Seguin 6.00 15.0
C3 Ryan Nugent-Hopkins 4.00 10.0
C4 Drew Doughty 4.00 10.0
C5 Phil Kessel 5.00 12.0
C6 Erik Karlsson 8.00 20.0
C7 James Neal 4.00 10.0
C8 Jonathan Quick 6.00 15.0
C9 Corey Perry 4.00 10.0
C10 Jeff Skinner 3.00 8.0
C11 Henrik Lundqvist 5.00 12.0
C12 Evgeni Malkin 12.00 30.0
C13 Taylor Hall 8.00 20.0
C14 Jordan Eberle 4.00 10.0
C15 Martin Brodeur 8.00 20.0
C16 Sidney Crosby 15.00 40.0
C17 Carey Price 20.00 50.0
C18 Alexander Ovechkin 25.00 60.0
C19 Steven Stamkos 12.00 30.0
C20 Jonathan Toews 12.00 30.0
C21 Paul Coffey 5.00 12.0
C22 Nicklas Lidstrom 5.00 12.0
C23 Mats Sundin 5.00 12.0
C24 Ray Bourque 8.00 20.0
C25 Larry Robinson 5.00 12.0
C26 Jean Beliveau 6.00 15.
C27 Guy Lafleur 6.00 15.
C28 Howie Morenz 4.00 10.
C29 Pelle Lindbergh 5.00 12.
C30 Mark Messier 6.00 15.
C31 Eric Lindros 6.00 15.
C32 Brett Hull 5.00 12.
C33 Bobby Hull 5.00 12.
C34 Ron Francis 6.00 15.
C35 Pavel Bure 8.00 20.
C36 Patrick Roy 20.00 50.
C37 Joe Sakic 12.00 30.
C38 Mario Lemieux 25.00 60.
C39 Bobby Orr 25.00 60.
C40 Wayne Gretzky 25.00 60.
C41 Petr Mrazek/225 8.00 20.
C42 Viktor Fasth/225 4.00 10.
C43 Quinton Howden/225 3.00 8.
C44 Jonas Brodin/225 3.00 8.
C45 Emerson Etem/225 4.00 10.
C46 Charlie Coyle/125 5.00 12.
C47 Brendan Gallagher/125 15.00 40.
C48 Ryan Spooner/125 5.00 12.
C49 Scott Laughton/125 8.00 20.
C50 Damien Brunner/125 8.00 20.

51 Cory Conacher/75 4.00 10.00
52 J.T. Miller/75 6.00 15.00
53 Dougie Hamilton/75 25.00 50.00
54 Mikhail Grigorenko/75 15.00 40.00
55 Jonathan Huberdeau/75 15.00 40.00
56 Mikael Granlund/75 10.00 25.00
57 Justin Schultz/75 6.00 15.00
58 Alex Galchenyuk/75 40.00 100.00
59 Vladimir Tarasenko/75 30.00 80.00
60 Nail Yakupov/75 50.00 100.00

2013-14 Upper Deck Trilogy Ice Scripts

ROUP A ODDS 1:186
ROUP B ODDS 1:130
ROUP C ODDS 1:56
ROUP D ODDS 1:13
VERALL ODDS 1:9
XCH EXPIRATION: 6/19/2015
AO Alexander Ovechkin A 30.00 60.00
BB Bill Barber D 6.00 15.00
BC Bobby Clarke B 20.00 40.00
BH Brett Hull A 20.00 50.00
BM Brad Marchand D 10.00 25.00
BO Bobby Orr C 60.00 120.00
CG Claude Giroux C EXCH 15.00 30.00
CH Cody Hodgson D 6.00 15.00
CJ Curtis Joseph B 20.00 40.00
CK Chris Kreider D 8.00 20.00
CP Carey Price B 25.00 50.00
CS Cory Schneider D 6.00 15.00
DG Doug Gilmour A 60.00 120.00
DH Dominik Hasek A EXCH 40.00 80.00
EB Ed Belfour A 15.00 40.00
EK Erik Karlsson D 10.00 25.00
EL Eric Lindros A 30.00 60.00
JA Jake Allen D 6.00 15.00
JB Jean Beliveau A 75.00 135.00
JE Jordan Eberle D 12.00 30.00
JH Jaroslav Halak D 8.00 20.00
JI Jarome Iginla A 15.00 40.00
JJ Jaromir Jagr A 40.00 80.00
JM Jacob Markstrom D 5.00 12.00
JS Joe Sakic A 30.00 60.00
KA Evander Kane D EXCH 8.00 20.00
KN Patrick Kane B 25.00 50.00
LE Lars Eller D 8.00 20.00
MB Mike Bossy A 40.00 80.00
MB Martin Brodeur A 40.00 80.00
MF Marc-Andre Fleury C 12.00 30.00
MG Mike Gartner D 8.00 20.00
ML Mario Lemieux A 75.00 135.00
MM Mark Messier A
PB Patrice Bergeron C 15.00 30.00
PD Pavel Datsyuk B 20.00 40.00
PK Phil Kessel C EXCH 10.00 25.00
PR Patrick Roy A 75.00 135.00
PS P.K. Subban C EXCH 15.00 40.00
RA Bill Ranford C 8.00 20.00
RB Ray Bourque A
RF Ron Francis A 20.00 50.00
RK Ryan Kesler D 8.00 20.00
RN Ryan Nugent-Hopkins B 30.00 60.00
SB Sven Baertschi D 6.00 15.00
SC Sean Couturier D 8.00 20.00
SD Sidney Crosby A 125.00 200.00
SW Jaden Schwartz D 6.00 15.00
TA Maxime Talbot D 5.00 12.00
TH Taylor Hall C 20.00 40.00
TL Trevor Linden D 8.00 20.00
TO Terry O'Reilly C 8.00 20.00
TS Tyler Seguin B 20.00 50.00
TV John Tavares C 12.00 30.00
TW Jonathan Toews B 25.00 60.00
WC Wendel Clark B 15.00 30.00
WG Wayne Gretzky A 150.00 250.00
ZK Zack Kassian D 6.00 15.00

2013-14 Upper Deck Trilogy Signature Pucks

ROUP A ODDS 1:200
ROUP B ODDS 1:92
ROUP C ODDS 1:70
ROUP D ODDS 1:38
ROUP E ODDS 1:24
VERALL ODDS 1:9
XCH EXPIRATION: 6/19/2015
PAG Alex Galchenyuk E 20.00 50.00
PAL Anders Lindback E 6.00 15.00
PAO Alexander Ovechkin A 40.00 80.00
PAS Andrew Shaw E 15.00 30.00
PBE Jean Beliveau A 75.00 150.00
PBG Brendan Gallagher D 20.00 50.00
PBH Bobby Hull B 30.00 60.00
PBM Brad Marchand E 12.00 30.00
PBO Bobby Orr C 75.00 150.00
PBR Bobby Ryan D 8.00 20.00
PBS Brayden Schenn D 8.00 20.00
PBT Bryan Trottier C 15.00 40.00
PCA Carl Hagelin D 8.00 20.00
PCC Cory Conacher E 5.00 12.00
PCH Cody Hodgson E 8.00 20.00
PCK Chris Kreider D 8.00 20.00
PCN Cam Neely B 20.00 40.00
PCP Carey Price B 40.00 80.00
PCS Cory Schneider B 8.00 20.00
PDA Dale Hawerchuk B 12.00 30.00
PDG Doug Gilmour B 25.00 50.00
PDH Dougie Hamilton E 10.00 25.00
PDS Darryl Sittler B 20.00 40.00
PEK Erik Karlsson A
PEL Eric Lindros A 30.00 60.00
PGA Jake Gardiner E 8.00 20.00
PGF Grant Fuhr B 15.00 40.00
PGG Mikhail Grigorenko E 10.00 25.00
PGL Gabriel Landeskog E EXCH 15.00 40.00
PGR Mikael Granlund E 12.00 30.00
PHA Dominik Hasek A
PHB Jonathan Huberdeau D 15.00 40.00
PHU Brett Hull A
PJA Jaden Schwartz E 10.00 25.00
PJB Jamie Benn E 10.00 25.00
PJD Jordan Schroeder D 8.00 20.00
PJE Jordan Eberle C 25.00 50.00
PJG Josh Gorges A
PJH Jaroslav Halak D 8.00 20.00
PJI Jarome Iginla A 15.00 40.00
PJJ Jaromir Jagr A 50.00 100.00
PJK Jake Allen E 10.00 25.00
PJQ Jonathan Quick D 15.00 30.00
PJS Jeff Skinner D 6.00 15.00
PJT Jonathan Toews B EXCH 40.00 80.00
PKE Phil Kessel C 12.00 30.00
PKU Jari Kurri A 20.00 50.00
PLA Guy Lafleur A 30.00 60.00
PLC Logan Couture D 8.00 20.00
PLL Louis Leblanc C 10.00 25.00
PMB Mikkel Boedker C 6.00 15.00
PMF Marc-Andre Fleury C 15.00 40.00
PMG Mike Gartner E 8.00 20.00
PMI Mike Bossy B 25.00 50.00

SPML Mario Lemieux A 90.00 150.00
SPMM Mark Messier A 30.00 60.00
SPMS Marc Staal D 8.00 20.00
SPNH Ryan Nugent-Hopkins B EXCH 20.00 50.00
SPNL Nicklas Lidstrom A 40.00 80.00
SPNY Nail Yakupov E EXCH 25.00 50.00
SPPB Patrice Bergeron C 15.00 40.00
SPPC Paul Coffey A 25.00 60.00
SPPD Pavel Datsyuk B 15.00 40.00
SPPR Patrick Roy A 60.00 120.00
SPPS P.K. Subban C 25.00 50.00
SPRA Bill Ranford C 15.00 30.00
SPRD Raphael Diaz C 6.00 15.00
SPRE Ryan Ellis D 5.00 12.00
SPRF Ron Francis B 15.00 40.00
SPRH Ron Hextall B 15.00 40.00
SPRI Pekka Rinne C 12.00 30.00
SPRJ Ryan Johansen D 10.00 25.00
SPRN Rick Nash C 15.00 30.00
SPRS Ryan Spooner D 12.00 30.00
SPRY Ryan Smyth B 10.00 25.00
SPSA Joe Sakic A 30.00 60.00
SPSB Sven Baertschi E 6.00 15.00
SPSC Sidney Crosby A EXCH 100.00 175.00
SPSH Brendan Smith E 6.00 15.00
SPSM Stan Mikita B 25.00 50.00
SPSV Jakob Silfverberg E 6.00 15.00
SPSZ Justin Schultz E 15.00 40.00
SPTA John Tavares E 20.00 50.00
SPTH Taylor Hall B 30.00 80.00
SPTL Trevor Linden A 25.00 50.00
SPTS Tyler Seguin C EXCH 12.00 30.00
SPTT Tony Tanti B 8.00 20.00
SPVT Vladimir Tarasenko E EXCH 12.00 30.00
SPWG Wayne Gretzky A 150.00 250.00
SPZP Zach Parise B 20.00 40.00

2013-14 Upper Deck Trilogy Three Star International Jerseys

GROUP A ODDS 1:555
GROUP B ODDS 1:52
GROUP C ODDS 1:30
GROUP D ODDS 1:17
OVERALL ODDS 1:9
CANGR8 Grtzky/Lmieux/Sakic A 40.00 80.00
CANNET Lngo/Brdr/Fleury D 5.00 12.00
CANYNG Hbrdeau/Lghtn/Cncher D 5.00 12.00
CZRFWD Jagr/Plknc/Elias D 10.00 25.00
CZRNET Vkoun/Hsek/Pvlec C 5.00 12.00
FINNET Rnne/Kprsff/Lhtnen C 5.00 12.00
RUSFWD Ovchkn/Dtsyk/Ykpv D 10.00 25.00
RUSNET Bryzglv/Vrlmv/Khbblin B 4.00 10.00
SLVGR8 Hssa/Gbrk/Chara C 5.00 12.00
SWEDEF Slmng/Ldstrm/Ekmn-Lrssn D 4.00 10.00
SWEDET Zttrbrg/Ldstrm/Frnzn B 5.00 12.00
SWEFWD Lndskg/Brglnd/Pjrvi D 4.00 10.00
SWEPTS Sndin/Ldstrm/Alfrdssn A 8.00 20.00
USAFWD Ststny/Drry/Brwn B 4.00 10.00
USANET Quick/Mller/Thmas C 6.00 15.00
USAYNG Glchnyk/Cyle/Etem D 5.00 12.00
RUSSTAR Bure/Ovchkn/Malkin C 15.00 40.00
SWEROOK Fsth/Brdin/Rkell C 4.00 10.00
SWESTAR Krlssn/Bckstrm/Zttrbrg B 8.00 20.00
SWEYDEF Ekmn-Lrssn/Lrssn/Brdn B 4.00 10.00
USASTAR Kne/Pvlski/Parise A 12.00 30.00
CANROOKD Hmltn/Olksk/Schltz D 4.00 10.00
CANROOKF Hbrdeau/Lghtn/Spner D 4.00 10.00

2013-14 Upper Deck Trilogy Three Star Past Present Future Jerseys

GROUP A ODDS 1:7006
GROUP B ODDS 1:1822
GROUP C ODDS 1:1001
GROUP D ODDS 1:51
GROUP E ODDS 1:35
GROUP F ODDS 1:16
OVERALL ODDS 1:9
PPFANA Ndrmyr/Gtzlf/Rkell F 6.00 15.00
PPFBOS Espsto/Brgrn/Sgin F 6.00 15.00
PPFCAR Frncs/Staal/Sknner D 5.00 12.00
PPFCGY McDnld/Ignla/Crvnka F 4.00 10.00
PPFDAL Mdno/Benn/Olksk D 6.00 15.00
PPFDRW Hsek/Hwrd/Mrzk E 8.00 20.00
PPFEDM Grtzky/Hall/Ykpv B 30.00 60.00
PPFFLA Bre/Vrstg/Hwdn C 5.00 12.00
PPFMON Koivu/Ellr/Glchnyk E 6.00 15.00
PPFMTL Rbnsn/Mrkv/Sbban F 6.00 15.00
PPFOIL Cffey/Whtny/Schltz F 4.00 10.00
PPFPHI Lndrs/Groux/Lghtn E 6.00 15.00
PPFSJS Thrntn/Cture/Ptrcki E 4.00 10.00
PPFSTL Fdrko/Brglnd/Trsnko D 5.00 12.00
PPFVAN Bure/Sdin/Schrder F 5.00 12.00
PPFBEES Bcyk/Hrtn/Spner F 4.00 10.00
PPFBOST Brque/Chra/Hmltn D 5.00 12.00
PPFEDMF Krri/Smyth/Ebrle D 4.00 10.00
PPFMINN Gbrik/Prise/Cyle E 4.00 10.00
PPFDUCKS Giguere/Hller/Fsth F 4.00 10.00
PPFPNTHR Bure/Flschmnn/Hbrd A 10.00 25.00
PPFWINGS Ldstrm/Zttrbrg/Brnner D 5.00 12.00

2014-15 Upper Deck Trilogy

COMP.SET w/o RC's (100) 15.00 40.00
101-133 ROOKIE PRINT RUN 799
134-166 ROOKIE AU PRINT RUN 399
EXCH EXPIRATION: 1/6/2017
1 Morgan Rielly .75 2.00
2 Anze Kopitar 1.25 3.00
3 Pekka Rinne 1.00 2.50
4 Sidney Crosby 3.00 8.00
5 Jonathan Quick 1.25 3.00
6 Chris Kunitz .75 2.00
7 Joe Thornton .75 2.00
8 Gabriel Landeskog .60 1.50
9 Milan Lucic .75 2.00
10 Sergei Bobrovsky .75 2.00
11 Alex Galchenyuk 1.25 3.00
12 Claude Giroux .75 2.00
13 Ryan Getzlaf 1.25 3.00
14 Cody Hodgson .75 2.00
15 Jacob Trouba .60 1.50
16 Jordan Eberle .75 2.00
17 Jamie Benn 1.00 2.50
18 Ryan Johansen 1.00 2.50
19 Pavel Datsyuk 1.00 2.50
20 Ryan McDonagh .75 2.00
21 Alexander Ovechkin 3.00 8.00
22 Vladimir Tarasenko 1.25 3.00
23 Nicklas Backstrom 1.25 3.00
24 Blake Wheeler .75 2.00
25 Corey Crawford 1.00 2.50
26 Rick Nash .75 2.00
27 Jonathan Bernier .75 2.00
28 Alexander Steen .75 2.00
29 Henrik Sedin .75 2.00
30 Joe Pavelski .75 2.00
31 Tuukka Rask .75 2.00
32 Antti Niemi .60 1.50
33 Henrik Lundqvist 1.00 2.50
34 Brent Seabrook .75 2.00
35 Taylor Hall 1.50 4.00
36 Zach Parise .75 2.00
37 Brendan Gallagher .75 2.00
38 Brad Marchand 1.00 2.50
39 Evgeni Malkin 2.50 6.00
40 Kyle Okposo .75 2.00
41 Logan Couture .75 2.00
42 Ryan Nugent-Hopkins .75 2.00
43 David Backes .75 2.00
44 Jonathan Huberdeau .75 2.00
45 Carey Price 2.50 6.00
46 P.K. Subban 1.25 3.00
47 Drew Doughty .75 2.00
48 Nazem Kadri .75 2.00
49 Corey Perry .75 2.00
50 John Gibson 1.00 2.50
51 Phil Kessel 1.00 2.50
52 James van Riemsdyk .75 2.00
53 Jeff Carter .75 2.00
54 Patrice Bergeron 1.00 2.50
55 Aleksander Barkov .75 2.00
56 Kari Lehtonen .60 1.50
57 Shea Weber .60 1.50
58 Daniel Sedin .75 2.00
59 Eric Staal 1.00 2.50
60 Ryan Suter .75 2.00
61 Patrick Kane 1.50 4.00
62 Jonathan Toews 1.50 4.00
63 Cam Ward .75 2.00
64 Cory Schneider .60 1.50
65 Boone Jenner .50 1.25
66 Dustin Byfuglien .75 2.00
67 John Tavares 1.50 4.00
68 Ryan Callahan .75 2.00
69 Steven Stamkos 1.50 4.00
70 Erik Karlsson 1.50 4.00
71 Martin St. Louis .75 2.00
72 Zemgus Girgensons .75 2.00
73 Tomas Hertl .75 2.00
74 Kyle Turris .75 2.00
75 Roberto Luongo .75 2.00
76 Max Pacioretty .75 2.00
77 Brandon Dubinsky .60 1.50
78 Mark Giordano .60 1.50
79 Semyon Varlamov .75 2.00
80 Nathan MacKinnon 1.50 4.00
81 Bryan Little .75 2.00
82 Henrik Zetterberg 1.00 2.50
83 Patrick Sharp .75 2.00
84 Sean Monahan .75 2.00
85 Mike Smith .75 2.00
86 T.J. Oshie 1.25 3.00
87 Jaromir Jagr 2.00 5.00
88 Matt Duchene .75 2.00
89 Tyler Seguin 1.25 3.00
90 Arturs Irbe .60 1.50
91 Bobby Orr 2.50 6.00
92 Teemu Selanne 1.50 4.00
93 Patrick Roy 2.00 5.00
94 Jeremy Roenick .75 2.00
95 Rob Blake .75 2.00
96 Mats Sundin .75 2.00
97 Mario Lemieux 2.50 6.00
98 Mike Bossy .75 2.00
99 Wayne Gretzky 4.00 10.00
100 Steve Yzerman 1.50 4.00
101 Oscar Klefbom/799 RC 4.00 10.00
102 Johnny Gaudreau/799 RC 6.00 15.00
103 Jonathan Drouin/799 RC 5.00 12.00
104 Teuvo Teravainen/799 RC 3.00 8.00
105 Greg McKegg/799 RC 1.50 4.00
106 Joey Hishon/799 RC 2.50 6.00
107 Marko Dano/799 RC 2.00 5.00
108 Ryan Sproul/799 RC 2.00 5.00
109 Evgeny Kuznetsov/799 RC 8.00 20.00
110 Brandon Gormley/799 RC 2.00 5.00
111 Aaron Ekblad/799 RC 8.00 20.00
112 Andre Burakovsky/799 RC 3.00 8.00
113 Curtis Lazar/799 RC 2.50 6.00
114 Victor Rask/799 RC 2.00 5.00
115 A.Khokhlachev/799 RC 2.00 5.00
116 Mark Visentin/799 RC 2.00 5.00
117 Vincent Trocheck/799 RC 2.50 6.00
118 Sam Reinhart/799 RC 6.00 15.00
119 Damon Severson/799 RC 2.00 5.00
120 Alexander Wennberg/799 RC 4.00 10.00
121 Colton Sissons/799 RC 2.00 5.00
122 William Karlsson/799 RC 8.00 20.00
123 Calle Jarnkrok/799 RC 2.00 5.00
124 Stuart Percy/799 RC 2.00 5.00
125 Anthony Duclair/799 RC 3.00 8.00
126 Griffin Reinhart/799 RC 2.50 6.00
127 Chris Tierney/799 RC 2.00 5.00
128 Jake McCabe/799 RC 2.00 5.00
129 Mirco Mueller/799 RC 2.00 5.00
130 V.Namestnikov/799 RC 3.00 8.00
131 Leon Draisaitl/799 RC 10.00 25.00
132 Bo Horvat/799 RC 6.00 15.00
133 Ty Rattie/799 RC 2.50 6.00
134 Oscar Klefbom AU/399 10.00 25.00
135 Johnny Gaudreau AU/399 25.00 50.00
136 Jonathan Drouin AU/399 12.00 30.00
137 Teuvo Teravainen AU/399 8.00 20.00
138 Greg McKegg AU/399 4.00 10.00
139 Joey Hishon AU/399 6.00 15.00
140 Marko Dano AU/399 5.00 12.00
141 Ryan Sproul AU/399 5.00 12.00
142 Evgeny Kuznetsov AU/399 15.00 30.00
143 Brandon Gormley AU/399 5.00 12.00
144 Aaron Ekblad AU/399 20.00 50.00
145 Andre Burakovsky AU/399 8.00 20.00
146 Curtis Lazar AU/399 6.00 15.00
147 Victor Rask AU/399 5.00 12.00
148 A.Khokhlachev AU/399 5.00 12.00
149 Mark Visentin AU/399 5.00 12.00
150 Vincent Trocheck AU/399 6.00 15.00
151 Sam Reinhart AU/399 15.00 40.00
152 Damon Severson AU/399 5.00 12.00
153 Alexander Wennberg AU/399 10.00 25.00
154 Colton Sissons AU/399 5.00 12.00
155 William Karlsson AU/399 20.00 50.00
156 Calle Jarnkrok AU/399 EXCH 5.00 12.00
157 Stuart Percy AU/399 5.00 12.00
158 Anthony Duclair AU/399 EXCH 8.00 20.00
159 Griffin Reinhart AU/399 6.00 15.00
160 Chris Tierney AU/399 5.00 12.00
161 Jake McCabe AU/399 EXCH 5.00 12.00
162 MIrco Mueller AU/399 5.00 12.00
163 V.Namestnikov AU/399 6.00 15.00
164 Leon Draisaitl AU/399 40.00 100.00
165 Bo Horvat AU/399 10.00 25.00
166 Ty Rattie AU/399 6.00 15.00
167 Oscar Klefbom AU/49 25.00 60.00
168 Johnny Gaudreau AU/49 125.00 250.00
169 Jonathan Drouin AU/49 60.00 120.00
170 Teuvo Teravainen AU/49 20.00 50.00
171 Greg McKegg AU/49 10.00 25.00
172 Joey Hishon AU/49 15.00 40.00
173 Marko Dano AU/49 12.00 30.00
174 Ryan Sproul AU/49 12.00 30.00
175 Evgeny Kuznetsov AU/49 30.00 80.00
176 Brandon Gormley AU/49 12.00 30.00
177 Aaron Ekblad AU/49 40.00 80.00
178 Andre Burakovsky AU/49 20.00 50.00
179 Curtis Lazar AU/49 20.00 50.00
180 Victor Rask AU/49 12.00 30.00
181 A.Khokhlachev AU/49 12.00 30.00
182 Mark Visentin AU/49 12.00 30.00
183 Vincent Trocheck AU/49 15.00 40.00
184 Sam Reinhart AU/49 40.00 100.00
185 Damon Severson AU/49 12.00 30.00
186 Alexander Wennberg AU/49 25.00 60.00
187 Colton Sissons AU/49 12.00 30.00
188 William Karlsson AU/49 50.00 120.00
189 Calle Jarnkrok AU/49 EXCH 12.00 30.00
190 Stuart Percy AU/49 12.00 30.00
191 Anthony Duclair AU/49 EXCH 20.00 50.00
192 Griffin Reinhart AU/49 15.00 40.00
193 Chris Tierney AU/49 12.00 30.00
194 Jake McCabe AU/49 EXCH 12.00 30.00
195 Mirco Mueller AU/49 12.00 30.00
196 V.Namestnikov AU/49 15.00 40.00
197 Leon Draisaitl AU/49 25.00 60.00
198 Bo Horvat AU/49 25.00 60.00
199 Ty Rattie AU/49 15.00 40.00
200 Drn/Ekb/Rnhrt AU/25 200.00 350.00

2014-15 Upper Deck Trilogy Radiant Blue

*VETS/200-367: 1.5X TO 4X BASIC CARDS
*VETS/102-196: 2X TO 5X BASIC CARDS
*VETS/54-99: 2.5X TO 6X BASIC CARDS
*101-133 ROOK/499: .4X TO 1X BASIC RC/799
*134-166 ROOK.AU/225: .5X TO 1.2X AUTO/399
*167-199 ROOK.AU/15: X TO X AUTO/49
EXCH EXPIRATION: 12/18/2017
23 Nicklas Backstrom/367 5.00 12.00
25 Corey Crawford/115 5.00 12.00
168 Johnny Gaudreau AU/15 250.00 400.00
169 Jonathan Drouin AU/15 175.00 300.00
177 Aaron Ekblad AU/15 125.00 200.00

2014-15 Upper Deck Trilogy Radiant Green

*VETS/54-99: 2.5X TO 6X BASIC CARDS
*VETS/30-48: 3X TO 8X BASIC CARDS
*VETS/15-29: 4X TO 10X BASIC CARDS
*101-133 ROOK/199: .5X TO 1.2X BASIC RC/799
*134-166 ROOK.AU/99: .6X TO 1.5X AUTO/399
23 Nicklas Backstrom/61 8.00 20.00
25 Corey Crawford/32 8.00 20.00
99 Wayne Gretzky/20 40.00 80.00
135 Johnny Gaudreau AU/99 75.00 150.00

2014-15 Upper Deck Trilogy Crystal

TCAK Anze Kopitar/275 6.00 15.00
TCAO Alexander Ovechkin/275 15.00 40.00
TCCG Claude Giroux/275 5.00 12.00
TCCP Carey Price/275 10.00 25.00
TCEM Evgeni Malkin/275 12.00 30.00
TCHL Henrik Lundqvist/275 5.00 12.00
TCHZ Henrik Zetterberg/275 5.00 12.00
TCJJ Jaromir Jagr/275 10.00 25.00
TCJQ Jonathan Quick/275 6.00 15.00
TCJT Jonathan Toews/275 8.00 20.00
TCMD Matt Duchene/275 4.00 10.00
TCPB Patrice Bergeron/275 5.00 12.00
TCPD Pavel Datsyuk/275 5.00 12.00
TCPK Phil Kessel/275 5.00 12.00
TCPS P.K. Subban/275 6.00 15.00
TCRG Ryan Getzlaf/275 6.00 15.00
TCSC Sidney Crosby/275 12.00 30.00
TCSS Steven Stamkos/275 8.00 20.00
TCTA John Tavares/275 8.00 20.00
TCZP Zach Parise/275 4.00 10.00
TCRAE1 Aaron Ekblad/399 12.00 30.00
TCRAE2 Aaron Ekblad/249 15.00 40.00
TCRAE3 Aaron Ekblad/125 20.00 50.00
TCRAK1 Alexander Khokhlachev/399 3.00 8.00
TCRAK2 Alexander Khokhlachev/249 4.00 10.00
TCRAK3 Alexander Khokhlachev/125 5.00 12.00
TCRBG1 Brandon Gormley/399 3.00 8.00
TCRBG2 Brandon Gormley/249 4.00 10.00
TCRBG3 Brandon Gormley/125 5.00 12.00
TCRBH1 Bo Horvat/399 6.00 15.00
TCRBH2 Bo Horvat/249 8.00 20.00
TCRBH3 Bo Horvat/125 10.00 25.00
TCRCJ1 Calle Jarnkrok/399 3.00 8.00
TCRCJ2 Calle Jarnkrok/249 4.00 10.00
TCRCJ3 Calle Jarnkrok/125 5.00 12.00
TCRCL1 Curtis Lazar/399 4.00 10.00
TCRCL2 Curtis Lazar/249 5.00 12.00
TCRCL3 Curtis Lazar/125 6.00 15.00
TCREK1 Evgeny Kuznetsov/399 12.00 30.00
TCREK2 Evgeny Kuznetsov/249 15.00 40.00
TCREK3 Evgeny Kuznetsov/125 20.00 50.00
TCRJD1 Jonathan Drouin/399 8.00 20.00
TCRJD2 Jonathan Drouin/249 10.00 25.00
TCRJD3 Jonathan Drouin/125 12.00 30.00
TCRJG1 Johnny Gaudreau/399 10.00 25.00
TCRJG2 Johnny Gaudreau/249 12.00 30.00
TCRJG3 Johnny Gaudreau/125 15.00 40.00
TCRJH1 Joey Hishon/399 4.00 10.00
TCRJH2 Joey Hishon/249 5.00 12.00
TCRJH3 Joey Hishon/125 6.00 15.00
TCRLD1 Leon Draisaitl/399 15.00 40.00
TCRLD2 Leon Draisaitl/249 20.00 50.00
TCRLD3 Leon Draisaitl/125 25.00 60.00
TCRMV1 Mark Visentin/399 3.00 8.00
TCRMV2 Mark Visentin/249 4.00 10.00
TCRMV3 Mark Visentin/125 5.00 12.00
TCRSR1 Sam Reinhart/399 10.00 25.00
TCRSR2 Sam Reinhart/249 12.00 30.00
TCRSR3 Sam Reinhart/125 15.00 40.00
TCRTR1 Ty Rattie/399 4.00 10.00
TCRTR2 Ty Rattie/249 5.00 12.00
TCRTR3 Ty Rattie/125 6.00 15.00
TCRTT1 Teuvo Teravainen/399 5.00 12.00
TCRTT2 Teuvo Teravainen/249 6.00 15.00
TCRTT3 Teuvo Teravainen/125 8.00 20.00
TCRVN1 V.Namestnikov/399 5.00 12.00
TCRVN2 V.Namestnikov/249 6.00 15.00
TCRVN3 Vladislav Namestnikov/125 8.00 20.00

2014-15 Upper Deck Trilogy Ice Scripts

GROUP A STATED ODDS 1:317
GROUP B STATED ODDS 1:269
GROUP C STATED ODDS 1:250
GROUP D STATED ODDS 1:97
OVERALL STATED ODDS 1:48
GRP A UPDATE ODDS 1:3024 '15-16 TRILOGY
GRP B UPDATE ODDS 1:594 '15-16 TRILOGY
OVERALL UPDATE ODDS 1:496 '15-16 TRILOGY
ISAO Alexander Ovechkin A 50.00 100.00
ISAT Alex Tanguay D 6.00 15.00
ISBH Bobby Hull A 30.00 60.00
ISBO Bobby Orr A 60.00 120.00
ISBO Sergei Bobrovsky D 10.00 25.00
ISBR Bobby Ryan B 10.00 25.00
ISCG Claude Giroux Upd. B 10.00 25.00
ISCL Claude Lemieux D 0.00 20.00
ISCN Cam Neely C 12.00 30.00
ISDB David Backes C 10.00 25.00
ISDG Doug Gilmour B 15.00 40.00
ISDS Darryl Sittler C 12.00 30.00
ISEK Evgeny Kuznetsov D 15.00 40.00
ISEM Evgeni Malkin A 30.00 60.00
ISJB Jonathan Bernier B 10.00 25.00
ISJB Johnny Bucyk C 8.00 20.00
ISJJ Jaromir Jagr C 40.00 80.00
ISJS Jaden Schwartz C 12.00 30.00
ISJT John Tavares D 20.00 50.00
ISLR Larry Robinson B 12.00 30.00
ISMB Mike Bossy B 12.00 30.00
ISMG Marian Gaborik D 10.00 25.00
ISMP Max Pacioretty D 10.00 25.00
ISNK Niklas Kronwall D 8.00 20.00
ISNL Nicklas Lidstrom B 12.00 30.00
ISPE Phil Esposito A 20.00 40.00
ISPS Patrick Sharp Upd. A 10.00 25.00
ISRB Ray Bourque A 25.00 50.00
ISRF Ron Francis D 12.00 30.00
ISRM Ryan McDonagh Upd. B 8.00 20.00
ISSB Scotty Bowman A 12.00 30.00
ISSM Stan Mikita B 30.00 60.00
ISSY Steve Yzerman A 60.00 100.00
ISTL Trevor Linden B 12.00 30.00
ISTT Teuvo Teravainen D 15.00 40.00
ISVL Vincent Lecavalier B 10.00 25.00
ISWG Wayne Gretzky A 150.00 250.00
ISZP Zach Parise A 12.00 30.00

2014-15 Upper Deck Trilogy Signature Pucks

GROUP A STATED ODDS 1:535
GROUP B STATED ODDS 1:136
GROUP C STATED ODDS 1:79
GROUP D STATED ODDS 1:73
GROUP E STATED ODDS 1:26
OVERALL STATED ODDS 1:14
SPAB Aleksander Barkov D 8.00 20.00
SPAG Alex Galchenyuk D 15.00 40.00
SPAI Arturs Irbe B
SPAO Alexander Ovechkin A EXCH 50.00 100.00
SPAR Antti Raanta E 12.00 30.00
SPBA David Backes D 8.00 20.00
SPBB Brian Bellows D 8.00 20.00
SPBG Brandon Gormley E 6.00 15.00
SPBH Bobby Hull B 15.00 40.00
SPBL Brian Leetch C 10.00 25.00
SPBO Bobby Orr B 60.00 100.00
SPBP Brad Park C 6.00 15.00
SPBR Martin Brodeur A
SPCG Claude Giroux B 20.00 40.00
SPCJ Calle Jarnkrok E EXCH 6.00 15.00
SPCP Corey Perry D EXCH 8.00 20.00
SPDB Dustin Brown D 6.00 15.00
SPDD Danny DeKeyser E 6.00 15.00
SPDG Doug Gilmour B 15.00 40.00
SPDI Dion Phaneuf C 8.00 20.00
SPDK Darcy Kuemper E 6.00 15.00
SPDS Denis Savard D 10.00 25.00
SPEK Evgeny Kuznetsov E 12.00 30.00
SPFP Felix Potvin C 20.00 40.00
SPGC Guy Carbonneau C 12.00 30.00
SPGF Grant Fuhr A 25.00 50.00
SPJA Jacob Trouba E 6.00 15.00
SPJB Jonathan Bernier C 8.00 20.00
SPJD Jonathan Drouin C EXCH 20.00 40.00
SPJG Johnny Gaudreau E EXCH 40.00 80.00
SPJH Joey Hishon D 8.00 20.00
SPJJ Jaromir Jagr A
SPJO Jonathan Toews A 40.00 80.00
SPJP Joe Pavelski E 10.00 25.00
SPJR Jeremy Roenick B 12.00 30.00
SPJS Joe Sakic A EXCH
SPJV James van Riemsdyk E EXCH 12.00 30.00
SPKD David Krejci B 12.00 30.00
SPKL Kari Lehtonen C 10.00 25.00
SPKO Olaf Kolzig C 10.00 25.00
SPLC Logan Couture D 10.00 25.00
SPLE John LeClair C 15.00 40.00
SPLR Larry Robinson C 10.00 25.00
SPLU Luc Robitaille B 25.00 50.00
SPMA Steve Mason E 8.00 20.00
SPMB Mike Bossy B
SPMD Matt Duchene C 8.00 20.00
SPMG Marian Gaborik C 12.00 30.00
SPMI Stan Mikita A
SPML Mario Lemieux B EXCH 40.00 80.00
SPMM Mike Modano B 20.00 40.00
SPMR Mike Richter C 12.00 30.00
SPMS Martin St. Louis B 12.00 30.00
SPNL Nicklas Lidstrom B 20.00 40.00
SPNM Nathan MacKinnon D 30.00 60.00
SPOA Adam Oates D 10.00 25.00
SPOM Olli Maatta D EXCH 8.00 20.00
SPPD Pavel Datsyuk B 15.00 40.00
SPPE Phil Esposito A
SPPJ Jason Pominville B 10.00 25.00
SPPK Phil Kessel B 15.00 40.00
SPPR Patrick Roy A 50.00 100.00
SPPT Pierre Turgeon C 12.00 30.00
SPRH Ron Hextall C 15.00 30.00
SPRM Ryan McDonagh E EXCH 12.00 30.00
SPRN Rick Nash B 15.00 40.00
SPRS Ryan Suter E 6.00 15.00
SPRV Rogie Vachon B 15.00 40.00
SPRY Bobby Ryan E 8.00 20.00
SPSC Sidney Crosby A EXCH 75.00 135.00
SPSM Sean Monahan E EXCH 12.00 30.00
SPST Ryan Strome E 6.00 15.00
SPSY Steve Yzerman A
SPTA John Tavares D EXCH 15.00 40.00
SPTE Teuvo Teravainen E 10.00 25.00
SPTJ Tomas Jurco E 8.00 20.00
SPTL Trevor Linden C 8.00 20.00
SPTO Terry O'Reilly C 12.00 30.00
SPTP Tomas Plekanec E 10.00 25.00
SPTR Ty Rattie E 8.00 20.00
SPTS Teemu Selanne B EXCH 40.00 80.00
SPTT Tomas Tatar E 10.00 25.00
SPTW Tom Wilson E 8.00 20.00
SPTY Tyler Toffoli E EXCH 8.00 20.00
SPVN Vladislav Namestnikov E 8.00 20.00
SPWG Wayne Gretzky B 175.00 300.00
SPZP Zach Parise B

2014-15 Upper Deck Trilogy Tryptichs

T1ST1 John Tavares JSY/400 8.00 20.00
T1ST2 Taylor Hall JSY/400 8.00 20.00
TANA1 Corey Perry AU/60 EXCH 12.00 30.00
TANA2 Ryan Getzlaf JSY/400 6.00 15.00
TANA3 Teemu Selanne PATCH/15
TAVS1 Patrick Roy JSY/250 10.00 25.00
TAVS2 Joe Sakic JSY/600 5.00 12.00
TAVS3 Alex Tanguay PATCH/100 5.00 12.00
TBB1 Bobby Orr AU/40 90.00 150.00
TBB2 Phil Esposito JSY/400 6.00 15.00
TBB3 Ray Bourque GLV/50 12.00 30.00
TBEES1 Ray Bourque STK/50 12.00 30.00
TBEES2 Cam Neely STK/50 8.00 20.00
TBEES3 Adam Oates JSY/400 4.00 10.00
TBH1 Brett Hull AU/60 20.00 40.00
TBH2 Brett Hull JSY/600 4.00 10.00
TBH3 Brett Hull PATCH/15
TBOS1 Tuukka Rask JSY/481 4.00 10.00
TBOS2 Zdeno Chara PATCH/150 8.00 20.00
TBOS3 P.Bergeron PATCH/100 10.00 25.00
TCAPS1 Braden Holtby JSY/400 6.00 15.00
TCAPS2 A.Ovechkin STK/150 30.00 80.00
TCAPS3 E.Kuznetsov AU/120 15.00 40.00
TCHI1 Corey Crawford JSY/600 5.00 12.00
TCHI2 Jonathan Toews AU/60 40.00 80.00
TCHI3 Duncan Keith JSY/400 4.00 10.00
TCP1 Carey Price JSY/600 12.00 30.00
TCP2 Carey Price GLV/50 25.00 60.00
TCP3 Carey Price BLK/300 10.00 25.00
TDAL1 Kari Lehtonen JSY/400 3.00 8.00
TDAL2 Tyler Seguin JSY/300 6.00 15.00
TDAL3 Jamie Benn PATCH/75 10.00 25.00
TDRW1 Nicklas Lidstrom JSY/103 5.00 12.00
TDRW2 Steve Yzerman JSY/400 8.00 20.00
TDRW3 Henrik Zetterberg JSY/400 5.00 12.00
TFLY1 Sean Couturier JSY/62 6.00 15.00
TFLY2 Claude Giroux JSY/600 4.00 10.00
TFLY3 Steve Mason JSY/400 3.00 8.00
TGOALIE1 Martin Brodeur JSY/600 8.00 20.00
TGOALIE2 Patrick Roy JSY/250 10.00 25.00
TGOALIE3 Dominik Hasek JSY/400 5.00 12.00
THL1 Henrik Lundqvist BLK/300 8.00 20.00
THL2 H.Lundqvist PATCH/50 10.00 25.00
THL3 Henrik Lundqvist BLK/50 10.00 25.00
THZ1 H.Zetterberg PATCH/50 10.00 25.00
THZ2 Henrik Zetterberg STK/150 10.00 25.00
THZ3 Henrik Zetterberg JSY/400 5.00 12.00
TJR1 Jeremy Roenick AU/60 20.00 40.00
TJR2 Jeremy Roenick JSY/600 4.00 10.00
TJR3 J.Roenick PATCH/100 10.00 25.00
TKINGS1 Wayne Gretzky AU/40 125.00 200.00
TKINGS2 Jari Kurri STK/150 8.00 20.00
TKINGS3 Luc Robitaille JSY/600 4.00 10.00
TLAK1 Jonathan Quick JSY/421 6.00 15.00
TLAK2 Anze Kopitar JSY/400 6.00 15.00
TLAK3 Dustin Brown JSY/400 3.00 8.00
TML1 Mario Lemieux GLV/50 25.00 60.00
TML2 Mario Lemieux AU/40 90.00 150.00
TML3 Mario Lemieux JSY/250 12.00 30.00
TMON1 P.K. Subban PATCH/25
TMON3 Max Pacioretty AU/90 8.00 20.00
TNET1 Curtis Joseph PAD/600 6.00 15.00
TNET2 Dominik Hasek PAD/600 8.00 20.00
TNET3 Grant Fuhr PAD/600 6.00 15.00
TNJD1 Adam Henrique JSY/400 4.00 10.00
TNJD2 Jaromir Jagr AU/40 25.00 50.00
TNJD3 Cory Schneider JSY/400 3.00 8.00
TNYR1 Rick Nash STK/142 8.00 20.00
TNYR2 Mats Zuccarello JSY/400 4.00 10.00
TNYR3 Chris Kreider JSY/90 5.00 12.00
TPB1 Pavel Bure AU/40 EXCH 20.00 50.00
TPB2 Pavel Bure TAG/25
TPB3 Pavel Bure PATCH/50 10.00 25.00
TPIT1 Ron Francis JSY/400 5.00 12.00
TPIT2 Mario Lemieux PATCH/15
TPIT3 Rob Brown PATCH/50 6.00 15.00
TPR1 Patrick Roy PAD/100 12.00 30.00
TPR2 Patrick Roy JSY/250 10.00 25.00
TPR3 Patrick Roy JSY/250 10.00 25.00
TRAN1 Mike Richter PATCH/25 10.00 25.00
TRAN2 Mark Messier STK/100 6.00 15.00
TRAN3 Henrik Lundqvist BLK/300 8.00 20.00
TRB1 Ray Bourque JSY/400 6.00 15.00
TRB2 Ray Bourque JSY/400 6.00 15.00
TRB3 Ray Bourque AU/60
TROOK1 Evgeny Kuznetsov JSY/600 10.00 25.00
TROOK2 Teuvo Teravainen JSY/600 4.00 10.00
TROOK3 Brandon Gormley JSY/600 4.00 10.00
TRUS1 A.Ovechkin JSY/400 15.00 40.00
TRUS2 Evgeni Malkin JSY/400 12.00 30.00
TRUS3 Pavel Datsyuk JSY/100 6.00 15.00
TSC1 Sidney Crosby JSY/400 15.00 40.00
TSC2 Sidney Crosby STK/150 30.00 80.00
TSC3 Sidney Crosby PATCH/15
TSJS1 Joe Thornton PATCH/50 8.00 20.00
TSJS2 Joe Pavelski AU/100 EXCH 8.00 20.00
TSJS3 Antti Niemi JSY/444 3.00 8.00
TSTAR1 Bobby Orr AU/40 90.00 150.00
TSTAR2 Wayne Gretzky BAG/75 25.00 50.00
TSTAR3 Mario Lemieux PATCH/25
TSY1 Steve Yzerman JSY/400 8.00 20.00
TSY2 Steve Yzerman AU/40 60.00 100.00
TSY3 Steve Yzerman STK/50 15.00 40.00
TTBL1 Jonathan Drouin JSY/400 10.00 25.00
TTBL3 Ben Bishop JSY/400 4.00 10.00
TTOR1 Nazem Kadri JSY/400 4.00 10.00
TTOR2 Phil Kessel STK/50 10.00 25.00
TTOR3 J.van Riemsdyk AU/80 8.00 20.00
TVET1 Jaromir Jagr STK/88 20.00 50.00
TVET2 Evgeni Malkin AU/60 25.00 50.00
TWG1 Wayne Gretzky BIB/100 20.00 40.00
TWG2 Wayne Gretzky AU/40 175.00 300.00
TWG3 Wayne Gretzky STK/50 40.00 80.00
TWINGS1 Henrik Zetterberg JSY/400 5.00 12.00
TWINGS2 Nicklas Lidstrom STK/15 15.00 40.00
TWINGS3 Pavel Datsyuk AU/60 20.00 40.00

2015-16 Upper Deck Trilogy

COMP.SET w/o RC's (100) 12.00 30.00
101-133 ROOKIE PRINT RUN 999
134-166 ROOKIE AU PRINT RUN 499
167-199 ROOKIE AU PRINT RUN 49
EXCH EXPIRATION: 12/17/2017
1 Ryan Getzlaf 1.00 2.50
2 Corey Perry .60 1.50
3 Frederik Andersen .50 1.25
4 Shane Doan .50 1.25
5 Oliver Ekman-Larsson .50 1.25
6 Mikkel Boedker .40 1.00
7 Zdeno Chara .60 1.50
8 Patrice Bergeron .75 2.00
9 Tuukka Rask .60 1.50
10 Sam Reinhart .60 1.50
11 Zemgus Girgensons .50 1.25
12 Matt Moulson .50 1.25
13 Johnny Gaudreau 1.00 2.50
14 Sean Monahan .60 1.50
15 Jiri Hudler .50 1.25
16 Eric Staal .75 2.00
17 Cam Ward .60 1.50
18 Elias Lindholm .40 1.00
19 Jonathan Toews 1.25 3.00
20 Duncan Keith .60 1.50
21 Corey Crawford .75 2.00
22 Nathan MacKinnon 1.25 3.00
23 Gabriel Landeskog .60 1.50
24 Matt Duchene .60 1.50
25 Ryan Johansen .75 2.00
26 Brandon Dubinsky .50 1.25
27 Scott Hartnell .60 1.50
28 Tyler Seguin 1.00 2.50
29 Jason Spezza .50 1.25
30 Kari Lehtonen .50 1.25
31 Henrik Zetterberg .75 2.00
32 Pavel Datsyuk .75 2.00
33 Gustav Nyquist .60 1.50
34 Taylor Hall 1.25 3.00
35 Ryan Nugent-Hopkins .60 1.50
36 Jordan Eberle .60 1.50
37 Aaron Ekblad .60 1.50
38 Jaromir Jagr 1.50 4.00
39 Jonathan Huberdeau .60 1.50
40 Jonathan Quick 1.00 2.50
41 Jeff Carter .60 1.50
42 Anze Kopitar 1.00 2.50
43 Zach Parise .60 1.50
44 Ryan Suter .40 1.00
45 Jason Pominville .50 1.25
46 Carey Price 2.00 5.00
47 P.K. Subban 1.00 2.50
48 Max Pacioretty .60 1.50
49 Shea Weber .50 1.25
50 Pekka Rinne .75 2.00
51 Calle Jarnkrok .50 1.25
52 Cory Schneider .50 1.25
53 Adam Henrique .60 1.50
54 Michael Cammalleri .50 1.25
55 John Tavares 1.25 3.00
56 Kyle Okposo .60 1.50
57 Ryan Strome .50 1.25
58 Henrik Lundqvist .75 2.00
59 Rick Nash .60 1.50
60 Mats Zuccarello .50 1.25
61 Mika Zibanejad .60 1.50
62 Craig Anderson .60 1.50
63 Erik Karlsson 1.25 3.00
64 Sean Couturier .60 1.50
65 Jakub Voracek .60 1.50
66 Claude Giroux .60 1.50
67 Sidney Crosby 2.50 6.00
68 Marc-Andre Fleury 1.00 2.50
69 Evgeni Malkin 2.00 5.00
70 Joe Thornton .60 1.50
71 Joe Pavelski .60 1.50
72 Logan Couture .60 1.50
73 Jake Allen .75 2.00
74 Vladimir Tarasenko 1.00 2.50
75 Jaden Schwartz .75 2.00
76 Steven Stamkos 1.25 3.00
77 Ben Bishop .60 1.50
78 Tyler Johnson .50 1.25
79 Jonathan Bernier .60 1.50
80 James van Riemsdyk .60 1.50
81 Nazem Kadri .50 1.25
82 Henrik Sedin .60 1.50
83 Ryan Miller .60 1.50
84 Bo Horvat 1.00 2.50
85 Alexander Ovechkin 2.50 6.00
86 Braden Holtby 1.00 2.50
87 Nicklas Backstrom 1.00 2.50
88 Blake Wheeler .60 1.50
89 Jacob Trouba .50 1.25
90 Mark Scheifele .75 2.00
91 Steve Yzerman 1.00 2.50
92 Felix Potvin 1.00 2.50
93 Mark Messier 1.00 2.50
94 Glenn Hall .50 1.25
95 Martin Brodeur 1.25 3.00
96 Ray Bourque 1.00 2.50
97 Mike Liut .40 1.00
98 Patrick Roy 1.50 4.00
99 Brett Hull .60 1.50
100 Wayne Gretzky 2.00 5.00
101 Connor McDavid RC 30.00 60.00
102 Henrik Samuelsson RC 1.25 3.00
103 Oscar Lindberg RC 1.50 4.00
104 Shane Prince RC 1.25 3.00
105 Robby Fabbri RC 2.00 5.00
106 Jacob de la Rose RC 1.50 4.00
107 Max Domi RC 3.00 8.00
108 Kevin Fiala RC 1.50 4.00
109 Emile Poirier RC 1.50 4.00
110 Sam Bennett RC 2.00 5.00
111 Brock McGinn RC 1.50 4.00
112 Antoine Bibeau RC 1.50 4.00
113 Derek Forbort RC 1.25 3.00
114 Noah Hanifin RC 2.00 5.00
115 Artemi Panarin RC 6.00 15.00
116 Ryan Hartman RC 2.00 5.00
117 Nick Cousins RC 1.50 4.00
118 Kyle Baun RC 1.50 4.00
119 Slater Koekkoek RC 1.25 3.00
120 Dylan Larkin RC 10.00 25.00
121 Daniel Sprong RC 3.00 8.00
122 Josh Anderson RC 1.50 4.00
123 Brendan Ranford RC 1.25 3.00
124 Nikolaj Ehlers RC 3.00 8.00
125 Stefan Noesen RC 1.25 3.00
126 Nicolas Petan RC 1.50 4.00
127 Nikolay Goldobin RC 1.50 4.00
128 Connor Hellebuyck RC 4.00 10.00
129 Anthony Stolarz RC 1.50 4.00
130 Matt Puempel RC 1.25 3.00
131 Jake Virtanen RC 2.00 5.00
132 Mikko Rantanen RC 3.00 8.00
133 Jack Eichel RC 12.00 30.00
134 Connor McDavid AU/499 150.00 250.00
135 Henrik Samuelsson AU/499 2.50 6.00
136 Oscar Lindberg AU/499 3.00 8.00
137 Shane Prince AU/499 2.50 6.00
138 Robby Fabbri AU/499 4.00 10.00
139 Jacob de la Rose AU/499 3.00 8.00
140 Max Domi AU/499 12.00 30.00
141 Kevin Fiala AU/499 3.00 8.00
142 Emile Poirier AU/499 3.00 8.00
143 Sam Bennett AU/499 8.00 20.00
144 Brock McGinn AU/499 3.00 8.00
145 Antoine Bibeau AU/499 3.00 8.00
146 Derek Forbort AU/499 2.50 6.00
147 Noah Hanifin AU/499 4.00 10.00
148 Artemi Panarin AU/499 30.00 60.00
149 Ryan Hartman AU/499 4.00 10.00
150 Nick Cousins AU/499 3.00 8.00
151 Kyle Baun AU/499 3.00 8.00
152 Slater Koekkoek AU/499 2.50 6.00
153 Dylan Larkin AU/499 50.00 100.00
154 Daniel Sprong AU/499 5.00 12.00
155 Josh Anderson AU/499 3.00 8.00
156 Brendan Ranford AU/499 2.50 6.00
157 Nikolaj Ehlers AU/499 6.00 15.00
158 Stefan Noesen AU/499 2.50 6.00
159 Nicolas Petan AU/499 3.00 8.00
160 Nikolay Goldobin AU/499 3.00 8.00
161 Connor Hellebuyck AU/499 10.00 25.00
162 Anthony Stolarz AU/499 3.00 8.00
163 Matt Puempel AU/499 2.50 6.00
164 Jake Virtanen AU/499 6.00 15.00
165 Mikko Rantanen AU/499 6.00 15.00
166 Jack Eichel/499 15.00 40.00
167 Connor McDavid AU/49 500.00 800.00
168 Henrik Samuelsson AU/49 8.00 20.00
169 Oscar Lindberg AU/49 10.00 25.00
170 Shane Prince AU/49 8.00 20.00
171 Robby Fabbri AU/49 12.00 30.00
172 Jacob de la Rose AU/49 10.00 25.00
173 Max Domi AU/49 20.00 50.00

174 Kevin Fiala AU/49 10.00 25.00
175 Emile Poirier AU/49 10.00 25.00
176 Sam Bennett AU/49 60.00 120.00
177 Brock McGinn AU/49 10.00 25.00
178 Antoine Bibeau AU/49 10.00 25.00
179 Derek Forbort AU/49 8.00 20.00
180 Noah Hanifin AU/49 12.00 30.00
181 Artemi Panarin AU/49 EXCH 125.00 200.00
182 Ryan Hartman AU/49 12.00 30.00
183 Nick Cousins AU/49 10.00 25.00
184 Kyle Baun AU/49 10.00 25.00
185 Slater Koekkoek AU/49 8.00 20.00
186 Dylan Larkin AU/49 200.00 350.00
187 Daniel Sprong AU/49 20.00 40.00
188 Josh Anderson AU/49 10.00 25.00
189 Brendan Ranford AU/49 8.00 20.00
190 Nikolaj Ehlers AU/49 20.00 50.00
191 Stefan Noesen AU/49 8.00 20.00
192 Nicolas Petan AU/49 10.00 25.00
193 Nikolay Goldobin AU/49 10.00 25.00
194 Connor Hellebuyck AU/49 40.00 80.00
195 Anthony Stolarz AU/49 10.00 25.00
196 Matt Puempel AU/49 8.00 20.00
197 Jake Virtanen AU/49 30.00 60.00
198 Mikko Rantanen AU/49 20.00 50.00
199 Jack Eichel/49 60.00 120.00
200 McDv/Lrkn/Dmi AU/25 800.00 1200.00
201 Colton Parayko/799 RC 3.00 8.00
Issued in SPx
202 Zachary Fucale/799 RC 2.50 6.00
Issued in SPx
203 Ben Hutton/799 RC 2.50 6.00
Issued in SPx
204 Matt O'Connor/799 RC 2.00 5.00
Issued in SPx
205 Jordan Weal/799 RC 2.50 6.00
Issued in SPx
206 Mattias Janmark/799 RC 2.50 6.00
Issued in SPx
207 Jared McCann/799 RC 2.50 6.00
Issued in SPx
208 Hunter Shinkaruk/799 RC 2.50 6.00
Issued in SPx
209 Andreas Athanasiou/799 RC 6.00 15.00
Issued in SPx
210 Mike Condon/799 RC 2.50 6.00
Issued in SPx
211 Colton Parayko AU/399 5.00 12.00
Issued in SPx
212 Zachary Fucale AU/399 4.00 10.00
Issued in SPx
213 Ben Hutton AU/399 4.00 10.00
Issued in SPx
214 Matt O'Connor AU/399 3.00 8.00
Issued in SPx
215 Jordan Weal AU/399 4.00 10.00
Issued in SPx
216 Mattias Janmark AU/399 4.00 10.00
Issued in SPx
217 Jared McCann AU/399 4.00 10.00
Issued in SPx
218 Hunter Shinkaruk AU/399 4.00 10.00
Issued in SPx
219 Andreas Athanasiou AU/399 10.00 25.00
Issued in SPx
220 Mike Condon AU/399 4.00 10.00
Issued in SPx
221 Colton Parayko AU/49 15.00 40.00
Issued in SPx
222 Zachary Fucale AU/49 12.00 30.00
Issued in SPx
223 Ben Hutton AU/49 12.00 30.00
Issued in SPx
224 Matt O'Connor AU/49 10.00 25.00
Issued in SPx
225 Jordan Weal AU/49 12.00 30.00
Issued in SPx
226 Mattias Janmark AU/49 12.00 30.00
Issued in SPx
227 Jared McCann AU/49 12.00 30.00
Issued in SPx
228 Hunter Shinkaruk AU/49 12.00 30.00
Issued in SPx
229 Andreas Athanasiou AU/49 30.00 80.00
Issued in SPx
230 Mike Condon AU/49 12.00 30.00
Issued in SPx

2015-16 Upper Deck Trilogy Rainbow Black

COMMON PATCH/40-78 6.00 15.00
PATCH UNL.STAR/40-78 8.00 20.00
COMMON PATCH/30-39 6.00 15.00
PATCH SEMISTAR/30-39 8.00 20.00
PATCH UNL.STAR/30-39 10.00 25.00
COMMON PATCH/15-29 8.00 20.00
PATCH SEMISTAR/15-29 10.00 25.00
PATCH UNL.STAR/15-29 12.00 30.00
*101-133 ROOK/49: 1.5X TO 4X BASIC RC/999
*ROOK.AU/130-209: .6X TO 1.5X BASIC AU/499
*ROOK.AU/57-95: .8X TO 2X BASIC AU/499
*ROOK.AU/30-47: 1X TO 2.5X BASIC AU/499
*ROOK.AU/15-27: 1.2X TO 3X BASIC AU/499
13 Johnny Gaudreau PATCH/40 12.00 30.00
19 Jonathan Toews PATCH/28 25.00 60.00
21 Corey Crawford PATCH/32 12.00 30.00
46 Carey Price PATCH/44 30.00 60.00
58 Henrik Lundqvist PATCH/33 12.00 30.00
67 Sidney Crosby PATCH/28 50.00 125.00
68 Marc-Andre Fleury PATCH/34 15.00 40.00
76 Steven Stamkos PATCH/29 25.00 60.00
87 Nicklas Backstrom PATCH/18 20.00 50.00
91 Steve Yzerman PATCH/14
95 Martin Brodeur PATCH/17 25.00 60.00
96 Ray Bourque PATCH/57 12.00 30.00
100 Wayne Gretzky PATCH/18 75.00 125.00
116 Ryan Hartman/49 8.00 20.00
148 Artemi Panarin AU/15 EXCH 125.00 200.00
149 Ryan Hartman AU/30 10.00 25.00
153 Dylan Larkin AU/15 200.00 350.00
161 Connor Hellebuyck AU/130 25.00 50.00

2015-16 Upper Deck Trilogy Rainbow Blue

*1-100 VETS/401-898: 1.2X TO 3X BASIC CARDS
*1-100 VETS/202-395: 1.5X TO 4X BASIC CARDS
*1-100 VETS/108-179: 2X TO 5X BASIC CARDS
*1-100 VETS/60-91: 2.5X TO 6X BASIC CARDS
*101-133 ROOK/399: .5X TO 1.2X BASIC RC/999
*134-166 RK.AU/199: .5X TO 1.2X BASIC AU/499
*167-198 RK.AU/64-97: .25X TO .6X BASIC AU/49
*167-198 RK.AU/41-56: .3X TO .8X BASIC AU/49
*167-198 RK.AU/30-39: .4X TO 1X BASIC AU/49
*167-198 RK.AU/15-29: .5X TO 1.2X BASIC AU/49
167-200 ROOKIE AU PRINT RUN 5-97
21 Corey Crawford/147 4.00 10.00
87 Nicklas Backstrom/572 3.00 8.00
100 Wayne Gretzky/91 20.00 40.00
116 Ryan Hartman/399 2.50 6.00
134 Connor McDavid AU/199 175.00 300.00
148 Artemi Panarin AU/199 50.00 100.00
149 Ryan Hartman AU/199 5.00 12.00
153 Dylan Larkin AU/199 90.00 150.00
166 Jack Eichel/199 15.00 40.00
167 Connor McDavid AU/97 350.00 600.00
181 Artemi Panarin AU/72 90.00 150.00
182 Ryan Hartman AU/38 12.00 30.00
186 Dylan Larkin AU/71 125.00 250.00
199 Jack Eichel/15

2015-16 Upper Deck Trilogy Rainbow Green

1-100 VET JSY PRINT RUN 52-114
101-133 ROOKIE JSY PRINT RUN 599
*134-166 PATCH/35: 1X TO 2.5X JSY/599
UNPRICED TAG PRINT RUN 3-5
1 Ryan Getzlaf JSY/105 6.00 15.00
2 Corey Perry JSY/105 4.00 10.00
3 Frederik Andersen JSY/113 3.00 8.00
4 Shane Doan JSY/95 3.00 8.00
5 Oliver Ekman-Larsson JSY/110 3.00 8.00
6 Mikkel Boedker JSY/108 2.50 6.00
7 Zdeno Chara JSY/97 4.00 10.00
8 Patrice Bergeron JSY/103 5.00 12.00
9 Tuukka Rask JSY/107 4.00 10.00
10 Sam Reinhart JSY/114 4.00 10.00
11 Zemgus Girgensons JSY/113 3.00 8.00
12 Matt Moulson JSY/107 3.00 8.00
13 Johnny Gaudreau JSY/114 6.00 15.00
14 Sean Monahan JSY/113 4.00 10.00
15 Jiri Hudler JSY/103 3.00 8.00
16 Eric Staal JSY/103 5.00 12.00
17 Cam Ward JSY/105 4.00 10.00
18 Elias Lindholm JSY/113 2.50 6.00
19 Jonathan Toews JSY/107 8.00 20.00
20 Duncan Keith JSY/105 4.00 10.00
21 Corey Crawford JSY/105 5.00 12.00
22 Nathan MacKinnon JSY/113 8.00 20.00
23 Gabriel Landeskog JSY/111 4.00 10.00
24 Matt Duchene JSY/109 4.00 10.00
25 Ryan Johansen JSY/111 5.00 12.00
26 Brandon Dubinsky JSY/106 3.00 8.00
27 Scott Hartnell JSY/100 4.00 10.00
28 Tyler Seguin JSY/110 6.00 15.00
29 Jason Spezza JSY/102 3.00 8.00
30 Kari Lehtonen JSY/103 3.00 8.00
31 Henrik Zetterberg JSY/102 5.00 12.00
32 Pavel Datsyuk JSY/101 5.00 12.00
33 Gustav Nyquist JSY/111 4.00 10.00
34 Taylor Hall JSY/110 8.00 20.00
35 Ryan Nugent-Hopkins JSY/111 4.00 10.00
36 Jordan Eberle JSY/110 4.00 10.00
37 Aaron Ekblad JSY/114 4.00 10.00
39 Jonathan Huberdeau JSY/112 4.00 10.00
40 Jonathan Quick JSY/107 6.00 15.00
41 Jeff Carter JSY/105 4.00 10.00
42 Anze Kopitar JSY/106 6.00 15.00
43 Zach Parise JSY/105 4.00 10.00
45 Jason Pominville JSY/103 3.00 8.00
46 Carey Price JSY/107 12.00 30.00
47 P.K. Subban JSY/109 6.00 15.00
48 Max Pacioretty JSY/108 4.00 10.00
49 Shea Weber JSY/105 3.00 8.00
50 Pekka Rinne JSY/105 5.00 12.00
51 Calle Jarnkrok JSY/113 3.00 8.00
52 Cory Schneider JSY/108 3.00 8.00
53 Adam Henrique JSY/110 4.00 10.00
54 Michael Cammalleri JSY/102 3.00 8.00
55 John Tavares JSY/109 8.00 20.00
56 Kyle Okposo JSY/107 4.00 10.00
57 Ryan Strome JSY/113 3.00 8.00
58 Henrik Lundqvist JSY/105 5.00 12.00
59 Rick Nash JSY/102 4.00 10.00
60 Mats Zuccarello JSY/110 3.00 8.00
61 Mika Zibanejad JSY/111 4.00 10.00
62 Craig Anderson JSY/102 4.00 10.00
63 Erik Karlsson JSY/109 8.00 20.00
64 Sean Couturier JSY/111 4.00 10.00
65 Jakub Voracek JSY/108 4.00 10.00
66 Claude Giroux JSY/107 4.00 10.00
67 Sidney Crosby JSY/105 15.00 40.00
68 Marc-Andre Fleury JSY/103 6.00 15.00
69 Evgeni Malkin JSY/106 12.00 30.00
70 Joe Thornton JSY/97 4.00 10.00
71 Joe Pavelski JSY/106 4.00 10.00
72 Logan Couture JSY/109 4.00 10.00
73 Jake Allen JSY/112 5.00 12.00
74 Vladimir Tarasenko JSY/112 6.00 15.00
75 Jaden Schwartz JSY/111 5.00 12.00
76 Steven Stamkos JSY/108 8.00 20.00
77 Ben Bishop JSY/108 4.00 10.00
79 Jonathan Bernier JSY/107 4.00 10.00
80 James van Riemsdyk JSY/109 4.00 10.00
81 Nazem Kadri JSY/109 3.00 8.00
82 Henrik Sedin JSY/100 4.00 10.00
83 Ryan Miller JSY/102 4.00 10.00
85 Alexander Ovechkin JSY/105 15.00 40.00
86 Braden Holtby JSY/110 6.00 15.00
87 Nicklas Backstrom JSY/107 6.00 15.00
88 Blake Wheeler JSY/108 4.00 10.00
89 Jacob Trouba JSY/113 3.00 8.00
90 Mark Scheifele JSY/111 5.00 12.00
91 Steve Yzerman JSY/83 6.00 15.00
93 Mark Messier JSY/79 6.00 15.00
94 Glenn Hall JSY/52 3.00 8.00
95 Martin Brodeur JSY/91 8.00 20.00
96 Ray Bourque JSY/79 6.00 15.00
98 Patrick Roy JSY/84 10.00 25.00
99 Brett Hull JSY/86 4.00 10.00
100 Wayne Gretzky JSY/79 12.00 30.00
101 Connor McDavid JSY/599 30.00 60.00
102 Henrik Samuelsson JSY/599 2.00 5.00
104 Shane Prince JSY/599 2.00 5.00
105 Robby Fabbri JSY/599 3.00 8.00
106 Jacob de la Rose JSY/599 2.50 6.00
107 Max Domi JSY/599 5.00 12.00
108 Kevin Fiala JSY/599 2.50 6.00
109 Emile Poirier JSY/599 2.50 6.00
110 Sam Bennett JSY/599 3.00 8.00
111 Brock McGinn JSY/599 2.50 6.00
112 Antoine Bibeau JSY/599 2.50 6.00
113 Derek Forbort JSY/599 2.00 5.00
114 Noah Hanifin JSY/599 3.00 8.00
116 Ryan Hartman JSY/599 3.00 8.00
117 Nick Cousins JSY/599 2.50 6.00
118 Kyle Baun JSY/599 2.50 6.00
119 Slater Koekkoek JSY/599 2.00 5.00
120 Dylan Larkin JSY/599 12.00 30.00
122 Josh Anderson JSY/599 2.50 6.00
124 Nikolaj Ehlers JSY/599 5.00 12.00
125 Stefan Noesen JSY/599 2.00 5.00
126 Nicolas Petan JSY/599 2.50 6.00
128 Connor Hellebuyck JSY/599 6.00 15.00
130 Matt Puempel JSY/599 2.00 5.00
131 Jake Virtanen JSY/599 3.00 8.00
133 Jack Eichel JSY/599 10.00 25.00
149 Ryan Hartman Patch/35 8.00 20.00

2015-16 Upper Deck Trilogy Ice Scripts

GROUP A ODDS 1:837
GROUP B ODDS 1:371
GROUP C ODDS 1:732
GROUP D ODDS 1:121
GROUP E ODDS 1:209
OVERALL STATED ODDS 1:48
EXCH EXPIRATION: 12/18/2017
ISAG Alex Galchenyuk B
ISAK Anze Kopitar C EXCH 15.00 40.00
ISAO Alexander Ovechkin A 60.00 100.00
ISBG Brendan Gallagher D 10.00 25.00
ISBO Bobby Orr A 60.00 100.00
ISBS Brandon Saad D 8.00 20.00
ISCC Chris Chelios B 12.00 30.00
ISCK Chris Kreider D 8.00 20.00
ISCM Connor McDavid D 175.00 300.00
ISCP Carey Price B 30.00 60.00
ISDP Derrick Pouliot E 6.00 15.00
ISDS Darryl Sittler B 10.00 25.00
ISFA Frederik Andersen B
ISGL Gabriel Landeskog D 8.00 20.00
ISJB Jonathan Bernier C 10.00 25.00
ISJB Jamie Benn A
ISJJ Jaromir Jagr A 30.00 60.00
ISJP Joe Pavelski B 10.00 25.00
ISJR James van Riemsdyk D 8.00 20.00
ISJT John Tavares C 20.00 50.00
ISJT John Tavares B
ISJV Jakub Voracek C 10.00 25.00
ISKT Kyle Turris D 6.00 15.00
ISMG Mike Gartner D 8.00 20.00
ISML Mario Lemieux A 100.00 175.00
ISMN Markus Naslund D 8.00 20.00
ISMR Morgan Rielly B
ISMS Mats Sundin A 20.00 40.00
ISNB Nick Bjugstad E 6.00 15.00
ISNM Nathan MacKinnon A
ISPD Pavel Datsyuk B 12.00 30.00
ISPM Patrick Marleau A 20.00 50.00
ISRB Rob Blake B 12.00 30.00
ISRJ Ryan Johansen D 10.00 25.00
ISRM Ryan Miller A
ISRN Rick Nash B 10.00 25.00
ISSC Sidney Crosby A 75.00 125.00
ISSP Jason Spezza B 10.00 25.00
ISSU Malcolm Subban E 10.00 25.00
ISSY Steve Yzerman A 60.00 100.00
ISTH Taylor Hall D 12.00 30.00
ISTJ Tyler Johnson E 6.00 15.00
ISWG Wayne Gretzky B 175.00 300.00

2015-16 Upper Deck Trilogy Signature Pucks

GROUP A ODDS 1:2237
GROUP B ODDS 1:147
GROUP C ODDS 1:156
GROUP D ODDS 1:85
GROUP E ODDS 1:70
GROUP F ODDS 1:48
OVERALL SIG.PUCK ODDS 1:14
SPAD Anthony Duclair B 8.00 20.00
SPAE Aaron Ekblad B 20.00 40.00
SPAI Arturs Irbe C 8.00 20.00
SPAL Anders Lee B
SPAO Alexander Ovechkin B 30.00 60.00
SPAV Andrei Vasilevskiy F 8.00 20.00
SPBB Ben Bishop E 6.00 15.00
SPBE Jonathan Bernier C 10.00 25.00
SPBG Brendan Gallagher D 10.00 25.00
SPBH Bo Horvat E 10.00 25.00
SPBR Brett Ritchie D 4.00 10.00
SPCC Chris Chelios B 10.00 25.00
SPCH Charles Hudon F 8.00 20.00
SPCM Connor McDavid C 150.00 250.00
SPCP Carey Price B 30.00 60.00
SPCS Cory Schneider C 8.00 20.00
SPDG Doug Gilmour B 15.00 40.00
SPDO Max Domi F 12.00 30.00
SPDP Derrick Pouliot F 5.00 12.00
SPFA Frederik Andersen D 5.00 12.00
SPFF Filip Forsberg A
SPFP Felix Potvin D 10.00 25.00
SPGA Mike Gartner D 6.00 15.00
SPGN Gustav Nyquist B 10.00 25.00
SPJB Jordan Binnington F 5.00 12.00
SPJI Jarome Iginla B 12.00 30.00
SPJK John Klingberg F 8.00 20.00
SPJL Jori Lehtera E 5.00 12.00
SPJP Joe Pavelski C 10.00 25.00
SPJT Jonathan Toews B 30.00 60.00
SPJV John Vanbiesbrouck C 10.00 25.00
SPKO Kyle Okposo B 10.00 25.00
SPKT Kyle Turris F 5.00 12.00
SPKY Keith Yandle B 10.00 25.00
SPLD Leon Draisaitl E 12.00 30.00
SPLE Mario Lemieux A 60.00 100.00
SPMA Martin Brodeur B 40.00 80.00
SPMB Martin Biron E 5.00 12.00
SPMC Marty McSorley D 10.00 25.00
SPMD Marcel Dionne C 12.00 30.00
SPMF Marc-Andre Fleury B 15.00 40.00
SPMG Mikael Granlund E 5.00 12.00
SPMK Mike Keane D 5.00 12.00
SPML Mike Liut E 4.00 10.00
SPMS Malcolm Subban F 15.00 40.00
SPMZ Mats Zuccarello D 6.00 15.00
SPNB Nick Bjugstad F 5.00 12.00
SPNE Nikolaj Ehlers F 8.00 20.00
SPNH Noah Hanifin C 12.00 30.00
SPNK Nikita Kucherov F EXCH 10.00 25.00
SPOR Bobby Orr B 60.00 120.00
SPPA David Pastrnak E 12.00 30.00
SPPD Pavel Datsyuk B 12.00 30.00
SPPM Patrick Marleau B 10.00 25.00
SPPO Jason Pominville D 5.00 12.00
SPPR Patrick Roy A 60.00 100.00
SPPS Patrick Sharp B 10.00 25.00
SPRB Rob Blake B 10.00 25.00
SPRJ Ryan Johansen D 8.00 20.00
SPRK Ryan Kesler D 8.00 20.00
SPRM Ryan Miller B 10.00 25.00
SPRN Rick Nash B 10.00 25.00
SPRY Bobby Ryan C 8.00 20.00
SPSB Sam Bennett E 20.00 40.00
SPSC Sidney Crosby A 60.00 100.00
SPSE Sean Couturier E 6.00 15.00
SPSL Steve Larmer D 5.00 12.00
SPSR Sam Reinhart C 10.00 25.00
SPSV Semyon Varlamov C 10.00 25.00
SPTA John Tavares B 20.00 50.00
SPTB Tom Barrasso D 6.00 15.00
SPTJ Tyler Johnson F 5.00 12.00
SPTK Torey Krug F 6.00 15.00
SPVI Jake Virtanen E 8.00 20.00
SPVO Jakub Voracek E 6.00 15.00
SPWG Wayne Gretzky B 175.00 300.00
SPZG Zemgus Girgensons F 5.00 12.00
SPZP Zach Parise B 10.00 25.00

2015-16 Upper Deck Trilogy Signature Pucks Draft Logo

SPCM1 Connor McDavid/21 300.00 450.00

2015-16 Upper Deck Trilogy Signature Pucks Dual

GROUP A ODDS 1:4187
GROUP B ODDS 1:1794
GROUP C ODDS 1:573
OVERALL STATED ODDS 1:432
EXCK EXPIRATION: 12/21/2017
SP2BK Burakovsky/Kuznetsov C 15.00 40.00
SP2FP Fleury/C.Price A EXCH 50.00 100.00
SP2GM Gretzky/C.McDavid B 700.00 1000.00
SP2JK T.Johnson/Kucherov C 20.00 50.00
SP2LM Lndeskg/McKinn B EXCH 40.00 80.00
SP2PG Pacioretty/Galchenyuk B 30.00 60.00
SP2RT B.Ryan/K.Turris C 10.00 25.00
SP2RW P.Rinne/S.Weber B 20.00 50.00
SP2SN R.Strome/B.Nelson C 10.00 25.00
SP2SS J.Sakic/M.Sundin A
SP2ST P.Sharp/J.Toews A 40.00 80.00
SP2TN T.Tatar/G.Nyquist C 12.00 30.00
SP2WR Wennberg/Rychel C EXCH 10.00 25.00

2015-16 Upper Deck Trilogy Tryptichs

AUTO STATED PRINT RUN 20-80
JSY STATED PRINT RUN 5-250
GLOVE STATED PRINT RUN 10-25
PATCH STATED PRINT RUN 5-75
STICK STATED PRINT RUN 5-75
TJJ1 Jaromir Jagr PATCH/50 25.00 50.00
TJJ2 Jaromir Jagr STK/25 25.00 60.00
TJJ3 Jaromir Jagr STK/75 20.00 50.00
TMB1 Martin Brodeur BLKR/50 20.00 50.00
TMB2 Martin Brodeur PATCH/25 20.00 50.00
TMB3 Martin Brodeur GLV/25 15.00 40.00
TON1 Owen Nolan PATCH/25 8.00 20.00
TON2 Owen Nolan AU/60 8.00 20.00
TON3 Owen Nolan JSY/150 2.50 6.00
TSC1 Sidney Crosby JSY/100 12.00 30.00
TSC2 Sidney Crosby AU/20 75.00 150.00
TSC3 Sidney Crosby STK/50 30.00 80.00
TWG1 Wayne Gretzky STK/25 60.00 120.00
TWG2 Wayne Gretzky AU/20 150.00 250.00
TWG3 Wayne Gretzky Socks/15 60.00 120.00
TBOS1 Bobby Orr AU/20
TBOS2 Ray Bourque AU/40 15.00 40.00
TBOS3 Zdeno Chara PATCH/75 8.00 20.00
TCBH1 Bobby Hull AU/40 12.00 30.00
TCBH2 Glenn Hall JSY/50 5.00 12.00
TCBH3 Tony Esposito AU/40 10.00 25.00
TCGY1 Jiri Hudler JSY/250 2.50 6.00
TCGY2 Sean Monahan JSY/200 3.00 8.00
TCGY3 Johnny Gaudreau JSY/150 5.00 12.00
TCHI1 Corey Crawford JSY/200 4.00 10.00
TCHI2 Patrick Kane PATCH/25 20.00 50.00
TCHI3 Jonathan Toews AU/20
TCOL1 Matt Duchene JSY/200 3.00 8.00
TCOL2 Gabriel Landeskog AU/60 8.00 20.00
TEDM1 Jari Kurri STK/25 10.00 25.00
TEDM2 Glenn Anderson AU/40 10.00 25.00
TEDM3 Grant Fuhr STK/25 10.00 25.00
TFLY1 Jakub Voracek AU/60 8.00 20.00
TFLY2 Claude Giroux PATCH/25 10.00 25.00
TFLY3 Steve Mason JSY/250 2.50 6.00
TLAK1 Drew Doughty GLV/25 8.00 20.00
TLAK2 Dustin Brown GLV/25
TLAK3 Jeff Carter GLV/25 8.00 20.00
TNET1 Terry Sawchuk STK/25 20.00 40.00
TNET3 Patrick Roy STK/50 20.00 50.00
TNYI1 Kyle Okposo PATCH/25 10.00 25.00
TNYI2 John Tavares GLV/25 15.00 40.00
TNYI3 Ryan Strome JSY/250 2.50 6.00
TOIL1 Nail Yakupov PATCH/50 6.00 15.00
TOIL2 Taylor Hall AU/80 10.00 25.00
TOIL3 Ryan Nugent-Hopkins JSY/200 3.00 8.00
TPHI1 Bobby Clarke AU/60 20.00 40.00
TPHI2 Pelle Lindbergh STK/15
TPHI3 Dave Schultz AU/80 8.00 20.00
TRC11 Connor McDavid JSY/250 30.00 60.00
TRC12 Jack Eichel JSY/250 10.00 25.00
TRC13 Sam Bennett JSY/250 3.00 8.00
TRC21 Kevin Fiala JSY/250 3.00 8.00
TRC22 Ryan Hartman JSY/250 4.00 10.00
TRC23 Henrik Samuelsson JSY/250 2.50 6.00
TRC31 Emile Poirier JSY/250 3.00 8.00
TRC32 Matt Puempel JSY/250 2.50 6.00
TRC33 Connor Hellebuyck JSY/250 6.00 15.00
TRUS1 Alexander Ovechkin AU/20 40.00 80.00
TRUS2 Evgeni Malkin PATCH/25 30.00 80.00
TRUS3 Pavel Datsyuk PAD/15 25.00 50.00
TTBL1 Steven Stamkos JSY/150 6.00 15.00
TTBL2 Jonathan Drouin AU/60 10.00 25.00
TTBL3 Ondrej Palat PATCH/50 6.00 15.00
TTML1 Nazem Kadri JSY/150 2.50 6.00
TTML2 Jonathan Bernier AU/60 8.00 20.00
TTML3 James van Riemsdyk PATCH/50 8.00 20.00
TTOR1 Felix Potvin AU/40 15.00 40.00
TTOR2 Doug Gilmour STK/25 12.00 30.00
TTOR3 Borje Salming AU/40 12.00 30.00
TVAN1 Henrik Sedin STK/50 8.00 20.00
TVAN2 Bo Horvat AU/80 12.00 30.00
TVAN3 Ryan Miller JSY/150 3.00 8.00
TBEES2 Phil Esposito AU/20
TBEES3 Ray Bourque GLV/15
TGOON1 Marty McSorley STK/25 10.00 25.00
TGOON2 Dave Schultz AU/60 8.00 20.00
TGOON3 Wendel Clark STK/50 10.00 25.00
TPENS2 Tom Barrasso AU/80 8.00 20.00
TPENS3 Paul Coffey PATCH/15 15.00 40.00
TSTAR1 Bobby Orr AU/20
TSTAR2 Wayne Gretzky AU/20 150.00 250.00
TSTAR3 Connor McDavid AU/60 250.00 400.00
TDRAFT1 Nathan MacKinnon PATCH/25 20.00 50.00
TDRAFT2 Aleksander Barkov JSY/250 3.00 8.00
TDRAFT3 Jonathan Drouin AU/80 10.00 25.00
TISLES1 Bob Bourne AU/40 8.00 20.00
TISLES2 Billy Smith PATCH/25 10.00 25.00
TISLES3 Mike Bossy AU/20 25.00 50.00
TWINGS1 Chris Chelios AU/40 10.00 25.00
TWINGS2 Nicklas Lidstrom AU/40 12.00 30.00
TWINGS3 Steve Yzerman AU/20 40.00 80.00
TGOALIE1 Carey Price BLKR/50 30.00 80.00
TGOALIE2 Jonathan Quick BLKR/50 12.00 30.00

2016-17 Upper Deck Trilogy

1 Patrick Kane 1.25 3.00
2 Steven Stamkos 1.25 3.00
3 Tyler Toffoli .60 1.50
4 Martin Jones .60 1.50
5 John Tavares 1.25 3.00
6 Joe Pavelski .60 1.50
7 Henrik Lundqvist .60 1.50
8 Ryan Getzlaf 1.00 2.50
9 Dylan Larkin 1.00 2.50
10 Evgeni Malkin 2.00 5.00
11 Braden Holtby 1.00 2.50
12 Jaromir Jagr 1.50 4.00
13 Morgan Rielly .50 1.25
14 Jarome Iginla .60 1.50
15 Jonathan Toews 1.25 3.00
16 Tuukka Rask .60 1.50
17 Erik Karlsson 1.25 3.00
18 Anze Kopitar 1.00 2.50
19 Matt Duchene .60 1.50
20 Carey Price 2.00 5.00
21 Tyler Seguin 1.00 2.50
22 Max Pacioretty .60 1.50
23 Filip Forsberg .75 2.00
24 Jaden Schwartz .75 2.00
25 Connor McDavid 3.00 8.00
26 John Klingberg .60 1.50
27 Duncan Keith .60 1.50
28 Aleksander Barkov .60 1.50
29 Nikita Kucherov 1.00 2.50
30 Alexander Ovechkin 2.50 6.00
31 Sam Bennett .75 2.00
32 Torey Krug .60 1.50
33 Claude Giroux .60 1.50
34 Noah Hanifin .60 1.50
35 Cory Schneider .50 1.25
36 Daniel Sedin .60 1.50
37 Jamie Benn .75 2.00
38 Ryan Kesler .60 1.50
39 Zach Parise .60 1.50
40 Johnny Gaudreau 1.00 2.50
41 Jack Eichel 1.25 3.00
42 Henrik Zetterberg .75 2.00
43 Blake Wheeler .60 1.50
44 Max Domi .75 2.00
45 Nick Leddy .40 1.00
46 Phil Kessel .75 2.00
47 Jack Johnson .40 1.00
48 Brent Burns .75 2.00
49 Vladimir Tarasenko 1.00 2.50
50 Sidney Crosby 2.50 6.00
51 Auston Matthews RC 30.00 80.00
52 Patrik Laine RC 12.00 30.00
53 Mitch Marner RC 12.00 30.00
54 Jesse Puljujarvi RC 4.00 10.00
55 Jimmy Vesey RC 3.00 8.00
56 Kyle Connor RC 4.00 10.00
57 Matthew Tkachuk RC 5.00 12.00
58 Ivan Provorov RC 3.00 8.00
59 Sebastian Aho RC 3.00 8.00
60 Travis Konecny RC 3.00 8.00
61 Christian Dvorak RC 1.50 4.00
62 Mathew Barzal RC 10.00 25.00
63 Thomas Chabot RC 3.00 8.00
64 Dylan Strome RC 3.00 8.00
65 Anthony Beauvillier RC 1.50 4.00
66 Zach Werenski RC 3.00 8.00
67 Pavel Buchnevich RC 2.50 6.00
68 Brayden Point RC 4.00 10.00
69 Danton Heinen RC 2.50 6.00
70 Nick Schmaltz RC 1.50 4.00
71 William Nylander RC 10.00 25.00
72 Oliver Bjorkstrand RC 1.25 3.00
73 Nikita Soshnikov RC 1.00 2.50
74 Anthony Mantha RC 4.00 10.00
75 Charlie Lindgren RC 3.00 8.00
76 Hudson Fasching RC 1.50 4.00
77 Ryan Pulock RC 1.50 4.00
78 Kasperi Kapanen RC 3.00 8.00
79 Sonny Milano RC 2.00 5.00
80 Daniel Altshuller RC 1.25 3.00
81 Connor Brown RC 2.50 6.00
82 Justin Bailey RC 1.50 4.00
83 Pavel Zacha RC 2.00 5.00
84 Auston Matthews AU/99 300.00 800.00
85 Patrik Laine AU/175 100.00 250.00
86 Mitch Marner AU/175 100.00 250.00
87 Jesse Puljujarvi AU/275 20.00 50.00
88 Jimmy Vesey AU/275 15.00 40.00
89 Kyle Connor AU/275 20.00 50.00
90 Matthew Tkachuk AU/275 25.00 60.00
91 Ivan Provorov AU/275 15.00 40.00
92 Sebastian Aho AU/275 15.00 40.00
93 Travis Konecny AU/275 15.00 40.00
94 Christian Dvorak AU/275 8.00 20.00
95 Mathew Barzal AU/275 25.00 60.00
96 Thomas Chabot AU/275 15.00 40.00
97 Dylan Strome AU/275 15.00 40.00
98 Anthony Beauvillier AU/275 8.00 20.00
99 Zach Werenski AU/275 20.00 50.00
100 Pavel Buchnevich AU/275 12.00 30.00
101 Brayden Point AU/275 20.00 50.00
102 Danton Heinen AU/275 12.00 30.00
103 Nick Schmaltz AU/275 8.00 20.00
104 William Nylander AU/275 30.00 80.00
105 Oliver Bjorkstrand AU/275 6.00 15.00
106 Nikita Soshnikov AU/275 5.00 12.00
107 Anthony Mantha AU/275 20.00 50.00
108 Charlie Lindgren AU/275 15.00 40.00
109 Hudson Fasching AU/275 8.00 20.00
110 Ryan Pulock AU/275 8.00 20.00
111 Kasperi Kapanen AU/275 15.00 40.00
112 Sonny Milano AU/275 10.00 25.00
113 Daniel Altshuller AU/275 6.00 15.00
114 Connor Brown AU/275 12.00 30.00
115 Justin Bailey AU/275 8.00 20.00
116 Pavel Zacha AU/275 10.00 25.00
117 Auston Matthews AU/25 500.00 900.00
118 Patrik Laine AU/49 150.00 300.00
119 Mitch Marner AU/49 150.00 300.00
120 Jesse Puljujarvi AU/49 40.00 100.00
121 Jimmy Vesey AU/49 40.00 100.00
122 Kyle Connor AU/49 30.00 80.00
123 Matthew Tkachuk AU/49 40.00 100.00
124 Ivan Provorov AU/49 25.00 60.00
125 Sebastian Aho AU/49 25.00 60.00
126 Travis Konecny AU/49 25.00 60.00
127 Christian Dvorak AU/49 12.00 30.00
128 Mathew Barzal AU/49 40.00 100.00
129 Thomas Chabot AU/49 25.00 60.00
130 Dylan Strome AU/49 25.00 60.00
131 Anthony Beauvillier AU/49 12.00 30.00
132 Zach Werenski AU/49 25.00 60.00
133 Pavel Buchnevich AU/49 20.00 50.00
134 Brayden Point AU/49 30.00 80.00
135 Danton Heinen AU/49 20.00 50.00
136 Nick Schmaltz AU/49 12.00 30.00
137 William Nylander AU/49 50.00 120.00
138 Oliver Bjorkstrand AU/49 10.00 25.00
139 Nikita Soshnikov AU/49 8.00 20.00
140 Anthony Mantha AU/49 30.00 80.00
141 Charlie Lindgren AU/49 25.00 60.00
142 Hudson Fasching AU/49 12.00 30.00
143 Ryan Pulock AU/49 12.00 30.00
144 Kasperi Kapanen AU/49 25.00 60.00
145 Sonny Milano AU/49 15.00 40.00
146 Daniel Altshuller AU/49 10.00 25.00
147 Connor Brown AU/49 20.00 50.00
148 Justin Bailey AU/49 12.00 30.00
149 Pavel Zacha AU/49 15.00 40.00
150 Matthews/Marner/Nylander AU/10 RC

2016-17 Upper Deck Trilogy Rainbow Black

1 Patrick Kane PATCH/17 8.00 20.00
3 Tyler Toffoli STK/58 10.00 25.00
4 Martin Jones PATCH/37 12.00 30.00
7 Henrik Lundqvist PATCH/65 10.00 25.00
9 Dylan Larkin PATCH/23 20.00 50.00
11 Braden Holtby PATCH/48 15.00 40.00
13 Morgan Rielly PATCH/36 10.00 25.00
14 Jarome Iginla STK/22 12.00 30.00
16 Tuukka Rask PATCH/64 10.00 25.00
17 Erik Karlsson GLV/66 20.00 50.00
18 Anze Kopitar STK/18 12.00 30.00
19 Matt Duchene PATCH/30 12.00 30.00
21 Tyler Seguin STK/40 15.00 40.00
22 Max Pacioretty SKATE/30 12.00 30.00
23 Filip Forsberg PATCH/64 12.00 30.00
24 Jaden Schwartz PATCH/33 15.00 40.00
25 Connor McDavid SOCK/16 25.00 60.00
26 John Klingberg PATCH/48 10.00 25.00
27 Duncan Keith PATCH/43 10.00 25.00
28 Aleksander Barkov PATCH/66 10.00 25.00
29 Nikita Kucherov PATCH/66 15.00 40.00
31 Sam Bennett PATCH/36 15.00 40.00
32 Torey Krug PATCH/44 10.00 25.00
33 Claude Giroux PATCH/67 10.00 25.00
34 Noah Hanifin PATCH/22 12.00 30.00
35 Cory Schneider PATCH/27 10.00 25.00
36 Daniel Sedin PATCH/33 12.00 30.00
37 Jamie Benn GLV/30 15.00 40.00
38 Ryan Kesler PATCH/50 10.00 25.00
39 Zach Parise PATCH/53 10.00 25.00
41 Jack Eichel PATCH/56 20.00 50.00
43 Blake Wheeler PATCH/82 10.00 25.00
44 Max Domi PATCH/18 10.00 25.00
45 Nick Leddy PATCH/40 6.00 15.00
46 Phil Kessel STK/26 15.00 40.00
47 Jack Johnson PATCH/86 6.00 15.00
48 Brent Burns PATCH/48 12.00 30.00
51 Auston Matthews 60.00 150.00
52 Patrik Laine 25.00 60.00
53 Mitch Marner 30.00 80.00
54 Jesse Puljujarvi 15.00 40.00
55 Jimmy Vesey 12.00 30.00
56 Kyle Connor 15.00 40.00
57 Matthew Tkachuk 20.00 50.00
58 Ivan Provorov 12.00 30.00
59 Sebastian Aho 12.00 30.00
60 Travis Konecny 12.00 30.00
61 Christian Dvorak 6.00 15.00
62 Mathew Barzal 20.00 50.00
63 Thomas Chabot 12.00 30.00
64 Dylan Strome 12.00 30.00
65 Anthony Beauvillier 6.00 15.00
66 Zach Werenski 12.00 30.00
67 Pavel Buchnevich 10.00 25.00
68 Brayden Point 15.00 40.00
69 Danton Heinen 10.00 25.00
70 Nick Schmaltz 6.00 15.00
71 William Nylander 25.00 60.00
72 Oliver Bjorkstrand 5.00 12.00
73 Nikita Soshnikov 4.00 10.00
74 Anthony Mantha 15.00 40.00
75 Charlie Lindgren 12.00 30.00
76 Hudson Fasching 6.00 15.00
77 Ryan Pulock 6.00 15.00
78 Kasperi Kapanen 12.00 30.00
79 Sonny Milano 8.00 20.00
80 Daniel Altshuller 5.00 12.00
81 Connor Brown 10.00 25.00
82 Justin Bailey 6.00 15.00
83 Pavel Zacha 8.00 20.00
88 Jimmy Vesey AU/66 20.00 50.00
89 Kyle Connor AU/17
93 Travis Konecny AU/24 25.00 60.00
94 Christian Dvorak AU/58 10.00 25.00
95 Mathew Barzal AU/16 20.00 50.00
96 Thomas Chabot AU/18 25.00 60.00
100 Pavel Buchnevich AU/75 15.00 40.00
101 Brayden Point AU/79 25.00 60.00
102 Danton Heinen AU/116 15.00 40.00
103 Nick Schmaltz AU/20 12.00 30.00
105 Oliver Bjorkstrand AU/89 8.00 20.00
107 Anthony Mantha AU/20 30.00 80.00
109 Hudson Fasching AU/118 10.00 25.00
111 Kasperi Kapanen AU/22 25.00 60.00
112 Sonny Milano AU/16
113 Daniel Altshuller AU/69 8.00 20.00
114 Connor Brown AU/156 15.00 40.00
115 Justin Bailey AU/52 10.00 25.00

2016-17 Upper Deck Trilogy Rainbow Green

1 Patrick Kane JSY/44 15.00 40.00
2 Steven Stamkos JSY/198 10.00 25.00
3 Tyler Toffoli JSY/230 4.00 10.00
4 Martin Jones JSY/205 4.00 10.00
5 John Tavares JSY/36 20.00 50.00
6 Joe Pavelski JSY/212 4.00 10.00
7 Henrik Lundqvist JSY/59 8.00 20.00
8 Ryan Getzlaf JSY/520 5.00 12.00
9 Dylan Larkin JSY/45 12.00 30.00
10 Evgeni Malkin JSY/108 15.00 40.00
11 Braden Holtby JSY/244 6.00 15.00
12 Jaromir Jagr JSY/133 12.00 30.00
13 Morgan Rielly JSY/236 3.00 8.00
14 Jarome Iginla JSY/190 5.00 12.00
15 Jonathan Toews JSY/51 15.00 40.00
16 Tuukka Rask JSY/167 5.00 12.00
18 Anze Kopitar JSY/243 6.00 15.00
19 Matt Duchene JSY/221 4.00 10.00
20 Carey Price JSY/36 30.00 80.00
21 Tyler Seguin JSY/163 8.00 20.00
22 Max Pacioretty JSY/84 6.00 15.00
23 Filip Forsberg JSY/182 6.00 15.00
24 Jaden Schwartz JSY/491 4.00 10.00
25 Connor McDavid JSY/48 40.00 100.00
26 John Klingberg JSY/269 4.00 10.00
27 Duncan Keith JSY/374 4.00 10.00
28 Aleksander Barkov JSY/381 4.00 10.00
29 Nikita Kucherov JSY/211 6.00 15.00
30 Alexander Ovechkin JSY/88 25.00 60.00
31 Sam Bennett JSY/137 6.00 15.00
33 Claude Giroux JSY/351 4.00 10.00
34 Noah Hanifin JSY/79 6.00 15.00
35 Cory Schneider JSY/270 3.00 8.00
36 Daniel Sedin JSY/123 5.00 12.00
37 Jamie Benn JSY/45 10.00 25.00
38 Ryan Kesler JSY/223 4.00 10.00
39 Zach Parise JSY/299 4.00 10.00
40 Johnny Gaudreau JSY/88 10.00 25.00
41 Jack Eichel JSY/81 12.00 30.00
42 Henrik Zetterberg JSY/97 8.00 20.00
43 Blake Wheeler JSY/440 3.00 8.00
44 Max Domi JSY/81 8.00 20.00
45 Nick Leddy JSY/417 2.00 5.00
46 Phil Kessel JSY/70 8.00 20.00
47 Jack Johnson JSY/629 2.00 5.00
49 Vladimir Tarasenko JSY/106 8.00 20.00
50 Sidney Crosby JSY/46 30.00 80.00
51 Auston Matthews JSY 30.00 80.00
52 Patrik Laine JSY 15.00 40.00
53 Mitch Marner JSY 20.00 50.00
54 Jesse Puljujarvi JSY 10.00 25.00
55 Jimmy Vesey JSY 8.00 20.00
56 Kyle Connor JSY 10.00 25.00
57 Matthew Tkachuk JSY 12.00 30.00
58 Ivan Provorov JSY 8.00 20.00
59 Sebastian Aho JSY 8.00 20.00
60 Travis Konecny JSY 8.00 20.00
61 Christian Dvorak JSY 4.00 10.00
62 Mathew Barzal JSY 12.00 30.00
63 Thomas Chabot JSY 8.00 20.00
64 Dylan Strome JSY 8.00 20.00
65 Anthony Beauvillier JSY 4.00 10.00
66 Zach Werenski JSY 8.00 20.00
67 Pavel Buchnevich JSY 6.00 15.00
68 Brayden Point JSY 10.00 25.00
70 Nick Schmaltz JSY 4.00 10.00
71 William Nylander JSY 15.00 40.00
72 Oliver Bjorkstrand JSY 3.00 8.00
73 Nikita Soshnikov JSY 2.50 6.00
74 Anthony Mantha JSY 10.00 25.00
75 Charlie Lindgren JSY 8.00 20.00
76 Hudson Fasching JSY 4.00 10.00
77 Ryan Pulock JSY 4.00 10.00
78 Kasperi Kapanen JSY 8.00 20.00
79 Sonny Milano JSY 5.00 12.00
80 Daniel Altshuller JSY 3.00 8.00
81 Connor Brown JSY 6.00 15.00
82 Justin Bailey JSY 4.00 10.00
83 Pavel Zacha JSY 5.00 12.00
84 Auston Matthews PATCH 100.00 200.00
85 Patrik Laine PATCH 40.00 100.00
86 Mitch Marner PATCH 50.00 125.00
87 Jesse Puljujarvi PATCH 25.00 60.00
88 Jimmy Vesey PATCH 20.00 50.00
89 Kyle Connor PATCH 25.00 60.00
90 Matthew Tkachuk PATCH 30.00 80.00
91 Ivan Provorov PATCH 20.00 50.00
92 Sebastian Aho PATCH 20.00 50.00
93 Travis Konecny PATCH 20.00 50.00
94 Christian Dvorak PATCH 10.00 25.00
95 Mathew Barzal PATCH 30.00 80.00
96 Thomas Chabot PATCH 20.00 50.00
97 Dylan Strome PATCH 20.00 50.00
98 Anthony Beauvillier PATCH 10.00 25.00
99 Zach Werenski PATCH 20.00 50.00
100 Pavel Buchnevich PATCH 15.00 40.00
101 Brayden Point PATCH 25.00 60.00
103 Nick Schmaltz PATCH 10.00 25.00
104 William Nylander PATCH 40.00 100.00
105 Oliver Bjorkstrand PATCH 8.00 20.00
106 Nikita Soshnikov PATCH 6.00 15.00
107 Anthony Mantha PATCH 25.00 60.00
108 Charlie Lindgren PATCH 20.00 50.00
109 Hudson Fasching PATCH 10.00 25.00
110 Ryan Pulock PATCH 10.00 25.00
111 Kasperi Kapanen PATCH 20.00 50.00
112 Sonny Milano PATCH 12.00 30.00
113 Daniel Altshuller PATCH 8.00 20.00
114 Connor Brown PATCH 15.00 40.00
115 Justin Bailey PATCH 10.00 25.00
116 Pavel Zacha PATCH 12.00 30.00

2016-17 Upper Deck Trilogy Hall of Fame Signature Pucks

HOFIBO Bobby Orr B 80.00 150.00
HOFIBS Borje Salming C 8.00 20.00
HOFIDG Doug Gilmour C 25.00 60.00
HOFIDH Dominik Hasek C 30.00 80.00
HOFIGH Glenn Hall A 20.00 50.00
HOFIJS Joe Sakic B 25.00 60.00
HOFILM Lanny McDonald C 15.00 40.00
HOFIML Mario Lemieux A 80.00 150.00
HOFIMM Mark Messier A 50.00 120.00
HOFINL Nicklas Lidstrom B 25.00 60.00
HOFIPB Pavel Bure B 30.00 80.00
HOFIPR Patrick Roy A 60.00 150.00
HOFISY Steve Yzerman A 50.00 120.00
HOFIWG Wayne Gretzky A 120.00 300.00

2016-17 Upper Deck Trilogy Ice Scripts

ISAH Adam Henrique D 10.00 25.00
ISAM Anthony Mantha D 25.00 60.00
ISBO Bobby Orr B 60.00 150.00
ISCM Connor McDavid B 120.00 300.00
ISLM Larry Murphy C 10.00 25.00
ISMF Marc-Andre Fleury D 12.00 30.00
ISMM Mark Messier A 60.00 150.00
ISOV Alexander Ovechkin A 40.00 100.00
ISPB Pavel Bure C 25.00 60.00
ISPZ Pavel Zacha D 12.00 30.00
ISTO Jonathan Toews B 30.00 80.00
ISTT Tyler Toffoli D 5.00 12.00
ISWG Wayne Gretzky A 150.00 300.00
ISWN William Nylander C 20.00 50.00

2016-17 Upper Deck Trilogy Signature Pucks

SPAA Andreas Athanasiou G 6.00 15.00
SPAH Adam Henrique E 6.00 15.00
SPAK Anze Kopitar C 15.00 40.00
SPAM Auston Matthews A 80.00 200.00
SPBB Brent Burns E 15.00 40.00
SPBJ Boone Jenner G 6.00 15.00
SPBS Brayden Schenn E 6.00 15.00
SPCM Connor McDavid C 100.00 250.00
SPCS Cory Schneider D 5.00 12.00
SPCW Cam Ward E 6.00 15.00
SPDK David Krejci E 6.00 15.00
SPDS Derek Stepan F 5.00 12.00
SPEK Aaron Ekblad G 6.00 15.00
SPGH Glenn Hall A 20.00 50.00
SPGI John Gibson G 6.00 15.00
SPHL Henrik Lundqvist B 30.00 80.00
SPHZ Henrik Zetterberg C 15.00 40.00
SPJA Jake Allen G 8.00 20.00
SPJH Jonathan Huberdeau D 6.00 15.00
SPJM Josh Morrissey G 8.00 20.00
SPJP Jesse Puljujarvi F 15.00 40.00
SPJT Joe Thornton C 10.00 25.00
SPJV James van Riemsdyk F 6.00 15.00
SPKP Kyle Palmieri F 5.00 12.00
SPLD Leon Draisaitl F 12.00 30.00
SPMA Anthony Mantha F 15.00 40.00
SPMB Matt Beleskey G 5.00 12.00
SPMD Matt Duchene C 6.00 15.00
SPMH Mike Hoffman G 5.00 12.00
SPMM Mark Messier B 15.00 40.00
SPMU Matt Murray E 15.00 40.00
SPNK Nikita Kucherov G 10.00 25.00
SPPB Peter Bondra C 8.00 20.00
SPPL Patrik Laine E 25.00 60.00
SPRF Robby Fabbri F 6.00 15.00
SPRM Ryan Miller D 6.00 15.00
SPRO Ryan O'Reilly G 6.00 15.00
SPSH Scott Hartnell D 6.00 15.00
SPSI Roman Josi G 6.00 15.00
SPSM Sean Monahan F 6.00 15.00
SPTL Trevor Linden C 10.00 25.00
SPTO Tyler Toffoli E 6.00 15.00
SPTS Tyler Seguin C 10.00 25.00
SPVR Victor Rask G 5.00 12.00
SPWG Wayne Gretzky B 150.00 250.00
SPWN William Nylander F 25.00 60.00

2016-17 Upper Deck Trilogy Signature Pucks Dual

P2AL A.Athanasiou/D.Larkin D 30.00 80.00
P2BL P.Bure/T.Linden B 50.00 120.00
P2DI J.Iginla/M.Duchene D 15.00 40.00
P2GM W.Gretzky/M.Messier A
P2MD C.McDavid/L.Draisaitl C 150.00 250.00
P2MN A.Matthews/W.Nylander C 175.00 300.00
P2SN R.Nash/D.Stepan C 20.00 50.00

2016-17 Upper Deck Trilogy Signature Pucks Team Logo

OMMON CARD 15.00 40.00
EMISTARS 20.00 50.00
NLISTED STARS 25.00 60.00
PAM Auston Matthews 250.00 400.00
PCM Connor McDavid 175.00 300.00
PWG Wayne Gretzky 200.00 300.00

2016-17 Upper Deck Trilogy Triple Relics

RBSS Benn/Seguin/Spezza/49 20.00 50.00
RBTB Bergeron/Thornton/Backstrom/125 12.0030.00
RCRS Carbonneau/Roy/Savard/25 40.00 100.00
RDGR Dionne/Gretzky/Robitaille/25 80.00 200.00
RHCL Hextall/Clarke/LeClair/49 12.00 30.00
RHYH Hull/Yzerman/Hasek/25 20.00 50.00
RJBL Jagr/Bure/Luongo/49 30.00 80.00
RJSS Milano/Dickinson/Bailey/125 10.00 25.00
RKDB Karlsson/Doughty/Burns/49 25.00 60.00
RKML Kessel/Malkin/Letang/25 50.00 125.00
RKOT Kane/Ovechkin/Tavares/25 60.00 150.00
RLCJ Brown/Lindgren/Morrissey/125 15.00 40.00
RPGP Price/Galchenyuk/Pacioretty/49 40.00 100.00
RPSG Perry/Selanne/Getzlaf/49 25.00 60.00
RQKC Quick/Kopitar/Carter/49 20.00 50.00
RSMS Sedin/Miller/Sedin/49 12.00 30.00
RZWS Zacha/Wood/Santini/125 10.00 25.00

2017-18 Upper Deck Trilogy

Connor McDavid 2.00 5.00
Oliver Ekman-Larsson .50 1.25
David Pastrnak .75 2.00
Alex Galchenyuk .60 1.50
Alexander Ovechkin 2.00 5.00
Mats Zuccarello .50 1.25
Wayne Simmonds .60 1.50
Brent Burns .60 1.50
Mark Scheifele .60 1.50
0 John Tavares 1.00 2.50
1 Henrik Zetterberg .50 1.25
2 Ryan Johansen .50 1.25
3 Aaron Ekblad .50 1.25
4 Jamie Benn .60 1.50
5 Sidney Crosby 2.00 5.00
6 Corey Perry .50 1.25
7 Mikael Granlund .50 1.25
8 Ryan O'Reilly .50 1.25
9 Sean Monahan .50 1.25
0 Auston Matthews 2.00 5.00
1 Jeff Carter .50 1.25
2 Nathan MacKinnon 1.00 2.50
3 Artemi Panarin .50 1.25
4 Nikita Kucherov .75 2.00
5 Patrick Kane 1.00 2.50
6 Erik Karlsson .60 1.50
7 Bo Horvat .50 1.25
8 Vladimir Tarasenko .75 2.00
9 Jordan Staal .50 1.25
0 Taylor Hall 1.00 2.50
1 Marc-Andre Fleury .75 2.00
2 Anze Kopitar .75 2.00
3 P.K. Subban .50 1.25
4 Milan Lucic .50 1.25
5 Jonathan Toews 1.00 2.50
6 William Karlsson 1.00 2.50
7 Jonathan Quick .75 2.00
8 Evgeny Kuznetsov .75 2.00
9 Leon Draisaitl .75 2.00
0 Carey Price 1.50 4.00
1 Mitch Marner .75 2.00
2 Sergei Bobrovsky .50 1.25
3 Tyler Seguin .75 2.00
4 Patrice Bergeron .60 1.50
5 Evgeni Malkin 1.50 4.00
6 Corey Crawford .60 1.50
7 Jonathan Drouin .50 1.25
8 Jack Eichel .75 2.00
9 Matt Murray .75 2.00
0 Wayne Gretzky 2.50 6.00
1 Christian Fischer RC 3.00 8.00
2 Jack Roslovic RC 3.00 8.00
3 Samuel Morin RC 2.50 6.00
4 Haydn Fleury RC 2.50 6.00
5 Colin White RC 2.50 6.00
6 Adrian Kempe RC 3.00 8.00
7 Alex Tuch RC 6.00 15.00
8 Nikita Scherbak RC 5.00 12.00
9 J.T. Compher RC 3.00 8.00
0 Vladislav Kamenev RC 4.00 10.00
1 Gabriel Carlsson RC 2.00 5.00
2 Riley Barber RC 2.00 5.00
3 Lucas Wallmark RC 2.50 6.00
4 Jon Gillies RC 2.50 6.00
5 Ivan Barbashev RC 2.50 6.00
6 Luke Kunin RC 2.50 6.00
7 Anders Bjork RC 3.00 8.00
8 Alex DeBrincat RC 6.00 15.00
9 Owen Tippett RC 5.00 12.00
0 Alexander Nylander RC 4.00 10.00
1 Jake DeBrusk RC 4.00 10.00
2 Tage Thompson RC 4.00 10.00
3 Tyson Jost RC 5.00 12.00
4 Logan Brown RC 2.50 6.00
5 Vadim Shipachyov RC 8.00 20.00
6 Evgeny Svechnikov RC 5.00 12.00
7 Josh Ho-Sang RC 3.00 8.00
8 Brock Boeser RC 15.00 40.00
9 Pierre-Luc Dubois RC 5.00 12.00
0 Charlie McAvoy RC 8.00 20.00
1 Clayton Keller RC 6.00 15.00
2 Nolan Patrick RC 5.00 12.00
3 Nico Hischier RC 8.00 20.00
4 Christian Fischer AU/349 10.00 25.00
5 Jack Roslovic AU/349 10.00 25.00
6 Samuel Morin AU/349 8.00 20.00
7 Haydn Fleury AU/349 8.00 20.00
8 Colin White AU/349 8.00 20.00
9 Adrian Kempe AU/349 10.00 25.00
0 Alex Tuch AU/349 20.00 50.00
1 Nikita Scherbak AU/349 15.00 40.00
2 J.T. Compher AU/349 10.00 25.00
3 Vladislav Kamenev AU/349 12.00 30.00
4 Gabriel Carlsson AU/349 6.00 15.00
5 Riley Barber AU/349 6.00 15.00
7 Jon Gillies AU/349 8.00 20.00
8 Ivan Barbashev AU/349 8.00 20.00
9 Luke Kunin AU/249 8.00 20.00
00 Anders Bjork AU/249 10.00 25.00
01 Alex DeBrincat AU/249 20.00 50.00
02 Owen Tippett AU/249 15.00 40.00
103 Alexander Nylander AU/249 12.00 30.00
105 Tage Thompson AU/249 12.00 30.00
106 Tyson Jost AU/249 15.00 40.00
108 Vadim Shipachyov AU/249 25.00 60.00
109 Evgeny Svechnikov AU/249 15.00 40.00
110 Josh Ho-Sang AU/249 10.00 25.00
111 Brock Boeser AU/149 150.00 300.00
112 Pierre-Luc Dubois 15.00 40.00
113 Charlie McAvoy AU/149 25.00 60.00
114 Clayton Keller AU/149 20.00 50.00
115 Nolan Patrick/149 12.00 30.00
116 Nico Hischier/149 20.00 50.00
117 Christian Fischer AU/49 20.00 50.00
118 Jack Roslovic AU/49 20.00 50.00
119 Samuel Morin AU/49 15.00 40.00
120 Haydn Fleury AU/49 15.00 40.00
121 Colin White AU/49 15.00 40.00
122 Adrian Kempe AU/49 20.00 50.00
123 Alex Tuch AU/49 40.00 100.00
124 Nikita Scherbak AU/49 30.00 80.00
125 J.T. Compher AU/49 20.00 50.00
126 Vladislav Kamenev AU/49 25.00 60.00
127 Gabriel Carlsson AU/49 12.00 30.00
128 Riley Barber AU/49 12.00 30.00
129 Lucas Wallmark AU/49 15.00 40.00
130 Jon Gillies AU/49 15.00 40.00
131 Ivan Barbashev AU/49 15.00 40.00
132 Luke Kunin AU/49 15.00 40.00
133 Anders Bjork AU/49 20.00 50.00
134 Alex DeBrincat AU/49 40.00 100.00
135 Owen Tippett AU/49 30.00 80.00
136 Alexander Nylander AU/49 25.00 60.00
138 Tage Thompson AU/49 25.00 60.00
139 Tyson Jost AU/49 30.00 80.00
141 Vadim Shipachyov AU/49 50.00 125.00
142 Evgeny Svechnikov AU/49 30.00 80.00
143 Josh Ho-Sang AU/49 20.00 50.00
144 Brock Boeser AU/49 350.00 500.00
145 Pierre-Luc Dubois AU/49 30.00 80.00
146 Charlie McAvoy AU/49 50.00 125.00
147 Clayton Keller AU/49 40.00 100.00
148 Nolan Patrick/25 20.00 50.00
149 Nico Hischier/25 30.00 80.00
150 Luc-DuBois AU/Keller AU/McAvoy AU/25 50.00 125.00

2017-18 Upper Deck Trilogy Black

COMMON CARD (1-50) 6.00 15.00
SEMISTARS 8.00 20.00
UNLISTED STARS 10.00 25.00
COMMON CARD (51-83) 4.00 10.00
SEMISTARS 5.00 12.00
UNLISTED STARS 6.00 15.00
COMMON CARD (84-150) 6.00 15.00
SEMISTARS 8.00 20.00
UNLISTED STARS 10.00 25.00
5 Alexander Ovechkin PATCH/17 20.00 50.00
6 Mats Zuccarello PATCH/44 15.00 40.00
15 Sidney Crosby PATCH/17 30.00 80.00
31 Marc-Andre Fleury PAD/18 30.00 80.00
41 Mitch Marner PATCH/42 25.00 60.00
54 Haydn Fleury 8.00 20.00
56 Adrian Kempe 15.00 40.00
72 Tage Thompson 12.00 30.00
78 Brock Boeser 60.00 150.00

2017-18 Upper Deck Trilogy Blue

*BLUE/999: 1.25X TO 3X BASIC CARDS
1 Connor McDavid 8.00 20.00
20 Auston Matthews 8.00 20.00

2017-18 Upper Deck Trilogy Green

COMMON CARD (1-83) 2.50 6.00
SEMISTARS 3.00 8.00
UNLISTED STARS 4.00 10.00
COMMON CARD (84-113) 6.00 15.00
SEMISTARS 8.00 20.00
UNLISTED STARS 10.00 25.00
78 Brock Boeser JSY/399 20.00 50.00
111 Brock Boeser PATCH/35 80.00 150.00

2017-18 Upper Deck Trilogy Combo Signature Pucks

SP2DT M.Dionne/D.Taylor B 40.00 100.00
SP2SK S.Stamkos/N.Kucherov A
SP2SL M.Scheifele/P.Laine B 50.00 125.00

2017-18 Upper Deck Trilogy Honorary Triple Swatches

HTSAE Aaron Ekblad/49 8.00 20.00
HTSAK Anze Kopitar/49 30.00 80.00
HTSAN Alexander Nylander/49 25.00 60.00
HTSCK Clayton Keller/25 25.00 60.00
HTSEK Erik Karlsson/25 20.00 50.00
HTSHA Noah Hanifin/25 12.00 30.00
HTSJB Jamie Benn/25 20.00 50.00
HTSJQ Jonathan Quick/49 15.00 40.00
HTSJS Jason Spezza/25 12.00 30.00
HTSLU Milan Lucic/25 30.00 80.00
HTSRL Roberto Luongo/25 25.00 60.00
HTSTJ Tyson Jost/49 15.00 40.00
HTSVT Vladimir Tarasenko/25 20.00 50.00

2017-18 Upper Deck Trilogy Ice Scripts

ISCK Clayton Keller C 25.00 60.00
ISCP Carey Price A 80.00 150.00
ISDS Derek Sanderson C 10.00 25.00
ISJJ Jaromir Jagr A 80.00 150.00
ISJK Jari Kurri B 10.00 25.00
ISLD Leon Draisaitl C 15.00 40.00
ISNK Nikita Kucherov C 15.00 40.00
ISNS Nikita Scherbak C 20.00 50.00
ISPL Patrik Laine B 30.00 80.00
ISRK Ryan Kesler B 15.00 40.00
ISSY Steve Yzerman A 80.00 150.00
ISWS Wayne Simmonds C 12.00 30.00

2017-18 Upper Deck Trilogy Personal Scripts

PSBO Bobby Orr B 250.00 350.00
PSCM Connor McDavid A
PSDS Dave Schultz C 25.00 60.00
PSHL Henrik Lundqvist B 50.00 125.00
PSSS Steven Stamkos B 80.00 200.00
PSTH Joe Thornton C 80.00 200.00
PSWG Wayne Gretzky A

2017-18 Upper Deck Trilogy Scripted Hall of Fame Plaques

SHOFMB Mike Bossy 60.00 150.00
SHOFPR Patrick Roy 250.00 350.00
SHOFTS Teemu Selanne 80.00 200.00
SHOFWG Wayne Gretzky 250.00 350.00

2017-18 Upper Deck Trilogy Signature Pucks

SPAB Aleksander Barkov B 8.00 20.00
SPAV Andrei Vasilevskiy C 10.00 25.00
SPBB Brock Boeser C 40.00 100.00
SPBR Bobby Ryan C 6.00 15.00
SPCA Cam Atkinson B 8.00 20.00
SPCB Connor Brown C 8.00 20.00
SPCH Carl Hagelin B 8.00 20.00
SPCS Conor Sheary B 8.00 20.00
SPDS Darryl Sittler A 8.00 20.00
SPES Evgeny Svechnikov C 15.00 40.00
SPFP Felix Potvin A 20.00 50.00
SPGF Grant Fuhr A 12.00 30.00
SPGI Mark Giordano B 8.00 20.00
SPGN Gustav Nyquist B 8.00 20.00
SPIB Ivan Barbashev C 8.00 20.00
SPIP Ivan Provorov C 8.00 20.00
SPJC John Carlson C 10.00 25.00
SPJH Jaroslav Halak B 8.00 20.00
SPJK Jari Kurri A 15.00 40.00
SPJM Jake Muzzin C 6.00 15.00
SPJP Joe Pavelski A 12.00 30.00
SPJR Jack Roslovic A 20.00 50.00
SPKM Kirk Muller C 6.00 15.00
SPKP Kyle Palmieri C 6.00 15.00
SPLC Logan Couture B 8.00 20.00
SPMI Mikael Granlund C 8.00 20.00
SPMM Michael Matheson C 6.00 15.00
SPMS Mark Scheifele A 15.00 40.00
SPMT Matthew Tkachuk C 8.00 20.00
SPNE Nikolaj Ehlers C 10.00 25.00
SPNN Nino Niederreiter C 6.00 15.00
SPNU Norm Ullman C 8.00 20.00
SPON Owen Nolan A 8.00 20.00
SPPL Pierre-Luc Dubois A 15.00 40.00
SPPM Petr Mrazek B 25.00 60.00
SPRB Rod Brind'Amour C 8.00 20.00
SPRK Ryan Kesler A 12.00 30.00
SPRS Ryan Spooner C 10.00 25.00
SPSI Charlie Simmer B 8.00 20.00
SPTB Tom Barrasso A 12.00 30.00
SPTT Teuvo Teravainen C 6.00 15.00
SPVA John Vanbiesbrouck A 20.00 50.00
SPVH Victor Hedman A 10.00 25.00
SPWS Wayne Simmonds A 10.00 25.00

2017-18 Upper Deck Trilogy Triple Relics

TRBDK Blake/Dionne/Kopitar/25 25.00 60.00
TRBKJ Boeser/Keller/Jost/49 80.00 200.00
TRCSR Clarke/Schultz/Recchi/25 20.00 50.00
TRDAW Dubinsky/Atkinson/Wennberg/49 15.00 40.00
TREKD Ekblad/Karlsson/Doughty/25 20.00 50.00
TRHBC Hasek/Belfour/Crawford/25 20.00 50.00
TRKTS Kane/Toews/Saad/25 30.00 80.00
TRLBC Lemieux/Barrasso/Coffey/25 50.00 125.00
TRLHH LaFontaine/Hawerchuk/Hasek/25 25.00 60.00
TRMDH McDavid/Draisaitl Nugent-Hopkins/25 60.00 150.00
TRMGF Messier/Gretzky/Fuhr/25 50.00 125.00
TRNSB Nylander/Svechnikov Barbashev/99 30.00 80.00
TROBM Ovechkin/Bure/Malkin/25 60.00 150.00
TRPLP Price/Lafleur/Roy/25 50.00 120.00
TRPSB Forsberg/Sakic/Bourque/25 25.00 60.00
TRSDT Shipachyov/DeBrincat/Tippett/49 50.00125.00
TRSMW Ho-Sang/McAvoy/White/49 50.00 125.00
TRTBS Tarasenko/Bouwmeester/Steen/49 25.00 60.00
TRVMD Varlamov/MacKinnon Duchene/49 30.00 80.00

2017-18 Upper Deck Trilogy Trophy Winners Signature Pucks

TWSBO Bobby Orr B 80.00 150.00
TWSCM Connor McDavid A
TWSCP Carey Price B
TWSHL Henrik Lundqvist C 60.00 150.00
TWSSS Steven Stamkos B 30.00 80.00

2017-18 Upper Deck Trilogy Tryptichs

TBOS1 Bobby Orr AU/49 80.00 150.00
TCAP2 Evgeny Kuznetsov PATCH/49 20.00 50.00
TCAP3 Braden Holtby JSY/149 6.00 15.00
TCBJ1 Cam Atkinson AU/199 10.00 25.00
TCBJ2 Alexander Wennberg PATCH/25 15.00 40.00
TCBJ3 Sergei Bobrovsky JSY/149 4.00 10.00
TDET1 Anthony Mantha AU/199 10.00 25.00
TDET2 Henrik Zetterberg PATCH/25 10.00 25.00
TDET3 Tomas Tatar JSY/149 4.00 10.00
TFLO2 Roberto Luongo STK/25
TFLO3 Aleksander Barkov JSY/149 4.00 10.00
THOF1 Mario Lemieux AU/20 80.00 200.00
THOF3 Joe Sakic JSY/25
TLAK2 Jonathan Quick BLKR/49 15.00 40.00
TLAK3 Jeff Carter JSY/149 4.00 10.00
TOTT1 Mike Hoffman AU/199 8.00 20.00
TOTT2 Erik Karlsson GLV/25 15.00 40.00
TOTT3 Mark Stone JSY/149 8.00 20.00
TPEN2 Phil Kessel JSY/49 6.00 15.00
TPEN3 Conor Sheary AU/199 10.00 25.00
TPRE1 P.K. Subban PATCH/49 5.00 12.00
TPRE2 Filip Forsberg JSY/149 5.00 12.00
TPRE3 Roman Josi JSY/149 4.00 10.00
TRC11 Nolan Patrick JSY/49 10.00 25.00
TRC12 Nico Hischier JSY/49 15.00 40.00
TRC13 Vadim Shipachyov JSY/149 15.00 40.00
TRC21 Brock Boeser JSY/149 15.00 40.00
TRC22 Clayton Keller JSY/49 12.00 30.00
TRC23 Charlie McAvoy JSY/149 12.00 30.00
TSTL1 Vladimir Tarasenko JSY/49 8.00 20.00
TSTL2 Alex Pietrangelo PATCH/49 4.00 10.00
TSTL3 Jake Allen PATCH/49 6.00 15.00
TTML1 Darryl Sittler AU/20
TTML3 Doug Gilmour JSY/25 25.00 60.00
TUSA2 Mike Modano PATCH/25 15.00 40.00
TVAN2 Henrik Sedin PATCH/49 5.00 12.00
TVAN3 Daniel Sedin JSY/49 5.00 12.00
TLEAF2 Mitch Marner PATCH/25
TLEAF3 William Nylander PATCH/49 15.00 40.00
TSTAR1 Connor McDavid AU/20
TSTAR3 Auston Matthews JSY/25 20.00 50.00

1996 Upper Deck U.S. Olympic

This multisport product was issued in June 1996, prior to the Centennial Olympic Games in Atlanta. Packs of 10 standard-size cards had a suggested retail price of $1.99. The set contains the following subsets: U.S. Olympic Moments (1-90), Future Champions (91-120) and Passing the Torch (121-135).

COMPLETE SET (135) 8.00 20.00
68 Jim Craig .20 .50
69 Mike Eruzione .25 .60

1996 Upper Deck U.S. Olympic Reflections of Gold

These cards were inserted in packs at a rate of 1:5. The photos are rendered in a bright metallic fashion on the fronts.

COMPLETE SET (10) 8.00 20.00
STATED ODDS 1:5
RG2 Mike Eruzione .60 1.50

1996 Upper Deck U.S. Olympic Reflections of Gold Signatures

These cards were distributed exclusively via mail-in redemption cards, which were inserted at a rate of 1:79 packs. Each redemption card identified which athlete's signature card it represented. There was an expiration date of Dec. 31, 1996. The Jordan card is extremely scarce; probably 25 or less were signed, and some never were redeemed. Kristi Yamaguchi apparently did not participate in this promotion.

COMPLETE SET (9) 3000.00 5000.00
STATED ODDS 1:79
RG2 Mike Eruzione 12.00 30.00

1999-00 Upper Deck Victory

Released as a 440-card set, 1999-00 Upper Deck Victory was comprised of 265 regular cards, 12 All Victory team cards showcasing top players, 30 Season Leaders, 40 Victory Prospects, 15 Stacking the Pads cards, 50 Hockey Legacy cards, and 28 Team Checklist cards. Base cards are white bordered with a red "Victory" logo. This brand contains no insert cards. Victory was packaged in 36-pack boxes where packs contained 12 cards and carried a suggested retail price of $.99.

COMPLETE SET (440) 20.00 50.00
1 Paul Kariya CL .12 .30
2 Paul Kariya .12 .30
3 Teemu Selanne .20 .50
4 Matt Cullen .05 .15
5 Steve Rucchin .05 .15
6 Oleg Tverdovsky .05 .15
7 Guy Hebert .10 .25
8 Fredrik Olausson .05 .15
9 Ted Donato .05 .15
10 Marty McInnis .05 .15
11 Damian Rhodes CL .05 .15
12 Jody Hull .05 .15
13 Damian Rhodes .05 .15
14 Kelly Buchberger .05 .15
15 Scott Langkow RC .05 .15
16 Norm Maracle .05 .15
17 Jason Botterill .05 .15
18 Randy Robitaille .05 .15
19 Ray Ferraro .05 .15
20 Ray Bourque CL .15 .40
21 Ray Bourque .15 .40
22 Sergei Samsonov .07 .20
23 Joe Thornton .15 .40
24 Shawn Bates .05 .15
25 Byron Dafoe .05 .15
26 Jonathan Girard .05 .15
27 Jason Allison .07 .20
28 Anson Carter .07 .20
29 Hal Gill .05 .15
30 Kyle McLaren .05 .15
31 Don Sweeney .05 .15
32 Dominik Hasek CL .15 .40
33 Dominik Hasek .15 .40
34 Michael Peca .07 .20
35 Miroslav Satan .07 .20
36 Dixon Ward .05 .15
37 Martin Biron .07 .20
38 Joe Juneau .07 .20
39 Cory Sarich .05 .15
40 Brian Holzinger .05 .15
41 Rhett Warrener .05 .15
42 Alexei Zhitnik .05 .15
43 Jean-Sebastien Giguere CL .10 .25
44 Valeri Bure .05 .15
45 Jean-Sebastien Giguere .10 .25
46 Jarome Iginla .10 .25
47 Rico Fata .05 .15
48 Derek Morris .05 .15
49 Rene Corbet .05 .15
50 Phil Housley .05 .15
51 Tyrone Garner RC .05 .15
52 Marc Savard .05 .15
53 Keith Primeau CL .05 .15
54 Sami Kapanen .05 .15
55 Bates Battaglia .05 .15
56 Arturs Irbe .07 .20
57 Keith Primeau .05 .15
58 Gary Roberts .05 .15
59 Ron Francis .12 .30
60 Paul Coffey .10 .25
61 Martin Gelinas .05 .15
62 Jeff O'Neill .05 .15
63 Glen Wesley .05 .15
64 Tony Amonte CL .07 .20
65 Tony Amonte .07 .20
66 J-P Dumont .07 .20
67 Doug Gilmour .12 .30
68 Ty Jones .05 .15
69 Anders Eriksson .05 .15
70 Remi Royer .05 .15
71 Jocelyn Thibault .07 .20
72 Alexei Zhamnov .05 .15
73 Eric Daze .07 .20
74 Bryan McCabe .07 .20
75 Peter Forsberg CL .10 .25
76 Chris Drury .07 .20
77 Peter Forsberg .10 .25
78 Patrick Roy .40 1.00
79 Joe Sakic .15 .40
80 Milan Hejduk .07 .20
81 Adam Deadmarsh .05 .15
82 Adam Foote .07 .20
83 Sandis Ozolinsh .05 .15
84 Claude Lemieux .07 .20
85 Brett Hull CL .15 .40
86 Ed Belfour .10 .25
87 Brett Hull .15 .40
88 Mike Modano .15 .40
89 Derian Hatcher .07 .20
90 Jamie Langenbrunner .05 .15
91 Joe Nieuwendyk .10 .25
92 Jon Sim RC .10 .25
93 Jere Lehtinen .07 .20
94 Darryl Sydor .07 .20
95 Sergei Zubov .05 .15
96 Steve Yzerman CL .30 .75
97 Brendan Shanahan .12 .30
98 Steve Yzerman .30 .75
99 Chris Chelios .10 .25
100 Sergei Fedorov .15 .40
101 Vyacheslav Kozlov .05 .15
102 Igor Larionov .10 .25
103 Nicklas Lidstrom .10 .25
104 Tomas Holmstrom .05 .15
105 Chris Osgood .10 .25
106 Kris Draper .07 .20
107 Darren McCarty .05 .15
108 Doug Weight CL .10 .25
109 Bill Guerin .10 .25
110 Tom Poti .05 .15
111 Mike Grier .05 .15
112 Tommy Salo .07 .20
113 Doug Weight .10 .25
114 Josef Beranek .05 .15
115 Fredrik Lindquist .05 .15
116 Roman Hamrlik .07 .20
117 Todd Marchant .05 .15
118 Janne Niinimaa .05 .15
119 Pavel Bure CL .12 .30
120 Pavel Bure .12 .30
121 Mark Parrish .05 .15
122 Scott Mellanby .05 .15
123 Viktor Kozlov .05 .15
124 Oleg Kvasha .05 .15
125 Rob Niedermayer .05 .15
126 Bret Hedican .05 .15
127 Trevor Kidd .05 .15
128 Robert Svehla .05 .15
129 Peter Worrell .05 .15
130 Rob Blake CL .10 .25
131 Rob Blake .10 .25
132 Pavel Rosa .05 .15
133 Donald Audette .05 .15
134 Luc Robitaille .10 .25
135 Vladimir Tsyplakov .05 .15
136 Jozef Stumpel .05 .15
137 Nathan Lafayette .05 .15
138 Glen Murray .07 .20
139 Zigmund Palffy .10 .25
140 Bryan Smolinski .05 .15
141 Jamie Storr .05 .15
142 Saku Koivu CL .10 .25
143 Saku Koivu .10 .25
144 Arron Asham .05 .15
145 Jeff Hackett .05 .15
146 Trevor Linden .10 .25
147 Eric Weinrich .05 .15
148 Vladimir Malakhov .05 .15
149 Martin Rucinsky .05 .15
150 Brian Savage .05 .15
151 Shayne Corson .05 .15
152 Scott Lachance .05 .15
153 Jose Theodore .10 .25
154 David Legwand CL .05 .15
155 Mike Dunham .05 .15
156 David Legwand .05 .15
157 Sergei Krivokrasov .05 .15
158 Cliff Ronning .05 .15
159 Kimmo Timonen .05 .15
160 Bob Boughner .05 .15
161 Mark Mowers RC .05 .15
162 Patrick Cote .05 .15
163 Tomas Vokoun .10 .25
164 Jan Vopat .05 .15
165 Martin Brodeur CL .20 .50
166 Martin Brodeur .20 .50
167 John Madden RC .10 .25
168 Vadim Sharifijanov .05 .15
169 Patrik Elias .10 .25
170 Scott Stevens .10 .25
171 Petr Sykora .07 .20
172 Jason Arnott .07 .20
173 Brendan Morrison .07 .20
174 Scott Niedermayer .10 .25
175 Bobby Holik .05 .15
176 Eric Brewer CL .05 .15
177 Eric Brewer .05 .15
178 Zdeno Chara .10 .25
179 Kenny Jonsson .05 .15
180 Dmitri Nabokov .05 .15
181 Mariusz Czerkawski .05 .15
182 Brad Isbister .05 .15
183 Olli Jokinen .07 .20
184 Felix Potvin .15 .40
185 Mike Watt .05 .15
186 Claude Lapointe .07 .20
187 Brian Leetch CL .10 .25
188 Manny Malhotra .07 .20
189 Mike Richter .10 .25
190 Theo Fleury .12 .30
191 Adam Graves .07 .20
192 Brian Leetch .10 .25
193 Petr Nedved .05 .15
194 Brent Fedyk .05 .15
195 Barry Richter .05 .15
196 Valeri Kamensky .05 .15
197 Kirk McLean .07 .20
198 Kevin Stevens .07 .20
199 Alexei Yashin CL .07 .20
200 Marian Hossa .07 .20
201 Alexei Yashin .07 .20
202 Shawn McEachern .05 .15
203 Sami Salo .07 .20
204 Daniel Alfredsson .10 .25
205 Magnus Arvedson .05 .15
206 Wade Redden .05 .15
207 Ron Tugnutt .07 .20
208 Chris Phillips .05 .15
209 Vaclav Prospal .05 .15
210 Eric Lindros CL .15 .40
211 John LeClair .10 .25
212 Eric Lindros .15 .40
213 Mark Recchi .12 .30
214 Rod Brind'Amour .10 .25
215 Eric Desjardins .07 .20
216 Jean-Marc Pelletier .05 .15
217 Ryan Bast RC .05 .15
218 Keith Jones .05 .15
219 John Vanbiesbrouck .07 .20
220 Brian Wesenberg RC .05 .15
221 Dan McGillis .05 .15
222 Keith Tkachuk CL .10 .25
223 Robert Esche RC .10 .25
224 Keith Tkachuk .10 .25
225 Nikolai Khabibulin .07 .20
226 Trevor Letowski .05 .15
227 Robert Reichel .05 .15
228 Jeremy Roenick .10 .25
229 Greg Adams .05 .15
230 Daniel Briere .07 .20
231 Rick Tocchet .07 .20
232 Stanislav Neckar .05 .15
233 Teppo Numminen .05 .15
234 Jaromir Jagr CL .25 .60
235 Jaromir Jagr .25 .60
236 Matthew Barnaby .07 .20
237 Tom Barrasso .10 .25
238 Jan Hrdina .05 .15
239 Martin Straka .05 .15
240 Jean-Sebastien Aubin .07 .20
241 Alexei Kovalev .07 .20
242 German Titov .05 .15
243 Kevin Hatcher .05 .15
244 Kip Miller .05 .15
245 Alexei Morozov .07 .20
246 Jeff Friesen CL .07 .20
247 Vincent Damphousse .07 .20
248 Jeff Friesen .07 .20
249 Scott Hannan .05 .15
250 Patrick Marleau .10 .25
251 Mike Ricci .07 .20
252 Owen Nolan .10 .25
253 Marco Sturm .07 .20
254 Gary Suter .05 .15
255 Jeff Norton .05 .15
256 Steve Shields .07 .20
257 Mike Vernon .07 .20
258 Al MacInnis CL .10 .25
259 Pavol Demitra .12 .30
260 Al MacInnis .10 .25
261 Lubos Bartecko .05 .15
262 Jochen Hecht RC .15 .40
263 Chris Pronger .07 .20
264 Grant Fuhr .10 .25
265 Michal Handzus .07 .20
266 Pierre Turgeon .10 .25
267 Jim Campbell .05 .15
268 Roman Turek .07 .20
269 Vincent Lecavalier CL .07 .20
270 Vincent Lecavalier .07 .20
271 Paul Mara .05 .15
272 Kevin Hodson .05 .15
273 Dan Cloutier .05 .15
274 Chris Gratton .05 .15
275 Pavel Kubina .05 .15
276 Darcy Tucker .05 .15
277 Alexandre Daigle .05 .15
278 Stephane Richer .07 .20
279 Niklas Sundstrom .05 .15
280 Mats Sundin CL .10 .25
281 Mats Sundin .10 .25
282 Bryan Berard .05 .15
283 Sergei Berezin .05 .15
284 Curtis Joseph .10 .25
285 Tomas Kaberle .05 .15
286 Daniil Markov .05 .15
287 Steve Thomas .05 .15
288 Mike Johnson .07 .20
289 Tie Domi .07 .20
290 Yanic Perreault .05 .15
291 Derek King .05 .15
292 Mark Messier CL .15 .40
293 Mark Messier .15 .40
294 Bill Muckalt .05 .15
295 Josh Holden .05 .15
296 Markus Naslund .10 .25
297 Kevin Weekes .05 .15
298 Ed Jovanovski .07 .20
299 Alexander Mogilny .07 .20
300 Mattias Ohlund .07 .20
301 Todd Bertuzzi .07 .20
302 Peter Schaefer .05 .15
303 Peter Bondra CL .07 .20
304 Peter Bondra .07 .20
305 Adam Oates .10 .25
306 Jan Bulis .05 .15
307 Jaroslav Svejkovsky .05 .15
308 Sergei Gonchar .05 .15
309 Olaf Kolzig .10 .25
310 Richard Zednik .05 .15
311 Benoit Gratton RC .05 .15
312 Matt Herr .05 .15
313 Nolan Baumgartner .05 .15
314 Peter Forsberg .10 .25
315 Jaromir Jagr .25 .60
316 Paul Kariya .12 .30
317 Ray Bourque .15 .40
318 Al MacInnis .10 .25
319 Dominik Hasek .15 .40
320 Steve Yzerman .30 .75
321 Teemu Selanne .20 .50
322 Brett Hull .15 .40
323 Chris Pronger .07 .20
324 Nicklas Lidstrom .10 .25
325 Patrick Roy .40 1.00
326 Teemu Selanne .20 .50
327 Tony Amonte .07 .20
328 Jaromir Jagr .25 .60
329 Alexei Yashin .07 .20
330 John LeClair .10 .25
331 Jaromir Jagr .25 .60
332 Peter Forsberg .10 .25
333 Paul Kariya .12 .30
334 Teemu Selanne .20 .50
335 Joe Sakic .15 .40
336 Jaromir Jagr .25 .60
337 Teemu Selanne .20 .50
338 Paul Kariya .12 .30
339 Peter Forsberg .10 .25
340 Joe Sakic .15 .40
341 Al MacInnis .10 .25
342 Nicklas Lidstrom .10 .25
343 Ray Bourque .15 .40
344 Fredrik Olausson .05 .15
345 Brian Leetch .10 .25
346 Martin Brodeur .20 .50
347 Ed Belfour .10 .25
348 Curtis Joseph .10 .25
349 Chris Osgood .10 .25
350 Patrick Roy .40 1.00
351 Milan Hejduk .07 .20
352 Brendan Morrison .07 .20
353 Chris Drury .07 .20
354 Jan Hrdina .05 .15
355 Mark Parrish .05 .15
356 Oleg Saprykin RC .10 .25
357 Patrik Stefan RC .10 .25
358 Pavel Brendl RC .15 .40
359 Roberto Luongo .12 .30
360 Scott Gomez .07 .20
361 Sheldon Keefe RC .10 .25
362 Simon Gagne .10 .25
363 Steve Kariya RC .10 .25
364 Alex Tanguay .07 .20
365 Brad Stuart .07 .20
366 Branislav Mezei RC .05 .15
367 Brian Campbell RC .10 .25
368 Daniel Sedin .25 .60
369 Henrik Sedin .25 .60
370 Mike Ribiero .07 .20
371 Ivan Novoseltsev RC .12 .30
372 Nick Boynton .07 .20
373 Nikos Tselios .05 .15
374 Tim Connolly .05 .15
375 J.F. Damphousse RC .05 .15
376 Patrick Roy .40 1.00
377 Ed Belfour .10 .25
378 Chris Osgood .10 .25
379 Arturs Irbe .07 .20
380 Nikolai Khabibulin .07 .20
381 Dominik Hasek .15 .40
382 Byron Dafoe .05 .15
383 Jean-Sebastien Giguere .10 .25
384 Olaf Kolzig .10 .25
385 John Vanbiesbrouck .07 .20
386 Martin Brodeur .20 .50
387 Dan Cloutier .05 .15
388 Damian Rhodes .05 .15
389 Curtis Joseph .10 .25
390 Mike Richter .10 .25
391 Wayne Gretzky .50 1.25
392 Wayne Gretzky .50 1.25
393 Wayne Gretzky .50 1.25
394 Wayne Gretzky .50 1.25
395 Wayne Gretzky .50 1.25
396 Wayne Gretzky .50 1.25
397 Wayne Gretzky .50 1.25
398 Wayne Gretzky .50 1.25
399 Wayne Gretzky .50 1.25
400 Wayne Gretzky .50 1.25
401 Wayne Gretzky .50 1.25
402 Wayne Gretzky .50 1.25
403 Wayne Gretzky .50 1.25
404 Wayne Gretzky .50 1.25
405 Wayne Gretzky .50 1.25
406 Wayne Gretzky .50 1.25
407 Wayne Gretzky .50 1.25
408 Wayne Gretzky .50 1.25
409 Wayne Gretzky .50 1.25
410 Wayne Gretzky .50 1.25
411 Wayne Gretzky .50 1.25
412 Wayne Gretzky .50 1.25
413 Wayne Gretzky .50 1.25
414 Wayne Gretzky .50 1.25
415 Wayne Gretzky .50 1.25
416 Wayne Gretzky .50 1.25
417 Wayne Gretzky .50 1.25
418 Wayne Gretzky .50 1.25
419 Wayne Gretzky .50 1.25
420 Wayne Gretzky .50 1.25
421 Wayne Gretzky .50 1.25
422 Wayne Gretzky .50 1.25
423 Wayne Gretzky .50 1.25
424 Wayne Gretzky .50 1.25
425 Wayne Gretzky .50 1.25
426 Wayne Gretzky .50 1.25
427 Wayne Gretzky .50 1.25
428 Wayne Gretzky .50 1.25
429 Wayne Gretzky .50 1.25
430 Wayne Gretzky .50 1.25
431 Wayne Gretzky .50 1.25
432 Wayne Gretzky .50 1.25
433 Wayne Gretzky .50 1.25
434 Wayne Gretzky .50 1.25
435 Wayne Gretzky .50 1.25
436 Wayne Gretzky .50 1.25
437 Wayne Gretzky .50 1.25
438 Wayne Gretzky .50 1.25
439 Wayne Gretzky .50 1.25
440 Wayne Gretzky .50 1.25

2000-01 Upper Deck Victory

Released as a 330-card set, Upper Deck Victory features 210 regular player cards, 20 Season Highlight cards, 30 Team Checklist cards, 20 NHL Prospect cards, and 50 NHL's Best cards. Victory was released in mid September and was packaged in 36-pack boxes with packs containing 12 cards and carried a suggested retail price of $.99. A contest card was also included in most packs, it allowed the collector to visit the Upper Deck website and enter a contest to win a Pavel Bure autographed jersey.

1 Paul Kariya CL .12 .30
2 Ladislav Kohn .05 .15
3 Vitali Vishnevsky .05 .15
4 Steve Rucchin .05 .15
5 Oleg Tverdovsky .05 .15
6 Guy Hebert .07 .20
7 Teemu Selanne .20 .50
8 Paul Kariya .12 .30
9 Patrik Stefan CL .07 .20
10 Andrew Brunette .05 .15
11 Patrik Stefan .07 .20
12 Donald Audette .07 .20
13 Damian Rhodes .05 .15
14 Maxim Galanov .05 .15
15 Dean Sylvester .05 .15
16 Ray Ferraro .05 .15
17 Joe Thornton CL .15 .40
18 Brian Rolston .07 .20
19 Sergei Samsonov .07 .20
20 Joe Thornton .15 .40
21 Byron Dafoe .07 .20
22 Jason Allison .07 .20
23 Anson Carter .07 .20
24 Hal Gill .05 .15
25 Dominik Hasek CL .15 .40
26 Dominik Hasek .15 .40
27 Michael Peca .07 .20
28 Miroslav Satan .05 .15
29 Doug Gilmour .12 .30
30 Chris Gratton .05 .15
31 Curtis Brown .05 .15
32 Maxim Afinogenov .05 .15
33 Jay McKee .05 .15
34 Valeri Bure CL .07 .20
35 Valeri Bure .07 .20
36 Fred Brathwaite .07 .20
37 Jarome Iginla .10 .25
38 Phil Housley .07 .20
39 Derek Morris .05 .15
40 Cory Stillman .05 .15
41 Marc Savard .07 .20
42 Ron Francis CL .12 .30
43 Sami Kapanen .05 .15
44 Arturs Irbe .07 .20
45 Rod Brind'Amour .10 .25
46 Gary Roberts .05 .15
47 Ron Francis .12 .30
48 Paul Coffey .10 .25
49 Jeff O'Neill .07 .20
50 Tony Amonte CL .07 .20
51 Tony Amonte .07 .20
52 Steve Sullivan .05 .15
53 Michal Grosek .05 .15
54 Boris Mironov .05 .15
55 Jocelyn Thibault .07 .20
56 Alexei Zhamnov .07 .20
57 Eric Daze .07 .20
58 Peter Forsberg CL .12 .30
59 Chris Drury .07 .20
60 Peter Forsberg .12 .30
61 Patrick Roy .25 .60
62 Joe Sakic .15 .40
63 Ray Bourque .15 .40

64 Adam Deadmarsh .07 .20
65 Milan Hejduk .07 .20
66 Sandis Ozolinsh .07 .20
67 Alex Tanguay .07 .20
68 Adam Foote .07 .20
69 Blue Jackets CL .05 .15
70 Mike Modano CL .15 .40
71 Ed Belfour .10 .25
72 Brett Hull .15 .40
73 Sergei Zubov .07 .20
74 Brenden Morrow .07 .20
75 Jamie Langenbrunner .07 .20
76 Joe Nieuwendyk .10 .25
77 Mike Modano .15 .40
78 Derian Hatcher .07 .20
79 Jere Lehtinen .07 .20
80 Roman Lyashenko .05 .15
81 Steve Yzerman CL .30 .75
82 Brendan Shanahan .12 .30
83 Steve Yzerman .30 .75
84 Chris Chelios .10 .25
85 Sergei Fedorov .15 .40
86 Slava Kozlov .07 .20
87 Pat Verbeek .07 .20
88 Nicklas Lidstrom .10 .25
89 Tomas Holmstrom .07 .20
90 Chris Osgood .10 .25
91 Martin Lapointe .07 .20
92 Doug Weight CL .10 .25
93 Bill Guerin .10 .25
94 Tom Poti .05 .15
95 Mike Grier .05 .15
96 Tommy Salo .07 .20
97 Doug Weight .10 .25
98 Ryan Smyth .07 .20
99 Alexander Selivanov .05 .15
100 Pavel Bure CL .12 .30
101 Pavel Bure .12 .30
102 Mark Parrish .05 .15
103 Scott Mellanby .05 .15
104 Viktor Kozlov .07 .20
105 Oleg Kvasha .05 .15
106 Ray Whitney .07 .20
107 Trevor Kidd .05 .15
108 Rob Blake CL .10 .25
109 Rob Blake .10 .25
110 Jere Karalahti .05 .15
111 Luc Robitaille .10 .25
112 Jozef Stumpel .05 .15
113 Glen Murray .05 .15
114 Zigmund Palffy .10 .25
115 Bryan Smolinski .07 .20
116 Minnesota Wild CL .05 .15
117 Saku Koivu CL .10 .25
118 Saku Koivu .10 .25
119 Sergei Zholtok .05 .15
120 Eric Weinrich .05 .15
121 Jose Theodore .12 .30
122 Martin Rucinsky .05 .15
123 Brian Savage .05 .15
124 Shayne Corson .05 .15
125 Dainius Zubrus .05 .15
126 David Legwand CL .05 .15
127 Mike Dunham .05 .15
128 David Legwand .10 .25
129 Greg Johnson .05 .15
130 Cliff Ronning .05 .15
131 Kimmo Timonen .05 .15
132 Patric Kjellberg .05 .15
133 Drake Berehowsky .05 .15
134 Martin Brodeur CL .20 .50
135 Martin Brodeur .20 .50
136 John Madden .07 .20
137 Scott Gomez .07 .20
138 Patrik Elias .10 .25
139 Scott Stevens .10 .25
140 Jason Arnott .07 .20
141 Alexander Mogilny .07 .20
142 Tim Connolly CL .05 .15
143 Dave Scatchard .05 .15
144 Tim Connolly .05 .15
145 Kenny Jonsson .05 .15
146 Claude Lapointe .05 .15
147 Mariusz Czerkawski .05 .15
148 Brad Isbister .05 .15
149 Olli Jokinen .07 .20
150 Theo Fleury CL .12 .30
151 Mike Richter .10 .25
152 Theo Fleury .12 .30
153 Adam Graves .07 .20
154 Brian Leetch .10 .25
155 Petr Nedved .07 .20
156 Radek Dvorak .07 .20
157 Mike York .05 .15
158 Marian Hossa CL .07 .20
159 Marian Hossa .07 .20
160 Radek Bonk .07 .20
161 Shawn McEachern .05 .15
162 Vaclav Prospal .05 .15
163 Daniel Alfredsson .10 .25
164 Magnus Arvedson .05 .15
165 Wade Redden .05 .15
166 John LeClair CL .10 .25
167 John LeClair .10 .25
168 Eric Lindros .15 .40
169 Mark Recchi .12 .30
170 Keith Primeau .07 .20
171 Eric Desjardins .07 .20
172 Brian Boucher .07 .20
173 Daymond Langkow .05 .15
174 Simon Gagne .10 .25
175 Jeremy Roenick CL .10 .25
176 Daniel Briere .05 .15
177 Keith Tkachuk .10 .25
178 Sean Burke .05 .15
179 Trevor Letowski .05 .15
180 Shane Doan .07 .20
181 Jeremy Roenick .10 .25
182 Travis Green .05 .15
183 Jaromir Jagr CL .25 .60
184 Jaromir Jagr .25 .60
185 Matthew Barnaby .07 .20
186 Robert Lang .05 .15
187 Jan Hrdina .05 .15
188 Martin Straka .07 .20
189 Ron Tugnutt .07 .20
190 Alexei Kovalev .07 .20
191 Jeff Friesen CL .05 .15
192 Vincent Damphousse .07 .20
193 Jeff Friesen .05 .15
194 Brad Stuart .07 .20
195 Patrick Marleau .10 .25
196 Mike Ricci .07 .20
197 Owen Nolan .10 .25
198 Steve Shields .05 .15
199 Chris Pronger CL .07 .20
200 Pavol Demitra .12 .30
201 Al MacInnis .10 .25
202 Lubos Bartecko .05 .15
203 Jochen Hecht .05 .15
204 Chris Pronger .07 .20
205 Roman Turek .07 .20
206 Michal Handzus .05 .15
207 Pierre Turgeon .10 .25
208 Vincent Lecavalier CL .07 .20
209 Vincent Lecavalier .07 .20
210 Paul Mara .05 .15
211 Mike Johnson .05 .15
212 Dan Cloutier .07 .20
213 Wayne Primeau .05 .15
214 Pavel Kubina .05 .15
215 Fredrik Modin .05 .15
216 Mats Sundin CL .10 .25
217 Mats Sundin .10 .25
218 Darcy Tucker .05 .15
219 Sergei Berezin .05 .15
220 Curtis Joseph .12 .30
221 Jonas Hoglund .05 .15
222 Nikolai Antropov .07 .20
223 Steve Thomas .05 .15
224 Tie Domi .15 .40
225 Mark Messier CL .15 .40
226 Mark Messier .15 .40
227 Andrew Cassels .05 .15
228 Brendan Morrison .10 .25
229 Markus Naslund .07 .20
230 Felix Potvin .15 .40
231 Ed Jovanovski .07 .20
232 Harold Druken .05 .15
233 Olaf Kolzig CL .10 .25
234 Peter Bondra .07 .20
235 Adam Oates .10 .25
236 Jan Bulis .05 .15
237 Jeff Halpern .05 .15
238 Sergei Gonchar .05 .15
239 Olaf Kolzig .10 .25
240 Chris Simon .05 .15
241 P.Bure/V.Bure HL .12 .30
242 P.Kariya/S.Kariya HL .12 .30
243 Dominik Hasek HL .15 .40
244 Patrick Roy HL .25 .60
245 Joe Sakic HL .15 .40
246 Ray Bourque HL .15 .40
247 Brett Hull HL .15 .40
248 Brendan Shanahan HL .12 .30
249 Steve Yzerman HL .30 .75
250 Pat Verbeek HL .07 .20
251 Pavel Bure HL .12 .30
252 Scott Gomez HL .07 .20
253 John LeClair HL .10 .25
254 Brian Boucher HL .07 .20
255 Jeremy Roenick HL .10 .25
256 Jaromir Jagr HL .25 .60
257 Chris Pronger HL .07 .20
258 Roman Turek HL .07 .20
259 Curtis Joseph HL .12 .30
260 Wayne Gretzky HL .50 1.25
261 S.Aubin RC/D.Hinote .07 .20
262 Brandon Smith RC .05 .15
Andre Savage
263 Keith Aldridge RC .05 .15
Ryan Christie
264 S.Reinprecht RC/B.Chartrand .10 .25
265 Petr Mika RC .05 .15
Jason Krog
266 Steve Valiquette RC .07 .20
Vladimir Orszagh
267 Kyle Freadrich RC .05 .15
Corey Sarich
268 Eric Nickulas RC .05 .15
Joel Prpic
269 David Gosselin RC .07 .20
Richard Lintner
270 Greg Andrusak RC .07 .20
Nathan Dempsey
271 Brent Sopel RC .10 .25
Alfie Michaud
272 Jeremy Stevenson RC .05 .15
Maxim Balmochnykh
273 Andreas Karlsson .05 .15
Scott Fankhouser
274 Dave Tanabe .05 .15
Byron Ritchie
275 Steven McCarthy .05 .15
Kyle Calder
276 Petr Schastlivy .07 .20
Mike Fisher
277 Andy Delmore .05 .15
Mark Eaton
278 Evgeni Nabokov .07 .20
Scott Hannan
279 D.Heatley RC/J.Svoboda RC 1.00 2.50
280 Matt Pettinger RC .05 .15
Chris Nielsen RC
281 Teemu Selanne NB .20 .50
282 Paul Kariya NB .12 .30
283 Patrik Stefan NB .07 .20
284 Sergei Samsonov NB .07 .20
285 Joe Thornton NB .15 .40
286 Dominik Hasek NB .15 .40
287 Doug Gilmour NB .12 .30
288 Valeri Bure NB .07 .20
289 Ron Francis NB .12 .30
290 Tony Amonte NB .07 .20
291 Peter Forsberg NB .12 .30
292 Patrick Roy NB .25 .60
293 Joe Sakic NB .15 .40
294 Ray Bourque NB .15 .40
295 Milan Hejduk NB .07 .20
296 Ed Belfour NB .10 .25
297 Brett Hull NB .15 .40
298 Mike Modano NB .15 .40
299 Brendan Shanahan NB .12 .30
300 Steve Yzerman NB .30 .75
301 Sergei Fedorov NB .15 .40
302 Chris Osgood NB .10 .25
303 Doug Weight NB .10 .25
304 Pavel Bure NB .12 .30
305 Zigmund Palffy NB .10 .25
306 Rob Blake NB .10 .25
307 Saku Koivu NB .10 .25
308 David Legwand NB .05 .15
309 Martin Brodeur NB .20 .50
310 Scott Gomez NB .07 .20
311 Tim Connolly NB .05 .15
312 Theo Fleury NB .12 .30
313 Marian Hossa NB .07 .20
314 John LeClair NB .10 .25
315 Eric Lindros NB .15 .40
316 Keith Tkachuk NB .10 .25
317 Jeremy Roenick NB .10 .25
318 Jaromir Jagr NB .25 .60
319 Jeff Friesen NB .05 .15
320 Owen Nolan NB .10 .25
321 Al MacInnis NB .10 .25
322 Pavol Demitra NB .05 .15
323 Chris Pronger NB .07 .20
324 Roman Turek NB .07 .20
325 Vincent Lecavalier NB .07 .20
326 Mats Sundin NB .10 .25
327 Curtis Joseph NB .12 .30
328 Mark Messier NB .15 .40
329 Peter Bondra NB .07 .20
330 Olaf Kolzig NB .10 .25
WCB Pavel Bure Jer Contest .05 .15

2001-02 Upper Deck Victory

Released in mid-August 2001, this 453-card set carried an SRP of $3.99 for a 10-card pack. The set was originally released as a 440-card set, and cards 441-453 were available in random packs of UD Rookie Update.

COMPLETE SET (453) 50.00 100.00
COMP.SERIES I (440) 30.00 60.00
1 Jean-Sebastien Giguere CL .10 .25
2 Steve Rucchin .10 .25
3 Oleg Tverdovsky .10 .25
4 Matt Cullen .10 .25
5 Vitali Vishnevsky .10 .25
6 Jean-Sebastien Giguere .12 .30
7 Mike LeClerc .10 .25
8 Petr Tenkrat .10 .25
9 Paul Kariya .20 .50
10 Samuel Pahlsson .10 .25
11 Jeff Friesen .10 .25
12 Milan Hnilicka CL .10 .25
13 Patrik Stefan .12 .30
14 Andrew Brunette .10 .25
15 Hnat Domenichelli .10 .25
16 Jiri Slegr .10 .25
17 Tomi Kallio .10 .25
18 Steve Staios .10 .25
19 Steve Guolla .10 .25
20 Milan Hnilicka .12 .30
21 Ray Ferraro .10 .25
22 Frantisek Kaberle .10 .25
23 Ladislav Kohn .10 .25
24 Byron Dafoe CL .10 .25
25 Sergei Samsonov .12 .30
26 Joe Thornton .20 .50
27 Per Johan Axelsson .10 .25
28 Brian Rolston .12 .30
29 Mikko Eloranta .10 .25
30 Jason Allison .12 .30
31 Mike Knuble .10 .25
32 Eric Weinrich .10 .25
33 Byron Dafoe .12 .30
34 Bill Guerin .15 .40
35 Kyle McLaren .10 .25
36 Dominik Hasek CL .20 .50
37 Curtis Brown .10 .25
38 Miroslav Satan .12 .30
39 Dominik Hasek .25 .60
40 Maxim Afinogenov .10 .25
41 Stu Barnes .12 .30
42 J-P Dumont .10 .25
43 Martin Biron .12 .30
44 Alexei Zhitnik .10 .25
45 Dimitri Kalinin .10 .25
46 Chris Gratton .10 .25
47 Denis Hamel .10 .25
48 Mike Vernon CL .10 .25
49 Jarome Iginla .15 .40
50 Marc Savard .10 .25
51 Jeff Cowan .10 .25
52 Derek Morris .10 .25
53 Dave Lowry .10 .25
54 Craig Conroy .10 .25
55 Robyn Regehr .10 .25
56 Oleg Saprykin .10 .25
57 Clarke Wilm .10 .25
58 Toni Lydman .10 .25
59 Arturs Irbe CL .10 .25
60 Rod Brind'Amour .15 .40
61 Ron Francis .20 .50
62 Sami Kapanen .10 .25
63 Jeff O'Neill .10 .25
64 Sandis Ozolinsh .10 .25
65 Arturs Irbe .12 .30
66 Dave Tanabe .10 .25
67 Shane Willis .10 .25
68 Josef Vasicek .10 .25
69 Tommy Westlund .10 .25
70 Bates Battaglia .10 .25
71 Jocelyn Thibault CL .10 .25
72 Steve Sullivan .10 .25
73 Tony Amonte .12 .30
74 Eric Daze .12 .30
75 Steven McCarthy .10 .25
76 Alexei Zhamnov .12 .30
77 Jaroslav Spacek .10 .25
78 Jocelyn Thibault .12 .30
79 Michael Nylander .10 .25
80 Kyle Calder .10 .25
81 Chris Herperger .10 .25
82 Ryan Vandenbussche .10 .25
83 Patrick Roy CL .30 .75
84 Peter Forsberg .20 .50
85 Ray Bourque .25 .60
86 Milan Hejduk .12 .30
87 Alex Tanguay .12 .30
88 David Aebischer .12 .30
89 Chris Drury .12 .30
90 Rob Blake .15 .40
91 Joe Sakic .25 .60
92 Patrick Roy .40 1.00
93 Ville Nieminen .10 .25
94 Steven Reinprecht .10 .25
95 Adam Foote .12 .30
96 Ron Tugnutt CL .10 .25
97 Geoff Sanderson .10 .25
98 Serge Aubin .10 .25
99 David Vyborny .10 .25
100 Ron Tugnutt .12 .30
101 Espen Knutsen .10 .25
102 Tyler Wright .10 .25
103 Lyle Odelein .10 .25
104 Marc Denis .12 .30
105 Blake Sloan .10 .25
106 Jean-Luc Grand-Pierre .10 .25
107 Mike Maneluk .10 .25
108 Ed Belfour CL .12 .30
109 Mike Modano .25 .60
110 Brett Hull .20 .50
111 Brenden Morrow .12 .30
112 Joe Nieuwendyk .15 .40
113 Sergei Zubov .12 .30
114 Ed Belfour .15 .40
115 Derian Hatcher .10 .25
116 Jamie Langenbrunner .10 .25
117 Grant Marshall .10 .25
118 Marty Turco .15 .40
119 Jere Lehtinen .12 .30
120 Darryl Sydor .10 .25
121 Chris Osgood CL .12 .30
122 Sergei Fedorov .25 .60
123 Steve Yzerman .50 1.25
124 Nicklas Lidstrom .15 .40
125 Mathieu Dandenault .10 .25
126 Slava Kozlov .12 .30
127 Chris Osgood .15 .40
128 Darren McCarty .10 .25
129 Kirk Maltby .10 .25
130 Boyd Devereaux .10 .25
131 Manny Legace .12 .30
132 Brendan Shanahan .20 .50
133 Tomas Holmstrom .10 .25
134 Tommy Salo CL .10 .25
135 Anson Carter .12 .30
136 Todd Marchant .10 .25
137 Ryan Smyth .12 .30
138 Tommy Salo .12 .30
139 Doug Weight .15 .40
140 Janne Niinimaa .10 .25
141 Rem Murray .12 .30
142 Daniel Cleary .12 .30
143 Tom Poti .10 .25
144 Georges Laraque .12 .30
145 Mike Grier .10 .25
146 Roberto Luongo CL .20 .50
147 Kevyn Adams .10 .25
148 Viktor Kozlov .10 .25
149 Marcus Nillson .10 .25
150 Robert Svehla .10 .25
151 Pavel Bure .20 .50
152 Anders Eriksson .10 .25
153 Vaclav Prospal .10 .25
154 Roberto Luongo .25 .60
155 Denis Shvidki .10 .25
156 Peter Worrell .10 .25
157 Olli Jokinen .12 .30
158 Felix Potvin CL .20 .50
159 Luc Robitaille .15 .40
160 Zigmund Palffy .15 .40
161 Jozef Stumpel .10 .25
162 Bryan Smolinski .10 .25
163 Glen Murray .12 .30
164 Aaron Miller .10 .25
165 Adam Deadmarsh .12 .30
166 Jaroslav Modry .10 .25
167 Felix Potvin .25 .60
168 Eric Belanger .10 .25
169 Ian Laperriere .10 .25
170 Manny Fernandez CL .10 .25
171 Marian Gaborik .25 .60
172 Stacy Roest .10 .25
173 Wes Walz .10 .25
174 Lubomir Sekeras .10 .25
175 Manny Fernandez .12 .30
176 Darby Hendrickson .10 .25
177 Aaron Gavey .10 .25
178 Roman Simicek .10 .25
179 Jamie McLennan .10 .25
180 Antti Laaksonen .10 .25
181 Andy Sutton .10 .25
182 Jose Theodore CL .12 .30
183 Richard Zednik .12 .30
184 Martin Rucinsky .10 .25
185 Saku Koivu .15 .40
186 Jose Theodore .15 .40
187 Brian Savage .10 .25
188 Oleg Petrov .10 .25
189 Patrice Brisebois .10 .25
190 Chad Kilger .10 .25
191 Craig Darby .10 .25
192 Andrei Markov .15 .40
193 Mike Dunham CL .10 .25
194 Cliff Ronning .10 .25
195 Vitali Yachmenev .10 .25
196 Scott Walker .10 .25
197 Kimmo Timonen .10 .25
198 Patric Kjellberg .10 .25
199 Mike Dunham .12 .30
200 Greg Johnson .10 .25
201 David Legwand .12 .30
202 Scott Hartnell .15 .40
203 Tom Fitzgerald .10 .25
204 Tomas Vokoun .12 .30
205 Martin Brodeur CL .25 .60
206 Scott Stevens .15 .40
207 Patrik Elias .15 .40
208 Randy McKay .10 .25
209 Jason Arnott .12 .30
210 Alexander Mogilny .12 .30
211 Petr Sykora .10 .25
212 Scott Gomez .12 .30
213 Sergei Brylin .10 .25
214 Bobby Holik .10 .25
215 Martin Brodeur .30 .75
216 John Madden .12 .30
217 Scott Niedermayer .15 .40
218 Rick DiPietro CL .10 .25
219 Mariusz Czerkawski .10 .25
220 Jason Krog .10 .25
221 Roman Hamrlik .10 .25
222 Jason Blake .10 .25
223 Rick DiPietro .12 .30
224 Dave Scatchard .10 .25
225 Brad Isbister .10 .25
226 Mark Parrish .10 .25
227 Kenny Jonsson .10 .25
228 Oleg Kvasha .10 .25
229 Mike Richter CL .12 .30
230 Mark Messier .25 .60
231 Mike York .10 .25
232 Theo Fleury .20 .50
233 Brian Leetch .15 .40
234 Petr Nedved .12 .30
235 Radek Dvorak .12 .30
236 Jan Hlavac .10 .25
237 Mike Richter .15 .40
238 Manny Malhotra .12 .30
239 Tomas Kloucek .10 .25
240 Sandy McCarthy .10 .25
241 Patrick Lalime CL .10 .25
242 Marian Hossa .12 .30
243 Shawn McEachern .10 .25
244 Wade Redden .10 .25
245 Daniel Alfredsson .15 .40
246 Radek Bonk .10 .25
247 Martin Havlat .12 .30
248 Patrick Lalime .12 .30
249 Magnus Arvedson .10 .25
250 Karel Rachunek .10 .25
251 Sami Salo .10 .25
252 Jani Hurme .12 .30
253 Roman Cechmanek CL .10 .25
254 John LeClair .15 .40
255 Daymond Langkow .12 .30
256 Keith Primeau .12 .30
257 Justin Williams .10 .25
258 Simon Gagne .15 .40
259 Roman Cechmanek .12 .30
260 Mark Recchi .20 .50
261 Ruslan Fedotenko .10 .25
262 Dan McGillis .10 .25
263 Eric Desjardins .12 .30
264 Brian Boucher .12 .30
265 Sean Burke CL .07 .20
266 Shane Doan .12 .30
267 Mike Johnson .10 .25
268 Michal Handzus .10 .25
269 Landon Wilson .10 .25
270 Jeremy Roenick .15 .40
271 Mika Alatalo .10 .25
272 Sean Burke .10 .25
273 Daniel Briere .12 .30
274 Trevor Letowski .10 .25
275 Teppo Numminen .10 .25
276 Ladislav Nagy .10 .25
277 Johan Hedberg CL .10 .25
278 Jaromir Jagr .40 1.00
279 Jan Hrdina .10 .25
280 Mario Lemieux .50 1.25
281 Alexei Kovalev .12 .30
282 Robert Lang .10 .25
283 Martin Straka .10 .25
284 Alexei Morozov .10 .25
285 Janne Laukkanen .10 .25
286 Rene Corbet .10 .25
287 Jean-Sebastien Aubin .12 .30
288 Darius Kasparaitis .10 .25
289 Evgeni Nabokov CL .10 .25
290 Teemu Selanne .30 .75
291 Patrick Marleau .15 .40
292 Owen Nolan .15 .40
293 Marcus Ragnarsson .10 .25
294 Brad Stuart .10 .25
295 Mike Ricci .12 .30
296 Vincent Damphousse .12 .30
297 Scott Thornton .12 .30
298 Mike Rathje .10 .25
299 Marco Sturm .10 .25
300 Evgeni Nabokov .12 .30
301 Alexander Korolyuk .10 .25
302 Brent Johnson CL .10 .25
303 Keith Tkachuk .15 .40
304 Cory Stillman .10 .25
305 Chris Pronger .12 .30
306 Scott Young .10 .25
307 Pavol Demitra .20 .50
308 Al MacInnis .15 .40
309 Jochen Hecht .10 .25
310 Pierre Turgeon .15 .40
311 Tyson Nash .10 .25
312 Jamal Mayers .10 .25
313 Dallas Drake .10 .25
314 Kevin Weekes CL .10 .25
315 Vincent Lecavalier .12 .30
316 Brad Richards .15 .40
317 Brian Holzinger .10 .25
318 Fredrik Modin .10 .25
319 Kevin Weekes .12 .30
320 Pavel Kubina .10 .25
321 Andrei Zyuzin .10 .25
322 Martin St. Louis .15 .40
323 Matthew Barnaby .10 .25
324 Nikolai Khabibulin .15 .40
325 Curtis Joseph CL .12 .30
326 Mats Sundin .15 .40
327 Gary Roberts .10 .25
328 Bryan McCabe .12 .30
329 Curtis Joseph .15 .40
330 Tomas Kaberle .10 .25
331 Jonas Hoglund .10 .25
332 Darcy Tucker .10 .25
333 Nikolai Antropov .10 .25
334 Tie Domi .12 .30
335 Aki Berg .10 .25
336 Dimitri Yushkevich .10 .25
337 Dan Cloutier CL .10 .25
338 Markus Naslund .15 .40
339 Donald Brashear .10 .25
340 Andrew Cassels .10 .25
341 Todd Bertuzzi .15 .40
342 Ed Jovanovski .12 .30
343 Brendan Morrison .12 .30
344 Daniel Sedin .15 .40
345 Henrik Sedin .15 .40
346 Dan Cloutier .12 .30
347 Peter Schaefer .10 .25
348 Harold Druken .10 .25
349 Olaf Kolzig CL .12 .30
350 Peter Bondra .15 .40
351 Sergei Gonchar .10 .25
352 Steve Konowalchuk .10 .25
353 Chris Simon .10 .25
354 Adam Oates .15 .40
355 Olaf Kolzig .15 .40
356 Jeff Halpern .10 .25
357 Trevor Linden .15 .40
358 Calle Johansson .12 .30
359 Dainius Zubrus .10 .25
360 Andrei Nikolishin .10 .25
361 Gregg Naumenko .10 .25
362 Tappr/Vigier/Snyder RC .12 .30
363 Kutlak RC/Goren/Kolarik .10 .25
364 Mika Noronen .10 .25
365 Murray/Fata/Petrovicky .10 .25
366 Hnkinsn RC/Lrcq RC/Bell .10 .25
367 Y.Babenko/R.Shearer .10 .25
368 Steve Gainey .10 .25
369 J.Williams/M.Kuznetsov .10 .25
370 Chimera RC/Comrie/Hajt .12 .30
371 Shelley RC/Spnhl RC/Kles .12 .30
372 M.Darche RC/M.Davidson .15 .40
373 Podkonicky RC/Thompson .10 .25
374 T.Scott/A.Lilja .10 .25
375 Pascal Dupuis RC .15 .40
376 Matteucci RC/Gustafson .10 .25
377 Francis Belanger RC .12 .30
378 C.Mason/P.Skrbek RC .10 .25
379 Dagenais/M.Jefferson RC .10 .25
380 Juraj Kolnik .10 .25
381 P.Smrek RC/Ulmer/Yerem .10 .25
382 Joel Kwiatkowski RC .10 .25
383 Maxime Ouellet .15 .40
384 David Cullen RC .10 .25
385 Tibb/Croz/Hedberg RC .12 .30
386 Kiprusoff/Samuelsson RC .15 .40
387 J.Obsut RC/M.Van Ryn .10 .25
388 Ziegler RC/Afanasenkov .12 .30
389 A.Ponikarovsky/J.Farkas .10 .25
390 K.Beech/M.Pettinger .10 .25
391 Mario Lemieux MHG .75 2.00
392 Jaromir Jagr MHG .30 .75
393 Chris Pronger MHG .15 .40
394 Peter Forsberg MHG .25 .60
395 Pavel Bure MHG .20 .50
396 Patrick Roy MHG 1.00 2.50
397 Joe Sakic MHG .40 1.00
398 Dominik Hasek MHG .30 .75
399 John Leclair MHG .20 .50
400 Sergei Fedorov MHG .30 .75
401 Nicklas Lidstrom MHG .20 .50
402 Martin Brodeur MHG .50 1.25
403 Ed Belfour MHG .20 .50
404 Steve Yzerman MHG .60 1.50
405 Owen Nolan MHG .15 .40
406 Keith Tkachuk MHG .20 .50
407 Olaf Kolzig MHG .15 .40
408 Rob Blake MHG .15 .40
409 Brett Hull MHG .25 .60
410 Brian Leetch MHG .15 .40
411 Ray Bourque MHG .30 .75
412 Pierre Turgeon MHG .15 .40
413 Alexei Yashin MHG .12 .30
414 Mike Modano MHG .20 .50
415 Curtis Joseph MHG .20 .50
416 Alexei Kovalev MHG .15 .40
417 Marian Hossa MHG .20 .50
418 Milan Hejduk MHG .20 .50
419 Markus Naslund MHG .20 .50
420 Theo Fleury MHG .20 .50
421 Bill Guerin MHG .15 .40
422 Doug Weight MHG .15 .40
423 Luc Robitaille MHG .15 .40
424 Zigmund Palffy MHG .15 .40
425 Jeremy Roenick MHG .25 .60
426 Mats Sundin MHG .20 .50
427 Alexander Mogilny MHG .15 .40
428 Ed Jovanovski MHG .15 .40
429 Adam Foote MHG .15 .40
430 Peter Bondra MHG .20 .50
431 Mark Recchi MHG .15 .40
432 Radek Bonk MHG .12 .30
433 Simon Gagne MHG .20 .50
434 Scott Stevens MHG .15 .40
435 Steve Sullivan MHG .12 .30
436 Martin Straka MHG .12 .30
437 Evgeni Nabokov MHG .15 .40
438 Keith Primeau MHG .15 .40
439 Brendan Shanahan MHG .20 .50
440 Vincent Lecavalier MHG .20 .50
441 Ilya Kovalchuk RC 5.00 12.00
442 Erik Cole RC 2.00 5.00
443 Pavel Datsyuk RC 5.00 12.00
444 Kristian Huselius RC 1.50 4.00
445 Marcel Hossa RC 1.50 4.00
446 Martin Erat RC 1.50 4.00
447 Christian Berglund RC 1.25 3.00
448 Raffi Torres RC 1.50 4.00
449 Dan Blackburn RC 1.25 3.00
450 Jiri Dopita RC
451 Krys Kolanos RC 1.00 2.50
452 Brian Sutherby RC 1.00 2.50
453 Olivier Michaud RC 1.50 4.00

2001-02 Upper Deck Victory Gold

Randomly inserted at 1:2 packs, this 440-card set paralleled the Series I base set but was printed on gold card stock.

*GOLD: 1X TO 2.5X BASIC CARDS
230 Mark Messier .60 1.50

2002-03 Upper Deck Victory

Released in late-July 2002, this 220-card set had an SRP of $.99 for a 10-card pack. A bronze bordered parallel was also created and inserted in 1:2 packs.

COMPLETE SET (220) 15.00 40.00
1 Vitali Vishnevsky .10 .25
2 Paul Kariya .20 .50
3 Jeff Friesen .10 .25
4 Jean-Sebastien Giguere .15 .40
5 Oleg Tverdovsky .10 .25
6 Matt Cullen .10 .25
7 Mike LeClerc .10 .25
8 Pasi Nurminen .10 .25
9 Dany Heatley .15 .40
10 Ilya Kovalchuk .20 .50
11 Pascal Rheaume .10 .25
12 Lubos Bartecko .10 .25
13 Mark Hartigan .10 .25
14 Frederic Cassivi .10 .25
15 Jozef Stumpel .10 .25
16 Sergei Samsonov .12 .30
17 P.J. Stock .10 .25
18 Joe Thornton .20 .50
19 Nick Boynton .10 .25
20 Brian Rolston .12 .30
21 Martin Lapointe .12 .30
22 Maxim Afinogenov .10 .25
23 Martin Biron .12 .30
24 J-P Dumont .10 .25
25 Stu Barnes .10 .25
26 Tim Connolly .10 .25
27 Miroslav Satan .15 .40
28 Taylor Pyatt .10 .25
29 Craig Conroy .10 .25
30 Roman Turek .15 .40
31 Jarome Iginla .15 .40
32 Dean McAmmond .10 .25
33 Marc Savard .10 .25
34 Derek Morris .10 .25
35 Micki Dupont RC .10 .25
36 Sami Kapanen .10 .25
37 Jeff O'Neill .10 .25
38 Ron Francis .20 .50
39 Rod Brind'Amour .15 .40
40 Erik Cole .12 .30
41 Bates Battaglia .10 .25
42 Arturs Irbe .12 .30
43 Alexei Zhamnov .12 .30
44 Jocelyn Thibault .12 .30
45 Eric Daze .10 .25
46 Steve Sullivan .10 .25
47 Phil Housley .12 .30
48 Kyle Calder .10 .25
49 Bob Probert .15 .40
50 Patrick Roy .40 1.00
51 Radim Vrbata .12 .30
52 Chris Drury .15 .40
53 Joe Sakic .25 .60
54 Milan Hejduk .12 .30
55 Alex Tanguay .12 .30
56 Peter Forsberg .20 .50
57 Rob Blake .15 .40
58 Ray Whitney .12 .30
59 Espen Knutsen .10 .25
60 Marc Denis .12 .30
61 Rostislav Klesla .10 .25
62 Ron Tugnutt .12 .30
63 Mike Sillinger .10 .25
64 Chris Nielsen .10 .25
65 Jason Arnott .12 .30
66 Marty Turco .15 .40
67 Jere Lehtinen .15 .40
68 Sergei Zubov .12 .30
69 Mike Modano .25 .60
70 Brenden Morrow .12 .30
71 Pierre Turgeon .15 .40
72 Derian Hatcher .12 .30
73 Brendan Shanahan .20 .50
74 Dominik Hasek .25 .60
75 Sergei Fedorov .25 .60
76 Pavel Datsyuk .20 .50
77 Steve Yzerman .30 .75
78 Brett Hull .20 .50
79 Chris Chelios .15 .40
80 Luc Robitaille .15 .40
81 Mike Comrie .15 .40
82 Anson Carter .12 .30
83 Ryan Smyth .12 .30
84 Tommy Salo .12 .30
85 Jochen Hecht .10 .25
86 Eric Brewer .10 .25
87 Mike York .10 .25
88 Kristian Huselius .10 .25
89 Stephen Weiss .15 .40
90 Roberto Luongo .25 .60
91 Sandis Ozolinsh .12 .30
92 Valeri Bure .12 .30
93 Marcus Nilsson .10 .25
94 Niklas Hagman .10 .25
95 Adam Deadmarsh .12 .30
96 Felix Potvin .25 .60
97 Jason Allison .12 .30
98 Eric Belanger .10 .25
99 Zigmund Palffy .15 .40
100 Cliff Ronning .10 .25
101 Mathieu Schneider .10 .25
102 Andrew Brunette .10 .25
103 Sylvain Blouin RC .10 .25
104 Marian Gaborik .25 .60
105 Wes Walz .10 .25
106 Filip Kuba .10 .25
107 Manny Fernandez .12 .30
108 Tony Virta .10 .25
109 Jose Theodore .15 .40
110 Saku Koivu .15 .40
111 Mike Ribeiro .12 .30
112 Yanic Perreault .10 .25
113 Oleg Petrov .10 .25
114 Joe Juneau .12 .30
115 Marcel Hossa .10 .25
116 Denis Arkhipov .10 .25
117 Scott Hartnell .15 .40
118 David Legwand .12 .30
119 Mike Dunham .12 .30
120 Kimmo Timonen .10 .25
121 Greg Johnson .10 .25
122 Andy Delmore .10 .25
123 Petr Sykora .12 .30
124 Scott Stevens .15 .40
125 Brian Gionta .12 .30
126 Scott Niedermayer .15 .40
127 Martin Brodeur .30 .75
128 Patrik Elias .15 .40
129 Joe Nieuwendyk .15 .40
130 Scott Gomez .12 .30
131 Ray Schultz RC .10 .25
132 Mark Parrish .10 .25
133 Raffi Torres .10 .25
134 Alexei Yashin .12 .30
135 Chris Osgood .15 .40
136 Michael Peca .12 .30
137 Shawn Bates .10 .25
138 Pavel Bure .20 .50
139 Mark Messier .25 .60
140 Eric Lindros .25 .60
141 Brian Leetch .15 .40
142 Petr Nedved .10 .25
143 Tom Poti .10 .25
144 Dan Blackburn .12 .30
145 Mike Richter .15 .40
146 Martin Havlat .12 .30
147 Patrick Lalime .12 .30
148 Daniel Alfredsson .15 .40
149 Marian Hossa .12 .30
150 Radek Bonk .12 .30
151 Wade Redden .10 .25
152 Magnus Arvedson .10 .25
153 Todd White .10 .25
154 Roman Cechmanek .12 .30
155 Mark Recchi .20 .50
156 Simon Gagne .15 .40
157 Jeremy Roenick .15 .40
158 John LeClair .15 .40
159 Keith Primeau .15 .40
160 Justin Williams .12 .30
161 Brian Boucher .12 .30
162 Krys Kolanos .10 .25
163 Sean Burke .10 .25
164 Teppo Numminen .12 .30
165 Shane Doan .12 .30
166 Ladislav Nagy .10 .25
167 Daymond Langkow .12 .30
168 Daniel Briere .12 .30
169 Kris Beech .10 .25
170 Johan Hedberg .15 .40
171 Martin Straka .12 .30
172 Mario Lemieux .50 1.25
173 Alexei Kovalev .15 .40
174 Jan Hrdina .10 .25
175 Alexei Morozov .10 .25
176 Vincent Damphousse .12 .30
177 Owen Nolan .15 .40
178 Patrick Marleau .15 .40
179 Evgeni Nabokov .12 .30
180 Brad Stuart .10 .25
181 Mike Ricci .12 .30
182 Scott Thornton .10 .25
183 Al MacInnis .15 .40
184 Pavol Demitra .20 .50
185 Chris Pronger .12 .30
186 Brent Johnson .12 .30
187 Doug Weight .15 .40
188 Keith Tkachuk .15 .40
189 Scott Young .10 .25
190 Cory Stillman .10 .25
191 Sheldon Keefe .10 .25
192 Brad Richards .15 .40
193 Nikolai Khabibulin .15 .40
194 Martin St. Louis .15 .40
195 Vincent Lecavalier .12 .30
196 Fredrik Modin .10 .25
197 Pavel Kubina .10 .25
198 Alexander Mogilny .12 .30
199 Tomas Kaberle .10 .25

0 Mats Sundin .15 .40
1 Gary Roberts .10 .25
2 Mikael Renberg .10 .25
3 Tie Domi .12 .30
4 Darcy Tucker .10 .25
5 Brendan Morrison .12 .30
6 Brent Sopel .10 .25
7 Trevor Linden .15 .40
8 Dan Cloutier .12 .30
9 Todd Bertuzzi .15 .40
0 Ed Jovanovski .12 .30
1 Markus Naslund .12 .30
2 Sergei Gonchar .12 .30
3 Jaromir Jagr .40 1.00
4 Peter Bondra .15 .40
5 Steve Konowalchuk .10 .25
6 Dainius Zubrus .10 .25
7 Brian Sutherby .10 .25
8 Olaf Kolzig .15 .40
9 Patrick Roy CL .25 .60
0 Pavel Bure CL .12 .30

2002-03 Upper Deck Victory Bronze

is 220-card set paralleled the base set with bronze n and was inserted at 1:2 packs.
RONZE: 1.2X TO 3X BASIC CARDS
9 Mark Messier .60 1.50

2002-03 Upper Deck Victory Gold

is 220-card set paralleled the base set with gold n. Each card was serial-numbered to 100.
OLD: 8X TO 20X BASIC CARDS
9 Mark Messier 4.00 10.00

2002-03 Upper Deck Victory Silver

is 220-card set paralleled the base set with silver n and was inserted at 1:36.
ILVER: 4X TO 10X BASIC CARDS
9 Mark Messier 2.00 5.00

2002-03 Upper Deck Victory National Pride

serted at 1:4, this 60-card set featured small color ayer photos over larger silhouettes.
OMPLETE SET 20.00 40.00
P1 Ruslan Salei .15 .40
P2 Paul Kariya .30 .75
P3 Jarome Iginla .40 1.00
P4 Joe Sakic .60 1.50
P5 Rob Blake .25 .60
P6 Steve Yzerman 1.50 4.00
P7 Brendan Shanahan .50 1.25
P8 Martin Brodeur .75 2.00
P9 Eric Lindros .30 .75
P10 Simon Gagne .30 .75
P11 Mario Lemieux 2.00 5.00
P12 Chris Pronger .25 .60
P13 Curtis Joseph .30 .75
P14 Milan Hejduk .30 .75
P15 Dominik Hasek .60 1.50
P16 Patrik Elias .25 .60
P17 Petr Sykora .15 .40
P18 Martin Rucinsky .15 .40
P19 Martin Havlat .25 .60
P20 Robert Lang .15 .40
P21 Jaromir Jagr .50 1.25
P22 Sami Kapanen .15 .40
P23 Ville Nieminen .15 .40
P24 Jere Lehtinen .25 .60
P25 Jani Hurme .25 .60
P26 Teppo Numminen .15 .40
P27 Teemu Selanne .30 .75
P28 Jochen Hecht .15 .40
P29 Marco Sturm .15 .40
P30 Olaf Kolzig .25 .60
P31 Ilya Kovalchuk .40 1.00
P32 Sergei Samsonov .25 .60
P33 Alexei Zhamnov .15 .40
P34 Sergei Fedorov .60 1.50
P35 Pavel Bure .50 1.25
P36 Alexei Yashin .15 .40
P37 Alexei Kovalev .25 .60
P38 Nikolai Khabibulin .30 .75
P39 Sergei Gonchar .15 .40
P40 Miroslav Satan .25 .60
P41 Zigmund Palffy .25 .60
P42 Marian Hossa .30 .75
P43 Pavol Demitra .25 .60
P44 Nicklas Lidstrom .30 .75
P45 Tomas Holmstrom .15 .40
P46 Tommy Salo .25 .60
P47 Daniel Alfredsson .25 .60
P48 Kim Johnsson .15 .40
P49 Mats Sundin .30 .75
P50 Markus Naslund .30 .75
P51 Bill Guerin .25 .60
P52 Tony Amonte .25 .60
P53 Chris Drury .25 .60
P54 Mike Modano .50 1.25
P55 Chris Chelios .30 .75
P56 Mike Dunham .25 .60
P57 Mike Richter .30 .75
P58 Jeremy Roenick .40 1.00
P59 Keith Tkachuk .30 .75
P60 Doug Weight .25 .60

2003-04 Upper Deck Victory

eleased in September, this 210-card set featured 200 se cards and a 10-card rookie redemption set. The okie redemption exchange card was inserted to 1:72. ease note that card #15 does not exist and card #27 as duplicated.
OMP.SET w/o RC's (200) 25.00 50.00
Paul Kariya .20 .50
Petr Sykora .12 .30
Adam Oates .15 .40
Stanislav Chistov .10 .25
Jean-Sebastien Giguere .15 .40
Dany Heatley .15 .40
Ilya Kovalchuk .15 .40
Marc Savard .12 .30
Patrik Stefan .10 .25
0 Simon Gamache .10 .25
Joe DiPenta RC .20 .50
2 Joe Thornton .20 .50
3 Glen Murray .12 .30
4 Bryan Berard .12 .30
5 P.J. Stock .10 .25
7 Jeff Hackett .12 .30
8 Steve Shields .12 .30
9 Miroslav Satan .12 .30
0 Daniel Briere .15 .40
1 Ales Kotalik .10 .25
2 Milan Bartovic RC .20 .50
3 Maxim Afinogenov .10 .25
4 Martin Biron .12 .30
5 Ryan Miller .15 .40
6 Rick Mrozik RC .10 .25
7 Sergei Samsonov .12 .30
27 Jarome Iginla .15 .40
28 Chris Drury .12 .30
29 Jordan Leopold .10 .25
30 Roman Turek .12 .30
31 Jamie McLennan .10 .25
32 Jeff O'Neill .10 .25
33 Ron Francis .20 .50
34 Rod Brind'Amour .15 .40
35 Erik Cole .12 .30
36 Pavel Brendl .10 .25
37 Steve Sullivan .10 .25
38 Alexei Zhamnov .12 .30
39 Eric Daze .12 .30
40 Kyle Calder .10 .25
41 Igor Radulov .10 .25
42 Jocelyn Thibault .12 .30
43 Peter Forsberg .20 .50
44 Milan Hejduk .12 .30
45 Alex Tanguay .12 .30
46 Joe Sakic .25 .60
47 Rob Blake .15 .40
48 David Aebischer .12 .30
49 Patrick Roy .40 1.00
50 Ray Whitney .12 .30
51 Andrew Cassels .10 .25
52 Geoff Sanderson .10 .25
53 Rick Nash .15 .40
54 Marc Denis .12 .30
55 Kent McDonell RC .20 .50
56 Mike Modano .25 .60
57 Bill Guerin .15 .40
58 Jere Lehtinen .12 .30
59 Jason Arnott .12 .30
60 Steve Ott .12 .30
61 Marty Turco .15 .40
62 Sergei Fedorov .25 .60
63 Brett Hull .20 .50
64 Brendan Shanahan .20 .50
65 Nicklas Lidstrom .15 .40
66 Pavel Datsyuk .20 .50
67 Henrik Zetterberg .20 .50
68 Steve Yzerman .40 1.00
69 Manny Legace .10 .25
70 Curtis Joseph .15 .40
71 Ryan Smyth .12 .30
72 Todd Marchant .10 .25
73 Mike Comrie .12 .30
74 Ales Hemsky .15 .40
75 Eric Brewer .10 .25
76 Fernando Pisani .10 .25
77 Tommy Salo .12 .30
78 Olli Jokinen .15 .40
79 Viktor Kozlov .10 .25
80 Stephen Weiss .10 .25
81 Jay Bouwmeester .15 .40
82 Roberto Luongo .25 .60
83 Zigmund Palffy .15 .40
84 Alexander Frolov .12 .30
85 Jason Allison .12 .30
86 Adam Deadmarsh .12 .30
87 Jamie Storr .12 .30
88 Cristobal Huet .12 .30
89 Marian Gaborik .25 .60
90 Pascal Dupuis .10 .25
91 P-M Bouchard .15 .40
92 Manny Fernandez .12 .30
93 Dwayne Roloson .12 .30
94 Wes Walz .10 .25
95 Saku Koivu .15 .40
96 Richard Zednik .10 .25
97 Marcel Hossa .10 .25
98 Jose Theodore .15 .40
99 Michael Komisarek .10 .25
100 Mathieu Garon .10 .25
101 Ron Hainsey .10 .25
102 David Legwand .12 .30
103 Denis Arkhipov .10 .25
104 Scott Hartnell .15 .40
105 Scottie Upshall .12 .30
106 Tomas Vokoun .12 .30
107 Patrik Elias .15 .40
108 Jamie Langenbrunner .12 .30
109 Scott Gomez .12 .30
110 Joe Nieuwendyk .15 .40
111 John Madden .10 .25
112 Scott Stevens .15 .40
113 Martin Brodeur .30 .75
114 Alexei Yashin .12 .30
115 Jason Blake .10 .25
116 Dave Scatchard .10 .25
117 Michael Peca .12 .30
118 Janne Niinimaa .10 .25
119 Rick DiPietro .12 .30
120 Garth Snow .12 .30
121 Alex Kovalev .12 .30
122 Anson Carter .12 .30
123 Eric Lindros .25 .60
124 Tom Poti .10 .25
125 Mark Messier .25 .60
126 Pavel Bure .20 .50
127 Brian Leetch .15 .40
128 Mike Dunham .12 .30
129 Dan Blackburn .12 .30
130 Marian Hossa .12 .30
131 Daniel Alfredsson .15 .40
132 Todd White .10 .25
133 Zdeno Chara .15 .40
134 Jason Spezza .15 .40
135 Patrick Lalime .12 .30
136 Ray Emery .12 .30
137 Jeremy Roenick .15 .40
138 Mark Recchi .20 .50
139 Tony Amonte .12 .30
140 Keith Primeau .15 .40
141 John LeClair .15 .40
142 Simon Gagne .15 .40
143 Robert Esche .10 .25
144 Mike Johnson .10 .25
145 Shane Doan .12 .30
146 Ladislav Nagy .10 .25
147 Chris Gratton .10 .25
148 Sean Burke .10 .25
149 Mario Lemieux .50 1.25
150 Martin Straka .10 .25
151 Rico Fata .10 .25
152 Johan Hedberg .12 .30
153 Sebastien Caron .12 .30
154 Brooks Orpik .12 .30
155 Teemu Selanne .30 .75
156 Vincent Damphousse .12 .30
157 Patrick Marleau .15 .40
158 Jim Fahey .10 .25
159 Niko Dimitrakos .10 .25
160 Kyle McLaren .10 .25
161 Evgeni Nabokov .12 .30
162 Peter Sejna RC .20 .50
163 Pavol Demitra .20 .50
164 Al MacInnis .15 .40
165 Doug Weight .15 .40
166 Keith Tkachuk .15 .40
167 Chris Pronger .12 .30
168 Chris Osgood .15 .40
169 Barret Jackman .10 .25
170 Vaclav Prospal .10 .25
171 Vincent Lecavalier .12 .30
172 Martin St. Louis .15 .40
173 Alexander Svitov .10 .25
174 Nikolai Khabibulin .15 .40
175 Matt Stajan RC .60 1.50
176 Alexander Mogilny .12 .30
177 Mats Sundin .15 .40
178 Owen Nolan .12 .30
179 Nik Antropov .12 .30
180 Doug Gilmour .20 .50
181 Tie Domi .12 .30
182 Gary Roberts .10 .25
183 Ed Belfour .15 .40
184 Carlo Colaiacovo .10 .25
185 Alexander Auld .10 .25
186 Markus Naslund .15 .40
187 Todd Bertuzzi .15 .40
188 Brendan Morrison .12 .30
189 Ed Jovanovski .12 .30
190 Matt Cooke .10 .25
191 Trevor Linden .15 .40
192 Henrik Sedin .15 .40
193 Daniel Sedin .15 .40
194 Dan Cloutier .12 .30
195 Jaromir Jagr .40 1.00
196 Sergei Gonchar .10 .25
197 Michael Nylander .10 .25
198 Peter Bondra .12 .30
199 Mike Grier .10 .25
200 Olaf Kolzig .15 .40
201 Joffrey Lupul RC 1.50 4.00
202 Eric Staal RC 3.00 8.00
203 Tuomo Ruutu RC 1.00 2.50
204 Nathan Horton RC 1.50 4.00
205 Dustin Brown RC 1.25 3.00
206 Jordin Tootoo RC 1.25 3.00
207 Joni Pitkanen RC 1.00 2.50
208 Milan Michalek RC 1.25 3.00
209 Sean Bergenheim RC .75 2.00
210 Marc-Andre Fleury RC 4.00 10.00

2003-04 Upper Deck Victory Bronze

*VETS/199: 4X TO 10X BASIC CARDS
*ROOKIES/199: 2.5X TO 6X BASIC RC

2003-04 Upper Deck Victory Gold

*VETS/25: 12X TO 30X BASIC CARDS
*ROOKIES: 1.5X TO 4X

2003-04 Upper Deck Victory Silver

*VETS50: 8X TO 20X BASIC CARDS
*ROOKIES/50: 5X TO 12X BASIC RC
STATED PRINT RUN 50 SER.#'d SETS

2003-04 Upper Deck Victory Freshman Flashback

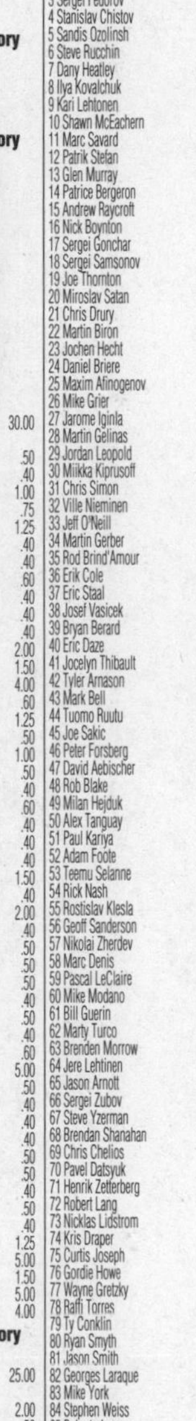

COMPLETE SET (50) 15.00 30.00
STATED ODDS 1:2
FF1 Paul Kariya .20 .50
FF2 Stanislav Chistov .15 .40
FF3 Ilya Kovalchuk .40 1.00
FF4 Dany Heatley .30 .75
FF5 Joe Thornton .50 1.25
FF6 Sergei Samsonov .15 .40
FF7 Ryan Miller .15 .40
FF8 Jarome Iginla .25 .60
FF9 Jordan Leopold .15 .40
FF10 Jocelyn Thibault .15 .40
FF11 Igor Radulov .15 .40
FF12 Peter Forsberg .75 2.00
FF13 Joe Sakic .60 1.50
FF14 Patrick Roy 1.50 4.00
FF15 Rick Nash .25 .60
FF16 Mike Modano .50 1.25
FF17 Henrik Zetterberg .20 .50
FF18 Brett Hull .40 1.00
FF19 Brendan Shanahan .20 .50
FF20 Dmitri Bykov .15 .40
FF21 Roberto Luongo .25 .60
FF22 Jay Bouwmeester .15 .40
FF23 Zigmund Palffy .15 .40
FF24 Cristobal Huet .15 .40
FF25 Marian Gaborik .60 1.50
FF26 Mike Komisarek .15 .40
FF27 Martin Brodeur .75 2.00
FF28 Alex Kovalev .15 .40
FF29 Pavel Bure .20 .50
FF30 Marian Hossa .20 .50
FF31 Jason Spezza .20 .50
FF32 Ray Emery .15 .40
FF33 John LeClair .20 .50
FF34 Tony Amonte .15 .40
FF35 Jeremy Roenick .25 .60
FF36 Mario Lemieux 2.00 5.00
FF37 Teemu Selanne .20 .50
FF38 Jim Fahey .15 .40
FF39 Niko Dimitrakos .15 .40
FF40 Chris Pronger .15 .40
FF41 Keith Tkachuk .20 .50
FF42 Vincent Lecavalier .20 .50
FF43 Owen Nolan .15 .40
FF44 Mats Sundin .20 .50
FF45 Alexander Mogilny .15 .40
FF46 Jaromir Jagr .50 1.25
FF47 Bobby Orr 2.00 5.00
FF48 Ray Bourque .60 1.50
FF49 Wayne Gretzky 2.00 5.00
FF50 Gordie Howe 1.50 4.00

2003-04 Upper Deck Victory Game Breakers

COMPLETE SET (50) 12.50 25.00
STATED ODDS 1:2
GB1 Peter Forsberg .75 2.00
GB2 Paul Kariya .20 .50
GB3 Ilya Kovalchuk .25 .60
GB4 Martin Brodeur 1.00 2.50
GB5 Sean Burke .15 .40
GB6 Bill Guerin .15 .40
GB7 Owen Nolan .15 .40
GB8 Alexei Yashin .15 .40
GB9 Marty Turco .15 .40
GB10 Dany Heatley .25 .60
GB11 Joe Sakic .40 1.00
GB12 Mike Comrie .15 .40
GB13 Jason Blake .15 .40
GB14 Nikolai Khabibulin .20 .50
GB15 Ed Belfour .20 .50
GB16 Chris Pronger .15 .40
GB17 Rick Nash .25 .60
GB18 Jaromir Jagr .30 .75
GB19 Vincent Lecavalier .20 .50
GB20 Olli Jokinen .15 .40
GB21 Alex Kovalev .15 .40
GB22 Mike Modano .30 .75
GB23 Henrik Zetterberg .20 .50
GB24 Roberto Luongo .25 .60
GB25 Teemu Selanne .20 .50
GB26 John LeClair .20 .50
GB27 Tie Domi .15 .40
GB28 Todd Bertuzzi .20 .50
GB29 Pavel Bure .20 .50
GB30 Mario Lemieux 1.25 3.00
GB31 Al MacInnis .15 .40
GB32 Joe Thornton .30 .75
GB33 Mats Sundin .20 .50
GB34 Keith Tkachuk .20 .50
GB35 Alexander Mogilny .15 .40
GB36 Marian Hossa .20 .50
GB37 Brett Hull .25 .60
GB38 Marian Gaborik .40 1.00
GB39 Tony Amonte .15 .40
GB40 Zigmund Palffy .15 .40
GB41 Patrick Roy 1.00 2.50
GB42 Sergei Samsonov .15 .40
GB43 Sergei Fedorov .25 .60
GB44 Markus Naslund .20 .50
GB45 Brendan Shanahan .20 .50
GB46 Saku Koivu .20 .50
GB47 Jarome Iginla .25 .60
GB48 Jocelyn Thibault .15 .40
GB49 Jason Spezza .20 .50
GB50 Jeremy Roenick .25 .60

2005-06 Upper Deck Victory

Victory was released in late-summer 2005, this 300-card set was one of the first of the 2005-06 season. The final 100 cards in the series were found in Upper Deck Series 2 packs.
COMP.SET w/o UPDATE (200) 15.00 30.00
COMP.UPDATE SET (100) 40.00 80.00
1 Jean-Sebastien Giguere .25 .60
2 Joffrey Lupul .20 .50
3 Sergei Fedorov .40 1.00
4 Stanislav Chistov .15 .40
5 Sandis Ozolinsh .15 .40
6 Steve Rucchin .15 .40
7 Dany Heatley .25 .60
8 Ilya Kovalchuk .25 .60
9 Kari Lehtonen .20 .50
10 Shawn McEachern .15 .40
11 Marc Savard .15 .40
12 Patrik Stefan .15 .40
13 Glen Murray .20 .50
14 Patrice Bergeron .30 .75
15 Andrew Raycroft .20 .50
16 Nick Boynton .15 .40
17 Sergei Gonchar .15 .40
18 Sergei Samsonov .20 .50
19 Joe Thornton .30 .75
20 Miroslav Satan .20 .50
21 Chris Drury .20 .50
22 Martin Biron .20 .50
23 Jochen Hecht .15 .40
24 Daniel Briere .25 .60
25 Maxim Afinogenov .15 .40
26 Mike Grier .15 .40
27 Jarome Iginla .25 .60
28 Martin Gelinas .15 .40
29 Jordan Leopold .15 .40
30 Miikka Kiprusoff .20 .50
31 Chris Simon .15 .40
32 Ville Nieminen .15 .40
33 Jeff O'Neill .15 .40
34 Martin Gerber .20 .50
35 Rod Brind'Amour .25 .60
36 Erik Cole .20 .50
37 Eric Staal .30 .75
38 Josef Vasicek .15 .40
39 Bryan Berard .15 .40
40 Eric Daze .20 .50
41 Jocelyn Thibault .20 .50
42 Tyler Arnason .15 .40
43 Mark Bell .15 .40
44 Tuomo Ruutu .25 .60
45 Joe Sakic .40 1.00
46 Peter Forsberg .30 .75
47 David Aebischer .20 .50
48 Rob Blake .25 .60
49 Milan Hejduk .20 .50
50 Alex Tanguay .25 .60
51 Paul Kariya .30 .75
52 Adam Foote .15 .40
53 Teemu Selanne .50 1.25
54 Rick Nash .25 .60
55 Rostislav Klesla .15 .40
56 Geoff Sanderson .15 .40
57 Nikolai Zherdev .15 .40
58 Marc Denis .20 .50
59 Pascal LeClaire .20 .50
60 Mike Modano .40 1.00
61 Bill Guerin .25 .60
62 Marty Turco .25 .60
63 Brenden Morrow .20 .50
64 Jere Lehtinen .20 .50
65 Jason Arnott .20 .50
66 Sergei Zubov .20 .50
67 Steve Yzerman .60 1.50
68 Brendan Shanahan .30 .75
69 Chris Chelios .25 .60
70 Pavel Datsyuk .30 .75
71 Henrik Zetterberg .30 .75
72 Robert Lang .15 .40
73 Nicklas Lidstrom .25 .60
74 Kris Draper .30 .75
75 Curtis Joseph .25 .60
76 Gordie Howe .75 2.00
77 Wayne Gretzky 1.25 3.00
78 Raffi Torres .15 .40
79 Ty Conklin .20 .50
80 Ryan Smyth .20 .50
81 Jason Smith .15 .40
82 Georges Laraque .20 .50
83 Mike York .15 .40
84 Stephen Weiss .15 .40
85 Roberto Luongo .40 1.00
86 Olli Jokinen .25 .60
87 Mike Van Ryn .15 .40
88 Kristian Huselius .15 .40
89 Jay Bouwmeester .25 .60
90 Eric Belanger .15 .40
91 Luc Robitaille .25 .60
92 Mathieu Garon .20 .50
93 Zigmund Palffy .25 .60
94 Lubomir Visnovsky .15 .40
95 Mike Cammalleri .25 .60
96 Marian Gaborik .40 1.00
97 Pascal Dupuis .15 .40
98 Andrew Brunette .15 .40
99 Brian Rolston .20 .50
100 Manny Fernandez .20 .50
101 Dwayne Roloson .20 .50
102 Jose Theodore .25 .60
103 Saku Koivu .25 .60
104 Michael Ryder .20 .50
105 Mike Ribeiro .20 .50
106 Sheldon Souray .15 .40
107 Richard Zednik .15 .40
108 Yanic Perreault .15 .40
109 David Legwand .20 .50
110 Scott Walker .15 .40
111 Tomas Vokoun .20 .50
112 Steve Sullivan .15 .40
113 Kimmo Timonen .15 .40
114 Martin Erat .15 .40
115 Martin Brodeur .50 1.25
116 Scott Stevens .25 .60
117 Scott Gomez .20 .50
118 Brian Rafalski .20 .50
119 Scott Niedermayer .25 .60
120 Patrik Elias .25 .60
121 Rick DiPietro .20 .50
122 Alexei Yashin .20 .50
123 Mark Parrish .15 .40
124 Michael Peca .20 .50
125 Trent Hunter .15 .40
126 Adrian Aucoin .15 .40
127 Bobby Holik .15 .40
128 Mark Messier .40 1.00
129 Mike Dunham .15 .40
130 Jaromir Jagr .60 1.50
131 Jamie Lundmark .15 .40
132 Tom Poti .15 .40
133 Daniel Alfredsson .25 .60
134 Martin Havlat .25 .60
135 Dominik Hasek .40 1.00
136 Jason Spezza .25 .60
137 Marian Hossa .20 .50
138 Peter Bondra .20 .50
139 Wade Redden .15 .40
140 Jeremy Roenick .25 .60
141 Simon Gagne .25 .60
142 Keith Primeau .25 .60
143 John LeClair .25 .60
144 Robert Esche .20 .50
145 Tony Amonte .20 .50
146 Donald Brashear .15 .40
147 Michal Handzus .20 .50
148 Brett Hull .30 .75
149 Shane Doan .20 .50
150 Ladislav Nagy .15 .40
151 Brian Boucher .20 .50
152 Mike Comrie .20 .50
153 Mike Ricci .20 .50
154 Milan Kraft .15 .40
155 Mario Lemieux .75 2.00
156 Marc-Andre Fleury .40 1.00
157 Mark Recchi .30 .75
158 Dick Tarnstrom .15 .40
159 Ryan Malone .15 .40
160 Patrick Marleau .25 .60
161 Nils Ekman .15 .40
162 Jonathan Cheechoo .25 .60
163 Evgeni Nabokov .20 .50
164 Marco Sturm .15 .40
165 Alyn McCauley .15 .40
166 Doug Weight .25 .60
167 Keith Tkachuk .25 .60
168 Chris Pronger .20 .50
169 Al MacInnis .25 .60
170 Patrick Lalime .20 .50
171 Pavol Demitra .30 .75
172 Barret Jackman .15 .40
173 Brad Richards .25 .60
174 Vincent Lecavalier .20 .50
175 Fredrik Modin .15 .40
176 Nikolai Khabibulin .25 .60
177 Ruslan Fedotenko .15 .40
178 Cory Stillman .20 .50
179 Martin St. Louis .25 .60
180 Dan Boyle .20 .50
181 Mats Sundin .25 .60
182 Bryan McCabe .15 .40
183 Joe Nieuwendyk .25 .60
184 Gary Roberts .15 .40
185 Tie Domi .20 .50
186 Ed Belfour .25 .60
187 Brian Leetch .25 .60
188 Darcy Tucker .20 .50
189 Markus Naslund .25 .60
190 Brendan Morrison .15 .40
191 Dan Cloutier .20 .50
192 Ed Jovanovski .20 .50
193 Matt Cooke .15 .40
194 Brent Sopel .15 .40
195 Trevor Linden .25 .60
196 Olaf Kolzig .25 .60
197 Jeff Halpern .15 .40
198 Alexander Semin .25 .60
199 Rastislav Stana .15 .40
200 Brendan Witt .15 .40
201 Teemu Selanne .50 1.25
202 Scott Niedermayer .25 .60
203 Marian Hossa .20 .50
204 Peter Bondra .20 .50
205 Brian Leetch .25 .60
206 Brad Boyes .20 .50
207 Ryan Miller .25 .60
208 Tony Amonte .20 .50
209 Justin Williams .20 .50
210 Nikolai Khabibulin .25 .60
211 Pavel Vorobiev .15 .40
212 Pierre Turgeon .25 .60
213 Sergei Fedorov .40 1.00
214 Antti Miettinen .15 .40
215 Niko Kapanen .15 .40
216 Manny Legace .25 .60
217 Jason Williams .15 .40
218 Chris Pronger .20 .50
219 Ales Hemsky .20 .50
220 Joe Nieuwendyk .25 .60
221 Nathan Horton .25 .60
222 Jeremy Roenick .25 .60
223 Pavol Demitra .30 .75
224 Pierre-Marc Bouchard .25 .60
225 Alex Kovalev .20 .50
226 Paul Kariya .30 .75
227 Scott Hartnell .25 .60
228 Brian Gionta .20 .50
229 Jamie Langenbrunner .15 .40
230 Miroslav Satan .20 .50
231 Alexei Zhitnik .15 .40
232 Steve Rucchin .15 .40
233 Kevin Weekes .20 .50
234 Dany Heatley .25 .60
235 Zdeno Chara .25 .60
236 Peter Forsberg .30 .75
237 Joni Pitkanen .15 .40
238 Curtis Joseph .25 .60
239 Geoff Sanderson .15 .40
240 Sergei Gonchar .15 .40
241 John LeClair .25 .60
242 Milan Michalek .15 .40
243 Petr Cajanek .15 .40
244 Sean Burke .15 .40
245 Vaclav Prospal .15 .40
246 Eric Lindros .40 1.00
247 Jason Allison .20 .50
248 Jeff O'Neill .15 .40
249 Todd Bertuzzi .25 .60
250 Jeff Friesen .15 .40
251 Peter Budaj RC 1.00 2.50
252 Wojtek Wolski RC .60 1.50
253 Brent Seabrook RC 1.50 4.00
254 Cam Barker RC .60 1.50
255 Gilbert Brule RC .75 2.00
256 Jay McClement RC .50 1.25
257 Jeff Woywitka RC .50 1.25
258 Andrew Alberts RC .50 1.25
259 Hannu Toivonen RC .75 2.00
260 Yann Danis RC .60 1.50
261 Alexander Perezhogin RC .60 1.50
262 Brad Winchester RC .75 2.00
263 Kyle Brodziak RC .50 1.25
264 Alexander Ovechkin RC 6.00 15.00
265 Jakub Klepis RC .50 1.25
266 Keith Ballard RC .60 1.50
267 David Leneveu RC .60 1.50
268 Zach Parise RC 2.00 5.00
269 Dion Phaneuf RC 1.25 3.00
270 Eric Nystrom RC .60 1.50
271 Mike Richards RC 1.50 4.00
272 Jeff Carter RC 1.25 3.00
273 R.J. Umberger RC .75 2.00
274 Cam Ward RC 1.25 3.00
275 Robert Nilsson RC .75 2.00
276 Chris Campoli RC .50 1.25
277 George Parros RC .50 1.25
278 Evgeny Artyukhin RC .60 1.50
279 Alexander Steen RC 1.50 4.00
280 Ryan Getzlaf RC 2.00 5.00
281 Corey Perry RC 3.00 8.00
282 Rostislav Olesz RC .60 1.50
283 Anthony Stewart RC .60 1.50
284 Ryan Whitney RC .75 2.00
285 Sidney Crosby RC 10.00 25.00
286 Maxime Talbot RC .75 2.00
287 Ryan Suter RC 1.00 2.50
288 Henrik Lundqvist RC 3.00 8.00
289 Alvaro Montoya RC .75 2.00
290 Jim Howard RC 2.50 6.00
291 Johan Franzen RC 1.25 3.00
292 Thomas Vanek RC 1.50 4.00
293 Andrej Meszaros RC .60 1.50
294 Christoph Schubert RC .50 1.25
295 Patrick Eaves RC .75 2.00
296 Steve Bernier RC .75 2.00
297 Jussi Jokinen RC .75 2.00
298 Braydon Coburn RC .75 2.00
299 Matt Foy RC .50 1.25
300 Mikko Koivu RC 1.00 2.50

2005-06 Upper Deck Victory Gold

*1-250 VETS/100: 6X TO 15X BASIC CARDS
*251-300 ROOKIES/100 : 3X TO 8X BASE RC
STATED PRINT RUN 100 SER.#'d SETS
128 Mark Messier 6.00 15.00
264 Alexander Ovechkin RC 50.00 125.00
269 Dion Phaneuf RC 10.00 25.00
285 Sidney Crosby RC 150.00 250.00

2005-06 Upper Deck Victory Silver

*1-200 SILVER/250: 3X TO 8X BASIC CARDS
PRINT RUN 250 SER.#'d SETS
128 Mark Messier 3.00 8.00

2005-06 Upper Deck Victory Jumbos

Available only in Canadian retail tins, this 42-card set paralleled the base set on jumbo-sized card stock.
BU1 Jean-Sebastien Giguere .75 2.00
BU2 Dany Heatley .75 2.00
BU3 Ilya Kovalchuk .75 2.00
BU4 Patrice Bergeron 1.00 2.50
BU5 Joe Thornton 1.00 2.50
BU6 Jarome Iginla .75 2.00
BU7 Miikka Kiprusoff .60 1.50
BU8 Joe Sakic 1.25 3.00
BU9 Peter Forsberg 1.00 2.50
BU10 Paul Kariya 1.00 2.50
BU11 Rick Nash .75 2.00
BU12 Mike Modano 1.25 3.00
BU13 Gordie Howe 2.50 6.00
BU14 Steve Yzerman 2.00 5.00
BU15 Brendan Shanahan 1.00 2.50
BU16 Wayne Gretzky 4.00 10.00
BU17 Ryan Smyth .60 1.50
BU18 Marian Gaborik 1.25 3.00
BU19 Jose Theodore .75 2.00
BU20 Saku Koivu .75 2.00
BU21 Michael Ryder .60 1.50
BU22 Martin Brodeur 1.50 4.00
BU23 Mark Messier 1.25 3.00
BU24 Jaromir Jagr 2.00 5.00
BU25 Dominik Hasek 1.25 3.00
BU26 Marian Hossa .60 1.50
BU27 Jason Spezza .75 2.00
BU28 Jeremy Roenick .75 2.00
BU29 Keith Primeau .75 2.00
BU30 Brett Hull 1.00 2.50
BU31 Mario Lemieux 2.50 6.00
BU32 Evgeni Nabokov .60 1.50
BU33 Patrick Marleau .75 2.00
BU34 Chris Pronger .60 1.50
BU35 Martin St. Louis .75 2.00
BU36 Vincent Lecavalier .60 1.50
BU37 Nikolai Khabibulin .75 2.00
BU38 Ed Belfour .75 2.00
BU39 Mats Sundin .75 2.00
BU40 Bryan McCabe .50 1.25
BU41 Markus Naslund .75 2.00
BU42 Ed Jovanovski .60 1.50

2005-06 Upper Deck Victory Game Breakers

COMPLETE SET (45) 8.00 20.00
STATED ODDS 1:2
GB1 Sergei Fedorov .60 1.50
GB2 Dany Heatley .40 1.00
GB3 Ilya Kovalchuk .40 1.00
GB4 Glen Murray .30 .75
GB5 Joe Thornton .50 1.25
GB6 Chris Drury .30 .75
GB7 Eric Daze .30 .75
GB8 Tuomo Ruutu .40 1.00
GB9 Peter Forsberg .50 1.25
GB10 Joe Sakic .60 1.50
GB11 Milan Hejduk .30 .75
GB12 Paul Kariya .50 1.25
GB13 Rick Nash .40 1.00
GB14 Mike Modano .60 1.50
GB15 Bill Guerin .40 1.00
GB16 Brendan Shanahan .50 1.25
GB17 Steve Yzerman 1.00 2.50
GB18 Kris Draper .50 1.25
GB19 Henrik Zetterberg .50 1.25
GB20 Ryan Smyth .30 .75
GB21 Olli Jokinen .40 1.00
GB22 Zigmund Palffy .40 1.00
GB23 Marian Gaborik .60 1.50
GB24 Michael Ryder .30 .75
GB25 Saku Koivu .40 1.00
GB26 Steve Sullivan .25 .60
GB27 Alexei Yashin .30 .75
GB28 Jaromir Jagr 1.00 2.50
GB29 Marian Hossa .30 .75
GB30 Martin Havlat .40 1.00
GB31 Peter Bondra .30 .75
GB32 Keith Primeau .40 1.00
GB33 Simon Gagne .40 1.00
GB34 Brett Hull .50 1.25
GB35 Shane Doan .30 .75
GB36 Mario Lemieux 1.25 3.00
GB37 Patrick Marleau .40 1.00
GB38 Pavol Demitra .50 1.25
GB39 Keith Tkachuk .40 1.00
GB40 Martin St. Louis .40 1.00
GB41 Vincent Lecavalier .30 .75
GB42 Brad Richards .40 1.00
GB43 Alexander Mogilny .30 .75
GB44 Mats Sundin .40 1.00
GB45 Markus Naslund .40 1.00

2005-06 Upper Deck Victory Stars on Ice

COMPLETE SET (45) 8.00 20.00
SI1 Jean-Sebastien Giguere .40 1.00
SI2 Dany Heatley .40 1.00
SI3 Ilya Kovalchuk .40 1.00
SI4 Joe Thornton .50 1.25
SI5 Andrew Raycroft .30 .75
SI6 Miroslav Satan .30 .75
SI7 Jarome Iginla .40 1.00
SI8 Miikka Kiprusoff .30 .75
SI9 Jeff O'Neill .25 .60
SI10 Jocelyn Thibault .30 .75
SI11 Joe Sakic .60 1.50
SI12 Peter Forsberg .50 1.25
SI13 Alex Tanguay .40 1.00
SI14 Rob Blake .40 1.00
SI15 David Aebischer .30 .75
SI16 Rick Nash .40 1.00
SI17 Marty Turco .40 1.00
SI18 Sergei Zubov .30 .75
SI19 Mike Modano .75 2.00
SI20 Nicklas Lidstrom .40 1.00
SI21 Steve Yzerman 1.00 2.50
SI22 Robert Lang .25 .60
SI23 Roberto Luongo .60 1.50
SI24 Luc Robitaille .40 1.00
SI25 Jose Theodore .40 1.00
SI26 Martin Brodeur .75 2.00
SI27 Scott Stevens .40 1.00
SI28 Eric Lindros .60 1.50
SI29 Dominik Hasek .60 1.50
SI30 Daniel Alfredsson .40 1.00
SI31 Jason Spezza .40 1.00
SI32 Jeremy Roenick .40 1.00
SI33 John LeClair .40 1.00
SI34 Brett Hull .50 1.25
SI35 Mario Lemieux 1.25 3.00
SI36 Evgeni Nabokov .30 .75
SI37 Keith Tkachuk .40 1.00
SI38 Doug Weight .40 1.00
SI39 Martin St. Louis .40 1.00
SI40 Nikolai Khabibulin .40 1.00
SI41 Ed Belfour .40 1.00
SI42 Brian Leetch .40 1.00
SI43 Mats Sundin .40 1.00
SI44 Markus Naslund .40 1.00
SI45 Ed Jovanovski .30 .75

2006-07 Upper Deck Victory

COMPLETE SET (230) 15.00 40.00
COMP.UPDATE SET (100) 10.00 25.00
231-330 ISSUED IN UD2 PACKS
1 Jean-Sebastien Giguere .25 .60
2 Joffrey Lupul .20 .50
3 Teemu Selanne .50 1.25
4 Andy McDonald .20 .50
5 Scott Niedermayer .25 .60
6 Ilya Bryzgalov .25 .60
7 Ilya Kovalchuk .25 .60
8 Kari Lehtonen .20 .50
9 Marian Hossa .20 .50
10 Marc Savard .15 .40
11 Slava Kozlov .15 .40
12 Patrice Bergeron .30 .75
13 Tim Thomas .30 .75
14 Brian Leetch .25 .60
15 Glen Murray .20 .50
16 Brad Boyes .15 .40
17 Marco Sturm .15 .40
18 Brad Stuart .15 .40
19 Andrew Raycroft .20 .50
20 Chris Drury .20 .50
21 Ryan Miller .25 .60
22 Thomas Vanek .30 .75
23 Tim Connolly .15 .40
24 Maxim Afinogenov .15 .40
25 Martin Biron .20 .50
26 Ales Kotalik .15 .40
27 Daniel Briere .25 .60
28 Miikka Kiprusoff .20 .50
29 Jarome Iginla .25 .60
30 Dion Phaneuf .25 .60
31 Daymond Langkow .15 .40
32 Chuck Kobasew .15 .40
33 Kristian Huselius .15 .40
34 Cam Ward .25 .60
35 Eric Staal .30 .75
36 Mark Recchi .30 .75

37 Doug Weight .25 .60
38 Justin Williams .20 .50
39 Erik Cole .20 .50
40 Rod Brind'Amour .25 .60
41 Tuomo Ruutu .25 .60
42 Nikolai Khabibulin .25 .60
43 Kyle Calder .15 .40
44 Brent Seabrook .25 .60
45 Mark Bell .15 .40
46 Pavel Vorobiev .15 .40
47 Joe Sakic .40 1.00
48 Jose Theodore .25 .60
49 Marek Svatos .15 .40
50 Milan Hejduk .20 .50
51 Alex Tanguay .15 .40
52 Rob Blake .25 .60
53 Andrew Brunette .15 .40
54 Rick Nash .25 .60
55 David Vyborny .15 .40
56 Marc Denis .20 .50
57 Nikolai Zherdev .15 .40
58 Sergei Fedorov .40 1.00
59 Pascal Leclaire .20 .50
60 Mike Modano .40 1.00
61 Marty Turco .25 .60
62 Jussi Jokinen .20 .50
63 Brenden Morrow .20 .50
64 Sergei Zubov .20 .50
65 Jere Lehtinen .15 .40
66 Bill Guerin .25 .60
67 Jason Arnott .20 .50
68 Steve Yzerman .60 1.50
69 Pavel Datsyuk .30 .75
70 Brendan Shanahan .30 .75
71 Manny Legace .20 .50
72 Nicklas Lidstrom .25 .60
73 Henrik Zetterberg .30 .75
74 Tomas Holmstrom .20 .50
75 Kris Draper .15 .40
76 Ryan Smyth .20 .50
77 Shawn Horcoff .15 .40
78 Ales Hemsky .20 .50
79 Chris Pronger .20 .50
80 Dwayne Roloson .20 .50
81 Michael Peca .20 .50
82 Raffi Torres .15 .40
83 Roberto Luongo .40 1.00
84 Nathan Horton .25 .60
85 Olli Jokinen .25 .60
86 Jay Bouwmeester .25 .60
87 Mike Van Ryn .15 .40
88 Joe Nieuwendyk .25 .60
89 Mathieu Garon .20 .50
90 Dustin Brown .25 .60
91 Alexander Frolov .15 .40
92 Pavol Demitra .30 .75
93 Craig Conroy .15 .40
94 Mike Cammalleri .15 .40
95 Lubomir Visnovsky .15 .40
96 Marian Gaborik .30 .75
97 Manny Fernandez .20 .50
98 Brian Rolston .20 .50
99 Pierre-Marc Bouchard .25 .60
100 Wes Walz .15 .40
101 Mikko Koivu .20 .50
102 David Aebischer .20 .50
103 Saku Koivu .25 .60
104 Alex Kovalev .20 .50
105 Michael Ryder .15 .40
106 Chris Higgins .15 .40
107 Mike Ribeiro .20 .50
108 Cristobal Huet .20 .50
109 Paul Kariya .30 .75
110 Tomas Vokoun .20 .50
111 Steve Sullivan .15 .40
112 Martin Erat .15 .40
113 Kimmo Timonen .15 .40
114 Scott Hartnell .25 .60
115 David Legwand .20 .50
116 Martin Brodeur .50 1.25
117 Brian Gionta .20 .50
118 Scott Gomez .20 .50
119 Patrik Elias .25 .60
120 Brian Rafalski .20 .50
121 Zach Parise .30 .75
122 Alexei Yashin .20 .50
123 Rick DiPietro .20 .50
124 Miroslav Satan .20 .50
125 Jason Blake .15 .40
126 Mike York .15 .40
127 Alexei Zhitnik .15 .40
128 Trent Hunter .15 .40
129 Henrik Lundqvist .50 1.25
130 Jaromir Jagr .60 1.50
131 Martin Straka .15 .40
132 Petr Prucha .20 .50
133 Michael Nylander .15 .40
134 Fedor Tyutin .15 .40
135 Jason Spezza .25 .60
136 Dany Heatley .25 .60
137 Dominik Hasek .30 .75
138 Daniel Alfredsson .25 .60
139 Zdeno Chara .25 .60
140 Wade Redden .15 .40
141 Martin Havlat .15 .40
142 Ray Emery .20 .50
143 Peter Forsberg .30 .75
144 Antero Niittymaki .20 .50
145 Simon Gagne .25 .60
146 Joni Pitkanen .15 .40
147 Keith Primeau .25 .60
148 Jeff Carter .25 .60
149 Mike Richards .25 .60
150 Robert Esche .20 .50
151 Shane Doan .20 .50
152 Curtis Joseph .25 .60
153 Ladislav Nagy .15 .40
154 Mike Comrie .20 .50
155 Geoff Sanderson .15 .40
156 Keith Ballard .15 .40
157 Sidney Crosby 1.00 2.50
158 Ryan Malone .15 .40
159 Marc-Andre Fleury .40 1.00
160 Sergei Gonchar .15 .40
161 Colby Armstrong .20 .50
162 Ryan Whitney .20 .50
163 Joe Thornton .30 .75
164 Evgeni Nabokov .20 .50
165 Patrick Marleau .25 .60
166 Jonathan Cheechoo .25 .60
167 Vesa Toskala .20 .50
168 Steve Bernier .15 .40
169 Curtis Sanford .20 .50
170 Lee Stempniak .15 .40
171 Keith Tkachuk .25 .60
172 Scott Young .15 .40
173 Petr Cajanek .15 .40
174 Barret Jackman .15 .40
175 Evgeni Artyukhin .15 .40
176 Vaclav Prospal .15 .40
177 Martin St. Louis .25 .60
178 Vincent Lecavalier .20 .50
179 Sean Burke .15 .40
180 Brad Richards .25 .60
181 Fredrik Modin .15 .40
182 Tie Domi .15 .40
183 Mats Sundin .25 .60
184 Ed Belfour .25 .60
185 Eric Lindros .40 1.00
186 Bryan McCabe .15 .40
187 Alexander Steen .25 .60
188 Darcy Tucker .20 .50
189 Jason Allison .20 .50
190 Henrik Sedin .25 .60
191 Alex Auld .15 .40
192 Markus Naslund .20 .50
193 Brendan Morrison .15 .40
194 Ed Jovanovski .20 .50
195 Mattias Ohlund .15 .40
196 Daniel Sedin .25 .60
197 Jeff Halpern .15 .40
198 Dainius Zubrus .15 .40
199 Alexander Ovechkin 1.00 2.50
200 Olaf Kolzig .25 .60
201 Tomas Kopecky RC .60 1.50
202 Billy Thompson RC .50 1.25
203 Dustin Byfuglien RC 1.25 3.00
204 Yan Stastny RC .50 1.25
205 Eric Fehr RC .75 2.00
206 Ben Ondrus RC .50 1.25
207 Rob Collins RC .50 1.25
208 Brendan Bell RC .50 1.25
209 Frank Doyle RC .60 1.50
210 Noah Welch RC .50 1.25
211 Filip Novak RC .50 1.25
212 Ian White RC .60 1.50
213 Konstantin Pushkarev RC .60 1.50
214 Dan Jancevski RC .50 1.25
215 Shea Weber RC 1.25 3.00
216 Michel Ouellet RC .60 1.50
217 Marc-Antoine Pouliot RC .50 1.25
218 Carsen Germyn RC .50 1.25
219 Matt Carle RC .50 1.25
220 Steve Regier RC .50 1.25
221 Mark Stuart RC .50 1.25
222 Bill Thomas RC .50 1.25
223 Jarkko Immonen RC .50 1.25
224 Erik Reitz RC .50 1.25
225 Joel Perrault RC .50 1.25
226 Ryan Potulny RC .50 1.25
227 Jeremy Williams RC .50 1.25
228 Masi Marjamaki RC .50 1.25
229 Miroslav Kopriva RC .50 1.25
230 Matt Koalska RC .50 1.25
231 Chris Pronger .25 .60
232 Zdeno Chara .30 .75
233 Marc Savard .20 .50
234 Hannu Toivonen .25 .60
235 Alex Tanguay .20 .50
236 Martin Havlat .20 .50
237 Michal Handzus .25 .60
238 Wojtek Wolski .25 .60
239 Jordan Leopold .20 .50
240 Fredrik Modin .20 .50
241 Gilbert Brule .25 .60
242 Anson Carter .25 .60
243 Mike Ribeiro .25 .60
244 Eric Lindros .50 1.25
245 Patrik Stefan .20 .50
246 Jeff Halpern .20 .50
247 Dominik Hasek .40 1.00
248 Joffrey Lupul .25 .60
249 Petr Sykora .25 .60
250 Todd Bertuzzi .30 .75
251 Ed Belfour .30 .75
252 Alexander Auld .20 .50
253 Rob Blake .30 .75
254 Dan Cloutier .25 .60
255 Pavol Demitra .40 1.00
256 Mark Parrish .20 .50
257 Sergei Samsonov .25 .60
258 Jason Arnott .25 .60
259 Mike Sillinger .20 .50
260 Brendan Shanahan .40 1.00
261 Matt Cullen .20 .50
262 Martin Gerber .25 .60
263 Kyle Calder .20 .50
264 Geoff Sanderson .20 .50
265 Owen Nolan .25 .60
266 Ed Jovanovski .25 .60
267 Jeremy Roenick .30 .75
268 Mark Recchi .40 1.00
269 Nils Ekman .20 .50
270 Mark Bell .20 .50
271 Mike Grier .20 .50
272 Doug Weight .30 .75
273 Bill Guerin .30 .75
274 Manny Legace .25 .60
275 Marc Denis .25 .60
276 Andrew Raycroft .25 .60
277 Michael Peca .25 .60
278 Kyle Wellwood .25 .60
279 Roberto Luongo .50 1.25
280 Alexander Semin .30 .75
281 Shane O'Brien RC .60 1.50
282 Jonas Johansson RC .60 1.50
283 Ryan Shannon RC .60 1.50
284 Patrick O'Sullivan RC 1.00 2.50
285 Anze Kopitar RC 2.50 6.00
286 John Oduya RC 1.00 2.50
287 Travis Zajac RC 1.25 3.00
288 Fredrik Norrena RC .60 1.50
289 Phil Kessel RC 2.50 6.00
290 Guillaume Latendresse RC 1.00 2.50
291 Nigel Dawes RC .60 1.50
292 Jordan Staal RC 1.50 4.00
293 Kristopher Letang RC 2.00 5.00
294 Paul Stastny RC 1.50 4.00
295 Niklas Backstrom RC 1.25 3.00
296 D.J. King RC .60 1.50
297 Marc-Edouard Vlasic RC .60 1.50
298 Patrick Thoresen RC .60 1.50
299 Ladislav Smid RC .60 1.50
300 Loui Eriksson RC 1.00 2.50
301 Patrick Fischer RC .60 1.50
302 Mikko Lehtonen RC .75 2.00
303 Roman Polak RC .75 2.00
304 Evgeni Malkin RC 6.00 15.00
305 Luc Bourdon RC 1.00 2.50
306 Alexei Kaigorodov RC .60 1.50
307 Alex Brooks RC .60 1.50
308 Nate Thompson RC .60 1.50
309 Janis Sprukts RC .60 1.50
310 Alexander Radulov RC 1.25 3.00
311 Keith Yandle RC 1.25 3.00
312 Enver Lisin RC .60 1.50
313 Cole Jarrett RC .60 1.50
314 Ryan Caldwell RC .60 1.50
315 David Printz RC .60 1.50
316 David Liffiton RC .60 1.50
317 Adam Burish RC 1.00 2.50
318 Dave Bolland RC 1.00 2.50
319 Michael Blunden RC .60 1.50
320 Matt Lashoff RC .60 1.50
321 Alexei Mikhnov RC .60 1.50
322 Jan Hejda RC .60 1.50
323 Lars Jonsson RC .60 1.50
324 Triston Grant RC .60 1.50
325 Alexander Edler RC 1.00 2.50
326 Brandon Prust RC .60 1.50
327 Dustin Boyd RC .60 1.50
328 Drew Stafford RC 1.00 2.50
329 Kelly Guard RC .75 2.00
330 Nathan McIver RC .60 1.50

2006-07 Upper Deck Victory Gold

*1-200 VETS: 5X TO 12X BASIC CARDS
*201-230 ROOK: 1.5X TO 4X BASIC RC

2006-07 Upper Deck Victory Game Breakers

COMPLETE SET (50) 60.00 125.00
STATED ODDS 1:4 PACKS
GB1 Jean-Sebastien Giguere 1.25 3.00
GB2 Ilya Kovalchuk 1.25 3.00
GB3 Marian Hossa 1.00 2.50
GB4 Patrice Bergeron 1.50 4.00
GB5 Jarome Iginla 1.25 3.00
GB6 Miikka Kiprusoff 1.00 2.50
GB7 Eric Staal 1.50 4.00
GB8 Martin Gerber 1.00 2.50
GB9 Nikolai Khabibulin 1.25 3.00
GB10 Joe Sakic 2.00 5.00
GB11 Alex Tanguay .75 2.00
GB12 Marek Svatos .75 2.00
GB13 Rick Nash 1.25 3.00
GB14 Mike Modano 2.00 5.00
GB15 Marty Turco 1.25 3.00
GB16 Henrik Zetterberg 1.50 4.00
GB17 Pavel Datsyuk 1.50 4.00
GB18 Brendan Shanahan 1.50 4.00
GB19 Roberto Luongo 2.00 5.00
GB20 Olli Jokinen 1.25 3.00
GB21 Alexander Frolov .75 2.00
GB22 Marian Gaborik 1.50 4.00
GB23 Saku Koivu 1.25 3.00
GB24 Alex Kovalev 1.00 2.50
GB25 Michael Ryder .75 2.00
GB26 Paul Kariya 1.50 4.00
GB27 Tomas Vokoun 1.00 2.50
GB28 Martin Brodeur 2.50 6.00
GB29 Patrik Elias 1.25 3.00
GB30 Jaromir Jagr 3.00 8.00
GB31 Henrik Lundqvist 2.50 6.00
GB32 Jason Spezza 1.25 3.00
GB33 Dany Heatley 1.25 3.00
GB34 Daniel Alfredsson 1.25 3.00
GB35 Dominik Hasek 1.50 4.00
GB36 Simon Gagne 1.25 3.00
GB37 Jeff Carter 1.25 3.00
GB38 Peter Forsberg 1.50 4.00
GB39 Shane Doan 1.00 2.50
GB40 Sidney Crosby 5.00 12.00
GB41 Marc-Andre Fleury 2.00 5.00
GB42 Joe Thornton 1.50 4.00
GB43 Patrick Marleau 1.25 3.00
GB44 Jonathan Cheechoo 1.25 3.00
GB45 Martin St. Louis 1.25 3.00
GB46 Vincent Lecavalier 1.00 2.50
GB47 Ed Belfour 1.25 3.00
GB48 Mats Sundin 1.25 3.00
GB49 Markus Naslund 1.00 2.50
GB50 Alexander Ovechkin 5.00 12.00

2006-07 Upper Deck Victory Next In Line

COMPLETE SET (50) 25.00 60.00
ODDS 1:4 PACKS
NL1 Corey Perry 1.00 2.50
NL2 Joffrey Lupul .75 2.00
NL3 Ryan Getzlaf 1.50 4.00
NL4 Ilya Kovalchuk 1.00 2.50
NL5 Kari Lehtonen .75 2.00
NL6 Patrice Bergeron 1.25 3.00
NL7 Andrew Raycroft .75 2.00
NL8 Brad Boyes .60 1.50
NL9 Thomas Vanek 1.25 3.00
NL10 Ryan Miller 1.00 2.50
NL11 Dion Phaneuf 1.00 2.50
NL12 Eric Staal 1.25 3.00
NL13 Cam Ward 1.00 2.50
NL14 Tuomo Ruutu 1.00 2.50
NL15 Marek Svatos .60 1.50
NL16 Rick Nash 1.00 2.50
NL17 Nikolai Zherdev .60 1.50
NL18 Gilbert Brule .75 2.00
NL19 Jussi Jokinen .75 2.00
NL20 Henrik Zetterberg 1.25 3.00
NL21 Ales Hemsky .75 2.00
NL22 Jarret Stoll .75 2.00
NL23 Nathan Horton 1.00 2.50
NL24 Rostislav Olesz .60 1.50
NL25 Alexander Frolov .60 1.50
NL26 Mike Cammalleri .60 1.50
NL27 Marian Gaborik 1.25 3.00
NL28 Mikko Koivu .75 2.00
NL29 Yann Danis .75 2.00
NL30 Alexander Perezhogin .60 1.50
NL31 Zach Parise 1.25 3.00
NL32 Rick DiPietro .75 2.00
NL33 Henrik Lundqvist 2.00 5.00
NL34 Petr Prucha .75 2.00
NL35 Jason Spezza 1.00 2.50
NL36 Dany Heatley 1.00 2.50
NL37 Jeff Carter 1.00 2.50
NL38 Mike Richards 1.00 2.50
NL39 Joni Pitkanen .60 1.50
NL40 Marc-Andre Fleury 1.50 4.00
NL41 Sidney Crosby 4.00 10.00
NL42 Jonathan Cheechoo 1.00 2.50
NL43 Evgeni Artyukhin .60 1.50
NL44 Matt Stajan .75 2.00
NL45 Alexander Steen 1.00 2.50
NL46 Ryan Kesler 1.25 3.00
NL47 Alex Auld .60 1.50
NL48 Alexander Ovechkin 4.00 10.00
NL49 Erik Cole .75 2.00
NL50 Kyle Wellwood .75 2.00

2006-07 Upper Deck Victory Jumbos

AF Alexander Frolov 2.00 5.00
AH Ales Hemsky 2.50 6.00
AO Alexander Ovechkin 12.00 30.00
AT Alex Tanguay 2.00 5.00
BB Brad Boyes 2.00 5.00
CP Chris Pronger 2.50 6.00
DA Daniel Alfredsson 3.00 8.00
DH Dany Heatley 3.00 8.00
ES Eric Staal 4.00 10.00
HL Henrik Lundqvist 6.00 15.00
HZ Henrik Zetterberg 4.00 10.00
IK Ilya Kovalchuk 3.00 8.00
JC Jonathan Cheechoo 3.00 8.00
JG Jean-Sebastien Giguere 3.00 8.00
JI Jarome Iginla 3.00 8.00
JJ Jaromir Jagr 8.00 20.00
JS Joe Sakic 5.00 12.00
JT Joe Thornton 4.00 10.00
KL Kari Lehtonen 2.50 6.00
MB Martin Brodeur 6.00 15.00
MG Marian Gaborik 4.00 10.00
MK Miikka Kiprusoff 2.50 6.00
MM Mike Modano 5.00 12.00
MN Markus Naslund 2.50 6.00
MR Michael Ryder 2.00 5.00
MS Martin St. Louis 3.00 8.00
MT Marty Turco 3.00 8.00
NK Nikolai Khabibulin 3.00 8.00
PB Patrice Bergeron 4.00 10.00
PD Pavel Datsyuk 4.00 10.00
PF Peter Forsberg 4.00 10.00
PK Paul Kariya 4.00 10.00
RL Roberto Luongo 5.00 12.00
RM Ryan Miller 3.00 8.00
RN Rick Nash 3.00 8.00
SC Sidney Crosby 12.00 30.00
SD Shane Doan 2.50 6.00
SG Simon Gagne 3.00 8.00
SK Saku Koivu 3.00 8.00
SP Jason Spezza 3.00 8.00
SU Mats Sundin 3.00 8.00
VL Vincent Lecavalier 2.50 6.00

2007-08 Upper Deck Victory

This 345-card set was released in August, 2007. The first 245 cards were issued into the hobby in six-card packs, with a 99 cent SRP, which came 36 packs to a box and 20 boxes to a case. In the first series, cards numbered 1-200 are veterans while cards 201-245 are Rookie Cards. There was an update set later issued, spilt into 50 veteran cards and 50 Rookie Cards. These cards were inserted one per Upper Deck Series 2 pack.

COMPLETE SET (345) 30.00 60.00
COMP.SET w/o SPs (200) 12.00 30.00
1 Martin Brodeur .50 1.25
2 Zach Parise .30 .75
3 Brian Rafalski .20 .50
4 Scott Gomez .20 .50
5 Brian Gionta .20 .50
6 Travis Zajac .20 .50
7 Patrik Elias .25 .60
8 Marc-Andre Fleury .40 1.00
9 Evgeni Malkin .75 2.00
10 Mark Recchi .30 .75
11 Jordan Staal .25 .60
12 Ryan Whitney .20 .50
13 Sergei Gonchar .15 .40
14 Sidney Crosby 1.00 2.50
15 Rick DiPietro .20 .50
16 Jason Blake .15 .40
17 Viktor Kozlov .15 .40
18 Ryan Smyth .20 .50
19 Alexei Yashin .20 .50
20 Miroslav Satan .20 .50
21 Henrik Lundqvist .30 .75
22 Martin Straka .15 .40
23 Brendan Shanahan .30 .75
24 Michael Nylander .15 .40
25 Sean Avery .15 .40
26 Jaromir Jagr .60 1.50
27 Martin Biron .20 .50
28 Jeff Carter .25 .60
29 Joni Pitkanen .15 .40
30 Mike Knuble .15 .40
31 Mike Richards .25 .60
32 Simon Gagne .25 .60
33 Ryan Miller .25 .60
34 Maxim Afinogenov .15 .40
35 Thomas Vanek .30 .75
36 Drew Stafford .20 .50
37 Jason Pominville .25 .60
38 Chris Drury .20 .50
39 Derek Roy .15 .40
40 Daniel Briere .25 .60
41 Ray Emery .20 .50
42 Jason Spezza .25 .60
43 Mike Fisher .15 .40
44 Wade Redden .15 .40
45 Daniel Alfredsson .25 .60
46 Dany Heatley .25 .60
47 Cristobal Huet .20 .50
48 Alex Kovalev .20 .50
49 Guillaume Latendresse .20 .50
50 Sheldon Souray .15 .40
51 Michael Ryder .15 .40
52 Chris Higgins .15 .40
53 Saku Koivu .25 .60
54 Andrew Raycroft .20 .50
55 Alexander Steen .25 .60
56 Tomas Kaberle .15 .40
57 Darcy Tucker .20 .50
58 Jeff O'Neill .15 .40
59 Bryan McCabe .15 .40
60 Mats Sundin .25 .60
61 Tim Thomas .30 .75
62 Marc Savard .15 .40
63 Marco Sturm .15 .40
64 Zdeno Chara .25 .60
65 Glen Murray .20 .50
66 Phil Kessel .30 .75
67 Patrice Bergeron .30 .75
68 Johan Holmqvist .20 .50
69 Dan Boyle .20 .50
70 Brad Richards .25 .60
71 Vaclav Prospal .15 .40
72 Vincent Lecavalier .20 .50
73 Martin St. Louis .25 .60
74 Kari Lehtonen .20 .50
75 Slava Kozlov .15 .40
76 Keith Tkachuk .25 .60
77 Marian Hossa .20 .50
78 Scott Mellanby .15 .40
79 Ilya Kovalchuk .25 .60
80 Cam Ward .25 .60
81 Erik Cole .20 .50
82 Justin Williams .20 .50
83 Cory Stillman .15 .40
84 Rod Brind'Amour .25 .60
85 Eric Staal .30 .75
86 Ed Belfour .25 .60
87 Nathan Horton .25 .60
88 Jay Bouwmeester .25 .60
89 Stephen Weiss .15 .40
90 Jozef Stumpel .15 .40
91 Olli Jokinen .20 .50
92 Olaf Kolzig .25 .60
93 Alexander Semin .25 .60
94 Chris Clark .15 .40
95 Matt Pettinger .15 .40
96 Eric Fehr .15 .40
97 Alexander Ovechkin 1.00 2.50
98 Dominik Hasek .30 .75
99 Tomas Holmstrom .20 .50
100 Pavel Datsyuk .30 .75
101 Nicklas Lidstrom .25 .60
102 Dan Cleary .20 .50
103 Kris Draper .15 .40
104 Henrik Zetterberg .30 .75
105 Tomas Vokoun .20 .50
106 Paul Kariya .30 .75
107 Chris Mason .20 .50
108 Kimmo Timonen .15 .40
109 Jason Arnott .20 .50
110 Steve Sullivan .15 .40
111 Peter Forsberg .30 .75
112 Manny Legace .20 .50
113 Brad Boyes .15 .40
114 Doug Weight .25 .60
115 Lee Stempniak .15 .40
116 Barret Jackman .15 .40
117 Jay McClement .15 .40
118 Nikolai Khabibulin .25 .60
119 Jason Williams .15 .40
120 Tuomo Ruutu .25 .60
121 Duncan Keith .25 .60
122 Radim Vrbata .20 .50
123 Martin Havlat .25 .60
124 Fredrik Norrena .15 .40
125 David Vyborny .15 .40
126 Sergei Fedorov .40 1.00
127 Fredrik Modin .15 .40
128 Pascal Leclaire .20 .50
129 Gilbert Brule .20 .50
130 Rick Nash .25 .60
131 Roberto Luongo .30 .75
132 Daniel Sedin .25 .60
133 Brendan Morrison .15 .40
134 Henrik Sedin .25 .60
135 Sami Salo .15 .40
136 Trevor Linden .25 .60
137 Markus Naslund .25 .60
138 Manny Fernandez .20 .50
139 Brian Rolston .20 .50
140 Pierre-Marc Bouchard .25 .60
141 Mikko Koivu .20 .50
142 Pavol Demitra .30 .75
143 Niklas Backstrom .25 .60
144 Marian Gaborik .30 .75
145 Miikka Kiprusoff .20 .50
146 Daymond Langkow .15 .40
147 Craig Conroy .15 .40
148 Dion Phaneuf .25 .60
149 Alex Tanguay .15 .40
150 Matthew Lombardi .15 .40
151 Jarome Iginla .25 .60
152 Peter Budaj .20 .50
153 Paul Stastny .25 .60
154 Milan Hejduk .20 .50
155 Wojtek Wolski .20 .50
156 Andrew Brunette .15 .40
157 Marek Svatos .15 .40
158 Jose Theodore .25 .60
159 Joe Sakic .40 1.00
160 Dwayne Roloson .20 .50
161 Raffi Torres .15 .40
162 Jarret Stoll .20 .50
163 Shawn Horcoff .15 .40
164 Joffrey Lupul .20 .50
165 Petr Sykora .20 .50
166 Ales Hemsky .20 .50
167 Jean-Sebastien Giguere .25 .60
168 Andy McDonald .20 .50
169 Scott Niedermayer .25 .60
170 Chris Kunitz .25 .60
171 Ryan Getzlaf .40 1.00
172 Chris Pronger .20 .50
173 Corey Perry .25 .60
174 Teemu Selanne .50 1.25
175 Vesa Toskala .20 .50
176 Jonathan Cheechoo .25 .60
177 Bill Guerin .25 .60
178 Evgeni Nabokov .20 .50
179 Milan Michalek .15 .40
180 Patrick Marleau .25 .60
181 Joe Thornton .30 .75
182 Marty Turco .25 .60
183 Philippe Boucher .15 .40
184 Mike Ribeiro .20 .50
185 Eric Lindros .40 1.00
186 Brenden Morrow .20 .50
187 Ladislav Nagy .15 .40
188 Mike Modano .40 1.00
189 Mathieu Garon .20 .50
190 Lubomir Visnovsky .15 .40
191 Rob Blake .25 .60
192 Anze Kopitar .40 1.00
193 Mike Cammalleri .20 .50
194 Alexander Frolov .15 .40
195 Curtis Joseph .25 .60
196 Owen Nolan .20 .50
197 Shane Doan .20 .50
198 Ed Jovanovski .20 .50
199 Mikael Tellqvist .20 .50
200 Zbynek Michalek .15 .40
201 Jack Johnson RC .60 1.50
202 Mark Mancari RC .60 1.50
203 Daniel Girardi RC .60 1.50
204 Rich Peverley RC .75 2.00
205 David Clarkson RC .75 2.00
206 Tomi Maki RC .50 1.25
207 Petr Kalus RC .50 1.25
208 Bryan Bickell RC 1.00 2.50
209 Marc Methot RC .50 1.25
210 Robbie Schremp RC .60 1.50
211 Yutaka Fukufuji RC .60 1.50
212 Frans Nielsen RC .75 2.00
213 Colin Fraser RC .50 1.25
214 Aaron Rome RC .60 1.50
215 Martin Lojek RC .50 1.25
216 Ryan Parent RC .50 1.25
217 David Moss RC .75 2.00
218 Ryan Callahan RC 1.00 2.50
219 Patrick Kaleta RC .50 1.25
220 Mark Fraser RC .50 1.25
221 Tobias Stephan RC .60 1.50
222 Tomas Popperle RC .60 1.50
223 Jeff Schultz RC .60 1.50
224 Tom Gilbert RC .60 1.50
225 Jonathan Sigalet RC .50 1.25
226 Brandon Dubinsky RC 1.00 2.50
227 Jaroslav Halak RC 1.25 3.00
228 David Krejci RC 1.50 4.00
229 Andy Greene RC .60 1.50
230 Lauri Tukonen RC .50 1.25
231 Jeff Finger RC .50 1.25
232 Daniel Carcillo RC .60 1.50
233 Kent Huskins RC .50 1.25
234 John Zeiler RC .50 1.25
235 Zack Stortini RC .50 1.25
236 Matt Ellis RC .60 1.50
237 Joel Lundqvist RC .50 1.25
238 Duncan Milroy RC .50 1.25
239 Bryan Young RC .50 1.25
240 Danny Bois RC .50 1.25
241 Drew Fata RC .50 1.25
242 Krys Barch RC .60 1.50
243 Pierre Parenteau RC .60 1.50
244 Mathieu Roy RC .50 1.25
245 Jannik Hansen RC .60 1.50
246 Dainius Zubrus .15 .40
247 Petr Sykora .20 .50
248 Darryl Sydor .15 .40
249 Bill Guerin .25 .60
250 Mike Comrie .20 .50
251 Chris Drury .20 .50
252 Scott Gomez .20 .50
253 Daniel Briere .25 .60
254 Joffrey Lupul .20 .50
255 Tim Connolly .15 .40
256 Andrew Peters .15 .40
257 Patrick Eaves .15 .40
258 Chris Neil .15 .40
259 Bryan Smolinski .15 .40
260 Roman Hamrlik .20 .50
261 Vesa Toskala .20 .50
262 Jason Blake .15 .40
263 Manny Fernandez .20 .50
264 Michel Ouellet .15 .40
265 Todd White .15 .40
266 Ray Whitney .20 .50
267 Mike Commodore .15 .40
268 Tomas Vokoun .20 .50
269 Richard Zednik .15 .40
270 Viktor Kozlov .15 .40
271 Michael Nylander .15 .40
272 Brian Rafalski .20 .50
273 Mikael Samuelsson .15 .40
274 Alexander Radulov .25 .60
275 Paul Kariya .30 .75
276 Keith Tkachuk .25 .60
277 Robert Lang .15 .40
278 Sergei Samsonov .20 .50
279 Nikolai Zherdev .15 .40
280 Brendan Morrison .15 .40
281 Mark Parrish .15 .40
282 Owen Nolan .20 .50
283 Adrian Aucoin .15 .40
284 Ryan Smyth .20 .50
285 Joni Pitkanen .15 .40
286 Geoff Sanderson .15 .40
287 Todd Bertuzzi .25 .60
288 Mathieu Schneider .15 .40
289 Matt Carle .15 .40
290 Jere Lehtinen .15 .40
291 Jussi Jokinen .15 .40
292 Ladislav Nagy .15 .40
293 Kyle Calder .15 .40
294 Fredrik Sjostrom .15 .40
295 Nick Boynton .15 .40
296 Andrew Cogliano RC 1.00 2.50
297 Anton Stralman RC .60 1.50
298 Bobby Ryan RC 1.50 4.00
299 Brett Sterling RC .60 1.50
300 Brian Elliott RC 1.25 3.00
301 Bryan Little RC 1.00 2.50
302 Cal Clutterbuck RC 1.00 2.50
303 Carey Price RC 8.00 20.00
304 Cory Murphy RC .60 1.50
305 Curtis McElhinney RC 1.00 2.50
306 Daniel Winnik RC .75 2.00
307 David Perron RC 1.00 2.50
308 Denis Tolpeko RC .60 1.50
309 Devin Setoguchi RC 1.00 2.50
310 Erik Johnson RC 1.00 2.50
311 James Sheppard RC .60 1.50
312 Jared Boll RC .75 2.00
313 Jaroslav Hlinka RC .75 2.00
314 Jiri Tlusty RC 1.00 2.50
315 Jonathan Bernier RC 1.50 4.00
316 Jonathan Toews RC 5.00 12.00
317 Kris Russell RC .75 2.00
318 Kyle Chipchura RC 1.00 2.50
319 Lukas Kaspar RC .60 1.50
320 Marc Staal RC 1.00 2.50
321 Martin Hanzal RC .75 2.00
322 Mason Raymond RC 1.00 2.50
323 Matt Keetley RC .75 2.00
324 Matt Moulson RC 1.00 2.50
325 Matt Niskanen RC 1.00 2.50
326 Matt Smaby RC .60 1.50
327 Mike Lundin RC .60 1.50
328 Mike Weber RC .60 1.50
329 Milan Lucic RC 3.00 8.00
330 Nick Foligno RC 1.25 3.00
331 Nicklas Backstrom RC 2.00 5.00
332 Nicklas Bergfors RC .60 1.50
333 Olli Malmivaara RC .60 1.50
334 Ondrej Pavelec RC 1.25 3.00
335 Patrick Kane RC 4.00 10.00
336 Peter Mueller RC .75 2.00
337 Petteri Wirtanen RC .60 1.50
338 Sam Gagner RC 1.25 3.00
339 Stefan Meyer RC .75 2.00
340 Steve Wagner RC .60 1.50
341 Tobias Stephan RC .75 2.00
342 Torrey Mitchell RC .75 2.00
343 Tyler Kennedy RC 1.00 2.50
344 Tyler Weiman RC .75 2.00
345 Ville Koistinen RC .60 1.50

2007-08 Upper Deck Victory Gold

*GOLD VETS: 6X TO 15X BASIC CARDS
1-200 GOLD VETS ODDS 1:24
*GOLD ROOKIES: 3X TO 8X RC
201-245 GOLD ROOKIE ODDS 1:240

2007-08 Upper Deck Victory EA Sports Face-Off

COMPLETE SET (6) 1.50 4.00
STATED ODDS 1:8
F01 Jarome Iginla .50 1.25
F02 Henrik Lundqvist .60 1.50
F03 Eric Staal .60 1.50
F04 Kris Draper .30 .75
F05 Chris Pronger .40 1.00
F06 Dion Phaneuf .50 1.25

2007-08 Upper Deck Victory GameBreakers

COMPLETE SET (50) 15.00 40.00
STATED ODDS 1:4
GB1 Sidney Crosby 2.50 6.0
GB2 Martin Brodeur 1.25 3.0
GB3 Joe Thornton .75 2.0
GB4 Saku Koivu .60 1.5
GB5 Daniel Alfredsson .60 1.5
GB6 Roberto Luongo .75 2.0
GB7 Chris Drury .50 1.2
GB8 Henrik Zetterberg .75 2.0
GB9 Ilya Kovalchuk .60 1.5
GB10 Jean-Sebastien Giguere .60 1.5
GB11 Mike Modano 1.00 2.5
GB12 Daniel Briere .60 1.5
GB13 Kari Lehtonen .50 1.2
GB14 Simon Gagne .60 1.5
GB15 Paul Kariya .75 2.0
GB16 Milan Hejduk .50 1.2
GB17 Dominik Hasek .75 2.0
GB18 Jonathan Cheechoo .60 1.5
GB19 Joe Sakic 1.00 2.5
GB20 Vincent Lecavalier .50 1.2
GB21 Cam Ward .60 1.5
GB22 Mats Sundin .60 1.5
GB23 Patrik Elias .60 1.5
GB24 Ryan Miller .60 1.5
GB25 Teemu Selanne 1.25 3.0
GB26 Jason Spezza .60 1.5
GB27 Tomas Vokoun .50 1.2
GB28 Ales Hemsky .50 1.2
GB29 Marian Hossa .50 1.2
GB30 Marc-Andre Fleury 1.00 2.5
GB31 Evgeni Malkin 2.00 5.0
GB32 Anze Kopitar 1.00 2.5
GB33 Olli Jokinen .50 1.2
GB34 Patrick Marleau .60 1.5
GB35 Dany Heatley .60 1.5
GB36 Paul Stastny .60 1.5
GB37 Marty Turco .60 1.5
GB38 Jarome Iginla .60 1.5
GB39 Eric Staal .75 2.0
GB40 Peter Forsberg .75 2.0
GB41 Andrew Raycroft .50 1.2
GB42 Martin St. Louis .60 1.5
GB43 Thomas Vanek .75 2.0
GB44 Pavel Datsyuk .75 2.0
GB45 Markus Naslund .60 1.5
GB46 Jaromir Jagr 1.50 4.0
GB47 Miikka Kiprusoff .50 1.2
GB48 Patrice Bergeron .75 2.0
GB49 Henrik Lundqvist .75 2.0
GB50 Alexander Ovechkin 2.50 6.0

2007-08 Upper Deck Victory Oversize Cards

COMPLETE SET (42) 30.00 60.0
OS1 Martin Brodeur 1.50 4.0
OS2 Marc-Andre Fleury 1.25 3.0
OS3 Evgeni Malkin 2.50 6.0
OS4 Sidney Crosby 3.00 8.0
OS5 Rick DiPietro .60 1.5
OS6 Henrik Lundqvist 1.00 2.5
OS7 Brendan Shanahan 1.00 2.5
OS8 Jaromir Jagr 2.00 5.0
OS9 Simon Gagne .75 2.0
OS10 Ryan Miller .75 2.0
OS11 Thomas Vanek 1.00 2.5
OS12 Jason Spezza .75 2.0
OS13 Dany Heatley .75 2.0
OS14 Michael Ryder .50 1.2
OS15 Saku Koivu .75 2.0
OS16 Andrew Raycroft .60 1.5
OS17 Mats Sundin .75 2.0
OS18 Patrice Bergeron 1.00 2.5
OS19 Vincent Lecavalier .60 1.5
OS20 Martin St. Louis .75 2.0
OS21 Kari Lehtonen .60 1.5
OS22 Ilya Kovalchuk .75 2.0
OS23 Eric Staal 1.00 2.5
OS24 Alexander Ovechkin 3.00 8.0
OS25 Dominik Hasek 1.00 2.5
OS26 Pavel Datsyuk 1.00 2.5
OS27 Henrik Zetterberg 1.00 2.5
OS28 Paul Kariya 1.00 2.5
OS29 Peter Forsberg 1.00 2.5
OS30 Rick Nash .75 2.0
OS31 Roberto Luongo 1.00 2.5
OS32 Markus Naslund .75 2.0
OS33 Marian Gaborik 1.00 2.5
OS34 Miikka Kiprusoff .60 1.5
OS35 Jarome Iginla .75 2.0
OS36 Joe Sakic 1.25 3.0
OS37 Dwayne Roloson .60 1.5
OS38 Jean-Sebastien Giguere .75 2.0
OS39 Jonathan Cheechoo .75 2.0
OS40 Joe Thornton 1.00 2.5
OS41 Mike Modano 1.25 3.0
OS42 Shane Doan .60 1.5

2007-08 Upper Deck Victory Stars on Ice

COMPLETE SET (50) 12.00 30.0
STATED ODDS 1:4
SI1 Roberto Luongo .60 1.5
SI2 Joe Thornton .60 1.5
SI3 Dion Phaneuf .50 1.2
SI4 Ryan Miller .50 1.2
SI5 Nicklas Lidstrom .50 1.2
SI6 Phil Kessel .60 1.5
SI7 Sergei Fedorov .75 2.0
SI8 Alexander Ovechkin 2.00 5.0
SI9 Jason Spezza .50 1.2
SI10 Brian Gionta .40 1.0
SI11 Dany Heatley .50 1.2
SI12 Eric Staal .60 1.5
SI13 Teemu Selanne 1.00 2.5
SI14 Jonathan Cheechoo .50 1.2
SI15 Cristobal Huet .40 1.0
SI16 Jaromir Jagr 1.25 3.0
SI17 Ilya Kovalchuk .50 1.2
SI18 Saku Koivu .50 1.2
SI19 Joe Sakic .75 2.0
SI20 Andy McDonald .40 1.0
SI21 Jay Bouwmeester .50 1.2
SI22 Ryan Getzlaf .75 2.0
SI23 Dominik Hasek .60 1.5
SI24 Scott Niedermayer .50 1.2
SI25 Simon Gagne .50 1.2
SI26 Martin St. Louis .50 1.2
SI27 Marian Hossa .40 1.0
SI28 Mats Sundin .50 1.2
SI29 Ryan Smyth .40 1.0
SI30 Martin Brodeur 1.00 2.5
SI31 Jordan Staal .50 1.2
SI32 Milan Hejduk .40 1.0
SI33 Rick Nash .50 1.2
SI34 Miikka Kiprusoff .40 1.0
SI35 Marty Turco .50 1.2
SI36 Patrice Bergeron .60 1.5
SI37 Vincent Lecavalier .40 1.0
SI38 Markus Naslund .50 1.2
SI39 Jarome Iginla .50 1.2
SI40 Henrik Zetterberg .60 1.5

41 Evgeni Malkin 1.50 4.00
42 Martin Havlat .50 1.25
43 Brendan Shanahan .60 1.50
44 Michael Ryder .30 .75
45 Patrick Marleau .50 1.25
46 Zach Parise .60 1.50
47 Daniel Briere .50 1.25
48 Marc-Andre Fleury .75 2.00
49 Tomas Kaberle .30 .75
50 Sidney Crosby 2.00 5.00

2008-09 Upper Deck Victory

COMPLETE SET (350) 25.00 60.00
COMP.SET w/o SPs (200) 12.00 30.00
COMP.UPDATE SET (100) 12.00 30.00
201-250 ROOKIE ODDS 1:4
UPDATES: ONE PER UD2 PACK A
RC UPDATE ODDS 1:4 UD2 PACKS
1 Olaf Kolzig .25 .60
2 Alexander Ovechkin 1.00 2.50
3 Nicklas Backstrom .40 1.00
4 Alexander Semin .25 .60
5 Cristobal Huet .20 .50
6 Sergei Fedorov .40 1.00
7 Roberto Luongo .30 .75
8 Daniel Sedin .25 .60
9 Henrik Sedin .25 .60
10 Ryan Kesler .30 .75
11 Alexander Edler .15 .40
12 Markus Naslund .20 .50
13 Brendan Morrison .15 .40
14 Mats Sundin .25 .60
15 Vesa Toskala .20 .50
16 Matt Stajan .20 .50
17 Darcy Tucker .20 .50
18 Tomas Kaberle .15 .40
19 Nikolai Antropov .20 .50
20 Alexander Steen .25 .60
21 Vincent Lecavalier .20 .50
22 Mike Smith .25 .60
23 Martin St. Louis .25 .60
24 Paul Ranger .15 .40
25 Jussi Jokinen .15 .40
26 Paul Kariya .30 .75
27 Manny Legace .25 .60
28 Lee Stempniak .15 .40
29 Erik Johnson .20 .50
30 Keith Tkachuk .25 .60
31 Brad Boyes .15 .40
32 Joe Thornton .30 .75
33 Milan Michalek .15 .40
34 Evgeni Nabokov .20 .50
35 Jonathan Cheechoo .25 .60
36 Patrick Marleau .25 .60
37 Brian Campbell .20 .50
38 Sidney Crosby 1.00 2.50
39 Marc-Andre Fleury .40 1.00
40 Ryan Malone .15 .40
41 Evgeni Malkin .75 2.00
42 Jordan Staal .25 .60
43 Ty Conklin .20 .50
44 Marian Hossa .20 .50
45 Ilya Bryzgalov .20 .50
46 Shane Doan .20 .50
47 Peter Mueller .20 .50
48 Radim Vrbata .20 .50
49 Ed Jovanovski .20 .50
50 Martin Hanzal .20 .50
51 Mike Richards .25 .60
52 Daniel Briere .25 .60
53 Mike Knuble .15 .40
54 Martin Biron .20 .50
55 Jeff Carter .25 .60
56 R.J. Umberger .15 .40
57 Simon Gagne .25 .60
58 Daniel Alfredsson .25 .60
59 Jason Spezza .25 .60
60 Ray Emery .20 .50
61 Wade Redden .15 .40
62 Dany Heatley .25 .60
63 Martin Gerber .20 .50
64 Henrik Lundqvist .30 .75
65 Scott Gomez .20 .50
66 Jaromir Jagr .60 1.50
67 Chris Drury .20 .50
68 Brendan Shanahan .30 .75
69 Marc Staal .25 .60
70 Michal Rozsival .15 .40
71 Rick DiPietro .20 .50
72 Bill Guerin .25 .60
73 Miroslav Satan .25 .60
74 Trent Hunter .15 .40
75 Mike Comrie .20 .50
76 Ruslan Fedotenko .15 .40
77 Martin Brodeur .50 1.25
78 Brian Gionta .20 .50
79 Travis Zajac .20 .50
80 Patrik Elias .25 .60
81 John Madden .15 .40
82 Zach Parise .25 .60
83 Jason Arnott .20 .50
84 Dan Ellis .15 .40
85 David Legwand .20 .50
86 J.P. Dumont .15 .40
87 Alexander Radulov .25 .60
88 Martin Erat .15 .40
89 Carey Price 1.00 2.50
90 Saku Koivu .25 .60
91 Andrei Kostitsyn .20 .50
92 Guillaume Latendresse .15 .40
93 Michael Ryder .15 .40
94 Alex Kovalev .20 .50
95 Chris Higgins .15 .40
96 Marian Gaborik .30 .75
97 Josh Harding .25 .60
98 Mikko Koivu .20 .50
99 Pierre-Marc Bouchard .25 .60
100 Brian Rolston .20 .50
101 Niklas Backstrom .25 .60
102 Anze Kopitar .40 1.00
103 Jack Johnson .15 .40
104 Patrick O'Sullivan .20 .50
105 Alexander Frolov .15 .40
106 Mike Cammalleri .20 .50
107 Dustin Brown .25 .60
108 Jason LaBarbera .20 .50
109 Olli Jokinen .20 .50
110 Tomas Vokoun .20 .50
111 Jay Bouwmeester .25 .60
112 Nathan Horton .20 .50
113 Stephen Weiss .15 .40
114 David Booth .15 .40
115 Dustin Penner .20 .50
116 Ales Hemsky .20 .50
117 Dwayne Roloson .20 .50
118 Sam Gagner .20 .50
119 Shawn Horcoff .15 .40
120 Jarret Stoll .20 .50
121 Andrew Cogliano .20 .50
122 Dominik Hasek .30 .75
123 Nicklas Lidstrom .25 .60
124 Dan Cleary .20 .50
125 Pavel Datsyuk .30 .75
126 Chris Osgood .25 .60
127 Valtteri Filppula .25 .60
128 Tomas Holmstrom .20 .50
129 Henrik Zetterberg .30 .75
130 Johan Holmqvist .20 .50
131 Brad Richards .25 .60
132 Mike Modano .40 1.00
133 Marty Turco .25 .60
134 Brenden Morrow .20 .50
135 Jere Lehtinen .15 .40
136 Sergei Zubov .20 .50
137 Mike Ribeiro .20 .50
138 Pascal Leclaire .20 .50
139 Rick Nash .25 .60
140 Nikolai Zherdev .15 .40
141 Gilbert Brule .15 .40
142 Michael Peca .20 .50
143 Peter Budaj .20 .50
144 Ryan Smyth .20 .50
145 Joe Sakic .40 1.00
146 Peter Forsberg .30 .75
147 Milan Hejduk .20 .50
148 Paul Stastny .25 .60
149 Wojtek Wolski .20 .50
150 Patrick Kane .50 1.25
151 Nikolai Khabibulin .25 .60
152 Martin Havlat .25 .60
153 Jonathan Toews .60 1.50
154 Patrick Sharp .25 .60
155 Duncan Keith .25 .60
156 Robert Lang .15 .40
157 Cam Ward .25 .60
158 Ray Whitney .20 .50
159 Eric Staal .30 .75
160 Justin Williams .20 .50
161 Rod Brind`Amour .25 .60
162 Erik Cole .20 .50
163 Miikka Kiprusoff .20 .50
164 Jarome Iginla .25 .60
165 Matthew Lombardi .15 .40
166 Dion Phaneuf .25 .60
167 Kristian Huselius .15 .40
168 Daymond Langkow .15 .40
169 Alex Tanguay .15 .40
170 Steve Bernier .15 .40
171 Derek Roy .15 .40
172 Ryan Miller .25 .60
173 Drew Stafford .20 .50
174 Jason Pominville .25 .60
175 Thomas Vanek .25 .60
176 Ales Kotalik .15 .40
177 Tim Thomas .25 .60
178 Patrice Bergeron .30 .75
179 Milan Lucic .40 1.00
180 Zdeno Chara .25 .60
181 Phil Kessel .30 .75
182 Glen Murray .20 .50
183 Marc Savard .15 .40
184 Colby Armstrong .15 .40
185 Ilya Kovalchuk .25 .60
186 Kari Lehtonen .20 .50
187 Slava Kozlov .15 .40
188 Bobby Holik .15 .40
189 Todd White .15 .40
190 Johan Hedberg .20 .50
191 Teemu Selanne .50 1.25
192 Ryan Getzlaf .40 1.00
193 Scott Niedermayer .25 .60
194 Jean-Sebastien Giguere .25 .60
195 Corey Perry .25 .60
196 Chris Kunitz .25 .60
197 Chris Pronger .20 .50
198 George Parros .15 .40
199 Sidney Crosby CL 1.00 2.50
200 Alexander Ovechkin CL 1.00 2.50
201 Derick Brassard RC .50 1.25
202 Mark Fistric RC .50 1.25
203 Alex Goligoski RC .75 2.00
204 Claude Giroux RC 1.25 3.00
205 Jon Filewich RC .50 1.25
206 Robbie Earl RC .40 1.00
207 Ilya Zubov RC .50 1.25
208 Steve Mason RC 1.00 2.50
209 Brian Boyle RC .50 1.25
210 Shawn Matthias RC .60 1.50
211 Ryan Stone RC .40 1.00
212 Teddy Purcell RC .75 2.00
213 Mike Iggulden RC .50 1.25
214 Tim Ramholt RC .50 1.25
215 Dan LaCosta RC .60 1.50
216 Sami Lepisto RC .50 1.25
217 Danny Taylor RC .50 1.25
218 Tom Cavanagh RC .50 1.25
219 Andrew Murray RC .50 1.25
220 Kevin Doell RC .40 1.00
221 Tim Conboy RC .50 1.25
222 Pascal Pelletier RC .40 1.00
223 Chris Minard RC .60 1.50
224 Joey Mormina RC .50 1.25
225 Darryl Boyce RC .50 1.25
226 Cody McLeod RC .50 1.25
227 Jordan Hendry RC .50 1.25
228 Corey Locke RC .50 1.25
229 Mike Brown RC .50 1.25
230 B.J. Crombeen RC .40 1.00
231 David Brine RC .40 1.00
232 Joe Jensen RC .60 1.50
233 Kyle Greentree RC .60 1.50
234 Peter Vandermeer RC .40 1.00
235 Marc-Andre Gragnani RC .50 1.25
236 Andrew Ebbett RC .40 1.00
237 Erik Ersberg RC .50 1.25
238 Jonathan Ericsson RC .60 1.50
239 Theo Peckham RC .60 1.50
240 Darren Helm RC .60 1.50
241 Mattias Ritola RC .50 1.25
242 Clay Wilson RC .40 1.00
243 Brian Lee RC .50 1.25
244 Alex Foster RC .50 1.25
245 Kyle Okposo RC .60 1.50
246 Kyle Turris RC 1.00 2.50
247 Tyler Plante RC .50 1.25
248 Matt D'Agostini RC .50 1.25
249 Adam Pineault RC .50 1.25
250 Boris Valabik RC .60 1.50
251 Brendan Morrison .15 .40
252 Mathieu Schneider .15 .40
253 Ron Hainsey .15 .40
254 Patrick Lalime .20 .50
255 Todd Bertuzzi .25 .60
256 Mike Cammalleri .20 .50
257 Joni Pitkanen .15 .40
258 Brian Campbell .20 .50
259 Cristobal Huet .20 .50
260 Adam Foote .15 .40
261 Darcy Tucker .20 .50
262 Andrew Raycroft .20 .50
263 Kristian Huselius .15 .40
264 R.J. Umberger .15 .40
265 Sean Avery .15 .40
266 Marian Hossa .20 .50
267 Ty Conklin .20 .50
268 Lubomir Visnovsky .15 .40
269 Erik Cole .20 .50
270 Keith Ballard .15 .40
271 Cory Stillman .15 .40
272 Jarret Stoll .20 .50
273 Andrew Brunette .15 .40
274 Owen Nolan .20 .50
275 Marek Zidlicky .15 .40
276 Georges Laraque .20 .50
277 Alex Tanguay .15 .40
278 Brian Rolston .20 .50
279 Doug Weight .25 .60
280 Mark Streit .15 .40
281 Markus Naslund .20 .50
282 Nikolai Zherdev .15 .40
283 Wade Redden .15 .40
284 Olli Jokinen .20 .50
285 Eric Godard .15 .40
286 Miroslav Satan .25 .60
287 Ruslan Fedotenko .15 .40
288 Rob Blake .25 .60
289 Chris Mason .20 .50
290 Mark Recchi .30 .75
291 Radim Vrbata .20 .50
292 Ryan Malone .15 .40
293 Andrej Meszaros .15 .40
294 Matt Carle .15 .40
295 Gary Roberts .15 .40
296 Olaf Kolzig .25 .60
297 Curtis Joseph .25 .60
298 Pavol Demitra .30 .75
299 Steve Bernier .15 .40
300 Jose Theodore .25 .60
301 Steve MacIntyre RC .60 1.50
302 Jason Garrison RC .60 1.50
303 Darroll Powe RC .60 1.50
304 Mitch Fritz RC .50 1.25
305 Fabian Brunnstrom RC .50 1.25
306 Petr Vrana RC .40 1.00
307 Nathan Oystrick RC .60 1.50
308 Brett Skinner RC .50 1.25
309 Matthew Halischuk RC .40 1.00
310 Pierre-Luc Letourneau-Leblond RC .40 1.00
311 Paul Bissonnette RC .75 2.00
312 Brad Staubitz RC .50 1.25
313 Tyler Sloan RC .75 2.00
314 Andreas Nodl RC .40 1.00
315 Derek Dorsett RC .75 2.00
316 Nikita Filatov RC .60 1.50
317 Dwight Helminen RC .60 1.50
318 Nikolai Kulemin RC .60 1.50
319 Viktor Tikhonov RC .50 1.25
320 Kevin Porter RC .50 1.25
321 Zach Boychuk RC .60 1.50
322 Patrik Berglund RC .50 1.25
323 Mikkel Boedker RC .75 2.00
324 Zach Bogosian RC .60 1.50
325 Drew Doughty RC 1.50 4.00
326 Michael Frolik RC .60 1.50
327 Colton Gillies RC .50 1.25
328 Jamie McGinn RC .60 1.50
329 Patric Hornqvist RC .60 1.50
330 Ryan Jones RC .60 1.50
331 Steve Mason RC 1.00 2.50
332 Ben Bishop RC 1.00 2.50
333 Vladimir Mihalik RC .40 1.00
334 Jonas Frogren RC .40 1.00
335 Oscar Moller RC .50 1.25
336 James Neal RC 1.25 3.00
337 Janne Niskala RC .60 1.50
338 T.J. Oshie RC 1.25 3.00
339 Adam Pardy RC .50 1.25
340 Alex Pietrangelo RC .75 2.00
341 Chris Porter RC .60 1.50
342 Jared Ross RC .60 1.50
343 Anssi Salmela RC .60 1.50
344 Luca Sbisa RC .40 1.00
345 Luke Schenn RC .75 2.00
346 Wayne Simmonds RC 1.00 2.50
347 Blake Wheeler RC 1.50 4.00
348 Brandon Sutter RC .60 1.50
349 Jakub Voracek RC 1.25 3.00
350 Steven Stamkos RC 4.00 10.00

2008-09 Upper Deck Victory Black

*VETS: 8X TO 20X BASIC CARDS
*ROOKIES: 2.5X TO 6X BASIC RC
STATED ODDS 1:720
UPDATE STATED ODDS 1:288
3 Nicklas Backstrom 8.00 20.00

2008-09 Upper Deck Victory Gold

*VETS: 4X TO 10X BASIC CARDS
*ROOKIES: 2X TO 5X BASIC RC
251-350 UPDATE ODDS 1:24
3 Nicklas Backstrom 4.00 10.00

2008-09 Upper Deck Victory Game Breakers

COMPLETE SET (50) 15.00 40.00
GB1 Sidney Crosby 2.00 5.00
GB2 Alexander Ovechkin 2.00 5.00
GB3 Roberto Luongo .60 1.50
GB4 Vincent Lecavalier .40 1.00
GB5 Miikka Kiprusoff .40 1.00
GB6 Joe Thornton .60 1.50
GB7 Ilya Kovalchuk .50 1.25
GB8 Martin Brodeur 1.00 2.50
GB9 Marian Gaborik .60 1.50
GB10 Henrik Zetterberg .60 1.50
GB11 Eric Staal .60 1.50
GB12 Mats Sundin .50 1.25
GB13 Anze Kopitar .75 2.00
GB14 Jaromir Jagr 1.25 3.00
GB15 Rick Nash .50 1.25
GB16 Patrick Kane 1.00 2.50
GB17 Dany Heatley .50 1.25
GB18 Paul Kariya .60 1.50
GB19 Jarome Iginla .50 1.25
GB20 Joe Sakic .75 2.00
GB21 Evgeni Malkin 1.50 4.00
GB22 Peter Mueller .40 1.00
GB23 Patrik Elias .50 1.25
GB24 Jean-Sebastien Giguere .50 1.25
GB25 Marian Hossa .40 1.00
GB26 Josh Harding .50 1.25
GB27 Marc-Andre Fleury .75 2.00
GB28 Nicklas Backstrom .75 2.00
GB29 Michael Ryder .30 .75
GB30 Carey Price 2.00 5.00
GB31 Sam Gagner .40 1.00
GB32 Jonathan Cheechoo .50 1.25
GB33 Patrice Bergeron .60 1.50
GB34 Tomas Vokoun .40 1.00
GB35 Daniel Sedin .50 1.25
GB36 Phil Kessel .60 1.50
GB37 Daniel Alfredsson .50 1.25
GB38 Olli Jokinen .40 1.00
GB39 Jack Johnson .30 .75
GB40 Paul Stastny .50 1.25
GB41 Ryan Miller .50 1.25
GB42 Pavel Datsyuk .60 1.50
GB43 Jonathan Toews 1.25 3.00
GB44 Simon Gagne .50 1.25
GB45 Teemu Selanne 1.00 2.50
GB46 Mike Richards .50 1.25
GB47 Shane Doan .40 1.00
GB48 Martin St. Louis .50 1.25
GB49 Henrik Lundqvist .60 1.50
GB50 Alexander Radulov .50 1.25

2008-09 Upper Deck Victory Jumbos

COMPLETE SET (42) 40.00 100.00
OS1 Alexander Ovechkin 4.00 10.00
OS2 Roberto Luongo 1.25 3.00
OS3 Mats Sundin 1.00 2.50
OS4 Vincent Lecavalier .75 2.00
OS5 Martin St. Louis 1.00 2.50
OS6 Paul Kariya 1.25 3.00
OS7 Joe Thornton 1.25 3.00
OS8 Sidney Crosby 4.00 10.00
OS9 Evgeni Malkin 3.00 8.00
OS10 Peter Mueller .75 2.00
OS11 Simon Gagne 1.00 2.50
OS12 Jason Spezza 1.00 2.50
OS13 Dany Heatley 1.00 2.50
OS14 Jaromir Jagr 2.50 6.00
OS15 Brendan Shanahan 1.25 3.00
OS16 Martin Brodeur 2.00 5.00
OS17 Carey Price 4.00 10.00
OS18 Saku Koivu 1.00 2.50
OS19 Marian Gaborik 1.25 3.00
OS20 Anze Kopitar 1.50 4.00
OS21 Ales Hemsky .75 2.00
OS22 Sam Gagner .75 2.00
OS23 Dominik Hasek 1.25 3.00
OS24 Pavel Datsyuk 1.25 3.00
OS25 Henrik Zetterberg 1.25 3.00
OS26 Mike Modano 1.50 4.00
OS27 Marty Turco 1.00 2.50
OS28 Rick Nash 1.00 2.50
OS29 Joe Sakic 1.50 4.00
OS30 Peter Forsberg 1.25 3.00
OS31 Paul Stastny 1.00 2.50
OS32 Patrick Kane 2.00 5.00
OS33 Jonathan Toews 2.50 6.00
OS34 Eric Staal 1.25 3.00
OS35 Miikka Kiprusoff .75 2.00
OS36 Jarome Iginla 1.00 2.50
OS37 Ryan Miller 1.00 2.50
OS38 Thomas Vanek 1.00 2.50
OS39 Patrice Bergeron 1.25 3.00
OS40 Ilya Kovalchuk 1.00 2.50
OS41 Teemu Selanne 2.00 5.00
OS42 Ryan Getzlaf 1.50 4.00

2008-09 Upper Deck Victory Stars of the Game

COMPLETE SET (50) 20.00 50.00
SG1 Teemu Selanne 1.00 2.50
SG2 Ilya Kovalchuk .50 1.25
SG3 Jonathan Toews 1.25 3.00
SG4 Jarome Iginla .50 1.25
SG5 Dominik Hasek .60 1.50
SG6 Marian Gaborik .60 1.50
SG7 Jason Spezza .50 1.25
SG8 Thomas Vanek .50 1.25
SG9 Henrik Lundqvist .60 1.50
SG10 Simon Gagne .50 1.25
SG11 Brad Boyes .30 .75
SG12 Sidney Crosby 2.00 5.00
SG13 Anze Kopitar .75 2.00
SG14 Martin Brodeur 1.00 2.50
SG15 Patrice Bergeron .60 1.50
SG16 Vincent Lecavalier .40 1.00
SG17 Saku Koivu .50 1.25
SG18 Roberto Luongo .60 1.50
SG19 Rick Nash .50 1.25
SG20 Henrik Zetterberg .60 1.50
SG21 Michael Ryder .30 .75
SG22 Joe Sakic .75 2.00
SG23 Jaromir Jagr 1.25 3.00
SG24 Dany Heatley .50 1.25
SG25 Ryan Miller .50 1.25
SG26 Eric Staal .60 1.50
SG27 Mats Sundin .50 1.25
SG28 Sam Gagner .40 1.00
SG29 Joe Thornton .60 1.50
SG30 Alexander Ovechkin 2.00 5.00
SG31 Miikka Kiprusoff .40 1.00
SG32 Mike Modano .75 2.00
SG33 Rick DiPietro .40 1.00
SG34 Paul Kariya .60 1.50
SG35 Patrick Kane 1.00 2.50
SG36 Alexander Radulov .50 1.25
SG37 Marty Turco .50 1.25
SG38 Ryan Getzlaf .75 2.00
SG39 Shane Doan .40 1.00
SG40 Evgeni Malkin 1.50 4.00
SG41 Pavel Datsyuk .60 1.50
SG42 Markus Naslund .40 1.00
SG43 Martin St. Louis .50 1.25
SG44 Paul Stastny .50 1.25
SG45 Tomas Vokoun .40 1.00
SG46 Zach Parise .50 1.25
SG47 Daniel Alfredsson .50 1.25
SG48 Marian Hossa .40 1.00
SG49 Carey Price 2.00 5.00
SG50 Brendan Shanahan .60 1.50

2009-10 Upper Deck Victory

COMPLETE SET (340) 75.00 150.00
COMP.SERIES 1 (250) 40.00 100.00
COMP.SET w/o SPs (200) 15.00 40.00
COMP.UPDATE SET (90) 20.00 50.00
RC STATED ODDS 1:2
UPDATE ODDS 1 PER UD2 PACK
1 Ryan Getzlaf .40 1.00
2 Scott Niedermayer .25 .60
3 Jean-Sebastien Giguere .25 .60
4 Corey Perry .25 .60
5 Chris Pronger .20 .50
6 Bryan Little .25 .60
7 Ilya Kovalchuk .25 .60
8 Kari Lehtonen .20 .50
9 Colby Armstrong .15 .40
10 Todd White .15 .40
11 Slava Kozlov .15 .40
12 Michael Ryder .15 .40
13 David Krejci .25 .60
14 Patrice Bergeron .30 .75
15 Blake Wheeler .25 .60
16 Zdeno Chara .25 .60
17 Phil Kessel .30 .75
18 Tim Thomas .25 .60
19 Marc Savard .15 .40
20 Clarke MacArthur .15 .40
21 Derek Roy .20 .50
22 Ryan Miller .25 .60
23 Drew Stafford .25 .60
24 Jason Pominville .25 .60
25 Thomas Vanek .25 .60
26 David Moss .20 .50
27 Mike Cammalleri .20 .50
28 Jarome Iginla .25 .60
29 Todd Bertuzzi .25 .60
30 Dion Phaneuf .30 .75
31 Miikka Kiprusoff .20 .50
32 Daymond Langkow .15 .40
33 Rene Bourque .15 .40
34 Olli Jokinen .20 .50
35 Cam Ward .25 .60
36 Ray Whitney .20 .50
37 Eric Staal .30 .75
38 Brandon Sutter .20 .50
39 Rod Brind`Amour .25 .60
40 Tuomo Ruutu .15 .40
41 Patrick Kane .50 1.25
42 Nikolai Khabibulin .25 .60
43 Martin Havlat .20 .50
44 Jonathan Toews .50 1.25
45 Patrick Sharp .25 .60
46 Brian Campbell .20 .50
47 Kris Versteeg .25 .60
48 John-Michael Liles .15 .40
49 Ryan Smyth .20 .50
50 T.J. Hensick .15 .40
51 Peter Budaj .20 .50
52 Milan Hejduk .20 .50
53 Paul Stastny .25 .60
54 Wojtek Wolski .15 .40
55 Jakub Voracek .25 .60
56 Derick Brassard .25 .60
57 Rick Nash .20 .50
58 Steve Mason .20 .50
59 R.J. Umberger .20 .50
60 Kristian Huselius .15 .40
61 Marty Turco .25 .60
62 Brad Richards .25 .60
63 Mike Modano .40 1.00
64 Loui Eriksson .20 .50
65 Brenden Morrow .20 .50
66 Mike Ribeiro .20 .50
67 Fabian Brunnstrom .20 .50
68 Johan Franzen .25 .60
69 Nicklas Lidstrom .25 .60
70 Jiri Hudler .20 .50
71 Pavel Datsyuk .30 .75
72 Ty Conklin .20 .50
73 Marian Hossa .20 .50
74 Tomas Holmstrom .20 .50
75 Henrik Zetterberg .30 .75
76 Ales Kotalik .15 .40
77 Andrew Cogliano .20 .50
78 Ales Hemsky .20 .50
79 Sheldon Souray .15 .40
80 Sam Gagner .20 .50
81 Shawn Horcoff .15 .40
82 Dustin Penner .15 .40
83 Dwayne Roloson .20 .50
84 Michael Frolik .20 .50
85 Tomas Vokoun .20 .50
86 Jay Bouwmeester .25 .60
87 Nathan Horton .25 .60
88 Stephen Weiss .15 .40
89 David Booth .15 .40
90 Anze Kopitar .40 1.00
91 Jack Johnson .15 .40
92 Alexander Frolov .20 .50
93 Drew Doughty .30 .75
94 Dustin Brown .20 .50
95 Erik Ersberg .20 .50
96 Marian Gaborik .30 .75
97 Marek Zidlicky .15 .40
98 Mikko Koivu .25 .60
99 Andrew Brunette .15 .40
100 Niklas Backstrom .25 .60
101 Antti Miettinen .15 .40
102 Andrei Kostitsyn .20 .50
103 Carey Price 1.00 2.50
104 Saku Koivu .25 .60
105 Andrei Markov .25 .60
106 Robert Lang .15 .40
107 Alex Tanguay .15 .40
108 Alex Kovalev .25 .60
109 Max Pacioretty .30 .75
110 Jason Arnott .20 .50
111 Dan Ellis .15 .40
112 Ryan Suter .25 .60
113 J.P. Dumont .15 .40
114 Shea Weber .20 .50
115 Martin Erat .15 .40
116 Martin Brodeur .50 1.25
117 Brian Gionta .20 .50
118 Travis Zajac .20 .50
119 Patrik Elias .25 .60
120 Scott Clemmensen .20 .50
121 Zach Parise .25 .60
122 Josh Bailey .20 .50
123 Rick DiPietro .20 .50
124 Doug Weight .25 .60
125 Kyle Okposo .25 .60
126 Mark Streit .15 .40
127 Henrik Lundqvist .40 1.00
128 Scott Gomez .20 .50
129 Wade Redden .15 .40
130 Chris Drury .20 .50
131 Marc Staal .25 .60
132 Nikolai Zherdev .15 .40
133 Markus Naslund .20 .50
134 Nik Antropov .20 .50
135 Daniel Alfredsson .25 .60
136 Jason Spezza .25 .60
137 Filip Kuba .15 .40
138 Antoine Vermette .15 .40
139 Dany Heatley .25 .60
140 Alex Auld .20 .50
141 Mike Richards .25 .60
142 Martin Biron .20 .50
143 Mike Knuble .15 .40
144 Daniel Briere .25 .60
145 Jeff Carter .25 .60
146 Scott Hartnell .25 .60
147 Simon Gagne .25 .60
148 Shane Doan .20 .50
149 Peter Mueller .20 .50
150 Mikkel Boedker .15 .40
151 Ilya Bryzgalov .20 .50
152 Kyle Turris .25 .60
153 Chris Kunitz .25 .60
154 Bill Guerin .25 .60
155 Petr Sykora .20 .50
156 Marc-Andre Fleury .40 1.00
157 Miroslav Satan .15 .40
158 Evgeni Malkin .75 2.00
159 Jordan Staal .25 .60
160 Sidney Crosby 1.00 2.50
161 Alex Goligoski .20 .50
162 Devin Setoguchi .20 .50
163 Joe Pavelski .25 .60
164 Ryane Clowe .20 .50
165 Evgeni Nabokov .20 .50
166 Patrick Marleau .25 .60
167 Dan Boyle .20 .50
168 Joe Thornton .25 .60
169 Manny Legace .20 .50
170 Paul Kariya .30 .75
171 Patrik Berglund .15 .40
172 Keith Tkachuk .25 .60
173 Brad Boyes .15 .40
174 Vincent Lecavalier .20 .50
175 Vaclav Prospal .15 .40
176 Steven Stamkos .50 1.25
177 Martin St. Louis .25 .60
178 Mike Smith .25 .60
179 Luke Schenn .20 .50
180 Matt Stajan .20 .50
181 Mikhail Grabovski .25 .60
182 Vesa Toskala .25 .60
183 Tomas Kaberle .15 .40
184 Alexei Ponikarovsky .15 .40
185 Nikolai Kulemin .20 .50
186 Kevin Bieksa .20 .50
187 Daniel Sedin .25 .60
188 Henrik Sedin .25 .60
189 Ryan Kesler .25 .60
190 Roberto Luongo .30 .75
191 Mats Sundin .25 .60
192 Steve Bernier .15 .40
193 Mike Green .25 .60
194 Alexander Ovechkin 1.00 2.50
195 Nicklas Backstrom .40 1.00
196 Alexander Semin .25 .60
197 Semen Varlamov .25 .60
198 Sergei Fedorov .40 1.00
199 Sidney Crosby CL .75 2.00
200 Alexander Ovechkin CL .75 2.00
201 Chris Durno RC .50 1.25
202 Peter Regin RC .50 1.25
203 Kevin Quick RC .40 1.00
204 Taylor Chorney RC .60 1.50
205 Mike Santorelli RC .60 1.50
206 Alexander Sulzer RC .40 1.00
207 Troy Bodie RC .50 1.25
208 Matt Beleskey RC .50 1.25
209 Kevin Westgarth RC .50 1.25
210 John Scott RC .60 1.50
211 Mikael Backlund RC .60 1.50
212 Byron Bitz RC .50 1.25
213 Matt Pelech RC .60 1.50
214 Tim Wallace RC .40 1.00
215 Ben Lovejoy RC .60 1.50
216 Riley Armstrong RC .50 1.25
217 Christian Hanson RC .60 1.50
218 Sean Collins RC .50 1.25
219 Riku Helenius RC .60 1.50
220 Ville Leino RC .50 1.25
221 Michal Neuvirth RC 1.00 2.50
222 Artem Anisimov RC .60 1.50
223 Davis Drewiske RC .60 1.50
224 David Schlemko RC .50 1.25
225 Luca Caputi RC .60 1.50
226 Jakub Petruzalek RC .60 1.50
227 Ryan Vesce RC .50 1.25
228 Jay Beagle RC .75 2.00
229 Jhonas Enroth RC .75 2.00
230 Brandon Segal RC .50 1.25
231 Tim Stapleton RC .60 1.50
232 Jesse Joensuu RC .50 1.25
233 John Negrin RC .60 1.50
234 Grant Lewis RC .50 1.25
235 Cal O'Reilly RC .50 1.25
236 Brian Salcido RC .50 1.25
237 Phil Oreskovic RC .60 1.50
238 Kris Chucko RC .50 1.25
239 Joel Rechlicz RC .40 1.00
240 Andrew MacDonald RC .40 1.00
241 Antti Niemi RC 1.00 2.50
242 Ivan Vishnevsky RC .50 1.25
243 Mike McKenna RC .50 1.25
244 Spencer Machacek RC .60 1.50
245 Tom Wandell RC .60 1.50
246 Michael Vernace RC .50 1.25
247 Yannick Weber RC .60 1.50
248 Matt Hendricks RC .50 1.25
249 Scott Lehman RC .40 1.00
250 T.J. Galiardi RC .60 1.50
251 Saku Koivu .25 .60
252 Joffrey Lupul .20 .50
253 Nik Antropov .20 .50
254 Maxim Afinogenov .15 .40
255 Mark Recchi .30 .75
256 Daniel Paille .20 .50
257 Tim Connolly .15 .40
258 Jay Bouwmeester .25 .60
259 Nigel Dawes .15 .40
260 Jussi Jokinen .15 .40
261 Marian Hossa .20 .50
262 Dustin Byfuglien .25 .60
263 Craig Anderson .25 .60
264 Antoine Vermette .15 .40
265 James Neal .25 .60
266 Jimmy Howard .30 .75
267 Dan Cleary .25 .60
268 Nikolai Khabibulin .25 .60
269 Patrick O'Sullivan .20 .50
270 Jordan Leopold .15 .40
271 Ryan Smyth .20 .50
272 Jonathan Quick .50 1.25
273 Owen Nolan .25 .60
274 Martin Havlat .20 .50
275 Mike Cammalleri .20 .50
276 Scott Gomez .20 .50
277 Brian Gionta .20 .50
278 Pekka Rinne .30 .75
279 Jamie Langenbrunner .15 .40
280 Matt Moulson .20 .50
281 Dwayne Roloson .20 .50
282 Marian Gaborik .30 .75
283 Vaclav Prospal .15 .40
284 Jonathan Cheechoo .25 .60
285 Alex Kovalev .25 .60
286 Milan Michalek .15 .40
287 Chris Pronger .20 .50
288 Ray Emery .20 .50
289 Matthew Lombardi .15 .40
290 Tyler Kennedy .20 .50
291 Dany Heatley .25 .60
292 Chris Mason .20 .50
293 Alex Tanguay .15 .40
294 Mattias Ohlund .15 .40
295 Mike Komisarek .20 .50
296 Francois Beauchemin .15 .40
297 Christian Ehrhoff .15 .40
298 Mikael Samuelsson .15 .40
299 Mike Knuble .15 .40
300 Brendan Morrison .20 .50
301 Evander Kane RC 1.00 2.50
302 Brad Marchand RC 1.50 4.00
303 Tyler Myers RC 1.00 2.50
304 Chris Butler RC .60 1.50
305 Matt Duchene RC 1.25 3.00
306 Ryan O'Reilly RC 1.00 2.50
307 Ryan Wilson RC .60 1.50
308 Jamie Benn RC 2.00 5.00
309 Perttu Lindgren RC .50 1.25
310 Aaron Gagnon RC .40 1.00
311 Francis Wathier RC .50 1.25
312 Dmitry Kulikov RC .60 1.50
313 Jakub Kindl RC .60 1.50
314 Teemu Laakso RC .40 1.00
315 Colin Wilson RC .60 1.50
316 Cody Franson RC .60 1.50
317 Ilkka Pikkarainen RC .60 1.50
318 John Tavares RC 4.00 10.00
319 Matt Gilroy RC .60 1.50
320 Michael Del Zotto RC .60 1.50
321 Erik Karlsson RC 2.00 5.00
322 James van Riemsdyk RC 1.25 3.00
323 Johan Backlund RC .60 1.50
324 Lars Eller RC .60 1.50
325 Jason Demers RC 1.00 2.50
326 Benn Ferriero RC .60 1.50
327 Frazer McLaren RC .50 1.25
328 Steven Zalewski RC .50 1.25
329 Logan Couture RC 1.25 3.00
330 James Wright RC .60 1.50
331 Victor Hedman RC 1.25 3.00
332 Viktor Stalberg RC .60 1.50
333 Jay Rosehill RC .60 1.50
334 Jonas Gustavsson RC 2.00 5.00
335 Tyler Bozak RC 1.00 2.50
336 James Reimer RC 2.50 6.00
337 Sergei Shirokov RC .40 1.00
338 Guillaume Desbiens RC .60 1.50
339 Michael Grabner RC .60 1.50
340 Braden Holtby RC 1.50 4.00

2009-10 Upper Deck Victory Black

*1-200 VETS: 15X TO 40X BASIC CARDS
STATED ODDS 1:720
*201-250 ROOK: 6X TO 15X BASIC CARDS
RC STATED ODDS 1:1,440
*251-300 VETS: 12X TO 30X BASIC CARDS
*301-350 ROOK: 4X TO 10X BASIC CARDS
UPDATE ODDS 1:288
195 Nicklas Backstrom 15.00 40.00

2009-10 Upper Deck Victory Gold

*GOLD: 4X TO 10X BASE
STATED ODDS 1:36
*GOLD RCs: 1.5X TO 4X BASE
RCs STATED ODDS 1:144
*GOLD UPDATE: 4X TO 10X BASE
*GOLD UPDATE RCs: 1.2X TO 3X BASE
GOLD UPDATE ODDS 1:24 UD2
121 Zach Parise 2.50 6.00
195 Nicklas Backstrom 4.00 10.00
318 John Tavares 8.00 20.00
334 Jonas Gustavsson 2.50 6.00
336 James Reimer 5.00 12.00

2009-10 Upper Deck Victory Game Breakers

COMPLETE SET (50) 15.00 40.00
STATED ODDS 1:4
GB1 Sidney Crosby 2.00 5.00
GB2 Patrick Sharp .50 1.25
GB3 Rick Nash .40 1.00
GB4 Phil Kessel .60 1.50
GB5 Brad Richards .50 1.25
GB6 Joe Thornton .50 1.25
GB7 Eric Staal .60 1.50
GB8 Simon Gagne .50 1.25
GB9 Paul Stastny .50 1.25
GB10 Thomas Vanek .50 1.25
GB11 Vincent Lecavalier .40 1.00
GB12 Martin St. Louis .50 1.25
GB13 Ilya Kovalchuk .50 1.25
GB14 David Krejci .50 1.25
GB15 Brad Boyes .30 .75
GB16 Alex Tanguay .30 .75
GB17 Jeff Carter .50 1.25
GB18 Patrick Kane 1.00 2.50
GB19 Devin Setoguchi .40 1.00
GB20 Jarome Iginla .50 1.25
GB21 Marian Gaborik .60 1.50
GB22 Pavel Datsyuk .60 1.50
GB23 Mikko Koivu .50 1.25
GB24 Markus Naslund .40 1.00
GB25 Loui Eriksson .40 1.00
GB26 Chris Drury .40 1.00
GB27 Dany Heatley .50 1.25
GB28 Jason Arnott .40 1.00
GB29 Evgeni Malkin 1.50 4.00
GB30 Peter Mueller .40 1.00
GB31 Bryan Little .50 1.25
GB32 Patrik Elias .50 1.25
GB33 Mats Sundin .50 1.25
GB34 Patrick Marleau .50 1.25
GB35 Patrice Bergeron .60 1.50
GB36 Shane Doan .40 1.00
GB37 Marian Hossa .40 1.00
GB38 Nicklas Backstrom .75 2.00
GB39 Alex Kovalev .50 1.25
GB40 Ryan Getzlaf .75 2.00
GB41 Mike Cammalleri .40 1.00
GB42 David Booth .30 .75
GB43 Jason Spezza .50 1.25
GB44 Jonathan Toews 1.00 2.50
GB45 Zach Parise .50 1.25
GB46 Ryane Clowe .40 1.00
GB47 Daniel Sedin .50 1.25
GB48 Henrik Zetterberg .60 1.50
GB49 Paul Kariya .60 1.50
GB50 Alexander Ovechkin 2.00 5.00

2009-10 Upper Deck Victory Jumbos

COMPLETE SET (42) 40.00 100.00
OS1 Ryan Getzlaf 1.50 4.00
OS2 Ilya Kovalchuk 1.00 2.50
OS3 Phil Kessel 1.25 3.00
OS4 Ryan Miller 1.00 2.50
OS5 Thomas Vanek 1.00 2.50
OS6 Jarome Iginla 1.00 2.50

OS7 Dion Phaneuf 1.25 3.00
OS8 Eric Staal 1.25 3.00
OS9 Patrick Kane 2.00 5.00
OS10 Jonathan Toews 2.00 5.00
OS11 Paul Stastny 1.00 2.50
OS12 Rick Nash .75 2.00
OS13 Steve Mason .75 2.00
OS14 Marty Turco 1.00 2.50
OS15 Mike Modano 1.50 4.00
OS16 Nicklas Lidstrom 1.00 2.50
OS17 Pavel Datsyuk 1.25 3.00
OS18 Henrik Zetterberg 1.25 3.00
OS19 Sam Gagner .75 2.00
OS20 Anze Kopitar 1.50 4.00
OS21 Drew Doughty 1.25 3.00
OS22 Marian Gaborik 1.25 3.00
OS23 Carey Price 4.00 10.00
OS24 Saku Koivu 1.00 2.50
OS25 Shea Weber .75 2.00
OS26 Martin Brodeur 2.00 5.00
OS27 Zach Parise 1.00 2.50
OS28 Rick DiPietro .75 2.00
OS29 Henrik Lundqvist 1.50 4.00
OS30 Jason Spezza 1.00 2.50
OS31 Dany Heatley 1.00 2.50
OS32 Mike Richards 1.00 2.50
OS33 Jeff Carter 1.00 2.50
OS34 Peter Mueller .75 2.00
OS35 Marc-Andre Fleury 1.50 4.00
OS36 Evgeni Malkin 3.00 8.00
OS37 Sidney Crosby 4.00 10.00
OS38 Joe Thornton 1.00 2.50
OS39 Vincent Lecavalier .75 2.00
OS40 Luke Schenn .75 2.00
OS41 Roberto Luongo 1.25 3.00
OS42 Alexander Ovechkin 4.00 10.00

2009-10 Upper Deck Victory Stars of the Game

COMPLETE SET (50) 20.00 50.00
STATED ODDS 1:4
SG1 Carey Price 2.00 5.00
SG2 Patrice Bergeron .60 1.50
SG3 Ilya Kovalchuk .50 1.25
SG4 Zach Parise .50 1.25
SG5 Vincent Lecavalier .40 1.00
SG6 Nicklas Lidstrom .50 1.25
SG7 Jean-Sebastien Giguere .50 1.25
SG8 Alexander Ovechkin 2.00 5.00
SG9 Joe Thornton .50 1.25
SG10 Patrick Kane 1.00 2.50
SG11 Marty Turco .50 1.25
SG12 Simon Gagne .50 1.25
SG13 Dany Heatley .50 1.25
SG14 Mats Sundin .50 1.25
SG15 Henrik Lundqvist .75 2.00
SG16 Eric Staal .60 1.50
SG17 Evgeni Malkin 1.50 4.00
SG18 Peter Mueller .40 1.00
SG19 Tomas Vokoun .40 1.00
SG20 Alex Kovalev .50 1.25
SG21 Henrik Zetterberg .60 1.50
SG22 Marian Gaborik .60 1.50
SG23 Martin Brodeur 1.00 2.50
SG24 Marc Savard .30 .75
SG25 Jarome Iginla .50 1.25
SG26 Vesa Toskala .50 1.25
SG27 Rick Nash .40 1.00
SG28 Pavel Datsyuk .60 1.50
SG29 Miikka Kiprusoff .40 1.00
SG30 Alex Tanguay .30 .75
SG31 Patrick Marleau .50 1.25
SG32 Jonathan Toews 1.00 2.50
SG33 Roberto Luongo .60 1.50
SG34 Thomas Vanek .50 1.25
SG35 Martin St. Louis .50 1.25
SG36 Jason Spezza .50 1.25
SG37 Paul Stastny .50 1.25
SG38 Marc-Andre Fleury .75 2.00
SG39 Alexander Semin .50 1.25
SG40 Mike Richards .50 1.25
SG41 Ryan Getzlaf .75 2.00
SG42 Mike Modano .75 2.00
SG43 Steve Mason .40 1.00
SG44 Markus Naslund .40 1.00
SG45 Marian Hossa .40 1.00
SG46 Anze Kopitar .75 2.00
SG47 Rick DiPietro .40 1.00
SG48 Saku Koivu .50 1.25
SG49 Paul Kariya .60 1.50
SG50 Sidney Crosby 2.00 5.00

2010-11 Upper Deck Victory

COMPLETE SET (350) 40.00 100.00
COMP.BASE SET (250) 25.00 60.00
COMP.SET w/o SPs (200) 12.00 30.00
COMP.UPD.SET (100) 15.00 40.00
COMP.UPD.w/o SPs (50) 8.00 20.00
201-250 ROOKIE STATED ODDS 1:2
UPDATE OVERALL ODDS 1:1 UD2
301-350 ROOK.UPDATE ODDS 1:3 UD2
1 Ryan Getzlaf .40 1.00
2 Jonas Hiller .20 .50
3 Corey Perry .25 .60
4 Bobby Ryan .25 .60
5 Lubomir Visnovsky .15 .40
6 Nik Antropov .20 .50
7 Zach Bogosian .20 .50
8 Evander Kane .25 .60
9 Bryan Little .25 .60
10 Rich Peverley .25 .60
11 Patrice Bergeron .30 .75
12 Zdeno Chara .20 .50
13 David Krejci .25 .60
14 Milan Lucic .25 .60
15 Marc Savard .15 .40
16 Tim Thomas .20 .50
17 Blake Wheeler .25 .60
18 Tim Connolly .15 .40
19 Ryan Miller .25 .60
20 Tyler Myers .25 .60
21 Jason Pominville .25 .60
22 Derek Roy .25 .60
23 Drew Stafford .25 .60
24 Thomas Vanek .25 .60
25 Erik Cole .20 .50
26 Jussi Jokinen .15 .40
27 Joni Pitkanen .20 .50
28 Eric Staal .30 .75
29 Brandon Sutter .20 .50
30 Cam Ward .25 .60
31 Jay Bouwmeester .30 .75
32 Rene Bourque .15 .40
33 Niklas Hagman .15 .40
34 Jarome Iginla .25 .60
35 Miikka Kiprusoff .20 .50
36 Daymond Langkow .15 .40
37 Matt Stajan .20 .50
38 Marian Hossa .20 .50
39 Patrick Kane .50 1.25
40 Duncan Keith .25 .60
41 Brent Seabrook .25 .60
42 Patrick Sharp .25 .60
43 Jonathan Toews .50 1.25
44 Kris Versteeg .20 .50
45 Derick Brassard .25 .60
46 Kristian Huselius .15 .40
47 Steve Mason .20 .50
48 Rick Nash .25 .60
49 Antoine Vermette .15 .40
50 Jakub Voracek .25 .60
51 Craig Anderson .25 .60
52 Matt Duchene .25 .60
53 T.J. Galiardi .20 .50
54 Milan Hejduk .20 .50
55 Ryan O'Reilly .25 .60
56 Paul Stastny .25 .60
57 Chris Stewart .20 .50
58 Jamie Benn .30 .75
59 Loui Eriksson .20 .50
60 Kari Lehtonen .20 .50
61 Brenden Morrow .20 .50
62 James Neal .25 .60
63 Mike Ribeiro .20 .50
64 Brad Richards .25 .60
65 Dan Cleary .25 .60
66 Pavel Datsyuk .30 .75
67 Johan Franzen .25 .60
68 Jim Howard .30 .75
69 Nicklas Lidstrom .25 .60
70 Brian Rafalski .15 .40
71 Henrik Zetterberg .30 .75
72 Andrew Cogliano .15 .40
73 Sam Gagner .20 .50
74 Ales Hemsky .20 .50
75 Shawn Horcoff .15 .40
76 Nikolai Khabibulin .20 .50
77 Dustin Penner .15 .40
78 David Booth .15 .40
79 Michael Frolik .15 .40
80 Nathan Horton .20 .50
81 Cory Stillman .15 .40
82 Tomas Vokoun .20 .50
83 Stephen Weiss .20 .50
84 Dustin Brown .25 .60
85 Drew Doughty .25 .60
86 Michal Handzus .20 .50
87 Anze Kopitar .40 1.00
88 Jonathan Quick .40 1.00
89 Wayne Simmonds .30 .75
90 Ryan Smyth .20 .50
91 Niklas Backstrom .25 .60
92 Andrew Brunette .15 .40
93 Brent Burns .30 .75
94 Cal Clutterbuck .25 .60
95 Martin Havlat .20 .50
96 Mikko Koivu .25 .60
97 Guillaume Latendresse .20 .50
98 Mike Cammalleri .25 .60
99 Scott Gomez .20 .50
100 Brian Gionta .20 .50
101 Jaroslav Halak .25 .60
102 Andrei Markov .25 .60
103 Tomas Plekanec .25 .60
104 Carey Price 1.00 2.50
105 Jason Arnott .20 .50
106 J.P. Dumont .15 .40
107 Martin Erat .15 .40
108 Patric Hornqvist .20 .50
109 Pekka Rinne .30 .75
110 Steve Sullivan .15 .40
111 Shea Weber .20 .50
112 Martin Brodeur .50 1.25
113 Patrik Elias .25 .60
114 Ilya Kovalchuk .25 .60
115 Jamie Langenbrunner .15 .40
116 Zach Parise .25 .60
117 Brian Rolston .20 .50
118 Travis Zajac .20 .50
119 Josh Bailey .20 .50
120 Blake Comeau .15 .40
121 Matt Moulson .20 .50
122 Kyle Okposo .25 .60
123 Mark Streit .15 .40
124 John Tavares .50 1.25
125 Ryan Callahan .25 .60
126 Chris Drury .20 .50
127 Brandon Dubinsky .20 .50
128 Marian Gaborik .30 .75
129 Henrik Lundqvist .40 1.00
130 Vaclav Prospal .15 .40
131 Marc Staal .25 .60
132 Daniel Alfredsson .25 .60
133 Mike Fisher .25 .60
134 Alex Kovalev .25 .60
135 Filip Kuba .15 .40
136 Brian Elliott .20 .50
137 Milan Michalek .15 .40
138 Jason Spezza .15 .40
139 Daniel Briere .25 .60
140 Jeff Carter .25 .60
141 Claude Giroux .25 .60
142 Scott Hartnell .25 .60
143 Chris Pronger .20 .50
144 Mike Richards .25 .60
145 James van Riemsdyk .40 1.00
146 Ilya Bryzgalov .20 .50
147 Shane Doan .20 .50
148 Scottie Upshall .15 .40
149 Radim Vrbata .20 .50
150 Wojtek Wolski .15 .40
151 Keith Yandle .25 .60
152 Sidney Crosby 1.00 2.50
153 Marc-Andre Fleury .40 1.00
154 Tyler Kennedy .15 .40
155 Kristopher Letang .25 .60
156 Evgeni Malkin .75 2.00
157 Jordan Staal .25 .60
158 Maxime Talbot .25 .60
159 Dan Boyle .20 .50
160 Ryane Clowe .15 .40
161 Dany Heatley .20 .50
162 Patrick Marleau .25 .60
163 Joe Pavelski .25 .60
164 Devin Setoguchi .20 .50
165 Joe Thornton .25 .60
166 David Backes .25 .60
167 Brad Boyes .15 .40
168 Erik Johnson .15 .40
169 Andy McDonald .20 .50
170 T.J. Oshie .40 1.00
171 David Perron .15 .40
172 Steve Downie .15 .40
173 Victor Hedman .30 .75
174 Vincent Lecavalier .20 .50
175 Ryan Malone .15 .40
176 Martin St. Louis .25 .60
177 Steven Stamkos .50 1.25
178 Tyler Bozak .25 .60
179 Jean-Sebastien Giguere .20 .50
180 Jonas Gustavsson .30 .75
181 Phil Kessel .30 .75
182 Nikolai Kulemin .20 .50
183 Dion Phaneuf .25 .60
184 Luke Schenn .20 .50
185 Alexandre Burrows .25 .60
186 Alexander Edler .15 .40
187 Ryan Kesler .25 .60
188 Roberto Luongo .25 .60
189 Mason Raymond .20 .50
190 Daniel Sedin .25 .60
191 Henrik Sedin .25 .60
192 Nicklas Backstrom .40 1.00
193 Tomas Fleischmann .15 .40
194 Mike Green .25 .60
195 Mike Knuble .15 .40
196 Alexander Ovechkin 1.00 2.50
197 Alexander Semin .25 .60
198 Semyon Varlamov .25 .60
199 Ryan Miller CL .20 .50
200 Steven Stamkos CL .40 1.00
201 Nick Bonino RC .60 1.50
202 Arturs Kulda RC .50 1.25
203 Andrew Bodnarchuk RC .50 1.25
204 Zach Hamill RC .50 1.25
205 Adam McQuaid RC .60 1.50
206 Jeff Penner RC .75 2.00
207 Jamie McBain RC .50 1.25
208 Jerome Samson RC .50 1.25
209 Justin Mercier RC .50 1.25
210 Brandon Yip RC .50 1.25
211 Grant Clitsome RC .50 1.25
212 Tomas Kana RC .50 1.25
213 Maxime Fortunus RC .40 1.00
214 Philip Larsen RC .50 1.25
215 Raymond Sawada RC .40 1.00
216 Dean Arsene RC .50 1.25
217 Johan Motin RC .40 1.00
218 Bryan Pitton RC .60 1.50
219 Alex Plante RC .50 1.25
220 Evgeny Dadonov RC .60 1.50
221 Mike Duco RC .50 1.25
222 Richard Clune RC .60 1.50
223 Cody Almond RC .50 1.25
224 Justin Falk RC .40 1.00
225 Maxim Noreau RC .40 1.00
226 Clayton Stoner RC .50 1.25
227 Casey Wellman RC .50 1.25
228 P.K. Subban RC 1.50 4.00
229 Brock Trotter RC 1.00 2.50
230 J.T. Wyman RC .50 1.25
231 Nick Spaling RC .50 1.25
232 Nick Palmieri RC .50 1.25
233 Dustin Kohn RC .50 1.25
234 Dylan Reese RC .50 1.25
235 Ilkka Heikkinen RC .75 2.00
236 Matt Zaba RC .60 1.50
237 Bobby Butler RC .50 1.25
238 Jared Cowen RC .50 1.25
239 Kaspars Daugavins RC .60 1.50
240 Derek Smith RC .50 1.25
241 Jeremy Duchesne RC .60 1.50
242 Nick Johnson RC .40 1.00
243 Alexander Pechurski RC .60 1.50
244 Eric Tangradi RC .50 1.25
245 John McCarthy RC .50 1.25
246 Dustin Tokarski RC .50 1.25
247 Brayden Irwin RC .50 1.25
248 Nazem Kadri RC 1.50 4.00
249 Evan Oberg RC .60 1.50
250 Kyle Wilson RC .60 1.50
251 Dustin Byfuglien .25 .60
252 Sergei Kostitsyn .15 .40
253 Ruslan Salei .15 .40
254 Marty Turco .25 .60
255 Zenon Konopka .20 .50
256 Alexei Ponikarovsky .15 .40
257 Ethan Moreau .15 .40
258 Nathan Horton .20 .50
259 Antero Niittymaki .20 .50
260 Raffi Torres .15 .40
261 Dominic Moore .15 .40
262 Jason Arnott .20 .50
263 Derek Boogaard .15 .40
264 Dan Ellis .20 .50
265 Milan Jurcina .15 .40
266 Andrew Raycroft .20 .50
267 Brent Sopel .15 .40
268 Olli Jokinen .20 .50
269 Matt Cullen .15 .40
270 Sergei Gonchar .15 .40
271 Dan Hamhuis .20 .50
272 Keith Ballard .15 .40
273 Sean O'Donnell .15 .40
274 Matt Hunwick .15 .40
275 Nikolai Zherdev .15 .40
276 Colby Armstrong .15 .40
277 Jeff Tambellini .15 .40
278 Chris Higgins .15 .40
279 Daniel Winnik .15 .40
280 Matthew Lombardi .15 .40
281 Todd White .15 .40
282 Alexander Frolov .15 .40
283 Brett Lebda .15 .40
284 Anton Volchenkov .15 .40
285 Jaroslav Halak .25 .60
286 Dennis Wideman .15 .40
287 Andrew Ladd .25 .60
288 Alex Tanguay .15 .40
289 Chris Mason .20 .50
290 Mike Modano .40 1.00
291 Manny Malhotra .20 .50
292 Martin Biron .20 .50
293 Paul Martin .15 .40
294 Pavel Kubina .15 .40
295 Sean Bergenheim .15 .40
296 Lars Eller .20 .50
297 John Madden .15 .40
298 Steve Bernier .15 .40
299 Jordan Leopold .15 .40
300 Willie Mitchell .15 .40
301 Kevin Shattenkirk RC 1.00 2.50
302 Mattias Tedenby RC .40 1.00
303 Ian Cole RC .50 1.25
304 Matt Kassian RC .50 1.25
305 Travis Hamonic RC .60 1.50
306 Eric Wellwood RC .60 1.50
307 Jeremy Morin RC .50 1.25
308 Keith Aulie RC .50 1.25
309 Stephen Gionta RC .60 1.50
310 Evgeny Grachev RC .50 1.25
311 Marco Scandella RC .50 1.25
312 Alexander Burmistrov RC .50 1.25
313 Ryan Reaves RC .60 1.50
314 Mike Moore RC .50 1.25
315 Tommy Wingels RC .50 1.25
316 Robin Lehner RC 1.00 2.50
317 Luke Adam RC .50 1.25
318 Derek Stepan RC 1.00 2.50
319 Mark Dekanich RC .50 1.25
320 Anders Lindback RC .50 1.25
321 Dana Tyrell RC .50 1.25
322 Jake Muzzin RC .50 1.25
323 Kyle Clifford RC .50 1.25
324 Brayden Schenn RC .75 2.00
325 Nino Niederreiter RC .60 1.50
326 Zac Dalpe RC .50 1.25
327 Jeff Skinner RC 3.00 8.00
328 Sergei Bobrovsky RC 1.25 3.00
329 T.J. Brodie RC .50 1.25
330 Henrik Karlsson RC .50 1.25
331 Cam Fowler RC .60 1.50
332 Alexander Vasyunov RC .50 1.25
333 Matt Taormina RC .50 1.25
334 Alexander Urbom RC .50 1.25
335 Olivier Magnan-Grenier RC .50 1.25
336 Jacob Josefson RC .50 1.25
337 Oliver Ekman-Larsson RC .75 2.00
338 Brian Fahey RC .50 1.25
339 Marcus Johansson RC .75 2.00
340 Tyler Seguin RC 3.00 8.00
341 Jordan Caron RC .75 2.00
342 Nick Holden RC .50 1.25
343 Evan Brophey RC .50 1.25
344 Brandon Pirri RC .50 1.25
345 Nick Leddy RC .50 1.25
346 Jonas Holos RC .50 1.25
347 Mark Olver RC .50 1.25
348 Magnus Paajarvi RC .60 1.50
349 Jordan Eberle RC 3.00 8.00
350 Taylor Hall RC 3.00 8.00

2010-11 Upper Deck Victory Black

*1-200 VETS: 15X TO 40X BASIC CARDS
1-200 VET STATED ODDS 1:720
*201-250 ROOK: 6X TO 15X BASIC CARDS
201-250 ROOKIE ODDS 1:1440
*251-300 VETS: 15X TO 40X BASIC CARDS
*301-350 ROOK: 5X TO 12X BASIC CARDS
192 Nicklas Backstrom 15.00 40.00

2010-11 Upper Deck Victory Gold

COMP.UPD.SET (100) 75.00 150.00
*GOLD VETS: 4X TO 10X BASE
VETERAN STATED ODDS 1:36
*GOLD ROOKIE: 1.5X TO 4X BASE
ROOKIE STATED ODDS 1:144
*GOLD UPD 251-300: 3X TO 8X BASE
*GOLD UPD ROOKIE 301-350: 1.5X TO 4X
OVERALL UPDATE ODDS 1:24 UD2
192 Nicklas Backstrom 4.00 10.00
248 Nazem Kadri 8.00 20.00

2010-11 Upper Deck Victory Red

*RED: 6X TO 15X BASE
*RED RCs: 4X TO 10X BASE
192 Nicklas Backstrom 6.00 15.00

2010-11 Upper Deck Victory Game Breakers

COMPLETE SET (50) 25.00 50.00
STATED ODDS 1:2
GBAK Anze Kopitar .60 1.50
GBAO Alexander Ovechkin 1.50 4.00
GBAS Alexander Semin .40 1.00
GBBA Nicklas Backstrom .60 1.50
GBCP Corey Perry .40 1.00
GBDA Daniel Alfredsson .40 1.00
GBDD Drew Doughty .40 1.00
GBDH Dany Heatley .30 .75
GBDR Derek Roy .40 1.00
GBDS Daniel Sedin .40 1.00
GBDU Pascal Dupuis .25 .60
GBEM Evgeni Malkin 1.25 3.00
GBES Eric Staal .50 1.25
GBGL Guillaume Latendresse .30 .75
GBHS Henrik Sedin .40 1.00
GBHZ Henrik Zetterberg .50 1.25
GBIK Ilya Kovalchuk .40 1.00
GBJC Jeff Carter .40 1.00
GBJI Jarome Iginla .40 1.00
GBJJ Jussi Jokinen .25 .60
GBJT John Tavares .75 2.00
GBJV James van Riemsdyk .60 1.50
GBKA Patrick Kane .75 2.00
GBMC Mike Cammalleri .40 1.00
GBMD Matt Duchene .40 1.00
GBMF Mike Fisher .40 1.00
GBMG Marian Gaborik .50 1.25
GBMH Michal Handzus .30 .75
GBMK Mikko Koivu .40 1.00
GBMM Matt Moulson .30 .75
GBMR Mike Richards .40 1.00
GBMS Martin St. Louis .40 1.00
GBNB Nicklas Bergfors .30 .75
GBPB Patrice Bergeron .50 1.25
GBPD Pavel Datsyuk .50 1.25
GBPH Patric Hornqvist .30 .75
GBPK Phil Kessel .50 1.25
GBPM Patrick Marleau .40 1.00
GBRG Ryan Getzlaf .60 1.50
GBRM Ryan Malone .25 .60
GBRN Rick Nash .40 1.00
GBRP Rich Peverley .40 1.00
GBSC Sidney Crosby 1.50 4.00
GBSD Shane Doan .30 .75
GBSS Steven Stamkos .75 2.00
GBTB Troy Brouwer .40 1.00
GBTH Joe Thornton .40 1.00
GBTO Jonathan Toews .75 2.00
GBWW Wojtek Wolski .25 .60
GBZP Zach Parise .40 1.00

2010-11 Upper Deck Victory Stars of the Game

COMPLETE SET (50) 20.00 50.00
STATED ODDS 1:2
SOGAK Anze Kopitar .60 1.50
SOGAM Andrei Markov .40 1.00
SOGAO Alexander Ovechkin 1.50 4.00
SOGBB Brad Boyes .25 .60
SOGBR Bobby Ryan .40 1.00
SOGCP Carey Price 1.50 4.00
SOGDA Daniel Alfredsson .40 1.00
SOGDD Drew Doughty .40 1.00
SOGDH Dany Heatley .30 .75
SOGDS Daniel Sedin .40 1.00
SOGEM Evgeni Malkin 1.25 3.00
SOGES Eric Staal .50 1.25
SOGGA Marian Gaborik .50 1.25
SOGHL Henrik Lundqvist .60 1.50
SOGHS Henrik Sedin .40 1.00
SOGHZ Henrik Zetterberg .50 1.25
SOGIB Ilya Bryzgalov .30 .75
SOGJC Jeff Carter .40 1.00
SOGJI Jarome Iginla .40 1.00
SOGJS Jason Spezza .25 .60
SOGJT John Tavares .75 2.00
SOGKE Phil Kessel .50 1.25
SOGMB Martin Brodeur .75 2.00
SOGMD Matt Duchene .40 1.00
SOGMF Marc-Andre Fleury .60 1.50
SOGMG Mike Green .40 1.00
SOGMK Mikko Koivu .40 1.00
SOGMR Mike Richards .40 1.00
SOGMS Martin St. Louis .40 1.00
SOGNB Nicklas Backstrom .60 1.50
SOGPB Patrice Bergeron .50 1.25
SOGPD Pavel Datsyuk .50 1.25
SOGPE Corey Perry .40 1.00
SOGPK Patrick Kane .75 2.00
SOGPR Chris Pronger .30 .75
SOGPS Paul Stastny .40 1.00
SOGRG Ryan Getzlaf .60 1.50
SOGRI Brad Richards .40 1.00
SOGRL Roberto Luongo .40 1.00
SOGRM Ryan Miller .40 1.00
SOGRN Rick Nash .40 1.00
SOGSC Sidney Crosby 1.50 4.00
SOGSD Shane Doan .30 .75
SOGSS Steven Stamkos .75 2.00
SOGSW Shea Weber .30 .75
SOGTH Joe Thornton .40 1.00
SOGTM Tyler Myers .40 1.00
SOGTO Jonathan Toews .75 2.00
SOGZC Zdeno Chara .30 .75
SOGZP Zach Parise .40 1.00

2011-12 Upper Deck Victory

COMPLETE SET (250) 25.00 60.00
COMP.SET w/o SPs (200) 12.00 30.00
COMP.UPDATE SET (60) 15.00 30.00
251-310 UPDATE ODDS 1:2 UD2 HOB
1 Ryan Getzlaf .40 1.00
2 Corey Perry .25 .60
3 Teemu Selanne .50 1.25
4 Bobby Ryan .25 .60
5 Cam Fowler .20 .50
6 Jonas Hiller .20 .50
7 Lubomir Visnovsky .15 .40
8 Evander Kane .25 .60
9 Dustin Byfuglien .25 .60
10 Alexander Burmistrov .20 .50
11 Ondrej Pavelec .25 .60
12 Andrew Ladd .25 .60
13 David Krejci .25 .60
14 Zdeno Chara .25 .60
15 Nathan Horton .25 .60
16 Patrice Bergeron .30 .75
17 Tyler Seguin .50 1.25
18 Tomas Kaberle .15 .40
19 Tim Thomas .25 .60
20 Milan Lucic .25 .60
21 Derek Roy .20 .50
22 Thomas Vanek .25 .60
23 Tyler Myers .25 .60
24 Tyler Ennis .20 .50
25 Drew Stafford .25 .60
26 Tim Connolly .15 .40
27 Ryan Miller .25 .60
28 Brad Boyes .15 .40
29 Jarome Iginla .25 .60
30 Alex Tanguay .15 .40
31 Rene Bourque .15 .40
32 Matt Stajan .20 .50
33 Jay Bouwmeester .25 .60
34 Miikka Kiprusoff .25 .60
35 Mikael Backlund .25 .60
36 Eric Staal .30 .75
37 Jeff Skinner .25 .60
38 Jussi Jokinen .15 .40
39 Cam Ward .25 .60
40 Joni Pitkanen .20 .50
41 Brandon Sutter .20 .50
42 Patrick Kane .50 1.25
43 Patrick Sharp .25 .60
44 Jonathan Toews .50 1.25
45 Marian Hossa .20 .50
46 Duncan Keith .25 .60
47 Brent Seabrook .25 .60
48 Michael Frolik .15 .40
49 Corey Crawford .30 .75
50 Milan Hejduk .20 .50
51 Matt Duchene .25 .60
52 Paul Stastny .25 .60
53 John-Michael Liles .15 .40
54 Erik Johnson .15 .40
55 David Jones .15 .40
56 Rick Nash .25 .60
57 Derick Brassard .25 .60
58 R.J. Umberger .15 .40
59 Antoine Vermette .15 .40
60 Jakub Voracek .25 .60
61 Steve Mason .20 .50
62 Brad Richards .25 .60
63 Loui Eriksson .20 .50
64 Mike Ribeiro .20 .50
65 Jamie Benn .30 .75
66 Kari Lehtonen .20 .50
67 Pavel Datsyuk .30 .75
68 Henrik Zetterberg .30 .75
69 Nicklas Lidstrom .25 .60
70 Dan Cleary .25 .60
71 Johan Franzen .25 .60
72 Jonathan Ericsson .20 .50
73 Jim Howard .25 .60
74 Jordan Eberle .25 .60
75 Sam Gagner .20 .50
76 Taylor Hall .50 1.25
77 Ales Hemsky .20 .50
78 Magnus Paajarvi .20 .50
79 Linus Omark .25 .60
80 Niclas Bergfors .20 .50
81 David Booth .15 .40
82 Tomas Vokoun .20 .50
83 Stephen Weiss .20 .50
84 Dustin Penner .20 .50
85 Anze Kopitar .40 1.00
86 Ryan Smyth .20 .50
87 Drew Doughty .25 .60
88 Jonathan Quick .40 1.00
89 Dustin Brown .25 .60
90 Jonathan Bernier .25 .60
91 Jack Johnson .15 .40
92 Mikko Koivu .20 .50
93 Martin Havlat .20 .50
94 Matt Cullen .15 .40
95 Brent Burns .30 .75
96 Niklas Backstrom .25 .60
97 Pierre-Marc Bouchard .25 .60
98 Andrei Kostitsyn .20 .50
99 Tomas Plekanec .25 .60
100 Brian Gionta .20 .50
101 Michael Cammalleri .20 .50
102 Benoit Pouliot .15 .40
103 P.K. Subban .50 1.25
104 Carey Price .75 2.00
105 Lars Eller .20 .50
106 Shea Weber .20 .50
107 Patric Hornqvist .20 .50
108 Cal O'Reilly .15 .40
109 Steve Sullivan .15 .40
110 Pekka Rinne .30 .75
111 Mike Fisher .25 .60
112 Zach Parise .25 .60
113 Patrik Elias .25 .60
114 Ilya Kovalchuk .25 .60
115 Martin Brodeur .50 1.25
116 Travis Zajac .20 .50
117 John Tavares .50 1.25
118 Blake Comeau .15 .40
119 Kyle Okposo .25 .60
120 Matt Moulson .20 .50
121 Michael Grabner .20 .50
122 Marian Gaborik .30 .75
123 Brandon Dubinsky .20 .50
124 Ryan Callahan .25 .60
125 Henrik Lundqvist .30 .75
126 Marc Staal .25 .60
127 Derek Stepan .25 .60
128 Wojtek Wolski .15 .40
129 Craig Anderson .25 .60
130 Jason Spezza .25 .60
131 Daniel Alfredsson .25 .60
132 Erik Karlsson .50 1.25
133 Mike Richards .25 .60
134 Jeff Carter .25 .60
135 Chris Pronger .20 .50
136 Claude Giroux .25 .60
137 Daniel Briere .25 .60
138 James van Riemsdyk .25 .60
139 Sergei Bobrovsky .25 .60
140 Scott Hartnell .25 .60
141 Kris Versteeg .20 .50
142 Kyle Turris .15 .40
143 Oliver Ekman-Larsson .25 .60
144 Shane Doan .20 .50
145 Ilya Bryzgalov .25 .60
146 Keith Yandle .25 .60
147 James Neal .25 .60
148 Sidney Crosby 1.00 2.50
149 Evgeni Malkin .75 2.00
150 Kristopher Letang .25 .60
151 Marc-Andre Fleury .40 1.00
152 Jordan Staal .25 .60
153 Maxime Talbot .20 .50
154 Tyler Kennedy .15 .40
155 Logan Couture .25 .60
156 Dany Heatley .20 .50
157 Joe Thornton .25 .60
158 Patrick Marleau .25 .60
159 Dan Boyle .20 .50
160 Joe Pavelski .25 .60
161 Ryane Clowe .15 .40
162 Antti Niemi .20 .50
163 Alex Pietrangelo .20 .50
164 Chris Stewart .20 .50
165 David Backes .25 .60
166 Patrik Berglund .20 .50
167 Jaroslav Halak .25 .60
168 David Perron .15 .40
169 Victor Hedman .30 .75
170 Steven Stamkos .50 1.25
171 Martin St. Louis .25 .60
172 Ryan Malone .15 .40
173 Vincent Lecavalier .20 .50
174 Luke Schenn .20 .50
175 Nazem Kadri .40 1.00
176 Clarke MacArthur .15 .40
177 Phil Kessel .30 .75
178 Nikolai Kulemin .25 .60
179 Jean-Sebastien Giguere .20 .50
180 Dion Phaneuf .25 .60
181 Alexander Edler .15 .40
182 Cory Schneider .20 .50
183 Christian Ehrhoff .15 .40
184 Daniel Sedin .25 .60
185 Henrik Sedin .25 .60
186 Ryan Kesler .25 .60
187 Roberto Luongo .25 .60
188 Alexandre Burrows .25 .60
189 Mason Raymond .20 .50
190 Michal Neuvirth .20 .50
191 Brooks Laich .15 .40
192 Jason Arnott .20 .50
193 Alexander Ovechkin 1.00 2.50
194 Alexander Semin .25 .60
195 Nicklas Backstrom .40 1.00
196 Mike Green .25 .60
197 Semyon Varlamov .25 .60
198 John Carlson .30 .75
199 Steven Stamkos CL .40 1.00
200 Sidney Crosby CL .75 2.00
201 Timo Pielmeier .60 1.50
202 Jean-Philippe Levasseur .50 1.25
203 Paul Postma RC .50 1.25
204 Andrei Zubarev RC .60 1.50
205 Carl Klingberg RC .50 1.25
206 Greg Nemisz RC .50 1.25
207 Lance Bouma RC .50 1.25
208 Marcus Kruger RC .75 2.00
209 Cameron Gaunce RC .40 1.00
210 John Moore RC .50 1.25
211 Tomas Kubalik RC .50 1.25
212 Tomas Vincour RC .50 1.25
213 Colton Sceviour RC .50 1.25
214 Teemu Hartikainen RC .50 1.25
215 Chris Vande Velde RC .75 2.00
216 Hugh Jessiman RC .50 1.25
217 Scott Timmins RC .50 1.25
218 Drew Bagnall RC .50 1.25
219 Carson McMillan RC .60 1.50
220 Aaron Palushaj RC .50 1.25
221 Brendon Nash RC .50 1.25
222 Jonathon Blum RC .50 1.25
223 Blake Geoffrion RC .50 1.25
224 Adam Henrique RC 1.25 3.00
225 Matt Campanale RC .50 1.25
226 Shane Sims RC .50 1.25
227 Mikko Koskinen RC .60 1.50
228 Todd Ford RC .60 1.50
229 Jamie Doornbosch RC .50 1.25
230 Mark Katic RC .50 1.25
231 Justin DiBenedetto RC .40 1.00
232 Cam Talbot RC 1.25 3.00
233 Patrick Wiercioch RC .50 1.25
234 Erik Condra RC .50 1.25
235 Roman Wick RC .60 1.50
236 Colin Greening RC .50 1.25
237 Andre Benoit RC .60 1.50
238 Stephane Da Costa RC .50 1.25
239 Erik Gustafsson RC .60 1.50
240 Ben Holmstrom RC .50 1.25
241 Zac Rinaldo RC .50 1.25
242 Brian Strait RC .60 1.50
243 Joe Vitale RC .50 1.25
244 Alex Stalock .50 1.25
245 Ben Scrivens RC .75 2.00
246 Matt Frattin RC .50 1.25
247 Joe Colborne RC .50 1.25
248 Yann Suave RC .50 1.25
249 Cody Hodgson RC 4.00 10.00
250 Cody Hodgson CL 1.00 2.50
251 Ville Leino .30 .75
252 Christian Ehrhoff .25 .60
253 Semyon Varlamov .40 1.00
254 Jean-Sebastien Giguere .30 .75
255 Jeff Carter .40 1.00
256 Tomas Fleischmann .25 .60
257 Kris Versteeg .30 .75
258 Jose Theodore .40 1.00
259 Mike Richards .40 1.00
260 Dany Heatley .30 .75
261 Devin Setoguchi .30 .75
262 Evgeni Nabokov .30 .75
263 Brad Richards .40 1.00
264 Ilya Bryzgalov .40 1.00
265 Jaromir Jagr 1.00 2.50
266 Maxime Talbot .30 .75
267 Brent Burns .50 1.25
268 Martin Havlat .30 .75
269 John-Michael Liles .25 .60
270 David Booth .25 .60
271 Tomas Vokoun .30 .75
272 Ondrej Pavelec .40 1.00
273 Evander Kane .40 1.00
274 Alexander Burmistrov .30 .75
275 Wayne Simmonds .50 1.25
276 Brayden Schenn .40 1.00
277 Dustin Byfuglien .40 1.00
278 Ryan Smyth .30 .75
279 Robyn Regehr .25 .60
280 Brian Campbell .25 .60
281 Devante Smith-Pelly RC 1.00 2.50
282 Peter Holland RC .60 1.50
283 Zack Kassian RC .75 2.00
284 Justin Faulk RC 1.00 2.50
285 Brandon Saad RC 1.25 3.00
286 Gabriel Landeskog RC 1.25 3.00
287 Ryan Johansen RC 1.25 3.00
288 Gustav Nyquist RC 1.50 4.00
289 Ryan Nugent-Hopkins RC 5.00 12.00
290 Anton Lander RC .60 1.50
291 Lennart Petrell RC .75 2.00
292 Colten Teubert RC .60 1.50
293 Erik Gudbranson RC .75 2.00
294 Louis Leblanc RC .60 1.50
295 Raphael Diaz RC .60 1.50
296 Alexei Emelin RC .60 1.50
297 Craig Smith RC .75 2.00
298 Adam Larsson RC .75 2.00
299 Keith Kinkaid RC .60 1.50
300 Tim Erixon RC .60 1.50
301 Calvin de Haan RC .60 1.50
302 Mika Zibanejad RC 1.50 4.00
303 Sean Couturier RC 1.25 3.00
304 Matt Read RC 1.25 3.00
305 Andy Miele RC .60 1.50
306 Brett Connolly RC .60 1.50
307 Jake Gardiner RC 1.00 2.50
308 Eddie Lack RC .60 1.50
309 Cody Eakin RC .75 2.00
310 Mark Scheifele RC 1.50 4.00

2011-12 Upper Deck Victory Black

*1-200 VETS: 15X TO 40X BASIC CARDS
*201-250 ROOK: 6X TO 15X BASIC CARDS
*251-280 VETS: 12X TO 30X BASIC CARDS
*281-310 ROOK: 4X TO 10X BASIC CARDS
49 Corey Crawford 12.00 30.00
195 Nicklas Backstrom 15.00 40.00

2011-12 Upper Deck Victory Red

*RED 1-200: 6X TO 15X BASE
*RED 201-250: 3X TO 8X BASE
49 Corey Crawford 5.00 12.00
195 Nicklas Backstrom 6.00 15.00
249 Cody Hodgson 8.00 20.00
250 Cody Hodgson CL 10.00 25.00

2011-12 Upper Deck Victory Game Breakers

COMPLETE SET (25) 10.00 25.00
GBAK Anze Kopitar .60 1.50
GBAO Alexander Ovechkin 1.50 4.00
GBAS Alexander Semin .40 1.00
GBBR Brad Richards .40 1.00
GBCG Claude Giroux .40 1.00
GBCP Chris Pronger .30 .75
GBDA Daniel Alfredsson .40 1.00
GBDB Dustin Byfuglien .40 1.00
GBDS Daniel Sedin .40 1.00
GBEM Evgeni Malkin 1.25 3.00
GBES Eric Staal .50 1.25
GBHZ Henrik Zetterberg .50 1.25
GBJI Jarome Iginla .40 1.00
GBJS Jeff Skinner .40 1.00
GBJT John Tavares .75 2.00
GBMK Mikko Koivu .30 .75
GBMS Martin St. Louis .40 1.00
GBNB Nicklas Backstrom .60 1.50
GBPK Phil Kessel .50 1.25
GBPS Patrick Sharp .40 1.00
GBRG Ryan Getzlaf .60 1.50
GBSC Sidney Crosby 1.50 4.00
GBSS Steven Stamkos .75 2.00
GBTH Taylor Hall .75 2.00
GBTO Jonathan Toews .75 2.00

2011-12 Upper Deck Victory Stars of the Game

COMPLETE SET (25) 10.00 25.00
SOGAO Alexander Ovechkin 1.50 4.00
SOGCP Carey Price 1.25 3.00
SOGDD Drew Doughty .40 1.00
SOGDH Dany Heatley .30 .75
SOGEM Evgeni Malkin 1.25 3.00
SOGES Eric Staal .50 1.25
SOGHS Henrik Sedin .40 1.00
SOGJT Jonathan Toews .75 2.00
SOGMB Martin Brodeur .75 2.00
SOGMD Matt Duchene .40 1.00
SOGMF Marc-Andre Fleury .60 1.50
SOGMG Marian Gaborik .50 1.25
SOGMR Mike Richards .40 1.00
SOGMS Martin St. Louis .40 1.00
SOGNB Nicklas Backstrom .60 1.50
SOGPD Pavel Datsyuk .50 1.25
SOGPK Patrick Kane .75 2.00
SOGRG Ryan Getzlaf .60 1.50
SOGRM Ryan Miller .40 1.00
SOGRN Rick Nash .40 1.00

OGSC Sidney Crosby 1.50 4.00
OGSS Steven Stamkos .75 2.00
OGTH Joe Thornton .40 1.00
OGTT Tim Thomas .40 1.00
OGZP Zach Parise .40 1.00

2015-16 Upper Deck Victory Black

VB1-VB16 ISSUED AT '15 TORONTO FALL EXPO
VB17-VB26 ISSUED VIA NATL CARD DAY PACKS
VB1 Shane Prince 1.00 2.50
VB2 Sam Bennett 1.50 4.00
VB3 Ryan Hartman 1.50 4.00
VB4 Ronalds Kenins 1.25 3.00
VB5 Matt Puempel 1.00 2.50
VB6 Malcolm Subban 3.00 8.00
VB7 Kevin Fiala 1.25 3.00
VB8 Jacob de la Rose 1.25 3.00
VB9 Emile Poirier 1.25 3.00
VB10 Antoine Bibeau 1.25 3.00
VB11 Brendan Ranford 1.00 2.50
VB12 Henrik Samuelsson 1.00 2.50
VB13 Stefan Noesen 1.00 2.50
VB14 Kyle Baun 1.25 3.00
VB15 Josh Anderson 1.25 3.00
VB16 Andrew Copp 1.25 3.00
VB17 Connor McDavid 40.00 80.00
VB18 Jake Virtanen 3.00 8.00
VB19 Nikolaj Ehlers 5.00 12.00
VB20 Robby Fabbri 3.00 8.00
VB21 Max Domi 5.00 12.00
VB22 Dylan Larkin 20.00 40.00
VB23 Artemi Panarin 8.00 20.00
VB24 Mike Condon 2.50 6.00
VB25 Noah Hanifin 3.00 8.00
VB26 Jack Eichel 20.00 40.00

2016-17 Upper Deck Victory Black

V1 William Nylander 8.00 20.00
V2 Miles Wood 1.50 4.00
V3 Kasperi Kapanen 4.00 10.00
V4 Sonny Milano 2.50 6.00
V5 Brendan Leipsic 2.00 5.00
V6 Nikita Soshnikov 1.25 3.00
V7 Tobias Lindberg 3.00 8.00
V8 Connor Brown 3.00 8.00
V9 Frederik Gauthier 1.50 4.00
V10 Zach Hyman 2.50 6.00
V11 Pavel Zacha 2.50 6.00
V12 Jason Dickinson 1.50 4.00
V13 Anthony Mantha 5.00 12.00
V14 Josh Morrissey 2.50 6.00
V15 Charlie Lindgren 4.00 10.00
V16 Hudson Fasching 2.00 5.00
V17 Auston Matthews 30.00 80.00
V18 Patrik Laine 20.00 50.00
V19 Matthew Tkachuk 6.00 15.00
V20 Mikhail Sergachev 4.00 10.00
V21 Mitch Marner 15.00 40.00
V22 Tyler Motte 2.00 5.00
V23 Nick Schmaltz 2.00 5.00
V24 Zach Werenski 4.00 10.00
V25 Ivan Provorov 4.00 10.00
V26 Jimmy Vesey 4.00 10.00

2000-01 Upper Deck Vintage

Released in mid January 2001, Upper Deck Vintage is a 400-card set comprised of 340 regular cards, 30 prospect cards and 30 triple player team checklists. Base cards are thick cardboard with a throwback vintage design. Backgrounds are white with a colored nameplate along the bottom. Vintage was packaged in 24-pack boxes with packs containing 10 cards and carried a suggested retail price of $1.99. NOTE: The Curtis Joseph promo was handed out as a single to announce the upcoming arrival of the product. It is card number 31 and has the word "sample" written across the back.

1 German Titov .10 .25
2 Teemu Selanne .30 .75
3 Matt Cullen .10 .25
4 Oleg Tverdovsky .10 .25
5 Jean-Sebastien Giguere .12 .30
6 Guy Hebert .12 .30
7 Mike Leclerc .10 .25
8 Jason Marshall .10 .25
9 Paul Kariya .20 .50
10 Steve Rucchin .10 .25
11 Paul Kariya .30 .75
Guy Hebert
Teemu Selanne
12 Paul Kariya .20 .50
Guy Hebert
13 Patrik Stefan .12 .30
14 Damian Rhodes .10 .25
15 Donald Audette .12 .30
16 Yannick Tremblay .10 .25
17 Hnat Domenichelli .10 .25
18 Dean Sylvester .10 .25
19 Steve Guolla .10 .25
20 Petr Buzek .10 .25
21 Andrew Brunette .10 .25
22 Ray Ferraro .10 .25
23 Patrik Stefan .12 .30
Damian Rhodes
Denny Lambert
24 Patrik Stefan .12 .30
Damian Rhodes
25 Joe Thornton .25 .60
26 Brian Rolston .12 .30
27 Kyle McLaren .10 .25
28 Sergei Samsonov .12 .30
29 Paul Coffey .15 .40
30 Andrei Kovalenko .10 .25
31 Jason Allison .12 .30
32 Bill Guerin .15 .40
33 Byron Dafoe .12 .30
34 Mikko Eloranta .10 .25
35 Don Sweeney .10 .25
36 Thrntn/Dafoe/McLar .25 .60
37 J.Thornton/Dafoe .25 .60
38 Miroslav Satan .10 .25
39 Dominik Hasek .25 .60
40 Stu Barnes .12 .30
41 Chris Gratton .10 .25
42 Doug Gilmour .20 .50
43 Curtis Brown .10 .25
44 James Patrick .10 .25
45 Alexei Zhitnik .12 .30
46 Rhett Warrener .10 .25
47 Dave Andreychuk .15 .40
48 Maxim Afinogenov .10 .25
49 Satan/Hasek/Ray CL .25 .60
50 M.Satan/D.Hasek .25 .60
51 Valeri Bure .12 .30
52 Mike Vernon .12 .30
53 Marc Savard .12 .30
54 Clarke Wilm .10 .25
55 Phil Housley .12 .30
56 Fred Brathwaite .12 .30
57 Cory Stillman .10 .25
58 Derek Morris .10 .25
59 Robyn Regehr .10 .25
60 Jarome Iginla .15 .40
61 Valeri Bure .12 .30
Fred Brathwaite
Jason Wiemer
62 Valeri Bure .12 .30
Fred Brathwaite
63 Bates Battaglia .10 .25
64 Sandis Ozolinsh .12 .30
65 Jeff O'Neill .12 .30
66 Ron Francis .20 .50
67 Sami Kapanen .10 .25
68 Martin Gelinas .10 .25
69 Arturs Irbe .12 .30
70 Dave Tanabe .10 .25
71 Rod Brind'Amour .15 .40
72 Glen Wesley .10 .25
73 Jeff O'Neill .20 .50
Arturs Irbe
Ron Francis
74 Ron Francis .20 .50
Arturs Irbe
75 Tony Amonte .12 .30
76 Steve Sullivan .10 .25
77 Eric Daze .12 .30
78 Boris Mironov .10 .25
79 Jocelyn Thibault .12 .30
80 Jean-Yves Leroux .10 .25
81 Valeri Zelepukin .10 .25
82 Alexei Zhamnov .12 .30
83 Josef Marha .10 .25
84 Michael Nylander .10 .25
85 Tony Amonte .12 .30
Jocelyn Thibault
Bob Probert
86 Tony Amonte .12 .30
Jocelyn Thibault
87 Patrick Roy .40 1.00
88 Joe Sakic .25 .60
89 Jon Klemm .10 .25
90 Adam Deadmarsh .12 .30
91 Ray Bourque .25 .60
92 Peter Forsberg .20 .50
93 Milan Hejduk .12 .30
94 Chris Drury .12 .30
95 Alex Tanguay .12 .30
96 Adam Foote .12 .30
97 Dave Reid .10 .25
98 Sakic/Roy/Bourque CL .40 1.00
99 J.Sakic/P.Roy .40 1.00
100 Marc Denis .12 .30
101 Geoff Sanderson .12 .30
102 Ron Tugnutt .12 .30
103 Lyle Odelein .10 .25
104 Krzysztof Oliwa .10 .25
105 Kevyn Adams .10 .25
106 Steve Heinze .10 .25
107 Jamie Pushor .10 .25
108 Bruce Gardiner .10 .25
109 Jan Caloun .10 .25
110 Kevyn Adams .12 .30
Marc Denis
Krzysztof Oliwa
111 Geoff Sanderson .12 .30
Ron Tugnutt
112 Mike Modano .25 .60
113 Jere Lehtinen .12 .30
114 Brett Hull .25 .60
115 Sergei Zubov .12 .30
116 Jamie Langenbrunner .12 .30
117 Shaun Van Allen .10 .25
118 Ed Belfour .15 .40
119 Brenden Morrow .12 .30
120 Darryl Sydor .12 .30
121 Joe Nieuwendyk .15 .40
122 Derian Hatcher .12 .30
123 Mike Modano .25 .60
Ed Belfour
Derian Hatcher
124 Mike Modano .25 .60
Ed Belfour
125 Steve Yzerman .50 1.25
126 Nicklas Lidstrom .15 .40
127 Sergei Fedorov .25 .60
128 Chris Osgood .15 .40
129 Brendan Shanahan .20 .50
130 Larry Murphy .12 .30
131 Darren McCarty .10 .25
132 Chris Chelios .15 .40
133 Kris Draper .10 .25
134 Tomas Holmstrom .12 .30
135 Slava Kozlov .12 .30
136 Yzerm/Osgood/Shanahn CL .50 1.25
137 S.Yzerman/C.Osgood .50 1.25
138 Doug Weight .15 .40
139 Todd Marchant .10 .25
140 Eric Brewer .10 .25
141 Mike Grier .10 .25
142 Tom Poti .10 .25
143 Ryan Smyth .12 .30
144 Tommy Salo .12 .30
145 Janne Niinimaa .10 .25
146 Daniel Cleary .12 .30
147 Bill Guerin .15 .40
148 Doug Weight .15 .40
Tommy Salo
Georges Laraque
149 Doug Weight .15 .40
Tommy Salo
150 Pavel Bure .20 .50
151 Ray Whitney .12 .30
152 Viktor Kozlov .12 .30
153 Igor Larionov .15 .40
154 Scott Mellanby .10 .25
155 Trevor Kidd .10 .25
156 Rob Niedermayer .12 .30
157 Robert Svehla .10 .25
158 Roberto Luongo .25 .60
159 Mike Sillinger .10 .25
160 Pavel Bure .25 .60
Roberto Luongo
Peter Worrell
161 Pavel Bure .20 .50
Trevor Kidd
162 Zigmund Palffy .15 .40
163 Luc Robitaille .15 .40
164 Stephane Fiset .10 .25
165 Rob Blake .15 .40
166 Bryan Smolinski .12 .30
167 Glen Murray .10 .25
168 Mattias Norstrom .10 .25
169 Jamie Storr .12 .30
170 Craig Johnson .10 .25
171 Nelson Emerson .10 .25
172 Zigmund Palffy .15 .40
Jamie Storr
Rob Blake
173 Luc Robitaille .15 .40
Stephane Fiset
174 Stacy Roest .10 .25
175 Manny Fernandez .12 .30
176 Jim Dowd .10 .25
177 Curtis Leschyshyn .10 .25
178 Jeff Nielsen .10 .25
179 Aaron Gavey .10 .25
180 Sergei Krivokrasov .10 .25
181 Brad Bombardir .10 .25
182 Cam Stewart .10 .25
183 Scott Pellerin .10 .25
184 Pell/Frndz/Gabrk CL .30 .75
185 Sergei Krivokrasov .12 .30
Manny Fernandez
186 Saku Koivu .15 .40
187 Eric Weinrich .10 .25
188 Sergei Zholtok .10 .25
189 Dainius Zubrus .10 .25
190 Brian Savage .10 .25
191 Jeff Hackett .10 .25
192 Patrick Poulin .10 .25
193 Jose Theodore .20 .50
194 Christian Laflamme .10 .25
195 Martin Rucinsky .10 .25
196 Trevor Linden .20 .50
Jose Theodore
Saku Koivu CL
197 Saku Koivu .20 .50
Jose Theodore
198 Greg Johnson .10 .25
199 Cliff Ronning .10 .25
200 Drake Berehowsky .10 .25
201 Mike Dunham .10 .25
202 David Legwand .15 .40
203 Tom Fitzgerald .10 .25
204 Patric Kjellberg .10 .25
205 Scott Walker .10 .25
206 Kimmo Timonen .10 .25
207 Bill Houlder .10 .25
208 David Legwand .15 .40
Mike Dunham
Todd Fitzgerald
209 David Legwand .15 .40
Mike Dunham
210 Scott Stevens .15 .40
211 Martin Brodeur .30 .75
212 Jason Arnott .12 .30
213 Patrik Elias .15 .40
214 Alexander Mogilny .12 .30
215 Scott Gomez .12 .30
216 John Madden .12 .30
217 Bobby Holik .10 .25
218 Petr Sykora .12 .30
219 Ken Sutton .10 .25
220 Randy McKay .10 .25
221 Gomz/Brodr/Stvns .30 .75
222 S.Gomez/M.Brodeur .30 .75
223 Tim Connolly .10 .25
224 Kevin Haller .10 .25
225 Brad Isbister .10 .25
226 Mariusz Czerkawski .10 .25
227 Roman Hamrlik .12 .30
228 Claude Lapointe .10 .25
229 Bill Muckalt .10 .25
230 John Vanbiesbrouck .12 .30
231 Kenny Jonsson .10 .25
232 Mark Parrish .10 .25
233 Tim Connolly .12 .30
John Vanbiesbrouck
Kenny Jonsson
234 Tim Connolly .12 .30
John Vanbiesbrouck
235 Theo Fleury .20 .50
236 Brian Leetch .15 .40
237 Mark Messier .25 .60
238 Adam Graves .12 .30
239 Mike Richter .15 .40
240 Vladimir Malakhov .10 .25
241 Mike York .10 .25
242 Radek Dvorak .12 .30
243 Petr Nedved .12 .30
244 Jan Hlavac .10 .25
245 Tim Taylor .10 .25
246 Mark Messier .25 .60
Mike Richter
Adam Graves
247 Mark Messier .25 .60
Mike Richter
248 Radek Bonk .12 .30
249 Marian Hossa .12 .30
250 Jason York .10 .25
251 Wade Redden .10 .25
252 Patrick Lalime .12 .30
253 Daniel Alfredsson .15 .40
254 Shawn McEachern .10 .25
255 Sami Salo .10 .25
256 Petr Schastlivy .10 .25
257 Vaclav Prospal .10 .25
258 Alexei Yashin .12 .30
Patrick Lalime
Marian Hossa
259 Marian Hossa .12 .30
Patrick Lalime
260 John LeClair .15 .40
261 Rick Tocchet .12 .30
262 Daymond Langkow .10 .25
263 Simon Gagne .15 .40
264 Keith Primeau .12 .30
265 Eric Desjardins .12 .30
266 Brian Boucher .12 .30
267 Andy Delmore .10 .25
268 Mark Recchi .20 .50
269 Keith Jones .10 .25
270 Chris Therien .10 .25
271 John LeClair .15 .40
Brian Boucher
Rick Tocchet
272 John LeClair .15 .40
Brian Boucher
273 Jeremy Roenick .15 .40
274 Teppo Numminen .10 .25
275 Brad May .10 .25
276 Keith Tkachuk .15 .40
277 Trevor Letowski .10 .25
278 Shane Doan .12 .30
279 Jyrki Lumme .10 .25
280 Joe Juneau .12 .30
281 Sean Burke .10 .25
282 Travis Green .10 .25
283 Jeremy Roenick .15 .40
Sean Burke
Keith Tkachuk
284 Keith Tkachuk .15 .40
Sean Burke
285 Jean-Sebastien Aubin .12 .30
286 Jaromir Jagr .40 1.00
287 Alexei Morozov .10 .25
288 Josef Beranek .10 .25
289 Jan Hrdina .10 .25
290 Milan Kraft .10 .25
291 Alexei Kovalev .12 .30
292 Robert Lang .10 .25
293 Janne Laukkanen .10 .25
294 Martin Straka .12 .30
295 J.Jagr/Aubin/Kasp .40 1.00
296 J.Jagr/J-S Aubin .40 1.00
297 Niklas Sundstrom .10 .25
298 Owen Nolan .15 .40
299 Jeff Friesen .10 .25
300 Vincent Damphousse .12 .30
301 Brad Stuart .12 .30
302 Marco Sturm .12 .30
303 Alexander Korolyuk .10 .25
304 Mike Ricci .12 .30
305 Patrick Marleau .15 .40
306 Steve Shields .10 .25
307 Jeff Friesen .15 .40
Steve Shields
Owen Nolan
308 Jeff Friesen .10 .25
Steve Shields
309 Chris Pronger .12 .30
310 Pavol Demitra .20 .50
311 Marty Reasoner .10 .25
312 Jochen Hecht .10 .25
313 Michal Handzus .10 .25
314 Al MacInnis .15 .40
315 Roman Turek .12 .30
316 Lubos Bartecko .10 .25
317 Jamal Mayers .10 .25
318 Dallas Drake .10 .25
319 Pierre Turgeon .15 .40
320 Pavol Demitra .20 .50
Roman Turek
Chris Pronger
321 Chris Pronger .12 .30
Roman Turek
322 Vincent Lecavalier .12 .30
323 Mike Johnson .10 .25
324 Brad Richards .15 .40
325 Dan Cloutier .12 .30
326 Paul Mara .10 .25
327 Fredrik Modin .10 .25
328 Bryan Muir .10 .25
329 Jassen Cullimore .10 .25
330 Todd Warriner .10 .25
331 Petr Svoboda .10 .25
332 Vincent Lecavalier .12 .30
Dan Cloutier
Petr Svoboda
333 Vincent Lecavalier .12 .30
Dan Cloutier
334 Mats Sundin .15 .40
335 Sergei Berezin .10 .25
336 Nikolai Antropov .12 .30
337 Steve Thomas .10 .25
338 Curtis Joseph .20 .50
339 Jonas Hoglund .10 .25
340 Dimitri Yushkevich .10 .25
341 Darcy Tucker .10 .25
342 Gary Roberts .10 .25
343 Jeff Farkas .10 .25
344 Tie Domi .25 .60
345 Mats Sundin .25 .60
Curtis Joseph
Tie Domi
346 Mats Sundin .20 .50
Curtis Joseph
347 Markus Naslund .12 .30
348 Brendan Morrison .15 .40
349 Todd Bertuzzi .12 .30
350 Adrian Aucoin .10 .25
351 Donald Brashear .10 .25
352 Murray Baron .10 .25
353 Daniel Sedin .30 .75
354 Andrew Cassels .10 .25
355 Henrik Sedin .25 .60
356 Mattias Ohlund .10 .25
357 Naslund/Potvin/Brash .25 .60
358 M.Naslund/F.Potvin .25 .60
359 Chris Simon .10 .25
360 Olaf Kolzig .15 .40
361 Jeff Halpern .10 .25
362 Andrei Nikolishin .10 .25
363 Steve Konowalchuk .10 .25
364 Peter Bondra .12 .30
365 Adam Oates .15 .40
366 Richard Zednik .10 .25
367 Sergei Gonchar .10 .25
368 Brendan Witt .10 .25
369 Peter Bondra .15 .40
Olaf Kolzig
Chris Simon
370 Adam Oates .15 .40
Olaf Kolzig
371 Rostislav Klesla RC .50 1.25
372 Jonas Ronnqvist RC .20 .50
373 Eric Nickulas RC .20 .50
374 Andrew Raycroft RC .50 1.25
375 Jeff Cowan RC .20 .50
376 Reto Von Arx RC .25 .60
377 Serge Aubin RC .25 .60
378 Tyler Bouck RC .20 .50
379 Michel Riesen RC .25 .60
380 Eric Belanger RC .25 .60
381 Marian Gaborik RC .60 1.50
382 Scott Hartnell RC .50 1.25
383 Greg Classen RC .20 .50
384 Willie Mitchell RC .30 .75
385 Colin White RC .20 .50
386 Steve Valiquette RC .25 .60
387 Jani Hurme RC .20 .50
388 Martin Havlat RC .60 1.50
389 Justin Williams RC .50 1.25
390 Petr Hubacek RC .20 .50
391 Roman Simicek RC .20 .50
392 Matt Elich RC .25 .60
393 Brent Sopel RC .30 .75
394 Marc-Andre Thinel RC .20 .50
395 Zdenek Blatny RC .20 .50
396 Michael Ryder RC 3.00 8.00
397 Jason Jaspers RC .20 .50
398 Jordan Krestanovich RC .20 .50
399 Fedor Fedorov RC .25 .60
400 Jeff Bateman RC .20 .50
31S Curtis Joseph SAMPLE .40 1.00

2000-01 Upper Deck Vintage All UD Team

COMPLETE SET (10) 6.00 15.00
STATED ODDS 1:23
UD1 Patrick Roy 2.00 5.00
UD2 Martin Brodeur 1.00 2.50
UD3 Chris Pronger .25 .60
UD4 Ray Bourque .75 2.00
UD5 Paul Kariya .25 .60
UD6 John LeClair .50 1.25
UD7 Steve Yzerman 2.00 5.00
UD8 Peter Forsberg 1.00 2.50
UD9 Jaromir Jagr .60 1.50
UD10 Pavel Bure .50 1.25

2000-01 Upper Deck Vintage Dynasty A Piece of History

Randomly inserted in packs at the rate of 1:72, this 11-card set features two swatches of game worn jerseys from some of the NHL's most dominating teams and player combinations. Two player photos are pictured in the middle of the card's horizontal design with jersey swatches on the outsides. Gold parallels to this set were also created and inserted randomly, these cards were numbered to just 50.

*GOLD/50: .6X TO 1.5X BASIC INSERTS
BG B.Bourne/C.Gillies 8.00 20.00
BK M.Bossy/A.Kallur 8.00 20.00
GC B.Goring/B.Carroll 8.00 20.00
GH C.Gillies/M.Hallin 8.00 20.00
GK W.Gretzky/M.Messier 40.00 100.00
LJ M.Lemieux/J.Jagr 25.00 60.00
LL P.Lafontaine/D.Langevin 8.00 20.00
NS B.Nystrom/B.Sutter 8.00 20.00
PR D.Potvin/C.Resch 8.00 20.00
TP B.Trottier/S.Persson 8.00 20.00
YO S.Yzerman/C.Osgood 10.00 25.00

2000-01 Upper Deck Vintage Great Gloves

COMPLETE SET (20) 4.00 10.00
STATED ODDS 1:12
GG1 Guy Hebert .40 1.00
GG2 Byron Dafoe .40 1.00
GG3 Dominik Hasek 1.25 2.50
GG4 Fred Brathwaite .40 1.00
GG5 Arturs Irbe .40 1.00
GG6 Patrick Roy 2.50 6.00
GG7 Ed Belfour .50 1.25
GG8 Chris Osgood .40 1.00
GG9 Tommy Salo .40 1.00
GG10 Trevor Kidd .40 1.00
GG11 Jose Theodore .60 1.50
GG12 Mike Richter .40 1.00
GG13 Brian Boucher .40 1.00
GG14 Jean-Sebastien Aubin .40 1.00
GG15 Steve Shields .40 1.00
GG16 Roman Turek .40 1.00
GG17 Dan Cloutier .40 1.00
GG18 Curtis Joseph .50 1.25
GG19 Felix Potvin .60 1.50
GG20 Olaf Kolzig .40 1.00

2000-01 Upper Deck Vintage Messier Heroes of Hockey

Randomly inserted in packs at the rate of 1:23, this 10-card set pays tribute to Mark Messier. Base cards are white bordered with an action photo set inside the NHL logo shield. The bottom of the card features a blue box containing the Mark Messier Heroes of Hockey logo.

COMPLETE SET (10) 10.00 20.00
COMMON MESSIER 1.25 3.00

2000-01 Upper Deck Vintage National Heroes

Randomly inserted in packs at the rate of 1:4, this 20-card set features top NHL players in action on a card with each respective player's home country flag set against a yellow background.

COMPLETE SET (20) 6.00 15.00
NH1 Paul Kariya .25 .60
NH2 Teemu Selanne .25 .60
NH3 Patrik Stefan .20 .50
NH4 Sergei Samsonov .20 .50
NH5 Dominik Hasek .50 1.25
NH6 Valeri Bure .20 .50
NH7 Tony Amonte .20 .50
NH8 Patrick Roy 1.25 3.00
NH9 Peter Forsberg .60 1.50
NH10 Mike Modano .40 1.00
NH11 Steve Yzerman 1.25 3.00
NH12 Pavel Bure .30 .75
NH13 Saku Koivu .25 .60
NH14 Martin Brodeur .60 1.50
NH15 Scott Gomez .20 .50
NH16 Mark Messier .30 .75
NH17 John LeClair .30 .75
NH18 Jeremy Roenick .30 .75
NH19 Jaromir Jagr .40 1.00
NH20 Mats Sundin .25 .60

2000-01 Upper Deck Vintage Original 6 Piece of History

Randomly inserted in packs at the rate of 1:72, this six card set features six top players from yesterday and today, each representing one of the NHL's original six teams. Cards have player action shots and a circular jersey swatch in the middle of the number six on the right side of the card front. Gold parallels to this set were also created and inserted randomly, these cards were limited to just 67 sets.

STATED ODDS 1:72
*GOLD/67: 1.2X TO 3X BASIC INSERTS
OCJ Curtis Joseph 6.00 15.00
OJT Jose Theodore 8.00 20.00
OMY Mike York 6.00 15.00
OSS Sergei Samsonov 6.00 15.00
OSY Steve Yzerman 12.50 30.00
OTE Tony Esposito 10.00 25.00

2000-01 Upper Deck Vintage Star Tandems

COMPLETE SET (10) 10.00 20.00
STATED ODDS 1:23
S1A Paul Kariya .50 1.25
S1B Teemu Selanne .50 1.25
S2A Joe Sakic .75 2.00
S2B Patrick Roy 2.00 5.00
S3A Steve Yzerman 2.00 5.00
S3B Brendan Shanahan .60 1.50
S4A Scott Gomez .50 1.25
S4B Martin Brodeur 1.00 2.50
S5A John LeClair .50 1.25
S5B Brian Boucher .50 1.25

2001-02 Upper Deck Vintage

Issued in late-December 2001, this 300-card set carried an SRP of $1.99 for a 10-card pack.

COMPLETE SET (300) 40.00 80.00
1 Jean-Sebastien Giguere .20 .50
2 Jeff Friesen .15 .40
3 Paul Kariya .30 .75
4 Oleg Tverdovsky .15 .40
5 Steve Rucchin .15 .40
6 Mike Leclerc .15 .40
7 Dan Bylsma .15 .40
8 Paul Kariya .30 .75
9 Mighty Ducks CL .20 .50
10 Patrik Stefan .20 .50
11 Tomi Kallio .15 .40
12 Chris Tamer .15 .40
13 Milan Hnilicka .20 .50
14 Ray Ferraro .15 .40
15 Stephen Guolla .15 .40
16 Ray Ferraro .15 .40
17 Thrashers CL .15 .40
18 Kyle McLaren .15 .40
19 Brian Rolston .20 .50
20 Byron Dafoe .20 .50
21 Mikko Eloranta .15 .40
22 Sergei Samsonov .20 .50
23 Joe Thornton .30 .75
24 Bill Guerin .25 .60
25 Joe Thornton .30 .75
26 Bruins CL .20 .50
27 Martin Biron .20 .50
28 Maxim Afinogenov .15 .40
29 J-P Dumont .15 .40
30 Chris Gratton .15 .40
31 Rhett Warrener .15 .40
32 Miroslav Satan .20 .50
33 Curtis Brown .15 .40
34 Miroslav Satan .20 .50
35 Sabres CL .15 .40
36 Marc Savard .15 .40
37 Jarome Iginla .25 .60
38 Derek Morris .15 .40
39 Oleg Saprykin .15 .40
40 Jeff Shantz .15 .40
41 Craig Conroy .15 .40
42 Jarome Iginla .25 .60
43 Flames CL .15 .40
44 Jeff O'Neill .15 .40
45 Arturs Irbe .20 .50
46 Shane Willis .15 .40
47 Dave Tanabe .15 .40
48 Rod Brind'Amour .25 .60
49 Sami Kapanen .15 .40
50 Ron Francis .30 .75
51 Jeff O'Neill .15 .40
52 Hurricanes CL .15 .40
53 Eric Daze .20 .50
54 Alexei Zhamnov .20 .50
55 Jaroslav Spacek .15 .40
56 Michael Nylander .15 .40
57 Tony Amonte .20 .50
58 Steve Sullivan .15 .40
59 Kevin Dean .15 .40
60 Steve Sullivan .15 .40
61 Blackhawks CL .15 .40
62 Chris Drury .20 .50
63 Rob Blake .25 .60
64 Joe Sakic .40 1.00
65 Peter Forsberg .30 .75
66 Ray Bourque .40 1.00
67 Milan Hejduk .20 .50
68 Patrick Roy .60 1.50
69 Joe Sakic .40 1.00
70 Avalanche CL .40 1.00
71 Ron Tugnutt .20 .50
72 Geoff Sanderson .15 .40
73 Espen Knutsen .15 .40
74 Tyler Wright .15 .40
75 Rostislav Klesla .15 .40
76 Jamie Heward .15 .40
77 Geoff Sanderson .15 .40
78 Blue Jackets CL .15 .40
79 Mike Modano .40 1.00
80 Ed Belfour .25 .60
81 Pierre Turgeon .25 .60
82 Joe Nieuwendyk .25 .60
83 Sergei Zubov .20 .50
84 Jere Lehtinen .20 .50
85 Donald Audette .15 .40
86 Mike Modano .40 1.00
87 Stars CL .25 .60
88 Steve Yzerman .75 2.00
89 Brendan Shanahan .30 .75
90 Sergei Fedorov .40 1.00
91 Luc Robitaille .25 .60
92 Dominik Hasek .40 1.00
93 Nicklas Lidstrom .25 .60
94 Darren McCarty .15 .40
95 Brendan Shanahan .30 .75
96 Red Wings CL .50 1.25
97 Tommy Salo .20 .50
98 Mike Comrie .20 .50
99 Tom Poti .15 .40
100 Mike Grier .15 .40
101 Janne Niinimaa .15 .40
102 Ryan Smyth .20 .50
103 Anson Carter .20 .50
104 Ryan Smyth .20 .50
105 Oilers CL .15 .40
106 Pavel Bure .30 .75
107 Viktor Kozlov .15 .40
108 Marcus Nilsson .15 .40
109 Denis Shvidki .15 .40
110 Bret Hedican .15 .40
111 Roberto Luongo .40 1.00
112 Pavel Bure .30 .75
113 Panthers CL .25 .60
114 Zigmund Palffy .25 .60
115 Felix Potvin .40 1.00
116 Adam Deadmarsh .20 .50
117 Glen Murray .20 .50
118 Eric Belanger .15 .40
119 Jason Holland .15 .40
120 Jozef Stumpel .15 .40
121 Zigmund Palffy .25 .60
122 Kings CL .25 .60
123 Marian Gaborik .40 1.00
124 Manny Fernandez .20 .50
125 Brad Bombardir .15 .40
126 Lubomir Sekeras .15 .40
127 Wes Walz .15 .40
128 Antti Laaksonen .15 .40
129 Marian Gaborik .40 1.00
130 Wild CL .25 .60
131 Saku Koivu .25 .60
132 Oleg Petrov .15 .40
133 Martin Rucinsky .15 .40
134 Jose Theodore .25 .60
135 Brian Savage .15 .40
136 Andrei Markov .25 .60
137 Richard Zednik .20 .50
138 Saku Koivu .25 .60
139 Canadiens CL .15 .40
140 David Legwand .20 .50
141 Mike Dunham .20 .50
142 Scott Walker .15 .40
143 Cliff Ronning .15 .40
144 Patric Kjellberg .15 .40
145 Greg Johnson .15 .40
146 Vitali Yachmenev .15 .40
147 Cliff Ronning .15 .40
148 Predators CL .15 .40
149 Martin Brodeur .50 1.25
150 Patrik Elias .25 .60
151 Jason Arnott .20 .50
152 Scott Niedermayer .25 .60
153 Petr Sykora .15 .40
154 Scott Gomez .20 .50
155 Scott Stevens .25 .60
156 Patrik Elias .25 .60
157 Devils CL .30 .75
158 Michael Peca .20 .50
159 Rick DiPietro .20 .50
160 Mariusz Czerkawski .15 .40
161 Roman Hamrlik .15 .40
162 Dave Scatchard .15 .40
163 Brad Isbister .15 .40
164 Mark Parrish .15 .40
165 Islanders CL .15 .40
166 Mark Messier .40 1.00
167 Theo Fleury .30 .75
168 Mike Richter .25 .60
169 Brian Leetch .25 .60
170 Kim Johnsson .15 .40
171 Radek Dvorak .20 .50
172 Theo Fleury .30 .75
173 Rangers CL .25 .60
174 Marian Hossa .20 .50
175 Radek Bonk .15 .40
176 Martin Havlat .20 .50
177 Daniel Alfredsson .25 .60
178 Magnus Arvedson .15 .40
179 Patrick Lalime .20 .50
180 Shawn McEachern .15 .40
181 Radek Bonk .15 .40
182 Senators CL .15 .40
183 Jeremy Roenick .25 .60
184 Roman Cechmanek .20 .50
185 Keith Primeau .20 .50
186 John LeClair .25 .60
187 Kent Manderville .15 .40
188 Mark Recchi .30 .75
189 Eric Desjardins .20 .50
190 Mark Recchi .30 .75
191 Flyers CL .20 .50
192 Sean Burke .15 .40
193 Shane Doan .20 .50
194 Michal Handzus .15 .40
195 Teppo Numminen .15 .40
196 Ladislav Nagy .15 .40
197 Landon Wilson .15 .40
198 Sean Burke .15 .40
199 Coyotes CL .15 .40
200 Alexei Kovalev .20 .50
201 Mario Lemieux .75 2.00
202 Johan Hedberg .20 .50
203 Robert Lang .15 .40
204 Martin Straka .15 .40
205 Andrew Ference .15 .40
206 Kevin Stevens .15 .40
207 Alexei Kovalev .20 .50
208 Penguins CL .50 1.25
209 Evgeni Nabokov .20 .50
210 Teemu Selanne .50 1.25
211 Owen Nolan .25 .60
212 Mike Ricci .20 .50
213 Scott Thornton .20 .50
214 Vincent Damphousse .20 .50
215 Brad Stuart .15 .40
216 Evgeni Nabokov .20 .50
217 Sharks CL .30 .75
218 Chris Pronger .20 .50
219 Keith Tkachuk .25 .60
220 Doug Weight .25 .60
221 Pavol Demitra .30 .75
222 Cory Stillman .15 .40
223 Al MacInnis .25 .60
224 Bryce Salvador .15 .40
225 Scott Young .15 .40
226 Blues CL .20 .50
227 Brad Richards .25 .60
228 Vincent Lecavalier .20 .50
229 Nikolai Khabibulin .25 .60
230 Fredrik Modin .15 .40
231 Martin St. Louis .25 .60
232 Pavel Kubina .15 .40
233 Brad Richards .25 .60
234 Lightning CL .15 .40
235 Curtis Joseph .25 .60
236 Mats Sundin .25 .60
237 Shayne Corson .15 .40
238 Darcy Tucker .15 .40
239 Nikolai Antropov .15 .40
240 Gary Roberts .15 .40
241 Bryan McCabe .20 .50
242 Mats Sundin .25 .60
243 Maple Leafs CL .15 .40
244 Markus Naslund .25 .60
245 Daniel Sedin .25 .60
246 Peter Schaefer .15 .40
247 Andrew Cassels .15 .40
248 Brendan Morrison .20 .50
249 Todd Bertuzzi .25 .60
250 Markus Naslund .25 .60
251 Canucks CL .15 .40
252 Steve Konowalchuk .15 .40
253 Sergei Gonchar .15 .40
254 Calle Johansson .20 .50
255 Peter Bondra .25 .60
256 Jaromir Jagr .60 1.50
257 Olaf Kolzig .25 .60
258 Andrei Nikolishin .15 .40
259 Olaf Kolzig .25 .60
260 Capitals CL .25 .60
261 P.Bure/J.Sakic/J.Jagr LL 1.00 2.50
262 J.Jagr/A.Oates/M.Straka LL 1.00 2.50
263 J.Jagr/J.Sakic/P.Elias LL 1.00 2.50
264 P.Bondra/P.Bure/J.Sakic LL .60 1.50
265 J.Sakic/P.Elias/S.Stevens LL .60 1.50
266 Barnaby/Worrell/Grimson LL .25 .60
267 Brodeur/Roy/Hasek LL 1.00 2.50
268 Turco/Cechmanek/Legace LL .40 1.00
269 Dunham/Burke/Turco LL .40 1.00
270 Hasek/Cechmanek/Brodeur LL .75 2.00
271 Timo Parssinen RC .60 1.50

272 Ilja Bryzgalov RC 1.25 3.00
273 Kevin Sawyer RC .50 1.25
274 Kamil Piros RC .50 1.25
275 Ilya Kovalchuk RC 2.50 6.00
276 Brian Pothier RC .50 1.25
277 Zdenek Kutlak RC .50 1.25
278 Vaclav Nedorost RC .50 1.25
279 Jaroslav Obsut RC .50 1.25
280 Niko Kapanen RC .75 2.00
281 Kristian Huselius RC .75 2.00
282 Jaroslav Bednar RC .50 1.25
283 Martin Erat RC .75 2.00
284 Josef Boumedienne RC .50 1.25
285 Scott Clemmensen RC .50 1.25
286 Andreas Salomonsson RC .50 1.25
287 Radek Martinek RC .50 1.25
288 Mikael Samuelsson RC .60 1.50
289 Peter Smrek RC .50 1.25
290 Ivan Ciernik RC .50 1.25
291 Chris Neil RC .60 1.50
292 Jiri Dopita RC .50 1.25
293 David Cullen RC .50 1.25
294 Krys Kolanos RC .50 1.25
295 Jeff Jillson RC .50 1.25
296 Mark Rycroft RC .60 1.50
297 Nikita Alexeev RC .50 1.25
298 Thomas Ziegler RC .60 1.50
299 Bob Wren RC .50 1.25
300 Brian Sutherby RC .50 1.25

2001-02 Upper Deck Vintage Jerseys

Randomly inserted at 1:144 packs, this 16-card set featured swatches of game-worn jerseys of the featured players. This set consisted of three subsets: Golden Goalies (denoted by a "GG" prefix), Stars of the Decades (denoted by a "SD" prefix), and Stanley Cup Stars (denoted by a "SC" prefix).

GGAM Andy Moog 10.00 25.00
GGBS Billy Smith 12.50 30.00
GGGC Gerry Cheevers 10.00 25.00
GGGF Grant Fuhr 10.00 25.00
GGRV Rogie Vachon 12.50 30.00
SCBS Billy Smith 10.00 25.00
SCBT Bryan Trottier 10.00 25.00
SCMB Mike Bossy 10.00 25.00
SCSY Steve Yzerman 6.00 15.00
SCWG Wayne Gretzky 40.00 100.00
SDBC Bobby Clarke 15.00 40.00
SDGH Gordie Howe 12.50 30.00
SDGL Guy Lafleur 10.00 25.00
SDGP Gilbert Perreault 10.00 25.00
SDMB Mike Bossy 10.00 25.00
SDPE Phil Esposito 10.00 25.00

2001-02 Upper Deck Vintage Next In Line

Serial-numbered to just 50-copies each, this 6-card set featured game-worn jersey swatches of NHL legends and their heir-apparents.

NLBL R.Bourque/N.Lidstrom 50.00 100.00
NLCO G.Cheevers/M.Ouellet 20.00 50.00
NLGS W.Gretzky/J.Sakic 100.00 200.00
NLHY G.Howe/S.Yzerman 125.00 250.00
NLLK G.Lafleur/P.Kariya 25.00 60.00
NLSC B.Smith/R.Cechmanek 15.00 40.00

2001-02 Upper Deck Vintage Sweaters of Honor

Inserted randomly in 1:96 hobby packs, this 4-card set featured game-used jersey swatches of the pictured players.

SHGL Guy Lafleur 8.00 20.00
SHLA Guy Lapointe 8.00 20.00
SHML Michel Larocque 6.00 15.00
SHSS Steve Shutt 6.00 15.00

2002-03 Upper Deck Vintage

This 350-card set consisted of 305 base cards (1-260/321-350); 30 checklist cards (261-290), 15 Achievements (291-305) and 15 statistical leaders cards (306-320). SP's were inserted at 1:5.

COMPLETE SET (350) 50.00 100.00
1 Vitali Vishnevski .12 .30
2 Paul Kariya SP .50 1.25
3 Samuel Pahlsson .12 .30
4 Mike LeClerc .12 .30
5 Matt Cullen .12 .30
6 Ruslan Salei .12 .30
7 Jean-Sebastien Giguere .20 .50
8 Andy McDonald .20 .50
9 Patrik Stefan .15 .40
10 Milan Hnilicka .15 .40
11 Lubos Bartecko .12 .30
12 Jeff Cowan .12 .30
13 Ilya Kovalchuk .25 .60
14 Frantisek Kaberle .12 .30
15 Dany Heatley .20 .50
16 Daniel Tjarnqvist .12 .30
17 Sergei Samsonov .15 .40
18 P.J. Stock .12 .30
19 Nick Boynton .12 .30
20 Martin Lapointe .15 .40
21 Jozef Stumpel .12 .30
22 John Grahame .12 .30
23 Joe Thornton SP .50 1.25
24 Glen Murray .15 .40
25 Brian Rolston .15 .40
26 Hal Gill .12 .30
27 Stu Barnes .12 .30
28 Tim Connolly .12 .30
29 Miroslav Satan .20 .50
30 Maxim Afinogenov .12 .30
31 Martin Biron .15 .40
32 Jay McKee .12 .30
33 J-P Dumont .12 .30
34 Curtis Brown .12 .30
35 Alexei Zhitnik .15 .40
36 Roman Turek .20 .50
37 Rob Niedermayer .15 .40
38 Marc Savard .12 .30
39 Jarome Iginla SP .40 1.00
40 Derek Morris .12 .30
41 Denis Gauthier .12 .30
42 Dave Lowry .12 .30
43 Craig Conroy .12 .30
44 Sami Kapanen .12 .30
45 Ron Francis .25 .60
46 Rod Brind'Amour .20 .50
47 Niclas Wallin .12 .30
48 Josef Vasicek .12 .30
49 Jeff O'Neill .12 .30
50 Erik Cole .15 .40
51 Dave Tanabe .12 .30
52 Arturs Irbe .15 .40
53 Steve Sullivan .12 .30
54 Ryan VandenBussche .12 .30
55 Michael Nylander .12 .30
56 Mark Bell .12 .30
57 Kyle Calder .12 .30
58 Jocelyn Thibault .15 .40
59 Eric Daze .12 .30
60 Alexei Zhamnov .15 .40
61 Steve Reinprecht .12 .30
62 Stephane Yelle .12 .30
63 Rob Blake .20 .50
64 Peter Forsberg .25 .60
65 Patrick Roy SP 1.00 2.50
66 Milan Hejduk .15 .40
67 Joe Sakic SP .60 1.50
68 Greg DeVries .12 .30
69 Chris Drury .20 .50
70 Alex Tanguay .15 .40
71 Adam Foote .12 .30
72 David Vyborny .12 .30
73 Rostislav Klesla .12 .30
74 Marc Denis .15 .40
75 Ray Whitney .15 .40
76 Jody Shelley .12 .30
77 Jean-Luc Grand-Pierre .12 .30
78 Geoff Sanderson .15 .40
79 Espen Knutsen .12 .30
80 Pierre Turgeon .20 .50
81 Mike Modano SP .60 1.50
82 Marty Turco .20 .50
83 Bill Guerin .20 .50
84 Jere Lehtinen .20 .50
85 Jason Arnott .15 .40
86 Derian Hatcher .15 .40
87 Brenden Morrow .15 .40
88 Steve Yzerman SP .75 2.00
89 Sergei Fedorov .30 .75
90 Pavel Datsyuk .25 .60
91 Nicklas Lidstrom .20 .50
92 Luc Robitaille .20 .50
93 Kris Draper .12 .30
94 Curtis Joseph .20 .50
95 Dominik Hasek SP .60 1.50
96 Brett Hull .25 .60
97 Brendan Shanahan .25 .60
98 Boyd Devereaux .12 .30
99 Tommy Salo .15 .40
100 Ryan Smyth .15 .40
101 Mike York .12 .30
102 Mike Comrie SP .40 1.00
103 Georges Laraque .15 .40
104 Ethan Moreau .12 .30
105 Daniel Cleary .15 .40
106 Anson Carter .15 .40
107 Viktor Kozlov .12 .30
108 Valeri Bure .15 .40
109 Olli Jokinen .20 .50
110 Sandis Ozolinsh .15 .40
111 Roberto Luongo .30 .75
112 Peter Worrell .12 .30
113 Niklas Hagman .12 .30
114 Kristian Huselius .12 .30
115 Zigmund Palffy .20 .50
116 Mattias Norstrom .12 .30
117 Mathieu Schneider .12 .30
118 Jason Allison .15 .40
119 Felix Potvin .30 .75
120 Bryan Smolinski .15 .40
121 Adam Deadmarsh .15 .40
122 Aaron Miller .12 .30
123 Richard Park .12 .30
124 Nick Schultz .12 .30
125 Marian Gaborik SP .60 1.50
126 Jim Dowd .12 .30
127 Hnat Domenichelli .12 .30
128 Filip Kuba .12 .30
129 Manny Fernandez .15 .40
130 Andrew Brunette .12 .30
131 Yanic Perreault .12 .30
132 Saku Koivu .20 .50
133 Richard Zednik .12 .30
134 Jose Theodore SP .20 .50
135 Donald Audette .12 .30
136 Craig Rivet .12 .30
137 Andrei Markov .20 .50
138 Andreas Dackell .12 .30
139 Stu Grimson .12 .30
140 Scott Hartnell .20 .50
141 Mike Dunham .15 .40
142 Martin Erat .12 .30
143 Kimmo Timonen .12 .30
144 Denis Arkhipov .12 .30
145 David Legwand .15 .40
146 Andy Delmore .12 .30
147 Sergei Brylin .12 .30
148 Scott Stevens .20 .50
149 Scott Niedermayer .20 .50
150 John Madden .12 .30
151 Patrik Elias .20 .50
152 Martin Brodeur SP .75 2.00
153 Joe Nieuwendyk .20 .50
154 Brian Rafalski .12 .30
155 Roman Hamrlik .12 .30
156 Raffi Torres .12 .30
157 Michael Peca .15 .40
158 Mark Parrish .12 .30
159 Oleg Kvasha .12 .30
160 Eric Cairns .12 .30
161 Dave Scatchard .12 .30
162 Chris Osgood .20 .50
163 Alexei Yashin SP .30 .75
164 Tom Poti .12 .30
165 Sandy McCarthy .12 .30
166 Radek Dvorak .15 .40
167 Petr Nedved .12 .30
168 Pavel Bure SP .50 1.25
169 Matthew Barnaby .12 .30
170 Mark Messier .30 .75
171 Eric Lindros .30 .75
172 Dan Blackburn .15 .40
173 Brian Leetch .20 .50
174 Wade Redden .12 .30
175 Radek Bonk .15 .40
176 Patrick Lalime .15 .40
177 Mike Fisher .12 .30
178 Martin Havlat .15 .40
179 Marian Hossa .15 .40
180 Magnus Arvedson .12 .30
181 Daniel Alfredsson .20 .50
182 Simon Gagne SP .40 1.00
183 Kim Johnsson .12 .30
184 Roman Cechmanek .15 .40
185 Mark Recchi .25 .60
186 Keith Primeau .20 .50
187 Justin Williams .15 .40
188 John LeClair .20 .50
189 Jeremy Roenick .20 .50
190 Eric Weinrich .12 .30
191 Donald Brashear .12 .30
192 Teppo Numminen .15 .40
193 Shane Doan .15 .40
194 Sean Burke .12 .30
195 Ladislav Nagy .12 .30
196 Daymond Langkow .15 .40
197 Daniel Briere .15 .40
198 Claude Lemieux .15 .40
199 Tony Amonte .15 .40
200 Ville Nieminen .12 .30
201 Martin Straka .15 .40
202 Mario Lemieux SP 1.50 4.00
203 Johan Hedberg .20 .50
204 Jan Hrdina .12 .30
205 Andrew Ference .12 .30
206 Alexei Kovalev .20 .50
207 Alexei Morozov .12 .30
208 Vincent Damphousse .15 .40
209 Scott Thornton .12 .30
210 Patrick Marleau .20 .50
211 Owen Nolan .20 .50
212 Mike Ricci .15 .40
213 Marcus Ragnarsson .12 .30
214 Marco Sturm .12 .30
215 Evgeni Nabokov SP .30 .75
216 Brad Stuart .12 .30
217 Tyson Nash .12 .30
218 Shjon Podein .12 .30
219 Pavol Demitra .25 .60
220 Keith Tkachuk SP .40 1.00
221 Doug Weight .20 .50
222 Cory Stillman .12 .30
223 Chris Pronger .15 .40
224 Brent Johnson .15 .40
225 Al MacInnis .20 .50
226 Vincent Lecavalier .15 .40
227 Vaclav Prospal .12 .30
228 Shane Willis .12 .30
229 Pavel Kubina .12 .30
230 Nikolai Khabibulin .20 .50
231 Martin St. Louis .20 .50
232 Fredrik Modin .12 .30
233 Brad Richards .20 .50
234 Tomas Kaberle .12 .30
235 Tie Domi .15 .40
236 Shayne Corson .12 .30
237 Mats Sundin SP .40 1.00
238 Gary Roberts .12 .30
239 Darcy Tucker .12 .30
240 Ed Belfour .20 .50
241 Bryan McCabe .12 .30
242 Alyn McCauley .12 .30
243 Alexander Mogilny .15 .40
244 Trevor Linden .20 .50
245 Todd Bertuzzi .20 .50
246 Markus Naslund .15 .40
247 Henrik Sedin .20 .50
248 Ed Jovanovski .15 .40
249 Daniel Sedin .20 .50
250 Dan Cloutier .15 .40
251 Brendan Morrison .15 .40
252 Brendan Witt .12 .30
253 Steve Konowalchuk .12 .30
254 Sergei Gonchar .15 .40
255 Peter Bondra .20 .50
256 Olaf Kolzig .20 .50
257 Jeff Halpern .12 .30
258 Jaromir Jagr SP 1.00 2.50
259 Andrei Nikolishin .12 .30
260 Robert Lang .12 .30
261 Mighty Ducks CL .15 .40
262 Thrashers CL .15 .40
263 Bruins CL .15 .40
264 Sabres CL .12 .30
265 Flames CL .12 .30
266 Hurricanes CL .15 .40
267 Blackhawks CL .10 .25
268 Avalanche CL .30 .75
269 Blue Jackets CL .10 .25
270 Stars CL .20 .50
271 Red Wings CL .25 .60
272 Oilers CL .12 .30
273 Panthers CL .20 .50
274 Kings CL .20 .50
275 Wild CL .20 .50
276 Canadiens CL .12 .30
277 Predators CL .12 .30
278 Devils CL .25 .60
279 Islanders CL .12 .30
280 Rangers CL .20 .50
281 Senators CL .12 .30
282 Flyers CL .12 .30
283 Coyotes CL .10 .25
284 Penguins CL .40 1.00
285 Sharks CL .12 .30
286 Blues CL .15 .40
287 Lightning CL .12 .30
288 Maple Leafs CL .12 .30
289 Cancucks CL .12 .30
290 Capitals CL .30 .75
291 Joe Sakic AA .40 1.00
292 Patrick Roy AA .60 1.50
293 Mike Modano AA .40 1.00
294 Brendan Shanahan AA .30 .75
295 Steve Yzerman AA .50 1.25
296 Detroit Red Wings AA .30 .75
297 Joe Nieuwendyk AA .25 .60
298 Martin Brodeur AA .50 1.25
299 Pavel Bure AA .30 .75
300 Brian Leetch AA .25 .60
301 Jeremy Roenick AA .25 .60
302 Mark Recchi AA .30 .75
303 Mario Lemieux AA .75 2.00
304 Teemu Selanne AA .50 1.25
305 Peter Bondra AA .25 .60
306 Iginla/Murray/Sundin SL .20 .50
307 Oates/Allison/Sakic SL .30 .75
308 Iginla/Naslund/Bertuzzi SL .20 .50
309 Bondra/Iginla/Yashin SL .20 .50
310 Gonchar/Lidstrom/Blake SL .20 .50
311 Rolston/Peca/Satan SL .20 .50
312 Chelios/Roenick/Gagne SL .20 .50
313 Worrell/Ference/Neil SL .12 .30
314 Briere/Hrdina/Deadmarsh SL .15 .40
315 Heatley/Kovlchk/Huslius SL .25 .60
316 Hasek/Brodeur/Nabokov SL .40 1.00
317 Roy/Cechmanek/Turco SL .50 1.25
318 Thdore/Roy/Cechmanek SL .50 1.25
319 Roy/Theodore/Khabibulin SL .50 1.25
320 Blckbrn/Kiprusof/Nornen SL .15 .40
321 Pasi Nurminen .12 .30
322 Mark Hartigan .12 .30
323 Henrik Tallinder .12 .30
324 Micki Dupont RC .30 .75
325 Jaroslav Svoboda .12 .30
326 Jordan Krestanovich .12 .30
327 Kelly Fairchild .12 .30
328 Riku Hahl .12 .30
329 Andrej Nedorost .12 .30
330 Blake Bellefeuille .12 .30
331 Ales Pisa .12 .30
332 Jani Rita .12 .30
333 Stephen Weiss .20 .50
334 Lukas Krajicek .15 .40
335 Sylvain Blouin RC .30 .75
336 Marcel Hossa .12 .30
337 Adam Hall RC .30 .75
338 Jonas Andersson .15 .40
339 Jan Lasak .15 .40
340 Ray Schultz RC .30 .75
341 Trent Hunter .12 .30
342 Martin Prusek .12 .30
343 Branko Radivojevic .12 .30
344 Shane Endicott .12 .30
345 Sebastien Centomo .12 .30
346 Karel Pilar .12 .30
347 Sebastien Charpentier .12 .30
348 Jean-Francois Fortin .12 .30
349 Ales Kotalik .12 .30
350 Kyle Rossiter .12 .30

2002-03 Upper Deck Vintage Green Backs

This skip-numbered 100-card set paralleled the base set with green card backs. This set was a hobby exclusive and each card was serial-numbered to just 199 copies.

*GREEN BACK/199: 5X TO 12X BASIC CARDS

2002-03 Upper Deck Vintage Jerseys

OS STATED ODDS 1:96 RETAIL
SO/EE/HS ODDS 1:96 HOB/RET
FS STATED ODDS 1:96 HOBBY
*GOLD/50: 1.2X TO 3X BASE JSY

EEBB Brian Boucher 3.00 8.00
EEDA David Aebischer 3.00 8.00
EEFP Felix Potvin 5.00 12.00
EEMB Martin Biron 3.00 8.00
EEMD Mike Dunham 3.00 8.00
EEMO Maxime Ouellet 3.00 8.00
EEMT Marty Turco 5.00 12.00
EEOK Olaf Kolzig 5.00 12.00
EERC Roman Cechmanek 3.00 8.00
EERT Ron Tugnutt 3.00 8.00
FSBM Brenden Morrow 5.00 12.00
FSCD Chris Drury 5.00 12.00
FSJJ Jaromir Jagr 6.00 15.00
FSKP Keith Primeau 3.00 8.00
FSMH Milan Hejduk 3.00 8.00
FSSY Steve Yzerman 12.00 30.00
HSJD J-P Dumont 3.00 8.00
HSJW Justin Williams 3.00 8.00
HSMD Marc Denis 3.00 8.00
HSPB Peter Bondra 5.00 12.00
HSRB Ray Bourque 8.00 20.00
HSRF Ruslan Fedotenko 3.00 8.00
HSRK Rostislav Klesla 3.00 8.00
HSSG Simon Gagne 5.00 12.00
HSSK Steve Konowalchuk 3.00 8.00
HSVN Ville Nieminen 3.00 8.00
OSED Eric Daze 3.00 8.00
OSGM Glen Murray 3.00 8.00
OSJT Jose Theodore SP 8.00 20.00
OSMS Mats Sundin 5.00 12.00
OSRD Radek Dvorak 3.00 8.00
OSSY Steve Yzerman 12.00 30.00
SOCD Chris Drury 5.00 12.00
SOEL Eric Lindros 6.00 15.00
SOJH Jeff Halpern 3.00 8.00
SOJI Jarome Iginla SP 8.00 20.00
SOJJ Jaromir Jagr SP 8.00 20.00
SOJL John LeClair 3.00 8.00
SOKP Keith Primeau 3.00 8.00
SOMR Mark Recchi 3.00 8.00
SOPF Peter Forsberg 5.00 15.00
SOPK Paul Kariya 5.00 12.00

2002-03 Upper Deck Vintage Tall Boys

Inserted 2 per hobby box, this 70-card set partially paralleled the base set on oversized cards. A gold version numbered out of 99 was also created.

*GOLD/99: 1.5X TO 4X BASIC INSERTS

T1 Paul Kariya .75 2.00
T2 Jean-Sebastien Giguere .60 1.50
T3 Dany Heatley 1.50 4.00
T4 Ilya Kovalchuk 1.00 2.50
T5 Joe Thornton 3.00 6.00
T6 Sergei Samsonov .60 1.50
T7 Miroslav Satan .60 1.50
T8 Maxim Afinogenov 1.50 4.00
T9 Roman Turek .60 1.50
T10 Jarome Iginla 1.00 2.50
T11 Arturs Irbe .60 1.50
T12 Ron Francis 1.00 2.50
T13 Eric Daze .60 1.50
T14 Jocelyn Thibault .60 1.50
T15 Patrick Roy 5.00 12.00
T16 Peter Forsberg 2.00 5.00
T17 Joe Sakic 1.50 4.00
T18 Chris Drury .60 1.50
T19 Alex Tanguay .60 1.50
T20 Espen Knutsen .60 1.50
T21 Rostislav Klesla .60 1.50
T22 Mike Modano 1.25 3.00
T23 Jason Arnott .60 1.50
T24 Steve Yzerman 3.00 8.00
T25 Brendan Shanahan .75 2.00
T26 Sergei Fedorov 1.25 3.00
T27 Curtis Joseph .75 2.00
T28 Mike Comrie .60 1.50
T29 Tommy Salo 1.00 2.50
T30 Roberto Luongo 1.50 4.00
T31 Stephen Weiss .60 1.50
T32 Jason Allison .60 1.50
T33 Zigmund Palffy .60 1.50
T34 Marian Gaborik 1.50 4.00
T35 Jose Theodore 1.00 2.50
T36 Saku Koivu .75 2.00
T37 Mike Dunham .60 1.50
T38 Scott Hartnell .60 1.50
T39 Martin Brodeur 2.00 5.00
T40 Patrik Elias .60 1.50
T41 Michael Peca .60 1.50
T42 Chris Osgood .60 1.50
T43 Eric Lindros .75 2.00
T44 Pavel Bure .75 2.00
T45 Daniel Alfredsson .60 1.50
T46 Marian Hossa .75 2.00
T47 Jeremy Roenick 1.00 2.50
T48 Simon Gagne .75 2.00
T49 Sean Burke .60 1.50
T50 Daniel Briere .60 1.50
T51 Tony Amonte .60 1.50
T52 Mario Lemieux 4.00 10.00
T53 Johan Hedberg .60 1.50
T54 Owen Nolan .60 1.50
T55 Evgeni Nabokov 1.00 2.50
T56 Keith Tkachuk .75 2.00
T57 Chris Pronger .60 1.50
T58 Vincent Lecavalier .75 2.00
T59 Nikolai Khabibulin .75 2.00
T60 Mats Sundin .75 2.00
T61 Alexander Mogilny .60 1.50
T62 Markus Naslund .75 2.00
T63 Todd Bertuzzi .75 2.00
T64 Jaromir Jagr 1.25 3.00
T65 Olaf Kolzig .60 1.50
T66 Gordie Howe 3.00 8.00
T67 Gordie Howe 3.00 8.00
T68 Gordie Howe 3.00 8.00
T69 Gordie Howe 3.00 8.00
T70 Gordie Howe 3.00 8.00

2000 Upper Deck Wayne Gretzky Master Collection

Released as a box set limited in production to 300 total sets (150 US and 150 Canada) the Upper Deck Wayne Gretzky Collection includes an 18-card base set where each card is sequentially numbered to 150, eight insert cards consisting of jersey cards and signed jersey cards sequentially numbered to 50, and one mystery pack containing an autograph, memorabilia card, or an autographed memorabilia card. Canadian versions are differentiated by the maple leaf they carry near each of the four corners of the card and the US version features stars instead.

COMPLETE SET (18) 200.00 400.00
COMMON GRETZKY (1-18) 12.00 30.00
*CANADIAN: .4X TO 1X US

2000 Upper Deck Wayne Gretzky Master Collection Inserts

Three versions of each card were released. Each Master Collection contains one of each of these three versions: One Edmonton autographed jersey card in Canadian issues and one unautographed Edmonton jersey card in USA sets, one Los Angeles jersey card, one All-Star jersey card, and one New York jersey card in Canadian sets and one autographed New York jersey card in American sets. Each card is sequentially numbered to 50.

1 Gretzky Ed.AU/50 Can 300.00 600.00
2 Gretzky Ed.AU/50 Can 300.00 600.00
3 Gretzky Ed.AU/50 Can 300.00 600.00
4 Gretzky Ed/50 USA 100.00 200.00
5 Gretzky Ed/50 USA 100.00 200.00
6 Gretzky Ed/50 USA 100.00 200.00
7 Gretzky LA/50 100.00 200.00
8 Gretzky LA/50 100.00 200.00
9 Gretzky LA/50 100.00 200.00
10 Gretzky AS/50 100.00 200.00
11 Gretzky AS/50 100.00 200.00
12 Gretzky AS/50 100.00 200.00
13 Gretzky NY AU/50 USA 300.00 600.00
14 Gretzky NY AU/50 USA 300.00 600.00
15 Gretzky NY AU/50 USA 300.00 600.00
16 Gretzky NY/50 Can 100.00 200.00
17 Gretzky NY/50 Can 100.00 200.00
18 Gretzky NY/50 Can 100.00 200.00

2000 Upper Deck Wayne Gretzky Master Collection Mystery Pack

One Mystery Pack was inserted into each Wayne Gretzky Master Collection which contained one of the following: one of 18 different Ultimate Gretzky Autograph 1/1's, one Great Gretzky Jersey card sequentially numbered to 99 , one Great Gretzky Signed Jersey card, one Great Gretzky Patch card, or one Great Gretzky Signed Patch card. Lower print runs are not priced due to scarcity.

ULTIMATE AU's #'D 1/1
US AND CANADA SAME VALUE
19 Gretzky Jersey/99 175.00 300.00
20 Gretzky Jersey AU/9
21 Gretzky Patch/15
22 Gretzky Patch AU/9

2011-12 Upper Deck Winter Classic

1 Sidney Crosby 8.00 20.00
2 Evgeni Malkin 6.00 15.00
3 Pascal Dupuis 1.25 3.00
4 Jordan Staal 2.00 5.00
5 Brooks Orpik 1.50 4.00
6 Chris Kunitz 2.00 5.00
7 Paul Martin 1.25 3.00
8 Eric Tangradi 1.25 3.00
9 Marc-Andre Fleury 3.00 8.00
10 Alex Ovechkin 8.00 20.00
11 Mike Green 2.00 5.00
12 Nicklas Backstrom 3.00 8.00
13 Alexander Semin 2.00 5.00
14 Mike Knuble 1.25 3.00
15 Brooks Laich 1.25 3.00
16 Tomas Fleischmann 1.25 3.00
17 Marcus Johansson 1.50 4.00
18 Semyon Varlamov 2.00 5.00
19 Pittsburgh 2011 1.25 3.00
20 City of Pittsburgh 1.25 3.00

2013-14 Upper Deck Winter Classic

COMPLETE SET (20) 40.00 80.00
WC1 Jimmy Howard 2.00 5.00
WC2 Henrik Zetterberg 2.50 6.00
WC3 Jonathan Ericsson 1.50 4.00
WC4 Dan Cleary 2.00 5.00
WC5 Johan Franzen 2.00 5.00
WC6 Daniel Alfredsson 2.00 5.00
WC7 Niklas Kronwall 1.50 4.00
WC8 Pavel Datsyuk 2.50 6.00
WC9 Danny DeKeyser 1.50 4.00
WC10 Petr Mrazek 2.50 6.00
WC11 Jonathan Bernier 2.00 5.00
WC12 Phil Kessel 2.50 6.00
WC13 James van Riemsdyk 2.00 5.00
WC14 Tyler Bozak 1.50 4.00
WC15 Nazem Kadri 2.00 5.00
WC16 Dion Phaneuf 2.00 5.00
WC17 Joffrey Lupul 1.50 4.00
WC18 James Reimer 2.00 5.00
WC19 Josh Leivo 2.00 5.00
WC20 Morgan Rielly 3.00 8.00

2015-16 Upper Deck Winter Classic Bruins

COMPLETE SET (5) 5.00 10.00
WCB1 Brad Marchand 1.25 3.00
WCB2 David Krejci .75 2.00
WCB3 David Pastrnak 1.50 4.00
WCB4 Tuukka Rask 1.00 2.50
WCB5 Zdeno Chara 1.00 2.50

2015-16 Upper Deck Winter Classic Canadiens

COMPLETE SET (5) 5.00 10.00
WCM1 P.K. Subban 1.50 4.00
WCM2 Andrei Markov 1.00 2.50
WCM3 Lars Eller .75 2.00
WCM4 Max Pacioretty 1.00 2.50
WCM5 Mike Condon .75 2.00

2016 Upper Deck World Cup of Hockey

WCH1 Jonathan Toews .50 1.25
WCH2 Carey Price .75 2.00
WCH3 Jamie Benn .30 .75
WCH4 John Tavares .50 1.25
WCH5 Sidney Crosby 1.00 2.50
WCH6 David Krejci .25 .60
WCH7 Radko Gudas .20 .50
WCH8 Petr Mrazek .25 .60
WCH9 Tomas Plekanec .25 .60
WCH10 Pavel Zacha .30 .75
WCH11 Leon Draisaitl .25 .60
WCH12 Marian Hossa .30 .75
WCH13 Tomas Tatar .20 .50
WCH14 Frederik Andersen .20 .50
WCH15 Roman Josi .25 .60
WCH16 Joe Pavelski .25 .60
WCH17 Patrick Kane .40 1.00
WCH18 Ben Bishop .25 .60
WCH19 Justin Abdelkader .20 .50
WCH20 John Carlson .30 .75
WCH21 Teuvo Teravainen .25 .60
WCH22 Joonas Donskoi .20 .50
WCH23 Aleksander Barkov .20 .50
WCH24 Pekka Rinne .30 .75
WCH25 Patrik Laine 1.00 2.50
WCH26 Connor McDavid .75 2.00
WCH27 Auston Matthews 1.50 4.00
WCH28 Matt Murray .30 .75
WCH29 Dylan Larkin .30 .75
WCH30 Johnny Gaudreau .30 .75
WCH31 Alexander Ovechkin 1.00 2.50
WCH32 Dmitry Orlov .25 .60
WCH33 Pavel Datsyuk .30 .75
WCH34 Nikita Kucherov .40 1.00
WCH35 Evgeni Malkin .75 2.00
WCH36 Erik Karlsson .50 1.25
WCH37 Henrik Zetterberg .30 .75
WCH38 Henrik Sedin .25 .60
WCH39 Nicklas Backstrom .40 1.00
WCH40 Henrik Lundqvist .30 .75

2016 Upper Deck World Cup of Hockey Autographs

WCHAAB Aleksander Barkov 20.00 50.00
WCHACP Carey Price 80.00 200.00
WCHADK David Krejci 25.00 60.00
WCHADL Dylan Larkin 30.00 80.00
WCHAFA Frederik Andersen 20.00 50.00
WCHAJD Joonas Donskoi 20.00 50.00
WCHAJP Joe Pavelski 25.00 60.00
WCHAMM Matt Murray 30.00 80.00
WCHAPZ Pavel Zacha 30.00 80.00
WCHASB Dmitry Orlov 25.00 60.00

2010 Upper Deck World of Sports

COMPLETE SET (375) 100.00 150.00
COMP.SET w/o SPs (300) 30.00 60.00
159 Sarah Davis .15 .40
160 Hannah Armstrong .15 .40
161 Jillian Saulnier .15 .40
162 Laurie Kingsbury .15 .40
163 Melodie Daoust .15 .40
164 Jamie Lee Rattray .15 .40
165 Jenna McParland .15 .40
166 Kelly Terry .15 .40
167 Emily Fulton .15 .40
168 Christine Bestland .15 .40
169 Carly Mercer .15 .40
170 Jessica Campbell .15 .40
171 Hayleigh Cudmore .15 .40
172 Brigette Lacquette .15 .40
173 Erin Ambrose .15 .40
174 Cassandra Poudrier .15 .40
175 Caitlin MacDonald .15 .40
176 Shannon Doyle .15 .40
177 Carmen MacDonald .15 .40
178 Erica Howe .15 .40
179 Stefan Elliott .15 .40
180 Curtis Hamilton .15 .40
181 Joey Hishon .25 .60
182 Stefan Della Rovere .15 .40
183 Brandon Kozun .15 .40
184 Zack Kassian .25 .60
185 Calvin Pickard .40 1.00
186 Olivier Roy .25 .60
187 Adam Henrique .25 .60
188 Erik Gudbranson .25 .60
189 Taylor Doherty .15 .40
190 Gabriel Bourque .25 .60
191 Taylor Hall 2.00 5.00
192 Scott Glennie .15 .40
193 Calvin de Haan .15 .40
194 Ethan Werek .15 .40
195 Ryan Ellis .15 .40
196 Cody Eakin .15 .40
197 Travis Hamonic .15 .40
198 Colten Teubert .15 .40
199 Martin Jones .25 .60
200 Jake Allen .40 1.00
236 Jennifer Botterill .25 .60
237 Cassie Campbell .40 1.00
238 Cammi Granato .25 .60
240 Hayley Wickenheiser .25 .60
242 Julie Chu .15 .40
246 Natalie Darwitz .15 .40
248 Kim St. Pierre .40 1.00
303 Taylor Hall SP 1.50 4.00
304 Sidney Crosby SP 2.00 5.00
305 Wayne Gretzky SP 2.00 5.00
306 Bobby Orr SP 1.00 2.50
307 John Tavares SP 1.50 4.00
308 Mark Messier SP 1.00 2.50
309 Gordie Howe SP 1.50 4.00
310 Mario Lemieux SP 1.00 2.50
311 Patrick Roy SP 1.50 4.00
312 Steve Yzerman SP 1.50 4.00
313 Phil Esposito SP 1.00 2.50
314 Tony Esposito SP 1.00 2.50
315 Ray Bourque SP 1.00 2.50
316 Luc Robitaille SP 1.00 2.50
317 Al MacInnis SP 1.00 2.50
318 Brian Leetch SP 1.00 2.50
319 Steven Stamkos SP 1.00 2.50
320 Grant Fuhr SP 1.00 2.50
321 Marc-Andre Fleury SP 1.00 2.50
322 Bobby Hull SP 1.00 2.50
323 Gilbert Perreault SP 1.00 2.50
324 Guy Lafleur SP 1.00 2.50
325 Joe Mullen SP 1.00 2.50
326 Lanny McDonald SP 1.00 2.50
327 Dale Hawerchuk SP 1.00 2.50
328 Denis Potvin SP 1.00 2.50
329 Dino Ciccarelli SP 1.00 2.50
330 Glenn Anderson SP 1.00 2.50

2010 Upper Deck World of Sports All-Sport Apparel Memorabilia

STATED ODDS ONE PER BOX
ASA33 John Tavares 5.00 12.00
ASA34 Sidney Crosby 12.00 30.00
ASA35 Wayne Gretzky 25.00 60.00
ASA36 Lanny McDonald 4.00 10.00
ASA37 Dale Hawerchuk 5.00 12.00
ASA38 Stefan Della Rovere 5.00 12.00
ASA39 Ryan Ellis 6.00 15.00
ASA40 Colten Teubert 4.00 10.00

2010 Upper Deck World of Sports All-Sport Apparel Memorabilia Autographs

OVERALL AUTO ODDS TWO PER BOX
STATED PRINT RUN 25 SER.#'d SETS
ASA33 John Tavares
ASA34 Sidney Crosby
ASA35 Wayne Gretzky
ASA36 Lanny McDonald
ASA37 Dale Hawerchuk
ASA38 Stefan Della Rovere
ASA39 Ryan Ellis
ASA40 Colten Teubert 10.00 25.00

2010 Upper Deck World of Sports Athletes of the World Autographs

OVERALL AUTO ODDS TWO PER BOX
AW91 Billy Smith 4.00 10.00
AW92 Dominik Hasek 10.00 25.00
AW93 Harry Howell 8.00 20.00
AW94 Elmer Lach 10.00 25.00
AW95 Jacques Lemaire
AW96 Igor Larionov
AW97 Jeremy Roenick 15.00 40.00
AW98 Michael Peca 6.00 15.00

2010 Upper Deck World of Sports Autographs

OVERALL AUTO ODDS TWO PER BOX
182 Stefan Della Rovere 5.00 12.00
188 Erik Gudbranson
191 Taylor Hall
192 Scott Glennie 5.00 12.00
193 Calvin de Haan 5.00 12.00
195 Ryan Ellis 12.00 30.00
198 Colten Teubert 5.00 12.00
236 Jennifer Botterill
237 Cassie Campbell 25.00 50.00
238 Cammi Granato 10.00 25.00
242 Julie Chu 6.00 15.00
246 Natalie Darwitz 6.00 15.00
303 Taylor Hall
304 Sidney Crosby 100.00 175.00
305 Wayne Gretzky
306 Bobby Orr
307 John Tavares
308 Mark Messier 25.00 50.00
309 Gordie Howe 60.00 120.00
310 Mario Lemieux
311 Patrick Roy
312 Steve Yzerman 40.00 80.00
313 Phil Esposito 15.00 30.00
314 Tony Esposito
315 Ray Bourque
316 Luc Robitaille
317 Al MacInnis
318 Brian Leetch
320 Grant Fuhr
321 Marc-Andre Fleury
322 Bobby Hull
323 Gilbert Perreault
324 Guy Lafleur 15.00 30.00
325 Joe Mullen
326 Lanny McDonald
327 Dale Hawerchuk 10.00 25.00
328 Denis Potvin
330 Glenn Anderson

2010 Upper Deck World of Sports Clear Competitors

STATED ODDS ONE PER BOX
STATED PRINT RUN 550 SER.#'d SETS
CC15 Sidney Crosby 5.00 12.00
CC16 Wayne Gretzky 12.00 30.00
CC17 Mark Messier 5.00 12.00
CC18 Taylor Hall 6.00 15.00
CC19 Patrick Roy 6.00 15.00
CC20 Steve Yzerman 5.00 12.00
CC21 John Tavares 4.00 10.00
CC22 Steven Stamkos 4.00 10.00
CC32 Cassie Campbell 3.00 8.00

2011 Upper Deck World of Sports

COMPLETE SET (400) 75.00 150.00
COMP.SET w/o SPs (300) 25.00 60.00
143 Sidney Crosby 1.00 2.50
144 Scott Niedermayer .15 .40
145 Bobby Hull .40 1.00
146 Joe Sakic .25 .60
147 Grant Fuhr .25 .60
148 Ron Francis .15 .40
149 Wayne Gretzky 2.00 5.00
150 Mike Gartner .15 .40
151 Dale Hawerchuk .15 .40
152 Al MacInnis .15 .40
153 Jaden Schwartz .25 .60
154 Gilbert Perreault .25 .60
155 Doug Wilson .15 .40
156 Greg McKegg .15 .40
157 Boone Jenner .15 .40
158 Dougie Hamilton .40 1.00
159 Brett Ritchie .15 .40
160 Matt Puempel .15 .40
161 Glenn Anderson .15 .40
162 Ron Hextall .25 .60
163 Brent Sutter .15 .40
164 Bill Ranford .15 .40
165 Curtis Joseph .25 .60
166 Ed Belfour .25 .60
167 Trevor Linden .15 .40
168 Nathan Beaulieu .15 .40
169 Neal Broten .15 .40
170 Jamie Oleksiak .15 .40
171 Ty Rattie .15 .40
172 Brendan Gallagher .40 1.00
173 Lucas Lessio .15 .40
174 Michael Bournival .15 .40
354 Bobby Clarke SP 1.00 2.50
355 Luc Robitaille SP 1.00 2.50
356 Mario Lemieux SP 1.25 3.00
357 Ray Bourque SP 1.00 2.50
358 Mark Messier SP 1.00 2.50
359 Mike Bossy SP 1.00 2.50
360 Larry Robinson SP 1.00 2.50
361 Denis Potvin SP 1.00 2.50
362 Phil Esposito SP 1.00 2.50
363 Brendan Shanahan SP 1.00 2.50
364 Darryl Sittler SP 1.00 2.50
365 Paul Coffey SP 1.00 2.50
366 Guy Lafleur SP 1.00 2.50
367 Doug Gilmour SP 1.00 2.50
368 Wayne Gretzky SP 2.00 5.00
369 Sidney Crosby SP 1.25 3.00
370 Bobby Orr SP 1.00 2.50
371 Gordie Howe SP 1.25 3.00
372 Cammi Granato SP 1.00 2.50
373 Eric Lindros SP 1.00 2.50
374 Patrick Roy SP 1.25 3.00

2011 Upper Deck World of Sports All-Sport Apparel Memorabilia

VERALL AUTO/MEM ODDS 3 PER BOX

Card	Low	High
SDH Dale Hawerchuk	4.00	10.00
SEL Eric Lindros	6.00	15.00

2011 Upper Deck World of Sports Athletes of the World Autographs

VERALL AUTO/MEM ODDS 3 PER BOX

Card	Low	High
WAR Alexander Radulov	6.00	15.00
WMN Markus Naslund	4.00	10.00
WPE Michael Peca	5.00	12.00

2011 Upper Deck World of Sports Autographs

Card	Low	High
43 Sidney Crosby A	75.00	125.00
44 Scott Niedermayer B	6.00	15.00
45 Bobby Hull B	20.00	40.00
46 Joe Sakic A		
47 Grant Fuhr B		
48 Ron Francis A		
49 Wayne Gretzky A		
50 Mike Gartner B	20.00	40.00
51 Dale Hawerchuk B	6.00	15.00
52 Al MacInnis C	10.00	25.00
53 Jaden Schwartz C	5.00	12.00
54 Gilbert Perreault B		
55 Doug Wilson C	5.00	12.00
61 Glenn Anderson A		
62 Ron Hextall C	20.00	40.00
64 Bill Ranford B		
65 Curtis Joseph		
54 Bobby Clarke A		
55 Luc Robitaille A		
56 Mario Lemieux A		
57 Ray Bourque B	25.00	50.00
58 Mark Messier A		
59 Mike Bossy A		
60 Larry Robinson A		
61 Denis Potvin A		
62 Phil Esposito A		
64 Darryl Sittler A		
65 Paul Coffey B		
67 Doug Gilmour B	12.00	30.00
68 Wayne Gretzky A		
69 Sidney Crosby A	75.00	125.00
70 Bobby Orr B	60.00	120.00
71 Gordie Howe B	75.00	150.00
72 Cammi Granato B	4.00	10.00
73 Eric Lindros		

1980 USA Olympic Team Mini Pics

Cards measure 1 3/4" x 2 3/4". Card fronts feature a black and white photo, players name, and position. Card backs feature card number and the words MINI PICS and 1980 GOLD MEDAL WINNERS.

Card	Low	High
COMPLETE SET (15)	25.00	50.00
1 Jim Craig	5.00	10.00
2 Mike Eruzione	5.00	10.00
3 John Harrington	.75	2.00
4 Mark Johnson	1.25	3.00
5 Rob McClanahan	.75	2.00
6 Jack O'Callahan	.75	2.00
7 Phil Verchota	.75	2.00
8 Bob Suter	.75	2.00
9 Eric Strobel	.75	2.00
10 Dave Silk	.75	2.00
11 Mike Ramsey	1.25	3.00
12 Marty Pavelich	.75	2.00
13 Steve Christoff	1.25	3.00
14 Dave Christian	1.25	3.00
15 Herb Brooks CO	2.50	5.00
NNO Score Card	2.50	5.00

1980 USSR Olympic Team Mini Pics

Cards measure 1 3/4" x 2 3/4". Card fronts feature a black and white photo, players name, and position. Card backs feature card number and the words MINI PICS.

Card	Low	High
COMPLETE SET (10)	17.50	35.00
1 Juri Fedorov	.75	2.00
2 Irek Gimayev	.75	2.00
3 Alexander Golikov	.75	2.00
4 Sergei Kapustin	.75	2.00
5 V.Kovin	.75	2.00
6 Boris Mikhailov	2.50	5.00
7 V.Myshkin	2.50	5.00
8 Vladimir Petrov	2.50	5.00
9 Vladislav Tretiak	5.00	10.00
10 Valeri Vasilijev	2.50	5.00

1983-84 Vachon

This set of 140 standard-size cards was issued by Vachon Foods as panels of two cards. The set includes players from the seven Canadian NHL teams. The cards were also available as a set directly from Vachon. The first printing contained an error in that number 96 pictures Peter Ihnacek instead of Walt Poddubny. The error was corrected for the second printing. The card backs are written in French and English. The Vachon logo is on the front of every card in the lower right corner. The set is difficult to collect in uncut panels of two; the prices below are for individual cards, the panel prices are 50 percent greater than the prices listed below.

Card	Low	High
COMPLETE SET (140)	80.00	200.00
1 Paul Baxter	.30	.75
2 Ed Beers	.20	.50
3 Steve Bozek	.20	.50
4 Mike Eaves	.20	.50
5 Don Edwards	.40	1.00
6 Kari Eloranta	.20	.50
7 Dave Hindmarch	.20	.50
8 Jamie Hislop	.20	.50
9 Steve Konroyd	.20	.50
10 Reggie Lemelin	.40	1.00
11 Hakan Loob	.75	2.00
12 Jamie Macoun	.20	.50
13 Lanny McDonald	1.25	3.00
14 Kent Nilsson	.75	2.00
15 Colin Patterson	.20	.50
16 Jim Peplinski	.40	1.00
17 Paul Reinhart	.40	1.00
18 Doug Risebrough	.40	1.00
19 Steve Tambellini	.20	.50
20 Mickey Volcan	.20	.50
21 Glenn Anderson	1.50	4.00
22 Paul Coffey	5.00	12.00
23 Lee Fogolin	.20	.50
24 Grant Fuhr	2.00	5.00
25 Randy Gregg	.20	.50
26 Wayne Gretzky	20.00	50.00
27 Charlie Huddy	.30	.75
28 Pat Hughes	.20	.50
29 Dave Hunter	.20	.50
30 Don Jackson	.20	.50
31 Jari Kurri	3.00	8.00
32 Willy Lindstrom	.20	.50
33 Ken Linseman	.30	.75
34 Kevin Lowe	.60	1.50
35 Dave Lumley	.20	.50
36 Mark Messier	10.00	25.00
37 Andy Moog	2.00	5.00
38 Jaroslav Pouzar	.20	.50
39 Tom Roulston	.20	.50
40 Dave Semenko	.30	.75
41 Guy Carbonneau	1.25	3.00
42 Kent Carlson	.20	.50
43 Gilbert Delorme	.20	.50
44 Bob Gainey	.75	2.00
45 Jean Hamel	.20	.50
46 Mark Hunter	.20	.50
47 Guy Lafleur	2.50	6.00
48 Craig Ludwig	.20	.50
49 Pierre Mondou	.20	.50
50 Mats Naslund	.75	2.00
51 Chris Nilan	.40	1.00
52 Greg Paslawski	.20	.50
53 Larry Robinson	.75	2.00
54 Richard Sevigny	.40	1.00
55 Steve Shutt	.75	2.00
56 Bobby Smith	.40	1.00
57 Mario Tremblay	.30	.75
58 Ryan Walter	.30	.75
59 Rick Wamsley	.40	1.00
60 Doug Wickenheiser	.20	.50
61 Bo Berglund	.20	.50
62 Dan Bouchard	.40	1.00
63 Alain Cote	.20	.50
64 Brian Ford	.20	.50
65 Michel Goulet	1.00	2.50
66 Dale Hunter	.75	2.00
67 Mario Marois	.30	.75
68 Tony McKegney	.30	.75
69 Randy Moller	.20	.50
70 Wilf Paiement	.40	1.00
71 Pat Price	.20	.50
72 Normand Rochefort	.20	.50
73 Andre Savard	.20	.50
74 Louis Sleigher	.20	.50
75 Anton Stastny	.30	.75
76 Marian Stastny	.30	.75
77 Peter Stastny	2.50	6.00
78 John Van Boxmeer	.20	.50
79 Wally Weir	.20	.50
80 Blake Wesley	.20	.50
81 John Anderson	.30	.75
82 Jim Benning	.20	.50
83 Dan Daoust	.20	.50
84 Bill Derlago	.30	.75
85 Dave Farrish	.20	.50
86 Miroslav Frycer	.20	.50
87 Stewart Gavin	.30	.75
88 Gaston Gingras	.20	.50
89 Billy Harris	.20	.50
90 Peter Inhacak	.40	1.00
91 Jim Korn	.20	.50
92 Terry Martin	.20	.50
93 Dale McCourt	.20	.50
94 Gary Nylund	.20	.50
95 Mike Palmateer	.75	2.00
96A Walt Poddubny ERR (Photo actually Peter Inhacek	4.00	10.00
96B Walt Poddubny COR (With mustache)	1.00	2.50
97 Borje Salming	1.25	3.00
98 Rick St.Croix	.40	1.00
99 Greg P. Terrion	.20	.50
100 Rick Vaive	.40	1.00
101 Richard Brodeur	.60	1.50
102 Jiri Bubla	.20	.50
103 Garth Butcher	.20	.50
104 Ron Delorme	.20	.50
105 John Garrett	.60	1.50
106 Jere Gillis	.20	.50
107 Thomas Gradin	.40	1.00
108 Doug Halward	.20	.50
109 Mark Kirton	.20	.50
110 Rick Lanz	.20	.50
111 Gary Lupul	.20	.50
112 Kevin McCarthy	.20	.50
113 Lars Molin	.20	.50
114 Jim Nill	.20	.50
115 Darcy Rota	.20	.50
116 Stan Smyl	.40	1.00
117 Harold Snepsts	.60	1.50
118 Patrik Sundstrom	.40	1.00
119 Tony Tanti	.40	1.00
120 Tiger Williams	.75	2.00
121 Scott Arniel	.20	.50
122 Dave Babych	.40	1.00
123 Laurie Boschman	.20	.50
124 Wade Campbell	.20	.50
125 Lucien DeBlois	.20	.50
126 Dale Hawerchuk	3.00	8.00
127 Brian Hayward	.40	1.00
128 Jim Kyte	.30	.75
129 Morris Lukowich	.20	.50
130 Bengt Lundholm	.20	.50
131 Paul MacLean	.40	1.00
132 Moe Mantha	.20	.50
133 Andrew McBain	.20	.50
134 Brian Mullen	.20	.50
135 Robert Picard	.20	.50
136 Doug Smail	.40	1.00
137 Doug Soetaert	.40	1.00
138 Thomas Steen	.60	1.50
139 Tim Watters	.20	.50
140 Tim Young	.30	.75

2000-01 Vanguard

In 2000-01 Pacific Vanguard was released as a 151-card set with cards 101-150 released as short-printed cards. The base set design consisted of card fronts that featured laser-etched technology to silhouette the player with silver blending into a team color. The short printed cards were serial numbered to 390.

Card	Low	High
1 Guy Hebert	.25	.60
2 Paul Kariya	.40	1.00
3 Teemu Selanne	.60	1.50
4 Ray Ferraro	.20	.50
5 Damian Rhodes	.20	.50
6 Patrik Stefan	.25	.60
7 Jason Allison	.25	.60
8 Bill Guerin	.30	.75
9 Sergei Samsonov	.25	.60
10 Joe Thornton	.50	1.25
11 Maxim Afinogenov	.20	.50
12 Doug Gilmour	.40	1.00
13 Dominik Hasek	.50	1.25
14 Miroslav Satan	.20	.50
15 Valeri Bure	.25	.60
16 Jarome Iginla	.30	.75
17 Marc Savard	.25	.60
18 Rod Brind'Amour	.30	.75
19 Ron Francis	.40	1.00
20 Arturs Irbe	.25	.60
21 Sami Kapanen	.20	.50
22 Tony Amonte	.25	.60
23 Jocelyn Thibault	.25	.60
24 Alexei Zhamnov	.25	.60
25 Ray Bourque	.50	1.25
26 Chris Drury	.25	.60
27 Peter Forsberg	.40	1.00
28 Milan Hejduk	.25	.60
29 Patrick Roy	.75	2.00
30 Joe Sakic	.50	1.25
31 Geoff Sanderson	.25	.60
32 Ron Tugnutt	.25	.60
33 Ed Belfour	.30	.75
34 Brett Hull	.50	1.25
35 Mike Modano	.50	1.25
36 Joe Nieuwendyk	.30	.75
37 Sergei Fedorov	.50	1.25
38 Nicklas Lidstrom	.30	.75
39 Chris Osgood	.30	.75
40 Brendan Shanahan	.40	1.00
41 Steve Yzerman	1.00	2.50
42 Anson Carter	.25	.60
43 Tommy Salo	.25	.60
44 Doug Weight	.30	.75
45 Pavel Bure	.40	1.00
46 Viktor Kozlov	.25	.60
47 Ray Whitney	.25	.60
48 Ziggy Palffy	.30	.75
49 Luc Robitaille	.30	.75
50 Sergei Krivokrasov	.20	.50
51 Saku Koivu	.30	.75
52 Trevor Linden	.30	.75
53 Jose Theodore	.40	1.00
54 David Legwand	.30	.75
55 Randy Robitaille	.20	.50
56 Jason Arnott	.25	.60
57 Martin Brodeur	.60	1.50
58 Patrik Elias	.30	.75
59 Scott Gomez	.25	.60
60 Alexander Mogilny	.25	.60
61 Tim Connolly	.20	.50
62 Mariusz Czerkawski	.20	.50
63 John Vanbiesbrouck	.25	.60
64 Theo Fleury	.40	1.00
65 Brian Leetch	.30	.75
66 Mark Messier	.50	1.25
67 Mike Richter	.30	.75
68 Daniel Alfredsson	.30	.75
69 Marian Hossa	.25	.60
70 Alexei Yashin	.25	.60
71 Brian Boucher	.25	.60
72 Simon Gagne	.30	.75
73 John LeClair	.30	.75
74 Eric Lindros	.50	1.25
75 Shane Doan	.25	.60
76 Jeremy Roenick	.30	.75
77 Keith Tkachuk	.30	.75
78 Jean-Sebastien Aubin	.25	.60
79 Jan Hrdina	.20	.50
80 Jaromir Jagr	.75	2.00
81 Martin Straka	.25	.60
82 Al MacInnis	.30	.75
83 Chris Pronger	.25	.60
84 Roman Turek	.25	.60
85 Pierre Turgeon	.30	.75
86 Vincent Damphousse	.25	.60
87 Jeff Friesen	.20	.50
88 Owen Nolan	.30	.75
89 Mike Johnson	.20	.50
90 Vincent Lecavalier	.25	.60
91 Nik Antropov	.25	.60
92 Tie Domi	.50	1.25
93 Curtis Joseph	.40	1.00
94 Mats Sundin	.30	.75
95 Andrew Cassels	.20	.50
96 Markus Naslund	.25	.60
97 Felix Potvin	.50	1.25
98 Peter Bondra	.25	.60
99 Olaf Kolzig	.30	.75
100 Adam Oates	.30	.75
101 Samuel Pahlsson	1.25	3.00
102 Jonas Ronnqvist RC	1.25	3.00
103 Milan Hnilicka	1.25	3.00
104 Andrew Raycroft RC	3.00	8.00
105 Dimitri Kalinin	1.25	3.00
106 Mika Noronen	1.25	3.00
107 Oleg Saprykin	1.25	3.00
108 Josef Vasicek RC	3.00	8.00
109 Shane Willis	1.25	3.00
110 Steve McCarthy	1.25	3.00
111 David Aebischer RC	2.50	6.00
112 Serge Aubin RC	1.50	4.00
113 Marc Denis	1.50	4.00
114 Rostislav Klesla RC	3.00	8.00
115 David Vyborny	1.25	3.00
116 Tyler Bouck RC	1.25	3.00
117 Marty Turco RC	2.50	6.00
118 Joaquin Gage	1.25	3.00
119 Michel Riesen RC	1.50	4.00
120 Brian Swanson RC	1.25	3.00
121 Roberto Luongo	3.00	8.00
122 Ivan Novoseltsev	1.25	3.00
123 Eric Belanger RC	1.50	4.00
124 Steven Reinprecht RC	2.00	5.00
125 Lubomir Visnovsky RC	2.50	6.00
126 Manny Fernandez	1.50	4.00
127 Marian Gaborik RC	4.00	10.00
128 Filip Kuba	1.25	3.00
129 Mathieu Garon	1.25	3.00
130 Andrei Markov	2.50	6.00
131 Scott Hartnell RC	3.00	8.00
132 Colin White RC	1.25	3.00
133 Rick DiPietro RC	5.00	12.00
134 Taylor Pyatt	1.25	3.00
135 Martin Havlat RC	4.00	10.00
136 Jani Hurme RC	1.25	3.00
137 Roman Cechmanek RC	1.50	4.00
138 Justin Williams RC	3.00	8.00
139 Robert Esche	1.25	3.00
140 Wyatt Smith	1.25	3.00
141 Ossi Vaananen RC	1.50	4.00
142 Milan Kraft	1.25	3.00
143 Brent Johnson	1.50	4.00
144 Ladislav Nagy	1.25	3.00
145 Evgeni Nabokov	1.50	4.00
146 Sheldon Keefe	1.25	3.00
147 Brad Richards	2.00	5.00
148 Petr Svoboda RC	1.50	4.00
149 Daniel Sedin	4.00	10.00
150 Henrik Sedin	3.00	8.00
151 Mario Lemieux	1.00	2.50

2000-01 Vanguard Holographic Gold

These cards were randomly inserted into packs of 2000-01 Pacific Vanguard retail at a rate of 1:25. These 100 cards were a parallel to the base set of Vanguard, and they were serial numbered to 60.

*1-151 VETS/60: 3X TO 8X BASIC CARDS

2000-01 Vanguard Holographic Purple

These cards were randomly inserted into packs of 2000-01 Pacific Vanguard hobby at a rate of 1:24. These 100 cards were a parallel to the base set of Vanguard, and they were serial numbered to 105.

*1-151 VETS/105: 2.5X TO 6X BASIC CARDS

2000-01 Vanguard Premiere Date

These cards were random inserts in 2000-01 Pacific Vanguard. This parallel set had the serial numbers on the bottom right corner on the front of the card. The cards were serial numbered to 100.

*1-150 VETS/100: 2.5X TO 6X BASIC CARDS

2000-01 Vanguard Cosmic Force

Randomly inserted in packs at a rate of 1:73, this 10-card set featured some of the top players from the NHL. The card design had a foilboard card front and used 30-point styrene. There was a photo of the players head over laying a full body photo faintly seen in the background.

Card	Low	High
COMPLETE SET (10)	30.00	80.00
1 Paul Kariya	2.50	6.00
2 Dominik Hasek	4.00	10.00
3 Peter Forsberg	4.00	10.00
4 Patrick Roy	10.00	25.00
5 Steve Yzerman	8.00	20.00
6 Pavel Bure	2.50	6.00
7 Martin Brodeur	6.00	15.00
8 Eric Lindros	2.50	6.00
9 Jaromir Jagr	4.00	10.00
10 Curtis Joseph	2.50	6.00

2000-01 Vanguard Dual Game-Worn Jerseys

These cards were inserted into packs of Pacific Vanguard at a rate of 2 per box. The 20-card set featured the some of the top players from the NHL. The cards featured 2 jersey swatches per card, one on the front and one on the back. The cards were highlighted with silver-foil markings and each was serial numbered.

STATED PRINT RUN 50-1500

Card	Low	High
1 J.Thrnton S.Samsnov/1500	6.00	15.00
2 P.Forsberg/M.Sundin/125	20.00	50.00
3 J.Sakic/E.Lindros/250	15.00	40.00
4 D.Hatcher/M.Modano/1500	6.00	15.00
5 B.Shanahan/C.Chelios/1500	6.00	15.00
6 S.Fedorov/C.Osgood/400	8.00	20.00
7 D.Weight/R.Smyth/1500	6.00	15.00
8 B.Holik/M.Czerkawski/1500	6.00	15.00
9 Vanbiesbrouck/Richter/50	25.00	60.00
10 A.Zhamnov/C.Stillman/1500	6.00	15.00
11 C.Ronning/V.Ychmnev/1500	6.00	15.00
12 T.Fitzgerald/K.Timonen/1400	6.00	15.00
13 B.Dafoe/D.McCarty/1400	6.00	15.00
14 K.McLarn/D.Sweeny/1400	6.00	15.00
15 J.Lehtinen/J.Lngnbrnnr/400	6.00	15.00
16 E.Daze/M.McInnis/300	6.00	15.00
17 A.Dackell/U.Dahlen/400	6.00	15.00
18 S.Corson/J.Hackett/400	6.00	15.00
19 C.Terreri/G.Hebert/400	6.00	15.00
20 S.Niedrmyr/M.Lapointe/400	6.00	15.00

2000-01 Vanguard Dual Game-Worn Patches

The 20-card set featured the some of the top players from the NHL. The cards featured 2 jersey-patch swatches per card, one on the front and one on the back. The cards were highlighted with silver-foil markings. The cards were serial numbered and the print runs vary, please see below for actual print runs. Note that card 9 does not exist.

Card	Low	High
1 J.Thornton/S.Samsnov/300	20.00	50.00
2 P.Forsberg/M.Sundin/100	40.00	100.00
3 J.Sakic/E.Lindros/100	25.00	60.00
4 D.Hatcher/M.Modano/300	15.00	40.00
5 B.Shanahan/C.Chelios/125	25.00	60.00
6 S.Fedorov/C.Osgood/25		
7 D.Weight/R.Smyth/300	10.00	25.00
8 B.Holik/M.Czerkawski/300	10.00	25.00
10 A.Zhamnov/C.Stillman/300	10.00	25.00
11 C.Ronning/V.Yachmnev/300	10.00	25.00
12 T.Fitzgerald/K.Timonen/300	10.00	25.00
13 B.Dafoe/D.McCarty/300	10.00	25.00
14 K.McLaren/D.Sweeney/300	10.00	25.00
15 J.Lehtinen/J.Langnbrnnr/100	10.00	25.00
16 E.Daze/M.McInnis/15		
17 A.Dackell/U.Dahlen/75	10.00	25.00
18 S.Corson/J.Hackett/75	10.00	25.00
19 C.Terreri/G.Hebert/75	10.00	25.00
20 S.Niedrmyr/M.Lapointe/100	10.00	25.00

2000-01 Vanguard High Voltage

These cards were randomly inserted in 2000-01 Pacific Vanguard at a rate of 1:1. The set consisted of 36 cards that featured some of the most prolific player from the NHL. Four different colored parallels were also created and randomly inserted. Parallel values can be found by using the multipliers below. Red parallels were serial numbered out of 299, gold parallels were serial numbered out of 199, green parallels were serial numbered out of 99, and silver parallels were serial numbered to just 10. Silver parallels are not priced due to scarcity.

Card	Low	High
COMPLETE SET (36)	8.00	20.00
*RED/299: 1.5X TO 4X BASIC INSERTS		
*GOLD/199: 2.5X TO 6X BASIC INSERTS		
*GREEN/99: 3X TO 8X BASIC INSERTS		
1 Paul Kariya	.30	.75
2 Teemu Selanne	.30	.75
3 Joe Thornton	.40	1.00
4 Jason Allison	.25	.60
5 Dominik Hasek	.60	1.50
6 Ray Bourque	.60	1.50
7 Peter Forsberg	.75	2.00
8 Patrick Roy	1.50	4.00
9 Joe Sakic	.60	1.50
10 Ed Belfour	.30	.75
11 Brett Hull	.40	1.00
12 Mike Modano	.50	1.25
13 Brendan Shanahan	.30	.75
14 Steve Yzerman	1.50	4.00
15 Doug Weight	.25	.60
16 Pavel Bure	.30	.75
17 Zigmund Palffy	.25	.60
18 Marian Gaborik	2.00	5.00
19 Martin Brodeur	.75	2.00
20 Scott Gomez	.25	.60
21 Rick DiPietro	2.00	5.00
22 Theo Fleury	.25	.60
23 Mark Messier	.30	.75
24 Marian Hossa	.30	.75
25 John LeClair	.30	.75
26 Eric Lindros	.30	.75
27 Jeremy Roenick	.40	1.00
28 Keith Tkachuk	.30	.75
29 Jaromir Jagr	.50	1.25
30 Pierre Turgeon	.25	.60
31 Vincent Lecavalier	.30	.75
32 Curtis Joseph	.30	.75
33 Mats Sundin	.30	.75
34 Daniel Sedin	.25	.60
35 Henrik Sedin	.25	.60
36 Peter Bondra	.30	.75

2000-01 Vanguard In Focus

Card	Low	High
COMPLETE SET (20)	20.00	40.00
STATED ODDS 1:25		
1 Paul Kariya	.60	1.50
2 Teemu Selanne	.60	1.50
3 Jason Allison	.50	1.25
4 Ray Bourque	1.25	3.00
5 Peter Forsberg	1.50	4.00
6 Patrick Roy	3.00	8.00
7 Brett Hull	.75	2.00
8 Sergei Fedorov	1.25	3.00
9 Steve Yzerman	3.00	8.00
10 Pavel Bure	.75	2.00
11 Marian Gaborik	3.00	8.00
12 Martin Brodeur	1.50	4.00
13 Theo Fleury	.50	1.25
14 John LeClair	.75	2.00
15 Jaromir Jagr	1.00	2.50
16 Vincent Lecavalier	.60	1.50
17 Curtis Joseph	.60	1.50
18 Mats Sundin	.60	1.50
19 Daniel Sedin	.50	1.25
20 Henrik Sedin	.50	1.25

2000-01 Vanguard Press East/West

Randomly inserted in packs of 2000-01 Pacific Vanguard, this 20-card set featured some of the top players from the NHL split into hobby-only cards and retail-only cards. The split was done on an East/West basis, the West players are hobby-only and the East players were retail-only. They were found in packs at a rate of 2:25 for either distribution channel.

Card	Low	High
COMPLETE SET (20)	30.00	60.00
1 Paul Kariya	.60	1.50
2 Teemu Selanne	.60	1.50
3 Peter Forsberg	1.50	4.00
4 Patrick Roy	3.00	8.00
5 Brett Hull	.75	2.00
6 Sergei Fedorov	1.25	3.00
7 Steve Yzerman	3.00	8.00
8 Zigmund Palffy	.50	1.25
9 Jeremy Roenick	.75	2.00
10 Pierre Turgeon	.50	1.25
11 Joe Thornton	2.50	6.00
12 Dominik Hasek	3.00	8.00
13 Pavel Bure	2.00	5.00
14 Martin Brodeur	4.00	10.00
15 Mark Messier	2.00	5.00
16 Alexei Yashin	1.50	4.00
17 Eric Lindros	1.50	4.00
18 Jaromir Jagr	2.50	6.00
19 Vincent Lecavalier	1.50	4.00
20 Curtis Joseph	1.50	4.00

2001-02 Vanguard

Released in early-February 2002, this 130-card set consisted of 100 regular base cards and 30 cards of first year players serial-numbered to 404 copies each.

Card	Low	High
1 Jeff Friesen	.20	.50
2 Paul Kariya	.40	1.00
3 Dany Heatley	.30	.75
4 Milan Hnilicka	.25	.60
5 Byron Dafoe	.25	.60
6 Glen Murray	.25	.60
7 Sergei Samsonov	.25	.60
8 Joe Thornton	.40	1.00
9 Martin Biron	.25	.60
10 Tim Connolly	.20	.50
11 J-P Dumont	.20	.50
12 Jarome Iginla	.30	.75
13 Marc Savard	.20	.50
14 Roman Turek	.25	.60
15 Ron Francis	.40	1.00
16 Arturs Irbe	.25	.60
17 Jeff O'Neill	.20	.50
18 Tony Amonte	.25	.60
19 Mark Bell	.20	.50
20 Kyle Calder	.20	.50
21 Eric Daze	.25	.60
22 Jocelyn Thibault	.25	.60
23 Rob Blake	.30	.75
24 Chris Drury	.25	.60
25 Milan Hejduk	.25	.60
26 Patrick Roy	.75	2.00
27 Joe Sakic	.50	1.25
28 Alex Tanguay	.25	.60
29 Rostislav Klesla	.20	.50
30 Ron Tugnutt	.25	.60
31 Ed Belfour	.30	.75
32 Mike Modano	.50	1.25
33 Pierre Turgeon	.30	.75
34 Sergei Fedorov	.50	1.25
35 Dominik Hasek	.50	1.25
36 Brett Hull	.40	1.00
37 Brendan Shanahan	.40	1.00
38 Steve Yzerman	1.00	2.50
39 Mike Comrie	.25	.60
40 Tommy Salo	.25	.60
41 Ryan Smyth	.25	.60
42 Pavel Bure	.40	1.00
43 Roberto Luongo	.50	1.25
44 Jason Allison	.25	.60
45 Zigmund Palffy	.30	.75
46 Felix Potvin	.50	1.25
47 Manny Fernandez	.25	.60
48 Marian Gaborik	.50	1.25
49 Doug Gilmour	.40	1.00
50 Yanic Perreault	.20	.50
51 Brian Savage	.20	.50
52 Jose Theodore	.30	.75
53 Mike Dunham	.25	.60
54 David Legwand	.25	.60
55 Jason Arnott	.25	.60
56 Martin Brodeur	.60	1.50
57 Patrik Elias	.30	.75
58 Rick DiPietro	.25	.60
59 Chris Osgood	.30	.75
60 Mark Parrish	.20	.50
61 Michael Peca	.25	.60
62 Alexei Yashin	.25	.60
63 Brian Leetch	.30	.75
64 Eric Lindros	.50	1.25
65 Mark Messier	.50	1.25
66 Mike Richter	.30	.75
67 Daniel Alfredsson	.30	.75
68 Martin Havlat	.25	.60
69 Marian Hossa	.25	.60
70 Patrick Lalime	.25	.60
71 Pavel Brendl	.20	.50
72 Roman Cechmanek	.25	.60
73 John LeClair	.30	.75
74 Jeremy Roenick	.30	.75
75 Sean Burke	.20	.50
76 Shane Doan	.25	.60
77 Daymond Langkow	.25	.60
78 Kris Beech	.20	.50
79 Johan Hedberg	.25	.60
80 Mario Lemieux	1.00	2.50
81 Brent Johnson	.25	.60
82 Chris Pronger	.25	.60
83 Keith Tkachuk	.30	.75
84 Doug Weight	.30	.75
85 Patrick Marleau	.30	.75
86 Evgeni Nabokov	.25	.60
87 Owen Nolan	.30	.75
88 Teemu Selanne	.60	1.50
89 Vincent Lecavalier	.25	.60
90 Brad Richards	.30	.75
91 Martin St. Louis	.30	.75
92 Curtis Joseph	.30	.75
93 Alexander Mogilny	.25	.60
94 Mats Sundin	.30	.75
95 Dan Cloutier	.25	.60
96 Brendan Morrison	.25	.60
97 Markus Naslund	.30	.75
98 Peter Bondra	.30	.75
99 Jaromir Jagr	.75	2.00
100 Olaf Kolzig	.30	.75
101 Ilja Bryzgalov RC	2.50	6.00
102 Timo Parssinen RC	1.25	3.00
103 Ilya Kovalchuk RC	5.00	12.00
104 Brian Pothier RC	1.00	2.50
105 Jukka Hentunen RC	1.00	2.50
106 Erik Cole RC	2.00	5.00
107 Vaclav Nedorost RC	1.00	2.50
108 Niko Kapanen RC	1.50	4.00
109 Pavel Datsyuk RC	5.00	12.00
110 Jason Chimera RC	1.00	2.50
111 Ty Conklin RC	1.50	4.00
112 Jussi Markkanen SP	1.00	2.50
113 Niklas Hagman RC	1.25	3.00
114 Kristian Huselius RC	1.50	4.00
115 Jaroslav Bednar RC	1.00	2.50
116 Pascal Dupuis RC	1.50	4.00
117 Nick Schultz RC	1.00	2.50
118 Martin Erat RC	1.50	4.00
119 Andreas Salomonsson RC	1.00	2.50
120 Radek Martinek RC	1.00	2.50
121 Raffi Torres RC	1.50	4.00
122 Dan Blackburn RC	1.25	3.00
123 Chris Neil RC	1.25	3.00
124 Jiri Dopita RC	1.00	2.50
125 David Cullen RC	1.00	2.50
126 Krystofer Kolanos RC	1.00	2.50
127 Mark Rycroft RC	1.25	3.00
128 Jeff Jillson RC	1.00	2.50
129 Nikita Alexeev RC	1.00	2.50
130 Brian Sutherby RC	1.00	2.50

2001-02 Vanguard Blue

Inserted in 1:49 hobby and 1:25 retail packs, this 130-card set paralleled the base set with blue foil highlights replacing the silver. Each card was serial-numbered out of 89.

*1-100 VETS: 3X TO 8X BASIC CARDS
*101-130 ROOK: .3X TO .8X BASIC RC/404

2001-02 Vanguard Premiere Date

Randomly inserted into hobby packs, this 130-card set paralleled the base set but each card carried a "Premier Date" stamp on the card front. Cards from this set were serial-numbered to 83 copies each.

*1-100 VETS: 3X TO 8X BASIC CARDS
*101-130 ROOK: .3X TO .8X BASIC RC/404

2001-02 Vanguard Red

Randomly inserted at 1:96 hobby and retail packs, this 130-card set paralleled the base set with red foil replacing the silver. Cards in this set were serial-numbered out of 38.

*1-100 VETS: 5X TO 12X BASIC CARDS
*101-130 ROOK: .4X TO 1X BASIC RC/404

2001-02 Vanguard East Meets West

This 10-card set was randomly inserted at 1:97 packs.

Card	Low	High
COMPLETE SET (10)	15.00	40.00
1 M.Lemieux/J.Jagr	5.00	12.00
2 P.Roy/D.Hasek	5.00	12.00
3 J.Sakic/P.Forsberg	4.00	10.00
4 M.Brodeur/J.Hedberg	4.00	10.00
5 E.Lindros/A.Yashin	2.00	5.00
6 P.Kariya/T.Selanne	2.00	5.00
7 S.Yzerman/S.Fedorov	4.00	10.00
8 B.Shanahan/P.Bure	2.00	5.00
9 J.Iginla/M.Sundin	2.50	6.00
10 C.Pronger/N.Lidstrom	2.00	5.00

2001-02 Vanguard In Focus

This 10-card set was randomly inserted at a rate of 1:481 hobby packs. Each card was serial-numbered to 55 copies each,

Card	Low	High
1 Patrick Roy	15.00	40.00
2 Joe Sakic	12.50	30.00
3 Dominik Hasek	12.50	30.00
4 Brendan Shanahan	10.00	25.00
5 Steve Yzerman	15.00	40.00
6 Pavel Bure	8.00	20.00
7 Martin Brodeur	15.00	40.00
8 Mario Lemieux	20.00	50.00
9 Mats Sundin	8.00	10.00
10 Jaromir Jagr	10.00	25.00

2001-02 Vanguard Memorabilia

This 50-card set featured pieces of game-used equipment. Cards 1-41 and 43-44 carried dual swatches of game jerseys. Card #42 carried a swatch of jersey and a piece of game-used stick. Cards 45-50 carried a piece of the goal net from the NHL All-Star game. Cards 1-44 were inserted at 2:25 hobby and 1:25 retail. Cards 45-50 were inserted at 1:97 hobby packs only.

Card	Low	High
1 P.Kariya/O.Tverdovsky	3.00	8.00
2 P.Kariya/G.Hebert	3.00	8.00
3 S.Samsonov/D.Sweeney	2.50	6.00
4 J.Iginla/M.Savard	3.00	8.00
5 F.Brathwaite/R.Turek	2.50	6.00
6 C.Stillman/C.Conroy	2.50	6.00
7 B.Mironov/M.Nylander	2.50	6.00
8 T.Amonte/S.Sullivan SP	5.00	12.00
9 J.Sakic/P.Forsberg	10.00	20.00
10 P.Roy/J.Sakic	8.00	20.00
11 M.Modano/D.Hatcher	5.00	12.00
12 J.Langenbrunner/D.Sydor	2.50	6.00
13 S.Yzerman/C.Chelios	8.00	20.00
14 N.Lidstrom/S.Fedorov SP	12.00	30.00
15 S.Koivu/T.Selanne	6.00	15.00
16 C.Ronning/V.Yachmenev	2.50	6.00
17 B.Holik/S.Niedermayer SP	2.50	6.00
18 M.Czerkawski/S.Bates	2.50	6.00
19 E.Lindros/P.Brendl	3.00	8.00
20 M.Richter/M.York	10.00	25.00
21 J.Roenick/E.Weinrich	8.00	20.00
22 J.Lehtinen/J.Lumme	2.50	6.00
23 M.Straka/J.Beranek	2.50	6.00
24 J.Hrdina/B.Boughner	2.50	6.00
25 A.Kovalev/D.Kasparaitis	2.50	6.00
26 M.Lemieux/R.Lang	8.00	20.00
27 M.Straka/R.Parent	2.50	6.00
28 D.Drake/M.Eastwood	2.50	6.00
29 J.Hecht/J.McLennan	2.50	6.00
30 P.Turgeon/V.Lecavalier	5.00	12.00
31 J.Dumont/S.Young	2.50	6.00
32 C.Joseph/J.Theodore	8.00	20.00
33 J.Jagr/P.Bondra	10.00	25.00
34 M.Sundin/A.Cassels	3.00	8.00
35 O.Kolzig/D.Cloutier SP	5.00	12.00
36 C.Lapointe/M.Lindgren	2.50	6.00
37 G.DeVries/E.Messier SP	5.00	12.00
38 S.Yzerman/E.Lindros SP	20.00	50.00
39 A.Kovalev/K.Miller	2.50	6.00
40 L.Odelein/A.Savage	2.50	6.00
41 M.Savard/R.Turek	2.50	6.00
42 J.Jagr JSY/I.Kovalchuk STK	12.50	30.00
43 P.Roy/J.Theodore	10.00	25.00
44 M.Lemieux/M.Sundin	10.00	25.00
45 T.Fleury/M.Hossa NET	12.50	30.00
46 B.Hull/P.Bure NET	20.00	50.00
47 D.Weight/P.Forsberg NET	10.00	25.00
48 J.Allsion/Z.Palffy NET	10.00	25.00
49 R.Blake/M.Hejduk NET	10.00	25.00
50 M.Brodeur/D.Hasek NET	25.00	60.00

2001-02 Vanguard Patches

Randomly inserted at 1:97 hobby packs, this 16-card set partially paralleled the base memorabilia set but featured swatches of jersey patches. The set is skip-numbered.

Card	Low	High
3 Samsonov/Sweeney	12.50	30.00
5 Brathwaite/R.Turek	12.50	30.00
6 C.Stillman/C.Conroy	12.50	30.00
10 P.Roy/J.Sakic	20.00	50.00
12 Langenbrunner/Sydor	12.50	30.00
21 J.Roenick/E.Weinrich	20.00	50.00
22 J.Lehtinen/J.Lumme	12.50	30.00
23 M.Straka/J.Beranek	12.50	30.00
25 Kovalev/D.Kasparaitis	12.50	30.00
27 M.Straka/R.Parent	12.50	30.00
28 D.Drake/M.Eastwood	12.50	30.00
33 J.Jagr/P.Bondra	15.00	40.00
37 G.DeVries/E.Messier	12.50	30.00
38 Yzerman/E.Lindros	30.00	80.00
39 A.Kovalev/K.Miller	12.50	30.00
41 M.Savard/R.Turek	12.50	30.00

2001-02 Vanguard Prime Prospects

This 20-card set was randomly inserted at 1:25 packs.

Card	Low	High
COMPLETE SET (20)	15.00	40.00
1 Dany Heatley	3.00	8.00
2 Ilya Kovalchuk	4.00	10.00
3 Vaclav Nedorost	.75	2.00
4 Rostislav Klesla	.75	2.00
5 Pavel Datsyuk	3.00	8.00
6 Mike Comrie	1.25	3.00
7 Kristian Huselius	.75	2.00
8 Jaroslav Bednar	.75	2.00
9 Marian Gaborik	3.00	8.00
10 Martin Erat	.75	2.00
11 Rick DiPietro	2.00	5.00
12 Dan Blackburn	.75	2.00
13 Martin Havlat	2.00	5.00
14 Pavel Brendl	.75	2.00
15 Krystofer Kolanos	.75	2.00
16 Brent Johnson	1.25	3.00
17 Jeff Jillson	.75	2.00
18 Nikita Alexeev	.75	2.00
19 Daniel Sedin	2.00	5.00
20 Henrik Sedin	2.00	5.00

2001-02 Vanguard Quebec Tournament Heroes

Cards from this 20-card set were split distributed. Cards 1-10 were found in packs at 1:25. Cards 11-20 were distributed as giveaways to fans attending the Quebec Tournament in Feb, 2002.

Card	Low	High
COMPLETE HOBBY SET (10)	20.00	40.00
1 Brett Hull	1.25	3.00
2 Mario Lemieux	5.00	12.00
3 Patrick Roy	4.00	10.00
4 Steve Yzerman	4.00	10.00
5 Mike Modano	1.50	4.00
6 Jeremy Roenick	1.25	3.00
7 Brendan Shanahan	1.50	4.00
8 Felix Potvin	1.00	2.50
9 Doug Weight	1.00	2.50
10 Eric Lindros	1.50	4.00
11 Jocelyn Thibault	4.00	10.00
12 Jason Allison	2.00	5.00
13 Chris Drury	2.00	5.00
14 Jeff O'Neill	2.00	5.00
15 Sergei Samsonov	10.00	25.00
16 Alex Tanguay	4.00	10.00
17 Marian Hossa	10.00	25.00
18 Simon Gagne	10.00	25.00
19 Vincent Lecavalier	6.00	15.00
20 Rick DiPietro	6.00	15.00

2001-02 Vanguard Stonewallers

This 20-card set was randomly inserted at 1:49 packs.

Card	Low	High
COMPLETE SET (20)	40.00	80.00
1 Milan Hnilicka	1.25	3.00
2 Byron Dafoe	1.25	3.00
3 Martin Biron	1.25	3.00
4 Roman Turek	1.25	3.00
5 Patrick Roy	6.00	15.00
6 Ed Belfour	1.50	4.00
7 Dominik Hasek	3.00	8.00
8 Tommy Salo	1.25	3.00
9 Roberto Luongo	2.00	5.00
10 Jose Theodore	2.00	5.00
11 Martin Brodeur	4.00	10.00
12 Chris Osgood	1.25	3.00
13 Mike Richter	1.50	4.00
14 Patrick Lalime	1.25	3.00
15 Roman Cechmanek	1.25	3.00
16 Johan Hedberg	1.25	3.00
17 Evgeni Nabokov	1.25	3.00
18 Nikolai Khabibulin	1.50	4.00
19 Curtis Joseph	1.50	4.00
20 Olaf Kolzig	1.25	3.00

2001-02 Vanguard V-Team

This 20-card set was randomly inserted at 1:25 hobby and retail packs. Cards 1-10 were hobby exclusives and cards 11-20 were retail exclusives.

Card	Low	High
COMPLETE SET (20)	12.00	30.00

1 Roman Turek .60 1.50
2 Patrick Roy 4.00 10.00
3 Ed Belfour .75 2.00
4 Dominik Hasek 1.50 4.00
5 Martin Brodeur 2.00 5.00
6 Chris Osgood .60 1.50
7 Roman Cechmanek .60 1.50
8 Johan Hedberg .60 1.50
9 Evgeni Nabokov .60 1.50
10 Curtis Joseph .75 2.00
11 Jarome Iginla 1.00 2.50
12 Joe Sakic 1.50 4.00
13 Brendan Shanahan 1.25 3.00
14 Steve Yzerman 4.00 10.00
15 Pavel Bure 1.00 2.50
16 Eric Lindros 1.25 3.00
17 Mario Lemieux 5.00 12.00
18 Teemu Selanne .75 2.00
19 Mats Sundin .75 2.00
20 Jaromir Jagr 1.25 3.00

2002-03 Vanguard

Released in March, this 136-card set consisted of 100 veteran base cards and 36 shortprinted rookie cards. Rookies were serial-numbered out of 1650. There were 6 cards per pack and 24 packs per box.

1 Jean-Sebastien Giguere .20 .50
2 Paul Kariya .25 .60
3 Steve Rucchin .12 .30
4 Byron Dafoe .15 .40
5 Dany Heatley .20 .50
6 Ilya Kovalchuk .25 .60
7 Glen Murray .15 .40
8 Brian Rolston .15 .40
9 Steve Shields .15 .40
10 Joe Thornton .25 .60
11 Martin Biron .15 .40
12 Chris Gratton .12 .30
13 Jochen Hecht .12 .30
14 Chris Drury .20 .50
15 Jarome Iginla .20 .50
16 Roman Turek .20 .50
17 Rod Brind'Amour .20 .50
18 Ron Francis .25 .60
19 Jeff O'Neill .12 .30
20 Kevin Weekes .15 .40
21 Tyler Arnason .20 .50
22 Eric Daze .12 .30
23 Theo Fleury .25 .60
24 Jocelyn Thibault .15 .40
25 Peter Forsberg .25 .60
26 Milan Hejduk .15 .40
27 Patrick Roy .50 1.25
28 Joe Sakic .30 .75
29 Andrew Cassels .12 .30
30 Marc Denis .15 .40
31 Geoff Sanderson .15 .40
32 Bill Guerin .20 .50
33 Mike Modano .30 .75
34 Marty Turco .20 .50
35 Sergei Fedorov .30 .75
36 Brett Hull .25 .60
37 Curtis Joseph .20 .50
38 Nicklas Lidstrom .20 .50
39 Brendan Shanahan .25 .60
40 Steve Yzerman .40 1.00
41 Anson Carter .15 .40
42 Mike Comrie .20 .50
43 Tommy Salo .15 .40
44 Kristian Huselius .12 .30
45 Olli Jokinen .20 .50
46 Roberto Luongo .30 .75
47 Jason Allison .15 .40
48 Adam Deadmarsh .15 .40
49 Ziggy Palffy .20 .50
50 Felix Potvin .30 .75
51 Andrew Brunette .12 .30
52 Marian Gaborik .30 .75
53 Dwayne Roloson .12 .30
54 Jeff Hackett .15 .40
55 Saku Koivu .20 .50
56 Yanic Perreault .12 .30
57 Jose Theodore .20 .50
58 Andreas Johansson .12 .30
59 David Legwand .15 .40
60 Martin Brodeur .40 1.00
61 Patrik Elias .20 .50
62 Jamie Langenbrunner .15 .40
63 Mark Parrish .12 .30
64 Michael Peca .15 .40
65 Alexei Yashin .15 .40
66 Dan Blackburn .15 .40
67 Pavel Bure .25 .60
68 Eric Lindros .30 .75
69 Daniel Alfredsson .20 .50
70 Marian Hossa .15 .40
71 Patrick Lalime .15 .40
72 Roman Cechmanek .15 .40
73 Simon Gagne .20 .50
74 John LeClair .20 .50
75 Jeremy Roenick .20 .50
76 Tony Amonte .15 .40
77 Brian Boucher .15 .40
78 Mike Johnson .15 .40
79 Johan Hedberg .20 .50
80 Alexei Kovalev .20 .50
81 Mario Lemieux .60 1.50
82 Eric Boguniecki .12 .30
83 Cory Stillman .12 .30
84 Doug Weight .20 .50
85 Evgeni Nabokov .15 .40
86 Owen Nolan .20 .50
87 Teemu Selanne .40 1.00
88 Nikolai Khabibulin .20 .50
89 Vincent Lecavalier .15 .40
90 Martin St. Louis .20 .50
91 Ed Belfour .20 .50
92 Alexander Mogilny .15 .40
93 Mats Sundin .20 .50
94 Todd Bertuzzi .20 .50
95 Dan Cloutier .15 .40
96 Brendan Morrison .15 .40
97 Markus Naslund .15 .40
98 Peter Bondra .20 .50
99 Jaromir Jagr .50 1.25
100 Olaf Kolzig .20 .50
101 Stanislav Chistov RC .60 1.50
102 Martin Gerber RC 1.00 2.50
103 Alexei Smirnov RC .75 2.00
104 Tim Thomas RC 2.50 6.00
105 Ryan Miller RC 4.00 10.00
106 Chuck Kobasew RC .75 2.00
107 Jordan Leopold RC 1.00 2.50
108 Pascal Leclaire RC .75 2.00
109 Rick Nash RC 5.00 12.00
110 Lasse Pirjeta RC .60 1.50
111 Steve Ott RC 1.25 3.00
112 Dmitri Bykov RC .60 1.50
113 Henrik Zetterberg RC 6.00 15.00
114 Ales Hemsky RC 2.50 6.00
115 Jay Bouwmeester RC 2.00 5.00
116 Mike Cammalleri RC 2.00 5.00
117 Alexander Frolov RC 1.25 3.00
118 P-M Bouchard RC 1.00 2.50
119 Stephane Veilleux RC .60 1.50
120 Sylvain Blouin RC .60 1.50
121 Ron Hainsey RC .60 1.50
122 Adam Hall RC .60 1.50
123 Scottie Upshall RC .75 2.00
124 Jason Spezza RC 4.00 10.00
125 Anton Volchenkov RC .60 1.50
126 Dennis Seidenberg RC 1.00 2.50
127 Patrick Sharp RC 2.00 5.00
128 Radovan Somik RC .60 1.50
129 Jeff Taffe RC .60 1.50
130 Dick Tarnstrom RC .60 1.50
131 Tom Koivisto RC .60 1.50
132 Curtis Sanford RC 1.00 2.50
133 Lynn Loyns RC .60 1.50
134 Alexander Svitov RC .60 1.50
135 Carlo Colaiacovo RC 1.00 2.50
136 Steve Eminger RC .60 1.50

2002-03 Vanguard LTD

Inserted at 1:5 hobby, this 136-card set paralleled the base set but each card was serial-numbered to 450.
*1-100 VETS: 3X TO 8X BASIC CARDS
*101-136 ROOKIES: .5X TO 1.2X

2002-03 Vanguard East Meets West

COMPLETE SET (10) 15.00 30.00
STATED ODDS 1:13
1 I.Kovalchuk/M.Naslund 2.00 5.00
2 J.Thornton/J.Iginla 2.50 6.00
3 M.Lemieux/S.Yzerman 4.00 10.00
4 P.Bure/S.Fedorov 2.00 5.00
5 J.LeClair/M.Modano 2.00 5.00
6 M.Sundin/P.Forsberg 2.00 5.00
7 V.Lecavalier/J.Sakic 2.00 5.00
8 M.Hossa/M.Gaborik 2.00 5.00
9 M.Brodeur/P.Roy 4.00 10.00
10 E.Belfour/M.Turco 2.00 5.00

2002-03 Vanguard In Focus

COMPLETE SET (10) 12.00 30.00
STATED ODDS 1:25
1 Paul Kariya 1.25 3.00
2 Ilya Kovalchuk 2.00 5.00
3 Peter Forsberg 2.00 5.00
4 Joe Sakic 2.00 5.00
5 Rick Nash 3.00 8.00
6 Steve Yzerman 4.00 10.00
7 Marian Gaborik 2.00 5.00
8 Jason Spezza 3.00 8.00
9 Mario Lemieux 4.00 10.00
10 Jaromir Jagr 1.50 4.00

2002-03 Vanguard Jerseys

STATED ODDS 3:25
*GOLD/50: 1X TO 2.5X BASIC JSY
1 Adam Oates 2.50 6.00
2 Dany Heatley 5.00 12.00
3 Ilya Kovalchuk 5.00 12.00
4 Patrik Stefan 2.50 6.00
5 Joe Thornton 6.00 15.00
6 J-P Dumont 2.50 6.00
7 Chris Drury 2.50 6.00
8 Jamie McLennan 2.50 6.00
9 Rod Brind'Amour 2.50 6.00
10 Sergei Berezin 2.50 6.00
11 Theo Fleury 3.00 8.00
12 Alexei Zhamnov SP 3.00 8.00
13 Joe Sakic 6.00 15.00
14 Rostislav Klesla 2.50 6.00
15 Mike Modano 6.00 15.00
16 Pierre Turgeon 2.50 6.00
17 Sergei Fedorov 4.00 10.00
18 Brett Hull 4.00 10.00
19 Curtis Joseph 3.00 8.00
20 Ryan Smyth 3.00 8.00
21 Kristian Huselius 2.50 6.00
22 Ziggy Palffy 3.00 8.00
23 Yanic Perreault 2.50 6.00
24 Jose Theodore 4.00 10.00
25 Scott Walker 2.50 6.00
26 Martin Brodeur 10.00 25.00
27 Scott Gomez 2.50 6.00
28 Michael Peca 2.50 6.00
29 Pavel Bure 3.00 8.00
30 Mark Messier 3.00 8.00
31 Daniel Alfredsson 3.00 8.00
32 Patrick Lalime 2.50 6.00
33 Tomi Kallio 2.50 6.00
34 John LeClair 2.50 6.00
35 Krystofer Kolanos 2.50 6.00
36 Johan Hedberg 2.50 6.00
37 Mario Lemieux 12.50 30.00
38 Pavol Demitra 2.50 6.00
39 Keith Tkachuk 2.50 6.00
40 Patrick Marleau 3.00 8.00
41 Evgeni Nabokov 3.00 8.00
42 Nikolai Khabibulin 3.00 8.00
43 Alexander Mogilny 2.50 6.00
44 Gary Roberts 2.50 6.00
45 Darcy Tucker 2.50 6.00
46 Dan Cloutier 2.50 6.00
47 Brendan Morrison 2.50 6.00
48 Markus Naslund 3.00 8.00
49 Peter Bondra 3.00 8.00
50 Jaromir Jagr 6.00 15.00

2002-03 Vanguard Prime Prospects

COMPLETE SET (20) 15.00 40.00
STATED ODDS 1:7
1 Stanislav Chistov .75 2.00
2 Alexei Smirnov .75 2.00
3 Ivan Huml .75 2.00
4 Ryan Miller 2.00 5.00
5 Chuck Kobasew 1.25 3.00
6 Jordan Leopold .75 2.00
7 Tyler Arnason .75 2.00
8 Rick Nash 4.00 10.00
9 Henrik Zetterberg 3.00 8.00
10 Ales Hemsky 1.50 4.00
11 Jay Bouwmeester 1.50 4.00
12 Stephen Weiss .75 2.00
13 Alexander Frolov 1.50 4.00
14 P-M Bouchard 1.50 4.00
15 Scottie Upshall .75 2.00
16 Justin Mapletoft .75 2.00
17 Jamie Lundmark .75 2.00
18 Jason Spezza 3.00 8.00
19 Petr Cajanek .75 2.00
20 Barret Jackman .75 2.00

2002-03 Vanguard Stonewallers

COMPLETE SET (12) 10.00 20.00
STATED ODDS 1:9
1 Patrick Roy 4.00 10.00
2 Marty Turco .60 1.50
3 Curtis Joseph .75 2.00
4 Roberto Luongo 1.00 2.50
5 Felix Potvin .75 2.00
6 Jose Theodore 1.00 2.50
7 Martin Brodeur 2.00 5.00
8 Mike Richter .75 2.00
9 Patrick Lalime .60 1.50
10 Roman Cechmanek .60 1.50
11 Nikolai Khabibulin .75 2.00
12 Ed Belfour .75 2.00

2002-03 Vanguard V-Team

Inserted at odds of 1:25, this 12-card set had split insertion. Cards 1-6 were found in hobby packs while cards 7-12 were found in retail packs.

COMPLETE SET (12) 20.00 40.00
1 Patrick Roy 4.00 10.00
2 Marty Turco .60 1.50
3 Curtis Joseph .75 2.00
4 Jose Theodore 1.00 2.50
5 Martin Brodeur 2.00 5.00
6 Ed Belfour .75 2.00
7 Ilya Kovalchuk 1.00 2.50
8 Joe Thornton 1.25 3.00
9 Joe Sakic 1.50 4.00
10 Steve Yzerman 4.00 10.00
11 Mario Lemieux 5.00 12.00
12 Jaromir Jagr 1.25 3.00

1924-26 V128-1 Paulin's Candy

This 70-card set was issued during the 1923-24 season and featured players from the WCHL. The horizontal back explains how to obtain either a hockey stick or a box of Paulin's chocolates by collecting and sending in the complete Famous Hockey Players set. The cards were to be returned to the collector with the hockey stick or chocolates. The cards are in black and white and measure approximately 1 3/8" by 2 3/4".

COMPLETE SET (70) 4500.00 9000.00
1 Bill Borland 75.00 150.00
2 Pete Speirs 50.00 100.00
3 Jack Hughes 50.00 100.00
4 Errol Gillis 50.00 100.00
5 Cecil Browne 50.00 100.00
6 W. Roberts 50.00 100.00
7 Howard Brandon 50.00 100.00
8 Fred Comfort 50.00 100.00
9 Cliff O'Meara 50.00 100.00
10 Leo Benard 50.00 100.00
11 Lloyd Harvey 50.00 100.00
12 Bobby Connors 50.00 100.00
13 Daddy Dalman 50.00 100.00
14 Dub Mackie 50.00 100.00
15 Lorne Chabot 150.00 300.00
16 Phat Wilson 75.00 125.00
17 Wilf L'Heureux 50.00 100.00
18 Danny Cox 50.00 100.00
19 Bill Brydge 50.00 100.00
20 Alex Gray 50.00 100.00
21 Albert Pudas 50.00 100.00
22 Jack Irwin 50.00 100.00
23 Puss Traub 50.00 100.00
24 Red McCusker 75.00 125.00
25 Jack Asseltine 75.00 125.00
26 Duke Dutkowski 50.00 100.00
27 Charley McVeigh 50.00 100.00
28 George Hay 125.00 250.00
29 Amby Moran 50.00 100.00
30 Barney Stanley 150.00 300.00
31 Art Gagne 50.00 100.00
32 Louis Berlinquette 50.00 100.00
33 P.C. Stevens 50.00 100.00
34 W.D. Elmer 50.00 100.00
35 Bill Cook 200.00 350.00
36 Leo Reise 50.00 100.00
37 Curly Headley 125.00 250.00
38 Newsy Lalonde 350.00 600.00
39 George Hainsworth 350.00 600.00
40 Laurie Scott 50.00 100.00
41 Joe Simpson 200.00 350.00
42 Bob Trapp 50.00 100.00
43 Joe McCormick 50.00 100.00
44 Ty Arbour 50.00 100.00
45 Duke Keats 75.00 125.00
46 Hal Winkler 50.00 100.00
47 Johnny Sheppard 50.00 100.00
48 Crutchy Morrison 50.00 100.00
49 Spunk Sparrow 50.00 100.00
50 Percy McGregor 50.00 100.00
51 Harry Tuckwell 50.00 100.00
52 Chubby Scott 50.00 100.00
53 Scotty Fraser 50.00 100.00
54 Bob Davis 50.00 100.00
55 Clucker White 50.00 100.00
56 Bob Armstrong 50.00 100.00
57 Doc Longtry 50.00 100.00
58 Darb Sommers 50.00 100.00
59 Frank Hacquoil 50.00 100.00
60 Stan Evans 50.00 100.00
61 Ed Oatman 50.00 100.00
62 Red Dutton 250.00 400.00
63 Herb Gardiner 125.00 250.00
64 Bernie Morris 50.00 100.00
65 Bobbie Benson 50.00 100.00
66 Ernie Anderson 50.00 100.00
67 Cully Wilson 50.00 100.00
68 Charlie Reid 75.00 125.00
69 Harry Oliver 125.00 250.00
70 Rusty Crawford 100.00 200.00

1928-29 V128-2 Paulin's Candy

This scarce set of 90 black and white cards was produced and distributed in Western Canada and features Western Canadian teams and players. The cards are numbered on the back and measure approximately 1 3/8" by 2 5/8". The card back details an offer (expiring June 1st, 1929) of a hockey stick prize (or box of chocolates for girls) if someone could bring in a complete set of 90 cards. Players on the Calgary Jimmies are not explicitly identified on the card so they are listed below without a specific player name.

COMPLETE SET (90) 2750.00 5500.00
1 Univ. of Man. Girls Hockey Team 50.00 100.00
2 Elgin Hockey Team 40.00 80.00
3 Brandon Schools Boy Champions 40.00 80.00
4 Port Arthur Hockey Team 40.00 80.00
5 Enderby Hockey Team 40.00 80.00
6 Humboldt High School Team 40.00 80.00
7 Regina Collegiate Hockey Team 40.00 80.00
8 Weyburn Beavers 40.00 80.00
9 Moose Jaw College Junior Hockey Team 50.00 100.00
10 M.A.C. Junior Hockey 40.00 80.00
11 Vermillion Agri-cultural School 40.00 80.00
12 Rovers& Cranbrook B.C. 40.00 80.00
13 Empire School& Moose Jaw 40.00 80.00
14 Arts Senior Hockey 40.00 80.00
15 Juvenile Varsity Hockey 40.00 80.00
16 St. Peter's College Hockey 40.00 80.00
17 Arts Girls Hockey 50.00 100.00
18 Swan River Hockey Team 40.00 80.00
19 U.M.S.U. Junior Hockey Team 40.00 80.00
20 Campion College Hockey Team 50.00 100.00
21 Drinkwater Hockey Team 40.00 80.00
22 Elks Hockey Team Biggar, Saskatchewan 40.00 80.00
23 South Calgary High School 40.00 80.00
24 Meota Hockey 40.00 80.00
25 Chartered Accountants 50.00 100.00
26 Nutana Collegiate Hockey Team 40.00 80.00
27 MacLeod Hockey Team 50.00 100.00
28 Arts Junior Hockey 40.00 80.00
29 Fort William Juniors 40.00 80.00
30 Swan Lake Hockey Team 40.00 80.00
31 Dauphin Hockey Team 40.00 80.00
32 Mount Royal Hockey Team 40.00 80.00
33 Port Arthur W. End Junior Hockey 40.00 80.00
34 Hanna Hockey Club 40.00 80.00
35 Vermillion Junior Hockey 40.00 80.00
36 Smithers Hockey Team 40.00 80.00
37 Lloydminster High School 40.00 80.00
38 Winnipeg Rangers 50.00 100.00
39 Delisle Intermediate Hockey 40.00 80.00
40 Moose Jaw College Senior Hockey 40.00 80.00
41 Art Bonneyman 25.00 50.00
42 Jimmy Graham 25.00 50.00
43 Pat O'Hunter 25.00 50.00
44 Leo Moret 25.00 50.00
45 Blondie McLennen 25.00 50.00
46 Red Beattie 40.00 80.00
47 Frank Peters 40.00 80.00
48 Lloyd McIntyre 25.00 50.00
49 Art Somers 40.00 80.00
50 Ikey Morrison 25.00 50.00
51 Calgary Jimmies 25.00 50.00
52 Don Cummings 25.00 50.00
53 Calgary Jimmies 25.00 50.00
54 P. Gerlitz 25.00 50.00
55 A. Kay 25.00 50.00
56 Paul Runge 40.00 80.00
57 J. Gerlitz 25.00 50.00
58 H. Gerlitz 25.00 50.00
59 C. Biles 25.00 50.00
60 Jimmy Evans 25.00 50.00
61 Ira Stuart 25.00 50.00
62 Berg Irving 50.00 100.00
63 Cecil Browne 40.00 80.00
64 Nick Wasnie 40.00 80.00
65 Gordon Teal 40.00 80.00
66 Jack Hughes 40.00 80.00
67 D. Yeatman 40.00 80.00
68 Connie Johanneson 25.00 50.00
69 S. Walters 25.00 50.00
70 Harold McMunn 40.00 80.00
71 Smokey Harris 25.00 50.00
72 Calgary Jimmies 25.00 50.00
73 Bernie Morris 25.00 50.00
74 J. Fowler 40.00 80.00
75 Calgary Jimmies 25.00 50.00
76 Pete Spiers 25.00 50.00
77 Bill Borland 40.00 80.00
78 Cliff O'Meara 40.00 80.00
79 F. Porteous 40.00 80.00
80 W. Brooks 40.00 80.00
81 Everett McGowan 25.00 50.00
82 Calgary Jimmies 25.00 50.00
83 George Dame 25.00 50.00
84 Calgary Jimmies 25.00 50.00
85 Calgary Jimmies 25.00 50.00
86 Calgary Jimmies 25.00 50.00
87 Norman Hec Fowler 40.00 80.00
88 Jimmy Hoyle 25.00 50.00
89 Charlie Gardiner 75.00 150.00
90 Calgary Jimmies 40.00 80.00

1933-34 V129

This 50-card set was issued anonymously during the 1933-34 season. Recent research may link the cards' distribution to British Consul Cigarettes. This has yet to be confirmed. The cards are sepia toned and measure approximately 1 5/8" by 2 7/8". The cards are numbered on the back with the capsule biography both in French and in English. Card number 39 is now known to exist but is quite scarce as it was the card that the company (allegedly) short-printed in order to make it difficult to complete the set. The short-printed Oliver card is not included in the complete set price below.

COMPLETE SET (49) 7500.00 15000.00
1 Red Horner RC 250.00 500.00
2 Hap Day 175.00 350.00
3 Ace Bailey RC 250.00 500.00
4 Buzz Boll RC 75.00 150.00
5 Charlie Conacher RC 500.00 1000.00
6 Busher Jackson RC 250.00 500.00
7 Joe Primeau RC 250.00 500.00
8 King Clancy 500.00 1000.00
9 Alex Levinsky RC 100.00 200.00
10 Bill Thoms RC 75.00 150.00
11 Andy Blair RC 75.00 150.00
12 Harold Cotton RC 100.00 200.00
13 George Hainsworth 250.00 500.00
14 Ken Doraty RC 75.00 150.00
15 Fred Robertson RC 75.00 150.00
16 Charlie Sands RC 75.00 150.00
17 Hec Kilrea RC 75.00 150.00
18 John Roach 100.00 200.00
19 Larry Aurie RC 75.00 150.00
20 Ebbie Goodfellow RC 150.00 300.00
21 Normie Himes RC 100.00 200.00
22 Bill Brydge RC 75.00 150.00
23 Red Dutton RC 150.00 300.00
24 Cooney Weiland RC 200.00 400.00
25 Bill Beveridge RC 100.00 200.00
26 Frank Finnigan 100.00 200.00
27 Albert Leduc RC 100.00 200.00
28 Babe Siebert RC 200.00 400.00
29 Murray Murdoch RC 75.00 150.00
30 Butch Keeling RC 75.00 150.00
31 Bill Cook RC 150.00 300.00
32 Cecil Dillon RC 75.00 150.00
33 Ivan Johnson RC 200.00 400.00
34 Ott Heller RC 100.00 200.00
35 Red Beattie RC 75.00 150.00
36 Dit Clapper 300.00 600.00
37 Eddie Shore RC 1000.00 2000.00
38 Marty Barry RC 150.00 300.00
39 Harry Oliver SP RC 7500.00 15000.00
40 Bob Gracie RC 75.00 150.00
41 Howie Morenz 1500.00 3000.00
42 Pit Lepine RC 75.00 150.00
43 Johnny Gagnon RC 75.00 150.00
44 Armand Mondou RC 75.00 150.00
45 Lorne Chabot RC 150.00 300.00
46 Bun Cook RC 150.00 300.00
47 Alex Smith RC 75.00 150.00
48 Danny Cox RC 75.00 150.00
49 Baldy Northcott RC UER 100.00 200.00
50 Paul Thompson RC 100.00 200.00

1924-25 V130 Maple Crispette

This 30-card set was issued during the 1924-25 season in the Montreal area. The cards are in black and white and measure approximately 1 3/8" by 2 3/8". There was a prize offer detailed on the reverse of every card offering a pair of hockey skates for a complete set of the cards. Card number 15 Cleghorn apparently was the "impossible" card that prevented most collectors of that day from ever getting the skates and it is considered one of the scarcest pre-war hockey cards. Since market sales data is too thin on the card we have not priced it below, but the very occassional reported sale is well over $10,000. The cards are numbered on the front in the lower right hand corner. The set is considered complete without the short-printed Cleghorn.

COMPLETE SET (29) 4000.00 8000.00
1 Dunc Munro RC 100.00 200.00
2 Clint Benedict 200.00 400.00
3 Norman Hec Fowler RC 100.00 200.00
4 Curly Headley RC 75.00 150.00
5 Alf Skinner RC 75.00 150.00
6 Lloyd Cook RC 150.00 300.00
7 Smokey Harris RC 75.00 150.00
8 Jim Herberts RC 75.00 150.00
9 Carson Cooper RC 75.00 150.00
10 Red Green 75.00 150.00
11 Billy Boucher 75.00 150.00
12 Howie Morenz 1000.00 2000.00
13 Georges Vezina 700.00 1400.00
14 Aurel Joliat 400.00 800.00
15 Sprague Cleghorn SP 6000.00 12000.00
16 Dutch Cain RC 75.00 150.00
17 Charlie Dinsmore RC 75.00 150.00
18 Punch Broadbent 150.00 300.00
19 Sam Rothschild RC 125.00 200.00
20 George Carroll RC 75.00 150.00
21 Billy Burch 150.00 300.00
22 Shorty Green 150.00 300.00
23 Mickey Roach 75.00 150.00
24 Ken Randall 75.00 150.00
25 Vernon Forbes 100.00 200.00
26 Charlie Langlois RC 75.00 150.00
27 Newsy Lalonde 300.00 600.00
28 Fred Lowrey RC 75.00 150.00
29 Ganton Scott RC 75.00 150.00
30 Louis Berlinquette RC 100.00 200.00
(spelled Berlinguette on front)

1923-24 V145-1

This relatively unattractive 40-card set is printed in sepia tone. The cards measure approximately 2" by 3 1/4". The cards have blank backs. The cards are numbered on the front in the lower left corner. The player's name, team, and National Hockey League are at the bottom of each card. The issuer of the set is not indicated in any way on the card, although speculation suggests it was William Patterson, Ltd, a Canadian confectioner. This set is easily confused with the other V145 set. Except for the tint and size differences and the different card name/number correspondence, these sets are essentially the same. Thankfully the only player with the same number in both sets is number 3 King Clancy. The Bert Corbeau card (#25) is extremely difficult to find in any condition, as it most likely was short printed. It is not included in the complete set price below.

COMPLETE SET (39) 6000.00 12000.00
1 Eddie Gerard 125.00 250.00
2 Frank Nighbor RC 175.00 350.00
3 King Clancy RC 900.00 1800.00
4 Jack Darragh 100.00 200.00
5 Harry Helman RC 50.00 100.00
6 George Boucher RC 100.00 200.00
7 Clint Benedict 150.00 300.00
8 Lionel Hitchman RC 100.00 200.00
9 Punch Broadbent 125.00 250.00
10 Cy Denneny RC 200.00 400.00
11 Sprague Cleghorn 150.00 300.00
12 Sylvio Mantha RC 125.00 250.00
13 Joe Malone 200.00 400.00
14 Aurel Joliat RC 650.00 1300.00
15 Howie Morenz RC 1500.00 3000.00
16 Billy Boucher RC 60.00 125.00
17 Billy Coutu RC 60.00 125.00
18 Odie Cleghorn 60.00 125.00
19 Georges Vezina 750.00 1500.00
20 Amos Arbour RC 50.00 100.00
21 Lloyd Andrews RC 50.00 100.00
22 Red Stuart RC 60.00 125.00
23 Cecil Dye RC 150.00 300.00
24 Jack Adams RC 200.00 400.00
25 Bert Corbeau RC SP 10000.00 20000.00
26 Reg Noble RC 150.00 300.00
27 Stan Jackson RC 50.00 100.00
28 John Roach RC 60.00 125.00
29 Vernon Forbes RC 60.00 125.00
30 Shorty Green RC 100.00 200.00
31 Red Green RC 50.00 100.00
32 Goldie Prodgers 50.00 100.00
33 Leo Reise RC 50.00 100.00
34 Ken Randall RC 50.00 100.00
35 Billy Burch RC 100.00 200.00
36 Jesse Spring RC 50.00 100.00
37 Eddie Bouchard RC 50.00 100.00
38 Mickey Roach RC 50.00 100.00
39 Chas. Fraser RC 50.00 100.00
40 Corbett Denneny RC 100.00 200.00

1924-25 V145-2

This 60-card set was issued anonymously during the 1924-25 season. The cards have a green-black tint and measure approximately 1 3/4" by 3 1/4". Cards are numbered in the lower left corner and have a blank back. The player's name, team, and National Hockey League are at the bottom of each card. The issuer of the set is not indicated in any way on the card, although speculation points to William Patterson, Ltd., a Canadian confectioner. This set is easily confused with the other V145 set. Except for the tint and size differences and the different card name/number correspondence, these sets are essentially the same. Thankfully the only player with the same number in both sets is number 3 King Clancy.

COMPLETE SET (60) 6000.00 12000.00
1 Joe Ironstone RC 250.00 500.00
2 George Boucher 100.00 200.00
3 King Clancy 750.00 1500.00
4 Lionel Hitchman 75.00 150.00
5 Hooley Smith RC 125.00 250.00
6 Frank Nighbor 100.00 200.00
7 Cy Denneny 125.00 250.00
8 Spiff Campbell RC 50.00 100.00
9 Frank Finnigan RC 75.00 150.00
10 Alex Connell RC 125.00 250.00
11 Vernon Forbes 60.00 125.00
12 Ken Randall 50.00 100.00
13 Billy Burch 100.00 200.00
14 Shorty Green 100.00 200.00
15 Red Green 50.00 100.00
16 Alex McKinnon RC 50.00 100.00
17 Charlie Langlois RC 50.00 100.00
18 Mickey Roach 50.00 100.00
19 Eddie Bouchard 50.00 100.00
20 Jesse Spring 50.00 100.00
21 Carson Cooper RC 50.00 100.00
22 Smokey Harris RC 50.00 100.00
23 Curly Headley RC 50.00 100.00
24 Lloyd Cook UER RC 200.00 400.00
(Bill on front)
25 Jim Herberts RC 50.00 100.00
26 Werner Schnarr RC 50.00 100.00
27 Alf Skinner RC 50.00 100.00
28 George Redding RC 50.00 100.00
29 Herbie Mitchell RC 50.00 100.00
30 Norman Hec Fowler RC 60.00 125.00
31 Red Stuart 50.00 100.00
32 Clint Benedict 100.00 200.00
33 Gerald Munro RC 50.00 100.00
34 Dunc Munro RC 60.00 125.00
35 Dutch Cain RC 50.00 100.00
36 Fred Lowrey RC 50.00 100.00
37 Sam Rothschild RC 75.00 135.00
38 Ganton Scott RC 50.00 100.00
39 Punch Broadbent 125.00 250.00
40 Charlie Dinsmore RC 50.00 100.00
41 Louis Berlinquette RC 50.00 100.00
42 George Carroll RC 50.00 100.00
43 Georges Vezina 600.00 1200.00
44 Billy Coutu 50.00 100.00
45 Odie Cleghorn 60.00 125.00
46 Billy Boucher 75.00 150.00
47 Howie Morenz 1000.00 2000.00
48 Aurel Joliat 500.00 1000.00
49 Sprague Cleghorn 125.00 250.00
50 Billy Mantha RC 75.00 150.00
51 Reg Noble 100.00 200.00
52 John Roach 60.00 125.00
53 Jack Adams 125.00 250.00
54 Cecil Dye 100.00 200.00
55 Reg Reid RC 50.00 100.00
56 Albert Holway RC 50.00 100.00
57 Bert McCaffery RC 50.00 100.00
58 Bert Corbeau 100.00 200.00
59 Lloyd Andrews RC 50.00 100.00
60 Stan Jackson 75.00 150.00

1933-34 V252 Canadian Gum

This unnumbered set of 50 cards was designated V252 by the American Card Catalog. Cards are black and white pictures with a red border. Backs are written in both French and English. Cards measure approximately 2 1/2" by 3 1/4" including a 3/4" tab at the bottom describing a premium (contest) offer and containing one large letter. When enough of these letters were saved so that the collector could spell out the names of five NHL teams, they could be redeemed for a free home hockey game according to the details given on the card backs. The cards are checklisted in alphabetical order.

COMPLETE SET (50) 4500.00 9000.00
1 Clarence Abel RC 100.00 200.00
2 Larry Aurie RC 90.00 150.00
3 Ace Bailey RC 200.00 400.00
4 Helge Bostrom RC 50.00 100.00
5 Bill Brydge RC 50.00 100.00
6 Glyn Brydson RC 50.00 100.00
7 Marty Burke RC 50.00 100.00
8 Gerald Carson RC 75.00 125.00
9 Lorne Chabot RC 200.00 400.00
10 King Clancy 450.00 800.00
11 Dit Clapper RC 200.00 400.00
12 Charlie Conacher RC 400.00 750.00
13 Lionel Conacher RC 200.00 400.00
14 Alex Connell 100.00 175.00
15 Bun Cook RC 100.00 175.00
16 Danny Cox RC 50.00 100.00
17 Hap Day 100.00 200.00
18 Cecil Dillon RC 50.00 100.00
19 Lorne Duguid RC 75.00 125.00
20 Duke Dutkowski RC 50.00 100.00
21 Red Dutton RC 100.00 175.00
22 Happy Emms RC 75.00 125.00
23 Frank Finnigan 75.00 125.00
24 Chuck Gardiner RC 100.00 175.00
25 Ebbie Goodfellow RC 100.00 175.00
26 Johnny Gottselig RC 75.00 125.00
27 Bob Gracie RC 50.00 100.00
28 George Hainsworth 200.00 400.00
29 Ott Heller RC 50.00 100.00
30 Normie Himes RC 75.00 125.00
31 Red Horner RC 150.00 300.00
32 Busher Jackson RC 200.00 400.00
33 Walter Jackson RC 50.00 100.00
34 Aurel Joliat 400.00 750.00
35 Dave Kerr RC 75.00 125.00
36 Pit Lepine RC 50.00 100.00
37 Georges Mantha RC 50.00 100.00
38 Howie Morenz 1000.00 2000.00
39 Murray Murdoch RC 50.00 100.00
40 Baldy Northcott RC 75.00 125.00
41 John Roach 90.00 150.00
42 Johnny Sheppard 50.00 100.00
43 Babe Siebert RC 125.00 250.00
44 Alex Smith RC 50.00 100.00
45 John Sorrell RC 90.00 150.00
46 Nelson Stewart RC 200.00 400.00
47 Dave Trottier RC 50.00 100.00
48 Bill Touhey RC 50.00 100.00
49 Jimmy Ward RC 50.00 100.00
50 Nick Wasnie RC 50.00 100.00

1933-34 V288 Hamilton Gum

This skip-numbered set of 21 cards was designated V288 by the American Card Catalog. Cards are black and white pictures with a beige, blue, green, or orange background. Backs are written in both French and English. Cards measure approximately 2 3/8" by 2 3/4".

COMPLETE SET (21) 3000.00 6000.00
1 Nick Wasnie 62.50 125.00
2 Joe Primeau 200.00 400.00
3 Marty Burke 50.00 100.00
7 Bill Thoms 50.00 100.00
8 Howie Morenz 1000.00 2000.00
9 Andy Blair 50.00 100.00
11 Ace Bailey 175.00 350.00
14 Wildor Larochelle 50.00 100.00
17 King Clancy 400.00 800.00
18 Sylvio Mantha 87.50 175.00
21 Red Horner 150.00 300.00
23 Pit Lepine 50.00 100.00
27 Aurel Joliat 400.00 800.00
29 Harvey(Busher) Jackson 175.00 350.00
30 Lorne Chabot 100.00 200.00
33 Hap Day 100.00 200.00
36 Alex Levinsky 62.50 125.00
39 Harold Cotton 75.00 150.00
42 Ebbie Goodfellow 87.50 175.00
44 Larry Aurie 50.00 100.00
49 Charlie Conacher 400.00 800.00

1937-38 V356 World Wide Gum

These greenish-gray cards feature the player's name and card number on the front and the card number, the player's name, his position and biographical data (in both English and French) on the back. Cards are approximately 2 3/8" by 2 7/8". Although the backs of the cards state that the cards were printed in Canada, no mention of the issuer, World Wide Gum, is apparent anywhere on the card.

COMPLETE SET (135) 11000.00 22000.00
1 Charlie Conacher 500.00 1000.00
2 Jimmy Ward 50.00 100.00
3 Babe Siebert 175.00 350.00
4 Marty Barry 100.00 200.00
5 Eddie Shore 750.00 1500.00
6 Paul Thompson 50.00 100.00
7 Roy Worters 150.00 300.00
8 Red Horner 100.00 200.00
9 Wilfred Cude 75.00 150.00
10 Lionel Conacher 175.00 350.00
11 Ebbie Goodfellow 125.00 250.00
12 Tiny Thompson 150.00 300.00
13 Mush March RC 60.00 125.00
14 Red Dutton 100.00 200.00
15 Butch Keeling 50.00 100.00
16 Frank Boucher RC 100.00 200.00
17 Tommy Gorman RC 50.00 100.00
18 Howie Morenz 1250.00 2500.00
19 Marvin Wentworth 75.00 150.00
20 Hooley Smith 100.00 200.00
21 Ivan Johnson RC 150.00 300.00
22 Baldy Northcott 75.00 150.00
23 Syl Apps 400.00 800.00
24 Hec Kilrea 50.00 100.00
25 John Sorrell 50.00 100.00
26 Lorne Carr RC 50.00 100.00
27 Charlie Sands 50.00 100.00
28 Nick Metz 50.00 100.00
29 King Clancy 500.00 1000.00
30 Russ Blinco 50.00 100.00
31 Pete Martin RC 50.00 100.00
32 Walter Buswell RC 50.00 100.00
33 Paul Haynes 50.00 100.00
34 Wildor Larochelle 60.00 125.00
35 Harold Cotton 60.00 125.00
36 Dit Clapper 200.00 400.00
37 Joe Lamb 50.00 100.00
38 Bob Gracie 50.00 100.00
39 Jack Shill 50.00 100.00
40 Buzz Boll 50.00 100.00
41 John Gallagher 50.00 100.00
42 Art Chapman 50.00 100.00
43 Tom Cook RC 50.00 100.00
44 Bill MacKenzie 50.00 100.00
45 Georges Mantha 50.00 100.00
46 Herb Cain 60.00 125.00
47 Mud Bruneteau RC 75.00 150.00
48 Bob Davidson 50.00 100.00
49 Doug Young RC 50.00 100.00
50 Paul Drouin RC 50.00 100.00
51 Busher Jackson 200.00 400.00
52 Hap Day 150.00 300.00
53 Dave Kerr 100.00 200.00
54 Al Murray 50.00 100.00
55 Johnny Gottselig 60.00 125.00
56 Andy Blair 50.00 100.00
57 Lynn Patrick 200.00 400.00
58 Sweeney Schriner 125.00 250.00
59 Happy Emms 60.00 125.00
60 Allan Shields 50.00 100.00
61 Alex Levinsky 60.00 125.00
62 Flash Hollett 50.00 100.00
63 Peggy O'Neil RC 50.00 100.00
64 Herbie Lewis RC 100.00 200.00
65 Aurel Joliat 400.00 800.00
66 Carl Voss RC 100.00 200.00
67 Stewart Evans 50.00 100.00
68 Bun Cook 125.00 250.00
69 Cooney Weiland 125.00 250.00
70 Dave Trottier 50.00 100.00
71 Louis Trudel RC 50.00 100.00
72 Marty Burke 50.00 100.00
73 Leroy Goldsworthy 50.00 100.00
74 Normie Smith RC 50.00 100.00
75 Syd Howe 150.00 300.00
76 Gordon Pettinger RC 50.00 100.00
77 Jack McGill 50.00 100.00
78 Pit Lepine 50.00 100.00
79 Sammy McManus RC 50.00 100.00
80 Phil Watson RC 75.00 150.00
81 Paul Runge 50.00 100.00
82 Bill Beveridge 60.00 125.00
83 Johnny Gagnon 50.00 100.00
84 Bucko MacDonald RC 60.00 125.00
85 Earl Robinson 50.00 100.00
86 Pep Kelly 50.00 100.00
87 Ott Heller 50.00 100.00
88 Murray Murdoch 50.00 100.00
89 Mac Colville RC 50.00 100.00
90 Alex Shibicky 75.00 150.00
91 Neil Colville 125.00 250.00
92 Normie Himes 60.00 125.00
93 Charley McVeigh 50.00 100.00
94 Lester Patrick 200.00 400.00
95 Connie Smythe 200.00 400.00
96 Art Ross 200.00 400.00
97 Cecil M.Hart RC 125.00 250.00
98 Dutch Gainor RC 50.00 100.00
99 Jack Adams 150.00 300.00
100 Howie Morenz Jr. 150.00 300.00
101 Buster Mundy RC 50.00 100.00

02 Johnny Wing RC 50.00 100.00
03 Morris Croghan RC 50.00 100.00
04 Pete Jotkus RC 50.00 100.00
05 Doug MacQuisten RC 50.00 100.00
06 Lester Brennan RC 50.00 100.00
07 Jack O'Connell RC 50.00 100.00
08 Ray Malentant RC 50.00 100.00
09 Ken Murray RC 50.00 100.00
10 Frank Stangle RC 50.00 100.00
11 Dave Neville RC 50.00 100.00
12 Claude Burke RC 50.00 100.00
13 Herman Murray RC 50.00 100.00
14 Buddy O'Connor RC 125.00 250.00
15 Albert Perreault RC 50.00 100.00
16 Johnny Taugher RC 50.00 100.00
17 Rene Boudreau RC 50.00 100.00
18 Kenny McKinnon RC 50.00 100.00
19 Alex Bolduc RC 50.00 100.00
20 Jimmy Keiller RC 50.00 100.00
21 Lloyd McIntyre RC 50.00 100.00
22 Emile Fortin RC 50.00 100.00
23 Mike Karakas 60.00 125.00
124 Art Wiebe 50.00 100.00
125 Louis St. Denis RC 50.00 100.00
126 Stan Pratt RC 50.00 100.00
127 Jules Cholette RC 50.00 100.00
128 Jimmy Muir RC 50.00 100.00
129 Pete Morin RC 50.00 100.00
130 Jimmy Heffernan RC 50.00 100.00
131 Morris Bastien RC 50.00 100.00
132 Tuffy Griffiths RC 50.00 100.00
133 Johnny Mahaffey RC 50.00 100.00
134 Trueman Donnelly RC 50.00 100.00
135 Bill Stewart RC 75.00 150.00

1933-34 V357 Ice Kings

This interesting and attractive set of 72 cards features black and white photos on the front, upon which the head of the player portrayed has been tinted in flesh tones. The cards measure approximately 2 3/8" by 2 7/8". The player's name appears on the front of the card. The card number, position, team and player's name is listed on the back as are brief biographies in both French and English. Most cards also appear in a second version with the resumes in English only. Printed in Canada and issued by World Wide Gum, the catalog designation for this set is V357.

COMP.SET (72) 9000.00 15000.00
*ENGLISH ONLY BACK: .5X TO 1X
1 Dit Clapper RC 350.00 600.00
2 Bill Brydge RC 50.00 100.00
3 Aurel Joliat UER 500.00 800.00
4 Andy Blair 50.00 100.00
5 Earl Robinson RC 50.00 100.00
6 Paul Haynes RC 50.00 100.00
7 Ronnie Martin RC 50.00 100.00
8 Babe Siebert RC 175.00 300.00
9 Archie Wilcox RC 50.00 100.00
10 Hap Day 150.00 250.00
11 Roy Worters RC 200.00 350.00
12 Nels Stewart RC 350.00 600.00
13 King Clancy 600.00 1000.00
14 Marty Burke RC 125.00 200.00
15 Cecil Dillon RC 50.00 100.00
16 Red Horner RC 175.00 300.00
17 Armand Mondou RC 50.00 100.00
18 Paul Raymond RC 50.00 100.00
19 Dave Kerr RC 75.00 125.00
20 Butch Keeling RC 50.00 100.00
21 Johnny Gagnon RC 50.00 100.00
22 Ace Bailey RC 300.00 500.00
23 Harry Oliver RC 150.00 250.00
24 Gerald Carson RC 50.00 100.00
25 Red Dutton RC 150.00 250.00
26 Georges Mantha RC 50.00 100.00
27 Marty Barry RC 150.00 250.00
28 Wildor Larochelle RC 75.00 125.00
29 Red Beattie RC 50.00 100.00
30 Bill Cook RC 150.00 250.00
31 Hooley Smith 150.00 250.00
32 Art Chapman RC 50.00 100.00
33 Harold Cotton RC 125.00 200.00
34 Lionel Hitchman 125.00 200.00
35 George Patterson RC 50.00 100.00
36 Howie Morenz 1200.00 2000.00
37 Jimmy Ward RC 50.00 100.00
38 Charley McVeigh RC 75.00 125.00
39 Glen Brydson RC 75.00 125.00
40 Joe Primeau RC 300.00 500.00
41 Joe Lamb RC 90.00 150.00
42 Sylvio Mantha 125.00 200.00
43 Cy Wentworth RC 75.00 125.00
44 Normie Himes RC 75.00 125.00
45 Doug Brennan RC 50.00 100.00
46 Pit Lepine RC 75.00 125.00
47 Alex Levinsky RC 75.00 125.00
48 Baldy Northcott RC 75.00 125.00
49 Ken Doraty RC 75.00 125.00
50 Bill Thoms RC 75.00 125.00
51 Vernon Ayres RC 75.00 125.00
52 Lorne Duguid RC 75.00 125.00
53 Wally Kilrea RC 75.00 125.00
54 Vic Ripley RC 75.00 125.00
55 Happy Emms RC 75.00 125.00
56 Duke Dutkowski RC 75.00 125.00
57 Tiny Thompson RC 300.00 500.00
58 Charlie Sands RC 75.00 125.00
59 Larry Aurie RC 75.00 125.00
60 Bill Beveridge RC 75.00 125.00
61 Bill McKenzie RC 75.00 125.00
62 Earl Roche RC 75.00 125.00
63 Bob Gracie RC 75.00 125.00
64 Hec Kilrea RC 75.00 125.00
65 Cooney Weiland RC 250.00 400.00
66 Bun Cook RC 200.00 350.00
67 John Roach 90.00 150.00
68 Murray Murdoch RC 75.00 125.00
69 Danny Cox RC 75.00 125.00
70 Desse Roche RC 75.00 125.00
71 Lorne Chabot RC 250.00 400.00
72 Syd Howe RC 250.00 400.00

1933-34 V357-2 Ice Kings Premiums

These six black-and-white large cards are actually premiums. The cards measure approximately 7" by 9". The cards are unnumbered and rather difficult to find now.

COMPLETE SET (6) 2000.00 4000.00
1 King Clancy 500.00 1000.00
2 Hap Day 175.00 350.00
3 Aurel Joliat 400.00 800.00
4 Howie Morenz 1000.00 2000.00
5 Allan Shields 87.50 175.00
6 Reginald Smith 125.00 250.00

1999-00 Wayne Gretzky Hockey

This Upper Deck-produced set features the top players in the NHL. Company spokesman Gretzky offered comments on each player on the card back. The product was packaged in 24-pack boxes with packs containing eight cards and carried a suggested retail price of $2.49. Please note that although card #GM1 was supposed to carry a piece of game-used puck, there have been several singles found with stick pieces instead.

1 Paul Kariya .20 .50
2 Guy Hebert .15 .40
3 Steve Rucchin .10 .25
4 Teemu Selanne .30 .75
5 Oleg Tverdovsky .10 .25
6 Matt Cullen .10 .25
7 Jeff Nielsen .10 .25
8 Patrik Stefan RC .15 .40
9 Kelly Buchberger .10 .25
10 Andrew Brunette .10 .25
11 Ray Ferraro .10 .25
12 Nelson Emerson .10 .25
13 Damian Rhodes .10 .25
14 Sergei Samsonov .12 .30
15 John Grahame RC .12 .30
16 Joe Thornton .25 .60
17 Jason Allison .12 .30
18 Kyle McLaren .10 .25
19 Rob DiMaio .10 .25
20 Ray Bourque .25 .60
21 Dominik Hasek .25 .60
22 Miroslav Satan .12 .30
23 Alexei Zhitnik .10 .25
24 Stu Barnes .12 .30
25 Curtis Brown .10 .25
26 Brian Campbell RC .15 .40
27 Michael Peca .12 .30
28 Marc Savard .10 .25
29 Valeri Bure .10 .25
30 Phil Housley .10 .25
31 Grant Fuhr .15 .40
32 Cory Stillman .10 .25
33 Oleg Saprykin RC .15 .40
34 Sami Kapanen .10 .25
35 Bates Battaglia .10 .25
36 Dave Tanabe .10 .25
37 Ron Francis .20 .50
38 Arturs Irbe .15 .40
39 Keith Primeau .10 .25
40 Doug Gilmour .20 .50
41 J-P Dumont .12 .30
42 Eric Daze .12 .30
43 Tony Amonte .12 .30
44 Alexei Zhamnov .10 .25
45 Kyle Calder RC .12 .30
46 Joe Sakic .25 .60
47 Chris Drury .12 .30
48 Milan Hejduk .12 .30
49 Adam Deadmarsh .12 .30
50 Patrick Roy .60 1.50
51 Peter Forsberg .15 .40
52 Alex Tanguay .12 .30
53 Mike Modano .25 .60
54 Brett Hull .25 .60
55 Ed Belfour .15 .40
56 Jamie Langenbrunner .10 .25
57 Pavel Patera RC .12 .30
58 Joe Nieuwendyk .15 .40
59 Jere Lehtinen .12 .30
60 Steve Yzerman .50 1.25
61 Jiri Fischer .10 .25
62 Brendan Shanahan .20 .50
63 Chris Osgood .15 .40
64 Chris Chelios .15 .40
65 Sergei Fedorov .25 .60
66 Nicklas Lidstrom .15 .40
67 Doug Weight .15 .40
68 Mike Grier .10 .25
69 Ryan Smyth .12 .30
70 Jason Smith .10 .25
71 Tom Poti .10 .25
72 Pavel Bure .20 .50
73 Mark Parrish .15 .40
74 Ivan Novoseltsev RC .20 .50
75 Trevor Kidd .10 .25
76 Viktor Kozlov .10 .25
77 Scott Mellanby .15 .40
78 Rob Blake .15 .40
79 Ian Lapperiere .10 .25
80 Zigmund Palffy .15 .40
81 Luc Robitaille .15 .40
82 Jozef Stumpel .10 .25
83 Aki Berg .10 .25
84 Stephane Fiset .12 .30
85 Saku Koivu .15 .40
86 Brian Savage .12 .30
87 Trevor Linden .15 .40
88 Jeff Hackett .10 .25
89 Eric Weinrich .10 .25
90 David Legwand .10 .25
91 Sergei Krivokrasov .10 .25
92 Randy Robitaille .10 .25
93 Kimmo Timonen .10 .25
94 Mike Dunham .15 .40
95 Brendan Morrison .12 .30
96 Scott Stevens .15 .40
97 Sheldon Souray .10 .25
98 Petr Sykora .12 .30
99 Wayne Gretzky .75 2.00
100 Martin Brodeur .30 .75
101 Scott Niedermayer .15 .40
102 Patrik Elias .15 .40
103 Tim Connolly .10 .25
104 Jorgen Jonsson RC .10 .25
105 Mathieu Biron .10 .25
106 Claude Lapointe .12 .30
107 Kenny Jonsson .10 .25
108 Roberto Luongo .20 .50
109 Theo Fleury .20 .50
110 Petr Nedved .10 .25
111 Valeri Kamensky .10 .25
112 Adam Graves .12 .30
113 Manny Malhotra .12 .30
114 Brian Leetch .15 .40
115 Mike Richter .15 .40
116 Marian Hossa .12 .30
117 Radek Bonk .10 .25
118 Joe Juneau .12 .30
119 Wade Redden .10 .25
120 Ron Tugnutt .12 .30
121 Daniel Alfredsson .15 .40
122 Eric Lindros .25 .60
123 John LeClair .15 .40
124 Marc Bureau .10 .25
125 Simon Gagne .15 .40
126 Mark Recchi .20 .50
127 Rod Brind'Amour .15 .40
128 John Vanbiesbrouck .12 .30
129 Keith Tkachuk .15 .40
130 Jeremy Roenick .15 .40
131 Daniel Briere .12 .30
132 Bob Essensa .10 .25
133 J.J. Daigneault .10 .25
134 Mika Alatalo RC .12 .30
135 Travis Green .10 .25
136 Jaromir Jagr .40 1.00
137 Martin Straka .10 .25
138 Alexei Morozov .12 .30
139 Jan Hrdina .10 .25
140 Alexei Kovalev .12 .30
141 Peter Skudra .12 .30
142 John Slaney .10 .25
143 Pierre Turgeon .15 .40
144 Roman Turek .15 .40
145 Pavol Demitra .20 .50
146 Al MacInnis .15 .40
147 Chris Pronger .12 .30
148 Jochen Hecht RC .25 .60
149 Jeff Friesen .12 .30
150 Steve Shields .10 .25
151 Patrick Marleau .15 .40
152 Vincent Damphousse .12 .30
153 Marco Sturm .12 .30
154 Brad Stuart .12 .30
155 Darcy Tucker .10 .25
156 Vincent Lecavalier .12 .30
157 Andrei Zyuzin .10 .25
158 Chris Gratton .10 .25
159 Fredrik Modin .10 .25
160 Mats Sundin .15 .40
161 Steve Thomas .10 .25
162 Sergei Berezin .10 .25
163 Mike Johnson .10 .25
164 Dimitri Khristich .10 .25
165 Bryan Berard .10 .25
166 Curtis Joseph .15 .40
167 Mark Messier .25 .60
168 Alexander Mogilny .12 .30
169 Garth Snow .12 .30
170 Markus Naslund .15 .40
171 Steve Kariya RC .12 .30
172 Peter Schaefer .12 .30
173 Peter Bondra .12 .30
174 Joe Sacco .10 .25
175 Adam Oates .15 .40
176 Olaf Kolzig .15 .40
177 Jan Bulis .10 .25
178 Alexander Volchkov RC .10 .25
179 Wayne Gretzky CL .75 2.00
180 Curtis Joseph CL .15 .40
GM1P Wayne Gretzky PUCK 25.00 60.00
GM1S Wayne Gretzky STICK 30.00 80.00

1999-00 Wayne Gretzky Hockey Changing The Game

Randomly inserted in packs at the rate of 1:27, this 10-card set highlights 10 top NHL stars who have left their mark on hockey. Each card is enhanced with silver foil stamping.

COMPLETE SET (10) 15.00 30.00
CG1 Peter Forsberg 1.50 4.00
CG2 Eric Lindros 1.25 3.00
CG3 Paul Kariya 1.25 3.00
CG4 Jaromir Jagr 1.50 4.00
CG5 Dominik Hasek 2.00 5.00
CG6 Sergei Samsonov 1.00 2.50
CG7 Theo Fleury 1.25 3.00
CG8 Al MacInnis 1.00 2.50
CG9 Pavel Bure 1.25 3.00
CG10 Patrick Roy 5.00 12.00

1999-00 Wayne Gretzky Hockey Elements of the Game

Randomly seeded in packs at the rate of 1:6, this 15-card set showcases top players on a card with purple foil borders with enhanced silver foil highlights.

COMPLETE SET (15) 8.00 15.00
EG1 Teemu Selanne .40 1.00
EG2 Mike Peca .30 .75
EG3 Sergei Samsonov .30 .75
EG4 Sergei Fedorov .60 1.50
EG5 Peter Forsberg 1.00 2.50
EG6 Brett Hull .50 1.25
EG7 Eric Lindros .40 1.00
EG8 Pavel Bure .40 1.00
EG9 Theo Fleury .30 .75
EG10 Martin Brodeur 1.00 2.50
EG11 Jaromir Jagr .60 1.50
EG12 Keith Tkachuk .40 1.00
EG13 Peter Bondra .40 1.00
EG14 Joe Sakic .75 2.00
EG15 Curtis Joseph .40 1.00

1999-00 Wayne Gretzky Hockey Great Heroes

Randomly inserted in packs at the rate of 1:27, this 10-card set showcases ten modern day heroes on a card with silver and purple foil borders and silver foil stamping.

COMPLETE SET (10) 20.00 40.00
GH1 Jaromir Jagr 2.00 5.00
GH2 Paul Kariya 2.00 5.00
GH3 Joe Sakic 2.50 6.00
GH4 Dominik Hasek 2.50 6.00
GH5 Patrick Roy 5.00 12.00
GH6 Steve Yzerman 5.00 12.00
GH7 Eric Lindros 2.00 5.00
GH8 Patrik Stefan 1.50 4.00
GH9 Teemu Selanne 2.00 5.00
GH10 Pavel Bure 1.50 4.00

1999-00 Wayne Gretzky Hockey Hall of Fame Career

Inserted one per pack this 30-card set traced Wayne Gretzky's career on a card with purple foil borders and silver foil stamping.

COMPLETE SET (30) 12.00 25.00
COMMON GRETZKY .40 1.00

1999-00 Wayne Gretzky Hockey Signs of Greatness

Randomly inserted in Retail packs at the rate of 1:15, this 15-card set features portrait photography and authentic player signatures.

AI Arturs Irbe 6.00 15.00
BH Brett Hull SP 30.00 60.00
CD Chris Drury 6.00 15.00
CJ Curtis Joseph SP 40.00 80.00
CO Chris Osgood 6.00 15.00
DL David Legwand 6.00 15.00
MP Mark Parrish 5.00 12.00
NK Nikolai Khabibulin 8.00 20.00
PB Pavel Bure SP 25.00 60.00
PM Paul Mara 5.00 12.00
PS Patrik Stefan 6.00 15.00
RB Ray Bourque 25.00 60.00
SS Sergei Samsonov SP 15.00 40.00
VS Vadim Sharifijanov 6.00 15.00
WG Wayne Gretzky SP 200.00 400.00

1999-00 Wayne Gretzky Hockey Tools of Greatness

Randomly inserted in Hobby packs at the rate of 1:139, this 20-card set features action player photography coupled with a swatch of a game used stick.

TGAI Arturs Irbe 10.00 25.00
TGBH Brett Hull 12.50 30.00
TGBS Brendan Shanahan 10.00 25.00
TGCJ Curtis Joseph 10.00 25.00
TGDW Doug Weight 10.00 25.00
TGEB Ed Belfour 10.00 25.00
TGEL Eric Lindros 10.00 25.00
TGLR Luc Robitaille 10.00 25.00
TGMR Mike Richter 10.00 25.00
TGMS Mats Sundin 10.00 25.00
TGNK Nikolai Khabibulin 10.00 25.00
TGPB Pavel Bure 10.00 25.00
TGPF Peter Forsberg 12.00 30.00
TGPK Paul Kariya 10.00 25.00
TGPR Patrick Roy 20.00 50.00
TGRB Ray Bourque 15.00 40.00
TGSS Sergei Samsonov 8.00 20.00
TGTA Tony Amonte 8.00 20.00
TGTS Teemu Selanne 10.00 25.00

1999-00 Wayne Gretzky Hockey Visionary

Randomly inserted in packs at the rate of 1:167, this 10-card set features none other than the Great One on an acetate holofoil insert card. Cards carry a "V" prefix.

COMPLETE SET (10) 75.00 150.00
COMMON GRETZKY (V1-V10) 10.00 25.00

1999-00 Wayne Gretzky Hockey Will to Win

Randomly seeded in packs at the rate of 1:13, this 10-card set features ten of the most dominant stars of the NHL. Cards are enhanced with silver foil highlights.

COMPLETE SET (10) 12.00 25.00
W1 Paul Kariya .60 1.50
W2 Steve Yzerman 3.00 8.00
W3 Jaromir Jagr 1.00 2.50
W4 Dominik Hasek 1.25 3.00
W5 Patrick Roy 3.00 8.00
W6 Jeremy Roenick .75 2.00
W7 Ray Bourque 1.00 2.50
W8 John LeClair .75 2.00
W9 Mats Sundin .60 1.50
W10 Mark Messier .75 2.00

1927 Werner and Mertz Field Hockey

Cards measure approximately 2 1/2 x 4 1/2 and feature full color drawings of field hockey action shots. Produced in Germany by Werner & Mertz Aktiengesellschaft, Mainz.

COMPLETE SET (6) 62.50 125.00
1 Womens Field Hockey 12.50 25.00
2 Womens Field Hockey 12.50 25.00
3 Mens Field Hockey Scrum at midfield 12.50 25.00
4 Mens Field Hockey Chasing the ball 12.50 25.00
5 Mens Field Hockey Pileup 12.50 25.00
6 Mens Field Hockey Goalie action shot 12.50 25.00

1982-83 Whalers Junior Hartford Courant

Sponsored by the Hartford Courant, this 23-card set measures approximately 3 1/4" by 6 3/8". The fronts feature borderless color action player photos. and the sponsor's name. The white backs carry a black-and-white headshot, player's name, jersey number, biography and statistics. The cards are unnumbered and checklisted below in alphabetical order. The card of Ron Francis appears in his Rookie Card year.

COMPLETE SET (22) 14.00 35.00
1 Greg Adams 1.50 4.00
2 Russ Anderson .75 2.00
3 Ron Francis 10.00 25.00
4 Michel Galarneau .75 2.00
5 Dan Fridgen .75 2.00
6 Archie Henderson .75 2.00
7 Ed Hospodar .75 2.00
8 Mark Johnson 1.25 3.00
9 Chris Kotsopoulos .75 2.00
10 Pierre Larouche 1.50 4.00
11 George Lyle .75 2.00
12 Greg Millen 2.00 5.00
13 Warren Miller .75 2.00
14 Ray Neufeld 1.25 3.00
15 Mark Renaud .75 2.00
16 Risto Siltanen 1.25 3.00
17 Stuart Smith .75 2.00
18 Blaine Stoughton 1.50 4.00
19 Doug Sulliman .75 2.00
20 Bob Sullivan .75 2.00
21 Mike Veisor 1.25 3.00
22 Mickey Volcan .75 2.00
23 Blake Wesley .75 2.00

1983-84 Whalers Junior Hartford Courant

Sponsored by the Hartford Courant, this 22-card set measures approximately 3 3/4" by 8 1/4". The fronts feature color action player photos and the sponsor's name. The white backs carry a black-and-white headshot, player's name, jersey number, biography and statistics. The cards are unnumbered and checklisted below in alphabetical order.

COMPLETE SET (22) 10.00 25.00
1 Bob Crawford .40 1.00
2 Mike Crombeen .40 1.00
3 Richie Dunn .40 1.00
4 Normand Dupont .40 1.00
5 Ron Francis 3.00 8.00
6 Ed Hospodar .40 1.00
7 Marty Howe .75 2.00
8 Mark Johnson .60 1.50
9 Chris Kotsopoulos .40 1.00
10 Pierre Lacroix .60 1.50
11 Greg Malone .60 1.50
12 Greg Malone .60 1.50
13 Ray Neufeld .60 1.50
14 Joel Quenneville .60 1.50
15 Torrie Robertson .60 1.50
16 Risto Siltanen .40 1.00
17 Blaine Stoughton .75 2.00
18 Steve Stoyanovich .40 1.00
19 Doug Sulliman .40 1.00
20 Sylvain Turgeon .60 1.50
21 Mike Veisor .60 1.50
22 Mike Zuke .40 1.00

1984-85 Whalers Junior Wendy's

This 22-card set was sponsored by Wendy's and The Civic Center Mall. The cards measure approximately 3 3/4" by 8 1/4" and feature color action player photos. The backs have a black and white head shot, biography, 1983-84 season summary, career summary, miscellaneous player information, and statistics. The cards are unnumbered and checklisted below in alphabetical order.

COMPLETE SET (22) 10.00 25.00
1 Jack Brownschidle .40 1.00
2 Sylvain Cote .40 1.00
3 Bob Crawford .40 1.00
4 Mike Crombeen .40 1.00
5 Tony Currie .40 1.00
6 Ron Francis 2.50 6.00
7 Mark Fusco .40 1.00
8 Dave Jensen .40 1.00
9 Mark Johnson .60 1.50
10 Chris Kotsopoulos .40 1.00
11 Greg Malone .60 1.50
12 Greg Millen .75 2.00
13 Ray Neufeld .40 1.00
14 Randy Pierce .40 1.00
15 Joel Quenneville .60 1.50
16 Torrie Robertson .60 1.50
17 Ulf Samuelsson 1.50 4.00
18 Risto Siltanen .40 1.00
19 Dave Tippett .40 1.00
20 Sylvain Turgeon .40 1.00
21 Steve Weeks .75 2.00
22 Mike Zuke .60 1.50

1985-86 Whalers Junior Wendy's

Sponsored by Wendy's, this 23-card set measures approximately 3 3/4" by 8 1/4". The fronts feature full-bleed color action player photos, along with the sponsor's name. The white backs carry a black-and-white headshot, biography, 1984-85 season summary, career summary, personal information, and statistics. The cards were issued to members of the team's Kid's Club. Since they are unnumbered, the cards are checklisted below in alphabetical order.

COMPLETE SET (23) 12.00 30.00
1 Jack Brownschidle .40 1.00
2 Sylvain Cote .40 1.00
3 Bob Crawford .40 1.00
4 Kevin Dineen 1.50 4.00
5 Paul Fenton .40 1.00
6 Ray Ferraro 1.25 3.00
7 Ron Francis 2.00 5.00
8 Scott Kleinendorst .40 1.00
9 Paul Lawless .40 1.00
10 Mike Liut 1.25 3.00
11 Paul MacDermid .40 1.00
12 Greg Malone .40 1.00
13 Dana Murzyn .40 1.00
14 Ray Neufeld .40 1.00
15 Jorgen Pettersson .40 1.00
16 Joel Quenneville .40 1.00
17 Torrie Robertson .60 1.50
18 Ulf Samuelsson 1.25 3.00
19 Risto Siltanen .40 1.00
20 Dave Tippett .40 1.00
21 Sylvain Turgeon .60 1.50
22 Steve Weeks .60 1.50
23 Mike Zuke .40 1.00

1986-87 Whalers Junior Thomas'

Sponsored by Thomas', this 23-card set measures approximately 3 3/4" by 8 1/4". The cards were issued only to members of the team's Kid's Club. The fronts feature color action player photos, along with the team and sponsor name. The white backs carry a black-and-white headshot, player's name, jersey number, biography, 1985-86 season summary, career summary, personal information, and statistics. The cards are unnumbered and checklisted below in alphabetical order.

COMPLETE SET (23) 12.00 30.00
1 John Anderson .40 1.00
2 Dave Babych .75 2.00
3 Wayne Babych .40 1.00
4 Sylvain Cote .40 1.00
5 Kevin Dineen 1.25 3.00
6 Dean Evason .40 1.00
7 Ray Ferraro .40 1.00
8 Ron Francis 2.50 6.00
9 Bill Gardner .40 1.00
10 Stewart Gavin .40 1.00
11 Doug Jarvis .40 1.00
12 Scot Kleinendorst .40 1.00
13 Paul Lawless .40 1.00
14 Mike Liut 1.25 3.00
15 Paul MacDermid .40 1.00
16 Mike McEwen .40 1.00
17 Dana Murzyn .40 1.00
18 Joel Quenneville .40 1.00
19 Torrie Robertson .50 1.25
20 Ulf Samuelsson 1.25 3.00
21 Dave Tippett .40 1.00
22 Sylvain Turgeon .40 1.00
23 Steve Weeks .60 1.50

1987-88 Whalers Jr. Burger King/Pepsi

This 21-card set was sponsored by Burger King restaurants and Pepsi Cola and measures approximately 3 3/4" by 8 1/4". The fronts feature color action player photos with the team name and sponsors' logos at the bottom. The backs carry a small headshot, biography, season summary, career summary, miscellaneous player information, and statistics. The cards, which were issued only to members of the team's Kid's Club, are unnumbered and checklisted below in alphabetical order.

COMPLETE SET (21) 10.00 25.00
1 John Anderson .40 1.00
2 Dave Babych .75 2.00
3 Sylvain Cote .40 1.00
4 Kevin Dineen 1.00 2.50
5 Dean Evason .40 1.00
6 Ray Ferraro 1.00 2.50
7 Ron Francis 1.50 4.00
8 Stew Gavin .40 1.00
9 Doug Jarvis .40 1.00
10 Scott Kleinendorst .40 1.00
11 Randy Ladouceur .40 1.00
12 Paul Lawless .40 1.00
13 Mike Liut 1.00 2.50
14 Paul MacDermid .40 1.00
15 Dana Murzyn .40 1.00
16 Joel Quenneville .40 1.00
17 Torrie Robertson .40 1.00
18 Ulf Samuelsson .75 2.00
19 Dave Tippett .40 1.00
20 Sylvain Turgeon .40 1.00
21 Steve Weeks .60 1.50

1988-89 Whalers Junior Ground Round

This 18-card set of Hartford Whalers was sponsored by Ground Round restaurants. The cards measure approximately 3 11/16" by 8 1/4". The front features a borderless full color photo of the player. The team logo and a Ground Round advertisement appear in the blue and green stripes that cut across the bottom of the card face. The back has a black and white head shot of the player at the upper left hand corner as well as extensive player information and career statistics. Another Ground Round advertisement and a Ground Round Drug Tip (an anti-drug and alcohol message) appear at the bottom of the card. The cards were issued to members of the team's Kid's Club. They are unnumbered and hence are checklisted below in alphabetical order.

COMPLETE SET (18) 8.00 20.00
1 John Anderson .40 1.00
2 Dave Babych .60 1.50
3 Sylvain Cote .40 1.00
4 Kevin Dineen .75 2.00
5 Dean Evason .40 1.00
6 Ray Ferraro .75 2.00
7 Ron Francis 1.50 4.00
8 Scot Kleinendorst .40 1.00
9 Randy Ladouceur .40 1.00
10 Mike Liut .75 2.00
11 Paul MacDermid .40 1.00
12 Brent Peterson .40 1.00
13 Joel Quenneville .40 1.00
14 Torrie Robertson .40 1.00
15 Ulf Samuelsson .75 2.00
16 Dave Tippett .40 1.00
17 Sylvain Turgeon .40 1.00
18 Carey Wilson .40 1.00

1989-90 Whalers Junior Milk

This 23-card set of Hartford Whalers was sponsored by Milk and issued to members of the team's Kid's Club. The cards measure approximately 3 11/16" by 8 1/4". The front features a borderless full color photo of the player. The team logo and a Milk advertisement appear in the blue and green stripes that cut across the bottom of the card face. The back has a black and white head shot of the player at the upper left hand corner as well as extensive player information and career statistics. A Junior Whaler Nutrition Tip and another Milk advertisement appear at the bottom of the card's reverse. The cards are unnumbered and hence are checklisted below in alphabetical order. Three cards (11, 12, 21) were added to the set at the end of the season and are marked as SP in the checklist below.

COMPLETE SET (23) 8.00 20.00
1 Mikael Andersson .20 .50
2 Dave Babych .30 .75
3 Sylvain Cote .20 .50
4 Randy Cunneyworth .20 .50
5 Kevin Dineen .60 1.50
6 Dean Evason .20 .50
7 Ray Ferraro .40 1.00
8 Ron Francis 1.25 3.00
9 Jody Hull .20 .50
10 Grant Jennings .20 .50
11 Ed Kastelic SP .75 2.00
12 Todd Krygier SP .75 2.00
13 Randy Ladouceur .20 .50
14 Mike Liut .60 1.50
15 Paul MacDermid .20 .50
16 Joel Quenneville .20 .50
17 Ulf Samuelsson .60 1.50
18 Brad Shaw .30 .75
19 Peter Sidorkiewicz .30 .75
20 Dave Tippett .20 .50
21 Mike Tomlak SP .75 2.00
22 Pat Verbeek .60 1.50
23 Scott Young .40 1.00

1990-91 Whalers Jr. 7-Eleven

This 27-card set of Hartford Whalers was issued by 7-Eleven and sent out as a premium to all members of the Hartford Junior Whalers. This set features full-color photographs on the front while the backs contain the same information about the players that is available in the media guides. The set has been checklisted alphabetically for convenient reference. The set measures approximately 3 3/4" by 8 1/4" and has the players of the Hartford Whalers along with a special Gordie Howe card. Four cards (3, 12, 19, 20) were added to the set at the end of the season and their backs are blank.

COMPLETE SET (27) 12.00 30.00
1 Mikael Andersson .20 .50
2 Dave Babych .20 .50
3 Rob Brown SP .75 2.00
4 Yvon Corriveau .20 .50
5 Sylvain Cote .20 .50
6 Doug Crossman .20 .50
7 Randy Cunneyworth .20 .50
8 Paul Cyr .20 .50
9 Kevin Dineen .40 1.00
10 Dean Evason .20 .50
11 Ron Francis 1.00 2.50
12 Chris Govedaris SP .75 2.00
13 Bobby Holik .60 1.50
14 Gordie Howe 2.00 5.00
15 Grant Jennings .20 .50
16 Ed Kastelic .20 .50
17 Todd Krygier .20 .50
18 Randy Ladouceur .20 .50
19 Jim McKenzie SP .75 2.00
20 Daryl Reaugh SP 1.00 2.50
21 Ulf Samuelsson .40 1.00
22 Brad Shaw .30 .75
23 Peter Sidorkiewicz .30 .75
24 Mike Tomlak .30 .75
25 Pat Verbeek .60 1.50
26 Carey Wilson .20 .50
27 Scott Young .30 .75

1991-92 Whalers Jr. 7-Eleven

This 28-card set of Hartford Whalers was issued by 7-Eleven and sent out as a premium to all members of the Hartford Junior Whalers. This set features full-color photographs on the front while the backs contain the same information about the players that is available in the media guides. The set has been checklisted alphabetically for convenient reference. The set measures approximately 3 3/4" by 8 1/4" and contains the players of the Hartford Whalers. Six cards (3, 6, 10, 12, 18, 19) were issued late in the season and their backs are blank.

COMPLETE SET (28) 8.00 20.00
1 Mikael Andersson .20 .50
2 Marc Bergevin .20 .50
3 James Black SP .60 1.50
4 Rob Brown .25 .60
5 Adam Burt .20 .50
6 Andrew Cassels SP 1.25 3.00
7 Murray Craven .30 .75
8 John Cullen .40 1.00
9 Randy Cunneyworth .20 .50
10 Paul Cyr SP .60 1.50
11 Joe Day .20 .50
12 Paul Gillis SP .60 1.50
13 Mark Greig .20 .50
14 Bobby Holik .30 .75
15 Doug Houda .20 .50
16 Mark Hunter .20 .50
17 Ed Kastelic .20 .50
18 Dan Keczmer SP .75 2.00
19 Steve Konroyd SP .60 1.50
20 Randy Ladouceur .20 .50
21 Jim McKenzie .20 .50
22 Michel Picard .20 .50
23 Geoff Sanderson 2.00 5.00
24 Brad Shaw .25 .60
25 Peter Sidorkiewicz .30 .75
26 Pat Verbeek .60 1.50
27 Kay Whitmore .30 .75
28 Zarley Zalapski .30 .75

1992-93 Whalers Dairymart

Sponsored by Dairymart, this 26-card set was issued to members of the team's Kid's Club. Each features a white-bordered glossy color studio head shot on a card that measures approximately 2 3/8" by 3 1/2". The Dairymart and Whalers logos are displayed above the player photo, and the player's name and position, along with "1992-93 Hartford Whalers," appear beneath his image. The white horizontal back carries the player's name, uniform number, position, and biography above a stat table. The cards are unnumbered and checklisted below in alphabetical order.

COMPLETE SET (26) 7.20 18.00
1 Jim Agnew .20 .50
2 Sean Burke .60 1.50
3 Adam Burt .20 .50
4 Andrew Cassels .40 1.00
5 Murray Craven .25 .60
6 Randy Cunneyworth .20 .50
7 Paul Gillis .20 .50
8 Paul Holmgren CO .20 .50
9 Doug Houda .20 .50
10 Mark Janssens .20 .50
11 Tim Kerr .30 .75
12 Steve Konroyd .20 .50
13 Nick Kypreos .20 .50
14 Randy Ladouceur .20 .50
15 Jim McKenzie .20 .50
16 Michael Nylander .40 1.00
17 Allen Pedersen .20 .50
18 Robert Petrovicky .20 .50
19 Frank Pietrangelo .30 .75
20 Patrick Poulin .20 .50
21 Geoff Sanderson 1.50 4.00
22 Pat Verbeek .60 1.50
23 Eric Weinrich .20 .50
24 Terry Yake .20 .50
25 Zarley Zalapski .20 .50
26 Junior Whalers Member Card .08 .25

1993-94 Whalers Coke

Sponsored by Coca-Cola, this 24-card set features white-bordered color studio head shots on cards that measure approximately 2 3/8" by 3 1/2". The white horizontal backs carry the player's name, uniform number, position, and biography above a stat table. The cards were issued to members of the Junior Whalers club, and as they are unnumbered, they are checklisted below in alphabetical order.

COMPLETE SET (24) 7.20 18.00
1 Sean Burke .75 2.00
2 Adam Burt .20 .50
3 Andrew Cassels .40 1.00
4 Randy Cunneyworth .20 .50
5 Alexander Godynyuk .20 .50
6 Mark Greig .20 .50
7 Mark Janssens .20 .50
8 Robert Kron .20 .50
9 Bryan Marchment .20 .50
10 Brad McCrimmon .20 .50
11 Pierre McGuire CO .08 .25
12 Michael Nylander .30 .75
13 James Patrick .20 .50
14 Frank Pietrangelo .30 .75
15 Marc Potvin .20 .50
16 Chris Pronger 1.25 3.00
17 Brian Propp .30 .75
18 Jeff Reese .30 .75
19 Geoff Sanderson .75 2.00
20 Jim Sandlak .20 .50
21 Jim Storm .20 .50
22 Darren Turcotte .20 .50
23 Pat Verbeek .60 1.50
24 Zarley Zalapski .20 .50

1995-96 Whalers Bob's Stores

This set features the Whalers of the NHL. The standard-sized cards were issued to members of the team's Junior Whalers kid's club. The cards are unnumbered, and so are listed below in alphabetical order.

COMPLETE SET (27) 4.80 12.00
1 Sean Burke .30 .75
2 Adam Burke .15 .40
3 Andrew Cassels .15 .40
4 Kelly Chase .15 .40
5 Scott Daniels .15 .40
6 Gerald Diduck .15 .40
7 Nelson Emerson .25 .60
8 Glen Featherstone .15 .40
9 Brian Glynn .15 .40
10 Mark Janssens .15 .40
11 Robert Kron .15 .40
12 Frantisek Kucera .15 .40
13 Jocelyn Lemieux .15 .40
14 Marek Malik .15 .40
15 Steve Martins .15 .40
16 Paul Maurice CO .08 .25
17 Brad McCrimmon .15 .40
18 Jason Muzzatti .15 .40
19 Andrei Nikolishin .15 .40
20 Jeff O'Neill .15 .40
21 Paul Ranheim .15 .40
22 Steven Rice .15 .40
23 Geoff Sanderson .15 .40

24 Brendan Shanahan 1.25 3.00
25 Kevin Smyth .15 .40
26 Glen Wesley .25 .60
27 Kids Club Discount Card .02 .10

1996-97 Whalers Kid's Club

This set features the Whalers of the NHL. The cards were produced by the team for distribution to members of its Kid's Club. The cards of Steve Chiasson and Kent Manderville were available only in sets issued late in the season. The Kevin Brown card is not necessary for the complete set. The photo features him with the Springfield Falcons, the Whalers' farm team, the background is a different color, and the stock is noticeably thinner.

COMPLETE SET (28) 14.00 35.00
1 Sean Burke .75 2.00
2 Jason Muzzatti .60 1.50
3 Kevin Dineen .60 1.50
4 Geoff Sanderson .60 1.50
5 Keith Primeau .75 2.00
6 Jeff O'Neill .75 2.00
7 Marek Malik .40 1.00
8 Paul Ranheim .40 1.00
9 Alexander Godynyuk .40 1.00
10 Robert Kron .40 1.00
11 Gerald Diduck .40 1.00
12 Kelly Chase .40 1.00
13 Glen Wesley .40 1.00
14 Andrew Cassels .60 1.50
15 Hnat Domenichelli .40 1.00
16 Sami Kapanen .75 2.00
17 Nelson Emerson .60 1.50
18 Mark Janssens .40 1.00
19 Stu Grimson .75 2.00
20 Nolan Pratt .40 1.00
21 Glen Featherstone .40 1.00
22 Curtis Leschyshyn .40 1.00
23 Jeff Brown .40 1.00
24 Adam Burt .40 1.00
25 Steven Rice .40 1.00
26 Kevin Brown 1.25 3.00
27 Steve Chiasson 1.25 3.00
28 Kent Manderville 1.25 3.00

1940 Wheaties M4

This set is referred to as the "Champs in the USA" The cards measure about 6" 8 1'4" and are numbered. The drawing portion (inside the dotted lines) measures approximately 6" X 6". There is a Baseball player on each card and they are joined by football players, football coaches, race car drivers, airline pilots, a circus clown, ice skater, hockey star and golfers. Each athlete appears in what looks like a stamp with a serrated edge. The stamps appear one above the other with a brief block of copy describing his or her achievements. There appears to have been three printings, resulting in some variation panels. The full panels tell the cereal buyer to look for either 27, 39, or 63 champ stamps. The first nine panels apparently were printed more than once, since all the unknown variations occur with those numbers.

COMPLETE SET (20) 400.00 800.00
1A R. Ruffing/B. Feller 40.00 80.00
1B R. Ruffing/L. Durocher 30.00 50.00

1962 Wheaties Great Moments in Canadian Sports

This 25 card set, which measure approximately 3 1/2" by 2 1/2" was issued in Canada one per cereal box. The fronts have a color drawing of an important event in Canadian sport history while the backs have a description in both English and French as to what the significance of the event was.

COMPLETE SET (25)
1 Bill Barilko 2.00 5.00
Scores winning goal in 1951 Stanley
7 Frank Mahovlich 3.00 8.00
1st Maple Leaf 40 goal scorer
12 Maurice Richard/1960 Stanley Cup 3.00 8.00
16 Bernie Geoffrion/1961 50th goal 3.00 8.00
22 Lionel Conacher 2.50 6.00
Hockey

2001-02 Wild Crime Prevention

These eight cards are part of a larger 24-card set that also features players from the Minnesota Twins and Vikings. The cards are standard sized and were issued by local police.

COMPLETE SET (8) 8.00 20.00
17 Willie Mitchell .40 1.00
18 Marian Gaborik 6.00 15.00
19 Darby Hendrickson .40 1.00
20 Andrew Brunette .40 1.00
21 Sergei Zholtok .40 1.00
22 Jim Dowd .40 1.00
23 Manny Fernandez .60 1.50
24 Nick Schultz .40 1.00

2001-02 Wild Team Issue

These oversized (5X8) team issues feature player photos on the front and stats on the back. The sponsor (SBC) appears on all three, but just two (Fernandez and Mitchell) have text reading Limited Edition, 1 of 2,500. It's not known whether these cards actually are from the same set (which is assumed) or not. The checklist is far from complete -- if you know of additional cards, please email us at hockeymag@beckett.com.

COMPLETE SET
1 Manny Fernandez .75 2.00
2 Stacy Roest .40 1.00
3 Willie Mitchell .40 1.00

2003-04 Wild Law Enforcement Cards

These cards were handed out by local police in the St. Paul area. They are unnumbered and listed below in alphabetical order. It's quite likely that more cards exist. Please contact us at hockeymag@beckett.com if you can confirm.

COMPLETE SET (11)
1 Brad Bombardir .40 1.00
2 Pierre-Marc Bouchard 1.25 3.00
3 Marian Gaborik 1.25 3.00
4 Filip Kuba .40 1.00
5 Willie Mitchell .40 1.00
6 Richard Park .40 1.00
7 Dwayne Roloson .75 2.00
8 Nick Schultz .40 1.00
9 Wes Walz .40 1.00
10 Sergei Zholtok .40 1.00
11 McGruff the Crime Dog .04 .10

2006-07 Wild Crime Prevention

1 Pavol Demitra .40 1.00
2 Kim Johnsson .40 1.00
3 Keith Carney .40 1.00
4 Mark Parrish .40 1.00
5 Brian Rolston .40 1.00
6 Kurtis Foster .40 1.00
7 Mikko Koivu .75 2.00
8 Marian Gaborik 2.00 5.00
9 McGruff the Crime Dog .10 .25

2007-08 Wild Crime Prevention

COMPLETE SET (9) 5.00 10.00
1 McGruff The Crime Dog .10 .25
2 Niklas Backstrom .75 2.00
3 Brent Burns .60 1.50
4 Pierre-Marc Bouchard .60 1.50
5 Nick Schultz .60 1.50
6 Stephane Veilleux .40 1.00
7 Josh Harding .75 2.00
8 Petteri Nummelin .40 1.00
9 Branko Radivojevic .40 1.00

2011-12 Minnesota Wild Team Issue Jumbo

1 Cody Almond .30 .75
2 Niklas Backstrom .50 1.25
3 Pierre-Marc Bouchard .50 1.25
4 Kyle Brodziak .30 .75
5 Cal Clutterbuck .50 1.25
6 Matt Cullen .30 .75
7 Justin Falk .30 .75
8 Josh Harding .50 1.25
9 Dany Heatley .40 1.00
10 Nick Johnson .40 1.00
11 Matt Kassian .30 .75
12 Mikko Koivu .40 1.00
13 Guillaume Latendresse .40 1.00
14 Warren Peters .50 1.25
15 Darroll Powe .30 .75
16 Nate Prosser .30 .75
17 Marco Scandella .30 .75
18 Devin Setoguchi .40 1.00
19 Jared Spurgeon .30 .75
20 Clayton Stoner

2011-12 Wild Team Issue Sony

1 Matt Cullen .50 1.25
2 Cal Clutterbuck .75 2.00
3 Devin Setoguchi .60 1.50
4 Mikko Koivu .60 1.50
5 Niklas Backstrom .75 2.00

1924 Willard's Chocolates Sports Champions V122

43 Harry Watson 125.00 250.00
45 Ernie Collett RC 75.00 150.00
47 Hooley Smith 125.00 250.00
52 Dunc Munro RC 100.00 200.00

1960-61 Wonder Bread Labels

Similar to Wonder Bread Premium Photos, these are the actual labels that were wrapped around the Wonder Bread packages. Little is known about them, and few are confirmed to exist, so no prices have been established.

1 Gordie Howe
2 Bobby Hull
3 Dave Keon
4 Maurice Richard

1960-61 Wonder Bread Premium Photos

Produced and issued in Canada, the 1960-61 Wonder Bread set features four hockey stars. This set of premium photos measure approximately 5" by 7" and are unnumbered. There were actually two sets produced: Bread Labels and Premium Photos. The bread labels are valued at 50 to 100 percent of the values listed below. Reportedly the premium photo was inside the bread package and there was also a small picture of the player on the end of the bread wrapper. Keon's photo is noteworthy for preceding his RC by one year.

COMPLETE SET (4) 300.00 600.00
1 Gordie Howe 150.00 300.00
2 Bobby Hull 100.00 200.00
3 Dave Keon 40.00 80.00
4 Maurice Richard 100.00 200.00

1960-61 York Photos

This set of 37 photos is very difficult to put together. These unnumbered photos measure approximately 5" by 7" and feature members of the Montreal Canadiens (MC) and Toronto Maple Leafs (TML). The checklist below is ordered alphabetically. These large black and white cards were supposedly available from York Peanut Butter as a mail-in premium in return for two proofs of purchase; unfortunately there are no identifying marking on the photo that indicate the producer or the year of issue. The photos are action shots with a facsimile autograph of the player on the photo. The cards were apparently issued very late in the 1960-61 season since the set includes Eddie Shack as a Maple Leaf (he was acquired by Toronto from the Rangers during the 1960-61 season), Gilles Tremblay (his first NHL season was 1960-61 with the Canadiens), and several players (Jean-Guy Gendron, Larry Regan, Bob Turner) who were with other teams for the 1961-62 season.

COMPLETE SET (37) 1200.00 2400.00
1 George Armstrong TML 30.00 60.00
2 Ralph Backstrom MC 25.00 50.00
3 Bob Baun TML 30.00 60.00
4 Jean Beliveau MC 87.50 175.00
5 Marcel Bonin MC 17.50 35.00
6 Johnny Bower TML 62.50 125.00
7 Carl Brewer TML 25.00 50.00
8 Dick Duff TML 25.00 50.00
9 Jean-Guy Gendron MC 17.50 35.00
10 Boom Boom Geoffrion MC 62.50 125.00
11 Phil Goyette MC 17.50 35.00
12 Billy Harris TML 17.50 35.00
13 Doug Harvey MC 50.00 100.00
14 Bill Hicke MC 17.50 35.00
15 Larry Hillman TML 17.50 35.00
16 Charlie Hodge MC 25.00 50.00
17 Tim Horton TML 87.50 175.00
18 Tom Johnson MC 25.00 50.00
19 Red Kelly TML 30.00 60.00
20 Dave Keon TML 62.50 125.00
21 Albert Langlois MC 17.50 35.00
22 Frank Mahovlich TML 62.50 125.00
23 Don Marshall MC 25.00 50.00
24 Dickie Moore MC 30.00 60.00
25 Bob Nevin TML 17.50 35.00
26 Bert Olmstead TML 30.00 60.00
27 Jacques Plante MC 175.00 350.00
28 Claude Provost MC 25.00 50.00
29 Bob Pulford TML 30.00 60.00
30 Larry Regan TML 17.50 35.00
31 Henri Richard MC 62.50 125.00
32 Eddie Shack TML 50.00 100.00
33 Allan Stanley TML 30.00 60.00
34 Ron Stewart TML 17.50 35.00
35 Jean-Guy Talbot MC 25.00 50.00
36 Gilles Tremblay MC 25.00 50.00
37 Bob Turner MC 17.50 35.00

1961-62 York Yellow Backs

This set of 42 octagonal cards was issued by York Peanut Butter. The cards are numbered on the backs at the top. An album was originally available as a send-in offer or at certain food stores for 25 cents. The cards measure approximately 2 1/2" in diameter. The set can be dated as a 1961-62 set by referring to the career totals given on the back of each player's cards. The card backs were written in both French and English. The set is considered complete without the album.

COMPLETE SET (42) 300.00 600.00
1 Bob Baun 7.50 15.00
2 Dick Duff 6.00 12.00
3 Frank Mahovlich 12.50 25.00
4 Gilles Tremblay 5.00 10.00
5 Dickie Moore 7.50 15.00
6 Don Marshall 5.00 10.00
7 Tim Horton 15.00 30.00
8 Johnny Bower 10.00 20.00
9 Allan Stanley 7.50 15.00
10 Jean Beliveau 20.00 40.00
11 Tom Johnson 7.50 15.00
12 Jean-Guy Talbot 6.00 12.00
13 Carl Brewer 5.00 10.00
14 Bob Pulford 7.50 15.00
15 Billy Harris 5.00 10.00
16 Bill Hicke 5.00 10.00
17 Claude Provost 6.00 12.00
18 Henri Richard 12.50 25.00
19 Bert Olmstead 7.50 15.00
20 Ron Stewart 5.00 10.00
21 Red Kelly 7.50 15.00
22 Toe Blake CO 7.50 15.00
23 Jacques Plante 25.00 50.00
24 Ralph Backstrom 6.00 12.00
25 Eddie Shack 10.00 20.00
26 Bob Nevin 5.00 10.00
27 Dave Keon 20.00 40.00
28 Boom Boom Geoffrion 10.00 20.00
29 Marcel Bonin 5.00 10.00
30 Phil Goyette 5.00 10.00
31 Larry Hillman 5.00 10.00
32 Larry Keenan 5.00 10.00
33 Al Arbour 7.50 15.00
34 J.C. Tremblay 6.00 12.00
35 Bobby Rousseau 5.00 10.00
36 Al McNeil 5.00 10.00
37 George Armstrong 7.50 15.00
38 Punch Imlach CO 6.00 12.00
39 King Clancy 10.00 20.00
40 Lou Fontinato 5.00 10.00
41 Cesare Maniago 7.50 15.00
42 Jean Gauthier 5.00 10.00
xx Album 20.00 40.00

1962-63 York Iron-On Transfers

These iron-on transfers are very difficult to find. They measure approximately 2 1/4" by 4 1/4". There is some dispute with regard to the year of issue but the 1962-63 season seems to be a likely date based on the careers of the players included in the set. These transfers are numbered at the bottom.

COMPLETE SET (36) 900.00 1800.00
1 Johnny Bower 25.00 50.00
2 Jacques Plante 75.00 150.00
3 Tim Horton 50.00 100.00
4 Jean-Guy Talbot 15.00 30.00
5 Carl Brewer 15.00 30.00
6 J.C. Tremblay 15.00 30.00
7 Dick Duff 15.00 30.00
8 Jean Beliveau 50.00 100.00
9 Dave Keon 25.00 50.00
10 Henri Richard 40.00 80.00
11 Frank Mahovlich 40.00 80.00
12 BoomBoom Geoffrion 25.00 50.00
13 Kent Douglas 12.50 25.00
14 Claude Provost 15.00 30.00
15 Bob Pulford 15.00 30.00
16 Ralph Backstrom 15.00 30.00
17 George Armstrong 20.00 40.00
18 Bobby Rousseau 12.50 25.00
19 Gordie Howe 125.00 250.00
20 Red Kelly 20.00 40.00
21 Alex Delvecchio 20.00 40.00
22 Dickie Moore 20.00 40.00
23 Marcel Pronovost 15.00 30.00
24 Doug Barkley 12.50 25.00
25 Terry Sawchuk 50.00 100.00
26 Billy Harris 12.50 25.00
27 Parker MacDonald 12.50 25.00
28 Don Marshall 12.50 25.00
29 Norm Ullman 25.00 50.00
30A Andre Pronovost 12.50 25.00
30B Vic Stasiuk 12.50 25.00
31 Bill Gadsby 15.00 30.00
32 Eddie Shack 25.00 50.00
33 Larry Jeffrey 12.50 25.00
34 Gilles Tremblay 12.50 25.00
35 Howie Young 12.50 25.00
36 Bruce MacGregor 12.50 25.00

1963-64 York White Backs

This set of 54 octagonal cards was issued with York Peanut Butter and York Salted Nuts. The cards are numbered on the backs at the top. The cards measure approximately 2 1/2" in diameter. The set can be dated as a 1963-64 set by referring to the career totals given on the back of each player's cards. The card backs were written in both French and English. An album was originally available for holding the set; the set is considered complete without the album.

COMPLETE SET (54) 375.00 750.00
1 Tim Horton 20.00 40.00
2 Johnny Bower 12.50 25.00
3 Ron Stewart 7.50 15.00
4 Eddie Shack 12.50 25.00
5 Frank Mahovlich 15.00 30.00
6 Dave Keon 15.00 30.00
7 Bob Baun 7.50 15.00
8 Bob Nevin 7.50 15.00
9 Dick Duff 7.50 15.00
10 Billy Harris 7.50 15.00
11 Larry Hillman 7.50 15.00
12 Red Kelly 10.00 20.00
13 Kent Douglas 7.50 15.00
14 Allan Stanley 7.50 15.00
15 Don Simmons 7.50 15.00
16 George Armstrong 10.00 20.00
17 Carl Brewer 7.50 15.00
18 Bob Pulford 7.50 15.00
19 Henri Richard 15.00 30.00
20 BoomBoom Geoffrion 12.50 25.00
21 Gilles Tremblay 7.50 15.00
22 Gump Worsley 12.50 25.00
23 Jean-Guy Talbot 7.50 15.00
24 J.C. Tremblay 7.50 15.00
25 Bobby Rousseau 7.50 15.00
26 Jean Beliveau 20.00 40.00
27 Ralph Backstrom 7.50 15.00
28 Claude Provost 7.50 15.00
29 Jean Gauthier 7.50 15.00
30 Bill Hicke 7.50 15.00
31 Terry Harper 7.50 15.00
32 Marc Reaume 7.50 15.00
33 Dave Balon 7.50 15.00
34 Jacques Laperriere 10.00 20.00
35 John Ferguson 10.00 20.00
36 Red Berenson 7.50 15.00
37 Terry Sawchuk 25.00 50.00
38 Marcel Pronovost 7.50 15.00
39 Bill Gadsby 10.00 20.00
40 Parker MacDonald 7.50 15.00
41 Larry Jeffrey 7.50 15.00
42 Floyd Smith 7.50 15.00
43 Andre Pronovost 7.50 15.00
44 Art Stratton 7.50 15.00
45 Gordie Howe 50.00 100.00
46 Doug Barkley 7.50 15.00
47 Norm Ullman 10.00 20.00
48 Eddie Joyal 7.50 15.00
49 Alex Faulkner 15.00 30.00
50 Alex Delvecchio 10.00 20.00
51 Bruce MacGregor 7.50 15.00
52 Ted Hampson 7.50 15.00
53 Pete Goegan 7.50 15.00
54 Ron Ingram 7.50 15.00
xx Album 20.00 40.00

1967-68 York Action Octagons

This 36-card set was issued by York Peanut Butter. Only cards 13-36 are numbered. The twelve unnumbered cards have been assigned the numbers 1-12 based on alphabetizing the names of the first player listed on each card. Each card shows an action scene involving two or three players. Uniform numbers are also given on the cards. The card backs give the details of a send-in contest ending June 30, 1968. Collecting four cards spelling "YORK" entitled one to receive a Bobby Hull Hockey Game. These octagonal cards measure approximately 2 7/8" in diameter. The card backs were written in both French and English.

COMPLETE SET (36) 300.00 600.00
1 Brian Conacher 22 7.50 15.00
Allan Stanley 26
Leon Rochefor
2 Terry Harper 19 10.00 20.00
Gump Worsley 30
Mike Walton 16
3 Tim Horton 7 20.00 40.00
George Armstrong 10
Jean Beliveau 4
4 Dave Keon 14 10.00 20.00
George Armstrong 10
Claude Provost 14
5 Jacques Laperriere 2 10.00 20.00
Rogatien Vachon 29
Bob Pulford 20
6 Bob Pulford 20 6.00 12.00
Brian Conacher 22
Claude Provost 14
7 Bob Pulford 20 6.00 12.00
Jim Pappin 18
Terry Harper 19
8 Pete Stemkowski 12 6.00 12.00
Jim Pappin 18
Harris 10
9 J.C. Tremblay 3 7.50 15.00
Rogatien Vachon 29
Pete Stemkowski 12
10 Rogatien Vachon 29 10.00 20.00
Ralph Backstrom 6
Bob Pulford 20
11 Rogatien Vachon 29 10.00 20.00
Jacques Laperriere 2
Mike Walton 16
12 Mike Walton 16 6.00 12.00
Pete Stemkowski 12
J.C. Tremblay 3
13 Dave Keon 14 7.50 15.00
Mike Walton 16
J.C. Tremblay 3
14 Pete Stemkowski 12 5.00 10.00
Ralph Backstrom 6
15 Rogatien Vachon 29 7.50 15.00
Bob Pulford 20
16 Johnny Bower 1 7.50 15.00
Ron Ellis 8
John Ferguson 22
17 Ron Ellis 8 7.50 15.00
Gump Worsley 30
18 Gump Worsley 30 12.50 25.00
Jacques Laperriere 2
Frank Mahovlich 27
19 J.C. Tremblay 3 7.50 15.00
Dave Keon 14
20 Claude Provost 14 10.00 20.00
Frank Mahovlich 27
21 John Ferguson 22 10.00 20.00
Tim Horton 7
22 Gump Worsley 30 7.50 15.00
Ron Ellis 8
23 Johnny Bower 1 10.00 20.00
Mike Walton 16
Jean Beliveau 4
24 J.C. Tremblay 3 7.50 15.00
Gump Worsley 30
Bob Pulford 20
25 Tim Horton 7 15.00 30.00
Johnny Bower 1
Jean Beliveau 4
26 Allan Stanley 26 7.50 15.00
Johnny Bower 1
Dick Duff 8
27 Ralph Backstrom 6 7.50 15.00
Johnny Bower 1
28 Yvan Cournoyer 12 20.00 40.00
Jean Beliveau 4
Frank Mahovlich 27
29 Johnny Bower 1 10.00 20.00
Larry Hillman 2
Yvan Cournoyer 12
30 Johnny Bower 1 10.00 20.00
Yvan Cournoyer 12
31 Tim Horton 7 10.00 20.00
Rogatien Vachon 29
32 Jim Pappin 18 7.50 15.00
Bob Pulford 20
Rogatien Vachon 29
33 Terry Harper 19 5.00 10.00
Bobby Rousseau 15
Pronovost 3
34 Johnny Bower 1 6.00 12.00
Pronovost 3
Ralph Backstrom 6
35 Frank Mahovlich 27 12.50 25.00
Gump Worsley 30
36 Claude Provost 14 6.00 12.00
Johnny Bower 1

1992-93 Zeller's Masters of Hockey

This seven-card "Signature Series" standard-size set, featuring former NHL greats, was a promotion by Zeller's. According to the certificate of authenticity, the production run was 1,000 sets. The cards have posed color player photos inside white borders. A blue stripe above the picture carries the player's name and is accented by a thin mustard stripe. A silver foil facsimile signature is inscribed across the picture. The backs have the blue and mustard stripes running down the left side and carrying the player's jersey number. In English and French, biography, career highlights, and statistics are included on a white background. A close-up color player photo with a shadow border partially overlaps the stripe near the top. The cards are unnumbered and checklisted below in alphabetical order. There was also a large Marcel Dionne card reportedly given out at various store signings.

COMPLETE SET (7) 8.00 20.00
1 Johnny Bower 1.25 3.00
2 Rod Gilbert 1.25 3.00
3 Ted Lindsay 1.25 3.00
4 Frank Mahovlich 1.50 4.00
5 Stan Mikita 1.50 4.00
6 Maurice Richard 2.50 6.00
7 Certificate of Authenticity

1992-93 Zeller's Masters of Hockey Signed

This set features cards signed by former NHL greats and was distributed by Canadian retailing giant Zeller's. It is believed that approximately 1,000 copies exist of each card. We cannot confirm exactly how they were distributed at this point, although it is believed they could be acquired through a Zeller's customer loyalty program. Any further information can be forwarded to hockeymag@beckett.com.

COMPLETE SET (7) 50.00 125.00
1 Johnny Bower 6.00 15.00
2 Rod Gilbert 6.00 15.00
3 Ted Lindsay 6.00 15.00
4 Frank Mahovlich 8.00 20.00
5 Stan Mikita 8.00 20.00
6 Maurice Richard 25.00 60.00
7 Certificate of Authenticity

1993-94 Zeller's Masters of Hockey

Featuring former NHL greats, this 8-card "Signature Series" marks the second consecutive year a promotion was issued by Zellers. The cards measure the standard size and have posed color player photos inside white borders. A blue stripe above the picture carries the player's name and is accented by a thin mustard stripe. A silver foil facsimile signature is inscribed across the picture. The backs have the blue and mustard stripes running down the left side and carrying the player's jersey number. In English and French, biography, career highlights, and statistics are included on a white background. A close-up color player photo with a shadow border partially overlaps the stripe near the top. The cards are unnumbered and checklisted below in alphabetical order.

COMPLETE SET (8) 6.00 15.00
1 Andy Bathgate .40 1.00
2 Johnny Bucyk .75 2.00
3 Yvan Cournoyer .75 2.00
4 Marcel Dionne .75 2.00
5 Bobby Hull 1.50 4.00
6 Brad Park .75 2.00
7 Jean Ratelle .75 2.00
8 Gump Worsley 1.00 2.50
NNO Marcel Dionne Large .40 1.00

1993-94 Zeller's Masters of Hockey Signed

This set features cards signed by former NHL greats and was distributed by Canadian retailing giant Zeller's. It is believed that approximately 2,000 copies of each card exist. It is believed they could be acquired through a Zeller's customer loyalty program.

COMPLETE SET (8) 60.00 150.00
1 Andy Bathgate 6.00 15.00
2 Johnny Bucyk 10.00 25.00
3 Yvan Cournoyer 10.00 25.00
4 Marcel Dionne 10.00 25.00
5 Bobby Hull 15.00 40.00
6 Brad Park 10.00 25.00
7 Jean Ratelle 6.00 15.00
8 Gump Worsley 10.00 25.00
NNO Marcel Dionne Large

1994-95 Zeller's Masters of Hockey

For the third consecutive year, Zeller's issued an 8-card "Signature Series" set, featuring former NHL greats. The cards measure the standard size and have posed color player photos inside white borders. A blue stripe above the picture carries the player's name and is accented by a thin mustard stripe. A silver foil facsimile signature is inscribed across the picture. The backs have the blue and mustard stripes running down the left side and carrying the player's jersey number. In English and French, biography, career highlights, and statistics are included on a white background. A close-up color player photo with a shadow border partially overlaps the stripe near the top. The cards are unnumbered and checklisted below in alphabetical order.

COMPLETE SET (8) 4.00 10.00
1 Jean Beliveau 1.50 4.00
2 Gerry Cheevers .75 2.00
3 Red Kelly .75 2.00
4 Dave Keon .75 2.00
5 Lanny McDonald .40 1.00
6 Pierre Pilote .40 1.00
7 Henri Richard .75 2.00
8 Norm Ullman .75 2.00
NNO Jean Beliveau Large .75 2.00

1994-95 Zeller's Masters of Hockey Signed

This set features cards signed by former NHL greats and was distributed by Canadian retailing giant Zeller's. It is believed that approximately 1,100 copies exist of each card. We cannot confirm exactly how they were distributed at this point, although it is believed they could be acquired through a Zeller's customer loyalty program. Any further information can be forwarded to hockeymag@beckett.com.

COMPLETE SET (8) 50.00 125.00
1 Jean Beliveau 25.00 50.00
2 Gerry Cheevers 6.00 15.00
3 Red Kelly 6.00 15.00
4 Dave Keon 6.00 15.00
5 Lanny McDonald 6.00 15.00
6 Pierre Pilote 6.00 15.00
7 Henri Richard 8.00 20.00
8 Norm Ullman 6.00 15.00

1995-96 Zeller's Masters of Hockey Signed

This set features cards signed by former NHL greats and was distributed by Canadian retailing giant Zeller's. It is believed that approximately 3,500 copies exist of each card. Unlike previous years, it is thought that there were no un-signed versions released. We cannot confirm exactly how they were distributed at this point, although it is believed they could be acquired through a Zeller's customer loyalty program. Any further information can be forwarded to hockeymag@beckett.com.

COMPLETE SET (8) 70.00 175.00
1 Mike Bossy 10.00 25.00
2 Eddie Giacomin 6.00 15.00
3 Gordie Howe 20.00 50.00
4 Jacques Laperriere 6.00 15.00
5 Gilbert Perreault 8.00 20.00
6 Serge Savard 6.00 15.00
7 Steve Shutt 6.00 15.00
8 Darryl Sittler 8.00 20.00

1995-96 Zenith

The 1995-96 Zenith set was issued in one series totaling 150 standard-size cards. The 6-card packs had a suggested retail of $3.99. The set features 24-point card stock with exclusive Dufex all-foil printing.

1 Brett Hull .20 .50
2 Paul Coffey .15 .40
3 Jaromir Jagr .40 1.00
4 Joe Murphy .10 .25
5 Jim Carey .12 .30
6 Eric Lindros .25 .60
7 Ulf Dahlen .10 .25
8 Mark Recchi .20 .50
9 Pavel Bure .20 .50
10 Adam Oates .15 .40
11 Theo Fleury .20 .50
12 Martin Brodeur .40 1.00
13 Wayne Gretzky .75 2.00
14 Geoff Sanderson .10 .25
15 Chris Gratton .10 .25
16 Owen Nolan .15 .40
17 Paul Kariya .20 .50
18 Mark Messier .25 .60
19 Mats Sundin .15 .40
20 Brian Savage .10 .25
21 Mathieu Schneider .10 .25
22 Alexandre Daigle .10 .25
23 Jason Arnott .12 .30
24 Mike Modano .25 .60
25 Scott Mellanby .12 .30
26 Alexei Zhamnov .15 .40
27 Scott Niedermayer .15 .40
28 Chris Pronger .15 .40
29 Ray Bourque .25 .60
30 Sergei Fedorov .25 .60
31 Alexander Mogilny .12 .30
32 Brian Leetch .15 .40
33 Adam Graves .12 .30
34 Jocelyn Thibault .12 .30
35 Ron Francis .20 .50
36 John Vanbiesbrouck .12 .30
37 Chris Chelios .15 .40
38 Pierre Turgeon .15 .40
39 Stephane Richer .12 .30
40 Al MacInnis .15 .40
41 Dave Andreychuk .15 .40
42 Mikael Renberg .12 .30
43 Nelson Emerson .10 .25
44 Kevin Hatcher .12 .30
45 Kirk Muller .12 .30
46 Bernie Nicholls .10 .25
47 Bill Ranford .12 .30
48 Luc Robitaille .15 .40
49 Peter Bondra .15 .40
50 Jari Kurri .15 .40
51 Dino Ciccarelli .12 .30
52 Kevin Stevens .12 .30
53 Mike Richter .15 .40
54 Doug Gilmour .20 .50
55 Kelly Hrudey .12 .30
56 Dave Gagner .10 .25
57 Kirk McLean .12 .30
58 Geoff Courtnall .10 .25
59 John LeClair .15 .40
60 Mike Vernon .12 .30
61 Cam Neely .15 .40
62 Mike Gartner .15 .40
63 Igor Korolev .10 .25
64 Joe Sakic .25 .60
65 Jeff Friesen .10 .25
66 Sergei Zubov .12 .30
67 Trevor Kidd .12 .30
68 Rod Brind'Amour .15 .40
69 John MacLean .12 .30
70 Peter Forsberg .40 1.00
71 Oleg Tverdovsky .15 .40
72 Jeremy Roenick .20 .50
73 Gary Suter .12 .30
74 Keith Tkachuk .15 .40
75 Todd Harvey .10 .25
76 Felix Potvin .15 .40
77 Vincent Damphousse .12 .30
78 Blaine Lacher .12 .30
79 Tomas Sandstrom .12 .30
80 Chris Osgood .12 .30
81 Arturs Irbe .12 .30
82 Pat Verbeek .12 .30
83 Keith Primeau .10 .25
84 Brett Lindros .10 .25
85 Pat LaFontaine .15 .40
86 Brendan Shanahan .20 .50
87 Trevor Linden .15 .40
88 Rob Blake .12 .30
89 Scott Stevens .15 .40
90 Tom Barrasso .12 .30
91 Mike Ricci .12 .30
92 Ray Sheppard .12 .30
93 Steve Yzerman .20 .50
94 Wendel Clark .15 .40
95 Ed Belfour .12 .30
96 Joe Juneau .12 .30
97 Ron Hextall .15 .40
98 Shayne Corson .10 .25
99 Guy Hebert .12 .30
100 Sean Burke .10 .25
101 Sandis Ozolinsh .12 .30
102 Teemu Selanne .30 .75
103 Petr Nedved .12 .30
104 Phil Housley .12 .30
105 Andy Moog .15 .40
106 Larry Murphy .15 .40
107 Grant Fuhr .15 .40
108 Mario Lemieux .50 1.25
109 Dominik Hasek .20 .50
110 Rob Niedermayer .12 .30
111 Steve Duchesne .10 .25
112 Joe Nieuwendyk .15 .40
113 Yanic Perreault .10 .25
114 Steve Thomas .12 .30
115 Russ Courtnall .10 .25
116 Claude Lemieux .15 .40
117 Patrick Roy .40 1.00
118 Rick Tocchet .12 .30
119 Stephane Fiset .12 .30
120 Daren Puppa .12 .30
121 Ed Jovanovski .15 .40
122 Eric Daze .30 .75
123 Cory Stillman .10 .25
124 Brendan Witt .15 .40
125 Valeri Bure .10 .25
126 Brian Holzinger RC .30 .75
127 Kyle McLaren RC .10 .25
128 Niklas Sundstrom .15 .40
129 Jamie Langenbrunner .10 .25
130 Jeff O'neill .15 .40
131 Vitali Yachmenev .15 .40
132 Shane Doan RC .50 1.25
133 Byron Dafoe .12 .30
134 Corey Hirsch .12 .30
135 Antti Tormanen RC .10 .25
136 Jason Bonsignore .10 .25
137 Ryan Smyth .12 .30
138 Bryan McCabe .15 .40
139 Chad Kilger RC .15 .40
140 Todd Bertuzzi RC .20 .50
141 Marcus Ragnarsson RC .20 .50
142 Marty Murray .15 .40
143 Daymond Langkow RC .15 .40
144 Saku Koivu .15 .40
145 Jere Lehtinen .12 .30
146 Aki Berg RC .15 .40
147 Radek Dvorak RC .20 .50
148 Robert Svehla RC .10 .25
149 Daniel Alfredsson RC .75 2.00
150 Miroslav Satan RC .20 .50

1995-96 Zenith Gifted Grinders

Randomly inserted in packs at a rate of 1:6, this 18-card set showcases some of the best tough-play wingers in the game.

COMPLETE SET (18) 6.00 15.00
1 Keith Tkachuk .60 1.50
2 Kevin Stevens .40 1.00
3 Wendel Clark .60 1.50
4 Claude Lemieux .40 1.00
5 Rick Tocchet .40 1.00
6 Trevor Linden .60 1.50
7 John LeClair .40 1.00
8 Mikael Renberg .40 1.00
9 Owen Nolan .40 1.00
10 Todd Harvey .40 1.00
11 Dave Gagner .40 1.00
12 Dale Hunter .40 1.00
13 Dave Andreychuk .40 1.00
14 Mark Recchi .40 1.00
15 Jason Arnott .40 1.00
16 Dino Ciccarelli .40 1.00
17 Adam Graves .40 1.00
18 Steve Thomas .40 1.00

1995-96 Zenith Rookie Roll Call

Randomly inserted in packs at a rate of 1:24, this 18-card set features the hottest 1995-96 rookies highlighted by the Dufex technology. A note on the card backs alluded to the total production run of these cards being no greater than 1,200 total sets.

COMPLETE SET (18) 8.00 20.00
1 Saku Koivu 1.25 3.00
2 Radek Dvorak .40 1.00
3 Brendan Witt .40 1.00
4 Antti Tormanen .40 1.00
5 Brian Holzinger .40 1.00
6 Aki Berg .40 1.00
7 Ed Jovanovski .75 2.00
8 Marcus Ragnarsson .40 1.00
9 Todd Bertuzzi 1.25 3.00
10 Daniel Alfredsson 1.25 3.00
11 Vitali Yachmenev .40 1.00
12 Chad Kilger .40 1.00
13 Eric Daze .40 1.00
14 Niklas Sundstrom .40 1.00
15 Shane Doan 1.25 3.00
16 Cory Stillman .40 1.00
17 Kyle McLaren .40 1.00
18 Jeff O'neill .40 1.00

1995-96 Zenith Z-Team

Randomly inserted in packs at a rate of 1:72, this 18-card set depicts the best players in hockey, using a modified Dufex-type foil style. Based on stated insertion odds and the information given on the backs of the Rookie Roll Call singles, it is believed that no more than 400 of each Z-Team card is in existence.

1 Patrick Roy 50.00 120.00
2 Martin Brodeur 50.00 125.00
3 Mario Lemieux 60.00 150.00
4 Wayne Gretzky 60.00 150.00
5 Mark Messier 30.00 80.00
6 Jeremy Roenick 25.00 60.00
7 Eric Lindros 30.00 80.00
8 Peter Forsberg 50.00 120.00
9 Sergei Fedorov 30.00 80.00
10 Mike Modano 30.00 80.00
11 Jaromir Jagr 50.00 120.00
12 Pavel Bure 25.00 60.00
13 Joe Sakic 30.00 80.00
14 Paul Kariya 25.00 60.00
15 Brett Hull 25.00 60.00
16 Brendan Shanahan 25.00 60.00
17 Felix Potvin 20.00 50.00
18 Jim Carey 15.00 40.00
S2 Martin Brodeur SAMPLE 6.00 15.00

1996-97 Zenith

The 1996-97 Zenith set was issued in one series totaling 150 cards and was distributed in six-card packs. Printed on thick card stock, the fronts feature color action player images on a gold foil background. The backs carry in-depth player statistics. Dainius Zubrus and Sergei Berezin are the key rookies in the set.

COMPLETE SET (150) 12.00 30.00
1 Mike Modano .30 .75
2 Martin Brodeur .40 1.00
3 Pavel Bure .25 .60
4 Ray Bourque .30 .75
5 Steve Yzerman .50 1.25
6 Keith Tkachuk .20 .50
7 Jim Carey .20 .50
8 Valeri Kamensky .15 .40
9 Valeri Bure .12 .30
10 Ron Francis .25 .60
11 Trevor Kidd .12 .30
12 Doug Weight .20 .50
13 Wayne Gretzky 1.00 2.50
14 Todd Gill .15 .40
15 Dominik Hasek .30 .75
16 Scott Mellanby .15 .40

7 John LeClair .20 .50
8 Al MacInnis .20 .50
9 Derian Hatcher .12 .30
20 Stephane Fiset .15 .40
21 Alexander Selivanov .12 .30
22 Vyacheslav Kozlov .12 .30
23 Alexei Yashin .15 .40
24 Wendel Clark .15 .40
25 Ed Belfour .20 .50
26 Travis Green .15 .40
27 Joe Juneau .12 .30
28 Teemu Selanne .40 1.00
29 Jeff O'Neill .12 .30
30 Jeremy Roenick .30 .75
31 Felix Potvin .20 .50
32 Bernie Nicholls .12 .30
33 Steve Thomas .12 .30
34 Alexander Mogilny .15 .40
35 Patrick Roy .50 1.25
36 Luc Robitaille .20 .50
37 Owen Nolan .20 .50
38 Sergei Zubov .12 .30
39 Pierre Turgeon .20 .50
40 Nikolai Khabibulin .15 .40
41 Adam Oates .20 .50
42 Stephane Richer .15 .40
43 Daren Puppa .15 .40
44 Joe Sakic .30 .75
45 Ed Jovanovski .15 .40
46 Ron Hextall .15 .40
47 Doug Gilmour .25 .60
48 Paul Coffey .20 .50
49 Craig Janney .15 .40
50 Brendan Witt .12 .30
51 Jere Lehtinen .12 .30
52 Vitali Yachmenev .12 .30
53 Damian Rhodes .15 .40
54 Petr Nedved .15 .40
55 Theo Fleury .40 1.00
56 Petr Sykora .12 .30
57 Kelly Hrudey .15 .40
58 Saku Koivu .20 .50
59 Brian Bradley .12 .30
60 Arturs Irbe .15 .40
61 Eric Lindros .30 .75
62 Michal Pivonka .12 .30
63 Joe Nieuwendyk .20 .50
64 Mats Sundin .20 .50
65 Jason Arnott .15 .40
66 Mike Richter .20 .50
67 Brett Hull 1.00 2.50
68 Chris Chelios .20 .50
69 Jocelyn Thibault .20 .50
70 Oleg Tverdovsky .15 .40
71 Peter Bondra .15 .40
72 Bill Ranford .15 .40
73 Scott Stevens .20 .50
74 Jaromir Jagr .50 1.25
75 Corey Hirsch .15 .40
76 Peter Forsberg .30 .75
77 Brendan Shanahan .25 .60
78 Antti Tormanen .12 .30
79 Marcus Ragnarsson .12 .30
80 Sergei Fedorov .30 .75
81 Todd Bertuzzi .20 .50
82 Grant Fuhr .20 .50
83 Pat LaFontaine .20 .50
84 Rob Niedermayer .15 .40
85 Brian Leetch .20 .50
86 Yanic Perreault .12 .30
87 Dino Ciccarelli .20 .50
88 Dimitri Khristich .12 .30
89 Jeff Friesen .12 .30
90 Paul Kariya .25 .60
91 John Vanbiesbrouck .20 .50
92 Roman Hamrlik .15 .40
93 Pat Verbeek .12 .30
94 Mark Messier .30 .75
95 Trevor Linden .15 .40
96 Igor Larionov .20 .50
97 Zigmund Palffy .20 .50
98 Tom Barrasso .15 .40
99 Eric Daze .15 .40
100 Vincent Damphousse .15 .40
101 Keith Primeau .12 .30
102 Claude Lemieux .12 .30
103 Daniel Alfredsson .20 .50
104 Ryan Smyth .15 .40
105 Chris Osgood .20 .50
106 Bill Guerin .20 .50
107 Shayne Corson .12 .30
108 Alexei Zhamnov .15 .40
109 Mikael Renberg .15 .40
110 Andy Moog .20 .50
111 Larry Murphy .15 .40
112 Curtis Joseph .20 .50
113 Cory Stillman .12 .30
114 Mario Lemieux .60 1.50
115 Scott Young .12 .30
116 Eric Fichaud .15 .40
117 Jonas Hoglund .12 .30
118 Tomas Holmstrom RC .60 1.50
119 Jarome Iginla .25 .60
120 Richard Zednik RC .25 .60
121 Andreas Dackell RC .20 .50
122 Anson Carter .15 .40
123 Dainius Zubrus RC .25 .60
124 Janne Niinimaa .20 .50
125 Jason Allison .15 .40
126 Bryan Berard .20 .50
127 Sergei Berezin RC .30 .75
128 Wade Redden .12 .30
129 Jim Campbell .12 .30
130 Darcy Tucker .12 .30
131 Harry York RC .20 .50
132 Brandon Convery .12 .30
133 Ethan Moreau RC .20 .50
134 Mattias Timander RC .20 .50
135 Christian Dube .12 .30
136 Kevin Hodson RC .20 .50
137 Anders Eriksson .12 .30
138 Chris O'Sullivan .12 .30
139 Jamie Langenbrunner .12 .30
140 Steve Sullivan RC .15 .40
141 Daymond Langkow .15 .40
142 Landon Wilson .12 .30
143 Scott Bailey .12 .30
144 Terry Ryan RC .20 .50
145 Curtis Brown .12 .30
146 Rem Murray RC .20 .50
147 Jamie Pushor .12 .30
148 Daniel Goneau RC .20 .50
149 Mike Prokopec RC .15 .40
150 Brad Smyth RC .15 .40

1996-97 Zenith Artist's Proofs

Randomly inserted in packs at a rate of 1:48, this 150-card set is parallel to the regular set and is similar in design. The difference is found in the gold, rainbow holographic foil stamp on each card.
*VETS: 20X TO 50X BASIC CARDS
*ROOKIES: 8X TO 20X

1996-97 Zenith Assailants

Randomly inserted in packs at a rate of 1:10, this 15-card set features color photos of some of the NHL's most deadly snipers (as well as a couple of guys who couldn't hit water from the beach) and is printed on silver, micro-etched, poly-laminate card stock.
COMPLETE SET (15) 10.00 25.00
1 Alexei Yashin .75 2.00
2 Mike Modano 2.00 5.00
3 Jason Arnott .75 2.00
4 Mikael Renberg .75 2.00
5 Saku Koivu 1.25 3.00
6 Todd Bertuzzi 1.25 3.00
7 Zigmund Palffy 1.25 3.00
8 Eric Lindros 1.25 3.00
9 Pat LaFontaine .75 2.00
10 John LeClair .75 2.00
11 Theo Fleury .75 2.00
12 Pierre Turgeon .75 2.00
13 Petr Nedved .75 2.00
14 Owen Nolan 1.25 3.00
15 Valeri Bure .75 2.00

1996-97 Zenith Champion Salute

Randomly inserted in packs at a rate of 1:23, this special commemorative insert set honors superstar veteran players who have played on a Stanley Cup championship team. The fronts feature color player photos printed on micro-etched, silver poly-laminate card stock, along with a faux "diamond" chip embedded in the Stanley Cup ring icon. A parallel to this set, entitled Champion Salute Extra, included an actual diamond chip.
COMPLETE SET (15) 25.00 60.00
*DIAMOND: 2X TO 5X BASIC INSERTS
1 Mark Messier 1.50 4.00
2 Wayne Gretzky 10.00 25.00
3 Grant Fuhr .75 2.00
4 Paul Coffey .75 2.00
5 Mario Lemieux 6.00 15.00
6 Jaromir Jagr 1.25 3.00
7 Ron Francis .75 2.50
8 Joe Sakic 2.50 6.00
9 Peter Forsberg 1.50 4.00
10 Claude Lemieux .75 2.00
11 Patrick Roy 5.00 12.00
12 Chris Chelios .75 2.00
13 Doug Gilmour .75 2.00
14 Mike Richter .75 2.00
15 Martin Brodeur 3.00 8.00
P3 Grant Fuhr PROMO 1.50 4.00
P9 Peter Forsberg PROMO 3.00 8.00
P15 Martin Brodeur PROMO 4.00 10.00

1996-97 Zenith Z-Team

Randomly inserted packs at a rate of 1:71, this 18-card set honors some of the NHL superstars by combining embossing, micro-etching, rainbow holographic and gold foil stamping on clear plastic card stock.
COMPLETE SET (18) 40.00 100.00
1 Eric Lindros 6.00 15.00
2 Paul Kariya 5.00 12.00
3 Teemu Selanne 8.00 20.00
4 Brendan Shanahan 6.00 15.00
5 Sergei Fedorov 6.00 15.00
6 Steve Yzerman 12.00 30.00
7 Brett Hull 6.00 15.00
8 Pavel Bure 5.00 12.00
9 Alexander Mogilny 4.00 10.00
10 Jeremy Roenick 5.00 12.00
11 Jocelyn Thibault 4.00 10.00
12 Keith Tkachuk 4.00 10.00
13 Daniel Alfredsson 4.00 10.00
14 Eric Daze 4.00 10.00
15 Jim Carey 4.00 10.00
16 Felix Potvin 6.00 15.00
17 John Vanbiesbrouck 4.00 10.00
18 Chris Osgood 5.00 12.00

1997-98 Zenith

The 1997-98 Zenith set was issued in one series totaling 100 cards and was distributed in packs of three 5" by 7" cards with one regular size card inside each of the jumbo cards. The jumbo cards had to be torn open to get to the regular cards inside. The fronts feature action color player photos. The backs carry player information and another photo.
COMPLETE SET (100) 50.00 125.00
1 Jarome Iginla .60 1.50
2 Peter Forsberg .75 2.00
3 Brendan Shanahan .50 1.25
4 Wayne Gretzky 2.00 5.00
5 Steve Yzerman 1.25 3.00
6 Eric Lindros .50 1.25
7 Keith Tkachuk .50 1.25
8 John LeClair .50 1.25
9 John Vanbiesbrouck .30 .75
10 Patrick Roy 1.25 3.00
11 Ray Bourque .60 1.50
12 Theo Fleury .20 .50
13 Brian Leetch .50 1.25
14 Chris Chelios .50 1.25
15 Paul Kariya .50 1.25
16 Mark Messier .50 1.25
17 Curtis Joseph .50 1.25
18 Mike Richter .50 1.25
19 Jeremy Roenick .60 1.50
20 Dominik Hasek .75 2.00
21 Martin Brodeur 1.00 2.50
22 Sergei Fedorov .60 1.50
23 Pierre Turgeon .30 .75
24 Teemu Selanne .50 1.25
25 Brett Hull .60 1.50
26 Saku Koivu .50 1.25
27 Owen Nolan .30 .75
28 Jozef Stumpel .20 .50
29 Joe Sakic .75 2.00
30 Zigmund Palffy .30 .75
31 Jaromir Jagr .75 2.00
32 Adam Oates .30 .75
33 Jeff Friesen .20 .50
34 Pavel Bure .50 1.25
35 Chris Osgood .30 .75
36 Mark Recchi .30 .75
37 Mike Modano .60 1.50
38 Felix Potvin .50 1.25
39 Vincent Damphousse .20 .50
40 Byron Dafoe .30 .75
41 Luc Robitaille .30 .75
42 Peter Bondra .30 .75
43 Daniel Alfredsson .30 .75
44 Pat LaFontaine .20 .50
45 Mikael Renberg .20 .50
46 Doug Gilmour .30 .75
47 Dino Ciccarelli .20 .50
48 Mats Sundin .50 1.25
49 Ed Belfour .50 1.25
50 Ron Francis .30 .75
51 Miroslav Satan .30 .75
52 Cory Stillman .20 .50
53 Bryan Berard .20 .50
54 Keith Primeau .20 .50
55 Eric Daze .30 .75
56 Chris Gratton .30 .75
57 Claude Lemieux .20 .50
58 Nicklas Lidstrom .50 1.25
59 Olaf Kolzig .30 .75
60 Grant Fuhr .30 .75
61 Jamie Langenbrunner .20 .50
62 Doug Weight .30 .75
63 Joe Nieuwendyk .20 .50
64 Yanic Perreault .20 .50
65 Jocelyn Thibault .30 .75
66 Guy Hebert .20 .50
67 Shayne Corson .20 .50
68 Bobby Holik .20 .50
69 Sami Kapanen .20 .50
70 Robert Reichel .20 .50
71 Ryan Smyth .20 .50
72 Alexei Yashin .20 .50
73 Trevor Linden .20 .50
74 Rod Brind'Amour .30 .75
75 Dave Gagner .20 .50
76 Nikolai Khabibulin .30 .75
77 Tom Barrasso .30 .75
78 Tony Amonte .30 .75
79 Alexander Mogilny .30 .75
80 Jason Allison .20 .50
81 Patrik Elias RC 1.25 3.00
82 Mike Johnson RC .30 .75
83 Richard Zednik .30 .75
84 Patrick Marleau .30 .75
85 Mattias Ohlund .30 .75
86 Sergei Samsonov .30 .75
87 Marco Sturm RC .75 2.00
88 Alyn McCauley .30 .75
89 Chris Phillips .30 .75
90 Brendan Morrison RC .75 2.00
91 Vaclav Prospal RC .40 1.00
92 Joe Thornton 1.50 4.00
93 Boyd Devereaux .30 .75
94 Alexei Morozov .30 .75
95 Vincent Lecavalier RC 10.00 25.00
96 Manny Malhotra RC .40 1.00
97 Roberto Luongo RC 10.00 25.00
98 Mathieu Garon .30 .75
99 Alex Tanguay RC 4.00 10.00
100 Josh Holden .30 .75

1997-98 Zenith Z-Gold

Randomly inserted in packs, this 100-card set is a parallel version of the base set printed on gold-foil card stock and sequentially numbered to 100.
*VETS: 15X TO 40X BASIC CARDS
*PROSPECTS: 10X TO 25X
4 Wayne Gretzky 150.00 300.00
9 John Vanbiesbrouck 20.00 50.00
95 Vincent Lecavalier 100.00 200.00
97 Roberto Luongo 100.00 200.00

1997-98 Zenith Z-Silver

Randomly inserted in packs at the rate of 1:7, this 100-card set is a parallel version of the base set printed on silver-foil board.
COMPLETE SET (100)
*VETS: 2X TO 5X BASIC CARDS
*PROSPECTS: 1X TO 2.5X
4 Wayne Gretzky 15.00 40.00
95 Vincent Lecavalier 15.00 40.00
97 Roberto Luongo 20.00 50.00

1997-98 Zenith 5x7

This 80-card set measuring 5" by 7" was distributed in three-card packs with a regular size card inside each jumbo card. The fronts feature color action player photos with another photo and player information on the backs.
COMPLETE SET (80) 75.00 150.00
PRICES REFLECT CLEANLY OPENED PACKS
1 Wayne Gretzky 4.00 10.00
2 Eric Lindros .60 1.50
3 Patrick Roy 3.00 8.00
4 John Vanbiesbrouck .50 1.25
5 Martin Brodeur 1.50 4.00
6 Teemu Selanne .60 1.50
7 Joe Sakic 1.25 3.00
8 Jaromir Jagr 1.00 2.50
9 Brendan Shanahan .60 1.50
10 Ed Belfour .60 1.50
11 Guy Hebert .50 1.25
12 Doug Gilmour .50 1.25
13 Keith Primeau .25 .60
14 Grant Fuhr .50 1.25
15 Joe Nieuwendyk .50 1.25
16 Ryan Smyth .50 1.25
17 Chris Osgood .50 1.25
18 Keith Tkachuk .60 1.50
19 Peter Forsberg 1.50 4.00
20 Jarome Iginla .75 2.00
21 Steve Yzerman 3.00 0.00
22 Jeremy Roenick .75 2.00
23 Jozef Stumpel .50 1.25
24 Mark Recchi .50 1.25
25 Daniel Alfredsson .50 1.25
26 Pat LaFontaine .60 1.50
27 Zigmund Palffy .50 1.25
28 Jason Allison .25 .60
29 Yanic Perreault .25 .60
30 Olaf Kolzig .50 1.25
31 Mikael Renberg .50 1.25
32 Bryan Berard .50 1.25
33 Jocelyn Thibault .50 1.25
34 Shayne Corson .50 1.25
35 Dave Gagner .25 .60
36 Claude Lemieux .25 .60
37 Saku Koivu .60 1.50
38 Curtis Joseph .60 1.50
39 Chris Chelios .60 1.50
40 Ray Bourque 1.00 2.50
41 Adam Oates .50 1.25
42 Felix Potvin .60 1.50
43 Peter Bondra .50 1.25
44 Sergei Fedorov 1.00 2.50
45 Paul Kariya .60 1.50
46 Theo Fleury .25 .60
47 John LeClair .60 1.50
48 Brett Hull .75 2.00
49 Rod Brind'Amour .50 1.25
50 Doug Weight .50 1.25
51 Jamie Langenbrunner .25 .60
52 Mats Sundin .60 1.50
53 Ron Francis .50 1.25
54 Eric Daze .50 1.25
55 Nicklas Lidstrom .60 1.50
56 Luc Robitaille .50 1.25
57 Vincent Damphousse .25 .60
58 Mike Modano 1.00 2.50
59 Pavel Bure .60 1.50
60 Owen Nolan .50 1.25
61 Pierre Turgeon .50 1.25
62 Dominik Hasek 1.25 3.00
63 Mike Richter .60 1.50
64 Mark Messier .60 1.50
65 Brian Leetch .60 1.50
66 Sergei Samsonov .30 .75
67 Alexei Morozov .30 .75
68 Marco Sturm 1.25 3.00
69 Patrik Elias 1.00 2.50
70 Eric Messier .30 .75
71 Mike Johnson .30 .75
72 Richard Zednik .30 .75
73 Mattias Ohlund .30 .75
74 Joe Thornton 1.50 4.00
75 Vincent Lecavalier 8.00 20.00
76 Manny Malhotra .75 2.00
77 Roberto Luongo 12.50 25.00
78 Mathieu Garon .30 .75
79 Alex Tanguay 2.50 6.00
80 Josh Holden .30 .75

1997-98 Zenith 5x7 Gold Impulse

Randomly inserted in packs, this 80-card set is a gold foil parallel version of the base set and is sequentially numbered to 100.
*VETS: 10X TO 25X BASIC 5x7
*PROPECTS: 2X TO 5X BASIC 5x7
PRICES REFLECT CLEANLY OPENED PACKS

1997-98 Zenith 5x7 Silver Impulse

Randomly inserted in packs at the rate of 1:7, this 80-card set is a silver foil parallel version of the base set.
*VETS: 2X TO 5X BASIC 5x7
*PROSPECTS: .3X TO .8X BASIC 5x7
PRICES REFLECT CLEANLY OPENED PACKS

1997-98 Zenith Chasing The Cup

Randomly inserted in packs at the rate of 1:25, this 15-card set features color photos of top players printed on rainbow-hued holographic foil with an image of the trophy in the background.
COMPLETE SET (15) 50.00 125.00
1 Patrick Roy 10.00 25.00
2 Wayne Gretzky 15.00 40.00
3 Jaromir Jagr 4.00 10.00
4 Eric Lindros 2.00 5.00
5 Mike Modano 4.00 10.00
6 Brendan Shanahan 2.00 5.00
7 Brett Hull 3.00 8.00
8 John LeClair 1.25 3.00
9 Jocelyn Thibault 1.25 3.00
10 Ed Belfour 2.00 5.00
11 Martin Brodeur 10.00 25.00
12 Peter Forsberg 6.00 15.00
13 Saku Koivu 2.00 5.00
14 Pat LaFontaine 1.25 3.00
15 Steve Yzerman 12.00 30.00

1997-98 Zenith Rookie Reign

Randomly inserted in packs at the rate of 1:25, this 15-card set features color photos of top young players printed on holographic foil.
COMPLETE SET (15) 30.00 60.00
1 Sergei Samsonov 4.00 10.00
2 Joe Thornton 8.00 20.00
3 Erik Rasmussen 1.25 3.00
4 Brendan Morrison 2.00 5.00
5 Magnus Arvedson 1.25 3.00
6 Vaclav Prospal 1.25 3.00
7 Brad Isbister 1.25 3.00
8 Alexei Morozov 1.25 3.00
9 Marco Sturm 2.00 5.00
10 Patrick Marleau 4.00 10.00
11 Alyn McCauley 2.00 5.00
12 Mike Johnson 1.25 3.00
13 Mattias Ohlund 1.25 3.00
14 Patrik Elias 2.00 5.00
15 Richard Zednik 1.25 3.00

1997-98 Zenith Z-Team

Randomly inserted in packs at the rate of 1:35 for cards #1-9 and 1:58 for #10-18, this 18-card set features color action photos of top NHL players and rookies in white, black, and colored borders. The backs carry player information.
COMPLETE SET (18) 100.00 200.00
*5X7: .5X TO 1.2X BASIC INSERTS
5X7 STATED ODDS 1:35
*GOLDS: 1X TO 2.5X BASIC INSERTS
GOLD STATED ODDS 1:175
1 Teemu Selanne 3.00 8.00
2 Wayne Gretzky 20.00 50.00
3 Patrick Roy 8.00 20.00
4 Eric Lindros 3.00 8.00
5 Peter Forsberg 6.00 15.00
6 Paul Kariya 3.00 8.00
7 John LeClair 2.00 5.00
8 Martin Brodeur 8.00 20.00
9 Brendan Shanahan 3.00 8.00
10 Joe Thornton 6.00 15.00
11 Mattias Ohlund 2.00 5.00
12 Mike Johnson 2.00 5.00
13 Vaclav Prospal 2.00 5.00
14 Sergei Samsonov 2.00 5.00
15 Marco Sturm 2.00 5.00
16 Patrik Elias 2.00 5.00
17 Richard Zednik 2.00 5.00
18 Alexei Morozov 2.00 5.00

2010-11 Zenith

COMP.SET w/o SPs (140) 20.00 50.00
(141-185) PRINT RUN 999 SER.#'d SETS
(186-210) PRINT RUN 999 SER.#'d SETS
(211-225) PRINT RUN 199 SER.#'d SETS
1 Claude Giroux .30 .75
2 Erik Johnson .20 .50
3 Roberto Luongo .30 .75
4 Joe Thornton .30 .75
5 Henrik Zetterberg .40 1.00
6 Dion Phaneuf .30 .75
7 Patrice Bergeron .40 1.00
8 Carey Price 1.25 3.00
9 Dustin Brown .30 .75
10 Martin Brodeur .60 1.50
11 Nicklas Backstrom .50 1.25
12 Patrick Marleau .30 .75
13 Sam Gagner .25 .60
14 Tomas Vokoun .25 .60
15 Teemu Selanne .60 1.50
16 Jonathan Quick .50 1.25
17 Steven Stamkos .60 1.50
18 Zach Parise .30 .75
19 Ryan Miller .30 .75
20 Henrik Sedin .30 .75
21 Alex Ovechkin 1.25 3.00
22 Shane Doan .25 .60
23 Phil Kessel .40 1.00
24 Patrick Sharp .30 .75
25 Sidney Crosby 1.25 3.00
26 Daniel Sedin .30 .75
27 Dany Heatley .25 .60
28 David Backes .30 .75
29 Tim Thomas .25 .60
30 Evgeni Malkin 1.00 2.50
31 Derick Brassard .30 .75
32 Simon Gagne .30 .75
33 Eric Staal .40 1.00
34 Tim Jackman .20 .50
35 Duncan Keith .30 .75
36 James Reimer .30 .75
37 Vincent Lecavalier .25 .60
38 Nicklas Lidstrom .30 .75
39 Jussi Jokinen .20 .50
40 Brad Marchand .50 1.25
41 Marc-Andre Fleury .50 1.25
42 Ryan Getzlaf .50 1.25
43 Steve Mason .25 .60
44 Ales Hemsky .25 .60
45 Niklas Backstrom .30 .75
46 Jonathan Toews .60 1.50
47 Rick Nash .30 .75
48 Jamie Langenbrunner .20 .50
49 Jimmy Howard .40 1.00
50 Mike Richards .30 .75
51 Jarome Iginla .30 .75
52 Pekka Rinne .40 1.00
53 Mikko Koivu .30 .75
54 Brad Richards .30 .75
55 Ilya Bryzgalov .25 .60
56 Thomas Vanek .30 .75
57 Marian Gaborik .40 1.00
58 Jaroslav Halak .30 .75
59 Paul Stastny .30 .75
60 Michael Cammalleri .30 .75
61 Nikolai Khabibulin .25 .60
62 Anze Kopitar .50 1.25
63 Dustin Byfuglien .30 .75
64 Daniel Alfredsson .30 .75
65 David Booth .20 .50
66 Wojtek Wolski .20 .50
67 Henrik Lundqvist .50 1.25
68 Craig Anderson .30 .75
69 Jeff Carter .30 .75
70 Jordan Leopold .20 .50
71 Ryan Kesler .30 .75
72 Mike Green .30 .75
73 Miikka Kiprusoff .25 .60
74 Jason Spezza .20 .50
75 Shea Weber .25 .60
76 Pierre-Alexandre Parenteau .20 .50
77 Antti Niemi .25 .60
78 Semyon Varlamov .30 .75
79 Matt Duchene .30 .75
80 Cam Ward .30 .75
81 John Tavares .60 1.50
82 Patrick Kane .60 1.50
83 Jordan Staal .30 .75
84 Brian Boucher .25 .60
85 T.J. Oshie .50 1.25
86 Corey Perry .30 .75
87 Clarke MacArthur .20 .50
88 Rick DiPietro .25 .60
89 Kari Lehtonen .25 .60
90 Brandon Dubinsky .25 .60
91 Stephen Weiss .25 .60
92 James Wisniewski .20 .50
93 Patrik Elias .30 .75
94 Rene Bourque .20 .50
95 Milan Lucic .30 .75
96 Andrew Ladd .30 .75
97 Bobby Ryan .30 .75
98 Dan Hamhuis .25 .60
99 Martin St. Louis .30 .75
100 Jason Pominville .30 .75
101 Brent Burns .40 1.00
102 Dwayne Roloson .25 .60
103 Peter Forsberg .40 1.00
104 Kris Letang .30 .75
105 Evander Kane .30 .75
106 Matthew Lombardi .20 .50
107 Corey Crawford .40 1.00
108 Dan Boyle .25 .60
109 Tomas Kaberle .20 .50
110 Andrej Meszaros .20 .50
111 Loui Eriksson .25 .60
112 Ryan Malone .20 .50
113 Mikhail Grabovski .25 .60
114 Michael Grabner .25 .60
115 Theo Peckham .20 .50
116 Rod Gilbert .30 .75
117 Steve Yzerman .75 2.00
118 Cam Neely .30 .75
119 Joe Sakic .50 1.25
120 Brian Leetch .30 .75
121 Darren Pang .30 .75
122 Curtis Joseph .40 1.00
123 Eric Lindros .50 1.25
124 Jeremy Roenick .30 .75
125 Mario Lemieux 1.00 2.50
126 Ray Bourque .50 1.25
127 Tiger Williams .25 .60
128 Doug Gilmour .40 1.00
129 Guy Lafleur .40 1.00
130 Felix Potvin .50 1.25
131 Dave Schultz .30 .75
132 Derek Sanderson .25 .60
133 Brett Hull .50 1.25
134 Dale Hawerchuk .40 1.00
135 Kelly Hrudey .25 .60
136 Nick Fotiu .40 1.00
137 Patrick Roy .75 2.00
138 Trevor Linden .30 .75
139 Jean Beliveau .30 .75
140 Ed Belfour .30 .75
141 Patrice Cormier RC 2.50 6.00
142 Jamie Arniel RC 2.00 5.00
143 Trevor Gillies RC 2.00 5.00
144 Nazem Kadri RC 10.00 25.00
145 Marcel Mueller RC 2.50 6.00
146 Jan Mursak RC 4.00 10.00
147 Cedrick Desjardins RC 2.50 6.00
148 Jon Matsumoto RC 2.00 5.00
149 Richard Bachman RC 2.50 6.00
150 Matt Calvert RC 3.00 8.00
151 Mark Dekanich RC 2.00 5.00
152 Matt Hackett RC 2.50 6.00
153 Chris Tanev RC 5.00 12.00
154 Eric Tangradi RC 2.00 5.00
155 Jim O'Brien RC 2.50 6.00
156 Andrew Desjardins RC 2.00 5.00
157 Brett MacLean RC 2.50 6.00
158 Brandon Mashinter RC 2.50 6.00
159 Dana Tyrell RC 2.00 5.00
160 Dale Weise RC 2.50 6.00
161 Linus Klasen RC 2.00 5.00
162 Brodie Dupont RC 2.50 6.00
163 Travis Hamonic RC 2.50 6.00
164 Alex Urbom RC 2.00 5.00
165 Jeff Petry RC 2.50 6.00
166 Aaron Volpatti RC 2.50 6.00
167 Cory Emmerton RC 2.50 6.00
168 Jordan Pearce RC 3.00 8.00
169 Timo Pielmeier RC 2.50 6.00
170 J.P. Anderson RC 2.50 6.00
171 Alex Stalock RC 2.50 6.00
172 Evgeny Grachev RC 2.00 5.00
173 Nathan Lawson RC 2.00 5.00
174 Andreas Engqvist RC 3.00 8.00
175 Alexander Vasyunov RC 2.00 5.00
176 Dwight King RC 2.00 5.00
177 Colby Cohen RC 2.00 5.00
178 Rhett Rakhshani RC 2.00 5.00
179 Travis Morin RC 1.50 4.00
180 Paul Byron RC 2.50 6.00
181 Brandon Pirri RC 2.00 5.00
182 Ian Cole RC 2.00 5.00
183 Stefan Della Rovere RC 2.00 5.00
184 Keith Aulie RC 2.00 5.00
185 Chris Mueller RC 2.00 5.00
186 Philip McRae AU RC 3.00 8.00
187 T.J. Brodie AU RC 3.00 8.00
188 Marcus Johansson AU RC 5.00 12.00
189 Eric Wellwood AU RC 4.00 10.00
190 Tommy Wingels AU RC 3.00 8.00
191 Robin Lehner AU RC 6.00 15.00
192 Mats Zuccarello AU RC 6.00 15.00
193 Mattias Tedenby AU RC 2.50 6.00
194 Ryan McDonagh AU RC 8.00 20.00
195 Tomas Tatar AU RC 12.00 30.00
196 Kyle Clifford AU RC 3.00 8.00
197 Matt Bartkowski AU RC 4.00 10.00
198 Kevin Poulin AU RC 4.00 10.00
199 Luke Adam AU RC 3.00 8.00
200 Anders Lindback AU RC 3.00 8.00
201 Zac Dalpe AU RC 3.00 8.00
202 Steven Kampfer AU RC 5.00 12.00
203 Jeremy Morin AU RC 3.00 8.00
204 Kyle Palmieri AU RC 6.00 15.00
205 Henrik Karlsson AU RC 3.00 8.00
206 Nick Leddy AU RC 3.00 8.00
207 Ekman-Larsson AU/499 RC 5.00 12.00
208 Nino Niederreiter AU RC 4.00 10.00
209 Jacob Markstrom AU RC 12.00 30.00
210 Jacob Josefson AU RC 3.00 8.00
211 Tyler Seguin AU/199 RC 40.00 100.00
212 Cam Fowler AU/199 RC 8.00 20.00
213 Jordan Eberle AU/199 RC 30.00 80.00
214 Jordan Caron AU/199 RC 10.00 25.00
215 Sergei Bobrovsky AU/199 RC 15.00 40.00
216 Taylor Hall AU/199 RC 25.00 60.00
217 Derek Stepan AU/199 RC 12.00 30.00
218 Magnus Paajarvi AU/99 RC 8.00 20.00
219 Jeff Skinner AU/199 RC 15.00 40.00
220 Brayden Schenn AU/199 RC 12.00 30.00
221 A.Burmistrov AU/199 RC 6.00 15.00
222 P.K. Subban AU/199 RC 40.00 80.00
223 K.Shattenkirk AU/199 RC 12.00 30.00
224 T.McCollum AU/199 RC 8.00 20.00
225 Linus Omark AU/199 RC 15.00 40.00

2010-11 Zenith Red Hot

*RED: 2X TO 5X BASE
11 Nicklas Backstrom 2.50 6.00
107 Corey Crawford 2.00 5.00

2010-11 Zenith White Hot

*WHITE: 6X TO 15X BASE
STATED PRINT RUN 25 SER.#'d SETS
11 Nicklas Backstrom 8.00 20.00
107 Corey Crawford 6.00 15.00

2010-11 Zenith Rookie Parallel

141-185 AUTO PRINT RUN 99
*NON-AU/186-210: .4X TO 1X BASIC CARD
186-210 NON-AU PRINT RUN 199
FOUND INSIDE DARE TO TEAR JUMBOS
144 Nazem Kadri AU 25.00 60.00
146 Jan Mursak AU 15.00 40.00
154 Eric Tangradi AU 20.00 50.00
163 Travis Hamonic AU 10.00 25.00
168 Jordan Pearce AU 12.00 30.00
171 Alex Stalock AU 10.00 25.00
184 Keith Aulie AU 8.00 20.00
209 Jacob Markstrom 8.00 20.00

2010-11 Zenith Behind The Bench Autographs

STATED PRINT RUN 199 SER.#'d SETS
1 Joel Quenneville 15.00 40.00
2 Mike Babcock 12.00 30.00
3 Ron Wilson 10.00 25.00
4 Barry Trotz 6.00 15.00
5 Bruce Boudreau 10.00 25.00
6 Lindy Ruff 10.00 25.00
7 Alain Vigneault 8.00 20.00
8 Peter Laviolette 8.00 20.00
9 Claude Julien 20.00 50.00
10 Jacques Martin 8.00 20.00

2010-11 Zenith Chasing The Cup

COMPLETE SET (20) 25.00 60.00
1 Roberto Luongo 1.50 4.00
2 Daniel Sedin 1.50 4.00
3 Jimmy Howard 2.00 5.00
4 Nicklas Lidstrom 1.50 4.00
5 Pekka Rinne 2.00 5.00
6 Brad Richards 1.50 4.00
7 Jonathan Toews 3.00 8.00
8 Corey Crawford 2.00 5.00
9 Joe Thornton 1.50 4.00
10 Ryane Clowe 1.00 2.50
11 Mike Richards 1.50 4.00
12 Claude Giroux 1.50 4.00
13 Tim Thomas 1.25 3.00
14 Patrice Bergeron 2.00 5.00
15 Sidney Crosby 6.00 15.00
16 Marc-Andre Fleury 2.50 6.00
17 Alex Ovechkin 6.00 15.00
18 Semyon Varlamov 1.50 4.00
19 Steven Stamkos 3.00 8.00
20 Carey Price 6.00 15.00

2010-11 Zenith Crease Is The Word

COMPLETE SET (10) 12.00 30.00
1 Jonas Hiller 1.25 3.00
2 Tim Thomas 1.25 3.00
3 Carey Price 6.00 15.00
4 Jimmy Howard 2.00 5.00
5 Kari Lehtonen 1.25 3.00
6 Marc-Andre Fleury 2.50 6.00
7 Cam Ward 1.50 4.00
8 Henrik Lundqvist 2.50 6.00
9 Ondrej Pavelec 1.50 4.00
10 Corey Crawford 2.00 5.00

2010-11 Zenith Dare To Tear Jumbo

PRICES FOR CLEANLY TORN CARDS
UNTORN CARD 15.00 40.00
226 Sidney Crosby 8.00 20.00
227 Steven Stamkos 4.00 10.00
228 Carey Price 8.00 20.00
229 Alex Ovechkin 8.00 20.00
230 Henrik Lundqvist 3.00 8.00
231 Martin St. Louis 2.00 5.00
232 Martin Brodeur 4.00 10.00
233 Henrik Sedin 2.00 5.00
234 Henrik Zetterberg 2.50 6.00
235 Roberto Luongo 2.00 5.00
236 Steve Yzerman 5.00 12.00
237 Joe Sakic 3.00 8.00
238 Mario Lemieux 6.00 15.00
239 Patrick Roy 5.00 12.00
240 Eric Lindros 3.00 8.00
241 Mark Messier 3.00 8.00
242 Ray Bourque 3.00 8.00
243 Tony Esposito 2.00 5.00
244 Jeremy Roenick 2.00 5.00
245 Felix Potvin 3.00 8.00
246 Ed Belfour 2.00 5.00
247 Doug Gilmour 2.50 6.00
248 Brian Leetch 2.00 5.00
249 Brendan Shanahan 2.50 6.00
250 Cam Neely 2.00 5.00

2010-11 Zenith Donruss Elite Autographs

STATED PRINT RUN 99 SER.#'d SETS
FOUND INSIDE ZENITH DARE TO TEAR JUMBOS
201 Taylor Hall 30.00 80.00
202 Tyler Seguin 40.00 100.00
203 Jeff Skinner 20.00 50.00
204 Jordan Eberle
205 Mattias Tedenby 6.00 15.00
206 P.K. Subban 40.00 100.00
207 Derek Stepan 15.00 40.00
208 Nino Niederreiter 10.00 25.00
209 Sergei Bobrovsky
210 Tomas Tatar 25.00 50.00
211 Cam Fowler 10.00 25.00
212 Robin Lehner 15.00 40.00
213 Mats Zuccarello 12.00 30.00
214 Nazem Kadri 20.00 50.00
215 Anders Lindback 8.00 20.00
216 Patrice Cormier 10.00 25.00
217 Jeremy Morin 8.00 20.00
218 Philip Larsen 8.00 20.00
219 Luke Adam 8.00 20.00
220 Linus Omark 15.00 40.00
221 Kyle Clifford 15.00 40.00
222 Keith Aulie 8.00 20.00
223 John McCarthy 8.00 20.00
224 Jacob Markstrom 25.00 60.00
225 Alexander Vasyunov 8.00 20.00
226 Brandon Pirri 8.00 20.00
227 Cory Emmerton 10.00 25.00
228 Evgeny Grachev 8.00 20.00
229 Kevin Shattenkirk 15.00 40.00
230 Maxim Noreau 6.00 15.00

2010-11 Zenith Epix

FOUND INSIDE ZENITH DARE TO TEAR JUMBOS
1 Loui Eriksson 2.50 6.00
2 Anze Kopitar 5.00 12.00
3 Ryan Kesler 3.00 8.00
4 Sidney Crosby 12.00 30.00
5 Daniel Sedin 3.00 8.00
6 Henrik Zetterberg 4.00 10.00
7 Brad Richards 3.00 8.00
8 Jarome Iginla 3.00 8.00
9 Milan Hejduk 2.50 6.00
10 Kris Letang 3.00 8.00
11 Thomas Vanek 3.00 8.00
12 Tyler Myers 3.00 8.00
13 Evgeni Malkin 10.00 25.00
14 Dustin Brown 3.00 8.00
15 Patrice Bergeron 4.00 10.00
16 Tobias Enstrom 2.00 5.00
17 Tomas Plekanec 3.00 8.00
18 James Neal 3.00 8.00
19 John Tavares 6.00 15.00
20 Stephen Weiss 2.50 6.00
21 Ryan Malone 2.00 5.00
22 Shane Doan 2.50 6.00
23 Patrik Elias 3.00 8.00
24 Phil Kessel 4.00 10.00
25 Milan Lucic 3.00 8.00
26 Ryan Smyth 2.50 6.00
27 Dustin Penner 2.00 5.00
28 Nikolai Kulemin 2.50 6.00
29 Danny Briere 3.00 8.00
30 Blake Comeau 2.00 5.00
31 Tomas Fleischmann 2.00 5.00
32 Michal Neuvirth 2.50 6.00
33 Ville Leino 2.50 6.00
34 Matthew Lombardi 2.00 5.00
35 Nikolay Zherdev 2.00 5.00
36 Sergei Gonchar 2.00 5.00
37 David Krejci 3.00 8.00
38 George Parros 2.50 6.00
39 Bryan Little 3.00 8.00
40 Tyler Ennis 2.50 6.00
41 Robyn Regehr 2.00 5.00
42 Duncan Keith 3.00 8.00
43 Ryan O'Reilly 3.00 8.00
44 Taylor Hall 10.00 25.00
45 Jacob Markstrom 6.00 15.00
46 Tomas Tatar 5.00 12.00
47 Mats Zuccarello 4.00 10.00
48 Ryan McDonagh 6.00 15.00
49 Jeff Skinner 5.00 12.00
50 Jordan Eberle 6.00 15.00

2010-11 Zenith Epix Materials

STATED PRINT RUN 100 SER.#'d SETS
1 Loui Eriksson 3.00 8.00
2 Anze Kopitar 6.00 15.00
3 Ryan Kesler 4.00 10.00
4 Sidney Crosby 15.00 40.00

5 Daniel Sedin 4.00 10.00
6 Henrik Zetterberg 5.00 12.00
7 Brad Richards 4.00 10.00
8 Jarome Iginla 4.00 10.00
9 Milan Hejduk 3.00 8.00
10 Kris Letang 4.00 10.00
11 Thomas Vanek 4.00 10.00
12 Tyler Myers 4.00 10.00
13 Evgeni Malkin 12.00 30.00
14 Dustin Brown 4.00 10.00
15 Patrice Bergeron 5.00 12.00
16 Tobias Enstrom 2.50 6.00
17 Tomas Plekanec 4.00 10.00
18 James Neal 4.00 10.00
19 John Tavares 8.00 20.00
20 Stephen Weiss 3.00 8.00
21 Ryan Malone 2.50 6.00
22 Shane Doan 3.00 8.00
23 Patrik Elias 4.00 10.00
24 Phil Kessel 5.00 12.00
25 Milan Lucic 4.00 10.00
26 Ryan Smyth 3.00 8.00
27 Dustin Penner 2.50 6.00
28 Nikolai Kulemin 3.00 8.00
29 Danny Briere 4.00 10.00
30 Blake Comeau 2.50 6.00
31 Tomas Fleischmann 2.50 6.00
32 Michal Neuvirth 3.00 8.00
33 Ville Leino 3.00 8.00
34 Matthew Lombardi 2.50 6.00
35 Nikolay Zherdev 2.50 6.00
36 Sergei Gonchar 2.50 6.00
37 David Krejci 4.00 10.00
38 George Parros 3.00 8.00
39 Bryan Little 4.00 10.00
40 Tyler Ennis 3.00 8.00
41 Robyn Regehr 2.50 6.00
42 Duncan Keith 4.00 10.00
43 Ryan O'Reilly 4.00 10.00
44 Taylor Hall 12.00 30.00
45 Jacob Markstrom 5.00 12.00
46 Tomas Tatar 6.00 15.00
47 Mats Zuccarello 5.00 12.00
48 Ryan McDonagh 8.00 20.00
49 Jeff Skinner 6.00 15.00
50 Jordan Eberle 8.00 20.00

2010-11 Zenith Gifted Grinders

COMPLETE SET (20) 15.00 40.00
1 Troy Brouwer 1.50 4.00
2 Alex Ovechkin 6.00 15.00
3 Luke Schenn 1.25 3.00
4 Brian Boyle 1.00 2.50
5 Chris Neil 1.00 2.50
6 Brenden Morrow 1.25 3.00
7 Shea Weber 1.25 3.00
8 David Backes 1.50 4.00
9 Cal Clutterbuck 1.50 4.00
10 Milan Lucic 1.50 4.00
11 James Neal 1.50 4.00
12 Ryan Getzlaf 2.50 6.00
13 Ryan Malone 1.00 2.50
14 Scott Hartnell 1.50 4.00
15 Shane Doan 1.25 3.00
16 Shawn Thornton 1.00 2.50
17 Dustin Brown 1.50 4.00
18 Derek Dorsett 1.00 2.50
19 Ryan Callahan 1.50 4.00
20 Marc Staal 1.50 4.00

2010-11 Zenith Gifted Grinders Scraps Jerseys

STATED PRINT RUN 99-299
*PRIME/24-50: .6X TO 1.5X JERSEYS
2 Alex Ovechkin 8.00 20.00
3 Luke Schenn 3.00 8.00
4 Brian Boyle 2.50 6.00
5 Chris Neil 2.50 6.00
6 Brenden Morrow 3.00 8.00
7 Shea Weber 3.00 8.00
8 David Backes 4.00 10.00
9 Cal Clutterbuck 4.00 10.00
10 Milan Lucic/99 5.00 12.00
11 James Neal 4.00 10.00
12 Ryan Getzlaf 6.00 15.00
13 Ryan Malone 2.50 6.00
14 Scott Hartnell 4.00 10.00
15 Shane Doan 3.00 8.00
16 Shawn Thornton 2.50 6.00
17 Dustin Brown/99 5.00 12.00
18 Derek Dorsett 2.50 6.00
19 Ryan Callahan 4.00 10.00
20 Marc Staal 4.00 10.00

2010-11 Zenith Mozaics

COMPLETE SET (20) 40.00 80.00
1 Pavelec/Boulton/Antropov 1.50 4.00
2 Thornton/Chara/Rask 1.50 4.00
3 Vanek/Pominville/Stafford 1.50 4.00
4 Kiprusoff/Iginla/Backlund 1.50 4.00
5 Galiardi/Stastny/Duchene 1.50 4.00
6 Vermette/Mason/Voracek 1.50 4.00
7 Richards/Benn/Daley 2.00 5.00
8 Tatar/Zetterberg/Lidstrom 2.50 6.00
9 Eberle/Hall/Paajarvi 4.00 10.00
10 Schenn/Kopitar/Doughty 2.50 6.00
11 Clutterbuck/Backstrom/Koivu 1.50 4.00
12 Price/Pouliot/Pacioretty 6.00 15.00
13 Weber/Rinne/Suter 2.00 5.00
14 Parise/Brodeur/Tedenby 3.00 8.00
15 Lundqvist/Callahan/Zuccarello 2.50 6.00
16 Malkin/Staal/Tangradi 5.00 12.00
17 Stamkos/Hedman/Malone 3.00 8.00
18 Kessel/Gustavsson/Kadri 4.00 10.00
19 Burrows/Kesler/Luongo 1.50 4.00
20 Knuble/Ovechkin/Fehr 6.00 15.00

2010-11 Zenith Mozaics Materials

*DOUBLE JSY: .5X TO 1.2X SINGLE JSY
1 Pavelec/Boulton/Antropov 4.00 10.00
2 Thornton/Chara/Rask 4.00 10.00
3 Vanek/Pominville/Stafford 4.00 10.00
4 Kiprusoff/Iginla/Backlund 4.00 10.00
5 Galiardi/Stastny/Duchene 4.00 10.00
6 Vermette/Mason/Voracek 4.00 10.00
7 Richards/Benn/Daley 5.00 12.00
8 Tatar/Zetterberg/Lidstrom 8.00 25.00
9 Eberle/Hall/Paajarvi 8.00 25.00
10 Schenn/Kopitar/Doughty 6.00 15.00
11 Clutterbuck/Backstrom/Koivu 4.00 10.00
12 Price/Pouliot/Pacioretty 15.00 40.00
13 Weber/Rinne/Suter 5.00 12.00
14 Parise/Brodeur/Tedenby 8.00 20.00
15 Lundqvist/Callahan/Zuccarello 6.00 15.00
16 Malkin/Staal/Tangradi 12.00 30.00
17 Stamkos/Hedman/Malone 8.00 20.00
18 Kessel/Gustavsson/Kadri 10.00 25.00
19 Burrows/Kesler/Luongo 4.00 10.00
20 Knuble/Ovechkin/Fehr 2.00 20.00

2010-11 Zenith Mozaics Materials Triple

*TRIPLE JSY: .6X TO 1.5X SINGLE JSY
9 Eberle/Hall/Paajarvi 20.00 50.00

2010-11 Zenith National Treasures Autographs

STATED PRINT RUN 99 SER.#'d SETS
FOUND INSIDE DARE TO TEAR JUMBOS
201 Zac Dalpe 12.00 30.00
202 Ryan McDonagh 20.00 50.00
203 Mats Zuccarello 25.00 60.00
204 Magnus Paajarvi
205 Cam Fowler 12.00 30.00
206 Ian Cole 20.00 50.00
207 Tyler Seguin 60.00 120.00
208 Jacob Markstrom 25.00 60.00
209 Jeff Skinner 30.00 80.00
210 Anders Lindback 10.00 25.00
211 Tomas Tatar 25.00 50.00
212 P.K. Subban 50.00 120.00
213 Taylor Hall 40.00 100.00
214 Nazem Kadri 30.00 80.00
215 Jordan Eberle 60.00 120.00
216 Kevin Shattenkirk 20.00 50.00
217 Mattias Tedenby 8.00 20.00
218 Jordan Caron 12.00 30.00
219 Nino Niederreiter 25.00 60.00
220 Jeremy Morin 10.00 25.00
221 Derek Stepan
222 Alexander Burmistrov 10.00 25.00
223 Marcus Johansson
224 Robin Lehner 15.00 40.00
225 Sergei Bobrovsky 40.00 80.00

2010-11 Zenith Rookie Roll Call

COMPLETE SET (20) 50.00 100.00
1 Logan Couture 1.50 4.00
2 Jeff Skinner 2.50 6.00
3 Taylor Hall 5.00 12.00
4 Derek Stepan 2.50 6.00
5 Cam Fowler 1.50 4.00
6 Jordan Eberle 3.00 8.00
7 Kevin Shattenkirk 2.50 6.00
8 Tyler Seguin 5.00 12.00
9 Tyler Ennis 1.25 3.00
10 Magnus Paajarvi 1.50 4.00
11 Mats Zuccarello 2.00 5.00
12 Tomas Tatar 2.50 6.00
13 Brad Marchand 2.50 6.00
14 Mark Letestu 1.50 4.00
15 Oliver Ekman-Larsson 2.00 5.00
16 Corey Crawford 2.00 5.00
17 Jonathan Bernier 1.50 4.00
18 Sergei Bobrovsky 3.00 8.00
19 Anders Lindback 1.25 3.00
20 James Reimer 1.50 4.00

2010-11 Zenith Rookie Roll Call Jerseys

*PATCH/25-50: .6X TO 1.5X BASIC JSY
2 Jeff Skinner 5.00 12.00
3 Taylor Hall 12.00 30.00
4 Derek Stepan 5.00 12.00
5 Cam Fowler 3.00 8.00
6 Jordan Eberle 6.00 15.00
7 Kevin Shattenkirk 8.00 20.00
8 Tyler Seguin 10.00 25.00
9 Tyler Ennis 2.50 6.00
10 Magnus Paajarvi 3.00 8.00
11 Mats Zuccarello 10.00 25.00
12 Tomas Tatar 5.00 12.00
14 Mark Letestu 6.00 15.00
15 Oliver Ekman-Larsson 4.00 10.00
16 Corey Crawford 4.00 10.00
17 Jonathan Bernier 3.00 8.00
18 Sergei Bobrovsky 6.00 15.00
19 Anders Lindback 2.50 6.00
20 James Reimer 8.00 20.00

2010-11 Zenith Team Logo Die-Cut Jerseys

AT Alex Tanguay 2.50 6.00
AV Antoine Vermette 2.50 6.00
BB Brian Boucher 3.00 8.00
BJ Brent Johnson 3.00 8.00
BS Brayden Schenn 5.00 12.00
CC Cal Clutterbuck 4.00 10.00
CG Claude Giroux 4.00 10.00
DB Dustin Brown 4.00 10.00
DC Daniel Carcillo 2.50 6.00
DK Duncan Keith 4.00 10.00
DKU Dmitry Kulikov 3.00 8.00
DL David Legwand 3.00 8.00
DP Dion Phaneuf 4.00 10.00
DS Drew Stafford 4.00 10.00
EM Evgeni Malkin 12.00 30.00
IB Ilya Bryzgalov 3.00 8.00
JB Jared Boll 2.50 6.00
JBO Jay Bouwmeester
JG Josh Gorges 2.50 6.00
JM Jacob Markstrom 5.00 12.00
JS Jordan Staal 4.00 10.00
JV Jakub Voracek 4.00 10.00
KL Kris Letang 8.00 20.00
LC Luca Caputi 3.00 8.00
ME Martin Erat 2.50 6.00
MH Martin Havlat 3.00 8.00
MP Max Pacioretty 4.00 10.00
MS Mikael Samuelsson 2.50 6.00
MSL Martin St. Louis 4.00 10.00
NB Niklas Backstrom 4.00 10.00
NL Nicklas Lidstrom 6.00 15.00
OE Oliver Ekman-Larsson 5.00 12.00
PB Peter Budaj 3.00 8.00
PD Pavel Datsyuk 5.00 12.00
PH Patric Hornqvist 3.00 8.00
PK Phil Kessel 5.00 12.00
RB Rene Bourque 2.50 6.00
RK Ryan Kesler 4.00 10.00
RL Roberto Luongo 4.00 10.00
RM Ryan Malone 2.50 6.00
RMI Ryan Miller 4.00 10.00
SD Shane Doan 3.00 8.00
SM Steve Mason 3.00 8.00
TC Tim Connolly 2.50 6.00
TE Tyler Ennis 3.00 8.00
TG T.J. Galiardi 3.00 8.00
TH Tomas Holmstrom 2.50 6.00
TP Tomas Plekanec 4.00 10.00
TPU Teddy Purcell 4.00 10.00
WS Wayne Simmonds 5.00 12.00

2010-11 Zenith Winter Warriors Materials

*PRIME/25-50: .6X TO 1.5X MATERIALS
VL Vincent Lecavalier 3.00 8.00
AF Alexander Frolov 2.50 6.00
AK Andrei Kostitsyn 3.00 8.00
AK Anze Kopitar 6.00 15.00
AV Antoine Vermette 2.50 6.00
BB Brent Burns 5.00 12.00
BS Brayden Schenn 5.00 12.00
CK Chris Kunitz 4.00 10.00
CP Carey Price 6.00 15.00
DB David Backes 4.00 10.00
DK David Krejci 4.00 10.00
DS Daniel Sedin 4.00 10.00
EB Eric Boulton 2.50 6.00
EK Evander Kane 4.00 10.00
GC Gregory Campbell 2.50 6.00
JB Jared Boll 2.50 6.00
JE Jordan Eberle 8.00 20.00
JI Jarome Iginla 4.00 10.00
JM Jacob Markstrom 5.00 12.00
JQ Jonathan Quick 4.00 10.00
KL Kari Lehtonen 3.00 8.00
KL Kris Letang 4.00 10.00
LE Loui Eriksson 3.00 8.00
MD Michael Del Zotto 3.00 8.00
MG Mark Giordano 3.00 8.00
MG Michael Grabner 3.00 8.00
MH Milan Hejduk 3.00 8.00
MH Martin Havlat 3.00 8.00
MP Magnus Paajarvi 4.00 10.00
MZ Mats Zuccarello 5.00 12.00
NK Nikolai Kulemin 3.00 8.00
PE Patrik Elias 4.00 10.00
PR Pekka Rinne 5.00 12.00
PR Peter Regin 3.00 8.00
RM Ryan McDonagh 8.00 20.00
SC Sidney Crosby 15.00 40.00
SG Sergei Gonchar 2.50 6.00
SG Scott Gomez 3.00 8.00
TE Tyler Ennis 3.00 8.00
TF Tomas Fleischmann 2.50 6.00
TH Tomas Holmstrom 2.50 6.00
TH Taylor Hall 10.00 25.00
TV Thomas Vanek 4.00 10.00
TZ Travis Zajac 3.00 8.00
VL Ville Leino 3.00 8.00
WB Wade Belak 3.00 8.00
WS Wayne Simmonds 5.00 12.00
ZB Zach Bogosian 3.00 8.00

2010-11 Zenith Yours Truly Autographs

UPDATES ISSUED IN 2011-12 PNNACLE
AA Artem Anisimov 5.00 12.00
AB Alexandre Burrows 8.00 20.00
AK Anze Kopitar 15.00 40.00
AO Alex Ovechkin Upd. 40.00 80.00
BB Brian Boucher 5.00 12.00
BE Jamie Benn 8.00 20.00
BK Mikael Backlund Upd. 4.00 10.00
BO Drayson Bowman 5.00 12.00
BS Brandon Sutter Upd. 5.00 12.00
BW Jay Bouwmeester 8.00 20.00
CM Chris Mason Upd. 5.00 12.00
CN Chris Neil 4.00 10.00
DB Dustin Brown 6.00 15.00
DC Daniel Carcillo 4.00 10.00
DP David Perron 4.00 10.00
DR Dwayne Roloson 5.00 12.00
EB Emile Bouchard 15.00 40.00
EK Evander Kane 6.00 15.00
EM Evgeni Malkin 30.00 60.00
GI Rod Gilbert 12.00 30.00
GP George Parros 5.00 12.00
GR Michael Grabner 8.00 20.00
GZ Greg Zanon 4.00 10.00
HO Tomas Holmstrom Upd. 5.00 12.00
JB Johnny Bower 8.00 20.00
JD Jeff Deslauriers 4.00 10.00
JF Johan Franzen 6.00 15.00
JG Jonas Gustavsson 8.00 20.00
JH Jimmy Howard 8.00 20.00
JM Joe Mullen 5.00 12.00
JN James Neal 6.00 15.00
JO Jonas Hiller 5.00 12.00
JT John Tavares 12.00 30.00
KA Erik Karlsson Upd. 8.00 20.00
KB Krys Barch 4.00 10.00
KL Kari Lehtonen 5.00 12.00
LC Luca Caputi 5.00 12.00
LE Loui Eriksson Upd. 6.00 15.00
LS Lee Stempniak 4.00 10.00
MB Mikkel Boedker Upd. 4.00 10.00
MF Michael Frolik Upd. 4.00 10.00
MG Marian Gaborik Upd.
MH Matt Hunwick 4.00 10.00
MM Matt Moulson 5.00 12.00
MR Mike Richards 20.00 50.00
MS Mikael Samuelsson 4.00 10.00
MT Max Talbot Upd. 6.00 15.00
NG Nathan Gerbe 4.00 10.00
NK Nikolai Khabibulin 5.00 12.00
NZ Nikolay Zherdev 4.00 10.00
OP Ondrej Pavelec Upd. 8.00 20.00
PH Patric Hornqvist 5.00 12.00
PK Patrick Kane 25.00 60.00
PM Peter Mueller Upd. 5.00 12.00
PR Patrick Roy Upd. 50.00 100.00
PS Paul Stastny Upd. 6.00 15.00
RB Ray Bourque Upd. 25.00 50.00
RC Ryan Callahan 10.00 25.00
RG Ryan Getzlaf 10.00 25.00
RI Pekka Rinne 8.00 20.00
RK Ryan Kesler Upd. 12.00 30.00
RM Ryan Miller Upd.
RP Rich Peverley 6.00 15.00
RR Rick Rypien 15.00 30.00
RS Ryan Smyth 5.00 12.00
RY Bobby Ryan 6.00 15.00
SA Sam Gagner Upd. 5.00 12.00
SC Sidney Crosby Upd. 75.00 150.00
SD Shane Doan Upd. 6.00 15.00
SG Scott Gomez 5.00 12.00
SM1 Steve Mason 5.00 12.00
SM2 Stan Mikita 12.00 30.00
SS Steven Stamkos 20.00 50.00
SW Stephen Weiss 5.00 12.00
TB Tyler Bozak Upd. 6.00 15.00
TH Jose Theodore 6.00 15.00
TM Tyler Myers 6.00 15.00
TT Tim Thomas 20.00 50.00
TU Marty Turco 6.00 15.00
TV Tomas Vokoun 5.00 12.00
TZ Travis Zajac Upd. 6.00 15.00
VA Semyon Varlamov 6.00 15.00
VL Vincent Lecavalier
VS Viktor Stalberg Upd. 5.00 12.00
WE Shea Weber Upd. 5.00 12.00
WW Wojtek Wolski 4.00 10.00
ZA Zach Bogosian Upd. 5.00 12.00
ZB Zach Boychuk 5.00 12.00
ZP Zach Parise
ZS Zack Stortini 4.00 10.00

2010-11 Zenith Z-Team

COMPLETE SET (10) 40.00 80.00
*RED HOT: .6X TO 1.5X Z-TEAM
*WHITE HOT/25: 1.2X TO 3X Z-TEAM
1 Steven Stamkos 4.00 10.00
2 Peter Forsberg 2.50 6.00
3 Sidney Crosby 8.00 20.00
4 Tim Thomas 1.50 4.00
5 Alex Ovechkin 8.00 20.00
6 Jarome Iginla 2.00 5.00
7 Jonathan Toews 4.00 10.00
8 Roberto Luongo 2.00 5.00
9 Taylor Hall 6.00 15.00
10 Jeff Skinner 3.00 8.00

1956 Austrian Platnik and Shone

This single comes from an Austrian-issued multi-sport series. The cards are oversized and feature black and white fronts with blue and white backs, highlighted by the Olympic rings.

NNO Ice Hockey 12.50 25.00

1995-96 Austrian National Team

This 24-card set of the Austrian national team was sold at the 1996 World Championships in Vienna. The cards measure approximately 2 7/8" by 4" and feature color player cut-outs on the left with a head shot and player information printed on the right. The backs are blank. The cards are unnumbered and checklisted below in alphabetical order.

COMPLETE SET (28) 6.00 15.00
1 Christoph Brander .40 1.00
2 Thomas Cijan .20 .50
3 Claus Dalpiaz .30 .75
4 Reinhard Divis 1.25 3.00
5 Konrad Dorn .20 .50
6 Robin Doyle .20 .50
7 Michael Guntner .20 .50
8 Karl Heinzle .20 .50
9 Herbert Hohenberger .30 .75
10 Dieter Kalt .20 .50
11 Peter Kasper .20 .50
12 Werner Kerth .20 .50
13 Martin Krainz .20 .50
14 Gunter Lanzinger .20 .50
15 Engelbert Linder .20 .50
16 Arthur Marczell .20 .50
17 Manfred Muhr .20 .50
18 Rick Nasheim .20 .50
19 Kraig Nienhuis .40 1.00
20 Christian Perthaler .20 .50
21 Michael Puschacher .20 .50
22 Gerhard Puschnik .20 .50
23 Andreas Puschnig .20 .50
24 Gerald Ressmann .20 .50
25 Mario Schaden .20 .50
26 Michael Shea .20 .50
27 Wolfgang Strauss .20 .50
28 Martin Ulrich .20 .50

1937 British Sporting Personalities

Card features black and white front with biographical information on back.

37 Joe Beaton 10.00 20.00

1994-95 Czech APS Extraliga

This 303-card set measures the standard size and features the players of the Czech Elite League. Several prominent NHLers, including Jaromir Jagr and Martin Straka appear in this set. They returned to their homeland to play for their old club teams during the 1994 NHL lockout.

COMPLETE SET (303) 60.00 150.00
1 Pavel Cagas .30 .75
2 Ladislav Blazek .20 .50
3 Ales Flasar .08 .25
4 Petr Tejkl .08 .25
5 Jaromir Latal .08 .25
6 Ales Tomasek .08 .25
7 Jiri Kuntos .08 .25
8 Jan Vavrecka .08 .25
9 Martin Smetak .08 .25
10 Patrik Rimmel .08 .25
11 Michal Slavik .08 .25
12 Milan Navratil .08 .25
13 Petr Fabian .15 .40
14 Zdenek Eichenmann .08 .25
15 Miroslav Chalanek .08 .25
16 Pavel Nohel .08 .25
17 Radim Radevic .08 .25
18 Tomas Martinec .08 .25
19 Ales Zima .08 .25
20 Ivo Hrstka .08 .25
21 Richard Brancik .08 .25
22 Martin Jenacek .08 .25
23 Robert Holy .08 .25
24 Radovan Biegl .20 .50
25 Dusan Salficky .30 .75
26 Jiri Malinsky .08 .25
27 Jan Filip .08 .25
28 Jaroslav Spelda .08 .25
29 Petr Jancarik .08 .25
30 Robert Kostka .08 .25
31 Kamil Toupal .08 .25
32 Tomas Pacal .08 .25
33 Ales Pisa .15 .40
34 Milan Hejduk 15.00 40.00
35 Josef Zajic .20 .50
36 Stanislav Prochazka .08 .25
37 Jiri Sejba .20 .50
38 Marek Zadina .08 .25
39 Milan Filipi .08 .25
40 David Pospisil .08 .25
41 Tomas Blazek .20 .50
42 Patrik Weber .15 .40
43 Richard Kral .15 .40
44 Martin Sekera .08 .25
45 Ladislav Lubina .08 .25
46 Jiri Provaznik .08 .25
47 Martin Chlad .20 .50
48 Tomas Vokoun 4.00 10.00
49 Pavel Trnka .30 .75
50 Petr Kuda .08 .25
51 Frantisek Kaberle .30 .75
52 Libor Prochazka .30 .75
53 Jan Dlouhy .08 .25
54 Otakar Cerny .08 .25
55 Martin Ancicka .08 .25
56 Marek Zidlicky .75 2.00
57 Martin Prochazka .20 .50
58 Pavel Patera .30 .75
59 Otakar Vejvoda .30 .75
60 Jan Blaha .08 .25
61 David Cermak .15 .40
62 Petr Ton .08 .25
63 Miroslav Mach .08 .25
64 Patrik Elias 6.00 15.00
65 Martin Stepanek .08 .25
66 Tomas Mikolasek .08 .25
67 Milan Ruchar .15 .40
68 Jaromir Jagr 20.00 50.00
69 Milos Kajer .08 .25
70 Jaromir Sindel .40 1.00
71 Ivo Capek .20 .50
72 Jan Bohacek .08 .25
73 Zdenek Touzimsky .08 .25
74 Jan Krulis .08 .25
75 Frantisek Musil .20 .50
76 Jaroslav Nedved .08 .25
77 Frantisek Ptacek .08 .25
78 Pavel Taborsky .08 .25
79 Frantisek Kucera .20 .50
80 Pavel Srek .08 .25
81 Martin Simek .08 .25
82 Zbynek Kukacka .08 .25
83 Jiri Zelenka .15 .40
84 Jan Hlavac .75 2.00
85 Patrik Martinec .08 .25
86 David Bruk .08 .25
87 Pavel Geffert .20 .50
88 Michal Sup .08 .25
89 Jaromir Kverka .08 .25
90 Miroslav Hlinka .08 .25
91 Milan Kastner .20 .50
92 Andrej Potajcuk .08 .25
93 Roman Turek 2.00 5.00
94 Ladislav Gula .20 .50
95 Robert Slavik .20 .50
96 Jiri Hala .08 .25
97 Jaroslav Modry .20 .50
98 Petr Sedy .08 .25
99 Petr Hodek .08 .25
100 Petr Mainer .08 .25
101 Michael Kubicek .08 .25
102 Milan Nedoma .20 .50
103 Rudolf Suchanek .08 .25
104 Libor Zabransky .20 .50
105 Jaroslav Brabec .08 .25
106 Lubos Rob .15 .40
107 Zdenek Sperger .08 .25
108 Ondrej Vosta .08 .25
109 Filip Turek .08 .25
110 Radek Belohlav .20 .50
111 Frantisek Sevcik .08 .25
112 Roman Bozek .15 .40
113 Roman Horak .20 .50
114 Pavel Pycha .08 .25
115 Arpad Gyori .08 .25
116 Tomas Vasicek .20 .50
117 Michal Hlinka .20 .50
118 Daniel Kysela .08 .25
119 Rudolf Wolf .08 .25
120 Antonin Planovsky .08 .25
121 Tomas Kramny .08 .25
122 Vitezslav Skuta .20 .50
123 Pavel Marecek .08 .25
124 Miroslav Javin .08 .25
125 Kamil Pribyla .08 .25
126 Michal Cerny .08 .25
127 Juris Opulskis .08 .25
128 Richard Smehlik .30 .75
129 Ales Badal .08 .25
130 Robert Simicek .08 .25
131 Vladimir Vujtek .20 .50
132 Tomas Chlubna .08 .25
133 Michal Piskor .15 .40
134 Petr Folta .15 .40
135 Roman Kadera .15 .40
136 Lumir Kotala .08 .25
137 Jan Peterek .15 .40
138 Roman Rysanek .08 .25
139 Rudolf Pejchar .20 .50
140 Jiri Kucera .20 .50
141 Stanislav Benes .08 .25
142 Karel Smid .20 .50
143 Martin Kovarik .08 .25
144 Jiri Jonak .08 .25
145 Alexander Savickij .08 .25
146 Vaclav Ruprecht .08 .25
147 Ivan Vlcek .08 .25
148 Jaroslav Spacek .20 .50
149 Peter Veselovsky .08 .25
150 Milan Cerny .08 .25
151 Milan Volak .08 .25
152 Dusan Huml .08 .25
153 Tomas Kucharcik .08 .25
154 Martin Zivny .08 .25
155 Martin Straka .75 2.00
156 Michal Straka .08 .25
157 Jiri Beranek .15 .40
158 Ondrej Steiner .20 .50
159 Josef Rybar .40 1.00
160 Jaroslav Kreuzmann .08 .25
161 David Trachta .08 .25
162 Marek Novotny .20 .50
163 Pavel Falta .20 .50
164 Antonin Necas .08 .25
165 Roman Cech .08 .25
166 Pavel Zmrhal .08 .25
167 Petr Buzek .20 .50
168 Jaroslav Benak .20 .50
169 Michael Vyhlidal .08 .25
170 Petr Kuchyna .08 .25
171 Josef Marha .40 1.00
172 Leos Pipa .08 .25
173 Jiri Poukar .08 .25
174 Libor Dolana .08 .25
175 Viktor Ujcik .30 .75
176 Ladislav Prokupek .20 .50
177 Jiri Cihlar .20 .50
178 Patrik Fink .08 .25
179 Oldrich Valek .08 .25
180 Zdenek Cely .08 .25
181 Jaroslav Kames .30 .75
182 Pavel Malac .20 .50
183 Martin Maskarinec .08 .25
184 Pavel Rajnoha .15 .40
185 Pavel Kowalczyk .08 .25
186 Miloslav Guren .20 .50
187 Radim Tesarik .08 .25
188 Jan Krajicek .08 .25
189 Patrik Hucko .08 .25
190 Roman Kankovsky .08 .25
191 Jaroslav Hub .08 .25
192 Petr Kankovsky .08 .25
193 Pavel Janku .20 .50
194 Miroslav Okal .08 .25
195 Zdenek Okal .08 .25
196 Roman Mejzlik .15 .40
197 Juraj Jurik .08 .25
198 Roman Meluzin .08 .25
199 Josef Straub .20 .50
200 Martin Kotasek .08 .25
201 Zdenek Sedlak .08 .25
202 Petr Cajanek 1.25 3.00
203 Zdenek Orct .40 1.00
204 Petr Franek .20 .50
205 Petr Svoboda .40 1.00
206 Angel Nikolov .20 .50
207 Petr Molnar .08 .25
208 Kamil Prachar .20 .50
209 Jiri Slegr .40 1.00
210 Radek Mrazek .08 .25
211 Jan Vopat .20 .50
212 Ondrej Zetek .08 .25
213 Martin Stelcich .08 .25
214 Zdenek Skorepa .08 .25
215 Stanislav Rosa .08 .25
216 Radek Sip .20 .50
217 Martin Rousek .08 .25
218 Tomas Vlasak .20 .50
219 Radim Piroutek .08 .25
220 Robert Kysela .20 .50
221 Martin Rucinsky .40 1.00
222 Robert Lang .75 2.00
223 Ivo Prorok .08 .25
224 Jan Alinc .15 .40
225 Vladimir Machulda .08 .25
226 Kamil Kolacek .08 .25
227 David Balazs .08 .25
228 Roman Cechmanek 4.00 10.00
229 Ivo Pesat .20 .50
230 Antonin Stavjana .20 .50
231 Pavel Augusta .08 .25
232 Daniel Vrla .08 .25
233 Alexej Jaskin .08 .25
234 Radek Mesicek .08 .25
235 Marek Tichy .08 .25
236 Stanislav Pavelec .08 .25
237 Jan Srdinko .08 .25
238 Zbynek Marak .08 .25
239 Andrej Galkin .08 .25
240 Miroslav Stavjana .08 .25
241 Libor Forch .08 .25
242 Roman Stantien .08 .25
243 Josef Beranek .30 .75
244 Lubos Jenacek .08 .25
245 Michal Tomek .08 .25
246 Rostislav Vlach .08 .25
247 Miroslav Barus .08 .25
248 Josef Podlaha .08 .25
249 Pavel Rohlik .08 .25
250 Martin Altrichter .20 .50
251 Radek Toth .30 .75
252 Vladimir Hudacek .20 .50
253 Miloslav Horava .20 .50
254 Petr Macek .08 .25
255 Pavel Blaha .08 .25
256 Radomir Brazda .08 .25
257 Jiri Hes .08 .25
258 Tomas Arnost .08 .25
259 Miroslav Hosek .08 .25
260 Jan Penk .08 .25
261 Tomas Jelinek .20 .50
262 Jiri Hlinka .08 .25
263 Lubos Pazler .08 .25
264 Roman Blazek .08 .25
265 Vladimir Ruzicka .40 1.00
266 Tomas Kupka .08 .25
267 Lubos Dopita .08 .25
268 Ladislav Slizek .08 .25
269 Milan Antos .08 .25
270 Vadim Kulabuchov .08 .25
271 Anatolij Najda .08 .25
272 Tomas Hyka .08 .25
273 Vaclav Eiselt .08 .25
274 Tomas Placatka .08 .25
275 Jan Nemecek .20 .50
276 Josef Augusta CO .08 .25
277 Lubomir Fischer CO .08 .25
278 Jaromir Precechtel CO .08 .25
279 Marek Sykora CO .08 .25
280 Petr Hemsky CO .08 .25
281 Jan Neliba CO .08 .25
282 Zdenek Muller CO .08 .25
283 Frantisek Vyborny CO .08 .25
284 Stanislav Berger CO .08 .25
285 Karel Prazak CO .08 .25
286 Vladimir Caldr CO .08 .25
287 Alois Hadamczik CO .08 .25
288 Bretislav Bochensky CO .08 .25
289 Karel Trachta CO .08 .25
290 Jindrich Setikovsky CO .08 .25
291 Jaroslav Holik CO .08 .25
292 Jan Hrbaty CO .08 .25
293 Vladimir Vujtek CO .08 .25
294 Zdenek Cech CO .08 .25
295 Frantisek Vorlicek CO .08 .25
296 Ondrej Weissmann CO .08 .25
297 Horst Valasek CO .08 .25
298 Zdislav Tabara CO .08 .25
299 Pavel Richter CO .08 .25
300 Bretislav Kopriva CO .08 .25
NNO Checklist 1 .02 .10
NNO Checklist 2 .02 .10
NNO Checklist 3 .02 .10

1995-96 Czech APS Extraliga

This 400-card set features color action player photos of members of the Czech Republic's Extraliga.

COMPLETE SET (400) 50.00 125.00
1 Horst Valasek .08 .25
2 Zdislav Tabara .08 .25
3 Roman Cechmanek 1.50 4.00
4 Ivo Pesat .30 .75
5 Alexej Jaskin .08 .25
6 Stanislav Pavelec .08 .25
7 Jan Srdinko .08 .25
8 Antonin Stavjana .20 .50
9 Pavel Taborsky .08 .25
10 Jiri Veber .08 .25
11 Daniel Vrla .08 .25
12 Miroslav Barus .08 .25
13 Ivan Padelek .08 .25
14 Libor Forch .08 .25
15 Andrej Galkin .08 .25
16 Lubos Jenacek .08 .25
17 Tomas Srsen .08 .25
18 Rostislav Vlach .08 .25
19 Zbynek Marak .08 .25
20 Jiri Dopita .40 1.00
21 Ales Polcar .30 .75
22 Roman Stantien .08 .25
23 Michal Tomek .08 .25
24 Jiri Zadrazil .08 .25
25 Pavel Augusta .08 .25
26 Tomas Jakes .08 .25
27 Vladimir Vujtek .20 .50
28 Zdenek Cech .08 .25
29 Jaroslav Kames .30 .75
30 Pavel Malac .30 .75
31 Jan Vavrecka .08 .25
32 Miroslav Javin .08 .25
33 Stanislav Medrik .08 .25
34 Pavel Kowalczyk .08 .25
35 Miloslav Guren .20 .50
36 Radim Tesarik .08 .25
37 Jan Krajicek .08 .25
38 Jiri Marusak .08 .25
39 Josef Straub .30 .75
40 Pavel Janku .08 .25
41 Roman Meluzin .30 .75
42 Miroslav Okal .08 .25
43 Zdenek Okal .08 .25
44 David Bruk .08 .25
45 Jaroslav Hub .08 .25
46 Petr Cajanek .40 1.00
47 Tomas Nemcicky .08 .25
48 Martin Kotasek .08 .25
49 Zdenek Sedlak .08 .25
50 Petr Leska .08 .25
51 Vladimir Caldr .08 .25
52 Jaroslav Liska .08 .25
53 Oldrich Svoboda .08 .25
54 Robert Slavik .20 .50
55 Rudolf Suchanek .08 .25
56 Milan Nedoma .30 .75
57 Lukas Zib .08 .25
58 Karel Soudek .08 .25
59 Petr Sedy .08 .25
60 Libor Zabransky .20 .50
61 Kamil Toupal .08 .25
62 Michal Kubicek .08 .25
63 Martin Masak .08 .25
64 Radek Belohlav .20 .50
65 Radek Toupal .15 .40
66 Pavel Pycha .08 .25
67 Lubos Rob .15 .40
68 Filip Turek .08 .25
69 Ondrej Vosta .08 .25
70 Roman Bozek .15 .40
71 Jaroslav Brabec .08 .25
72 Petr Sailer .08 .25
73 Martin Strba .08 .25
74 Zdenek Sperger .08 .25
75 Jan Neliba .08 .25
76 Zdenek Muller .08 .25
77 Martin Chlad .30 .75
78 Jiri Kucera .08 .25
79 Jan Dlouhy .08 .25
80 Tomas Kaberle .75 2.00
81 Petr Kasik .08 .25
82 Jan Krulis .08 .25
83 Petr Kuda .08 .25
84 Libor Prochazka .20 .50
85 Martin Stepanek .08 .25
86 Marek Zidlicky .40 1.00
87 Jiri Beranek .15 .40
88 Jiri Burger .08 .25
89 David Cermak .08 .25
90 Milos Kajer .08 .25
91 Miroslav Mach .08 .25
92 Tomas Mikolasek .08 .25
93 Pavel Patera .30 .75
94 Martin Prochazka .30 .75
95 Petr Ton .08 .25
96 Otakar Vejvoda .30 .75
97 Josef Zajic .30 .75
98 Josef Augusta .08 .25
99 Lubomir Fischer .08 .25
100 Jaromir Precechtel .08 .25
101 Pavel Cagas .20 .50
102 Ladislav Blazek .20 .50
103 Jaromir Latal .08 .25
104 Jiri Latal .15 .40
105 Petr Tejkl .08 .25
106 Jiri Kuntos .08 .25
107 Patrik Rimmel .08 .25
108 Robert Machalek .08 .25
109 Jiri Polak .08 .25
110 Martin Bakula .08 .25
111 Michal Slavik .08 .25
112 Pavel Nohel .08 .25
113 Igor Cikl .08 .25
114 Zdenek Eichenmann .08 .25
115 Milan Navratil .08 .25
116 Ales Zima .08 .25
117 Tomas Martinec .15 .40
118 Richard Brancik .08 .25
119 Ondrej Kratena .30 .75
120 Michal Bros .20 .50
121 Juraj Jurik .08 .25
122 Jan Tomajko .08 .25
123 Richard Farda .15 .40
124 Bretislav Kopriva .08 .25
125 Martin Altrichter .30 .75
126 Radek Toth .20 .50
127 Miloslav Horava .30 .75
128 Martin Maskarinec .08 .25
129 Jakub Ficenec .20 .50
130 Jiri Hes .08 .25
131 Andrej Jakovenko .15 .40
132 Petr Macek .08 .25
133 Jan Penk .08 .25
134 Robert Kostka .08 .25
135 Vladimir Ruzicka .30 .75
136 Viktor Ujcik .30 .75
137 Ivo Prorok .08 .25
138 Tomas Jelinek .20 .50
139 Michal Sup .08 .25
140 Milan Antos .08 .25
141 Roman Blazek .08 .25
142 Jiri Hlinka .08 .25
143 Tomas Kupka .08 .25
144 Vaclav Eiselt .08 .25
145 Jaroslav Bednar .75 2.00
146 Ladislav Svoboda .08 .25
147 Ladislav Kudrna .08 .25
148 Josef Beranek .20 .50
149 Vladimir Kyhos .08 .25
150 Zdenek Orct .30 .75
151 Petr Franek .30 .75
152 Kamil Prachar .15 .40
153 Angel Nikolov .20 .50
154 Ondrej Zetek .08 .25
155 Tomas Arnost .08 .25
156 Normunds Sejejs .08 .25
157 Petr Kratky .08 .25
158 Sergej Butko .08 .25
159 Petr Molnar .08 .25
160 Radek Mrazek .08 .25
161 Radim Piroutek .08 .25
162 David Balazs .08 .25
163 Jindrich Kotrla .08 .25
164 Jaroslav Buchal .08 .25
165 Josef Straka .30 .75
166 Michail Fadejev .08 .25
167 Radek Sip .08 .25
168 Martin Rousek .08 .25
169 Tomas Vlasak .20 .50
170 Robert Kysela .30 .75
171 Jan Alinc .15 .40
172 Vladimir Machulda .08 .25
173 Vladimir Jerabek .08 .25
174 Frantisek Vorlicek .08 .25
175 Jan Hrbaty .08 .25
176 Marek Novotny .20 .50
177 Lukas Sablik .08 .25
178 Roman Kankovsky .08 .25
179 Michael Vyhlidal .08 .25
180 Jan Bohacek .08 .25
181 Roman Cech .30 .75
182 Zdenek Touzimsky .08 .25
183 Marek Posmyk .20 .50
184 Pavel Rajnoha .15 .40
185 Martin Tupa .08 .25
186 Libor Dolana .08 .25
187 Petr Vlk .15 .40

188 Petr Kankovsky .08 .25
189 Jiri Cihlar .30 .75
190 Jiri Poukar .08 .25
191 Jaromir Kverka .08 .25
192 Leos Pipa .08 .25
193 Ladislav Prokupek .30 .75
194 Patrik Fink .08 .25
195 Marek Melenovsky .30 .75
196 Jiri Holik .08 .25
197 Miroslav Bruna .08 .25
198 Jaroslav Walter .08 .25
199 Otto Zelezny .08 .25
200 Libor Barta .08 .25
201 Pavel Nestak .08 .25
202 Leo Gudas .08 .25
203 Karel Beran .08 .25
204 Richard Adam .08 .25
205 Pavel Zubicek .08 .25
206 Alexandr Elsner .08 .25
207 Robert Kantor .08 .25
208 Ladislav Tresl .20 .50
209 Frantisek Sevcik .20 .50
210 Michal Konecny .08 .25
211 Richard Sebestu .08 .25
212 Roman Mejzlik .15 .40
213 Zdenek Cely .08 .25
214 Jiri Vitek .08 .25
215 Radek Haman .08 .25
216 Tomas Krasny .08 .25
217 Jiri Suhrada .08 .25
218 Jaroslav Smolik .08 .25
219 Alois Hadamczik CO .08 .25
220 Karel Suchanek .08 .25
221 Michal Hlinka .30 .75
222 Josef Lucak .08 .25
223 Karel Pavlik .08 .25
224 Stanislav Meciar .30 .75
225 Petr Mainer .08 .25
226 Petr Pavlas .08 .25
227 Lubomir Sekeras .40 1.00
228 Roman Sindel .20 .50
229 Vaclav Slaby .08 .25
230 Miroslav Cihal .08 .25
231 Martin Palinek .08 .25
232 Petr Zajonc .08 .25
233 Michal Piskor .15 .40
234 Roman Kadera .30 .75
235 Marek Zadina .08 .25
236 Richard Kral .15 .40
237 Miroslav Skovira .08 .25
238 Vladimir Michalek .08 .25
239 Libor Zatopek .08 .25
240 Dusan Adamcik .08 .25
241 Jiri Novotny .08 .25
242 Karel Trachta .08 .25
243 Jindrich Setikovsky .08 .25
244 Rudolf Pejchar .30 .75
245 Michal Marik .08 .25
246 Karel Smid .30 .75
247 Martin Kovarik .08 .25
248 Jiri Hanzlik .08 .25
249 Jaroslav Spacek .20 .50
250 Stanislav Benes .08 .25
251 Robert Jindrich .20 .50
252 Vaclav Ruprecht .08 .25
253 Tomas Kucharcik .08 .25
254 Michal Straka .08 .25
255 Ondrej Steiner .20 .50
256 Tomas Klimt .20 .50
257 Martin Zivny .08 .25
258 Milan Volak .08 .25
259 Pavel Metlicka .08 .25
260 Josef Rybar .30 .75
261 Jaroslav Kreuzmann .08 .25
262 David Trachta .08 .25
263 Anatolij Najda .08 .25
264 Tomas Ruprecht .08 .25
265 Dalibor Sanda .08 .25
266 Jaroslav Brabec .08 .25
267 Frantisek Vyborny .08 .25
268 Stanislav Berger .08 .25
269 Ivo Capek .30 .75
270 David Volek .30 .75
271 Jiri Vykoukal .20 .50
272 Vaclav Burda .08 .25
273 Petr Kuchyna .08 .25
274 Pavel Srek .08 .25
275 Frantisek Ptacek .08 .25
276 Radek Hamr .15 .40
277 Jiri Krocak .08 .25
278 Jaroslav Nedved .08 .25
279 Jiri Zelenka .15 .40
280 David Vyborny .30 .75
281 Checklist 1 .02 .10
282 Checklist 2 .02 .10
283 Checklist 3 .02 .10
284 Checklist 4 .02 .10
285 Zbynek Kukacka .08 .25
286 Miroslav Hlinka .08 .25
287 Jaroslav Hlinka .08 .25
288 Jan Hlavac .40 1.00
289 Andrej Potajcuk .08 .25
290 Richard Zemlicka .40 1.00
291 Vladimir Stransky .08 .25
292 Ladislav Svozil .08 .25
293 Martin Prusek 4.00 10.00
294 Vladimir Hudacek .15 .50
295 Pavel Marecek .08 .25
296 Rudolf Wolf .08 .25
297 Tomas Kramny .08 .25
298 Pavel Kubina 1.25 3.00
299 Rene Sevecek .08 .25
300 Filip Kuba .30 .75
301 Ales Tomasek .08 .25
302 Roman Rysanek .08 .25
303 Vladimir Vujtek .20 .50
304 Petr Folta .08 .25
305 Jan Peterek .08 .25
306 Roman Simicek .20 .50
307 Pavel Zdrahal .08 .25
308 Pavel Sebesta .08 .25
309 David Moravec .40 1.00
310 Tomas Chlubna .08 .25
311 Ludek Krayzel .08 .25
312 Waldemar Klisiak .08 .25
313 Petr Fabian .08 .25
314 Josef Palacek .08 .25
315 Florian Strida .08 .25
316 Radovan Biegl .08 .25
317 Dusan Salficky .30 .75
318 Petr Jancarik .08 .25
319 Tomas Pacal .08 .25
320 Radomir Brazda .08 .25
321 Radek Mesicek .08 .25
322 Jiri Antonin .08 .25
323 Alexander Terechov .08 .25
324 Milan Beranek .08 .25
325 Ladislav Lubina .08 .25
326 David Pospisil .08 .25
327 Milan Kastner .08 .25
328 Stanislav Prochazka .08 .25
329 Patrik Weber .08 .25
330 Milan Hejduk 10.00 20.00
331 Tomas Blazek .08 .25
332 Jiri Jantovsky .08 .25
333 Jaroslav Kudrna .08 .25
334 Tomas Pisa .08 .25
335 Ales Pisa .08 .25
336 Ivan Vasilev .08 .25
337 Milan Hnilicka 2.00 5.00
338 Ales Flasar .08 .25
339 Martin Smetak .08 .25
340 Libor Polasek .20 .50
341 Vitezslav Skuta .08 .25
342 Ladislav Benysek .40 1.00
343 Jaroslav Smolik .08 .25
344 Igor Cikl .08 .25
345 Jan Czerlinski .08 .25
346 Marek Vorel .08 .25
347 Martin Ancicka .08 .25
348 Pavel Skrbek .20 .50
349 Petr Kadlec .08 .25
350 Tomas Kucharcik .08 .25
351 Ludek Bukac .30 .75
352 Zdenek Uher .08 .25
353 Roman Cechmanek 1.50 4.00
354 Roman Turek .75 2.00
355 Petr Briza .75 2.00
356 Jaroslav Kames .30 .75
357 Antonin Stavjana .20 .50
358 Bedrich Scerban .30 .75
359 Petr Kuchyna .08 .25
360 Jiri Vykoukal .30 .75
361 Frantisek Kaberle .30 .75
362 Jan Vopat .30 .75
363 Libor Prochazka .20 .50
364 Jiri Kucera .20 .50
365 Tomas Jelinek .20 .50
366 Richard Zemlicka .40 1.00
367 Martin Hostak .20 .50
368 Tomas Srsen .08 .25
369 Jiri Dopita .40 1.00
370 Martin Prochazka .30 .75
371 Pavel Patera .20 .50
372 Otakar Vejvoda .30 .75
373 Roman Horak .08 .25
374 Radek Belohlav .20 .50
375 Pavel Geffert .08 .25
376 Jan Alinc .08 .25
377 Roman Kadera .08 .25
378 Viktor Ujcik .30 .75
379 Roman Meluzin .20 .50
380 Pavel Janku .08 .25
381 Tomas Kucharcik .08 .25
382 Zbynek Marak .08 .25
383 Ales Zima .08 .25
384 Jaromir Jagr 10.00 25.00
385 Pavel Patera .30 .75
386 Martin Prochazka .30 .75
387 Pavel Janku .08 .25
388 Roman Cechmanek 1.50 4.00
389 Antonin Stavjana .20 .50
390 Rostislav Vlach .08 .25
391 Lubos Jenacek .08 .25
392 Dominik Hasek 6.00 15.00
393 Jiri Holik .08 .25
394 Frantisek Pospisil .08 .25
395 Ivan Hlinka .30 .75
396 Vladimir Martinec .08 .25
397 Jaroslav Pouzar .08 .25
398 Karel Gut .08 .25
399 Jan Benda .30 .75
400 unknown .08 .25

1996-97 Czech APS Extraliga

This 350-card set features the players of the top division in the Czech Republic, the Extraliga. They were produced by APS cards and sponsored by Fuji Film. Key cards in the set include Roman Turek, Marek Posmyk and Robert Reichel.

COMPLETE SET (350) 36.00 90.00
1 Marek Sykora CO .02 .10
2 Vladimir Kolek .02 .10
3 Rudolf Pejchar .15 .40
4 Ladislav Kudrna .15 .40
5 Miloslav Horava .08 .25
6 Petr Kadlec .08 .25
7 Jaromir Latal .08 .25
8 Jiri Hes .08 .25
9 Andrei Jakovenko .08 .25
10 Martin Maskarinec .08 .25
11 Jaroslav Horacek .08 .25
12 Robert Kostka .08 .25
13 Jiri Dolezal .08 .25
14 Tomas Kucharcik .08 .25
15 Ivo Prorok .08 .25
16 Roman Kadera .08 .25
17 Jiri Hlinka .08 .25
18 Tomas Kupka .08 .25
19 Viktor Ujcik .30 .75
20 Vladimir Ruzicka .15 .40
21 Ladislav Slizek .08 .25
22 Jaroslav Bednar .40 1.00
23 Michal Sup .08 .25
24 Radek Matejovsky .08 .25
25 Horst Valasek .02 .10
26 Jiri Vodak .02 .10
27 Jaroslav Kames .30 .75
28 Petr Kubena .15 .40
29 Petr Kuchyna .08 .25
30 Jiri Marusak .08 .25
31 Radim Tesarik .08 .25
32 Vadim Podrezov .08 .25
33 Stanislav Medrik .08 .25
34 Jan Krajicek .08 .25
35 Pavel Kowalczyk .08 .25
36 David Bruk .08 .25
37 Tomas Nemcicky .08 .25
38 Zdenek Sedlak .08 .25
39 Ales Zima .08 .25
40 Zbynek Marak .08 .25
41 Ales Polcar .08 .25
42 Roman Meluzin .08 .25
43 Pavel Janku .08 .25
44 Miroslav Okal .08 .25
45 Petr Cajanek .40 1.00
46 Martin Kotasek .08 .25
47 Petr Leska .08 .25
48 Alois Hadamczik CO .02 .10
49 Ales Mach .02 .10
50 Radovan Biegl .20 .50
51 Josef Lukac .20 .50
52 Petr Jancarik .08 .25
53 Lubomir Sekeras .40 1.00
54 Jiri Kuntos .08 .25
55 Stanislav Pavelec .08 .25
56 Patrik Hucko .08 .25
57 Miroslav Cihal .08 .25
58 Karel Pavlik .08 .25
59 Ondrej Zetek .08 .25
60 Richard Kral .08 .25
61 Petr Folta .08 .25
62 Josef Straub .08 .25
63 Petr Zajonc .08 .25
64 Roman Kontsek .08 .25
65 Marek Zadina .08 .25
66 Roman Blazek .08 .25
67 Michal Piskor .08 .25
68 Jozef Dano .08 .25
69 Vladimir Machulda .08 .25
70 Jiri Novotny .08 .25
71 Petr Lipina .08 .25
72 Jan Novotny CO .02 .10
73 Lubomir Bauer .02 .10
74 Milan Hnilicka 2.00 5.00
75 Martin Chlad .20 .50
76 Petr Kasik .08 .25
77 Jan Krulis .08 .25
78 Libor Prochazka .20 .50
79 Jan Dlouhy .08 .25
80 Marek Zidlicky .40 1.00
81 Tomas Kaberle .60 1.50
82 Pavel Skrbek .20 .50
83 Tomas Trachta .08 .25
84 Zdenek Eichenmann .08 .25
85 Josef Zajic .20 .50
86 David Cermak .08 .25
87 Ladislav Svoboda .08 .25
88 Tomas Mikolasek .08 .25
89 Petr Ton .08 .25
90 Jiri Beranek .15 .40
91 Vaclav Eiselt .08 .25
92 Jiri Burger .08 .25
93 Petr Tenkrat .30 .75
94 Petr Vogeltanz .08 .25
95 Filip Klapac .08 .25
96 Karel Suchanek .08 .25
97 Kamil Konecny .08 .25
98 Rostislav Haas .08 .25
99 Roman Slupina .08 .25
100 Milos Hrubes .08 .25
101 Petr Tejkl .08 .25
102 Martin Bakula .08 .25
103 Radek Mesicek .08 .25
104 Karel Frydl .08 .25
105 David Galvas .08 .25
106 Denis Tsygurov .15 .40
107 Juraj Jurik .08 .25
108 Petr Fabian .08 .25
109 Radim Radevic .08 .25
110 Jiri Zadrazil .08 .25
111 Martin Filip .08 .25
112 Karel Horny .08 .25
113 Zdenek Pavelek .08 .25
114 Eduard Gorbachev .15 .40
115 Valerij Belov .08 .25
116 Dalibor Rimsky .08 .25
117 Marek Harazim .08 .25
118 David Dostal .08 .25
119 Slavomir Lener .15 .40
120 Vaclav Sykora .08 .25
121 Robert Schistad .15 .40
122 Martin Cinibulk .08 .25
123 Jiri Vykoukal .20 .50
124 Jan Bohacek .08 .25
125 Jaroslav Nedved .08 .25
126 Jiri Krocak .08 .25
127 Vaclav Burda .08 .25
128 Radek Hamr .15 .40
129 Frantisek Ptacek .08 .25
130 Roman Horak .08 .25
131 Pavel Geffert .08 .25
132 Richard Zemlicka .20 .50
133 Jiri Zelenka .15 .40
134 Patrik Martinec .08 .25
135 David Vyborny .20 .50
136 Miroslav Hlinka .08 .25
137 Martin Hostak .15 .40
138 Jan Hlavac .40 1.00
139 Jaroslav Hinka .08 .25
140 Jan Benda .15 .40
141 Josef Palecek .08 .25
142 Milos Riha CO .08 .25
143 Libor Barta .08 .25
144 Dusan Salficky .30 .75
145 Radomir Brazda .08 .25
146 Pavel Augusta .08 .25
147 Jiri Malinsky .08 .25
148 Tomas Pacal .08 .25
149 Ales Pisa .08 .25
150 Pavel Kriz .15 .40
151 Alexander Tsyplakov .20 .50
152 Petr Mudroch .08 .25
153 Ladislav Lubina .08 .25
154 David Pospisil .08 .25
155 Stanislav Prochazka .08 .25
156 Tomas Martinec .08 .25
157 Milan Hejduk 7.50 15.00
158 Tomas Martinec .08 .25
159 Jiri Jantovsky .08 .25
160 Martin Koudelka .08 .25
161 Pavel Kabrt .08 .25
162 Petr Sykora .20 .50
163 Milan Prochazka .15 .40
164 Karel Plasek .08 .25
165 Josef Beranek .20 .50
166 Vladimir Kyhos .08 .25
167 Zdenek Orct .30 .75
168 Richard Hrazdira .08 .25
169 Kamil Prachar .15 .40
170 Radek Mrazek .08 .25
171 Roman Cech .20 .50
172 Angel Nikolov .20 .50
173 Martin Stepanek .08 .25
174 Sergej Butko .08 .25
175 Normunds Sejejs .08 .25
176 Petr Kratky .08 .25
177 Vladimir Jerabek .08 .25
178 Kamil Kastak .15 .40
179 Robert Kysela .08 .25
180 Petr Hrbek .08 .25
181 Martin Rousek .08 .25
182 Tomas Krasny .08 .25
183 Tomas Vlasak .20 .50
184 David Balazs .08 .25
185 Jindrich Kotrla .08 .25
186 Josef Straka .20 .50
187 Jaroslav Buchal .08 .25
188 Kamil Piros .60 1.50
189 Vladimir Vujtek .08 .25
190 Ladislav Svozil .08 .25
191 Martin Prusek 2.00 5.00
192 Tomas Vasicek .08 .25
193 Jiri Jonak .08 .25
194 Ales Tomasek .08 .25
195 Daniel Kysela .08 .25
196 Vitezslav Skuta .08 .25
197 Tomas Kramny .08 .25
198 Rene Sevecek .08 .25
199 Dmitrij Jerofejev .08 .25
200 Pavel Kumstat .08 .25
201 Roman Rysanek .08 .25
202 Roman Simicek .20 .50
203 Martin Smetak .08 .25
204 Tomas Chlubna .08 .25
205 Ludek Krayzel .08 .25
206 David Moravec .20 .50
207 Alexander Prokopjev .08 .25
208 Ales Kratoska .08 .25
209 Libor Pavlis .08 .25
210 Radek Klauda .08 .25
211 Libor Polasek .15 .40
212 Jan Neliba .08 .25
213 Zdislav Tabara .08 .25
214 Roman Cechmanek .75 2.00
215 Ivo Pesat .20 .50
216 Antonin Stavjana .20 .50
217 Bedrich Scerban .15 .40
218 Jiri Veber .08 .25
219 Alexej Jaskin .08 .25
220 Jan Srdinko .08 .25
221 Tomas Jakes .08 .25
222 Petr Kubox .08 .25
223 Michal Divisek .08 .25
224 Rostislav Vlach .08 .25
225 Michal Tomek .08 .25
226 Oto Hascak .20 .50
227 Tomas Kapusta .20 .50
228 Tomas Srsen .08 .25
229 Roman Stantien .08 .25
230 Jiri Dopita .30 .75
231 Ivan Padelek .08 .25
232 Andrej Galkin .08 .25
233 Ondrej Kratena .20 .50
234 David Hruska .08 .25
235 Daniel Tesarik .08 .25
236 Lukas Duba .08 .25
237 Vladimir Caldr .08 .25
238 Jaroslav Liska .08 .25
239 Oldrich Svoboda .08 .25
240 Robert Slavik .20 .50
241 Rudolf Suchanek .08 .25
242 Karel Soudek .08 .25
243 Milan Nedoma .20 .50
244 Kamil Toupal .08 .25
245 Petr Sedy .08 .25
246 Lukas Zib .08 .25
247 Martin Masak .08 .25
248 Radek Martinek .40 1.00
249 Vladimir Antipin .08 .25
250 Radek Toupal .15 .40
251 Pavel Pycha .08 .25
252 Lubos Rob .15 .40
253 Filip Turek .08 .25
254 Arpad Gyori .08 .25
255 Radek Belohlav .20 .50
256 Ondrej Vosta .08 .25
257 Milan Navratil .08 .25
258 Frantisek Sevcik .08 .25
259 Petr Sailer .08 .25
260 Michal Horak .08 .25
261 Kamil Brabenec .15 .40
262 Miroslav Barus .08 .25
263 Jiri Latal .15 .40
264 Miroslav Venkrbec .08 .25
265 Ladislav Blazek .20 .50
266 Robert Horyna .15 .40
267 Petr Pavlas .08 .25
268 Roman Veber .08 .25
269 Marek Tichy .08 .25
270 Jergus Baca .15 .40
271 Ladislav Benysek .20 .50
272 Jiri Polak .08 .25
273 Marek Cernosek .08 .25
274 Michal Slavik .08 .25
275 Pavel Nohel .08 .25
276 Radek Sip .08 .25
277 Jan Tomajko .08 .25
278 Michal Bros .15 .40
279 Radek Prochazka .08 .25
280 Radek Svoboda .08 .25
281 Michal Dvorak .08 .25
282 Ales Lipensky .08 .25
283 Filip Dvorak .08 .25
284 Milan Jurak .08 .25
285 Adam Drabek .08 .25
286 Bohuslav Ebermann .08 .25
287 Radim Rulik .08 .25
288 Martin Altrichter .20 .50
289 Michal Marik .08 .25
290 Ivan Vlcek .08 .25
291 Josef Reznicek .08 .25
292 Karel Smid .20 .50
293 Vaclav Ruprecht .08 .25
294 Jaroslav Spacek .20 .50
295 Jiri Hanzlik .08 .25
296 Robert Jindrich .20 .50
297 Tomas Jelinek .08 .25
298 Milan Volak .08 .25
299 Radek Kampf .08 .25
300 Miroslav Mach .08 .25
301 Petr Korinek .20 .50
302 Jiri Kucera .15 .40
303 Michal Straka .08 .25
304 Tomas Klimt .20 .50
305 Josef Rybar .20 .50
306 Dalibor Sanda .08 .25
307 Jiri Novotny .08 .25
308 Pavel Vostrak .08 .25
309 Frantisek Vorlicek .08 .25
310 Jan Hrbaty .08 .25
311 Ivo Capek .20 .50
312 Marek Novotny .08 .25
313 Roman Kankovsky .08 .25
314 Miroslav Javin .08 .25
315 Michael Vyhlidal .08 .25
316 Zdenek Touzimsky .08 .25
317 Martin Tupa .08 .25
318 Marian Morava .08 .25
319 Filip Vanecek .08 .25
320 Marek Posmyk .20 .50
321 Libor Dolana .08 .25
322 Petr Vlk .15 .40
323 Petr Kankovsky .08 .25
324 Jaroslav Hub .08 .25
325 Jiri Poukar .08 .25
326 Leos Pipa .08 .25
327 Ladislav Prokupek .20 .50
328 Patrik Fink .08 .25
329 Marek Melenovsky .15 .40
330 Milan Antos .08 .25
331 Jiri Holik .08 .25
332 Miroslav Bruna .08 .25
333 Michail Fadejev .08 .25
334 Ludek Bukac .15 .40
335 Slavomir Lener .15 .40
336 Zdenek Uher .08 .25
337 Roman Cechmanek .75 2.00
338 Roman Turek .75 2.00
339 Robert Sysela .08 .25
340 Jiri Veber .08 .25
341 Pavel Patera .20 .50
342 Radek Bonk .40 1.00
343 Radek Belohlav .20 .50
344 Drahomir Kadlec .15 .40
345 Michal Sykora .20 .50
346 Jiri Vykoukal .20 .50
347 Viktor Ujcik .20 .50
348 Stanislav Neckar .20 .50
349 Robert Reichel .30 .75
350 Roman Meluzin .15 .40

1997-98 Czech APS Extraliga

This standard-sized set features the players of the Czech Republic's Extraliga and was produced by APS. The set features early or even first cards of several top NHLers including Milan Hejduk, Patrik Stefan and Roman Cechmanek.

COMPLETE SET (380) 50.00 125.00
1 Slavomir Lener CO .20 .50
2 Vaclav Sykora CO .08 .25
3 Milan Hnilicka 2.00 5.00
4 Martin Cinibulk .08 .25
5 Frantisek Ptacek .08 .25
6 Frantisek Kucera .08 .25
7 Jaroslav Nedved .08 .25
8 Jiri Krocak .08 .25
9 Martin Holy .08 .25
10 Jaromir Kverka .08 .25
11 Jiri Zelenka .08 .25
12 Richard Zemlicka .20 .50
13 Jaroslav Hlinka .08 .25
14 Jaroslav Bednar .40 1.00
15 Ivo Novotny .08 .25
16 Radek Duda .20 .50
17 Michal Sivek .75 2.00
18 Jan Hlavac .40 1.00
19 Miroslav Hlinka .08 .25
20 Patrik Stefan ERC 1.25 3.00
21 Vaclav Burda .08 .25
22 Patrik Martinec .08 .25
23 Ladislav Benysek .20 .50
24 Jiri Vykoukal .20 .50
25 Petr Nedved .75 2.00
26 Jan Neliba CO .08 .25
27 Zdislav Tabara CO .08 .25
28 Roman Cechmanek 2.00 5.00
29 Ivo Pesat .30 .75
30 Radim Tesarik .08 .25
31 Antonin Stavjana .20 .50
32 Jiri Veber .08 .25
33 Michal Bros .08 .25
34 Alexej Jaskin .08 .25
35 Andrej Galkin .08 .25
36 Rostislav Vlach .08 .25
37 Ivan Padelek .08 .25
38 Tomas Srsen .08 .25
39 Jiri Dopita .30 .75
40 Ondrej Kratena .08 .25
41 Tomas Kapusta .08 .25
42 Pavel Zubicek .08 .25
43 Radek Belohlav .20 .50
44 Tomas Demel .08 .25
45 Michal Divisek .08 .25
46 Michal Safarik .08 .25
47 Josef Beranek .20 .50
48 Jan Tomajko .08 .25
49 Jan Srdinko .08 .25
50 Roman Stantien .08 .25
51 Eduard Novak CO .08 .25
52 Zdenek Cech CO .08 .25
53 Jaroslav Kames .40 1.00
54 Robert Hamrla .08 .25
55 Pavel Kowalczyk .08 .25
56 Jan Krajicek .08 .25
57 Petr Kuchyna .08 .25
58 Pavel Rajnoha .08 .25
59 Martin Hamrlik .08 .25
60 Jiri Marusak .08 .25
61 Karel Rachunek .40 1.00
62 Roman Meluzin .20 .50
63 Ales Zima .08 .25
64 Pavel Janku .20 .50
65 Tomas Nemcicky .08 .25
66 Petr Cajanek .30 .75
67 Miroslav Okal .08 .25
68 Zdenek Sedlak .08 .25
69 Ales Polcar .08 .25
70 Petr Leska .08 .25
71 Martin Spanhel .30 .75
72 Branislav Janos .08 .25
73 Marek Vorel .08 .25
74 Tomas Zizka .08 .25
75 Ondrej Weissman CO .08 .25
76 Vladimir Jerabek CO .08 .25
77 Zdenek Orct .30 .75
78 Richard Hrazdira .08 .25
79 Angel Nikolov .08 .25
80 Drahomir Kadlec .30 .75
81 Frantisek Prochazka .08 .25
82 Radek Mrazek .08 .25
83 Petr Molnar .08 .25
84 Martin Stepanek .08 .25
85 Roman Cech .08 .25
86 Vladimir Gyna .08 .25
87 Tomas Vlasak .08 .25
88 Robert Kysela .08 .25
89 Martin Rousek .08 .25
90 Petr Hrbek .08 .25
91 Vladimir Petrovka .08 .25
92 Ivo Prorok .08 .25
93 Tomas Krasny .08 .25
94 David Balazs .08 .25
95 Josef Straka .08 .25
96 Kamil Piros .40 1.00
97 Denis Afinogenov .20 .50
98 Rail Muftijev .08 .25
99 Dmitrij Denisov .08 .25
100 Karel Franek CO .08 .25
101 Petr Pelucha CO .08 .25
102 Rostislav Haas .08 .25
103 Pavel Nestak .08 .25
104 Martin Maskarinec .08 .25
105 David Galvas .08 .25
106 Milos Hrubes .08 .25
107 Pavel Sebesta .08 .25
108 Tomas Kramny .08 .25
109 Pavel Marecek .08 .25
110 Vaclav Slaby .08 .25
111 Petr Suchanek .08 .25
112 Zbynek Marak .08 .25
113 Michal Tomek .08 .25
114 Michal Piskor .08 .25
115 Juraj Jurik .08 .25
116 Karel Horny .08 .25
117 Jiri Zurek .08 .25
118 Martin Sychra .08 .25
119 Zdenek Pavelek .08 .25
120 Richard Brancik .08 .25
121 Milan Ministr .08 .25
122 Martin Sekera .08 .25
123 Vladimir Vujtek CO .20 .50
124 Ladislav Svozil CO .08 .25
125 Martin Prusek 1.50 4.00
126 Zdenek Dobes .08 .25
127 Jiri Jonak .08 .25
128 Vitezslav Skuta .08 .25
129 Dmitrij Jerofejev .08 .25
130 Petr Jurecka .08 .25
131 Pavel Kumstat .08 .25
132 Roman Simicek .20 .50
133 Roman Rysanek .08 .25
134 David Moravec .30 .75
135 Alexander Prokopjev .08 .25
136 Alexander Cherbajev .08 .25
137 Libor Pavlis .08 .25
138 Jan Matejny .08 .25
139 Libor Polasek .08 .25
140 Martin Kotasek .08 .25
141 Petr Zajonc .08 .25
142 Martin Lamich .08 .25
143 Daniel Vilasek .08 .25
144 Martin Tomasek .08 .25
145 Ales Kratoska .08 .25
146 Richard Farda CO .08 .25
147 Ladislav Slizek CO .08 .25
148 Martin Altrichter .08 .25
149 Ladislav Blazek .20 .50
150 Robert Kostka .08 .25
151 Jiri Hes .08 .25
152 Andrej Jakovenko .08 .25
153 Pavel Kolarik .20 .50
154 Martin Bakula .08 .25
155 Petr Kadlec .08 .25
156 Jan Novak .08 .25
157 Jan Hejda .08 .25
158 Vladimir Ruzicka .20 .50
159 Viktor Ujcik .20 .50
160 Jiri Dolezal .08 .25
161 Jiri Poukar .08 .25
162 Tomas Kucharcik .08 .25
163 Michal Sup .08 .25
164 Jiri Hlinka .08 .25
165 Tomas Kupka .08 .25
166 Radek Matejovsky .08 .25
167 Robert Kucera .08 .25
168 Jan Fadrny .08 .25
169 Jan Sochor .08 .25
170 Marek Sykora CO .08 .25
171 Radim Rulik CO .08 .25
172 Michal Marik .08 .25
173 Dusan Salficky .40 1.00
174 Josef Reznicek .08 .25
175 Ivan Vlcek .08 .25
176 Robert Jindrich .20 .50
177 Jiri Hanzlik .08 .25
178 Pavel Srek .08 .25
179 Ondrej Zetek .08 .25
180 Pavel Geffert .08 .25
181 David Pospisil .08 .25
182 Martin Filip .08 .25
183 Tomas Jelinek .08 .25
184 Michal Straka .08 .25
185 Milan Volak .08 .25
186 Pavel Vostrak .08 .25
187 Dalibor Sanda .08 .25
188 Milan Navratil .08 .25
189 Mojmir Musil .08 .25
190 Milan Kraft 2.00 5.00
191 Jiri Jelen .08 .25
192 Martin Cech .08 .25
193 Jan Novotny CO .08 .25
194 Lubomir Bauer CO .08 .25
195 Radek Toth .08 .25
196 Martin Bilek .08 .25
197 Jan Krulis .08 .25
198 Marek Zidlicky .08 .25
199 Tomas Kaberle 1.25 3.00
200 Pavel Skrbek .20 .50
201 Jan Penk .08 .25
202 Jan Dlouhy .08 .25
203 Jan Hranac .08 .25
204 Josef Zajic .08 .25
205 Zdenek Eichenmann .08 .25
206 Petr Ton .08 .25
207 Jiri Beranek .08 .25
208 Ladislav Svoboda .08 .25
209 Vaclav Eiselt .08 .25
210 Jiri Burger .08 .25
211 Petr Tenkrat .30 .75
212 Jiri Kuchler .08 .25
213 Tomas Trachta .08 .25
214 Jiri Holsan .08 .25
215 Milan Novy .08 .25
216 Jiri Kloboucek .08 .25
217 Tomas Mikolasek .08 .25
218 Milan Kasparek CO .08 .25
219 Karel Trachta CO .08 .25
220 Vladimir Hudacek .08 .25
221 Robert Horyna CO .08 .25
222 Petr Pavlas .08 .25
223 Petr Mainer .08 .25
224 Ales Tomasek .08 .25
225 Pavel Blaha .08 .25
226 Jiri Polak .08 .25
227 Martin Richter .08 .25
228 Martin Rejthar .08 .25
229 Michal Cerny .08 .25
230 Zbynek Kukacka .08 .25
231 Ondrej Steiner .08 .25
232 Pavel Metlicka .08 .25
233 Martin Streit .08 .25
234 Radek Prochazka .08 .25
235 Radek Svoboda .08 .25
236 Michal Porak .08 .25
237 Michal Horak .08 .25
238 Jan Lipiansky .08 .25
239 Jaroslav Buchal .08 .25
240 Tomas Klimt .20 .50
241 Petr Fical .08 .25
242 Milos Riha CO .08 .25
243 Josef Palecek CO .08 .25
244 Libor Barta .08 .25
245 Adam Svoboda .40 1.00
246 Patrik Rozsival .08 .25
247 Jiri Malinsky .08 .25
248 Ales Pisa .08 .25
249 Tomas Pacal .08 .25
250 Pavel Kriz .20 .50
251 Pavel Augusta .08 .25
252 Petr Murdoch .08 .25
253 Robert Pospisil .08 .25
254 Tomas Blazek .20 .50
255 Milan Hejduk 8.00 20.00
256 Jiri Jantovsky .08 .25
257 Stanislav Prochazka .08 .25
258 Tomas Martinec .08 .25
259 Pavel Kabrt .08 .25
260 Jaroslav Kudrna .20 .50
261 Karel Plasek .08 .25
262 Petr Sykora 2.00 5.00
263 Lukas Palecek .08 .25
264 Vladimir Caldr CO .08 .25
265 Jaroslav Liska CO .08 .25
266 Oldrich Svoboda .40 1.00
267 Robert Slavik .08 .25
268 Rudolf Suchanek .08 .25
269 Karel Soudek .08 .25
270 Milan Nedoma .08 .25
271 Kamil Toupal .08 .25
272 Lukas Zib .08 .25
273 Jan Bohacek .08 .25
274 Filip Vanecek .08 .25
275 Radek Martinek .30 .75
276 Radek Toupal .08 .25
277 Lubos Rob .08 .25
278 Pavel Pycha .08 .25
279 David Bruk .08 .25
280 Filip Turek .08 .25
281 Ondrej Vosta .08 .25
282 Arpad GyÃ¶ri .08 .25
283 Petr Sailer .08 .25
284 Martin Strba .08 .25
285 Petr Sachl .08 .25
286 Miroslav Barus .08 .25
287 Vaclav Kral .08 .25
288 Ales Kotalik ERC 2.00 5.00
289 Josef Augusta CO .20 .50
290 Karel Dvorak CO .08 .25
291 Marek Novotny .20 .50
292 Lukas Sablik .08 .25
293 Michael Vyhlidal .08 .25
294 Miroslav Javin .08 .25
295 Martin Tupa .08 .25
296 Marian Morava .08 .25
297 Jaroslav Horacek .08 .25
298 Tomas Jakes .08 .25
299 Daniel Zapotocny .08 .25
300 Miroslav Duben .08 .25
301 Petr Vlk .08 .25
302 Roman Mejzlik .08 .25
303 Jiri Cihlar .08 .25
304 Jaroslav Hub .08 .25
305 Leos Pipa .08 .25
306 Ladislav Prokupek .08 .25
307 Marek Melenovsky .08 .25
308 Milan Antos .08 .25
309 Vaclav Adamec .08 .25
310 Ales Sochorec .08 .25
311 Ales Polcar .08 .25
312 Daniel Hodek .08 .25
313 Alois Hadamczik CO .08 .25
314 Kamil Konecny CO .08 .25
315 Radovan Biegl .20 .50
316 Vlastimil Lakosil .08 .25
317 Lubomir Sekeras .30 .75
318 Miroslav Cihal .08 .25
319 Petr Jancarik .08 .25
320 Stanislav Pavelec .08 .25
321 Jiri Kuntos .08 .25
322 Patrik Hucko .08 .25
323 Petr Gregorek .08 .25
324 Filip Stefanka .08 .25
325 Vladimir Machulda .08 .25
326 Marek Zadina .08 .25
327 Richard Kral .08 .25
328 Jozef Dano .08 .25
329 Ladislav Lubina .08 .25
330 Tomas Chlubna .08 .25
331 Jan Peterek .08 .25
332 Petr Folta .08 .25
333 Josef Straub .08 .25
334 Roman Kadera .08 .25
335 Marian Kacir .08 .25
336 Robert Kantor .08 .25
337 Roman Kontsek .08 .25
338 Miloslav Horava .08 .25
339 Ladislav Kudrna .08 .25
340 Ivan Hlinka CO .30 .75
341 Slavomir Lener CO .20 .50
342 Roman Cechmanek 2.00 5.00
343 Milan Hnilicka 2.00 5.00
344 Martin Prusek 1.50 4.00
345 Frantisek Kaberle .20 .50
346 Jiri Slegr .20 .50
347 Jiri Vykoukal .20 .50
348 Jiri Veber .08 .25
349 Ladislav Benysek .20 .50
350 Frantisek Kucera .08 .25
351 Libor Prochazka .08 .25
352 Jaroslav Spacek .20 .50
353 Vlastimil Kroupa .08 .25
354 Robert Reichel .30 .75
355 Robert Lang .40 1.00
356 Pavel Patera .20 .50
357 Martin Prochazka .20 .50
358 Jiri Dopita .30 .75
359 Josef Beranek .20 .50
360 Viktor Ujcik .20 .50
361 David Vyborny .20 .50
362 Vladimir Vujtek .20 .50
363 Roman Simicek .20 .50
364 Jan Alinc .08 .25
365 Rostislav Vlach .08 .25
366 Ondrej Kratena .08 .25
367 Richard Zemlicka .20 .50
368 Dominik Hasek POY 4.00 10.00
369 Jiri Dopita .30 .75
370 Roman Cechmanek 2.00 5.00
371 Roman Horak .08 .25
372 Richard Zemlicka .20 .50
373 Antonin Stavjana .20 .50
374 Ondrej Kratena .08 .25
375 Richard Farda .08 .25
376 Frantisek Cernik .08 .25
377 Ludek Cajka .08 .25
378 Vlastimil Bubnik .08 .25
379 Josef Mikolas .08 .25
380 Stanislav Konopasek .08 .25

1997-98 Czech DS Extraliga

This set features the top players of the Czech Extraliga. The first 13 cards are short printed. Card No. 1, Roman Cechmanek Super Chase, was issued 1:48, while the Golden All-Stars cards No. 2-12 came 1:4.

COMPLETE SET (120) 20.00 75.00
1 Roman Cechmanek 4.00 10.00
2 Milan Hnilicka 4.00 10.00
3 Josef Beranek .30 .75
4 Milan Nedoma .40 1.00
5 Lubomir Sekeras .40 1.00
6 Jiri Vykoukal .75 2.00
7 Jiri Dopita .75 2.00
8 Robert Kysela .40 1.00
9 Roman Meluzin .75 2.00
10 Roman Simicek .20 .50
11 Petr Ton .40 1.00
12 Viktor Ujcik .75 2.00
13 Vladimir Hudacek .20 .50
14 Petr Pavlas .08 .25
15 Ales Tomasek .08 .25
16 Pavel Blaha .08 .25
17 Pavel Nohel .08 .25
18 Tomas Klimt .20 .50
19 Radek Prochazka .08 .25
20 Rostislav Haas .08 .25
21 Karel Smid .20 .50

22 Milos Hrubes .08 .25
23 Martin Maskarinec .08 .25
24 Zbynek Marak .08 .25
25 Michal Tomek .08 .25
26 Juraj Jurik .08 .25
27 Oldrich Svoboda .40 1.00
28 Rudolf Suchanek .08 .25
29 Karel Soudek .08 .25
30 Radek Martinek .30 .75
31 Radek Toupal .08 .25
32 Lubos Rob .08 .25
33 Pavel Pycha .08 .25
34 Marek Novotny .08 .25
35 Michael Vyhlidal .08 .25
36 Petr Vlk .08 .25
37 Roman Mejzlik .08 .25
38 Jiri Cihlar .08 .25
39 Jaroslav Hub .08 .25
40 Marek Melenovsky .08 .25
41 Zdenek Orct .30 .75
42 Angel Nikolov .20 .50
43 Frantisek Prochazka .08 .25
44 Martin Stepanek .08 .25
45 Tomas Vlasak .08 .25
46 Martin Rousek .08 .25
47 Petr Hrbek .08 .25
48 Ivo Prorok .08 .25
49 Dusan Salficky .30 .75
50 Josef Reznicek .08 .25
51 Ivan Vlcek .08 .25
52 Robert Jindrich .20 .50
53 Pavel Geffert .08 .25
54 Tomas Jelinek .08 .25
55 David Pospisil .08 .25
56 Milan Volak .08 .25
57 Antonin Stavjana .20 .50
58 Radim Tesarik .08 .25
59 Alexej Jaskin .08 .25
60 Tomas Srsen .08 .25
61 Tomas Kapusta .08 .25
62 Radek Belohlav .20 .50
63 Ondrej Kratena .08 .25
64 Jan Tomajko .08 .25
65 Michal Bros .08 .25
66 Rostislav Vlach .08 .25
67 Libor Barta .08 .25
68 Pavel Augusta .08 .25
69 Tomas Blazek .08 .25
70 Milan Hejduk 4.00 10.00
71 Stanislav Prochazka .08 .25
72 Tomas Martinec .08 .25
73 Jaroslav Kudrna .20 .50
74 Ladislav Blazek .08 .25
75 Martin Bakula .08 .25
76 Vladimir Ruzicka .20 .50
77 Jiri Dolezal .08 .25
78 Jiri Poukar .08 .25
79 Tomas Kucharcik .08 .25
80 Frantisek Kucera .08 .25
81 Vaclav Burda .08 .25
82 Jaroslav Nedved .08 .25
83 Richard Zemlicka .20 .50
84 Jiri Zelenka .08 .25
85 Patrik Martinec .08 .25
86 Jan Hlavac .40 1.00
87 Patrik Stefan ERC .75 2.00
88 Jaroslav Bednar .40 1.00
89 Radek Toth .08 .25
90 Jan Krulis .08 .25
91 Pavel Skrbek .20 .50
92 Josef Zajic .08 .25
93 Zdenek Eichenmann .08 .25
94 Ladislav Svoboda .08 .25
95 Martin Prusek .75 2.00
96 Jiri Jonak .08 .25
97 Vitezslav Skuta .08 .25
98 Dimitri Jerofejev .08 .25
99 Roman Rysanek .08 .25
100 David Moravec .20 .50
101 Alexander Prokopjev .08 .25
102 Jaroslav Kames .30 .75
103 Pavel Kowalczyk .08 .25
104 Petr Kuchyna .08 .25
105 Ales Zima .08 .25
106 Pavel Janku .08 .25
107 Tomas Nemcicky .08 .25
108 Petr Cajanek .40 1.00
109 Branislav Janos .08 .25
110 Radovan Biegl .20 .50
111 Richard Kral .08 .25
112 Roman Kontsek .08 .25
113 Jozef Dano .08 .25
114 Ladislav Lubina .08 .25
115 Tomas Chlubna .08 .25
116 Jozef Straub .08 .25
117 Roman Kadera .08 .25
118 Marek Zadina .08 .25
119 Checklist .02 .10
120 Premium card

1997-98 Czech DS Stickers

This set of stickers features many of the players in the Czech Republic Extraliga. The stickers are about 1/3 the size of a standard card. Because many of them were placed into sticker albums, they are difficult to find in their original condition.

COMPLETE SET (283) 35.00 90.00
1 Roman Cechmanek .60 1.50
2 Jiri Veber .08 .25
3 Jiri Vykoukal .20 .50
4 Miloslav Horava .08 .25
5 Martin Stepanek .08 .25
6 Antonin Stavjana .20 .50
7 Bedrich Scerban .08 .25
8 Radek Belohlav .20 .50
9 League Logo .08 .25
10 Jiri Dopita .30 .75
11 David Vyborny .20 .50
12 Josef Beranek .20 .50
13 Vladimir Jerabek .08 .25
14 Viktor Ujcik .20 .50
15 Roman Meluzin .20 .50
16 Jiri Kucera .08 .25
17 Robert Lang .40 1.00
18 Roman Cechmanek .60 1.50
19 Antonin Stavjana .20 .50
20 Tomas Jakes .08 .25
21 Alexej Jaskin .08 .25
22 Jan Srdinko .08 .25
23 Jiri Veber .08 .25
24 Bedrich Scerban .08 .25
25 Ivan Padelek .08 .25
26 HC Petra Vsetin Logo .08 .25
27 HC Petra Vsetin Team Card .08 .25
28 HC Petra Vsetin Team Card .08 .25
29 Rostislav Vlach .08 .25
30 Josef Beranek .20 .50
31 Ondrej Kratena .08 .25
32 Jiri Dopita .30 .75
33 Tomas Kapusta .08 .25
34 Tomas Srsen .08 .25
35 Andrej Galkin .08 .25
36 Oto Hascak .08 .25
37 Zdenek Orct .30 .75
38 Martin Stepanek .08 .25
39 Normunds Sejejs .08 .25
40 Sergej Butko .08 .25
41 Roman Cech .08 .25
42 Radek Mrazek .08 .25
43 Angel Nikolov .20 .50
44 Robert Kysela .08 .25
45 HC Litvinov Logo .08 .25
46 HC Litvinov Team Card .08 .25
47 HC Litvinov Team Card .08 .25
48 Vladimir Jerabek .08 .25
49 Martin Rousek .08 .25
50 Jaroslav Buchal .08 .25
51 Petr Hrbek .08 .25
52 Tomas Vlasak .08 .25
53 Tomas Krasny .08 .25
54 Josef Straka .08 .25
55 Kamil Kastak .08 .25
56 Robert Schistad .08 .25
57 Radek Hamr .08 .25
58 Jaroslav Nedved .08 .25
59 Jan Bohacek .08 .25
60 Vaclav Burda .08 .25
61 Jiri Vykoukal .20 .50
62 Frantisek Ptacek .08 .25
63 Jan Benda .08 .25
64 HC Sparta Praha Logo .08 .25
65 HC Sparta Praha Team Card .08 .25
66 HC Sparta Praha Team Card .08 .25
67 Richard Zemlicka .20 .50
68 Roman Horak .20 .50
69 Patrik Martinec .08 .25
70 Martin Hostak .08 .25
71 David Vyborny .20 .50
72 Pavel Geffert .08 .25
73 Robert Lang .40 1.00
74 Andrej Potajcuk .08 .25
75 Oldrich Svoboda .40 1.00
76 Karel Soudek .08 .25
77 Kamil Toupal .08 .25
78 Milan Nedoma .08 .25
79 Radek Martinek .20 .50
80 Vladimir Antipin .08 .25
81 Rudolf Suchanek .08 .25
82 Pavel Pycha .08 .25
83 HC Ceske Budejovice Logo .08 .25
84 HC Ceske Budejovice Team .08 .25
85 HC Ceske Budejovice Team .08 .25
86 Radek Toupal .08 .25
87 Lubos Rob .08 .25
88 Milan Navratil .08 .25
89 Filip Turek .08 .25
90 Radek Belohlav .20 .50
91 Miroslav Barus .08 .25
92 Frantisek Sevcik .08 .25
93 Arpad GyA¶ri .08 .25
94 Jaroslav Kames .30 .75
95 Petr Kuchyna .08 .25
96 Pavel Kowalczyk .08 .25
97 Stanislav Medrik .08 .25
98 Jan Krajicek .08 .25
99 Radim Tesarik .08 .25
100 Jiri Marusak .08 .25
101 Pavel Janku .08 .25
102 HC ZPS Zlin Logo .08 .25
103 HC ZPS Zlin Team Card .08 .25
104 HC ZPS Zlin Team Card .08 .25
105 Ales Polcar .08 .25
106 David Bruk .08 .25
107 Zbynek Marak .08 .25
108 Ales Zima .08 .25
109 Roman Meluzin .20 .50
110 Miroslav Okal .08 .25
111 Petr Cajanek .40 1.00
112 Tomas Nemcicky .08 .25
113 Rudolf Pejchar .08 .25
114 Jaromir Latal .08 .25
115 Robert Kostka .08 .25
116 Jiri Hes .08 .25
117 Petr Kadlec .08 .25
118 Martin Maskarinec .08 .25
119 Miloslav Horava .08 .25
120 Roman Kadera .08 .25
121 HC Slavia Praha Logo .08 .25
122 HC Slavia Praha Team Card .08 .25
123 HC Slavia Praha Team Card .08 .25
124 Tomas Kucharcik .08 .25
125 Jiri Dolezal .08 .25
126 Jaroslav Bednar .40 1.00
127 Ladislav Slizek .08 .25
128 Tomas Kupka .08 .25
129 Viktor Ujcik .20 .50
130 Vladimir Ruzicka .20 .50
131 Ivo Prorok .08 .25
132 Milan Hnilicka .60 1.50
133 Jan Krulis .08 .25
134 Jan Dlouhy .08 .25
135 Libor Prochazka .08 .25
136 Tomas Kaberle .60 1.50
137 Marek Zidlicky .40 1.00
138 Petr Kasik .08 .25
139 Jiri Beranek .08 .25
140 HC Poldi Kladno Logo .08 .25
141 HC Poldi Kladno Team Card .08 .25
142 HC Poldi Kladno Team Card .08 .25
143 Josef Zajic .08 .25
144 Tomas Mikolasek .08 .25
145 Ladislav Svoboda .08 .25
146 Zdenek Eichenmann .08 .25
147 Vaclev Eiselt .08 .25
148 Petr Ton .08 .25
149 Jiri Burger .08 .25
150 David Cermak .08 .25
151 Ivo Capek .08 .25
152 Marian Morava .08 .25
153 Michael Vyhlidal .08 .25
154 Roman Kankovsky .08 .25
155 Zdenek Touzimsky .08 .25
156 Marek Posmyk .08 .25
157 Miroslav Javin .08 .25
158 Miroslav Bruna .08 .25
159 HC Dukla Jihlava Logo .08 .25
160 HC Dukla Jihlava Team Card .08 .25
161 HC Dukla Jihlava Team Card .08 .25
162 Jaroslav Hub .08 .25
163 Petr Vlk .08 .25
164 Jiri Poukar .08 .25
165 Petr Kankovsky .08 .25
166 Ladislav Prokupek .08 .25
167 Milan Antos .08 .25
168 Leos Pipa .08 .25
169 Michail Fadejev .08 .25
170 Ladislav Blazek .08 .25
171 Petr Pavlas .20 .50
172 Marek Cernosek .08 .25
173 Ladislav Benysek .20 .50
174 Jergus Baca .08 .25
175 Marek Tichy .08 .25
176 Roman Veber .08 .25
177 Martin Streit .08 .25
178 Hockey Olomouc Logo .08 .25
179 Hockey Olomouc Team Card .08 .25
180 Hockey Olomouc Team Card .08 .25
181 Michal Bros .08 .25
182 Radek Svoboda .08 .25
183 Pavel Nohel .08 .25
184 Radek Prochazka .08 .25
185 Jan Tomajko .08 .25
186 Michal Slavik .08 .25
187 Radek Sip .08 .25
188 Filip Dvorak .08 .25
189 Martin Prusek .60 1.50
190 Jiri Jonak .08 .25
191 Pavel Kumstat .08 .25
192 Vitezslav Skuta .08 .25
193 Dmitri Jerofejev .08 .25
194 Rene Sevecek .08 .25
195 Ales Tomasek .08 .25
196 Roman Simicek .20 .50
197 HC Vitkovice Logo .08 .25
198 HC Vitkovice Team Card .08 .25
199 HC Vitkovice Team Card .08 .25
200 Alexander Prokopjev .08 .25
201 Jan Peterek .08 .25
202 David Moravec .20 .50
203 Tomas Chlubna .08 .25
204 Libor Polasek .08 .25
205 Ales Kratoska .08 .25
206 Roman Rysanek .08 .25
207 Martin Smetak .08 .25
208 Martin Altrichter .08 .25
209 Karel Smid .20 .50
210 Josef Reznicek .08 .25
211 Jaroslav Spacek .20 .50
212 Ivan Vlcek .08 .25
213 Jiri Hanzlik .08 .25
214 Robert Jindrich .20 .50
215 Milan Volak .08 .25
216 HC ZKZ Plzen Logo .08 .25
217 HC ZKZ Plzen Team Card .08 .25
218 HC ZKZ Plzen Team Card .08 .25
219 Jiri Kucera .08 .25
220 Tomas Klimt .20 .50
221 Tomas Jelinek .08 .25
222 Michal Straka .08 .25
223 Miroslav Mach .08 .25
224 Pavel Vostrak .08 .25
225 Petr Korinek .08 .25
226 Radek Kampf .08 .25
227 Radovan Biegl .20 .50
228 Jiri Kuntos .08 .25
229 Lubomir Sekeras .30 .75
230 Petr Jancarik .08 .25
231 Stanislav Pavelec .08 .25
232 Ondrej Zetek .08 .25
233 Patrik Hucko .08 .25
234 Vladimir Machulda .08 .25
235 HC Zelezarny Trinec Logo .08 .25
236 HC Zelezarny Trinec Team .08 .25
237 HC Zelezarny Trinec Team .08 .25
238 Jozef Dano .08 .25
239 Roman Blazek .08 .25
240 Marek Zadina .08 .25
241 Richard Kral .08 .25
242 Petr Folta .08 .25
243 Michal Piskor .08 .25
244 Josef Straub .08 .25
245 Petr Zajonc .08 .25
246 Dusan Salficky .30 .75
247 Pavel Augusta .08 .25
248 Tomas Pacal .08 .25
249 Jiri Malinsky .08 .25
250 Pavel Kriz .08 .25
251 Radomir Brazda .08 .25
252 Ales Pisa .08 .25
253 Ladislav Lubina .08 .25
254 HC IB Pardubice Logo .08 .25
255 HC IB Pardubice Team .08 .25
256 HC IB Pardubice Team .08 .25
257 Tomas Blazek .08 .25
258 Jiri Jantovsky .08 .25
259 Milan Hejduk 4.00 10.00
260 Tomas Martinec .08 .25
261 David Pospisil .08 .25
262 Stanislav Prochazka .08 .25
263 Milan Prochazka .08 .25
264 Milan Kastner .08 .25
265 Rostislav Haas .08 .25
266 Denis Tsygurov .08 .25
267 Martin Bakula .08 .25
268 David Galvas .08 .25
269 Petr Tejkl .08 .25
270 Radek Mesicek .08 .25
271 Milos Hrubes .08 .25
272 Eduard Gorbachev .08 .25
273 HC Slezan Opava Logo .08 .25
274 HC Slezan Opava Team .08 .25
275 HC Slezan Opava Team .08 .25
276 Petr Fabian .08 .25
277 Zdenek Pavelek .08 .25
278 Karel Horny .08 .25
279 Martin Filip .08 .25
280 Juraj Jurik .08 .25
281 Radim Radevic .08 .25
282 Jan Zurek .08 .25
283 Valerij Belov .08 .25

1998-99 Czech DS

This set features the top players of the Czech Republic's Extraliga. The set features several short prints. Card no. 1 is 1:125, cards no. 2-11 are 1:30 and cards no. 12-25 are 1:20.

COMPLETE SET (125) 75.00 150.00
1 Jiri Dopita 10.00 25.00
2 Pavel Patera 2.00 5.00
3 Martin Prochazka 2.00 5.00
4 Martin Rucinsky 2.00 5.00
5 Vladimir Vujtek 2.00 5.00
6 David Moravec 2.00 5.00
7 Libor Prochazka 2.00 5.00
8 Viktor Ujcik 2.00 5.00
9 Vladimir Ruzicka 2.00 5.00
10 Frantisek Kucera 2.00 5.00
11 David Vyborny 2.00 5.00
12 Rudolf Pejchar 4.00 10.00
13 Oldrich Svoboda 2.00 5.00
14 Marek Novotny 2.00 5.00
15 Zdenek Orct 2.00 5.00
16 Libor Barta 2.00 5.00
17 Dusan Salficky 2.00 5.00
18 Pavel Cagas 2.00 5.00
19 Ladislav Blazek 2.00 5.00
20 Roman Cechmanek 2.00 5.00
21 Milan Hnilicka 2.00 5.00
22 Martin Cinibulk 2.00 5.00
23 Martin Prusek 2.00 5.00
24 Jaroslav Kames 2.00 5.00
25 Radovan Biegl 2.00 5.00
26 Petr Pavlas .08 .25
27 Ondrej Steiner .08 .25
28 Pavel Janku .08 .25
29 Jaromir Kverka .08 .25
30 Martin Rousek .08 .25
31 Milan Nedoma .08 .25
32 Radek Martinek .20 .50
33 Rudolf Suchanek .08 .25
34 Radek Toupal .15 .40
35 Filip Turek .08 .25
36 Miroslav Barus .08 .25
37 Miroslav Duben .08 .25
38 Petr Vlk .08 .25
39 Marek Melenovsky .08 .25
40 Jiri Cihlar .08 .25
41 Roman Mejzlik .08 .25
42 Ales Polcar .08 .25
43 Angel Nikolov .20 .50
44 Martin Stepanek .08 .25
45 Petr Hrbek .08 .25
46 Ivo Prorok .08 .25
47 Vladimir Petrovka .08 .25
48 Robert Kysela .08 .25
49 Josef Straka .08 .25
50 Ales Pisa .08 .25
51 Pavel Kriz .08 .25
52 Tomas Blazek .08 .25
53 Tomas Martinec .08 .25
54 Jiri Jantovsky .08 .25
55 Stanislav Prochazka .08 .25
56 Jaroslav Kudrna .08 .25
57 Josef Reznicek .08 .25
58 Pavel Geffert .08 .25
59 Petr Korinek .15 .40
60 Pavel Vostrak .08 .25
61 Michal Straka .08 .25
62 David Pospisil .08 .25
63 Milan Volak .08 .25
64 Milan Navratil .08 .25
65 Vitezslav Skuta .08 .25
66 Michael Vyhlidal .08 .25
67 Petr Kuchyna .08 .25
68 Drahomir Kadlec .08 .25
69 Petr Kadlec .08 .25
70 Martin Bakula .08 .25
71 Andrej Jakovenko .08 .25
72 Marian Kacir .20 .50
73 Vladimir Machulda .08 .25
74 Michal Sup .08 .25
75 Jiri Dolezal .15 .40
76 Tomas Kucharcik .08 .25
77 Jiri Veber .08 .25
78 Jan Srdinko .08 .25
79 Radim Tesarik .08 .25
80 Ondrej Kratena .08 .25
81 Michal Bros .08 .25
82 Jan Tomajko .08 .25
83 Tomas Srsen .08 .25
84 Zbynek Marak .08 .25
85 Radek Belohlav .15 .40
86 Roman Stantien .08 .25
87 Alexej Jaskin .08 .25
88 Vaclav Burda .08 .25
89 Ladislav Benysek .20 .50
90 Frantisek Ptacek .08 .25
91 Roman Horak .08 .25
92 Richard Zemlicka .20 .50
93 Jan Hlavac .40 1.00
94 Jiri Zelenka .08 .25
95 Patrik Martinec .08 .25
96 Jaroslav Bednar .40 1.00
97 Marek Zidlicky .40 1.00
98 Ladislav Svoboda .08 .25
99 Vaclav Eiselt .08 .25
100 Zdenek Eichenmann .08 .25
101 Jiri Burger .08 .25
102 Ales Tomasek .08 .25
103 Tomas Jelinek .08 .25
104 Rene Sevecek .08 .25
105 Pavel Kowalczyk .08 .25
106 Alexander Cherbajev .08 .25
107 Martin Kotasek .08 .25
108 Ales Kratoska .08 .25
109 Martin Hamrlik .08 .25
110 Roman Meluzin .08 .25
111 Petr Cajanek .40 1.00
112 Tomas Nemcicky .15 .40
113 Josef Straub .08 .25
114 Miroslav Okal .08 .25
115 Lubomir Sekeras .30 .75
116 Jiri Kuntos .08 .25
117 Stanislav Pavelec .08 .25
118 Richard Kral .08 .25
119 Ladislav Lubina .08 .25
120 Roman Kadera .08 .25
121 Jozef Dano .08 .25
122 Tomas Chlubna .08 .25
123 Ales Zima .08 .25
124 Branislav Janos .08 .25
125 Checklist .02 .10

1998-99 Czech DS Stickers

This set features many of the top stars of the Czech Extraliga in fun sticker form. The stickers are approximately 1-by-1 1/2 inches and feature color fronts and blank backs.

COMPLETE SET 30.00 60.00
1 HC Petra Vsetin .08 .25
2 HC Petra Vsetin .08 .25
3 HC Petra Vsetin .08 .25
4 HC Petra Vsetin .08 .25
5 HC Petra Vsetin .08 .25
6 HC Petra Vsetin .08 .25
7 League Logo .08 .25
8 Roman Cechmanek .40 1.00
10 Antonin Stavjana .15 .40
11 Milan Nedoma .08 .25
12 Jiri Vykoukal .20 .50
14 Martin Stepanek .08 .25
15 Vitezslav Skuta .08 .25
16 Jiri Zelenka .08 .25
17 Robert Lang .40 1.00
18 Ondrej Kratena .08 .25
19 Viktor Ujcik .15 .40
24 Team Logo .02 .10
25 Team Photo .08 .25
26 Team Photo .08 .25
27 Vladimir Hudacek .20 .50
28 Robert Horyna .08 .25
29 Petr Pavlas .08 .25
30 Ales Tomasek .08 .25
31 Pavel Blaha .08 .25
32 Jiri Polak .08 .25
33 Martin Richter .08 .25
34 Marek Cernosek .08 .25
35 Pavel Nohel .08 .25
36 Michal Cerny .08 .25
37 Tomas Klimt .20 .50
38 Ondrej Steiner .08 .25
39 Zbynek Kukacka .08 .25
40 Martin Streit .08 .25
41 Radek Prochazka .08 .25
42 Radek Svoboda .08 .25
43 Jan Lipiansky .08 .25
44 Team Logo .02 .10
45 Team Photo .08 .25
46 Team Photo .08 .25
47 Rostislav Haas .08 .25
48 Pavel Nestak .08 .25
49 Martin Maskarinec .08 .25
50 David Galvas .08 .25
51 Milos Hrubes .08 .25
52 Karel Smid .20 .50
53 Tomas Kramny .08 .25
54 Pavel Marecek .08 .25
55 Zbynek Marak .08 .25
56 Michal Tomek .08 .25
57 Juraj Jurik .08 .25
58 Michal Piskor .08 .25
59 Karel Horny .08 .25
60 Pavel Sebesta .08 .25
61 Martin Sychra .08 .25
62 Zdenek Pavelek .08 .25
63 Milan Kubis .08 .25
64 Team Logo .02 .10
65 Team Photo .08 .25
66 Team Photo .08 .25
67 Oldrich Svoboda .20 .50
68 Rudolf Suchanek .08 .25
69 Karel Soudek .08 .25
70 Milan Nedoma .08 .25
71 Radek Martinek .20 .50
72 Jan Bohacek .08 .25
73 Kamil Toupal .08 .25
74 Radek Toupal .08 .25
75 Lubos Rob .08 .25
76 Pavel Pycha .08 .25
77 Filip Turek .08 .25
78 David Bruk .08 .25
79 Ondrej Vosta .08 .25
80 Arpad GyA¶ri .08 .25
81 Miroslav Barus .08 .25
82 Petr Sailer .08 .25
83 Petr Sachl .08 .25
84 Team Logo .02 .10
85 Team Photo .08 .25
86 Team Photo .08 .25
87 Zdenek Orct .30 .75
88 Richard Hrazdira .08 .25
89 Frantisek Prochazka .08 .25
90 Angel Nikolov .20 .50
91 Martin Stepanek .08 .25
92 Roman Cech .08 .25
93 Radek Mrazek .08 .25
94 Robert Kysela .08 .25
95 Tomas Vlasak .08 .25
96 Martin Rousek .08 .25
97 Petr Hrbek .08 .25
98 Vladimir Petrovka .08 .25
99 Ivo Prorok .08 .25
100 Denis Afinogenov .20 .50
101 Rail Muftijev .08 .25
102 Dmitrij Denisov .08 .25
103 Kamil Piros .40 1.00
104 Team Logo .02 .10
105 Team Photo .08 .25
106 Team Photo .08 .25
107 Marek Novotny .08 .25
108 Lukas Sablik .08 .25
109 Michael Vyhlidal .08 .25
110 Miroslav Javin .08 .25
111 Martin Tupa .08 .25
112 Marian Morava .08 .25
113 Tomas Jakes .08 .25
114 Miroslav Duben .08 .25
115 Petr Vlk .08 .25
116 Roman Mejzlik .08 .25
117 Jiri Cihlar .08 .25
118 Jaroslav Hub .08 .25
119 Leos Pipa .08 .25
120 Ladislav Prokupek .08 .25
121 Marek Melenovsky .08 .25
122 Milan Antos .08 .25
123 Miroslav Stavjana .08 .25
124 Team Logo .02 .10
125 Team Photo .08 .25
126 Team Photo .08 .25
127 Libor Barta .08 .25
128 Adam Svoboda .30 .75
129 Michal Sykora .15 .40
130 Pavel Augusta .08 .25
131 Tomas Pacal .08 .25
132 Ales Pisa .08 .25
133 Petr Mudroch .08 .25
134 Alexander Cypljakov .08 .25
135 Jiri Malinsky .08 .25
136 Milan Hejduk 4.00 10.00
137 Tomas Blazek .08 .25
138 Jaroslav Kudrna .08 .25
139 Tomas Maskarinec .08 .25
140 Stanislav Prochazka .08 .25
141 Jiri Jantovsky .08 .25
142 Pavel Kabrt .08 .25
143 Martin Koudelka .08 .25
144 Team Logo .02 .10
145 Team Photo .08 .25
146 Team Photo .08 .25
147 Dusan Salficky .30 .75
148 Michal Marik .08 .25
149 Josef Reznicek .08 .25
150 Ivan Vlcek .08 .25
151 Robert Jindrich .20 .50
152 Martin Cech .08 .25
153 Jiri Hanzlik .08 .25
154 Pavel Srek .08 .25
155 Tomas Jelinek .08 .25
156 Pavel Geffert .08 .25
157 David Pospisil .08 .25
158 Martin Filip .08 .25
159 Milan Volak .08 .25
160 Michal Straka .08 .25
161 Milan Navratil .08 .25
162 Mojmir Musil .08 .25
163 Pavel Vostrak .08 .25
164 Team Logo .02 .10
165 Team Photo .08 .25
166 Team Photo .08 .25
167 Roman Cechmanek .40 1.00
168 Antonin Stavjana .15 .40
169 Jan Srdinko .08 .25
170 Radim Tesarik .08 .25
171 Alexej Jaskin .08 .25
172 Michal Divisek .08 .25
173 Pavel Zubicek .08 .25
174 Rostislav Vlach .08 .25
175 Jiri Dopita .30 .75
176 Tomas Srsen .08 .25
177 Radek Belohlav .15 .40
178 Tomas Kapusta .08 .25
179 Ondrej Kratena .08 .25
180 Michal Bros .08 .25
181 Jan Tomajko .08 .25
182 Andrej Galkin .08 .25
183 Josef Beranek .20 .50
184 Team Logo .02 .10
185 Team Photo .08 .25
186 Team Photo .08 .25
187 Ladislav Blazek .20 .50
188 Martin Altrichter .08 .25
189 Robert Kostka .08 .25
190 Andrej Jakovenko .08 .25
191 Pavel Kolarik .20 .50
192 Martin Bakula .08 .25
193 Petr Kadlec .08 .25
194 Jan Hejda .08 .25
195 Vladimir Ruzicka .20 .50
196 Viktor Ujcik .15 .40
197 Jiri Dolezal .15 .40
198 Jiri Poukar .08 .25
199 Tomas Kucharcik .08 .25
200 Michal Sup .08 .25
201 Jiri Hlinka .08 .25
202 Tomas Kupka .08 .25
203 Radek Matejovsky .08 .25
204 Team Logo .02 .10
205 Team Photo .08 .25
206 Team Photo .08 .25
207 Milan Hnilicka .75 2.00
208 Martin Cinibulk .08 .25
209 Jiri Vykoukal .20 .50
210 Vaclav Burda .08 .25
211 Frantisek Kucera .08 .25
212 Jaroslav Nedved .08 .25
213 Frantisek Ptacek .08 .25
214 Richard Zemlicka .20 .50
215 Jiri Zelenka .08 .25
216 Patrik Martinec .08 .25
217 Jaroslav Bednar .40 1.00
218 Jaromir Kverka .08 .25
219 Jan Hlavac .40 1.00
220 Miroslav Hlinka .08 .25
221 Jaroslav Hlinka .08 .25
222 Patrik Stefan .75 2.00
223 Petr Nedved .40 1.00
224 Team Logo .02 .10
225 Team Photo .08 .25
226 Team Photo .08 .25
227 Radek Toth .08 .25
228 Martin Bilek .20 .50
229 Jan Krulis .08 .25
230 Marek Zidlicky .40 1.00
231 Tomas Kaberle .40 1.00
232 Pavel Skrbek .20 .50
233 Jan Penk .08 .25
234 Jan Dlouhy .08 .25
235 Josef Zajic .08 .25
236 Zdenek Eichenmann .08 .25
237 Petr Ton .08 .25
238 Jiri Beranek .08 .25
239 Tomas Mikolasek .08 .25
240 Ladislav Svoboda .08 .25
241 Vaclav Eiselt .08 .25
242 Jiri Burger .08 .25
243 Petr Tenkrat .40 1.00
244 Team Logo .02 .10
245 Team Photo .08 .25
246 Team Photo .08 .25
247 Martin Prusek .75 2.00
248 Zdenek Dobes .08 .25
249 Vitezslav Skuta .08 .25
250 Pavel Kumstat .08 .25
251 Jiri Jonak .08 .25
252 Rene Sevecek .08 .25
253 Dmitrij Jerofejev .08 .25
254 Petr Jurecka .08 .25
255 Roman Simicek .20 .50
256 Roman Rysanek .08 .25
257 David Moravec .20 .50
258 Alexander Prokopjev .08 .25
259 Libor Polasek .08 .25
260 Martin Kotasek .08 .25
261 Alexander Cherbajev .08 .25
262 Libor Pavlis .08 .25
263 Petr Zajonc .08 .25
264 Team Logo .02 .10
265 Team Photo .08 .25
266 Team Photo .08 .25
267 Radovan Biegl .20 .50
268 Lubomir Sekeras .30 .75
269 Jiri Kuntos .08 .25
270 Stanislav Pavelec .08 .25
271 Patrik Hucko .08 .25
272 Petr Jancarik .08 .25
273 Robert Kantor .08 .25
274 Richard Kral .08 .25
275 Ladislav Lubina .08 .25
276 Tomas Chlubna .08 .25
277 Roman Kadera .08 .25
278 Josef Straub .08 .25
279 Jozef Dano .08 .25
280 Roman Kontsek .08 .25
281 Marek Zadina .08 .25
282 Petr Folta .08 .25
283 Jan Peterek .08 .25
284 Team Logo .02 .10
285 Team Photo .08 .25
286 Team Photo .08 .25
287 Jaroslav Kames .30 .75
288 Pavel Kowalczyk .08 .25
289 Jan Krajicek .08 .25
290 Petr Kuchyna .08 .25
291 Martin Hamrlik .08 .25
292 Pavel Rajnoha .08 .25
293 Jiri Marusak .08 .25
294 Roman Meluzin .20 .50
295 Pavel Janku .08 .25
296 Ales Zima .08 .25
297 Miroslav Okal .08 .25
298 Petr Cajanek .40 1.00
299 Tomas Nemcicky .08 .25
300 Branislav Janos .08 .25
301 Ales Polcar .08 .25
302 Zdenek Sedlak .08 .25
303 Petr Leska .08 .25

1998-99 Czech OFS

This expansive set covers the entire Czech Extraliga. Cards 1-249 comprise Series I, while cards 250-490 make up Series II. Each series also has four NNO checklists. The set is noteworthy for including early cards of Martin Havlat and Roman Cechmanek, among others.

COMPLETE SET (490) 60.00 150.00
1 Ondrej Weissmann .08 .25
2 Zdenek Orct .20 .50
3 Angel Nikolov .20 .50
4 Radek Mrazek .08 .25
5 Martin Stepanek .08 .25
6 Sergej Butko .08 .25
7 Oleg Romanov .08 .25
8 Marian Menhart .20 .50
9 Vladimir Petrovka .08 .25
10 Ivo Prorok .08 .25
11 Jindrich Kotrla .08 .25
12 Josef Straka .08 .25
13 Vadim Bekbulatov .08 .25
14 Daniel Branda .08 .25
15 Vojtech Kubincak .08 .25
16 Michal Travnicek .20 .50
17 Zdenek Venera .08 .25
18 Jaroslav Kames .30 .75
19 Pavel Augusta .08 .25
20 Patrik Hucko .08 .25
21 Martin Hamrlik .08 .25
22 Jiri Marusak .08 .25
23 Pavel Mojzis .08 .25
24 Tomas Zizka .08 .25
25 Roman Meluzin .08 .25
26 Michal Tomek .08 .25
27 Josef Straub .08 .25
28 Tomas Nemcicky .15 .40
29 Petr Cajanek .40 1.00
30 Miroslav Okal .08 .25
31 Petr Leska .08 .25
32 Petr Vala .08 .25
33 Radim Rulik .08 .25
34 Dusan Salficky .30 .75
35 Josef Reznicek .08 .25
36 Robert Jindrich .20 .50
37 Jiri Hanzlik .08 .25
38 Ondrej Kriz .08 .25
39 Vladimir Zajic .08 .25
40 Pavel Geffert .08 .25
41 David Pospisil .08 .25
42 Milan Antos .08 .25
43 Petr Korinek .15 .40
44 Michal Straka .08 .25
45 Milan Volak .08 .25
46 Pavel Vostrak .08 .25
47 Milan Navratil .08 .25
48 Martin Spanhel .40 1.00
49 Josef Augusta .08 .25
50 Jaroslav Suchan .08 .25
51 Martin Tupa .08 .25
52 Marian Morava .08 .25
53 Michal Divisek .08 .25
54 Petr Svoboda .15 .40
55 Zdenek Fuksa .08 .25
56 Petr Vlk .08 .25
57 Jiri Cihlar .08 .25
58 Leos Pipa .08 .25
59 Marek Melenovsky .08 .25
60 Miroslav Bruna .08 .25
61 Petr Mokrejs .08 .25
62 Vaclav Adamec .08 .25
63 Richard Cachnin .08 .25
64 Jan Kloboucek .08 .25
65 Stanislav Nevesely .08 .25
66 Radek Masny .08 .25
67 Jan Krajicek .08 .25
68 Ales Tomasek .08 .25
69 Vladimir Holik .08 .25
70 Tomas Jelinek .08 .25
71 Pavel Nohel .08 .25
72 Jaroslav Hub .08 .25
73 Robert Kucera .08 .25
74 Andrej Galkin .08 .25
75 Pavel Selingr .08 .25
76 Pavel Bacho .08 .25
77 Jiri Zurek .08 .25
78 Pavel Zdrahal .08 .25
79 Bogdan Savenko .08 .25
80 Zdenek Sedlak .08 .25
81 Karel Trachta .08 .25
82 Rudolf Pejchar .20 .50
83 Petr Pavlas .08 .25
84 Pavel Blaha .08 .25
85 Martin Richter .08 .25
86 Jan Snopek .15 .40
87 Martin Filip .08 .25
88 Jaromir Kverka .08 .25
89 Pavel Janku .08 .25
90 Martin Rousek .08 .25
91 Ondrej Steiner .08 .25
92 Pavel Metlicka .08 .25
93 Streit Martin .08 .25
94 Ladislav Prokupek .08 .25
95 Richard Richter .08 .25
96 Martin Maskarinec .08 .25
97 Zdislav Tabara .08 .25
98 Miroslav Venkrbec .08 .25
99 Roman Cechmanek .40 1.00
100 Jiri Veber .08 .25
101 Radim Tesarik .08 .25
102 Jan Srdinko .08 .25
103 Alexej Jaskin .08 .25
104 Pavel Zubicek .08 .25
105 Jiri Dopita .30 .75
106 Martin Prochazka .20 .50
107 Pavel Patera .20 .50
108 Radek Belohlav .15 .40
109 Ondrej Kratena .08 .25
110 Michal Bros .08 .25
111 Jan Tomajko .08 .25
112 Roman Stantien .08 .25
113 Ladislav Svozil .08 .25
114 Jiri Trvaj .08 .25
115 Rene Sevecek .08 .25
116 Vitezslav Skuta .08 .25
117 Pavel Kowalczyk .08 .25
118 Radek Philipp .08 .25
119 Vladimir Vujtek .20 .50
120 Alexander Cherbajev .08 .25
121 Libor Pavlis .08 .25
122 Libor Polasek .08 .25
123 Martin Kotasek .08 .25
124 Zdenek Pavelek .08 .25
125 Martin Lamich .08 .25
126 Igor Varickij .08 .25
127 Petr Hubacek .08 .25
128 Zbynek Irgl .08 .25
129 Julius Supler .08 .25
130 Milan Hnilicka .40 1.00
131 Frantisek Ptacek .08 .25
132 Ladislav Benysek .20 .50
133 Richard Adam .08 .25
134 Frantisek Kucera .08 .25
135 Pavel Srek .08 .25
136 Jiri Zelenka .08 .25
137 David Vyborny .20 .50
138 Patrik Martinec .08 .25
139 Jaroslav Bednar .40 1.00
140 Jan Hlavac .40 1.00
141 Miroslav Hlinka .08 .25
142 Jaroslav Hlinka .08 .25
143 Martin Chabada .08 .25
144 Vaclav Novak .08 .25
145 Michal Chalupa .08 .25
146 Adam Svoboda .30 .75
147 Jiri Malinsky .08 .25
148 Ales Pisa .08 .25
149 Tomas Pacal .08 .25
150 Pavel Kriz .08 .25
151 Petr Jancarik .08 .25
152 Petr Mudroch .08 .25

153 Tomas Blazek .08 .25
154 Jiri Jantovsky .08 .25
155 Stanislav Prochazka .08 .25
156 Tomas Martinec .08 .25
157 Pavel Kabrt .08 .25
158 Jaroslav Kudrna .20 .50
159 Karel Plasek .08 .25
160 Michal Mikeska .08 .25
161 Zdenek Sindler .08 .25
162 Martin Cinibulk .20 .50
163 Marek Zidlicky .40 1.00
164 Jan Dlouhy .08 .25
165 Pavel Taborsky .08 .25
166 Michal Madl .08 .25
167 Jiri Jelinek .08 .25
168 Tomas Mikolasek .08 .25
169 Ladislav Svoboda .08 .25
170 Jiri Burger .08 .25
171 Petr Tenkrat .40 1.00
172 Tomas Kupka .08 .25
173 Marke Vorel .08 .25
174 Michal Kanka .08 .25
175 Tomas Horna .08 .25
176 Zdenek Mraz .08 .25
177 Kamil Konecny .08 .25
178 Radovan Biegl .20 .50
179 Stanislav Pavelec .08 .25
180 Jiri Kuntos .08 .25
181 Petr Gregorek .08 .25
182 Miroslav Cihal .08 .25
183 Robert Prochazka .08 .25
184 Viktor Ujcik .20 .50
185 Ladislav Lubina .08 .25
186 Jan Peterek .08 .25
187 Petr Folta .08 .25
188 Ales Zima .08 .25
189 Roman Kadera .08 .25
190 Vaclav Pletka .20 .50
191 Patrik Moskal .08 .25
192 David Appel .08 .25
193 Jaroslav Parizek CO .08 .25
194 Michal Marik .08 .25
195 Rudolf Suchanek .08 .25
196 Milan Nedoma .08 .25
197 Kamil Toupal .08 .25
198 Roman Cech .08 .25
199 Radek Martinek .20 .50
200 Vladimir Sicak .08 .25
201 Radek Toupal .15 .40
202 Filip Turek .08 .25
203 Petr Sailer .08 .25
204 Martin Strba .08 .25
205 Miroslav Barus .08 .25
206 Vaclav Kral .08 .25
207 Milan Filipi .08 .25
208 Peter Bartos .08 .25
209 Richard Farda .08 .25
210 Roman Malek .08 .25
211 Robert Kostka .08 .25
212 Pavel Kolarik .20 .50
213 Martin Bakula .08 .25
214 Petr Kadlec .08 .25
215 Jan Novak .08 .25
216 Vladimir Ruzicka .20 .50
217 Jiri Dolezal .15 .40
218 Tomas Kucharcik .08 .25
219 Michal Sup .08 .25
220 Vladimir Machulda .08 .25
221 Petr Mika .30 .75
222 Tomas Divisek .30 .75
223 Jan Kopecky .08 .25
224 Jiri Polak .08 .25
225 Ivan Hlinka OLY .30 .75
226 Slavomir Lener OLY .15 .40
227 Dominik Hasek OLY 4.00 10.00
228 Roman Cechmanek OLY .40 1.00
229 Milan Hnilicka OLY .40 1.00
230 Richard Smehlik OLY .15 .40
231 Petr Svoboda OLY .15 .40
232 Roman Hamrlik OLY .30 .75
233 Jiri Slegr OLY .15 .40
234 Frantisek Kucera OLY .08 .25
235 Libor Prochazka OLY .20 .50
236 Jaroslav Spacek OLY .20 .50
237 Robert Reichel OLY .40 1.00
238 Robert Lang OLY .40 1.00
239 Pavel Patera OLY .30 .75
240 Martin Prochazka OLY .20 .50
241 Jiri Dopita OLY .30 .75
242 Josef Beranek OLY .20 .50
243 David Moravec OLY .30 .75
244 Jan Caloun OLY .20 .50
245 Martin Rucinsky OLY .30 .75
246 Martin Straka OLY .40 1.00
247 Jaromir Jagr OLY 8.00 20.00
248 Vladimir Ruzicka OLY .20 .50
249 Milan Hejduk OLY 4.00 10.00
250 Ladislav Slizek .08 .25
251 Ladislav Blazek .08 .25
252 Andrej Jakovenko .08 .25
253 Jan Hejda .08 .25
254 Marian Kacir .20 .50
255 Robin Bacul .08 .25
256 Jan Sochor .08 .25
257 Petr Hrbek .08 .25
258 Jan Sebor .08 .25
259 Michal Slavik .08 .25
260 Vladimir Jerabek .08 .25
261 Marek Pinc .08 .25
262 Vladimir Gyna .08 .25
263 Martin Znojemsky .08 .25
264 Robert Kysela .08 .25
265 Petr Hrbek .08 .25
266 Kamil Piros .40 1.00
267 Viktor Hubl .08 .25
268 Marian Kacir .20 .50
269 Miloslav Horava .08 .25
270 Michal Pinc .08 .25
271 Zdenek Skorepa .08 .25
272 Vaclav Sykora .08 .25
273 Antonin Stavjana .15 .40
274 Richard Hrazdira .08 .25
275 Karel Rachunek .40 1.00
276 David Brezik .08 .25
277 Marek Zadina .08 .25
278 Jaroslav Balastik .08 .25
279 Martin Ambruz .08 .25
280 Ondrej Vesely .08 .25
281 Tomas Kapusta .08 .25
282 Tomas Martinek .08 .25
283 Ivan Rachunek .20 .50
284 Karel Sefcik .08 .25
285 Marek Sykora .08 .25
286 Vladimir Hudacek .20 .50
287 Ivan Vlcek .08 .25
288 Martin Cech .08 .25
289 Michal Vasicek .08 .25
290 Michal Jelinek .08 .25
291 Vladimir Bednar .08 .25
292 Pavel Augusta .08 .25
293 Ladislav Slizek .08 .25
294 Karel Dvorak .08 .25
295 Marek Novotny .08 .25
296 Lukas Sablik .08 .25
297 Daniel Zapotocny .08 .25
298 Miroslav Duben .08 .25
299 Ales Polcar .08 .25
300 Roman Mejzlik .08 .25
301 Radek Matejovsky .08 .25
302 Daniel Hodek .08 .25
303 Ales Padelek .08 .25
304 Ivan Padelek .08 .25
305 Pavel Rajnoha .08 .25
306 Richard Adam .08 .25
307 Vladimir Caldr .08 .25
308 Jiri Dobrovolny .08 .25
309 Lukas Novak .08 .25
310 Ivo Novotny .08 .25
311 Jan Smarda .08 .25
312 Lubomir Oslizlo .08 .25
313 Pavel Cagas .20 .50
314 Petr Kuchyna .08 .25
315 Drahomir Kadlec .08 .25
316 Michael Vyhlidal .08 .25
317 Miroslav Javin .08 .25
318 Petr Suchanek .08 .25
319 Vitezslav Skuta .08 .25
320 Libor Polasek .08 .25
321 Jiri Poukal .08 .25
322 Michal Cech .08 .25
323 Lukas Fiala .08 .25
324 Milota Florian .08 .25
325 Milan Kubis .08 .25
326 Jiri Latal .08 .25
327 Libor Pavlis .08 .25
328 Ivan Puncochar .08 .25
329 Rostislav Vlach .08 .25
330 Tomas Zapletal .08 .25
331 Josef Beranek .20 .50
332 Robert Hamrla .08 .25
333 Marek Cernosek .08 .25
334 Normunds Sejejs .08 .25
335 Tomas Klimt .08 .25
336 Radek Prochazka .08 .25
337 Radek Svoboda .08 .25
338 Michal Horak .08 .25
339 Jakub Kraus .08 .25
340 Ivo Pesat .08 .25
341 Tomas Jakes .08 .25
342 Michal Safarik .08 .25
343 Tomas Srsen .08 .25
344 Zbynek Marak .08 .25
345 Tomas Demel .08 .25
346 Ondrej Kavulic .08 .25
347 Petr Suchy .08 .25
348 Libor Zabransky .15 .40
349 Vladimir Vujtek .20 .50
350 Martin Prusek .40 1.00
351 Lukas Galvas .08 .25
352 Petr Jurecka .08 .25
353 Vadim Brezgunov .08 .25
354 Lukas Zatopek .08 .25
355 David Moravec .20 .50
356 Ludek Krayzel .08 .25
357 Ales Kratoska .08 .25
358 Ales Tomasek .08 .25
359 Milos Holan .15 .40
360 Roman Kelner .08 .25
361 Frantisek Vyborny .08 .25
362 Petr Prikryl .08 .25
363 Zdenek Touzimsky .08 .25
364 Vaclav Burda .08 .25
365 Vaclav Benak .08 .25
366 Michal Dobron .08 .25
367 Richard Zemlicka .20 .50
368 Roman Horak .08 .25
369 Michal Sivek .40 1.00
370 Jaroslav Kalla .08 .25
371 Pavel Richter .08 .25
372 Jaroslav Roubik .08 .25
373 Michal Sykora .15 .40
374 Milos Riha .08 .25
375 Libor Barta .08 .25
376 Alexander Cypljakov .08 .25
377 Robert Pospisil .08 .25
378 Petr Caslava .08 .25
379 Martin Koudelka .08 .25
380 Patrik Rozsival .08 .25
381 Michal Tvrdik .08 .25
382 Tomas Vak .08 .25
383 Alois Hadamczik CO .08 .25
384 Vlastimil Lakosil .08 .25
385 Lubomir Sekeras .20 .50
386 Libor Prochazka .20 .50
387 Robert Kantor .08 .25
388 Mario Cartelli .08 .25
389 Richard Kral .08 .25
390 Jozef Dano .08 .25
391 Branislav Janos .08 .25
392 Tomas Chlubna .08 .25
393 Martin Havlat 10.00 25.00
394 Jaroslav Jagr .20 .50
395 Lubomir Bauer .08 .25
396 Martin Bilek .20 .50
397 Lubos Horcicka .08 .25
398 Jiri Krocak .08 .25
399 Martin Taborsky .08 .25
400 Zdenek Eichenmann .08 .25
401 Vaclav Eiselt .08 .25
402 Premysl Sedlak .08 .25
403 Jiri Holsan .08 .25
404 Jiri Kames .08 .25
405 Jiri Habacek .08 .25
406 Stanislav Lapacek .08 .25
407 Lukas Poznik .08 .25
408 Otakar Vejvoda .15 .40
409 Jaroslav Liska .08 .25
410 Oldrich Svoboda .20 .50
411 Lukas Zib .08 .25
412 Michal Klimes .08 .25
413 Kamil Brabenec .08 .25
414 Ales Kotalik 1.00 2.50
415 Jiri Broz .08 .25
416 Zdenek Kutlak .20 .50
417 Vaclav Nedorost .40 1.00
418 Lubos Rob .10 .25
419 Martin Prusek .40 1.00
420 Frantisek Kaberle .20 .50
421 Jiri Vykoukal .20 .50
422 Jiri Veber .08 .25
423 Ladislav Benysek .20 .50
424 Martin Stepanek .08 .25
425 Jan Srdinko .08 .25
426 Radek Belohlav .15 .40
427 David Vyborny .20 .50
428 Viktor Ujcik .20 .50
429 Roman Meluzin .08 .25
430 Vladimir Vujtek .20 .50
431 Ondrej Kratena .08 .25
432 Michal Bros .08 .25
433 Marian Kacir .20 .50
434 Jan Hlavac .40 1.00
435 Richard Kral .08 .25
436 Roman Kadera .08 .25
437 Ivan Hlinka .40 1.00
438 Roman Cechmanek .40 1.00
439 Milan Hnilicka .40 1.00
440 Libor Prochazka .20 .50
441 Pavel Patera .20 .50
442 Martin Prochazka .20 .50
443 Josef Augusta .08 .25
444 Pavel Richter .08 .25
445 Marek Sykora .08 .25
446 Milan Hnilicka .40 1.00
447 Dusan Salficky .30 .75
448 Frantisek Kucera .08 .25
449 Ladislav Benysek .20 .50
450 Josef Reznicek .08 .25
451 Martin Richter .08 .25
452 Ales Pisa .08 .25
453 Ivan Vlcek .08 .25
454 Martin Stepanek .08 .25
455 Petr Jancarik .08 .25
456 David Vyborny .20 .50
457 Jan Hlavac .40 1.00
458 Jiri Zelenka .08 .25
459 Petr Tenkrat .40 1.00
460 Vaclav Kral .08 .25
461 David Pospisil .08 .25
462 Vaclav Eiselt .08 .25
463 Tomas Kucharcik .08 .25
464 Petr Korinek .15 .40
465 Pavel Janku .08 .25
466 Radek Toupal .15 .40
467 Ivo Prorok .08 .25
468 Zdislav Tabara .08 .25
469 Jaroslav Jagr .20 .50
470 Roman Cechmanek .40 1.00
471 Libor Prochazka .20 .50
472 Jiri Veber .08 .25
473 Milos Holan .15 .40
474 Jan Srdinko .08 .25
475 Robert Kantor .08 .25
476 Ales Tomasek .08 .25
477 Miroslav Duben .08 .25
478 Jiri Dopita .30 .75
479 Martin Prochazka .20 .50
480 Pavel Patera .20 .50
481 Radek Belohlav .15 .40
482 David Moravec .20 .50
483 Roman Meluzin .08 .25
484 Jiri Poukar .08 .25
485 Andrej Galkin .08 .25
486 Ivo Padelek .08 .25
487 Marek Zadina .08 .25
488 Petr Cajanek .40 1.00
489 Miroslav Javin .08 .25
490 Ondrej Kratena .08 .25
NNO Checklist .02 .10
NNO Checklist .02 .10
NNO Checklist .02 .10
NNO Checklist .02 .10
NNO Checklist .02 .10
NNO Checklist .02 .10
NNO Checklist .02 .10
NNO Checklist .02 .10

1998-99 Czech OFS Legends

This series of insert cards honoring some of the greatest players in Czech history were randomly included in series II packs.

COMPLETE SET (20) 12.00 30.00
1 Vaclav Nedomansky .75 2.00
2 Miroslav Horava .75 2.00
3 Peter Stastny 4.00 10.00
4 Jiri Sejba .40 1.00
5 Ivan Hlinka 1.25 3.00
6 Vladimir Martinec .40 1.00
7 Jaroslav Pouzar .40 1.00
8 Jiri Holecek .40 1.00
9 Ludek Cajka .40 1.00
10 Ludek Bukac .40 1.00
11 Milan Novy .75 2.00
12 Jiri Kralik .40 1.00
13 Jiri Hrdina .40 1.00
14 Frantisek Cernik .40 1.00
15 Frantisek Pospisil .40 1.00
16 Jiri Lala .40 1.00
17 Antonin Stavjana .75 2.00
18 Jaromir Sindel .75 2.00
19 Vincent Lukac .40 1.00
20 Dusan Pasek 1.25 3.00

1998-99 Czech OFS Olympic Winners

This insert series commemorates the members of the Czech Republic's gold medal-winning Olympic squad. Cards 1-10 were found in Series I packs, while cards 11-20 were found in Series II.

COMPLETE SET (20) 30.00 75.00
1 Jiri Dopita .75 2.00
2 Dominik Hasek 8.00 20.00
3 Jaromir Jagr 15.00 40.00
4 Frantisek Kucera .75 2.00
5 Pavel Patera .75 2.00
6 Robert Reichel .75 2.00
7 Martin Rucinsky .75 2.00
8 Vladimir Ruzicka .75 2.00
9 Jiri Slegr .75 2.00
10 Petr Svoboda .75 2.00
11 David Moravec .75 2.00
12 Richard Smehlik .75 2.00
13 Jaroslav Spacek .75 2.00
14 Martin Prochazka .75 2.00
15 Roman Hamrlik .75 2.00
16 Ivan Hlinka .75 2.00
17 Roman Cechmanek 1.25 3.00
18 Josef Beranek .75 2.00
19 Robert Lang 1.25 3.00
20 Martin Straka 1.25 3.00

1998 Czech Bonaparte

This unusual set features many members of the 1998 Czech Gold medal winning Olympic team. The cards are the size of playing cards, feature a photo on the front, and the word Bonaparte on the back. The numbering assigned to each is found on the front of the cards.

COMPLETE SET (33) 14.00 35.00
1A Martin Prochazka .20 .50
1B Robert Reichel .20 .50
1C Robert Lang .20 .50
1D Milan Hejduk 1.50 4.00
2A Martin Rucinsky .20 .50
2B Jaromir Jagr 2.00 5.00
2C Richard Smehlik .20 .50
2D Dominik Hasek 1.25 3.00
3A Josef Beranek .20 .50
3B Jaroslav Spacek .20 .50
3C Jaromir Jagr 2.00 5.00
3D Jiri Slegr .20 .50
4A Vladimir Ruzicka .20 .50
4B Roman Cechmanek .40 1.00
4C Jan Caloun .20 .50
4D Milan Hnilicka .75 2.00
5A Jiri Dopita .30 .75
5B Frantisek Kucera .20 .50
5C Jaromir Jagr 2.00 5.00
5D Petr Svoboda .20 .50
6A Petr Svoboda .20 .50
6B Ivan Hlinka .20 .50
6C Slavomir Lener .20 .50
6D Jaromir Jagr 2.00 5.00
7A Jiri Slegr .20 .50
7B Martin Straka .20 .50
7C Pavel Patera .20 .50
7D David Moravec .20 .50
8A Vladimir Ruzicka .20 .50
8B Libor Prochazka .20 .50
8C Roman Hamrlik .20 .50
8D Dominik Hasek 1.25 3.00
HOKEJ Jaromir Jagr

1998 Czech Bonaparte Tall

These Tall Boy-type cards feature Czech's Olympic champs from 1998. The cards have a small colour photo surrounded by plenty of white space, a large Czech flag and the Bonaparte 1998.

COMPLETE SET ?
1 Dominik Hasek
2 Jaromir Jagr
3 Robert Reichel

1998 Czech Pexeso

This set of undersized cards features members of the Olympic Gold medal-winning Czech squad. It is believed that the cards were issued as a premium with some sort of food item.

COMPLETE SET (28) 8.00 20.00
1 Martin Prochazka .08 .25
2 Robert Reichel .20 .50
3 Robert Lang .20 .50
4 Milan Hejduk 1.50 4.00
5 Martin Rucinsky .08 .25
6 Richard Smehlik .08 .25
7 Dominik Hasek 1.25 3.00
8 Josef Beranek .08 .25
9 Jaroslav Spacek .08 .25
10 Jaromir Jagr 2.00 5.00
11 Roman Cechmanek .40 1.00
12 Martin Rucinsky .08 .25
13 Jiri Slegr .08 .25
14 Jan Caloun .08 .25
15 Milan Hnilicka .75 2.00
16 Jiri Dopita .20 .50
17 Jiri Kucera .08 .25
18 Jaromir Jagr 2.00 5.00
19 Petr Svoboda .08 .25
20 Ivan Hlinka .08 .25
21 Slavomir Lener .08 .25
22 Jiri Slegr .08 .25
23 Martin Straka .08 .25
24 Pavel Patera .08 .25
25 David Moravec .08 .25
26 Libor Prochazka .08 .25
27 Roman Hamrlik .08 .25
28 Dominik Hasek 1.25 3.00

1998 Czech Spaghetti

This undersized set honors the members of the Czech team that won the Olympic Gold medal. The cards were issued as a premium on boxes of pasta products, and were licensed by the NHLPA.

COMPLETE SET (12) 8.00 20.00
1 Jaromir Jagr 4.00 10.00
2 Dominik Hasek 2.00 5.00
3 Josef Beranek .40 1.00
4 Roman Hamrlik .40 1.00
5 Robert Lang .60 1.50
6 Martin Straka .60 1.50
7 Robert Reichel .60 1.50
8 Martin Rucinsky .60 1.50
9 Jiri Slegr .40 1.00
10 Petr Svoboda .40 1.00
11 Richard Smehlik .40 1.00
12 Martin Prochazka .40 1.00

1999-00 Czech DS

This set features the stars of the Czech Republic's top league. The set includes cards of NHLers Patrik Elias and Brendan Morrison, who began that season in the Czech league whilst in the midst of a contract dispute. Checklist courtesy of Hockey Heaven.

COMPLETE SET (196) 30.00 75.00
1 Richard Hrazdira .20 .50
2 Vladimir Hudacek .20 .50
3 Roman Hamrlik .30 .75
4 Martin Hamrlik .08 .25
5 Jiri Marusak .08 .25
6 Tomas Zizka .20 .50
7 Petr Cajanek .30 .75
8 Miroslav Okal .08 .25
9 Josef Straub .08 .25
10 Petr Leska .08 .25
11 Michal Tomek .08 .25
12 Martin Kotasek .08 .25
13 Ondrej Vesely .08 .25
14 Petr Vala .08 .25
15 Rudolf Pejchar .08 .25
16 Zdenek Smid .30 .75
17 Martin Richter .08 .25
18 Petr Pavlas .08 .25
19 Martin Maskarinec .08 .25
20 Jan Snopek .08 .25
21 Michal Divisek .08 .25
22 Pavel Janku .08 .25
23 Jaromir Kverka .08 .25
24 Martin Rousek .08 .25
25 Miroslav Barus .08 .25
26 Martin Streit .08 .25
27 Martin Filip .08 .25
28 Radek Prochazka .08 .25
29 Ivo Capek .20 .50
30 Michal Marik .08 .25
31 Milan Nedoma .08 .25
32 Radek Martinek .20 .50
33 Rudolf Suchanek .20 .50
34 Roman Cech .08 .25
35 Vaclav Kral .08 .25
36 Filip Turek .08 .25
37 Peter Bartos .08 .25
38 Radek Toupal .08 .25
39 Lubos Rob .08 .25
40 Martin Strba .08 .25
41 Petr Sailer .08 .25
42 Kamil Brabenec .08 .25
43 Pavel Cagas .20 .50
44 Robert Horyna .08 .25
45 Michael Vyhlidal .08 .25
46 Miroslav Javin .08 .25
47 Libor Pivko .08 .25
48 Ales Tomasek .08 .25
49 Roman Horak .20 .50
50 Pavel Nohel .08 .25
51 Ales Aima .08 .25
52 Marek Melanovsky .08 .25
53 Jaroslav Hub .08 .25
54 Pavel Zdrahal .08 .25
55 Bogdan Savenko .08 .25
56 Robert Kantor .08 .25
57 Zdenek Orct .20 .50
58 Marek Pinc .08 .25
59 Miloslav Horava .08 .25
60 Angel Nikolov .20 .50
61 Petr Kratky .08 .25
62 Radek Mrazek .08 .25
63 Robert Reichel .20 .50
64 Robert Kysela .08 .25
65 Ivo Prorok .08 .25
66 Jan Alinc .20 .50
67 Jindrich Kotrla .08 .25
68 Zdenek Skorepa .20 .50
69 Josef Straka .08 .25
70 Michal Travnicek .20 .50
71 Libor Barta .08 .25
72 Adam Svoboda .30 .75
73 Ales Pisa .08 .25
74 Tomas Pacal .08 .25
75 Jiri Malinsky .08 .25
76 Petr Jancarik .08 .25
77 Patrik Elias .75 2.00
78 Brendan Morrison 1.25 3.00
79 Radek Bonk .40 1.00
80 Jaroslav Kudrna .20 .50
81 Tomas Blazek .08 .25
82 Ladislav Lubina .08 .25
83 Stanislav Prochazka .08 .25
84 Jiri Jantovsky .08 .25
85 Dusan Salficky .30 .75
86 Radek Masny .08 .25
87 Josef Reznicek .08 .25
88 Ivan Vlcek .08 .25
89 Martin Cech .08 .25
90 Jiri Hanzlik .08 .25
91 Martin Spanhel .30 .75
92 Michal Straka .08 .25
93 Zdenek Sedlak .08 .25
94 Pavel Vostrak .08 .25
95 Petr Korinek .20 .50
96 Pavel Geffert .08 .25
97 David Pospisil .08 .25
98 Milan Volak .08 .25
99 Vlastimil Lakosil .20 .50
100 Marek Novotny .08 .25
101 Jiri Kuntos .08 .25
102 Petr Gregorek .08 .25
103 Milos Holan .08 .25
104 Lubomir Sekeras .20 .50
105 Richard Kral .08 .25
106 Marek Zadina .08 .25
107 Martin Havlat 6.00 15.00
108 Roman Dadera .08 .25
109 Tomas Chlubna .08 .25
110 Petr Folta .08 .25
111 Ondrej Zetek .08 .25
112 Branislav Janos .08 .25
113 Ladislav Blazek .08 .25
114 Roman Malek .08 .25
115 Vitezslav Skuta .08 .25
116 Jan Krajicek .08 .25
117 Pavel Kolarik .20 .50
118 Martin Bakula .08 .25
119 Vladimir Ruzicka .20 .50
120 Tomas Kucharcik .08 .25
121 Michal Sup .08 .25
122 Jiri Dolezal .08 .25
123 Jan Kopecky .08 .25
124 Petr Hrbek .08 .25
125 Radek Matejovsky .08 .25
126 Vladimir Machulda .08 .25
127 Roman Cechmanek .40 1.00
128 Ivo Pesat .08 .25
129 Jan Srdinko .08 .25
130 Libor Zabransky .08 .25
131 Jiri Veber .08 .25
132 Radim Tesarik .08 .25
133 Jiri Dopita .20 .50
134 Radek Belohlav .15 .40
135 Jan Tomajko .08 .25
136 Jan Pardavy .08 .25
137 Roman Stantien .08 .25
138 Zbynek Marak .08 .25
139 Alexei Jaskin .08 .25
140 Pavel Zubicek .08 .25
141 Petr Briza .30 .75
142 Petr Prikryl .08 .25
143 Frantisek Kucera .07 .20
144 Ladislav Benysek .20 .50
145 Michal Sykora .20 .50
146 Jaroslav Nedved .08 .25
147 David Vyborny .20 .50
148 Patrik Martinec .08 .25
149 Jaroslav Hlinka .08 .25
150 Ondrej Kratena .08 .25
151 Michal Bros .08 .25
152 Richard Zemlicka .20 .50
153 Jiri Zelenka .08 .25
154 Vaclav Eiselt .08 .25
155 Martin Bilek .20 .50
156 Lubos Horcicka .08 .25
157 Michal Madl .08 .25
158 Jan Krulis .08 .25
159 Jiri Krocak .08 .25
160 Jan Dlouhy .08 .25
161 Tomas Horna .08 .25
162 Ladislav Svoboda .08 .25
163 Zdenek Eichenmann .08 .25
164 Jiri Burger .08 .25
165 Tomas Kupka .08 .25
166 Jiri Kames .20 .50
167 Juri Holdan .08 .25
168 Ondrej Kriz .08 .25
169 Martin Prusek .75 2.00
170 Jiri Trvaj .08 .25
171 Dmitrij Jerofejev .08 .25
172 Lukas Galvas .08 .25
173 Pavel Kowalczyk .08 .25
174 Petr Jurecka .08 .25
175 Ludik Krayzel .08 .25
176 Libor Polasek .08 .25
177 Martin Lamich .08 .25
178 Petr Hubacek .08 .25
179 Serej Petrenko .08 .25
180 Zdenik Pavelek .08 .25
181 Martin Tomasek .08 .25
182 Zbynik Irgi .08 .25
183 Ladislav Kudrna .20 .50
184 Pavol Rybar .20 .50
185 Pavel Kumstat .08 .25
186 Tomas Jakes .08 .25
187 Karel Soudek .08 .25
188 Jiri Hes .08 .25
189 Petr Kankovsky .08 .25
190 Milan Kastner .08 .25
191 Jiri Poukar .08 .25
192 Peter Pucher .08 .25
193 Marek Vorel .08 .25
194 Radek Haman .08 .25
195 Karel Plasek .08 .25
196 Milan Prochazka .08 .25
GC Jaromir Jagr Gold 20.00 50.00

1999-00 Czech DS Goalies

This set, featuring the top goalies of the Czech league, were random inserts in packs. The set includes a key pre-NHL card of Roman Cechmanek.

COMPLETE SET (14) 16.00 40.00
G1 Richard Hrazdira 1.25 3.00
G2 Rudolf Pejchar 1.25 3.00
G3 Ivo Capek 1.25 3.00
G4 Pavel Cagas 1.25 3.00
G5 Zdenek Orct 1.25 3.00
G6 Libor Barta 1.25 3.00
G7 Dusan Salficky 1.50 4.00
G8 Vlastimil Lakosil 1.25 3.00
G9 Ladislav Blazek 1.25 3.00
G10 Roman Cechmanek 1.50 4.00
G11 Petr Briza 1.50 4.00
G12 Martin Bilek 1.25 3.00
G13 Martin Prusek 4.00 10.00
G14 Pavol Rybar 1.25 3.00

1999-00 Czech DS National Stars

These cards, featuring the members of the Czech Republic's gold medal winning team, were randomly inserted in packs.

COMPLETE SET (23) 50.00 125.00
NS1 Dominik Hasek 8.00 20.00
NS2 Milan Hnilicka 2.00 5.00
NS3 Jaromir Jagr 15.00 40.00
NS4 Jiri Slegr 1.25 3.00
NS5 Jaroslav Spacek 1.25 3.00
NS6 Frantisek Kucera 1.25 3.00
NS7 Roman Hamrlik 1.50 4.00
NS8 Petr Svoboda 1.50 4.00
NS9 Viktor Ujcik 1.25 3.00
NS10 Frantisek Kaberle 1.25 3.00
NS11 Libor Prochazka 1.25 3.00
NS12 Robert Reichel 1.25 3.00
NS13 Martin Rucinsky 1.25 3.00
NS14 Martin Straka 1.50 4.00
NS15 Martin Prochazka 1.25 3.00
NS16 Pavel Patera 1.25 3.00
NS17 Vladimir Ruzicka 1.25 3.00
NS18 Josef Beranek 1.25 3.00
NS19 David Moravec 1.25 3.00
NS20 Jan Hlavac 1.50 4.00
NS21 David Vyborny 1.25 3.00
NS22 Jiri Dopita 1.25 3.00
NS23 Petr Sykora 2.00 5.00

1999-00 Czech DS Premium

This insert set features the top Czech-born players and was randomly seeded into packs. The cards were limited to 150 copies each.

COMPLETE SET (12) 36.00 75.00
P1 Dominik Hasek 10.00 25.00
P2 Roman Turek 1.50 4.00
P3 Roman Cechmanek 1.50 4.00
P4 Milan Hnilicka 2.00 5.00
P5 Martin Prochazka 1.25 3.00
P6 Jaromir Jagr 20.00 50.00
P7 Jiri Slegr 1.25 3.00
P8 Jaroslav Spacek 1.25 3.00
P9 Pavel Patera 1.25 3.00
P10 Jiri Dopita 1.25 3.00
P11 Robert Reichel 1.25 3.00
P12 Martin Rucinsky 1.50 4.00

1999-00 Czech OFS

This set features every player from the Czech Elite League.

COMPLETE SET (560) 30.00 75.00
1 Libor Barta .08 .25
2 Martin Bilek .20 .50
3 Ladislav Blazek .08 .25
4 Petr Briza .30 .75
5 Ivo Capek .20 .50
6 Roman Cechmanek .40 1.00
7 Robert Horyna .20 .50
8 Vladimir Hudacek .20 .50
9 Ladislav Kudrna .20 .50
10 Vlastimil Lakosil .20 .50
11 Michal Marik .20 .50
12 Zdenek Orct .20 .50
13 Rudolf Pejchar .20 .50
14 Martin Prusek .75 2.00
15 Dusan Salficky .30 .75
16 Richard Farda .07 .20
17 Marian Jelinek .07 .20
18 Josef Beranek .07 .20
19 Leo Gudas .07 .20
20 Milan Hnilicka .40 1.00
21 Milos Holan .07 .20
22 Jan Hrdina .75 2.00
23 Jaromir Jagr 4.00 10.00
24 Frantisek Kaberle .20 .50
25 Tomas Kaberle .30 .75
26 Pavel Kubina .40 1.00
27 Marek Malik .07 .20
28 Pavel Patera .20 .50
29 Martin Prochazka .07 .20
30 Vaclav Prospal .20 .50
31 Robert Reichel .20 .50
32 Martin Rucinsky .20 .50
33 Vladimir Ruzicka .20 .50
34 Pavel Skrbek .20 .50
35 Jiri Slegr .20 .50
36 Jaroslav Spacek .20 .50
37 Martin Straka .40 1.00
38 Vaclav Varada .20 .50
39 David Volek .20 .50
40 Jan Vopat .20 .50
41 Vladimir Caldr .07 .20
42 Martin Bakula .07 .20
43 Miroslav Hajek .07 .20
44 Petr Hrbek .07 .20
45 Petr Kadlec .07 .20
46 Jan Kopecky .07 .20
47 Jan Krajicek .07 .20
48 Angel Krstev .07 .20
49 Radek Matejovsky .07 .20
50 Jan Novak .07 .20
51 Vladimir Pojkar .07 .20
52 Vladimir Ruzicka .20 .50
53 Jan Slavik .07 .20
54 Jan Sochor .07 .20
55 Michal Sup .07 .20
56 Zdislav Tabara .07 .20
57 Jiri Dopita .20 .50
58 Ondrej Kavulic .07 .20
59 Petr Kubos .07 .20
60 Radim Kucharczyk .07 .20
61 Marko Palo .07 .20
62 Jukka Seppo .07 .20
63 Lukas Slaby .07 .20
64 Roman Stantien .07 .20
65 Petr Suchy .07 .20
66 Radim Tesarik .07 .20
67 Jan Tomajko .07 .20
68 Martin Vozdecky .07 .20
69 Petr Zajgla .07 .20
70 Pavel Zubicek .07 .20
71 Pavel Pazourek .07 .20
72 Petr Belohlavek .07 .20
73 Radim Freibauer .07 .20
74 Radek Haman .07 .20
75 David Havir .07 .20
76 Jiri Hes .07 .20
77 Jiri Hradecky .07 .20
78 Jan Kloboucek .07 .20
79 David Pazourek .07 .20
80 David Petlak .07 .20
81 Karel Plasek .07 .20
82 Jiri Poukar .07 .20
83 Milan Prochazka .07 .20
84 Peter Pucher .07 .20
85 Marek Vorel .07 .20
86 Pavel Marek .07 .20
87 Martin Barek .07 .20
88 Tomas Blazek .07 .20
89 Jan Dusanek .07 .20
90 Patrik Elias .75 2.00
91 Petr Jancarik .07 .20
92 Jaroslav Kudrna .20 .50
93 Tomas Martinec .07 .20
94 Brendan Morrison .40 1.00
95 Andrej Novotny .07 .20
96 Tomas Pacal .07 .20
97 Rastislav Palov .07 .20
98 Patrik Rozsival .07 .20
99 Michael Tvrdik .07 .20
100 Tomas Vak .07 .20
101 Pavel Richter .07 .20
102 Michal Bros .08 .25
103 Vaclav Eiselt .07 .20
104 Petr Havelka .07 .20
105 Martin Holy .07 .20
106 Pavel Kasparik .07 .20
107 Ondrej Kratena .08 .25
108 Frantisek Kucera .07 .20
109 Jaroslav Nedved .07 .20
110 Frantisek Ptacek .07 .20
111 Miha Rebolj .07 .20
112 Pavel Srek .07 .20
113 David Vyborny .07 .20
114 Jiri Zelenka .07 .20
115 Richard Zemlicka .20 .50
116 Marek Sykora .07 .20
117 Milan Antos .07 .20
118 Martin Cech .07 .20
119 Marek Cernosek .07 .20
120 Petr Chvojka .07 .20
121 Pavel Geffert .07 .20
122 Jiri Hanzlik .07 .20
123 Jiri Jelen .07 .20
124 Michal Jelinek .07 .20
125 Petr Korinek .20 .50
126 Josef Reznicek .07 .20
127 Radek Svoboda .07 .20
128 Petr Ulehla .07 .20
129 Ivan Vlcek .07 .20
130 Pavel Vostrak .07 .20
131 Martin Pesout .07 .20
132 Michal Dobron .07 .20
133 Martin Filip .07 .20
134 Pavel Janku .07 .20
135 Jaroslav Kalla .07 .20
136 Jan Kostal .07 .20
137 Jaromir Kverka .07 .20
138 Petr Macek .07 .20
139 Martin Maskarinec .07 .20
140 Petr Pavlas .07 .20
141 Josef Podlaha .07 .20
142 Michal Porak .07 .20
143 Martin Richter .07 .20
144 Jan Snopek .07 .20
145 Martin Streit .07 .20
146 Vaclav Sykora .07 .20
147 David Balazs .07 .20
148 Viktor Hubl .07 .20
149 Petr Kratky .07 .20
150 Vojtech Kubincak .07 .20
151 Robert Kysela .07 .20
152 Marian Menhart .20 .50
153 Radek Mrazek .07 .20
154 Angel Nikolov .20 .50
155 Karel Pilar .40 1.00
156 Ivo Prorok .07 .20
157 Robert Reichel .20 .50
158 Zdenek Skorepa .20 .50
159 Josef Straka .07 .20
160 Martin Strbak .07 .20
161 Otakar Vejvoda .07 .20
162 Jan Dlouhy .07 .20
163 Zdenek Eichenmann .07 .20
164 Jiri Holsan .07 .20
165 Tomas Horna .07 .20
166 Ondrej Kriz .07 .20
167 Jiri Krocak .07 .20
168 Tomas Kupka .07 .20
169 Michal Madl .07 .20
170 Milan Novy .07 .20
171 Tomas Polansky .07 .20
172 Lukas Poznik .07 .20
173 Ladislav Svoboda .07 .20
174 Tomas Ullrych .07 .20
175 Martin Vejvoda .07 .20
176 Jaroslav Liska .07 .20
177 Kamil Brabenec .07 .20
178 Roman Cech .07 .20
179 Milan Filipi .07 .20
180 Stanislav Jasecko .07 .20
181 Josef Jindra .07 .20
182 Michal Klimes .07 .20
183 Zdenek Kutlak .20 .50
184 Milan Nedoma .07 .20
185 David Nedorost .07 .20
186 Lubos Rob .07 .20
187 Petr Sailer .07 .20
188 Jiri Simanek .07 .20
189 Rudolf Suchanek .07 .20
190 Radek Toupal .07 .20
191 Alois Hadamczik CO .07 .20
192 Mario Cartelli .07 .20
193 Petr Gregorek .07 .20
194 Martin Havlat 6.00 15.00
195 Branislav Janos .07 .20
196 Roman Kadera .07 .20
197 Richard Kral .07 .20
198 Jiri Kuntos .07 .20
199 David Nosek .07 .20
200 Vaclav Pletka .20 .50
201 Pavel Selinger .07 .20
202 Petr Svoboda .15 .40
203 Viktor Ujcik .15 .40
204 Marek Zadina .07 .20
205 Jiri Zurek .07 .20
206 Antonin Stavjana .07 .20
207 Jaroslav Balastik .07 .20
208 Roman Hamrlik .30 .75
209 Lubomir Korhon .07 .20

210 Martin Kotasek .07 .20
211 Petr Leska .07 .20
212 Patrik Luza .07 .20
213 Jiri Marusak .07 .20
214 Pavel Mojzis .07 .20
215 Milan Navratil .07 .20
216 Miroslav Okal .07 .20
217 Michal Tomek .07 .20
218 Petr Vala .07 .20
219 Pavol Valko .07 .20
220 Tomas Zizka .07 .20
221 Vladimir Vujtek .07 .20
222 Lukas Galvas .07 .20
223 Dmitrij Gogolev .07 .20
224 Zbynek Irgl .07 .20
225 Dmitri Jerofejev .07 .20
226 Petr Jurecka .07 .20
227 Ludek Krayzel .07 .20
228 Daniel Kysela .07 .20
229 Zdenek Pavelek .07 .20
230 Sergei Petrenko .07 .20
231 Daniel Seman .07 .20
232 Lukas Smolka .07 .20
233 Vaclav Varada .20 .50
234 Jan Vytisk .07 .20
235 Lukas Zatopek .07 .20
236 Richard Farda .07 .20
237 Michal Cech .07 .20
238 Vladimir Holik .07 .20
239 Andrei Yakovenko .07 .20
240 Marek Melenovsky .07 .20
241 Martin Miklik .07 .20
242 Pavel Nohel .07 .20
243 Libor Pivko .07 .20
244 Bogdan Savenko .07 .20
245 Petr Suchanek .07 .20
246 Kamil Suchanek .07 .20
247 Petr Tejkl .07 .20
248 Petr Vlasanek .07 .20
249 Michael Vyhlidal .07 .20
250 Tomas Zapletal .07 .20
251 Josef Augusta .07 .20
252 Ivan Hlinka .20 .50
253 Vladimir Martinec .07 .20
254 Roman Cechmanek .40 1.00
255 Martin Prusek .75 2.00
256 Radek Belohlav .15 .40
257 Ladislav Benysek .20 .50
258 Petr Cajanek .30 .75
259 Jan Caloun .20 .50
260 Jiri Dopita .20 .50
261 Vaclav Kral .07 .20
262 Frantisek Kucera .07 .20
263 Tomas Kucharcik .07 .20
264 Radek Martinek .20 .50
265 Ales Pisa .07 .20
266 Robert Reichel .20 .50
267 Martin Richter .07 .20
268 Roman Simicek .20 .50
269 Jan Srdinko .07 .20
270 Martin Stepanek .07 .20
271 Petr Tenkrat .30 .75
272 Jan Tomajko .07 .20
273 Viktor Ujcik .15 .40
274 Tomas Vlasak .07 .20
275 David Vyborny .07 .20
276 Jiri Vykoukal .07 .20
277 Jaroslav Parizek CO .07 .20
278 Peter Bartos .07 .20
279 Jiri Broz .07 .20
280 Ales Kotalik 1.25 3.00
281 Lukas Zib .07 .20
282 Vaclav Kral .07 .20
283 Radek Martinek .20 .50
284 Vaclav Nedorost .75 2.00
285 Martin Strba .07 .20
286 Filip Turek .07 .20
287 Ivo Pestuka CO .07 .20
288 Jaroslav Hub .07 .20
289 Miroslav Javin .07 .20
290 Roman Kontsek .07 .20
291 Rostislav Pilavka .07 .20
292 Ivan Puncochar .07 .20
293 Roman Rysanek .07 .20
294 Petr Sykora .07 .20
295 Ales Tomasek .07 .20
296 Daniel Vilasek .07 .20
297 David Kriz .07 .20
298 Michal Mikeska .07 .20
299 Pavol Pekarik .07 .20
300 Jan Peterek .07 .20
301 Radek Philipp .07 .20
302 Pavel Zdrahal .07 .20
303 Ales Zima .07 .20
304 Filip Stefanka .07 .20
305 Tomas Sykora .07 .20
306 Marcel Hanzal .07 .20
307 Roman Horak .07 .20
308 Milos Riha CO .07 .20
309 Ladislav Prokupek .07 .20
310 Roman Prosek .07 .20
311 Martin Rousek .07 .20
312 Miroslav Barus .07 .20
313 Michal Divisek .07 .20
314 David Hruska .07 .20
315 Pavel Metlicka .07 .20
316 Radek Prochazka .07 .20
317 Tomas Martinec .07 .20
318 Zdenek Pavelek .07 .20
319 Jiri Polak .07 .20
320 Tomas Chlubna .07 .20
321 Jiri Malinsky .07 .20
322 Petr Fiala .07 .20
323 Eduard Novak CO .07 .20
324 Lubomir Bauer .07 .20
325 Petr Bohunicky .07 .20
326 Jiri Burger .07 .20
327 Jiri Hubacek .07 .20
328 Jiri Kames .07 .20
329 Michal Kanka .07 .20
330 Petr Kounovsky .07 .20
331 Jan Krulis .07 .20
332 Radim Skuhrovec .07 .20
333 Martin Taborsky .07 .20
334 Ladislav Vlcek .07 .20
335 Radek Gardon .07 .20
336 Vladimir Jerabek CO .07 .20
337 Jan Alinc .07 .20
338 Vladimir Gyna .07 .20
339 Jindrich Kotrla .07 .20
340 Michal Travnicek .07 .20
341 Lukas Bednarik .07 .20
342 Daniel Branda .07 .20
343 Marek Cernosek .07 .20
344 Jan Liska .07 .20
345 Kamil Piros .40 1.00
346 Petr Rosol .07 .20
347 Josef Palecek CO .07 .20
348 Petr Hemsky CO .07 .20
349 Milan Chalupa CO .07 .20
350 Ales Hemsky 8.00 20.00
351 Jiri Jantovsky .07 .20
352 Robert Kantor .07 .20
353 Marek Cernosek .07 .20
354 Jiri Malinsky .07 .20
355 Miroslav Mosnar .07 .20
356 Ales Pisa .07 .20
357 Stanislav Prochazka .07 .20
358 Petr Sykora .07 .20
359 Jan Archalous .07 .20
360 Martin Filip .07 .20
361 Pavel Kabrt .07 .20
362 Jan Kolar .07 .20
363 Martin Koudelka .07 .20
364 Radek Matejovsky .07 .20
365 Michal Mikeska .07 .20
366 Petr Mudroch .07 .20
367 Petr Caslava .07 .20
368 Radim Rulik CO .07 .20
369 Jiri Dobrovolny .07 .20
370 Mojmir Musil .07 .20
371 David Pospisil .07 .20
372 Martin Spanhel .40 1.00
373 Jaroslav Spelda .07 .20
374 Michal Straka .07 .20
375 Milan Volak .07 .20
376 Zdenek Sedlak .07 .20
377 Jan Fiala .07 .20
378 Petr Kadlec .07 .20
379 Josef Straka .07 .20
380 Jiri Kalous CO .07 .20
381 Josef Beranek CO .07 .20
382 Jiri Dolezal .07 .20
383 Jan Hejda .07 .20
384 Pavel Kolarik .20 .50
385 Tomas Kucharcik .07 .20
386 Vladimir Machulda .07 .20
387 Jan Bohac .07 .20
388 Pavel Geffert .07 .20
389 Jiri Jantovsky .07 .20
390 Zdenek Skorepa .07 .20
391 Vitezslav Skuta .07 .20
392 Robin Bacul .07 .20
393 Marek Tomica .07 .20
394 Frantisek Vyborny CO .07 .20
395 Ladislav Benysek .20 .50
396 Jaroslav Hlinka .07 .20
397 Vaclav Novak .07 .20
398 Patrik Martinec .07 .20
399 Vaclav Novak .07 .20
400 Josef Slanec .07 .20
401 Michal Sykora .08 .25
402 Vladimir Vujtek .07 .20
403 Kamil Konecny CO .07 .20
404 Jozef Dano .07 .20
405 Petr Folta .07 .20
406 Tomas Chlubna .07 .20
407 Robert Kantor .07 .20
408 Jan Marek .07 .20
409 Lubomir Sekeras .20 .50
410 Ondrej Zetek .07 .20
411 David Appel .07 .20
412 Pavel Janku .07 .20
413 Dmitrij Jerofejev .07 .20
414 David Nosek .07 .20
415 Vladimir Vlk .07 .20
416 Kamil Konecny .07 .20
417 Jan Sterbak CO .07 .20
418 Mojmir Trlicik .07 .20
419 Pavel Bacho .07 .20
420 Ondrej Zetek .07 .20
421 Roman Kadera .07 .20
422 Petr Hubacek .07 .20
423 Roman Kelner .07 .20
424 Pavel Kowalczyk .07 .20
425 Martin Lamich .07 .20
426 Jan Matejny .07 .20
427 Libor Pavlis .07 .20
428 Radek Philipp .07 .20
429 Libor Polasek .07 .20
430 Martin Tomasek .07 .20
431 Libor Gelacek .07 .20
432 Martin Louzek .07 .20
433 Martin Maskarinec .07 .20
434 David Moravec .20 .50
435 Ivan Padelek .07 .20
436 Martin Streit .07 .20
437 Miroslav Venkrbec .07 .20
438 Radek Belohlav .15 .40
439 Alexej Jaskin .07 .20
440 Zbynek Marak .07 .20
441 Oleg Antonenko .07 .20
442 Josef Mikes .07 .20
443 Jan Pardavy .07 .20
444 Jan Srdinko .07 .20
445 Jiri Veber .07 .20
446 Libor Zabransky .07 .20
447 Pavel Patera .20 .50
448 Martin Prochazka .07 .20
449 Zbynek Spitzer .07 .20
450 S. Prikryl CO .07 .20
451 Petr Cajanek .30 .75
452 Jiri David .07 .20
453 Martin Hamrlik .07 .20
454 Marek Ivan .07 .20
455 Josef Straub .07 .20
456 Ondrej Vesely .07 .20
457 Martin Ambruz .07 .20
458 Jan Homer .07 .20
459 Rostislav Malena .07 .20
460 S. Barada CO .07 .20
461 Pavol Valko .07 .20
462 Marek Uram .07 .20
463 Patrik Fink .07 .20
464 Tomas Hradecky .07 .20
465 Tomas Jakes .07 .20
466 Petr Kankovsky .07 .20
467 Milan Kastner .07 .20
468 David Kudelka .07 .20
469 Pavel Kumstat .07 .20
470 Karel Soudek .07 .20
471 Jan Kopecky .07 .20
472 Michal Bros .08 .25
473 Martin Cech .07 .20
474 Petr Gregorek .07 .20
475 Jiri Hanzlik .07 .20
476 Jaroslav Hlinka .07 .20
477 Petr Korinek .07 .20
478 Ludek Krayzel .07 .20
479 David Moravec .20 .50
480 Angel Nikolov .20 .50
481 Pavel Patera .20 .50
482 Kamil Piros .40 1.00
483 Vaclav Pletka .20 .50
484 Martin Spanhel .40 1.00
485 Radim Tesarik .07 .20
486 Libor Zabransky .07 .20
487 Petr Briza .30 .75
488 Dusan Salficky .30 .75
489 Roman Cechmanek .40 1.00
490 Vladimir Hudacek .20 .50
491 Peter Bartos .07 .20
492 Vladimir Vujtek .07 .20
493 David Vyborny .07 .20
494 Ladislav Benysek .20 .50
495 Tomas Blazek .08 .25
496 Frantisek Kucera .07 .20
497 Jiri Burger .07 .20
498 Jan Kopecky .07 .20
499 Vaclav Kral .07 .20
500 Jan Krulis .07 .20
501 Ivo Prorok .07 .20
502 Radek Martinek .20 .50
503 Jaroslav Nedved .07 .20
504 Petr Pavlas .07 .20
505 Ales Pisa .07 .20
506 Michal Sykora .08 .25
507 Robert Reichel .20 .50
508 Miroslav Buras .07 .20
509 Martin Spanhel .40 1.00
510 Michal Sup .07 .20
511 Petr Cajanek .40 1.00
512 Jiri Dopita .20 .50
513 Martin Hamrlik .07 .20
514 Roman Horak .07 .20
515 Zbynek Irgl .07 .20
516 Tomas Jakes .07 .20
517 Ludek Krayzel .07 .20
518 Jiri Kuntos .07 .20
519 Petr Leska .07 .20
520 Jiri Marusak .07 .20
521 David Moravec .20 .50
522 Jan Pardavy .07 .20
523 Pavel Patera .20 .50
524 Jan Peterek .07 .20
525 Martin Prochazka .07 .20
526 Karel Soudek .07 .20
527 Jan Srdinko .07 .20
528 Radim Tesarik .07 .20
529 Viktor Ujcik .15 .40
530 Libor Zabransky .08 .25
531 Pavel Cagas .20 .50
532 Zdenek Smid .20 .75
533 Lubos Horcicka .20 .50
534 Pavel Krizek .20 .50
535 Marek Pinc .20 .50
536 Petr Jez .08 .25
537 Radek Masny .20 .50
538 Roman Malek .20 .50
539 Tomas Duba .20 .50
540 Petr Prikryl .20 .50
541 Jiri Kratochvil .20 .50
542 Marek Novotny .08 .25
543 Jiri Trvaj .20 .50
544 Ivo Pesat .20 .50
545 Richard Hrazdira .20 .50
546 Petr Kubena .20 .50
547 Pavol Rybar .20 .50
548 Adam Svoboda .30 .75
549 Radek Masny .20 .50
550 Petr Tucek .20 .50
551 Vladimir Hudacek .20 .50
552 Dusan Salficky .30 .75
NNO Ladislav Blazek CL .08 .25
NNO Martin Prusek CL .40 1.00
NNO Zdenek Orct CL .40 1.00
NNO Petr Briza CL .30 .75
NNO Vladimir Hudacek CL .20 .50
NNO Roman Cechmanek CL .40 1.00
NNO Rudolf Pejchar CL .40 1.00
NNO Dusan Salficky CL .30 .75

1999-00 Czech OFS All-Star Game Blue

A blue-foil enhanced parallel to the 44-card All-Star Game subset. These cards were random inserts in packs.

COMPLETE SET (44) 15.00 25.00
487 Petr Briza .40 1.00
488 Dusan Salficky .40 1.00
489 Roman Cechmanek .75 2.00
490 Vladimir Hudacek .20 .50
491 Peter Bartos .20 .50
492 Vladimir Vujtek .20 .50
493 David Vyborny .20 .50
494 Ladislav Benysek .40 1.00
495 Tomas Blazek .40 1.00
496 Frantisek Kucera .20 .50
497 Jiri Burger .20 .50
498 Jan Kopecky .20 .50
499 Vaclav Kral .20 .50
500 Jan Krulis .20 .50
501 Ivo Prorok .20 .50
502 Radek Martinek .40 1.00
503 Jaroslav Nedved .20 .50
504 Petr Pavlas .20 .50
505 Ales Pisa .20 .50
506 Michal Sykora .20 .50
507 Robert Reichel .40 1.00
508 Miroslav Buras .20 .50
509 Martin Spanhel .30 .75
510 Michal Sup .20 .50
511 Petr Cajanek 1.25 3.00
512 Jiri Dopita .40 1.00
513 Martin Hamrlik .20 .50
514 Roman Horak .20 .50
515 Zbynek Irgl .20 .50
516 Tomas Jakes .20 .50
517 Ludek Krayzel .20 .50
518 Jiri Kuntos .20 .50
519 Petr Leska .20 .50
520 Jiri Marusak .20 .50
521 David Moravec .20 .50
522 Jan Pardavy .20 .50
523 Pavel Patera .20 .50
524 Jan Peterek .20 .50
525 Martin Prochazka .20 .50
526 Karel Soudek .20 .50
527 Jan Srdinko .20 .50
528 Radim Tesarik .20 .50
529 Viktor Ujcik .20 .50
530 Libor Zabransky .30 .75

1999-00 Czech OFS All-Star Game Gold

These cards are a further parallel of the Embossed Blue parallel. Odds are not known and no pricing information is available. Forward any information on these cards to hockeymag@beckett.com.

1999-00 Czech OFS All-Star Game Red

These cards are a further parallel of the Embossed Blue parallel. Odds are not known and no pricing information is available. Forward any information on these cards to hockeymag@beckett.com.

1999-00 Czech OFS All-Star Game Silver

These cards are a further parallel of the Embossed Blue parallel. Odds are not known and no pricing information is available. Forward any information on these cards to hockeymag@beckett.com.

1999-00 Czech OFS Goalie Die-Cuts

These randomly inserted cards parallel the first 15 cards in the base set and feature a distinctive die-cutting.

COMPLETE SET (15) 40.00 80.00
1 Libor Barta 2.00 5.00
2 Martin Bilek 2.00 5.00
3 Ladislav Blazek 2.00 5.00
4 Petr Briza 3.00 8.00
5 Ivo Capek 2.00 5.00
6 Roman Cechmanek 4.00 10.00
7 Robert Horyna 2.00 5.00
8 Vladimir Hudacek 2.00 5.00
9 Ladislav Kudrna 2.00 5.00
10 Vlastimil Lakosil 2.00 5.00
11 Michal Marik 2.00 5.00
12 Zdenek Orct 2.00 5.00
13 Rudolf Pejchar 2.00 5.00
14 Martin Prusek 8.00 20.00
15 Dusan Salficky 3.00 8.00

1999-00 Czech OFS Jagr Team Embossed

This set parallels cards #16-40 of the base OFS set, which features the Jagr Team subset. The cards are distinguishable from base cards by an embossed feature.

COMPLETE SET (25) 15.00 30.00
16 Richard Farda .20 .50
17 Marian Jelinek .20 .50
18 Josef Beranek .20 .50
19 Leo Gudas .20 .50
20 Milan Hnilicka 1.25 3.00
21 Milos Holan .20 .50
22 Jan Hrdina .75 2.00
23 Jaromir Jagr 8.00 20.00
24 Frantisek Kaberle .20 .50
25 Tomas Kaberle .60 1.50
26 Pavel Kubina .75 2.00
27 Marek Malik .20 .50
28 Pavel Patera .20 .50
29 Martin Prochazka .20 .50
30 Vaclav Prospal .40 1.00
31 Robert Reichel .40 1.00
32 Martin Rucinsky .40 1.00
33 Vladimir Ruzicka .20 .50
34 Pavel Skrbek .40 1.00
35 Jiri Slegr .40 1.00
36 Jaroslav Spacek .40 1.00
37 Martin Straka .75 2.00
38 Vaclav Varada .40 1.00
39 David Volek .40 1.00
40 Jan Vopat .40 1.00

1999-00 Czech Score Blue 2000

This set features players from the Czech second division. The set is noteworthy for the inclusion of cards of NHLers Brendan Morrison and Patrik Elias, who were holding out from the New Jersey Devils at the time. A parallel version of the set, Red Ice 2000, also exists. At this time, we believe there is no price difference between the two versions.

COMPLETE SET (165) 20.00 50.00
1 Roman Malek .30 .75
2 Roman Hrubes .20 .50
3 Ladislav Slizek .20 .50
4 Jaroslav Roubik .20 .50
5 Jiri Kuchler .20 .50
6 Petr Mudroch .20 .50
7 Jiri Cmunt .20 .50
8 Lukas Palecek .20 .50
9 Pavel Malecek .20 .50
10 Vaclav Drabek .20 .50
11 Dalibor Sanda .20 .50
12 Jiri Novotny .20 .50
13 Dalimil Svoboda .20 .50
14 Petr Kubena .20 .50
15 Martin Svetlik .20 .50
16 Jakub Ziska .20 .50
17 Richard Kolacek .20 .50
18 Tomas Trachta .20 .50
19 Patrik Weber .20 .50
20 Ales Sochorec .20 .50
21 Alexandr Elsner .20 .50
22 Michal Safarik .20 .50
23 Michal Safarik .20 .50
24 Tomas Mikolasek .20 .50
25 Pavel Malac .20 .50
26 Kamil Jarina .20 .50
27 Petr Martinek .20 .50
28 Ladislav Bousek .20 .50
29 Kamil Kolacek .20 .50
30 Jiri Gombar .20 .50
31 David Hajek .20 .50
32 Martin Tupa .20 .50
33 Stanislav Stavensky .20 .50
34 Martin Stelcich .20 .50
35 Radek Sip .20 .50
36 Petr Altrichter .20 .50
37 Lukas Stabl .20 .50
38 Lukas Sablik .20 .50
39 Marian Morava .20 .50
40 Zdenek Fuksa .20 .50
41 Petr Mokrejs .20 .50
42 Miroslav Duben .20 .50
43 Jiri Cihlar .20 .50
44 Vaclav Adamec .20 .50
45 Daniel Hodek .20 .50
46 Ales Polcar .20 .50
47 Daniel Zapotocny .20 .50
48 Richard Cachnin .20 .50
49 Roman Spiler .20 .50
50 Filip Sindelar .20 .50
51 Petr Jaros .20 .50
52 Marek Dvorak .20 .50
53 Jaroslav Mares .20 .50
54 Robert Vavroch .20 .50
55 Vratislav Hreben .20 .50
56 Petr Cerveny .20 .50
57 Jaroslav Kocar .20 .50
58 Ales Skokan .20 .50
59 Michal Horak .20 .50
60 Jakub Kraus .20 .50
61 Marcel Kucera .20 .50
62 Miroslav Sedlacek .20 .50
63 Richard Richter .20 .50
64 Rudolf Mudra .20 .50
65 Jaroslav Muller .20 .50
66 Evzen Gal .20 .50
67 Petr Spojcar .20 .50
68 Jaroslav Kreuzman .20 .50
69 Premysl Sedlak .20 .50
70 Martin Nosek .20 .50
71 Tomas Vyskocil .20 .50
72 Michal Lanicek .20 .50
73 Pavel Malac .20 .50
74 Ales Vala .20 .50
75 Martin Vyborny .20 .50
76 Tomas Vozka .20 .50
77 Petr Hocicka .20 .50
78 Jan Plodek .20 .50
79 Oldrich Nyc .20 .50
80 Filip Pesan .20 .50
81 Milan Plodek .20 .50
82 Jiri Matousek .20 .50
83 Vitezslav Jankovych .20 .50
84 Petr Kus .20 .50
85 Martin Chlad .20 .50
86 Hiroyuki Murakami .20 .50
87 Lukas Bednarik .20 .50
88 Michal Oliverius .20 .50
89 Tomas Pisa .20 .50
90 Jan Hranac .20 .50
91 Jan Bohacek .20 .50
92 Tomas Klimt .20 .50
93 Martin Zivny .20 .50
94 Michal Havel .20 .50
95 Martin Rejthar .20 .50
96 Karl Rakovsky .20 .50
97 Martin Vojtek .20 .50
98 Robert Prochazka .20 .50
99 Daniel Vilasek .20 .50
100 Jan Kasik .20 .50
101 Jevgenij Alipov .20 .50
102 Ales Kretinsky .20 .50
103 Pavel Sebesta .20 .50
104 David Kostelnak .20 .50
105 Karel Harazim .20 .50
106 Richard Brancik .20 .50
107 Petr Rozum .20 .50
108 Michal Pinkas .20 .50
109 Robert Slavik .20 .50
110 Josef Vachulka .20 .50
111 Lubos Pindiak .20 .50
112 Robert Zak .20 .50
113 David Mika .20 .50
114 Jiri Kudrna .20 .50
115 Vaclav Benak .20 .50
116 Roman Bezpalec .20 .50
117 Pavel Hejl .20 .50
118 Michal Janiga .20 .50
119 Vladimir Mizera .20 .50
120 David Plsek .20 .50
121 Petr Tucek .20 .50
122 Martin Palinek .20 .50
123 Jiri Polak .20 .50
124 Michal Cerny .20 .50
125 Milan Ministr .20 .50
126 Tomas Hradecky .20 .50
127 David Svec .20 .50
128 Filip Janecek .20 .50
129 Tomas Hradecky .20 .50
130 Radomir Brazda .20 .50
131 Petr Hrachovina .20 .50
132 Martin Altrichter .20 .50
133 Jaromir Pichal .20 .50
134 Jiri Bures .20 .50
135 Jiri Mifek .20 .50
136 Jaroslav Smolik .20 .50
137 Milota Florian .20 .50
138 Robert Holy .20 .50
139 Josef Drabek .20 .50
140 Michal Slavik .20 .50
141 Tomas Kramny .20 .50
142 Jan Konecny .20 .50
143 Radek Lukes .20 .50
144 Robert Hamrla .20 .50
145 Petr Lustinec .20 .50
146 Radek Kucera .20 .50
147 Petr Sakarov .20 .50
148 Pavel Kormunda .20 .50
149 Petr Suchy .20 .50
150 David Brezik .20 .50
151 Michal Nohejl .20 .50
152 Martin Jenacek .20 .50
153 Dusan Barica .20 .50
154 Zdenek Kucirek .20 .50
155 Stanislav Neruda .20 .50
156 Robert Pospisil .20 .50
157 Brendan Morrison .75 2.00
158 Frantisek Sevcik .20 .50
159 Roman Hlouch .20 .50
160 Patrik Elias .75 2.00
161 Oldrich Bakus .20 .50
162 Jiri Oliva .20 .50
163 Karel Sefcik .20 .50
164 Marcel Hrbacek .20 .50
165 Rostislav Malena .20 .50

2000 Czech Stadion

This set was issued in conjunction with Stadion, a Czech sports magazine. It was released in two series totaling 216 cards and featuring athletes of several different sports. The hockey cards from the set are listed below in checklist order.

COMPLETE SET (216) 100.00 200.00
5 Dominik Hasek 1.25 3.00
13 Roman Turek .20 .50
57 Jaromir Jagr 2.00 5.00
61 Mike Ricci .20 .50
64 Marty McSorley .20 .50
65 Martin Brodeur 4.00 10.00
66 Olaf Kolzig .60 1.50
67 Mark Messier 1.50 4.00
68 Eric Lindros 1.25 3.00
69 Robert Lang .20 .50
71 Milan Hejduk 1.25 3.00
72 Alexei Yashin .20 .50
74 Owen Nolan .40 1.00
75 Patrick Roy 6.00 15.00
76 Petr Svoboda .10 .25
77 Martin Straka .20 .50
79 Mario Lemieux 6.00 15.00
80 Petr Nedved .20 .50
81 Mats Sundin 1.25 3.00
82 Wayne Gretzky 10.00 25.00
83 Jaromir Jagr 2.00 5.00
84 Saku Koivu 1.25 3.00
85 Steve Yzerman 6.00 15.00
87 Mike Modano 1.25 3.00
90 Brian Leetch .75 2.00
91 Patrik Stefan .20 .50
92 Ed Belfour 1.50 4.00
93 Curtis Joseph 1.25 3.00
94 Brett Hull 1.50 4.00
95 Scott Stevens .40 1.00
96 Patrik Elias .40 1.00
99 Pavel Bure 1.25 3.00
109 Roman Turek .30 .50
110 Arturs Irbe .20 .50
111 Radek Dvorak .20 .50
112 Valeri Kamensky .20 .50
113 Jiri Slegr .20 .50
114 Alexander Mogilny .40 1.00
115 Peter Forsberg 2.00 5.00
116 Martin Havlat 4.00 10.00
117 Daniel Alfredsson .40 1.00
118 Theo Fleury .75 2.00
119 Sergei Brylin .10 .25
120 Patrick Roy 6.00 15.00
121 Patrick Lalime .60 1.50
122 Tomas Vokoun .60 1.50
123 Marian Hossa 1.25 3.00
124 Zigmund Palffy .40 1.00
125 Evgeni Nabokov .75 2.00
126 Jaroslav Modry .10 .25
145 Rob Blake .40 1.00
146 Jaromir Jagr 2.00 5.00
147 Mario Lemieux 6.00 15.00
148 Mario Lemieux 6.00 15.00
149 Al MacInnis .40 1.00
150 Mark Messier 1.50 4.00
151 Chris Pronger .75 2.00
152 Mike Richter 1.25 3.00
153 Brian Savage .20 .50
154 Maxim Afinogenov .40 1.00
155 Martin Biron .75 2.00
156 Martin Brodeur 4.00 10.00
157 Paul Coffey .75 2.00
158 Mariusz Czerkawski .20 .50
159 Wayne Gretzky 10.00 25.00
160 Michal Grosek .10 .25
161 Adam Graves .20 .50
162 J.Jagr 6.00 15.00
M.Lemieux
190 Dominik Hasek 1.25 3.00
191 Milan Hnilicka .40 1.00
192 Joe Sakic 2.00 5.00
193 Jocelyn Thibault .75 2.00
194 Vladimir Chebaturkin .10 .25
195 Bill Guerin .40 1.00
196 Krzysztof Oliwa .40 1.00
197 Bob Probert .75 2.00
198 Rick Tocchet .40 1.00

2000-01 Czech DS Extraliga

This set features the top players of the Czech Elite league. The cards feature an action photo on the front surrounded by a white border, with two more photos and stats on the back.

COMPLETE SET (168) 25.00 60.00
1 Petr Briza .40 1.00
2 Petr Prikryl .20 .50
3 Libor Zabransky .20 .50
4 Vlastimil Kroupa .20 .50
5 Frantisek Ptacek .20 .50
6 Michal Dobron .20 .50
7 Vladimir Vujtek .20 .50
8 Jaroslav Hlinka .20 .50
9 Martin Chabada .20 .50
10 Ondrej Kratena .20 .50
11 Michal Bros .20 .50
12 Richard Zemlicka .30 .75
13 Jaroslav Kames .40 1.00
14 Ivo Pesat .20 .50
15 Jan Srdinko .20 .50
16 Milan Nedoma .20 .50
17 Martin Strbak .20 .50
18 Radim Tesarik .20 .50
19 Jan Pardavy .20 .50
20 Jiri Dopita .40 1.00
21 Jan Sochor .20 .50
22 Jan Lipiansky .20 .50
23 Jiri Hudler 6.00 15.00
24 Ondrej Vesely .20 .50
25 Dusan Salficky .40 1.00
26 Petr Kus .20 .50
27 Josef Reznicek .20 .50
28 Martin Cech .20 .50
29 Ivan Vlcek .20 .50
30 Jiri Hanzlik .20 .50
31 Pavel Vostrak .20 .50
32 Petr Korinek .20 .50
33 Milan Volak .20 .50
34 Michal Straka .20 .50
35 David Pospisil .20 .50
36 Milan Antos .20 .50
37 Zdenek Orct .40 1.00
38 Michal Podolka .40 1.00
39 Angel Nikolov .30 .75
40 Karel Pilar .40 1.00
41 Radek Mrazek .20 .50
42 Vladimir Gyna .20 .50
43 Robert Reichel .30 .75
44 Petr Rosol .20 .50
45 Vojtech Kubincak .20 .50
46 Kamil Piros .40 1.00
47 Vesa Karjalainen .20 .50
48 Robert Kysela .20 .50
49 Vladimir Hudacek .40 1.00
50 Richard Hrazdira .20 .50
51 Tomas Zizka .40 1.00
52 Jiri Marusak .20 .50
53 Martin Hamrlik .20 .50
54 Miroslav Barus .20 .50
55 Miroslav Okal .20 .50
56 Petr Cajanek .30 .75
57 Jaroslav Balastik .20 .50
58 Petr Vala .20 .50
59 Martin Ambruz .20 .50
60 Petr Leska .20 .50
61 Marek Novotny .20 .50
62 Vlastimil Lakosil .40 1.00
63 Marek Zadina .20 .50
64 Mario Cartelli .20 .50
65 Vladimir Vlk .20 .50
66 Jiri Kuntos .20 .50
67 Richard Kral .20 .50
68 Viktor Ujcik .30 .75
69 Jozef Dano .20 .50
70 Petr Gregorek .20 .50
71 Richard Kapus .20 .50
72 Pavel Janku .20 .50
73 Michal Marik .20 .50
74 Ivo Capek .40 1.00
75 Radek Martinek .40 1.00
76 Rudolf Suchanek .20 .50
77 Stanislav Jasecko .20 .50
78 Vaclav Kral .20 .50
79 Filip Turek .20 .50
80 Lubos Rob .20 .50
81 Radek Belohlav .30 .75
82 Jiri Simanek .20 .50
83 Ales Kotalik .20 .50
84 Kamil Brabenec .20 .50
85 Libor Barta .20 .50
86 Adam Svoboda .40 1.00
87 Ales Pisa .40 1.00
88 Jiri Malinsky .20 .50
89 Petr Jancarik .20 .50
90 Otakar Janecky .30 .75
91 Ladislav Lubina .20 .50
92 Tomas Blazek .20 .50
93 Jaroslav Kudrna .30 .75
94 Michal Mikeska .20 .50
95 Stanislav Prochazka .20 .50
96 Michal Tvrdik .20 .50
97 Oldrich Svoboda .40 1.00
98 Ladislav Kudrna .20 .50
99 Tomas Jakes .20 .50
100 Jiri Hes .20 .50
101 Pavel Kumstat .20 .50
102 Karel Soudek .20 .50
103 Peter Pucher .20 .50
104 David Havir .20 .50
105 Zbynek Marak .20 .50
106 Milan Prochazka .20 .50
107 Radek Haman .20 .50
108 David Pazourek .20 .50
109 Ladislav Blazek .20 .50
110 Roman Malek .40 1.00
111 Petr Kadlec .20 .50
112 Jan Novak .20 .50
113 Angel Krstev .20 .50
114 Jan Snopek .20 .50
115 Daniel Branda .20 .50
116 Jan Alinc .20 .50
117 Viktor Hubl .20 .50
118 Petr Hrbek .20 .50
119 Jan Bohac .20 .50
120 Zdenek Skorepa .20 .50
121 Petr Franek .20 .50
122 Zdenek Smid .40 1.00
123 Libor Prochazka .20 .50
124 Normunds Sejejs .20 .50
125 Jiri Polak .20 .50
126 Roman Zak .20 .50
127 Jaromir Kverka .20 .50
128 Tomas Chlubna .20 .50
129 Radek Prochazka .20 .50
130 David Hruska .20 .50
131 Robert Tomik .20 .50
132 Pavel Kasparik .20 .50
133 Lubos Horcicka .20 .50
134 Marek Pinc .30 .75
135 Jan Krulis .20 .50
136 Michal Madl .20 .50
137 Radek Gardon .20 .50
138 Jan Bohacek .20 .50
139 Ladislav Svoboda .20 .50
140 Tomas Horna .20 .50
141 Jiri Holsan .20 .50
142 Ondrej Kriz .20 .50
143 Ladislav Vlcek .20 .50
144 Jozef Voskar .20 .50
145 Radovan Biegl .30 .75
146 Radek Masny .20 .50
147 Michael Vyhlidal .20 .50
148 Miroslav Javin .20 .50
149 Petr Pavlas .20 .50
150 Tomas Srsen .20 .50
151 Petr Folta .20 .50
152 Libor Pivko .20 .50
153 Daniel Bohac .20 .50
154 Roman Horak .20 .50
155 Jan Peterek .20 .50
156 Richard Pavlikovsky .20 .50
157 Martin Prusek .40 1.00
158 Jiri Trvaj .20 .50
159 Zdenek Pavelek .20 .50
160 Vitezslav Skuta .20 .50
161 Dimitri Jerofejev .20 .50
162 David Moravec .40 1.00
163 Roman Kadera .20 .50
164 Zbynek Irgl .20 .50
165 Marek Ivan .20 .50
166 Martin Prochazka .30 .75
167 Josef Straub .20 .50
168 Ivan Padelek .20 .50

2000-01 Czech DS Extraliga Best of the Best

This insert set features the two best Czech-born players ever. The autograph cards are serial numbered out of 200.

COMPETE SET (4) 25.00 60.00
PRINT RUN 200 SER.#'d SETS
BBH1 Dominik Hasek 4.00 10.00
BBH2 Dominik Hasek 4.00 10.00
BBJ1 Jaromir Jagr 6.00 15.00
BBJ2 Jaromir Jagr 6.00 15.00
BBH1 D.Hasek AU/200 40.00 100.00
BBJ2 J.Jagr AU/200 60.00 150.00

2000-01 Czech DS Extraliga Goalies

This insert set features the top stoppers in the Czech Extraliga.

COMPLETE SET (14) 25.00 60.00
G1 Petr Briza 3.00 8.00
G2 Jaroslav Kames 2.00 5.00
G3 Dusan Salficky 2.00 5.00
G4 Zdenek Orct 2.00 5.00
G5 Vladimir Hudacek 2.00 5.00
G6 Vlastimil Lakosil 2.00 5.00
G7 Ivo Capek 2.00 5.00
G8 Adam Svoboda 2.00 5.00
G9 Oldrich Svoboda 2.00 5.00
G10 Roman Malek 2.00 5.00
G11 Zdenek Smid 2.00 5.00
G12 Marek Pinc 2.00 5.00
G13 Radovan Biegl 2.00 5.00
G14 Martin Prusek 4.00 10.00

2000-01 Czech DS Extraliga National Team

This insert set features members of the Czech Republic's gold medal-winning World Championships team.

COMPLETE SET (10) 25.00 60.00
NT1 Dusan Salficky 2.00 5.00
NT2 Roman Cechmanek 3.00 7.50
NT3 Martin Stepanek 1.25 3.00
NT4 Vladimir Vujtek 1.25 3.00
NT5 Robert Reichel 2.00 5.00
NT6 Jiri Dopita 2.00 5.00
NT7 Martin Rucinsky 2.00 5.00
NT8 Martin Havlat 10.00 25.00
NT9 Tomas Vlasak 1.25 3.00
NT10 Michal Bros 1.25 3.00

2000-01 Czech DS Extraliga Team Jagr

This players for this insert set were chosen by Jagr himself as his favorite Czech stars. The cards are slightly thicker than the base cards of this season.

COMPETE SET (16) 40.00 80.00
JT1 Roman Turek 2.00 5.00
JT2 Milan Hnilicka 2.00 5.00
JT3 Petr Sykora 1.50 4.00
JT4 Roman Hamrlik 1.25 3.00
JT5 Martin Straka 1.50 4.00
JT6 Pavel Kubina 1.25 3.00
JT7 Petr Nedved 1.50 4.00
JT8 Martin Prochazka 1.25 3.00
JT9 Vaclav Prospal 1.25 3.00
JT10 David Volek 1.25 3.00
JT11 Milan Hejduk 6.00 15.00
JT12 Jaromir Jagr 8.00 25.00
JT13 Jan Hlavac 1.50 4.00
JT14 Pavel Patera 1.25 3.00
JT15 Tomas Vlasak 1.25 3.00
JT16 Vaclav Varada 1.25 3.00

2000-01 Czech DS Extraliga Team Jagr Parallel

This partial parallel set features Jagr's favorite Czech players in the NHL. The cards were serial numbered out of 300.

COMPLETE SET (9) 50.00 125.00
STATED PRINT RUN 300 SER.#'d SETS
JT1 Roman Turek 8.00 20.00
JT2 Milan Hnilicka 4.00 10.00
JT3 Petr Sykora 4.00 15.00
JT4 Roman Hamrlik 4.00 10.00
JT5 Martin Straka 4.00 10.00
JT6 Petr Nedved 4.00 10.00
JT7 Milan Hejduk 12.50 30.00
JT8 Jaromir Jagr 20.00 50.00
JT9 Jan Hlavac 4.00 10.00

2000-01 Czech DS Extraliga Top Stars

This set features the first All-Star team of the Czech Extraliga.

TS1 Petr Briza 3.00 8.00
TS2 Radek Martinek 2.00 5.00
TS3 Petr Cajanek 2.00 5.00
TS4 Jiri Dopita 3.00 8.00
TS5 Robert Reichel 3.00 8.00
TS6 Martin Prochazka 2.00 5.00

2000-01 Czech DS Extraliga Valuable Players

Yet another insert set featuring the Extraliga's top stars.

COMPLETE SET (6) 12.00 20.00
VP1 Vladimir Hudacek 2.00 5.00
VP2 Frantisek Kucera 1.00 3.00
VP3 Michal Sykora 1.00 3.00
VP4 Robert Reichel 2.00 5.00
VP5 Jiri Dopita 2.00 5.00
VP6 Petr Cajanek 1.00 3.00

2000-01 Czech DS Extraliga World Champions

This insert set features more members of the Czech World Championship team.

COMPLETE SET (11) 30.00 75.00
WCH1 Roman Cechmanek 6.00 8.00
WCH2 Dusan Salficky 2.00 5.00
WCH3 Radek Martinek 2.00 5.00
WCH4 Martin Stepanek 2.00 5.00
WCH5 Frantisek Kucera 2.00 5.00
WCH6 Michal Sykora 2.00 5.00
WCH7 Martin Havlat 10.00 25.00
WCH8 Robert Reichel 2.00 5.00
WCH9 Tomas Vlasak 2.00 5.00
WCH10 David Vyborny 2.00 5.00
WCH11 Michal Bros 2.00 5.00

2000-01 Czech OFS

This set was released in pack form in the Czech Republic and features every member of that country's elite league.

COMPLETE SET (421) 32.00 80.00
1 Team Logo .04 .10
2 Jaroslav Liska CO .04 .10
3 Jaroslav Parizek CO .04 .10
4 Jan Tlacil CO .04 .10
5 Jaroslav Pouzar CO .04 .10
6 Michal Marik .10 .25
7 Ivo Capek .20 .50
8 Radek Martinek .30 .50
9 Rudolf Suchanek .20 .50
10 Stanislav Jasecko .10 .25
11 Pavel Mojzis .10 .25
12 Vaclav Benak .10 .25
13 Ladislav Cierny .20 .50
14 Josef Jindra .10 .25
15 Vaclav Kral .10 .25
16 Filip Turek .10 .25
17 Lubos Rob .10 .25
18 Radek Belohlav .15 .40
19 Ales Kotalik .75 2.00
20 Kamil Brabenec .10 .25
21 Jiri Simanek .10 .25
22 Martin Strba .10 .25
23 Petr Sailer .10 .25
24 Milan Filipi .04 .25
25 Jiri Broz .10 .25
26 Jiri Novotny .20 .50
27 Michal Vondrka .10 .25
28 Team Logo .04 .10
29 Josef Palacek CO .04 .10
30 Petr Hemsky CO .04 .10
31 Libor Barta .20 .25
32 Adam Svoboda .30 .75
33 Martin Barek .10 .25
34 Ales Pisa .10 .25
35 Jiri Malinsky .10 .25
36 Petr Jancarik .10 .25
37 Miroslav Duben .10 .25
38 Tomas Pacal .10 .25
39 Michal Divisek .10 .25
40 Andrej Novotny .10 .25
41 Petr Mudroch .10 .25
42 Otakar Janecky .20 .50
43 Ladislav Lubina .10 .25
44 Tomas Blazek .20 .25
45 Jaroslav Kudrna .20 .50
46 Michal Mikeska .10 .25
47 Stanislav Prochazka .10 .25
48 Michal Tvrdik .10 .25
49 Martin Filip .10 .25
50 Martin Koudelka .10 .25
51 Pavel Kabrt .10 .25
52 Petr Sykora .20 .50
53 Tomas Rolinek .10 .25
54 Jan Kolar .10 .25
55 Team Logo .04 .10
56 Marek Sykora CO .04 .10
57 Dusan Salficky .30 .75
58 Petr Kus .10 .25
59 Josef Reznicek .10 .25
60 Martin Cech .10 .25
61 Ivan Vlcek .10 .25
62 Jiri Hanzlik .10 .25
63 Jaroslav Spelda .10 .25
64 Zdenek Touzimsky .10 .25
65 Jiri Dobrovolny .10 .25
66 Jan Choteborsky .10 .25
67 Pavel Vostrak .10 .25
68 Petr Korinek .20 .50
69 Milan Volak .10 .25
70 Michal Straka .10 .25
71 David Pospisil .10 .25
72 Josef Straka .10 .25
73 Milan Antos .10 .25
74 Andrej Nedorost .40 1.00
75 Vaclav Eiselt .10 .25
76 Jiri Jelen .10 .25
77 Michal Dvorak .10 .25
78 Jiri Zurek .10 .25
79 Dusan Andrasovsky .10 .25
80 Team Logo .04 .10
81 Jaromir Sindel CO .10 .25
82 Ondrej Weissmann CO .04 .10
83 Ladislav Blazek .20 .25
84 Roman Malek .10 .25
85 Petr Kadlec .10 .25
86 Jan Novak .10 .25
87 Angel Krstev .10 .25
88 Jan Snopek .10 .25
89 Jan Kloboucek .10 .25
90 Jan Hejda .10 .25
91 Petr Martinek .10 .25
92 Jan Slavik .10 .25
93 Daniel Branda .10 .25
94 Jan Alinc .20 .50
95 Viktor Hubl .10 .25
96 Jan Kopecky .10 .25
97 Jan Bohac .10 .25
98 Zdenek Skorepa .20 .50
99 Michal Sup .10 .25
100 Radek Matejovsky .10 .25
101 Robin Bacul .10 .25
102 Leos Cermak .10 .25
103 Petr Jira .10 .25
104 Marek Tomica .10 .25
105 Petr Hrbek .10 .25
106 Team Logo .04 .10
107 Eduard Novak CO .04 .10
108 Petr Fiala CO .04 .10
109 Lubos Horcicka .10 .25
110 Marek Pinc .10 .25
111 Jan Pospisil .10 .25
112 Jan Krulis .10 .25
113 Michal Madl .10 .25
114 Ondrej Kriz .10 .25
115 Jan Bohacek .10 .25
116 David Hajek .10 .25
117 Jan Dlouhy .10 .25
118 Martin Taborsky .10 .25
119 Jiri Kames .20 .50
120 Ladislav Svoboda .10 .25
121 Pavel Geffert .10 .25
122 Tomas Horna .10 .25
123 Jiri Holsan .10 .25
124 Radek Gardon .10 .25
125 Ladislav Vlcek .10 .25
126 Jozef Voskar .10 .25
127 Tomas Klimt .20 .50
128 Premysl Sedlak .10 .25
129 Tomas Plekanec ERC .10 .25
130 Michal Havel .10 .25
131 Vaclav Skuhravy .10 .25
132 Team Logo .04 .10
133 Vaclav Sykora CO .04 .10
134 Otakar Vejvoda CO .04 .10
135 Zdenek Orct .20 .50
136 Michal Podolka .30 .75
137 Angel Nikolov .20 .50
138 Karel Pilar .40 1.00
139 Radek Mrazek .10 .25
140 Marek Cernosek .10 .25
141 Vladimir Gyna .10 .25
142 Martin Tupa .10 .25
143 Jan Hranac .10 .25
144 Petr Suchy .10 .25
145 Robert Reichel .31 .50
146 Petr Rosol .10 .25
147 Vojtech Kubincak .10 .25
148 Kamil Piros .40 1.00
149 Jindrich Kotrla .10 .25
150 Vesa Karjalainen .10 .25
151 Robert Kysela .10 .25
152 Stanislav Stavensky .10 .25
153 Tomas Martinec .10 .25
154 Zdenek Zak .10 .25
155 Martin Tvrznik .10 .25
156 Lukas Bednarik .10 .25
157 Team Logo .04 .10
158 Radim Rulik CO .04 .10
159 Martin Pesout CO .04 .10
160 Petr Franek .10 .25
161 Zdenek Smid .30 .75
162 Pavel Csipka .10 .25
163 Libor Prochazka .10 .25
164 Robert Kantor .10 .25
165 Jiri Polak .10 .25
166 Normunds Sejejs .10 .25
167 Roman Prosek .10 .25
168 Roman Zak .10 .25
169 Ivan Puncochar .10 .25
170 Petr Puncochar .10 .25
171 Jakub Grof .10 .25
172 Jaromir Kverka .10 .25
173 Tomas Chlubna .10 .25
174 Radek Prochazka .10 .25
175 David Hruska .10 .25
176 Robert Tomik .10 .25
177 Pavel Kasparik .10 .25
178 Martin Rousek .10 .25
179 Jaroslav Kalla .10 .25
180 Peter Bohunicky .10 .25
181 Jan Kostal .10 .25
182 Petr Domin .10 .25
183 Petr Sinagl .10 .25
184 Team Logo .04 .10
185 Milan Chalupa CO .10 .25
186 Pavel Pazourek CO .04 .10
187 Oldrich Svoboda .10 .25
188 Ladislav Kudrna .20 .50
189 Miloslav Bahensky .10 .25
190 Tomas Jakes .10 .25
191 Jiri Hes .10 .25
192 Pavel Kumstat .10 .25
193 Karel Soudek .10 .25
194 Pavol Valko .10 .25
195 David Havir .10 .25
196 David Petlak .10 .25
197 Vladimir Holik .10 .25
198 Peter Pucher .10 .25
199 Marek Uram .10 .25
200 Karel Plasek .10 .25
201 Zbynek Marak .10 .25
202 Milan Prochazka .10 .25
203 Patrik Fink .10 .25
204 David Pazourek .10 .25
205 Marek Vorel .10 .25
206 Radek Haman .10 .25
207 Petr Lipina .10 .25
208 Petr Kumstat .10 .25
209 Team Logo .04 .10
210 Vladimir Vujtek CO .04 .10
211 Ales Mach CO .04 .10
212 Marek Novotny .10 .25
213 Vlastimil Lakosil .20 .50
214 Mario Cartelli .10 .25
215 Vladimir Vlk .10 .25
216 Jiri Kuntos .10 .25
217 Petr Gregorek .10 .25
218 Robert Prochazka .10 .25
219 Ondrej Zetek .10 .25
220 David Nosek .10 .25
221 Tomas Houdek .10 .25
222 Tomas Harant .10 .25
223 Richard Kral .10 .25
224 Viktor Ujcik .15 .40
225 Jozef Dano .10 .25
226 Richard Kapus .10 .25
227 Pavel Janku .20 .25
228 Marek Zadina .10 .25
229 Branislav Janos .10 .25
230 Tomas Nemcicky .10 .25
231 Patrik Moskal .10 .25
232 David Appel .10 .25
233 Jan Marek .10 .25
234 Jiri Hasek .10 .25
235 Team Logo .04 .10
236 Alois Hadamczik CO .04 .10
237 Kamil Konecny CO .04 .10
238 Mojmir Trlicik CO .04 .10
239 Martin Prusek .75 2.00
240 Jiri Trvaj .10 .25
241 Lukas Smolka .10 .25
242 Vitezslav Skuta .10 .25
243 Dmitrij Jerofejev .10 .25
244 Daniel Kapotocny .10 .25
245 Petr Jurecka .10 .25
246 Radek Philipp .10 .25
247 Lukas Zatopek .10 .25
248 Daniel Seman .10 .25
249 Jan Vytisk .10 .25
250 David Moravec .20 .50
251 Martin Prochazka .10 .25
252 Ivan Padelek .10 .25
253 Josef Straub .10 .25
254 Roman Kadera .10 .25
255 Marek Ivan .10 .25
256 Zdenek Pavelek .10 .25
257 Martin Tomasek .10 .25
258 Pavel Selinger .10 .25
259 Jan Pleva .10 .25
260 Ales Padelek .10 .25
261 Team Logo .04 .10
262 Ivo Pestuka CO .04 .10
263 Jiri Reznar CO .04 .10
264 Radovan Biegl .10 .25
265 Radek Masny .10 .25
266 Michael Vyhlidal .10 .25
267 Miroslav Javin .10 .25
268 Richard Pavlikovsky .10 .25
269 Petr Pavlas .10 .25
270 Patrik Rimmel .10 .25
271 Ales Tomasek .10 .25
272 Petr Suchanek .10 .25
273 Tomas Srsen .10 .25
274 Petr Folta .10 .25
275 Libor Pivko .10 .25
276 Daniel Bohac .10 .25
277 Roman Horak .20 .50
278 Jan Peterek .10 .25
279 Marek Melenovsky .10 .25
280 Pavel Zdrahal .10 .25
281 Roman Kontsek .10 .25
282 Michal Cech .10 .25
283 Tomas Sykora .10 .25
284 Martin Streit .10 .25
285 Milos Melicherik .10 .25
286 Team Logo .04 .10
287 Milos Riha CO .04 .10
288 Frantisek Vyborny CO .04 .10
289 Pavel Hynek CO .04 .10
290 Petr Briza .30 .75
291 Petr Prikryl .10 .25
292 Tomas Duba .10 .25
293 Libor Zabransky .20 .25
294 Vlastimil Kroupa .20 .50
295 Frantisek Ptacek .10 .25
296 Michal Dobron .10 .25
297 Pavel Srek .10 .25
298 Jaroslav Nedved .10 .25
299 Martin Holy .10 .25
300 Miha Rebolj .10 .25
301 Jan Hanzlik .10 .25
302 Vladimir Vujtek .20 .50
303 Jaroslav Hlinka .10 .25
304 Martin Chabada .10 .25
305 Ondrej Kratena .10 .25
306 Michal Bros .20 .25
307 Patrik Martinec .10 .25
308 Richard Zemlicka .20 .50
309 Jiri Zelenka .10 .25
310 Vaclav Novak .10 .25
311 Petr Havelka .10 .25
312 Michal Sivek .60 1.50
313 Petr Hrbek .10 .25
314 Radek Duda .10 .25
315 Josef Slanec .10 .25
316 Petr Kanko .75 2.00
317 Team Logo .04 .10
318 Zdislav Tabara CO .04 .10
319 Miroslav Venkrbec CO .04 .10
320 Jaroslav Kames .30 .75
321 Ivo Pesat .10 .25
322 Lukas Plsek .10 .25
323 Jan Srdinko .10 .25
324 Milan Nedoma .10 .25
325 Martin Strbak .10 .25
326 Radim Tesarik .10 .25
327 Pavel Zubicek .10 .25
328 Alexej Jaskin .10 .25
329 Petr Kubos .10 .25
330 Zbynek Spitzer .10 .25
331 Michal Safarik .10 .25
332 Pavel Augusta .10 .25
333 Jan Pardavy .10 .25
334 Jiri Dopita .20 .50
335 Jan Tomajko .10 .25
336 Roman Stantien .10 .25
337 Jan Sochor .10 .25
338 Martin Paroulek .10 .25
339 Jan Lipiansky .10 .25
340 Jiri Hudler ERC 6.00 15.00
341 Ondrej Vesely .10 .25
342 Jiri Jantovsky .10 .25
343 Petr Zajgla .10 .25
344 Tomas Demel .10 .25
345 Petr Vampola .10 .25
346 Team Logo .04 .10
347 Antonin Stavjana CO .10 .25
348 Zdenek Venera CO .04 .10
349 Vladimir Hudacek .20 .50
350 Richard Hrazdira .20 .50
351 Petr Tucek .10 .25
352 Tomas Zizka .10 .25
353 Jiri Marusak .10 .25
354 Martin Hamrlik .10 .25
355 Patrik Luza .10 .25
356 Rostislav Malena .08 .20
357 Jan Homer .10 .25
358 Lukas Zib .10 .25
359 Boris Zabka .10 .25
360 Miroslav Okal .08 .20
361 Petr Cajanek .30 .75
362 Jaroslav Balastik .10 .25
363 Petr Vala .10 .25
364 Martin Ambruz .10 .25
365 Petr Leska .10 .25
366 Miroslav Barus .10 .25
367 Martin Kotasek .10 .25
368 Lubomir Korhon .20 .50
369 Ivan Rachunek .40 1.00
370 Radovan Somik .10 .25
371 Filip Cech .10 .25
372 Martin Jenacek .10 .25
373 Pavel Mojzis .10 .25
374 Milan Navratil .10 .25
375 Michal Safarik .10 .25
376 Miroslav Blatak .10 .25
377 Team Logo .04 .10
378 Roman Turek .40 1.00
379 Milan Hnilicka .40 1.00
380 Tomas Kaberle .30 .75
381 Frantisek Kaberle .20 .50
382 Roman Hamrlik .30 .75
383 Pavel Kubina .40 1.00
384 Jaromir Jagr 2.00 5.00
385 Patrik Elias .75 2.00
386 Milan Hejduk 2.00 5.00
387 Radek Dvorak .40 1.00
388 Petr Nedved .30 .75
389 Vaclav Prospal .40 1.00
390 Pavel Patera .20 .50
391 Petr Sykora 1.25 3.00
392 Vaclav Varada .20 .50
393 Martin Straka .40 1.00
394 Jan Hrdina .40 1.00
395 David Volek .20 .50
396 Tomas Vlasak .10 .25
397 Michal Rozsival .30 .75
398 Team Logo .04 .10
399 Ladislav Blazek .20 .25
400 Miloslav Horava .10 .25
401 Frantisek Kucera .20 .20
402 Lubomir Sekeras .20 .50
403 Petr Kadlec .10 .25
404 Jaroslav Spacek .20 .50
405 Frantisek Prochazka .20 .50
406 Antonin Stavjana .10 .25
407 Vladimir Ruzicka .20 .50
408 Petr Rosol .10 .25
409 Robert Reichel .31 .50
410 Martin Rucinsky .20 .50
411 Josef Beranek .20 .50
412 Viktor Ujcik .15 .40
413 Michal Sup .10 .25
414 Ivo Prorok .10 .25
415 Zdeno Ciger .20 .50
416 Jiri Hrdina .10 .25
417 J.Jagr/V.Ruzicka 2.00 5.00
418 Checklist .04 .10
419 Checklist .04 .10
420 Checklist .04 .10
421 Checklist .04 .10

2000-01 Czech OFS Star Emerald

This is one of three versions of this insert set, found exclusively in packs of Czech OFS. The Emerald version was found 1:2 packs. The Violet parallels were found 1:3 packs and the Pink parallels were found 1:6 packs.

COMPLETE SET (36) 10.00 25.00
EMERALD ODDS 1:2
*VIOLET PARALLELS: 1X to 2X
VIOLET ODDS 1:3
PINK PARALLELS : 2X to 3X
PINK ODDS 1:6
1 Jaroslav Kames .40 1.00
2 Jiri Dopita .40 1.00
3 Jan Pardavy .20 .50
4 Vladimir Hudacek .20 .50
5 Petr Cajanek .75 2.00
6 Richard Hrazdira .40 1.00
7 Petr Briza .75 2.00
8 Jiri Zelenka .20 .50
9 Richard Zemlicka .40 1.00
10 Libor Barta .40 1.00
11 Adam Svoboda .40 1.00
12 Otakar Janecky .40 1.00
13 Vaclav Kral .20 .50
14 Rudolf Suchanek .40 1.00
15 Michal Marik .20 .50
16 Dusan Salficky .60 1.50
17 Petr Korinek .40 1.00
18 Ivan Vlcek .20 .50
19 Zdenek Orct .40 1.00
20 Robert Reichel .40 1.00
21 Petr Franek .20 .50
22 Libor Prochazka .20 .50
23 Vlastimil Lakosil .40 1.00
24 Richard Kral .20 .50
25 Viktor Ujcik .20 .50
26 Martin Prusek 1.00 2.50
27 Martin Prochazka .20 .50
28 Josef Straub .20 .50
29 Radek Gardon .20 .50
30 Lubos Horcicka .20 .50
31 Tomas Srsen .20 .50
32 Radovan Biegl .20 .50
33 Oldrich Svoboda .20 .50
34 Marek Uram .20 .50
35 Ladislav Blazek .40 1.00
36 Roman Malek .20 .50

2001 Czech Stadion

This set was issued in conjunction with the Czech sports magazine Stadion. It is a multi-sport issue. We have only included hockey players, so it is listed below in skip-numbered form.

COMPLETE SET (45) 30.00 60.00
217 Ray Bourque 2.00 5.00
218 Patrik Elias .75 2.00
219 Milan Hejduk .75 2.00
220 Bobby Holik .40 1.00
221 Tomas Kaberle .40 1.00
222 Nick Lidstrom 1.25 3.00
223 Petr Sykora .40 1.00
224 Martin Skoula .40 1.00
225 Alex Tanguay .75 2.00
226 Daniel Alfredsson .75 2.00
227 Jason Allison .40 1.00
228 Adam Deadmarsh .40 1.00
229 Chris Drury .75 2.00
230 Bob Essensa .40 1.00
231 Scott Gomez .40 1.00
233 Tomas Holmstrom .75 2.00
234 Darius Kasparaitis .40 1.00
235 Pavel Brendl .40 1.00
236 Eric Lindros 1.25 3.00
237 Rostislav Klesla .40 1.00
238 Scott Niedermayer .40 1.00
239 Brett Hull 1.25 3.00
240 Paul Kariya 1.25 3.00
241 Chris Gratton .40 1.00
242 Doug Gilmour .75 2.00
243 Alexei Yashin .40 1.00
244 Saku Koivu .75 2.00
245 Randy McKay .40 1.00
246 Markus Naslund .75 2.00
247 Keith Primeau .40 1.00
248 Dainius Zubrus .40 1.00
249 Dominik Hasek 1.50 4.00
250 Frantisek Kaberle .40 1.00
251 Jaromir Jagr 2.00 5.00
252 Jaromir Jagr (Tennis) 2.00 5.00
253 Rob Blake .40 1.00
254 Adam Oates .40 1.00
255 Joe Sakic 2.00 5.00
256 Alexei Kovalev .40 1.00
257 Ivan Hlinka .40 1.00
258 Martin Straka .40 1.00
259 Milan Hnilicka .40 1.00
260 Miroslav Satan .40 1.00
261 Peter Bondra .40 1.00
324 John Leclair .40 1.00

2001-02 Czech DS

COMPLETE SET (61) 15.00 30.00
1 Dominik Hasek 2.00 5.00
2 Vladimir Hudacek .20 .50
3 Roman Malek .10 .25
4 Mario Cartelli .10 .25
5 Tomas Kaberle .30 .75
6 Petr Kadlec .10 .25
7 Angel Nikolov .20 .50
8 Radek Philipp .10 .25
9 Libor Prochazka .10 .25
10 Michal Sykora .10 .25
11 Libor Zabransky .10 .25
12 Kamil Brabenec .10 .25
13 Michal Bros .10 .25
14 Jiri Burger .10 .25
15 Petr Cajanek .30 .75
16 Jaroslav Hlinka .10 .25
17 Viktor Hubl .10 .25
18 David Moravec .20 .50
19 Martin Prochazka .10 .25
20 Petr Sykora .10 .25
21 Jan Tomajko .10 .25
22 Viktor Ujcik .15 .35
23 Pavel Vostrak .10 .25
24 Jaroslav Bednar .20 .50
25 Martin Rucinsky .20 .50
26 Tomas Vokoun 1.25 3.00
27 Milan Hnilicka .20 .50
28 Josef Melichar .20 .50
29 Michal Rozsival .20 .50
30 Karel Pilar .20 .50
31 Jan Horacek .10 .25
32 Robert Schnabel .20 .50
33 Pavel Kolarik .20 .50
34 Petr Mika .20 .50
35 Petr Tenkrat .20 .50
36 Jaromir Jagr 2.00 5.00
37 Pavel Patera .20 .50
38 Josef Beranek .20 .50
39 Martin Straka .30 .75
40 Petr Nedved .30 .75
41 Martin Rucinsky .20 .50
42 Robert Reichel .20 .50
43 David Vyborny .40 1.00
44 Roman Hamrlik .30 .75
45 Milan Hejduk 1.25 3.00
46 Patrik Elias .75 2.00
47 Vaclav Prospal .20 .50
48 Vaclav Varada .20 .50
49 Petr Sykora .10 .25
50 Dusan Salficky .30 .75
51 Petr Briza .30 .75
52 Martin Prusek .40 1.00
53 Radek Martinek .20 .50
54 Karel Pilar .20 .50
55 Viktor Ujcik .15 .35
56 Vaclav Nedorost .40 1.00
57 Ales Kotalik .60 1.50
58 Jiri Dopita .20 .50
59 Robert Reichel .20 .50
60 Petr Cajanek .30 .75
61 David Moravec .20 .50

2001-02 Czech DS Best of the Best

COMPLETE SET (9) 5.00 10.00
STATED ODDS 1:3
BB1 Dominik Hasek 2.00 5.00
BB2 Tomas Kaberle .60 1.50
BB3 Michal Sykora .20 .50
BB4 Petr Cajanek .60 1.50
BB5 David Moravec .40 1.00
BB6 Martin Prochazka .20 .50
BB7 Martin Rucinsky .40 1.00
BB8 Robert Reichel .40 1.00
BB9 Jiri Dopita .40 1.00

2001-02 Czech DS Goalies

COMPLETE SET (5) 6.00 15.00
STATED ODDS 1:4
G1 Dominik Hasek 4.00 10.00
G2 Milan Hnilicka .75 2.00
G3 Petr Briza .75 2.00
G4 Roman Cechmanek .75 2.00
G5 Roman Malek .75 2.00

2001-02 Czech DS Ice Heroes

COMPLETE SET (10) 8.00 15.00
STATED ODDS 1:2
IH1 Tomas Vokoun 2.00 5.00
IH2 Jaromir Jagr 3.00 8.00
IH3 Pavel Patera .40 1.00
IH4 Josef Beranek .40 1.00
IH5 Martin Straka .75 2.00
IH6 Petr Nedved .60 1.50
IH7 Martin Rucinsky .40 1.00
IH8 Robert Reichel .40 1.00
IH9 David Vyborny .20 .50
IH10 Petr Tenkrat .60 1.50

2001-02 Czech DS Legends

COMPLETE SET (12) 3.00 6.00
STATED ODDS 1:2
L1 Jiri Holocek .40 1.00
L2 Jiri Kralik .20 .50
L3 Vlastimil Bubnik .40 1.00
L4 Vaclav Rozinak .20 .50
L5 Vladimir Zabrodsky .40 1.00
L6 Vladimir Martinec .40 1.00
L7 Ivan Hlinka .40 1.00
L8 Jan Havel .20 .50
L9 Frantisek Pospisil .20 .50
L10 Jaroslav Holik .20 .50
L11 Milan Novy .40 1.00
L12 Jiri Lala .20 .50

2001-02 Czech DS Top Gallery

COMPLETE SET (2) 8.00 15.00
STATED ODDS 1:10
1 Jaromir Jagr 4.00 10.00
2 Jaromir Jagr 4.00 10.00

2001-02 Czech National Team Postcards

COMPLETE SET (17) 20.00 40.00
1 Josef Beranek .75 2.00
2 Petr Briza .75 2.00
3 Josef Beranek .75 2.00
4 Radek Duda .75 2.00
5 Jiri Hudler 2.00 5.00
6 Jaromir Jagr 4.00 10.00
7 Richard Kral .75 2.00
8 Frantisek Kucera .75 2.00
9 David Moravec .75 2.00
10 Karel Rachunek .75 2.00
11 Martin Richter .75 2.00
12 Dusan Salficky .75 2.00
13 Michal Sykora .75 2.00
14 Viktor Ujcik .75 2.00
15 Tomas Vlasak .75 2.00
16 Vladimir Vujtek .75 2.00
17 Michal Bros .75 2.00

2001-02 Czech OFS

This set features the top players of the Czech Elite League. The cards were sold in pack form. The set is noteworthy for including an early card of Jiri Hudler.

COMPLETE SET (284) 25.00 50.00
1 Lukas Hronek .08 .20
2 Petr Martinek .08 .20
3 Petr Kadlec .08 .20
4 Roman Malek .08 .20
5 Jan Alinc .20 .50
6 Josef Beranek .20 .50
7 Viktor Hubl .08 .20
8 Martin Rousek .08 .20
9 Radek Matejovsky .08 .20
10 Jan Kloboucek .08 .20
11 Daniel Brandl .08 .20
12 Viktor Ujcik .20 .50
13 Milan Antos .08 .20
14 Radek Belohlav .08 .20
15 Michal Bros .20 .50
16 Petr Briza .20 .50
17 Radek Hamr .08 .20
18 Jaroslav Hlinka .08 .20
19 Martin Chabada .08 .20
20 Pavel Kasparik .08 .20
21 Marek Ivan .08 .20
22 Lukas Galvas .08 .20
23 Radek Simicek .08 .20
24 Robert Tomanek .08 .20
25 Jan Tomajko .08 .20
26 Ivan Padelek .08 .20
27 Zdenek Pavelek .08 .20
28 Radek Philipp .08 .20
29 Pavel Srek .08 .20
30 David Moravec .20 .50
31 Jan Srdinko .08 .20
32 Marek Melenovsky .20 .50
33 Frantisek Ptacek .08 .20
34 Vaclav Novak .08 .20
35 Jaroslav Nedved .20 .50
36 Ludek Krayzel .08 .20
37 Roman Kadera .08 .20
38 Petr Jurecka .08 .20
39 Lukas Smolka .08 .20
40 Vitezslav Skuta .08 .20
41 Josef Straub .08 .20
42 Jiri Trvaj .08 .20
43 Jan Vytisk .08 .20
44 Daniel Zapotocny .08 .20
45 Pavel Selingr .08 .20
46 Martin Prochazka .20 .50
47 Vlastimil Lakosil .08 .20
48 Petr Gregorek .08 .20
49 Mario Cartelli .08 .20
50 Miloslav Guren .20 .50
51 Petr Jancarik .08 .20
52 Libor Prochazka .20 .50
53 Jan Slavik .08 .20
54 Pavel Janku .08 .20
55 Branislav Janos .08 .20
56 Marek Zadina .08 .20
57 Jiri Polak .08 .20
58 Ondrej Nemec .08 .20
59 Petr Kubos .08 .20
60 Slavomir Hrina .08 .20
61 Ivo Pesat .08 .20
62 Radovan Biegl .20 .50
63 Zdenek Skorepa .20 .50
64 Roman Meluzin .08 .20
65 Jan Marek .08 .20
66 Richard Kral .08 .20
67 Rostislav Vlach .08 .20
68 Ondrej Vetchy .08 .20
69 Petr Vampola .08 .20
70 Lukas Valko .08 .20
71 Michal Sararcik .08 .20
72 Martin Streit .08 .20
73 Radim Kucharczyk .08 .20
74 Jiri Hudler 8.00 20.00
75 Jiri Burger .08 .20
76 Martin Strbak .08 .20
77 Martin Ambruz .08 .20
78 Jakub Blazek .08 .20
79 Pavel Mojzis .08 .20
80 Jiri Marusak .08 .20
81 Rostislav Malena .08 .20
82 Jan Homer .08 .20
83 Martin Hamrlik .08 .20
84 Petr Tucek .08 .20
85 Vladimir Hubacek .08 .20
86 Ales Zacha .08 .20
87 Radovan Somik .40 1.00
88 Ivan Rachunek .08 .20
89 Libor Pivko .08 .20
90 Milan Ministr .08 .20
91 Petr Leska .08 .20
92 Martin Jenacek .08 .20
93 Petr Cajanek .30 .75
94 Karol Bartanus .20 .50
95 Jaroslav Balastik .08 .20
96 Petr Havelka .08 .20
97 Jan Hanzlik .08 .20
98 Petr Prikryl .08 .20
99 Libor Zabransky .20 .50
100 David Hnat .08 .20
101 David Pazourek .08 .20
102 Zbynek Marak .08 .20
103 Radek Haman .08 .20
104 Karel Soudek .08 .20
105 Pavel Kumstat .08 .20
106 Tomas Jakes .08 .20
107 Vladimir Holik .08 .20
108 Jiri Hes .08 .20
109 David Havir .08 .20
110 Oldrich Svoboda .20 .50
111 Ladislav Kudrna .20 .50
112 Valdemar Jirus .08 .20
113 Miroslav Okal .08 .20
114 Peter Bohunicky .08 .20
115 Patrik Hucko .08 .20
116 Miroslav Blatak .08 .20
117 Tomas Netik .08 .20
118 Richard Zemlicka .20 .50
119 Marek Uram .08 .20
120 Peter Pucher .08 .20
121 Lukas Krajicek ERC .75 2.00
122 Michal Klimes .08 .20
123 Josef Jindra .08 .20
124 Ladislav Cierny .08 .20
125 Michal Marik .08 .20
126 Josef Kucera .08 .20
127 Michal Kolarik .08 .20
128 Jiri Hasek .08 .20
129 David Nosek .08 .20
130 Martin Vojtek .08 .20
131 Milan Nedoma .08 .20
132 Rudolf Suchanek .08 .20
133 Filip Vanecek .08 .20
134 Pavel Zubicek .08 .20
135 Kamil Brabenec .08 .20
136 Jiri Broz .08 .20
137 Dan Hlavka .08 .20
138 Stepan Hrebejk .08 .20
139 Roman Horak .08 .20
140 Milan Michalek ERC 6.00 15.00
141 Peter Bartos .20 .50
142 Michal Vondrka .08 .20
143 Jiri Simanek .08 .20
144 Petr Sailer .08 .20
145 Lubos Rob .08 .20
146 Jan Rehor .08 .20
147 Martin Strba .08 .20
148 Marek Pinc .08 .20
149 Vladimir Gyna .08 .20
150 Jan Hranac .08 .20
151 Martin Nosek .08 .20
152 Lukas Pozivil .08 .20
153 Vojtech Kubincak .08 .20
154 Anton Lezo .08 .20
155 Martin Tupa .08 .20
156 Vlastimil Kroupa .20 .50
157 Jindrich Kotrla .08 .20
158 David Hruska .08 .20
159 Petr Jira .08 .20
160 Michal Oliverius .08 .20
161 Lukas Havel .08 .20
162 Jaroslav Buchal .08 .20
163 Jan Sulc .08 .20
164 Pavol Rieciciar .08 .20
165 Petr Klima .20 .50
166 Jiri Gombar .08 .20
167 Tomas Kaberle .20 .50
168 Ladislav Svoboda .08 .20
169 Pavel Geffert .08 .20
170 Tomas Horna .08 .20
171 Zdenek Orct .20 .50
172 Robert Kysela .08 .20
173 Radek Gardon .08 .20
174 Ondrej Kriz .20 .50
175 Tomas Klimt .20 .50
176 Jan Bohacek .20 .50
177 Michal Havel .08 .20
178 David Hajek .08 .20
179 Vaclav Skuhravy .08 .20
180 Radim Skuhrovec .08 .20
181 Tomas Plekanec .40 1.00
182 Jan Dlouhy .08 .20
183 David Patera .08 .20
184 Jan Krulis .08 .20
185 Jan Pospisil .08 .20
186 David Appel .08 .20
187 Jakub Kraus .08 .20
188 Petr Machulda .08 .20
189 Petr Franek .08 .20
190 Jaromir Kverka .08 .20
191 Michal Madl .08 .20
192 Marcel Kucera .08 .20
193 Jakub Grof .08 .20
194 Michal Dobron .08 .20
195 Jan Kopecky .08 .20
196 Dmitrij Rodine .08 .20
197 David Balasz .08 .20
198 Roman Prosek .08 .20
199 Jan Kostal .08 .20
200 Petr Domin .08 .20
201 Jan Choteborsky .08 .20
202 Vaclav Benak .08 .20
203 Miroslav Simonovic .08 .20
204 Jiri Hanzlik .08 .20
205 Josef Reznicek .08 .20
206 Ivan Vlcek .08 .20
207 Libor Barta .08 .20
208 Ondrej Steiner .08 .20
209 Dusan Andrasovsky .08 .20
210 Martin Vyborny .08 .20
211 Juraj Stefanka .08 .20
212 Radek Duda .08 .20
213 Josef Slanec .08 .20
214 Michal Dvorak .08 .20
215 Libor Pavlis .08 .20
216 Vaclav Eiselt .08 .20
217 Tomas Nemcicky .08 .20
218 Petr Mudroch .08 .20
219 Patrik Moskal .08 .20
220 Zdenek Sedlak .08 .20
221 Pavel Vostrak .08 .20
222 Milan Volak .08 .20
223 Petr Mudroch .08 .20
224 Jiri Malinsky .08 .20
225 Jan Svik .08 .20
226 Petr Caslava .08 .20
227 Michal Straka .08 .20
228 Adam Svoboda .20 .50
229 Josef Straka .20 .50
230 Patrik Rimmel .08 .20
231 Petr Pavlas .08 .20
232 Michael Prochazka .20 .50
233 Miroslav Javin .08 .20
234 Robin Bacul .08 .20
235 Marek Cernosek .08 .20
236 Petr Folta .08 .20
237 Pavel Malac .08 .20
238 Radek Krestan .08 .20
239 Lubomir Korhon .08 .20
240 Pavel Cagas .20 .50
241 Radoslav Kropac .08 .20
242 Dusan Pohorelec .08 .20
243 Petr Vala .08 .20
244 Pavel Zdrahal .08 .20
245 Otakar Janecky .20 .50
246 Tomas Blazek .20 .50
247 Michael Vyhlidal .20 .50
248 Michal Sykora .20 .50
249 Tomas Pacal .08 .20
250 Andrej Novotny .08 .20
251 Tomas Rolinek .08 .20
252 Stanislav Prochazka .08 .20
253 David Pospisil .08 .20
254 Michal Mikeska .08 .20
255 Ladislav Lubina .08 .20
256 Jaroslav Kudrna .20 .50

257 Tomas Vak .08 .20
258 Michal Tvrdik .08 .20
259 Petr Sykora .20 .50
260 Jan Bokoc .08 .20
261 Milan Prochazka .08 .20
262 Patrik Fink .08 .20
263 Richard Kuckrek .08 .20
264 Marek Vorel .08 .20
265 Tomas Klimes .08 .20
266 Premysl Sedlak .08 .20
267 David Hajek .08 .20
268 Ladislav Vlcek .08 .20
269 Jiri Kames .20 .50
270 Radek Krestan .08 .20
271 Jan Hejda .08 .20
272 Borek Stagma .08 .20
273 Leos Cermak .08 .20
274 Jan Novak .08 .20
275 Zbynek Tuma .08 .20
276 Daniel Bohac .08 .20
277 Michal Sup .08 .20
278 Jan Snopek .08 .20
279 Adam Saffer .08 .20
280 David Pojkar .08 .20
281 Marek Tomica .08 .20
282 Petr Jurecka .08 .20
283 Lukas Krenzelok .08 .20
284 Michael Prochazka .20 .50

2001-02 Czech OFS All Stars

These cards were randomly inserted into packs of Czech OFS.

COMPLETE SET (41) 20.00 40.00
1 Martin Hamrlik .40 1.00
2 Petr Gregorek .40 1.00
3 Oldrich Svoboda .75 2.00
4 Radim Tesarik .40 1.00
5 Jiri Dopita 1.25 3.00
6 Petr Cajanek .75 2.00
7 Marek Uram .40 1.00
8 Michael Vyhlidal .40 1.00
9 Mario Cartelli .40 1.00
10 Pavel Zdrahal .40 1.00
11 Libor Prochazka .75 2.00
12 Ales Pisa .75 2.00
13 Robert Reichel .75 2.00
14 Josef Reznicek .40 1.00
15 Karel Pilar 1.25 3.00
16 Dusan Salficky .75 2.00
17 Patrik Martinec .40 1.00
18 Rudolf Suchanek .40 1.00
19 Jaromir Kverka .40 1.00
20 Ladislav Svoboda .40 1.00
21 Daniel Branda .40 1.00
22 Jan Pardavy .40 1.00
23 David Moravec .75 2.00
24 Zbynek Marak .40 1.00
25 Petr Leska .40 1.00
26 Jiri Marusak .40 1.00
27 Roman Stantien .40 1.00
28 Jan Srdinko .40 1.00
29 Martin Prusek 2.00 5.00
30 Libor Pivko .40 1.00
31 Zdenek Pavelek .40 1.00
32 Jaroslav Hlinka .40 1.00
33 Otakar Janecky .75 2.00
34 Petr Kadlec .75 2.00
35 Ales Kotalik 1.25 3.00
36 Jan Krulis .40 1.00
37 Robert Tomik .40 1.00
38 Petr Sykora .75 2.00
39 Ivan Vlcek .40 1.00
40 Pavel Vostrak .40 1.00
41 Vladimir Vujtek .40 1.00

2001-02 Czech OFS Gold Inserts

These cards were randomly inserted into packs of Czech OFS. We have no confirmation on insertion rate.

COMPLETE SET (11) 20.00 40.00
G1 Roman Malek 2.00 5.00
G2 Petr Franek 2.00 5.00
G3 Petr Prikryl 2.00 5.00
G4 Vlastimil Lakosil 2.00 5.00
G5 Radovan Biegl 2.00 5.00
G6 Vladimir Hudacek 2.00 5.00
G7 Oldrich Svoboda 2.00 5.00
G8 Josef Kucera 2.00 5.00
G9 Michal Marik 2.00 5.00
G10 Miroslav Simonovic 2.00 5.00
G11 Pavel Malac 2.00 5.00

2001-02 Czech OFS H Inserts

These cards were randomly inserted into packs of Czech OFS. We have no confirmation on insertion rate.

COMPLETE SET (15) 25.00 50.00
H1 Lukas Hronek 1.50 4.00
H2 Marcel Kucera 1.50 4.00
H3 Zdenek Orct 2.00 5.00
H4 Martin Vojtek 1.50 4.00
H5 Jan Pospisil 1.50 4.00
H6 Lukas Smolka 1.50 4.00
H7 Jiri Trvaj 1.50 4.00
H8 Ivo Pesat 1.50 4.00
H9 Petr Tucek 1.50 4.00
H10 Ladislav Kudrna 1.50 4.00
H11 Marek Pinc 1.50 4.00
H12 Pavel Cagas 1.50 4.00
H13 Adam Svoboda 2.00 5.00
H14 Libor Barta 1.50 4.00
H15 Petr Briza 2.50 6.00

2001-02 Czech OFS Red Inserts

These cards were randomly inserted into packs of Czech OFS. We have no confirmation on insertion rate.

COMPLETE SET (24) 25.00 50.00
RE1D Viktor Ujcik .75 2.00
RE2D Josef Beranek .75 2.00
RE3D Tomas Plekanec .75 2.00
RE4D Tomas Kaberle 1.25 3.00
RE5D Jiri Zelenka .75 2.00
RE6D Martin Prochazka .75 2.00
RE7D David Moravec .75 2.00
RE8D Petr Klima .75 2.00
RE9D Rudolf Suchanek .75 2.00
RE10D Frantisek Kucera .75 2.00
RE11D Michal Sykora .75 2.00
RE12D Otakar Janecky .75 2.00
RE13D Pavel Zdrahal .75 2.00
RE14D Radoslav Kropac .75 2.00
RE15D Rostislav Vlach .75 2.00
RE16D Marek Uram .75 2.00
RE17D Petr Leska .75 2.00
RE18D Petr Cajanek 1.25 3.00
RE19D Ondrej Kratena 1.25 3.00
RE20D Petr Korinek .75 2.00
RE21D Jiri Hudler 6.00 15.00
RE22D Pavel Janku .75 2.00
RE23D Richard Kral .75 2.00
RE24D Miloslav Guren .75 2.00

2002 Czech National Team Postcards

COMPLETE SET (15) 10.00 20.00
1 Jaroslav Balastik .75 2.00
2 Jaroslav Bednar .75 2.00
3 Petr Briza .75 2.00
4 Jan Hlavac .75 2.00
5 Jindrich Kotrla .40 1.00
6 Tomas Kucharcik .40 1.00
7 Jan Marek .40 1.00
8 Zbynek Michalek 1.25 3.00
9 Jaroslav Modry .40 1.00
10 Vaclav Pletka .40 1.00
11 Jaroslav Spacek .40 1.00
12 Petr Tenkrat .40 1.00
13 Radim Tesarik .40 1.00
14 Marek Vorel .40 1.00
15 David Vyborny .75 2.00

2002 Czech Stadion Cup Finals

This set features stars from the World Cup and Stanley Cup. Only hockey players are listed below.

COMPLETE SET (9)
484 Scotty Bowman .75 2.00
485 Jiri Fischer .75 2.00
486 Ron Francis .75 2.00
487 Dominik Hasek 2.00 5.00
488 Arturs Irbe .75 2.00
489 Marek Malik .40 1.00
490 Jaroslav Svoboda .40 1.00
491 Jiri Slegr .40 1.00
492 Josef Vasicek .40 1.00

2002 Czech Stadion Olympics

This set was issued in conjunction with the Czech sports magazine Stadion. It features athletes who represented the Czech Republic at the 2002 Winter Olympics. We only include hockey players, so the set is listed in skip-number form below.

325 Petr Cajanek .75 2.00
326 Roman Cechmanek .40 1.00
327 Jiri Dopita .40 1.00
328 Radek Dvorak .40 1.00
329 Patrik Elias 1.25 3.00
330 Roman Hamrlik .40 1.00
331 Milan Hejduk 1.25 3.00
332 Martin Havlat 2.00 5.00
333 Dominik Hasek 2.00 5.00
334 Jan Hrdina .40 1.00
335 Jaromir Jagr 2.00 5.00
336 Tomas Kaberle .75 2.00
337 Pavel Patera .40 1.00
338 Robert Lang .40 1.00
339 Pavel Kubina .40 1.00
340 Petr Sykora .40 1.00
341 Martin Rucinsky .40 1.00
342 Robert Reichel .40 1.00
347 Roman Turek .40 1.00
348 Jaroslav Spacek .40 1.00
349 Richard Smehlik .40 1.00
350 Martin Skoula .40 1.00
351 Michal Sykora .40 1.00

2002-03 Czech DS

This set features the top Czech players in the world. The first 40 cards in the set are base cards. 41-54 are Young Heroes (1:2); 55-75 are Jagr Team base cards; 76-82 are Goalies (1:3); 83-89 are Best Shooters (1:3); 90-96 are Power Stars (1:3) and 97-100 are Stanley Cup Champs (1:7).

COMPLETE SET (100) 30.00 60.00
41-54 ODDS 1:2
55-96 ODDS 1:3
97-100 ODDS 1:7
1 Milan Hnilicka .40 1.00
2 Dusan Salficky .30 .75
3 Petr Briza .30 .75
4 Adam Svoboda .30 .75
5 Frantisek Kucera .10 .25
6 Petr Kadlec .10 .25
7 Karel Rachunek .30 .75
8 Richard Kral .10 .25
9 Josef Beranek .20 .50
10 Radek Duda .10 .25
11 Petr Mudroch .10 .25
12 Milan Michalek 2.00 5.00
13 Tomas Kucharcik .10 .25
14 Frantisek Kaberle .10 .25
15 Rostislav Klesla .75 2.00
16 Filip Kuba .20 .50
17 Pavel Kubina .30 .75
18 Jaroslav Spacek .20 .50
19 Michal Sykora .10 .25
20 Martin Richter .10 .25
21 Michal Bros .10 .25
22 Petr Cajanek .30 .75
23 Jaroslav Hlinka .10 .25
24 Jan Hrdina .40 1.00
25 Jaromir Jagr 2.00 5.00
26 David Moravec .20 .50
27 Pavel Patera .20 .50
28 Martin Prochazka .10 .25
29 Zdenek Sedlak .10 .25
30 Viktor Ujcik .20 .50
31 Tomas Vlasak .10 .25
32 Ondrej Kratena .10 .25
33 David Vyborny .10 .25
34 Vladimir Vujtek .20 .50
35 Petr Leska .10 .25
36 Marek Zidlicky .30 .75
37 Jaroslav Balastik .10 .25
38 Libor Pivko .10 .25
39 David Hruska .10 .25
40 Jiri Marusak .10 .25
41 Milan Hnilicka 2.00 5.00
42 Tomas Vokoun .20 .50
43 Jaroslav Spacek .10 .25
44 Jaroslav Bednar .10 .25
45 Martin Rucinsky .10 .25
46 Jaromir Jagr .20 .50
47 Karel Pilar 2.00 5.00
48 David Vyborny .10 .25
49 Frantisek Kaberle .20 .50
50 Tomas Kaberle .10 .25
51 Vaclav Prospal .40 1.00
52 Jan Hrdina .10 .25
53 Robert Reichel .20 .50
54 Josef Melichar .10 .25
55 Jan Hlavac .40 1.00
56 Jiri Fischer .75 2.00
57 Milan Hejduk .20 .50
58 Jiri Dopita .40 1.00
59 Vaclav Varada .20 .50
60 Patrik Stefan 2.00 5.00
61 Milan Kraft .20 .50
62 Jiri Hudler .10 .25
63 Libor Ustrnul .10 .25
64 Lukas Hronek .30 .75
65 Miroslav Blatak .20 .50
66 Jan Hanzlik .40 1.00
67 Jiri Novotny .20 .50
68 Ales Hemsky .20 .50
69 Tomas Plekanec .40 1.00
70 Filip Novak .75 2.00
71 Miloslav Horava 1.50 4.00
72 Lukas Krajicek .20 .50
73 Tomas Mojzis .20 .50
74 Jiri Jakes .40 1.00
75 Jan Bohac .40 1.00
76 Milan Hnilicka .40 1.00
77 Dusan Salficky .30 .75
78 Roman Malek .10 .25
79 Tomas Vokoun .75 2.00
80 Lukas Hronek .10 .25
81 Petr Briza .30 .75
82 Adam Svoboda .30 .75
83 Viktor Ujcik .20 .50
84 Martin Prochazka .10 .25
85 Petr Cajanek .30 .75
86 Pavel Patera .20 .50
87 Radek Duda .10 .25
88 Tomas Vlasak .10 .25
89 Jaromir Jagr 2.00 5.00
90 Jaromir Jagr 2.00 5.00
91 Robert Reichel .20 .50
92 Frantisek Kaberle .10 .25
93 Jaroslav Spacek .20 .50
94 Jan Hlavac .20 .50
95 Martin Rucinsky .20 .50
96 Tomas Kaberle .30 .75
97 Dominik Hasek 1.25 3.00
98 Dominik Hasek 1.25 3.00
99 Dominik Hasek 1.25 3.00
100 Checklist .10 .25

2002-03 Czech OFS Plus

COMPLETE SET (369) 75.00 125.00
1 Daniel Branda .20 .50
2 Michal Bros .20 .50
3 Petr Briza .30 .75
4 Jan Hanzlik .20 .50
5 Petr Havelka .20 .50
6 Valdemar Jirus .20 .50
7 Pavel Kasparik .20 .50
8 Ondrej Kratena .20 .50
9 Petr Leska .20 .50
10 Patrik Martinec .20 .50
11 Jaroslav Nedved .20 .50
12 Petr Prikryl .20 .50
13 Frantisek Ptacek .20 .50
14 Martin Richter .20 .50
15 Jan Srdinko .20 .50
16 Martin Spanhel .20 .50
17 Pavel Srek .20 .50
18 Jan Tomajko .20 .50
19 Robert Tomik .20 .50
20 Roman Vondracek .20 .50
21 Jiri Zelenka .20 .50
22 Richard Zemlicka .20 .50
23 Jaroslav Balastik .60 1.50
24 Miroslav Blatak .20 .50
25 Martin Cech .20 .50
26 Lukas Galvas .20 .50
27 Martin Hamrlik .20 .50
28 Jan Homer .20 .50
29 Slavomir Hrina .20 .50
30 Petr Hubacek .20 .50
31 Patrik Hucko .20 .50
32 Martin Jenacek .20 .50
33 Jiri Marusak .20 .50
34 Milan Ministr .20 .50
35 Petr Mokrejs .20 .50
36 Miroslav Okal .20 .50
37 Ivo Pesat .20 .50
38 Libor Pivko .20 .50
39 Ivan Rachunek .20 .50
40 Petr Tucek .20 .50
41 Ondrej Vesely .20 .50
42 Rostislav Vlach .20 .50
43 Ladislav Vlcek .20 .50
44 Martin Zahorovsky .20 .50
45 Pavel Zubicek .20 .50
46 Jiri Burger .20 .50
47 Marek Cernosek .20 .50
48 Martin Falter .20 .50
49 Stanislav Gron .40 1.00
50 Jakub Hulva .20 .50
51 Lukas Chmelir .20 .50
52 Zbynek Irgl .30 .75
53 Petr Jurecka .20 .50
54 Roman Kadera .20 .50
55 Ludek Krayzel .20 .50
56 Leszek Laszkiewicz .20 .50
57 Marek Melenovsky .20 .50
58 David Moravec .20 .50
59 Ales Padelek .20 .50
60 Ivan Padelek .20 .50
61 Radek Philipp .20 .50
62 Martin Ambruz .20 .50
63 Peter Bartek .20 .50
64 Radovan Biegl .30 .75
65 Tomas Demel .20 .50
66 Marek Dubec .20 .50
67 Jiri Hudler 10.00 25.00
68 Alexej Jaskin .20 .50
69 Petr Kubos .20 .50
70 Radim Kucharczyk .20 .50
71 Patrik Luza .20 .50
72 Ondrej Nemec .20 .50
73 Lukas Plsek .20 .50
74 Jiri Polak .20 .50
75 Bohuslav Ptacek .20 .50
76 Jan Sochor .20 .50
77 Roman Stantien .20 .50
78 Martin Streit .20 .50
79 Tomas Vak .20 .50
80 Lukas Valko .20 .50
81 Petr Vampola .20 .50
82 Jiri Hasek .20 .50
83 Lubos Horcicka .20 .50
84 Tomas Houdek .20 .50
85 Jiri Hunkes .20 .50
86 Marek Ivan .20 .50
87 Petr Jancarik .20 .50
88 Pavel Janku .20 .50
89 Richard Kral .20 .50
90 Vlastimil Lakosil .20 .50
91 Jiri Malinsky .20 .50
92 Jan Marek .20 .50
93 Rostislav Martynek .20 .50
94 Roman Meluzin .20 .50
95 Marian Morava .20 .50
96 David Nosek .20 .50
97 Zdenek Pavelek .20 .50
98 Gregor Poloncic .20 .50
99 Libor Prochazka .20 .50
100 Marek Zadina .20 .50
101 Tomas Zboril .20 .50
102 Boris Zabka .20 .50
103 Martin Altrichter .20 .50
104 Miroslav Barus .20 .50
105 Vaclav Benak .20 .50
106 Roman Erat .20 .50
107 Radek Haman .20 .50
108 David Havir .20 .50
109 Ales Kretinsky .20 .50
110 Pavel Kumstat .20 .50
111 Petr Kumstat .20 .50
112 David Ludvik .20 .50
113 Jan Mikulik .20 .50
114 Karel Plasek .20 .50
115 Jan Plch .20 .50
116 Milan Prochazka .20 .50
117 Peter Pucher .20 .50
118 Jaroslav Sklenar .20 .50
119 Jan Snopek .20 .50
120 Karel Soudek .20 .50
121 Oldrich Svoboda .20 .50
122 Milan Toman .20 .50
123 Marek Uram .20 .50
124 Marek Vorel .20 .50
125 Lukas Bednarik .20 .50
126 Daniel Bohac .20 .50
127 Jakub Cech .20 .50
128 Michal Cech .20 .50
129 Vratislav Cech .20 .50
130 Ales Cerny .20 .50
131 Juraj Durco .20 .50
132 Martin Filip .20 .50
133 Petr Folta .20 .50
134 Tomas Harant .20 .50
135 Martin Holy .20 .50
136 Jan Kopecky .20 .50
137 Jiri Kucera .20 .50
138 Michal Marik .20 .50
139 Petr Pavlas .20 .50
140 Albin Podstavek .20 .50
141 Radek Prochazka .20 .50
142 Rene Pucher .20 .50
143 Tomas Srsen .20 .50
144 Ales Stanek .20 .50
145 Vaclav Studeny .20 .50
146 Filip Stefanka .20 .50
147 Milan Beranek .20 .50
148 Martin Cakajik .20 .50
149 Pavel Falta .20 .50
150 Miroslav Hajek .20 .50
151 Jan Holub .20 .50
152 Vitezslav Jankovych .20 .50
153 Pavel Kabrt .20 .50
154 Vaclav Koci .20 .50
155 Radoslav Kropac .20 .50
156 Angel Krstev .20 .50
157 Vojtech Kubincak .20 .50
158 Jiri Kudrna .20 .50
159 Pavel Malecek .20 .50
160 Jiri Moravec .20 .50
161 Mojmir Musil .20 .50
162 Vaclav Novak .20 .50
163 Jan Plodek .20 .50
164 Robert Pospisil .20 .50
165 Stanislav Prochazska .20 .50
166 Patrik Rozsival .20 .50
167 Michal Straka .20 .50
168 Daniel Babka .20 .50
169 Michal Barinka .20 .50
170 Peter Bartos .20 .50
171 Jiri Broz .20 .50
172 Petr Gregorek .20 .50
173 Stepan Hrebejk .20 .50
174 Vladimir Hudacek .20 .50
175 Josef Jindra .20 .50
176 Ivo Kotaska .20 .50
177 Josef Kucera .20 .50
178 Milan Michalek 4.00 10.00
179 Frantisek Mrazek .20 .50
180 Jan Mucha .20 .50
181 Milan Nedoma .20 .50
182 Zdenek Ondrej .20 .50
183 Lubos Rob .20 .50
184 Petr Sailer .20 .50
185 Rudolf Suchanek .20 .50
186 Jiri Simanek .20 .50
187 Martin Strba .20 .50
188 Filip Turek .20 .50
189 Michal Vondrka .20 .50
190 Jan Alinc .20 .50
191 Jiri Gombar .20 .50
192 Vladimir Gyna .20 .50
193 Lukas Havel .20 .50
194 Jan Hranac .20 .50
195 Petr Klima .20 .50
196 Jan Kloboucek .20 .50
197 Jindrich Kotrla .20 .50
198 Vlastimil Kroupa .20 .50
199 Jiri Kuntos .20 .50
200 Petr Macholda .20 .50
201 Tomas Martinec .20 .50
202 Marek Pinc .20 .50
203 Michal Podolka .20 .50
204 Lukas Pozivil .20 .50
205 Ivo Prorok .20 .50
206 Lukas Riha .20 .50
207 Stanislav Stavensky .20 .50
208 Jiri Slegr .20 .50
209 Jan Sulc .20 .50
210 Martin Tupa .20 .50
211 Martin Barek .20 .50
212 Jakub Barton .20 .50
213 Tomas Blazek .20 .50
214 Tomas Divisek .40 1.00
215 Miroslav Duben .20 .50
216 Otakar Janecky .20 .50
217 Jan Kolar .20 .50
218 Petr Koukal .20 .50
219 Ladislav Lubina .20 .50
220 Michal Mikeska .20 .50
221 Petr Mocek .20 .50
222 Petr Mudroch .20 .50
223 Andrej Novotny .20 .50
224 Lubomir Pistek .20 .50
225 David Pospisil .20 .50
226 Petr Prucha 6.00 15.00
227 Tomas Rolinek .20 .50
228 Petr Caslava .20 .50
229 Adam Svoboda .30 .75
230 Michal Sykora .20 .50
231 Petr Sykora .20 .50
232 Michael Vyhlidal .20 .50
233 Milan Antos .20 .50
234 Josef Beranek .20 .50
235 Dominik Granak .20 .50
236 Jan Hejda .40 1.00
237 Lukas Hronek .20 .50
238 David Hruska .20 .50
239 Petr Jaros .20 .50
240 Petr Kadlec .20 .50
241 Jakub Klepis ERC 1.25 3.00
242 Pavel Kolarik .20 .50
243 Frantisek Kucera .20 .50
244 Roman Malek .20 .50
245 Petr Mika .30 .75
246 Jan Novak .20 .50
247 Marek Posmyk .20 .50
248 Ondrej Steiner .20 .50
249 Michal Sup .20 .50
250 Adam Saffer .20 .50
251 Josef Straub .20 .50
252 Marek Tomica .20 .50
253 Viktor Ujcik .20 .50
254 Dusan Andrasovsky .20 .50
255 Libor Barta .20 .50
256 Michal Dobron .20 .50
257 Radek Duda .20 .50
258 Michal Dvorak .20 .50
259 Robert Hamrla .20 .50
260 Jiri Hanzlik .20 .50
261 Petr Chvojka .20 .50
262 Vaclav Kral .20 .50
263 Ales Kratoska .20 .50
264 Radek Matejovsky .20 .50
265 Josef Reznicek .20 .50
266 Josef Straka .20 .50
267 Jaroslav Spelda .20 .50
268 Juraj Stefanka .20 .50
269 Jan Svik .20 .50
270 Ivan Vlcek .20 .50
271 Milan Voboril .20 .50
272 Milan Volak .20 .50
273 Josef Voskar .20 .50
274 Martin Vyborny .20 .50
275 Robin Bacul .20 .50
276 David Balasz .20 .50
277 Richard Bauer .20 .50
278 Petr Franek .20 .50
279 Jakub Grof .20 .50
280 Martin Hlavacka .20 .50
281 Jan Kostal .20 .50
282 Lukas Krajicek .60 1.50
283 Jakub Kraus .20 .50
284 Marcel Kucera .20 .50
285 Jaromir Kverka .20 .50
286 Michal Madl .20 .50
287 Tomas Nemcicky .20 .50
288 Martin Opatovsky .20 .50
289 Libor Pavlis .20 .50
290 Petr Puncochar .20 .50
291 Dmitri Rodine .20 .50
292 Vaclav Skuhravy .20 .50
293 Ladislav Svoboda .20 .50
294 Petr Sinagl .20 .50
295 Marek Topoli .20 .50
296 Kamil Tvrdek .20 .50
297 Pavel Selinger .20 .50
298 Radim Tesarik .20 .50
299 Jiri Trvaj .20 .50
300 Jan Vytisk .20 .50
301 Danniel Zapotocny .20 .50
302 Michal Divisek .20 .50
303 Jiri Dobrovolny .20 .50
304 Michal Kello .20 .50
305 Radek Krestan .20 .50
306 Tomas Micka .20 .50
307 Petr Mika .20 .50
308 Jan Dresler .20 .50
309 Rostislav Olesz ERC 4.00 10.00
310 Lukas Zatopek .20 .50
311 Vaclav Pletka .30 .75
312 Lukas Krenzelok .20 .50
313 Lukas Smolka .20 .50
314 Jaroslav Sklenar .20 .50
315 Richard Bordowski .20 .50
316 Mario Cartelli .20 .50
317 Tomas Horna .20 .50
318 Petr Hrbek .20 .50
319 Martin Kotasek .20 .50
320 Jan Korotvicka .20 .50
321 Michal Tvrdik .20 .50
322 David Pojkar .20 .50
323 Martin Adamsky .20 .50
324 Jaroslav Kracik .20 .50
325 Miloslav Topol .20 .50
326 Vojtech Polak .20 .50
327 Lukas Pech .20 .50
328 Jaroslav Hasek .20 .50
329 Jan Kudrna .20 .50
330 Jan Visek .20 .50
331 Patrik Moskal .20 .50
332 Zdenek Smid .20 .50
333 Michal Travnicek .20 .50
334 Martin Nosek .20 .50
335 Zdenek Skorepa .20 .50
336 Jan Horacek .20 .50
337 David Appel .20 .50
338 Petr Svoboda .20 .50
339 Jan Nemecek .20 .50
340 Jan Kotatko .20 .50
341 Ales Vala .20 .50
342 Radek Mrazek .20 .50
343 Viktor Hubl .20 .50
344 Jaroslav Kudrna .20 .50
345 Tomas Pacal .20 .50
346 David Mazanec .20 .50
347 Radek Prochazka .20 .50
348 Ales Kratoska .20 .50
349 Michal Marik .20 .50
350 Ladislav Vlcek .20 .50
351 Jiri Hanzlik .20 .50
352 Jaroslav Hubl .20 .50
353 Martin Tuma .20 .50
354 Petr Martinek .20 .50
355 Michal Divisek .20 .50
356 Lubomir Hurtaj .20 .50
357 Jakub Koreis ERC .75 2.00
358 Ondrej Kubes .20 .50
359 Viktor Ujcik .20 .50
360 Radek Dlouhy .20 .50
361 Radek Duda .20 .50
362 Milan Kopecky .20 .50
363 Patrik Stejskal .20 .50
364 Vaclav Pletka .30 .75
365 Radek Masny .20 .50
366 Zbynek Spitzer .20 .50
367 Tomas Frolo .20 .50
368 Martin Filip .20 .50
369 Ivan Rachunek .20 .50
370 Tomas Klimes .20 .50

2002-03 Czech OFS Plus All-Star Game

COMPLETE SET (43) 30.00 75.00
H1 Jaroslav Balastik 2.00 5.00
H2 Jiri Burger .75 2.00
H3 Petr Cajanek 1.25 3.00
H4 Petr Gregorek .75 2.00
H5 Miloslav Guren .75 2.00
H6 Martin Hamrlik .75 2.00
H7 Vladimir Hudacek .75 2.00
H8 Jiri Hudler 4.00 10.00
H9 Tomas Jakes .75 2.00
H10 Miroslav Javin .75 2.00
H11 Lubomir Korhon .75 2.00
H12 Richard Kral .75 2.00
H13 Petr Leska .75 2.00
H14 Jiri Marusak .75 2.00
H15 Marek Melenovsky .75 2.00
H16 David Moravec .75 2.00
H17 David Nosek .75 2.00
H18 Karel Soudek .75 2.00
H19 Jiri Trvaj .75 2.00
H20 Marek Uram .75 2.00
H21 Petr Vala .75 2.00
H22 Ondrej Vesely .75 2.00
H23 Peter Bartos .75 2.00
H24 Petr Briza 1.25 3.00
H25 Vladimir Gyna .75 2.00
H26 Martin Hlavacka .75 2.00
H27 Jaroslav Hlinka .75 2.00
H28 Otakar Janecky .75 2.00
H29 Petr Kadlec .75 2.00
H30 Ladislav Lubina .75 2.00
H31 Jaroslav Nedved .75 2.00
H32 Tomas Nemcicky .75 2.00
H33 Josef Reznicek .75 2.00
H34 Vaclav Skuhravy .75 2.00
H35 Jan Srdinko .75 2.00
H36 Josef Straka .75 2.00
H37 Adam Svoboda 1.25 3.00
H38 Ladislav Svoboda .75 2.00
H39 Michal Sykora .75 2.00
H40 Viktor Ujcik .75 2.00
H41 Unknown .75 2.00
H42 Jiri Zelenka .75 2.00
H43 Daniel Branda .75 2.00

2002-03 Czech OFS Plus Checklists

COMPLETE SET (12) 5.00 10.00
C1 Jakub Cech .40 1.00
C2 Marek Pinc .40 1.00
C3 Pavel Falta .40 1.00
C4 Petr Prikril .40 1.00
C5 Lukas Hronek .40 1.00
C6 Robert Hamrla .40 1.00
C7 Adam Svoboda .75 2.00
C8 Petr Franek .40 1.00
C9 Petr Tucek .40 1.00
C10 Lubos Horcicka .40 1.00
C11 Jiri Trvaj .40 1.00
C12 Radovan Biegl .75 2.00

2002-03 Czech OFS Plus Masks

Those numbers not listed below remain unknown.

M2 Ivo Pesat 4.00 10.00
M3 Petr Tucek 4.00 10.00
M4 Jiri Trvaj 4.00 10.00
M5 Lukas Plsek 4.00 10.00
M6 Radovan Biegl 4.00 10.00
M7 Marek Pinc 4.00 10.00
M8 Petr Prikril 4.00 10.00
M9 Lukas Hronek 4.00 10.00
M10 Roman Malek 4.00 10.00
M11 Pavel Falta 4.00 10.00
M14 Vladimir Hudacek 4.00 10.00
M16 Adam Svoboda 6.00 15.00
M17 Robert Hamrla 4.00 10.00
M18 Marcel Kucera 4.00 10.00
M24 Jakub Cech 4.00 10.00

2002-03 Czech OFS Plus Trios

STATED ODDS 1:8
T1 Vladimir Hudacek 2.50 6.00
Rudolf Suchanek
Peter Bartos
T2 Michal Marik 2.50 6.00
Filip Stefanka
Michal Cech
T3 Jakub Cech 2.50 6.00
Tomas Harant
Daniel Bohac
T4 Petr Franek 2.50 6.00
Dmitri Rodine
TomasNemcicky
T5 Pavel Falta 2.50 6.00
Angel Krstev
Vitezslav Jankovych
T6 Marek Pinc 2.50 6.00
Jiri Slegr
Martin Rucinsky
T7 Michal Podolka 2.50 6.00
{ Petr Martinek
Petr Klima
T8 Adam Svoboda 2.50 6.00
Michal Sykora
Petr Sykora
T9 Tomas Maly 2.50 6.00
Michael Vyhlidal
Ladislav Lubina
T10 Libor Barta 2.50 6.00
Josef Reznicek
Radek Duda
T11 Robert Hamrla 2.50 6.00
Ivan Vlcek
Josef Straka
T12 Roman Malek 2.50 6.00
Frantisek Kucera
Josef Beranek
T13 Lukas Hronek 2.50 6.00
Petr Kadlec
Viktor Ujcik
T14 Petr Briza 2.50 6.00
Jaroslav Nedved
Richard Zemlicka
T15 Petr Prikril 2.50 6.00
Jan Srdinko
Petr Leska
T16 Vlastimil Lakosil 2.50 6.00
Libor Prochazka
Richard Kral
T17 Lubos Horcicka 2.50 6.00
David Nosek
Vaclav Pletka
T18 Jiri Trvaj 2.50 6.00
Radim Tesarik
David Moravec
T19 Martin Falter 2.50 6.00
Marek Cernosek
Roman Kadera
T20 Radovan Biegl 8.00 20.00
Alexej Jaskin
Jiri Hudler
T21 Radek Masny 2.50 6.00
Petr Kubos
Radim Kucharczyk
T22 Ivo Pesat 2.50 6.00
Martin Hamrlik
Miroslav Okal
T23 Petr Tucek 2.50 6.00
Jirin Marusak
Ladislav Vlach
T24 Petr Svoboda 2.50 6.00
Jan Snopek
Peter Pucher
T25 Martin Altrichter 2.50 6.00
Karel Soudek
Marek Uram

2002-03 Czech OFS Plus Znaky Klubu

COMPLETE SET (14) 5.00 10.00
Z1 Ceske Budejovice .40 1.00
Z2 Havirov Panthers .40 1.00
Z3 Energie Karlovy Vary .40 1.00
Z4 Bili Tygri Liberec .40 1.00
Z5 Chemopetrol Litvinov .40 1.00
Z6 IPB Pojistovna Pardubice .40 1.00
Z7 Keramika Plzen .40 1.00
Z8 Slavia Praha .40 1.00
Z9 Sparta Praha .40 1.00
Z10 Ocelari Trinec .40 1.00
Z11 Vitkovice .40 1.00
Z12 Vsetin .40 1.00
Z13 Hame Zlin .40 1.00
Z14 ME Znojemsti Orli .40 1.00

2002-03 Czech OFS Plus Duos

COMPLETE SET (25) 40.00 80.00
STATED ODDS 1:8
D1 Radovan Biegl 6.00 15.00
Jiri Hudler
D2 Petr Briza 2.00 5.00
Jiri Zelenka
D3 Martin Richter 2.00 5.00
Jan Tomajko
D4 Josef Beranek 2.00 5.00
Roman Malek
D5 Frantisek Kucera 2.00 5.00
Viktor Ujcik
D6 Jiri Trvaj 2.00 5.00
David Moravec
D7 Jiri Burger 2.00 5.00
Roman Kadera
D8 Libor Prochazska 2.00 5.00
Richard Kral
D9 Vaclav Pletka 2.00 5.00
Vlastimil Lakocil
D10 Adam Svoboda 2.00 5.00
Michal Vyhlidal
D11 Michal Sykora 2.00 5.00
Ladislav Lubina
D12 Oldrich Svoboda 3.00 8.00
Marek Uram
D13 Peter Pucher 2.00 5.00
Martin Altrichter
D14 Martin Vyborny 2.00 5.00
Libor Barta
D15 Radek Duda 2.00 5.00
Robert Hamrla
D16 Martin Hamrlik 2.00 5.00
Jiri Marusak
D17 Rostislav Vlach 2.00 5.00
Petr Tucek
D18 Petr Ranek 2.00 5.00
Robin Bacul
D19 Vladimir Hudacek 2.00 5.00
Milan Nedoma
D20 Vlastimil Kroupa 2.00 5.00
Marek Pinc
D21 Martin Rucinsky 2.00 5.00
Jiri Slegr
D22 Radoslav Kropac 2.00 5.00
Pavel Falta
D23 Angel Krstev 2.00 5.00
Vitezslav Jankovych
D24 Tomas Srsen 2.00 5.00
Jakub Cech
D25 Jan Kopecky 2.00 5.00
Michal Marik

2003 Czech National Team Postcards

This postcard-sized issue features members of the Czech team from the 2003 World Championships.

COMPLETE SET (17) 20.00 40.00
17 David Vyborny 1.25 3.00
1 Jaroslav Balastik 1.25 3.00
2 Jan Hejda .75 2.00
3 Milan Hejduk 2.00 5.00
4 Jan Hlavac .75 2.00
5 Ivan Hlinka CO .40 1.00
6 Jiri Hudler 4.00 10.00
7 Frantisek Kaberle .75 2.00
8 Jindrich Kotrla .75 2.00
9 Jaroslav Modry .75 2.00
10 Robert Reichel .75 2.00
11 Martin Straka .75 2.00
12 Radek Sup .75 2.00
13 Martin Tomasek .75 2.00
14 Josef Vasicek .75 2.00
15 Tomas Vokoun 2.00 5.00
16 Radim Vrbata 1.25 3.00
18 Tomas Kaberle 2.00 5.00
19 Michal Sup .75 2.00
20 Jaroslav Hlinka .75 2.00

2003 Czech Stadion

This multi-sport set was issued in conjunction with the Czech magazine Stadion. It is listed below in skip-numbered form.

COMPLETE SET 15.00 40.00
529 Anson Carter .40 1.00
530 Peter Bondra .40 1.00
531 Magnus Arvedson .40 1.00
532 Sandy McCarthy .40 1.00
533 Mikko Eloranta .40 1.00
534 Tie Domi .75 2.00
535 Bates Battaglia .40 1.00
536 Jaromir Jagr 4.00 10.00
Mario Lemieux
537 Darcy Tucker .40 1.00
538 Brian Rafalski .40 1.00
539 Jozef Stumpel .40 1.00
540 Marco Sturm .40 1.00
541 Eric Lindros 1.25 3.00
542 Ed Jovanovski .40 1.00
543 Darren McCarty .40 1.00
544 Zigmund Palffy .40 1.00
545 Luc Robitaille 1.25 3.00
546 Keith Primeau .40 1.00
547 Bobby Clarke .40 1.00
548 Marcel Dionne .40 1.00
549 Ken Dryden 2.00 5.00
550 Frank Mahovlich .75 2.00
551 Valeri Kharlamov .75 2.00
552 Phil Esposito 2.00 5.00
553 Boris Mikhailov .75 2.00
554 Stan Mikita .75 2.00
555 Bobby Orr 4.00 10.00
556 Vladimir Petrov .40 1.00
557 Vladislav Tretiak 1.25 3.00
562 Chuck Kobasew .40 1.00
565 Bobby Holik .40 1.00

2003-04 Czech National Team

This partial checklist represents what appears to be a set produced by World Sport of the 2003-04 Czech National Team. If anyone has additional information, please forward it to hockeymag@beckett.com

COMPLETE SET

Dusan Salficky .40 1.00
Jan Hejda .20 .50
Martin Cech .20 .50
Pavel Patera .20 .50

2003-04 Czech OFS Plus

COMPLETE SET (398) 40.00 80.00
1 Jiri Burger .20 .50
2 Marek Cernosek .20 .50
3 Jan Dresler .20 .50
4 Martin Falter .20 .50
5 Petr Hubacek .20 .50
6 Jakub Hulva .20 .50
7 Lukas Chmelir .20 .50
8 Zbynek Irgl .20 .50
9 Roman Kadera .20 .50
10 Rostislav Olesz 1.25 3.00
11 Ludek Krayzel .20 .50
12 Lukas Krenzelok .20 .50
13 Pavel Kumstat .20 .50
14 Jiri Trvaj .20 .50
15 Petr Vala .20 .50
16 Ales Padelek .20 .50
17 Ivan Padelek .20 .50
18 Tomas Ficenc .20 .50
19 Pavel Kowalczyk .20 .50
20 Petr Mika .20 .50
21 Daniel Zapotocny .20 .50
22 Daniel Seman .20 .50
23 Martin Tomasek .20 .50
24 Martin Ambruz .20 .50
25 Marek Dubec .20 .50
26 Radovan Biegl .30 .75
27 Michal Horak .20 .50
28 Tomas Demel .20 .50
29 Radim Hruska .20 .50
30 Petr Kubos .20 .50
31 Alexej Jaskin .20 .50
32 Ondrej Nemec .20 .50
33 Jiri Polak .20 .50
34 Roman Stantien .20 .50
35 Jan Sochor .20 .50
36 Radek Masny .20 .50
37 Tomas Vak .20 .50
38 Petr Vampola .20 .50
39 Pavel Selinger .20 .50
40 Jiri Hasek .20 .50
41 Michal Hudec .20 .50
42 Lubomir Stach .20 .50
43 Martin Vyrubalik .20 .50
44 Patrik Luza .20 .50
45 Otakar Janecky .20 .50
46 Martin Barek .20 .50
47 Tomas Blazek .20 .50
48 Petr Caslava .20 .50
49 Tomas Divisek .20 .50
50 Miroslav Duben .20 .50
51 Petr Koukal .20 .50
52 Jaroslav Kudrna .20 .50
53 Frantisek Mrazek .20 .50
54 Petr Mudroch .20 .50
55 Andrej Novotny .20 .50
56 Tomas Pacal .20 .50
57 Lubomir Pistek .20 .50
58 Petr Prucha 2.00 5.00
59 Adam Svoboda .30 .75
60 Jan Kolar .20 .50
61 Michal Sykora .20 .50
62 Petr Sykora .20 .50
63 Jiri Dopita .20 .50
64 Peter Podhradsky .20 .50
65 Tomas Razingar .20 .50
66 Jan Alinc .20 .50
67 Robin Bacul .20 .50
68 Richard Bauer .20 .50
69 Lukas Bednarik .20 .50
70 Jakub Kraus .20 .50
71 Lukas Galvas .20 .50
72 Jan Kostal .20 .50
73 Lukas Krajicek .40 1.00
74 Petr Kumstat .20 .50
75 Tomas Mencicky .20 .50
76 Rudolf Pejchar .20 .50
77 Dmitrij Rodin .20 .50
78 Vaclav Skuhravy .20 .50
79 Frantisek Ptacek .20 .50
80 Vojtech Polak .20 .50
81 Ladislav Svoboda .20 .50
82 Michal Tvrdik .20 .50
83 Lukas Sablik .20 .50
84 Tomas Netik .20 .50
85 Miroslav Vantroba .20 .50
86 Martin Kivon .20 .50
87 Jan Lipiansky .20 .50
88 David Balaze .20 .50
89 Frantisek Bojnic .20 .50
90 Viktor Hubl .20 .50
91 Jan Hranac .20 .50
92 Jiri Gombar .20 .50
93 Lukas Havel .20 .50
94 Marian Kacir .20 .50
95 Lukas Kaspar .20 .50
96 Jan Kloboucek .20 .50
97 Vlastimil Kroupa .20 .50
98 Vojtech Kubincak .20 .50
99 Tomas Martinec .20 .50
100 Petr Martinek .20 .50
101 Lukas Riha .20 .50
102 Richard Zemlicka .20 .50
103 Tomas Rolinek .20 .50
104 Miha Rebolj .20 .50
105 Michal Travnicek .20 .50
106 Marek Pinc .20 .50
107 Lukas Pozivil .20 .50
108 Ivo Prorok .20 .50
109 Martin Cakajik .20 .50
110 Miroslav Hajek .20 .50
111 Jan Holub .20 .50
112 Richard Jares .20 .50
113 Waldemar Jirus .20 .50
114 Pavel Kasparik .20 .50
115 Vaclav Koci .20 .50
116 Radoslav Kropac .20 .50
117 Angel Krstev .20 .50
118 Vaclav Novak .20 .50
119 Jiri Moravec .20 .50
120 Lukas Pabiska .20 .50
121 Mojmir Musil .20 .50
122 Jan Plodek .20 .50
123 Stanislav Prochazka .20 .50
124 Patrik Rozsival .20 .50
125 Michal Straka .20 .50
126 Oldrich Svoboda .20 .50
127 Ladislav Smid ERC 2.00 5.00
128 Lubomir Korhon .20 .50
129 Rudolf Vercik .20 .50
130 Jaroslav Balastik .40 1.00
131 Miroslav Blatak .20 .50
132 Martin Cech .20 .50
133 Martin Cech .20 .50
134 Martin Hamrlik .20 .50
135 Martin Jenacek .20 .50
136 Petr Leska .20 .50
137 Petr Macholda .20 .50
138 Petr Mokrejs .20 .50
139 Martin Nosek .20 .50
140 Miroslav Okal .20 .50
141 Martin Altrichter .20 .50
142 Radim Tesarik .20 .50
143 Petr Tucek .20 .50
144 Ondrej Vesely .20 .50
145 Rostislav Vlach .20 .50
146 Martin Zahorovsky .20 .50
147 Pavel Zubicek .20 .50
148 Peter Barinka .20 .50
149 Erik Weissemann .20 .50
150 Pavel Zavrtalek .20 .50
151 Michal Bros .20 .50
152 Petr Briza .30 .75
153 Jan Hanzlik .20 .50
154 Jaroslav Mrazek .20 .50
155 Jakub Sindel .30 .75
156 Ondrej Kratena .30 .75
157 Jan Marek .20 .50
158 Martin Paroulek .20 .50
159 Petr Ton .20 .50
160 David Vrbata .20 .50
161 Libor Prochazka .20 .50
162 Josef Reznicek .20 .50
163 Marek Schwarz ERC 2.00 5.00
164 Jan Srdinko .20 .50
165 Jan Tomajko .20 .50
166 Roman Vondracek .20 .50
167 Jan Vytisk .20 .50
168 Karel Hromas .20 .50
169 Jiri Jakes .20 .50
170 Radek Mika .20 .50
171 Milan Antos .20 .50
172 Josef Beranek .20 .50
173 Radek Dlouhy .20 .50
174 Jan Fadrny .20 .50
175 Dominik Granak .20 .50
176 Lukas Hronek .20 .50
177 David Hruska .20 .50
178 Jiri Kuntos .20 .50
179 Roman Malek .20 .50
180 Patrik Martinec .20 .50
181 Petr Jaros .20 .50
182 Jakub Klepis .40 1.00
183 Pavel Kolarik .20 .50
184 Milan Kopecky .20 .50
185 Frantisek Kucera .20 .50
186 Jan Novak .20 .50
187 David Pojkar .20 .50
188 Ondrej Stanek .20 .50
189 Michal Sup .20 .50
190 Adam Saffer .20 .50
191 Stanislav Gron .40 1.00
192 Petr Kadlec .20 .50
193 Marek Tomica .20 .50
194 Leos Cermak .20 .50
195 Ivan Dropa .20 .50
196 Martin Adamsky .20 .50
197 Michal Dobron .20 .50
198 Michal Dvorak .20 .50
199 Libor Barta .20 .50
200 Mario Cartelli .20 .50
201 Jiri Hanzlik .20 .50
202 Ales Kratoska .20 .50
203 Ondrej Kubes .20 .50
204 Josef Straka .20 .50
205 Radek Matejovsky .20 .50
206 Jan Svik .20 .50
207 Milan Voboril .20 .50
208 Milan Volak .20 .50
209 Zdenek Smid .20 .50
210 David Pospisil .20 .50
211 Roman Bilek .20 .50
212 Jiri Dobrovolny .20 .50
213 Michal Duraz .20 .50
214 Patrik Rimmel .20 .50
215 Zdenek Sedlak .20 .50
216 Vitezslav Bilek .20 .50
217 Jakub Evan .20 .50
218 Martin Frolik .20 .50
219 Radek Gardon .20 .50
220 Tomas Horna .20 .50
221 Miloslav Horava .20 .50
222 Vitezslav Jankovych .20 .50
223 Jaroslav Kalla .20 .50
224 David Pazourek .20 .50
225 Jan Pospisil .20 .50
226 Tomas Klimt .20 .50
227 Jan Krulis .20 .50
228 Robert Kysela .20 .50
229 Rostislav Malena .20 .50
230 Zdenek Orct .20 .50
231 Jiri Zeman .20 .50
232 Jan Dlouhy .20 .50
233 Petr Horava .20 .50
234 Petr Kasik .20 .50
235 Miroslav Lazo .20 .50
236 Martin Prochazka .20 .50
237 Juraj Stefanka .20 .50
238 Miroslav Barus .20 .50
239 Vaclav Benak .20 .50
240 Roman Erat .20 .50
241 Radek Haman .20 .50
242 David Havir .20 .50
243 Ales Kretinsky .20 .50
244 David Ludvik .20 .50
245 Roman Nemecek .20 .50
246 Karel Plasek .20 .50
247 Jan Snopek .20 .50
248 Milan Prochazka .20 .50
249 Peter Pucher .20 .50
250 Robert Slavik .20 .50
251 Pavel Mojzis .20 .50
252 Tomas Duba .20 .50
253 Igor Rataj .20 .50
254 Jan Pardavy .20 .50
255 Lukas Vomela .20 .50
256 Daniel Babka .20 .50
257 Radek Belohlav .20 .50
258 Stepan Hrebejk .20 .50
259 Vladimir Hudacek .20 .50
260 Stanislav Jasecko .20 .50
261 Josef Jindra .20 .50
262 Vaclav Koci .20 .50
263 Jaroslav Kristek .20 .50
264 Josef Kucera .20 .50
265 Lukas Kveton .20 .50
266 Jan Mucha .20 .50
267 Zbynek Neckar .20 .50
268 Zdenek Ondrej .20 .50
269 Ivan Rachunek .20 .50
270 Lubos Rob .20 .50
271 Petr Sailer .20 .50
272 Jiri Simanek .20 .50
273 Vladimir Skoda .20 .50
274 Rudolf Suchanek .20 .50
275 Filip Turek .20 .50
276 Michal Vondra .20 .50
277 Robert Prochazka .20 .50
278 Marek Schwarz 2.00 5.00
279 Zdenek Skorepa .20 .50
280 Filip Stefanka .20 .50
281 Richard Bordowski .20 .50
282 Michal Holes .20 .50
283 Lubos Horcicka .20 .50
284 Tomas Houdek .20 .50
285 Jiri Hunkes .20 .50
286 Marek Ivan .20 .50
287 Petr Jancarik .20 .50
288 Pavel Janku .20 .50
289 Richard Kral .20 .50
290 Jan Kudrna .20 .50
291 Vlastimil Lakosil .20 .50
292 Marek Melenovsky .20 .50
293 Jiri Malinsky .20 .50
294 Rostislav Martynek .20 .50
295 Roman Meluzin .20 .50
296 Zdenek Pavelek .20 .50
297 Vaclav Pletka .20 .50
298 Michal Podolka .20 .50
299 Jiri Polansky .20 .50
300 Gregor Poloncic .20 .50
301 Josef Vitek .20 .50
302 Boris Zabka .20 .50
303 Marek Zadina .20 .50
304 Tomas Zboril .20 .50
305 Tomas Frolo .20 .50
306 Martin Vyborny .20 .50
307 Marok Posmyk .20 .50
308 Milan Nedoma .20 .50
309 Dusan Andrasovsky .20 .50
310 Ladislav Lubina .20 .50
311 Alexandr Hylak .20 .50
312 Jaroslav Nedved .20 .50
313 Pavel Falta .20 .50
314 Leos Cermak .20 .50
315 Tomas Vlcek .20 .50
316 Igor Murin .20 .50
317 Tomas Karny .20 .50
318 Patrik Hucko .20 .50
319 Michal Mikeska .20 .50
320 Pavel Srek .20 .50
321 Gabriel Spilar .20 .50
322 Petr Havelka .20 .50
323 Martin Richter .20 .50
324 Radovan Sloboda .20 .50
325 Peter Bartos .20 .50
326 Vladimir Gyna .20 .50
327 Jan Chabera .20 .50
328 Andrej Mezin .20 .50
329 Jan Rehor .20 .50
330 Martin Strba .20 .50
331 Miroslav Durak .20 .50
332 Kamil Jarina .20 .50
333 Roman Kadera .20 .50
334 Angel Krstev .20 .50
335 Michal Marik .20 .50
336 Jakub Petruzalek .20 .50
337 Lubos Bartecko .20 .50
338 Petr Buzek .20 .50
339 Vaclav Eiselt .20 .50
340 Martin Chabada .20 .50
341 Tomas Popperle .20 .50
342 Zdenek Sedlak .20 .50
343 Ladislav Svoboda .20 .50
344 Roman Simicek .20 .50
345 Martin Havlat 2.00 5.00
346 Martin Vojtek .20 .50
347 Martin Jurecka .20 .50
348 Petr Jurecka .20 .50
349 David Mocek .20 .50
350 Patrik Rimmel .20 .50
351 Juraj Stefanka .20 .50
352 Filip Turek .20 .50
353 Pavel Zdrahal .20 .50
354 Daniel Mracka .20 .50
355 Libor Pavlis .20 .50
356 Tomaz Razingar .20 .50
357 Pavel Sebesta .20 .50
358 Dalibor Sochorek .20 .50
359 Radim Tesarik .20 .50
360 Juraj Prokop .20 .50
361 Josef Hrabal .20 .50
362 Stefan Zigardy .20 .50
363 Jan Kudrna .20 .50
364 Vaclav Skuhravy .20 .50
365 Ivan Droppa .20 .50
366 Michal Hreus .20 .50
367 Radim Skuhrovec .20 .50
368 Jiri Veber .20 .50
369 Jan Dlouhy .20 .50
370 Marek Dubec .20 .50
371 Miroslav Hlinka .20 .50
372 Jiri Beroun .20 .50
373 Tomas Duba .20 .50
374 Tomas Hradecky .20 .50
375 Jaroslav Mares .20 .50
376 Petr Puncochar .20 .50
377 Michal Straka .20 .50
378 Marek Uram .20 .50
379 Jakub Kindl .20 .50
380 Libor Zabransky .20 .50
381 Lubomir Jurtaj .20 .50
382 Petr Jez .20 .50
383 Robert Jindrich .20 .50
384 Roman Malek .20 .50
385 Martin Paroulek .20 .50
386 Adam Saffer .20 .50
387 Michal Straka .20 .50
388 Martin Klaus .20 .50
389 Tomas Kapusta .20 .50
390 Lubomir Vosatko .20 .50
391 Jiri Hanzlik .20 .50
392 Jiri Hasek .20 .50
393 Ctibor Jech .20 .50
394 Ctirad Ovcacik .20 .50
395 Tomas Rolinek .20 .50
396 Martin Tupa .20 .50
397 Libor Barta .20 .50
398 Jiri Jantovsky .20 .50
399 Petr Jaros .20 .50
400 Martin Havlat CL .75 2.00

2003-04 Czech OFS Plus All-Star Game

COMPLETE SET (45) 30.00 75.00
H1 Miroslav Simonovic .75 2.00
H2 Normunds Sejejs .75 2.00
H3 Jiri Hes .75 2.00
H4 Marcel Hanzal .75 2.00
H5 Roman Kukumberg .75 2.00
H6 Arne Krotak .75 2.00
H7 Karol Krizan .75 2.00
H8 Juraj Kledrowetz .75 2.00
H9 Miroslav Vantroba .75 2.00
H10 Miroslav Skovira .75 2.00
H11 Jaroslav Kmit .75 2.00
H12 Lubomir Kolnik .75 2.00
H13 Pavel Kowalczyk .75 2.00
H14 Martin Ivicic .75 2.00
H15 Branislav Janos .75 2.00
H16 Zdeno Ciger .75 2.00
H17 Petr Korinek .75 2.00
H18 Tomas Starosta .75 2.00
H19 Tomas Nadazdi .75 2.00
H20 Igor Rataj .75 2.00
H21 Richard Kapus .75 2.00
H22 Erik Weissmann .75 2.00
H23 Adam Svoboda 1.25 3.00
H24 Michal Sykora .75 2.00
H25 Petr Sykora .75 2.00
H26 Roman Malek 1.25 3.00
H27 Petr Kadlec .75 2.00
H28 Jan Hejda .75 2.00
H29 Michal Sup .75 2.00
H30 Frantisek Kucera .75 2.00
H31 Frantisek Ptacek .75 2.00
H32 Ondrej Kratena .75 2.00
H33 Libor Prochazka .75 2.00
H34 Richard Kral .75 2.00
H35 Marek Zadina .75 2.00
H36 Jan Marek .75 2.00
H37 Vaclav Pletka .75 2.00
H38 Martin Hlavacka .75 2.00
H39 Jan Vytisk .75 2.00
H40 David Moravec .75 2.00
H41 Jiri Burger .75 2.00
H42 Jiri Hudler 6.00 15.00
H43 Marek Uram .75 2.00
H44 Peter Pucher .75 2.00
H45 A.Svoboda .75 2.00
M.Sykora CL

2003-04 Czech OFS Plus Checklists

COMPLETE SET (14) 15.00 30.00
1 Jiri Trvaj 1.25 3.00
2 Radovan Biegl 1.25 3.00
3 Adam Svoboda 1.25 3.00
4 Petr Franek 1.25 3.00
5 Marek Pinc 1.25 3.00
6 Oldrich Svoboda 1.25 3.00
7 Petr Tucek 1.25 3.00
8 Petr Briza 1.25 3.00
9 Roman Malek 1.25 3.00
10 Libor Barta 1.25 3.00
11 Josef Kucera 1.25 3.00
12 Martin Altrichter 1.25 3.00
13 Josef Kucera 1.25 3.00
14 Vlastimil Lakosil 1.25 3.00

2003-04 Czech OFS Plus MS Praha

COMPLETE SET (50) 30.00 75.00
SE1 Martin Havlat 4.00 10.00
SE2 Roman Simicek .75 2.00
SE3 Petr Briza 1.25 3.00
SE4 Jan Marek .75 2.00
SE5 Petr Buzek .75 2.00
SE6 Ondrej Kratena .75 2.00
SE7 Michal Sykora .75 2.00
SE8 Petr Sykora .75 2.00
SE9 Adam Svoboda 1.25 3.00
SE10 Jiri Dopita .75 2.00
SE11 Michal Mikeska .75 2.00
SE12 Petr Prucha 4.00 10.00
SE13 Martin Prochazka .75 2.00
SE14 Zdenek Orct 1.25 3.00
SE15 Petr Leska .75 2.00
SE16 Jaroslav Balastik 1.25 3.00
SE17 Jan Snopek .75 2.00
SE18 Jiri Burger .75 2.00
SE19 Rostislav Olesz 4.00 10.00
SE20 Jiri Trvaj .75 2.00
SE21 Zdenek Pavelek .75 2.00
SE22 Frantisek Ptacek .75 2.00
SE23 Roman Malek .75 2.00
SE24 Marek Posmyk .75 2.00
SE25 Petr Kadlec .75 2.00
SE26 Oldrich Svoboda .75 2.00
SE27 Josef Beranek .75 2.00
SE28 Michal Travnicek .75 2.00
SE29 Lukas Havel .75 2.00
SE30 Jiri Hudler 4.00 10.00
SE31 David Moravec .75 2.00
SE32 Radim Tesarik .75 2.00
SE33 Jan Hejda .75 2.00
SE34 Vlastimil Lakosil .75 2.00
SE35 Martin Chabada .75 2.00
SE36 Petr Franek .75 2.00
SE37 Radovan Biegl 1.25 3.00
SE38 Tomas Duba .75 2.00
SE39 Lukas Hronek .75 2.00
SE40 Jan Novak .75 2.00
SE41 Martin Altrichter .75 2.00
SE42 Marek Schwarz 2.00 5.00
SE43 Josef Kucera .75 2.00
SE44 Tomas Divisek .75 2.00
SE45 Jakub Klepis 2.00 5.00
SE46 Michal Sup .75 2.00
SE47 Michal Marik .75 2.00
SE48 Richard Kral .75 2.00
SE49 Marek Pinc .75 2.00
SE50 Pavel Falta .75 2.00

2003-04 Czech Pardubice Postcards

This team-issued set features postcard sized (4X6) collectibles of the Pardubice squad from the Czech Elite League. They are listed below in alphabetical order.

COMPLETE SET (16) 8.00 15.00
1 Martin Barek .40 1.00
2 Tomas Blazek .40 1.00
3 Tomas Divisek .40 1.00
4 Jiri Dopita .40 1.00
5 Otakar Janecky .40 1.00
6 Petr Koukal .40 1.00
7 Jaroslav Kudrna .40 1.00
8 Ladislav Lubina .40 1.00
9 Michal Mikeska .40 1.00
10 Frantisek Mrazek .40 1.00
11 Andrej Novotny .40 1.00
12 Tomas Pacal .40 1.00
13 Petr Prucha 2.00 5.00
14 Tomaz Razingar .40 1.00
15 Adam Svoboda .75 2.00
16 Michal Sykora .40 1.00

2003-04 Czech Stadion

These cards were issued as part of a multi-sport set by a Czech athletic magazine.

601 Scott Stevens .75 2.00
603 Patrik Elias .75 2.00
604 Jeff Friesen .40 1.00
605 Grant Marshall .40 1.00
606 Jamie Langenbrunner .40 1.00
607 Martin Brodeur 4.00 10.00
608 Scott Niedermayer .40 1.00
609 Mike Rupp .40 1.00
610 Ruslan Salei .40 1.00
611 Guy Lafleur 1.50 4.00
612 Petr Sykora .40 1.00
613 Steve Rucchin .40 1.00
614 Jean-Sebastien Giguere 1.25 3.00
615 Adam Oates .40 1.00
616 Paul Kariya 1.50 4.00
617 Steve Thomas .40 1.00
618 Rob Niedermayer .40 1.00
622 Vladimir Zabrodsky .40 1.00
637 Vsevolod Bobrov .40 1.00
638 Vlastimil Bubnik .40 1.00
639 Leif Holmqvist .40 1.00
640 Vladimir Dzurilla .75 2.00
641 Anatoli Firsov .40 1.00
642 Josef Golonka .40 1.00
643 Jiri Holecek .40 1.00
644 Jaroslav Holik .40 1.00
645 Jiri Holik .40 1.00
646 Bobby Hull 2.00 5.00
647 Alexander Yakushev .75 2.00
648 Sven Tumba Johansson .40 1.00
649 Alexander Maltsev .75 2.00
650 Vaclav Nedomansky .40 1.00
651 Alexander Ragulin .75 2.00
652 Maurice Richard 2.00 5.00
653 Vladimir Martinek .40 1.00
654 Frantisek Pospisil .40 1.00

2004 Czech World Championship Postcards

This series was issued to commemorate the 2004 World Championships, which were held in Prague and Ostrava, Czech Republic. They are postcard sized and unnumbered.

COMPLETE SET (24) 10.00 25.00
1 Josef Beranek .40 1.00
2 Roman Cechmanek .60 1.50
3 Jiri Dopita .40 1.00
4 Radek Dvorak .40 1.00
5 Radek Hamr .40 1.00
6 Roman Hamrlik .40 1.00
7 Jan Hejda .40 1.00
8 Jan Hlavac .40 1.00
9 Jaroslav Hlinka .40 1.00
10 Jaromir Jagr 2.00 5.00
11 Frantisek Kaberle .40 1.00
12 Milan Kraft .40 1.00
13 Jan Novak .40 1.00
14 Vaclav Prospal .40 1.00
15 Petr Prucha 1.50 4.00
16 Martin Rucinsky .40 1.00
17 Dusan Salficky .60 1.50
18 Jiri Slegr .40 1.00
19 Jaroslav Spacek .40 1.00
20 Martin Straka .40 1.00
21 Michal Sup .40 1.00
22 Tomas Vokoun 1.50 4.00
23 David Vyborny .60 1.50

2004-05 Czech HC Plzen Postcards

This postcard issue features members of HC Plzen, one of the top teams in the Czech Extraliga. The set is noteworthy for the inclusion of several NHLers who joined the team during the 2004-05 lockout.

COMPLETE SET (23) 10.00 20.00
1 Martin Adamsky .40 1.00
2 Dusan Andrasovsky .40 1.00
3 Mario Cartelli .40 1.00
4 Martin Cibak .60 1.50
5 Tomas Duba .40 1.00
6 Michal Duras .40 1.00
7 Robert Jindrich .60 1.50
8 Jaroslav Kracik .40 1.00
9 Jaroslav Kudrna .40 1.00
10 Radek Matejovsky .40 1.00
11 Frank Mrazek .40 1.00
12 Milan Nedoma .40 1.00
13 Martin Paroulek .40 1.00
14 Rudolf Pejchar .40 1.00
15 David Pospisil .40 1.00
16 Jaroslav Spacek .40 1.00
17 Pavel Srek .40 1.00
18 Josef Straka .40 1.00
19 Martin Straka .60 1.50
20 Michal Straka .40 1.00
21 Pavel Trnka .40 1.00
22 Martin Vyborny .40 1.00
23 Jan Vytisk .40 1.00

2004-05 Czech HC Slavia Praha Postcards

This postcard issue features HC Slavia Praha from the Czech Extraliga. The set is noteworthy for the inclusion of several well-known NHL stars who played with the team during the 2004-05 lockout. but if you know of others, please contact us via email at hockeymag@beckett.com.

COMPLETE SET (22) 15.00 25.00
1 Milan Antos .40 1.00
2 Radek Duda .40 1.00
3 Petr Franek .40 1.00
4 Petr Kadlec .40 1.00
5 Tomas Kloucek .60 1.50
6 Zigmund Palffy 1.50 4.00
7 Vladimir Ruzicka .40 1.00
8 Jozef Stumpel .60 1.50
9 Radek Sup .40 1.00
10 Josef Vasicek .60 1.50
11 Tomas Vlasak .40 1.00
12 Team Card .60 1.50
13 Josef Beranek .40 1.00
14 Jan Novak .40 1.00
15 Pavel Kolarik .40 1.00
16 David Hruska .40 1.00
17 Michal Sup .40 1.00
18 Jaroslav Spacek .40 1.00
19 Dominik Granak .40 1.00
20 Lukas Havel .40 1.00
21 Zdenek Smid .40 1.00
22 Tomas Zizka .40 1.00

2004-05 Czech HC Sparta Praha Postcards

This postcard issue features Sparta Praha, a top team in the Czech Extraliga. It features a number of well-known NHLers who ventured overseas during the lockout of 2004-05.

COMPLETE SET (24) 15.00 30.00
1 Petr Briza .75 2.00
2 Michal Bros .40 1.00
3 Martin Chabada .40 1.00
4 Michal Dobron .40 1.00
5 Michal Dragoun .40 1.00
6 Jan Hanzlik .40 1.00
7 Jan Hlavac .75 2.00
8 Pavel Kasparik .40 1.00
9 Jindrich Kotrla .40 1.00
10 Ondrej Kratena .40 1.00
11 Jan Marek .40 1.00
12 Petr Nedved .75 2.00
13 Tomas Netik .40 1.00
14 Rostislav Olesz 1.25 3.00
15 Karel Pilar .75 2.00
16 Tomas Popperle .40 1.00
17 Libor Prochazka .40 1.00
18 Jozef Reznicek .40 1.00
19 Martin Richter .40 1.00
20 Robert Schnabel .40 1.00
21 Jakub Sindel .40 1.00
22 Michal Sivek .75 2.00
23 Petr Ton .40 1.00
24 David Vyborny .75 2.00

2004-05 Czech NHL ELH Postcards

This series of 16 postcards features NHL players who spent all or part of the 2004-05 season in the Czech Extraliga. The cards feature full-colour photos on the fronts showing the players in their Czech sweaters. The cards are unnumbered and listed below alphabetically.

COMPLETE SET (16) 15.00 30.00
1 Jan Bulis .75 2.00
2 Petr Cajanek .75 2.00
3 Roman Hamrlik .75 2.00
4 Milan Hejduk 1.50 4.00
5 Ales Hemsky 1.50 4.00
6 Jan Hlavac .75 2.00
7 Jaromir Jagr 2.00 5.00
8 Ales Kotalik .75 2.00
9 Petr Nedved .75 2.00
10 Karel Pilar .75 2.00
11 Robert Reichel .75 2.00
12 Martin Rucinsky .75 2.00
13 Jiri Slegr .75 2.00
14 Jaroslav Spacek .75 2.00
15 Martin Straka .75 2.00
16 David Vyborny .75 2.00

2004-05 Czech OFS

COMPLETE SET (372) 40.00 100.00
1 Petr Altrichter .08 .20
2 Oldrich Bakus .08 .20
3 Petr Buzek .08 .20
4 Tomas Cachotsky .08 .20
5 Dusan Devecka .08 .20
6 Jiri Dobrovolny .08 .20
7 Tomas Ficenc .08 .20
8 Marian Havel .08 .20
9 Roman Hlouch .08 .20
10 Lukas Hronek .08 .20
11 Jiri Jantovsky .08 .20
12 Petr Kuchyna .08 .20
13 Rostislav Malena .08 .20
14 Jaroslav Mares .08 .20
15 Ales Padelek .08 .20
16 Vojtech Polak .08 .20
17 Petr Puncochar .08 .20
18 Ladislav Rytnauer .08 .20
19 Jaroslav Suchan .08 .20
20 Petr Vala .08 .20
21 Rudolf Vercik .08 .20
22 Martin Zajac .08 .20
23 Richard Bauer .08 .20
24 Michal Dvorak .08 .20
25 Martin Hlavacka .08 .20
26 Martin Kivon .08 .20
27 Jan Kostal .08 .20
28 Petr Kumstat .08 .20
29 Edgars Masalskis .08 .20
30 Petr Mika .08 .20
31 Lukas Pech .08 .20
32 Milan Prochazka .08 .20
33 Frantisek Ptacek .08 .20
34 Vaclav Skuhravy .08 .20
35 Zdenek Smid .08 .20
36 Dmitrij Suur .08 .20
37 Robert Tomik .08 .20
38 Jiri Polak .08 .20
39 Lukas Krajicek .40 1.00
40 Lukas Bednarik .08 .20
41 Jakub Kraus .08 .20
42 Jan Alinc .08 .20
43 Jan Lipiansky .08 .20
44 Lubomir Hurtaj .08 .20
45 Zdenek Kutlak .08 .20
46 Lukas Mensator .20 .50
47 Vitezslav Bilek .08 .20
48 Vratislav Cech .08 .20
49 Jakub Evan .08 .20
50 Martin Frolik .08 .20
51 Michael Frolik 2.00 5.00
52 Radek Gardon .08 .20
53 Miloslav Horava .08 .20
54 Petr Horava .08 .20
55 Tomas Horna .08 .20
56 Jaromir Jagr 2.00 5.00
57 Jiri Jelinek .08 .20
58 Tomas Kaberle .20 .50
59 Jaroslav Kalla .08 .20
60 Tomas Klimt .08 .20
61 Jakub Lev .08 .20
62 Zdenek Orct .20 .50
63 Pavel Patera .08 .20
64 Martin Prochazka .08 .20
65 Martin Sevc .08 .20
66 Jaroslav Spelda .08 .20
67 Josef Zajic .08 .20
68 Jan Holub .08 .20
69 Richard Jares .08 .20
70 Valdemar Jirus .08 .20
71 Ales Kotalik .60 1.50
72 Jiri Moravec .08 .20
73 Vaclav Nedorost .40 1.00
74 Vaclav Novak .08 .20
75 Jan Plodek .08 .20
76 Andrej Podkonicky .08 .20
77 Stanislav Prochazka .08 .20
78 Igor Rataj .08 .20
79 Patrik Rozsival .08 .20
80 Ladislav Smid ERC .75 2.00
81 Jan Tomajko .08 .20
82 Lubomir Vaic .20 .50
83 Radim Vrbata .40 1.00
84 Pavel Falta .08 .20
85 Leos Cermak .08 .20
86 Miroslav Duben .08 .20
87 Milan Hnilicka .40 1.00
88 Jiri Hanzlik .08 .20
89 David Balaze .08 .20
90 Frantisek Bombic .08 .20
91 Daniel Branda .08 .20
92 Jiri Gombar .08 .20
93 Lukas Havel .08 .20
94 Viktor Hubl .08 .20
95 Kamil Jarina .08 .20
96 Jan Kloboucek .08 .20
97 Vlastimil Kroupa .08 .20
98 Vojtech Kubincak .08 .20
99 Tomas Kurka .08 .20
100 Michal Marik .08 .20
101 Lukas Pozivil .08 .20
102 Robert Reichel .20 .50
103 Lukas Riha .08 .20
104 Martin Rucinsky .20 .50
105 Zbynek Sklenicka .08 .20
106 Martin Skoula .20 .50
107 Radim Skuhrovec .08 .20
108 Jiri Slegr .08 .20
109 Michal Travnicek .08 .20
110 Martin Tupa .08 .20
111 Tomas Blazek .08 .20
112 Jan Bulis .08 .20
113 Petr Caslava .08 .20
114 Tomas Divisek .20 .50
115 Jiri Dopita .20 .50
116 David Havir .08 .20
117 Milan Hejduk .75 2.00
118 Alexandr Hylak .08 .20
119 Jaroslav Kames .20 .50
120 Jan Kolar .08 .20
121 Petr Koukal .08 .20
122 Tomas Linhart .08 .20
123 Ladislav Lubina .08 .20
124 Michal Mikeska .08 .20
125 Petr Mudroch .08 .20
126 Andrej Novotny .08 .20
127 Tomas Pacal .08 .20
128 Petr Prucha .75 2.00
129 Tomaz Razingar .08 .20
130 Tomas Rolinek .08 .20
131 Jan Snopek .08 .20
132 Petr Sykora .40 1.00
133 Jan Lasak .75 2.00
134 Ales Hemsky 1.25 3.00
135 Michal Tvrdik .08 .20
136 Lubomir Korhon .08 .20
137 Martin Adamsky .08 .20
138 Dusan Andrasovsky .08 .20
139 Mario Cartelli .08 .20
140 Tomas Duba .08 .20
141 Michal Duraz .08 .20
142 Petr Havelka .08 .20
143 Robert Jindrich .20 .50
144 Josef Straka .08 .20
145 Jaroslav Kracik .08 .20
146 Milan Kraft .40 1.00
147 Martin Straka .40 1.00
148 Radek Matejovsky .08 .20
149 Michal Straka .08 .20
150 Milan Nedoma .08 .20
151 Rudolf Pejchar .08 .20
152 David Pospisil .08 .20
153 Adam Saffer .08 .20
154 Jaroslav Spacek .08 .20
155 Pavel Trnka .08 .20
156 Martin Vyborny .08 .20
157 Jan Vytisk .08 .20
158 Milan Antos .08 .20
159 Radek Dlouhy .08 .20
160 Radek Duda .08 .20
161 Petr Franek .08 .20
162 Dominik Granak .08 .20
163 David Hruska .08 .20
164 Petr Kadlec .08 .20
165 Tomas Kloucek .20 .50
166 Pavel Kolarik .08 .20
167 Milan Kopecky .08 .20
168 Ales Kratoska .08 .20
169 Frantisek Kucera .08 .20
170 Lukas Musil .08 .20
171 Jan Novak .08 .20
172 Zigmund Palffy .75 2.00
173 Jozef Stumpel .20 .50
174 Michal Sup .08 .20
175 Marek Tomica .08 .20
176 Josef Vasicek .20 .50
177 Michal Vondrka .08 .20
178 Boris Zabka .08 .20
179 Petr Jaros .08 .20
180 David Pojkar .08 .20
181 Patrik Martinec .08 .20
182 Vladimir Sobotka .08 .20
183 Petr Briza .20 .50
184 Michal Dobron .08 .20
185 Jan Hanzlik .08 .20
186 Jan Hlavac .20 .50
187 Martin Chabada .08 .20
188 Pavel Kasparik .08 .20
189 Jindrich Kotrla .08 .20
190 Jan Marek .08 .20
191 Petr Nedved .20 .50
192 Tomas Netik .08 .20
193 Rostislav Olesz 1.25 3.00
194 Karel Pilar .20 .50
195 Tomas Popperle .08 .20
196 Libor Prochazka .08 .20
197 Josef Reznicek .08 .20
198 Martin Richter .08 .20
199 Robert Schnabel .08 .20
200 Jakub Sindel .08 .20
201 Michal Sivek .08 .20
202 Petr Ton .08 .20
203 David Vyborny .20 .50
204 Radek Bonk .20 .50
205 Richard Bordowski .08 .20
206 Martin Cakajik .08 .20
207 Miroslav Durak .08 .20
208 Jiri Hasek .08 .20
209 Pavel Janku .08 .20
210 Vladislav Koutsky .08 .20
211 Richard Kral .08 .20
212 Vlastimil Lakosil .08 .20
213 Jiri Malinsky .08 .20
214 Rostislav Martynek .08 .20
215 Marek Melenovsky .08 .20
216 Zdenek Pavelek .08 .20
217 Jan Peterek .08 .20
218 Vaclav Pletka .20 .50
219 Peter Podhradsky .08 .20
220 Jiri Polansky .08 .20
221 Michal Rozsival .20 .50
222 Zdenek Skorepa .08 .20
223 Filip Stefanka .08 .20
224 Jiri Burger .08 .20
225 Marek Cernosek .08 .20
226 Petr Hubacek .08 .20
227 Stanislav Hudec .08 .20
228 Jakub Hulva .08 .20
229 Zbynek Irgl .08 .20
230 Martin Krayzel .08 .20
231 Lukas Krenzelok .08 .20
232 Pavel Kumstat .08 .20
233 Marek Malik .08 .20
234 David Moravec .08 .20
235 Ivan Padelek .08 .20
236 Radek Philipp .08 .20
237 Marek Pinc .08 .20
238 Martin Prusek .40 1.00
239 Patrik Rimmel .08 .20
240 Martin Tomasek .08 .20
241 Filip Turek .08 .20
242 Vaclav Varada .20 .50

Card	Low	High
243 Kamil Brabenec	.08	.20
244 Roman Cechmanek	.20	.50
245 Tomas Demel	.08	.20
246 Marek Dubec	.08	.20
247 Tomas Frolo	.08	.20
248 Ladislav Gengel	.08	.20
249 Josef Hrabal	.08	.20
250 Alexej Jaskin	.08	.20
251 Rostislav Klesla	.40	1.00
252 Robin Kovar	.08	.20
253 Pavel Kowalczyk	.08	.20
254 Radek Masny	.08	.20
255 Ondrej Nemec	.08	.20
256 Libor Pavlis	.08	.20
257 Lukas Plsek	.08	.20
258 Branko Radivojevic	.40	1.00
259 Pavel Selingr	.08	.20
260 Roman Stantien	.08	.20
261 Tomas Vak	.08	.20
262 Martin Vasut	.08	.20
263 Rostislav Vlach	.08	.20
264 Marek Zadina	.08	.20
265 Robert Horak	.08	.20
266 Radovan Somik	.08	.20
267 Jan Koroptvicka	.08	.20
268 Ondrej Vesely	.08	.20
269 Martin Altrichter	.08	.20
270 Martin Ambruz	.08	.20
271 Jaroslav Balastik	.40	1.00
272 Peter Barinka	.20	.50
273 Miroslav Blatak	.08	.20
274 Petr Cajanek	.20	.50
275 Martin Cech	.08	.20
276 Martin Erat	.40	1.00
277 Lukas Galvas	.08	.20
278 Roman Hamrlik	.20	.50
279 Martin Jenacek	.08	.20
280 Miroslav Kovacik	.08	.20
281 Jaroslav Kristek	.08	.20
282 Tomas Kudelka	.08	.20
283 Petr Leska	.08	.20
284 Petr Mokrejs	.08	.20
285 Igor Murin	.08	.20
286 David Nosek	.08	.20
287 Miroslav Okal	.08	.20
288 Radim Tesarik	.08	.20
289 Martin Vosatko	.08	.20
290 Martin Zahorovsky	.08	.20
291 Pavel Zubicek	.08	.20
292 Vaclav Benak	.08	.20
293 Radim Bicanek	.08	.20
294 Roman Erat	.08	.20
295 Radek Haman	.08	.20
296 Tomas Kucharcik	.08	.20
297 Branislav Kvetan	.08	.20
298 Zdenek Ondrej	.08	.20
299 Jan Pardavy	.08	.20
300 Peter Pucher	.08	.20
301 Ivan Rachunek	.08	.20
302 Milan Toman	.08	.20
303 Marek Vorel	.08	.20
304 Marek Uram	.08	.20
305 Karel Plasek	.08	.20
306 Ales Kretinsky	.08	.20
307 Miroslav Barus	.08	.20
308 David Ludvik	.08	.20
309 Robert Slavik	.08	.20
310 Pavel Mojzis	.08	.20
311 Tomas Vokoun	1.25	3.00
312 Patrik Elias	.40	1.00
313 Martin Havlat	.75	2.00
314 David Vsetecka	.08	.20
315 Josef Vitek	.08	.20
316 Jiri Hunkes	.08	.20
317 Radim Kucharczyk	.08	.20
318 Branislav Mezei	.20	.50
319 Karel Rachunek	.20	.50
320 Ivan Majesky	.20	.50
321 David Vrbata	.08	.20
322 Jaroslav Kasik	.08	.20
323 Ondrej Malinsky	.08	.20
324 Michal Dragoun	.08	.20
325 Michal Bros	.08	.20
326 Ondrej Kratena	.08	.20
327 Petr Kasik	.08	.20
328 Jiri Zeman	.08	.20
329 Miroslav Kopriva	.08	.20
330 Robert Kysela	.08	.20
331 Frantisek Kaberle	.08	.20
332 Jan Hrdina	.20	.50
333 Jiri Jelinek	.08	.20
334 Milan Hluchy	.08	.20
335 Jiri Stejskal	.08	.20
336 Jiri Fischer	.20	.50
337 Angel Krstev	.08	.20
338 Tomas Klimenta	.08	.20
339 Lukas Pabiska	.08	.20
340 Petr Vampola	.08	.20
341 Jan Visek	.08	.20
342 Jaroslav Modry	.20	.50
343 Martin Strba	.08	.20
344 David Stich	.08	.20
345 Jakub Korinek	.08	.20
346 Martin Paroulek	.08	.20
347 Frantisek Mrazek	.08	.20
348 Martin Cibak	.20	.50
349 David Moravec	.08	.20
350 Lukas Pulpan	.08	.20
351 Josef Beranek	.08	.20
352 Tomas Vlasak	.08	.20
353 Tomas Zizka	.08	.20
354 Vladimir Vujtek	.08	.20
355 Daniel Seman	.08	.20
356 Roman Simicek	.08	.20
357 Juraj Stefanka	.08	.20
358 Tomas Dolana	.08	.20
359 Pavel Vostrak	.08	.20
360 Radovan Biegl	.20	.50
361 Karol Sloboda	.08	.20
362 Vladimir Gyna	.08	.20
363 Petr Gregorek	.08	.20
364 Jiri Hudler	1.50	4.00
365 Pavel Kubina	.40	1.00
366 Ludek Krayzel	.08	.20
367 Martin Hamrlik	.08	.20
368 Michal Hrazdira	.08	.20
369 Connor Dunlop	.40	1.00
370 Miroslav Hanuljak	.08	.20
371 Miroslav Zalesak	.40	1.00
372 Radovan Biegl	.20	.50
373 Martin Vojtek	.08	.20
374 TomÃ¡Å¡ Zboril	.08	.20
375 TomÃ¡Å¡ Kloucek	.20	.50
376 TomÃ¡Å¡ PospÃÅ¡il	.20	.50
377 Jaroslav Kudrna	.20	.50
378 TomÃ¡Å¡ Harant	.20	.50
379 Milan Kraft	.20	.50
380 Radim Kucharczyk	.08	.20
381 Roman MÃ¡lek	.20	.50
382 Andrej Nedorost	.20	.50
383 Vojtech PolÃ¡k	.30	.75
384 FrantiÅ¡ek MrÃ¡zek	.08	.20
385 Jan Caloun	.08	.20
386 Radek Fiala	.08	.20
387 Martin Heinisch	.08	.20
388 Peter Jansky	.08	.20
389 Jindrich Kotrla	.08	.20
390 Jaroslav Å pacek	.08	.20
391 Matej Badiura	.08	.20
392 Å tepÃ¡n Hrebejk	.08	.20
393 Radek HubÃ¡cek	.08	.20
394 Radek HubÃ¡cek	.08	.20
395 MojmÃr Musil	.08	.20
396 Robert Najdek	.08	.20
397 Michal NedbÃ¡lek	.08	.20
398 Michal Å afarÃk	.08	.20
399 Radek Bonk	.20	.50
400 Ondrej VeselÃ½	.08	.20
401 Martin Ambruz	.08	.20
402 JirÃ Beroun	.08	.20
403 Martin CakajÃk	.08	.20
404 Petr KuboÅ¡	.08	.20
405 Milan MikulÃk	.08	.20
406 Roman Nemecek	.08	.20
407 Ondrej Å mach	.08	.20
408 Josef Straka	.08	.20
409 RÃ³bert Filc	.08	.20
410 Pavel MojzÃÅ¡	.08	.20
411 Jan Peterek	.08	.20
412 Radek ProchÃ¡zka	.08	.20
NNO Frantisek Kaberle CL	.08	.20

2004-05 Czech OFS Assist Leaders

Card	Low	High
COMPLETE SET (15)	15.00	35.00
1 Josef Beranek	1.25	3.00
2 Petr Leska	1.25	3.00
3 Peter Pucher	1.25	3.00
4 Josef Straka	1.25	3.00
5 Jan Marek	1.25	3.00
6 Zdenek Pavelek	1.25	3.00
7 Jiri Dopita	1.25	3.00
8 Jiri Burger	1.25	3.00
9 Martin Hamrlik	1.25	3.00
10 Michal Bros	1.25	3.00
11 Pavel Janku	1.25	3.00
12 Marek Uram	1.25	3.00
13 Tomas Divisek	1.25	3.00
14 Dusan Andrasovsky	1.25	3.00
15 Petr Sykora	1.25	3.00

2004-05 Czech OFS Checklist Cards

Card	Low	High
COMPLETE SET	10.00	25.00
1 Petr Buzek	.75	2.00
2 Frantisek Ptacek	.75	2.00
3 Jaromir Jagr	2.00	5.00
4 Patrik Rozsival	.75	2.00
5 Martin Skoula	.75	2.00
6 Milan Hejduk	1.25	3.00
7 Jaroslav Spacek	.75	2.00
8 Zigmund Palffy	1.25	3.00
9 Petr Nedved	.75	2.00
10 Radek Bonk	.75	2.00
11 David Moravec	.75	2.00
12 Rostislav Klesla	.75	2.00
13 Petr Cajanek	.75	2.00
14 Patrik Elias	1.25	3.00

2004-05 Czech OFS Czech/Slovak

Card	Low	High
COMPLETE SET (46)	20.00	40.00
1 Jaroslav Balastik	.75	2.00
2 Jiri Burger	.40	1.00
3 Tomas Demel	.40	1.00
4 Michal Dobron	.40	1.00
5 Jiri Dopita	.40	1.00
6 Tomas Duba	.40	1.00
7 Martin Chabada	.40	1.00
8 Waldemar Jirus	.40	1.00
9 Jiri Malinsky	.40	1.00
10 Jan Novak	.40	1.00
11 Frantisek Ptacek	.40	1.00
12 Peter Pucher	.40	1.00
13 Petr Sailer	.40	1.00
14 Jan Srdinko	.40	1.00
15 Josef Straka	.40	1.00
16 Michal Sup	.40	1.00
17 Adam Svoboda	.75	2.00
18 Michal Sykora	.40	1.00
19 Petr Sykora	.40	1.00
20 Michal Travnicek	.40	1.00
21 Marek Uram	.40	1.00
22 Libor Zabransky	.40	1.00
23 Daniel Babka	.40	1.00
24 Martin Bartek	.40	1.00
25 Zdeno Ciger	.40	1.00
26 Peter Fabus	.40	1.00
27 Miroslav Hala	.40	1.00
28 Juraj Halaj	.40	1.00
29 Richard Hartmann	.40	1.00
30 Jiri Hes	.40	1.00
31 Martin Ivicic	.40	1.00
32 Juraj Kledrowetz	.40	1.00
33 Jaroslav Kmit	.40	1.00
34 Arne Krotak	.40	1.00
35 Roman Kukumberg	.40	1.00
36 Igor Majesky	.40	1.00
37 Petr Pavlas	.40	1.00
38 Slavomir Pavlicko	.40	1.00
39 Pavol Rybar	.40	1.00
40 Michal Segla	.40	1.00
41 Richard Sechny	.40	1.00
42 Marcel Simurda	.40	1.00
43 Tomas Starosta	.40	1.00
44 Rastislav Stork	.40	1.00
45 Adam Svoboda CL	.75	2.00
46 Pavol Rybar CL	.40	1.00

2004-05 Czech OFS Defence Points

Card	Low	High
COMPLETE SET (15)	15.00	25.00
1 Martin Hamrlik	1.00	2.50
2 David Havir	1.00	2.50
3 Jan Novak	1.00	2.50
4 Stanislav Jasecko	1.00	2.50
5 Michal Sykora	1.00	2.50
6 Josef Reznicek	1.00	2.50
7 Frantisek Ptacek	1.00	2.50
8 Alexej Jaskin	1.00	2.50
9 Valdemar Jirus	1.00	2.50
10 Petr Kadlec	1.00	2.50
11 Jiri Malinsky	1.00	2.50
12 Patrik Luza	1.00	2.50
13 Radim Tesarik	1.00	2.50
14 Pavel Kowalczyk	1.00	2.50
15 Petr Jancarik	1.00	2.50

2004-05 Czech OFS Goals-Against Leaders

Card	Low	High
COMPLETE SET (16)	25.00	60.00
1 Igor Murin	2.00	5.00
2 Adam Svoboda	2.50	6.00
3 Petr Briza	2.00	5.00
4 Jiri Trvaj	2.00	5.00
5 Roman Malek	2.00	5.00
6 Petr Franek	2.00	5.00
7 Radovan Biegl	2.00	5.00
8 Tomas Duba	2.00	5.00
9 Zdenek Orct	2.00	5.00
10 Lukas Hronek	2.00	5.00
11 Martin Vojtek	2.00	5.00
12 Martin Altrichter	2.00	5.00
13 Oldrich Svoboda	2.00	5.00
14 Michal Marik	2.00	5.00
15 Marek Pinc	2.00	5.00
NNO Altrichter Murin CL	2.00	5.00

2004-05 Czech OFS Goals Leaders

Card	Low	High
COMPLETE SET (15)	12.00	30.00
1 Jaroslav Balastik	1.50	4.00
2 Michal Sup	1.00	2.50
3 Marek Uram	1.00	2.50
4 Josef Straka	1.00	2.50
5 Jiri Burger	1.00	2.50
6 Petr Sykora	1.00	2.50
7 Marek Melenovsky	1.00	2.50
8 Jan Marek	1.00	2.50
9 Lukas Havel	1.00	2.50
10 Jiri Dopita	1.00	2.50
11 Tomas Divisek	1.00	2.50
12 Peter Barinka	1.00	2.50
13 Zbynek Irgl	1.00	2.50
14 David Hruska	1.00	2.50
15 Ondrej Vesely	1.00	2.50

2004-05 Czech OFS Jaromir Jagr

Card	Low	High
COMPLETE SET (6)	20.00	50.00
JO1 Jaromir Jagr	4.00	10.00
JO2 Jaromir Jagr	4.00	10.00
JO3 Jaromir Jagr	4.00	10.00
JO4 Jaromir Jagr	4.00	10.00
JO5 Jaromir Jagr	4.00	10.00
JO6 Jaromir Jagr	4.00	10.00

2004-05 Czech OFS Points Leaders

Card	Low	High
COMPLETE SET (15)	20.00	40.00
1 Josef Beranek	1.25	3.00
2 Petr Leska	1.25	3.00
3 Josef Straka	1.25	3.00
4 Peter Pucher	1.25	3.00
5 Jan Marek	1.25	3.00
6 Marek Uram	1.25	3.00
7 Jiri Burger	1.25	3.00
8 Jiri Dopita	1.25	3.00
9 Jaroslav Balastik	1.25	3.00
10 Petr Sykora	1.25	3.00
11 Michal Sup	1.25	3.00
12 Tomas Divisek	1.25	3.00
13 Marek Melenovsky	1.25	3.00
14 Zdenek Pavelek	1.25	3.00
15 Michal Bros	1.25	3.00

2004-05 Czech OFS Save Percentage Leaders

Card	Low	High
COMPLETE SET (15)	25.00	60.00
1 Igor Murin	2.00	5.00
2 Petr Briza	2.00	5.00
3 Zdenek Orct	2.00	5.00
4 Petr Franek	2.00	5.00
5 Roman Malek	2.00	5.00
6 Jiri Trvaj	2.00	5.00
7 Adam Svoboda	2.50	6.00
8 Radovan Biegl	2.00	5.00
9 Martin Vojtek	2.00	5.00
10 Tomas Duba	2.00	5.00
11 Martin Altrichter	2.00	5.00
12 Marek Pinc	2.00	5.00
13 Lukas Hronek	2.00	5.00
14 Libor Barta	2.00	5.00
15 Michal Marik	2.00	5.00

2004-05 Czech OFS Stars

Card	Low	High
COMPLETE SET (51)	30.00	60.00
1 Tomas Kaberle	.75	2.00
2 Jaromir Jagr	4.00	10.00
3 Radim Vrbata	1.25	3.00
4 Vaclav Nedorost	.75	2.00
5 Tomas Kurka	.40	1.00
6 Martin Rucinsky	.40	1.00
7 Martin Skoula	.40	1.00
8 Robert Reichel	.40	1.00
9 Jiri Slegr	.40	1.00
10 Jan Bulis	.40	1.00
11 Milan Hejduk	1.50	4.00
12 Ales Hemsky	2.00	5.00
13 Jiri Dopita	.40	1.00
14 Jan Lasak	.75	2.00
15 Martin Straka	.40	1.00
16 Jaroslav Spacek	.40	1.00
17 Milan Kraft	.75	2.00
18 Zigmund Palffy	1.25	3.00
19 Josef Stumpel	.40	1.00
20 Josef Vasicek	.40	1.00
21 Tomas Kloucek	.40	1.00
22 Radek Duda	.40	1.00
23 Jan Hlavac	.40	1.00
24 Karel Pilar	.40	1.00
25 David Vyborny	.75	2.00
26 Petr Nedved	.40	1.00
27 Michal Rozsival	.40	1.00
28 Radek Bonk	.40	1.00
29 Branislav Mezei	.40	1.00
30 Martin Prusek	.75	2.00
31 Marek Malik	.40	1.00
32 Pavel Kubina	.40	1.00
33 Vaclav Varada	.40	1.00
34 Rostislav Klesla	.40	1.00
35 Roman Cechmanek	.40	1.00
36 Branko Radivojevic	.40	1.00
37 Radovan Somik	.40	1.00
38 Martin Erat	.40	1.00
39 Roman Hamrlik	.40	1.00
40 Petr Cajanek	.40	1.00
41 Patrik Elias	.75	2.00
42 Martin Havlat	1.50	4.00
43 Karel Rachunek	.40	1.00
44 Tomas Vokoun	2.00	5.00
45 Petr Buzek	.40	1.00
46 David Moravec	.40	1.00
47 Martin Hlavacka	.40	1.00
48 Ales Kotalik	1.25	3.00
49 Robert Schnabel	.40	1.00
50 Michal Sivek	.40	1.00
51 Jaromir Jagr CL	4.00	10.00

2004-05 Czech OFS Stars II

Card	Low	High
COMPLETE SET (16)	20.00	50.00
1 Frantisek Kaberle	1.50	4.00
2 Jan Hrdina	1.50	4.00
3 Ivan Majesky	1.50	4.00
4 Jiri Hudler	6.00	15.00
5 Connor Dunlop	1.50	4.00
6 Vladimir Vujtek	1.50	4.00
7 Josef Beranek	1.50	4.00
8 Tomas Vlasak	1.50	4.00
9 Roman MÃ¡lek	1.50	4.00
10 Jan Caloun	1.50	4.00
11 JirÃ Fischer	2.00	5.00
12 Jaroslav ModrÃ½	1.50	4.00
13 Roman Å imÃcek	1.50	4.00
14 TomÃ¡Å¡ Harant	1.50	4.00
15 Martin HamrlÃk	1.50	4.00
16 Pavel Kubina CL	1.50	4.00

2004-05 Czech OFS Team Cards

Card	Low	High
COMPLETE SET (14)	6.00	15.00
1 Jaroslav Suchan	.40	1.00
2 Zdenek Smid	.40	1.00
3 Zdenek Orct	.75	2.00
4 Milan Hnilicka	.75	2.00
5 Michal Marik	.40	1.00
6 Jan Lasak	1.25	3.00
7 Tomas Duba	.40	1.00
8 Petr Franek	.40	1.00
9 Petr Briza	.75	2.00
10 Vlastimil Lakosil	.40	1.00
11 Martin Prusek	.75	2.00
12 Roman Cechmanek	.75	2.00
13 Martin Altrichter	.40	1.00
14 Robert Slavik	.40	1.00

2005 Czech World Champions Postcards

Standard postcard-sized issue was released to commemorate the Czech Republic's victory at the 2005 WC. The cards are unnumbered.

Card	Low	High
COMPLETE SET (23)	15.00	40.00
1 Frantisek Kaberle	.40	1.00
2 Jiri Slegr	.40	1.00
3 David Vyborny	.40	1.00
4 Jiri Fischer	.40	1.00
5 Jan Hlavac	.40	1.00
6 Josef Vasicek	.40	1.00
7 Vaclav Prospal	.40	1.00
8 Vaclav Varada	.40	1.00
9 Pavel Kubina	.40	1.00
10 Radek Dvorak	.40	1.00
11 Ales Hemsky	1.50	4.00
12 Radim Vrbata	.75	2.00
13 Martin Rucinsky	.40	1.00
14 Martin Straka	.40	1.00
15 Jaromir Jagr	4.00	10.00
16 Marek Zidlicky	.40	1.00
17 Milan Hnilicka	.75	2.00
18 Petr Sykora	.40	1.00
19 Tomas Kaberle	.40	1.00
20 Petr Cajanek	.40	1.00
21 Tomas Vokoun	2.00	5.00
22 Jaroslav Spacek	.40	1.00
23 Jan Hejda	.40	1.00

2005-06 Czech HC Ceski Budejovice

Card	Low	High
COMPLETE SET (16)	8.00	20.00
1 Kamil Brabenec	.60	1.50
2 Petr Gregorek	.60	1.50
3 Tomas Harant	.60	1.50
4 Stepan Hrebejk	.60	1.50
5 Viktor Hubl	.60	1.50
6 Michal Hudec	.60	1.50
7 Milan Kopecky	.60	1.50
8 Jindrich Kotrla	.60	1.50
9 Ales Kratoska	.60	1.50
10 Zdenek Kutlak	.60	1.50
11 Jan Mucha	.60	1.50
12 Marek Posmyk	.60	1.50
13 Petr Sailer	.60	1.50
14 Roman Turek	.75	2.00
15 Tomas Vak	.60	1.50
16 Rene Vydareny	.60	1.50

2005-06 Czech HC Hame Zlin

Card	Low	High
COMPLETE SET (16)	8.00	20.00
1 Martin Altrichter	.60	1.50
2 Petr Barinka	.60	1.50
3 Jan Benda	.60	1.50
4 Miroslav Blatak	.60	1.50
5 Lukas Galvas	.60	1.50
6 Martin Hamrlik	.60	1.50
7 Richard Kral	.60	1.50
8 Petr Leska	.60	1.50
9 Marek Melenovsky	.60	1.50
10 Petr Mokrejs	.60	1.50
11 Igor Murin	.60	1.50
12 David Nosek	.60	1.50
13 Miroslav Okal	.60	1.50
14 Ivan Rachunek	.60	1.50
15 Michal Travnicek	.60	1.50
16 Martin Zahorovsky	.60	1.50

2005-06 Czech HC Karlovy Vary

Card	Low	High
COMPLETE SET (16)	8.00	20.00
1 Jan Alinc	.60	1.50
2 Roman Cechmanek	.75	2.00
3 Miroslav Duben	.60	1.50
4 Michal Dvorak	.60	1.50
5 Lubomir Hurtaj	.60	1.50
6 Jan Kostal	.60	1.50
7 Lukas Krajicek	.60	1.50
8 Petr Kumstat	.60	1.50
9 Lukas Mensator	.60	1.50
10 Andrej Nedorost	.60	1.50
11 Ondrej Nemec	.60	1.50
12 Lukas Pech	.60	1.50
13 Frantisek Ptacek	.60	1.50
14 Josef Reznicek	.60	1.50
15 Vaclav Skuhravy	.60	1.50
16 Libor Ustrnul	.60	1.50

2005-06 Czech HC Kladno

Card	Low	High
COMPLETE SET (15)	10.00	25.00
1 Jan Besser	.60	1.50
2 Martin Frolik	.60	1.50
3 Michael Frolik	2.00	5.00
4 Radek Gardon	.60	1.50
5 Tomas Horna	.60	1.50
6 Ivan Huml	1.00	2.50
7 Jaroslav Kalla	.60	1.50
8 Jakub Lev	.60	1.50
9 Zdenek Orct	.75	2.00
10 Libor Prochazka	.60	1.50
11 Martin Prochazka	.60	1.50
12 Jaroslav Spelda	.60	1.50
13 Ladislav Vlcek	.60	1.50
14 Josef Zajic	.60	1.50
15 Jiri Zeman	.60	1.50

2005-06 Czech HC Liberec

Card	Low	High
COMPLETE SET (16)	8.00	20.00
1 Leos Cermak	.60	1.50
2 Pavel Falta	.60	1.50
3 Jiri Hanzlik	.60	1.50
4 Milan Hnilicka	.75	2.00
5 Valdemar Jirus	.60	1.50
6 Angel Krstev	.60	1.50
7 Lukas Pabiska	.60	1.50
8 Andrej Podkonicky	.60	1.50
9 Stanislav Prochazka	.60	1.50
10 Igor Rataj	.60	1.50
11 Martin Richtr	.60	1.50
12 Patrik Rozsival	.60	1.50
13 Martin Rygl	.60	1.50
14 Jan Tomajko	.60	1.50
15 Lubomir Vaic	.60	1.50
16 Petr Vampola	.60	1.50

2005-06 Czech HC Pardubice

Card	Low	High
COMPLETE SET (16)	8.00	20.00
1 Tomas Blazek	.60	1.50
2 Jan Caloun	.60	1.50
3 Petr Caslava	.60	1.50
4 David Havir	.60	1.50
5 Robert Kantor	.60	1.50
6 Jan Kolar	.60	1.50
7 Lubomir Korhon	.60	1.50
8 Jan Lasak	1.25	3.00
9 Ladislav Lubina	.60	1.50
10 Michal Mikeska	.60	1.50
11 Frantisek Mrazek	.60	1.50
12 Petr Mudroch	.75	2.00
13 Andrej Novotny	.75	2.00
14 Tomas Rolinek	.60	1.50
15 Jan Snopek	.60	1.50
16 Michal Tvrdik	.60	1.50

2005-06 Czech HC Plzen

Card	Low	High
COMPLETE SET (16)	8.00	20.00
1 Martin Adamsky	.60	1.50
2 Mario Cartelli	.60	1.50
3 Michal Duras	.60	1.50
4 Petr Jez	.60	1.50
5 Robert Jindrich	.60	1.50
6 Jaroslav Kracik	.60	1.50
7 Roman Malek	.60	1.50
8 Radek Matejovsky	.60	1.50
9 David Moravec	.60	1.50
10 Martin Stepanek	.60	1.50
11 Josef Straka	.60	1.50
12 Michal Straka	.60	1.50
13 Pavel Trnka	.60	1.50
14 Matej Trojovsky	.60	1.50
15 Roman Tvrdon	.60	1.50
16 Marek Vorel	.60	1.50

2005-06 Czech HC Slavia Praha

Card	Low	High
COMPLETE SET (16)	8.00	20.00
1 Jaroslav Bednar	.60	1.50
2 Josef Beranek	.60	1.50
3 Roman Cervenka	.60	2.00
4 Radek Dlouhy	.60	1.50
5 Jiri Drtina	.60	1.50
6 Radek Duda	.60	1.50
7 Petr Franek	.60	1.50
8 David Hruska	.60	1.50
9 Petr Kadlec	.60	1.50
10 Pavel Kolarik	.60	1.50
11 Jan Novak	.60	1.50
12 Michal Sup	.60	1.50
13 Tomas Vlasak	.60	1.50
14 Michal Vondrka	.60	1.50
15 Boris Zabka	.60	1.50
16 Tomas Zizka	.60	1.50

2005-06 Czech HC Sparta Praha

Card	Low	High
COMPLETE SET (16)	8.00	20.00
1 Petr Briza	1.25	3.00
2 Marek Cernosek	.60	1.50
3 Michal Dobron	.60	1.50
4 Jan Hanzlik	.60	1.50
5 Martin Hlavacka	.60	1.50
6 Martin Chabada	.60	1.50
7 Ondrej Kratena	.60	1.50
8 Jan Marek	.60	1.50
9 Jakub Sindel	.60	1.50
10 Michal Sivek	.75	2.00
11 Martin Spanhel	.75	2.00
12 Josef Straka	.60	1.50
13 Milan Toman	.60	1.50
14 Petr Ton	.60	1.50
15 Roman Vopat	.60	1.50
16 Jiri Vykoukal	.60	1.50

2005-06 Czech HC Trinec

Card	Low	High
COMPLETE SET (15)	8.00	20.00
1 Richard Bordowski	.60	1.50
2 Lukas Danecek	.60	1.50
3 Jiri Hasek	.60	1.50
4 Jiri Hunkes	.60	1.50
5 Tomas Jurdic	.60	1.50
6 Jaroslav Kudrna	.60	1.50
7 Tomas Pacal	.60	1.50
8 Jan Peterek	.60	1.50
9 Lubomir Pistek	.60	1.50
10 Vaclav Pletka	1.00	2.50
11 Jiri Polansky	.60	1.50
12 Radim Tesarik	.60	1.50
13 David Vsetecka	.60	1.50
14 Martin Vojtek	.60	1.50
15 Tomas Zboril	.60	1.50

2005-06 Czech HC Vitkovice

Card	Low	High
COMPLETE SET (16)	8.00	20.00
1 Jiri Burger	.60	1.50
2 Jan Dresler	.60	1.50
3 Petr Hubacek	.60	1.50
4 Stanislav Hudec	.60	1.50
5 Jakub Hulva	.60	1.50
6 Zbynek Irgl	.60	1.50
7 Petr Jurecka	.60	1.50
8 Jaroslav Kames	.75	2.00
9 Bedrich Kohler	.60	1.50
10 Lukas Krenzelok	.60	1.50
11 Radoslav Kropac	.60	1.50
12 Radek Philipp	.60	1.50
13 Marek Pinc	.75	2.00
14 Radek Prochazka	.60	1.50
15 Roman Simicek	.60	1.50
16 Martin Tomasek	.60	1.50

2005-06 Czech HC Vsetin

Card	Low	High
COMPLETE SET (15)	8.00	20.00
1 Richard Bauer	.60	1.50
2 Tomas Demel	.60	1.50
3 Roman Gorev	.60	1.50
4 Michal Horak	.60	1.50
5 Josef Hrabal	.60	1.50
6 Ondrej Hruska	.60	1.50
7 Radim Hruska	.60	1.50
8 Josef Kucera	.60	1.50
9 David Kveton	.60	1.50
10 Havi Sasu	.60	1.50
11 Zdenek Spitzer	.60	1.50
12 Roman Stantien	.60	1.50
13 Filip Stefanka	.60	1.50
14 Ondrej Steiner	.60	1.50
15 Patrik Luza	.60	1.50

2005-06 Czech HC Znojmo

Card	Low	High
COMPLETE SET (14)	8.00	20.00
1 Radim Bicanek	.60	1.50
2 Martin Cakajik	.60	1.50
3 Jiri Dopita	.60	1.50
4 Roman Erat	.60	1.50
5 Radek Haman	.60	1.50
6 Richard Jares	.60	1.50
7 Ales Kretinsky	.60	1.50
8 Milan Ministr	.60	1.50
9 Pavel Mojzis	.60	1.50
10 Zdenek Ondrej	.60	1.50
11 Karel Plasek	.60	1.50
12 Peter Pucher	.60	1.50
13 Jiri Trvaj	.60	1.50
14 Marek Uram	.60	1.50

2006-07 Czech CP Cup Postcards

Card	Low	High
COMPLETE SET (23)	20.00	40.00
1 Miroslav Blatak	.75	2.00
2 Jiri Burger	.75	2.00
3 Radek Hamr	.75	2.00
4 Jaroslav Hlinka	.75	2.00
5 Milan Hnilicka	1.25	3.00
6 Miloslav Horava	.75	2.00
7 Petr Hubacek	.75	2.00
8 Jiri Hunkes	.75	2.00
9 Martin Chabada	.75	2.00
10 Zbynek Irgl	.75	2.00
11 Zdenek Kutlak	.75	2.00
12 Roman Malek	.75	2.00
13 Jan Marek	.75	2.00
14 Josef Marha	.75	2.00
15 Vaclav Pletka	.75	2.00
16 Tomas Rolinek	.75	2.00
17 Michal Sivek	.75	2.00
18 Vaclav Skuhravy	.75	2.00
19 Petr Sykora	.75	2.00
20 Martin Sevc	.75	2.00
21 Ivan Rachunek	.75	2.00
22 Lukas Zib	.75	2.00
23 Tomas Zizka	.75	2.00

2006-07 Czech HC Ceske Budejovice Postcards

Card	Low	High
COMPLETE SET (14)	15.00	25.00
1 Petr Gregorek	.75	2.00
2 Viktor Hubl	.75	2.00
3 Michal Hudec	.75	2.00
4 Jindrich Kotrla	.75	2.00
5 Jan Mucha	.75	2.00
6 Vaclav Nedorost	1.25	3.00
7 Petr Sailer	.75	2.00
8 Jiri Simanek	.75	2.00
9 Milan Toman	.75	2.00
10 Roman Turek	1.25	3.00
11 Martin Vagner	.75	2.00
12 Tomas Vak	.75	2.00
13 Ondrej Vesely	.75	2.00
14 Rene Vydareny	.75	2.00

2006-07 Czech HC Kladno Postcards

It is quite likely that this checklist is incomplete. If you know if additional postcards, please email us at hockeymag@beckett.com.

Card	Low	High
COMPLETE SET (11)	10.00	20.00
1 Ales Pavlas	.75	2.00
2 Jakub Lev	.75	2.00
3 Jaroslav Kalla	.75	2.00
4 Martin Frolik	.75	2.00
5 Martin Prochazka	.75	2.00
6 Martin Sevc	.75	2.00
7 Michal Havel	.75	2.00
8 Milan Hluchy	.75	2.00
9 Pavel Patera	.75	2.00
10 Radek Gardon	.75	2.00
11 Zdenek Orct	1.25	3.00

2006-07 Czech HC Liberec Postcards

It is likely this checklist is incomplete. Please forward additional information to hockeymag@beckett.com.

Card	Low	High
COMPLETE SET (12)	10.00	20.00
1 Jakub Cutta	.75	2.00
2 Ondrej Hruska	.75	2.00
3 Waldemar Jirus	.75	2.00
4 Angel Krstev	.75	2.00
5 Michal Nedvidek	.75	2.00
6 Vaclav Novak	.75	2.00
7 Vaclav Pletka	.75	2.00
8 Filip Sindelar	.75	2.00
9 Jan Tomajko	.75	2.00
10 Lubomir Vaic	.75	2.00
11 Jan Visek	.75	2.00
12 Lukas Zib	.75	2.00

2006-07 Czech HC Pardubice Postcards

Card	Low	High
COMPLETE SET (23)	20.00	40.00
1 Dusan Andrasovsky	.75	2.00
2 Tomas Blazek	1.25	3.00
3 Jan Caloun	1.25	3.00
4 Petr Caslava	.75	2.00
5 David Havir	.75	2.00
6 Miroslav Hlinka	.75	2.00
7 Jan Kolar	.75	2.00
8 Jaroslav Koma	.75	2.00
9 Petr Koukal	.75	2.00
10 Vladislav Koutsky	.75	2.00
11 Jan Lasak	1.25	3.00
12 Tomas Linhart	.75	2.00
13 Frantisek Mrazek	.75	2.00
14 Andrej Novotny	.75	2.00
15 Ales Pisa	.75	2.00
16 Libor Pivko	.75	2.00
17 Tomas Rolinek	.75	2.00
18 Michal Seda	.75	2.00
19 Jan Snopek	.75	2.00
20 Adam Svoboda	1.25	3.00
21 Petr Sykora	.75	2.00
22 Michal Tvrdik	.75	2.00
23 Jan Stary	.75	2.00

2006-07 Czech HC Plzen Postcards

Card	Low	High
COMPLETE SET (16)	15.00	30.00
1 Adam Saffer	.75	2.00
2 Ales Padelek	.75	2.00
3 David Ludvik	.75	2.00
4 Jiri Malinsky	.75	2.00
5 Jiri Zelenka	.75	2.00
6 Lukas Derner	.75	2.00
7 Lukas Pulpan	.75	2.00
8 Roman Malek	1.25	3.00
9 Martin Adamsky	.75	2.00
10 Michal Duras	.75	2.00
11 Milan Nedoma	.75	2.00
12 Peter Fabus	.75	2.00
13 Petr Jez	.75	2.00
14 Tomas Divisek	.75	2.00
15 Tomas Kubalik	.75	2.00
16 Vaclav Benak	.75	2.00

2006-07 Czech HC Slavia Praha Postcards

Card	Low	High
COMPLETE SET (16)	15.00	30.00
1 Jaroslav Bednar	.75	2.00
2 Josef Beranek	.75	2.00
3 Leos Cermak	.75	2.00
4 Roman Cervenka	.75	2.00
5 Radek Dlouhy	.75	2.00
6 Jiri Drtina	.75	2.00
7 Dominik Granak	.75	2.00
8 Martin Hlavacka	.75	2.00
9 David Hruska	.75	2.00
10 Pavel Kolarik	.75	2.00
11 Igor Rataj	.75	2.00
12 Vladimir Sobotka	.75	2.00
13 Michal Sup	.75	2.00
14 Adam Svoboda	1.25	3.00
15 Tomas Vlasak	.75	2.00
16 Tomas Zizka	.75	2.00

2006-07 Czech HC Sparta Praha Postcards

Card	Low	High
COMPLETE SET (15)	15.00	30.00
1 Ladislav Benysek	.75	2.00
2 Marek Cernosek	.75	2.00
3 David Vrbata	.75	2.00
4 Dusan Salficky	1.25	3.00
5 Frantisek Ptacek	.75	2.00
6 Jan Hanzlik	.75	2.00
7 Jan Hlavac	1.25	3.00
8 Jaroslav Hlinka	.75	2.00
9 Jakub Langhammer	.75	2.00
10 Michal Sivek	1.25	3.00
11 Ondrej Kratena	.75	2.00
12 Petr Ton	.75	2.00
13 Martin Strba	.75	2.00
14 Tomas Netik	.75	2.00
15 Tomas Protivny	.75	2.00

2006-07 Czech HC Vsetin Postcards

This listing is likely to be incomplete.

Card	Low	High
COMPLETE SET (12)	10.00	25.00
1 Lukas Bolf	.75	2.00
2 Guntis Galvins	.75	2.00
3 Josef Hrabal	.75	2.00
4 Jiri Kucny	.75	2.00
5 Lukas Duba	.75	2.00
6 Lubos Rob	.75	2.00
7 Lubomir Sabol	.75	2.00
8 Vladimir Skoda	.75	2.00
9 Lubomir Stach	.75	2.00
10 Roman Stantien	.75	2.00
11 Martin Stefl	.75	2.00
12 Tomas Demel	.75	2.00

2006-07 Czech HC Zlin Hame Postcards

Card	Low	High
COMPLETE SET (15)	15.00	30.00
1 Martin Cech	.75	2.00
2 Martin Hamrlik	.75	2.00
3 Jan Horacek	.75	2.00
4 Robin Kovar	.75	2.00
5 Jaroslav Kristek	.75	2.00
6 Pavel Kubis	.75	2.00
7 Petr Leska	.75	2.00
8 Marek Melenovsky	1.25	3.00
9 Igor Murin	.75	2.00
10 Roman Psurny	.75	2.00
11 Ivan Rachunek	.75	2.00
12 Robert Tomik	.75	2.00
13 Lubomir Sekeras	.75	2.00
14 Martin Zahorovsky	.75	2.00
15 Pavel Zubicek	.75	2.00

2006-07 Czech IIHF World Championship Postcards

Card	Low	High
COMPLETE SET (23)	20.00	40.00
1 Jaroslav Balastik	.75	2.00
2 Jaroslav Bednar	.60	1.50
3 Jan Bulis	.60	1.50
4 Martin Erat	.75	2.00
5 Jan Hejda	.60	1.50
6 Jan Hlavac	.60	1.50
7 Jaroslav Hlinka	.60	1.50
8 Milan Hnilicka	.75	2.00
9 Petr Hubacek	.60	1.50
10 Zbynek Irgl	.60	1.50
11 Tomas Kaberle	.75	2.00
12 Lukas Krajicek	.75	2.00
13 Zdenek Kutlak	.60	1.50
14 Zbynek Michalek	.60	1.50
15 Tomas Plekanec	1.25	3.00
16 Ivo Prorok	.60	1.50
17 Martin Richter	.60	1.50
18 Tomas Rolinek	.60	1.50
19 Martin Skoula	.60	1.50
20 Patrik Stefan	.60	1.50
21 Adam Svoboda	.60	1.50
22 Petr Tenkrat	.60	1.50
23 David Vyborny	.75	2.00

2006-07 Czech LG Hockey Games Postcards

Card	Low	High
COMPLETE SET (22)	15.00	30.00
1 Jaroslav Balastik	.75	2.00
2 Jaroslav Bednar	.40	1.00
3 Miroslav Blatak	.40	1.00
4 Petr Hubacek	.40	1.00
5 Jiri Hunkes	.40	1.00
6 Zbynek Irgl	.75	2.00
7 Jaroslav Kracik	.40	1.00
8 Lukas Krajicek	.75	2.00
9 Jaroslav Kudrna	.75	2.00
10 Zdenek Kutlak	.40	1.00
11 Jan Marek	.40	1.00
12 Zbynek Michalek	.40	1.00
13 Jan Novak	.40	1.00
14 Jan Peterek	.40	1.00
15 Tomas Popperle	.75	2.00
16 Ivo Prorok	.40	1.00
17 Tomas Rolinek	.40	1.00
18 Martin Sevc	.40	1.00
19 Martin Skoula	.40	1.00
20 Patrik Stefan	.40	1.00
21 Adam Svoboda	.75	2.00
22 Petr Tenkrat	.40	1.00

2006-07 Czech OFS

Card	Low	High
COMPLETE SET (326)	75.00	125.00
1 Kamil Brabenec	.20	.50
2 Petr Gregorek	.20	.50
3 Milan Gulas	.20	.50
4 Stepan Hrebejk	.20	.50
5 Viktor Hubl	.20	.50
6 Michal Hudec	.20	.50
7 Jan Chabera	.30	.75
8 Jindrich Kotrla	.20	.50
9 Zdenek Kutlak	.30	.75
10 Lukas Kveton	.20	.50
11 Petr Machacek	.20	.50
12 Jan Mucha	.20	.50

13 Vaclav Nedorost .40 1.00
14 Marek Posmyk .30 .75
15 Petr Sailer .20 .50
16 Jiri Simanek .20 .50
17 Milan Toman .20 .50
18 Roman Turek .40 1.00
19 Martin Vagner .30 .75
20 Tomas Vak .20 .50
21 Ondrej Vesely .20 .50
22 Rene Vydareny .20 .50
23 David Balasz .20 .50
24 Michal Borovansky .20 .50
25 Michal Dobron .20 .50
26 Miroslav Duben .20 .50
27 Michal Dvorak .20 .50
28 Jiri Hanzlik .20 .50
29 Vojtech Kloz .20 .50
30 Jan Kostal .20 .50
31 Milan Kraft .40 1.00
32 Petr Kumstat .20 .50
33 Vladimir Machulda .20 .50
34 Lukas Mensator .30 .75
35 Petr Mudroch .20 .50
36 Ondrej Nemec .20 .50
37 Lukas Pech .20 .50
38 Milan Prochazka .20 .50
39 Josef Reznicek .20 .50
40 Lukas Sablik .30 .75
41 Frantisek Skladany .20 .50
42 Vaclav Skuhravy .20 .50
43 Kamil Tvrdek .20 .50
44 Libor Ustrnul .30 .75
45 Jiri Burger .20 .50
46 Jan Dresler .20 .50
47 Michal Gulasi .20 .50
48 Petr Hubacek .20 .50
49 Stanislav Hudec .20 .50
50 Lukas Chmelir .20 .50
51 Zbynek Irgl .30 .75
52 Stanislav Jasecko .20 .50
53 Petr Jurecka .20 .50
54 Tomas Kana .20 .50
55 Bedrich Kohler .20 .50
56 Lukas Krenzelok .20 .50
57 Radoslav Kropac .20 .50
58 Petr Kubos .20 .50
59 Milan Mikulik .20 .50
60 Marek Pinc .30 .75
61 Radek Prochazka .20 .50
62 Filip Seman .20 .50
63 Roman Simicek .20 .50
64 Jakub Stepanek .30 .75
65 Martin Tomasek .20 .50
66 Lukas Klimek .20 .50
67 Jiri Vykoukal .20 .50
68 David Vrbata .20 .50
69 Petr Ton .20 .50
70 Jan Tabacek .20 .50
71 Michal Sivek .40 1.00
72 Dusan Salficky .60 1.50
73 Frantisek Ptacek .20 .50
74 Petr Prikryl .30 .75
75 Tomas Protivny .20 .50
76 Martin Podlesak .20 .50
77 Tomas Netik .20 .50
78 Jaroslav Mrazek .20 .50
79 Jakub Langhammer .20 .50
80 Ondrej Kratena .30 .75
81 Karel Hromas .20 .50
82 Jaroslav Hlinka .20 .50
83 Jan Hlavac .40 1.00
84 Jan Hanzlik .20 .50
85 Michal Dragoun .20 .50
86 Marek Cernosek .20 .50
87 Ladislav Benysek .20 .50
88 Jan Holub .20 .50
89 Ondrej Hruska .20 .50
90 Ctibor Jech .20 .50
91 Valdemar Jirus .20 .50
92 Tomas Klimenta .20 .50
93 Vaclav Koci .20 .50
94 Angel Krstev .20 .50
95 Jiri Moravec .20 .50
96 Michal Nedvidek .30 .75
97 Lukas Pabiska .20 .50
98 Rok Pajic .20 .50
99 Vaclav Pletka .30 .75
100 Jan Plodek .20 .50
101 Andrej Podkonicky .20 .50
102 Stanislav Prochazka .20 .50
103 Jiri Stejskal .30 .75
104 Petr Sachl .20 .50
105 Lubomir Vaic .20 .50
106 Petr Vampola .20 .50
107 Jan Visek .20 .50
108 Lukas Zib .20 .50
109 Boris Zabka .20 .50
110 Dusan Andrasovsky .20 .50
111 Tomas Blazek .20 .50
112 Jan Caloun .30 .75
113 Petr Caslava .20 .50
114 David Havir .20 .50
115 Miroslav Hlinka .20 .50
116 Jan Kolar .20 .50
117 Jaroslav Koma .20 .50
118 Petr Koukal .20 .50
119 Vladislav Koutsky .30 .75
120 Jan Lasak .75 2.00
121 Tomas Linhart .20 .50
122 Andrej Novotny .20 .50
123 Zdenek Ondrej .20 .50
124 Tomas Rolinek .20 .50
125 Jan Snopek .20 .50
126 Petr Sykora .20 .50
127 Michal Seda .20 .50
128 Lukas Bednarik .20 .50
129 Jan Benda .20 .50
130 Frantisek Bombic .20 .50
131 Daniel Branda .20 .50
132 Jakub Cerny .20 .50
133 Vladimir Gyna .20 .50
134 Jan Hranac .20 .50
135 Jaroslav Hubl .30 .75
136 Peter Jansky .20 .50
137 Martin Jenacek .20 .50
138 Milan Kopecky .20 .50
139 Vojtech Kubincak .20 .50
140 Frantisek Lukes .20 .50
141 Marian Morava .20 .50
142 Angel Nikolov .20 .50
143 Lukas Pozivil .20 .50
144 Ivo Prorok .20 .50
145 Robert Reichel .40 1.00
146 Zbynek Sklenicka .20 .50
147 Radim Skuhrovec .20 .50
148 Jiri Slegr .30 .75
149 Michal Travnicek .20 .50
150 Michal Podolka .40 1.00
151 Jaroslav Barton .20 .50
152 Radovan Biegl .30 .75
153 Jan Danecek .20 .50
154 Lukas Danecek .40 1.00
155 Tomas Frolo .20 .50
156 Jiri Hasek .20 .50
157 Alexandr Hegegy .20 .50
158 Marcin Kolusz .20 .50
159 Lubomir Korhon .20 .50
160 Vlastimil Kroupa .20 .50
161 Jaroslav Kudrna .20 .50
162 Rostislav Martynek .20 .50
163 Tomas Pacal .20 .50
164 Jan Peterek .20 .50
165 Jiri Polansky .20 .50
166 Tomaz Razingar .20 .50
167 Zdenek Skorepa .20 .50
168 Radim Tesarik .20 .50
169 Roman Tomas .20 .50
170 Tomas Vrba .20 .50
171 Jan Vytisk .20 .50
172 Stefan Zigardy .30 .75
173 Armands Berzins .20 .50
174 Lukas Bolf .20 .50
175 Martin Davidek .20 .50
176 Tomas Demel .20 .50
177 Lukas Duba .20 .50
178 Marek Dubec .20 .50
179 Guntis Galvins .20 .50
180 Marek Grill .20 .50
181 Michal Horak .20 .50
182 Josef Hrabal .20 .50
183 Jakub Kraus .20 .50
184 Jiri Kucny .20 .50
185 David Kveton .20 .50
186 Radim Ostrcil .20 .50
187 Lubos Rob .20 .50
188 Lubomir Sabol .20 .50
189 Petr Sakrajda .20 .50
190 Roman Stantien .20 .50
191 Matej Stritesky .20 .50
192 Vladimir Skoda .20 .50
193 Lubomir Stach .20 .50
194 Martin Stefl .20 .50
195 Simo Vehvilainen .30 .75
196 Dusan Brincko .20 .50
197 Waldemar Pelikovsky .20 .50
198 Jiri Beroun .20 .50
199 Radim Bicanek .20 .50
200 Martin Cakajik .20 .50
201 Jiri Dopita .30 .75
202 Roman Erat .20 .50
203 Radek Haman .20 .50
204 Christoph Harand .20 .50
205 Richard Jares .20 .50
206 Ivo Kotaska .20 .50
207 Radim Kucharczyk .20 .50
208 Pavel Mojzis .20 .50
209 Roman Nemecek .20 .50
210 Karel Plasek .20 .50
211 Peter Pucher .20 .50
212 Martin Ruzicka .20 .50
213 Pavel Selingr .20 .50
214 Jaroslav Svoboda .20 .50
215 Ondrej Smach .20 .50
216 Jiri Trvaj .30 .75
217 David Turon .20 .50
218 Lubomir Vaskovic .20 .50
219 David Adamec .30 .75
220 Stanislav Balan .20 .50
221 Jakub Cech .30 .75
222 Martin Cech .20 .50
223 Lukas Galvas .20 .50
224 Martin Hamrlik .20 .50
225 Jan Horacek .20 .50
226 Pavel Kasparik .20 .50
227 Robin Kovar .20 .50
228 Jaroslav Kristek .20 .50
229 Pavel Kubis .20 .50
230 Petr Leska .20 .50
231 Martin Lucka .20 .50
232 Jiri Marusak .20 .50
233 Marek Melenovsky .20 .50
234 Pavel Mokrejs .20 .50
235 Igor Murin .30 .75
236 David Nosek .20 .50
237 Miroslav Okal .20 .50
238 Michal Psurny .20 .50
239 Roman Psurny .20 .50
240 Ivan Rachunek .20 .50
241 Dalibor Sedlar .30 .75
242 Lubomir Sekeras .20 .50
243 Robert Tomik .20 .50
244 Lubomir Vosatko .20 .50
245 Martin Zahorovsky .20 .50
246 Pavel Zubicek .20 .50
247 Vitezslav Bilek .20 .50
248 Vratislav Cech .20 .50
249 Marek Curilla .20 .50
250 Richard Divis .20 .50
251 Martin Frolik .20 .50
252 Radek Gardon .20 .50
253 David Hajek .20 .50
254 Michal Havel .20 .50
255 Milan Hluchy .20 .50
256 Tomas Horna .20 .50
257 Petr Jaros .20 .50
258 Jaroslav Kalla .20 .50
259 Jiri Kuchler .20 .50
260 Jakub Lev .30 .75
261 Zdenek Orct .30 .75
262 Pavel Patera .20 .50
263 Ales Pavlas .20 .50
264 Libor Prochazka .20 .50
265 Martin Prochazka .20 .50
266 Martin Sevc .20 .50
267 Martin Stepanek .20 .50
268 Jiri Zeman .20 .50
269 Vaclav Benak .20 .50
270 Mario Cartelli .20 .50
271 Michal Duraz .20 .50
272 Jan Herman .20 .50
273 Petr Jez .30 .75
274 Richard Kepl .20 .50
275 Richard Kral .20 .50
276 Roman Malek .30 .75
277 Jiri Malinsky .20 .50
278 Radek Matejovsky .20 .50
279 David Mazanec .20 .50
280 Milan Nedoma .20 .50
281 Ales Padelek .20 .50
282 Igor Rataj .20 .50
283 Adam Saffer .20 .50
284 Jakub Sindel .20 .50
285 Pavel Trnka .20 .50
286 Milan Voboril .20 .50
287 Jiri Zelenka .20 .50
288 Jaroslav Bednar .40 1.00
289 Josef Beranek .20 .50
290 Roman Cervenka .20 .50
291 Tomas Divisek .40 1.00
292 Radek Dlouhy .20 .50
293 Jiri Drtina .20 .50
294 Petr Franek .30 .75
295 Dominik Granak .20 .50
296 Lukas Hronek .30 .75
297 David Hruska .20 .50
298 Jiri Jebavy .20 .50
299 Petr Kadlec .20 .50
300 David Pojkar .20 .50
301 Vladimir Ruzicka .20 .50
302 Jakub Sklenar .20 .50
303 Vladimir Sobotka .20 .50
304 Michal Sup .20 .50
305 Tomas Spila .20 .50
306 Tomas Vlasak .20 .50
307 Michal Vondrka .20 .50
308 Tomas Zizka .20 .50
309 Radek Hubacek .20 .50
310 Petr Tucek .30 .75
311 Andrej Novotny .20 .50
312 Petr Puncochar .20 .50
313 Jan Stary .20 .50
314 Michal Tvrdik .20 .50
315 Libor Pivko .20 .50
316 Jan Kolar .20 .50
317 Martin Cech .20 .50
318 Jan Kana .20 .50
319 Tomas Voracek .20 .50
320 Marek Novotny .20 .50
321 Tomas Brnak .20 .50
322 Martin Zatovic .30 .75
323 Tomas Chrenko .20 .50
324 Ales Pisa .20 .50
325 Frantisek Mrazek .20 .50
326 Josef Kucera .20 .50
327 Frantisek Mrazek .20 .50
328 Josef Kucera .20 .50

2006-07 Czech OFS All Stars

1 Milan Hnilicka 2.00 5.00
2 Roman Malek 2.00 5.00
3 Jan Novak 1.50 4.00
4 Miroslav Blatak 1.50 4.00
5 Frantisek Ptacek 1.50 4.00
6 Josef Reznicek 1.50 4.00
7 Radim Tesarik 1.50 4.00
8 Stanislav Hudec 1.50 4.00
9 Valdemar Jirus 1.50 4.00
10 Martin Richter 1.50 4.00
11 Ivan Rachunek 1.50 4.00
12 Lubomir Vaic 1.50 4.00
13 Petr Sykora 1.50 4.00
14 Michal Mikeska 1.50 4.00
15 Jan Marek 1.50 4.00
16 Marek Tomica 1.50 4.00
17 Jiri Burger 1.50 4.00
18 Michal Travnicek 1.50 4.00
19 Radek Gardon 1.50 4.00
20 David Moravec 1.50 4.00
21 Jan Peterek 1.50 4.00
22 Ales Kretinsky 1.50 4.00

2006-07 Czech OFS Brothers

1 M.Herman/J.Herman 2.00 5.00
2 J.Kana/T.Kana 2.00 5.00
3 L.Danecek/J.Danecek 2.00 5.00
4 R.Hubacek/P.Hubacek 2.00 5.00
5 M.Psurny/R.Psurny 2.00 5.00

2006-07 Czech OFS Coaches

1 Ernest Bokros .40 1.00
2 Milos Holan .40 1.00
3 Miloslav Horava .40 1.00
4 Josef Jandac .40 1.00
5 Jiri Jurik .40 1.00
6 Zdenek MÃ¼ller .40 1.00
7 Josef Palecek .40 1.00
8 Vladimir Ruzicka .40 1.00
9 Milos Riha .40 1.00
10 Marek Sykora .40 1.00
11 Vaclav Sykora .40 1.00
12 Zdenek Venera .40 1.00
13 Rostislav Vlach .40 1.00
14 Frantisek Vyborny .40 1.00

2006-07 Czech OFS Defenders

1 Martin Hamrlik .75 2.00
2 Jan Novak .75 2.00
3 Stanislav Hudec .75 2.00
4 Martin Richter .75 2.00
5 Valdemar Jirus .75 2.00
6 Petr Gregorek .75 2.00
7 Marek Posmyk .75 2.00
8 Martin Sevc .75 2.00
9 Josef Reznicek .75 2.00
10 Miroslav Blatak .75 2.00
11 Petr Kadlec .75 2.00
12 Radim Tesarik .75 2.00
13 Angel Krstev .75 2.00
14 Radim Bicanek .75 2.00
15 Frantisek Ptacek .75 2.00

2006-07 Czech OFS Goalies I

1 Igor Murin 2.00 5.00
2 Lukas Mensator 2.00 5.00
3 Petr Franek 2.00 5.00
4 Milan Hnilicka 2.00 5.00
5 Jiri Trvaj 2.00 5.00
6 Marek Pinc 2.00 5.00
7 Roman Malek 2.00 5.00
8 Jan Chabera 2.00 5.00
9 Radek Fiala 2.00 5.00
10 Sasu Hovi 2.00 5.00
11 Jan Lasak 2.50 6.00
12 Kamil Jarina 2.00 5.00
13 Petr Briza 2.50 6.00
14 Martin Altrichter 2.00 5.00
15 Roman Turek 2.00 5.00

2006-07 Czech OFS Goalies II

1 Milan Hnilicka 2.00 5.00
2 Igor Murin 2.00 5.00
3 Petr Franek 2.00 5.00
4 Jan Chabera 2.00 5.00
5 Jiri Trvaj 2.00 5.00
6 Lukas Mensator 2.00 5.00
7 Marek Pinc 2.00 5.00
8 Roman Turek 2.00 5.00
9 Radek Fiala 2.00 5.00
10 Roman Malek 2.00 5.00
11 Kamil Jarina 2.00 5.00
12 Martin Altrichter 2.00 5.00
13 Jan Lasak 2.50 6.00
14 Petr Briza 2.50 6.00
15 Radovan Biegl 2.00 5.00

2006-07 Czech OFS Goals Leaders

1 Petr Ton 1.25 3.00
2 Michal Sup 1.25 3.00
3 Jan Marek 1.25 3.00
4 Jaroslav Kudrna 1.25 3.00
5 Jaroslav Bednar 1.25 3.00
6 Ales Padelek 1.25 3.00
7 Lubomir Vaic 1.25 3.00
8 Jan Caloun 1.25 3.00
9 Igor Rataj 1.25 3.00
10 Peter Pucher 1.25 3.00
11 Radek Duda 1.25 3.00
12 Petr Hubacek 1.25 3.00
13 Ondrej Kratena 1.25 3.00
14 Jiri Zelenka 1.25 3.00
15 Jan Benda 1.25 3.00

2006-07 Czech OFS Jagr Team

1 Marek Schwarz 3.00 8.00
2 Jaroslav Kames 1.25 3.00
3 Jiri Tlusty 4.00 10.00
4 Petr Taticek 1.25 3.00
5 Jakub Koreis 2.00 5.00
6 Jiri Novotny 1.25 3.00
7 Lukas Krajicek 1.25 3.00
8 Martin Richter 1.25 3.00
9 Rostislav Klesla 1.25 3.00
10 Josef Melichar 1.25 3.00
11 Michal Rozsival 1.25 3.00
12 Petr Tenkrat 1.25 3.00
13 Tomas Plekanec 2.50 6.00
14 Jaroslav Hlinka 1.25 3.00
15 Jan Hrdina 1.25 3.00
16 Ales Kotalik 2.00 5.00
17 Tomas Kaberle 2.00 5.00
18 David Vyborny 1.25 3.00
19 Martin Straka 1.25 3.00
20 Martin Rucinsky 1.25 3.00
21 Jaromir Jagr 4.00 10.00
22 Jaroslav Svoboda 1.25 3.00
23 Jiri Hudler 2.50 6.00

2006-07 Czech OFS Points Leaders

1 Jan Marek 1.25 3.00
2 Lubomir Vaic 1.25 3.00
3 Josef Beranek 1.25 3.00
4 Petr Ton 1.25 3.00
5 Jaroslav Kudrna 1.25 3.00
6 Jaroslav Bednar 1.25 3.00
7 Radek Duda 1.25 3.00
8 Jan Peterek 1.25 3.00
9 Peter Pucher 1.25 3.00
10 Jan Benda 1.25 3.00
11 Petr Hubacek 1.25 3.00
12 Jan Caloun 1.25 3.00
13 Tomas Vlasak 1.25 3.00
14 Martin Strba 1.25 3.00
15 Michal Sup 1.25 3.00

2006-07 Czech OFS Stars

1 Jiri Stejskal 1.25 3.00
2 Andrej Podkonicky 1.25 3.00
3 Daniel Branda 1.25 3.00
4 Lukas Mensator 1.25 3.00
5 Milan Kraft 1.25 3.00
6 Igor Murin 1.25 3.00
7 Petr Leska 1.25 3.00
8 Martin Hamrlik 1.25 3.00
9 Roman Malek 1.25 3.00
10 Richard Kral 1.25 3.00
11 Petr Sykora 1.25 3.00
12 Miroslav Hlinka 1.25 3.00
13 Roman Turek 1.50 4.00
14 Vaclav Nedorost 1.25 3.00
15 Jiri Polansky 1.25 3.00
16 Zdenek Orct 1.50 4.00
17 Jaroslav Bednar 1.25 3.00
18 Dusan Salficky 1.50 4.00
19 Jiri Vykoukal 1.25 3.00
20 Tomas Demel 1.25 3.00
21 Martin Stefl 1.25 3.00
22 Roman Erat 1.25 3.00
23 Pavel Mojzis 1.25 3.00
24 Jiri Trvaj 1.50 4.00
25 Zbynek Irgl 1.50 4.00

2006-07 Czech OFS Team Cards

1 R.Turek/V.Nedorost 1.50 4.00
2 L.Mansator/P.Kumstat 1.50 4.00
3 P.Patera/Z.Orct 1.50 4.00
4 J.Stejskal/J.Plodek 1.50 4.00
5 R.Reichel/J.Hubl 1.50 4.00
6 P.Sykora/J.Lasak 2.00 5.00
7 J.Zelenka/R.Malek 1.50 4.00
8 T.Vlasak/P.Franek 1.50 4.00
9 D.Salficky/J.Hlinka 1.50 4.00
10 R.Biegl/J.Vytisk 1.50 4.00
11 M.Pinc/J.Burger 1.50 4.00
12 M/Stefl/R.Stantien 1.50 4.00
13 I.Murin/P.Leska 1.50 4.00
14 J.Trvaj/J.Dopita 1.50 4.00

2006-07 Czech NHL ELH Postcards

COMPLETE SET (15) 15.00 30.00
1 Martin Havlat .75 2.00
2 Milan Hnilicka .75 2.00
3 Jan Hrdina .75 2.00
4 Milan Kraft .75 2.00
5 Pavel Kubina .75 2.00
6 Jason Marshall .75 2.00
7 Vaclav Nedorost .75 2.00
8 Zigmund Palffy 1.25 3.00
9 Michal Rozsival .75 2.00
10 Jaroslav Spacek .75 2.00
11 Josef Stumpel .75 2.00
12 Pavel Trnka .75 2.00
13 Vaclav Varada .75 2.00
14 Radim Vrbata .75 2.00
15 Josef Vasicek .75 2.00

2006-07 Czech Super Six Postcards

1 Niklas Backstrom 2.00 5.00
2 Michal Bros .75 2.00
3 Mikhail Grabovskij 1.25 3.00
4 David Havir .75 2.00
5 Miroslav Hlinka .75 2.00
6 Robert Kantor .75 2.00
7 Jan Lasak 1.25 3.00
8 Michal Mikeska .75 2.00
9 Vaclav Pletka .75 2.00
10 Tomasz Razingar 1.25 3.00
11 Tomas Rolinek .75 2.00
12 Pavel Rosa .75 2.00
13 Maxim Susinskij .75 2.00
14 Petr Tenkrat .75 2.00
15 Viktor Ujcik .75 2.00
16 Jari Viuhkola .75 2.00

1999-00 Danish Hockey League

Little is known about this set beyond the checklist and thus it is not priced. Several cards are marked below as unknown. If you have information about the identities of these cards or have sales information, write hockeymag@beckett.com.

COMPLETE SET (225)
1 Jan Jensen
2 Kenneth Jensen
3 Torben Schultz
4 Michael Pedersen
5 Henrik Benjaminsen
6 Mikkel Bjerrum
7 Todd Sparks
8 Keld Frederiksen
9 Alexander Weinrich
10 Kristian Lodberg
11 Lars T. Pedersen
12 Oleg Starkov
13 Andreas Andreasen
14 Mikko Suvanto
15 Anders Skov
16 Jacques Joubert
17 Thomas Bjerrum
18 Bjorn Eden
19 Jesper Madsen
20 Thomas Kjogx
21 Anders Johansson
22 Mats Diberius
23 Bill Stewart
24 Robert Nordberg
25 Peter Nordstrom
26 Rasmus Aradsson
27 Ole Valipirtti
28 Mathias Frelin
29 Bo Larsen
30 Mikko Niemi
31 Michel Olsen
32 Rasmus Jacobsen
33 Jens Maribo
34 Brian Jensen
35 Claus Esmark
36 Rasmus Olsen
37 Brian Schultz
38 Christian Jorgensen
39 Johan Marklund
40 Rene Sloth
41 Ronni Dahlsten
42 Ronni Thomassen
43 Thor Dresler
44 Poul B. Andersson
45 Steen Bengtson
46 Peter Therkildsen
47 unknown
48 Claus Mortensen
49 Daniel Nielsen
50 Jan Philipsen
51 Kasper Degn
52 Martin Kristiansen
53 Jarmo Kuusisto
54 unknown
55 Rasmus Hartung
56 Todd Bjorkstrand
57 Rico Larsen
58 unknown
59 Martin Struzinski
60 Christian Kjaergaard
61 Jesper Molby
62 Rasmus Pander
63 Dan Jensen
64 Lasse Degn
65 Sami Wikstrom
66 unknown
67 Michael Madsen
68 Mikael Wiklander
69 Lars Bach
70 Christian Erntgaard
71 unknown
72 Claus Jensen
73 Henrik Lundin
74 Mikko Honkonen
75 Morten Callesen
76 Ray Podloski
77 Sami Simonen
78 Stefan Nyman
79 Soren Nielsen
80 Valeri Chierny
81 Brian Foder
82 Rasmus Kubel
83 Jan Jensen
84 Ole Christiansen
85 Kim Foder
86 Dan Jensen
87 Thomas Carlsson
88 Jiri Podesva
89 Jens Sonny Thomsen
90 Alexanders Shishkovich
91 Jesper Pedersen
92 Carsten Ronnest
93 Alexanders Macijevskis
94 Jacek Nowakowski
95 Mads Moller
96 unknown
97 Ronnie Sorensen
98 Thomas Englund
99 Tomas Placatka
100 unknown
101 Kasper Haslund Knudsen
102 Thomas Mortensen
103 Bo Nordby Andersen
104 Rasmus Kristiansen
105 Jens Christian Gregersen
106 Jesper Pedersen
107 Thomas Pedersen
108 Johan Allringer
109 Casper Nilsson
110 Peter Skraem
111 Henrik B. Madsen
112 Curt Regnier
113 Dean Seymour
114 Mario Simioni
115 Jens Hellsten
116 Henrik Oxholm
117 Ntsika Shange
118 Dmitri Lavrentiev
119 Marku Kyllonen
120 Lars Oxholm
121 Pavel Tolstik
122 Anders Holst
123 Rasmus Holst
124 Pierre Dufour
125 Soren Tranholm
126 unknown
127 Rene B. Madsen
128 Rene Jensen
129 Bill Morrison
130 Michael Senderovitz
131 Michael Sauffaus
132 Christian Fabricius
133 Pavel Lazerev
134 unknown
135 Soren Koziol
136 Boris Bykovsky
137 Igor A. Knyazev
138 Henrik Borner
139 Jannik Sonderby
140 Michael Thomsen
141 Magnus Sorensen
142 Anatoli Chistyakov
143 Filip Faurholm
144 Ulrich Hansen
145 Magnus Sundquist
146 Soren Lykke-Jorgensen
147 unknown
148 Ulrick Sinding Olsen
149 Martin Skygge
150 Rasmus Nielsen
151 Lars Bundgaard
152 Johan Westermark
153 Mads Johnsen
154 Mike Grey
155 Anders Thomsen
156 Kasper Kristensen
157 Lars Molgaard
158 Karel Smid
159 Soren Jensen
160 Martin E. Andersen
161 Ilja Dubkov
162 Mads Brandt
163 Radim Piroutek
164 Thomas Reinert
165 Christian Schioldan
166 Bent Christensen
167 Sergejs Senins
168 Hasse Olsen
169 Simon Pedersen
170 Klaus Nielsen
171 Torbin Benjaminsen
172 Andreas Borup
173 Henrik Bjerring
174 unknown
175 Andres V. Jensen
176 Michael Widenborg
177 Ruby Flomo
178 unknown
179 Marco Poulsen
180 unknown
181 Sergejs Cubars
182 Andreas Sabroe
183 Christian Dall-Hansen
184 unknown
185 Lars-Peter Drewsen
186 Michael Lauridsen
187 Morten Ovesen
188 Thomas Hansen
189 Dan Vollertzen
190 unknown
191 Casper Brandis
192 Casper Skovby
193 unknown
194 Thomas Wahlgren
195 Dan Jensen
196 Thomas Robbert
197 Benny Nielsen
198 Troels Biltoft
199 unknown
200 Jimmy Nielsson
201 Mikkel Schmidt
202 Anders Hansen
203 unknown
204 Morten Hagen
205 unknown
206 Morten Dahlmann
207 Nicklas Plampeck
208 Randy Maxwell
209 Soren True
210 Leonid Truhno
211 Mads True
212 Nikolai Clausen
213 Alexander Alexeev
214 Pavel Kostichkin
215 Thomas Johansen
216 Jens Johansson
217 Jesper Gram
218 Alexander Sundberg
219 Christian Mourier
220 Kristian Just Petersen
221 Dennis Olsson
222 Andreas Mattsson
223 Andre Clausen
224 Hakan Falkenhall
225 Nicklas Monberg

2005-06 Dutch Vadeko Flyers

COMPLETE SET (20) 8.00 15.00
1 Kevin Bruijsten .30 .75
2 Andriy Butochnov .30 .75
3 Anton Butochnov .30 .75
4 Sander Dijkstra .30 .75
5 James Easter .30 .75
6 Brent Janssen .30 .75
7 Matt Korthuis .30 .75
8 Petr Kratky .30 .75
9 Hans Kroon .30 .75
10 Paul Kroon .30 .75
11 Jacco Landman .30 .75
12 Don Nichols .30 .75
13 Marcel Nijland .30 .75
14 Tyler Palmiscno .30 .75
15 Marco Postma .30 .75
16 Brad Smulders .30 .75
17 Ruud vander Holst .30 .75
18 Jeroen van Olphen .30 .75
19 Stanislav Vernikov .30 .75
20 Brain de Bruijn HC .10 .25

1966 Finnish Jaakiekkosarja

This early Finnish set is presented for checklisting purposes only. We have no confirmed sales info and thus the set is unpriced.

COMPLETE SET (220)
1 Jukka Haapala
2 Simo Saimo
3 Hannu Torma
4 Jukka Savunen
5 Tenho Lotila
6 Tapani Koskimaki
7 Matti Saurio
8 Risto Kaitala
9 Raimo Tiainen
10 Esa Isaksson
11 Pentti Rautalin
12 Heikko Stenvall
13 Teppo Rastio
14 Jorma Vehmanen
15 Raimo Kilpio
16 Veikko Ukkonen
17 Lauri Lehtonen
18 Heikki Veravainen
19 Pentti Riitahaara
20 Pekka Kuusisto
21 Tapio Rautalammi
22 Raimo Tuli
23 Matti Paivinen
24 Matti Harju
25 Kari Sillanpaa
26 Matti Keinonen
27 Pekka Lahti
28 Johannes Karttunen
29 Sakari Isomaki
30 Samu Leikko
31 Tapani Suominen
32 Esa Vesslin
33 Pekka Jalava
34 Pertti Makela
35 Juha Rantasila
36 Jukka Haanpaa
37 Teuvo Helenius
38 Anto Virtanen
39 Kimmo Nokikuru
40 Jaakko Honkanen
41 Seppo Nystrom
42 Tuomo Pirskainen
43 Matti Jansson
44 Alpo Suhonen
45 Matti Varpela
46 Kaj Matalamaki
47 Antti Heikkila
48 Jaakko Jaskari
49 Jouko Ojansuu
50 Mikko Myllyniemi
51 Veli-Pekka Ketola
52 Matti Salmi
53 Pentti Vihanto
54 Hannu Luojola
55 Seppo Parikka
56 Martti Salonen
57 Risto Forss
58 Hannu Niittoaho
59 Kari Johansson
60 Henry Leppa
61 Jarmo Rantanen
62 Kari Torkkel
63 Seppo Vikstrom
64 Veijo Saarinen
65 Pekka Lahtela
66 Risto Vainio
67 Reijo Paksal
68 Erkan Nasib
69 Matti Breilin
70 Voitto Soini
71 Urpo Ylonen
72 Rauno Heinonen
73 Heikki Heino
74 Lasse Killi
75 Ilkka Mesikammen
76 Timo Nummelin
77 Pertti Kuismanen
78 Juhani Wahlsten
79 Rauli Ottila
80 Pertti Karelius
81 Teuvo Andelmin
82 Kari Varjanen
83 Kalevi Leppanen
84 Juhani Iso-Eskeli
85 Hannu Koivunen
86 Yrjo Hakala
87 Kari Ruontimo
88 Raimo Lohko
89 Markku Eiskonen
90 Hannu Lemander
91 Timo Vaatamoinen
92 Pekka Moisio
93 Martti Makia
94 Risto Heinvirta
95 Taisto Jahma
96 Veikko Makia
97 Raimo Helppolainen
98 Lalli Partinen
99 Keijo Sinkkonen
100 Antti Ravi
101 Martti Sinkkonen
102 Heikki Juselius
103 Timo Rantala
104 Heikki Mikkola
105 Jaakko Siren
106 Matti Korhonen
107 Erkki Mononen
108 Pertti Valkonen
109 Ilpo Koskela
110 Bengt Wilenius
111 Hannu Lindberg
112 Kristen Bertell
113 Veikko Kuusisto
114 Tapio Majaniemi
115 Leo Vankka
116 Pentti Harju
117 Ari Myllymaki
118 Matti Koskinen
119 Pentti Andersson
120 Pertti Heikkinen
121 Pekka Peltoniemi
122 Jouko Jarvinen
123 Matti Vartiainen
124 Esko Reijonen
125 Erkki Rasanen
126 Timo Viskari
127 Raimo Turkulainen
128 Paavo Tirkkonen
129 Orvo Paatero
130 Juhani Leirivaara
131 Jyrki Turunen
132 Timo Tuomainen
133 Pentti Karkkainen
134 Jussi Piuhola
135 Pentti Pihlapuro
136 Pentti Pennanen
137 Esa Viskari
138 Timo Luostarinen
139 Seppo Iivonen
140 Risto Alho
141 Esko Kiuru
142 Jaakko Hovinheimo
143 Jaakko Koikkalainen
144 Juhani Sodervik
145 Seppo Makinen
146 Teuvo Peltola
147 Antti Alenius
148 Kalevi Numminen
149 Esko Kaonpaa
150 Lauri Salomaa
151 Risto Pirttiaho
152 Antti Leppanen
153 Kari Makinen
154 Jorma Oksala
155 Pekka Marjamaki
156 Jouni Seistamo
157 Pertti Ansakorpi
158 Erkki Jarkko
159 Juhani Peltola
160 Erkki Mannikko
161 Keijo Mannisto
162 Matti Peltonen
163 Hannu Heikkonen
164 Pentti Hyytiainen
165 Antti Virtanen
166 Seppo Nurmi
167 Matti Reunamaki
168 Mikko Raikkonen
169 Esko Rantanen
170 Eero Holopainen
171 Juhani Ruohonen
172 Veikko Savolainen
173 Heikki Sivonen
174 Markku Pulli
175 Pekka Uitus

176 Heikki Keinonen
177 Jorma Saarikorpi
178 Rauno Lehtio
179 Kalevi Toivonen
180 Jorma Vilen
181 Pentti Kuusinen
182 Olavi Haapalainen
183 Seppo Nikkila
184 Jorma Suokko
185 Heino Pulli
186 Risto Lehtio
187 Pekka Lehtolainen
188 Timo Hirsimaki
189 Kari Palo-Oja
190 Pekka Leimu
191 Ali Saadetin
192 Erkki Jarvinen
193 Markku Hakanen
194 Jorma Kallio
195 Vaino Kolkka
196 Timo Saari
197 Jorma Peltonen
198 Pentti Pynnonen
199 Pentti Uotila
200 Timo Lahtinen
201 Juhani Lahtinen
202 Reijo Hakanen
203 Lasse Oksanen
204 Juhani Aromaki
205 Jukka Alkula
206 Pekka Olkkonen
207 Tapani Salo
208 Vesa Kartsalo
209 Antti Komsi
210 Asko Sallamaa
211 Juhani Tarkiainen
212 Antero Hakala
213 Ulf Slotte
214 Raimo Savolainen
215 Matias Savolainen
216 Risto Savolainen
217 Keijo Makinen
218 Tapio Makinen
219 Ossi Peltoniemi
220 Matti Valikangas

1971-72 Finnish Suomi Stickers

COMPLETE SET (384)	200.00	400.00
1 Vitaly Davydov	.30	.75
2 Anatoli Firsov	2.00	5.00
3 Valeri Kharlamov	6.00	15.00
4 Viktor Konovalenko	.30	.75
5 Viktor Kuzkin	.30	.75
6 Yuri Liapkin	.40	1.00
7 Vladimir Lutchenko	.30	.75
8 Alexander Maltsev	2.00	5.00
9 Alexander Martiniuk	.40	1.00
10 Boris Mikhailov	2.00	5.00
11 Evgeni Mishakov	.30	.75
12 Vladimir Petrov	2.00	5.00
13 Alexander Ragulin	.75	2.00
14 Igor Romishevski	.30	.75
15 Vladimir Shadrin	.40	1.00
16 Viatjeslav Starshinov	.40	1.00
17 Vladislav Tretiak	10.00	20.00
18 Gennady Tsygankov	.40	1.00
19 Vladimir Vikulov	.40	1.00
20 Evgeni Zimin	.40	1.00
21 Bedrich Brunschk	.20	.50
22 Jiri Bubla	.75	2.00
23 Josef Cerny	.30	.75
24 Richard Farda	.20	.50
25 Jan Havel	.20	.50
26 Ivan Hnlicka	.20	.50
27 Jiri Holecek	.40	1.00
28 Jiri Holik	.30	.75
29 Josef Horesovsky	.20	.50
30 Jiri Kochta	.20	.50
31 Oldrich Machac	.20	.50
32 Vladimir Martinec	.30	.75
33 Vaclav Nedomansky	.75	2.00
34 Eduard Novak	.20	.50
35 Frantisek Panchartek	.20	.50
36 Frantisek Pospisil	.30	.75
37 Marcel Sakac	.20	.50
38 Bohuslav Stastny	.40	1.00
39 Jan Suchy	.30	.75
40 Christer Abrahamsson	.75	2.00
41 Thommy Abrahamsson	.40	1.00
42 Thommie Bergman	1.25	3.00
43 Arne Carlsson	.20	.50
44 Inge Hammarstrom	4.00	10.00
45 Anders Hedberg	3.00	8.00
46 Leif Holmqvist	.75	2.00
47 Stig-Goran Johansson	.40	1.00
48 Stefan Karlsson	.20	.50
49 Hans Lindberg	.20	.50
50 Tord Lundstrom	.20	.50
51 William Lofqvist	.40	1.00
52 Kjell-Rune Milton	.20	.50
53 Lars-Goran Nilsson	.20	.50
54 Bert-Ola Nordlander	.40	1.00
55 Hakan Nygren	.20	.50
56 Bjorn Palmqvist	.20	.50
57 Hakan Pettersson	.20	.50
58 Ulf Sterner	.20	.50
59 Lennart Svedberg	.40	1.00
60 Hakan Wickberg	.20	.50
61 Esa Isaksson	.20	.50
62 Heikki Jarn	.20	.50
63 Veli-Pekka Ketola	.75	2.00
64 Ilpo Koskela	.20	.50
65 Seppo Lindstrom	.20	.50
66 Harri Linnonmaa	.20	.50
67 Hannu Luojola	.20	.50
68 Pekka Mononen	.20	.50
69 Erkki Mononen	.20	.50
70 Lauri Mononen	.20	.50
71 Matti Murto	.40	1.00
72 Lasse Oksanen	.20	.50
73 Esa Peltonen	.20	.50
74 Seppo Repo	.20	.50
75 Tommi Salmelainen	.20	.50
76 Juhani Tamminen	.20	.50
77 Jorma Valtonen	.40	1.00
78 Jorma Vehmanen	.20	.50
79 Urpo Ylonen	.40	1.00
80 Jouko Oystila	.20	.50
81 Tapio Flinck	.20	.50
82 Antti Heikkila	.20	.50
83 Reijo Heinonen	.20	.50
84 Jaakko Honkanen	.20	.50
85 Veli-Pekka Ketola	.75	2.00
86 Raimo Kilpio	.20	.50
87 Tapio Koskinen	.20	.50
88 Kaj Matalamaki	.20	.50
89 Pertti Makela	.20	.50
90 Pekka Rautakallio	.20	.50
91 Markku Riihimaki	.20	.50
92 Matti Salmi	.20	.50
93 Jorma Valtonen	.40	1.00
94 Anto Virtanen	.20	.50
95 Erkki Vakiparta	.20	.50
96 Pertti Ahokas	.20	.50
97 Pertti Arvaja	.20	.50
98 Olli Hietanen	.20	.50
99 Pentti Hiiros	.20	.50
100 Eero Holopainen	.20	.50
101 Kari Kinnunen	.20	.50
102 Ilpo Koskela	.20	.50
103 Timo Kyntola	.20	.50
104 Henry Leppa	.20	.50
105 Erkki Mononen	.20	.50
106 Pertti Nurmi	.20	.50
107 Timo Relas	.20	.50
108 Timo Sutinen	.20	.50
109 Timo Turunen	.20	.50
110 Jouko Oystila	.20	.50
111 Juhani Bostrom	.20	.50
112 Kimmo Heino	.20	.50
113 Esa Isaksson	.20	.50
114 Juhani Jylha	.20	.50
115 Heikki Jarn	.20	.50
116 Mauri Kaukorari	.20	.50
117 Vaino Kolkka	.20	.50
118 Harri Linnonmaa	.20	.50
119 Jaakko Marttinen	.20	.50
120 Matti Murto	.40	1.00
121 Lalli Partinen	.20	.50
122 Juha Rantasila	.20	.50
123 Heikki Riihiranta	.20	.50
124 Jorma Rikala	.20	.50
125 Tommi Salmelainen	.20	.50
126 Jorma Thusberg	.20	.50
127 Matti Vaisanen	.20	.50
128 Jukka Alkula	.20	.50
129 Pertti Ansakorpi	.20	.50
130 Keijo Jarvinen	.20	.50
131 Pertti Koivulahti	.20	.50
132 Ilpo Kuisma	.20	.50
134 Antti Leppanen	.20	.50
135 Pekka Marjamaki	.20	.50
136 Mikko Mynttien	.20	.50
137 Pekka Makinen	.20	.50
138 Seppo Makinen	.20	.50
139 Keijo Mannisto	.20	.50
140 Antti Perttula	.20	.50
141 Tuomo Rautiainen	.20	.50
142 Juhani Saarelainen	.20	.50
143 Jorma Saarikorpi	.20	.50
144 Risto Seesvuori	.20	.50
145 Jorma Siitarinen	.20	.50
146 Raimo Suoniemi	.20	.50
147 Juhani Aaltonen	.20	.50
148 Matti Ahvenharju	.20	.50
149 Hannu Auvinen	.20	.50
150 Jorma Borgstrom	.20	.50
151 Martti Immonen	.20	.50
152 Matti Keinonen	.20	.50
153 Seppo Laakkio	.20	.50
154 Timo Lahtinen	.20	.50
155 Esa Peltonen	.20	.50
156 Keijo Puhakka	.20	.50
157 Antti Ravi	.20	.50
158 Timo Saari	.20	.50
159 Esa Siren	.20	.50
160 Erkki Suni	.20	.50
161 Seppo Suoraniemi	.20	.50
162 Juhani Tamminen	.20	.50
163 Jorma Vehmanen	.20	.50
164 Stig Wetzell	.20	.50
165 Olli Viilma	.20	.50
166 Leo Aikas	.20	.50
167 Sakari Ahlberg	.20	.50
168 Seppo Ahokainen	.20	.50
169 Jorma Aro	.20	.50
170 Esko Eriksson	.20	.50
171 Marku Hakanen	.20	.50
172 Matti Hakanen	.20	.50
173 Reijo Hakanen	.20	.50
174 Martti Helle	.20	.50
175 Timo Hirsimaki	.20	.50
176 Jorma Kallio	.20	.50
177 Esko Kaonpaa	.20	.50
178 Pentti Koskela	.20	.50
179 Pekka Kuusisto	.20	.50
180 Pekka Leimu	.20	.50
181 Jukka Mattila	.20	.50
182 Lasse Oksanen	.20	.50
183 Kari Palooja	.20	.50
184 Jorma Peltonen	.40	1.00
185 Tuomo Sillman	.20	.50
186 Jaakko Siren	.20	.50
187 Veikkoi Suominen	.20	.50
188 Matti Jakonen	.20	.50
189 Kari Johansson	.20	.50
190 Arto Kaunonen	.20	.50
191 Timo Kokkonen	.20	.50
192 Reijo Leppanen	.20	.50
193 Seppo Lindstrom	.20	.50
194 Hannu Luojola	.20	.50
195 Hannu Niittoaho	.20	.50
196 Reijo Paksal	.20	.50
197 Seppo Parikka	.20	.50
198 Jarmo Rantanen	.20	.50
199 Veijo Saarinen	.20	.50
200 Martti Salonen	.20	.50
201 Voitto Soini	.20	.50
202 Kari Torkkel	.20	.50
203 Risto Vainio	.20	.50
204 Pentti Vihanto	.20	.50
205 Seppo Wikstrom	.20	.50
206 Urpo Ylonen	.40	1.00
207 Hannu Haapalainen	.20	.50
208 Jukka-Pekka Jarvenpaa	.20	.50
209 Timo Jarvinen	.20	.50
210 Heikki Keinonen	.20	.50
211 Heimo Keinonen	.20	.50
212 Rauno Lehtio	.20	.50
213 Markku Moisio	.20	.50
214 Seppo Nurmi	.20	.50
215 Esko Rantanen	.20	.50
216 Juhani Ruohonen	.20	.50
217 Mikkp Raikkonen	.20	.50
218 Lauri Salomaa	.20	.50
219 Veikko Savolainen	.20	.50
220 Leo Seppanen	.20	.50
221 Pekka Uitus	.20	.50
222 Jorma Vilen	.20	.50
223 Tapio Virhimo	.20	.50
224 Kauko Fomin	.20	.50
225 Heikki Hurme	.20	.50
226 Eero Juntunen	.20	.50
227 Lauri Jamsen	.20	.50
228 Lasse Kiili	.20	.50
229 Hannu Koivunen	.20	.50
230 Jarmo Koivunen	.20	.50
231 Pekka Lahtela	.20	.50
232 Ilkka Mesikammen	.20	.50
233 Timo Nummelin	.20	.50
234 Rauli Ottila	.20	.50
235 Matti Rautee	.20	.50
236 Pekka Rautee	.20	.50
237 Jari Rosberg	.20	.50
238 Jouni Samuli	.20	.50
239 Harry Silver'	.20	.50
240 Rauli Tammelin	.20	.50
241 Bengt Wilenius	.20	.50
242 Mikko Erholm	.20	.50
243 Veikko Ihalainen	.20	.50
244 Heikki Kauhanen	.20	.50
245 Tapani Koskimaki	.20	.50
246 Antti Laine	.20	.50
247 Arto Laine	.20	.50
248 Timo Lehtorinne	.20	.50
249 Hannu Lunden	.20	.50
250 Teppo Rastio	.20	.50
251 Pentti Rautalin	.20	.50
252 Kai Rosvall	.20	.50
253 Ilkka Saarikko	.20	.50
254 Jari Sarronlahti	.20	.50
255 Matti Saurio	.20	.50
256 Hannu Siivonen	.20	.50
257 Erkki Sundelin	.20	.50
258 Simo Suoknuuti	.20	.50
259 Martti Haapala	.20	.50
260 Yrjo Hakulinen	.20	.50
261 Pentti Hirvonen	.20	.50
262 Antero Honkanen	.20	.50
263 Pekka Lavkainen	.20	.50
264 Pentti Lavkainen	.20	.50
265 Pertti Martikainen	.20	.50
266 Pentti Martikainen	.20	.50
267 Seppo Nevalainen	.20	.50
268 Tapio Pohtinen	.20	.50
269 Kari Puustinen	.20	.50
270 Markku Rouhiainen	.20	.50
271 Jarmo Sahlmann	.20	.50
272 Seppo Saros	.20	.50
273 Juha Silvennoinen	.20	.50
274 Unto Turpeinen	.20	.50
275 Kari Viitakahti	.20	.50
276 Erkki Airaksinen	.20	.50
277 Kauko Alkunen	.20	.50
278 Jarmo Gummerus	.20	.50
279 Bjorn Herbert	.20	.50
280 Jarmo Jaakkola	.20	.50
281 Hannu Kapanen	.20	.50
282 Matti Koskinen	.20	.50
283 Martti Kuokkanen	.20	.50
284 Juhani Laine	.20	.50
285 Heikki Leppik	.20	.50
286 Juhani Langstrom	.20	.50
287 Osmo Lotjonen	.20	.50
288 Lauri Mononen	.20	.50
289 Christer Nordblad	.20	.50
290 Juha Poikolainen	.20	.50
291 Kimmo Rantanen	.20	.50
292 Seppo Repo	.20	.50
293 Ilpo Ruokosalmi	.20	.50
294 Arto Siisala	.20	.50
295 Bo Sjostedt	.20	.50
296 Pentti Viitanen	.20	.50
297 Pekka Arbelius	.40	1.00
298 Olli Engvist	.20	.50
299 Hannu Hiltunen	.20	.50
300 Paavo Holopainen	.20	.50
301 Juha Huikari	.20	.50
302 Ari Jalonen	.20	.50
303 Kari Jalonen	.20	.50
304 Ari Kaikkonen	.20	.50
305 Ari Kalmokoski	.20	.50
306 Arto Lehtinen	.20	.50
307 Markku Narhi	.20	.50
308 Ilkka Okkonen	.20	.50
309 Matti Perhonma	.20	.50
310 Juha-Pekka Porvari	.20	.50
311 Arto Ruotanen	.20	.50
312 Reijo Ruotsalainen	.20	.50
313 Matti Ruutti	.20	.50
314 Pertti Raisanen	.20	.50
315 Ari Timosaari	.20	.50
316 Janne Oro	.20	.50
317 Anssi Eronen	.20	.50
318 Seppo Hirvonen	.20	.50
319 Jari Hannu Hamalainen	.20	.50
320 Jari Pekka Hamalainen	.20	.50
321 Timo Harkonen	.40	1.00
322 Jouko Ikonen	.20	.50
323 Lasse Kaiponen	.20	.50
324 Jyri Kemppinen	.20	.50
325 Jouni Kostiainen	.20	.50
326 Kai Kulhoranta	.20	.50
327 Olli Lemola	.20	.50
328 Jari Lopponen	.20	.50
329 Pasi Makkonen	.20	.50
330 Vesa Massinen	.20	.50
331 Timo Minkkila	.20	.50
332 Petri Pellinen	.20	.50
333 Juhan Rasanen	.20	.50
334 Pasi Sallinen	.20	.50
335 Kauko Tamminen	.20	.50
336 Olli Teijonmaa	.20	.50
337 Ismo Tolvanen	.20	.50
338 Timo Vaahtoluoto	.20	.50
339 Kari Heikkila	.20	.50
340 Pekka Helander	.20	.50
341 Jari Hirsimaki	.20	.50
342 Jari Huotari	.20	.50
343 Ilkka Huura	.20	.50
344 Tero Juojarvi	.20	.50
345 Jari Jarvinen	.20	.50
346 Mika Laine	.20	.50
347 Marko Lepaus	.20	.50
348 Pertti Lundberg	.20	.50
349 Tino Minetti	.20	.50
350 Jarom Partanen	.20	.50
351 Olli-Pekka Perala	.20	.50
352 Ari Ruuska	.20	.50
353 Kai Saario	.20	.50
354 Olli-Pekka Turunen	.20	.50
355 Veli-Matti Uusimaa	.20	.50
356 Mauri Viita	.20	.50
357 Timo Virtanen	.20	.50
358 Jarmo Viteli	.20	.50
359 Petri Viteli	.20	.50
360 Ari Havukainen	.20	.50
361 Ismo Heinonen	.20	.50
362 Riku Hoyden	.20	.50
363 Jari Jokinen	.20	.50
364 Timo Joutsenvuori	.20	.50
365 Jyrki Jantti	.20	.50
366 Kimmo Jantti	.20	.50
367 Toni Ketola	.20	.50
368 Juha Korhonen	.20	.50
369 Ari Laine	.20	.50
370 Kari Lainio	.20	.50
371 Juha Makinen	.20	.50
372 Reima Numminen	.20	.50
373 Mika Pirila	.20	.50
374 Kai Pulli	.20	.50
375 Tero Tommila	.20	.50
376 Harri Tuohimaa	.20	.50
377 Pasi Tuohimaa	.20	.50
378 Ari Veijalainen	.20	.50
379 Jean Beliveau	10.00	25.00
380 Phil Esposito	15.00	40.00
381 Tony Esposito	15.00	40.00
382 Gordie Howe	30.00	60.00
383 Bobby Hull	15.00	40.00
384 Bobby Orr	50.00	100.00

1972-73 Finnish Jaakiekko

COMPLETE SET (360)	100.00	200.00
1 Vladimir Bednar	.40	1.00
2 Jiri Bubla	.40	1.00
3 Vladimir Dzurilla	1.25	3.00
4 Richard Farda	.20	.50
5 Julius Haas	.20	.50
6 Ivan Hlinka	.75	2.00
7 Jiri Holecek	.75	2.00
8 Jaroslav Holik	.40	1.00
9 Jiri Holik	.40	1.00
10 Josef Horesovsky	.20	.50
11 Jan Klapac	.20	.50
12 Jiri Kochta	.20	.50
13 Milan Kuzela	.20	.50
14 Oldrich Machac	.20	.50
15 Vladimir Martinec	.20	.50
16 Vaclav Nedomansky	2.00	5.00
17 Josef Palecek	.20	.50
18 Frantisek Pospisil	.20	.50
19 Bohuslav Stastny	.20	.50
20 Rudolf Tajcnar	.20	.50
21 Vjatsjeslav Anisin	.40	1.00
22 Juri Blinov	.40	1.00
23 Aleksandr Gusev	.75	2.00
24 Valeri Kharlamov	6.00	15.00
25 Aleksandr Yakushev	4.00	10.00
26 Viktor Kuzkin	.40	1.00
27 Vladimir Lutshenko	.40	1.00
28 Aleksandr Maltsev	2.00	5.00
29 Boris Mikhailov	2.00	5.00
30 Jevgeni Mishakov	.75	2.00
31 Vladimir Petrov	2.00	5.00
32 Aleksandr Ragulin	.75	2.00
33 Igor Romishevski	.40	1.00
34 Vladimir Shadrin	.75	2.00
35 Vladimir Shepovalov	.40	1.00
36 Vjatsjeslav Soloduhin	.40	1.00
37 Vladislav Tretjak	8.00	20.00
38 Gennadi Tsigankov	.40	1.00
39 Valeri Vasiljev	2.00	5.00
40 Vladimir Vikulov	.40	1.00
41 Christer Abrahamsson	1.25	3.00
42 Tommy Abrahamsson	1.25	3.00
43 Thommie Bergman	2.00	5.00
44 Inge Hammarstrom	3.00	8.00
45 Anders Hedberg	3.00	8.00
46 Leif Holmqvist	.75	2.00
47 Bjorn Johansson	.20	.50
48 Stig-Goran Johansson	.40	1.00
49 Stefan Karlsson	.20	.50
50 Stig Larsson	.20	.50
51 Mats Lind	.20	.50
52 Tord Lundstrom	.20	.50
53 Lars-Goran Johansson	.20	.50
54 Bjorn Palmqvist	.20	.50
55 Hakan Pettersson	.20	.50
56 Borje Salming	8.00	20.00
57 Lars-Erik Sjoberg	1.25	3.00
58 Carl Sundqvist	.20	.50
59 Hakan Wickberg	.20	.50
60 Stig Ostling	.20	.50
61 Seppo Ahokainen	.20	.50
62 Matti Keinonen	.20	.50
63 Veli-Pekka Ketola	1.25	3.00
64 Harri Linnonmaa	.20	.50
65 Pekka Marjamaki	.20	.50
66 Lauri Mononen	.20	.50
67 Matti Murto	.20	.50
68 Timo Nummelin	.20	.50
69 Lasse Oksanen	.20	.50
70 Esa Peltonen	.20	.50
71 Juha Rantasila	.20	.50
72 Pekka Rautakallio	1.25	3.00
73 Seppo Repo	.20	.50
74 Heikki Riihiranta	.20	.50
75 Juhani Tamminen	.40	1.00
76 Timo Turunen	.20	.50
77 Pertti Valkeapaa	.20	.50
78 Jorma Valtonen	.20	.50
79 Stig Wetzell	.20	.50
80 Jouko Oystila	.20	.50
81 Juhani Bostrom	.20	.50
82 Kimmo Heino	.20	.50
83 Penti Karlsson	.20	.50
84 Mauri Kaukokari	.20	.50
85 Jarmo Koivunen	.20	.50
86 Heikki Kojola	.20	.50
87 Vaino Kolkka	.20	.50
88 Harri Linnonmaa	.20	.50
89 Jaakko Marttinen	.20	.50
90 Matti Murto	.20	.50
91 Lalli Partinen	.20	.50
92 Juha Rantasila	.20	.50
93 Heikki Riihiranta	.20	.50
94 Jorma Rikala	.20	.50
95 Henry Saleva	.20	.50
96 Tommi Salmelainen	.20	.50
97 Jorma Thusberg	.20	.50
98 Jorma Virtanen	.20	.50
99 Matti Vaisanen	.20	.50
100 Juhani Aaltonen	.20	.50
101 Jorma Immonen	.20	.50
102 Martti Immonen	.20	.50
103 Heikki Jarn	.20	.50
104 Matti Keinonen	.20	.50
105 Seppo Laakkio	.20	.50
106 Timo Lahtinen	.20	.50
107 Esa Peltonen	.20	.50
108 Keijo Puhakka	.20	.50
109 Seppo Railio	.20	.50
110 Antti Ravi	.20	.50
111 Timo Saari	.20	.50
112 Esa Siren	.20	.50
113 Seppo Suoraniemi	.20	.50
114 Juhani Tamminen	.20	.50
115 Jorma Vehmanen	.20	.50
116 Stig Wetzell	.20	.50
117 Leo Aikas	.20	.50
118 Sakari Ahlberg	.20	.50
119 Seppo Ahokainen	.20	.50
120 Jorma Aro	.20	.50
121 Esko Eriksson	.20	.50
122 Markku Hakanen	.20	.50
123 Timo Hirsimaki	.20	.50
124 Jorma Kallio	.20	.50
125 Esko Kaonpaa	.20	.50
126 Pentti Koskela	.20	.50
127 Pekka Kuusisto	.20	.50
128 Pekka Leimu	.20	.50
129 Len Lunde	.20	.50
130 Jukka Mattila	.20	.50
131 Lasse Oksanen	.20	.50
132 Hannu Palmu	.20	.50
133 Kari Palo-oja	.20	.50
134 Jorma Peltonen	.20	.50
135 Tuomo Sillman	.20	.50
136 Veikko Suominen	.20	.50
137 Pertti Ahokass	.20	.50
138 Pertti Arvaja	.20	.50
139 Christer Bergenheim	.20	.50
140 Jorma Borgstrom	.20	.50
141 Olli Hietanen	.20	.50
142 Pentti Hiiros	.20	.50
143 Eero Holopainen	.20	.50
144 Kari Kinnunen	.20	.50
145 Keijo Koivunen	.20	.50
146 Ilpo Koskela	.20	.50
147 Timo Kyntola	.20	.50
148 Henry Leppa	.20	.50
149 Erkki Mononen	.20	.50
150 Pertti Nurmi	.20	.50
151 Tero Raty	.20	.50
152 Timo Sutinen	.20	.50
153 Timo Turunen	.20	.50
154 Jouko Oystila	.20	.50
155 Hannu Haapalainen	.20	.50
156 Olavi Haapalainen	.20	.50
157 Jukka-Pekka Jarvenpaa	.20	.50
158 Heimo Keinonen	.20	.50
159 Markku Moisio	.20	.50
160 Heikki Nurmi	.20	.50
161 Seppo Nurmi	.20	.50
162 Oiva Oijennus	.20	.50
163 Reino Pulkkinen	.20	.50
164 Esko Rantanen	.20	.50
165 Juhani Ruohonen	.20	.50
166 Mikko Raikkonen	.20	.50
167 Lauri Salomaa	.20	.50
168 Leo Seppanen	.20	.50
169 Pekka Uitus	.20	.50
170 Jorma Vilen	.20	.50
171 Tapio Virhimo	.20	.50
172 Leo Haakana	.20	.50
173 Seppo Hyvonen	.20	.50
174 Heikki Juselius	.20	.50
175 Hannu Lemander	.20	.50
176 Kyosti Lahde	.20	.50
177 Ari Mikkola	.20	.50
178 Martti Makia	.20	.50
179 Martti Narinen	.20	.50
180 Pekka Nieminen	.20	.50
181 Teijo Rasanen	.20	.50
182 Timo Sartiala	.20	.50
183 Pekka Sartjarvi	.20	.50
184 Keijo Sinkkonen	.20	.50
185 Martti Sinkkonen	.20	.50
186 Arto Summanen	.20	.50
187 Erkki Suni	.20	.50
188 Seppo Urpalainen	.20	.50
189 Matti Vaatamoinen	.20	.50
190 Timo Vaatamoinen	.20	.50
191 Jukka Alkula	.20	.50
192 Pertti Ansakorpi	.20	.50
193 Keijo Jarvinen	.20	.50
194 Pertti Koivulahti	.20	.50
195 Ilpo Kuisma	.20	.50
196 Vesa Lehtoranta	.20	.50
197 Antti Leppanen	.20	.50
198 Pekka Marjamaki	.20	.50
199 Mikko Mynttinen	.20	.50
200 Pekka Makinen	.20	.50
201 Seppo Makinen	.20	.50
202 Antti Perttula	.20	.50
203 Tuomo Rautiainen	.20	.50
204 Jorma Saarikorpi	.20	.50
205 Jorma Siitarinen	.20	.50
206 Raimo Suoniemi	.20	.50
207 Pertti Valkeapaa	.20	.50
208 Kari Horkko	.20	.50
209 Eero Juntunen	.20	.50
210 Lauri Jamsen	.20	.50
211 Kari Kauppila	.20	.50
212 Lasse Kiili	.20	.50
213 Olli Kokkonen	.20	.50
214 Pekka Lahtela	.20	.50
215 Robert Lamoureux	.20	.50
216 Ilkka Mesikammen	.20	.50
217 Timo Nummelin	.20	.50
218 Rauli Ottila	.20	.50
219 Matti Rautee	.20	.50
220 Pekka Rautee	.20	.50
221 Jari Rosberg	.20	.50
222 Jouni Samuli	.20	.50
223 Harri Silver	.20	.50
224 Rauli Tammelin	.20	.50
225 Bengt Wilenius	.20	.50
226 Pertti Hasanen	.20	.50
227 Kari Johansson	.20	.50
228 Arto Kaunonen	.20	.50
229 Timo Kokkonen	.20	.50
230 Reijo Leppanen	.20	.50
231 Seppo Lindstrom	.20	.50
232 Hannu Luojola	.20	.50
233 Hannu Niittoaho	.20	.50
234 Reijo Paksal	.20	.50
235 Seppo Parikka	.20	.50
236 Jarmo Rantanen	.20	.50
237 Kari Salonen	.20	.50
238 Tapani Sura	.20	.50
239 Kari Torkkel	.20	.50
240 Risto Vainio	.20	.50
241 Pentti Vihanto	.20	.50
242 Seppo Wikstrom	.20	.50
243 Urpo Ylonen	.20	.50
244 Tapio Flinck	.20	.50
245 Antti Heikkila	.20	.50
246 Reijo Heinonen	.20	.50
247 Jaakko Honkanen	.20	.50
248 Veli-Pekka Ketola	1.25	3.00
249 Raimo Kilpio	.20	.50
250 Tapio Koskinen	.20	.50
251 Jarkko Levonen	.20	.50
252 Kaj Matalamaki	.20	.50
253 Pertti Makela	.20	.50
254 Hannu Pulkkinen	.20	.50
255 Pekka Rautakallio	1.25	3.00
256 Markku Riihimaki	.20	.50
257 Matti Salmi	.20	.50
258 Jorma Valtonen	.20	.50
259 Anto Virtanen	.20	.50
260 Erkki Vakiparta	.20	.50
261 Martti Jarkko	.20	.50
262 Torsti Jarvenpaa	.20	.50
263 Tapio Kallio	.20	.50
264 Jussi Kiansten	.20	.50
265 Kimmo Korpela	.20	.50
266 Jarmo Kuisma	.20	.50
267 Antero Lehtonen	.20	.50
268 Mikko Leinonen	.20	.50
269 Tuomas Leinonen	.20	.50
270 Lasse Litma	.20	.50
271 Seppo Makinen	.20	.50
272 Heikki Niemi	.20	.50
273 Reijo Narvanen	.20	.50
274 Kalevi Paakkonen	.20	.50
275 Reijo Rossi	.20	.50
276 Seppo Sevon	.20	.50
277 Jorma Siren	.20	.50
278 Risto Sirkkola	.20	.50
279 Risto Hevonkorpi	.20	.50
280 Veijo Hukkanen	.20	.50
281 Timo Hytti	.20	.50
282 Kalle Impola	.20	.50
283 Pertti Jarvenpaa	.20	.50
284 Rauno Jarvinen	.20	.50
285 Antti Kaivola	.20	.50
286 Jorma Karvonen	.20	.50
287 Pekka Karvonen	.20	.50
288 Seppo Kettunen	.20	.50
289 Kari Niemi	.20	.50
290 Timo Niiniviita	.20	.50
291 Jari Nurminen	.20	.50
292 Pentti Poussu	.20	.50
293 Matti Rautiainen	.20	.50
294 Vesa Ronkainen	.20	.50
295 Mauri Salminen	.20	.50
296 Kari Silius	.20	.50
297 Kimo Turtiainen	.20	.50
298 Juha Wikman	.20	.50
299 Juha-Pekka Aho	.20	.50
300 Matti Estola	.20	.50
301 Markku Heinonen	.20	.50
302 Mauri Heinonen	.20	.50
303 Jukka Hirsimaki	.20	.50
304 Jarmo Huhtala	.20	.50
305 Harri Huotari	.20	.50
306 Kari Jarvinen	.20	.50
307 Jari Kaarela	.20	.50
308 Kai Lehto	.20	.50
309 Jari Leppanen	.20	.50
310 Jarmo Lilius	.20	.50
311 Markus Matsson	.20	.50
312 Jari Niinimaki	.20	.50
313 Hannu Oksanen	.20	.50
314 Sakari Pehu	.20	.50
315 Mika Rajala	.20	.50
316 Risto Siltanen	.20	.50
317 Jarmo Siro	.20	.50
318 Jukka Siro	.20	.50
319 Jari Uusikartano	.20	.50
320 Seppo Vartiainen	.20	.50
321 Mika Weissman	.20	.50
322 Seppo Aro	.20	.50
323 Jari Huotari	.20	.50
324 Ilkka Huura	.20	.50
325 Jari Hytti	.20	.50
326 Jarmo Jamalainen	.20	.50
327 Jari Jokinen	.20	.50
328 Tero Juojarvi	.20	.50
329 Jari Jarvinen	.20	.50
330 Lauri Kosonen	.20	.50
331 Aki Laakso	.20	.50
332 Ismo Laine	.20	.50
333 Matti Lisko	.20	.50
334 Dale Lunde	.20	.50
335 Markku Pirkkalanniemi	.20	.50
336 Rauno Saarnio	.20	.50
337 Jukka Silander	.20	.50
338 Olli-Pekka Turunen	.20	.50
339 Mauri Unkila	.20	.50
340 Jarmo Viteli	.20	.50
341 Jukka Ahonen	.20	.50
342 Jari Hallila	.20	.50
343 Jari Helle	.20	.50
344 Jari Hirsimaki	.20	.50
345 Petri Jokinen	.20	.50
346 Kari Jarvinen	.20	.50
347 Arto Laine	.20	.50
348 Ari Leinonen	.20	.50
349 Jukka Oksanen	.20	.50
350 Sten Pakarinen	.20	.50
351 Jyrki Seppa	.20	.50
352 Jari Simola	.20	.50
353 Olli Sarkilahti	.20	.50
354 Kari-Pekka Tarko	.20	.50
355 Timo Toivonen	.20	.50
356 Veli-Matti Uusimaa	.20	.50
357 Risto Viljanen	.20	.50
358 Timo Virtanen	.20	.50
359 Teppo Valimaki	.20	.50
360 Juha Yrjola	.20	.50

1972 Finnish Hellas

This vintage Finnish set appears to feature players who appeared in the previous World Championships.

COMPLETE SET (99)	50.00	125.00
1 Seppo Ahokainen	.20	.50
2 Veli-Pekka Ketola	.60	1.50
3 Henry Leppa	.20	.50
4 Harri Linnonmaa	.20	.50
5 Pekka Marjamaki	.20	.50
6 Lauri Mononen	.20	.50
7 Matti Murto	.20	.50
8 Timo Nummelin	.20	.50
9 Lasse Oksanen	.20	.50
10 Esa Peltonen	.20	.50
11 Pekka Rautakallio	.60	1.50
12 Seppo Repo	.20	.50
13 Heikki Riihiranta	.40	1.00
14 Tommi Salmelainen	.20	.50
15 Leo Seppanen	.20	.50
16 Juhani Tamminen	.40	1.00
17 Timo Turunen	.20	.50
18 Pertti Valkeapaa	.20	.50
19 Jorma Valtonen	.40	1.00
20 Jouko Oystila	.20	.50
21 Timo Saari	.20	.50
22 Seppo Suoraniemi	.20	.50
23 Leif Holmqvist	.40	1.00
24 Thommy Abrahamsson	.40	1.00
25 Thommie Bergman	.75	2.00
26 Stig Ostling	.40	1.00
27 Lars Sjoberg	.75	2.00
28 Carl Sundquist	.20	.50
29 Bjorn Johansson	.20	.50
30 Tord Lundstrom	.20	.50
31 Stig-Goran Johansson	.20	.50
32 Stefan Karlsson	.20	.50
33 Lars-Goran Nilsson	.20	.50
34 Stig Larsson	.20	.50
35 Mats Lindh	.20	.50
36 Bjorn Palmqvist	.20	.50
37 Inge Hammarstrom	4.00	10.00
38 Anders Hedberg	2.00	5.00
39 Kurt Larsson	.20	.50
40 Hakan Pettersson	.20	.50
41 Hakan Wickberg	.20	.50
42 Borje Salming	6.00	15.00
43 Franz Funk	.20	.50
44 Otto Schneitberger	.20	.50
45 Josef Volk	.20	.50
46 Rudolph Thanner	.20	.50
47 Paul Langner	.20	.50
48 Harald Kadow	.20	.50
49 Anton Pohl	.20	.50
50 Karl-Heinz Egger	2.00	5.00
51 Lorenz Funk	.20	.50
52 Alois Schloder	.20	.50
53 Gustav Hanig	.20	.50
54 Philips Reiner	.20	.50
55 Bernd Kuhn	.20	.50
56 Johan Eimansberger	.20	.50
57 Rainer Makatsch	.20	.50
58 Michael Eibl	.20	.50
59 Hans Schichti	.20	.50
60 Anrton Hoffher	.20	.50
61 Valdimir Lutchenko	.40	1.00
62 Aleksandr Gusev	.30	.75
63 Vladimir Lutchenko	.40	1.00
64 Viktor Kuzkin	.20	.50
65 Aleksandr Ragulin	.40	1.00
66 Igor Romishevski	.20	.50
67 Gennadi Tsigankov	.40	1.00
68 Valeri Vasiliev	.40	1.00
69 Yuri Blinov	.20	.50
70 Alexander Maltsev	2.00	5.00
71 Evgeny Mishakov	.30	.75
72 Boris Mikhailov	2.00	5.00
73 Vjatseslav Anisin	.30	.75
74 Alexander Yakushev	2.00	5.00
75 Vladimir Petrov	1.25	3.00
76 Valeri Kharlamov	4.00	10.00
77 Vladimir Vikulov	.30	.75
78 Vladimir Shadrin	.30	.75
79 Vladislav Tretiak	6.00	15.00
80 Vladimir Dzurilla	.60	1.50
81 Jiri Holecek	.40	1.00
82 Josef Horesovsky	.20	.50
83 Oldrich Machac	.20	.50
84 Jaroslav Holik	.30	.75
85 Rudolf Tajcnar	.20	.50
86 Frantisek Pospisil	.30	.75
87 Jiri Kochta	.20	.50
88 Jan Klapac	.20	.50
89 Vladimir Martinec	.20	.50
90 Richard Farda	.30	.75
91 Bohuslav Stastny	.30	.75
92 Vaclav Nedomansky	.60	1.50
93 Julius Haas	.20	.50
94 Josef Palecek	.20	.50
95 Jiri Bubla	.40	1.00
96 Milan Kuzela	.20	.50
97 Vladimir Bednar	.20	.50
98 Jiri Holik	.40	1.00
99 Ivan Hlinka	.30	.75

1972 Finnish Panda Toronto

COMPLETE SET (118)	50.00	100.00
1 Juhani Bostrom	.40	1.00
2 Gary Engberg	.40	1.00
3 Kimmo Heino	.40	1.00
4 Mauri Kaukokari	.40	1.00
5 Vaino Kolkka	.40	1.00
6 Harri Linnonmaa	.40	1.00
7 Jaakko Marttinen	.40	1.00
8 Matti Murto	.40	1.00
9 Lalli Partinen	.40	1.00
10 Juha Rantasila	.40	1.00
11 Heikki Riihiranta	.40	1.00
12 Jorma Rikala	.40	1.00
13 Tommi Salmelainen	.40	1.00
14 Jorma Thusberg	.40	1.00
15 Jorma Virtanen	.40	1.00
16 Matti Vaisanen	.40	1.00
17 Sakari Ahlberg	.40	1.00
18 Jorma Aro	.40	1.00
19 Esko Eriksson	.40	1.00
20 Markku Hakanen	.40	1.00
21 Matti Hakanen	.40	1.00
22 Reijo Hakanen	.40	1.00
23 Timo Hirsimaki	.40	1.00
24 Jorma Kallio	.40	1.00
25 Esko Kaonpaa	.40	1.00
26 Pentti Koskela	.40	1.00
27 Pekka Kuusisto	.40	1.00
28 Pekka Leimu	.40	1.00
29 Lasse Oksanen	.40	1.00
30 Kari Palo-oja	.40	1.00
31 Jorma Peltonen	.40	1.00
32 Veikko Suominen	.40	1.00
33 Tapio Flinck	.40	1.00
34 Pentti Hakamaki	.40	1.00
35 Antti Heikkila	.40	1.00
36 Reijo Heinonen	.40	1.00
37 Jaakko Honkanen	.40	1.00
38 Veli-Pekka Ketola	.40	1.00
39 Raimo Kilpio	.40	1.00
40 Tapio Koskinen	.40	1.00
41 Kaj Matalamaki	.40	1.00
42 Pekka Rautakallio	.40	1.00
43 Matti Salmi	.40	1.00
44 Kari-Pekka Toivonen	.40	1.00
45 Jorma Valtonen	.40	1.00
46 Anto Virtanen	.40	1.00
47 Erkki Vakiparta	.40	1.00
48 Vitaly Davydov	.75	2.00
49 Anatoly Firsov	.75	2.00
50 Valeri Kharlamov	8.00	20.00
51 Victor Konovalenko	.75	2.00
52 Victor Kuzkin	.75	2.00
53 Yuri Liapkin	.75	2.00
54 Vladimir Lutchenko	.75	2.00
55 Alexander Maltsev	2.00	5.00
56 Alexander Martyniuk	.75	2.00
57 Boris Mikhailov	2.00	5.00
58 Aleksander Ragulin	.75	2.00
59 Igor Romishevskyi	.75	2.00
60 Vladimir Shadrin	.75	2.00
61 Viacheslav Starshinov	.75	2.00
62 Vladislav Tretiak	8.00	20.00
63 Evgenyi Zimin	.75	2.00
64 Christer Abrahamsson	.75	2.00
65 Tommy Abrahamsson	.75	2.00
66 Arne Carlsson	.40	1.00
67 Inge Hammarstrom	2.00	5.00
68 Leif Holmqvist	.75	2.00
69 Stig-Goran Johansson	.40	1.00
70 Stefan Karlsson	.40	1.00
71 Hans Lindberg	.40	1.00
72 Tord Lundstrom	.40	1.00
73 Lars-Goran Nilsson	.40	1.00
74 Bert-Ola Nordlander	.40	1.00
75 Hakan Nygren	.40	1.00
76 Bjorn Palmqvist	.40	1.00
77 Ulf Sterner	.40	1.00
78 Lennart Svedberg	.40	1.00
79 Hakan Wickberg	.40	1.00
80 Josef Cerny	.40	1.00
81 Richard Farda	.40	1.00
82 Ivan Hlinka	.40	1.00
83 Jiri Holecek	.40	1.00
84 Jiri Holik	.40	1.00
85 Josef Horesovsky	.40	1.00
86 Milan Kuzela	.40	1.00

7 Oldrich Machac .40 1.00
8 Vladimir Martinec .40 1.00
9 Vladimir Nadrchal .40 1.00
0 Vaclav Nedomansky 1.50 4.00
1 Frantisek Panchartek .40 1.00
2 Frantisek Pospisil .40 1.00
3 Marcel Sakac .40 1.00
4 Bohuslav Stastny .40 1.00
5 Rudolf Tajcnar .40 1.00
6 Esa Isaksson .40 1.00
7 Heikki Jarn .40 1.00
8 Veli-Pekka Ketola 1.50 4.00
9 Ilpo Koskela .40 1.00
00 Seppo Lindstrom .40 1.00
01 Harri Linnonmaa .40 1.00
102 Pekka Marjamaki .40 1.00
03 Erkki Mononen .40 1.00
04 Lauri Mononen 1.00
05 Matti Murto .40 1.00
06 Lasse Oksanen .40 1.00
107 Esa Peltonen .40 1.00
08 Seppo Repo .40 1.00
109 Tommi Salmelainen .40 1.00
110 Jorma Valtonen .40 1.00
111 Urpo Ylonen .40 1.00
12 Jouko Oystila .40 1.00
13 Sovjet - Finland .40 1.00
114 Sverige - Tjeckoslovakien .40 1.00
115 Finland - Svergie .40 1.00
116 Tjeckoslovakien - Sovjet .40 1.00
117 USA - Sovjet .40 1.00
118 Hockey Sticks .40 1.00

1972 Finnish Semic World Championship

Printed in Italy by Semic Press, the 233 cards comprising this set measure 1 7/8" by 2 1/2" and feature posed color player photos on their white-bordered fronts.

1973-74 Finnish Jaakiekko

COMPLETE SET (325) 125.00 250.00
Vjatsjeslav Anisin .75 2.00
2 Aleksandr Bodunov .75 2.00
3 Aleksandr Gusev .75 2.00
4 Valeri Kharlamov 6.00 15.00
5 Aleksandr Yakushev 2.00 5.00
6 Juri Lebedev .75 2.00
7 Juri Liapkin .75 2.00
8 Vladimir Lutshenko .75 2.00
9 Aleksandr Maltsev 2.00 5.00
10 Aleksandr Martiniuk .75 2.00
11 Boris Mikhailov 2.00 5.00
12 Jevgeni Paladiev .75 2.00
13 Vladimir Petrov 2.00 5.00
14 Aleksandr Ragulin .75 2.00
15 Vladimir Shadrin .75 2.00
16 Aleksandr Sidelnikov .75 2.00
17 Vladislav Tretiak 8.00 20.00
18 Gennadi Tsigankov .75 2.00
19 Valeri Vasiljev 2.00 5.00
20 Vladimir Vikulov .75 2.00
21 Aleksandr Voltshkov .75 2.00
22 Christer Abrahamsson 1.25 3.00
23 Thommy Abrahamsson 1.25 3.00
24 Roland Bond .40 1.00
25 Arne Carlsson .40 1.00
26 Inge Hammarstrom 2.00 5.00
27 Anders Hedberg 2.00 5.00
28 Bjorn Johansson .40 1.00
29 Stefan Karlsson .40 1.00
30 Curt Larsson .40 1.00
31 Tord Lundstrom .40 1.00
32 William Lofqvist .40 1.00
33 Ulf Nilsson 2.00 5.00
34 Borje Salming 6.00 15.00
35 Lars-Erik Sjoberg 1.25 3.00
36 Ulf Sterner .40 1.00
37 Karl-Johan Sundqvist .40 1.00
38 Dan Soderstrom .40 1.00
39 Hakan Wickberg .40 1.00
40 Kjell-Arne Wickstrom .40 1.00
41 Dick Yderstrom .40 1.00
42 Mats Ahlberg .40 1.00
43 Peter Adamik .40 1.00
44 Jiri Bubla .40 1.00
45 Jiri Crha 1.25 3.00
46 Richard Farda .40 1.00
47 Ivan Hlinka .75 2.00
48 Jiri Holecek .75 2.00
49 Jaroslav Holik .40 1.00
50 Jiri Holik .40 1.00
51 Josef Horesovsky .40 1.00
52 Jan Klapac .40 1.00
53 Jiri Kochta .40 1.00
54 Milan Kuzela .40 1.00
55 Oldrich Machac .40 1.00
56 Vladimir Martinec .40 1.00
57 Vaclav Nedomansky 1.25 3.00
58 Jiri Novak .40 1.00
59 Josef Palecek .40 1.00
60 Frantisek Pospisil .40 1.00
61 Bohuslav Stastny .40 1.00
62 Karel Vohralik .40 1.00
63 Seppo Ahokainen .40 1.00
64 Matti Keinonen .40 1.00
65 Veli-Pekka Ketola 1.25 3.00
66 Ilpo Koskela .40 1.00
67 Ilpo Kuisma .40 1.00
68 Pekka Kuusisto .40 1.00
69 Henry Leppa .40 1.00
70 Antti Leppanen .40 1.00
71 Seppo Lindstrom .40 1.00
72 Lauri Mononen .40 1.00
73 Timo Nummelin .40 1.00
74 Lalli Partinen .40 1.00
75 Esa Peltonen .40 1.00
76 Pekka Rautakallio 1.25 3.00
77 Seppo Repo .40 1.00
78 Heikki Riihiranta .40 1.00
79 Timo Sutinen .40 1.00
80 Juhani Tamminen .40 1.00
81 Timo Turunen .40 1.00
82 Jorma Valtonen .40 1.00
83 Jorma Vehmanen .40 1.00
84 Jouko Oystila .40 1.00
85 Josef Batkiewicz .40 1.00
86 Krzysztof Bialynicki .40 1.00
87 Stefan Chowaniec .40 1.00
88 Ludwik Czachovski .40 1.00
89 Andrzej Czczepaniec .40 1.00
90 Stanislav Fryzlewicz .40 1.00
91 Robert Goralczyk .40 1.00
92 Mieczyslaw Jaskierski .40 1.00
93 Tadeusz Kacik .40 1.00
94 Adam Kopczynski .40 1.00
95 Valery Kosyl .40 1.00
96 Tadeusz Obloj .40 1.00
97 Jerzy Potz .40 1.00
98 Andrzej Slowakiewicz .40 1.00
99 Josef Slowakiewicz .40 1.00
100 Jan Szeja .40 1.00
101 Leszek Tokarz .40 1.00
102 Wieslav Tokarz .40 1.00
103 Henryk Vojtynek .40 1.00
104 Walenty Zietara .40 1.00
105 Pertti Arvaja .40 1.00
106 Olli J. Hietanen .40 1.00
107 Olli T. Hietanen .40 1.00
108 Pentti Hiiros .40 1.00
109 Eero Holopainen .40 1.00
110 Kari Kinnunen .40 1.00
111 Ilpo Koskela .40 1.00
112 Timo Kyntola .40 1.00
113 Henry Leppa .40 1.00
114 Jan Lindberg .40 1.00
115 Lauri Mononen .40 1.00
116 Mika Rajala .40 1.00
117 Pertti Nurmi .40 1.00
118 Jyrki Seivo .40 1.00
119 Jorma Siitarinen .40 1.00
120 Seppo Suoraniemi .40 1.00
121 Timo Sutinen .40 1.00
122 Timo Turunen .40 1.00
123 Jorma Valtonen .40 1.00
124 Seppo Vartiainen .40 1.00
125 Jouko Oystila .40 1.00
126 Juhani Bostrom .40 1.00
127 Matti Hagman 1.25 3.00
128 Kimmo Heino .40 1.00
129 Jorma Immonen .40 1.00
130 Pentti Karlsson .40 1.00
131 Mauri Kaukokari .40 1.00
132 Jarmo Koivunen .40 1.00
133 Vaino Kolkka .40 1.00
134 Harri Linnonmaa .40 1.00
135 Jaakko Marttinen .40 1.00
136 Matti Murto .40 1.00
137 Lalli Partinen .40 1.00
138 Esa Peltonen .40 1.00
139 Juha Rantasila .40 1.00
140 Heikki Riihiranta .40 1.00
141 Jorma Rikala .40 1.00
142 Tommi Salmelainen .40 1.00
143 Henry Saleva .40 1.00
144 Juhani Tamminen .75 2.00
145 Jorma Thusberg .40 1.00
146 Jorma Virtanen .40 1.00
147 Matti Vaisanen .40 1.00
148 Stig Wetzell .40 1.00
149 Jukka Alkula .40 1.00
150 Pertti Ansakorpi .40 1.00
151 Hannu Haapalainen .40 1.00
152 Martti Jarkko .40 1.00
153 Keijo Jarvinen .40 1.00
154 Pertti Koivulahti .40 1.00
155 Ilpo Kuisma .40 1.00
156 Antero Lehtonen .40 1.00
157 Antti Leppanen .40 1.00
158 Lasse Litma .40 1.00
159 Pekka Marjamaki .40 1.00
160 Mikko Myrttinen .40 1.00
161 Pekka Makinen .40 1.00
162 Seppo I. Makinen .40 1.00
163 Seppo S. Makinen .40 1.00
164 Keijo Mannisto .40 1.00
165 Antti Perttula .40 1.00
166 Tuomo Rautiainen .40 1.00
167 Jorma Saarikorpi .40 1.00
168 Juha Silvennoinen .40 1.00
169 Jorma Siren .40 1.00
170 Raimo Suoniemi .40 1.00
171 Pertti Valkeapaa .40 1.00
172 Sakari Ahlberg .40 1.00
173 Seppo Ahokainen .40 1.00
174 Jorma Aro .40 1.00
175 Esko Eriksson .40 1.00
176 Markku Hakanen .40 1.00
177 Reijo Hakanen .40 1.00
178 Martti Helle .40 1.00
179 Erkki Jarvinen .40 1.00
180 Jorma Kallio .40 1.00
181 Erkki Kesalainen .40 1.00
182 Pekka Kuusisto .40 1.00
183 Pekka Leimu .40 1.00
184 Jukka Mattila .40 1.00
185 Esko Makinen .40 1.00
186 Lassse Oksanen .40 1.00
187 Kari Palo-oja .40 1.00
188 Jorma Peltonen .40 1.00
189 Pekka Rampa .40 1.00
190 Heikki Salminen .40 1.00
191 Tuomo Sillman .40 1.00
192 Veikko Suominen .40 1.00
193 Tapio Virhimo .40 1.00
194 Juhani Aaltonen .40 1.00
195 Bjorn Herbert .40 1.00
196 Hannu Kapanen .40 1.00
197 Matti Keinonen .40 1.00
198 Lasse Kiili .40 1.00
199 Matti Koskinen .40 1.00
200 Martti Kuokkanen .40 1.00
201 Urpo Kuukauppi .40 1.00
202 Seppo Laakkio .40 1.00
203 Timo Lahtinen .40 1.00
204 Juhani Laine .40 1.00
205 Heikki Leppik .40 1.00
206 Osmo Lotjonen .40 1.00
207 Kyosti Majava .40 1.00
208 Keijo Puhakka .40 1.00
209 Antti Ravi .40 1.00
210 Seppo Repo .40 1.00
211 Timo Saari .40 1.00
212 Arto Siissala .40 1.00
213 Jorma Vehmanen .40 1.00
214 Pentti Viitanen .40 1.00
215 Leo Aikas .40 1.00
216 Raine Heinonen .40 1.00
217 Vladimir Jursinov .40 1.00
218 Jukka-Pekka Jarvenpaa .40 1.00
219 Pertti Jarvenpaa .40 1.00
220 Heimo Keinonen .40 1.00
221 Seppo Kettunen .40 1.00
222 Veikko Kirveskoski .40 1.00
223 Reijo Laksola .40 1.00
224 Raimo Majapuro .40 1.00
225 Markku Moisio .40 1.00
226 Heikki Nurmi .40 1.00
227 Seppo Nurmi .40 1.00
228 Oiva Oijennus .40 1.00
229 Esko Rantanen .40 1.00
230 Matti Rautiainen .40 1.00
231 Juhani Ruohonen .40 1.00
232 Mikko Raikkonen .40 1.00
233 Lauri Salomaa .40 1.00
234 Veikko Savolainen .40 1.00
235 Leo Seppanen .40 1.00
236 Veikko Seppanen .40 1.00
237 Pekka Uitus .40 1.00
238 Kari Viitalahti .40 1.00
239 Jorma Vilen .40 1.00
240 Asko Ahonen .40 1.00
241 Tapio Flinck .40 1.00
242 Matti Hakanen .40 1.00
243 Antti Heikkila .40 1.00
244 Reijo Heinonen .40 1.00
245 Jaakko Honkanen .40 1.00
246 Jari Kaski .40 1.00
247 Veli-Pekka Ketola .40 1.00
248 Raimo Kilpio .40 1.00
249 Tapio Koskinen .40 1.00
250 Jarkko Levonen .40 1.00
251 Kaj Matalamaki .40 1.00
252 Pertti Makela .40 1.00
253 Jaakko Niemi .40 1.00
254 Hannu Pulkkinen .40 1.00
255 Pekka Rautakallio .40 1.00
256 Markku Riihimaki .40 1.00
257 Anto Virtanen .40 1.00
258 Erkki Vakiparta .40 1.00
259 Pertti Hasanen .40 1.00
260 Rainer Holmroos .40 1.00
261 Kari Johansson .40 1.00
262 Arto Kaunonen .40 1.00
263 Timo Kokkonen .40 1.00
264 Reijo Leppanen .40 1.00
265 Seppo Lindstrom .40 1.00
266 Hannu Luojola .40 1.00
267 Hannu Niittoaho .40 1.00
268 Reijo Paksal .40 1.00
269 Seppo Parikka .40 1.00
270 Jarmo Rantanen .40 1.00
271 Kari Hyokki .40 1.00
272 Kari Salonen .40 1.00
273 Tapani Sura .40 1.00
274 Kari Torkkel .40 1.00
275 Risto Vainio .40 1.00
276 Pentti Vihanto .40 1.00
277 Urpo Ylonen .40 1.00
278 Lars Ellfolk .40 1.00
279 Kari Horkko .40 1.00
280 Hannu Jortikka .40 1.00
281 Eero Juntunen .40 1.00
282 Lauri Jamsen .40 1.00
283 Jari Kapanen .40 1.00
284 Jari Kauppila .40 1.00
285 Matti Kauppila .40 1.00
286 Jukka Koskilahti .40 1.00
287 Jukka Koivu .40 1.00
288 Ilkka Laaksonen .40 1.00
289 Robert Lamoureux .40 1.00
290 Hannu Lunden .40 1.00
291 Ilkka Mesikammen .40 1.00
292 Timo Nummelin .40 1.00
293 Timo Nurminen .40 1.00
294 Rauli Ottila .40 1.00
295 Matti Rautee .40 1.00
296 Pekka Rautee .40 1.00
297 Jari Rosberg .40 1.00
298 Tarmo Saarni .40 1.00
299 Asko Salminen .40 1.00
300 Jouni Samuli .40 1.00
301 Rauli Tammelin .40 1.00
302 Veijo Wahlsten .40 1.00
303 Bengt Wilenius .40 1.00
304 Denis Bavaudin .40 1.00
305 Mikko Erholm .40 1.00
306 Matti Forss .40 1.00
307 Esa Hakkarainen .40 1.00
308 Veikko Ihalainen .40 1.00
309 Esa Isaksson .40 1.00
310 Juhani Jylha .40 1.00
311 Heikki Kauhanen .40 1.00
312 Jari Laiho .40 1.00
313 Arto Laine .40 1.00
314 Jouni Peltonen .40 1.00
315 Jouni Rinne .40 1.00
316 Kai Rosvall .40 1.00
317 Seppo Santala .40 1.00
318 Jari Sarronlahti .40 1.00
319 Matti Saurio .40 1.00
320 Ari Sjoman .40 1.00
321 Erkki Sundelin .40 1.00
322 Ismo Villa .40 1.00
323 Mikko Ylaja .40 1.00
324 Veijo Ylanen .40 1.00
NNO Album 25.00 50.00

1974 Finnish Jenkki

COMPLETE SET (120) 50.00 100.00
1 Sakari Ahlberg .30 .75
2 Seppo Ahokainen .30 .75
3 Jukka Alkula .30 .75
4 Jorma Aro .30 .75
5 Hannu Haapalainen .30 .75
6 Veli-Pekka Ketola 1.25 3.00
7 Tapio Koskinen .30 .75
8 Henry Leppa .30 .75
9 Antti Leppanen .30 .75
10 Reijo Leppanen .30 .75
11 Pekka Marjamaki .30 .75
12 Matti Murto .30 .75
13 Esa Peltonen .30 .75
14 Pekka Rautakallio 1.25 3.00
15 Leo Seppanen .30 .75
16 Juha Silvennoinen .30 .75
17 Raimo Suoniemi .30 .75
18 Seppo Suoraniemi .30 .75
19 Timo Sutinen .30 .75
20 Juhani Tamminen .75 2.00
21 Pertti Valkeapaa .30 .75
22 Christer Abrahamsson 1.25 3.00
23 Thommie Bergman 1.25 3.00
24 Roland Bond .30 .75
25 Anders Hedberg 2.00 5.00
26 Bjorn Johansson .30 .75
27 Stefan Karlsson .30 .75
28 Mats Lind .30 .75
29 Tord Lundstrom .30 .75
30 William Lofqvist .30 .75
31 Ulf Nilsson 2.00 5.00
32 Bjorn Palmqvist .30 .75
33 Hakan Pettersson .30 .75
34 Lars-Erik Sjoberg .75 2.00
35 Ulf Sterner .30 .75
36 Karl-Johan Sundqvist .30 .75
37 Hakan Wickberg .30 .75
38 Kjell-Arne Wickstrom .30 .75
39 Dick Yderstrom .30 .75
40 Mats Ahlberg .30 .75
41 Stig Ostling .30 .75
42 Vjatseslav Anisin .40 1.00
43 Aleksandr Bodunov .40 1.00
44 Aleksandr Gusev .40 1.00
45 Valeri Kharlamov 6.00 15.00
46 Aleksandr Yakushev 2.00 5.00
47 Juri Liapkin .40 1.00
48 Vladimir Lutshenko .40 1.00
49 Aleksandr Maltsev 2.00 5.00
50 Aleksandr Martiniuk .40 1.00
51 Boris Mikhailov 2.00 5.00
52 Jevgeni Paladiev .40 1.00
53 Vladimir Petrov 2.00 5.00
54 Aleksandr Ragulin .40 1.00
55 Vladimir Shadrin .40 1.00
56 Aleksandr Sidelnikov .40 1.00
57 Vladislav Tretiak 6.00 15.00
58 Gennadi Tsigankov .40 1.00
59 Valeri Vasiljev 2.00 5.00
60 Vladimir Vikulov .40 1.00
61 Aleksandr Voltshkov .40 1.00
62 Julij Blinov .40 1.00
63 Vladimir Sepovalov .40 1.00
64 Josef Horesovsky .30 .75
65 Peter Adamik .30 .75
66 Vladimir Bednar .30 .75
67 Jiri Bubla .75 2.00
68 Richard Farda .30 .75
69 Julius Haas .30 .75
70 Ivan Hlinka .75 2.00
71 Jiri Holecek .75 2.00
72 Jaroslav Holik .30 .75
73 Jiri Holik .30 .75
74 Jan Klapac .30 .75
75 Jiri Kochta .30 .75
76 Milan Kuzela .30 .75
77 Oldrich Machac .30 .75
78 Vladimir Martinec .30 .75
79 Vaclav Nedomansky 1.50 4.00
80 Josef Palecek .30 .75
81 Frantisek Pospisil .30 .75
82 Bohuslav Stastny .30 .75
83 Rudolf Tajcnar .30 .75
84 Karl Vohralik .30 .75
85 Jerzy Potz .30 .75
86 Andrzej Slowakiewicz .30 .75
87 Josef Slowakiewicz .30 .75
88 Leszek Tokarz .30 .75
89 Wieslav Tokarz .30 .75
90 Henryk Vojtynek .30 .75
91 Walenty Zietara .30 .75
92 Josef Batkiewicz .30 .75
93 Stefan Chowaniec .30 .75
94 Ludvik Czachovski .30 .75
95 Andrzej Czczepaniec .30 .75
96 Robert Goralczyk .30 .75
97 Mieczyslaw Jaskierski .30 .75
98 Tadeusz Kacik .30 .75
99 Adam Kopczynski .30 .75
100 Valery Kosyl .30 .75
101 Tadeusz Obloj .30 .75
102 Joachim Stasche .30 .75
103 Roland Peters .30 .75
104 Dietmar Peters .30 .75
105 Bernd Karrenbauer .30 .75
106 Peter Prusa .30 .75
107 Rainer Patschinski .30 .75
108 Hartmut Nickel .30 .75
109 Dieter Dewitz .30 .75
110 Harald Felber .30 .75
111 Joachim Hurbanek .30 .75
112 Wolfgang Fischer .30 .75
113 Frank Braun .30 .75
114 Dieter Huschto .30 .75
115 Ruediger Hoack .30 .75
116 Dieter Simon .30 .75
117 Hartwig Schur .30 .75
118 Jochen Philip .30 .75
119 Rolf Bielas .30 .75
120 Peter Slapke .30 .75

1974 Finnish Typotor

COMPLETE SET (120) 30.00 80.00
1 Matti Murto .40 1.00
2 Esa Peltonen .20 .50
3 Juha Rantasila .40 1.00
4 Heikki Riihiranta .75 2.00
5 Juhani Tamminen .75 2.00
6 Jorma Virtanen .40 1.00
7 Seppo Ahokainen .40 1.00
8 Jorma Kallio .20 .50
9 Ari Kankaanpera .20 .50
10 Lasse Oksanen .20 .50
11 Jorma Peltonen .40 1.00
12 Tapio Virhimo .20 .50
13 Ilpo Kokela .20 .50
14 Henry Leppa .20 .50
15 Seppo Suoraniemi .20 .50
16 Timo Sutinen .20 .50
17 Timo Turunen .20 .50
18 Jorma Valtonen .40 1.00
19 Mikko Erholm .20 .50
20 Esa Isaksson .20 .50
21 Juhani Jylha .20 .50
22 Tapani Koskimaki .20 .50
23 Hannu Siivonen .20 .50
24 Jorma Vehmanen .40 1.00
25 Jukka Alkula .20 .50
26 Hannu Haapalainen .20 .50
27 Martti Jarkko .20 .50
28 Antti Leppannen .20 .50
29 Pekka Marjamaki .20 .50
30 Raimo Suoniemi .20 .50
31 Lasse Kiili .20 .50
32 Timo Nummelin .20 .50
33 Matti Rautee .20 .50
34 Pekka Rautee .20 .50
35 Seppo Repo .20 .50
36 Jouko Oystila .20 .50
37 Kari Johansson .20 .50
38 Reijo Leppanen .20 .50
39 Seppo Lindstrom .20 .50
40 Hannu Niittoaho .20 .50
41 Pentti Vihanto .20 .50
42 Urpo Ylonen .20 .50
43 Antti Heikkila .20 .50
44 Reijo Heinonen .20 .50
45 Veli-Pekka Ketola .60 1.50
46 Raimo Kilpio .20 .50
47 Tapio Koskinen .20 .50
48 Pekka Rautakallio .75 2.00
49 Seppo Ahokainen .20 .50
50 Henry Leppa .20 .50
51 Antti Leppanen .20 .50
52 Pekka Marjamaki .20 .50
53 Matti Murto .20 .50
54 Esa Peltonen .20 .50
55 Heikki Riihiranta .40 1.00
56 Timo Sutinen .20 .50
57 Juhani Tamminen .75 2.00
58 Rolf Bielas .20 .50
59 Joachim Hurbanek .20 .50
60 Reinhard Karger .20 .50
61 Hartmut Nickel .20 .50
62 Rudiger Noack .20 .50
63 Helmut Novy .20 .50
64 Dietmar Peters .20 .50
65 Peter Prusa .20 .50
66 Peter Slapke .20 .50
67 Vakeri Kharlamov 4.00 10.00
68 Alexander Yakushev 1.50 4.00
69 Alexander Maltsev 1.50 4.00
70 Boris Mikhailov 1.50 4.00
71 Vladimir Petrov 1.50 4.00
72 Vladimir Shadrin .40 1.00
73 Vladislav Tretiak 6.00 15.00
74 Gennady Tsygankov .40 1.00
75 Valeri Vasiljev 1.25 3.00
76 Per-Erik Ingier .20 .50
77 Morten Johansen .20 .50
78 Hakan Lundenes .20 .50
79 N. Nilsen .20 .50
80 Morten Sethereng .20 .50
81 T. Skar .20 .50
82 J-E. Solberg .20 .50
83 K. Thorkildsen .20 .50
84 T. Troymark .20 .50
85 J. Borovicz .20 .50
86 L. Czachovski .20 .50
87 Michael Jaskierski .20 .50
88 Tadeusz Kacik .20 .50
89 Adam Kopczynski .20 .50
90 Tadeusz Obtoj .20 .50
91 Jan Szeja .20 .50
92 Leszek Tokarz .20 .50
93 Walenty Zietara .20 .50
94 Christer Abrahamsson .50 1.50
95 Tommy Abrahamsson .75 2.00
96 Anders Hedberg 1.50 4.00
97 Stefan Karlsson .20 .50
98 Kjell-Rune Milton .20 .50
99 Ulf Nilsson 1.50 4.00
100 Bjorn Palmqvist .20 .50
101 Dan Soderstrom .20 .50
102 Mats Ahlberg .30 .75
103 Guy Dubois .40 1.00
104 C. Friedrich .20 .50
105 Charly Henzen .20 .50
106 Ueli Hofmann .20 .50
107 Mirco Horisberger .20 .50
108 M. Lindenmann .20 .50
109 Alfio Molina .20 .50
110 Tony Neininger .20 .50
111 U. Williman .20 .50
112 Richard Farda .20 .50
113 Ivan Hlinka .40 1.00
114 Jiri Holecek .40 1.00
115 Jiri Holik .40 1.00
116 Josef Horesovsky .20 .50
117 Jiri Kochta .20 .50
118 Oldrich Machac .20 .50
119 Vladimir Martinec .20 .50
120 Bohuslav Stastny .30 .75

1978-79 Finnish SM-Liiga

This set features the top players from Finland's elite league. These odd-sized cards measure 2 X 2 3/8. The set is noteworthy for including the first known card of Hall of Famer Jari Kurri. It is believed the cards were issued in pack form, but that cannot be ascertained at this point.

COMPLETE SET (240) 50.00 125.00
1 Hannu Kamppuri .40 1.00
2 Pekka Rautakallio .75 2.00
3 Timo Nummelin .20 .50
4 Pertti Valkeapaa .20 .50
5 Risto Siltanen .40 1.00
6 Hannu Haapalainen .20 .50
7 Markku Kiimalainen .20 .50
8 Tapio Levo .40 1.00
9 Lasse Litma .20 .50
10 Reijo Ruotsalainen .75 2.00
11 Jukka Porvari .20 .50
12 Matti Rautiainen .20 .50
13 Veli-Pekka Ketola .75 2.00
14 Antero Lehtonen .20 .50
15 Martti Jarkko .20 .50
16 Juhani Tamminen .75 2.00
17 Pertti Koivulahti .20 .50
18 Kari Makkonen .20 .50
19 Antero Kivela .20 .50
20 Veli-Matti Ruisma .20 .50
21 Stig Wetzell .20 .50
22 Kyosti Majava .20 .50
23 Seppo Pakelo .20 .50
24 Reijo Laksola .20 .50
25 Heikki Riihiranta .20 .50
26 Raimo Hirvonen .20 .50
27 Jorma Immonen .20 .50
28 Terry Ball .20 .50
29 Pertti Lehtonen .20 .50
30 Jaakko Marttinen .20 .50
31 Esa Peltonen .40 1.00
32 Lauri Mononen .40 1.00
33 Tommi Salmelainen .20 .50
34 Hannu Kapanen .20 .50
35 Matti Forss .20 .50
36 Harri Linnonmaa .20 .50
37 Matti Murto .20 .50
38 Juhani Bostrom .20 .50
39 Matti Hagman .40 1.00
40 Ilkka Sinisalo .75 2.00
41 Tomi Taimio .20 .50
42 Ari Lahteenmaki .20 .50
43 Tapio Virhimo .20 .50
44 Jukka Airaksinen .20 .50
45 Hannu Helander .20 .50
46 Jorma Aro .20 .50
47 Jouko Urvikko .20 .50
48 Hannu Pulkkinen .20 .50
49 Olli Pennanen .20 .50
50 Ari Kankaanpera .20 .50
51 Risto Siltanen .40 1.00
52 Jari Jarvinen .20 .50
53 Sakari Ahlberg .20 .50
54 Keijo Kivela .20 .50
55 Lasse Oksanen .20 .50
56 Risto Kankaanpera .20 .50
57 Kari Jarvinen .20 .50
58 Pekka Orimus .20 .50
59 Jarmo Huhtala .20 .50
60 Hannu Oksanen .20 .50
61 Jari Viitala .20 .50
62 Veikko Suominen .20 .50
63 Antti Heikkila .20 .50
64 Seppo Hiitela .20 .50
65 Hannu Kamppuri .40 1.00
66 Patrik Wainio .20 .50
67 Timo Blomqvist .40 1.00
68 Ilmo Uotila .20 .50
69 Pertti Savolainen .20 .50
70 Jussi Lepisto .20 .50
71 Jorma Piisinen .20 .50
72 Robert Barnes .20 .50
73 Ari Makinen .20 .50
74 David Conte .40 1.00
75 Juha Jyrkkio .20 .50
76 Jari Kurri 20.00 40.00
77 Matti Heikkila .20 .50
78 Henry Leppa .20 .50
79 Pekka Kaski .20 .50
80 Jari Kapanen .20 .50
81 Ari Mikkola .20 .50
82 Vesa Rajaniemi .20 .50
83 Ari Blomqvist .20 .50
84 Erkki Korhonen .20 .50
85 Rainer Risku .20 .50
86 Henry Saleva .20 .50
87 Leo Seppanen .20 .50
88 Rauli Sohlman .20 .50
89 Juhani Ruohonen .20 .50
90 Tuomo Martin .20 .50
91 Reijo Mansikka .20 .50
92 Reino Pulkkinen .20 .50
93 Mauri Kultakuusi .20 .50
94 Kari Saarikko .20 .50
95 Kari Viitalahti .20 .50
96 Barry Salovaara .20 .50
97 Auvo Vaananen .20 .50
98 Pauli Pyykko .20 .50
99 Ari Jortikka .20 .50
100 Jukka-Pekka Jarvenpaa .20 .50
101 Seppo Sevon .20 .50
102 Pekka Koskela .20 .50
103 Arto Jokinen .20 .50
104 Timo Niinivirta .20 .50
105 Matti Rautiainen .20 .50
106 Pertti Jarvenpaa .20 .50
107 Reima Pullinen .20 .50
108 Jukka-Pekka Vuorinen .20 .50
109 Petteri Kanerva .20 .50
110 Kalevi Rantanen .20 .50
111 Jorma Virtanen .20 .50
112 Matti Kaario .20 .50
113 Frank Neal .20 .50
114 Eero Mantere .20 .50
115 Harri Nyman .20 .50
116 Olli Saarinen .20 .50
117 Jari Saarela .20 .50
118 Pasi Virta .20 .50
119 Dave Chalk .20 .50
120 Hannu Koskinen .20 .50
121 Harri Toivonen .20 .50
122 Jarmo Makitalo .20 .50
123 Kari Makitalo .20 .50
124 Olavi Niemenranta .20 .50
125 Pekka Laine .20 .50
126 Markku Hakulinen .20 .50
127 Pekka Nissinen .20 .50
128 Yrjo Hakulinen .20 .50
129 Timo Heino .20 .50
130 Hannu Savolainen .20 .50
131 Ari Hellgren .20 .50
132 Matti Saikkonen .20 .50
133 Ilpo Kukkola .20 .50
134 Pentti Karlsson .20 .50
135 Pekka Karjala .20 .50
136 Juha Tuohimaa .20 .50
137 Pekka Makinen .20 .50
138 Reijo Ruotsalainen .75 2.00
139 Seppo Tenhunen .20 .50
140 Hannu Jalonen .20 .50
141 Jari Virtanen .20 .50
142 Juha Huikuri .20 .50
143 Veikko Torkkeli .20 .50
144 Markku Kiimalainen .20 .50
145 Kalevi Hongisto .20 .50
146 Eero Vartiainen .20 .50
147 Jouko Kamarainen .20 .50
148 Kai Suikkanen .20 .50
149 Ilkka Alatalo .20 .50
150 Markku Perkkio .20 .50
151 Jorma Torkkeli .20 .50
152 Kari Jalonen .20 .50
153 Hannu Siivonen .20 .50
154 Kari Kaupinsalo .20 .50
155 Teppo Mattsson .20 .50
156 Esa Hakkarainen .20 .50
157 Jouni Peltonen .20 .50
158 Timo Peltonen .20 .50
159 Hannu Luojola .20 .50
160 Tapani Koskimaki .20 .50
161 Tuomo Jormakka .20 .50
162 Mika Rajala .20 .50
163 Pekka Santanen .20 .50
164 Jorma Vehmanen .20 .50
165 Olli Tuominen .20 .50
166 Hannu Kemppainen .20 .50
167 Ismo Villa .20 .50
168 Matti Tynkkynen .20 .50
169 Jouni Rinne .20 .50
170 Jari Rastio .20 .50
171 Harri Tuohimaa .20 .50
172 Jari Laiho .20 .50
173 Juhani Wallenius .20 .50
174 Pekka Strander .20 .50
175 Pertti Hasanen .20 .50
176 Petri Karjalainen .20 .50
177 Jorma Kallio .20 .50
178 Pekka Marjamaki .20 .50
179 Hannu Haapalainen .20 .50
180 Pertti Valkeapaa .20 .50
181 Lasse Litma .20 .50
182 Jukka Hirsimaki .20 .50
183 Oiva Oijennus .20 .50
184 Jukka Aikula .20 .50
185 Timo Susi .20 .50
186 Jukka Porvari .20 .50
187 Erkki Lehtonen .20 .50
188 Antero Lehtonen .20 .50
189 Juha Solvennoinen .20 .50
190 Pertti Koivulahti .20 .50
191 Keijo Mannisto .20 .50
192 Jorma Sevon .20 .50
193 Martti Jarkko .20 .50
194 Jari Lindgren .20 .50
195 Tapio Kallio .20 .50
196 Tero Kapynen .20 .50
197 Urpo Ylonen .20 .50
198 Jorma Valtonen .20 .50
199 Harri Kari .20 .50
200 Hannu Jortikka .20 .50
201 Timo Nummelin .20 .50
202 Seppo Suoraniemi .20 .50
203 Ilkka Mesikammen .20 .50
204 Pertti Ahokas .20 .50
205 Hannu Niitoaho .20 .50
206 Arto Kaunonen .20 .50
207 Pekka Rautee .20 .50
208 Juhani Tamminen .20 .50
209 Timo Viljanen .20 .50
210 Kari Kauppila .20 .50
211 Bengt Willenius .20 .50
212 Reijo Leppanen .20 .50
213 Rauli Tammelin .20 .50
214 Jukka Koskilahtl .20 .50
215 Markku Haapaniemi .20 .50
216 Kari Horkko .20 .50
217 Kalevi Aho .20 .50
218 Hakan Hjerpe .20 .50
219 Antero Kivela .20 .50
220 Pertti Lehti .20 .50
221 Antti Heikkila .20 .50
222 Tapio Flinck .20 .50
223 Pekka Rautakallio .75 2.00
224 Jaakko Niemi .20 .50
225 Tapio Levo .40 1.00
226 Jyrki Levonen .20 .50
227 Harry Nikander .20 .50
228 Arto Javanainen .20 .50
229 Pekka Makela .20 .50
230 Tapio Koskinen .20 .50
231 Pekka Stenfors .20 .50
232 Ari Peltola .20 .50
233 Veli-Pekka Ketola .75 2.00
234 Erkki Vakiparta .20 .50
235 Rauli Levonen .20 .50
236 Martti Nenonen .20 .50
237 Jouni Makitalo .20 .50
238 Veli-Matti Ruisma .20 .50
239 Tauno Makela .20 .50
240 Kari Makkonen .20 .50

1982 Finnish Skopbank

Little is known about this sticker set beyond the checklist and values, provided by Finnish collector Janne Harvula. The cards are unnumbered and are checklisted below in alphabetical order.

COMPLETE SET (8) 24.00 60.00
1 Pekka Arbelius 2.00 5.00
2 Ari Hellgren 2.00 5.00
3 Raimo Hirvonen 2.00 5.00
4 Hannu Kamppuri 3.00 8.00
5 Markku Kiimalainen 2.00 5.00
6 Pertti Koivulahti 2.00 5.00
7 Hannu Koskinen 2.00 5.00
8 Mikko Leinonen 2.00 5.00
9 Reijo Leppanen 2.00 5.00
10 Tapio Levo 2.00 5.00
11 Timo Nummelin 2.00 5.00
12 Jukka Porvari 2.00 5.00
13 Reijo Ruotsalainen 3.00 8.00
14 Seppo Suoraniemi 2.00 5.00
15 Timo Susi 2.00 5.00
16 Juhani Tamminen 3.00 8.00

1989 Finnish Pelimiehen

Little is known about this six-sticker set beyond the accuracy of the checklist, which was provided by collector Ray Bayless. Any additional information can be forwarded to hockeymag@beckett.com

COMPLETE SET (6) 12.00 30.00
1 Kari Eloranta 1.25 3.00
2 Jari Kurri 6.00 15.00
3 Reijo Ruotsalainen 1.25 3.00
4 Christian Ruuttu 1.25 3.00
5 Kari Takko 2.00 5.00
6 Esa Tikkanen 3.00 8.00

1990-91 Finnish Jyvas-Hyva Stickers

Size about 1 2/3 X 4 1/6. These stickers were inserted inside chocolate bar wrappers (one sticker per bar).

COMPLETE SET (12) 10.00 25.00
NNO JypHT Jyvaskyla .75 2.00
NNO Jokerit .75 2.00
NNO Lukko Rauma 1.25 3.00
NNO Kalpa Kuopio .75 2.00
NNO HIFK .75 2.00
NNO HPK Hameenlinna .75 2.00
NNO Ilves Tampere .75 2.00
NNO Hockey Reipas Lahti .75 2.00
NNO Saipa Lappeenranta .75 2.00
NNO Tappara Tampere .75 2.00
NNO TPS Turku .75 2.00
NNO Assat Pori .75 2.00

1991 Finnish Semic World Championship Stickers

These hockey stickers, which measure approximately 2 1/8" by 2 7/8", were sold five to a packet. Also an album was available to display all 250 stickers. The fronts display color posed player shots framed by a red inner border studded with yellow miniature stars and a white outer border. The team flag, the player's name, and the sticker number appear in the white border below the picture. The backs were different based on distribution; blank backs were sold in Czechoslovakia; Marabou Choclolate ads were on the backs of cards sold in Finland and Milky Way ads were on the back of cards sold in Sweden. The stickers are grouped according to country. Teemu Selanne and Nicklas Lidstrom each appears in his Rookie Card year.

COMPLETE SET (250) 50.00 100.00
1 Finnish Emblem .02 .10
2 Markus Ketterer .20 .50
3 Sakari Lindfors .20 .50
4 Jukka Tammi .20 .50
5 Timo Jutila .08 .25
6 Hannu Virta .08 .25
7 Simo Saarinen .08 .25
8 Jukka Marttila .08 .25
9 Ville Siren .08 .25
10 Pasi Huura .08 .25
11 Hannu Henriksson .08 .25
12 Arto Ruotanen .08 .25
13 Ari Haanpaa .08 .25
14 Pauli Jarvinen .08 .25
15 Teppo Kivela .08 .25
16 Risto Kurkinen .08 .25
17 Mika Nieminen .08 .25
18 Jari Kurri .75 2.00
19 Esa Keskinen .08 .25
20 Raimo Summanen .08 .25
21 Teemu Selanne 4.00 10.00
22 Jari Torkki .08 .25
23 Hannu Jarvenpaa .08 .25
24 Raimo Helminen .08 .25
25 Timo Peltomaa .08 .25
26 Swedish Emblem .02 .10
27 Peter Lindmark .20 .50
28 Rolf Ridderwall .20 .50
29 Tommy Soderstrom .20 .50
30 Thomas Eriksson .08 .25
31 Nicklas Lidstrom 4.00 10.00
32 Tomas Jonsson .08 .25
33 Tommy Samuelsson .08 .25
34 Fredrik Stillman .08 .25
35 Peter Andersson .08 .25
36 Peter Andersson .08 .25
37 Kenneth Kennholt .08 .25
38 Hakan Loob .40 1.00
39 Thomas Rundqvist .08 .25
40 Hakan Ahlund .08 .25
41 Jan Viktorsson .08 .25
42 Charles Berglund .08 .25
43 Mikael Johansson .08 .25
44 Robert Burakovsky .08 .25
45 Bengt-Ake Gustafsson .08 .25
46 Patrik Carnback .08 .25
47 Patrik Erickson .08 .25
48 Anders Carlsson .08 .25
49 Mats Naslund .75 2.00
50 Kent Nilsson .75 2.00
51 Canadian Emblem .40 1.00
52 Patrick Roy 10.00 25.00
53 Ed Belfour 2.00 5.00
54 Daniel Berthiaume .40 1.00

55 Ray Bourque 4.00 10.00
56 Scott Stevens .40 1.00
57 Al MacInnis .75 2.00
58 Paul Coffey .75 2.00
59 Paul Cavallini .40 1.00
60 Zarley Zalapski .40 1.00
61 Steve Duchesne .40 1.00
62 Dave Ellett .40 1.00
63 Mark Messier 4.00 10.00
64 Wayne Gretzky 12.00 30.00
65 Steve Yzerman 8.00 20.00
66 Pierre Turgeon .40 1.00
67 Bernie Nicholls .40 1.00
68 Cam Neely 2.00 5.00
69 Joe Nieuwendyk .40 1.00
70 Luc Robitaille 2.00 5.00
71 Kevin Dineen .40 1.00
72 John Cullen .40 1.00
73 Steve Larmer .40 1.00
74 Mark Recchi .75 2.00
75 Joe Sakic 4.00 10.00
76 Soviet Emblem .02 .10
77 Arturs Irbe .40 1.00
78 Alexei Marin .20 .50
79 Mikhail Shtalenkov .20 .50
80 Vladimir Malakhov .08 .25
81 Vladimir Konstantinov 1.25 3.00
82 Igor Kravchuk .08 .25
83 Ilya Byakin .08 .25
84 Dimitri Mironov .08 .25
85 Vladimir Turikov .08 .25
86 Vjatjeslav Uvajev .08 .25
87 Vladimir Fedosov .08 .25
88 Valeri Kamensky .08 .25
89 Pavel Bure 2.00 5.00
90 Vyacheslav Butsayev .08 .25
91 Igor Maslennikov .08 .25
92 Evgeny Davydov .08 .25
93 Andrei Kovalev .08 .25
94 Alexander Semak .08 .25
95 Alexei Zhamnov .08 .25
96 Sergei Nemchinov .08 .25
97 Viktor Gordijuk .08 .25
98 Vyacheslav Kozlov .08 .25
99 Andrei Khomotov .08 .25
100 Vyacheslav Bykov .08 .25
101 Czech Emblem .02 .10
102 Petr Briza .20 .50
103 Dominik Hasek 4.00 10.00
104 Eduard Hartmann .20 .50
105 Bedrich Scerban .08 .25
106 Jiri Slegr .08 .25
107 Josef Reznicek .08 .25
108 Petr Pavlas .08 .25
109 Peter Slanina .08 .25
110 Martin Maskarinec .08 .25
111 Antonin Stavjana .08 .25
112 Stanislav Medrik .08 .25
113 Dusan Pasek .08 .25
114 Jiri Lala .08 .25
115 Darius Rusnak .08 .25
116 Oto Hascak .08 .25
117 Radek Toupal .08 .25
118 Pavel Pycha .08 .25
119 Lubomir Kolnik .08 .25
120 Libor Dolana .08 .25
121 Ladislav Lubina .08 .25
122 Tomas Jelinek .08 .25
123 Petr Vlk .08 .25
124 Vladimir Petrovka .08 .25
125 Richard Zemlicka .08 .25
126 U.S.A. Emblem .02 .10
127 John Vanbiesbrouck .75 2.00
128 Mike Richter .75 2.00
129 Chris Terreri .40 1.00
130 Chris Chelios 2.00 5.00
131 Brian Leetch 1.25 3.00
132 Gary Suter .40 1.00
133 Phil Housley .40 1.00
134 Mark Howe .40 1.00
135 Al Iafrate .40 1.00
136 Kevin Hatcher .40 1.00
137 Mathieu Schneider .40 1.00
138 Pat LaFontaine .75 2.00
139 Darren Turcotte .40 1.00
140 Neal Broten .75 2.00
141 Mike Modano 2.00 5.00
142 Dave Christian .40 1.00
143 Craig Janney .40 1.00
144 Brett Hull 2.00 5.00
145 Kevin Stevens .40 1.00
146 Joe Mullen .40 1.00
147 Tony Granato .40 1.00
148 Ed Olczyk .40 1.00
149 Jeremy Roenick 2.00 5.00
150 Jimmy Carson .40 1.00
151 West German Emblem .02 .10
152 Helmut De Raaf .20 .50
153 Josef Heiss .20 .50
154 Karl Friesen .20 .50
155 Uli Hiemer .08 .25
156 Harold Kreis .08 .25
157 Udo Kiessling .08 .25
158 Michael Schmidt .08 .25
159 Michael Heidt .08 .25
160 Andreas Pokorny .08 .25
161 Bernd Wagner .08 .25
162 Uwe Krupp .08 .25
163 Gerd Truntschka .08 .25
164 Bernd Truntschka .08 .25
165 Thomas Brandl .08 .25
166 Peter Draisaitl .08 .25
167 Andreas Brockmann .08 .25
168 Ulrich Liebsch .08 .25
169 Ralf Hantschke .08 .25
170 Thomas Schinko .08 .25
171 Anton Krinner .08 .25
172 Thomas Werner .08 .25
173 Dieter Hegen .08 .25
174 Helmut Steiger .08 .25
175 Georg Franz .08 .25
176 Swiss Emblem .02 .10
177 Renato Tosio .20 .50
178 Reto Pavoni .20 .50
179 Dino Stecher .20 .50
180 Sven Leuenberger .08 .25
181 Rick Tschumi .08 .25
182 Patrice Brasey .08 .25
183 Didier Massy .08 .25
184 Sandro Bertaggia .08 .25
185 Samuel Balmer .08 .25
186 Martin Rauch .08 .25
187 Marc Leuenberger .08 .25
188 Jorg Eberle .08 .25
189 Fredy Luthi .08 .25
190 Andy Ton .08 .25
191 Raymond Walder .08 .25
192 Manuele Celio .08 .25
193 Roman Wager .08 .25
194 Felix Hollenstein .08 .25
195 Andre Rotheli .08 .25
196 Christian Weber .08 .25
197 Peter Jaks .08 .25
198 Gil Montandon .08 .25
199 Oliver Hoffmann .08 .25
200 Thomas Vrabec .08 .25
201 Teppo Numminen .08 .25
202 Jyrki Lumme .08 .25
203 Esa Tikkanen .08 .25
204 Petri Skriko .08 .25
205 Christian Ruutu .08 .25
206 Ilkka Sinisalo .08 .25
207 Calle Johansson .08 .25
208 Tomas Sandstrom .08 .25
209 Thomas Steen .08 .25
210 Per-Erik Eklund .08 .25
211 Mats Sundin 1.25 3.00
212 Johan Garpenlov .08 .25
213 Slava Fetisov .08 .25
214 Alexei Kasatonov .08 .25
215 Mikhail Tatarinov .08 .25
216 Sergei Makarov .20 .50
217 Igor Larionov .40 1.00
218 Alexander Mogilny .40 1.00
219 Sergei Fedorov 1.25 3.00
220 Petr Klima .08 .25
221 David Volek .08 .25
222 Michal Pivonka .08 .25
223 Robert Reichel .08 .25
224 Robert Holik .08 .25
225 Jaromir Jagr 4.00 10.00
226 Urpo Ylonen .08 .25
227 Ilpo Koskela .08 .25
228 Pekka Rautakallio .20 .50
229 Lasse Oksanen .08 .25
230 Veli-Pekka Ketola .20 .50
231 Leif Holmqvist .20 .50
232 Lennart Svedberg .08 .25
233 Sven Tumba Johansson .08 .25
234 Ulf Sterner .08 .25
235 Anders Hedberg .20 .50
236 Ken Dryden 2.00 5.00
237 Bobby Orr 10.00 25.00
238 Gordie Howe 4.00 10.00
239 Bobby Hull 3.00 8.00
240 Phil Esposito 2.00 5.00
241 Vladislav Tretiak 4.00 10.00
242 Alexander Ragulin .08 .25
243 Anatoli Firsov .08 .25
244 Valeri Kharlamov 2.00 5.00
245 Alexander Maltsev .75 2.00
246 Jiri Holecek .08 .25
247 Jan Suchy .08 .25
248 Jozef Golonka .08 .25
249 Vaclav Nedomansky .08 .25
250 Ivan Hlinka .08 .25

1991-92 Finnish Jyvas-Hyva Stickers

This set features the players of Finland's SM-Liiga. The stickers were inserted as premiums in candy products. They measured 1 2/3 X 4 1/6. The set is noteworthy for the inclusion of a sticker of Teemu Selanne in his RC year. A poster on which to place the stickers was also issued for this set.

COMPLETE SET (84) 20.00 50.00
1 Sakari Lindfors .40 1.00
2 Jukka Seppo .08 .25
3 Pekka Tuomisto .05 .15
4 Harri Tuohimaa .05 .15
5 Pertti Lehtonen .05 .15
6 Simo Saarinen .05 .15
7 Timo Lehkonen .05 .15
8 Teppo Kivela .05 .15
9 Markku Piikkila .05 .15
10 Pekka Peltola .05 .15
11 Hannu Henriksson .05 .15
12 Jari Haapamaki .05 .15
13 Jukka Tammi .40 1.00
14 Risto Jalo .05 .15
15 Timo Peltomaa .05 .15
16 Raimo Summanen .40 1.00
17 Ville Siren .20 .50
18 Risto Siltanen .40 1.00
19 Markus Ketterer .30 .75
20 Pekka Jarvela .05 .15
21 Teemu Selanne 15.00 40.00
22 Keijo Sailynoja .05 .15
23 Mika Stromberg .08 .25
24 Waltteri Immonen .05 .15
25 Ari-Pekka Siekkinen .08 .25
26 Jari Lindroos .08 .25
27 Ari Haanpaa .05 .15
28 Jiri Dolezal .08 .25
29 Harri Laurila .05 .15
30 Leo Gudas .08 .25
31 Mika Rautio .05 .15
32 Pekka Tirkkonen .05 .15
33 Jarmo Kekalainen .20 .50
34 Juha Jokiharju .05 .15
35 Juha Tuohimaa .05 .15
36 Erik Hamalainen .08 .25
37 Juha Jaaskelainen .05 .15
38 Rostislav Vlach .05 .15
39 Jouni Mustonen .05 .15
40 Marku Kyllonen .05 .15
41 Antonin Stavjana .08 .25
42 Ossi Piitulainen .05 .15
43 Petr Briza .40 1.00
44 Mika Nieminen .20 .50
45 Jari Torkki .05 .15
46 Tommi Pullola .05 .15
47 Jarmo Kuusisto .05 .15
48 Pasi Huura .05 .15
49 Jaromir Sindel .20 .50
50 Marko Jantunen .08 .25
51 Erkki Laine .05 .15
52 Erkki Makela .05 .15
53 Niko Marttila .05 .15
54 Erik Kakko .05 .15
55 Jari Halme .05 .15
56 Kari Heikkinen .05 .15
57 Jiri Kucera .08 .25
58 Vesa Viitakoski .20 .50
59 Jukka Marttila .05 .15
60 Pekka Laksola .05 .15
61 Jouni Rokama .08 .25
62 Esa Keskinen .20 .50
63 Jukka Vilander .05 .15
64 Jari Pulliainen .05 .15
65 Jouko Narvanmaa .05 .15
66 Hannu Virta .08 .25
67 Kari Takko .40 1.00
68 Janne Virtanen .05 .15
69 Arto Javanainen .05 .15
70 Oleg Znarok .08 .25
71 Tapio Levo .05 .15
72 Harry Nikander .05 .15
NNO Hockey Reipat Lahti .05 .15
NNO Joensuun Kiekkopojat .05 .15
NNO Rauman Luoko .05 .15
NNO Turun Palloseura .05 .15
NNO Jokerit Helsinki .08 .25
NNO HPK Hameenlinna .05 .15
NNO JyPHT Jyvaskyla .05 .15
NNO KaiPa Kupio .05 .15
NNO Assat Pori .05 .15
NNO Ilves Tampere .05 .15
NNO Tappara Tampere .05 .15
NNO HIFK Helsinki .05 .15

1992 Finnish Semic

COMPLETE SET (288) 50.00 100.00
1 Finland .02 .10
2 Pentti Matikainen .20 .50
3 Markus Ketterer .20 .50
4 Sakari Lindfors .20 .50
5 Teppo Numminen .08 .25
6 Jyrki Lumme .08 .25
7 Janne Laukkanen .08 .25
8 Ville Siren .08 .25
9 Mikko Haapakoski .08 .25
10 Simo Saarinen .08 .25
11 Teemu Selanne 2.00 5.00
12 Petri Skriko .08 .25
13 Iiro Jarvi .08 .25
14 Esa Tikkanen .08 .25
15 Christian Ruuttu .08 .25
16 Raimo Summanen .08 .25
17 Jari Kurri .75 2.00
18 Timo Peltomaa .08 .25
19 Mika Nieminen .08 .25
20 Mikko Makela .08 .25
21 Janne Ojanen .08 .25
22 Jarmo Kekalainen .08 .25
23 Keijo Sailynoja .08 .25
24 Esa Keskinen .08 .25
25 Norge .02 .10
26 Bengt Ohlsson .20 .50
27 Jim Marthinsen .20 .50
28 Steve Allman .20 .50
29 Petter Salsten .08 .25
30 Age Ellingsen .08 .25
31 Kim Sogaard .08 .25
32 Jan Roar Fagerli .08 .25
33 Tommy Jakobsen .08 .25
34 Cato Tom Andersen .08 .25
35 Arne Billkvam .08 .25
36 Oystein Olsen .08 .25
37 Geir Hoff .08 .25
38 Erik Kristiansen .08 .25
39 Orjan Lovdal .08 .25
40 Espen Knutsen .75 2.00
41 Ole Eskild Dahlstrom .08 .25
42 Rune Gulliksen .08 .25
43 Marius Rath .08 .25
44 Petter Thoresen .08 .25
45 Tom Johansen .08 .25
46 Stephen Foyn .08 .25
47 Stig Johansen .08 .25
48 Per Christian Knold .08 .25
49 Svierge .02 .10
50 Conny Evensson .02 .10
51 Tommy Soderstrom .20 .50
52 Fredrik Andersson .20 .50
53 Thomas Eriksson .08 .25
54 Peter Andersson .08 .25
55 Peter Andersson .08 .25
56 Nicklas Lidstrom 2.00 5.00
57 Calle Johansson .08 .25
58 Ulf Samuelsson .08 .25
59 Fredrik Olausson .08 .25
60 Borje Salming .40 1.00
61 Hakan Loob .08 .25
62 Thomas Rundqvist .08 .25
63 Mats Naslund .08 .25
64 Mikael Johansson .08 .25
65 Bengt-Ake Gustavsson .08 .25
66 Peter Ottosson .08 .25
67 Markus Naslund .08 .25
68 Daniel Rydmark .08 .25
69 Tomas Sandstrom .08 .25
70 Thomas Steen .08 .25
71 Per-Erik Eklund .08 .25
72 Mats Sundin .75 2.00
73 Kanada .20 .50
74 Dave King .02 .10
75 Bill Ranford .75 2.00
76 Ed Belfour 1.25 3.00
77 Al MacInnis .75 2.00
78 Scott Stevens .40 1.00
79 Steve Smith .40 1.00
80 Ray Bourque 3.00 8.00
81 Paul Coffey .75 2.00
82 Larry Murphy .40 1.00
83 Mark Tinordi .40 1.00
84 Wayne Gretzky 10.00 25.00
85 Mark Messier 3.00 8.00
86 Mario Lemieux 8.00 20.00
87 Steve Yzerman 6.00 15.00
88 Eric Lindros 1.25 3.00
89 Luc Robitaille 1.25 3.00
90 Theoren Fleury .75 2.00
91 Steve Larmer .40 1.00
92 Brent Sutter .40 1.00
93 Shayne Corson .40 1.00
94 Dale Hawerchuk .75 2.00
95 Russ Courtnall .40 1.00
96 Rick Tocchet .40 1.00
97 Soviet .02 .10
98 Victor Tikhonov .02 .10
99 Andrei Trefilov .20 .50
100 Mikhail Shtalenkov .20 .50
101 Alexei Kasatonov .08 .25
102 Mikhail Tatarinov .08 .25
103 Igor Kravchuk .08 .25
104 Vladimir Malakhov .08 .25
105 Alex Gusarov .08 .25
106 Dimitri Filimonov .08 .25
107 Dimitri Mironov .08 .25
108 Vladimir Konstantinov .75 2.00
109 Sergei Fedorov 1.25 3.00
110 Alexei Zhamnov .08 .25
111 Vyatcheslav Kozlov .08 .25
112 Valery Kamesky .08 .25
113 Alexander Semak .08 .25
114 Vjatcheslav Butsayev .08 .25
115 Andrei Lomakin .08 .25
116 Pavel Bure 2.00 5.00
117 Andrei Kovalenko .08 .25
118 Ravil Khaidarov .08 .25
119 Victor Gordiuk .08 .25
120 Vitali Prokhorov .08 .25
121 Tjeckoslovakien .02 .10
122 Ivan Hlinka .02 .10
123 Oldrich Svoboda .20 .50
124 Dominik Hasek 4.00 10.00
125 Leo Gudas .08 .25
126 Frantisek Musil .08 .25
127 Kamil Prachar .08 .25
128 Frantisek Kucera .08 .25
129 Richard Smehlik .08 .25
130 Jergus Baca .08 .25
131 Jiri Slegr .08 .25
132 Petr Hrbek .08 .25
133 Kamil Kastak .08 .25
134 Richard Zemlicka .08 .25
135 Jaromir Jagr 3.00 8.00
136 Martin Rucinsky .08 .25
137 Josef Beranek .08 .25
138 Michael Pivonka .08 .25
139 Robert Kron .08 .25
140 Zigmund Palffy .75 2.00
141 Tomas Jelinek .08 .25
142 Robert Reichel .08 .25
143 Lubomir Kolnik .08 .25
144 Zdeno Ciger .08 .25
145 USA .02 .10
146 Tim Taylor .02 .10
147 John Vanbiesbrouck .75 2.00
148 Mike Richter .75 2.00
149 Phil Housley .08 .25
150 Brian Leetch .40 1.00
151 Kevin Hatcher .08 .25
152 Gary Suter .08 .25
153 Chris Chelios .75 2.00
154 Eric Weinrich .08 .25
155 Jim Johnson .08 .25
156 Brett Hull 2.00 5.00
157 Mike Modano 2.00 5.00
158 Jeremy Roenick 2.00 5.00
159 Pat LaFontaine .40 1.00
160 Craig Janney .08 .25
161 Ed Olczyk .08 .25
162 Tony Granato .08 .25
163 Joe Mullen .08 .25
164 Dave Christian .08 .25
165 Doug Brown .08 .25
166 Kevin Miller .08 .25
167 Joel Otto .08 .25
168 Randy Wood .08 .25
169 Tyskland .02 .10
170 Ludek Bukac .08 .25
171 Klaus Merk .08 .25
172 Josef Heiss .08 .25
173 Harold Kreiss .08 .25
174 Michael Heidt .08 .25
175 Jorg Mayr .08 .25
176 Marco Rentzsch .08 .25
177 Heinrich Schiffel .08 .25
178 Stefan Steinecker .08 .25
179 Torsten Kienass .08 .25
180 Raimund Hilger .08 .25
181 Ernst Kopf .08 .25
182 Peter Draisatl .08 .25
183 Axel Kammerer .08 .25
184 Michael Rumrich .08 .25
185 Jurgen Rumrich .08 .25
186 Georg Holzmann .08 .25
187 Lorenz Funk .08 .25
188 Thomas Schinko .08 .25
189 Andreas Lupzig .08 .25
190 Tobias Abstreiter .08 .25
191 Michael Pohl .08 .25
192 Antony Vogel .08 .25
193 Schweiz .02 .10
194 Juhani Tamminen .02 .10
195 Renato Tosio .20 .50
196 Reto Pavoni .20 .50
197 Rick Tschumi .08 .25
198 Patrice Brasey .08 .25
199 Didier Massy .08 .25
200 Sandro Bertaggia .08 .25
201 Sven Leuenberger .08 .25
202 Samuel Palmer .08 .25
203 Martin Rauch .08 .25
204 Dino Kessler .08 .25
205 Raymond Walder .08 .25
206 Peter Jaks .08 .25
207 Andy Ton .08 .25
208 Jorg Eberle .08 .25
209 Felix Hollenstein .08 .25
210 Fredy Luthi .08 .25
211 Manuele Celio .08 .25
212 Christian Weber .08 .25
213 Andre Rotheli .08 .25
214 Gil Montandon .08 .25
215 Thomas Vrabec .08 .25
216 Patrick Howald .08 .25
217 Frankrike .02 .10
218 Kjell Larsson .02 .10
219 Jean-Marc Djian .20 .50
220 Petri Ylonen .20 .50
221 Stephane Botteri .08 .25
222 Michel Leblanc .08 .25
223 Jean-Philippe Lemoine .08 .25
224 Denis Perez .08 .25
225 Bruno Saunier .08 .25
226 Steven Woodburn .08 .25
227 Serge Poudrier .08 .25
228 Michael Babin .08 .25
229 Stephane Barin .08 .25
230 Philippe Bozon .40 1.00
231 Arnaud Briand .08 .25
232 Yves Crettenand .08 .25
233 Patrick Dunn .08 .25
234 Yannick Goicoechea .08 .25
235 Benoit Laporte .08 .25
236 Christian Pouget .08 .25
237 Antoine Richer .08 .25
238 Christophe Ville .08 .25
239 Peter Almasy .08 .25
240 Pierre Pousse .08 .25
241 Italien .02 .10
242 Gene Ubriaco .02 .10
243 David Delfino .40 1.00
244 Mike Zanier .40 1.00
245 Erwin Kostner .08 .25
246 Roberto Oberrauch .08 .25
247 Jim Camazzola .08 .25
248 Anthony Circelli .08 .25
249 Michael de Angelis .08 .25
250 Giovanni Marchetti .08 .25
251 Alessandro Batiani .08 .25
252 Georg Comploi .08 .25
253 Gaetano Orlando .08 .25
254 Bruno Zarrillo .08 .25
255 Emilio Iovio .08 .25
256 Frank Nigro .08 .25
257 Marco Scapinello .08 .25
258 Giuseppe Foglietta .08 .25
259 Rick Morocco .08 .25
260 Santino Pellegrino .08 .25
261 Lucio Topatigh .08 .25
262 Mario Simioni .08 .25
263 Ivano Cloch .08 .25
264 Martino Soracreppa .08 .25
265 Polen .02 .10
266 Leszek Lejcyk .02 .10
267 Andrzej Hanisz .20 .50
268 Mariusz Kieca .20 .50
269 Henryk Gruth .08 .25
270 Janusz Syposz .08 .25
271 Robert Szopinski .08 .25
272 Mark Cholewa .08 .25
273 Jacek Zamojski .08 .25
274 Rafal Stroka .08 .25
275 Dariusz Garbocz .08 .25
276 Stanislaw Cyrwus .08 .25
277 Janusz Adamiec .08 .25
278 Miloslaw Copija .08 .25
279 Piotr Zdunek .08 .25
280 Krzysztof Bujar .08 .25
281 Ludwik Czapka .08 .25
282 Andrzej Kotonski .08 .25
283 Janusz Hajnos .08 .25
284 Slawomir Wieloch .08 .25
285 Wojciech Matczak .08 .25
286 Jedrzej Kasperczyk .08 .25
287 Wojciech Tkacs .08 .25
288 Mariusz Czerkawski .20 .50

1992-93 Finnish Jyvas-Hyva Stickers

This sticker set features the players of the SM-Liiga. The odd-sized stickers (about 2 x 3 1/3) were inserted as premiums with candy products and came in strips of three. The set is noteworthy for early appearances of Saku Koivu and Sami Kapanen.

COMPLETE SET (204) 19.56 48.89
1 Harri Rindell .05 .15
2 Sakari Lindfors .40 1.00
3 Simo Saarinen .05 .15
4 Pertti Lehtonen .05 .15
5 Kari Laitinen .05 .15
6 Teppo Kivela .05 .15
7 Darren Boyko .20 .50
8 Kai Rautio .08 .25
9 Drahomir Kadlec .08 .25
10 Mika Kortelainen .05 .15
11 Jukka Seppo .08 .25
12 Pekka Tuomisto .05 .15
13 Pasi Sormunen .05 .15
14 Kai Tervonen .05 .15
15 Ville Peltonen .40 1.00
16 Valeri Krykov .05 .15
17 Iiro Jarvi .20 .50
18 Hannu Jortikka .05 .15
19 Timo Lehkonen .05 .15
20 Timo Nykopp .05 .15
21 Janne Laukkanen .40 1.00
22 Marko Palo .08 .25
23 Juha Ylonen 1.25 3.00
24 Jarkko Varvio .20 .50
25 Marko Allen .05 .15
26 Marko Tuulola .05 .15
27 Jarkko Nikander .08 .25
28 Radek Toupal .05 .15
29 Tommi Varjonen .05 .15
30 Niko Marttila .05 .15
31 Jari Haapamaki .05 .15
32 Pasi Kivela .05 .15
33 Tony Virta .05 .15
34 Markku Piikkila .05 .15
35 Anatoli Bogdanov .05 .15
36 Jukka Tammi .40 1.00
37 Jani Nikko .08 .25
38 Jukka Ollila .05 .15
39 Tommi Kiiski .05 .15
40 Mikko Luovi .08 .25
41 Juha Jarvenpaa .05 .15
42 Juha Lampinen .05 .15
43 Janne Siva .05 .15
44 Timo Peltomaa .08 .25
45 Mika Arvaja .05 .15
46 Esa Tommila .05 .15
47 Kristian Taubert .05 .15
48 Jarkko Glad .05 .15
49 Hannu Mattila .05 .15
50 Pasi Maattanen .05 .15
51 Petri Sullamaa .05 .15
52 Boris Majorov .05 .15
53 Markus Ketterer .40 1.00
54 Waltteri Immonen .05 .15
55 Mika Stromberg .08 .25
56 Keijo Sailynoja .05 .15
57 Otakar Janecky .08 .25
58 Jiri Sejba .08 .25
59 Kari Martikainen .05 .15
60 Erik Hamalainen .08 .25
61 Timo Norppa .05 .15
62 Pekka Jarvela .05 .15
63 Juha Salo .05 .15
64 Heikki Riihijarvi .05 .15
65 Ari Salo .05 .15
66 Hannu Jarvenpaa .20 .50
67 Jali Wahlsten .05 .15
68 Juha Jokiharju .05 .15
69 Hannu Aravirta .05 .15
70 Ari-Pekka Siekkinen .08 .25
71 Jarmo Jokilahti .05 .15
72 Harri Laurila .05 .15
73 Juha Riihijarvi .20 .50
74 Jari Lindroos .08 .25
75 Marko Virtanen .05 .15
76 Jari Munck .05 .15
77 Markku Heikkinen .05 .15
78 Lasse Nieminen .05 .15
79 Tero Lehikoinen .05 .15
80 Ari Haanpaa .05 .15
81 Jarmo Rantanen .05 .15
82 Veli-Pekka Hard .05 .15
83 Mika Paananen .05 .15
84 Joni Lius .08 .25
85 Risto Kurkinen .05 .15
86 Juha Junno .05 .15
87 Pasi Kuivalainen .20 .50
88 Jari Jarvinen .05 .15
89 Vesa Salo .05 .15
90 Vesa Karjalainen .05 .15
91 Darius Rusnak .05 .15
92 Arto Sirvio .05 .15
93 Vesa Ruotsalainen .05 .15
94 Juha Tuohimaa .05 .15
95 Jari Hamalainen .05 .15
96 Pekka Tirkkonen .05 .15
97 Jari Laukkanen .05 .15
98 Antti Tuomenoksa .05 .15
99 Janne Leppanen .05 .15
100 Marko Jantunen .08 .25
101 Dusan Pasek .40 1.00
102 Sami Kapanen 1.25 3.00
103 Martti Merra .05 .15
104 Sami Aikaa .05 .15
105 Teemu Sillanpaa .05 .15
106 Sami Nuutinen .05 .15
107 Jere Lehtinen 3.00 8.00
108 Jan Langbacka .05 .15
109 Tero Lehtera .08 .25
110 Robert Salo .05 .15
111 Jimi Helin .05 .15
112 Sami Kokko .05 .15
113 Riku Kuusisto .05 .15
114 Markku Tiinus .05 .15
115 Pasi Heinisto .05 .15
116 Petri Pulkkinen .05 .15
117 Tom Laaksonen .05 .15
118 Jarmo Muukkonen .05 .15
119 Petro Koivunen .08 .25
120 Matti Keinonen .05 .15
121 Petr Briza .40 1.00
122 Timo Kulonen .05 .15
123 Allan Measures .05 .15
124 Harri Suvanto .05 .15
125 Timo Saarikoski .05 .15
126 Mika Alatalo .75 2.00
127 Kari-Pekka Friman .05 .15
128 Jarmo Kuusisto .05 .15
129 Mika Valila .05 .15
130 Jari Torkki .05 .15
131 Pekka Peltola .05 .15
132 Pasi Huura .05 .15
133 Matti Forss .05 .15
134 Kalle Sahlstedt .08 .25
135 Tommi Pullola .05 .15
136 Tero Arkiomaa .05 .15
137 Esko Nokelainen .05 .15
138 Petri Engman .05 .15
139 Timo Kahelin .05 .15
140 Pasi Ruponen .05 .15
141 Petteri Sihvonen .05 .15
142 Toni Sihvonen .05 .15
143 Sami Wikstrom .05 .15
144 Erik Kakko .05 .15
145 Jari Parviainen .05 .15
146 Jonni Vauhkonen .08 .25
147 Jari Kauppila .05 .15
148 Erkki Makela .05 .15
149 Jarkko Hamalainen .05 .15
150 Petri Koski .05 .15
151 Sami Lekkerimaki .05 .15
152 Toni Koivunen .05 .15
153 Jani Uski .05 .15
154 Pertti Hasanen .05 .15
155 Jaromir Sindel .20 .50
156 Tommi Haapsaari .05 .15
157 Jukka Marttila .05 .15
158 Jarmo Kekalainen .20 .50
159 Tommi Pohja .05 .15
160 Pauli Jarvinen .05 .15
161 Timo Jutila .20 .50
162 Janne Gronvall .08 .25
163 Jussi-Pekka Jarvinen .05 .15
164 Kari Heikkinen .05 .15
165 Marko Ek .05 .15
166 Veli-Pekka Kautonen .05 .15
167 Pekka Laksola .05 .15
168 Pasi Forsberg .05 .15
169 Marko Lapinkoski .05 .15
170 Mikko Peltola .05 .15
171 Vladimir Jursinov .05 .15
172 Jouni Rokama .08 .25
173 Mikko Haapakoski .05 .15
174 Kari Harila .05 .15
175 Kari Kanervo .05 .15
176 Esa Keskinen .20 .50
177 Saku Koivu 6.00 15.00
178 Jouko Narvanmaa .05 .15
179 Alexander Smirnov .05 .15
180 Reijo Mikkolainen .05 .15
181 Mikko Makela .30 .75
182 Raimo Summanen .20 .50
183 Hannu Virta .08 .25
184 Jukka Virtanen .05 .15
185 German Titov .20 .50
186 Jukka Vilander .05 .15
187 Ari Vuori .05 .15
188 Vasili Tikhonov .20 .50
189 Kari Takko .40 1.00
190 Sami Saarinen .05 .15
191 Marko Sten .05 .15
192 Arto Javanainen .05 .15
193 Janne Virtanen .05 .15
194 Arto Heiskanen .05 .15
195 Jouni Vento .05 .15
196 Olli Kaski .05 .15
197 Vyacheslav Fandul .05 .15
198 Jokke Hainanen .05 .15
199 Petri Varis .20 .50
200 Harry Nikander .05 .15
201 Jarno Miikkulainen .05 .15
202 Jari Korpisalo .08 .25
203 Rauli Raitanen .05 .15
204 Jari Levonen .05 .15

1993-94 Finnish Jyvas-Hyva Stickers

This 349-sticker set features the players of Finland's SM-Liiga. The odd-sized stickers (1 X 1 1/2") were inserted as premiums with candy products. The set skips the following numbers: 30, 60, 90, 120, 150, 180, 210, 240, 270, 300, 330. There are no spaces for these cards in the binder produced to store the set, and the cards were never issued. The set is noteworthy for early appearances of Saku Koivu and Janne Niinimaa.

COMPLETE SET (359) 24.00 60.00
1 HIFK Team Photo .02 .10
2 HIFK Team Photo .02 .10
3 HIFK Team Photo .02 .10
4 HIFK Team Photo .02 .10
5 HIFK Team Photo .02 .10
6 HIFK Team Photo .02 .10
7 HIFK Team Photo .02 .10
8 HIFK Team Photo .02 .10
9 HIFK Team Photo .02 .10
10 HIFK Team Photo .02 .10
11 HIFK Team Photo .02 .10
12 HIFK Team Photo .02 .10
13 Harri Rindell .05 .15
14 Sakari Lindfors .40 1.00
15 Simo Saarinen .05 .15
16 Pertti Lehtonen .05 .15
17 Jari Laukkanen .05 .15
18 Valeri Krykov .05 .15
19 Iiro Jarvi .20 .50
20 Jari Munck .05 .15
21 Pasi Sormunen .05 .15
22 Pekka Peltola .05 .15
23 Teppo Kivela .05 .15
24 Pekka Tuomisto .05 .15
25 Kai Tervonen .05 .15
26 Dan Lambert .20 .50
27 Marco Poulsen .05 .15
28 Ville Peltonen .40 1.00
29 Kim Ahlroos .05 .15
31 HPK Team Photo .02 .10
32 HPK Team Photo .02 .10
33 HPK Team Photo .02 .10
34 HPK Team Photo .02 .10
35 HPK Team Photo .02 .10
36 HPK Team Photo .02 .10
37 HPK Team Photo .02 .10
38 HPK Team Photo .02 .10
39 HPK Team Photo .02 .10
40 HPK Team Photo .02 .10
41 HPK Team Photo .02 .10
42 HPK Team Photo .02 .10
43 Pentti Matikainen .05 .15
44 Kari Rosenberg .08 .25
45 Mikko Myllykoski .05 .15
46 Janne Laukkanen .40 1.00
47 Jarkko Nikander .08 .25
48 Tomas Kapusta .05 .15
49 Mika Lartama .05 .15
50 Niko Marttila .05 .15
51 Jari Haapamaki .05 .15
52 Tommi Varjonen .05 .15
53 Tony Virta .05 .15
54 Marko Palo .08 .25
55 Marko Allen .05 .15
56 Miikka Ruokonen .05 .15
57 Jani Hassinen .05 .15
58 Pasi Kivila .05 .15
59 Markku Piikkila .05 .15
61 Ilves Team Photo .02 .10
62 Ilves Team Photo .02 .10
63 Ilves Team Photo .02 .10
64 Ilves Team Photo .02 .10
65 Ilves Team Photo .02 .10
66 Ilves Team Photo .02 .10
67 Ilves Team Photo .02 .10
68 Ilves Team Photo .02 .10
69 Ilves Team Photo .02 .10
70 Ilves Team Photo .02 .10
71 Ilves Team Photo .02 .10
72 Ilves Team Photo .02 .10
73 Jukka Jalonen .05 .15
74 Jukka Tammi .40 1.00
75 Jani Nikko .08 .25
76 Hannu Henriksson .05 .15
77 Juha Jarvenpaa .05 .15
78 Hannu Mattila .05 .15
79 Timo Peltomaa .08 .25
80 Jukka Ollila .05 .15
81 Juha-Matti Marijarvi .05 .15
82 Mikko Louvi .08 .25
83 Jarno Peltonen .05 .15
84 Pasi Maattanen .05 .15
85 Juha Lampinen .05 .15
86 Allan Measures .05 .15
87 Janne Seva .05 .15
88 Risto Jalo .05 .15
89 Esa Tommila .05 .15
91 Jokerit Team Photo .02 .10
92 Jokerit Team Photo .02 .10
93 Jokerit Team Photo .02 .10
94 Jokerit Team Photo .02 .10
95 Jokerit Team Photo .02 .10
96 Jokerit Team Photo .02 .10
97 Jokerit Team Photo .02 .10
98 Jokerit Team Photo .02 .10
99 Jokerit Team Photo .02 .10
100 Jokerit Team Photo .02 .10
101 Jokerit Team Photo .02 .10
102 Jokerit Team Photo .02 .10
103 Alpo Suhonen .20 .50
104 Ari Sulander .40 1.00
105 Kari Martikainen .08 .25
106 Erik Hamalainen .08 .25
107 Juha Jokiharju .05 .15
108 Otakar Janecky .08 .25
109 Petri Varis .20 .50
110 Waltteri Immonen .05 .15
111 Mika Stromberg .08 .25
112 Keijo Sailynoja .05 .15
113 Timo Saarikoski .05 .15
114 Juha Ylonen .75 2.00
115 Ari Salo .05 .15
116 Heikki Riihijarvi .05 .15
117 Timo Norppa .05 .15
118 Jali Wahlsten .05 .15
119 Rami Koivisto .05 .15
121 JYP HT Team Photo .02 .10
122 JYP HT Team Photo .02 .10
123 JYP HT Team Photo .02 .10
124 JYP HT Team Photo .02 .10
125 JYP HT Team Photo .02 .10
126 JYP HT Team Photo .02 .10
127 JYP HT Team Photo .02 .10
128 JYP HT Team Photo .02 .10
129 JYP HT Team Photo .02 .10
130 JYP HT Team Photo .02 .10
131 JYP HT Team Photo .02 .10
132 JYP HT Team Photo .02 .10
133 Kari Savolainen .05 .15
134 Ari-Pekka Siekkinen .08 .25
135 Harri Laurila .05 .15
136 Markku Heikkinen .05 .15
137 Jari Lindroos .08 .25
138 Lasse Nieminen .05 .15
139 Risto Kurkinen .05 .15
140 Jarmo Jokilahti .06 .15
141 Veli-Pekka Hard .05 .15
142 Joni Lius .08 .25
143 Jyrki Jokinen .05 .15
144 Mika Arvaja .05 .15
145 Vesa Ponto .05 .15
146 Jarmo Rantanen .05 .15
147 Mika Paananen .05 .15
148 Marko Virtanen .08 .25
149 Marko Ek .05 .15
151 Kalpa Team Photo .02 .10
152 Kalpa Team Photo .02 .10
153 Kalpa Team Photo .02 .10
154 Kalpa Team Photo .02 .10
155 Kalpa Team Photo .02 .10
156 Kalpa Team Photo .02 .10
157 Kalpa Team Photo .02 .10
158 Kalpa Team Photo .02 .10
159 Kalpa Team Photo .02 .10
160 Kalpa Team Photo .02 .10
161 Kalpa Team Photo .02 .10
162 Kalpa Team Photo .02 .10
163 Hannu Kapanen .05 .15
164 Pasi Kuivalainen .20 .50
165 Kimmo Timonen .60 1.50
166 Vesa Salo .05 .15
167 Jani Rautio .05 .15
168 Pekka Tirkkonen .05 .15
169 Dimitri Zinine .05 .15
170 Antti Tuomenoksa .05 .15
171 Jari Jarvinen .05 .15
172 Tuomas Kalliomaki .05 .15
173 Tommi Miettinen .08 .25
174 Sami Kapanen .75 2.00
175 Vesa Ruotsalainen .05 .15
176 Mikko Tavi .05 .15
177 Sami Mettovaara .05 .15
178 Veli-Pekka Pekkarinen .05 .15
179 Arto Sirvio .05 .15
181 Kiekko-Espoo Team Photo .02 .10
182 Kiekko-Espoo Team Photo .02 .10
183 Kiekko-Espoo Team Photo .02 .10
184 Kiekko-Espoo Team Photo .02 .10
185 Kiekko-Espoo Team Photo .02 .10
186 Kiekko-Espoo Team Photo .02 .10
187 Kiekko-Espoo Team Photo .02 .10

188 Kiekko-Espoo Team Photo .02 .10
189 Kiekko-Espoo Team Photo .02 .10
190 Kiekko-Espoo Team Photo .02 .10
191 Kiekko-Espoo Team Photo .02 .10
192 Kiekko-Espoo Team Photo .02 .10
193 Martti Merra .05 .15
194 Timo Maki .05 .15
195 Sami Nuutinen .05 .15
196 Teemu Sillanpaa .05 .15
197 Tero Lehtera .08 .25
198 Jan Langbacka .05 .15
199 Jukka Tiilikainen .05 .15
200 Petri Pulkkinen .05 .15
201 Robert Salo .05 .15
202 Petro Koivunen .08 .25
203 Juha Ikonen .05 .15
204 Mikko Lempiainen .05 .15
205 Marko Halonen .05 .15
206 Jimi Helin .05 .15
207 Timo Hirvonen .05 .15
208 Mikko Halonen .05 .15
209 Kimmo Maki-Kokkila .05 .15
211 Lukko Team Photo .02 .10
212 Lukko Team Photo .02 .10
213 Lukko Team Photo .02 .10
214 Lukko Team Photo .02 .10
215 Lukko Team Photo .02 .10
216 Lukko Team Photo .02 .10
217 Lukko Team Photo .02 .10
218 Lukko Team Photo .02 .10
219 Lukko Team Photo .02 .10
220 Lukko Team Photo .02 .10
221 Lukko Team Photo .02 .10
222 Lukko Team Photo .02 .10
223 Vaclav Sykora .05 .15
224 Jarmo Myllys .40 1.00
225 Kari-Pekka Friman .05 .15
226 Timo Kulonen .05 .15
227 Pasi Saarela .05 .15
228 Kalle Sahlstedt .08 .25
229 Kimmo Rintanen .20 .50
230 Jarmo Kuusisto .05 .15
231 Tuomas Gronman .08 .25
232 Tero Arkiomaa .05 .15
233 Petr Korinek .08 .25
234 Mika Alatalo .60 1.50
235 Marko Tuulola .05 .15
236 Pasi Huura .05 .15
237 Tommi Pullola .05 .15
238 Mika Valila .05 .15
239 Jari Torkki .05 .15
241 Reipas Lahti Team Photo .02 .10
242 Reipas Lahti Team Photo .02 .10
243 Reipas Lahti Team Photo .02 .10
244 Reipas Lahti Team Photo .02 .10
245 Reipas Lahti Team Photo .02 .10
246 Reipas Lahti Team Photo .02 .10
247 Reipas Lahti Team Photo .02 .10
248 Reipas Lahti Team Photo .02 .10
249 Reipas Lahti Team Photo .02 .10
250 Reipas Lahti Team Photo .02 .10
251 Reipas Lahti Team Photo .02 .10
252 Reipas Lahti Team Photo .02 .10
253 Kari Makinen .05 .15
254 Oldrich Svoboda .05 .15
255 Timo Kahelin .05 .15
256 Pasi Ruponen .05 .15
257 Tommy Kiviaho .05 .15
258 Jari Multanen .05 .15
259 Erkki Makela .05 .15
260 Jari Parviainen .05 .15
261 Petri Koski .05 .15
262 Jouni Vauhkonen .08 .25
263 Toni Koivunen .05 .15
264 Sami Wikstrom .05 .15
265 Jarkko Hamalainen .05 .15
266 Sami Helenius .20 .50
267 Sami Lekkerimaki .05 .15
268 Jari Kauppila .05 .15
269 Jani Uski .05 .15
271 Tappara Team Photo .02 .10
272 Tappara Team Photo .02 .10
273 Tappara Team Photo .02 .10
274 Tappara Team Photo .02 .10
275 Tappara Team Photo .02 .10
276 Tappara Team Photo .02 .10
277 Tappara Team Photo .02 .10
278 Tappara Team Photo .02 .10
279 Tappara Team Photo .02 .10
280 Tappara Team Photo .02 .10
281 Tappara Team Photo .02 .10
282 Tappara Team Photo .02 .10
283 Boris Majorov .05 .15
284 Timo Hankela .05 .15
285 Timo Jutila .20 .50
286 Samuli Rautio .05 .15
287 Ari Haanpaa .05 .15
288 Mikko Peltola .05 .15
289 Pauli Jarvinen .05 .15
290 Pekka Laksola .05 .15
291 Janne Gronvall .08 .25
292 Kari Heikkinen .05 .15
293 Tommi Pohja .05 .15
294 Petri Aaltonen .05 .15
295 Petri Kalteva .05 .15
296 Tommi Haapsaari .05 .15
297 Teemu Numminen .05 .15
298 Pasi Forsberg .05 .15
299 Veli-Pekka Kautonen .05 .15
301 TPS Team Photo .02 .10
302 TPS Team Photo .02 .10
303 TPS Team Photo .02 .10
304 TPS Team Photo .02 .10
305 TPS Team Photo .02 .10
306 TPS Team Photo .02 .10
307 TPS Team Photo .02 .10
308 TPS Team Photo .02 .10
309 TPS Team Photo .02 .10
310 TPS Team Photo .02 .10
311 TPS Team Photo .02 .10
312 TPS Team Photo .02 .10
313 Vladimir Jursinov .05 .15
314 Jouni Rokama .08 .25
315 Hannu Virta .08 .25
316 Erik Kakko .05 .15
317 Jukka Vilander .05 .15
318 Esa Keskinen .20 .50
319 Ari Vuori .05 .15
320 Jouko Narvanmaa .05 .15
321 Marko Kiprusoff .08 .25
322 Jere Lehtinen 2.00 5.00
323 Saku Koivu 4.00 10.00
324 Marko Jantunen .08 .25
325 Kari Harila .05 .15
326 Alexander Smirnov .05 .15
327 Toni Sihvonen .05 .15
328 Harri Sillgren .05 .15
329 Kai Nurminen .40 1.00
331 Assat Team Photo .02 .10
332 Assat Team Photo .02 .10
333 Assat Team Photo .02 .10
334 Assat Team Photo .02 .10
335 Assat Team Photo .02 .10
336 Assat Team Photo .02 .10
337 Assat Team Photo .02 .10
338 Assat Team Photo .02 .10
339 Assat Team Photo .02 .10
340 Assat Team Photo .02 .10
341 Assat Team Photo .02 .10
342 Assat Team Photo .02 .10
343 Veli-Pekka Ketola .08 .25
344 Kari Takko .40 1.00
345 Olli Kaski .05 .15
346 Karri Kivi .05 .15
347 Arto Heiskanen .05 .15
348 Janne Virtanen .05 .15
349 Mikael Kotkaniemi .05 .15
350 Stanislav Meciar .05 .15
351 Jarno Miikkulainen .05 .15
352 Jokke Heinanen .05 .15
353 Vjatseslav Fandul .08 .25
354 Ari Saarinen .05 .15
355 Jouni Vento .05 .15
356 Arto Javanainen .05 .15
357 Jari Korpisalo .08 .25
358 Rauli Raitanen .05 .15
359 Jari Levonen .05 .15
NNO Binder 4.00 10.00

1993-94 Finnish SISU

The 396 standard-size cards comprising this first series of players from the Finnish Hockey League feature on-ice color player photos on their fronts. The photos are bordered in a gray lithic, and each carries the player's name, uniform number, and team logo near the bottom. The gray lithic design continues on the horizontal back, which carries the player's team name in a yellow stripe across the top, followed below by his name, position, biography, and statistics. With a few exceptions, all text is in Finnish. Cards 301-396 differ from the others in that the design is orange lithic instead of gray, and some have horizontal fronts. The cards are numbered on the front. There are several new errors and variations in this edition, as provided by Finnish collector Heikki Silvennoinen.

COMPLETE SET (396) 20.00 50.00
1 Jokerit Team Card .08 .25
2 Alpo Suhonen .20 .50
3 Ari Sulander .40 1.00
4 Marko Rantanen .05 .15
5 Ari Salo .02 .10
6 Kalle Koskinen .05 .15
7 Sebastian Sulku .02 .10
8 Waltteri Immonen .05 .15
9 Mika Stromberg .08 .25
10 Heikki Riihijarvi .02 .10
11 Kari Martikainen .05 .15
12 Erik Hamalainen .08 .25
13 Juha Jokiharju .05 .15
14 Timo Norppa .02 .10
15 Rami Koivisto .02 .10
16 Antti Tormanen .30 .75
17 Keijo Sailynoja .05 .15
18 Jere Keskinen .02 .10
19 Jali Wahlsten .02 .10
20 Mikko Kontilla .02 .10
21 Juha Ylonen .60 1.50
22 Jussi Vienonen ERR .02 .10
{wrong photo
22B Jussi Vienonen COR .08 .25
23 Petri Varis .20 .50
24 Juha Lind .40 1.00
25 Timo Saarikoski .02 .10
26 Otakar Janecky .08 .25
27 TPS Team Card .05 .15
28 Vladimir Jursinov CO .02 .10
29 Jouni Rokama .05 .15
30 Kimmo Lecklin .02 .10
31 Jouko Narvanmaa .02 .10
32 Petteri Nummelin .05 .15
33 Erik Kakko .02 .10
34 Tom Koivisto .02 .10
35 Marko Kiprusoff .08 .25
36 Kari Harila .02 .10
37 Hannu Virta .08 .25
38 Aki Berg .40 1.00
39 Aleksander Smirnov .02 .10
40 Esa Keskinen .08 .25
41 Saku Koivu 4.00 10.00
42 Jukka Vilander .02 .10
43 Antti Aalto .40 1.00
44 Mika Karapuu ERR .02 .10
{wrong photo
44B Mika Karapuu COR .08 .25
45 Toni Sihvonen .02 .10
46 Pavel Torgajev .08 .25
47 Jere Lehtinen 1.25 3.00
48 Kai Nurminen .08 .25
49 Harri Sillgren .02 .10
50 Niko Mikkola .02 .10
51 Ari Vuori .02 .10
52 Lasse Pirjeta .02 .10
53 Reijo Mikkolainen .02 .10
54 Marko Jantunen .08 .25
55 Mikko Virolainen ERR .02 .10
{wrong photo
55B Mikko Virolainen COR .08 .25
56 Tappara Team Card .05 .15
57 Boris Majorov CO .02 .10
58 Jaromir Sindel .08 .25
59 Timo Hankela .02 .10
60 Teemu Kivinen .02 .10
61 Petri Kalteva .02 .10
62 Jari Harjumaki .02 .10
63 Timo Jutila .08 .25
64 Janne Gronvall .08 .25
65 Jari Gronstrand .05 .15
66 Pekka Laksola .02 .10
67 Tommi Haapsaari .02 .10
68 Veli-Pekka Kautonen .02 .10
69 Mikko Peltola .02 .10
70 Kari Heikkinen .02 .10
71 Teemu Numminen .02 .10
72 Jiri Kucera .05 .15
73 Pauli Jarvinen .02 .10
74 Pasi Forsberg .02 .10
75 Tero Toivola .02 .10
76 Ari Haanpaa .05 .15
77 Tommi Pohja .02 .10
78 Samuli Rautio .02 .10
79 Markus Oijennus .02 .10
80 Petri Aaltonen .02 .10
81 HIFK Team Card .05 .15
82 Harri Rindell CO .02 .10
83 Sakari Lindfors .08 .25
84 Mikael Granlund .02 .10
85 Kimmo Hyttinen .02 .10
86 Jere Karalahti .20 .50
87 Dan Lambert .20 .50
88 Simo Saarinen .02 .10
89 Pasi Sormunen .02 .10
90 Tommi Hamalainen .02 .10
91 Pertti Lehtonen .02 .10
92 Jari Munck .02 .10
93 Kai Tervonen .02 .10
94 Kim Ahlroos .02 .10
95 Teppo Kivela .02 .10
96 Darren Boyko .05 .15
97 Pekka Peltola .02 .10
98 Marco Poulsen .02 .10
99 Valeri Krykov .02 .10
100 Jari Laukkanen .02 ..10
101 Ville Peltonen .40 1.00
102 Pekka Tuomisto .02 .10
103 Miro Haapaniemi .02 .10
104 Mika Kortelainen .02 .10
105 Marko Ojanen .02 .10
106 Iiro Jarvi .05 .15
107 Ilves Tampere Team Card .05 .15
108 Jukka Jalonen CO .02 .10
109 Jukka Tammi .20 .50
110 Mika Manninen .05 .15
111 Jani Nikko .08 .25
112 Jukka Ollila .02 .10
113 Juha Lampinen .02 .10
114 Hannu Henriksson .02 .10
115 Sami Lehtonen .02 .10
116 Mikko Niemi .02 .10
117 Juha-Matti Marijarvi .02 .10
118 Jarkko Glad .02 .10
119 Allan Measures .02 .10
120 Mikko Luovi .05 .15
121 Risto Jalo .05 .15
122 Juha Jarvenpaa .05 .15
123 Jarno Peltonen .02 .10
124 Matti Kaipainen .02 .10
125 Timo Peltomaa .05 .15
126 Esa Tommila .02 .10
127 Hannu Mattila .02 .10
128 Jari Neuvonen .02 .10
129 Pasi Maattanen .02 .10
130 Juha Hautamaa .02 .10
131 Janne Seva .02 .10
132 Sami Ahlberg .02 .10
133 Jari Virtanen .02 .10
134 JyP HT Team Card .05 .15
135 Kari Savolainen CO .02 .10
136 Ari-Pekka Siekkinen .05 .15
137 Marko Leinonen .02 .10
138 Jan Latvala .02 .10
139 Markku Heikkinen .02 .10
140 Jarmo Jokilahti .02 .10
141 Veli-Pekka Hard .02 .10
142 Kalle Koskinen .02 .10
143 Vesa Ponto .02 .10
144 Petri Kujala .02 .10
145 Jarmo Rantanen .02 .10
146 Harri Laurila .02 .10
147 Lasse Nieminen .02 .10
148 Mika Paananen .02 .10
149 Mika Arvaja .02 .10
150 Marko Virtanen .05 .15
151 Marko Ek .02 .10
152 Joni Lius .02 .10
153 Teemu Kohvakka .02 .10
154 Jari Lindroos .05 .15
155 Marko Kupari .02 .10
156 Markku Ikonen .02 .10
157 Jyrki Jokinen .02 .10
158 Risto Kurkinen .02 .10
159 KalPa Team Card .05 .15
160 Hannu Kapanen CO .02 .10
161 Pasi Kuivalainen .05 .15
162 Kimmo Kapanen .02 .10
163 Kimmo Timonen .40 1.00
164 Jari Jarvinen .02 .10
165 Mikko Tavi .02 .10
166 Jermu Pisto .02 .10
167 Antti Tuomenoksa .02 .10
168 Vesa Ruotsalainen .02 .10
169 Vesa Salo .02 .10
170 Veli-Pekka Pekkarinen .02 .10
171 Tuomas Kalliomaki .02 .10
172 Dimitri Zinine .02 .10
173 Jani Rautio .02 .10
173B Marko Virtanen ERR .08 .25
{incorrect numbering
174 Janne Kekalainen .02 .10
174B Marko Ek ERR .08 .25
{incorrect numbering
175 Arto Sirvio .02 .10
176 Sami Mettovaara .02 .10
177 Sami Simonen .02 .10
178 Pekka Tirkkonen .05 .15
179 Sami Kapanen .75 2.00
180 Jussi Tarvainen .02 .10
181 Lukko Team Card .05 .15
182 Vaclav Sykora .02 .10
183 Jarmo Myllys .40 1.00
183B Petri Kujala ERR .08 .25
{incorrect numbering
184 Kimmo Vesa .02 .10
185 Mika Yli-Maenpaa .05 .15
185B Jarmo Rantanen ERR .08 .25
{incorrect numbering
186 Jarmo Kuusisto .02 .10
187 Marko Tuulola .02 .10
188 Tuomas Gronman .08 .25
189 Timo Kulonen .02 .10
189B Mika Arvaja ERR .08 .25
{incorrect numbering
190 Kari-Pekka Friman VAR .02 .10
{name on front smaller font
190B Kari-Pekka Friman VAR .08 .25
{name on front larger font
191 Pasi Huura .05 .15
192 Harri Suvanto .02 .10
193 Kamil Kastak .02 .10
194 Jari Torkki .02 .10
195 Kalle Sahlstedt .05 .15
196 Tommi Pullola .02 .10
197 Mika Valila .02 .10
198 Tero Arkiomaa .02 .10
199 Pasi Saarela .02 .10
200 Matti Forss .02 .10
201 Jussi Kiuru ERR .02 .10
{wrong photo
201B Jussi Kiuru COR .08 .25
202 Mika Alatalo .75 2.00
203 Kimmo Rintanen .08 .25
204 Petri Latti ERR .02 .10
{wrong photo
204B Petri Latti COR .08 .25
205 Petr Korinek .05 .15
206 Assat Team Card .05 .15
207 Veli-Pekka Ketola CO .05 .15
208 Kari Takko .08 .25
209 Timo Jarvinen .02 .10
210 Marko Sten .02 .10
211 Pasi Peltonen .02 .10
212 Olli Kaski .02 .10
213 Jarno Miikkulainen .02 .10
214 Jouni Vento .02 .10
215 Karri Kivi .05 .15
215B HIFK Team Card ERR .02 .10
{incorrect numbering
215C Jouni Vento ERR .08 .25
{incorrect numbering
216 Stanislav Meciar .02 .10
217 Nemo Nokkosmaki .02 .10
218 Arto Javanainen .02 .10
219 Janne Virtanen .02 .10
220 Vjatseslav Fandul .05 .15
221 Jari Levonen .02 .10
222 Jarno Levonen .02 .10
223 Jari Korpisalo .08 .25
224 Jokke Heinanen .02 .10
225 Harri Lonnberg .02 .10
226 Ari Saarinen .02 .10
227 Kari Syvasalmi .02 .10
228 Jarno Makela .02 .10
229 Rauli Raitanen .02 .10
230 Arto Heiskanen .02 .10
231 Mikael Kotkaniemi .02 .10
232 HPK Team Card .05 .15
233 Pentti Matikainen .02 .10
234 Kari Rosenberg .05 .15
235 Petri Vilen .02 .10
236 Marko Allen .02 .10
237 Mikko Myllykoski .02 .10
238 Kim Vahanen .02 .10
239 Janne Laukkanen .30 .75
240 Jari Haapamaki .02 .10
241 Niko Marttila .02 .10
242 Esa Sateri .02 .10
243 Toni Virta .02 .10
244 Marko Palo .05 .15
245 Markku Piikkila .02 .10
246 Jani Hassinen .02 .10
247 Jarkko Nikander .05 .15
248 Pasi Kivila .02 .10
249 Mika Lartama .02 .10
250 Tomas Kapusta .05 .15
251 Tommi Varjonen .02 .10
252 Teemu Tamminen .02 .10
253 Jukka Seppo .05 .15
254 Kiekko-Espoo Team Card .05 .15
255 Martti Merra .02 .10
256 Scott Brower .20 .50
257 Timo Maki .02 .10
258 Petri Pulkkinen .02 .10
259 Robert Salo .02 .10
260 Sami Nuutinen .02 .10
261 Teemu Sillanpaa .02 .10
262 Marko Halonen .02 .10
263 Jimi Helin .02 .10
264 Kari Haakana .02 .10
265 Jukka Tiilikainen .02 .10
266 Jan Langbacka .02 .10
267 Jarmo Muukkonen .02 .10
268 Timo Hirvonen .05 .15
269 Pasi Heinisto .02 .10
270 Kimmo Maki-Kokkila .02 .10
271 Mikko Lempiainen .02 .10
272 Tero Lehtera .05 .15
273 Hannu Jarvenpaa .05 .15
274 Riku Kuusisto .02 .10
275 Mikko Halonen .02 .10
276 Markku Takala .02 .10
277 Petro Koivunen .05 .15
278 Reipas Lahti Team Card .05 .15
279 Kari Makinen CO .02 .10
280 Oldrich Svoboda .02 .10
281 Pekka Ilmivalta .02 .10
282 Matti Vuorio .02 .10
283 Jari Parviainen .02 .10
284 Timo Kahelin .02 .10
285 Ville Skinnari .02 .10
286 Petri Koski .02 .10
287 Jarkko Hamalainen .02 .10
288 Pasi Ruponen .02 .10
289 Oldrich Valek .02 .10
290 Juha Nurminen .02 .10
291 Erkki Laine .02 .10
292 Sami Lekkerimaki .02 .10
293 Tommy Kiviaho .02 .10
293B Ville Skinnari ERR .08 .25
{incorrect numbering
294 Jyrki Poikolainen .02 .10
295 Sami Wikstrom .02 .10
296 Jonni Vauhkonen .08 .25
297 Erkki Laine .02 .10
298 Jani Uski .02 .10
299 Jari Multanen .02 .10
300 Toni Koivunen .02 .10
301 Runkosarjan 1 .02 .10
302 Runkosarjan 2 .02 .10
303 Runkosarjan 3 .02 .10
304 Runkosarjan 4 .02 .10
305 Runkosarjan 5 .02 .10
306 Runkosarjan 6 .02 .10
307 Runkosarjan 7 .02 .10
308 Runkosarjan 8 .02 .10
309 Runkosarjan 9 .02 .10
310 Runkosarjan 10 .02 .10
311 Runkosarjan 11 .02 .10
312 Runkosarjan 12 .02 .10
313 Runkosarjan 13 .02 .10
314 Runkosarjan 14 .02 .10
315 Runkosarjan 15 .02 .10
316 Runkosarjan 16 .02 .10
317 Runkosarjan 17 .02 .10
318 Runkosarjan 18 .02 .10
319 Runkosarjan 19 .02 .10
320 Runkosarjan 20 .02 .10
321 Runkosarjan 21 .02 .10
322 Runkosarjan 22 .02 .10
323 Runkosarjan 23 .02 .10
324 Runkosarjan 24 .02 .10
325 Runkosarjan 25 .02 .10
326 Runkosarjan 26 .02 .10
327 Runkosarjan 27 .02 .10
328 Runkosarjan 28 .02 .10
329 Runkosarjan 29 .02 .10
330 Runkosarjan 30 .02 .10
331 Runkosarjan 31 .02 .10
332 Runkosarjan 32 .02 .10
333 Runkosarjan 33 .02 .10
334 Runkosarjan 34 .02 .10
335 Runkosarjan 35 .02 .10
336 Runkosarjan 36 .02 .10
337 Runkosarjan 37 .02 .10
338 Runkosarjan 38 .02 .10
339 Runkosarjan 39 .02 .10
340 Runkosarjan 40 .02 .10
341 Runkosarjan 41 .02 .10
342 Runkosarjan 42 .02 .10
343 Runkosarjan 43 .02 .10
344 Runkosarjan 44 .02 .10
345 Paikallisottelut .02 .10
(HIFK/
346 Paikallisottelut .02 .10
(Lukko
347 Paikallisottelut .02 .10
(HPK
I
348 Paikallisottelut .02 .10
(JyP H
349 Puolivaliera .02 .10
(HPK
Lukko)
350 Puolivaliera .02 .10
(Jokerit
A
351 Puolivaliera .02 .10
(Jokerit
Assat)
352 Puolivaliera .02 .10
(TPS
Ilves
353 Valiera .02 .10
(HPK
JyP HT)
354 Valiera .02 .10
(TPS
Assat)
355 Pronssiottelu .02 .10
356 1.Finaali .02 .10
(TPS 9& HPK 3
357 2. Finalli .02 .10
358 3.Finalli .02 .10
(TPS 3& HPK 2
360 Esa Keskinen LL .08 .25
361 Tomas Kapusta LL .02 .10
362 Erik Hamalainen LL .05 .15
363 Brian Tutt LL .02 .10
364 Otakar Janecky LL ERR .05 .15
364B Otakar Janecky LL COR .08 .25
365 Ville Peltonen LL .40 1.00
366 Petr Briza AS .40 1.00
367 Janne Laukkanen AS .20 .50
368 Timo Jutila AS .08 .25
369 Juha Riihijarvi AS ERR .08 .25
{card back from 384
369B Juha Riihijarvi AS COR .20 .50
370 Esa Keskinen AS ERR .08 .25
{card back from 372
370B Esa Keskinen AS COR
371 Jarkko Varvio AS .05 .15
372 Esa Keskinen AW .08 .25
Fair Pl
372B Esa Keskinen AW COR .20 .50
373 Vladimir Jursinov AW .02 .10
Be
374 Erik Hamalainen AW .05 .15
Best
375 Timo Lehkonen AW .05 .15
Best G
376 German Titov AW .08 .25
Most Pl
377 Raimo Summanen AW .05 .15
378 Mikko Haapakoski AW .02 .10
Bes
379 Marko Palo AW .02 .10
380 Seppo Makela AW .02 .10
381 TPS, Turku Team Card .02 .10
382 HPK Hameenlinna .02 .10
Hopeami
383 JyP HT Jyvaskyla .02 .10
384 Juha Riihijarvi MVP ERR .05 .15
{card back from 369
384B Juha Riihijarvi MVP COR .08 .25
385 Jukka Virtanen .02 .10
386 Kari Jalonen .05 .15
387 Matti Forss .02 .10
388 Arto Javanainen .02 .10
389 Saku Koivu/1993 NHL Dra 4.00 10.00
390 Janne Niinimaa/1993 NHL .40 1.00
391 Ville Peltonen/1993 NHL .40 1.00
392 Jonni Vauhkonen .08 .25
393 Petri Varis/1993 NHL Dr .20 .50
394 Antti Aalto/1993 NHL Dr .40 1.00
395 Jere Karalahti/1993 NHL .20 .50
396 Kimmo Timonen/1993 NHL .40 1.00

1993-94 Finnish SISU Autographs

These cards were issued as random inserts in packs of 1993-94 SISU. Essentially, they are the same as the base cards, save for the autograph and serial numbering. We do not have confirmed serial numbers for any of these cards. If you can provide them, please contact us at hockeymag@beckett.com. Thanks to collector Heikki Silvennoinen for providing the checklist.

COMPLETE SET (12) 90.00 150.00
8 Waltteri Immonen 4.00 10.00
41 Saku Koivu 20.00 50.00
73 Pauli Jarvinen 4.00 10.00
83 Sakari Lindfors 10.00 25.00
121 Risto Jalo 4.00 10.00
173 Marko Virtanen 4.00 10.00
178 Pekka Tirkkonen 6.00 15.00
203 Kimmo Rintanen 4.00 10.00
223 Jari Korpisalo 4.00 10.00
239 Janne Laukkanen 6.00 15.00
260 Sami Nuutinen 4.00 10.00
296 Jonni Vauhkonen 4.00 10.00

1993-94 Finnish SISU Promos

Produced by Leaf, this 12-card promo set was handed out to members of the Finnish media before the 1993-94 season to introduce North American style hockey cards to the fanatical hockey followers of Finland. The card design mirrors that of the base cards, but the cards are not numbered on the back.

COMPLETE SET (12) 4.00 125.00
NNO Rami Koivisto 4.00 10.00
NNO Janne Laukkanen 6.00 15.00
NNO Pekka Tirkkonen 6.00 15.00
NNO Timo Peltomaa 4.00 10.00
NNO Jari Lindroos 4.00 10.00
NNO Petri Skriko 6.00 15.00
NNO Mika Alatalo 6.00 15.00
NNO Timo Jutila 4.00 10.00
NNO Pasi Ruponen 4.00 10.00
NNO German Titov 4.00 10.00
NNO Rauli Raitanen 4.00 10.00
NNO Simo Saarinen 4.00 10.00

1994 Finnish Jaa Kiekko

This 360-card set was issued in Finland by Semic in conjunction with the 1994 World Championships. The set includes players from the traditional hockey powers, as well as Great Britain, Austria, Norway and France, shown in action for their countries. A number of NHL players who had participated in previous Canada Cups or World Championships are also pictured. The cards were distributed in 5-card packets. A binder also was available to house the collection.

COMPLETE SET (360) 30.00 50.00
1 Jarmo Myllys .08 .25
2 Pasi Kuivalainen .02 .10
3 Jukka Tammi .07 .20
4 Markus Ketterer .08 .25
5 Timo Jutila .05 .15
6 Mikko Haapakoski .02 .10
7 Marko Tuulola .02 .10
8 Jyrki Lumme .08 .25
9 Kari Harila .02 .10
10 Teppo Numminen .08 .25
11 Pasi Sormunen .02 .10
12 Petteri Nummelin .02 .10
13 Harri Laurila .02 .10
14 Mika Stromberg .05 .15
15 Ville Siren .05 .15
16 Pekka Laksola .02 .10
17 Janne Laukkanen .07 .20
18 Marko Kiprusoff .05 .15
19 Waltteri Immonen .05 .15
20 Teemu Selanne .60 1.50
21 Mika Alatalo .08 .25
22 Vesa Viitakoski .05 .15
23 Tero Arkiomaa .02 .10
24 Jari Kurri .20 .50
25 Pekka Tirkkonen .02 .10
26 Jarmo Kekalainen .05 .15
27 Saku Koivu .40 1.00
28 Antti Tormanen .07 .20
29 Jere Lehtinen .20 .50
30 Raimo Helminen .05 .15
31 Mikko Makela .05 .15
32 Marko Jantunen .05 .15
33 Ville Peltonen .08 .25
34 Esa Tikkanen .08 .25
35 Janne Ojanen .05 .15
36 Mika Nieminen .02 .10
37 Marko Palo .02 .10
38 Rauli Raitanen .02 .10
39 Sami Kapanen .40 1.00
40 Juha Riihijarvi .02 .10
41 Esa Keskinen .02 .10
42 Jari Korpisalo .02 .10
43 Christian Ruuttu .05 .15
44 Jarkko Varvio .05 .15
45 Sami Wahlsten .02 .10
46 Petri Varis .08 .25
47 Timo Saarikoski .02 .10
48 Timo Norppa .02 .10
49 Marko Virtanen .02 .10
50 Pauli Jarvinen .02 .10
51 Hakan Algotsson .07 .20
52 Tommy Soderstrom .08 .25
53 Rolf Ridderwall .05 .15
54 Tomas Jonsson .05 .15
55 Christian Due-Boje .02 .10
56 Peter Popovic .05 .15
57 Fredrik Stillman .02 .10
58 Magnus Svensson .07 .20
59 Fredrik Nilsson .02 .10
60 Tommy Albelin .05 .15
61 Joacim Esbjors .02 .10
62 Roger Johansson .05 .15
63 Stefan Nilsson .02 .10
64 Hakan Loob .08 .25
65 Peter Ottosson .02 .10
66 Daniel Rydmark .02 .10
67 Mikael Renberg .08 .25
68 Patrik Juhlin .07 .20
69 Thomas Rundqvist .05 .15
70 Andreas Johansson .08 .25
71 Stefan Ornskog .05 .15
72 Nillas Eriksson .02 .10
73 Jonas Bergqvist .08 .25
74 Mats Sundin .40 1.00
75 Peter Forsberg .75 2.00
76 Stefan Elvenes .02 .10
77 Tomas Forslund .05 .15
78 Patric Kjellberg .08 .25
79 Bill Ranford .20 .50
80 Corey Hirsch .08 .25
81 Larry Murphy .08 .25
82 Mark Tinordi .05 .15
83 Scott Stevens .20 .50
84 Al Macinnis .40 1.00
85 Steve Smith .08 .25
86 Paul Coffey .40 1.00
87 Eric Desjardins .08 .25
88 Eric Lindros .60 1.50
89 Dale Hawerchuk .20 .50
90 Steve Larmer .08 .25
91 Brent Sutter .07 .20
92 Luc Robitaille .40 1.00
93 Shayne Corson .08 .25
94 Mark Messier .60 1.50
95 Rick Tocchet .20 .50
96 Theo Fleury .40 1.00
97 Dirk Graham .08 .25
98 Russ Courtnall .08 .25
99 Wayne Gretzky 2.00 5.00
100 Brendan Shanahan .60 1.50
101 Mark Recchi .40 1.00
102 David Harlock .05 .15
103 Craig Woodcroft .02 .10
104 Paul Kariya .75 2.00
105 Jason Marshall .05 .15
106 Brett Lindros .08 .25
107 Mike Richter .40 1.00
108 Mike Dunham .20 .50
109 Craig Wolanin .05 .15
110 Jim Johnson .05 .15
111 Chris Chelios .40 1.00
112 Eric Weinrich .05 .15
113 Brian Leetch .40 1.00
114 Kevin Hatcher .08 .25
115 Ed Olczyk .08 .25
116 Kevin Miller .07 .20
117 Doug Brown .02 .10
118 Joe Mullen .08 .25
119 Craig Janney .08 .25
120 Pat LaFontaine .20 .50
121 Gary Suter .08 .25
122 Jeremy Roenick .40 1.00
123 Brett Hull .60 1.50
124 Joel Otto .08 .25
125 Mike Modano .60 1.50
126 Tony Granato .08 .25
127 Dave Christian .07 .20
128 Brian Mullen .05 .15
129 Chris Ferraro .07 .20
130 John Lilley .05 .15
131 Jeff Lazaro .05 .15
132 Peter Ferraro .08 .25
133 Brian Rolston .08 .25
134 David Roberts .05 .15
135 Nikolai Khabibulin .40 1.00
136 Andrei Trefilov .08 .25
137 Vladimir Malakhov .08 .25
138 Alexander Karpovtsev .07 .20
139 Alexander Kmirnov .02 .10
140 Sergei Zubov .08 .25
141 Sergei Seljanin .02 .10
142 Sergei Shendelev .02 .10
143 Alexei Kasatonov .07 .20
144 Sergei Sorokin .02 .10
145 Vjatseslav Bykov .02 .10
146 Sergei Fedorov 60 1.50
147 Alexei Yashin .08 .25
148 Vjatseslav Butsajev .05 .15
149 Konstantin Astrahantsev .02 .10
150 Alexei Zhamnov .08 .25
151 Dimitri Frolov .02 .10
152 Slava Kozlov .08 .25
153 Sergei Pushkov .02 .10
154 Andrei Khomutov .02 .10
155 Sergei Makarov .08 .25
156 Igor Larionov .20 .50
157 Valeri Kamenski .08 .25
158 Alexander Semak .05 .15
159 Alexei Gusarov .05 .15
160 Andrei Lomakin .05 .15
161 Igor Korolev .05 .15
162 Ravil Haidarov .02 .10
163 Dominik Hasek .60 1.50
164 Oldrich Svoboda .02 .10
165 Petr Briza .08 .25
166 Leo Gudas .02 .10
167 Kamil Prachar .02 .10
168 Richard Smehlik .07 .20
169 Frantisek Kucera .05 .15
170 Drahomir Kadlec .05 .15
171 Jan Vopat .02 .10
172 Frantisek Prochazka .02 .10
173 Antonin Stavjana .02 .10
174 Bedrich Scerban .02 .10
175 Kamil Kastak .02 .10
176 Josef Beranek .08 .25
177 Martin Rucinsky .08 .25
178 Michal Pivonka .08 .25
179 Tomas Jelinek .02 .10
180 Richard Zemlicka .02 .10
181 Robert Kron .07 .20
182 Jiri Slegr .08 .25
183 Jaromir Jagr .75 2.00
184 Robert Reichel .08 .25
185 David Vyborny .05 .15
186 Robert Lang .08 .25
187 Petr Rosol .02 .10
188 Otakar Janecky .05 .15
189 Martin Hostak .02 .10
190 Jiri Kucera .05 .15
191 Eduard Hartmann .08 .25
192 Lubomir Sekeras .02 .10
193 Marian Smerciak .02 .10
194 Jan Varholik .02 .10
195 Lubomir Rybovic .02 .10
196 Miroslav Marcinko .02 .10
197 Stanislav Medrik .02 .10
198 Zdeno Ciger .07 .20
199 Jergus Baca .05 .15
200 Peter Stastny .08 .25
201 Peter Veselovsky .02 .10
202 Anton Stastny .07 .20
203 Lubomir Kolnik .05 .15
204 Roman Kontsek .02 .10
205 Rene Pucher .02 .10
206 Slavomir Ilvasky .02 .10
207 Zigmund Palffy .40 1.00
208 Vlastimil Plavucha .02 .10
209 Dusan Pohorelec .02 .10
210 Robert Petrovicky .05 .15
211 Michel Valliere .02 .10
212 Petri Ylonen .08 .25
213 Jean-Philippe Lemoine .02 .10
214 Christophe Moyon .02 .10
215 Denis Perez .02 .10
216 Bruno Saunier .02 .10
217 Stephane Botteri .02 .10
218 Michel Breistroff .02 .10
219 Geralf Guennelon .02 .10
220 Serge Poudrier .02 .10
221 Benjamin Agnel .02 .10
222 Stephane Arcangeloni .02 .10
223 Pierrick Maia .02 .10
224 Antoine Richer .02 .10
225 Christoph Ville .02 .10
226 Michael Babin .02 .10
227 Lionel Orsolini .02 .10
228 Stephane Barin .02 .10
229 Arnaud Briand .02 .10
230 Franck Pajonkowski .07 .20
231 Claus Dalpiaz .07 .20
232 Brian Stankiewicz .02 .10
233 Rob Doyle .02 .10
234 Michael Guntner .02 .10
235 Martin Krainz .02 .10
236 Michael Shea .02 .10
237 Martin Ulrich .02 .10
238 Erich Solderer .02 .10
239 Wayne Groulx .02 .10
240 Andreas Puschnig .02 .10
241 Dieter Kalt .02 .10
242 Gerhard Puschnik .02 .10
243 Werner Kerth .02 .10
244 Richard Nasheim .02 .10
245 Arno Maier .02 .10
246 Mario Schaden .02 .10
247 Reinhard Lampert .02 .10
248 Karl Heinzle .02 .10
249 Wolfgang Kromp .02 .10
250 Marty Dallman .02 .10
251 Jim Marthinsen .07 .20
252 Rob Schistad .02 .10
253 Tom Cato Andersen .02 .10
254 Anders Myrvold .07 .20
255 Svein Enok Norstebo .02 .10
256 Tommy Jakobsen .02 .10
257 Pal Kristiansen .02 .10
258 Petter Salsten .02 .10
259 Ole Eskild Dahlstrom .02 .10
260 Morten Finstad .02 .10
261 Espen Knutsen .08 .25
262 Erik Kristiansen .02 .10
263 Geir Hoff .02 .10
264 Roy Johansen .02 .10
265 Trond Magnussen .02 .10
266 Marius Rath .02 .10
267 Vegar Barlie .02 .10
268 Arne Billkvam .02 .10
269 Tom Johansen .02 .10
270 Petter Thoresen .02 .10
271 Klaus Merk .08 .25
272 Josef Heiss .07 .20
273 Rikhard Amann .02 .10
274 Torsten Kienass .02 .10
275 Mirco Ludemann .02 .10
276 Jason Meyer .02 .10
277 Uli Hiemer .02 .10
278 Karsten Mende .02 .10
279 Andreas Niederberger .02 .10
280 Thomas Brandl .02 .10
281 Benoit Doucet .05 .15
282 Robert Hock .02 .10
283 Georg Franz .02 .10
284 Ernst Kopf, Jr. .02 .10
285 Reemt Pyka .05 .15
286 Jurgen Rumrich .02 .10
287 Dieter Hegen .02 .10

288 Raimund Hilger .02 .10
289 Thomas Schinko .02 .10
290 Leo Stefan .02 .10
291 David Delfino .07 .20
292 Elmar Parth .02 .10
293 Luigi Da Corte .02 .10
294 Phil De Gaetano .02 .10
295 Ralph Di Fiore .02 .10
296 Giorgio Comploi .02 .10
297 Alexander Thaler .02 .10
298 Giovanni Marchetti .02 .10
299 Gaetano Orlando .05 .15
300 Frank Di Muzio .02 .10
301 Giuseppe Foglietta .02 .10
302 Stefano Figliuzzi .02 .10
303 John Vecchiarelli .02 .10
304 Maurizio Mansi .02 .10
305 Santino Pellegrino .02 .10
306 Lino De Toni .02 .10
307 Mario Chitarroni .02 .10
308 Bruno Zarillo .02 .10
309 Armando Chelodi .02 .10
310 Carmine Vani .02 .10
311 Martin McKay .02 .10
312 Scott O'Connor .02 .10
313 John McCrone .02 .10
314 Stephen Cooper .02 .10
315 Mike O'Connor .02 .10
316 Chris Kelland .02 .10
317 Graham Waghorn .02 .10
318 Nicky Chinn .02 .10
319 Damian Smith .02 .10
320 Tim Cranston .02 .10
321 Scott Morrisson .02 .10
322 Antony Johnson .02 .10
323 Tony Hand .05 .15
324 Kevin Conway .02 .10
325 Rick Fera .02 .10
326 Doug McEwen .02 .10
327 Scott Neil .02 .10
328 John Iredale .02 .10
329 Iain Robertson .02 .10
330 Ian Cooper .02 .10
331 Bill Ranford DT .08 .25
332 Jarmo Myllys DT .08 .25
333 Dominik Hasek DT .60 1.50
334 Tommy Soderstrom DT .08 .25
335 Teppo Numminen DT .08 .25
336 Mihail Tatarinov DT .05 .15
337 Paul Coffey DT .40 1.00
338 Chris Chelios DT .40 1.00
339 Brian Leetch DT .40 1.00
340 Al MacInnis DT .40 1.00
341 Vladimir Malakhov DT .08 .25
342 Kevin Hatcher DT .08 .25
343 Jiri Slegr DT .05 .15
344 Wayne Gretzky DT 2.00 5.00
345 Teemu Selanne DT .60 1.50
346 Jari Kurri DT .20 .50
347 Brett Hull DT .60 1.50
348 Sergei Fedorov DT .60 1.50
349 Esa Tikkanen DT .08 .25
350 Mark Messier DT .60 1.50
351 Jaromir Jagr DT .75 2.00
352 Jeremy Roenick DT .40 1.00
353 Luc Robitaille DT .40 1.00
354 Tomas Sandstrom DT .08 .25
355 Peter Forsberg DT .75 2.00
356 Alexei Zhamnov DT .08 .25
357 Theo Fleury DT .40 1.00
358 Rick Tocchet DT .20 .50
359 Pat LaFontaine DT .20 .50
360 Eric Lindros DT .60 1.50
NNO Album 4.00 10.00

1994-95 Finnish SISU

Manufactured by Leaf in Turku, Finland, this set consists of 400 standard-size cards and features Finnish Hockey League players. The cards were sold in eight-card foil packs. The Canada Bowl Super Chase Card was inserted in first series foil packs. The Saku Koivu Super Chase Card was randomly inserted in second series foil packs at a rate of one in 192 packs. Several notable NHLers, including Teemu Selanne, Jari Kurri and Esa Tikkanen returned to Finland during the 1994 NHL lockout and thus appear in the second series.

COMPLETE SET (400) 20.00 50.00
COMPLETE SERIES 1 (200) 6.00 15.00
COMPLETE SERIES 2 (200) 14.00 35.00
1 Pasi Kuivolainen .07 .20
2 Jere Karalahti .20 .50
3 Markku Heikkinen .02 .10
4 Marko Allen .02 .10
5 Jarmo Kuusisto .02 .10
6 Marko Tuulola .02 .10
7 Marko Kiprusoff .08 .25
8 Vesa Ponto .02 .10
9 Tero Lehtera .07 .20
10 Darren Boyko .02 .10
11 Kari Heikkinen .02 .10
12 Niko Marttila .02 .10
13 Jari Torkki .02 .10
14 Jiri Kucera .07 .20
15 Jari Levonen .02 .10
16 Juha Ikonen .02 .10
17 Joni Lius .02 .10
18 Pekka Tuomisto .02 .10
19 Petri Kokku .02 .10
20 Jere Lehtinen 1.25 3.00
21 Janne Kekalainen .02 .10
22 Ari Haanpaa .02 .10
23 Hannu Jarvenpaa .07 .20
24 Waltteri Immonen .07 .20
25 Jari Lindroos .07 .20
26 Jan Langbacka .02 .10
27 Kari Takko .20 .50
28 Pasi Maattanen .02 .10
29 Jan Latvala .02 .10
30 Arto Heiskanen .02 .10
31 Iiro Jarvi .08 .25
32 Igor Boldin .02 .10
33 Sami Simonen .02 .10
34 Kari Rosenberg .07 .20
35 Sakari Lindfors .20 .50
36 Veli-Pekka Hard .02 .10
37 Jari Halme .08 .25
38 Jukka Tammi .20 .50
39 Kalle Koskinen .02 .10
40 Pekka Tirkkonen .02 .10
41 Ari Sulander .20 .50
42 Joni Hassinen .02 .10
43 Timo Peltomaa .02 .10
44 Sami Mettovaara .02 .10
45 Mika Yli-Maenpaa .08 .25
46 Toni Virta .02 .10
47 Kimmo Lecklin .07 .20
48 Rauli Raitanen .02 .10
49 Juha Lind .20 .50
50 Ari-Pekka Siekkinen .07 .20
51 Kim Ahlroos .02 .10
52 Jarkko Nikander .02 .10
53 Jouni Vento .02 .10
54 Juha Lampinen .02 .10
55 Kalle Sahlstedt .02 .10
56 Teemu Sillanpaa .02 .10
57 Lasse Nieminen .02 .10
58 Janne Niinimaa .40 1.00
59 Timo Jutila .07 .20
60 Tommi Haapsaari .02 .10
61 Allan Measures .02 .10
62 Petteri Nummelin .02 .10
63 Antti Tormanen .08 .25
64 Pekka Laksola .02 .10
65 Esa Sateri .02 .10
66 Petro Koivunen .02 .10
67 Janne Virtanen .02 .10
68 Pekka Peltola .02 .10
69 Matti Kaipainen .02 .10
70 Semi Pekki .02 .10
71 Jussi Tarvainen .02 .10
72 Jari Virtanen .02 .10
73 Kimmo Salminen .02 .10
74 Tommi Varjonen .02 .10
75 Pauli Jarvinen .02 .10
76 Hannu Mattila .02 .10
77 Aleksander Smirnov .02 .10
78 Arto Kulmala .02 .10
79 Roland Carlsson .02 .10
80 Jarma Miikkulainen .02 .10
81 Jarmo Muukkonen .02 .10
82 Mika Paananen .02 .10
83 Pasi Kivila .02 .10
84 Jari Laukkanen .02 .10
85 Tero Arkiomaa .02 .10
86 Tommi Miettinen .07 .20
87 Juha Jarvenpaa .02 .10
88 Niko Mikkola .02 .10
89 Antti Tuomenoksa .02 .10
90 Ilkka Sinisalo .08 .25
91 Otakar Janecky .07 .20
92 Arto Sirvio .02 .10
93 Robert Salo .02 .10
94 Ari Saarinen .02 .10
95 Kari Martikainen .02 .10
96 Miro Haapaniemi .02 .10
97 Fredrik Norrena .07 .20
98 Erik Hamalainen .07 .20
99 Simo Saarinen .02 .10
100 Harri Suvanto .02 .10
101 Kai Nurminen .20 .50
102 Rami Koivisto .02 .10
103 Pasi Peltonen .02 .10
104 Kari-Pekka Friman .02 .10
105 Mika Kortelainen .07 .20
106 Timo Hirvanen .02 .10
107 Jari Haapamaki .02 .10
108 Mika Manninen .02 .10
109 Ari Vuori .02 .10
110 Markku Ikonen .02 .10
111 Mikko Konttila .02 .10
112 Harri Sillgren .02 .10
113 Mikko Teui .02 .10
114 Markus Oijennus .02 .10
115 Kimmo Hyttinen .02 .10
116 Jokke Heinanen .02 .10
117 Sami Ahlberg .02 .10
118 Mika Rautio .07 .20
119 Ari Salo .07 .20
120 Juha Hautamaa .02 .10
121 Kari Haakana .02 .10
122 Sami Nuutinen .02 .10
123 Lasse Pirjeta .02 .10
124 Koijo Sailynoja .07 .20
125 Mikael Kotkaniemi .02 .10
126 Samuli Rautio .02 .10
127 Veli-Pekka Pekkarinen .02 .10
128 Hannu Henriksson .02 .10
129 Antti Aalto .30 .75
130 Jyrki Jokinen .02 .10
131 Marko Ek .02 .10
132 Marko Ojanen .02 .10
133 Mika Arvaja .02 .10
134 Karri Kivi .02 .10
135 Timo Saarikoski .02 .10
136 Toni Sihvonen .02 .10
137 Mika Laaksonen .02 .10
138 HIFK Helsinki Team Card .02 .10
139 HPK Team Card .02 .10
140 Ilves Team Card .02 .10
141 Jokerit Team Card .08 .25
142 JyP HT Team Card .02 .10
143 KalPa Team Card .02 .10
144 Kiekko-Espoo Team Card .02 .10
145 Lukko Team Card .02 .10
146 Tappara Team Card .02 .10
147 TPS Turku Team Card .02 .10
148 TuTo Turku Team Card .02 .10
149 Assat Team Card .02 .10
150 Petteri Nummelin CL .02 .10
151 Kari Takko CL .08 .25
152 Vladimir Jursinov CL .02 .10
153 Juha Lind CL .08 .25
154 Marko Jantunen .07 .20
Goals
R
155 Jere Lehtinen .75 2.00
Goals
Pl
156 Esa Keskinen .08 .25
Points
Re
157 Jere Lehtinen .75 2.00
Points
P
158 Timo Peltomaa .08 .25
Penalties
159 Janne Gronvall Pena .08 .25
160 Jarmo Myllys .20 .50
All Stars#
161 Markko Kiprusoff .08 .25
All St
162 Timo Jutila .07 .20
All Stars/
163 Sami Kapanen .40 1.00
All Stars#
164 Esa Keskinen .08 .25
All Stars#
165 Mika Alatalo .20 .50
All Stars#
166 Ville Peltonen .20 .50
HIFK
Te
167 Igor Boldin .02 .10
168 Sami Lehtonen .02 .10
169 Juha Jokiharju .02 .10
170 Harri Laurila .02 .10
171 Pekka Tirkkonen .02 .10
KalPa/
172 Mikko Halonen .02 .10
173 Tero Arkiomaa .02 .10
174 Jonni Vauhkonen .08 .25
Reipas#
175 Janne Gronvall .08 .25
Tappara#
176 Marko Jantunen .02 .10
177 Jouni Vento .07 .20
Assat
Team
178 HIFK .02 .10
179 HPK .02 .10
180 Ilves Tampere .02 .10
Team Performance
Final Position 7t
181 JyP HT .02 .10
182 Jokerit .02 .10
183 KalPa .02 .10
184 Kiekko-Espoo .02 .10
185 Lukko .02 .10
186 Tappara .02 .10
187 TPS .02 .10
188 Reipas .02 .10
189 Assat .02 .10
190 Jokerit .08 .25
Finnish Champio
191 Lukko/2nd Place Nationa .02 .10
192 TPS .08 .25
European Champions
193 TPS .08 .25
European Cup Champi
194 Playoffs .02 .10
195 Playoffs .02 .10
196 Playoffs .02 .10
197 Finals Game 1 .02 .10
198 Finals Game 2 .02 .10
199 Finals Game 3 .02 .10
200 Finals Game 4 .02 .10
201 Jouni Rokama .07 .20
202 Sami Leinonen .02 .10
203 Jani Nikko .08 .25
204 Arto Vuoti .02 .10
205 Petr Pavlas .02 .10
206 Reijo Mikkolainen .02 .10
207 Jari Kurri .75 2.00
208 Janne Ojanen .20 .50
209 Sami Kapanen .75 2.00
210 Teppo Kivela .02 .10
211 Saku Koivu 2.00 5.00
212 Pekka Virta .02 .10
213 Risto Jalo .07 .20
214 Sergei Prjakhin .08 .25
215 Aleksander Barkov .02 .10
216 Ville Peltonen .30 .75
217 Jari Korpisalo .07 .20
218 Jari Liikkanen .02 .10
219 Timo Lehkonen .07 .20
220 Juha Ylonen .20 .50
221 Harri Lonnberg .02 .10
222 Teemu Vuorinen .02 .10
223 Pertti Lehtonen .02 .10
224 Tommi Pullola .02 .10
225 Tomas Kapusta .07 .20
226 Joonas Jaaskelainen .02 .10
227 Jukka Tiilikainen .02 .10
228 Jarno Kultanen .20 .50
229 Kimmo Kapanen .08 .25
230 Jari Kauppila .02 .10
231 Jarkko Glad .02 .10
232 Nemo Nokkosmaki .02 .10
233 Petri Matikainen .02 .10
234 Christian Ruutu .20 .50
235 Martti Jarventie .30 .75
236 Sami Salo .20 .50
237 Timo Kulonen .02 .10
238 Pasi Sormunen .02 .10
239 Timo Nurmberg .02 .10
240 Jari Hirsimaki .02 .10
241 Tommi Hamalainen .02 .10
242 Vesa Salo .08 .25
243 Juha Nurminen .02 .10
244 Petr Korinek .02 .10
245 Kimmo Vesa .07 .20
246 Jukka Seppo .02 .10
247 Jarno Makela .02 .10
248 Petri Varis .20 .50
249 Marko Virtanen .02 .10
250 Risto Siltanen .08 .25
251 Juha Jarvenpaa .02 .10
252 Raimo Summanen .08 .25
253 Markus Hatinen .02 .10
254 Kimmo Nurro .02 .10
255 Timo Salonen .02 .10
256 Jari Munck .02 .10
257 Kimmo Rintanen .08 .25
258 Jarno Levonen .02 .10
259 Jarno Peltonen .02 .10
260 Valeri Krykov .02 .10
261 Kai Rautio .02 .10
262 Timo Blomqvist .08 .25
263 Teemu Selanne 2.00 5.00
264 Juha Virtanen .02 .10
265 Veli-Pekka Kautonen .02 .10
266 Mikko Koivunoro .02 .10
267 Mikko Luovi .08 .25
268 Jaroslav Otevrel .02 .10
269 Erik Kakko .02 .10
270 Peter Ahola .07 .20
271 Miikka Kemppi .02 .10
272 Toni Makiaho .02 .10
273 Pekka Poikolainen .02 .10
274 Timo Norppa .02 .10
275 Sebastian Sulku .02 .10
276 Esa Tikkanen .40 1.00
277 Pasi Saarela .02 .10
278 Ilpo Kauhanen .20 .50
279 Mika Alatalo .20 .50
280 Jukka Suomalainen .02 .10
281 Tony Arima .02 .10
282 Mika Puhakka .02 .10
283 Jussi Kiuru .02 .10
284 Jarkko Isotalo .02 .10
285 Esa Tommila .02 .10
286 Jouni Loponen .02 .10
287 Jermu Pisto .02 .10
288 Pasi Heinisto .02 .10
289 Toni Porkka .02 .10
290 Juha Vuorivirta .08 .25
291 Vesa Karjalainen .02 .10
292 Tom Koivisto .02 .10
293 Markku Hurme .02 .10
294 Mika Kannisto .02 .10
295 Marko Rantanen .07 .20
296 Petri Kalteva .02 .10
297 Pasi Huura .02 .10
298 Miikka Ruokonen .02 .10
299 Tuomo Raty .02 .10
300 Vadim Shaidullin .02 .10
301 Juha Riihijarvi .07 .20
302 Brad Turner .02 .10
303 Marko Toivola .02 .10
304 Kimmo Timonen .30 .75
305 Kai Nurminen .20 .50
306 Vesa Lehtonen .02 .10
307 Mika Niittymaki .02 .10
308 Sami Wahlsten .02 .10
309 Pavel Torgajev .08 .25
310 Pasi Kemppainen .02 .10
311 Markku Kallio .02 .10
312 Timo Maki .07 .20
313 Mika Stromberg .08 .25
314 Tuomas Gronman .08 .25
315 Tommi Rajamaki .08 .25
316 Juri Kuznetsov .07 .20
317 Mikko Myllykoski .02 .10
318 Brian Tutt .02 .10
319 Teemu Numminen .07 .20
320 Juha Jokiharju .02 .10
321 Mika Lehtinen .02 .10
322 Jari Pulliainen .02 .10
323 Kimmo Maki-Kokkila .02 .10
324 Mikko Peltola .02 .10
325 Risto Kurkinen .02 .10
326 Harri Laurila .02 .10
327 Vjatcheslav Fandul .02 .10
328 Niklas Hede .02 .10
329 Boris Rousson .20 .50
330 Jukka Ollila .08 .25
331 Jouni Tuominen .02 .10
332 Marko Harkonen .07 .20
333 Petri Engman .07 .20
334 Mikko Halonen .02 .10
335 Aki Berg .30 .75
336 Kristian Fagerstrom .02 .10
337 Jiri Veber .02 .10
338 Tommy Kiviaho .02 .10
339 Konstantin Astrahantsev .02 .10
340 Jukka Makitalo .07 .20
341 Timo Nykopp .02 .10
342 Sami Lehtonen .02 .10
343 Joni Lehto .07 .20
344 Jouko Myrra .02 .10
345 Mikko Makela .20 .50
346 Marco Poulsen .02 .10
347 Janne Seva .02 .10
348 Shawn McEachern .20 .50
349 Jarkko Varvio .07 .20
350 Mikko Konttila .02 .10
351 Veli-Pekka Ahonen .02 .10
352 Michael Nylander .30 .75
353 Kristian Taubert .02 .10
354 Ismo Kuoppala .02 .10
355 Kimmo Hyttinen .02 .10
356 Petri Latti .02 .10
357 Ted Donato .20 .50
358 Jari Harjumaki .02 .10
359 Teppo Numminen .20 .50
360 Jyrki Lumme .20 .50
361 German Titov .20 .50
362 Kari Eloranta .08 .25
363 Raimo Helminen .08 .25
364 Marko Jantunen .08 .25
365 Olli Kaski .02 .10
366 Jarmo Kekalainen .07 .20
367 Esa Keskinen .08 .25
368 Jarmo Makitalo .02 .10
369 Mika Nieminen .08 .25
370 Marko Palo .02 .10
371 Ville Siren .08 .25
372 Kari Suoraniemi .02 .10
373 Otakar Janecky .08 .25
Playmake
374 Jari Lindroos PM .02 .10
375 Teppo Kivela PM .02 .10
376 Petri Varis PM .08 .25
377 Pekka Laksola PM .02 .10
378 Jari Korpisalo PM .07 .20
379 Iiro Jarvi PM .08 .25
380 Timo Saarikoski PM .02 .10
381 Rauli Raitanen PM .02 .10
382 Juha Riihijarvi .02 .10
Playmak
383 Juha Jokiharju PM .02 .10
384 Vesa Salo PM .02 .10
385 Mika Nieminen CL .08 .25
386 Marko Jantunen CL .02 .10
387 Checklist 301-350 .40 1.00
Mika
388 Checklist 351-400 .08 .25
Ari S
389 Hannu Kapanen CO .02 .10
390 Hannu Savolainen CO .02 .10
391 Heikki Vesala CO .02 .10
392 Hannu Aravirta CO .02 .10
393 Kari Savolainen CO .02 .10
394 Anatoli Bogdanov CO .02 .10
395 Harri Rindell CO .02 .10
396 Vaclav Sykora CO .02 .10
397 Boris Majorov CO .02 .10
398 Vladimir Jursinov CO .05 .15
399 Seppo Suoraniemi CO .02 .10
400 Veli-Pekka Ketola CO .08 .25
NNO1 Canada Bowl 8.00 20.00
Super Chase
NNO1B Canada Bowl Super Chase ERR
{card back text not f
NNO2 Saku Koivu 20.00 50.00
Super Chase

1994-95 Finnish SISU Fire On Ice

This 20-card set highlights players who had multiple games of three or more points during the 1993-94 Finnish season. The cards were randomly inserted in first series packs.

COMPLETE SET (20) 12.00 30.00
1 Tero Arkiomoa .40 1.00
2 Igor Boldin .40 1.00
3 Vjatseslav Fandul .40 1.00
4 Otakar Janecky .75 2.00
5 Marko Jantunen .75 2.00
6 Timo Jutila .40 1.00
7 Pauli Jarvinen .40 1.00
8 Sami Kapanen 1.25 3.00
9 Tomas Kapusta .40 1.00
10 Esa Keskinen .75 2.00
11 Saku Koivu 4.00 10.00
12 Petro Koivunen .40 1.00
13 Petr Korinek .40 1.00
14 Jari Karpisolo .40 1.00
15 Risto Kurkinen .40 1.00
16 Tero Lehtera .75 2.00
17 Juha Nurminen .40 1.00
18 Kai Nurminen .75 2.00
19 Janne Ojanen .75 2.00
20 Jari Torkki .40 1.00

1994-95 Finnish SISU Guest Specials

Randomly inserted at a rate of one in thirteen series two foil packs, this 12-card standard-size set focuses on NHL stars who signed on to play in the Finnish league during the 1994 NHL lockout.

COMPLETE SET (12) 16.00 30.00
1 Ted Donato .75 2.00
2 Jari Kurri 2.00 5.00
3 Jyrki Lumme .75 2.00
4 Shawn McEachern .75 2.00
5 Mikko Makela .75 2.00
6 Teppo Numminen .75 2.00
7 Michael Nylander .75 2.00
8 Christian Ruuttu .75 2.00
9 Teemu Selanne 10.00 20.00
10 Esa Tikkanen .75 2.00
11 German Titov .40 1.00
12 Jarkko Varvio .40 1.00

1994-95 Finnish SISU Horoscopes

Randomly inserted at a rate of one in four second series foil packs, this 20-card standard-size set describes the players' personalities according to the astrological signs they were born under.

COMPLETE SET (20) 4.80 12.00
1 Juha Lind .40 1.00
2 Jukka Seppo .40 1.00
3 Antti Tuomenoksa .20 .50
4 Tuomas Gronman .40 1.00
5 Peter Ahola .20 .50
6 Ville Peltonen .75 2.00
7 Timo Saarikoski .20 .50
8 Timo Peltomaa .40 1.00
9 Jari Levonen .20 .50
10 Teppo Kivela .20 .50
11 Valeri Krykov .20 .50
12 Juha Riihijarvi .20 .50
13 Kai Nurminen .40 1.00
14 Mikko Luovi .20 .50
15 Raimo Summanen .40 1.00
16 Tommy Kiviaho .20 .50
17 Hannu Jarvenpaa .20 .50
18 Marko Virtanen .20 .50
19 Sami Lehtonen .20 .50
20 Mika Alatalo .75 2.00

1994-95 Finnish SISU Junior

These standard size cards feature ten of Finland's brightest young stars as they appeared as youth hockey players. The cards were randomly inserted into series I packs.

COMPLETE SET (10) 6.00 15.00
1 Saku Koivu 3.00 8.00
2 Jekke Heimanen .40 1.00
3 Tommi Miettinen .40 1.00
4 Jere Karalahti .75 2.00
5 Kalle Koskinen .40 1.00
6 Kari Rosenberg .40 1.00
7 Mika Manninen .40 1.00
8 Jussi Tarvainen .40 1.00
9 Mika Stromberg .40 1.00
10 Kalle Sahlstedt .40 1.00

1994-95 Finnish SISU Magic Numbers

This ten-card standard-size set was randomly inserted at a rate of one in eight second series foil packs.

COMPLETE SET (10) 4.80 12.00
1 Pasi Kuivalainen .40 1.00
2 Petteri Nummelin .75 2.00
3 Jarmo Kuusisto .40 1.00
4 Janne Ojanen .40 1.00
5 Sami Kapanen 1.25 3.00
6 Pekka Virta .40 1.00
7 Antti Tormanen .40 1.00
8 Jari Korpisalo .40 1.00
9 Kimmo Salminen .40 1.00
10 Jukka Tammi 1.25 3.00

1994-95 Finnish SISU NHL Draft

Randomly inserted at a rate of one in twenty foil second series packs, this eight-card standard-size set spotlights seven Finns who were drafted by NHL teams in 1994.

COMPLETE SET (8) 2.00 5.00
1 Title Card .20 .50
2 Marko Kiprusoff .40 1.00
3 Jussi Tarvainen .40 1.00
4 Arto Kuki .40 1.00
5 Tommi Rajamaki .40 1.00
6 Tero Lehtera .40 1.00
7 Tommi Miettinen .40 1.00
8 Antti Tormanen .40 1.00

1994-95 Finnish SISU NIL Phenoms

These standard size cards feature ten goaltenders who posted multiple shutouts during the 1993-94 Finnish campaign. The cards show the netminder cutout photo of the netminder over a brown backdrop.

COMPLETE SET (10) 12.00 30.00
1 Mika Manninen 1.25 3.00
2 Kari Takko 2.00 5.00
3 Ari Sulander 2.00 5.00
4 Jouni Rokama 1.25 3.00
5 Kari Rosenberg 1.25 3.00
6 Mika Rautio 1.25 3.00
7 Ari-Pekka Siekkinen 1.25 3.00
8 Allain Roy 1.25 3.00
9 Pasi Kuivalainen 1.25 3.00
10 Sakari Lindfors 1.25 3.00

1994-95 Finnish SISU Specials

These ten standard sized cards were random inserts in Leaf first series packs and showcase winners of the player of the month award, among other titles. The main cards are white. The B cards are black. The B suffix does not appear on the actual card: it is included here for checklisting purposes only. The Koivu Jumbo was available as a redemption to those who sent in the Koivu Super Bonus card. It mirrors the white version of the Koivu card.

COMPLETE SET (10) 8.00 20.00
1 Mika Alatalo .75 2.00
1B Mika Alatalo
2 Jari Korpisalo .40 1.00
2B Jari Korpisalo
3 Petteri Nummelin .75 2.00
3B Petteri Nummelin
4 Janne Ojanen .40 1.00
4B Janne Ojanen
5 Sami Kapanen 1.25 3.00
5B Sami Kapanen
6 Kari Takko .75 2.00
6B Kari Takko
7 Esa Keskinen .40 1.00
7B Esa Keskinen
8 Ari Sulander .75 2.00
8B Ari Sulander
9 Jarmo Myllys .75 2.00
9B Jarmo Myllys
10 Saku Koivu 4.00 10.00
10B Saku Koivu
10J Saku Koivu JUMBO

1995 Finnish Karjala World Championship Labels

This unusual set is comprised of 24 odd-sized (2 1/2 by 2 1/2") labels that were issued on the front of Karjala beer bottles in Finland to commemorate that country's first World Championship. Each label features an action photo of the player superimposed over the gold medal, with his name underneath. The Finnish national team logo is in the upper left corner, and World Champions, 1995 (in Finnish) is in the right. The labels are blank backed. As they are unnumbered, the labels are listed below in alphabetical order.

COMPLETE SET (24) 16.00 40.00
1 Erik Hamalainen .40 1.00
2 Raimo Helminen .40 1.00
3 Timo Jutila .60 1.50
4 Sami Kapanen .75 2.00
5 Esa Keskinen .40 1.00
6 Marko Kiprusoff .40 1.00
7 Saku Koivu 2.00 5.00
8 Tero Lehtera .40 1.00
9 Jere Lehtinen 1.25 3.00
10 Curt Lindstrom .40 1.00
11 Jarmo Myllys .75 2.00
12 Mika Nieminen .40 1.00
13 Janne Niinimaa .75 2.00
14 Petteri Nummelin .40 1.00
15 Janne Ojanen .40 1.00
16 Marko Palo .40 1.00
17 Ville Peltonen .60 1.50
18 Mika Stromberg .40 1.00
19 Ari Sulander .75 2.00
20 Raimo Summanen .40 1.00
21 Jukka Tammi .75 2.00
22 Antti Tormanen .40 1.00
23 Hannu Virta .60 1.50
24 Juha Ylonen .60 1.50

1995 Finnish Kellogg's

This six-card set was issued as a one-card-per-box premium in Kellogg's cereals in Finland. The cards are about half the size of a standard card.

COMPLETE SET (6) 12.00 30.00
1 Jarmo Myllys 2.00 5.00
2 Marko Kiprusoff 1.25 3.00
3 Hannu Virta 1.25 3.00
4 Ville Peltonen 1.25 3.00
5 Saku Koivu 6.00 15.00
6 Sami Kapanen 2.00 5.00

1995 Finnish Semic World Championships

This 240 standard-size card set features players from Finland and other countries who have taken part in international competition. Subsets include All Stars, Maalivahti Extra and Future Stars.

COMPLETE SET (240) 20.00 50.00
1 Pasi Kuivalainen .07 .20
2 Marko Kiprusoff .05 .15
3 Tuomas Gronman .05 .15
4 Erik Hamalainen .02 .10
5 Timo Jutila .05 .15
6 Pasi Sormunen .02 .10
7 Waltteri Immonen .05 .15
8 Janne Ojanen .05 .15
9 Esa Keskinen .05 .15
10 Kimmo Timonen .08 .25
11 Saku Koivu .40 1.00
12 Janne Laukkanen .08 .25
13 Marko Palo .02 .10
14 Raimo Helminen .05 .15
15 Mika Alatalo .08 .25
16 Ville Peltonen .15 .40
17 Jari Kurri .30 .75
18 Jari Korpisalo .05 .15
19 Kimmo Rintanen .05 .15
20 Jere Lehtinen .40 1.00
21 Kalle Sahlstedt .05 .15
22 Christian Ruuttu .05 .15
23 Hannu Virta .05 .15
24 Sami Kapanen .20 .50
25 Marko Tuulola .02 .10
26 Mika Stromberg .05 .15
27 Tero Lehtera .05 .15
28 Petri Varis .05 .15
29 Mikko Peltola .02 .10
30 Jukka Tammi .08 .25
31 Tero Arkiomaa .02 .10
32 Olli Kaski .02 .10
33 Pekka Laksola .02 .10
34 Mika Valila .02 .10
35 Jarmo Myllys .08 .25
36 Harri Laurila .02 .10
37 Teppo Numminen .08 .25
38 Jyrki Lumme .07 .20
39 Petteri Nummelin .02 .10
40 Mika Nieminen .08 .25
41 Teemu Selanne .60 1.50
42 Mikko Makela .05 .15
43 Esa Tikkanen .15 .40
44 Jarkko Varvio .05 .15
45 Vesa Viitakoski .05 .15
46 Juha Riihijarvi .05 .15
47 Markus Ketterer .08 .25
48 Mikko Haapakoski .02 .10
49 Antti Tormanen .05 .15
50 Timo Peltomaa .02 .10
51 Rauli Raitanen .02 .10
52 Roger Nordstrom .02 .10
53 Tommy Salo .20 .50
54 Tommy Soderstrom .20 .50
55 Magnus Svensson .05 .15
56 Fredrik Stillman .02 .10
57 Nicklas Lidstrom .40 1.00
58 Roger Johansson .02 .10
59 Kenny Jonsson .20 .50
60 Peter Andersson .02 .10
61 Tommy Sjodin .05 .15
62 Mats Sundin .40 1.00
63 Jonas Bergqvist .05 .15
64 Peter Forsberg .75 2.00
65 Roger Hansson .02 .10
66 Jorgen Jonsson .02 .10
67 Charles Berglund .02 .10
68 Mikael Johansson .02 .10
69 Tomas Forslund .05 .15
70 Andreas Dackell .08 .25
71 Stefan Ornskog .02 .10
72 Mikael Andersson .05 .15
73 Jan Larsson .02 .10
74 Patrik Carnback .05 .15
75 Hakan Loob .08 .25
76 Patrik Juhlin .08 .25
77 Bill Ranford .20 .50
78 Ed Belfour .60 1.50
79 Rob Blake .20 .50
80 Yves Racine .05 .15
81 Steve Smith .05 .15
82 Paul Coffey .40 1.00
83 Larry Murphy .20 .50
84 Mark Tinordi .05 .15
85 Al MacInnis .40 1.00
86 Paul Kariya .75 2.00
87 Joe Sakic .75 2.00
88 Brendan Shanahan .60 1.50
89 Luc Robitaille .40 1.00
90 Rod Brind'Amour .30 .75
91 Shayne Corson .08 .25
92 Mike Ricci .08 .25
93 Mario Lemieux ERR 2.00 5.00
Name
94 Eric Lindros .75 2.00
95 Russ Courtnall .08 .25
96 Theo Fleury .40 1.00
97 Mark Messier .60 1.50
98 Rick Tocchet .20 .50
99 Wayne Gretzky 2.00 5.00
100 Steve Larmer .08 .25
101 Brett Lindros .08 .25
102 John Vanbiesbrouck .40 1.00
103 Craig Wolanin .05 .15
104 Chris Chelios .40 1.00
105 Brian Leetch .40 1.00
106 Kevin Hatcher .07 .20
107 Craig Janney .08 .25
108 Tim Sweeney .05 .15
109 Shawn Chambers .05 .15
110 Scott Young .08 .25
111 John Lilley .05 .15
112 Joe Sacco .05 .15
113 Brett Hull .60 1.50
114 Pat LaFontaine .20 .50
115 Joel Otto .08 .25
116 Mike Modano .60 1.50
117 Tony Granato .05 .15
118 Jeremy Roenick .60 1.50
119 Jeff Lazaro .05 .15
120 Brian Mullen .05 .15
121 Mihail Shtalenkov .20 .50
122 Valeri Ivannikov .02 .10
123 Andrei Nikolishin .08 .25
124 Ilya Byakin .05 .15
Spelled Ilj
125 Alexander Smirnov .02 .10
126 Dimitri Yushkevich .08 .25
127 Sergei Shendelev .02 .10
128 Alexei Zhitnik .05 .15
Spelled
129 Igor Ulanov .05 .15
130 Dmitri Frolov .02 .10
131 Valeri Kamensky .15 .40
Spelled
132 Igor Fedulov .02 .10
133 Andrei Kovalenko .08 .25
134 Valeri Bure .20 .50
135 Sergei Berezin .15 .40
136 Alexei Yashin .20 .50
Spelled A
137 Vyatcheslav Kozlov .15 .40
Spel
138 Vyatcheslav Bykov .08 .25
Spell
139 Andrei Khomutov .08 .25
Spelled
140 Petr Briza .08 .25
141 Dominik Hasek .60 1.50
142 Roman Turek .30 .75
143 Jan Vopat .05 .15
144 Drahomir Kadlec .05 .15
145 Petr Pavlas .02 .10
146 Frantisek Kucera .05 .15
147 Jiri Veber .02 .10
148 David Vyborny .05 .15
149 Radek Toupal .05 .15
150 Jiri Kucera .05 .15
151 Richard Zemlicka .05 .15
152 Martin Rucinsky .08 .25
153 Jiri Dolezal .02 .10
154 Josef Beranek .05 .15
155 Martin Prochazka .02 .10
156 Tomas Srsen .05 .15
157 David Bruk .02 .10
158 Jaromir Jagr .75 2.00
159 Jan Caloun .05 .15
160 Martin Straka .20 .50
161 Roman Horak .02 .10
162 Frantisek Musil .05 .15
163 Peter Hrbek .02 .10
164 Jan Alino .02 .10
165 Joseph Heiss .07 .20
166 Peter Gulda .02 .10
167 Jayson Meyer .02 .10
168 Ernst Kopf .02 .10
169 Raimund Hilger .02 .10
170 Richard Bohm .02 .10
171 Michael Rosati .08 .25
172 Michael DeAngelis .02 .10
173 Anthony Circelli .02 .10
174 Gaetano Orlando .02 .10
175 Lucio Topatigh .02 .10
176 Martin Pavlu .02 .10
177 Jim Marthinsen .08 .25
178 Petter Salsten .02 .10
179 Tommy Jacobson .02 .10
180 Morten Finsted .02 .10
181 Tom Andersen .02 .10
182 Manus Rath .02 .10
183 Michael Puschacher .05 .15
184 James Burton .02 .10
185 Michael Shea .02 .10
186 Dieter Kalt .02 .10
187 Manfred Muhr .02 .10
188 Andreas Puschnig .02 .10
189 Renato Tosio .02 .10
190 Doug Honneger .02 .10
191 Felix Hollenstein .02 .10
192 Jorg Eberle .02 .10
193 Gil Montandon .02 .10
194 Roberto Triulzi .02 .10
195 Petri Ylonen .05 .15
196 Bruno Maynort .02 .10
197 Michel LeBlanc .02 .10
198 Benoit Laborte .04 .10
199 Christophe Ville .02 .10
200 Antoine Richer .02 .10
201 Bill Ranford .20 .50
MM 94 All
202 Timo Jutila AS .05 .15
203 Magnus Svensson AS .05 .15
204 Jari Kurri .30 .75
MM 94 All St
205 Saku Koivu .40 1.00
MM 94 All St
206 Paul Kariya .75 2.00
MM 94 All S
207 Jarmo Myllys .08 .25
Maalivahti
208 Bill Ranford .20 .50
Maalivahti
209 Roger Nordstrom ME .02 .10
210 Guy Hebert .30 .75
Maalivahti E
211 Mihail Shtalenkov .20 .50
Maali
212 Tommy Soderstrom .20 .50
Maaliv

3 Petr Briza .08 .25
Maalivahti E
4 Dominik Hasek .60 1.50
Maalivaht
5 Tom Barrasso .15 .40
Maalivahti
6 Jukka Tammi ME .05 .15
7 John Vanbiesbrouck .40 1.00
Maal
8 Mike Richter .40 1.00
Maalivahti
9 Saku Koivu Special .40 1.00
0 Saku Koivu Special .40 1.00
1 Saku Koivu Special .40 1.00
2 Saku Koivu Special .40 1.00
3 Saku Koivu Special .40 1.00
4 Saku Koivu Special .40 1.00
5 Tuomas Gronman FS .05 .15
6 Jani Nikko FS .02 .10
7 Janne Niinimaa .40 1.00
Future S
8 Jukka Tiilikainen FS .02 .10
9 Kimmo Rintanen FS .05 .15
0 Ville Peltonen .15 .40
Future S
1 Sami Kapanen .30 .75
Future Sta
2 Jere Lehtinen .40 1.00
Future St
3 Kimmo Timonen .05 .15
Future St
4 Jonni Vauhkonen .05 .15
Future
5 Juha Lind FS .08 .25
6 Tommi Miettinen FS .05 .15
7 Jere Karalahti .08 .25
Future S
8 Antti Aalto .08 .25
Future Star
9 Teemu Kohvakka FS .02 .10
0 Niko Mikkola FS .02 .10

1995-96 Finnish Beckett Ad Cards

is eight-card set features color action player photos a perforated sheet which measures approximately 3" 9". The top half of the sheet contains the photo ile the bottom half is a form to subscribe to the nnish Beckett Hockey Monthly magazine. The backs e blank. Although these look like cards, they actually re meant to be folded in half and used as a otective covering for trading cards which were spensed through vending machines in Finland ring the 1995-96 season. The cards were not anufactured by Beckett, but by Semic, the company ich produced the Finnish and Swedish versions of ckett Hockey Monthly.

OMPLETE SET (8) 10.00 25.00
Saku Koivu 4.00 10.00
Jere Lehtinen 2.00 5.00
Ville Peltonen .75 2.00
Erik Hamalainen .75 2.00
Sami Kapanen 2.00 5.00
Marko Kiprusoff .75 2.00
Mika Stromberg .75 2.00
Marko Palo .75 2.00

1995-96 Finnish Jaa Kiekko Lehti Ad Cards

is eight-card set features color action photos on a rforated sheet which measures approximately 3" by . The top half of the sheet contains the photo of a pular Finnish national team member, while the ttom half is a form to subscribe to Jaa Kiekko Lehti, e leading hockey magazine in that country. The backs e blank. Although these look like cards when parated, they actually were meant to be folded in half d used as a protective barrier for trading cards which ere dispensed through vending machines in Finland ring the 1995-96 season. The cards were produced Semic, and were numbered out of 8 on the front.

OMPLETE SET (8) 14.00 35.00
Jarmo Myllys 1.25 3.00
Jari Kurri 1.50 4.00
Saku Koivu 3.00 8.00
Teemu Selanne 6.00 15.00
Esa Tikkanen 1.25 3.00
Christian Ruuttu .75 2.00
Mika Nieminen .75 2.00
Timo Jutila .75 2.00

1995-96 Finnish SISU

is 400-card set features the players of Finland's top ckey circuit, the SM-Liiga. The cards were stributed in two series of 200 cards each, and in cks of eight cards. The fronts feature a full-bleed oto with the player's name ghosted along the ttom. The Saku Koivu Super Chase card was ndomly inserted in series 1 packs at a rate of 1:600. e Koivu Super Bonus and Niinimaa Super Chase rds were found in series 2 packs at a rate of 1:480. e latter Koivu card could be redeemed to Leaf in nland for an exclusive Koivu SISU Specials jumbo rd. If redeemed, the Super Bonus card was returned th a punch hole. These cards trade for about half the punched.

OMPLETE SET (400) 20.00 50.00
OMPLETE SERIES 1 (200) 12.00 30.00
OMPLETE SERIES 2 (200) 8.00 20.00
HIFK, Team Card .02 .10
Kimmo Kapanen .02 .10
Juri Kuznetsov .02 .10
Simo Saarinen .02 .10
Roland Carlsson .02 .10
Veli-Pekka Fagerstrom .02 .10
Kristian Fagerstrom .02 .10
Mika Kortelainen .02 .10
Jari Laukkanen .02 .10
Juha Nurminen .02 .10
Markku Hurme .02 .10
Sami Kapanen .40 1.00
Darren Boyko .02 .10
Marko Ojanen .02 .10
HPK, Team Card .02 .10
Kari Rosenberg .08 .25
Petri Engman .02 .10
Niko Marttila .02 .10
Jari Haapamaki .02 .10
Marko Allen .02 .10
Erik Kakko .02 .10
Mikko Myllykoski .02 .10
Jani Hassinen .02 .10
Risto Jalo .08 .25
Juha Jarvenpaa .02 .10
Jari Kauppila .02 .10
Toni Makiaho .02 .10
Ilves, Team Card .02 .10
Mika Manninen .08 .25
Hannu Henriksson .02 .10
Petri Kokko .02 .10
Martti Jarventie .20 .50
Allan Measures .02 .10
34 Pasi Huura .02 .10
35 Janne Seva .02 .10
36 Tommy Kiviaho .02 .10
37 Reijo Mikkolainen .02 .10
38 Hannu Mattila .02 .10
39 Jari Virtanen .02 .10
40 Sami Ahlberg .02 .10
41 Juha Hautamaa .02 .10
42 Jokerit, Team Card .02 .10
43 Ari Sulander .20 .50
44 Santeri Immonen .02 .10
45 Pasi Sormunen .02 .10
46 Waltteri Immonen .02 .10
47 Mika Stromberg .08 .25
48 Kari Martikainen .02 .10
49 Tommi Sova .08 .25
50 Juha Lind .20 .50
51 Niko Halttunen .02 .10
52 Keijo Sailynoja .08 .25
53 Otakar Janecky .08 .25
54 Timo Saarikoski .02 .10
55 JYP HT, Team Card .02 .10
56 Ari-Pekka Siekkinen .08 .25
57 Vesa Ponto .02 .10
58 Kalle Koskinen .02 .10
59 Jouni Loponen .02 .10
60 Miska Kangasniemi .08 .25
61 Mika Paananen .02 .10
62 Markku Ikonen .02 .10
63 Kimmo Salminen .02 .10
64 Joni Lius .02 .10
65 Lasse Nieminen .02 .10
66 Janne Kurjenniemi .02 .10
67 Marko Virtanen .02 .10
68 KalPa, Team Card .02 .10
69 Jarkko Kortesoja .02 .10
70 Petri Matikainen .02 .10
71 Mika Laaksonen .02 .10
72 Kai Rautio .02 .10
73 Jarno Kultanen .20 .50
74 Miikka Ruokonen .02 .10
75 Jussi Tarvainen .02 .10
76 Mikko Honkonen .02 .10
77 Sami Simonen .02 .10
78 Petr Korinek .02 .10
79 Veli-Pekka Pekkarinen .02 .10
80 Pekka Tirkkonen .02 .10
81 Kiekko-Espoo, Team Card .02 .10
82 Iiro Itamies .08 .25
83 Tommi Nyyssonen .02 .10
84 Robert Salo .02 .10
85 Sami Nuutinen .02 .10
86 Timo Blomqvist .02 .10
87 Ismo Kuoppala .02 .10
88 Mikko Koivunoro .02 .10
89 Petro Koivunen .08 .25
90 Jarmo Muukkonen .02 .10
91 Sergei Prjahin .02 .10
92 Teemu Riihijarvi .08 .25
93 Juha Ikonen .02 .10
94 Lukko, Team Card .02 .10
95 Boris Rousson .20 .50
96 Vesa Salo .08 .25
97 Toni Porkka .02 .10
98 Mika Yli-Maenpaa .08 .25
99 Juha Riihijarvi .08 .25
100 Petri Latti .02 .10
101 Veli-Pekka Ahonen .02 .10
102 Mikko Peltola .02 .10
103 Kalle Sahlstedt .08 .25
104 Jari Torkki .02 .10
105 Jussi Kiuru .02 .10
106 Sakari Palsola .02 .10
107 Tappara, Team Card .02 .10
108 Ilpo Kauhanen .20 .50
109 Sami Lehtonen .02 .10
110 Pasi Petrilainen .02 .10
111 Pekka Laksola .02 .10
112 Tommi Haapsaari .02 .10
113 Ville Nieminen 1.25 3.00
114 Arto Kulmala .02 .10
115 Valeri Krykov .02 .10
116 Timo Nurmberg .02 .10
117 Aleksander Barkov .02 .10
118 Miikka Kemppi .02 .10
119 Marko Toivola .02 .10
120 Juha Vuorivirta .08 .25
121 TPS, Team Card .02 .10
122 Miikka Kiprusoff 4.00 10.00
123 Kimmo Timonen .20 .50
124 Sami Salo .02 .10
125 Kari Harila .02 .10
126 Tuomas Gronman .08 .25
127 Vjatsheslav Fandul .02 .10
128 Mika Alatalo .20 .50
129 Jukka Tiilikainen .02 .10
130 Kimmo Rintanen .15 .40
131 Hannes Hyvonen .20 .50
132 Simo Rouvali .02 .10
133 Harri Sillgren .02 .10
134 Harri Suvanto .02 .10
135 TuTo, Team Card .02 .10
136 Markus Korhonen .02 .10
137 Sebastian Sulku .02 .10
138 Jukka Suomalainen .02 .10
139 Timo Kulonen .02 .10
140 Risto Siltanen .08 .25
141 Sami Leinonen .02 .10
142 Juha Virtanen .02 .10
143 Jari Hirsimaki .02 .10
144 Jouni Tuominen .02 .10
145 Vesa Karjalainen .02 .10
146 Pekka Virta .02 .10
147 Jouko Myrra .02 .10
148 Assat, Team Card .02 .10
149 Kari Takko .20 .50
150 Timo Nykopp .02 .10
151 Harri Laurila .02 .10
152 Jarno Miikkulainen .02 .10
153 Pasi Peltonen .02 .10
154 Jari Korpisalo .02 .10
155 Teppo Kivela .02 .10
156 Jari Levonen .02 .10
157 Janne Virtanen .02 .10
158 Jarno Makela .02 .10
159 Mikael Kotkaniemi .02 .10
160 Ari Saarinen .02 .10
161 Boris Rousson AS .20 .50
162 Joni Lehto AS .05 .15
163 Marko Kiprusoff AS .08 .25
164 Jere Lehtinen AS .40 1.00
165 Saku Koivu AS 1.25 3.00
166 Kai Nurminen AS .20 .50
167 Ari Sulander AS .20 .50
168 Mika Stromberg AS .08 .25
169 All Stars .02 .10
Kuusisto
170 All Stars .02 .10
Arkiomaa
171 Otakar Janecky AS .08 .25
172 Ville Peltonen AS .20 .50
173 Milestones .02 .10
Arima
174 Milestones .02 .10
Boyko
175 Milestones .02 .10
Friman
176 Milestones .02 .10
Heiskanen
177 Milestones .02 .10
Henriksson
178 Milestones .02 .10
Hamalainen
179 Milestones .02 .10
Jalo
180 Timo Jutila AS .07 .20
181 Milestones .02 .10
Jarvenpaa
182 Milestones .02 .10
Kuusisto
183 Milestones .02 .10
Laksola
184 Milestones .02 .10
Laurila
185 Milestones .02 .10
Lehtonen
186 Milestones .02 .10
Lindroos
187 Milestones .02 .10
Mikkolainen
188 Milestones .02 .10
Tommila
189 Milestones .02 .10
Torkki
190 Milestones .02 .10
Tuomenoksa
191 Milestones .02 .10
Vuori
192 TPS, SM-kultaa .02 .10
193 Jokerit, SM-hopeaa .02 .10
194 Assat, SM-pronssia .02 .10
195 Jokerit, EM-kultaa .02 .10
196 TPS, EM-pronssia .02 .10
197 Checklist 1-50, Nurminen .15 .40
198 Veli-Pekka Kautonen CL .02 .10
199 Koivu Checklist .40 1.00
200 Kiprusoff Checklist .08 .25
201 HIFK, Fan Card .02 .10
202 Sakari Lindfors .20 .50
203 Lauri Puolanne .02 .10
204 Pertti Lehlonen .02 .10
205 Peter Ahola .02 .10
206 Jere Karalahti .20 .50
207 Kimmo Maki-Kokkila .02 .10
208 Tom Laaksonen .02 .10
209 Tero Hamalainen .02 .10
210 Miro Haapaniemi .02 .10
211 Toni Sihvonen .02 .10
212 Sami Laine .02 .10
213 Iiro Jarvi .08 .25
214 Pekka Tuomisto .02 .10
215 HPK, Fan Card .02 .10
216 Mika Pictila .08 .25
217 Tom Koivisto .02 .10
218 Tommi Hamalainen .02 .10
219 Kai Rautio .02 .10
220 Jani Nikko .08 .25
221 Mika Kannisto .02 .10
222 Jason Miller .02 .10
223 Niklas Hede .02 .10
224 Tony Virta .02 .10
225 Aleksander Andrijevski .02 .10
226 Mika Puhakka .02 .10
227 Timo Peltomaa .02 .10
228 Toni Saarinen .02 .10
229 Ilves, Fan Card .02 .10
230 Vesa Toskala 1.25 3.00
231 Pekka Kangasalusta .02 .10
232 Juha Lampinen .02 .10
233 Pasi Saarinen .02 .10
234 Teemu Vuorinen .02 .10
235 Jarno Peltonen .02 .10
236 Matti Kaipainen .02 .10
237 Semi Pekki .02 .10
238 Sami Karjalainen .02 .10
239 Juoni Lahtinen .02 .10
240 Pasi Maatanen .02 .10
241 Petri Murtovaara .02 .10
242 Tomi Hirvonen .02 .10
243 Mikko Eloranta .20 .50
244 Mika Arvaja .02 .10
245 Juha Jarvenpaa .08 .25
246 Jokerit, Fan Card .02 .10
247 Marko Rantanen .02 .10
248 Marko Tuulola .02 .10
249 Jani-Matti Loikala .02 .10
250 Antti-Jussi Niemi .20 .50
251 Janne Niinimaa .30 .75
252 Jari Lindroos .02 .10
253 Paso Saarela .02 .10
254 Juha Ylonen .30 .75
255 Mika Asikainen .08 .25
256 Eero Somervuori .40 1.00
257 Tero Lehtera .02 .10
258 Jukka Penttinen .02 .10
259 Petri Varis .20 .50
260 JyP HT, Fan Card .02 .10
261 Marko Leinonen .02 .10
262 Jan Latvala .02 .10
263 Jukka Laamanen .02 .10
264 Pekka Poikolainen .02 .10
265 Thomas Sjogren .02 .10
266 Pasi Kangas .08 .25
267 Tini Koivunen .02 .10
268 Lasse Jamsen .02 .10
269 Petri Kujala .02 .10
270 Mikko Inkinen .02 .10
271 Kalpa, Fan Card .02 .10
272 Pasi Kuivalainen .20 .50
273 Pasi Kolehmainen .02 .10
274 Reijo Ruotsalainen .08 .25
275 Jarkko Glad .02 .10
276 Ivan Vizek .02 .10
277 Jarmo Levonen .02 .10
278 Janne Kekalainen .02 .10
279 Veli-Pekka Nutikka .20 .50
280 Mikko Konttila .08 .25
281 Janne Virtanen .02 .10
282 Pasi Kemppainen .02 .10
283 Kiekko-Espoo, Fan Card .02 .10
284 Mika Rautio .08 .25
285 Kari Haakana .02 .10
286 Teemu Sillanpaa .02 .10
287 Timo Nykopp .02 .10
288 Miikka Teimonen .02 .10
289 Tero Tiainen .02 .10
290 Joonas Jaaskelainen .02 .10
291 Lubomir Kolnik .08 .25
292 Arto Sirvio .02 .10
293 Iikka Sinisalo .08 .25
294 Timo Hirvonen .02 .10
295 Arto Kuki .02 .10
296 Timo Norppa .02 .10
297 Lukko, Fan Card .02 .10
298 Timo Kauharren .02 .10
299 Joni Lehto .02 .10
300 Jarno Miikkulainen .02 .10
301 Kimmo Lotvonen .02 .10
302 Robert Nordmark .02 .10
303 Riku Kallioniemi .02 .10
304 Matti Raunio .02 .10
305 Tommi Turunen .02 .10
306 Jarkko Varvio .05 .15
307 Tero Arkiomaa .02 .10
308 Harri Lonnberg .08 .25
309 Mikko Luovi .02 .10
310 Tappara, Fan Card .02 .10
311 Jussi Markkanen .75 2.00
312 Timo Jutila .02 .10
313 Jukka Ollila .02 .10
314 Antti Rahkonen .02 .10
315 Derek Mayer .02 .10
316 Petri Kalteva .02 .10
317 Jarkko Nikander .02 .10
318 Pauli Jarvinen .02 .10
319 Mikko Helisten .02 .10
320 Ari Haanpaa .02 .10
321 Markus Oijennus .02 .10
322 Janne Ojanen .15 .40
323 TPS, Fan Card .02 .10
324 Fredrik Norrena .15 .40
325 Mika Lehtinen .02 .10
326 Karlis Skrastins .20 .50
327 Marru Laapas .02 .10
328 Antti Aalto .20 .50
329 Teemu Numminen .02 .10
330 Tommi Miettinen .02 .10
331 Lasse Pirjeta .02 .10
332 Miikka Rousu .02 .10
333 Marko Makinen .02 .10
334 Mikko Markkanen .02 .10
335 Tomi Kallio .40 1.00
336 Miika Elomo .20 .50
337 Sami Mettovaara .02 .10
338 TuTo, Fan Card .02 .10
339 Jukka Tammi .15 .40
340 Kari-Pekka Friman .02 .10
341 Veli-Pekka Hard .02 .10
342 Antti Tirkkonen .02 .10
343 Jukka Seppo .02 .10
344 Kim Ahlroos .02 .10
345 Marto Poulsen .02 .10
346 Juha Kuusisaari .02 .10
347 Mikko Laaksonen .02 .10
348 Tuomas Jalava .02 .10
349 Tommi Pullola .08 .25
350 Tuomas Kalliomaki .02 .10
351 Assat, Fan Card .02 .10
352 Karri Kivi .02 .10
353 Olli Kaski .02 .10
354 Jouni Vento .02 .10
355 Tommi Rajamaki .08 .25
356 Jokke Heinanen .02 .10
357 Tomas Kapusta .02 .10
358 Jaroslav Otevrel .02 .10
359 Timo Salonen .02 .10
360 Pekka Virta .02 .10
361 Vesa Goman .02 .10
362 Pekka Peltola .02 .10
363 Rauli Raitanen .02 .10
364 Pasi Tuominen .02 .10
365 Kari Syvasalmi .02 .10
366 Timo Hakanen .02 .10
367 Foreigners .02 .10
Andrijevski
368 Foreigners .02 .10
Barkov
369 Foreigners .02 .10
Boyko
370 Foreigners .02 .10
Fandul
371 Foreigners .02 .10
Janecky
372 Foreigners .02 .10
Kapusta
373 Foreigners .02 .10
Kolnik
374 Foreigners .02 .10
Korinek
375 Foreigners .02 .10
Mayer
376 Foreigners .02 .10
Measures
377 Foreigners .02 .10
Miller
378 Foreigners .02 .10
Nordmark
379 Foreigners .02 .10
Otevrel
380 Foreigners .02 .10
Prjahin
381 Foreigners .08 .25
Rousson
382 Foreigners .02 .10
Sjogren
383 Foreigners .02 .10
Skrastins
384 Foreigners .02 .10
Vlzek
385 Vladimir Jursinov .02 .10
386 Hannu Aravirta .02 .10
387 Veli-Pekka Ketola .08 .25
388 Vaclav Sykora .02 .10
389 Hannu Kapanen .02 .10
390 Kari Savolainen .02 .10
391 Harri Rindell .02 .10
392 Anatoli Bogdanov .02 .10
393 Sakari Pietilla .02 .10
394 Jukka Rautakorpi .02 .10
395 Harri Jalava .02 .10
396 Vladimir Jursinov Jr. .02 .10
397 Checklist 201-250 .20 .50
398 Checklist 251-300 .02 .10
399 Checklist 301-350 .02 .10
400 Koivu Checklist .40 1.00
NNOA Saku Koivu Super Bonus 10.00 20.00
(SISU logo upper right
NNOB Saku Koivu Super Bonus
(SISU logo upper left
NNO Saku Koivu Jumbo 2.00 5.00
NNO Saku Koivu Super Chase 10.00 25.00
NNO Janne Niinimaa Super Chase 4.00 10.00

1995-96 Finnish SISU Double Trouble

This eight-card set features action shots of the top two players from the teams of the SM-Liiga. The cards were randomly inserted at a rate of 1:17 series 2 packs.

COMPLETE SET (8) 8.00 20.00
1 T.Gronman 1.25 3.00
K.Timonen
2 W.Immonen 1.25 3.00
M.Stromberg
3 O.Kaski 1.25 3.00
K.Kivi
4 J.Lehto 1.25 3.00
R.Nordmark
5 P.Ahola 1.25 3.00
P.Lehtonen
6 T.Blomqvist 1.25 3.00
S.Nuutinen
7 R.Ruotsalainen 1.25 3.00
I.Vizek
8 T.Jutila 1.25 3.00
P.Laksola

1995-96 Finnish SISU Drafted Dozen

Randomly inserted at a rate of 1:19 series 2 packs, this set depicts a dozen players from the SM-Liiga who were selected in the NHL Entry Draft.

COMPLETE SET (12) 8.00 25.00
1 Aki Berg .75 2.00
2 Teemu Riihijarvi .40 1.00
3 Miika Elomo .75 2.00
4 Marko Makinen .40 1.00
5 Tomi Kallio 1.25 3.00
6 Sami Kapanen 1.50 4.00
7 Vesa Toskala 2.00 5.00
8 Miikka Kiprusoff 6.00 15.00
9 Timo Hakanen .40 1.00
10 Juha Vuorivirta .40 1.00
11 Tomi Hirvonen .40 1.00
12 Mikko Markkanen .40 1.00

1995-96 Finnish SISU Ghost Goalies

This 10-card set focuses on the top netminders of the SM-Liiga. The cards were randomly inserted at a rate of 1:24 series 1 packs.

COMPLETE SET (10) 16.00 40.00
1 Sakari Lindfors 2.00 5.00
2 Boris Rousson 1.50 4.00
3 Ari Sulander 2.00 5.00
4 Kari Takko 1.50 4.00
5 Fredrik Norrena 1.50 4.00
6 Kari Rosenberg 1.50 4.00
7 Ari-Pekka Siekkinen 1.50 4.00
8 Jukka Tammi 1.50 4.00
9 Pasi Kuivalainen 1.50 4.00
10 Ilpo Kauhanen 1.50 4.00

1995-96 Finnish SISU Gold Cards

This 24-card set celebrates the players who earned Finland's first major title by winning the 1995 World Championship. The cards were distributed over both series in a scattered (i.e., not 1-12 and 13-24) fashion. The cards were randomly inserted at a rate of 1:10 series 1 packs and 1:9 series 2 packs.

COMPLETE SET (24) 24.00 60.00
1 Title Card .75 2.00
2 Jarmo Myllys 1.50 4.00
3 Ari Sulander 1.50 4.00
4 Jukka Tammi 1.50 4.00
5 Erik Hamalainen .75 2.00
6 Timo Jutila .75 2.00
7 Marko Kiprusoff .75 2.00
8 Janne Niinimaa 1.50 4.00
9 Petteri Nummelin .75 2.00
10 Mika Stromberg .75 2.00
11 Hannu Virta .75 2.00
12 Raimo Helminen .75 2.00
13 Sami Kapanen 2.00 5.00
14 Esa Keskinen .75 2.00
15 Saku Koivu 6.00 15.00
16 Tero Lehtera .75 2.00
17 Jere Lehtinen 3.00 8.00
18 Mika Nieminen .75 2.00
19 Janne Ojanen .75 2.00
20 Marko Palo .75 2.00
21 Ville Peltonen 1.25 3.00
22 Raimo Summanen .75 2.00
23 Antti Tormanen .75 2.00
24 Juha Ylonen 1.25 3.00

1995-96 Finnish SISU Limited

This 108-card set is the first super-premium issue released in Europe. The cards are printed on 24-point stock and picture the elite athletes of the Finnish SM-Liiga. Production was announced as 7,500 individually numbered boxes. Each box contained 18, 5-card "packs". These packs were actually boxes themselves, and pictured either Saku Koivu, Teemu Selanne or Esa Tikkanen. The card fronts have a color photo of the player over his ghosted close-up in the background. The back contains another photo as well as a brief bio in Finnish and the Leaf trademark. Several NHLers who played here during the 1994 lockout are featured, including Selanne, Jari Kurri, and Koivu. The Koivu Line super chase card was randomly inserted 1:219 and was serial numbered out of 720.

COMPLETE SET (108) 20.00 40.00
1 Fredrik Norrena .20 .50
2 Hannu Virta .15 .40
3 Petteri Nummelin .07 .20
4 Tuomas Gronman .15 .40
5 Marko Kiprusoff .15 .40
6 Saku Koivu 2.00 5.00
7 Raimo Summanen .15 .40
8 Esa Keskinen .15 .40
9 Jere Lehtinen 1.25 3.00
10 Ari Sulander .30 .75
11 Waltteri Immonen .07 .20
12 Mika Stromberg .15 .40
13 Janne Niinimaa .40 1.00
14 Otakar Janecky .15 .40
15 Teemu Selanne 4.00 10.00
16 Jari Kurri 1.25 3.00
17 Antti Tormanen .15 .40
18 Petri Varis .30 .75
19 Kari Takko .30 .75
20 Olli Kaski .07 .20
21 Rauli Raitanen .07 .20
22 Jari Korpisalo .07 .20
23 Teppo Kivela .07 .20
24 Jokke Heinanen .07 .20
25 Arto Javanainen .07 .20
26 Jari Levonen .07 .20
27 Arto Heiskanen .07 .20
28 Jarmo Myllys .40 1.00
29 Boris Rousson .20 .50
30 Jarmo Kuusisto .07 .20
31 Joni Lehto .07 .20
32 Robert Nordmark .07 .20
33 Tero Arkiomaa .07 .20
34 Jari Torkki .07 .20
35 Juha Riihijarvi .15 .40
36 Matti Forss .07 .20
37 Sakari Lindfors .30 .75
38 Pertti Lehtonen .07 .20
39 Simo Saarinen .07 .20
40 Esa Tikkanen .40 1.00
41 Ville Peltonen .40 1.00
42 Christian Ruuttu .15 .40
43 Mika Kortelainen .07 .20
44 Darren Boyko .07 .20
45 Iiro Jarvi .15 .40
46 Ari-Pekka Siekkinen .20 .50
47 Harri Laurila .07 .20
48 Jouni Loponen .07 .20
49 Joni Lius .07 .20
50 Jari Lindroos .07 .20
51 Risto Kurkinen .07 .20
52 Thomas Sjorgren .07 .20
53 Marko Virtanen .07 .20
54 Michael Nylander .40 1.00
55 Mika Rautio .20 .50
56 Sami Nuutinen .07 .20
57 Peter Ahola .07 .20
58 Timo Blomqvist .07 .20
59 Ikka Sinisalo .15 .40
60 Petro Koivunen .15 .40
61 Sergei Prjahin .07 .20
62 Tero Lehtera .07 .20
63 Mariusz Czerkawski .40 1.00
64 Pasi Kuivalainen .30 .75
65 Kimmo Timonen .40 1.00
66 Reijo Ruotsalainen .15 .40
67 Vesa Salo .15 .40
68 Petr Korinek .07 .20
69 Marko Jantunen .15 .40
70 Pekka Tirkkonen .07 .20
71 Janne Kekalainen .07 .20
72 Sami Kapanen .75 2.00
73 Timo Jutila .07 .20
74 Pekka Laksola .07 .20
75 Janne Gronvall .15 .40
76 Jiri Kucera .07 .20
77 Janne Ojanen .20 .50
78 Pauli Jarvinen .07 .20
79 Ari Haanpaa .07 .20
80 Aleksander Barkov .07 .20
81 Theo Fleury 1.25 3.00
82 Kari Rosenberg .15 .40
83 Janne Laukkanen .20 .50
84 Jani Nikko .15 .40
85 Mika Lartama .07 .20
86 Kai Nurminen .30 .75
87 Tomas Kapusta .07 .20
88 Marko Palo .07 .20
89 Jarkko Varvio .15 .40
90 Risto Jalo .15 .40
91 Jukka Tammi .20 .50
92 Risto Siltanen .15 .40
93 Teppo Numminen .30 .75
94 Marco Poulsen .07 .20
95 Jukka Seppo .07 .20
96 Vesa Karjalainen .07 .20
97 Ted Donato .15 .40
98 Juha Virtanen .07 .20
99 Jari Hirsimaki .07 .20
100 Vesa Toskala 2.50 5.00
101 Jyrki Lumme .40 1.00
102 Hannu Henriksson .07 .20
103 Allan Measures .07 .20
104 Timo Peltomaa .07 .20
105 Juha Hautamaa .07 .20
106 Mikko Makela .15 .40
107 Juha Jarvenpaa .07 .20
108 Semi Pekki .07 .20
NNO Koivu Line Super Chase 10.00 25.00

1995-96 Finnish SISU Limited Leaf Gallery

The nine cards in this set were randomly inserted at a rate of 1 in 6 packs of SISU Limited. The fronts feature a dynamic action photo surrounded by a refractive holofoil border. The cards are numbered of 9 on the front. The backs display a gold-foil etched portrait of the player.

COMPLETE SET (9) 10.00 15.00
1 Jyrki Lumme .75 2.00
2 Janne Laukkanen .75 2.00
3 Michael Nylander 1.25 3.00
4 Janne Ojanen .75 2.00
5 Peter Ahola .75 2.00
6 Kari Takko 1.25 3.00
7 Hannu Virta .75 2.00
8 Juha Lind .75 2.00
9 Sakari Lindfors 1.25 3.00

1995-96 Finnish SISU Limited Signed and Sealed

The nine cards in this set were randomly inserted at a rate of 1 in 9 SISU Limited packs. The set features a number of current and former NHLers. The cards feature an action photo printed on a silver foil background. The player's "signature" is embossed in gold foil across the bottom of the photo. The backs feature another photo and are numbered out of 9.

COMPLETE SET (9) 20.00 25.00
1 Sami Kapanen 1.25 3.00
2 Christian Ruuttu .75 2.00
3 Teemu Selanne 7.50 15.00
4 Aki Berg .75 2.00
5 Joni Lehto .75 2.00
6 Teppo Numminen .75 2.00
7 Jari Kurri 2.00 5.00
8 Esa Tikkanen 1.25 3.00
9 Theo Fleury 2.00 5.00

1995-96 Finnish SISU Painkillers

Randomly inserted in series 1 packs at a rate of 1:15, these eight cards highlight some of the dominant snipers of the SM-Liiga.

COMPLETE SET (8) 3.00 8.00
1 Jokke Heinanen .40 1.00
2 Mika Alatalo .40 1.00
3 Joni Lehto .40 1.00
4 Harri Lonnberg .40 1.00
5 Ville Peltonen .75 2.00
6 Harri Sillgren .40 1.00
7 Petri Varis .75 2.00
8 Marko Virtanen .40 1.00

1995-96 Finnish SISU Specials

Randomly inserted at a rate of 1:24 series 1 packs, these cards picture some of the most popular players in the SM-Liiga, including several NHLers who played there during the 1994 lockout.

COMPLETE SET (10) 16.00 40.00
1 Petri Varis 1.25 3.00
2 Boris Rousson 1.25 3.00
3 Saku Koivu 6.00 15.00
4 Jari Kurri 3.00 8.00
5 Jarmo Kuusisto .75 2.00
6 Janne Ojanen .75 2.00
7 Jere Lehtinen 3.00 8.00
8 Peter Ahola .75 2.00
9 Jukka Seppo .75 2.00
10 Michael Nylander 1.25 3.00

1995-96 Finnish SISU Spotlights

This eight-card series shines the -- yes -- spotlight on some of the most offensively gifted players in the SM-Liiga. The cards were randomly inserted in series 2 packs at a rate of 1.8.

COMPLETE SET (8) 2.00 5.00
1 Otakar Janecky .40 1.00
2 Jari Korpisalo .40 1.00
3 Juha Riihijarvi .40 1.00
4 Iiro Jarvi .40 1.00
5 Thomas Sjogren .40 1.00
6 Risto Jalo .40 1.00
7 Jari Hirsimaki .40 1.00
8 Juha Hautamaa .40 1.00

1996-97 Finnish SISU Redline

This set featuring players of Finland's SM-Liiga is complete at 200 cards; although a second series was intended, it was not produced as a result of disappointing sales for the first series. The Super Chase and Super Bonus cards were randomly inserted at the rate of 1:240 packs. If found, they could be exchanged by mail with Leaf for one of five Silver Signature goalie cards that were limited to 400 copies. We have no further information on these Silver Signature cards. Anyone who can provide photocopies or other documentation of these cards is asked to email hockeymag@beckett.com.

COMPLETE SET (200) 8.00 20.00
1 Checklist (1-50) .02 .10
2 Sakari Lindfors .20 .50
3 Peter Ahola .05 .15
4 Jere Karalahti .20 .50
5 Pertti Lehtonen .02 .10
6 Lauri Puolanne .02 .10
7 Sami Laine .08 .25
8 Tommy Kiviaho .02 .10
9 Markku Hurme .02 .10
10 Jari Laukkanen .02 .10
11 Tero Nyman .02 .10
12 Toni Sihvonen .02 .10
13 Mika Kortelainen .05 .15
14 Tero Hamalainen .02 .10
15 Mika Pietila .08 .25
16 Erik Kakko .02 .10
17 Tom Koivisto .02 .10
18 Jani Nikko .08 .25
19 Risto Jalo .08 .25
20 Aleksander Andrievski .05 .15
21 Jari Kauppila .02 .10
22 Jarkko Savijoki .02 .10
23 Toni Makiaho .02 .10
24 Mika Kannisto .02 .10
25 Mika Puhakka .02 .10
26 Toni Saarinen .02 .10
27 Vesa Toskala .40 1.00
28 Teemu Vuorinen .02 .10
29 Petri Kokko .02 .10
30 Pekka Kangasalusta .02 .10
31 Tommi Kahiluoto .02 .10
32 Jarno Peltonen .02 .10
33 Mika Arvaja .02 .10
34 Matti Kaipainen .02 .10
35 Hannu Mattila .02 .10
36 Tomi Hirvonen .02 .10
37 Jouni Lahtinen .02 .10
38 Jari Suorsa .02 .10
39 Juha Jarvenpaa .07 .20
40 Semi Pekki .02 .10
41 Ari Sulander .20 .50
42 Mika Stromberg .08 .25
43 Marko Tuulola .02 .10
44 Pasi Sormunen .02 .10
45 Waltteri Immonen .05 .15
46 Jukka Penttinen .02 .10
47 Petri Varis .20 .50
48 Keijo Sailynoja .08 .25
49 Tero Lehtera .05 .15
50 Checklist (51-100) .02 .10
51 Jari Lindroos .05 .15
52 Ismo Kuoppala .02 .10
53 Juha Ylonen .20 .50
54 Pasi Saarela .05 .15
55 Marko Leinonen .02 .10
56 Kalle Koskinen .02 .10
57 J-P Laamanen .02 .10
58 Jouni Loponen .02 .10
59 Pekka Poikolainen .02 .10
60 Jan Latvala .02 .10
61 Timo Ahmaoja .02 .10
62 Mika Paananen .02 .10
63 Kimmo Salminen .02 .10
64 Lasse Jamsen .02 .10
65 Thomas Sjogren .07 .20
66 Juha Viinikainen .02 .10
67 Mikko Inkinen .02 .10
68 Toni Koivunen .02 .10
69 Pasi Kuivalainen .08 .25
70 Tommi Kovanen .02 .10
71 Jermu Pisto .02 .10
72 Ivan Vlzek .02 .10
73 Mika Laaksonen .02 .10
74 Miikka Ruokonen .02 .10
75 Sami Simonen .02 .10
76 Mikko Honkonen .02 .10
77 Veli-Pekka Nutikka .20 .50
78 Arto Sirvio .02 .10
79 Janne Kekalainen .02 .10
80 Jarno Levonne .02 .10
81 Jussi Tarvainen .02 .10
82 Iiro Itamies .08 .25
83 Tommi Nyyssonen .02 .10
84 Kari Haakana .02 .10
85 Jarmo Muukkonen .02 .10
86 Tero Nissinen .02 .10
87 Tero Tiainen .02 .10
88 Joonas Jaaskelainen .02 .10
89 Juha Ikonen .02 .10
90 Timo Norppa .02 .10
91 Teemu Riihijarvi .08 .25
92 Mikko Koivunoro .02 .10
93 Sergei Priakhin .05 .15
94 Timo Hirvonen .02 .10
95 Boris Rousson .20 .50
96 Kimmo Lotvonen .02 .10
97 Riku Kallioniemi .02 .10
98 Martti Jarventie .15 .40
99 Mikko Luovi .07 .20
100 Checklist (101-150) .02 .10
101 Kalle Sahlstedt .08 .25
102 Sakari Palsola .02 .10
103 Tommi Turunen .02 .10
104 Petri Latti .02 .10
105 Jonni Vauhkonen .05 .15
106 Veli-Pekka Ahonen .02 .10
107 Jari Torkki .05 .15
108 Jarkko Varvio .05 .15
109 Matti Viitakoski .02 .10
110 Mikko Myllykoski .02 .10
111 Petri Peronmaa .02 .10
112 Vesa Ruotsalainen .02 .10
113 Timo Lohko .02 .10
114 Simo Liukka .02 .10
115 Juha-Pekka Rinkinen .02 .10
116 Timo Makinen .02 .10
117 Marko Ek .05 .15
118 Matti Nevalainen .02 .10

119 Ari Santanen .02 .10
120 Jonas Hemming .02 .10
121 Mika Karapuu .02 .10
122 Ilpo Kauhanen .20 .50
123 Sami-Ville Salomaa .02 .10
124 Antti Rahkonen .02 .10
125 Harri Laurilla .02 .10
126 Sami Lehtonen .02 .10
127 Pasi Petrilainen .08 .25
128 Arto Kulmala .02 .10
129 Jarkko Nikander .02 .10
130 Timo Nurmberg .02 .10
131 Tuomas Reijonen .02 .10
132 Aleksander Barkov .02 .10
133 Mika Niittymaki .02 .10
134 Valeri Krykov .02 .10
135 Fredrik Norrena .20 .50
136 Mika Lehtinen .02 .10
137 Sami Salo .20 .50
138 Riku-Petteri Lehtonen .02 .10
139 Mikko Sokka .02 .10
140 Manu Laapas .02 .10
141 Hannes Hyvonen .15 .40
142 Miikka Rousu .02 .10
143 Simo Rouvali .02 .10
144 Tommi Miettinen .02 .10
145 Kimmo Rintanen .20 .50
146 Tomi Kallio .20 .50
147 Antti Aalto .20 .50
148 Miika Elomo .20 .50
149 Kari Takko .20 .50
150 Checklist (151-200) .02 .10
151 Tommi Rajemaki .08 .25
152 Pasi Peltonen .02 .10
153 Karri Kivi .07 .20
154 Jokke Heinanen .02 .10
155 Teppo Kivela .02 .10
156 Vesa Goman .02 .10
157 Pekka Virta .02 .10
158 Pasi Tuominen .02 .10
159 Timo Hakanen .02 .10
160 Jari Levonen .02 .10
161 Jari Korpisalo .05 .15
162 Timo Salonen .02 .10
163 Jokerit .08 .25
164 Jokerit .02 .10
165 Jokerit .02 .10
166 Jokerit .02 .10
167 Jokerit .02 .10
168 Jokerit .02 .10
169 Jokerit .02 .10
170 Jokerit .02 .10
171 Jokerit .02 .10
172 Jokerit .02 .10
173 Jokerit .02 .10
174 Jokerit .02 .10
175 Ari Sulander .20 .50
176 Joni Lehto .05 .15
177 Timo Jutila .05 .15
178 Mikko Peltola .02 .10
179 Juha Riihijarvi .08 .25
180 Petri Varis .20 .50
181 Boris Rousson .20 .50
182 Kimmo Timonen .20 .50
183 Mika Stromberg .08 .25
184 Jari Korpisalo .05 .15
185 Otakar Janecky .08 .25
186 Juha Lind .08 .25
187 Aarne Honkavaara .20 .50
188 Esko Niemi .02 .10
189 Raimo Kilpio .02 .10
190 Jarmo Wasama .02 .10
191 Lalli Partinen .02 .10
192 Urpo Ylonen .08 .25
193 Ilpo Koskela .20 .50
194 Jorma Vehmanen .02 .10
195 Pekka Marjamaki .02 .10
196 Veli-Pekka Ketola .08 .25
197 Matti Murto .02 .10
198 Juhani Tamminen .08 .25
199 Matti Hagman .07 .20
200 Checklist (inserts) .08 .25
NNO Kari Takko Super Bonus 2.00 5.00
NNO Juha Riihijarvi Chase 2.00 5.00

1996-97 Finnish SISU Redline At The Gala

This set of inserts showcases the 1995-96 award winners from the SM-Liiga. The cards were randomly inserted at a rate of 1:6 packs. The card fronts display the players in the tuxedos accepting the awards, while the backs show the player in action.

COMPLETE SET (8) 5.00 10.00
STATED ODDS 1:6
1 Petri Varis .75 2.00
2 Juha Riihijarvi .40 1.00
3 Waltteri Immonen .40 1.00
4 Jani Hurme 1.25 3.00
5 Pasi Kuivalainen .75 2.00
6 Mika Stromberg .40 1.00
7 Sakari Pietila .40 1.00
8 Ari Sulander .75 2.00

1996-97 Finnish SISU Redline Keeping It Green

This most difficult of the SISU inserts (1:60) features four top netminders in a set promoting environmental awareness, as well as keeping the light behind their nets from turning red.

COMPLETE SET (4) 15.00 30.00
STATED ODDS 1:60
1 Ari Sulander 4.00 10.00
2 Jani Hurme 7.50 15.00
3 Boris Rousson 4.00 10.00
4 Mika Pietila 4.00 10.00

1996-97 Finnish SISU Redline Mighty Adversaries

This 9-card set with a two-front format was inserted at a rate of 1:8 packs. Each side featured either a forward or a goalie, with the ghosted image of the counterpart's face in the background. Each side also had text addressing their adversarial relationship.

COMPLETE SET (9) 10.00 25.00
STATED ODDS 1:8
1 K.Takko 1.25 3.00
K.Rintanen
2 B.Rousson 1.25 3.00
P.Saarela
3 I.Kauhanen 1.25 3.00
A.Andrijevski
4 A.Sulander 1.25 3.00
M.Kortelainen
5 P.Kuivalainen 1.25 3.00
T.Sjogren
6 V.Toskala 2.00 5.00
J.Ojanen
7 F.Norrena 1.25 3.00
O.Janecky
8 S.Lindfors 1.25 3.00
J.Korpisalo
9 A.Siekkinen 1.25 3.00
J.Lindroos

1996-97 Finnish SISU Redline Promos

These cards were handed out at a hockey event in Finland to promote the upcoming series. Checklist courtesy of collector Heikki Silvenoinen.

COMPLETE SET (12) 15.00
1 Mika Kortelainen .40 1.00
2 Alexander Andrievski .40 1.00
3 Vesa Toskala 1.25 3.00
4 Jari Lindroos .40 1.00
5 Thomas Sjogren .40 1.00
6 Pasi Kuivalainen .75 2.00
7 Iiro Itamies .75 2.00
8 Kalle Sahlstedt .75 2.00
9 Mika Karapuu .40 1.00
10 Valeri Krykov .40 1.00
11 Kimmo Rintanen .40 1.00
12 Jari Levonen .40 1.00

1996-97 Finnish SISU Redline Rookie Energy

This 9-card set features the top rookies from the SM-Liiga's 95-96 campaign. The cards were randomly inserted into packs at a rate of 1:6. The card fronts feature an image of the player over a colored sky highlighted by lightning bolts. The backs include a head shot as well as some text relating the player's fine season

COMPLETE SET (9) 8.00 15.00
STATED ODDS 1:6
1 Jani Hurme 2.00 5.00
2 Mikko Eloranta .75 2.00
3 Sami Salo .75 2.00
4 Tero Hamalainen .40 1.00
5 Miika Elomo .75 2.00
6 Mika Pietila .40 1.00
7 Arto Kuki .40 1.00
8 Vesa Toskala 2.00 5.00
9 Miikka Rousu .40 1.00

1996-97 Finnish SISU Redline Silver Signatures

These cards were available as a redemption only to those who mailed in their Kari Takko Super Bonus card. Thanks to collector Heikki Silvennoinen for providing the checklist.

COMPLETE SET (5) 60.00 125.00
1 Jani Hurme 12.00 30.00
2 Pasi Kuivalainen 8.00 20.00
3 Boris Rousson 12.00 30.00
4 Ari Sulander 12.00 30.00
5 Vesa Toskala 15.00 40.00

1996-97 Finnish SISU Redline Sledgehammers

These 9 cards were randomly inserted into packs at a rate of 1:6. The cards are essentially double-fronted, with both sides picturing the player in action, superimposed over a Sledgehammer logo.

COMPLETE SET (9) 2.00 5.00
STATED ODDS 1:6
1 Hannu Henriksson .40 1.00
2 Robert Nordmark .40 1.00
3 Pasi Sormunen .40 1.00
4 Tuomas Gronman .40 1.00
5 Derek Mayer .40 1.00
6 Toni Porkka .40 1.00
7 Timo Peltomaa .40 1.00
8 Iiro Jarvi .40 1.00
9 Joni Lehto .40 1.00

1998-99 Finnish Kerailysarja

This set features many of the players of Finland's SM-Liiga. The cards feature a colour action photo on the front, while the backs feature another photo and stats.

COMPLETE SET (270) 16.00 40.00
1 Checklist 1-60 .07 .20
2 Checklist 61-120 .07 .20
3 Checklist 121-180 .07 .20
4 Checklist 181-240 .07 .20
5 Checklist 241-270 .07 .20
6 Inserts Checklist .07 .20
7 Ari-Pekka Siekkinen .15 .40
8 Jani Riihinen .07 .20
9 Riku Varjamo .07 .20
10 Jiri Vykoukal .07 .20
11 Jonas Andersson-Junkka .15 .40
12 Riku-Petteri Lehtonen .07 .20
13 Pasi Sormunen .07 .20
14 Robert Salo .07 .20
15 Juha Gustafsson .15 .40
16 Christian Ruuttu .15 .40
17 Tero Hamalainen .07 .20
18 Juha Ikonen .07 .20
19 Hannes Hyvonen .20 .50
20 Timo Hirvonen .20 .50
21 Petr Ton .07 .20
22 Nils Ekman .30 .75
23 Joonas Jaaskelainen .07 .20
24 Tommy Kiviaho .07 .20
25 Tomas Kapusta .07 .20
26 Tero Tiainen .07 .20
27 Teemu Riihijarvi .15 .40
28 Jan Lundell .07 .20
29 Niklas Backstrom .07 .20
30 Ville Siren .07 .20
31 Marko From .07 .20
32 Brian Rafalski .40 1.00
33 Jarno Kultanen .20 .50
34 Toni Lydman .20 .50
35 Jani Nikko .15 .40
36 Jere Karalahti .15 .40
37 Kari Rajala .07 .20
38 Kari Kalto .07 .20
39 Kimmo Kuhta .07 .20
40 Jan Caloun .15 .40
41 Markku Hurme .07 .20
42 Tom Laaksonen .07 .20
43 Niklas Hagman .40 1.00
44 Luciano Borsato .07 .20
45 Toni Sihvonen .07 .20
46 Mika Kortelainen .15 .40
47 Toni Makiaho .07 .20
48 Mika Nieminen .15 .40
49 Jarkko Ruutu .30 .75
50 Marko Tuomainen .15 .40
51 Pasi Nurminen 1.50 4.00
52 Kari Rosenberg .07 .20
53 Aki Heino .07 .20
54 Erik Kakko .07 .20
55 Tom Koivisto .07 .20
56 Ari Vallin .07 .20
57 Tomi Kallarsson .07 .20
58 Jaroslav Nedved .07 .20
59 Kai Rautio .07 .20
60 Mikko Kuparinen .15 .40
61 Mika Kannisto .07 .20
62 Juha Virtanen .07 .20
63 Jani Keinanen .07 .20
64 Jyrki Louhi .07 .20
65 Roman Simicek .20 .50
66 Semi Pekki .07 .20
67 Timo Parssinen .07 .20
68 Jarkko Savijoki .07 .20
69 Marko Palo .07 .20
70 Antti Virtanen .07 .20
71 Niko Kapanen .75 2.00
72 Tomas Vlasak .15 .40
73 Riku Hahl .40 1.00
74 Vesa Toskala .75 2.00
75 Markus Korhonen .07 .20
76 Timo Willman .07 .20
77 Veli-Pekka Hard .07 .20
78 Pekka Kangasalusta .07 .20
79 Oscar Ackestrom .07 .20
80 Allan Measures .07 .20
81 Pasi Puistola .07 .20
82 Pasi Saarinen .15 .40
83 Mikko Haapakoski .07 .20
84 Martti Jarventie .20 .50
85 Mika Arvaja .07 .20
86 Juha Hautamaa .07 .20
87 Raimo Helminen .15 .40
88 Tomi Hirvonen .07 .20
89 Matti Kaipainen .07 .20
90 Peter Larsson .07 .20
91 Vesa Viitakoski .15 .40
92 Mikko Peltola .07 .20
93 Timo Peltomaa .07 .20
94 Hannu Mattila .07 .20
95 Sami Ahlberg .07 .20
96 Juha Jarvenpaa .07 .20
97 Markus Ketterer .15 .40
98 Ari Kumpula .07 .20
99 Waltteri Immonen .07 .20
100 Antti-Jussi Niemi .15 .40
101 Sami Nuutinen .07 .20
102 Yves Racine .15 .40
103 Rami Alanko .07 .20
104 Mika Stromberg .15 .40
105 Ossi Vaananen .40 1.00
106 Jani Rita .40 1.00
107 Sami Mettovaara .07 .20
108 Fredrik Nilsson .07 .20
109 Kimmo Rintanen .15 .40
110 Jari Kauppila .07 .20
111 Pasi Saarela .15 .40
112 Timo Saarikoski .07 .20
113 Eero Somervuori .15 .40
114 Jukka Tiilikainen .07 .20
115 Jarkko Vaananen .07 .20
116 Otakar Janecky .15 .40
117 Patrik Juhlin .15 .40
118 Juha Lind .20 .50
119 Marko Leinonen .07 .20
120 Tommi Satosaari .07 .20
121 Mikko Luoma .07 .20
122 Jan Latvala .07 .20
123 Kevin Wortman .07 .20
124 Kalle Koskinen .07 .20
125 Jyrki Valivaara .07 .20
126 Markus Kankaanpera .07 .20
127 Jarkko Glad .07 .20
128 Marko Kauppinen .07 .20
129 Robert Nordberg .07 .20
130 Juha Viinikainen .07 .20
131 Marko Ojanen .07 .20
132 Toni Koivunen .07 .20
133 Mikko Rantala .07 .20
134 Jussi Tarvainen .07 .20
135 Tommi Turunen .07 .20
136 Timo Vertala .07 .20
137 Veli-Pekka Nutikka .15 .40
138 Stefan Ornskog .07 .20
139 Marko Virtanen .07 .20
140 Lasse Jamsen .07 .20
141 Kimmo Kapanen .07 .20
142 Ari Luostarinen .07 .20
143 Tobias Ablad .07 .20
144 Derry Menard .07 .20
145 Jermu Pisto .07 .20
146 Sebastian Sulku .07 .20
147 Timo Ahmaoja .07 .20
148 Teemu Tuomainen .07 .20
149 Pekka Poikolainen .07 .20
150 Aki Korhonen .07 .20
151 Pekka Tirkkonen .07 .20
152 Petro Koivunen .07 .20
153 Marko Levanen .07 .20
154 Janne Kekalainen .07 .20
155 Antti Riekkinen .07 .20
156 Mikko Honkonen .07 .20
157 Timo Sikkula .07 .20
158 Sami Simonen .07 .20
159 Mikko Konttila .07 .20
160 Jaakko Uhlback .07 .20
161 Lubos Rob .07 .20
162 Kimmo Vesa .07 .20
163 Sinuhe Wallinheimo .07 .20
164 Jaakko Harikkala .15 .40
165 Atvars Tribuntsovs .07 .20
166 Ismo Kuoppala .07 .20
167 Kimmo Lotvonen .07 .20
168 Marko Toivonen .07 .20
169 Erik Hamalainen .15 .40
170 Mikael Tjallden .07 .20
171 Roland Carlsson .07 .20
172 Niko Halttunen .07 .20
173 Jouni Vauhkonen .07 .20
174 Matti Raunio .07 .20
175 Ville Mikkonen .07 .20
176 Petri Pakaslahti .07 .20
177 Janne Seva .07 .20
178 Harri Sillgren .07 .20
179 Leonids Tambijevs .07 .20
180 Jari Hyvarinen .07 .20
181 Patrik Wallenberg .07 .20
182 Jarkko Nikander .07 .20
183 Aigars Cipruss .07 .20
184 Jussi Markkanen .60 1.50
185 Pasi Hakkinen .07 .20
186 Harri Tikkanen .07 .20
187 Juri Kuznetsov .07 .20
188 Riku Kallioniemi .07 .20
189 Jussi Pekkala .07 .20
190 Mikko Myllykoski .07 .20
191 Vesa Ruotsalainen .07 .20
192 Tommi Sova .07 .20
193 Dale McTavish .07 .20
194 Pasi Maattanen .07 .20
195 Aleksander Matsijevski .07 .20
196 Sami Kaartinen .07 .20
197 Ari Saarinen .07 .20
198 Joel Salonen .07 .20
199 Ari Santanen .07 .20
200 Mika Skytta .07 .20
201 Mika Kauppinen .07 .20
202 Keijo Sailynoja .07 .20
203 Eric Weilleux .07 .20
204 Ville Immonen .07 .20
205 Mika Noronen 2.00 5.00
206 Iiro Itamies .07 .20
207 Josef Boumedienne .20 .50
208 Miska Kangasniemi .15 .40
209 Mikko Tamminen .07 .20
210 Timo Jutila .07 .20
211 Janne Gronvall .15 .40
212 Sami-Ville Salomaa .07 .20
213 Janne Vuorela .07 .20
214 Pasi Petrilainen .15 .40
215 Pasi Tuominen .07 .20
216 Jani Hassinen .07 .20
217 Valeri Krykov .07 .20
218 Juha Vuorivirta .07 .20
219 Aleksander Barkov .07 .20
220 Harri Lonnberg .07 .20
221 Arto Kumala .07 .20
222 Janne Ojanen .15 .40
223 Lasse Pirjeta .07 .20
224 Sami Salonen .07 .20
225 Johannes Alanen .07 .20
226 Mikko Makela .15 .40
227 Fredrik Norrena .15 .40
228 Miikka Kiprusoff 2.00 5.00
229 Kimmo Eronen .07 .20
230 Marko Kiprusoff .07 .20
231 Jouni Loponen .07 .20
232 Ilkka Mikkola .15 .40
233 Aki Berg .20 .50
234 Tommi Rajamaki .15 .40
235 Peter Ahola .07 .20
236 Mika Lehtinen .07 .20
237 Tony Virta .07 .20
238 Joni Lius .07 .20
239 Mikko Eloranta .20 .50
240 Marco Tuokko .07 .20
241 Juha Joninen .07 .20
242 Tomi Kallio .15 .40
243 Mikko Rautio .07 .20
244 Jani Kiviharju .07 .20
245 Tommi Miettinen .20 .50
246 Simo Rouvali .07 .20
247 Kalle Sahlstedt .15 .40
248 Teemu Elomo .15 .40
249 Mika Alatalo .20 .50
250 Miika Elomo .15 .40
251 Pasi Kuivalainen .15 .40
252 Mika Lehto .07 .20
253 Joachim Esbjors .07 .20
254 Mikko Sokka .07 .20
255 Pasi Peltonen .15 .40
256 Vesa Salo .07 .20
257 Mika Laaksonen .07 .20
258 Santeri Immonen .07 .20
259 Jonas Esbjors .07 .20
260 Vjatcheslav Fandul .07 .20
261 Kimmo Salminen .07 .20
262 Jokke Heinanen .07 .20
263 Jari Levonen .07 .20
264 Niko Mikkola .07 .20
265 Andrei Potaitshuk .07 .20
266 Rauli Raitanen .07 .20
267 Timo Hakanen .07 .20
268 Jan Benda .07 .20
269 Tero Arkiomaa .15 .40
270 Marko Kivenmaki .07 .20

1998-99 Finnish Kerailysarja 90's Top 12

These inserts honor the decade's best Finnish players. They were randomly inserted into packs. Unfortunately, the wrappers do not reveal the insertion odds.

COMPLETE SET (12) 16.00 30.00
1 Jere Lehtinen 1.25 3.00
2 Pertti Lehtonen .75 2.00
3 Janne Laukkanen .75 2.00
4 Jukka Tammi .75 2.00
5 Teemu Selanne 4.00 10.00
6 Jari Lindroos .75 2.00
7 Sami Kapanen 1.25 3.00
8 Jarmo Kuusisto .75 2.00
9 Ari Santanen .75 2.00
10 Timo Jutila .75 2.00
11 Saku Koivu 2.00 5.00
12 Kari Takko .75 2.00

1998-99 Finnish Kerailysarja Dream Team

These inserts honor the best of Finland's current talent pool. The cards were randomly inserted into packs. Unfortunately, the packs do not reveal the insertion odds.

COMPLETE SET (7) 16.00 20.00
1 Jari Kurri 2.00 5.00
2 Ari Sulander 1.25 3.00
3 Jyrki Lumme .75 2.00
4 Janne Niinimaa .75 2.00
5 Jere Lehtinen 1.50 4.00
6 Saku Koivu 2.00 5.00
7 Teemu Selanne 4.00 10.00

1998-99 Finnish Kerailysarja Leijonat

These inserts honor players who have performed for The Lions, the nickname of Finland's national team. The cards were randomly inserted into packs. Unfortunately, the packs do not reveal the insertion odds.

COMPLETE SET (47) 6.00 15.00
1 Markus Ketterer .20 .50
2 Jarmo Myllys .20 .50
3 Jukka Tammi .20 .50
4 Peter Ahola .08 .25
5 Erik Hamalainen .08 .25
6 Timo Jutila .08 .25
7 Jere Karalahti .20 .50
8 Marko Kiprusoff .08 .25
9 Janne Laukkanen .20 .50
10 Joni Lehto .08 .25
11 Kaj Linna .08 .25
12 Jouni Loponen .08 .25
13 Toni Lydman .15 .40
14 Antti-Jussi Niemi .20 .50
15 Petteri Nummelin .08 .25
16 Mika Stromberg .08 .25
17 Kimmo Timonen .20 .50
18 Hannu Virta .08 .25
19 Mika Alatalo .20 .50
20 Mikko Eloranta .20 .50
21 Raimo Helminen .08 .25
22 Juha Ikonen .08 .25
23 Marko Jantunen .08 .25
24 Olli Jokinen .75 2.00
25 Joonas Jaaskelainen .08 .25
26 Sami Kapanen .75 2.00
27 Esa Keskinen .08 .25
28 Jari Korpisalo .08 .25
29 Tero Lehtera .08 .25
30 Juha Lind .08 .25
31 Joni Lius .08 .25
32 Toni Makiaho .08 .25
33 Mika Nieminen .20 .50
34 Janne Ojanen .08 .25
35 Marko Palo .08 .25
36 Ville Peltonen .30 .75
37 Juha Riihijarvi .08 .25
38 Kimmo Rintanen .08 .25
39 Christian Ruuttu .15 .40
40 Jarkko Ruutu .08 .25
41 Jukka Seppo .08 .25
42 Raimo Summanen .08 .25
43 Esa Tikkanen .40 1.00
44 Marko Tuomainen .08 .25
45 Antti Tormanen .08 .25
46 Jarkko Varvio .08 .25
47 Juha Ylonen .20 .50

1998-99 Finnish Kerailysarja Mad Masks

These inserts honor the best goalies in Finland. The cards were randomly inserted into packs. Unfortunately, the packs do not reveal the insertion odds.

COMPLETE SET (12) 24.00 75.00
1 Ari-Pekka Siekkinen 2.00 5.00
2 Jan Lundell 2.00 5.00
3 Pasi Nurminen 6.00 15.00
4 Vesa Toskala 4.00 10.00
5 Markus Ketterer 2.00 5.00
6 Marko Leinonen 2.00 5.00
7 Kimmo Kapanen 2.00 5.00
8 Sinuhe Wallinheimo 2.00 5.00
9 Jussi Markkanen 4.00 10.00
10 Mika Noronen 6.00 15.00
11 Fredrik Norrena 2.00 5.00
12 Pasi Kuivalainen 2.00 5.00

1998-99 Finnish Kerailysarja Off Duty

These inserts show players away from the ice. The cards were randomly inserted into packs. Unfortunately, the packs do not reveal the insertion odds.

COMPLETE SET (12) 8.00 20.00
1 Juha Ikonen .75 2.00
2 Toni Sihvonen .75 2.00
3 Tom Koivisto .75 2.00
4 Juha Hautamaa .75 2.00
5 Kimmo Rintanen .75 2.00
6 Marko Leinonen .75 2.00
7 Sami Simonen .75 2.00
8 Sinuhe Wallinheimo 1.25 3.00
9 Jussi Markkanen 1.50 4.00
10 Arto Kulmala .75 2.00
11 Marko Kiprusoff .75 2.00
12 Pasi Kuivalainen .75 2.00

1999 Finnish Valio World Championships

Little is known about this Finnish issued set other than the confirmed checklist. Any additional information can be forwarded to hockeymag@beckett.com.

COMPLETE SET (6) 6.00 15.00
1 Kari Eloranta .75 2.00
2 Jari Kurri 3.00 8.00
3 Tapio Levo .75 2.00
4 Markus Mattsson 1.25 3.00
5 Jukka Porvari .75 2.00
6 Pekka Rautakallio .75 2.00

1999-00 Finnish Cardset

This set features the top players of the Finnish SM-Liiga. It was issued in foil packs over two series. The cards feature action photos over a computer generated background. Cards #158-177 comprise a Sharpshooters subset while cards #178-200 form a Flaming Patriots subset. The Jere Lehtinen Triple Threat card was a long-odds insert that was hand serial numbered out of 1,000 copies. The Teemu Selanne Global Glory card was a long-odds insert that was hand serial numbered out of 1,000 copies as well. Neither card is considered part of the complete set.

COMPLETE SET (346) 30.00 75.00
1 Checklist 1-40 .07 .20
2 Checklist 41-80 .07 .20
3 Checklist 81-120 .07 .20
4 Checklist 121-160 .07 .20
5 Checklist 161-200 .07 .20
6 Inserts Checklist .07 .20
7 Ari-Pekka Siekkinen .15 .40
8 Jiri Vykoukal .07 .20
9 Riku Varjamo .07 .20
10 Riku-Petteri Lehtonen .07 .20
11 Juha Gustafsson .15 .40
12 Arto Laatikainen .30 .75
13 Hannes Hyvonen .20 .50
14 Timo Hirvonen .20 .50
15 Tommy Kiviaho .07 .20
16 Tero Tiainen .07 .20
17 Joonas Jaaskelainen .07 .20
18 Teemu Riihijarvi .15 .40
19 Olli Ahonen .07 .20
20 Santeri Heiskanen .07 .20
21 Jarno Kultanen .20 .50
22 Marko From .07 .20
23 Kimmo Kuhta .07 .20
24 Tom Laaksonen .07 .20
25 Kari Kalto .07 .20
26 Jan Caloun .15 .40
27 Markku Hurme .07 .20
28 Toni Makiaho .07 .20
29 Mika Nieminen .15 .40
30 Luciano Borsato .07 .20
31 Aki Heino .07 .20
32 Jonas Andersson-Junkka .15 .40
33 Tomi Kallarsson .07 .20
34 Roman Simicek .20 .50
35 Juha Virtanen .07 .20
36 Antti Virtanen .07 .20
37 Jyrki Louhi .07 .20
38 Jarkko Savijoki .07 .20
39 Jukka Hentunen .20 .50
40 Timo Parssinen .40 1.00
41 Niko Kapanen .40 1.00
42 Tomas Vlasak .15 .40
43 Kristian Antila .07 .20
44 Pasi Puistola .07 .20
45 Pasi Saarinen .15 .40
46 Pekka Kangasalusta .07 .20
47 Martti Jarventie .07 .20
48 Sami Karjalainen .07 .20
49 Riku Niemela .07 .20
50 Mikko Peltola .07 .20
51 Juha Hautamaa .07 .20
52 Raimo Helminen .15 .40
53 Tomi Hirvonen .07 .20
54 Sami Ahlberg .07 .20
55 Vesa Viitakoski .07 .20
56 Mika Arvaja .07 .20
57 Rami Alanko .07 .20
58 Antti-Jussi Niemi .15 .40
59 Antti Hulkkonen .10 .30
60 Jani Rita .40 1.00
61 Jarkko Vaananen .07 .20
62 Fredrik Nilsson .07 .20
63 Jari Kauppila .07 .20
64 Eero Somervuori .20 .50
65 Jukka Tiilikainen .07 .20
66 Patrik Juhlin .15 .40
67 Tommi Satosaari .07 .20
68 Jarkko Glad .07 .20
69 Jyrki Valivaara .07 .20
70 Markus Kankaanpera .07 .20
71 Kalle Koskinen .07 .20
72 Juha Viinikainen .07 .20
73 Marko Ojanen .07 .20
74 Toni Koivunen .07 .20
75 Veli-Pekka Nutikka .15 .40
76 Stefan Ornskog .07 .20
77 Marko Virtanen .07 .20
78 Lasse Jamsen .07 .20
79 Petri Vehanen .07 .20
80 Kimmo Lotvonen .07 .20
81 Jaakko Harikkala .15 .40
82 Ismo Kuoppala .07 .20
83 Erik Hamalainen .15 .40
84 Zdenek Nedved .07 .20
85 Harri Suvanto .07 .20
86 Jouni Vauhkonen .07 .20
87 Ville Mikkonen .07 .20
88 Janne Seva .07 .20
89 Petri Latti .07 .20
90 Harri Sillgren .07 .20
91 Leonids Tambijevs .07 .20
92 Sami Lehtinen .07 .20
93 Jussi-Antti Reimari .07 .20
94 Marko Ahonen .07 .20
95 Veli-Pekka Laitinen .07 .20
96 Mika Niskanen .07 .20
97 Jan Latvala .07 .20
98 Mika Asikainen .07 .20
99 Aigars Cipruss .07 .20
100 Michael Johansson .07 .20
101 Tomi-Pekka Kolu .07 .20
102 Jarkko Ollikainen .07 .20
103 Toni Saarinen .07 .20
104 Jussi Vienonen .07 .20
105 Jouko Mytta .07 .20
106 Jussi Markkanen .40 1.00
107 Harri Tikkanen .07 .20
108 Riku Kallioniemi .07 .20
109 Jussi Pekkala .07 .20
110 Mikko Myllykoski .07 .20
111 Vesa Ruotsalainen .07 .20
112 Tommi Sova .07 .20
113 Ari Santanen .07 .20
114 Pasi Maattanen .07 .20
115 Tero Hamalainen .07 .20
116 Mika Skytta .07 .20
117 Ville Immonen .07 .20
118 Keijo Sailynoja .07 .20
119 Miska Kangasniemi .15 .40
120 Josef Boumedienne .20 .50
121 Janne Vuorela .07 .20
122 Janne Gronvall .15 .40
123 Valeri Krykov .07 .20
124 Arto Kumala .07 .20
125 Aleksander Barkov .07 .20
126 Johannes Alanen .07 .20
127 Jani Hassinen .07 .20
128 Janne Ojanen .15 .40
129 Tuomas Reijonen .07 .20
130 Sami Salonen .07 .20
131 Fredrik Norrena .15 .40
132 Kimmo Eronen .07 .20
133 Marko Kiprusoff .08 .25
134 Jouni Loponen .07 .20
135 Ilkka Mikkola .15 .40
136 Jani Kiviharju .07 .20
137 Tony Virta .07 .20
138 Kalle Sahlstedt .15 .40
139 Tomi Kallio .40 1.00
140 Joni Lius .07 .20
141 Teemu Elomo .15 .40
142 Ville Vahalahti .07 .20
143 Marco Tuokko .07 .20
144 Kai Nurminen .15 .40
145 Petr Kuchyna .07 .20
146 Tuomo Kyha .07 .20
147 Pasi Peltonen .15 .40
148 Santeri Immonen .07 .20
149 Pauli Levokari .07 .20
150 Vesa Salo .07 .20
151 Timo Salonen .07 .20
152 Marko Kivenmaki .07 .20
153 Niko Mikkola .07 .20
154 Andrei Potaitshuk .07 .20
155 Tero Arkiomaa .15 .40
156 Timo Hakanen .07 .20
157 Jan Peterek .07 .20
158 Jan Caloun .15 .40
159 Pasi Saarela .15 .40
160 Tomas Vlasak .15 .40
161 Brian Rafalski .40 1.00
162 Peter Larsson .07 .20
163 Roman Simicek .20 .50
164 Raimo Helminen .15 .40
165 Leonids Tambijevs .07 .20
166 Mika Nieminen .15 .40
167 Janne Ojanen .15 .40
168 Otakar Janecky .15 .40
169 Juha Ikonen .07 .20
170 Jari Kauppila .07 .20
171 Jan Benda .07 .20
172 Tony Virta .07 .20
173 Niko Kapanen .40 1.00
174 Aleksander Barkov .07 .20
175 Hannes Hyvonen .20 .50
176 Lasse Pirjeta .07 .20
177 Jussi Tarvainen .07 .20
178 Miikka Kiprusoff 2.00 5.00
179 Ari Sulander .30 .75
180 Vesa Toskala .75 2.00
181 Aki Berg .20 .50
182 Jere Karalahti .20 .50
183 Marko Kiprusoff .08 .25
184 Toni Lydman .20 .50
185 Kari Martikainen .07 .20
186 Antti-Jussi Niemi .15 .40
187 Petteri Nummelin .15 .40
188 Kimmo Timonen .30 .75
189 Mikko Eloranta .20 .50
190 Raimo Helminen .15 .40
191 Olli Jokinen .40 1.00
192 Tomi Kallio .40 1.00
193 Saku Koivu 1.25 3.00
194 Juha Lind .20 .50
195 Ville Peltonen .20 .50
196 Kimmo Rintanen .15 .40
197 Teemu Selanne 2.00 5.00
198 Toni Sihvonen .07 .20
199 Marko Tuomainen .15 .40
200 Antti Tormanen .20 .50
201 Tom Draper .15 .4
202 Timo Leinonen .07 .2
203 Pasi Nurminen 1.25 3.0
204 Tommi Satosaari .07 .2
205 Mika Oksa .07 .2
206 Jermu Pisto .07 .2
207 Niclas Hedberg .15 .4
208 Peter Ahola .07 .2
209 Aki Korhonen .07 .2
210 Mikko Kaukokari .07 .2
211 Esa Pirnes .07 .2
212 Arto Kuki .07 .2
213 Dale McTavish .15 .4
214 Ari Katavisto .07 .2
215 Teemu Siren .07 .2
216 Mikael Jamsanen .07 .2
217 Otakar Janecky .15 .4
218 Niklas Backstrom .07 .2
219 Ari Ahonen ERC 1.25 3.0
220 Jere Karalahti .20 .5
221 Marek Zidlicky .07 .2
222 Toni Lydman .07 .2
223 Pekka Kangasalusta .07 .2
224 Kari Rajala .07 .2
225 Mike Gaffney .07 .2
226 Timo Ahmaoja .07 .2
227 Aki Tuominen .07 .2
228 Aki Uusikartano .07 .2
229 Mika Kortelainen .15 .4
230 Toni Sihvonen .07 .2
231 Pasi Nielikainen .07 .2
232 Lasse Pirjeta .07 .2
233 Kimmo Kapanen .07 .2
234 Ari Kumpula .07 .2
235 Kimmo Peltonen .07 .2
236 Sebastian Sulku .07 .2
237 Harri Laurila .07 .2
238 Teemu Aalto .07 .2
239 Oscar Ackestrom .07 .2
240 Antti Miettinen ERC .30 .7
241 Marko Palo .07 .2
242 Riku Hahl .40 1.0
243 Petr Tenkrat .30 .7
244 Pasi Kuivalainen .15 .4
245 Arto Tukio .07 .2
246 Hannu Henriksson .07 .2
247 Teemu Kesa .07 .2
248 Antti Bruun .07 .2
249 Tomi Pettinen .07 .2
250 Tapio Sammalkangas .07 .2
251 Rodrigo Lavins .15 .4
252 Ilkka Laitinen .07 .2
253 Tommi Miettinen .15 .4
254 Jarkko Nikander .07 .2
255 Daniel Marois .15 .4
256 Antti Hilden .07 .2
257 Kimmo Vesa .07 .2
258 Pasi Nurminen 1.25 3.0
259 Ossi Vaananen .40 1.0
260 Sean Gagnon .15 .4
261 Marko Kauppinen .15 .4
262 Tuomas Gronman .07 .2
263 Tom Koivisto .07 .2
264 Tomek Valtonen .07 .2
265 Esa Tikkanen .40 1.0
266 Jan Benda .07 .2
267 Tommi Santala .07 .2
268 Petri Varis .15 .4
269 Tuomas Eskelinen .07 .2
270 Tero Lehtera .15 .4
271 Markus Hatinen .07 .2
272 Pekka Poikolainen .07 .2
273 Mikko Luoma .07 .2
274 Vesa Ponto .07 .2
275 Nik Zupancic .07 .2
276 Pasi Kangas .15 .4
277 Topi Riutta .07 .2
278 Jussi Pesonen .07 .2
279 Petr Ton .07 .2
280 Jaroslav Bednar .30 .7
281 Tom Draper .20 .5
282 Mika Laaksonen .07 .2
283 Allan Measures .07 .2
284 Martin Stepanek .07 .2
285 Marko Toivonen .07 .2
286 Petteri Lotila .07 .2
287 Jari Hyvarinen .07 .2
288 Timo Peltomaa .07 .2
289 Petri Pakaslahti .07 .2
290 Jokke Heinanen .07 .2
291 Matti Kaipainen .07 .2
292 Ville Koivula .07 .2
293 Veli-Pekka Kautonen .07 .2
294 Daniel Johansson .07 .2
295 Tommi Kovanen .07 .2
296 Roland Carlsson .07 .2
297 Jani Keinanen .07 .2
298 Mikko Juutilainen .07 .2
299 Aki Kaskinen .07 .2
300 Tommi Turunen .07 .2
301 Mathias Bosson .07 .2
302 Teemu Riihijarvi .07 .2
303 Pasi Hakkinen .07 .2
304 Jani-Matti Loikala .07 .2
305 Juri Kuznetsov .15 .4
306 Mikko Jokela .07 .2
307 Ville Hamalainen .07 .2
308 Joel Salonen .07 .2
309 Timo Saarikoski .07 .2
310 Pekka Tirkkonen .07 .2
311 Mika Kauppinen .15 .4
312 Sami Kaartinen .07 .2
313 Timo Jarvinen .07 .2
314 Jason Muzzatti .20 .5
315 Per Lofstrom .07 .2
316 Ari Vallin .07 .2
317 Asko Rantanen .07 .2
318 Tuukka Mantyla .07 .2
319 Pasi Petrilainen .20 .5
320 Pasi Tuominen .07 .2
321 Roman Meluzin .07 .2
322 Miikka Mannikko .07 .2
323 Jussi Tarvainen .07 .2
324 Timo Vertala .07 .2
325 Jaakko Uhlback .07 .2
326 Antero Niittymaki ERC 1.25 3.0
327 Kimmo Lecklin .07 .2
328 Tommi Rajamaki .07 .2
329 Mika Lehtinen .07 .2
330 Kari Harila .07 .2
331 Petri Tahtisalo .07 .2
332 Esa Keskinen .07 .2
333 Kimmo Rintanen .15 .4
334 Michael Holmkvist .20 .5
335 Mikko Rautee .07 .2
336 Mika Lehto .07 .2
337 Timo Leinonen .07 .2
338 Timo Willman .07 .2
339 Olli Kaski .07 .2
340 Samu Wesslin .07 .2
341 Mika Kannisto .07 .2

2 Ales Kratoska .07 .20
3 Marko Luomala .07 .20
4 Jaakko Makela .07 .20
5 Ondreji Steiner .07 .20
6 Markku Tahtinen .07 .20
0 Teemu Selanne GG 10.00 25.00
0 Jere Lehtinen TT 4.00 10.00

1999-00 Finnish Cardset Aces High

is insert set was created in the form of playing cards. veral great stars of Finland's past, as well as four eerleaders from the SM-Liiga are featured alongside day's heroes. The fronts feature action photos with mbols in the corners of typical playing cards. As the rds are not traditionally numbered, they have been ted below according to their suits. C stands for ubs, D for Diamonds, H for Hearts and S for Spades.

MPLETE SET (54) 8.00 25.00
Jari Kurri .75 2.00
Teemu Selanne 2.00 5.00
Peter Ahola .07 .20
Teppo Numminen .20 .50
Janne Laukkanen .07 .20
Risto Siltanen .07 .20
Iiro Jarvi .07 .20
Antti Aalto .07 .20
Theo Fleury .75 2.00
Ilkka Sinsalo .07 .20
0 Michael Nylander .07 .20
Timo Blomqvist .07 .20
Sami Salo .07 .20
Marko Kiprusoff .07 .20
Aki Berg .20 .50
Jan Caloun .07 .20
Olli Jokinen .40 1.00
Patrik Juhlin .07 .20
Dale McTavish .07 .20
0 Sami Kapanen .40 1.00
Hannu Virta .07 .20
Tuomas Gronman .07 .20
Timo Jutila .07 .20
Jyrki Lumme .20 .50
Juha Ylonen .30 .75
Janne Ojanen .07 .20
Juha Lind .20 .50
Antti Tormanen .07 .20
0 Jarkko Varvio .07 .20
Reijo Ruotsalainen .07 .20
Janne Niinimaa .20 .50
Brian Rafalski .20 .50
Kimmo Timonen .20 .50
Kai Nurminen .07 .20
Raimo Helminen .07 .20
Raimo Summanen .07 .20
Petri Varis .15 .40
0 Christian Ruuttu .07 .20
Jani Hurme .40 1.00
Mika Alatalo .20 .50
Ville Peltonen .15 .40
Paivi Ylitile .40 1.00
Jarmo Myllys .20 .50
Mikko Eloranta .20 .50
Jere Lehtinen .60 1.50
Carissa Chan .40 1.00
Boris Rousson .20 .50
Jan Benda .07 .20
Saku Koivu 1.50 4.00
Ann Bjorklof .40 1.00
Kari Takko .20 .50
Marko Tuomainen .07 .20
Esa Tikkanen .40 1.00
Satu Jokinen .40 1.00

999-00 Finnish Cardset Blazing Patriots

is insert set is a partial parallel of the Flaming triots subset and features the top performers for land's national team. The cards were inserted at a e of 1:10 packs.

MPLETE SET (6) 20.00 30.00
ATED ODDS 1:10
Miikka Kiprusoff 4.00 10.00
Jere Karalahti 1.25 3.00
Kimmo Timonen 1.25 3.00
Teemu Selanne 4.00 10.00
Saku Koivu 4.00 8.00
Marko Tuomainen 1.25 3.00

1999-00 Finnish Cardset Jere Lehtinen Triple Threat

is is a single card tribute to Finnish hockey hero e Lehtinen. The card is hand numbered on the back t of 1,000.

Jere Lehtinen 4.00 10.00

1999-00 Finnish Cardset Most Wanted

is insert set features the players drafted earliest in NHL draft. The cards were inserted at a rate of 1:4 cks.

MPLETE SET (12) 20.00 30.00
ATED ODDS 1:4
Aki Berg .75 2.00
Olli Jokinen .75 2.00
Teemu Selanne 4.00 10.00
Teemu Riihuarvi .40 1.00
Jani Rita .75 2.00
Saku Koivu 4.00 8.00
Mika Noronen 2.00 5.00
Miika Elomo .75 2.00
Jukka Seppo .40 1.00
Ari Ahonen 2.00 5.00
Tuomas Gronman .40 1.00
Ville Siren .40 1.00

1999-00 Finnish Cardset Par Avion

is insert set focuses on some of the best Finnish yers who have moved on to play in North America. e cards were inserted 1:4 packs.

MPLETE SET (12) 14.00 25.00
ATED ODDS 1:4
Mika Alatalo .75 2.00
Toni Lydman .75 2.00
Brian Rafalski .75 2.00
Jere Karalahti .75 2.00
Juha Lind .75 2.00
Mikko Kuparinen .40 1.00
Marko Tuomainen .40 1.00
Miikka Kiprusoff 4.00 10.00
Mika Noronen 2.00 5.00
Vesa Toskala 2.00 5.00
Mikko Eloranta .75 2.00
Jarkko Ruutu .75 2.00

1999-00 Finnish Cardset Puck Stoppers

is six-card set features the top netminders in the -Liiga. The cards were inserted at a rate of 1:10.

MPLETE SET (6) 12.00 25.00
ATED ODDS 1:10
1 Antero Niittymaki 4.00 10.00
2 Ari-Pekka Siekkinen 2.00 5.00
3 Pasi Kuivalainen 2.00 5.00
4 Sami Lehtinen 2.00 5.00
5 Jason Muzzatti 2.00 5.00
6 Kimmo Kapanen 2.00 5.00

2000-01 Finnish Cardset

This brand features the players from Finland's tip league, the SM-Liiga. It was issued in foil packs across three separate series. The cards are brightly colored with an action photo on the front, another on the back, and a bizarre ranking system on the back which tabulates how great the player is. The brand is noteworthy for including cards of several prominent Finnish players currently in the NHL, as well as several 2001 draft picks such as Mikko Koivu and Tuomo Ruutu. There were three special cards hand numbered to 1,000 copies available: Saku Koivu Millennium Thunder was found in series 1 packs, Pasi Nurminen Masked Marvel was found in series 2, and Ari Ahonen Masked Marvel card was inserted into series 3 packs.

COMPLETE SET (360) 30.00 60.00
1 Checklist .04 .10
2 Checklist .04 .10
3 Checklist .04 .10
4 Mika Oksa .04 .10
5 Peter Ahola .04 .10
6 Jermu Pisto .04 .10
7 Jiri Vykoukal .04 .10
8 Niclas Hedberg .04 .10
9 Teemu Siren .04 .10
10 Joonas Jaaskelainen .20 .50
11 Timo Hirvonen .04 .10
12 Mikko Kaukokari .04 .10
13 Ari Ahonen 1.25 3.00
14 Marek Zidlicky .04 .10
15 Jarno Kultanen .08 .20
16 Toni Sihvonen .04 .10
17 Aki Uusikartano .04 .10
18 Pasi Nlelikainen .04 .10
19 Hannes Hyvonen .20 .50
20 Mika Nieminen .20 .50
21 Mika Kortelainen .04 .10
22 Kimmo Kapanen .04 .10
23 Jonas Andersson-Junkka .08 .20
24 Kimmo Peltonen .04 .10
25 Sebastian Sulku .04 .10
26 Teemu Aalto .04 .10
27 Antti Miettinen .30 .75
28 Riku Hahl .40 1.00
29 Marko Palo .04 .10
30 Juha Pitkamaki .04 .10
31 Arto Tukio .20 .50
32 Tapio Sammalkangas .04 .10
33 Tomi Pettinen .04 .10
34 Jarkko Nikander .04 .10
35 Raimo Helminen .08 .20
36 Juha Hautamaa .04 .10
37 Sami Karjalainen .04 .10
38 Pasi Nurminen .75 2.00
39 Ossi Vaananen .30 .75
40 Marko Kauppinen .20 .50
41 Tom Koivisto .04 .50
42 Rami Alanko .04 .10
43 Petri Varis .20 .50
44 Jan Benda .08 .20
45 Jani Rita .40 1.00
46 Markus Kankaanpera .20 .50
47 Jarkko Glad .04 .10
48 Jyrki Valivaara .04 .10
49 Tuomas Pihlman ERC .04 .10
50 Jussi Pesonen .04 .10
51 Petr Ton .04 .10
52 Markus Korhonen .20 .50
53 Harri Aho .04 .10
54 Karri Kivi .08 .20
55 Mikko Haapakoski .04 .10
56 Jakko Niskavaara .08 .20
57 Niklas Hagman .40 1.00
58 Sakari Palsola .04 .10
59 Jari Laukkanen .04 .10
60 Petri Isotalus .20 .50
61 Jari Viuhkola .04 .10
62 Allan Measures .04 .10
63 Mika Laaksonen .04 .10
64 Marko Toivonen .04 .10
65 Matti Kaipainen .04 .10
66 Petri Latti .04 .10
67 Sami Torkki .04 .10
68 Jokke Hainanen .04 .10
69 Sami Lehtinen .20 .50
70 Veli-Pekka Laitinen .04 .10
71 Kaj Lindstrom .04 .10
72 Mika Niskanen .04 .10
73 Jani Keinanen .04 .10
74 Tommi Turunen .04 .10
75 Mikko Juutilainen .04 .10
76 Veli-Pekka Nutikka .08 .20
77 Mikko Jokela .20 .50
78 Martin Richter .04 .10
79 Pekka Tirkkonen .08 .20
80 Vladimir Machulda .04 .10
81 Ville Hamalainen .04 .10
82 Mika Skytta .04 .10
83 Ville Immonen .04 .10
84 Sami Kaartinen .04 .10
85 Tuukka Mantyla .20 .50
86 Miska Kangasniemi .08 .20
87 Janne Gronvall .08 .20
88 Jussi Tarvainen .08 .20
89 Janne Ojanen .04 .10
90 Jaakko Uhlback .04 .10
91 Johannes Alanen .04 .10
92 Jani Hassinen .04 .10
93 Fredrik Norrena .20 .50
94 Jouni Loponen .04 .10
95 Tommi Rajamaki .04 .10
96 Kimmo Eronen .04 .10
97 Kimmo Rintanen .04 .10
98 Tony Virta .04 .10
99 Jani Kiviharju .04 .10
100 Teemu Elomo .04 .10
101 Mikko Rautee .04 .10
102 Jim Hrivnak .20 .50
103 Pasi Peltonen .04 .10
104 Timo Willman .04 .10
105 Pauli Levokari .04 .10
106 Tuomo Kyha .04 .10
107 Janne Laitila .04 .10
108 Janne Makela .04 .10
109 Samu Wesslin .04 .10
110 Hannu Tala .04 .10
111 Vesa Toskala .40 1.00
112 Aki Berg .20 .50
113 Antti-Jussi Niemi .08 .20
114 Janne Niinimaa .20 .50
115 Ville Peltonen .30 .75
116 Olli Jokinen .40 1.00
117 Teemu Selanne 1.25 3.00
118 Marko Tuomainen .08 .20
119 Juha Lind .20 .50
120 Niko Kapanen .40 1.00
121 Checklist 1 .04 .10
122 Checklist 2 .04 .10
123 Checklist 3 .04 .10
124 Arto Laatikainen .20 .50
125 Tero Maatta .30 .50
126 Juha Gustafsson .04 .10
127 Toni Koivunen .04 .10
128 Teemu Virkkunen .04 .10
129 Valeri Krykov .04 .10
130 Frank Banham .20 .50
131 Semir Ben-Amor .04 .10
132 Jiri Burger .04 .10
133 Aki Tuominen .04 .10
134 Ray Giroux .08 .20
135 Mikko Kurvinen .04 .10
136 Patrik Hucko .04 .10
137 Jari Kauppila .04 .10
138 Tony Salmelainen .04 .10
139 Kimmo Kuhta .04 .10
140 Jaroslav Bednar .40 .50
141 Ari Vallin .04 .10
142 Sami Nuutinen .04 .10
143 Jani Virtanen .04 .10
144 Timo Ahmaoja .04 .10
145 Tomi Suoniemi .04 .10
146 Jari Kesti .04 .10
147 Tommi Santala .04 .10
148 Pavel Rosa .20 .50
149 Eero Somervuorl .08 .20
150 Mika Pietila .04 .10
151 Ivan Majesky ERC .04 .10
152 Antti Bruun .04 .10
153 Matt Smith .08 .20
154 Jari-Pekka Pajula .04 .10
155 Kimmo Vaha-Ruohola .04 .10
156 Toni Dahlman .04 .10
157 Antti Hilden .04 .10
158 Timo Koskela .04 .10
159 Vesa Viitakoski .08 .20
160 Kari Haakana .04 .10
161 Pasi Saarinen .08 .20
162 Santeri Heiskanen .04 .10
163 Antti Tormanen .08 .20
164 Juha Virtanen .04 .10
165 Tuomo Ruutu ERC 4.00 10.00
166 Niko Mikkola .04 .10
167 Aigars Cipruss .04 .10
168 Mika Lehto .04 .10
169 Chris MacKenzie .08 .20
170 Pekka Poikolainen .04 .10
171 Riku Varjamo .04 .10
172 Markku Paukkunen .04 .10
173 Mika Paananen .04 .10
174 Juha-Pekka Hytonen .04 .10
175 Janne Hauhtonen .04 .10
176 Jouni Kulonen .04 .10
177 Antti Virtanen .04 .10
178 Kristian Taubert .04 .10
179 Mikko Lehtonen .20 .50
180 Lasse Kukkonen ERC .04 .10
181 Kimmo Koskenkorva .04 .10
182 Tuomo Harjula .04 .10
183 Juha Joenvaara .04 .10
184 Brett Lievers .04 .10
185 Miikka Rousu .04 .10
186 Bruce Racine .20 .50
187 Ismo Kuoppala .04 .10
188 Topi Lehtonen .04 .10
189 Toni Koivisto .04 .10
190 Jouni Vauhkonen .08 .20
191 Jimmy Provencher .04 .10
192 Pasi Saarela .04 .10
193 Pasi Kuivalainen .20 .50
194 Jussi-Antti Reimari .04 .10
195 Jan Latvala .04 .10
196 Roman Vopat .08 .20
197 Janne Sinkkonen .04 .10
198 Ales Kratoska .04 .10
200 Niklas Backstrom .04 .10
201 Oleg Romanov .04 .10
202 Riku Kallioniemi .04 .10
203 Petri Kokko .04 .10
204 Juha Pursiainen .04 .10
205 Joni Yli-Torkko .04 .10
206 Pasi Tuominen .04 .10
207 Ludek Krayzel .04 .10
208 Mika Kauppinen .08 .20
209 Jussi Markkanen .40 1.00
210 Alain Cote .08 .20
211 Pekka Saravo .04 .10
212 Niki Siren .04 .10
213 Timo Vertala .04 .10
214 Tero Lehtera .08 .20
215 Arto Kuki
216 Henrik Tallinder .20 .50
217 Martti Jarventie .30 .50
218 Marco Tuokko .04 .10
219 Joni Lius .04 .10
220 Jarkko Varvio .08 .20
221 Michael Holmqvist
222 Mikko Koivu ERC 6.00 15.00
223 Ari Vapola .04 .10
224 Curtis Sheptak .04 .10
225 Marcus Kristoffersson .40 1.00
226 Jari Korpisalo .04 .10
227 Gabriel Karlsson .20 .50
228 Sami Salonen .04 .10
229 Jarkko Vaananen .04 .10
230 Niklas Hede .04 .10
231 Ari Sulander .20 .50
232 Jere Karalahti .20 .50
233 Toni Lydman .20 .50
234 Petteri Nummelin .20 .50
235 Raimo Helminen .20 .50
236 Tomi Kallio .30 .50
237 Toni Sihvonen .04 .10
238 Jukka Hentunen .20 .50
239 Tony Virta .04 .10
240 Esa Tikkanen .20 .50
241 Checklist 1 .04 .10
242 Checklist 2 .04 .10
243 Checklist 3 .04 .10
244 Tom Draper .20 .50
245 Timo Willman .04 .10
246 Asko Rantanen .04 .10
247 Jukka Tiilikainen .04 .10
248 Mikael Jamsanen .04 .10
249 Kari Kalto .04 .10
250 Esa Pirnes .04 .10
251 Johan Davidsson .20 .50
252 Shayne Toporowski .20 .50
253 Sakari Lindfors .20 .50
254 Tomi Nyman .04 .10
255 Kari Rajala .04 .10
256 Martin Stepanek .04 .10
257 Veli-Pekka Kautonen .04 .10
258 Toni Makiaho .04 .10
259 Lasse Pirjeta .04 .10
260 Markku Hurme .04 .10
261 Erkki Rajamaki .04 .10
262 Jan Caloun .20 .50
263 Joonas Vihko .04 .10
264 Jan Lundell .04 .10
265 Dan Ratushny .08 .20
266 Darcy Werenka .08 .20
267 Timo Parssinen .30 .50
268 Tomas Vlasak .04 .10
269 Jyrki Louhi .04 .10
270 Pasi Maattanen .04 .10
271 Petr Kuchyna .04 .10
272 Jani Nikko .04 .10
273 Tommi Miettinen .30 .50
274 Jesse Welling .04 .10
275 Oliver Setzinger .04 .50
276 Jarno Peltonen .04 .10
277 Tony Salmelainen .04 .10
278 Kari Lehtonen ERC 8.00 20.00
279 Pauli Levokari .04 .10
280 Thomas Johansson .04 .10
281 Lee Sorochan .20 .50
282 Tomek Valtonen .04 .10
283 Jukka Hentunen .20 .50
284 Mikko Ruutu .20 .50
285 Timo Saarikoski .04 .10
286 Teemu Sainomaa .04 .10
287 Ari-Pekka Siekkinen .04 .10
288 Tomi Hirvonen .04 .10
289 Jarno Tiilikainen .04 .10
290 Radoslav Kropac .04 .10
291 Zdenek Sedlak .04 .10
292 Tuomo Jaaskelainen .04 .10
203 Antti Kangas .04 .10
294 Steve Shierreffs .04 .10
295 Pekka Kangasalusta .04 .10
296 Vjatsheslav Fandul .04 .10
297 Kimmo Salminen .04 .10
298 Sami Alalauri .04 .10
299 Andrei Potaitshuk .04 .10
300 Petri Vehanen .04 .10
301 Erik Hamalainen .04 .10
302 Tuomas Gronman .04 .10
303 Kimmo Lotvonen .04 .10
304 Janne Siivonen .04 .10
305 Marko Kivenmaki .04 .10
306 Zdenek Nedved .04 .10
307 Petri Pakaslahti .04 .10
308 Harri Sillgren .04 .10
309 Samu Isosalo .04 .10
310 Henri Laurila .04 .10
311 Jussi Salminen .04 .10
312 Kalle Koskinen .04 .10
313 Jarkko Ollikainen .04 .10
314 Toni Saarinen .04 .10
315 Teemu Riihijarvi .08 .20
316 Lasse Jamsen .04 .10
317 Jouko Myrra .04 .10
318 Pasi Hakkinen .04 .10
319 Juha Kuokkanen .04 .10
320 Roland Carlsson .04 .10
321 Harri Tikkanen .04 .10
322 Juri Kuznetsov .20 .50
323 Ville Kiiskinen .04 .10
324 Olli Sipilainen .04 .10
325 Tuomas Reijonen .04 .10
326 Joel Salonen .04 .10
327 Sami Ahlberg .04 .10
328 Sasu Hovi .04 .10
329 Janne Vourela .04 .10
330 Mikko Luoma .04 .10
331 Miro Laitinen .04 .10
332 Sami Venalainen .04 .10
333 Marko Ojanen .04 .10
334 Marko Makinen .04 .10
335 Aleksander Barkov .04 .10
336 Antero Niittymaki 1.25 3.00
337 Markus Seikola .04 .10
338 Ilkka Mikkola .04 .10
339 Mika Lehtinen .04 .10
340 Niko Kapanen .40 1.00
341 Ville Vahalahti .04 .10
342 Kalle Sahlstedt .20 .50
343 Kristian Antila .04 .10
344 Pasi Puistola .04 .10
345 Vesa Salo .04 .10
346 Veli-Pekka Hard .04 .10
347 Eric Perrin .04 .10
348 Tomas Kucharcik .04 .10
349 Markku Tahtinen .04 .10
350 Mikko Konttila .04 .10
351 Pasi Nurminen .75 2.00
352 Kimmo Timonen .20 .50
353 Jyrki Lumme .20 .50
354 Janne Laukkanen .20 .50
355 Kimmo Rintanen .20 .50
356 Saku Koivu .75 2.00
357 Jere Lehtinen .40 1.00
358 Sami Kapanen .40 1.00
359 Antti Aalto .20 .50
360 Mika Alatalo .20 .50
NNO Ari Ahonen MM 8.00 20.00
NNO Saku Koivu MT 10.00 25.00
NNO Pasi Nurminen MM 10.00 25.00

2000-01 Finnish Cardset Masquerade

These singles feature the masks of the top netminders of the SM-Liiga. They were inserted approximately 1:5 packs in series three only.

COMPLETE SET (9) 24.00 40.00
STATED ODDS 1:5 SERIES 3
1 Mika Pietila 2.00 5.00
2 Bruce Racine 4.00 10.00
3 Sami Lehtinen 2.00 5.00
4 Niklas Backstrom 2.00 5.00
5 Antero Niittymaki 6.00 15.00
6 Markus Korhonen 2.00 5.00
7 Jussi Markkanen 6.00 15.00
8 Tom Draper 4.00 10.00
9 Kristian Antila 2.00 5.00

2000-01 Finnish Cardset Master Blasters

This nine-card set honors the Finnish league's top snipers. The cards were inserted 1:5 packs in series one.

COMPLETE SET (9) 12.50 20.00
STATED ODDS 1:5 SERIES 1
1 Kai Nurminen 1.20 3.00
2 Jan Caloun 1.20 3.00
3 Petr Tenkrat 2.00 5.00
4 Jaroslav Bednar 2.00 5.00
5 Dale McTavish .80 2.00
6 Kalle Sahlstedt 1.20 3.00
7 Zdenek Nedved .80 2.00
8 Tomi Kallio 2.00 5.00
9 Timo Parssinen 2.00 5.00

2000-01 Finnish Cardset Next Generation

This set features the top newcomers to the Finnish Elite League. The cards were inserted at a rate of 1:5 packs in series two only.

COMPLETE SET (9) 30.00 30.00
STATED ODDS 1:5 SERIES 2
1 Mikko Koivu 4.00 10.00
2 Tuukka Mantyla .60 1.50
3 Tuomo Ruutu 3.00 8.00
4 Jani Rita 1.00 2.50
5 Ari Ahonen 1.50 4.00
6 Arto Tukio .60 1.50
7 Antti Miettinen 1.50 4.00
8 Markus Kankaanpera .60 1.50
9 Antero Niittymaki 2.00 5.00

2001 Finnish Cardset Teemu Selanne

NNO Teemu Selanne 8.00 20.00

2001-02 Finnish Cardset

This set features the top players of the Finnish SM-Liiga. The series was divided into two sets, with 180 cards in the first series, and 200 in the second. The set is noteworthy for containing early cards of first-rounders such as Mikko Koivu, Tuomo Ruutu and Hannu Toivonen. The autographs of Koivu and Ruutu, along with the American Dream card of Ville Nieminen, were random inserts in series 1 packs. The Niittymaki and Lehtonen autographs, along with the Kurri insert, were found in series 2 packs. There were 200 copies of each autograph, and 999 copies of the Nieminen and Kurri inserts.

COMPLETE SET (380) 35.00 70.00
1 Espoo Blues .04 .10
2 Mika Oksa .08 .20
3 Tero Maatta .20 .50
4 Jermu Pisto .08 .20
5 Niclas Hedberg .08 .20
6 Arto Laatikainen .20 .50
7 Valeri Krykov .08 .20
8 Teemu Virkkunen .08 .20
9 Teemu Siren .08 .20
10 Timo Hirvonen .08 .20
11 Mikael Jamsanen .08 .20
12 Kari Kalto .08 .20
13 HIFK Helsinki .04 .10
14 Sakari Lindfors .20 .50
15 Marek Zidlicky .40 1.00
16 Tuomas Eskelinen .08 .20
17 Aki Tuominen .08 .20
18 Mikko Kurvinen .08 .20
19 Hannes Hyvonen .20 .50
20 Kimmo Kuhta .08 .20
21 Toni Happola .08 .20
22 Pasi Nielikainen .08 .20
23 Mika Nieminen .20 .50
24 Toni Makiaho .08 .20
25 Jaroslav Bednar .20 .50
26 HPK Hameenlinna .04 .10
27 Kimmo Peltonen .08 .20
28 Teemu Aalto .08 .20
29 Eero Somervuori .08 .20
30 Riku Hahl .20 .50
31 Antti Miettinen .75 2.00
32 Tommi Santala .08 .20
33 Kasper Kenig .08 .20
34 Pasi Maattanen .08 .20
35 Ilves Tampere .04 .10
36 Mika Pietila .08 .20
37 Jani Nikko .08 .20
38 Antti Bruun .08 .20
39 Tomi Pettinen .08 .20
40 Matt Smith .08 .20
41 Oliver Setzinger .20 .50
42 Toni Dahlman .08 .20
43 Timo Koskela .08 .20
44 Kimmo Vaha-Ruohola .08 .20
45 Jarkko Nikander .08 .20
46 Jari-Pekka Pajula .08 .20
47 Antti Hilden .08 .20
48 Jokerit Helsinki .04 .10
49 Pasi Nurminen .60 1.50
50 Kari Haakana .20 .50
51 Rami Alanko .08 .20
52 Tomek Valtonen .08 .20
53 Teemu Sainomaa .08 .20
54 Antti Tormanen .08 .20
55 Timo Saarikoski .08 .20
56 Teemu Laine .20 .50
57 Mikko Ruutu .08 .20
58 Tuomo Ruutu 1.50 4.00
59 Niko Mikkola .08 .20
60 JYP Jyvaskala .04 .10
61 Mika Lehto .08 .20
62 Pekka Poikolainen .08 .20
63 Jarkko Glad .08 .20
64 Tuomo Jaaskelainen .08 .20
65 Juha-Pekka Hytonen .08 .20
66 Tuomas Pihlman .20 .50
67 Janne Hauhtonen .08 .20
68 Jouni Kulonen .08 .20
69 Tomi Hirvonen .08 .20
70 Antti Virtanen .08 .20
71 Oulun Karpat .04 .10
72 Antti Kangas .08 .20
73 Lasse Kukkonen .20 .50
74 Joni Pitkanen ERC .75 2.00
75 Harri Aho .08 .20
76 Kristian Taubert .08 .20
77 Mikko Lehtonen .20 .50
78 Kimmo Koskenkorva .08 .20
79 Jari Laukkanen .08 .20
80 Juha Joenvaara .08 .20
81 Brett Lievers .08 .20
82 Jari Viuhkola .08 .20
83 Andrei Potaitshuk .08 .20
84 Rauman Lukko .04 .10
85 Mika Laaksonen .08 .20
86 Topi Lehtonen .08 .20
87 Marko Toivonen .08 .20
88 Tuomas Gronman .08 .20
89 Petteri Lotila .08 .20
90 Toni Koivisto .08 .20
91 Sami Torkki .08 .20
92 Samu Isosalo .08 .20
93 Petri Latti .08 .20
94 Janne Siivonen .08 .20
95 Matti Kaipainen .08 .20
96 Lahden Pelicans .04 .10
97 Pasi Kuivalainen .20 .50
98 Mika Niskanen .08 .20
99 Jan Latvala .08 .20
100 Kaj Lindstrom .08 .20
101 Mikko Peltola .08 .20
102 Teemu Riihijarvi .08 .20
103 Jani Keinanen .08 .20
104 Lasse Jamsen .08 .20
105 Toni Saarinen .08 .20
106 Veli-Pekka Nutikka .08 .20
107 SaiPa Lappeenranta .04 .10
108 Harri Tikkanen .08 .20
109 Riku Kallioniemi .08 .20
110 Juri Kuznetsov .20 .50
111 Petri Kokko .08 .20
112 Mikko Jokela .20 .50
113 Ville Hamalainen .08 .20
114 Pasi Tuominen .08 .20
115 Pekka Tirkkonen .08 .20
116 Mika Kauppinen .08 .20
117 Vladimir Machulda .20 .50
118 Olli Sipilainen .08 .20
119 Joni Yli-Torkko .08 .20
120 Tappara Tampere .04 .10
121 Jussi Markkanen .40 1.00
122 Miska Kangasniemi .08 .20
123 Miikko Luoma .08 .20
124 Pekka Saravo .08 .20
125 Miro Laitinen .08 .20
126 Aleksander Barkov .08 .20
127 Jussi Tarvainen .08 .20
128 Marko Ojanen .08 .20
129 Johannes Alanen .08 .20
130 Timo Vertala .08 .20
131 Jaakko Uhlback .08 .20
132 Arto Kuki .08 .20
133 TPS Turku .04 .10
134 Antero Niittymaki .75 2.00
135 Tuomo Karjalainen .08 .20
136 Mika Lehtinen .08 .20
137 Henrik Tallinder .20 .50
138 Markus Seikola .08 .20
139 Kimmo Eronen .08 .20
140 Martti Jarventie .20 .50
141 Mikko Rautee .08 .20
142 Mikko Koivu 2.00 5.00
143 Marco Tuokko .08 .20
144 Michael Holmqvist .40 1.00
145 Ville Vahalahti .08 .20
146 Porin Assat .04 .10
147 Kristian Antila .08 .20
148 Pasi Peltonen .08 .20
149 Curtis Sheptak .08 .20
150 Sami Karjalainen .08 .20
151 Jari Korpisalo .08 .20
152 Mikko Konttila .08 .20
153 Juha Viinikainen .08 .20
154 Eric Perrin .08 .20
155 Markku Tahtinen .08 .20
156 Finnish National Team .04 .10
157 Pasi Nurminen .60 1.50
158 Miikka Kiprusoff .75 2.00
159 Jarmo Myllys .20 .50
160 Marko Kiprusoff .08 .20
161 Petteri Nummelin .20 .50
162 Kimmo Timonen .20 .50
163 Sami Salo .20 .50
164 Ossi Vaananen .20 .50
165 Aki Berg .20 .50
166 Antti-Jussi Niemi .08 .20
167 Janne Gronvall .08 .20
168 Raimo Helminen .08 .20
169 Antti Laaksonen .20 .50
170 Tomi Kallio .20 .50
171 Niko Kapanen .40 1.00
172 Sami Kapanen .40 1.00
173 Jukka Hentunen .20 .50
174 Timo Parssinen .20 .50
175 Juha Lind .20 .50
176 Toni Sihvonen .08 .20
177 Kimmo Rintanen .08 .20
178 Tony Virta .08 .20
179 Juha Ylonen .20 .50
180 Jarkko Ruutu .20 .50
181 Espoo Blues .04 .10
182 Jarmo Myllys .20 .50
183 Juha Gustafsson .08 .20
184 Matti Kuusisto .08 .20
185 Jani Virtanen .08 .20
186 Jiri Vykoukal .08 .20
187 Jan Caloun .20 .50
188 Markku Hurme .08 .20
189 Jiri Zelenka .08 .20
190 Tero Lehtera .08 .20
191 Janne Seva .08 .20
192 Teemu Elomo .08 .20
193 Filip Turek .08 .20
194 HIFK Helsinki .04 .10
195 Mikko Stromberg .08 .20
196 Antti-Pekka Lamberg .08 .20
197 Robert Kantor .08 .20
198 Jonas Junkka .08 .20
199 Mikko Ilkka .08 .20
200 Pauli Levokari .08 .20
201 Kari Rajala .08 .20
202 Joonas Vihko .08 .20
203 Carlo Grunn .08 .20
204 Jonni Vauhkonen .20 .50
205 Mika Kortelainen .08 .20
206 Kimmo Salminen .08 .20
207 Aigars Cipruss .08 .20
208 Ilkka Pikkarainen .08 .20
209 Andrej Podkonicky .20 .50
210 Kim Hirschovits .08 .20
211 HPK Hameenlinna .04 .10
212 Zdenek Smid .20 .50
213 Hannu Toivonen ERC 1.25 3.00
214 Joni Puurula .08 .20
215 Vladimir Sicak .08 .20
216 Janne Juppo .08 .20
217 Sebastian Sulku .08 .20
218 Markus Kankaanpera .20 .50
219 Marko Tuulola .08 .20
220 Tuukka Makela .40 1.00
221 Erkki Rajamaki .08 .20
222 Olli Sillanpaa .08 .20
223 Vladimir Vujtek .08 .20
224 Tomas Kucharcik .08 .20
225 Harri Suutarinen .08 .20
226 Jarkko Savijoki .08 .20
227 Zdenek Nedved .08 .20
228 Janne Lahti .08 .20
229 Ilves Tampere .04 .10
230 Bruce Racine .20 .50
231 Juha Pitkamaki .08 .20
232 Kari Takko .20 .50
233 Ville Koistinen .08 .20
234 Arto Tukio .20 .50
235 Teemu Jaaskelainen .08 .20
236 Ivan Majesky .20 .50
237 Roman Vopat .08 .20
238 Tommi Miettinen .20 .50
239 Riku Rahikainen .08 .20
240 Ville Hirvonen .08 .20
241 Tony Salmelainen .08 .20
242 Vesa Viitakoski .08 .20
243 Mika Nieminen .20 .50
244 Raimo Helminen .08 .20
245 Jokerit Helsinki .04 .10
246 Markus Helanen .08 .20
247 Jamie Ram .20 .50
248 Kari Lehtonen 4.00 10.00
249 Ari Vallin .08 .20
250 Pasl Saarlnen .08 .20
251 Tuomas Luotonen .08 .20
252 Ilkka Mikkola .08 .20
253 Tom Koivisto .08 .20
254 Olli Malmivaara .08 .20
255 Rob Cowie .20 .50
256 Alex Brooks .08 .20
257 Sean Bergenheim ERC .60 1.50
258 Antti Aalto .20 .50
259 Ville Peltonen .20 .50
260 Petri Pakaslahti .08 .20
261 Petri Varis .20 .50
262 Jussi Pesonen .08 .20
263 Frank Banham .20 .50
264 Pavel Rosa .20 .50
265 JYP Jyvaskyla .04 .10
266 Tero Leinonen .08 .20
267 Jani-Matti Loikala .08 .20
268 Martin Cech .08 .20
269 Sami Siltavirta .08 .20
270 Jyri Marttinen .08 .20
271 Petri Virolainen .08 .20
272 Angel Nikolov .20 .50
273 Olli Ahonen .08 .20
274 Jari Jaaskelainen .08 .20
275 Harri Sillgren .08 .20
276 Petr Ton .08 .20
277 Tomas Chlubna .08 .20
278 Oulun Karpat .04 .10
279 Markus Korhonen .20 .50
280 Kimmo Lotvonen .08 .20
281 Mikko Myllykoski .08 .20
282 Pekka Saarenheimo .08 .20
283 Mika Pyorala .08 .20
284 Tuomo Harjula .08 .20
285 Harri Korpela .08 .20
286 Janne Pesonen .08 .20
287 Juha-Pekka Haataja .08 .20
288 Sakari Palsola .08 .20
289 Lasse Pirjeta .08 .20
290 Jussi Jokinen ERC 2.00 5.00
291 Rauman Lukko .04 .10
292 Petri Vehanen .08 .20
293 Jaakko Harikkala .08 .20
294 Mikko Purontakanen .08 .20
295 Ville Piekkola .20 .50
296 Janne Niskala .08 .20
297 Teemu Kesa .08 .20
298 Jaakko Hagelberg .08 .20
299 Jari Hyvarinen .08 .20
300 Mika Viinanen .08 .20
301 Joel Salonen .08 .20
302 Teemu Normio .08 .20
303 Hermani Vidman .08 .20
304 Aki Uusikartano .08 .20
305 Pasi Saarela .08 .20
306 Markus Jamsa .08 .20
307 Lahden Pelicans .04 .10
308 Mikko Ramo .08 .20
309 Kalle Koskinen .08 .20
310 Jussi-Antti Reimari .08 .20
311 Veli-Pekka Laitinen .08 .20
312 Henri Laurila .08 .20
313 Teemu Viherva .08 .20
314 Jussi Saarinen .08 .20
315 Olli Sinkkonen .08 .20
316 Jarkko Vaananen .08 .20
317 Jarkko Ollikainen .08 .20
318 Joonas Jaaskelainen .20 .50
319 Niki Siren .08 .20
320 Tommi Turunen .08 .20
321 Toni Koivunen .08 .20
322 SaiPa Lappeenranta .04 .10
323 Juha Kuokkanen .08 .20
324 Sami Lehtinen .20 .50
325 Tomas Duba .08 .20
326 Antti Hulkkonen .08 .20
327 Juha Pursiainen .08 .20
328 Jan Huokko .08 .20
329 Ville Immonen .08 .20
330 Mikko Kinnunen .08 .20
331 Mika Skytta .08 .20
332 Juuso Vakkilainen .08 .20
333 Jesse Welling .08 .20
334 Ville Koho .08 .20
335 Tappara Tampere .04 .10
336 Tom Draper .20 .50
337 Tuukka Mantyla .20 .50
338 Pasi Puistola .08 .20
339 Jyrki Valivaara .08 .20
340 Janne Gronvall .08 .20
341 Esa Pirnes .08 .20
342 Christian Sjogren .08 .20
343 Marko Makinen .08 .20
344 Sami Venalainen .08 .20
345 Janne Ojanen .08 .20
346 Tuomas Reijonen .08 .20
347 Jani Hassinen .08 .20
348 TPS Turku .04 .10
349 Fredrik Norrena .20 .50
350 Matti Tahkapaa .08 .20
351 Marko Kauppinen .20 .50
352 Pasi Petrilainen .08 .20
353 Pekka Kangasalusta .08 .20
354 Markku Paukkunen .08 .20
355 Chris Joseph .20 .50
356 Peter Schaefer .20 .50
357 Kai Nurminen .20 .50
358 Miika Elomo .20 .50
359 Janne Jokila .08 .20
360 Mikko Kankaanpera .08 .20
361 Tommi Hannus .08 .20
362 Mika Alatalo .20 .50
363 Rob Shearer .20 .50
364 Jani Kiviharju .08 .20
365 Porin Assat .04 .10
366 Tommi Satosaari .08 .20
367 Matti Jarvinen .08 .20
368 Mika Rontti .08 .20
369 Timo Willman .08 .20
370 Stanislav Jasecko .08 .20
371 Jukka-Pekka Laamanen .08 .20
372 Timo Ahmaoja .08 .20
373 Tapio Sammalkangas .08 .20
374 Jan Lipiansky .08 .20
375 Jani Vaananen .08 .20
376 Jarkko Immonen .08 .20
377 Sandy Moger .20 .50
378 Marko Palo .08 .20
379 Semir Ben-Amor .08 .20
380 Samu Wesslin .08 .20
NNO Jari Kurri HOF 8.00 20.00
NNO Mikko Koivu AU 30.00 80.00
NNO Antero Niittymaki AU 12.00 30.00
NNO Tuomo Ruutu AU 25.00 60.00
NNO Ville Nieminen DREAM 2.00 5.00
NNO Kari Lehtonen AU 60.00 125.00

2001-02 Finnish Cardset Adrenaline Rush

This set features some of the top young talent in Finland's SM-Liiga. The odds for these series 1 inserts is not confirmed at this time.

COMPLETE SET (6) 16.00 35.00
RANDOM INSERTS IN SERIES 1 PACKS
1 Kari Lehtonen 6.00 15.00
2 Tero Maatta 1.25 3.00
3 Tuukka Mantyla 1.25 3.00
4 Tony Salmelainen 1.25 3.00
5 Mikko Koivu 4.00 10.00
6 Tuomo Ruutu 4.00 10.00

2001-02 Finnish Cardset Dueling Aces

This set features a pair of arch-enemies from the Finnish SM-Liiga. The cards were random inserts in series 2 packs. The exact odds of insertion are not confirmed at this time.

COMPLETE SET (8) 6.00 15.00
RANDOM INSERTS IN SERIES 2 PACKS
1 Joonas Jaaskelainen .75 2.00
Vladimir Machulda
2 Ville Peltonen 1.25 3.00
Janne Ojanen
3 Jan Caloun .75 2.00
Kai Nurminen
4 Toni Happola .75 2.00
Mika Viinanen
5 Vladimir Vujtek .75 2.00
Raimo Helminen
6 Petr Ton .75 2.00
Pavel Rosa
7 Marek Zidlicky .75 2.00
Jiri Vykoukal
8 Tom Draper 1.25 3.00
Jari Korpisalo

2001-02 Finnish Cardset Haltmeisters

This set features the top Finnish-born goaltenders, many of whom were employed in North America during this season. The odds on these series 1 inserts are unconfirmed at this time.

COMPLETE SET (12) 30.00 75.00
RANDOM INSERTS IN SERIES 1 PACKS
1 Pasi Nurminen 4.00 10.00
2 Miikka Kiprusoff 6.00 15.00
3 Jani Hurme 4.00 10.00
4 Vesa Toskala 4.00 10.00
5 Mika Noronen 4.00 10.00
6 Jarmo Myllys 2.00 5.00
7 Ari Sulander 2.00 5.00
8 Ari Ahonen 4.00 10.00
9 Jussi Markkanen 4.00 10.00
10 Fredrik Norrena 2.00 5.00
11 Sakari Lindfors 2.00 5.00
12 Pasi Kuivalainen 2.00 5.00

2001-02 Finnish Cardset Salt Lake City

This set features 12 members of Finland's Olympic team. The cards were inserted in series 2 packs. The odds of insertion cannot be confirmed at this time.

COMPLETE SET (12) 20.00 30.00
RANDOM INSERTS IN SERIES 2 PACKS
1 Jani Hurme 1.25 3.00
2 Miikka Kiprusoff 3.00 8.00
3 Teppo Numminen .75 2.00
4 Kimmo Timonen .75 2.00
5 Janne Niinimaa .75 2.00
6 Jyrki Lumme .75 2.00
7 Teemu Selanne 4.00 10.00
8 Juha Ylonen .75 2.00
9 Jere Lehtinen 1.25 3.00
10 Tomi Kallio .75 2.00
11 Raimo Helminen .75 2.00
12 Sami Kapanen 1.25 3.00

2002-03 Finnish Cardset

This set was issued in two series and features the top players of the SM-Liiga.

COMPLETE SET (300) 30.00 80.00
1 Peter Ahola .08 .20
2 Mika Alatalo .08 .20
3 Kristian Antila .08 .20
4 Frank Banham .25 .60
5 Jaroslav Bednar .25 .60
6 Jan Benda .08 .20
7 Frantisek Bombic .08 .20
8 Jan Caloun .08 .20
9 Martin Cech .08 .20
10 Tomas Chlubna .08 .20
11 Toni Dahlman .08 .20
12 Johan Davidsson .08 .20
13 Tom Draper .25 .60
14 Tomas Duba .08 .20
15 Miika Elomo .25 .60
16 Mikko Eloranta .25 .60
17 Vjatsheslav Fandul .08 .20
18 Theo Fleury .40 1.00
19 Janne Gronvall .08 .20
20 Kari Haakana .08 .20
21 Niklas Hagman .25 .60
22 Riku Hahl .40 1.00
23 Jaakko Harikkala .25 .60
24 Jani Hassinen .08 .20
25 Timo Hirvonen .08 .20
26 Sasu Hovi .08 .20
27 Markku Hurme .08 .20
28 Ville Immonen .08 .20
29 Otakar Janecky .25 .60
30 Olli Jokinen .25 .60
31 Martti Jarventie .25 .60
32 Erik Kakko .08 .20
33 Tomi Kallio .25 .60
34 Kimmo Kapanen .08 .20
35 Niko Kapanen .25 .60
36 Sami Kapanen .25 .60
37 Jari Kauppila .08 .20
38 Markus Ketterer .25 .60
39 Marko Kiprusoff .08 .20
40 Miikka Kiprusoff .40 1.00
41 Tom Koivisto .25 .60
42 Markus Korhonen .25 .60
43 Jari Korpisalo .08 .20
44 Mika Kortelainen .08 .20
45 Kimmo Koskenkorva .08 .20
46 Valeri Krykov .08 .20
47 Kimmo Kuhta .08 .20
48 Pasi Kuivalainen .25 .60
49 Jarno Kultanen .08 .20
50 Mikko Kuparinen .08 .20
51 Jari Kurri .40 1.00
52 Jarmo Kuusisto .08 .20
53 Juri Kuznetsov .08 .20
54 Arto Laatikainen .25 .60
55 Veli-Pekka Laitinen .08 .20
56 Peter Larsson .08 .20
57 Mikko Lehtonen .08 .20
58 Pertti Lehtonen .08 .20
59 Jari Levonen .08 .20
60 Brett Lievers .08 .20
61 Juha Lind .08 .20
62 Sakari Lindfors .25 .60
63 Kimmo Lotvonen .08 .20
64 Jyrki Lumme .25 .60
65 Petri LA¤tti .08 .20
66 Vladimir Machulda .08 .20
67 Ivan Majesky .25 .60
68 Olli Malmivaara .08 .20
69 Jussi Markkanen .25 .60
70 Kari Martikainen .08 .20
71 Dale McTavish .08 .20
72 Sami Mettovaara .08 .20
73 Antti Miettinen 3.00 8.00
74 Niko Mikkola .08 .20
75 Cory Murphy .08 .20
76 Jason Muzzatti .25 .60
77 Tuukka Makela .25 .60
78 Marko MA¤kinen .25 .60
79 David Nemirovsky .08 .20
80 Ville Nieminen .25 .60
81 Antero Niittymaki .40 1.00
82 Angel Nikolov .08 .20
83 Janne Niskala .25 .60
84 Fredrik Norrena .25 .60
85 Petteri Nummelin .25 .60
86 Kai Nurminen .25 .60
87 Janne Ojanen .08 .20
88 Mika Oksa .08 .20
89 Petri Pakaslahti .08 .20
90 Mikko Peltola .08 .20
91 Kimmo Peltonen .08 .20
92 Pasi Peltonen .08 .20
93 Tomi Pettinen .08 .20
94 Tuomas Pihlman .40 1.00
95 Ilkka Pikkarainen .08 .20
96 Lasse Pirjeta .08 .20
97 Esa Pirnes .08 .20
98 Andrei Potaitshuk .08 .20
99 Pasi Puistola .08 .20
100 Joni Puurula .40 1.00
101 Timo Parssinen .08 .20
102 Bruce Racine .25 .60
103 Brian Rafalski .25 .60
104 Jamie Ram .25 .60
105 Martin Richter .25 .60
106 Juha Riihijarvi .08 .20
107 Teemu Riihijarvi .08 .20
108 Kimmo Rintanen .08 .20
109 Pavel Rosa .08 .20
110 Boris Rousson .25 .60
111 Christian Ruuttu .08 .20
112 Pasi Saarela .08 .20
113 Peter Schaefer .08 .20
114 Markus Seikola .08 .20
115 Teemu Selanne .75 2.00
116 Oliver Setzinger .25 .60
117 Vladimir Sicak .08 .20
118 Ari-Pekka Siekkinen .08 .20
119 Toni Sihvonen .08 .20
121 Ari Sulander .25 .60
122 Sebastian Sulku .08 .20
123 Mike Stapleton .08 .20
123 Kari Takko .25 .60
124 Jussi Tarvainen .08 .20
125 Esa Tikkanen .25 .60
126 Harri Tikkanen .08 .20
127 Petr Ton .08 .20
128 Vesa Toskala .25 .60
129 Arto Tukio .08 .20
130 Tommi Turunen .08 .20
131 Marko Tuulola .08 .20
132 Markku TA¤htinen .08 .20
133 Antti Tormanen .08 .20
134 Ville Vahalahti .08 .20
135 Ari Vallin .08 .20
136 Petri Varis .25 .60
137 Timo Vertala .08 .20
138 Joonas Vihko .08 .20
139 Mika Viinanen .08 .20
140 Vesa Viitakoski .08 .20
141 Tony Virta .08 .20
142 Tomas Vlasak .08 .20
143 Pavel Vostrak .08 .20
144 Vladimir Vujtek .08 .20
145 Jiri Vykoukal .08 .20
146 Marek Zidlicky .08 .20
147 Kari Lehtonen CL 2.50 6.00
148 Niklas Backstrom CL .08 .20
149 Petri Vehanen CL .08 .20
150 Tomas Duba CL .08 .20
151 Antti Aalto .25 .60
152 Teemu Aalto .08 .20
153 Ari Ahonen .75 2.00
154 Rami Alanko .08 .20
155 Drew Bannister .08 .20
156 Aleksander Barkov .08 .20
157 Aki Berg .25 .60
158 Sean Bergenheim .25 .60
159 Tom Bissett .25 .60
160 Niklas Backstrom .08 .20
161 Aigars Cipruss .08 .20
162 Parris Duffus .25 .60
163 Jason Elliott .25 .60
164 Teemu Elomo .08 .20
165 Jarkko Glad .08 .20
166 Carlo Grunn .08 .20
167 Tuomas Gronman .08 .20
168 Juha Gustafsson .08 .20
169 Timo Hakanen .08 .20
170 Quinn Hancock .08 .20
171 Markus Helanen .08 .20
172 Raimo Helminen .08 .20
173 Jukka Hentunen .08 .20
174 Michael Holmkvist .25 .60
175 Antti Hulkkonen .08 .20
176 Jani Hurme .40 1.00
177 Hannes Hyvonen .25 .60
178 Erik Hamalainen .08 .20
179 Toni Happola .08 .20
180 Juha Ikonen .08 .20
181 Jarkko Immonen .08 .20
182 Mikko Jokela .25 .60
183 Jussi Jokinen .40 1.00
184 Timo Jutila .08 .20
185 Lasse Jamsen .08 .20
186 Joonas Jaaskelainen .08 .20
187 Matti Kaipainen .08 .20
188 Robert Kantor .08 .20
189 Jere Karalahti .08 .20
190 Marko Kauppinen .08 .20
191 Mika Kauppinen .08 .20
192 Jani Keinanen .08 .20
193 Max Kenig .08 .20
194 Esa Keskinen .08 .20
195 Jani Kiviharju .08 .20
196 Toni Koivisto .08 .20
197 Mikko Koivu 2.00 5.00
198 Saku Koivu 1.25 3.00
199 Toni Koivunen .08 .20
200 Tomas Kucharcik .08 .20
201 Arto Kuki .08 .20
202 Lasse Kukkonen .08 .20
203 Juha Kuokkanen .08 .20
204 Janne Laakkonen .08 .20
205 Antii Laaksonen .25 .60
206 Jukka-Pekka Laamanen .08 .20
207 Scott Langkow .25 .60
208 Jan Latvala .08 .20
209 Janne Laukkanen .08 .20
210 Jari Laukkanen .08 .20
211 Tero Lehtera .25 .60
212 Jere Lehtinen .40 1.00
213 Mika Lehto .08 .20
214 Kari Lehtonen 5.00 12.00
215 Tero Leinonen .08 .20
216 Pauli Levokari .08 .20
217 Joni Lius .08 .20
218 Jouni Loponen .08 .20
219 Mikko Luoma .08 .20
220 Toni Lydman .08 .20
221 Jyri Marttinen .08 .20
222 Ilkka Mikkola .08 .20
223 Mikko Myllykoski .08 .20
224 Jere Myllyniemi .08 .20
225 Jarmo Myllys .25 .60
226 Toni Makiaho .08 .20
227 Tuuka Mantyla .08 .20
228 Tero Maatta .25 .60
229 Antti-Jussi Niemi .08 .20
230 Mika Nieminen .08 .20
231 Janne Niinimaa .25 .60
232 Jesse Niinimaki .40 1.00
233 Tuomas Nissinen .08 .20
234 Mika Noronen .40 1.00
235 Teppo Numminen .25 .60
236 Pasi Nurminen .25 .60
237 Michael Nylander .25 .60
238 Matti Naatanen .08 .20
239 Marko Ojanen .08 .20
240 Marko Palo .08 .20
241 Sakari Palsola .08 .20
242 Jan Pardavy .08 .20
243 Timo Peltomaa .08 .20
244 Ville Peltonen .08 .20
245 Eric Perrin .08 .20
246 Jussi Pesonen .08 .20
247 Pasi Petrilainen .08 .20
248 Juha Pitkamaki .08 .20
249 Joni Pitkanen 1.25 3.00
250 Toni Porkka .08 .20
251 Mika Pyorala .08 .20
252 Erkki Rajamaki .08 .20
253 Jani Rita .25 .60
254 Jarkko Ruutu .25 .60
255 Mikko Ruutu .40 1.00
256 Tuomo Ruutu 1.00 2.50
257 Mikko Ramo .08 .20
258 Timo Saarikoski .08 .20
259 Pasi Saarinen .08 .20
260 Kalle Sahlstedt .08 .20
261 Teemu Sainomaa .08 .20
262 Tony Salmelainen .08 .20
263 Sami Salo .25 .60
264 Timo Salonen .08 .20
265 Tommi Santala .08 .20
266 Peter Sarno .25 .60
267 Tommi Satosaari .08 .20
268 Steve Shirreffs .08 .20
269 Harri Sillgren .08 .20
270 Roman Simicek .08 .20
271 Eero Somervuori .25 .60
272 Dave Stathos .08 .20
273 Mika Stromberg .25 .60
274 Raimo Summanen .25 .60
275 Henrik Tallinder .25 .60
276 Petr Tenkrat .25 .60
277 Tim Thomas .40 1.00
278 Kimmo Timonen .08 .20
279 Pekka Tirkkonen .08 .20
280 Hannu Toivonen 1.00 2.50
281 Sami Torkki .08 .20
282 Marco Tuokko .08 .20
283 Marko Tuomainen .08 .20
284 Aki Uusikartano .08 .20
285 Lubomir Vaic .08 .20
286 Tomek Valtonen .08 .20
287 Petri Vehanen .08 .20
288 Samu Wesslin .08 .20
289 Hannu Virta .08 .20
290 Antii Virtanen .08 .20
291 Jari Viuhkola .08 .20
292 Roman Vopat .08 .20
293 Julkka Voutilainen .08 .20
294 Jyrki Valivaara .08 .20
295 Ossi Vaananen .25 .60
296 Juha Ylonen .25 .60
297 Dave Stathos .08 .20
298 Scott Langkow .25 .60
299 Tero Leinonen .08 .20
300 Mika Lehto .08 .20

2002-03 Finnish Cardset Bound for Glory

Random inserts in series two packs. Insertion odds unknown.

COMPLETE SET (10) 12.00 30.00
1 Sean Bergenheim .75 2.00
2 Jussi Jokinen 1.50 4.00
3 Mikko Koivu 3.00 8.00
4 Kari Lehtonen 4.00 10.00
5 Jesse Niinimaki .40 1.00
6 Joni Pitkanen 1.25 3.00
7 Tuomo Ruutu 2.00 5.00
8 Oliver Setzinger .40 1.00
9 Jussi Timonen .75 2.00
10 Hannu Toivonen 2.00 5.00

2002-03 Finnish Cardset Dynamic Duos

Randomly inserted in series 2 packs. Insertion ratios unknown.

COMPLETE SET (10) 15.00 40.00
1 Saku Koivu 4.00 10.00
Mikko Koivu
2 Pasi Nurminen 4.00 10.00
Kari Lehtonen
3 Sami Kapanen 2.00 5.00
Tuomo Ruutu
4 Janne Niinimaa 1.25 3.00
Joni Pitkanen
5 Olli Jokinen 1.25 3.00
Jukka Voutilainen
6 Ville Nieminen 1.25 3.00
Tuukka Mantyla
7 Tomi Kallio 1.25 3.00
Tuomas Pihlman
8 Jani Hurme 1.25 3.00
Tomas Duba
9 Niko Kapanen 2.00 5.00
Antti Miettinen
10 Teemu Selanne 4.00 10.00
Sean Bergenheim

2002-03 Finnish Cardset Kari Lehtonen Honors

Random inserts in series 2 packs. Odds unconfirmed, but believed to be 1:64.

COMPLETE SET (3) 10.00 25.00
1 Kari Lehtonen 4.00 10.00
U-18 top goalie
2 Kari Lehtonen 4.00 10.00
U-18 All-Stars
3 Kari Lehtonen 4.00 10.00
{U-20 top goalie

2002-03 Finnish Cardset Kari Lehtonen Trophies

Random inserts in series 1 packs. Odds were 1:64.

COMPLETE SET (3) 10.00 25.00
1 Kari Lehtonen 4.00 10.00
2 Kari Lehtonen 4.00 10.00
3 Kari Lehtonen 4.00 10.00

2002-03 Finnish Cardset Signatures

STATED ODDS 1:128 SERIES 1
STATED PRINT RUN 120 SER.#'d SETS
1 Sean Bergenheim 10.00 25.00
2 Jussi Jokinen 15.00 40.00
3 Mikko Koivu 20.00 50.00
4 Kari Lehtonen 100.00 200.00
5 Jesse Niinimaki

25.00

2002-03 Finnish Cardset Signatures

6 Joni Pitkanen 20.00 50.00
7 Tuomo Ruutu 25.00 60.00
8 Oliver Setzinger 10.00 25.00
9 Jussi Timonen 10.00 25.00
10 Hannu Toivonen 15.00 40.00

2002-03 Finnish Cardset Solid Gold

COMPLETE SET (6) 6.00 15.00
STATED ODDS 1:16 SERIES 1
1 Pasi Nurminen .75 2.00
2 Janne Niinimaa .75 2.00
3 Sami Salo .75 2.00
4 Sami Kapanen .75 2.00
5 Saku Koivu 2.00 5.00
6 Teemu Selanne 2.00 5.00

2002-03 Finnish Cardset Solid Gold Six-Pack

Randomly inserted in series 2 packs. Insertion ratios unknown.

COMPLETE SET (6) 3.00 8.00
1 Jussi Markkanen 1.25 3.00
2 Toni Lydman .40 1.00
3 Ossi Vaananen .40 1.00
4 Niklas Hagman .40 1.00
5 Olli Jokinen 1.25 3.00
6 Niko Kapanen 1.25 3.00

2003-04 Finnish Cardset

COMPLETE SET (182) 20.00 40.00
1 Jere Myllyniemi .20 .50
2 Sami Heinonen .20 .50
3 Sebastien Sulku .08 .20
4 Tero Maatta .08 .20
5 Rami Alanko .08 .20
6 Arto Laatikainen .08 .20
7 Jan Caloun .08 .20
8 Markku Hurme .08 .20
9 Jukka Tiilikainen .08 .20
10 Ladislav Kohn .08 .20
11 Miika Elomo .08 .20
12 Bruce Gardiner .20 .50
13 Marko Tuomainen .08 .20
14 Teemu Elomo .08 .20
15 Dave Stathos .30 .75
16 Ladislav Benysek .08 .20
17 Jere Karalahti .08 .20
18 Jarno Kultanen .08 .20
19 Toni Soderholm .08 .20
20 Pasi Saarinen .08 .20
21 Kim Hirschovits .08 .20
22 Kimmo Kuhta .08 .20
23 Joonas Vihko .08 .20
24 Toni Happola .08 .20
25 Carlo Grunn .08 .20
26 Timo Parssinen .20 .50
27 Brett Harkins .20 .50
28 Martin Spanhel .08 .20
29 Joni Puurula .20 .50
30 Rob Tallas .20 .50
31 Vladimir Sicak .08 .20
32 Aki Heino .08 .20
33 Tomas Eskeleinen .08 .20
34 Marko Tuulola .08 .20
35 Teemu Aalto .08 .20
36 Jyrki Louhi .08 .20
37 Tony Virta .08 .20
38 Vladimir Vujtek .08 .20
39 Tomas Kucharcik .08 .20
40 Janne Laakkonen .08 .20
41 Janne Lahti .08 .20
42 Anders Burstrom .08 .20
43 Juha Pitkamaki .20 .50
44 Tuomas Nissinen .20 .50
45 Cory Murphy .08 .20
46 Ismo Siren .08 .20
47 Martin Hlavacka .08 .20
48 Jukka-Pekka Laamanen .08 .20
49 Jesse Niinimaki .30 .75
50 Ville Snellman .08 .20
51 Toni Dahlman .08 .20
52 Erkki Rajamaki .08 .20
53 Marek Vorel .08 .20
54 Mikko Suvanto .08 .20
55 Vesa Viitakoski .08 .20
56 Raimo Helminen .08 .20
57 Markus Helanen .20 .50
58 Pasi Hakkinen .20 .50
59 Sami Helenius .20 .50
60 Jan Latvala .08 .20
61 Martti Jarventie .20 .50
62 Arto Tukio .08 .20
63 Tomek Valtonen .08 .20
64 Petri Pakaslahti .08 .20
65 Jussi Pesonen .08 .20
66 Timo Vertala .08 .20
67 Tommi Turunen .08 .20
68 Glen Metropolit .30 .75
69 Marko Jantunen .08 .20
70 Teemu Laine .08 .20
71 Tero Leinonen .20 .50
72 Tommi Nikkila .20 .50
73 Tuomo Kortelainen .08 .20
74 Tommi Kovanen .08 .20
75 Jari Korhonen .08 .20
76 Jyri Marttinen .08 .20
77 Ilari Filppula .08 .20
78 Tuomo Jaaskelainen .08 .20
79 Alexandre Tremblay .08 .20
80 Jari Jaaskelainen .08 .20
81 Jarkko Immonen .08 .20
82 Jaakko Uhlback .08 .20
83 Antti Virtanen .08 .20
84 P.C. Drouin .20 .50
85 Niklas Backstrom .30 .75
86 Ari Vallin .08 .20
87 Ilkka Mikkola .08 .20
88 Martin Stepanek .08 .20
89 Mikko Lehtonen .08 .20
90 Kimmo Lotvonen .08 .20
91 Mikko Myllykoski .08 .20
92 Jussi Jokinen .08 .20
93 Lasse Jamsen .08 .20
94 Mika Pyorala .08 .20
95 Janne Pesonen .08 .20
96 Brett Lievers .08 .20
97 Jari Viuhkola .08 .20
98 Sakari Palsola .08 .20
99 Antti Jokela .20 .50
100 Petri Vehanen .20 .50
101 Jaakko Harikkala .08 .20
102 Toni Porkka .08 .20
103 Janne Niskala .08 .20
104 Erik Hamalainen .08 .20
105 Mikko Luovi .08 .20
106 Mika Viinanen .08 .20
107 Toni Koivisto .08 .20
108 Sami Torkki .08 .20
109 Joe Murphy .20 .50
110 Markku Tahtinen .08 .20
111 Quinn Hancock .20 .50
112 Pasi Saarela .08 .20
113 Mikko Ramo .08 .20
114 Martin Cech .08 .20
115 Tero Paappanen .08 .20
116 Santeri Heiskanen .08 .20
117 Jermu Pisto .08 .20
118 Radek Philipp .08 .20
119 Tommi Hannus .08 .20
120 Daniel Widing .08 .20
121 Jari Kauppila .08 .20
122 Ville Hirvonen .08 .20
123 Toni Saarinen .08 .20
124 Toni Makiaho .08 .20
125 Shayne Toporowski .20 .50
126 Oliver Setzinger .20 .50
127 Juha Kuokkanen .08 .20
128 Jarmo Myllys .20 .50
129 Jussi Pekkala .08 .20
130 Petri Kokko .08 .20
131 Antti Bruun .08 .20
132 Sami Kaartinen .08 .20
133 Ville Immonen .08 .20
134 Kalle Kerman .08 .20
135 Mika Kauppinen .08 .20
136 Vladimir Machulda .08 .20
137 Pasi Nielikainen .08 .20
138 Petr Sachl .08 .20
139 Aki Uusikartano .08 .20
140 Timo Hirvonen .08 .20
141 Sasu Hovi .20 .50
142 Mika Lehto .20 .50
143 Pekka Saravo .08 .20
144 Pasi Puistola .08 .20
145 Pasi Petrilainen .08 .20
146 Miska Kangasniemi .08 .20
147 Janne Ojanen .08 .20
148 Aleksander Barkov .08 .20
149 Petri Varis .08 .20
150 Marko Ojanen .08 .20
151 Marko Makinen .08 .20
152 Sami Venalainen .08 .20
153 Stefan Ohman .08 .20
154 Arto Kuki .08 .20
155 Teemu Lassila .20 .50
156 Tuomo Karjalainen .20 .50
157 Kimmo Peltonen .08 .20
158 Marko Kauppinen .08 .20
159 David Schneider .08 .20
160 Jiri Vykoukal .08 .20
161 Antti Hulkkonen .08 .20
162 Mikko Koivu 1.25 3.00
163 Marko Tuokko .08 .20
164 Antti Aalto .08 .20
165 Kai Nurminen .08 .20
166 Ville Vahalahti .08 .20
167 Mikko Eloranta .08 .20
168 Niko Mikkola .08 .20
169 Scott Langkow .30 .75
170 Steve Shierreffs .20 .50
171 Pasi Peltonen .08 .20
172 Oleg Sorokin .08 .20
173 Jarkko Glad .08 .20
174 Samu Wesslin .08 .20
175 Vyacheslav Fandul .08 .20
176 Jari Korpisalo .08 .20
177 Pasi Tuominen .08 .20
178 Marko Kivenmaki .08 .20
179 Tomi Pollanen .08 .20
180 Timo Salonen .08 .20
181 Juha Kiilholma .08 .20
182 Martin Bergeron .20 .50

2003-04 Finnish Cardset D-Day

Featuring Finnish prospects drafted highly by the NHL, these cards were inserted 1:8 packs.

COMPLETE SET (16) 15.00 40.00
DD1 Sean Bergenheim .75 2.00
DD2 Mikael Holmqvist .75 2.00
DD3 Lasse Kukkonen .75 2.00
DD4 Kari Lehtonen 5.00 12.00
DD5 Mikko Luoma .40 1.00
DD6 Antti Miettinen .75 2.00
DD7 Eric Perrin 1.25 3.00
DD8 Tuomas Pihlman .75 2.00
DD9 Ilkka Pikkarainen .40 1.00
DD10 Esa Pirnes .40 1.00
DD11 Joni Pitkanen 1.25 3.00
DD12 Tuomo Ruutu 3.00 8.00
DD13 Tomi Santala .40 1.00
DD14 Eero Somervuori .40 1.00
DD15 Hannu Toivonen 3.00 8.00
DD16 Marek Zidlicky 1.25 3.00

2003-04 Finnish Cardset Globetrotters

These cards were inserted 1:16.

COMPLETE SET (9) 6.00 15.00
GR1 Toni Dahlman .75 2.00
GR2 Mikko Eloranta .75 2.00
GR3 Sami Helenius .75 2.00
GR4 Marko Jantunen .75 2.00
GR5 Jere Karalahti .75 2.00
GR6 Martin Stepanek .75 2.00
GR7 Petri Varis .75 2.00
GR8 Tony Virta .75 2.00
GR9 Vladimir Vujtek .75 2.00

2003-04 Finnish Cardset Vintage 1983

Featuring three top prospects born in 1983, these cards were inserted 1:32.

COMPLETE SET (3) 10.00 25.00
V1 Mikko Koivu 6.00 15.00
V2 Joni Pitkanen 2.00 5.00
V3 Tuomo Ruutu 4.00 10.00

2004-05 Finnish Cardset

Includes cards from a 200-card main set plus a 117-card update series.

COMPLETE SET (317) 30.00 60.00
1 Jere Myllyniemi .20 .50
2 Mika Oksa .20 .50
3 Kari Haakana .08 .20
4 Arto Laatikainen .08 .20
5 Mika Lehtinen .08 .20
6 Landon Wilson .20 .50
7 Donald MacLean .20 .50
8 Krystofer Kolanos .20 .50
9 Joni Toykkala .08 .20
10 Olli Ahonen .08 .20
11 Ladislav Kohn .08 .20
12 Lauri Tukonen ERC 1.25 3.00
13 Teemu Elomo .08 .20
14 Dave Stathos .20 .50
15 Marek Zidlicky .20 .50
16 Jere Karalahti .08 .20
17 Jarno Kultanen .08 .20
18 Toni Soderholm .08 .20
19 Pasi Saarinen .08 .20
20 Kim Hirschovits .08 .20
21 Kimmo Kuhta .08 .20
22 Joonas Vihko .08 .20
23 Jarkko Ruutu .20 .50
24 Timo Parssinen .08 .20
25 Arttu Luttinen .08 .20
26 Lennart Petrell .08 .20
27 Brett Harkins .20 .50
28 Eetu Holma .08 .20
29 Roman Vopat .08 .20
30 Miika Wiikman .20 .50
31 Vladimir Sicak .20 .50
32 Tuomas Eskelinen .08 .20
33 Mikko Jokela .08 .20
34 Veli-Pekka Laitinen .08 .20
35 Tuukka Makela .08 .20
36 Jyrki Louhi .08 .20
37 Jani Hassinen .08 .20
38 Hannu Vaisanen .08 .20
39 Riku Hahl .20 .50
40 Jani Keinanen .08 .20
41 Janne Laakkonen .08 .20
42 Jani Rita .20 .50
43 Jukka Voutilainen .08 .20
44 Toni Makiaho .08 .20
45 Oliver Setzinger .20 .50
46 Juha Pitkamaki .08 .20
47 Tuukka Rask ERC 2.00 5.00
48 Ville Koistinen .08 .20
49 Cory Murphy .08 .20
50 Sami Helenius .20 .50
51 Ismo Kuoppala .08 .20
52 Jesse Niinimaki .20 .50
53 Marko Luomala .08 .20
54 Timo Peltomaa .08 .20
55 Ville Leino .08 .20
56 Steve Kariya .40 1.00
57 Patrik Stefan .20 .50
58 Jussi Pesonen .08 .20
59 Tommi Turunen .08 .20
60 Raimo Helminen .08 .20
61 Simo Vidgren .08 .20
62 Pasi Hakkinen .20 .50
63 Tim Thomas .40 1.00
64 Kevin Kantee .08 .20
65 Kari Martikainen .08 .20
66 Jan Latvala .08 .20
67 Sami Lepisto .08 .20
68 Martti Jarventie .08 .20
69 Marko Jantunen .08 .20
70 Tomek Valtonen .08 .20
71 Toni Dahlman .08 .20
72 Petri Pakaslahti .08 .20
73 Petri Varis .08 .20
74 Juha Lind .08 .20
75 Timo Vertala .08 .20
76 Quinn Hancock .08 .20
77 Glen Metropolit .20 .50
78 Valtteri Filppula ERC .50 1.25
79 Tommi Nikkila .20 .50
80 Sinuhe Wallinheimo .20 .50
81 Tommi Kovanen .08 .20
82 Duvie Westcott .20 .50
83 Jari Korhonen .08 .20
84 Ilari Filppula .08 .20
85 Arsi Piispanen .08 .20
86 Steve Martins .20 .50
87 Jarkko Immonen .20 .50
88 Janne Hauhtonen .08 .20
89 Jaakko Uhlback .08 .20
90 Antti Virtanen .08 .20
91 Niklas Backstrom .40 1.00
92 Oskari Korpikari .08 .20
93 Lasse Kukkonen .20 .50
94 Ari Vallin .08 .20
95 Mikko Lehtonen .20 .50
96 Janne Niinimaa .08 .20
97 Jussi Jokinen .40 1.00
98 Viktor Ujcik .08 .20
99 Pekka Saarenheimo .08 .20
100 Mika Pyorala .08 .20
101 Janne Pesonen .08 .20
102 Jari Viuhkola .08 .20
103 Toni Sihvonen .08 .20
104 Sakari Palsola .08 .20
105 Petr Tenkrat .08 .20
106 Eero Somervuori .08 .20
107 Michael Nylander .20 .50
108 Dwayne Roloson .75 2.00
109 Petri Vehanen .08 .20
110 Toni Porkka .08 .20
111 Tomi Pettinen .08 .20
112 Janne Niskala .08 .20
113 Otto Honkaheimo .08 .20
114 Erik Hamalainen .08 .20
115 Steve Larouche .20 .50
116 Esa Pirnes .08 .20
117 Ville Snellman .08 .20
118 Shayne Toporowski .08 .20
119 Martin Bartek .08 .20
120 Toni Koivisto .08 .20
121 Sami Torkki .08 .20
122 Markku Tahtinen .08 .20
123 Pasi Saarela .08 .20
124 Pasi Nurminen .20 .50
125 Santeri Heiskanen .08 .20
126 Topi Lehtonen .08 .20
127 Erik Kakko .08 .20
128 Daniel Widing .08 .20
129 Sami Salonen .08 .2
130 Lasse Jamsen .08 .2
131 Ville Hirvonen .08 .2
132 Toni Saarinen .08 .2
133 Jesse Saarinen .08 .2
134 Jesse Welling .08 .2
135 Toni Koivunen .08 .2
136 Jarmo Myllys .20 .5
137 Jussi Pekkala .08 .2
138 Jussi Timonen .08 .2
139 Olli Malmivaara .08 .2
140 Petri Kokko .08 .2
141 Justin D. Forrest .08 .2
142 Eetu Qvist .08 .2
143 Kalle Kerman .08 .2
144 Mika Kauppinen .08 .2
145 Petr Sachl .08 .2
146 Petteri Nokelainen ERC 1.25 3.0
147 Timo Hirvonen .08 .2
148 Frank Banham .20 .5
149 Ville Viitaluoma .08 .2
150 Mika Lehto .20 .5
151 Anssi Salmela .08 .2
152 Pekka Saravo .08 .2
153 Juha Gustafsson .08 .2
154 Pasi Puistola .08 .2
155 Robert Kantor .08 .2
156 Mikko Myllykoski .08 .2
157 Janne Ojanen .08 .2
158 Johannes Alanen .08 .2
159 Mika Viinanen .08 .2
160 Marko Ojanen .08 .2
161 Petri Kontiola .08 .2
162 Ville Nieminen .20 .5
163 Sami Venalainen .08 .2
164 Stefan Ohman .08 .2
165 Tomas Chlubna .08 .2
166 Teemu Laine .08 .2
167 Teemu Lassila .20 .5
168 Tuomo Karjalainen .08 .2
169 Marko Kiprusoff .08 .2
170 Kimmo Eronen .08 .2
171 Markus Seikola .08 .2
172 David Schneider .08 .2
173 Jiri Vykoukal .08 .2
174 Antti Hulkkonen .08 .2
175 Marco Tuokko .08 .2
176 Antti Aalto .08 .2
177 Joni Lius .08 .2
178 Kai Nurminen .08 .2
179 Ville Vahalahti .08 .2
180 Lauri Korpikoski ERC 1.25 3.0
181 Mika Alatalo .08 .2
182 Jari Kauppila .08 .2
183 Arttu Virtanen .08 .2
184 Tuomas Nissinen .08 .2
185 Scott Langkow .20 .5
186 Pasi Peltonen .08 .2
187 Olegs Sorokins .08 .2
188 Pauli Levokari .08 .2
189 Greg Classen .20 .5
190 Samu Wesslin .08 .2
191 Mika Niemi .08 .2
192 Jari Korpisalo .08 .2
193 Jesse Joensuu .08 .2
194 Pasi Tuominen .08 .2
195 Marko Kivenmaki .08 .2
196 Teemu Virkkunen .08 .2
197 Pasi Nielikainen .08 .2
198 Jason Williams .20 .5
199 Aki Uusikartano .08 .2
200 Juha Kiilholma .08 .2
201 Janne Jalasvaara .08 .2
202 Tommi Pelkonen .08 .2
203 Tero Maatta .08 .2
204 Antti Pihlstrom .08 .2
205 Miika Elomo .08 .2
206 Jarkko Almmonen .08 .2
207 Mike Ribeiro .20 .5
208 Matti Naatanen .08 .2
209 Jani Nieminen .08 .2
210 Tomas Vokoun .75 2.0
211 Mikko Turunen .08 .2
212 Mikko Kurvinen .08 .2
213 Hannu Pikkarainen .08 .2
214 Lasse Pirjeta .08 .2
215 Juha Fagerstedt .08 .2
216 Jermu PorthA¨n .08 .2
217 Mikko Laine .08 .2
218 Mika Noronen .20 .5
219 Jarno Virkki .08 .2
220 Tuomas Immonen .08 .2
221 Jukka-Pekka Laamanen .08 .2
222 Josh Holden .08 .2
223 Petteri Virtanen .08 .2
224 Joni Lappalainen .08 .2
225 Joni Lindlof .08 .2
226 Juha-Pekka Loikas .08 .2
227 Janne Lahti .08 .2
228 Juuso Riksman .08 .2
229 Teemu Jaaskelainen .08 .2
230 Henri Laurila .08 .2
231 Ossi Pellinen .08 .2
232 Antti Miettinen .40 1.0
233 Hannes Hyvonen .08 .2
234 Jukka Tiilikainen .08 .2
235 Tommi Jaminki .08 .2
236 Mikko Suvanto .08 .2
237 Samuli Jalkanen .08 .2
238 Brian Campbell .20 .5
239 Mikko Kalteva .08 .2
240 Markus Kankaanpera .08 .2
241 Tero Konttinen .08 .2
242 Ossi Vaananen .08 .2
243 Tomi Maki .08 .2
244 Arto Koivisto .08 .2
245 Arto Kuki .08 .2
246 Roni Andersson .08 .2
247 Teemu Kuusisto .08 .2
248 Petri Virolainen .08 .2
249 Ilkka Vaarasuo .08 .2
250 Carlo GrA¼nn .08 .2
251 Juha-Pekka Hytonen .08 .2
252 Jari Jaaskelainen .08 .2
253 Ossi Louhivaara .08 .2
254 Tuomas Mikkonen .08 .2
255 Eero Hyvarinen .08 .2
256 Jody Shelley .40 1.0
257 Pekka Rinne 4.00 10.0
258 Ilkka Mikkola .08 .2
259 Topi Jaakola .08 .2
260 Kimmo Lotvonen .08 .2
261 Josef Boumedienne .08 .2
262 Juha-Pekka Haataja .08 .2
263 Antti Aarnio .08 .2
264 Mikael Vuorio .08 .2
265 Jaakko Harikkala .08 .2
266 Antti Bruun .08 .2
267 Ilkka Saarela .08 .2
268 Jarkko Kauvosaari .08 .2
269 Teemu Normio .08 .2

70 Janne Siivonen .08 .20
71 Juhamatti Yli-Junnila .08 .20
72 Joni Yli-Torkko .08 .20
73 Jaakko Suomalainen .08 .20
74 Karri Ramo .08 .20
75 Markus Helanen .08 .20
76 Olli Korkeavuori .08 .20
77 Antti-Pekka Lamberg .08 .20
78 Mikko Niinikoski .08 .20
79 Petri Koskinen .08 .20
80 Tommi Hannus .08 .20
81 Tuomas Santavuori .08 .20
82 Juha Kuokkanen .08 .20
83 Thomas Innerwinkler .08 .20
84 Harri Tikkanen .08 .20
85 Matti Hana .08 .20
86 Ossi-Petteri Gronholm .08 .20
87 Mike Gabinet .08 .20
88 Kalle Kaijomaa .08 .20
89 Ville Koho .08 .20
90 Mika Skytta .08 .20
91 Tuomas Vanttinen .08 .20
92 Andrew Raycroft .60 1.50
93 Sasu Hovi .08 .20
94 Mikko Pukka .08 .20
95 Kimmo Koskenkorva .08 .20
96 Teemu Nurmi .08 .20
97 Robert Tomik .08 .20
98 Jarkko Pyymaki .08 .20
99 Marko Makinen .08 .20
00 Timo Vertala .08 .20
01 Juho Santanen .08 .20
02 Simon Backman .08 .20
03 Markku Paukkunen .08 .20
04 Craig Rivet .08 .20
05 Tomi Sykko .08 .20
06 Saku Koivu .75 2.00
07 Matias Metsaranta .08 .20
08 Markus Ojala .08 .20
09 Tyler Bouck .20 .50
10 Matti Aho .08 .20
11 Marko Toivonen .08 .20
12 Mika Rontti .08 .20
13 Atte Pentikainen .08 .20
14 Aki Heino .08 .20
15 Kristian Kuusela .08 .20
16 Matti Kuparinen .08 .20
17 Juha-Pekka Ketola .08 .20

2004-05 Finnish Cardset Parallel

X to 5X BASE CARD VALUE

2004-05 Finnish Cardset Saku Koivu Golden Signatures

Random inserts in series II packs.
COMPLETE SET (3) 10.00 25.00
Saku Koivu 4.00 10.00
Saku Koivu 4.00 10.00
Saku Koivu 4.00 10.00

2004-05 Finnish Cardset Signatures

Random inserts in series II packs. Inserted approximately one per box.
Joni Toykkala 8.00 20.00
Ladislav Kohn 8.00 20.00
Lauri Tukonen 12.00 30.00
Marek Zidlicky 12.00 30.00
Jere Karalahti 8.00 20.00
Jarno Kultanen 8.00 20.00
Brett Harkins 8.00 20.00
Vladimir Sicak 8.00 20.00
Tuomas Eskelinen 8.00 20.00
0 Riku Hahl 8.00 20.00
1 Jani Rita 8.00 20.00
2 Tuukka Rask 25.00 60.00
3 Jussi Pesonen 8.00 20.00
4 Simo Vidgren 8.00 20.00
5 Toni Dahlman 8.00 20.00
6 Valtteri Filppula 15.00 30.00
7 Duvie Westcott 12.00 30.00
8 Arsi Piispanen 8.00 20.00
9 Steve Martins 8.00 20.00
0 Jarkko Immonen 12.00 30.00
1 Niklas Backstrom 15.00 40.00
2 Jussi Jokinen 25.00 60.00
3 Dwayne Roloson 15.00 40.00
4 Esa Pirnes 8.00 20.00
5 Erik Kakko 8.00 20.00
6 Jarmo Myllys 8.00 20.00
7 Petteri Nokelainen 12.00 30.00
8 Frank Banham 12.00 30.00
9 Pekka Saravo 8.00 20.00
0 Pasi Puistola 8.00 20.00
1 Mikko Myllykoski 8.00 20.00
2 Petri Kontiola 8.00 20.00
3 Ville Nieminen 8.00 20.00
4 Marko Kiprusoff 8.00 20.00
5 David Schneider 8.00 20.00
6 Lauri Korpikoski 12.00 30.00
7 Olegs Sorokins 8.00 20.00
8 Mika Niemi 8.00 20.00
9 Jesse Joensuu 8.00 20.00
0 Teemu Virkkunen 8.00 20.00
1 Jason Williams 12.00 30.00

2004-05 Finnish Cardset Stars of the Game

COMPLETE SET (14) 10.00 25.00
Riku Hahl 1.25 3.00
Hannes Hyvonen .40 1.00
Jarkko Immonen 1.25 3.00
Scott Langkow .75 2.00
Teemu Lassila .40 1.00
Ville Nieminen .75 2.00
Janne Niinimaa .75 2.00
Mika Noronen 1.25 3.00
Pasi Nurminen 1.25 3.00
0 Michael Nylander .75 2.00
1 Jarkko Ruutu .75 2.00
2 Patrik Stefan .75 2.00
3 Tim Thomas 1.25 3.00
4 Marek Zidlicky .75 2.00

2004-05 Finnish Cardset Tribute to Koivu

Random inserts in series II packs.
COMPLETE SET (3) 10.00 25.00
Saku Koivu 4.00 10.00
Saku Koivu 4.00 10.00
Saku Koivu 4.00 10.00

2004-05 Finnish Cardset Tribute to Nieminen

COMMON CARD 1.25 3.00

2005 Finnish Tappara Legendat

COMPLETE SET (32) 10.00 25.00
Antti Leppanen .40 1.00
Seppo Liitsola .40 1.00
Aleksander Barkov .40 1.00
Jukka Porvari .40 1.00
Mikko Leinonen .40 1.00
6 Martti Jarkko .40 1.00
7 Kiira Korpi .40 1.00
8 Ville Nieminen .40 1.00
9 Esko Niemi .40 1.00
10 Teppo Numminen .40 1.00
11 Erkki Lehtonen .40 1.00
12 Jarl Ohlson .40 1.00
13 Timo Susi .40 1.00
14 Kiira Korpi .40 1.00
15 Timo Jutila .40 1.00
16 Hannu Kamppuri .75 2.00
17 Lasse Litma .40 1.00
18 Pertti Valkeapaa .40 1.00
19 Yrjo Hakala .40 1.00
20 Jouni Seistamo .40 1.00
21 Kiira Korpi .40 1.00
22 Pekka Marjamaki .40 1.00
23 Markus Mattsson .40 1.00
24 Seppo Ahokainen .40 1.00
25 Hannu Haapalainen .40 1.00
26 Esko Luostarinen .40 1.00
27 Pertti Koivulahti .40 1.00
28 Kiira Korpi .40 1.00
29 Janne Ojanen .40 1.00
30 Kalevi Numminen .40 1.00
31 Jukka Rautakorpi .40 1.00
32 Rauno Korpi .40 1.00

2005-06 Finnish Cardset

COMPLETE SET (352) 25.00 60.00
1 Janne Jalasvaara .10 .25
2 Kari Haakana .10 .25
3 Arto Laatikainen .10 .25
4 Joni TÃ¶ykkÃ¤lÃ¤ .10 .25
5 Olli Ahonen .10 .25
6 Ladislav Kohn .10 .25
7 Lauri Tukonen .20 .50
8 Mike Ribeiro .20 .50
9 Niko Nieminen .10 .25
10 Jan Lundell .10 .25
11 Marek Zidlicky .20 .50
12 Mikko Turunen .10 .25
13 Toni Lydman .10 .25
14 Mikko Kurvinen .10 .25
15 Pasi Saarinen .10 .25
16 Kim Hirschovits .10 .25
17 Joonas Vihko .10 .25
18 Toni HÃ¤ppÃ¶lÃ¤ .10 .25
19 Juha Fagerstedt .10 .25
20 Turo JÃ¤rvinen .10 .25
21 Arttu Luttinen .10 .25
22 Eetu Holma .10 .25
23 Olli Jokinen .20 .50
24 Mika Noronen .20 .50
25 Miika Wiikman .10 .25
26 Tuomas Immonen .10 .25
27 Mikko Jokela .10 .25
28 Veli-Pekka Laitinen .10 .25
29 Jyrki Louhi .10 .25
30 Petteri Wirtanen .10 .25
31 Joni Lappalainen .10 .25
32 Hannu VÃ¤isÃ¤nen .10 .25
33 Riku Hahl .10 .25
34 Jani KeinÃ¤nen .10 .25
35 Juha-Pekka Loikas .10 .25
36 Janne Lahti .10 .25
37 Oliver Setzinger .10 .25
38 Juha PitkÃ¤mÃ¤ki .10 .25
39 Vesa Toskala .40 1.00
40 Tuukka Rask 1.25 3.00
41 Joonas RÃ¶nnberg .10 .25
42 Ville Koistinen .20 .50
43 Ossi Pellinen .10 .25
44 Marko Anttila .10 .25
45 Marko Luomala .10 .25
46 Patrik Stefan .10 .25
47 Jussi Pesonen .10 .25
48 Raimo Helminen .10 .25
49 Simo Vidgren .10 .25
50 Pasi HÃ¤kkinen .10 .25
51 Tim Thomas .75 2.00
52 Brian Campbell .20 .50
53 Markus KankaanperÃ¤ .10 .25
54 Kevin Kantee .10 .25
55 Kari Martikainen .10 .25
56 Ossi VÃ¤Ã¤nÃ¤nen .10 .25
57 Martti JÃ¤rventie .10 .25
58 Tomi MÃ¤ki .10 .25
59 Toni Dahlman .10 .25
60 Petri Pakaslahti .10 .25
61 Petri Varis .10 .25
62 Teemu Kuusisto .10 .25
63 Tommi NikkilÃ¤ .10 .25
64 Tommi Kovanen .10 .25
65 Duvie Westcott .20 .50
66 Ilkka Vaarasuo .10 .25
67 Carlo Crunn .10 .25
68 Juha-Pekka HytÃ¶nen .10 .25
69 Arsi Piispanen .10 .25
70 Jari JÃ¤Ã¤skelÃ¤inen .10 .25
71 Ossi Louhivaara .10 .25
72 Tuomas Mikkonen .10 .25
73 Jarkko Immonen .20 .50
74 Antti Virtanen .10 .25
75 Ari Luostarinen .10 .25
76 Jermu Pisto .10 .25
77 Mikko Saavinen .10 .25
78 Samuli Suhonen .10 .25
79 Ville HÃ¤mÃ¤lÃ¤inen .10 .25
80 Tuomas Kiiskinen .10 .25
81 Henri Huohvanainen .10 .25
82 Sami Salonen .10 .25
83 Max Kenig .10 .25
84 Saku KekÃ¤lÃ¤inen .10 .25
85 Sami Kaartinen .10 .25
86 Timo Kuuluvainen .10 .25
87 Pekka Rinne .60 1.50
88 Oskari Korpikari .10 .25
89 Lasse Kukkonen .10 .25
90 Ilkka Mikkola .10 .25
91 Topi Jaakola .10 .25
92 Janne Niinimaa .10 .25
93 Jussi Jokinen .40 1.00
94 Viktor Ujcik .10 .25
95 Pekka Saarenheimo .10 .25
96 Mika PyÃ¶rÃ¤lÃ¤ .10 .25
97 Juha-Pekka Haataja .10 .25
98 Petr Tenkrat .10 .25
99 Antti Jokela .10 .25
100 Dwayne Roloson .40 1.00
101 Toni Porkka .10 .25
102 Antti Bruun .10 .25
103 Otto Honkaheimo .10 .25
104 Ilkka Heikkinen .10 .25
105 Tommi Hannus .10 .25
106 Ville Snellman .10 .25
107 Jarkko Kauvosaari .10 .25
108 Jaakko Hagelberg .10 .25
109 Teemu Normio .10 .25
110 Markku TÃ¤htinen .10 .25
111 Juhamatti Yli-Junnila .10 .25
112 Pasi Nurminen .15 .40
113 Olli Korkeavuori .10 .25
114 Kimmo Pikkarainen .10 .25
115 Santeri Heiskanen .10 .25
116 Matias Loppi .10 .25
117 Tuomas Santavuori .10 .25
118 Toni Sihvonen .10 .25
119 Henri Heino .10 .25
120 Marcus Paulsson .10 .25
121 Tommi Turunen .10 .25
122 Ville-Matti Koponen .10 .25
123 Jesse Saarinen .10 .25
124 Jussi Timonen .10 .25
125 Harri Tikkanen .10 .25
126 Olli Malmivaara .10 .25
127 Ossi-Petteri GrÃ¶nholm .10 .25
128 Petri Kokko .10 .25
129 Kalle Kaijomaa .10 .25
130 Ville Koho .10 .25
131 Teemu Paakkarinen .10 .25
132 Mika SkyttÃ¤ .10 .25
133 Tuomas VÃ¤nttinen .10 .25
134 Eetu Qvist .10 .25
135 Ville Viitaluoma .10 .25
136 Mikko Silvennoinen .10 .25
137 Mika Lehto .10 .25
138 Anssi Salmela .10 .25
139 Ville MÃ¤ntymaa .10 .25
140 Pasi Puistola .10 .25
141 Mikko Pukka .10 .25
142 Janne Ojanen .10 .25
143 Mika Viinanen .10 .25
144 Marko Ojanen .10 .25
145 Petri Kontiola .10 .25
146 Marko MÃ¤kinen .10 .25
147 Ville Nieminen .10 .25
148 Sami VenÃ¤lÃ¤inen .10 .25
149 Stefan Ã–hman .10 .25
150 Teemu Laine .10 .25
151 Juho Santanen .10 .25
152 Tuomo Karjalainen .10 .25
153 Marko Kiprusoff .10 .25
154 Kimmo Eronen .10 .25
155 Antti Hulkkonen .10 .25
156 Saku Koivu .40 1.00
157 Antti Aalto .10 .25
158 Kai Nurminen .10 .25
159 Ville Vahalahti .10 .25
160 Lauri Korpikoski .40 1.00
161 Jari Kauppila .10 .25
162 Arttu Virtanen .10 .25
163 Matti Aho .10 .25
164 Tuomas Nissinen .10 .25
165 Pasi Peltonen .10 .25
166 Marko Toivonen .10 .25
167 Kristian Kuusela .10 .25
168 Mika Niemi .10 .25
169 Matti Kuparinen .10 .25
170 Marko KivenmÃ¤ki .10 .25
171 Pasi NielikÃ¤inen .10 .25
172 Jason Williams .40 1.00
173 Aki Uusikartano .10 .25
174 Juha Kiilholma .10 .25
175 Neil Little .40 1.00
176 Matti Kaltiainen .10 .25
177 Tuomas Eskelinen .10 .25
178 Tero Maatta .10 .25
179 Kimmo Peltonen .10 .25
180 Joakim Eriksson .10 .25
181 Esa Pirnes .10 .25
182 Markku Hurme .10 .25
183 Pentti Noyranen .10 .25
184 Steve Kariya .40 1.00
185 Timo Hirvonen .10 .25
186 Jaakko Uhlback .10 .25
187 Kari Kalto .10 .25
188 Tom Askey .20 .50
189 Robert Schnabel .10 .25
190 Jere Karalahti .10 .25
191 Hannu Pikkarainen .10 .25
192 Patrik Lostedt .10 .25
193 Tony Salmelainen .20 .50
194 Miika Jouhkimainen .10 .25
195 Jermu Porthen .10 .25
196 Janne Hauhtonen .10 .25
197 Tobias Salmelainen .10 .25
198 Lennart Petrell .10 .25
199 Pasi Salonen .10 .25
200 Heikki Laine .10 .25
201 Juha Toivonen .10 .25
202 David Schneider .10 .25
203 Juuso Hietanen .10 .25
204 Jukka-Pekka Laamanen .10 .25
205 Kaspars Astashenko .10 .25
206 Jani Hassinen .10 .25
207 Jari Sailio .10 .25
208 Mikko Laine .10 .25
209 Antti Hilden .10 .25
210 Jukka Voutilainen .10 .25
211 Janis Sprukts .10 .25
212 Ville Leino .10 .25
213 Toni Niemi .10 .25
214 Jyrki Lumme .10 .25
215 Juha Alen .10 .25
216 Mikko Kuukka .10 .25
217 Jonas Andersson .10 .25
218 Perttu Lindgren .40 1.00
219 Ville Korhonen .10 .25
220 Tommi Huhtala .10 .25
221 Toni Koivisto .10 .25
222 Jason Guerriero .10 .25
223 Tomi Hirvonen .10 .25
224 Henrik Juntunen .10 .25
225 Vesa Viitakoski .10 .25
226 Joonas Hallikainen .10 .25
227 Samuli Jalkanen .10 .25
228 Mikko Kalteva .10 .25
229 Jan Latvala .10 .25
230 Sami Lepisto .10 .25
231 Tero Konttinen .10 .25
232 Tony Virta .10 .25
233 Marko Jantunen .10 .25
234 Tomek Valtonen .10 .25
235 Jesse Niinimaki .10 .25
236 Arto Koivisto .10 .25
237 Ilari Filppula .10 .25
238 Tommi Santala .10 .25
239 Arto Kuki .10 .25
240 Sinuhe Wallinheimo .20 .50
241 Miika Huczkowski .10 .25
242 Jaako Niskavaara .10 .25
243 Eerikki Koivu .10 .25
244 Juha Salmu .10 .25
245 Jyri Marttinen .10 .25
246 Johannes Alanen .10 .25
247 Filip Riska .10 .25
248 Miikka Mannikko .10 .25
249 Valtteri Tenkanen .10 .25
250 Lucas Lawson .10 .25
251 Tero Koponen .10 .25
252 Miika Lahti .10 .25
253 Juha Jaaskelainen .10 .25
254 Kimmo Kapanen .10 .25
255 Juha Alastalo .10 .25
256 Juho Kuronen .10 .25
257 Jussi Savolainen .10 .25
258 Matti Kuusisto .10 .25
259 Mikko Hakkarainen .10 .25
260 Jani Tuppurainen .10 .25
261 Tomi Pollanen .10 .25
262 Kasper Kenig .10 .25
263 Tomas Kurka .10 .25
264 Matti Tiihonen .10 .25
265 Niklas Backstrom .75 2.00
266 Mika Pietila .10 .25
267 Antti Ylonen .10 .25
268 Ari Vallin .10 .25
269 Mikko Lehtonen .15 .40
270 Jouni Loponen .10 .25
271 Janne Pesonen .10 .25
272 Tommi Paakkolanvaara .10 .25
273 Jari Viuhkola .10 .25
274 Mikko Alikoski .10 .25
275 Michal Bros .10 .25
276 Kalle Sahlstedt .10 .25
277 Juhamatti Aaltonen .10 .25
278 Tomi Mustonen .10 .25
279 Scott Langkow .20 .50
280 Topi Lehtonen .10 .25
281 Markku Paukkunen .10 .25
282 Tuukka Makela .10 .25
283 Pauli Levokari .10 .25
284 Erik Hamalainen .10 .25
285 Jamie Wright .10 .25
286 Petri Lammassaari .10 .25
287 Shayne Toporowski .10 .25
288 Miikka Tuomainen .10 .25
289 Pasi Saarela .10 .25
290 Joni Yli-Torkko .10 .25
291 Antti Niemi .10 .25
292 Esa Saksinen .10 .25
293 Sami Helenius .10 .25
294 Jarkko Glad .10 .25
295 Erik Kakko .10 .25
296 Kari Sihvonen .10 .25
297 Toni Koivunen .10 .25
298 Olli Julkunen .10 .25
299 Jussi Saarinen .10 .25
300 Lasse Jamsen .10 .25
301 Mikko Stromberg .10 .25
302 Rob Zepp .20 .50
303 Mikko Palomaki .10 .25
304 Juha Jokiraita .10 .25
305 Joni Tuominen .10 .25
306 Kristian Kudroc .10 .25
307 Antti Pihlstrom .10 .25
308 Kimmo Koskenkorva .10 .25
309 Jaska Vilen .10 .25
310 Morten Ask .10 .25
311 Jarkko Immonen .20 .50
312 Peter Nylander .10 .25
313 Janne Kolehmainen .10 .25
314 Teemu Seppanen .10 .25
315 Pekka Tuokkola .10 .25
316 Brian White .10 .25
317 Marko Kauppinen .10 .25
318 Tuukka Mantyla .10 .25
319 Jussi Halme .10 .25
320 Greg Hawgood .20 .50
321 Janne Gronvall .10 .25
322 Teemu Nurmi .10 .25
323 Jarkko Pyymaki .10 .25
324 Teemu Virkkunen .10 .25
325 Timo Vertala .10 .25
326 Quinn Hancock .10 .25
327 Mika Lehtinen .10 .25
328 Henri Palmroth .10 .25
329 Simon Backman .10 .25
330 Markus Seikola .10 .25
331 Tomi Sykko .10 .25
332 Joni Lius .10 .25
333 Jussi Makkonen .10 .25
334 Mika Alatalo .10 .25
335 Jarmo Jokila .10 .25
336 Daniel Widing .10 .25
337 Andreas Jamtin .10 .25
338 Tuukka Pulliainen .10 .25
339 Juuso Riksman .10 .25
340 Jussi Rynnas .10 .25
341 Justin Forrest .10 .25
342 Atte Pentikainen .10 .25
343 Matt Nickerson .20 .50
344 Jesse Saarinen .10 .25
345 Mikko Rautee .10 .25
346 Jesse Joensuu .20 .50
347 Tuomas Takala .10 .25
348 Rob Hisey .10 .25
349 Patrik Forsbacka .10 .25
350 Petteri Tasku .10 .25
351 Leo Komarov .10 .25
352 Matti Kaipainen .10 .25

2005-06 Finnish Cardset Magicmakers

COMPLETE SET (18) 15.00 40.00
STATED ODDS 1:4
1 Mike Ribeiro .75 2.00
2 Toni Lydman .75 2.00
3 Olli Jokinen 1.25 3.00
4 Jarkko Ruutu .75 2.00
5 Riku Hahl .75 2.00
6 Josh Holden .75 2.00
7 Steve Kariya 1.25 3.00
8 Patrik Stefan .75 2.00
9 Sami LepistÃ¶ .75 2.00
10 Ossi VÃ¤Ã¤nÃ¤nen .75 2.00
11 Valtteri Filppula 2.00 5.00
12 Jarkko Immonen 1.50 4.00
13 Jussi Jokinen 2.00 5.00
14 Jari Viuhkola .75 2.00
15 Ville Nieminen .75 2.00
16 Saku Koivu 2.00 5.00
17 Craig Rivet .75 2.00
18 Jason Williams 1.50 4.00

2005-06 Finnish Cardset Super Snatchers

COMPLETE SET (18) 20.00 50.00
STATED ODDS 1:4
1 Jan Lundell 1.25 3.00
2 Tomas Vokoun 2.50 6.00
3 Mika Noronen 1.25 3.00
4 Miika Wiikman 1.25 3.00
5 Juha PitkÃ¤mÃ¤ki 1.25 3.00
6 Vesa Toskala 2.50 6.00
7 Tim Thomas 2.50 6.00
8 Sinuhe Wallinheimo 1.25 3.00
9 Kimmo Kapanen 1.25 3.00
10 Niklas Backstrom 1.50 4.00
11 Dwayne Roloson 1.50 4.00
12 Pasi Nurminen 1.25 3.00
13 Jarmo Myllys 1.25 3.00
14 Andrew Raycroft 2.00 5.00
15 Mika Lehto 1.25 3.00
16 Tuomo Karjalainen 1.25 3.00
17 Teemu Lassila 1.25 3.00
18 Tuomas Nissinen 1.25 3.00

2006-07 Finnish Cardset

COMPLETE SERIES 1 (180) 40.00 80.00
1 Juha Gustafsson .20 .50
2 Tuomas Eskelinen .20 .50
3 Arto Laatikainen .20 .50
4 Kimmo Peltonen .20 .50
5 Jari Korhonen .20 .50
6 Markku Hurme .20 .50
7 Olli Ahonen .20 .50
8 Ladislav Kohn .20 .50
9 Erkki RajamÃ¤ki .20 .50
10 Mikko Lehtonen .20 .50
11 Pentti NÃ¶yrÃ¤nen .20 .50
12 Kari Kalto .20 .50
13 Jan Lundell .30 .75
14 Teemu Laakso .20 .50
15 Jere Karalahti .20 .50
16 Mikko Turunen .20 .50
17 Hannu Pikkarainen .20 .50
18 Tony Salmelainen .20 .50
19 Turo JÃ¤rvinen .20 .50
20 Jermu PorthÃ©n .20 .50
21 Janne Hauhtonen .20 .50
22 Arttu Luttinen .20 .50
23 Pasi Salonen .20 .50
24 Heikki Laine .20 .50
25 Karri RÃ¤mÃ¶ .75 2.00
26 Juha Toivonen .20 .50
27 David Schneider .20 .50
28 Juuso Hietanen .20 .50
29 Mikko Jokela .20 .50
30 Veli-Pekka Laitinen .20 .50
31 Jani Hassinen .20 .50
32 Jari Sailio .20 .50
33 Petteri Wirtanen .20 .50
34 Iivo Hokkanen .20 .50
35 Joni Lappalainen .20 .50
36 Hannu VÃ¤isÃ¤nen .20 .50
37 Juha-Pekka Loikas .20 .50
38 Ville Leino .20 .50
39 Tuukka Rask 2.00 5.00
40 Toni Niemi .20 .50
41 Jyrki Lumme .20 .50
42 Ville Koistinen .20 .50
43 Juha AlÃ©n .20 .50
44 Juho Mielonen .20 .50
45 Perttu Lindgren .60 1.50
46 Marko Anttila .20 .50
47 Ville Korhonen .20 .50
48 Toni Koivisto .20 .50
49 Jussi Pesonen .20 .50
50 Tomi Hirvonen .20 .50
51 Vesa Viitakoski .20 .50
52 Raimo Helminen .20 .50
53 Joonas Hallikainen .20 .50
54 Mikko Kalteva .20 .50
55 Markus KankaanperÃ¤ .20 .50
56 Kevin Kantee .20 .50
57 Jan Latvala .20 .50
58 Sami LepistÃ¶ .20 .50
59 Tony Virta .20 .50
60 Tomek Valtonen .20 .50
61 Arto Koivisto .20 .50
62 Petri Pakaslahti .20 .50
63 Tommi Santala .20 .50
64 Petri Varis .20 .50
65 Jesse Uronen .20 .50
66 Roni Andersson .20 .50
67 Sinuhe Wallinheimo .30 .75
68 Miika Huczkowski .20 .50
69 Jaako Niskavaara .20 .50
70 Erkka LeppÃ¤nen .20 .50
71 Eerikki Koivu .20 .50
72 Juha Salmu .20 .50
73 Jyrki Marttinen .20 .50
74 Carlo GrÃ¼nn .20 .50
75 Johannes Alanen .20 .50
76 Miikka MÃ¤nnikkÃ¶ .20 .50
77 Juha-Pekka HytÃ¶nen .20 .50
78 Arsi Piispanen .20 .50
79 Jari JÃ¤Ã¤skelÃ¤inen .20 .50
80 Ossi Louhivaara .20 .50
81 Kimmo Kapanen .30 .75
82 Jermu Pisto .20 .50
83 Matti Kuusisto .20 .50
84 Juha Alastalo .20 .50
85 Ville HÃ¤mÃ¤lÃ¤inen .20 .50
86 Jani Tuppurainen .20 .50
87 Kasper Kenig .20 .50
88 Henri Huohvanainen .20 .50
89 Sami Salonen .20 .50
90 Tuomas Kiiskinen .20 .50
91 Sami Kaartinen .20 .50
92 Niklas Backstrom 1.50 4.00
93 Oskari Korpikari .20 .50
94 Ari Vallin .20 .50
95 Ilkka Mikkola .20 .50
96 Mikko Lehtonen .20 .50
97 Jouni Loponen .20 .50
98 Viktor Ujcik .20 .50
99 Janne Pesonen .20 .50
100 Tommi Paakkolanvaara .20 .50
101 Jyri Junnila .20 .50
102 Jari Viuhkola .20 .50
103 Michal Bros .20 .50
104 Kalle Sahlstedt .20 .50
105 Tomi Mustonen .20 .50
106 Markus Nordlund .20 .50
107 Otto Honkaheimo .20 .50
108 Tuukka MÃ¤kelÃ¤ .20 .50
109 Ilkka Heikkinen .20 .50
110 Pauli Levokari .20 .50
111 Erik HÃ¤mÃ¤lÃ¤inen .20 .50
112 Tommi Hannus .20 .50
113 Ville-Vesa Vainiola .20 .50
114 Petri Lammassaari .20 .50
115 Shayne Toporowski .20 .50
116 Jarkko Kauvosaari .20 .50
117 Miikka Tuomainen .20 .50
118 Juhamatti Yli-Junnila .20 .50
119 Antti Niemi .30 .75
120 Esa Saksinen .20 .50
121 Olli Korkeavuori .20 .50
122 Sami Helenius .20 .50
123 Jarkko Glad .20 .50
124 Erik Kakko .20 .50
125 Matias Loppi .20 .50
126 Olli Julkunen .20 .50
127 Jesse Saarinen .20 .50
128 Jussi Saarinen .20 .50
129 Tuomas Santavuori .20 .50
130 Henri Heino .20 .50
131 Ville-Matti Koponen .20 .50
132 Toni Koivunen .20 .50
133 Mikko StrÃ¶mberg .20 .50
134 Jussi Timonen .30 .75
135 Harri Tikkanen .20 .50
136 Mikko PalomÃ¤ki .20 .50
137 Ossi-Petteri GrÃ¶nholm .20 .50
138 Ville Koho .20 .50
139 Kimmo Koskenkorva .20 .50
140 Teemu Paakkarinen .20 .50
141 Jaska Vilen .20 .50
142 Jarkko Immonen .30 .75
143 Janne Kolehmainen .20 .50
144 Mika Lehto .30 .75
145 Marko Kauppinen .20 .50
146 Ville MÃ¤ntymaa .20 .50
147 Tuukka MÃ¤ntylÃ¤ .20 .50
148 Mikko Pukka .20 .50
149 Janne GrÃ¶nvall .20 .50
150 Teemu Nurmi .20 .50
151 Mika Viinanen .20 .50
152 Petri Kontiola .20 .50
153 Sami VenÃ¤lÃ¤inen .20 .50
154 Stefan Ã–hman .20 .50
155 Quinn Hancock .20 .50
156 Teemu Laine .20 .50
157 Marko Kiprusoff .20 .50
158 Simon Backman .20 .50
159 Tomi SykkÃ¶ .20 .50
160 Kai Nurminen .20 .50
161 Jussi Makkonen .20 .50
162 Ville Vahalahti .20 .50
163 Lauri Korpikoski .60 1.50
164 Mika Alatalo .20 .50
165 Arttu Virtanen .20 .50
166 Matti Aho .20 .50
167 Tuukka Pulliainen .20 .50
168 Jussi RynnÃ¤s .20 .50
169 Pasi Peltonen .20 .50
170 Marko Toivonen .20 .50
171 Mika Rontti .20 .50
172 Juhamatti HietamÃ¤ki .20 .50
173 Matt Nickerson .40 1.00
174 Kristian Kuusela .20 .50
175 Jesse Joensuu .20 .50
176 Marko KivenmÃ¤ki .20 .50
177 Matti Kuparinen .20 .50
178 Tuomas Takala .20 .50
179 Rob Hisey .20 .50
180 Patrik Forsbacka .20 .50
181 Bernd BrÃ¼ckler .30 .75
182 Ari Ahonen .40 1.00
183 Tomi KÃ¤llarsson .20 .50
184 Kimmo Pikkarainen .20 .50
185 Ismo Kuoppala .20 .50
186 Samuli Suhonen .20 .50
187 Tomas Sinisalo .20 .50
188 Joni TÃ¶ykkÃ¤lÃ¤ .20 .50
189 Jari Tolsa .20 .50
190 Semir Ben-Amor .20 .50
191 Ville Viitaluoma .20 .50
192 Mikko Laine .20 .50
193 Martin Kariya .20 .50
194 Toni KÃ¤hkÃ¶nen .20 .50
195 Aleksis Ahlqvist .30 .75
196 Robert Schnabel .20 .50
197 Cory Murphy .20 .50
198 Patrik Lostedt .20 .50
199 Pasi Saarinen .20 .50
200 Kimmo Kuhta .20 .50
201 Miikka Jouhkimainen .20 .50
202 Raymond Murray .20 .50
203 Juha Fagerstedt .20 .50
204 Janne Laakkonen .20 .50
205 Lennart Petrell .20 .50
206 Ilkka Pikkarainen .20 .50
207 Jan Hrdina .20 .50
208 Pasi NielikÃ¤inen .20 .50
209 Mika Oksa .30 .75
210 Miika Wiikman .30 .75
211 Risto Korhonen .20 .50
212 Mikko MÃ¤enpÃ¤Ã¤ .20 .50
213 Philippe Seydoux .20 .50
214 Mika StrÃ¶mberg .30 .75
215 Fredrik Svensson .20 .50
216 Jani KeinÃ¤nen .20 .50
217 Janne Lahti .20 .50
218 Joonas Vihko .20 .50
219 Aki Uusikartano .20 .50
220 Antti PihlstrÃ¶m .20 .50
221 Jonas Andersson .20 .50
222 Toni MÃ¤kiaho .20 .50
223 Riku Helenius .60 1.50
224 Teemu JÃ¤Ã¤skelÃ¤inen .20 .50
225 Mikko Kuukka .20 .50
226 Teppo Tuomanen .20 .50
227 Kristian Kudroc .20 .50
228 Pasi PetrilÃ¤inen .20 .50
229 Mikko Peltola .20 .50
230 Sami Sandell .20 .50
231 Tommi Huhtala .20 .50
232 Pasi MÃ¤Ã¤ttÃ¤nen .20 .50
233 Lauris Darzins .20 .50
234 Tomas Kurka .20 .50
235 Niko Hovinen .30 .75
236 Juuso Riksman .30 .75
237 Mikko Kuparinen .20 .50
238 Marko Tuulola .20 .50
239 Martti JÃ¤rventie .20 .50
240 Tim Stapleton .20 .50
241 Jyrki Louhi .20 .50
242 Jani Rita .20 .50
243 Arto Kuki .20 .50
244 Kim Hirschovits .20 .50
245 Ryan VandenBussche .40 1.00
246 Jori LehterÃ¤ .20 .50
247 Samuli Jalkanen .20 .50
248 Pekka Tuokkola .20 .50
249 Miska Kangasniemi .20 .50
250 Henrik Forsberg .20 .50
251 Valtteri Tenkanen .20 .50
252 Miika Lahti .20 .50
253 Tuomas VÃ¤nttinen .20 .50
254 Samuli Piiroinen .20 .50
255 Olli SipilÃ¤inen .20 .50
256 Riku Rahikainen .20 .50
257 Ilari Filppula .20 .50
258 Tuomas Nissinen .30 .75
259 Janne Jalasvaara .20 .50
260 Kyle Peto .20 .50
261 Mats Hansson .20 .50
262 Mikko Purontakanen .20 .50
263 Eetu Qvist .20 .50
264 Timo Koskela .20 .50
265 Martin Sonnenberg .20 .50
266 Matt Davidson .20 .50
267 Aatu HÃ¤mÃ¤lÃ¤inen .20 .50
268 Jaakko Suomalainen .30 .75
269 Tuomas Tarkki .30 .75
270 Tommi Leinonen .20 .50
271 Topi Jaakola .20 .50
272 Ivan Majesky .20 .50
273 Atvars Tribuncovs .20 .50
274 Jukka-Pekka Laamanen .20 .50
275 Antti YlÃ¶nen .20 .50
276 Teemu Normio .20 .50
277 Veikko Karppinen .20 .50
278 Mika PyÃ¶rÃ¤lÃ¤ .20 .50
279 Antti Aarnio .20 .50
280 Juhamatti Aaltonen .20 .50
281 Markus Korhonen .30 .75
282 Petri TÃ¤htisalo .20 .50
283 Kari Martikainen .20 .50
284 Jiri Hunkes .20 .50
285 Otto Honkaheimo .20 .50
286 Jan Platil .20 .50
287 Pekka Saarenheimo .20 .50
288 Toni Dahlman .20 .50
289 Juha-Pekka Haataja .20 .50
290 Henrik Juntunen .20 .50
291 Marko Luomala .20 .50
292 Josef Straka .20 .50
293 Tommi Satosaari .20 .50
294 Jani ForsstrÃ¶m .20 .50
295 Mikko Heiskanen .20 .50
296 Anssi Salmela .20 .50
297 Ville Uusitalo .20 .50
298 Vili Sopanen .20 .50
299 Karo Koivunen .20 .50
300 Toni Sihvonen .20 .50
301 Kari Sihvonen .20 .50
302 Leo Komarov .20 .50
303 Marko Jantunen .20 .50
304 Rob Zepp .30 .75
305 Jarno Virkki .20 .50
306 Joonas RÃ¶nnberg .20 .50
307 Pauli Levokari .20 .50
308 Kalle Kaijomaa .20 .50
309 Henrik PetrÃ© .20 .50
310 Sami RyhÃ¤nen .20 .50
311 Petri Koskinen .20 .50
312 Mikko Hakkarainen .20 .50
313 Janne Jokila .20 .50
314 Eetu Holma .20 .50
315 Emil Lundberg .20 .50
316 Ville Snellman .20 .50
317 Jens BergenstrÃ¶m .20 .50
318 Tommi NikkilÃ¤ .30 .75
319 Burke Henry .20 .50
320 Matti Koistinen .20 .50
321 Harri Ilvonen .20 .50
322 Dale Clarke .20 .50
323 Teemu Aalto .20 .50
324 Janne Ojanen .20 .50
325 Niko Nieminen .20 .50
326 Jarkko PyymÃ¤ki .20 .50
327 Marko Ojanen .20 .50
328 Jonas Enlund .20 .50
329 Antti HÃ¶lli .20 .50
330 Teemu Virkkunen .20 .50
331 Juho Santanen .20 .50
332 Jani Hurme .40 1.00
333 Juho Jokinen .20 .50
334 Aki Berg .20 .50
335 Vladimir Sicak .20 .50
336 Jesse Saarinen .20 .50
337 Mikko Rautee .20 .50
338 Tommi Laine .20 .50
339 Layne Ulmer .20 .50
340 Tuomas Suominen .20 .50
341 Ivan Huml .30 .75
342 Teemu Ramstedt .20 .50
343 Joni Yli-Torkko .20 .50
344 Matti Kaltiainen .30 .75
345 Eero KilpelÃ¤inen .30 .75
346 Peter Aston .20 .50
347 Anssi Tieranta .20 .50
348 Eetu Heikkinen .20 .50
349 Ilkka TÃ¶rnvall .20 .50
350 Tapio Sammalkangas .20 .50
351 Toni HÃ¤ppÃ¶lÃ¤ .20 .50
352 Tom Wandell .20 .50
353 Aleksandr Naurov .20 .50
354 Joonas Kemppainen .20 .50
355 Ville Hirvonen .20 .50
356 Brandon Crombeen .30 .75

2006-07 Finnish Cardset Between the Pipes

1 Ari Ahonen 3.00 8.00
2 Bernd BrÃ¼ckler 2.00 5.00
3 Aleksis Ahlqvist 2.00 5.00
4 Jan Lundell 2.00 5.00
5 Mika Oksa 2.00 5.00
6 Miika Wiikman 2.00 5.00
7 Riku Helenius 2.50 6.00
8 Tuukka Rask 5.00 12.00
9 Niko Hovinen 2.00 5.00
10 Juuso Riksman 2.00 5.00
11 Sinuhe Wallinheimo 2.00 5.00
12 Kimmo Kapanen 2.00 5.00
13 Tuomas Nissinen 2.00 5.00
14 Jaakko Suomalainen 2.00 5.00
15 Tuomas Tarkki 2.00 5.00
16 Markus Korhonen 2.00 5.00
17 Antti Niemi 4.00 10.00
18 Mikko StrÃ¶mberg 2.00 5.00
19 Rob Zepp 2.00 5.00
20 Mika Lehto 2.00 5.00
21 Tommi NikkilÃ¤ 2.00 5.00
22 Jani Hurme 2.50 6.00
23 Matti Kaltiainen 2.00 5.00
24 Eero KilpelÃ¤inen 2.00 5.00

2006-07 Finnish Cardset Enforcers

1 Sami Helenius 1.25 3.00
2 Kristian Kudroc 1.25 3.00
3 Ryan VandenBussche 2.00 5.00
4 Robert Schnabel 1.25 3.00
5 Burke Henry 1.25 3.00
6 Jan Platil 1.25 3.00
7 Toni MÃ¤kiaho 1.25 3.00
8 Markus KankaanperÃ¤ 1.25 3.00
9 Aki Berg 1.25 3.00
10 Pasi Peltonen 1.25 3.00
11 Pasi NielikÃ¤inen 1.25 3.00
12 Jere Karalahti 1.25 3.00

2006-07 Finnish Cardset Playmakers Rookies

1 Perttu Lindgren 2.00 5.00
2 Juhamatti Aaltonen 1.25 3.00
3 Jussi Makkonen 1.25 3.00
4 Pasi Salonen 1.25 3.00
5 Juuso Hietanen 1.25 3.00
6 Petteri Wirtanen 1.25 3.00
7 Petri Lammassaari 1.25 3.00
8 Patrick Forsbacka 1.25 3.00
9 Juha AlÃ©n 1.25 3.00
10 Miika Lahti 1.25 3.00
11 Jari Sailio 1.25 3.00
12 Leo Komarov 1.25 3.00

2006-07 Finnish Cardset Playmakers Rookies Gold

COMPLETE SET (12) 40.00 80.00
STATED PRINT RUN 100 SER.#'d SETS
1 Perttu Lindgren 6.00 15.00
2 Juhamatti Aaltonen 4.00 10.00
3 Jussi Makkonen 4.00 10.00
4 Pasi Salonen 4.00 10.00
5 Juuso Hietanen 4.00 10.00
6 Petteri Wirtanen 4.00 10.00
7 Petri Lammassaari 4.00 10.00
8 Patrick Forsbacka 4.00 10.00
9 Juha AlA©n 4.00 10.00
10 Miika Lahti 4.00 10.00
11 Jari Sailio 4.00 10.00
12 Perttu Lindgren 4.00 10.00

2006-07 Finnish Cardset Playmakers Rookies Silver

COMPLETE SET (12) 15.00 40.00
STATED PRINT RUN 200 SER.#'d SETS
1 Perttu Lindgren 4.00 10.00
2 Juhamatti Aaltonen 2.00 5.00
3 Jussi Makkonen 2.00 5.00
4 Pasi Salonen 2.00 5.00
5 Juuso Hietanen 2.00 5.00
6 Petteri Wirtanen 2.00 5.00
7 Petri Lammassaari 2.00 5.00
8 Patrick Forsbacka 2.00 5.00
9 Juha AlA©n 2.00 5.00
10 Miika Lahti 2.00 5.00
11 Jari Sailio 2.00 5.00
12 Leo Komarov 2.00 5.00

2006-07 Finnish Cardset Signature Sensations

1 Mikko Lehtonen 15.00 40.00
2 Erkki RajamÃ¤ki 15.00 40.00
3 Miika Wiikman 15.00 40.00
4 Juuso Hietanen 15.00 40.00
5 Petteri Wirtanen 15.00 40.00
6 Tuukka Rask 40.00 80.00
7 Ville Koistinen 15.00 40.00
8 Perttu Lindgren 25.00 60.00
9 Joonas Hallikainen 15.00 40.00
10 Sami LepistA¶ 15.00 40.00
11 Tommi Santala 15.00 40.00
12 Sinuhe Wallinheimo 15.00 40.00
13 Miika Lahti 15.00 40.00
14 Arsi Piispanen 15.00 40.00
15 Kimmo Kapanen 15.00 40.00
16 Tuomas Kiiskinen 15.00 40.00
17 Mikko Alikoski 15.00 40.00
18 Lasse Kukkonen 15.00 40.00
19 Juhamatti Aaltonen 15.00 40.00
20 Otto Honkaheimo 15.00 40.00
21 Petri Lammassaari 15.00 40.00
22 Miikka Tuomainen 15.00 40.00
23 Antti Niemi 30.00 60.00
24 Jesse Saarinen 15.00 40.00
25 Mikko StrA¶mberg 15.00 40.00
26 Jarkko Immonen 15.00 40.00
27 Mika Lehto 15.00 40.00
28 Petri Kontiola 15.00 40.00
29 Juho Santanen 15.00 40.00
30 Jussi Makkonen 15.00 40.00
31 Tuukka Pulliainen 15.00 40.00
32 Kristian Kuusela 15.00 40.00
33 Jesse Joensuu 15.00 40.00
34 Marko KivenmÃ¤ki 15.00 40.00
35 Patrick Forsbacka 15.00 40.00

2006-07 Finnish Cardset Superior Snatchers

1 Niklas Backstrom 4.00 10.00
2 Joonas Hallikainen 2.00 5.00
3 Kimmo Kapanen 2.00 5.00
4 Mika Lehto 2.00 5.00
5 Jan Lundell 2.00 5.00
6 Antti Niemi 4.00 10.00
7 Tuukka Rask 5.00 12.00
8 Juuso Riksman 2.00 5.00
9 Karri RÃ¤mA¶ 3.00 8.00
10 Sinuhe Wallinheimo 2.00 5.00
11 Miika Wiikman 2.00 5.00
12 Rob Zepp 2.00 5.00

2006-07 Finnish Cardset Superior Snatchers Gold

COMPLETE SET (12) 60.00 150.00
STATED PRINT RUN 100 SER.#'d SETS
1 Niklas Backstrom 12.00 30.00
2 Joonas Hallikainen 6.00 15.00
3 Kimmo Kapanen 6.00 15.00
4 Mika Lehto 6.00 15.00
5 Jan Lundell 6.00 15.00
6 Antti Niemi 6.00 15.00
7 Tuukka Rask 15.00 40.00
8 Juuso Riksman 6.00 15.00
9 Karri RÃ¤mA¶ 8.00 20.00
10 Sinuhe Wallinheimo 6.00 15.00
11 Miika Wiikman 6.00 15.00
12 Rob Zepp 6.00 15.00

2006-07 Finnish Cardset Superior Snatchers Silver

COMPLETE SET (12) 50.00 100.00
STATED PRINT RUN 200 SER.#'d SETS
1 Niklas Backstrom 8.00 20.00
2 Joonas Hallikainen 4.00 10.00
3 Kimmo Kapanen 4.00 10.00
4 Mika Lehto 4.00 10.00
5 Jan Lundell 4.00 10.00
6 Antti Niemi 4.00 10.00
7 Tuukka Rask 12.00 30.00
8 Juuso Riksman 4.00 10.00
9 Karri RÃ¤mA¶ 6.00 15.00
10 Sinuhe Wallinheimo 4.00 10.00
11 Miika Wiikman 4.00 10.00
12 Rob Zepp 4.00 10.00

2006-07 Finnish Cardset Trophy Winners

COMPLETE SET (7) 6.00 15.00
1 Jukka Jalonen 1.25 3.00
2 Perttu Lindgren 2.00 5.00
3 Esa Pirnes 1.25 3.00
4 Juuso Riksman 1.25 3.00
5 Lasse Kukkonen 1.25 3.00
6 Miika Wiikman 1.25 3.00
7 Tony Salmelainen 1.25 3.00

2006-07 Finnish Ilves Team Set

1 Juha Alen .20 .50
2 Juuso Antonen .20 .50
3 Marko Anttila .20 .50
4 Lauris Darzins .20 .50
5 Riku Helenius .75 2.00
6 Tomi Hirvonen .20 .50
7 Tommi Huhtala .20 .50
8 Teemu Jaaskelainen .20 .50
9 Toni Koivisto .20 .50
10 Ville Korhonen .20 .50
11 Kristian Kudroc .20 .50
12 Tomas Kurka .20 .50
13 Mikko Kuukka .20 .50
14 Jarno Laitinen .20 .50
15 Joonas Lehtivuori .20 .50
16 Perttu Lindgren .60 1.50
17 Juho Mielonen .20 .50
18 Pasi Maattanen .20 .50
19 Toni Niemi .20 .50
20 Mikko Peltola .20 .50
21 Jussi Pesonen .20 .50
22 Pasi Petrilainen .20 .50
23 Tuukka Rask 4.00 10.00
24 Sami Sandell .20 .50
25 Teppo Tuomanen .20 .50
26 Vesa Viitakoski .20 .50
27 Kari Eloranta CO .10 .25
28 Petteri Hirvonen CO .10 .25

2006-07 Finnish Porin Assat Pelaajakortit

COMPLETE SET (32) 10.00 25.00
1 Matti Kaltiainen .30 .75
2 Eero Kilpelainen .60 1.50
3 Jussi Rynnas .30 .75
4 Pasi Peltonen .30 .75
5 Marko Toivonen .30 .75
6 Mika Rontti .30 .75
7 Peter Aston .30 .75
8 Tero Konttinen .30 .75
9 Juhamatti Hietamaki .30 .75
10 Anssi Tieranta .30 .75
11 Eetu Heikkinen .30 .75
12 Iikka Tornvall .30 .75
13 Tapio Samalkangas .30 .75
14 Toni Happola .30 .75
15 Kristian Kuusela .30 .75
16 Tom Wandell .30 .75
17 Tuomas Huhtanen .30 .75
18 Jesse Joensuu .30 .75
19 Marko Kivenmaki .30 .75
20 Matti Kuparinen .30 .75
21 Tuomas Takala .30 .75
22 Patrick Forsbacka .30 .75
23 Petteri Tasku .30 .75
24 Alexander Naurov .30 .75
25 Joonas Kemppainen .30 .75
26 Jussi Peltomaa .30 .75
27 Ville Hirvonen .30 .75
28 Brandon BJ Crombeen .40 1.00
29 Teemu Kesa .30 .75
30 Tobias Salmelainen .30 .75
31 David Bararuk .30 .75
32 Jari Harkala .30 .75

2007-08 Finnish Cardset MVP

1 Martin Kariya 1.00 2.50
2 Cory Murphy 1.00 2.50
3 Mikko MÃ¤enpÃ¤Ã¤ 1.00 2.50
4 Tuukka Rask 2.50 6.00
5 Jani Rita 1.00 2.50
6 Sinuhe Wallinheimo 1.00 2.50
7 Jani Tuppurainen 1.00 2.50
8 Jari Viuhkola 1.00 2.50
9 Juha-Pekka Haataja 1.00 2.50
10 Antti Niemi 4.00 10.00
11 Kimmo Koskenkorva 1.00 2.50
12 Petri Kontiola 1.00 2.50
13 Aki Berg 1.00 2.50
14 Marko KivenmÃ¤ki 1.00 2.50

2007-08 Finnish Cardset Twirls

1 Bernd BrÃ¼ckler 1.00 2.50
2 Jere Karalahti 1.00 2.50
3 Antti PihlstrA¶m 1.00 2.50
4 Perttu Lindgren 1.25 3.00
5 Kim Hirschovits 1.00 2.50
6 Juuso Riksman 1.00 2.50
7 Janne Pesonen 1.00 2.50
8 Tuomas Tarkki 1.00 2.50
9 Tuomas Suominen 1.00 2.50

2008-09 Finnish Cardset Goalie Tandems

GT1 B.Bruckler/M.Koskinen
GT2 J.Pitkamaki/J.Nieminen
GT3 T.Lassila/M.Stromberg
GT4 H.Toivonen/M.Patsi
GT5 J.Riksman/J.Hallikainen
GT6 S.Wallinheimo/P.Tuokkola
GT7 M.Jarvinen/M.Oksa
GT8 T.Tarkki/P.Koivisto
GT9 P.Vehanen/J.Myllykoski
GT10 T.Nikkila/N.Hovinen
GT11 I.Tarkki/V.Hostikka
GT12 M.Lehto/H.Sateri
GT13 A.Salak/J.Kuokkanen
GT14 E.Kilpelainen/T.Duba

2008-09 Finnish Cardset International Stars

IS1 Jonas Andersson
IS2 Shawn Bates
IS3 Jiri Bicek
IS4 Mike Bishai
IS5 Kip Brennan
IS6 Bernd Bruckler
IS7 Dale Clarke
IS8 Daniel Corso
IS9 Derek Damon
IS10 Tomas Duba
IS11 Ben Eaves
IS12 Colby Genoway
IS13 Quinn Hancock
IS14 Duane Harmer
IS15 Steve Kariya
IS16 Ryan Keller
IS17 Kyle Klubbertanz
IS18 Troy Milam
IS19 Dmitri Nabokov
IS20 Patrik Nevalainen
IS21 Matt Nickerson
IS22 Geoff Platt
IS23 Alexander Salak
IS24 Steve Saviano
IS25 Joey Tenute
IS26 Shayne Toporowski

2008-09 Finnish Cardset Show Exclusive Dual Game Worn Jerseys

SEHK J.Haataja/M.Kivenmaki
SEHR S.Helenius/J.Ruutu
SEJK O.Jokinen/S.Kapanen
SENR V.Nieminen/T.Rask

2008-09 Finnish Cardset Signatures

AA Antti Aarnio S1
AE Antti Erkinjuntti S1
AE Antti Erkinjuntti S2
AL Arttu Luttinen S2
AS Alexander Salak S1
AY Antti Ylonen S1
DD Derek Damon S2
DI Dan Iliakis S1
DN Dmitri Nabokov S2
ER Erkki Rajamaki S1
HF Henrik Forsberg S1
HL Henri Laurila S1
HT Hannu Toivonen/85 S2
IF Ilari Filppula S2
IM Ilkka Mikkola S1
IT Iiro Tarkki S1
JA Jerry Ahtola S1
JE Jonas Enlund S2
JI Jarkko Immonen S2
JK Joonas Kemppainen S2
JL Janne Lahti S2
JN Jani Nieminen S1
JP Juuso Puustinen S2
JR Jani Rita S1
JR Juuso Riksman S2
JT Joey Tenute S2
KH Kim Hirschovits S2
KK Kristian Kuusela S2
KS Kalle Sahlstedt S2
LK Leo Komarov S1
LP Lennart Petrell S2
LT Lauri Tukonen/85 S2
MA Marko Anttila S1
ME Mikko Eloranto S2
MJ Mika Jarvinen S1
MK Marko Kivenmaki S2
ML Mika Lehto S1
MM Mikko Maenpaa S2
MO Mika Oksa S1
MS Mika Stromberg S2
MT Markku Tahtinen S2
OM Olli Malmivaara S2
PK Petri Koivisto S2
PL Petri Lammassaari S2
PT Pekka Tuokkola S2
RK Ryan Keller S2
SK Steve Kariya S2
SM Simo Malkia S1
ST Sami Torkki S1
ST Shayne Toporowski S2
SW Sinuhe Wallinheimo S2
TJ Toni Jalo S1
TK Tuomas Kiiskinen S1
TK Toni Koivisto S2
TL Teemu Lassila S1
TM Tomi Maki S2
TN Teemu Nurmi S1
TP Tomi Pettinen S2
TS Tomi Sallinen S1
TV Tuomas Vanttinen S1
TV Tony Virta S2
VM Ville Mantymaa S1
VN Ville Nieminen S2
AnL Antti Laaksonen S2
JAI Jarkko Immonen S2
JAK Jarkko Kauvosaari S2
JeJ Jesse Jyrkkio S1
JLe Jori Lehtera S1
JoL Joonas Lehtivuori S1
JPL Juha-Pekka Loikas S1
JuJ Juha Jarvenpaa S1
JuT Jussi Tarvainen S2
KAK Kalle Kerman S1
KiK Kimmo Kuhta S1
MAM Masi Marjamaki/85 S2
MKA Mikko Kalteva S1
Mku Mikael Kurki S1
PAS Pasi Saarela S1
PeS Pekka Saarenheimo S1
PLi Perttu Lindgren/85 S2
SAK Sami Kapanen S2
SBA Semir Ben-Amor S1
SsA Sakari Salminen S1
Ssu Samuli Suhonen S1

2009-10 Finnish Cardset The Mask

MASK1 Jani Nieminen
MASK2 Juuso Riksman
MASK3 Petri Vehanen
MASK4 Tuomas Tarkki
MASK5 Mika Jarvinen
MASK6 Juha Pitkamaki
MASK7 Eero Kilpelainen
MASK8 David Leggio
MASK9 Sinuhe Wallinheimo

2009-10 Finnish Upper Deck Victory

COMPLETE SET (250) 75.00 150.00
COMP.SET w/o SPS (200) 30.00 60.00
*FINNISH: .6X TO 1.5X BASIC VICTORY
ROOKIE STATED ODDS 1:2
195 Nicklas Backstrom .60 1.50

2009-10 Finnish Upper Deck Victory Suomalaisia Supertahtia

COMPLETE SET (20) 10.00 25.00
STATED ODDS 1 PER PACK
FF1 Kari Lehtonen .60 1.50
FF2 Niklas Hagman .50 1.25
FF3 Niklas Backstrom .75 2.00
FF4 Sami Salo .75 2.00
FF5 Jarkko Ruutu .50 1.25
FF6 Vesa Toskala .75 2.00
FF7 Antti Miettinen .50 1.25
FF8 Jere Lehtinen .60 1.50
FF9 Mikko Koivu .75 2.00
FF10 Teppo Numminen .60 1.50
FF11 Saku Koivu .75 2.00
FF12 Olli Jokinen .60 1.50
FF13 Teemu Selanne 1.50 4.00
FF14 Kimmo Timonen .60 1.50
FF15 Tuomo Ruutu .50 1.25
FF16 Miikka Kiprusoff .60 1.50
FF17 Joni Pitkanen .60 1.50
FF18 Valtteri Filppula .75 2.00
FF19 Pekka Rinne 1.00 2.50
FF20 Jussi Jokinen .50 1.25

1994-95 French National Team

These standard-size cards were made available to fans at venues where the national team was appearing in France. The cards feature simulated action photography, surrounded by red, white and blue borders. The player's name is at the top of the card, while the words "Equipe de France 94-95" line the bottom. Card backs contain a color headshot, and international statistics. The cards are unnumbered and checklisted below in alphabetical order.

COMPLETE SET (35) 8.00 20.00
1 Benjamin Agnel .20 .50
2 Richard Aimonetto .20 .50
3 Stephane Arcangeloni .20 .50
4 Mickael Babin .20 .50
5 Alain Beaule .20 .50
6 J. Francois Bonnard .20 .50
7 Arnaud Briand .20 .50
8 Karl DeWolf .20 .50
9 Serge Djelloul .20 .50
10 Roger Dube .20 .50
11 Patrick Dunn .20 .50
12 J. Christophe Filippin .20 .50
13 Michel Galarneau .20 .50
14 Gerald Guennelon .20 .50
15 Eric Lemarque .20 .50
16 J. Philippe Lemoine .20 .50
17 Fabrice LHenry .30 .75
18 Pierrick Maia .20 .50
19 Antoine Mindjimba .75 2.00
20 Christophe Moyon .20 .50
21 Lionel Orsolini .20 .50
22 Franck Pajonkowski .30 .75
23 Denis Perez .20 .50
24 Eric Pinard .20 .50
25 Serge Poudrier .30 .75
26 Christian Pouget .20 .50
27 Pierre Pousse .20 .50
28 Antoine Richer .20 .50
29 Franck Saunier .20 .50
30 J. Marc Soghomonian .20 .50
31 Juhani Tamminen .30 .75
32 Michel Valliere .30 .75
33 Andre Vittenberg .20 .50
34 Steven Woodburn .20 .50
35 Petri Ylonen .60 1.50

1936 German Jaszmatzi

Full color card from the Deutscher Sports series of Germany. Thin paper stock, with back in German.

208 Ice Hockey 15.00 30.00

1994-95 German DEL

This 440-card set of the German hockey league was produced (apparently) by International Hockey Archives. The cards feature an action photo on the front, with player and team name along the borders. The back contain a space for autographing, as well as another photo and player bio in German. The set includes NHL prospects Florian Keller and Jochen Hecht, as well as several ex-NHL players.

COMPLETE SET (440) 20.00 50.00
1 International Hockey Association .02 .10
2 DEL 1994/95 .02 .10
3 Season 1994-95 .02 .10
4 Augsburger Panther Team .02 .10
5 Gunnar Leidborg .02 .10
6 Gary Prior .08 .25
7 Scott Campbell .02 .10
8 Dieter Medicus .02 .10
9 Duanne Moeser .02 .10
10 Daniel Naud .02 .10
11 Andy Romer .02 .10
12 Thomas Groger .02 .10
13 Sven Zywitza .02 .10
14 Fritz Meyer .02 .10
15 Christian Curth .02 .10
16 Toni Krinner .02 .10
17 Patrik Pysz .02 .10
18 Heinrich Romer .02 .10
19 Ales Polcar .02 .10
20 Philip Kukuk .02 .10
21 Dietrich Adam .02 .10
22 Tim Schnobrich .02 .10
23 Tim Ferguson .08 .25
24 Robert Heidt .02 .10
25 Alfred Burkhard .02 .10
26 Charly Fliegauf .02 .10
27 Robert Paclik .02 .10
28 Stefan Mayer .02 .10
29 Reinhard Haider .02 .10
30 Dennis Schrapp .02 .10
31 Eisbaren Berlin Team Card .02 .10
32 Walter Jaroslav .02 .10
33 Klaus Schroder .02 .10
34 Andre Dietzsch .02 .10
35 Juri Stumpf .02 .10
36 Torsten Deutscher .02 .10
37 Frank Kannewurf .02 .10
38 Thomas Graul .02 .10
39 Sven Felski .02 .10
40 Moritz Schmidt .02 .10
41 Marco Swibenko .02 .10
42 Holger Mix .02 .10
43 Jiri Dopita .40 1.00
44 Dirk Perschau .02 .10
45 Guido Hiller .02 .10
46 Daniel Held .02 .10
47 Richard Zemlicka .08 .25
48 Jan Schertz .02 .10
49 Mike Losch .02 .10
50 Patrick Solf .02 .10
51 Rupert Meister .02 .10
52 BSC Preussen Team Card .02 .10
53 Billy Flynn .08 .25
54 Tony Tanti .08 .25
55 Jochen Molling .02 .10
56 Andreas Schubert .02 .10
57 Stefan Steinecker .02 .10
58 Josef Lehner .02 .10
59 Tom O'Regan .08 .25
60 Gaetan Malo .02 .10
61 Michael Komma .02 .10
62 Marco Schinko .02 .10
63 Marco Rentzsch .02 .10
64 Georg Holzmann .02 .10
65 Mark Kosturik .02 .10
66 Jurgen Rumrich .02 .10
67 John Chabot .20 .50
68 Harald Windler .02 .10
69 Mark Teevens .08 .25
70 Klaus Merk .08 .25
71 Stephan Sinner .02 .10
72 Mark Gronau .02 .10
73 Bruce Hardy .08 .25
74 Fabian Brannstrom .02 .10
75 Daniel Poudrier .08 .25
76 Dusseldorfer EG Team Card .02 .10
77 Hans Zach .02 .10
78 Helmut DeRaaf .02 .10
79 Markus Kehle .02 .10
80 Christian Schmitz .02 .10
81 Lorenz Funk .02 .10
82 Chris Valentine .20 .50
83 Rafael Jedamzik .02 .10
84 Torsten Kienass .08 .25
85 Christopher Kreutzer .02 .10
86 Benoit Doucet .08 .25
87 Bernd Kuhnhauser .02 .10
88 Andreas Niederberger .02 .10
89 Rick Amann .08 .25
90 Thorsten Van Leyen .02 .10
91 Bruce Eakin .02 .10
92 Pierre Rioux .08 .25
93 Andreas Brockmann .02 .10
94 Uli Hiemer .02 .10
95 Bernd Truntschka .08 .25
96 Wolfgang Kummer .02 .10
97 Carsten Gossmann .02 .10
98 Ernst Kopf .08 .25
99 Robert Sterflinger .02 .10
100 Kevin LaVallee .08 .25
101 Rainer Zerwesz .02 .10
102 Frankfurt Lions Team Card .02 .10
103 Pjotr Vorobjev .02 .10
104 Peter Obresa .02 .10
105 Vladimir Quapp .02 .10
106 Florian Storf .02 .10
107 Alexander Wedl .02 .10
108 Olaf Scholz .02 .10
109 Ilya Vorobjev .02 .10
110 Ladislav Strompf .02 .10
111 Udo Dohler .02 .10
112 Alexander Wunsch .02 .10
113 Jiri Lala .02 .10
114 Andrej Jaufmann .02 .10
115 Thomas Muhlbauer .02 .10
116 Markus Kempf .02 .10
117 Igor Schultz .02 .10
118 Martin Schultz .02 .10
119 Michael Raubal .02 .10
120 Rudi Gorgenlander .02 .10
121 Jurgen Schaal .02 .10
122 Patrick Vozar .02 .10
123 Rochus Schneider .02 .10
124 Toni Raubal .02 .10
125 Stefan Koniger .02 .10
126 EC Hannover Team Card .02 .10
127 Hartmut Nickel .02 .10
128 Joachim Lempio .02 .10
129 Torsten Hanusch .02 .10
130 Thomas Jungwirth .02 .10
131 David Reierson .02 .10
132 Friedhelm Bogelsack .02 .10
133 Thomas Werner .02 .10
134 Dirk Rohrbach .02 .10
135 Harald Kuhnke .02 .10
136 Florian Funk .02 .10
137 Mark Maroste .02 .10
138 Anton Maidl .02 .10
139 Rene Reuter .02 .10
140 Rene Ledock .02 .10
141 Marco Herbst .02 .10
142 Milos Vanik .02 .10
143 Gunther Preuss .02 .10
144 Troy Tumbach .02 .10
145 Marc Wittbrock .02 .10
146 Roger Mede .02 .10
147 Craig Topolnisky .02 .10
148 Josef Schlickenrieder .02 .10
149 Marcus Bleicher .02 .10
150 EC Kassel Team Card .02 .10
151 Ross Yates .02 .10
152 Josef Kontny .02 .10
153 Milan Mokros .02 .10
154 Alexander Engel .02 .10
155 Greg Johnston .08 .25
156 Jedrzej Kasperczyk .02 .10
157 Dave Morrison .02 .10
158 Jaro Mucha .02 .10
159 Mike Millar .08 .25
160 Ireneusz Pacula .02 .10
161 Vitalij Grossmann .02 .10
162 Murray McIntosh .02 .10
163 Manfred Ahne .02 .10
164 Peter Kwasigroch .02 .10
165 Georg Guttler .02 .10
166 Falk Ozellis .02 .10
167 Mario Naster .02 .10
168 Sergej Wikulow .02 .10
169 Gerhard Hegen .02 .10
170 Brian Hannon .02 .10
171 Tino Boos .02 .10
172 Kaufbeurer Adler Team Card .02 .10
173 Peter Kathan .02 .10
174 Kenneth Karouk .02 .10
175 Michael Olbrich .02 .10
176 Drahomir Kadlec .08 .25
177 Christian Seeberger .02 .10
178 Elmar Boiger .02 .10
179 Oto Hascak .02 .10
180 Thorsten Rau .02 .10
181 Tomas Martinec .02 .10
182 Norbert Zabel .02 .10
183 Daniel Kunce .02 .10
184 Hans-Jorg Mayer .02 .10
185 Manfred Jorde .02 .10
186 Roland Timoschuk .02 .10
187 Jim Hoffmann .02 .10
188 Andreas Volland .02 .10
189 Rolf Hammer .02 .10
190 Manuel Hess .02 .10
191 Timo Gschwill .02 .10
192 Marc Pethke .02 .10
193 Axel Kammerer .02 .10
194 Jurgen Simon .02 .10
195 Patrick Lange .02 .10
196 Ronny Martin .02 .10
197 Kolner EC Team Card .02 .10
198 Vladimir Vassiliev .02 .10
199 Bernd Haake .02 .10
200 Joseph Heiss .30 .75
201 Jorg Mayr .02 .10
202 Thomas Brandl .02 .10
203 Stephan Mann .02 .10
204 Tonny Reddo .02 .10
205 Mirco Ludemann .08 .25
206 Leo Stefan .08 .25
207 Andreas Pokorny .02 .10
208 Peter Draisaitl .08 .25
209 Ralf Dobrzynski .02 .10
210 Andreas Lupzig .02 .10
211 Karsten Mende .02 .10
212 Frank Hohenadl .02 .10
213 Marco Heinrichs .02 .10
214 Michael Rumrich .02 .10
215 Martin Ondrejka .02 .10
216 Herbert Hohenberger .08 .25
217 Thorsten Sendt .02 .10
218 Thorsten Koslowski .02 .10
219 Olaf Grundmann .02 .10
220 Franz Demmel .02 .10
221 Sergej Berezin .75 2.00
222 Krefelder EV Team Card .02 .10
223 Michael Zettel .02 .10
224 Frank Brunsing .02 .10
225 Karel Lang .02 .10
226 Markus Kranwinkel .02 .10
227 Earl Spry .02 .10
228 Andre Grein .02 .10
229 Greg Evtushevski .08 .25
230 Herberts Vasiljevs .02 .10
231 Ken Petrash .02 .10
232 Greg Thomson .02 .10
233 Reemt Pyka .08 .25
234 Brad Bergen .08 .25
235 Chris Lindberg .08 .25
236 Markus Kranwinkel .02 .10
237 Martin Gebel .02 .10
238 Francois Sills .02 .10
239 Klaus Micheller .02 .10
240 Peter Ihnacak .20 .50
241 Marek Stebnicki .02 .10
242 Johnny Walker .02 .10
243 Gunter Oswald .02 .10
244 James Hanlon .02 .10
245 Rene Bielke .02 .10
246 EV Landshut Team Card .02 .10
247 Bernahrd Johnston .02 .10
248 Mark Stuckey .02 .10
249 Michael Bresagk .02 .10
250 Bernd Wagner .02 .10
251 Eduard Uvria .02 .10
252 Mike Smazal .02 .10
253 Jacek Plachta .02 .10
254 Georg Franz .02 .10
255 Stephan Retzer .02 .10
256 Henri Marcoux .02 .10
257 Andreas Loth .02 .10
258 Mike Bullard .02 .10
259 Markus Berwanger .02 .10
260 Petr Briza .40 1.00
261 Wally Schreiber .20 .50
262 Peter Gulda .02 .10
263 Ralf Hantschke .02 .10
264 Steve McNeil .02 .10
265 Christian Kunast .02 .10
266 Jorg Hendrick .02 .10
267 Helmut Steiger .02 .10
268 Udo Kiessling .02 .10
269 Mike Lay .02 .10
270 Adler Mannheim Team Card .02 .10
271 Lance Nethery .08 .25
272 Marcus Kuhl .02 .10
273 Joachim Appel .02 .10
274 Harold Kreis .02 .10
275 Mike Heidt .02 .10
276 Mario Gehrig .02 .10
277 Pavel Gross .02 .10
278 Steffen Michel .02 .10
279 Daniel Korber .02 .10
280 Robert Cimetta .08 .25
281 Dale Krentz .08 .25
282 Jochen Hecht 4.00 10.00
283 Till Feser .02 .10
284 Lars Bruggemann .02 .10
285 Toni Plattner .02 .10
286 Alexander Schuster .02 .10
287 Dieter Willmann .02 .10
288 Markus Flemming .02 .10
289 Rick Goldmann .20 .50
290 Damian Adamus .02 .10
291 Frederik Ledlin .02 .10
292 David Musial .02 .10
293 Michael Gabler .02 .10
294 Sven Valenti .02 .10
295 Maddogs Munchen Team Card .02 .10
296 Robert Murdoch .02 .10
297 Alexander Genze .02 .10
298 Greg Muller .02 .10
299 Mike Schmidt .02 .10
300 Zdenek Travnicek .02 .10
301 Christian Lukes .02 .10
302 Gordon Sherven .08 .25
303 Anthony Vogel .02 .10
304 Michael Hreuss .02 .10
305 Dale Derkatch .08 .25
306 Sergej Schendelew .02 .10
307 Christian Brittig .02 .10
308 Harald Waibel .02 .10
309 Rainer Lutz .02 .10
310 Ewald Steiger .02 .10
311 Didi Hegen .02 .10
312 Ralf Reisinger .02 .10
313 Henrik Holscher .02 .10
314 Karl Friesen .20 .50
315 Christian Frutel .02 .10
316 Tobias Abstreiter .02 .10
317 Christopher Sandner .02 .10
318 Harald Birk .02 .10
319 Chris Straube .02 .10
320 EHC 80 Nurnberg Team Card .02 .10
321 Josef Golonka .02 .10
322 Christian Gerum .02 .10
323 Paul Geddes .02 .10
324 Ian Young .02 .10
325 Stefan Steinbock .02 .10
326 Doug Irwin .02 .10
327 Christian Flugge .02 .10
328 Klaus Birk .02 .10
329 Jurgen Lechl .02 .10
330 Thomas Popiesch .02 .10
331 Miroslav Maly .02 .10
332 Stephan Eder .02 .10
333 Arno Brux .02 .10
334 Jiri Dolezal .02 .10
335 Reiner Vorderbruggen .02 .10
336 Thomas Sterflinger .02 .10
337 Bernhard Engelbrecht .02 .10
338 Michael Weinfurter .02 .10
339 Sepp Wassermann .02 .10
340 Stephan Bauer .02 .10
341 Otto Sykora .02 .10
342 Ratingen Die Lowen Team Card .02 .10
343 Bill Lochead .08 .25
344 Pavel Mann .02 .10
345 Christian Kohmann .02 .10
346 Sven Prusa .02 .10
347 Otto Keresztes .02 .10
348 Frank Kovacs .02 .10
349 Jiri Smicek .02 .10
350 Richard Brodnicke .02 .10
351 Andrej Fuchs .02 .10
352 Oliver Kasper .02 .10
353 Michael Kratz .02 .10
354 Klaus Striemitzer .02 .10
355 Oliver Schwarz .02 .10
356 Boris Fuchs .02 .10
357 Christian Althoff .02 .10
358 Waldemar Novosjolov .02 .10
359 Thomas Imdahl .02 .10
360 Helmut Elters .02 .10
361 Andrej Hanisz .02 .10
362 Peter Lutter .02 .10
363 Martem Janov .02 .10
364 Mark Bassen .02 .10
365 Udo Schmid .02 .10
366 Mark Bassen .08 .25
367 Rosenheim Star Bulls Team Card .02 .10
368 Ernst Hofner .02 .10
369 Ludek Bukac .02 .10
370 Markus Wieland .02 .10
371 Andreas Schneider .02 .10
372 Raphael Kruger .02 .10
373 Michael Tattner .02 .10
374 Rick Boehm .02 .10
375 Robert Hock .02 .10
376 Joachim Reil .02 .10
377 Radek Toupal .02 .10
378 Martin Reichel .02 .10
379 Ron Fischer .02 .10
380 Raimund Hilger .08 .25
381 Petr Hrbek .02 .10
382 Oliver Hausler .02 .10
383 Christian Gegenfurther .02 .10
384 Marc Seliger .08 .25
385 Venci Sebek .02 .10
386 Florian Keller .08 .25
387 Heinrich Schiffl .02 .10
388 Michael Pohl .02 .10
389 Fuchse Sachsen Team Card .02 .10
390 Jiri Kochta .02 .10
391 Boris Capla .02 .10
392 Matthias Kliemann .02 .10
393 Josef Rednicek .02 .10
394 Branjo Heisig .02 .10
395 Jens Schwabe .08 .25
396 Frank Peschke .02 .10
397 Thomas Schubert .02 .10
398 Torsten Eisebitt .02 .10
399 Marcel Lichnovsky .02 .10
400 Jari Gronstrand .08 .25
401 Thomas Knobloch .02 .10
402 Falk Herzig .02 .10
403 Thomas Wagner .02 .10
404 Jan Tabor .02 .10
405 Sebastian Klenner .02 .10
406 Peter Hofmann .02 .10
407 Terry Cambell .08 .25
408 Antonio Fonso .02 .10
409 Thomas Bresagk .02 .10
410 Peter Franke .02 .10
411 Andreas Ott .02 .10
412 Michael Flemming .02 .10
413 Janusz Janikowski .02 .10
414 Schwenningen Wild Wings Team Card .02 .10
415 Miroslav Berek .02 .10
416 Bob Burns .02 .10
417 Thomas Gaus .02 .10
418 Richard Trojan .02 .10
419 Ilmar Toman .02 .10
420 Alan Young .02 .10
421 Michael Pastika .02 .10
422 Thomas Schadler .02 .10
423 Andrei Kovalev .02 .10
424 Alexander Horn .02 .10
425 Petr Kopta .02 .10
426 Robert Brezina .02 .10
427 Wayne Hynes .08 .25
428 Frantisek Frosch .02 .10
429 Carsten Solbach .02 .10
430 George Fritz .02 .10
431 Mike Bader .02 .10
432 Thomas Deiter .02 .10
433 Daniel Nowak .08 .25
434 Peter Heinold .02 .10
435 Matthias Hoppe .02 .10
436 Grant Martin .08 .25
437 Roger Bruns .02 .10
438 Andreas Renz .02 .10
439 Karsten Schulz .02 .10
440 Alfie Turcotte .08 .25

1994-95 German First League

This set features players of the German First League, a division one lower than the DEL. The set is noteworthy for the inclusion of several NHLers who performed briefly on this circuit during the 1994 NHL lockout, including Jaromir Jagr, Petr Klima and Vladimir Konstantinov.

COMPLETE SET (665) 30.00 80.00
33 Jorn Seuthe .08 .25
34 Pietro Vacca .08 .25
35 Gunther Eisenhut .08 .25
36 Thomas Kulzer .08 .25
37 Christian Zessak .08 .25
38 Peter Sterz .08 .25
39 Michael Maass .08 .25
40 Thomas Brandl .08 .25
41 Thomas Daffner .08 .25
42 Volker Kollmeder .08 .25
43 Thomas Haiti .08 .25
44 Hans Eberhard .08 .25
45 Enrico Kock .08 .25
46 Peter Hampl .08 .25
47 German Wolgin .08 .25
48 Andrej Balandin .08 .25
49 Rainer Wohlmann .08 .25
50 Teamcard Checklist .08 .25
51 Michael Eibl .08 .25
52 Sven Schubert .08 .25
53 Franz Steer .08 .25
54 Ottmar Schluttenhofer .08 .25
55 Wolfgang Oswald .08 .25
56 John Samanski .08 .25
57 Marty Irvine .08 .25
58 Herbert Schadler .08 .25
59 Jeff Vaive .08 .25
60 Markus Neumuller .08 .25
61 Norbert Arians .08 .25
62 Alfred Weiss .08 .25
63 Gert Heubach .08 .25
64 Hans-Georg Eder .08 .25
65 Hansi Bader .08 .25
66 Franz Futtner .08 .25
67 Klaus Pillmaier .08 .25
68 Donar Dotzauer .08 .25
69 Bertil Filgis .08 .25
70 Roman Zaborowski .08 .25
71 Thomas Dahlem .08 .25
72 Markus Faistenhammer .08 .25
73 Teamcard Checklist .08 .25
74 Thomas Dolak .08 .25
75 Oliver Kratt .08 .25
76 Klaus Muller .08 .25
77 Ralf Lux .08 .25
78 Igor Dorochin .08 .25
79 Ravil Khaidarov .08 .25
80 Peter Hejma .08 .25
81 Thomas Geldreich .08 .25
82 Christian Helber .08 .25
83 Marc Schonfeld .08 .25
84 Christian Wolfgramm .08 .25
85 Leos Zajic .08 .25
86 Rick Laycock .08 .25
87 Stefan Lahn .08 .25
88 Thomas Steinberg .08 .25
89 Jan Repka .08 .25
90 Joseph Peroutka .08 .25
91 Andreas Mockl .08 .25
92 Peter Salmik .08 .25
93 Jorg Lettgen .08 .25
94 Frank Furderer .08 .25
95 Christian Ott .08 .25
96 Teamcard Checklist .08 .25
97 Rodion Pauels .08 .25
98 Aaron Strasser .08 .25

9 Ernst Messthaler .08 .25
00 Juri Starkhov .08 .25
01 Nikolai Varianov .08 .25
02 Tomas Krejcir .08 .25
03 Stefan Zellhuber .08 .25
04 Markus Gmeiner .08 .25
05 Richard Schnetz .08 .25
06 Wolfgang Koziol .08 .25
07 Christian Hauserer .08 .25
08 Gerhard Dittrich .08 .25
09 Christopher Zweng .08 .25
10 Peter Hartung .08 .25
11 Robert Scharpf .08 .25
12 Florian Schneider .08 .25
13 Tauno Zobel .08 .25
14 Matthias Sanger .08 .25
15 Peter Asanger .08 .25
16 Christian Gansenender .08 .25
17 Hans-Jorg Stetter .08 .25
18 Thomas Frohlich .08 .25
19 Karl Streit .08 .25
20 Stefan Bardzinski .08 .25
21 Teamcard .08 .25
Checklist
22 Josef Capla .08 .25
23 Jorg Zinnecker .08 .25
24 Peter Harrer .08 .25
25 Heinrich Korph .08 .25
26 Martin Kirsch .08 .25
27 Michael Freissmann .08 .25
28 Peter Rappold .08 .25
29 Daniel Piechaczek .08 .25
30 Bernd Gossinger .00 .25
31 Michael Hogl .08 .25
32 Hubert Jellen .08 .25
33 Hans Hansch .08 .25
34 Steven Schafer .08 .25
35 Harald Wust .08 .25
36 Jean-Claude Brehm .08 .25
37 Olaf Bjorner .08 .25
38 Dusan Canik .08 .25
39 Martin Gessinger .08 .25
40 Martin Tschichoflos .08 .25
41 Ultich Liebsch .08 .25
42 Svyatoslav Khalizov .08 .25
43 Michael Pescheck .08 .25
44 Roland Seckler .08 .25
45 Teamcard .08 .25
Checklist
46 Gerd Wittmann .08 .25
47 Vladimir Macholda .08 .25
48 Sascha Bernhardt .08 .25
49 Michael Thurner .08 .25
50 Norbert Haslach .08 .25
51 Vitus ner Mitterfell .08 .25
52 Thorsten Haaf .08 .25
53 Michael Stejskal .08 .25
54 Klaus Jansen .08 .25
55 Oliver Hackert .08 .25
56 Ladislav Svozil .08 .25
57 Karsten Neumann .08 .25
58 Alexander Ulmer .08 .25
59 Joseph West .08 .25
60 Oliver Weissenberger .08 .25
61 Manfred Schuster .08 .25
62 Oliver Vost .08 .25
63 Peter Stankovic .08 .25
64 Uwe Geisert .08 .25
65 Peter Holdschick .08 .25
66 Ralf Hartfuss .08 .25
67 Bernhard Kopf .08 .25
68 Teamcard .08 .25
Checklist
69 Kim Collins .08 .25
70 Josef Wieser .08 .25
71 Frank Fischer .08 .25
72 Peter Geier .08 .25
73 Glenn Goodall .40 1.00
74 Patrick Fertich .08 .25
75 Mathias Wieser .08 .25
76 Maximilian Schindler .08 .25
77 Bastian Kammerloher .08 .25
78 James Quinlan .08 .25
79 Dirk Heick .08 .25
80 Walter Deisenberger .08 .25
81 Christoph Sauter .08 .25
82 Christian Walleitner .08 .25
83 Martin Sauter .08 .25
84 Oliver Mayer .08 .25
85 Roland Floss .08 .25
86 Maximilian Ahammer .08 .25
87 Robert Schumacher .08 .25
88 Ludvik Kopecky .08 .25
89 Florian Eder .10 .25
90 Teamcard .08 .25
Checklist
91 Ewalds Grabowskis .08 .25
92 Gerhard Petrussek .08 .25
93 Robert Bockler .08 .25
94 Markus Epple .08 .25
95 Mivhael Weisenbach .08 .25
96 Michael Billmaier .08 .25
97 Joachim Ried .08 .25
98 Holger Micheller .08 .25
99 Igor Pavlov .08 .25
0 Rudiger Weis .08 .25
1 Alexander Zittlau .08 .25
2 Michael Schaeufl .08 .25
3 Oleg Znarok .08 .25
4 Armin Fohry .08 .25
5 Franz-Xaver Ibelherr .08 .25
6 Karl Sajdl .08 .25
7 Daniel Schury .08 .25
8 Manfred Korb .08 .25
9 Christian Baier .08 .25
0 Christian Reuter .08 .25
1 Paul Haringer .08 .25
2 Erwin Haiusa .08 .25
3 Roland Hanemann .08 .25
4 Joachim Jais .08 .25
5 Teamcard .08 .25
Checklist
6 Eduard Giblak .08 .25
7 Robert Bohm .08 .25
8 Paul Greiter .08 .25
9 Max Ostermeier .08 .25
0 Florian Schmid .08 .25
1 Alexander Meyer .08 .25
2 Michael Lehmann .08 .25
3 Andi Ostermeier .08 .25
4 Manfred Braun .08 .25
5 Franz Daxner .08 .25
6 Michael Hock .08 .25
7 Oliver Kleininger .08 .25
8 Chris Clarke .08 .25
9 Andreas Paukner .08 .25
0 Florian Jager .08 .25
1 Patrick Gerber .08 .25
2 Karl Huttl .08 .25
3 Brad Belland .08 .25
4 Christian Lex .08 .25
235 Anton Hager .08 .25
236 Uli Stadier .08 .25
237 Teamcard .08 .25
Checklist
238 Florian Strida .08 .25
239 Peter Freissl .08 .25
240 Peter Engel .08 .25
241 Georg Weckerle .08 .25
242 Reiner Bauerle .08 .25
243 Johann Fischer .08 .25
244 Christian Kratzmeir .08 .25
245 Martin Strida .08 .25
246 Wolfgang Obermeier .08 .25
247 Franz Bruckl .08 .25
248 Robert Schmidt .08 .25
249 Jiri Jiroutek .08 .25
250 Bjorn Lehner .08 .25
251 Florian Rohde .08 .25
252 Paul Ruzicka .08 .25
253 Andreas Kraus .08 .25
254 Oliver Ciganovic .08 .25
255 Christian Steidl .08 .25
256 Klaus Strobl .08 .25
257 Robert Hauck .08 .25
258 Thomas Reitmeir .08 .25
259 Joachim Hagelsperger .08 .25
260 Florian Steidl .08 .25
261 Teamcard .08 .25
Checklist
262 Alexej Sulak .08 .25
263 Markus Mayer .08 .25
264 Thomas Brenzig .08 .25
265 Sven Erhart .08 .25
266 Holger Lieb .08 .25
267 Josef Maier .08 .25
268 Paul Huber .08 .25
269 Rainer Hain .08 .25
270 Peter Kothmayr .08 .25
271 Denis Hanko .08 .25
272 Manfred Muhlegger .08 .25
273 James Johannsen .08 .25
274 Michael Kteitl .08 .25
275 Reiner Sangl .08 .25
276 Rainer Hirschvogel .08 .25
277 Markus Weiss .08 .25
278 Herbert Gmeinder .08 .25
279 Gunther Hartmann .08 .25
280 Jorg Peters .08 .25
281 Sergej Boldavesko .08 .25
282 Peter Dorn .08 .25
283 Markus Kothmayr .08 .25
284 Teamcard .08 .25
Checklist
285 Georg Kink .08 .25
286 Gerhard Stranka .08 .25
287 Michael Pump .08 .25
288 Tom Gobel .08 .25
289 Vladimir Fedossov .08 .25
290 Andreas Oswald .08 .25
291 Andreas Ludwig .08 .25
292 Martin Leuthner .08 .25
293 Jurgen Reindl .08 .25
294 Karl Ostler .08 .25
295 Martin Holzer .08 .25
296 Peter Fischer .08 .25
297 Jens Feller .08 .25
298 Henry Domke .08 .25
299 Markus Kossig .08 .25
300 Andreas Maurer .08 .25
301 Georg Grunauer .08 .25
302 Andreas Wittig .08 .25
303 Andreas Gebauer .08 .25
304 Hubert Buchwieser .08 .25
305 Andreas Raubal .08 .25
306 Christian Winkler .08 .25
307 Brett Stewart .08 .25
308 Christoph Sandner .08 .25
309 Rainer Lutz .08 .25
310 Alfred Burkhard .08 .25
311 Dale Derkatch .20 .50
312 Teamcard .08 .25
Checklist
313 Rudolf Sindelar .08 .25
314 Thomas Hobek .08 .25
315 Jason Hall .08 .25
316 Jochen Hordler .08 .25
317 Mark Armstrong .08 .25
318 Peter Netsch .08 .25
319 Armin Hanke .08 .25
320 Jaroslav Peska .08 .25
321 Steve Neumann .08 .25
322 Markus Trendl .08 .25
323 Daniel Gardner .08 .25
324 Marek Kurowski .08 .25
325 Markus Albrecht .08 .25
326 Sascha Groger .08 .25
327 Stefan Leuschner .08 .25
328 Andreas Kimker .08 .25
329 Roland Schneider .08 .25
330 Elko Porzi .08 .25
331 Stefan Wegmann .08 .25
332 Holger Cecco .08 .25
333 Ralf Gaess .08 .25
334 EHC Straubing .08 .25
335 Franz Hejcik .08 .25
337 Achim Sipmeier .08 .25
338 Christian Penzkofer .08 .25
339 Thomas Schambeck .08 .25
340 Douglas Kirton .08 .25
341 Rainer Schuster .08 .25
342 Vaclav Mandous .08 .25
343 Christian Knott .08 .25
344 Edward Zawatsky .08 .25
345 Christian Heitzer .08 .25
346 RA¼diger Metsch .08 .25
347 Christian Setz .08 .25
348 Sascha Werner .08 .25
349 Martin Ebenburger .08 .25
350 Daniel Vogl .08 .25
351 Stephan Meier .08 .25
352 Sven Barnet .08 .25
353 Robert Steinmann .08 .25
354 1. EV Weiden .08 .25
355 Wilbert Duszenko .08 .25
356 Alexander Becker .08 .25
357 Frank Gentges .08 .25
358 Anton Doll .08 .25
359 Stefan Peschek .08 .25
360 Oliver Hecht .08 .25
361 Dirk Salinger .08 .25
362 Yuri Chipitsyn .08 .25
363 Marco Zimmermann .08 .25
364 Christian Martin .08 .25
365 Lubos Thur .08 .25
366 Andreas Frysztacki .08 .25
367 Sergej Agejkin .08 .25
368 Roman Bartosch .08 .25
369 Ales Volek .08 .25
370 Josef PreuÃŸ .08 .25
371 Thomas Pokorny .00 .25
372 Roman Zilka .08 .25
373 Dietmar Habnitt .08 .25
374 Horst BÃornreuther .08 .25
375 Stefan Breitner .08 .25
376 Teamcard .08 .25
Checklist
377 Ricki Alexander .08 .25
378 Ingo Schwarz .08 .25
379 Serge Lajoie .08 .25
380 Thomas Barczikowski .08 .25
381 Rik Schaefer .08 .25
382 Markus Reiter .08 .25
383 Todd Goodwin .08 .25
384 Thorsten Wolf .08 .25
385 Volker Lindenzweig .08 .25
386 Sven Paschek .08 .25
387 Markus Jehner .08 .25
388 Jurgen Engels .08 .25
389 Martin Prada .08 .25
390 Norbert Scholz .08 .25
391 Gregory Pruden .08 .25
392 Oliver Vieten .08 .25
393 Robert Vozar .08 .25
394 Martin Williams .08 .25
395 Jan Schier .08 .25
396 Michael Eckert .08 .25
397 Thomas Krebs .08 .25
398 Teamcard .08 .25
Checklist
399 Gerald Mull .08 .25
400 Juris Kruminsch .08 .25
401 Frank Strauss .08 .25
402 Peter Kaluza .08 .25
403 Dirk Sobottka .08 .25
404 Alwin Wever .08 .25
405 Jerzey Christ .08 .25
406 Andreas Kemper .08 .25
407 Andre Wilmshofer .08 .25
408 Olaf Busch .08 .25
409 Rico Petrick .08 .25
410 Kurt Wickenheiser .20 .50
411 Marc Muller .20 .50
412 Steffen Klau .08 .25
413 Zsolt Heffler .08 .25
414 Martin Bergeron .08 .25
415 Willi Tesch .08 .25
416 Frank Fischoder .08 .25
417 Darius Wonschweski .08 .25
418 Teamcard .08 .25
Checklist
419 Eduard Nocak .08 .25
420 Stephan Schafer .08 .25
421 Michael Schmitz .08 .25
422 Jochen Hecker .08 .25
423 Axel Gesser .08 .25
424 Heinz-Gerd Albers .08 .25
425 Markus Bak .08 .25
426 Bernd Deske .08 .25
427 Ron Noak .08 .25
428 Darren Colbourne .08 .25
429 Frank Pribil .08 .25
430 Holger Rimroth .08 .25
431 Lars Tannhof .08 .25
432 Ulrik Kuhnekath .08 .25
433 Jorg Deske .08 .25
434 Guy Phillips .08 .25
435 Jorg Bohme .08 .25
436 Udo Sofan .08 .25
437 Matthias Starke .08 .25
438 Oliver Walde .08 .25
439 Teamcard .08 .25
Checklist
440 Dieter Bruggemann .08 .25
441 Julian Binavince .08 .25
442 Kai Kemper .08 .25
443 Raimund Peschke .08 .25
444 Frank Besser .08 .25
445 Frank Blanke .08 .25
446 John Neeld .08 .25
447 Alexander Knoff .08 .25
448 Brad Scott .08 .25
449 Bodo Mischer .08 .25
450 Jiri Kovarik .08 .25
451 Markus Kolloch .08 .25
452 Carsten Plate .08 .25
453 Thomas Hesse .08 .25
454 Jorg Loschek .08 .25
455 Dirk Voss .08 .25
456 Detlev Eltermann .08 .25
457 Volker Loscheck .08 .25
458 Richard Drewniak .08 .25
459 Teamcard .08 .25
Checklist
460 Erwin Materna .08 .25
461 Ingmar Kracht .08 .25
462 Michael Meixner .08 .25
463 Dirk Rossbach .08 .25
464 Karsten Scherping .08 .25
465 Mark Mahon .08 .25
466 Wolfgang Hofbauer .08 .25
467 Uwe Geiselmann .08 .25
468 Sean Krakivsky .08 .25
469 Douglas Murray .08 .25
470 Marek Gajewski .08 .25
471 Mario Feigl .08 .25
472 Frank Liebert .08 .25
473 Miroslav Mago .08 .25
474 Mirsolav Sakmirda .08 .25
475 Dirk Nieleck .08 .25
476 Jan Furd .08 .25
477 Ralf Kubiak .08 .25
478 Marek Adamec .08 .25
479 Douglas Murray .08 .25
480 Teamcard .08 .25
Checklist
481 Sergej Svetlov .08 .25
482 Christian Berlin .08 .25
483 Marek Adamek .08 .25
484 Ralf Cassebaum .08 .25
485 Ingo Rdurch .08 .25
486 Sergej Hatkevitsch .08 .25
487 Thomas Otto .08 .25
488 Riccardo Siegert .08 .25
489 Willy Reinhard .08 .25
490 Jorn Sigmansky .08 .25
491 Guido Drongowski .08 .25
492 Carsten Boss .08 .25
493 Jacek Plechutta .08 .25
494 Thorsten Peters .08 .25
495 Lutz Bongers .08 .25
496 Armin Schnitzler .08 .25
497 Teamcard .08 .25
Checklist
498 Walter Koberle .08 .25
499 Carsten Lange .08 .25
500 Jurgen Schultz .08 .25
501 Jan Raspel .08 .25
502 Christoph Gelzinus .08 .25
503 Markus Kamman .08 .25
504 Markus Buchhart .08 .25
505 Holger Schmitz .08 .25
506 Ladislav Kolda .08 .25
507 Arndt Kons .08 .25
508 Boris Morsch .08 .25
509 Darius Wonschewski .08 .25
510 Benedikt Kons .08 .25
511 James Dressler .08 .25
512 Dirk Scholz .08 .25
513 Marco Scharf .08 .25
514 Mike van Hauten .08 .25
515 Max Bander .08 .25
516 Gilbert Schroder .08 .25
517 Teamcard .08 .25
Checklist
518 Alexander Wolkow .08 .25
519 Sven Schmitz .08 .25
520 Andrej Ovtschinnikov .08 .25
521 Boguslav Kuta .08 .25
522 Sergej Zaitsev .08 .25
523 Rene Naroska .08 .25
524 Markus Menschig .08 .25
525 Milos Piperski .08 .25
526 Andreas Halfmann .08 .25
527 Marcus Golabek .08 .25
528 Peter Kraus .08 .25
529 Peter Juchem .08 .25
530 Marius Cissewski .08 .25
531 Falk Elzner .08 .25
532 Jens Herget .08 .25
533 Fabian Dahlem .08 .25
534 Jurgen Trattner .08 .25
535 Daniel Walther .08 .25
536 Peter Burfant .08 .25
537 Eduard Lorer .08 .25
538 Andreas Keiler .08 .25
539 Haie Schalker GEV .08 .25
540 Charly Stenner CO .08 .25
541 Thomas Blasche .08 .25
542 Dietmar Schramm .08 .25
543 Achim Blaar .08 .25
544 Graischa Pietsch .08 .25
545 Robert Simon .08 .25
546 Bruce Bonner .08 .25
547 Ladislav Hospodar .08 .25
548 Martin Jilek .08 .25
549 Michael Scanu .08 .25
550 Phil Berger .08 .25
551 Christoph Kleckers .08 .25
552 Patrick Schmitz .08 .25
553 Gregor Wilk .08 .25
554 Jens Casten .08 .25
555 Andre Jucknischke .08 .25
556 Vladimir Kames .08 .25
557 Petr Fiala .08 .25
558 Marco Blazyczek .08 .25
559 Trajan Cazacu .08 .25
560 Robert Schutz .08 .25
561 Jaromir Jagr 20.00 50.00
562 ETC Timmendorf .08 .25
563 Jeff Pyle .08 .25
564 Gerd Vogel .08 .25
565 Andrzej Bielenink .08 .25
566 Marvin Glaser .08 .25
567 Harald Bolke .08 .25
568 Christian Spaan .08 .25
569 Henry Thom .08 .25
570 Matthias Schnabel .08 .25
571 Mike Bukowski .08 .25
572 Jeff Tomlinson .20 .50
573 Steffen Thau .08 .25
574 Mark MacKay .20 .50
575 Olaf Brull .08 .25
576 Moe Lemay .40 1.00
577 Michael Mai .08 .25
578 Peter Hiller .08 .25
579 Christoph Hadraschek .08 .25
580 Mike Wehrmann .08 .25
581 Lars Wunsche .08 .25
582 Maj Boguslaw .08 .25
583 Sven Rampf .08 .25
584 Teamcard .08 .25
Checklist
585 Helmut Bauer .08 .25
586 Guido Titzhoff .08 .25
587 Lubomir Lang .08 .25
588 Guy Rouleau .08 .25
589 Andreas Naumann .20 .50
590 Marc Otten .08 .25
591 Kenneth Filgis .08 .25
592 Dimitri Matuschow .08 .25
593 Markus Pollock .08 .25
594 Mario Plack .08 .25
595 Herbert Plattner .08 .25
596 Roman Sindelar .20 .50
597 Herbert Ott .08 .25
598 Reik Blasche .08 .25
599 Vladimir Lukscheider .08 .25
600 Christof Grunthal .08 .25
601 Hermann Retzer .08 .25
602 Adam Gedyk .08 .25
603 Ralf Lamberty .08 .25
604 Teamcard .08 .25
Checklist
605 Kevin Gaudet .08 .25
606 Dale Reinig .08 .25
607 Jorg Meyer .08 .25
608 Bruce Keller .08 .25
609 Laszlo Csata .08 .25
610 Douglas Murray .08 .25
611 Garry Schwindt .08 .25
612 Fred Carroll .08 .25
613 Len Soccio .20 .50
614 Michail Lemmer .08 .25
615 Dieter Reiss .08 .25
616 Jirko Seib .08 .25
617 Matthias Kuhnel .08 .25
618 Heinrich Synowietz .08 .25
619 Paul Synowietz .08 .25
620 Justyn Denisiuk .08 .25
621 Slawomir Osinski .08 .25
622 Jari Pasanen .08 .25
623 Marcus Beeck .08 .25
624 Vladimir Konstantinov 4.00 10.00
625 Teamcard .08 .25
Checklist
626 Josef Vimmer .08 .25
627 Torsten Kluin .08 .25
628 Dieter Frenzel .08 .25
629 Harald Hebig .08 .25
630 Jorg Volkle .08 .25
631 Alexander Gorsdorf .08 .25
632 Roman Slezak .08 .25
633 Jan Baron .08 .25
634 Sergej Jaschin .08 .25
635 Robert Eylert .08 .25
636 Anatoli Antipov .08 .25
637 Heiko Tabor .08 .25
638 Jan-Hans Pokorny .08 .25
639 Roman Blazek .08 .25
640 Alexander Purschel .08 .25
641 Bernd Timmer .08 .25
642 Tomasz Mieszkowski .08 .25
643 Vaclav Drobny .08 .25
644 Teamcard .08 .25
Checklist
645 Nikolai Besprosvannych .08 .25
646 Dimitri Ritthaler .08 .25
647 Dimitri Konjuchov .08 .25
648 Erwin Forster .08 .25
649 Olaf-Bjorn Kolle .08 .25
650 Gary Cummins .08 .25
651 Garth Bannatyne .08 .25
652 Jamie Hartnett .08 .25
653 Cory Holden .08 .25
654 Andreas Henkel .08 .25
655 Janusz Wielgus .08 .25
656 Douglas Morton .08 .25
657 Kebin McGibney .08 .25
658 Daniel Poudrier .20 .50
659 Peter Just .08 .25
660 Lumir Mikesz .08 .25
661 Kenneth Filbey .08 .25
662 Richard Jelsovsky .08 .25
663 Petr Klima .40 1.00
664 Jiri Jiroutek .08 .25
665 Mark MacKay .20 .50

1995-96 German DEL

This 450-card set features the players of Germany's top hockey division, the DEL. The cards measure the standard size, and were issued in six-card packs for 2.5 marks. The card fronts feature action photography with the player name, position and team logo along the bottom. The back includes another photo along with stats. The set is highlighted by the inclusion of several NHLers who played in the DEL during the 1994 lockout including Pavel Bure, Jeremy Roenick and Brendan Shanahan. The hologram chase card was randomly inserted in 1:375 packs. A collector's album to house the cards was available through a wrapper offer for 45 marks.

COMPLETE SET (450) 50.00 125.00
1 Gary Prior .05 .15
2 R. Meister .02 .10
3 D. Schrapp .02 .10
4 S. Campbell .02 .10
5 F. Meyer .02 .10
6 R. Mendel .02 .10
7 K. Collins .05 .15
8 S. Mayer .02 .10
9 T. Fendt .02 .10
10 Andrei Skopintsev .05 .15
11 B. Wilkie .02 .10
12 D. Moeser .02 .10
13 Martin Nagler .02 .10
14 Sven Zywitza .02 .10
15 Marc Habscheid .08 .25
16 D. Held .02 .10
17 H.Romer .02 .10
18 Rick Laycock .02 .10
19 Robert Francz .02 .10
20 Tim Ferguson .02 .10
21 R. Heidt .05 .15
22 Eric Dylla .02 .10
23 H. Birk .02 .10
24 R. Schneider .02 .10
25 B. Flynn .02 .10
26 A. Dietzsch .02 .10
27 U. Dohler .02 .10
28 J. Stumpf .02 .10
29 T. Deutscher .02 .10
30 F. Kannewurf .02 .10
31 T. Graul .02 .10
32 D. Perschau .02 .10
33 P. Solf .02 .10
34 D. Poudrier .02 .10
35 Bernhard Kaminski .02 .10
36 Christoph Hadraschek .02 .10
37 S. Felski .02 .10
38 M. Swibenko .02 .10
39 H. Mix .02 .10
40 M. Maroste .02 .10
41 T. Tumbach .02 .10
42 J. Schertz .02 .10
43 M. Losch .02 .10
44 Andreas Naumann .05 .15
45 Marc Garthe .02 .10
46 I. Dorochin .02 .10
47 Thomas Mitew .02 .10
48 Claes Lundmark .02 .10
49 C. Panek .02 .10
50 K. Merk .20 .50
51 M. Gronau .02 .10
52 S. Steinecker .02 .10
53 J. Lehner .02 .10
54 T. O'Regan .05 .15
55 F. Stillmann .02 .10
56 M. Rentzsch .02 .10
57 S. Sinner .02 .10
58 A. Schubert .05 .15
59 T. Tanti .08 .25
60 G. Malo .02 .10
61 M. Komma .02 .10
62 T. Schinko .02 .10
63 G. Holzmann .02 .10
64 M. Kosturik .02 .10
65 C. Brittig .02 .10
66 J. Rumrich .02 .10
67 J. Chabot .20 .50
68 A. Dimbat .02 .10
69 U. Liebsch .02 .10
70 M. Teevens .05 .15
71 F. Brannstom .02 .10
72 Dennis Meyer .02 .10
73 Lars Hoffmann .02 .10
74 H. Nilsson .02 .10
75 M. Karlsson .02 .10
76 Helmut De Raaf .08 .25
77 K. Fischer .30 .75
78 C. Gossmann .02 .10
79 T. Kienas .08 .25
80 C. Kreutzer .02 .10
81 B. Bergen .02 .10
82 A. Niederberger .05 .15
83 R. Amann .02 .10
84 U. Hiemer .05 .15
85 S. Sorokin .05 .15
86 R. Sterflinger .02 .10
87 L. Funk .02 .10
88 C. Valentine .20 .50
89 G. Sherven .05 .15
90 B. Lingemann .02 .10
91 B. Doucet .08 .25
92 B. Kuhnhauser .02 .10
93 B. Eakin .05 .15
94 D. Hegen .08 .25
95 A. Brockmann .02 .10
96 B. Truntschka .08 .25
97 W. Kummer .02 .10
98 M. Makela .08 .25
99 N. Mondt .02 .10
100 P. Vorobjew .05 .15
101 P. Obresa .02 .10
102 T. Mayer .02 .10
103 M. Seliger .40 1.00
104 F. Storf .02 .10
105 L. Strompf .02 .10
106 G. Thomson .02 .10
107 S. Schendelev .02 .10
108 Martin Duris .02 .10
109 Rudi Gorgenlander .02 .10
110 Andreas Raubal .02 .10
111 S. Ziesche .05 .15
112 P. Kopta .02 .10
113 T. Popiesch .02 .10
114 F. Sills .02 .10
115 J. Lala .05 .15
116 R. Reichel .40 1.00
117 M. Kempf .02 .10
118 I. Schultz .02 .10
119 M. Schultz .02 .10
120 B. Hannon .02 .10
121 J. Schaal .02 .10
122 P. Vozar .02 .10
123 R. Kennedy .02 .10
124 F. Bogelsack .05 .15
125 M. Herbst .02 .10
126 J. Schlickenrieder .02 .10
127 T. Hanusch .02 .10
128 T. Jungwirth .02 .10
129 D. Reierson .02 .10
130 C. Curth .02 .10
131 A. Maidl .02 .10
132 M. Wittbrock .02 .10
133 B. Schlegel .08 .25
134 T. Werner .02 .10
135 D. Rohrbach .02 .10
136 B. Hardy .02 .10
137 H. Kuhnke .02 .10
138 F. Funk .02 .10
139 R. Reuter .02 .10
140 M. Vanik .02 .10
141 G. Preuss .02 .10
142 K. LaVallee .05 .15
143 M. Bleicher .02 .10
144 A. Krinner .02 .10
145 H. Waibel .02 .10
146 H. Zach .02 .10
147 J. Kontny .02 .10
148 G. Hegen .02 .10
149 M. Mokros .02 .10
150 V. Sebek .02 .10
151 A. Engel .02 .10
152 A. Wedl .02 .10
153 J. Mucha .02 .10
154 M. McIntosh .02 .10
155 G. Guttler .02 .10
156 G. Johnston .05 .15
157 J. Kaspercyk .02 .10
158 D. Morrison .02 .10
159 M. Millar .05 .15
160 I. Pacula .02 .10
161 Vitalij Grossmann .02 .10
162 Igor Varitsky .02 .10
163 P. Kwasigroch .02 .10
164 B. Heisig .02 .10
165 G. Evtushevski .05 .15
166 F. Ozellis .02 .10
167 T. Boos .02 .10
168 J. Tolvanen .02 .10
169 D. Medicus .02 .10
170 M. Olbrich .02 .10
171 M. Pethke .02 .10
172 D. Kadlec .05 .15
173 C. Seeberger .02 .10
174 G. Kunce .02 .10
175 D. Kunce .02 .10
176 T. Gschwill .02 .10
177 Marco Eltner .02 .10
178 J. Simon .02 .10
179 Alexander Herbst .02 .10
180 E. Boiger .02 .10
181 O. Hascak .08 .25
182 T. Schnobrich .02 .10
183 A. Vogel .02 .10
184 T. Martinec .02 .10
185 H. Mayer .05 .15
186 R. Timoschuk .02 .10
187 J. Hoffmann .02 .10
188 A. Volland .02 .10
189 R. Hammer .02 .10
190 M. Hess .02 .10
191 D. Derkatch .20 .50
192 Sebastian Schwele .02 .10
193 R.J. Murdoch .08 .25
194 B. Haake .02 .10
195 J. Heiss .30 .75
196 O. Grundmann .02 .10
197 A. Genze .02 .10
198 A. von Trzcinski .02 .10
199 J. Mayr .05 .15
200 M. Ludemann .08 .25
201 A. Pokorny .02 .10
202 J. Meyer .02 .10
203 K. Mende .02 .10
204 H. Hohenberger .20 .50
205 T. Brandl .02 .10
206 S. Mann .02 .10
207 L. Borsato .08 .25
208 L. Stefan .08 .25
209 P. Draisaitl .08 .25
210 A. Lupzig .08 .25
211 R. Reisinger .02 .10
212 R. Zerwesz .02 .10
213 M. Rumrich .02 .10
214 M. Ondrejka .02 .10
215 T. Abstreiter .02 .10
216 F. Demmel .02 .10
217 Sergei Berezin .40 1.00
218 M. Berek .02 .10
219 K. Lang .02 .10
220 R. Bieike .02 .10
221 M. Krawinkel .02 .10
222 K. Karpuk .02 .10
223 K. Micheller .02 .10
224 E. Spry .02 .10
225 A. Ott .02 .10
226 P. Limatainen .02 .10
227 A. Grein .02 .10
228 K. Petrash .02 .10
229 J. Hanlon .02 .10
230 R. Pyka .08 .25
231 T. Imdahl .02 .10
232 C. Lindberg .08 .25
233 Jay Luknowsky .02 .10
234 P. Ihnacak .08 .25
235 M. Stebnicki .02 .10
236 J. Walker .02 .10
237 A. Brux .02 .10
238 Robert Busch .02 .10
239 M. Bassen .02 .10
240 M. Gebel .02 .10
241 B. Johnston .02 .10
242 P. Briza .30 .75
243 C. Kunast .02 .10
244 M. Bresagk .02 .10
245 E. Uvira .02 .10
246 M. Heidt .02 .10
247 P. Gulda .02 .10
248 U. KieBling .08 .25
249 D. Bloem .02 .10
250 T. Vogl .02 .10
251 J. Plachta .02 .10
252 G. Franz .02 .10
253 S. Retzer .02 .10
254 H. Marcoux .02 .10
255 A. Loth .02 .10
256 M. Bullard .08 .25
257 J. Charbonneau .08 .25
258 W. Schreiber .08 .25
259 J. Handrick .02 .10
260 H. Steiger .02 .10
261 Marco Sturm 6.00 15.00
262 L. Nethery .05 .15
263 M. Kuhl .02 .10
264 J. Appel .02 .10
265 M. Flemming .02 .10
266 H. Kreis .02 .10
267 P. Stanton .08 .25
268 C. Lukes .02 .10
269 S. Michel .02 .10
270 S. Richer .05 .15
271 J. Hanft .02 .10
272 E. Goldmann .02 .10
273 M. Gehrig .02 .10
274 P. Gross .02 .10
275 D. Korber .02 .10
276 R. Cimetta .08 .25
277 Jochen Hecht 1.25 3.00
278 T. Feser .02 .10
279 Alexander Serikow .40 1.00
280 P. Pysz .05 .15
281 D. Adamus .02 .10
282 David Musial .02 .10
283 M. Hreus .02 .10
284 C. Straube .02 .10
285 S. Valenti .02 .10
286 S. Thivierge .02 .10
287 J. Eysselt .02 .10
288 Richard Neubauer .02 .10
289 Roman Turek .40 1.00
290 S. Lahn .02 .10
291 C. Gerum .02 .10
292 H. Smazal .02 .10
293 M. Maly .02 .10
294 T. Sterflinger .02 .10
295 Michael Weinfurter .02 .10
296 S. Bauer .02 .10
297 L. Bruggemann .02 .10
298 M. Kehle .02 .10
299 P. Geddes .02 .10
300 I. Young .02 .10
301 S. Steinbock .02 .10
302 J. Lechl .02 .10
303 Markus Goerlitz .02 .10
304 J. Dolozal .08 .25
305 H. Holscher .02 .10
306 S. Wassermann .02 .10
307 O. Sykora .02 .10
308 B. Lochead .05 .15
309 P. Lange .02 .10
310 I. Wood .02 .10
311 H. Thorn .02 .10
312 D. Irwin .02 .10
313 C. Schmitz .02 .10
314 A. Wunsch .02 .10
315 C. Holden .02 .10
316 Jamie Bartman .02 .10
317 P. Lutter .02 .10
318 P. Mann .02 .10
319 G. Muller .02 .10
320 C. Kohmann .02 .10
321 P. Beraldo .05 .15
322 T. Groger .02 .10
323 A. Fuchs .02 .10
324 K. Birk .02 .10
325 Dave Rich .02 .10
326 B. Fuchs .02 .10
327 T. Muhlbauer .02 .10
328 A. Kammerer .02 .10
329 J. Lazaro .20 .50
330 O. Scholz .02 .10
331 B. Reynolds .02 .10
332 J. Sevcik .08 .25
333 P.M. Arnholt .02 .10
334 Gerhard Stranka .02 .10
335 V. Riendeau .20 .50
336 M. Schmidt .02 .10
337 T. Gobel .02 .10
338 V. Fedosov .02 .10
339 R. Jadamzik .02 .10
340 F. Hohendahl .02 .10
341 Anton Raubal .02 .10
342 C. Schonmoser .02 .10
343 Andreas Ludwig .02 .10
344 Karl Ostler .02 .10
345 M. Berwanger .02 .10
346 Martin Holzer .02 .10
347 Jens Feller .02 .10
348 Henry Domke .02 .10
349 Andreas Maurer .02 .10
350 Andreas Gebauer .02 .10
351 G. Oswald .02 .10
352 Hubert Buchwieser .02 .10
353 Brett Stewart .02 .10
354 C. Sandner .02 .10
355 Joachim Hagelsperger .02 .10
356 R. Hock .02 .10
357 Mark Jooris .02 .10
358 E. Hofner .02 .10
359 G. Clark .02 .10
360 K. Friesen .30 .75
361 K. Dalpiaz .08 .25
362 M. Wieland .02 .10
363 C. Clarke .02 .10
364 M. Pottinger .02 .10
365 R. Kruger .02 .10
366 R. Fischer .02 .10
367 C. Gegenfurter .02 .10
368 H. Schiffl .02 .10
369 A. Schneider .02 .10
370 Vitus Mitterfellner .02 .10
371 R. Bohm .02 .10
372 D. Krentz .08 .25
373 Tobias Schraven .02 .10
374 F. Keller .40 1.00
375 D. Derraugh .04 .10
376 M. Reichel .05 .15
377 Markus Draxler .02 .10
378 R. Hilger .05 .15
379 M. Pohl .02 .10
380 M. Kropf .02 .10
381 J. Savage .20 .50
382 J. Eckmaier .02 .10
383 R.R. Burns .02 .10
384 G. Leidborg .02 .10

385 C. Solbach .02 .10
386 M. Hoppe .02 .10
387 G. Hynes .08 .25
388 T. Gaus .02 .10
389 Z. Travnicek .02 .10
390 R. Trojan .02 .10
391 F. Frosch .02 .10
392 D. Nowak .02 .10
393 A. Renz .02 .10
394 A. Young .02 .10
395 R. Brezina .02 .10
396 W. Hynes .02 .10
397 G. Fritz .02 .10
398 M. Bader .02 .10
399 G. Martin .02 .10
400 K. Schulz .02 .10
401 M. Lay .02 .10
402 J. Penney .05 .15
403 R. Cernomaz .05 .15
404 M. MacKay .30 .75
405 S. Hasan .02 .10
406 J. Kochta .02 .10
407 T. Bresagk .02 .10
408 P. Franke .02 .10
409 J. Molling .02 .10
410 F. Prochazka .02 .10
411 J. Reznicek .02 .10
412 T. Schubert .02 .10
413 R. Martin .02 .10
414 M. Lichnovsky .02 .10
415 M. Kliemann .02 .10
416 Ronny Reddo .02 .10
417 F. Peschke .02 .10
418 T. Eisebitt .02 .10
419 J. Janikowski .02 .10
420 T. Knobloch .02 .10
421 F. Herzig .02 .10
422 T. Wagner .02 .10
423 J. Tabor .05 .15
424 Jorg Pohling .02 .10
425 R. Vit .02 .10
426 V. Kulabuchov .02 .10
427 D. Cup Meister 1995 .08 .25
428 Kingston Kuhnhauser .08 .25
Genze
429 Heib .08 .25
Lupzig
430 Brandl .08 .25
Mann
431 Doucet .08 .25
Nowak
432 Meyer .08 .25
Pyka
433 Hegen .08 .25
Kunce
434 Humrich .08 .25
Ludemann
435 Benda .08 .25
Kosturik
436 Kienass Brockmann .05 .15
Hanft
437 Draisaitl Simon .08 .25
Schneider
438 Niederberger .08 .25
439 Martin Reichel .05 .15
440 Klaus Merk .20 .50
441 Glenn Anderson 1.25 3.00
442 Pavel Bure 12.00 30.00
443 Vincent Damphousse 2.00 5.00
444 Uwe Krupp .20 .50
445 Robert Reichel .40 1.00
446 Jeremy Roenick 12.00 30.00
447 Brendan Shanahan 12.00 30.00
448 Jozef Stumpel .75 2.00
449 Doug Weight 2.00 5.00
450 Scott Young .75 2.00
NNO Hologram Karte 4.00 10.00

1996-97 German DEL

This 360-card set features the players of Germany's top division, the DEL. The cards measure the standard size and were issued in six-card packs. The card fronts feature full-bleed action photography, along with the player's name, team logo and logo of the manufacturer. The back includes another photo, affiliated logos, and stats for the '95-96 season, along with career totals and, in some cases, NHL totals. In a few instances, no stats are provided in the case of those players making their debuts in the DEL.

COMPLETE SET (360) 16.00 40.00
1 Gary Prior CO .05 .15
2 Bruno Campese .08 .25
3 Leonardo Conti .05 .15
4 Scott Campbell .05 .15
5 Robert Mendel .05 .15
6 Serge Poudrier .05 .15
7 Torsten Fendt .05 .15
8 Shawn Rivers .05 .15
9 Stefan Mayer .05 .15
10 Michael Bakos .05 .15
11 Tommy Jakobsen .05 .15
12 Duanne Moeser .05 .15
13 Tero Arkiomaa .05 .15
14 Sven Zywitza .05 .15
15 Craig Streu .05 .15
16 Terry Campbell .05 .15
17 Timothy Ferguson .05 .15
18 Yves Heroux .05 .15
19 Max Boldt .05 .15
20 Andre Faust .05 .15
21 Rochus Schneider .05 .15
22 Ron Kennedy CO .05 .15
23 Barry Lewis ASST CO .05 .15
24 Mario Brunetta .20 .50
25 Udo Dohler .05 .15
26 Dirk Perschau .05 .15
27 Darren Durdle .05 .15
28 Greg Andrusak .08 .25
29 Leif Carlsson .05 .15
30 Derek Mayer .08 .25
31 Rob Leask .05 .15
32 Chad Biafore .05 .15
33 Thomas Steen .05 .15
34 Lorenz Funk .05 .15
35 Florian Funk .05 .15
36 Sven Felski .05 .15
37 Peter John Lee .08 .25
38 Andrew McKim .20 .50
39 Andrei Lomakin .08 .25
40 Pelle Svensson .05 .15
41 Jan Schertz .05 .15
42 Kraig Nienhuis .20 .50
43 Niklas Hede .05 .15
44 Mario Chitarroni .08 .25
45 Chris Govedaris .20 .50
46 Pentti Matikainen CO .05 .15
47 Jukka Tammi .08 .25
48 Rupert Meister .05 .15
49 Florian Storf .05 .15
50 Greg Thomson .05 .15
51 Toni Porkka .05 .15
52 Sergej Schendelev .05 .15
53 Kai Rautio .05 .15
54 Rudi Gorgenlander .05 .15
55 Petr Kopta .05 .15
56 Tony Virta .08 .25
57 Ilja Vorobjev .05 .15
58 Thomas Popiesch .05 .15
59 Francois Sills .05 .15
60 Jiro Jarvi .05 .15
61 Jurgen Schaal .05 .15
62 Pavel Vit .05 .15
63 Timo Peltomaa .05 .15
64 Igor Schultz .05 .15
65 Dave Archibald .08 .25
66 Joni Lehto .05 .15
67 Brad Jones .05 .15
68 Miroslav Berek CO .05 .15
69 Karel Lang .05 .15
70 Peter Franke .05 .15
71 Markus Krawinkel .05 .15
72 Zdenek Travnicek .05 .15
73 Martin Gebel .05 .15
74 Klaus Micheller .05 .15
75 Earl Spry .05 .15
76 Frantisek Frosch .05 .15
77 Petri Liimatainen .05 .15
78 Andre Grein .05 .15
79 Ken Petrash .05 .15
80 James Hanlon .05 .15
81 Andrej Kovalev .05 .15
82 Reemt Pyka .05 .15
83 Chris Lindberg .08 .25
84 Jay Luknowsky .05 .15
85 Peter Ihnacak .08 .25
86 Marek Stebnicki .05 .15
87 Johnny Walker .05 .15
88 Danton Cole .08 .25
89 Michael Hreus .05 .15
90 Damian Adamus .05 .15
91 Bill Lochead CO .08 .25
92 Joakim Persson .08 .25
93 Ian Wood .05 .15
94 Pierre Jonsson .05 .15
95 Juha Lampinen .05 .15
96 Christian Schmitz .05 .15
97 Cory Holden .05 .15
98 Peter Lutter .05 .15
99 Dieter Bloem .05 .15
100 Maurizio Catenacci .05 .15
101 Andrej Fuchs .05 .15
102 Mark Montanari .05 .15
103 Boris Fuchs .05 .15
104 Andreas Salomonsson .05 .15
105 Robert Reynolds .05 .15
106 Axel Kammerer .05 .15
107 Jeffrey Lazaro .08 .25
108 Olaf Scholz .05 .15
109 Tony Cimellaro .05 .15
110 Kenneth Hodge .08 .25
111 Gregory Burke .05 .15
112 Tom Coolen CO .05 .15
113 Marc Pethke .05 .15
114 Christian Kunast .05 .15
115 Drahomir Kadlec .08 .25
116 Florian Kuhn .08 .25
117 Erich Goldmann .08 .25
118 Jurgen Simon .05 .15
119 Jeff Winstanley .05 .15
120 Stefano Figliuzzi .05 .15
121 Maurice Mansi .05 .15
122 Agostino Casale .05 .15
123 Hans-Jorg Mayer .05 .15
124 Dino Felicetti .05 .15
125 Roland Timoschuk .05 .15
126 Jim Hoffmann .05 .15
127 John Porco .05 .15
128 Rolf Hammer .05 .15
129 Manuel Hess .05 .15
130 Andy Rymsha .08 .25
131 Wolfgang Kummer .05 .15
132 Trevor Burgess .05 .15
133 Daniel Kunce .05 .15
134 Timo Sutinen .05 .15
135 Petr Briza .30 .75
136 Markus Nachtmann .05 .15
137 Markus Wieland .05 .15
138 Mike Heidt .05 .15
139 Peter Gulda .05 .15
140 Jacek Plachta .05 .15
141 Georg Franz .05 .15
142 Stephan Retzer .05 .15
143 Henry Marcoux .05 .15
144 Mike Bullard .30 .75
145 Jose Charbonneau .08 .25
146 Wally Schreiber .08 .25
147 Jorg Handrick .05 .15
148 Helmut Steiger .05 .15
149 Marco Sturm 4.00 10.00
150 Jonas Johnsson .05 .15
151 Vesa Salo .05 .15
152 Gino Cavallini .08 .25
153 Lars Hurtig .05 .15
154 Olli Kaski .05 .15
155 007 Charly .05 .15
156 Lance Nethery CO .05 .15
157 Ross Yates ASST CO .05 .15
158 Joachim Appel .05 .15
159 Mike Rosati .20 .50
160 Harold Kreis .05 .15
161 Paul Stanton .08 .25
162 Christian Lukes .05 .15
163 Robert Nardella .05 .15
164 Alexander Erdmann .05 .15
165 Stephane J.G. Richer .08 .25
166 Martin Ulrich .05 .15
167 Mike Pellegrims .05 .15
168 Mario Gehrig .05 .15
169 Pavel Gross .05 .15
170 Dave Tomlinson .08 .25
171 Daniel Korber .05 .15
172 Francois Guay .05 .15
173 Jochen Hecht 1.25 3.00
174 Florian Keller .20 .50
175 Till Feser .05 .15
176 Alexander Serikow .20 .50
177 Christian Pouget .05 .15
178 Dieter Kalt .05 .15
179 Paul Beraldo .05 .15
180 Steven Thornton .05 .15
181 Robert Cimetta .20 .50
182 Gary Clark CO .05 .15
183 Bjorn Leonhardt .05 .15
184 Claus Dalpiaz .08 .25
185 Jesper Duus .05 .15
186 Manuel Hiemer .05 .15
187 Markus Pottinger .05 .15
188 Chris Bartolone .05 .15
189 Christian Gegenfurther .05 .15
190 Heinrich Schiffl .05 .15
191 Per Lundell .05 .15
192 Joel Savage .08 .25
193 Josef Muller .05 .15
194 Jari Torkki .05 .15
195 James Hiller .05 .15
196 Doug Derraugh .05 .15
197 Pekka Tirkkonen .05 .15
198 Martin Reichel .05 .15
199 Raimond Hilger .08 .25
200 Michael Schneidawind .05 .15
201 Scott Beattie .05 .15
202 Paris Proft .05 .15
203 Kevin Gaudet .05 .15
204 Wayne Cowley .05 .15
205 Marco Herbst .05 .15
206 Andreas Schubert .05 .15
207 Stephan Sinner .05 .15
208 Heinrich Synowietz .05 .15
209 Paul Synowietz .05 .15
210 Dimitri Frolov .05 .15
211 Andrej Saposhnikov .05 .15
212 Jedrzej Kasperczyk .05 .15
213 Joseph West .05 .15
214 Fabian Ahrens .05 .15
215 Maurice Lemay .05 .15
216 Mark Kosturik .05 .15
217 Mark Jooris .05 .15
218 Len Soccio .05 .15
219 Mark Mahon .05 .15
220 Frank LaScala .05 .15
221 Jari Pasanen .05 .15
222 Ralph Vos .05 .15
223 Anthony Cirelli .05 .15
224 Emilio Iovio .05 .15
225 Gerhard Brunner CO .05 .15
226 Pavel Cagas .05 .15
227 Jonas Eriksson .05 .15
228 Alexander Engel .05 .15
229 Gregory Johnston .08 .25
230 Alexander Wedl .05 .15
231 Jouni Vento .05 .15
232 Roger Ohman .05 .15
233 David Morrison .05 .15
234 Bruce Eakin .05 .15
235 Michael Millar .05 .15
236 Roger Hansson .02 .10
237 Peter Kwasigroch .05 .15
238 Branjo Heisig .05 .15
239 Jukka Seppo .05 .15
240 Greg Evtushevski .05 .15
241 Falk Ozellis .05 .15
242 Daniel Larin .05 .15
243 Tino Boos .05 .15
244 Toni Krinner .05 .15
245 Milan Mokros .05 .15
246 Peter Ustorf CO .05 .15
247 Klaus Merk .08 .25
248 David Berge .05 .15
249 Georg Holzmann .05 .15
250 Tom O'Regan .05 .15
251 Jochen Molling .05 .15
252 Joseph Lehner .05 .15
253 Marco Rentzsch .05 .15
254 Pekka Laksola .05 .15
255 Petri Matikainen .05 .15
256 Tony Tanti .30 .75
257 Gaetan Malo .05 .15
258 Thomas Schinko .05 .15
259 Vitali Karamnow .05 .15
260 Gunther Oswald .05 .15
261 Christian Brittig .05 .15
262 Jurgen Rumrich .05 .15
263 John Chabot .20 .50
264 Andreas Dimbat .05 .15
265 Mark Teevens .05 .15
266 Veli-Pekka Kautonen .05 .15
267 Jarno-Sakari Peltonen .05 .15
268 Hardy Nilsson CO .05 .15
269 Martin Karlsson ASST CO .05 .15
270 Ake Lilljebjorn .05 .15
271 Kai Fischer .08 .25
272 Brad Bergen .05 .15
273 Andreas Niederberger .05 .15
274 Sergej Sorokin .05 .15
275 Robert Sterflinger .05 .15
276 Peter Andersson .05 .15
277 Viktor Gordiouk .08 .25
278 Gordon Sherven .08 .25
279 Benoit Doucet .20 .50
280 Bernd Kuhnhauser .08 .25
281 Dieter Hegen .05 .15
282 Andreas Brockmann .05 .15
283 Ernst Kopf .05 .15
284 Alexej Kudashov .05 .15
285 Bernd Truntschka .08 .25
286 Mikko Makela .05 .15
287 Nikolaus Mondt .05 .15
288 Boris Lingemann .05 .15
289 Thomas Brandl .08 .25
290 Leo Stefan .08 .25
291 Bob Burns .05 .15
292 Carsten Solbach .05 .15
293 Matthias Hoppe .05 .15
294 Sascha Goc .20 .50
295 Gordon Hynes .20 .50
296 Thomas Gaus .05 .15
297 Brian Tutt .05 .15
298 Richard Trojan .05 .15
299 Daniel Nowak .05 .15
300 Andreas Renz .05 .15
301 Sana Hassan .05 .15
302 Alan Young .05 .15
303 Mike Bader .05 .15
304 Robert Brezina .05 .15
305 Wayne Hynes .05 .15
306 Mark Bassen .05 .15
307 Andrew Clark .05 .15
308 Grant Martin .05 .15
309 Michael Lay .05 .15
310 Jackson Penney .05 .15
311 Rich Chernomaz .15 .40
312 Mark MacKay .20 .50
313 Vladimir Fedosov .05 .15
314 Emanuel Viveiros .08 .25
315 Jan Eysselt CO .05 .15
316 Michel Valliere .05 .15
317 Stefan Lahn .05 .15
318 Christian Gerum .05 .15
319 Heiko Smazal .05 .15
320 Christian Curth .05 .15
321 Miroslav Maly .05 .15
322 Torsten Kienass .05 .15
323 Thomas Sterflinger .05 .15
324 Lars Bruggemann .05 .15
325 Paul Geddes .05 .15
326 Rolan Ramoser .05 .15
327 Martin Jiranek .05 .15
328 Stefan Steinbock .05 .15
329 Martin Ekrt .05 .15
330 Jurgen Lechl .05 .15
331 Dion Del Monte .05 .15
332 Markus Welz .05 .15
333 Henrik Holscher .05 .15
334 Otto Sykora .05 .15
335 Milos Vanik .05 .15
336 Robert Murdoch CO .05 .15
337 Bernd Haake ASST CO .05 .15
338 Joseph Heiss .08 .25
339 Olaf Grundmann .05 .15
340 Alexander Genze .05 .15
341 Jorg Mayr .05 .15
342 Mirco Ludemann .05 .15
343 Jayson Meyer .05 .15
344 Karsten Mende .05 .15
345 Herbert Hohenberger .08 .25
346 Joe Cirella .08 .25
347 Petter Nilsson .05 .15
348 Jim Montgomery .20 .50
349 Stefan Mann .05 .15
350 Luciano Borsato .08 .25
351 Dwayne Norris .08 .25
352 Bruno Zarrillo .05 .15
353 Peter Draisaitl .08 .25
354 Joe Busillo .05 .15
355 Andreas Lupzig .05 .15
356 Rainer Zerwesz .05 .15
357 Thomas Forslund .08 .25
358 Tobias Abstreiter .05 .15
359 Patrick Carnback .08 .25
360 Franz Demmel .05 .15

1998-99 German DEL

This set features members of Germany's top hockey circuit. The card stock is very thin, and the words Schirner Edition appear on the front. The backs feature sponsor information (including Eishockey News), stats, and a reproduced signature.

COMPLETE SET (344) 20.00 50.00
1 Burke Murphy .07 .20
2 Marc Seliger .20 .50
3 Jason Clark .07 .20
4 Mike McNeill .07 .20
5 Norm Matherson .07 .20
6 Jeff Sebastien .07 .20
7 Phil Huber .07 .20
8 Todd Wtzel .07 .20
9 Jesper Morin .07 .20
10 Marc Pethke .07 .20
11 Jacek Plachta .07 .20
12 Marcus Adolfson .07 .20
13 Christian Schmitz .07 .20
14 Bob Marshall .07 .20
15 Peter Lutter .07 .20
16 Stefan Mayer .07 .20
17 Daniel Korber .07 .20
18 Carsten Gosdeck .07 .20
19 Jiri Kochta .07 .20
20 Petri Liimatainen .07 .20
21 Thomas Brandl .07 .20
22 Andrej Kovalev .08 .25
23 Johnny Walker .07 .20
24 Neil Eisenhut .20 .50
25 Karel Lang .07 .20
26 Marek Stebnicki .07 .20
27 Chris Bartolone .07 .20
28 John Van Kessel .07 .20
29 Lars Bruggemann .07 .20
30 Jason Meyer .07 .20
31 Reemt Pyka .07 .20
32 Mark Pederson .07 .20
33 Veli-Pekka Kautonen .07 .20
34 Tommie Hartogs .07 .20
35 Frantisek Frosch .07 .20
36 Leo van den Thillart .07 .20
37 Vitali Karamnov .08 .25
38 Stephane Barin .07 .20
39 Roger Nordstrom .07 .20
40 Robert Ouellet .07 .20
41 Doug Mason .07 .20
42 Francois Guay .07 .20
43 Greg Johnston .20 .50
44 Greg Evtushevski .07 .20
45 Shane Peacock .07 .20
46 Chris Rogles .30 .75
47 Gunter Oswald .07 .20
48 Jukka Seppo .07 .20
49 Jurgen Rumrich .07 .20
50 Roger Hansson .07 .20
51 Stephane Robitaille .07 .20
52 Orjan Lindmark .07 .20
53 Jeff MacLeod .07 .20
54 Alexander Wedl .07 .20
55 Jochen Molling .07 .20
56 Paul Cohen .07 .20
57 Daniel Kreutzer .07 .20
58 Nikolaus Mondt .07 .20
59 John Lilley .20 .50
60 Roland Ramoser .07 .20
61 Thomas Dolak .07 .20
62 Tino Boos .07 .20
63 Tobias Abstreiter .07 .20
64 Hans Zach .07 .20
65 Petr Briza .30 .75
66 Wally Schreiber .20 .50
67 Chris Luongo .20 .50
68 Dean Evason .20 .50
69 David Bruce .20 .50
70 Peter Douris .20 .50
71 Jason Herter .20 .50
72 Jorg Hendrick .07 .20
73 Rob Murphy .20 .50
74 Mike Casselmann .07 .20
75 Steve Junker .07 .20
76 Zbynek Kukacka .07 .20
77 Mark Krys .07 .20
78 Markus Wieland .07 .20
79 Evan Marble .07 .20
80 Jari Korpisalo .07 .20
81 Peter Gulda .07 .20
82 Bob Joyce .20 .50
83 Johan Rosen .07 .20
84 Christian Kunast .07 .20
85 Olli Kaski .07 .20
86 Chris Valentine .30 .75
87 Corey Millen .20 .50
88 Tomas Forslund .15 .40
89 Bruno Zarrillo .20 .50
90 Igor Alexandrov .07 .20
91 Bob Halkidis .20 .50
92 Petri Varis .20 .50
93 Joseph Heiss .20 .50
94 Greg Brown .20 .50
95 Dwayne Norris .20 .50
96 Mirko Ludemann .07 .20
97 John Miner .07 .20
98 Boris Rousson .30 .75
99 Craig Woodcroft .07 .20
100 Jorg Mayr .07 .20
101 Steve Wilson .07 .20
102 Rainer Zerwesz .07 .20
103 Brian McReynolds .07 .20
104 Andreas Lupzig .07 .20
105 Giuseppe Busillo .07 .20
106 Jeff Ricciardi .07 .20
107 Mike Hartman .20 .50
108 Timo Lahtinen .07 .20
109 Stephane Morin .20 .50
110 Paul Broten .20 .50
111 Robert Guillet .07 .20
112 Clayton Beddoes .15 .40
113 Robert Cimetta .20 .50
114 Dave MacIntyre .07 .20
115 Johan Norgren .07 .20
116 Todd Nelson .07 .20
117 Guy Phillips .07 .20
118 Craig Martin .20 .50
119 Parris Duffus .30 .75
120 Christian Brittig .07 .20
121 Thomas Schinko .07 .20
122 Mario Gehrig .07 .20
123 Fredrik Ytfeldt .07 .20
124 Lawrence Rucchin .07 .20
125 Heinz Ehlers .07 .20
126 Heinrich Schiffl .07 .20
127 Sylvain Couturier .08 .25
128 Hakan Galiamoutsas .07 .20
129 David Berge .07 .20
130 Marc Savard .07 .20
131 Dale McCourt .20 .50
132 Jukka Tammi .20 .50
133 Chris Snell .20 .50
134 John Chabot .20 .50
135 Len Barrie .20 .50
136 Lija Vorobjev .07 .20
137 Steve Palmer .07 .20
138 Fabrice L'Henry .07 .20
139 Rob Doyle .07 .20
140 Victor Gervais .07 .20
141 Jose Charbonneau .08 .25
142 Thorsten Apel .07 .20
143 Michael Bresagk .07 .20
144 Rick Hayward .08 .25
145 Phil von Steffenelli .07 .20
146 Martin Williams .07 .20
147 Toni Porkka .07 .20
148 Jean-Marc Richard .07 .20
149 Douglas Kirton .07 .20
150 Joel Savage .20 .50
151 Ralf Hantschke .07 .20
152 Ken Quinney .15 .40
153 Marcus Bleicher .07 .20
154 Bob Manno .08 .25
155 Rob Cowie .07 .20
156 Mike Bullard .30 .75
157 Maren Valenti .07 .20
158 Sven Felski .07 .20
159 Andrew McKim .20 .50
160 Derek Mayer .08 .25
161 Niklas Hede .07 .20
162 Thomas Steen .20 .50
163 Mario Brunetta .20 .50
164 Marc Fortier .20 .50
165 Thomas Rhodin .07 .20
166 Nico Pyka .07 .20
167 Chris Govedaris .08 .25
168 Lorenz Funk .07 .20
169 Florian Funk .07 .20
170 Yvon Corriveau .20 .50
171 Mikael Wahlberg .07 .20
172 Darren Durdle .07 .20
173 Pelle Svensson .07 .20
174 Greg Andrusak .08 .25
175 Leif Carlsson .07 .20
176 Andreas Brockmann .07 .20
177 Robert Leask .07 .20
178 Mario Chitaroni .07 .20
179 Chad Biafore .07 .20
180 Peter John Lee .07 .20
181 Len Soccio .20 .50
182 Jason Lafreniere .20 .50
183 Joe West .07 .20
184 Brent Tully .20 .50
185 Mark Kosturik .07 .20
186 David Haas .07 .20
187 Darcy Martini .07 .20
188 Gary Leeman .20 .50
189 Lee Davidson .07 .20
190 Scott Metcalfe .20 .50
191 Tom Pederson .20 .50
192 Francois Gravel .07 .20
193 Bjorn Leonhardt .07 .20
194 Mike Johnson .07 .20
195 Claudio Scremin .07 .20
196 Mike Ware .07 .20
197 Jurgen Trattner .07 .20
198 Dan Currie .20 .50
199 Patrick Curcio .07 .20
200 Patrick Senger .07 .20
201 Frank Di Muzio .07 .20
202 Kevin Gaudet .07 .20
203 Mark MacKay .20 .50
204 Claude Vilgrain .20 .50
205 Rich Chernomaz .07 .20
206 Daniel Laperriere .20 .50
207 Wayne Hynes .07 .20
208 Todd Harkins .07 .20
209 Scott McCrory .20 .50
210 Andrew Rymsha .15 .40
211 Daniel Nowak .07 .20
212 Andy Schneider .15 .40
213 David Marcinshyn .07 .20
214 Marc Laniel .07 .20
215 Guy Lehoux .07 .20
216 Matthias Vater .07 .20
217 Jens Stramkowski .07 .20
218 Alexander Dexheimer .07 .20
219 Mark Bassen .07 .20
220 Steffen Karg .07 .20
221 Randy Perry .07 .20
222 Robert Schistad .20 .50
223 Andreas Renz .07 .20
224 Matthias Hoppe .07 .20
225 Ron Ivany .07 .20
226 Phillippe Bozon .40 1.00
227 Dave Tomlinson .20 .50
228 Stephane Richer .07 .20
229 Paul Stanton .20 .50
230 Pavel Gross .07 .20
231 Christian Pouget .07 .20
232 Jackson Penney .07 .20
233 Gordon Hynes .20 .50
234 Jason Young .07 .20
235 Alexander Serikow .20 .50
236 Mike Stevens .07 .20
237 Mike Pellegrims .07 .20
238 Reid Simonton .07 .20
239 Christian Lukes .07 .20
240 Ron Pasco .07 .20
241 Mike Hudson .30 .75
242 Denis Perez .07 .20
243 Svan Rampf .07 .20
244 Danny Lorenz .20 .50
245 Brian Tutt .07 .20
246 Jan Alston .07 .20
247 Lance Nethery .07 .20
248 Sergio Momesso .20 .50
249 Andrej Mezin .40 1.00
250 Jarno Peltonen .07 .20
251 Martin Reichel .07 .20
252 Sergej Stas .07 .20
253 Martin Jiranek .07 .20
254 Jason Miller .07 .20
255 Jozef Cierny .07 .20
256 Liam Garvey .07 .20
257 Kevin Grant .07 .20
258 Chris Strausse .07 .20
259 Heiko Smazal .07 .20
260 Vadim Shakhraichuk .07 .20
261 Leszek Laszkiewicz .07 .20
262 Sven Valenti .07 .20
263 Michel Valliere .07 .20
264 Per Lundell .07 .20
265 Dimitri Dudik .07 .20
266 Daniel Kunce .07 .20
267 Ivan Droppa .07 .20
268 Peter Ihnacak .20 .50
269 Harald Birk .07 .20
270 Bradley Bergen .07 .20
271 Pierre Rioux .07 .20
272 Jim Camazzola .07 .20
273 Klaus Merk .20 .50
274 Rick Girard .07 .20
275 Andre Faust .07 .20
276 Hakan Ahlund .07 .20
277 Kyosti Karjalainen .20 .50
278 Leonardo Conti .07 .20
279 Leo Gudas .07 .20
280 Mathias Ahxner .07 .20
281 Francois Groleau .07 .20
282 Michael Bakos .07 .20
283 Alan Reader .07 .20
284 Nordin Harfaoui .07 .20
285 Dale Craigwell .20 .50
286 Dimitri Gromling .07 .20
287 Duanne Moeser .07 .20
288 Tommy Jakobsen .07 .20
289 Patrik Degerstedt .07 .20
290 Greg Bullock .07 .20
291 Gunnar Leidborg .07 .20
292 Dieter Hegen .07 .20
293 Derek Cormier .07 .20
294 Jim Hiller .07 .20
295 Gordon Sherven .08 .25
296 Eric Murana .07 .20
297 Robert Muller .07 .20
298 Klaus Kathan .07 .20
299 Raimond Hilger .07 .20
300 Christian Due-Boje .07 .20
301 Jesper Duus .07 .20
302 Michael Pohl .07 .20
303 Bernd Kuhnhauser .15 .40
304 Frank Hohenadl .07 .20
305 Alexander Jansen .07 .20
306 Teemu Sillanpaa .07 .20
307 Hans Abranamsson .07 .20
308 Claus Dalpiaz .08 .25
309 Kari Haakana .07 .20
310 Christian Gegenfurtner .07 .20
311 Peter Ottosson .07 .20
312 Wolfgang Kummer .07 .20
313 Beppi Eckmaier .07 .20
314 Gerhard Brunner .07 .20
315 Mirko Ludemann .08 .25
316 Sven Felski .07 .20
317 Reemt Pyka .07 .20
318 Jorg Mayr .07 .20
319 Michael Bresagk .07 .20
320 Andraes Lupzig .07 .20
321 Jurgen Rumrich .07 .20
322 Josef Lehner .07 .20
323 Peter Draisaitl .07 .20
324 Leo Stefan .07 .20
325 Joseph Heiss .08 .25
326 Klaus Kathan .07 .20
327 Klaus Merk .08 .25
328 Peter Gulda .07 .20
329 Daniel Nowak .07 .20
330 Bradley Bergen .07 .20
331 Thomas Dolak .07 .20
332 Martin Reichel .07 .20
333 Alexander Serikow .20 .50
334 Harold Birk .07 .20
335 Michael Bakos .07 .20
336 Mario Gehrig .07 .20
337 Mark Mackay .20 .50
338 Dieter Hegen .15 .40
339 Hans Zach .07 .20
340 Erich Kuhnackl .15 .40
341 Ernst Hofner .07 .20
NNO Gerhard Leinauer CL .07 .20
NNO Rick Amann CL .08 .25
NNO Robert Muller CL .07 .20

1999-00 German DEL

This 434-card set features the players of Germany's elite hockey league. The regulation-sized cards feature a color photo on the front, along with two photos and stats on the back. The set was sponsored by Eishockey News and Skoda and may have been produced by a company named Eberswalder.

COMPLETE SET (434) 24.00 60.00
1 Mannheim .05 .15
2 Gordon Hynes .20 .50
3 Paul Stanton .20 .50
4 Christian Lukes .05 .15
5 Clayton Beddoes .20 .50
6 Shawn McCosh .05 .15
7 Dave Tomlinson .20 .50
8 Patrice Lefebvre .20 .50
9 Steve Junker .20 .50
10 Ralph Intranuovo .20 .50
11 Joel Savage .20 .50
12 Stephane J.G. Richer .20 .50
13 Rainer Zerwesz .05 .15
14 Yves Racine .20 .50
15 Mike Stevens .20 .50
16 Markus Wieland .05 .15
17 Bjorn Leonhardt .05 .15
18 Mike Rosati .20 .50
19 Philip Schumacher .05 .15
20 Jan Alston .05 .15
21 Kevin Grant .05 .15
22 Chris Straube .05 .15
23 Dennis Seidenberg .05 .15
24 Chris Valentine TR .20 .50
25 NA¼rnberg .05 .15
26 Stefan Mann .05 .15
27 Vadim Shakhraichuk .05 .15
28 Roland Ramoser .05 .15
29 Martin Jiranek .05 .15
30 Hannes KA¶rber .05 .15
31 Jarno Peltonen .05 .15
32 Dimitri Dudik .05 .15
33 Viktors Ignatjevs .05 .15
34 Alexander Cherbayev .08 .25
35 Martin Reichel .05 .15
36 Russ Romaniuk .08 .25
37 Jason Miller .05 .15
38 Sergej Bautin .05 .15
39 Jozef Cierny .05 .15
40 Marc Seliger .40 1.00
41 Daniel Kunce .05 .15
42 Pasi Sormunen .05 .15
43 Christian SchA¶nmoser .05 .15
44 Stefan Mayer .05 .15
45 Alain Cote .08 .25
46 Liam Garvey .05 .15
47 John Craighead .05 .15
48 Petr Franek .05 .15
49 Peter Ihnacak TR .20 .50
50 Eisbaren .05 .15
51 Nico Pyka .05 .15
52 Robert Leask .20 .50
53 Alexander Godynyuk .08 .25
54 Lorenz Funk .05 .15
55 Sven Felski .05 .15
56 Giuseppe Busillo .05 .15
57 Yvon Corriveau .20 .50
58 Mikael Wahlberg .05 .15
59 Udo Dohler .05 .15
60 Sandy Smith .20 .50
61 Jaroslav Kames .05 .15
62 Rob Murphy .08 .25
63 Marc Fortier .20 .50
64 Mario Chitaroni .05 .15
65 Leif Carlsson .05 .15
66 Derek Mayer .20 .50
67 Sebastian Elwing .05 .15
68 Thomas Schinko .05 .15
69 Rob Cowie .05 .15
70 Thomas Rhodin .05 .15
71 Peter Hammarstrom .05 .15
72 Chris Govedaris .20 .50
73 Mike Bullard .20 .50
74 Peter John Lee TR .05 .15
75 Frankfurt .05 .15
76 Michael Bresagk .05 .15
77 Joachim Appel .05 .15
78 Rick Hayward .20 .50
79 Robin Doyle .05 .15
80 Christian Langer .05 .15
81 Bob Bassen .20 .50
82 John Chabot .20 .50
83 Devin Edgerton .05 .15
84 Toni Porkka .05 .15
85 Jean-Marc Richard .05 .15
86 Jose Charbonneau .08 .25
87 Douglas Kirton .05 .15
88 Andrej Vasilyev .05 .15
89 Ralf Hantschke .05 .15
90 Steve Palmer .05 .15
91 Jason Ruff .20 .50
92 Bastian Niedermeier .05 .15
93 Chris Hynes .05 .15
94 Victor Gervais .05 .15
95 Ken Quinney .20 .50
96 Mark Bassen .05 .15
97 Chris Snell .20 .50
98 Eldon Reddick .20 .50
99 Peter Obresa TR .05 .15
100 Koln .05 .15
101 Joseph Heiss .20 .50
102 Steve Wilson .05 .15
103 Mario Doyon .20 .50
104 Jorg Mayr .05 .15
105 Marty Murray .20 .50
106 Mirko Ludemann .05 .15
107 Dwayne Norris .20 .50
108 Christoph Paepke .05 .15
109 Bruno Zarrillo .20 .50
110 Dan Lambert .20 .50
111 Anders Huusko .05 .15
112 George Zajankala .05 .15
113 Andreas Lupzig .05 .15
114 Jean-Yves Roy .20 .50
115 Tomas Forslund .08 .25
116 Jason Young .08 .25
117 Todd Hlushko .20 .50
118 Andrew Verner .20 .50
119 Corey Millen .20 .50
120 Greg Brown .05 .15
121 John Miner .08 .25
122 Sergio Momesso .20 .50
123 Lance Nethery TR .05 .15
124 Krefeld .05 .15
125 Karel Lang .05 .15
126 Andy Roach .05 .15
127 Tomas Brandl .05 .15
128 Neil Eisenhut .20 .50
129 Ilja Vorobjev .05 .15
130 Andrey Kovalev .05 .15
131 Mark Pederson .08 .25
132 Shayne Wright .05 .15
133 Reemt Pyka .05 .15
134 Andrew Rymsha .05 .15
135 Lars Bruggemann .05 .15
136 Tommie Hartogs .05 .15
137 Marek Stebnicki .05 .15
138 Johnny Walker .05 .15
139 Chris Bartolone .05 .15
140 Stephane Barin .05 .15
141 Mickey Elick .05 .15
142 Phil von Stefenelli .08 .25
143 Jean-Francois Jomphe .20 .50
144 Robert Ouellet .05 .15
145 Roger Nordstrom .05 .15
146 Martin Lindman .05 .15
147 Doug Mason TR .05 .15
148 Augsburg .05 .15
149 Vladislav Boulin .05 .15
150 Leo Gudas .05 .15
151 Duane Moeser .05 .15
152 Sergej Vostrikov .05 .15
153 Igor Maslennikov .05 .15
154 Kyosti Karjalainen .05 .15
155 Kurtis Miller .05 .15
156 Bradley Bergen .05 .15
157 Scott Allison .05 .15
158 Hakan Ahlund .05 .15
159 Peter Larsson .05 .15
160 Brian Loney .05 .15
161 Michael Bakos .05 .15
162 Sven Rampf .05 .15
163 Jim Camazzola .05 .15
164 Andre Faust .05 .15
165 Harald Birk .05 .15
166 Tommy Jakobsen .05 .15
167 Sergej Klimovich .05 .15
168 Klaus Merk .20 .50
169 Bob Manno TR .08 .25
170 Kassel .05 .15
171 Jochen Molling .05 .15
172 David Cooper .20 .50
173 Thomas Dolak .05 .15
174 Stephane Robitaille .05 .15
175 Jeff MacLeod .05 .15
176 Roger Hansson .05 .15

77 Francois Guay .05 .15
78 Nikolaus Mondt .05 .15
79 Andreas Loth .05 .15
80 Ron Pasco .05 .15
81 Jurgen Rumrich .05 .15
82 Greg Evtushevski .05 .15
83 Daniel Kreutzer .05 .15
84 Brent Tully .05 .15
85 Ivan Droppa .05 .15
86 Tobias Abstreiter .05 .15
87 Sylvain Turgeon .20 .50
88 Chris Rogles .20 .50
89 Leonardo Conti .05 .15
90 Tino Boos .05 .15
91 Benjamin Hinterstocker .05 .15
92 Craig Woodcroft .20 .50
93 Orjan Lindmark .05 .15
94 Hans Zach TR .05 .15
95 Schwenningen .05 .15
96 Kevin Wortman .05 .15
97 Marc Laniel .20 .50
98 Daniel Laperriere .20 .50
99 Marcel Goc 1.25 3.00
00 Guy Lehoux .05 .15
01 Steffen Oder .05 .15
02 Jens Stramkowski .05 .15
03 Mark Kolesar .15 .40
04 Scott McCrory .05 .15
05 John Lilley .20 .50
06 Patrik Augusta .05 .15
07 Randy Perry .05 .15
08 Daniel Nowak .05 .15
09 Todd Harkins .05 .15
10 Robert Schistad .05 .15
11 Andreas Renz .05 .15
12 Stephane Beauregard .20 .50
13 Rick Girard .05 .15
14 Iain Fraser .20 .50
15 Andy Schneider .20 .50
16 Mark Mackay .20 .50
17 Rich Chernomaz TR .20 .50
18 Hannover .05 .15
19 Lars Jansson .05 .15
20 Tom Pederson .20 .50
21 Juri Gunko .05 .15
22 Mattias Loof .05 .15
23 Joseph West .05 .15
24 Egor Bashkatov .08 .25
25 Grigori Panteleyev .20 .50
26 Mark Kosturik .05 .15
27 Len Soccio .05 .15
28 Dominic Lavoie .20 .50
29 Peter Willmann .05 .15
30 Wally Schreiber .20 .50
31 Scott Metcalfe .20 .50
32 David Haas .05 .15
33 Ildar Mukhometov .20 .50
34 Igor Chibirev .08 .25
35 Michael Thurner .05 .15
36 Jan Munster .05 .15
37 Jakob Karlsson .05 .15
38 David Sulkovsky .05 .15
39 Brian Tutt .05 .15
40 Igor Alexandrov .05 .15
41 Kevin Gaudet TR .05 .15
42 Rosenheim .05 .15
43 Hakan Algotsson .20 .50
44 Trevor Burgess .05 .15
45 Christian Due-Boje .05 .15
46 Teemu Sillanpaa .05 .15
47 Curtis Fry .05 .15
48 Gordon Sherven .20 .50
49 Frank Hohenadl .05 .15
50 Bernd Kuhnhauser .05 .15
51 Michael Pohl .05 .15
52 Derek Cormier .05 .15
53 Jean-Francois Quintin .20 .50
54 Dieter Hegen .05 .15
55 Peter Ottosson .05 .15
56 Raimond Hilger .08 .25
57 Niklas Brannstrom .05 .15
58 Wolfgang Kummer .05 .15
59 Kari Haakana .05 .15
60 Paul Weismann .05 .15
61 Klaus Kathan .05 .15
62 Sami Nuutinen .05 .15
63 Patrik Hucko .05 .15
64 Robert Muller .05 .15
65 Gerhard Brunner TR .05 .15
66 Capitals .05 .15
67 Andrej Mezin .40 1.00
68 Fredrik Stillman .20 .50
69 Fredrik Ytfeldt .05 .15
70 Markus Pottinger .05 .15
71 Niklas Hede .05 .15
72 Alexander Kuzminski .05 .15
73 Thomas Sjogren .05 .15
74 Dennis Meyer .05 .15
75 Robert Cimetta .20 .50
76 Jim Hiller .05 .15
77 Doug Derraugh .05 .15
78 Patrick Senger .05 .15
79 Pavel Gross .05 .15
80 Robert Guillet .05 .15
81 Sylvain Couturier .05 .15
82 Heinrich Schiffl .05 .15
83 Heinz Ehlers .05 .15
84 Larry Rucchin .05 .15
85 Gregory Johnston .20 .50
86 David Berge .05 .15
87 Johan Norgren .05 .15
88 Martin Ulrich .05 .15
89 Benjamin Hecker .05 .15
90 Mike Pellegrims .05 .15
91 Michael Komma TR .05 .15
92 Oberhausen .05 .15
93 Peter Gulda .05 .15
94 Jergus Baca .05 .15
95 Bob Marshall .05 .15
96 Mike Sullivan .20 .50
97 Jacek Plachta .05 .15
98 Andrei Fuchs .05 .15
99 Mike McNeill .20 .50
00 Aleksandrs Kerch .05 .15
01 Robert Hock .05 .15
02 Albert Malgin .05 .15
03 Kai Fischer .20 .50
04 Burke Murphy .05 .15
05 Jeff Sebastian .05 .15
06 Sergej Stas .05 .15
07 Sebastian Klenner .05 .15
08 Boris Fuchs .05 .15
09 Ivo Jan .05 .15
10 Francois Gravel .05 .15
11 Alexander Makritzky .05 .15
12 Viktor Karatchun .05 .15
13 Gunnar Leidborg TR .05 .15
14 Munchen .05 .15
15 Boris Rousson .20 .50
16 Hans Lodin .05 .15
17 Chris Luongo .20 .50
318 Mike Casselman .05 .15
319 Heiko Smazal .05 .15
320 Peter Abstreiter .05 .15
321 Simon Wheeldon .20 .50
322 Phil Huber .05 .15
323 Peter Douris .20 .50
324 Jari Korpisalo .05 .15
325 Kent Fearns .05 .15
326 Markus Jocher .05 .15
327 Pelle Svensson .05 .15
328 Sven Wiele .05 .15
329 Wayne Hynes .05 .15
330 Bill McDougall .20 .50
331 Alexander Serikow .20 .50
332 Robert Joyce .20 .50
333 Jorg Handrick .05 .15
334 Jason Herter .08 .25
335 Johan Rosen .05 .15
336 Mike Kennedy .20 .50
337 Christian Kunast .05 .15
338 Shane Peacock .05 .15
339 Sean Simpson TR .05 .15
340 Essen .05 .15
341 Oldrich Svoboda .05 .15
342 Bodo Mueller-Boenigk .05 .15
343 Vlastimil Kroupa .05 .15
344 Zdenek Touzimsky .05 .15
345 Pavel Augusta .05 .15
346 Christian Kohmann .05 .15
347 Martin Sychra .05 .15
348 Torsten Kienass .08 .25
349 Peter Draisaitl .05 .15
350 Marian Kacir .05 .15
351 Terry Campbell .05 .15
352 Roland Verwey .05 .15
353 Radek Toth .05 .15
354 Josef Zajic .05 .15
355 Jochen Vollmer .05 .15
356 Jiri Sejba .05 .15
357 Jukka Seppo .05 .15
358 Marc Savard .20 .50
359 Enrico Ciccone .08 .25
360 Michael Dvorak .05 .15
361 Tomas Nemcicky .05 .15
362 Andrej Nederost .40 1.00
363 Tomas Srsen .05 .15
364 Bedrich Scerban .05 .15
365 Jan Benda TR .15 .40
366 3ffi National .05 .15
367 Robert Muller .05 .15
368 Torsten Kienass .08 .25
369 Markus Pottinger .05 .15
370 Lorenz Funk .05 .15
371 Nico Pyka .05 .15
372 Sven Felski .05 .15
373 Jochen Molling .05 .15
374 Christian Langer .05 .15
375 Nikolaus Mondt .05 .15
376 Bernd Kuhnhauser .05 .15
377 Jurgen Rumrich .05 .15
378 Lars Bruggemann .05 .15
379 Alexander Serikow .20 .50
380 Klaus Kathan .05 .15
381 Terry Campbell .05 .15
382 Tino Boos .05 .15
383 Michael Bresagk .05 .15
384 Christian Lukes .05 .15
385 Heiko Smazal .05 .15
386 Tobias Abstreiter .05 .15
387 Thomas Dolak .05 .15
388 Udo Dohler .05 .15
389 Andreas Loth .05 .15
390 David Berge .05 .15
391 Mark MacKay .20 .50
392 Hans Zach TR .05 .15
393 Moderatoren .05 .15
394 Marc Hindelang .05 .15
395 Peter Kohl .05 .15
396 Sven Kukulies .05 .15
397 Claus Muller .05 .15
398 Gerhard Leinauer .05 .15
399 Michael Leopold .05 .15
400 Rick Amann .05 .15
401 Schiris .05 .15
402 Holger Gerstberger .05 .15
403 Ralph Dimmers .05 .15
404 Harald Deubert .05 .15
405 Petr Chvatal .05 .15
406 Frank Awizus .05 .15
407 Axel Rademaker .05 .15
408 Wolfgang Hellwig .05 .15
409 Gerhard Muller .05 .15
410 Gerhard Lichtnecker .05 .15
411 Rainer Kluge .05 .15
412 Stefan TR .05 .15
413 Richard SchÃ¼tz .05 .15
414 Willi Schimm .05 .15
415 Peter Slapke .05 .15
416 TW 1 .05 .15
417 TW 2 .05 .15
418 TW 3 .05 .15
419 TW 4 .05 .15
420 TW 5 .05 .15
421 TW 6 .05 .15
422 TW 7 .05 .15
423 TW 8 .05 .15
424 TW 9 .05 .15
425 RS 1 .05 .15
426 RS 2 .05 .15
427 RS 3 .05 .15
428 RS 4 .05 .15
429 RS 5 .05 .15
430 RS 6 .05 .15
431 RS 7 .05 .15
432 RS 8 .05 .15
433 RS 9 .05 .15
434 SK .05 .15

1999-00 German Bundesliga 2

COMPLETE SET (330) 30.00 60.00
1 EC Bad Nauheim Team Card .02 .10
2 Darryl Olsen .20 .50
3 Sven Gerbig .08 .25
4 Gaetan Malo .08 .25
5 Steffen Michel .08 .25
6 Dennis Cardona .08 .25
7 Marco Rentzsch .08 .25
8 Dino Felicetti .08 .25
9 David Matsos .08 .25
10 Sven Paschek .08 .25
11 Marco Heinrichs .08 .25
12 Larry Mitchell .08 .25
13 Ingo Schwarz .08 .25
14 Dale Jago .08 .25
15 Claus Dalpiaz .20 .50
16 Marc West .08 .25
17 Christian Seeberger .08 .25
18 Olaf Scholz .08 .25
19 Carsten Gosdeck .08 .25
20 Dan Olsen .08 .25
21 EC Bad TÃ¶lz Team Card .02 .10
22 Christian Proulx .20 .50
23 Michael Teltscher .08 .25
24 Florian Keller .08 .25
25 Christian Curth .08 .25
26 Yanick Dube .20 .50
27 Markus Witting .08 .25
28 Axel Kammerer .08 .25
29 Dave Flanagan .08 .25
30 Ilpo Kauhanen .20 .50
31 Johan SÃ¤lle .08 .25
32 Ambrosius Fichtner .08 .25
33 David St. Pierre .08 .25
34 Mathias Hart .08 .25
35 Franz Demmel .08 .25
36 Markus Feierabend .08 .25
37 Florian Zeller .08 .25
38 Sven Valenti .08 .25
39 Christian Gegenfurtner .08 .25
40 Josef Schlickenrieder .08 .25
41 SC Bietigheim-Bissingen Team Card .02 .10
42 David Belitski .20 .50
43 Frank Appel .08 .25
44 Markus Rohde .08 .25
45 Milos Vanik .08 .25
46 Marc Mundil .08 .25
47 Ulrich Liebsch .08 .25
48 Darren Ritchie .08 .25
49 Mike Bader .08 .25
50 Daniel Held .08 .25
51 Andrej Jaufmann .08 .25
52 Tim Leahy .08 .25
53 Martin Ancicka .08 .25
54 Christian Baader .08 .25
55 Craig Teeple .08 .25
56 Ralf StÃ¤rk .08 .25
57 Andreas Naumann .08 .25
58 Stephan Sinner .08 .25
59 Timo Nykopp .08 .25
60 Vaclav Drobny .08 .25
61 Thomas Mieszkowski .08 .25
62 Tom Pokel .08 .25
63 Braunlager EHC Harz Team Card .02 .10
64 Jarno Miikkulainen .20 .50
65 Peter Lundmark .20 .50
66 Josef Beppi Eckmair .08 .25
67 Douglas Murray .08 .25
68 Chris Clarke .08 .25
69 Ron Gaudet .08 .25
70 Sven Gerike .08 .25
71 Marek Gajewski .08 .25
72 Markus Draxler .08 .25
73 Frederik Andersson .08 .25
74 Timo Gschwill .08 .25
75 Georg Gailer .08 .25
76 Frank Richardt .08 .25
77 Johan Silfwerplatz .08 .25
78 Marcus Bleicher .08 .25
79 Anton Krinner .08 .25
80 Sebastian Buchwieser .08 .25
81 Bastian Niedermeier .08 .25
82 Anton Raubal .08 .25
83 Peter Gailer .08 .25
84 DÃ¼sseldorfer EG Team Card .02 .10
85 Chad Biafore .20 .50
86 Fabian BrÃ¤nnstrÃ¶m .20 .50
87 Zdenek Travnicek .08 .25
88 Victor Gordiouk .08 .25
89 Leo Stefan .08 .25
90 Till Feser .08 .25
91 Andreas Pokorny .08 .25
92 Andreas Brockmann .08 .25
93 Ralf Reisinger .08 .25
94 Marc Dillmann .08 .25
95 Sergej Sorokin .08 .25
96 Peter Franke .08 .25
97 Udo Schmid .08 .25
98 Rafael Jedamzik .08 .25
99 Jouni Vento .08 .25
100 Torsten Kunz .08 .25
101 Sebastian Odenthal .08 .25
102 Anders Gozzi .08 .25
103 Maurizio Mansi .08 .25
104 Boris Lingemann .08 .25
105 Czeslaw Panek .08 .25
106 EHC Freiburg Team Card .02 .10
107 Rostislav Haas .20 .50
108 Alexander Semak .08 .25
109 Oleg Znarok .08 .25
110 David Danner .08 .25
111 Igor Dorochin .08 .25
112 Tobias Samendinger .08 .25
113 Ravil Khaidarov .08 .25
114 Evgeni Sultanowitsch .08 .25
115 Thomas Jetter .08 .25
116 Rudolf GorgenlÃ¤nder .08 .25
117 Andrej Strakhov .08 .25
118 Vitalij Grossmann .08 .25
119 Max Bauer .08 .25
120 Peter Mares .08 .25
121 Josef Peroutka .08 .25
122 Peter Precan .08 .25
123 Michael Vasicek .08 .25
124 Patrick Vozar .08 .25
125 Frantisek Frosch .08 .25
126 Thomas Dolak sen. .08 .25
127 Grefrather EV Team Card .02 .10
128 Frank Gentges .20 .50
129 Jochen Hecker .08 .25
130 Dirk Kuhnekath .08 .25
131 Bill Trew .08 .25
132 Thomas Popiesch .08 .25
133 Christoph Kleckers .08 .25
134 Henrik HÃ¶lscher .08 .25
135 Arno Brux .08 .25
136 Ashlin Halfnight .08 .25
137 Nolan McDonald .08 .25
138 Gilbert SchrÃ¶der .08 .25
139 Nicklas Norlander .08 .25
140 Steve Smillie .08 .25
141 Tobias Grossecker .08 .25
142 Marcel Sakac .08 .25
143 Elmar Schmitz .08 .25
144 Hamburg Crocodiles Team Card .02 .10
145 Alexander Genze .08 .25
146 Derek Booth .08 .25
147 Alexander Engel .08 .25
148 John Johnson .08 .25
149 Jason Dunham .08 .25
150 Mike Millar .08 .25
151 Jay Luknowsky .08 .25
152 Andy Pritchard .08 .25
153 Mark Mahon .08 .25
154 Patrick Pysz .08 .25
155 Karsten Mende .08 .25
156 Phil Bourque .20 .50
157 JÃ¼rgen Trattner .08 .25
158 Carsten Solbach .08 .25
159 Maurice Lemay .30 .75
160 Jayson Meyer .08 .25
161 Marius Cissewski .08 .25
162 Christoph Sandner .08 .25
163 Harald Waibel .08 .25
164 Mario Gehrig .08 .25
165 Ross Yates .08 .25
166 Heilbronner EC Team Card .02 .10
167 Mikael Granlund .20 .50
168 Alexander Schuster .08 .25
169 Niklas Rinaldo .08 .25
170 Todd Sparks .08 .25
171 Thomas SchÃ¤dler .08 .25
172 Martin Williams .08 .25
173 Kenneth Filbey .08 .25
174 Ronny Martin .08 .25
175 Henri Marcoux .08 .25
176 Christian Martin .08 .25
177 Felix Feeser .08 .25
178 Brad Scott .08 .25
179 Alexander Semjonov .08 .25
180 Michael Rumrich .08 .25
181 Layne Roland .08 .25
182 BjÃ¶rn Barta .08 .25
183 Markus Eberl .08 .25
184 Rainer Suchan .08 .25
185 Johan Lindh .08 .25
186 Gary Prior .08 .25
187 ERC Ingolstadt Team Card .02 .10
188 Marco Thommes .08 .25
189 Stephane Julien .08 .25
190 Agostino Casale .08 .25
191 Kevin Ryan .08 .25
192 Harald SchÃ¤fler .08 .25
193 Markus Welz .08 .25
194 Wolfgang Fries .08 .25
195 Petr Bares .08 .25
196 Thomas Daffner .08 .25
197 Clayton Young .08 .25
198 Samuel Groleau .08 .25
199 Philippe DeRouville .30 .75
200 Cory Holden .08 .25
201 Sven Zywitza .08 .25
202 Frank Kannewurf .08 .25
203 Fabian Dahlem .08 .25
204 JÃ¼rgen Simon .08 .25
205 Roland Timoschuk .08 .25
206 Glenn Goodall .40 1.00
207 Giacinto Boni .08 .25
208 Iserlohner EC Team Card .02 .10
209 Cory Laylin .08 .25
210 Oliver Bernhardt .08 .25
211 Robert Gratza .08 .25
212 Collin Danielsmeier .08 .25
213 Pat Mikesch .08 .25
214 Tomas Martinec .08 .25
215 Teal Fowler .08 .25
216 Michael Hackert .08 .25
217 Mike Muller .08 .25
218 Oliver Hackert .08 .25
219 Peter Hellmann .08 .25
220 Steve Potvin .08 .25
221 Torsten Fendt .08 .25
222 Manuel Kofler .08 .25
223 Lars MÃ¼ller .08 .25
224 Elvis Beslagic .08 .25
225 Ronny Arendt .08 .25
226 Christian Franz .08 .25
227 Ian Wood .20 .50
228 Greg Poss .08 .25
229 EHC Neuwied Team Card .02 .10
230 Juri Stumpf .08 .25
231 Dean Fedorchuk .08 .25
232 Andrej Teljukin .08 .25
233 Alexander Andrievsky .08 .25
234 Ladislav Strompf .08 .25
235 Richard Baptist .08 .25
236 Otto Keresztes .08 .25
237 Klaus Micheller .08 .25
238 Todd Johnson .08 .25
239 Mario Naster .08 .25
240 Jens Hergt .08 .25
241 Falk Ozellis .08 .25
242 Craig Streu .08 .25
243 Marc Gronau .08 .25
244 Ole Kopitz .08 .25
245 Vitalij Semenchenko .08 .25
246 Radek Vit .08 .25
247 Sinuhe Wallinheimo .30 .75
248 Michael Weinfurter .08 .25
249 Petteri Lehmussaari .08 .25
250 GEC Nordhorn Team Card .02 .10
251 Christian von Trzcinski .08 .25
252 Jedrzej Kasperczyk .08 .25
253 Peter Kwasigroch .08 .25
254 Christian Spaan .08 .25
255 Gabriel KrÃ¼ger .08 .25
256 Moritz Schmidt .08 .25
257 Alexej Pogodin .08 .25
258 Markus Kempf .08 .25
259 Sergej Zvyagin .08 .25
260 Christian Brittig .08 .25
261 Juris Opulskis .08 .25
262 Andreas Morczinietz .08 .25
263 Andrzej Hanisz .08 .25
264 Sami Leinonen .08 .25
265 Sergej Tchoudinov .08 .25
266 Mikka Kemppi .08 .25
267 Anton Weissgerber .08 .25
268 SC Riessersee Team Card .02 .10
269 Michael Pump .08 .25
270 Georg GÃ¼ttler .08 .25
271 Christoph Klotz .08 .25
272 Tim Regan .08 .25
273 Alexander Wedl .08 .25
274 Mika Puhakka .08 .25
275 Martin Holzer .08 .25
276 Hubert Buchwieser .08 .25
277 Michael Raubal .08 .25
278 Josef Lehner .08 .25
279 Christian Mayr .08 .25
280 Tobias Netter .08 .25
281 Tom OÂ´Grady .08 .25
282 Samuli Peltosara .08 .25
283 Leonhard Wild .08 .25
284 Florian Brandl .08 .25
285 Duane Dennis .08 .25
286 Mark Zdan .08 .25
287 Florian Storf .08 .25
288 Ron Chyzowski .08 .25
289 ES Weisswasser Team Card .02 .10
290 Torsten Hanusch .08 .25
291 Daniel Sikorski .08 .25
292 Alexej Jefimov .08 .25
293 Alexandre Vinogradov .08 .25
294 Ronny Reddo .08 .25
295 Frank Peschke .08 .25
296 Ronny Glaser .08 .25
297 JÃ¶rgen Hermansson .08 .25
298 Robert Brezina .08 .25
299 Sven Steinecke .08 .25
300 David Musial .08 .25
301 Pekka Virta .08 .25
302 Thomas Knobloch .08 .25
303 Daniel Bartell .08 .25
304 Falk Herzig .08 .25
305 Dimitri Alekhin .08 .25
306 Joakim Wiberg .08 .25
307 Martin Wiita .08 .25
308 JÃ¶rg Pohling .08 .25
309 Bror Hansson .08 .25
310 EC Wilhelmshaven-Stickhausen Team Card .02 .10
311 Vadim Finko .08 .25
312 Harald Hebig .08 .25
313 Kai Ahlroth .08 .25
314 Boris Blank .08 .25
315 Eduard Lewandowski .08 .25
316 Alexander Rusch .08 .25
317 Dimitry Dudarev .08 .25
318 Vitali Janke .08 .25
319 Ilja Stachenkov .08 .25
320 JÃ¼rgen Schaal .08 .25
321 Andrej Dmitriev .08 .25
322 Iiro ItÃ¤mies .08 .25
323 Sergej Jaschin .08 .25
324 Martin Ekrt .08 .25
325 Marian Horvarth .08 .25
326 Mario SchÃ¼ssel .08 .25
327 Alexander Herbst .08 .25
328 Andrej Naumann .08 .25
329 Peter Kalinowski .08 .25
330 Anatoli Antipov .08 .25

2000-01 German Berlin Polar Bears Postcards

This team-issued set is standard postcard size. Cards are unnumbered and listed below in alphabetical order. Thanks to collector Andy Hatzos for this and other Polar Bears checklist.

COMPLETE SET (22) 10.00 20.00
1 John Chabot .40 1.00
2 Derek Cormier .40 1.00
3 Rob Cowie .40 1.00
4 Uli Egen .40 1.00
5 Sven Felski .40 1.00
6 Marc Fortier .40 1.00
7 Alexander Godynyuk .40 1.00
8 Rich Gosselin .40 1.00
9 Peter Hammarstrom .40 1.00
10 Todd Harkins .40 1.00
11 Alex Hicks .40 1.00
12 Alexander Jung .40 1.00
13 Daniel Laperriere .40 1.00
14 Rob Leask .40 1.00
15 Martin Lindman .40 1.00
16 Derek Mayer .40 1.00
17 Klaus Merk .40 1.00
18 Nico Pyka .40 1.00
19 Sandy Smith .40 1.00
20 Jeff Tomlinson .40 1.00
21 Lubomir Vaic .40 1.00
22 Steve Walker .40 1.00

2000-01 German DEL Upper Deck

This set features the top players in Germany's elite league. The cards were produced by Upper Deck and feature an action photo on the front, with a head shot and stats on the back.

COMPLETE SET (240) 15.00 40.00
1 Gordon Hynes .10 .25
2 Dave Tomlinson .20 .50
3 Stephane Richer .05 .15
4 Steve Junker .05 .15
5 Wayne Hynes .05 .15
6 Bradley Bergen .05 .15
7 Devin Edgerton .05 .15
8 Ron Pasco .05 .15
9 Francois Groleau .05 .15
10 Todd Hlushko .20 .50
11 Mike Rosati .20 .50
12 Chris Straube .05 .15
13 Jean-Francois Jomphe .20 .50
14 Jan Alston .05 .15
15 Sven Rampf .05 .15
16 Sergej Vostrikov .05 .15
17 Igor Maslennikov .05 .15
18 Reemt Pyka .05 .15
19 Dave Chyzowski .20 .50
20 Arnaud Briand .05 .15
21 Sergej Stas .05 .15
22 Sebastian Klenner .05 .15
23 Vasily Pankov .05 .15
24 Duane Moeser .05 .15
25 Jason Muzzatti .40 1.00
26 Herbert Hohenberger .20 .50
27 Ryan Savoia .05 .15
28 Jim Camazzola .05 .15
29 Tommy Jakobsen .05 .15
30 Andrei Mezin .40 1.00
31 Markus Pottinger .05 .15
32 Thomas Sjogren .05 .15
33 Jim Hiller .05 .15
34 Pavel Gross .05 .15
35 Robert Guillet .05 .15
36 Udo Dohler .05 .15
37 Anders Huusko .05 .15
38 Heinz Ehlers .05 .15
39 Gregory Johnston .20 .50
40 Petri Liimatainen .05 .15
41 Johan Norgren .05 .15
42 Martin Ulrich .05 .15
43 Iain Fraser .10 .25
44 Gary Shuchuk .10 .25
45 Torsten Kienass .10 .25
46 Niki Mondt .05 .15
47 Bernd Kuhnhauser .05 .15
48 Craig Reichert .10 .25
49 Niclas Sundblad .10 .25
50 Sergey Sorokin .05 .15
51 Peter Franke .05 .15
52 Ivan Droppa .05 .15
53 Christopher Bartolone .05 .15
54 Leo Stefan .05 .15
55 Victor Gordiouk .10 .25
56 Lorenz Funk .05 .15
57 Boris Lingemann .05 .15
58 Andrei Trefilov .20 .50
59 Nico Pyka .05 .15
60 Alexander Jung .05 .15
61 Alexander Godynyuk .10 .25
62 Derek Mayer .10 .25
63 Sven Felski .05 .15
64 Marc Fortier .10 .25
65 John Chabot .20 .50
66 Derek Cormier .05 .15
67 Steve Walker .05 .15
68 Lubomir Vaic .10 .25
69 Klaus Merk .20 .50
70 Dan Laperriere .20 .50
71 Rob Cowie .05 .15
72 Martin Lindman .05 .15
73 Chris Govedaris .20 .50
74 Michael Bresagk .05 .15
75 Leonardo Conti .05 .15
76 Robin Doyle .05 .15
77 Toni Porkka .05 .15
78 John Walker .05 .15
79 Jean-Marc Richard .05 .15
80 Jason Ruff .10 .25
81 Jason Cirone .10 .25
82 Jose Charbonneau .10 .25
83 Victor Gervais .05 .15
84 Patrice Lefebvre .20 .50
85 Martin Gendron .20 .50
86 Ken Quinney .20 .50
87 Keith Aldridge .20 .50
88 Eldon Reddick .20 .50
89 Oscar Ackestrom .05 .15
90 Mattias Loof .05 .15
91 Egor Bashkatov .10 .25
92 Mark Kosturik .05 .15
93 Wallace Schreiber .20 .50
94 Dominic Lavoie .10 .25
95 Rob Murphy .10 .25
96 Pavel Cagas .05 .15
97 Igor Chibirev .10 .25
98 Kevin Grant .05 .15
99 Jan Munster .05 .15
100 Chris Snell .10 .25
101 Patrik Zetterberg .05 .15
102 Colin Beardsmore .05 .15
103 Calle Carlsson .05 .15
104 Tomas Martinec .05 .15
105 Teal Fowler .05 .15
106 Alexander Kuzminski .05 .15
107 Terence Campbell .05 .15
108 Duane Derksen .20 .50
109 Peter Roed .05 .15
110 Torsten Fendt .05 .15
111 Shawn Anderson .05 .15
112 Manuel Kofler .05 .15
113 Radek Toth .05 .15
114 Steve Potvin .05 .15
115 Brent Tully .05 .15
116 Ted Crowley .05 .15
117 Pat Mikesch .05 .15
118 Stephane Robitaille .05 .15
119 Francois Guay .05 .15
120 Andreas Loth .05 .15
121 Patrice Tardif .20 .50
122 Scott Levins .05 .15
123 Joachim Appel .05 .15
124 Chris Rogles .20 .50
125 Thomas Daffner .05 .15
126 Klaus Kathan .05 .15
127 Sylvain Turgeon .10 .25
128 Andrew Verner .20 .50
129 Bruno Zarrillo .05 .15
130 Dwayne Norris .20 .50
131 Christoph Paepke .05 .15
132 Mirko Ludemann .05 .15
133 Andreas Lupzig .05 .15
134 Jason Young .10 .25
135 Joseph Heiss .20 .50
136 Tomas Forslund .10 .25
137 Andre Faust .05 .15
138 Tino Boos .05 .15
139 John Miner .10 .25
140 Dave McIlwain .20 .50
141 Dieter Kalt .05 .15
142 Corey Millen .20 .50
143 Marc Hussey .05 .15
144 Brent Severyn .20 .50
145 Christian Ehrhoff .05 .15
146 Neil Eisenhut .10 .25
147 Ilja Vorobjev .05 .15
148 Shayne Wright .05 .15
149 Dan Lambert .20 .50
150 Brad Purdie .05 .15
151 Christoph Brandner .05 .15
152 Roger Nordstrom .05 .15
153 Jeff Christian .10 .25
154 Karel Lang .05 .15
155 Thomas Brandl .05 .15
156 Martin Sychra .05 .15
157 Jason McBain .05 .15
158 Ralph Intranuovo .20 .50
159 Jarkko Savijoki .05 .15
160 Marc Savard .20 .50
161 Roman Meluzin .05 .15
162 Todd Simon .10 .25
163 Jean-Francois Quintin .10 .25
164 Scott Pearson .20 .50
165 Kevin Wortman .05 .15
166 Geoff Sarjeant .20 .50
167 Leonard Wild .05 .15
168 Erich Goldmann .20 .50
169 Marc Laniel .20 .50
170 Esa Tikkanen .75 2.00
171 Hans Lodin .05 .15
172 Rick Girard .05 .15
173 Christian Kunast .05 .15
174 Simon Wheeldon .15 .40
175 Shane Peacock .05 .15
176 Christoph Schubert .05 .15
177 Peter Douris .10 .25
178 Alexander Serikow .20 .50
179 Peter Larsson .05 .15
180 Thomas Dolak .05 .15
181 Jorg Handrick .05 .15
182 Jason Herter .10 .25
183 Andrew Schneider .10 .25
184 Parris Duffus .20 .50
185 Luciano Borsato .10 .25
186 Jurgen Rumrich .05 .15
187 Dimitri Dudik .05 .15
188 Alexander Cherbayev .10 .25
189 Martin Jiranek .05 .15
190 Martin Reichel .05 .15
191 Mario Chitarroni .05 .15
192 Jason Miller .05 .15
193 Bjorn Nord .05 .15
194 Kevin Miehm .10 .25
195 Marc Seliger .20 .50
196 Daniel Kunce .05 .15
197 Paul Stanton .10 .25
198 Peter Gulda .05 .15
199 Christian Kohmann .05 .15
200 Mika Arvaja .05 .15
201 Carsten Gosdeck .05 .15
202 Aleksandrs Kercs .05 .15
203 Alexandre Andrievski .10 .25
204 Robert Hock .05 .15
205 Josef Zajic .05 .15
206 Marek Stebnicki .05 .15
207 Andrej Kovalev .05 .15
208 Ladislav Karabin .05 .15
209 Peter Draisaitl .05 .15
210 Sinuhe Wallinheimo .10 .25
211 Jergus Baca .05 .15
212 Peter Allen .05 .15
213 Alexander Duck .05 .15
214 Marcel Goc .60 1.50
215 Jens Stramkowski .05 .15
216 Mark MacKay .10 .25
217 Vadym Slivchenko .05 .15
218 Jacek Plachta .05 .15
219 Alexei Yegorov .20 .50
220 Patrik Augusta .05 .15
221 Brad Schlegel .10 .25
222 Andreas Renz .05 .15
223 Thomas Greilinger .05 .15
224 Ian Gordon .10 .25
225 Mike Bullard .20 .50
226 Robert Muller .05 .15
227 Mike Pellegrims .05 .15
228 Mike Casselman .05 .15
229 Leonardo Soccio .05 .15
230 Andreas Pokorny .10 .25
231 Tim Schnelle .05 .15
232 Daniel Kreutzer .05 .15
233 Tobias Abstreiter .05 .15
234 Tomas Hartogs .05 .15
235 Stephane Barin .05 .15
236 Boris Rousson .20 .50
237 Mike Kennedy .10 .25
238 John Craighead .05 .15
239 Marc Pethke .05 .15
240 Markus Janka .05 .15

2000-01 German DEL Upper Deck All-Star Class

This series was an insert found in the 2000-01 German DEL set and features the league's top scorers. They were inserted at a rate of 1:17.

COMPLETE SET (10) 8.00 20.00
STATED ODDS 1:17
A1 Martin Jiranek .80 2.00
A2 Patrice Lefebvre 1.60 4.00
A3 Peter Douris .80 2.00
A4 Sergej Vostrikov .80 2.00
A5 Gregory Johnston 1.20 3.00
A6 Chris Govedaris .80 2.00
A7 Mike Casselman .80 2.00
A8 Corey Millen 1.20 3.00
A9 Shawn Anderson 1.20 3.00
A10 Sylvain Turgeon 1.20 3.00

2000-01 German DEL Upper Deck Game Jersey

This insert set features a swatch of actual game-worn jersey on each card. Because the jerseys in the DEL are laden with ads, multi-colored swatches are plentiful. As such, they do not draw significant premiums as similar swatches might earn in North American sets. The cards were inserted 1:144 packs.

COMPLETE SET (16) 160.00 400.00
STATED ODDS 1:144
BZ Bruno Zarrillo 16.00 40.00
DM Duane Moeser 10.00 25.00
JB Jergus Baca 12.00 30.00
JR Jurgen Rumrich 10.00 25.00
LE Leonard Soccio 12.00 30.00
LS Leo Stefan 12.00 30.00
MF Marc Fortier 12.00 30.00
MM Mark MacKay 12.00 30.00
MS Marc Savard 20.00 50.00
PG Pavel Gross 12.00 30.00
SR Stephane Richer 12.00 30.00
SW Simon Wheeldon 16.00 40.00
TA Tobias Abstreiter 16.00 40.00
TF Teal Fowler 12.00 30.00
TH Tomas Hartogs 12.00 30.00
TP Toni Porkka 10.00 25.00

2000-01 German DEL Upper Deck Profiles

Inserted 1:8 packs of German DEL, these cards picture the league's top performers.

COMPLETE SET (11) 8.00 20.00
STATED ODDS 1:8
P1 Jan Alston .80 2.00
P2 Andrei Mezin 2.00 5.00
P3 John Chabot 1.20 3.00
P4 Wallace Schreiber 1.20 3.00
P5 Shane Peacock .80 2.00
P6 Mike Bullard 1.20 3.00
P7 Mirko Ludemann .80 2.00
P8 Boris Rousson 1.25 3.00
P9 Andrej Kovalev .80 2.00
P10 Mike Pellegrims .40 1.00
P11 Andrei Trefilov .80 2.00

2000-01 German DEL Upper Deck Star Attractions

This set profiles the most popular players in the German DEL. The cards were inserted 1:17 packs.

COMPLETE SET (10) 10.00 25.00
STATED ODDS 1:17
S1 Ivan Droppa 1.25 3.00
S2 Gordon Hynes 1.20 3.00
S3 Marek Stebnicki 1.20 3.00
S4 Daniel Kreutzer 1.20 3.00
S5 Thomas Brandl 1.20 3.00
S6 Esa Tikkanen 2.00 5.00
S7 Bob Sweeney 1.20 3.00
S8 Paul Stanton 1.20 3.00
S9 Dave Tomlinson 1.20 3.00
S10 Brent Severyn 2.00 5.00

2001-02 German Adler Mannheim Eagles Postcards

1 Robert Muller .75 2.00
2 Eric Charron .75 2.00
3 Devin Edgerton .75 2.00
4 Mike Rosati .75 2.00
5 Chris Straube .75 2.00
6 Francois Groleau .75 2.00
7 Rene Corbet .75 2.00
8 Stephane Richer 1.25 3.00
9 Stefan Ustorf .75 2.00

2001-02 German Berlin Polar Bears Postcards

COMPLETE SET (27) 10.00 25.00
1 Keith Aldridge .40 1.00
2 Alex Barta .40 1.00
3 Boris Blank .40 1.00
4 David Cooper .40 1.00
5 Patrick Czajka .40 1.00
6 Uli Egen .40 1.00
7 Sven Felski .40 1.00
8 Marc Fortier .40 1.00
9 Daniel Laperriere .40 1.00
10 Steve Larouche .40 1.00
11 Rob Leask .40 1.00
12 Scott Levins .40 1.00
13 Eduard Lewandoski .40 1.00
14 Martin Lindman .40 1.00
15 Chris Marinucci .40 1.00
16 Klaus Merk .40 1.00
17 Hartmut Nickel .40 1.00
18 Fabio Patrzek .40 1.00
19 Ed Patterson .40 1.00
20 Nico Pyka .40 1.00
21 David Roberts .40 1.00
22 Jan Schertz .40 1.00

23 Richard Shulmistra .40 1.00
24 Tom Skinner .40 1.00
25 Lee Sorochan .40 1.00
26 Jeff Tomlinson .40 1.00
27 Steve Walker .40 1.00

2001-02 German DEL Upper Deck

This set features the top players of the German DEL. The cards were produced by Upper Deck and sold only in Germany. The design mirrors that of the base NHL 2001-02 Upper Deck series.

COMPLETE SET (270) 15.00 40.00
1 Igor Alexandrov .08 .20
2 Marc Beaucage .15 .40
3 Eric Dylla .20 .50
4 Mickey Elick .15 .40
5 Magnus Eriksson .08 .20
6 Jakub Ficenec .20 .50
7 Robert Guillet .08 .20
8 Tommy Jakobsen .08 .20
9 Christian Lukes .08 .20
10 Igor Maslennikov .08 .20
11 Duanne Moeser .15 .40
12 Vasily Pankov .08 .20
13 Reemt Pyka .08 .20
14 Reid Simonton .15 .40
15 Sergej Vostrikov .08 .20
16 Alexander Cherbayev .08 .20
17 Heinz Ehlers .08 .20
18 Ronny Arendt .08 .20
19 Andrej Vassilyev .08 .20
20 Francois Leroux .20 .50
21 Andrei Mezin .40 1.00
22 Jan MÃ¼nster .08 .20
23 Markus PÃ¶ttinger .08 .20
24 Patrick Senger .08 .20
25 Aleksandrs Kercs .08 .20
26 Gordon Hynes .20 .50
27 Greg Andrusak .20 .50
28 Vjatcheslav Fanduls .08 .20
29 Yvon Corriveau .20 .50
30 Frederik Ã–berg .08 .20
31 Keith Aldridge .20 .50
32 David Cooper .15 .40
33 Sven Felski .08 .20
34 Marc Fortier .20 .50
35 Dan Laperriere .20 .50
36 Steve LaRouche .20 .50
37 Scott Levins .20 .50
38 Chris Marinucci .20 .50
39 Klaus Merk .20 .50
40 Nico Pyka .08 .20
41 David Roberts .20 .50
42 Jan Schertz .08 .20
43 Richard Shulmistra .20 .50
44 Lee Sorochan .20 .50
45 Steve Walker .15 .40
46 Chris Bartolone .15 .40
48 Ivan Droppa .08 .20
49 Neil Eisenhut .15 .40
50 Tore Vikingstad .08 .20
51 Torsten Kienass .08 .20
52 Bernd KÃ¼hnhauser .08 .20
53 Trond Magnussen .08 .20
54 Mike Pellegrims .15 .40
55 Jean-Francois Quintin .15 .40
56 Ralf Reisinger .08 .20
57 Leo Stefan .08 .20
58 Andrej Trefilov .20 .50
59 Martin Ulrich .08 .20
60 Rainer Zerwesz .08 .20
61 Frank Appel .15 .40
62 Lars BrÃ¼ggemann .08 .20
63 Mike Casselman .15 .40
64 Ted Crowley .15 .40
65 Liam Garvey .08 .20
66 Erich Goldmann .20 .50
67 Todd Hawkins .15 .40
68 Ralph Intranuovo .20 .50
69 Martin Sychra .08 .20
70 Riku-Petteri Lehtonen .08 .20
71 Doug MacDonald .15 .40
72 Marc Savard .20 .50
73 Todd Simon .15 .40
74 Jimmy Waite .30 .75
75 Craig Woodcroft .15 .40
76 Michael Bresagk .08 .20
77 Brent Cullaton .15 .40
78 Rob Doyle .08 .20
79 Greg Evtushevski .15 .40
80 Victor Gervais .15 .40
81 Rick Girard .15 .40
82 Stewart Malgunas .15 .40
83 Rob Pearson .20 .50
84 Eldon Reddick .20 .50
85 Ian Fraser .15 .40
86 Alexander Selivanov .08 .20
87 Vadim Slivchenko .08 .20
88 Chris Snell .15 .40
89 Brent Tully .15 .40
90 John Walker .15 .40
91 Oscar AckestrÃ¶m .20 .50
92 Egor Bashkatov .08 .20
93 Igor Chibirev .08 .20
94 Kevin Grant .15 .40
95 David Haas .15 .40
96 Peter Jakobsson .08 .20
97 Dominic Lavoie .20 .50
98 Mattias LÃ¶Ã¶f .08 .20
99 Rob Murphy .15 .40
100 Mark Pederson .15 .40
101 Wally Schreiber .15 .40
102 Len Soccio .20 .50
103 Andrew Verner .20 .50
104 Steve Wilson .15 .40
105 Patrik Zetterberg .08 .20
106 Doug Ast .15 .40
107 Colin Beardsmore .15 .40
108 Guy Dupuis .15 .40
109 Oliver Bernhardt .08 .20
110 Rusty Fitzgerald .20 .50
111 Terry Hollinger .20 .50
112 Kimmo Kapanen .08 .20
113 Dmitrij Kotschnew .08 .20
114 Cory Laylin .15 .40
115 Paul Dyck .20 .50
116 Tomas Martinec .08 .20
117 Colin Danielsmeier .08 .20
118 David Musial .15 .40
119 Andreas Pokorny .08 .20
120 Sean Tallaire .15 .40
121 Tobias Abstreiter .20 .50
122 Thomas Daffner .08 .20
123 Doug Derraugh .15 .40
124 Leonid Fatikov .08 .20
125 Tommie Hartogs .08 .20
126 Klaus Kathan .08 .20
127 Ilpo Kauhanen .20 .50
128 Ã–rjan Lindmark .08 .20
129 Andreas Loth .08 .20
130 Jeff MacLeod .15 .40
131 Pat Mikesch .08 .20
132 Jochen Molling .08 .20
133 Brent Peterson .20 .50
134 Shayne Wright .15 .40
135 Jeff Tory .15 .40
136 Tino Boos .08 .20
137 AndrÃ© Faust .20 .50
138 Alex Hicks .20 .50
139 Petri Liimatainen .08 .20
140 Mirko LÃ¼demann .20 .50
141 JÃ¶rg Mayr .08 .20
142 Dave McLlwain .20 .50
143 Corey Millen .20 .50
144 John Miner .15 .40
145 Dwayne Norris .15 .40
146 Toni Porkka .08 .20
147 Andreas Renz .08 .20
148 Chris Rogles .20 .50
149 Niklas Sundblad .20 .50
150 Jason Young .15 .40
151 Patrik Augusta .08 .20
152 StÃ©phane Barin .08 .20
153 Thomas Brandl .08 .20
154 Steffen Ziesche .08 .20
156 Jeff Christian .15 .40
157 Gilbert Dionne .20 .50
158 Mario Doyon .20 .50
159 Daniel Kunce .08 .20
160 Dan Lambert .30 .75
161 Roger NordstrÃ¶m .08 .20
162 Brad Purdie .20 .50
163 Gary Shuchuk .20 .50
164 Sergej Stas .08 .20
165 Phil von Stefenelli .20 .50
166 Brad Bergen .15 .40
167 Fabian BrÃ¤nnstrÃ¶m .08 .20
168 Devin Edgerton .15 .40
169 Todd Hlushko .20 .50
170 Wayne Hynes .15 .40
171 FranÃ§ois Groleau .15 .40
172 Michel Picard .20 .50
173 Yves Racine .20 .50
174 StÃ©phane Richer .15 .40
175 Andy Roach .15 .40
176 Mike Rosati .30 .75
177 Mike Stevens .15 .40
178 Dave Tomlinson .15 .40
179 Steve Junker .15 .40
180 Stefan Ustorf .20 .50
181 Kent Fearns .15 .40
182 Jason Herter .15 .40
183 Mike Kennedy .20 .50
184 Derek King .20 .50
185 Christian KÃ¼nast .08 .20
186 Hans Lodin .08 .20
187 David Oliver .15 .40
188 Shane Peacock .15 .40
189 Derek PlantÃ© .20 .50
190 Johan RosÃ©n .08 .20
191 Boris Rousson .20 .50
192 Andy Schneider .15 .40
193 Peter Douris .20 .50
194 Heiko Smazal .08 .20
195 Simon Wheeldon .20 .50
196 Shawn Anderson .15 .40
197 Luciano Borsato .20 .50
198 Frederic Chabot .60 1.50
199 Mario Chitarroni .20 .50
200 Kevin Dahl .15 .40
201 David Emma .20 .50
202 Martin Jiranek .08 .20
203 Chris Luongo .20 .50
204 Guy Lehoux .20 .50
205 Jacek Plachta .08 .20
206 Martin Reichel .08 .20
207 JÃ¼rgen Rumrich .08 .20
208 Christian SchÃ¶nmoser .08 .20
209 Jan Nemecek .08 .20
210 Bruno Zarrillo .20 .50
211 Andreas Lupzig .08 .20
212 Jergus Baca .08 .20
213 Derek Cormier .15 .40
214 John Craighead .30 .75
215 Jesper Damgaard .08 .20
216 Peter Gulda .08 .20
217 Robert Hock .08 .20
218 Martin Hohenberger .08 .20
219 Ladislav Karabin .08 .20
220 Christian Kohmann .08 .20
221 Andrej Kovalev .08 .20
222 Jason McBain .15 .40
223 Andrei Teljukin .08 .20
224 Sinuhe Wallinheimo .20 .50
225 Josef Zajic .08 .20
226 Micah Aivazoff .30 .75
227 Peter Allen .15 .40
228 Mike Bullard .20 .50
229 Dave Chyzowski .20 .50
230 Eric Dubois .15 .40
231 Ian Gordon .15 .40
232 Markus Janka .08 .20
233 Mark MacKay .20 .50
234 Neal Martin .15 .40
235 Jeff Nelson .15 .40
236 Jackson Penney .15 .40
237 Kent Simpson .15 .40
238 Jason Deleurme .15 .40
239 Gerhard Unterluggauer .08 .20
240 Darcy Werenka .20 .50
241 Andreas Morczinietz .08 .20
242 Christian Rohde .08 .20
243 Jonas Lanier .08 .20
244 Boris Blank .08 .20
245 Eduard Lewandowski .08 .20
246 Niki Mondt .08 .20
247 Leonard Wild .08 .20
248 Leonardo Conti .08 .20
249 Philip Schumacher .08 .20
250 BjÃ¶rn Leonhardt .20 .50
251 Christian Franz .20 .50
252 Manuel Kofler .20 .50
253 Daniel Kreutzer .20 .50
254 Markus Guggemos .20 .50
255 Dimitri PÃ¤tzold .20 .50
256 Benjamin Hinterstocker .20 .50
257 Christian Ehrhoff .40 1.00
258 Adrian Grygiel .20 .50
259 Benjamin Voigt .20 .50
260 Robert MÃ¼ller .20 .50
261 Dennis Seidenberg .60 1.50
262 Peter Abstreiter .20 .50
263 Christoph Schubert .20 .50
264 Andrej Strakhov .20 .50
265 Benjamin Hecker .20 .50
266 Vitalij Aab .20 .50
267 Carsten Gosdeck .20 .50
268 Lasse Kopitz .20 .50
269 Marcel Goc .75 2.00
270 Alexander DÃ¼ck .20 .50

2001-02 German DEL Upper Deck Gate Attractions

This set features the most exciting players in the DEL. The cards were inserted one in every 17 packs.

COMPLETE SET (10) 10.00 25.00
STATED ODDS 1:17
GA1 Sergej Vostrikov 1.25 3.00
GA2 Aleksandrs Kercs 1.25 3.00
GA3 Sven Felski 1.25 3.00
GA4 Mark MacKay 1.25 3.00
GA5 Alexander Selivanov 1.25 3.00
GA6 Len Soccio 2.00 5.00
GA7 Ivan Droppa 1.25 3.00
GA8 Gilbert Dionne 2.00 5.00
GA9 Stefan Ustorf 1.25 3.00
GA10 Jason Miller 1.25 3.00

2001-02 German DEL Upper Deck Goalies in Action

This set features the top stoppers in the DEL. The cards were inserted one in every 17 packs

COMPLETE SET (10) 20.00 40.00
STATED ODDS 1:17
G1 Andrei Mezin 2.50 6.00
G2 Klaus Merk 2.00 5.00
G3 Andrej Trefilov 2.50 6.00
G4 Andrew Verner 2.00 5.00
G5 Chris Rogles 2.00 5.00
G6 Roger Nordstrom 2.00 5.00
G7 Mike Rosati 2.00 5.00
G8 Christian Kunast 2.00 5.00
G9 Marc Seliger 3.00 8.00
G10 Sinuhe Wallinheimo 2.00 5.00

2001-02 German DEL Upper Deck Jerseys

The cards in this set feature a swatch of a jersey worn in an actual DEL game. Singles were inserted one in every 144 packs.

COMPLETE SET (6) 150.00 400.00
AMJ Andrei Mezin 20.00 50.00
ATJ Andrej Trefilov 12.00 30.00
AVJ Andrew Verner 12.00 30.00
CKJ Christian Kunast 8.00 20.00
CRJ Chris Rogles 12.00 30.00
ERJ Eldon Reddick 12.00 30.00
FCJ Frederic Chabot 20.00 50.00
IGJ Ian Gordon 8.00 20.00
JWJ Jimmy Waite 20.00 50.00
KKJ Kimmo Kapanen 8.00 20.00
LFJ Leonid Fatikov 8.00 20.00
MEJ Magnus Eriksson 8.00 20.00
MRJ Mike Rosati 12.00 30.00
RNJ Roger Nordstrom 8.00 20.00
RSJ Richard Shulmistra 12.00 30.00
SWJ Sinuhe Wallinheimo 12.00 30.00

2001-02 German DEL Upper Deck Skilled Stars

This series features some of the DEL's top players. The cards were inserted one in every eight packs.

COMPLETE SET (11) 6.00 15.00
SS1 Robert Hock .75 2.00
SS2 David Cooper 1.25 3.00
SS3 Brad Purdie 1.25 3.00
SS4 Todd Simon .75 2.00
SS5 Oscar Ackestrom .75 2.00
SS6 Tomas Martinec .75 2.00
SS7 Pat Mikesch .75 2.00
SS8 Mirko Ludemann .75 2.00
SS9 Stephane Richer .75 2.00
SS10 Shane Peacock .75 2.00
SS11 Paul Stanton .75 2.00

2002-03 German Adler Mannheim Eagles Postcards

1 Todd Hlushko .40 1.00
2 Thomas Schenkel .40 1.00
3 Danny Aus Den Birken .40 1.00
4 Mike Rosati .40 1.00
5 Thomas Fischer .40 1.00
6 Klaus Kathan .40 1.00
7 Sachar Blank .40 1.00
8 Yannic Seidenberg .40 1.00
9 Rico Rossi .40 1.00
10 Bill Stewart .40 1.00
11 Fabio Carciola .40 1.00
12 Rene Corbet .40 1.00
13 Sascha Goc .40 1.00
14 Nick Naumenko .40 1.00
15 Ilja Vorobiev .40 1.00
16 Steve Junker .40 1.00
17 Wayne Hynes .40 1.00
18 Devin Edgerton .40 1.00

2002-03 German Berlin Polar Bears Postcards

COMPLETE SET (28) 10.00 25.00
1 Keith Aldridge .40 1.00
2 Alex Barta .40 1.00
3 Marc Beaufait .40 1.00
4 Brad Bergen .40 1.00
5 Boris Blank .40 1.00
6 David Cooper .40 1.00
7 Yvon Corriveau .40 1.00
8 Kelly Fairchild .40 1.00
9 Sven Felski .40 1.00
10 John Gruden .40 1.00
11 Thorsten Heine .40 1.00
12 Martin Hoffmann .40 1.00
13 Oliver Jonas .40 1.00
14 Florian Katz .40 1.00
15 Florian Keller .40 1.00
16 Mark Kosick .40 1.00
17 Rob Leask .40 1.00
18 Klaus Merk .40 1.00
19 Hartmut Nickel .40 1.00
20 Pierre Page CO .40 1.00
21 Ricard Persson .40 1.00
22 Daniel Pyka .40 1.00
23 Nico Pyka .40 1.00
24 David Roberts .40 1.00
25 Rob Shearer .40 1.00
26 Richard Shulmistra .40 1.00
27 Jeff Tomlinson .40 1.00
28 Steve Walker .40 1.00

2002-03 German DEL City Press

COMPLETE SET (290) 50.00 100.00
1 Ronny Arendt .20 .50
2 Philippe Audet .20 .50
3 Bjorn Barta .20 .50
4 Frederic Bouchard .20 .50
6 Shawn Carter .20 .50
7 Igor Dorochin .20 .50
8 P.C. Drouin .40 1.00
9 Magnus Eriksson .20 .50
10 Thorsten Fendt .20 .50
11 Maxim Galanov .20 .50
12 Patrick Koslow .20 .50
13 Greg Leeb .40 1.00
14 Christian Lukes .20 .50
15 Shayne McCosh .20 .50
16 Duanne Moeser .20 .50
17 Christopher Oravec .20 .50
18 Reid Simonton .20 .50
19 Andrej Strakhov .20 .50
20 Chris Straube .20 .50
21 Sergej Vostrikov .20 .50
22 Keith Aldridge .20 .50
23 Alexander Barta .20 .50
24 Mark Beaufait .20 .50
25 Bradley Bergen .20 .50
26 Boris Blank .20 .50
27 David Cooper .20 .50
28 Yvon Corriveau .20 .50
29 Kelly Fairchild .20 .50
30 Sven Felski .20 .50
31 John Gruden .20 .50
32 Oliver Jonas .20 .50
33 Florian Keller .20 .50
34 Robert Leask .20 .50
35 Ricard Persson .20 .50
36 Nico Pyka .20 .50
37 David Roberts .20 .50
38 Rob Shearer .20 .50
39 Richard Shulmistra .20 .50
40 Jeff Tomlinson .20 .50
41 Steve Walker .20 .50
42 Marc Beaucage .20 .50
43 Fabian Brannstrom .20 .50
44 Jeff Christian .20 .50
45 Neil Eisenhut .20 .50
46 Jakub Ficenec .40 1.00
47 Michael Hackert .20 .50
48 Mathias Hart .20 .50
49 Tommy Jakobsen .20 .50
50 Alexander Jung .20 .50
51 Torsten Kienass .20 .50
52 Daniel Kreutzer .20 .50
53 Bernd Kuhnhauser .20 .50
54 Trond Magnussen .20 .50
55 Nikolaus Mondt .20 .50
56 Mike Pellegrims .20 .50
57 Markus Pottinger .20 .50
58 Jean-Francois Quintin .20 .50
59 Leo Stefan .20 .50
60 Andrei Trefilov .20 .50
61 Martin Ulrich .20 .50
62 Gerhard Unterluggauer .20 .50
63 Tore Vikingstad .20 .50
64 Rainer Zerwesz .20 .50
65 Greg Adams .20 .50
66 Pascal Appel .20 .50
67 Michael Bresagk .20 .50
68 Robert Busch .20 .50
69 Collin Danielsmeier .20 .50
70 Jason Dunham .20 .50
71 Rusty Fitzgerald .20 .50
72 Marc Fortier .20 .50
73 Robert Francz .20 .50
74 Matthias Frenzel .20 .50
75 Victor Gervais .20 .50
76 Rick Girard .20 .50
77 Cory Laylin .20 .50
78 Stewart Malgunas .20 .50
79 Jackson Penney .20 .50
80 Marc Pethke .20 .50
81 Stephane Richer .20 .50
82 Dominic Roussel .40 1.00
83 Christoph Sandner .20 .50
84 Chris Snell .20 .50
85 Paul Stanton .20 .50
86 Jonas Stopfgeshoff .20 .50
87 Peter Abstreiter .20 .50
88 Greg Andrusak .20 .50
89 Ted Crowley .20 .50
90 Thomas Dolak .20 .50
91 Ted Drury .20 .50
92 Bobby House .20 .50
93 Manuel Kofler .20 .50
94 Patrick Koppchen .20 .50
95 Christian Kunast .20 .50
96 Bob Lachance .20 .50
97 Jason Miller .20 .50
98 Jacek Plachta .20 .50
99 Boris Rousson .40 1.00
100 Andrew Schneider .20 .50
101 Heiko Smazal .20 .50
102 Mike Stevens .20 .50
103 David Sulkovsky .20 .50
104 Jeff Tory .20 .50
105 Christian Volk .20 .50
106 Phil von Stefenelli .20 .50
107 Gilbert Dionne .20 .50
108 Patrick Ehelechner .20 .50
109 Edvin Frylen .20 .50
110 Lorenz Funk Jr. .20 .50
111 Todd Hawkins .20 .50
112 Stefan Hellkvist .20 .50
113 Peter Jakobsson .20 .50
114 Peter Johansson .20 .50
115 Torbjorn Johansson .20 .50
116 Jakob Karlsson .20 .50
117 Sebastian Klenner .20 .50
118 Mattias Loof .20 .50
119 Rob Murphy .20 .50
120 Fredrik Oberg .20 .50
121 Daniel Reiss .20 .50
122 Wallace Schreiber .20 .50
123 Patrick Senger .20 .50
124 Leonard Soccio .20 .50
125 Andrew Verner .20 .50
126 Steve Wilson .20 .50
127 Chad Allan .20 .50
128 Mike Bales .40 1.00
129 Petr Bares .20 .50
130 Francois Bouchard .20 .50
131 Brad Burym .20 .50
132 Terry Campbell .20 .50
133 Kent Fearns .20 .50
134 Alexander Genze .20 .50
135 Erich Goldman .20 .50
136 Glen Goodall .40 1.00
137 Samuel Groleau .20 .50
138 Jean-Francois Jomphe .20 .50
139 Ilpo Kauhanen .20 .50
140 Steve Lingren .20 .50
141 Christoph Melischko .20 .50
142 Neville Rautert .20 .50
143 Jason Ruff .20 .50
144 Reiner Suchan .20 .50
145 Sean Tallaire .20 .50
146 Shayne Toporowski .20 .50
147 Jason Young .20 .50
148 Igor Alexandrov .20 .50
149 Doug Ast .20 .50
150 Christopher Bartolone .20 .50
151 Colin Beardsmore .20 .50
152 Oliver Bernhardt .20 .50
153 Lars Bruggemann .20 .50
154 Markus Draxler .20 .50
155 Jorgen Eriksson .20 .50
156 Petr Fical .20 .50
157 Christian Franz .20 .50
158 Carsten Gosdeck .20 .50
159 Justin Harney .20 .50
160 Christian Hommel .20 .50
161 Scott King .20 .50
162 Lasse Kopitz .20 .50
163 Dimitrij Kotschnew .20 .50
164 Chris Lipsett .20 .50
165 Andrej Podkonicky .20 .50
166 Roland Verwey .20 .50
167 Jimmy Waite .40 1.00
168 Steve Washburn .20 .50
169 Tobias Abstreiter .20 .50
170 Gert Acker .20 .50
171 Frank Appel .20 .50
172 Alexander Cherbayev .20 .50
173 Thomas Daffner .20 .50
174 Doug Deraugh .20 .50
175 Markus Janka .20 .50
176 Lars Jansson .20 .50
177 Orjan Lindmark .20 .50
178 Andreas Loth .20 .50
179 Jeffrey John MacLeod .20 .50
180 Pat Mikesch .20 .50
181 Zdenek Nedved .20 .50
182 Rich Parent .40 1.00
183 Brent Peterson .20 .50
184 Stephan Retzer .20 .50
185 StÃ©phane Robitaille .20 .50
186 Alexander Serikow .20 .50
187 Andrej Teljukin .20 .50
188 Sven Valenti .20 .50
189 Mikael Wahlberg .20 .50
190 Shayne Wright .20 .50
191 Tino Boos .20 .50
192 Mickey Elick .20 .50
193 Sebastian Furchner .20 .50
194 Alex Hicks .20 .50
195 Robert Hock .20 .50
196 Markus Jocher .20 .50
197 Eduard Lewandowski .20 .50
198 Mirko Ludemann .20 .50
199 Dave McLlwain .20 .50
200 Andreas Morczinietz .20 .50
201 Frederik Nilsson .20 .50
202 Dwayne Norris .20 .50
203 Ron Pasco .20 .50
204 Shane Peacock .20 .50
205 Andreas Renz .20 .50
206 Chris Rogles .40 1.00
207 Stefan Schauer .20 .50
208 Brad Schlegel .20 .50
209 Niklas Sundblad .20 .50
210 Christoph Ullmann .20 .50
211 Darcy Werenka .20 .50
212 Leonard Wild .20 .50
213 Patrick Augusta .20 .50
214 Stephane Barin .20 .50
215 Thomas Brandl .20 .50
216 Christoph Brandner .20 .50
217 Mario Doyon .20 .50
218 Paul Dyck .20 .50
219 Christian Ehrhoff 1.25 3.00
220 Adrian Grygiel .20 .50
221 Daniel Kunce .20 .50
222 Dan Lambert .20 .50
223 Jonas Lanier .20 .50
224 Sandy Moger .20 .50
225 Robert Muller .20 .50
226 David Musial .20 .50
227 Roger Nordstrom .20 .50
228 Gunther Oswald .20 .50
229 Brad Purdie .20 .50
230 Andreas Raubal .20 .50
231 Darryl Shannon .20 .50
232 Gary Shuchuk .20 .50
233 Sergej Stas .20 .50
234 Steffen Ziesche .20 .50
235 Michael Bakos .20 .50
236 Rene Corbet .20 .50
237 Devin Edgerton .20 .50
238 Sascha Goc .20 .50
239 Marcel Goc .75 2.00
240 Francois Groleau .20 .50
241 Todd Hlushko .20 .50
242 Wayne Hynes .20 .50
243 Chris Joseph .20 .50
244 Steve Junker .20 .50
245 Klaus Kathan .20 .50
246 Mike Kennedy .20 .50
247 Tomas Martinec .20 .50
248 Anders Myrvold .20 .50
249 Nick Naumenko .20 .50
250 Dimitri Patzold .75 2.00
251 Jason Podollan .20 .50
252 Yves Racine .20 .50
253 Andy Roach .40 1.00
254 Mike Rosati .40 1.00
255 Yannic Seidenberg .20 .50
256 Stefan Ustorf .20 .50
257 Ilja Vorobiev .20 .50
258 Vitalij Aab .20 .50
259 Shawn Anderson .20 .50
260 Frederic Chabot .75 2.00
261 Kevin Dahl .20 .50
262 Ivan Droppa .20 .50
263 Thomas Greilinger .20 .50
264 Robert Guillet .20 .50
265 Martin Jiranek .20 .50
266 Steve Larouche .20 .50
267 Guy Lehoux .20 .50
268 Christopher Luongo .20 .50
269 Martin Reichel .20 .50
270 Jurgen Rumrich .20 .50
271 Marc Savard .20 .50
272 Thomas Schinko .20 .50
273 Christian Schonmoser .20 .50
274 Marc Seliger .20 .50
275 Martin Sychra .20 .50
276 Dave Tomlinson .20 .50
277 Terry Yake .20 .50
278 Paul Brousseau .20 .50
279 Markus Busch .20 .50
280 Dave Chyzowski .20 .50
281 Alexander Duck .20 .50
282 Mark Etz .20 .50
283 Francois Fortier .20 .50
284 Ian Gordon .20 .50
285 Eric Houde .20 .50
286 Ladislav Karabin .20 .50
287 Steffen Karg .20 .50
288 Rainer Kosttstorfer .20 .50
289 Christian Kohmann .20 .50
290 Alexander Kuzminski .20 .50
291 Neal Martin .20 .50
292 Jochen Molling .20 .50
293 Curtis Sheptak .20 .50
294 Vadim Slivchenko .20 .50
295 Ralf Stark .20 .50
296 Jens Stramkowski .20 .50
297 Mathias Svedberg .20 .50
298 Lukas Zib .20 .50

2002-03 German DEL City Press Top Stars

COMPLETE SET (10)
GT1 Marc Seliger
GT2 Tobias Abstreiter
GT3 Christian Ehrhoff
GT4 Jurgen Rumrich
GT5 Mirko Ludemann
GT6 Christian Kunast
GT7 Sven Felski
GT8 Daniel Kreutzer
GT9 Wayne Hynes
GT10 Klaus Kathan

2003-04 German Berlin Polar Bears Postcards

COMPLETE SET (31) 10.00 25.00
1 Keith Aldridge .40 1.00
2 Nils Antons .40 1.00
3 Alex Barta .40 1.00
4 Jens Baxmann .40 1.00
5 Mark Beaufait .40 1.00
6 Brad Bergen .40 1.00
7 Florian Busch .40 1.00
8 Yvon Corriveau .40 1.00
9 Tobias Draxinger .40 1.00
10 Micki DuPont .40 1.00
11 Kelly Fairchild .40 1.00
12 Sven Felski .40 1.00
13 Tom Fiedler .40 1.00
14 Patrick Flynn .40 1.00
15 Mathias Forster .40 1.00
16 Martin Hoffmann .40 1.00
17 Frank Hordler .40 1.00
18 Oliver Jonas .40 1.00
19 Florian Keller .40 1.00
20 Rob Leask .40 1.00
21 Hartmut Nickel .40 1.00
22 Pierre Page CO .40 1.00
23 Rich Parent .75 2.00
24 Denis Pederson .40 1.00
25 Ricard Persson .40 1.00
26 Andre Rankel .40 1.00
27 David Roberts .40 1.00
28 Darryl Shannon .40 1.00
29 Rob Shearer .40 1.00
30 Jeff Tomlinson .40 1.00
31 Steve Walker .40 1.00

2003-04 German Deg Metro Stars

This was a team-issued set featuring a club from the top German league.

COMPLETE SET (23) 10.00 20.00
1 Fabian Brannstrom .40 1.00
2 Christian Brittig .40 1.00
3 Mathias Hart .40 1.00
4 Tommy Jakobsen .40 1.00
5 Thomas Jorg .40 1.00
6 Alexander Jung .40 1.00
7 Florian Jung .40 1.00
8 Walter Koberle .40 1.00
9 Michael Komma .40 1.00
10 Daniel Kreutzer .40 1.00
11 Bobo Kuhnhauser .40 1.00
12 Trond Magnussen .40 1.00
13 Pat Mikesch .40 1.00
14 Johan Molin .40 1.00
15 Mike Pellegrims .40 1.00
16 Markus Pottinger .40 1.00
17 Alexander Sulzer .40 1.00
18 Jeff Tory .40 1.00
19 Andrej Trefilov .40 1.00
20 Martin Ulrich .40 1.00
21 Gerhard Unterluggauer .40 1.00
22 Tore Vikingstad .40 1.00
23 Clayton Young .40 1.00

2003-04 German DEL

COMPLETE SET (210) 15.00 40.00
1 Rene Corbet .10 .25
2 Devin Edgerton .10 .25
3 Sascha Goc .10 .25
4 Francois Groleau .10 .25
5 Robert Hock .10 .25
6 Chris Joseph .10 .25
7 Klaus Kathan .10 .25
8 Tomas Martinec .10 .25
9 Jochen Molling .10 .25
10 Derek Plante .10 .25
11 Jason Podollan .10 .25
12 Andy Roach .20 .50
13 Marc Seliger .10 .25
14 Richard Shulmistra .10 .25
15 Christoph Ullmann .10 .25
16 Ronny Arendt .10 .25
17 Bjorn Barta .10 .25
18 Colin Beardsmore .10 .25
19 Shawn Carter .10 .25
20 Eric Dandenault .10 .25
21 Xavier Delisle .10 .25
22 Magnus Eriksson .10 .25
23 Francois Fortier .10 .25
24 Rick Girard .10 .25
25 John Miner .10 .25
26 Duanne Moeser .10 .25
27 Arvids Rekis .10 .25
28 Marc Savard .10 .25
29 Andrej Strakhov .10 .25
30 Bob Wren .10 .25
31 Fabian Brannstrom .10 .25
32 Christian Brittig .10 .25
33 Tommy Jakobsen .10 .25
34 Alexander Jung .10 .25
35 Daniel Kreutzer .10 .25
36 Trond Magnussen .10 .25
37 Pat Mikesch .10 .25
38 Mike Pellegrims .10 .25
39 Marcus Thuresson .10 .25
40 Jeff Tory .10 .25
41 Andrej Trefilov .10 .25
42 Martin Ulrich .10 .25
43 Gerhard Unterluggauer .10 .25
44 Tore Vikingstad .10 .25
45 Clayton Young .10 .25
46 Peter Boon .10 .25
47 Dany Bousquet .10 .25
48 Olivier Coqueux .10 .25
49 David Danner .10 .25
50 Juraj Faith .10 .25
51 Dusan Frosch .10 .25
52 Rudolf Gorgenlander .10 .25
53 Rostislav Haas .10 .25
54 Henrik Holscher .10 .25
55 Thomas Jetter .10 .25
56 Ravil Khaidarov .10 .25
57 Vadim Slivchenko .10 .25
58 Sergej Stas .10 .25
59 Bastian Steingross .10 .25
60 Jiri Zelenka .10
61 Keith Aldridge .10
62 Alexander Barta .10
63 Mark Beaufait .10
64 Micki Dupont .10
65 Kelly Fairchild .10
66 Sven Felski .10
67 Oliver Jonas .10
68 Florian Keller .10
69 Robert Leask .10
70 Rich Parent .40
71 Denis Pederson .10
72 Ricard Persson .10
73 David Roberts .10
74 Rob Shearer .10
75 Steve Walker .10
76 Doug Ast .10
77 Craig Ferguson .10
78 Jakub Ficenec .20
79 Glenn Goodall .40
80 Samuel Groleau .10
81 Justin Harney .10
82 Cameron Mann .40
83 Nikolaus Mondt .10
84 Gunther Oswald .10
85 Yves Racine .10
86 Thomas Schinko .10
87 Ken Sutton .10
88 Sean Tallaire .10
89 Phil von Stefenelli .10
90 Jimmy Waite .40
91 Christian Kohmann .10
92 Jesse Belanger .10
93 Francois Bouchard .10
94 Michael Bresagk .10
95 Ian Gordon .10
96 David Gosselin .10
97 Michael Hackert .10
98 Mike Harder .10
99 Sebastian Klenner .10
100 Patrick Lebeau .40
101 Dwayne Norris .10
102 Peter Ratchuk .10
103 Martin Reichel .10
104 Paul Stanton .10
105 Jason Young .10
106 Darren van Impe .10
107 Mark Greig .10
108 Robert House .10
109 Wayne Hynes .10
110 Christian Kunast .10
111 Patrick Koppchen .10
112 Dan Lambert .10
113 Paul Manning .10
114 Shane Peacock .10
115 Jacek Plachta .10
116 Brad Purdie .10
117 Boris Rousson .40
118 Andrew Schneider .10
119 Heiko Smazal .10
120 Dave Tomlinson .10
121 Patrik Augusta .10
122 Bjorn Bombis .10
123 Jeff Christian .10
124 Gordon Borberg .10
125 Edvin Frylen .10
126 Lorenz Funk .10
127 David Haas .10
128 Peter Jakobsson .10
129 Ilpo Kauhanen .10
130 Mattias Loof .10
131 Zdenek Nedved .10
132 Frederik Oberg .10
133 Leonard Soccio .10
134 Andrej Teljukin .10
135 Steve Wilson .10
136 David Cooper .10
137 Bryan Adams .10
138 Chris Bartolone .10
139 James Black .10
140 Lars Bruggemann .10
141 Jason Cipolla .10
142 Michael Fountain .10
143 Erich Goldmann .10
144 Matt Henderson .10
145 Matt Higgins .10
146 Christian Hommel .10
147 Scott King .10
148 Dimitrij Kotschnew .10
149 Rob Sandrock .10
150 Roland Verwey .10
151 Tobias Abstreiter .10
152 Paul Brousseau .10
153 Ted Crowley .10
154 Josh DeWolf .10
155 Ted Drury .10
156 Joaquin Gage .10
157 Orjan Lindmark .10
158 Andreas Loth .10
159 Jeff MacLeod .10
160 Brent Peterson .10
161 Stephan Retzer .10
162 Stephane Robitaille .10
163 Alexander Serikow .10
164 Matthias Trattnig .10
165 Mikael Wahlberg .10
166 Jeremy Adduono .10
167 Tino Boos .10
168 Jeff Dessner .10
169 Mickey Elick .10
170 Sebastian Furchner .10
171 Alex Hicks .10
172 Mirko Ludemann .10
173 Eduard Lewandowski .10
174 Dave McLlwain .10
175 Andreas Morczinietz .10
176 Andreas Renz .10
177 Chris Rogles .10
178 Jean-Yves Roy .10
179 Brad Schlegel .10
180 Leo Stefan .10
181 Pascal Appel .10
182 Marc Beaucage .10
183 Eric Bertrand .10
184 Adrian Grygiel .10
185 Robert Guillet .10
186 Christopher Kelleher .10
187 Daniel Kunce .10
188 Justin Kurtz .10
189 Chris Luongo .10
190 Robert Muller .10
191 Alexander Selivanov .10
192 Stefan Ustorf .10
193 Shayne Wright .10
194 Terry Yake .10
195 Steffen Ziesche .10
196 Vitalij Aab .10
197 Frederic Chabot .40
198 Marian Cisar .10
199 Petr Fical .10
200 Liam Garvey .10

01 Thomas Greilinger .10 .25
02 Martin Jiranek .10 .25
03 Stephane Julien .10 .25
04 Lasse Kopitz .10 .25
05 Steve Larouche .10 .25
06 Greg Leeb .20 .50
07 Guy Lehoux .10 .25
08 Alfie Michaud .10 .25
09 Yan Stastny ERC 1.25 3.00
10 Robert Tomik .10 .25

2003-04 German DEL All-Stars

OMPLETE SET (22) 15.00 30.00
S1 Jimmy Waite 1.25 3.00
S2 Andrej Trefilov 1.25 3.00
S3 Chris Rogles 1.25 3.00
S4 Justin Harney .75 2.00
S5 Paul Stanton .75 2.00
S6 Andy Roach 1.25 3.00
S7 Christoph Brandner .75 2.00
S8 Dwayne Norris .75 2.00
S9 Francois Fortier .75 2.00
S10 Philippe Audet .75 2.00
S11 Doug Ast .75 2.00
S12 Brad Purdie .75 2.00
S13 Kelly Fairchild .75 2.00
S14 Wally Schreiber .75 2.00
S15 Terry Yake .75 2.00
S16 Jean-Francois Jomphe .75 2.00
S17 Andrew Schneider .75 2.00
S18 Tommy Jakobsen .75 2.00
S19 Dave McLlwain .75 2.00
S20 Trond Magnussen .75 2.00
S21 Shawn Anderson .75 2.00
S22 Jeff Tory .75 2.00

2003-04 German Mannheim Eagles Postcards

ese 4X6 postcards were issued by the team in set rm. All cards are autographed by the players, though the Sachar Blank autograph was scratched ut in our set. Perhaps the auto was determined to ave been signed by someone else???

OMPLETE SET (29) 30.00 75.00
Richard Shulmistra 1.50 4.00
Marc Seliger 1.50 4.00
Marco Schutz 1.50 4.00
Sachar Blank .40 1.00
Yannic Seidenberg 1.50 4.00
Bill Stewart 1.50 4.00
Christoph Ullmann 1.50 4.00
Stefan Ustorf 1.50 4.00
Rico Rossi 1.50 4.00
Andy Roach 2.50 6.00
Yves Racine 1.50 4.00
Nico Pyka 1.50 4.00
Jason Podollan 2.50 6.00
Derek Plante 2.50 6.00
Jochen Molling 1.50 4.00
Tomas Martinec 1.50 4.00
Mike Kennedy 1.50 4.00
Klaus Kathan 1.50 4.00
Steve Junker 1.50 4.00
Chris Joseph 1.50 4.00
Robert Hock 1.50 4.00
Todd Hlushko 1.50 4.00
Francois Groleau 1.50 4.00
Sascha Goc 1.50 4.00
Devin Edgerton 1.50 4.00
Rene Corbet 1.50 4.00
Fabio Carciola 1.50 4.00
Michael Bakos 1.50 4.00
Danny Aus Den Birken 1.50 4.00
Marc Bruns 1.50 4.00
Markus Koch 1.50 4.00
Andy Roach 2.50 6.00
Christoph Ullmann 1.50 4.00

2003-04 German Nuremberg Ice Tigers Postcards

ese 4X6 postcards were issued in set form by the am. They are unnumbered and listed below in habetical order.

MPLETE SET (26) 10.00 25.00
Vitalij Aab .40 1.00
Benjamin Barz .40 1.00
Frederic Chabot 1.25 3.00
Marian Cisar .40 1.00
Kevin Dahl .40 1.00
Jon DiSalvatore .40 1.00
Petr Fical .40 1.00
Konstantin Firsanov .40 1.00
Liam Garvey .40 1.00
Thomas Greilinger .40 1.00
Tobias Guttner .40 1.00
Martin Jiranek .40 1.00
Stephane Julien .40 1.00
Lasse Kopitz .40 1.00
Steve Larouche .40 1.00
Greg Leeb .75 2.00
Guy Lehoux .40 1.00
Josef Menauer .40 1.00
Alfie Michaud .40 1.00
Sebastian Osterloh .40 1.00
Felix Petermann .40 1.00
Greg Poss .40 1.00
Jurgen Rumrich .40 1.00
Christian Schonmoser .40 1.00
Otto Sykora GM .40 1.00
Robert Tomik .40 1.00

2004-05 German Augsburg Panthers Postcards

ese cards are unnumbered and so are listed below in habetical order.

MPLETE SET (27) 10.00 25.00
Pascal Appel .40 1.00
Ronny Arendt .40 1.00
Steve Bancroft .40 1.00
Bjorn Barta .40 1.00
Rich Brennan .40 1.00
Robert Brezina .40 1.00
Marc Brown .40 1.00
Robert Busch .40 1.00
Shawn Carter .40 1.00
David Danner .40 1.00
Dennis Endras .40 1.00
Brian Felsner .40 1.00
Torsten Fendt .40 1.00
Francois Fortier .40 1.00
Rick Girard .40 1.00
Manuel Kopfler .40 1.00
Jean-Francois Labbe .75 2.00
Benoit Laporte CO .20 .50
Roland Mayr .40 1.00
Francois Methot .40 1.00
John Miner .40 1.00
Duanne Moeser .40 1.00
Mike Pudlick .40 1.00
Daniel Rau .40 1.00
Arvids Rekis .40 1.00

26 Steffen Tolzer .40 1.00
27 Benjamin Voigt .40 1.00

2004-05 German Berlin Eisbarens 50th Anniversary

Standard-sized card set features top players from the past and present of Germany's most famous team.

COMPLETE SET (75) 15.00 30.00
1 Header .04 .10
2 Mike Losch .20 .50
3 Dave Morrison .20 .50
4 Roland Peters .20 .50
5 Mario Plack .20 .50
6 Joachim Stasche .20 .50
7 Detlef Radant .20 .50
8 Pelle Svensson .20 .50
9 Egon Schmeisser .20 .50
10 Klaus Merk .20 .50
11 Rainer Patschinski .20 .50
12 Franz Steer .20 .50
13 Sergej Jaschin .20 .50
14 Steffen Ziesche .20 .50
15 Wolfgang Kraske .20 .50
16 Torsten Deutscher .20 .50
17 Magnus Roupe .20 .50
18 Heinz Pohland .20 .50
19 Mark Jooris .20 .50
20 Wolfgang Beuthner .20 .50
21 Uwe Geisert .20 .50
22 Rene Bielke .20 .50
23 Reinhard Fengler .20 .50
24 Dietmar Peters .20 .50
25 Helmut Senftleben .20 .50
26 Peter Prusa .20 .50
27 Thomas Swibenko .20 .50
28 Marc Fortier .20 .50
29 Andre Dietzch .20 .50
30 Holger Mix .20 .50
31 Werner Thomas .20 .50
32 Hanne Frenzel .20 .50
33 Thomas Mitew .20 .50
34 Jeff Tomlinson .20 .50
35 Fred Freitag .20 .50
36 Bernd Karrenbauer .20 .50
37 Friedhelm Bogelsack .20 .50
38 Thomas Graul .20 .50
39 Sven Felski .20 .50
40 Dirk Perschau .20 .50
41 Gerhard Muller .20 .50
42 Jurgen Schmutzler .20 .50
43 Wilhelm Kopatz .20 .50
44 Dieter Janke .20 .50
45 Jurgen Geisert .20 .50
46 Rob Cowie .20 .50
47 Dieter Dewitz .20 .50
48 Joachim Lempio .20 .50
49 Leif Carlsson .20 .50
50 Joachim Hurbanek .20 .50
51 Gerhard Klugel .20 .50
52 Udo Dohler .20 .50
53 Frank Proske .20 .50
54 Wolfgang Plotka .20 .50
55 Hartmut Nickel .20 .50
56 Andrew McKim .20 .50
57 Jens Ziesche .20 .50
58 Wilfried Rohrbach .20 .50
59 Dieter Frenzel .20 .50
60 Jurgen Breitschuh .20 .50
61 Peter-John Lee .20 .50
62 Mike Bullard .20 .50
63 Guido Hiller .20 .50
64 Gunther Katzur .20 .50
65 Peter Lehnigk .20 .50
66 Matthias Dietz .20 .50
67 Harald Kuhnke .20 .50
68 Frank Krause .20 .50
69 Joachim Ziesche .20 .50
70 Dieter Voigt .20 .50
71 Thomas Steen .20 .50
72 Daniel Held .20 .50
73 Derek Mayer .20 .50
74 Nico Pyka .20 .50
75 Checklist .04 .10

2004-05 German Berlin Polar Bears Postcards

These cards are unnumbered and are listed below in alphabetical order.

COMPLETE SET (32) 10.00 25.00
1 Alexander Barta .30 .75
2 Jens Baxmann .30 .75
3 Mark Beaufait .30 .75
4 Florian Busch .30 .75
5 Erik Cole .75 2.00
6 Nathan Dempsey .40 1.00
7 Tobias Draxinger .30 .75
8 Danier Dshunussow .30 .75
9 Micki Dupont .40 1.00
10 Kelly Fairchild .40 1.00
11 Sven Felski .30 .75
12 Christoph Gawlik .30 .75
13 Shawn Heins .40 1.00
14 Martin Hoffmann .30 .75
15 Frank Hordler .30 .75
16 Kay Hurbanek .30 .75
17 Oliver Jonas .30 .75
18 Florian Keller .30 .75
19 Olaf Kolzig 2.00 5.00
20 Rob Leask .30 .75
21 Hartmut Nickel ACO .10 .25
22 Pierre Page CO .10 .25
23 Denis Pederson .40 1.00
24 Ricard Persson .30 .75
25 Andre Rankel .30 .75
26 Rob Shearer .30 .75
27 Stefan Ustorf .30 .75
28 Steve Walker .30 .75
29 Derrick Walser .40 1.00
30 Yourri Ziffzer .30 .75
31 Bully MASCOT .10 .25
32 Team Photo .10 .25

2004-05 German Cologne Sharks Postcards

The cards are unnumbered, so they are listed below alphabetically.

COMPLETE SET (28) 10.00 25.00
1 Jeromy Adduono .40 1.00
2 Colin Beardsmore .40 1.00
3 Markus Berwanger CO .10 .25
4 Dan Djornlie .40 1.00
5 Boris Blank .40 1.00
6 Tino Boos .40 1.00
7 Jon Coleman .40 1.00
8 Thomas Fischer .40 1.00
9 Sebastian Furchner .40 1.00
10 Philip Gogulla .40 1.00
11 Thomas Greiss .40 1.00
12 Mattias Hart .40 1.00
13 Alex Hicks .40 1.00
14 Kai Hospelt .40 1.00
15 Michael Hrstka .40 1.00
16 Stephane Julien .40 1.00
17 Eduard Lewandowski .40 1.00
18 Mirko Ludemann .40 1.00
19 Dave McLlwain .40 1.00
20 Rupert Meister ACO .10 .25
21 Moritz Muller .40 1.00
22 Andreas Renz .40 1.00
23 Chris Rogles .60 1.50
24 Jean-Yves Roy .40 1.00
25 Brad Schlegel .40 1.00
26 Yannic Seidenberg .40 1.00
27 Paul Traynor .40 1.00
28 Hans Zach CO .10 .25

2004-05 German DEL

COMPLETE SET (283) 25.00 50.00
1 Vitalij Aab .10 .25
2 Danny aus den Birken .10 .25
3 Michael Bakos .10 .25
4 Sven Butenschon .10 .25
5 Rene Corbet .20 .50
6 Andy Delmore .20 .50
7 Devin Edgerton .10 .25
8 Sascha Goc .20 .50
9 Francois Groleau .10 .25
10 Eric Healey .20 .50
11 Jochen Hecht .40 1.00
12 Christopher Joseph .10 .25
13 Steve Kelly .10 .25
14 Markus Kink .10 .25
15 Derek Plante .10 .25
16 Jason Podollan .10 .25
17 Nico Pyka .10 .25
18 John Tripp .10 .25
19 Cristobal Huet 1.25 3.00
20 Thomas Greilinger .10 .25
21 Christoph Ullmann .10 .25
22 Ronny Arendt .10 .25
23 Bjorn Barta .10 .25
24 Robert Brezina .10 .25
25 Marc Brown .10 .25
26 Shawn Carter .10 .25
27 Brian Felsner .10 .25
28 Thorsten Fendt .10 .25
29 Francois Fortier .10 .25
30 Rick Girard .10 .25
31 Manuel Kofler .10 .25
32 Jean Francois Labbe .20 .50
33 Roland Mayr .10 .25
34 Francois Methot .10 .25
35 John Miner .10 .25
36 Duanne Moeser .10 .25
37 Arvids Rekis .10 .25
38 Steve Bancroft .10 .25
39 Mike Pudlick .10 .25
40 David Danner .10 .25
41 Daniel Rau .10 .25
42 Christian Brittig .10 .25
43 Fabian Brannstrom .10 .25
44 Eric Dandenault .10 .25
45 Matt Davidson .10 .25
46 Matt Herr .20 .50
47 Tommy Jakobsen .10 .25
48 Alexander Jung .10 .25
49 Klaus Kathan .10 .25
50 Bernd Kuhnhauser .10 .25
51 Daniel Kreutzer .10 .25
52 Trond Magnussen .10 .25
53 Mike Pellegrims .10 .25
54 Andrew Schneider .10 .25
55 Jeff Tory .10 .25
56 Andrej Trefilov .20 .50
57 Martin Ulrich .10 .25
58 Tore Vikingstad .10 .25
59 Clayton Young .10 .25
60 Florian Jung .10 .25
61 Alexander Sulzer .10 .25
62 Jens Baxmann .10 .25
63 Mark Beaufait .10 .25
64 Tobias Draxinger .10 .25
65 Micki DuPont .20 .50
66 Kelly Fairchild .20 .50
67 Sven Felski .10 .25
68 Shawn Heins .20 .50
69 Frank Hordler .10 .25
70 Oliver Jonas .10 .25
71 Florian Keller .10 .25
72 Robert Leask .10 .25
73 Denis Pederson .10 .25
74 Ricard Persson .10 .25
75 Rob Shearer .10 .25
76 Stefan Ustorf .10 .25
77 Steve Walker .10 .25
78 Derrick Walser .20 .50
79 Youri Ziffzer .10 .25
80 Alexander Barta .10 .25
81 Florian Busch .10 .25
82 Chris Armstrong .10 .25
83 Doug Ast .20 .50
84 Brad Burym .10 .25
85 Craig Ferguson .10 .25
86 Jakub Ficenec .20 .50
87 Glenn Goodall .20 .50
88 Justin Harney .10 .25
89 Martin Jiranek .10 .25
90 Andreas Loth .10 .25
91 Cameron Mann .40 1.00
92 Nikolaus Mondt .10 .25
93 Gunther Oswald .10 .25
94 Aleksander Polaczek .10 .25
95 Marco Sturm .40 1.00
96 Ken Sutton .10 .25
97 Phil von Stefenelli .10 .25
98 Jimmy Waite .20 .50
99 Andy McDonald .40 1.00
100 Daniel Hilpert .10 .25
101 Christoph Melischko .10 .25
102 Boris Ackers .10 .25
103 Marc Beaucage .10 .25
104 Francois Bouchard .10 .25
105 Mihael Bresagk .10 .25
106 Ian Gordon .10 .25
107 Markus Jocher .10 .25
108 Sebastian Klenner .10 .25
109 Christian Kohmann .10 .25
110 Patrick Lebeau .20 .50
111 Mikael Magnusson .10 .25
112 Dwayne Norris .10 .25
113 Sean Pronger .10 .25
114 Peter Ratchuk .10 .25
115 Martin Reichel .10 .25
116 Andrej Strakhov .10 .25
117 David Sulkovsky .10 .25
118 Jason Young .10 .25
119 Stephane Robidas .20 .50
120 Michael Hackert .10 .25
121 Neville Rautert .10 .25
122 Nils Antons .10 .25
123 Robert Francz .10 .25
124 Robert House .10 .25
125 Wayne Hynes .10 .25
126 Craig Johnson .10 .25
127 Alan Letang .10 .25
128 Paul Manning .10 .25
129 Jochen Molling .10 .25
130 Shane Peacock .10 .25
131 Jacek Plachta .10 .25
132 Brad Purdie .10 .25
133 Brandon Reid .40 1.00
134 Boris Rousson .40 1.00
135 Jurgen Rumrich .10 .25
136 Heiko Smazal .10 .25
137 Dave Tomlinson .10 .25
138 Darren van Impe .10 .25
139 Leonhard Wild .10 .25
140 Jim Dowd .20 .50
141 Christopher Oravec .10 .25
142 Martin Walter .10 .25
143 Peter Abstreiter .10 .25
144 Patrick Augusta .10 .25
145 Gordon Borberg .10 .25
146 Lars Bruggemann .10 .25
147 Jason Cipolla .10 .25
148 Thomas Dolak .10 .25
149 Edvin Frylen .10 .25
150 Robert Hock .10 .25
151 Christian Kunast .10 .25
152 Lipo Kauhanen .10 .25
153 Patrick Koppchen .10 .25
154 Dan Lambert .10 .25
155 Andreas Morczienitz .10 .25
156 Frederik Oberg .10 .25
157 Len Soccio .10 .25
158 Andrej Teljukin .10 .25
159 Steve Wilson .10 .25
160 Michael Nemirovski .10 .25
161 Rene Rothke .10 .25
162 Benedikt Schopper .10 .25
163 Bryan Adams .10 .25
164 Igor Alexandrov .10 .25
165 Oliver Bernhardt .10 .25
166 Leonardo Conti .10 .25
167 Collin Danielsmeier .10 .25
168 Sven Gerbig .10 .25
169 Erich Goldmann .10 .25
170 Rhett Gordon .10 .25
171 Matt Higgins .20 .50
172 Ralph Intrnuovo .20 .50
173 Martin Knold .10 .25
174 Dimitij Kotschew .10 .25
175 Brett Lysak .10 .25
176 Mike Martin .10 .25
177 Kevin Mitchell .10 .25
178 Roland Verwey .10 .25
179 Brian White .10 .25
180 Mike York .20 .50
181 Mark Etz .10 .25
182 Franz Fritzmeier .10 .25
183 Tobias Abstreiter .10 .25
184 Gert Acker .10 .25
185 Dany Bousquet .20 .50
186 Daniel Corso .20 .50
187 Kirk Furey .10 .25
188 Joaquin Gage .20 .50
189 David Gosselin .10 .25
190 Christian Hommel .10 .25
191 Sebastian Jones .10 .25
192 Mark Greig .10 .25
193 Christian Laflamme .10 .25
194 Jan Munster .10 .25
195 Dean Melanson .10 .25
196 Alexander Serikow .10 .25
197 Brian Swanson .10 .25
198 Martin Sychra .10 .25
199 Sven Valent .10 .25
200 Nick Schultz .20 .50
201 Stephan Retzer .10 .25
202 Petr Macholda .10 .25
203 Christian Retzer .10 .25
204 Jeremy Adduono .20 .50
205 Colin Beardsmore .10 .25
206 Dan Bjornlie .10 .25
207 Boris Blank .10 .25
208 Tino Boos .10 .25
209 Thomas Fischer .10 .25
210 Thomas Greiss .10 .25
211 Matthias Hart .10 .25
212 Alex Hicks .10 .25
213 Stephane Julien .10 .25
214 Mirko Ludemann .10 .25
215 Eduard Lewandowski .10 .25
216 Dave McLlwain .10 .25
217 Andreas Renz .10 .25
218 Chris Rogles .20 .50
219 Jean-Yves Roy .10 .25
220 Brad Schlegel .10 .25
221 Leo Stefan .10 .25
222 Yannic Seidenberg .10 .25
223 Sebastian Furchner .10 .25
224 Steve Brule .10 .25
225 Alexander Dueck .10 .25
226 Paul Dyck .10 .25
227 Carsten Gosdeck .10 .25
228 Robert Guillet .10 .25
229 Chris Herperger .10 .25
230 Christian Rhode .10 .25
231 Ivo Jan .10 .25
232 Markus Janka .10 .25
233 Scott King .10 .25
234 Daniel Kunce .10 .25
235 Justin Kurtz .10 .25
236 Guy Lehoux .10 .25
237 Robert Muller .10 .25
238 Florian Schnitzer .10 .25
239 Alexander Selivanov .10 .25
240 Shayne Wright .10 .25
241 Steffen Ziesche .10 .25
242 Adrian Grygiel .10 .25
243 Rainer Kottstorfer .10 .25
244 Drew Bannister .10 .25
245 Benjamin Barz .10 .25
246 Petr Fical .10 .25
247 Konstantin Firsanov .10 .25
248 Christian Franz .10 .25
249 Mike Green .10 .25
250 Lasse Kopitz .10 .25
251 Greg Leeb .10 .25
252 Tomas Martinec .10 .25
253 Ulrich Maurer .10 .25
254 Josef Menauer .10 .25
255 Stefan Schauer .10 .25
256 Lubomir Sekeras .10 .25
257 Yan Stastny 1.25 3.00
258 Adam Svoboda .20 .50
259 Sean Tallaire .10 .25
260 Brad Tapper .20 .50
261 Pascal Trepanier .20 .50
262 Bjorn Bombis .10 .25
263 Felix Petermann .10 .25
264 Ivan Ciernik .10 .25
265 Dale Clarke .10 .25
266 Xavier Delisle .10 .25
267 Alexander Genze .10 .25
268 Ladislav Karabin .10 .25
269 Andrej Kaufmann .10 .25
270 Boris Lingemann .10 .25
271 Per-Anton Lundstrom .10 .25
272 Marek Mastic .10 .25
273 David Musial .10 .25
274 Christoph Paepke .10 .25
275 Richard Pavlikovsky .10 .25
276 Marc Seliger .10 .25
277 Todd Simon .10 .25
278 Peter Smrek .10 .25
279 Rainer Suchan .10 .25
280 Roman Veber .10 .25
281 Jan Zurek .10 .25
282 Markus Guggemos .10 .25
283 Tobias Samendinger .10 .25
NNO Deutscher Meister 2004 Frankfurt Lions 4.00 10.00

2004-05 German DEL All-Stars

COMPLETE SET (19) 15.00 30.00
AS1 Jimmy Waite 2.00 5.00
AS2 Andrej Trefilov .75 2.00
AS3 Stephane Julien .75 2.00
AS4 Ricard Persson .75 2.00
AS5 Peter Ratchuk .75 2.00
AS6 Jakub Ficenec 1.25 3.00
AS7 Mike Pellegrims .75 2.00
AS8 John Miner .75 2.00
AS9 Cameron Mann 1.25 3.00
AS10 Marian Cisar .75 2.00
AS11 Ted Drury .75 2.00
AS12 Rene Corbet .75 2.00
AS13 Kelly Fairchild .75 2.00
AS14 Danny Bousquet .75 2.00
AS15 Patrick Augusta .75 2.00
AS16 Alexander Selivanov .75 2.00
AS17 Dave McLlwain .75 2.00
AS18 Brad Purdie .75 2.00
AS19 Scott King .75 2.00

2004-05 German DEL Global Players

COMPLETE SET (5) 10.00 20.00
GP1 Olaf Kolzig 4.00 10.00
GP2 Christian Ehrhoff 1.25 3.00
GP3 Jochen Hecht 1.25 3.00
GP4 Marco Sturm 1.25 3.00
GP5 Dennis Seidenberg 1.25 3.00
GP6 Checklist .40 1.00

2004-05 German DEL Superstars

COMPLETE SET (23) 20.00 40.00
SU01 Sven ButenschÃ¶n .75 2.00
SU02 Jochen Hecht 1.25 3.00
SU03 Cristobal Huet 2.00 5.00
SU04 Yannick Tremblay .75 2.00
SU05 Erik Cole 1.25 3.00
SU06 Olaf KÃ¶lzig 2.00 5.00
SU07 Nathan Dempsey .75 2.00
SU08 Stephane Robidas .75 2.00
SU09 Doug Weight .75 2.00
SU10 Andy McDonald .75 2.00
SU11 Marco Sturm 1.25 3.00
SU12 Jamie Langenbrunner .75 2.00
SU13 Aaron Ward .75 2.00
SU14 Mike York .75 2.00
SU15 John-Michael Liles .75 2.00
SU16 Jean-Sebastien Giguere .75 2.00
SU17 Paul Mara .75 2.00
SU18 Nick Schultz .75 2.00
SU19 Tom Preissing .75 2.00
SU20 Krys Kolanos .75 2.00
SU21 Ty Conklin 1.25 3.00
SU22 Kevyn Adams .75 2.00
SU23 Superstars Checklist .40 1.00

2004-05 German DEL Update

284 Fabio Carciola .10 .25
285 Steven Passmore .20 .50
286 Adler Manheim CL .04 .10
287 Richard Brennan .10 .25
288 Augsburger Panther CL .04 .10
289 Markus Pottinger .10 .25
290 Patrick Reimer .10 .25
291 Thomas Jorg .10 .25
292 DEG Metro Stars CL .04 .10
293 Andre Rankel .10 .25
294 Norman Martens .10 .25
295 Christoph Gawlik .10 .25
296 Daniar Dshunussov .10 .25
297 Richard Mueller .10 .25
298 Marcus Sommerfeld .10 .25
299 Ehc EisBaren Berlin CL .04 .10
300 Mike Harder .10 .25
301 Markus Schroder .10 .25
302 Steffen Karg .10 .25
303 ERC Ingolstadt CL .04 .10
304 Joseph Murray .10 .25
305 Chad Bassen .10 .25
306 Frankfurt Lions CL .04 .10
307 Sasha Martinovic .10 .25
308 Clayton Young .10 .25
309 Hamburg Freezers CL .04 .10
310 Todd Hlushko .10 .25
311 Marian Cisar .10 .25
312 Bastian Steingrog .04 .10
313 Alexander Serikow .10 .25
314 Jonas Lanier .10 .25
315 Michael Kozhenikov .10 .25
316 Wayne Hynes .10 .25
317 Rich Parent .40 1.00
318 Hannover Scorpions CL .04 .10
319 Tobias Schwab .10 .25
320 Iserluhn Roosters CL .04 .10
321A Paul Traynor .10 .25
322A John Coleman .10 .25
322B Ted Drury .20 .50
323A Kai Hospelt .10 .25
323B Corey Hirsch .20 .50
324A Andreas Loth .10 .25
324B Peter Abstreiter .10 .25
325A Marquis Mathieu .40 1.00
325B Mark Kosick .10 .25
326 Manuel Klinge .10 .25
326A Manuel Klinge .10 .25
326b Kolner Haie CL .04 .10
327 Kassel Huskies CL .04 .10
334 Stefan Schroder .10 .25
335 Martin Hyun .10 .25
336 Martin Schymainski .10 .25
337 Vadim Slivchenko .10 .25
338 Krefeld Checklist .04 .10
339 Herbert Vasiljievs .10 .25
340 Lukas Lang .10 .25
341 Robert Tomik .10 .25
342 Nuremberg Checklist .04 .10
343 Sebastian Osterioh .10 .25
344 Lars Bruggemann .10 .25
345 Artjom Kostyrev .10 .25
346 Eric Wolfsburg CL .04 .10
NNO Kolner Haie Checklist .04 .10

2004-05 German Dusseldorf Metro Stars Postcards

COMPLETE SET (25) 10.00 20.00
1 Fabian Brannstrom .40 1.00
2 Christian Brittig .40 1.00
3 Eric Dandenault .40 1.00
4 Matt Davidson .40 1.00
5 Matt Herr .75 2.00
6 Tommy Jakobsen .40 1.00
7 Thomas Jorg .40 1.00
8 Alexander Jung .40 1.00
9 Florian Jung .40 1.00
10 Klaus Kathan .40 1.00
11 Walter Koberle CO .10 .25
12 Daniel Kreutzer .40 1.00
13 Bernd Kuhnhauser .40 1.00
14 Trond Magnussen .40 1.00
15 Mike Pellegrims .40 1.00
16 Markus Pottinger .40 1.00
17 Patrick Reimer .40 1.00
18 Andy Schneider .40 1.00
19 Alexander Sulzer .40 1.00
20 Jeff Tory .40 1.00
21 Andrei Trefilov .60 1.50
22 Martin Ulrich .40 1.00
23 Tore Vikingstad .40 1.00
24 Clayton Young .40 1.00
25 Dussi MASCOT .04 .10

2004-05 German Hamburg Freezers Postcards

The cards are unnumbered and so are listed below in alphabetical order.

COMPLETE SET (22) 10.00 20.00
1 Nils Antons .40 1.00
2 Robert Francz .40 1.00
3 Jean-Sebastien Giguere 2.00 5.00
4 Bobby House .40 1.00
5 Craig Johnson .40 1.00
6 Alan Letang .40 1.00
7 Paul Manning .40 1.00
8 Sasha Martinovic .40 1.00
9 Jochen Molling .40 1.00
10 Christopher Oravec .40 1.00
11 Shane Peacock .40 1.00
12 Jacek Plachta .40 1.00
13 Brad Purdie .40 1.00
14 Brandon Reid .75 2.00
15 Boris Rousson .75 2.00
16 Jorgen Rumrich .40 1.00
17 Mike Schmidt CO .40 1.00
18 Mike Smazal .40 1.00
19 Dave Tomlinson .40 1.00
20 Darren Van Impe .40 1.00
21 Martin Walter .40 1.00
22 Clayton Young .40 1.00

2004-05 German Hannover Scorpions Postcards

Cards are unnumbered and so are listed below alphabetically.

COMPLETE SET (29) 10.00 25.00
1 Peter Abstreiter .40 1.00
2 Patrik Augusta .40 1.00
3 Gordon Borberg .40 1.00
4 Lars Bruggemann .40 1.00
5 Jason Cipolla .40 1.00
6 Marian Cisar .40 1.00
7 Thomas Dolak .40 1.00
8 Edvin Frylen .40 1.00
9 Axel Hackert .40 1.00
10 Todd Hlushko .40 1.00
11 Robert Hock .40 1.00
12 Wayne Hynes .40 1.00
13 Ilpo Kauhanen .75 2.00
14 Patrick Koppchen .40 1.00
15 Mikhail Kozhevnikov .40 1.00
16 Christian Kunast .40 1.00
17 Dan Lambert .40 1.00
18 Jonas Lanier .40 1.00
19 Paul Mara .75 2.00
20 Andreas Morczinietz .40 1.00
21 Fredrik Oberg .40 1.00
22 Andy Reiss .40 1.00
23 Rene Rothke .40 1.00
24 Benedikt Schopper .40 1.00
25 Alexander Serikow .40 1.00
26 Lenny Soccio .40 1.00
27 Bastian Steingross .40 1.00
28 Andrei Teljukin .40 1.00
29 Steve Wilson .40 1.00

2004-05 German Ingolstadt Panthers

Cards are unnumbered and are listed below alphabetically.

COMPLETE SET (29) 10.00 25.00
1 Chris Armstrong .30 .75
2 Doug Ast .30 .75
3 Jamie Bartman CO .10 .25
4 Brad Burym .30 .75
5 Craig Ferguson .30 .75
6 Jakub Ficenec .30 .75
7 Glen Goodall .30 .75
8 Mike Harder .30 .75
9 Justin Harney .30 .75
10 Daniel Hilpert .30 .75
11 Martin Jiranek .30 .75
12 Steffen Karg .30 .75
13 Ron Kennedy CO .10 .25
14 Jamie Langenbrunner .30 .75
15 Cameron Mann .75 2.00
16 Andy McDonald .75 2.00
17 Christoph Melischko .30 .75
18 Nikolaus Mondt .30 .75
19 Gunther Oswald .30 .75
20 Alexander Polaczek .30 .75
21 Markus Schroder .30 .75
22 Marco Sturm 1.25 3.00
23 Ken Sutton .30 .75
24 Phil von Stefenelli .30 .75
25 Jimmy Waite .75 2.00
26 Aaron Ward .75 2.00
27 Xavier MASCOT .04 .10
28 Drew Omicioli .30 .75
29 Andreas Loth .30 .75

2004-05 German Krefeld Penguins Postcards

COMPLETE SET (24) 12.00 30.00
1 Steve Brule .60 1.50
2 Alexander Duck .60 1.50
3 Paul Dyck .60 1.50
4 Franz Fritzmeier CO .10 .25
5 Carsten Gosdeck .60 1.50
6 Adrien Grygiel .60 1.50
7 Robert Guillet .60 1.50
8 Chris Herperger .60 1.50
9 Martin Hyun .60 1.50
10 Ivo Jan .60 1.50
11 Markus Janka .60 1.50
12 Scott King .60 1.50
13 Rainer Kottstorfer .60 1.50
14 Daniel Kunce .60 1.50
15 Justin Kurtz .60 1.50
16 Guy Lehoux .60 1.50
17 Robert Muller .60 1.50
18 Christian Rohde .60 1.50
19 Florian Schnitzer .60 1.50
20 Alexander Selivanov .60 1.50
21 Mario Simioni CO .10 .25
22 Ferdinand Stradter MD .10 .25
23 Shayne Wright .60 1.50
24 Steffen Ziesche .60 1.50

2004-05 German Nuremburg Ice Tigers Postcards

Set is unnumbered and cards are listed below alphabetically.

COMPLETE SET (19) 10.00 25.00
1 Drew Bannister .60 1.50
2 Benjamin Barz .60 1.50
3 Bjorn Bombis .60 1.50
4 Robert Dietrich .60 1.50
5 Petr Fical .60 1.50
6 Konstantin Firsanov .60 1.50
7 Christian Franz .60 1.50
8 Mike Green .60 1.50
9 Lasse Kopitz .60 1.50
10 Lukas Lang .60 1.50
11 Tomas Martinec .60 1.50
12 Ulrich Maurer .60 1.50
13 Felix Petermann .60 1.50
14 Greg Poss CO .10 .25
15 Stefan Schauer .60 1.50
16 Yan Stastny 1.25 3.00
17 Adam Svoboda 1.25 3.00
18 Otto Sykora MG .10 .25
19 Brad Tapper .60 1.50

2004-05 German Weiden Blue Devils

Team-issued set from the German Second Division.

COMPLETE SET (27) 10.00 20.00
1 Florian Bartels .30 .75
2 Michal Bartosch .30 .75
3 J.F. Boutin .30 .75
4 Christian Franz .30 .75
5 Roman Goeldner .30 .75
6 Christian Grosch .30 .75
7 Peter Gruhle .30 .75
8 Benjamin Grunwald .30 .75
9 Stephan Hagn .30 .75
10 Reinhard Haider .30 .75
11 Alexander Herbst .30 .75
12 Michael Hoeck .30 .75
13 Thomas Kastner .30 .75
14 Stefan Keski-Kungas .30 .75
15 Christian Kinateder .30 .75
16 Holger Koenig .30 .75
17 Christian Meiler .30 .75
18 Florian Ondruschka .30 .75
19 Jan Penk .30 .75
20 Michal Piskor .30 .75
21 Daniel Rappl .30 .75
22 Samuel St. Pierre .30 .75
23 Damiel Strom .30 .75
24 Sebastian Wolsch .30 .75
25 Florian Zellner .30 .75
26 Josef Hefner ACO .10 .25
27 Leos Sulak CO .10 .25

2005-06 German DEL

COMPLETE SET (381) 30.00 60.00
1 Patrick Aufiero .10 .25
2 Christian Eklund .10 .25
3 Dennis Endrass .10 .25
4 Thorsten Fendt .10 .25
5 Rick Girard .10 .25
6 Scott King .20 .50
7 Manuel Kofler .10 .25
8 Martin Lindmann .10 .25
9 Roland Mayr .10 .25
10 Josef Menauer .10 .25
11 Steve Potvin .10 .25
12 Daniel Rau .10 .25
13 Arvids Rekis .10 .25
14 Rainer Suchan .10 .25
15 Jayme Filipowicz .10 .25
16 Rolf Wanhainen .10 .25
17 Stefan Endrass .10 .25
18 Brendan Yarema .10 .25
19 David Danner .10 .25
20 Konstantin Firsanov .10 .25
21 Jens Baxmann .10 .25
22 Mark Beaufait .10 .25
23 Tobias Draxinger .10 .25
24 Daniar Dshunussow .10 .25
25 Micki DuPont .20 .50
26 Kelly Fairchild .20 .50
27 Sven Felski .10 .25
28 Steve Walker .10 .25
29 Christoph Gawlik .10 .25
30 Frank HÃ¶rdler .10 .25
31 Rob Leask .10 .25
32 Norman Martens .10 .25
33 Richard Mueller .10 .25
34 Rene Kramer .10 .25
35 Stefan Ustorf .10 .25
36 Derrick Walser .20 .50
37 Denis Pederson .20 .50
38 Youri Ziffzer .10 .25
39 Florian Busch .10 .25
40 Andre Rankel .10 .25
41 Steve Brule .10 .25
42 Mathieu Darche .20 .50
43 Robert Francz .10 .25
44 Thorsten Kienass .10 .25
45 Patrick Koslow .10 .25
46 Petri Kujala .10 .25
47 Trond Magnussen .10 .25
48 Shawn McNeill .20 .50
49 Stephane Robitaille .10 .25
50 Christian Rohde .10 .25
51 Martin Schymainski .10 .25
52 Niklas Sundblad .10 .25
53 Andrej Teljukin .10 .25
54 Michael Waginger .10 .25
55 Jean-Luc Grand-Pierre .20 .50
56 Radek Vit .10 .25
57 Francois Groleau .10 .25
58 Mika Puhakka .10 .25
59 BjÃ¶rn Reiser .10 .25
60 Anton Bader .10 .25
61 Alexander Jung .10 .25
62 Marian Bazany .10 .25
63 Fabian BrÃ¤nnstrÃ¶m .10 .25
64 Chris Ferraro .20 .50
65 Florian Jung .10 .25
66 Thomas JÃ¶rg .10 .25
67 Craig Johnson .20 .50

68 Klaus Kathan .10 .25
69 Daniel Kreutzer .10 .25
70 Peter Ferraro .20 .50
71 Mike Pellegrims .10 .25
72 Chris Schmidt .10 .25
73 Andrew Schneider .20 .50
74 Jeff Tory .10 .25
75 Andrej Trefilov .20 .50
76 Tore Vikingstad .10 .25
77 Todd Reirden .10 .25
78 Tommy Jakobsen .10 .25
79 Patrick Reimer .10 .25
80 Alexander Sulzer .10 .25
81 Patrick Boileau .10 .25
82 Francois Bouchard .10 .25
83 Michael Bresagk .10 .25
84 Daniel Corso .20 .50
85 Ian Gordon .10 .25
86 David Gosselin .20 .50
87 Markus Jocher .10 .25
88 Sebastian Klenner .10 .25
89 Christian Kohmann .10 .25
90 Patrick Lebeau .20 .50
91 Dwayne Norris .20 .50
92 Philippe Plante .10 .25
93 Neville Rautert .10 .25
94 Jonas StÃ¶pfgeshoff .10 .25
95 David Sulkovsky .10 .25
96 Jason Young .10 .25
97 Boris Ackers .10 .25
98 Chad Bassen .10 .25
99 Simon Danner .10 .25
100 Jan Barta .10 .25
101 Marc Beaucage .10 .25
102 BjÃ¶rn Bombis .10 .25
103 Francois Fortier .10 .25
104 Benoit Gratton .20 .50
105 Tobias GÃ¼ttner .10 .25
106 Benjamin Hinterstocker .10 .25
107 Martin Hinterstocker .10 .25
108 Christian Hommel .10 .25
109 Alan Letang .10 .25
110 Paul Manning .10 .25
111 Sasa Martinovic .10 .25
112 Shane Peacock .10 .25
113 Jacek Plachta .10 .25
114 Boris Rousson .20 .50
115 Heiko Smazal .10 .25
116 Christopher Oravec .10 .25
117 Jeff Ulmer .10 .25
118 Darren van Impe .10 .25
119 Alexander Barta .10 .25
120 Martin Walter .10 .25
121 Patrick Augusta .10 .25
122 Brad Burym .10 .25
123 Jason Cipolla .10 .25
124 Thomas Dolak .10 .25
125 Sascha Goc .20 .50
126 Mike Green .20 .50
127 Shawn Heins .20 .50
128 Robert Hock .10 .25
129 Marcel Juhasz .10 .25
130 Trevor Kidd .20 .50
131 Patrick KÃ¶ppchen .10 .25
132 Christian KÃ¼nast .10 .25
133 Dan Lambert .20 .50
134 Andreas Morczinietz .10 .25
135 Brad Tapper .20 .50
136 Todd Warriner .20 .50
137 Jeff Finley .10 .25
138 Steve Guolla .20 .50
139 Rene RÃ¶thke .10 .25
140 Michael HÃ¶ck .10 .25
141 Chris Armstrong .10 .25
142 Doug Ast .10 .25
143 BjÃ¶rn Barta .10 .25
144 Craig Ferguson .10 .25
145 Jakub Ficenec .20 .50
146 Glenn Goodall .20 .50
147 Daniel Hilpert .10 .25
148 Jason Holland .10 .25
149 Martin Jiranek .10 .25
150 Florian Keller .10 .25
151 Cameron Mann .20 .50
152 Christoph Melischko .10 .25
153 GÃ¼nther Oswald .10 .25
154 Sebastian Vogl .10 .25
155 Ken Sutton .10 .25
156 Sean Tallaire .10 .25
157 Phil von Stefenelli .20 .50
158 Jimmy Waite .20 .50
159 Christoph HÃ¶henleitner .10 .25
160 Yannic Seidenberg .10 .25
161 Vitalij Aab .10 .25
162 Bryan Adams .10 .25
163 Collin Danielsmeier .10 .25
164 Mark Etz .10 .25
165 Linus Fagemo .10 .25
166 Kirk Furey .10 .25
167 Erich Goldmann .10 .25
168 Michael Wolf .10 .25
169 Matt Higgins .20 .50
170 Raffaele Intranuovo .20 .50
171 Sebastian Jonas .10 .25
172 Ladislav Karabin .10 .25
173 Martin Knold .10 .25
174 Leonardo Conti .10 .25
175 Dimitrij Kotschnew .10 .25
176 Markus PÃ¶ttinger .10 .25
177 Bruce Richardson .10 .25
178 Mats Trygg .10 .25
179 Tobias Schwab .10 .25
180 Alexej Dmitriev .10 .25
181 Tobias Abstreiter .10 .25
182 Drew Bannister .20 .50
183 Eric Bertrand .10 .25
184 Joaquin Gage .20 .50
185 Sven Gerbig .10 .25
186 Domminik Hammer .10 .25
187 Justin Harney .10 .25
188 Guy Lehoux .10 .25
189 Alexander Serikow .10 .25
190 Martin Sychra .10 .25
191 Sven Valenti .10 .25
192 Steffen Ziesche .10 .25
193 Dale Clarke .10 .25
194 Danny Groulx .10 .25
195 Ryan Kraft .10 .25
196 Adam Ondraschek .10 .25
197 Jason Ulmer .10 .25
198 Alexander Heinrich .10 .25
199 Manuel Klinge .10 .25
200 Tobias WÃ¶rle .10 .25
201 Jeremy Adduono .10 .25
202 Tino Boos .10 .25
203 Ivan Ciernik .10 .25
204 Sebastian Furchner .10 .25
205 Thomas Greiss .10 .25
206 Kai Hospelt .10 .25
207 Oliver Jonas .10 .25
208 Stephane Julien .10 .25
209 Lasse Kopitz .10 .25
210 Eduard Lewandowski .10 .25
211 Mirko LÃ¼demann .10 .25
212 Dave McLlwain .10 .25
213 Nikolaus Mondt .10 .25
214 Andreas Renz .10 .25
215 Jean-Yves Roy .10 .25
216 Paul Traynor .10 .25
217 Brad Schlegel .10 .25
218 Alex Hicks .10 .25
219 Philip Gogulla .10 .25
220 Moritz MÃ¼ller .10 .25
221 Boris Blank .10 .25
222 Alexander DÃ¼ck .10 .25
223 Franz Fritzmeier .10 .25
224 Robert Guillet .10 .25
225 Chris Herperger .10 .25
226 Andre Huebscher .10 .25
227 Ivo Jan .10 .25
228 Rainer KÃ¶ttsdorfer .10 .25
229 Daniel Kunce .10 .25
230 Richard Pavlikovski .10 .25
231 Ken Passmann .10 .25
232 Alexander Selivanov .10 .25
233 Herberts Vasiljevs .10 .25
234 Roland Verwey .10 .25
235 Markus Witting .10 .25
236 Robert MÃ¼ller .10 .25
237 Philip Hendle .10 .25
238 Andy Hedlund .10 .25
239 Adrian Grygiel .10 .25
240 Daniel Pietta .10 .25
241 Ronny Arendt .10 .25
242 Patrick Ehelechner .20 .50
243 Michael Bakos .10 .25
244 Lonny Bohonos .20 .50
245 Shawn Carter .10 .25
246 Karl Dykhuis .10 .25
247 Devin Edgerton .10 .25
248 Pierre Hedin .10 .25
249 Steve Kelly .20 .50
250 Marcus Kink .10 .25
251 Peter Ratchuk .10 .25
252 Sefan Retzer .10 .25
253 Jeff Shantz .10 .25
254 John Tripp .10 .25
255 Marco SchÃ¼tz .10 .25
256 Sachar Blank .10 .25
257 Fredrik Chabot .20 .50
258 Rene Corbet .20 .50
259 Fabio Carciola .10 .25
260 Christoph Ullmann .10 .25
261 Benjamin Barz .10 .25
262 Colin Beardsmore .10 .25
263 Rich Brennan .10 .25
264 Matt Davidson .20 .50
265 Robert DÃ¶me .20 .50
266 Petr Fical .10 .25
267 Christian Franz .10 .25
268 Lukas Lang .10 .25
269 Jean-Francois Labbe .20 .50
270 Christian Laflamme .10 .25
271 Greg Leeb .10 .25
272 Thomas Martinec .10 .25
273 Francois Methot .10 .25
274 Michel Periard .10 .25
275 Alexander Polaczek .10 .25
276 Jame Pollock .10 .25
277 Christian Retzer .10 .25
278 Brian Swanson .10 .25
279 Felix Petermann .10 .25
280 Stefan Schauer .10 .25
281 Olaf KÃ¶lzig 2.00 5.00
282 Alexander Jung .10 .25
283 Rob Leask .10 .25
284 Christian Erhoff .30 .75
285 Chritoph Schubert .10 .25
286 Andreas Renz .10 .25
287 Lasse Kopitz .10 .25
288 Dennis Seidenberg .20 .50
289 Sven Felski .10 .25
290 Jochen Hecht .40 1.00
291 Marco Sturm .40 1.00
292 Stefan Ustorf .10 .25
293 Daniel Kreutzer .10 .25
294 Alexander Barta .10 .25
295 Thomas Martinec .10 .25
296 Klaus Kathan .10 .25
297 Michael Hackert .10 .25
298 Tino Boos .10 .25
299 Andreas Morczinietz .10 .25
300 Jan Benda .10 .25
301 Patrick Buzas .10 .25
302 Jay Henderson .20 .50
303 Marc Savard .10 .25
304 Steffen TÃ¶lzer .10 .25
305 Drake Berehowsky .10 .25
306 Constantin Braun .10 .25
307 Sean Fischer .10 .25
308 Patrick Jarrett .20 .50
309 TomÃ¡s PÃ¶pperle .10 .25
310 Deron Quint .20 .50
311 Thomas Schenkel .10 .25
312 Hugo Boisvert .10 .25
313 Patrick Ehelechner .20 .50
314 Kari Haakana .10 .25
315 Martin Hamann .10 .25
316 Michael Henrich .10 .25
317 Markus Schmidt .10 .25
318 Chris Bright .10 .25
319 Michael Hackert .10 .25
320 Steve Kelly .10 .25
321 James Patrick .10 .25
322 Martin Reichel .10 .25
323 Andrej Strakhov .10 .25
324 Roman Cechmanek .20 .50
325 Matthias Forster .10 .25
326 Niklas Hede .10 .25
327 Ryan Jardine .10 .25
328 Steffen Karg .10 .25
329 Max Lingemann .10 .25
330 Florian Schnitzer .10 .25
331 Lukas Slavetinsky .10 .25
332 BjÃ¶rn Bombis .10 .25
333 Dominik Hammer .10 .25
334 Jonas Lanier .10 .25
335 Marty Murray .10 .25
336 AndrÃ© Reiss .10 .25
337 Benedikt Schopper .10 .25
338 Wally Schreiber .10 .25
339 Matt Kinch .10 .25
340 Bastian Steingrog .10 .25
341 Rob Valicevic .20 .50
342 Mark Greig .10 .25
343 Brad Purdie .10 .25
344 Rich Parent .40 1.00
345 Steve Brule .10 .25
346 Brad Burym .10 .25
347 Martin Hlinka .10 .25
348 Sinsa Martinovic .10 .25
349 Chris Nielsen .10 .25
350 Sebastian Osterloh .10 .25
351 Torsten Ankert .10 .25
352 Daniel Hatterscheid .10 .25
353 William Lindsay .10 .25
354 Henry Martens .10 .25
355 Ted Drury .10 .25
356 Mike Pudlick .10 .25
357 Igor Alexandrov .10 .25
358 Anthony Aquino .10 .25
359 David Cespiva .10 .25
360 Daniel Del Monte .10 .25
361 Ilpo Kauhanen .20 .50
362 Stefan Langwieder .10 .25
363 Thomas Pielmeier .10 .25
364 Yannick Tremblay .10 .25
365 Gert Acker .10 .25
366 Ulrich Maurer .10 .25
367 Florian Ondruschka .10 .25
368 BjÃ¶rn Barta .10 .25
369 Michael Bresagk .10 .25
370 Petr Fical .10 .25
371 Sebastian Furchner .10 .25
372 Marcel Goc .20 .50
373 Dimitrij Kotschnew .10 .25
374 Eduard Lewandowski .10 .25
375 Robert MÃ¼ller .10 .25
376 Alexander Sulzer .10 .25
377 Christoph Ullmann .10 .25
378 Thomas Greiss .10 .25
379 Nico Pyka .10 .25
NNO EisbÃ¤ren Berlin Deutscher Meister 2005 4.00 10.00
NNO DEG Metro Stars DEB Pokalsieger 2006 4.00 10.00

2005-06 German DEL All-Star Jerseys

AS01 Andy Delmore 8.00 20.00
AS02 Micki DuPont 8.00 20.00
AS03 Jakub Ficenec 8.00 20.00
AS04 Darren van Impe 8.00 20.00
AS05 Stepahne Julien 8.00 20.00
AS06 Ladislav Karabin 8.00 20.00
AS07 Ivan Ciernik 8.00 20.00
AS08 Patrick Lebeau 8.00 20.00
AS09 Dave McLlwain 8.00 20.00
AS10 Francois Methot 8.00 20.00
AS11 Duanne Moeser 8.00 20.00
AS12 Dwayne Norris 8.00 20.00
AS13 Mike Pellegrims 8.00 20.00
AS14 Brad Purdie 8.00 20.00
AS15 Chris Rogles 8.00 20.00
AS16 Boris Rousson 10.00 25.00
AS17 Alexander Selivanov 8.00 20.00
AS18 Yan Stastny 12.00 30.00
AS19 Steve Walker 8.00 20.00
AS20 Pascal Trepanier 8.00 20.00
AS21 All Star Game 2006 20.00 50.00

2005-06 German DEL DEB-Jerseys

TR01 Jan Benda 8.00 20.00
TR02 Jochen Hecht 12.00 30.00
TR03 Olaf KÃ¶lzig 20.00 50.00
TR04 Marco Sturm 12.00 30.00

2005-06 German DEL Goalies

COMPLETE SET (14) 20.00 40.00
G01 Roman Cechmanek 1.25 3.00
G02 Patrick Ehelechner 2.00 5.00
G03 Joaquin Gage 1.25 3.00
G04 Ian Gordon 1.25 3.00
G05 Thomas Greiss 1.25 3.00
G06 Trevor Kidd 2.00 5.00
G07 Alexander Jung 1.25 3.00
G08 Ilpo Kauhanen 1.25 3.00
G09 Jean-François LabbÃ© 1.25 3.00
G10 Robert MÃ¼ller 1.25 3.00
G11 Rich Parent 2.00 5.00
G12 TomÃ¡s PÃ¶pperle 1.25 3.00
G13 Jimmy Waite 2.00 5.00
G14 Rolf Wanhainen 1.25 3.00

2005-06 German DEL Star Attack

COMPLETE SET (10) 8.00 20.00
ST01 Ivan Ciernik .75 2.00
ST02 Jochen Hecht 1.25 3.00
ST03 Daniel Kreutzer .75 2.00
ST04 Patrick Lebeau .75 2.00
ST05 Dwayne Norris .75 2.00
ST06 Yan Stastny 1.50 4.00
ST07 Brad Tapper .75 2.00
ST08 Pascal Trepanier .75 2.00
ST09 Mike York 1.25 3.00
ST10 Jason Young .75 2.00

2005-06 German DEL Team Checklists

COMPLETE SET (20) 6.00 15.00
CL01 Augsburger Panther Checklist .40 1.00
CL02 EisbÃ¤ren Berlin Checklist .40 1.00
CL03 DEG Metro Stars Checklist .40 1.00
CL04 EV Duisburg Checklist .40 1.00
CL05 Frankfurt Lions Checklist .40 1.00
CL06 Hamburg Freezers Checklist .40 1.00
CL07 Hannover Scorpions Checklist .40 1.00
CL08 ERC Ingolstadt Checklist .40 1.00
CL09 Iserlohn Roosters Checklist .40 1.00
CL10 Kassel Huskies Checklist .40 1.00
CL11 KÃ¶lner Haie Checklist .40 1.00
CL12 Krefeld Pinguine Checklist .40 1.00
CL13 Adler Mannheim Checklist .40 1.00
CL14 NÃ¼rnberg Ice Tigers Checklist .40 1.00
CL15 Nationalmannschaft Checklist .40 1.00
CL16 Defender Checklist .40 1.00
CL17 Star Attack Checklist .40 1.00
CL18 Allstars 05 Checklist .40 1.00
CL19 Goalies Checklist .40 1.00
CL20 Trikotkarten DEB Checklist .40 1.00

2006-07 German DEL All-Star Jerseys

AS1 Doug Ast 10.00 25.00
AS2 Francois Bouchard 10.00 25.00
AS3 Ivan Ciernik 10.00 25.00
AS4 Ted Drury 10.00 25.00
AS5 Jakub Ficenec 15.00 40.00
AS6 Andy Hedlund 10.00 25.00
AS7 Matt Higgins 10.00 25.00
AS8 Martin Hlinka 10.00 25.00
AS9 Stephane Julien 10.00 25.00
AS10 Trevor Kidd 15.00 40.00
AS11 Scott King
AS12 Pat Lebeau
AS13 Dave McLlwain
AS14 Shane Peacock
AS15 Denis Pederson
AS16 StÃ©phane Robitaille
AS17 Alexander Selivanov
AS18 Jeff Shantz
AS19 Jimmy Waite
AS20 Derrick Walser

2006-07 German DEL German Forwards

GF1 Tomas Martinec 1.25 3.00
GF2 Michael Hackert 1.25 3.00
GF3 Andreas Morczinietz 1.25 3.00
GF4 Daniel Kreutzer 1.25 3.00
GF5 Manuel Kofler 1.25 3.00
GF6 Sven Felski 1.25 3.00
GF7 Markus Jocher 1.25 3.00
GF8 Robert Hock 1.25 3.00
GF9 Robert Francz 1.25 3.00
GF10 Petr Fical 1.25 3.00
GF11 Tino Boos 1.25 3.00
GF12 Boris Blank 1.25 3.00
GF13 Alexander Barta 1.25 3.00
GF14 Michael Waginger 1.25 3.00

2006-07 German DEL New Arrivals

NA1 Travis Brigley 1.25 3.00
NA2 Cory Cross 1.25 3.00
NA3 Per Eklund 1.25 3.00
NA4 Scott King 1.25 3.00
NA5 Jason Marshall 1.25 3.00
NA6 Dusan Milo 1.25 3.00
NA7 Eric Nickulas 2.00 5.00
NA8 Andy Roach 2.00 5.00
NA9 Nathan Robinson 2.00 5.00
NA10 Jamie Storr 1.50 4.00
NA11 Levente Szuper 1.50 4.00
NA12 Chris Taylor 1.25 3.00
NA13 Brad Tiley 1.25 3.00
NA14 Daniel Tkaczuk 1.25 3.00

2006-07 German DEL Team Leaders

TL1 Craig Darby 1.25 3.00
TL2 Ted Drury 1.25 3.00
TL3 Glen Goodall 2.00 5.00
TL4 Torsten Kienass 1.25 3.00
TL5 Alan Letang 1.25 3.00
TL6 Greg Leeb 1.25 3.00
TL7 Dave McIlwain 1.25 3.00
TL8 Jimmy Roy 1.25 3.00
TL9 William Trew 1.25 3.00
TL10 Stefan Ustorf 1.25 3.00
TL11 Todd Warriner 1.50 4.00
TL12 Pascal Trepanier 1.25 3.00
TL13 Craig Johnson 1.25 3.00
TL14 Jason Young 1.25 3.00

2006-07 German DEL Wings

1 Martin Bartek
2 Rob Collins
3 Stefan Ustorf
4 Shane Joseph
5 Thomas Dolak
6 Ivan Ciernik
7 Brad Smyth
8 Chris Taylor
9 Herberts Vasiljevs
10 Greg Leeb
11 Nathan Robinson
12 William Trew
13 John Tripp
14 Michael Wolf

2006-07 German DEL Young-Stars

1 Patrick Buzas
2 Robert Dietrich
3 AndrÃ© Huebscher
4 Michail Kozhevnikov
5 Moritz MÃ¼ller
6 Florian Ondruschka
7 Felix Petermann
8 Matthias Potthoff
9 Markus Schmidt
10 Florian Schnitzer
11 Yannic Seidenberg
12 Alexander Weiss
13 Thomas Wilhelm
14 Tobias WÃ¶rle

2007-08 German DEL Adler Mannheim Eagles Postcards

1 Martin Ancicka
2 Ronny Arendt
3 Danny Aus Den Birken
4 Francois Bouchard
5 Sven Butenschon
6 Rene Corbet
7 Rico Fata
8 Christopher Fischer
9 Colin Forbes
10 Teal Fowler
11 Rick Girard
12 Michael Hackert
13 Adam Hauser
14 Jason Jaspers
15 Ilpo Kauhanen
16 Marcus Kink
17 Benedikt Kohl
18 Stefan Langwieder
19 Eduard Lewandowski
20 Tomas Martinec
21 Frank Mauer
22 Francois Methot
23 Robert Muller
24 Felix Petermann
25 Greg Poss
26 Philipp Schlager
27 Jeff Shantz
28 Blake Sloan
29 Pascal Trepanier
30 Christoph Ullmann

2007-08 German DEL Cologne Sharks

COMPLETE SET (27)
1 Marcel MÃ¼ller
2 Alexej Dmitriev
3 Mirko LÃ¼demann
4 Daniel Rudslatt
5 Todd Warriner
6 Sean Tallaire
7 Sebastian Furchner
8 Kai Hospelt
9 Bryan Adams
10 Mats Schobel
11 StÃ©phane Julien
12 Mats Trygg
13 Soren Sturm
14 Ivan Ciernik
15 Andreas Renz
16 Stefan Horneber
17 Kamil Piros
18 Travis Scott
19 Dave McLlwain
20 Torsten Ankert
21 Philip Gogulla
22 Moritz Muller
23 Jerome Flaake
24 Rupert Meister
25 Clayton Beddoes
26 Doug Mason
27 Team Photo

2007-08 German DEL Doublepack

DP01 Christian Chartier
Rhett Gordon
DP02 Deron Quint
Steve Walker
DP03 Andrej Teljukin
Jade Galbraith
DP04 Peter Ratchuk
Rob Collins
DP05 Jason Marshall
Jeff Ulmer
DP06 Andy Delmore
Francois Fortier
DP07 Sascha Goc
Chris Herperger
DP08 Jason Holland
Doug Ast
DP09 Paul Traynor
Michael Wolf
DP10 Stephane Julien
Ivan Ciernik
DP11 Richard Pavlikovsky
Herberts Vasiljevs
DP12 Pascal Trepanier
Colin Forbes
DP13 Brian Swanson
Rich Brennan
DP14 Josef Lehner
William Trew
DP15 Jean-Francois Fortin
Michael Henrich
DP16 Sascha Goc
{ Daniel Kreutzer
DP17 Sven Felski
{ Alexander Barta
DP18 Robert Dietrich
{ Philip Gogulla
DP19 Dimitrij Kotschnew
{ Alexander Sulzer
DP20 Doublepack Checkliste

2007-08 German DEL Frankfurt Lions Postcards

1 Tobias Worle
2 Jason Young
3 Jason Marshall
4 Michael Bresagk
5 Simon Danner
6 Jay Henderson
7 Chris Armstrong
8 Chris Taylor
9 Jeff Heerema
10 Martin Reichel
11 Peter Smrek
12 Boris Ackers
13 Pavel Gross
14 Rich Chernomaz
15 Layne Ulmer
16 Jeff Ulmer
17 Derek Hahn
18 Radek Krestan
19 Ilia Vorobiev
20 Lasse Kopitz

2007-08 German DEL Masked Marvels

COMPLETE SET (16)
MM01 Jamie Storr
MM02 Jean-Marc Pelletier
MM03 Mike Bales
MM04 Dimitrij Kotschnew
MM05 Jimmy Waite
MM06 Norm Maracle
MM07 Adam Hauser
MM08 Alexander Jung
MM09 Rob Zepp
MM10 Ian Gordon
MM11 Chris Rogles
MM12 Patrick Desrochers
MM13 Travis Scott
MM14 Reto Pavoni
MM15 Christian Rohde
MM16 Checkliste

2007-08 German DEL Meisterkarte

MK01 Mannheim Adler

2007-08 German DEL Playmakers

COMPLETE SET (15)
PM01 Shane Joseph
PM02 Mark Beaufait
PM03 Dan Tessier
PM04 Daniel Kreutzer
PM05 Chris Taylor
PM06 Brad Smyth
PM07 Thomas Dolak
PM08 Jakub Ficenec
PM09 Robert Hock
PM10 Dave McLlwain
PM11 Jan Alinc
PM12 Francois Methot
PM13 Scott King
PM14 Trevor Gallant
PM15 Chad Wiseman

2007-08 German DEL Pokalsiegerkarte

PK01 Deutscher Pokalsieger

2007-08 German DEL Signatures

SI01 Denis Pederson
SI02 Jamie Storr
SI03 Jason Young
SI04 Sascha Goc
SI05 Jimmy Waite
SI06 Norm Maracle
SI07 Dave McLlwain
SI08 Jeff Shantz
SI09 Dimitrij Kotschnew
SI10 Chris Rogles
SI11 Signatures Checkliste

2007-08 German DEL Skills Competition

SC01 Andy Roach
SC02 Jakub Ficenec
SC03 Dimitrij Kotschnew
SC04 Eduard Lewandowski
SC05 Brad Smyth
SC06 Checkliste

2008-09 German DEL Preview

1 N.Maracle/I.Gordon
2 F.Bouchard/F.Fortier
3 H.Pratt/R.Regehr
4 P.Ratchuk/A.Hedlund
5 A.Roach/D.Quint
6 Gardner/Ramsay/Courchaine
7 Ulmer/Chouinard/Brigley
8 Robinson/Bellissimo/Feeb
9 King/Sarno/Methot
10 M.Marik/R.Muller
11 M.Bresagk/L.Kopitz
12 J.Ficenec/R.Pavlikovsky
13 P.Koppchen/M.Bakos
14 Lewandowski/Barta/Felski
15 Spylo/Hock/Wolf
16 Ciernik/Alinc/Vasiljevs
17 Sikora/Ullmann/Fical
18 Robert MÃ¼ller
19 Andreas Renz
20 Michael Bakos
21 Christoph Ullmann
22 Sven Felski
23 Daniel Kreutzer
24 Philip Gogulla
25 Michael Wolf
26 Michael Hackert
42 Norm Maracle
43 Ian Gordon
44 Deron Quint
45 Andy Roach
46 Andy Hedlund
47 Francois Bouchard
48 Peter Ratchuk
49 Harlan Pratt
50 Richie Regehr
51 Nathan Robinson
52 Adam Courchaine
53 Scott King
54 Ryan Ramsay
55 Francois Fortier
56 Eric Chouinard
57 Peter Sarno
58 Kevin Gardner
59 Vince Bellissimo
60 Brad Leeb
61 Francois Methot
62 Travis Brigley
63 Jason Ulmer
64 Teamfoto Nordamerika
65 Michal Marik
66 Robert MÃ¼ller
67 Michael Bresagk
68 Lasse Kopitz
69 Michael Bakos
70 Jakub Ficenec
71 Richard Pavlikovsky
72 Patrick KÃ¶ppchen
73 Sven Felski
74 Michael Wolf
75 Christoph Ullmann
76 Ahren Spylo
77 Herberts Vasiljevs
78 Petr Sikora
79 Ivan Ciernik
80 Alexander Barta
81 Eduard Lewandowski
82 Petr Fical
83 Jan Alinc
84 Robert Hock
85 Freiberger Arena
86 Teamfoto Team Europa
87 Dimitrij Kotschnew
88 Robert MÃ¼ller
89 Patrick Ehelechner
90 Dimitri PÃ¤tzold
91 Michael Bakos
92 Andreas Renz
93 Dennis Seidenberg
94 Christoph Schubert
95 Rainer KÃ¶ttstorfer
96 Sebastian Osterloh
97 Chris Schmidt
98 Frank HÃ¶rdler
99 Andre Reiss
100 Sven Felski
101 Michael Wolf
102 Christoph Ullmann
103 Michael Hackert
104 Philip Gogulla
105 Aleksander Polaczek
106 Manuel Klinge
107 Andre Rankel
108 Stefan Ustorf
109 Felix SchÃ¼tz
110 Yannic Seidenberg
111 John Tripp
112 Petr Fical
113 Marco Sturm
114 Uwe Krupp
115 Ernst HÃ¶fner
116 Klaus Merk
129 Checkliste Reihenkarten Team
130 Checkliste Reihenkarten Team
131 Checkliste DEB Reihenkarten
133 Checkliste Team Nordamerika
134 Checkliste Team Europa
135 Checkliste Team Nationalmannschaft

2007-08 Italian Ritten Renon Team Set

COMPLETE SET (23) 4.00 10.00
1 Josh Olson .25 .60
2 Mark Smith .25 .60
3 Enrico Dorigatti .25 .60
4 Shawn Mather .25 .60
5 Dan Tudin .25 .60
6 Alex Egger .25 .60
7 Tony Tuzzolino .25 .60
8 Ingemar Gruber .25 .60
9 Kaspars Astashenko .25 .60
10 Emanuel Scelfo .25 .60
11 Jan Vodrazka .25 .60
12 Paolo Bustreo .25 .60
13 Matteo Rasom .25 .60
14 Alex Rottensteiner .25 .60
15 Lorenz Daccordo .25 .60
16 Marcus Hafner .25 .60
17 Fritz Ploner .25 .60
18 Thomas Unterfrauner .25 .60
19 Benjamin Bregenzer .25 .60
20 Frederic Cloutier .25 .60
21 Niederstaetter .25 .60
22 Paul Adey .25 .60
23 Herbert Frisch .25 .60

1992-93 Norwegian Elite Series

COMPLETE SET (242) 20.00 50.00
1 Jim Marthinsen .20 .50
2 Jarl Eriksen .07 .20
3 Erik Tveten .07 .20
4 Carl Gunnar Gundersen .07 .20
5 Nick Carone .07 .20
6 Jaromir Latal .07 .20
7 Tom Johansen .07 .20
8 Asgaut Moe .07 .20
9 Oystein Olsen .07 .20
10 Atle Olsen .07 .20
11 Roy Johansen .07 .20
12 Marius Rath .07 .20
13 Svenn Erik Bjornstad .07 .20
14 Jon Magne Karlstad .07 .20
15 Pal Kristiansen .07 .20
16 Espen Knutsen 2.00 5.00
17 Stig Johansen .07 .20
18 Geir Myhre .07 .20
19 Remo Martinsen .07 .20
20 Jan Tore Ronningen .07 .20
21 Jon Hroar Nordstrom .07 .20
22 Tom Erik Olsen .07 .20
23 Peter Madach .07 .20
24 Rune Gulliksen .07 .20
25 Carl Oscar Boe Andersen .07 .20
26 Martin Ahlberg .07 .20
27 Erik Kristiansen .07 .20
28 Tommy Larsen .07 .20
29 Age Ellingsen .07 .20
30 Patric Eide .07 .20
31 Svein Harald Arnesen .07 .20
32 Petter Thoresen .07 .20
33 Pal Marthinsen .07 .20
34 Ole Eskild Dahlstrom .07 .20
35 Nikolai Davydkin .07 .20
36 Lennart Ahlberg .07 .20
37 Tommie Eriksen .07 .20
38 Jan Roar Fagerli .07 .20
39 Erik Nerell .07 .20
40 Knut Walbye .07 .20
41 Pal Dahlstrom .07 .20
42 Martin Andresen .07 .20
43 Geir Hoff .07 .20
44 Cato Andersen .07 .20
45 Per Oddvar Walbye .07 .20
46 Cato Tom Andersen .07 .20
47 Frode Hansen .20 .50
48 Petter Salsten .07 .20
49 Arne Billkvam .07 .20
50 Jarle Friis .07 .20
51 Steve Allmann .07 .20
52 Torbjorn Orskau .07 .20
53 Christian Kjeldsberg .07 .20
54 Bjorn Mathisrud .07 .20
55 Pal Gjermundsen .07 .20
56 Ketil Martinsen .07 .20
57 Vidar Andersen .07 .20
58 Rene Hansen .07 .20
59 Martin Friis .07 .20
60 Orjan Lovdal .07 .20
61 Lars Hakon Andersen .07 .20
62 Robert Sundt .07 .20
63 Henrik Buskoven .07 .20
64 Morten Finstad .20 .50
65 Magnus Christoffersen .07 .20
66 Roar Larsen .07 .20
67 Zdenek Albrecht .07 .20
68 Oldrich Valek .07 .20
69 Fredrik Jacobsen .07 .20
70 Rune Hansen .07 .20
71 Lars Jacobsen .07 .20
72 Staffan Tholsson .07 .20
73 Lase Syversen .07 .20
74 Kim Sogaard .07 .20
75 Jan Erik Thoresen .07 .20
76 Pal Andre Eriksen .07 .20
77 Bjorn Freddy Bekkerud .07 .20
78 Kjell Erik Myreng .07 .20
79 Lars Eilertsen .07 .20
80 Reino Johansen .07 .20
81 Igor Mishukov .07 .20
82 Ole Petter Dalene .07 .20
83 Jon Gundersen .07 .20
84 Pal Raab Lien .07 .20
85 Vadim Tunikov .07 .20
86 Tommy Skaarberg .07 .20
87 Per Christian Knold .07 .20
88 Stephen Foyn .07 .20
89 Glenn Asland .07 .20
90 Bjorte Olsson .07 .20
91 Gorm Gundersen .07 .20
92 Morgan Andersen .07 .20
93 Vegar Barlie .07 .20
94 Oystein Tronrud .07 .20
95 Kim Fagerhoi .07 .20
96 Tor Nilsen .07 .20
97 Arne Bergseng .07 .20
98 Timo Laituri .07 .20
99 Sjur Robert Nilsen .07 .20
100 Mattis Haakensen .07 .20
101 Lars Bergseng .07 .20
102 Svein Enok Norstebo .20 .50
103 Tor Anders Jacobsen .07 .20
104 Jorgen Salsten .07 .20
105 Tommy Jakobsen .07 .20
106 Tim Budy .07 .20
107 Martin Wiita .07 .20
108 Lenny Eriksson .07 .20
109 Stale Berg .07 .20
110 Bjorn Anders Dahl .07 .20
111 Geir Tore Dahl .07 .20
112 Dallas Gaume .07 .20
113 Geir Haugen .07 .20
114 Roar Husby .07 .20
115 Robert Nielsen .07 .20
116 Lars Erik Lunde .07 .20
117 Kare Nordnes .07 .20
118 Magne Nordnes .07 .20
119 Geir Leknes .07 .20
120 Rob Doroshuk .07 .20
121 Roger Olsen .07 .20
122 Oyvind Sorli .07 .20
123 Gunnar Bye .07 .20
124 Per Kristian Vellan .07 .20
125 Marc Laniel .20 .50
126 Dallas Gaume .07 .20
127 Robert Schistad .07 .20
128 Jan Petter Loschbrandt .07 .20
129 Tore Kristensen .07 .20
130 Eskil Eide .07 .20
131 Erik Brodahl .07 .20
132 Morten Nordhus .07 .20
133 Erik Pettersen .07 .20
134 Hans Bekken .07 .20
135 Jan Bekken .07 .20
136 Jon Erik Haaland .07 .20
137 Richard Little .07 .20
138 Eivind Olsen .07 .20
139 Morten Gilje .07 .20
140 Sverre Hogemark .07 .20
141 Eirik Paulsen .07 .20
142 Kyle McDonough .07 .20
143 Steffen Trettenes .07 .20
144 Richard David .07 .20
145 Odd Nilsen .07 .20
146 Per Marthinsen .07 .20
147 Johnny Nilsen .07 .20
148 Per Christian Fjeldstad .07 .20
149 Christian Hafsmoe .07 .20

Raymond Lunde .07 .20
Rene Lemire .07 .20
Thomas Kristiansen .07 .20
Vidar Wold .07 .20
Hans Petter Halla .07 .20
Michael Smithurst .07 .20
Lars Erik Solberg .07 .20
Kenneth Fjell .07 .20
Morten Hem .07 .20
Dag Hoyem .07 .20
Vince Guidotti .07 .20
Glen Engevik .07 .20
Joe Clarke .07 .20
Lars Erik Kjaer .07 .20
Gorm Laursen .07 .20
Per Reidar Johansen .07 .20
Anders Martinsen .07 .20
Jorn Arild Flatha .07 .20
Rune Hansen .07 .20
Stian Kraft .07 .20
Geir Svendsberget .07 .20
Andre Aas .07 .20
Erik Skoglund Nilsen .07 .20
Frode Sletner .07 .20
Petter Syversne .07 .20
Jarle Gundersen .07 .20
Terje Wikstrom .07 .20
Steve MacDonald .07 .20
Sjur Kinder .07 .20
Morten Fjeldstad .07 .20
George Tower .07 .20
Espen Knutsen 2.00 5.00
Jon Magne Karlstad .07 .20
Tommy Jakobsen .07 .20
Valerengen .02 .10
Trondheim .02 .10
Dallas Gaume .20 .50
Bjorn Anders Dahl .02 .10
Jarl Eriksen .02 .10
Mark Fioretti .02 .10
Brian Tutt .20 .50
Jim Marthinsen .20 .50
Brian Tutt .20 .50
Jaromir Latal .07 .20
Espen Knutsen 2.00 5.00
Dallas Gaume .20 .50
Oldrich Valek .07 .20
Bjorn Skaare .07 .20
Knut Walbye .07 .20
Age Ellingsen .07 .20
Espen Knutsen 2.00 5.00
Ole Eskild Dahlstrom .07 .20
Tommie Eriksen .07 .20
Vegar Barlie .07 .20
Glenn Jessesen .07 .20
Tor Arne Alseth .07 .20
Per Kristian Vellan .07 .20
Jone Hatteland .07 .20
Henrik Aaby .07 .20
Johnny Nilsen .07 .20
Geir Svendsberget .07 .20
Pal Kristian Eggen .07 .20
Andreas Brunvoll .07 .20
Andre Manscov Hansen .07 .20
Frode Christiansen .07 .20
Jan Morten Dahl .07 .20
Stian Kraft .07 .20
Lubos Sikela .07 .20
Rune Fjeldstad .07 .20
Sven Arild Olsen .07 .20
Kent Inge Kristiansen .07 .20
Sjur Rakstad Larsen .07 .20
Borre Ostvang .07 .20
Harald Bastiansen .07 .20
Jon Warset .07 .20
Jo Espen Leibnitz .07 .20
Arild Syversen .07 .20
Terje Haukali .07 .20
Geir Dalene .07 .20
Jonas Larsen .07 .20
Thomas Hansen .07 .20
Stig Olsen .07 .20
Lars Hansen .07 .20
Hans M. Anonsen .07 .20
Ketil Kristiansen .07 .20
Bjornar Sorensen .07 .20
Tom Jostne .07 .20
John Klears .07 .20
Arve Jansen .07 .20
Orjan Gjertsen .07 .20
Checklist (1-81) .02 .10
Checklist (82-162) .02 .10
Checklist (163-242) .02 .10

1999-00 Norwegian National Team

MPLETE SET (24) 10.00 25.00
bert Schistad .75 2.00
eir Svendsberget .40 1.00
enrik Aaby .40 1.00
mmy Jacobsen .40 1.00
mmy Jacobsen .40 1.00
ndre Manskov Hansen .40 1.00
orten Fjeldstad .40 1.00
rs Hakon Andersen .40 1.00
arius Trygg .40 1.00
vein Enok Norstebo .75 2.00
arl Oscar Boe Andersen .40 1.00
le Eskild Dalstrom .40 1.00
er Age Skroder .40 1.00
al Johnsen .40 1.00
rond Vegar Magnussen .40 1.00
lats Trygg .40 1.00
etil Wold .40 1.00
jur Robert Nilsen .40 1.00
nders Myrvold .75 2.00
ore Vikingstad .40 1.00
jorge Josefsen .40 1.00
yvind Sorli .40 1.00
ard Sorlie .40 1.00
eif Boork CO .20 .50

69-70 Russian National Team Postcards

PLETE SET (27) 75.00 150.00
tor Zinger 1.50 4.00
ali Davydov 1.50 4.00
adimir Lutchenko 1.50 4.00
tor Kuzkin 1.50 4.00
exander Ragulin 4.00 10.00
r Romishevski 1.50 4.00
ris Mikhailov 6.00 15.00
cheslav Starshinov 1.50 4.00
geny Zimin 1.50 4.00
exander Maltsev 6.00 15.00
natoli Firsov 4.00 10.00
vgeny Paladiev 1.50 4.00
exander Yakushev 6.00 15.00
adimir Petrov 6.00 15.00
aleri Kharlamov 10.00 25.00
vgeny Mishakov 1.50 4.00

17 Vladimir Vikulov 1.50 4.00
18 Vladimir Yursinov 1.50 4.00
19 Viktor Pushkov 1.50 4.00
20 Arkady Chernishev 1.50 4.00
21 Anatoli Tarasov 4.00 10.00
22 USSR vs Sweden .75 2.00
23 USSR vs Sweden .75 2.00
24 USSR vs Sweden .75 2.00
25 USSR vs Finland, Sweden .75 2.00
26 USSR vs Canada, Sweden 1.50 4.00
27 Team Photo 1.50 4.00

1970-71 Russian National Team Postcards

This set measures 3 1/2" by 5 3/4". The horizontal fronts feature a color head shot and a preprint blue ink autograph on the left, and a black and white action photo on the right. The backs look like standard postcards. A protective sleeve featuring Russia in action against Sweden is usually found with the set.

COMPLETE SET (20) 100.00 150.00
1 Viktor Konovalenko 2.00 5.00
2 Vitali Davydov 2.00 5.00
3 Vladimir Lutchenko 2.00 5.00
4 Valeri Nikitin 2.00 5.00
5 Alexander Ragulin 4.00 10.00
6 Igor Romishevski 2.00 5.00
7 Evgeni Paladiev 2.00 5.00
8 Viacheslav Starshinov 2.00 5.00
9 Viktor Polupanov 2.00 5.00
10 Alexander Maltsev 6.00 15.00
11 Anatoli Firsov 6.00 15.00
12 Evgeni Mishakov 2.00 5.00
13 Boris Mikhailov 6.00 15.00
14 Valeri Vasiliev 4.00 10.00
15 Alexander Yakushev 6.00 15.00
16 Vladimir Petrov 6.00 15.00
17 Valeri Kharlamov 10.00 25.00
18 Vladimir Vikulov 2.00 5.00
19 Vladimir Shadrin 2.00 5.00
20 Vladislav Tretiak 10.00 25.00

1973-74 Russian National Team

This set comes in a commemorative folder and features "cards" that are 4 1/16 by 5 3/4.

COMPLETE SET (25) 60.00 125.00
1 Team Photo 1.50 4.00
2 Vladislav Tretiak 8.00 20.00
3 Alexander Sidelnikov 1.50 4.00
4 Alexander Gusev 1.50 4.00
5 Valeri Vasiliev 3.00 8.00
6 Boris Mikhailov 3.00 8.00
7 Vladimir Petrov 3.00 8.00
8 Valeri Kharlamov 6.00 15.00
9 Kharlamov, Petrov, Mikhailov 4.00 10.00
10 Vladimir Lutchenko 1.50 4.00
11 Gennady Tsygankov 1.50 4.00
12 Alexander Ragulin 1.50 4.00
13 Alexander Volchkov 1.50 4.00
14 Viacheslav Anisin 1.50 4.00
15 Yuri Lebedev 1.50 4.00
16 Alexander Bodunov 1.50 4.00
17 Alexander Martinyuk 1.50 4.00
18 Vladimir Shadrin 1.50 4.00
19 Alexander Yakushev 3.00 8.00
20 Alexander Maltsev 3.00 8.00
21 Evgeny Paladiev 1.50 4.00
22 Yuri Liapkin 1.50 4.00
23 Bobrov .75 2.00
Kulagin CO
24 Boris Mikhailov 3.00 8.00
25 Viktor Kuzkin 1.50 4.00

1974 Russian National Team

Unusually sized (8.25 X 3.5) postcard-type collectibles feature members of the powerful CCCP club. Often found in a folder.

COMPLETE SET (25) 50.00 100.00
1 Vyacheslav Anisin 1.50 4.00
2 Vsevolod Bobrov CO 1.50 4.00
3 Alexander Bodunov 1.50 4.00
4 Alexander Gusev 1.50 4.00
5 Sergei Kapustin 1.50 4.00
6 Valeri Kharlamov 5.00 12.00
7 Boris Kulagin CO 1.50 4.00
8 Viktor Kuzkin 1.50 4.00
9 Yuri Lebedev 1.50 4.00
10 Yuri Liapkin 1.50 4.00
11 Vladimir Lutchenko 1.50 4.00
12 Alexander Maltsev 3.00 8.00
13 Boris Mikhailov 3.00 8.00
14 Boris Mikhailov 3.00 8.00
15 Vladimir Petrov 3.00 8.00
16 Vladimir Repneev 1.50 4.00
17 Vladimir Shadrin 1.50 4.00
18 Yuri Shatalov 1.50 4.00
19 Alexander Sidelnikov 1.50 4.00
20 Vladislav Tretiak 6.00 15.00
21 Gennady Tsygankov 1.50 4.00
22 Valeri Vasiliev 3.00 8.00
23 Alexander Yakushev 3.00 8.00
24 USSR .40 1.00
25 USSR .40 1.00

1979 Russian National Team

This set features the Soviet National Team. The cards measure 8 1/4 by 5 7/8 and were issued in a folder.

COMPLETE SET (24) 37.50 100.00
1 Team Photo .50 1.00
2 Viktor Tikhonov CO 1.00 2.00
3 Vladimir Yursinov CO .50 2.00
4 Vladislav Tretiak 5.00 15.00
5 Alexander Pashkov 1.50 3.00
6 Vladimir Lutchenko 1.00 3.00
7 Valeri Vasiliev 1.00 5.00
8 Gennady Tsygankov 1.00 3.00
9 Yuri Fedorov 1.00 2.00
10 Slava Fetisov 5.00 15.00
11 Zinetula Bilyaletinov 2.50 5.00
12 Vasili Pervukhin 1.00 3.00
13 Boris Mikhailov 2.50 8.00
14 Vladimir Petrov 2.50 8.00
15 Valeri Kharlamov 5.00 15.00
16 Alexander Maltsev 2.50 8.00
17 Sergei Kapustin 1.00 3.00
18 Yuri Lebedev 1.00 2.00
19 Viktor Zhluktov 1.00 3.00
20 Helmut Balderis 1.50 5.00
21 Alexander Golikov 1.00 2.00
22 Sergei Makarov 4.00 15.00
23 Vladimir Golikov 1.00 2.00
24 Team Photo .50 1.00

1984 Russian National Team

This 23-card set presents Russian hockey players. The cards were packaged in a cardboard sleeve that displays a photo of the 1983 Russian national team. The cards measure approximately 5 1/2" by 7" and feature full-bleed head and shoulders shots of the players dressed in civilian clothing. On the left portion, the backs carry three action shots in a filmstrip format while the right portion has player information in Russian. The cards are unnumbered and checklisted below in alphabetical order.

COMPLETE SET (23) 40.00 80.00
1 Sergei Babinov .75 2.00
2 Helmut Balderis 1.25 3.00
3 Zinetula Bilyaletinov 1.25 3.00
4 Vyacheslav Bykov 2.00 5.00
5 Slava Fetisov 4.00 10.00
6 Irek Gimaev .75 2.00
7 Sergei Kapustin .75 2.00
8 Alexei Kasatonov 2.00 5.00
9 Andrei Khomotov 2.00 5.00
10 Vladimir Krutov 4.00 10.00
11 Igor Larionov 6.00 15.00
12 Sergei Makarov 4.00 10.00
13 Alexander Maltsev 2.00 5.00
14 Vladimir Myshkin 2.00 5.00
15 Vasily Pervukhin .75 2.00
16 Sergei Shepelev .75 2.00
17 Alexander Skvorstsov .75 2.00
18 Sergei Starikov 1.25 3.00
19 Viktor Tikhonov CO .75 2.00
20 Vladislav Tretiak 4.00 10.00
21 Mikhael Vasiliev .75 2.00
22 Vladimir Yursinov CO .40 1.00
23 Viktor Zhluktov .75 2.00
24 Vladimir Zubkov .75 2.00

1987 Russian National Team

This 24-card set presents Russian hockey players and is subtitled "The USSR 1987 National Hockey Team." The cards were printed in the USSR, released by Panorama Publishers (USSR), and distributed in North America by Tri-Globe International, Inc. The production run was reportedly 25,000 sets. The cards were packaged in a cardboard sleeve that displays a team photo from the world championships. The cards measure approximately 4 1/8" by 5 13/16" and feature full-bleed head and shoulders shots of the players dressed in coat and tie. The player's autograph and uniform number are printed on the lower portion of the picture in gold lettering. The backs are in Russian and present player profile and statistics. The cards are unnumbered and checklisted below in alphabetical order.

COMPLETE SET (24) 18.00 45.00
1 Sergei Ageikin .40 1.00
2 Evgeny Belosheikin .75 2.00
3 Zinetula Belyaletdinov .40 1.00
4 Viachesiav Bykov .75 2.00
5 Slava Fetisov 2.00 5.00
6 Alexei Gusarov .60 1.50
7 Valeri Kamensky 1.25 3.00
8 Alexei Kasatonov .75 2.00
9 Yuri Khmylev .60 1.50
10 Andrei Khomutov .75 2.00
11 Vladimir Konstantinov 2.00 5.00
12 Vladimir Krutov 1.25 3.00
13 Igor Larionov 2.00 5.00
14 Sergei Makarov 1.25 3.00
15 Sergei Mylnikov .75 2.00
16 Vasili Pervukhin .40 1.00
17 Sergei Starikov .40 1.00
18 Igor Stelnov .40 1.00
19 Sergei Svetlov .40 1.00
20 Viktor Tikhonov CO .75 2.00
21 Viktor Tjumenev .40 1.00
22 Michael Varnakov .40 1.00
23 Sergei Yashin .40 1.00
24 Vladimir Yursinov CO .40 1.00

1989 Russian National Team

This set of 24 postcards was released by Plakat Publishers, USSR. The cards measure approximately 4 1/8" by 5 13/16" and features some of the best Russian players of modern years. The set features 22 player cards and two coach cards. The cards were packaged in a cardboard sleeve that displays an action photo of Valeri Kamensky. Reportedly 100,000 sets were printed but most were sold in the USSR and fewer sets made it to the U.S. and Canada. The fronts have head and shoulder shots of Russian Team players in coat and tie (street clothes) with a superimposed facsimile autograph while the backs contain biographical information in Russian. An unauthorized reprint of the set was issued in 1991, but the size was reduced to 2 1/2" by 3 1/2". The players in the reprint set who had since played in the NHL were given English biographies on labels added to the back. The cards are listed below alphabetically since they are unnumbered.

COMPLETE SET (24) 14.00 35.00
1 Ilya Byakin .30 .75
2 Viacheslav Bykov .40 1.00
3 Alexandr Chernik .20 .50
4 Igor Dmitriev CO .20 .50
5 Sergei Fedorov 3.00 8.00
6 Slava Fetisov 1.25 3.00
7 Alexei Gusarov .30 .75
8 Arturs Irbe 2.00 5.00
9 Valeri Kamensky .75 2.00
10 Alexei Kasatonov .60 1.50
11 Svatoslav Khalizov .20 .50
12 Yuri Khmylev .30 .75
13 Andrei Khomutov .40 1.00
14 Vladimir Konstantinov 2.00 5.00
15 Vladimir Krutov .75 2.00
16 Dimitri Kvartalnov .40 1.00
17 Igor Larionov 1.50 4.00
18 Sergei Makarov .75 2.00
19 Vladimir Mishkin .40 1.00
20 Sergei Mylnikov .40 1.00
21 Sergei Nemchinov .40 1.00
22 Valeri Shirjaev .20 .50
23 Viktor Tikhonov CO .40 1.00
24 Sergei Yashin .20 .50

1991 Russian Sports Unite Hearts

A boxed set of standard-sized cards of Russian players in the NHL, this issue was limited to 50,000 sets produced.

COMPLETE SET (10) 6.00 15.00
1 Sergei Fedorov 2.00 5.00
2 Viacheslav Fetisov .75 2.00
3 Alexei Gusarov .40 1.00
4 Alexei Kasatonov .40 1.00
5 Vladimir Konstantinov .75 2.00
6 Igor Larionov .75 2.00
7 Sergei Makarov .40 1.00
8 Alexander Mogilny .75 2.00
9 Mikhail Tatarinov .40 1.00
10 Vladislav Tretiak 1.25 3.00

1991 Russian Stars in NHL

This 11-card standard-size set was reportedly printed in Leningrad by Ivan Fiodorov Press as a special limited edition; it is claimed that there were only 50,000 sets issued. The cards essentially feature Russian players in the NHL. The front has a full-color player photo, bordered on the two sides by hockey sticks (with hockey gloves below). A red banner is draped across the top of the picture, with the player's name in between USSR (sickle and hammer) and USA (US flag) emblems. In contrast to the dark purple background, the bottom is light purple and presents the message "Sports Unites Hearts" in English and Russian. The horizontally-oriented back provide player information in two colored panels (English and Russian) and has a head shot of the player as well.

COMPLETE SET (11) 3.00 8.00
1 Sergei Fedorov 1.50 4.00
2 Slava Fetisov .40 1.00
3 Alexei Gusarov .08 .25
4 Alexei Kasatonov .20 .50
5 Vladimir Konstantinov .40 1.00
6 Igor Larionov .40 1.00
7 Sergei Makarov .40 1.00
8 Alexander Mogilny .60 1.50
9 Mikhail Tatarinov .08 .25
10 Vladislav Tretiak .75 2.00
11 Team Photo .15 .40
USSR National Team

1991-92 Russian Stars Red Ace

This 17-card standard-size set, featuring Russian stars in the NHL, was produced by Red Ace. The cards were packaged in a box, on which it is claimed that the production run was limited to 50,000 sets. The fronts feature borderless action shots with the player's name. Printed on white cover stock, the horizontal backs feature a close-up photograph as well as biographical and statistical information in Russian and English. The cards are unnumbered and checklisted below in alphabetical order.

COMPLETE SET (17) 4.00 10.00
1 Pavel Bure 1.25 3.00
2 Evgeny Davydov .08 .25
3 Sergei Fedorov 1.25 3.00
4 Slava Fetisov .40 1.00
5 Alexei Gusarov .08 .25
6 Valeri Kamensky .30 .75
7 Alexei Kasatonov .20 .50
8 Ravil Khaidarov .08 .25
9 Vladimir Konstantinov .40 1.00
10 Igor Kravchuk .15 .40
11 Igor Larionov .40 1.00
12 Andrei Lomakin .08 .25
13 Sergei Makarov .30 .75
14 Alexander Mogilny .40 1.00
15 Sergei Nemchinov .15 .40
16 Anatoli Semenov .08 .25
17 Mikhail Tatarinov .08 .25

1991-92 Russian Tri-Globe Bure

This standard-size five-card set was produced by Tri-Globe as part of the "The Magnificent Five" series. These sets spotlight five Russian hockey stars currently playing in the NHL, with set 2 featuring Pavel Bure. It is claimed that 5,000 numbered display boxes were produced, each containing 40 sets (ten for each player). Printed in Russia on heavy laminated textured stock, card fronts feature full-color action shots in various formats and accented predominantly in green. Each set includes a checklist on the back of a Sergei Fedorov promo card.

COMPLETE SET (6) 3.00 8.00
COMMON CARD (6-10) .60 1.50
NNO Sergei Fedorov .20 .50
Checklist

1991-92 Russian Tri-Globe Fedorov

This five-card set honoring Sergei Fedorov is the product of a joint venture between Tri-Globe International, Inc. and Ivan Fiodorov Press. The cards measure approximately 2 1/2" by 3 3/4" and are printed on a grainy cardboard stock. The fronts feature color action game shots. The cards are numbered on the back. According to Tri-Globe, 600 uncut, numbered sheets were printed, producing the equivalent of 3,000 sets, as well as 1,000 uncut, numbered five-card strips. Moreover, 100,000 five-card sets were reportedly produced.

COMPLETE SET (5) 2.50 6.00
COMMON CARD (1-5) .50 1.25

1991-92 Russian Tri-Globe Irbe

This standard-size five-card set was produced by Tri-Globe as part of the "The Magnificent Five" series. These sets spotlight five Russian hockey stars currently playing in the NHL, with set four featuring Arturs Irbe.

COMPLETE SET (6) 1.50 4.00
COMMON CARD (16-20) .30 .75
NNO Sergei Fedorov .20 .50
Checklist

1991-92 Russian Tri-Globe Kamensky

This standard-size five-card set was produced by Tri-Globe as part of the "The Magnificent Five" series. These sets spotlight five Russian hockey stars currently playing in the NHL, with set 1 featuring Valeri Kamensky.

COMPLETE SET (6) .60 1.50
COMMON CARD (1-5) .30 .75
NNO Sergei Fedorov .20 .50
Checklist

1991-92 Russian Tri-Globe Semenov

This standard-size five-card set was produced by Tri-Globe as part of the "The Magnificent Five" series. These sets spotlight five Russian hockey stars currently playing in the NHL, with set three featuring Anatoli Semenov.

COMPLETE SET (6) .60 1.50
COMMON CARD (11-15) .08 .25
NNO Sergei Fedorov .20 .50
Checklist

1992 Russian Stars Red Ace

The 1992 Red Ace Russian Hockey Stars boxed set was co-sponsored by the World of Hockey Magazine and World Sport. The cards were sold in a light blue box with production limited supposedly to 25,000 sets. The cards are printed on thin card stock and measure approximately 2 1/2" by 3 3/8". The light blue bordered fronts feature color action player photos. The player's name appears on a light green diagonal stripe in an upper corner, accented with a red triangle containing a white star. The Red Ace logo is printed in a lower corner of the picture. The white backs display a small head shot next to the player's name on a green bar. In a pale pink panel below is the player's biography and career highlights in Russian and English. The cards are numbered on the back.

COMPLETE SET (36) 2.00 5.00
1 Darius Kasparaitis .10 .25
2 Alexei Zhamnov .10 .25
3 Dimitri Khristich .20 .50
4 Andrei Trefilov .20 .50
5 Vitali Prokhorov .02 .10
6 Dmitri Filimonov .02 .10
7 Valeri Zelepukin .10 .25
8 Alexei Kovalev .30 .75
9 Dmitri Kvartalnov .10 .25
10 Igor Korolev .10 .25
11 Nikolai Borschevsky .10 .25
12 Igor Boldin .02 .10
13 Arturs Irbe .30 .75
14 Viacheslav Butsayev .02 .10
15 Boris Mironov .10 .25
16 Sergei Bautin .02 .10
17 Alexander Kharlamov .10 .25
18 Viacheslav Kozlov .20 .50
19 Mikhail Shtalenkov .20 .50
20 Roman Oksyuta .02 .10
21 Sandis Ozolinsh .20 .50
22 Dmitri Mironov .10 .25
23 Sergei Brylin .10 .25
24 Vladimir Grachev .02 .10
25 Dmitri Starostenko .02 .10
26 Andrei Nazarov .10 .25
27 Alexei Yashin .20 .50
28 Vladimir Malakhov .10 .25
29 Ravil Jakubov .02 .10
30 Sergei Klimovich .02 .10
31 Artur Oktjabrev .02 .10
32 Lev Berdichevski .02 .10
33 Ian Kaminski .10 .25
34 Andrei Kovalenko .10 .25
35 Dmitri Yushkevich .10 .25
36 Checklist .02 .10

1992 Russian Tri-Globe From Russia With Puck

Twelve Russian hockey stars who are currently playing in the NHL are featured in this 24-card boxed standard-size set, with two cards devoted to each player. The production run was reportedly 50,000 sets. The fronts of all cards display color action player photos. On the player's first card (i.e., an odd-numbered card), his name appears at the top in a silver stripe, and red, white, and blue stripes accent the picture on three sides. On his second card (i.e., an even-numbered card), black-and-white speckled stripes edge the picture above and below. The back of the player's first card carries a second color action photo and biographical information, while the back of his second card has a close-up color photo and career statistics. All text is in French and English.

COMPLETE SET (24) 4.00 10.00
1 Igor Larionov .20 .50
2 Igor Larionov .20 .50
3 Andrei Lomakin .08 .25
4 Andrei Lomakin .08 .25
5 Pavel Bure .75 2.00
6 Pavel Bure .75 2.00
7 Alexei Zhamnov .08 .25
8 Alexei Zhamnov .08 .25
9 Sergei Krivokrasov .08 .25
10 Sergei Krivokrasov .08 .25
11 Valeri Kamensky .08 .25
12 Valeri Kamensky .08 .25
13 Viacheslav Kozlov .20 .50
14 Viacheslav Kozlov .20 .50
15 Valeri Zelepukhin .08 .25
16 Valeri Zelepukhin .08 .25
17 Igor Kravchuk .08 .25
18 Igor Kravchuk .08 .25
19 Vladimir Malakhov .08 .25
20 Vladimir Malakhov .08 .25
21 Boris Mironov .08 .25
22 Boris Mironov .08 .25
23 Arturs Irbe .20 .50
24 Arturs Irbe .20 .50

1992-93 Russian Stars Red Ace

This 37-card, standard-size set features action color player photos bordered in white. The player's name and the Red Ace logo appear in a gradated violet stripe at the bottom. A red triangle at the upper left corner of the picture carries a white star outline. In a red box with rounded corners, the back provides biography in Cyrillic (Russian) and English. The top portion of the back has a yellow background and displays a close-up photo in a circular format and the player's name in Russian and English. The cards are numbered on the back essentially alphabetically.

COMPLETE SET (37) 2.00 5.00
1 Aleksander Barkov .02 .10
2 Sergei Bautin .02 .10
3 Igor Boldin .02 .10
4 Nikolai Borchevsky .08 .25
5 Sergei Brylin .08 .25
6 Viacheslav Butsayev .02 .10
7 Alexander Cherbajev .02 .10
8 Evgeny Garanin .02 .10
9 Sergei Gonchar .20 .50
10 Alexander Karpovtsev .08 .25
11 Darius Kasparaitis .08 .25
12 Alexander Kharlamov .08 .25
13 Yuri Khmylev .08 .25
14 Sergei Klimovich .02 .10
15 Igor Korolev .08 .25
16 Andrei Kovalenko .08 .25
17 Alexei Kovalev UER .30 .75
(Bac
18 Dmitri Kvartalnov .08 .25
19 Vladimir Malakhov .08 .25
20 Maxim Mikhailovsky .02 .10
21 Boris Mironov .08 .25
22 Dmitri Mironov .08 .25
23 Andrei Nazarov .08 .25
24 Roman Oksyuta .02 .10
25 Artur Oktyabrev .02 .10
26 Sergei Petrenko .02 .10
27 Oleg Petrov .08 .25
28 Andrei Potaichuk .02 .10
29 Vitali Prokhorov .02 .10
30 Alexander Semak .08 .25
31 Dmitri Starostenko .02 .10
32 Ravil Yakubov .02 .10
33 Alexei Yashin .20 .50
34 Dmitri Yushkevich .08 .25
35 Alexei Zhamnov .08 .25
36 Alexei Zhitnik .08 .25
NNO Checklist Card .02 .10

1998-99 Russian Hockey League

This set features the elite of the Russian Hockey League. The cards feature blue borders around action shots. The set is notable for featuring 2001 first-overall draft pick Ilya Kovalchuk.

COMPLETE SET (167) 24.00 60.00
1 Sergei Gomolyako .20 .50
2 Sergei Zemchenok .20 .50
3 Oleg Mikulchik .20 .50
4 Evgueni Koreshkov .20 .50
5 Andrei Razin .20 .50
6 Ravil Gusmanov .20 .50
7 Dmitri Popov .20 .50
8 Valeri Karpov .30 .75
9 Andrei Sokolov .20 .50
10 Makhail Borodulin .20 .50
11 Konstantin Shafranov .30 .75
12 Vladimir Antipin .20 .50
13 Igor Zemlyanoi .20 .50
14 Sergei Tertyshny .20 .50
15 Vadim Glovatski .20 .50
16 AlexanderÂ Golts .30 .75
17 AlexanderÂ Koreshkov .20 .50
18 Boris Tortunov .20 .50
19 Valeri Nikulin .20 .50
20 Andrei Sapoznikov .20 .50
21 Dmitri Maksimov .20 .50
22 Dmitri Mylnikov .75 2.00
23 Maxim Sushinski .40 1.00
24 Yuri Panov .20 .50
25 AlexanderÂ erekhov .20 .50
26 Vladimir Zorkin .20 .50
27 Eduard Gorbachev .20 .50
28 Leonid Kaparekin .20 .50
29 AlexanderÂ Savchenkov .20 .50
30 Maxim Chukanov .20 .50
31 Evgueni Fedorov .20 .50
32 Yaroslav Lyuzenkov .20 .50
33 Oleg Leontiev .20 .50
34 Sergei Osipov .20 .50
35 Andrei Kudinov .20 .50
36 Dmitri Krasotkin .20 .50
37 Ravil Yakubov .40 1.00
38 Dmitri Zatonski .20 .50
39 Konstantin Maslyukov .20 .50
40 Andrei Subbotin .30 .75
41 Pavel Kamentsev .20 .50
42 Evgueni Tarasov .20 .50
43 Oleg Kryazhev .20 .50
44 Igor Nikitin .20 .50
45 Denis Arkhipov 1.25 3.00
46 Albert Loginov .20 .50
47 Andrei Samokhvalov .20 .50
48 Igor Dorofeev .20 .50
49 Sergei Bautin .20 .50
50 Evgueni Varlamov .20 .50
51 Sergei Korobkin .20 .50
52 Rafik Yakubov .20 .50
53 Alexei Chupin .20 .50
54 Dmitri Ryabikin .20 .50
55 Alexei Kudashav .20 .50
56 AlexanderÂ rofimov .20 .50
57 Igor Andryushchenko .20 .50
58 Igor Gorbenko .20 .50
59 Dmitri Gorenko .20 .50
60 AlexanderÂ Kazakov .20 .50
61 Evgueni Kuveko .20 .50
62 Igor Nikolaev .20 .50
63 Mikhail Pereyaslov .20 .50
64 AlexanderÂ Filippov .20 .50
65 Igor Mikhailov .20 .50
66 Roman Shipulin .20 .50
67 Dmitri Shpakovski .20 .50
68 Dmitri Shulakov .20 .50
69 Konstantin Golokhvastov .20 .50
70 Yuri Fimin .20 .50
71 Sergei Yasakov .20 .50
72 Oleg Filimonov .20 .50
73 Anatoli Ustyugov .20 .50
74 Andrei Skabelka .30 .75
75 Sergei Zolotov .20 .50
76 Dmitri Bezrukov .20 .50
77 Dmitri Vanyasov .20 .50
78 Evgueni Zakharov .20 .50
79 Arat Kadyekin .20 .50
80 Evgueni Mlinchenko .20 .50
81 Leonid Labzov .20 .50
82 Andrei Mazhugin .20 .50
83 Vladislav Makarov .20 .50
84 Remir Khaidarov .20 .50
85 Pavel Agarkov .20 .50
86 Igor Belyavski .20 .50
87 Dmitri Dubrovski .20 .50
88 Vyacheslav Zavalnyuk .20 .50
89 Yuri Zuev .20 .50
90 Andrei Evstafiev .20 .50
91 Vadim Epanchintsev .40 1.00
92 Igor Zelenchev .20 .50
93 Dmitri Klevakin .20 .50
94 Alexei Koledaev .20 .50
95 Nikolai Kurochkin .20 .50
96 Boris Kuzmin .20 .50
97 Roman Kukhtinov .20 .50
98 Sergei Moskalev .20 .50
99 Evgueni Pupkov .20 .50
100 Alexei Tkachuk .20 .50
101 Rinat Khasanov .20 .50
102 Sergei Shalamai .20 .50
103 Vadim Tarasov .75 2.00
104 Vladislav Morozov .20 .50
105 Almaz Garifullin .30 .75
106 Ilnur Gizatullin .20 .50
107 AlexanderÂ Zavyalov .20 .50
108 Oleg Vevcherenko .20 .50
109 AlexanderÂ Savitski .20 .50
110 Mikhail Sarmatin .20 .50
111 Igor Stepanov .20 .50
112 Konstantin Butsenko .20 .50
113 Alexei Murzin .20 .50
114 Andrei Nikolaev .20 .50
115 Dmitri Plekhanov .20 .50
116 Roman Salnikov .20 .50
117 Vyacheslav Timchenko .20 .50
118 Anitoli Stepanishev .20 .50
119 Roman Baranov .20 .50
120 Artem Anisimov .20 .50
121 Yuri Guniko .20 .50
122 Eduard Kudermetov .20 .50
123 Dmitri Balmin .20 .50
124 Igor Dyakiv .20 .50
125 Ramil Saifullin .20 .50
126 AlexanderÂ Vyukhin .20 .50
127 Oleg Leontiev .20 .50
128 Evgueni Koreshkov .20 .50
129 Sergei Gomolyako .20 .50
130 Oleg Mikulchik .20 .50
131 Andrei Petrakov .20 .50
132 Alexei Stepanov .20 .50
133 Dmitri Verzhinin .20 .50
134 Artem Ostroushko .20 .50
135 Sergei Berdnikov .20 .50
136 Konstantin Koltsov .20 .50
137 Vladimir Tarasov .20 .50
138 Sergei Shimkovski .20 .50
139 Oleg Pchelyakov .20 .50
140 Oleg Burlutski .20 .50
141 Oleg Bratash .20 .50
142 Sergei Voronov .20 .50
143 Uldar Mukhometov .30 .75
144 Alexei Egorov .40 1.00
145 Vladimir Kopat .20 .50
146 Vladimir Kochin .20 .50
147 Alexei Putilin .20 .50
148 Andrei Rasolko .20 .50
149 Vadim Molotilov .20 .50
150 Dmitri Nazarov .20 .50
151 Igor Vyazmikin .20 .50
152 Alexei Kalyukhny .20 .50
153 Denis Kartsev .20 .50
154 AlexanderÂ Kuvaldin .20 .50
155 Alexei Troschinsky .20 .50
156 AlexanderÂ Kharitonov .40 1.00
157 Valeri Cherny .20 .50
158 Yuri Dobrishkin .20 .50
159 Evgueni Pavlov .20 .50
160 Nikolai Antropov 1.25 3.00
161 AlexanderÂ Zhurik .20 .50
162 Valeri Belousov .20 .50
163 Artem Chubarov .40 1.00
164 Boris Zelenko .20 .50
165 Dmitri Frolov .40 1.00
166 Vladimir Kirik .20 .50
167 Alexei Danilov .20 .50

1999 Russian Fetisov Tribute

This set commemorates a game held in Russia in tribute of Slava Fetisov, perhaps the most important Russian-born player ever. It featured both Russian and NHL stars.

COMPLETE SET (41) 6.00 15.00
1 Alexander Korolyuk .07 .20
2 Pavel Bure .75 2.00
3 Alexei Morozov .07 .20
4 Viktor Kozlov .07 .20
5 Sergei Makarov .20 .50
6 Valeri Kamensky .07 .20
7 Maxim Afinogenov .20 .50
8 Slava Fetisov .20 .50
9 Maxim Sokolov .20 .50
10 Vladimir Malakhov .07 .20
11 Alexei Yashin .07 .20
12 Sergei Vyshedkevich .07 .20
13 Oleg Tverdovsky .07 .20
14 Sergei Brylin .07 .20
15 Vladimir Krutov .20 .50
16 Gennadi Tsygankov .07 .20
17 Egor Podomatski .20 .50
18 Vitali Vishnevski .07 .20
19 Sergei Nemchinov .07 .20
20 Daniil Markov .07 .20
21 Alexander Kharitonov .07 .20
22 Slava Bykov .07 .20
23 Bobby Carpenter .07 .20
24 Scott Stevens .20 .50
25 Ken Daneyko .07 .20
26 Jari Kurri .75 2.00
27 Slava Kozlov .20 .50
28 Anders Eriksson .07 .20
29 Darius Kasparaitis .07 .20
30 Doug Brown .07 .20
31 Ilkka Sinisalo .07 .20
32 Valeri Shiryaev .07 .20
33 Martin Brodeur 2.00 5.00
34 Christian Ruuttu .07 .20
35 Randy McKay .07 .20
36 Gino Odjick .20 .50
37 Igor Larionov .20 .50
38 Martin Lapointe .07 .20
39 Larry Robinson CO .20 .50
40 Viktor Tikhonov CO .07 .20
41 Scotty Bowman CO .20 .50

1999-00 Russian Dynamo Moscow

This team-issued set features Dynamo Moscow of the Russian League. The cards were sold by the team at its souvenir stands.

COMPLETE SET (27) 6.00 15.00
1 Alexei Tereshenko .20 .50
2 Igor Shadilov .20 .50
3 Alexei Ponikarovski .30 .75
4 Alexei Litvinenko .20 .50
5 Roman Zolotov .20 .50
6 Andrei Markov .75 2.00
7 Alexander Khavanov .30 .75
8 Vitali Proshkin .20 .50
9 Alexei Troschinsky .20 .50
10 Oleg Orekhovski .20 .50
11 Marat Davydov .20 .50
12 Dmitri Kokorev .20 .50
13 Alexander Kharitonov .30 .75
14 Alexander Prokopiev .20 .50
15 Mikhail Ivanov .20 .50
16 Alexei Kudashov .30 .75
17 Alexander Kuvaldin .20 .50
18 Denis Kartsev .20 .50
19 Stanislav Romanov .20 .50
20 Alexander Savchenkov .20 .50
21 Lev Berdichevski .20 .50
22 Alexei Kalyuzhni .20 .50
23 Alexander Stepanov .20 .50
24 Boris Zelenko .20 .50
25 Vitali Yeremeev .60 1.50
26 Alexei Yegorov .40 1.00
NNO Team Photo .20 .50

1999-00 Russian Hockey League

This set features the top players of the sprawling Russian Hockey League. The cards feature a color action photo on the front and player information on the back in Cyrillic. The set is noteworthy for featuring the first ever card of 2001 first overall pick, Ilya Kovalchuk.

COMPLETE SET (270) 60.00 100.00
1 Valeri Karpov .40 1.00
2 Igor Zemlyanoi .08 .25
3 Mikhail Borodulin .08 .25
4 Vladimir Antipin .08 .25
5 Vadim Glovatskin .08 .25
6 Alexei Stepanov .08 .25
7 Sergei Gomolyako .08 .25
8 Andrei Sokolov .08 .25
9 Andrei Razin .08 .25
10 Dmitri Popov .08 .25
11 Valeri Nikulin .08 .25
12 Andrei Petrakov .08 .25
13 Evgueni Koreshkov .08 .25
14 Alexander Koreshkov .08 .25
15 Andrei Sapozhnikov .20 .50
16 Oleg Mikulchik .40 1.00
17 Ravil Gusmanov .30 .75
18 Vitali Prokhorov .20 .50
19 Boris Tortunov .08 .25
20 Sergei Zemchenok .08 .25
21 Sergei Tertyshny .08 .25
22 Yuri Kuznetsov .08 .25
23 Maxim Bets .40 1.00
24 Sergei Osipov .08 .25
25 Oleg Leontiev .08 .25
26 Andrei Kudinov .08 .25
27 Konstantin Bezborodov .08 .25
28 Maxim Stepanov .08 .25
29 Alexei Lazarenko .08 .25
30 Vladimir Tyurikov .08 .25
31 Alexei Komarov .08 .25
32 Oleg Polkovinkov .08 .25
33 Dmitri Vershinin .08 .25
34 Vladimir Dumnov .08 .25
35 Oleg Smirnov .08 .25
36 Denis Ivanov .08 .25
37 Alexander Grishin .08 .25
38 Sergei Luchinkin .08 .25

39 Sergei Reshetnikov .08 .25
40 Denis Martiniuk .08 .25
41 Igor Boldin .08 .25
42 Nikolai Semin .08 .25
43 Alexander Zhdan .30 .75
44 Denis Metliuk .08 .25
45 Sergei Zolotov .08 .25
46 Yuri Dobryshkin .08 .25
47 Sergei Milnikov .40 1.00
48 Anton Ulyanov .08 .25
49 Yakov Deev .08 .25
50 Dmitri Bykov .08 .25
51 Dmitri Milnikov .40 1.00
52 Rinat Kasyanov .08 .25
53 Dmitri Balmin .08 .25
54 Alexei Chupin .08 .25
55 Artem Anisimov .08 .25
56 Sergei Smirnov .08 .25
57 Ivan Andriyashev .08 .25
58 Sergei Shilov .08 .25
59 Vladislav Makarov .08 .25
60 Dmitri Mylnikov .75 2.00
(Sergei Mylnikov Jr.
61 Rafik Yakubov .08 .25
62 Dmitri Shandurov .08 .25
63 Vladimir Pozdnyakov .08 .25
64 Alexei Ivashkin .08 .25
65 Valeri Ivannikov .08 .25
66 Egor Mikhailov .08 .25
67 Alexander Zibin .08 .25
68 Igor Averchenkov .08 .25
69 Alexei Sheblanov .08 .25
70 Dmitri Yachanov .08 .25
71 Oleg Romanov .08 .25
72 Denis Arkhipov 1.25 3.00
73 Almaz Garifullin .08 .25
74 Evgueni Varlamov .08 .25
75 Igor Stepanov .08 .25
76 Alexander Zavyalov .08 .25
77 Ilinur Gizhatullin .08 .25
78 Alexander Trofimov .08 .25
79 Eduard Kudermetov .08 .25
80 Remir Khaidarov .08 .25
81 Nikolai Pronin .08 .25
82 Andrei Glebov .08 .25
83 Andrei Savchenko .08 .25
84 Andrei Mukhachev .08 .25
85 Maxim Ossipov .20 .50
86 Sergei Mozyakin .08 .25
87 Alexei Gubarev .08 .25
88 Oleg Filimonov .30 .75
89 Igor Nikolaev .08 .25
90 Eduard Polyakov .08 .25
91 Konstantin Tatarintsev .08 .25
92 Anitoli Ustyugov .08 .25
93 Victor Dronov .08 .25
94 Sergei Yasakov .08 .25
95 Oleg Gorbenko .08 .25
96 Igor Andryushenko .08 .25
97 Alexei Plotinkov .08 .25
98 Igor Bakhmutov .08 .25
99 Dmitri Shandurov .08 .25
100 Dmitri Bezrukov .08 .25
101 Airat Kadeikin .08 .25
102 Leonid Labzov .08 .25
103 Alexei Vakhrushev .08 .25
104 Denis Tsigurov .08 .25
105 Roman Baranov .08 .25
106 Vladimir Zorkin .08 .25
107 Dmitri Maksimov .08 .25
108 Dmitri Kulikov .08 .25
109 Alexander Guskov .08 .25
110 Dmitri Khomutov .08 .25
111 Alexander Skugarev .08 .25
112 Mikhail Pereyaslov .08 .25
113 Artem Argokov .08 .25
114 Alexei Strakhov .08 .25
115 Dmitri Shulakov .08 .25
116 Oleg Vevcherenko .08 .25
117 Yuri Fimin .08 .25
118 Ruslan Bernikov .08 .25
119 Alexander Titov .08 .25
120 Dmitri Gorenko .08 .25
121 Alexander Filippov .08 .25
122 Konstantin Mitroshkin .08 .25
123 Alexander Zevakhin .08 .25
124 Steve Plouffe .40 1.00
125 Nikolai Tsulgin .30 .75
126 Alexei Tertyshny .08 .25
127 Nikolai Zavarykhin .30 .75
128 Evgueni Zakharov .08 .25
129 Sergei Klimentiev .20 .50
130 Pavel Duma .30 .75
131 Maxim Vasyuchkov .08 .25
132 Rustem Amirov .08 .25
133 Matvei Belpusov .08 .25
134 AlexanderÂ€chev .08 .25
135 Evgueni Muratov .08 .25
136 Andrei Buldakov .08 .25
137 Andrei Tsareev .08 .25
138 Vladimir Zavyalov .08 .25
139 Andrei Pchelyakov .08 .25
140 Igor Knyazev 1.25 3.00
141 Ilya Kovalchuk 25.00 50.00
142 Alexei Chervyakov .08 .25
143 Vladimir Kulikov .08 .25
144 Andrei Bushan .08 .25
145 Ravil Yakubov .20 .50
146 Sergei Shitkovski .08 .25
147 Sergei Berdnikov .08 .25
148 Ramil Saifullin .08 .25
149 Konstantin Golokhvastov .08 .25
150 Konstantin Maslyukov .08 .25
151 Alexei Bulatov .08 .25
152 Dmitri Kirilenko .08 .25
153 Sergei Makarov .08 .25
154 Rustem Kamaletdinov .08 .25
155 Maxim Mikhailovski .30 .75
156 Denis Khlopotnov .40 1.00
157 Albert Loginov .08 .25
158 Dmitri Nazarov .08 .25
159 Alexei Miroshnikov .08 .25
160 Sergei Zimakov .08 .25
161 Valeri Belov .08 .25
162 Alexei Kochegarov .08 .25
163 Alexei Pogonin .08 .25
164 Andrei Rasolko .08 .25
165 Dmitri Denisov .20 .50
166 Dmitri Tarasov .08 .25
167 Vadim Pokotilo .08 .25
168 Evgueni Fedorov .08 .25
169 Maxim Sushinski .30 .75
170 Alexander Popov .08 .25
171 Dmitri Parkhomenko .08 .25
172 Oleg Kryazhev .08 .25
173 Vitali Lyutkevich .08 .25
174 Dmitri Zatonski .08 .25
175 Oleg Ugolnikov .08 .25
176 Alexander Svitov 1.50 4.00
177 Dmitri Ryabkin .08 .25
178 Nikolai Babenko .08 .25
179 Yuri Panov .08 .25
180 Andrei Samokhvalov .08 .25
181 Alexander Ermakov .08 .25
182 Sergei Kagaikin .08 .25
183 Anvar Gatiyatulin .08 .25
184 Vladimir Tarasov .08 .25
185 Igor Varitskin .08 .25
186 Oleg Bolkov .08 .25
187 Rail Muftiev .08 .25
188 Vitali Yeremeev 1.25 3.00
189 Vladislav Brizgalov .30 .75
190 Dmitri Teplyakov .08 .25
191 Vladimir Kopat .08 .25
192 Denis Kuzmenko .08 .25
193 Evgueni Petrochinin .08 .25
194 Sergei Arekaev .08 .25
195 Pavel Agarkov .08 .25
196 Evgueni Pupkov .08 .25
197 Vadim Tarasov .40 1.00
198 Andrei Smirnov .08 .25
199 Alexander Maksimov .08 .25
200 Vitali Valui .08 .25
201 Sergei Petrenko .08 .25
202 Alexei Chistyakov .08 .25
203 Alexei Murzin .08 .25
204 Oleg Komissarov .08 .25
205 Mikhail Buturlin .08 .25
206 Konstantin Frolov .08 .25
207 Igor Zhelenchev .08 .25
208 Oleg Shargorodski .40 1.00
209 Sergei Selyutin .08 .25
210 Alexei Kupreenkov .08 .25
211 Roman Kukhtinov .08 .25
212 Vladislav Morozov .08 .25
213 Igor Belyavski .08 .25
214 Sergei Moskalev .08 .25
215 Alexei Tkachuk .08 .25
216 Sergei Chernyavski .08 .25
217 Vitali Kabanov .08 .25
218 Dmitri Klevakin .08 .25
219 Alexei Koledaev .08 .25
220 Oleg Glebov .08 .25
221 Georgi Evtyukhin .08 .25
222 Alexei Koznev .08 .25
223 Alexei Rubov .08 .25
224 Sergei Zinovjev 2.00 5.00
225 Evgueni Petrochinin .08 .25
226 Valeri Pokrovski .08 .25
227 Sergei Fedotov .08 .25
228 Vyacheslav Kurochkin .08 .25
229 Oleg Boltunov .08 .25
230 Alexei Baranov .08 .25
231 Igor Emeleev .08 .25
232 Roman Krivomazov .08 .25
233 Sergei Tikhonov .08 .25
234 Vladislav Brizgalov .30 .75
235 Dmitri Dubrovski .08 .25
236 Stepan Mokhov .08 .25
237 Dmitri Gogolev .08 .25
238 Evgueni Filinov .08 .25
239 Alexander Yudin .20 .50
240 Alexander Drozdetskin .08 .25
241 Sergei Shalamai .08 .25
242 Timofei Shishkanov .40 1.00
243 Alexander Sivov .08 .25
244 Vadim Musatov .08 .25
245 Andrei Chernoskutov .08 .25
246 Ruslan Shafikov .08 .25
247 Maxim Sokolov .20 .50
248 Alexander Matvichuk .08 .25
249 Andrei Evstafiev .08 .25
250 Vyacheslav Zavalnyuk .08 .25
251 Andrei Korolev .08 .25
252 Alexander Yudin .20 .50
253 Dmitri Mikhailov .08 .25
254 Artem Ostroushko .08 .25
255 Rinat Khasanov .08 .25
256 Vadim Epanchintsev .30 .75
257 Pavel Komarov .08 .25
258 Alexander Vyukhin .08 .25
259 Alfred Fatkullin .08 .25
260 Danis Zaripov .08 .25
261 Andrei Zubkov .08 .25
262 Marat Askarov .08 .25
263 Alexei Myagkikh .08 .25
264 Alexander Yudin .20 .50
265 Eduard Dmitriev .08 .25
266 Oleg Saltikov .08 .25
267 Oleg Grachev .08 .25
268 Valeri Oleinik .08 .25
269 Konstantin Koltsov .40 1.00
NNO Andrei Raiski .08 .25
NNO I.Koreshkov .20 .50
Alexander Koreshkov
Evgeni Koreshk

1999-00 Russian Metallurg Magnetogorsk

This team set features Metallurg of the Russian Hockey League. The cards are numbered sequentially to those in the Dynamo Moscow set.

COMPLETE SET 6.00 15.00
27 Sergei Gomolyako .20 .50
28 Vadim Glovatski .20 .50
29 Sergei Tertyshny .20 .50
30 Igor Zemlyanoi .20 .50
31 Valeri Nikulin .20 .50
32 Andrei Sapozhnikov .30 .75
33 Boris Tortunov .20 .50
34 Sergei Zemchenok .20 .50
35 Oleg Mikulchuk .30 .75
36 Andrei Razin .30 .75
37 Ravil Gusmanov .30 .75
38 Maxim Bets .30 .75
39 Andrei Petrakov .20 .50
40 Andrei Kudinov .20 .50
41 Mikhail Borodulin .20 .50
42 Sergei Osipov .20 .50
43 Valeri Karpov .30 .75
44 Evgeni Koreshkov .20 .50
45 Alexander Koreshkov .20 .50
46 Dmitri Popov .20 .50
47 Andrei Sokolov .20 .50
48 Oleg Leontiev .20 .50
49 Vladimir Antipin .20 .50
50 Alexei Stelanov .20 .50
51 Vitali Prokhorov .30 .75
52 Alexander Golts .20 .50
53 Konstantin Shafranov .40 1.00
54 Team Card .20 .50

1999-00 Russian Stars of Hockey

This 42-card set was issued in May of 2000 in conjunction with the Russian Championship tournament. It was created to commemorate stars of past championship tournaments.

COMPLETE SET (42) 12.00 30.00
1 Alexei Chupin .08 .25
2 Alexander Prokopiev .08 .25
3 Alexei Kudashov .08 .25
4 Alexander Khavanov .20 .50
5 Andrei Markov .60 1.50
6 Maxim Sushinski .08 .25
7 Dmitri Krasotkin .08 .25
8 Sergei Petrenko .08 .25
9 Valeri Karpov .08 .25
10 Sergei Tertyshny .08 .25
11 Ravil Gusmanov .08 .25
12 Egor Podomatski .20 .50
13 Alexei Chervyakov .08 .25
14 Valeri Ivannikov .08 .25
15 Maxim Mikhailovski .08 .25
16 Alexander Kharitonov .20 .50
17 Denis Arkhipov .30 .75
18 Yuri Dobryshkin .08 .25
19 Alexander Kuvaldin .08 .25
20 Dmitri Vlasenkov .08 .25
21 Evgeny Petrochinin .08 .25
22 Alexei Koznev .08 .25
23 Oleg Shargorodski .08 .25
24 Maxim Bets .08 .25
25 Dmitri Filimonov .08 .25
26 Alexei Yashin .20 .50
27 Pavel Bure 1.00 2.50
28 Sergei Fedorov 1.25 3.00
29 Alexander Mogilny .40 1.00
30 Alexei Kovalev .40 1.00
31 Maxim Sokolov .08 .25
32 Vyacheslav Kozlov .30 .75
33 Alexander Yakushev .40 1.00
34 Valeri Kharlamov 1.00 2.50
35 Alexei Kasatonov .20 .50
36 Vladislav Tretiak 2.00 5.00
37 Vyacheslav Fetisov .75 2.00
38 Valeri Vasiliev .40 1.00
39 Boris Mikhailov .40 1.00
40 Vyacheslav Anisin .08 .25
41 Vladimir Petrov .40 1.00
42 Alexander Maltsev .40 1.00

1999-00 Russian Stars Postcards

These postcards picture Russian stars with their club teams. It's likely that the listing below is not complete. The cards feature only the player's jersey number, so they are listed below in alphabetical order.

1 Maxim Afinogenov .75 2.00
2 Maxim Balmochnykh .40 1.00
3 Maxim Bets .40 1.00
4 Alexander Boikov .40 1.00
5 Victor Chistov .40 1.00
6 Marat Davydov .40 1.00
7 Kirill Golubev .40 1.00
8 Alexei Gorshkov .40 1.00
9 Airat Kadeikin .40 1.00
10 Svyatoslav Khalizov .40 1.00
11 Igor Khatsej .40 1.00
12 Viacheslav Kurochkin .40 1.00
13 Evgeny Kuveko .40 1.00
14 Albert Lecshev .40 1.00
15 Egor Mikhailov .75 2.00
16 Ildar Mukhametov .75 2.00
17 Andrei Pchelyakov .40 1.00
18 Sergey Petrenko .40 1.00
19 Alexander Prokopiev .40 1.00
20 Maxim Rybin .40 1.00
21 Vener Safin .40 1.00
22 Evgeny Shtepa .40 1.00
23 Dmitry Starostenko .40 1.00
24 Maxim Stepanov .40 1.00
25 Andrei Subbotin .40 1.00
26 Vadim Tarasov .75 2.00
27 Alexei Tkachuk .40 1.00
28 Andrei Tsarev .40 1.00
29 Vasily Turkovsky .40 1.00
30 Vladimir Tyurikov .40 1.00
31 Alexander Vyukhin .40 1.00
32 Sergei Yasakov .40 1.00

2000 Russian Champions

This Russian-produced set features players who have won the big one back in the ol' USSR.

COMPLETE SET (6) 4.00 10.00
1 Alexander Khavanov .80 2.00
2 Alexei Troschinsky .80 2.00
3 Andrei Markov 1.25 3.00
4 Alexander Kharitonov .80 2.00
5 Alexander Prokopiev .40 1.00
6 Vitali Yeremeyev 1.20 3.00

2000-01 Russian Dynamo Moscow

This set features players from the top Russian club team, Dynamo Moscow. The cards were produced in Russia and apparently were sold at home games. Some sets made their way to North America via the Internet.

COMPLETE SET (33) 6.00 15.00
1 Alexey Yegorov .30 .75
2 Oleg Shevtsov .20 .50
3 Alexander Yeremenko .30 .75
4 Mikhail Shtalenkov .40 1.00
5 Roman Zolotov .20 .50
6 Oleg Orekhovsky .20 .50
7 Igor Stchadilov .20 .50
8 Oleg Polkovnikov .20 .50
9 Ilya Nikulin .30 .75
10 Evgeny Gribko .20 .50
11 Marat Davydov .20 .50
12 Mikhail Donika .20 .50
13 Andrei Kuzmin .20 .50
14 Mikhail Ivanov .20 .50
15 Alexander Kuvaldin .20 .50
16 Sergei Klimovich .20 .50
17 Alexander Kharlamov .30 .75
18 Alexander Savchenkov .20 .50
19 Alexei Smirnov .40 1.00
20 Oleg Smirnov .20 .50
21 Stanislav Romanov .20 .50
22 Alexei Kudashov .30 .75
23 Boris Zelenko .20 .50
24 Alexei Tereshenko .20 .50
25 Alexander Stepanov .20 .50
26 Dmitri Dudarev .20 .50
27 Denis Kartsev .20 .50
28 Dmitri Subbotin .20 .50
29 Igor Bakhmutov .20 .50
30 Alexander Karpovtsev .30 .75
31 Alexander Klebnikov .20 .50
32 Dmitri Semenov .20 .50
33 Dmitriy Kokorev .30 .75

2000-01 Russian Dynamo Moscow Blue-White

Little is known about this Russian-produced set beyond the checklist. Additional information can be forwarded to hockeymag@beckett.com

COMPLETE SET (5) 2.50 6.00
1 Mikhail Shtalenkov 1.25 3.00
2 Alexei Kudashov .75 2.00
3 Oleg Orekhovsky .40 1.00
4 Mikhail Ivanov .40 1.00
5 Dmitri Subbotin .40 1.00

2000-01 Russian Goalkeepers

As the title suggests, this Russian-produced set features top stoppers from the RHL. Any additional information can be forwarded to hockeymag@beckett.com.

COMPLETE SET (9) 5.00 12.00
1 Maxim Sokolov .40 1.00
2 Mikhail Shtalenkov .75 2.00
3 Ilja Bryzgalov 1.50 4.00
4 Andrei Tsareev .40 1.00
5 Oleg Shevtsov .40 1.00
6 Andrei Malkov .40 1.00
7 Sergey Nikolaev .40 1.00
8 Alexei Yegorov .40 1.00
9 Maxim Mikhailovsky .40 1.00

2000-01 Russian Hockey League

This set features the top players in Russia's elite league. The set is noteworthy for including early or first cards of top Russian prospects Ilya Kovalchuk, Stan Chistov, Alexander Svitov, Andrei Medvedev, Pavel Datsyuk, etc. It is worth noting that card #260 is misnumbered at #199.

COMPLETE SET (394) 75.00 175.00
COMMON CARD (1-394) .10 .25
SEMISTARS .20 .50
UNLISTED STARS .30 .75
1 Oleg Filimonov .10 .25
2 Alexei Lazarenko .10 .25
3 Sergei Yasakov .10 .25
4 Steve Plouffe .30 .75
5 Alexander Tichkin .10 .25
6 Igor Boldin .10 .25
7 Vitali Evdokimov .10 .25
8 Igor Andryiotshenko .10 .25
9 Alexander Grishin .10 .25
10 Andrei Kyselev .10 .25
11 Dmitri Tarasov .10 .25
12 Anatoli Ustyugov .10 .25
13 Ruslan Bernikov .10 .25
14 Oleg Naumenko .10 .25
15 Igor Nikolaev .10 .25
16 Renat Khairetdinov .10 .25
17 Vadim Pokotilo .10 .25
18 Vladimir Tyorikov .10 .25
19 Dmitri Uchaikin .10 .25
20 Konstantin Mitroshkin .10 .25
21 Alexei Plotnikov .10 .25
22 Oleg Vevcherenko .10 .25
23 Dmitri Shulakov .10 .25
24 Sergei Butko .10 .25
25 Dmitri Levinski .10 .25
26 Vladimir Gusev .30 .75
27 Denis Martiniuk .10 .25
28 Ross Harris .10 .25
29 Nikolai Pronin .10 .25
30 Sergei Zholotov .10 .25
31 Dmitri Bykov .75 2.00
32 Remir Khaidarov .10 .25
33 Eduard Kudermetov .10 .25
34 Dmitri Yachanov .10 .25
35 Dmitri Balmin .10 .25
36 Alexander Zhdan .30 .75
37 Alexei Chupin .10 .25
38 Almaz Gariffillin .10 .25
39 Alexander Zavyalov .10 .25
40 Ilnur Gizhatullin .10 .25
41 Alexei Tertyshny .10 .25
42 Evgeni Varlamov .10 .25
43 Oleg Glebov .10 .25
44 Sergei Mylnikov Jr. .30 .75
45 Leonid Kanaryekin .10 .25
46 Ildar Yobin .10 .25
47 Anton Volchenkov ERC 2.00 5.00
48 Andrei Loginov .10 .25
49 Vitali Drindeyen .10 .25
50 Pavel Khanarski .10 .25
51 Vladimir Kramskoy .10 .25
52 Oleg Mikulchik .10 .25
53 Vyacheslav Zhavaliuk .10 .25
54 Sergei Soin ERC .75 2.00
55 Andrei Galkin .10 .25
56 Valeri Cherni .10 .25
57 Andrei Posnov .10 .25
58 Alexander Ardashev .10 .25
59 Roman Salnikov .10 .25
60 Eduard Gorbachev .10 .25
61 Sergei Martinov .10 .25
62 Dmitri Perozhkov .10 .25
63 Alexander Frolov ERC 6.00 15.00
64 Vladimir Zhavyalov .10 .25
65 Lev Berdischevski .10 .25
66 Andrei Maximenko .10 .25
67 Dmitri Teplyakov .10 .25
68 Boris Kuzmin .10 .25
69 Nikolai Ruzhenikov .10 .25
70 Maxim Ossipov .20 .50
71 Vladimir Loginov .10 .25
72 Andrei Kuzmin .20 .50
73 Ilya Dokshin .10 .25
74 Sergei Yakimovich .10 .25
75 Oleg Kuzmin .10 .25
76 Yuri Truvacheev .10 .25
77 Fedor Tjutin ERC .10 .25
78 Alexei Tsvetkov .10 .25
79 Alexander Shenkar .10 .25
80 Gyori Kabanov .10 .25
81 Vitali Chumicheev .10 .25
82 Artem Chernov .30 .75
83 Dmitri Khramchenko .20 .50
84 Andrei Sharapov .10 .25
85 Oleg Antonenko .10 .25
86 Oleg Namestnikov .10 .25
87 Andrei Poddyakon .10 .25
88 Vasili Smirnov .10 .25
89 Vitali Novopashin .10 .25
90 Roman Malov .10 .25
91 Vadim Averkin .10 .25
92 Nikolai Voevodin .10 .25
93 Vladimir Fedosov .10 .25
94 Vasili Chestokletov .10 .25
95 Anatoli Filatov .10 .25
96 Igor Safonov .10 .25
97 Mikhail Belobragin .10 .25
98 Maxim Ovchinikov .10 .25
99 Alexei Vorobiev .10 .25
100 Igor Shevtsov .10 .25
101 Sergei Fadeyev .10 .25
102 Dmitri Pankov .10 .25
103 Sergei Berdnikov .10 .25
104 Georgi Evtyiokhin .10 .25
105 Sergei Voronov .10 .25
106 Alexei Kaliozhni .10 .25
107 Yuri Kuznetsov .10 .25
108 Alexander Golts .20 .50
109 Sergei Klyshin .10 .25
110 Igor Melyakov .10 .25
111 Sergei Kiseleev .10 .25
112 Igor Karpenko .30 .75
113 Igor Karpenko .30 .75
114 Sergei Nikolayev .10 .25
115 Igor Sipchenko .10 .25
116 Valeri Pokrovski .10 .25
117 Sergei Gubernatorov .10 .25
118 Igor Samoylov .10 .25
119 Alexander Urakin .10 .25
120 Oleg Eremeyev .10 .25
121 Paolo Della Bella .20 .50
122 Slava Bezhukladnikov .10 .25
123 Alexei Troschinsky .20 .50
124 Vladimir Antipin .10 .25
125 Alexander Yudin .10 .25
126 Vitali Proshkin .10 .25
127 Ilya Kovalchuk 6.00 15.00
128 Dmitri Ryabikin .10 .25
129 Alexander Zhurik .10 .25
130 Igor Shastin .10 .25
131 Mikhail Shukaev .10 .25
132 Anvar Gatiyatulin .10 .25
133 Andrei Anisimov .10 .25
134 Maxim Soloviev .10 .25
135 Konstantin Bezborodov .10 .25
136 Ravil Yakubov .10 .25
137 Alexander Prokopiev .10 .25
138 Oleg Shargorodsky .20 .50
139 Ruslan Batyrshin .20 .50
140 Alexei Kypreyenkov .10 .25
141 Pavel Komarov .10 .25
142 Alexei Sharnin .10 .25
143 Sergei Fedotov .10 .25
144 Denis Khlistov .10 .25
145 Mikhail Potapov .10 .25
146 Alexander Semak .20 .50
147 Andrei Vasilesvki .30 .75
148 Azhat Sharipov .10 .25
149 Andrei Sidyakin .10 .25
150 Sergei Shikhanov .10 .25
151 Sergei Gomolyako .10 .25
152 Dmitri Nabokov .20 .50
153 Valentin Morozov .10 .25
154 Denis Metliuk .20 .50
155 Ilja Bryzgalov ERC 2.00 5.00
156 Alexander Lyubimov .20 .50
157 Ilya Byakin .20 .50
158 Sergei Tertyshny .10 .25
159 Valeri Karpov .20 .50
160 Andrei Tarasenko .10 .25
161 Alexander Yudin .20 .50
162 Nikolai Zavarukin .20 .50
163 Oleg Belkin .10 .25
164 Andrei Skabelka .10 .25
165 Leonid Fatikov .10 .25
166 Oleg Khmylev .10 .25
167 Denis Afinogenov .10 .25
168 Alexander Nesterov .10 .25
169 Andrei Kruchinin .10 .25
170 Andrei Petrunin .20 .50
171 Vladimir Malenkikh .10 .25
172 Sergei Shabanov .10 .25
173 Vadim Tarasov .30 .75
174 Igor Zhelenchev .10 .25
175 Sergei Shalamai .10 .25
176 Yuri Zhuev .10 .25
177 Artem Argokov .10 .25
178 Evgeni Pupkov .10 .25
179 Sergei Moskaleev .10 .25
180 Alexander Filippov .10 .25
181 Igor Dyakiv .10 .25
182 Stanislav Pinevski .10 .25
183 Alexander Agnevtshikov .10 .25
184 Sergei Sherevtsov .10 .25
185 Roman Kuhtinov .10 .25
186 Evgeni Lapin .10 .25
187 Nikolai Kurochkin .10 .25
188 Alexei Alekeev .10 .25
189 Alexei Koledaev .10 .25
190 Sergei Berenikin .10 .25
191 Denis Tyurin .10 .25
192 Rail Rozakov .10 .25
193 Vladimir Pozdnyakov .10 .25
194 Pavel Desyatkov .10 .25
195 Alexei Krovopuskov .10 .25
196 Sergei Sevastyanov .10 .25
197 Mikhail Yakubov ERC 1.50 4.00
198 Mikhail Sevastyanov .10 .25
199 Pavel Torgaev .10 .25
200 Denis Tyulyapkin .10 .25
201 Dmitri Altareev .10 .25
202 Maxim Savosin .10 .25
203 Leonid Toropchenko .10 .25
204 Stanislav Timakov .10 .25
205 Valeri Emelyanov .10 .25
206 Igor Gracheev .10 .25
207 Stanislav Udyachski .10 .25
208 Yuris Ozols .10 .25
209 Alexander Galkin .10 .25
210 Sergei C. Makarov .10 .25
211 Sergei Seliutin .10 .25
212 Alexander Popov .10 .25
213 Sergei Zhadeleyenov .10 .25
214 Alexei Litvinenko .10 .25
215 Dmitri Shulga .10 .25
216 Denis Sokolov .10 .25
217 Maxim Krayev .10 .25
218 Renat Hasanov .10 .25
219 Boris Tortunov .10 .25
220 Dmitri Krasotkin .10 .25
221 Maxim Velikov .10 .25
222 Yuri Panov .10 .25
223 Alexander Vyukhin .10 .25
224 Vadim Shakhraichuk .10 .25
225 Alexei Badyukov .10 .25
226 Alexander Korobolin .10 .25
227 Dmitri Zatonski .10 .25
228 Kirill Koltsov .75 2.00
229 Alexander Svitov 1.25 3.00
230 Ilya Gorbushin .10 .25
231 Andrei Samokhvalov .10 .25
232 Igor Nikitin .10 .25
233 Ramil Saifullin .10 .25
234 Viktor Chistov .10 .25
235 Vladimir Vorobiev .10 .25
236 Igor Niklulin .10 .25
237 Alexander Sidorovski .10 .25
238 Oleg Polkovnikov .10 .25
239 Dmitri Dudarev .10 .25
240 Andrei Sapozhnikov .10 .25
241 Andrei Kudinov .10 .25
242 Alik Gareev .10 .25
243 Ruslan Nurtdinov .10 .25
244 Alexander Ageev .10 .25
245 Andrei Yakhanov .10 .25
246 Vener Safin .10 .25
247 Sergei Komarov .10 .25
248 Nail Shayakhmetov .10 .25
249 Vladislav Ozolin .10 .25
250 Nikolai Tsuligin .10 .25
251 Albert Letsvheyev .10 .25
252 Stanislav Shalnov .10 .25
253 Maxim Orlov .10 .25
254 Alexei Chernikov .10 .25
255 Sergei B. Makarov .10 .25
256 Sergei Zimakov .20 .50
257 Gennady Savilov .10 .25
258 Vasili Turkovski .10 .25
259 Igor Mikhailov .10 .25
260 Vadim Glovatskin .10 .25
261 Alexei Tkachuk .10 .25
262 Mikhail Volkov .10 .25
263 Dmitri Gogolev .10 .25
264 Pavel Agarkov .10 .25
265 Vladimir Korsunov .10 .25
266 Andrei Medvedev 1.50 4.00
267 Dmitri Bykov .75 2.00
268 Ruslan Zainullin .20 .50
269 Dmitri Starostenko .10 .25
270 Alexander Schev .10 .25
271 Andrei Petrakov .10 .25
272 Sergei Klimentiev .10 .25
273 Yuri Kuznetsov .10 .25
274 Igor Knyazev .60 1.50
275 Vladimir Tikhomirov .10 .25
276 Vladimir Repneev .10 .25
277 Alexander Boikov .10 .25
278 Sergei Voronov .10 .25
279 Rustem Kamaletdinov .10 .25
280 Konstantin Molodstov .10 .25
281 Andrei Frolkin .10 .25
282 Vladimir Terekhov .10 .25
283 Dmitri Klevakin .10 .25
284 Denis Denisov .20 .50
285 Vladislav Korneev .20 .50
286 Evgeni Muratov .20 .50
287 Pavel Duma .30 .75
288 Egor Shastin .75 2.00
289 Artem Chernov .30 .75
290 Rail Rozakov .30 .75
291 Alexander Chagodaev .30 .75
292 Alexander Buturlin .75 2.00
293 Mikhail Yakubov 1.50 4.00
294 Alexei Petrov .30 .75
295 Pavel Vorobiev ERC 1.50 4.00
296 Ilya Kovalchuk 6.00 15.00
297 Vladimir Tikhomirov .20 .50
298 Igor Bakhmutov .20 .50
299 Sergei Zholotov .20 .50
300 Vadim Tarasov .30 .75
301 Andrei Medvedev 1.50 4.00
302 Anton Volchenkov ERC 2.00 5.00
303 Denis Grebeshkov ERC .40 1.00
304 Andrei Shefer .75 2.00
305 Alexander Seluyanov .20 .50
306 Ivan Nepryaev .30 .75
307 Stanislav Chistov ERC 2.00 5.00
308 Alexander Barkunov .30 .75
309 Alexander Svitov 1.25 3.00
310 Igor Boriskov .20 .50
311 Alexander Zhdan .30 .75
312 Ilya Nikulin .20 .50
313 Mikhail Donika .20 .50
314 Andrei Kuzmin .20 .50
315 Alexei Smirnov .75 2.00
316 Vadim Brezhgunov .75 2.00
317 Mikhail Shtalenkov .30 .75
318 Sergei Klimovich .20 .50
319 Alexander Kharlamov .20 .50
320 Dmitri Subbotin .10 .25
321 Alexander Karpovstev .10 .25
322 Oleg Shevtsov .10 .25
323 Evgeni Gribko .10 .25
324 Denis Khlopotnov .30 .75
325 Pavel Boichenko .10 .25
326 Alexander Stepanov .10 .25
327 Nikolai Ignatov .10 .25
328 Alexander Skoptsov .10 .25
329 Mikhail Mikhailovski .10 .25
330 Sergei Semin .10 .25
331 Pavel Trakhanov .10 .25
332 Dmitri Riabkin .10 .25
333 Ravil Yakubov .10 .25
334 Pavel Datsyuk ERC 15.00 40.00
335 Andrei Evstafiev .10 .25
336 Andrei Razin .10 .25
337 Denis Afinogenov .10 .25
338 Oleg Orekhovsky .10 .25
339 Ilya Gorbushin .10 .25
340 Viktor Tchistov .10 .25
341 Valeri Oleinik .10 .25
342 Sergei Shumykin .10 .25
343 Oleg Romashko .10 .25
344 Yuri Bogusevich .10 .25
345 Nikolai Koptin .10 .25
346 Vladislav Pustovalov .10 .25
347 Andrei Gavrylin .10 .25
348 Dmitri Chikin .10 .25
349 Evgeni Letov .10 .25
350 Vadim Navrotskin .10 .25
351 Vitali Chumichev .10 .25
352 Sergei Mozyakin .10 .25
353 Alexei Simakov .10 .25
354 Vadim Gusev .10 .25
355 Sergei Kutyavin .10 .25
356 Lev Trifonov .10 .25
357 Roman Oksiuta .10 .25
358 Alexei Chervyakov .10 .25
359 Sergei Erkovich .10 .25
360 Oleg Volkov .10 .25
361 Sergei Gomolyako .10 .25
362 Evgeni Bobariko .10 .25
363 Evgeni Bobariko .10 .25
364 Igor Boldin .10 .25
365 Oleg Komissarov .10 .25
366 Yuri Zlov .10 .25
367 Andrei Pchelyakov .10 .25
368 Oleg Boltunov .10 .25
369 Nikolai Babenko .10 .25
370 Igor Varitskin .10 .25
371 Andrei Rasolko .10 .25
372 Dmitri Denisov .10 .25
373 Konstantin Maslyukov .10 .25
374 Vadim Epanchintsev .20 .50
375 Alexei Krivchenkov .10 .25
376 Maxim Sokolov .10 .25
377 Alexei Koznev .10 .25
378 Evgeni Petrochinin .10 .25
379 Vladislav Luchkin .10 .25
380 Artur Oktyabriev .10 .25
381 Vladimir Kopat .10 .25
382 Vladimir Kochin .10 .25
383 Igor Emeleev .10 .25
384 Sergei Shitkovski .10 .25
385 Andrei Kozrev .10 .25
386 Alexander Smagin .10 .25
387 Rafik Yakubov .10 .25
388 Ildar Mukhometov .30 .75
389 Ivan Tkachenko .10 .25
390 Evgeni Akhmetov .10 .25
391 Vitali Lyutkevich .10 .25
392 Alexander Vinogradov .10 .25
393 Evgeni Artyukhin .10 .25
394 Andrei Tsareev .10 .25

2001-02 Russian Dynamo Moscow

This set features the players of Moscow's top team, Dynamo. The cards were sold in set form, apparently home games.

COMPLETE SET (22) 15.00 35.
1 Oleg Orekhovskiy .20
2 Alexei Troschinsky .30
3 Andrey Razin .20
4 Dmitriy Starostenko .20
5 Andrey Skopintsev .20
6 Evgeniy Gribko .20
7 Alexey Kudashov .20
8 Evgeniy Lapin .20
9 Iliy Nikulin .20
10 Valeriy Karpov .20
11 Alexander Kuvaldin .20
12 Ravil Yakubov .20
13 Alexander Nizivij .20
14 Dmitriy Semenov .20
15 Alexander Ovechkin 10.00 25.
16 Marat Davydov .20
17 Mikhail Shtalenkov .30
18 Vladimir Korolkov .20
19 Igor Mirnov .20
20 Vitaliy Yeremeev .40 1.
21 Alexander Savchenkov .30
22 Sergei Vishedkevich .30

2001-02 Russian Dynamo Moscow Mentos

This set also features Dynamo Moscow and is distinguishable from the other set by the prominent placement of the Mentos trademark. Little else is known about this set; additional information can be forwarded to hockeymag@beckett.com.

COMPLETE SET (16) 3.00 8.
1 Sergey Vishedkevich .20
2 Evgeniy Lapin .20
3 Alexander Savtchenkov .20
4 Alexander Stepanov .20
5 Mikhail Ivanov .20
6 Mikhail Shtalenkov .30
7 Dmitriy Starostenko .20
8 Alexei Troschinsky .20
9 Ravil Yakubov .20
10 Oleg Orekhovskiy .20
11 Andrey Skopintsev .20
12 Andrey Razin .20
13 Marat Davydov .20
14 Iliy Nikulin .20
15 Alexander Yudin .20
16 Evgeniy Gribko .20

2001-02 Russian Hockey League

COMPLETE SET (173) 30.00 60.
1 Dmitri Spirin .08
2 Alexander Yakovenko .08
3 Ivan Sakharov .08
4 Andrei Mukhachev .08
5 Anatoli Stepanov .08
6 Nikolai Pronin .08
7 Igor Boiko .08
8 Alexander Borovkov .08
9 Dmitri Sergeev .08
10 Stepanov Brothers .08
11 Renat Kharetdinov .08
12 Alexander Andrievsky .08
13 Evgeni Bobariko .08
14 Andrei Galkin .08
15 Evgeni Gamalei .08
16 Oleg Grachev .08
17 Dmitri Yevdokimov .08
18 Andrei Yershov .08
19 Sergei Kiselev .08
20 Maxim Korobov .08
21 Denis Kuzmenko .08
22 Denis Makarov .08
23 Sergei Makarov .08
24 Oleg Mikulchik .08
25 Roman Oksiuta .08
26 Slava Polikarkin .08
27 Andrei Ponomarev .08
28 Dmitri Popov .08
29 Vitali Prokhorov .08
30 Alexander Romanov .08
31 Sergei Selyutin .08
32 Alexander Smirnov .75 2.
33 Sergei Sorokin .08
34 Mikhail Strelkov .08
35 Stanislav Timakov .08
36 Dmitri Timofeev .08
37 Vladimir Fedossov .08
38 Alexei Chrevyakov .08
39 Vitali Chinakhov .08
40 Oleg Yashin .08
41 Sergei Gomolyako .08
42 Vasili Chistokletov .08
43 Alexander Yudin .08
44 Alexander Yudin .08
45 Alexander Yudin .08
46 Artem Anisimov .08
47 Sergei Shikhanov .08
48 Evgeni Akhmetov .08
49 Igor Varitsky .08
50 Vladimir Antipin .08
51 Vadim Sharifjanov .20
52 Rail Muftiev .08
53 Maxim Bets .20
54 Viktor Ignatiev .20
55 Yuri Trubachev .08
56 Igor Shadilov .08
57 Sergei Gusev .08
58 Viktor Chistov .20
59 Maxim Sokolov .40 1
60 Alexander Semak .08
61 Ruslan Akhmadullin .08
62 Igor Volkov .08
63 Sergei Shalamai .08
64 Vitali Karamnov .08
65 Vladislav Ozolin .08
66 Vladislav Makarov .08
67 Igor Karpenko .40 1
68 Parris Duffus .75 2
69 Igor Shastin .08
70 Evgeny Muratov .08
71 Nikolai Bardin .08
72 Roman Baranov .08
73 Artem Chernov .08
74 Konstantin Mikhailov .08
75 Dmitri Parkhomenko .08
76 Igor Mikhailov .08
77 Vladimir Korsunov .08
78 Alexei Livinenko .08
79 Alexander Vyukhin .20
80 Dmitri Zatonski .08
81 Kirill Koltsov .75 2
82 Alexander Kharitonov .08
83 Renat Kharetdinov .08
84 Alexander Levenyuk .08
85 Alexei Volkov .40 1

Sergei Yasakov .08 .20
Andrei Dylevsky .08 .20
Sergei Kutyavin .08 .20
Sergei Yerkovich .08 .20
Sergei Berdnikov .08 .20
Oleg Shargorodsky .20 .50
Oleg Vevcherenko .08 .20
Stanislav Shalnov .08 .20
Alexei Gorshkov .08 .20
Andrei Subbotin .60 1.50
Ramil Saifullin .08 .20
Ilya Gorbushin .08 .20
Alexander Svitov 1.25 3.00
Sergei Tertyshny .08 .20
Alexander Popov .08 .20
Alexander Korobolin .08 .20
Denis Zaripov .08 .20
Sergei Klimentiev .08 .20
Dmitri Kirilenko .08 .20
Maxim Rybin .08 .20
Konstantin Gorovikov .08 .20
Denis Khlystov .08 .20
Andrei Tsareev .20 .50
Alexei Chupin .08 .20
Alexander Drozdetski .08 .20
Vadim Brezgunov .08 .20
Alexei Podalinski .08 .20
Konstantin Shafronov .08 .20
Alexander Golts .08 .20
Ilya Gorokhov .08 .20
Dmitri Zatonski .08 .20
Vadim Epanchinsev .08 .20
Dmitri Gogolev .08 .20
Alexander Yudin .08 .20
Maxim Sokolov .40 1.00
Boris Tortunov .20 .50
Vladimir Antipov .08 .20
Vladimir Kretchin .08 .20
Sergei Zinovjev 1.25 3.00
Andrei Kruchinin .08 .20
Sergei Zhukov .08 .20
Yuri Kuznetsov .08 .20
Anton But .08 .20
Denis Khlopotnov .20 .50
Yuri Kuznetsov .08 .20
Oleg Shvetsov .20 .50
Andrei Loginov .08 .20
Stanislav Udiansky .08 .20
Denis Baev .08 .20
Sergei Semin .08 .20
Maxim Soloviev .08 .20
Dmitri Dubrovsky .08 .20
Vitali Drynin .08 .20
Lev Berdischevski .08 .20
Alexei Sergievsky .08 .20
Evgeni Artyukhin .08 .20
Alexei Kochegarov .08 .20
Evgeny Lapenkov .08 .20
Alexander Borozenko .08 .20
Dmitri Vershinin .08 .20
Yaroslav Lyuzenkov .08 .20
Artem Rybin .08 .20
Alexander Skoptsev .08 .20
Alexei Pogonin .08 .20
Vladislav Poperechny .08 .20
Dmitri Plekhanov .08 .20
Alexei Krovopuskov .08 .20
Alexei Yegorov .20 .50
Oleg Voschenikin .08 .20
Vitali Trigubov .20 .50
Jan Benda .08 .20
Patrik Martinec .08 .20
Dmitri Yachanov .20 .50
Almaz Garifullin .08 .20
Alexei Murzin .08 .20
Vladimir Loginov .08 .20
Khalim Nigmatullin .08 .20
Alexander Dolishnya .08 .20
Igor Fadeev .08 .20
Dmitri Kulikov .08 .20
Andrei Yemelin .08 .20
Oleg Yashin .08 .20
Andrei Zabolotnev .08 .20
Alexander Semak .08 .20
Sergei Askimov .08 .20
Rinat Khasanov .08 .20

2001-02 Russian Legions

e is known about this set, which features top sian players. It is believed that the checklist below complete. Any additional information can be arded to hockeymag@beckett.com.

IPLETE SET (3) .75 2.00
exei Troschinsky .40 1.00
nitriy Starostenko .40 1.00
adimir Tsiplakov .40 1.00

2001-02 Russian Lightnings

is known about this Russian set, which features layers of the RHL. Any additional information can rwarded to hockeymag@beckett.com.

IPLETE SET (8) 2.00 5.00
xim Sushinskiy .40 1.00
r Varitskiy .40 1.00
exey Kudashov .40 1.00
drey Razin .40 1.00
nitriy Gogolev .40 1.00
nitriy Kvartalnov .40 1.00
nis Metlyuk .40 1.00
drei Kovalenko .40 1.00

001-02 Russian Ultimate Line

is known about this Russian set, which features oaltneders of the RHL. Any additional information be forwarded to hockeymag@beckett.com.

IPLETE SET (5)
aliy Yeremeev .75 2.00
r Podomatskiy .75 2.00
ke Fountain .75 2.00
oslav Kamesh .40 1.00
xander Yeremenko .40 1.00

001-02 Russian Young Lions

is known about this Russian set, which features layers of the RHL. Any additional information can rwarded to hockeymag@beckett.com.

PLETE SET (11) 10.00 40.00
Kovalchuk 6.00 15.00
xander Svitov .75 2.00
xander Ovechkin 6.00 15.00
r Grigorenko 1.50 4.00
ll Koltsov .75 2.00
ton Babchuk .75 2.00
xander Frolov 1.25 3.00
olai Zherdev 1.25 3.00
xander Perezhogin .40 1.00
a Nikulin .40 1.00
axim Sheviev .40 1.00

002 Russian Olympic Faces

set was released in Russia to celebrate key players e Russian Olympic club. It is believed that the list v is incomplete. Please forward additional information to hockeymag@beckett.com.

COMPLETE SET (4) 2.76 6.89
1 Nikolai Khabibulin .80 2.00
2 Nikolai Khabibulin .80 2.00
3 Sergei Fedorov 1.20 2.50
4 Sergei Fedorov 1.20 2.50

2002 Russian Olympic Team

This set was released in Russia to celebrate members of its Olympic Team. It is believed that the listing below could be incomplete. Please forward information of additional cards to hockeymag@beckett.com.

COMPLETE SET (9) 6.00 15.00
1 Sergei Samsonov .80 2.00
2 Sergei Fedorov 1.25 3.00
3 Pavel Bure 1.00 2.50
4 Ilya Kovalchuk 3.00 8.00
5 Valeri Bure .20 .50
6 Alexei Kovalev .20 .50
7 Nikolai Khabibulin .80 2.00
8 Maxim Afinogenov .75 2.00
9 Darius Kasparaitis .10 .25

2002 Russian World Championships

This Russian-produced set honors members of that country's World Championship team.

COMPLETE SET (20) 3.00 8.00
1 Egor Podomatski .40 1.00
2 Alexander Yudin .20 .50
3 Maxim Sushinski .20 .50
4 Maxim Sokolov .40 1.00
5 Ivan Tkachenko .20 .50
6 Vladimir Antipov .20 .50
7 Roman Lyashenko .30 .75
8 Maxim Afinogenov .75 2.00
9 Alexander Guskov .20 .50
10 Alexei Koznev .20 .50
11 Sergei Gusev .20 .50
12 Slava Butsayev .20 .50
13 Ravil Gusmanov .20 .50
14 Dmitri Kalinin .20 .50
15 Valeri Karpov .20 .50
16 Andrei Kovalenko .20 .50
17 Alexander Prokopiev .20 .50
18 Sergei Vyshedkevich .20 .50
19 Dmitri Zatonsky .20 .50
20 Sergei Zhukov .20 .50

2002-03 Russian Future Stars

This Russian-produced set features many of that country's top young stars.

COMPLETE SET (20) 10.00 25.00
1 Alexander Ovechkin 6.00 15.00
2 Igor Grigorenko 1.25 3.00
3 Vladislav Evseev .75 2.00
4 Konstantin Glazachev .40 1.00
5 Fedor Tyutin .40 1.00
6 Denis Grebeshkov .40 1.00
7 Alexander Perezhogin .75 2.00
8 Kiril Koltsov .40 1.00
9 Yuri Trubachev .20 .50
10 Andrei Taratukhin .20 .50
11 Igor Mirnov .20 .50
12 Dmitri Chernykh .20 .50
13 Dmitri Shitikov .20 .50
14 Dmitri Semin .20 .50
15 Andrei Medvedev .40 1.00
16 Alexei Volkov .30 .75
17 Sergei Zinovjev .75 2.00
18 Sergei Soin .40 1.00
19 Alexei Mikhnov .20 .50
20 Ilya Nikulin .20 .50

2002-03 Russian Hockey League

This set, produced by World Sport, features the top players in the Russian circuit. Many players have multiple cards in the set from a variety of subsets including All-Stars, Team Russia and World Juniors. Card #184 appears twice.

COMPLETE SET (273) 75.00 150.00
COMMON CARD (1-273) .08 .20
SEMISTARS .20 .50
UNLISTED STARS .40 1.00
1 Evgeni Krutov .08 .20
2 Sergei Zhurikov .08 .20
3 Alexei Medvedev .08 .20
4 Juri Bogusevich .08 .20
5 Gleb Klimenko .08 .20
6 Alexei Petrov .08 .20
7 Andrei Tsarev .20 .50
8 Victor Lee .08 .20
9 Slava Zavalnyuk ENG .20 .50
10 Slava Zavalnyuk RUS .20 .50
11 Dmitri Klevakin .20 .50
12 Dmitri Semin .08 .20
13 Evgeny Fedorov .08 .20
14 Evgeny Fedorov .08 .20
15 Dmitri Yachanov .20 .50
16 Dmitri Balmin .08 .20
17 Konstantin Maslyukov .08 .20
18 Vitali Atyushov .08 .20
19 Denis Metliuk .08 .20
20 Andrei Kudinov .08 .20
21 Anton Babchuk ERC 1.25 3.00
22 Alexei Badyukov .08 .20
23 Dmitri Gogolev .08 .20
24 Alexei Chupin .08 .20
25 Denis Platonov .08 .20
26 Sergei Zolotov .08 .20
27 Jan Benda .08 .20
28 Steve Plouffe .75 2.00
29 Artem Chernov .08 .20
30 Dmitri Khomutov .20 .50
31 Sergei Zvyagin .20 .50
32 Vladimir Malenjkih .08 .20
33 Oleg Minakov .08 .20
34 Stanislav Yasechko .08 .20
35 Mike Fountain .75 2.00
36 Oleg Volkov .08 .20
37 Maxim Mikhailovsky .20 .50
38 Oleg Belkin .08 .20
39 Alexander Buturlin .08 .20
40 Alexander Bobkin .08 .20
41 Sergei Sevostjanov .08 .20
42 Andrei Frolkin .08 .20
43 Alexander Boikov .08 .20
44 Richard Shekhny .08 .20
45 Petr Vorobiev CO .04 .10
46 Andrei Esipov .08 .20
47 Mikhail Sevostjanov .08 .20
48 Alexander Semin ERC 6.00 15.00
49 Alexander Yudin .08 .20
50 Rail Rozakov .08 .20
51 Sergei Berdnikov .08 .20
52 Philip Metliuk .08 .20
53 Vadim Averkin .08 .20
54 Alexander Gutov .08 .20
55 Ilya Gorokov .08 .20
56 Maxim Kondratiev .20 .50
57 Alexander Nesterov .08 .20
58 Igor Grigorenko ERC 5.00 12.00
59 Vladislav Boulin .08 .20
60 Artur Oktyabrev .08 .20
61 Ladislav Chierny .08 .20
62 Alexander Yudin .08 .20
63 Alex Westlund .75 2.00
64 Alexander Fomitchev .40 1.00
65 David MacIsaac .20 .50
66 Andrei Tsarev .20 .50
67 Maxim Spiridonov .08 .20
68 Vadim Pokotilo .08 .20
69 Konstantin Chaschukhin .20 .50
70 Evgeni Safronov .08 .20
71 Albert Vishnyakov .08 .20
72 Christian Bronsard .75 2.00
73 Alexei Mikhnov .20 .50
74 Askhat Rakhmatullin .08 .20
75 Andrei Tarasenko .08 .20
76 Alexei Korshkov .08 .20
77 Leo Chermak .08 .20
78 Kirill Sidorenko .08 .20
79 Sergei Gomolyako .08 .20
80 Ildar Mukhometov .20 .50
81 Dmitri Dudarev .08 .20
82 Artem Ternavsky .08 .20
83 Igor Kamaev .08 .20
84 Sergei Rozin .08 .20
85 Roman Gorev .08 .20
86 Dmitri Kokorev .08 .20
87 Martin Tomasek .08 .20
88 Roman Popov .08 .20
89 Vladimir Antipin .08 .20
90 Vadim Tarasov .20 .50
91 Sergei Mikhailev CO .04 .10
92 Nikolai Zherdev ERC 6.00 15.00
93 Andrei Mukhachev .08 .20
94 Ilya Byakin .08 .20
95 Miroslav Guren .08 .20
96 Nikolai Pronin .08 .20
97 Sergei Mozyakin .08 .20
98 Maxim Ossipov .08 .20
99 Alexei Kolkunov .08 .20
100 Albert Leschev .08 .20
101 Alexander Polushin ERC 2.00 5.00
102 Igor Emeleev .08 .20
103 Sergei Luchinkin .08 .20
104 Rail Muftiev .08 .20
105 Nikolai Semin .08 .20
106 Sergei Anshakov .20 .50
107 Vadim Khomitsky .08 .20
108 Pavel Trakhanov .08 .20
109 Yan Golubovsky .20 .50
110 Dusan Salficky .40 1.00
111 Dmitri Kosmachev .08 .20
112 Vladimir Kramskoy .08 .20
113 Alexander Drozdetsky .08 .20
114 Alexei Shotkov .08 .20
115 Maxim Velikov .08 .20
116 Evgeni Akhmetov .08 .20
117 Vladimir Gorbunov .08 .20
118 Pavel Patera .08 .20
119 Maxim Sokolov .40 1.00
120 Martin Prochazka .08 .20
121 Tomas Vlasak .08 .20
122 Alexander Perezhogin .75 2.00
123 Dmitri Zatonsky .08 .20
124 Andrei Subbotin .40 1.00
125 Ravil Yakubov .08 .20
126 Valeri Pokrovsky .08 .20
127 Kirill Koltsov 1.25 3.00
128 Ramil Saifullin .08 .20
129 Maxim Sokolov .40 1.00
130 Igor Varitsky .08 .20
131 Maxim Balmochnykh .20 .50
132 Marcel Cousineau .75 2.00
133 Yuri Kuznetsov .08 .20
134 Ruslan Nurtdinov .08 .20
135 Andrei Sidyakin .08 .20
136 Sergei Zvyagin .20 .50
137 Patrik Guchko .08 .20
138 Andrei Yakhanov .08 .20
139 Evgeni Muratov .08 .20
140 Alexei Simakov .08 .20
141 Roman Baranov .08 .20
142 Alexander Zavyalov .08 .20
143 Evgeni Varlamov .08 .20
144 Alexei Tertyshny .08 .20
145 Danis Zaripov .08 .20
146 Vasili Turkovsky .08 .20
147 Alexander Guskov .08 .20
148 Alexander Zhurik .08 .20
149 Yuri Kuznetsov .08 .20
150 Maxim Balmochnykh .20 .50
151 Marat Davydov .08 .20
152 Alexei Koznev .08 .20
153 Valeri Karpov .08 .20
154 Oleg Shargorodsky .20 .50
155 Sergei Gomolyako .08 .20
156 Vladimir Tikhomirov .20 .50
157 Alexei Yegorov .20 .50
158 Konstantin Simchuk .20 .50
159 Sergei Shalamai .08 .20
160 Alexei Danilov .08 .20
161 Vadim Epanchintsev .08 .20
162 Vasily Tikhonov ACO .04 .10
163 Viktor Tikhonov CO .08 .20
164 Andrei Sapozhnikov .08 .20
165 Yuri Dobryshkin .08 .20
166 Vasili Turkovsky .08 .20
167 Evgeni Petrochinin .08 .20
168 Sergei Gimaev .08 .20
169 Alexander Yudin .08 .20
170 Alexander Shinin .08 .20
171 Yuri Trubachev .08 .20
172 Evgeny Isakov .08 .20
173 Andrei Nikitenko .08 .20
174 Alexander Shinkar .08 .20
175 Viktor Chistov .20 .50
176 Andrei Shefer .20 .50
177 Igor Shadilov .08 .20
178 Martin Brochu .75 2.00
179 Alexei Kalyuzhny .08 .20
180 Alexander Shinin .08 .20
181 Maxim Balmochnykh .20 .50
182 Vladimir Antipov .08 .20
183 Boris Tortunov .08 .20
184 Vadim Epanchintsev .08 .20
184B Yuri Trubachev .08 .20
185 Fedor Tyutin 1.25 3.00
186 Sergei Anshakov .20 .50
187 Timofei Shishkanov 2.00 5.00
188 Igor Grigorenko ERC 6.00 15.00
189 Maxim Kondratiev ERC .20 .50
190 Kirill Koltsov .75 2.00
191 Evgeny Artyukhin .08 .20
192 Konstantin Barulin ERC .40 1.00
193 Andrei Taratukhin .08 .20
194 Dmitri Fakhrutdinov .08 .20
195 Dmitri Pestunov .08 .20
196 Andrei Medvedev .75 2.00
197 Nikolai Zherdev ERC 6.00 15.00
198 Alexander Ovechkin ERC 25.00 60.00
199 Alexander Polushin ERC 2.00 5.00
200 Alexei Kaigorodov .08 .20
201 Alexander Perezhogin ERC .75 2.00
202 Mikhail Lyubushin .08 .20
203 Konstantin Korneev .20 .50
204 Denis Grebeshkov 1.25 3.00
205 Konstantin Gorovikov .08 .20
206 Vitali Proshkin .08 .20
207 Alexander Suglobov ERC .40 1.00
208 Alexei Chupin .08 .20
209 Sergei Soin .20 .50
210 Andrei Subbotin .40 1.00
211 Dmitri Vlasenkov .08 .20
212 Sergei Gusev .08 .20
213 Vladimir Vujtek .08 .20
214 Vasily Turkovsky .08 .20
215 Igor Shadilov .08 .20
216 Yuri Dobryshin .08 .20
217 Igor Podomatski .40 1.00
218 Alexander Semak .08 .20
219 Ilya Byakin .08 .20
220 Alexander Guskov .08 .20
221 Alexander Guskov .08 .20
222 Nikolai Zavarukhin .08 .20
223 Andrei Petrunin .08 .20
224 Konstantin Gorovikov .08 .20
225 Alexei Gorshkov .08 .20
226 Rustem Kamaletdinov .08 .20
227 Alexander Zavakhin .08 .20
228 Vladislav Ozolin .08 .20
229 Dmitri Krasotkin .08 .20
230 Sergei Nemchinov .20 .50
231 Alexei Chupin .08 .20
232 Andrei Kovalenko .08 .20
233 Sergei Gomolyako .08 .20
234 Vitali Yeremeyev .40 1.00
235 Sergei Zholotov .08 .20
236 Dmitri Kirilenko .08 .20
237 Sergei Askimov .08 .20
238 Ruslan Berdnikov .08 .20
239 Yuri Butsayev .08 .20
240 Sergei Zinovjev 2.00 5.00
241 Radim Tesarik .08 .20
242 Dmitri Zatonsky .08 .20
243 Konstantin Baranov .08 .20
244 Vladimir Popov CO .04 .10
245 Sergei Piskunov .08 .20
246 Vladimir Antipin .08 .20
247 Alexander Drozdetksy .08 .20
248 Sergei Vyshedkevich .20 .50
249 Timofei Shishkanov 2.00 5.00
250 Alexander Kharitonov .08 .20
251 Dmitri Fakhrutdinov .08 .20
252 Vladimir Tsyplakov .08 .20
253 Evgeni Namestnikov .20 .50
254 Vitali Atyushov .08 .20
255 Dmitri Erofeev .08 .20
256 Sergei Korolev .08 .20
257 Dmitri Erofeev .08 .20
258 Vladislav Gushin .08 .20
259 Vadim Glovatskin .08 .20
260 Renat Khasanov .08 .20
261 Nikolai Zherdev ERC 6.00 15.00
262 Dmitri Zatonsky .08 .20
263 Yan Peterik .08 .20
264 Alexei Petrov .08 .20
265 Lev Trifonov .08 .20
266 Almaz Garifullin .08 .20
267 Mikhail Sarmatin .08 .20
268 Rail Rozakov .08 .20
269 Patrick Labrecque .75 2.00
270 Oleg Khmyl .08 .20
271 Alexander Blokhin .08 .20
272 Leonid Labzov .08 .20

2002-03 Russian Lightnings

COMPLETE SET (3) 10.00 25.00
1 Alexander Ovechkin 10.00 25.00
2 Alexander Polushin .75 2.00
3 Alexander Stepanov .20 .50

2002-03 Russian SL

Little is known about the background of this set. If you have any information, please forward it to hockeymag@beckett.com.

COMPLETE SET (52) 20.00 40.00
1 Andrei Razin .20 .50
2 Dusan Salficky .40 1.00
3 Alexander Polushin .75 2.00
4 Alexander Guskov .20 .50
5 Vladimir Vujtek CO .04 .10
6 Evgeni Varlamov .20 .50
7 Andrei Skopintsev .20 .50
8 Vladimir Plyustchev CO .04 .10
9 Valeri Karpov .20 .50
10 Igor Mirnov .20 .50
11 Egor Podomatskiy .30 .75
12 Mike Fountain .30 .75
13 Mikhail Donika .20 .50
14 Vyacheslav Butsaev .20 .50
15 Andrei Esipov .20 .50
16 Igor Grigorenko 1.25 3.00
17 Yuri Moiseev CO .04 .10
18 Alexander Zhdan .20 .50
19 Maxim Sokolov .20 .50
20 Alexander Selivanov .20 .50
21 Mikhail Ivanov .20 .50
22 Ivan Hlinka CO .10 .25
23 Andrei Tsareev .20 .50
24 Dmitri Ryabykin .20 .50
25 Jiri Slegr .20 .50
26 Sergei Soin .30 .75
27 Anton But .20 .50
28 Alexander Ovechkin 10.00 25.00
29 Vladimir Antipov .20 .50
30 Evgeni Makarov .20 .50
31 Sergei Naumov .20 .50
32 Andrei Pyatanov CO .04 .10
33 Sergei Gusev .20 .50
34 Viktor Tikhonov CO .04 .10
35 Mikhail Lyubushin .20 .50
36 Dmitri Yachanov .20 .50
37 Tomas Vlasak .20 .50
38 Alex Westlund .40 1.00
39 Vladislav Boulin .20 .50
40 Jan Peterek .20 .50
41 Vladimir Vorobiev .20 .50
42 Petr Vorobiev CO .04 .10
43 Vasily Turkovski .20 .50
44 Nikolai Zherdev 1.50 4.00
45 Andrei Taratukhin .20 .50
46 Viktor Aleksandrov .20 .50
47 Yuri Dobryshkin .20 .50
48 Alexander Savchenkov .20 .50
49 Sergei Voronov .20 .50
50 Alexei Terestchenko .20 .50
51 Alexei Shkotov .20 .50
52 Alexander Zevakhin .20 .50

2002-03 Russian Transfert

COMPLETE SET (31) 6.00 15.00
1 Alexander Semin .40 1.00
2 Alexander Golts .20 .50
3 Georgi Evtyukhin .20 .50
4 Alexander Korolyuk .20 .50
5 Marcel Cousineau .30 .75
6 Sergei Bautin .20 .50
7 Vitali Lutkevich .20 .50
8 Valeri Zelepukin .20 .50
9 Nikolai Zherdev 1.25 3.00
10 Vladimir Vorobiev .20 .50
11 Sergei Petrenko .20 .50
12 Osmo Soutukorva .20 .50
13 Sergei Korolev .20 .50
14 Alex Westlund .20 .50
15 Denis Afinogenov .20 .50
16 Vadim Tarasov .40 1.00
17 Alexander Zhdan .20 .50
18 Alexander Selivanov .20 .50
19 Vladislav Boulin .20 .50
20 Maxim Sokolov .20 .50
21 Dmitri Gogolev .20 .50
22 Alexei Volkov .30 .75
23 Ravil Yakubov .20 .50
24 Mikhail Ivanov .20 .50
25 Alexei Egorov .20 .50
26 Viktor Gordiyuk .20 .50
27 Alexander Semak .20 .50
28 Bruce Gardiner .20 .50
29 Rodrigo Lavins .20 .50
30 Steve Plouffe .30 .75
31 Sergei Krivokrasov .20 .50

2002-03 Russian Transfert Promos

COMPLETE SET (6) 2.00 5.00
1 Vladimir Vorobiev .40 1.00
2 Osmo Soutukorvo .40 1.00
3 Vitali Lutkevich .40 1.00
4 Denis Afinogenov .40 1.00
5 Alexei Volkov .75 2.00
6 Maxim Sokolov .75 2.00

2002-03 Russian Ultimate Line

COMPLETE SET (13) 6.00 15.00
1 Sergei Zvyagin .40 1.00
2 Dusan Salficky .75 2.00
3 Alexander Yeremenko .40 1.00
4 Sergei Nikolaev .40 1.00
5 Mike Fountain 1.25 3.00
6 Steve Plouffe 1.25 3.00
7 Igor Karpenko .75 2.00
8 Oleg Glebov .40 1.00
9 Patrick Labrecque 1.25 3.00
10 Alexei Volkov .75 2.00
11 Vadim Tarasov .75 2.00
12 Andrei Medvedev .75 2.00
13 Vitali Yeremeyev .75 2.00

2002-03 Russian Young Lions

COMPLETE SET (17) 10.00 25.00
1 Dmitri Kazionov .20 .50
2 Alexander Ovechkin 6.00 15.00
3 Igor Mirnov .20 .50
4 Alexander Semin .40 1.00
5 Igor Grigorenko 1.25 3.00
6 Sergei Soin .30 .75
7 Denis Grebeshkov .40 1.00
8 Alexei Kaigorodov .20 .50
9 Dmitry Pestunov .20 .50
10 Alexander Polushin .75 2.00
11 Konstantin Mikhailov .20 .50
12 Iliy Nikulin .20 .50
13 Alexander Perezhogin .75 2.00
14 Alexei Mikhnov .20 .50
15 Nikolai Zherdev 1.25 3.00
16 Fedor Tyutin .40 1.00
NNO Alexander Ovechkin PROMO 6.00 15.00

2003 Russian Under-18 Team

COMPLETE SET (22) 15.00 35.00
1 Grigori Shafigulin .20 .50
2 Dmitri Petrov .20 .50
3 Alexei Ivanov .20 .50
4 Evgeni Malkin 6.00 15.00
5 Dmitri Pestunov .20 .50
6 Vitali Anikienko .20 .50
7 Dmitri Chernykh .20 .50
8 Anton Dubinin .20 .50
9 Rustan Sidikov .30 .75
10 Alexander Naurov .20 .50
11 Denis Pervyshin .20 .50
12 Alexander Ovechkin 6.00 15.00
13 Denis Ezhov .20 .50
14 Georgi Misharin .20 .50
15 Anton Belov .20 .50
16 Artem Nosov .20 .50
17 Denis Loginov .20 .50
18 Dmitri Kosmachev .20 .50
19 Konstantin Makarov .20 .50
20 Sergei Gorelov .30 .75
21 Konstantin Glazachev .60 1.50
22 Dmitri Shitikov .20 .50

2003 Russian World Championship Stars

COMPLETE SET (35) 10.00 25.00
1 Jan Benda .10 .25
2 Leonid Tambievs .10 .25
3 Jan Lasak .30 .75
4 Miroslav Hlinka .10 .25
5 Sergei Naumov .20 .50
6 Atvars Tribuntsovs .10 .25
7 Peter Forsberg 1.25 3.00
8 Tommy Salo .30 .75
9 Mats Sundin .60 1.50
10 Henrik Zetterberg .60 1.50
11 Mikael Tellqvist .60 1.50
12 Dany Heatley .75 2.00
13 Sean Burke .40 1.00
14 Mike Comrie .30 .75
15 Kris Draper .40 1.00
16 Roberto Luongo 1.25 3.00
17 Anson Carter .40 1.00
18 Miroslav Satan .40 1.00
19 Peter Bondra .40 1.00
20 Zigmund Palffy .40 1.00
21 Robert Svehla .10 .25
22 Richard Zednik .10 .25
23 Arturs Irbe .40 1.00
24 Milan Hejduk .60 1.50
25 Jiri Hudler .75 2.00
26 Robert Reichel .10 .25
27 Martin Straka .20 .50
28 Radek Duda .10 .25
29 Alexander Khavanov .10 .25
30 Ilya Kovalchuk 1.00 2.50
31 Maxim Sokolov .20 .50
32 Tomas Vokoun .60 1.50
33 Ryan Smith .60 1.50
34 Rodrigo Lavins .10 .25
35 Eric Brewer .20 .50

2003 Russian World Championship Team 2003

COMPLETE SET (24) 6.00 15.00
1 Maxim Sokolov .20 .50
2 Igor Podomatski .20 .50
3 Alexander Frolov .75 2.00
4 Alexander Semin 1.00 2.50
5 Pavel Datsyuk 1.25 3.00
6 Ivan Novoseltsev .10 .25
7 Sergei Zinovjev .40 1.00
8 Vladimir Antipov .10 .25
9 Dmitri Kalinin .10 .25
10 Vitali Proshkin .10 .25
11 Sergei Soin .10 .25
12 Alexander Suglobov .20 .50
13 Alexander Zhdan .10 .25
14 Sergei Vyshedkevich .10 .25
15 Sergei Gusev .10 .25
16 Oleg Saprykin .20 .50
17 Denis Arkhipov .20 .50
18 Dmitri Erofeev .10 .25
19 Igor Grigorenko .75 2.00
20 Alexander Guskov .10 .25
21 Vasily Turkovsky .10 .25
22 Alexander Khavanov .10 .25
23 Ilya Kovalchuk 2.00 5.00
24 Alexei Kaigorodov .40 1.00

2003 Russian World Championships Preview

COMPLETE SET (5) 6.00 15.00
1 Alexander Ovechkin 6.00 15.00
2 Pavel Datsyuk .75 2.00
3 Denis Loginov .20 .50
4 Denis Arkhipov .20 .50
5 Ilya Kovalchuk 1.50 4.00

2003-04 Russian Avangard Omsk

This 28-card set honours the 2002-03 champions of the Russian league. It was produced by World Sport.

COMPLETE SET (28) 4.00 10.00
1 Maxim Sokolov .20 .50
2 Konstantin Baranov .10 .25
3 Maxim Sushinski .10 .25
4 Dmitri Zatonsky .10 .25
5 Tomas Vlasak .10 .25
6 Oleg Tverdovsky .10 .25
7 Sergei Krivokrasov .10 .25
8 Stanislav Shalnov .10 .25
9 Dmitri Subbotin .10 .25
10 Dmitri Ryabikin .10 .25
11 Valeri Belousov CO .04 .10
12 Igor Nikitin .10 .25
13 Pavel Patera .10 .25
14 Alexander Popov .10 .25
15 Ramil Saifullin .10 .25
16 Yuri Yermolin .10 .25
17 Alexander Golovin .10 .25
18 Alexander Prokopiev .10 .25
19 Evgeni Khatsei .10 .25
20 Oleg Grachev .10 .25
21 Jaroslav Bednar .20 .50
22 Oleg Orekhovsky .10 .25
23 Yuri Panov .10 .25
24 Anton Kuzmin .10 .25
25 Vladimir Antipin .10 .25
26 Vitali Semenchenko .20 .50
27 Anatoli Bardin GM .04 .10
28 Checklist .04 .10

2003-04 Russian Hockey League

This set was produced by World Sport in Russia.

COMPLETE SET (283) 50.00 125.00
1 Roman Salnikov .08 .20
2 Denis Tyrin .08 .20
3 Almaz Garifullin .08 .20
4 Sergei Shalamai .08 .20
5 Andrei Evstafiev .08 .20
6 Nikolai Zherdev 2.00 5.00
7 Mikhail Sarmatin .08 .20
8 Dusan Salficky .40 1.00
9 Sergei Mozyakin .08 .20
10 Andrei Razin .08 .20
11 Yuri Butsayev .08 .20
12 Oleg Romashko .20 .50
13 Evgeny Fedorov .08 .20
14 Danis Zaripov .08 .20
15 Gennady Razin .08 .20
16 Oleg Filimonov .20 .50
17 Dmitri Tarasov .08 .20
18 Vitali Shulakov .08 .20
19 Oleg Minakov .08 .20
20 Jan Benda .08 .20
21 Alexander Zevakhin .08 .20
22 Alexander Yudin .08 .20
23 Alexander Yudin .08 .20
24 SKA St. Pete's .04 .10
25 Dynamo Moscow .04 .10
26 Vitali Yeremeev .20 .50
27 Alexei Volkov .20 .50
28 Alexander Yeremenko .20 .50
29 Mikhail Lyubishin .08 .20
30 Ilya Nikulin .08 .20
31 Alexei Troschinsky .08 .20
32 Igor Mirnov .08 .20
33 Alexander Kuvaldin .08 .20
34 Igor Schyadilov .08 .20
35 Andrei Skopintsev .08 .20
36 Alexander Kharitonov .08 .20
37 Alexei Chupin .08 .20
38 Vadim Shakhrajchuk .08 .20
39 Alexander Savchenkov .08 .20
40 Vladislav Boulin .08 .20
41 Alexei Kudashov .08 .20
42 Alexander Zhdan .08 .20
43 Alexei Tereschenko .08 .20
44 Alexander Stepanov .08 .20
45 Alexander Ovechkin 10.00 25.00
46 Sergei Vyshedkevich .20 .50
47 Miroslav Hlinka .08 .20
48 Dmitri Starostenko .08 .20
49 Alexander Stepanov .08 .20
50 Alexander Ovechkin 10.00 25.00
51 Tomas Garant .20 .50
52 Vladimir Vorobiev .08 .20
53 Yuri Babenko .08 .20
54 Ruslan Zainullin .20 .50
55 Robert Kantor .08 .20
56 Denis Kartsev .08 .20
57 Vladislav Evseev .40 1.00
58 Zinatula Bilyaletdinov CO .08 .20
59 Alexei Yegorov .20 .50
60 Sergei Naumov .40 1.00
61 Sergei Semin .08 .20
62 Valeri Pokrovski .08 .20
63 Torbjorn Johansson .08 .20
64 Artem Ostroushko .08 .20
65 Andrei Spiridonov .08 .20
66 Marat Davydov .08 .20
67 Nikolai Syrtsov .08 .20
68 Vyacheslav Zavalnyuk .08 .20
69 Andrei Kozyrev .08 .20
70 Yan Golubovsky .20 .50
71 Jan Lasak .75 2.00
72 Konstantin Kasjyanchuk .08 .20
73 Egor Bashkatov .08 .20
74 Andrei Potaichuk .08 .20
75 Egor Mikhailov .08 .20
76 Andrei Galushkin .08 .20
77 Mike Watt .20 .50
78 Alexei Akifjev .08 .20
79 Andrei Pchelyakov .08 .20
80 Evgeni Tunik .08 .20
81 Pavel Boichenko .08 .20
82 Valeri Zelepukin .08 .20
83 Oleg Boltunov .08 .20
84 Alexei Tsvetkov .08 .20
85 Boris Mikhailov CO .20 .50
86 Eduard Kudermetov .08 .20
87 Sergei Berdnikov .08 .20
88 Vladimir Antipin .08 .20
89 Oleg Tverdovsky .08 .20
90 Denis Khlopotnov .08 .20
91 Fedor Tyutin .40 1.00
92 Andrei Shurupov .08 .20
93 Evgeny Koronov .08 .20
94 Albert Leschev .08 .20
95 Sergei Yerkovich .08 .20
96 Vladimir Tyurikov .08 .20
97 Dmitri Vershinin .08 .20
98 Alexei Krutov .08 .20
99 German Titov .08 .20
100 Igor Nikolaev .08 .20
101 Maxim Shevyev .08 .20
102 Andrei Ershov .08 .20
103 Ilya Krikunov .08 .20
104 Peter Skudra .40 1.00
105 Andrei Galkin .08 .20
106 Andei Dylevski .08 .20
107 Ondrej Steiner .08 .20
108 Vadim Brezgunov .08 .20
109 Roman Oksiuta .08 .20
110 Oleg Belkin .08 .20
111 Alexander Boikov .08 .20
112 Dmitri Kazionov .08 .20
113 Vladimir Malenkikh .08 .20
114 Ruslan Bernikov .08 .20
115 Alexander Buturlin .08 .20
116 Andrei Esipov .08 .20
117 Maxim Semenov .08 .20
118 Yakov Rachinsky .08 .20
119 Mikhail Balandin .08 .20
120 Dmitri Vorobiev .08 .20
121 J.F. Labbe .40 1.00
122 Rinat Khasanov .08 .20
123 Vladimir Loginov .08 .20
124 Alexei Deev .08 .20
125 Alexander Grishin .08 .20
126 Sergei Gomolyako .08 .20
127 Anatoli Filatov .08 .20
128 Vasili Koshechkin .20 .50
129 Alexander Seluyanov .08 .20
130 Ladislav Cherny .08 .20
131 Igor Varitski .08 .20
132 Maxim Yakutsenya .08 .20
133 Alexander Gutov .08 .20
134 Stanislav Zhmakin .08 .20
135 Mikhail Sevostjanov .08 .20
136 Alexander Skugarev .08 .20
137 Sergei Sevostjanov .08 .20
138 Petr Vorobiev CO .04 .10
139 Yevgeni Safronov .08 .20
140 Ilya Vorobiev .08 .20
141 Alexander Titov .08 .20
142 Ruslan Nurtdinov .08 .20
143 Alexander Zavjalov .08 .20
144 Vadim Epanchinsev .08 .20
145 Jamie Ram .75 2.00
146 Viktor Chistov CO .04 .10
147 Tomas Hlubna .08 .20
148 Alexander Semak .08 .20
149 Sergei Gimaev .08 .20
150 Nikolai Makarov CO .04 .10
151 Atvars Tribuntsovs .08 .20
152 Vladislav Ozolin .08 .20
153 Nikolai Semin .08 .20
154 Vitali Proshkin .08 .20
155 Vassiliy Turkovsky .08 .20
156 Denis Platonov .08 .20
157 Radek Duda .08 .20
158 Sergei Korolev .08 .20
159 Konstantin Korneev .20 .50
160 Sergei Arakaev .08 .20
161 Denis Denisov .08 .20
162 Alexander Drozdetsky .08 .20
163 Alexander Cherbayev .08 .20
164 Maxim Mikhailovsky .20 .50
165 Mikhail Tyulyapkin .08 .20
166 Valeri Kamensky .08 .20
167 Vladimir Vujtek .08 .20
168 Konstanin Glazachev .20 .50
169 Konstantin Mikhailov .08 .20
170 Egor Shastin .08 .20
171 Alexei Mikhnov .40 1.00
172 Alexander Fomitchev .30 .75
173 Daniel Branda .08 .20
174 Eric Charron .20 .50
175 Miroslav Guren .08 .20
176 Ravil Yakubov .08 .20
177 Dmitri Dudarev .08 .20
178 Ruslan Batyrshin .08 .20
179 Ruslan Shafikov .08 .20
180 Martin Cech .08 .20
181 Tero Lehtera .08 .20
182 Egor Mikhailov .08 .20
183 Valeri Pokrovsky .08 .20
184 Vadim Sharifjanov .20 .50
185 David Pospisil .08 .20
186 Yan Golubovsky .20 .50
187 Angel Nikolov .20 .50
188 Viktor Alexandrov .20 .50
189 Dmitri Pankov .08 .20
190 Jiri Marushak .08 .20
191 Oleg Gross CO .04 .10
192 Sergei Moskalev .08 .20
193 Alexei Medvedev .08 .20
194 Vadim Tarasov .30 .75
195 Evgeny Shaiger .08 .20
196 Nikolai Soloviev CO .04 .10
197 Evgeny Lapin .08 .20
198 Mikhail Chernov .08 .20
199 Zdenek Skorepa .08 .20
200 Sergei Mikhailev CO .04 .10
201 Sergei Naumov .40 1.00
202 Evgeny Korolev .08 .20
203 Rail Rozakov .08 .20
204 Yuri Kuznetsov .20 .50
205 Sergei Berdnikov .08 .20
206 Yuri Kuznetsov .20 .50
207 Andrei Sapozhnikov .08 .20
208 Andrei Nikitenko .08 .20
209 Andrei Petrunin .08 .20

210 Yuri Dobryshkin .08 .20
211 Sergei Gimaev .08 .20
212 Alexander Astashev CO .04 .10
213 Vadim Khomitsky .08 .20
214 Maxim Yakutsenya .08 .20
215 Martin Richter .08 .20
216 Sergei Anshakov .20 .50
217 Denis Parshin .20 .50
218 Sergei Berezin .08 .20
219 Jan Hejda .08 .20
220 Dmitri Levinsky .08 .20
221 Norm Maracle .75 2.00
222 Pavel Patera .08 .20
223 Tomas Vlasak .08 .20
224 Jaroslav Bednar .20 .50
225 Konstantin Baranov .08 .20
226 Maxim Sokolov .30 .75
227 Denis Kuzmenko .20 .50
228 Oleg Burlitsky .08 .20
229 Alexei Potemkin .08 .20
230 Alexander Zhukov .08 .20
231 Ilnaz Zagitov .08 .20
232 Dmitri Yushkevich .08 .20
233 Martin Hlavacka .08 .20
234 Alexander Guskov .08 .20
235 Robert Kantor .08 .20
236 Marat Vailullin .08 .20
237 Zdenek Orct .20 .50
238 David Nemirovsky .20 .50
239 Jiri Hudler 2.00 5.00
240 Maxim Krivonozhkin .08 .20
241 Yuri Butsayev .20 .50
242 Andrei Esipov .08 .20
243 Rudolf Guna .08 .20
244 Philip Metliuk .08 .20
245 Alexander Lyubimov .08 .20
246 Jiri Trvaj .20 .50
247 Dmitri Cherhukh .08 .20
248 Renat Khairetdinov .08 .20
249 Artem Vostrikov .08 .20
250 Peter Skudra .40 1.00
251 Evgeny Malkin 15.00 40.00
252 Nikolai Tsulygin .08 .20
253 Andrei Kostitsyn 4.00 10.00
254 Denis Belsky .08 .20
255 Andrei Davletov .08 .20
256 Sergei Konkov .08 .20
257 Denis Loginov .08 .20
258 Michael Martin .08 .20
259 David Moravec .08 .20
260 Yan Peterik .08 .20
261 Lubomir Sekeras .08 .20
262 Toivo Suursoo .08 .20
263 Marat Salimov .08 .20
264 Sergei Fadeev .08 .20
265 Mikhail Shukaev .08 .20
266 Dmitri Yachanov .20 .50
267 Lukas Zib .08 .20
268 Butsayev Brothers .08 .20
269 Sergei Sevostjanov .08 .20
270 Mikhail Sevostjanov .08 .20
271 Ruslan Nurtdinov .08 .20
272 Frank Banham .20 .50
273 Herbert Vasiliev .08 .20
274 Dave Karpa .20 .50
275 Kirill Lyamin .20 .50
276 Mikhail Chernov .08 .20
277 Ildar Mukhometov .20 .50
278 Ilya Zubov .08 .20
279 Sergei Shinkar .08 .20
280 Sergei Voronov .08 .20
281 Sergei Borisov .20 .50
282 Yuri Trubachev .08 .20
283 Sergei Bernatsky .08 .20

2003-04 Russian Metallurg Magnitogorsk

COMPLETE SET (9) 3.00 8.00
1 Vitali Atyushov .40 1.00
2 Alexander Boikov .40 1.00
3 Evgeni Gladskikh .40 1.00
4 Oleg Davydov .40 1.00
5 Nikolia Ignatov .40 1.00
6 Dmitri Pestunov .40 1.00
7 Ivan Sidorov .40 1.00
8 Martin Cech .40 1.00
9 Lubomir Vaic .40 1.00

2003-04 Russian National Team

Produced by World Sport, this set highlights 36 players who wore the jersey of Russia's various national teams over the 2003-04 season.

COMPLETE SET (36) 10.00 25.00
1 Alexei Badyukov .20 .50
2 Danis Zaripov .20 .50
3 Sergei Mozyakin .20 .50
4 Andrei Mukhachev .20 .50
5 Igor Emeleev .20 .50
6 Denis Gusmanov .20 .50
7 Maxim Spiridonov .20 .50
8 Alexei Yegorov .20 .50
9 Alexander Stepanov .20 .50
10 Nikolai Semin .20 .50
11 Alexander Drozdetsky .20 .50
12 Alexander Skugarev .20 .50
13 Sergei Korolev .20 .50
14 Vladimir Chebaturkin .20 .50
15 Andrei Kovalenko .20 .50
16 Vitali Yachmenev .20 .50
17 Igor Volkov .20 .50
18 Alexander Boikov .20 .50
19 Yuri Dobryshkin .20 .50
20 Alexander Ryazantsev .20 .50
21 Maxim Sushinsky .30 .75
22 Alexander Prokopiev .20 .50
23 Oleg Tverdovsky .20 .50
24 Alexander Ovechkin 6.00 15.00
25 Viktor Tikhonov .20 .50
26 Vladimir Malenkikh .20 .50
27 Valeri Zelepukin .20 .50
28 Dmitri Yushkevich .20 .50
29 Andrei Bashkirov .20 .50
30 Alexander Buturlin .20 .50
31 Leonid Kanareikin .20 .50
32 Artur Oktyabrev .20 .50
33 Maxim Kondratiev .20 .50
34 Vyacheslav Butsayev .20 .50
35 Alexander Savchenkov .20 .50
36 Sergei Krivokrasov .20 .50

2003-04 Russian Postcards

This postcard-sized set features 12 members of Russia's national team. The cards feature only jersey numbers, so they are listed below alphabetically.

COMPLETE SET (12) 8.00 20.00
1 Viacheslav Butsayev .75 2.00
2 Alexander Guskov .75 2.00
3 Andrei Kovalenko .75 2.00
4 Sergei Mozyakin .75 2.00
5 Egor Podomatsky .75 2.00
6 Alexander Prokopiev .75 2.00
7 Maxim Sokolov .75 2.00
8 Maxim Sushinsky .75 2.00
9 Oleg Tverdovsky .75 2.00
10 Igor Volkov .75 2.00
11 Vitali Yachmenev .75 2.00
12 Dmitry Zatonsky .75 2.00

2003-04 Russian SL

COMPLETE SET (40) 15.00 30.00
1 Alexei Chupin .20 .50
2 Radek Duda .20 .50
3 Alexei Yegorov .40 1.00
4 Tomas Harant .20 .50
5 Miroslav Hlinka .20 .50
6 Tomas Hlubna .20 .50
7 J.F. Labbe .30 .75
8 Oleg Orekhovsky .20 .50
9 Alexander Ovechkin 4.00 10.00
10 Andrei Razin .20 .50
11 Dmitri Ryabykin .20 .50
12 Konstantin Simchuk .40 1.00
13 Andrei Subbotin .20 .50
14 Yuri Trubachev .20 .50
15 Ravil Yakubov .20 .50
16 Nikolai Zherdev 1.25 3.00
17 Vadim Tarasov .40 1.00
18 Sergei Naumovs .40 1.00
19 Christian Bronsard .40 1.00
20 Dmitri Kazionov .20 .50
21 Sergei Gomolyako .20 .50
22 Alexander Kuvaldin .20 .50
23 Peter Skudra .40 1.00
24 Alex Westlund .40 1.00
25 Sergei Shalamai .20 .50
26 Atvars Tribuntsovs .20 .50
27 Alexei Kudashov .20 .50
28 Ruslan Nurtdinov .20 .50
29 David Moravec .20 .50
30 Alexei Tertyshny .20 .50
31 Mikhail Shukaev .40 1.00
32 Alexei Vasiliev .20 .50
33 Kirill Lyamin .40 1.00
34 Daniel Branda .20 .50
35 Vadim Khomitsky .20 .50
36 Vitali Yeremeev .40 1.00
37 Lubomir Vaic .20 .50
38 Ruslan Zainullin .20 .50
39 Alexander Savchenkov .20 .50
40 Sergei Mozyakin .20 .50

2003-04 Russian Young Lions

COMPLETE SET (7) 5.00 12.00
1 Dmitri Chernykh .40 1.00
2 Alexander Semin .60 1.50
3 Alexander Ovechkin 4.00 10.00
4 Maxim Shevjev .40 1.00
5 Dmitri Pestunov .40 1.00
6 Maxim Krivonozhkin .40 1.00
7 Kirill Lyamin .40 1.00

2004 Russian Super League All-Stars

COMPLETE SET (31) 6.00 15.00
1 Egor Podomatsky .40 1.00
2 Viktor Chistov .40 1.00
3 Dmitry Krasotkin .20 .50
4 Alexei Troschinsky .20 .50
5 Vladimir Tyurikov .20 .50
6 Alexander Yudin .20 .50
7 Alexander Semak .20 .50
8 Marat Davydov .20 .50
9 Dmitry Gogolev .20 .50
10 Andrei Razin .20 .50
11 Valeri Zelepukin .20 .50
12 Egor Mikhailov .20 .50
13 Pavel Boichenko .20 .50
14 Vladimir Samylin .20 .50
15 Vladimir Vorobiev .20 .50
16 Alexei Chupin .20 .50
17 Konstantin Simchuk .40 1.00
18 Alexander Fomitchev .40 1.00
19 Sergei Klimentiev .20 .50
20 Andrei Evstafiev .20 .50
21 Jiri Marushak .20 .50
22 Nikolai Tsulygin .20 .50
23 Oleg Khmylev .20 .50
24 Jan Benda .20 .50
25 Sergei Gomolyako .20 .50
26 Igor Varitsky .20 .50
27 Andrei Skabelka .20 .50
28 Evgeny Koreshkov .20 .50
29 Sergei Moskalev .20 .50
30 Dmitri Kvartalnov .20 .50
31 Vadim Epanchintsev .20 .50

2004 Russian Under-18 Team

COMPLETE SET (23) 15.00 40.00
1 Adgur Dzhugelia .20 .50
2 Evgeni Biryukov .20 .50
3 Sergei Salnikov .20 .50
4 Kirill Lyamin .30 .75
5 Dmitri Shitikov UER .20 .50
(first name listed as Sergei
6 Rinat Ibragimov .20 .50
7 Anton Belov .20 .50
8 Sergei Shirokov .20 .50
9 Nikolai Kulemin .20 .50
10 Ivan Kasutin .30 .75
11 Evgeni Malkin 10.00 25.00
12 Roman Voloshenko .40 1.00
13 Alexander Aksenenko .20 .50
14 Sergei Karetin .20 .50
15 Enver Lisin .40 1.00
16 Denis Parshin .20 .50
17 Alexander Plyuschev .20 .50
18 Mikhail Yunkov .20 .50
19 Sergei Ogorodnikov .20 .50
20 Anton Khudobin .30 .75
21 Alexei Yemelin .40 1.00
22 Alexander Radulov 4.00 10.00
NNO Checklist .02 .10

2004 Russian World Championship Team

This set, produced by World Sport, features the 2004 World Championship team.

COMPLETE SET (25) 15.00 30.00
1 Maxim Afinogenov .60 1.50
2 Alexei Yashin .20 .50
3 Nikolai Pronin .20 .50
4 Maxim Kondratiev .20 .50
5 Andrei Skopintsev .20 .50
6 Alexander Prokopiev .20 .50
7 Alexei Morozov .20 .50
8 Alexander Ovechkin 8.00 20.00
9 Maxim Sushinski .20 .50
10 Alexander Guskov .20 .50
11 Alexander Skugarev .20 .50
12 Vasili Turkovski .20 .50
13 Alexander Fomitchev .30 .75
14 Andrei Bashkirov .20 .50
15 Valeri Zelepukin .20 .50
16 Vitali Proshkin .20 .50
17 Ilya Kovalchuk 2.00 5.00
18 Maxim Sokolov .20 .50
19 Dmitri Bykov .20 .50
20 Oleg Tverdovsky .20 .50
21 Slava Butsayev .20 .50
22 Dmitri Yushkevich .20 .50
23 Dmitri Kalinin .20 .50
24 Vladimir Antipov .20 .50
25 Egor Podomatski .30 .75

2004 Russian World Junior Team

This team set was sold in Russia after the team won the WJC Gold medal in Finland. Produced by World Sport.

COMPLETE SET (22) 15.00 40.00
1 Konstantin Korneev .20 .50
2 Denis Grot .20 .50
3 Alexander Ovechkin 8.00 20.00
4 Dmitry Pestunov .20 .50
5 Alexei Shkotov .20 .50
6 Sergei Gimaev .20 .50
7 Andrei Spiridonov .20 .50
8 Ilya Krikunov .20 .50
9 Evgeni Malkin 8.00 20.00
10 Sergei Anshakov .20 .50
11 Mikhail Tyulyapkin .20 .50
12 Sergei Karpov .20 .50
13 Grigory Shafigulin .20 .50
14 Alexander Kozhevnikov .20 .50
15 Yuri Ermolin .20 .50
16 Dmitry Kosmachev .20 .50
17 Denis Ezhov .20 .50
18 Evgeny Tunik .20 .50
19 Dmitry Kazionov .20 .50
20 Alexander Semin 1.25 3.00
21 Konstantin Barulin .40 1.00
22 Denis Khudyakov .40 1.00

2004-05 Russian Back to Russia

COMPLETE SET (41) 12.00 30.00
1 Alexander Frolov .75 2.00
2 Pavel Datsyuk 1.50 4.00
3 Konstantin Koltsov .20 .50
4 Andrei Markov .40 1.00
5 Slava Kozlov .40 1.00
6 Dmitri Afanasenkov .20 .50
7 Igor Korolev .20 .50
8 Ilya Kovalchuk 4.00 10.00
9 Artem Chubarov .20 .50
10 Nikolai Zherdev 1.00 2.50
11 Alexander Semin 1.50 4.00
12 Maxim Kuznetsov .20 .50
13 Andrei Nikolishin .20 .50
14 Alexei Ponikarovsky .40 1.00
15 Maxim Afinogenov .75 2.00
16 Oleg Saprykin .20 .50
17 Viktor Kozlov .40 1.00
18 Andrei Nazarov .20 .50
19 Fedor Fedorov .40 1.00
20 Maxim Kondratiev .20 .50
21 Alexei Morozov .20 .50
22 Dmitry Kalinin .20 .50
23 Alexander Karpovtsev .20 .50
24 Nikolai Khabibulin .75 2.00
25 Oleg Kvasha .20 .50
26 Vitaly Vishnevsky .40 1.00
27 Sergei Gonchar .40 1.00
28 Darius Kasparaitis .20 .50
29 Alexander Perezhogin .40 1.00
30 Kirill Safronov .20 .50
31 Fedor Tyutin .20 .50
32 Nikolai Antropov .40 1.00
33 Evgeny Nabokov 1.00 2.50
34 Sergei Brylin .20 .50
35 Alexei Kovalev .40 1.00
36 Alexei Yashin .40 1.00
37 Ruslan Salei .20 .50
38 Sergei Samsonov 1.00 2.50
39 Alexei Zhitnik .20 .50
40 Igor Radulov .20 .50
41 Denis Arkhipov .40 1.00

2004-05 Russian Hope

COMPLETE SET (6) 15.00 30.00
1 Alexander Ovechkin 8.00 20.00
2 Evgeni Malkin
3 Enver Lisin .40 1.00
4 Anton Belov .40 1.00
5 Yakov Rylov .40 1.00
6 Viacheslav Seluyanov .40 1.00

2004-05 Russian Legion

COMPLETE SET (41) 15.00 40.00
1 Pavel Rosa .20 .50
2 Jaromir Jagr 6.00 15.00
3 Lubomir Bartecko .20 .50
4 Martin Strbak .20 .50
5 Martin Havlat 1.50 4.00
6 Fred Brathwaite .75 2.00
7 Tomas Harant .20 .50
8 Vladimir Tsyplakov .20 .50
9 Joni Puurula .20 .50
10 Dainius Zubrus .20 .50
11 Vadim Shakhraichuk .20 .50
12 Jussi Markkanen .40 1.00
13 Vladimir Hudacek .20 .50
14 Curtis Murphy .20 .50
15 Roman Tomas .20 .50
16 Jiri Trvaj .20 .50
17 Jaroslav Bednar .20 .50
18 Miroslav Lipovsky .20 .50
19 Martin Cech .20 .50
20 Jaroslav Hlinka .20 .50
21 Lukas Zib .20 .50
23 Jan Hejda .20 .50
24 Vincent Lecavalier 6.00 15.00
25 Miroslav Guren .20 .50
27 Petr Sykora .40 1.00
28 Kamil Piros .20 .50
29 Patrik Elias .40 1.00
30 Petr Kubos .20 .50
31 Marc Lamothe .40 1.00
32 Roman Malek .20 .50
33 Aigars Cipruss .20 .50
34 Markus Korhonen .20 .50
35 Jan Benda .20 .50
36 Dusan Salficky .40 1.00
37 Dany Heatley 6.00 15.00
38 Mika Pietila .20 .50
39 Pauli Jaks .20 .50
41 Atvars Tribuntsovs .20 .50

2004-05 Russian Moscow Dynamo

COMPLETE SET (36) 15.00 35.00
1 Maxim Afinogenov .75 2.00
2 Yuri Babenko .20 .50
3 Lubomir Bartecko .20 .50
4 Vladislav Boulin .20 .50
5 Albert Vishnyakov .20 .50
6 Vladimir Vorobiev .20 .50
7 Sergey Vyshedkevich .20 .50
8 Martin Havlat 1.50 4.00
9 Tomas Harant .20 .50
10 Pavel Datsyuk 1.25 3.00
11 Vladislav Evseev .20 .50
12 Vitaly Yeremeev .40 1.00
13 Alexander Yeremenko .40 1.00
14 Vladimir Karpov .20 .50
15 Denis Kartsev .20 .50
16 Alexei Komarov .20 .50
17 Alexei Kudashov .20 .50
18 Maxim Kuznetsov .20 .50
19 Andrei Markov .20 .50
20 Igor Mirnov .20 .50
21 Ilya Nikulin .20 .50
22 Alexander Ovechkin 8.00 20.00
23 Oleg Orekhovsky .20 .50
24 Konstantin Romanov .20 .50
25 Pavel Rosa .20 .50
26 Yakov Rylov .20 .50
27 Alexander Savchenkov .20 .50
28 Andrei Skopintsev .20 .50
29 Alexander Stepanov .20 .50
30 Alexei Tereschenko .20 .50
31 Alexei Troschinsky .20 .50
32 Alexander Kharitonov .20 .50
33 Artem Chubarov .20 .50
34 Alexei Chupin .20 .50
35 Igor Shadilov .20 .50
36 Vladimir Krikunov CO .20 .50

2004-05 Russian RHL

COMPLETE SET (22) 15.00 30.00
1 Sergey Borisov .20 .50
2 Andrei Kovalenko .20 .50
3 Maxim Potapov .20 .50
4 Roman Sychev .20 .50
5 Andrei Taratukhin .20 .50
6 Maxim Ovchinikov .20 .50
7 Denis Mashanov .20 .50
8 Alexander Zavyzlov .20 .50
9 Andrei Petrunin .20 .50
10 Mikhail Varnakov .20 .50
11 Sergey Zhurikov .20 .50
12 Evgeni Malkin 10.00 25.00
13 Igor Grigorenko 1.25 3.00
14 Vladimir Popov .20 .50
15 Ruslan Khasanshin .20 .50
16 Dmitry Dudarev .20 .50
17 Valery Pokrovsky .20 .50
18 Andrei Tsareev .20 .50
19 Roman Malov .20 .50
20 Sergey Korolev .20 .50
21 Maxim Ossipov .20 .50
22 Vladimir Antipin .20 .50

2005 Russian Avangard Omsk Calendars

These oversized cards (4X3) feature players from the 2003-04 Russian champs on the front, and a calendar on the back. It's possible other cards exist in this series.

COMPLETE SET (5) 4.00 8.00
1 Alexander Prokopiev .75 2.00
2 Dmitry Subbotin .75 2.00
3 Maxim Sushinsky .75 2.00
4 Oleg Tverdovsky .75 2.00
5 Team photo .75 2.00

2005-06 Russian Hockey League RHL

COMPLETE SET (60) 20.00 40.00
1 Denis Kulyash .20 .50
2 Alexander Bumagin .20 .50
3 Alexei Kaigorodov .40 1.00
4 Anton Krysanov .20 .50
5 Alexander Budkin .20 .50
6 Denis Bodrov .20 .50
7 Stanislav Chistov .30 .75
8 Mikhail Grabovsky .30 .75
9 Nikita Alexeev .30 .75
10 Dmitri Shitikov .20 .50
11 Igor Ignatushkin .20 .50
12 Vladislav Bouljin .20 .50
13 Fred Brathwaite .40 1.00
14 Alexander Korolyuk .30 .75
15 Alexei Troschinsky .20 .50
16 Alexei Shkotov .20 .50
17 Eugeni Birukov .20 .50
18 Alexei Chupin .20 .50
19A Dmitri Bykov .20 .50
19B Alexander Ryazantsev .20 .50
20 Vadim Epanchintsev .20 .50
21 Milan Kraft .30 .75
22 Andrei Mukhachev .20 .50
23 Eugeni Fedorov .30 .75
24 Alexander Semin 1.25 3.00
25 Vladimir Vorobiev .20 .50
26 Eugeni Ryasenski .20 .50
28 Travis Scott .40 1.00
30 Maxim Sushinsky .30 .75
31 David Nemirovsky .30 .75
32 David Ling .30 .75
33 Vyacheslav Buravchikov .20 .50
34 Sergei Zvyagin .20 .50
35 Raymond Giroux .30 .75
36 Kirill Koltsov .40 1.00
37 Eugeni Malkin 8.00 20.00
38 Atrem Bikkinyaev .20 .50
39 Ilya Zubov .40 1.00
40 Nikolai Kulemin .40 1.00
41 Oleg Romashko .20 .50
42 Alexander Rybakov .20 .50
43 Dusan Sakficky .40 1.00
44 Maxim Yakutsenya .20 .50
45 Boris Tortunov .20 .50
46 Ilya Nikulin .20 .50
48 Radik Zakiyev .20 .50
49 Ruslan Nurtdinov .20 .50
50 Tyler Moss .40 1.00
51 Dmitri Obukhov .20 .50
52 Andrei Nikolishin .20 .50
53 Alexander Yunkov / Mikhail Yunkov .20 .50
54 Alexander Yudin .20 .50
55 Eugeni Konstantinov .40 1.00
C1 Milos Rziga .20 .50
C2 Jan Zachurla .20 .50
C3 Vladimir Kapulovsky .20 .50

2006 Russian Sport Collection Olympic Stars

1 Maxim Afinogenov 1.00 2.50
2 Ilya Bryzgalov 1.00 2.50
3 Anton Volchenkov 1.00 2.50
4 Sergei Gonchar 1.00 2.50
5 Pavel Datsyuk 2.00 5.00
6 Darius Kasparaitis 1.00 2.50
7 Alexei Kovalev 1.00 2.50
8 Ilya Kovalchuk 4.00 10.00
9 Evgeny Malkin 8.00 20.00
10 Andrei Markov 1.00 2.50
11 Evgeny Nabokov 2.00 5.00
12 Alexander Ovechkin 8.00 20.00
13 Maxim Sokolov 1.00 2.50
14 Fedor Tyutin 1.00 2.50
15 Alexei Yashin 1.00 2.50
16 Daniel Alfredson 2.00 5.00
17 Henrik Zetterberg 2.00 5.00
18 Nicklas Lidstrom 2.00 5.00
19 Henrik Lundqvist 4.00 10.00
20 Mats Sundin 2.00 5.00
21 Peter Forsberg 4.00 10.00
22 Jussi Jokinen 1.00 2.50
23 Saku Koivu 2.00 5.00
24 Jere Lehtinen 2.00 5.00
25 Antero Niittymaki 2.00 5.00
26 Ville Peltonen 1.00 2.50
27 Teemu Selanne 4.00 10.00
28 Tomas Vokoun 2.00 5.00
29 Tomas Kaberle 1.00 2.50
30 Martin Straka 1.00 2.50
31 Milan Hejduk 2.00 5.00
32 Ales Hemsky 2.00 5.00
33 Jaromir Jagr 4.00 10.00
34 Martin Brodeur 6.00 15.00
35 Jarome Iginla 4.00 10.00
36 Vincent Lecavalier 4.00 10.00
37 Rick Nash 4.00 10.00
38 Brad Richards 2.00 5.00
39 Joe Sakic 6.00 15.00
40 Joe Thornton 4.00 10.00
41 Dany Heatley 4.00 10.00
42 Peter Bondra 1.00 2.50
43 Peter Budaj 1.00 2.50
44 Marian Gaborik 4.00 10.00
45 Pavol Demitra 1.00 2.50
46 Richard Zednik 1.00 2.50
47 Zdeno Chara 1.00 2.50
48 Marian Hossa 2.00 5.00
49 Miroslav Satan 1.00 2.50
50 Rick Dipietro 2.00 5.00
51 Mike Modano 3.00 8.00
52 Keith Tkachuk 2.00 5.00
53 Vitali Yeremeyev 1.00 2.50

2006 Russian Torino Olympic Team

COMPLETE SET (26) 15.00 25.00
1 Alexander Ovechkin 4.00 10.00
2 Evgeny Malkin 4.00 10.00
3 Maxim Sokolov .20 .50
4 Ilya Bryzgalov .40 1.00
5 Fedor Tyutin .20 .50
6 Vitaly Vishenvsky .20 .50
7 Maxim Sushinski .20 .50
8 Alexei Yashin .20 .50
9 Alexei Kovalev .40 1.00
10 Alexander Korolyuk .20 .50
11 Ilya Kovalchuk 1.25 3.00
12 Maxim Afinogenov .40 1.00
13 Alexander Kharitonov .20 .50
14 Pavel Datsyuk .75 2.00
15 Viktor Kozlov .20 .50
16 Ivan Nepryaev .20 .50
17 Andrei Markov .20 .50
18 Alexander Frolov .40 1.00
19 Sergei Zhukov .20 .50
20 Evgeny Nabokov .40 1.00
21 Darius Kasparaitis .20 .50
22 Andrei Taratukhin .20 .50
23 Sergei Gonchar .20 .50
24 Anton Volchenkov .20 .50
25 Daniil Markov .20 .50
26 Russian Team CL .02 .10

1995-96 Slovakian APS National Team

This set of 28-cards features the 1996 Slovakian national team. The cards were sold in team set form at home games. The cards feature an action photo complemented by national and federation logos. The card backs reprise the front photo along with international statistics. The set is notable for the inclusion of sniper Peter Bondra, among other NHLers.

COMPLETE SET (28) 20.00 40.00
1 Dr. Jan Mitosinka CO .02 .10
2 Dusan Pasek CO .08 .25
3 Julius Supler CO .08 .25
4 Jan Selvek .08 .25
5 Jaromir Dragan .08 .25
6 Eduard Hartmann .08 .25
7 Roman Cunderlik .08 .25
8 Stanislav Jasecko .08 .25
9 Lubomir Sekeras .40 1.00
10 Stanislav Medrik .08 .25
11 Jan Varholik .08 .25
12 Marian Smerciak .08 .25
13 Robert Svehla .40 1.00
14 Slavomir Vorobel .20 .50
15 Vlastimil Plavucha .08 .25
16 Oto Hascak .20 .50
17 Peter Bondra 6.00 15.00
18 Rene Pucher .08 .25
19 Miroslav Satan 6.00 15.00
20 Branislav Janos .08 .25
21 Lubomir Kolnik .20 .50
22 Peter Stastny 2.00 5.00
23 Zdeno Ciger .20 .50
24 Zigmund Palffy 6.00 15.00
25 Josef Dano .08 .25
26 Robert Petrovicky .20 .50
27 Dusan Pohorelec .08 .25
28 Jozef Stumpel .75 2.00

1995 Slovakian-Quebec Pee-Wee Tournament

This 29-card set features the group of youngsters who represented Slovakia at the 1995 Quebec Pee Wee Tournament. The cards were sold at the tournament to help finance the team's trip. The cards have color player photos with red inside and faded purple outside borders. The backs carry player information. The cards are unnumbered and checklisted below in alphabetical order.

COMPLETE SET (29) 3.00 8.00
1 Jozef Balej 1.25 3.00
2 Patrik Behan .08 .25
3 Michal Bela .08 .25
4 Ivan Dobry .08 .25
5 Milan Dornic CO .02 .10
6 Vladimir Dubek .08 .25
7 Ladislav Gero CO .02 .10
8 Marian Hutyra .08 .25
9 Peter Hutyra .08 .25
10 Dr. Leopold Karafiat MG .02 .10
11 Miroslav Karafiat CO .02 .10
12 Vladimir Kulich .08 .25
13 Marek Laco .08 .25
14 Michal Loksa .08 .25
15 Igor Martak .08 .25
16 Branislav Medzihorsky .08 .25
17 Miroslav Micuda .08 .25
18 Tomas Mihalik .08 .25
19 Stanislav Mistrik .08 .25
20 Andrej Mrena .08 .25
21 Marian Nemeth .08 .25
22 Vladimir Polacek .08 .25
23 Rastislav Sendrey .08 .25
24 Norbert Skorvaga .08 .25
25 Tomas Surovy .60 1.50
26 Michal Turcer .08 .25
27 Sponsor Card .10 .25
28 Team Card .02 .10
29 Title Card .10 .25

1996 Slovakian Quebec Pee-Wee Tournament Team

This 30-card set features color player photos with red inside and faded purple outside borders. The backs carry player information. The cards are unnumbered and checklisted below in alphabetical order.

COMPLETE SET (30) 5.60 15.00
1 Jozef Balej .75 2.00
2 Michal Baranka .20 .50
3 Jan Behan CO .02 .10
4 Martin Bonda .20 .50
5 Robert Cerny .20 .50
6 Peter Duris .20 .50
7 Jan Frkan .20 .50
8 Milan Fujerik CO .02 .10
9 Michal Gunis .20 .50
10 Stefan Hlusek .20 .50
11 Peter Holecko .20 .50
12 Dr. Leopold Karafial GM .02 .10
13 Lukas Krejci .20 .50
14 Miroslav Kristin .20 .50
15 Andrej Kucko .20 .50
16 Roman Kyndl .20 .50
17 Michal Macho .20 .50
18 Tomas Mikus .30 .75
19 Juraj Nemcak .30 .75
20 Viliam Ondrejik .20 .50
21 Miroslav Pistek .20 .50
22 Marek Pollak .30 .75
23 Tomas Psenka .20 .50
24 Milan Sitar CO .02 .10
25 Frantisek Skladany .40 1.00
26 Peter Steklac .20 .50
27 Richard Svrbik .20 .50
28 Michal Sykora .20 .50
29 Martin Wala .20 .50
30 Team Picture .02 .10

1998-99 Slovakian Eurotel

This set of cards was released in Slovakia to promote Eurotel. The slightly undersized issues feature a number of NHL stars -- primarily of European origin.

COMPLETE SET (29) 32.00 80.00
1 Peter Bondra 1.25 3.00
2 Sergei Fedorov 2.00 5.00
3 Peter Forsberg 3.00 8.00
4 Wayne Gretzky 8.00 20.00
5 Bill Guerin .75 2.00
6 Brett Hull 1.50 4.00
7 Jaromir Jagr 2.00 5.00
8 Saku Koivu 1.25 3.00
9 Jari Kurri .75 2.00
10 Pat Lafontaine .75 2.00
11 Janne Laukkanen .40 1.00
12 Robert Lang .40 1.00
13 John LeClair .75 2.00
14 Eric Lindros 1.50 4.00
15 Al MacInnis .75 2.00
16 Joe Nieuwendyk .75 2.00
17 Zigmund Palffy .75 2.00
18 Mike Richter 1.25 3.00
19 Patrick Roy 6.00 15.00
20 Joe Sakic 2.00 5.00
21 Tommy Salo .75 2.00
22 Miroslav Satan .75 2.00
23 Teemu Selanne 1.50 4.00
24 Mikhail Shtalenkov .40 1.00
25 Martin Straka .40 1.00
26 Mats Sundin .75 2.00
27 Alexei Yashin .40 1.00
28 Steve Yzerman 6.00 15.00
29 Alexei Zhamnov .40 1.00

1999-00 Slovakian Challengers

This odd-sized set was produced as a promotional incentive by a Slovakian candy bar manufacturer. The checklist for this set provided by www.hockeyheaven.com.

COMPLETE SET (30) 30.00 60.00
1 Rob Niedermayer .20 .50
2 Robert Svehla .20 .50
3 Richard Zednik .20 .50
4 Steve Sullivan .20 .50
5 Alexei Yashin .20 .50
6 Alexander Mogilny .30 .75
7 Zigmund Palffy .40 1.00
8 Martin Brodeur 6.00 15.00
9 Sandis Ozolinsh .20 .50
10 Adam Deadmarsh .30 .75
11 Peter Forsberg 2.50 6.00
12 Martin Rucinsky .20 .50
13 Shayne Corson .20 .50
14 Grant Fuhr .75 2.00
15 Al MacInnis .75 2.00
16 Paul Kariya 2.00 5.00
17 Teemu SelAonne 2.00 5.00
18 Steve Yzerman 8.00 20.00
19 Chris Osgood .75 2.00
20 Brendan Shanahan 1.25 3.00
21 Vaclav Varada .20 .50
22 Brian Holzinger .20 .50
23 Dominik Hasek 2.50 6.00
24 Michael Peca .30 .75
25 Ed Belfour 1.25 3.00
26 Jere Lehtinen .75 2.00
27 Jaromir Jagr 3.00 8.00
28 Kevin Hatcher .20 .50
29 John LeClair .75 2.00
30 Alexei Zhamnov .20 .50

2001 Slovakian Kvarteto

This set features players who routinely suit up for Slovakia in key international events. The cards are shaped like playing cards, with a photo on front and the words Kvarteto on the back.

COMPLETE SET (33) 10.00 25.00
1A Jergus Baca .20 .50
1B Josef Dano .20 .50
1C Peter Bondra .40 2.00
1D Jaromir Dragan .40 1.00
2A Zdeno Ciger .20 .50
2B Peter Bondra .60 2.00
2C Pavol Demitra .60 2.00
2D Stanislav Jasecko .20 .50
3A Ivan Droppa .20 .50
3B Otto Hascak .20 .50
3C Branislav Janos .20 .50
3D Peter Bondra .60 2.00
4A Stanislav Jasecko .20 .50
4B Lubomir Kolnik .20 .50
4C Zigmund Palffy .60 2.00
4D Roman Kontsek .20 .50
5A Igor Murin .20 .50
5B Lubomir Visnovsky .30 .75
5C Lubomir Kolnik .20 .50
5D Jan Pardavy .20
6A Robert Petrovicky .20
6B Vlastimil Plavucha .20
6C Peter Pucher .20
6D Rene Pucher .20
7A Pavol Rybar .20
7B Miroslav Satan .60 2.
7C Lubomir Sekeras .30
7D Roman Stantien .20
8A Roman Stantien .20
8B Jozef Stumpel .30
8C Robert Svehla .20
8D Marian Varolik .20
HOKEJ Peter Bondra 2.00 5.

2002 Slovakian Kvarteto

This set features the world champion Slovaks. They look like playing cards with a player photo on the fr and the word Kvarteto on the back. We have a comp list of players, but the numbering was randomly assigned. If you have the correct numbering, please in touch.

COMPLETE SET (32) 8.00 20.
1 Miroslav Satan .75 2.
2 Peter Bondra .75 2.
3 Zigmund Palffy .75 2.
4 Jan Lasak .40 1.
5 Rastislav Stana .40 1.
6 Radoslav Hecl .20
7 Richard Lintner .20
8 Dusan Milo .20
9 Peter Smrek .20
10 Martin Strbak .20
11 Lubomir Visnovsky .20
12 Jergus Baca .20
13 Michael Handzus .20
14 Rastislav Pavlikovsky .20
15 Robert Petrovicky .20
16 Jozef Stumpel .20
17 Radovan Somik .20
18 Robert Tomik .20
19 Miroslav Hlinka .20
20 Lubos Bartecko .20
21 Ladislav Nagy .40 1.
22 Vladimir Orszagh .20
23 Peter Stastny GM .20
24 Samuel Petras .20
25 Dalimir Jancovic .20
26 Ernest Bokros .20
27 Marek Uram .20
28 Peter Pucher .20
29 Ladislav Cierny .20
30 Vladimir Stastny .20
31 Miroslav Simonovic .20
32 Jan Filc .20

2004-05 Slovakian Poprad Tea Set

COMPLETE SET (30) 10.00 25.
1 Ladislav Svozil .30
2 Vladimir Klinga .30
3 Stanislav Kozuch .30
4 Radovan Hurajt .30
5 Miroslav Javin .30
6 Stefan Rusnak .30
7 Miroslav Turan .30
8 Lukas Bambuch .30
9 Stefan Fabian .30
10 Ridvan Sadiki .30
11 Tomas Jurco .30
12 Radoslav Suchy .30
13 Tomas Valecko .30
14 Pavol Gurcik .30
15 Peter Bondra 1.25 3.
16 Miroslav Skovira .30
17 Slavomir Pavlicko .30
18 Juraj Halaj .30
19 Pavol Zavacky .30
20 Miroslav Ihnacak .30
21 Juraj Faith .30
22 Peter Misal .30
23 Ludovit Jurinyi .30
24 Jozef Slaninak .30
25 Richard Zemlicka .30
26 Stefan Rusnak .30
27 Miroslav Stolc .30
28 Viktor Kubenko .30
29 Erik Piatak .30
30 Roman Soltys .30

2004-05 Slovakian Skalica Tea Set

COMPLETE SET (28) 10.00 25
1 Martin Kucera .40 1
2 Matej Bukna .40 1
3 Tibor Visnovsky .40 1
4 Josef Mrena .40 1
5 Jaroslav Prosvic .40 1
6 Roman Chatrnuch .40 1
7 Milan Carsky .40 1
8 Miroslav Zalesak .60 1
9 Davis Galvas .40 1
10 Rene Jarolin .40 1
11 Richard Hartmann .40 1
12 Peter Kocak .40 1
13 Roman Kelner .40 1
14 Milan Malik .40 1
15 Marek Grill .40 1
16 Robert Liscak .40 1
17 Zigmund Palffy 1.25 3
18 Ladislav Paciga .40 1
19 Jozef Liska .40 1
20 Radovan Sloboda .40 1
21 Boris Flamik .40 1
22 Juraj Mikus .40 1
23 Peter Ivicic .40 1
24 Richard Stehlik .40 1
25 Martin Ivicic .40 1
26 Petr Tucek .40 1
27 Lukas Komarek .40 1
28 Martin Skadra .40 1

2004-05 South Surrey Eagles

COMPLETE SET (30) 15
1 Tyson Angus
2 Tim Crowder
3 Chris Defrancescanto
4 Korey Diehl
5 Korey Diehl PROMO
6 Tyler Eckford
7 Tyler Eckford PROMO
8 Matthew Girling
9 Daniel Idema
10 Andrew Kozek
11 Andrew Kozek PROMO
12 Kyle Kuehner
13 Aaron McKenzie
14 Brock Meadows
15 T.J. Miller
16 David Moncur
17 Tyrell Moulton
18 T.J. Mulock

9 T.J. Mulock PROMO 1.00
0 Kyle Nason .50
1 Blake Rielly PROMO 1.00
2 Blake Rielly PROMO 1.00
3 David Rutherford .50
4 David Rutherford PROMO 1.00
5 Cody Rymut .50
5 Dustin Slade .50
7 Stewart Thiessen .50
3 Matt Wiest .50
9 Rick Hillier HC .10
0 Team Card .10

1932-33 Swedish Marabou

his multi-sport Swedish issue is believed to contain ust six hockey players. The singles are very small, easuring about 1/2" by 1". It is believed that two ersions of the set exist, one with white borders and nother without. The fronts feature a photo, while the acks have the player's name, history, and the set ame, Marabou-Sportserie. If anyone knows of other ockey players in this set, please contact us at ockeymag@beckett.com
ockey players in set (6)
C. Abrahamsson
16 Herman Carlsson
17 Folke Wohlin
18 Carl-Erik Furst
19 Bertil Linde
50 Olof Johansson

1964 Swedish Coralli ISHockey

hese tiny cards (1 7/8" by 1 1/4") feature players from e Swedish national team, Tre Kroner, as well as many ub teams. The cards apparently were distributed as emiums in chocolate bars. According to reports, uch sets existed in Sweden as far back as 1955. The rd fronts have a posed player photo, name and card umber. The backs offer a brief biography in Swedish. n album to hold these cards is believed to exist; this, owever, has not been confirmed.

OMPLETE SET (165) 150.00 300.00
Sven Johansson 1.50 3.00
Ove Malmberg 1.00 2.00
Bjorn Larsson 1.00 2.00
Ulf Sterner 1.00 2.00
Bertil Karlsson 1.00 2.00
Leif Holmqvist 5.00 10.00
Uno Ohrlund 1.00 2.00
Mats Lonn 1.00 2.00
Bjorn Palmqvist 1.00 2.00
Nils Johansson 1.00 2.00
Ander Andersson 1.00 2.00
Lennart Haggroth 2.00 4.00
Hans Svedberg 1.00 2.00
Ronald Pettersson 1.00 2.00
Lars Eric Lundvall 1.00 2.00
Gert Blome 1.00 2.00
Bo Englund 1.00 2.00
Folke Bengtsson 1.00 2.00
Nils Nilsson 1.00 2.00
Lennart Johansson 1.00 2.00
Lennart Svedberg 2.50 5.00
Lars Ake Sivertsson 1.00 2.00
Hakan Wickberg 1.00 2.00
Tord Lundstrom 1.00 2.00
Ove Andersson 1.00 2.00
Bert Ola Nordlander 1.50 3.00
Jan Erik Nilsson 1.00 2.00
Eilert Maatta 1.00 2.00
Roland Stoltz 1.00 2.00
Kurt Thulin 1.00 2.00
Ove Andersson 1.00 2.00
Ingemar Johansson 1.00 2.00
Rune Lind 1.00 2.00
Bert Ola Nordlander 1.50 3.00
Hans Eriksson 1.00 2.00
Antik Johansson 1.00 2.00
Bo Hansson 1.00 2.00
Jan Back 1.00 2.00
Lennart Soderberg 1.00 2.00
Benny Soderling 1.00 2.00
Anders Parmstrom 1.00 2.00
Lennart Selinder 1.00 2.00
Bjorn Larsson 1.00 2.00
Jorma Salmi 1.00 2.00
Berndt Arvidsson 1.00 2.00
P.A. Karlstrom 1.00 2.00
Lars Erik Sjoberg 5.00 10.00
Vilgot Larsson 1.00 2.00
Gunnar Andersson 1.00 2.00
Roland Bond 1.00 2.00
Goran Lysen 1.00 2.00
Bosse Englund 1.00 2.00
Stig Pavels 1.00 2.00
Bengt Bornstrom 1.00 2.00
Nisse Nilsson 1.00 2.00
Lennart Lange 1.00 2.00
Des Moroney 1.00 2.00
Folke Bengtsson 1.00 2.00
Olle Sjogren 1.00 2.00
Knut Knutsson 1.00 2.00
Kjell Svensson 1.00 2.00
Rickard Fagerlund 2.50 5.00
Arne Loong 1.00 2.00
Stig Carlsson 1.00 2.00
Lars Hagg 1.00 2.00
Olle Stenar 1.00 2.00
Einar Granath 1.00 2.00
Leif Andersson 1.00 2.00
Hans Soderstrom 1.00 2.00
Kalle Lilja 1.00 2.00
Soren Maatta 1.00 2.00
Sven Bystrom 1.00 2.00
Hans Karlsson 1.00 2.00
Stig Goran Johansson 1.50 3.00
Jan Allinger 1.00 2.00
Kjell Larsson 1.00 2.00
Hakan Wickberg 1.00 2.00
Tord Lundstrom 1.00 2.00
Lennart Svedberg 2.50 5.00
Jan Erik Lyck 1.00 2.00
Hans Eriksson 1.00 2.00
Kjell Jonsson 1.00 2.00
Lars Hedenstrom 1.00 2.00
Lars Ake Sivertsson 1.00 2.00
Lennart Johansson 1.00 2.00
Hans Sjoberg 1.00 2.00
Hans Dahllof 1.00 2.00
Leif Jansson 1.00 2.00
Lars Byling 1.00 2.00
Bertil Lindstrom 1.00 2.00
Arne Eriksson 1.00 2.00
Gert Blomer 1.00 2.00
Kjell Adrian 1.00 2.00
Jan Olsen 1.00 2.00
Benny Karlsson 1.00 2.00
Tommy Carlsson 1.00 2.00
Ulf Sterner 1.00 2.00
Kjell-Ove Gustafsson 1.00 2.00
Lars Erik Lundvall 1.00 2.00
Kjell-Ronny Pettersson 1.00 2.00
101 Ronald Pettersson 1.00 2.00
102 Kjell Jonsson 1.00 2.00
103 Gote Hansson 1.00 2.00
104 Rolf Eklof 1.00 2.00
105 Eine Olsson 1.00 2.00
106 Hans-Erik Fernstrom 1.00 2.00
107 Leif Holmkvist 1.00 2.00
108 Bo Zetterberg 1.00 2.00
109 Ake Zattlin 1.00 2.00
110 Bengt-Olov Andreasson 1.00 2.00
111 Borje Mohlander 1.00 2.00
112 Sture Sundin 1.00 2.00
113 Bertil Karlsson 1.00 2.00
114 Lars Molander 1.00 2.00
115 Benno Persson 1.00 2.00
116 Gert Nystrom 1.00 2.00
117 Sune Bohlin 1.00 2.00
118 Olle Westlund 1.00 2.00
119 Goran Wallin 1.00 2.00
120 Ingemar Persson 1.00 2.00
121 Tommy Bjorkman 1.00 2.00
122 Eddie Wingren 1.00 2.00
123 Lars Bjorn 1.00 2.00
124 Roland Stoltz 1.00 2.00
125 Sven Johansson 1.50 3.00
126 Leif Skold 1.00 2.00
127 Hans Mild 1.00 2.00
128 Kurt Thulin 1.00 2.00
129 Ake Rydberg 1.00 2.00
130 Ove Malmberg 1.00 2.00
131 Lars Lundqvist 1.00 2.00
132 Kurt Svensson 1.00 2.00
133 Gosta Westerlund 1.00 2.00
134 Lars Andersson 1.00 2.00
135 Ulf Rydin 1.00 2.00
136 Lennart Haggroth 2.00 4.00
137 Jan Hedberg 1.00 2.00
138 Karl Soren Hedlund 1.00 2.00
139 Hans Svedberg 1.00 2.00
140 Sture Hoverberg 1.00 2.00
141 Anders Ronnblom 1.00 2.00
142 Ulf Eriksson 1.00 2.00
143 Anders Andersson 1.00 2.00
144 Henrik Hedlund 1.00 2.00
145 Per Lundstrom 1.00 2.00
146 Hakan Nygren 1.00 2.00
147 Bo Berglund, Sr 2.00 4.00
148 Lars Ake Warning 1.00 2.00
149 Sven-Olov Johansson 1.00 2.00
150 Ove Stenlund 1.00 2.00
151 Ivar Larsson 1.00 2.00
152 Nils Johansson 1.00 2.00
153 Sten Olsen 1.00 2.00
154 Lars Gidlund 1.00 2.00
155 Tor Haarstad 1.00 2.00
156 K-O Barrefjord 1.00 2.00
157 Bjorn Palmqvist 1.00 2.00
158 Soren Lindstrom 1.00 2.00
159 Henna Svensson 1.00 2.00
160 Lars Hagstrom 1.00 2.00
161 Ake Eklof 1.00 2.00
162 Ulf Lindstrom 1.00 2.00
163 Ronny Nordstrom 1.00 2.00
164 Paul Stahl 1.00 2.00
165 Kenneth Sahlen 1.50 3.00

1965 Swedish Coralli ISHockey

These tiny (1 7/8" by 1 1/4") feature players from the Swedish National Team, Tre Kroner, as well as many club teams. The cards apparently were issued as premiums with chocolate bars. The card fronts have a posed player photo, name and card number. The backs offer a brief biography in Swedish.

COMPLETE SET (214) 125.00 300.00
1 Sven Johansson 1.25 3.00
2 Ove Malmberg .75 2.00
3 Bjorn Larsson .75 2.00
4 Ulf Sterner .75 2.00
5 Bertil Karlsson 1.00 3.00
6 Leif Holmqvist 4.00 8.00
7 Uno Ohrlund .75 2.00
8 Mats Lonn .75 2.00
9 Bjorn Palmqvist .75 2.00
10 Nils Johansson .75 2.00
11 Anders Andersson .75 2.00
12 Lennart Haggroth 1.50 4.00
13 Hans Svedberg .75 2.00
14 Ronald Pettersson .75 2.00
15 Lars Eric Lundvall .75 2.00
16 Gert Blome .75 2.00
17 Bo Englund .75 2.00
18 Folke Bengtsson .75 2.00
19 Nils Nilsson .75 2.00
20 Lennart Johansson .75 2.00
21 Lennart Svedberg 1.75 4.00
22 Lars Ake Sivertsson .75 2.00
23 Hakan Wickberg .75 2.00
24 Tord Lundstrom .75 2.00
25 Ove Andersson .75 2.00
26 Bert Ola Nordlander 1.25 3.00
27 Jan Erik Nilsson .75 2.00
28 Eilert Maatta .75 2.00
29 Roland Stoltz .75 2.00
30 Kurt Thulin .75 2.00
31 Leif Holmqvist 4.00 8.00
32 Ingemar Johansson 1.00 3.00
33 Rune Lind .75 2.00
34 Bert-Ola Nordlander 1.25 3.00
35 Hans Eriksson .75 2.00
36 Antik Johansson .75 2.00
37 Bo Hansson .75 2.00
38 Hans-Ake Carlsson .75 2.00
39 Lennart Soderberg .75 2.00
40 Benny Soderling .75 2.00
41 Anders Parmstrom .75 2.00
42 Lennart Selinder .75 2.00
43 Bjorn Larsson .75 2.00
44 Ove Hedberg .75 2.00
45 Berndt Arvidsson .75 2.00
46 P.A. Carlstrom .75 2.00
47 Lars Erik Sjoberg 4.00 8.00
48 Kjell Fhinn .75 2.00
49 Gunnar Andersson .75 2.00
50 Roland Bond .75 2.00
51 Goran Lysen .75 2.00
52 Bosse Englund .75 2.00
53 Stig Pavels .75 2.00
54 Bengt Bornstrom .75 2.00
55 Nisse Nilsson .75 2.00
56 Lennart Lange .75 2.00
57 Tommy Abrahamsson 4.00 8.00
58 Folke Bengtsson .75 2.00
59 Olle Sjogren .75 2.00
60 Knut Knutsson .75 2.00
61 Kjell Svensson .75 2.00
62 Rickard Fagerlund 1.75 4.00
63 Eilert Maatta .75 2.00
64 Stig Carlsson .75 2.00
65 Lars Hagg .75 2.00
66 Olle Stenar .75 2.00
67 Einar Andersson .75 2.00
68 Leif Andersson .75 2.00
69 Percy Lind .75 2.00
70 Gunnar Tallberg .75 2.00
71 Soren Maatta .75 2.00
72 Sven Bystrom .75 2.00
73 Hans Carlsson .75 2.00
74 Stig Goran Johansson 1.25 3.00
75 Thomas Warming .75 2.00
76 Kjell Larsson .75 2.00
77 Hakan Wickberg .75 2.00
78 Tord Lundstrom .75 2.00
79 Lennart Svedberg 2.00 4.00
80 Jan Erik Lyck .75 2.00
81 Stefan Carlsson .75 2.00
82 Kjell Jonsson .75 2.00
83 Lars Hedenstrom .75 2.00
84 Lars Ake Sivertsson .75 2.00
85 Lennart Johansson .75 2.00
86 Hans Sjoberg .75 2.00
87 Hans Dahllof .75 2.00
88 Hans Lindberg .75 2.00
89 Lars Bylund .75 2.00
90 Sten Edqvist .75 2.00
91 Arne Ericsson .75 2.00
92 Gert Blomer .75 2.00
93 Kjell Adrian .75 2.00
94 Jan Olsen .75 2.00
95 Benny Karlsson .75 2.00
96 Jorma Salmi .75 2.00
97 Ulf Sterner .75 2.00
98 Kjell-Ove Gustafsson .75 2.00
99 Lars Erik Lundvall .75 2.00
100 Kjell-Ronny Pettersson 1.00 3.00
101 Ronald Pettersson .75 2.00
102 Kjell Jonsson .75 2.00
103 Gote Hansson .75 2.00
104 Ove Sterner .75 2.00
105 Eine Olsson .75 2.00
106 Hans-Frik Fernstrom .75 2.00
107 Per-Olov Hardin .75 2.00
108 Bo Zetterberg .75 2.00
109 Ake Zettlin .75 2.00
110 Bengt-Olov Andreasson .75 2.00
111 Borje Molander .75 2.00
112 Sture Sundin .75 2.00
113 Bertil Karlsson 1.00 3.00
114 Lars Molander .75 2.00
115 Benno Persson .75 2.00
116 Ake Eklof .75 2.00
117 Ronny Francis .75 2.00
118 Olle Westlund .75 2.00
119 Goran Wallin .75 2.00
120 Ingemar Persson .75 2.00
121 Tommy Bjorkman .75 2.00
122 Eddie Wingren .75 2.00
123 Lars Bjorn .75 2.00
124 Roland Stoltz .75 2.00
125 Sven Johansson 1.25 3.00
126 Arne Loong .75 2.00
127 Hans Mild .75 2.00
127 Per Lundstrom .75 2.00
128 Kurt Thulin .75 2.00
129 Ake Rydberg .75 2.00
130 Ove Malmberg .75 2.00
131 Lars Lundqvist .75 2.00
132 Kurt Svensson .75 2.00
133 Gosta Westerlund .75 2.00
134 Lars Andersson .75 2.00
135 Ulf Rydin .75 2.00
136 Lennart Haggroth 1.50 4.00
137 Jan Hedberg .75 2.00
138 Anders Carlberg .75 2.00
139 Hans Svedberg .75 2.00
140 Sture Hofverberg .75 2.00
141 Anders Ronnblom .75 2.00
142 Ulf Eriksson .75 2.00
143 Anders Andersson .75 2.00
144 Henrik Hedlund .75 2.00
145 Roger Boman .75 2.00
146 Bo Astrom .75 2.00
147 Bo Berglund 1.50 3.00
148 Lars Ake Warning .75 2.00
149 Sven-Olov Johansson .75 2.00
150 Ove Stenlund .75 2.00
151 Ivar Larsson .75 2.00
152 Nicke Johansson .75 2.00
153 Sten Olsen .75 2.00
154 Lars Gidlund .75 2.00
155 Tor Haarstad .75 2.00
156 Hakan Nygren .75 2.00
157 Bjorn Palmqvist .75 2.00
158 Soren Lindgren .75 2.00
159 Henry Svensson .75 2.00
160 Lars Hagstrom .75 2.00
161 Ake Eklof .75 2.00
162 Ulf Lundstrom .75 2.00
163 Ronny Nordstrom .75 2.00
164 Paul Stahl .75 2.00
165 Kenneth Sahlen 1.25 3.00
166 Anders Hedlund .75 2.00
167 Ingemar Caris .75 2.00
168 Arne Carlsson .75 2.00
169 Gote Bostrom .75 2.00
170 Roger Olsson .75 2.00
171 Ole Jacobson .75 2.00
172 Curt Edenvik .75 2.00
173 Goran Svensson .75 2.00
174 Eje Lindstrom .75 2.00
175 Curt Larsson 2.50 5.00
176 Gunnar Backman .75 2.00
177 Anders Nordin .75 2.00
178 Ulf Torstensson .75 2.00
179 Kent Lindgren .75 2.00
180 Kent Sjalin .75 2.00
181 Lars Goran Nilsson .75 2.00
182 Helmo Klockare .75 2.00
183 Lars Sattare .75 2.00
184 Lars-Ake Lundell .75 2.00
185 Kjell Savstrom .75 2.00
186 Carl-Goran Oberg .75 2.00
187 Bjorn Larsson .75 2.00
188 Leif Eriksson .75 2.00
189 Dag Olsson .75 2.00
190 Lars Lohman .75 2.00
191 unknown .75 2.00
192 unknown .75 2.00
193 unknown .75 2.00
194 unknown .75 2.00
195 unknown .75 2.00
196 unknown .75 2.00
197 unknown .75 2.00
198 unknown .75 2.00
199 unknown .75 2.00
200 Hans Aleblad .75 2.00
201 Karl Soren Hedlund .75 2.00
202 Clarence Carlsson .75 2.00
203 Bjorn Johansson .75 2.00
204 Kent Persson .75 2.00
205 Goran Thelin .75 2.00
206 Leif Ohrlund .75 2.00
207 Mats Davidsson .75 2.00
208 Leif Artursson .75 2.00
209 Karl Gunnar Backman .75 2.00
210 Hans Mellinger .75 2.00
211 Hans Inge Lund .75 2.00
212 Kent Jansson .75 2.00
213 Anders Ronnkvist .75 2.00
214 Bo Olofsson .75 2.00

1967-68 Swedish Hockey

This 300-card set features the skaters from the Swedish first and second division teams from the 1967-68 season, as well as the national team, Tre Kronor. The cards measure 2" by 3 1/8" and feature posed color photos on the front. The national team cards have the words Tre Kronor and the three crown logo across the top. The backs have the card number, player stats and an invitation to purchase a collectors album, all in Swedish. The album for the set includes numerous pages of text and photos about Swedish hockey, and is valued at $35. Although short on widely recognizable names, the set does include early -- if not first -- cards of Inge Hammarstrom and Christer Abrahamsson.

COMPLETE SET (300) 62.50 150.00
1 Christer Abrahamsson 2.00 4.00
2 Tommy Abrahamsson 1.00 2.00
3 Folke Bengtsson .25 1.00
4 Arne Carlsson .25 1.00
5 Bengt-Ake Gustavsson .25 1.00
6 Anders Hagstrom .25 1.00
7 Inge Hammarstrom 2.50 5.00
8 Leif Henriksson .25 1.00
9 Leif Holmqvist 1.00 2.00
10 Per-Arne Hubinette .25 1.00
11 Mats Hysing .25 1.00
12 Nils Johansson .25 1.00
13 Stig-Goran Johansson .25 1.00
14 Hans Lindberg .25 1.00
15 Tord Lundstrom .25 1.00
16 Lars-Goran Nilsson .25 1.00
17 Anders Nordin .25 1.00
18 Bert-Ola Nordlander .25 1.00
19 Roger Olsson .25 1.00
20 Bjorn Palmqvist .25 1.00
21 Kjell Sundstrom .25 1.00
22 Lennart Svedberg .50 2.00
23 Hakan Wickberg .25 1.00
24 Carl-Goran Oberg .25 1.00
25 Lasse Ohman .25 1.00
26 Curt Edenvik .25 1.00
27 Hans Eriksson .25 1.00
28 Rolf Hallgren .25 1.00
29 Bo Hansson .25 1.00
30 Ove Hedberg .25 1.00
31 Kjell Hedman .50 2.00
32 Leif Holmqvist 1.00 2.00
33 Anders Johansson .25 1.00
34 Bengt Larsson .25 1.00
35 Bjorn Larsson .25 1.00
36 Rune Lindh .25 1.00
37 Borje Molander .25 1.00
38 Kjell Nilsson .25 1.00
39 Bert-Ola Nordlander .25 1.00
40 Anders Parmstrom .25 1.00
41 Lennart Sellinder .25 1.00
42 Kjell Savstrom .25 1.00
43 Lars Bylund .25 1.00
44 Hans Dahllof .50 2.00
45 Lennart Gustafsson .25 1.00
46 Lars Hedenstrom .25 1.00
47 Lennart Johansson .25 1.00
48 Kjell Johansson .25 1.00
49 Stefan Karlsson .25 1.00
50 Nisse Larsson .25 1.00
51 Lennart Lind .25 1.00
52 Hans Lindberg .25 1.00
53 Tord Lundstrom .25 1.00
54 Jan-Erik Lyck .25 1.00
55 Lars-Goran Nilsson .25 1.00
56 Anders Sahlin .25 1.00
57 Lars-Ake Sivertsson .25 1.00
58 Hans Sjoberg .25 1.00
59 Hakan Wickberg .25 1.00
60 Tommy Bjorkman .50 2.00
61 Lasse Bjorn .25 1.00
62 Thomas Carlsson .25 1.00
63 Roland Einarsson .50 2.00
64 Kjell Keijser .25 1.00
65 Stig Larsson .25 1.00
66 Kent Lindgren .25 1.00
67 Tommie Lindgren .25 1.00
68 Lars-Ake Lundell .25 1.00
69 Per Lundstrom .25 1.00
70 Bjorn Palmqvist .25 1.00
71 Ulf Rydin .25 1.00
72 Lars-Eric Sjoberg 2.00 4.00
73 Lars Starck .25 1.00
74 Roland Stoltz .25 1.00
75 Henry Svensson .25 1.00
76 Kurt Thulin .25 1.00
77 Gosta Westerlund .25 1.00
78 Eddie Wingren .25 1.00
79 Carl-Goran Oberg .25 1.00
80 Anders Andersson .25 1.00
81 Hasse Andersson .25 1.00
82 Hakan Andersson .25 1.00
83 Anders Asplund .25 1.00
84 Hans Bergqvist .25 1.00
85 Hans Bostrom .25 1.00
86 Kjell Eklov .50 2.00
87 Conny Evensson .50 2.00
88 Bjorn Fagerlund .50 2.00
89 Ingemar Magnusson .25 1.00
90 Hans-Ake Nilsson .25 1.00
91 Rune Nilsson .25 1.00
92 Kent Olsson .25 1.00
93 Lars Stalberg .25 1.00
94 Christer Sundqvist .25 1.00
95 Christer Abrahamsson 2.00 4.00
96 Tommy Abrahamsson 1.00 2.00
97 Bosse Andersson .25 1.00
98 Gunnar Andersson .25 1.00
99 Lars Andersson .25 1.00
100 Folke Bengtsson .25 1.00
101 Roland Bond .25 1.00
102 Kjell Fihnn .25 1.00
103 Jan-Olof Kroon .25 1.00
104 Lennart Lange .25 1.00
105 Sture Loksell .50 2.00
106 Goran Lysen .25 1.00
107 Ulf Martensson .25 1.00
108 Nisse Nilsson .25 1.00
109 Dag Ohlsson .25 1.00
110 Olle Sjogren .25 1.00
111 Ake Sunesson .25 1.00
112 Dan Soderstrom .25 1.00
113 Goran Winge .25 1.00
114 Mats Ahlberg .25 1.00
115 Olle Ost .25 1.00
116 Gunnar Backman .25 1.00
117 Lage Edin .25 1.00
118 Ake Eklof .25 1.00
119 Torbjorn Hubinette .25 1.00
120 Nils Johansson .25 1.00
121 Ulf Kroon .25 1.00
122 Ivar Larsson .50 2.00
123 Christer Nilsson .25 1.00
124 Anders Nordin .25 1.00
125 Hakan Nygren .25 1.00
126 Sten Olsen .25 1.00
127 Paul Stahl .25 1.00
128 Gunnar Safsten .25 1.00
129 Ulf Torstensson .25 1.00
130 Ulf Wigren .25 1.00
131 Lars Ohman .25 1.00
132 Tore Ohman .25 1.00
133 Bengt Andersson .25 1.00
134 Nils Carlsson .25 1.00
135 Kjell Eklind .25 1.00
136 Allan Fernstrom .25 1.00
137 Bengt Gustavsson .25 1.00
138 Bengt-Ake Gustavsson .50 2.00
139 Gote Hansson .25 1.00
140 Per-Arne Hubinette .25 1.00
141 Sven-Ake Jakobsson .25 1.00
142 Goran Johansson .50 2.00
143 Mats Lind .25 1.00
144 Mats Lonn .25 1.00
145 Ulf Nises .25 1.00
146 Bo Olsson .25 1.00
147 Lennart Svedberg .50 2.00
148 Evert Tysk .25 1.00
149 Stig Ostling .25 1.00
150 Ulf Berglund .25 1.00
151 Clarence Carlsson .25 1.00
152 Arne Ekenberg .25 1.00
153 Kenneth Ekman .25 1.00
154 Tom Haugh .50 2.00
155 Rolf Joelsson .25 1.00
156 Bjorn Johanesson .25 1.00
157 Arne Johansson .25 1.00
158 Bengt-Goran Karlsson .25 1.00
159 Kjell Larsson .25 1.00
160 Lasse Larsson .25 1.00
161 Barry Murman .25 1.00
162 Klas Goran Nilsson .25 1.00
163 Rolf Norell .25 1.00
164 Lennart Skordaker .25 1.00
165 Ulf Sterner .50 2.00
166 Arne Wickstrom .25 1.00
167 Bengt-Olov Andreasson .50 2.00
168 Leif Eriksson .25 1.00
169 Ove Evaldson .25 1.00
170 Hans-Erik Fernstrom .25 1.00
171 Kenneth Hillgren .25 1.00
172 Per-Olof Hardin .25 1.00
173 Bertil Karlsson .25 1.00
174 Torsten Karlsson .25 1.00
175 Rolf Larsson .25 1.00
176 William Lofqvist 1.00 2.00
177 Lars Mollander .25 1.00
178 Gert Nystrom .25 1.00
179 Olle Westlund .25 1.00
180 Bo Zetterberg .25 1.00
181 Leif Andersson .25 1.00
182 Borje Burlin .25 1.00
183 Hans Carlsson .25 1.00
184 Stig Carlsson .25 1.00
185 Einar Granath .25 1.00
186 Kjell-Ake Hedstrom .25 1.00
187 Mats Hysing .25 1.00
188 Stig-Goran Johansson .25 1.00
189 Curt Larsson 1.25 2.50
190 Eilert Maatta .25 1.00
191 Soren Maatta .25 1.00
192 Nils-Olof Schilstrom .25 1.00
193 Jan Schullstrom .25 1.00
194 Kjell Svensson .50 2.00
195 Gunnar Tallberg .25 1.00
196 Dick Yderstrom .25 1.00
197 Sten Andersson .50 2.00
198 Lars Arne Bergkvist .25 1.00
199 Anders Edstrom .25 1.00
200 Lars Bertil Ericsson .25 1.00
201 Charles Gustavsson .25 1.00
202 Ake Johansson .25 1.00
203 Lars Karestal .25 1.00
204 Rolf Karlsson .25 1.00
205 Erik Lindahl .25 1.00
206 Freddy Lindfors .50 2.00
207 Lennart Lindkvist .25 1.00
208 Kjell Rune Milton .25 1.00
209 Olle Nilsater .25 1.00
210 Birger Nordlund .25 1.00
211 Inge Tornlund .25 1.00
212 Jan Roger Oberg .25 1.00
213 Kjell Sture Oberg .25 1.00
214 Tommy Andersson .25 1.00
215 Soren Bostrom .25 1.00
216 Anders Bryner .25 1.00
217 Anders Claesson .50 2.00
218 Svante Granholm .25 1.00
219 Inge Hammarstrom 2.50 5.00
220 Borje Holmstrom .25 1.00
221 Jan Johansson .25 1.00
222 Antero Jonasson .25 1.00
223 Ove Jonsson .25 1.00
224 Lennart Lind .50 2.00
225 Jan-Erik Nilsson .25 1.00
226 Kurt Olofsson .25 1.00
227 Gosta Sjokvist .25 1.00
228 Jan Stolpe .25 1.00
229 Kjell Westerlund .25 1.00
230 Olle Ahman .25 1.00
231 Jan-Ivar Bergqvist .25 1.00
232 Lars-Ake Brannlund .50 2.00
233 Hans Bohlmark .25 1.00
234 Jan Christiansson .25 1.00
235 Bengt Eriksson .25 1.00
236 Arne Grenemo .25 1.00
237 Lars-Olof Henriksson .25 1.00
238 Kurt Jakobsson .25 1.00
239 Leif Jakobsson .25 1.00
240 Lars-Goran Johansson .25 1.00
241 Kimo Kivela .25 1.00
242 Borje Maatta .25 1.00
243 Anders Rapp .25 1.00
244 Tommy Sahlsten .25 1.00
245 Stig-Olof Zetterbg .25 1.00
246 Lennart Abrahamsson .25 1.00
247 John Andersson .25 1.00
248 Ove Andersson .50 2.00
249 Kjell-olov Barrefjord .25 1.00
250 Ulf Barrefjord .25 1.00
251 Kent Bjork .25 1.00
252 Lars Dahlgren .25 1.00
253 Karl-Ove Eriksson .25 1.00
254 Osten Folkesson .25 1.00
255 Anders Hagstrom .25 1.00
256 Eric Jarvholm .25 1.00
257 Ulf Lindstrom .25 1.00
258 Bengt Lovgren .25 1.00
259 Roger Nilsson .25 1.00
260 Bengt Persson .50 2.00
261 Kjell Sundstrom .25 1.00
262 Roger Osterlund .25 1.00
263 Hans Aleblad .50 2.00
264 Ake Bolander .25 1.00
265 Karl-Gunnar Backman .25 1.00
266 Mats Davidsson .25 1.00
267 Bosse Englund .25 1.00
268 Tommy Eriksson .25 1.00
269 Karl-Soren Hedlund .25 1.00
270 Don Hughes .25 1.00
271 Krister Lindgren .25 1.00
272 Hans Mellinger .25 1.00
273 Des Moroney .25 1.00
274 Bo Olofsson .25 1.00
275 Hakan Olsson .25 1.00
276 Kent Persson .25 1.00
277 Ove Stenlund .25 1.00
278 Goran Thelin .25 1.00
279 Ove Thelin .25 1.00
280 Leif Ohrlund .25 1.00
281 Uno Ohrlund .25 1.00
282 Jan Ostling .25 1.00
283 Gert Blome .25 1.00
284 Ingemar Caris .50 2.00
285 Arne Carlsson .25 1.00
286 Kjell-Ove Gustafsson .25 1.00
287 Henric Hedlund .25 1.00
288 Leif Henriksson .25 1.00
289 Kjell Jonsson .25 1.00
290 Berny Karlsson .25 1.00
291 Goran Lindberg .25 1.00
292 Bernt Lundqvist .25 1.00
293 Lars Eric Lundvall .25 1.00
294 Carl-Fredrik Montan .25 1.00
295 Eine Ohlsson .50 2.00
296 Jan Olsen .25 1.00
297 Roger Olsson .25 1.00
298 Kjell-Ronnie Pettersson .50 2.00
299 Ronald Pettersson .25 1.00
300 Roland Sarnholm .25 1.00

1969-70 Swedish Hockey

This 384-card set was released in Sweden by Williams Forlags AB to commemorate the players and nations competing in the World Championships, as well as club teams from Sweden. The cards measured 1 7/8" by 2 1/2" and featured a small portrait on the front, along with team name and emblem. The backs gave the player's name, vital stats (in Swedish) and sticker number. Early (first?) appearances by many legends make this set notable: look for Valeri Kharlamov, Alexander Yakushev and Ulf Nilsson. An album was available which not only housed the set, but offered stories, photos and stats to wrap up the previous season. This album is valued at $50.

COMPLETE SET (384) 200.00 400.00
1 Valeri Charlamov 7.50 15.00
2 Vitalij Davydov .75 1.50
3 Anatolij Firsov 3.00 6.00
4 Alexander Jakusjev 5.00 10.00
5 Vladimir Jursinov 1.00 2.00
6 Victor Kuzkin .38 .75
7 Vladimir Lutjenko 1.00 2.00
8 Alexander Maltsev 5.00 10.00
9 Boris Michailov 5.00 10.00
10 Jevgenij Misjakov 1.50 3.00
11 Vladimir Petrov 5.00 10.00
12 Jevgenij Poladjev .38 .75
13 Victor Putjkov .50 1.00
14 Alexander Ragulin 1.50 3.00
15 Igor Romisjevskij .38 .75
16 Vjatjeslav Starsjinov 1.25 2.50
17 Vladimir Vikulov .75 1.50
18 Jevgenij Zimin .75 1.50
19 Victor Zinger .50 1.00
20 Josef Augusta .38 .75
21 Vladimir Bednar .38 .75
22 Josef Cerny .50 1.00
23 Vladimir Dzurilla 5.00 10.00
24 Richard Farda .38 .75
25 Josef Golonka .75 1.50
26 Jan Havel .38 .75
27 Jaroslav Holik .75 1.50
28 Jiri Holik .50 1.00
29 Josef Horesovsky .38 .75
30 Jan Hrbaty .38 .75
31 Jaroslav Jirik .38 .75
32 Jan Klapac .38 .75
33 Miroslav Lacky .75 1.50
34 Oldrich Machac .38 .75
35 Vaclav Nedomansky 2.50 5.00
36 Frantisek Pospisil 1.00 2.00
37 Frantisek Sevcik .50 1.00
38 Jan Suchy .50 1.00
39 Ake Carlsson .38 .75
40 Curt Edenvik .38 .75
41 Hans Eriksson .38 .75
42 Bo Hansson .38 .75
43 Ove Hedberg .38 .75
44 Kjell Hedman .75 1.50
45 Leif Holmqvist 1.50 3.00
46 Anders Johansson .38 .75
47 Bjorn Larsson .38 .75
48 Borje Molander .38 .75
49 Ulf Nilsson 10.00 20.00
50 Bert-Ola Nordlander .50 1.00
51 Bo Olofsson .38 .75
52 Anders Parmstrom .38 .75
53 Lennart Selinder .38 .75
54 Hans Stromberg .38 .75
55 Kjell Savstrom .38 .75
56 Lars-Ake Warning .38 .75
57 Lars Bylund .38 .75
58 Inge Hammarstrom 2.50 5.00
59 Hans Dahllof .75 1.50
60 Lars Hedenstrom .38 .75
61 Kjell Johnsson .38 .75
62 Lennart Johansson .38 .75
63 Bertil Karlsson .38 .75
64 Stefan Karlsson .38 .75
65 Lennart Lind .38 .75
66 Hans Lindberg .38 .75
67 Tord Lundstrom .38 .75
68 Jan-Erik Lyck .38 .75
69 William Lovqvist 1.00 2.00
70 Lars-Goran Nilsson .38 .75
71 Stig Salming .50 1.00
72 Lars-Ake Sivertsson .38 .75
73 Lars-Goran Tano .38 .75
74 Hakan Wickberg .38 .75
75 Rolf Berglund .38 .75
76 Lars Alserydh .75 1.50
77 Tage Blom .38 .75
78 Alf Granstrom .38 .75
79 Lennart Haggroth .75 1.50
80 Bertil Karlsson .38 .75
81 Sven-Bertil Lindstrom .38 .75
82 Anders Lundberg .38 .75
83 Goran Lundmark .75 1.50
84 Sven-Erik Lundqvist .38 .75
85 Hans Lundstrom .38 .75
86 Kjell Lang .38 .75
87 Borje Lofstedt .38 .75
88 Olle Nilsson .38 .75
89 Jan-Olof Nordin .38 .75
90 Kjell Rehnstrom .38 .75
91 Peder Rehnstrom .38 .75
92 Leif Tjernstrom .38 .75
93 Kjell-Arne Wikstrom .38 .75
94 Anders Andren .38 .75
95 Thomas Carlsson .38 .75
96 Roland Einarsson 1.00 2.00
97 Lars Granlund .38 .75
98 Stig Larsson .38 .75
99 Lars-Ake Lundell .38 .75
100 Per Lundstrom .38 .75
101 Bjorn Palmquist .38 .75
102 Ulf Rydin .38 .75
103 Christer Sehlstedt .75 1.50
104 Lars Starck .38 .75
105 Roland Stoltz .38 .75
106 Billy Sundstrom .38 .75
107 Henry Svensson .38 .75
108 Ove Svensson .38 .75
109 Ulf Torstensson .38 .75
110 Christer Abrahamsson 2.50 5.00
111 Tommy Abrahamsson 1.00 2.00
112 Gunnar Andersson .38 .75
113 Folke Bengtsson .38 .75
114 Kjell Brus .38 .75
115 Ake Danielsson .38 .75
116 Bo Englund .38 .75
117 Lennart Gustavsson .38 .75
118 Hans Jax .38 .75
119 Jan-Olof Kroon .38 .75
120 Roger Lindqvist .38 .75
121 Gunnar Mars .75 1.50
122 Ulf Martensson .38 .75
123 Nisse Nilsson .38 .75
124 Lars-Erik Sjoberg 2.50 5.00
125 Olle Sjogren .38 .75
126 Dan Soderstrom .38 .75
127 Mats Ahlberg .38 .75
128 Gunnar Backman 1.00 2.00
129 Ulf Croon .38 .75
130 Lage Edin .38 .75
131 Ake Eklof .38 .75
132 Anders Hedberg 10.00 20.00
133 Torbjorn Hubinette .38 .75
134 Nils Johansson .38 .75
135 Ivar Larsson 1.00 2.00
136 Christer Nilsson .38 .75
137 Lennart Norberg .38 .75
138 Anders Nordin .38 .75
139 Hakan Nygren .38 .75
140 Sten Olsen .38 .75
141 Anders Schahlin .38 .75
142 Gunnar Safsten .38 .75
143 Ulf Wigren .38 .75
144 Lars Ohman .38 .75
145 Tore Ohman .38 .75
146 Nils Carlsson .38 .75
147 Kjell Eklund .38 .75
148 Bengt Gustavsson .38 .75
149 Bengt-Ake Gustavsson 1.00 2.00
150 Gote Hansson .38 .75
151 Hans Hansson .38 .75
152 Per-Arne Hubinette .38 .75
153 Sven-Ake Jakobsson .38 .75
154 Goran Johansson .75 1.50
155 Mats Lind .38 .75
156 Mats Lonn .38 .75
157 Borje Marcus .38 .75
158 Lars Mjoberg .38 .75
159 Ulf Nises .38 .75
160 Bo Olsson .38 .75
161 Erling Sundblad .38 .75
162 Lennart Svedberg 1.00 2.00
163 Evert Tysk .38 .75
164 Stig Ostling .38 .75
165 Magnus Andersson .38 .75
166 Erling Bergmark .38 .75
167 Kenneth Hellman .38 .75
168 Bjorn Johansson .38 .75
169 Ulf Johansson .38 .75
170 Berny Karlsson .38 .75
171 Nils-Erik Karlsson .38 .75
172 Rolf Larsson .38 .75
173 Tore Larsson .38 .75
174 Roland Lestander .75 1.50
175 Lennart Lindgren .38 .75
176 Finn Lundstrom .38 .75
177 Kenneth Manberg .38 .75
178 Lars Molander .38 .75
179 Lennart Rudby .38 .75
180 Sven-Ake Rudby .38 .75
181 Curt Svensson .38 .75
182 Sverker Torstensson .38 .75
183 Gunnar Backman 1.00 2.00
184 Arne Carlsson .38 .75
185 Leif Henriksson .38 .75
186 Leif Holmqvist 1.50 3.00
187 Mats Hysing .38 .75
188 Nils Johansson .38 .75
189 Stig-Goran Johansson .75 1.50
190 Stefan Karlsson .38 .75
191 Tord Lundstrom .38 .75
192 Kjell-Rune Milton .38 .75
193 Lars-Goran Nilsson .38 .75
194 Bert-Ola Nordlander .50 1.00
195 Hakan Nygren .38 .75
196 Roger Olsson .38 .75
197 Bjorn Palmquist .38 .75
198 Lars-Erik Sjoberg 2.00 4.00
199 Ulf Sterner .38 .75
200 Lennart Svedberg .75 1.50
201 Dick Yderstrom .38 .75
202 Lennart Abrahamsson .38 .75
203 Anders Bengtsson .75 1.50
204 Agne Bylund .38 .75
205 Jan Edlund .38 .75
206 Goran Hedberg .38 .75
207 Christer Johansson .38 .75
208 Rolf Jager .38 .75
209 Per-Erik Kall .38 .75
210 Anders Norberg .38 .75
211 Janne Pettersson .75 1.50
212 Bo Sjostrom .38 .75
213 Dick Sjostrom .38 .75
214 Lasse Sjostrom .38 .75
215 Ulf Steckser .38 .75
216 Lennart Strohm .38 .75
217 Kurt Tillander .38 .75
218 Roger Osterlund .38 .75
219 Hans-Ake Andersson .38 .75
220 Hans Bejbom .38 .75
221 Carl-Axel Berglund .38 .75
222 Goran Borell .38 .75
223 Bjarne Brostrom .38 .75
224 Per Backman .38 .75

Card	Low	High
225 Kennet Calen	.38	.75
226 Lennart Carlsson	.38	.75
227 Mats Davidasson	.38	.75
228 Curt Ferding	.38	.75
229 Lars-Olof Granstrom	.38	.75
230 Rolf Hansson	.38	.75
231 Rune Holmgren	.38	.75
232 Rune Norrstrom	.38	.75
233 Bert-Ake Olsson	.38	.75
234 Olle Olsson	.38	.75
235 Jan Svedman	.38	.75
236 Walter Winsth	.38	.75
237 Goran Akerlund	.38	.75
238 Borje Burlin	.38	.75
239 Hans Carlsson	.38	.75
240 Stig Carlsson	.38	.75
241 Gunnar Granberg	.38	.75
242 Allan Helenefors	.38	.75
243 Mats Hysing	.38	.75
244 Bertil Jacobsson	.38	.75
245 Stig-Goran Johansson	.75	1.50
246 Curt Larsson	1.25	2.50
247 Eilert Maatta	.38	.75
248 Soren Maatta	.38	.75
249 Tommy Bergman	.38	.75
250 Nils-Olof Schilstrom	.38	.75
251 Jan Schullstrom	.38	.75
252 Kjell Svensson	.75	1.50
253 Gunnar Tallberg	.38	.75
254 Borje Ulweback	.38	.75
255 Dick Yderstrom	.38	.75
256 Tommy Andersson	.38	.75
257 Bulla Berggren	.38	.75
258 Anders Bryner	.38	.75
259 Anders Claesson	.75	1.50
260 Jan Johansson	.38	.75
261 Ove Jonsson	.38	.75
262 Lennart Lind	.38	.75
263 Arne Lundstrom	.38	.75
264 Ake Lundstrom	.38	.75
265 Jan-Erik Nilsson	.38	.75
266 Lennart Norberg	.38	.75
267 Sten-Olov Olsson	.38	.75
268 Hakan Pettersson	.38	.75
269 Stefan Pettersson	.38	.75
270 Gosta Sjokvist	.38	.75
271 Jan Stolpe	.38	.75
272 Ake Soderberg	.38	.75
273 Kjell Westerlund	.38	.75
274 Olle Ahman	.38	.75
275 Krister Andersson	.75	1.50
276 Bert Danielsson	.38	.75
277 Gert Danielsson	.38	.75
278 Bengt Eriksson	.38	.75
279 Lars-Anders Gustavsson	.38	.75
280 Curt Jacobsson	.38	.75
281 Leif Jacobsson	.38	.75
282 Lars-Erik Jakobsson	.38	.75
283 Lars-Goran Johansson	.38	.75
284 Des Moroney	.38	.75
285 Borje Maatta	.38	.75
286 Lars-Ake Nordin	.38	.75
287 Kenneth Pedersen	.38	.75
288 Anders Rapp	.38	.75
289 Benny Runesson	.38	.75
290 Jonny Ryman	.38	.75
291 Ake Ryman	.38	.75
292 Goran Ahstrom	.75	1.50
293 John Andersson	.38	.75
294 Kjell-Olov Barrefjord	.38	.75
295 Ulf Barrefjord	.38	.75
296 Kent Bjork	.38	.75
297 Lars Dahlgren	.38	.75
298 Karl-Olof Eriksson	.38	.75
299 Osten Folkesson	.38	.75
300 Anders Hagstrom	.38	.75
301 Eric Jarvholm	.38	.75
302 Ulf Larsson	.38	.75
303 Bo Leong	.75	1.50
304 Bengt Lofgren	.38	.75
305 Roger Nilsson	.38	.75
306 Bengt Persson	.75	1.50
307 Ulf Stromsoe	.38	.75
308 Kjell Sundstrom	.38	.75
309 Leif Andersson	.38	.75
310 Bernt Augustsson	.38	.75
311 Kjell Augustsson	.38	.75
312 Tommy Eriksson	1.00	2.00
313 Lars-Olof Feltendahl	.38	.75
314 Karl-Soren Hedlund	.38	.75
315 Penti Hyytiainen	.38	.75
316 Arne Johansson	.38	.75
317 Bengt-Goran Karlsson	.38	.75
318 Curt Lundmark	1.00	2.00
319 Hakan Olsson	.75	1.50
320 Kent Persson	.38	.75
321 Ove Stenlund	.38	.75
322 Goran Thelin	.38	.75
323 Ove Thelin	.38	.75
324 Bo Astrom	.38	.75
325 Hasse Mellinger	.38	.75
326 Uno Ohrlund	.38	.75
327 Jan Ostling	.38	.75
328 Kjell Andersson	.38	.75
329 Ronny Andersson	1.00	2.00
330 Gert Blome	.38	.75
331 Ingemar Caris	1.00	2.00
332 Arne Carlsson	.38	.75
333 Svante Granholm	.38	.75
334 Henric Hedlund	.38	.75
335 Leif Henriksson	.38	.75
336 Anders Johansson	.38	.75
337 Kjell Jonsson	.38	.75
338 Bjorn Lindberg	.38	.75
339 Goran Lindberg	.38	.75
340 Carl-Fredrik Montan	.38	.75
341 Leif Nilsson	.38	.75
342 Kurt Olofsson	.38	.75
343 Jan Olsen	.38	.75
344 Roger Olsson	.38	.75
345 Kjell-Ronnie Petterson	.38	.75
346 Ulf Sterner	.38	.75
347 Rickie Bayes	1.25	2.50
348 Gary Begg	.75	1.50
349 Roger Bourbonnais	1.00	2.00
350 Jack Bownass	1.00	2.00
351 Terry Caffery	1.25	2.50
352 Steve Carlyle	1.25	2.50
353 Ab Demarco	1.50	3.00
354 Ted Hargreaves	1.00	2.00
355 Bill Heindl	1.25	2.50
356 Fran Huck	.75	1.50
357 Steve King	1.25	2.50
358 Chuck Lefley	2.00	4.00
359 Morris Mott	1.25	2.50
360 Terry O'Malley	1.00	2.00
361 Kevin O'Shea	1.25	2.50
362 Gerry Pinder	2.00	4.00
363 Steve Rexe	1.50	3.00
364 Ken Stephenson	1.25	2.50
365 Wayne Stephenson	5.00	10.00
366 Matti Harju	.38	.75
367 Esa Isaksson	.38	.75
368 Kari Johansson	.38	.75
369 Juhani Jylha	.38	.75
370 Matti Keinonen	.38	.75
371 Veli-Pekka Ketola	1.50	3.00
372 Lasse Kiili	.75	1.50
373 Ilpo Koskela	.38	.75
374 Pekka Leimu	.38	.75
375 Seppo Lindstrom	.38	.75
376 Pekka Marjamaki	.38	.75
377 Lauri Mononen	.38	.75
378 Lasse Oksanen	.38	.75
379 Lalli Partanen	.38	.75
380 Esa Peltonen	.38	.75
381 Jorma Peltonen	.38	.75
382 Juhani Rantasila	.38	.75
383 Juhani Wahlsten	.38	.75
384 Urpo Ylonen	1.25	2.50

1970-71 Swedish Mastar Serien

This 200-card set was released in Sweden to commemorate the 1970 World Championships held in Bern and Geneva, Switzerland. The cards in the set are inconsistent in their appearance. Cards 1-50 measure approximately 2 3/4" by 3 3/4". Cards 51-100 are 3" by 4". Cards 101-200 are 3" by 3 3/4". All feature color action photos on the front, but only the first and third groupings have numbers on the front. Cards 51-100 were not numbered on the cards but only in the collector's album. The cards were distributed in 5-card, clear plastic packages. The key cards in the set are two of HOFer Ken Dryden as a member of Team Canada. The cards precede his RC by two years. An album was available to store the cards; it is valued at $30.

Card	Low	High
COMPLETE SET (200)	175.00	350.00
1 Vladimir Dzurila	4.00	8.00
2 Jozef Golonka	.50	1.00
3 Jiri Holik	.38	.75
4 Vaclav Nedomansky	1.25	2.50
5 Vaclav Nedomansky	1.25	2.50
6 Jaroslav Holik	.50	1.00
7 Jozef Golonka	.50	1.00
8 Vaclav Nedomansky	1.25	2.50
9 Vladimir Bednar	.25	.50
10 Jan Havel	.25	.50
11 Jan Hrbaty	.25	.50
12 Jan Suchy	.38	.75
13 Lasse Oksanen	.25	.50
14 Urpo Ylonen	.50	1.00
15 Michael Curran	.75	1.50
16 Gary Begg	.50	1.00
17 Carl Lackey	.50	1.00
18 Terry O'Malley	.75	1.50
19 Gary Gamuicci	.50	1.00
20 Seppo Lindstrom	.25	.50
21 Lucenko	.75	1.50
Misjakov		
Davidov		
22 Victor Putjkov	.38	.75
23 Alexandr Ragulin	1.00	2.00
24 Gerry Pinder	1.25	2.50
25 Fran Huck	.50	1.00
26 Ken Dryden	50.00	100.00
27 Viktor Zinger	.38	.75
28 Vladimir Petrov	2.50	5.00
29 Igor Romisjevsky	.50	1.00
Viktor Zinger		
30 Valerij Charlamov	5.00	10.00
31 Alexandr Ragulin	1.00	2.00
32 Ab Demarco	1.00	2.00
33 Morris Mott	.75	1.50
34 Fran Huck	.50	1.00
35 Vjatjeslav Starsinov	.75	1.50
36 Lars-Goran Nilsson	.50	1.00
37 Stig-Goran Stisse Johansson	.50	1.00
38 Leif Honken Holmqvist	1.00	2.00
39 Hakan Nygren	.25	.50
40 Tord Lundstrom	.25	.50
41 Ulf Sterner	.25	.50
42 Lars-Erik Sjoberg	1.50	3.00
43 Kjell-Rune Milton	.25	.50
44 Leif Honken Holmqvist	1.00	2.00
45 Stefan Lill-Prosten Karlsson	.25	.50
46 Lennart Lill-Strimma Svedberg	.50	1.00
47 Tord Lundstrom	.25	.50
48 Ulf Sterner	.25	.50
49 Tord Lundstrom	.25	.50
50 Lennart Lill-Strimma Svedberg	.50	1.00
51 Sverige (12 st)	.25	.50
52 Bert-Ola Nordlander	.38	.75
53 Leif Honken Holmqvist	1.00	2.00
54 Lars-Erik Sjoberg	1.50	3.00
55 Lars-Erik Sjoberg	1.50	3.00
56 Nils Nicke Johansson	.25	.50
57 Ulf Sterner	.25	.50
58 Ulf Sterner	.25	.50
Leif Blixten Henriksson		
59 Tord Lundstrom	.25	.50
60 Mats Hysing	.25	.50
Nils Johansson		
61 Lars-Goran Nilsson	.25	.50
62 Hakan Nygren	.25	.50
63 USSR vs. Team Canada	1.25	2.50
Gerry Pinder		
Anatolij Firsov		
Alexandre Jakusjev		
Alexandr Ragulin		
Igor Romisjevsky		
Stephenson		
Ken Dryden		
Bill Heindl		
Vitalij Misjakov		
64 Evgenij Misjakov	.50	1.00
65 Vjatjaslav Starsinov	.75	1.50
66 Alexandr Ragulin	1.00	2.00
67 Alexandr Maltsev	2.50	5.00
68 Anatolij Firsov	2.00	4.00
69 Vladimir Lucenko	.75	1.50
70 Vladimir Petrov	2.50	5.00
71 Vladimir Petrov	2.50	5.00
72 Vjatjeslav Starsinov	.75	1.50
73 Vladimir Vikulov	.50	1.00
74 Vitaly Davidov	.50	1.00
75 Evgenij Zimin	.38	.75
76 Vladimir Bednar	1.25	2.50
Vladimir Dzurila		
77 Jan Suchy	.38	.75
78 Jaroslav Holik	.50	1.00
79 Josef Horesovsky	.25	.50
80 Jozef Golonka	.50	1.00
81 Richard Farda	.25	.50
82 Frantisek Pospisil	.50	1.00
Oldrich Machac		
83 Ilop Koskela	.25	.50
84 Juhani Jylha	.25	.50
85 Esa Peltonen	.25	.50
86 Lasse Oksanen	.25	.50
87 Juhani Wahlsten	.25	.50
88 Juha Rantasila	.25	.50
89 Bob Paradise	.50	1.00
90 Bob Paradise	.50	1.00
91 Tim Sheehy	.50	1.00
92 Michael Curran	.75	1.50
93 Ken Dryden	50.00	100.00
94 Morris Mott	.75	1.50
95 Fran Huck	.50	1.00
96 unknown	.25	.50
97 unknown	.25	.50
98 unknown	.25	.50
99 unknown	.25	.50
100 unknown	.25	.50
101 Arne Carlsson	.25	.50
102 Nils Nicke Johansson	.25	.50
103 Leif Holmqvist	1.00	2.00
104 Leif Henriksson	.25	.50
105 Lennart Svedberg	.50	1.00
106 Hakan Wickberg	.25	.50
107 Gennar Backman	.25	.50
108 Roger Olsson	.25	.50
109 Kjell-Rune Milton	.25	.50
110 Mats Hysing	.25	.50
111 Lars-Erik Sjoberg	1.50	3.00
112 Anders Hedberg	5.00	10.00
113 Bjorn Palmqvist	.25	.50
114 Tord Lundstrom	.25	.50
115 Ulf Sterner	.25	.50
116 Stig-Goran Johansson	.50	1.00
117 Lars-Goran Nilsson	.25	.50
118 Stefan Karlsson	.25	.50
119 Anders Nordin	.25	.50
120 Hans Virus Lindberg	.25	.50
121 Davidov	.50	1.00
Starshinov		
Polupanov		
Jakushev		
Maltsev		
Firsov		
122 Vitaly Davidov	.50	1.00
123 Alexandr Jakusjev	2.50	5.00
Valtonen O. Rantasila		
124 Alexandr Maltsev	2.50	5.00
125 Valerij Charlamov	5.00	10.00
126 Alexandr Ragulin	1.00	2.00
127 Igor Romisjevskij	.25	.50
128 Boris Michailov	2.50	5.00
129 Vyatcheslav Starsinov	.50	1.00
Victor Polupanov		
Alexander Ragulin		
Vladimir Lucenko		
130 Victor Konovalenko	.25	.50
131 Jakusjev	2.00	4.00
Vitalij Davidov		
Boris Michailov		
Vladislav Tretiak		
Alexander Maltsev		
Evgenji Paladjev		
132 Vladimir Lucenko	1.50	3.00
Vladimir Petrov		
Anatoli Firsov		
Valerij Nikitin		
Igor Romishevski		
Vikulov		
Alexander Yakushev		
133 Alexandr Maltsev	2.50	5.00
134 Valerij Nikitin	.25	.50
135 Vladimir Vikulov	.50	1.00
136 Vjatjeslav Starsinov	.75	1.50
137 Evgenij Paladjev	.25	.50
138 Vladimir Shapovalov	.25	.50
139 Anatolij Firsov	2.00	4.00
140 Victor Polupanov	.25	.50
141 Jaroslav Jirik	.25	.50
142 Miroslav Lacky	.50	1.00
143 Jan Suchy	.38	.75
144 Lubomir Ujvary	.25	.50
145 Vladimir Bednar	.25	.50
146 Richard Farda	.25	.50
147 Josef Cernyh	.38	.75
148 Vaclav Nedomansky	1.25	2.50
149 Jaroslav Holik	.75	1.50
150 Jiri Holik	.38	.75
151 Julius Haas	.38	.75
Vladislav Martinec		
152 Vaclav Nedomansky	1.25	2.50
153 Josef Horesovsky	.25	.50
154 Oldrich Machac	.25	.50
155 Tommy Abrahamsson	.50	1.00
Jiri Kochta		
156 Vladimir Dzurila	2.00	4.00
Jan Suchy		
Vladimir Bednar		
157 Jorma Valtonen	.50	1.00
158 Veli-Pekka Ketola	1.00	2.00
159 Matti Murto	.25	.50
Lauri Mononen		
160 Heikki Riihiranta	.50	1.00
161 Pekka Leimu	.25	.50
162 Lasse Oksanen	.25	.50
163 Jorma Valtonen	.25	.50
Vaino Kolkka		
Pekka Marjamaki		
164 Urpo Ylonen	.50	1.00
165 Matti Keinonen	.25	.50
166 Juha Rantasila	.75	1.50
Anatolij Firsov		
167 Jorma Vehmanen	.25	.50
168 Matti Murto	.25	.50
169 Peter Slapke	.25	.50
170 Claus Hirche	.25	.50
171 Frank Braun	.25	.50
172 Rolf Bielas	.25	.50
173 Kargar	.25	.50
Hiller		
Ziesche		
Braun		
174 Beilas	.25	.50
Braun		
Hirche		
Kolbe		
175 Wilfried Rohrbach	.25	.50
Hartmut Nickel		
176 Plotka	.25	.50
Karrenbauer		
Rohrbach		
Patschinski		
177 John Mayasich	.25	.50
(James Branch		
178 Larry Skime	.50	1.00
179 Paul Coppo	.50	1.00
180 Larry Pleau	.50	1.00
181 Bruce Riutta	.50	1.00
Ron Nasland		
John Lothrop		
182 Jerry Lackey	.50	1.00
183 Bob Paradise	.75	1.50
Michael Curran		
Carl Lackey		
184 Paul Coppo	.50	1.00
Peter Markle		
185 Roger Bourbonnais	.75	1.50
186 Ted Hargreaves	.75	1.50
187 Fran Huck	.50	1.00
188 Wayne Stephenson	2.50	5.00
189 Morris Mott	.75	1.50
190 Gerry Pinder	1.25	2.50
191 Gary Begg	.50	1.00
192 Ken Dryden	50.00	100.00
Blank Back		
193 Felix Goralczyk	.25	.50
194 Andrzej Tkacz	.25	.50
195 Jan Modzelewski	.25	.50
196 Marian Kajzerek	.25	.50
197 Josef Stefaniak	.25	.50
198 Walery Kosyl	.25	.50
199 Jan Modzelewski	.25	.50
200 Pajerski	.25	.50
Goralzcyk		
Chachowski		
Polen		

1970-71 Swedish Hockey

This set of 384-cards was issued by Williams Forlags AB and printed by Panini in Italy. The cards, which measure approximately 2 1/2" by 1 3/4", feature teams from the Swedish first and second divisions, as well as national team members from Tre Kroner, Russia, Czechoslovakia, Finland and East Germany. The card fronts feature a small player portrait along with the team emblem. The backs give player name, a brief bio and card number. The set includes many well known international stars, most prominently the first appearance of HOFer Borje Salming. An album to house the stickers was available as well; it also included text and photos to give a brief history of the teams involved. It is valued at approximately $40. Note: Spellings are as they appear on the cards and, in the case of Russian players, are not necessarily the spellings typically used for these players.

Card	Low	High
COMPLETE SET (384)	200.00	400.00
1 Leif (Honken) Holmqvist	1.25	2.50
2 Kjell Hedman	.75	1.50
3 Lars Danielsson	.38	.75
4 Ake Fagerstrom	.38	.75
5 Per-Arne Hubinette	.38	.75
6 Hakan Lindgren	.38	.75
7 Bert-Ola Nordlander	.50	1.00
8 Rolf (Rattan) Edberg	.38	.75
9 Bo Hansson	.38	.75
10 Jan-Olov Kroon	.38	.75
11 Ulf Nilsson	5.00	10.00
12 Bosse Olofsson	.38	.75
13 Lennart Selinder	.38	.75
14 Hans Stromberg	.38	.75
15 Kjell Savstrom	.38	.75
16 Lars-Ake Warning	.38	.75
17 Lars-Goran Nilsson	.75	1.50
Alexander Yakushev		
18 William Lofqvist	.75	1.50
19 Hans Dahllof	.75	1.50
20 Lars Bylund	.38	.75
21 Lars Hedenstrom	.38	.75
22 Kjell Johnsson	.38	.75
23 Borje Salming	12.50	25.00
24 Stig Salming	.38	.75
25 Stig Ostling	.38	.75
26 Inge Hammarstrom	2.50	5.00
27 Lennart Johansson	.38	.75
28 Stefan Karlsson	.38	.75
29 Lennart Lind	.38	.75
30 Hans (Virus) Lindberg	.38	.75
31 Tord Lundstrom	.38	.75
32 Jan-Erik Lyck	.38	.75
33 Lars-Goran Nilsson	.38	.75
34 Lars-Ake Sivertsson	.38	.75
35 Hakan Wickberg	.38	.75
36 puzzle	.38	.75
37 puzzle	.38	.75
38 puzzle	.38	.75
39 puzzle	.38	.75
40 puzzle	.38	.75
41 puzzle	.38	.75
42 puzzle	.50	.75
43 puzzle	.50	.75
44 puzzle	.38	.75
45 puzzle	.38	.75
46 puzzle	.50	.75
47 puzzle	.50	.75
48 Roland Einarsson	.75	1.50
49 Ake Eklof	.38	.75
50 Christer Ahlstrand	.38	.75
51 Thomas Carlsson	.38	.75
52 Anders Rylin	.38	.75
53 Billy Sundstrom	.38	.75
54 Folke Bengtsson	.38	.75
55 Stig Larsson	.38	.75
56 Lars-Ake Lundell	.38	.75
57 Per Lundstrom	.38	.75
58 Bjorn Palmqvist	.38	.75
59 Ulf Rydin	.38	.75
60 Ove Svensson	.38	.75
61 Jan Zabrodsky	.38	.75
62 Leif Holmqvist PUZ	1.00	2.00
63 Leif Holmqvist PUZ	1.00	2.00
64 Leif Holmqvist PUZ	1.00	2.00
65 Leif Holmqvist PUZ	1.00	2.00
66 Christer Abrahamsson	1.50	3.00
67 Christer Sterner	.75	1.50
68 Thommy Abrahamsson	.75	1.50
69 Karl-Gustaf Alander	.38	.75
70 Gunnar Andersson	.38	.75
71 Roland Bond	.38	.75
72 Ake Danielsson	.38	.75
73 Per-Olov Brasar	1.50	3.00
74 Kjell Brus	.38	.75
75 Hans Jax	.38	.75
76 Dan Labraaten	1.50	3.00
77 Roger Lindqvist	.38	.75
78 Ulf Martensson	.38	.75
79 Olle Sjogren	.38	.75
80 Ingemar Snis	.38	.75
81 Dan Soderstrom	.38	.75
82 Mats Ahlberg	.38	.75
83 Gunnar Backman	.75	1.50
84 Ivar Larsson	.75	1.50
85 Lage Edin	.38	.75
86 Kjell-Rune Milton	.38	.75
87 Ulf Torstensson	.38	.75
88 Ulf Wigren	.38	.75
89 Ulf Croon	.38	.75
90 Hakan Dahllof	.38	.75
91 Anders Hedberg	5.00	10.00
92 Torbjorn Hubinette	.38	.75
93 Christer Nilsson	.38	.75
94 Lennart Norberg	.38	.75
95 Anders Nordin	.38	.75
96 Hakan Nygren	.38	.75
97 Per-Olof Uusitalo	.38	.75
98 Lars Ohman	.38	.75
99 Tore Ohman	.38	.75
100 V. Dzurilla PUZ	.75	1.50
101 V. Dzurilla PUZ	.75	1.50
102 V. Dzurilla PUZ	.75	1.50
103 V. Dzurilla PUZ	.75	1.50
104 V. Dzurilla PUZ	.75	1.50
105 V. Dzurilla PUZ	.75	1.50
106 V. Dzurilla PUZ	.75	1.50
107 V. Dzurilla PUZ	.75	1.50
108 V. Dzurilla PUZ	.75	1.50
109 V. Dzurilla PUZ	.75	1.50
110 V. Dzurilla PUZ	.75	1.50
111 V. Dzurilla PUZ	.75	1.50
112 Bengt-Ake Gustavsson	.75	1.50
113 Lars Gustavsson	.75	1.50
114 Tommy Andersson	.38	.75
115 Hans-Olov Ernlund	.38	.75
116 Lars Mjoberg	.38	.75
117 Gote Hansson	.38	.75
118 L. Svedberg PUZ	.50	1.00
119 B. Mikhailov PUZ	1.50	3.00
120 L. Holmqvist PUZ	1.00	2.00
121 Hans Hansson	.38	.75
122 Sven-Ake Jakobsson	.38	.75
123 Mats Lind	.38	.75
124 Mats Lonn	.38	.75
125 Borje Marcus	.38	.75
126 Ulf Nises	.38	.75
127 Borje Skoog	.38	.75
128 Erling Sundblad	.38	.75
129 Kent Sundkvist	.38	.75
130 Curt Larsson	1.00	2.00
131 Torbjorn Hellsing	.75	1.50
132 Tommie Bergman	2.00	4.00
133 Arne Carlsson	.38	.75
134 Allan Helenefors	.38	.75
135 Eilert Maatta	.38	.75
136 Jan Schullstrom	.38	.75
137 Hans Carlsson	.38	.75
138 Tommy Carlsson	.38	.75
139 Gunnar Granberg	.38	.75
140 Mats Hysing	.38	.75
141 Bertil Jacobsson	.38	.75
142 Stig-Goran Johansson	.38	.75
143 Soren Maatta	.38	.75
144 Nils-Olov Schilstrom	.38	.75
145 Dick Yderstrom	.38	.75
146 Carl-Goran Oberg	.38	.75
147 Lennart Svedberg	.50	1.00
148 Anders Claesson	.75	1.50
149 Kent Othberg	.75	1.50
150 Jan Johansson	.38	.75
151 Jan-Erik Nilsson	.38	.75
152 Stefan Pettersson	.38	.75
153 Lennart Svedberg	.75	1.50
154 Bo Berggren	.38	.75
155 Arne Lundstrom	.38	.75
156 Finn Lundstrom	.38	.75
157 I. Romisjevskij PUZ	.38	.75
158 I. Romisjevskij PUZ	.50	1.00
159 Ake Lundstrom	.38	.75
160 V. Tretiak PUZ	4.00	8.00
161 V. Tretiak PUZ	4.00	8.00
162 Lennart Norberg	.38	.75
163 Hakan Pettersson	.38	.75
164 Ake Soderberg	.50	1.00
165 Olle Ahman	.38	.75
166 puzzle	.38	.75
167 puzzle	.38	.75
168 puzzle	.38	.75
169 puzzle	.38	.75
170 puzzle	.38	.75
171 puzzle	.38	.75
172 puzzle	.38	.75
173 puzzle	.38	.75
174 puzzle	.38	.75
175 puzzle	.38	.75
176 puzzle	.38	.75
177 puzzle	.38	.75
178 Christer Andersson	.75	1.50
179 Goran Astrom	.75	1.50
180 Kenneth Ekman	.38	.75
181 Lars Erik Jakobsson	.38	.75
182 Des Moroney	.38	.75
183 Borje Maatta	.38	.75
184 Kenneth Pedersen	.38	.75
185 Anders Rapp	.38	.75
186 Sven Crabo	.38	.75
187 Lars Anders Gustavsson	.38	.75
188 Kurt Jacobsson	.38	.75
189 Leif Jacobsson	.38	.75
190 Lars Goran Johansson	.38	.75
191 Bernt Karlsson	.38	.75
192 Benny Runesson	.38	.75
193 Jonny Ryman	.38	.75
194 Ake Ryman	.38	.75
195 Christer Grahn	.75	1.50
196 Ronny Sandstrom	.38	.75
197 John Andersson	.38	.75
198 Karl-Olof Eriksson	.38	.75
199 Anders Hagstrom	.38	.75
200 Rolf Jager	.38	.75
201 Erik Jarvholm	.38	.75
202 Lars Nordin	.38	.75
203 Ulf Barrefjord	.38	.75
204 Lars Dahlgren	.38	.75
205 Ulf Ingvarsson	.38	.75
206 Ulf Larsson	.38	.75
207 Jan Lundqvist	.38	.75
208 Ulf Lundstrom	.38	.75
209 Bengt Lovgren	.38	.75
210 Lars SJostrom	.38	.75
211 Kjell Sundstrom	.38	.75
212 Ulf Stromsoe	.38	.75
213 Hakan Olsson	.75	1.50
214 Leif Andersson	.38	.75
215 Tommy Eriksson	.75	1.50
216 Karl-Soren Hedlund	.38	.75
217 Curt Lundmark	.75	1.50
218 Ove Nystrom	.38	.75
219 Gote Gustavsson	.38	.75
220 Hans Hjelm	.38	.75
221 Pennti Hyytiainen	.38	.75
222 Arne Johansson	.38	.75
223 Bengt-Goran Karlsson	.38	.75
224 Kent Persson	.38	.75
225 Ove Stenlund	.38	.75
226 Goran Thelin	.38	.75
227 Ove Thelin	.38	.75
228 Bo Astrom	.38	.75
229 Jan Ostling	.38	.75
230 V. Tretiak action	10.00	20.00
231 V. Konovalenko PUZ	.38	.75
232 V. Konovalenko PUZ	.38	.75
233 V. Konovalenko PUZ	.38	.75
234 V. Konovalenko PUZ	.38	.75
235 V. Konovalenko PUZ	.38	.75
236 V. Konovalenko PUZ	.38	.75
237 V. Konovalenko PUZ	.38	.75
238 V. Konovalenko PUZ	.38	.75
239 V. Konovalenko PUZ	.38	.75
240 V. Konovalenko PUZ	.38	.75
241 V. Konovalenko PUZ	.38	.75
242 V. Konovalenko PUZ	.38	.75
243 Ingemar Caris	.75	1.50
244 Ronny Andersson	.75	1.50
245 Gert Blome	.38	.75
246 Anders Johansson	.38	.75
247 Goran Lindberg	.38	.75
248 Jan Olsen	.38	.75
249 Lars-Erik Sjoberg	2.00	4.00
250 Kjell Andersson	.38	.75
251 Svante Granholm	.38	.75
252 Henrik Hedlund	.38	.75
253 Leif Henriksson	.38	.75
254 Bjorn Lindberg	.38	.75
255 Billy Lindstrom	.38	.75
256 Carl-Fredrik Montan	.38	.75
257 Leif Nilsson	.38	.75
258 Kurt Olofsson	.38	.75
259 Roger Olsson	.38	.75
260 Kjell-Ronnie Pettersson	.38	.75
261 Soviet team PUZ	.38	.75
262 Soviet team PUZ	.38	.75
263 Soviet team PUZ	.38	.75
264 Soviet team PUZ	.38	.75
265 Soviet team PUZ	.38	.75
266 Soviet team PUZ	.38	.75
267 Soviet team PUZ	.38	.75
268 Soviet team PUZ	.38	.75
269 Soviet team PUZ	.38	.75
270 Soviet team PUZ	.38	.75
271 Soviet team PUZ	.38	.75
272 Soviet team PUZ	.38	.75
273 Leif Holmqvist	1.00	2.00
274 Gunnar Backman	.75	1.50
275 Christer Abrahamsson	1.50	3.00
276 Thommy Abrahamsson	.75	1.50
277 Arne Carlsson	.38	.75
278 Nils Johansson	.38	.75
279 Ljell-Rune Milton	.38	.75
280 Lars-Erik Sjoberg	2.00	4.00
281 Lennart Svedberg	.75	1.50
282 Anders Hedberg	5.00	10.00
283 Stig-Goran Johansson	.38	.75
284 Stefan Karlsson	.38	.75
285 Hans Lindberg	.38	.75
286 Tord Lundstrom	.38	.75
287 Lars-Goran Nilsson	.38	.75
288 Anders Nordin	.38	.75
289 Roger Olsson	.38	.75
290 Bjorn Palmqvist	.38	.75
291 Ulf Sterner	.38	.75
292 Hakan Wickberg	.38	.75
293 Urpo Ylonen	1.00	2.00
294 Jorma Valtonen	.75	1.50
295 Ilpo Koskela	.38	.75
296 Seppo Lindstrom	.38	.75
297 Pekka Marjamaki	.38	.75
298 Lalli Partinen	.38	.75
299 Juha Rantasila	.38	.75
300 Heikki Riihiranta	1.00	2.00
301 Pekka Keimu	.38	.75
302 Matti Keinonen	.38	.75
303 Veli-Pekka Ketola	1.50	3.00
304 Vaino Kolkka	.38	.75
305 Harri Linnonmaa	.38	.75
306 Lauri Mononen	.38	.75
307 Matti Murto	.75	1.50
308 Lasse Oksanen	.38	.75
309 Esa Peltonen	.38	.75
310 Jorma Peltonen	.38	.75
311 Juhani Tamminen	.75	1.50
312 Jorma Vehmanen	.38	.75
313 Viktor Konovalenko	.75	1.50
314 Vladislav Tretjak	20.00	40.00
315 Vitalij Davidov	.75	1.50
316 Vladimir Lutjenko	.75	1.50
317 Jevgenij Paladjev	.38	.75
318 Alexander Ragulin	1.50	3.00
319 Igor Romisjevski	.50	1.00
320 Valerij Vasiljev	2.50	5.00
321 Valerij Nikitin	.50	1.00
322 Valerij Charlamov	7.50	15.00
323 Anatolij Firsov	4.00	8.00
324 Alexander Jakusjev	4.00	8.00
325 Alexander Maltsev	4.00	8.00
326 Boris Michailov	4.00	8.00
327 Jevgenij Misjakov	1.25	2.50
328 Vladimir Petrov	2.50	5.00
329 Viktor Polupanov	.38	.75
330 Vladimir Sjadrin	1.50	3.00
331 Vjatjeslav Starsinov	1.25	2.50
332 Vladimir Vikulov	.50	1.00
333 puzzle	.38	.75
334 puzzle	.38	.75
335 puzzle	.38	.75
336 puzzle	.38	.75
337 puzzle	.38	.75
338 puzzle	.38	.75
339 puzzle	.38	.75
340 puzzle	.38	.75
341 puzzle	.38	.75
342 puzzle	.38	.75
343 puzzle	.38	.75
344 puzzle	.38	.75
345 Vladimir Dzurilla	2.50	5.00
346 Miroslav Lacky	.75	1.50
347 Vladimir Bednar	.38	.75
348 Josef Horesovsky	.38	.75
349 Oldrich Machac	.38	.75
350 Frantisek Pospisil	.75	1.50
351 Jan Suchy	.50	1.00
352 Lubomir Ujvary	.38	.75
353 Josef Cerny	.50	1.00
354 Richard Farda	.38	.75
355 Julius Haas	.38	.75
356 Ivan Hlinka	.75	1.50
357 Jaroslav Holik	.50	1.00
358 Jiri Holik	.50	1.00
359 Jan Hrbaty	.38	.75
360 Jiri Kochta	.38	.75
361 Vladislav Martinec	.38	.75
362 Vaclav Nedomansky	1.50	3.00
363 Stanislav Pryl	.38	.75
364 Frantisek Sevcik	.38	.75
365 Klaus Hirche	.75	1.50
366 Diter Purschel	.75	1.50
367 Frank Braun	.38	.75
368 Dieter Dewitz	.38	.75
369 Bernd Karrenbauer	.38	.75
370 Helmut Novy	.38	.75
371 Dietmar Peters	.38	.75
372 Wolfgang Plotka	.38	.75
373 Peter Slapke	.38	.75
374 Rolf Bielas	.38	.75
375 Lothar Fuchs	.38	.75
376 Bernd Hiller	.38	.75
377 Reinhard Karger	.38	.75
378 Hartmut Nickel	.38	.75
379 Rudiger Noack	.38	.75
380 Rainer Patschinski	.38	.75
381 Peter Prusa	.38	.75
382 Wilfried Rohrbach	.38	.75
383 Dieter Rohl	.38	.75
384 Joachim Ziesche	.38	.75

1971-72 Swedish Hockey

This set of 400 cards was printed by Panini and released in Sweden by Williams Forlags AB. The cards-- which measure approximately 2 1/2" by 1 3/4" -- feature players from Sweden's top league, as well as from several national teams and NHL clubs. The fronts offer a simple player portrait; the backs contain sticker number and a brief player bio in Swedish. An album to house the set can be found; it is valued approximately at $40. Key stars in this loaded set include Bobby Orr, Gordie Howe and Vladislav Tretiak. NOTE: Spellings used are those found on the sticker. In the case of the Russian players, these spellings may differ from those in common usage.

Card	Low	High
COMPLETE SET (400)	225.00	450.00
1 Christer Abrahamsson	1.00	2.00
2 Leif (Honken) Holmqvist	.50	1.00
3 William (Loken) Lofqvist	.50	1.00
4 Thommy Abrahamsson	.50	1.00
5 Gunnar Andersson	.25	.50
6 Thommie Bergman	1.50	3.00
7 Arne Carlsson	.25	.50
8 Kjell-Rune Milton	.25	.50
9 Bert-Ola Nordlander	.50	1.00
10 Lennart Svedberg	.50	1.00
11 Lars-Erik Sjoberg	1.00	2.00
12 Stig Ostling	.25	.50
13 Inge Hammarstrom	1.50	10.00
14 Anders Hedberg	4.00	8.00
15 Stig-Goran Johansson	.50	1.00
16 Stefan Karlsson	.25	.50
17 Dan Labraaten	1.00	2.00
18 Hans (Virus) Lindberg	.25	.50
19 Tord Lundstrom	.25	.50
20 Lars-Goran Nilsson	.25	.50
21 Hakan Nygren	.25	.50
22 Bjorn Palmqvist	.25	.50
23 Hakan Pettersson	.25	.50
24 Ulf Sterner	.25	.50
25 Hakan Wickberg	.25	.50
26 Viktor Konovalenko	.30	.75
27 Vladislav Tretjak	10.00	20.00
28 Gennadij Cigannkov	.30	.75
29 Vitali Davidov	.30	.75
30 Victor Kuskin	.25	.50
31 Vladimir Lutjenko	.30	.75
32 Alexander Ragulin	1.00	2.00
33 Igor Romisjevskij	.30	.75
34 Valerij Kharlamov	5.00	15.00
35 Anatolij Firsov	2.50	5.00
36 Alexander Maltsev	2.50	5.00
37 Boris Michailov	2.50	5.00
38 Jevgenij Misjakov	1.00	2.00
39 Vladimir Petrov	2.50	5.00
40 Vjatjeslav Starshinov	.50	1.0
41 Vladimir Vikulov	.30	.7
42 Evgenij Zimin	.50	1.0
43 Jiri Holecek	.50	1.0
44 Josef Horesovsky	.25	.5
45 Oldrich Machac	.25	.5
46 Frantisek Panchartek	.25	.5
47 Frantisek Pospisil	.30	.7
48 Jan Suchy	.30	.7
49 Josef Cerny	.30	.7
50 Richard Farda	.25	.5
51 Jan Havel	.25	.5
52 Ivan Hlinka	.50	1.0
53 Jiri Holik	.30	.7
54 Jiri Kochta	.25	.5
55 Vladimir Martinec	.30	.7
56 Vaclav Nedomansky	1.00	2.0
57 Eduard Novak	.25	.5
58 Bohuslav Stastny	.50	1.0
59 Jorma Valtonen	.50	1.0
60 Urpo Ylonen	.50	1.0
61 Ilpo Koskela	.25	.5
62 Seppo Lindstrom	.25	.5
63 Hannu Luojola	.25	.5
64 Pekka Marjamaki	.25	.5
65 Esa Isaksson	.25	.5
66 Veli-Pekka Ketola	1.00	2.0
67 Harri Linnonmaa	.25	.5
68 Erkki Mononen	.25	.5
69 Lauri Mononen	.25	.5
70 Matti Murto	.50	1.0
71 Lasse Oksanen	.25	.5
72 Esa Peltonen	.25	.5
73 Juhanni Tamminen	.50	1.0
74 Jorma Vehmanen	.25	.5
75 Leif (Honken) Holmqvist	.50	1.0
76 Bert Jattne	.50	1.0
77 Lars Danielsson	.25	.5
78 Ake Fagerstrom	.25	.5
79 Per-Arne (Hybbe) Hubinette	.25	.5
80 Hakan (Flamman) Lindgren	.25	.5
81 Bert-Ola Nordlander	.50	1.0
82 Lennart (Petter) Pettersson	.25	.5
83 Rolf (Rattan) Edberg	.25	
84 Bo Hansson	.25	
85 Jan-Olov Kroon	.25	
86 Gunnar (Gurra) Lindkvist	.25	
87 Christer Lundberg	.25	
88 Ulf (Projsarn) Nilsson	4.00	8.0
89 Bo Olofsson	.25	
90 Jan Olsson	.25	
91 Lennart (Sillen) Selinder	.25	
92 Soren Sjogren	.25	
93 Hans (Strumpan) Stromberg	.25	
94 Jan Ostling	.25	
95 Kjell Helling	.50	1.
96 William (Loken) Lofqvist	.50	1.
97 Lars (Bylle) Bylund	.25	
98 Kjell (Kulan) Johnsson	.25	
99 Par Malmstrom	.25	
100 Borje Salming	5.00	10.
101 Stig Salming	.25	
102 Stig Ostling	.25	
103 Inge Hammarstrom	1.50	10.
104 Lennart Johansson	.25	
105 Stefan Karlsson	.25	
106 Lennart (Huppa) Lind	.25	
107 Hans (Virus) Lindberg	.25	
108 Tord Lundstrom	.25	
109 Jan-Erik Lyck	.25	
110 Lars-Goran Nilsson	.25	
111 Leif Olsson	.25	
112 Lars-Ake (Sivert) Sivertsson	.25	
113 Hakan Wickberg	.25	
114 Lars Oberg	.25	
115 Roland Einarsson	.50	1.
116 Peder Nilsson	.50	1.
117 Kent Olsson	.50	1.
118 Thomas Carlsson	.25	
119 Lars-Ake Lundell	.25	
120 Jorgen Palm	.25	
121 Anders Rylin	.25	
122 Billy Sundstrom	.25	
123 Kent Soderlund	.25	
124 Folke (Totte) Bengtsson	.25	
125 Ake Eklof	.25	

26 Stig Larsson	.25	.50
27 Sven-Bertil Lindstrom	.25	.50
28 Thomas Palm	.25	.50
29 Bjorn Palmqvist	.25	.50
30 Ulf Rydin	.25	.50
31 Ove Svensson	.25	.50
32 Per-Allan Wikstrom	.25	.50
33 Anders Andren	.25	.50
34 Per Lundstrom	.25	.50
5 Lennart Andersson	.50	1.00
6 Kent Bodin	.50	1.00
7 Bjorn Fagerlund	.50	1.00
8 Ake Carlsson	.25	.50
9 Nils (Nicke) Johansson	.25	.50
0 Lars-Goran Nilsson	.25	.50
1 Kent Olsson	.50	1.00
2 Hans-Ake Rosendahl	.25	.50
3 Karl-Johan Sundqvist	.25	.50
4 Benny Andersson	.25	.50
5 Hasse Andersson	.25	.50
6 Kent-Erik Andersson	.25	.50
7 Berndt Augustsson	.25	.50
8 Kjell Augustsson	.25	.50
9 Per-Ole Backman	.25	.50
0 Conny Evensson	.50	1.00
1 Sten Johansson	.25	.50
2 Leif Labraaten	.25	.50
3 Sven-Ove (Nutte) Olsson	.25	.50
4 Ulf Sterner	.25	.50
5 Christer Abrahamsson	1.00	2.00
6 Krister Sterner	.50	1.00
7 Thommy Abrahamsson	.50	1.00
8 Karl-Gustaf Alander	.25	.50
9 Gunnar Andersson	.25	.50
0 Roland Bond	.25	.50
1 Ake Danielsson	.25	.50
2 Ulf Weinstock	.25	.50
3 Per-Olov Brasar	1.00	2.00
4 Kjell Brus	.25	.50
5 Hans (Jacken) Jax	.25	.50
6 Dan Labraaten	1.00	2.00
7 Roger (Stoarn) Lindqvist	.25	.50
8 Ulf (Marten) Martensson	.25	.50
9 Stig Nordin	.25	.50
0 Olle (Mapa) Sjogren	.25	.50
1 Ingemar Snis	.25	.50
2 Dan Soderstrom	.25	.50
3 Bo Theander	.30	.75
4 Mats (Matta) Ahlberg	.25	.50
5 Gunnar (Backis) Backman	.25	.50
Ivar Larsson	.50	1.00
Sture Andersson	.25	.50
Lage Edin	.25	.50
Kjell-Rune (Mille) Milton	.25	.50
Per-Olof Uusitalo	.25	.50
Ulf Wigren	.25	.50
Hakan Dahlof	.25	.50
Anders Hedberg	4.00	8.00
Torbjorn Hubinette	.25	.50
Assar Lundgren	.25	.50
Per Lundqvist	.25	.50
Christer Nilsson	.25	.50
Kenneth Nordenberg	.25	.50
Anders (Ante) Nordin	.25	.50
Hakan Nygren	.25	.50
Ulf Thors	.25	.50
Ulf Torstensson	.25	.50
Lars Ohman	.25	.50
Tore Ohman	.25	.50
Tony Esposito	17.50	35.00
Bobby Orr	50.00	100.00
Jean Beliveau	12.50	35.00
Gordie Howe	40.00	75.00
Phil Esposito	12.50	35.00
Bobby Hull	20.00	40.00
Bengt-Ake Gustavsson	.50	1.00
Lars Gustavsson	.50	1.00
Tommy Andersson	.25	.50
Hans-Olov Ernlund	.25	.50
Tord Johansson	.25	.50
Lars Mjoberg	.25	.50
Per-Erik (Plattis) Olsson	.25	.50
Tord Svensson	.25	.50
Jan (Bambis) Danielsson	.25	.50
Tommy Eriksson	.50	1.00
Gote Hansson	.25	.50
Hans Hansson	.25	.50
Sven-Ake (Saja) Jacobsson	.25	.50
Mats (Tuppen) Lonn	.25	.50
Borje Marcus	.25	.50
Lars Munther	.25	.50
Ulf Nises	.25	.50
Anders Rosen	.25	.50
Borje Skogs	.25	.50
Kent Sundkvist	.25	.50
Mikael Collin	.50	1.00
Bjorn Jansson	.50	1.00
Curt Larsson	.50	1.00
Tommie Bergman	1.50	3.00
Arne Carlsson	.25	.50
Christer Karlsson	.25	.50
Eilert (Garvis) Maatta	.25	.50
Jan Schullstrom	.25	.50
Borje (Poppen) Burlin	.25	.50
Hans Carlsson	.25	.50
Tommy Carlsson	.25	.50
Mats Hysing	.25	.50
Bertil Jacobsson	.25	.50
Stig-Goran Johansson	.50	1.00
Dan Landegren	.25	.50
Kjell Landstrom	.25	.50
Soren Maatta	.25	.50
Nils-Olov Schilstrom	.25	.50
Dick Yderstrom	.25	.50
Carl Goran (Lillstoveln) Oberg	.25	.50
Anders Claesson	.50	1.00
Kent Othberg	.50	1.00
Jan Johansson	.25	.50
Jan-Erik (Biffen) Nilsson	.25	.50
Stefan Pettersson	.25	.50
Tord Salomonsson	.25	.50
Lennart Svedberg	.50	1.00
Bo (Bulla) Berggren	.25	.50
Bjorn Broman	.25	.50
Lennart Broman	.25	.50
Ove Larsson	.25	.50
Rolf Larsson	.25	.50
Orjan Lindstrom	.25	.50
Arne Lundstrom	.25	.50
Thinn Lundstrom	.25	.50
Ake Lundstrom	.25	.50
Lennart Norberg	.25	.50
Hakan Pettersson	.25	.50
Ake (Taget) Soderberg	.25	.50
Olle Ahman	.25	.50
Christer Andersson	.50	1.00
Bengt Gustavsson	.25	.50
Goran (Klasse) Astrom	.25	.50
Anders Brostrom	.25	.50
Kenneth Ekman	.25	.50
Soren Gunnarsson	.25	.50
267 Lars-Erik Jacobsson	.25	.50
268 Des Moroney	.25	.50
269 Borje Maatta	.25	.50
270 Tommy Pettersson	.25	.50
271 Bengt Alm	.25	.50
272 Sven Crabo	.25	.50
273 Bengt (Benken) Eriksson	.25	.50
274 Kurt Jakobsson	.25	.50
275 Leif (Tvilling) Jakobsson	.25	.50
276 Lars-Goran Johansson	.25	.50
277 Bert (Berra) Karlsson	.25	.50
278 Benny (Nacka) Runesson	.25	.50
279 Ake Ryman	.25	.50
280 Jan Roger (Joje) Strand	.25	.50
281 Christer (Slim) Grahn	.30	.75
282 Ronny (Centis) Sandstrom	.25	.50
283 John Andersson	.25	.50
284 Karl-Olov (Kalle) Eriksson	.25	.50
285 Anders (Hagge) Hagstrom	.25	.50
286 Ulf (Ingo) Ingvarsson	.25	.50
287 Rolf Jager	.25	.50
288 Erik (Jarvis) Jarvholm	.25	.50
289 Bo Westling	.25	.50
290 Ulf (Lill-Barre) Barrefjord	.25	.50
291 Kent Bjork	.25	.50
292 Lars (Dallas) Dahlgren	.25	.50
293 Ulf (Pygge) Larsson	.25	.50
294 Jan Lundqvist	.25	.50
295 Ulf Lundstrom	.25	.50
296 Bengt (Lovet) Lovgren	.25	.50
297 Leif Martensson	.25	.50
298 Lars-Ake (Nollan) Nordin	.25	.50
299 Lars Sjostrom	.25	.50
300 Kjell Sundstrom	.25	.50
301 Ronny Andersson	.50	1.00
302 Ingemar (Sparris) Caris	.50	1.00
303 Anders (Johan) Johansson	.25	.50
304 Hakan (Norsen) Norstrom	.25	.50
305 Jan Olsen	.25	.50
306 Lars-Erik Sjoberg	.50	1.00
307 Bengt (Bengan) Sjoholm	.25	.50
308 Kjell Andersson	.25	.50
309 Svante Granholm	.25	.50
310 Kjell-Ove Gustavsson	.25	.50
311 Henrik (Tosse) Hedlund	.25	.50
312 Leif (Blixten) Henriksson	.25	.50
313 Lars-Erik Johansson	.25	.50
314 Bjorn (Nalle) Lindberg	.25	.50
315 Evert Lindstrom	.25	.50
316 Willy Lindstrom	1.00	2.00
317 Leif (Nisse) Nilsson	.25	.50
318 Kurt (Kulle) Olofsson	.25	.50
319 Roger (Viking) Olsson	.25	.50
320 Kjell-Ronnie Pettersson	.25	.50
321 Kenneth Holmstedt	.50	1.00
322 Lars-Erik Larsson	.25	.50
323 Lennart (Sly) Eriksson	.25	.50
324 Lennart Gustavsson	.25	.50
325 Jan-Ake Karlsson	.25	.50
326 Rolf Karlsson	.25	.50
327 Bengt Lundberg	.25	.50
328 Anders Thelander	.25	.50
329 Kent Bengtsson	.25	.50
330 Gunnar Backman	.50	1.00
331 Stefan Canderyd	.25	.50
332 Curt Edenvik	.25	.50
333 Per Edenvik	.25	.50
334 Weine Gullberg	.25	.50
335 Nils-Arne Hedqvist	.25	.50
336 Bengt-Ake Karlsson	.25	.50
337 Christer Kihlstrom	.25	.50
338 Stig-Olof (Bullen) Persson	.25	.50
339 Christer Sjoberg	.25	.50
340 Roddy Skyllqvist	.25	.50
341 Lars Blomqvist	.50	1.00
342 Bjorn Forsberg	.50	1.00
343 Anders Hedlund	.25	.50
344 Lennart Johansson	.25	.50
345 Martin Kruger	.25	.50
346 Harry Namd	.25	.50
347 Lennart Strohm	.25	.50
348 Peter Bejemark	.25	.50
349 Bertil Bond	.25	.50
350 Nils Carlsson	.25	.50
351 Ulf Pilo	.25	.50
352 Claes-Ove Fjallby	.25	.50
353 Lars Granlund	.25	.50
354 Kjell Keijser	.25	.50
355 Lennart Lange	.25	.50
356 Bo Mellbin	.25	.50
357 Lars Starck	.25	.50
358 Leif Svensson	.25	.50
359 Kjell Ahlen	.25	.50
360 Henry (Henna) Svensson	.25	.50
361 Sven-Allan Ellstrom	.50	1.00
362 Tommy Eriksson	.50	1.00
363 Walter Winsth	.50	1.00
364 Hans-Ake Andersson	.25	.50
365 Jan Andersson	.25	.50
366 Hans Bejbom	.25	.50
367 Goran Borell	.25	.50
368 Bo Schilstrom	.25	.50
369 Bjarne Brostrom	.25	.50
370 Kenneth Calen	.25	.50
371 Lennart Carlsson	.25	.50
372 Mats Davidsson	.25	.50
373 Rolf Hansson	.25	.50
374 Rune Norrstrom	.25	.50
375 Gunther Rauch	.25	.50
376 Jan Vestberg	.25	.50
377 Bengt Wistling	.25	.50
378 Kent Zetterberg	.25	.50
379 Goran Akerlund	.25	.50
380 Uno (Garvis) Ohrlund	.25	.50
381 Goran Hogosta	.60	1.50
382 Juha Raninen	.50	1.00
383 Bert Backman	.25	.50
384 Christer Collin	.25	.50
385 Dag Olsson	.25	.50
386 Bjorn Resare	.25	.50
387 Lars Thoreus	.25	.50
388 Stig Andersson	.25	.50
389 Borje Engblom	.25	.50
390 Christer Englund	.25	.50
391 Bo Eriksson	.25	.50
392 Mats Eriksson	.25	.50
393 Roland Eriksson	.25	.50
394 Olle Henriksson	.25	.50
395 Yngve Hindrikes	.25	.50
396 Kjell Jansson	.25	.50
397 Jan Johansson	.25	.50
398 Jan Karlsson	.25	.50
399 Agne Norberg	.25	.50
400 Christian Reuthie	.25	.50

1972 Swedish Semic World Championship

Printed in Italy by Semic Press, the 233 cards comprising this set measure 1 7/8" by 2 1/2" and feature posed color player photos on their white-bordered fronts. The white back carries the player's name and text in Swedish. The cards are numbered on the back and arranged by national teams as follows: Soviet Union (1-20), Czechoslovakia (21-41), Sweden (42-70), Finland (71-92), Germany (93-117), United States (118-137), France (138-162), and Canada (163-233).

COMPLETE SET (233)	200.00	400.00
1 Viktor Konovalenko	.38	.75
2 Vitalij Davydov	.38	.75
3 Vladimir Lutjenko	.38	.75
4 Viktor Kuskin	.38	.75
5 Alexander Ragulin	.75	3.00
6 Igor Romitjevskij	.38	.75
7 Gennadij Tsigankov	.38	.75
8 Vjatsjeslav Starsjinov	.75	1.50
9 Evgenij Zimin	.50	1.00
10 Alexander Maltsev	2.50	5.00
11 Anatolij Firsov	1.25	2.00
12 Evgenij Misjakov	.38	.75
13 Boris Michailov	2.00	4.00
14 Juri Ljapkin	.50	1.00
15 Alexander Martinyk	.38	.75
16 Vladimir Petrov	2.00	4.00
17 Valeri Kharlamov	5.00	10.00
18 Vladimir Vikulov	.38	.75
19 Vladimir Sjadrin	.50	1.00
20 Vladislav Tretiak	10.00	20.00
21 Marcel Sakac	.25	.50
22 Jiri Holecek	.50	1.00
23 Josef Horesovsky	.25	.50
24 Oldrich Machac	.25	.50
25 Rudolf Tajcnar	.25	.50
26 Frantisek Panchartek	.25	.50
27 Frantisek Pospisil	.38	.75
28 Jiri Kochta	.25	.50
29 Jan Havel	.25	.50
30 Vladimir Martinec	.25	.50
31 Richard Farda	.25	.50
32 Bohuslav Stastny	.38	.75
33 Vaclav Nedomansky	.75	1.50
34 Josef Cerny	.25	.50
35 Bedrich Brunchk	.25	.50
36 Jan Suchy	.25	.50
37 Eduard Novak	.25	.50
38 Jiri Bubla	.75	1.50
39 Jiri Holik	.38	.75
40 Ivan Hlinka	1.00	2.00
41 Vladimir Bednar	.25	.50
42 Leif Holmqvist	.50	1.00
43 Christer Abrahamsson	1.00	2.00
44 Christer Andersson	.50	1.00
45 Lars-Erik Sjoberg	.75	1.50
46 Lennart Svedberg	.50	1.00
47 Stig-Goran Johansson	.25	.50
48 Bert-Ola Nordlander	.25	.50
49 Thommy Abrahamsson	.50	1.00
50 Arne Carlsson	.25	.50
51 Stefan Karlsson	.25	.50
52 Hakan Wickberg	.25	.50
53 Hakan Nygren	.25	.50
54 Lars-Goran Nilsson	.25	.50
55 Thommie Bergman	1.00	2.00
56 Ulf Sterner	.38	.75
57 Hans Lindberg	.25	.50
58 Tord Lundstrom	.25	.50
59 Gunnar Andersson	.25	.50
60 Bjorn Palmqvist	.25	.50
61 Inge Hammarstrom	1.00	2.00
62 Kjell-Rune Milton	.25	.50
63 Kjell Brus	.25	.50
64 Kenneth Ekman	.25	.50
65 Bengt-Goran Karlsson	.25	.50
66 Hakan Pettersson	.25	.50
67 Dan Labraaten	.75	1.50
68 Dan Soderstrom	.25	.50
69 Anders Hedberg	2.50	5.00
70 Ake Soderberg	.25	.50
71 Urpo Ylonen	.25	.50
72 Ilpo Koskela	.25	.50
73 Seppo Lindstrom	.25	.50
74 Hannu Luojola	.25	.50
75 Pekka Marjamaki	.25	.50
76 Jouko Oystila	.25	.50
77 Heikki Jarn	.25	.50
78 Esa Isaksson	.25	.50
79 Veli-Pekka Ketola	.75	1.50
80 Harri Linnonmaa	.25	.50
81 Erkki Mononen	.25	.50
82 Lauri Mononen	.25	.50
83 Matti Murto	.25	.50
84 Lasse Oksanen	.25	.50
85 Esa Peltonen	.25	.50
86 Seppo Repo	.25	.50
87 Tommi Salmelainen	.25	.50
88 Juhani Tamminen	.25	.50
89 Jorma Vehmanen	.25	.50
90 Jorma Valtonen	.38	.75
91 Matti Keinonen	.25	.50
92 Juha Rantasila	.25	.50
93 Toni Kehle	.25	.50
94 Josef Schramm	.25	.50
95 Walter Stadler	.25	.50
96 Josef Volk	.25	.50
97 Hans Schichtl	.25	.50
98 Erwin Riedmeier	.25	.50
99 Werner Modes	.25	.50
100 Johann Eimannsberger	.25	.50
101 Karlheinz Egger	.25	.50
102 Lorenz Funk, Sr.	.25	.50
103 Klaus Ego	.25	.50
104 Anton Hofherr	.25	.50
105 Otto Schneitberger	.25	.50
106 Heinz Weisenbach	.25	.50
107 Alois Schloder	.25	.50
108 Gustav Hanig	.25	.50
109 Rainer Philipp	.25	.50
110 Bernd Kuhn	.25	.50
111 Paul Langner	.25	.50
112 Franz Hofherr	.25	.50
113 Reinhold Bauer	.25	.50
114 Johann Rotkirch	.25	.50
115 Walter Koberle	.25	.50
116 Rainer Makatsch	.25	.50
117 Carl Wetzel	.38	.75
118 Mike Curran	.38	.75
119 Jim McElmury	.38	.75
120 Bruce Riutta	.38	.75
121 Tom Mellor	.38	.75
122 Don Ross	.38	.75
123 Gary Gambucci	.38	.75
124 Keith Christiansen	.38	.75
125 Len Lilyholm	.38	.75
126 Henry Boucha	.75	3.00
127 Craig Falkman	.38	.75
128 Tim Sheehy	.38	.75
129 Kevin Ahearn	.38	1.00
130 Craig Patrick	1.00	2.00
131 Pete Fichuk	.38	1.00
132 George Konik	.38	1.00
133 Dick McGlynn	.38	1.00
134 Dick Toomey	.38	1.00
135 Paul Schilling	.38	1.00
136 Bob Lindberg	.38	1.00
137 Dick Tomasoni	.38	1.00
138 Nando Mathieu	.25	.50
139 Francis Reinhard	.25	.50
140 Gaston Furrer	.25	.50
141 Bruno Wittwer	.25	.50
142 Andre Berra	.25	.50
143 Hans Keller	.25	.50
144 Peter Luthi	.25	.50
145 Peter Aeschlimann	.25	.50
146 Werner Kuenzi	.25	.50
147 Tony Neininger	.25	.50
148 Jacques Pousaz	.25	.50
149 Roger Chappot	.25	.50
150 Charly Henzen	.25	.50
151 Paul Probst	.25	.50
152 Guy Dubois	.25	.50
153 Rene Squaldo	.25	.50
154 Rene Huegenin	.25	.50
155 Gaston Pelletier	.25	.50
156 Beat Kaufmann	.25	.50
157 Alfio Molina	.25	.50
158 Gerald Rigolet	.25	.50
159 Harald Jones	.25	.50
160 Gilbert Mathieu	.25	.50
161 Michel Turler	.25	.50
162 Reto Taillens	.25	.50
163 Norm Ullman	1.50	5.00
164 Dave Keon	2.50	10.00
165 Roger Crozier	2.50	5.00
166 Ron Ellis	1.50	5.00
167 Paul Henderson	2.50	10.00
168 Jim Dorey	.50	1.00
169 Jacques Plante	15.00	30.00
170 Jean-Guy Gendron	.50	1.00
171 Gary Smith	1.50	3.00
172 Dennis Hextall	.50	2.00
173 Norm Ferguson	.50	1.00
174 Simon Nolet	.50	1.00
175 Bernie Parent	5.00	10.00
176 Ted Hampson	.50	1.00
177 Earl Ingarfield	.50	1.00
178 Larry Hillman	.50	2.00
179 Gary Dornhoefer	1.00	3.00
180 Gary Croteau	.50	1.00
181 Carol Vadnais	.50	2.00
182 Jim Roberts	.50	2.00
183 Red Berenson	1.50	5.00
184 Phil Esposito	12.50	25.00
185 John McKenzie	1.00	3.00
186 Barclay Plager	1.00	3.00
187 Glenn Hall	7.50	15.00
188 Gerry Cheevers	7.50	15.00
189 Jim McKenny	.50	1.00
190 Gordie Howe	25.00	50.00
191 Garry Unger	1.00	3.00
192 Roy Edwards	1.50	5.00
193 Alex Delvecchio	2.50	5.00
194 Brad Park	2.50	10.00
195 Frank Mahovlich	5.00	10.00
196 Phil Goyette	.50	1.00
197 Don Marshall	.50	1.00
198 Henri Richard	5.00	10.00
199 Claude Larose	.50	1.00
200 Bobby Rousseau	.50	1.00
201 Lorne Worsley	5.00	10.00
202 Gilles Marotte	.75	1.50
203 Bob Pulford	1.50	5.00
204 Yvan Cournoyer	2.50	5.00
205 Eddie Joyal	.50	1.00
206 Ross Lonsberry	.50	1.00
207 Jean Beliveau	10.00	20.00
208 Jacques Lemaire	2.50	5.00
209 Orland Kurtenbach	.75	1.50
210 Andre Boudrias	.50	1.00
211 Jim Neilson	.50	2.00
212 Walter Tkaczuk	1.00	3.00
213 Ed Giacomin	5.00	10.00
214 Jean Ratelle	2.50	5.00
215 Les Binkley	1.50	5.00
216 Jean Pronovost	.50	1.00
217 Bryan Watson	.50	2.00
218 Dean Prentice	.50	1.00
219 Jean-Paul Parise	1.00	3.00
220 Bill Goldsworthy	.75	3.00
221 Wayne Maki	.50	2.00
222 Dale Tallon	.75	3.00
223 Bobby Orr	37.50	75.00
224 Pit Martin	.50	2.00
225 Jacques Laperriere	1.50	3.00
226 Bill Flett	.50	2.00
227 Stan Mikita	7.50	15.00
228 Bobby Hull	15.00	30.00
229 Larry Pleau	.50	2.00
230 Keith Magnuson	1.00	2.00
231 Tony Esposito	7.50	15.00
232 Rogatien Vachon	4.00	10.00
233 Mickey Redmond	7.50	15.00

1972-73 Swedish Stickers

This 300-sticker set was issued in Sweden by Williams Forlags AB for the 1972-73 season. While the majority of the set is taken up by players from the Swedish Elitserien, there also are stickers featuring stars from Russia, Czechoslovakia, Finland and the NHL. Key stickers include pre-NHL appearances from Anders Hedberg, Borje Salming and Ulf Nilsson. NHL stars such as Bobby Orr, Ken Dryden and Bobby Hull also are featured, along with Soviet greats such as Tretiak and Kharlamov. The card fronts feature a posed color photo, while the backs have the sticker number and player information in Swedish. A book to hold the stickers was available at the time for 3.5 kroner, or about fifty cents. It is filled with stories about the teams, league schedules and photos, along with spaces for the stickers. It is valued now at $25. The prices below are for unused stickers; because it was the habit then to put them in the album, relatively few remain in their original state.

COMPLETE SET (300)	150.00	300.00
1 Christer Abrahamsson	1.00	2.00
2 Leif Holmqvist	.50	1.00
3 Tommy Abrahamsson	.50	1.00
4 Thommie Bergman	1.00	2.00
5 Bjorn Johansson	.25	.50
6 Kjell-Rune Milton	.25	.50
7 Borje Salming	5.00	10.00
8 Lars-Erik Sjoberg	1.00	2.00
9 Karl-Johan Sundqvist	.25	.50
10 Stig Ostling	.25	.50
11 Inge Hammarstrom	1.00	2.00
12 Anders Hedberg	2.50	5.00
13 Stig-Goran Johansson	.25	.50
14 Stefan Karlsson	.25	.50
15 Hans Lindberg	.25	.50
16 Mats Lindh	.25	.50
17 Tord Lundstrom	.25	.50
18 Lars-Goran Nilsson	.25	.50
19 Bjorn Palmqvist	.25	.50
20 Hakan Wickberg	.25	.50
21 Jiri Holecek	.50	1.00
22 Josef Horesovsky	.25	.50
23 Frantisek Pospisil	.38	.75
24 Jaroslav Holik	.25	.50
25 Jiri Holik	.38	.75
26 Vaclav Nedomansky	1.00	2.00
27 Vladislav Tretiak	10.00	20.00
28 Gennadi Tsigankov	.38	.75
29 Igor Romisjevskij	.38	.75
30 Valeri Kharlamov	5.00	10.00
31 Alexander Maltsev	2.50	5.00
32 Vladimir Vikulov	.38	.75
33 Jorma Valtonen	.38	.75
34 Pekka Marjamaki	.25	.50
35 Matti Keinonen	.25	.50
36 Veli-Pekka Ketola	1.00	2.00
37 Lauri Mononen	.25	.50
38 Lasse Oksanen	.25	.50
39 Krister Sterner	.50	1.00
40 Sten-Ake Bark	.25	.50
41 Jan-Erik Silfverberg	.25	.50
42 Steffan Andersson	.25	.50
43 Roland Eriksson	.25	.50
44 Gunnar Johansson	.25	.50
45 Jiri Holecek	.50	1.00
46 Thommie Bergman	1.00	2.00
47 Josef Horesovsky	.25	.50
48 Vladimir Vikulov	.38	.75
49 Alexander Maltsev	2.50	5.00
50 Valeri Kharlamov	5.00	10.00
51 Leif Holmqvist	.50	1.00
52 Lars Danielsson	.25	.50
53 Ake Fagerstrom	.25	.50
54 Per-Arne Hubinette	.25	.50
55 Hakan Lindgren	.25	.50
56 Bert-Ola Nordlander	.25	.50
57 Bo Olofsson	.25	.50
58 Soren Sjogren	.25	.50
59 Jan Olsson	.25	.50
60 Lennart Sellnder	.25	.50
61 Jan Olof Kroon	.25	.50
62 Rolf Edberg	.25	.50
63 Ulf Nilsson	2.50	5.00
64 Leif Holmgren	.25	.50
65 Jan Ostling	.25	.50
66 Christer Grahn	.50	1.00
67 Karl-Olov Grahn	.50	1.00
68 Anders Hagstrom	.25	.50
69 Erik Jarvholm	.25	.50
70 Bo Westling	.25	.50
71 Ulf Ingvarsson	.25	.50
72 Bengt Lovgren	.25	.50
73 Kjell Sundstrom	.25	.50
74 Kent Bjork	.25	.50
75 Ulf Lundstrom	.25	.50
76 Mats Lundmark	.25	.50
77 Ulf Barrefjord	.25	.50
78 Lars Dahlgren	.25	.50
79 Olle Nilsson	.25	.50
80 Roger Nilsson	.25	.50
81 Willie Lofqvist	.50	1.00
82 Jan-Erik Silfverberg	.25	.50
83 Kjell Johnsson	.25	.50
84 Jan-Olof Svensson	.25	.50
85 Stig Salming	.25	.50
86 Borje Salming	5.00	10.00
87 Stig Ostling	.25	.50
88 Tord Lundstrom	.25	.50
89 Inge Hammarstrom	1.00	2.00
90 Lars-Goran Nilsson	.25	.50
91 Hans Lindberg	.25	.50
92 Hakan Wickberg	.25	.50
93 Jan-Erik Lyck	.25	.50
94 Stefan Karlsson	.25	.50
95 Lars Oberg	.25	.50
96 Roland Einarsson	.50	1.00
97 Billy Sundstrom	.25	.50
98 Anders Rylin	.25	.50
99 Tomas Carlsson	.25	.50
100 Ulf Ojerklint	.25	.50
101 L-A Gustavsson	.50	1.00
102 Jorgen Palm	.25	.50
103 Lars-Ake Lundell	.25	.50
104 Ake Eklof	.25	.50
105 Bengt-Ake Karlsson	.25	.50
106 Bjorn Palmqvist	.25	.50
107 Per-Allan Wickstrom	.25	.50
108 Sven-Bertil Lindstrom	.25	.50
109 Totte Bengtsson	.25	.50
110 Stig Larsson	.25	.50
111 Ken Dryden	20.00	40.00
112 Jacques Laperriere	1.50	3.00
113 Bobby Orr	37.50	75.00
114 Brad Park	2.50	5.00
115 Phil Esposito	10.00	20.00
116 Rod Gilbert	2.50	5.00
117 Vic Hadfield	1.50	3.00
118 Bobby Hull	15.00	30.00
119 Frank Mahovlich	5.00	10.00
120 Jean Ratelle	2.50	5.00
121 Lennart Andersson	.50	1.00
122 Karl-Johan Sundqvist	.25	.50
123 Nicke Johansson	.25	.50
124 Lars-Goran Nilsson	.25	.50
125 Ake Carlsson	.25	.50
126 Hans-Ake Rosendahl	.25	.50
127 Sten-Ake Bark	.25	.50
128 Par Backman	.25	.50
129 Leif Labraaten	.25	.50
130 Berndt Augustsson	.25	.50
131 Uffe Sterner	.25	.50
132 Benny Andersson	.25	.50
133 Conny Evensson	.50	1.00
134 Kjell Augustsson	.25	.50
135 Hans Andersson	.25	.50
136 Kenneth Holmstedt	.50	1.00
137 Lennart Gustavsson	.25	.50
138 Lennart Eriksson	.25	.50
139 Rolf Carlsson	.25	.50
140 Bengt Lundberg	.25	.50
141 Jan-Ake Karlsson	.25	.50
142 Curt Edenvik	.25	.50
143 Per Edenvik	.25	.50
144 Weine Gullberg	.25	.50
145 Gunnar Backman	.50	1.00
146 Roddy Skyllqvist	.25	.50
147 Stefan Canderyd	.25	.50
148 Christer Kihlstrom	.25	.50
149 Nils-Arne Hedqvist	.25	.50
150 Stig-Olof Persson	.25	.50
151 Christer Abrahamsson	1.00	2.00
152 Thommy Abrahamsson	.50	1.00
153 Roland Bond	.25	.50
154 Gunnar Andersson	.25	.50
155 Ulf Weinstock	.25	.50
156 Ake Danielsson	.25	.50
157 Peter Gudmundsson	.25	.50
158 Olle Sjogren	.25	.50
159 Hans Jax	.25	.50
160 Mats Ahlberg	.25	.50
161 Dan Labraaten	1.00	2.00
162 Ulf Martensson	.25	.50
163 Kjell Brus	.25	.50
164 Dan Soderstrom	.25	.50
165 Per Olof Brasar	1.00	2.00
166 Ivar Larsson	.50	1.00
167 Sture Andersson	.25	.50
168 Lage Edin	.25	.50
169 Kjell Rune Milton	.25	.50
170 Ulf Wigren	.25	.50
171 Hakan Dahllof	.25	.50
172 Anders Hedberg	2.50	5.00
173 Assar Lundgren	.25	.50
174 Christer Nilsson	.25	.50
175 Anders Nordin	.25	.50
176 Hakan Nygren	.25	.50
177 Ulf Thors	.25	.50
178 Ulf Torstensson	.25	.50
179 Lasse Ohman	.25	.50
180 Tore Ohman	.25	.50
181 Bengt Ake Gustafsson	.38	.75
182 Tommy Andersson	.25	.50
183 Hans-Olof Ernlund	.25	.50
184 Tord Johansson	.25	.50
185 Tord Svensson	.25	.50
186 Jan Danielsson	.25	.50
187 Tommy Eriksson	.50	1.00
188 Gote Hansson	.25	.50
189 Hans Hansson	.25	.50
190 Sven-Ake Jacobsson	.25	.50
191 Mats Lonn	.25	.50
192 Lars Mjoberg	.25	.50
193 Lars Munther	.25	.50
194 Ulf Nises	.25	.50
195 Borje Skogs	.25	.50
196 Roland Lestander	.25	.50
197 Bosse Andersson	.25	.50
198 Hakan Dahlin	.25	.50
199 Martin Johansson	.25	.50
200 Anders Lindberg	.25	.50
201 Lars-Fredrik Nystrom	.25	.50
202 Hans Gunnar Skarin	.25	.50
203 Jerry Aberg	.25	.50
204 Anders Almqvist	.25	.50
205 Christer Johansson	.25	.50
206 Per Johansson	.25	.50
207 Martin Karlsson	.25	.50
208 Lars-Gunnar Lundberg	.25	.50
209 Hardy Nilsson	.25	.50
210 Kjell-Arne Wikstrom	.25	.50
211 Mikael Collin	.50	1.00
212 Curt Larsson	.50	1.00
213 Arne Carlsson	.25	.50
214 Bjorn Johansson	.25	.50
215 Nils-Olov Schilstrom	.25	.50
216 Jan Schullstrom	.25	.50
217 Borje Burlin	.25	.50
218 Hans Carlsson	.25	.50
219 Mats Hysing	.25	.50
220 Bertil Jacobsson	.25	.50
221 Stisse Johansson	.25	.50
222 Dan Landegren	.25	.50
223 Kjell Landstrom	.25	.50
224 Dick Yderstrom	.25	.50
225 Carl-Goran Oberg	.25	.50
226 Christer Sehlstedt	.25	.50
227 Tommie Lindgren	.25	.50
228 Jan-Erik Nilsson	.25	.50
229 Stefan Pettersson	.25	.50
230 Tord Nansen	.25	.50
231 Bo Berggren	.25	.50
232 Bjorn Broman	.25	.50
233 Ove Larsson	.25	.50
234 Kent Lindgren	.25	.50
235 Orjan Lindstrom	.25	.50
236 Lennart Norberg	.25	.50
237 Arne Lundstrom	.25	.50
238 Hakan Pettersson	.25	.50
239 Ake Soderberg	.25	.50
240 Olle Ahman	.25	.50
241 Christer Andersson	1.00	2.00
242 Anders Brostrom	.25	.50
243 Kenneth Ekman	.25	.50
244 Soren Gunnarsson	.25	.50
245 Borje Maatta	.25	.50
246 Tommy Pettersson	.25	.50
247 Kurt Jakobsson	.25	.50
248 Leif Jakobsson	.25	.50
249 Lars-Goran Johansson	.25	.50
250 Bengt-Goran Karlsson	.25	.50
251 Berndt Karlsson	.25	.50
252 Tadeusz Niedomyst	.25	.50
253 Benny Runesson	.25	.50
254 Ake Ryman	.25	.50
255 Jan-Roger Strand	.25	.50
256 Goran Hogosta	.50	1.00
257 Bert Backman	.25	.50
258 Christer Collin	.25	.50
259 Bo Eriksson	.25	.50
260 Hakan Norstrom	.25	.50
261 Lars Thoreus	.25	.50
262 Stig Andersson	.25	.50
263 Mats Eriksson	.25	.50
264 Roland Eriksson	.25	.50
265 Kjell Fhinn	.25	.50
266 Olle Henriksson	.25	.50
267 Yngve Hindrikes	.25	.50
268 Jan Karlsson	.25	.50
269 Kjell Jansson	.25	.50
270 Ingemar Snis	.25	.50
271 Christer Stahl	.25	.50
272 Leif Andersson	.25	.50
273 Tommy Eriksson	.50	1.00
274 Christer Holmstrom	.25	.50
275 Curt Lundmark	1.00	2.00
276 Dennis Pettersson	.25	.50
277 Ove Thelin	.25	.50
278 Bo Wahlberg	.25	.50
279 Gote Gustavsson	.25	.50
280 Christer Lindgren	.25	.50
281 Kent Persson	.25	.50
282 Par Marts	.25	.50
283 Ove Stenlund	.25	.50
284 Bo Olsson	.25	.50
285 Bo Astrom	.25	.50
286 Ronny Andersson	.50	1.00
287 Roger Bergman	.25	.50
288 Thommie Bergman	1.00	2.00
289 Anders Johansson	.25	.50
290 Jan Olsen	.25	.50
291 Lars Erik Sjoberg	1.00	2.00
292 Kjell Andersson	.25	.50
293 Svante Granholm	.25	.50
294 Henrik Hedlund	.25	.50
295 Leif Henriksson	.25	.50
296 Mats Lindh	.25	.50
297 Evert Lindstrom	.25	.50
298 Willy Lindstrom	1.00	2.00
299 Roger Olsson	.25	.50
300 Kjell-Ronnie Pettersson	.25	.50

1973-74 Swedish Stickers

This 243-sticker set was produced in Sweden by Williams Forlags AB. It features players from the top Swedish league, as well as several Russian teams. The set includes such legendary figures as Valeri Kharlamov, Vladislav Tretiak and a rare card of notorious head coach Vselvolod Bobrov. The fronts feature a color player photo, while the backs have sticker number and information in Swedish. There was an album available to store the set; it currently retails for around $20.

COMPLETE SET (243)	100.00	175.00
1 Christer Abrahamsson	1.00	2.00
2 William Lofqvist	.50	1.00
3 Arne Karlsson	.25	.50
4 Lars-Erik Sjoberg	1.00	2.00
5 Bjorn Johansson	.25	.50
6 Thommy Abrahamsson	.50	1.00
7 Borje Salming	5.00	10.00
8 Karl Johan Sundqvist	.25	.50
9 Ulf Sterner	.25	.50
10 Ulf Nilsson	2.50	5.00
11 Kjell-Arne Wickstrom	.25	.50
12 Inge Hammarstrom	2.50	5.00
13 Hakan Wickberg	.25	.50
14 Tord Lundstrom	.25	.50
15 Dan Soderstrom	.25	.50
16 Mats Ahlberg	.50	1.00
17 Anders Hedberg	2.50	5.00
18 Dick Yderstrom	.30	.75
19 Stefan Karlsson	.25	.50
20 Roland Bond	.25	.50
21 Kjell-Rune Milton	.25	.50
22 Willy Lindstrom	.75	1.50
23 Kurt Carlsson	.30	.75
24 Mats Waltin	.25	.50
25 Roland Eriksson	.25	.50
26 Martin Karlsson	.25	.50
27 Jiri Holecek	.50	1.00
28 Josef Horesovsky	.25	.50
29 Oldrich Machac	.25	.50
30 Vladimir Martinec	.50	1.00
31 Vaclav Nedomansky	.75	1.50
32 Jiri Kochta	.25	.50
33 Jorma Waltonen	.50	1.00
34 Heikki Riihiranta	.50	1.00
35 Lauri Mononen	.25	.50
36 Timo Turunen	.25	.50
37 Matti Keinonen	.25	.50
38 Seppo Repo	.25	.50
39 Christer Abrahamsson	.75	1.50
40 Lars Stenvall	.25	.50
41 Per Karlsson	.25	.50
42 Roland Bond	.25	.50
43 Thommy Abrahamsson	.50	1.00
44 Ulf Weinstock	.25	.50
45 Gunnar Andersson	.25	.50
46 Hans Eriksson	.25	.50
47 Peter Gudmundsson	.25	.50
48 Mats Ahlberg	.50	1.00
49 Per-Olov Brasar	.75	1.50
50 Roger Lindqvist	.25	.50
51 Dan Soderstrom	.25	.50
52 Ulf Martensson	.25	.50
53 Kjell Brus	.25	.50
54 Hans Jax	.25	.50
55 Dan Labraaten	.75	1.50
56 Nils-Olov Olsson	.25	.50
57 Stig Nordin	.25	.50
58 Bo Theander	.25	.50
59 Curt Larsson	.50	1.00
60 Mikael Collin	.50	1.00
61 Arne Carlsson	.25	.50
62 Leif Svensson	.25	.50
63 Sverker Torstensson	.25	.50
64 Bjorn Johansson	.25	.50
65 Stisse Johansson	.25	.50
66 Carl-Goran Oberg	.25	.50
67 Mats Hysing	.25	.50
68 Mats Walltin	.25	.50
69 Hans Carlsson	.25	.50
70 Nils-Olov Schilstrom	.25	.50
71 Kjell-Arne Wickstrom	.25	.50
72 Jan Schullstrom	.25	.50
73 Borje Burlin	.25	.50
74 Dick Yderstrom	.30	.75
75 Dan Landegren	.25	.50
76 Kjell Landstrom	.25	.50
77 Vladislav Tretjak	10.00	20.00
78 Alexander Sidelnikov	1.00	2.00
79 Alexander Ragulin	1.25	2.50
80 Vladimir Luttjenko	1.00	2.00
81 Gennadij Tsygankov	.75	1.50
82 Alexander Gusev	.50	1.00
83 Jevgenij Poladiev	.30	.75
84 Jurij Liapkin	.75	1.50
85 Valerij Vasiljev	1.50	3.00
86 Boris Michailov	2.50	5.00
87 Valeri Kharlamov	5.00	10.00
88 Vladimir Petrov	2.50	5.00
89 Alexander Maltsev	2.50	5.00
90 Vladimir Sjadrin	1.25	2.50
91 Alexander Yakusjev	2.50	5.00
92 Alexander Martynjuk	.30	.75
93 Vjateslav Anissin	.50	1.00
94 Jurij Lebedev	1.00	2.00
95 Alexander Bodunov	.50	1.00
96 Alexander Volchkov	1.00	2.00
97 Vsevolod Bobrov	2.00	4.00
98 Konstantin Loktev	.25	.50
99 Anatolij Firsov	1.50	3.00
100 Viktor Kuzkin	.50	1.00
101 Jurij Blochin	.25	.50
102 Vladimir Vikulov	.50	1.00
103 Jurij Blinov	.50	1.00
104 Jevgenij Misjakov	1.00	2.00
105 Vladimir Trunov	.25	.50
106 Sergej Glazov	.25	.50
107 Vladimir Popov	.75	1.50
108 Viktor Zinger	.50	1.00
109 Viktor Krivolapov	.30	.75
110 Jevgenij Kazatjkin	.25	.50
111 Viktor Korotkov	.75	1.50
112 Valentin Markov	.25	.50
113 Alexander Sapjolkin	.25	.50
114 Leonid Borzov	.25	.50
115 Gennadij Krylov	.25	.50
116 Konstantin Klimov	.25	.50
117 Jevgenij Zimin	.50	1.00
118 Vladimir Gurejev	.25	.50
119 Viktor Jaroslavtsev	.25	.50
120 Alexander Pasjkov	.30	.75
121 Vladimir Polupanov	.50	1.00
122 Vitalij Davydov	.75	1.50
123 Michail Alexeenko	.25	.50
124 Alexander Filippov	.50	1.00
125 Valerij Nazarov	.25	.50
126 Vladimir Orlov	.25	.50
127 Stanislav Sitjegolev	.25	.50
128 Anatolij Bjelonozjkin	.25	.50

129 Vladimir Devjatov .25 .50
130 Jevgenij Kotlov .25 .50
131 Anatolij Motovilov .25 .50
132 Jurij Reps .25 .50
133 Igor Samotjernov .25 .50
134 Alexander Sevidov .25 .50
135 Viktor Sjilov .25 .50
136 Jurij Tjitjurin .30 .75
137 Sune Odling .25 .50
138 Lars-Erik Sjoberg 1.00 2.00
139 Bengt Sjoholm .25 .50
140 Leif Henriksson .25 .50
141 Henric Hedlund .25 .50
142 Roger Olsson .25 .50
143 Kjell-Rune Milton .25 .50
144 Kjell-Ronnie Pettersson .25 .50
145 Svante Granholm .25 .50
146 Kjell Andersson .25 .50
147 Lars-Erik Esbjorn .25 .50
148 Bjorn Lindberg .25 .50
149 Willy Lindstrom .75 1.50
150 Evert Lindstrom .25 .50
151 Lars-Erik Johansson .25 .50
152 Krister Sterner .30 .75
153 Mats Lindh .25 .50
154 Roger Bergman .25 .50
155 Willie Lofqvist .50 1.00
156 Jan Olov Svensson .25 .50
157 Jan Erik Silfverberg .25 .50
158 Stig Ostling .50 1.00
159 Kjell Johansson .25 .50
160 Borje Salming 5.00 10.00
161 Stig Salming .50 1.00
162 Tord Lundstrom .25 .50
163 Hakan Wickberg .25 .50
164 Inge Hammarstrom 2.50 5.00
165 Lars Goran Nilsson .25 .50
166 Jan Erik Lyck .25 .50
167 Stefan Karlsson .25 .50
168 Lennart Lind .50 1.00
169 Hans Ake Persson .25 .50
170 Lars Oberg .25 .50
171 Lars Erik Eriksson .25 .50
172 Bjorn Fagerlund .30 .75
173 Nicke Johansson .25 .50
174 Lars Goran Nilsson .25 .50
175 Hans Erik Jansson .25 .50
176 Per Backman .25 .50
177 Jorgen Palm .25 .50
178 Conny Evensson .30 .75
179 Ulf Sterner .25 .50
180 Sven Ake Rudby .25 .50
181 Lennart Andersson .30 .75
182 Kent Erik Andersson .25 .50
183 Hans Ake Rosendahl .25 .50
184 Karl Johan Sundqvist .25 .50
185 Hasse Andersson .25 .50
186 Benny Andersson .25 .50
187 Gunnar Johansson .25 .50
188 Sten Ake Bark .25 .50
189 Lasse Zetterstrom .25 .50
190 Leif Holmqvist .50 1.00
191 Bert Jattne .50 1.00
192 Lars Danielsson .50 1.00
193 Hakan Lindgren .25 .50
194 Ake Fagerstrom .25 .50
195 Bert-Ola Nordlander .30 .75
196 Leif Holmgren .25 .50
197 Soren Sjogren .25 .50
198 Hans Lindberg .25 .50
199 Jan-Olov Kroon .25 .50
200 Rolf Edberg .25 .50
201 Lennart Selinder .50 1.00
202 Ulf Nilsson 2.50 5.00
203 Jan Olsson .25 .50
204 Jan Ostling .25 .50
205 Christer Lundberg .25 .50
206 Christer Englund .25 .50
207 Bo Olofsson .25 .50
208 Roland Einarsson .50 1.00
209 Ake Danielsson .25 .50
210 Billy Sundstrom .25 .50
211 Thomas Carlsson .25 .50
212 Stig Larsson .25 .50
213 Lars Ake Gustavsson .50 1.00
214 Bjorn Palmqvist .25 .50
215 Anders Hedberg 2.50 5.00
216 Anders Rylin .25 .50
217 Sven Bertil Lindstrom .25 .50
218 Kjell Nilsson .25 .50
219 Claes Goran Wallin .25 .50
220 Ake Eklof .25 .50
221 Peder Nilsson .30 .75
222 Lars Ake Lundell .25 .50
223 Bengt Ake Karlsson .25 .50
224 Ove Svensson .25 .50
225 Soren Johansson .25 .50
226 Christer Sehlstedt .30 .75
227 Lage Edin .25 .50
228 Tommy Andersson .25 .50
229 Janerik Nilsson .25 .50
230 Tommie Lindgren .25 .50
231 Bo Bergman .25 .50
232 Lennart Norberg .25 .50
233 Olle Ahman .25 .50
234 Arne Lundstrom .30 .75
235 Kent Lindgren .25 .50
236 Orjan Lindstrom .25 .50
237 Kent Othberg .30 .75
238 Finn Lundstrom .25 .50
239 Ake Soderberg .25 .50
240 Jan Kock .25 .50
241 Ove Larsson .25 .50
242 Hakan Pettersson .25 .50
243 Stefan Pettersson .25 .50

1974 Swedish Semic World Championship Stickers

This 100-sticker set featuring World Championship players was produced by Semic of Sweden. The stickers measure approximately 2" by 3", and were designed to be placed on one of four team-specific posters. The cards were issued in sheets of two.

COMPLETE SET (100) 40.00 80.00
1 Christer Abrahamsson .75 1.50
2 William Lofqvist .50 1.00
3 Arne Carlsson .25 .50
4 Lars-Erik Sjoberg 1.00 2.00
5 Bjorn Johansson .25 .50
6 Tommy Abrahamsson .50 1.00
7 Karl-Johan Sundqvist .25 .50
8 Ulf Nilsson 2.00 4.00
9 Hakan Wickberg .25 .50
10 Dan Soderstrom .25 .50
11 Mats Ahlberg .30 .75
12 Anders Hedberg 2.00 4.00
13 Dick Yderstrom .25 .50
14 Stefan Karlsson .25 .50
15 Roland Bond .25 .50
16 Kjell-Rune Milton .25 .50
17 Willy Lindstrom .50 1.00
18 Mats Waltin .25 .50
19 Lars-Goran Nilsson .25 .50
20 Bjorn Palmquist .25 .50
21 Stig-Goran Johansson .25 .50
22 Bo Berggren .25 .50
23 Dan Labraaten .75 1.50
24 Curt Larsson .30 .75
25 Mats Lindh .25 .50
26 Vladislav Tretiak 7.50 15.00
27 Alexander Ragulin .50 1.00
28 Vladimir Luttjenko .50 1.00
29 Gennadij Tsygankov .50 1.00
30 Alexander Gusev .50 1.00
31 Jevgenij Poladiev .25 .50
32 Jurij Ljapkin .50 1.00
33 Boris Michailov 2.00 4.00
34 Valeri Kharlamov 3.00 10.00
35 Vladimir Petrov 2.00 3.00
36 Alexander Maltsev 2.00 4.00
37 Vladimir Sjadrin .30 .75
38 Alexander Yakusjev 2.00 4.00
39 Alexander Martynjuk .30 .75
40 Jurij Lebedev .75 1.50
41 Alexander Bodunov .50 1.00
42 Anatolij Firsov .75 1.50
43 Vitalij Davydov .30 .75
44 Vjateslav Starsjinov .30 .75
45 Viktor Kuzkin .25 .50
46 Igor Romitjevskij .25 .50
47 Jevgenij Zimin .30 .75
48 Jevgenij Misjakov .50 1.00
49 Vladimir Vikulov .30 .75
50 Viktor Konovalenko .50 1.00
51 Jiri Holecek .50 1.00
52 Frantisek Pospisil .30 .75
53 Jiri Bubla .50 1.00
54 Josef Horesovsky .25 .50
55 Oldrich Machac .25 .50
56 Vladimir Martinec .25 .50
57 Vaclav Nedomansky .75 1.50
58 Jiri Kochta .25 .50
59 Milan Novy .50 1.00
60 Jaroslav Holik .30 .75
61 Jiri Holik .50 1.00
62 Jiri Klapac .25 .50
63 Richard Farda .30 .75
64 Bohuslav Stastny .30 .75
65 Jiri Novak .25 .50
66 Ivan Hlinka .30 .75
67 Jan Suchy .30 .75
68 Vladimir Bednar .25 .50
69 Rudolf Tajcnar .25 .50
70 Josef Cerny .25 .50
71 Jan Havel .30 .75
72 Marcel Sakac .25 .50
73 Frantisek Pancharek .25 .50
74 Bedrich Brunchk .25 .50
75 Edvard Novak .25 .50
76 Jorma Valtonen .50 1.00
77 Seppo Lindstrom .25 .50
78 Pekka Marjamaki .25 .50
79 Pekka Rautakallio .75 1.50
80 Heikki Riihiranta .50 1.00
81 Seppo Suoraniemi .25 .50
82 Jouko Oystila .25 .50
83 Veli-Pekka Ketola .75 1.50
84 Henry Leppa .25 .50
85 Harri Linnonmaa .25 .50
86 Matti Murto .25 .50
87 Lasse Oksanen .25 .50
88 Esa Peltonen .25 .50
89 Seppo Repo .25 .50
90 Raimo Suoniemi .25 .50
91 Timo Sutinen .25 .50
92 Juhani Tamminen .50 1.00
93 Leo Seppanen .25 .50
94 Hannu Haapalainen .25 .50
95 Pertti Valkeapaa .25 .50
96 Sakari Ahlberg .25 .50
97 Antti Leppanen .25 .50
98 Kalevi Numminen .25 .50
99 Lauri Mononen .25 .50
100 Ilpo Koskela .30 .75
NNO Ulf Nilsson poster
NNO Valeri Kharlamov poster
NNO Vaclav Nedomansky poster
NNO Timo Sutinen poster

1974-75 Swedish Stickers

This set of 324 stickers commemorates the competitors on the 1974-75 World Championship, along with players from club teams across Europe. The stickers -- which measure approximately 3" by 2" -- feature action photography on the front, with player name and card number along the bottom. The backs have the set logo, a reprise of the card number and encouragement in Swedish to build the entire set. The last six cards were recently identified by Swedish collector Per Vedin.

COMPLETE SET (324) 100.00 175.00
1 Vladislav Tretiak 7.50 15.00
2 Gennadij Tsigannkov .50 1.00
3 Valerij Vasiljev 1.50 3.00
4 Alexander Gusev .50 1.00
5 Valeri Kharlamov 3.00 10.00
6 Vladimir Petrov 2.00 4.00
7 Boris Michailov 2.00 4.00
8 Alexander Maltsev 2.00 4.00
9 Alexander Yakusjev 2.00 4.00
10 Jiri Chra 1.50 3.00
11 Jiri Bubla .50 1.00
12 Milan Kuzela .25 .50
13 Oldrich Machac .25 .50
14 Ivan Hlinka .50 1.00
15 Vaclav Nedomansky .75 1.50
16 Boshulav Stastny .75 1.50
17 Vladimir Martinec .25 .50
18 Richard Farda .25 .50
19 Curt Larsson .30 .75
20 Lars-Erik Sjoberg 1.00 2.00
21 Thommy Abrahamsson .50 1.00
22 Kjell-Rune Milton .25 .50
23 Anders Hedberg 2.00 4.00
24 Mats Ahlberg .30 .75
25 Dan Soderstrom .25 .50
26 Ulf Nilsson 2.00 4.00
27 Per-Olof Brassar .75 1.50
28 Stig Wetzell .25 .50
29 Juha Rantasila .25 .50
30 Heikki Riihiranta .50 1.00
31 Timo Saari .25 .50
32 Seppo Repo .25 .50
33 Esa Peltonen .25 .50
34 Juhani Tamminen .50 1.00
35 Matti Murto .25 .50
36 Harri Linnonmaa .25 .50
37 Gennadij Lapsjenkov .50 1.00
38 Pjotr Zjulin .25 .50
39 Vladimir Merinov .25 .50
40 Sergej Tyznych 1.00 2.00
41 Valerij Kostin .25 .50
42 Valerij Nikitin .50 1.00
43 Sergej Gusev .50 1.00
44 Valentin Kozin .25 .50
45 Viktor Liksiutkin .25 .50
46 Alexander Golikov .50 1.00
47 Viktor Zhluktov .50 1.00
48 Anatolij Frolov .75 1.50
49 Vladimir Golikov 1.00 2.00
50 Nikolaj Epstein .25 .50
51 Alexander Kasjajev .25 .50
52 Alexander Sidelnikov 1.00 2.00
53 Valerij Kuzmin .50 1.00
54 Viktor Kuznetsov .50 1.00
55 Jurij Terechin .30 .75
56 Jurij Tjitjurin .30 .75
57 Jurij Sjatavalov .30 .75
58 Vjatjeslav Anissin .30 .75
59 Alexander Bodunov .50 1.00
60 Jurij Lebedev .75 1.50
61 Igor Dmitriev 2.00 4.00
62 Konstantin Klimov .30 .75
63 Sergej Kapustin .30 .75
64 Vladimir Repnjov .30 .75
65 Jevgenij Kucharzj .30 .75
66 Boris Kulagin 1.00 2.00
67 Viktor Afonin .25 .50
68 Juris Liberts .30 .75
69 Igor Kobzev .30 .75
70 Valerij Odintsov .30 .75
71 Vjatjeslav Nazarov .50 1.00
72 Andris Hendelis .30 .75
73 Alexander Sokolovskij .30 .75
74 Michail Denisov .30 .75
75 Helmut Balderis 2.00 4.00
76 Vladimir Sorokin .25 .50
77 Vladimir Sernjajev .25 .50
78 Viktor Verizjnikov .25 .50
79 Vladimir Markov .25 .50
80 Viktor Tichonov 2.50 5.00
81 Edgar Rosenberg .25 .50
82 Alexander Kotomkin .25 .50
83 Vladimir Astafjev .50 1.00
84 Alexander Kulikov .25 .50
85 Sergej Mosjkarov .25 .50
86 Vjatjeslav Usjmakov .25 .50
87 Jurij Fjodorov .50 1.00
88 Victor Dobrochotov .25 .50
89 Vitalij Krajov .25 .50
90 Alexej Masjin .25 .50
91 Vladimir Orlov .25 .50
92 Vladimir Smagin .25 .50
93 Alexander Usov .25 .50
94 Alexander Fedotov .50 1.00
95 Alexander Prilepskij .25 .50
96 Alexander Rogov .25 .50
97 Seppo Ahokainen .25 .50
98 Lasse Oksanen .25 .50
99 Jorma Peltonen .50 1.00
100 Henry Leppa .25 .50
101 Seppo Suoraniemi .25 .50
102 Timi Sutinen .25 .50
103 Jorma Valtonen .50 1.00
104 Antti Leppanen .25 .50
105 Pekka Marjamaki .25 .50
106 Juoko Oystila .25 .50
107 Seppo Lindstrom .25 .50
108 Veli-Pekka Ketola .75 1.50
109 Jiri Holecek .50 1.00
110 Jiri Kochta .25 .50
111 Josef Horesovsky .25 .50
112 Jaroslav Sima .25 .50
113 Frantisek Vorlicek .25 .50
114 Vladimir Kostka .25 .50
115 Jaroslav Holik .30 .75
116 Jiri Holik .50 1.00
117 Jan Suchy .30 .75
118 Josef Augusta, .25 .50
119 Miroslav Dvorak .50 1.00
120 Jan Hrbaty .25 .50
121 AIK .25 .50
122 If Bjorkloven .25 .50
123 Brynas IF .25 .50
124 Djurgardens IF .25 .50
125 Farjestads BK .25 .50
126 IF Karlskoga .25 .50
127 Leksands IF .25 .50
128 MoDo AIK .25 .50
129 Mora IK .25 .50
130 Skelleftea AIK .25 .50
131 Sodertalje SK .25 .50
132 Timra IK .25 .50
133 Tingsryds AIF .25 .50
134 V. Frolunda IF .25 .50
135 Vasteras IK .25 .50
136 Orebro IK .25 .50
137 Christer Abrahamsson .75 1.50
138 Christer Andersson .25 .50
139 Mikael Collin .50 1.00
140 Bjorn Fagerlund .25 .50
141 Christer Grahn .50 1.00
142 Kenneth Holmstedt .25 .50
143 Goran Hogosta .50 1.00
144 Bert Jattne .25 .50
145 Curt Larsson .30 .75
146 Ivar Larsson .25 .50
147 Wille Lofqvist .50 1.00
148 Peder Nilsson .25 .50
149 Christer Sehlstedt .25 .50
150 Krister Sterner .30 .75
151 Christer Stahl .25 .50
152 Sune Odling .25 .50
153 Thommy Abrahamsson .50 1.00
154 Gunnar Andersson .25 .50
155 Jan Andersson .25 .50
156 Leif Andersson .25 .50
157 Sture Andersson .25 .50
158 Tommy Andersson .25 .50
159 Sten Ake Bark .25 .50
160 Roger Bergman .25 .50
161 Roland Bond .25 .50
162 Arne Carlsson .25 .50
163 Thomas Carlsson .25 .50
164 Lasse Danielsson .25 .50
165 Ake Danielsson .25 .50
166 Kenneth Ekman .25 .50
167 Lars Erik Esbjors .25 .50
168 Soren Gunnarsson .25 .50
169 Mats Hysing .25 .50
170 Bjorn Johansson .25 .50
171 Martin Johansson .25 .50
172 Jan Kock .25 .50
173 Hakan Lindgren .25 .50
174 Larsake Lundell .25 .50
175 Mats Lundmark .25 .50
176 Kjell-Rune Milton .25 .50
177 Jan Erik Nilsson .25 .50
178 Lars Goran Nilsson .25 .50
179 Hakan Nygren .25 .50
180 Jan Olsson .25 .50
181 Jorgen Palm .25 .50
182 Dennis Pettersson .25 .50
183 Stefan Pettersson .25 .50
184 Anders Rylin .25 .50
185 Stig Salming .30 .75
186 Nils-Olof Schilstrom .25 .50
187 Jan Erik Silfverberg .25 .50
188 Lars Erik Sjoberg 1.50 3.00
189 Karl-Johan Sundqvist .25 .50
190 Jan-Olof Svensson .25 .50
191 Leif Svensson .25 .50
192 Tord Svensson .25 .50
193 Sverker Torstensson .25 .50
194 Mats Walltin .25 .50
195 Ulf Weinstock .25 .50
196 Jan Ove Wiberg .25 .50
197 Lars Zetterstrom .25 .50
198 Stig Ostling .30 .75
199 Hans Andersson .25 .50
200 Kent-Erik Andersson .25 .50
201 Kjell Andersson .25 .50
202 Ulf Barrefjord .25 .50
203 Kent Bengtsson .25 .50
204 Bo Berggren .25 .50
205 Kjell Brus .25 .50
206 Per-Olof Brasar .75 1.50
207 Borje Burlin .25 .50
208 Per Backman .25 .50
209 Stefan Canderyd .25 .50
210 Hans Carlsson .25 .50
211 Hakan Dahlov .25 .50
212 Rolf Edberg .25 .50
213 Ake Eklof .25 .50
214 Roland Eriksson .25 .50
215 Conny Evensson .50 1.00
216 Svante Granholm .25 .50
217 Peter Gudmundsson .25 .50
218 Hans Hansson .25 .50
219 Anders Hedberg 2.00 4.00
220 Henric Hedlund .25 .50
221 Nils Arne Hedqvist .25 .50
222 Leif Henriksson .25 .50
223 Leif Holmgren .25 .50
224 Sven-Ake Jacobsson .25 .50
225 Hans Jax .25 .50
226 Christer Johansson .25 .50
227 Gunnar Johansson .25 .50
228 Lars Erik Johansson .25 .50
229 Stig-Goran Johansson .25 .50
230 Soren Johansson .25 .50
231 Bengt Goran Karlsson .25 .50
232 Bengt-Ake Karlsson .25 .50
233 Martin Karlsson .25 .50
234 Stefan Karlsson .25 .50
235 Jan-Olov Kroon .25 .50
236 Dan Labraaten .75 1.50
237 Dan Landegren .25 .50
238 Kjell Landstrom .25 .50
239 Ove Larsson .25 .50
240 Stig Larsson .25 .50
241 Hans Lindberg .25 .50
242 Mats Lindh .25 .50
243 Willy Lindstrom .50 1.00
244 Orjan Lindstrom .25 .50
245 Christer Lundberg .25 .50
246 Lars-Gunnar Lundberg .25 .50
247 Per Lundqvist .25 .50
248 Arne Lundstrom .50 1.00
249 Fhinn Lundstrom .25 .50
250 Bengt Lovgren .25 .50
251 Ulf Martensson .25 .50
252 Par Marts .25 .50
253 Tadeusz Niedomysl .25 .50
254 Hardy Nilsson .25 .50
255 Lars Goran Nilsson .25 .50
256 Ulf Nilsson 2.00 4.00
257 Anders Nordin .25 .50
258 Nils-Olof Olsson .25 .50
259 Bjorn Palmqvist .25 .50
260 Kent Persson .25 .50
261 Hakan Pettersson .25 .50
262 Sven-Ake Rudby .25 .50
263 Benny Runesson .25 .50
264 Jan Roger Strand .25 .50
265 Ake Soderberg .50 1.00
266 Dan Soderstrom .25 .50
267 Ulf Torstensson .25 .50
268 Claes Goran Wallin .25 .50
269 Hakan Wickberg .25 .50
270 Kjell Arne Wickstrom .25 .50
271 Per Allan Wickstrom .25 .50
272 Dick Yderstrom .25 .50
273 Mats Ahlberg .30 .75
274 Olle Ahman .25 .50
275 Lars Oberg .25 .50
276 Jan Ostling .25 .50
277 Akning .25 .50
278 Akning .25 .50
279 Akning .25 .50
280 Skott .25 .50
281 Skott .25 .50
282 Skott .25 .50
283 Puckforing .25 .50
284 Tekning .25 .50
285 Malvaktsspel .50 1.00
286 Malvaktsspel .50 1.00
287 Forsvarsspel .25 .50
288 Forsvarsspel .25 .50
289 Forsvarsspel .25 .50
290 Forsvarsspel .25 .50
291 Forsvarsspel .25 .50
292 Forsvarsspel .25 .50
293 Forsvarsspel .25 .50
294 Forsvarsspel .25 .50
295 Forsvarsspel .25 .50
296 Forsvarsspel .25 .50
297 Forsvarsspel .25 .50
298 Forsvarsspel .25 .50
299 Forsvarsspel .25 .50
300 Forsvarsspel .25 .50
301 Forsvarsspel .25 .50
302 Forsvarsspel .25 .50
303 Anfallsspel .25 .50
304 Anfallsspel .25 .50
305 Anfallsspel .25 .50
306 Anfallsspel .25 .50
307 Anfallsspel .25 .50
308 Anfallsspel .25 .50
309 Anfallsspel .25 .50
310 Anfallsspel .25 .50
311 Anfallsspel .25 .50
312 Anfallsspel .25 .50
313 Inge Hammarstrom 1.00 2.00
314 Borje Salming 3.00 6.00
315 Thommie Bergman 1.25 2.50
316 Leif Holmqvist .50 1.00
317 Ulf Sterner .25 .50
318 Tord Lundstrom .25 .50
319 Tre Kroner puzzle .25 .50
320 Tre Kroner puzzle .25 .50
321 Tre Kroner puzzle .25 .50
322 Tre Kroner puzzle .25 .50
323 Tre Kroner puzzle .25 .50
324 Tre Kroner puzzle .25 .50

1981 Swedish Semic Hockey VM Stickers

This 144-sticker set was released in conjunction with the 1981 World Championships. The stickers, which measure 3" by 2 1/8", feature a color photo on the front along with the player name, country and national flag. The backs contain the card number and a remainder to place the stickers in the special set album (which retails now in the $25 range). The set is notable for the inclusion of Glenn Anderson in his RC year, as well as Mats Naslund and Neal Broten prior to their RCs. The set also features members of the American "Miracle On Ice" Olympic team; in some cases, these are the only "legitimate" card-like elements of players such as Mike Eruzione, Buzz Schneider, etc.

COMPLETE SET (144) 50.00 125.00
1 Goran Hogosta .20 .50
2 Tomas Jonsson .20 .50
3 Ulf Weinstock .08 .25
4 Goran Nilsson .08 .25
5 Jan Eriksson .08 .25
6 Tommy Samuelsson .08 .25
7 Mats Waltin .08 .25
8 Peter Helander .08 .25
9 Per Lundqvist .08 .25
10 Conny Silfverberg .08 .25
11 Mats Naslund 2.00 5.00
12 Lennart Norberg .08 .25
13 Bengt Lundholm .40 1.00
14 Leif Holmgren .08 .25
15 Bo Berglund .40 1.00
16 Dan Soderstrom .08 .25
17 Lars Molin .30 .75
18 Tore Oqvist .08 .25
19 Ari Hellgren .08 .25
20 Hannu Lassila .08 .25
21 Kari Eloranta .40 1.00
22 Lasse Litma .08 .25
23 Seppo Suoraniemi .08 .25
24 Tapio Levo .20 .50
25 Timo Nummelin .08 .25
26 Reijo Ruotsalainen .60 1.50
27 Markku Kiimalainen .08 .25
28 Mikko Leinonen .30 .75
29 Reijo Leppanen .08 .25
30 Hannu Koskinen .08 .25
31 Timo Susi .08 .25
32 Jukka Porvari .08 .25
33 Arto Javanainen .08 .25
34 Juhanni Tamminen .40 1.00
35 Pertti Koivulahti .08 .25
36 Antero Lehtonen .08 .25
37 Vladislav Tretiak 4.00 10.00
38 Vladimir Mysjkin .60 1.50
39 Slava Fetisov 2.50 6.00
40 Vladimir Luttjenko .30 .75
41 Sergei Babinov .20 .50
42 Vasilij Pervuchin .30 .75
43 Sergej Starikov .30 .75
44 Zinetula Biljaletdinov .30 .75
45 Vladimir Krutov 2.00 5.00
46 Alexander Maltsev 1.25 3.00
47 Jurij Lebedev .30 .75
48 Viktor Tiumenev .20 .50
49 Nikolaj Drozdetskij .08 .25
50 Valeri Kharlamov 2.50 6.00
51 Sergej Makarov 2.00 5.00
52 Vladimir Golikov .30 .75
53 Alexander Skvortsov .20 .50
54 Michail Varnakov .30 .75
55 Jiri Kralik .20 .50
56 Jaromir Sindel .60 1.50
57 Miroslav Dvorak .30 .75
58 Frantisek Kaberle .20 .50
59 Arnold Kadlec .20 .50
60 Jan Neliba .08 .25
61 Radoslav Svoboda .08 .25
62 Jaroslav Lycka .08 .25
63 Milan Novy .40 1.00
64 Jaroslav Pouzar .40 1.00
65 Miroslav Frycer .60 1.50
66 Karel Holy .08 .25
67 Ladislav Svozil .08 .25
68 Marian Bezak .08 .25
69 Jindrich Kokrment .08 .25
70 Jiri Lala .30 .75
71 Ludos Penicka .08 .25
72 Ivan Hlinka .75 2.00
73 Wayne Stephenson .75 2.00
74 Ron Paterson .30 .75
75 Warren Anderson .30 .75
76 Brad Pirie .30 .75
77 Randy Gregg .60 1.50
78 Tim Watters .40 1.00
79 Joe Grant .30 .75
80 Don Spring .30 .75
81 Ron Davidson .30 .75
82 Glenn Anderson 4.00 10.00
83 Kevin Maxwell .30 .75
84 Jim Nill .40 1.00
85 John Devaney .30 .75
86 Paul MacLean .60 1.50
87 Dan D'Alvise .30 .75
88 Ken Berry .30 .75
89 David Hindmarch .30 .75
90 Kevin Primeau .40 1.00
91 Steve Janaszak 2.00 5.00
92 Bob Suter 2.00 5.00
93 Ken Morrow 2.00 5.00
94 Mike Ramsey 2.00 5.00
95 Bill Baker 2.00 5.00
96 Dave Christian 2.00 5.00
97 Les Auge .40 1.00
98 Dave Silk 2.00 5.00
99 Neal Broten 2.00 5.00
100 Mark Johnson 2.00 5.00
101 Steve Christoff 2.00 5.00
102 Mark Pavelich 2.00 5.00
103 Eric Strobel 2.00 5.00
104 Mike Eruzione 10.00 25.00
105 Rob McClanahan 2.00 5.00
106 Buzz Schneider 2.00 5.00
107 Phil Verchota 2.00 5.00
108 John Harrington 2.00 5.00
109 Leif Holmqvist .40 1.00
110 Kjell Svensson .30 .75
111 Roland Stoltz .08 .25
112 Bert-Ola Nordlander .08 .25
113 Nils Johansson .08 .25
114 Lennart Svedberg .20 .50
115 Ulf Sterner .08 .25
116 Hakan Wickberg .08 .25
117 Tord Lundstrom .08 .25
118 Carl-Goran Oberg .08 .25
119 Eilert Maatta .08 .25
120 Lars-Goran Nilsson .08 .25
121 Nils Nilsson .08 .25
122 Hans Oberg .08 .25
123 Lars-Erik Lundvall .08 .25
124 Sven Tumba Johansson .20 .50
125 Lars Bjorn .08 .25
126 Ronald Pettersson .08 .25
127 World Championships 1981 .08 .25
128 Sweden .08 .25
129 Finland .08 .25
130 Soviet Union .08 .25
131 CSSR .08 .25
132 Canada .30 .75
133 U.S.A. .30 .75
134 West Germany .08 .25
135 Holland .08 .25
136 Referee's Signs .08 .25
137 Referee's Signs .08 .25
138 Referee's Signs .08 .25
139 Referee's Signs .08 .25
140 Referee's Signs .08 .25
141 Referee's Signs .08 .25
142 Referee's Signs .08 .25
143 Referee's Signs .08 .25
144 Referee's Signs .08 .25

1982 Swedish Semic VM Stickers

This 162-sticker set was released in 1982 to commemorate the World Championships held in Helsinki and Tampere, Finland. The stickers measure 3" by 2 1/8" and feature color photos along with the player's name and emblem (national or NHL) on the front. The backs have the sticker number, along with text in both Finnish and Swedish. The set does not include any North American-born NHLers, but does have several prominent Swedish NHL stars, including Hakan Loob, Mats Naslund, and Kent Nilsson.

COMPLETE SET (162) 24.00 60.00
1 Peter Lindmark .40 1.00
2 Gote Walitalo .08 .25
3 Gunnar Leidborg .08 .25
4 Goran Lindblom .08 .25
5 Thomas Eriksson .08 .25
6 Mats Waltin .08 .25
7 Jan Eriksson .08 .25
8 Mats Thelin .30 .75
9 Peter Helander .08 .25
10 Tommy Samuelsson .08 .25
11 Bo Ericsson .08 .25
12 Peter Andersson .20 .50
13 Mats Naslund 2.00 5.00
14 Ulf Isaksson .08 .25
15 Patrik Sundstrom .75 2.00
16 Peter Sundstrom .60 1.50
17 Thomas Rundqvist .30 .75
18 Mats Ulander .08 .25
19 Tommy Morth .08 .25
20 Ove Olsson .08 .25
21 Rolf Edberg .08 .25
22 Hakan Loob 1.50 4.00
23 Leif Holmgren .40 1.00
24 Jan Erixon .60 1.50
25 Harald Luckner .08 .25
26 Hannu Kamppuri .40 1.00
27 Hannu Issila .20 .50
28 Kari Heikkila .08 .25
29 Timo Nummelin .08 .25
30 Pertti Lehtonen .08 .25
31 Raimo Hirvonen .08 .25
32 Seppo Suoraniemi .08 .25
33 Juha Huikari .08 .25
34 Hannu Helander .08 .25
35 Lasse Litma .08 .25
36 Hakan Hjerpe .08 .25
37 Kari Jalonen .20 .50
38 Arto Javanainen .08 .25
39 Jari Lindgren .08 .25
40 Markku Kiimalainen .08 .25
41 Jarmo Makitalo .08 .25
42 Jorma Sevon .08 .25
43 Erkki Laine .08 .25
44 Hannu Koskinen .08 .25
45 Reijo Leppanen .08 .25
46 Pekka Arbelius .08 .25
47 Markku Hakulinen .08 .25
48 Timo Susi .08 .25
49 Esa Peltonen .08 .25
50 Juhani Tamminen .40 1.00
51 Vladislav Tretiak 4.00 10.00
52 Vladimir Mysjkin .30 .75
53 Slava Fetisov 2.00 5.00
54 Sergej Babinov .20 .50
55 Vasilij Pervuchin .20 .50
56 Valerij Vasiljev .30 .75
57 Alexei Kasatonov .75 2.00
58 Zinetula Biljaletdinov .40 1.00
59 Sergej Starikov .30 .75
60 Sergej Makarov 1.25 3.00
61 Sergej Sjepelev .30 .75
62 Vladimir Krutov 1.25 3.00
63 Nikolaj Drozdetskij .30 .75
64 Viktor Zjluktov .20 .50
65 Viktor Sjalimov .20 .50
66 Vladimir Golikov .20 .50
67 Aleksandr Maltsev 1.00 2.50
68 Andrej Khomutov .75 2.00
69 Sergej Svetlov .20 .50
70 Helmut Balderis .30 .75
71 Sergej Kapustin .20 .50
72 Vladimir Zubkov .20 .50
73 Aleksandr Kozjevnikov .20 .50
74 Jurij Lebedev .20 .50
75 Nikolaj Makarov .20 .50
76 Jiri Kralik .20 .50
77 Karel Lang .20 .50
78 Jaromir Sindel .40 1.00
79 Miloslav Horava .20 .50
80 Milan Chalupa .20 .50
81 Stanislav Hajdusek .08 .25
82 Arnold Kadlec .20 .50
83 Miroslav Dvorak .20 .50
84 Jan Neliba .08 .25
85 Petr Misek .08 .25
86 Eduard Uvira .08 .25
87 Milan Novy .20 .50
88 Frantisek Cerny .20 .50
89 Jiri Lala .20 .50
90 Jindrich Kokrment .08 .25
91 Frantisek Cernik .20 .50
92 Darius Rusnak .08 .25
93 Dusan Pasek .20 .50
94 Lubomir Penicka .08 .25
95 Jaroslav Korbela .08 .25
96 Peter Ihnacak .40 1.00
97 Jaroslav Hrdina .08 .25
98 Igor Liba .20 .50
99 Peter Slania .08 .25
100 Vincent Lukac .08 .25
101 Erich Weishaupt .20 .50
102 Bernhard Engelbrecht .20 .50
103 Robert Murray .20 .50
104 Peter Gailer .08 .25
105 Udo Kiessling .20 .5
106 Harold Kreis .20 .5
107 Joachim Reil .08 .2
108 Harald Krull .08 .2
109 Ulrich Egen .08 .2
110 Marcus Kuhl .08 .2
111 Peter Schiller .08 .2
112 Erich Kuhnhackl .20 .5
113 Holger Meitinger .08 .2
114 Ernst Hofner .08 .2
115 Vladimir Vacatko .08 .2
116 Manfred Wolf .08 .2
117 Johann Morz .08 .2
118 Franz Reindl .08 .2
119 Helmut Steiger .08 .2
120 Georg Holzmann .08 .2
121 Roy Roedger .08 .2
122 Jim Corsi .40 1.0
123 Nick Sanza .08 .2
124 Guido Tenisi 8.00 20.0
125 Erwin Kostner .08 .2
126 Mike Amodeo .20 .5
127 John Bellio .08 .2
128 Dave Tomassoni .08 .2
129 Daniel Pupillo .08 .2
130 Giulio Francella .08 .2
131 Fabio Polloni .08 .2
132 Adolf Insam .08 .2
133 Patrick Dell'Jannone .08 .2
134 Rick Bragnalo .08 .2
135 Michael Mair .08 .2
136 Alberto DiFazio .08 .2
137 Cary Farelli .08 .2
138 Tom Milani .08 .2
139 Martin Pavlu .08 .2
140 Bob De Piero .08 .2
141 Grant Goegan .08 .2
142 Jerry Ciarcia .08 .2
143 Borje Salming 2.00 5.0
144 Lars Lindgren .20
145 Ulf Nilsson .75 2.0
146 Bengt-Ake Gustavsson .60 1.5
147 Kent Nilsson 1.50 4.0
148 Thomas Gradin 1.25 3.0
149 Lars Molin .30
150 Thomas Steen 1.25 3.
151 Bengt Lundholm .30
152 Jorgen Pettersson .30
153 Jukka Porvari .20
154 Tapio Levo .20
155 Reijo Ruotsalainen .30
156 Matti Hagman .30
157 Risto Siltanen .30
158 Ilkka Sinisalo .40 1.0
159 Markus Mattsson .30
160 Mikko Leinonen .20
161 Pekka Rautakallio .40 1.
162 Veli-Pekka Ketola .40 1.

1983 Swedish Semic VM Stickers

COMPLETE SET (162) 40.00 80.
1 Peter Lindmark .40 1.
2 Gote Walitalo .08
3 Lars Eriksson .08
4 Roger Hagglund .08
5 Thomas Eriksson .30
6 Mats Waltin .08
7 Jan Eriksson .08
8 Mats Thelin .30
9 Michael Thelven .20
10 Peter Andersson .40 1.
11 Bo Ericson .08
12 Bo Berglund .20
13 Tomas Sandstrom 1.25 3.
14 Per-Erik Eklund .75 2.
15 Roland Eriksson .08
16 Peter Sundstrom .40 1.
17 Thomas Rundqvist .60 1.
18 Mats Ulander .08
19 Tommy Morth .08
20 Ove Olsson .08
21 HÅ¥kan Sodergren .08
22 HÅ¥kan Loob 2.00 5.
23 Leif Holmgren .08
24 Jan Erixon .40 1.
25 Tom Eklund .08
26 Hannu Kamppuri .40 1.
27 Rauli Sohlman .08
28 Kari Takko .40 1
29 Pekka Rautakallio .40 1
30 Pertti Lehtonen .08
31 Hannu Haapalainen .08
32 Markus Lehto .08
33 Juha Huikari .08
34 Hannu Helander .08
35 Lasse Litma .08
36 Arto Routanen .08
37 Raimo Summanen .20
38 Arto Javaninen .08
39 Jari Lindgren .08
40 Risto Jalo .20
41 Petri Skriko .08
42 Juha Nurmi .08
43 Erkki Laine .20
44 Anssi Melametsa .08
45 Reijo Leppanen .08
46 Matti Hagman .40
47 Kari Makkonen .08
48 Timo Susi .08
49 Harri Touhimaa .08
50 Arto Jokinen .08
51 Vladislav Tretiak 6.00 15
52 Vladimir Mysjkin .40 1
53 Vjatjeslav Fetisov 2.00 5
54 Sergej Babinov .08
55 Vasilij Pervuchin .30
56 Sergej Gimajev .08
57 Aleksej Kasatonov .40
58 Zinetula Biljaletdinov .20
59 Sergej Starikov .08
60 Sergej Makarov 2.00 5
61 Sergej Sjepelev .08
62 Vladimir Krutov 2.00 5
63 Nikolaj Drozdetskij .08
64 Viktor Zjluktov .08
65 Viktor Sjalimov .08
66 Vladimir Golikov .08
67 Aleksandr Maltsev 1.25
68 Andrej Chomutov .40
69 Vjatjeslav Bykov .30
70 Michail Vasiljev .08
71 Sergej Kapustin .20
72 Aleksandr Gerasimov .08
73 Aleksandr Kozjevnikov .08
74 Igor Larionov 4.00 1
75 Vladimir Zubkov .08
76 Jiri Kralik .08
77 Karel Lang .20
78 Jaromir Sindel .20
79 Miloslav Horava .20

80 Milan Chalupa	.20	.50
81 Stanislav Hajdusek	.08	.25
82 Arnold Kadlec	.20	.50
83 Ladislav Kolda	.08	.25
84 Jaroslav Benak	.08	.25
85 Radoslav Svoboda	.08	.25
86 Eduard Uvira	.08	.25
87 Antonin Planovsky	.08	.25
88 Petr Slanina	.08	.25
89 Jiri Lala	.20	.50
90 Jindrich Kokrment	.08	.25
91 Frantisek Cernik	.08	.25
92 Darius Rusnak	.08	.25
93 Dusan Pasek	.30	.75
94 Pavel Richtr	.08	.25
95 Jaroslav Korbela	.08	.25
96 Ivan Dornic	.08	.25
97 Jiri Hrdina	.08	.25
98 Igor Liba	.20	.50
99 Jiri Dudacek	.20	.50
100 Vincent Lukac	.08	.25
101 Erich Weishaupt	.08	.25
102 Bernhard Engelbrecht	.08	.25
103 Karl-Heinz Friesen	.30	.75
104 Ignaz Berndaner	.08	.25
105 Udo Kiessling	.20	.50
106 Harold Kreis	.08	.25
107 Joachim Reil	.08	.25
108 Gerd Truntschka	.20	.50
109 Ulrich Egen	.08	.25
110 Marcus Kuhl	.08	.25
111 Peter Schiller	.08	.25
112 Erich KA¼hnhackl	.20	.50
113 Holger Meitinger	.08	.25
114 Ernst Hofner	.08	.25
115 Dieter Hegen	.08	.25
116 Manfred Wolf	.08	.25
117 Johann Morz	.08	.25
118 Franz Reindl	.08	.25
119 Helmut Steiger	.08	.25
120 Horst-Peter Kretschmer	.08	.25
121 Roy Roedger	.08	.25
122 Jim Corsi	.08	.25
123 Nick Sanza	.08	.25
124 Guido Tenisi	8.00	20.00
125 Erwin Kostner	.08	.25
126 Mike Amodeo	.20	.50
127 John Bellio	.08	.25
128 Dave Tomassoni	.08	.25
129 Bob Manno	.30	.75
130 Gino Pasqualotto	.08	.25
131 Fabio Polloni	.08	.25
132 Adolf Insam	.08	.25
133 Constant Priondolo	.08	.25
134 Rick Bragnalo	.08	.25
135 Michael Mair	.08	.25
136 Alberto Di Fazio	.08	.25
137 Cary Farelli	.08	.25
138 Tom Milani	.08	.25
139 Martin Pavlu	.08	.25
140 Bob De Piero	.08	.25
141 Grant Goegan	.08	.25
142 Jerry Ciarcia	.08	.25
143 Rene Bielke	.08	.25
144 Ingolf Spantig	.08	.25
145 Frank Braun	.08	.25
146 Joachim Lempio	.08	.25
147 Reinhardt Fengler	.08	.25
148 Dieter Frenzel	.08	.25
149 Klaus Schroder	.08	.25
150 Dietmar Peters	.08	.25
151 Dieter Simon	.08	.25
152 Andreas Ludwig	.08	.25
153 Detlef Radant	.08	.25
154 Friedhelm Bogelsack	.08	.25
155 Thomas Graul	.08	.25
156 Roland Peters	.08	.25
157 Frank Pruske	.08	.25
158 Fred Bartell	.08	.25
159 Harald Kuhnke	.08	.25
160 Gerhard MA¼ller	.08	.25
161 Harald Bolke	.08	.25
162 Dieter Kinzel	.08	.25

1983-84 Swedish Semic Elitserien

Card fronts feature action photos from players in the Swedish Elite League. Many players have cards in this set that predate their NHL Rookie Cards, which make for unique and challenging collectibles.

COMPLETE SET (243)	24.00	60.00
1 Gunnar Leidborg	.20	.50
2 Peter Aslin	.40	1.00
3 Mats Thelin	.40	1.00
4 Jan Eriksson	.08	.25
5 Hans Cederholm	.08	.25
6 Bo Ericsson	.08	.25
7 Bjorn Hellman	.08	.25
8 Tomas Nord	.08	.25
9 Anders Wallin	.08	.25
10 Mats Alba	.08	.25
11 Ronny Jansson	.08	.25
12 Roger Lindstrom	.08	.25
13 Mats Hessel	.08	.25
14 Peter Gradin	.08	.25
15 Mats Ulander	.08	.25
16 Per-Erik Eklund	1.25	3.00
17 Ulf Isaksson	.08	.25
18 Rolf Eriksson	.08	.25
19 Michael Wikstrom	.08	.25
20 Leif Holmgren	.08	.25
21 Per Martinelle	.08	.25
22 Tommy Lehmann	.30	.75
23 Hans Norberg	.08	.25
24 Jan Ericsson	.08	.25
25 Per Backman	.08	.25
26 Gote Walitalo	.08	.25
27 Jakob Gustavsson	.08	.25
28 Staffan Andersson	.08	.25
29 Torbjorn Andersson	.08	.25
30 Anders Bostrom	.08	.25
31 Jan Lindholm	.08	.25
32 Ulf Nilsson	2.00	5.00
33 Par Sjolander	.08	.25
34 Lennart Dahlberg	.08	.25
35 Rolf Berglund	.08	.25
36 Patrik Aberg	.08	.25
37 Tom Eklund	.08	.25
38 Stefan Nilsson	.08	.25
39 Matti Pauna	.08	.25
40 Jan Lundstrom	.08	.25
41 Mikael Andersson	1.25	3.00
42 Hans Edlund	.08	.25
43 Jon Lundstrom	.08	.25
44 Tony Lundgren	.08	.25
45 Ulf Wikgren	.08	.25
46 Tomas Hedin	.08	.25
47 Lars-Gunnar Pettersson	.08	.25
48 Peter Edstrom	.08	.25
49 Tore Okvist	.08	.25
50 Tommy Sandlin	.30	.75
51 Lars Eriksson	.08	.25
52 Ake Lilljebjorn	.20	.50
53 Anders Backstrom	.08	.25
54 Goran Grundstrom	.08	.25
55 Jan Kock	.08	.25
56 Gunnar Persson	.08	.25
57 Torbjorn Mattsson	.08	.25
58 Stig Ostling	.08	.25
59 Hans Johansson	.08	.25
60 Robert Nordmark	.40	1.00
61 Mikael Sandstrom	.08	.25
62 Anders Carlsson	.08	.25
63 Christer Andersson	.08	.25
64 Per Hedenstrom	.08	.25
65 Bjorn Akerblom	.08	.25
66 Conny Silfverberg	.08	.25
67 Jonny Stridh	.08	.25
68 Goran Sjoberg	.08	.25
69 Kenneth Andersson	.08	.25
70 Fredrik Lundstrom	.08	.25
71 Henrik Cedergren	.08	.25
72 Tomas Sandstrom	1.25	3.00
73 Anders Huss	.08	.25
74 Stig Salming	.20	.50
75 Rolf Ridderwall	.40	1.00
76 Bo Larsson	.08	.25
77 Mikael Westling	.08	.25
78 Tord Nansen	.08	.25
79 Tommy Albelin	1.25	3.00
80 Orvar Stambert	.08	.25
81 Karl-Erik Lilja	.08	.25
82 Mats Waltin	.08	.25
83 Stefan Perlstrom	.08	.25
84 Michael Thelven	.20	.50
85 Stefan Jansson	.08	.25
86 Jens Ohling	.08	.25
87 Peter Nilsson	.08	.25
88 Hakan Eriksson	.08	.25
89 Jorgen Holmberg	.08	.25
90 Tommy Morth	.08	.25
91 Jan Claesson	.08	.25
92 Per Goransson	.08	.25
93 Martin Linse	.08	.25
94 Bjorn Carlsson	.08	.25
95 Hakan Sodergren	.08	.25
96 Anders Johnsson	.08	.25
97 Jan Viktorsson	.20	.50
98 Jeff Hallegard	.08	.25
99 Leif Boork	.08	.25
100 Hakan Hermansson	.08	.25
101 Thomas Blom	.08	.25
102 Christer Dalgard	.08	.25
103 Tommy Samuelsson	.08	.25
104 Lars-Goran Nilsson	.08	.25
105 Peter Andersson	.40	1.00
106 Mats Lusth	.08	.25
107 Tommy Moller	.08	.25
108 Leif Carlsson	.08	.25
109 Urban Larsson	.08	.25
110 Hakan Nordin	.08	.25
111 Harald Luckner	.08	.25
112 Thomas Rundqvist	.60	1.50
113 Kjell Dahlin	.75	2.00
114 Robin Eriksson	.08	.25
115 Jan Ingman	.08	.25
116 Stefan Persson	.08	.25
117 Peter Berndtsson	.08	.25
118 Anders Steen	.08	.25
119 Claes-HEnrik Silfver	.08	.25
120 Magnus Roupe	.40	1.00
121 Jan Wickberg	.08	.25
122 Dan Mohlin	.08	.25
123 Kent Olsson	.08	.25
124 Stefan Lunner	.08	.25
125 Niklas Holmberg	.08	.25
126 Anders Alverud	.08	.25
127 Stefan Svensson	.08	.25
128 Lars Karlsson	.08	.25
129 Ulf Weinstock	.08	.25
130 Kjell Samuelsson	1.25	3.00
131 Magnus Svensson	.40	1.00
132 Ove Pettersson	.08	.25
133 Hans Eriksson	.08	.25
134 Ulf Samuelsson	1.25	3.00
135 Roland Eriksson	.08	.25
136 Kjell Bond	.08	.25
137 Per Nordlinder	.08	.25
138 Ivan Hansen	.08	.25
139 Sivert Andersson	.08	.25
140 Jonas Bergkvist	.40	1.00
141 Per-Olof Carlsson	.08	.25
142 Dan Labraaten	.60	1.50
143 Ulf Skoglund	.08	.25
144 Ove Olsson	.08	.25
145 Mikael Leek	.08	.25
146 Mats Loov	.08	.25
147 Lennart Ahlberg	.08	.25
148 Hardy Astrom	2.00	5.00
149 Anders Bergman	.08	.25
150 Per Forsberg	.08	.25
151 Sture Andersson	.08	.25
152 Mikael Good	.08	.25
153 Jan Nyman	.08	.25
154 Roger Eliasson	.08	.25
155 Jan Karlsson	.08	.25
156 Lennart Jonsson	.08	.25
157 Robert Frestadius	.08	.25
158 Juha Tuohimaa	.08	.25
159 Jerry Lundberg	.08	.25
160 Tommy Sjalin	.08	.25
161 Ulf Norberg	.08	.25
162 Michael Hjalm	.08	.25
163 Per Nilsson	.08	.25
164 Lars Nyberg	.08	.25
165 Ulf Odmark	.08	.25
166 Ingemar Strom	.08	.25
167 Erik Holmberg	.08	.25
168 Lars Bystrom	.08	.25
169 Lars Hellstrom	.08	.25
170 Henry Saleva	.08	.25
171 Hardy Nilsson	.08	.25
172 Mats Abrahamsson	.08	.25
173 Ulf Nilsson	2.00	5.00
174 Jens Johansson	.08	.25
175 Lars Marklund	.08	.25
176 Robert Ohman	.08	.25
177 Goran Lindblom	.08	.25
178 Ola Stenlund	.08	.25
179 Ulf Agren	.08	.25
180 Thomas Ahlen	.08	.25
181 Tomas Jonsson	.75	2.00
182 Mikael Granstedt	.08	.25
183 Mats Lundstrom	.08	.25
184 Per Andersson	.08	.25
185 Johnny Forsman	.10	.25
186 Lars Nystrom	.08	.25
187 Niklas Mannberg	.08	.25
188 Peter Lundmark	.75	2.00
189 Claes Lindblom	.08	.25
190 Leif Hedlund	.08	.25
191 Roland Stoltz	.08	.25
192 Martin Pettersson	.08	.25
193 Jorgen Marklund	.08	.25
194 Mats Lundstrom	.08	.25
195 Tommy Andersson	.08	.25
196 Ake Andersson	.08	.25
197 Lars Fernqvist	.08	.25
198 Anders Eldebrink	.40	1.00
199 Ulf Borg	.08	.25
200 Mats Kihlstrom	.30	.75
201 Bo Andersson	.08	.25
202 Peter Ekroth	.08	.25
203 Jukka Hirsimaki	.08	.25
204 Stefan Jonsson	.08	.25
205 Peter Loob	.20	.50
206 Tomas Jernberg	.08	.25
207 Dan Hermansson	.08	.25
208 Glenn Johansson	.08	.25
209 Leif R. Carlsson	.08	.25
210 Johan Mellstrom	.08	.25
211 Tomas Gustavsson	.08	.25
212 Olof Johansson	.08	.25
213 Peter Wallin	.08	.25
214 Hans Sarkijarvi	.08	.25
215 Reine Karlsson	.08	.25
216 Conny Jansson	.08	.25
217 Jarmo Makitalo	.08	.25
218 Mikael Johansson	.08	.25
219 Timo Lahtinen	.08	.25
220 Goran Nilsson	.08	.25
221 Joakim Hokegard	.08	.25
222 Peter Pettersson	.08	.25
223 Goran Nilsson	.08	.25
224 Jan Carlsson	.08	.25
225 Soren Johansson	.08	.25
226 Thomas Lundin	.08	.25
227 Calle Johansson	.75	2.00
228 Anders Brostrom	.08	.25
229 Stefan Larsson	.08	.25
230 Thomas Karrbrandt	.08	.25
231 Roger Hagglund	.08	.25
232 Christer Kellgren	.08	.25
233 Kent Eriksson	.08	.25
234 Mikael Andersson	1.25	3.00
235 Ove Karlsson	.08	.25
236 Peter Elander	.08	.25
237 Hans Jonsson	.08	.25
238 Hasse Sjoo	.08	.25
239 Ulf Labraaten	.08	.25
240 Jens Hellgren	.08	.25
241 Roger Ahsberg	.08	.25
242 Kurt Carlsson	.08	.25
243 Peter Gustavsson	.08	.25

1984-85 Swedish Semic Elitserien

This 243-sticker set captures the top players in the Swedish Elitserien. The stickers were produced by Semic Press AB, and measure approximately 3" by 2 1/4". The fronts display a color portrait along with player name, card number and team emblem. The backs have ordering information for the set album (valued at $10) and more stickers.

COMPLETE SET (243)	20.00	50.00
1 Gunnar Leidborg	.20	.50
2 Thomas Ostlund	.75	2.00
3 Jan Eriksson	.08	.25
4 Tomas Nord	.08	.25
5 Bjorn Hellman	.08	.25
6 Hans Cederholm	.08	.25
7 Mats Alba	.08	.25
8 Roger Hellgren	.08	.25
9 Peter Zetterholm	.08	.25
10 Tony Barthelsson	.08	.25
11 Roger Lindstrom	.08	.25
12 Mats Hessel	.08	.25
13 Peter Gradin	.08	.25
14 Per-Erik Eklund	.75	2.00
15 Ulf Isaksson	.08	.25
16 Harri Tiala	.08	.25
17 Michael Wikstrom	.08	.25
18 Per Backe	.08	.25
19 Per Martinelle	.08	.25
20 Tommy Lehmann	.20	.50
21 Hans Norberg	.08	.25
22 Odd Nilsson	.08	.25
23 Henrik Cedergren	.08	.25
24 Stefan Sandin	.08	.25
25 Per Backman	.08	.25
26 Gote Walitalo	.08	.25
27 Jakob Gustavsson	.08	.25
28 Torbjorn Andersson	.08	.25
29 Anders Bostrom	.08	.25
30 Jan Lindholm	.08	.25
31 Lars Karlsson	.08	.25
32 Rolf Berglund	.08	.25
33 Lennart Dahlberg	.08	.25
34 Patric Aberg	.08	.25
35 Ulf Nilsson	1.50	4.00
36 Mats Jacobsson	.08	.25
37 Michael Hjalm	.08	.25
38 Stefan Nilsson	.08	.25
39 Matti Pauna	.08	.25
40 Jan Lundstrom	.08	.25
41 Mikael Andersson	.40	1.00
42 Hans Edlund	.08	.25
43 Jon Lundstrom	.08	.25
44 Tony Lundgren	.08	.25
45 Ulf Wikgren	.08	.25
46 Thomas Hedin	.08	.25
47 Lars-Gunnar Pettersson	.08	.25
48 Peter Edstrom	.08	.25
49 Tommy Sandlin	.20	.50
50 Lars Eriksson	.08	.25
51 Ake Lilljebjorn	.20	.50
52 Mats Kihlstrom	.20	.50
53 Anders Backstrom	.08	.25
54 Lars Ivarsson	.40	1.00
55 Jan Kock	.08	.25
56 Gunnar Persson	.08	.25
57 Torbjorn Mattsson	.08	.25
58 Per Jarnberg	.08	.25
59 Hans Johansson	.08	.25
60 Anders Huss	.08	.25
61 Per Nilsson	.08	.25
62 Owe Eriksson	.08	.25
63 Christer Andersson	.08	.25
64 Per Hedenstrom	.08	.25
65 Jan Larsson	.08	.25
66 Conny Silfverberg	.08	.25
67 Jonny Stridh	.08	.25
68 Erik Holmberg	.08	.25
69 Kenneth Andersson	.08	.25
70 Fredrik Lundstrom	.08	.25
71 Peter Eriksson	.08	.25
72 Peter Eriksson	.08	.25
73 Stig Salming	.20	.50
74 Rolf Ridderwall	.40	1.00
75 Mats Ytter	.08	.25
76 Michael Thelven	.30	.75
77 Stefan Perlstrom	.08	.25
78 Tord Nansen	.08	.25
79 Tommy Albelin	.75	2.00
80 Orvar Stambert	.08	.25
81 Karl-Erik Lilja	.08	.25
82 Kristian Henriksson	.08	.25
83 Arto Blomsten	.30	.75
84 Anders Johnsson	.08	.25
85 Pontus Molander	.08	.25
86 Jens Ohling	.08	.25
87 Peter Nilsson	.08	.25
88 Hakan Sodergren	.08	.25
89 Jorgen Holmberg	.08	.25
90 Tommy Morth	.08	.25
91 Jan Claesson	.08	.25
92 Per Goransson	.08	.25
93 Jan Viktorsson	.20	.50
94 Bjorn Carlsson	.08	.25
95 Erik Ahlstrom	.08	.25
96 Peter Schank	.08	.25
97 Ake Eksell	.08	.25
98 Gunnar Svensson	.08	.25
99 Peter Lindmark	.08	.25
100 Christer Dalgard	.08	.25
101 Hakan Nordin	.08	.25
102 Fredrik Olausson	1.25	3.00
103 Tommy Samuelsson	.08	.25
104 Anders Svensson	.08	.25
105 Peter Andersson	.30	.75
106 Mats Lusth	.08	.25
107 Tommy Moller	.08	.25
108 Leif Carlsson	.08	.25
109 Kent-Erik Andersson	.08	.25
110 Erkki Laine	.08	.25
111 Harald Luckner	.08	.25
112 Staffan Lundh	.08	.25
113 Kjell Dahlin	.75	2.00
114 Dan Mohlin	.08	.25
115 Jan Ingman	.08	.25
116 Stefan Persson	.40	1.00
117 Peter Berndtsson	.08	.25
118 Lars Karlsson	.08	.25
119 Claes-Henrik Silfver	.08	.25
120 Magnus Roupe	.30	.75
121 Conny Evensson	.30	.75
122 Bo Larsson	.08	.25
123 Hans-Goran Elo	.08	.25
124 Carsten Bokstrom	.08	.25
125 Claes Norstrom	.08	.25
126 Alf Tornqvist	.08	.25
127 Bruno Ohlzon	.08	.25
128 Peter Lindgren	.08	.25
129 Christian Due-Boije	.20	.50
130 Tony Landeskog	.08	.25
131 Tomas Lunden	.08	.25
132 Lars Lindskog	.08	.25
133 Anders Karlsson	.08	.25
134 Morgan Craas	.08	.25
135 Ulf Andersson	.08	.25
136 Timo Salomaa	.08	.25
137 Ulf Radbjer	.08	.25
138 Hans Segerberg	.08	.25
139 Roger Melin	.08	.25
140 Rolf Edberg	.08	.25
141 Lasse Bjork	.08	.25
142 Robin Eriksson	.08	.25
143 Thomas Jagenstedt	.08	.25
144 Jan Lindberg	.08	.25
145 Bjorn Berggren	.08	.25
146 Tommy Nilsson	.08	.25
147 Stefan Lunner	.08	.25
148 Niklas Holmberg	.08	.25
149 Anders Alverud	.08	.25
150 Stefan Svensson	.08	.25
151 Jussi Lepisto	.08	.25
152 Kjell Samuelsson	.75	2.00
153 Magnus Svensson	.30	.75
154 Ove Pettersson	.08	.25
155 Stefan Nilsson	.08	.25
156 Jens Christiansson	.08	.25
157 Orjan Lindmark	.08	.25
158 Tomas Gustafsson	.08	.25
159 Jan Segersten	.08	.25
160 Jonas Bergqvist	.40	1.00
161 Per-Olof Carlsson	.08	.25
162 Hannu Oksanen	.08	.25
163 Dan Labraaten	.60	1.50
164 Ulf Skoglund	.08	.25
165 Ove Olsson	.08	.25
166 Mats Loov	.08	.25
167 Hakan Olsson	.08	.25
168 Carl-Erik Larsson	.08	.25
169 Dan Soderstrom	.08	.25
170 Mats Blomqvist	.08	.25
171 Robert Skoog	.08	.25
172 Lars Lindgren	.08	.25
173 Robert Nordmark	.30	.75
174 Kjell-Ake Johansson	.08	.25
175 Kari Heikkila	.08	.25
176 Torbjorn Wirf	.08	.25
177 Lars Modig	.08	.25
178 Bo Eriksson	.08	.25
179 Roger Ohman	.30	.75
180 Mats Ohman	.08	.25
181 Matti Ruisma	.08	.25
182 Erik Stalnacke	.08	.25
183 Jari Lindgren	.08	.25
184 Jens Hellgren	.08	.25
185 Lars-Goran Niemi	.08	.25
186 Tore Okvist	.08	.25
187 Ingemar Mikko	.08	.25
188 Roger Mikko	.08	.25
189 Rolf Karlsson	.08	.25
190 Petter Antti	.08	.25
191 Johan Stromvall	.08	.25
192 Tomas Backstrom	.08	.25
193 Jan Nilsson	.08	.25
194 Freddy Lindfors	.08	.25
195 Mats Abrahamsson	.08	.25
196 Ulf Nilsson	1.50	4.00
197 Goran Lindblom	.08	.25
198 Thomas Ahlen	.08	.25
199 Jens Johansson	.08	.25
200 Lars Marklund	.08	.25
201 Ola Stenlund	.08	.25
202 Ulf Lindblom	.08	.25
203 Olle Haggstrom	.08	.25
204 Ulf Agren	.08	.25
205 Mikael Granstedt	.08	.25
206 Hans Nilsson	.08	.25
207 Per Andersson	.08	.25
208 Jonny Forsman	.08	.25
209 Lars Nystrom	.08	.25
210 Niklas Mannberg	.08	.25
211 Peter Lundmark	.40	1.00
212 Claes Lindblom	.08	.25
213 Leif Hedlund	.08	.25
214 Roland Stoltz	.08	.25
215 Martin Pettersson	.08	.25
216 Jorgen Marklund	.08	.25
217 Mats Lundstrom	.08	.25
218 Tommy Andersson	.08	.25
219 Hardy Astrom	1.25	3.00
220 Sam Lindstahl	.30	.75
221 Jari Luoma	.08	.25
222 Anders Eldebrink	.30	.75
223 Ulf Borg	.08	.25
224 Bo Ericson	.08	.25
225 Tomas Jernberg	.08	.25
226 Peter Ekroth	.08	.25
227 Stefan Jonsson	.08	.25
228 Niklas Gallstedt	.08	.25
229 Jonas Heed	.08	.25
230 Jarmo Makitalo	.08	.25
231 Thom Eklund	.08	.25
232 Dan Hermansson	.08	.25
233 Glenn Johansson	.08	.25
234 Leif R. Carlsson	.08	.25
235 Johan Mellstrom	.08	.25
236 Niclas Lindgren	.08	.25
237 Peter Wallin	.08	.25
238 Hans Sarkijarvi	.08	.25
239 Anders Carlsson	.08	.25
240 Reine Karlsson	.08	.25
241 Conny Jansson	.08	.25
242 Stefan Karlsson	.08	.25
243 Timo Lahtinen	.08	.25

1985-86 Swedish Panini Stickers

This set of 240 stickers was produced by Panini Italy for distribution in Sweden. The stickers feature the top players of the Swedish elite league and were packaged five per pack. The 2 1/2" by 2" stickers feature a player portrait on the front. An album for housing the stickers also was available; it now trades in the $10 range. North American collectors may not rave about the player selection, but some of Sweden's best are represented including Peter Lindmark, Tomas Rundqvist and Anders Eldebrink. Some sticker are half of a larger image -- these are designated by U (upper), L (lower or left) and R (right).

COMPLETE SET (240)	25.00	60.00
1 AIK Team Emblem	.08	.25
2 Per Backman	.08	.25
3 Tomas Ostlund	.75	2.00
4 Gunnar Leidborg	.08	.25
5 Jari Munck	.08	.25
6 Jan Eriksson	.08	.25
7 Hans Cederholm	.08	.25
8 Bjorn Hellman	.08	.25
9 Tomas Ahlen	.08	.25
10 Roger Hellgren	.08	.25
11 Mats Alba	.08	.25
12 Roger Lindstrom	.08	.25
13 Team Picture Left	.08	.25
14 Team Picture Right	.08	.25
15 Mats Hessel	.08	.25
16 Peter Gradin	.08	.25
17 Thomas Bjuhr	.08	.25
18 Per Martinelle	.08	.25
19 Tommy Lehman	.20	.50
20 Thomas Jagenstedt	.08	.25
21 Hans Segerberg	.08	.25
22 Odd Nilsson	.08	.25
23 Bjorkloven Team Picture L	.08	.25
24 Bjorkloven Team Picture U	.08	.25
25 Jakob Gustavsson	.08	.25
26 Gote Walitalo	.08	.25
27 Torbjorn Andersson	.08	.25
28 Jan Lindholm	.08	.25
29 Lars Karlsson	.08	.25
30 Calle Johansson	.75	2.00
31 Ulf Nilsson	1.25	3.00
32 Rolf Berglund	.08	.25
33 Matti Pauna	.08	.25
34 Mikael Andersson	.75	2.00
35 Tommy Sandlin	.08	.25
36 Team Emblem	.08	.25
37 Hans Edlund	.08	.25
38 Ulf Dahlen	1.25	3.00
39 Mikael Hjalm	.08	.25
40 Jon Lundstrom	.08	.25
41 Lars-Gunnar Pettersson	.08	.25
42 Peter Edstrom	.08	.25
43 Tore Oqvist	.08	.25
44 Par Edlund	.08	.25
45 Brynas Team Emblem	.08	.25
46 Stig Salming	.08	.25
47 Lars Eriksson	.08	.25
48 Ake Lilljebjorn	.08	.25
49 Anders Backstrom	.08	.25
50 Lars Ivarsson	.08	.25
51 Mats Kihlstrom	.08	.25
52 Jan Ove Mettavainio	.08	.25
53 Gunnar Persson	.08	.25
54 Torbjorn Mattsson	.08	.25
55 Christer Andersson	.08	.25
56 Per Hedenstrom	.08	.25
57 Team Picture L	.08	.25
58 Team Picture R	.08	.25
59 Per Nilsson	.08	.25
60 Conny Silfverberg	.08	.25
61 Jonny Stridh	.08	.25
62 Owe Eriksson	.08	.25
63 Kenneth Andersson	.08	.25
64 Erik Holmberg	.08	.25
65 Joakim Pehrson	.08	.25
66 Anders Huss	.20	.50
67 Djurgarden Team Picture L	.08	.25
68 Djurgarden Team Picture R	.08	.25
69 Rolf Ridderwall	.40	1.00
70 Mats Ytter	.20	.50
71 Orvar Stambert	.08	.25
72 Karl-Erik Lilja	.08	.25
73 Arto Blomsten	.20	.50
74 Stefan Perlstrom	.08	.25
75 Peter Lindgren	.08	.25
76 Tommy Albelin	.30	.75
77 Jens Ohling	.08	.25
78 Peter Nilsson	.08	.25
79 Gunnar Svenson	.08	.25
80 Team Emblem	.08	.25
81 Jorgen Holmberg	.08	.25
82 Tommy Morth	.08	.25
83 Bjorn Carlsson	.08	.25
84 Hakan Sodergren	.20	.50
85 Anders Johnson	.08	.25
86 Mikael Johansson	.08	.25
87 Jan Viktorsson	.08	.25
88 Erik Ahlstrom	.08	.25
89 Farjestad Team Emblem	.08	.25
90 Conny Evensson	.20	.50
91 Peter Lindmark	.60	1.50
92 Christer Dalgard	.08	.25
93 Tommy Samuelsson	.08	.25
94 Peter Andersson	.30	.75
95 Mats Lusth	.08	.25
96 Leif Karlsson	.08	.25
97 Fredrik Olausson	.75	2.00
98 Hakan Nordin	.08	.25
99 Harald Luckner	.08	.25
100 Tomas Rundqvist	.20	.50
101 Team Picture L	.08	.25
102 Team Picture R	.08	.25
103 Jan Ingman	.08	.25
104 Erkki Laine	.08	.25
105 Stefan Persson	.40	1.00
106 Claes-Henrik Silfver	.08	.25
107 Magnus Roupe	.30	.75
108 Mikael Holmberg	.08	.25
109 Kent-Erik Andersson	.08	.25
110 Staffan Lundh	.08	.25
111 Kjell Dahlin U	.20	.50
112 Kjell Dahlin L	.20	.50
113 Kjell Samuelsson U	.40	1.00
114 Kjell Samuelsson L	.40	1.00
115 Peter Lindmark U	.20	.50
116 Peter Lindmark L	.20	.50
117 Pelle Lindberg U	4.00	10.00
118 Pelle Lindberg L	4.00	10.00
119 Per-Erik Eklund U	.30	.75
120 Per-Erik Eklund L	.30	.75
121 Anders Eldebrink L	.15	.40
122 Anders Eldebrink R	.15	.40
123 Michael Thelven U	.15	.40
124 Michael Thelven L	.15	.40
125 Dan Labraaten L	.20	.50
126 Dan Labraaten R	.20	.50
127 Ove Olsson L	.08	.25
128 Ove Olsson R	.08	.25
129 Kent-E Andersson L	.08	.25
130 Kent-E Andersson R	.08	.25
131 Leksand Team Emblem	.08	.25
132 Dan Soderstrom	.08	.25
133 Stefan Lunner	.08	.25
134 Peter Aslin	.40	1.00
135 Jussi Lepisto	.08	.25
136 Magnus Svensson	.30	.75
137 Owe Pettersson	.08	.25
138 Stefan Nilsson	.08	.25
139 Orjan Lindmark	.08	.25
140 Tomas Nord	.08	.25
141 Robert Burakovsky	.20	.50
142 Jan Segersten	.08	.25
143 Team Picture L	.08	.25
144 Team Picture R	.08	.25
145 Jonas Bergkvist	.30	.75
146 Per-Olof Carlsson	.08	.25
147 Dan Labraaten	.40	1.00
148 Ulf Skoglund	.08	.25
149 Ove Olsson	.08	.25
150 Heinz Ehlers	.08	.25
151 Mats Loov	.08	.25
152 Jarmo Makitalo	.08	.25
153 Lulea Team Picture L	.08	.25
154 Lulea Team Picture R	.08	.25
155 Mats Blomqvist	.08	.25
156 Robert Skoog	.08	.25
157 Lars Modig	.08	.25
158 Kjell-Ake Johansson	.08	.25
159 Bo Eriksson	.08	.25
160 Robert Nordmark	.20	.50
161 Kari Heikkila	.08	.25
162 Lars Lindgren	.08	.25
163 Roger Mikko	.08	.25
164 Kari Jaako	.08	.25
165 Hans Lindberg	.08	.25
166 Team Emblem	.08	.25
167 Petter Antti	.08	.25
168 Johan Stromvall	.08	.25
169 Juha Nurmi	.08	.25
170 Erik Stalnacke	.08	.25
171 Lars Hurtig	.08	.25
172 Jari Lindgren	.08	.25
173 Jens Hellgren	.08	.25
174 Hans Norberg	.08	.25
175 HV 71 Team Emblem	.08	.25
176 Curt Lundmark	.40	1.00
177 Kenneth Johansson	.08	.25
178 Tomas Javeblad	.08	.25
179 Nils-G Svensson	.08	.25
180 Bert-Roland Naslund	.08	.25
181 Kevan Beaton	.08	.25
182 Jan Hedell	.08	.25
183 Fredrik Stillman	.15	.40
184 Kari Eloranta	.30	.75
185 Klas Heed	.08	.25
186 Hans Sallin	.08	.25
187 Team Picture L	.08	.25
188 Team Picture R	.08	.25
189 Ove Tornberg	.08	.25
190 Thomas Ljungberg	.08	.25
191 Bengt Kinell	.08	.25
192 Roland Eriksson	.08	.25
193 Uno Johansson	.08	.25
194 Ivan Hansen	.08	.25
195 Thomas Lindster	.08	.25
196 Per Martinsson	.08	.25
197 MoDo Team Picture L	.08	.25
198 MoDo Team Picture R	.08	.25
199 Anders Bergman	.08	.25
200 Goran Arnmark	.08	.25
201 Thomas Olofsson	.08	.25
202 Jorgen Palm	.08	.25
203 Ulf Agren	.08	.25
204 Roger Eliasson	.08	.25
205 Juha Tuohimaa	.08	.25
206 Jan Karlsson	.08	.25
207 Lennart Jonsson	.08	.25
208 Ulf Norberg	.08	.25
209 Hakan Nygren	.08	.25
210 Team Emblem	.08	.25
211 Hakan Hierpe	.08	.25
212 Anders Wikberg	.08	.25
213 P-A Alexandersson	.08	.25
214 Ingemar Strom	.08	.25
215 Tommy Eriksson	.08	.25
216 Lars Molin	.20	.50
217 Lars Bystrom	.08	.25
218 Pekka Arbelius	.08	.25
219 Sodertalje Team Emblem	.08	.25
220 Kjell Larsson	.08	.25
221 Sam Lindstal	.08	.25
222 Hardy Astrom	1.25	3.00
223 Anders Eldebrink	.30	.75
224 Niklas Gallstedt	.08	.25
225 Jonas Heed	.08	.25
226 Peter Ekroth	.08	.25
227 Bo Eriksson	.08	.25
228 Stefan Jonsson	.08	.25
229 Thom Eklund	.08	.25
230 Glenn Johansson	.08	.25
231 Team Picture L	.08	.25
232 Team Picture R	.08	.25
233 Leif Carlsson	.08	.25
234 Jan Claesson	.08	.25
235 Niclas Lindgren	.08	.25
236 Peter Wallin	.08	.25
237 Hans Sarkijarvi	.08	.25
238 Reine Karlsson	.08	.25
239 Conny Jansson	.08	.25
240 Anders Carlsson	.08	.25

1986-87 Swedish Panini Stickers

This 270-sticker set features the top players in Sweden for the '86-87 season. The stickers -- which measure approximately 2 1/2" by 2" -- were produced by Panini in Italy. The fronts feature a portrait along with name and team logo. The backs are numbered and include information about completing the set and the available album (valued at $10).The set is short on recognizable names, but does include early appearances by Ulf Dahlen and Calle Johansson, among others.

COMPLETE SET (270)	20.00	50.00
1 Bjorkloven Team Emblem	.08	.25
2 Hans Lindberg	.08	.25
3 Gote Walitalo	.08	.25
4 Jakob Gustavsson	.08	.25
5 Torbjorn Andersson	.08	.25
6 Lars Karlsson	.08	.25
7 Calle Johansson	.40	1.00
8 Rolf Berglund	.08	.25
9 Patrik Aberg	.08	.25
10 Niclas Holmgren	.08	.25
11 Roger Hagglund	.08	.25
12 Team Picture Left	.08	.25
13 Team Picture Right	.08	.25
14 Peter Andersson	.30	.75
15 Tore Oqvist	.08	.25
16 Johan Tornqvist	.08	.25
17 Par Edlund	.08	.25
18 Stefan Nilsson	.08	.25
19 Matti Pauna	.08	.25
20 Lars-Gunnar Pettersson	.08	.25
21 Mikael Hjalm	.08	.25
22 Hans Edlund	.08	.25
23 Peter Sundstrom	.40	1.00
24 Jon Lundstrom	.08	.25
25 Peter Edstrom	.08	.25
26 Mikael Andersson	.40	1.00
27 Ulf Dahlen	.75	2.00
28 Brynas Team Emblem	.08	.25
29 Stig Salming	.08	.25
30 Ake Lilljebjorn	.08	.25
31 Lars Eriksson	.08	.25
32 Christer Lundqvist	.08	.25
33 Lars Ivarsson	.08	.25
34 Torbjorn Mattsson	.08	.25
35 Gunnar Persson	.08	.25
36 Anders Backstrom	.08	.25
37 Team Picture L	.08	.25
38 Team Picture R	.08	.25
39 Jan Ove Mettavainio	.08	.25
40 Par Djoos	.20	.50
41 Tommy Sjodin	.40	1.00
42 Conny Silfverberg	.08	.25
43 Christer Andersson	.08	.25
44 Kenneth Andersson	.08	.25
45 Lars Andersson	.08	.25
46 Anders Huss	.08	.25
47 Joakim Pehrson	.08	.25
48 Jonny Stridh	.08	.25
49 Patrik Eriksson	.08	.25
50 Anders Ivarsson	.08	.25
51 Mikael Lindholm	.08	.25
52 Jan Larsson	.08	.25
53 Peter Eriksson	.08	.25
54 Jan Gronberg	.08	.25
55 Djurgarden Team Emblem	.08	.25
56 Leif Boork	.08	.25
57 Rolf Ridderwall	.40	1.00
58 Hans-Goran Elo	.08	.25
59 Tommy Albelin	.40	1.00
60 Orvar Stambert	.08	.25
61 Tomas Eriksson	.08	.25
62 Stefan Perlstrom	.08	.25
63 Arto Blomsten	.20	.50
64 Christian Due-Boije	.20	.50
65 Kalle Lilja	.08	.25
66 Team Picture L	.08	.25
67 Team Picture R	.08	.25
68 Stefan Jansson	.08	.25
69 Hakan Sodergren	.08	.25
70 Jens Ohling	.08	.25
71 Peter Nilsson	.08	.25
72 Tommy Morth	.08	.25
73 Bjorn Carlsson	.08	.25
74 Per Goransson	.08	.25
75 Pontus Molander	.08	.25
76 Jeff Hallegard	.08	.25
77 Tomaz Eriksson	.08	.25
78 Mikael Johansson	.08	.25
79 Anders Johnson	.08	.25
80 Jan Viktorsson	.08	.25
81 Johan Garpenlov	.40	1.00
82 Farjestad Team Emblem	.08	.25
83 Conny Evensson	.20	.50
84 Peter Lindmark	.40	1.00
85 Christer Dalgard	.08	.25
86 Tommy Samuelsson	.08	.25
87 Mats Lusth	.08	.25
88 Peter Andersson	.08	.25
89 Hakan Nordin	.08	.25
90 Leif Carlsson	.08	.25
91 Team Picture L	.08	.25
92 Team Picture R	.08	.25
93 Patrik Lundback	.08	.25
94 Anders Berglund	.08	.25
95 Roger Johansson	.08	.25
96 Thomas Rundqvist	.20	.50
97 Harald Luckner	.08	.25
98 Erkki Laine	.08	.25
99 Jan Ingman	.08	.25
100 Staffan Lund	.08	.25
101 Claes-Henrik Silfver	.08	.25
102 Magnus Roupe	.20	.50
103 Stefan Persson	.40	1.00
104 Daniel Rydmark	.08	.25
105 Bo Svanberg	.08	.25
106 Mikael Holmberg	.08	.25
107 Tomas Tallberg	.08	.25
108 Kjell Augustsson	.08	.25
109 HV 71 Team Emblem	.08	.25
110 Curt Lundmark	.20	.50
111 Thomas Javeblad	.08	.25
112 Kenneth Johansson	.08	.25
113 Kari Eloranta	.30	.75
114 Jan Hedell	.08	.25
115 Arto Routanon	.08	.25
116 Klas Heed	.08	.25
117 Bert-Roland Naslund	.08	.25
118 Nils-Gunnar Svensson	.08	.25
119 Fredrik Stillman	.08	.25
120 Team Picture L	.08	.25
121 Team Picture R	.08	.25
122 Nicklas Carlsson	.08	.25
123 Ivan Hansen	.08	.25
124 Thomas Ljungberg	.08	.25
125 Peter Eriksson	.08	.25
126 Hans Wallin	.08	.25
127 Ove Thornberg	.08	.25
128 Per Martinsson	.08	.25
129 Mats Loov	.08	.25

130 Stefan Nilsson .08 .25
131 Peter Eriksson .08 .25
132 Thomas Lindster .08 .25
133 Boo Peterzen .08 .25
134 Stefan Falk .08 .25
135 Torgny Karlsson .08 .25
136 Leksand Team Emblem .08 .25
137 Kalle Alander .08 .25
138 Peter Aslin .30 .75
139 Bengt-Ake Pers .08 .25
140 Magnus Svensson .20 .50
141 Ove Pettersson .08 .25
142 Stefan Nilsson .08 .25
143 Jens Christiansson .08 .25
144 Leif Eriksson .08 .25
145 Team Picture L .08 .25
146 Team Picture R .08 .25
147 Orjan Lindmark .08 .25
148 Thomas Nord .08 .25
149 Peter Imhauser .08 .25
150 Dan Labraaten .40 1.00
151 Ulf Skoglund .08 .25
152 Jarmo Makitalo .08 .25
153 Per-Olof Carlsson .08 .25
154 Ove Olsson .08 .25
155 Heinz Ehlers .08 .25
156 Jonas Bergqvist .20 .50
157 Robert Burakovsky .20 .50
158 Carl-Erik Larsson .08 .25
159 Cenneth Soderlund .08 .25
160 Ola Sundberg .08 .25
161 Ronny Reichenberg .08 .25
162 Hans Jax .08 .25
163 Lulea Team Emblem .08 .25
164 Freddy Lindfors .08 .25
165 Mats Blomqvist .08 .25
166 Robert Skoog .08 .25
167 Robert Nordmark .20 .50
168 Lars Lindgren .08 .25
169 Lars Modig .08 .25
170 Bo Eriksson .08 .25
171 Kjell-Ake Johansson .08 .25
172 Roger Akerstrom .08 .25
173 Juha Tuohimaa .08 .25
174 Team Picture L .08 .25
175 Team Picture R .08 .25
176 Mats Ohman .08 .25
177 Erik Stalnacke .08 .25
178 Juha Nurmi .08 .25
179 Lars-Goran Niemi .08 .25
180 Hans Norberg .08 .25
181 Jari Lindgren .08 .25
182 Roger Mikko .08 .25
183 Lars Hurtig .08 .25
184 Johan Stromvall .08 .25
185 Jens Hellgren .08 .25
186 Kari Jaako .08 .25
187 Stefan Nilsson .08 .25
188 Ulf Taavola .08 .25
189 Tomas Edstrom .08 .25
190 MoDo Team Emblem .08 .25
191 Hakan Nygren .08 .25
192 Anders Bergman .08 .25
193 Fredrik Andersson .08 .25
194 Robert Frestadius .08 .25
195 Jouko Narvanmaa .08 .25
196 Jan Asplund .08 .25
197 Ulf Agren .08 .25
198 Jorgen Palm .08 .25
199 Team Picture L .08 .25
200 Team Picture R .08 .25
201 Per Forsberg .08 .25
202 Jens Johansson .08 .25
203 Hans Lodin .08 .25
204 Lars Molin .08 .25
205 Per-Arne Alexandersson .08 .25
206 Pecka Arbelius .08 .25
207 Per Nilsson .08 .25
208 Anders Wikberg .08 .25
209 Lars Bystrom .08 .25
210 Ulf Odmark .08 .25
211 Robert Tedenby .08 .25
212 Kent Lantz .08 .25
213 Ulf Sandstrom .08 .25
214 Mikael Pettersson .08 .25
215 Peter Smedberg .08 .25
216 Mikael Stahl .08 .25
217 Skelleftea Team Emblem .08 .25
218 Christer Abrahamsson .40 1.00
219 Mats Abrahamsson .08 .25
220 Ulf Nilsson 1.00 2.50
221 Goran Lindblom .08 .25
222 Lars Marklund .08 .25
223 Ola Stenlund .08 .25
224 Serge Roy .20 .50
225 Mikael Lindman .08 .25
226 Robert Larsson .08 .25
227 Stefan Svensson .08 .25
228 Team Picture L .08 .25
229 Team Picture R .08 .25
230 Roland Stoltz .08 .25
231 Martin Pettersson .08 .25
232 Jonny Forsman .08 .25
233 Tomas Hedin .08 .25
234 Mikael Granstedt .08 .25
235 Randy Heath .08 .25
236 Peter Lundmark .30 .75
237 Niklas Mannberg .08 .25
238 Claes Lindblom .20 .50
239 Mats Lundmark .08 .25
240 Jorgen Marklund .08 .25
241 Daniel Pettersson .08 .25
242 Mats Lundstrom .08 .25
243 Hans Hjalmar .08 .25
244 Sodertalje Team Emblem .08 .25
245 Dan Hober .08 .25
246 Sam Lindstahl .08 .25
247 Reino Sundberg .08 .25
248 Anders Eldebrink .20 .50
249 Mats Kihlstrom .08 .25
250 Ulf Borg .08 .25
251 Bo Ericsson .08 .25
252 Peter Ekroth .08 .25
253 Team Picture L .08 .25
254 Team Picture R .08 .25
255 Jonas Heed .08 .25
256 Stefan Jonsson .08 .25
257 Hans Pettersson .08 .25
258 Hans Sarkijarvi .08 .25
259 Thom Eklund .08 .25
260 Glenn Johansson .08 .25
261 Peter Loob .08 .25
262 Niklas Lindgren .08 .25
263 Conny Jansson .08 .25
264 Tomas Jernberg .08 .25
265 Reine Karlsson .08 .25
266 Anders Frykbo .08 .25
267 Jan Loob .08 .25
268 Peter Larsson .08 .25
269 Erik Holmberg .08 .25
270 Jorgen Winborg .08 .25

1987-88 Swedish Panini Stickers

This 270-sticker set features the top players from the Elitserien. The stickers -- which measure approximately 2 1/2" by 2" -- were produced by Panini in Italy. The fronts feature a portrait along with player name and team logo. The backs are numbered and contain information about completing the set and acquiring a collector's album (valued now at about $10).

COMPLETE SET (270) 20.00 50.00
1 AIK Team Emblem .08 .25
2 AIK Team Picture Left .08 .25
3 AIK Team Picture Right .08 .25
4 Lars-Gunnar Jansson .08 .25
5 Ake Liljebjorn .08 .25
6 Thomas Ostlund .40 1.00
7 Jan Eriksson .08 .25
8 Hans Cederholm .08 .25
9 Rickard Franzen .08 .25
10 Thomas Ahlen .08 .25
11 Mats Thelin .20 .50
12 Bjorn Hellman .08 .25
13 Peter Gradin .20 .50
14 Bjorn Carlsson .08 .25
15 Anders Gozzi .08 .25
16 Per Martinelle .08 .25
17 Bo Berglund .20 .50
18 Thomas Gradin .40 1.00
19 Hans Segerberg .08 .25
20 Odd Nilsson .08 .25
21 Mats Hessel .08 .25
22 IF Bjorkloven Team Emblem .08 .25
23 IF Bjorkloven Team Picture Left .08 .25
24 IF Bjorkloven Team Picture Right .08 .25
25 Rolf Jager .08 .25
26 Gote Walitalo .08 .25
27 Staffan Andersson .08 .25
28 Torbjorn Andersson .08 .25
29 Lars Karlsson .08 .25
30 Roger Hagglund .08 .25
31 Rolf Berglund .08 .25
32 Peter Andersson .08 .25
33 Age Ellingsen .08 .25
34 Matti Pauna .08 .25
35 Tore Oqvist .08 .25
36 Mikael Andersson .40 1.00
37 Hans Edlund .08 .25
38 Johan Tornqvist .08 .25
39 Peter Edstrom .08 .25
40 Par Edlund .08 .25
41 Erik Kristiansen .08 .25
42 Ulf Andersson .08 .25
43 Brynas IF Team Emblem .08 .25
44 Brynas IF Team Picture Left .08 .25
45 Brynas IF Team Picture Right .08 .25
46 Tord Lundstrom .08 .25
47 Lars Eriksson .08 .25
48 Michael Sundlov .40 1.00
49 Lars Ivarsson .08 .25
50 Par Djoos .20 .50
51 Jan Ove Mettavainio .08 .25
52 Anders Backstrom .08 .25
53 Gunnar Persson .08 .25
54 Christer Andersson .08 .25
55 Conny Silfverberg .08 .25
56 Jonny Stridh .08 .25
57 Kyosti Karjalainen .20 .50
58 Willy Lindstrom .30 .75
59 Joakim Pehrson .08 .25
60 Patrik Erickson .08 .25
61 Anders Huss .08 .25
62 Peter Eriksson .08 .25
63 Jan Larsson .08 .25
64 Djurgardens IF Team Emblem .08 .25
65 Djurgardens IF Team Picture Left .08 .25
66 Djurgardens IF Team Picture Right .08 .25
67 Ingvar Karlsson .08 .25
68 Rolf Ridderwall .40 1.00
69 Hans-Goran Elo .08 .25
70 Orvar Stambert .08 .25
71 Kalle Lilja .08 .25
72 Arto Blomsten .20 .50
73 Stefan Jansson .08 .25
74 Tomas Eriksson .08 .25
75 Christian Due-Boije .20 .50
76 Jens Ohling .08 .25
77 Pontus Molander .08 .25
78 Tommy Morth .08 .25
79 Johan Garpenlov .40 1.00
80 Hakan Sodergren .08 .25
81 Anders Johnson .08 .25
82 Mikael Johansson .08 .25
83 Jan Viktorsson .08 .25
84 Peter Nilsson .08 .25
85 Farjestads BK Team Emblem .08 .25
86 Farjestads BK Team Picture Left .08 .25
87 Farjestads BK Team Picture Right .08 .25
88 Per Backman .08 .25
89 Peter Lindmark .40 1.00
90 Christer Dalgard .08 .25
91 Tommy Samuelsson .08 .25
92 Peter Andersson .08 .25
93 Mats Lusth .08 .25
94 Leif Carlsson .08 .25
95 Jesper Duus .08 .25
96 Hakan Nordin .08 .25
97 Thomas Rundqvist .20 .50
98 Staffan Lund .08 .25
99 Harald Luckner .08 .25
100 Erkki Laine .08 .25
101 Stefan Persson .30 .75
102 Bo Svanberg .08 .25
103 Claes-Henrik Silfver .08 .25
104 Mikael Holmberg .08 .25
105 Roger Johansson .08 .25
106 HV 71 Team Emblem .08 .25
107 HV 71 Team Picture Left .08 .25
108 HV 71 Team Picture Right .08 .25
109 Curt Lundmark .40 1.00
110 Kenneth Johansson .08 .25
111 Boo Peterzen .08 .25
112 Arto Routanen .08 .25
113 Jan Hedell .08 .25
114 Fredrik Stillman .08 .25
115 Reijo Ruotsalainen .40 1.00
116 Bert-Roland Naslund .08 .25
117 Peter Eriksson .08 .25
118 Hans Wallin .08 .25
119 Peter Berndtsson .08 .25
120 Mats Loov .08 .25
121 Thomas Lindster .08 .25
122 Peter Eriksson .08 .25
123 Hasse Sjoo .08 .25
124 Stefan Nilsson .08 .25
125 Stefan Falk .08 .25
126 Ove Thornberg .08 .25
127 Wash Out .08 .25
128 Butt-Ending .08 .25
129 Fordrojd Signal .08 .25
130 Hakning .08 .25
131 Charging .08 .25
132 Olampligt Upptradande .08 .25
133 Fasthallning .08 .25
134 Hog Klubba .08 .25
135 Tripping .08 .25
136 Cross Checking .08 .25
137 Armbagstackling .08 .25
138 Icing .08 .25
139 Icing .08 .25
140 Boarding .08 .25
141 Slashing .08 .25
142 Roughing .08 .25
143 Spearing .08 .25
144 Interference .08 .25
145 Leksands IF Team Emblem .08 .25
146 Leksands IF Team Picture Left .08 .25
147 Leksands IF Team Picture Right .08 .25
148 Christer Abrahamsson .40 1.00
149 Peter Aslin .20 .50
150 Bengt-Ake Pers .08 .25
151 Magnus Svensson .20 .50
152 Stefan Nilsson .08 .25
153 Orjan Lindmark .08 .25
154 Thomas Nord .08 .25
155 Peter Imhauser .08 .25
156 Stefan Larsson .08 .25
157 Robert Burakovsky .20 .50
158 Jonas Bergqvist .20 .50
159 Heinz Ehlers .08 .25
160 Ivan Hansen .08 .25
161 Jarmo Makitalo .08 .25
162 Dan Labraaten .30 .75
163 Per-Olof Carlsson .08 .25
164 Carl-Erik Larsson .08 .25
165 Ulf Skoglund .08 .25
166 Lulea Hockey Team Emblem .08 .25
167 Lulea Hockey Team Picture Left .08 .25
168 Lulea Hockey Team Picture Right .08 .25
169 Freddy Lindfors .08 .25
170 Tomas Javeblad .08 .25
171 Robert Skoog .08 .25
172 Juha Tuohimaa .08 .25
173 Bo Eriksson .08 .25
174 Roger Akerstrom .08 .25
175 Lars Lindgren .08 .25
176 Lars Modig .08 .25
177 Erik Stalnacke .08 .25
178 Johan Stromvall .08 .25
179 Juha Nurmi .08 .25
180 Lars-Goran Niemi .08 .25
181 Jari Lindgren .08 .25
182 Lars-Gunnar Pettersson .08 .25
183 Hans Norberg .08 .25
184 Kari Jaako .08 .25
185 Lars Hurtig .08 .25
186 Jens Hellgren .08 .25
187 MoDo Hockey Team Emblem .08 .25
188 MoDo Hockey Team Picture Left .08 .25
189 MoDo Hockey Team Picture Right .08 .25
190 Anders Nordin .08 .25
191 Anders Bergman .08 .25
192 Fredrik Andersson .08 .25
193 Hans Lodin .08 .25
194 Jens Johansson .08 .25
195 Juouko Narvanmaa .08 .25
196 Robert Frestadius .08 .25
197 Per Forsberg .08 .25
198 Mikael Hjalm .08 .25
199 Ulf Sandstrom .08 .25
200 Ulf Odmark .08 .25
201 Per Nilsson .08 .25
202 Anders Wikberg .08 .25
203 Lars Molin .20 .50
204 Per-Arne Alexandersson .08 .25
205 Lars Bystrom .08 .25
206 Mikael Stahl .08 .25
207 Ove Pettersson .08 .25
208 Skelleftea Hockey Team Emblem .08 .25
209 Skelleftea Hockey Team Picture Left .08 .25
210 Skelleftea Hockey Team Picture Right .08 .25
211 Tommie Bergman .40 1.00
212 Ulf Nilsson .75 2.00
213 Sam Lindstahl .08 .25
214 Lars Marklund .08 .25
215 Goran Lindblom .08 .25
216 Ola Stenlund .08 .25
217 Stefan Svensson .08 .25
218 Kari Suoraniemi .08 .25
219 Hans Hjalmar .08 .25
220 Mikael Granstedt .08 .25
221 Mats Lundstrom .08 .25
222 Jonny Forsman .08 .25
223 Kari Jalonen .20 .50
224 Claes Lindblom .20 .50
225 Tomas Hedin .08 .25
226 Martin Pettersson .08 .25
227 Jorgen Marklund .08 .25
228 Niklas Mannberg .08 .25
229 Sodertalje SK Team Emblem .08 .25
230 Sodertalje SK Team Picture Left .08 .25
231 Sodertalje SK Team Picture Right .08 .25
232 John Pettersson .08 .25
233 Reino Sundberg .08 .25
234 Jari Luoma .08 .25
235 Anders Eldebrink .20 .50
236 Mats Kihlstrom .08 .25
237 Jonas Heed .08 .25
238 Bo Ericsson .08 .25
239 Ulf Borg .08 .25
240 Stefan Jonsson .08 .25
241 Mats Hallin .08 .25
242 Glenn Johansson .08 .25
243 Thomas Ljungberg .08 .25
244 Hans Sarkijarvi .08 .25
245 Thom Eklund .08 .25
246 Peter Larsson .08 .25
247 Conny Jansson .08 .25
248 Niklas Lindgren .08 .25
249 Reine Karlsson .08 .25
250 Vasby IK Team Emblem .08 .25
251 Vasby IK Team Picture Left .08 .25
252 Vasby IK Team Picture Right .08 .25
253 Anders Jacobsen .08 .25
254 Jorgen Larsson .08 .25
255 Stefan Sohlin .08 .25
256 Torbjorn Mattsson .08 .25
257 Hakan Persson .08 .25
258 Kenneth Lindqvist .08 .25
259 Jens Mackegard .08 .25
260 Anders Lindberg .08 .25
261 Mats Edholm .08 .25
262 Mats Poppler .08 .25
263 Claes Gustafsson .08 .25
264 Per Bergman .08 .25
265 Peter Wallen .08 .25
266 Hans-Rickard Andersson .08 .25
267 Arto Heinola .08 .25
268 Mats Lindberg .08 .25
269 Urban Jakobsson .08 .25
270 Stefan Sandin .08 .25

1989 Swedish Semic World Championship Stickers

This 200-sticker set captures some of the players who have represented their country at the World Championships. The stickers, which came in packs of five, measure 3" by 2 1/8" and feature color photos, along with player name, card number and national flag. The backs contain an ad for Pepsi. The NHL players are pictured in their team sweaters, including stars such as Wayne Gretzky and Patrick Roy.

COMPLETE SET (200) 60.00 125.00
1 Sweden National Emblem .02 .10
2 Tommy Sandlin .08 .25
3 Peter Lindmark .08 .25
4 Rolf Ridderwall .08 .25
5 Tomas Jonsson .08 .25
6 Tommy Albelin .08 .25
7 Mats Kihlstrom .02 .10
8 Tommy Samuelsson .02 .10
9 Anders Eldebrink .05 .15
10 Fredrik Olausson .08 .25
11 Peter Andersson .05 .15
12 Thomas Eriksson .02 .10
13 Thom Eklund .02 .10
14 Bo Berglund .05 .15
15 Thomas Steen .15 .40
16 Ulf Sandstrom .02 .10
17 Jonas Bergkvist .08 .25
18 Thomas Rundqvist .05 .15
19 Per-Erik Eklund .20 .50
20 Bengt-Ake Gustavsson .05 .15
21 Patrik Sundstrom .15 .40
22 Mikael Johansson .05 .15
23 Hakan Sodergren .02 .10
24 Kent Nilsson .20 .50
25 Lars-Gunnar Pettersson .02 .10
26 Finland National Emblem .02 .10
27 Pentti Matikainen .08 .25
28 Jukka Tammi .08 .25
29 Sakari Lindfors .08 .25
30 Reijo Ruotsalainen .08 .25
31 Kari Eloranata .08 .25
32 Timo Blomqvist .08 .25
33 Simo Saarinen .02 .10
34 Hannu Virta .08 .25
35 Jouko Narvanmaa .02 .10
36 Jarmo Kuusisto .02 .10
37 Kari Suoraniemi .02 .10
38 Reijo Mikkolainen .02 .10
39 Raimo Helminen .08 .25
40 Raimo Summanen .08 .25
41 Mikko Makela .08 .25
42 Kari Jalonen .02 .10
43 Kari Laitinen .02 .10
44 Petri Skriko .15 .40
45 Erkki Laine .02 .10
46 Pauli Jarvinen .02 .10
47 Jukka Vilander .02 .10
48 Esa Keskinen .15 .40
49 Ari Vuori .02 .10
50 Mika Nieminen .15 .40
51 Canada National Emblem .08 .25
52 Dave King .08 .25
53 Grant Fuhr .75 2.00
54 Patrick Roy 12.00 30.00
55 Ron Hextall .75 2.00
56 Al MacInnis .60 1.50
57 Ray Bourque 4.00 10.00
58 Scott Stevens .20 .50
59 Paul Coffey 1.25 3.00
60 Zarley Zalapski .15 .40
61 James Patrick .15 .40
62 Kevin Lowe .15 .40
63 Brad McCrimmon .15 .40
64 Mario Lemieux 12.00 30.00
65 Wayne Gretzky 20.00 50.00
66 Denis Savard .30 .75
67 Dale Hawerchuk .40 1.00
68 Luc Robitaille .75 2.00
69 Mark Messier 4.00 10.00
70 Michel Goulet .20 .50
71 Cam Neely 2.00 5.00
72 Steve Yzerman 10.00 25.00
73 Bernie Nicholls .30 .75
74 Joe Nieuwendyk .40 1.00
75 Mike Gartner .40 1.00
76 USSR National Emblem .08 .25
77 Viktor Tichonov .07 .20
78 Jevgenij Belosjejkin .20 .50
79 Sergei Mylnikov .20 .50
80 Sergei Golosjumov .08 .25
81 Alexei Kasatonov .20 .50
82 Aleksej Gusarov .08 .25
83 Andrej Smirnov .05 .15
84 Valerij Sjirjajev .05 .15
85 Igor Stelnov .05 .15
86 Vladimir Konstantinov 1.25 3.00
87 Slava Fetisov .40 1.00
88 Sergei Jasjin .05 .15
89 Vladimir Krutov .30 .75
90 Igor Larionov .75 2.00
91 Valerij Kamenskij .20 .50
92 Vjatjeslav Bykov .20 .50
93 Andrej Chomutov .20 .50
94 Yuri Khmylev .20 .50
95 Sergei Nemchinov .20 .50
96 Sergei Makarov .40 1.00
97 Igor Jesmantovitj .05 .15
98 Andrei Lomakin .07 .20
99 Anatolij Semjonov .08 .25
100 Aleksandr Tjernych .05 .15
101 West Germany National Emblem .02 .10
102 Xaver Unsinn .08 .25
103 Karl Friesen .08 .25
104 Josef Schlickenrieder .02 .10
105 Matthias Hoppe .02 .10
106 Andreas Niederberger .02 .10
107 Udo Kiessling .05 .15
108 Uli Hiemer .05 .15
109 Harold Kreis .05 .15
110 Manfred Schuster .02 .10
111 Jorg Hanft .02 .10
112 Ron Fischer .02 .10
113 Michael Heidt .05 .15
114 Dieter Hegen .05 .15
115 Gerd Truntschka .05 .15
116 Helmut Steiger .02 .10
117 Georg Franz .02 .10
118 Georg Holzmann .02 .10
119 Peter Obresa .02 .10
120 Bernd Truntschka .05 .15
121 Manfred Wolf .02 .10
122 Roy Roedger .02 .10
123 Axel Kammerer .02 .10
124 Peter Draisaitl .07 .20
125 Daniel Held .02 .10
126 Poland National Emblem .02 .10
127 Leszek Lejczyk .07 .20
128 Jerzy Mruk .07 .20
129 Andrezej Hanisz .02 .10
130 Dariusz Wieczorek .02 .10
131 Jacek Zamojski .02 .10
132 Marek Cholewa .02 .10
133 Henryk Gruth .02 .10
134 Robert Szopinski .02 .10
135 Jerzy Potz .02 .10
136 Andrzej Swiatek .02 .10
137 Ludvik Czapka .02 .10
138 Piotr Zdunek .02 .10
139 Jedrzej Kasperczyk .02 .10
140 Krzysztof Podsiadlo .02 .10
141 Miroslaw Copija .02 .10
142 Krzysztof Bujar .02 .10
143 Janusz Adamiec .02 .10
144 Jacek Solinski .02 .10
145 Roman Steblecki .02 .10
146 Adam Fraszko .02 .10
147 Leszek Minge .02 .10
148 Piotr Kwasigroch .02 .10
149 Ireneusz Pacula .02 .10
150 1989 World Championship Emblem .02 .10
151 USA National Emblem .08 .25
152 Art Berglund .02 .10
153 Tom Barrasso .20 .50
154 John Vanbiesbrouck 1.25 3.00
155 Gary Suter .20 .50
156 Phil Housley .20 .50
157 Chris Chelios 1.25 3.00
158 Mike Ramsey .08 .25
159 Rod Langway .08 .25
160 Mark Howe .15 .40
161 Brian Leetch .75 2.00
162 Al Iafrate .15 .40
163 Jimmy Carson .05 .15
164 Pat LaFontaine .40 1.00
165 Neal Broten .20 .50
166 Dave Christian .15 .40
167 Brett Hull 4.00 10.00
168 Bob Carpenter .08 .25
169 Ed Olczyk .08 .25
170 Joe Mullen .20 .50
171 Bob Brooke .05 .15
172 Brian Lawton .05 .15
173 Craig Janney .20 .50
174 Mark Johnson .08 .25
175 Chris Nilan .08 .25
176 CSSR National Emblem .02 .10
177 Pavel Wohl .08 .25
178 Dominik Hasek 6.00 15.00
179 Jaromir Sindel .08 .25
180 Petr Briza .40 1.00
181 Antonin Stavjana .08 .25
182 Bedrich Scerban .07 .20
183 Petr Slanina .02 .10
184 Frantisek Kucera .07 .20
185 Jergus Baca .05 .15
186 Leo Gudas .05 .15
187 Drahomir Kadlec .05 .15
188 Mojmir Bozik .02 .10
189 Petr Vlk .02 .10
190 Vladimir Ruzicka .08 .25
191 Otakar Janecky .08 .25
192 Jan Vodila .02 .10
193 Jiri Dolezal .02 .10
194 Rostislav Vlach .02 .10
195 Jiri Kucera .07 .20
196 Jiri Sejba .05 .15
197 Oldrich Valek .02 .10
198 Jiri LaLa .05 .15
199 Robert Kron .08 .25
200 Petr Rosol .05 .15
NNO Sticker Album 4.00 10.00

1989-90 Swedish Semic Elitserien Stickers

This 285-sticker set captures the excitement of the Elitserien in thrilling posed color photos. The 3" by 2 1/8" sticker fronts are complemented by player name, sticker number and team emblem. the backs contain an ad for Pripp's Energy drink. The set is notable for the first "card" appearances of Mats Sundin and Nicklas Lidstrom.

COMPLETE SET (285) 20.00 50.00
1 AIK .08 .25
2 Ake Lilljebjorn .08 .25
3 Thomas Ostlund .30 .75
4 Mats Thelin .08 .25
5 Thomas Ahlen .08 .25
6 Petri Liimatainen .08 .25
7 Roger Ohman .08 .25
8 Rikard Franzen .08 .25
9 Stefan Claesson .08 .25
10 Tommy Hedlund .08 .25
11 Stefan Jansson .08 .25
12 Peter Gradin .08 .25
13 Thomas Gradin .20 .50
14 Bo Berglund .08 .25
15 Heinz Ehlers .08 .25
16 Robert Burakovsky .08 .25
17 Alexander Kozjevnikov .08 .25
18 Peter Hammarstrom .08 .25
19 Anders Gozzi .08 .25
20 Thomas Bjuhr .08 .25
21 Patric Englund .08 .25
22 Odd Nilsson .08 .25
23 Mats Lindberg .08 .25
24 Peter Johansson .08 .25
25 Patric Kjellberg .30 .75
26 Brynas IF .08 .25
27 Lars Eriksson .08 .25
28 Michael Sundlov .08 .25
29 Par Djoos .08 .25
30 Tommy Sjodin .08 .25
31 Nikolaj Davydkin .08 .25
32 Niklas Gallstedt .08 .25
33 Mikael Lindman .08 .25
34 Jan-Erik Stormqvist .08 .25
35 Tommy Melkersson .08 .25
36 Mikael Enander .08 .25
37 Anders Huss .08 .25
38 Anders Carlsson .08 .25
39 Willy Lindstrom .20 .50
40 Kyosti Karjalainen .08 .25
41 Jan Larsson .08 .25
42 Patrik Erickson .08 .25
43 Joakim Pehrson .08 .25
44 Johan Brummer .08 .25
45 Peter Eriksson .08 .25
46 Peter Gustafsson .08 .25
47 Tomas Olund .08 .25
48 Magnus Asberg .08 .25
49 Djurgardens IF .08 .25
50 Rolf Ridderwall .20 .50
51 Tommy Soderstrom .60 1.50
52 Thomas Eriksson .08 .25
53 Arto Blomsten .08 .25
54 Orvar Stambert .08 .25
55 Christian Due-Boje .08 .25
56 Kenneth Kennholt .08 .25
57 Mats Waltin .08 .25
58 Karl-Erik Lilja .08 .25
59 Marcus Ragnarsson .20 .50
60 Hakan Sodergren .08 .25
61 Mikael Johansson .08 .25
62 Jens Ohling .08 .25
63 Jan Viktorsson .08 .25
64 Peter Nilsson .08 .25
65 Charles Berglund .08 .25
66 Kent Johansson .08 .25
67 Johan Garpenlov .20 .50
68 Ola Andersson .08 .25
69 Anders Johnson .08 .25
70 Bengt Akerblom .08 .25
71 Ola Josefsson .08 .25
72 Mats Sundin 4.00 10.00
73 Farjestads BK .08 .25
74 Anders Bergman .08 .25
75 Jorgen Ryden .08 .25
76 Tommy Samuelsson .08 .25
77 Fredrik Olausson .30 .75
78 Peter Hasselblad .08 .25
79 Jesper Duus .08 .25
80 Anders Berglund .08 .25
81 Mattias Andersson .08 .25
82 Mattias Olsson .08 .25
83 Greger Artursson .08 .25
84 Jakob Karlsson .08 .25
85 Thomas Rundqvist .08 .25
86 Staffan Lundh .08 .25
87 Jan Ingman .08 .25
88 Kjell Dahlin .08 .25
89 Bengt-Ake Gustafsson .20 .50
90 Magnus Roupe .08 .25
91 Hakan Loob .40 1.00
92 Mikael Holmberg .08 .25
93 Daniel Rydmark .08 .25
94 Lars Karlsson .08 .25
95 Peter Ottosson .08 .25
96 HV 71 .08 .25
97 Kenneth Johansson .08 .25
98 Claes Heljemo .08 .25
99 Lars Ivarsson .08 .25
100 Arto Ruotanen .08 .25
101 Fredrik Stillman .08 .25
102 Klas Heed .08 .25
103 Nils-Gunnar Svensson .08 .25
104 Per Gustafsson .08 .25
105 Tommy Fritz .08 .25
106 Mats Nilsson .08 .25
107 Hasse Sjoo .08 .25
108 Mats Loov .08 .25
109 Ove Thornberg .08 .25
110 Eddy Ericsson .08 .25
111 Ivan Avdejev .08 .25
112 Stefan Persson .20 .50
113 Rick Erdall .08 .25
114 Stefan Nilsson .08 .25
115 Stefan Ornskog .08 .25
116 Patrik Ross .08 .25
117 Stefan Falk .08 .25
118 Claes Roupe .08 .25
119 Peter Ekelund .08 .25
120 Leksands IF .08 .25
121 Peter Aslin .30 .75
122 Olow Sundstrom .08 .25
123 Jonas Leven .08 .25
124 Tomas Jonsson .20 .50
125 Magnus Svensson .08 .25
126 Ricard Persson .20 .50
127 Per Lundell .08 .25
128 Tomas Nord .08 .25
129 Peter Wallin .08 .25
130 Orjan Lindmark .08 .25
131 Henric Bjorkman .08 .25
132 Anders Pettersson .08 .25
133 Per-Olof Carlsson .08 .25
134 Tomas Forslund .20 .50
135 Niklas Eriksson .08 .25
136 Richard Kromm .08 .25
137 Jarmo Makitalo .08 .25
138 Peter Lundmark .30 .75
139 Ronny Reichenberg .08 .25
140 Cenneth Soderlund .08 .25
141 Jens Nielsen .08 .25
142 Marcus Thuresson .08 .25
143 Anders Broms .08 .25
144 Joakim Backlund .08 .25
145 Lulea HF .08 .25
146 Robert Skoog .08 .25
147 Tomas Javeblad .08 .25
148 Lars Modig .08 .25
149 Jan-Ove Mettavainio .08 .25
150 Osmo Soutokorva .08 .25
151 Torbjorn Lindberg .08 .25
152 Timo Jutila .20 .50
153 Roger Akerstrom .08 .25
154 Per Ljusterang .08 .25
155 Tomas Lilja .08 .25
156 Johan Stromvall .08 .25
157 Lars-Gunnar Pettersson .08 .25
158 Lars Hurtig .08 .25
159 Morgan Samuelsson .08 .25
160 Stefan Nilsson .08 .25
161 Vesa Kangas .08 .25
162 Kari Jaako .08 .25
163 Juha Nurmi .08 .25
164 Jens Hellgren .08 .25
165 Tomas Berglund .08 .25
166 Lars Edstrom .08 .25
167 Petter Antti .08 .25
168 MoDo HK .08 .25
169 Fredrik Andersson .08 .25
170 Goran Arnmark .08 .25
171 Timo Blomqvist .08 .25
172 Hakan Stromqvist .08 .25
173 Robert Frestadius .08 .25
174 Lars Jansson .08 .25
175 Hans Lodin .08 .25
176 Ove Pettersson .08 .25
177 Tony Olofsson .08 .25
178 Jorgen Eriksson .08 .25
179 Ulf Sandstrom .08 .25
180 Michael Hjalm .08 .25
181 Urban Nordin .08 .25
182 Lars Bystrom .08 .25
183 Jens Ohman .08 .25
184 Ulf Odmark .08 .25
185 Mikael Stahl .08 .25
186 Per Nilsson .08 .25
187 Ingemar Strom .08 .25
188 Kent Lantz .08 .25
189 Kent Norberg .08 .25
190 Patrik Soderholm .08 .25
191 Skelleftea HC .08 .25
192 Sam Lindstahl .08 .25
193 Dick Andersson .08 .25
194 Kari Suoraniemi .08 .25
195 Robert Larsson .08 .25
196 Kari Yli-Maenpaa .08 .25
197 Ola Stenlund .08 .25
198 Tony Barthelson .08 .25
199 Lars Marklund .08 .25
200 Glenn Hedman .08 .25
201 Dick Burlin .08 .25
202 Michael Granstedt .08 .25
203 Pekka Jarvela .08 .25
204 Hans Hjalmar .08 .25
205 Mats Lundstrom .08 .25
206 Martin Pettersson .08 .25
207 Johnny Forsman .08 .25
208 Daniel Pettersson .08 .25
209 Niklas Mannberg .08 .25
210 Niklas Brannstrom .08 .25
211 Jan Johansson .08 .25
212 Jorgen Wannstrom .08 .25
213 Leif Johansson .08 .25
214 Par Mikaelsson .08 .25
215 Fredrik Andersson .08 .25
216 Sodertalje SK .08 .25
217 Reino Sundberg .08 .25
218 Jari Luoma .08 .25
219 Anders Eldebrink .08 .25
220 Mats Kilstrom .08 .25
221 Jonas Heed .08 .25
222 Hans Pettersson .08 .25
223 Jan Bergman .08 .25
224 Thomas Carlsson .08 .25
225 Stefan Jonsson .08 .25
226 Thom Eklund .08 .25
227 Ola Rosander .08 .25
228 Bjorn Carlsson .08 .25
229 Thomas Sjogren .08 .25
230 Thomas Ljungbergh .08 .25
231 Stefan Olsson .08 .25
232 Reine Landgren .08 .25
233 Anders Frykbo .08 .25
234 Conny Jansson .08 .25
235 Peter Larsson .08 .25
236 Tomaz Eriksson .08 .25
237 Erik Holmberg .08 .25
238 Patrik Lindh .08 .25
239 Vasteras IK .08 .25
240 Mats Ytter .08 .25
241 Par Hellenberg .08 .25
242 Jan Eriksson .08 .25
243 Peter Popovic .20 .50
244 Tore Lindgren .08 .25
245 Leif Rohlin .20 .50
246 Henrik Andersson .08 .25
247 Nicklas Lidstrom 4.00 10.00
248 Jan Karlsson .08 .25
249 Peter Jacobsson .08 .25
250 Patrik Juhlin .20 .50
251 Goran Sjoberg .08 .25
252 Fredrik Nilsson .08 .25
253 Stefan Hellkvist .08 .25
254 Tomas Strandberg .08 .25
255 Anders Berglund .08 .25
256 Claes Lindblom .08 .25
257 Magnus Wallin .08 .25
258 Bjorn Akerblom .08 .25
259 Joakim Lundholm .08 .25
260 Jorgen Holmberg .08 .25
261 Ronny Hansen .08 .25
262 Misjat Fachrutdinov .08 .25
263 Vastra Frolunda HC .08 .25
264 Hakan Algotsson .30 .75
265 Per Lundbergh .08 .25
266 Jan Karlsson .08 .25
267 Joacim Esbjors .08 .25
268 Leif Carlsson .08 .25
269 Stefan Axelsson .08 .25
270 Peter Ekroth .08 .25
271 Jorgen Palm .08 .25
272 Hakan Nordin .08 .25
273 Stefan Larsson .08 .25
274 Mikael Andersson .20 .50
275 Terho Koskela .08 .25
276 Patrik Carnback .20 .50
277 Serge Boisvert .08 .25
278 Arto Sirvio .08 .25
279 Peter Berndtsson .08 .25
280 Jorgen Pettersson .08 .25
281 Niklas Andersson .08 .25
282 Peter Gustavsson .08 .25
283 Paul Andersson .08 .25
284 Mats Graesen .08 .25
285 Kent Orrgren .08 .25

1990-91 Swedish Semic Elitserien Stickers

This 294-sticker set features the players of the Swedish Elitserien. The stickers measure 3" by 2 1/8" and utilize posed color player photos on the front, along with sticker number, name and club emblem. The backs feature consumer ads. The set includes the first "card" of players such as Mikael Renberg and Markus Naslund.

COMPLETE SET (294) 16.00 40.00
1 MoDo Hockey Team Team Emblem .02 .10
2 MoDo Hockey Team Picture .02 .10
3 Fredrik Andersson .08 .25
4 Goran Arnmark .08 .25
5 Ari Salo .02 .10
6 Anders Berglund .02 .10
7 Lars Jansson .02 .10
8 Hans Lodin .02 .10
9 Ove Pettersson .02 .10
10 Jorgen Eriksson .02 .10
11 Tony Olofsson .02 .10
12 Tomas Nanzen .02 .10
13 Michael Hjalm .02 .10
14 Erik Holmberg .02 .10
15 Urban Nordin .02 .10
16 Kent Lantz .02 .10
17 Lars Bystrom .02 .10
18 Jens Ohman .02 .10
19 Ulf Odmark .02 .10
20 Mikael Stahl .02 .10
21 Ingemar Strom .02 .10
22 Tommy Pettersson .02 .10
23 Markus Naslund 2.00 5.00
24 Per Wallin .05 .15
25 Vastra Frolunda HC Team Emblem .02 .10
26 Vastra Frolunda HC .02 .10

Team Picture
Ake Lilljebjorn .20 .50
Hakan Algotsson .20 .50
Leif Carlsson .02 .10
Jonas Heed .02 .10
Hakan Nordin .02 .10
Joacim Esbjors .05 .15
Stefan Axelsson .15 .40
Stefan Larsson .05 .15
Jorgen Palm .02 .10
Oscar Ackerstrom .02 .10
Patrik Carnback .20 .50
Mats Lundstrom .02 .10
Niklas Andersson .08 .25
Serge Boisvert .07 .20
Arto Sirvio .02 .10
Terho Koskela .02 .10
Kari Jaako .02 .10
Peter Berndtsson .02 .10
Mikael Andersson .08 .25
Par Edlund .02 .10
Jonas Andersson .02 .10
Johan Witehall .20 .50
Sodertalje SK .02 .10
eam Emblem
Sodertalje SK .02 .10
eam Picture
Reino Sundberg .08 .25
Jari Luoma .08 .25
Mats Kilstrom .02 .10
Stefan Jonsson .02 .10
Peter Ekroth .02 .10
Mats Waltin .02 .10
Jan Bergman .02 .10
Hans Pettersson .02 .10
Stefan Nyman .02 .10
Conny Jansson .02 .10
Thom Eklund .02 .10
Otakar Hascak .07 .20
Morgan Samuelsson .05 .15
Reine Landgren .02 .10
Bjorn Carlsson .02 .10
Ola Andersson .02 .10
Tomaz Eriksson .02 .10
Bert-Olav Karlsson .02 .10
Ola Rosander .02 .10
Stefan Olsson .02 .10
Scott Moore .02 .10
Anders Frykbo .02 .10
AIK .02 .10
eam Emblem
AIK .02 .10
eam Picture
Thomas Ostlund .20 .50
Sam Lindstahl .08 .25
Borje Salming 1.25 3.00
Mats Thelin .08 .25
Petter Salsten .02 .10
Petri Liimatainen .02 .10
Rikard Franzen .05 .15
Stefan Claesson .02 .10
Torbjorn Mattsson .02 .10
Daniel Jardemyr .02 .10
Robert Burakovsky .07 .20
Peter Gradin .02 .10
Thomas Bjuhr .02 .10
Heinz Ehlers .02 .10
Tommy Lehmann .07 .20
Peter Hammarstrom .02 .10
Patric Kjellberg .40 1.00
Patric Englund .02 .10
Mats Lindberg .02 .10
Peter Johansson .02 .10
Kristian Gahn .07 .20
Niklas Sundblad .08 .25
Erik Andersson .02 .10
HV 71 .02 .10
eam Emblem
HV 71 .02 .10
eam Picture
Peter Aslin .20 .50
Kenneth Johansson .08 .25
Arto Ruotanen .02 .10
Fredrik Stillman .05 .15
Lars Ivarsson .02 .10
Klas Heed .02 .10
Per Gustafsson .20 .50
Mathias Svedberg .02 .10
Tommy Fritz .02 .10
Mats Nilsson .02 .10
Peter Eriksson .02 .10
Risto Kurkinen .02 .10
Thomas Ljungbergh .02 .10
Ove Thornberg .02 .10
Mats Loov .02 .10
Eddy Ericsson .02 .10
Stefan Ornskog .08 .25
Patrik Ross .02 .10
Stefan Persson .08 .25
Dennis Strom .02 .10
Peter Ekelund .02 .10
Jonas Jonsson .02 .10
Torbjorn Persson .02 .10
Malmo IF .02 .10
eam Emblem
Malmo IF .02 .10
am Picture
Peter Lindmark .20 .50
Roger Nordstrom .08 .25
Timo Blomqvist .08 .25
Peter Andersson .08 .25
Mats Lusth .02 .10
Johan Salle .02 .10
Roger Ohman .05 .15
Anders Svensson .02 .10
Peter Imhauser .02 .10
Johan Norgren .02 .10
Raimo Helminen .20 .50
Peter Sundstrom .08 .25
Mats Hallin .02 .10
Matti Pauna .02 .10
Patrik Gustavsson .02 .10
Hakan Ahlund .02 .10
Daniel Rydmark .05 .15
Lennart Hermansson .02 .10
Carl-Erik Larsson .02 .10
Rick Erdall .02 .10
Bo Svanberg .02 .10
Fredrik Johansson .02 .10
Jens Hemstrom .02 .10
Vasteras IK .02 .10
am Emblem
Vasteras IK .02 .10
am Picture
Mats Ytter .08 .25
Par Hellenberg .08 .25
Nicklas Lidstrom 2.00 5.00
Leif Rohlin .15 .40
Peter Popovic .20 .50
Jan Karlsson .02 .10
Henrik Andersson .02 .10

157 Tore Lindgren .02 .10
158 Peter Jacobsson .02 .10
159 Pierre Ivarsson .02 .10
160 Jan Eriksson .02 .10
161 Goran Sjoberg .02 .10
162 Misjat Fachrutdinov .05 .15
163 Anders Berglund .02 .10
164 Claes Lindblom .02 .10
165 Jorgen Holmberg .02 .10
166 Stefan Hellkvist .02 .10
167 Tomas Strandberg .02 .10
168 Bjorn Akerblom .02 .10
169 Ronny Hansen .02 .10
170 Fredrik Nilsson .05 .15
171 Patrik Juhlin .20 .50
172 Henrik Nilsson .02 .10
173 Brynas IF .02 .10
Team Emblem
174 Brynas IF .02 .10
Team Picture
175 Michael Sundlov .20 .50
176 Lars Eriksson .08 .25
177 Tommy Sjodin .08 .25
178 Brad Berry .02 .10
179 Niklas Gallstedt .02 .10
180 Mikael Lindman .02 .10
181 Urban Molander .02 .10
182 Jan-Erik Stormqvist .02 .10
183 Stefan Klockare .07 .20
184 Tommy Melkersson .02 .10
185 Anders Carlsson .02 .10
186 Patrik Erickson .02 .10
187 Anders Huss .02 .10
188 Jan Larsson .02 .10
189 Peter Larsson .02 .10
190 Anders Gozzi .05 .15
191 Joakim Pehrson .05 .15
192 Peter Gustafsson .02 .10
193 Peter Eriksson .02 .10
194 Johan Brummer .02 .10
195 Tomas Olund .02 .10
196 Kenneth Andersson .02 .10
197 Leksands IF .02 .10
Team Emblem
198 Leksands IF .02 .10
Team Picture
199 Olow Sundstrom .08 .25
200 Lars-Erik Lord .08 .25
201 Jonas Leven .02 .10
202 Tomas Jonsson .08 .25
203 Ricard Persson .08 .25
204 Per Lundell .02 .10
205 Tomas Nord .02 .10
206 Mattias Andersson .02 .10
207 Henric Bjorkman .02 .10
208 Orjan Lindmark .02 .10
209 Tomas Forslund .08 .25
210 Niklas Eriksson .02 .10
211 Peter Lundmark .05 .15
212 Per-Olof Carlsson .02 .10
213 Marcus Thuresson .02 .10
214 Jens Nielsen .02 .10
215 Cenneth Soderlund .02 .10
216 Markus Akerblom .05 .15
217 Ronny Reichenberg .02 .10
218 Fredrik Olsson .02 .10
219 Niklas Hillblom .02 .10
220 Magnus Gustafsson .02 .10
221 Fredrik Jax .05 .15
222 Lulea HF .02 .10
Team Emblem
223 Lulea HF .02 .10
Team Picture
224 Robert Skoog .08 .25
225 Tomas Javeblad .08 .25
226 Timo Jutila .08 .25
227 Per Ljusterang .02 .10
228 Lars Modig .02 .10
229 Torbjorn Lindberg .02 .10
230 Tomas Lilja .20 .50
231 Osmo Soutukorva .02 .10
232 Jan-Ove Mettavainio .02 .10
233 Roger Akerstrom .02 .10
234 Johan Stromvall .02 .10
235 Ulf Sandstrom .02 .10
236 Lars-Gunnar Pettersson .02 .10
237 Pauli Jarvinen .02 .10
238 Lars Hurtig .02 .10
239 Tomas Berglund .02 .10
240 Stefan Nilsson .02 .10
241 Mikael Renberg .75 2.00
242 Hans Hjalmar .02 .10
243 Jens Hellgren .02 .10
244 Lars Edstrom .02 .10
245 Robert Nordberg .08 .25
246 Farjestads BK .02 .10
Team Emblem
247 Farjestads BK .02 .10
Team Picture
248 Anders Bergman .08 .25
249 Jorgen Ryden .08 .25
250 Patrik Haltia .20 .50
251 Tommy Samuelsson .02 .10
252 Jim Leavins .02 .10
253 Peter Hasselblad .02 .10
254 Jesper Duus .02 .10
255 Mattias Olsson .02 .10
256 Greger Artursson .02 .10
257 Jakob Karlsson .02 .10
258 Thomas Rhodin .02 .10
259 Bengt-Ake Gustafsson .15 .40
260 Hakan Loob .40 1.00
261 Thomas Rundqvist .08 .25
262 Kjell Dahlin .08 .25
263 Magnus Roupe .08 .25
264 Jan Ingman .02 .10
265 Lars Karlsson .02 .10
266 Mikael Holmberg .02 .10
267 Staffan Lundh .02 .10
268 Peter Ottosson .02 .10
269 Jonas Hoglund 1.25 3.00
270 Clas Eriksson .02 .10
271 Djurgardens IF .02 .10
Team Emblem
272 Djurgardens IF .02 .10
Team Picture
273 Tommy Soderstrom .40 1.00
274 Joakim Persson .20 .50
275 Thomas Eriksson .02 .10
276 Arto Blomsten .08 .25
277 Kenneth Kennholt .05 .15
278 Christian Due-Boje .07 .20
279 Orvar Stambert .02 .10
280 Per Nygards .02 .10
281 Marcus Ragnarsson .20 .50
282 Thomas Johansson .02 .10
283 Ronnie Pettersson .02 .10
284 Charles Berglund .02 .10
285 Jan Viktorsson .07 .20
286 Jens Ohling .05 .15
287 Ola Josefsson .02 .10

288 Peter Nilsson .02 .10
289 Andres Johnson .02 .10
290 Hakan Sodergren .02 .10
291 Stefan Gustavson .02 .10
292 Magnus Jansson .02 .10
293 Mikael Johansson .02 .10
294 Johan Lindstedt .02 .10

1991 Swedish Semic World Championship Stickers

These hockey stickers, which measure approximately 2 1/8" by 2 7/8", were sold five to a packet. Also an album was available to display all 250 stickers. The fronts display color posed player shots framed by a red inner border studded with yellow miniature stars and a white outer border. The team flag, the player's name, and the sticker number appear in the white border below the picture. The backs were different based on distribution; blank backs were sold in Czechoslovakia; Marabou Chocolate ads were on the backs of cards sold in Finlands and Milky Way ads were on the back of cards sold in Sweden. The stickers are grouped according to country. Teemu Selanne appears in his Rookie Card year.

COMPLETE SET (250) 50.00 125.00
1 Finnish Emblem .02 .10
2 Markus Ketterer .20 .50
3 Sakari Lindfors .08 .25
4 Jukka Tammi .08 .25
5 Timo Jutila .05 .15
6 Hannu Virta .05 .15
7 Simo Saarinen .02 .10
8 Jukka Marttila .02 .10
9 Ville Siren .05 .15
10 Pasi Huura .05 .15
11 Hannu Henriksson .02 .10
12 Arto Ruotanen .02 .10
13 Ari Haanpaa .02 .10
14 Pauli Jarvinen .02 .10
15 Teppo Kivela .02 .10
16 Risto Kurkinen .02 .10
17 Mika Nieminen .05 .15
18 Jari Kurri .40 1.00
19 Esa Keskinen .08 .25
20 Raimo Summanen .02 .10
21 Teemu Selanne 3.00 8.00
22 Jari Torkki .02 .10
23 Hannu Jarvenpaa .05 .15
24 Raimo Helminen .05 .15
25 Timo Peltomaa .05 .15
26 Swedish Emblem .02 .10
27 Peter Lindmark .08 .25
28 Rolf Ridderwall .05 .15
29 Tommy Soderstrom .20 .50
30 Thomas Eriksson .05 .15
31 Nicklas Lidstrom 2.00 5.00
32 Tomas Jonsson .05 .15
33 Tommy Samuelsson .02 .10
34 Fredrik Stillman .05 .15
35 Peter Andersson .05 .15
36 Peter Andersson .05 .15
37 Kenneth Kennholt .05 .15
38 Hakan Loob .08 .25
39 Thomas Rundqvist .05 .15
40 Hakan Ahlund .02 .10
41 Jan Viktorsson .02 .10
42 Charles Berglund .05 .15
43 Mikael Johansson .02 .10
44 Robert Burakovsky .02 .10
45 Bengt-Ake Gustafsson .05 .15
46 Patrik Carnback .02 .10
47 Patrik Erickson .02 .10
48 Anders Carlsson .02 .10
49 Mats Naslund .15 .40
50 Kent Nilsson .15 .40
51 Canadian Emblem .40 1.00
52 Patrick Roy 6.00 15.00
53 Ed Belfour .75 2.00
54 Daniel Berthiaume .05 .15
55 Ray Bourque 2.00 5.00
56 Scott Stevens .30 .75
57 Al MacInnis .60 1.50
58 Paul Coffey .75 2.00
59 Paul Cavallini .05 .15
60 Zarley Zalapski .05 .15
61 Steve Duchesne .05 .15
62 Dave Ellett .05 .15
63 Mark Messier 1.50 4.00
64 Wayne Gretzky 10.00 25.00
65 Steve Yzerman 6.00 15.00
66 Pierre Turgeon .60 1.50
67 Bernie Nicholls .20 .50
68 Cam Neely 1.50 4.00
69 Joe Nieuwendyk .30 .75
70 Luc Robitaille .60 1.50
71 Kevin Dineen .05 .15
72 John Cullen .05 .15
73 Steve Larmer .07 .20
74 Mark Recchi .60 1.50
75 Joe Sakic 2.00 5.00
76 Soviet Emblem .20 .50
77 Arturs Irbe .40 1.00
78 Alexei Marin .02 .10
79 Mikhail Shtalenkov .08 .25
80 Vladimir Malakhov .08 .25
81 Vladimir Konstantinov .40 1.00
82 Igor Kravchuk .05 .15
83 Ilya Byakin .05 .15
84 Dimitri Mironov .07 .20
85 Vladimir Turikov .02 .10
86 Vjatjeslav Uvajev .02 .10
87 Vladimir Fedosov .02 .10
88 Valeri Kamensky .20 .50
89 Pavel Bure 1.50 4.00
90 Vyacheslav Butsayev .05 .15
91 Igor Maslennikov .02 .10
92 Evgeny Davydov .05 .15
93 Andrei Kovalev .02 .10
94 Alexander Semak .05 .15
95 Alexei Zhamnov .15 .40
96 Sergei Nemchinov .05 .15
97 Viktor Gordijuk .02 .10
98 Vyacheslav Kozlov .30 .75
99 Andrei Khomotov .20 .50
100 Vyacheslav Bykov .15 .40
101 Czech Emblem .02 .10
102 Petr Briza .08 .25
103 Dominik Hasek 2.00 5.00
104 Eduard Hartmann .05 .15
105 Bedrich Scerban .05 .15
106 Jiri Slegr .07 .20
107 Josef Reznicek .02 .10
108 Petr Pavlas .02 .10
109 Peter Slanina .02 .10
110 Martin Maskarinec .02 .10
111 Antonin Stavjana .05 .15
112 Stanislav Medrik .02 .10
113 Dusan Pasek .07 .20
114 Jiri Lala .05 .15
115 Darius Rusnak .02 .10
116 Oto Hascak .05 .15
117 Radek Toupal .05 .15
118 Pavel Pycha .02 .10
119 Lubomir Kolnik .02 .10
120 Libor Dolana .02 .10
121 Ladislav Lubina .05 .15
122 Tomas Jelinek .02 .10
123 Petr Vlk .02 .10
124 Vladimir Petrovka .02 .10
125 Richard Zemlicka .05 .15
126 U.S.A. Emblem .20 .50
127 John Vanbiesbrouck .75 2.00
128 Mike Richter .75 2.00
129 Chris Terreri .08 .25
130 Chris Chelios .75 2.00
131 Brian Leetch .40 1.00
132 Gary Suter .07 .20
133 Phil Housley .08 .25
134 Mark Howe .05 .15
135 Al Iafrate .08 .25
136 Kevin Hatcher .08 .25
137 Mathieu Schneider .08 .25
138 Pat LaFontaine .30 .75
139 Darren Turcotte .05 .15
140 Neal Broten .07 .20
141 Mike Modano 1.50 4.00
142 Dave Christian .05 .15
143 Craig Janney .15 .40
144 Brett Hull 1.50 4.00
145 Kevin Stevens .15 .40
146 Joe Mullen .08 .25
147 Tony Granato .07 .20
148 Ed Olczyk .05 .15
149 Jeremy Roenick 1.50 4.00
150 Jimmy Carson .05 .15
151 West German Emblem .02 .10
152 Helmut De Raaf .02 .10
153 Josef Heiss .07 .20
154 Karl Friesen .07 .20
155 Uli Hiemer .05 .15
156 Harold Kreis .02 .10
157 Udo Kiessling .05 .15
158 Michael Schmidt .02 .10
159 Michael Heidt .05 .15
160 Andreas Pokorny .02 .10
161 Bernd Wagner .02 .10
162 Uwe Krupp .08 .25
163 Gerd Truntschka .05 .15
164 Bernd Truntschka .05 .15
165 Thomas Brandl .02 .10
166 Peter Draisaitl .02 .10
167 Andreas Brockmann .02 .10
168 Ulrich Liebsch .02 .10
169 Ralf Hantschke .02 .10
170 Thomas Schinko .02 .10
171 Anton Krinner .02 .10
172 Thomas Werner .02 .10
173 Dieter Hegen .05 .15
174 Helmut Steiger .02 .10
175 Georg Franz .02 .10
176 Swiss Emblem .02 .10
177 Renato Tosio .02 .10
178 Reto Pavoni .05 .15
179 Dino Stecher .02 .10
180 Sven Leuenberger .02 .10
181 Rick Tschumi .02 .10
182 Patrice Brasey .02 .10
183 Didier Massy .02 .10
184 Sandro Bertaggia .02 .10
185 Samuel Balmer .02 .10
186 Martin Rauch .02 .10
187 Marc Leuenberger .02 .10
188 Jorg Eberle .02 .10
189 Fredy Luthi .02 .10
190 Andy Ton .02 .10
191 Raymond Walder .02 .10
192 Manuele Celio .02 .10
193 Roman Wager .02 .10
194 Felix Hollenstein .02 .10
195 Andre Rotheli .02 .10
196 Christian Weber .02 .10
197 Peter Jaks .02 .10
198 Gil Montandon .02 .10
199 Oliver Hoffmann .02 .10
200 Thomas Vrabec .02 .10
201 Teppo Numminen .07 .20
202 Jyrki Lumme .05 .15
203 Esa Tikkanen .15 .40
204 Petri Skriko .05 .15
205 Christian Ruutu .07 .20
206 Ilkka Sinisalo .07 .20
207 Calle Johansson .07 .20
208 Tomas Sandstrom .07 .20
209 Thomas Steen .07 .20
210 Per-Erik Eklund .07 .20
211 Mats Sundin .60 1.50
212 Johan Garpenlov .07 .20
213 Slava Fetisov .40 1.00
214 Alexei Kasatonov .15 .40
215 Mikhail Tatarinov .02 .10
216 Sergei Makarov .20 .50
217 Igor Larionov .40 1.00
218 Alexander Mogilny .60 1.50
219 Sergei Fedorov 1.50 4.00
220 Petr Klima .05 .15
221 David Volek .07 .20
222 Michal Pivonka .08 .25
223 Robert Reichel .08 .25
224 Robert Holik .20 .50
225 Jaromir Jagr 2.00 5.00
226 Urpo Ylonen .02 .10
227 Ilpo Koskela .02 .10
228 Pekka Rautakallio .07 .20
229 Lasse Oksanen .02 .10
230 Veli-Pekka Ketola .07 .20
231 Leif Holmqvist .05 .15
232 Lennart Svedberg .04 .10
233 Sven Tumba Johansson .02 .10
234 Ulf Sterner .02 .10
235 Anders Hedberg .08 .25
236 Ken Dryden 2.00 5.00
237 Bobby Orr 6.00 15.00
238 Gordie Howe 2.00 5.00
239 Bobby Hull 1.25 3.00
240 Phil Esposito 1.50 4.00
241 Vladislav Tretiak 1.50 4.00
242 Alexander Ragulin .08 .25
243 Anatoli Firsov .08 .25
244 Valeri Kharlamov .40 1.00
245 Alexander Maltsov .20 .50
246 Jiri Holecek .07 .20
247 Jan Suchy .02 .10
248 Jozef Golonka .02 .10
249 Vaclav Nedomansky .07 .20
250 Ivan Hlinka .07 .20

1991-92 Swedish Semic Elitserien Stickers

This 360-sticker series captures the players of the Swedish Elitserien. The sticker, which measure 3" by 2 1/8", have posed color photos on the front, along with player name, team emblem and sticker number. The backs note the set's sponsor "Cloetta" -- a Swedish confectioner. The set includes early appearances by Mats Sundin, Peter Forsberg and Mikael Renberg.

COMPLETE SET (360) 20.00 50.00
1 AIK .02 .10
Team Emblem
2 Thomas Ostlund .08 .25
3 Sam Lindstahl .08 .25
4 Borje Salming .30 .75
5 Petri Liimatainen .02 .10
6 Mats Thelin .08 .25
7 Rikard Franzen .05 .15
8 Petter Sahlsten .02 .10
9 Daniel Jardemyr .02 .10
10 Thomas Nilsson .02 .10
11 Niclas Havelid .02 .10
12 Mattias Norstrom .08 .25
13 Peter Gradin .02 .10
14 Peter Hammarstrom .02 .10
15 Patrik Ericksson .05 .15
16 Thomas Bjuhr .02 .10
17 Thomas Strandberg .02 .10
18 Tommy Lehmann .07 .20
19 Mats Lindberg .02 .10
20 Patric Kjellberg .20 .50
21 Michael Nylander .40 1.00
22 Patric Englund .02 .10
23 Niclas Sundblad .20 .50
24 Kristian Gahn .08 .25
25 Erik Andersson .02 .10
26 Bjorn Ahlstrom .02 .10
27 Brynas .02 .10
Team Emblem
28 Michael Sundlov .08 .25
29 Lars Eriksson .08 .25
30 Lars Karlsson .02 .10
31 Tommy Sjodin .07 .20
32 Nikolaj Davydkin .02 .10
33 Niklas Gallstedt .02 .10
34 Mikael Lindman .02 .10
35 Tommy Melkersson .02 .10
36 Mikael Enander .02 .10
37 Urban Molander .02 .10
38 Stefan Klockare .05 .15
39 Anders Huss .05 .15
40 Mikael Lindholm .02 .10
41 Jan Larsson .02 .10
42 Anders Gozzi .05 .15
43 Peter Larsson .02 .10
44 Thomas Tallberg .05 .15
45 Peter Gustafsson .02 .10
46 Joakim Persson .20 .50
47 Peter Eriksson .02 .10
48 Ove Mohlin .05 .15
49 Jonas Johnsson .02 .10
50 Johan Schillgard .02 .10
51 Andreas Dackell .08 .25
52 Tom Bissett .05 .15
53 Djurgarden .02 .10
Team Emblem
54 Tommy Soderstrom .30 .75
55 Joakim Persson .20 .50
56 Petter Ronnqvist .08 .25
57 Thomas Eriksson .02 .10
58 Kenneth Kennholt .05 .15
59 Arto Blomsten .07 .20
60 Orvar Stambert .02 .10
61 Christian Due-Boje .05 .15
62 Marcus Ragnarsson .20 .50
63 Per Nygards .02 .10
64 Thomas Johansson .02 .10
65 Mikael Johansson .02 .10
66 Charles Berglund .05 .15
67 Jan Viktorsson .05 .15
68 Ola Josefsson .02 .10
69 Jens Ohling .05 .15
70 Magnus Jansson .02 .10
71 Peter Nilsson .02 .10
72 Fredrik Lindquist .08 .25
73 Mariusz Czerkawski .60 1.50
74 Johan Lindstedt .02 .10
75 Stefan Ketola .08 .25
76 Erik Huusko .05 .15
77 Anders Huusko .05 .15
78 Farjestad .02 .10
Team Emblem
79 Anders Bergman .08 .25
80 Jorgen Ryden .08 .25
81 Patrik Haltia .15 .40
82 Tommy Samuelsson .02 .10
83 Per Lundell .02 .10
84 Leif Carlsson .02 .10
85 Jesper Duus .02 .10
86 Mattias Olsson .02 .10
87 Thomas Rhodin .02 .10
88 Jakob Karlsson .02 .10
89 Greger Artursson .02 .10
90 Thomas Rundqvist .05 .15
91 Bengt-Ake Gustafsson .08 .25
92 Hakan Loob .40 1.00
93 Lars Karlsson .02 .10
94 Magnus Roupe .07 .20
95 Kjell Dahlin .08 .25
96 Staffan Lundh .02 .10
97 Peter Ottosson .02 .10
98 Niklas Brannstrom .02 .10
99 Jonas Hoglund .75 2.00
100 Clas Eriksson .02 .10
101 Andreas Johansson .20 .50
102 Mathias Johansson .02 .10
103 HV 71 .02 .10
Team Emblem
104 Peter Aslin .15 .40
105 Boo Ahl .20 .50
106 Stefan Magnusson .02 .10
107 Fredrik Stillman .07 .20
108 Lars Ivarsson .02 .10
109 Klas Heed .02 .10
110 Arto Ruotanen .02 .10
111 Per Gustafsson .02 .10
112 Tommy Fritz .02 .10
113 Mathias Svedberg .02 .10
114 Kristian Pedersen .02 .10
115 Peter Eriksson .02 .10
116 Risto Kurkinen .02 .10
117 Ove Thornberg .02 .10
118 Stefan Ornskog .08 .25
119 Thomas Ljungberg .02 .10
120 Patrik Ross .02 .10
121 Eddy Ericsson .02 .10
122 Dennis Strom .02 .10
123 Torbjorn Persson .02 .10
124 Jonas Jonsson .02 .10
125 Peter Ekelund .02 .10
126 Stefan Falk .08 .25
127 Ronny Nilsson .02 .10
128 Leksand .02 .10
Team Emblem
129 Olow Sundstrom .08 .25
130 Jonas Leven .08 .25
131 Tomas Jonsson .08 .25
132 Ricard Persson .08 .25
133 Magnus Svensson .15 .40
134 Mattias Andersson .02 .10
135 Henric Bjorkman .02 .10
136 Orjan Lindmark .02 .10
137 Orjan Nilsson .02 .10
138 Tomas Ring .02 .10
139 Roger Johansson .02 .10
140 Marcus Thuresson .02 .10
141 Per-Olof Carlsson .02 .10
142 Jens Nielsen .02 .10
143 Cenneth Soderlund .02 .10
144 Markus Akerblom .07 .20
145 Fredrik Jax .07 .20
146 Reine Rauhala .05 .15
147 Niklas Eriksson .02 .10
148 Martin Wiita .02 .10
149 Jonas Bergqvist .07 .20
150 Hannu Jarvenpaa .08 .25
151 Lulea .02 .10
Team Emblem
152 Robert Skoog .08 .25
153 Erik Granqvist .08 .25
154 Timo Jutila .08 .25
155 Tomas Lilja .02 .10
156 Lars Modig .02 .10
157 Per Ljusterang .02 .10
158 Jari Gronstrand .02 .10
159 Torbjorn Lindberg .02 .10
160 Patrik Hoglund .07 .20
161 Petter Nilsson .02 .10
162 Daniel Behm .02 .10
163 Johan Stromvall .02 .10
164 Pauli Jarvinen .02 .10
165 Lars Edstrom .02 .10
166 Lars-Gunnar Pettersson .02 .10
167 Stefan Nilsson .02 .10
168 Lars Hurtig .02 .10
169 Tomas Berglund .02 .10
170 Robert Nordberg .08 .25
171 Mikael Renberg .75 2.00
172 Ulf Sandstrom .02 .10
173 Jens Hellgren .02 .10
174 Mikael Engstrom .02 .10
175 Malmo .02 .10
Team Emblem
176 Peter Lindmark .15 .40
177 Roger Nordstrom .15 .40
178 Johan Mansson .02 .10
179 Timo Blomqvist .15 .40
180 Peter Andersson .08 .25
181 Mats Lusth .02 .10
182 Roger Ohman .02 .10
183 Johan Salle .02 .10
184 Anders Svensson .02 .10
185 Johan Norgren .02 .10
186 Raimo Helminen .15 .40
187 Mats Hallin .08 .25
188 Mats Naslund .40 1.00
189 Robert Burakovsky .08 .25
190 Hakan Ahlund .02 .10
191 Peter Sundstrom .15 .40
192 Daniel Rydmark .07 .20
193 Matti Pauna .02 .10
194 Roger Hansson .02 .10
195 Patrik Gustavsson .02 .10
196 Rick Erdall .02 .10
197 Bo Svanberg .02 .10
198 Jesper Mattsson .20 .50
199 Jonas Hakansson .02 .10
200 MoDo .02 .10
Team Emblem
201 Fredrik Andersson .08 .25
202 Goran Arnmark .08 .25
203 Miloslav Horava .08 .25
204 Hans Lodin .02 .10
205 Lars Jansson .02 .10
206 Jorgen Eriksson .02 .10
207 Anders Berglund .02 .10
208 Osmo Soutokorva .02 .10
209 Tomas Nanzen .02 .10
210 Hans Jonsson .20 .50
211 Fredrik Bergqvist .02 .10
212 Erik Holmberg .02 .10
213 Peter Forsberg 4.00 10.00
214 Markus Naslund 1.25 3.00
215 Magnus Wernblom .02 .10
216 Lars Bystrom .02 .10
217 Kent Lantz .02 .10
218 Per Wallin .07 .20
219 Lennart Henriksson .02 .10
220 Ingemar Strom .02 .10
221 Ulf Odmark .02 .10
222 Jens Ohman .02 .10
223 Tommy Pettersson .02 .10
224 Andreas Salomonsson .05 .15
225 Sodertalje .02 .10
Team Emblem
226 Reino Sundberg .08 .25
227 Stefan Dernestal .08 .25
228 Mats Kihlstrom .02 .10
229 Stefan Jonsson .02 .10
230 Jan Bergman .02 .10
231 Peter Ekroth .02 .10
232 Stefan Nyman .02 .10
233 Thomas Carlsson .02 .10
234 Stefan Claesson .02 .10
235 Oto Hascak .07 .20
236 Morgan Samuelsson .02 .10
237 Tomaz Eriksson .02 .10
238 Thom Eklund .02 .10
239 Conny Jansson .02 .10
240 Bjorn Carlsson .02 .10
241 Scott Moore .02 .10
242 Reine Landgren .02 .10
243 Ola Rosander .02 .10
244 Stefan Olsson .02 .10
245 Anders Frykbo .02 .10
246 Ola Andersson .02 .10
247 Joe Tracy .02 .10
248 Christer Ljungberg .02 .10
249 Patrik Nyberg .02 .10
250 Joakim Skold .02 .10
251 Vasteras .02 .10
Team Emblem
252 Mats Ytter .08 .25
253 Par Hellenberg .08 .25
254 Tommy Salo 1.50 4.00
255 Nicklas Lidstrom 1.50 4.00
256 Robert Nordmark .08 .25
257 Leif Rohlin .15 .40
258 Roger Akerstrom .05 .15
259 Peter Popovic .08 .25
260 Jan Karlsson .02 .10
261 Tore Lindgren .02 .10
262 Peter Jacobsson .02 .10
263 Pierre Ivarsson .02 .10
264 Misjat Fachrutdinov .02 .10
265 Paul Andersson .02 .10
266 Patrik Juhlin .20 .50
267 Henrik Nilsson .02 .10
268 Anders Berglund .02 .10
269 Claes Lindblom .02 .10
270 Jorgen Holmberg .02 .10
271 Stefan Hellkvist .02 .10
272 Fredrik Nilsson .08 .25
273 Johan Brummer .02 .10
274 Micael Karlberg .02 .10
275 Niclas Lundberg .02 .10
276 Vastra Frolunda .02 .10
Team Emblem
277 Ake Lilljebjorn .08 .25
278 Hakan Algotsson .15 .40
279 Hakan Nordin .02 .10
280 Jonas Heed .02 .10
281 Joacim Esbjors .05 .15
282 Stefan Larsson .02 .10
283 Stefan Axelsson .08 .25
284 Oscar Ackestrom .02 .10
285 Jerk Hogstrom .02 .10
286 Patric Aberg .02 .10
287 Patrik Carnback .08 .25
288 Serge Boisvert .08 .25
289 Mats Lundstrom .02 .10
290 Mikael Andersson .20 .50
291 Kari Jaako .02 .10
292 Terho Koskela .02 .10
293 Lars Dahlstrom .02 .10
294 Jerry Persson .02 .10
295 Peter Berndtsson .02 .10
296 Thomas Sjogren .05 .15
297 Par Edlund .02 .10
298 Christian Lechtaler .02 .10
299 Jonas Esbjors .05 .15
300 Dennis Fredriksson .02 .10
301 Mats Hjalmarsson .02 .10
302 Leif Holmgren CO .02 .10
303 Tommy Sandlin CO .02 .10
304 Lars Falk CO .02 .10
305 Harald Luckner CO .02 .10
306 Lars-Erik Lundstrom CO .02 .10
307 Staffan Tholson CO .02 .10
308 Freddy Lindfors CO .02 .10
309 Timo Lahtinen CO .02 .10
310 Jan-Ake Andersson CO .02 .10
311 Claes-Goran Wallin CO .02 .10
312 Mikael Lundstrom CO .02 .10
313 Leif Boork CO .02 .10
314 Thomas Rundqvist .08 .25
315 Hakan Loob .40 1.00
316 Tommy Soderstrom .30 .75
317 Niklas Andersson .08 .25
318 Hakan Loob .40 1.00
319 Tomas Sandstrom .20 .50
320 Rolf Ridderwall .08 .25
321 Thomas Eriksson .02 .10
322 Nicklas Lidstrom 1.50 4.00
323 Mats Sundin 1.50 4.00
324 Thomas Rundqvist .08 .25
325 Hakan Loob .40 1.00
326 Marcus Karlsson .02 .10
327 Anders Eriksson .02 .10
328 Mats Lindgren .20 .50
329 Mikael Hakansson .08 .25
330 Mathias Johansson .02 .10
331 Niclas Sundstrom .40 1.00
332 Jesper Mattsson .20 .50
333 Anders Soderberg .20 .50
334 Swedish IHF Emblem .02 .10
335 1991 World Champions .02 .10
336 Rolf Ridderwall .08 .25
337 Peter Lindmark .15 .40
338 Tommy Soderstrom .30 .75
339 Kjell Samuelsson .08 .25
340 Calle Johansson .20 .50
341 Nicklas Lidstrom 1.50 4.00
342 Tomas Jonsson .08 .25
343 Peter Andersson .08 .25
344 Kenneth Kennholt .05 .15
345 Fredrik Stillman .07 .20
346 Thomas Rundqvist .08 .25
347 Hakan Loob .40 1.00
348 Bengt-Ake Gustafsson .08 .25
349 Mats Naslund .40 1.00
350 Mikael Johansson .02 .10
351 Charles Berglund .05 .15
352 Jan Viktorsson .05 .15
353 Johan Garpenlov .02 .10
354 Anders Carlsson .02 .10
355 Patrik Ericksson .05 .15
356 Jonas Bergqvist .07 .20
357 Mats Sundin 1.50 4.00
358 Per-Erik Eklund .02 .10
359 Conny Evensson .02 .10
360 Curt Lundmark .02 .10
NNO Sticker Album 4.00 10.00

1992-93 Swedish Semic Elitserien Stickers

This 356-sticker set covers the Swedish Elitserien. The stickers, which measure 3" by 2 1/8", feature posed color photos and player name on the front. The back has card number, and a cartoon ad for Buster, a sports magazine for Swedish boys. The set is highlighted by the pre-NHL appearances of Peter Forsberg, Mikael Renberg and Tommy Salo, as well as former greats such as Borje Salming and Hakan Loob.

COMPLETE SET (356) 30.00 75.00
1 AIK Team Picture .02 .10
2 AIK Team Picture .02 .10
3 Brynas Team Picture .02 .10
4 Brynas Team Picture .02 .10
5 Djurgarden Team Picture .02 .10
6 Djurgarden Team Picture .02 .10
7 Farjestad Team Picture .02 .10
8 Farjestad Team Picture .02 .10
9 HV 71 Team Picture .02 .10
10 HV 71 Team Picture .02 .10
11 Leksand Team Picture .02 .10
12 Leksand Team Picture .02 .10
13 Lulea Team Picture .02 .10
14 Lulea Team Picture .02 .10
15 Malmo Team Picture .02 .10
16 Malmo Team Picture .02 .10
17 MoDo Team Picture .02 .10
18 MoDo Team Picture .02 .10
19 Rogle Team Picture .02 .10
20 Rogle Team Picture .02 .10
21 Vasteras Team Picture .02 .10
22 Vasteras Team Picture .02 .10
23 Vastra Frolunda Team .02 .10
24 Vastra Frolunda Team .02 .10
25 AIK Team Emblem .02 .10
26 Rolf Ridderwall .08 .25
27 Sam Lindstahl .07 .20
28 Ronnie Karlsson .02 .10
29 Mats Thelin .08 .25
30 Mattias Norstrom .30 .75
31 Dick Tarnstrom .08 .25
32 Petri Liimatainen .02 .10
33 Rikard Franzen .05 .15
34 Daniel Jardemyr .02 .10

35 Niclas Havelid .40 1.00
36 Borje Salming .75 2.00
37 Thomas Bjuhr .02 .10
38 Peter Hammarstrom .02 .10
39 Thomas Strandberg .02 .10
40 Mats Lindberg .02 .10
41 Anders Bjork .02 .10
42 Anders Johnson .02 .10
43 Patrik Erickson .05 .15
44 Torbjorn Ohrlund .02 .10
45 Bjorn Ahlstrom .02 .10
46 Niclas Sundblad .05 .15
47 Patric Englund .02 .10
48 Kritian Gahn .02 .10
49 Morgan Samuelsson .05 .15
50 Brynas Team Emblem .02 .10
51 Michael Sundlov .20 .50
52 Lars Karlsson .08 .25
53 Bedrich Scerban .05 .15
54 Mikael Lindman .02 .10
55 Tommy Melkersson .02 .10
56 Stefan Klockare .05 .15
57 Mikael Enander .02 .10
58 Roger Karlsson .02 .10
59 Niklas Gallstedt .02 .10
60 Christer Olsson .20 .50
61 Anders Carlsson .02 .10
62 Thomas Tallberg .05 .15
63 Tom Bissett .05 .15
64 Andreas Dackell .40 1.00
65 Mikael Wahlberg .02 .10
66 Jan Larsson .02 .10
67 Anders Gozzi .02 .10
68 Ove Molin .02 .10
69 Anders Huss .05 .15
70 Peter Gustafsson .02 .10
71 Jonas Johnsson .02 .10
72 Peter Larsson .02 .10
73 Mikael Lindholm .02 .10
74 Djurgarden Team Emblem .02 .10
75 Thomas Ostlund .20 .50
76 Petter Ronnquist .07 .20
77 Christian Due-Boje .05 .15
78 Arto Blomsten .05 .15
79 Kenneth Kennholt .07 .20
80 Marcus Ragnarsson .20 .50
81 Thomas Johansson .02 .10
82 Joakim Lundberg .02 .10
83 Thomas Eriksson .02 .10
84 Bjorn Nord .08 .25
85 Mikael Magnusson .02 .10
86 Charles Berglund .02 .10
87 Erik Huusko .05 .15
88 Anders Huusko .02 .10
89 Tony Skopac .02 .10
90 Jens Ohling .07 .20
91 Peter Nilsson .02 .10
92 Magnus Jansson .02 .10
93 Kent Nilsson .30 .75
94 Mikael Hakansson .02 .10
95 Ola Josefsson .02 .10
96 Jerry Friman .02 .10
97 Fredrik Lindquist .15 .40
98 Mathias Hallback .02 .10
99 Jan Viktorsson .02 .10
100 Farjestad Team Emblem .02 .10
101 Anders Bergman .08 .25
102 Jonas Eriksson .07 .20
103 Patrik Haltia .20 .50
104 Tommy Samuelsson .02 .10
105 Jesper Duus .02 .10
106 Leif Carlsson .02 .10
107 Per Lundell .02 .10
108 Jakob Karlsson .02 .10
109 Thomas Rhodin .02 .10
110 Mattias Olsson .02 .10
111 Hakan Loob .40 1.00
112 Thomas Rundqvist .02 .10
113 Andreas Johansson .20 .50
114 Staffan Lundh .02 .10
115 Jonas Hoglund .40 1.00
116 Bengt-Ake Gustafsson .15 .40
117 Mattias Johansson .02 .10
118 Clas Eriksson .02 .10
119 Peter Ottosson .02 .10
120 Niklas Brannstrom .02 .10
121 Lars Karlsson .08 .25
122 Peter Hagstrom .02 .10
123 Kjell Dahlin .15 .40
124 HV 71 Team Emblem .02 .10
125 Peter Aslin .08 .25
126 Boo Ahl .20 .50
127 Antonin Stavjana .07 .20
128 Klas Heed .02 .10
129 Tommy Fritz .02 .10
130 Kristian Pedersen .02 .10
131 Per Gustafsson .20 .50
132 Mathias Svedberg .02 .10
133 Niclas Rahm .02 .10
134 Martin Danielsson .02 .10
135 Fredrik Stillman .02 .10
136 Lars Ivarsson .02 .10
137 Ove Thornberg .02 .10
138 Peter Ekelund .02 .10
139 Eddy Eriksson .02 .10
140 Stefan Ornskog .07 .20
141 Patrik Ross .02 .10
142 Torbjorn Persson .02 .10
143 Kamil Kastak .07 .20
144 Dennis Strom .02 .10
145 Peter Eriksson .02 .10
146 Magnus Axelsson .07 .20
147 Stefan Falk .07 .20
148 Thomas Ljungberg .02 .10
149 Leksand Team Emblem .02 .10
150 Ake Lilljebjorn .08 .25
151 Jonas Leven .08 .25
152 Johan Hedberg 1.25 3.00
153 Tomas Jonsson .15 .40
154 Henric Bjorkman .02 .10
155 Mattias Andersson .02 .10
156 Rickard Persson .08 .25
157 Orjan Nilsson .02 .10
158 Magnus Svensson .08 .25
159 Orjan Lindmark .02 .10
160 Jan Huokko .02 .10
161 Reine Rauhala .02 .10
162 Emil Skoglund .02 .10
163 Jens Nielsen .02 .10
164 Marcus Thuresson .02 .10
165 Niklas Eriksson .02 .10
166 Tomas Srsen .05 .15
167 Jonas Bergqvist .08 .25
168 Per-Olof Carlsson .02 .10
169 Markus Akerblom .02 .10
170 Greg Parks .05 .15
171 Mattias Loof .02 .10
172 Cenneth Soderlund .02 .10
173 Jarmo Makitalo .02 .10
174 Lulea Team Emblem .02 .10
175 Robert Skoog .07 .20
176 Erik Grankvist .07 .20
177 Lars Modig .02 .10
178 Patrik Hoglund .02 .10
179 Niklas Bjornfot .02 .10
180 Torbjorn Lindberg .02 .10
181 Ville Siren .08 .25
182 Petter Nilsson .02 .10
183 Joakim Gunler .02 .10
184 Tomas Lilja .02 .10
185 Stefan Jonsson .02 .10
186 Stefan Nilsson .07 .20
187 Johan Stromvall .02 .10
188 Robert Nordberg .05 .15
189 Tomas Berglund .05 .15
190 Mikael Renberg .75 2.00
191 Lars-Gunnar Pettersson .02 .10
192 Lars Edstrom .02 .10
193 Kyosti Karjalainen .07 .20
194 Lars Hurtig .02 .10
195 Fredrik Oberg .02 .10
196 Mikael Engstrom .02 .10
197 Mika Nieminen .20 .50
198 Malmo Team Emblem .02 .10
199 Peter Lindmark .20 .50
200 Roger Nordstrom .08 .25
201 Johan Mansson .02 .10
202 Anders Svensson .02 .10
203 Timo Blomqvist .08 .25
204 Johan Norgren .02 .10
205 Mats Lusth .02 .10
206 Peter Hasselblad .02 .10
207 Robert Svehla .20 .50
208 Johan Salle .02 .10
209 Roger Ohman .02 .10
210 Raimo Helminen .20 .50
211 Roger Hansson .07 .20
212 Per Rosenqvist .02 .10
213 Bo Svanberg .02 .10
214 Daniel Rydmark .07 .20
215 Patrik Sylvegard .02 .10
216 Jonas Hakansson .02 .10
217 Jesper Mattsson .20 .50
218 Hakan Ahlund .02 .10
219 Peter Sundstrom .15 .40
220 Mats Naslund .75 2.00
221 Robert Burakovsky .05 .15
222 MoDo Team Emblem .02 .10
223 Fredrik Andersson .07 .20
224 Anders Nasstrom .07 .20
225 Anders Berglund .02 .10
226 Miloslav Horava .05 .15
227 Hans Lodin .02 .10
228 Lars Jansson .02 .10
229 Jorgen Eriksson .02 .10
230 Anders Eriksson .40 1.00
231 Hans Jonsson .02 .10
232 Tomas Nanzen .02 .10
233 Mattias Timander .20 .50
234 Fredrik Bergqvist .02 .10
235 Magnus Wernblom .07 .20
236 Martin Hostak .05 .15
237 Mikael Pettersson .02 .10
238 Lennart Hermansson .02 .10
239 Tommy Lehmann .07 .20
240 Markus Naslund .40 1.00
241 Ulf Odmark .02 .10
242 Peter Forsberg 6.00 15.00
243 Andreas Salomonsson .02 .10
244 Niklas Sundstrom .40 1.00
245 Lars Bystrom .02 .10
246 Erik Holmberg .02 .10
247 Henrik Gradin .02 .10
248 Rogle Team Emblem .02 .10
249 Kenneth Johansson .08 .25
250 Billy Nilsson .08 .25
251 Orjan Jacobsson .02 .10
252 Daniel Johansson .20 .50
253 Kenny Jonsson .60 1.50
254 Kari Eloranta .08 .25
255 Kari Suoraniemi .02 .10
256 Hakan Persson .02 .10
257 Rikard Gronborg .02 .10
258 Stefan Nilsson .02 .10
259 Per Ljusterang .02 .10
260 Igor Stelnov .02 .10
261 Peter Lundmark .08 .25
262 Heinz Ehlers .02 .10
263 Michael Hjalm .02 .10
264 Jan Ericson .02 .10
265 Pelle Svensson .02 .10
266 Mats Loov .05 .15
267 Stefan Elvenes .05 .15
268 Roger Elvenes .07 .20
269 Peter Wennberg .02 .10
270 Per Wallin .08 .25
271 Torgny Lowgren .02 .10
272 Jorgen Jonsson .02 .10
273 Vasteras Team Emblem .02 .10
274 Mats Ytter .08 .25
275 Tommy Salo .75 2.00
276 Erik Bergstrom .02 .10
277 Pierre Ivarsson .02 .10
278 Peter Popovic .20 .50
279 Sergei Fokin .02 .10
280 Edvin Frylen .08 .25
281 Leif Rohlin .15 .40
282 Peter Karlsson .02 .10
283 Peter Jacobsson .02 .10
284 Roger Akerstrom .05 .15
285 Robert Nordmark .07 .20
286 Patrik Juhlin .20 .50
287 Misjat Fachrutdinov .05 .15
288 Henrik Nilsson .02 .10
289 Mikael Pettersson .02 .10
290 Fredrik Nilsson .05 .15
291 Stefan Hellkvist .02 .10
292 Henrik Pettersson .02 .10
293 Micael Karlberg .02 .10
294 Anders Berglund .02 .10
295 Claes Lindblom .05 .15
296 Johan Brummer .02 .10
297 Patrik Ulin .02 .10
298 Paul Andersson .02 .10
299 Vastra Frolunda Team Emblem .02 .10
300 Hakan Algotsson .20 .50
301 Mikael Sandberg .08 .25
302 Patric Aberg .02 .10
303 Joacim Esbjors .05 .15
304 Oscar Ackestrom .02 .10
305 Jonas Heed .02 .10
306 Stefan Axelsson .08 .25
307 Ronnie Sundin .20 .50
308 Stefan Larsson .02 .10
309 Jonathan Hagrenius .02 .10
310 Serge Boisvert .05 .15
311 Jerry Persson .02 .10
312 Trond Magnussen .02 .10
313 Terho Koskela .02 .10
314 Peter Berndtsson .02 .10
315 Mikael Persson .02 .10
316 Mats Hjalmarsson .02 .10
317 Henrik Lundin .02 .10
318 Jonas Esbjors .02 .10
319 Daniel Alfredsson 1.00 2.50
320 Stefan Ketola .02 .10
321 Lars Dahlstrom .02 .10
322 Par Edlund .02 .10
323 Thomas Sjogren .05 .15
324 Leif Holmgren CO .02 .10
325 Tommy Sandlin CO .02 .10
326 Lars Falk CO .02 .10
327 Harald Luckner CO .02 .10
328 Lars-Erik Lundstrom CO .02 .10
329 Wayne Fleming CO .02 .10
330 Freddy Lindfors CO .02 .10
331 Timo Lahtinen CO .02 .10
332 Kent Forsberg CO .08 .25
333 Christer Abrahamsson CO .08 .25
334 Mikael Lundstrom CO .02 .10
335 Leif Boork CO .02 .10
336 Tommy Sjodin .08 .25
337 Hakan Loob .40 1.00
338 Michael Nylander .40 1.00
339 Michael Nylander .40 1.00
340 Hakan Loob .40 1.00
341 Calle Johansson .20 .50
342 Tommy Sandlin .02 .10
343 Tommy Soderstrom .40 1.00
344 Tommy Sjodin .08 .25
345 Peter Andersson .05 .15
346 Hakan Loob .40 1.00
347 Peter Forsberg 6.00 15.00
348 Mats Sundin 2.00 5.00
349 Jonas Forsberg .20 .50
350 Stefan Bjork .05 .15
351 Edvin Frylen .08 .25
352 Mikael Tjallden .05 .15
353 Johan Davidsson .20 .50
354 Markus Eriksson .05 .15
355 Fredrik Lindh .05 .15
356 Peter Nylander .05 .15

1993 Swedish Semic World Championships Stickers

This 1993 issue of 288-stickers was issued in Sweden to commemorate the 1993 World Championships. The stickers measure 3" by 2 1/8" and feature players from ten nations, mostly in action shots in their national team garb. The NHL players (#169-208) are shown in the club team sweaters. The backs bear the sticker number, as well as player information in Swedish. An album to hold the stickers is valued at about $10.

COMPLETE SET (288) 24.00 60.00
1 Peter Aslin .08 .25
2 Hakan Algotsson .08 .25
3 Kenneth Kennholt .02 .10
4 Arto Blomsten .05 .15
5 Tomas Jonsson .02 .10
6 Fredrik Stillman .02 .10
7 Stefan Larsson .02 .10
8 Peter Popovic .08 .25
9 Hakan Loob .08 .25
10 Thomas Rudqvist .02 .10
11 Patrik Juhlin .08 .25
12 Mikael Renberg .20 .50
13 Peter Forsberg 2.00 5.00
14 Markus Naslund .60 1.50
15 Bengt-Ake Gustafsson .08 .25
16 Jan Larsson .02 .10
17 Fredrik Nilsson .02 .10
18 Roger Hansson .02 .10
19 Tommy Soderstrom .08 .25
20 Anders Eldebrink .05 .15
21 Ulf Samuelsson .02 .10
22 Kjell Samuelsson .08 .25
23 Nicklas Lidstrom 1.25 3.00
24 Tommy Sjodin .05 .15
25 Calle Johansson .08 .25
26 Fredrik Olausson .08 .25
27 Peter Andersson .05 .15
28 Tommy Albelin .05 .15
29 Roger Johansson .05 .15
30 Par Djoos .05 .15
31 Mikael Johansson .02 .10
32 Tomas Sandstrom .08 .25
33 Mats Sundin .60 1.50
34 Ulf Dahlen .08 .25
35 Jan Erixon .05 .15
36 Thomas Steen .08 .25
37 Mikael Andersson .05 .15
38 Johan Garpenlov .08 .25
39 Per-Erik Eklund .08 .25
40 Michael Nylander .08 .25
41 Tomas Forslund .02 .10
42 Patric Kjellberg .20 .50
43 Patrik Carnback .02 .10
44 Niclas Andersson .02 .10
45 Markus Ketterer .08 .25
46 Sakari Lindfors .08 .25
47 Jarmo Myllys .20 .50
48 Peter Ahola .05 .15
49 Mikko Haapakoski .02 .10
50 Kai Harila .02 .10
51 Pasi Huura .05 .15
52 Waltteri Immonen .05 .15
53 Timo Jutila .02 .10
54 Janne Laukkanen .08 .25
55 Harri Laurila .02 .10
56 Jyrki Lumme .08 .25
57 Teppo Numminen .08 .25
58 Sami Nuutinen .02 .10
59 Ville Siren .05 .15
60 Pasi Sormunen .02 .10
61 Mika Stromberg .05 .15
62 Mika Alatalo .20 .50
63 Raimo Helminen .02 .10
64 Pauli Jarvinen .02 .10
65 Jarmo Kekalainen .05 .15
66 Jari Korpisalo .05 .15
67 Jari Kurri .40 1.00
68 Mikko Makela .08 .25
69 Mika Nieminen .08 .25
70 Timo Norppa .02 .10
71 Janne Ojanen .02 .10
72 Timo Peltomaa .02 .10
73 Rauli Raitanen .02 .10
74 Juha Riihijarvi .08 .25
75 Christian Ruuttu .08 .25
76 Timo Saarikoski .02 .10
77 Teemu Selanne 2.00 5.00
78 Jukka Seppo .05 .15
79 Petri Skriko .08 .25
80 Esa Tikkanen .20 .50
81 Pekka Tuomisto .02 .10
82 Petri Varis .08 .25
83 Jarkko Varvio .05 .15
84 Vesa Viitakoski .05 .15
85 Marko Virtanen .02 .10
86 Jali Wahlsten .02 .10
87 Sami Wahlsten .02 .10
88 Pentti Matikainen .02 .10
89 Petr Briza .08 .25
90 Roman Turek .40 1.00
91 Milos Holan .02 .10
92 Drahomir Kadlec .05 .15
93 Bedrick Scerban .05 .15
94 Frantisek Prochazka .02 .10
95 Richard Zemlicka .08 .25
96 Roman Horak .40 1.00
97 Lubos Rob .02 .10
98 Jiri Kucera .05 .15
99 Tomas Kapusta .02 .10
100 Roman Rysanek .02 .10
101 Roman Hamrlik .08 .25
102 Robert Svehla .08 .25
103 Tomas Jelinek .05 .15
104 Petr Klima .08 .25
105 Josef Beranek .07 .20
106 Robert Petrovicky .05 .15
107 Kamil Kastak .05 .15
108 David Volek .05 .15
109 Renato Tosio .02 .10
110 Patrick Schopf .02 .10
111 Samuel Balmer .02 .10
112 Andreas Beutler .02 .10
113 Patrice Brasey .02 .10
114 Rick Tschumi .02 .10
115 Sven Leuenberger .02 .10
116 Sandro Bertaggia .02 .10
117 Patrick Howald .02 .10
118 Andy Ton .02 .10
119 Keith Fair .02 .10
120 Mario Brodmann .02 .10
121 Fredy Luhti .02 .10
122 Jorg Eberle .05 .15
123 Roman Wager .02 .10
124 Manuele Celio .02 .10
125 Christian Weber .02 .10
126 Roger Thony .02 .10
127 Felix Hollenstein .02 .10
128 Gil Montandon .02 .10
129 Nikolai Khabibulin .60 1.50
130 Alexei Cherviakov .02 .10
131 Ilja Biakin .05 .15
132 Dmitri Filimonov .05 .15
133 Alexander Karpovtsev .08 .25
134 Sergei Sorokin .05 .15
135 Andrei Sapozhnikov .02 .10
136 Alexei Yashin .20 .50
137 Alexander Cherbayev .02 .10
138 Konstantin Astrakhantsev .05 .15
139 Sergei Petrenko .05 .15
140 Viktor Kozlov .08 .25
141 Roman Oksyuta .02 .10
142 Vladimir Malakhov .08 .25
143 Andrei Lomakin .05 .15
144 Dimitri Yushkevich .08 .25
145 Igor Korolev .02 .10
146 Darius Kasparaitis .08 .25
147 Vyacheslav Bykov .08 .25
148 Andrei Khomutov .08 .25
149 Helmut De Raaf .02 .10
150 Klaus Merk .08 .25
151 Michael Heidt .08 .25
152 Michael Schmidt .02 .10
153 Uli Hiemer .02 .10
154 Andreas Niederberger .02 .10
155 Rick Amann .02 .10
156 Andreas Brockmann .02 .10
157 Gerd Truntschka .05 .15
158 Dieter Hegen .05 .15
159 Stefan Ustorf .05 .15
160 Georg Holzmann .02 .10
161 Ernst Kopf Jr. .02 .10
162 Bernd Truntschka .05 .15
163 Raimund Hilger .02 .10
164 Wolfgang Kummer .02 .10
165 Georg Franz .02 .10
166 Thomas Brandl .02 .10
167 Michael Rumrich .02 .10
168 Uwe Krupp .08 .25
169 Tom Barrasso .20 .50
170 Mike Richter .60 1.50
171 Brian Leetch .60 1.50
172 Chris Chelios .60 1.50
173 Al Iafrate .08 .25
174 Phil Housley .08 .25
175 Kevin Hatcher .08 .25
176 Gary Suter .08 .25
177 Mathieu Schneider .08 .25
178 Joe Mullen .08 .25
179 Kevin Stevens .08 .25
180 Jeremy Roenick 1.50 4.00
181 Tony Granato .08 .25
182 Mike Modano 1.25 3.00
183 Pat LaFontaine .30 .75
184 Ed Olczyk .05 .15
185 Brett Hull 1.50 4.00
186 Craig Janney .08 .25
187 Jimmy Carson .05 .15
188 Tony Amonte .40 1.00
189 Patrick Roy 5.00 12.00
190 Kirk McLean .20 .50
191 Larry Murphy .20 .50
192 Ray Bourque 2.00 5.00
193 Al MacInnis .60 1.50
194 Steve Duchesne .08 .25
195 Eric Desjardins .20 .50
196 Scott Stevens .30 .75
197 Paul Coffey .60 1.50
198 Mario Lemieux 5.00 12.00
199 Wayne Gretzky 6.00 15.00
200 Rick Tocchet .20 .50
201 Eric Lindros 1.25 3.00
202 Mark Messier 1.25 3.00
203 Steve Yzerman 4.00 10.00
204 Luc Robitaille .60 1.50
205 Mark Recchi .60 1.50
206 Joe Sakic 2.00 5.00
207 Owen Nolan .40 1.00
208 Gary Roberts .20 .50
209 David Delfino .08 .25
210 Mike Rosati .08 .25
211 Robert Oberrauch .02 .10
212 Jim Camazzola .02 .10
213 Bill Stewart .02 .10
214 Mike DeAngelis .02 .10
215 Anthony Circelli .02 .10
216 Georg Comploy .02 .10
217 Frank DiMuzio .02 .10
218 Gates Orlando .05 .15
219 John Vecchiarelli .02 .10
220 Joe Foglietta .02 .10
221 Lucio Topatigh .02 .10
222 Carmine Vani .05 .15
223 Lino DeToni .02 .10
224 Mario Chitarron .02 .10
225 Bruno Zarrillo .02 .10
226 Maurizio Mansi .02 .10
227 Stefan Figliuzzi .02 .10
228 Santino Pellegrino .02 .10
229 Jim Marthinsen .08 .25
230 Rob Schistad .08 .25
231 Petter Salsten .02 .10
232 Cato Tom Andersen .02 .10
233 Tommy Jakobsen .02 .10
234 Svein E Norstebo .02 .10
235 Jon Magne Karlstad .02 .10
236 Kim Sogaard .02 .10
237 Geir Hoff .02 .10
238 Erik Kristiansen .02 .10
239 Petter Thoresen .02 .10
240 Ole Eskild Dahlstrom .02 .10
241 Espen Knutsen .20 .50
242 Oystein Olsen .02 .10
243 Roy Johansen .02 .10
244 Trond Magnussen .02 .10
245 Arne Billkvam .02 .10
246 Marius Rath .02 .10
247 Tom Erik Olsen .02 .10
248 Morten Finstad .02 .10
249 Petri Ylonen .08 .25
250 Michel Valliere .08 .25
251 Stephane Botteri .02 .10
252 Serge Poudrier .05 .15
253 Eric Durand .02 .10
254 Jean-Philippe Lemoine .05 .15
255 Denis Perez .05 .15
256 Sebastien Marquet .02 .10
257 Michael Babin .02 .10
258 Stephane Barin .02 .10
259 Arnaud Briand .02 .10
260 Yves Crettenand .02 .10
261 Laurent Deschaume .02 .10
262 Roger Dube .02 .10
263 Patrick Dunn .02 .10
264 Franck Pajonkowski .05 .15
265 Pierre Pousse .02 .10
266 Antoine Richer .02 .10
267 Christophe Ville .02 .10
268 Philippe Bozon .40 1.00
269 Brian Stankiewicz .02 .10
270 Claus Dalpiaz .08 .25
271 Michael Shea .08 .25
272 Robin Doyle .02 .10
273 Martin Ulrich .02 .10
274 Martin Krainz .02 .10
275 Erich Solderer .02 .10
276 Michael Guntner .02 .10
277 Friedrich Ganster .02 .10
278 Wayne Groulx .02 .10
279 Dieter Kalt .02 .10
280 Werner Kerth .02 .10
281 Arno Maier .02 .10
282 Richard Nasheim .02 .10
283 Christian Perthaler .02 .10
284 Andreas Puschnig .02 .10
285 Gerhard Puschnik .02 .10
286 Walter Putnik .02 .10
287 Reinhard Lampert .02 .10
288 Mario Schaden .02 .10

1993-94 Swedish Semic Elitserien

This 320-sticker set was the collectible to own for fans of the Elitserien. This comprehensive issue had a posed player photo and name on the front, with card number and a cartoon ad for the whimsical boy's sports magazine, "Buster" on the back.

COMPLETE SET (320) 24.00 60.00
1 Bjorkloven Team Emblem .02 .10
2 Patrik Hofbauer .02 .10
3 Jorgen Wikstrom .02 .10
4 Mattias Hedlund .02 .10
5 Yuri Kuznetsov .07 .20
6 Ulf Odling .02 .10
7 Jorgen Eriksson .02 .10
8 Jorgen Hermansson .02 .10
9 Peter Andersson .02 .10
10 Joakim Lindgren .02 .10
11 Glenn Hedman .02 .10
12 Roger Kyro .02 .10
13 Niklas Norberg .02 .10
14 Alexander Belyavsky .05 .15
15 Anders Nejdsater .02 .10
16 Stefan Olofsson .02 .10
17 Mikael Andersson .08 .25
18 Ulf Andersson .02 .10
19 Patrik Sundstrom .08 .25
20 Hakan Hermansson .02 .10
21 Micael Karlberg .02 .10
22 Peder Bejegard .02 .10
23 Johan Boman .02 .10
24 Joakim Lindgren .02 .10
25 Brynas Team Emblem .02 .10
26 Michael Sundlov .07 .20
27 Lars Karlsson .07 .20
28 Bedrich Scerban .02 .10
29 Mikael Lindman .02 .10
30 Johan Tornberg .02 .10
31 Tommy Melkersson .02 .10
32 Stefan Klockare .05 .15
33 Mikael Enander .02 .10
34 Mikael Wiklander .02 .10
35 Christer Olsson .08 .25
36 Thomas Tallberg .05 .15
37 Andreas Dackell .40 1.00
38 Mikael Wahlberg .02 .10
39 Anders Gozzi .02 .10
40 Niklas Gallstedt .02 .10
41 Per-Johan Johansson .02 .10
42 Joakim Persson .08 .25
43 Branislav Janos .02 .10
44 Ove Molin .02 .10
45 Anders Huss .02 .10
46 Jonas Johnsson .02 .10
47 Peter Larsson .02 .10
48 Anders Carlsson .02 .10
49 Djurgarden Team Emblem .02 .10
50 Thomas Ostlund .08 .25
51 Petter Ronnquist .05 .15
52 Christian Due-Boje .05 .15
53 Marcus Ragnarsson .20 .50
54 Joakim Musakka .02 .10
55 Thomas Johansson .02 .10
56 Thomas Eriksson .02 .10
57 Bjorn Nord .08 .25
58 Mikael Magnusson .02 .10
59 Robert Nordmark .05 .15
60 Charles Berglund .02 .10
61 Erik Huusko .05 .15
62 Anders Huusko .02 .10
63 Jens Ohling .05 .15
64 Peter Nilsson .02 .10
65 Magnus Jansson .02 .10
66 Mikael Hakansson .02 .10
67 Ola Josefsson .02 .10
68 Jerry Friman .02 .10
69 Mariusz Czerkawski .40 1.00
70 Fredrik Lindquist .07 .20
71 Mattias Hallback .02 .10
72 Patrik Erickson .02 .10
73 Farjestad Team Emblem .02 .10
74 Anders Bergman .08 .25
75 Jonas Eriksson .07 .20
76 Tommy Samuelsson .02 .10
77 Jesper Duus .02 .10
78 Leif Carlsson .02 .10
79 Per Lundell .02 .10
80 Brian Tutt .05 .15
81 Jakob Karlsson .02 .10
82 Thomas Rhodin .02 .10
83 Mattias Olsson .02 .10
84 Hakan Loob .30 .75
85 Andreas Johansson .20 .50
86 Magnus Arvedsson .40 1.00
87 Anders Oberg .02 .10
88 Mattias Johansson .02 .10
89 Mats Lindgren .20 .50
90 Clas Eriksson .02 .10
91 Patrik Degerstedt .02 .10
92 Peter Ottosson .02 .10
93 Niklas Brannstrom .02 .10
94 Lars Karlsson .07 .20
95 Kjell Dahlin .08 .25
96 Jonas Hoglund .40 1.00
97 HV 71 Team Emblem .02 .10
98 Peter Aslin .08 .25
99 Boo Ahl .08 .25
100 Antonin Stavjana .07 .20
101 Kenneth Kennholt .05 .15
102 Hans Abrahamsson .02 .10
103 Andreas Schultz .02 .10
104 Per Gustafsson .08 .25
105 Mathias Svedberg .02 .10
106 Niklas Rahm .02 .10
107 Fredrik Stillman .02 .10
108 Owe Thornberg .02 .10
109 Thomas Gustavsson .02 .10
110 Stefan Ornskog .05 .15
111 Peter Hammarstrom .02 .10
112 Torbjorn Persson .02 .10
113 John Byce .05 .15
114 Peter Eriksson .02 .10
115 Magnus Axelsson .05 .15
116 Stefan Falk .05 .15
117 Patric Kjellberg .07 .20
118 Johan Davidsson .20 .50
119 Thomas Ljungberg .02 .10
120 Patrik Ross .02 .10
121 Leksand Team Emblem .02 .10
122 Johan Hedberg .75 2.00
123 Ake Lilljebjorn .05 .15
124 Tomas Jonsson .08 .25
125 Stefan Bergkvist .05 .15
126 Henric Bjorkman .02 .10
127 Hans Lodin .02 .10
128 Magnus Svensson .05 .15
129 Orjan Lindmark .02 .10
130 Jan Huokko .02 .10
131 Roger Johansson .02 .10
132 Per Widmark .02 .10
133 Marcus Thuresson .02 .10
134 Niklas Eriksson .02 .10
135 Peter Ciavaglia .05 .15
136 Jonas Bergkvist .08 .25
137 Martin Wiita .02 .10
138 Markus Akerblom .02 .10
139 Greg Parks .05 .15
140 Mattias Loof .02 .10
141 Andreas Karlsson .02 .10
142 Markus Eriksson .02 .10
143 Tomas Forslund .08 .25
144 Jarmo Makitalo .02 .10
145 Lulea Team Emblem .02 .10
146 Robert Skoog .05 .15
147 Erik Grankvist .07 .20
148 Lars Modig .02 .10
149 Patrik Hoglund .02 .10
150 Niklas Bjornfot .02 .10
151 Torbjorn Lindberg .02 .10
152 Ville Siren .07 .20
153 Petter Nilsson .02 .10
154 Tomas Lilja .02 .10
155 Stefan Jonsson .02 .10
156 Stefan Nilsson .02 .10
157 Joakim Gunler .02 .10
158 Johan Stromvall .02 .10
159 Kyosti Karjalainen .07 .20
160 Robert Nordberg .02 .10
161 Tomas Berglund .02 .10
162 Lars-Gunnar Pettersson .02 .10
163 Lars Edstrom .02 .10
164 Lars Hurtig .02 .10
165 Fredrik Oberg .02 .10
166 Mikael Engstrom .02 .10
167 Johan Rosen .02 .10
168 Mika Nieminen .08 .25
169 Malmo Team Emblem .02 .10
170 Peter Lindmark .08 .25
171 Roger Nordstrom .05 .15
172 Daniel Granqvist .05 .15
173 Johan Norgren .02 .10
174 Johan Salle .02 .10
175 Petri Liimatainen .02 .10
176 Peter Hasselblad .02 .10
177 Robert Svehla .08 .25
178 Ricard Persson .08 .25
179 Roger Ohman .02 .10
180 Raimo Helminen .08 .25
181 Marcus Magnertoft .02 .10
182 Mattias Bosson .02 .10
183 Roger Hansson .02 .10
184 Bo Svanberg .02 .10
185 Daniel Rydmark .07 .20
186 Patrik Sylvegard .02 .10
187 Jens Hemstrom .02 .10
188 Jesper Mattsson .08 .25
189 Hakan Ahlund .02 .10
190 Peter Sundstrom .08 .25
191 Mats Naslund .40 1.00
192 Mikko Makela .07 .20
193 MoDo Team Emblem .02 .10
194 Henrik Arvsell .02 .10
195 Fredrik Andersson .05 .15
196 Anders Berglund .02 .10
197 Mattias Timander .08 .25
198 Miloslav Horava .05 .15
199 Lars Jansson .02 .10
200 Anders Eriksson .20 .50
201 Hans Jonsson .20 .50
202 Tomas Nanzen .02 .10
203 Fredrik Bergqvist .02 .10
204 Magnus Wernblom .05 .15
205 Anders Soderberg .08 .25
206 Martin Hostak .05 .15
207 Lennart Hermansson .02
208 Ulf Odmark .02
209 Peter Forsberg 4.00 10.0
210 Per Svartvadet .20
211 Andreas Salomonsson .02
212 Niklas Sundstrom .40 1.0
213 Lars Bystrom .02
214 Mats Lundstrom .02
215 Erik Holmberg .02
216 Henrik Gradin .02
217 Rogle Team Emblem .02
218 Kenneth Johansson .07
219 Magnus Swardh .02
220 Daniel Johansson .08
221 Kari Suoraniemi .02
222 Pierre Johnsson .02
223 Kenny Jonsson .40 1.0
224 Per Ljusterang .02
225 Arto Ruotanen .02
226 Daniel Tjarnquist .08
227 Kari Eloranta .05
228 Per Wallin .08
229 Peter Lundmark .05
230 Roger Elvenes .05
231 Michael Hjalm .02
232 Mattias Olivestedt .02
233 Jan Ericsson .02
234 Tomas Srsen .02
235 Pelle Svensson .02
236 Jorgen Jonsson .02
237 Stefan Elvenes .05
238 Fredrik Moller .02
239 Tord Elvenes .02
240 Mats Loov .02
241 Vasteras Team Emblem .02
242 Mats Ytter .07
243 Tommy Salo .40 1.0
244 Sergei Fokin .02
245 Edvin Frylen .07
246 Leif Rohlin .08
247 Peter Karlsson .02
248 Peter Jacobsson .02
249 Thomas Carlsson .02
250 Lars Ivarsson .02
251 Roger Akerstrom .05
252 Patrik Juhlin .08
253 Alexei Salomatin .05
254 Mishat Fahrutdinov .05
255 Henrik Nilsson .02
256 Mikael Pettersson .02
257 Stefan Hellkvist .02
258 Jens Nielsen .02
259 Hans Huczkowski .02
260 Claes Lindblom .02
261 Johan Brummer .02
262 Dejan Kostic .02
263 Paul Andersson .02
264 Henrik Nordfeldt .02
265 Vastra Frolunda Team Emblem .02
266 Hakan Algotsson .08
267 Mikael Sandberg .07
268 Stefan Nyman .02
269 Joacim Esbjors .05
270 Oscar Ackestrom .02
271 Vladimir Kramskoy .02
272 Richard Sohrman .02
273 Stefan Axelsson .05
274 Ronnie Sundin .08
275 Stefan Larsson .02
276 Thomas Sjogren .02
277 Serge Boisvert .05
278 Jerry Persson .02
279 Terho Koskela .02
280 Peter Strom .02
281 Peter Berndtsson .02
282 Henrik Lundin .02
283 Jonas Esbjors .02
284 Daniel Alfredsson 1.00 2.5
285 Stefan Ketola .02
286 Lars Dahlstrom .02
287 Par Edlund .02
288 Oto Hascak .05
289 Lars-Gunnar Jansson CO .02
290 Tommy Sandlin CO .02
291 Tommy Boustedt CO .02
292 Jorgen Palm CO .02
293 Hakan Nygren CO .02
294 Wayne Fleming CO .02
295 Sakari Pietila CO .02
296 Timo Lahtinen CO .02
297 Kent Forsberg CO .07
298 Christer Abrahamsson CO .08
299 Mikael Lundstrom CO .02
300 Leif Boork CO .02
301 Peter Forsberg 4.00 10.0
302 Peter Forsberg 4.00 10.0
303 Hakan Loob .30
304 Kenny Jonsson .40 1.0
305 Peter Forsberg 4.00 10.
306 Mats Sundin 1.50 4.
307 Micheal Sundlov AS .07
308 Roger Akerstrom AS .05
309 Fredrik Stillman AS .02
310 Mikael Renberg AS .40 1.
311 Peter Forsberg AS 4.00 10.
312 Ulf Dahlen AS .08
313 Pal Grotnes FS .07
314 Daniel Tjarnquist FS .08
315 Henrik Rehnberg FS .05
316 Mattias Ohlund FS .40 1.
317 Jan Labraaten FS .08
318 Patrik Wallenberg FS .07
319 Niklas Wallin FS .07
320 Tobias Thermell FS .07

1994 Swedish Olympics Lillehammer

This listing includes only the hockey cards from a larger Swedish issue that was released to commemorate the 1994 Olympic Games, which were held in Lillehammar.

COMPLETE HOCKEY SET (56) 15.00 30.
273 Ice Hockey Logo .02
274 Russian Team Puzzle .07
275 Russian Team Puzzle .07
276 Russian Team Puzzle .07
277 Russian Team Puzzle .07
278 Russian Team Puzzle .07
279 Russian Team Puzzle .07
280 Konstantin Astrakhantsev .20
281 Viacheslav Bykov .20
282 Sergei Sorokin .20
283 Alexander Smirnov .20
284 Swedish Team Sticker .07
285 Swedish Team Sticker .07
286 Swedish Team Sticker .07
287 Swedish Team Sticker .07
288 Swedish Team Sticker .07
289 Swedish Team Sticker .07
290 Markus Naslund .75 2.
291 Peter Forsberg 4.00 10.

292 Mats Sundin 1.50 4.00
293 Mikael Renberg .20 .50
294 Tommy Soderstrom .20 .50
295 Finnish Team Puzzle .07 .20
296 Finnish Team Puzzle .07 .20
297 Finnish Team Puzzle .07 .20
298 Finnish Team Puzzle .07 .20
299 Finnish Team Puzzle .07 .20
300 Finnish Team Puzzle .07 .20
301 Markus Ketterer .20 .50
302 Vesa Viitakoski .07 .20
303 Esa Tikkanen .20 .50
304 Erik Hamalainen .07 .20
305 Norwegian Team Puzzle .07 .20
306 Norwegian Team Puzzle .07 .20
307 Norwegian Team Puzzle .07 .20
308 Norwegian Team Puzzle .07 .20
309 Norwegian Team Puzzle .07 .20
310 Norwegian Team Puzzle .07 .20
311 Jim Marthinsen .20 .50
312 Erik Kristiansen .07 .20
313 Petter Salsten .07 .20
314 Eric Lindros 1.50 4.00
315 Greg Johnson .20 .50
316 Allain Roy .20 .50
317 Hank Lammens .30 .75
318 Leo Gudas .20 .50
319 Petr Briza .30 .75
320 Petr Rosol .20 .50
321 Otakar Janecky .20 .50
322 Mike Richter .75 2.00
323 Brett Hull 2.00 5.00
324 Chris Chelios .75 2.00
325 Pat Lafontaine .75 2.00
326 Claus Dalpiaz .20 .50
327 Stephane Barin .07 .20
328 Gerd Truntschka .07 .20

1994-95 Swedish Leaf

The 1994-95 Leaf Swedish hockey set consists of 320 standard-size cards that were issued in two series. The fronts feature color action player photos that are full-bleed except on the left, where a team color-coded stripe carries the player's name and his team's name. Leaf's logo in gold-foil appears in one of the corners. The team color-coded backs carry a color player close-up with a short biography, career stats and the team logo. Each series closes with team cards (135-158, 307-318) and checklists (159-160, 319-320).

COMPLETE SET (320) 26.00 65.00
COMPLETE SERIES 2 (161-320) 16.00 40.00
COMPLETE SERIES 1 (1-160) 10.00 25.00
1 Thomas Tallberg .02 .10
2 Hakan Algotsson .08 .25
3 Mikael Magnusson .02 .10
4 Per Lundell .02 .10
5 Kenneth Kennholt .02 .10
6 Jan Huokko .02 .10
7 Petter Nilsson .02 .10
8 Johan Norgren .02 .10
9 Anders Berglund .02 .10
10 Kari Eloranta .07 .20
11 Sam Lindstahl .02 .10
12 Johan Rosen .02 .10
13 Jonas Johnsson .02 .10
14 Erik Huusko .07 .20
15 Thomas Rhodin .02 .10
16 Patric Kjellberg .15 .40
17 Fredrik Andersson .02 .10
18 Stefan Nilsson .02 .10
19 Petri Liimatainen .02 .10
20 Lars Jansson .02 .10
21 Per Wallin .02 .10
22 Mika Nieminen .15 .40
23 Lars Ivarsson .02 .10
24 Ronnie Sundin .15 .40
25 Bedrich Scerban .02 .10
26 Anders Huusko .02 .10
27 Erik Grenkvist .02 .10
28 Stefan Ornskog .07 .20
29 Marcus Thuresson .02 .10
30 Johan Stromvall .02 .10
31 Peter Hasselblad .02 .10
32 Anders Eriksson .20 .50
33 Roger Elvenes .02 .10
34 Stefan Larsson .02 .10
35 Alexei Salomatin .02 .10
36 Niclas Havelid .40 1.00
37 Mikael Lindman .02 .10
38 Jens Ohling .02 .10
39 Hakan Loob .30 .75
40 Johan Hedberg .60 1.50
41 Niklas Eriksson .02 .10
42 Robert Nordberg .05 .15
43 Robert Svehla .40 1.00
44 Hans Jonsson .30 .75
45 Thomas Srsen .02 .10
46 Thomas Sjogren .02 .10
47 Mishat Fahrutdinov .02 .10
48 Thomas Strandberg .02 .10
49 Andreas Dackell .30 .75
50 Peter Nilsson .02 .10
51 Andreas Johansson .30 .75
52 Stefan Falk .02 .10
53 Marcus Akerblom .02 .10
54 Peter Aslin .08 .25
55 Ricard Persson .15 .40
56 Tomas Nanzen .02 .10
57 Per-Johan Svensson .02 .10
58 Terho Koskela .02 .10
59 Henrik Nilsson .02 .10
60 Mats Lindberg .02 .10
61 Anders Huss .02 .10
62 Magnus Jansson .02 .10
63 Mats Lindgren .20 .50
64 Thomas Ljungberg .02 .10
65 Tomas Forslund .08 .25
66 Thomas Ostlund .15 .40
67 Raimo Helminen .08 .25
68 Magnus Wernblom .02 .10
69 Jorgen Jonsson .02 .10
70 Peter Berndtsson .02 .10
71 Stefan Hellkvist .02 .10
72 Tommy Lehmann .07 .20
73 Stefan Klockare .02 .10
74 Ola Josefsson .02 .10
75 Peter Lindmark .08 .25
76 Owe Thornberg .02 .10
77 Jarmo Makitalo .02 .10
78 Tomas Berglund .02 .10
79 Bo Svanberg .02 .10
80 Lennart Hermansson .02 .10
81 Stefan Elvenes .02 .10
82 Daniel Alfredsson 1.50 4.00
83 Claes Lindblom .02 .10
84 Bjorn Ahlstrom .02 .10
85 Ove Molin .02 .10
86 Fredrik Lindquist .20 .50
87 Clas Eriksson .02 .10
88 Peter Hammarstrom .02 .10
89 Magnus Swardh .02 .10
90 Lars Hurtig .02 .10
91 Daniel Rydmark .02 .10
92 Lars Bystrom .02 .10
93 Mats Loov .02 .10
94 Lars Dahlstrom .02 .10
95 Johan Brummer .02 .10
96 Patric Englund .02 .10
97 Christer Olsson .15 .40
98 Patrik Erickson .02 .10
99 Peter Ottosson .02 .10
100 Tomas Jonsson .08 .25
101 Lars Modig .02 .10
102 Ake Lilljebjorn .02 .10
103 Patrik Sylvegard .02 .10
104 Daniel Johansson .20 .50
105 Edvin Frylen .08 .25
106 Par Edlund .02 .10
107 Paul Andersson .02 .10
108 Rikard Franzen .02 .10
109 Christian Due-Boje .08 .25
110 Tommy Samuelsson .02 .10
111 Mathias Svedberg .02 .10
112 Hans Lodin .02 .10
113 Jonas Eriksson .08 .25
114 Mikael Engstrom .02 .10
115 Hakan Ahlund .02 .10
116 Kari Suoraniemi .02 .10
117 Peter Jacobsson .02 .10
118 Kristian Gahn .02 .10
119 Tommy Melkersson .02 .10
120 Oscar Ackestrom .02 .10
121 Thomas Johansson .02 .10
122 Jesper Duus .02 .10
123 Hans Abrahamsson .02 .10
124 Orjan Lindmark .02 .10
125 Torbjorn Lindberg .02 .10
126 Michael Sundlov .08 .25
127 Peter Sundstrom .08 .25
128 Pierre Johnsson .02 .10
129 Thomas Carlsson .02 .10
130 Stefan Axelsson .02 .10
131 Robert Nordmark .07 .20
132 Torbjorn Persson .02 .10
133 Bjorn Nord .02 .10
134 Mats Ytter .02 .10
135 AIK Team Statistics .02 .10
136 Brynas IF Team Statistics .02 .10
137 Djurgardens IF Team Statistics .02 .10
138 Vastra Frolunda Team Statistics .02 .10
139 Farjestad BK Team Statistics .02 .10
140 HV-71 Team Statistics .02 .10
141 Leksand IF Team Statistics .02 .10
142 Lulea HF Team Statistics .02 .10
143 Malmo IF Team Statistics .02 .10
144 MoDo Hockey Team Statistics .02 .10
145 Rogle BK Team Statistics .02 .10
146 Varsteras IK Team Statistics .02 .10
147 AIK Logo .02 .10
148 Brynas IF Logo .02 .10
149 Djurgardens IF .02 .10
150 Vastra Frolunda Logo .02 .10
151 Farjestads BK .02 .10
152 HV-71 Logo .02 .10
153 Leksands IF Logo .02 .10
154 Lulea HF .02 .10
155 Malmo IF .02 .10
156 MoDo Hockey .02 .10
157 Rogle BK .02 .10
158 Vasteras IK .02 .10
159 Checklist 1-80 .02 .10
160 Checklist 81-160 .02 .10
161 Kenneth Johansson .08 .25
162 Stefan Jonsson .02 .10
163 Mikael Wahlberg .02 .10
164 Per Djoos .08 .25
165 Andreas Schultz .02 .10
166 Sacha Molin .02 .10
167 Marcus Ramen .02 .10
168 Jergus Baca .02 .10
169 Erik Bergstrom .02 .10
170 Jonas Forsberg .15 .40
171 Olli Kaski .02 .10
172 Morgan Samuelsson .02 .10
173 Anders Burstrom .02 .10
174 Stanislav Meciar .02 .10
175 Leif Rohlin .15 .40
176 Lars Edstrom .02 .10
177 Esa Keskinen .08 .25
178 Daniel Casselstahl .02 .10
179 Mattias Timander .20 .50
180 Peter Nordstrom .02 .10
181 Patric Aberg .02 .10
182 Mikael Enander .02 .10
183 Charles Berglund .08 .25
184 Jonas Andersson-Junkka .15 .40
185 Sergei Fokin .02 .10
186 Boo Ahl .15 .40
187 Jiri Kucera .08 .25
188 Roger Nordstrom .02 .10
189 Peter Forsberg 6.00 15.00
190 Arto Ruotanen .02 .10
191 Mikael Wiklander .02 .10
192 Joakim Persson .08 .25
193 Peter Larsson .02 .10
194 Per Eklund .15 .40
195 Joacim Esbjors .02 .10
196 Magnus Arvedsson .60 1.50
197 Marko Palo .02 .10
198 Mikael Holmberg .02 .10
199 Mikael Renberg .75 2.00
200 Tero Lehtera .15 .40
201 Fredrik Lindh .02 .10
202 Joham Finnstrom .02 .10
203 Peter Popovic .08 .25
204 Tnny Barthelson .02 .10
205 Stefan Polla .02 .10
206 Jonas Esbjors .02 .10
207 Roger Hansson .02 .10
208 Mikael Hakanson .02 .10
209 Daniel Tjarnqvist .15 .40
210 Anders Carlsson .08 .25
211 Dick Tarnstrom .15 .40
212 Johan Tornberg .02 .10
213 Joakim Lundberg .02 .10
214 Marko Jantunen .15 .40
215 Patrik Haltia .02 .10
216 Fredrik Stillman .02 .10
217 Andy Schneider .02 .10
218 Thomas Holmstrom ERC 2.00 5.00
219 Jens Hemstrom .02 .10
220 Anders Soderberg .20 .50
221 Peter Lundmark .02 .10
222 Patrik Juhlin .15 .40
223 Anders Gozzi .02 .10
224 Marcus Ragnarsson .30 .75
225 Mattias Olsson .02 .10
226 Andreas Karlsson .20 .50
227 Tomas Lilja .02 .10
228 Stefan Ohman .02 .10
229 Jarmo Kekalainen .08 .25
230 Tony Skopac .02 .10
231 Lars Karlsson .08 .25
232 Mats Sundin 1.00 2.50
233 Peter Strom .02 .10
234 Mattias Johansson .02 .10
235 Johan Lindbom .02 .10
236 Mats Lusth .02 .10
237 Marcus Magnertoft .02 .10
238 Martin Hostak .02 .10
239 Mikael Pettersson .02 .10
240 Johan Akerman .02 .10
241 Mathias Hallback .02 .10
242 Johan Davidsson .20 .50
243 Per-Erik Eklund .15 .40
244 Johan Salle .02 .10
245 Per Svartvadet .20 .50
246 Ville Siren .08 .25
247 Mattias Loof .02 .10
248 Per-Johan Axelsson .60 1.50
249 Peter Gerhardsson .02 .10
250 Jonas Bergqvist .08 .25
251 Per-Johan Johansson .40 1.00
252 Mattias Bosson .02 .10
253 Andreas Olsson .02 .10
254 Patrik Zetterberg .02 .10
255 Michael Johansson .02 .10
256 Stefan Gustavson .02 .10
257 Jerry Persson .02 .10
258 Stefan Nilsson .02 .10
259 Roger Johansson .02 .10
260 Jarmo Myllys .20 .50
261 Kyosti Karjalainen .02 .10
262 Thomas Eriksson .02 .10
263 Michael Hjalm .02 .10
264 Espen Knutsen .40 1.00
265 Andreas Salomonsson .02 .10
266 Patrik Hoglund .02 .10
267 Peter Andersson .02 .10
268 Brett Hauer .08 .25
269 Stefan Ketola .02 .10
270 Patrik Carnback .08 .25
271 Petter Ronnqvist .02 .10
272 Roger Ohman .02 .10
273 Fredrik Modin .75 2.00
274 Alexander Beliavski .02 .10
275 Niklas Brannstrom .02 .10
276 Per Gustafsson .15 .40
277 Nicklas Nordqvist .02 .10
278 Roger Akerstrom .02 .10
279 Jiri Vykoukal .08 .25
280 Jesper Mattsson .15 .40
281 Henrik Nordfeldt .02 .10
282 Joakim Musakka .02 .10
283 Anders Johnson .02 .10
284 Niklas Sundstrom .40 1.00
285 Nicklas Lidstrom 1.00 2.50
286 Tomas Sandstrom .40 1.00
287 Jens Nielsen .02 .10
288 Mattias Ohlund .75 2.00
289 Markus Eriksson .02 .10
290 Mikael Sandberg .08 .25
291 Sergeij Pushkov .02 .10
292 Jonas Hoglund .40 1.00
293 Peter Ekelund .02 .10
294 Fredrik Bergqvist .02 .10
295 Torgny Bendelin .02 .10
296 Tommy Sandlin .02 .10
297 Tommy Boustedt .02 .10
298 Conny Evensson .02 .10
299 Sune Bergman .02 .10
300 Wayne Fleming .02 .10
301 Lars Bergstrom .02 .10
302 Hannu Jortikka .02 .10
303 Leif Boork .02 .10
304 Christer Abrahamsson .08 .25
305 Randy Edmonds .02 .10
306 Ulf Labraaten .02 .10
307 AIK .02 .10
308 Brynas IF .02 .10
309 Djurgardens IF .02 .10
310 Farjestads BK .02 .10
311 HV 71 .02 .10
312 Leksands IF .02 .10
313 Lulea HF .02 .10
314 Malmo IF .02 .10
315 MoDo .02 .10
316 Rogle BK .02 .10
317 Vasteras IK .02 .10
318 Vastra Frolunda .02 .10
319 Checklist 161-240 .02 .10
320 Checklist 241-320 .02 .10
NNO1 Malmo IF SuperChase 10.00 25.00
NNO2 M.Lindgren SuperChase 6.00 15.00

1994-95 Swedish Leaf Clean Sweepers

This 10-card standard size set highlights 10 of the top goalies in the Swedish Elitserien. The cards were randomly inserted into series one packs. The fronts have a color photo with the player's name in yellow on a red background at the bottom. The word "Cleansweepers" is at the top in gold-foil as are the words "Elit Set" in the bottom right corner. The backs have player information in green with a blue background. The cards are numbered "X of 10."

COMPLETE SET (10) 10.00 25.00
1 Peter Lindmark 1.25 3.00
2 Michael Sundlov 1.25 3.00
3 Thomas Ostlund 1.25 3.00
4 Jonas Eriksson 1.25 3.00
5 Peter Aslin 1.25 3.00
6 Ake Lilljebjorn 1.25 3.00
7 Johan Hedberg 2.00 5.00
8 Henrik Arvsell 1.25 3.00
9 Fredrik Andersson 1.25 3.00
10 Hakan Algotsson 1.25 3.00

1994-95 Swedish Leaf Foreign Affairs

Featuring foreign-born players competing in the Elitserien, this ten-card set was inserted in series two foil packs. The fronts feature a color player cutout superimposed over his country's flag. The words "Foreign Affairs" in foil letters are printed on the bottom, while the player's name and his team's name appear vertically on the right. The backs carry player profile. All information is printed in Swedish.

COMPLETE SET (10) 8.00 20.00
1 Espen Knutsen 2.00 5.00
2 Esa Keskinen .75 2.00
3 Marko Jantunen .75 2.00
4 Jarmo Myllys 1.25 3.00
5 Jiri Kucera .75 2.00
6 Jiri Vykoukal .75 2.00
7 Jarmo Kekalainen .75 2.00
8 Olli Kaski .75 2.00
9 Jergus Baca .75 2.00
10 Tero Lehtera .75 2.00

1994-95 Swedish Leaf Gold Cards

This 24-card standard size set commemorates the members of Sweden's 1994 Olympic gold medal team. The cards were randomly inserted into series one packs. The fronts have a full-color photo ghosted over an image of the gold medal with the player's name at the bottom. The words "Gold Cards" are at the bottom in gold-foil as are the words "Elit Set" in the top right corner. The backs have the player's name and information with a stick figure playing hockey numerous times being the background. The cards are numbered "X of 24."

COMPLETE SET (24) 30.00 75.00
1 Title Card 2.00 5.00
2 Andreas Dackell 1.25 3.00
3 Charles Berglund .75 2.00
4 Christian Due-Boje .75 2.00
5 Daniel Rydmark .75 2.00
6 Fredrik Stillman .75 2.00
7 Hakan Algotsson 1.25 3.00
8 Hakan Loob 1.25 3.00
9 Jonas Bergqvist .75 2.00
10 Jorgen Jonsson .75 2.00
11 Kenny Jonsson 1.25 3.00
12 Leif Rohlin .75 2.00
13 Magnus Svensson .75 2.00
14 Mats Naslund 1.25 3.00
15 Michael Sundlov 1.25 3.00
16 Niklas Eriksson .75 2.00
17 Patric Kjellberg .75 2.00
18 Patrick Juhlin .75 2.00
19 Peter Forsberg 15.00 40.00
20 Roger Hansson .75 2.00
21 Roger Johansson .75 2.00
22 Stefan Ornskog .75 2.00
23 Tomas Jonsson .75 2.00
24 Tommy Salo 2.00 5.00

1994-95 Swedish Leaf Guest Special

Featuring players who joined the Elitserien during the 1994 NHL lockout, this eight card set was inserted in second-series foil packs. The fronts feature a color player action shot. The words "Guest Special" appear in a foil bar above the photo, while the player's name is printed in a foil bar below. The horizontal backs carry a color player cut-out superimposed over a drawing of the world.

COMPLETE SET (8) 16.00 40.00
1 Mats Sundin 4.00 10.00
2 Tomas Sandstrom .75 2.00
3 Peter Forsberg 10.00 25.00
4 Nicklas Lidstrom 4.00 10.00
5 Mikael Renberg 1.25 3.00
6 Roger Johansson .40 1.00
7 Peter Popovic .40 1.00
8 Patrick Juhlin .40 1.00

1994-95 Swedish Leaf NHL Draft

This ten-card standard-size set featuring players drafted by NHL teams in 1994 was inserted in second-series foil packs. The fronts feature a color player action shot. The year 1994 is separated by the NHL draft logo. The backs contain information in Swedish about the player's selection in the 1994 NHL draft.

COMPLETE SET (10) 12.00 30.00
1 Mattias Ohlund 1.50 4.00
2 Johan Davidsson .40 1.00
3 Fredrik Modin 1.50 4.00
4 Johan Finnstrom .40 1.00
5 Edvin Frylen .40 1.00
6 Daniel Alfredsson 3.00 8.00
7 Patrik Haltia 1.25 3.00
8 Peter Strom .40 1.00
9 Thomas Holmstrom 4.00 10.00
10 Dick Tarnstrom .75 2.00

1994-95 Swedish Leaf Playmakers

This six-card standard size set shines the spotlight on five of the top goal scorers in the Swedish Elitserien. The cards were randomly inserted into series one packs. The fronts have a full-color photo with an orange and black background. The words "Play Makers" are on the left side and the words "Elit Set" is in the bottom right corner in gold-foil. The backs have "Play Makers" at the top in silver with an orange background. The player's name and number of assists he had in each of the previous three seasons with a black background. Card #1 is different in that it is a title card and has a picture of all five players in the set. The cards are numbered "X of 6."

COMPLETE SET (6) 2.00 5.00
1 Title Card .75 2.00
2 Stefan Nilsson .40 1.00
3 Mika Nieminen .40 1.00
4 Raimo Helminen .40 1.00
5 Peter Larsson .40 1.00
6 Hakan Loob .75 2.00

1994-95 Swedish Leaf Rookie Rockets

Inserted in second-series foil packs, this 10-card set features rookies in the Swedish league. Borderless horizontal fronts feature a color player cut-out along with "Rookie" in big foil letters. The player's name and his team's name appears in a red bar on the bottom. The horizontal back carry another color player cut-out along with player profile.

COMPLETE SET (10) 8.00 20.00
1 Fredrik Modin 1.25 3.00
2 Jonas Andersson-Junkka .75 2.00
3 Thomas Holmstrom 4.00 10.00
4 Mattias Ohlund 1.25 3.00
5 Per Eklund .40 1.00
6 Daniel Tjarnqvist .40 1.00
7 Joakim Persson .75 2.00
8 Patrik Haltia .75 2.00
9 Andreas Karlsson .40 1.00
10 Stefan Nilsson .40 1.00

1994-95 Swedish Leaf Studio Signatures

This 12-card standard-size set was inserted in second-series foil packs. The fronts feature borderless color studio photos. The player's facsimile autograph in foil letters appears at the bottom. The backs carry a drawing of the player in close-up.

COMPLETE SET (12) 4.00 10.00
1 Rikard Franzen .40 1.00
2 Anders Huss .40 1.00
3 Jens Ohling .40 1.00
4 Tommy Samuelsson .40 1.00
5 Fredrik Stillman .40 1.00
6 Jonas Bergqvist .40 1.00
7 Johan Stromvall .40 1.00
8 Roger Nordstrom .40 1.00
9 Lars Bystrom .40 1.00
10 Roger Elvenes .40 1.00
11 Leif Rohlin .75 2.00
12 Tero Koskela .40 1.00

1994-95 Swedish Leaf Top Guns

This 10-card standard size set consists of some of the top goal scorers in the Swedish Elitserien. The cards were randomly inserted into series one packs. The fronts have a full-color photo with a background that looks like fire works. In one of the top corners the words "Top Gun" are in gold-foil as are the words "Elit Set" in the bottom right corner. The backs have "Top Gun" in red at the top as if it were underneath rippling water. At the bottom is the number of goals they scored each of the previous three seasons. The cards are numbered "X of 10."

COMPLETE SET (10) 4.80 12.00
1 Thomas Srsen .40 1.00
2 Hakan Loob 1.25 3.00
3 Lars Hurtig .40 1.00
4 Stefan Elvenes .40 1.00
5 Jorgen Jonsson .40 1.00
6 Robert Svehla 1.25 3.00
7 Daniel Rydmark .40 1.00
8 Owe Thornberg .40 1.00
9 Patric Kjellberg .75 2.00
10 Mats Loov .40 1.00

1995 Swedish Globe World Championships

This 270-card set was produced by Semic Press to commemorate the 1995 World Championships, which were held in Stockholm. The players pictured have represented their countries at some point in international competition, and thus are shown wearing their national team garb. Card fronts feature a variegated yellow-orange border, with the Globe and World Championships logo (VM '95) along the top. Player name and country are listed in a blue bar and in Swedish text, along the bottom. A silver foil Globe '95 icon is set in the lower left corner. Card backs include a small reprise of the front photo, along with personal information, including all statistics from major international tournaments. No card number 85 is in the set - Mike Gartner was misnumbered 86. An NNO two-sided card of Peter Forsberg and Mats Sundin was randomly inserted in packs. It is believed that there are less than 2,000 of these cards in circulation. A special binder was released to store the set; it is valued at $5.

COMPLETE SET (270) 20.00 50.00
1 Tommy Soderstrom .08 .25
2 Roger Nordstrom .02 .10
3 Tommy Salo .40 1.00
4 Hakan Algotsson .07 .20
5 Thomas Ostlund .08 .25
7 Ulf Samuelsson .05 .15
8 Calle Johansson .07 .20
9 Nicklas Lidstrom .60 1.50
10 Tommy Albelin .05 .15
11 Peter Andersson .02 .10
12 Magnus Svensson .05 .15
13 Mats Sundin .40 1.00
14 Tomas Jonsson .05 .15
15 Kenny Jonsson .08 .25
16 Tommy Sjodin .05 .15
17 Fredrik Stillman .02 .10
18 Marcus Ragnarsson .08 .25
19 Peter Popovic .05 .15
20 Arto Blomsten .02 .10
21 Peter Forsberg 1.25 3.00
22 Roger Johansson .02 .10
23 Leif Rohlin .05 .15
24 Bjorn Nord .02 .10
25 Stefan Larsson .02 .10
26 Fredrik Olausson .05 .15
27 Kjell Samuelsson .05 .15
28 Tomas Sandstrom .08 .25
29 Mikael Renberg .08 .25
30 Mikael Johansson .02 .10
31 Patrik Juhlin .05 .15
32 Roger Hansson .02 .10
33 Daniel Rydmark .05 .15
34 Jonas Bergqvist .05 .15
35 Michael Nylander .08 .25
36 Johan Garpenlov .05 .15
37 Charles Berglund .02 .10
38 Jorgen Jonsson .02 .10
39 Stefan Ornskog .02 .10
40 Thomas Steen .05 .15
41 Patrik Carnback .05 .15
42 Mikael Andersson .05 .15
43 Markus Naslund .30 .75
44 Andreas Dackell .08 .25
45 Erik Huusko .02 .10
46 Tomas Forslund .05 .15
47 Daniel Alfredsson .20 .50
48 Ulf Dahlen .08 .25
49 Anders Huusko .02 .10
50 Tomas Holmstrom .40 1.00
51 Niklas Andersson .02 .10
52 Hakan Loob .08 .25
53 Per-Erik Eklund .05 .15
54 Patrik Erickson .02 .10
55 Jonas Forsberg .08 .25
56 Daniel Johansson .05 .15
57 Mattias Ohlund .08 .25
58 Anders Eriksson .08 .25
59 Fredrik Modin .20 .50
60 Niklas Sundstrom .08 .25
61 Jesper Mattsson .08 .25
62 Johan Davidsson .08 .25
63 Mats Lindgren .08 .25
64 Leif Holmqvist .02 .10
65 Pelle Lindbergh .40 1.00
66 Lennart Svedberg .02 .10
67 Borje Salming .08 .25
68 Sven Tumba Johansson .02 .10
69 Ulf Sterner .02 .10
70 Anders Hedberg .08 .25
71 Kent Nilsson .08 .25
72 Mats Naslund .08 .25
73 Patrick Roy 2.50 6.00
74 Ed Belfour .60 1.50
75 Bill Ranford .20 .50
76 Paul Coffey .40 1.00
77 Ray Bourque .75 2.00
78 Steve Smith .05 .15
79 Al MacInnis .30 .75
80 Mark Tinordi .05 .15
81 Scott Stevens .08 .25
82 Rob Blake .30 .75
83 Theo Fleury .40 1.00
84 Mark Messier .60 1.50
85 Mike Gartner UER card n .20 .50
86 Brendan Shanahan .60 1.50
87 Mario Lemieux 2.50 6.00
88 Eric Lindros 1.25 3.00
89 Steve Yzerman 2.50 6.00
90 Adam Oates .20 .50
91 Paul Kariya 1.50 4.00
92 Rick Tocchet .20 .50
93 Doug Gilmour .40 1.00
94 Luc Robitaille .30 .75
95 Jason Arnott .20 .50
96 Adam Graves .20 .50
97 Petr Nedved .08 .25
98 Mark Recchi .30 .75
99 Wayne Gretzky 3.00 8.00
100 Mike Richter .60 1.50
101 John Vanbiesbrouck .40 1.00
102 Tom Barrasso .08 .25
103 Brian Leetch .30 .75
104 Gary Suter .08 .25
105 Kevin Hatcher .05 .15
106 Phil Housley .08 .25
107 Chris Chelios .40 1.00
108 Eric Weinrich .05 .15
109 Derian Hatcher .08 .25
110 Craig Wolanin .05 .15
111 Mike Modano .60 1.50
112 Joe Mullen .08 .25
113 Joel Otto .08 .25
114 Doug Brown .08 .25
115 Brett Hull .60 1.50
116 Pat LaFontaine .20 .50
117 Jeremy Roenick .60 1.50
118 Craig Janney .08 .25
119 Kevin Miller .05 .15
120 Tony Granato .08 .25
121 Tony Amonte .30 .75
122 Kevin Stevens .08 .25
123 Darren Turcotte .05 .15
124 Scott Young .20 .50
125 Doug Weight .30 .75
126 Phil Bourque .05 .15
127 Markus Ketterer .05 .15
128 Jarmo Myllys .20 .50
129 Jyrki Lumme .08 .25
130 Timo Jutila .05 .15
131 Marko Kiprusoff .05 .15
132 Hannu Virta .05 .15
133 Teppo Numminen .08 .25
134 Janne Laukkanen .08 .25
135 Mika Nieminen .08 .25
136 Janne Ojanen .05 .15
137 Jari Kurri .20 .50
138 Esa Tikkanen .08 .25
139 Saku Koivu .40 1.00
140 Teemu Selanne .75 2.00
141 Raimo Helminen .05 .15
142 Mikko Makela .05 .15
143 Christian Ruuttu .05 .15
144 Esa Keskinen .05 .15
145 Dominik Hasek .60 1.50
146 Petr Briza .08 .25
147 Richard Smehlik .05 .15
148 Leo Gudas .02 .10
149 Roman Hamrlik .08 .25
150 Antonin Stavjana .05 .15
151 Jiri Slegr .05 .15
152 Jiri Vykoukal .05 .15
153 Tomas Jelinek .05 .15
154 Richard Zemlicka .05 .15
155 Robert Lang .08 .25
156 Michal Pivonka .08 .25
157 Jaromir Jagr 1.25 3.00
158 Josef Beranek .05 .15
159 Robert Reichel .05 .15
160 Petr Hrbek .02 .10
161 Jiri Kucera .05 .15
162 Kamil Kastak .02 .10
163 Andrei Trefilov .08 .25
164 Mikhail Shtalenkov .08 .25
165 Sergei Zubov .08 .25
166 Vladimir Malakhov .05 .15
167 Igor Kravchuk .05 .15
168 Alexei Gusarov .05 .15
169 Alexei Zhitnik .08 .25
170 Alexander Smirnov .02 .10
171 Dimitri Yushkevich .08 .25
172 Alexei Yashin .15 .40
173 Alexei Zhamnov .08 .25
174 Pavel Bure .75 2.00
175 Sergei Fedorov .75 2.00
176 Andrei Kovalenko .08 .25
177 Alexei Kovalev .20 .50
178 Andrei Khomutov .05 .15
179 Valeri Kamensky .08 .25
180 Viacheslav Bykov .07 .20
181 Claus Dalpiaz .05 .15
182 Michael Puschacher .05 .15
183 Ken Strong .02 .10
184 Martin Ulrich .02 .10
185 Andreas Puschnig .02 .10
186 Herbert Hohenberger .08 .25
187 Marty Dallmann .02 .10
188 James Burton .02 .10
189 Michael Shea .02 .10
190 Jim Marthinsen .08 .25
191 Orjan Lovdal .02 .10
192 Cato Tom Andersen .02 .10
193 Geir Hoff .02 .10
194 Tommy Jakobsen .02 .10
195 Marius Rath .02 .10
196 Trond Magnussen .02 .10
197 Svein Enok Norstebo .02 .10
198 Espen Knutsen .20 .50
199 Petri Ylonen .05 .15
200 Michel Valliere .02 .10
201 Franck Pajonkowski .05 .15
202 Pierrick Maia .02 .10
203 Christophe Ville .02 .10
204 Serge Poudrier .02 .10
205 Philippe Bozon .05 .15
206 Gerald Guennelon .02 .10
207 Antoine Richer .02 .10
208 Reto Pavoni .05 .15
209 Renato Tosio .05 .15
210 Jorg Eberle .02 .10
211 Fredy Luthi .02 .10
212 Christian Weber .02 .10
213 Sandro Bertaggia .02 .10
214 Patrick Howald .02 .10
215 Gil Montandon .02 .10
216 Rick Tschumi .02 .10
217 Klaus Merk .07 .20
218 Josef Heiss .08 .25
219 Rick Amann .02 .10
220 Michael Rumrich .02 .10
221 Thomas Brandl .02 .10
222 Andreas Niederberger .02 .10
223 Leo Stefan .02 .10
224 Stefan Ustorf .05 .15
225 Dieter Hegen .05 .15
226 Michael Rosati .05 .15
227 Bruno Campese .05 .15
228 Roberto Oberrauch .02 .10
229 Anthony Circelli .02 .10
230 Bill Stewart .02 .10
231 Bruno Zarillo .02 .10
232 Gaetano Orlando .02 .10
233 Stefan Figliuzzi .02 .10
234 Jimmy Carnazzola .02 .10
235 Vladislav Tretiak .40 1.00
236 Slava Fetisov .20 .50
237 Alexei Kasatonov .08 .25
238 Sergei Makarov .08 .25
239 Igor Larionov .30 .75
240 Vladimir Krutov .08 .25
241 Valeri Kharlamov .08 .25
242 Vladimir Petrov .05 .15
243 Boris Mikhailov .08 .25
244 Sweden Olympic Gold 94 .08 .25
245 Sweden Olympic Gold 94 .08 .25
246 Sweden Olympic Gold 94 .08 .25
247 Canada World Champions .30 .75
248 Canada World Champions .08 .25
249 Canada World Champions .20 .50
250 Manon Rheaume 1.25 3.00
251 Sundin and Andersson .20 .50
252 Brolin and Knutsen .08 .25
253 Peter Forsberg Special 1.25 3.00
254 Peter Forsberg Special 1.25 3.00
255 Peter Forsberg Special 1.25 3.00
256 Mats Sundin Special .40 1.00
257 Mats Sundin Special .40 1.00
258 Mats Sundin Special .40 1.00
259 Mikael Renberg Special .08 .25
260 Mikael Renberg Special .08 .25
261 Mikael Renberg Special .08 .25
262 Eric Lindros Special 1.25 3.00
263 Eric Lindros Special 1.25 3.00
264 Eric Lindros Special 1.25 3.00
265 Wayne Gretzky Special 3.00 8.00
266 Wayne Gretzky Special 3.00 8.00
267 Wayne Gretzky Special 3.00 8.00
268 Checklist 1-90 (Renberg .08 .25
269 Checklist 91-180 (Sundi .40 1.00
270 Checklist 181-270 (Fors 1.25 3.00
XX Binder 2.00 5.00
NNO Peter Forsberg Mats Sundin 10.00 20.00

1995 Swedish World Championships Stickers

This set recently was confirmed by collector Per Vedin. Checklist is likely incomplete.

1 Bill Ranford .02 .10
2 Stephane Fiset .20 .50
3 Steve Duchesne .08 .25
4 Brad Schlegel .02 .10
5 Luke Richardson .02 .10
6 Darryl Sydor .02 .10
7 Yves Racine .02 .10
8 Rob Blake .20 .50
9 Marc Bergevin .02 .10
10 Paul Coffey .60 1.50
11 Jason Arnott .20 .50
12 Geoff Sanderson .20 .50
13 Shayne Corson .20 .50
14 Mike Ricci .20 .50
15 Kelly Buchberger .20 .50
16 Brendan Shanahan .75 2.00
17 Patrick Verbeek .20 .50
18 Nelson Emerson .20 .50
19 Rod Brindâ€™Amour .20 .50
20 Joe Sakic 2.00 5.00
21 Luc Robitaille .60 1.50
22 Stephen Thomas .08 .25
23 Paul Kariya 1.50 4.00
24 Theo Fleury .50 1.25
25 Dave Gagner .20 .50
26 Valeri Ivannikov .02 .10
27 Mikhail Shtalenkov .20 .50
28 Nikolai Tsulygin .02 .10
29 Dmitri Krasotkin .02 .10
30 Morat Davydov .02 .10
31 Andrei Sklopintsev .02 .10
32 Oleg Davydov .02 .10
33 Evgeni Gribko .02 .10
34 Andrei Yakhanov .02 .10
35 Igor Nikulin .02 .10
36 Valeri Kamensky .02 .10
37 Boris Timofeev .02 .10
38 Dmitri Denisov .02 .10
39 Rail Muftiev .02 .10
40 Andrei Tarasenko .02 .10
41 Oleg Belov .02 .10
42 Andrei Kovalenko .02 .10
43 Igor Varitski .02 .10
44 Ravil Yakubov .02 .10
45 Viacheslav Kozlov .20 .50
46 Alexander Vinogradov .02 .10
47 Yuri Tsyplakov .02 .10
48 Stanislav Romanov .02 .10
49 Slava Bykov .08 .25
50 Andrei Khomutov .08 .25
51 Joseph Heiss .02 .10
52 Klaus Merk .08 .25
53 Mirko LÃ¼demann .02 .10
54 Ulrich Hiemer .02 .10
55 Torsten Kienass .02 .10
56 Jayson Meyer .02 .10
57 Josef Lehner .02 .10
58 Ron Fischer .08 .25
59 Michael Bresagk .02 .10
60 Andreas Niederberger .02 .10
61 Peter Gulda .02 .10
62 Jan Benda .08 .25
63 Thomas Brandl .02 .10
64 Andreas Lupzig .02 .10
65 Michael Rumrich .02 .10
66 Benoit Doucet .08 .25
67 Raimond Hilger .02 .10
68 Georg Franz .02 .10
69 Jorg Handrick .02 .10
70 Dieter Hegen .08 .25
71 Ernst Kopf .02 .10
72 Gunter Oswald .02 .10
73 Georg Holzmann .02 .10
74 JÃ¼rgen Rumrich .02 .10
75 Leo Stefan .02 .10
76 Bruno Campese .08 .25
77 Michael Rosati .20 .50
78 Giovanni Marchetti .02 .10
79 Georg Comploj .02 .10
80 Luigi da Corte .02 .10
81 Robert Oberrauch .02 .10

82 Anthony Circelli .02 .10
83 Alex Thaler .02 .10
84 Carlo Lorenzi .02 .10
85 Michael de Angelis .02 .10
86 Emilio Iovio .02 .10
87 Gaetano Orlando .08 .25
88 Lucio Topatigh .02 .10
89 Stefano Figliuzzi .02 .10
90 Bruno Zarrillo .02 .10
91 Mark Montanari .02 .10
92 Armando Chelodi .02 .10
93 Mirko Moroder .02 .10
94 Alex Gschliesser .02 .10
95 Maurizio Mansi .02 .10
96 Petri YlÃ¶nen .08 .25
97 Michel Valliere .08 .25
98 Serge Djelloul .02 .10
99 Christophe Moyon .02 .10
100 Gerald Guennelon .02 .10
101 Philippe Lemoine .02 .10
102 Denis Perez .08 .25
103 Serge Poudrier .08 .25
104 Steven Woodburn .02 .10
105 Michael Babin .02 .10
106 Benjamin Agnel .02 .10
107 Stephane Arcangeloni .02 .10
108 Laurent Deschaume .02 .10
109 Pierre Pousse .02 .10
110 Patrick Dunn .02 .10
111 Pierrick Maia .02 .10
112 Philippe Bozon .20 .50
113 Christian Pouget .02 .10
114 Antoine Richer .02 .10
115 Richard Aimonetto .02 .10
116 Reto Pavoni .02 .10
117 Renato Tosio .02 .10
118 Marco Bayer .02 .10
119 Sandro Bertaggia .02 .10
120 Fredy Bobillier .02 .10
121 Dino Kessler .02 .10
122 Sven Leuenberger .02 .10
123 Martin Steinegger .02 .10
124 Andreas Zehnder .02 .10
125 Misko Antisin .02 .10
126 Gian-Marco Crameri .08 .25
127 JÃ¶rg Eberle .08 .25
128 Patrick Fischer .02 .10
129 Patrick Howald .02 .10
130 Marcel Jenni .02 .10
131 Gil Montandon .02 .10
132 Pascal Schaller .02 .10
133 Andy Ton .02 .10
134 Roberto Triulzi .02 .10
135 Theo Wittman .02 .10
136 Roger Nordstrom .02 .10
137 Thomas Ostlund .08 .25
138 Magnus Svensson .02 .10
139 Tommy Sjodin .08 .25
140 Fredrik Stillman .02 .10
141 Tomas Jonsson .02 .10
142 Stefan Larsson .02 .10
143 Leif Rohlin .02 .10
144 Marcus Ragnarsson .02 .10
145 Christer Olsson .02 .10
146 Morgan Samuelsson .02 .10
147 Andreas Dackell .02 .10
148 Jonas Johnsson .02 .10
149 Charles Berglund .02 .10
150 Erik Huusko .02 .10
151 Daniel Rydmark .02 .10
152 Patrik CarnbÃ¤ck .02 .10
153 Mats Lindgren .02 .10
154 Jonas Bergkvist .02 .10
155 Stefan Ornskog .02 .10
156 Per-Erik Eklund .08 .25
157 Thomas Forslund .02 .10
158 Roger Hansson .02 .10
159 Hakan Ahlund .02 .10
160 Daniel Alfredsson .20 .50
161 Jarmo Myllys .20 .50
162 Jukka Tammi .08 .25
163 Mika Stromberg .08 .25
164 Erik Hamalainen .02 .10
165 Karri Kivi .02 .10
166 Timo Jutila .02 .10
167 Petteri Nummelin .02 .10
168 Hannu Virta .02 .10
169 Marko Kiprusov .02 .10
170 Waltteri Immonen .08 .25
171 Janne Ojanen .02 .10
172 Esa Keskinen .02 .10
173 Marko Jantunen .02 .10
174 Saku Koivu .40 1.00
175 Marko Palo .02 .10
176 Tero Lehtera .02 .10
177 Mika Alatalo .20 .50
178 Ville Peltonen .08 .25
179 Raimo Helminen .02 .10
180 Petri Varis .08 .25
181 Jokke HeinÃ¤nen .02 .10
182 Timo Saarikoski .02 .10
183 Sami Kapanen .20 .50
184 Tero Arkiomaa .02 .10
185 Mika Nieminen .08 .25
186 Peter Briza .20 .50
187 Roman Turek .20 .50
188 Milos Holan .02 .10
189 Drahomir Kadlec .08 .25
190 Frantisek Kaberle .02 .10
191 Bedrich Scerban .08 .25
192 Roman Hamrlik .08 .25
193 Jan Vopat .02 .10
194 Antonin Stavjana .02 .10
195 Jiri Vykoukal .02 .10
196 Jiri Veber .02 .10
197 Frantisek Musil .02 .10
198 Richard Zemlicka .08 .25
199 Kamil Kastak .08 .25
200 Jiri Kucera .08 .25
201 Roman Horak .02 .10
202 Martin Rucinsky .08 .25
203 Josef Beranek .08 .25
204 Bobby Holik .08 .25
205 Otakar Janecky .08 .25
206 Jiri Dolezal .02 .10
207 Martin Straka .08 .25
208 Martin HostakÂ• .02 .10
209 Radek Toupal .02 .10
210 Tomas Kapusta .02 .10
211 Guy Hebert .40 1.00
212 Mike Richter .60 1.50
213 Shawn Chambers .02 .10
214 Sean Hill .02 .10
215 Don McSween .02 .10
216 Pat Neaton .02 .10
217 Barry Richter .02 .10
218 Craig Wolanin .02 .10
219 Gary Suter .08 .25
220 Robert Beers .08 .25
221 Brett Hauer .02 .10
222 Peter Ciavaglia .02 .10
223 Phil Bourque .02 .10
224 Shjon Podein .08 .25
225 John Lilley .08 .25
226 Tim Sweeney .08 .25
227 Scott Young .08 .25
228 Craig Janney .08 .25
229 Joe Sacco .08 .25
230 Jeffrey Lazaro .08 .25
231 Doug Weight .40 1.00
232 Thomas Bissett .20 .50
233 James Campbell .08 .25
234 Mark Beaufait .08 .25
235 Peter Ferraro .08 .25
236 Jim Marthinsen .08 .25
237 Robert Schistad .08 .25
238 Jan Roar Fagerli .02 .10
239 Petter Salsten .02 .10
240 Carl Oscar Boe Andersen .02 .10
241 Svein Enok Norstebo .02 .10
242 Tommie Eriksen .02 .10
243 Tom Erik Olsen .02 .10
244 Geir Hoff .02 .10
245 Bjorn Anders Dahl .02 .10
246 Trond Magnussen .02 .10
247 Orjan Lovdahl .02 .10
248 Espen Knutsen .20 .50
249 Rune Gulliksen .02 .10
250 Eirik Paulsen .02 .10
251 Sjur Robert Nilsen .02 .10
252 Petter Thoresen .02 .10
253 Rune Fjeldstad .02 .10
254 Erik Tveten .02 .10
255 Henrik Aaby .02 .10
256 Michael Puschacher .02 .10
257 Claus Dalpiaz .08 .25
258 Michael Guntner .02 .10
259 Martin Ulrich .02 .10
260 Peter Kasper .02 .10
261 Engelbert Linder .02 .10
262 Herbert Hohenberger .02 .10
263 Gerhard Unterluggauer .02 .10
264 Martin Krainz .02 .10
265 Helmut Karel .02 .10
266 Werner Kerth .02 .10
267 Dieter Kalt .02 .10
268 Patrick Pilloni .02 .10
269 Mario Schaden .02 .10
270 Wolfgang Kromp .02 .10
271 Gunter Lanzinger .02 .10
272 Manfred Muhr .02 .10
273 Gerald Ressman .02 .10
274 Siegfried Haberl .02 .10
275 Christoph Brandner .02 .10
276 Wayne Gretzky 6.00 15.00
277 Mario Lemieux 5.00 12.00
278 Eric Lindros 1.50 4.00
279 Mark Messier 1.25 3.00
280 Steve Yzerman 4.00 10.00
281 Pavel Bure 1.00 2.50
282 Sergei Fedorov 1.25 3.00
283 Igor Larionov .40 1.00
284 Sergei Makarov .40 1.00
285 Alexander Mogilny .40 1.00
286 Ulf Dahlen .08 .25
287 Peter Forsberg 2.00 5.00
288 Mikael Renberg .20 .50
289 Ulf Samuelsson .10 .25
290 Tomas SandstrÃ¶m .08 .25
291 Thomas Steen .08 .25
292 Mats Sundin .60 1.50
293 Jari Kurri .40 1.00
294 Teemu Selanne 2.00 5.00
295 Esa Tikkanen .20 .50
296 Dominik Hasek 1.25 3.00
297 Jaromir Jagr 1.50 4.00
298 Robert Reichel .10 .25
299 Brett Hull 1.50 4.00
300 Brian Leetch .60 1.50

1995-96 Swedish Leaf

The 1995-96 Leaf Elit set was issued in two series (150 and 160 cards, respectively) and featured the players of Sweden's top league, the Elitserien. The cards feature a full-bleed design, with the player's name ghosted along the bottom. The set was distributed in 8-card packs. The NNO Per-Erik (Pelle) Eklund card was randomly inserted in series 1 packs, while the HV71 card, commemorating the team's 1994-95 championship, could be found in series 2 packs.

COMPLETE SET (310) 16.00 40.00
COMPLETE SERIES 1 (150) 8.00 20.00
COMPLETE SERIES 2 (160) 8.00 20.00
1 Hakan Loob .20 .50
2 AIK .08 .25
3 AIK, Season Stats .05 .15
4 Joakim Persson .08 .25
5 Niclas Havelid .30 .75
6 Tony Barthelson .05 .15
7 Patric Aberg .05 .15
8 Johan Akerman .05 .15
9 Dick Tarnstrom .08 .25
10 Stefan Gustavson .05 .15
11 Anders Gozzi .05 .15
12 Morgan Samuelsson .08 .25
13 Brynas IF .05 .15
14 Brynas, Season Stats .05 .15
15 Michael Sundlov .08 .25
16 Stefan Klockare .08 .25
17 Bedrick Scerban .05 .15
18 Andreas Dackell .30 .75
19 Fredrik Modin .75 2.00
20 Ove Molin .05 .15
21 Mikael Wahlberg .05 .15
22 Thomas Tallberg .05 .15
23 Peter Larsson .05 .15
24 Stefan Ketola .08 .25
25 Djurgardens IF .08 .25
26 Djurgarden, Season Stats .05 .15
27 Jonas Forsberg .15 .40
28 Christian Due-Boje .08 .25
29 Mikael Magnusson .05 .15
30 Thomas Johansson .05 .15
31 Joakim Musakka .05 .15
32 Erik Hussko .08 .25
33 Jens Ohling .05 .15
34 Per Eklund .08 .25
35 Espen Knutsen .40 1.00
36 Patrik Erickson .05 .15
37 Farjestads BK .05 .15
38 Farjestad, Season Stats .05 .15
39 Patrik Haltia .08 .25
40 Sergei Fokin .05 .15
41 Thomas Rhodin .05 .15
42 Stefan Nilsson .05 .15
43 Magnus Arvedsson .30 .75
44 Mattias Johansson .05 .15
45 Clas Eriksson .05 .15
46 Peter Ottosson .05 .15
47 HV 71 .05 .15
48 HV 71, Season Stats .05 .15
49 Boo Ahl .15 .40
50 Kenneth Kennholt .05 .15
51 Hans Abrhamsson .05 .15
52 Peter Hammarstrom .05 .15
53 Johan Davidsson .20 .50
54 Stefan Falk .05 .15
55 Johan Lindbom .05 .15
56 Esa Keskinen .08 .25
57 Stefan Ornskog .08 .25
58 Peter Ekelund .05 .15
59 Leksands IF .05 .15
60 Leksand, Season Stats .05 .15
61 Johan Hedberg 1.50 4.00
62 Tomas Jonsson .08 .25
63 Hans Lodin .05 .15
64 Orjan Lindmark .05 .15
65 Jan Huokko .05 .15
66 Markus Eriksson .05 .15
67 Andreas Karlsson .05 .15
68 Mikael Holmberg .05 .15
69 Jonas Bergqvist .08 .25
70 Niklas Eriksson .05 .15
71 Per-Erik Eklund .08 .25
72 Lulea HF .05 .15
73 Lulea, Season Stats .05 .15
74 Jarmo Myllys .20 .50
75 Mattias Ohlund .40 1.00
76 Lars Modig .05 .15
77 Torbjorn Lindberg .05 .15
78 Roger Akerstrom .05 .15
79 Stefan Jonsson .05 .15
80 Johan Rosen .05 .15
81 Tomas Berglund .05 .15
82 Robert Nordberg .05 .15
83 Jiri Kucera .08 .25
84 Thomas Holmstrom .75 2.00
85 Malmo IF .05 .15
86 Malmo, Season Stats .05 .15
87 Peter Andersson .05 .15
88 Roger Ohman .05 .15
89 Marcus Magnertoft .05 .15
90 Patrik Sylvegard .05 .15
91 Hakan Ahlund .05 .15
92 Jesper Mattsson .08 .25
93 Roger Hansson .05 .15
94 Mattias Bosson .05 .15
95 Bo Svanberg .05 .15
96 Raimo Helminen .08 .25
97 MoDo Hockey .08 .25
98 MoDo, Season Stats .05 .15
99 Petter Ronnqvist .08 .25
100 Lars Jansson .05 .15
101 Mattias Timander .20 .50
102 Hans Jonsson .05 .15
103 Anders Soderberg .15 .40
104 Martin Hostak .05 .15
105 Kyosti Karjalainen .08 .25
106 Mikael Hakanson .05 .15
107 Per Svartvadet .15 .40
108 Andreas Salomonsson .40 1.00
109 Lars Bystrom .05 .15
110 Magnus Wernblom .05 .15
111 Rogle BK .05 .15
112 Rogle, Season Stats .05 .15
113 Magnus Swardh .08 .25
114 Arto Ruotanen .05 .15
115 Johan Finnstrom .08 .25
116 Daniel Tjarnqvist .20 .50
117 Pierre Johnsson .05 .15
118 Per Wallin .08 .25
119 Michael Johansson .05 .15
120 Per-Johan Svensson .05 .15
121 Roger Elvenes .05 .15
122 Mats Loov .05 .15
123 Michael Hjalm .08 .25
124 Vasteras IK .05 .15
125 Vasteras, Season Stats .05 .15
126 Mats Ytter .08 .25
127 Erik Bergstrom .08 .25
128 Lars Ivarsson .05 .15
129 Mishat Fahrutdinov .05 .15
130 Claes Lindblom .05 .15
131 Paul Andersson .05 .15
132 Henrik Nordfeldt .05 .15
133 Alexei Salomatin .05 .15
134 Mikael Pettersson .05 .15
135 Vastra Frolunda HC .05 .15
136 Frolunda, Season Stats .05 .15
137 Hakan Algotsson .08 .25
138 Jonas Andersson-Junkka .08 .25
139 Stefan Larsson .05 .15
140 Par Djoos .08 .25
141 Ronnie Sundin .08 .25
142 Par Edlund .08 .25
143 Peter Berndtsson .05 .15
144 Joacim Esbjors .05 .15
145 Alexander Beliavski .05 .15
146 Jonas Esbjors .05 .15
147 Marko Jantunen .08 .25
148 Peter Strom .05 .15
149 Checklist 1-75 .05 .15
150 Checklist 76-150 .05 .15
151 AIK .08 .25
152 AIK, Captains .05 .15
153 Mikael Nilsson .05 .15
154 Juha Jokiharju .08 .25
155 Stefan Andersson .05 .15
156 Thomas Strandberg .05 .15
157 Mats Lindberg .05 .15
158 Peter Gerhardsson .05 .15
159 Tommy Lehmann .08 .25
160 Tommy Hedlund .05 .15
161 Peter Wallin .08 .25
162 Bjorn Ahlstrom .05 .15
163 Erik Hamalainen .08 .25
164 Patric Englund .05 .15
165 Rikard Franzen .05 .15
166 BRYNAS IF .05 .15
167 Brynas, Captains .05 .15
168 Lars Karlsson .05 .15
169 Jonas Lofstrom .05 .15
170 Stefan Polla .05 .15
171 Mikael Lind .05 .15
172 Brian Rafalski .75 2.00
173 Roger Kyro .05 .15
174 Per-Johan Johansson .05 .15
175 Greg Parks .05 .15
176 Per Lofstrom .05 .15
177 Jonas Johnsson .05 .15
178 Mikael Lindman .05 .15
179 Mikael Wiklander .05 .15
180 Tommy Melkersson .05 .15
181 DJURGARDENS IF .08 .25
182 Djurgarden, Captains .05 .15
183 Thomas Ostlund .20 .50
184 Patrik Hofbauer .05 .15
185 Magnus Jansson .05 .15
186 Niklas Falk .05 .15
187 Ola Josefsson .05 .15
188 Joakim Lundberg .05 .15
189 Fredrik Lindquist .15 .40
190 Patrik Kjellberg .20 .50
191 Jan Viktorsson .08 .25
192 Bjorn Nord .05 .15
193 Tommy Jacobsen .05 .15
194 Anders Huusko .05 .15
195 Kristofer Ottosson .05 .15
196 VASTRA FROLUNDA HC .05 .15
197 Frolunda, Captains .05 .15
198 Mikael Sandberg .05 .15
199 Jerry Persson .05 .15
200 Peter Hogardh .05 .15
201 Stefan Axelsson .08 .25
202 Lars Edstrom .05 .15
203 Lars-Goran Wiklander .08 .25
204 Per-Johan Axelsson .40 1.00
205 Henrik Nilsson .05 .15
206 Petteri Nummelin .08 .25
207 Christian Ruuttu .20 .50
208 Oscar Ackestrom .05 .15
209 FARJESTADS BK .05 .15
210 Farjestad, Captains .05 .15
211 Markus Ketterer .08 .25
212 Bjorn Eriksson .05 .15
213 Jonas Hoglund .40 1.00
214 Peter Nordstrom .05 .15
215 Jorgen Jonsson .05 .15
216 Greger Artursson .05 .15
217 Jesper Duus .05 .15
218 Roger Johansson .05 .15
219 Leif Carlsson .05 .15
220 Per Lundell .05 .15
221 Vitali Prokhorov .08 .25
222 HV 71 .05 .15
223 HV 711, Captains .05 .15
224 Kenneth Johansson .05 .15
225 Thomas Gustavsson .05 .15
226 Marcus Thuresson .05 .15
227 Vesa Salo .08 .25
228 Kai Nurminen .20 .50
229 Johan Brummer .05 .15
230 Daniel Johansson .08 .25
231 Per Gustafsson .08 .25
232 Niklas Rahm .05 .15
233 LIKSANDS IF .05 .15
234 Leksand, Captains .05 .15
235 Per-Ragnar Bergkvist .08 .25
236 Anders Carlsson .05 .15
237 Micael Karlberg .05 .15
238 Torgny Lowgren .05 .15
239 Stefan Hellkvist .05 .15
240 Markus Akerblom .05 .15
241 Joakim Lidgren .05 .15
242 Tomas Froslund .08 .25
243 Torbjorn Johansson .05 .15
244 Nicklas Nordqvist .05 .15
245 LULEA HF .05 .15
246 Lulea, Captains .05 .15
247 Erik Grankvist .05 .15
248 Mikael Lindholm .05 .15
249 Johan Stromvall .05 .15
250 Anders Burstrom .05 .15
251 Lars Hurtig .05 .15
252 Stefan Nilsson .05 .15
253 Jan Mertzig .08 .25
254 Petter Nilsson .05 .15
255 Malmo IF .05 .15
256 Malmo IF, Captains .05 .15
257 Peter Lindmark .08 .25
258 Roger Nordstrom .08 .25
259 Andreas Lilja .05 .15
260 Brian McReynolds .05 .15
261 Ilja Byakin .08 .25
262 Robert Burakovsky .05 .15
263 Mikael Burakovsky .05 .15
264 Stefan Elvenes .08 .25
265 Johan Salle .05 .15
266 Kim Johnsson .05 .15
267 Peter Hasselblad .05 .15
268 Marko Palo .05 .15
269 MODO Hockey .08 .25
270 MoDo, Captains .08 .25
271 Fredrik Andersson .05 .15
272 Frantisek Kaberle .08 .25
273 Samuel Pahlsson .30 .75
274 Jan Larsson .05 .15
275 Per-Anton Lundstrom .08 .25
276 Tomas Nansen .05 .15
277 Marcus Karlsson .05 .15
278 Jan-Axel Alavaara .08 .25
279 Kristian Gahn .08 .25
280 ROGLE BK .05 .15
281 Rogle, Captains .05 .15
282 Patrik Backlund .05 .15
283 Peter Lundmark .05 .15
284 Anders Berglund .05 .15
285 Harijs Vitolins .05 .15
286 Jens Nielsen .05 .15
287 Greg Brown .08 .25
288 Bjorn Linden .05 .15
289 VASTERAS IK .05 .15
290 Vasteras, Captains .05 .15
291 Jakob Karlsson .05 .15
292 Patrik Zetterberg .05 .15
293 Mattias Loof .05 .15
294 Johan Tornberg .05 .15
295 Andrei Korolev .05 .15
296 Mattias Olsson .05 .15
297 Roger Rosen .05 .15
298 Andrei Lulin .05 .15
299 Edvin Fylen .08 .25
300 Mats Lusth .05 .15
301 Fredrik Oberg .05 .15
302 All Stars Myllys .20 .50
303 All Stars Jonsson .08 .25
304 All Stars Andersson .08 .25
305 All Stars Loob .20 .50
306 All Stars Keskinen .08 .25
307 All Stars Ruuttu .08 .25
308 Checklist 151-230 .05 .15
309 Checklist 231-310 .05 .15
310 Checklist Insert Cards .05 .15
NNO HV71, Svenska Mastare 4.00 10.00
NNO Per-Erik Eklund 4.00 10.00

1995-96 Swedish Leaf Champs

Randomly inserted in series 1 packs at a rate of 1:11, this 15-card set celebrates members of Sweden's championship team. The cards are individually serially numbered on the back. It is believed that 1,000 of each were produced.

COMPLETE SET (15) 10.00 25.00
1 Tomas Jonsson .75 2.00
2 Patrik Kjellberg 1.25 3.00
3 Hakan Loob 1.25 3.00
4 Peter Lindmark 1.25 3.00
5 Anders Carlsson .75 2.00
6 Raimo Helminen 1.25 3.00
7 Esa Keskinen .75 2.00
8 Jan Larsson .75 2.00
9 Roger Johansson .75 2.00
10 Andreas Dackell 1.25 3.00
11 Stefan Ornskog .75 2.00
12 Michael Sundlov 1.25 3.00
13 Per-Erik Eklund .75 2.00
14 Kenneth Kennholt .75 2.00
15 Jan Viktorsson .75 2.00

1995-96 Swedish Leaf Face to Face

Randomly inserted in series two packs at a rate of 1:5, this 15-card set features the top two talents on each of the Elitserien teams.

COMPLETE SET (15) 6.00 15.00
1 M.Samuelsson .40 1.00
T.Strandberg
2 B.Scerban .40 1.00
G.Parks
3 E.Huusko .40 1.00
A.Hussko
4 S.Larsson .40 1.00
M.Jantunen
5 H.Loob .75 2.00
R.Johansson
6 K.Kennholt .40 1.00
P.Gustafsson
7 Stefan Hellkvist .40 1.00
T.Forslund
8 T.Holmstrom 2.00 5.00
R.Akerstrom
9 S.Elvenes .40 1.00
R.Burakovsky
10 M.Hostak .40 1.00
M.Timander
11 M.Loov .40 1.00
M.Hjalm
12 A.Salomatin .40 1.00
F.Oberg
13 P.Erickson 1.25 3.00
E.Knutsen
14 P.Andersson .40 1.00
P.Hasselblad
15 T.Jonsson .40 1.00
M.Akerblom

1995-96 Swedish Leaf Goldies

Randomly inserted in series 1 packs at a rate of 1:14, this 10-card set captures some of the top young scorers in Sweden.

COMPLETE SET (10) 6.00 15.00
1 Morgan Samuelsson .75 2.00
2 Ove Molin .75 2.00
3 Fredrik Lindquist .75 2.00
4 Peter Strom .75 2.00
5 Mattias Johansson .75 2.00
6 Stefan Ornskog .75 2.00
7 Niklas Eriksson .75 2.00
8 Johan Rosen .75 2.00
9 Roger Ohman .75 2.00
10 Anders Soderberg .75 2.00

1995-96 Swedish Leaf Mega

The fifteen cards in this set were randomly inserted at a rate of 1:20 series 1 packs.

COMPLETE SET (15) 12.00 30.00
1 Michael Sundlov 1.25 3.00
2 Jonas Bergqvist 1.25 3.00
3 Marko Jantunen .75 2.00
4 Thomas Ostlund 1.25 3.00
5 Tomas Jonsson .75 2.00
6 Esa Keskinen .75 2.00
7 Roger Nordstrom .75 2.00
8 Mattias Ohlund 1.50 4.00
9 Hakan Loob 1.25 3.00
10 Raimo Helminen .75 2.00
11 Per-Erik Eklund 1.25 3.00
12 Jarmo Myllys 1.50 4.00
13 Rikard Franzen .75 2.00
14 Christer Olsson .75 2.00
15 Per Gustafsson .75 2.00

1995-96 Swedish Leaf Rookies

Randomly inserted in series one packs at a rate of 1:6, this nine card set reveals Leaf's picks as the top frosh in the Elitserien.

COMPLETE SET (9) 6.00 15.00
1 Peter Wallin .75 2.00
2 Jan-Axel Alavaara .75 2.00
3 Niklas Falk .75 2.00
4 Lars-Goran Wiklander .75 2.00
5 Torbjorn Johansson .75 2.00
6 Jan Mertzig .75 2.00
7 Mikael Burakovsky .75 2.00
8 Marcus Karlsson .75 2.00
9 Roger Rosen .75 2.00

1995-96 Swedish Leaf Spidermen

The stingiest netminders in Sweden are the focus of this 14-card set. The cards were randomly inserted at the rate of 1:8 series one packs.

COMPLETE SET (14) 20.00 40.00
1 Joakim Persson 1.25 3.00
2 Michael Sundlov 1.25 3.00
3 Thomas Ostlund 1.50 4.00
4 Hakan Algotsson 1.25 3.00
5 Patrik Haltia 1.25 3.00
6 Boo Ahl 1.50 4.00
7 Johan Hedberg 2.00 5.00
8 Jarmo Myllys 1.50 4.00
9 Jonas Forsberg 1.50 4.00
10 Petter Ronnqvist 1.25 3.00
11 Magnus Swardh 1.25 3.00
12 Mats Ytter 1.25 3.00
13 Mikael Sandberg 1.25 3.00
14 Roger Nordstrom 1.25 3.00

1995-96 Swedish Upper Deck

The 1995-96 Upper Deck Swedish Elit set was issued in one series totaling 260 cards. The set was issued in 10-card packs and features players from the Swedish Elitserien and was endorsed by its Players Association (SICO). The highlight is the subset Where Are They Now? (234-248) which showcases a number of former Swedish stars now in the NHL.

COMPLETE SET (260) 16.00 40.00
1 Joakim Persson .08 .25
2 Erik Hamalainen .08 .25
3 Dick Tarnstrom .08 .25
4 Rikard Franzen .02 .10
5 Niclas Havelid .30 .75
6 Tony Barthelson .02 .10
7 Tommy Hedlund .02 .10
8 Patric Aberg .02 .10
9 Stefan Gustavson .02 .10
10 Anders Gozzi .02 .10
11 David Engblom .02 .10
12 Stefan Andersson .02 .10
13 Tomas Strandberg .02 .10
14 Mats Lindberg .02 .10
15 Tommy Lehmann .08 .25
16 Bjorn Ahlstrom .02 .10
17 Patrik Englund .02 .10
18 Morgan Samuelsson .08 .25
19 Michael Sundlov .20 .50
20 Bedrich Scerban .02 .10
21 Mikael Lindman .02 .10
22 Mikael Wiklander .02 .10
23 Tommy Melkersson .02 .10
24 Stefan Klockare .08 .25
25 Per Lofstrom .02 .10
26 Jonas Johnsson .02 .10
27 Roger Kyro .02 .10
28 Jonas Lofstrom .02 .10
29 Stefan Ketola .08 .25
30 Mikael Wahlberg .02 .10
31 Stefan Polla .02 .10
32 Greg Parks .02 .10
33 Ove Molin .02 .10
34 Peter Larsson .02 .10
35 Fredrik Modin .40 1.00
36 Andreas Dackell .30 .75
37 Thomas Ostlund .20 .50
38 Tommy Jakobsen .02 .10
39 Christian Due-Boje .08 .25
40 Thomas Johansson .02 .10
41 Joakim Lundberg .02 .10
42 Bjorn Nord .02 .10
43 Mikael Magnusson .02 .10
44 Erik Huusko .08 .25
45 Anders Huusko .02 .10
46 Kristofer Ottosson .02 .10
47 Magnus Jansson .02 .10
48 Niklas Falk .08 .25
49 Ola Josefsson .02 .10
50 Per Eklund .08 .25
51 Espen Knutsen .40 1.00
52 Jens Ohling .02 .10
53 Patric Kjellberg .30 .75
54 Patrik Erickson .02 .10
55 Jan Viktorsson .08 .25
56 Markus Ketterer .20 .50
57 Jesper Duus .02 .10
58 Sergei Fokin .02 .10
59 Per Lundell .02 .10
60 Thomas Rhodin .02 .10
61 Henrik Rehnberg .02 .10
62 Roger Johansson .02 .10
63 Leif Carlsson .02 .10
64 Hakan Loob .20 .50
65 Stefan Nilsson .02 .10
66 Vitali Prokhorov .08 .25
67 Magnus Arvedsson .02 .10
68 Jonas Hoglund .40 1.00
69 Mathias Johansson .02 .10
70 Patrik Wallenberg .02 .10
71 Claes Eriksson .02 .10
72 Jorgen Jonsson .02 .10
73 Peter Nordstrom .02 .10
74 Peter Ottosson .02 .10
75 Boo Ahl .15 .40
76 Per Gustafsson .08 .25
77 Niklas Rahm .02 .10
78 Hans Abrahamsson .02 .10
79 Kenneth Kennholt .02 .10
80 Daniel Johansson .08 .25
81 Vesa Salo .08 .25
82 Thomas Gustavsson .02 .10
83 Stefan Ornskog .08 .25
84 Stefan Falk .02 .10
85 Peter Hammarstrom .02 .10
86 Johan Davidsson .20 .50
87 Peter Ekelund .02 .10
88 Johan Lindbom .02 .10
89 Esa Keskinen .08 .25
90 Kai Nurminen .20 .50
91 Magnus Eliasson .02 .10
92 Marcus Thuresson .02 .10
93 Johan Brummer .02 .10
94 Johan Hedberg .40 1.00
95 Tomas Jonsson .08 .25
96 Torbjorn Johansson .02 .10
97 Hans Lodin .02 .10
98 Orjan Lindmark .02 .10
99 Jan Huokko .02 .10
100 Joakim Lidgren .02 .10
101 Per-Erik Eklund .08 .25
102 Anders Carlsson .02 .10
103 Niklas Eriksson .02 .10
104 Mikael Karlberg .02 .10
105 Jonas Bergqvist .08 .25
106 Torgny Lowgren .02 .10
107 Stefan Hellkvist .02 .10
108 Markus Akerblom .02 .10
109 Mikael Holmberg .02 .10
110 Andreas Karlsson .02 .10
111 Markus Akerblom .02 .10
112 Tomas Forslund .08 .25
113 Jarmo Myllys .20 .50
114 Lars Modig .02 .10
115 Patrik Hoglund .02 .10
116 Torbjorn Lindberg .02 .10
117 Jan Mertzig .08 .25
118 Petter Nilsson .02 .10
119 Mattias Ohlund .40 1.00
120 Roger Akerstrom .02 .10
121 Stefan Jonsson .02 .10
122 Stefan Nilsson .02 .10
123 Tomas Holmstrom .75 2.00
124 Mikael Lindholm .02 .10
125 Johan Stromvall .02 .10
126 Jiri Kucera .08 .25
127 Joakim Backlund .02 .10
128 Robert Nordberg .02 .10
129 Tomas Berglund .02 .10
130 Frederik Johansson .02 .10
131 Lars Hurtig .02 .10
132 Johan Rosen .02 .10
133 Roger Nordstrom .08 .25
134 Kim Johnsson .40 1.00
135 Peter Hasselblad .02 .10
136 Ilya Byakin .08 .25
137 Johan Salle .02 .10
138 Peter Andersson .02 .10
139 Roger Ohman .02 .10
140 Marko Palo .02 .10
141 Raimo Helminen .08 .25
142 Mattias Bosson .02 .10
143 Markus Magnertoft .02 .10
144 Roger Hansson .02 .10
145 Bo Svanberg .02 .10
146 Patrik Sylvegard .02 .10
147 Brian McReynolds .02 .10
148 Hakan Ahlund .02 .10
149 Robert Burakovsky .02 .10
150 Stefan Elvenes .08 .25
151 Patrik Boij .02 .10
152 Petter Ronnqvist .08 .25
153 Mattias Timander .20 .50
154 Lars Jansson .02 .10
155 Frantisek Kaberle .20 .50
156 Hans Jonsson .02 .10
157 Tomas Nansen .02 .10
158 Marcus Karlsson .02 .10
159 Kristian Gahn .08 .25
160 Magnus Wernblom .02 .10
161 Anders Soderberg .15 .40
162 Martin Hostak .02 .10
163 Kyosti Karjalainen .08 .25
164 Mikael Hakanson .02 .10
165 Jan Larsson .02 .10
166 Per Svartvadet .15 .40
167 Andreas Salomonsson .40 1.00
168 Samuel Pahlsson .60 1.50
169 Lars Bystrom .02 .10
170 Magnus Swardh .08 .25
171 Anders Berglund .02 .10
172 Pierre Johnsson .02 .10
173 Johan Finnstrom .08 .25
174 Arto Ruotanen .02 .10
175 Daniel Tjarnqvist .20 .50
176 Greg Brown .08 .25
177 Per Wallin .08 .25
178 Peter Lundmark .02 .10
179 Roger Elvenes .02 .10
180 Michael Hjalm .08 .25
181 Jens Hemstrom .02 .10
182 Pelle Svensson .02 .10
183 Harijs Vitolins .02 .10
184 Jens Nielsen .02 .10
185 Mats Loov .02 .10
186 Mats Ytter .08 .25
187 Lars Ivarsson .02 .10
188 Edvin Frylen .08 .25
189 Andrei Lyulin .02 .10
190 Johan Tornberg .02 .10
191 Mattias Olsson .02 .10
192 Mats Lusth .02 .10
193 Fredrik Oberg .02 .10
194 Alexei Salomatin .02 .10
195 Mishat Fahrutdinov .02 .10
196 Mikael Pettersson .02 .10
197 Andrei Korolev .02 .10
198 Mattias Loof .02 .10
199 Claes Lindblom .02 .10
200 Paul Andersson .02 .10
201 Roger Rosen .02 .10
202 Hakan Algotsson .08 .25
203 Par Djoos .08 .25
204 Mikael Sandberg .02 .10
205 Joachim Esbjors .02 .10
206 Stefan Axelsson .08 .25
207 Ronnie Sundin .15 .40
208 Stefan Larsson .02 .10
209 Petteri Nummelin .08 .25
210 Christian Ruuttu .20 .50
211 Marko Jantunen .08 .25
212 Peter Strom .02 .10
213 Peter Berndtsson .02 .10
214 Lars Edstrom .02 .10
215 Peter Hogardh .02 .10
216 Par Edlund .02 .10
217 Lars-Goran Wiklander .08 .25
218 Henrik Nilsson .02 .10
219 Rikard Franzen .02 .10
220 Fredrik Modin .30 .75
221 Anders Soderberg .15 .40
222 Per Eklund .08 .25
223 Hakan Loob .20 .50
224 Markus Ketterer .08 .25
225 Esa Keskinen .08 .25
226 Per Gustafsson .08 .25
227 Tomas Jonsson .08 .25
228 Per-Erik Eklund .08 .25
229 Mattias Ohlund .40 1.00
230 Jarmo Myllys .20 .50
231 Peter Andersson .02 .10
232 Raimo Helminen .08 .25
233 Christian Ruuttu .20 .50
234 Peter Forsberg 3.00 8.00
235 Mikael Renberg .20 .50
236 Mats Sundin 1.00 2.50
237 Michael Nylander .20 .50
238 Tommy Soderstrom .20 .50
239 Nicklas Lidstrom .75 2.00
240 Kenny Jonsson .30 .75
241 Patrik Carnback .08 .25
242 Johan Garpenlov .20 .50
243 Magnus Svensson .15 .40
244 Patrik Juhlin .15 .40
245 Markus Naslund .75 2.00
246 Tommy Salo .40 1.00
247 Fredrik Olausson .20 .50
248 Tommy Albelin .08 .25
249 Rikard Franzen .02 .10
250 Jonas Johnsson .02 .10
251 Thomas Ostlund .20 .50
252 Hakan Loob .20 .50
253 Per Gustafsson .08 .25
254 Per-Erik Eklund .08 .25
255 Tomas Jonsson .08 .25
256 Mattias Ohlund .40 1.00
257 Peter Andersson .02 .10
258 Christian Ruuttu .20 .50
259 Checklist .02 .10
260 Checklist .02 .10

1995-96 Swedish Upper Deck 1st Division Stars

This 20-card insert series, which was included in packs at indeterminate odds (estimated at 1:8) features players from the Swedish First Division, a league one step below the Elitserien.

COMPLETE SET (20) 6.00 15.00
DS1 Anders Huss .40 1.00
DS2 Igor Vlasov .40 1.00
DS3 Ulf Sandstrom .40 1.00
DS4 Hans Huczkowski .40 1.00
DS5 Johan Ramstedt .40 1.00
DS6 Anders Eldebrink .40 1.00
DS7 Niklas Brannstrom .40 1.00
DS8 Peter Nilsson .40 1.00
DS9 Sam Lindstahl .40 1.00
DS10 Tony Skopac .40 1.00
DS11 Jonas Eriksson .40 1.00
DS12 Anders Lonn .40 1.00
DS13 Peter Hagstrom .40 1.00
DS14 Magnus Roupe .40 1.00
DS15 Peter Pettersson .40 1.00
DS16 Peter Eriksson .40 1.00
DS17 Fredrik Bergqvist .40 1.00
DS18 Larry Pilut .40 1.00
DS19 Peter Olsson .40 1.00
DS20 Staffan Lundh .40 1.00

1995-96 Swedish Upper Deck Ticket to North America

This 20-card set was randomly inserted in packs at indeterminate odds (estimated at 1:10) and features athletes whose strong play has led to them being selected in the draft and may earn them a shot at the NHL.

COMPLETE SET (20) 12.00 30.00
NA1 Joakim Persson .75 2.00
NA2 Dick Tarnstrom .75 2.00
NA3 Andreas Dackell .75 2.00
NA4 Fredrik Modin 1.25 3.00
NA5 Per Eklund .40 1.00

NA6 Espen Knutsen 1.25 3.00
NA7 Fredrik Lindquist .40 1.00
NA8 Jonas Hoglund .75 2.00
NA9 Jorgen Jonsson .40 1.00
NA10 Johan Davidsson .75 2.00
NA11 Per Gustafsson .40 1.00
NA12 Johan Lindbom .40 1.00
NA13 Markus Akerblom .40 1.00
NA14 Jan Huokko .40 1.00
NA15 Tomas Holmstrom 4.00 10.00
NA16 Mattias Ohlund 1.25 3.00
NA17 Johan Rosen .40 1.00
NA18 Frantisek Kaberle .75 2.00
NA19 Mattias Timander .75 2.00
NA20 Magnus Wernblom .40 1.00

1996 Swedish Semic Wien

The 1996 Semic Wien set was issued in one series totaling 240 cards to commemorate the 1996 World Championships held in Vienna. The set features players who have competed for their countries in various tournaments, wearing their national team colors. Many top NHLers are featured, including Wayne Gretzky, Eric Lindros and Ray Bourque. The cards were distributed in ten-card packs.

COMPLETE SET (240) 16.00 40.00
1 Jarmo Myllys .08 .25
2 Marko Kiprusoff .05 .15
3 Petteri Nummelin .02 .10
4 Erik Hamalainen .02 .10
5 Timo Jutila .05 .15
6 Janne Ninimaa .08 .25
7 Raimo Summanen .05 .15
8 Janne Ojanen .05 .15
9 Esa Keskinen .05 .15
10 Ari Sulander .08 .25
11 Saku Koivu .20 .50
12 Jukka Tammi .08 .25
13 Marko Palo .02 .10
14 Raimo Helminen .05 .15
15 Antti Tormanen .07 .20
16 Ville Peltonen .08 .25
17 Tero Lehtera .05 .15
18 Mika Stromberg .05 .15
19 Sami Kapanen .15 .40
20 Jere Lehtinen .15 .40
21 Juha Ylonen .07 .20
22 Mika Nieminen .07 .20
23 Hannu Virta .05 .15
24 Jari Kurri .15 .40
25 Christian Ruuttu .05 .15
26 Jyrki Lumme .05 .15
27 Teppo Numminen .08 .25
28 Esa Tikkanen .08 .25
29 Janne Laukkanen .07 .20
30 Aki Berg .08 .25
31 Teemu Selanne .60 1.50
32 Markus Ketterer .08 .25
33 Joni Lehto .02 .10
34 Juha Riihijarvi .05 .15
35 Sakari Lindfors .08 .25
36 Kai Nurminen .08 .25
37 Huey, Dewey, Louie .20 .50
38 Tommy Soderstrom .08 .25
39 Tommy Salo .20 .50
40 Thomas Ostlund .07 .20
41 Boo Ahl .07 .20
42 Calle Johansson .07 .20
43 Tommy Albelin .05 .15
44 Ulf Samuelsson .05 .15
45 Nicklas Lidstrom .40 1.00
46 Magnus Svensson .05 .15
47 Tomas Jonsson .05 .15
48 Tommy Sjodin .05 .15
49 Marcus Ragnarsson .08 .25
50 Christer Olsson .02 .10
51 Rikard Franzen .02 .10
52 Mattias Ohlund .08 .25
53 Kenny Jonsson .08 .25
54 Roger Johansson .02 .10
55 Anders Eriksson .08 .25
56 Mats Sundin .30 .75
57 Peter Forsberg .75 2.00
58 Mikael Renberg .08 .25
59 Tomas Sandstrom .07 .20
60 Ulf Dahlen .05 .15
61 Michael Nylander .05 .15
62 Patrik Juhlin .05 .15
63 Patrik Carnback .05 .15
64 Andreas Johansson .07 .20
65 Mikael Johansson .02 .10
66 Per-Erik Eklund .05 .15
67 Tomas Forslund .05 .15
68 Andreas Dackell .07 .20
69 Per Eklund .05 .15
70 Tomas Holmstrom .20 .50
71 Jonas Bergqvist .05 .15
72 Daniel Alfredsson .15 .40
73 Fredrik Modin .08 .25
74 Magic Moment .40 1.00
75 Ed Belfour .40 1.00
76 Bill Ranford .08 .25
77 Sean Burke .08 .25
78 Ray Bourque .60 1.50
79 Paul Coffey .20 .50
80 Scott Stevens .08 .25
81 Al MacInnis .20 .50
82 Larry Murphy .08 .25
83 Eric Desjardins .08 .25
84 Steve Duchesne .07 .20
85 Mario Lemieux 1.50 4.00
86 Mark Messier .40 1.00
87 Theo Fleury .30 .75
88 Eric Lindros .60 1.50
89 Rick Tocchet .15 .40
90 Brendan Shanahan .40 1.00
91 Claude Lemieux .15 .40
92 Joe Juneau .08 .25
93 Luc Robitaille .30 .75
94 Paul Kariya .75 2.00
95 Joe Sakic .75 2.00
96 Mark Recchi .20 .50
97 Jason Arnott .15 .40
98 Rod Brind'Amour .15 .40
99 Wayne Gretzky 2.00 5.00
100 Adam Oates .20 .50
101 Steve Yzerman 1.50 4.00
102 Roman Turek .20 .50
103 Dominik Hasek .40 1.00
104 Petr Briza .08 .25
105 Antonin Stavjana .05 .15
106 Frantisek Kaberle .07 .20
107 Jiri Vykoukal .05 .15
108 Jan Vopat .07 .20
109 Libor Prochazka .02 .10
110 Petr Kuchyna .05 .15
111 Frantisek Musil .05 .15
112 Leo Gudas .02 .10
113 Jiri Slegr .07 .20
114 Pavel Patera .08 .25
115 Otakar Vejvoda .08 .25
116 Martin Prochazka .08 .25
117 Jiri Kucera .02 .10
118 Pavel Janku .07 .20
119 Roman Meluzin .02 .10
120 Richard Zemlicka .02 .10
121 Martin Hostak .02 .10
122 Jiri Dopita .07 .20
123 Radek Belohlav .07 .20
124 Roman Horak .02 .10
125 Jaromir Jagr .60 1.50
126 Michal Pivonka .08 .25
127 Josef Beranek .05 .15
128 Robert Reichel .08 .25
129 Nikolai Khabibulin .20 .50
130 Sergei Abramov .07 .20
131 Yevgeny Tarasov .02 .10
132 Igor Kravchuk .07 .20
133 Dmitri Mironov .08 .25
134 Alexei Zhitnik .08 .25
135 Vladimir Malakhov .07 .20
136 Sergei Zubov .08 .25
137 Dimitri Yushkevich .08 .25
138 Ilya Byakin .02 .10
139 Alexander Smirnov .02 .10
140 Andrei Skopintsev .02 .10
141 Sergei Fedorov .60 1.50
142 Pavel Bure .75 2.00
143 Alexei Zhamnov .08 .25
144 Andrei Kovalenko .08 .25
145 Igor Korolev .05 .15
146 Vyacheslav Kozlov .15 .40
147 Viktor Kozlov .08 .25
148 Alexei Yashin .15 .40
149 Valeri Kamensky .08 .25
150 Stanislav Romanov .02 .10
151 Viacheslav Bykov .07 .20
152 Andrei Khomutov .08 .25
153 Sergei Berezin .15 .40
154 German Titov .08 .25
155 Dmitri Denisov .02 .10
156 John Vanbiesbrouck .20 .50
157 Jim Carey .08 .25
158 Mike Richter .30 .75
159 Chris Chelios .30 .75
160 Brian Leetch .30 .75
161 Phil Housley .08 .25
162 Gary Suter .07 .20
163 Kevin Hatcher .07 .20
164 Brett Hull .40 1.00
165 Pat LaFontaine .15 .40
166 Mike Modano .40 1.00
167 Jeremy Roenick .40 1.00
168 Keith Tkachuk .30 .75
169 Joe Mullen .07 .20
170 Craig Janney .08 .25
171 Joel Otto .07 .20
172 Doug Weight .20 .50
173 Scott Young .08 .25
174 Michael Rosati .05 .15
175 Bruno Campese .05 .15
176 Robert Oberrauch .02 .10
177 Robert Nardella .02 .10
178 Stefano Figluzzi .02 .10
179 Maurizio Mansi .02 .10
180 Gaetano Orlando .02 .10
181 Mario Chitarroni .02 .10
182 Martin Pavlu .02 .10
183 Petri Ylonen .07 .20
184 Michel Valliere .02 .10
185 Serge Poudrier .02 .10
186 Denis Perez .02 .10
187 Antoine Richer .02 .10
188 Philippe Bozon .05 .15
189 Christian Pouget .02 .10
190 Franck Pajonkowski .05 .15
191 Stephane Barin .02 .10
192 Klaus Merk .07 .20
193 Marc Seliger .05 .15
194 Mirco Ludermann .02 .10
195 Jayson Meyer .02 .10
196 Benoit Doucet .05 .15
197 Thomas Brandl .02 .10
198 Dieter Hegen .05 .15
199 Martin Reichel .02 .10
200 Leo Stefan .02 .10
201 Robert Schistad .02 .10
202 Jim Marthinsen .07 .20
203 Tommy Jakobsen .02 .10
204 Petter Salsten .02 .10
205 Svein Norstebo .02 .10
206 Espen Knutsen .08 .25
207 Trond Magnussen .02 .10
208 Henrik Aaby .02 .10
209 Marius Rath .02 .10
210 Claus Dalpiaz .05 .15
211 Michael Puschacher .05 .15
212 Robin Doyle .02 .10
213 James Burton .02 .10
214 Herbert Hohenberger .02 .10
215 Andreas Pusnik .02 .10
216 Richard Nasheim .02 .10
217 Deiter Kalt .02 .10
218 Werner Kerth .02 .10
219 Eduard Hartmann .05 .15
220 Jaromir Dragan .08 .25
221 Robert Svehla .08 .25
222 Lubomir Sekeras .08 .25
223 Marian Smerciak .02 .10
224 Jergus Baca .05 .15
225 Stanslav Medrik .02 .10
226 Miroslav Marcinko .02 .10
227 Peter Stastny .08 .25
228 Peter Bondra .20 .50
229 Zdeno Ciger .08 .25
230 Jozef Stumpel .08 .25
231 Miroslav Satan .20 .50
232 Lubomir Kolnik .07 .20
233 Robert Petrovicky .05 .15
234 Zigmund Palffy .20 .50
235 Oto Hascak .05 .15
236 Jozef Dano .02 .10
237 Checklist .08 .25
238 Checklist .08 .25
239 Checklist .08 .25
240 Checklist .08 .25
NNO Super Chase Card 10.00 25.00

1996 Swedish Semic Wien All-Stars

Randomly inserted in packs at a rate of 1:20, this 6-card , double-sided set acknowledges the first and second team all-stars from the 1995 WC. Both sides share similar designs; the player on the side with the gold foil stars across the top was the first team selection.

COMPLETE SET (6) 3.00 8.00
AS1 Roman Turek .75 2.00
Jarmo Myllys
AS2 Timo Jutila .20 .50
Christer Olsson
AS3 Tommy Sjodin .20 .50
Marko Kiprusoff
AS4 Jere Lehtinen .75 2.00
Sergei Berezin
AS5 Saku Koivu 2.00 5.00
Pelle Eklund
AS6 Ville Peltonen .40 1.00
Andrew McKim

1996 Swedish Semic Wien Coca-Cola Dream Team

This 12-card set was created as a promotion to tie in with both the World Championships and the Semic Wien set. The cards were issued four to a pack at participating Shell gas stations in Sweden with the purchase of a Coca-Cola product. The cards mirror their counterparts in the regular Semic Wien set, save for the numbering and the silver Dream Team icon on the upper corner of each.

COMPLETE SET (12) 20.00 50.00
1 Tommy Soderstrom .75 2.00
2 Boo Ahl .75 2.00
3 Tomas Jonsson .40 1.00
4 Rikard Franzen .40 1.00
5 Mattias Ohlund 1.25 3.00
6 Roger Johansson .40 1.00
7 Mats Sundin 4.00 10.00
8 Peter Forsberg 12.00 30.00
9 Mikael Renberg 1.25 3.00
10 Per-Erik Eklund .40 1.00
11 Andreas Dackell 1.25 3.00
12 Jonas Bergqvist .75 2.00

1996 Swedish Semic Wien Hockey Legends

Randomly inserted in packs at a rate of 1:6, this 18-card set recalls some of the best to lace 'em up on either side of the pond. The card front features a period action photo, with the Hockey Legends logo above in gold foil. The backs display another vintage photo, along with career notes and international play totals. The cards are numbered with an HL prefix.

COMPLETE SET (18) 14.00 35.00
HL1 Ken Dryden 4.00 10.00
HL2 Guy Lafleur 2.00 5.00
HL3 Mike Bossy 1.50 4.00
HL4 Valeri Vasiliev .40 1.00
HL5 Anatoli Firosov .40 1.00
HL6 Alexander Maltsev .75 2.00
HL7 Tony Esposito 2.00 5.00
HL8 Rod Langway .40 1.00
HL9 Bryan Trottier 1.25 3.00
HL10 Lennart Haggroth .40 1.00
HL11 Ulf Nilsson .75 2.00
HL12 Lars-Gunnar Lundberg .40 1.00
HL13 Veli-Pekka Ketola .40 1.00
HL14 Lasse Oksanen .40 1.00
HL15 Pekka Rautakallio .40 1.00
HL16 Jiri Holecek .75 2.00
HL17 Jan Suchy .40 1.00
HL18 Vaclav Nedomansky .75 2.00

1996 Swedish Semic Wien Nordic Stars

Randomly inserted in packs at a rate of 1:48, this 6-card set heaps praise on Scandinavia's best. Card fronts utilize an action photo over a stylized background with an apt description of the player prominently featured. The backs display international totals, with a brief bio in English. The cards are numbered with an NS prefix.

COMPLETE SET (6) 10.00 25.00
NS1 Peter Forsberg 4.00 10.00
NS2 Teemu Selanne 2.50 6.00
NS3 Mats Sundin 2.00 5.00
NS4 Jari Kurri 2.00 5.00
NS5 Nicklas Lidstrom 2.00 5.00
NS6 Esa Tikkanen .75 2.00

1996 Swedish Semic Wien Super Goalies

Randomly inserted in packs at a rate of 1:12, this 9-card set captures the last line of defense of some elite hockey nations. The fronts have an action photo over a ghosted, maskless image. The back has another photo and a brief bio in English. The cards are numbered with an SG prefix out of 9. The key card is a rare shot of Patrick Roy from a Team Canada training camp session.

COMPLETE SET (9) 15.00 30.00
SG1 Dominik Hasek 4.00 8.00
SG2 Ed Belfour 2.00 5.00
SG3 Jarmo Myllys .75 2.00
SG4 Tommy Soderstrom .75 2.00
SG5 Jim Carey .75 2.00
SG6 Roman Turek 1.25 3.00
SG7 Patrick Roy 8.00 20.00
SG8 Markus Ketterer .75 2.00
SG9 Tommy Salo .75 2.00

1997-98 Swedish Alfabilder Autographs

These cards are part of a larger multi-sport set of autographs issued within Sweden. We have listed just the hockey players in the set, below. If anyone has information on other hockey players in this set, or on the set itself, please forward it to hockeymag@beckett.com.

1 Sven Tumba Johansson 8.00 20.00
2 Roland Stoltz 4.00 10.00
3 Eilert Maatta 4.00 10.00
4 Lennart Haggroth 6.00 15.00
5 Nisse Nilsson 4.00 10.00
6 Ulf Sterner 8.00 20.00
7 Leif Holmqvist 8.00 20.00
8 Tord Lundstrom 4.00 10.00
9 Borje Salming 20.00 50.00
10 Anders Hedberg 12.00 30.00
11 Anders Kallur 6.00 15.00
12 Stefan Persson 6.00 15.00
13 Goran Hogosta 4.00 10.00
14 Bengt-Ake Gustafsson 8.00 20.00
15 Mats Naslund 12.00 30.00
16 Kent Nilsson 12.00 30.00
17 Hakan Loob 12.00 30.00
18 Peter Lindmark 10.00 25.00

1997-98 Swedish Collector's Choice

This set was produced by Upper Deck for the Swedish SEL. The cards came in 10-card packs for about $1.50 per pack. It is noteworthy for featuring early cards of Daniel and Henrik Sedin.

COMPLETE SET (225) 10.00 25.00
1 Miikka Kiprusoff 1.25 3.00
2 Karri Kivi .02 .10
3 Erik Hamalainen .07 .20
4 Libor Prochazka .02 .10
5 Dick Tarnstrom .20 .50
6 Niclas Havelid .20 .50
7 Tomas Strandberg .02 .10
8 Stefan Gustavsson .02 .10
9 Anders Gozzi .02 .10
10 Pavel Patera .15 .40
11 David Engblom .02 .10
12 Peter Hammarstrom .02 .10
13 Mats Lindberg .02 .10
14 Fredrik Krekula .02 .10
15 Otakar Vejvoda .02 .10
16 Bjorn Ahlstrom .02 .10
17 Michael Sundlov .08 .25
18 PÅor Djoos .02 .10
19 Tommy Melkersson .02 .10
20 Stefan Klockare .02 .10
21 Johan Hansson .02 .10
22 Per Lofstrom .02 .10
23 Tommy Westlund .08 .25
24 Teppo Kivela .02 .10
25 Niclas Wallin .30 .75
26 Roger Kyro .02 .10
27 Ove Molin .02 .10
28 Mikko Luovi .02 .10
29 Evgenij Davydov .02 .10
30 Anders Huss .02 .10
31 Peter Nylander .02 .10
32 Jan Larsson .02 .10
33 Tommy Soderstrom .20 .50
34 Marcus Matthiasson .02 .10
35 Daniel Carlsson .02 .10
36 Ronnie Pettersson .02 .10
37 Kenneth Kennholt .02 .10
38 Bjorn Nord .07 .20
39 Mikael Hakansson .07 .20
40 Daniel Tjarnqvist .20 .50
41 Charles Berglund .02 .10
42 Mikael Johansson .02 .10
43 Marcus Nilsson .20 .50
44 Nichlas Falk .08 .25
45 Fredrik Lindqvist .08 .25
46 Patric Kjellberg .20 .50
47 Patrik Erickson .02 .10
48 Jan Viktorsson .02 .10
49 Niklas Anger .08 .25
50 Boris Rousson .08 .25
51 Peter Jakobsson .02 .10
52 Peter Nordstrom .08 .25
53 Sergei Fokin .02 .10
54 Niklas Sjokvist .02 .10
55 Jaroslav Spacek .08 .25
56 Greger Artursson .02 .10
57 Roger Johansson .02 .10
58 Stefan Nilsson .02 .10
59 Pelle Prestberg .02 .10
60 Kristian Huselius .75 2.00
61 Mathias Johansson .02 .10
62 Trond Magnussen .02 .10
63 Claes Eriksson .02 .10
64 Jorgen Jonsson .15 .40
65 Atle Olsen .02 .10
66 Patrik Wallenberg .02 .10
67 Lars-Goran Wiklander .02 .10
68 Mikael Sandberg .08 .25
69 Christer Olsson .02 .10
70 Joachim Esbjors .02 .10
71 Henrik Nilsson .02 .10
72 Arto Blomsten .02 .10
73 Magnus Johansson .02 .10
74 Stefan Larsson .02 .10
75 Par Edlund .02 .10
76 Marko Jantunen .02 .10
77 Joni Lius .02 .10
78 Patrik Carnback .07 .20
79 Ville Peltonen .20 .50
80 Peter Berndtsson .02 .10
81 Kai Nurminen .07 .20
82 Jonas Esbjors .02 .10
83 Peter Strom .02 .10
84 Kari Takko .08 .25
85 Johan Forsander .08 .25
86 Jouni Loponen .02 .10
87 David Petrasek .02 .10
88 Daniel Johansson .07 .20
89 Fredrik Stillman .02 .10
90 Anatoly Fedotov .02 .10
91 Stefan Ornskog .02 .10
92 Stefan Falk .02 .10
93 Peter Ekelund .02 .10
94 Esa Keskinen .02 .10
95 Patrik Lundback .02 .10
96 Anders Huusko .02 .10
97 Magnus Svensson .02 .10
98 Alexei Salomatin .02 .10
99 Patrik Englund .02 .10
100 Ake Lilljebjorn .08 .25
101 Tomas Jonsson .02 .10
102 Torbjorn Johansson .02 .10
103 Hans Lodin .02 .10
104 Magnus Svensson .02 .10
105 Andreas Karlsson .20 .50
106 Joakim Lidgren .02 .10
107 Fredrik Jonsson .02 .10
108 Per-Erik Eklund .02 .10
109 Anders Carlsson .02 .10
110 Johan Witehall .02 .10
111 Jens Nielsen .02 .10
112 Niklas Eriksson .02 .10
113 Jonas Bergqvist .07 .20
114 Stefan Hellkvist .02 .10
115 Markus Akerblom .07 .20
116 Anders Lonn .02 .10
117 Jarmo Myllys .08 .25
118 Johan Finnstrom .07 .20
119 Sergei Bautin .02 .10
120 Jan Mertzig .07 .20
121 Osmo Soutokorva .02 .10
122 Roger Akerstrom .02 .10
123 Stefan Jonsson .07 .20
124 Stefan Nilsson .02 .10
125 Jonas Ronnqvist .08 .25
126 Joakim Backlund .02 .10
127 Robert Nordberg .02 .10
128 Mikael Lovgren .02 .10
129 Anders Burstrom .02 .10
130 Fredrik Johansson .02 .10
131 Mika Alatalo .20 .50
132 Fredrik Nilsson .02 .10
133 Roger Nordstrom .08 .25
134 Andrew Verner .08 .25
135 Marko Kiprusoff .08 .25
136 Kim Johnsson .20 .50
137 Magnus Nilsson .02 .10
138 Jesper Damgaard .02 .10
139 Marek Malik .07 .20
140 Mats Lusth .02 .10
141 Janne Ojanen .07 .20
142 Mikko Peltola .02 .10
143 Mathias Bosson .02 .10
144 Daniel Rydmark .02 .10
145 Patrik Sylvegard .02 .10
146 Juha Riihijarvi .07 .20
147 Fredrik Oberg .02 .10
148 Mikael Burakovsky .02 .10
149 Petter Ronnqvist .08 .25
150 Pierre Hedin .15 .40
151 Jan-Axel Alavaara .02 .10
152 Frantisek Kaberle .20 .50
153 Hans Jonsson .20 .50
154 Jonas Junkka .07 .20
155 Marcus Karlsson .02 .10
156 Kristian Gahn .08 .25
157 Magnus Wernblom .08 .25
158 Anders Soderberg .08 .25
159 Daniel Sedin 1.25 3.00
160 Henrik Sedin 1.25 3.00
161 Samuel Pahlsson .30 .75
162 Per Svartvadet .15 .40
163 Andreas Salomonsson .20 .50
164 Ravil Yakubov .02 .10
165 David Vyborny .20 .50
166 Magnus Lindqvist .08 .25
167 Anders Eldebrink .02 .10
168 Johan Norgren .02 .10
169 Christian Due-Boje .02 .10
170 Jonas Heed .02 .10
171 Josef Boumedienne .15 .40
172 Marko Virtanen .02 .10
173 Kyosti Karjalainen .02 .10
174 Jorgen Bemstrom .02 .10
175 Joakim Ericsson .02 .10
176 Jens Ohling .02 .10
177 Martin Hostak .02 .10
178 Lars Dahlstrom .02 .10
179 Niklas Brannstrom .02 .10
180 Mikko Makela .02 .10
181 Petr Korinek .07 .20
182 Joakim Persson .08 .25
183 Tobias Lilja .02 .10
184 Edvin Frylen .07 .20
185 Jakob Karlsson .07 .20
186 Johan Tornberg .02 .10
187 Patrik Hoglund .02 .10
188 Mattias Loof .02 .10
189 Mikael Pettersson .02 .10
190 Johan Molin .02 .10
191 Fredrik Eriksson .02 .10
192 Henrik Nordfeldt .02 .10
193 Jonas Olsson .02 .10
194 Roger Jonsson .02 .10
195 Roger Rosen .02 .10
196 Henric Bjorkman .02 .10
197 Harri Sillgren .02 .10
198 Paul Andersson-Everberg .02 .10
199 Tommy Soderstrom .20 .50
200 Stefan Nilsson .02 .10
201 Tomas Jonsson .02 .10
202 Jonas Bergqvist .07 .20
203 Christer Olsson .02 .10
204 Per Svartvadet .15 .40
205 Anders Huss .02 .10
206 Roger Johansson .02 .10
207 Stefan Ornskog .02 .10
208 Anders Eldebrink .02 .10
209 Niclas Havelid .20 .50
210 Charles Berglund .02 .10
211 Kai Nurminen .07 .20
212 Stefan Nilsson .02 .10
213 Per-Erik Eklund .02 .10
214 Janne Ojanen .07 .20
215 Per Svartvadet .15 .40
216 Michael Sundlov .08 .25
217 Roger Johansson .02 .10
218 Stefan Ornskog .02 .10
219 Kyosti Karjalainen .02 .10
220 Roger Rosen .02 .10
221 Jonas Bergqvist .07 .20
222 Esa Keskinen .02 .10
223 Christer Olsson .02 .10
224 Checklist .05
225 Checklist .05

1997-98 Swedish Collector's Choice Crash the Game

Mirroring the chase program first used in North America, these interactive cards allowed fans a chance to redeem them for specially foiled complete Crash sets. The cards were inserted 1:8 packs.

COMPLETE SET (30) 8.00 20.00
*PRIZE CARDS: .3X TO .8X BASIC INSERTS
C1 Patric Kjellberg .60 1.50
C2 Mikael Johansson .25 .60
C3 Daniel Tjarnqvist .40 1.00
C4 Christer Olsson .25 .60
C5 Ville Peltonen .60 1.50
C6 Kai Nurminen .40 1.00
C7 Stefan Nilsson .25 .60
C8 Jan Mertzig .25 .60
C9 Anders Carlsson .25 .60
C10 Jonas Bergqvist .25 .60
C11 Magnus Svensson .25 .60
C12 Janne Ojanen .40 1.00
C13 Marko Kiprusoff .60 1.50
C14 Juha Riihijarvi .25 .60
C15 Daniel Sedin 1.50 4.00
C16 Henrik Sedin 1.50 4.00
C17 Evgenij Davydov .25 .60
C18 Anders Huss .25 .60
C19 Jan Larsson .25 .60
C20 Roger Johansson .25 .60
C21 Jorgen Jonsson .40 1.00
C22 Kristian Huselius 1.25 3.00
C23 Stefan Ornskog .25 .60
C24 Anders Huusko .25 .60
C25 Esa Keskinen .25 .60
C26 Joakim Eriksson .25 .60
C27 Anders Eldebrink .25 .60
C28 Mikko Makela .25 .60
C29 Henric Bjorkman .25 .60
C30 Roger Rosen .25 .60

1997-98 Swedish Collector's Choice Select

This chase set features elite players from the past and present of the SEL. The cards were inserted 1:8 packs.

COMPLETE SET (15) 40.00 80.00
UD1 Peter Forsberg 12.00 30.00
UD2 Daniel Sedin 4.00 10.00
UD3 Nichlas Falk .75 2.00
UD4 Marko Jantunen .40 1.00
UD5 Ville Peltonen 1.25 3.00
UD6 Jorgen Jonsson .75 2.00
UD7 Roger Johansson .40 1.00
UD8 Stefan Ornskog .75 2.00
UD9 Henrik Sedin 4.80 10.00
UD10 Jonas Bergqvist .40 1.00
UD11 Tomas Jonsson .40 1.00
UD12 Stefan Nilsson .40 1.00
UD13 Janne Ojanen .40 1.00
UD14 Magnus Wernblom .40 1.00
UD15 Edvin Frylen .40 1.00
NNO Peter Forsberg Elite 20.00 50.00

1997-98 Swedish Collector's Choice Stick'Ums

These stickers were inserted 1:4 packs and feature top players of the SEL.

COMPLETE SET (15) 4.00 10.00
S1 Miikka Kiprusoff 1.25 3.00
S2 Marcus Nilsson .40 1.00
S3 Christer Olsson .08 .25
S4 Jorgen Jonsson .20 .50
S5 Fredrik Stillman .08 .25
S6 Per-Erik Eklund .20 .50
S7 Jarmo Myllys .20 .50
S8 Daniel Rydmark .08 .25
S9 Henric Bjorkman .08 .25
S10 Henrik Sedin 1.00 2.50
S11 Daniel Sedin 1.00 2.50
S12 Anders Huss .08 .25
S13 Patrik Carnback .08 .25
S14 Daniel Tjarnqvist .20 .50
S15 Jonas Bergqvist .20 .50

1998-99 Swedish UD Choice

This Upper Deck-produced issue features the players of the Swedish Elitserien. The design mimics that of the 1998-99 North American UD Choice set. It is noteworthy for featuring early cards of Daniel and Henrik Sedin, along with Johan Hedberg and Mattias Karlin. The final two cards in the listing are the first-ever memorabilia cards issued in Sweden. Both feature a pair of swatches from the jerseys of the Sedin Twins, but the second also is graced by the autograph of both players on the jersey swatches.

COMPLETE SET (225) 10.00 25.00
1 Jonas Forsberg .08 .25
2 Rikard Franzen .02 .10
3 Mathias Svedberg .02 .10
4 Dick Tarnstrom .20 .50
5 Jan Sandstrom .02 .10
6 Johan Silfwerplatz .02 .10
7 Henrik Tallinder .20 .50
8 Stefan Gustavson .02 .10
9 Kristian Gahn .20 .50
10 Bjorn Ahlstrom .02 .10
11 Peter Hammarstrom .02 .10
12 Anders Gozzi .02 .10
13 Fredrik Krekula .02 .10
14 Erik Norback .02 .10
15 Niklas Anger .20 .50
16 Mats Lindberg .02 .10
17 Jorgen Wikstrom .02 .10
18 Per-Anton Lundstrom .08 .25
19 Mattias Hedlund .02 .10
20 Jorgen Hermansson .02 .10
21 Fredrik Bergqvist .02 .10
22 Joakim Lidgren .02 .10
23 Robert Karlsson .02 .10
24 Christian Lechtaler .02 .10
25 Aleksandrs Beljavskis .02 .10
26 Jens Ohman .02 .10
27 Stefan Ohman .02 .10
28 Martin Wiita .02 .10
29 Johan Ramstedt .08 .25
30 Per Ledin .02 .10
31 Jukka Penttinen .02 .10
32 Aleksandrs Semjonovs .02 .10
33 Johan Holmqvist .60 1.50
34 Tommy Melkersson .02 .10
35 Marko Tuulola .02 .10
36 Johan Hansson .02 .10
37 Par Djoos .02 .10
38 Per Lofstrom .02 .10
39 Niclas Wallin .20 .50
40 Roger Kyro .02 .10
41 Ove Molin .02 .10
42 Stefan Lundqvist .02 .10
43 Peter Nylander .02 .10
44 Jan Larsson .02 .10
45 Teppo Kivela .02 .10
46 Tom Bissett .08 .25
47 Anders Huss .02 .10
48 Mikko Luovi .08 .25
49 Tommy Soderstrom .30 .75
50 Bjorn Nord .08 .25
51 Ronnie Pettersson .02 .10
52 Thomas Johansson .02 .10
53 Daniel Tjarnqvist .20 .50
54 Anders Myrvold .08 .25
55 Mikael Magnusson .02 .10
56 Mikael Johansson .02 .10
57 Nichlas Falk .08 .25
58 Mikael Hakanson .02 .10
59 Charles Berglund .08 .25
60 Lars-Goran Wiklander .02 .10
61 Per Eklund .07 .20
62 Jan Viktorsson .02 .10
63 Patrik Erickson .02 .10
64 Espen Knutsen .40 1.00
65 Jimmie Olvestad .20 .50
66 Mikael Sandberg .02 .10
67 Christer Olsson .02 .10
68 Petter Nilsson .02 .10
69 Magnus Johansson .02 .10
70 Ronnie Sundin .08 .25
71 Radek Hamr .02 .10
72 Stefan Larsson .02 .10
73 Mattias Nilimaa .02 .10
74 Linus Fagemo .02 .10
75 Marko Jantunen .02 .10
76 Patrik Carnback .02 .10
77 Peter Berndtsson .02 .10
78 Mikael Samuelsson .30 .75
79 Peter Strom .02 .10
80 Par Edlund .02 .10
81 Henrik Nilsson .20 .50
82 Jonas Johnsson .02 .10
83 Kimmo Lecklin .02 .10
84 Roger Johansson .02 .10
85 Sergei Fokin .02 .10
86 Greger Artursson .02 .10
87 Jonas Elofsson .20 .50
88 Peter Jakobsson .02 .10
89 Dimitri Erofeev .02 .10
90 Patrik Zetterberg .02 .10
91 Niklas Sjokvist .02 .10
92 Trond Magnussen .02 .10
93 Peter Hagstrom .02 .10
94 Pelle Prestberg .02 .10
95 Mathias Johansson .08 .25
96 Michael Holmqvist .20 .50
97 Clas Eriksson .02 .10
98 Kristian Huselius 1.00 2.50
99 Jorgen Jonsson .20 .50
100 Kari Takko .08 .25
101 David Petrasek .02 .10
102 Daniel Johansson .20 .50
103 Per Gustafsson .02 .10
104 Fredrik Stillman .02 .10
105 Nicklas Rahm .02 .10
106 Mikael Lindman .02 .10
107 Jerry Persson .02 .10
108 Esa Keskinen .02 .10
109 Peter Ekelund .02 .10
110 Antti Tormanen .08 .25
111 Marcus Kristoffersson .20 .50
112 Anders Huusko .02 .10
113 Erik Huusko .02 .10
114 Johan Lindbom .08 .25
115 Jarkko Varvio .02 .10
116 Ulf Dahlen .08 .25
117 Johan Hedberg .40 1.00
118 Jan Huokko .02 .10
119 Torbjorn Johansson .02 .10
120 Hans Lodin .02 .10
121 Nicklas Nordqvist .02 .10
122 Stefan Bergqvist .02 .10
123 Magnus Svensson .02 .10
124 Andreas Karlsson .20 .50
125 Per-Erik Eklund .08 .25
126 Anders Carlsson .02 .10
127 Niklas Eriksson .02 .10
128 Stefan Hellkvist .02 .10
129 Jens Nielsen .02 .10
130 Anders Lonn .02 .10
131 Markus Akerblom .02 .10
132 Mikael Karlberg .02 .10
133 Jarmo Myllys .08 .25
134 Stefan Jonsson .02 .10
135 Osmo Soutokorva .02 .10
136 Johan Finnstrom .02 .10
137 Roger Akerstrom .08 .25
138 Igor Matushkin .02 .10
139 Jonas Ronnqvist .20 .50
140 Thomas Sjogren .02 .10
141 Tomas Berglund .02 .10
142 Mikael Lovgren .02 .10
143 Anders Burstrom .02 .10
144 Jorgen Bemstrom .02 .10
145 Martin Hostak .02 .10
146 Bert-Olav Karlsson .02 .10
147 Lars Edstrom .02 .10
148 Jiri Kucera .02 .10
149 Andrew Verner .08 .25
150 Kim Johnsson .08 .25
151 Kari Harila .02 .10
152 Niclas Havelid .40 1.00
153 Jesper Damgaard .02 .10
154 Johan Tornberg .02 .10
155 Mats Lusth .02 .10
156 Jan Hammar .02 .10
157 Marcus Magnertoft .02 .10
158 Marcus Thuresson .08 .25
159 Magnus Nilsson .02 .10
160 Mikael Lindholm .08 .25
161 Patrik Sylvegard .02 .10
162 Juha Riihijarvi .08 .25
163 Jesper Mattsson .08 .25
164 Niklas Sundblad .02 .10
165 Toivo Suursoo .02 .10
166 Petter Ronnquist .08 .25
167 Pierre Hedin .20 .50
168 Per Hallberg .02 .10
169 Jan-Axel Alavaara .02 .10
170 Hans Jonsson .20 .50
171 Lars Jansson .02 .10
172 Frantisek Kaberle .20 .50
173 Andreas Salomonsson .08 .25
174 Magnus Wernblom .08 .25
175 Mikael Pettersson .02 .10
176 Per Svartvadet .20 .50
177 Daniel Sedin .75 2.00
178 Henrik Sedin .75 2.00
179 Jan Alinc .02 .10
180 Samuel Pahlsson .40 1.00
181 Anders Soderberg .20 .50
182 Magnus Eriksson .02 .10
183 Andrei Lulin .02 .10
184 Jakob Karlsson .08 .25
185 Patrik Hoglund .02 .10
186 Joakim Lundberg .02 .10
187 Arto Blomsten .02 .10
188 Mattias Loof .02 .10
189 Mikael Pettersson .02 .10
190 Joakim Backlund .02 .10
191 Daniel Rydmark .02 .10
192 Johan Molin .02 .10
193 Paul Andersson-Everberg .02 .10
194 Henrik Nordfeldt .02 .10
195 Jonas Olsson .02 .10
196 Fredrik Oberg .02 .10
197 Roger Rosen .02 .10
198 Roland Stoltz .02 .10
199 Lars Bjorn .02 .10
200 Ulf Sterner .02 .10
201 Leif Holmqvist .08 .25
202 Hans Mild .02 .10
203 Bert-Ola Nordlander .02 .10
204 Eilert Maatta .02 .10
205 Ronald Pettersson .02 .10
206 Tord Lundstrom .02 .10
207 Lennart Svedberg .08 .25
208 Roland Stoltz .02 .10
209 Eilert Maatta .02 .10
210 Lennart Svedberg .08 .25
211 Tord Lundstrom .02 .10
212 Leif Holmqvist .08 .25
213 Magnus Nilsson .20 .50
214 Mikael Holmqvist .20 .50
215 Mattias Karlin .20 .50
216 Pierre Hedin .20 .50
217 Henrik Petre .20 .50
218 Johan Forsander .08 .25
219 Daniel Sedin .75 2.00
220 Henrik Sedin .75 2.00
221 Markus Nilsson .40 1.00
222 Checklist .02 .10
223 Checklist .02 .10
224 Checklist .02 .10
225 Checklist .02 .10
GJ1 D.Sedin 20.00 50.00
H.Sedin
GJA1 D.Sedin 75.00 200.00
H.Sedin

1998-99 Swedish UD Choice Day in the Life

This insert set captures moments in the regular lives of the SEL's biggest stars.

COMPLETE SET (10) 4.00 10.00
1 Rikard Franzen .40 1.00
2 Par Djoos .40 1.00
3 Tommy Soderstrom .75 2.00
4 Pelle Prestberg .40 1.00
5 Esa Keskinen .40 1.00
6 Johan Hedberg .75 2.00
7 Jarmo Myllys .75 2.00
8 Marcus Thuresson .40 1.00
9 Samuel Pahlsson 1.00 2.50
10 Christer Olsson .40 1.00

1999-00 Swedish Upper Deck

This 220-card set captures the heroes of Sweden's Elitserien. The cards were produced by Upper Deck and mirror the UD MVP set produced earlier in the year for NHL fans.

COMPLETE SET (220) 10.00 25.00
1 Mattias Pettersson .07 .20
2 Rikard Franzen .08 .25

3 Mattias Svedberg .07 .20
4 Dick Tarnstrom .30 .75
5 Jan Sandstrom .07 .20
6 Anders Myrvold .08 .25
7 Henrik Tallinder .20 .50
8 Per-Anton Lundstrom .07 .20
9 Kristian Gahn .07 .20
10 BjÃ¶rn Ahlstrom .07 .20
11 Stefan Gustavsson .07 .20
12 Jarkko Varvio .08 .25
13 Fredrik Krekula .07 .20
14 Erik Norback .07 .20
15 Niklas Anger .15 .40
16 Mats Lindberg .07 .20
17 Erik Andersson .07 .20
18 Johan Holmqvist .60 1.50
19 Tommy Sjodin .08 .25
20 Marko Tuulola .07 .20
21 Henrik Petre .15 .40
22 Par Djoos .08 .25
23 Niclas Wallin .40 1.00
24 Roger Kyro .07 .20
25 Ove Molin .07 .20
26 Stefan Lundqvist .07 .20
27 Goran Hermansson .07 .20
28 Jan Larsson .07 .20
29 Daniel RudslÃ¤tt .07 .20
30 Tom Bisset .15 .40
31 Kenneth Bergqvist .07 .20
32 Mikko Luovi .07 .20
33 Johan Lindstrom .07 .20
34 Daniel Olsson .07 .20
35 Tommy Soderstrom .20 .50
36 Bjorn Nord .15 .40
37 Niklas Kronwall 1.00 2.50
38 Thomas Johansson .07 .20
39 Daniel Tjarnqvist .20 .50
40 Mikael Magnusson .07 .20
41 Mikael Johansson .07 .20
42 Niklas Falk .15 .40
43 Mikael Hakansson .15 .40
44 Charles Berglund .08 .25
45 Lars-Goran Wiklander .07 .20
46 Per Eklund .08 .25
47 Kristofer Johansson .07 .20
48 Mathias Tjarnqvist .15 .40
49 Espen Knutsen .40 1.00
50 Jimmie Olvestad .20 .50
51 Mikko Konttila .07 .20
52 Vesa Toskala .75 2.00
53 Roger Johansson .07 .20
54 Sergei Fokin .07 .20
55 Greger Artursson .07 .20
56 Jonas Elofsson .15 .40
57 Radek Hamr .07 .20
58 Henrik Rehnberg .07 .20
59 Peter Nordstrom .08 .25
60 Niklas Sjokvist .07 .20
61 Trond Magnussen .07 .20
62 Peter Hagstrom .07 .20
63 Pelle Prestberg .07 .20
64 Mathias Johansson .15 .40
65 Tore Vikingstad .07 .20
66 Clas Eriksson .07 .20
67 Marko Jantunen .07 .20
68 Christian Berglund .20 .50
69 Mario Brunetta .15 .40
70 Petter Nilsson .07 .20
71 Magnus Johansson .07 .20
72 Ronnie Sundin .15 .40
73 Stefan Larsson .07 .20
74 Christian Backman .15 .40
75 Par Edlund .08 .25
76 Reid Simonton .07 .20
77 Kristian Huselius .40 1.00
78 Pasi Saarela .07 .20
79 Juha Ikonen .07 .20
80 Linus Fagemo .07 .20
81 Patrik Carnback .08 .25
82 Peter Berndtsson .07 .20
83 Peter Strom .07 .20
84 Henrik Nilsson .07 .20
85 Jonas Johnsson .07 .20
86 Kari Takko .15 .40
87 David Petrasek .07 .20
88 Joacim Esbjors .07 .20
89 Per Gustafsson .08 .25
90 Jani Nikko .07 .20
91 Mikael Lindman .07 .20
92 Oleg Belov .08 .25
93 Jonas Esbjors .07 .20
94 Jonas Forsander .15 .40
95 Peter Ekelund .07 .20
96 Antti Tormanen .08 .25
97 Anders Lonn .07 .20
98 Gabriel Karlsson .07 .20
99 Johan Hult .07 .20
100 Mattias Remstam .07 .20
101 Daniel Wallin .07 .20
102 Johan Lindbom .07 .20
103 Reinhard Divis .40 1.00
104 Jan Huokko .07 .20
105 Torbjorn Johansson .07 .20
106 Per Lundell .07 .20
107 David Ytfeldt .07 .20
108 Stefan Bergkvist .07 .20
109 Patrik Allvin .07 .20
110 Niklas Persson .07 .20
111 Martin Jansson .07 .20
112 Anders Carlsson .07 .20
113 Niklas Eriksson .07 .20
114 Stefan Hellkvist .07 .20
115 Jens Nielsen .07 .20
116 Morten Green .07 .20
117 Markus Akerblom .07 .20
118 Mikael Karlberg .07 .20
119 Mattias Elm .07 .20
120 Edvin Frylen .07 .20
121 Martin Knold .07 .20
122 Erkki Saramaa .07 .20
123 Nicklas Nordqvist .07 .20
124 Jesper Andersson .07 .20
125 Henrik Andersson .07 .20
126 Henrik Nordfeldt .07 .20
127 Ulf Soderstrom .07 .20
128 Ragnar Karlsson .07 .20
129 Fredrik Elmvall .07 .20
130 Peter Casparsson .07 .20
131 Dennis Ejdeholm .07 .20
132 Mattias Nilimaa .07 .20
133 Mike Helber .07 .20
134 Johan Bylow .07 .20
135 Jarmo Myllys .15 .40
136 Vaclav Burda .07 .20
137 Osmo Soutukorva .07 .20
138 Johan Finnstrom .08 .25
139 Roger Akerstrom .07 .20
140 Torbjorn Lindberg .07 .20
141 Jonas Ronnqvist .40 1.00
142 Jonathan Hedstrom .15 .40
143 Tomas Berglund .07 .20
144 Mikael Lovgren .07 .20
145 Anders Burstrom .07 .20
146 JÃ¶rgen Bemstrom .07 .20
147 Martin Hostak .07 .20
148 Hans Huczkowski .07 .20
149 Lars Edstrom .07 .20
150 Jiri Kucera .08 .25
151 Andreas Hadelov .07 .20
152 Johan Tornberg .07 .20
153 Mats Lusth .07 .20
154 Andreas Lilja .07 .20
155 Peter Jakobsson .07 .20
156 Henrik Malmstrom .07 .20
157 Tomas Sandstrom .20 .50
158 Kim Staal .07 .20
159 Jan Hammar .07 .20
160 Marcus Magnertoft .07 .20
161 Marcus Thuresson .07 .20
162 Magnus Nilsson .07 .20
163 Mikael Lindholm .07 .20
164 Juha Riihijarvi .07 .20
165 Jesper Mattsson .08 .25
166 Niklas Sundblad .08 .25
167 Toivo Suursoo .07 .20
168 Tobias Lundstrom .07 .20
169 Pierre Hedin .15 .40
170 Per Hallberg .07 .20
171 Jan-Axel Alavaara .07 .20
172 Jesper Duus .07 .20
173 Francois Bouchard .07 .20
174 Andreas Pihl .07 .20
175 Andreas Salomonsson .30 .75
176 Magnus Wernblom .07 .20
177 Mikael Pettersson .07 .20
178 Mattias Weinhandl .30 .75
179 Daniel Sedin .60 1.50
180 Henrik Sedin .60 1.50
181 Tommy Pettersson .07 .20
182 Samuel Pahlsson .40 1.00
183 Anders Soderberg .15 .40
184 Mattias Karlin .15 .40
185 Magnus Eriksson .07 .20
186 Andrei Lulin .07 .20
187 Denis Chervyakov .07 .20
188 Dimitri Chikin .07 .20
189 Joakim Lundberg .07 .20
190 Henric Bjorkman .07 .20
191 Roger Jonsson .07 .20
192 Peter Nylander .07 .20
193 Mikael Pettersson .07 .20
194 Patrik Zetterberg .07 .20
195 Daniel Rydmark .08 .25
196 Johan Molin .07 .20
197 Paul Andersson-Everberg .07 .20
198 Jonas Finn-Olsson .07 .20
199 Fredrik Oberg .07 .20
200 Roger Rosen .07 .20
201 Henrik Tallinder .15 .40
202 Kenneth Bergqvist .07 .20
203 Mathias Tjarnqvist .15 .40
204 Jimmie Olvestad .30 .75
205 Jonas Elofsson .15 .40
206 Christian Berglund .30 .75
207 Johan Forsander .15 .40
208 David Ytfeldt .07 .20
209 Niklas Persson .07 .20
210 Henrik Andersson .07 .20
211 Jonathan HedstrÃ¶m .20 .50
212 Kim Staal .07 .20
213 Pierre Hedin .15 .40
214 Mattias Weinhandl .30 .75
215 Rikard Ekstrom .07 .20
216 Christian Backman .20 .50
217 Daniel Sedin CL .20 .50
218 Peter Ekelund CL .07 .20
219 Tommy Soderstrom CL .15 .40
220 Henrik Sedin CL .20 .50

1999-00 Swedish Upper Deck Hands of Gold

This set, featuring the top snipers in the Elitserien, was randomly inserted into packs of 1999-2000 UD SHL.

COMPLETE SET (15) 12.00 30.00
H1 Mats Lindberg .75 2.00
H2 Tom Bissett 1.25 3.00
H3 Jan Larsson .75 2.00
H4 Per Eklund 1.25 3.00
H5 Thomas Johansson .75 2.00
H6 Mathias Johansson .75 2.00
H7 Peter Ekelund .75 2.00
H8 Anders Carlsson .75 2.00
H9 Ulf Soderstrom .75 2.00
H10 Jonas Ronnqvist 1.25 3.00
H11 Marcus Thuresson 1.25 3.00
H12 Daniel Sedin 2.00 5.00
H13 Henrik Sedin 2.00 5.00
H14 Daniel Rydmark .75 2.00
H15 Kristian Huselius 2.00 5.00

1999-00 Swedish Upper Deck Lasting Impressions

This insert set features a number of Sweden's top young stars and veterans.

COMPLETE SET (12) 12.00 30.00
1 Rikard Franzen 1.25 3.00
2 Par Djoos 1.25 3.00
3 Charles Berglund 1.25 3.00
4 Roger Johansson 1.25 3.00
5 Kari Takko 1.50 4.00
6 Anders Carlsson 1.25 3.00
7 Mike Helber 1.25 3.00
8 Jiri Kucera 1.25 3.00
9 Juha Riihijarvi 1.25 3.00
10 Samuel Pahlsson 2.00 5.00
11 Magnus Eriksson 1.25 3.00
12 Patrik Carnback 1.25 3.00

1999-00 Swedish Upper Deck PowerDeck

Like the NHL versions that preceded them, these small CD-ROMs offer video action, still shots and statistics when loaded onto your home PC.

COMPLETE SET (2) 3.00 8.00
1 SHL 2.00 5.00
2 D.Sedin 2.00 5.00
H.Sedin

1999-00 Swedish Upper Deck SHL Signatures

These sweet inserts feature a genuine autograph from a star of the Swedish Elitserien.

COMPLETE SET (20) 70.00 150.00
1 Stefan Gustavsson 2.00 5.00
2 Rikard Franzen 2.00 5.00
3 Johan Holmqvist 6.00 12.00
4 Espen Knutsen 6.00 12.00
5 Peter Nordstrom 2.00 5.00
6 Marko Jantunen 2.00 5.00
7 Kristian Huselius 8.00 20.00
8 Jonas Johnsson 2.00 5.00
9 Per Gustafsson 2.00 5.00
10 Johan Lindbom 4.00 10.00
11 Stefan Hellkvist 2.00 5.00
12 Ulf Soderstrom 2.00 5.00
13 Jarmo Myllys 4.00 10.00
14 Johan Tornberg 2.00 5.00
15 Daniel Sedin 10.00 20.00
16 Henrik Sedin 10.00 20.00
17 Magnus Eriksson 2.00 5.00
18 Tommy Sjodin 2.00 5.00
19 Tommy Soderstrom 4.00 10.00
20 Tomas Sandstrom 4.00 10.00

1999-00 Swedish Upper Deck Snapshots

This insert set features more of the top performers of the SHL.

COMPLETE SET (15) 12.00 30.00
1 Anders Myrvold .75 2.00
2 Johan Holmqvist 1.25 3.00
3 Ove Molin .40 1.00
4 Tommy Soderstrom 1.25 3.00
5 Espen Knutsen 1.50 4.00
6 Peter Nordstrom .40 1.00
7 Per Gustafsson .40 1.00
8 Stefan Bergkvist .40 1.00
9 Mattias Elm .40 1.00
10 Jarmo Myllys 1.50 4.00
11 Tomas Sandstrom 1.50 4.00
12 Magnus Wernblom .40 1.00
13 Mattias Weinhandl 1.50 4.00
14 Denis Chervyakov .40 1.00
15 Kristian Huselius 4.00 10.00

2000-01 Swedish Upper Deck

This set was produced by Upper Deck for distribution in the Swedish market and features the top players of the SHL. The design for the set mimics the one used for 2000-01 UD MVP in North America.

COMPLETE SET (220) 10.00 25.00
1 Tim Thomas .60 1.50
2 Per-Anton Lundstrom .15 .40
3 Dick Tarnstrom .20 .50
4 Rikard Franzen .04 .10
5 Rikard Ekstrom .04 .10
6 Jan Sandstrom .04 .10
7 Stefan Gustavson .04 .10
8 Anders Gozzi .04 .10
9 Stefan Hellkvist .04 .10
10 Mats Lindberg .04 .10
11 Bjorn Danielsson .04 .10
12 Erik Andersson .04 .10
13 Bjorn Ahlstrom .04 .10
14 Kristian Gahn .04 .10
15 Petter Sandstrom .04 .10
16 Mattias Hedlund .04 .10
17 Tommi Hamalainen .04 .10
18 Jorgen Hermansson .04 .10
19 Jesper Jager .04 .10
20 Christian Lechtaler .04 .10
21 Aleksanders Beliavskis .04 .10
22 Johan Ramstedt .04 .10
23 Lars Briell .04 .10
24 Johan Boman .04 .10
25 Aleksanders Semjonovs .04 .10
26 Mathias Bosson .04 .10
27 Niko Halttunen .04 .10
28 Fredrik Nasvall .04 .10
29 Johan Asplund .15 .40
30 Henrik Petre .04 .10
31 Par Djoos .04 .10
32 Tommy Sjodin .04 .10
33 Christer Olsson .04 .10
34 Marko Tuulola .04 .10
35 Johan Molin .04 .10
36 Tony Martensson .04 .10
37 Tom Bissett .15 .40
38 Roger Kyro .04 .10
39 Ove Molin .04 .10
40 Mikko Luovi .04 .10
41 Daniel Rudslatt .04 .10
42 Kenneth Bergqvist .04 .10
43 Jan Larsson .04 .10
44 Mikael Tellqvist .75 2.00
45 Niklas Kronwall 1.00 2.50
46 Francois Bouchard .04 .10
47 Edvin Frylen .04 .10
48 Mikael Magnusson .04 .10
49 Daniel Tjarnqvist .20 .50
50 Charles Berglund .04 .10
51 Kristofer Ottosson .04 .10
52 Kyosti Karjalainen .04 .10
53 Nichlas Falk .04 .10
54 Mathias Tjarnqvist .15 .40
55 Jimmie Olvestad .20 .50
56 Johan Garpenlov .04 .10
57 Andreas Salomonsson .20 .50
58 Mikael Johansson .04 .10
59 Vladimir Orszagh .15 .40
60 Henrik Lundqvist 8.00 20.00
61 Magnus Johansson .04 .10
62 Christian Backman .04 .10
63 Nicklas Rahm .04 .10
64 Ronnie Sundin .04 .10
65 Par Edlund .04 .10
66 Magnus Kahnberg .04 .10
67 Pelle Prestberg .04 .10
68 Patrik Carnback .04 .10
69 Juha Ikonen .04 .10
70 Jari Tolsa .04 .10
71 Kristian Huselius .40 1.00
72 Peter Strom .04 .10
73 Henrik Nilsson .04 .10
74 Jonas Johnsson .04 .10
75 Mikael Andersson .04 .10
76 Magnus Eriksson .04 .10
77 Sergei Fokin .04 .10
78 Jonas Frogren .04 .10
79 Thomas Rhodin .04 .10
80 Greger Artursson .04 .10
81 Radek Hamr .04 .10
82 Roger Johansson .04 .10
83 Marko Jantunen .04 .10
84 Ulf Soderstrom .04 .10
85 Christian Berglund .04 .10
86 Mathias Johansson .04 .10
87 Trond Magnussen .04 .10
88 Peter Nordstrom .15 .40
89 Clas Eriksson .04 .10
90 Jorgen Jonsson .04 .10
91 Marcel Jenni .04 .10
92 Stefan Liv .60 1.50
93 Joacim Esbjors .04 .10
94 Per Gustafsson .04 .10
95 Fredrik Stillman .04 .10
96 Mikael Lindman .04 .10
97 Peter Ottosson .04 .10
98 Oleg Belov .04 .10
99 Peter Ekelund .04 .10
100 Johan Hult .04 .10
101 Johan Lindbom .04 .10
102 Jonas Esbjors .04 .10
103 Johan Forsander .04 .10
104 Mattias Remstam .04 .10
105 Fredrik Oberg .04 .10
106 Reinhard Divis .40 1.00
107 Magnus Svensson .04 .10
108 Jan Huokko .04 .10
109 Stefan Bergkvist .04 .10
110 Lars Jonsson .20 .50
111 Per Lofstrom .04 .10
112 Jens Nielsen .04 .10
113 Niklas Eriksson .04 .10
114 Daniel Widing .04 .10
115 Niklas Persson .04 .10
116 Henrik Nordfeldt .04 .10
117 Tore Vikingstad .15 .40
118 Mikael Karlberg .04 .10
119 Robert Burakovsky .04 .10
120 Jarmo Myllys .20 .50
121 Torbjorn Lindberg .04 .10
122 Petter Nilsson .04 .10
123 Osmo Soutukorva .04 .10
124 Roger Akerstrom .04 .10
125 Johan Finnstrom .04 .10
126 Jiri Kucera .04 .10
127 Jonathan Hedstrom .20 .50
128 Tomas Berglund .04 .10
129 Mikael Renberg .20 .50
130 Anders Burstrom .04 .10
131 Hans Huczkowski .04 .10
132 Martin Hostak .04 .10
133 Lars Edstrom .04 .10
134 Sami Mettovaara .04 .10
135 Andreas Hadelov .04 .10
136 David Petrasek .04 .10
137 Peter Jakobsson .04 .10
138 Joakim Lundberg .04 .10
139 Christian Due-Boje .04 .10
140 Johan Tornberg .04 .10
141 Henrik Malmstrom .04 .10
142 Marcus Thuresson .04 .10
143 Daniel Rydmark .04 .10
144 Juha Riihijarvi .04 .10
145 Jesper Mattsson .04 .10
146 Fredrik Lindquist .04 .10
147 Tomas Sandstrom .04 .10
148 Kim Staal .04 .10
149 Jan Hammar .04 .10
150 Tobias Lundstrom .04 .10
151 Andreas Pihl .04 .10
152 Pierre Hedin .04 .10
153 Jan-Axel Alavaara .04 .10
154 Lars Jansson .04 .10
155 Per Hallberg .04 .10
156 Jesper Duus .04 .10
157 Magnus Wernblom .04 .10
158 Anders Soderberg .15 .40
159 Tommy Pettersson .04 .10
160 Mattias Weinhandl .40 1.00
161 Peter Hogardh .04 .10
162 Patrik Wallenberg .04 .10
163 Jorgen Bemstrom .04 .10
164 Stefan Ohman .04 .10
165 Boo Ahl .15 .40
166 Pasi Petrilainen .15 .40
167 Stefan Klockare .04 .10
168 Daniel Casselstahl .04 .10
169 Marcus Karlsson .04 .10
170 Robert Carlsson .04 .10
171 Per Hallin .04 .10
172 Nik Zupancic .04 .10
173 Timo Peltomaa .04 .10
174 Linus Fagemo .04 .10
175 Henrik Zetterberg ERC 4.00 10.00
176 Mikael Lind .04 .10
177 Anders Huss .04 .10
178 Markus Matthiasson .04 .10
179 Stefan Hellkvist SS .04 .10
180 Kristian Gahn SS .04 .10
181 Bjorn Ahlstrom SS .04 .10
182 Aleksanders Beliavskis SS .04 .10
183 Tom Bissett SS .15 .40
184 Tommy Sjodin SS .04 .10
185 Ove Molin SS .04 .10
186 Mikael Tellqvist SS .75 2.00
187 Mikael Johansson SS .04 .10
188 Vladimir Orszagh SS .15 .40
189 Johan Garpenlov SS .04 .10
190 Christian Berglund SS .04 .10
191 Jorgen Jonsson SS .04 .10
192 Radek Hamr SS .04 .10
193 Kristian Huselius SS .40 1.00
194 Mikael Andersson SS .04 .10
195 Patrik Carnback SS .04 .10
196 Per Gustafsson SS .04 .10
197 Johan Lindbom SS .04 .10
198 Oleg Belov SS .04 .10
199 Robert Burakovsky SS .04 .10
200 Mikael Renberg SS .20 .50
201 Petter Nilsson SS .04 .10
202 Jarmo Myllys SS .20 .50
203 Tomas Sandstrom SS .15 .40
204 Marcus Thuresson SS .04 .10
205 Fredrik Lindquist SS .04 .10
206 Magnus Wernblom SS .04 .10
207 Mattias Weinhandl SS .20 .50
208 Henrik Zetterberg SS 4.00 10.00
209 Mats Lindberg CL .04 .10
210 Jorgen Hermansson CL .04 .10
211 Par Djoos CL .04 .10
212 Jimmie Olvestad CL .15 .40
213 Christian Backman CL .04 .10
214 Radek Hamr CL .04 .10
215 Peter Ekelund CL .04 .10
216 Lars Jonsson CL .20 .50
217 Mikael Renberg CL .20 .50
218 Fredrik Lindquist CL .04 .10
219 Mattias Weinhandl CL .20 .50
220 Marcus Karlsson CL .04 .10

2000-01 Swedish Upper Deck Game Jerseys

This pair of memorabilia cards featuring Sweden's top young prospects were randomly inserted in packs at a rate of 1:216.

COMPLETE SET (2) 40.00 50.00
DS Daniel Sedin 20.00 30.00
HS Henrik Sedin 20.00 30.00

2000-01 Swedish Upper Deck Masked Men

This set features the top goaltenders in the Swedish Elitserien. The cards were randomly inserted at a rate of 1:24 packs.

COMPLETE SET (7) 20.00 40.00
M1 Tim Thomas 3.00 8.00
M2 Mikael Tellqvist 6.00 15.00
M3 Magnus Eriksson 2.50 6.00
M4 Reinhard Divis 4.00 10.00
M5 Jarmo Myllys 2.50 6.00
M6 Andreas Hadelov 2.00 5.00
M7 Boo Ahl 2.00 5.00

2000-01 Swedish Upper Deck SHL Excellence

This set honors two players on the same team who achieved excellence in the SHL. The cards were inserted 1:24 packs.

COMPLETE SET (5) 15.00 30.00
S1 V.Orszagh 2.00 5.00
J.Garpenlov
S2 C.Berglund 2.00 5.00
J.Jonsson
S3 P.Carnback 4.00 10.00
K.Huselius
S4 M.Renberg 2.50 6.00
J.Myllys
S5 M.Weinhandl 3.00 8.00
M.Wernblom

2000-01 Swedish Upper Deck SHL Signatures

This set of signed cards featuring the top stars of the Swedish Elite League were inserted 1:17 packs. The cards ape the design used earlier in the year in Upper Deck's MVP Pro Sign issue.

COMPLETE SET (42) 225.00 450.00
AB Alexander Beliavski 4.00 10.00
AG Anders Gozzi 4.00 10.00
AH Andreas Hadelov 4.00 10.00
AS Alexander Semjonovs 4.00 10.00
BA Boo Ahl 4.00 10.00
CB Christian Backman 4.00 10.00
CH Christian Berglund 4.00 10.00
DR Daniel Rydmark 4.00 10.00
FL Fredrik Lindquist 4.00 10.00
GA Greger Artursson 4.00 10.00
HZ Henrik Zetterberg 30.00 60.00
JE Jonas Esbjors 4.00 10.00
JG Johan Garpenlov 4.00 10.00
JH Jorgen Hermansson 4.00 10.00
JJ Jorgen Jonsson 4.00 10.00
JL Jan Larsson 4.00 10.00
JN Jens Nielsen 4.00 10.00
JO Jonathan Hedstrom 8.00 20.00
KG Kristian Gahn 4.00 10.00
KH Kristian Huselius 12.50 30.00
MA Mikael Andersson 4.00 10.00
ME Mikael Tellqvist 12.50 30.00
MH Martin Hostak 4.00 10.00
MI Mattias Weinhandl 8.00 20.00
MJ Mikael Johansson 4.00 10.00
ML Mats Lindberg 4.00 10.00
MN Mikael Renberg 8.00 20.00
MR Mattias Remstam 4.00 10.00
MS Magnus Svensson 4.00 10.00
MT Marcus Thuresson 4.00 10.00
MW Magnus Wernblom 4.00 10.00
NK Niklas Kronwall 20.00 50.00
OB Oleg Belov 4.00 10.00
OM Ove Molin 4.00 10.00
PC Patrik Carnback 4.00 10.00
PD Par Djoos 4.00 10.00
PN Petter Nilsson 4.00 10.00
RD Reinhard Divis 10.00 25.00
RJ Roger Johansson 4.00 10.00
SH Stefan Hellkvist 4.00 10.00
TB Tom Bissett 4.00 10.00
TL Tobias Lundstrom 4.00 10.00

2000-01 Swedish Upper Deck Top Draws

This set highlights the most popular players in the SHL. Singles were inserted 1:8 packs.

COMPLETE SET (11) 7.50 15.00
T1 Bjorn Ahlstrom .40 1.00
T2 Ove Molin .40 1.00
T3 Mikael Tellqvist 2.00 5.00
T4 Patrik Carnback .40 1.00
T5 Roger Johansson .40 1.00
T6 Oleg Belov .40 1.00
T7 Jens Nielsen .40 1.00
T8 Jonathan Hedstrom .40 1.00
T9 Fredrik Lindquist .40 1.00
T10 Mattias Weinhandl .75 2.00
T11 Anders Huss .40 1.00

2000-01 Swedish Upper Deck Top Playmakers

This insert set honors athletes who consistently top the SHL scoring charts. Cards were inserted at a rate of 1:24 packs.

COMPLETE SET (8) 15.00 30.00
P1 Mats Lindberg 1.50 4.00
P2 Jan Larsson 1.50 4.00
P3 Mikael Johansson 1.50 4.00
P4 Jonas Johnsson 1.50 4.00
P5 Jorgen Jonsson 1.50 4.00
P6 Martin Hostak 1.50 4.00
P7 Juha Riihijarvi 1.50 4.00
P8 Mattias Weinhandl 2.50 6.00

2001-02 Swedish Alfabilder

COMPLETE SET (18) 10.00 25.00
1 Sven Tumba Johansson .40 1.00
2 Roland Rolle Stoltz .40 1.00
3 Eilert Mattaa .40 1.00
4 Lennart Klimpen Haggroth .40 1.00
5 Nisse Nilsson .40 1.00
6 Ulf Sterner .40 1.00
7 Leif Honken Holmqvist .75 2.00
8 Tord Lundstrom .40 1.00
9 Borje Salming 2.00 5.00
10 Anders Hedberg 1.25 3.00
11 Anders Kallur .75 2.00
12 Stefan Persson .75 2.00
13 Goran Hogosta .40 1.00
14 Bengt-Ake Gustavsson .40 1.00
15 Mats Naslund 1.25 3.00
16 Kent Nilsson 1.25 3.00
17 Hakan Loob 1.25 3.00
18 Peter Lindmark .75 2.00

2001-02 Swedish Brynas Tigers

This set features the Tigers of the Swedish Elite League. The set is postcard-styled and sized, with a posed photo on the front, and a b/w head shot and brief stats on the back.

COMPLETE SET (27) 10.00 25.00
1 Adam Andersson .40 1.00
2 Johan Asplund .75 2.00
3 Kenneth Bergqvist .40 1.00
4 Tom Bissett .60 1.50
5 Bjorn Danielsson .40 1.00
6 Par Djoos .40 1.00
7 Jonas Floberg .40 1.00
8 Kristoffer Jobs .40 1.00
9 Daniel Johansson .40 1.00
10 Roger Kyro .40 1.00
11 Jan Larsson .40 1.00
12 Mikko Luovi .40 1.00
13 Per Mars .40 1.00
14 Tony Martensson .40 1.00
15 Roger Melin .40 1.00
16 Ove Molin .40 1.00
17 Christer Olsson .40 1.00
18 Jussi Pekkala .40 1.00
19 Gunnar Persson .40 1.00
20 Henrik Petre .40 1.00
21 Mattias Pettersson .40 1.00
22 Henrik Rehnberg .40 1.00
23 Daniel Rudslatt .40 1.00
24 Tommy Sjodin .40 1.00
25 Jonas Soling .40 1.00
26 Daniel Wagstrom .40 1.00
27 Team Card .40 1.00

2002-03 Swedish Malmo Red Hawks

1 Joakim Lundberg .40 1.00
2 Johan Bjork .40 1.00
3 Peter Hasselbald .40 1.00
4 Henrik Malmstrom .40 1.00
5 Jan Hammer .40 1.00
6 Marcus Magnertoft .40 1.00
7 Marcus Thuresson .40 1.00
8 Frans Nielsen .40 1.00
9 Daniel Rydmark .40 1.00
10 Juha Riihijarvi .40 1.00
11 Jesper Mattsson .40 1.00
12 David Petrasek .40 1.00
13 Mikael Wahlberg .40 1.00
14 Toivo Suursoo .40 1.00
15 Janos Vas .40 1.00
16 Robert Borgqvist .40 1.00
17 Petri Liimatainen .40 1.00
18 Johan Norgren .40 1.00
19 Andreas Valdix .40 1.00
20 Peter Andersson .40 1.00
21 Roger Ohman .40 1.00

2002-03 Swedish SHL

This set features the top players of the Swedish Elite league.

COMPLETE SET (292) 20.00 50.00
1 Johan Asplund .20 .50
2 Par Djoos .08 .20
3 Tommy Sjodin .08 .20
4 Henrik Rehnberg .08 .20
5 Adam Andersson .08 .20
6 Tony Martensson .08 .20
7 Roger Kyro .08 .20
8 Ove Molin .08 .20
9 Bjorn Danielsson .08 .20
10 Jan Larsson .08 .20
11 Jonas Soling .08 .20
12 Sergei Naumov .20 .50
13 Ronnie Pettersson .08 .20
14 Bjorn Nord .08 .20
15 Mikael Magnusson .08 .20
16 Tomas Strandberg .08 .20
17 Peter Lindelof .08 .20
18 Mikael Johansson .08 .20
19 Christian Eklund .08 .20
20 Johan Forsander .08 .20
21 Mikael Hakanson .08 .20
22 Nils Ekman .20 .50
23 Martin Gerber .40 1.00
24 Mats Trygg .08 .20
25 Jonas Frogren .08 .20
26 Thomas Rhodin .08 .20
27 Greger Artursson .08 .20
28 Marko Jantunen .08 .20
29 Claes Eriksson .08 .20
30 Rickard Wallin .08 .20
31 Marcel Jenni .08 .20
32 Mathias Johansson .08 .20
33 Peter Hammarstrom .08 .20
34 Boo Ahl .20 .50
35 Daniel Ljungqvist .08 .20
36 Per Gustafsson .08 .20
37 Jouni Loponen .08 .20
38 Richard Pavlikovsky .08 .20
39 Peter Ekelund .08 .20
40 Anders Huusko .08 .20
41 Mattias Remstam .08 .20
42 Johan Hult .08 .20
43 Bjorn Melin .08 .20
44 Kalle Sahlstedt .08 .20
45 Fredrik Jensen .08 .20
46 Mathias Ahxner .08 .20
47 Martin Knold .08 .20
48 Christoffer Norgren .08 .20
49 Johan Bulow .08 .20
50 Fredrik Johansson .08 .20
51 Henrik Andersson .08 .20
52 Fredrik Emvall .08 .20
53 Per Eklund .08 .20
54 Stefan Pettersson .08 .20
55 Magnus Gastrin .08 .20
56 Daniel Henriksson .20 .50
57 Jonas Andersson-Junkka .08 .20
58 Jan Sandstrom .08 .20
59 Petter Nilsson .08 .20
60 Roger Akerstrom .08 .20
61 Stefan Nilsson .08 .20
62 Jonathan Hedstrom .08 .20
63 Per Ledin .08 .20
64 Anders Burstrom .08 .20
65 Hans Huczkowski .08 .20
66 Emil Lundberg .08 .20
67 Andreas Hadelov .20 .50
68 Peter Hasselblad .08 .20
69 Peter Andersson .08 .20
70 Roger Ohman .08 .20
71 Henrik Malmstrom .08 .20
72 Marcus Thuresson .08 .20
73 Daniel Rydmark .08 .20
74 Juha Riihijarvi .08 .20
75 Marcus Magnertoft .08 .20
76 Mika Hannula .08 .20
77 Jesper Mattsson .08 .20
78 Peter Hirsch .20 .50
79 Pierre Hedin .08 .20
80 Jan Oberg .08 .20
81 Magnus Wernblom .08 .20
82 Tommy Pettersson .08 .20
83 Peter Hogardh .20 .50
84 Peter Oberg .08 .20
85 Joakim Lindstrom .08 .20
86 Magnus Hedlund .08 .20
87 Mattias Wennerberg .08 .20
88 Stefan Ohman .08 .20
89 Rolf Wanhainen .20 .50
90 Ola Mollerstedt .08 .20
91 Stefan Bernstrom .08 .20
92 Peter Popovic .08 .20
93 Peter Ahola .08 .20
94 Jesper Bjorck .08 .20
95 Jukka Tiilikainen .08 .20
96 Erik Norback .08 .20
97 Juha Lind .20 .50
98 Peter Gerhardsson .08 .20
99 Jorgen Bernstrom .08 .20
100 Fredrik Andersson .08 .20
101 Tommi Rajamaki .08 .20
102 David Halvardsson .08 .20
103 Daniel Casselstahl .08 .20
104 Niklas Nordgren .08 .20
105 Markus Matthiasson .20 .50
106 Robert Carlsson .08 .20
107 Per Hallin .08 .20
108 Henrik Zetterberg 1.00 2.50
109 Mikael Lind .08 .20
110 Ed Ward .08 .20
111 Henrik Lundqvist 2.00 5.00
112 Jan-Axel Alavaara .08 .20
113 Christian Backman .08 .20
114 Ronnie Sundin .08 .20
115 Magnus Kahnberg .08 .20
116 Jens Karlsson .08 .20
117 Juha Ikonen .08 .20
118 Jari Tolsa .08 .20
119 Niklas Andersson .08 .20
120 Jonas Johnsson .08 .20
121 Peter Strom .08 .20
122 Brynas IF Logo .08 .20
123 Djurgardens Logo .08 .20
124 Farjestads Logo .08 .20
125 HV 71 Logo .08 .20
126 Leksands Logo .08 .20
127 Linkopings Logo .08 .20
128 Lulea Logo .08 .20
129 Malmo Logo .08 .20
130 MoDo Logo .08 .20
131 Sodertalje Logo .08 .20
132 Timra Logo .08 .20
133 Vastra Frolunda Logo .08 .20
134 Christer Olsson CL .08 .20
135 Thomas Ostlund CL .08 .20
136 Jorgen Jonsson CL .08 .20
137 Johan Davidsson CL .08 .20
138 Mikael Sandberg CL .15 .40
139 Tomas Berglund CL .08 .20
140 Tomas Sandstrom CL .08 .20
141 Richard Lintner CL .08 .20
142 Peter Larsson CL .08 .20
143 Henrik Zetterberg CL .75 2.00
144 Joel Lundqvist CL .08 .20
145 Jamie Ram .20 .50
146 Daniel Johansson .08 .20
147 Jussi Pekkala .08 .20
148 Veli-Pekka Laitinen .08 .20
149 Kristoffer Jobs .08 .20
150 Jonas Floberg .08 .20
151 Simon Ostlund .08 .20
152 Tommi Miettinen .08 .20
153 Niklas Anger .15 .40
154 Daniel Wagstrom .08 .20
155 Joaquin Gage .15 .40
156 Bjorn Bjurling .08 .20
157 Niklas Kronwall .40 1.00
158 Per-Anton Lundstrom .20 .50
159 Kristofer Ottosson .08 .20
160 Joakim Eriksson .08 .20
161 Daniel Rudslatt .08 .20
162 Nichlas Falk .08 .20
163 Matthias Trattnig .08 .20
164 Fredrik Lindquist .08 .20
165 Johan Lindstrom .08 .20
166 Mikael Gerden .08 .20
167 Sinuhe Wallinheimo .08 .20
168 Per Lundell .08 .20
169 Per Hallberg .08 .20
170 Radek Hamr .08 .20
171 Ulf Soderstrom .08 .20
172 Marius Trygg .08 .20
173 Peter Nordstrom .08 .20
174 Jorgen Jonsson .08 .20
175 Par Backer .08 .20
176 Pelle Prestberg .08 .20
177 Dieter Kalt .08 .20
178 Stefan Liv .60 1.50
179 Mika Niskanen .08 .20
180 Timmy Pettersson .08 .20
181 Daniel Josefsson .08 .20
182 Jani Hassinen .08 .20
183 Sebastian Meijer .08 .20
184 Niklas Brannstrom .08 .20
185 Par Arlbrandt .08 .20
186 Pasi Maattanen .08 .20
187 Johan Davidsson .15 .40
188 Jonas Fransson .08 .20
189 Sean Gauthier .15 .40
190 Christer Olsson .08 .20
191 Niklas Gallstedt .08 .20
192 Hans Lodin .08 .20
193 Per Lofstrom .08 .20
194 Mike Stapleton .08 .20
195 Jens Nielsen .08 .20
196 Niklas Eriksson .08 .20
197 Mikael Karlberg .08 .20
198 Mikael Pettersson .08 .20
Robert Nilsson
199 Tobias Holm .08 .20
200 Niklas Persson .08 .20
201 Goran Hermansson .08 .20
202 Tomas Forslund .08 .20
203 Henrik Nordfeldt .08 .20
204 Johan Rosen .08 .20
205 Joel Davis .08 .20
206 Mikael Sandberg .15 .40
207 Andreas Pihl .08 .20
208 Jan Mertzig .08 .20
209 Thomas Johansson .08 .20
210 Andreas Holmqvist .08 .20
211 Barry Richter .15 .40
212 Stefan Gustavson .08 .20
213 Brian Felsner .15 .40
214 Johan Franzen ERC 1.00 2.50
215 Tim Eriksson .08 .20
216 Mikael Hakanson .08 .20
217 Gusten Tornqvist .08 .20
218 Pavel Skrbek .08 .20
219 Patrik Bjaarnhjelm .08 .20
220 Johan Finnstrom .20 .50
221 Fredrik Svensson .08 .20
222 Linus Fagemo .08 .20
223 Patrik Tano .08 .20
224 Kamil Brabenec .08 .20
225 Thomas Berglund .08 .20
226 Jonas Hagerback .08 .20
227 Magnus Nilsson .08 .20
228 Robert Borgqvist .08 .20
229 Joakim Lundberg .08 .20
230 David Petrasek .08 .20
231 Petri Liimatainen .08 .20
232 Johan Norgren .08 .20
233 Jan Hammar .08 .20
234 Frans Nielsen .08 .20
235 Mikael Wahlberg .08 .20
236 Toivo Suursoo .08 .20
237 Juuso Riksman .08 .20
238 Tobias Enstrom .08 .20
239 Jesper Damgaard .08 .20
240 Erik Leverstrom .08 .20
241 Dusan Milo .08 .20

242 Martin Johansson .08 .20
243 Anders Soderberg .15 .40
244 Jonas Almtorp .08 .20
245 Fredrik Warg .08 .20
246 Joakim Lindstrom .08 .20
247 Morten Green .08 .20
248 Miroslav Hlinka .08 .20
249 Magnus Lindquist .08 .20
250 Alexander Blomqvist .08 .20
251 Anders Back .08 .20
252 Leif Rohlin .08 .20
253 Robert Carlsson .08 .20
254 Antti Tormanen .08 .20
255 David Svee .08 .20
256 Gabriel Karlsson .08 .20
257 Mattias Carlsson .08 .20
258 Peter Larsson .08 .20
259 Patrik Zetterberg .08 .20
260 Kristian Gahn .08 .20
261 Kimmo Kapanen .08 .20
262 Martin Lindman .08 .20
263 Kalle Koskinen .08 .20
264 Robert Jindrich .08 .20
265 Par Styf .08 .20
266 Patrik Wallenberg .08 .20
267 Christian Soderstrom .08 .20
268 Henrik Eriksson .08 .20
269 Valeri Krykov .08 .20
270 Toni Koivunen .08 .20
271 Markus Akerblom .08 .20
272 Fredrik Norrena .40 1.00
273 Magnus Johansson .08 .20
274 Kimmo Eronen .08 .20
275 Oscar Ackestrom .08 .20
276 Erik Kakko .08 .20
277 Mattias Luukkonen .08 .20
278 Patrik Carnback .08 .20
279 Alexander Steen ERC 1.50 4.00
280 Joel Lundqvist .08 .20
281 Jonas Esbjors .08 .20
282 Mikael Andersson .08 .20
283 Jamie Ram .20 .50
284 Joaquin Gage .20 .50
285 Sinuhe Wallinheimo .20 .50
286 Stefan Liv .60 1.50
287 Sean Gauthier .15 .40
288 Mikael Sandberg .08 .20
289 Daniel Henriksson .08 .20
290 Andreas Hadelov .08 .20
291 Peter Hirsch .20 .50
292 Magnus Lindquist .08 .20
293 Kimmo Kapanen .08 .20
294 Fredrik Norrena .40 1.00

2002-03 Swedish SHL Dynamic Duos

These cards were randomly inserted at a rate of 1:16 series two packs.
COMPLETE SET (9) 6.00 15.00
1 Par Djoos .75 2.00
Tommy Sjodin
2 Mikael Johansson .75 2.00
Kristofer Ottosson
3 Par Backer .75 2.00
Jorgen Jonsson
4 Lars Jonsson 1.25 3.00
Daniel Widing
5 Petr Nilsson .75 2.00
Stefan Nilsson
6 Mika Hannula .75 2.00
Juha Riihijarvi
7 Juha Lind .75 2.00
Antti Tormanen
8 Markus Matthiasson .75 2.00
Markus Akerblom
9 Joel Lundqvist 2.00 5.00
Alexander Steen

2002-03 Swedish SHL Masks

These cards were randomly inserts in series 2 packs at a rate of 1:32.
COMPLETE SET (9) 25.00 50.00
1 Sinuhe Wallinheimo 3.00 8.00
2 Stefan Liv 4.00 10.00
3 Sean Gauthier 3.00 8.00
4 Mikael Sandberg 3.00 8.00
5 Andreas Hadelov 3.00 8.00
6 Peter Hirsch 3.00 8.00
7 Magnus Lindquist 3.00 8.00
8 Kimmo Kapanen 3.00 8.00
9 Fredrik Norrena 4.00 10.00

2002-03 Swedish SHL Netminders

This set features top Swedish goalies and was inserted 1:8 series one packs.
COMPLETE SET (9) 15.00 20.00
NM1 Martin Gerber 2.00 5.00
NM2 Sergei Naumov .75 2.00
NM3 Stefan Liv 2.00 5.00
NM4 Rolf Wanhainen .75 2.00
NM5 Peter Hirsch .75 2.00
NM6 Daniel Henriksson .75 2.00
NM7 Mikael Sandberg .75 2.00
NM8 Johan Asplund .75 2.00
NM9 Andreas Hadelov .75 2.00

2002-03 Swedish SHL Next Generation

This set features the top young players in the SHL and was inserted 1:16 series one packs.
COMPLETE SET (9) 15.00 30.00
NG1 Joel Lundqvist 1.50 4.00
NG2 Par Backer 1.50 4.00
NG3 Magnus Hedlund 1.50 4.00
NG4 Adam Andersson 1.50 4.00
NG5 Henrik Lundqvist 1.50 4.00
NG6 Joakim Lindstrom 1.50 4.00
NG7 Jonas Johansson 3.00 8.00
NG8 Bjorn Melin 1.50 4.00
NG9 Jens Karlsson 2.00 5.00

2002-03 Swedish SHL Parallel

These cards were issued as random inserts in packs.
*PARALLEL: 2X TO 5X BASIC CARDS

2002-03 Swedish SHL Promos

This 11-card set was created to promote the new series of SHL cards, produced by Sweden's The Card Cabinet. The cards feature different photos and numbering than those of the same players in the base set.
COMPLETE SET (11) 8.00 20.00
TCC1 Tommy Sjodin .40 1.00
TCC2 Christian Eklund .40 1.00
TCC3 Martin Gerber .75 2.00
TCC4 Stefan Liv .75 2.00
TCC5 Per Eklund .40 1.00
TCC6 Jonas Andersson-Junkka .40 1.00
TCC7 Mika Hannula .40 1.00
TCC8 Mattias Weinhandl .75 2.00
TCC9 Peter Popovic .40 1.00
TCC10 Henrik Zetterberg 6.00 15.00
TCC11 Jan-Axel Alavaara .40 1.00

2002-03 Swedish SHL Sharpshooters

This set features the best snipers in the SHL and was inserted 1:8 series one packs.
COMPLETE SET (9) 20.00 40.00
SS1 Peter Hogardh 1.50 4.00
SS2 Jorgen Jonsson 1.50 4.00
SS3 Dieter Kalt 1.50 4.00
SS4 Per-Age Skroder 2.50 6.00
SS5 Juha Riihijarvi 1.50 4.00
SS6 Peter Larsson 1.50 4.00
SS7 Markus Matthiasson 1.50 4.00
SS8 Mattias Weinhandl 2.50 6.00
SS9 Nils Ekman 2.50 6.00

2002-03 Swedish SHL Signatures

This set features autographs of many of the top stars of the SHL. The cards were inserted 1:32 series one packs.
STATED ODDS 1:32
1 Jonas Soling 4.00 10.00
2 Ove Molin 4.00 10.00
3 Nils Ekman 6.00 15.00
4 Kristofer Ottosson 4.00 10.00
5 Jorgen Jonsson 6.00 15.00
6 Rickard Wallin 6.00 15.00
7 Johan Davidsson 6.00 15.00
8 Mikael Sandberg 6.00 15.00
9 Stefan Nilsson 4.00 10.00
10 Andreas Hadelov 6.00 15.00
11 Jesper Mattsson 4.00 10.00
12 Peter Hogardh 6.00 15.00
13 Rolf Wanhainen 6.00 15.00
14 Juha Lind 6.00 15.00
15 Henrik Zetterberg 40.00 80.00
16 Per Hallin 4.00 10.00
17 Niklas Andersson 4.00 10.00
18 Alexander Steen 15.00 40.00

2002-03 Swedish SHL Signatures Series II

Inserted at a rate of 1:32 series 2 packs. The cards are unnumbered and listed below in checklist order.
STATED ODDS 1:32 SERIES II PACKS
1 Stefan Pettersson 6.00 15.00
2 Daniel Henriksson 6.00 15.00
3 Erik Nordback 6.00 15.00
4 Bjorn Nord 6.00 15.00
5 Ulf Soderstrom 6.00 15.00
6 Stefan Liv 10.00 25.00
7 Mikael Hakansson 6.00 15.00
8 Joel Lundqvist 10.00 25.00
9 Robert Carlsson 6.00 15.00
10 Peter Popovic 6.00 15.00
11 Magnus Wernblom 6.00 15.00
12 Juha Riihijarvi 6.00 15.00
13 Jonathan Hedstrom 8.00 20.00
14 Marcus Thuresson 6.00 15.00
15 Per Eklund 6.00 15.00
16 Antti Tormanen 6.00 15.00
17 Fredrik Lindqvist 6.00 15.00
18 Jens Nielsen 6.00 15.00
19 Sean Gauthier 6.00 15.00
20 Niklas Eriksson 6.00 15.00
21 Leif Rohlin 6.00 15.00
22 Lars Jonsson 8.00 20.00
23 Kalle Sahlstedt SP 15.00 40.00
24 Per-Age Skroder SP 15.00 40.00
25 Dieter Kalt 6.00 15.00
26 Johan Asplund 8.00 20.00

2002-03 Swedish SHL Team Captains

Inserted in series two at a rate of 1:8 packs.
COMPLETE SET (9) 6.00 15.00
1 Jan Larsson .75 2.00
2 Nichlas Falk .75 2.00
3 Jorgen Jonsson .75 2.00
4 Johan Davidsson .75 2.00
5 Christer Olsson .75 2.00
6 Stefan Gustavson .75 2.00
7 Roger Akerstrom .75 2.00
8 Pierre Hedin .75 2.00
9 Peter Popovic .75 2.00

2003-04 Swedish Elite

Sold in two series, with each containing 144 cards.
COMPLETE SET (288) 20.00 40.00
COMMON CARD (1-144) .02 .05
SEMISTARS .08 .20
UNLISTED STARS .20 .50
1 Joakim Lundstrom .08 .20
2 Daniel Johansson .08 .20
3 Tommy Sjodin .08 .20
4 Adam Andersson .08 .20
5 Veli-Pekka Laitinen .08 .20
6 Jonas Soling .08 .20
7 Simon Ostlund .08 .20
8 Roger Kyro .08 .20
9 Ove Molin .08 .20
10 Bjorn Danielsson .08 .20
11 Tommi Miettinen .08 .20
12 Joaquin Gage .20 .50
13 Ronnie Pettersson .08 .20
14 Niklas Kronwall .40 1.00
15 Bjorn Nord .08 .20
16 Kristofer Ottosson .08 .20
17 Daniel Rudslatt .08 .20
18 Nichlas Falk .08 .20
19 Mathias Tjarnqvist .20 .50
20 Christian Eklund .08 .20
21 Fredrik Lindqvist .20 .50
22 Mikael Johansson .08 .20
23 Fredrik Norrena .20 .50
24 Kimmo Eronen .08 .20
25 Ronnie Sundin .08 .20
26 Erik Kakko .08 .20
27 Mattias Luukkonen .08 .20
28 Magnus Kahnberg .08 .20
29 Jari Tolsa .08 .20
30 Joel Lundqvist .08 .20
31 Niklas Andersson .08 .20
32 Peter Strom .08 .20
33 Jens Karlsson .08 .20
34 Sinuhe Wallinheimo .20 .50
35 Per Hallberg .08 .20
36 Mats Trygg .08 .20
37 Gregor Artursson .08 .20
38 Radek Hamr .08 .20
39 Peter Nordstrom .08 .20
40 Claes Eriksson .08 .20
41 Par Backer .08 .20
42 Marcel Jenni .08 .20
43 Peter Hammarstrom .08 .20
44 Dieter Kalt .08 .20
45 Boo Ahl .20 .50
46 Daniel Ljungqvist .08 .20
47 Ola Thorwalls .08 .20
48 Timmy Pettersson .08 .20
49 Jouni Loponen .08 .20
50 Jani Hassinen .08 .20
51 Peter Ekelund .08 .20
52 Kalle Sahlstedt .08 .20
53 Pasi Maattanen .08 .20
54 Mattias Remstam .08 .20
55 Johan Davidsson .08 .20
56 Jonas Elofsson .08 .20
57 Christer Olsson .08 .20
58 Lars Jonsson .30 .75
59 Hans Lodin .08 .20
60 Jens Nielsen .08 .20
61 Niklas Eriksson .08 .20
62 Mikael Pettersson .08 .20
63 Tobias Holm .08 .20
64 Niklas Persson .08 .20
65 Goran Hermansson .08 .20
66 Henrik Nordfeldt .08 .20
67 Andreas Pihl .08 .20
68 Jan Mertzig .08 .20
69 Martin Knold .08 .20
70 Andreas Holmqvist .08 .20
71 Barry Richter .08 .20
72 Johan Bulow .08 .20
73 Fredrik Johansson .08 .20
74 Tim Eriksson .08 .20
75 Fredrik Emvall .08 .20
76 Mikael Hakanson .08 .20
77 Per Eklund .08 .20
78 Gusten Tornqvist .08 .20
79 Jonas Andersson-Junkka .08 .20
80 Petter Nilsson .08 .20
81 Pavel Skrbek .08 .20
82 Johan Finnstrom .08 .20
83 Stefan Nilsson .08 .20
84 Kamil Brabenec .08 .20
85 Thomas Berglund .08 .20
86 Hans Huczkowski .08 .20
87 Per Ledin .08 .20
88 Andreas Hadelov .20 .50
89 Joakim Lundberg .08 .20
90 David Petrasek .08 .20
91 Petri Liimatainen .08 .20
92 Peter Andersson .08 .20
93 Frans Nielsen .08 .20
94 Daniel Rydmark .08 .20
95 Juha Riihijarvi .08 .20
96 Jesper Mattsson .08 .20
97 Toivo Suursoo .08 .20
98 Mika Hannula .08 .20
99 Juuso Riksman .08 .20
100 Jan Oberg .08 .20
101 Dusan Milo .08 .20
102 Magnus Hedlund .08 .20
103 Martin Wilde .08 .20
104 Mika Lehtinen .08 .20
105 Anders Soderberg .08 .20
106 Tommy Pettersson .08 .20
107 Peter Hogardh .08 .20
108 Peter Oberg .08 .20
109 Joakim Lindstrom .08 .20
110 Mattias Wennerberg .08 .20
111 Magnus Lindquist .08 .20
112 Anders Back .08 .20
113 Stefan Bemstrom .08 .20
114 Peter Popovic .08 .20
115 Peter Ahola .08 .20
116 Robert Carlsson .08 .20
117 Antti Tormanen .08 .20
118 Gabriel Karlsson .08 .20
119 Jorgen Bemstrom .08 .20
120 Peter Larsson .08 .20
121 Patrik Zetterberg .08 .20
122 Kimmo Kapanen .20 .50
123 David Halvardsson .08 .20
124 Tommi Rajamaki .08 .20
125 Kalle Koskinen .08 .20
126 Par Styf .08 .20
127 Christian Soderstrom .08 .20
128 Niklas Nordgren .08 .20
129 Valeri Krykov .08 .20
130 Per Hallin .08 .20
131 Christian Sjogren .08 .20
132 Markus Matthiasson .08 .20
133 Brynas IF .04 .10
134 Djurgardens IF .04 .10
135 Frolunda Indians .04 .10
136 Farjestads BK .04 .10
137 HV 71 .04 .10
138 Leksands IF .04 .10
139 Linkopings HC .04 .10
140 Lulea Hockey .04 .10
141 MIF Redhawks .04 .10
142 MoDo Hockey .04 .10
143 Sodertalje SK .04 .10
144 Timra IK .04 .10
145 Markus Korhonen .20 .50
146 Mikko Kuparinen .08 .20
147 Jesper Bjorck .08 .20
148 Daniel Casselstahl .08 .20
149 Henrik Malmstrom .08 .20
150 Nicklas Danielsson .08 .20
151 Jacob Johansson .08 .20
152 Patrik Ronnqvist .08 .20
153 Peter Nylander .08 .20
154 Niklas Anger .08 .20
155 Mikael Lind .08 .20
156 Bjorn Bjurling .08 .20
157 Staffan Kronwall .08 .20
158 Johnny Oduya .08 .20
159 Mika Stromberg .08 .20
160 Richard Lintner .08 .20
161 Christopher Thorn .08 .20
162 Jonathan Hedstrom .08 .20
163 Tomas Kollar .08 .20
164 Johannes Salmonsson .08 .20
165 Fredrik Bremberg .08 .20
166 Mikael Johansson .08 .20
167 Marcus Kristoffersson .08 .20
168 Stefan Pettersson .08 .20
169 Kenneth Bergqvist .08 .20
170 Henrik Lundqvist .75 2.00
171 Jan-Axel Alavaara .08 .20
172 Antti-Jussi Niemi .08 .20
173 Oscar Ackestrom .08 .20
174 Alexander Steen 2.00 5.00
175 Loui Eriksson .40 1.00
176 Jonas Esbjors .08 .20
177 Jonas Johnson .40 1.00
178 Tomi Kallio .20 .50
179 Robin Jonsson .08 .20
180 Jonas Frogren .08 .20
181 Janne Gronvall .08 .20
182 Hannes Hyvonen .08 .20
183 Pelle Prestberg .08 .20
184 Ulf Soderstrom .08 .20
185 Mathias Johansson .08 .20
186 Jorgen Jonsson .08 .20
187 Fredrik Eriksson .08 .20
188 Calle Steen .08 .20
189 Stefan Liv .40 1.00
190 Fredrik Olausson .20 .50
191 Simon Skoog .08 .20
192 Mika Niskanen .08 .20
193 Johan Halvardsson .08 .20
194 Stefan Hellkvist .08 .20
195 Per-age Skroder .08 .20
196 Martin Thornberg .08 .20
197 Anders Huusko .08 .20
198 Bjorn Melin .08 .20
199 Andreas Jamtin .08 .20
200 Mike Bales .20 .50
201 Johan Backlund .08 .20
202 Richard Pavlikovsky .08 .20
203 Tommy Westlund .08 .20
204 Robert Nilsson .08 .20
205 Johan Witehall .08 .20
206 Christopher Lindholm .08 .20
207 Joonas Jaaskelainen .08 .20
208 Johan RosA©n .08 .20
209 Daniel Sperrle .08 .20
210 Fredrik Norrena .20 .50
211 Thomas Johansson .08 .20
212 Peter Casparsson .08 .20
213 Christoffer Norgren .08 .20
214 Jyrki Valivaara .08 .20
215 Johan FranzA©n .40 1.00
216 Mikko Peltola .08 .20
217 Ragnar Karlsson .08 .20
218 Pekka Tirkkonen .08 .20
219 Mikael von der Geest .08 .20
220 Andreas Sundin .08 .20
221 Jussi Tarvainen .08 .20
222 Johan Lindstrom .08 .20
223 Daniel Henriksson .20 .50
224 Jonas Johansson .08 .20
225 Johan Fransson .40 1.00
226 Jan Sandstrom .08 .20
227 Tuukka Mantyla .08 .20
228 Roger Akerstrom .08 .20
229 Jonas Ronnqvist .08 .20
230 Linus Fagemo .08 .20
231 Emil Lundberg .08 .20
232 Jonas Nordquist .08 .20
233 Jonas Hagerback .08 .20
234 Magnus Nilsson .08 .20
235 Johan Tellstrom .08 .20
236 Pierre Berggren .08 .20
237 Christopher Nilstorp .20 .50
238 Johan Bjork .08 .20
239 Magnus Osterby .08 .20
240 Johan Norgren .08 .20
241 Jens Olsson .08 .20
242 Jan Hammar .08 .20
243 Marcus Magnertoft .08 .20
244 Niklas Sundblad .08 .20
245 Mikael Wahlberg .08 .20
246 Kim Staal .08 .20
247 Andreas Valdix .08 .20
248 Kimmo Vesa .08 .20
249 Jesper Damgaard .08 .20
250 Martin Johansson .08 .20
251 Lars Jansson .08 .20
252 Magnus Wernblom .08 .20
253 Fredrik Warg .08 .20
254 Morten Green .08 .20
255 Per Svartvadet .20 .50
256 Magnus Gustafsson .08 .20
257 Rolf Wanhainen .20 .50
258 Johan Berggren .08 .20
259 Bert Robertsson .08 .20
260 Peter Messa .08 .20
261 Jan Huokko .08 .20
262 Joakim Eriksson .08 .20
263 Urban Omark .08 .20
264 Juha Lind .08 .20
265 Bobbie Hagelin .08 .20
266 Kristian Gahn .08 .20
267 Mattias Ohrling .08 .20
268 Jesper Jager .08 .20
269 Jan Nemecek .08 .20
270 Sanny Lindstrom .08 .20
271 Mats Hansson .08 .20
272 Robert Carlsson .08 .20
273 Yared Hagos .30 .75
274 Lee Jinman .08 .20
275 Fredrik Sundin .08 .20
276 Toni Koivunen .08 .20
277 Brynas IF .04 .10
278 Djurgardens IF .04 .10
279 Frolunda Indians .04 .10
280 Farjestads BK .04 .10
281 HV 71 .04 .10
282 Leksands IF .04 .10
283 Linkopings HC .04 .10
284 Lulea Hockey .04 .10
285 MIF Redhawks .04 .10
286 MoDo Hockey .04 .10
287 Sodertalje SK .04 .10
288 Timra IK .04 .10

2003-04 Swedish Elite Enforcers

COMPLETE SET (12) 5.00 10.00
STATED ODDS 1:8 SERIES 2
EF1 Hannes Hyvonen .40 1.00
EF2 Oscar Ackestrom .40 1.00
EF3 Thomas Berglund .40 1.00
EF4 Andreas Pihl .40 1.00
EF5 Joel Lundqvist .75 2.00
EF6 Par Styf .40 1.00
EF7 Bert Robertsson .40 1.00
EF8 Bjorn Nord .40 1.00
EF9 Henrik Nordfeldt .40 1.00
EF10 Christian Sjogren .40 1.00
EF11 Niklas Sundblad .40 1.00
EF12 Magnus Wernblom .40 1.00

2003-04 Swedish Elite Global Impact

COMPLETE SET (12) 6.00 15.00
STATED ODDS 1:8 SERIES 2
GI1 Markus Korhonen .75 2.00
GI2 Richard Lintner .40 1.00
GI3 Tomi Kallio .75 2.00
GI4 Sinuhe Wallinheimo .75 2.00
GI5 Per-age Skroder .40 1.00
GI6 Mike Bales 1.25 3.00
GI7 Brian Felsner 1.00 2.50
GI8 Kamil Brabenec .40 1.00
GI9 Toivo Suursoo .40 1.00
GI10 Jesper Damgaard .40 1.00
GI11 Juha Lind .40 1.00
GI12 Jan Nemecek .40 1.00

2003-04 Swedish Elite Hot Numbers

COMPLETE SET (12) 8.00 20.00
STATED ODDS 1:16 SERIES 2
HN1 Stefan Liv 1.50 4.00
HN2 Robert Nilsson .75 2.00
HN3 Nicklas Falk .40 1.00
HN4 Alexander Steen 3.00 8.00
HN5 Jorgen Jonsson .40 1.00
HN6 Rolf Wanhainen .75 2.00
HN7 Markus Matthiasson .40 1.00
HN8 Thomas Johansson .40 1.00
HN9 Daniel Henriksson .75 2.00
HN10 Mikael Lind .40 1.00
HN11 Petri Liimatainen .40 1.00
HN12 Per Svartvadet .75 2.00

2003-04 Swedish Elite Jerseys

COMPLETE SET (5) 25.00 60.00
1 Kimmo Kapanen 4.00 10.00
2 Sinuhe Wallinheimo 8.00 20.00
3 Daniel Henriksson 4.00 10.00
4 Henrik Lundqvist 8.00 20.00
5 Magnus Johansson 4.00 10.00

2003-04 Swedish Elite Masks

COMPLETE SET (4) 15.00 30.00
1 Sinuhe Wallinheimo 4.00 10.00
2 Stefan Liv 5.00 12.00
3 Andreas Hadelov 4.00 10.00
4 Kimmo Kapanen 4.00 10.00

2003-04 Swedish Elite Masks II

COMPLETE SET (4) 15.00 30.00
STATED ODDS 1:32 SERIES 2
1 Stefan Liv 5.00 12.00
2 Kimmo Kapanen 4.00 10.00
3 Andreas Hadelov 4.00 10.00
4 Sinuhe Wallinheimo 4.00 10.00

2003-04 Swedish Elite Rookies

These cards were inserted at a rate of 1:8 packs.
COMPLETE SET (9) 6.00 15.00
STATED ODDS 1:8
1 Adam Andersson .40 1.00
2 Joakim Lundstrom .40 1.00
3 Nicklas Eckerblom .40 1.00
4 Alexander Steen 3.00 8.00
5 Sebastian Meijer .40 1.00
6 Robert Nilsson 1.00 2.50
7 Frans Nielsen 1.00 2.50
8 Tobias Enstrom .40 1.00
9 Joakim Lindstrom .40 1.00

2003-04 Swedish Elite Signatures

These authentic signatures were inserted at a rate of 1:32 Series 1 packs.
COMPLETE SET (16) 50.00 125.00
STATED ODDS 1:32 SERIES 1
1 Antti Tormanen 4.00 10.00
2 Tommy Sjodin 4.00 10.00
3 Joel Lundqvist 8.00 20.00
4 Daniel Henriksson 4.00 10.00
5 Tobias Enstrom 4.00 10.00
6 Jonas Johnsson 4.00 10.00
7 Mika Lehtinen 4.00 10.00
8 Tommi Miettinen 4.00 10.00
9 Peter Popovic 4.00 10.00
10 Fredrik Norrena 8.00 20.00
11 Jonas Andersson-Junkka 4.00 10.00
12 Magnus Wernblom 4.00 10.00
13 Niklas Anger 4.00 10.00
14 Patrik Bjaarnhjelm 4.00 10.00
15 Mattias Wennerberg 4.00 10.00
16 Robert Nilsson SP 10.00 25.00

2003-04 Swedish Elite Signatures II

STATED ODDS 1:32 SERIES 2
1 Sinuhe Wallinheimo 6.00 15.00
2 Per Hallberg 4.00 10.00
3 Par Backer 4.00 10.00
4 Jorgen Jonsson 4.00 10.00
5 Par Styf 4.00 10.00
6 Markus Matthiasson 4.00 10.00
7 Kimmo Kapanen 6.00 15.00
8 Niklas Kronwall 15.00 40.00
9 Bjorn Nord 4.00 10.00
10 Daniel Rudslatt 4.00 10.00
11 Per Eklund 4.00 10.00
12 Pasi Maatanen 4.00 10.00
13 Peter Ekelund 4.00 10.00
14 Stefan Liv 12.00 30.00
15 Johan Davidsson SP 20.00 50.00
16 Daniel Rydmark 4.00 10.00
17 Petri Liimatainen 4.00 10.00
18 Andreas Hadelov 6.00 15.00
19 Christer Olsson 4.00 10.00
20 Niklas Eriksson 4.00 10.00
21 Jens Nielsen 4.00 10.00

2003-04 Swedish Elite Silver

These parallels to the base set were inserted at a rate of 1:4 packs. Value is 1X to 2X the value of the comparable base card.

2003-04 Swedish Elite Stars of the Game

COMPLETE SET (9) 8.00 20.00
STATED ODDS 1:32
1 Kristofer Ottosson 1.25 3.00
2 Niklas Andersson 1.25 3.00
3 Jorgen Jonsson 1.25 3.00
4 Johan Davidsson 1.25 3.00
5 Per Eklund 1.25 3.00
6 Jonas Ronnqvist 1.25 3.00
7 Juha Riihijarvi 1.25 3.00
8 Antti Tormanen 1.25 3.00
9 Niklas Nordgren 1.25 3.00

2003-04 Swedish Elite Zero Hero

COMPLETE SET (9) 15.00 40.00
STATED ODDS 1:16
1 Henrik Lundqvist 5.00 12.00
2 Rolf Wanhainen 2.00 5.00
3 Andreas Hadelov 2.00 5.00
4 Joaquin Gage 2.00 5.00
5 Sinuhe Wallinheimo 2.00 5.00
6 Stefan Liv 2.50 6.00
7 Sean Gauthier 2.00 5.00
8 Juuso Riksman 2.00 5.00
9 Kimmo Kapanen 2.00 5.00

2004-05 Swedish Alfabilder Alfa Stars

COMPLETE SET (54) 10.00 25.00
1 Johan Hedberg .20 .50
2 Mattias Ohlund .20 .50
3 Kim Johnsson .20 .50
4 Kenny Jonsson .20 .50
5 Nicklas Lidstrom .40 1.00
6 Mikael Renberg .20 .50
7 Stefan Liv .40 1.00
8 Christian Backman .20 .50
9 Magnus Kahnberg .20 .50
10 Andreas Johansson .20 .50
11 Daniel Alfredsson .40 1.00
12 Daniel Sedin .40 1.00
13 Mats Sundin .75 2.00
14 Mattias Norstrom .20 .50
15 Johan Davidsson .20 .50
16 Tomas Holmstrom .40 1.00
17 Marcus Ragnarsson .20 .50
18 Marcus Nilson .20 .50
19 Markus Naslund .75 2.00
20 Henrik Sedin .40 1.00
21 Peter Forsberg 2.00 5.00
22 Per-Johan Axelsson .20 .50
23 Kristian Huselius .20 .50
24 Michael Nylander .20 .50
25 Mattias Weinhandl .20 .50
26 Samuel Pahlsson .20 .50
27 Jorgen Jonsson .20 .50
28 Dick Tarnstrom .20 .50
29 Nils Ekman .20 .50
30 Henrik Lundqvist 3.00 8.00
31 Fredrik Olausson .20 .50
32 Mikael Tellqvist .40 1.00
33 Fredrik Modin .20 .50
34 Niklas Sundstrom .20 .50
35 Tommy Salo .20 .50
36 Daniel Tjarnqvist .20 .50
37 Fredrik Sjostrom .20 .50
38 Robert Nilsson .20 .50
39 Alexander Steen 2.00 5.00
40 Henrik Zetterberg .75 2.00
41 Tomas Sandstrom .20 .50
42 Tomas Jonsson .20 .50
43 Jonas Bergqvist .20 .50
44 Magnus Svensson .20 .50
45 Challe Berglund .20 .50
46 Leif Holmqvist .20 .50
47 Borje Salming .40 1.00
48 Sven Tumba Johansson .20 .50
49 Ulf Sterner .20 .50
50 Anders Kallur .20 .50
51 Mats Naslund .20 .50
52 Hakan Loob .20 .50
53 Kent Nilsson .20 .50
54 Pekka Lindmark .20 .50

2004-05 Swedish Alfabilder Alfa Stars Golden Ice

COMPLETE SET (12) 10.00 25.00
1 Jonas Bergqvist .75 2.00
2 Sven Tumba .75 2.00
3 Hakan Loob .75 2.00
4 Peter Forsberg 4.00 10.00
5 Pekka Lindmark .75 2.00
6 Tomas Jonsson .75 2.00
7 Challe Berglund .75 2.00
8 Tommy Salo .75 2.00
9 Jorgen Jonsson .75 2.00
10 M.Renberg 1.25 3.00
N.Sundstrom
11 M.Norstrom 1.25 3.00
M.Ohlund
12 F.Modin 1.25 3.00
K.Johnsson

2004-05 Swedish Alfabilder Autographs

Random inserts in Swedish product, limited to 200 copies each.
COMPLETE SET (28) 150.00 300.00
101 Markus Naslund 12.00 30.00
102 Henrik Zetterberg 12.00 30.00
103 Peter Forsberg 25.00 60.00
104 Per-Johan Axelsson 3.00 8.00
105 Henrik Sedin 5.00 12.00
106 Mikael Renberg 3.00 8.00
107 Nicklas Lidstrom 12.00 30.00
108 Tomas Sandstrom 4.00 10.00
109 Johan Hedberg 4.00 10.00
110 Tomas Jonsson 3.00 8.00
111 Michael Nylander 4.00 10.00
112 Mikael Tellqvist 10.00 25.00
113 Nils Ekman 3.00 8.00
114 Mattias Ohlund 3.00 8.00
115 Fredrik Modin 3.00 8.00
116 Jonas Bergqvist 3.00 8.00
117 Tommy Salo 4.00 10.00
118 Dick Tarnstrom 3.00 8.00
119 Niklas Sundstrom 3.00 8.00
120 Tomas Holmstrom 8.00 20.00
121 Charles Berglund 3.00 8.00
122 Christian Backman 3.00 8.00
123 Magnus Svensson 3.00 8.00
124 Marcus Nilson 4.00 10.00
125 Samuel Pahlsson 4.00 10.00
126 Daniel Tjarnqvist 3.00 8.00
127 Kristian Huselius 4.00 10.00
128 Mattias Weinhandl 3.00 8.00

2004-05 Swedish Alfabilder Limited Autographs

Parallel to the basic autographs, these cards are limited to just 50 copies.
COMPLETE SET (28) 500.00 700.00
101 Markus Naslund 20.00 50.00
102 Henrik Zetterberg 20.00 50.00
103 Peter Forsberg 100.00 200.00
104 Per-Johan Axelsson 8.00 20.00
105 Henrik Sedin 10.00 25.00
106 Mikael Renberg 8.00 20.00
107 Nicklas Lidstrom 20.00 50.00
108 Tomas Sandstrom 8.00 20.00
109 Johan Hedberg 8.00 20.00
110 Tomas Jonsson 8.00 20.00
111 Michael Nylander 8.00 20.00
112 Mikael Tellqvist 15.00 40.00
113 Nils Ekman 8.00 20.00
114 Mattias Ohlund 8.00 20.00
115 Fredrik Modin 12.00 30.00
116 Jonas Bergqvist 8.00 20.00
117 Tommy Salo 8.00 20.00
118 Dick Tarnstrom 8.00 20.00
119 Niklas Sundstrom 8.00 20.00
120 Tomas Holmstrom 15.00 40.00
121 Charles Berglund 8.00 20.00
122 Christian Backman 8.00 20.00
123 Magnus Svensson 8.00 20.00
124 Marcus Nilson 8.00 20.00
125 Samuel Pahlsson 8.00 20.00
126 Daniel Tjarnqvist 8.00 20.00
127 Kristian Huselius 8.00 20.00
128 Mattias Weinhandl 8.00 20.00

2004-05 Swedish Alfabilder Next In Line

COMPLETE SET (6) 15.00 40.00
1 Leif Holmqvist 2.00 5.00
Tommy Salo
2 Borje Salming 4.00 10.00
Nick Lidstrom
3 Sven Johansson 6.00 15.00
Peter Forsberg
4 Ulf Sterner 4.00 10.00
Henrik Zetterberg
5 Hakan Loob 4.00 10.00
Mats Naslund
6 Kent Nilsson 2.00 5.00
Robert Nilsson

2004-05 Swedish Alfabilder Proof Parallels

3X to 5X BASE CARD

2004-05 Swedish Djurgardens Postcards

These standard postcard-sized collectibles were issued by the team. All copies we've seen have been signed, so it's likely that's the only way they were made available. It's likely that more singles exist than listed below.
COMPLETE SET
1 Mariusz Czerkawski .75 2.00
2 Daniel Fernholm .75 2.00
3 Espen Knutsen 1.25 3.00
4 Marcus Kristofferson .75 2.00
5 Staffan Kronwall 1.25 3.00
6 Robert Nilsson 1.25 3.00
7 Jimmie Olvestad .75 2.00
8 Kristofer Ottosson .75 2.00
9 Mika Stromberg .75 2.00
10 Daniel Tjarnqvist .75 2.00

2004-05 Swedish Elitset

COMPLETE SET (288) 15.00 40.00
1 Markus Korhonen .08 .20
2 Daniel Johansson .08 .20
3 Tommy Sjodin .08 .20
4 Daniel Casselstahl .08 .20
5 Henrik Malmstrom .08 .20
6 Jakob Johansson .08 .20
7 Patrik Ronnqvist .08 .20
8 Roger Kyro .08 .20
9 Ove Molin .08 .20
10 Bjorn Danielsson .08 .20
11 Tommi Miettinen .08 .20
12 Bjorn Bjurling .08 .20
13 Staffan Kronwall .08 .20
14 Johnny Oduya .20 .50
15 Daniel Rudslatt .08 .20
16 Nichlas Falk .08 .20
17 Tomas Kollar .08 .20
18 Christian Eklund .08 .20
19 Fredrik Bremberg .08 .20
20 Mikael Johansson .08 .20
21 Marcus Kristoffersson .20 .50
22 Kenneth Bergqvist .08 .20
23 Johan Jonfeldt .08 .20
24 Jan-Axel Alavaara .08 .20
25 Antti-Jussi Niemi .08 .20
26 Ronnie Sundin .08 .20
27 Magnus Kahnberg .08 .20
28 Alexander Steen 1.50 4.00
29 Jari Tolsa .08 .20
30 Jonas Esbjors .08 .20
31 Niklas Andersson .08 .20
32 Peter Strom .08 .20
33 Jonas Johnson .30 .75
34 Jens Karlsson .08 .20
35 Fredrik Eriksson .08 .20
36 Martin Lindman .08 .20
37 Jonas Frogren .08 .20
38 Greger Artursson .08 .20
39 Radek Hamr .08 .20
40 Janne Gronvall .08 .20
41 Hannes Hyvonen .08 .20
42 Peter Nordstrom .08 .20
43 Par Backer .08 .20
44 Marcel Jenni .08 .20
45 Peter Hammarstrom .08 .20
46 Dieter Kalt .08 .20
47 Stefan Liv .40 1.00
48 Fredrik Olausson .08 .20
49 Ola Thorwalls .08 .20
50 Jouni Loponen .08 .20
51 Stefan Hellkvist .08 .20
52 Per-Age Skroder .08 .20
53 Peter Ekelund .08 .20
54 Martin Thornberg .08 .20
55 Anders Huusko .08 .20
56 Kalle Sahlstedt .08 .20
57 Pasi Maattanen .08 .20
58 Mattias Remstam .08 .20
59 Johan Davidsson .08 .20
60 Fredrik Norrena .20 .50
61 Peter Casparsson .08 .20
62 Martin Knold .08 .20
63 Jyrki Valivaara .08 .20
64 Mikko Peltola .08 .20
65 Tim Eriksson .08 .20
66 Fredrik Emvall .08 .20
67 Jussi Tarvainen .08 .20
68 Mikael Hakanson .08 .20
69 Per Eklund .08 .20
70 Gusten Tornqvist .08 .20
71 Jonas Andersson-Junkka .08 .20
72 Jan Sandstrom .08 .20
73 Tuukka Mantyla .08 .20
74 Stefan Nilsson .08 .20
75 Linus Fagemo .08 .20
76 Emil Lundberg .08 .20
77 Thomas Berglund .08 .20
78 Hans Huczkowski .08 .20
79 Per Ledin .08 .20
80 Johan Tellstrom .08 .20
81 Pierre Berggren .08 .20
82 Robert Borgqvist .08 .20
83 David Petrasek .08 .20
84 Magnus Osterby .08 .20
85 Petri Liimatainen .08 .20
86 Johan Norgren .08 .20
87 Peter Andersson .08 .20
88 Marcus Magnertoft .08 .20
89 Frans Nielsen .08 .20
90 Daniel Rydmark .08 .20
91 Mikael Wahlberg .08 .20
92 Kim Staal .08 .20
93 Jan Oberg .08 .20
94 Martin Johansson .08 .20
95 Lars Jansson .08 .20
96 Anders Soderberg .08 .20
97 Tommy Pettersson .08 .20
98 Fredrik Warg .08 .20
99 Magnus Hedlund .08 .20
100 Morten Green .08 .20
101 Magnus Gastrin .08 .20
102 Bengt Hoglund .08 .20
103 Adam Andersson .08 .20
104 Henrik Petre .08 .20
105 Daniel Back .08 .20
106 Hakan Bogg .08 .20
107 Jonas Westerling .08 .20
108 Magnus Sandberg .08 .20
109 Magnus Lindquist .08 .20
110 Bert Robertsson .08 .20
111 Jonathan Ericsson ERC .08 .20
112 Stefan Bemstrom .08 .20
113 Erik Norback .08 .20
114 Joakim Eriksson .08 .20
115 Robert Dome .08 .20
116 Robert Carlsson .08 .20

117 Teemu Riihijarvi .08 .20
118 Gabriel Karlsson .08 .20
119 Jorgen Bemstrom .08 .20
120 Peter Larsson .08 .20
121 Kimmo Kapanen .20 .50
122 Tommi Rajamaki .08 .20
123 Jesper Jager .08 .20
124 Sanny Lindstrom .08 .20
125 Kalle Koskinen .08 .20
126 Par Styf .08 .20
127 Christian Soderstrom .08 .20
128 Niklas Nordgren .08 .20
129 Valeri Krykov .08 .20
130 Per Hallin .08 .20
131 Christian Sjogren .08 .20
132 Fredrik Sundin .08 .20
133 Peter Andersson .08 .20
134 Ove Molin .08 .20
135 Daniel Rydmark .08 .20
136 Johan Davidsson .08 .20
137 Thomas Berglund .08 .20
138 Pelle Prestberg .08 .20
139 Mathias Johansson .08 .20
140 Roger Kyro .08 .20
141 Kristofer Ottosson .08 .20
142 Nichlas Falk .08 .20
143 Dieter Kalt .08 .20
144 Tomi Kallio .20 .50
145 Johan Holmqvist .20 .50
146 Niklas Andersson .08 .20
147 Mikko Kuparinen .08 .20
148 Mattias Karlsson .08 .20
149 Sebastian Sulku .08 .20
150 Jonas Soling .08 .20
151 Nicklas Danielsson .08 .20
152 Andreas Dackell .20 .50
153 Mikko Luovi .08 .20
154 Mikael Lind .08 .20
155 Vesa Viitakoski .08 .20
156 Rolf Wanhainen .08 .20
157 Mika Stromberg .08 .20
158 Daniel Fernholm .08 .20
159 Daniel Tjarnqvist .08 .20
160 Rikard Franzen .08 .20
161 Nils Ekman .20 .50
162 Kristofer Ottosson .08 .20
163 Robert Nilsson .08 .20
164 Johannes Salmonsson .08 .20
165 Marcus Nilson .30 .75
166 Jimmie Olvestad .08 .20
167 Espen Knutsen .30 .75
168 Mariusz Czerkawski .20 .50
169 Henrik Lundqvist 2.00 5.00
170 Tom Koivisto .08 .20
171 Arto Tukio .08 .20
172 Christian Backman .08 .20
173 Peter Hogardh .08 .20
174 Joel Lundqvist .08 .20
175 Loui Eriksson .30 .75
176 Samuel Pahlsson .20 .50
177 Martin Pluss .08 .20
178 Per-Johan Axelsson .20 .50
179 Tomi Kallio .20 .50
180 Daniel Henriksson .20 .50
181 Robin Jonsson .08 .20
182 Per Hallberg .08 .20
183 Mats Trygg .08 .20
184 Pelle Prestberg .08 .20
185 Jesper Mattsson .08 .20
186 Christian Berglund .08 .20
187 Jonas Hoglund .20 .50
188 Mathias Johansson .08 .20
189 Jorgen Jonsson .08 .20
190 Fredrik Eriksson .08 .20
191 Calle Steen .08 .20
192 Boo Ahl .20 .50
193 Daniel Ljungqvist .08 .20
194 Per Gustafsson .08 .20
195 Johan Halvardsson .08 .20
196 Kimmo Peltonen .08 .20
197 Mathias Tjarnqvist .20 .50
198 Andreas Karlsson .08 .20
199 Andreas Jamtin .08 .20
200 Stefan Pettersson .08 .20
201 Daniel Sperrle .08 .20
202 Magnus Johansson .08 .20
203 Henrik Tallinder .20 .50
204 Christoffer Norgren .08 .20
205 Jakob Karlsson .08 .20
206 Johan Franzen .40 1.00
207 Tony Martensson .08 .20
208 Ulf Soderstrom .08 .20
209 Brendan Morrison .20 .50
210 Kristian Huselius .20 .50
211 Mike Knuble .20 .50
212 Johan Lindstrom .08 .20
213 Kristian Antila .08 .20
214 Johan Fransson .20 .50
215 Niclas Wallin .08 .20
216 Roger Akerstrom .08 .20
217 Jaroslav Obsut .08 .20
218 Jonas Ronnqvist .08 .20
219 Thomas Koch .08 .20
220 Justin Williams .20 .50
221 Jonas Nordquist .08 .20
222 Fredrik Hynning .08 .20
223 Karl Fabritius .08 .20
224 Tomas Holmstrom .40 1.00
225 Andreas Hadelov .20 .50
226 Christopher Nilstorp .20 .50
227 Miska Kangasniemi .08 .20
228 Bjorn Melin .08 .20
229 Jan Hammar .08 .20
230 Jason Deleurme .08 .20
231 Carl Soderberg .60 1.50
232 Andreas Valdix .08 .20
233 Mika Hannula .08 .20
234 Peter Hammarstrom .08 .20
235 Markus Matthiasson .08 .20
236 Tommy Salo .20 .50
237 Mattias Timander .08 .20
238 Hans Jonsson .08 .20
239 Tobias Enstrom .08 .20
240 Jesper Damgaard .08 .20
241 Oscar Hedman .08 .20
242 Pierre Hedin .08 .20
243 Daniel Sedin .40 1.00
244 Mattias Weinhandl .20 .50
245 Andreas Salomonsson .20 .50
246 Peter Oberg .08 .20
247 Henrik Sedin .40 1.00
248 Peter Forsberg 1.25 3.00
249 Alexander Steen 1.50 4.00
250 Per Svartvadet .20 .50
251 Tero Leinonen .08 .20
252 Andreas Lilja .08 .20
253 Marko Kauppinen .08 .20
254 Pavel Skrbek .08 .20
255 Calle Bergstrom .08 .20
256 Peter Nolander .08 .20
257 Jonathan Granstrom .08 .20
258 Marcus Eriksson .08 .20
259 Shawn Horcoff .20 .50
260 Kenneth Bergqvist .08 .20
261 Anders Nilsson .08 .20
262 Martin Jansson .08 .20
263 Mikael Simons .08 .20
264 Peter Nylander .08 .20
265 Rastislav Stana .30 .75
266 Niclas Havelid .08 .20
267 Dick Tarnstrom .20 .50
268 Peter Popovic .08 .20
269 Petri Liimatainen .08 .20
270 Timmy Pettersson .08 .20
271 Jan Huokko .08 .20
272 Anders Burstrom .08 .20
273 Nicklas Bergfors .40 1.00
274 Jonas Andersson .08 .20
275 Peter Ferraro .20 .50
276 Chris Ferraro .20 .50
277 Miikka Kiprusoff .75 2.00
278 Jimmy Danielsson .08 .20
279 Johan Svedberg .08 .20
280 Mats Hansson .08 .20
281 Lars Jonsson .20 .50
282 Teemu Aalto .08 .20
283 Robert Carlsson .08 .20
284 Kristian Gahn .08 .20
285 Yared Hagos .20 .50
286 Henrik Zetterberg .75 2.00
287 Magnus Nilsson .08 .20
288 Jonathan Hedstrom .20 .50

2004-05 Swedish Elitset Dominators

Inserted at a rate of 1:16 series 2 packs.
COMPLETE SET (9) 25.00 50.00
STATED ODDS 1:16 SERIES 2
1 Kahnberg 1.25 3.00
Prestberg
Eriksson
2 Forsberg 6.00 15.00
Zetterberg
Huselius
3 Kiprusoff 6.00 15.00
Salo
Holmqvist
4 Fransson 4.00 10.00
Steen
Lundqvist
5 Morrison 3.00 8.00
Williams
Horcoff
6 Tallinder 3.00 8.00
Holmstrom
Lilja
7 Knutsen 1.25 3.00
Pluss
Kallio
8 Tarnstrom 1.25 3.00
Olausson
Tjarnqvist
9 Sedin 6.00 15.00
Sedin
Forsberg

2004-05 Swedish Elitset Forsberg Tribute

Inserted 1:8 series 1 packs.
COMPLETE SET (6) 10.00 25.00
STATED ODDS 1:8
1 Peter Forsberg 2.00 5.00
2 Peter Forsberg 2.00 5.00
3 Peter Forsberg 2.00 5.00
4 Peter Forsberg 2.00 5.00
5 Peter Forsberg 2.00 5.00
6 Peter Forsberg 2.00 5.00

2004-05 Swedish Elitset Future Stars

Inserted 1:8 series 1 packs.
COMPLETE SET (12) 15.00 30.00
STATED ODDS 1:8 SERIES 1
1 Carl Soderberg 1.50 4.00
2 Loui Eriksson 2.00 5.00
3 Linus Videll .75 2.00
4 Johan Fransson 2.00 5.00
5 Robert Nilsson 2.00 5.00
6 Nicklas Danielsson .75 2.00
7 Andreas Valdix .75 2.00
8 Alexander Steen 4.00 10.00
9 Joakim Lundstrom .75 2.00
10 Daniel Fernholm .75 2.00
11 Joakim Lindstrom .75 2.00
12 Mats Hansson .75 2.00

2004-05 Swedish Elitset Gold

3X to 5X BASE CARD VALUE

2004-05 Swedish Elitset High Expectations

Inserted 1:16 in series 1 packs.
COMPLETE SET (10) 10.00 25.00
STATED ODDS 1:16 SERIES 1
1 Jonas Soling .75 2.00
2 Tomas Kollar .75 2.00
3 Henrik Lundqvist 6.00 15.00
4 Mathias Johansson .75 2.00
5 Bjorn Melin .75 2.00
6 Tim Eriksson .75 2.00
7 Jonas Ronnqvist .75 2.00
8 Mattias Wennerberg .75 2.00
9 Peter Popovic .75 2.00
10 Yared Hagos 1.25 3.00

2004-05 Swedish Elitset In The Crease

Inserted 1:32 series 1 packs.
COMPLETE SET (10) 15.00 40.00
STATED ODDS 1:32 SERIES 1
1 Markus Korhonen 1.25 3.00
2 Bjorn Bjurling 1.25 3.00
3 Henrik Lundqvist 10.00 25.00
4 Sinuhe Wallinheimo 1.25 3.00
5 Stefan Liv 2.00 5.00
6 Fredrik Norrena 2.00 5.00
7 Daniel Henriksson 1.25 3.00
8 Andreas Hadelov 1.25 3.00
9 Rolf Wanhainen 1.25 3.00
10 Kimmo Kapanen 1.25 3.00

2004-05 Swedish Elitset Jerseys Series 1

STATED PRINT RUN 35 SETS
1 Markus Korhonen 12.00 30.00
2 Kimmo Kapanen 12.00 30.00
3 Sinuhe Wallinheimo 12.00 30.00
4 Henrik Lundqvist 30.00 75.00
5 Per Gustavsson 12.00 30.00

2004-05 Swedish Elitset Jerseys Series 2

STATED PRINT RUN 35 SETS
AH Andreas Hadelov 12.00 30.00
PP Peter Popovic 12.00 30.00
SL Stefan Liv 20.00 50.00
TJ Thomas Johansson 12.00 30.00

2004-05 Swedish Elitset Limited Signatures

Random inserts in series 2 packs, limited to 50 copies each.
STATED PRINT RUN 50 SETS
INSERTED RANDOMLY SERIES 2
1 Daniel Henriksson 10.00 25.00
2 Jorgen Jonsson 10.00 25.00
3 Per Gustavsson 10.00 25.00
4 Andreas Lilja 10.00 25.00
5 Niclas Havelid 10.00 25.00
6 Jonas Ronnqvist 10.00 25.00

2004-05 Swedish Elitset Masks

Inserted 1:32 series 2 packs.
COMPLETE SET (8) 50.00 100.00
STATED ODDS 1:32 SERIES 2
1 Johan Holmqvist 4.00 10.00
2 Bjorn Bjurling 4.00 10.00
3 Henrik Lundqvist 12.00 30.00
4 Stefan Liv 6.00 15.00
5 Andreas Hadelov 4.00 10.00
6 Gusten Tornqvist 4.00 10.00
7 Rastislav Stana 6.00 15.00
8 Miikka Kiprusoff 12.00 30.00

2004-05 Swedish Elitset Signatures

Inserted 1:32 series 1 packs.
COMPLETE SET (15) 100.00 175.00
STATED ODDS 1:32 SERIES 1
1 Andreas Hadelov 6.00 15.00
2 Andreas Valdix 6.00 15.00
3 Joakim Eriksson 6.00 15.00
4 Rolf Wanhainen 6.00 15.00
5 Jonas Ronnqvist 6.00 15.00
6 Johan Fransson 10.00 25.00
7 Per Svartvadet 6.00 15.00
8 Bjorn Bjurling 6.00 15.00
9 Niklas Falk 6.00 15.00
10 Robert Carlsson 6.00 15.00
11 Yared Hagos 6.00 15.00
12 Joakim Lundstrom 6.00 15.00
13 Mikael Lind 6.00 15.00
14 Pelle Prestberg 6.00 15.00
15 Hannes Hyvonen 6.00 15.00

2004-05 Swedish Elitset Signatures Series A

STATED ODDS 1:32 SERIES 2
1 Frans Nielsen 4.00 10.00
2 Kim Staal 4.00 10.00
3 Per Eklund 4.00 10.00
4 Fredrik Norrena 6.00 15.00
5 Mikko Peltola 4.00 10.00
6 Tim Eriksson 4.00 10.00
7 Roger Akerstrom 4.00 10.00
8 Daniel Henriksson 4.00 10.00
9 Mats Hansson 4.00 10.00
10 Kimmo Kapanen 6.00 15.00
11 Tommi Miettinen 4.00 10.00
12 Bjorn Danielsson 4.00 10.00
13 Marcel Jenni 4.00 10.00
14 Henrik Lundqvist 20.00 50.00
15 Tomi Kallio 4.00 10.00
16 Niklas Andersson 4.00 10.00
17 Antti-Jussi Niemi 4.00 10.00

2004-05 Swedish Elitset Signatures Series B

STATED ODDS 1:32 SERIES 2
1 Andreas Dackell 4.00 10.00
2 Johan Holmqvist 6.00 15.00
3 Daniel Henriksson 4.00 10.00
4 Jonas Hoglund 4.00 10.00
5 Jorgen Jonsson 4.00 10.00
6 Mathias Johansson 4.00 10.00
7 Kimmo Peltonen 4.00 10.00
8 Mathias Tjarnqvist 6.00 15.00
9 Stefan Pettersson 4.00 10.00
10 Andreas Lilja 6.00 15.00
11 Mikael Simons 4.00 10.00
12 Peter Nylander 4.00 10.00
13 Dick Tarnstrom 4.00 10.00
14 Niclas Havelid 6.00 15.00
15 Peter Forsberg 30.00 75.00
16 Tommy Salo 6.00 15.00
17 Tomas Holmstrom 10.00 25.00

2004-05 Swedish HV71 Postcards

We have confirmed a handful of cards from this Swedish issue, thanks to collector Vinnie Montalbano. It's a certainty that others exist. If you know of others, please email hockeymag@beckett.com.
COMPLETE SET
1 Brian Boucher 1.25 3.00
2 Andreas Jamtin .75 2.00
3 Simon Skoog .75 2.00
4 David Fredriksson .75 2.00
5 Fredrik Olausson .75 2.00
6 Per Gustafsson .75 2.00
7 Peter Ekelund .75 2.00
8 Anders Huusko .75 2.00

2004-05 Swedish MoDo Postcards

These 5X7 postcards were issued by the team, apparently in set form. They are unnumbered and feature more than a dozen moonlighting NHLers.
COMPLETE SET (30) 20.00 40.00
1 Peter Forsberg 4.00 10.00
2 Henrik Sedin 2.00 5.00
3 Daniel Sedin 2.00 5.00
4 Mattias Weinhandl .75 2.00
5 Adrian Aucoin .75 2.00
6 Mattias Timander .75 2.00
7 Per Svartvadet .75 2.00
8 Alexander Steen 4.00 10.00
9 Tommy Salo .75 2.00
10 Markus Naslund 2.00 5.00
11 Andreas Salomonsson .75 2.00
12 Frantisek Kaberle .75 2.00
13 Hans Jonsson .40 1.00
14 Joakim Lindstrom .40 1.00
15 Pierre Hedin .40 1.00
16 Dan Hinote .75 2.00
17 Lars Jansson .40 1.00
18 Magnus Gastrin .40 1.00
19 Mattias Hellstrom .40 1.00
20 Tobias Viklund .40 1.00
21 Michael Zajkowski .40 1.00
22 Morten Green .40 1.00
23 Mattias Wennerberg .40 1.00
24 Magnus Hedlund .40 1.00
25 Peter Oberg .40 1.00
26 Fredrik Warg .40 1.00
27 Jarmo Hedman .40 1.00
28 Tobias Enstrom .40 1.00
29 Jan Oberg .40 1.00
30 Jesper Damgaard .40 1.00

2004-05 Swedish Pure Skills

COMPLETE SET (144) 20.00 50.00
1 Johan Holmqvist .20 .50
2 Chris Phillips .08 .20
3 Tommy Sjodin .08 .20
4 Andreas Dackell .08 .20
5 Tommi Miettinen .08 .20
6 Ronald Petrovicky .08 .20
7 Mikael Lind .08 .20
8 Jose Theodore 1.25 3.00
9 Daniel Tjarnqvist .08 .20
10 Dan Boyle .08 .20
11 Nils Ekman .08 .20
12 Marcus Nilson .08 .20
13 Espen Knutsen .08 .20
14 Mariusz Czerkawski .08 .20
15 Henrik Lundqvist 1.50 4.00
16 Tom Koivisto .08 .20
17 Sami Salo .08 .20
18 Christian Backman .08 .20
19 Daniel Alfredsson .40 1.00
20 Niklas Andersson .08 .20
21 Samuel Pahlsson .20 .50
22 Martin Pluss .08 .20
23 Jonas Johnson .08 .20
24 Tomi Kallio .08 .20
25 Martin Gerber .30 .75
26 Zdeno Chara .30 .75
27 Sheldon Souray .08 .20
28 Pelle Prestberg .08 .20
29 Christian Berglund .08 .20
30 Jonas Hoglund .08 .20
31 Peter Nordstrom .08 .20
32 Jorgen Jonsson .08 .20
33 Marian Gaborik 1.25 3.00
34 Stefan Liv .40 1.00
35 Anders Eriksson .08 .20
36 Per Gustafsson .08 .20
37 Manny Malhotra .08 .20
38 Andreas Karlsson .08 .20
39 Jonathan Cheechoo .60 1.50
40 Johan Davidsson .08 .20
41 Fredrik Norrena .40 1.00
42 Magnus Johansson .08 .20
43 Thomas Johansson .08 .20
44 Mikko Peltola .08 .20
45 Tony Martensson .08 .20
46 Brendan Morrison .20 .50
47 Michael Knuble .20 .50
48 Kristian Antila .20 .50
49 Niclas Wallin .08 .20
50 Roger Akerstrom .08 .20
51 Jaroslav Obsut .08 .20
52 Jonas Ronnqvist .08 .20
53 Justin Williams .20 .50
54 Per Ledin .08 .20
55 Tomas Holmstrom .40 1.00
56 Andreas Hadelov .20 .50
57 David Petrasek .08 .20
58 Peter Andersson .08 .20
59 Bjorn Melin .08 .20
60 Carl Soderberg .40 1.00
61 Mika Hannula .08 .20
62 Tommy Salo .20 .50
63 Mattias Timander .08 .20
64 Adrian Aucoin .20 .50
65 Daniel Sedin .30 .75
66 Mattias Weinhandl .20 .50
67 Markus Naslund .75 2.00
68 Henrik Sedin .30 .75
69 Peter Forsberg 2.00 5.00
70 Alexander Steen .75 2.00
71 Per Svartvadet .08 .20
72 Dan Hinote .20 .50
73 Tero Leinonen .20 .50
74 Pavel Skrbek .08 .20
75 Daniel Cleary .08 .20
76 Rastislav Pavlikovsky .20 .50
77 Marian Hossa .75 2.00
78 Shawn Horcoff .30 .75
79 Ladislav Nagy .30 .75
80 Marcel Hossa .30 .75
81 Rastislav Stana .30 .75
82 Dick Tarnstrom .20 .50
83 Peter Popovic .08 .20
84 Joakim Eriksson .08 .20
85 Kyle Calder .20 .50
86 Mikael Samuelsson .08 .20
87 Scott Thornton .20 .50
88 Dragan Umicevic .08 .20
89 Miikka Kiprusoff .75 2.00
90 Aki-Petteri Berg .08 .20
91 Teemu Aalto .08 .20
92 Niklas Nordgren .08 .20
93 Yared Hagos .20 .50
94 Henrik Zetterberg .75 2.00
95 Kent Manderville .08 .20
96 Jonathan Hedstrom .20 .50
97 Landon Wilson .20 .50
98 Ladislav Kohn .08 .20
99 Mike Ribeiro .20 .50
100 Tomas Vokoun .75 2.00
101 Marek Zidlicky .20 .50
102 Jere Karalahti .08 .20
103 Jarno Kultanen .08 .20
104 Lasse Pirjeta .20 .50
105 Jarkko Ruutu .20 .50
106 Timo Parssinen .08 .20
107 Brett Harkins .20 .50
108 Mika Noronen .20 .50
109 Josh Holden .20 .50
110 Riku Hahl .20 .50
111 Jani Rita .20 .50
112 Juuso Riksman .08 .20
113 Sami Helenius .08 .20
114 Steve Kariya .40 1.00
115 Patrik Stefan .20 .50
116 Hannes Hyvonen .08 .20
117 Tim Thomas .40 1.00
118 Ossi Vaananen .20 .50
119 Marko Jantunen .08 .20
120 Toni Dahlman .08 .20
121 Glen Metropolit .20 .50
122 Sinuhe Wallinheimo .20 .50
123 Steve Martins .20 .50
124 Jarkko Immonen .20 .50
125 Jody Shelley .40 1.00
126 Niklas Backstrom 1.00 2.50
127 Janne Niinimaa .20 .50
128 Josef Boumedienne .08 .20
129 Petr Tenkrat .08 .20
130 Michael Nylander .20 .50
131 Dwayne Roloson .75 2.00
132 Erik Hamalainen .08 .20
133 Esa Pirnes .08 .20
134 Pasi Nurminen .20 .50
135 Jarmo Myllys .20 .50
136 Andrew Raycroft 1.00 2.50
137 Ville Nieminen .20 .50
138 Stefan Ohman .08 .20
139 Teemu Lassila .08 .20
140 Craig Rivet .20 .50
141 Saku Koivu .60 1.50
142 Antti Aalto .08 .20
143 Scott Langkow .08 .20
144 Jason Williams .30 .75

2004-05 Swedish Pure Skills Jerseys

Limited to 35 copies each.
COMPLETE SET (4) 30.00 80.00
JR Jarkko Ruutu 10.00 25.00
PS Per Svartvadet 10.00 25.00
TS Tommy Salo 10.00 25.00
VN Ville Nieminen 10.00 25.00

2004-05 Swedish Pure Skills Parallel

Inserted at a rate of 1:4 packs and limited to just 100 copies.
5X to 8X BASE CARD VALUE

2004-05 Swedish Pure Skills Professional Power

COMPLETE SET (25) 30.00 75.00
AB Aki-Petteri Berg .75 2.00
CR Craig Rivet 1.25 3.00
DA Daniel Alfredsson 2.00 5.00
DS Daniel Sedin 1.25 3.00
DT Daniel Tjarnqvist .75 2.00
DT Dick Tarnstrom 1.25 3.00
HS Henrik Sedin 1.25 3.00
HZ Henrik Zetterberg 4.00 10.00
JN Janne Niinimaa .75 2.00
MC Mariusz Czerkawski .75 2.00
MG Marian Gaborik 6.00 15.00
MH Marian Hossa 4.00 10.00
MN Marcus Nilson .75 2.00
MN Markus Naslund 4.00 10.00
MN Michael Nylander 1.25 3.00
MZ Marek Zidlicky .75 2.00
OV Ossi Vaananen .75 2.00
PF Peter Forsberg 10.00 25.00
PS Patrik Stefan .75 2.00
RH Raimo Helminen .75 2.00
SK Saku Koivu 4.00 10.00
SP Samuel Pahlsson .75 2.00
SS Sami Salo .75 2.00
VN Ville Nieminen .75 2.00
ZC Zdeno Chara 1.25 3.00

2004-05 Swedish Pure Skills Signatures Limited

Limited to just 50 copies each.
PRINT RUN 50 SER.#'d SETS 100.00 200.00
1 Andreas Dackell 10.00 25.00
2 Peter Forsberg 60.00 125.00
3 Henrik Zetterberg 20.00 50.00
4 Miikka Kiprusoff 20.00 50.00

2004-05 Swedish Pure Skills The Wall

Inserted at a rate of 1:40.
COMPLETE SET (10) 40.00 100.00
AR Andrew Raycroft 8.00 20.00
FN Fredrik Norrena 2.00 5.00
HL Henrik Lundqvist 8.00 20.00
JT Jose Theodore 10.00 25.00
MG Martin Gerber 4.00 10.00
MK Miikka Kiprusoff 10.00 25.00
MN Mika Noronen 2.00 5.00
NB Niklas Backstrom 4.00 10.00
TS Tommy Salo 2.00 5.00
TT Tim Thomas 6.00 15.00

2005-06 Swedish SHL Elitset

COMPLETE SET (288) 25.00 60.00
1 Johan Holmqvist .40 1.00
2 Niklas Andersson .20 .50
3 Mikko Kuparinen .10 .25
4 Tommy Sjodin .10 .25
5 Sebastian Sulku .10 .25
6 Henrik Malmstrom .10 .25
7 Andreas Dackell .10 .25
8 Ove Molin .10 .25
9 Bjorn Danielsson .10 .25
10 Tommi Miettinen .10 .25
11 Mikael Lind .10 .25
12 Vesa Viitakoski .10 .25
13 Jose Theodore 1.25 3.00
14 Ronnie Pettersson .10 .25
15 Daniel Tjarnqvist .20 .50
16 Christopher Thorn .10 .25
17 Robert Nilsson .75 2.00
18 Daniel Rudslat .10 .25
19 Nichlas Falk .10 .25
20 Marcus Nilson .20 .50
21 Jimmie Olvestad .10 .25
22 Patrick Thoresen .40 1.00
23 Tom Koivisto .10 .25
24 Antti-Jussi Niemi .10 .25
25 Sami Salo .10 .25
26 Daniel Alfredsson .75 2.00
27 Magnus Kahnberg .10 .25
28 Peter Hogardh .10 .25
29 Jari Tolsa .10 .25
30 Joel Lundqvist .20 .50
31 Jonas Esbjors .10 .25
32 Niklas Andersson .10 .25
33 Samuel Pahlsson .20 .50
34 Martin Pluss .10 .25
35 Jonas Johnsson .10 .25
36 Tomi Kallio .10 .25
37 Martin Gerber .40 1.00
38 Daniel Henriksson .10 .25
39 Robin Jonsson .10 .25
40 Jonas Frogren .10 .25
41 Radek Hamr .10 .25
42 Zdeno Chara .75 2.00
43 Pelle Prestberg .10 .25
44 Jesper Mattsson .10 .25
45 Jonas Hoglund .10 .25
46 Mathias Johansson .10 .25
47 Peter Nordstrom .10 .25
48 Fredrik Eriksson .10 .25
49 Par Backer .10 .25
50 Stefan Liv .40 1.00
51 Anders Eriksson .10 .25
52 Daniel Ljungqvist .10 .25
53 Per Gustafsson .10 .25
54 Simon Skoog .10 .25
55 Ola Svanberg .10 .25
56 Johan Halvardsson .10 .25
57 Anders Huusko .10 .25
58 Andreas Karlsson .10 .25
59 Pasi Maattanen .10 .25
60 Stefan Pettersson .10, .25
61 Johan Davidsson .10 .25
62 Johan Backlund .10 .25
63 Stefan Bemstrom .10 .25
64 A–rjan Lindmark .10 .25
65 Jens Bergenstrom .10 .25
66 Niklas Eriksson .10 .25
67 Niklas Persson .10 .25
68 Johan Rosen .10 .25
69 Fredrik Norrena .40 1.00
70 Magnus Johansson .10 .25
71 Thomas Johansson .10 .25
72 Christoffer Norgren .10 .25
73 Jyrki VĤlivaara .10 .25
74 Mikko Peltola .10 .25
75 Ulf Soderstrom .10 .25
76 Johan Andersson .10 .25
77 Tim Eriksson .10 .25
78 Michael Knuble .20 .50
79 Fredrik Emwall .10 .25
80 Jussi Tarvainen .10 .25
81 Mikael Hakanson .10 .25
82 Gusten Tornqvist .10 .25
83 Johan Fransson .10 .25
84 Jan Sandstrom .10 .25
85 Jaroslav Obsut .10 .25
86 Jonas Ronnqvist .10 .25
87 Thomas Koch .10 .25
88 Emil Lundberg .10 .25
89 Jonas Nordquist .10 .25
90 Fredrik Hynning .10 .25
91 Karl Fabricius .10 .25
92 Michael Zajkowski .10 .25
93 Hans Jonsson .10 .25
94 Tobias Enstrom .10 .25
95 Jesper Damgaard .10 .25
96 Oscar Hedman .10 .25
97 Daniel Sedin .40 1.00
98 Mattias Weinhandl .10 .25
99 Andreas Salomonsson .10 .25
100 Markus Naslund .75 2.00
101 Henrik Sedin .40 1.00
102 Peter Forsberg 2.00 5.00
103 Morten Green .10 .25
104 Per Svartvadet .10 .25
105 Magnus Gastrin .10 .25
106 Calle BergstrĶm .10 .25
107 Peter Nolander .10 .25
108 Jonathan Granstrom .10 .25
109 Hakan Bogg .10 .25
110 Shawn Horcoff .40 1.00
111 Jonas Westerling .10 .25
112 Marian Hossa .75 2.00
113 Marcus Eriksson .10 .25
114 Magnus Sandberg .10 .25
115 Kenneth Bergkvist .10 .25
116 Anders Nilsson .10 .25
117 Mikael Simons .10 .25
118 Magnus Lindquist .10 .25
119 Bert Robertsson .10 .25
120 Nicklas Grossman .10 .25
121 Dick Tarnstrom .10 .25
122 Petri Liimatainen .10 .25
123 Timmy Pettersson .10 .25
124 Jan Huokko .10 .25
125 Anders Burstrom .10 .25
126 Robert Carlsson .10 .25
127 Nicklas Bergfors .40 1.00
128 Erik Norback .10 .25
129 Gabriel Karlsson .10 .25
130 Jorgen Bemstrom .10 .25
131 Miikka Kiprusoff 1.25 3.00
132 Johan Svedberg .10 .25
133 Sanny Lindstrom .10 .25
134 Kalle Koskinen .10 .25
135 Mats Hansson .10 .25
136 Teemu Aalto .10 .25
137 Christian Soderstrom .10 .25
138 Robert Carlsson .10 .25
139 Niklas Nordgren .20 .50
140 Per Hallin .10 .25
141 Kristian Gahn .10 .25
142 Henrik Zetterberg .75 2.00
143 Magnus Nilsson .10 .25
144 Jonathan Hedstrom .10 .25
145 Markus Korhonen .10 .25
146 Daniel Johansson .10 .25
147 Martin Ohrstedt .10 .25
148 Jorgen Sundqvist .10 .25
149 Daniel Casselstahl .10 .25
150 Rodrigo Lavins .10 .25
151 Antti Aarnio .10 .25
152 Jonas Almtorp .10 .25
153 Mathias Mansson .10 .25
154 Nicklas Backstom ERC 4.00 10.00
155 Lars-Erik Spets .10 .25
156 Mikael Wahlberg .10 .25
157 Petter Ronnquist .10 .25
158 Teemu Lassila .10 .25
159 Andre Mattsson .10 .25
160 Jonas Liwing .10 .25
161 Erik Ryman .10 .25
162 Adam Andersson .10 .25
163 Jesper Bjorck .10 .25
164 Henrik Nordfeldt .10 .25
165 Johan Eneqvist .10 .25
166 Christofer Lofberg .10 .25
167 Patric Hornqvist .10 .25
168 Fredrik Bremberg .10 .25
169 Marcus Kristoffersson .10 .25
170 Per Eklund .10 .25
171 Mikael Sandberg .10 .25
172 Tommy Salo .20 .50
173 Jan-Axel Alavaara .10 .25
174 Arto Tukio .10 .25
175 Richard Demen-Willaume .10 .25
176 Ronnie Sundin .10 .25
177 Johnny Oduya .20 .50
178 Sebastian Karlsson .10 .25
179 Kirill Starkov .10 .25
180 Johan Witehall .10 .25
181 Christopher Heino-Lindberg .10 .25
182 Rami Alanko .10 .25
183 Per Hallberg .10 .25
184 Thomas Rhodin .10 .25
185 Mikael Johansson .10 .25
186 Rickard Wallin .10 .25
187 Jorgen Jonsson .10 .25
188 Fredrik Eriksson .10 .25
189 Johan Olsson .10 .25
190 Emil Kaberg .10 .25
191 Per Ledin .10 .25
192 Erik Ersberg ERC 1.00 2.50
193 Fredrik Olausson .10 .25
194 Lars Jonsson .20 .50
195 Mika Niskanen .10 .25
196 David Petrasek .10 .25
197 Martin Thornberg .10 .25
198 David Fredriksson .10 .25
199 Bjorn Melin .10 .25
200 Jens Karlsson .10 .25
201 Mattias Remstam .10 .25
202 Mika Hannula .10 .25
203 Tomas Duba .10 .25
204 Elias Granat .10 .25
205 Magnus Osterby .10 .25
206 Yan Golubovsky .10 .25
207 Jan Srdinko .10 .25
208 Patrik Hucko .10 .25
209 Patrik Wallenberg .10 .25
210 Mike Watt .10 .25
211 Sebastian Meijer .10 .25
212 Jesper Ollas .10 .25
213 Niklas Broms .10 .25
214 Magnus Hedlund .10 .25
215 Oscar Steen .10 .25
216 Jimmie Ericsson .10 .25
217 Jukka Tiilikainen .10 .25
218 Jiri Bicek .10 .25
219 Jonas Fransson .10 .25
220 Andreas Pihl .10 .25
221 Mikko Luoma .10 .25
222 Victor Ringberg .10 .25
223 Tony Martensson .10 .25
224 Jonas Soling .10 .25
225 Sami Torkki .10 .25
226 Johan Lindstrom .10 .25
227 Patric Blomdahl .10 .25
228 David Rautio .10 .25
229 Mattias Modig .10 .25
230 Erik Lindberg .10 .25
231 Pekka Saravo .10 .25
232 Pavel Skrbek .10 .25
233 Per Savilahti-Nagander .10 .25
234 Johan Harju .10 .25
235 Mikael Renberg .20 .50
236 Ragnar Karlsson .10 .25
237 Vladimir Machulda .10 .25
238 Lubomir Bartecko .10 .25
239 Magnus Isaksson .10 .25
240 Christopher Konigsson .10 .25
241 Karol Krizan .10 .25
242 Mattias Timander .10 .25
243 Vladimir Sicak .10 .25
244 Tobias Viklund .10 .25
245 Mattias Hellstrom .10 .25
246 Pasi Tuominen .10 .25
247 Rastislav Pavlikovsky .10 .25
248 Peter Oberg .10 .25
249 Mikael Pettersson .10 .25
250 Miloslav Horava .10 .25
251 Jan Pardavy .10 .25
252 Daniel Sperrle .10 .25
253 Petri Vehanen .10 .25
254 Peter Smrek .10 .25
255 Atvars Tribuntsovs .10 .25
256 Ross Lupaschuk .10 .25
257 Pierre Johnsson .10 .25
258 Jarno Kultanen .10 .25
259 Thomas Skogs .10 .25
260 Jordan Krestanovich .10 .25
261 Marco Tuokko .10 .25
262 Eric Johansson .10 .25
263 Kalle Kerman .10 .25
264 Peter Fabus .10 .25
265 Teemu Elomo .10 .25
266 Martin Jansson .10 .25
267 Rastislav Stana .20 .50
268 Stanislav Neckar .10 .25
269 Henrik Petre .10 .25
270 Jonathan Ericsson .10 .25
271 Daniel Ljungqvist .10 .25
272 Pasi Petrilainen .10 .25
273 Per-Ake Skroder .10 .25
274 Christoph Brandner .10 .25
275 Anze Kopitar 6.00 15.00
276 Tomas Kollar .10 .25
277 Dragan Umicevic .10 .25
278 Petr Leska .10 .25
279 Johan Asplund .10 .25
280 Mika Oksa .10 .25
281 Par Styf .10 .25
282 Carl-Johan Johansson .10 .25
283 Peter Regin .10 .25
284 Frans Nielsen .40 1.00
285 Mattias Wennerberg .10 .25
286 Peter Strom .10 .25
287 Valeri Krykov .10 .25
288 Fredrik Warg .10 .25

2005-06 Swedish SHL Elitset Catchers

COMPLETE SET (12) 40.00 80.00
STATED ODDS 1:16 SER. 2 PACKS
1 Johan Holmqvist 3.00 8.00
2 Teemu Lassila 3.00 8.00
3 Tommy Salo 3.00 8.00
4 Daniel Henriksson 3.00 8.00
5 Stefan Liv 4.00 10.00
6 Johan Backlund 3.00 8.00
7 Fredrik Norrena 4.00 10.00
8 David Rautio 3.00 8.00
9 Karol Krizan 3.00 8.00
10 Petri Vehanen 3.00 8.00
11 Rastislav Stana 4.00 10.00
12 Mika Oksa 3.00 8.00

2005-06 Swedish SHL Elitset Icons

COMPLETE SET (9) 15.00 30.00
STATED ODDS 1:32 SER. 2 PACKS
1 Peter HammarstrĶm 2.00 5.00
2 Jorgen Jonsson 2.00 5.00
3 Mathias Johansson 2.00 5.00
4 Thomas Johansson 2.00 5.00
5 Jonas Johnsson 2.00 5.00
6 Kristian Gahn 2.00 5.00
7 Ove Molin 2.00 5.00
8 Per Gustafsson 2.00 5.00
9 Fredrik Bremberg 2.00 5.00

2005-06 Swedish SHL Elitset Playmakers

COMPLETE SET (12) 25.00 60.00
STATED ODDS 1:32 SER. 1 PACKS
1 Mikael Lind 2.00 5.00
2 Marcus Nilson 2.00 5.00
3 Niklas Andersson 2.00 5.00
4 Daniel Alfredsson 4.00 10.00
5 Jorgen Jonsson 2.00 5.00
6 Johan Davidsson 2.00 5.00
7 Brendan Morrison 2.00 5.00
8 Daniel Sedin 3.00 8.00
9 Henrik Sedin 3.00 8.00
10 Marian Hossa 6.00 15.00
11 Scott Thornton 2.00 5.00
12 Henrik Zetterberg 6.00 15.00

2005-06 Swedish SHL Elitset Rookies

COMPLETE SET (9) 12.00 30.00
STATED ODDS 1:32 SER. 2 PACKS
1 Alexander Ribbenstrand 1.50 4.00
2 Anton Axelsson 1.50 4.00
3 Christopher Heino-Lindberg 1.50 4.00
4 Erik Andersson 1.50 4.00
5 Mattias Ritola 1.50 4.00
6 Robin Lindqvist 1.50 4.00

7 Tommy Enstrom 1.50 4.00
8 Jens Jakobs 1.50 4.00
9 Anton Stralman 2.50 6.00

2005-06 Swedish SHL Elitset Series One Signatures

COMPLETE SET (15) 100.00 200.00
1 Ulf Soderstrom 6.00 15.00
2 Tim Eriksson 6.00 15.00
3 Petri Liimatainen 6.00 15.00
4 Nicklas Grossman 6.00 15.00
5 Oscar Hedman 6.00 15.00
6 Tobias Viklund 6.00 15.00
7 Johan Davidsson 6.00 15.00
8 Ola Svanberg 6.00 15.00
9 Anders Huusko 6.00 15.00
10 Jonas Hoglund 6.00 15.00
11 Daniel Henriksson 6.00 15.00
12 Johan Fransson 6.00 15.00
13 Karl Fabricius 6.00 15.00
14 Gusten Tornqvist 6.00 15.00
15 Christopher Thorn 6.00 15.00

2005-06 Swedish SHL Elitset Series Two Signatures

The short printed autographs are not priced due to a lack of market activity.
1 Mathias Mansson SP
2 Mikael Wahlberg SP
3 Adam Andersson 6.00 15.00
4 Patrick Thoresen 8.00 20.00
5 Niklas Andersson 6.00 15.00
6 Magnus Kahnberg 6.00 15.00
7 Tomi Kallio 8.00 20.00
8 Mathias Johansson 6.00 15.00
9 Jesper Mattsson 6.00 15.00
10 Thomas Rhodin 6.00 15.00
11 Per Gustafsson 6.00 15.00
12 Stefan Liv 10.00 25.00
13 Stefan Pettersson 6.00 15.00
14 Tomas Duba 6.00 15.00
15 Ã–rjan Lindmark 6.00 15.00
16 Niklas Persson 6.00 15.00
17 Fredrik Emwall 6.00 15.00
18 Tony Martensson 6.00 15.00
19 Fredrik Norrena 8.00 20.00
20 Lubomir Bartecko 6.00 15.00
21 David Rautio 6.00 15.00
22 Mikael Renberg 10.00 25.00
23 Christoph Brandner 6.00 15.00
24 Anze Kopitar 75.00 125.00
25 Jan Huokko 6.00 15.00
26 Peter Strom 6.00 15.00
27 Christian Soderstrom 6.00 15.00
28 Mattias Wennerberg 6.00 15.00
29 Mats Hansson SP
30 Henrik Lundqvist SP
31 Jorgen Jonsson SP
32 Joel Lundqvist SP

2005-06 Swedish SHL Elitset Star Potential

COMPLETE SET (18) 15.00 40.00
STATED ODDS 1:8 SER. 1 PACKS
1 Niklas Andersson .75 2.00
2 Nicklas Backstrom 2.50 6.00
3 Robert Nilsson .75 2.00
4 Christopher Thorn 1.50 4.00
5 Loui Eriksson 1.50 4.00
6 Henrik Lundqvist 4.00 10.00
7 Robin Jonsson .75 2.00
8 Ola Svanberg .75 2.00
9 Tony Martensson .75 2.00
10 Johan Fransson .75 2.00
11 Tobias Enstrom .75 2.00
12 Oscar Hedman .75 2.00
13 Jonathan Granstrom .75 2.00
14 Nicklas Bergfors 1.50 4.00
15 Dragan Umisevic .75 2.00
16 Linus Videll .75 2.00
17 Yared Hagos .75 2.00
18 Mats Hansson .75 2.00

2005-06 Swedish SHL Elitset Stoppers

COMPLETE SET (12) 30.00 75.00
STATED ODDS 1:16 SER. 1 PACKS
1 Johan Holmqvist 3.00 8.00
2 Jose Theodore 6.00 15.00
3 Rolf Wanhainen 2.00 5.00
4 Henrik Lundqvist 6.00 15.00
5 Martin Gerber 3.00 8.00
6 Daniel Henriksson 2.00 5.00
7 Stefan Liv 3.00 8.00
8 Fredrik Norrena 3.00 8.00
9 Tommy Salo 2.00 5.00
10 Tero Leinonen 2.00 5.00
11 Rastislav Stana 2.00 5.00
12 Miikka Kiprusoff 6.00 15.00

2005-06 Swedish SHL Elitset Teammates

COMPLETE SET (12) 8.00 20.00
STATED ODDS 1:8 SER. 2 PACKS
1 Andreas Dackell / Mikael Lind .75 2.00
2 Nichlas Falk / Patrick Thoresen .75 2.00
3 Jonas Hoglund / Pelle Prestberg .75 2.00
4 Niklas Andersson / Tomi Kallio .75 2.00
5 Johan Davidsson / Mattias Remstam .75 2.00
6 Niklas Person / Patrik Wallenberg .75 2.00
7 Fredrik Emwall / Ulf SÃ¶derstrÃ¶m .75 2.00
8 Karl Fabricius / Mikael Renberg 1.25 3.00
9 Andreas Salomonsson / Per Svartvadet .75 2.00
10 Anders Nilsson / Kalle Kerman .75 2.00
11 Jorgen Bemstrom / Timmy Pettersson .75 2.00
12 Robert Carlsson / Valeri Krykov .75 2.00

2006-07 Swedish HockeyAllsvenskan Future Stars

1 John Wikner
2 Martin Gudmundsson
3 Emil Axelsson
4 Alexander HellstrÃ¶m
5 Johan Larsson
6 Mikael Owilli
7 Linus Klasen
8 Mattias Ritola
9 Marcus Olsson
10 Magnus Svensson
11 Linus BladstrÃ¶m
12 Mattias SjÃ¶gren
13 Tommy EnstrÃ¶m
14 Fredric Andersson
15 Mikael Backlund
16 Robert RosÃ©n

2006-07 Swedish HockeyAllsvenskan Hot Numbers

1 Ivan Puncochar
2 Andreas Lindahl
3 Johan Ã„lgekrans
4 Robin Jalkerud
5 Alexander Johansson
6 Robert Carlsson
7 Knut Henrik Spets
8 Marcus Ragnarsson
9 Sebastian Lauritzen
10 Jonny Ã…gren
11 Johan Markusson
12 PÃ¤r Arlbrandt
13 Pasi Saarela
14 Patrik Juhlin
15 Patric Hucko
16 Jonas Westerling

2006-07 Swedish HockeyAllsvenskan In the Crease

1 Jimmy Danielsson
2 Gusten TÃ¶rnqvist
3 Mikael Bohman
4 Thomas Sehlstedt
5 David Rautio
6 Carl-Johan Klint
7 Pontus SjÃ¶gren
8 Peter Hirsch
9 Antti Jokela
10 Martin Holst
11 Ari Luostarinen
12 Andreas Andersson
13 Nestor LÃ¶gdal
14 Magnus Lindquist
15 Johan Thalberg
16 Peter Andersson

2006-07 Swedish HockeyAllsvenskan Jerseys

1 Peter Hirsch
2 Magnus Lindquist

2006-07 Swedish HockeyAllsvenskan Signatures

1 Christoffer From-BjÃ¶rk
2 Niklas Andersson
3 Petter Sandberg
4 Andreas Dahlberg
5 Andreas Nordfeldt
6 Jesse Pehu
7 Jens Jakobs
8 Olof Svensson
9 Robert Ã…ndberg
10 Andreas Valdix
11 Fredrik HÃ¥kansson
12 Patrik RÃ¶nnqvist
13 Calle Steen
14 Carter Trevisani
15 Fredrik Sonntag
16 Henric BjÃ¶rkman
17 Marcus SÃ¶derkvist
18 Robin Persson
19 Brandon Nolan
20 David Holmqvist
21 Eric Yngve

2006-07 Swedish SHL Elitset

COMPLETE SET (288) 25.00 50.00
1 Johan Holmqvist .40 1.00
2 Daniel Johansson .10 .25
3 Tommy Sodin .10 .25
4 Jorgen Sundqvist .10 .25
5 Rodrigo Lavins .10 .25
6 Henrik Malmstrom .10 .25
7 Jonas Almtorp .10 .25
8 Andreas Dackel .10 .25
9 Mathias Mansson .10 .25
10 Ove Molin .10 .25
11 Lars-Erik Spets .10 .25
12 Mikael Lind .10 .25
13 Petter Ronnquist .10 .25
14 Ronnie Pettersson .10 .25
15 Alexander Ribbenstrand .10 .25
16 Jonas Liwing .10 .25
17 Jesper Bjorck .10 .25
18 Henrik Nordfeldt .10 .25
19 Johan Eneqvist .10 .25
20 Nichlas Falk .10 .25
21 Christofer Lofberg .10 .25
22 Patric Hornqvist .10 .25
23 Jimmie Olvestad .10 .25
24 Patrick Thoresen .60 1.50
25 Per Eklund .10 .25
26 Mikael Sandberg .10 .25
27 Tom Koivisto .10 .25
28 Antti-Jussi Niemi .10 .25
29 Arto Tukio .10 .25
30 Richard Demen-Willaume .10 .25
31 Johnny Oduya .30 .75
32 Magnus Kahnberg .10 .25
33 Peter Hogardh .10 .25
34 Kirill Starkov .10 .25
35 Joel Lundqvist .60 1.50
36 Jonas Esbjors .10 .25
37 Niklas Andersson .10 .25
38 Martin Plass .10 .25
39 Tomi Kallio .10 .25
40 Daniel Henriksson .10 .25
41 Rami Alanko .10 .25
42 Robin Jonsson .10 .25
43 Jonas Frogren .10 .25
44 Thomas Rhodin .10 .25
45 Jesper Mattsson .10 .25
46 Jonas Hoglund .20 .50
47 Rickard Wallin .10 .25
48 Mathias Johansson .10 .25
49 Peter Nordstrom .10 .25
50 Jorgen Jonsson .10 .25
51 Per Ledin .10 .25
52 Pelle Prestberg .10 .25
53 Stefan Liv .40 1.00
54 Fredrik Olausson .10 .25
55 Per Gustafsson .10 .25
56 Ola Svanberg .10 .25
57 David Petrasek .10 .25
58 Johan Halvardsson .10 .25
59 Martin Thornberg .10 .25
60 Erik Andersson .10 .25
61 David Fredriksson .10 .25
62 Andreas Karlsson .10 .25
63 Bjorn Melin .10 .25
64 Mattias Remstam .10 .25
65 Johan Davidsson .10 .25
66 Stefan Pettersson .10 .25
67 Mika Hannula .10 .25
68 Jonas Fransson .10 .25
69 Mikko Luoma .10 .25
70 Magnus Johansson .10 .25
71 Christoffer Norgren .10 .25
72 Jyrki Valivaara .10 .25
73 Tony Martensson .10 .25
74 Jonas Soling .10 .25
75 Ulf Soderstrom .10 .25
76 Tim Eriksson .10 .25
77 Sami Torkki .10 .25
78 Fredrik Emwall .10 .25
79 Jussi Tarvainen .10 .25
80 Johan Lindstrom .10 .25
81 Mikael Hakansson .10 .25
82 David Rautio .10 .25
83 Johan Fransson .10 .25
84 Erik Lindberg .10 .25
85 Jan Sandstrom .10 .25
86 Pekka Saravo .10 .25
87 Thomas Koch .10 .25
88 Emil Lundberg .10 .25
89 Fredrik Hynning .10 .25
90 Mikael Renberg .20 .50
91 Ragnar Karlsson .10 .25
92 Vladimir Machulda .10 .25
93 Lubomir Bartecko .10 .25
94 Robin Lindqvist .10 .25
95 Gustaf Wesslau .10 .25
96 Edvin Frylen .10 .25
97 Jan oberg .10 .25
98 Juha Riihijarvi .10 .25
99 Mikael Wahlberg .10 .25
100 Robert Tomik .10 .25
101 Markus Matthiasson .10 .25
102 Karol Krizan .10 .25
103 Mattias Timander .10 .25
104 Hans Jonsson .10 .25
105 Tobias Enstrom .10 .25
106 Jesper Damgaard .10 .25
107 Oscar Hedman .10 .25
108 Tobias Viklund .10 .25
109 Pasi Tuominen .10 .25
110 Morten Green .10 .25
111 Andreas Salomonsson .10 .25
112 Peter Oberg .10 .25
113 Mikael Pettersson .10 .25
114 Per Svartvadet .10 .25
115 Magnus Gastrin .10 .25
116 Petri Vehanen .10 .25
117 Atvars Tribuntsovs .10 .25
118 Jarno Kultanen .10 .25
119 Thomas Skogs .10 .25
120 Calle Bergstrom .10 .25
121 Eric Johansson .10 .25
122 Kenneth Bergqvist .10 .25
123 Andreas Nilsson .10 .25
124 Teemu Elomo .10 .25
125 Martin Jansson .10 .25
126 Mikael Simons .10 .25
127 Andreas Hadelov .10 .25
128 Fredrik Bergqvist .10 .25
129 Libor Prochazka .10 .25
130 Johan Ramstedt .10 .25
131 Pontus Petterstrom .10 .25
132 Daniel Welser .10 .25
133 Brett Harkins .10 .25
134 Johan Asplund .10 .25
135 Anton Stralman .40 1.00
136 Carl-Johan Johansson .10 .25
137 Peter Regin .10 .25
138 Frans Nielsen .40 1.00
139 Per Hallin .10 .25
140 Kristian Gahn .10 .25
141 Magnus Nilsson .10 .25
142 Mattias Wennerberg .10 .25
143 Peter Strom .10 .25
144 Fredrik Warg .10 .25
145 Robert Kristan .10 .25
146 Daniel Sperrle .20 .50
147 Antti Hulkkonen .10 .25
148 Nicholas Angell .10 .25
149 Peter Nolander .10 .25
150 Daniel Casselstahl .10 .25
151 Daniel Hermansson .10 .25
152 Nicklas Backstrom 2.00 5.00
153 Johannes Salmonsson .10 .25
154 Bjorn Danielsson .10 .25
155 Mads Hansen .10 .25
156 Sebastian Karlsson .10 .25
157 Jiri Bicek .10 .25
158 Daniel Larsson .10 .25
159 Teemu Lassila .20 .50
160 Martin Lindman .10 .25
161 Thomas Johansson .10 .25
162 Timmy Pettersson .10 .25
163 Fredrik Ericson .10 .25
164 Kristofer Ottosson .10 .25
165 Christian Eklund .10 .25
166 Fredrik Bremberg .10 .25
167 Par Backer .10 .25
168 Morten Ask .10 .25
169 Nicklas Danielsson .10 .25
170 Dragan Umicevic .10 .25
171 Tommy Salo .20 .50
172 Jan-Axel Alavaara .10 .25
173 Markus Seikola .10 .25
174 Ronnie Sundin .10 .25
175 Tomi Pettinen .10 .25
176 Jonas Ahnelov .10 .25
177 Johan Fransson .10 .25
178 Fredrik Johansson .10 .25
179 Karl Fabricius .10 .25
180 Anton Axelsson .10 .25
181 Steve Kariya .40 1.00
182 Johan Ryno .10 .25
183 Christopher Heino-Lindberg .20 .50
184 Atte Pentikainen .10 .25
185 Janne Niskala .10 .25
186 Esa Pirnes .10 .25
187 Per Aslund .10 .25
188 Emil Kaberg .10 .25
189 Christian Soderstrom .10 .25
190 Mikael Johansson .10 .25
191 Erik Ersberg .10 .25
192 Scott Langkow .20 .50
193 Johan Akerman .10 .25
194 Daniel Grillfors .10 .25
195 Pasi Puistola .10 .25
196 Lance Ward .10 .25
197 Erik Andersson .10 .25
198 Andreas Falk .10 .25
199 Jari Kauppila .10 .25
200 Timo Vertala .10 .25
201 Jukka Voutilainen .10 .25
202 Andreas Jamtin .10 .25
203 Roman Cechmanek .20 .50
204 Christopher Kelleher .10 .25
205 Carl Gunnarsson .10 .25
206 Andreas Holmqvist .10 .25
207 Oscar Ackestrom .10 .25
208 Joakim Eriksson .10 .25
209 Martin Samuelsson .20 .50
210 Niklas Olausson .10 .25
211 Patric Blomdahl .10 .25
212 Tero Leinonen .10 .25
213 Pavel Skrbek .10 .25
214 Roger Akerstrom .10 .25
215 Per Savilahti-Nagander .10 .25
216 Jaroslav Obsut .10 .25
217 Tomas Wallgren .10 .25
218 Martin Chabada .10 .25
219 Jesse Niinimaki .10 .25
220 Anders Burstrom .10 .25
221 Kalle Kerman .10 .25
222 Johan Harju .10 .25
223 Viktor Lindgren .10 .25
224 Tomas Surovy .20 .50
225 Rastislav Stana .10 .25
226 Patrik Hersley .10 .25
227 Johan Bjork .10 .25
228 Ross Lupaschuk .10 .25
229 Simon Skoog .10 .25
230 Andreas Thuresson .10 .25
231 Lasse Pirjeta .10 .25
232 Milan Bartovic .10 .25
233 Nicklas Jadeland .10 .25
234 Marcus Paulsson .10 .25
235 Mikael Johansson .10 .25
236 David Moravec .10 .25
237 Linus Fagemo .10 .25
238 Michal Zajkowski .10 .25
239 Tommy Wargh .10 .25
240 Adam Andersson .10 .25
241 Mattias Hellstrom .10 .25
242 Per-Ake Skroder .10 .25
243 Oscar Steen .10 .25
244 Niklas Sundstrom .10 .25
245 Miloslav Horava .10 .25
246 Johan Nilsson .10 .25
247 Robert Dome .10 .25
248 Juha Pitkamaki .10 .25
249 Mikko Ramo .10 .25
250 Tomas Slovak .10 .25
251 Pierre Johnsson .10 .25
252 Anton Stralman .10 .25
253 Mikko Kurvinen .10 .25
254 Miroslav Blatek .10 .25
255 Hakan Bogg .10 .25
256 Anders Bastiansen .10 .25
257 Marco Tuokko .10 .25
258 Ryan Jardine .10 .25
259 Eric Beaudoin .10 .25
260 Pavel Brendl .20 .50
261 Dave Stathos .10 .25
262 Per Helmersson .10 .25
263 Per-Anton Lundstrom .10 .25
264 Fredrik Lindgren .10 .25
265 Daniel Sondell .10 .25
266 Kari Haakana .10 .25
267 Richard Lintner .10 .25
268 Magnus Wernblom .10 .25
269 Fredrik Krekula .10 .25
270 Jason King .10 .25
271 Jimmie Eriksson .10 .25
272 Anders Soderberg .10 .25
273 Marcus Kristoffersson .10 .25
274 Markku Tahtinen .10 .25
275 Fredrik Oberg .10 .25
276 Johan Backlund .10 .25
277 Sanny Lindstrom .10 .25
278 Kalle Koskinen .10 .25
279 Kimmo Lotvonen .10 .25
280 Petri Kokko .10 .25
281 Par Styf .10 .25
282 Oscar Sundh .10 .25
283 Peter Nordstrom .10 .25
284 Robert Carlsson .10 .25
285 Johan Andersson .10 .25
286 Timo Parssinen .10 .25
287 Riku Hahl .20 .50
288 Jonathan Hedstrom .10 .25
NNO Nicklas Backstrom ROY SIL
NNO Nicklas Backstrom ROY Gold

2006-07 Swedish SHL Elitset Goal Patrol

1 Johan Holmqvist 5.00 12.00
2 Markus Korhonen 4.00 10.00
3 Teemu Lassila 4.00 10.00
4 Tommy Salo 4.00 10.00
5 Mikael Sandberg 4.00 10.00
6 Christopher Heino-Lindberg 4.00 10.00
7 Daniel Henriksson 4.00 10.00
8 Stefan Liv 5.00 12.00
9 Tomas Duba 4.00 10.00
10 Jonas Fransson 4.00 10.00
11 Fredrik Norrena 6.00 15.00
12 Mattias Modig 4.00 10.00
13 David Rautio 4.00 10.00
14 Karol Krizan 4.00 10.00
15 Daniel Sperrle 4.00 10.00
16 Petri Vehanen 4.00 10.00
17 Magnus Lindquist 4.00 10.00
18 Mika Oksa 4.00 10.00

2006-07 Swedish SHL Elitset In The Crease

1 Johan Holmqvist 5.00 12.00
2 Teemu Lassila 4.00 10.00
3 Tommy Salo 4.00 10.00
4 Daniel Henriksson 4.00 10.00
5 Stefan Liv 5.00 12.00
6 Fredrik Norrena 6.00 15.00
7 Mattias Modig 4.00 10.00
8 Karol Krizan 4.00 10.00
9 Petri Vehanen 4.00 10.00

2006-07 Swedish SHL Elitset Performers

1 Nicklas Backstrom 6.00 15.00
2 Dragan Umicevic 1.50 4.00
3 Niklas Andersson 1.50 4.00
4 Tomi Kallio 1.50 4.00
5 Mathias Johansson 1.50 4.00
6 Mika Hannula 1.50 4.00
7 Johan Davidsson 1.50 4.00
8 Tony Martensson 1.50 4.00
9 Mikael Hakansson 1.50 4.00
10 Mikael Renberg 2.00 5.00
11 Lasse Pirjeta 1.50 4.00
12 Juha RiihijÃ¤rvi 1.50 4.00
13 Per Svartvadet 1.50 4.00
14 Pavel Brendl 1.50 4.00
15 Magnus Wernblom 1.50 4.00
16 Anders Soderberg 1.50 4.00
17 Timo Parssinen 1.50 4.00
18 Jonathan Hedstrom 1.50 4.00

2006-07 Swedish SHL Elitset Playmakers

1 Mikael Lind 1.50 4.00
2 Fredrik Bremberg 1.50 4.00
3 Niklas Andersson 1.50 4.00
4 Joel Lundqvist 2.50 6.00
5 Jorgen Jonsson 1.50 4.00
6 Rickard Wallin 1.50 4.00
7 Andreas Karlsson 1.50 4.00
8 Tony Martensson 1.50 4.00
9 Lubomir Bartecko 1.50 4.00
10 Andreas Salomonsson 1.50 4.00
11 Hakan Bogg 1.50 4.00
12 Frans Nielsen 2.50 6.00

2007-08 Swedish Lulea Postcards

COMPLETE SET (21) 15.00 30.00
1 Robin Olsson .75 2.00
2 Mikko Pukka .75 2.00
3 Jan Sandstrom .75 2.00
4 Johan Ejdepalm .75 2.00
5 Tommi Miettinen .75 2.00
6 Pekka Saravo .75 2.00
7 Pavel Skrbek .75 2.00
8 Martin Chabada .75 2.00
9 Cory Larose .75 2.00
10 Anders Burstrom .75 2.00
11 Johan Harju .75 2.00
12 Lubos Bartecko .75 2.00
13 Mats Lavander .75 2.00
14 Robin Lindqvist .75 2.00
15 Viktor Lindgren .75 2.00
16 Linus Omark .75 2.00
17 Mikael Lidhammer .75 2.00
18 Per Savilahti-Nagander .75 2.00
19 Mattias Modig .75 2.00
20 Jaroslav Obsut .75 2.00
21 Gusten Tornqvist .75 2.00

2007-08 Swedish Malmo Red Hawks

COMPLETE SET (23) 15.00 30.00
1 Robin Weihager .75 2.00
2 Johan Bjork .75 2.00
3 Daniel Casselstahl .75 2.00
4 Jonathan Sjolund .75 2.00
5 Jan Oberg .75 2.00
6 Robin Alvarez .75 2.00
7 Kim Johansson .75 2.00
8 Martin Samuelsson .75 2.00
9 Marcus Paulsson .75 2.00
10 Mikael Wahlberg .75 2.00
11 Carl Soderberg 1.25 3.00
12 Emil Lundgren .75 2.00
13 Antti Bruun .75 2.00
14 Jani Hurme 1.25 3.00
15 Jyrki Valivaara .75 2.00
16 Calle Steen .75 2.00
17 Mikko Eloranta .75 2.00
18 Andreas Bystrom .75 2.00
19 Ville Nieminen 1.25 3.00
20 Patrik Lundh .75 2.00
21 Jens Svensson .75 2.00
22 Fredrik Eriksson .75 2.00
23 Tomas Wallgren .75 2.00

2007-08 Swedish SHL Elitset

Issued in two 144-card series.
COMPLETE SET (288) 30.00 60.00
1 Daniel Sperrle .10 .25
2 Daniel Johansson .10 .25
3 Antti Hulkkonen .10 .25
4 Nicholas Angell .10 .25
5 Peter Nolander .10 .25
6 Mathias Mansson .10 .25
7 Daniel Hermansson .10 .25
8 Johannes Salmonsson .10 .25
9 Bjorn Danielsson .10 .25
10 Mads Hanssen .10 .25
11 Sebastian Karlsson .10 .25
12 Daniel Larsson .10 .25
13 Ronnie Pettersson .10 .25
14 Dennis Persson .10 .25
15 Thomas Johansson .10 .25
16 Jonas Liwing .10 .25
17 Timmy Pettersson .10 .25
18 Fredrik Ericson .10 .25
19 Kristofer Ottosson .10 .25
20 Nichlas Falk .10 .25
21 Jimmie Olvestad .10 .25
22 Christian Eklund .10 .25
23 Par Backer .10 .25
24 Morten Ask .10 .25
25 Nicklas Danielsson .10 .25
26 Joel Gistedt .20 .50
27 Ronnie Sundin .10 .25
28 Fredrik Johansson .10 .25
29 Karl Fabricius .10 .25
30 Steve Kariya .40 1.00
31 Jonas EsbjÃ¶rs .10 .25
32 Niklas Andersson .10 .25
33 Martin Pluss .10 .25
34 Johan Ryno .10 .25
35 Tomi Kallio .10 .25
36 Christopher Heino-Lindberg .10 .25
37 Jonas Frogren .10 .25
38 Thomas Rhodin .10 .25
39 Pelle Prestberg .10 .25
40 Jesper Mattsson .10 .25
41 Esa Pirnes .10 .25
42 Jonas Hoglund .10 .25
43 Peter Nordstrom .10 .25
44 Emil Kaberg .10 .25
45 Christian SoderstrÃ¶m .10 .25
46 Mathias Johansson .10 .25
47 Mikael Johansson .10 .25
48 Erik Ersberg .10 .25
49 Johan Akerman .10 .25
50 Per Gustafsson .10 .25
51 Pasi Puistola .10 .25
52 David Petrasek .10 .25
53 Martin Thornberg .10 .25
54 Andreas Falk .10 .25
55 David Fredriksson .10 .25
56 Jari Kauppila .10 .25
57 Timo Vertala .10 .25
58 Jukka Voutilainen .10 .25
59 Andreas Jamtin .10 .25
60 Johan Davidsson .10 .25
61 Jonas Fransson .10 .25
62 Magnus Johansson .10 .25
63 Tony Martensson .10 .25
64 Ulf Soderstrom .10 .25
65 Joakim Eriksson .10 .25
66 Tim Eriksson .10 .25
67 Niklas Olausson .10 .25
68 Sami Torkki .10 .25
69 Fredrik Emvall .10 .25
70 Johan Lindstrom .10 .25
71 Mikael Hakansson .10 .25
72 Patric Blomdahl .10 .25
73 Jan Sandstrom .10 .25
74 Pekka Saravo .10 .25
75 Pavel Skrbek .10 .25
76 Jaroslav Obsut .10 .25
77 Tomas Wallgren .10 .25
78 Martin Chabada .10 .25
79 Jesse Niinimaki .10 .25
80 Andreas Burstrom .10 .25
81 Kalle Kerman .10 .25
82 Johan Harju .10 .25
83 Robin Lindqvist .10 .25
84 Viktor Lindgren .10 .25
85 Linus Omark .10 .25
86 Karol Krizan .10 .25
87 Mattias Timander .10 .25
88 Hans Jonsson .10 .25
89 Oscar Hedman .10 .25
90 Adam Andersson .10 .25
91 Mattias Hellstrom .10 .25
92 Per-Ake Skroder .10 .25
93 Andreas Salomonsson .10 .25
94 Peter Oberg .10 .25
95 Mikael Pettersson .10 .25
96 Niklas Sundstrom .10 .25
97 Miloslav Horava .10 .25
98 Magnus Gastrin .10 .25
99 Juha Pitkamaki .10 .25
100 Pierre Johnsson .10 .25
101 Jarno Kultanen .10 .25
102 Thomas Skogs .10 .25
103 Antti Bruun .10 .25
104 Anders Bastiansen .10 .25
105 Marco Tuokko .10 .25
106 Eric Beaudoin .10 .25
107 Kenneth Bergqvist .10 .25
108 Anders Nilsson .10 .25
109 Teemu Elomo .10 .25
110 Martin Jansson .10 .25
111 Andreas Hadelov .10 .25
112 Per-Anton Lundstrom .10 .25
113 Fredrik Lindgren .10 .25
114 Kari Haakana .10 .25
115 Fredrik Krekula .10 .25
116 Johan Ramstedt .10 .25
117 Pontus Pettersson .10 .25
118 Jimmie Eriksson .10 .25
119 Anders Soderberg .10 .25
120 Marcus Kristoffersson .10 .25
121 Fredrik Oberg .10 .25
122 Jhonas Enroth .40 1.00
123 Martin Thelander .10 .25
124 Daniel Josefsson .10 .25
125 Fredric Andersson .10 .25
126 Robert Carlsson .10 .25
127 Jorgen Bemstrom .10 .25
128 Tony Lagerstrom .10 .25
129 Ragnar Karlsson .10 .25
130 Tomas Kollar .10 .25
131 Johan Sjodell-Wiklander .10 .25
132 AndrÃ©e Persson .10 .25
133 Johan Backlund .10 .25
134 Anton Stralman .75 2.00
135 Sanny Lindstrom .10 .25
136 Kimmo Lotvonen .10 .25
137 Petri Kokko .10 .25
138 Par Styf .10 .25
139 Peter Regin .10 .25
140 Johan Andersson .10 .25
141 Bjorn Svensson .10 .25
142 Timo Parssinen .10 .25
143 Riku Hahl .10 .50
144 Jonathan Hedstrom .20 .50
145 Markus Korhonen .10 .25
146 Tommy Sjodin .10 .25
147 Niclas Andersen .10 .25
148 Pavel Brendl .20 .50
149 Andreas Dackell .10 .25
150 Daniel Widing .10 .25
151 Markus Kankaanpera .10 .25
152 Alexander Sundstrom .10 .25
153 Lars Erik Spets .10 .25
154 Jusso Hietanen .10 .25
155 Ove Molin .10 .25
156 Janne Hauhtonen .10 .25
157 Jorgen Sundqvist .10 .25
158 Daniel Larsson .10 .25
159 David Printz .20 .50
160 Fredrik Bremberg .10 .25
161 Patric Hornqvist .10 1.00
162 Dick Axelsson .10 .25
163 Andreas Engqvist .10 .25
164 Niklas Anger .10 .25
165 Edvin Frylen .10 .25
166 Oscar Eklund .10 .25
167 Mark Owuya .40 1.00
168 Jiri Marusak .10 .25
169 Ari Ahonen .40 1.00
170 Toni Soderholm .10 .25
171 Jonas Johnson .10 .25
172 Jonas Nordquist .10 .25
173 Philip Larsen .10 .25
174 Fredrik Pettersson .10 .25
175 Magnus Kahnberg .10 .25
176 Antti-Jussi Niemi .10 .25
177 Jonas Ahnelov .10 .25
178 Andreas Holmqvist .10 .25
179 Johan Andersson .10 .25
180 Tomi Kallio .10 .25
181 Oscar Ackestrom .10 .25
182 Michael Holmqvist .10 .25
183 Jonas Gustavsson .10 .25
184 Johan Motin .10 .25
185 Jens Skalberg .10 .25
186 Dominik Granak .10 .25
187 Rickard Wallin .10 .25
188 Per Aslund .10 .25
189 Jorgen Jonsson .10 .25
190 Martin Johansson .10 .25
191 Eero Somervuori .10 .25
192 Fabian Brunnstrom .10 2.50
193 Dave Cullen .10 .25
194 Stefan Liv .40 1.00
195 Mikko Luoma .10 .25
196 Daniel Grillfors .10 .25
197 Per Ledin .10 .25
198 Stefan Pettersson .10 .25
199 Jan Hrdina .10 .25
200 Jonas Johansson .10 .25
201 Andreas Jamtin .10 .25
202 Lance Ward .10 .25
203 Andreas Falk .10 .25
204 Andreas Andersson .10 .25
205 Rastislav Stana .10 .25
206 Fredrik Emvall .10 .25
207 Daniel Fernholm .10 .25
208 Calle Gunnarsson .10 .25
209 Mattias Weinhandl .10 .50
210 Ville Vahalahti .10 .25
211 Niklas Persson .10 .25
212 Patrik Zackrisson .10 .25
213 Kim Staal .10 .25
214 Tony Martensson .10 .25
215 Mattias Carlsson .10 .25
216 Andreas Pihl .10 .25
217 Mattias Modig .10 .25
218 Gusten Tornqvist .10 .25
219 Mikko Pukka .10 .25
220 Jan Sandstrom .10 .25
221 Jussi Tarvainen .10 .25
222 Tommi Miettinen .10 .25
223 Magnus Isaksson .10 .25
224 Mats Lavander .10 .25
225 Mikael Lidhammar .10 .25
226 Johan Ejdepalm .10 .25
227 Robin Olsson .10 .25
228 Michal Zajkowski .10 .25
229 Per Hallberg .10 .25
230 Victor Hedman .75 2.00
231 Tommy Wargh .10 .25
232 Pierre Hedin .10 .25
233 Magnus Wernblom .10 .25
234 Fredrik Warg .10 .25
235 Per Svartvadet .10 .25
236 Jari Tolsa .10 .25
237 Andreas Molinder .10 .25
238 Oscar Steen .10 .25
239 Lars Johansson .10 .25
240 Marco Tuokko .10 .25
241 Yared Hagos .20 .50
242 Ivan Huml .20 .50
243 Jonathan Granstrom .10 .25
244 Toni Dahlman .10 .25
245 Hakan Bogg .10 .25
246 Johan Lindstrom .10 .25
247 Tero Maatta .10 .25
248 Mikko Kurvinen .10 .25
249 Adam Andersson .10 .25
250 Martti Jarventie .10 .25
251 Nicklas Dahlberg .10 .25
252 Jan Novak .10 .25
253 Christoffer Norgren .10 .25
254 Tobias Viklund .10 .25
255 Pontus PetterstrÃ¶m .10 .25
256 Lee Goren .40 1.00
257 Thomas Larsson .10 .25
258 Mikael Renberg .40 1.00
259 Kimmo Koskenkorva .10 .25
260 Kent McDonnell .20 .50
261 Erik Andersson .10 .25
262 Erik Forssell .10 .25
263 Jimmie Ericsson .10 .25
264 Bjorn Bjurling .10 .25
265 Linus Klasen .10 .25
266 Stefan Grahns .10 .25
267 Per Hallin .10 .25
268 Par Arlbrandt .10 .25
269 Linus Videll .10 .25
270 Petri Pakaslahti .10 .25
271 Martin Cibak .10 .25
272 Jens Olsson .10 .25
273 KristianÂ Kudroc .10 .25
274 Jarno Kultanen .10 .25
275 Stefan Bemstrom .10 .25
276 Duane Harmer .10 .25
277 Magnus Akerlund .10 .25
278 Par Styf .10 .25
279 Anton Axelsson .10 .25
280 Oscar Sundh .10 .25
281 Jonathan Hedstrom .10 1.00
282 Erik Andersson .10 .25
283 Mika Pyorala .10 .25
284 Robert Carlsson .10 .25
285 Robin Jonsson .10 .25
286 Sanny Lindstrom .10 .25
287 Riku Hahl .10 .25
288 Kalle Koskinen Timra .10 .25

2007-08 Swedish SHL Elitset Complete Players

1 Nicklas Backstrom 4.00 10.00
2 Fredrik Bremberg 1.25 3.00
3 Steve Kariya 1.50 4.00
4 Martin Pluss 1.25 3.00
5 Peter Nordstrom 1.25 3.00
6 Andreas Jamtin 1.25 3.00
7 Johan Davidsson 1.25 3.00
8 Joakim Eriksson 1.25 3.00
9 Tony Martensson 1.25 3.00
10 Jaroslav Obsut 1.25 3.00
11 Tomas Surovy 1.25 3.00
12 Anders Bastiansen 1.25 3.00
13 Robert Dome 1.25 3.00
14 Per Svartvadet 1.25 3.00
15 Jimmie Eriksson 1.25 3.00
16 Linus Videll 1.25 3.00
17 Johan Backlund 1.25 3.00
18 Jonathan Hedstrom 2.00 5.00

2007-08 Swedish SHL Elitset Double Impact

COMPLETE SET (12) 12.00 30.00
1 P.Hornqvist/F.Bremberg 2.00 5.00
2 T.Sjodin/M.Mansson 1.25 3.00
3 A.Holmqvist/M.Holmqvist 1.25 3.00
4 P.Skroder/N.Sundstrom 1.25 3.00
5 T.Eriksson/F.Emwall 1.25 3.00
6 E.Somervuori/J.Jonsson 1.25 3.00
7 L.Omark/J.Harju 1.25 3.00
8 T.Dahlman/J.Pitkamaki 1.25 3.00
9 M.Renberg/J.Ericsson 1.50 4.00
10 J.Enroth/L.Klasen 2.00 5.00
11 J.Hedstrom/R.Hahl 2.00 5.00
12 A.Jamtin/P.Ledin 1.25 3.00

2007-08 Swedish SHL Elitset Future Watch

COMPLETE SET (12) 20.00 50.00
1 Niclas Andersen 2.50 6.00
2 Dick Axelsson 2.50 6.00
3 Philip Larsen 2.50 6.00
4 Johan Motin 2.50 6.00
5 Fredrik Pettersson 2.50 6.00
6 Patrik Zackrisson 2.50 6.00
7 Mattias Modig 2.50 6.00
8 Victor Hedman 6.00 15.00
9 Alexander Sundstrom 2.50 6.00
10 Thomas Larsson 2.50 6.00
11 Linus Klasen 2.50 6.00
12 Tobias Forsberg 2.50 6.00

2007-08 Swedish SHL Elitset Great Gloves

COMPLETE SET (9) 15.00 40.00
1 Daniel Sperrle 2.50 6.00
2 Daniel Larsson 2.50 6.00
3 Christopher Heino-Lindberg 2.50 6.00
4 Erik Ersberg 2.50 6.00
5 Jonas Fransson 2.50 6.00
6 Karol Krizan 2.50 6.00
7 Juha Pitkamaki 2.50 6.00
8 Andreas Hadelov 2.50 6.00
9 Johan Backlund 2.50 6.00

2007-08 Swedish SHL Elitset Jersey Autographs

1 Tony Martensson
2 Mikael Renberg

2007-08 Swedish SHL Elitset Jerseys

1 Kristofer Ottosson 10.00 25.00
2 Arto Tukio 10.00 25.00
3 Dennis Persson 10.00 25.00
4 Mathias Johansson 10.00 25.00
5 Stefan Liv 15.00 40.00

2007-08 Swedish SHL Elitset Signatures

1 Jimmie Olvestad 4.00 10.00
2 Dragan Umicevic 4.00 10.00
3 Peter Nordstrom 4.00 10.00
4 Tero Leinonen 4.00 10.00
5 Martin Chabada 4.00 10.00
6 Johan Harju 4.00 10.00
7 Rickard Lintner 4.00 10.00
8 Johan Backlund 4.00 10.00
9 Jonathan Hedstrom 8.00 20.00
10 Riku Hahl 4.00 10.00
11 Timo Parssinen 4.00 10.00
12 Mikael Johansson 4.00 10.00
13 Esa Pirnes 4.00 10.00
14 Johan Davidsson 4.00 10.00
15 Tony Martensson 4.00 10.00
16 Joakim Eriksson 4.00 10.00
17 Karol Krizan 4.00 10.00
18 Juha Pitkamaki 5.00 12.00
19 Mikael Simons 4.00 10.00
20 Tomas Skogs 4.00 10.00
21 Jhonas Enroth 8.00 20.00
22 Johan Sjodell-Wiklander 5.00 12.00
23 Fredrik Sonntag 4.00 10.00
24 Robert Carlsson 4.00 10.00
25 Jimmie Olvestad 4.00 10.00
26 Daniel Larsson 4.00 10.00
27 Patric Hornqvist 6.00 15.00
28 Nicklas Sundstrom 4.00 10.00
29 Tommy Wargh 4.00 10.00
30 Andreas Falk 4.00 10.00
31 Johan Akerman 4.00 10.00
32 Johan Backlund 4.00 10.00
33 Riku Hahl 6.00 15.00
34 Oscar Sundh 4.00 10.00
35 Timo Parssinen 4.00 10.00
36 Christian SoderstrÃ¶m 4.00 10.00
37 Eric Beaudoin 4.00 10.00
38 Bjorn Danielsson 4.00 10.00
39 Mathias Mansson 4.00 10.00
40 Martin Chabada 4.00 10.00
41 Linus Omark 4.00 10.00
42 Johan Harju 4.00 10.00
43 Johan Ramstedt 4.00 10.00
44 Pontus Pettersson 4.00 10.00
45 Andreas Hadelov 4.00 10.00
46 Jimmie Eriksson 4.00 10.00

2007-08 Swedish SHL Elitset The Dominators

COMPLETE SET (18) 25.00 50.00
1 Pavel Brendl 2.00 5.00
2 Patric Hornqvist 2.00 5.00
3 Jimmie Olvestad 1.50 4.00
4 Jonas Nordquist 1.50 4.00
5 Rickard Wallin 1.50 4.00
6 Martin Thornberg 1.50 4.00
7 Jan Hrdina 1.50 4.00
8 Mattias Weinhandl 1.50 4.00
9 Jan Sandstrom 1.50 4.00
10 Jari Tolsa 1.50 4.00
11 Niklas Sundstrom 1.50 4.00
12 Juha Pitkamaki 2.00 5.00
13 Fredrik Lindgren 1.50 4.00
14 Sanny Lindstrom 1.50 4.00
15 Per Hallin 1.50 4.00
16 Riku Hahl 2.00 5.00
17 Esa Pirnes 1.50 4.00
18 Mathias Mansson 1.50 4.00

2007-08 Swedish SHL Elitset The Guardians

COMPLETE SET (12) 30.00 75.00
1 Markus Korhonen 3.00 8.00
2 Daniel Larsson 3.00 8.00
3 Joel Gistedt 3.00 8.00
4 Stefan Liv 3.00 8.00
5 Rastislav Stana 3.00 8.00
6 Mattias Modig 3.00 8.00
7 Karol Krizan 3.00 8.00
8 Juha Pitkamaki 3.00 8.00
9 Jhonas Enroth 3.00 8.00
10 Magnus Akerlund 3.00 8.00
11 Andreas Hadelov 3.00 8.00
12 Christopher Heino-Lindberg 3.00 8.00

2007-08 Swedish SHL Elitset The Specialists

COMPLETE SET (9) 20.00 40.00
1 Karol Krizan 2.00 5.00
2 Juha Pitkamaki 2.50 6.00
3 Janne Niskala 2.00 5.00
4 Johan Akerman 2.00 5.00
5 Fredrik Bremberg 2.00 5.00
6 Nicklas Backstrom 6.00 15.00
7 Fredrik Emvall 2.00 5.00
8 Tomi Kallio 2.00 5.00
9 Mikael Renberg 2.50 6.00

2007-08 Swedish SHL Elitset Wave of the Future

COMPLETE SET (9) 20.00 50.00
1 Patric Hornqvist 4.00 10.00
2 Joel Gistedt 2.50 6.00
3 Niklas Olausson 2.50 6.00
4 Linus Omark 2.50 6.00
5 Tommy Wargh 2.50 6.00
6 Lars Johansson 2.50 6.00
7 Jhonas Enroth 4.00 10.00
8 Oscar Sundh 2.50 6.00
9 Anton Stralman 5.00 12.00

2009-10 Swedish Upper Deck Victory

COMPLETE SET (250) 75.00 150.00
COMP.SET w/o SPS (200) 30.00 60.00
*SWEDISH: .6X TO 1.5X BASIC VICTORY
ROOKIE STATED ODDS 1:4
195 Nicklas Backstrom .60 1.50

2009-10 Swedish Upper Deck Victory Svenska Superstjarnor

COMPLETE SET (20) 12.00 30.00
STATED ODDS 1:6
SS1 Henrik Lundqvist 1.25 3.00
SS2 Loui Eriksson .60 1.50
SS3 Alexander Edler .50 1.25
SS4 P.J. Axelsson .75 2.00
SS5 Nicklas Lidstrom .75 2.00
SS6 Mattias Ohlund .50 1.25
SS7 Mikael Samuelsson .50 1.25
SS8 Henrik Zetterberg 1.00 2.50
SS9 Michael Nylander .50 1.25
SS10 Niklas Kronwall .60 1.50
SS11 Daniel Alfredsson .75 2.00
SS12 Kim Johnsson .50 1.25
SS13 Mats Sundin .75 2.00
SS14 Tomas Holmstrom .60 1.50
SS15 Fredrik Modin .50 1.25
SS16 Henrik Sedin .75 2.00
SS17 Daniel Sedin .75 2.00
SS18 Kristian Huselius .50 1.25
SS19 Nicklas Backstrom 1.25 3.00
SS20 Johan Franzen .75 2.00

1993-94 Swiss HNL

This large set, released by Jurg Ochsner and sponsored by Ford and Sport newspaper, appears to include everyone who performed in the Swiss National League in 1992-93. The set is highlighted by bright, team-color coordinated design elements and sharp photography, as well as the presence of several ex-NHLers. The set appears to use three languages on the card fronts, varying as to the main language in the team's home locale. All coaches cards below are marked TR (the abbreviation for the French "traineur"). A limited number of factory sets were available; each was serially numbered out of 3,000 and registered to the person making the purchase. A collectible binder to hold the set is valued at $5.

COMPLETE SET (510) 24.00 60.00
1 Title Card .05 .15
2 Title Card .05 .15
3 Title Card .05 .15
4 EHC-Kloten .05 .15
5 EHC-Kloten .05 .15
6 Conny Evensson CO .07 .20
7 Ernst Bruderer ACO .05 .15
8 Reto Pavoni .20 .50
9 Claudio Bayer .20 .50
10 Martin Bruderer .05 .15
11 Anders Eldebrink .08 .25
12 Marco Kloti .05 .15
13 Marco Knecht .05 .15
14 Martin Kout .05 .15
15 Fausto Mazzoleni .05 .15
16 Daniel Sigg .05 .15
17 Daniel Weber .05 .15
18 Manuele Celio .05 .15
19 Patric Della Rossa .20 .50
20 Michael Diener .05 .15
21 Bruno Erni .05 .15
22 Oliver Hoffmann .05 .15
23 Felix Hollenstein .08 .25
24 Mikael Johansson .08 .25
25 Daniel Knecht .05 .15
26 Roger Meier .05 .15
27 Sacha Ochsner .08 .25
28 Peter Schlagenhauf .05 .15
29 Roman Wager .08 .25
30 HC Fribourg-Gotteron .05 .15
31 HC Fribourg-Gotteron .05 .15
32 Paul-Andre Cadieux CO .05 .15
33 Francois Huppe ACO .05 .15
34 Dino Stecher .20 .50
35 Marc Gygli .20 .50
36 Patrice Brasey .05 .15
37 Fredy Bobillier .05 .15
38 Antoine Descloux .05 .15
39 Christian Hofstetter .05 .15
40 Douglas M. Honegger .05 .15
41 Olivier Keller .05 .15
42 David Leibzig .05 .15
43 Didier Princi .05 .15
44 Joel Aeschlimann .05 .15
45 Christophe Brown .05 .15
46 Slava Bykov .20 .50
47 Stefan Grogg .05 .15
48 Andrej Khomutov .20 .50
49 Marc Leuenberger .05 .15
50 Bruno Maurer .05 .15
51 Frank Monnier .05 .15
52 Alain Reymond .05 .15
53 Mario Rottaris .05 .15
54 Pascal Schaller .05 .15
55 Chad Silver .05 .15
56 SC Bern .05 .15
57 SC Bern .05 .15
58 Hannu Jortikka CO .05 .15
59 Jim Koleff ACO .05 .15
60 Renato Tosio .20 .50
61 Roland Meyer .20 .50
62 Raoul Baumgartner .05 .15
63 Andreas Beutler .05 .15
64 Martin Brich .05 .15
65 Mikko Haapakoski .05 .15
66 Martin Rauch .05 .15
67 Jorg Reber .05 .15
68 Daniel Rutschi .05 .15
69 Gaetan Voisard .08 .25
70 Peter Bartschi .05 .15
71 Michael Buhler .05 .15
72 Rene Friedli .05 .15
73 Regis Fuchs .05 .15
74 Gregor Horak .05 .15
75 Michael Meier .05 .15
76 Gil Montandon .05 .15
77 Dan Quinn .20 .50
78 Harry Rogenmoser .05 .15
79 Roberto Triulzi .05 .15
80 Thomas C. Vrabec .05 .15
81 HC Lugano .05 .15
82 HC Lugano .05 .15
83 John Slettvoll CO .05 .15
84 Bruno Rogger ACO .05 .15
85 Lars Weibel .20 .50
86 Christophe Wahl .20 .50
87 Samuel Balmer .05 .15
88 Sandro Bertaggia .20 .50
89 Per Djoos .08 .25
90 Claudio Ghillioni .05 .15
91 Davide Jelmini .05 .15
92 Sven Leuenberger .05 .15
93 Ruedi Niderost .05 .15
94 Patrick Sutter .05 .15
95 Jean-Jacques Aeschlimann .08 .25
96 Jorg Eberle .08 .25
97 Ruben Fontana .05 .15
98 Axel Heim .05 .15
99 Christian Hofstetter .05 .15
100 Patrick Howald .08 .25
101 Marcel Jenni .05 .15
102 Andreas Keller .05 .15
103 Jan Larsson .05 .15
104 Andre Rotheli .05 .15
105 Matthias Schenkel .05 .15
106 Raymond Walder .05 .15
107 EV Zug .05 .15
108 EV Zug .05 .15
109 Bjorn Kinding CO .05 .15
110 Sean Simpson ACO .05 .15
111 Patrick Schopf .20 .50
112 Tony Koller .20 .50
113 Jakub Horak .05 .15
114 Dino Kessler .08 .25
115 Andre Kunzi .05 .15
116 Thomas Kunzi .05 .15
117 Andreas Ritsch .05 .15
118 Bill Schafhauser .05 .15
119 Pat Schafhauser .05 .15
120 Misko Antisin .08 .25
121 Mario Brodmann .05 .15
122 Tom Fergus .20 .50
123 Andreas Fischer .05 .15
124 Patrick Fischer .05 .15
125 Daniel Giger .05 .15
126 Daniel Meier .05 .15
127 Colin Muller .05 .15
128 Neuenschwander Ph. .05 .15
129 Daniel Schaltegger .05 .15
130 Franz Steffen .05 .15
131 Ken Yaremchuk .20 .50
132 HC Ambri-Piotta .05 .15
133 HC Ambri-Piotta .05 .15
134 Perry Pearn CO .08 .25
135 Dale McCourt ACO .08 .25
136 Markus Bachschmied .20 .50
137 Marco Baron .20 .50
138 Mark Astley .08 .25
139 Brenno Celio .05 .15
140 Filippo Celio .05 .15
141 Ivan Gazzaroli .05 .15
142 Tiziano Gianini .08 .25
143 Blair Muller .05 .15
144 Luigi Riva .05 .15
145 Rick Tschumi .05 .15
146 Nicola Celio .08 .25
147 Keith Fair .05 .15
148 Igor Fedulov .05 .15
149 Mathias Holzer .05 .15
150 Peter Jaks .05 .15
151 Vincent Lechenne .05 .15
152 Juri Leonov .05 .15
153 Petr Malkov .05 .15
154 Markus Studer .05 .15
155 Stefano Togni .05 .15
156 Luca Vigano .05 .15
157 Theo Wittmann .05 .15
158 Zurcher SC .05 .15
159 Zurcher SC .05 .15
160 Arno Del Curto CO .05 .15
161 Ueli Hofmann ACO .05 .15
162 Daniel Riesen .20 .50
163 Rolf Simmen .20 .50
164 Marco Bayer .08 .25
165 Jiri Faic .05 .15
166 Yvan Griga .05 .15
167 Noel Guyaz .05 .15
168 Edgar Salis .05 .15
169 Christian Sigrist .05 .15
170 Bruno Vollmer .05 .15
171 Andreas Zehnder .05 .15
172 Matthias Baechler .05 .15
173 Vjeran Ivankovic .05 .15
174 Peter Kobel .05 .15
175 Ronnie Leuthold .05 .15
176 Claudio Micheli .05 .15
177 Patrizio Morger .05 .15
178 Sergei Priakhin .08 .25
179 Roger Thony .05 .15
180 Andy Ton .05 .15
181 Christian Weber .05 .15
182 Vladimir Yeremin .05 .15
183 Michel Zeiter .05 .15
184 EHC Biel-Bienne .05 .15
185 EHC Biel-Bienne .05 .15
186 Jakob Kolliker CO .05 .15
187 Lautenschlager ASST TR .05 .15
188 Oliver Anken .20 .50
189 Christian Cretin .20 .50
190 Beat Cattaruzza .05 .15
191 Jean-Michel Clavien .05 .15
192 Sven Dick .05 .15
193 Daniel Dubois .05 .15
194 Leo Gudas .08 .25
195 Bjorn Schneider .05 .15
196 Martin Steinegger .05 .15
197 Gaetan Boucher .05 .15
198 Thomas Burillo .05 .15
199 Reynald De Ritz .05 .15
200 Patrick Glanzmann .05 .15
201 Freddy Luthi .05 .15
202 Beat Nuspliger .05 .15
203 Cyrill Pasche .05 .15
204 Robert Yannick .05 .15
205 Andre Rufener .05 .15
206 Bernhard Schuemperli .08 .25
207 Marc Weber .08 .25
208 Ramil Yuldashev .05 .15
209 HC Davos .05 .15
210 HC Davos .05 .15
211 Mats Waltin CO .05 .15
212 Marcus Theus ACO .05 .15
213 Nando Wieser .20 .50
214 Marino Buriola .20 .50
215 Thomi Derungs .05 .15
216 Andy Egli .05 .15
217 Beat Equilino .05 .15
218 Marc Gianola .05 .15
219 Andrea Haller .05 .15
220 Didier Massy .05 .15
221 Roland Ruedi .05 .15
222 Roger Sigg .05 .15
223 Mica Blaha .08 .25
224 Gian Marco Crameri .05 .15
225 Remo Gross .05 .15
226 Martin Hanggi .05 .15
227 Markus Morf .05 .15
228 Rene Muller .05 .15
229 Andi Naser .05 .15
230 Oliver Roth .05 .15
231 Rato Schneider .05 .15
232 Serge Soguel .05 .15
233 Gilles Thibaudeau .20 .50
234 Steve Tsujiura .08 .25
235 EHC Olten .05 .15
236 EHC Olten .05 .15
237 Dick Decloe CO .05 .15
238 Beat Aebischer .20 .50
239 Sascha Friedli .20 .50
240 Matthias Aregger .05 .15
241 Eric Bourquin .05 .15
242 Fabian Gull .05 .15
243 Urs Hirschi .05 .15
244 Alessandro Reinhart .05 .15
245 Christian Schuster .05 .15
246 Christian Silling .05 .15
247 Richard Stucki .05 .15
248 Adrian Bachofner .05 .15
249 Markus Butler .05 .15
250 Ralph Donghi .05 .15
251 Guido Egli .05 .15
252 Paul Gagne .20 .50
253 Thomas Loosli .05 .15
254 Steve Metzger .05 .15
255 Viktor Muller .05 .15
256 Mike Richard .05 .15
257 Kevin Schlapfer .05 .15
258 Peter Trummer .05 .15
259 Andre Von Rohr .05 .15
260 HC Ajoie .05 .15
261 HC Ajoie .05 .15
262 Michael McNamara CO .05 .15
263 Claude Fugere ACO .05 .15
264 Nicola Fraschina .20 .50
265 Didier Tosi .20 .50
266 Dave Baechler .05 .15
267 Sandro Capaul .05 .15
268 Romain Fleury .05 .15
269 Carl Lapointe .05 .15
270 John Miner .05 .15
271 Daniel Rohrbach .05 .15
272 Ralph Tanner .05 .15
273 Yann Voillat .05 .15
274 Mauro Bornet .05 .15
275 Kalle Furer .05 .15
276 Thomas Griga .05 .15
277 Patrice Heiz .05 .15
278 Willy Kohler .05 .15
279 Daniel Lamminger .05 .15
280 Francois Marquis .05 .15
281 Marco Mozzini .05 .15
282 Giovanni Pestrin .05 .15
283 Ken Priestlay .08 .25
284 Frederic Rothen .05 .15
285 EHC Chur .05 .15
286 EHC Chur .05 .15
287 Bengt Ericsson CO .05 .15
288 Roberto Lavoie ACO .05 .15
289 Peter Martin .20 .50
290 Thomas Liesch .20 .50
291 Marco Capaul .05 .15
292 Marco Gazzola .05 .15
293 Bruno Habisreutinger .05 .15
294 Markus Knobel .05 .15
295 Thomas Locher .05 .15
296 Roger Schnoz .05 .15
297 Roland Simonet .05 .15
298 Ivo Stoffel .05 .15
299 Rene Ackermann .05 .15
300 Patrice Bosch .05 .15
301 Harry Derungs .05 .15
302 Marco Ferrari .05 .15
303 Miguel Fondado .05 .15
304 Claudio Kalser .05 .15
305 Claudio Krattli .05 .15
306 Zbysek Kurylowski .05 .15
307 Andrei Kwartalnov .05 .15
308 Albert Malgin .05 .15
309 Wayne Manley .05 .15
310 Riccardo Signorell .05 .15
311 HC Martigny .05 .15
312 HC Martigny .05 .15
313 Bob Mongrain CO .05 .15
314 Thierry Andrey .20 .50
315 Florian Garnier .20 .50
316 Thierry Evequoz .05 .15
317 Alexandre Formaz .05 .15
318 Tom Jaeggi .05 .15
319 Adrian Jezzone .05 .15
320 Jaques Mauron .05 .15
321 Patrick Neukom .05 .15
322 Brian Rueger .05 .15
323 Bruno Steck .05 .15
324 Steve Aebersold .05 .15
325 Nicolas Baumann .05 .15
326 Alain Bernard .05 .15
327 Jean-Daniel Bonito .05 .15
328 Olivier Ecoeur .05 .15
329 Kelly Glowa .05 .15
330 Thomas Heldner .05 .15
331 Thierry Moret .05 .15
332 Stefan Nussberger .05 .15
333 Petr Rosol .08 .25
334 Gabriel Taccoz .05 .15
335 SC Herisau .05 .15
336 SC Herisau .05 .15
337 Mike McParland CO .05 .15
338 Mark McGregor ACO .05 .15
339 Stephan Morf .20 .50
340 Stefan Allenspach .20 .50
341 Urs Balzarek .05 .15
342 Sascha Bleiker .05 .15
343 Damian Freitag .05 .15
344 Karl Knopf .05 .15
345 Andy Krapf .05 .15
346 Andreas Maag .05 .15
347 Paul Summermatter .05 .15
348 Markus Wetter .05 .15
349 Marco Beer .05 .15
350 Bernhard Blochliger .05 .15
351 Libor Dolana .05 .15
352 Philipp Egli .05 .15
353 Marco Fischer .05 .15
354 Reto Germann .05 .15
355 Urs Hartmann .05 .15
356 Markus Keller .05 .15
357 Trevor Meier .05 .15
358 Roger Nater .05 .15
359 Petr Vlk .08 .25
360 Gerd Zenhausern .05 .15
361 SC Rapperswil-Jona .05 .15
362 SC Rapperswil-Jona .05 .15
363 Pekka Rautakallio CO .20 .50
364 Ueli Scheidegger ACO .05 .15
365 Marius Boesch .05 .15
366 Michael Habig .08 .25
367 Armin Berchtold .05 .15
368 Daniel Bunzli .05 .15
369 Erich Frey .05 .15
370 Patrick Gotz .05 .15
371 Marc Haueter .05 .15
372 Christian Langer .05 .15
373 Markus Naef .05 .15
374 Daniel Aeschbacher .05 .15
375 Ray Allison .05 .15
376 Tom Bissett .20 .50
377 Warren Bruetsch .05 .15
378 Turi Camenzind .05 .15
379 Jean-Noel Honegger .05 .15
380 Roman Kessler .05 .15
381 Hans Kossman .05 .15
382 Marco Seeholzer .05 .15
383 Laurent Stehlin .05 .15
384 Marco Werder .05 .15
385 EHC Bulach .05 .15
386 EHC Bulach .05 .15
387 Lars-Erik Lundstrom CO .05 .15
388 Urs Liljequist ACO .05 .15
389 Ronnie Rueger .20 .50
390 Carlo Buriola .20 .50
391 Rolf Bunter .05 .15
392 David Erny .05 .15
393 Urs Gull .05 .15
394 Thomas Jaggli .05 .15
395 Stefan Meier .05 .15
396 Marco Schellenberg .05 .15
397 Marcel Schonhaar .05 .15
398 Robin Bauer .05 .15
399 Daniele Celio .05 .15
400 Peter Ekelund .05 .15
401 Urs Luthi .05 .15
402 Don McLaren .08 .25
403 Kim Pedersen .05 .15
404 Matthias Pittet .05 .15
405 Ercan Sahin .05 .15
406 Thomas Studer .05 .15
407 Markus Suter .05 .15
408 Martin Caretta .05 .15
409 Mike Tschumi .05 .15
410 Lausanne HC .05 .15
411 Lausanne HC .05 .15
412 Jean Lussier CO .05 .15
413 Beat Kindler .08 .25
414 Michel Pilet .05 .15
415 Urs Burkart .05 .15
416 Jean Gagnon .05 .15
417 Nicolas Goumaz .05 .15
418 Fabian Guignard .05 .15
419 Benedict Sapin .05 .15
420 Raymond Wyssen .05 .15
421 Laurent Bucher .05 .15
422 Olivier Chenuz .05 .15
423 Alain Comte .05 .15
424 Martin Desjardins .05 .15
425 Gaby Epiney .05 .15
426 Stephane Gasser .05 .15
427 Nicolas Gauch .05 .15
428 Gilles Guyaz .05 .15
429 Dan Hodgson .20 .50
430 Maxime Lapointe .05 .15
431 Laurent Pasquini .05 .15
432 Gilles Prince .05 .15
433 Yannick Theler .05 .15
434 HC Thurgau .05 .15
435 HC Thurgau .05 .15
436 Anders Sorensen CO .05 .15
437 Max Baumann .05 .15
438 Martin Studer .20 .50
439 Thomas Berger .20 .50
440 Andy Gasser .05 .15
441 Patrick Henry .05 .15
442 Reto Muller .05 .15
443 Ralph Ott .05 .15
444 Mike Posma .05 .15
445 Hadrian Rosenberg .05 .15
446 Marcel Stocker .05 .15
447 Robert Wiesmann .05 .15
448 Gianni Dalla Vecchia .05 .15
449 Dan Daoust .20 .50
450 Matthias Keller .05 .15
451 Roger Keller .05 .15
452 Peter Kostli .05 .15
453 Bernhard Lauber .05 .15
454 Benjamin Mueller .05 .15
455 Silvio Schai .05 .15
456 Rolf Schrepfer .05 .15
457 Robert Slehofer .05 .15
458 Thomas Steger .05 .15
459 Cuno Weisser .05 .15
460 Grasshoppers-Club Zurich .05 .15
461 Grasshoppers-Club Zurich .05 .15
462 Esa Siren CO .05 .15
463 Bruno Aegerter ACO .05 .15
464 Marcel Kohli .20 .50
465 Olivier Leuenberger .20 .50
466 Giorgio Giacomelli .05 .15
467 Roman Honegger .05 .15
468 Sandro Just .05 .15
469 Mats Lusth .05 .15
470 Marcel Wick .05 .15
471 Lukas Zehnder .05 .15
472 Rolf Ziegler .05 .15
473 Jerry Zuurmond .05 .15
474 Alain Ayer .05 .15
475 Leo Cadisch .05 .15
476 Pascal Fah .05 .15
477 Roman Furrer .05 .15
478 Marco Hagmann .05 .15
479 Peter Hofmann .05 .15
480 Adrian Hotz .05 .15
481 Patrick Looser .05 .15
482 Oliver Muffler .05 .15
483 Keith Osborne .08 .25
484 Thierry Paterlini .05 .15
485 Markus Schellenberg .05 .15
486 HC La Chaux-de-Fonds .05 .15
487 HC LaChaux-de-Fonds .05 .15
488 Ricardo Fuhrer CO .05 .15
489 Jean-Luc Schnegg .08 .25
490 Thierry Loup .08 .25
491 Thierry Baume .05 .15
492 Jean-Luc Christen .05 .15
493 Thierry Murisier .05 .15
494 Danny Ott .05 .15
495 Guido Pfosi .05 .15
496 Rene Raess .05 .15
497 Valeri Shirajev .08 .25
498 Frank Vuillemin .05 .15
499 Marco Dick .05 .15
500 Michael Ferrari .05 .15
501 Olivier Gazzaroli .05 .15
502 Sandy Jeannin .05 .15
503 Lane Lambert .08 .25
504 Guido Laczko .05 .15
505 Boris Leimgruber .05 .15
506 Claude Luthi .05 .15
507 Patrick Oppliger .05 .15
508 Jean-Luc Rod .05 .15
509 Gabriel Rohrbach .05 .15
510 Yvan Zimmermann .05 .15

1995-96 Swiss HNL

This very large set, released by Jurg Ochsner and sponsored by the Swiss Bank Society appears to include everyone who performed in the Swiss national hockey league in 1994-95. They were distributed in 6-card packs for 2 francs. The set is highlighted by marvelous color action photography, a subset of six NNO referee cards, and the inclusion of six NHLers who played in Switzerland during the NHL lockout including Doug Gilmour and Chris Chelios. Of interest is the usage of three languages (French, German and Italian) on the card fronts, which varies by the main language in the team's home locale. Note: the TR suffix in this case is the direct translation of coach (traineur). A collector's album also was available by mail. It is valued at $5.00.

COMPLETE SET (545) 30.00 75.00
1 Kloten .02 .10
2 Kloten .02 .10
3 Alpo Suhonen CO .20 .50
4 Ernst Bruderer ACO .02 .10
5 Matthias Muller .08 .25
6 Reto Pavoni .20 .50
7 Marco Bayer .02 .10
8 Martin Bruderer .02 .10
9 Marco Kloti .02 .10
10 Michael Kress .02 .10
11 Marc Ochsner .02 .10
12 Bjorn Schneider .02 .10
13 Daniel Sigg .02 .10
14 Daniel Weber .02 .10
15 Charles Berglund .02 .10
16 Manuele Celio .02 .10
17 Patrik Della Rossa .02 .10
18 Michael Diener .02 .10
19 Bruno Erni .02 .10
20 Oliver Hoffmann .02 .10
21 Felix Hollenstein .02 .10
22 Mathias Holzer .02 .10
23 Mikael Johansson .02 .10
24 Roger Meier .02 .10
25 Sacha Oscsner .02 .10
26 Frederic Rothen .02 .10
27 Roman Wager .02 .10
28 ZSC .02 .10
29 ZSC .02 .10
30 Larry Huras TR .02 .10
31 Ted Snell ATR .02 .10
32 Thomas Papp .15 .40
33 Dino Stecher .15 .40
34 Patrick Hager .02 .10
35 Martin Kout .02 .10
36 Didier Princi .02 .10
37 Edgar Salis .02 .10
38 Bruno Steck .02 .10
39 Nicholas Steiger .02 .10
40 Andreas Zehnder .02 .10
41 Mario Brodmann .02 .10
42 Marc Fortier .08 .25
43 Nicholas Gauch .02 .10
44 Vjeran Ivankovic .02 .10
45 Sandy Jeannin .02 .10
46 Patrick Lebeau .20 .50
47 Phillipp Luber .02 .10
48 Don McLaren .08 .25
49 Claudio Micheli .02 .10
50 Patrizio Morger .02 .10
51 Marco Seeholzer .02 .10
52 Bruno Vollmer .02 .10
53 Michel Zeiter .02 .10
54 Fribourg .02 .10
55 Fribourg .02 .10
56 Kjell Larsson TR .02 .10
57 Ueli Hofmann ATR .02 .10
58 David Aebischer ERC 15.00 40.00
59 Thomas Berger .15 .40
60 Steve Meuwly .07 .20
61 Johan Bertholet .02 .10
62 Fredy Bobillier .02 .10
63 Patrice Brasey .02 .10
64 Antoine Descloux .02 .10
65 Andy Egli .02 .10
66 Christian Hofstetter .02 .10
67 Olivier Keller .02 .10
68 Andrei Lomakin .08 .25
69 Mark Streit .02 .10
70 Christophe Brown .02 .10
71 Slava Bykov .20 .50
72 Matthias Bachler .02 .10
73 Axel Heim .02 .10
74 Andrej Khomutov .20 .50
75 Marc Leuenberger .02 .10
76 Alfred Luthi .04 .10
77 Daniel Meier .02 .10
78 Mario Rottaris .02 .10
79 Pascal Schaller .02 .10
80 Sacha Schneider .02 .10
81 Joel Aeschlimann .02 .10
82 Bern .02 .10
83 Bern .02 .10
84 Brian Lefley CO .02 .10
85 Ueli Schwarz ATR .02 .10
86 Reto Schurch .15 .40
87 Renato Tosio .15 .40
88 Mikko Haapakoski .02 .10
89 Christian Langer .02 .10
90 Sven Leuenberger .02 .10
91 Phillippe Portner .02 .10
92 Martin Rauch .02 .10
93 Pascal Sommer .02 .10
94 Martin Steinegger .02 .10
95 Gaeton Voisard .02 .10
96 Rene Friedli .02 .10
97 Regis Fuchs .02 .10
98 Patrick Howald .02 .10
99 Andy Keller .02 .10
100 Vincent Lechenne .02 .10
101 Lars Leuenberger .02 .10
102 Trevor Meier .02 .10
103 Gilles Montandon .02 .10
104 Philippe Muller .02 .10
105 Gaetano Orlando .08 .25
106 Roberto Triuizi .02 .10
107 Thomas Vrabec .02 .10
108 Davos .02 .10
109 Davos .02 .10
110 Mats Waltin TR .02 .10
111 Evgeni Popichin ACO .02 .10
112 Ivo Kleeb .15 .40
113 Nando Wiesser .15 .40
114 Samuel Balmer .02 .10
115 Martin Brich .02 .10
116 Beat Equilino .02 .10
117 Ivan Gazzaroli .02 .10
118 Marc Gianola .02 .10
119 Andrea Haeller .02 .10
120 Doug Honegger .02 .10
121 Andrej Kovalev .02 .10
122 Jan Alston .02 .10
123 Gian-Marco Crameri .02 .10
124 Dan Hodgson .20 .50
125 Rene Muller .02 .10
126 Andy Naser .02 .10
127 Oliver Roth .02 .10
128 Ivo Ruthemann .02 .10
129 Reto Stirnimann .02 .10
130 Reto Von Arx .02 .10
131 Christian Weber .02 .10
132 Lugano .02 .10
133 Lugano .02 .10
134 John Slettvoll TR .02 .10
135 Nicola Fraschina .15 .40
136 Lars Weibel .30 .75
137 Sandro Bertaggia .07 .20
138 Francesco Bizzozero .02 .10
139 Michel Kamber .02 .10
140 Ruedi Niderost .02 .10
141 Pat Schafhauser .02 .10
142 Tommy Sjodin .08 .25
143 Patrick Sutter .02 .10
144 Rick Tschumi .02 .10
145 J. Jacques Aeschlimann .02 .10
146 Markus Butler .02 .10
147 Jorg Eberle .02 .10
148 Keith Fair .02 .10
149 Marcel Jenni .02 .10
150 Stephan Lebeau .40 1.00
151 Patrick Looser .02 .10
152 Stefano Togni .02 .10
153 Andy Ton .02 .10
154 Remo Walder .02 .10
155 EVZ .02 .10
156 EVZ .02 .10
157 Jim Koleff TR .02 .10
158 Bob Lesley ACO .02 .10
159 Sacha Friedli .15 .40
160 Patrick Schopf .15 .40
161 Livio Fazio .02 .10
162 Stefan Grauwiler .02 .10
163 Dino Kessler .02 .10
164 Andre Kunzi .02 .10
165 Thomas Kunzi .02 .10
166 Fausto Mazzoleni .02 .10
167 John Miner .02 .10
168 Bill Schafhauser .02 .10
169 Steve Aebersold .02 .10
170 Misko Antisin .02 .10
171 Patrick Fischer .02 .10
172 Daniel Giger .02 .10
173 Mathias Keller .02 .10
174 Marco Koppel .02 .10
175 Colin Muller .02 .10
176 Philipp Neuenschwander .02 .10
177 Andre Rotheli .02 .10
178 Chad Silver .02 .10
179 Franz Steffen .02 .10
180 Ken Yaremchuk .20 .50
181 Ambri Piotta .02 .10
182 Ambri Piotta .02 .10
183 Alexander Yakushev CO .08 .25
184 Petr Malkov ATR .02 .10
185 Markus Bachschmied .15 .40
186 Paolo Della Bella .15 .40
187 Pauli Jaks .20 .50
188 Brenno Celio .02 .10
189 Tiziano Gianini .07 .20
190 Fabian Gull .02 .10
191 Noel Guyaz .02 .10
192 Jakub Horak .02 .10
193 Alessandro Reinhart .02 .10
194 Luigi Riva .02 .10
195 Gianni Sanese .02 .10
196 Oskar Szczepaniec .02 .10
197 Mattia Baldi .02 .10
198 Nicola Celio .02 .10
199 Dmitri Denisov .02 .10
200 Gaby Epiney .02 .10
201 John Fritsche .02 .10
202 Patrick Glanzmann .02 .10
203 Thomas Heldner .02 .10
204 Paolo Imperatori .02 .10
205 Peter Jaks .02 .10
206 Dimitri Kvartalnov .20 .50
207 Omar Tognini .02 .10
208 Nicola Pini .02 .10
209 Luca Vigano .02 .10
210 Theo Wittmann .02 .10
211 Rapperswil .02 .10
212 Rapperswil .02 .10
213 Pekka Rautakallio TR .08 .25
214 Ueli Scheidegger ATR .02 .10
215 Claudio Bayer .15 .40
216 Christian Cretin .15 .40
217 Daniel Bunzli .02 .10
218 Marco Capaul .02 .10
219 Roland Kradolfer .02 .10
220 Blair Muller .02 .10
221 Andreas Ritsch .02 .10
222 Daniel Rutschi .02 .10
223 Roger Sigg .02 .10
224 Adrian Bachofner .02 .10
225 Arthur Camenzind .02 .10
226 Christian Hofstetter .02 .10
227 Michael Meier .02 .10
228 Mike Richard .07 .20
229 Harry Rogenmoser .02 .10
230 Andy Rufener .02 .10
231 Sergio Soguel .02 .10
232 Gilles Thibaudeau .08 .25
233 Roger Thony .02 .10
234 Marc Weber .02 .10
235 Marco Werder .02 .10
236 Lausanne HC .02 .10
237 Jean Lussier TR .02 .10
238 Thierry Andrey .15 .40
239 Beat Kindler .15 .40
240 Jean Gagnon .02 .10
241 Fabian Guignard .02 .10
242 Philippe Marquis .02 .10
243 Stephan Schneider .02 .10
244 Roland Simonet .02 .10
245 Ivo Stoffel .02 .10
246 Marcel Wick .02 .10
247 Raymond Wyssen .02 .10
248 Martin Desjardins .02 .10
249 Maxime Lapointe .02 .10
250 Bruno Maurer .02 .10
251 Frank Monnier .02 .10
252 Cyrill Pasche .02 .10
253 Laurent Pasquini .02 .10
254 Alain Reymond .02 .10
255 Yannick Robert .02 .10
256 Kevin Schlapfer .02 .10
257 Gabriel Taccoz .02 .10
258 Claude Verret .02 .10
259 Gerd Zenhausern .02 .10
260 Biel .02 .10
261 Biel .02 .10
262 Barry Jenkins TR .02 .10
263 Sacha Devaux .15 .40
264 Christoph Wahl .15 .40
265 Beat Cattaruzza .02 .10
266 Sven Dick .02 .10
267 Claudio Ghillioni .02 .10
268 Stefan Lutz .02 .10
269 Guido Pfosi .02 .10
270 Sven Schmid .02 .10
271 Daniel Schneider .02 .10
272 Frank Aeschlimann .02 .10
273 Thomas Burillo .02 .10
274 Stefan Choffat .02 .10
275 Reynald DeRitz .02 .10
276 Marco Dick .02 .10
277 Ralph Donghi .02 .10
278 Stefan Groff .02 .10
279 Andrej Kwartalnov .02 .10
280 Albert Malgin .02 .10
281 Oliver Muller .02 .10
282 Michel Riesen .75 2.00
283 Bernhard Schumperli .08 .25
284 Mike Tschumi .02 .10
285 Grasshoppers .02 .10
286 Grasshoppers .02 .10
287 Bruno Aegerter CO .02 .10
288 Matti Alatalo ATR .02 .10
289 Marcel Kohli .15 .40
290 Stephan Morf .15 .40

291 Michel Faeh .02 .10
292 Marc Haueter .02 .10
293 Roman Honegger .02 .10
294 Arne Ramholt .02 .10
295 Hannu Virta .08 .25
296 Rolf Ziegler .02 .10
297 Jerry Zuurmond .02 .10
298 Alain Ayer .02 .10
299 Andre Baumann .02 .10
300 Warren Bruetsch .02 .10
301 Pascal Faeh .02 .10
302 Roman Furrer .02 .10
303 Marco Hagmann .02 .10
304 Dominik Jenny .02 .10
305 Mika Nieminen .02 .10
306 Fabio Obrist .02 .10
307 Thierry Paterlini .02 .10
308 Marco Schellenberg .02 .10
309 Mathias Schenkel .02 .10
310 Peter Schlagenhauf .02 .10
311 Markus Studer .02 .10
312 Thomas Ziegler .02 .10
313 Thurgau .02 .10
314 Thurgau .02 .10
315 Mike McParland TR .02 .10
316 Fritz Lanz ATR .02 .10
317 Roger Hugentobler .15 .40
318 Peter Martin .15 .40
319 Dominik Schmid .02 .10
320 Andrea Baumgartner .02 .10
321 Nicolas Goumaz .02 .10
322 Martin Granicher .02 .10
323 Ralph Ott .02 .10
324 Henry Patrick .02 .10
325 Mike Posma .02 .10
326 Marcel Schmid .02 .10
327 Robert Wiesmann .02 .10
328 Dan Daoust .20 .50
329 Slaven Imhof .02 .10
330 Roger Keller .02 .10
331 Martin Knopfli .02 .10
332 Guido Laczko .02 .10
333 Bernhard Lauber .02 .10
334 Gery Othman .02 .10
335 Rolf Schrepfer .02 .10
336 Thomas Seitz .02 .10
337 Robert Slehofer .02 .10
338 Rene Stussi .02 .10
339 Cuno Weisser .02 .10
340 Benjamin Winkler .02 .10
341 Langnau .02 .10
342 Langnau .02 .10
343 Paul Andre Cadieux TR .02 .10
344 Jakob Kolliker ATR .02 .10
345 Thomas Dreier .15 .40
346 Toni Koller .15 .40
347 Daniel Aegerter .02 .10
348 Raoul Baumgartner .02 .10
349 Andreas Beutler .02 .10
350 Urs Hirschi .02 .10
351 Stefan Probst .02 .10
352 Raphael Schneider .02 .10
353 Pascal Stoller .02 .10
354 Rolf Badertscher .02 .10
355 Peter Bartschi .02 .10
356 Beat Friedrich .02 .10
357 Walter Gerber .02 .10
358 Kelly Glowa .02 .10
359 Alan Hirschi .02 .10
360 Markus Hirschi .02 .10
361 Gregor Horak .02 .10
362 Lane Lambert .08 .25
363 Beat Nuspliger .02 .10
364 Stefan Tschiemer .02 .10
365 Chaux De Fonds .02 .10
366 Chaux De Fonds .02 .10
367 Riccardo Fuhrer TR .02 .10
368 Roland Meyer .15 .40
369 Jean-Luc Schnegg .15 .40
370 Eric Bourquin .02 .10
371 Daniel Dubois .02 .10
372 Andres Egger .02 .10
373 Daniel Elsener .02 .10
374 Thierry Murisier .02 .10
375 Daniel Ott .02 .10
376 Jorg Reber .02 .10
377 Valeri Chiriaev .02 .10
378 Michele Bizzozero .02 .10
379 Philippe Bozon .40 1.00
380 Jean-Marc Brunner .02 .10
381 Florian Chappot .02 .10
382 Gilles Dubois .02 .10
383 Willy Kohler .02 .10
384 Boris Leimgruber .02 .10
385 Patrick Oppliger .02 .10
386 Benoit Pont .02 .10
387 Laurent Stehlin .02 .10
388 Olivier Wuthrich .02 .10
389 Herisau .02 .10
390 Herisau .02 .10
391 Mark McGregor TR .02 .10
392 Reto Roveda ATR .02 .10
393 Michael Habig .15 .40
394 Ronald Rueger .15 .40
395 Urs Balzarek .02 .10
396 Thomas Derungs .02 .10
397 Damian Freitag .02 .10
398 Roland Habisreutinger .02 .10
399 Marco Knecht .02 .10
400 Karl Knopf .02 .10
401 Andy Maag .02 .10
402 Krister Cantoni .02 .10
403 Rico Enzler .02 .10
404 John Fust .02 .10
405 Remo Gastaldo .02 .10
406 Reto German .02 .10
407 Frank Guay .02 .10
408 Daniel Knecht .02 .10
409 Andy Krapf .02 .10
410 Roger Nater .02 .10
411 Marco Tanner .02 .10
412 Claude Vilgrain .40 1.00
413 Chur .02 .10
414 Chur .02 .10
415 Juri Voshakov TR .02 .10
416 Thomas Liesch .15 .40
417 Reto Zuccolini .15 .40
418 Sacha Bleiker .02 .10
419 Patrick Fischer .02 .10
420 Bruno Habisreutinger .02 .10
421 Jurg Hardegger .02 .10
422 Dominic Meier .02 .10
423 Loris Papa .02 .10
424 Robert Papp .02 .10
425 Valery Belov .02 .10
426 Valery Cherny .02 .10
427 Miguel Fondado .02 .10
428 Oliver Gazzaroli .02 .10
429 Claudio Krattli .02 .10
430 Claudio Peer .02 .10
431 Michael Putzi .02 .10
432 Roger Rieder .02 .10
433 Riccardo Signorell .02 .10
434 Peter Thoma .02 .10
435 Patrick Werthan .02 .10
436 Olten .02 .10
437 Olten .02 .10
438 Milan Mrukvia ATR .02 .10
439 Beat Aebischer .15 .40
440 Thierry Loup .15 .40
441 Ralph Gugelmann .02 .10
442 Roland Ruedi .02 .10
443 Andre Schneeberger .02 .10
444 Richard Stucki .02 .10
445 Thomas Studer .02 .10
446 Ville Siren .08 .25
447 Pius Weber .02 .10
448 Rene Ackermann .02 .10
449 Lars Aebi .02 .10
450 Andreas Fischer .02 .10
451 Marcel Franzi .02 .10
452 Paul Gagne .20 .50
453 Stephane Gasser .02 .10
454 Pirmin Keller .02 .10
455 Claude Luthi .02 .10
456 Patrick Siegwart .02 .10
457 Patrik Traber .02 .10
458 Andre Van Rohr .02 .10
459 HCM .02 .10
460 Kent Ruhnke TR .02 .10
461 Patrick Grand .15 .40
462 Didier Tosi .15 .40
463 Pascal Avanthay .02 .10
464 Bernard Bauer .02 .10
465 Ayocholos Escher .02 .10
466 Thierry Evequoz .02 .10
467 David Jelmini .02 .10
468 Xavier Kappeler .02 .10
469 Patrik Neukom .02 .10
470 Pierre-Alain Ancay .02 .10
471 Florian Andenmatten .02 .10
472 J-Daniel Bonito .02 .10
473 Alain Darbellay .02 .10
474 Olivier Ecoeur .02 .10
475 Igor Fedulov .02 .10
476 Nicolas Gastaldo .02 .10
477 Thierry Moret .02 .10
478 Stephan Nussberger .02 .10
479 Achim Pleschberger .02 .10
480 Petr Rosol .02 .10
481 Fabrizio Silietti .02 .10
482 Yannick Theler .02 .10
483 Geneve .02 .10
484 Geneve .02 .10
485 Francois Huppe TR .02 .10
486 Gary Shennan ATR .02 .10
487 Jean-Philippe Challande .15 .40
488 Jerome Hagmann .15 .40
489 Claude Cienciala .02 .10
490 Chris Felix .02 .10
491 Romain Fleury .02 .10
492 Daniel Herlea .02 .10
493 Camille Meylan .02 .10
494 Toni Nelli .02 .10
495 Christian Serena .02 .10
496 David Leibzig .02 .10
497 Antoine Cloux .02 .10
498 Nicolas Corthay .02 .10
499 Marc Hinni .02 .10
500 Olivier Honsberger .02 .10
501 Gael Kertudo .02 .10
502 Jorg Ledermann .02 .10
503 Andrew McKim .20 .50
504 Benjamin Muller .02 .10
505 Martin Stastny .02 .10
506 Michel Wicky .02 .10
507 Schwiezer .08 .25
508 Christian Weber .20 .50
509 Jean-Jacques Aeschlimann .08 .25
510 Sandro Bertaggia .20 .50
511 Lars Weibel .20 .50
512 Tommy Sjodin .08 .25
513 Andrei Khomutov .20 .50
514 Lars Weibel .20 .50
515 Anders Eldebrink .08 .25
516 Ken Yaremchuk .20 .50
517 Reto Pavoni .20 .50
518 Dino Kessler .02 .10
519 Fausto Mazzoleni .02 .10
520 Andy Ton .02 .10
521 Dan Hodgson .20 .50
522 Roman Wager .02 .10
523 Reto Pavoni .20 .50
524 Reijo Ruotsalainen .20 .50
525 Tommy Sjodin .08 .25
526 Andrej Kwartalnov .02 .10
527 Mikael Johansson .02 .10
528 Ken Yaremchuk .40 1.00
529 Reto Pavoni .20 .50
530 Dino Kessler .02 .10
531 Marco Bayer .02 .10
532 Misko Antisin .02 .10
533 Sacha Ochsner .02 .10
534 Roman Wager .02 .10
535 Reto Pavoni .20 .50
536 Reijo Ruotsalainen .20 .50
537 Andreas Eldebrink .08 .25
538 Ken Yaremchuk .40 1.00
539 Mikael Johansson .02 .10
540 Tom Fergus .40 1.00
541 Dan Quinn .20 .50
542 Valeri Kamenski .40 1.00
543 Phil Housley .40 1.00
544 Chris Chelios 6.00 15.00
545 Doug Gilmour 6.00 15.00
NNO Beat Eichmann .02 .10
NNO Danny Kurmann .02 .10
NNO Reto Bertolotti .02 .10
NNO Roland Stadler .02 .10
NNO Beat Eichmann .02 .10

1996-97 Swiss HNL

This set features the players from both the A and B leagues from Switzerland. We've been unable to identify all of the players completely. If you can provide additional information, please forward it to hockeymag@beckett.com

COMPLETE SET (588) 40.00 80.00
1 EHC Kloten .02 .10
2 Fleming CO .02 .10
3 Schumacher .02 .10
4 Reto Pavoni .02 .10
5 Walter .02 .10
6 Marco Bayer .02 .10
7 Greg Brown .02 .10
8 Martin Bruderer .02 .10
9 Marco Kloti .02 .10
10 Marco Knecht .02 .10
11 Michael Kress .02 .10
12 Bjorn Schneider .02 .10
13 Daniel Weber .02 .10
14 Robin Bauer .02 .10
15 Charles Berglund .02 .10
16 Matthias Bachler .02 .10
17 Manuele Celio .02 .10
18 Patrick Della Rossa .02 .10
19 Jorg Eberle .02 .10
20 Felix Hollenstein .02 .10
21 Mathias Holzer .02 .10
22 Mikael Johansson .02 .10
23 Martin Pluss .02 .10
24 Frederic Rothen .02 .10
25 Roman Wager .02 .10
26 SC Bern .02 .10
27 Chuck Lefley CO .02 .10
28 Schwarz .02 .10
29 Renato Tosio .02 .10
30 Alex Reinhard .02 .10
31 Timo Jutila .02 .10
32 Christian Langer .02 .10
33 Sven Leuenberger .02 .10
34 Martin Rauch .02 .10
35 Ville Siren .02 .10
36 Martin Steinegger .02 .10
37 Gaetan Voisard .02 .10
38 Rene Friedli .02 .10
39 Regis Fuchs .02 .10
40 Patrick Howald .02 .10
41 Vincent Lechenne .02 .10
42 Stefan Moser .02 .10
43 Trevor Meier .02 .10
44 Gil Montandon .02 .10
45 Michael Mouther .02 .10
46 Laurent Muller .02 .10
47 Philppe Mueller .02 .10
48 Gates Orlando .20 .50
49 Thierry Paterlini .02 .10
50 Roberto Triulzi .02 .10
51 EV Zug .02 .10
52 Jim Koleff CO .02 .10
53 Simpson .02 .10
54 Patrick Schopf .02 .10
55 Ronnie Rueger .02 .10
56 Livio Fazio .02 .10
57 Stefan Grauwiler .02 .10
58 Dino Kessler .02 .10
59 Andre Kunzi .02 .10
60 Thomas Kunzi .02 .10
61 John Miner .02 .10
62 Patrick Sutter .02 .10
63 Steve Aebersold .02 .10
64 Misko Antisin .02 .10
65 Patrick Fischer .02 .10
66 Daniel Giger .02 .10
67 Stephen Grogg .02 .10
68 Bill McDougall .02 .10
69 Colin Muller .02 .10
70 Phil Neuenschwander .02 .10
71 Philipp Orlandi .02 .10
72 Andre Rotheli .02 .10
73 Chad Silver .02 .10
74 Franz Steffen .02 .10
75 Wes Walz .75 2.00
76 HC Ambri Piotta .02 .10
77 Alexander Jakushev CO .20 .50
78 Pauli Jaks .20 .50
79 Paolo Della Bella .02 .10
80 Brenno Celio .02 .10
81 Ivan Gazzaroli .02 .10
82 Tiziano Gianini .02 .10
83 Noel Guyaz .02 .10
84 Jakub Horak .02 .10
85 Alessandro Reinhart .02 .10
86 Oskar Szczepaniec .02 .10
87 Dmitri Tsygurov .02 .10
88 Mattia Baldi .02 .10
89 Nicola Celio .02 .10
90 John Fritsche .02 .10
91 Patrick Glanzmann .02 .10
92 Thomas Heldner .02 .10
93 Peter Jaks .02 .10
94 Dmitri Kvartalnov .20 .50
95 Oleg Petrov .02 .10
96 Omar Tognini .02 .10
97 Igor Chibirev .02 .10
98 Luca Vigano .02 .10
99 Theo Wittmann .02 .10
100 HC Davos .02 .10
101 Del Curto CO .02 .10
102 Evgeni Popichin ACO .02 .10
103 Nando Wieser .02 .10
104 Thomas Berger .02 .10
105 Samuel Balmer .02 .10
106 Beat Equilino .02 .10
107 Marc Gianola .02 .10
108 Malier .02 .10
109 Valeri Shiryaev .02 .10
110 Daniel Sigg .02 .10
111 Mark Streit .40 1.00
112 Jan Von Arx .02 .10
113 Dan Hodgson .02 .10
114 Philipp Luber .02 .10
115 Rene Mueller .02 .10
116 Andy Naser .02 .10
117 Sergei Petrenko .02 .10
118 Oliver Roth .02 .10
119 Ivo Ruthemann .02 .10
120 Mario Schocher .02 .10
121 Reto Stirnimann .02 .10
122 Reto Von Arx .20 .50
123 Christian Weber .02 .10
124 Ken Yaremchuk .20 .50
125 SC Rapperswil Jona .02 .10
126 Pekka Rautakallio CO .02 .10
127 Ueli Scheidegger .02 .10
128 Claudio Bayer .02 .10
129 Remo Wehrli .02 .10
130 Daniel Buenzli .02 .10
131 Marko Capaul .02 .10
132 Kari Martikainen .02 .10
133 Dominic Meier .02 .10
134 Blair Muller .02 .10
135 Mathias Seger .02 .10
136 Roger Sigg .02 .10
137 Adrian Bachofner .02 .10
138 Arthur Camenzind .02 .10
139 Oliver Hoffmann .02 .10
139 Daniel Bunzli .02 .10
140 Christian Hofstetter .02 .10
141 Michael Meler .02 .10
142 Mike Richard .02 .10
143 Harry Rogenmoser .02 .10
144 Sergio Soguel .02 .10
145 Gilles Thibaudeau .02 .10
146 Roger Thony .02 .10
147 Mark Weber .02 .10
148 Christian Wolhwend .02 .10
149 HC Lugano .02 .10
150 Mats Waltin CO .02 .10
151 Gunnar Leidborg .02 .10
152 Lars Weibel .20 .50
153 Davide Gislimberti .02 .10
154 Sandro Bertaggia .02 .10
155 Fabian Guignard .02 .10
156 David Jelmini .02 .10
157 Rudi Niderost .02 .10
158 Luigi Riva .02 .10
159 Tommy Sjodin .02 .10
160 Rick Tschumi .02 .10
161 Jerry Zuurmond .02 .10
162 J.-J. Aeschlimann .02 .10
163 Markus Butler .02 .10
164 Gian-Marco Crameri .02 .10
165 Bruno Erni .02 .10
166 Keith Fair .02 .10
167 Marcel Jenni .02 .10
168 Marcel Franzi .02 .10
169 Stephan Lebeau .20 .50
170 Stefano Togni .02 .10
171 Andy Ton .02 .10
172 Raymond Walder .02 .10
173 Marco Werder .02 .10
174 Michael Nylander .20 .50
175 Zurcher SC .02 .10
176 Alpo Suhonen CO .02 .10
177 Frutiger .02 .10
178 Thomas Papp .02 .10
179 M. Muller .02 .10
180 Patrick Hager .02 .10
181 Martin Kout .02 .10
182 Robert Nordmark .02 .10
183 Didier Princi .02 .10
184 Edgar Salis .02 .10
185 Bruno Steck .02 .10
186 Nicolas Steiger .02 .10
187 Andreas Zehnder .02 .10
188 Mario Brodmann .02 .10
189 Marc Fortier .02 .10
190 Axel Heim .02 .10
191 Vjeran Ivankovic .02 .10
192 Sandy Jeannin .02 .10
193 Peter Kobel .02 .10
194 Patrick Lebeau .20 .50
195 Claudio Micheli .02 .10
196 Patrizio Morger .02 .10
197 Bruno Vollmer .02 .10
198 Michel Zeiter .02 .10
199 Gerd Zenhausern .02 .10
200 HC Fribourg .02 .10
201 Larsson CO .02 .10
202 Courvoisier .02 .10
203 Thomas Ostlund .02 .10
204 Steve Meuwly .02 .10
205 David Aebischer 4.00 10.00
206 Fredy Bobillier .02 .10
207 Patrice Brasey .02 .10
208 Antoine Descloux .02 .10
209 Andi Egli .02 .10
210 Christian Hofstetter .02 .10
211 Olivier Keller .02 .10
212 Philippe Marquis .02 .10
213 Marc Werlen .02 .10
214 Christophe Brown .02 .10
215 Slava Bykov .20 .50
216 David Dousse .02 .10
217 Stefan Choffat .02 .10
218 Andrei Khomutov .20 .50
219 Daniel Meier .02 .10
220 Patrick Oppliger .02 .10
221 Mario Rottaris .02 .10
222 Pascal Schaller .02 .10
223 Didier Schafer .02 .10
224 Al Raymond .02 .10
225 HC La Chaux De Fonds .02 .10
226 Ricardo Fuhrer CO .02 .10
227 Jean-Luc Schnegg .02 .10
228 Roland Meyer .02 .10
229 Eric Bourquin .02 .10
230 Rob Cowie .02 .10
231 Daniel Dubois .02 .10
232 Dan Eisener .02 .10
233 Thierry Murisier .02 .10
234 Dany Ott .02 .10
235 Jorg Reber .02 .10
236 Pascal Sommer .02 .10
237 Jan Alston .40 1.00
238 Florian Andenmatten .02 .10
239 Loic Burkhalter .02 .10
240 Christer Cantoni .02 .10
241 Florian Chappot .02 .10
242 Michael Diener .02 .10
243 Gilles Dubois .02 .10
244 Rob Gaudreau .02 .10
245 Boris Liemgruber .02 .10
246 Benoit Pont .02 .10
247 Bernhard Schumperli .02 .10
248 Michel Wicky .02 .10
249 HC Lausanne .02 .10
250 Johnston .02 .10
251 Beat Kindler .02 .10
252 Bernhard Lauber .02 .10
253 Sebastien De Allegri .02 .10
254 Thierry Evequoz .02 .10
255 Nicolas Goumaz .02 .10
256 Cull .02 .10
257 Ivo Stoffel .02 .10
258 Turcotte .02 .10
259 Philippe Bozon .40 1.00
260 Johan Bertholet .02 .10
261 Andre Doll .02 .10
262 Rolf Ziegler .02 .10
263 Horvath .02 .10
264 Bruno Maurer .02 .10
265 Alfie Michaud .20 .50
266 Frank Monnier .02 .10
267 Patrice Pellet .02 .10
268 Mario Seeholzer .02 .10
269 Robert Slehofer .02 .10
270 Laurent Stehlin .02 .10
271 Grasshoppers .02 .10
272 Bruno Aegerter .02 .10
273 Alatalo .02 .10
274 Marcel Kohli .02 .10
275 Olivier Wissmann .02 .10
276 Martin Brich .02 .10
277 Marc Haueter .02 .10
278 FahM. .02 .10
279 Roman Honegger .02 .10
280 Arne Ramholt .02 .10
281 Daniel Rutschi .02 .10
282 Alain Ayer .02 .10
283 Andre Baumann .02 .10
284 Warren Brutsch .02 .10
285 Roman Furrer .02 .10
286 Marco Hagmann .02 .10
287 Patrick Looser .02 .10
288 Lasse Nieminen .02 .10
289 Andy Rufener .02 .10
290 Christian Ruuttu .20 .50
291 Mathias Schenkel .02 .10
292 Peter Schlagenhauf .02 .10
293 HC Thurgau .02 .10
294 Mike McParland .02 .10
295 Peter Martin .02 .10
296 Sutter .02 .10
297 Martin Granicher .02 .10
298 Henry .02 .10
299 Ralph Ott .02 .10
300 Mike Posma .02 .10
301 Marcel Schmid .02 .10
302 Christian Schuster .02 .10
303 Robert Wiesmann .02 .10
304 Dan Daoust .02 .10
305 Slaven Imhof .02 .10
306 Matthias Keller .02 .10
307 Ronny Keller .02 .10
308 Guido Laczko .02 .10
309 Don McLaren .02 .10
310 Gery Othman .02 .10
311 Rolf Schrepfer .02 .10
312 Rene Stussi .02 .10
313 Cuno Weisser .02 .10
314 Benjamin Winkler .02 .10
315 SC Langnau .02 .10
316 Paul-Andre Cadieux .02 .10
317 Jakub Kolliker .02 .10
318 Martin Gerber ERC 4.00 10.00
319 Thomas Dreier .02 .10
320 Daniel Aegerter .02 .10
321 Raoul Baumgartner .02 .10
322 Andreas Beutler .02 .10
323 Mario Doyon .02 .10
324 Roland Kradolfer .02 .10
325 Raphael Schneider .02 .10
326 Pascal Stoller .02 .10
327 Rolf Badertscher .02 .10
328 Bruno Brechbuhl .02 .10
329 Peter Bartschi .02 .10
330 Walter Gerber .02 .10
331 Markus Hirschi .02 .10
332 Jakub Horak .02 .10
333 Andreas Keller .02 .10
334 Beat Nuspliger .02 .10
335 Greg Parks .02 .10
336 Kevin Schlapfer .02 .10
337 Stefan Tschiemer .02 .10
338 SC Herisau .02 .10
339 McGregor .02 .10
340 Markus Bachschmied .02 .10
341 Schiess .02 .10
342 Urs Balzarek .02 .10
343 Damien Freitag .02 .10
344 Fritz .02 .10
345 Thomas Jaggli .02 .10
346 Karl Knopf .02 .10
347 Andy Krapf .02 .10
348 Andy Maag .02 .10
349 Devin Edgerton .02 .10
350 Rico Enzler .02 .10
351 John Fust .02 .10
352 Martin Hanggi .02 .10
353 Francois Marquis .02 .10
354 Ludwig Marek .02 .10
355 Pinelli .02 .10
356 Ivo Ruthemann .02 .10
357 Scheiwiller .02 .10
358 Claude Vilgrain .40 1.00
359 Sacha Weibel .02 .10
360 HC Martigny .02 .10
361 Steve Pochon .02 .10
362 Patrick Grand .02 .10
363 Didier Tosi .02 .10
364 Pascal Avanthay .02 .10
365 Jean-Michel Clavien .02 .10
366 Ayocholos Escher .02 .10
367 Alan Hirschi .02 .10
368 Patrik Neukom .02 .10
369 Benedikt Sapin .02 .10
370 Marc Zurbriggen .02 .10
371 Jean-Daniel Bonito .02 .10
372 Igor Fedulov .02 .10
373 Nicolas Gastaldo .02 .10
374 Paolo Imperatori .02 .10
375 Thierry Moret .02 .10
376 Stephan Nussberger .02 .10
377 Petr Rosol .02 .10
378 Fabrizio Silietti .02 .10
379 Yannick Theler .02 .10
380 Natal Zurbriggen .02 .10
381 EHC Biel-Bienne .02 .10
382 Michael Zettel .02 .10
383 Christoph Wahl .02 .10
384 Devaux .02 .10
385 Sven Dick .02 .10
386 Romain Fleury .02 .10
387 Claudio Ghillioni .02 .10
388 Urs Hirschi .02 .10
389 Sven Schmid .02 .10
390 Daniel Schneider .02 .10
391 Alain Villard .02 .10
392 Thomas Burillo .02 .10
393 Reynald De Ritz .02 .10
394 Marco Dick .02 .10
395 Paul Gagne .02 .10
396 Gabriel Taccoz .02 .10
397 Shawn Heaphy .02 .10
398 Maxime Lapointe .02 .10
399 Luthi .02 .10
400 Serge Meyer .02 .10
401 Cyrill Pasche .02 .10
402 Michel Riesen .20 .50
403 HC Geneve-Servette .02 .10
404 Huppe .02 .10
405 Hagmann .02 .10
406 Michel Pilet .02 .10
407 Francesco Bizzozero .02 .10
408 Daniel Herlea .02 .10
409 Pascal Lamprecht .02 .10
410 Thevoz .02 .10
411 Daniel Zieri .02 .10
412 Christian Serena .02 .10
413 Nicolas Studer .02 .10
414 Joel Aeschlimann .02 .10
415 Antoine Cloux .02 .10
416 Claude Verret .02 .10
417 Martin Desjardins .02 .10
418 Olivier Ecoeur .02 .10
419 Gaby Epiney .02 .10
420 Laurent Faller .02 .10
421 Nicholas Gauch .02 .10
422 Olivier Honsberger .02 .10
423 Gael Kertudo .02 .10
424 Jorg Ledermann .02 .10
425 EHC Olten .02 .10
426 Hoffmann .02 .10
427 Beat Aebischer .02 .10
428 Thierry Loup .02 .10
429 Ralph Gugelmann .02 .10
430 Bruno Habisreutinger .02 .10
431 Phillippe Portner .02 .10
432 Gianni Sanese .02 .10
433 Schonauer .02 .10
434 Richard Stucki .02 .10
435 Thomas Studer .02 .10
436 Dobler .02 .10
437 Yanick Dube .02 .10
438 Mario Koppel .02 .10
439 Luthi .02 .10
440 Muller .02 .10
441 Nicola Pini .02 .10
442 Thomas Seitz .02 .10
443 Patrick Siegwart .02 .10
444 Pirmin Keller .02 .10
445 Andre Von Rohr .02 .10
446 Andre Von Rohr .02 .10
447 EHC Chur .02 .10
448 Voschakov .02 .10
449 Thomas Liesch .02 .10
450 Reto Zuccolini .02 .10
451 Armin Berchtold .02 .10
452 Sacha Bleiker .02 .10
453 Sandro Capaul .02 .10
454 Patrick Fischer .02 .10
455 Andreas Ritsch .02 .10
456 Stefan Schneider .02 .10
457 Roland Simonet .02 .10
458 Rene Ackermann .02 .10
459 Andreas Fischer .02 .10
460 Miguel Fondado .02 .10
461 Claudio Peer .02 .10
462 Reto Germann .02 .10
463 Albert Malgin .02 .10
464 Roger Rieder .02 .10
465 Michael Rosenast .02 .10
466 Riccardo Signorell .02 .10
467 Harijs Vitolinsh .02 .10
468 Patrick Werthan .02 .10
469 Nussle .02 .10
470 SC Luzern .02 .10
471 Hansson .02 .10
472 Beat Lautenschlager .02 .10
473 Patrice Bosch .02 .10
474 Rosset .02 .10
475 Alain Comte .02 .10
476 Dominik Jenny .02 .10
477 Samuelsson .02 .10
478 Ron Stillhardt .02 .10
479 Marco Tanner .02 .10
480 Markus Wetter .02 .10
481 Martin Bahnik .02 .10
482 Baiada .02 .10
483 Buchel .02 .10
484 Marco Fischer .02 .10
485 P. Giger .02 .10
486 Daniel Lamminger .02 .10
487 M. Ledermann .02 .10
488 Daniel Mares .02 .10
489 P. Mares .02 .10
490 Marco Mozzini .02 .10
491 Mario Schocher .02 .10
492 Ramil Yuldaschev .02 .10
493 Ron Stillhardt .02 .10
494 HC Ajoie .02 .10
495 Hans Kossmann .02 .10
496 Christian Cretin .02 .10
497 Rosado .02 .10
498 Rapheal Berger .02 .10
499 Matthias Bachler .02 .10
500 Erich Frey .02 .10
501 Heusler .02 .10
502 M. Reinhard .02 .10
503 Julien Vauclair ERC .40 1.00
504 Yann Voillat .02 .10
505 Patrick Adami .02 .10
506 Denis Chalifoux .02 .10
507 Guyaz .02 .10
508 Alexandre Von Arb .02 .10
509 Holmberg .02 .10
510 Honegger .02 .10
511 Herve Meyer .02 .10
512 Marc Fritsche .02 .10
513 Migy .02 .10
514 Giovanni Pestrin .02 .10
515 Geoffrey Vauclair .02 .10
516 Reto Pavoni .02 .10
517 Gaeten Voisard .02 .10
518 Martin Bruderer .02 .10
519 Felix Hollenstein .02 .10
520 Gil Montandon .02 .10
521 Patrick Howald .02 .10
522 National Team .02 .10
523 Schenk .02 .10
524 Paul-Andre Cadieux .02 .10
525 Jakub Kolliker .02 .10
526 Reto Pavoni .02 .10
527 Pauli Jaks .20 .50
528 Samuel Balmer .02 .10
529 Marco Bayer .02 .10
530 Sandro Bertaggia .02 .10
531 Martin Bruderer .02 .10
532 Tiziano Gianini .02 .10
533 Sven Leuenberger .02 .10
534 Gaetan Voisard .02 .10
535 Andreas Zehnder .02 .10
536 Manuele Celio .02 .10
537 Nicola Celio .02 .10
538 Patrick Fischer .02 .10
539 Felix Hollenstein .02 .10
540 Peter Jaks .02 .10
541 Sandy Jeannin .02 .10
542 Marcel Jenni .02 .10
543 Harry Rogenmoser .02 .10
544 Frederic Rothen .02 .10
545 Reto Von Arx .20 .50
546 Christian Weber .02 .10
547 Michel Zeiter .02 .10
548 SIHL .02 .10
549 Swiss National Inline Team .02 .10
550 Alan Wittwer .02 .10
551 Markus Bachschmied .02 .10
552 Waber .02 .10
553 Ochsner .02 .10
554 Mueller .02 .10
555 Bauer .02 .10
556 Ivo Ruthemann .02 .10
557 Sven Lindemann .02 .10
558 Alexandre Von Arb .02 .10
559 Ronnie Rueger .02 .10
561 Klaus .02 .10
562 Guido Lindemann .02 .10
563 Rico Enzler .02 .10
564 Andres Egger .02 .10
565 Kuendig .02 .10
566 Wild .02 .10
567 Johansson .02 .10
568 Patrick Howald .02 .10
569 Muller .02 .10
570 Tschibirev .02 .10
571 Jan Alston .40 1.00
572 Mike Richard .02 .10
573 Stephan Lebeau .20 .50
574 Marc Fortier .02 .10
575 Slava Bykov .20 .50
576 Frank Monnier .02 .10
577 Patrick Oppliger .02 .10
578 Lasse Nieminen .02 .10
579 Dan Daoust .20 .50
580 Glowa .02 .10
581 Claude Vilgrain .40 1.00
582 Petr Rosol .02 .10
583 Dmitri Kvartalnov .20 .50
584 Andrew McKim .20 .50
585 Rene Ackermann .02 .10
586 Valery Cherny .02 .10
587 Referees .02 .10
588 Referees .02 .10

1998-99 Swiss Power Play Stickers

COMPLETE SET (382) 40.00 80.00
1 Team Ambri Left .07 .20
2 Team Ambri Right .07 .20
3 Larry Hurras .07 .20
4 Pauli Jaks .07 .20
5 Peter Martin .07 .20
6 Fredy Bobillier .07 .20
7 Ivan Gazzaroli .07 .20
8 Tiziano Gianini .07 .20
9 Giordano Guidotti .07 .20
10 Leif Rohlin .07 .20
11 Edgar Salis .07 .20
12 Bruno Steck .07 .20
13 Oliver Tschanz .07 .20
14 Mattia Baldi .07 .20
15 Krister Cantoni .07 .20
16 Manuele Celio .07 .20
17 Nicola Celio .07 .20
18 Paul DiPietro .20 .50
19 John Fritsche .07 .20
20 Vjeran Ivankovic .07 .20
21 Oleg Petrov .07 .20
22 Franz Steffen .07 .20
23 Omar Tognini .07 .20
24 Theo Wittmann .07 .20
25 Thomas Ziegler .07 .20
26 Team Bern Left .07 .20
27 Team Bern Right .07 .20
28 Ueli Schwarz .07 .20
29 Renato Tosio .07 .20
30 Reto Schurch .07 .20
31 Alexander Godynyuk .07 .20
32 Sven Leuenberger .07 .20
33 Martin Rauch .07 .20
34 Bjorn Schneider .07 .20
35 Stefan Schneider .07 .20
36 Pascal Sommer .07 .20
37 Martin Steinegger .07 .20
38 Gregor Thommen .07 .20
39 Bjorn Christen .07 .20
40 David Jobin .07 .20
41 Patrick Howald .07 .20
42 Boris Leimgruber .07 .20
43 Lars Leuenberger .07 .20
44 Dave McLlwain .07 .20
45 Gil Montandon .07 .20
46 Daniel Marois .07 .20
47 Michel Mouther .07 .20
48 Thierry Paterlini .07 .20
49 Roberto Triulzi .07 .20
50 Marc Weber .07 .20
51 Team Davos Left .07 .20
52 Team Davos Right .07 .20
53 Arno Del Curto .07 .20
54 Stephane Beauregard .20 .50
55 Marco Wegmuller .07 .20
56 Beat Equilino .07 .20
57 Marc Gianola .07 .20
58 Andrea Haller .07 .20
59 Michael Kress .07 .20
60 Pettri Nummelin .07 .20
61 Mark Streit .40 1.00
62 Jan Von Arx .07 .20
63 Andre Baumann .07 .20
64 Sandy Jeannin .07 .20
65 Rene Muller .07 .20
66 Kai Nurminen .07 .20
67 Peter Kobel .07 .20
68 Sandro Rizzi .07 .20
69 Oliver Roth .07 .20
70 Ivo Ruthemann .07 .20
71 Mario Schocher .07 .20
72 Reto Stirnimann .07 .20
73 Reto Von Arx .20 .50
74 Beat Helbstab .07 .20
75 Timo Helbling .20 .50
76 Team Fribourg Left .07 .20
77 Team Fribourg Right .07 .20
78 Andre Peloffy .07 .20
79 David Aebischer 2.00 5.00
80 Thomas Ostlund .20 .50
81 Alain Sansonnens .07 .20
82 Patrice Brasey .07 .20
83 Antoine Descloux .07 .20
84 Livio Fazio .07 .20
85 Romain Fleury .07 .20
86 Olivier Keller .07 .20
87 Philippe Marquis .07 .20
88 Marc Werlen .07 .20
89 Igor Chibirev .07 .20
90 Flavien Conne .07 .20
91 David Dousse .07 .20
92 Rene Furler .07 .20
93 Daniel Giger .07 .20
94 Goran Bezina .07 .20
95 Philipp Orlandi .07 .20
96 Mario Rottaris .07 .20
97 Pascal Schaller .07 .20
98 Robert Slehofer .07 .20
99 Pavel Torgajev .07 .20
100 Gerd Zenhausern .07 .20
101 Team Kloten Left .07 .20
102 Team Kloten Right .07 .20
103 Reto Pavoni .07 .20
104 Marco Buhrer .07 .20
105 Samuel Balmer .07 .20
106 Marco Bayer .07 .20
107 Martin Bruderer .07 .20
108 Marco Kloti .07 .20
109 Beat Meier .07 .20
110 Tommy Sjodin .07 .20
111 Daniel Weber .07 .20
112 Benjamin Winkler .07 .20
113 Philipp Folghera .07 .20
114 Thomas Heldner .07 .20
115 Felix Hollenstein .07 .20
116 Sven Lindemann .07 .20
117 Bill McDougall .07 .20
118 Martin Pluss .07 .20
119 Frederic Rothen .07 .20
120 Andy Rufener .07 .20
121 Matthias Schenkel .07 .20
122 Rene Stussi .07 .20
123 Chris Tancill .07 .20
124 Adrian Wichser .07 .20
125 Team Langnau Left .07 .20
126 Team Langnau Right .07 .20
127 Jakob Kolliker .07 .20

128 Martin Gerber 2.00 5.00
129 Ivo Kleeb .07 .20
130 Daniel Aegerter .07 .20
131 Mario Doyon .07 .20
132 Marco Knecht .07 .20
133 Pascal Muller .07 .20
134 Wesley Snell .07 .20
135 Oskar Szczepaniec .07 .20
136 Markus Wuthrich .07 .20
137 Alexis Vacheron .07 .20
138 Rolf Bradertscher .07 .20
139 Peter Bartschi .07 .20
140 Bruno Brechbuhl .07 .20
141 Marc Buhlmann .07 .20
142 Todd Elik .07 .20
143 Marco Fischer .07 .20
144 John Fust .07 .20
145 Andy Keller .07 .20
146 Michael Liniger .07 .20
147 Greg Parks .07 .20
148 Benoit Pont .07 .20
149 Stefan Tschiemer .07 .20
150 Team Lugano Left .07 .20
151 Team Lugano Right .07 .20
152 Jim Koleff CO .07 .20
153 Cristobal Huet 6.00 15.00
154 Lars Weibel .07 .20
155 Peter Andersson .07 .20
156 Mark Astley .07 .20
157 Sandro Bertaggia .07 .20
158 Fabian Guignard .07 .20
159 Rick Tschumi .07 .20
160 Julien Vauclair .20 .50
161 Gaetan Voisard .07 .20
162 Rolf Ziegler .07 .20
163 Jean Jacques Aeschlimann .07 .20
164 Misko Antisin .07 .20
165 Gian Marco Crameri .07 .20
166 Andre Doll .07 .20
167 Keith Fair .07 .20
168 Patrick Fischer .07 .20
169 Regis Fuchs .07 .20
170 Marcel Jenni .07 .20
171 Trevor Meier .07 .20
172 Andy Naser .07 .20
173 Gaetano Orlando .20 .50
174 Geoffrey Vauclair .07 .20
175 Team Rapperswil Left .07 .20
176 Team Rapperswil Right .07 .20
177 Mark McGregor .07 .20
178 Claudio Bayer .07 .20
179 Remo Wehrli .07 .20
180 Marco Capaul .07 .20
181 Christian Langer .07 .20
182 Dominic Meier .07 .20
183 Jorg Reber .07 .20
184 Matthias Seger .07 .20
185 Daniel Sigg .07 .20
186 Roger Sigg .07 .20
187 Adrian Bachofner .07 .20
188 Markus Butler .07 .20
189 Rene Friedli .07 .20
190 Oliver Hoffmann .07 .20
191 Christian Hofstetter .07 .20
192 Chris Lindberg .07 .20
193 Frank Monnier .07 .20
194 Mark Ouimet .07 .20
195 Mike Richard .07 .20
196 Harry Rogenmoser .07 .20
197 Bernhard Schumperli .07 .20
198 Ken Yaremchuk .07 .20
199 Team EVZ Left .07 .20
200 Team EVZ Right .07 .20
201 Sean Simpson .07 .20
202 Ronald Rueger .07 .20
203 Patrick Schopf .07 .20
204 Raphael Berger .07 .20
205 Matthias Holzer .07 .20
206 Jakub Horak .07 .20
207 Dino Kessler .07 .20
208 Reto Kobach .07 .20
209 Andre Kunzi .07 .20
210 Thomas Kunzi .07 .20
211 Patrick Sutter .07 .20
212 Christoph Brown .07 .20
213 Jorg Eberle .07 .20
214 Devin Edgerton .07 .20
215 Stefan Grogg .07 .20
216 Daniel Meier .07 .20
217 Colin Muller .07 .20
218 Patrick Oppliger .07 .20
219 Andre Rotheli .07 .20
220 Sacha Schneider .07 .20
221 Kevin Todd .07 .20
222 Samuel Villiger .07 .20
223 Wes Walz .40 1.00
224 Team ZSC Left .07 .20
225 Team ZSC Right .07 .20
226 Kent Ruhnke .07 .20
227 Thomas Papp .07 .20
228 Ari Sulander .20 .50
229 Martin Brich .07 .20
230 Marc Haueter .07 .20
231 Michel Kamber .07 .20
232 Martin Kout .07 .20
233 Kari Martikainen .07 .20
234 Adrien Plavsic .07 .20
235 Pascal Stoller .07 .20
236 Andreas Zehnder .07 .20
237 Patrik Della Rossa .07 .20
238 Axel Heim .07 .20
239 Dan Hodgson .07 .20
240 Peter Jaks .07 .20
241 Claudio Micheli .07 .20
242 Patrizio Morger .07 .20
243 Laurent Muller .07 .20
244 Rolf Schrepfer .07 .20
245 Chad Silver .07 .20
246 Christian Weber .07 .20
247 Michel Zeiter .07 .20
248 National Team Left .07 .20
249 National Team Right .07 .20
250 Raphael Kruger .07 .20
251 David Aebischer 2.00 5.00
252 Misko Antisin .07 .20
253 Mattia Baldi .07 .20
254 Gian Marco Crameri .07 .20
255 Patrick Fischer .07 .20
256 Peter Jaks .07 .20
257 Sandy Jeannin .07 .20
258 Marcel Jenni .07 .20
259 Dino Kessler .07 .20
260 Claudio Micheli .07 .20
261 Reto Pavoni .07 .20
262 Martin Pluss .07 .20
263 Martin Rauch .07 .20
264 Ivo Ruthemann .07 .20
265 Edgar Salis .07 .20
266 Matthias Seger .07 .20
267 Franz Steffen .07 .20
268 Martin Steinegger .07 .20
269 Mark Streit .20 .50
270 Patrick Sutter .07 .20
271 Reto Von Arx .20 .50
272 Michel Zeiter .07 .20
273 Bill Gilligan .07 .20
274 Marco Buhrer .07 .20
275 Ralph Bundi .07 .20
276 Alex Chatelain .07 .20
277 Bjorn Christen .07 .20
278 Flavien Conne .07 .20
279 Patrick Fischer .07 .20
280 Sven Lindemann .07 .20
281 Michel Mouther .07 .20
282 Laurent Muller .07 .20
283 Marc Reichert .07 .20
284 Alain Reist .07 .20
285 Michel Riesen .20 .50
286 Sandro Rizzi .07 .20
287 Mario Schocher .07 .20
288 Rene Stussi .07 .20
289 Julien Vauclair .20 .50
290 Jan Von Arx .07 .20
291 Marc Werlen .07 .20
292 Adrian Wichser .07 .20
293 Markus Wuthrich .07 .20
294 Thomas Ziegler .07 .20
295 Team Biel Left .07 .20
296 Team Biel Right .07 .20
297 Christian Cretin .07 .20
Alain Reist
298 Sven Schmid .07 .20
Paul Gagne
299 Paul-Andre Cadieux .07 .20
300 Shawn Heaphy .07 .20
Cyrill Pasche
301 Team La Chaux de Fonds Left .07 .20
302 Team La Chaux de Fonds Right .07 .20
303 Thomas Berger .07 .20
Valeri Schirjaev
304 Lugio Riva .07 .20
Steve Aebersold
305 Riccardo Fuhrer .07 .20
306 Stephan Lebeau .07 .20
Stefano Togni
307 Team Chur Left .07 .20
308 Team Chur Right .07 .20
309 Thomas Liesch .07 .20
Patrick Fischer
310 Mike Posma .07 .20
Mario Brodmann
311 Mike McParland .07 .20
312 Harijs Vitolinsh .07 .20
Reymond Walder
313 Team GC Left .07 .20
314 Team GC Right .07 .20
315 Olivier Wissmann .07 .20
Arne Ramholt
316 Marco Schellenberg .07 .20
Domenic Amodeo
317 Dave Tietzen .07 .20
318 Mark Kaufman .07 .20
Riccardo Signorell
319 Team Servette Left .07 .20
320 Team Servette Right .07 .20
321 Steve Meuwly .07 .20
David Leibzig
322 Maxime Lapointe .07 .20
Christian Serena
323 Jean Perron CO .07 .20
324 Mark Jorris .07 .20
Sandy Smith
325 Team Herisau Left .07 .20
326 Team Herisau Right .07 .20
327 Fabian Gull .07 .20
Robert Burakowsky
328 Markus Bachschmied .07 .20
Urs Balzarek
329 Evgeny Popichin .07 .20
330 Alain Fraser .07 .20
Cuno Weisser
331 Team Lausanne Left .07 .20
332 Team Lausannne Right .07 .20
333 Beat Kindler .07 .20
Serge Poudrier
334 Andy Krapf .07 .20
Jorg Ledermann
335 Benoit Laporte .07 .20
336 Slava Bykov .07 .20
Daniel Nakaoka
337 Team Martigny Left .07 .20
338 Team Martigny Right .07 .20
339 Didier Tosi .07 .20
Jean-Michel Clavien
340 Benedict Sapin .07 .20
Jean-Daniel Bonito
341 Petr Rosol .07 .20
342 Nicolas Gastaldo .07 .20
Thierry Moret
343 Team Olten Left .07 .20
344 Team Olten Right .07 .20
345 Beat Aebischer .07 .20
Richard Stucki
346 Igor Boriskov .07 .20
Albert Malgin
347 Markus Graf .07 .20
348 Luca Vigano .07 .20
Andre Von Rohr
349 Team Sierre Left .07 .20
350 Team Sierre Right .07 .20
351 Matthias Lauber .07 .20
Michel Fah
352 Philippe Faust .07 .20
Bruno Erni
353 Christian Wittwer .07 .20
354 Marco Poulsen .07 .20
Gilles Thibaudeau
355 Team Thurgau Left .07 .20
356 Team Thurgau Right .07 .20
357 Marius Bosch .07 .20
Patrick Henry
358 Ralph Ott .07 .20
Scott Beattie
359 Henryk Gruth .07 .20
360 Kevin Miehm .07 .20
Roman Wager
A SEHV .07 .20
{ LSHG
B HC Ambri Piotta .07 .20
C SC Bern .07 .20
D HC Davos .07 .20
E HC Fribourg Gotteron .07 .20
F EHC Kloten .07 .20
G SC Langnau .07 .20
H HC Lugano .07 .20
I SC Rapperswil-Jona .07 .20
J EV Zug .07 .20
K ZSC Lions .07 .20
L EHC Biel-Bienne .07 .20
M HC La Chaux De Fonds .07 .20
N EHC Chur .07 .20
O Grasshoppers .07 .20
P HC Geneve Servette .07 .20
Q SC Herisau .07 .20
R HC Lausanne .07 .20
S EHC Martigny .07 .20
T EHC Olten .07 .20
U HC Sierre .07 .20
V HC Thurgau .07 .20

1999-00 Swiss Panini Stickers

COMPLETE SET (380) 40.00 80.00
1 Team Ambri Left .07 .20
2 Team Ambri Right .07 .20
3 Larry Huras .07 .20
4 Pauli Jaks .07 .20
5 Peter Martin .07 .20
6 Fredy Bobillier .07 .20
7 Ivan Gazzaroli .07 .20
8 Tiziano Gianini .07 .20
9 John Gobbi .07 .20
10 Thomas Kunzi .07 .20
11 Leif Rohlin .07 .20
12 Bruno Steck .07 .20
13 Krister Cantoni .07 .20
14 Manuele Celio .07 .20
15 Nicola Celio .07 .20
16 Luca Cereda .20 .50
17 Alain Demuth .07 .20
18 Paolo Duca .07 .20
19 John Fritsche .07 .20
20 Ryan Gardner .07 .20
21 Vitaly Lakhmatov .07 .20
22 Stephan Lebeau .20 .50
23 Patrick Lebeau .20 .50
24 Franz Steffen .07 .20
25 Thomas Ziegler .07 .20
26 Team Bern Left .07 .20
27 Team Bern Right .07 .20
28 Pekka Rautakallio CO .07 .20
29 Martin Kilchor .07 .20
30 Renato Tosio .07 .20
31 David Jobin .07 .20
32 Sven Leuenberger .07 .20
33 Petri Liimatainen .07 .20
34 Martin Rauch .07 .20
35 Pascal Sommer .07 .20
36 Martin Steinegger .07 .20
37 Fabian Stephan .07 .20
38 Gregor Thommen .07 .20
39 Alex Chatelain .07 .20
40 Bjorn Christen .07 .20
41 Patrick Howald .07 .20
42 Roland Kaser .07 .20
43 Boris Leimgruber .07 .20
44 Lars Leuenberger .07 .20
45 Dave McLlwain .07 .20
46 Thierry Paterlini .07 .20
47 Jackson Penney .07 .20
48 Marc Reichert .07 .20
49 Ivo Ruthemann .07 .20
50 Marc Weber .07 .20
51 Team Davos Left .07 .20
52 Team Davos Right .07 .20
53 Arno Del Curto .07 .20
54 Petter Ronnqvist .07 .20
55 Marco Wegmuller .07 .20
56 Beat Equilino .07 .20
57 Marc Gianola .07 .20
58 Andreas Haller .07 .20
59 Timo Helbling .20 .50
60 Beat Heldstab .07 .20
61 Petteri Nummelin .07 .20
62 Jan Von Arx .07 .20
63 Andre Baumann .07 .20
64 Patrick Fischer .07 .20
65 Marc Heberlein .07 .20
66 Sandy Jeannin .07 .20
67 Michael Kress .07 .20
68 Fredrik Lindquist .07 .20
69 Rene Muller .07 .20
70 Claudio Neff .07 .20
71 Sandro Rizzi .07 .20
72 Oliver Roth .07 .20
73 Frederic Rothen .07 .20
74 Mario Schocher .07 .20
75 Reto Von Arx .20 .50
76 Team Fribourg Left .07 .20
77 Team Fribourg Right .07 .20
78 Ueli Schwarz .07 .20
79 Thomas Ostlund .20 .50
80 Alain Sansonnens .07 .20
81 Goran Bezina .07 .20
82 Livio Fazio .07 .20
83 Romain Fleury .07 .20
84 Fabian Guignard .07 .20
85 Philippe Marquis .07 .20
86 Mika Stromberg .07 .20
87 Marc Werlen .07 .20
88 Rolf Ziegler .07 .20
89 Robert Burakowski .07 .20
90 Flavien Conne .07 .20
91 Rene Furler .07 .20
92 Daniel Giger .07 .20
93 Gil Montandon .07 .20
94 Colin Muller .07 .20
95 Michael Neininger .07 .20
96 Real Raemy .07 .20
97 Mario Rottaris .07 .20
98 Pascal Schaller .07 .20
99 Robert Slehofer .07 .20
100 Gerd Zenhausern .07 .20
101 Team Kloten Left .07 .20
102 Team Kloten Right .07 .20
103 Vladimir Jursinov CO .07 .20
104 Reto Pavoni .07 .20
105 Samuel Balmer .07 .20
106 Andre Bielmann .07 .20
107 Martin Bruderer .07 .20
108 Martin Hohener .07 .20
109 Marco Kloti .07 .20
110 Arne Ramholt .07 .20
111 Oskar Szczepaniec .07 .20
112 Benjamin Winkler .07 .20
113 Mathias Wuest .07 .20
114 Thomas Heldner .07 .20
115 Felix Hollenstein .07 .20
116 Peter Kobel .07 .20
117 Sven Lindemann .07 .20
118 Andrew McKim .20 .50
119 Andreas Nauser .07 .20
120 Martin Pluss .07 .20
121 Sebastien Reuille .07 .20
122 Andy Rufener .07 .20
123 Matthias Schenkel .07 .20
124 Tomas Strandberg .07 .20
125 Adrian Wichser .07 .20
126 Team Langnau Left .07 .20
127 Team Langnau Right .07 .20
128 Bengt-Ake Gustafsson .07 .20
129 Alfred Bohren .07 .20
130 Martin Gerber 2.00 5.00
131 Adrian Hunziker .07 .20
132 Daniel Aegeter .07 .20
133 Antoine Descloux .07 .20
134 Steve Hirschi .07 .20
135 Erik Kakko .07 .20
136 Pascal Muller .07 .20
137 Markus Wuthrich .07 .20
138 Rolf Badertscher .07 .20
139 Daniel Bieri .07 .20
140 Bruno Brechbuhl .07 .20
141 Marc Buhlmann .07 .20
142 Todd Elik .07 .20
143 John Fust .07 .20
144 Daniel Gauthier .07 .20
145 Bjorn Guazzini .07 .20
146 Matthias Holzer .07 .20
147 Michael Liniger .07 .20
148 Benoit Pont .07 .20
149 Stefan Tschiemer .07 .20
150 Team Lugano Left .07 .20
151 Team Lugano Right .07 .20
152 Jim Koleff CO .07 .20
153 Cristobal Huet 4.00 10.00
154 Lars Weibel .20 .50
155 Peter Andersson .07 .20
156 Mark Astley .07 .20
157 Sandro Bertaggia .07 .20
158 Olivier Keller .07 .20
159 Rick Tschumi .07 .20
160 Julien Vauclair .20 .50
161 Gaetan Voisard .20 .50
162 J.Jacques Aeschlimann .07 .20
163 Misko Antisin .07 .20
164 Philippe Bozon .40 1.00
165 Gian Marco Crameri .07 .20
166 Andre Doll .07 .20
167 Christian Dube .07 .20
168 Keith Fair .07 .20
169 Igor Fedulov .07 .20
170 Regis Fuchs .07 .20
171 Marcel Jenni .07 .20
172 Trevor Meier .07 .20
173 Andy Naser .07 .20
174 Geoffrey Vauclair .07 .20
175 Team Rapperswil Left .07 .20
176 Team Rapperswil Right .07 .20
177 Evgeny Popichin .07 .20
178 Claudio Bayer .07 .20
179 Remo Wehrli .07 .20
180 Marco Capaul .07 .20
181 Dominic Meier .07 .20
182 Jorg Reber .07 .20
183 Alain Reist .07 .20
184 Daniel Sigg .07 .20
185 Roger Sigg .07 .20
186 Magnus Svensson .07 .20
187 Loic Burkhalter .07 .20
188 Markus Butler .07 .20
189 Rene Friedli .07 .20
190 Sandro Haberlin .07 .20
191 Axel Heim .07 .20
192 Oliver Hoffmann .07 .20
193 Vjeran Ivankovic .07 .20
194 Frank Monnier .07 .20
195 Mark Ouimet .07 .20
196 Mike Richard .07 .20
197 Bernhard Schumperli .07 .20
198 Marcel Sommer .07 .20
199 Paul Ysebaert .07 .20
200 Team EVZ Left .07 .20
201 Team EVZ Right .07 .20
202 Rauno Korpi .07 .20
203 Ronnie Rueger .07 .20
204 Patrick Schopf .07 .20
205 Marco Bayer .07 .20
206 Raphael Berger .07 .20
207 Patrick Fischer .07 .20
208 Jakub Horak .07 .20
209 Dino Kessler .07 .20
210 Reto Kobach .07 .20
211 Andre Kunzi .07 .20
212 Patrick Sutter .07 .20
213 Christophe Brown .07 .20
214 Paul Di Pietro .20 .50
215 Stefan Grogg .07 .20
216 Daniel Meier .07 .20
217 Stefan Niggli .07 .20
218 Patrick Oppliger .07 .20
219 Andre Rotheli .07 .20
220 Sascha Schneider .07 .20
221 Rene Stussi .07 .20
222 Chris Tancill .07 .20
223 Samuel Villiger .07 .20
224 Dave Roberts .07 .20
225 Team ZSC Left .07 .20
226 Team ZSC Right .07 .20
227 Kent Ruhnke .07 .20
228 Thomas Papp .07 .20
229 Ari Sulander .20 .50
230 Ronny Keller .07 .20
231 Martin Kout .07 .20
232 Kari Martikainen .07 .20
233 Adrien Plavsic .07 .20
234 Edgar Salis .07 .20
235 Mathias Seger .07 .20
236 Pascal Stoller .07 .20
237 Andreas Zehnder .07 .20
238 Mattia Baldi .07 .20
239 Robin Bauer .07 .20
240 Patric Della Rossa .07 .20
241 Dan Hodgson .07 .20
242 Peter Jaks .07 .20
243 Claudio Micheli .07 .20
244 Patrizio Morger .07 .20
245 Laurent Muller .07 .20
246 Rolf Schrepfer .07 .20
247 Reto Stirnimann .07 .20
248 Christian Weber .07 .20
249 Michel Zeiter .07 .20
250 Ralph Krueger .07 .20
251 National Team Left .07 .20
252 National Team Right .07 .20
253 David Aebischer 2.00 5.00
254 Pauli Jaks .20 .50
255 Reto Pavoni .07 .20
256 Olivier Keller .07 .20
257 Philippe Marquis .07 .20
258 Ivo Ruthemann .07 .20
259 Mathias Seger .07 .20
260 Martin Steinegger .07 .20
261 Mark Streit .20 .50
262 Patrick Sutter .07 .20
263 Benjamin Winkler .07 .20
264 Mattia Baldi .07 .20
265 Gian Marco Crameri .07 .20
266 Patric Della Rossa .07 .20
267 Patrick Fischer .07 .20
268 Sandy Jeannin .07 .20
269 Marcel Jenni .07 .20
270 Laurent Muller .07 .20
271 Martin Pluss .07 .20
272 Sandro Rizzi .07 .20
273 Geoffrey Vauclair .07 .20
274 Reto Von Arx .20 .50
275 Michel Zeiter .07 .20
276 John Slettvoll .07 .20
277 National U20 TeamLeft .07 .20
278 National U20 Team Right .07 .20
279 Marco Buhrer .07 .20
280 Oliver Wissmann .07 .20
281 Goran Bezina .07 .20
282 David Jobin .07 .20
283 Pascal Muller .07 .20
284 Alain Reist .07 .20
285 Gregor Thommen .07 .20
286 Alex Vacheron .07 .20
287 Julien Vauclair .20 .50
288 Fabio Beccarelli .07 .20
289 Luca Cereda .20 .50
290 Bjorn Christen .07 .20
291 Flavien Conne .07 .20
292 Alain Demuth .07 .20
293 Philipp Folghera .07 .20
294 Roland Kaser .07 .20
295 Cornel Prinz .07 .20
296 Marc Reichert .07 .20
297 Michel Riesen .20 .50
298 Sandro Tschour .07 .20
299 Adrian Wichser .07 .20
300 Team Biel Left .07 .20
301 Team Biel Right .07 .20
302 Paul Gagne .07 .20
303 Sebastien Kohler .07 .20
Sven Schmid
304 Gilles Dubois .07 .20
Michel Mongeau
305 Cyrill Pasche .20 .50
Claude Vilgrain
306 La Chaux De Fonds Left .07 .20
307 La Chaux De Fonds Right .07 .20
308 Jaroslav Jagr .07 .20
309 Thomas Berger .07 .20
Ruedi Niderost
310 Luigi Riva .07 .20
Valeri Shiryayev
311 Steve Aebersold .07 .20
Christian Pouget
312 Team Chur Left .07 .20
313 Team Chur Right .07 .20
314 Mike McParland .07 .20
315 Nando Wieser .07 .20
Matthias Bachler
316 Michael Meier .07 .20
Roger Rieder
317 Sandro Tschour .07 .20
Theo Wittmann
318 Team GC Left .07 .20
319 Team GC Right .07 .20
320 Riccardo Fuhrer .07 .20
321 Oliver Wissmann .07 .20
Pascal Fah
322 David Fehr .07 .20
Oliver Kamber
323 Patrick Looser .07 .20
Riccardo Signorell
324 Team Lausanne Left .07 .20
325 Team Lausanne Right .07 .20
326 Benoit Laporte .07 .20
327 Beat Kindler .07 .20
Slava Bykov
328 Patrick Giove .07 .20
Maxime Lapointe
329 Jorg Ledermann .07 .20
Valentin Wirz
330 Team Olten Left .07 .20
331 Team Olten Right .07 .20
332 Markus Graf .07 .20
333 Beat Aebischer .07 .20
Andy Egli
334 Richard Stucki .07 .20
Evgeny Davydov
335 Michel Mouther .07 .20
Mikhail Volkov
336 Team Servette Left .07 .20
337 Team Servette Right .07 .20
338 Francois Huppe .07 .20
339 David Bochy .07 .20
Christian Serena
340 Sott Beatti .07 .20
Shawn Heaphy
341 Paul Savary .07 .20
Michel Wicky
342 Team Sierre Left .07 .20
343 Team Sierre Right .07 .20
344 Kevin Primeau .07 .20
345 Matthias Lauber .07 .20
Adrian Jezzone
346 Patrick Neukom .07 .20
Philipp Luber
347 Dimitri Shamolin .07 .20
Gilles Thibaudeau
348 Team Thurgau Left .07 .20
349 Team Thurgau Right .07 .20
350 Robert Wiesmann .07 .20
351 Marco Buhrer .07 .20
Stefan Grauwiler
352 Domenic Amodeo .07 .20
Matthias Keller
353 Patrick Meier .07 .20
Morgan Samuelsson
354 Team Visp Left .07 .20
355 Team Visp Right .07 .20
356 Bruno Zenhausern .07 .20
357 Reiner Karlen .07 .20
Wesley Snell
358 Marc Zurbriggen .07 .20
Franziskus Heinzmann
359 Andy Egli .07 .20
Gabriel Taccoz
A SEHV/LSHG .07 .20
B HC Ambri Piotta .07 .20
C SC Bern .07 .20
D HC Davos .07 .20
E HC Fribourg Gotteron .07 .20
F EHC Kloten .07 .20
G SC Langnau .07 .20
H HC Lugano .07 .20
I SC Rapperswil-Jona .07 .20
J EV Zug .07 .20
K ZSC Lions .07 .20
L EHC Biel-Bienne .07 .20
M HC La Chaux De Fonds .07 .20
N EHC Chur .07 .20
O Grasshoppers .07 .20
P HC Lausanne .07 .20
Q EHC Olten .07 .20
R HC Geneve Servette .07 .20
S HC Sierre .07 .20
T HC Thurgau .07 .20
U Visp .07 .20

2000-01 Swiss Panini Stickers

COMPLETE SET (322) 20.00 50.00
1 Logo Swiss Hockey Federation .08 .20
2 Ambri Team Card .08 .20
3 Ambri Team Card .08 .20
4 Ambri Logo .08 .20
5 Pietre Page .08 .20
6 Pauli Jaks .08 .20
7 Gianluca Mona .08 .20
8 Fredy Bobillier .08 .20
9 Ivan Gazzaroli .08 .20
10 Tiziano Gianini .08 .20
11 Thomas Kunzi .08 .20
12 Leif Rohlin .08 .20
13 Krister Cantoni .08 .20
14 Manuele Celio .08 .20
15 Nicola Celio .08 .20
16 Alain Demuth .08 .20
17 Paolo Duca .08 .20
18 John Fritsche .08 .20
19 Ryan Gardner .08 .20
20 Paolo Imperatori .08 .20
21 Vitaly Lakhmatov .08 .20
22 Stephan Lebeau .08 .20
23 Dan Marois .08 .20
24 Omar Tognini .08 .20
25 Thomas Ziegler .08 .20
26 Logo SCB .08 .20
27 Team Card SCB .08 .20
28 Team Card SCB .08 .20
29 Pekka Rautakallio .08 .20
30 Renato Tosio .08 .20
31 David Jobin .08 .20
32 Marc Leuenberger .08 .20
33 Sven Leuenberger .08 .20
34 Dominic Meier .08 .20
35 Frederik Olausson .08 .20
36 Martin Steinegger .08 .20
37 Fabian Stephan .08 .20
38 Rolf Ziegler .08 .20
39 Alex Chatelain .08 .20
40 Bjorn Christen .08 .20
41 Patrick Howald .08 .20
42 Andreas Johansson .08 .20
43 Patrick Juhlin .08 .20
44 Rolan Kasar .08 .20
45 Boris Leimgruber .08 .20
46 Marc Reichert .08 .20
47 Ivo Ruthemann .08 .20
48 Franz Steffen .08 .20
49 Marc Weber .08 .20
50 La Chaux De Fonds Logo .08 .20
51 Chaux Fonds Team Card .08 .20
52 Chaux Fonds Team Card .08 .20
53 Dan Hober .08 .20
54 Thomas Berger .08 .20
55 Gilles Cattela .08 .20
56 Pascal Avanthay .08 .20
57 Raphael Brusa .08 .20
58 Fabian Guignard .08 .20
59 Ruedi Niderost .08 .20
60 Roger Ohmann .08 .20
61 Valery Schirjaev .08 .20
62 Alexis Vacheron .08 .20
63 Steve Aebersold .08 .20
64 Thomas Derungs .08 .20
65 Claude Luthi .08 .20
66 Fabrice Maillat .08 .20
67 Thibaut Monnet .08 .20
68 Daniel Nakaota .08 .20
69 Stefan Nilsson .08 .20
70 Steve Pochon .08 .20
71 Philippe Halmann .08 .20
72 Julien Turler .08 .20
73 Sami Villiger .08 .20
74 Chur Logo .08 .20
75 Chur Team Card .08 .20
76 Chur Team Card .08 .20
77 Mike McParland .08 .20
78 Marco Buhrer .08 .20
79 Nando Wieser .08 .20
80 Noel Guyaz .08 .20
81 Christian Langer .08 .20
82 Ivo Stoffel .08 .20
83 Pasi Sormunen .08 .20
84 Mika Stromberg .08 .20
85 Matthias Bachler .08 .20
86 Fabio Beccarelli .08 .20
87 Patrick Kruger .08 .20
88 Michael Meier .08 .20
89 Daniel Peer .08 .20
90 Roger Rieder .08 .20
91 Michael Rosenast .08 .20
92 Oliver Roth .08 .20
93 Rene Stussi .08 .20
94 Sandro Tschuor .08 .20
95 Harijs Vitolinsh .08 .20
96 Raymond Walder .08 .20
97 Theo Wittmann .08 .20
98 HC Davos Logo .08 .20
99 HC Davos Team Card .08 .20
100 HC Davos Team Card .08 .20
101 Arno Del Curto .08 .20
102 Petter Ronnquist .08 .20
103 Lars Weibel .08 .20
104 Beat Equilino .08 .20
105 Marc Gianola .08 .20
106 Andrea Haller .08 .20
107 Michael Kress .08 .20
108 Kevin Miller .08 .20
109 Ralph Ott .08 .20
110 Jan Von Arx .08 .20
111 Andre Baumann .08 .20
112 Lonny Bohonos .08 .20
113 Pat Falloon .08 .20
114 Patrick Fischer .08 .20
115 Marc Heberlein .08 .20
116 Rene Muller .08 .20
117 Claudio Neff .08 .20
118 Thierry Paterlini .08 .20
119 Sandro Rizzi .08 .20
120 Frederic Rothen .08 .20
121 Mario Schocher .08 .20
122 Gotteron Logo .08 .20
123 Gotteron Team Card .08 .20
124 Gotteron Team Card .08 .20
125 Serge Pelletier .08 .20
126 Thomas Ostlund .20 .50
127 Alain Sansonnens .08 .20
128 Raphael Berger .08 .20
129 Goran Bezina .08 .20
130 Christoph Decurtins .08 .20
131 Antoine Descloux .08 .20
132 Livio Fazio .08 .20
133 Philippe Marquis .08 .20
134 Martin Rauch .08 .20
135 Marc Werlen .08 .20
136 Craig Ferguson .08 .20
137 Lars Leuenberger .08 .20
138 Silvan Lussy .08 .20
139 Gil Montandon .08 .20
140 Michel Mouther .08 .20
141 Mario Rottaris .08 .20
142 Jean Yves Roy .08 .20
143 Pascal Schaller .08 .20
144 Robert Slehofer .08 .20
145 Gerd Zenhausern .08 .20
146 Kloten Logo .08 .20
147 Kloten Team Card .08 .20
148 Kloten Team Card .08 .20
149 Vladimir Yursinov CO .08 .20
150 Reto Pavoni .20 .50
151 Martin Hohener .08 .20
152 Ronny Keller .08 .20
153 Marko Kiprusoff .08 .20
154 Marco Kloti .08 .20
155 Dejan Lozanov .08 .20
156 Oskar Szczepaniec .08 .20
157 Beni Winkler .08 .20
158 Sven Helfenstein .08 .20
159 Felix Hollenstein .08 .20
160 Andy Keller .08 .20
161 Sven Lindemann .08 .20
162 Andreas Nauser .08 .20
163 Fredrik Nilsson .08 .20
164 Martin Pluss .08 .20
165 Sebastian Reuille .08 .20
166 Andy Rufener .08 .20
167 Adi Wichser .08 .20
168 Thomas Widmer .08 .20
169 Mathias Wust .08 .20
170 Langnau Logo .08 .20
171 Langnau Team Card .08 .20
172 Langnau Team Card .08 .20
173 Bengt Ake Gustafsson .08 .20
174 Martin Gerber .75 2.00
175 Martin Zerzuben .08 .20
176 Daniel Aegerter .08 .20
177 Samuel Balmer .08 .20
178 Steve Hirschi .08 .20
179 Erik Kakko .08 .20
180 Pascal Muller .08 .20
181 Pascal Stoller .08 .20
182 Florian Andenmatten .08 .20
183 Rolf Badertscher .08 .20
184 Bruno Brechbuhl .08 .20
185 John Fust .08 .20
186 Daniel Gauthier .08 .20
187 Thomas Heldner .08 .20
188 Matthias Holzer .08 .20
189 Michael Neininger .08 .20
190 Benoit Pont .08 .20
191 Vlastimil Plavucha .08 .20
192 Daniel Steiner .08 .20
193 Stefan Tschiemer .08 .20
194 Lugano Logo .08 .20
195 Lugano Team Card .08 .20
196 Lugano Team Card .08 .20
197 Jim Koleff .08 .20
198 Cristobal Huet .08 5.00
199 Peter Martin .08 .20
200 Peter Andersson .08 .20
201 Mark Astley .08 .20
202 Sandro Bertaggia .08 .20
203 Olivier Keller .08 .20
204 Rick Tschumi .08 .20
205 Gaetan Voisard .08 .20
206 Jean-Jacques Aeschlimann .08 .20
207 Misko Antisin .08 .20
208 Philippe Bozon .40 1.00
209 Flavien Conne .08 .20
210 Christian Dube .08 .20
211 Keith Fair .08 .20
212 Igor Fedulov .08 .20
213 Regis Fuchs .08 .20
214 Sandy Jeannin .08 .20
215 Trevor Meier .08 .20
216 Andy Naser .08 .20
217 Geoffrey Vauclair .08 .20
218 Rapperswil Logo .08 .20
219 Rapperswil Team Card .08 .20
220 Rapperswil Team Card .08 .20
221 Evgeny Popikhin .08 .20
222 Claudio Bayer .08 .20
223 Matthias Lauber .08 .20
224 Marco Capaul .08 .20
225 Jakub Horak .08 .20
226 Kari Martikainen .08 .20
227 Jorg Reber .08 .20
228 Alain Reist .08 .20
229 Roger Sigg .08 .20
230 Loic Burkhalter .08 .20
231 Markus Butler .08 .20
232 Rene Friedli .08 .20
233 Rene Furler .08 .20
234 Dani Giger .08 .20
235 Sandro Haberlin .08 .20
236 Axel Heim .08 .20
237 Philppe Luber .08 .20
238 Dale McTavish .08 .20
239 Patrizio Morger .08 .20
240 Mike Richard .08 .20
241 Bernhard Schumperli .08 .20
242 EVZ Logo .08 .20
243 EVZ Team Card .08 .20
244 EVZ Team Card .08 .20
245 Andre Peloffy .08 .20
246 Ronnie Rueger .08 .20
247 Patrick Schopf .08 .20
248 Marco Bayer .08 .20
249 Ralph Bundi .08 .20
250 Patrick Fischer .08 .20
251 Dino Kessler .08 .20
252 Andre Kunzi .08 .20
253 Reto Kobach .08 .20
254 Patrick Sutter .08 .20
255 Christophe Brown .08 .20
256 Paul Di Pietro .20 .50
257 Todd Elik .08 .20
258 Stefan Grogg .08 .20
259 Vjeran Ivankovic .08 .20
260 Daniel Meier .08 .20
261 Stefan Niggli .08 .20
262 Patrick Oppliger .08 .20
263 Andre Rotheli .08 .20
264 Sascha Schneider .08 .20
265 Chris Tancill .08 .20
266 ZSC Logo .08 .20
267 ZSC Team Card .08 .20
268 ZSC Team Card .08 .20
269 Larry Hurras .08 .20
270 Thomas Papp .08 .20
271 Ari Sulander .20 .50
272 Martin Kout .08 .20
273 Adrien Plavsic .08 .20
274 Edgar Salis .08 .20
275 Mathias Seger .08 .20
276 Bruno Seck .08 .20

277 Andreas Zehnder	.08	.20
278 Mattia Baldi	.08	.20
279 Gian Marco Crameri	.08	.20
280 Partric Della Rossa	.08	.20
281 Daniel Hodgson	.08	.20
282 Peter Jaks	.08	.20
283 Andrew McKim	.20	.50
284 Claudio Micheli	.08	.20
285 Laurent Muller	.08	.20
286 Mark Ouimet	.08	.20
287 Rolf Schrepfer	.08	.20
288 Reto Stirnimann	.08	.20
289 Michel Zeiter	.08	.20
290 HC Ajoie Logo	.08	.20
291 Yann Voillat	.08	.20
292 Chris Belanger	.08	.20
293 EHC Basel Logo	.08	.20
294 Todd Wetzel	.08	.20
295 Patrick Girard	.08	.20
296 EHC Biel Logo	.08	.20
297 Sven Schmid	.08	.20
298 Kevin Schlapfer	.08	.20
299 GCK Lions Logo	.08	.20
300 Patrick Looser	.08	.20
301 Mikko Myllykoski	.08	.20
302 HC Geneve Logo	.08	.20
303 Patrice Brasey	.08	.20
304 Scott Beattie	.08	.20
305 SC Herisau Logo	.08	.20
306 Andy Karpf	.08	.20
307 Patrick Amann	.08	.20
308 HC Lausanne Logo	.08	.20
309 Beat Kindler	.08	.20
310 Serge Poudrier	.08	.20
311 EHC Olten Logo	.08	.20
312 Beat Aebischer	.08	.20
313 Richard Stucki	.08	.20
314 HC Sierre Logo	.08	.20
315 Jean Michel Clavien	.08	.20
316 Gaby Epiney	.08	.20
317 HC Thurgau Logo	.08	.20
318 Martin Bruderer	.08	.20
319 Morgan Samuelsson	.08	.20
320 EHC Visp Logo	.08	.20
321 Stefan Ketola	.08	.20
322 Gabriel Taccoz	.08	.20

2000-01 Swiss Panini Stickers National Team Insert

P1 Martin Gerber	1.00	2.50
P2 David Aebischer	1.00	2.50
P3 Relo Pavoni	.40	1.00
P4 Patrick Fisher	.40	1.00
P5 Olivier Keller	.40	1.00
P6 Martin Steinegger	.40	1.00
P7 Edgar Salis	.40	1.00
P8 Mark Streit	.40	1.00
P9 Julien Vavclair	.40	1.00
P10 Patrick Sutter	.40	1.00
P11 Mathias Seger	.40	1.00
P12 Rolf Ziegler	.40	1.00
P13 Flavien Conne	.40	1.00
P14 Jean-Jaques Aeschlimann	.40	1.00
P15 Mattia Baldi	.40	1.00
P16 Patric Della Rossa	.40	1.00
P17 Marcel Jenni	.40	1.00
P18 Gian Marco Crameri	.40	1.00
P19 Claudio Micheli	.40	1.00
P20 Alain Demuth	.40	1.00
P21 Thomas Ziegler	.40	1.00
P22 Patrick Fischer	.40	1.00
P23 Ivo Ruthemann	.40	1.00
P24 Reto Von Arx	.40	1.00
P25 Michel Zeiter	.40	1.00
P26 Michel Riesen	.40	1.00
P27 Sandy Jeannin	.40	1.00
P28 Lurent Muller	.40	1.00
P29 Martin Pluss	.40	1.00
P30 Adi Wichser	.40	1.00

2000-01 Swiss Slapshot Mini-Cards

COMPLETE SET (192)	20.00	40.00
LT1 Martin Gerber	2.00	5.00
LT2 Daniel Aegerter	.10	.25
LT3 Samuel Balmer	.10	.25
LT4 Beat Gerber	.10	.25
LT5 Steve Hirschi	.10	.25
LT6 Erik Kakko	.10	.25
LT7 Pascal Muller	.10	.25
LT8 Pascal Stoller	.10	.25
LT9 Rolf Badertscher	.10	.25
LT10 Bruno Brechbuhl	.10	.25
LT11 John Fust	.10	.25
LT12 Daniel Gauthier	.10	.25
LT13 Thomas Heldner	.10	.25
LT14 Matthias Holzer	.10	.25
LT15 Vlastimil Plavucha	.10	.25
LT16 Benoit Pont	.10	.25
RJ1 Claudio Bayer	.10	.25
RJ2 Marco Capaul	.10	.25
RJ3 Kari Martikainen	.10	.25
RJ4 Roger Sigg	.10	.25
RJ5 Jorg Reber	.10	.25
RJ6 Loic Burkhalter	.10	.25
RJ7 Markus Butler	.10	.25
RJ8 Rene Friedli	.10	.25
RJ9 Rene Furler	.10	.25
RJ10 Daniel Giger	.10	.25
RJ11 Axel Heim	.10	.25
RJ12 Philipp Luber	.10	.25
RJ13 Dale McTavish	.10	.25
RJ14 Patrizio Morger	.10	.25
RJ15 Mike Richard	.10	.25
RJ16 Bernhard Schumperli	.10	.25
EVZ1 Ronnie Rueger	.10	.25
EVZ2 Patrick Schopf	.10	.25
EVZ3 Marco Bayer	.10	.25
EVZ4 Patrick Fischer	.10	.25
EVZ5 Dino Kessler	.10	.25
EVZ6 Andre Kunzi	.10	.25
EVZ7 Patrick Sutter	.10	.25
EVZ8 Paul Di Pietro	.20	.50
EVZ9 Todd Elik	.20	.50
EVZ10 Stefan Grogg	.10	.25
EVZ11 Vjeran Ivankovic	.10	.25
EVZ12 Daniel Meier	.10	.25
EVZ13 Patrick Oppliger	.10	.25
EVZ14 Andre Rotheli	.10	.25
EVZ15 Sascha Schneider	.10	.25
EVZ16 Chris Tancill	.10	.25
HCD1 Lars Welbel	.20	.50
HCD2 Beat Equilino	.10	.25
HCD3 Marc Gianola	.10	.25
HCD4 Andreas Häller	.10	.25
HCD5 Ralph Ott	.10	.25
HCD6 Jan Von Arx	.10	.25
HCD7 Andre Baumann	.10	.25
HCD8 Lonny Bohonos	.20	.50
HCD9 Patrick Fischer	.10	.25
HCD10 Kevin Miller	.20	.50
HCD11 Rene Muller	.10	.25
HCD12 Thierry Paterlini	.10	.25
HCD13 Sandro Rizzi	.10	.25
HCD14 Frederic Rothen	.10	.25
HCD15 Mario Schocher	.10	.25
HCD16 Pat Falloon	.20	.50
HCL1 Cristobal Huet	2.00	5.00
HCL2 Peter Anderson	.10	.25
HCL3 Igor Fedulov	.10	.25
HCL4 Sandro Bertaggia	.10	.25
HCL5 Olivier Keller	.10	.25
HCL6 Julien Vauclair	.10	.25
HCL7 Gaetan Voisard	.10	.25
HCL8 J.-Jacques Aeschlimann	.10	.25
HCL9 Misko Antisin	.10	.25
HCL10 Philippe Bozon	.40	1.00
HCL11 Jan-Philippe Cadieux	.10	.25
HCL12 Flavien Conne	.10	.25
HCL13 Christian Dube	.10	.25
HCL14 Regis Fuchs	.10	.25
HCL15 Sandy Jeannin	.10	.25
HCL16 Keith Fair	.10	.25
SCB1 Renato Tosio	.10	.25
SCB2 David Jobin	.10	.25
SCB3 Sven Leuenberger	.10	.25
SCB4 Dominic Meier	.10	.25
SCB5 Frederik Olausson	.10	.25
SCB6 Martin Steinegger	.10	.25
SCB7 Rolf Ziegler	.10	.25
SCB8 Bjorn Christen	.10	.25
SCB9 Patrick Howald	.10	.25
SCB10 Andreas Johansson	.10	.25
SCB11 Patrick Juhlin	.10	.25
SCB12 Alex Chatelain	.10	.25
SCB13 Boris Leimgruber	.10	.25
SCB14 Ivo Ruthemann	.10	.25
SCB15 Franz Steffen	.10	.25
SCB16 Marc Weber	.10	.25
EHCC1 Nando Wieser	.10	.25
EHCC2 Noel Guyaz	.10	.25
EHCC3 Christian Langer	.10	.25
EHCC4 Ivo Stoffel	.10	.25
EHCC5 Mika Stromberg	.10	.25
EHCC6 Pasi Sormunen	.10	.25
EHCC7 Matthias Bachler	.10	.25
EHCC8 Patrick Kruger	.10	.25
EHCC9 Michael Meier	.10	.25
EHCC10 Michael Rosenast	.10	.25
EHCC11 Oliver Roth	.10	.25
EHCC12 Marc Haueter	.10	.25
EHCC13 Sandro Tschuor	.10	.25
EHCC14 Raymond Walder	.10	.25
EHCC15 Theo Wittmann	.10	.25
EHCC16 UNKNOWN	.10	.25
EHCK1 Reto Pavoni	.10	.25
EHCK2 Martin Hohener	.10	.25
EHCK3 Marko Kiprusoff	.10	.25
EHCK4 Marco Kloti	.10	.25
EHCK5 Oskar Szczepaniec	.10	.25
EHCK6 UNKNOWN	.10	.25
EHCK7 Fredrik Nilsson	.10	.25
EHCK8 Sven Helfenstein	.10	.25
EHCK9 Felix Hollenstein	.10	.25
EHCK10 Andy Keller	.10	.25
EHCK11 Sven Lindemann	.10	.25
EHCK12 Martin Pluss	.10	.25
EHCK13 Sebastien Reuille	.10	.25
EHCK14 Andre Rufener	.10	.25
EHCK15 Steve Washburn	.10	.25
EHCK16 Adrian Wichser	.10	.25
HCAP1 Pauli Jaks	.10	.25
HCAP2 Fredy Bobillier	.10	.25
HCAP3 Ivan Gazzaroli	.10	.25
HCAP4 Tiziano Gianini	.10	.25
HCAP5 Thomas Kunzi	.10	.25
HCAP6 Leif Rohlin	.10	.25
HCAP7 Krister Cantoni	.10	.25
HCAP8 Manuele Celio	.10	.25
HCAP9 Nicola Celio	.10	.25
HCAP10 Alain Demuth	.10	.25
HCAP11 Paolo Duca	.10	.25
HCAP12 John Fritsche	.10	.25
HCAP13 Ryan Gardner	.10	.25
HCAP14 Paolo Imperatori	.10	.25
HCAP15 Stephan Lebeau	.20	.50
HCAP16 Daniel Marois	.20	.50
HCCF1 Thomas Berger	.10	.25
HCCF2 Raphael Brusa	.10	.25
HCCF3 Fabian Guignard	.10	.25
HCCF4 Valeri Shiryaev	.10	.25
HCCF5 Ruedi Niderost	.10	.25
HCCF6 Roger Ohmann	.10	.25
HCCF7 Alexis Vacheron	.10	.25
HCCF8 Steve Aebersold	.10	.25
HCCF9 Thomas Derungs	.10	.25
HCCF10 Claude Luthi	.10	.25
HCCF11 Fabrice Maillat	.10	.25
HCCF12 Daniel Nakaoka	.10	.25
HCCF13 Stefan Nilsson	.10	.25
HCCF14 Julien Turler	.10	.25
HCCF15 Samuel Villiger	.10	.25
HCCF16 Thibaut Monnet	.10	.25
HCFG1 Thomas Ostlund	.20	.50
HCFG2 Goran Bezina	.10	.25
HCFG3 Antonie Descloux	.10	.25
HCFG4 Livio Fazio	.10	.25
HCFG5 Philippe Marquis	.10	.25
HCFG6 Martin Rauch	.10	.25
HCFG7 Marc Werlen	.10	.25
HCFG8 Craig Ferguson	.10	.25
HCFG9 Lars Leuenberger	.10	.25
HCFG10 Gil Montandon	.10	.25
HCFG11 Mario Rottaris	.10	.25
HCFG12 Jean-Yves Roy	.10	.25
HCFG13 Pascal Schaller	.10	.25
HCFG14 Robert Slehofer	.10	.25
HCFG15 Gerd Zenhäusern	.10	.25
HCFG16 Michel Mouther	.10	.25
ZSCL1 Ari Sulander	.20	.50
ZSCL2 Adrien Plavsic	.10	.25
ZSCL3 Edgar Salis	.10	.25
ZSCL4 Matthias Seger	.10	.25
ZSCL5 Mark Streit	.20	.50
ZSCL6 Andreas Zehnder	.10	.25
ZSCL7 Mattia Baldi	.10	.25
ZSCL8 Gian Marco Crameri	.10	.25
ZSCL9 Patric Della Rossa	.10	.25
ZSCL10 Dan Hodgson	.10	.25
ZSCL11 Peter Jaks	.10	.25
ZSCL12 Andrew McKim	.20	.50
ZSCL13 Claudio Micheli	.10	.25
ZSCL14 Laurent Muller	.10	.25
ZSCL15 Rolf Schrepfer	.10	.25
ZSCL16 Michel Zeiter	.10	.25

2001-02 Swiss EV Zug Postcards

These unnumbered 4X6 postcards were issued by the team and feature stylized action photos.

COMPLETE SET (27)	10.00	25.00
1 Team photo	.40	1.00
2 Doug Mason	.40	1.00
3 Richmond Gosselin	.40	1.00
4 Patrick Schopf	.40	1.00
5 Ronnie Rueger	.40	1.00
6 Ruedi Niderost	.40	1.00
7 Ralf Bundi	.40	1.00
8 Patrick Fischer	.40	1.00
9 Fabio Schumacher	.40	1.00
10 Pascal Muller	.40	1.00
11 Arne Ramholt	.40	1.00
12 Kevin Gloor	.40	1.00
13 Andre Kunzi	.40	1.00
14 Reto Kobach	.40	1.00
15 Thomas Nussli	.40	1.00
16 Stefan Voegele	.40	1.00
17 Stefan Niggli	.40	1.00
18 Duri Camichel	.40	1.00
19 Vjeran Ivankovic	.40	1.00
20 Patrick Oppliger	.40	1.00
21 Frederic Rothen	.40	1.00
22 Stefan Grogg	.40	1.00
23 Christoph Brown	.40	1.00
24 Chris Tancill	.75	2.00
25 Todd Elik	.75	2.00
26 Joel Savage	.75	2.00
27 Paul DiPietro	.75	2.00

2001-02 Swiss HNL

This series features the top players in the Swiss Elite League, one of the top European circuits.

COMPLETE SET (480)	30.00	75.00
1 Larry Huras	.10	.25
2 Thomas Papp	.10	.25
3 Ari Sulander	.40	1.00
4 Martin Kout	.10	.25
5 Adrian Plavsic	.10	.25
6 Tim Ramholt	.60	1.50
7 Edgar Salis	.10	.25
8 Mathias Seger	.10	.25
9 Bruno Steck	.10	.25
10 Mark Streit	.10	.25
11 Jan Alston	.20	.50
12 Mattia Baldi	.10	.25
13 Gian-Marco Crameri	.10	.25
14 Patric Della Rossa	.10	.25
15 Paolo Duca	.10	.25
16 Dan Hodgson	.20	.50
17 Peter Jaks	.10	.25
18 Claudio Micheli	.10	.25
19 Mark Ouimet	.20	.50
20 Morgan Samuelsson	.10	.25
21 Stefan Schnyder	.10	.25
22 Reto Stirnimann	.10	.25
23 Petri Varis	.20	.50
24 Michel Zeiter	.10	.25
25 Zinetoula Bilyaletdinov	.10	.25
26 Paolo Della Bella	.10	.25
27 Cristobal Huet ERC	2.00	5.00
28 Mark Astley	.20	.50
29 Sandro Bertaggia	.10	.25
30 Olivier Keller	.10	.25
31 Petteri Nummelin	.10	.25
32 Patrick Sutter	.10	.25
33 Rick Tschumi	.10	.25
34 Gaetan Voisard	.10	.25
35 Jean-Jacques Aeschlimann	.10	.25
36 Jan Cadieux	.10	.25
37 Gregory Christen	.10	.25
38 Flavien Conne	.10	.25
39 Christian Dube	.10	.25
40 Keith Fair	.10	.25
41 Regis Fuchs	.10	.25
42 Ryan Gardner	.20	.50
43 Sandy Jeannin	.10	.25
44 Mike Maneluk	.20	.50
45 Andy Naser	.10	.25
46 Andre Rotheli	.10	.25
47 Raffaele Sannitz	.30	.75
48 Geoffrey Vauclair	.10	.25
49 Kloten-Flyers	.10	.25
50 Vladimir Jursinov	.10	.25
51 Flavio Ludke	.10	.25
52 Reto Pavoni	.20	.50
53 Severin Blindenbacher	.10	.25
54 Manuel Gossweiler	.10	.25
55 Fabian Guignard	.10	.25
56 Roman Hardmeier	.10	.25
57 Martin Hohener	.10	.25
58 Ronny Keller	.10	.25
59 Chris O'Sullivan	.20	.50
60 Gregor Thommen	.10	.25
61 Mathias Wust	.10	.25
62 Andre Bielmann	.10	.25
63 Patrik Bartschi	.10	.25
64 Andreas Cellar	.10	.25
65 Felix Hollenstein	.10	.25
66 Andy Keller	.10	.25
67 Dario Kostovic	.10	.25
68 Sven Lindemann	.10	.25
69 Fredrik Nilsson	.10	.25
70 Emanuel Peter	.10	.25
71 Martin Pluss	.10	.25
72 Kimmo Rintanen	.10	.25
73 Adrian Wichser	.30	.75
74 Thomas Widmer	.10	.25
75 Riccardo Fuhrer	.10	.25
76 Marco Buhrer	.20	.50
77 Andreas Schweizer	.10	.25
78 Rikard Franzen	.10	.25
79 David Jobin	.10	.25
80 Sven Leuenberger	.10	.25
81 Marc Leuenberger	.10	.25
82 Dominic Meier	.10	.25
83 Martin Steinegger	.10	.25
84 Rolf Ziegler	.10	.25
85 Derek Armstrong	.20	.50
86 Andre Baumann	.10	.25
87 Alex Chatelain	.10	.25
88 Sven Helfenstein	.10	.25
89 Patrik Juhlin	.20	.50
90 Laurent Muller	.10	.25
91 Philippe Muller	.10	.25
92 Marc Reichert	.10	.25
93 Ivo Ruthemann	.10	.25
94 Rolf Schrepfer	.10	.25
95 Franz Steffen	.10	.25
96 Fabian Sutter	.10	.25
97 Marc Weber	.10	.25
98 Arno Del Curto	.10	.25
99 Jonas Hiller	1.00	2.50
100 Lars Weibel	.20	.50
101 Beat Equilino	.10	.25
102 Beat Forster	.10	.25
103 Marc Gianola	.10	.25
104 Andrea Haller	.10	.25
105 Michael Kress	.10	.25
106 Ralph Ott	.10	.25
107 Jan von Arx	.10	.25
108 Benjamin Winkler	.10	.25
109 Andres Ambuhl	.10	.25
110 Lonny Bohonos	.20	.50
111 Andreas Camenzind	.10	.25
112 Bjorn Christen	.10	.25
113 Patrick Fischer	.10	.25
114 Joel Frohlicher	.10	.25
115 Stefan Gahler	.10	.25
116 Marc Heberlein	.10	.25
117 Josef Marha	.10	.25
118 Kevin Miller	.20	.50
119 Rene Muller	.10	.25
120 Sandro Rizzi	.10	.25
121 Serge Pelletier	.10	.25
122 Matthias Lauber	.20	.50
123 Gianluca Mona	.20	.50
124 Raphael Berger	.10	.25
125 Antoine Descloux	.10	.25
126 Mike Gaul	.20	.50
127 Lukas Gerber	.10	.25
128 Philippe Marquis	.10	.25
129 Martin Rauch	.10	.25
130 Marc Werlen	.10	.25
131 Craig Ferguson	.20	.50
132 Gilbert Flueler	.10	.25
133 Christof Hiltebrand	.10	.25
134 Patrick Howald	.10	.25
135 Lars Leuenberger	.10	.25
136 Silvan Lussy	.10	.25
137 David Maurer	.10	.25
138 Thibaut Monnet	.10	.25
139 Gil Montandon	.10	.25
140 Michel Mouther	.10	.25
141 Mario Rottaris	.10	.25
142 Jean-Yves Roy	.20	.50
143 Robert Slehofer	.10	.25
144 Colin Muller	.10	.25
145 Evgeni Popichin	.10	.25
146 Thomas Berger	.20	.50
147 Simon Zuger	.20	.50
148 Marco Capaul	.10	.25
149 Livio Fazio	.10	.25
150 Jakub Horak	.10	.25
151 Kari Martikainen	.10	.25
152 Alain Reist	.10	.25
153 Marc Schefer	.10	.25
154 Fabian Stephan	.10	.25
155 Markus Butler	.10	.25
156 Rene Friedli	.10	.25
157 Daniel Giger	.10	.25
158 Axel Heim	.10	.25
159 Philipp Luber	.10	.25
160 Dale McTavish	.20	.50
161 Claudio Moggi	.10	.25
162 Sandro Moggi	.10	.25
163 Patrizio Morger	.10	.25
164 Sebastien Reuille	.10	.25
165 Mike Richard	.10	.25
166 Morgan Samuelsson	.10	.25
167 Doug Mason	.10	.25
168 Ronnie Rueger	.20	.50
169 Patrick Schopf	.20	.50
170 Ralf Bundi	.10	.25
171 Patrick Fischer	.10	.25
172 Reto Kobach	.10	.25
173 Andre Kunzi	.10	.25
174 Pascal Muller	.10	.25
175 Ruedi Niderost	.10	.25
176 Arne Ramholt	.10	.25
177 Fabio Schumacher	.10	.25
178 Christophe Brown	.10	.25
179 Duri Camichel	.10	.25
180 Paul Di Pietro	.20	.50
181 Todd Elik	.20	.50
182 Stefan Grogg	.10	.25
183 Vjeran Ivankovic	.10	.25
184 Stefan Niggli	.10	.25
185 Thomas Nussli	.10	.25
186 Patrick Oppliger	.10	.25
187 Frederic Rothen	.10	.25
188 Joel Savage	.20	.50
189 Chris Tancill	.20	.50
190 Vassily Tikhonov	.10	.25
191 Claudio Bayer	.20	.50
192 Marco Streit	.20	.50
193 Daniel Aegerter	.10	.25
194 Samuel Balmer	.10	.25
195 Beat Gerber	.10	.25
196 Steve Hirschi	.10	.25
197 Erik Hamalainen	.10	.25
198 Thomas Kunzi	.10	.25
199 Pascal Stoller	.10	.25
200 Rolf Badertscher	.10	.25
201 Brian Bonin	.20	.50
202 Bruno Brechbuhl	.10	.25
203 John Fust	.10	.25
204 Daniel Gauthier	.10	.25
205 Thomas Heldner	.10	.25
206 Matthias Holzer	.10	.25
207 Benjamin Pluss	.10	.25
208 Benoit Pont	.10	.25
209 Bernhard Schumperli	.10	.25
210 Daniel Steiner	.10	.25
211 Rostislav Cada	.10	.25
212 Lorenzo Barenco	.10	.25
213 Pauli Jaks	.20	.50
214 Marco Bayer	.10	.25
215 Nicola Celio	.10	.25
216 Ivan Gazzaroli	.10	.25
217 Tiziano Gianini	.10	.25
218 John Gobbi	.10	.25
219 Andreas Hanni	.10	.25
220 Martin Stepanek	.10	.25
221 Loic Burkhalter	.10	.25
222 Corsin Camichel	.10	.25
223 Krister Cantoni	.10	.25
224 Manuele Celio	.10	.25
225 Alain Demuth	.10	.25
226 John Fritsche	.10	.25
227 Paolo Imperatori	.10	.25
228 Roland Kaser	.10	.25
229 Vitaly Lakhmatov	.10	.25
230 Michel Liniger	.10	.25
231 Robert Petrovicky	.10	.25
232 Omar Tognini	.10	.25
233 Tomas Vlasak	.10	.25
234 Niklas Wikegard	.10	.25
235 Tobias Stephan	1.25	3.00
236 Nando Wieser	.10	.25
237 Rene Back	.10	.25
238 Cyrill Geyer	.10	.25
239 Noel Guyaz	.10	.25
240 Marc Haueter	.10	.25
241 Ivo Stoffel	.10	.25
242 Mika Stromberg	.10	.25
243 Andreas Zehnder	.10	.25
244 Fabio Beccarelli	.10	.25
245 Matthias Bachler	.10	.25
246 Kristian Gahn	.10	.25
247 Patrick Kruger	.10	.25
248 Michael Meier	.10	.25
249 Daniel Peer	.10	.25
250 Roger Rieder	.10	.25
251 Oliver Roth	.10	.25
252 Ivo Simeon	.10	.25
253 Rene Stussi	.10	.25
254 Sandro Tschuor	.10	.25
255 Johan Witehall	.10	.25
256 Theo Wittmann	.10	.25
257 HC Lausanne	.10	.25
258 Mike McParland	.10	.25
259 Beat Kindler	.20	.50
260 Reto Schurch	.20	.50
261 Malik Benturqui	.10	.25
262 Michel Kamber	.10	.25
263 Dejan Lozanov	.10	.25
264 Michel N'Goy	.10	.25
265 Serge Poudrier	.10	.25
266 Roger Sigg	.10	.25
267 Thomas Studer	.10	.25
268 Oliver Tschanz	.10	.25
269 Florian Andenmatten	.10	.25
270 Andrei Bashkirov	.20	.50
271 Daniel Bieri	.10	.25
272 Thierry Bornand	.10	.25
273 Sandro Haberlin	.10	.25
274 Oliver Kamber	.10	.25
275 Trevor Meier	.10	.25
276 Philippe Orlandi	.10	.25
277 Dmitri Shamolin	.10	.25
278 Samuel Villiger	.10	.25
279 Sacha Weibel	.20	.50
280 Gerd Zenhausern	.10	.25
281 Michel Lussier	.10	.25
282 Gilles Cattela	.10	.25
283 Thierry Noel	.10	.25
284 Oliver Amadio	.10	.25
285 Pascal Avanthay	.10	.25
286 Nicolas Bernasconi	.10	.25
287 Raphael Brusa	.10	.25
288 Valeri Chiriaev	.10	.25
289 Marc Tschudy	.10	.25
290 Alexis Vacheron	.10	.25
291 Steve Aebersold	.10	.25
292 Jesse Belanger	.20	.50
293 Thomas Deruns	.10	.25
294 Jamie Heinrich	.10	.25
295 Vincent Lechenne	.10	.25
296 Claude Luethi	.10	.25
297 Fabrice Maillat	.10	.25
298 Daniel Nakaoka	.10	.25
299 Michael Neininger	.10	.25
300 Philippe Thalmann	.10	.25
301 Markus Graf	.10	.25
302 Marco Wegmuller	.20	.50
303 Martin Zerzuben	.10	.25
304 Sven Dick	.10	.25
305 Serge Meyer	.10	.25
306 Jorg Reber	.10	.25
307 Sven Schmid	.10	.25
308 Bjorn Schneider	.10	.25
309 Pascal Sommer	.10	.25
310 Mauro Beccarelli	.10	.25
311 Philipp Folghera	.10	.25
312 Rene Furler	.10	.25
313 Stefan Moser	.10	.25
314 Andreas Nauser	.10	.25
315 Cyrill Pasche	.10	.25
316 Reggie Savage	.20	.50
317 Ryan Savoia	.20	.50
318 Kevin Schlapfer	.10	.25
319 Marco Signer	.10	.25
320 Stefan Tschiemer	.10	.25
321 Chris McSorley	.10	.25
322 David Bochy	.20	.50
323 Flavio Streit	.10	.25
324 Fredy Bobillier	.10	.25
325 Patrice Brasey	.10	.25
326 Fabian Gull	.10	.25
327 David Leibzig	.10	.25
328 Todd Richards	.20	.50
329 Nicolas Studer	.10	.25
330 Misko Antisin	.10	.25
331 Philippe Bozon	.75	2.00
332 Igor Fedulov	.10	.25
333 Marco Fischer	.10	.25
334 Xavier Gattuso	.10	.25
335 Maxime Lapointe	.10	.25
336 Boris Leimgruber	.10	.25
337 Paul Savary	.10	.25
338 Didier Schafer	.10	.25
339 Pascal Schaller	.10	.25
340 Mario Schocher	.10	.25
341 Bruno Aegerter	.10	.25
342 Rainer Karlen	.10	.25
343 Marc Zimmermann	.20	.50
344 Beat Heldstab	.10	.25
345 Karl Knopf	.10	.25
346 Philipp Portner	.10	.25
347 Francis Reichmuth	.10	.25
348 Marco Schupbach	.10	.25
349 Marc Zurbriggen	.10	.25
350 Patrick Aeberli	.10	.25
351 Sergio Biner	.10	.25
352 Marc Buhlmann	.10	.25
353 Nicolas Gastaldo	.10	.25
354 Stefan Ketola	.10	.25
355 Swen Kohler	.10	.25
356 Richard Laplante	.10	.25
357 Cedric Metrailler	.10	.25
358 Detlef Prediger	.10	.25
359 Gabriel Taccoz	.10	.25
360 Ken Zurfluh	.10	.25
361 Arnold Lortscher	.10	.25
362 Beat Aebischer	.10	.25
363 Rainer Kalin	.10	.25
364 Francesco Bizzozero	.10	.25
365 Christoph Decurtins	.10	.25
366 Mark Emmenegger	.10	.25
367 Ruedi Forster	.10	.25
368 Jurg Hardegger	.10	.25
369 Richard Stucki	.10	.25
370 Stefan Wuthrich	.10	.25
371 Alain Ayer	.10	.25
372 Yanick Dube	.10	.25
373 Reto Germann	.10	.25
374 Patrick Giroud	.10	.25
375 Bjorn Guazzini	.10	.25
376 Albert Malgin	.10	.25
377 Oliver Muller	.10	.25
378 Patrick Siegwart	.10	.25
379 Andre von Rohr	.10	.25
380 Matti Alatalo	.10	.25
381 Christian Weber	.10	.25
382 Marc Eichmann	.10	.25
383 Matthias Schoder	.20	.50
384 Stefan Badrutt	.10	.25
385 Chris Belanger	.10	.25
386 Thomi Derungs	.10	.25
387 Michael Hofer	.10	.25
388 Andri Stoffel	.10	.25
389 Andreas Furrer	.10	.25
390 Lukas Grauwiler	.10	.25
391 Rolf Hildebrand	.10	.25
392 Alex Krstic	.10	.25
393 Patrick Landolt	.10	.25
394 Patrick Looser	.10	.25
395 Dean Seymour	.10	.25
396 Riccardo Signorell	.10	.25
397 Pascal Tiegermann	.10	.25
398 Thomas Walser	.10	.25
399 Simon Wanner	.10	.25
400 Merlin Malinowski	.10	.25
401 Olivier Gigon	.10	.25
402 Sebastien Kohler	.20	.50
403 Ludovic Aubry	.10	.25
404 Eric Bourquin	.10	.25
405 Dany Ott	.10	.25
406 Christian Schuster	.10	.25
407 Wes Snell	.10	.25
408 Markus Wuthrich	.10	.25
409 Steven Barras	.10	.25
410 Martin Bergeron	.10	.25
411 Scott Biser	.10	.25
412 Florian Conz	.10	.25
413 Real Gerber	.10	.25
414 Sacha Guerne	.10	.25
415 Shawn Heaphy	.10	.25
416 Jerome Kohler	.10	.25
417 Jean-Charles Lapaire	.10	.25
418 Boe Leslie	.10	.25
419 Steve Pochon	.10	.25
420 Yann Voillat	.10	.25
421 Didier Massy	.10	.25
422 Gregory Berclaz	.10	.25
423 Roland Meyer	.10	.25
424 Johan Bertholet	.10	.25
425 Lionel D'Urso	.10	.25
426 Cedric Favre	.10	.25
427 Jonathan Lussier	.10	.25
428 Pietro Ottini	.10	.25
429 Emmanuel Tacchini	.10	.25
430 Beat Brantschen	.10	.25
431 Elvis Clavien	.10	.25
432 Gaby Epiney	.10	.25
433 Kelly Glowa	.10	.25
434 Pietro Juri	.10	.25
435 Daniel Mares	.10	.25
436 Cedric Melly	.10	.25
437 Thierry Metrailler	.10	.25
438 Fabrizio Silietti	.10	.25
439 Daniel Wobmann	.10	.25
440 Raymond Zahnd	.10	.25
441 Christian Ruegg	.10	.25
442 Matthias Muller	.10	.25
443 Pascal Sievert	.10	.25
444 Claude Amstutz	.10	.25
445 Roland Kradolfer	.10	.25
446 Pascal Lamprecht	.10	.25
447 Patrick Mader	.10	.25
448 Michael Marki	.10	.25
449 Alessandro Sellitto	.10	.25
450 Daniel Sigg	.10	.25
451 Rico Beltrame	.10	.25
452 Marius Brugger	.10	.25
453 Joel Camenzind	.10	.25
454 Michael Diener	.10	.25
455 Timmy Hoppe	.10	.25
456 Roland Korsch	.10	.25
457 Real Raemy	.10	.25
458 Marco Seeholzer	.10	.25
459 Harijs Vitolinsch	.10	.25
460 Jacques Zimmermann	.10	.25
461 Beat Lautenschlager	.10	.25
462 Davide Gislimberti	.10	.25
463 Peter Mettler	.20	.50
464 Marc Gautschi	.10	.25
465 Zbynek Hybler	.10	.25
466 Stephane Julien	.10	.25
467 Kim Scheidegger	.10	.25
468 Olivier Schaublin	.10	.25
469 Dominik Z'berg	.10	.25
470 Philipp Dornbierer	.10	.25
471 Patrick Girod	.10	.25
472 Marco Graf	.10	.25
473 Andreas Haner	.10	.25
474 Michael Murer	.10	.25
475 Robert Othmann	.10	.25
476 Steve Potvin	.10	.25
477 David Raissle	.10	.25
478 Jarkko Schaublin	.10	.25
479 Lovis Schonenberger	.10	.25
480 Marcel Sommer	.10	.25

2002-03 Swiss EV Zug Postcards

These unnumbered 4X6 postcards were issued by the team and feature stylized action photos on the front.

COMPLETE SET (26)	10.00	25.00
1 Team photo	.40	1.00
2 Doug Mason	.40	1.00
3 Chris Tancill	.75	2.00
4 Paul DiPietro	.75	2.00
5 Richmond Gosselin	.40	1.00
6 Patrick Schopf	.40	1.00
7 Peter Mettler	.40	1.00
8 Ruedi Niderost	.40	1.00
9 Ralf Bundi	.40	1.00
10 Charles Simard	.40	1.00
11 Patrick Fischer	.40	1.00
12 Fabio Schumacher	.40	1.00
13 Pascal Muller	.40	1.00
14 Gaetan Voisard	.40	1.00
15 Lovis Schonenberger	.40	1.00
16 Stefan Voegele	.40	1.00
17 Stefan Niggli	.40	1.00
18 Duri Camichel	.40	1.00
19 Patrick Oppliger	.40	1.00
20 Paolo Duca	.40	1.00
21 Andre Rufener	.40	1.00
22 Alain Demuth	.40	1.00
23 Oliver Kamber	.40	1.00
24 Frederic Rothen	.40	1.00
25 Joel Savage	.75	2.00
26 Chris Armstrong	.40	1.00

2002-03 Swiss HNL

This series features the top players in the Swiss Elite League, one of the top European circuits. The set features top prospects Tobias Stephan and Tim Ramholt.

COMPLETE SET (499)	30.00	75.00
1 Lars Weibel	.20	.50
2 Andrea Haller	.10	.25
3 Jonas Hiller	1.00	2.50
4 Jan von Arx	.10	.25
5 Lonny Bohonos	.20	.50
6 Marco Gruber	.10	.25
7 Marc Gianola	.10	.25
8 Josef Marha	.10	.25
9 Michel Riesen	.40	1.00
10 Reto von Arx	.20	.50
11 Ralph Ott	.10	.25
12 Ari Sulander	.40	1.00
13 Martin Kout	.10	.25
14 Edgar Salis	.10	.25
15 Andres Ambuhl	.10	.25
16 Jan Alston	.20	.50
17 Gian-Carlo Hendry	.10	.25
18 Peter Jaks	.10	.25
19 Patrick Fischer	.10	.25
20 Mark Ouimet	.20	.50
21 Reto Stirnimann	.10	.25
22 Davide Gislimberti	.10	.25
23 Marc Heberlein	.10	.25
24 Sandro Bertaggia	.10	.25
25 Olivier Keller	.10	.25
26 Jean-Jacques Aeschlimann	.10	.25
27 Thierry Paterlini	.10	.25
28 Flavien Conne	.10	.25
29 Ryan Gardner	.20	.50
30 Corey Millen	.20	.50
31 Fabian Sutter	.10	.25
32 Andre Rotheli	.10	.25
33 Vladimir Jursinov	.10	.25
34 Lukas Baumgartner	.10	.25
35 Matthias Schoder	.20	.50
36 Martin Hohener	.10	.25
37 Alain Reist	.10	.25
38 Deny Bartschi	.10	.25
39 Jakub Horak	.10	.25
40 Jaroslav Hlinka	.10	.25
41 Sven Lindemann	.10	.25
42 Marc Reichert	.10	.25
43 Tim Ramholt	.40	1.00
44 Thomas Widmer	.10	.25
45 Gianluca Mona	.20	.50
46 Mike Gaul	.20	.50
47 Mark Streit	.10	.25
48 Philippe Marquis	.10	.25
49 Patrick Howald	.10	.25
50 David Maurer	.10	.25
51 Patric Della Rossa	.10	.25
52 Michel Mouther	.10	.25
53 Robert Slehofer	.10	.25
54 Pauli Jaks	.20	.50
55 Dan Hodgson	.20	.50
56 Ivan Gazzaroli	.10	.25
57 Martin Rauch	.10	.25
58 Loic Burkhalter	.10	.25
59 Claudio Micheli	.10	.25
60 Nicola Celio	.10	.25
61 Paolo Imperatori	.10	.25
62 Robert Petrovicky	.10	.25
63 Raeto Raffainer	.10	.25
64 Doug Mason	.10	.25
65 Chris Armstrong	.10	.25
66 Ruedi Niderost	.10	.25
67 Jim Koleff	.10	.25
68 Duri Camichel	.10	.25
69 Paolo Duca	.10	.25
70 Patrick Oppliger	.10	.25
71 Mark Astley	.20	.50
72 Joel Savage	.20	.50
73 Stefan Voegele	.10	.25
74 Marc Eichmann	.10	.25
75 Andreas Hanni	.10	.25
76 Marc Leuenberger	.10	.25
77 Martin Steinegger	.10	.25
78 Alex Chatelain	.10	.25
79 Patrick Sutter	.10	.25
80 Patrik Juhlin	.20	.50
81 Laurent Muller	.10	.25
82 Rolf Schrepfer	.10	.25
83 Krister Cantoni	.10	.25
84 Beat Kindler	.20	.50
85 Fredy Bobillier	.10	.25
86 Serge Poudrier	.10	.25
87 Regis Fuchs	.10	.25
88 Florian Andenmatten	.10	.25
89 Thierry Bornand	.10	.25
90 Philipp Orlandi	.10	.25
91 Mike Maneluk	.20	.50
92 Sacha Weibel	.20	.50
93 Kari Eloranta	.20	.50
94 Livio Fazio	.10	.25
95 Andy Naser	.10	.25
96 Kari Martikainen	.10	.25
97 Patrick Aeberli	.10	.25
98 Axel Heim	.10	.25
99 Adrian Wichser	.20	.50
100 Patrizio Morger	.10	.25
101 Jarno Peltonen	.10	.25
102 Thomas Walser	.10	.25
103 Tobias Stephan	.75	2.00
104 Marco Streit	.20	.50
105 Beat Gerber	.10	.25
106 Pascal Stoller	.10	.25
107 Fabian Guignard	.10	.25
108 Bruno Brechbuhl	.10	.25
109 Todd Elik	.20	.50
110 Benjamin Pluss	.10	.25
111 Marco Kloti	.10	.25
112 Bernhard Schumperli	.10	.25
113 Fabien Hecquet	.10	.25
114 Brett Hauer	.20	.50
115 Cyrill Buhler	.10	.25
116 Wes Snell	.10	.25
117 Misko Antisin	.10	.25
118 Gian-Marco Crameri	.10	.25
119 Andreas Camenzind	.10	.25
120 Daniel Meier	.10	.25
121 Paul Savary	.10	.25
122 Dario Kostovic	.10	.25
123 Michel Lussier	.10	.25
124 Romano Lemm	.10	.25
125 Oliver Amadio	.10	.25
126 Dejan Lozanov	.10	.25
127 Emanuel Peter	.10	.25
128 Steve Aebersold	.10	.25
129 Martin Pluss	.10	.25
130 Boris Leimgruber	.10	.25
131 Daniel Nakaoka	.10	.25
132 Roger Rieder	.10	.25
133 Julien Turler	.10	.25
134 Kimmo Rintanen	.10	.25
135 Martin Zerzuben	.10	.25
136 Sven Dick	.10	.25
137 Colin Muller	.10	.25
138 Bjorn Schneider	.10	.25
139 Matthias Lauber	.20	.50
140 Mauro Beccarelli	.10	.25
141 Stefan Moser	.10	.25
142 Raphael Berger	.10	.25

143 Kevin Schlapfer .10 .25
144 Alain Birbaum .10 .25
145 Thomas Papp .10 .25
146 Michael Hofer .10 .25
147 Lukas Gerber .10 .25
148 Andri Stoffel .10 .25
149 Tiziano Gianini .10 .25
150 Sandro Moggi .10 .25
151 Riccardo Signorell .10 .25
152 Oliver Tschanz .10 .25
153 Simon Wanner .10 .25
154 Craig Ferguson .20 .50
155 Rainer Karlen .10 .25
156 Beat Heldstab .10 .25
157 Vjeran Ivankovic .10 .25
158 Marco Schupbach .10 .25
159 Silvan Lussy .10 .25
160 Michael Gerber .10 .25
161 Cedric Metrailler .10 .25
162 Thibaut Monnet .10 .25
163 Stephane Roy .10 .25
164 Gil Montandon .10 .25
165 Merlin Malinowski .10 .25
166 Olivier Devaux .10 .25
167 Mario Rottaris .10 .25
168 Dany Ott .10 .25
169 Jean-Yves Roy .20 .50
170 Markus Wuthrich .10 .25
171 Florian Conz .10 .25
172 Valentin Wirz .10 .25
173 Jerome Kohler .10 .25
174 Rostislav Cada .10 .25
175 Yann Voillat .10 .25
176 Rainer Kalin .10 .25
177 Simon Zuger .20 .50
178 Jurg Hardegger .10 .25
179 Robin Breitbach .10 .25
180 Richard Stucki .10 .25
181 Reto Germann .10 .25
182 John Gobbi .10 .25
183 Claude Luethi .10 .25
184 Reto Kobach .10 .25
185 Robert Othmann .10 .25
186 Matthias Muller .10 .25
187 Martin Stepanek .10 .25
188 Pascal Lamprecht .10 .25
189 Alan Tallarini .10 .25
190 Andre Nussbaum .10 .25
191 Michael Diener .10 .25
192 Corsin Camichel .10 .25
193 Timmy Hoppe .10 .25
194 Manuele Celio .10 .25
195 Marco Signer .10 .25
196 Beat Lautenschlager .10 .25
197 John Fritsche .10 .25
198 Marco Knecht .10 .25
199 John Fust .10 .25
200 Alexis Vacheron .10 .25
201 Martin Bergeron .10 .25
202 Vitaly Lakhmatov .10 .25
203 Andreas Haner .10 .25
204 Michel Liniger .10 .25
205 Marco Seeholzer .10 .25
206 Samuel Villiger .10 .25
207 Zdenek Sedlak .10 .25
208 Roland Meyer .10 .25
209 Egor Shastin .10 .25
210 Cedric Favre .10 .25
211 Roland Kradolfer .10 .25
212 Peter Mettler .20 .50
213 Severin Cavegn .10 .25
214 Patrick Schopf .20 .50
215 Antoine Lussier .10 .25
216 Oleg Siritsa .10 .25
217 Patrick Fischer .10 .25
218 Sascha Friedli .10 .25
219 Pascal Muller .10 .25
220 Rolf Diethelm .10 .25
221 Alan Hirschi .10 .25
222 Charles Simard .10 .25
223 Mario Heiniger .10 .25
224 Gaetan Voisard .10 .25
225 Marco Pistolato .10 .25
226 Mischa von Gunten .10 .25
227 Alain Demuth .10 .25
228 Ralph Krueger .10 .25
229 Paul Di Pietro .20 .50
230 Flavien Conne .10 .25
231 Alain Demuth .10 .25
232 Oliver Kamber .10 .25
233 Martin Hohener .10 .25
234 Stefan Niggli .10 .25
235 David Jobin .10 .25
236 Marc Reichert .10 .25
237 Frederic Rothen .10 .25
238 Mathias Seger .10 .25
239 Andre Rufener .10 .25
240 Patrick Sutter .10 .25
241 Winners Pluss .10 .25
242 Lovis Schonenberger .10 .25
243 Lonny Bohonos .20 .50
244 Chris Tancill .20 .50
245 Mike Maneluk .20 .50
246 Martin Pluss .10 .25
247 Kent Ruhnke .10 .25
248 Arno Del Curto .10 .25
249 Marco Buhrer .20 .50
250 Florian Blatter .10 .25
251 Michael Kress .10 .25
252 Rikard Franzen .10 .25
253 Benjamin Winkler .10 .25
254 David Jobin .10 .25
255 Bjorn Christen .10 .25
256 Steivan Hasler .10 .25
257 Sven Leuenberger .10 .25
258 Kevin Miller .20 .50
259 Dominic Meier .10 .25
260 Sandro Rizzi .10 .25
261 Pekka Rautakallio .20 .50
262 Rolf Ziegler .10 .25
263 Rene Back .10 .25
264 Sebastien Bordeleau .20 .50
265 Arne Ramholt .10 .25
266 Mathias Seger .10 .25
267 Christian Dube .10 .25
268 Mattia Baldi .10 .25
269 Sven Helfenstein .10 .25
270 Rolf Hildebrand .10 .25
271 Christian Matte .20 .50
272 Andy Keller .10 .25
273 Derek Plante .20 .50
274 Lars Leuenberger .10 .25
275 Michel Zeiter .10 .25
276 Ronnie Rueger .20 .50
277 Philippe Muller .10 .25
278 Noel Guyaz .10 .25
279 Ivo Ruthemann .10 .25
280 Petteri Nummelin .10 .25
281 Jan Cadieux .10 .25
282 Thomas Ziegler .10 .25
283 Keith Fair .10 .25
284 Mike McParland .10 .25
285 Sandy Jeannin .10 .25
286 Mirko Murovic .20 .50
287 Reto Schurch .20 .50
288 Raffaele Sannitz .20 .50
289 Malik Benturqui .10 .25
290 Flavio Ludke .10 .25
291 Severin Blindenbacher .10 .25
292 Ronny Keller .10 .25
293 Marko Kiprusoff .10 .25
294 Michel N'Goy .10 .25
295 Gregor Thommen .10 .25
296 Patrik Bartschi .10 .25
297 Thomas Studer .10 .25
298 Marc Werlen .10 .25
299 Andrei Bashkirov .20 .50
300 Daniel Bieri .10 .25
301 Mathias Holzer .10 .25
302 Trevor Meier .10 .25
303 Dmitri Shamolin .10 .25
304 Jarrod Skalde .20 .50
305 Michel Wicky .10 .25
306 Gerd Zenhausern .10 .25
307 Thomas Berger .20 .50
308 Marco Capaul .10 .25
309 Cyrill Geyer .10 .25
310 Michel Kamber .10 .25
311 Marc Schefer .10 .25
312 Fabian Stephan .10 .25
313 Markus Butler .10 .25
314 Daniel Giger .10 .25
315 Philipp Luber .10 .25
316 Dale McTavish .20 .50
317 Thomas Nussli .10 .25
318 Mikko Peltola .10 .25
319 Sebastien Reuille .10 .25
320 Niki Siren .10 .25
321 Alfred Bohren .10 .25
322 Claudio Bayer .20 .50
323 Daniel Aegerter .10 .25
324 Samuel Balmer .10 .25
325 Steve Hirschi .10 .25
326 Thomas Kunzi .10 .25
327 Mathias Wust .10 .25
328 Brian Bonin .20 .50
329 Marc Buhlmann .10 .25
330 Mike Craig .20 .50
331 Stefan Grogg .10 .25
332 Thomas Heldner .10 .25
333 Benoit Pont .10 .25
334 Sascha Schneider .10 .25
335 Daniel Steiner .10 .25
336 Chris McSorley .10 .25
337 Reto Pavoni .20 .50
338 Patrice Brasey .10 .25
339 Jamie Heward .20 .50
340 Dino Kessler .10 .25
341 Nicolas Studer .10 .25
342 Pierre-Alain Ancay .10 .25
343 Yvan Benoit .10 .25
344 Philippe Bozon .40 1.00
345 Thomas Derungs .10 .25
346 Igor Fedulov .10 .25
347 Michael Neininger .10 .25
348 Kevin Romy .10 .25
349 Pascal Schaller .10 .25
350 Theo Wittmann .10 .25
351 Florien Bruegger .10 .25
352 Gilles Cattela .10 .25
353 Nicolas Bernasconi .10 .25
354 Valeri Chiriaev .10 .25
355 Jonathan Pan .10 .25
356 Marc Tschudy .10 .25
357 Philippe Fontana .10 .25
358 Jamie Heinrich .10 .25
359 Fabrice Maillat .10 .25
360 Damien Micheli .10 .25
361 Philippe Thalmann .10 .25
362 Omar Tognini .10 .25
363 Bror Hansson .10 .25
364 Simon Rytz .10 .25
365 Fabian Beck .10 .25
366 Chris Belanger .10 .25
367 Serge Meyer .10 .25
368 Jorg Reber .10 .25
369 Remo Altorfer .10 .25
370 Fabio Beccarelli .10 .25
371 Rene Furler .10 .25
372 Vincent Lechenne .10 .25
373 Steve Pochon .10 .25
374 Ryan Savoia .20 .50
375 Christian Weber .10 .25
376 Yves Burlimann .10 .25
377 Marco Baumann .10 .25
378 Andreas Furrer .10 .25
379 Patrick Meichtry .10 .25
380 Daniel Schnyder .10 .25
381 Lukas Grauwiler .10 .25
382 Claudio Moggi .10 .25
383 Andreas Nauser .10 .25
384 Mike Richard .10 .25
385 Pascal Tiegermann .10 .25
386 Petri Varis .20 .50
387 Alexis Weber .10 .25
388 Bruno Aegerter .10 .25
389 Marc Zimmermann .20 .50
390 Stefan Badrutt .10 .25
391 Philipp Portner .10 .25
392 Kim Scheidegger .10 .25
393 Marc Zurbriggen .10 .25
394 Nicolas Gastaldo .10 .25
395 Stefan Gahler .10 .25
396 Stefan Ketola .10 .25
397 Marcel Moser .10 .25
398 Detlef Prediger .10 .25
399 Adrian Witschi .10 .25
400 Ken Zurfluh .10 .25
401 Michael Fluckiger .10 .25
402 Ludovic Aubry .10 .25
403 John Miner .10 .25
404 Jonathan Miner .10 .25
405 Christian Schuster .10 .25
406 Martin Schupbach .10 .25
407 Steven Barras .10 .25
408 Elvis Clavien .10 .25
409 Gilbert Flueler .10 .25
410 Sacha Guerne .10 .25
411 Christoph Lindberg .10 .25
412 Cyrill Pasche .10 .25
413 Arnold Lortscher .10 .25
414 Beat Aebischer .10 .25
415 Francesco Bizzozero .10 .25
416 Ruedi Forster .10 .25
417 Karl Knopf .10 .25
418 Francis Reichmuth .10 .25
419 Stefan Wuthrich .10 .25
420 Martin Gendron .20 .50
421 Kevin Gloor .10 .25
422 Bjorn Guazzini .10 .25
423 Albert Malgin .10 .25
424 Oliver Muller .10 .25
425 Patrick Siegwart .10 .25
426 Christian Ruegg .10 .25
427 Pasqual Sievert .10 .25
428 Christoph Decurtins .10 .25
429 Patrick Mader .10 .25
430 Michael Marki .10 .25
431 Raphael Schoop .10 .25
432 Daniel Sigg .10 .25
433 Philipp Dornbierer .10 .25
434 Curdin Grischott .10 .25
435 Roland Korsch .10 .25
436 Mikko Liukonnen .10 .25
437 Christian Strasser .10 .25
438 Harijs Vitolinsch .10 .25
439 Flavio Streit .10 .25
440 Stephane Julien .10 .25
441 Roland Kaser .10 .25
442 Olivier Schaublin .10 .25
443 Andreas Zehnder .10 .25
444 Rolf Badertscher .10 .25
445 Marco Fischer .10 .25
446 Marco Graf .10 .25
447 Cornel Prinz .10 .25
448 David Raissle .10 .25
449 Marcel Sommer .10 .25
450 Rene Stussi .10 .25
451 Kim Collins .10 .25
452 Thomas Baumle .10 .25
453 Lionel D'Urso .10 .25
454 Philippe Faust .10 .25
455 Fabian Gull .10 .25
456 Terry Hollinger .10 .25
457 Andre Bielmann .10 .25
458 Joel Camenzind .10 .25
459 Derek Cormier .10 .25
460 Maxime Lapointe .10 .25
461 Thierry Metrailler .10 .25
462 Didier Schafer .10 .25
463 Daniel Wobmann .10 .25
464 Ernst Bruderer .10 .25
465 Andreas Schweizer .10 .25
466 Simon Born .10 .25
467 Bernhard Fankhauser .10 .25
468 Marcel Habisreutinger .10 .25
469 Reto Klay .10 .25
470 Lars Sommer .10 .25
471 Eric Lecompte .20 .50
472 Martin Meyer .10 .25
473 Tassilo Schwarz .10 .25
474 Zeno Schwarz .10 .25
475 Martin Wuthrich .10 .25
476 Bruno Zarrillo .20 .50
477 Jean-Jacques Aeschlimann .10 .25
478 Reto von Arx .20 .50
479 Gian-Marco Crameri .10 .25
480 Patric Della Rossa .10 .25
481 Patrick Fischer .10 .25
482 Martin Gerber 2.00 5.00
483 Sandy Jeannin .10 .25
484 Marcel Jenni .10 .25
485 Olivier Keller .10 .25
486 Martin Pluss .10 .25
487 Michel Riesen .40 1.00
488 Ivo Ruthemann .10 .25
489 Martin Steinegger .10 .25
490 Mark Streit .10 .25
491 Lars Weibel .20 .50
492 Rolf Ziegler .10 .25
493 Cristobal Huet 1.25 3.00
494 Mark Streit .10 .25
495 Charly Oppliger .10 .25
496 Fredy Pargatzi .10 .25
497 Lonny Bohonos .20 .50
498 Patrik Juhlin .20 .50
499 Felix Hollenstein .10 .25

2002-03 Swiss SCL Tigers

COMPLETE SET
1 Johan Fransson .75 2.00
2 Pavel Skrbek .75 2.00
3 Jonas Ronnqvist .75 2.00
4 Magnus Nilsson .75 2.00
5 Gusten Tornqvist .75 2.00
6 Daniel Henriksson .75 2.00
7 Todd Elik .75 2.00

2003-04 Swiss EV Zug Postcards

These unnumbered 4X6 postcards were issued by the team and feature a colour headshot on the front. The two Patrick Fischers are different players with the same name. The Claude Lemieux single was issued as an update later in the season and so the set is considered complete without it.

COMPLETE SET (27) 10.00 25.00
1 Team Photo .40 1.00
2 Silvan Anthamatten .40 1.00
3 Duri Camichel .40 1.00
4 Corsin Casutt .40 1.00
5 Alain Demuth .40 1.00
6 Rafael Diaz .40 1.00
7 Paul Dipietro .40 1.00
8 Thomas Dommen .40 1.00
9 Paolo Duca .40 1.00
10 Livio Fazio .40 1.00
11 Patrick Fischer .40 1.00
12 Patrick Fischer .40 1.00
13 Daniel Giger .40 1.00
14 Andreas Kung .40 1.00
15 Colin Muller .40 1.00
16 Pascal Muller .40 1.00
17 Patrick Oppliger .40 1.00
18 Barry Richter .40 1.00
19 Frederic Rothen .40 1.00
20 Joel Savage .40 1.00
21 Lovis Schonenberger .40 1.00
22 Patrick Schopf .40 1.00
23 Fabio Schumacher .40 1.00
24 Sean Simpson .40 1.00
25 Chris Tancill .40 1.00
26 Michael Tobler .40 1.00
27 Gaetan Voisard .40 1.00
28 Claude Lemieux 4.00 10.00

2004-05 Swiss Davos Postcards

Cards measure 4X6 and feature a head shot on the front. All cards are autographed except for the group cards. Set is noteworthy for the inclusion of Joe Thornton and Rick Nash.

COMPLETE SET (30) 40.00 80.00
1 Team photo .40 1.00
2 Team history .40 1.00
3 Andres Ambuhl 1.25 3.00
4 Thomas Baumle 1.25 3.00
5 Florian Blatter 1.25 3.00
6 Daniell Boss 1.25 3.00
7 Bjorn Christen 1.25 3.00
8 Franco Collenberg 1.25 3.00
9 Arno Del Curto 1.25 3.00
10 Beat Forster 1.25 3.00
11 Marc Gianola 1.25 3.00
12 Peter Guggisberg 1.25 3.00
13 Niklas Hagman 2.00 5.00
14 Andreas Haller 1.25 3.00
15 Stevan Hasler 1.25 3.00
16 Marc Heberlein 1.25 3.00
17 Jonas Hiller 2.00 5.00
18 Michael Kress 1.25 3.00
19 Josef Marha 1.25 3.00
20 Laurent Muller 1.25 3.00
21 Rick Nash 12.00 30.00
22 Claudio Neff 1.25 3.00
23 Arne Ramholt 1.25 3.00
24 Michel Riesen 1.25 3.00
25 Sandro Rizzi 1.25 3.00
26 Fabian Sutter 1.25 3.00
27 Joe Thornton 15.00 40.00
28 Jan Von Arx 1.25 3.00
29 Reto Von Arx 1.25 3.00
30 Benjamin Winkler 1.25 3.00

2004-05 Swiss EV Zug Postcards

The cards are approximately 4X6. We've seen signed versions of the cards as well, but it's not known whether they were issued that way officially, or signed afterwards.

COMPLETE SET (28) 10.00 25.00
1 Brett Hauer .75 2.00
2 Niko Kapanen .75 2.00
3 Mike Fisher 1.25 3.00
4 Barry Richter .40 1.00
5 Oleg Petrov .40 1.00
6 Lars Weibel .40 1.00
7 Rafael Walter .40 1.00
8 Jan Feldmann .40 1.00
9 Livio Fazio .40 1.00
10 Pascal Muller .40 1.00
11 Rafael Diaz .40 1.00
12 Rene Back .40 1.00
13 Gaetan Voisard .40 1.00
14 Silvan Anthamatten .40 1.00
15 Patric Della Rosa .40 1.00
16 Gian-Marco Crameri .40 1.00
17 Patrick Fisher .40 1.00
18 Duri Camichel .40 1.00
19 Patrick Oppliger .40 1.00
20 Duca Paolo .40 1.00
21 Fabian Schnyder .40 1.00
22 Corsin Casutt .40 1.00
23 Daniel Giger .40 1.00
24 Frederic Rothen .40 1.00
25 Beat Schuler .40 1.00
26 Sean Simpson CO .40 1.00
27 Colin Muller ACO .40 1.00
28 Team Photo .40 1.00

2004-05 Swiss Lausanne HC Postcards

Standard postcard-sized collectibles were sold by the team in set form. The series in noteworthy for the inclusion of reigning NHL scoring champ Martin St. Louis. The cards are unnumbered. Checklist courtesy of collector Vincent Montalbano.

COMPLETE SET (25) 10.00 25.00
1 Pascal Schaller .40 1.00
2 Robert Slehofer .40 1.00
3 Alain Reist .40 1.00
4 Bruno Steck .40 1.00
5 Andy Roach .75 2.00
6 Thomas Berger .40 1.00
7 Patrick Boileau .75 2.00
8 Florian Andenmatten .40 1.00
9 Sunshine Romerio .40 1.00
10 Julien Turler .40 1.00
11 Gerd Zenhausern .40 1.00
12 Loic Merz .40 1.00
13 Martin St. Louis 4.00 10.00
14 Christophe Brown .40 1.00
15 Michael Ngoy .40 1.00
16 Mathias Holzer .40 1.00
17 Laurent Emery .40 1.00
18 Florian Conz .40 1.00
19 Marko Tuomainen .40 1.00
20 Michael Kamber .40 1.00
21 Lovis Schonenberger .40 1.00
22 Sacha Weibel .40 1.00
23 Eric Landry .40 1.00
24 Bill Stewart CO .10 .25
25 Gary Sheehan ACO .10 .25

2007-08 Swiss HC Lugano

COMPLETE SET (27) 15.00 30.00
1 Krister Cantoni .60 1.50
2 Alessandro Chiesa .60 1.50
3 Flavien Conne .60 1.50
4 Fabrizio Conte .60 1.50
5 Andreas Hanni .60 1.50
6 Timo Helbling .60 1.50
7 Jukka Hentunen .60 1.50
8 Steve Hirschi .60 1.50
9 Sandy Jeannin .60 1.50
10 Mike Knoepfli .60 1.50
11 Dario Kostovic .60 1.50
12 Marty Murray .60 1.50
13 Andy Naser .60 1.50
14 Thierry Paterlini .60 1.50
15 Kevin Romy .60 1.50
16 Raffaele Sannitz .60 1.50
17 Yannick Tremblay .60 1.50
18 Julien Vauclair .60 1.50
19 Tristan Vauclair .60 1.50
20 Raffael Walter .60 1.50
21 Landon Wilson .60 1.50
22 Valentin Wirz .60 1.50
23 Simon Zuger .60 1.50
24 Ivano Zanatta HC .10 .25
25 Diego Scandella AC .10 .25
26 Dusan Sidor .60 1.50
27 Tiziano Muzio .60 1.50

2012-13 Swiss EV Zug Postcards

1 Yannick Blaser
2 Damien Brunner
3 Corsin Casutt
4 Alessandro Chiesa
5 Bjorn Christen
6 Raphael Diaz
7 Nolan Diem
8 Samuel Erni
9 Patrick Fischer
10 Andreas Furrer
11 Timo Helbling
12 Josh Holden
13 Kevin Huber
14 Waltteri Immonen
15 Dominic Lammer
16 Sven Lindemann
17 Fabian Luth
18 Jussi Markkanen
19 Lino Martschini
20 Linus Omark
21 Mattias Rossi
22 Florian Schmuckli
23 Cedric Schneuwly
24 Fabian Schnyder
25 Doug Shedden
26 Reto Suri
27 Fabian Sutter
28 Andy Wozniewski
29 Henrik Zetterberg
30 Patrick Zubler
31 Sandro Zurkirchen
32 Team Postcard

2012-13 Swiss HC Biel Postcards

1 Eric Beaudoin
2 Reto Berra
3 Gianni Ehrensperger
4 Jeffrey Fuglister
5 Kevin Gloor
6 Manuel Gossweiler
7 Marc Grieder
8 Gaetan Haas
9 Anthony Huguenin
10 Patrick Kane
11 Steve Kellenberger
12 Clarence Kparghai
13 Andrien Lauper
14 Dominic Meier
15 Jacob Micflikier
16 Emanuel Peter
17 Marc-Antoine Pouliot
18 Anthony Rouiller
19 Rajan Sataric
20 Kevin Schlapfer
21 Marc Schmid
22 Tyler Seguin
23 Ahren Spylo
24 Dino Stecher
25 Marco Streit
26 Dario Trutmann
27 Mathieu Tschantre
28 Ramon Untersander
29 Thomas Wellinger
30 Philipp Wetzel
31 Marc Wieser
32 Silvan Wyss

2012-13 Swiss Rapperswill Lakers Postcards

1 David Aebisscher
2 Nils Berger
3 Sven Berger
4 Loic Burkhalter
5 Thomas Busser
6 Andreas Camenzind
7 Duri Camichel
8 Michael Del Zotto
9 Robbie Earl
10 Marc Geiger
11 Cyrill Geyer
12 Sandro Gmur
13 Lukas Grauwiler
14 Stefan Hurlimann
15 Mauro Jorg
16 Juraj Kolnik
17 Jonas Muller
18 Benjamin Neukom
19 Michel Reisen
20 Antonio Rizzello
21 Harry Rogenmoser
22 Roland Schmid
23 Peter Sejna
24 Jason Spezza
25 Nicolas Thibaudeau
26 Derrick Walser
27 Marco Welti
28 Adrian Wichser
29 Benjamin Winkler

2012-13 Swiss SNL

SNL001 Nolan Schaefer .40 1.00
SNL002 Lorenzo Croce .20 .50
SNL003 Julien Bonnet .20 .50
SNL004 Reto Kobach .20 .50
SNL005 Zdenek Kutlak .30 .75
SNL006 Maxim Noreau .40 1.00
SNL007 Marc Schulthess .20 .50
SNL008 Patrick Sidler .20 .50
SNL009 Adrian Trunz .20 .50
SNL010 Elias Bianchi .20 .50
SNL011 Mattia Bianchi .20 .50
SNL012 Paolo Duca .30 .75
SNL013 Daniele Grassi .20 .50
SNL014 Vitali Lakhmatov .20 .50
SNL015 Alain Mieville .20 .50
SNL016 Max Pacioretty .75 2.00
SNL017 Richard Park .40 1.00
SNL018 Marco Pedretti .30 .75
SNL019 Inti Pestoni .40 1.00
SNL020 Marc Reichert .20 .50
SNL021 Roman Schlagenhauf .20 .50
SNL022 Jason Williams .75 2.00
SNL023 Tim Weber .20 .50
SNL024 Serge Pelletier .20 .50
SNL025 Checklist Ambri-Piotta .20 .50
SNL026 Marco Buhrer .40 1.00
SNL027 Olivier Gigon .20 .50
SNL028 Franco Collenberg .20 .50
SNL029 Philippe Furrer .30 .75
SNL030 Beat Gerber .20 .50
SNL031 Andreas Hanni .20 .50
SNL032 Martin Hohener .20 .50
SNL033 David Jobin .20 .50
SNL034 Roman Josi 1.25 3.00
SNL035 Geoff Kinrade .40 1.00
SNL036 Travis Roche .40 1.00
SNL037 Mark Streit 1.25 3.00
SNL038 Pascal Berger .20 .50
SNL039 Christoph Bertschy .30 .75
SNL040 Nicklas Danielsson .30 .75
SNL041 Thomas Deruns .20 .50
SNL042 Ryan Gardner .40 1.00
SNL043 Caryl Neuenschwander .20 .50
SNL044 Martin Pluss .40 1.00
SNL045 Flurin Randegger .20 .50
SNL046 Byron Ritchie .40 1.00
SNL047 Daniel Rubin .20 .50
SNL048 Ivo Ruthemann .30 .75
SNL049 Tristan Scherwey .20 .50
SNL050 John Tavares 1.50 4.00
SNL051 Joel Vermin .40 1.00
SNL052 Antti Tormanen .40 1.00
SNL053 Lars Leuenberger .20 .50
SNL054 Checklist SC Bern .20 .50
SNL055 Reto Berra .60 1.50
SNL056 Marco Streit .20 .50
SNL057 Marc Schmid .20 .50
SNL058 Manuel Gossweiler .20 .50
SNL059 Marc Grieder .20 .50
SNL060 Anthony Huguenin .20 .50
SNL061 Clarence Kphargai .20 .50
SNL062 Dominic Meier .20 .50
SNL063 Dario Trutmann .30 .75
SNL064 Ramon Untersander .20 .50
SNL065 Thomas Wellinger .30 .75
SNL066 Eric Beaudoin .40 1.00
SNL067 Gianni Ehrensperger .20 .50
SNL068 Jeffrey Fuglister .20 .50
SNL069 Kevin Gloor .20 .50
SNL070 Gaetan Haas .30 .75
SNL071 Patrick Kane 1.50 4.00
SNL072 Steve Kellenberger .20 .50
SNL073 Adrien Lauper .20 .50
SNL074 Jacob Micflikier .40 1.00
SNL075 Emanuel Peter .20 .50
SNL076 Marc-Antoine Pouliot .40 1.00
SNL077 Tyler Seguin 1.50 4.00
SNL078 Ahren Spylo .40 1.00
SNL079 Mathieu Tschantre .30 .75
SNL080 Philipp Wetzel .20 .50
SNL081 Marc Wieser .20 .50
SNL082 Kevin Schlapfer .40 1.00
SNL083 Dino Stecher .20 .50
SNL084 Checklist Biel .20 .50
SNL085 Leonardo Genoni .40 1.00
SNL086 Janick Schwendener .20 .50
SNL087 Santeri Alatalo .30 .75
SNL088 Rene Back .20 .50
SNL089 Beat Forster .30 .75
SNL090 Robin Grossmann .30 .75
SNL091 Samuel Guerra .20 .50
SNL092 Mathias Joggi .20 .50
SNL093 Tim Ramholt .30 .75
SNL094 Noah Schneeberger .20 .50
SNL095 Jan Von Arx .20 .50
SNL096 Dario Burgler .40 1.00
SNL097 Corsin Camichel .20 .50
SNL098 Peter Guggisberg .20 .50
SNL099 Gregory Hofmann .30 .75
SNL100 Rick Nash 1.50 4.00
SNL101 Josef Marha .40 1.00
SNL102 Sandro Rizzi .20 .50
SNL103 Sven Ryser .20 .50
SNL104 Patrick Schommer .20 .50
SNL105 Gregory Sciaroni .20 .50
SNL106 Jannick Steinmann .20 .50
SNL107 Petr Sykora .40 1.00
SNL108 Petr Taticek .40 1.00
SNL109 Joe Thornton 1.50 4.00
SNL110 Reto Von Arx .40 1.00
SNL111 Dino Wieser .20 .50
SNL112 Arno Del Curto .40 1.00
SNL113 Checklist Davos .20 .50
SNL114 Benjamin Conz .40 1.00
SNL115 Simon Rytz .20 .50
SNL116 Marc Abplanalp .20 .50
SNL117 Alain Birbaum .20 .50
SNL118 Lukas Gerber .20 .50
SNL119 Shawn Heins .30 .75
SNL120 Joel Kwiatkowski .30 .75
SNL121 Romain Loeffel .20 .50
SNL122 Michael Ngoy .20 .50
SNL123 Sebastian Schilt .20 .50
SNL124 Cedric Botter .20 .50
SNL125 Andrey Bykov .40 1.00
SNL126 Jan Cadieux .20 .50
SNL127 David Desharnais 1.25 3.00
SNL128 Christian Dube .40 1.00
SNL129 Simon Gamache .40 1.00
SNL130 Adam Hasani .20 .50
SNL131 Sandy Jeannin .30 .75
SNL132 Mike Knoepfli .20 .50
SNL133 Greg Mauldin .40 1.00
SNL134 Melvin Merola .20 .50
SNL135 Benjamin Pluss .30 .75
SNL136 Pavel Rosa .40 1.00
SNL137 Julien Sprunger .40 1.00
SNL138 Tristan Vauclair .20 .50
SNL139 Hans Kossmann .40 1.00
SNL140 Rene Matte .20 .50
SNL141 Checklist Fribourg .20 .50
SNL142 Tobias Stephan .40 1.00
SNL143 Federico Tamo .20 .50
SNL144 Eliot Antonietti .20 .50
SNL145 Goran Bezina .30 .75
SNL146 Marc Gautschi .20 .50
SNL147 Kevin Hecquefeuille .30 .75
SNL148 Jonathan Mercier .20 .50
SNL149 Gian-Andrea Randegger .20 .50
SNL150 Daniel Vukovic .20 .50
SNL151 Yannick Weber 1.25 3.00
SNL152 Cody Almond .60 1.50
SNL153 Logan Couture 1.50 4.00
SNL154 Rico Fata .40 1.00
SNL155 Samuel Friedli .20 .50
SNL156 Dan Fritsche .60 1.50
SNL157 John Fritsche .20 .50
SNL158 Roland Gerber .20 .50
SNL159 Ryan Keller .40 1.00
SNL160 Alexandre Picard .60 1.50
SNL161 Christopher Rivera .20 .50
SNL162 Kevin Romy .30 .75
SNL163 Juraj Simek .30 .75
SNL164 Julian Walker .30 .75
SNL165 Chris McSorley .40 1.00
SNL166 Louis Matte .20 .50
SNL167 Checklist Servette Geneve .20 .50
SNL168 Lukas Meili .20 .50
SNL169 Ronnie Rueger .40 1.00
SNL170 Christopher Bagnoud .20 .50
SNL171 Eric Blum .30 .75
SNL172 Felicien Du Bois .20 .50
SNL173 Micki Dupont .60 1.50
SNL174 Philippe Schelling .20 .50
SNL175 Nicholas Steiner .20 .50
SNL176 Lukas Stoop .20 .50
SNL177 Patrick Von Gunten .40 1.00
SNL178 Matthias Bieber .30 .75
SNL179 Simon Bodenmann .30 .75
SNL180 Yannick Herren .20 .50
SNL181 Denis Hollenstein .40 1.00
SNL182 Marcel Jenni .40 1.00
SNL183 Kamil Kreps .30 .75
SNL184 Brooks Laich 1.50 4.00
SNL185 Romano Lemm .20 .50
SNL186 Robin Leone .20 .50
SNL187 Michael Liniger .20 .50
SNL188 Emil Lundberg .30 .75
SNL189 Lars Neher .20 .50
SNL190 Raffaele Sannitz .30 .75
SNL191 Tommi Santala .40 1.00
SNL192 Victor Stancescu .30 .75
SNL193 Samuel Walser .20 .50
SNL194 Tomas Tamfal .20 .50
SNL195 Frederic Rothen .20 .50
SNL196 Checklist Kloten .20 .50
SNL197 Thomas Baumle .40 1.00
SNL198 Remo Giovannini .20 .50
SNL199 Jaroslav Hubl .40 1.00
SNL200 Federico Lardi .20 .50
SNL201 Kim Lee Lindemann .20 .50
SNL202 Simon Luthi .20 .50
SNL203 Christian Moser .20 .50
SNL204 Mark Popovic .40 1.00
SNL205 Jorg Reber .20 .50
SNL206 Philippe Rytz .20 .50
SNL207 Jared Spurgeon .75 2.00
SNL208 Martin Stettler .20 .50
SNL209 Adrian Brunner .20 .50
SNL210 Tobias Bucher .20 .50
SNL211 Tyler Ennis 1.25 3.00
SNL212 Etienne Froidevaux .20 .50
SNL213 Joel Genazzi .20 .50
SNL214 Adrian Gerber .20 .50
SNL215 Lukas Haas .20 .50
SNL216 Arnaud Jacquemet .20 .50
SNL217 Robin Leblanc .20 .50
SNL218 Kurtis McLean .40 1.00
SNL219 Claudio Moggi .20 .50
SNL220 Sandro Moggi .20 .50
SNL221 Simon Moser .40 1.00
SNL222 Pascal Pelletier .40 1.00
SNL223 Alban Rexha .20 .50
SNL224 John Fust .20 .50
SNL225 Alex Reinhard .20 .50
SNL226 Checklist SCL Tigers .20 .50
SNL227 Michael Fluckiger .20 .50
SNL228 Daniel Manzato .30 .75
SNL229 Florian Blatter .20 .50
SNL230 Ilkka Heikkinen .60 1.50
SNL231 Steve Hirschi .20 .50
SNL232 Lorenz Kienzle .20 .50
SNL233 Johan Morant .20 .50
SNL234 Matteo Nodari .20 .50
SNL235 Petteri Nummelin .40 1.00
SNL236 Luca Sbisa 1.25 3.00
SNL237 Dominik Schlumpf .20 .50
SNL238 Stefan Ulmer .20 .50
SNL239 Julien Vauclair .40 1.00
SNL240 Patrice Bergeron 1.50 4.00
SNL241 Flavien Conne .20 .50
SNL242 Hnat Domenichelli .30 .75
SNL243 Luca Fazzini .20 .50
SNL244 Oliver Kamber .20 .50
SNL245 Diego Kostner .20 .50
SNL246 Brett McLean .40 1.00
SNL247 Glen Metropolit .60 1.50
SNL248 Brady Murray .30 .75
SNL249 Jordy Murray .30 .75
SNL250 Leandro Profico .20 .50
SNL251 Sebastien Reuille .20 .50
SNL252 Thomas Rufenacht .20 .50
SNL253 Dario Simion .20 .50
SNL254 Daniel Steiner .30 .75
SNL255 Larry Huras .40 1.00
SNL256 Patrick Fischer .30 .75
SNL257 Checklist Lugano .20 .50
SNL258 David Aebischer .40 1.00
SNL259 Jonas Muller .20 .50
SNL260 Sven Berger .20 .50
SNL261 Thomas Busser .20 .50
SNL262 Andreas Camenzind .20 .50
SNL263 Michael Del Zotto 1.25 3.00
SNL264 Cyrill Geyer .20 .50
SNL265 Sandro Gmur .20 .50
SNL266 Nicolas Marzan .20 .50
SNL267 Derrick Walser .40 1.00
SNL268 Marc Welti .20 .50
SNL269 Benjamin Winkler .20 .50
SNL270 Nils Berger .20 .50
SNL271 Loic Burkhalter .20 .50
SNL272 Duri Camichel .20 .50
SNL273 Robbie Earl .60 1.50
SNL274 Jeremy Gaillard .20 .50
SNL275 Lukas Grauwiler .20 .50
SNL276 Stefan Hurlimann .20 .50
SNL277 Mauro Jorg .30 .75
SNL278 Juraj Kolnik .40 1.00
SNL279 Benjamin Neukom .20 .50
SNL280 Michel Riesen .30 .75
SNL281 Antonio Rizzello .20 .50
SNL282 Peter Sejna .40 1.00
SNL283 Jason Spezza 1.50 4.00
SNL284 Nicholas Thibaudeau .20 .50
SNL285 Gian-Andrea Thony .20 .50
SNL286 Adrian Wichser .20 .50
SNL287 Harry Rogenmoser .20 .50
SNL288 Checklist Rapperswil .20 .50
SNL289 Lukas Flueler .40 1.00
SNL290 Tim Wolf .20 .50
SNL291 Severin Blindenbacher .40 1.00
SNL292 Luca Camperchioli .20 .50
SNL293 Patrick Geering .20 .50
SNL294 John Gobbi .20 .50
SNL295 Matt Lashoff .40 1.00
SNL296 Marco Maurer .20 .50
SNL297 Daniel Schnyder .20 .50
SNL298 Mathias Seger .40 1.00
SNL299 Andri Stoffel .20 .50
SNL300 Andres Ambuhl .40 1.00
SNL301 Chris Baltisberger .20 .50
SNL302 Mark Bastl .20 .50
SNL303 Dustin Brown 1.50 4.00
SNL304 Cyrill Buhler .20 .50
SNL305 Patrik Bartschi .20 .50
SNL306 Luca Cunti .40 1.00
SNL307 Ronalds Kenins .40 1.00
SNL308 Thibaut Monnet .40 1.00
SNL309 Reto Schappi .20 .50
SNL310 Ryan Shannon .40 1.00
SNL311 Jeff Tambellini .40 1.00
SNL312 Morris Trachsler .30 .75
SNL313 Roman Wick .40 1.00
SNL314 Sandro Zangger .20 .50
SNL315 Marc Crawford .40 1.00
SNL316 Rob Cookson .20 .50
SNL317 Checklist ZSC Lions .20 .50
SNL318 Jussi Markkanen .40 1.00
SNL319 Sandro Zurkirchen .20 .50
SNL320 Robin Kuonen .20 .50
SNL321 Yannick Blaser .20 .50
SNL322 Alessandro Chiesa .20 .50
SNL323 Raphael Diaz 1.25 3.00
SNL324 Patrick Fischer II .20 .50
SNL325 Andreas Furrer .20 .50
SNL326 Timo Helbling .30 .75
SNL327 Andy Wozniewski .30 .75
SNL328 Patrick Zubler .20 .50
SNL329 Damien Brunner 1.25 3.00
SNL330 Corsin Casutt .20 .50
SNL331 Bjorn Christen .20 .50
SNL332 Josh Holden .60 1.50
SNL333 Dominic Lammer .20 .50
SNL334 Sven Lindemann .20 .50
SNL335 Fabian Luthi .20 .50

SNL336 Lino Martschini .30 .75
SNL337 Linus Omark .75 2.00
SNL338 Matthias Rossi .20 .50
SNL339 Cedric Schneuwly .20 .50
SNL340 Fabian Schnyder .30 .75
SNL341 Reto Suri .40 1.00
SNL342 Fabian Sutter .20 .50
SNL343 Henrik Zetterberg 1.50 4.00
SNL344 Doug Shedden .40 1.00
SNL345 Waltteri Immonen .20 .50
SNL346 Checklist EV Zug .20 .50
SNL347 Reto Berra .60 1.50
SNL348 Martin Gerber .60 1.50
SNL349 Alessandro Chiesa .20 .50
SNL350 Tim Ramholt .30 .75
SNL351 Patrick Von Gunten .40 1.00
SNL352 Clarence Kphargai .20 .50
SNL353 Robin Grossmann .30 .75
SNL354 Patrick Geering .20 .50
SNL355 Eric Blum .30 .75
SNL356 Romain Loeffel .20 .50
SNL357 Fabian Schnyder .30 .75
SNL358 Andres Ambuhl .40 1.00
SNL359 Simon Bodenmann .30 .75
SNL360 Inti Pestoni .30 .75
SNL361 Victor Stancescu .30 .75
SNL362 Reto Suri .40 1.00
SNL363 Daniel Rubin .20 .50
SNL364 Ryan Gardner .40 1.00
SNL365 Patrik Bartschi .20 .50
SNL366 Denis Hollenstein .40 1.00
SNL367 Dario Burgler .40 1.00
SNL368 Kevin Romy .30 .75
SNL369 Julian Walker .30 .75
SNL370 Roman Wick .40 1.00
SNL371 Sean Simpson .40 1.00
SNL372 Checklist Team Switzerland .20 .50
SNL373 Cory Schneider 1.50 4.00
SNL374 Matt Duchene 1.50 4.00
SNL375 Jaroslav Bednar .60 1.50
SNL376 Alain Berger .30 .75
SNL377 Petr Sykora .75 2.00
SNL378 Chris Campoli .75 2.00
SNL379 Nikolaj Ehlers .40 1.00
SNL380 Ryan MacMurchy .30 .75
SNL381 Sebastian Sutter .20 .50
SNL382 Martin Ulmer .20 .50
SNL383 Enzo Corvi .20 .50
SNL384 Radek Dvorak .75 2.00
SNL385 Loui Eriksson 1.50 4.00
SNL386 Lukas Sieber .20 .50
SNL387 Maxim Sushinsky .40 1.00
SNL388 Mathieu Carle .40 1.00
SNL389 Tony Salmelainen .40 1.00
SNL390 Paul Savary .30 .75
SNL391 Eric Walsky .30 .75
SNL392 Pascal Muller .20 .50
SNL393 Alexandre Giroux .40 1.00
SNL394 Felix Hollenstein .40 1.00
SNL395 Sami El-Assaoui .20 .50
SNL396 Bryce Lampman .40 1.00
SNL397 Thomas Nussli .20 .50
SNL398 Mark Bomersback .30 .75
SNL399 Charles Linglet .40 1.00
SNL400 Pierrick Pivron .20 .50
SNL401 Pavel Rosa .40 1.00
SNL402 Steve McCarthy .40 1.00
SNL403 Mikko Lehtonen .40 1.00
SNL404 Fabrice Herzog .20 .50
SNL405 Raphael Diaz 1.50 4.00
SNL406 Roman Josi 1.25 3.00
SNL407 Luca Sbisa 1.25 3.00
SNL408 Mark Streit 1.25 3.00
SNL409 Yannick Weber 1.25 3.00
SNL410 Damien Brunner 2.00 5.00

2012-13 Swiss SNL Captains

SNLCA01 Paolo Duca 2.00 5.00
SNLCA02 Martin Pluss 2.00 5.00
SNLCA03 Mathieu Tschantre 2.00 5.00
SNLCA04 Sandro Rizzi 2.00 5.00
SNLCA05 Sandy Jeannin 2.00 5.00
SNLCA06 Goran Bezina 2.00 5.00
SNLCA07 Victor Stancescu 2.00 5.00
SNLCA08 Simon Moser 2.00 5.00
SNLCA09 Julien Vauclair 2.00 5.00
SNLCA10 Cyrill Geyer 2.00 5.00
SNLCA11 Mathias Seger 2.00 5.00
SNLCA12 Fabian Schnyder 2.00 5.00

2012-13 Swiss SNL Global Impact

SNLGI01 Jason Williams 4.00 10.00
SNLGI02 Nicklas Danielsson 3.00 8.00
SNLGI03 Marc-Antoine Pouliot 3.00 8.00
SNLGI04 Petr Taticek 3.00 8.00
SNLGI05 Simon Gamache 3.00 8.00
SNLGI06 Cody Almond 3.00 8.00
SNLGI07 Micki Dupont 3.00 8.00
SNLGI08 Mark Popovic 3.00 8.00
SNLGI09 Ilkka Heikkinen 3.00 8.00
SNLGI10 Robbie Earl 3.00 8.00
SNLGI11 Ryan Shannon 3.00 8.00
SNLGI12 Linus Omark 4.00 10.00

2012-13 Swiss SNL Lockout Memories

SNLLM01 Matt Duchene 6.00 15.00
SNLLM02 John Tavares 6.00 15.00
SNLLM03 Patrick Kane 6.00 15.00
SNLLM04 Tyler Seguin 6.00 15.00
SNLLM05 Joe Thornton 6.00 15.00
SNLLM06 Rick Nash 6.00 15.00
SNLLM07 Logan Couture 6.00 15.00
SNLLM08 Brooks Laich 6.00 15.00
SNLLM09 Patrice Bergeron 6.00 15.00
SNLLM10 Jason Spezza 6.00 15.00
SNLLM11 Dustin Brown 6.00 15.00
SNLLM12 Henrik Zetterberg 6.00 15.00

2012-13 Swiss SNL Lockout Stars

SNLLS01 John Tavares 12.00 30.00
SNLLS02 Mark Streit 8.00 20.00
SNLLS03 Roman Josi 8.00 20.00
SNLLS04 Tyler Seguin 12.00 30.00
SNLLS05 Patrick Kane 12.00 30.00
SNLLS06 Joe Thornton 10.00 25.00
SNLLS07 Rick Nash 12.00 30.00
SNLLS08 Logan Couture 10.00 25.00
SNLLS09 Yannick Weber 8.00 20.00
SNLLS10 Brooks Laich 12.00 30.00
SNLLS11 Tyler Ennis 8.00 20.00
SNLLS12 Patrice Bergeron 12.00 30.00
SNLLS13 Luca Sbisa 8.00 20.00
SNLLS14 Jason Spezza 10.00 25.00
SNLLS15 Michael Del Zotto 10.00 25.00
SNLLS16 Dustin Brown 10.00 25.00
SNLLS17 Henrik Zetterberg 12.00 30.00
SNLLS18 Raphael Diaz 8.00 20.00

2012-13 Swiss SNL Masked Men

*BLACK/30: 1X TO 2.5X BASIC INSERT/600
SNLMM01 Nolan Schaefer 4.00 10.00
SNLMM02 Marco Buhrer 4.00 10.00
SNLMM03 Reto Berra 4.00 10.00
SNLMM04 Leonardo Genoni 4.00 10.00
SNLMM05 Benjamin Conz 4.00 10.00
SNLMM06 Tobias Stephan 4.00 10.00
SNLMM07 Ronnie Rueger 4.00 10.00
SNLMM08 Thomas Baumle 4.00 10.00
SNLMM09 Daniel Manzato 4.00 10.00
SNLMM10 David Aebischer 4.00 10.00
SNLMM11 Lukas Flueler 4.00 10.00
SNLMM12 Jussi Markkanen 4.00 10.00

2012-13 Swiss SNL Meisterkarte

*BLACK/30: 1X TO 2.5X BASIC INSERT/600
SNLMK01 ZSC Lions 5.00 12.00

2012-13 Swiss SNL Meisterpokal

SNLMP01 Meisterpokal 2.50 6.00

2012-13 Swiss SNL Playmakers

SNLPM01 Inti Pestoni 2.00 5.00
SNLPM02 John Tavares 5.00 12.00
SNLPM03 Tyler Seguin 5.00 12.00
SNLPM04 Joe Thornton 4.00 10.00
SNLPM05 Christian Dube 2.00 5.00
SNLPM06 Kevin Romy 2.00 5.00
SNLPM07 Denis Hollenstein 3.00 8.00
SNLPM08 Pascal Pelletier 2.00 5.00
SNLPM09 Glen Metropolit 3.00 8.00
SNLPM10 Jason Spezza 4.00 10.00
SNLPM11 Roman Wick 2.00 5.00
SNLPM12 Henrik Zetterberg 5.00 12.00

2012-13 Swiss SNL Scoring Kings

*PINK/30: 1X TO 2.5X BASIC INSERT/600
SNLSK01 Maxim Noreau 3.00 8.00
SNLSK02 Byron Ritchie 3.00 8.00
SNLSK03 Ahren Spylo 3.00 8.00
SNLSK04 Petr Sykora 3.00 8.00
SNLSK05 Julien Sprunger 3.00 8.00
SNLSK06 Rico Fata 3.00 8.00
SNLSK07 Tommi Santala 3.00 8.00
SNLSK08 Kurtis McLean 3.00 8.00
SNLSK09 Jaroslav Bednar 3.00 8.00
SNLSK10 Loic Burkhalter 3.00 8.00
SNLSK11 Jeff Tambellini 3.00 8.00
SNLSK12 Damien Brunner 6.00 15.00

2012-13 Swiss SNL Swiss Heroes

*PINK/30: 1X TO 2.5X BASIC INSERT/600
SNLSH01 Damien Brunner 6.00 15.00

2012-13 Swiss SNL Top Prospects

*BLACK/30: 1X TO 2.5X BASIC INSERT/600
SNLTP01 Daniele Grassi 3.00 8.00
SNLTP02 Christoph Bertschy 4.00 10.00
SNLTP03 Dario Trutmann 4.00 10.00
SNLTP04 Gregory Hofmann 4.00 10.00
SNLTP05 Melvin Merola 3.00 8.00
SNLTP06 Eliot Antonietti 3.00 8.00
SNLTP07 Lukas Meili 3.00 8.00
SNLTP08 Alban Rexha 3.00 8.00
SNLTP09 Luca Fazzini 3.00 8.00
SNLTP10 Tim Wolf 3.00 8.00
SNLTP11 Dominic Lammer 3.00 8.00
SNLTP12 Lino Martschini 4.00 10.00

1954 UK A and BC Chewing Gum

The cards listed below were part of a multi-sport set issued in England, possibly with packs of A and BC Chewing Gum. They feature b&w headshots and blank backs. The players appear to be from an early English league. It's quite possible that other hockey players were featured. If you can address this checklist, please contact us at hockeymag@beckett.com.

COMPLETE SET (?)
35 Chick Zamick 8.00 20.00
36 Cliff Ryan 8.00 20.00
37 Sonny Rost 8.00 20.00
38 Malcolm Davidson 8.00 20.00
39 Ray Gariepy 12.00 30.00
40 George Beach 8.00 20.00
41 Lefty Wilmot 8.00 20.00
74 Bill Johnson 8.00 20.00
75 Joe Shack 8.00 20.00
76 Tony Licari 8.00 20.00

1998-99 UK Basingstoke Bison

This set features the Bison of the British Hockey League. The set was produced by Armchair Sports, an English card shop, and was sold by that store and the team. The print run has been confirmed at 200 sets.

COMPLETE SET (24) 4.00 10.00
1 Rick Strachan .25 .60
2 Joe Baird .25 .60
3 Chris Crombie .25 .60
4 Steve Smillie .25 .60
5 Chris Bailey .25 .60
6 Bjarne Levison .25 .60
7 Mike Ellis .25 .60
8 Chris Chard .25 .60
9 Anthony Page .25 .60
10 Adam Cathcart .25 .60
11 Rick Fera .25 .60
12 Gary Clark .25 .60
13 Tony Redmond .25 .60
14 Alec Field .25 .60
15 Hakan Klys .25 .60
16 Mitch Grant .25 .60
17 Jake Armstrong .25 .60
18 Don Deopoe CO .02 .10
19 Garfunkel's MASCOT .02 .10
20 The Puck .02 .10
21 The Goal .02 .10
22 Penalty Shots .02 .10
23 Team CL .02 .10
NNO Competition .02 .10

1999-00 UK Basingstoke Bison

This set features the Bison of Britain's top hockey league. The set was produced by Armchair Sports, a card shop in the UK, and was sold by the team at home games. The print run has been confirmed at 200 sets.

COMPLETE SET (22) 4.00 10.00
1 Rick Strachan .20 .50
2 Dru Burgess .20 .50
3 Danny Meyers .20 .50
4 Gary Clark .20 .50
5 Peter Romeo .20 .50
6 Mike Ellis .20 .50
7 Joey Baird .20 .50
8 Charlie Colon .20 .50
9 Wayne Crawford .20 .50
10 Alec Field .20 .50
11 Tony Redmond .20 .50
12 Mitch Grant .20 .50
13 Duncan Paterson .20 .50
14 Dwayne Newman .20 .50
15 Mark Barrow .20 .50
16 Adam Greener .20 .50
17 Face Off .08 .25
18 Goal Mouth Scramble .08 .25
19 Joe Watkins .20 .50
20 Michael Knights .20 .50
21 Jeff Daniels .20 .50
22 Team CL .02 .10

2003-04 UK Basingstoke Bison

COMPLETE SET (21) 4.00 10.00
1 Curtis Cruickshank .30 .75
2 Dean Skinns .30 .75
3 David Geris .30 .75
4 James Hutchinson .20 .50
5 Phil Roy .20 .50
6 Doug Schueller .20 .50
7 Kim Vahanen .20 .50
8 Joe Ciccarello .20 .50
9 Martin Filip .20 .50
10 Richard Hargreaves .20 .50
11 Darren Hurley .20 .50
12 Jaromir Kverka .20 .50
13 Steve Moria .20 .50
14 Blake Sorensen .20 .50
15 Shaun Thompson .20 .50
16 Nicky Watt .30 .75
17 Christian Widauer .20 .50
18 Chris Slater .20 .50
19 Luc Chabot .20 .50
20 Matt Reid .20 .50
21 Checklist .04 .10

2001-02 UK Belfast Giants

This 35-card set featured the Belfast Giants of the British Ice Hockey Superleague for the seasons of 2001-02 and 2002-03. Please note that card #13 was not produced.This set was produced by Armchair Sports in England.

COMPLETE SET (35) 8.00 20.00
1 Mike Bales .40 1.00
2 Terran Sandwith .30 .75
3 Dave Whistle CO .04 .10
4 Shane Johnson .30 .75
5 Colin Ward .30 .75
6 Kevin Riehl .30 .75
7 Rob Stewart .30 .75
8 Jason Ruff .30 .75
9 Sean Berens .30 .75
10 Jeff Hoad .30 .75
11 David Matsos .30 .75
12 Curtis Bowen .30 .75
14 Chad Allan .30 .75
15 Rod Stevens .30 .75
16 Paxton Schulte .40 1.00
17 Jason Bowen .40 1.00
18 Mark Cavallin .30 .75
19 Todd Kelman .30 .75
20 Checklist .04 .10
21 Tom Blatchford TR .04 .10
22 Redemption Card .04 .10
23 Shayne Toporowski .40 1.00
24 Derek Wilkinson .30 .75
25 Paul Ferone .30 .75
26 Todd Goodwin .30 .75
27 Kory Karlander .30 .75
28 Doug Searle .30 .75
29 Jerry Keefe .30 .75
30 Jason Wright .30 .75
31 Steve Roberts .30 .75
32 Mark Cavallin .30 .75
33 Mike Bales NM .40 1.00
34 Front Office .04 .10
35 Checklist .04 .10

2003-04 UK Belfast Giants

Unnumbered cards, listed in alphabetical order.

COMPLETE SET (19) 5.00 10.00
1 Sean Berens .20 .50
2 Curt Bowen .30 .75
3 Jason Bowen .20 .50
4 Mark Finney .20 .50
5 Leigh Jamieson .20 .50
6 Shane Johnson .20 .50
7 Todd Kelman .20 .50
8 Brad Kenny .20 .50
9 Gareth Martin .20 .50
10 Chris McGimpsey .30 .75
11 Mark Morrison .20 .50
12 Jason Ruff .20 .50
13 Colin Ryder .30 .75
14 Paul Sample .20 .50
15 Paxton Schulte .20 .50
16 Rob Stewart .20 .50
17 Grant Taylor .20 .50
18 Graeme Walton .20 .50
19 Colin Ward .20 .50

2004-05 UK Brent Bobyck Testimonial

COMPLETE SET (12) 2.00 5.00
COMMON CARD (1-12)
1 Brent Bobyck 1994-95 .20 .50
2 Brent Bobyck 1995-96 .20 .50
3 Brent Bobyck 1996-97 .20 .50
4 Brent Bobyck 1997-98 .20 .50
5 Brent Bobyck 1998-99 .20 .50
6 Brent Bobyck 1999-00 .20 .50
7 Brent Bobyck 2000-01 .20 .50
8 Brent Bobyck 2001-02 .20 .50
9 Brent Bobyck 2002-03 .20 .50
10 Brent Bobyck 2003-04 .20 .50
11 Brent Bobyck 2004-05 .20 .50
12 Brent Bobyck CL .04 .10

2000-01 UK Cardiff Devils

This set features the Devils of the British league. It is believed that this is an incomplete checklist and so is not priced in set form. If you know of additional singles, please contact us at hockeymag@beckett.com.

COMPLETE SET (14)
1 Derek Herlofsky .20 .50
2 Alan Schuler .20 .50
3 Vezio Sacratini .20 .50
4 Clayton Norris .20 .50
5 Rick Strachan .20 .50
6 John Parco .20 .50
7 Kip Noble .20 .50
8 Steve Thornton .20 .50
9 Denis Chasse .20 .50
10 Mike Ware .20 .50
11 Steve Moria .20 .50
12 Frank Evans .20 .50
13 Jonathan Phillips .20 .50
14 Ian McIntyre .20 .50

2001-02 UK Cardiff Devils

This set was produced by Armchair Sports in England.

COMPLETE SET (19) 5.00 10.00
1 Clayton Norris .30 .75
2 Rick Strachan .20 .50
3 Alan Schuler .20 .50
4 Kim Ahlroos .20 .50
5 John Parco .20 .50
6 Frank Evans .20 .50
7 Denis Chasse .40 1.00
8 Steve Thornton .30 .75
9 Dwight Parrish .20 .50
10 Steve Moria .20 .50
11 Jonathan Phillips .20 .50
12 Ian McIntyre .20 .50
13 Ivan Matulik .20 .50
14 Mike Ware .30 .75
15 Vezio Sacratini .20 .50
16 Steve Lyle .30 .75
17 Derek Herlofsky .40 1.00
18 Kip Noble .20 .50
19 Checklist .04 .10

2002-03 UK Cardiff Devils

This 19-card set featured the Cardiff Devils of the British Ice Hockey Superleague. Each card was numbered at the bottom of the card back. This set was available during home games.

COMPLETE SET (19) 5.00 10.00
1 Clayton Norris .20 .50
2 Rick Strachan .20 .50
3 Alan Schuler .20 .50
4 Kim Ahlroos .20 .50
5 John Parco .20 .50
6 Frank Evans .20 .50
7 Denis Chasse .40 1.00
8 Steve Thornton .30 .75
9 Dwight Parrish .20 .50
10 Steve Moria .20 .50
11 Jonathan Phillips .20 .50
12 Ian McIntyre .20 .50
13 Ivan Matulik .20 .50
14 Mike Ware .30 .75
15 Vezio Sacratini .20 .50
16 Stevie Lyle .30 .75
17 Derek Herlofsky .30 .75
18 Kip Noble .20 .50
19 Checklist .04 .10

2003-04 UK Cardiff Devils

COMPLETE SET (21) 5.00 10.00
1 Jason Cugnet .30 .75
2 Jeff Burgoyne .20 .50
3 Matt Myers .20 .50
4 Jason Stone .20 .50
5 David James .20 .50
6 Phil Manny .20 .50
7 Russ Romaniuk .40 1.00
8 Phil Hill .20 .50
9 Jonathan Phillips .20 .50
10 Jeff Brown .20 .50
11 Ivan Matulik .20 .50
12 Ed Patterson .20 .50
13 Mike Ware .30 .75
14 Vezio Sacratini .20 .50
15 Neil Francis .20 .50
16 James Manson .20 .50
17 Jason Becker .20 .50
18 Dennis Maxwell .20 .50
19 Doug McEwen .20 .50
20 Dave Whistle CO .04 .10
21 Checklist .04 .10

2002-03 UK Coventry Blaze

This 24-card set featured the Coventry Blaze of the Findus British National League. They were available at home games. Cards were unnumbered and are listed below in checklist order.

COMPLETE SET (24) 5.00 12.00
1 Greg Rockman .20 .50
2 Jody Lehman .20 .50
3 Steve Carpenter .20 .50
4 Alan Levers .20 .50
5 James Pease .20 .50
6 Andreas Moborg .20 .50
7 Mathias Soderstrom .20 .50
8 Adam Radmall .20 .50
9 Ron Shudra .30 .75
10 Shaun Johnson .20 .50
11 Steve Chartrand .20 .50
12 Kurt Irvine .20 .50
13 Russ Cowley .20 .50
14 Tom Watkins .20 .50
15 Ashley Tait .30 .75
16 Gareth Owens .20 .50
17 Joel Poirier .30 .75
18 Hilton Ruggles .20 .50
19 Lee Richardson .20 .50
20 Michael Tasker .20 .50
21 Paul Thompson CO .04 .10
22 Steve Small .04 .10
Phil Hadley
John Crook
23 Blaze Dancers .20 .50
24 Checklist .04 .10

2003-04 UK Coventry Blaze

COMPLETE SET (18) 5.00 12.00
1 Alan Levers .25 .60
2 Mathias Soderstrom .25 .60
3 Steve Carpenter .30 .75
4 Jody Lehman .25 .60
5 Steve O'Brien .25 .60
6 Steve Gallace .25 .60
7 Adam Radmall .25 .60
8 Shaun Johnson .25 .60
9 Graham Schlender .25 .60
10 Steve Chartrand .25 .60
11 Russ Cowley .25 .60
12 Tom Watkins .25 .60
13 Ashley Tait .30 .75
14 Gareth Owen .25 .60
15 Joel Poirier .30 .75
16 Hilton Ruggles .25 .60
17 Lee Richardson .25 .60
18 Michael Tasker .25 .60

2003-04 UK Coventry Blaze Calendars

COMPLETE SET (12) 5.00 10.00
1 Mathias Soderstrom .40 1.00
2 Ashley Tait .40 1.00
3 Steve Carpenter .40 1.00
4 Steve Chartrand .40 1.00
Shaun Johnson
5 Russ Cowley .40 1.00
Tom Watkins
6 Graham Schlender .40 1.00
7 Jody Lehman .40 1.00
8 Michael Tasker .40 1.00
Hilton Ruggles
9 Lee Richardson .40 1.00
Alan Levers
10 Joel Poirier .40 1.00
11 Garth Owen .40 1.00
Adam Radmall
12 Steve Gallace .40 1.00
Steve O'Brien

2003-04 UK Coventry Blaze History

COMPLETE SET (18) 5.00 10.00
1 Steve Chartrand .20 .50
2 Kurt Irvine .20 .50
3 Mathias Soderstrom .20 .50
4 Michael Tasker .20 .50
5 A.J. Kelham .20 .50
6 Hilton Ruggles .20 .50
7 Luc Chabot .20 .50
8 Paul Thompson CO .20 .50
9 Steve Carpenter .30 .75
10 Shaun Johnson .20 .50
11 Andrew McNiven .20 .50
12 Jody Lehman .30 .75
13 Justin George .20 .50
14 Claude Dumas .20 .50
15 Craig Chapman .20 .50
16 Stephen Cooper .30 .75
17 Mike Shewan .20 .50
18 Ron Shudra .30 .75

2004-05 UK Coventry Blaze

Produced by Cardtraders.co.UK.

COMPLETE SET (25) 5.00 10.00
1 Wade Belak .30 .75
2 Adam Brittle .20 .50
3 Adam Calder .20 .50
4 Tom Carlon .20 .50
5 Dan Carlson .20 .50
6 Luc Chabot ACO .04 .10
7 Russ Cowley .20 .50
8 Jody Lehman .20 .50
9 Neal Martin .20 .50
10 Chris McNamara .20 .50
11 Pavol Mihalik .20 .50
12 Andre Payette .20 .50
13 James Pease .20 .50
14 Joel Poirier .20 .50
15 Graham Schlender .20 .50
16 Doug Schueller .20 .50
17 Dan Shea .20 .50
18 Ashley Tait .30 .75
19 Paul Thompson CO .04 .10
20 Michal Vrabel .20 .50
21 Tom Watkins .20 .50
22 Nathanael Williams .20 .50
23 S.Small .20 .50
A.Henry
24 A.Buxton .20 .50
M.Cowley
25 Kix Kat MASCOT .04 .10

2004-05 UK Coventry Blaze Champions

COMPLETE SET (20) 5.00 10.00
1 Jody Lehman .30 .75
2 Dan Shea .20 .50
3 Wade Belak .40 1.00
4 Neal Martin .20 .50
5 Doug Schueller .20 .50
6 Pavol Mahalik .20 .50
7 Jozef Lukac .20 .50
8 James Pease .20 .50
9 Andre Payette .20 .50
10 Dan Carlson .20 .50
11 Graham Schlender .20 .50
12 Adam Calder .20 .50
13 Ashley Tait .30 .75
14 Joel Poirier .20 .50
15 Russ Cowley .20 .50
16 Chris McNamara .20 .50
17 Nathanael Williams .20 .50
18 Tom Watkins .20 .50
19 Card List .04 .10
20 Paul Thompson CO .20 .50

2006-07 UK Coventry Blaze

COMPLETE SET (20) 8.00 15.00
1 Neal Martin .30 .75
2 Joe Henry .30 .75
3 Reid Simonton .30 .75
4 Samy Nasreddine .30 .75
5 Tom Pease .30 .75
6 Barrie Moore .30 .75
7 Tom Watkins .30 .75
8 Ashley Tait .30 .75
9 James Pease .30 .75
10 Tom Carlon .30 .75
11 Adam Calder .30 .75
12 Dan Carlson .30 .75
13 Steve Fone .30 .75
14 Gareth Owen .30 .75
15 Trevor Koenig .30 .75
16 Danny Stewart .30 .75
17 Michael Wales .30 .75
18 Rumun Ndur .30 .75
19 Sylvain Cloutier .30 .75
20 Paul Thompson CO .30 .75

2007-08 UK Coventry Blaze

COMPLETE SET (43) 15.00 25.00
1 Hayden Laverick .30 .75
2 James Archer .30 .75
3 Josh Bruce .30 .75
4 Neal Martin .30 .75
5 Joe Henry .30 .75
6 Ryan Selwood .30 .75
7 James Cooke .30 .75
8 Tom Ledgard .30 .75
9 Scott Murray .30 .75
10 Ian Hunt .30 .75
11 Jonathan Weaver .30 .75
12 Russell Cowley .30 .75
13 Barrie Moore .30 .75
14 Tom Watkins .30 .75
15 James Pease .30 .75
16 Luke Curtis .30 .75
17 Chris Wilcox .30 .75
18 Adam Calder .30 .75
19 Dan Carlson .30 .75
20 Kieran Papps .30 .75
21 Steve Fone .30 .75
22 Stuart Dayton .30 .75
23 Dan Shea .30 .75
24 Trevor Koenig .30 .75
25 Aram Todd .30 .75
26 Danny Stewart .30 .75
27 Ollie Nabbs .30 .75
28 KC Timmons .30 .75
29 Matt Halford .30 .75
30 Tom Pease .30 .75
31 Scott Mulholland .30 .75
32 Rumun Ndur .30 .75
33 Tom Hooper .30 .75
34 Matt Soderstrom .30 .75
35 Michael Tasker .30 .75
36 Sylvain Cloutier .30 .75
37 Daniel Burgess .30 .75
38 Curtis Huppe .30 .75
39 David Vychodil .30 .75
40 Paul Thompson HC .02 .10
41 Luc Chabot AC .02 .10
42 Joel Poirier HC .02 .10
43 Reg Wilcox AC .02 .10

2001-02 UK Dundee Stars

This set was produced by Armchair Sports in England.

COMPLETE SET (18) 5.00 10.00
1 Checklist .04 .10
2 Nate Leslie .25 .60
3 Scott Young .25 .60
4 Tony Hand .30 .75
5 Paul Berrington .25 .60
6 Gary Dowd .25 .60
7 Teeder Wynne .25 .60
8 Mikko Inkinen .25 .60
9 Andrew Finlay .25 .60
10 Jan Mikel .25 .60
11 Craig Nelson .25 .60
12 Dominic Hopkins .25 .60
13 Stewart Rugg .25 .60
14 Patrick Lochi .25 .60
15 Stephen Murphy .25 .60
16 Slava Koulikov .25 .60
17 Martin Wiita .25 .60
18 Scott Kirton .25 .60

2002-03 UK Dundee Stars

This 18-card set was produced by cardtraders.co.uk to commerorate the champions of the 2001-02 British National League, the Dundee Stars. The sets were limited to a production run of 495 total.

COMPLETE SET (18) 5.00 10.00
1 Checklist .04 .10
2 Nate Leslie .25 .60
3 Scott Young .25 .60
4 Tony Hand .30 .75
5 Paul Berrington .25 .60
6 Gary Dowd .25 .60
7 Teeder Wynne .25 .60
8 Mikko Inkinen .25 .60
9 Andy Finlay .25 .60
10 Jan Mikel .25 .60
11 Craig Nelson .25 .60
12 Dominic Hopkins .25 .60
13 Stewart Rugg .25 .60
14 Patric Lochi .25 .60
15 Stephen Murphy .25 .60
16 Viatcheslav Koulikov .25 .60
17 Martin Wiita .25 .60
18 Scott Kirton .25 .60

2004-05 UK Edinburgh Capitals

Produced by Cardtraders.co.UK.

COMPLETE SET (18) 5.00 12.00
1 Jan Krajicek .30 .75
2 Mindraugas Kieras .40 1.00
3 Laurie Dunbar .30 .75
4 Steven Francey .30 .75
5 Marty Johnston .30 .75
6 Craig Wilson .30 .75
7 David Beatson .30 .75
8 Ross Hay .30 .75
9 Steven Lynch .30 .75
10 Daniel McIntyre .30 .75
11 Neil Hay .30 .75
12 Martin Cingel .30 .75
13 Dino Bauba .30 .75
14 David Trofimenkoff .40 1.00
15 Rastislav Bohme .30 .75
16 Miroslav Droppa .30 .75
17 Ryan Ford .40 1.00
18 Checklist .04 .10

2007-08 UK Edinburgh Capitals

COMPLETE SET (19) 7.00 15.00
1 Kyle Horne .40 1.00
2 Mark Garside .40 1.00
3 Jordan Steele .40 1.00
4 Ryan Crane .40 1.00
5 Colin Hemingway .40 1.00
6 Mark Wires .40 1.00
7 Neil Hay .40 1.00
8 Ross Dalgleish .40 1.00
9 Mike Stutzel .40 1.00
10 Adam Stefishen .40 1.00
11 Doug Christiansen .40 1.00
12 Martin Cingel .40 1.00
13 Dino Bauba .40 1.00
14 Mark Paterson .40 1.00
15 Iain Bowie .40 1.00
16 J.F. Perras .40 1.00
17 Ryan Ford .40 1.00
18 Patrik Luza .40 1.00
19 Ben O'Connor .40 1.00

2004-05 UK EIHL All-Stars

COMPLETE SET (18) 5.00 12.00
1 Jody Lehman .30 .75
2 Wade Belak .40 1.00
3 Neal Martin .20 .50
4 Tony Hand .40 1.00
5 Adam Calder .20 .50
6 Jon Cullen .20 .50
7 Martin Klempa .20 .50
8 Rob Davison .40 1.00
9 Dion Darling .20 .50
10 Dan Carlson .20 .50
11 George Awarda .20 .50
12 Vezio Sacratini .20 .50
13 Curtis Cruickshank .30 .75
14 Eric Cairns .40 1.00
15 Nick Boynton .40 1.00
16 Shawn Maltby .40 1.00
17 David Clarke .20 .50
18 Scott Nichol .40 1.00

1996-97 UK Fife Flyers

This set features the Flyers of Britain's top league. It was produced by the team and sold at home games.

COMPLETE SET (20) 5.00 12.00
1 Gavin Fleming .30 .75
2 John Reid .30 .75
3 Russ Parent .30 .75
4 Derek E. King .30 .75
5 Colin Grubb .30 .75
6 Colin Hamilton .30 .75
7 Andy Finlay .30 .75
8 Richard Dingwall .30 .75
9 Andy Samuel .30 .75
10 Wayne Maxwell .30 .75
11 Craig Wilson .30 .75
12 Daryl Venters .30 .75
13 Gordon Latto .30 .75
14 Richard Danskin .30 .75
15 Martin McKay .30 .75
16 Kyle Horne .30 .75
17 Mark Morrison CO .20 .50
18 Frank Morris .30 .75
19 Steven E. King .30 .75
20 Lee Mercer .30 .75

1997-98 UK Fife Flyers

This set features the Flyers of the British Ice Hockey League. The sets were sold by the team at its souvenir stands on game nights.

COMPLETE SET (20) 4.80 12.00
1 Team Photo .20 .50
2 Bernie McCrone .30 .75
3 Wayne Maxwell .30 .75
4 Derek E. King .30 .75
5 Mark Slater .30 .75
6 Bill Moody .30 .75
7 Lee Cowmedow .30 .75
8 Richard Charles .30 .75
9 Andy Finlay .30 .75
10 Daryl Venters .30 .75
11 Steven E. King .30 .75
12 Andy Samuel .30 .75
13 Gordon Latto .30 .75
14 Mark Morrison CO .20 .50
15 John Haig .30 .75
16 Lee Mercer .30 .75
17 Gary Wishart .30 .75
18 Colin Hamilton .30 .75
19 Frank Morris .30 .75
20 David Smith .30 .75

2001-02 UK Fife Flyers

This 12-card sticker set featured the Fife Flyors of the British National League. Each sticker was approximately 2"x 2" and were issued one per week during the season. A limited edition wall chart to affix the stickers to was also available. The stickers are not numbered and are listed below in order of the player's jersey number.

COMPLETE SET (12) 4.00 10.00
1 Shawn Silver .40 1.00
2 Derek King .40 1.00
3 Kyle Horner .40 1.00
4 Todd Dutiaume .40 1.00
5 Steven King .40 1.00
6 Mark Morrison .40 1.00
7 Mark Dutiaume .40 1.00
8 Gary Wishart .40 1.00
9 Iain Robertson .40 1.00
10 Karry Biette .40 1.00
11 Russell Monteith .40 1.00
12 Frank Morris .40 1.00

1994-95 UK Guildford Flames

This set features the Flames of the British Hockey League. The set was produced by Armchair Sports, an English card shop, and was sold by that store and the team on game nights.

COMPLETE SET (25) 4.00 10.00
1 Ben Challice .20 .50
2 Wayne Trunchion .20 .50
3 Terry Kurtenbach .20 .50
4 Fred Perlini .20 .50
5 Andy Sparks .20 .50
6 Rob Friesen .20 .50
7 Drew Chapman .20 .50
8 Kevin Parish .20 .50
9 John Noctor .20 .50
10 Ron Charbonneau GM .02 .10
11 Peter Morley .20 .50
12 Andy Allan .20 .50
13 Ryan Campbell .20 .50
14 Ronnie Evans-Harvey .20 .50
15 Paul Thompson .20 .50
16 Bill Rawles .20 .50
17 Nicky Landoli .20 .50
18 Elliott Andrews .20 .50
19 Dean Russell-Samways .20 .50
20 Home Kit .02 .10
21 Away Kit .02 .10
22 5 Imports .20 .50
23 3 Letters .02 .10
24 Spectrum .02 .10
25 Checklist .02 .10

1995-96 UK Guildford Flames

This set features the Flames of the British Hockey League. The set was produced by Armchair Sports, an English card shop, and was sold by that store and the team on game nights.

COMPLETE SET (30) 6.00 15.00
1 Dave Gregory .20 .50
2 Wayne Trunchion .20 .50
3 Andy Allan .20 .50
4 Terry Kurtenbach .20 .50
5 Ryan Campbell .20 .50
6 Fred Perlini .20 .50
7 Ronnie Evans-Harvey .20 .50
8 Andy Sparks .20 .50
9 Paul Thompson .20 .50
10 Nick Rothwell .20 .50
11 Drew Chapman .20 .50
12 Troy Kennedy .20 .50
13 Barrie Aisbitt .20 .50
14 Elliott Andrews .20 .50
15 Darrin Zinger .20 .50
16 Dean Russell-Samways .20 .50
17 Dave Graham .20 .50
18 Ivan Brown .20 .50
19 Home Kit .20 .50
20 Away Kit .20 .50
21 Spectrum .20 .50
22 Checklist .20 .50
23 Home Action .20 .50
24 Away Action .20 .50
25 P.C. Jim Bennett .20 .50
26 Terry Kurtenbach GOLD .20 .50
27 Paul Thompson GOLD .20 .50
28 Fred Perlini GOLD .20 .50
29 Future GOLD .20 .50
30 Celebration GOLD .20 .50

1996-97 UK Guildford Flames

This set features the Flames of the British Hockey League. The set was produced by Armchair Sports, an English card shop, and was sold by that store and the team on game nights.

COMPLETE SET (30) 5.00 12.00
1 John Wolfe .20 .50
2 Rob Lamey .20 .50
3 Wayne Crawford .20 .50
4 Terry Kurtenbach .20 .50
5 Ryan Campbell .20 .50
6 Fred Parlini .20 .50
7 Paul Thompson .20 .50
8 Mike Bettens .20 .50
9 Mark Finney .20 .50
10 Ryan Ferster .20 .50
11 Nick Cross .20 .50
12 Damian Smith .20 .50
13 Mike Mowbray .20 .50
14 Elliott Andrews .20 .50
15 Darrin Zinger .20 .50

16 Brad Kirkwood .20 .50
17 Derek DeCosty .20 .50
18 Mark Hazelhurst .20 .50
19 Lee Saunders .20 .50
20 Barrie Aisbitt .20 .50
21 Paul McCallion .20 .50
22 Valeri Vasie .20 .50
23 Goalies .20 .50
24 Capt. & Ast.Capt. .20 .50
25 Celebration .08 .25
26 Pep Talk .08 .25
27 Home Kit .08 .25
28 Away Kit .08 .25
29 Spectrum .08 .25
30 Training Staff .08 .25

1997-98 UK Guildford Flames

This set features the Flames of the British Hockey League. The set was produced by Armchair Sports, an English card shop, and was sold by that store and the team on game nights.

COMPLETE SET (30) 4.80 12.00
1 Peter Morley .20 .50
2 Rob Larney .30 .75
3 Andrew Hannah .30 .75
4 Joe Johnson .30 .75
5 Terry Kurtenbach .30 .75
6 Ryan Campbell .20 .50
7 Scott Adair .20 .50
8 Paul Thompson .20 .50
9 Ricky Plant .20 .50
10 Pete Kasowski .20 .50
11 Andrew Einhorn .20 .50
12 Bobby Brown .20 .50
13 Anthony Page .20 .50
14 Nick Rothwell .20 .50
15 Mike Harding .20 .50
16 Darrin Zinger .30 .75
17 Jamie Organ .20 .50
18 Barcley Pearce .20 .50
19 Simon Smith .20 .50
20 Russ Plant .20 .50
21 Stan Marple CO .02 .10
22 Home Kit .02 .10
23 Away Kit .02 .10
24 Dressing Room .02 .10
25 Capt. & Ast. Capt. .20 .50
26 Celebration .02 .10
27 Checklist .02 .10
28 Spectrum .02 .10
29 Sizzler .02 .10
30 Training Staff .02 .10

1998-99 UK Guildford Flames

This set features the Flames of the British Hockey League. The set was produced by Armchair Sports, an English card shop, and was sold by that store and the team on game nights.

COMPLETE SET (30) 4.00 10.00
1 Team CL .02 .10
2 Ryan Campbell .20 .50
3 Robin Davison .20 .50
4 Derek DeCosty .20 .50
5 Dominic Hopkins .20 .50
6 Simon Howard .20 .50
7 Kirk Humphreys .20 .50
8 Andy Johnston .20 .50
9 Rob Johnston .20 .50
10 Peter Kasowski .20 .50
11 Terry Kurtenbach .20 .50
12 Rob Lamey .20 .50
13 Adrian Lomonaco .20 .50
14 Sam Mager .20 .50
15 Stan Marple CO .02 .10
16 Brian Mason .20 .50
17 Peter Morley .20 .50
18 Jamey Organ .20 .50
19 Barcley Pearce .20 .50
20 Andy Pickles .20 .50
21 Greg Randall .20 .50
22 Sizzler MASCOT .02 .10
23 Simon Smith .20 .50
24 Scott Stephenson .20 .50
25 Paul Thompson .20 .50
26 Captain & Assistants .02 .10
27 GB Uniform .02 .10
28 Trophies .02 .10
29 Home Kit .02 .10
30 Away Kit .02 .10

1999-00 UK Guildford Flames

This set features the Flames of the British Hockey League. The set was produced by Armchair Sports, an English card shop, and was sold by that store and the team on game nights.

COMPLETE SET (30) 4.00 10.00
1 Team CL .02 .10
2 Biette, Crombie, Dixon .20 .50
3 Team Photo (home) .20 .50
4 Team Photo (away) .20 .50
5 Celebration .02 .10
6 Karry Biette .20 .50
7 Tom Brown .20 .50
8 Ryan Campbell .20 .50
9 Gary Clark .20 .50
10 Chris Crombie .20 .50
11 Derek Decosty .20 .50
12 Paul Dixon .20 .50
13 GB Uniform .02 .10
14 Patrick Flanagan .20 .50
15 Dominic Hopkins .20 .50
16 Simon Howard .20 .50
17 Adrian Jenkinson TR .02 .10
18 Peter Kasowski .20 .50
19 Grant King .20 .50
20 Rob Lamey .20 .50
21 James Manson .20 .50
22 Stan Marple CO .02 .10
23 Stan Marple CO .02 .10
24 Jamey Organ .20 .50
25 Barcley Pearce .20 .50
26 Rick Plant .20 .50
27 Russ Plant .20 .50
28 Sizzlers MASCOT .02 .10
29 Jamie Thompson .20 .50
30 Mike Urquhart ACO .02 .10

2000-01 UK Guildford Flames

This set features the Bison of the British Hockey League. The set was produced by Armchair Sports, an English card shop, and was sold by that store and the team.

COMPLETE SET (30) 4.00 10.00
1 Karry Biette .14 .40
2 Tom Brown .14 .40
3 Ryan Campbell .14 .40
4 Scott Campbell .14 .40
5 Wayne Crawford .14 .40
6 Chris Crombie .14 .40
7 Derek DeCosty .14 .40
8 Paul Dixon .14 .40
9 John Haig .14 .40
10 Adrian Jenkinson TR .10 .25
11 Jason Jennings .14 .40
12 Grant King .14 .40
13 Rob Lamey .14 .40
14 Stan Marple CO .10 .25
15 Stan Marple CO .10 .25
16 Mark McArthur .20 .50
17 Tyrone Miller .14 .40
18 Jason Moses .14 .40
19 Barcley Pearce .14 .40
20 Ricky Plant .14 .40
21 Sizzler MASCOT .10 .25
22 Jason Stone .14 .40
23 David Smith .14 .40
24 Mike Urquhart .14 .40
25 Team Photo (home) .14 .40
26 Team Photo (away) .14 .40
27 Captain & Assistants .14 .40
28 Home Grown .14 .40
29 Celebration .10 .25
30 Logo Card .10 .25

2001-02 UK Guildford Flames

This team set was produced to honor Guildford's tenth anniversary season. The set was co-sponsored by the Surrey Police Department and was available at Flames' home games. The cards were unnumbered and are listed below in checklist order.

COMPLETE SET (30) 5.00 12.00
1 Checklist .04 .10
2 Mark McArthur .30 .75
3 Michael Plenty .20 .50
4 Stan Marple .20 .50
5 Regan Stocco .20 .50
6 Derek DeCosty .20 .50
7 Todd Wetzel .20 .50
8 Ricky Plant .20 .50
9 John Haig .20 .50
10 Tony Redmond .20 .50
11 Paul Dixon .20 .50
12 Grant King .30 .75
13 Greg Burke .20 .50
14 Scott Campbell .20 .50
15 Nicky Chinn .30 .75
16 Mark Galazzi .20 .50
17 David Smith .20 .50
18 Jason Dailey .20 .50
19 Michael Timms .20 .50
20 Mikko Koivunoro .20 .50
21 Stan Marple HCO .04 .10
22 Mike Urquhart ACO .04 .10
23 Adrian Jenkinson TR .04 .10
24 Paul Dixon .20 .50
Derek DeCosty
Nicky Chinn
25 Team Photo Home .20 .50
26 Team Photo Away .20 .50
27 Sizzler MASCOT .04 .10
28 Jason Dailey .20 .50
Celebration
29 Trophies .04 .10
30 Mark McArthur .20 .50
Grant King

2002-03 UK Guildford Flames

This 30-card set featured players from the Guildford Flames of the Bristish National League. The cards were available at home games. The cards were not numbered and were listed below in checklist order.

COMPLETE SET (30) 5.00 12.00
1 Ian Herbers .20 .50
2 Stan Marple HCO .20 .50
3 David Clarke .20 .50
4 Derek DeCosty .20 .50
5 Craig Lyons .20 .50
6 Ricky Plant .20 .50
7 Tony Redmond .20 .50
8 Paul Dixon .20 .50
9 Jason Lafreniere .30 .75
10 Jason Bowen .20 .50
11 Grant King .20 .50
12 Mike Torchia .30 .75
13 Corey Lyons .20 .50
14 Nicky Chinn .30 .75
15 Jeff White .20 .50
16 Mark Galazzi .20 .50
17 Ricky Skene .20 .50
18 Mike Urquhart ACO .04 .10
19 Stan Marple HCO .04 .10
20 Adrian Jenkinson TR .04 .10
21 Paul Dixon .20 .50
Corey Lyons
Jason Lafreniere
22 Team Photo .20 .50
Home
23 Team Photo .20 .50
Away
24 Team Photo .20 .50
Alternate
25 Sizzler MASCOT .04 .10
26 Grant King .30 .75
Mike Torchia
27 Ricky Plant GB .20 .50
28 David Clarke GB .20 .50
29 Andy Sparks .20 .50
Fred Perlini
Ryan Campbell
Retired Numbers
30 Checklist .04 .10

2003-04 UK Guildford Flames

COMPLETE SET (30) 5.00 12.00
1 Header Card .04 .10
2 Peter Michnac .20 .50
3 Stan Marple .20 .50
4 Marian Smerciak .20 .50
5 Neil Liddiard .20 .50
6 Ryan Vince .20 .50
7 Ricky Plant .30 .75
8 Michael Timms .20 .50
9 Tony Redmond .20 .50
10 Milos Melicherik .20 .50
11 Paul Dixon .20 .50
12 Rastislav Palov .20 .50
13 Jozef Kohut .20 .50
14 Joe Dollin .20 .50
15 Stevie Lyle .40 1.00
16 Peter Konder .20 .50
17 Mark Galazzi .20 .50
18 Nick Cross .20 .50
19 Paul Dixon ACO .04 .10
20 Stan Marple HCO .04 .10
21 Dave Wiggins AM .04 .10
22 Captains & Assistants .20 .50
23 Home Kit .04 .10
24 Away Kit .04 .10
25 Mascot .04 .10
26 Action Card .04 .10
27 Flames Goalies .30 .75
28 Flames Eastern Europeans .20 .50
29 British Line .30 .75
30 Ricky Plant .20 .50
Leading British Points

2004-05 UK Guildford Flames

Produced by the team and available through the team's store and Armchair Sports.

COMPLETE SET (30) 5.00 12.00
1 Guildford Flames .04 .10
2 Peter Michnac .20 .50
3 Neil Liddiard .20 .50
4 Marian Smerciak .20 .50
5 David Savage .20 .50
6 Jason Reilly .20 .50
7 Stuart Potts .20 .50
8 Adam Walker .20 .50
9 Milos Melicherik .20 .50
10 Paul Dixon .20 .50
11 Andrew Hemmings .20 .50
12 Rastislav Palov .20 .50
13 Dusan Pohorelec .20 .50
14 Jozef Kohut .20 .50
15 Simon Lavis .20 .50
16 Miroslav Bielik .20 .50
17 Tom Annetts .20 .50
18 Peter Konder .20 .50
19 Nick Cross .20 .50
20 Paul Dixon .20 .50
21 Stan Marple CO .04 .10
22 Dave Wiggin ACO .04 .10
23 Captains and Assistants .20 .50
24 Home Jersey Team Photo .04 .10
25 Away Jersey Team Photo .04 .10
26 Sizzler MASCOT .04 .10
27 Celebration .04 .10
28 Netminders .30 .75
29 Playoff Trophy .04 .10
30 Terry Kurtenbach JSY RET .20 .50

2006-07 UK Guildford Flames

COMPLETE SET (24) 8.00 15.00
1 Neil Liddiard .25 .60
2 Marian Smerciak .25 .60
3 David Savage .25 .60
4 Ben Johnson .25 .60
5 Rob Lamey .25 .60
6 Stuart Potts .25 .60
7 Andrew Hemmings .25 .60
8 Rick Plant .25 .60
9 Robert Young .25 .60
10 Ben Duggan .25 .60
11 Milos Melicherik .25 .60
12 Paul Dixon .25 .60
13 Vaclav Zavoral .25 .60
14 Simon James .25 .60
15 Joe Watkins .40 1.00
16 Tom Annetts .40 1.00
17 Chris Wiggins .25 .60
18 Ben Austin .25 .60
19 Jozef Kohut .25 .60
20 Adam Hyman .25 .60
21 Rick Skene .25 .60
22 Ollie Bronniman .25 .60
23 Stan Marple .25 .60
24 Paul Dixon .25 .60

2007-08 UK Guildford Flames

COMPLETE SET (22) 7.00 15.00
1 Neil Liddiard .30 .75
2 David Savage .30 .75
3 Ben Johnson .30 .75
4 Rob Lamey .30 .75
5 Stuart Potts .30 .75
6 Rick Plant .30 .75
7 Ben Duggan .30 .75
8 Terry Miles .30 .75
9 Milos Melicherik .30 .75
10 Paul Dixon .30 .75
11 Vaclav Zavoral .30 .75
12 Dominic Hopkins .30 .75
13 Joe Watkins .60 1.50
14 Alexander Mettam .30 .75
15 Lukas Smital .30 .75
16 Ben Austin .30 .75
17 Jozef Kohut .30 .75
18 Nick Cross .30 .75
19 Rick Skene .30 .75
20 Taras Foremsky .30 .75
21 Ollie Bronnimann .30 .75
22 Paul Dixon HC .10 .25

1999-00 UK Hull Thunder

This set features the Thunder of the British league. The set was produced by card shop Armchair Sports and was sold at the store and at home games. The print run has been confirmed at 500 sets.

COMPLETE SET (20) 4.00 10.00
1 Team CL .02 .10
2 Don Depoe CO .08 .25
3 Ian Defty .20 .50
4 Simon Greaves .20 .50
5 Mark Florence .20 .50
6 Dan Carney .20 .50
7 Stephen Johnson .20 .50
8 Anthony Johnson .20 .50
9 Scott Stephenson .20 .50
10 Tam Watkins .20 .50
11 Paul Thompson .20 .50
12 Jason Tatarnic .20 .50
13 Mark Pallister .20 .50
14 Ron Shudra .20 .50
15 Pasi Raitanen .30 .75
16 Steve Morden .20 .50
17 Slava Koulikov .20 .50
18 Steve Brown .20 .50
19 Chris Douglas .20 .50
20 Chris Bailey .20 .50

2001-02 UK Hull Thunder

Produced and sold by Armchair Sports, a British card shop, this 25-card set was sold at that shop and also at Thunder home games. The total print run has been confirmed at only just sets.

COMPLETE SET (25) 4.00 10.00
1 Checklist .04 .10
2 Mike Bishop CO .04 .10
3 Stephen Foster .20 .50
4 Andy Moffat .20 .50
5 Mike Bishop .20 .50
6 Corey Lyons .20 .50
7 Andy Munroe .20 .50
8 Mark Florence .20 .50
9 Stephen Johnson .20 .50
10 Anthony Johnson .20 .50
11 Anthony Payne .20 .50
12 Ryan Lake .20 .50
13 Karl Hopper UER .20 .50
14 Michael Bowman .20 .50
15 Stephen Wallace .20 .50
16 Ian Defty .20 .50
17 Oleg Synkov .20 .50
18 Steve Smillie .20 .50
19 Rob McCaig .20 .50
20 Darren Houghton .20 .50
21 Daryl Lavoie .20 .50
22 Eric Lavigne .20 .50
23 Mike O'Connor GM .04 .10
24 Terry Ward ACO .04 .10
25 Vanessa Brown TR .04 .10

2002-03 UK Hull Thunder

This 25-card set featured the Hull Thunder of the British National League. This set was produced by Armchair Sports and was available through them or the club shops on game nights.

COMPLETE SET (25) 5.00 12.00
1 Checklist .04 .10
2 Mike Bishop HCO .04 .10
3 Stephen Foster .20 .50
4 Keith Leyland .20 .50
5 Anthony Payne .20 .50
6 Scott Young .20 .50
7 Nathan Hunt .20 .50
8 Paul Ferone .20 .50
9 Andy Munroe .20 .50
10 Mark Florence .20 .50
11 Paul Wallace .20 .50
12 Mike Morin .20 .50
13 Ryan Lake .20 .50
14 Karl Hopper .20 .50
15 Mark Bultje .20 .50
16 Jonathan Weaver .20 .50
17 Steve Smillie .20 .50
18 Dominic Parlatore .20 .50
19 Dan Currie .30 .75
20 Sam Roberts .20 .50
21 Eoin McInerney .40 1.00
22 Marc West .20 .50
23 Mike Bishop .20 .50
24 Eric Lavigne .30 .75
25 Mike O'Connor GM .04 .10

1993-94 UK Humberside Hawks

This postcard set commemorates a now-defunct club in the British Ice Hockey League. The set was sponsored by BAE Aerospace and was given away during the season on game nights.

COMPLETE SET (18) 6.00 15.00
1 Kenny Johnson .40 1.00
2 Gavin De Jonge .40 1.00
3 Chris Hobson .40 1.00
4 Mike Bishop .40 1.00
6 Paul Simpson .40 1.00
7 Stewart Carvil .40 1.00
8 Shaun Johnson .40 1.00
9 Arren Burn .40 1.00
10 Stephen Johnson .40 1.00
12 Anthony Johnson .40 1.00
15 Anthony Payne .40 1.00
16 Andy Giles .40 1.00
17 Mike O'Conner .40 1.00
19 Andy Steel .40 1.00
20 Frank Killen .40 1.00
21 Dan Dorian .40 1.00
23 Alexander Koulikov .40 1.00
NNO Peter Johnson CO .40 1.00

1994-95 UK Humberside Hawks

This postcard set commemorates a now-defunct club in the British Ice Hockey League. The set was sponsored by BAE Aerospace and was given away during the season on game nights.

COMPLETE SET (20) 8.00 20.00
2 Malcolm Bell .40 1.00
4 Mike Bishop .40 1.00
5 Scott Young .40 1.00
6 Paul Simpson .40 1.00
8 Shaun Johnson .40 1.00
9 Wayne Anchikoski .60 1.50
10 Stephen Johnson .40 1.00
12 Anthony Johnson .40 1.00
14 Tony Saxby .40 1.00
15 Darcy Cahill .40 1.00
16 Chris Hobson .40 1.00
17 Danny Parkin .40 1.00
19 Scott Morrison .40 1.00
20 Danny Thompson .40 1.00
21 Paul Cast .40 1.00
22 Andy Port .40 1.00
23 Dominik Love .40 1.00
NNO Peter Johnson CO .20 .50
NNO Gavin De Jonge .40 1.00
NNO David Standling .40 1.00

2002-03 UK Ivan Matulik Testimonial

Set features prominent UK star Ivan Matulik, with one card for each season he played in England.

COMPLETE SET (12) 2.00 5.00
1 Header .20 .50
2 Sheffield Steelers .20 .50
3 Murrayfield Racers .20 .50
4 Cardiff Devils .20 .50
5 Cardiff Devils .20 .50
6 Cardill Devils .20 .50
7 Cardiff Devils .20 .50
8 Cardiff Devils .20 .50
9 Cardiff Devils .20 .50
10 Manchester Storm .20 .50
11 Manchester Storm .20 .50
12 Cardiff Devils .20 .50

1998-99 UK Kingston Hawks

This set features the Hawks of the British league. The set was produced by Armchair Sports, a local card shop, and sold at that store and at home games. The print run has been confirmed at 500 sets.

COMPLETE SET (25) 4.00 10.00
1 Dale Lambert CO .15 .40
2 Ian Defty .15 .40
3 Mikka Pynnonen .20 .50
4 Simon Greaves .15 .40
5 Kelly Reed .15 .40
6 Dominic Love .20 .50
7 Bjorn Widmark .20 .50
8 Steve Nemeth .20 .50
9 Christer Widmark .20 .50
10 Stephen Johnson .15 .40
11 Mark Florence .15 .40
12 Anthony Payne .15 .40
13 Chris Hobson .15 .40
14 Mark McCoy .20 .50
15 Andy Steel .15 .40
16 Paddy O'Conner .15 .40
17 Ashley Tait .15 .40
18 Matt Staunton .15 .40
19 Pasi Raitanen .20 .50
20 Jason Coles .15 .40
21 Simon Leach .15 .40
22 Lucas Miller .15 .40
23 Michael Tasker .15 .40
24 Keith Milhench GM .02 .10
25 Team CL .02 .10

1997-98 UK Kingston Hawks Stickers

Produced by the team owner, this 20-sticker set came with a wall chart and the stickers could be bought as a set or singles.

COMPLETE SET (20) 4.80 12.00
1 Keith Milhench CO .08 .25
2 Bobby McEwen ACO .08 .25
3 Malcolm Bell .30 .75
4 Michael Knights .30 .75
5 Paul Simpson .30 .75
6 Kelly Reid .30 .75
7 Dominic Love .30 .75
8 Phil Brook .30 .75
9 Anthony Payne .30 .75
10 Chris Hobson .30 .75
11 Steve Smillie .30 .75
12 Andy Steel .30 .75
13 Ashley Tait .30 .75
14 Slava Koulikov .30 .75
15 Norman Pinnington .30 .75
16 Tony McAleavy .30 .75
17 Pasi Raitinen .30 .75
18 The Kingston Kid .08 .25
19 Ian Defty .30 .75
20 Michael Tasker .30 .75

2000-01 UK Kudos ISL

COMPLETE SET (169) 12.00 30.00
1 Ice Hockey Superleague .10 .30
2 Jim Lynch .10 .30
3 Paul Heavey .10 .30
4 Philippe Derouville .10 .30
5 Colin Ryder .10 .30
6 Trevor Doyle .10 .30
7 Derek Eberle .10 .30
8 Anders Hillstorm .10 .30
9 Jan Mikel .10 .30
10 Johan Silfwerplatz .10 .30
11 Scott Young .10 .30
12 Dainius Bauyba .10 .30
13 Cam Bristow .10 .30
14 Shawn Bryam .10 .30
15 Ed Courtenay .10 .30
16 Tony Hand .10 .30
17 Rhett Gordon .10 .30
18 Mike Harding .10 .30
19 Mark Montanari .10 .30
20 Jonathon Weaver .10 .30
21 Teeder Wynne .10 .30
22 Dave Whistle .10 .30
23 Mark Cavallin .10 .30
24 Todd Kelman .10 .30
25 Kevin Riehl .10 .30
26 Paxton Schulte .10 .30
27 Colin Ward .10 .30
28 Jeff Hoad .10 .30
29 Shane Johnson .10 .30
30 Enio Sacilotto .10 .30
31 Brian Greer .10 .30
32 Joe Watkins .10 .30
33 Matej Bukna .10 .30
34 Jimmy Drolet .10 .30
35 Jason Mansoff .10 .30
36 Mark Matier .10 .30
37 Steve O'Rourke .10 .30
38 Reid Simonton .10 .30
39 Brent Bobyck .10 .30
40 Chris Brant .10 .30
41 Mark Bultje .10 .30
42 Joe Cardarelli .10 .30
43 Dan Ceman .10 .30
44 Joe Ciccarello .10 .30
45 Darren Hurley .10 .30
46 Blaxe Knox .10 .30
47 Stephane Roy .10 .30
48 Bard Wingfield .10 .30
49 Doug McCarthy .10 .30
50 Troy Walkington .10 .30
51 Stevie Lyle .10 .30
52 Derek Herlofsky .10 .30
53 Frank Evans .10 .30
54 Kip Noble .10 .30
55 Claton Norris .10 .30
56 Dwight Parrish .10 .30
57 Alan Schuler .10 .30
58 Rick Strachan .10 .30
59 Denis Chasse .10 .30
60 James Hanlon .10 .30
61 Rick Kowalsky .10 .30
62 Ivan Matulik .10 .30
63 Ian Macintyre .10 .30
64 Steve Moria .10 .30
65 John Parco .10 .30
66 Vezio Sacratini .10 .30
67 Steve Thornton .10 .30
68 Mike Ware .10 .30
69 Chris McSorley .10 .30
70 Trevor Robins .10 .30
71 Shawn Silver .10 .30
72 Rich Bronilla .10 .30
73 Martin Neal .10 .30
74 Randy Perry .10 .30
75 Mikael Tjallden .10 .30
76 Nicky Chinn .10 .30
77 Pat Ferschweiler .10 .30
78 Claude Jutras .10 .30
79 Mikko Koivynoro .10 .30
80 Mark Kolesar .10 .30
81 Jay Neal .10 .30
82 Ryan Richardson .10 .30
83 Paul Rushforth .10 .30
84 David Vallieres .10 .30
85 Darby Walker .10 .30
86 Brendan Yarema .10 .30
87 Terry Cristensen .10 .30
88 Daryl Lipsey .10 .30
89 Frank Pietrangelo .10 .30
90 Dave Trofimenkoff .10 .30
91 Curtis Bowen .10 .30
92 Matt Eldred .10 .30
93 Perry Johnson .10 .30
94 Troy Neumeier .10 .30
95 Rob Robinson .10 .30
96 Blair Scott .10 .30
97 Pierre Allard .10 .30
98 Kevin Brown .10 .30
99 Greg Bullock .10 .30
100 Doug Doull .10 .30
101 Marty Flichel .10 .30
102 Trevor Gallant .10 .30
103 Jason Glover .10 .30
104 Mike Morin .10 .30
105 Corey Spring .10 .30
106 Shyne Stevenson .10 .30
107 Rob Trumbly .10 .30
108 Jukka Jalonen .10 .30
109 Jimmy Hibbert .10 .30
110 Tommi Satosaari .10 .30
111 Craig Binns .10 .30
112 Santeri Immonen .10 .30
113 Arttu Kaykho .10 .30
114 Miroslav Mosnar .10 .30
115 Darren Mcausland .10 .30
116 Rob Wilson .10 .30
117 Tero Arkiomaa .10 .30
118 Louis Bedard .10 .30
119 Tomas Kupka .10 .30
120 Matt Oates .10 .30
121 Joel Poirer .10 .30
122 Timo Salonen .10 .30
123 Tommi Sova .10 .30
124 Alex Dampier .10 .30
125 Edin Mcinerney .10 .30
126 Willis Jordan .10 .30
127 Greg Burke .10 .30
128 Ryan Gillis .10 .30
129 Eric Lavigne .10 .30
130 Daryl Lavoie .10 .30
131 Jim Paek .10 .30
132 Duncan Paterson .10 .30
133 Pierre Claude Drouin .10 .30
134 Graham Garden .10 .30
135 Greg Hadden .10 .30
136 Jamie Leach .10 .30
137 Daryl Moxam .10 .30
138 Barry Nieckar .10 .30
139 David Struch .10 .30
140 Ashley Tait .10 .30
141 Randall Weber .10 .30
142 Mike Blaisdell .10 .30
143 Mike O'Neill .10 .30
144 Steve Carpenter .10 .30
145 Shayne McCosh .10 .30
146 Jeff Sebastian .10 .30
147 Kayle Short .10 .30
148 Adam Smith .10 .30
149 Dennis Vial .10 .30
150 Scott Allison .10 .30
151 Paul Beraldo .10 .30
152 Rick Brebant .10 .30
153 Dale Craigwell .10 .30
154 David Longstaff .10 .30
155 Scott Metcalfe .10 .30
156 Warren Norris .10 .30
157 Steve Roberts .10 .30
158 Kent Simpson .10 .30
159 Jason Weaver .10 .30
160 Brent Bobyck .10 .30
161 Ayr Scottish Eagles .02 .10
162 Belfast Giants .02 .10
163 Bracknell Bees .02 .10
164 Bt Cardif Devils .02 .10
165 London Knights .02 .10
166 Manchester Storm .02 .10
167 Newcastle Jesters .02 .10
168 Nottingham Panthers .02 .10
169 Sheffield Steelers .02 .10

1999-00 UK London Knights

This postcard sized set features the Knights of the top British league. The set was produced by Armchair Sports and sold by that card shop, as well as by the team at home games.

COMPLETE SET (17) 3.60 9.00
1 Tom Ashe .20 .50
2 Mark Bultje .20 .50
3 John Byce .30 .75
4 Scott Campbell .20 .50
5 Mark Cavallin .30 .75
6 Ryan Duthie .20 .50
7 Jeff Hoad .20 .50
8 Marc Hussey .30 .75
9 Guy Leveque .20 .50
10 Neal Martin .20 .50
11 Chris McSorley CO .20 .50
12 Tim Murray .20 .50
13 Scott Rex CO .08 .25
14 Paul Rushforth .20 .50
15 Claudio Scremin .30 .75
16 Mike Ware .30 .75
17 Todd Wetzel .20 .50

2001-02 UK London Knights

This set was produced by Armchair Sports in England.

COMPLETE SET (34) 5.00 12.00
1 Logo and Checklist .04 .10
2 Doug Serle .20 .50
3 Gerald Adams .20 .50
4 Kim Ahlroos .20 .50
5 Sean Blanchard .20 .50
6 Trevor Roenick .30 .75
7 David Struch .20 .50
8 Dave Clark .20 .50
9 Nathan Leslie .20 .50
10 Maurizio Mansi .20 .50
11 Steve Thornton .20 .50
12 Mark Kolesar .20 .50
14 Mike Barrie .20 .50
15 Greg Burke .20 .50
16 Bob Leslie HCO .04 .10
17 Ian McIntyre .20 .50
18 Ritchie Bronilla .20 .50
19 Vezio Sacratini .20 .50
20 Trevor Robins .20 .50
21 Jason Ellery EQM .04 .10
22 Mike Ware .20 .50
23 Rob Donovan .20 .50
24 David Trofimenkoff .20 .50
25 Dominic Amodeo .30 .75
26 Scott Bailey .30 .75
27 Paul Rushforth .20 .50
28 Mighty Knight MASCOT .04 .10
29 Dave Struch .20 .50
Mark Kolesar
30 Vez .20 .50
Mo
Dom
31 London Knights Logo .04 .10
32 Mark Kolesar .20 .50
Mike Barrie
33 Rob Donovan .20 .50
Mo Mansi
34 Ian McIntyre .20 .50
Dave Trofimenkoff
35 Mo Mansi .20 .50
Sue Chetham

2002-03 UK London Knights

This set was produced by Armchair Sports in England.

COMPLETE SET (24) 5.00 10.00
1 Checklist .04 .10
2 Ake Lilljebjorn .20 .50
3 Gerald Adams .20 .50
4 Kim Ahlroos .20 .50
5 Nathan Leslie .20 .50
6 Moe Mansi .20 .50
7 Mark Kolesar .30 .75
8 A.J. Kelham .20 .50
9 Jeff Hoad .20 .50
10 Chris Slater .20 .50
11 Ian McIntyre .20 .50
12 Greg Burke .20 .50
13 Steve Aronson .20 .50
14 Rich Bronilla .20 .50
15 Vezio Sacratini .20 .50
16 Dave Trofimenkoff .30 .75
17 Paul Rushforth .20 .50
18 Sean Blanchard .30 .75
19 Dennis Maxwell .30 .75
20 Ed Patterson .30 .75
21 Bob Leslie CO .04 .10
22 Mighty Knight .04 .10
23 Jim Brithen CO .04 .10
24 Jason Ellery EQM .04 .10

2003-04 UK London Racers

COMPLETE SET (20) 5.00 10.00
1 Chris Bailey .20 .50
2 Noel Burkitt .20 .50
3 Nick Burton .20 .50
4 Lukas Filip .20 .50
5 Kalle Konsti .20 .50
6 Zoran Kozic .20 .50
7 Evan Lindsay .30 .75
8 Marc Long .20 .50
9 Mike McKinnon .20 .50
10 Brian McLaughlin .20 .50
11 Sean Murdoch .20 .50
12 Mojmir Musil .20 .50
13 Oscar MASCOT .04 .10
14 Jason Robinson .20 .50
15 Mark Scott .20 .50
16 Jani Touminen .20 .50
17 Warren Tait .20 .50
18 Matt Van der Velden .30 .75
19 Erik Zachrisson .20 .50

2004-05 UK London Racers Playoffs

COMPLETE SET (18) 6.00 15.00
1 Eric Cairns .60 1.50
2 Joe Ciccarello .30 .75
3 Jeremy Cornish .30 .75
4 Adam Dobson .40 1.00
5 Matt Foord .30 .75
6 Mark Gouett .30 .75
7 Richard Hargreaves .30 .75
8 Jason Hewitt .30 .75
9 Denis Ladouceur .30 .75
10 Dennis Maxwell .30 .75
11 J.J. McGrath .30 .75
12 Ian McIntyre .30 .75
13 Steve Moria .30 .75
14 Scott Nichol .60 1.50
15 Jason Robinson .30 .75
16 Mark Thomas .30 .75
17 Jim Vickers .30 .75
18 Joe Watkins .30 .75

2003-04 UK Manchester Phoenix

COMPLETE SET (22) 5.00 10.00
1 Jayme Platt .30 .75
2 Rick Brebant .20 .50
3 Dave Clancy .30 .75
4 Dwight Parrish .20 .50
5 Mike Lankshear .20 .50
6 Mark Thomas .20 .50
7 Carl Greenhous .20 .50
8 Mark Bultje .20 .50
9 David Kozier .20 .50
10 Mike Morin .20 .50
11 Petteri Lotila .20 .50
12 Chad Brandimore .20 .50
13 George Awada .20 .50
14 Marc Lovell .20 .50
15 Jason Hewitt .20 .50
16 Aaron Davies .20 .50
17 Darcy Anderson .20 .50
18 Mika Skytta .20 .50
19 Jeff Sebastian .20 .50
20 Nick Poole .20 .50
21 Manace MASCOT .04 .10
NNO Checklist .04 .10
NNO Checklist .04 .10

2001-02 UK Manchester Storm

Produced by Cardtraders.com, this 24-card set was available at Storm home games. The production run was limited to just 495 sets. Card #13 was not printed for superstitious reasons. Card #24 card was redeemable for a limited edition 12"x12" team card that was individually serial-numbered to 125.

COMPLETE SET (24) 4.80 12.00
1 Paul Ferone .20 .50
2 Dan Preston .20 .50
3 Trevor Gallant .20 .50
4 Mike Morin .20 .50
5 Dwight Parrish .20 .50
6 Mark Bultje .20 .50
7 Joe Busillo .20 .50
8 Ivan Matulik .20 .50
9 Pierre Allard .20 .50
10 Russ Romaniuk .20 .50
11 Joe Cardarelli .20 .50
12 Stevie Lyle .30 .75
14 Mike Torchia .40 1.00
15 Kayle Short .20 .50
16 Justin Hocking .30 .75
17 Kris Miller .20 .50
18 Russ Richardson .20 .50
19 Daryl Lipsey HCO .04 .10
20 Mike Torchia .30 .75
21 Stevie Lyle .30 .75
22 Lightning Jack MASCOT .04 .10
23 Rob Wilson .04 .10
24 Redemption Card .04 .10
25 Checklist .04 .10

2001-02 UK Manchester Storm Retro

This 21-card set featured some of the most popular players from the history of the Manchster Storm of the British Ice Hockey Superleague. Cards are not numbered and are listed below by jersey number.

COMPLETE SET (21) 5.00 10.00
1 Dale Jago .20 .50
2 Craig Woodcroft .20 .50
3 Trevor Gallant .20 .50
4 Kelly Askew .20 .50
5 Jeff Tomlinson .20 .50
6 Daryl Lipsey .20 .50
7 Mike Morin .20 .50
8 Shawn Byram .20 .50
9 Pierre Allard .20 .50
10 Mark Bernard .20 .50
11 John Finnie .20 .50
12 Blair Scott .20 .50

13 Hilton Ruggles .20 .50
14 David Trofimenkoff .20 .50
15 Jim Hrivnak .30 .75
16 Frank Pietrangelo .30 .75
17 Brad Rubachuk .20 .50
18 Stefan Ketola .20 .50
19 Jeff Jablonski .20 .50
20 Kris Miller .20 .50
21 Logo Card .04 .10

2002-03 UK Manchester Storm

This set was produced by Armchair Sports in England.

COMPLETE SET (21) 5.00 10.00
1 Colin Pepperall .20 .50
2 Dan Preston .20 .50
3 Shawn Maltby .20 .50
4 Geoff Peters .20 .50
5 Mike Perna .20 .50
6 Pasi Nielikainen .20 .50
7 Dwight Parrish .20 .50
8 Mark Bultje .20 .50
9 Rob Wilson .20 .50
10 Ivan Matulik .20 .50
11 Pierre Allard .20 .50
12 David Longstaff .20 .50
13 Ryan Stewart .20 .50
14 Joe Cardarelli .20 .50
15 Stevie Lyle .30 .75
16 Mike Torchia .30 .75
17 Dan Hodge .20 .50
18 Daryl Lipsey HCO .04 .10
19 Mike Torchia .30 .75
20 Stevie Lyle .30 .75
21 Checklist .04 .10

2000-01 UK Nottingham Panthers

This set features the Panthers of Britain's top hockey league. The cards were produced by Cardtraders.com, and available from the team on game nights. Card #13 does not exist due to superstitious reasons.

COMPLETE SET (30) 4.80 12.00
1 Checklist .04 .10
2 Jordan Willis .30 .75
3 Paul Moran .16 .40
4 Duncan Paterson .16 .40
5 Kevin Hoffman .16 .40
6 David Struch .16 .40
7 Randall Weber .16 .40
8 Greg Hadden .16 .40
9 Daryl Lavoie .16 .40
10 P.C. Drouin .20 .50
11 Marc Levers .16 .40
12 Darryl Moxam .20 .50
14 Greg Burke .16 .40
15 Ashley Tait .16 .40
16 Ryan Gillis .16 .40
17 Jim Paek .20 .50
18 Chris Baxter .16 .40
19 Jamie Leach .30 .75
20 Eoin McInerney .30 .75
21 Robert Nordmark .16 .40
22 Graham Garden .16 .40
23 Casson Masters .16 .40
24 Barry Nieckar .20 .50
25 Eric Lavigne .20 .50
27 Peter Woods CO .04 .10
28 Redemption Voucher .02 .10
29 Alex Dampier DOH .04 .10
30 Gary Moran GM .04 .10
31 Team Photo .16 .40
32 Player Awards .16 .40
NA Robert Nordmark .16 .40

2001-02 UK Nottingham Panthers

Produced by Cardtraders.com, this 28-card set was available at Panthers home games. The production run was limited to just 495 sets, and each card states that on the card back. Card #13 was not printed for superstitious reasons.

COMPLETE SET (31) 4.80 12.00
1 Team Logo .04 .10
2 Brent Pope .20 .50
3 Clayton Norris .20 .50
4 Patrick Wallenberg .20 .50
5 Randall Weber .20 .50
6 Greg Hadden .20 .50
7 Frank Evans .20 .50
8 Claude Savoie .20 .50
9 P.C. Drouin .30 .75
10 Steve Moira .20 .50
11 Ashley Tait .30 .75
12 Paul Adey CO .04 .10
14 Jimmy Drolet .30 .75
15 Danny Lorenz .30 .75
16 Joel Poirier .30 .75
17 Paul Moran .20 .50
18 Barry Nieckar .30 .75
19 Darren Maloney .20 .50
20 Calle Carlsson .20 .50
21 Pasi Hakkinen .20 .50
22 A.J. Kelham .20 .50
23 Alex Dampier CO .04 .10
24 Lee Jinman .30 .75
25 Gary Moran GM .04 .10
26 Paws MASCOT .04 .10
27 Equipment Managers .04 .10
28 Trainers .04 .10
29 Head Office .04 .10
30 Christian Sjogren .20 .50
31 Jim Paek .20 .50
32 Danny Lorenz .20 .50

2002-03 UK Nottingham Panthers

Produced by cardtraders.uk, this 22-card set featured the Nottingham Panthers of the British Ice Hockey Superleague. The cards are unnumbered and are listed below in checklist order.

COMPLETE SET (22) 4.00 10.00
1 Mika Pietila .20 .50
2 Jim Paek .20 .50
3 Marc Hussey .20 .50
4 Eric Charron .20 .50
5 Greg Hadden .20 .50
6 Dody Wood .30 .75
7 Briane Thompson .20 .50
8 Jason Elders .20 .50
9 Kristian Taubert .20 .50
10 Scott Allison .20 .50
11 Mark Cadotte .20 .50
12 Petter Sandstrom .20 .50
13 John Purves .30 .75
14 Paul Moran .20 .50
15 Barry Nieckar .30 .75
16 Jason Clarke .20 .50
17 Lee Jinman .30 .75
18 Paul Adey .20 .50
19 Mascot .04 .10
20 Gary Moran GM .04 .10
21 Checklist .04 .10
22 Front Office .04 .10

2003-04 UK Nottingham Panthers

COMPLETE SET (18) 5.00 10.00
1 Niklas Sundberg .30 .75
2 David Clarke .20 .50
3 Kim Ahlroos .20 .50
4 James Morgan .20 .50
5 David Struch .20 .50
6 Robert Stancok .20 .50
7 Briane Thompson .20 .50
8 Marc Levers .20 .50
9 Kristian Taubert .20 .50
10 Mikko Koivunoro .20 .50
11 Geoff Woolhouse .30 .75
12 Joel Salonen .20 .50
13 Mark Cadotte .30 .75
14 Paul Moran .20 .50
15 Daniel Scott .20 .50
16 Calle Carlsson .20 .50
17 John Craighead .30 .75
18 Paul Addey CO .04 .10

2004-05 UK Nottingham Panthers

Produced by the team and sold in the club shop.

COMPLETE SET (20) 5.00 10.00
1 Paul Adey CO .04 .10
2 Kim Ahlroos .20 .50
3 Calle Carlsson .20 .50
4 David Clarke .20 .50
5 Mark Cadotte .30 .75
6 John Craighead .30 .75
7 Curtis Cruickshank .20 .50
8 Marek Ivan .20 .50
9 Konstantin Kalmikov .20 .50
10 Jan Krulis .20 .50
11 Jan Mandosko .20 .50
12 Steve McKenna .40 1.00
13 Gary Moran GM .04 .10
14 Paul Moran .20 .50
15 Matt Myers .20 .50
16 Scott Ricci .20 .50
17 Daniel Scott .20 .50
18 Roman Tvrdon .20 .50
19 Richard Wojciak .20 .50
20 Geoff Woolhouse .20 .50

2006-07 UK Nottingham Panthers

COMPLETE SET (20) 8.00 15.00
1 Joe Cardarelli .30 .75
2 David Clarke .30 .75
3 James Cooke .30 .75
4 James Ferrara .30 .75
5 Jan Krajicek .30 .75
6 Sean McAslan .30 .75
7 Danny Meyers .30 .75
8 Paul Moran .30 .75
9 Matt Myers .30 .75
10 James Neil .30 .75
11 Corey Neilson .30 .75
12 Matus Petricko .30 .75
13 Mike Rees .30 .75
14 Rastislav Rovnianek .30 .75
15 Ryan Shmyr .30 .75
16 Steve Silmes .30 .75
17 Rod Stevens .30 .75
18 Geoff Woolhouse .60 1.50
19 Mike Ellis CO .02 .10
20 Calle Carlsson ACO .02 .10

2007-08 UK Nottingham Panthers

COMPLETE SET (19) 7.00 15.00
1 Tom Askey .40 1.00
2 Geoff Woolhouse .40 1.00
3 Patrik Wallenberg .30 .75
4 Matt Myers .30 .75
5 Jon Coleman .30 .75
6 James Neil .30 .75
7 Robert Stancok .30 .75
8 Johan Molin .30 .75
9 Marc Levers .30 .75
10 James Ferrara .30 .75
11 Danny Meyers .30 .75
12 Mark Richardson .30 .75
13 Kevin Bergin .30 .75
14 Ryan Shmyr .30 .75
15 Eric Nelson .30 .75
16 Steve Pelletier .30 .75
17 Sean McAslan .30 .75
18 Corey Neilson .30 .75
19 Mike Ellis .30 .75

2002-03 UK Peterborough Phantoms

This set was produced by Armchair Sports in England.

COMPLETE SET (18) 5.00 10.00
1 Luc Chabot .30 .75
2 James Moore .25 .60
3 David Whitwell .25 .60
4 Craig Britton .25 .60
5 Jon Fone .25 .60
6 Pete Morley .25 .60
7 Jessie Hammill .25 .60
8 Jason Buckman .25 .60
9 Lewis Buckman .25 .60
10 Russell Coleman .25 .60
11 Duncan Cook .25 .60
12 Darren Cotton .25 .60
13 Jon Cotton .25 .60
14 James Ellwood .25 .60
15 Grant Hendry .25 .60
16 Doug McEwen .25 .60
17 Shaun Yardley .25 .60
18 Checklist .10 .25

2004-05 UK Ron Shudra Testimonial

COMPLETE SET (16) 3.00 8.00
1 Ron Shudra 1990-91 .20 .50
2 Ron Shudra 1991-92 .20 .50
3 Ron Shudra 1992-93 .20 .50
4 Ron Shudra 1993-94 .20 .50
5 Ron Shudra 1994-95 .20 .50
6 Ron Shudra 1995-96 .20 .50
7 Ron Shudra 1996-97 .20 .50
8 Ron Shudra 1997-98 .20 .50
9 Ron Shudra 1998-99 .20 .50
10 Ron Shudra 1999-00 .20 .50
11 Ron Shudra 2000-01 .20 .50
12 Ron Shudra 2001-02 .20 .50
13 Ron Shudra 2002-03 .20 .50
14 Ron Shudra 2003-04 .20 .50
15 Ron Shudra 2004-05 .20 .50
16 Ron Shudra CL .20 .50

2000-01 UK Sekonda Superleague

This 206-card set produced by Kudos featured the players of the British Superleague. The cards were unnumbered, and so are listed in team set order below. The last 36 cards of the set were available as an update set to the original 170-card base set. Cards were available at most Superleague venues in 5-card cello packs or as team sets or the complete league set.

COMPLETE SET (170) 20.00 50.00
COMPLETE UPDATE SET (36) 4.00 10.00
1 Ice Hockey Superleague .10 .25
2 Jim Lynch CO .10 .25
3 Paul Heavey ACO .10 .25
4 Philippe DeRouville .40 1.00
5 Colin Ryder .30 .75
6 Trevor Doyle .20 .50
7 Derek Eberle .20 .50
8 Anders Hillstrom .20 .50
9 Jan Mikel .20 .50
10 Johan Silfwerplatz .20 .50
11 Scott Young .20 .50
12 Dainius Bauyba .20 .50
13 Cam Bristow .20 .50
14 Shawn Byram .20 .50
15 Ed Courtenay .30 .75
16 Tony Hand .30 .75
17 Rhett Gordon .20 .50
18 Mike Harding .20 .50
19 Mark Montanari .20 .50
20 Jonathan Weaver .20 .50
21 Teeder Wynne .20 .50
22 David Whistle CO .10 .25
23 Mark Cavallin .20 .50
24 Todd Kelman .20 .50
25 Kevin Riehl .20 .50
26 Paxton Schulte .20 .50
27 Colin Ward .20 .50
28 Jeff Hoad .20 .50
29 Shane Johnson .20 .50
30 Enio Sacilotto CO .10 .25
31 Brian Greer .20 .50
32 Joe Watkins .20 .50
33 Matej Bukna .20 .50
34 Jimmy Drolet .20 .50
35 Jason Mansoff .20 .50
36 Mark Matier .20 .50
37 Steve O'Rourke .20 .50
38 Reid Simonton .20 .50
39 Brent Bobyck .20 .50
40 Chris Brant .20 .50
41 Mark Bultje .20 .50
42 Joe Cardarelli .20 .50
43 Dan Ceman .20 .50
44 Joe Ciccarello .20 .50
45 Darren Hurley .20 .50
46 Blake Knox .20 .50
47 Stephane Roy .20 .50
48 Brad Wingfield .20 .50
49 Doug McCarthy CO .10 .25
50 Troy Walkington CO .10 .25
51 Stevie Lyle .80 2.00
52 Derek Herlofsky .40 1.00
53 Frank Evans .20 .50
54 Kip Noble .20 .50
55 Clayton Norris .20 .50
56 Dwight Parrish .20 .50
57 Alan Schuler .20 .50
58 Rick Strachan .20 .50
59 Denis Chasse .20 .50
60 James Hanlon .20 .50
61 Rick Kowalsky .20 .50
62 Ivan Matulik .20 .50
63 Ian McIntyre .20 .50
64 Steve Moria .20 .50
65 John Parco .20 .50
66 Vezio Sacratini .20 .50
67 Steve Thornton .20 .50
68 Mike Ware .20 .50
69 Chris McSorley CO .10 .25
70 Trevor Robins .20 .50
71 Shawn Silver .20 .50
72 Rich Bronilla .20 .50
73 Neal Martin .20 .50
74 Randy Perry .20 .50
75 Mikael Tjallden .20 .50
76 Nicky Chinn .30 .75
77 Pat Ferschweiler .20 .50
78 Claude Jutras .20 .50
79 Mikko Koivunoro .20 .50
80 Mark Kolesar .20 .50
81 Jay Neal .20 .50
82 Bryan Richardson .20 .50
83 Paul Rushforth .20 .50
84 David Vallieres .20 .50
85 Darby Walker .20 .50
86 Brendan Yarema .20 .50
87 Terry Cristensen CO .10 .25
88 Daryl Lipsey ACO .10 .25
89 Frank Pietrangelo .40 1.00
90 Dave Trofimenkoff .40 1.00
91 Curtis Bowen .20 .50
92 Matt Eldred .20 .50
93 Perry Johnson .20 .50
94 Troy Neumeier .20 .50
95 Rob Robinson .20 .50
96 Blair Scott .20 .50
97 Pierre Allard .20 .50
98 Kevin Brown .20 .50
99 Greg Bullock .20 .50
100 Doug Doull .20 .50
101 Marty Flichel .20 .50
102 Trevor Gallant .20 .50
103 Jason Glover .20 .50
104 Mike Morin .20 .50
105 Corey Spring .20 .50
106 Shayne Stevenson .20 .50
107 Rob Trumbley .20 .50
108 Jukka Jalonen CO .10 .25
109 Jim Hibbert .20 .50
110 Tommi Satosaari .20 .50
111 Craig Binns .20 .50
112 Santeri Immonen .20 .50
113 Arttu Kayhko .20 .50
114 Miroslav Mosnar .20 .50
115 Darren McAusland .20 .50
116 Rob Wilson .20 .50
117 Tero Arkiomaa .20 .50
118 Louis Bedard .20 .50
119 Tomas Kupka .20 .50
120 Matt Oates .20 .50
121 Joel Poirer .20 .50
122 Timo Salonen .20 .50
123 Tommi Sova .20 .50
124 Alex Dampier CO .10 .25
125 Eoin McInerney .40 1.00
126 Jordan Willis .40 1.00
127 Greg Burke .20 .50
128 Ryan Gillis .20 .50
129 Eric Lavigne .20 .50
130 Daryl Lavoie .20 .50
131 Jim Paek .20 .50
132 Duncan Paterson .20 .50
133 P. C. Drouin .20 .50
134 Graham Garden .20 .50
135 Greg Hadden .20 .50
136 Jamie Leach .20 .50
137 Daryl Moxam .20 .50
138 Barry Nieckar .20 .50
139 David Struch .20 .50
140 Ashley Tait .20 .50
141 Randall Weber .20 .50
142 Mike Blaisdell CO .10 .25
143 Mike O'Neill .40 1.00
144 Steve Carpenter .20 .50
145 Shayne McCosh .20 .50
146 Jeff Sebastian .20 .50
147 Kayle Short .20 .50
148 Adam Smith .20 .50
149 Dennis Vial .40 1.00
150 Scott Allison .20 .50
151 Paul Beraldo .20 .50
152 Rick Brebant .20 .50
153 Dale Craigwell .20 .50
154 David Longstaff .20 .50
155 Scott Metcalfe .20 .50
156 Warren Norris .20 .50
157 Steve Roberts .20 .50
158 Kent Simpson .20 .50
159 Jason Weaver .20 .50
160 Brent Bobyck .20 .50
161 Ayr Eagles .10 .25
162 Belfast Giants .10 .25
163 Bracknell Bees .10 .25
164 Cardiff Devils .10 .25
165 London Knights .10 .25
166 Manchester Storm .10 .25
167 Newcastle Jesters .10 .25
168 Nottingham Panthers .10 .25
169 Sheffield Steelers .10 .25
170 Lucky Card .40 1.00
171 Tony Hand .20 .50
172 Jason Bowen .20 .50
173 Paul Ferone .20 .50
174 Todd Goodwin .20 .50
175 Kory Karlander .20 .50
176 Jerry Keefe .20 .50
177 Steve Roberts .20 .50
178 Doug Searle .20 .50
179 Rod Stevens .20 .50
180 Rob Stewart .20 .50
181 Derek Wilkinson .40 1.00
182 Jason Wright .20 .50
183 Bob Maudie .20 .50
184 Jason Heywood .20 .50
185 Frank Defrenza .20 .50
186 J-F Tremblay .10 .25
187 Kim Ahlroos .10 .25
188 Aaron Boh .20 .50
189 Terry Marchant .10 .25
190 Grant Richison .10 .25
191 Mikael Tjallden .20 .50
192 Brendan Yarema .20 .50
193 Brent Bobyck .10 .25
194 Pat Mazzoli .10 .25
195 Barrie Moore .10 .25
196 Eric Fenton .20 .50
197 Daniel Lacroix .20 .50
198 Chris Baxter .10 .25
199 Casson Masters .10 .25
200 Robert Nordmark .10 .25
201 Paul Adey .20 .50
202 Kent Simpson .20 .50
203 Mike Torchia .40 1.00
204 Checklist .04 .10
205 Checklist .04 .10
206 Checklist .04 .10

1993-94 UK Sheffield Steelers

This 19-card set was produced as part of a Drugs Freeze program and originally came with a collector's album.

COMPLETE SET (19) 4.00 10.00
1 Andy Havenhand .20 .50
2 Alan Hague .20 .50
3 Tim Cranston .20 .50
4 Neil Abel .20 .50
5 Scott Neil .20 .50
6 Steve Nemeth .20 .50
7 Tommy Plommer .20 .50
8 Ivan Matulik .20 .50
9 Danny Boome .20 .50
10 Mark Wright .20 .50
11 Chris Kelland .20 .50
12 Les Millie .20 .50
13 Selmar Odeline .20 .50
14 Ron Shudra .20 .50
15 Martin McKay .20 .50
16 Dampier w Tuyl .20 .50
17 Netminders .30 .75
18 Team Photo .30 .75
19 Sheffield Scimitars .20 .50

1994-95 UK Sheffield Steelers

This set features the Steelers of the British league. The cards are regulation size and were sold by the team at home games as part of a Drugs Freeze program.

COMPLETE SET (25) 4.00 10.00
1 Alex Dampier MGR .08 .25
2 Clyde Tuyl CO .08 .25
3 Paul Jackson .30 .75
4 Scott Neil .20 .50
5 Team Photo .20 .50
6 Ron Handy .20 .50
7 Patrick O'Conner .20 .50
8 Dean Smith .20 .50
9 Mike O'Conner .20 .50
10 Backroom Staff .08 .25
11 Tim Cranston .20 .50
12 Les Millie .20 .50
13 Alan Hague .20 .50
14 Perry Doyle .20 .50
15 Ron Shudra .20 .50
16 Mark Wright .20 .50
17 Tommy Plommer .20 .50
18 Scott Heaton .20 .50
19 Neil Abel .20 .50
20 Steeler Dan .08 .25
21 Rob Wilson .20 .50
22 Chris Kelland .20 .50
23 Andy Havenhand .20 .50
24 Martin McKay .20 .50
25 Steve Nemeth .30 .75

1995-96 UK Sheffield Steelers

This set features the Steelers of the British league. This 24-card set was produced as part of a Drugs Freeze program and originally came with a collector's album.

COMPLETE SET (24) 4.00 10.00
1 Martin McKay .15 .40
2 Ron Shudra .15 .40
3 Ken Priestlay .20 .50
4 Steve Nemeth .20 .50
5 Tommy Plommer .15 .40
6 Nicky Chinn .40 1.00
7 Tony Hand .40 1.00
8 Mike O'Conner .15 .40
9 Mark Wright .15 .40
10 Chris Kelland .15 .40
11 Andre Malo .15 .40
12 Les Millie .15 .40
13 Sheffield Arena .08 .25
14 Team Photo .15 .40
15 Scott Heaton .15 .40
16 Tim Cranston .15 .40
17 Neil Abel .15 .40
18 Scott Neil .15 .40
19 Perry Doyle .15 .40
20 Backroom Staff .08 .25
21 Alex Dampier MGR .08 .25
22 Clyde Tuyl CO .08 .25
23 The Silverware .08 .25
24 Steeler Foggy Dan .08 .25

1997-98 UK Sheffield Steelers

This set features the Steelers of the British Ice Hockey League. This 25-card set was produced as part of a Drugs Freeze program and originally came with a collector's album. The sets were available on game nights.

COMPLETE SET (25) 4.80 12.00
1 James Hibbert .20 .50
2 Tim Cranston .20 .50
3 Rob Wilson .20 .50
4 Ken Priestlay .30 .75
5 Tommy Plommer .20 .50
6 Frank Kovacs .20 .50
7 Nicky Chinn .30 .75
8 David Longstaff .20 .50
9 Tony Hand .30 .75
10 Dion Del Monte .20 .50
11 Scott Allison .20 .50
12 Chris Kelland .20 .50
13 Sheffield Arena .08 .25
14 Team Photo .08 .25
15 Andre Malo .20 .50
16 Jamie Van Der Horst .20 .50
17 Andre Malo .20 .50
18 Mike Ware .20 .50
19 Ron Shudra .20 .50
20 Ed Courteney .30 .75
21 Piero Greco .20 .50
22 Corey Beaulieu .20 .50
23 Steeler Foggy Dan .08 .25
24 Alex Dampier MGR .08 .25
25 Clyde Tuyl CO .08 .25

1999-00 UK Sheffield Steelers

This postcard size set features the Steelers of the top British league. The cards were produced by Armchair Sports, a British card shop, and sold there and by the team.

COMPLETE SET (22) 4.80 12.00
1 Mike Blaisdell CO .20 .50
2 Dan Ceman .30 .75
3 Greg Clancy .20 .50
4 Ed Courtenay .40 1.00
5 Dale Craigwell .40 1.00
6 Matt Hoffman .20 .50
7 Dale Junkin .20 .50
8 Derek Laxdal .30 .75
9 David Longstaff .20 .50
10 Andre Malo .20 .50
11 Mark Matier .20 .50
12 Shayne McCosh .20 .50
13 Don McKee CO .02 .10
14 Kip Noble .20 .50
15 Thomas Plommer .20 .50
16 Kayle Short .20 .50
17 Shawn Silver .20 .50
18 Grant Sjerven .20 .50
19 Dennis Vial .40 1.00
20 Jason Weaver .20 .50
21 Rob Wilson .20 .50
22 Teeder Wynne .20 .50

2000-01 UK Sheffield Steelers

This set features the Steelers of the British Sekonda league, the top division in the UK. The cards were sold in set form by the team.

COMPLETE SET (27) 4.00 10.00
1 Logo Card .10 .25
2 Champions .14 .40
3 Team Photo .14 .40
4 Paul Adey .14 .40
5 Scott Allison .14 .40
6 Andy & Paul .04 .10
7 Paul Beraldo .20 .50
8 Mike Blaisdell .20 .50
9 Brent Bobyck .14 .40
10 Rick Brebant .14 .40
11 Steve Carpenter .14 .40
12 Dale Craigwell .14 .40
13 Steeler Dan MASCOT .10 .25
14 David Longstaff .14 .40
15 Shayne McCosh .14 .40
16 Scott Metcalfe .14 .40
17 Warren Norris .14 .40
18 Mike O'Neill .30 .75
19 Steve Roberts .14 .40
20 Jeff Sebastian .14 .40
21 Kayle Short .14 .40
22 David Simms CO .10 .25
23 Kent Simpson .14 .40
24 Adam Smith .14 .40
25 Mike Torchia .40 1.00
26 Dennis Vial .20 .50
27 Jason Weaver .14 .40

2000-01 UK Sheffield Steelers Centurions

Produced by Cardtraders.com, this 18- card set celebrates the players who have represented Sheffield in more than 100 games. The set was sold on game nights and was also available through Armchair Sports.

COMPLETE SET (18) 4.00 10.00
1 Ed Courtenay .40 1.00
2 Tommy Plommer .20 .50
3 David Longstaff .20 .50
4 Rob Wilson .20 .50
5 Ron Shudra .20 .50
6 Tim Cranston .20 .50
7 Chris Kelland .20 .50
8 Andre Malo .20 .50
9 Ken Priestlay .30 .75
10 Scott Neil .20 .50
11 Tony Hand .40 1.00
12 Kayle Short .20 .50
13 Mike O'Connor .20 .50
14 Scott Allison .20 .50
15 Neil Abel .20 .50
16 Steve Nemeth .20 .50
17 Checklist .04 .10
18 Ron Shudra Player of the Decade .20 .50

2001-02 UK Sheffield Steelers

COMPLETE SET (19) 5.00 10.00
1 Scott Allison .20 .50
2 Ryan Bach .30 .75
3 Cal Benazic .20 .50
4 Mike Blaisdell CO .20 .50
5 Brent Bobyck .20 .50
6 Chris Brant .20 .50
7 Rick Brebant .20 .50
8 Jeff Brown .20 .50
9 Mark Dutiaume .20 .50
10 Paul Kruse .30 .75
11 Mark Laniel .20 .50
12 Brad Lauer .20 .50
13 Peter Leboutillier .30 .75
14 Chris Lipsett .20 .50
15 Jason Mansoff .20 .50
16 Bob Maudie .20 .50
17 Kevin Miehm .20 .50
18 Jeff Sebastian .20 .50
19 Ron Shudra .20 .50

2002-03 UK Sheffield Steelers

COMPLETE SET (19) 5.00 10.00
1 Mike Blaisdell CO .20 .50
2 Brent Bobyck .20 .50
3 Rick Brebant .20 .50
4 Jeff Brown .20 .50
5 Calle Carlsson .20 .50
6 Dion Darling .20 .50
7 Mark Dutiaume .20 .50
8 Iain Fraser .20 .50
9 Rhett Gordon .20 .50
10 Joel Laing .30 .75
11 Marc Laniel .20 .50
12 Scott Levins .20 .50
13 Mike Morin .20 .50
14 Warren Norris .20 .50
15 Trevor Prior .30 .75
16 Jason Sessa .30 .75
17 Kent Simpson .20 .50
18 Chris Szysky .20 .50
19 Timo Willman .20 .50

2003-04 UK Sheffield Steelers

COMPLETE SET (21) 5.00 10.00
1 Gerald Adams .20 .50
2 Erik Anderson .20 .50
3 Mike Blaisdell CO .20 .50
4 Ben Bliss .20 .50
5 Brent Bobyck .20 .50
6 Kevin Bolibruck .20 .50
7 Christian Bronsard .30 .75
8 Dion Darling .20 .50
9 Kirk DeWaele .20 .50
10 Rob Dopson .30 .75
11 Steve Duncombe .20 .50
12 Mark Dutiaume .20 .50
13 Steve Ellis .20 .50
14 Gavin Farrand .20 .50
15 Joel Irving .20 .50
16 Ryan Lake .20 .50
17 David Lawrence .30 .75
18 Marc Lefebvre .20 .50
19 Mike Peron .20 .50
20 Pasi Raitanan UER .30 .75
21 Ron Shudra .20 .50

2003-04 UK Sheffield Steelers Stickers

COMPLETE SET (18) 3.00 6.00
1 Mark Dutiaume .20 .50
2 Gavin Farrand .20 .50
3 Mike Peron .20 .50
4 Ryan Lake .20 .50
5 Dion Darling .20 .50
6 Davey Lawrence .20 .50
7 Rob Dopson .30 .75
8 Steve Ellis .20 .50
9 Ron Shudra .20 .50
10 Brent Bobyck .20 .50
11 Erik Anderson .20 .50
12 Kirk DeWaele .20 .50
13 Joel Irving .20 .50
14 Steve Duncombe .20 .50
15 Dan Hughes .20 .50
16 Marc Lefebvre .20 .50
17 Ben Bliss .20 .50
18 Gerald Adams .20 .50

2004-05 UK Sheffield Steelers

COMPLETE SET (20) 5.00 10.00
1 Jayme Platt .20 .50
2 David Lawrence .20 .50
3 Daryl Andrews .20 .50
4 Gerad Adams .20 .50
5 Steve Duncombe .20 .50
6 Ron Shudra .30 .75
7 Dion Darling .20 .50
8 David Cousineau .30 .75
9 Marc Lefebvre .20 .50
10 Mike Peron .20 .50
11 Mark Dutiaume .20 .50
12 Rob Stewart .20 .50
13 Erik Anderson .20 .50
14 Gavin Farrand .20 .50
15 Joe Ciccarello .20 .50
16 Ben Bliss .20 .50
17 Paul Sample .20 .50
18 Jeff Christian .20 .50
19 Brent Bobyck .20 .50
20 Checklist .04 .10

1994-95 UK Solihul Barons

This set features the Barons of the British league. Any additional information can be forwarded to hockeymag@beckett.com.

COMPLETE SET (15) 5.00 10.00
1 Jake Armstrong .30 .75
2 Stephen Doyle .30 .75
3 Paul Frankum .30 .75
4 Justin George .30 .75
5 Andy Havenhand .30 .75
6 Nick Henry .30 .75
7 Richard Hillas .30 .75
8 Phil Lee .30 .75
9 Declan McNaughton .30 .75
10 Joel Pickering .30 .75
11 Dan Prachar .30 .75
12 Gareth Roddis .30 .75
13 Jamie Van der Horst .30 .75
14 Dave Wilkie .30 .75
15 Liam Young .30 .75

1995-96 UK Solihull Barons

This set features the Barons of the British league. Little is known about this set beyond the confirmed checklist. Additional information can be forwarded to hockeymag@beckett.com.

COMPLETE SET (13) 2.00 5.00
1 Jamie Van Der Horst .20 .50
2 Nick Henry .20 .50
3 Gareth Roddis .20 .50
4 Jake Armstrong .20 .50
5 Andy Havenhand .20 .50
6 Paul Frankum .20 .50
7 David Wilkie .20 .50
8 Phil Lee .20 .50
9 Dan Pracher .20 .50
10 Alan Hague .20 .50
11 Justin George .20 .50
12 Liam Young .20 .50
13 Stephen Doyle .20 .50

2004-05 UK Steven Carpenter Testimonial

COMPLETE SET (10) 2.00 5.00
1 Steven Carpenter 1996-97 .20 .50
2 Steven Carpenter 1997-98 .20 .50
3 Steven Carpenter 1998-99 .20 .50
4 Steven Carpenter 1999-00 .20 .50
5 Steven Carpenter 2000-01 .20 .50
6 Steven Carpenter 2001-02 .20 .50
7 Steven Carpenter 2002-03 .20 .50
8 Steven Carpenter 2003-04 .20 .50
9 Steven Carpenter 2004-05 .20 .50
10 Steven Carpenter CL .20 .50

2004-05 UK Thommo's Top 10

COMPLETE SET (10) 5.00 10.00
1 Greg Hadden .40 1.00
2 Tony Hand .60 1.50
3 Claudio Scremin .40 1.00
4 Rick Brebant .40 1.00
5 Mike Blaisdell .40 1.00
6 Joel Laing .40 1.00
7 Darryl Olsen .40 1.00
8 Marty Dallman .40 1.00
9 Dennis Vial .60 1.50
10 Patrice Lefebvre .60 1.50

2004-05 UK U-20 Team

COMPLETE SET (23) 5.00 10.00
1 David Lawrence .20 .50
2 Kevin Phillips .20 .50
3 Simon Butterworth .20 .50
4 Shaun Thompson .20 .50
5 Kurt Reynolds .20 .50
6 Shane Moore .20 .50
7 Steven Duncombe .20 .50
8 Leigh Jamieson .20 .50
9 Adam Brittle .20 .50
10 Chad Reekie .20 .50
11 Chace Ferrand .20 .50
12 David Phillips .20 .50
13 Bari McKenzie .20 .50
14 Lee Mitchell .20 .50
15 Tom Carlon .20 .50
16 Mark Richardson .20 .50
17 Adam Walker .20 .50
18 Euan Forsyth .20 .50
19 Andrew Thornton .20 .50
20 Luke Boothroyd .20 .50
21 Lewis Day .20 .50
22 Geoffrey Woolhouse .20 .50
23 Checklist .04 .10

1998-99 Abilene Aviators

This set features the Aviators of the WPHL. The set was issued as a promotional giveaway in set form. The Don Margettie card was issued separately at another promotional event and is not part of the complete set proper. The cards are unnumbered and are listed alphabetically.

COMPLETE SET (21) 8.00 20.00
1 Erik Noack .40 1.00
2 Jeff Triano CO .20 .50
3 Don Margettie .40 1.00
4 Tony Martino .40 1.00
5 Mathieu Raby .60 1.50
6 Derek Booth .40 1.00
7 Mario Dumoulin .40 1.00
8 Charlie Lawson .40 1.00
9 Jean-Francois Gregoire .40 1.00
10 Craig Perrett .40 1.00
11 Eric Naud .60 1.50
12 Stephane Roy .40 1.00
13 Charles Poulin .40 1.00
14 Jayson Brunette .40 1.00
15 Stephen Maltby .40 1.00
16 Terho Koskela .40 1.00
17 Francois Archambault .40 1.00
18 Marty Dallman .40 1.00
19 Mario Cormier .40 1.00
20 Eric Brule .40 1.00
21 Don Margettie PROMO 2.00 5.00

1995-96 Adirondack Red Wings

This 25-card set produced by Split Second features the Adirondack Red Wings of the AHL. The sets were available at games and by mail. The cards feature a glossy action photo along with team and manufacturer logos on the front. The cards are unnumbered and listed below in alphabetical order.

COMPLETE SET (25) 4.80 12.00
1 Jeff Bloemberg .15 .40
2 Curtis Bowen .15 .40
3 Dave Chyzowski .15 .40
4 Sylvain Cloutier .15 .40
5 Ryan Duthie .15 .40
6 Anders Eriksson .20 .50
7 Yan Golubovski .30 .75
8 Ben Hankinson .15 .40
9 Kevin Hodson .40 1.00
10 Scott Hollis .15 .40
11 Mike Knuble .40 1.00
12 Jason MacDonald .20 .50
13 Mark Major .15 .40
14 Norm Maracle .40 1.00
15 Kurt Miller .15 .40
16 Mike Needham .15 .40
17 Troy Neumeier .15 .40
18 Mark Ouimet .15 .40
19 Jamie Pushor .20 .50
20 Stacy Roest .40 1.00
21 Brandon Smith .20 .50
22 Kerry Toporowski .15 .40
23 Wes Walz .40 1.00
24 Aaron Ward .30 .75
25 Hockeye Mascot .02 .10

1999-00 Adirondack IceHawks

This set features the IceHawks of the UHL. The cards were produced by Blue Line Sports and were sold at

home games.
COMPLETE SET (25) 4.00 10.00
1 Header .08 .25
Checklist
2 Stephan Brochu .20 .50
3 Eric Boyte .20 .50
4 David Dartsch .20 .50
5 John Batten .20 .50
6 Larry Empey .20 .50
7 Chris Ross .20 .50
8 Trent Schachle .20 .50
9 Checklist .08 .25
10 Shawn Yakimishyn .20 .50
11 Francois Sasseville .20 .50
12 Guillaume Rodrigue .20 .50
13 Trevor Jobe .20 .50
14 Tony Cimellaro .20 .50
15 Cameron MacDonald .20 .50
16 Bobby Cunningham .20 .50
17 Checklist .08 .25
18 Alexei Deev .20 .50
19 Wade Welte .20 .50
20 Alexei Yegorov .30 .75
21 Chad Ford .20 .50
22 Jack Greig .20 .50
23 Ben Metzger .20 .50
24 Robbie Nichols .20 .50
25 Hawkeye .08 .25

1999-00 AHL All-Stars

This 12-card set showcases the 2000 AHL All-Stars with full-color action photos. The cards were available at the rink the day of the AS Game. The cards are not numbered and are listed below alphabetically.

COMPLETE SET (12) 8.00 20.00
1 Martin Brochu .60 1.50
2 Craig Ferguson .40 1.00
3 Peter Ferraro .40 1.00
4 Michael Gaul .40 1.00
5 Miikka Kiprusoff 2.00 5.00
6 Christian Matte .60 1.50
7 Chris O'Sullivan .40 1.00
8 Martin St. Louis 2.00 5.00
9 Brad Tiley .40 1.00
10 Daniel Trebil .40 1.00
11 Alexandre Volchkov .40 1.00
12 Bob Wren .40 1.00

2004-05 AHL All-Stars

COMPLETE SET (49) 10.00 20.00
1 Keith Ballard .10 .25
2 Nolan Baumgartner .10 .25
3 Sean Bergenheim .10 .25
4 Patrice Bergeron 1.25 3.00
5 Brandon Bochenski .30 .75
6 Rene Bourque .20 .50
7 Jay Bouwmeester .40 1.00
8 Dustin Brown .40 1.00
9 Mike Cammalleri .40 1.00
10 Craig Darby .10 .25
11 Christian Ehrhoff .10 .25
12 Steve Eminger .10 .25
13 Simon Gamache .20 .50
14 Mathieu Garon .30 .75
15 Denis Grebeshkov .10 .25
16 Dan Hamhuis .10 .25
17 Andy Hilbert .10 .25
18 Michael Holmqvist .10 .25
19 Andrew Hutchinson .10 .25
20 Ryan Kesler .10 .25
21 Jason King .10 .25
22 Chuck Kobasew .30 .75
23 Mikko Koivu .40 1.00
24 Niklas Kronwall .30 .75
25 Jason Labarbera .20 .50
26 Kari Lehtonen 1.25 3.00
27 Joey MacDonald .40 1.00
28 Ryan Miller .60 1.50
29 Antero Niittymaki .40 1.00
30 Lawrence Nycholat .10 .25
31 Michel Ouellet .10 .25
32 Zach Parise 1.25 3.00
33 Eric Perrin .10 .25
34 Joni Pitkanen .20 .50
35 Tomas Plekanec .20 .50
36 Brian Pothier .10 .25
37 Travis Roche .10 .25
38 Tony Salmelainen .10 .25
39 Patrick Sharp .10 .25
40 Jason Spezza .75 2.00
41 Eric Staal .60 1.50
42 Alexander Svitov .10 .25
43 Brad Tiley .10 .25
44 Anton Volchenkov .10 .25
45 Kyle Wellwood .30 .75
46 Dennis Wideman .10 .25
47 Finland Representatives .20 .50
48 Manchester Monarchs .10 .25
49 Checklist .04 .10

2002-03 AHL Top Prospects

This series was produced by Choice Marketing in conjunction with the PHPA and the AHL. The set was sold online and at rinks around the league. The set features a number of top prospects on their first pro cards.

COMPLETE SET (45) 8.00 20.00
1 Ramzi Abid .10 .25
2 Alex Auld .30 .75
3 Jared Aulin .20 .50
4 Jason Bacashihua .20 .50
5 Kris Beech .10 .25
6 Brad Boyes .30 .75
7 Scott Clemmensen .20 .50
8 Ty Conklin .20 .50
9 Niko Dimitrakos .10 .25
10 Rick DiPietro .60 1.50
11 Micki Dupont .10 .25
12 Ray Emery .40 1.00
13 Shane Endicott .10 .25
14 Garnet Exelby .20 .50
15 Jim Fahey .10 .25
16 Ron Hainsey .20 .50
17 Darren Haydar .20 .50
18 Jonathan Hedstrom .10 .25
19 Jeff Heerema .10 .25
20 Andy Hilbert .10 .25
21 Trent Hunter .20 .50
22 Mike Komisarek .20 .50
23 Tomas Kopecky .20 .50
24 Pascal Leclaire .40 1.00
25 Guillaume Lefebvre .10 .25
26 Michael Leighton .20 .50
27 Roman Lyashenko .10 .25
28 Tomas Malec .10 .25
29 Ryan Miller .75 2.00
30 Shaone Morrisonn .20 .50
31 Filip Novak .10 .25
32 Steve Ott .40 1.00
33 Maxime Ouellet .20 .50
34 Justin Papineau .10 .25
35 John Pohl .10 .25
36 Brandon Reid .10 .25
37 Jani Rita .10 .25
38 Phillippe Sauve .20 .50
39 Jason Spezza 1.25 3.00
40 Charlie Stephens .10 .25
41 Jeff Taffe .10 .25
42 J.P. Vigier .10 .25
43 Kyle Wanvig .10 .25
44 Duvie Westcott .10 .25
45 Tomas Zizka .10 .25

2003-04 AHL Top Prospects

This series was produced by Choice Marketing and sold in complete set form at AHL rinks.

COMPLETE SET (46) 6.00 15.00
1 Anton Babchuk .10 .25
2 Jason Bacashihua .20 .50
3 Ryan Bayda .10 .25
4 Brad Boyes .20 .50
5 Ilja Bryzgalov .20 .50
6 Peter Budaj .20 .50
7 Carlo Colaiacovo .10 .25
8 Ray Emery .40 1.00
9 Kurtis Foster .10 .25
10 Denis Grebeshkov .10 .25
11 Chris Higgins .40 1.00
12 Jiri Hudler .40 1.00
13 Ryan Kesler .20 .50
14 Mike Komisarek .10 .25
15 Lukas Krajicek .10 .25
16 Niklas Kronwall .30 .75
17 Brooks Laich .10 .25
18 Pascal Leclaire .20 .50
19 Kari Lehtonen .75 2.00
20 David LeNeveu .20 .50
21 Ross Lupaschuk .10 .25
22 Justin Mapletoft .10 .25
23 Jay McClement .10 .25
24 Ryan Miller .40 1.00
25 Shaone Morrisonn .10 .25
26 Maxime Ouellet .20 .50
27 Johnny Pohl .20 .50
28 Jason Pominville .40 1.00
29 Mark Popovic .10 .25
30 Jani Rita .10 .25
31 Derek Roy .40 1.00
32 Patrick Sharp .10 .25
33 Charlie Stephens .10 .25
34 Alexander Suglobov .10 .25
35 Tomas Surovy .10 .25
36 Jeff Taffe .10 .25
37 Petr Taticek .10 .25
38 Hannu Toivonen .40 1.00
39 Fedor Tyutin .10 .25
40 Scott Upshall .20 .50
41 Stephane Veilleux .10 .25
42 Kyle Wanvig .10 .25
43 Stephen Weiss .20 .50
44 Kyle Wellwood .40 1.00
45 Jeff Woywitka .10 .25
NNO Checklist .04 .10

2004-05 AHL Top Prospects

COMPLETE SET (61) 10.00 25.00
1 Zach Parise 1.00 2.50
2 Alexander Suglobov .10 .25
3 Jason Spezza .60 1.50
4 Antoine Vermette .20 .50
5 Anton Volchenkov .10 .25
6 Sean Bergenheim .10 .25
7 Kari Lehtonen 1.00 2.50
8 Karl Stewart .10 .25
9 Joffrey Lupul .30 .75
10 Stanislav Chistov .10 .25
11 Marcel Goc .10 .25
12 Brad Winchester .10 .25
13 Doug Lynch .10 .25
14 Niklas Kronwall .30 .75
15 Nathan Robinson .10 .25
16 Tomas Plekanec .20 .50
17 Trevor Daley .10 .25
18 Jozef Balej .10 .25
19 Jason Labarbera .20 .50
20 Peter Budaj .20 .50
21 Pierre-Marc Bouchard .30 .75
22 Brent Burns .20 .50
23 Mikko Koivu .40 1.00
24 Eric Staal .60 1.50
25 Chuck Kobasew .20 .50
26 Brent Krahn .20 .50
27 Yanick Lehoux .10 .25
28 Mike Cammalleri .40 1.00
29 Dustin Brown .20 .50
30 Denis Grebeshkov .10 .25
31 Jason King .10 .25
32 Ryan Kesler .10 .25
33 Timofei Shishkanov .10 .25
34 Scottie Upshall .20 .50
35 Jordin Tootoo .40 1.00
36 Mikhail Yakubov .10 .25
37 Anton Babchuk .10 .25
38 R.J. Umberger .20 .50
39 Joni Pitkanen .20 .50
40 Antero Niittymaki .40 1.00
41 Steve Eminger .10 .25
42 Jakub Klepis .10 .25
43 Patrice Bergeron 1.00 2.50
44 Hannu Toivonen .40 1.00
45 Derek Roy .20 .50
46 Thomas Vanek 1.00 2.50
47 Stephen Weiss .20 .50
48 Jay Bouwmeester .30 .75
49 Nathan Horton .30 .75
50 Adam Henrich .10 .25
51 Kyle Wellwood .30 .75
52 Matthew Stajan .30 .75
53 Carlo Colaiacovo .20 .50
54 Alexander Svitov .10 .25
55 David LeNeveu .20 .50
56 Michel Ouellet .10 .25
57 Ryan Whitney .30 .75
58 Marc-Andre Fleury .60 1.50
59 Mike Glumac .10 .25
60 Peter Sejna .10 .25
NNO Checklist .04 .10

2005-06 AHL All-Stars

COMPLETE SET (45) 10.00 25.00
1 Keith Aucoin .20 .50
2 Sven Butenschon .20 .50
3 Braydon Coburn .20 .50
4 Yann Danis .40 1.00
5 Andy Delmore .20 .50
6 Eric Fehr .20 .50
7 Valtteri Filppula .50 1.25
8 Wade Flaherty .40 1.00
9 Bruno Gervais .20 .50
10 Denis Grebeshkov .20 .50
11 Denis Hamel .20 .50
12 Mark Hartigan .20 .50
13 Eric Healey .20 .50
14 Jiri Hudler .40 1.00
15 Vitaly Kolesnik .40 1.00
16 Kirby Law .20 .50
17 Junior Lessard .40 1.00
18 Corey Locke .20 .50
19 Donald MacLean .20 .50
20 Al Montoya .75 2.00
21 Mike Mottau .20 .50
22 Curtis Murphy .20 .50
23 Filip Novak .20 .50
24 Lawrence Nycholat .20 .50
25 Patrick O'Sullivan .40 1.00
26 Nathan Paetsch .20 .50
27 Libor Pivko .20 .50
28 Thomas Pock .20 .50
29 Johnny Pohl .20 .50
30 Richie Regehr .20 .50
31 Pekka Rinne .40 1.00
32 Pat Rissmiller .20 .50
33 Jimmy Roy .20 .50
34 Dany Sabourin .40 1.00
35 Ryan Shannon .20 .50
36 John Slaney .20 .50
37 Martin St. Pierre .20 .50
38 Alexander Suglobov .20 .50
39 Jeff Tambellini .20 .50
40 Layne Ulmer .20 .50
41 Ryan Vesce .20 .50
42 Noah Welch .20 .50
43 Erik Westrum .40 1.00
44 AHL All-Stars .20 .50
NNO Checklist .01 .01

2005-06 AHL Top Prospects

COMPLETE SET (50) 15.00 25.00
1 Nicklas Bergfors .20 .50
2 Steve Bernier .40 1.00
3 Kevin Bieksa .20 .50
4 Chris Bourque .40 1.00
5 Alexandre Burrows .40 1.00
6 Braydon Coburn .20 .50
7 Jeremy Colliton .20 .50
8 Ryan Craig .20 .50
9 Yann Danis .40 1.00
10 Nigel Dawes .20 .50
11 Patrick Eaves .40 1.00
12 Dan Ellis .40 1.00
13 Eric Fehr .20 .50
14 Valtteri Filppula .50 1.25
15 Tomas Fleischmann .20 .50
16 Bruno Gervais .20 .50
17 Mike Glumac .20 .50
18 Josh Harding .40 1.00
19 Jim Howard .40 1.00
20 Jean-Francois Jacques .20 .50
21 Matt Jones .20 .50
22 Vitaly Kolesnik .40 1.00
23 Staffan Kronwall .20 .50
24 Ryan Lannon .20 .50
25 Al Montoya .75 2.00
26 Eric Nystrom .20 .50
27 Patrick O'Sullivan .40 1.00
28 Nathan Paetsch .20 .50
29 Dustin Penner .40 1.00
30 Alexandre Picard .20 .50
31 Libor Pivko .20 .50
32 Geoff Platt .20 .50
33 Konstantin Pushkarev .20 .50
34 Tyler Redenbach .20 .50
35 Pekka Rinne .40 1.00
36 Peter Sejna .20 .50
37 Ryan Shannon .20 .50
38 Brian Sipotz .20 .50
39 Martin St. Pierre .20 .50
40 Yan Stastny .20 .50
41 Barry Tallackson .20 .50
42 Jeff Tambellini .20 .50
43 Chris Thorburn .20 .50
44 Lauri Tukonen .20 .50
45 Ryan Vesce .20 .50
46 Roman Voloshenko .20 .50
47 Ben Walter .20 .50
48 Noah Welch .20 .50
49 Jeremy Williams .40 1.00
50 Checklist .01 .01

2006-07 AHL Top Prospects

1 Kyle Cumiskey .20 .50
2 Justin Peters .20 .50
3 Andrew Ebbett .20 .50
4 Josh Hennessy .30 .75
5 Jeff Tambellini .20 .50
6 Robert Nilsson .20 .50
7 Blake Comeau .20 .50
8 Brett Stirling .30 .75
9 Nathan Oystrick .20 .50
10 Boris Valabik .20 .50
11 Jonathan Ericsson .20 .50
12 Jimmy Howard .40 1.00
13 Jaroslav Halak .75 2.00
14 Ryan Callahan .20 .50
15 Daniel Girardi .30 .75
16 Jeff Schultz .20 .50
17 Benoit Pouliot .40 1.00
18 Joel Lundqvist .40 1.00
19 Vojtech Polak .20 .50
20 Andy Greene .20 .50
21 Matt Moulson .20 .50
22 Peter Harrold .20 .50
23 Colby Genoway .20 .50
24 Alex Edler .30 .75
25 Rich Peverley .20 .50
26 Cal O'Reilly .20 .50
27 Troy Brouwer .30 .75
28 Dustin Byfuglien .20 .50
29 Corey Crawford .30 .75
30 Dustin Boyd .30 .75
31 Curtis McElhinney .20 .50
32 Roman Polak .20 .50
33 Marek Schwarz .40 1.00
34 Stefan Ruzicka .20 .50
35 Ryan Shannon .20 .50
36 David Krejci .30 .75
37 Matt Lashoff .30 .75
38 Clarke MacArthur .20 .50
39 Drew Stafford .75 2.00
40 Bill Thomas .20 .50
41 Blair Jones .20 .50
42 Karri Ramo .30 .75
43 Tomas Popperle .20 .50
44 Colin Murphy .20 .50
45 Justin Pogge .75 2.00
46 Jon Filewich .20 .50
47 Rob Schremp .60 1.50
48 Jeff Drouin-Deslauriers .30 .75
49 Joe Pavelski .40 1.00
50 Thomas Greiss .30 .75

2007-08 AHL Top Prospects

COMPLETE SET (50) 12.00 20.00
1 Bobby Hughes .20 .50
2 Brian Lee .20 .50
3 Nick Foligno .20 .50
4 Frans Nielsen .20 .50
5 Blake Comeau .20 .50
6 Brett Sterling .20 .50
7 Ondrej Pavelec .30 .75
8 Jonathan Ericsson .40 1.00
9 Jakub Kindl .20 .50
10 Sergei Kostitsyn .40 1.00
11 Ryan O'Byrne .20 .50
12 Greg Moore .20 .50
13 Brodie Dupont .20 .50
14 Kyle Wilson .20 .50
15 Daren Machesney .20 .50
16 Petr Kalus .20 .50
17 Cal Clutterbuck .20 .50
18 Mark Fistric .20 .50
19 T.J. Hensick .20 .50
20 Chris Stewart .20 .50
21 Mark Fraser .20 .50
22 Teddy Purcell .30 .75
23 Brian Boyle .60 1.50
24 Luc Bourdon .30 .75
25 Michael Grabner .20 .50
26 Cal O'Reilly .20 .50
27 Cody Franson .20 .50
28 Vladimir Mihalik .20 .50
29 Roman Polak .20 .50
30 Marek Schwarz .25 .60
31 Jonathan Matsumoto .30 .75
32 Ryan Parent .30 .75
33 Bobby Ryan .30 .75
34 Brian Salcido .20 .50
35 Matt Hunwick .20 .50
36 Tuukka Rask .30 .75
37 Kris Chucko .20 .50
38 Matt Pelech .20 .50
39 Stefan Meyer .20 .50
40 Marek Zagrapan .20 .50
41 Cam Barker .20 .50
42 Jack Skille .30 .75
43 Keith Yandle .20 .50
44 Colin McDonald .20 .50
45 Marc Pouliot .20 .50
46 Derick Brassard .20 .50
47 Justin Pogge .40 1.00
48 Kristopher Letang .20 .50
49 Mike Iggulden .20 .50
50 Lukas Kaspar .20 .50

2010-11 AHL Top Prospects

COMPLETE SET (50) 8.00 20.00
1 Luke Adam .20 .50
2 Jake Allen .40 1.00
3 Alexander Avtsin .15 .40
4 Johan Backlund .20 .50
5 Kyle Beach .25 .60
6 Mikkel Boedker .15 .40
7 Robert Bortuzzo .20 .50
8 Zach Boychuk .20 .50
9 Bobby Butler .20 .50
10 Taylor Chorney .20 .50
11 Joe Colborne .25 .60
12 Ian Cole .20 .50
13 Kaspars Daugavins .25 .60
14 Corey Elkins .15 .40
15 Benn Ferriero .15 .40
16 Cameron Gaunce .20 .50
17 Blake Geoffrion .25 .60
18 Colton Gillies .15 .40
19 Evgeny Grachev .20 .50
20 Cody Hodgson .75 2.00
21 Braden Holtby .50 1.25
22 Jesse Joensuu .20 .50
23 Nick Johnson .15 .40
24 Linus Klasen .20 .50
25 Mikko Koskinen .25 .60
26 Philip Larsen .20 .50
27 Nick Leddy .20 .50
28 Jacob Markstrom .30 .75
29 Alec Martinez .20 .50
30 Thomas McCollum .25 .60
31 John Moore .20 .50
32 Greg Nemisz .20 .50
33 Kyle Palmieri .40 1.00
34 Aaron Palushaj .25 .60
35 Mathieu Perreault .20 .50
36 Alex Plante .20 .50
37 Paul Postma .25 .60
38 Kevin Quick .15 .40
39 Michal Repik .15 .40
40 Jussi Rynnas .25 .60
41 Maxime Sauve .25 .60
42 Marco Scandella .20 .50
43 Jordan Schroeder .25 .60
44 Zac Dalpe .20 .50
45 Alex Stalock .25 .60
46 Tomas Tatar .40 1.00
47 Mattias Tedenby .15 .40
48 Viktor Tikhonov .20 .50
49 James Wright .15 .40
50 Mats Zuccarello .30 .75

1995-96 AHCA

This 10-card set was produced by the American Hockey Coaches Association for the College Hockey Centennial and features black-and-white photos in a tan border. The backs carry information about the events pictured on the front, which all are key in the history of the development of hockey in the United States.

COMPLETE SET (10) 3.00 8.00
1 The Pioneers .20 .50
2 The Inspiration Hobey Baker .60 1.50
3 The Personalities .20 .50
John Mariucci
4 The Champions Michigan .40 1.00
5 The Colleges .20 .50
Edward Jeremiah
6 The Coaches Ron Mason .20 .50
7 The Records 1970 Cornell squad .20 .50
8 The Moments Dean Talafous .20 .50
9 The Traditions .20 .50
1978 Boston University Champions
10 The Future Cammi Granato .60 1.50

1991-92 Air Canada SJHL

This 250-card standard-size set features players in the Saskatchewan Junior Hockey League. The set included an entry form for a contest sponsored by Air Canada and Old Dutch, which entitled the winner to a trip for two to anywhere in North America. The cards features posed color player photos with team color-coded shadow borders. The pictures are set on thin, white card stock with the team name in a yellow bar at the top. The player's name appears in the white margin at the bottom. The backs are white and carry biographical information and a player profile. The cards are numbered on the back and were issued in five series denoted by the letters A, B, C, D, and E as card number prefixes.

COMPLETE SET (250) 14.00 35.00
A1 Dean Normand .10 .30
Humboldt Broncos
A2 Dan Meyers .08 .25
Estevan Brui
A3 Tyson Balog .07 .20
Weyburn Red Wings
A4 Tyler McMillan .07 .20
Weyburn Red Wings
A5 Jason Selkirk .07 .20
Saskatoon Titans
A6 Bryce Bohun .07 .20
A7 Blaire Hornung .07 .20
Saskatoon Titans
A8 Craig McKechnie .07 .20
Melville Millionaires
A9 Rejean Stringer .07 .20
A10 Corri Moffat .07 .20
Melville Millionaires
A11 Dion Johnson .07 .20
A12 Rod Krushel .07 .20
Melville Millionaires
A13 Mike Langen .07 .20
Weyburn Red Wings
A14 Jeff Hassman .07 .20
Melville Millionaires
A15 Dean Moore .07 .20
Notre Dame Hounds
A16 Trevor Wathen .07 .20
Minot Americans
A17 Curtis Knight .07 .20
Humboldt Broncos
A18 Chris Morgan .07 .20
Minot Americans
A19 Trevor Thurstan .07 .20
Flin Flon Bombers
A20 Wayne Filipenko .07 .20
Minot Americans
A21 Jason Feiffer .07 .20
Weyburn Red Wings
A22 Layne Douglas .07 .20
Minot Americans
A23 Dave Gardner .07 .20
A24 Ryan Sandholm .07 .20
Notre Dame Hounds
A25 Corey McKee .07 .20
Melfort Mustangs
A26 Trevor Schmiess .07 .20
Humboldt Broncos
A27 Todd Hollinger .20 .50
Saskatoon Titans
A28 Jay Dunn .07 .20
A29 Jamie Ling .10 .30
Notre Dame Hounds
A30 Todd Small .07 .20
Saskatoon Titans
A31 Barret Kropf .07 .20
Melfort Mustangs
A32 Dean Gerard .07 .20
Melfort Mustangs
A33 Christian Dutil .07 .20
Yorkton Terriers
A34 Tyler Scheidt .07 .20
Aaron Campbell
Melfort Mustangs
A35 Dean Sideroff .07 .20
Humboldt Broncos
A36 Dan Dufresne .07 .20
Notre Dame Hounds
A37 Cam Yager .07 .20
A38 Richard Nagy .08 .25
Flin Flon
A39 Aaron Cain .20 .50
Flin Flon Bombers
A40 Rob Beck .07 .20
Flin Flon Bombers
A41 Blair Wagar .07 .20
Yorkton Terriers
A42 Kim Maier .07 .20
Estevan Bruins
A43 Brent Hoiness .07 .20
A44 Troy Edwards .07 .20
Estevan Bruins
A45 Evan Anderson .07 .20
Estevan Bruins
A46 Carlin Nordstrom .07 .20
A47 Dean Seymour .07 .20
Yorkton Terriers
A48 Scott Wotton .10 .30
Yorkton Terriers
A49 Curtis Joseph 4.00 10.00
SJHL All Star
B1 Richard Boscher .07 .20
Saskatoon Titans
B2 James Schaeffler .07 .20
Saskatoon Titans
B3 Wes Rommel .07 .20
B4 Corey Thompson .07 .20
B5 Rob Phillips .10 .30
B6 Jim McLean .07 .20
B7 Trevor Warrener .20 .50
Saskatoon Titans
B8 Peter Boake .07 .20
Weyburn Red Wings
B9 Kevin Riffel .07 .20
Estevan Bruins
B10 Tom Perry .07 .20
Humboldt Broncos
B11 Mark Baird .07 .20
Humboldt Broncos
B12 Stacy Prevost .07 .20
Yorkton Terriers
B13 Taras Lendzyk .07 .20
Humboldt Broncos
B14 Shawn Reis .07 .20
Melfort Mustangs
B15 Shawn Thompson .07 .20
Future Prospect
B16 Curtis Kleisinger .07 .20
Notre Dame Hounds
B17 Kent Rogers .07 .20
Saskatoon Titans
B18 Scott Christion .10 .30
Notre Dame Hounds
B19 Gerald Tallaire .10 .30
Estevan Bruins
B20 Kelly Hollingshead .10 .30
Este
B21 Mike Savard .07 .20
B22 Darren Maloney .07 .20
Melville Millionaires
B23 Jason Hynd .07 .20
B24 Scott Stewart .07 .20
Flin Flon Bombers
B25 Scott Beattie .10 .30
SJHL All Star
B26 Dave McAmmond .07 .20
Flin Flon Bombers
B27 Myles Gibb .07 .20
B28 Ryan Bach .20 .50
Notre Dame Hounds
B29 Martin Smith .07 .20
B30 Leigh Brookbank .07 .20
Yorkton Terriers
B31 Todd Markus .07 .20
Melfort Mustangs
B32 The Boys From PA .10 .30
Dean Gerard
Darryn Listwan
Sco
B33 Randy Muise .07 .20
Weyburn Red Wings
B34 George Gervais .07 .20
Estevan Bruins
B35 Keith Harris .07 .20
Weyburn Red Wings
B36 Jamie Stelmak .07 .20
Melville Millionaires
B37 Bart Vanstaalduinen .07 .20
Notre Dame Hounds
B38 Scott Murray .07 .20
Minot Americans
B39 Danny Galarneau .07 .20
Yorkton Terriers
B40 Keith Murphy .07 .20
Melville Millionaires
B41 Jeff Kungle .10 .30
Melfort Mustangs
B42 Michel Cook .07 .20
Yorkton Terriers
B43 Daryl Krauss .07 .20
Weyburn Red Wings
B44 Derek Wynne .07 .20
Minot Americans
B45 Derek Crimin .07 .20
Minot Americans
B46 Jason Brown .07 .20
Flin Flon Bombers
B47 Bruce Matatall .07 .20
Minot Americans
B48 Chris Hatch .07 .20
Flin Flon Bombers
B49 Kurtise Souchotte .07 .20
Melville Millionaires
B50 Michael Brennan .07 .20
Humboldt Broncos
B51 Orrin Hergott .07 .20
Future Prospect
C1 Craig Matatall .07 .20
Notre Dame Hounds
C2 Brad Prefontaine .07 .20
Melville Millionaires
C3 Mike Evans .07 .20
Notre Dame Hounds
C4 Jody Reiter .07 .20
C5 Jeremy Mylymok .07 .20
Notre Dame Hounds
C6 Dave Doucet .10 .30
Melville Mi
C7 Randy Kerr .07 .20
Melville Millionaires
C8 Gordon McCann .07 .20
Melville Millionaires
C9 Quinn Fair .07 .20
Notre Dame Hounds
C10 Kyle Niemegeers .07 .20
Estevan Bruins
C11 Ryan Smith .10 .30
North Battle
C12 Mike Hillock .07 .20
Minot Americans
C13 Vern Anderson .07 .20
C14 Trent Hamm .07 .20
C15 Curtis Folkett ACO .07 .20
Estevan Bruins
C16 Warren Pickford .07 .20
C17 Craig Volstad .07 .20
C18 Sean Tallaire .10 .30
Estevan B
C19 Jason Yaganiski .07 .20
Minot Americans
C20 Jim McLarty .07 .20
C21 Jamie Fyfuglien .07 .20
Minot Americans
C22 Terry Metro .07 .20
Minot Americans
C23 Todd Kozak .07 .20
C24 Jeff Huckle .07 .20
Saskatoon Titans
C25 Darren McLean .07 .20
Estevan Bruins
C26 Bret Mohninger .07 .20
Saskatoon Titans
C27 Tim Slukynsky .07 .20
Yorkton Terriers
C28 Roman Mrhalek .07 .20
Yorkton Terriers
C29 Joel Martinson .07 .20
Humboldt Broncos
C30 Ron Patterson .07 .20
Flin Flon Bombers
C31 Mark Gorgi .07 .20
Melfort Mustangs
C32 Tom Thomson .07 .20
Saskatoon Titans
C33 Greg Wahl .07 .20
Saskatoon Titans
C34 Craig Perrett .07 .20
Melfort Mustangs
C35 Mike Harder .07 .20
Weyburn Red Wings
C36 Jeff Cole .07 .20
Humboldt Broncos
C37 Justin Christoffer .07 .20
Humboldt Broncos
C38 Nolan Weir .07 .20
Flin Flon Bombers
C39 Jeff Knight .07 .20
Melfort Mustangs
C40 Lyle Vaughan .07 .20
Yorkton Terriers
C41 Scott Bellefontaine .07 .20
Yorkton Terriers
C42 Trevor Mathias .07 .20
Weyburn Red Wings
C43 Chris Schinkel .10 .30
Humboldt
C44 Scott Rogers .08 .20
Melfort Mustangs
C45 Shane Holunga .07 .20
Weyburn Red Wings
C46 Dwayne Rhinehart .07 .20
Flin Flon Bombers
C47 Eddy Marchant .07 .20
Flin Flon Bombers
C48 Travis Smith .07 .20
Weyburn Red Wings
C49 Not Known .07 .20
C50 Mike Hidlebaugh .07 .20
Future Prospect
D1 Darcy Herlick .07 .20
Weyburn Red Wings
D2 Joel Appleton .07 .20
Humboldt Broncos
D3 Bobby Standish .07 .20
Melfort Mustangs
D4 Kory Karlander .10 .30
Saskatoon Titans
D5 Brett Kinaschuk .07 .20
Humboldt Broncos
D6 Kevin Messer .07 .20
D7 Jason Martin .07 .20
Weyburn Red Wings
D8 Devin Zimmer .07 .20
Minot Americans
D9 David Foster .07 .20
Humboldt Broncos
D10 Bob Schwark .07 .20
Melfort Mustangs
D11 Ted Grayling .07 .20
Melville Millionaires
D12 Travis Vantighem .10 .30
Melvil
D13 Darren Houghton .07 .20
Melville Millionaires
D14 Wade Welte .07 .20
Melville Millionaires
D15 1991 NB All Stars .20 .50
Martin Smith
Ron Gunville
Der
D16 Kevin Powell .07 .20
Minot Americans
D17 Returning Hounds .07 .20
Dave Lovesin
Bernie Adlys
Bart
D18 Dennis Budeau .07 .20
Minot Americans
D19 Darren Opp .07 .20
D20 Jeff Greenwood .07 .20
D21 Mark Daniels .20 .50
Saskatoon Titans
D22 Todd Murphy .07 .20
D23 Scott Weaver .07 .20
Minot Americans
D24 Robby Bear .07 .20
Yorkton Terriers
D25 Nigel Werenka .10 .30
Yorkton Terriers
D26 Sean Timmins .07 .20
Notre Dame Hounds
D27 Ken Malenfant .07 .20
Saskatoon Titans
D28 Greg Taylor .07 .20
Melfort Mustangs
D29 Sheldon Bylsma .07 .20
Yorkton Terriers
D30 Clint Hooge .07 .20
Flin Flon Bombers
D31 Bob McIntosh .07 .20
Notre Dame Hounds
D32 Dave Lovsin .07 .20
Notre Dame Hounds
D33 Jeremy Mathies .07 .20
D34 Blaine Fomradas .07 .20
Weyburn Red Wings
D35 Cory Borys .07 .20
Yorkton Terriers
D36 Brad Purdie .07 .20
Weyburn Red Wings
D37 J. Sotropa .07 .20
Saskatoon Titans
D38 Duane Vardale .07 .20
D39 Jim Nellis .07 .20
D40 Brent Sheppard .07 .20
Humboldt Broncos
D41 Cam Bristow .07 .20
Melfort Mustangs
D42 Steven Brent .07 .20
Estevan Bruins
D43 Mike Matteucci .07 .20
Estevan Bruins
D44 Bryan Cossette .07 .20
Estevan Bruins
D45 Tyler Kuhn .07 .20
Flin Flon Bombers
D46 Dave Debusschere .07 .20
Esteva
D47 Darryl Dickson .07 .20
Flin Flon Bombers
D48 Derek Meikle .07 .20
Flin Flon Bombers
D49 Parris Duffus .20 .50
Ex SJHLer
D50 Lance Wakefield .10 .30
Future Prospect
E1 Brooke Battersby .07 .20
Estevan Bruins
E2 Jay Dobrescu .07 .20
Estevan Bruins
E3 Blair Allison .07 .20
Estevan Bruins
E4 Shane Johnson .07 .20
Estevan Bruins
E5 Carson Cardinal .07 .20
Estevan Bruins
E6 Dean Pooyak .07 .20
Flin Flon Bombers
E7 Mark Loeppky .07 .20
Flin Flon Bombers
E8 Travis Cheyne .07 .20
Flin Flon Bombers
E9 Karl Johnson .07 .20
Flin Flon Bombers
E10 Jason Ahenakew .07 .20
Flin Flon Bombers
E11 Darren Schmidt .10 .30
Humboldt Broncos
E12 Larry Empey .07 .20
Humboldt Broncos
E13 Colin Froese .07 .20
Humboldt Broncos
E14 Darryn Listwan .07 .20
Melfort Mustangs
E15 Todd MacMillan .07 .20
Melfort Mustangs
E16 Ken Ruddock .07 .20
Melfort Mustangs
E17 Derek Simonson .07 .20
Melfort Mustangs
E18 Lyle Ehrmantraut .07 .20
Minot Americans

19 Jody Weller .07 .20
20 Danny Dennis .07 .20
Melville Millionaires
21 Trent Harper .07 .20
Melville Millionaires
22 Jason Prokopetz .10 .30
Melvill
23 Tom Thomson .07 .20
Saskatoon Titans
24 Trent Dumaine .07 .20
25 Mike Wevers .07 .20
Saskatoon Titans
26 Darren Duncalfe .07 .20
Weyburn Red Wings
27 Regan Simpson .07 .20
28 Jeff Bloski .07 .20
29 Blake Sutton .07 .20
30 Darcy Blair .10 .30
North Battl
31 Marty Craigdallie .07 .20
Notre Dame Hounds
32 Jason Krug .07 .20
Notre Dame Hounds
33 Mark Hansen .07 .20
Notre Dame Hounds
34 Bernie Adlys .07 .20
Notre Dame Hounds
35 Brett Colborne .07 .20
Notre Dame Hounds
36 Tony Bergin .07 .20
Notre Dame Hounds
37 Ian Adamson .07 .20
38 Darren MacMillan .07 .20
39 Rob Neighbour .07 .20
40 Jeff Lawson .07 .20
41 Derrick Brucks .07 .20
Saskatoon Titans
42 Todd Schoenroth .07 .20
Saskatoon Titans
43 Jody Forseth .07 .20
Weyburn Red Wings
44 Derek Beuselinck .07 .20
Weyburn Red Wings
45 Clint Wensley .07 .20
Weyburn Red Wings
46 Darren Donald .07 .20
Weyburn Red Wings
47 Shane Stangby .07 .20
Yorkton Terriers
48 Jamie Dunn .07 .20
Yorkton Terriers
49 Steve Sabo .07 .20
Yorkton Terriers
50 Anthony Toth .07 .20
Yorkton Terriers

1991-92 Air Canada SJHL All-Stars

This 50-card standard-size set features Saskatchewan Junior Hockey League All-Stars. The set included an entry form for a contest sponsored by Air Canada and Old Dutch, which entitled the winner to a trip for two to anywhere in North America. The cards feature posed color player photos with yellow shadow borders. The pictures are set against a white card face accented with an screened pale purple star pattern. The words "All Star" appear in red within a yellow and black striped bar at the top, while the player's name is printed below the photo. The backs carry the player's name, biographical information, and a player profile.

COMPLETE SET (50) 4.80 12.00
1 Jeff Kungle .15 .40
2 Jay Dunn .08 .25
3 Kevin Dickie .08 .25
4 Martin Smith .08 .25
5 Jeff Cole .08 .25
6 Trent Hamm .08 .25
7 Kent Rogers .08 .25
8 Dean Gerard .08 .25
9 Jim McLarty .08 .25
10 Malcolm Kostuchenko .08 .25
11 Mark Scollan .08 .25
12 Brad Federenko .20 .50
13 Rob Beck .08 .25
14 Bryce Bohun .08 .25
15 Kory Karlander .15 .40
16 Scott Christion .15 .40
17 Tyler Kuhn .08 .25
18 Corri Moffatt .08 .25
19 Layne Douglas .08 .25
20 Shane Holunga .08 .25
21 Mike Matteucci .08 .25
22 Bart Vanstaalduinen .08 .25
23 Brad McEwen .08 .25
24 Kim Maier .08 .25
25 Jamie Ling .20 .50
26 Dean Seymour .08 .25
27 Derek Crimin .08 .25
28 Evan Anderson .08 .25
29 Craig Matatall .08 .25
30 Keith Murphy .08 .25
31 Jason Feiffer .08 .25
32 Michel Cook .08 .25
33 Rod Krushel .08 .25
34 Tyler Rice .15 .40
35 Gerald Tallaire .20 .50
36 Richard Nagy .08 .25
37 Taras Lendzyk .08 .25
38 Jeff Knight .08 .25
39 Darren Opp .08 .25
40 Dwayne Rhinehart .08 .25
41 Minot Americans .08 .25
Layne Douglas
Derek Crimin
42 Scott Bellefontaine .08 .25
43 Darren Maloney .08 .25
44 North Division .20 .50
All-Star Team
Team Photo
45 Yorkton Terriers .20 .50
All Stars
Michel Cook
Dean Seymour
Scott Bellefontaine
46 Melville Millionaires .20 .50
All Stars
Team Photo
47 Best 1992 All-Stars .20 .50
Kevin Dickie CO
Mike Matteucci
Kory Karlander
Kim Maier
Darren Opp
Richard Nagy
Mark Scollan
48 Estevan Bruins .20 .50
All Stars
Gerald Tallaire
Kim Maier
Mike Matteucci
Evan Anderson
49 Notre Dame Hounds .20 .50
All Stars
Tyler Rice
Scott Christion
Bart Van Staalduinen
Jamie Ling
Craig Matatall
50 Bob Robson CO .08 .25

2003-04 Alaska Aces

Produced by RBI Sports and sold at the team's rink.

COMPLETE SET (16) 10.00 20.00
1 Jordan Cameron .50 1.25
2 Kimbi Daniels .50 1.25
3 Bret DeCecco .50 1.25
4 Wes Dorey .50 1.25
5 Jonathan Gauthier .50 1.25
6 Malcolm Hutt .50 1.25
7 Mike Jones .50 1.25
8 Charles Linglet .50 1.25
9 Chris Lipsett .50 1.25
10 Lance Mayes .75 2.00
11 Keith McCambridge .50 1.25
12 Ryan Moren .50 1.25
13 Dan Murphy .75 2.00
14 Shane Palahicky .50 1.25
15 Garrett Prosofsky .50 1.25
16 Mark Smith .50 1.25

2010-11 Alaska Aces

COMPLETE SET (20) 4.00 10.00
1 Scott Burt .30 .75
2 Wes Goldie .60 1.50
3 Bryan Miller .30 .75
4 Brian Swanson .60 1.50
5 Chad Anderson .30 .75
6 Ethan Cox .30 .75
7 Alex Dzielski .30 .75
8 Adam Courchaine .30 .75
9 Scott Howes .30 .75
10 Kory Falite .30 .75
11 Garry Nunn .30 .75
12 Maxime Tanguay .30 .75
13 Gerald Coleman .30 .75
14 Mark Isherwood .30 .75
15 Steve Ward .30 .75
16 Chris Langkow .30 .75
17 Jerad Stewart .30 .75
18 Zach Harrison .30 .75
19 Brandon Gentile .30 .75
20 Russ Sinkewich .30 .75

1995-96 Alaska Gold Kings

This 19-card set of the Alaska Gold Kings appears to be the first set produced for a club in the West Coast Hockey League. The set was manufactured and distributed by Jessen Associates. The fronts feature action color photos, complemented by the player's name, number and position, the team logo and the league name. The backs contain biographical and statistical data. The set is unnumbered, and listed in alphabetical order.

COMPLETE SET (19) 3.60 9.00
1 Title Card .08 .25
2 Derby Bognar .20 .50
3 Geoff Bumstead .30 .75
4 Chris Cahill .20 .50
5 Warren Carter .20 .50
6 John Haddad .20 .50
7 Todd Henderson .20 .50
8 Wade Klippenstein .20 .50
9 Matt Koleski .20 .50
10 Donald Lester .20 .50
11 Derek Linnell .20 .50
12 Jamie Loewen .20 .50
13 Travis MacMillan .20 .50
14 Kirk Patton .20 .50
15 Guy Prince .20 .50
16 Rob Proffitt .20 .50
17 Ryan Reynard .20 .50
18 Wayne Sawchuk CO .02 .10
19 Shawn Ulrich .20 .50

1996-97 Alaska Gold Kings

This 14-card set of "Alaska's 1st Professional Hockey Team" features the Gold Kings of the West Coast Hockey League. The set was produced by Split Second, using unusually heavy card stock, and features grainy action photos on the front, along with the player's name and jersey number, and the team logo. The backs all include the team logo, as well as those of sponsors Coca-Cola of Fairbanks, Winchell's, Club Golf and Twisted Stitches. No player info is included. The cards are unnumbered, and are listed below alphabetically.

COMPLETE SET (14) 3.00 8.00
1 Mark Costea .30 .75
2 Shane Fisher .30 .75
3 Colin Foley .30 .75
4 Chris French .30 .75
5 Yoshifumi Fujtsawa .30 .75
6 Todd Henderson .30 .75
7 Kelly Hrycun .30 .75
8 Shawn Lofroth .30 .75
9 Brad McCaughey CO .02 .10
10 Billy McGuigan .30 .75
11 Jay Murphy .30 .75
12 Sergei Olympiev .30 .75
13 Orion The Lion .02 .10
Mascot
14 Shawn Ulrich .30 .75

1996-97 Albany River Rats

This set features the River Rats of the AHL. The set was produced by Split Second and sold by the team at the rink for $5.

COMPLETE SET (26) 6.00 15.00
1 Eric Bertrand .20 .50
2 Brad Bombardir .20 .50
3 Steve Brule .20 .50
4 Mike Dunham .40 1.00
5 Patrik Elias .75 2.00
6 Bryan Helmer .20 .50
7 Bobby House .20 .50
8 Geordie Kinnear .20 .50
9 Chris McAlpine .20 .50
10 Krzysztof Oliwa .40 1.00
11 Jay Pandolfo .40 1.00
12 Denis Pederson .30 .75
13 Pascal Rheaume .30 .75
14 Vadim Sharifijanov .20 .50
15 Richard Shulmistra .30 .75
16 Peter Sidorkiewicz .30 .75
17 Zdenek Skorepa .20 .50
18 Sheldon Souray .20 .50
19 Mark Strobel .20 .50
20 Steve Sullivan .40 1.00
21 Sergei Vyshedkevich .20 .50
22 John Cunniff CO .02 .10
23 Dennis Gendron CO .02 .10
24 Rowdy MASCOT .02 .10
25 AHL Web Site .02 .10
26 PHPA Web Site .02 .10

1997-98 Albany River Rats

This set features the River Rats of the AHL. The set was produced by SplitSecond and was sold by the team at home games.

COMPLETE SET (26) 6.00 15.00
1 Eric Bertrand .15 .40
2 Jiri Bicek .40 1.00
3 Steve Brule .15 .40
4 Bryan Helmer .15 .40
5 Bobby House .15 .40
6 Geordie Kinnear .20 .50
7 Sasha Lakovic .20 .50
8 Judd Lambert .20 .50
9 John Madden .75 2.00
10 Brendan Morrison .75 2.00
11 Jay Pandolfo .20 .50
12 Richard Rochefort .15 .40
13 Vadim Sharifijanov .20 .50
14 Peter Sidorkiewicz .20 .50
15 Zdenek Skorepa .15 .40
16 Rob Skrlac .15 .40
17 Ken Sutton .15 .40
18 Paul Traynor .15 .40
19 Sergei Vyshedkevich .20 .50
20 Colin White .30 .75
21 Jeff Williams .15 .40
22 Peter Zezel .40 1.00
23 John Cunnitt CO .10 .25
24 Dennis Gendron CO .10 .25
25 PHPA Web Site .02 .10
26 AHL Web Site .02 .10

1998-99 Albany River Rats

This set features the River Rats of the AHL. The set was produced by Split Second and was sold by the team at its souvenir stands.

COMPLETE SET (25) 4.80 12.00
1 Eric Bertrand .15 .40
2 Jiri Bicek .30 .75
3 Steve Brule .20 .50
4 Mike Buzak .15 .40
5 David Cunniff .15 .40
6 Pierre Dagenais .30 .75
7 Josh DeWolf .15 .40
8 Sascha Goc .30 .75
9 Frederic Henry .15 .40
10 Geordie Kinnear .20 .50
11 John Madden .75 2.00
12 Rob Pattison .15 .40
13 Henrik Rehnberg .15 .40
14 Richard Rochefort .15 .40
15 Alexander Semak .15 .40
16 Rob Skrlac .15 .40
17 Ken Sutton .15 .40
18 Chris Thompson .15 .40
19 Sergei Vyshedkevich .15 .40
20 Colin White .30 .75
21 Jeff Williams .15 .40
22 Red Gendron CO .02 .10
23 John Cunniff CO .02 .10
24 Rowdy MASCOT .02 .10
25 AHL Web Site .02 .10

1999-00 Albany River Rats

This 26-card set showcases the AHL River Rats, and was sold by the team at its souvenir shop. The cards are not numbered so they are listed alphabetically.

COMPLETE SET (26) 4.80 12.00
1 George Awada .15 .40
2 Jiri Bicek .30 .75
3 Steve Brule .20 .50
4 Bobby Carpenter ACO .20 .50
5 Sylvain Cloutier .15 .40
6 David Cunniff .15 .40
7 John Cunniff CO .15 .40
8 Pierre Dagenais .30 .75
9 Jean-Francois Damphousse .60 1.50
10 Josh DeWolf .20 .50
11 Dennis Gendron ACO .15 .40
12 Sascha Goc .30 .75
13 Stanislav Gron .40 1.00
14 Frederic Henry .30 .75
15 Steve Kelly .20 .50
16 Andre Lakos .15 .40
17 Sasha Lakovic .20 .50
18 Carlyle Lewis .15 .40
19 David Maley .15 .40
20 Willie Mitchell .15 .40
21 Richard Rochefort .15 .40
22 Rob Skrlac .15 .40
23 Ken Sutton .15 .40
24 Rowdy MASCOT .02 .10
25 Colin White .30 .75
26 Jeff Williams .15 .40

2000-01 Albany River Rats

This set features the River Rats of the AHL and was produced by Choice Marketing. The cards were sold in set form by the team at its souvenir stands.

COMPLETE SET (27) 4.00 10.00
1 Daryl Andrews .15 .40
2 Jiri Bicek .30 .75
3 Max Birbraer .20 .50
4 Josef Boumedienne .15 .40
5 Sylvain Cloutier .15 .35
6 Mike Commodore .20 .50
7 Pierre Dagenais .30 .75
8 Chris Ferraro .15 .35
9 Sascha Goc .20 .50
10 Stanislav Gron .40 1.00
11 Mike Jefferson .20 .50
12 Andre Lakos .15 .35
13 Jason Lehoux .15 .35
14 Carlyle Lewis .15 .35
15 Willie Mitchell .20 .50
16 Lucas Nehrling .15 .35
17 Henrik Rehnberg .15 .35
18 Richard Rochefort .15 .35
19 Michael Rupp .40 1.00
20 Rob Skrlac .15 .35
21 Ed Ward .15 .35
22 Jean-Francois Damphousse .30 .75
23 Frederic Henry .20 .50
24 John Cunniff CO .04 .10
25 Bobby Carpenter ACO .10 .25
26 Alex Zinevych .15 .35
27 Team CL .04 .10

2001-02 Albany River Rats

This set features the River Rats of the AHL. The cards were produced by Choice Marketing and sold at home games.

COMPLETE SET (28) 6.00 12.00
1 Checklist .04 .10
2 Sylvain Cloutier .10 .25
3 Jean-Francois Damphousse .20 .50
4 Mike Commodore .10 .25
5 Daryl Andrews .10 .25
6 Andre Lakos .10 .25
7 Mikko Jokela .20 .50
8 Joel Dezainde .10 .25
9 Jiri Bicek .30 .75
10 Stanislav Gron .30 .75
11 Brian Gionta .40 1.00
12 Richard Rochefort .10 .25
13 Michael Rupp .30 .75
14 Ted Drury .10 .25
15 Max Birbraer .20 .50
16 Christian Berglund .10 .25
17 Scott Cameron .10 .25
18 Jason Lehoux .10 .25
19 Brett Clouthier .10 .25
20 Bruce Gardiner .10 .25
21 Stephen Guolla .20 .50
22 Victor Uchevatov .10 .25
23 Joel Bouchard .10 .25
24 Ari Ahonen 1.25 3.00
25 Scott Clemmensen .40 1.00
26 Bob Carpenter CO .04 .10
27 Geordie Kinnear ACO .04 .10
28 Rowdy .04 .10

2002-03 Albany River Rats

This set was produced by Choice Marketing and sold at home games.

COMPLETE SET (28) 5.00 12.00
1 Ari Ahonen .40 1.00
2 Alex Brooks .20 .50
3 Brett Clouthier .20 .50
4 Christian Berglund .20 .50
5 Craig Darby .20 .50
6 Chris Hartsburg .20 .50
7 Daryl Andrews .20 .50
8 David Roche .20 .50
9 Eric Johansson .20 .50
10 Jiri Bicek .20 .50
11 Joe Hulbig .20 .50
12 Jason Lehoux .20 .50
13 Krisjanis Redlihs .20 .50
14 Ken Sutton .20 .50
15 Max Birbraer .40 1.00
16 Mikko Jokela .20 .50
17 Mike Matteucci .20 .50
18 Michael Rupp .40 1.00
19 Ray Giroux .20 .50
20 Rob Skrlac .20 .50
21 Scott Cameron .20 .50
22 Scott Clemmensen .40 1.00
23 Victor Uchevatov .20 .50
24 Greg Crozier .20 .50
25 Dennis Gendron HCO .04 .10
26 Geordie Kinnear ACO .04 .10
27 Gates Orlando ACO .04 .10
NNO Checklist .04 .10

2002-03 Albany River Rats AAP

This set was issued as a promotional giveaway at a late-season game. The card backs all feature an ad for Advance Auto Parts. The cards are unnumbered and so are listed below in alphabetical order.

COMPLETE SET (25) 8.00 20.00
1 Checklist card .04 .10
2 Ari Ahonen .50 1.25
3 Daryl Andrews .40 1.00
4 Max Birbraer .50 1.25
5 Alex Brooks .40 1.00
6 Scott Cameron .40 1.00
7 Scott Clemmensen .50 1.25
8 Brett Clouthier .40 1.00
9 Greg Crozier .40 1.00
10 Craig Darby .40 1.00
11 Ray Giroux .40 1.00
12 Red Gendron CO .04 .10
13 Chris Hartsburg .40 1.00
14 Joe Hulbig .40 1.00
15 Eric Johansson .40 1.00
16 Mikko Jokela .40 1.00
17 Jason Lehoux .40 1.00
18 Mike Matteucci .40 1.00
19 Krisjanis Redlihs .40 1.00
20 Dave Roche .40 1.00
21 Rowdy MASCOT .04 .10
22 Michael Rupp .50 1.25
23 Rob Skrlac .40 1.00
24 Ken Sutton .40 1.00
25 Victor Uchevatov .40 1.00

2003-04 Albany River Rats

This set was produced by Choice Marketing and sold at home games.

COMPLETE SET (30) 5.00 12.00
1 Checklist .04 .10
2 Ari Ahonen .30 .75
3 Maxim Balmochnykh .15 .40
4 Jiri Bicek .15 .40
5 Alex Brooks .15 .40
6 Scott Clemmensen .30 .75
7 Brett Clouthier .15 .40
8 Greg Crozier .15 .40
9 Craig Darby .15 .40
10 Matt DeMarchi .15 .40
11 Adrian Foster .15 .40
12 Ray Giroux .15 .40
13 Tyler Hanchuck .15 .40
14 Chris Hartsburg .15 .40
15 Joe Hulbig .15 .40
16 Eric Johansson .15 .40
17 Steve Kariya .60 1.50
18 Matus Kostur .15 .40
19 Mike Matteucci .15 .40
20 Ryan Murphy .15 .40
21 Ahren Nittel .30 .75
22 Tuomas Pihlman .30 .75
23 Ilkka Pikkarainen .15 .40
24 Krisjanis Redlihs .15 .40
25 Rob Skrlac .15 .40
26 Alexander Suglobov .15 .40
27 Victor Uchevatov .15 .40
28 Dennis Gendron CO .04 .10
29 Gates Orlando ACO .04 .10
30 Geordie Kinnear ACO .04 .10

2003-04 Albany River Rats Kinko's

COMPLETE SET (26) 15.00 30.00
1 Ari Ahonen .60 1.50
2 Maxim Balmochnykh .40 1.00
3 Jiri Bicek .40 1.00
4 Alex Brooks .40 1.00
5 Scott Clemmensen .60 1.50
6 Brett Clouthier .40 1.00
7 Greg Crozier .40 1.00
8 Craig Darby .40 1.00
9 Matt DeMarchi .40 1.00
10 Adrian Foster .40 1.00
11 Ray Giroux .40 1.00
12 Tyler Hanchuck .40 1.00
13 Chris Hartsburg .40 1.00
14 Joe Hulbig .40 1.00
15 Eric Johansson .40 1.00
16 Steve Kariya 1.25 3.00
17 Matus Kostur .40 1.00
18 Mike Matteucci .40 1.00
19 Ryan Murphy .40 1.00
20 Ahren Nittel .75 2.00
21 Tuomas Pihlman .40 1.00
22 Ilkka Pikkarainen .40 1.00
23 Krisjanis Redlihs .40 1.00
24 Rob Skrlac .40 1.00
25 Alexander Suglobov .40 1.00
26 Victor Uchevatov .40 1.00

2004-05 Albany River Rats

COMPLETE SET (25) 6.00 15.00
1 Ari Ahonen .30 .75
2 Bobby Allen .15 .40
3 Alex Brooks .15 .40
4 Scott Clemmensen .30 .75
5 Brett Clouthier .15 .40
6 Matt DeMarchi .15 .40
7 Adrian Foster .15 .40
8 David Hale .40 1.00
9 Cam Janssen .40 1.00
10 Eric Johansson .15 .40
11 Teemu Kesa .15 .40
12 Ivan Khomutov .15 .40
13 Dean McAmmond .15 .40
14 Ryan Murphy .15 .40
15 Ahren Nittel .30 .75
16 Zach Parise 2.00 5.00
17 Tuomas Pihlman .15 .40
18 Ilkka Pikkarainen .15 .40
19 Krisjanis Redlihs .15 .40
20 Pascal Rheaume .15 .40
21 Ray Schultz .15 .40
22 Rob Skrlac .15 .40
23 Aaron Voros .15 .40
24 Aleksander Suglobov .15 .40
25 Robbie Ftorek CO .04 .10

2005-06 Albany River Rats

COMPLETE SET (28) 6.00 15.00
1 Ari Ahonen .40 1.00
2 Bobby Allen .20 .50
3 Nicklas Bergfors .20 .50
4 Alex Brooks .20 .50
5 Ben Carpentier .20 .50
6 David Clarkson .20 .50
7 Matt DeMarchi .20 .50
8 Frank Doyle .40 1.00
9 Adrian Foster .20 .50
10 David Hale .20 .50
11 Cam Janssen .40 1.00
12 Teemu Kesa .20 .50
13 Ivan Khomutov .20 .50
14 Bryan Miller .20 .50
15 Ryan Murphy .20 .50
16 Ahren Nittel .40 1.00
17 Tuomas Pihlman .20 .50
18 Ilkka Pikkarainen .20 .50
19 Krisjanis Redlihs .20 .50
20 Pascal Rheaume .20 .50
21 Jason Ryznar .20 .50
22 Ray Schultz .20 .50
23 Mike Sgroi .20 .50
24 Aleksander Suglobov .20 .50
25 Barry Tallackson .40 1.00
26 Aaron Voros .20 .50
27 Petr Vrana .20 .50
28 Robbie Ftorek .02 .10

2006-07 Albany River Rats

COMPLETE SET (27) 5.00 12.00
1 Kevin Estrada .20 .50
2 Keith Aucoin .20 .50
3 Ryan Bayda .20 .50
4 Joe Barnes .20 .50
5 Jesse Boulerice .20 .50
6 Johnny Boychuck .20 .50
7 Tim Conboy .20 .50
8 Kyle Cumiskey .20 .50
9 Dan DaSilva .20 .50
10 Pat Dwyer .20 .50
11 Jeff Finger .20 .50
12 Dave Gove .20 .50
13 Ben Guite .20 .50
14 Scott Kelman .20 .50
15 Mitch Love .20 .50
16 Cody McLeod .20 .50
17 Matt Murley .20 .50
18 Justin Peters .30 .75
19 Jakub Petruzalek .20 .50
20 Peter Tsimikalis .20 .50
21 Tyler Weiman .30 .75
22 Shane Willis .20 .50
23 Brett Carson .20 .50
24 Tom Rowe HC .02 .10
25 Joe Sacco CO .02 .10
NNO Rowdy MASCOT .02 .10
NNO Checklist .01 .01

2013-14 Alberni Valley Bulldogs

COMPLETE SET (22) 6.00 15.00
1 Hunter Stewart .30 .75
2 Nathan Warren .30 .75
3 Harlan Orr .30 .75
4 Craig Martin .30 .75
5 Robert Click .30 .75
6 Quinton Wunder .30 .75
7 Brett Stewart .30 .75
8 Ryan Buse .30 .75
9 Jake Kauppila .30 .75
10 Mitch Owsley .30 .75
11 Tryg Strand .30 .75
12 Darian Henry .30 .75
13 Zach Funk .30 .75
14 Scott Clark .30 .75
15 Mitch Makin .30 .75
16 Josh Adkins .30 .75
17 Justin Georgeson .30 .75
18 Zak Bowles .30 .75
19 Dylan Haugen .30 .75
20 Kurt Gosselin .30 .75
21 Garrett Halls .30 .75
22 Connor LaCouvee .30 .75

1999-00 Alexandria Warthogs

This set features the Warthogs of the WPHL. The singles were handed out one per home game throughout the season. The card of Jason Leveille was not widely distributed to the public because of an early season trade. A few copies, however, have made their way onto the secondary market.

COMPLETE SET (23) 20.00 50.00
1 Mark Biesenthal .75 2.00
2 Jeff Blair .75 2.00
3 Jason Desloover .75 2.00
4 Josh Dobbyn .75 2.00
5 Valeri Ermolov .75 2.00
6 Dion Hagan .75 2.00
7 Daniel Korber .75 2.00
8 Chris Low .75 2.00
9 Jay Mazur .75 2.00
10 Jim Mroz .75 2.00
11 Matt Osiecki .75 2.00
12 Chris Peach .75 2.00
13 Marc Pethke .75 2.00
14 Robert Plante .75 2.00
15 Regan Stocco .75 2.00
16 Matt Turek .75 2.00
17 Colby Van Tassel .75 2.00
18 Miles Van Tassel .75 2.00
19 Mike Zruna CO .40 1.00
20 Jason Leveille 4.00 10.00
21 Marcus Adolfsson .75 2.00
22 Bill Weir .75 2.00
23 Chad Wilchynski .75 2.00

1998-99 Amarillo Rattlers

This 21-card set was a promotional giveaway that was handed out over five Rattlers home games.

COMPLETE SET (21) 10.00 25.00
1 Matt Brenner .60 1.50
2 Chris Brooks .60 1.50
3 Stephen Douglas .60 1.50
4 Steve Ferranti .60 1.50
5 Bob Gohde .60 1.50
6 Brad Haelzle .60 1.50
7 Derek Innanen .60 1.50
8 Trevor Janicki .60 1.50
9 Brendan Kenny .60 1.50
10 Todd Laurin .60 1.50
11 Adam Lord .60 1.50
12 Cal McGowan .75 2.00
13 Jim McLean .60 1.50
14 David Rattray .60 1.50
15 Jaynen Rissling .60 1.50
16 Per Schlyter .60 1.50
17 Scott W. Stevens .60 1.50
18 Neil Gondek ACO .08 .25
19 Ken Karpuk CO .08 .25
20 Amarillo Rattlers .08 .25
21 Greg Sieg TR .08 .25

2000-01 Amarillo Rattlers

This set features the Rattlers of the WPHL. It is believed that the set was a promotional giveaway, but that cannot be confirmed.

COMPLETE SET (20) 8.00 20.00
1 Eric Andersen .40 1.00
2 Chris Bell .40 1.00
3 Rodney Bowers .40 1.00
4 Jeff Cheeseman .40 1.00
5 Marc Dupuis .40 1.00
6 Larry Empey .40 1.00
7 Vincent Grant .40 1.00
8 Brad Haelzle .40 1.00
9 Toby Harris .40 1.00
10 Robert Holsinger .75 2.00
11 Todd MacDonald .75 2.00
12 Jeff Mancini .40 1.00
13 Jodi Murphy .75 2.00
14 Billy Newson .40 1.00
15 Jay Pecora .40 1.00
16 Doug Shepherd .40 1.00
17 Tony White .40 1.00
18 Chad Wilchynski .40 1.00
19 Kevin Abrams CO .08 .25
20 Team Card .08 .25

1993-94 Amos Les Forestiers

This 26-card standard-size set features Les Forestiers, a Midget AAA team in the province of Quebec. Les Forestiers is one of ten teams in the province from which the junior teams pick their players. The production run was reportedly 505 sets, including 60 autographed sets randomly placed in the lot. On a white card face, the fronts display posed color player photos framed by blue on the left and top and by magenta on the right and bottom. Player identification is printed in the top border, and the team name is printed in the left border. The backs present biographical and trivia information. The set includes 1995 NHL first rounder, Martin Biron.

COMPLETE SET (26) 14.00 35.00
1 Jean-Francois Belley .40 1.00
2 Carl Benoit .40 1.00
3 Martin Biron 6.00 15.00
4 David Bolduc .40 1.00
5 Martin Bradette .40 1.00
6 Dave Fontaine .40 1.00
7 Paul-Sebastien Gagnon .40 1.00
8 Eric Germain .40 1.00
9 Eric Houle .40 1.00
10 Jacques Larrivee ACO .08 .25
11 Yannick Lavoie .40 1.00
12 Mathieu Letourneau .40 1.00
13 Vincent Levasseur .40 1.00
14 Jonathan Levesque .40 1.00
15 Eric Naud .40 1.00
16 Christian Neveu .40 1.00
17 Patrick Pelchat .40 1.00
18 John Pyliotis .40 1.00
19 Luc St-Germain .40 1.00
20 Frederick Servant .40 1.00
21 Philippe Tremblay .40 1.00
22 Serge Trepanier CO .08 .25
23 Dany Villeneuve .40 1.00
24 Les Veterans .40 1.00
Christian Neveu
Mathieu Letourneau
25 Team Photo .40 1.00
CL
26 Title card .08 .25

1992-93 Anaheim Bullfrogs RHI

This set features the Bullfrogs of Roller Hockey International. The set was sold by the team at home games.

COMPLETE SET (20) 4.00 10.00
1 Header Card .02 .10
2 Maury Silver .20 .50
3 Stuart Silver .20 .50
4 Marc Lyons .20 .50
5 Kevin Kerr .20 .50
6 Grant Sonier ACO .08 .25
7 Darry Potomski .30 .75
8 Bob McKillop .20 .50
9 Rob Laurie .30 .75
10 Bill Horn .20 .50
11 Savo Mitrovic .20 .50
12 Chris McSorley CO .20 .50
13 Victor Gervais .30 .75
14 Darren Perkins .20 .50
15 Christian LaLonde .20 .50
16 Joe Cook .20 .50
17 Ken Murchison .20 .50
18 Brad McCaghey .20 .50
19 Devin Edgerton .20 .50
20 Mike Dutters .20 .50

1993-94 Anaheim Bullfrogs RHI

This 21-piece set commemorates one of the most successful teams in the brief-lived Roller Hockey International. Along with traditional cards, each set also came with a POG slammer. The cards are unnumbered, and so are listed below alphabetically

COMPLETE SET (21) 3.20 10.00
1 Shayne Arsenault .20 .50
2 Steve Beadle .20 .50
3 Jim Brown .20 .50
4 Joe Cook .20 .50
5 Victor Gervais .20 .50
6 Chris Gordon .20 .50
7 Kevin Kerr .30 .75
8 Yuri Krivokhija .20 .50
9 Christian Lalonde .20 .50
10 Darren Langdon .30 .75
11 Rob Laurie .30 .75
12 Brad McCaughey .20 .50
13 Bobby McKillop .30 .75
14 Savo Mitrovic .20 .50
15 Ken Murchison .20 .50
16 Darren Perkins .20 .50
17 Grant Sonier CO .08 .25
NNO The Mask .30 .75
NNO 1993 RHI World Champions .20 .50
NNO Header .02 .10
NNO Medallion Slammer .20 .50

1994-95 Anaheim Bullfrogs RHI

This set features the Bullfrogs of Roller Hockey Intl. The 20-card set was sold by the team at home games. Because the singles are not numbered, the players appear alphabetically.

COMPLETE SET (20) 3.60 10.00
1 Darren Banks .30 .75
2 Jared Bednar .20 .50
3 Steve Cadieux .20 .50
4 Joe Cook .20 .50
5 Mark Deazeley .20 .50
6 Victor Gervais .30 .75
7 Chris Gordon .20 .50
8 Fredrik Jax .20 .50
9 Rick Judson .20 .50
10 Rob Laurie .30 .75
11 BJ MacPherson .20 .50
12 Brad McCaughey .20 .50
13 Savo Mitrovic .20 .50
14 Marc Ouimet .30 .75
15 Darren Perkins .20 .50
16 Daniel Shank .30 .75
17 Grant Sonier CO .02 .10
18 Brad Tiley .20 .50
19 Todd Wetzel .20 .50
20 Header/Checklist .02 .10

1995-96 Anaheim Bullfrogs RHI

Little is known about this set beyond the confirmed checklist. Any additional information can be forwarded to hockeymag@beckett.com.

COMPLETE SET (20) 3.00 8.00
1 Checklist .02 .10
2 Grant Sonier CO .02 .10
3 Brad McCaughey ACO .02 .10
4 Victor Gervais .15 .40
5 Darren Perkins .15 .40
6 Savo Mitrovic .15 .40
7 Joe Cook .15 .40
8 Todd Wetzel .15 .40
9 Scott Bell .15 .40
10 Rick Judson .15 .40
11 BJ MacPherson .15 .40
12 Rob Laurie .15 .40
13 Darren Banks .20 .50
14 Sean O'Brien .15 .40
15 Jakub Ficenec .15 .40
16 Mark Stitt .15 .40
17 Glenn Stewart .15 .40
18 Mark DeSantis .15 .40
19 Tom Menicci .15 .40
20 Eric Raymond .15 .40

1996-97 Anaheim Bullfrogs RHI

This 21-card set was available late in the season, and could only be purchased at games. The cards are unnumbered, and are listed below in the order they were packaged. They were produced by Star Images Assoc.

COMPLETE SET (21) 3.60 9.00
1 Bullfrogs Logo .02 .10
2 Zeus Mascot .02 .10
3 Rob Laurie .20 .50
4 Victor Gervais .20 .50
5 Doug McCarthy .20 .50
6 Kurt Seher .20 .50
7 Marty Yewchuk .20 .50
8 David Goverde .25 .60
9 BJ MacPherson .02 .10
10 Rick Judson .25 .60
11 Jakub Ficenec .20 .50
12 Tom Menicci .20 .50
13 Glenn Stewart .20 .50
14 Mark Stitt .20 .50
15 Jim Bermingham .20 .50
16 Todd Wetzel .20 .50
17 Joe Cook .20 .50
18 Ray Edwards .20 .50
19 Chris Newans .20 .50
20 Darren Perkins .20 .50
21 Brad McCaughey CO .02 .10

1994-95 Anchorage Aces

This set features the Aces of the WCHL. Little is known about this set beyond the checklist, which was provided by Ralph Slate of www.hockeydb.com. Any additional information can be forwarded to hockeymag@beckett.com.

COMPLETE SET (27) 4.80 12.00
1 Kevin Fitzgerald .20 .50
2 Tony Link .20 .50
3 Zack Westin .20 .50
4 Kory Wright .20 .50
5 Kord Cernich .20 .50
6 Darrin Semeniuk .20 .50
7 Brian Kraft .20 .50
8 Raymond Blackadar .20 .50
9 Jim Tobin .20 .50
10 Tracy Link .20 .50
11 Michael Warde .20 .50
12 Garvin Federenko .20 .50
13 Jim Mayes .20 .50
14 Vern Hickel .20 .50
15 Derek Donald .20 .50
16 Brian Majeske .20 .50
17 Chad Meyhoff .20 .50
18 Doug Spooner .20 .50
19 Maurice Hall .20 .50
20 Pete McEnaney .20 .50
21 Keith Street .20 .50
22 Georg Thiele .20 .50

23 Tim Molle .20 .50
24 Brian Bethard .20 .50
25 Dean Trboyevich .20 .50
26 Logo Card .04 .10
27 Team Photo .20 .50
Checklist

1996-97 Anchorage Aces

This 16-card set was produced as a promotional giveaway for the Anchorage Aces of the WCHL. The fronts feature posed photos with the players blatantly shilling for the Subway chain; that company's logo is prominently displayed in the lower left corner, along with those of the local FOX TV outlet and KWHL radio. The backs feature sketchy bio information. As the cards are unnumbered, they are listed below in alphabetical order.

COMPLETE SET (16) 3.00 8.00
1 Alaska's Morning Show .02 .10
2 Derek Donald .30 .75
3 Kiddie Fox .02 .10
4 Dean Larson .30 .75
5 Steve MacSwain .30 .75
6 Mark The Hitman .02 .10
7 J.J. Michaels .30 .75
8 Black Mike .02 .10
9 Craig Mittleholt .30 .75
10 Chris Newans .30 .75
11 Frank Ouellette .30 .75
12 Chad Richard .30 .75
13 Sean Rowe .30 .75
14 Keith Street .30 .75
15 Dean Trboyevich .30 .75
16 Free Q-Zar Game Card .02 .10

1997-98 Anchorage Aces

This set features the Aces of the WCHL. The set was produced by the team and sold at home games.

COMPLETE SET (25) 3.60 9.00
1 Title Card .02 .10
2 Walt Poddubny CO .20 .50
3 Kenny Huizenga .20 .50
4 Kord Cernich .20 .50
5 Bobby Cunningham .20 .50
6 Derek Donald .20 .50
7 Dallas Ferguson .20 .50
8 Derek Gauthier .20 .50
9 Jason Gibson .20 .50
10 Marc LaForge .20 .50
11 Dean Larson .20 .50
12 Dave Latta .20 .50
13 Steve MacSwain .20 .50
14 Chris Newans .20 .50
15 Hayden O'Rear .20 .50
16 Brian Renfrew .20 .50
17 Sean Rowe .20 .50
18 Jason Shmyr .20 .50
19 Keith Street .20 .50
20 Sergei Tkachenko .20 .50
21 George Wilcox .20 .50
22 Paul Williams .20 .50
23 Mascot .02 .10
24 Mascot .02 .10
25 Mascot .02 .10

1998-99 Anchorage Aces

This set features the Aces of the WHL. The cards measure 2 1/2 by 3 1/2 and feature a full-bleed color photo on the front. The team logo is blown up in the lower left corner. The backs feature stats over a ghosted player head shot.

COMPLETE SET (26) 4.00 10.00
1 Checklist .20 .50
Team Photo
2 Dean Trboyevich .20 .50
3 Kevin Epp .20 .50
4 Hayden O'Rear .20 .50
5 Richard Peacock .20 .50
6 Sean Rowe .20 .50
7 Boomer Mascot .02 .10
8 George Wilcox .20 .50
9 Sergei Tkachenko .20 .50
10 Frank Jury TR .02 .10
11 Walt Poddubny HCO .20 .50
12 Kent Baumbach .20 .50
13 Wade Brookbank .20 .50
14 Keith Street .20 .50
15 Bob Cunningham .20 .50
16 Kord Cernich .20 .50
17 Paul Williams .20 .50
18 Evgeny Kourilin .20 .50
19 Jason Gibson .20 .50
20 Steve MacSwain .20 .50
21 Dean Larson .20 .50
22 Dallas Ferguson .20 .50
23 Derek Gauthier .20 .50
24 Yvan Corbin .20 .50
25 Sponsor Card .02 .10
26 Fred Rannard BR .02 .10

1999-00 Anchorage Aces

This set features the Aces of the WCHL. The card fronts feature a full-bleed color photo, along with the logos of sponsors Subway and Wideo City. The backs contain a b/w head shot and stats from the previous season.

COMPLETE SET (28) 4.00 10.00
1 Bob Wilkie HCO .08 .25
2 Fred Rannard .20 .50
3 Paul Williams .20 .50
4 Steve MacSwain .20 .50
5 Marc Charbonneau .20 .50
6 Chad Power .20 .50
7 Brian Elder .20 .50
8 Tim Lozinik .20 .50
9 Sponsor Card .02 .10
10 Sponsor Card .02 .10
11 Kord Cernich .20 .50
12 George Wilcox .20 .50
13 Keith Street .20 .50
14 Derek Gauthier .20 .50
15 Ruslan Batyrshin .30 .75
16 Sean Rowe .20 .50
17 Dean Larson .20 .50
18 Team Photo .20 .50
19 Sponsor Card .02 .10
20 Sponsor Card .02 .10
21 Walt Poddubny HCO .08 .25
22 Dallas Ferguson .20 .50
23 Chad Richard .20 .50
24 Denis Pigolitsyn .20 .50
25 Clayton Read .20 .50
26 Marc Delmore .20 .50
27 Lada Hampeis .20 .50
28 Sponsor Card .02 .10

2001-02 Anchorage Aces

This set features the Aces of the WCHL. The set was given away at a home game late in the season.

COMPLETE SET (22) 8.00 20.00
1 Shane Calder .40 1.00
2 Bob Cunningham .40 1.00
3 Kimbi Daniels .40 1.00
4 Simon Duplessis .40 1.00
5 Yuri Krivokhija .40 1.00
6 Brian LaFleur .40 1.00
7 Dean Larson .40 1.00
8 Michael Marostega .40 1.00
9 Jamie McCaig .60 1.50
10 Chris Newans .40 1.00
11 Denis Pigolitsin .40 1.00
12 Tobin Praznik .40 1.00
13 Chad Richard .60 1.50
14 Olie Sundstrom .60 1.50
15 Paul Williams .40 1.00
16 J.J. Wrobel .40 1.00
17 Jami Yoder .40 1.00
18 B.J. Young .40 1.00
19 Walt Poddubny CO .10 .25
20 Boomer MASCOT .04 .10
21 ACS Wireless .04 .10
22 Team Photo .20 .50

1990-91 Arizona Icecats

Produced by the Ninth Inning, this 16-card standard-size set features members of the Arizona Icecats. Production was reportedly limited to 2,150 sets, obtainable either at the Tucson Convention Center Ice Arena on game days or at the Ninth Inning (a card shop). The front features a posed color photo of the player, with thin black border on white card stock. The upper left and lower right hand corners of the picture are cut out, with the year and the team logo inserted in these spaces respectively. The back presents biographical information in a black box. Although the individual cards are unnumbered, they are checklisted below according to the numbering assigned to them on the checklist card.

COMPLETE SET (16) 3.00 8.00
1 Leo Golembiewski CO .30 .75
2 Icecat Leaders .40 1.00
Kevin Sheehan
John Allen
Leo Golembiewski CO
Kelly Walker
John Wegener
3 John Allen .30 .75
4 Don Carlson .20 .50
5 Dan Divjak .30 .75
6 Frank DeMaio .20 .50
7 Jeremy Goltz .30 .75
8 Aaron Joffe .20 .50
9 Dan O'Day .20 .50
10 Dan Olberg .20 .50
11 Cory Oleson .30 .75
12 Kevin Sheehan .30 .75
13 Dean Sives .20 .50
14 Kelly Walker .30 .75
15 John Wegener .30 .75
16 Logo Card .20 .50
Checklist

1991-92 Arizona Icecats

This 20-card standard-size set features members of the Arizona Icecats. The front features a posed color photo of the player, with thin blue border and a blue shadow-border on white card stock. The player's name appears in the bottom shadow- border. The back presents biographical information and statistics in a black shadow-bordered box. Though the individual cards are unnumbered, they are checklisted below according to the numbering assigned to them on the checklist card.

COMPLETE SET (20) 4.00 10.00
1 Leo Golembiewski CO .08 .25
2 Don Carlson .20 .50
3 Kelly Walker .30 .75
4 Cory Oleson .30 .75
5 Drew Sibr .20 .50
6 Dan Divjak .30 .75
7 Jeremy Goltz .30 .75
8 Aaron Joffe .20 .50
9 Tommy Smith .20 .50
10 Dan Anderson .20 .50
11 Dean Sives .20 .50
12 Steve Hutchings .20 .50
13 Shane Fausel .20 .50
14 Greg Mitchell .20 .50
15 Ricky Pope .20 .50
16 Nate Soules .20 .50
17 Flavio Gentile .20 .50
18 Icecats Leaders .20 .50
Leo Golembiewski CO
Kelly Walker
Cory Oleson
Jeremy Goltz
Dan Divjak
19 Glenn Hall 1.00 2.50
Honorary Captain
20 Logo Card .08 .25
Checklist

1992-93 Arizona Icecats

This 16-card standard-size set features the Arizona Icecats hockey team. The fronts display a posed color player photo with multiple blue drop borders. The player's name appears in a royal blue stripe across the bottom of the picture. The backs carry biographical information and statistics in a black shadow-bordered box. Though the individual cards are unnumbered, they are checklisted below according to the numbering assigned to them on the checklist card.

COMPLETE SET (20) 3.00 8.00
1 Leo Golembiewski CO .08 .25
2 Kelly Walker .25 .60
3 Cory Oleson .25 .60
4 Tommy Smith .20 .50
5 John Allen .20 .50
6 Dan Anderson .20 .50
7 Aaron Joffe .20 .50
8 Dan Divjak .25 .60
9 Jeremy Goltz .20 .50
10 Steve Hutchings .20 .50
11 Greg Mitchell .20 .50
12 Ricky Pope .20 .50
13 Nate Soules .20 .50
14 Matt Glines .20 .50
15 Mark Thawley .20 .50
16 Andre Zafrani .20 .50
17 Chris Noga .20 .50
18 Jim Kolbe .08 .25
Honorary Captain
19 Coach and Top Gun Line .30 .75
Cory Oleson
Leo Golembiew
20 Logo Card .08 .25
Checklist

1993-94 Arizona Icecats

Yet another set issued by the most hobby-friendly club hockey team in the United States. This year's celebrity captain is that exemplary American, Oliver North. The set was sold by the team to raise money for the program.

COMPLETE SET (20) 3.00 8.00
1 Header Card .08 .25
2 Leo Golembiewski CO .08 .25
3 Greg Mitchell .20 .50
4 Ricky Pope .20 .50
5 Dan Divjak .25 .60
6 Brian Consolino .20 .50
7 Matt Gines .20 .50
8 Steve Hutchings .20 .50
9 Joel Nusbaum .20 .50
10 Sam Battaglia .20 .50
11 Kiva Gippo .20 .50
12 Jeremy Goltz .20 .50
13 Peter Scott .20 .50
14 Kevin Oztekin .20 .50
15 Nate Soules .20 .50
16 Chris Noga .20 .50
17 Dennis Hands .20 .50
18 Mark Thawley .20 .50
19 Leader Card .08 .25
20 Oliver North .30 .75

1994-95 Arizona Icecats

This low-tech set features the Icecats of the NCAA. The fronts offer a posed on-ice photo, taken in front of a bad backdrop. The backs feature 1993-94 stats and a pre-printed autograph.

COMPLETE SET (24) 10.00 25.00
1 Title Card/CL .02 .10
2 Leo Golembiewski CO .40 1.00
3 Steve Hutchings .40 1.00
4 Nate Soules .40 1.00
5 Chris Noga .40 1.00
6 Kevin Oztekin .40 1.00
7 Greg Mitchell .40 1.00
8 Ricky Pope .40 1.00
9 Brian Consolino .40 1.00
10 John Muntz .40 1.00
11 Joel Nusbaum .40 1.00
12 Sam Battaglia .40 1.00
13 Kiva Gippo .40 1.00
14 Peter Scott .40 1.00
15 Dennis Hands .60 1.50
16 Mark Thawley .40 1.00
17 Ryan Rockabrand .40 1.00
18 Joe Joyce .40 1.00
19 Jeremy Walters .40 1.00
20 Ethan Kaulas .40 1.00
21 Reg Kerr/Glen Hall .75 2.00
22 Leo Golembiewski .60 1.50
Keith Magnuson
23 Stan Mikita 2.00 5.00
Glen Hall
Keith Magnuson
Al Secord
24 Madhouse on Main Street .10 .25

1995-96 Arizona Icecats

This set features the Icecats of the ACHA. The cards feature a posed photo on the front, framed by a purple border. The sparse backs offer peronsal data and stats.

COMPLETE SET (23) 25.00
1 Title Card/CL .02 .10
2 Leo Golembiewski CO .10 .25
3 Chris Noga .40 1.00
4 John Muntz .40 1.00
5 Kevin Oztekin .40 1.00
6 Mark Thawley .40 1.00
7 Sam Battaglia .40 1.00
8 Peter Scott .40 1.00
9 Joel Nusbaum .40 1.00
10 Ryan Rockabrand .40 1.00
11 Andy Knick .40 1.00
12 Brian Meehan .40 1.00
13 Bob Majka .40 1.00
14 Ben Ruston .40 1.00
15 Jeff Rice .40 1.00
16 Brian Consolino .40 1.00
17 Bryan Fork .40 1.00
18 Joel Hilshey .50 1.25
19 Joe Joyce .40 1.00
20 Jeremy Goltz ACO .10 .25
21 Icecat Leaders .20 .50
22 Scotty Bowman 2.00 5.00
23 Scotty Bowman Hon Capt. 2.00 5.00

1996-97 Arizona Icecats

This set features the Icecats of the ACHA. The cards are standard-sized and feature a posed shot framed by a thick red border. The sparse backs list personal data and last season's stats.

COMPLETE SET (25) 4.00 25.00
1 Title Card/CL .02 .10
2 Leo Golembiewski HCO .10 .25
3 Kevin Baskel .40 1.00
4 Sam Battaglia .40 1.00
5 Brian Consolino .40 1.00
6 Josh Flett .40 1.00
7 Eric Holton .40 1.00
8 Paul Juran .40 1.00
9 Andy Knick .40 1.00
10 Eliot Komar .40 1.00
11 Beau Lemire .50 1.25
12 Joe McCaffrey .40 1.00
13 Brian Meehan .40 1.00
14 Joel Nusbaum .40 1.00
15 Ace Pascual .40 1.00
16 Rob Poupard .40 1.00
17 Ben Ruston .40 1.00
18 Peter Scott .40 1.00
19 Mike Tesi .40 1.00
20 Tom Thompson .40 1.00
21 Dave Weiss .40 1.00
22 Bob Majka .40 1.00
23 Leo Golembiewski HCO .10 .25
24 Jeremy Goltz ACO .10 .25
25 Stan Mikita Hon Capt. 2.00 5.00

1997-98 Arizona Icecats

This set features the Icecats of the ACHA. The cards feature a posed color photo framed by a thick white border. Card numbers are found on the front, lower right. The sparse backs list player personal data.

COMPLETE SET (26) 10.00 25.00
1 Title Card/CL .02 .10
2 Leo Golembiewski HCO .20 .50
3 Benedictine HOF .10 .25
4 Kevin Baskel .40 1.00
5 Jordan Bolton .60 1.50
6 Tyler Brush .40 1.00
7 Ed Carfora .40 1.00
8 Paul Dorn .40 1.00
9 Chad Dyjak .40 1.00
10 Rodney Glassman .40 1.00
11 Mike Graves .40 1.00
12 Marc Harris .40 1.00
13 Joe McCaffrey .40 1.00
14 Charles McCarty .40 1.00
15 Bob Majka .40 1.00
16 Brian Meehan .40 1.00
17 Ace Pascual .40 1.00
18 Joe Peplinski .60 1.50
19 Ben Ruston .40 1.00
20 Mike Tesi .40 1.00
21 Tom Thompson .40 1.00
22 Kory Wagstaff .40 1.00
23 Max Wilkie .40 1.00
24 Jim Wilkey .40 1.00
25 Jeremy Goltz ACO .20 .50
26 Rex Allen, Jr. Hon Capt. .40 1.00

1998-99 Arizona Icecats

COMPLETE SET (27) 10.00 25.00
1 Tyler Brush .40 1.00
2 Ed Carfora .40 1.00
3 Quinn Carter .40 1.00
4 Hunter Cherenack .40 1.00
5 Paul Dorn .40 1.00
6 Andrew Edwards .40 1.00
7 Rodney Glassman .40 1.00
8 Leo Golembiewski CO .02 .10
9 Jeremy Goltz ACO .02 .10
10 Mike Graves .40 1.00
11 Marc Harris .40 1.00
12 Bobby Hull HON CPT 2.00 5.00
13 Pavel Jandura .40 1.00
14 Bob Majka .40 1.00
15 Joe McCaffrey .40 1.00
16 Kyle McNeilance .40 1.00
17 Brian Meehan .40 1.00
18 Kevin Meehan .40 1.00
19 Mark Meister .40 1.00
20 Eugene Mesh .40 1.00
21 Jason Morgan .40 1.00
22 Kyle Neary .40 1.00
23 Jason Royce .40 1.00
24 Mike Tesi .40 1.00
25 Tom Thompson .40 1.00
26 Team Leaders .40 1.00
27 Checklist .02 .10

1999-00 Arizona Icecats

COMPLETE SET (28) 8.00 20.00
1 Tyler Brush .40 1.00
2 Ed Carfora .40 1.00
3 Hunter Cherenack .40 1.00
4 Paul Dorn .40 1.00
5 Andrew Edwards .40 1.00
6 Dave Galardini .40 1.00
7 Leo Golembiewski CO .02 .10
8 Jeremy Goltz ACO .02 .10
9 Mike Graves .40 1.00
10 Marc Harris .40 1.00
11 Chase Hoyt .40 1.00
12 Pavel Jandura .40 1.00
13 Dave Loftus .40 1.00
14 Bob Majka .40 1.00
15 Joe McCaffrey .40 1.00
16 Kyle McNeilance .40 1.00
17 Brian Meehan .40 1.00
18 Kevin Meehan .40 1.00
19 Mark Meister .40 1.00
20 Jason Morgan .40 1.00
21 Kyle Neary .40 1.00
22 Ryan Roth .40 1.00
23 Jason Royce .40 1.00
24 Sgt. Slaughter HON CPT .75 2.00
25 Tom Thompson .40 1.00
26 Team Leaders .40 1.00
27 L. Golembiewski Golf Classic .02 .10
28 Checklist .02 .10

2000-01 Arizona Icecats

COMPLETE SET (30) 8.00 20.00
1 Header .02 .10
Checklist
2 Joe Boysen .40 1.00
3 Tyler Brush .40 1.00
4 Ed Carfora .40 1.00
5 Paul Dorn .40 1.00
6 Andrew Edwards .40 1.00
7 Andrew Fredericks .40 1.00
8 Dave Galardini .40 1.00
9 Mike Graves .40 1.00
10 Marc Harris .40 1.00
11 Pavel Jandura .40 1.00
12 Braden Koprivica .40 1.00
13 Wes Krisay .40 1.00
14 Dave Loftus .40 1.00
15 Kyle McNeilance .40 1.00
16 Kevin Meehan .40 1.00
17 Jason Morgan .40 1.00
18 Kyle Neary .40 1.00
19 Bill Pardue .40 1.00
20 Jason Royce .40 1.00
21 John Saunders .40 1.00
22 Stefan Thomasson .40 1.00
23 Bill Veasey .40 1.00
24 Tom Wood .40 1.00
25 Leo Golembiewski CO .02 .10
26 Brian Meehan ACO .02 .10
27 Bob Leoni ACO .02 .10
28 Team Leaders .20 .50
29 Golf Classic .02 .10
30 Joe Cristiani HON CAPT .02 .10

2001-02 Arizona Icecats

COMPLETE SET (26) 8.00 20.00
1 Bryan Aronchick .40 1.00
2 Shaun Brooks .40 1.00
3 Papa Joe Chevalier HON CPT .20 .50
4 Andrew Fredericks .40 1.00
5 Dave Galardini .40 1.00
6 Leo Golembiewski CO .04 .10
7 Pavel Jandura .40 1.00
8 Matt Johnson .40 1.00
9 Braden Koprivica .40 1.00
10 Wes Krisay .40 1.00
11 Dave Loftus .40 1.00
12 Brian Meehan ACO .04 .10
13 Kevin Meehan .40 1.00
14 Mickey Meehan .40 1.00
15 Mickey Meehan .40 1.00
16 Matt Naylor .40 1.00
17 Kyle Neary .40 1.00
18 Bill Pardue .40 1.00
19 John Saunders .40 1.00
20 Mike Smith .40 1.00
21 Tom Wolf .40 1.00
22 Tom Wood .40 1.00
23 Nick Woods .40 1.00
24 Jerald Zivic .40 1.00
25 Team Leaders .20 .50
26 Checklist .04 .10

2002-03 Arizona Icecats

COMPLETE SET (32) 10.00 25.00
1 Bryan Aronchick .40 1.00
2 Matt Baumann .40 1.00
3 Shaun Brooks .40 1.00
4 Banks Concepcion .40 1.00
5 Cole Dunlop .40 1.00
6 Andrew Fredericks .40 1.00
7 Justin Guerra .40 1.00
8 Don Holtz .40 1.00
9 Matt Johnson .40 1.00
10 Rick Karasch .40 1.00
11 Braden Koprivica .40 1.00
12 Wes Krisay .40 1.00
13 Dave Loftus .40 1.00
14 Mickey Meehan .40 1.00
15 Keith Mitchell .40 1.00
16 Matt Muller .40 1.00
17 Matt Naylor .40 1.00
18 Eric Ormson .40 1.00
19 Bill Pardue .40 1.00
20 Mike Pelletier .40 1.00
21 Brian Pollock .40 1.00
22 Mike Smith .40 1.00
23 Dan Whitlock .40 1.00
24 Drew Williamson .40 1.00
25 Tim Wochok .40 1.00
26 Nick Woods .40 1.00
27 Leo Golembiewski CO .04 .10
28 Brian Meehan ACO .04 .10
29 Team Leaders .20 .50
30 Dwain Pipe MASCOT .04 .10
31 Don Rickles HON CPT .40 1.00
32 Checklist .04 .10

2003-04 Arizona Icecats

COMPLETE SET (31) 8.00 20.00
1 Bryan Aronchick .40 1.00
2 Shaun Brooks .40 1.00
3 Anthony Capone .40 1.00
4 Banks Concepion .40 1.00
5 Kevin Conners .40 1.00
6 Dave Cwik .40 1.00
7 Cole Dunlop .40 1.00
8 Andrew Fredericks .40 1.00
9 Don Holtz .40 1.00
10 Rick Karasch .40 1.00
11 Jerod Keene .40 1.00
12 Eric Kowalek .40 1.00
13 Casey Leyva .40 1.00
14 Bryan Meagher .40 1.00
15 Mickey Meehan .40 1.00
16 Jeff Merritt .40 1.00
17 Keith Mitchell .40 1.00
18 Josh Parry .40 1.00
19 D.J Pelletier .40 1.00
20 Brian Pollock .40 1.00
21 Mike Smith .40 1.00
22 Dan Whitlock .40 1.00
23 Drew Williamson .40 1.00
24 Tim Wochok .40 1.00
25 Leo Golembiewski CO .04 .10
26 Brian Meehan ACO .04 .10
27 Team Leaders .20 .50
28 Dwain Pipe MASCOT .04 .10
29 Don Rickles .40 1.00
30 John McCain HON CPT .40 1.00
31 Header Card .04 .10

2004-05 Arizona Icecats

COMPLETE SET (34) 6.00 15.00
1 Bryan Aronchick .30 .75
2 Anthony Capone .30 .75
3 Cole Dunlop .30 .75
4 Luke Edwall .30 .75
5 Leo Golembiewski CO .04 .10
6 Don Holtz .30 .75
7 Craig Irwin .30 .75
8 Eric Kowalek .30 .75
9 Dave Lawrence .30 .75
10 Casey Leyva .30 .75
11 Scott Marshall .30 .75
12 Brian Meehan ACO .04 .10
13 Mickey Meehan .30 .75
14 Keith Mitchell .30 .75
15 Josh Parry .30 .75
16 D.J. Pelletier .30 .75
17 Mike Pelletier .30 .75
18 Mark Perzi .30 .75
19 Jay Punsky .30 .75
20 Max Sliwinski .30 .75
21 Mike Smith .30 .75
22 Doug Wilson .30 .75
23 Tim Wochok .30 .75
24 Jerald Zivic .30 .75
25 Team Leaders .20 .50
26 Equipment Managers .04 .10
27 Sgt. Slaughter .40 1.00
28 L. Gombiewski Celebrity Golf .04 .10
29 Dwain Pipe MASCOT .04 .10
30 Sons of the Pioneers .04 .10
31 Team Picture .04 .10
32 Sen. John McCain .40 1.00
33 Willie Nelson HON CPT .40 1.00
34 Header Card .04 .10

2002-03 Arkansas Riverblades

COMPLETE SET (24) 10.00 25.00
1 Jason Bermingham .40 1.00
2 Mike Cirillo .40 1.00
3 Ryan Coole .40 1.00
4 Aaron Davis .40 1.00
5 Scott Fankhouser .75 2.00
6 Ernie Hartlieb .40 1.00
7 Maxim Linnik .40 1.00
8 Eric Long .40 1.00
9 Terry Marchant .40 1.00
10 Matt Pagnutti .20 .50
11 Samuel Paquet .40 1.00
12 Mike Renzi .40 1.00
13 Jason Saal .75 2.00
14 Mike Sandbeck .40 1.00
15 Mark Scott .40 1.00
16 Bud Smith .40 1.00
17 Jimi St. John .40 1.00
18 Dean Stock .40 1.00
19 Dean Stork .04 .10
20 Garry Toor .40 1.00
21 Damon Whitton .40 1.00
22 Chris Cichocki HCO .10 .25
23 RiverBabes .40 1.00
24 Rocky Bear-Boa Mascot .04 .10

1999-00 Asheville Smoke

This set was given out in three series at home games. The cards feature jersey numbers on the back, but are listed below in alphabetical order because of duplicate and skipped numbers.

COMPLETE SET (27) 30.00 75.00
1 Checklist .08 .25
2 Francois Bourdeau 1.25 3.00
3 Dan Brenzavich 1.25 3.00
4 Peter Cermak 1.25 3.00
5 Frank DeFrenza 1.25 3.00
6 Paul Giblin 1.25 3.00
7 Brent Gretzky 2.00 5.00
8 Francois Leroux 1.25 3.00
9 Dan McIntyre 1.25 3.00
10 Rob Milliken 1.25 3.00
11 Hayden O'Rear 1.25 3.00
12 Vaclav Pazourek 1.25 3.00
13 Cory Peterson 1.25 3.00
14 Jon Pirrong 2.00 5.00
15 Ken Plaquin 1.25 3.00
16 Ryan Prentice 1.25 3.00
17 Josh Tymchak 1.25 3.00
18 Shawn Ulrich 1.25 3.00
19 Lindsay Vallis 1.25 3.00
20 Richie Walcott 1.25 3.00
21 Bruce Watson 1.25 3.00
22 Cory Peterson 1.25 3.00
Josh Tymchak
Bruce Watson
23 Keith Gretzky HCO 1.25 3.00
24 Aaron Fackler EM .08 .25
25 Smoky Mascot .08 .25
26 Sponsor Card .01
27 Team Photo .40 1.00

2000-01 Asheville Smoke

This set features the Smoke of the UHL. The set was produced by Roox, and was distributed as a promotional giveaway over the course of three home games.

COMPLETE SET (27) 6.00 15.00
1 Ryan Aikia .30 .75
2 Brent Belecki .30 .75
3 Blue Bennefield .30 .75
4 Derek Crimin .30 .75
5 Alexandre Fomitchev .40 1.00
6 John Hewitt .30 .75
7 Olaf Kjenstad .40 1.00
8 Dominic Maltais .40 1.00
9 Tyler Prosofsky .30 .75
10 Bobby Rapoza .30 .75
11 Bogdan Rudenko .30 .75
12 J.C. Ruid .30 .75
13 Lee Svangstu .30 .75
14 Shawn Ulrich .30 .75
15 Pat Bingham CO .20 .50
16 Smoky MASCOT .04 .10
17 Ingles Zamboni SPONSOR .04 .10
18 Manager TR .04 .10
19 Tom Wilson .30 .75
20 Brett Colborne .30 .75
21 Robert Marshall .30 .75
22 Alex Dumas .30 .75
23 Vitali Andreev .30 .75
24 Evan Lindsay .40 1.00
25 Bruce Watson .40 1.00
26 Asheville Smoke .04 .10
27 He Shoots Team Card .10 .25

2001-02 Asheville Smoke

This set features the Smoke of the UHL. The cards were issued as a promotional giveaway, apparently at three different home games. Any additional information on this set can be forwarded to hockeymag@beckett.com.

COMPLETE SET (24) 8.00 20.00
1 Team Photo .20 .50
2 Kris Mallette .60 1.50
3 Tyler McMillan .40 1.00
4 Mike Payne .40 1.00
5 Chad Wagner .60 1.50
6 Forrest Gore .40 1.00
7 Tom Wilson .40 1.00
8 Todd Bisson .40 1.00
9 Geoff Derouin .60 1.50
10 Bobby Rapoza .40 1.00
11 Kamil Kuriplach .40 1.00
12 Todd MacIsaac .40 1.00
13 Sean Fitzgerald .40 1.00
14 Samuel Paquet .40 1.00
15 Kris Schultz .40 1.00
16 Bob Dalessio EQMG .04 .10
17 Smoky MASCOT .04 .10
18 Curtis Menzul .40 1.00
19 Cory Peterson .40 1.00
20 Jean-Francois Dufour .40 1.00
21 Jeff Petruic .40 1.00
22 J.C. Ruid .40 1.00
23 Blaine Russell .60 1.50
24 Shawn Ulrich CO .04 .10

1992-93 Atlanta Knights

Released by the team, this 24-card set features the 1992-93 Atlanta Knights. Base cards feature full color action photography and white borders. The set's print run was limited to 5000, and they were sold at the Omni Arena during the season for $5. This set is not numbered so it appears in packing order.

COMPLETE SET (24) 4.80 12.00
1 Header Card .02 .10
2 Manon Rheaume 2.00 5.00
3 Jeff Buchanan .08 .25
4 Matt Hervey .08 .25
5 Rick Lanz .08 .25
6 Colin Miller .08 .25
7 Keith Osborne .08 .25
8 Jason Lafreniere .08 .25
9 Jock Callander .40 1.00
10 Brent Gretzky .20 .50
11 Steve Maltais .40 1.00
12 Serguei Ossipov .40 1.00
13 Shayne Stevenson .20 .50
14 Scott Boston .08 .25
15 Jean Blouin .08 .25
16 Shawn Rivers .20 .50
17 Dan Vincelette .08 .25
18 Chris Lipuma .08 .25
19 Don Burke .08 .25
20 Christian Campeau .08 .25
21 Tim Bergland .08 .25
22 J.C. Bergeron .20 .50
23 David Littman .20 .50
24 Gene Ubriaco HCO .02 .10

1993-94 Atlanta Knights

Released by the team, this 24-card set features the 1992-93 Atlanta Knights. Base cards feature full color action photography and white borders. Set print run was limited to 5000, and were sold at the Omni Arena during the season for $5.00.

COMPLETE SET (24) 6.00 15.00
1 Mike Greenlay .20 .50
2 Jeff Buchanan .15 .40
3 Eric Charron .15 .40
4 Colin Miller .15 .40
5 Brent Gretzky .30 .75
6 Steve LaRouche .15 .40
7 Marc Tardif .20 .50
8 Jeff Madill .15 .40
9 Devin Edgerton .15 .40
10 Bill McDougall .15 .40
11 Jason Ruff .15 .40
12 Eric Dubois .15 .40
13 Martin Tanguay .15 .40
14 Stan Drulia .30 .75
15 Normand Rochefort .15 .40
16 Shawn Rivers .20 .50
17 Chris Lipuma .15 .40
18 Cory Cross .15 .40
19 Christian Campeau .15 .40
20 Tim Bergland .15 .40
21 J.C. Bergeron .20 .50
22 Manon Rheaume 2.50 6.00
23 Gene Ubriaco HCO .02 .10
CL Header Card .02 .10

1994-95 Atlanta Knights

Released by the team, this 24-card set features the 1992-93 Atlanta Knights. Base cards feature full color action photography and white borders. Set print run was limited to 5000, and were sold at the Omni Arena during the season for $5.00. This set is not numbered so it appears in packing order

COMPLETE SET (27) 4.00 10.00
1 Header Card .02 .10
2 Mike Greenlay .30 .75
3 Chris Nelson .15 .40
4 Derek Mayer .15 .40
5 Drew Bannister .15 .40
6 Allen Pedersen .15 .40
7 Colin Miller .15 .40
8 Brent Gretzky .30 .75
9 Peter Ferraro .15 .40
10 Devin Edgerton .15 .40
11 Chris Ferraro .30 .75
12 Jason Ruff .15 .40
13 Eric Dubois .15 .40
14 Stan Drulia .30 .75
15 Allen Egeland .15 .40
16 Aaron Gavey .15 .40
17 Yves Heroux .15 .40
18 Brian Straub .15 .40
19 Jeff Toms .15 .40
20 Chris Lipuma .15 .40
21 Cory Cross .15 .40
22 Christian Campeau .15 .40
23 Derek Wilkinson .30 .75
24 Brantt Myhres .30 .75
25 John Paris Jr. HCO .02 .10
26 Scott Gordon ACO .02 .10
27 Sir Hat Trick Mascot .02 .10

1995-96 Atlanta Knights

This set features the Knights of the IHL. The set was produced by Edge Ice.

COMPLETE SET (25) 5.00 12.00
1 Drew Bannister .20 .50
2 Doug Barrault .20 .50
3 Corey Beaulieu .20 .50
4 Ryan Brown .20 .50
5 Christian Campeau .20 .50
6 Stan Drulia .30 .75
7 Eric Dubois .20 .50
8 Allan Egeland .20 .50
9 Brantt Myhres .30 .75
10 Mark Greig .20 .50
11 Bob Halkidis .20 .50
12 Alexandre LaPorte .20 .50
13 Chris LiPuma .20 .50
14 Tyler Moss .30 .75
15 Brent Peterson .20 .50
16 Adrien Plavsic .20 .50
17 Jason Ruff .20 .50
18 Reggie Savage .20 .50
19 Corey Spring .20 .50
20 Jeff Toms .20 .50
21 Derek Wilkinson .30 .75
22 John Paris CO .08 .25
23 Scott Gordon CO .08 .25
24 Kurt Harvey TR .02 .10
25 Sir Hat Trick MAS .02 .10

2001-02 Atlantic City Boardwalk Bullies

These cards were handed out by the team at home games and player appearances. They appear to be hand cut and, therefore are varying sizes. The checklist may be incomplete.

COMPLETE SET (26) 10.00 20.00
1 Checklist .04 .10
2 Shane Belter .40 1.00
3 John Campbell .40 1.00
4 J.F. Caudron .40 1.00
5 Vratislav Cech .40 1.00
6 Kevin Colley .40 1.00
7 Sasha Cucuz .40 1.00
8 Luke Curtin .40 1.00
9 Shawn Degagne .60 1.50
10 Keith Dupee .40 1.00
11 Kirk Furey .40 1.00
12 Tyler Johnston .40 1.00
13 Jerry Keefe .40 1.00
14 Daniel Lacroix .40 1.00
15 Mark Loeding .40 1.00
16 Scott Matzka .40 1.00
17 Jamie O'Leary .40 1.00
18 Stefan Rivard .60 1.50
19 Rob Stanfield .40 1.00
20 Scott Stirling .60 1.50
21 Ian Walterson .40 1.00
22 Mike Haviland HCO .04 .10
23 Leigh Mendelson ACO .04 .10
24 Rick Bronwell EQM .04 .10
25 Woolly MASCOT .04 .10
26 Damien Hess TR .04 .10

2002-03 Atlantic City Boardwalk Bullies

It is believed these cards were handed out as singles by the team at home games and at public appearances. The checklist below may not be complete. Please forward any additional info to hockeymag@beckett.com.

COMPLETE SET (25) 10.00 20.00
1 Rick Bronwell EQM .04 .10
2 J.F. Caudron .40 1.00
3 Steve Cheredaryk .40 1.00
4 Kevin Colley .60 1.50
5 Luke Curtin .40 1.00
6 Kirk Furey .40 1.00
7 Jade Galbraith .75 2.00
8 Jerry Galway .40 1.00
9 Mike Haviland HCO .04 .10
10 Jimmy Henkel .40 1.00
11 Damien Hess TR .04 .10
12 Mark Loeding .40 1.00
13 Shawn Maltby .60 1.50
14 Scott Matzka .40 1.00
15 Leigh Mendelson ACO .04 .10
16 Ryan Mougenel .40 1.00
17 Steve Munn .40 1.00
18 Mike Nicholishen .40 1.00
19 Stefan Rivard .40 1.00
20 Paul Spadafora .40 1.00
21 Scott Stirling .60 1.50
22 Ian Walterson .40 1.00
23 Matthew Yeats .60 1.50

24 Wooly MASCOT .04 .10
25 Checklist .04 .10

2003-04 Atlantic City Boardwalk Bullies

Little is known about this set, beyond the checklist information provided by the great Ralph Slate.

COMPLETE SET (30) 10.00 25.00
1 Bujar Amidovski .75 2.00
2 Jon Cullen .40 1.00
3 Luke Curtin .40 1.00
4 Chad Dameworth .40 1.00
5 Danny Eberly .40 1.00
6 Brian Fahey .40 1.00
7 Aaron Foster .40 1.00
8 Kirk Furey .40 1.00
9 Jim Henkel .40 1.00
10 Scott Horvath .40 1.00
11 Matt Hubbauer .40 1.00
12 Jim Leger .40 1.00
13 John Longo .40 1.00
14 Preston Mizzi .40 1.00
15 Jake Moreland .40 1.00
16 Steve Munn .40 1.00
17 Sam Paolini .40 1.00
18 Joshua Prudden .40 1.00
19 Dave Reid .40 1.00
20 Stefan Rivard .40 1.00
21 John Sabo .40 1.00
22 Pierre-Luc Sleigher .40 1.00
23 Marc St. Jean .40 1.00
24 Scott Stirling .40 1.00
25 Ian Walterson .40 1.00
26 Kam White .40 1.00
27 Mike Haviland HCO .04 .10
28 Matt Thomas ACO .04 .10
29 Mascot .04 .10
30 Checklist .04 .10

2003-04 Atlantic City Boardwalk Bullies RBI Sports

This team set was sold at home games.

COMPLETE SET (16) 3.00 8.00
17 Jon Cullen .20 .50
18 Luke Curtin .20 .50
19 Danny Eberly .20 .50
20 Brian Fahey .20 .50
21 Aaron Foster .20 .50
22 Scott Horvath .20 .50
23 Jake Moreland .20 .50
24 Steve Munn .20 .50
25 Sam Paolini .20 .50
26 Joshua Prudden .20 .50
27 Dave Reid .20 .50
28 Stefan Rivard .20 .50
29 Pierre-Luc Sleigher .20 .50
30 Scott Stirling .20 .50
31 Ian Walterson .20 .50
32 Kam White .20 .50

2004-05 Atlantic City Boardwalk Bullies

These cards were given away over the course of the season. It's believed the checklist is complete, and the card numbering may be inaccurate. If you know of other cards, please email us at hockeymag@beckett.com.

COMPLETE SET (30) 10.00 25.00
1 Dave Reid .40 1.00
2 Ian Walterson .40 1.00
3 Fraser Clair .40 1.00
4 Brad Both .40 1.00
5 Colin Shields .40 1.00
6 Scott Horvath .40 1.00
7 Kelsey Muench .40 1.00
8 Derek Edwardson .40 1.00
9 Jason Notermann .40 1.00
10 Dustan Heintz .40 1.00
11 Tom Reimann .40 1.00
12 Paul Caponigri .40 1.00
13 Luke Curtin .40 1.00
14 Eric Nelson .40 1.00
15 Trevor Koenig .60 1.50
16 Brian Maddox TR .04 .10
17 Matt Thomas CO .04 .10
18 Mark French ACO .04 .10
19 Chris Burke EQM .04 .10
20 Brian Fahey .40 1.00
21 Vincent Macri .40 1.00
22 Jake Moreland .60 1.50
23 Dan Peters .40 1.00
24 Brett Peterson .40 1.00
25 Peter Bournazakis .40 1.00
26 Shawn Mather .40 1.00
27 Brett Nowak .40 1.00
28 Jean-Francois Plourde .40 1.00
29 Ryan Reid .40 1.00
30 Woolly MASCOT .04 .10

2004-05 Atlantic City Boardwalk Bullies Kinko's

COMPLETE SET (30) 10.00 25.00
1 Kelly Cup CL .02 .10
2 Jake Moreland .40 1.00
3 Bujar Amidovski .75 2.00
4 Steve Munn .40 1.00
5 Brian Fahey .40 1.00
6 Kam Whie .40 1.00
7 Dave Reid .40 1.00
8 Ian Walterson .40 1.00
9 Pierre-Luc Sleigher .40 1.00
10 Danny Eberly .40 1.00
11 Jim Henkel .40 1.00
12 Scott Horvath .40 1.00
13 Sam Paolini .40 1.00
14 John Sabo .40 1.00
15 Josh Prudden .40 1.00
16 John Longo .40 1.00
17 Matt Hubbaer .40 1.00
18 Marc St.Jean .40 1.00
19 Stefan Rivard .40 1.00
20 Chad Dameworth .40 1.00
21 Preston Mizzi .40 1.00
22 Jim Leger .40 1.00
23 Kirk Furey .40 1.00
24 Aaron Foster .40 1.00
25 Luke Curtin .40 1.00
26 Jon Cullan .40 1.00
27 Scott Stirling .40 1.00
28 Mike Haviland .40 1.00
29 Matt Thomas .40 1.00
30 Wooly .02 .10

2001-02 Augusta Lynx

This set features the Lynx of the ECHL. The cards were given away at eight different games, one per night.

COMPLETE SET (8) 6.00 15.00
1 Patrick Yetman .75 2.00
2 Scott Morrow .75 2.00
3 Cris Classen .75 2.00
4 Tyler Willis 1.25 3.00
5 Jeff Bes 1.25 3.00
6 Wes Swinson .75 2.00
7 Guy Larose .75 2.00
8 John Whitwell .75 2.00

2002-03 Augusta Lynx

COMPLETE SET (18) 10.00 20.00
61 Ryan Crane .40 1.00
62 Curtis Cruickshank .60 1.50
63 Tom Draper .60 1.50
64 Chris Gustafson .40 1.00
65 Tyson Holly .40 1.00
66 Andrew Ianiero .40 1.00
67 Martin Lapointe .40 1.00
68 Ryan Lauzon .40 1.00
69 Jay Leach .40 1.00
70 Mike Legg .40 1.00
71 Vince Malts .40 1.00
72 Brad Ralph .40 1.00
73 Philippe Roy .40 1.00
74 Josh St. Louis .40 1.00
75 Jim Shepherd .40 1.00
76 Chris Thompson .40 1.00
77 Mark Thompson .40 1.00
78 Andrew Williamson .40 1.00

2003-04 Augusta Lynx

This set was sold by the team at home games. The odd numbering reflects this portion of the entire league run produced by RBI Sports. Production supposedly was limited to 250 sets.

COMPLETE SET (16) 10.00 25.00
33 Todd Bennett .60 1.50
34 Scott Corbott .60 1.50
35 John Cronin .60 1.50
36 Brandon Doria .60 1.50
37 Matt Dzieduszycki .60 1.50
38 Paul Elliott .60 1.50
39 Jonathan Gagnon .60 1.50
40 Louis Goulet .60 1.50
41 Nick Greenough .60 1.50
42 Peter Hamerlik .75 2.00
43 Greg Jacina .60 1.50
44 Scott Kelman .60 1.50
45 Robert Liscak .60 1.50
46 Gregg Naumenko .75 2.00
47 Treavor Peterson .60 1.50
48 Shawn Weiman .60 1.50

2006-07 Augusta Lynx

COMPLETE SET (21) 15.00 30.00
1 Garrett Bembridge .75 2.00
2 Sean Blanchard .60 1.50
3 Mike Erickson .60 1.50
4 Louis Goulet .60 1.50
5 Shane Hynes .60 1.50
6 Jamie Johnson .60 1.50
7 Jason Kostadine .60 1.50
8 Nick Kuiper .60 1.50
9 Ryan Lang .60 1.50
10 Eric Lundberg .60 1.50
11 Roman Marakhovski .60 1.50
12 Nathan Marsters 1.25 3.00
13 David McKee 1.25 3.00
14 Brian Passmore .75 2.00
15 Joe Pereira .60 1.50
16 Jason Platt .60 1.50
17 Nathan Saunders .60 1.50
18 Ken Scuderi .60 1.50
19 Aaron Slattengren .60 1.50
20 Dirk Southern .60 1.50
21 Weston Tardy .60 1.50

2010-11 Augusta Riverhawks

COMPLETE SET (20) 4.00 10.00
1 Matt Auffrey .60 1.50
2 Adam Avramenko .30 .75
3 Drew Baker .30 .75
4 Nick Bydal .30 .75
5 Derek Fisher .30 .75
6 Kevin Fukala .30 .75
7 Jim Gehring .30 .75
8 Neil Graham .30 .75
9 Brandon Kosolofsky .30 .75
10 Lucas LaBelle .30 .75
11 Luke Lucyk .30 .75
12 Gus .30 .75
13 Aaron McGill .30 .75
14 Jordan McLaughlin .30 .75
15 Curtis Megginson .30 .75
16 Egor Mironov .30 .75
17 Ryan Olidis .30 .75
18 Jon Olthuis .30 .75
19 Jason Price .30 .75
20 Brad Ralph .30 .75

1997-98 Austin Ice Bats

This 24-card set featuring the Ice Bats of the WPHL was sold at the final home game and during the playoffs.

COMPLETE SET (24) 5.00 10.00
1 Ryan Anderson .20 .50
2 Chad Erickson .30 .75
3 Tim Findlay .30 .75
4 Todd Harris .20 .50
5 Rob Hartnell .20 .50
6 Chris Haskett .20 .50
7 Kyle Haviland .20 .50
8 Mike Jackson .20 .50
9 Jeff Kungle .20 .50
10 Darrin MacKay .20 .50
11 Dean Mando .20 .50
12 Keith Moran .20 .50
13 Ryan Pawluk .20 .50
14 Derek Riley .20 .50
15 Jason Rose .20 .50
16 Andy Ross .20 .50
17 Brett Seguin .20 .50
18 Christian Soucy .30 .75
19 Jeremy Thompson .20 .50
20 Richard Uniacke .20 .50
21 Joe Van Volsen .20 .50
22 Paul Lawless CO .08 .25
23 Fang Mascot .02 .10
24 Ice Bats Hummer PROMO .02 .10

1999-00 Austin Ice Bats

This set features the Ice Bats of the WPHL. The cards were handed out as promotional giveaways at two home games. The set features two cards (Nos. 29 & 30) that were only given out at Lowe's Home Improvement when a redemption card from the set was turned in.

COMPLETE SET (34) 12.00 30.00
1 Andy Ross .40 1.00
2 Shawn Legault .40 1.00
3 Craig Stahl .40 1.00
4 Ryan Pisiak .40 1.00
5 David Moore .40 1.00
6 David Brosseau .40 1.00
7 Jeff Greenlaw .40 1.00
8 Jeff Kungle .40 1.00
9 Bryan McMullen .40 1.00
10 Dan Price .40 1.00
11 Brent Hughes CO .08 .25
12 Glen Norman .40 1.00
13 Clint Shuman TR .08 .25
14 The IceBatmobile .08 .25
15 Rob Laurie .60 1.50
16 Brent Currie .40 1.00
17 Stu Kulak .40 1.00
18 Kelly Smart .40 1.00
19 Jim Shepherd .40 1.00
20 Ryan Anderson .40 1.00
21 Laird Lidster .40 1.00
22 Matt Sharuga .40 1.00
23 Derek Nicolson .40 1.00
24 Ryan Brindley .40 1.00
25 Tyler Perry .40 1.00
26 Fang MAS .08 .25
27 Ken McRae CO .08 .25
28 Gunner Garrett TR .08 .25
29 Ryan Pisiak 1.25 3.00
30 Ryan Anderson 1.25 3.00
31 Shawn Legault .40 1.00
32 Ryan Anderson .40 1.00
33 David Moore .40 1.00
34 Andy Ross .40 1.00

2000-01 Austin Ice Bats

This set features the Ice Bats of the WPHL. The set was released as a promotional giveaway, and was handed out over the course of two home games. Cards # 29 and 30 were redemption cards that could be acquired at a local hardware store.

COMPLETE SET (30) 8.00 30.00
1 Ryan Anderson .30 1.00
2 David Brosseau .30 1.00
3 Bobby Brown .30 1.00
4 Jonathan Forest .30 1.00
5 Mike Gaffney .40 1.50
6 Jeff Greenlaw .30 1.00
7 Daniel Kletke .30 1.00
8 Jeff Kungle .30 1.00
9 Eric Landry .40 1.50
10 Roger Lewis .30 1.00
11 Josh Maser .30 1.00
12 Bryan McMullen .30 1.00
13 Derek Nicolson .30 1.00
14 Erik Noack .30 1.00
15 Keith O'Brien .30 1.00
16 Tyler Perry .30 1.00
17 Philippe Plante .30 1.00
18 Dan Price .30 1.00
19 Brett Seguin .40 1.50
20 Kelly Smart .30 1.00
21 Troy Stonier .30 1.00
22 Daniel Tetrault .30 1.00
23 Brent Hughes CO .20 .50
24 Ken McRae CO .20 .50
25 Clint Shuman TR .10 .10
26 CC Comedy Club .01 .02
27 Hooters Hot Shot .20 .50
28 Fang MASCOT .04 .10
29 Redemption .04 .10
29R Spike & Fang MASCOTS .15 3.00
30 Redemption .04 .10
30R Ice Bats All Stars .15 3.00

2001-02 Austin Ice Bats

This set features the Ice Bats of the WPHL. The set was handed out to fans at a single home game early in 2002.

COMPLETE SET (25) 8.00 20.00
1 Ryan Anderson .40 1.00
2 Bobby Brown .40 1.00
3 Patrick Brownlee .40 1.00
4 Jeff Greenlaw .40 1.00
5 Ian LaRocque .40 1.00
6 Eric Labelle .40 1.00
7 Tab Lardner .40 1.00
8 Darryl McArthur .60 1.50
9 Dan McIntyre .40 1.00
10 Bryan McMullen .40 1.00
11 Dominic Periard .40 1.00
12 Ryan Pisiak .40 1.00
13 Dan Price .40 1.00
14 Brett Seguin .40 1.00
15 Kelly Smart .40 1.00
16 Gerald Tallaire .60 1.50
17 Daniel Tetrault .60 1.50
18 Greg Willers .40 1.00
19 Jeff Worlton .40 1.00
20 Brent Hughes CO .10 .25
21 Ken McRae ACO .10 .25
22 Fang MASCOT .04 .10
23 Glen Norman DB .04 .10
24 Gunner Garrett EQMG .04 .10
24 Clint Shuman TR .04 .10
25 Hootie Celebrates .04 .10

2002-03 Austin Ice Bats

COMPLETE SET (24) 10.00 20.00
1 Matt Barnes .60 1.50
2 Peter Brady .60 1.50
3 Patrick Brownlee .40 1.00
4 Mike Gaffney .40 1.00
5 Jeff Greenlaw .40 1.00
6 Doug Johnson .40 1.00
7 Tab Lardner .40 1.00
8 Shawn Legault .60 1.50
9 Darryl McArthur .40 1.00
10 Scott McCallum .40 1.00
11 Mike Olynyk .40 1.00
12 Randy Ponte .40 1.00
13 Dan Price .40 1.00
14 Mike Rees .40 1.00
15 Brett Seguin .40 1.00
16 Matt Sharuga .40 1.00
17 Kelly Smart .40 1.00
18 Gerald Tallaire .40 1.00
19 Brent Hughes HCO .10 .25
20 Jeff Kungle ACO .10 .25
21 Gunner Garrett EQM .04 .10
22 Fang Mascot .04 .10
23 Fang's Gang .04 .10
24 Clint Shuman TR .04 .10

2003-04 Austin Ice Bats

This set was issued as a promotional giveaway and split over two home games, making it difficult to complete. The cards are unnumbered and listed below in alphabetical order.

COMPLETE SET (24) 15.00 30.00
1 Peter Brady .60 1.50
2 Patrick Brownlee .60 1.50
3 Brandon Carper .60 1.50
4 Shawn Conschafter .60 1.50
5 Jonathan Forest .60 1.50
6 Brent Hughes .60 1.50
7 Tab Lardner .60 1.50
8 Shawn Legault .75 2.00
9 Chris Legg .60 1.50
10 Darryl McArthur .75 2.00
11 Scott McCallum .60 1.50
12 Mike Olynyk .60 1.50
13 Brett Seguin .60 1.50
14 Kelly Smart .60 1.50
15 Josh St. Louis .60 1.50
16 Derek Stone .60 1.50
17 Gerald Tallaire .60 1.50
18 Daniel Tetrault .60 1.50
19 Clint Way .60 1.50
20 Jeff Greenlaw HCO .10 .25
21 Gunner Garrett EQM .04 .10
22 Cheerleaders .10 .25
23 Mascot .04 .10
24 Clint Shuman TR .04 .10

2004-05 Austin Ice Bats

Issued as a stadium giveaway in two parts.

COMPLETE SET (23) 15.00 30.00
1 Peter-Emmanuel Brady .75 2.00
2 Brian Pasko .60 1.50
3 Kelly Smart .60 1.50
4 Ryan Leasa .60 1.50
5 Kris Knoblauch .60 1.50
6 Chris Richards .60 1.50
7 Dallas Anderson 1.25 3.00
8 John McNabb .75 2.00
9 Mike Olynyk .75 2.00
10 Sponsor Card .04 .10
11 Clint Shuman TR .04 .10
12 Fang MASCOT .04 .10
13 Matt Barnes .75 2.00
14 Benoit Genesse .60 1.50
15 Jonathan Jolette .60 1.50
16 Jeff Neufeld .60 1.50
17 Jared Dumba .60 1.50
18 Mike Mohr .60 1.50
19 Arturs Kupaks .60 1.50
20 Vinnie Jonasson .60 1.50
21 Greg Gatto CO .04 .10
22 Gunner Garrett EQM .04 .10
23 Bat Girls .20 .50

2006-07 Austin Ice Bats

Set was issued in two, 12-card perforated sheets. The cards are oversized.

1 Miguel Beaudry .60 1.50
2 Adam Holmgren .60 1.50
3 Chad McIver .60 1.50
4 Chris Murphy .60 1.50
5 Chris Ovington .60 1.50
6 Tony Quesada .60 1.50
7 John Ronan .60 1.50
8 Ray Smegal .60 1.50
9 Julian Smith .60 1.50
10 Mike Tucciarone .60 1.50
11 Terry Virtue .60 1.50
12 Logo Card .10 .25
13 Jordan Biachin .75 2.00
14 Kevin Couture .60 1.50
15 Aaron Davis .60 1.50
16 Britt Dougherty .60 1.50
17 Jason Kenyon .60 1.50
18 Henry Kuster .60 1.50
19 John McNabb .60 1.50
20 J.F. Picard .60 1.50
21 Mike Possin .60 1.50
22 Aaron Wilson .60 1.50
23 Fang MASCOT .10 .25
24 Logo Card .10 .25

1999-00 Baie-Comeau Drakkar

This set features the Drakkar of the QMJHL. The set was produced by card store CTM Ste-Foy and was sold at that shop and at home games.

COMPLETE SET (28) 4.00 10.00
1 Daniel Bergeron .15 .40
2 Jerome Bergeron .15 .40
3 Eric Bleau .15 .40
4 Marco Charpentier .15 .40
5 Jean-Philippe Chartier .30 .75
6 Serge Crochetiere .15 .40
7 Sylvain Deschatelets .15 .40
8 Kevin Deslauriers .15 .40
9 Maxime Fortunus .15 .40
10 Jonathan Gautier .15 .40
11 Duilio Grande .15 .40
12 Evgeny Gusakov .15 .40
13 Paul Lavoie .15 .40
14 Robin Leblanc .15 .40
15 Yannick Lehoux .30 .75
16 Charles Linglet .15 .40
17 Andre Mercure .15 .40
18 Chris Page .15 .40
19 Dominic Periard .15 .40
20 Jerome Petit .15 .40
21 Ghyslain Rousseau .30 .75
22 Bruno St. Jacques .30 .75
23 Eric Tremblay .15 .40
24 Guy Turmel .15 .40
25 Patrick Daviault CO .02 .10
26 Richard Martel CO .02 .10
27 Michel Larocque TR .02 .10
28 Brian St.Louis TR .02 .10

2000-01 Baie-Comeau Drakkar

This set features the Drakkar of the QMJHL. The set was produced by CTM-Ste-Foy and was sold through that shop and at home games.

COMPLETE SET (26) 4.00 10.00
1 Jonathan Walsh .15 .40
2 Joel Perrault .15 .40
3 Pierre-Andre Leblanc .15 .40
4 Dominic Periard .15 .40
5 Maxime Fortunus .15 .40
6 Pascal Pelletier .15 .40
7 Robin Leblanc .15 .40
8 Luis Tremblay .15 .40
9 Thierry Douville .15 .40
10 Marco Charpentier .15 .40
11 Premysl Duben .15 .40
12 Yanick Lehoux .40 1.00
13 Duilio Grande .15 .40
14 Kevin Deslauriers .15 .40
15 Matthew Hyde .15 .40
16 Guy Turmel .15 .40
17 Evgeny Gusakov .15 .40
18 Ghyslain Rousseau .20 .50
19 David St. Germain .20 .50
20 Jonathan Jolette .15 .40
21 Martin Mandeville .15 .40
22 Daniel Bergeron .15 .40
23 Charles Linglet .15 .40
24 Jonathan Gautier .15 .40
25 Richard Martel CO CL .02 .10
NNO Snorri MASCOT .02 .10

2000-01 Baie-Comeau Drakkar Signed

This set is exactly the same as the base Drakkar set from this season, save that every card has been hand signed by the player pictured. Each card also is serial numbered out of just 100.

COMPLETE SET (26) 20.00 50.00
1 Jonathan Walsh .80 2.00
2 Joel Perrault .80 2.00
3 Pierre-Andre Leblanc .80 2.00
4 Dominic Periard .80 2.00
5 Maxime Fortunus .80 2.00
6 Pascal Pelletier .80 2.00
7 Robin Leblanc .80 2.00
8 Luis Tremblay .80 2.00
9 Thierry Douville .80 2.00
10 Marco Charpentier .80 2.00
11 Premysl Duben .80 2.00
12 Yanick Lehoux 2.00 5.00
13 Duilio Grande .80 2.00
14 Kevin Deslauriers .80 2.00
15 Matthew Hyde .80 2.00
16 Guy Turmel .80 2.00
17 Evgeny Gusakov .80 2.00
18 Ghyslain Rousseau 2.00 5.00
19 David St. Germain 2.00 5.00
20 Jonathan Jolette .80 2.00
21 Martin Mandeville .80 2.00
22 Daniel Bergeron .80 2.00
23 Charles Linglet .80 2.00
24 Jonathan Gautier .80 2.00
25 Richard Martel CO CL .04 .10
NNO Snorri MASCOT .04 .10

2001-02 Baie-Comeau Drakkar

This set features les Drakkar of the QMJHL. The set was produced by well-known card shop CTM Ste-Foy, and was sold at the team's home games. It was reported that less than 1,000 sets were produced.

COMPLETE SET (25) 5.00 12.00
1 Joel Perrault .20 .50
2 Louis-Philippe Martin .20 .50
3 Jonathan Lachance .20 .50
4 Maxime Fortunus .20 .50
5 Pascal Pelletier .20 .50
6 Robin Leblanc .20 .50
7 Luis Tremblay .20 .50
8 Thierry Douville .20 .50
9 Martin Kuna .20 .50
10 Yanick Lehoux .30 .75
11 Duilio Grande .20 .50
12 Kevin Deslauriers .20 .50
13 Matthew Hyde .20 .50
14 Jean Junior Morin .20 .50
15 Ghyslain Rousseau .30 .75
16 Jonathan Dupras .20 .50
17 Caleb Moffat .20 .50
18 Marc-Andre Roy .20 .50
19 Martin Mandeville .20 .50
20 Daniel Bergeron .30 .75
21 Charles Linglet .20 .50
22 Jean-Francois Savage .20 .50
23 Benoit Mondou .30 .75
24 Jean-Francois Jacques .20 .50
NNO Richard Martel CO/CL .04 .10

2002-03 Baie-Comeau Drakkar

COMPLETE SET (26) 5.00 12.00
1 Maxime Belanger .20 .50
2 Joel Perrault .30 .75
3 Alexandre Lamarche .20 .50
4 Jean-Philippe Gauthier .20 .50
5 Louis-Philippe Martin .20 .50
6 Maxime Fortunus .20 .50
7 Pascal Pelletier .20 .50
8 Robin Leblanc .20 .50
9 Luis Tremblay .20 .50
10 Thierry Douville .20 .50
11 Jimmy Arsenault .20 .50
12 Travis Antler .20 .50
13 Kevin Deslauriers .20 .50
14 Patrick Lepage .30 .75
15 Sebastien Leonard .20 .50
16 Philip Lacroix .30 .75
17 Michel Bergevin-Robinson .30 .75
18 Caleb Moffat .20 .50
19 Marc-Andre Roy .20 .50
20 Patrick Thoresen .40 1.00
21 Martin Mandeville .20 .50
22 Charles Linglet .20 .50
23 Benoit Mondou .30 .75
24 Jean-Francois Jacques .20 .50
25 Richard Martel CO/CL .02 .10
26 Snorri MASCOT .02 .10

2003-04 Baie-Comeau Drakkar

This set was produced by CTM Sports and sold at home games.

COMPLETE SET (27) 5.00 12.00
1 Ryan-James Hand .20 .50
2 Patrick Simaro .20 .50
3 Ryan Lehr .20 .50
4 Maxime Belanger .20 .50
5 Martin Krayzel .20 .50
6 Alexandre Blais .20 .50
7 Jonathan Duchesneau .20 .50
8 Alexandre Lamarche Froelich .20 .50
9 Maxime Fortunas .20 .50
10 Robin Leblanc .20 .50
11 Luis Tremblay .20 .50
12 Frederic Gariepy .20 .50
13 Vitaly Lanochkin .20 .50
14 Olivier Furlong .20 .50
15 Simon Lepage .20 .50
16 Loic Lacasse .30 .75
17 Patrick Laurin .20 .50
18 Julien Walsh .30 .75
19 Pierre-Luc Leblond-Letourneau .20 .50
20 Martin Mandeville .20 .50
21 Nicolas Robillard .20 .50
22 Petr Preucil .20 .50
23 Philippe Cote .20 .50
24 Jean-Francois Jacques .30 .75
25 Alexandre Dulac Lemelin .20 .50
26 Maxime Fortunas TL .20 .50
27 Jean-Francois Jacques TL .30 .75

2004-05 Baie-Comeau Drakkar

A total of 350 team sets were produced.

COMPLETE SET (24) 4.00 10.00
1 Alexandre Blais .20 .50
2 Alexandre Dulac-Lemelin .20 .50
3 Alexandre Picard-Hooper .20 .50
4 Banjamin Breault .20 .50
5 Erick Lajoie .20 .50
6 Francois Bouchard .20 .50
7 Jean-Francois Jacques .20 .50
8 Joakim Jensen .20 .50
9 Jonathan Duchesneau .20 .50
10 Loic Lacasse .30 .75
11 Martin Aubin .20 .50
12 Martin Mandeville .20 .50
13 Mathieu Gravel .20 .50
14 Maxime Belanger .20 .50
15 Michael Dupont .30 .75
16 Nicolas Robillard .20 .50
17 Patrick Simard .20 .50
18 Philippe Cote .20 .50
19 Pierre-Luc Leblond-Letourneau .20 .50
20 Ryan Lehr .20 .50
21 Ryan-James Hand .20 .50
22 Sebastien Blouin .20 .50
23 Tomas Fendek .20 .50
24 Vitaly Lanochkin .20 .50

2005-06 Baie-Comeau Drakkar

COMPLETE SET (22) 5.00 10.00
1 Benjamin Breault .20 .50
2 Charles-Antoine Messier .20 .50
3 Patrick Simard .20 .50
4 Ryan Lehr .20 .50
5 Tomas Fendek .20 .50
6 Alexandre Blais .20 .50
7 Jonathan Duchesneau .20 .50
8 Christian Landry .20 .50
9 Francois Chabot .20 .50
10 Alexandre Picard-Hooper .20 .50
11 Francois Bouchard .20 .50
12 Jean-Sebastien Hogg .20 .50
13 Adam Bourque-Leblanc .20 .50
14 Joakim Jensen .20 .50
15 Alexandre Dulac-Lemelin .20 .50
16 Maxime D. Ouimet .20 .50
17 Oliver Donais .20 .50
18 Samuel Beland .20 .50
19 Francois Filion .20 .50
20 Loic Lacasse .20 .50
21 Michael Dupont .20 .50
22 Martin Aubin .20 .50

1998-99 Bakersfield Condors

This set features the Condors of the WCHL. The cards measure 2 5/8 by 3 5/8 and feature a full-bleed color photo on the front. The backs feature player stats and the logo of sponsor KRAB radio

COMPLETE SET (24) 4.00 10.00
1 Jamie Adams .30 .75
2 Kevin Barrett .30 .75
3 Brady Blain .30 .75
4 Marc Boxer .30 .75
5 Steve Chelios .40 1.00
6 Jamie Cooke .30 .75
7 Steve Dowhy .30 .75
8 Brad Guzda .30 .75
9 Nick Hriczov .30 .75
10 Kelly Hrycun .30 .75
11 Marcel Kuris .30 .75
12 Dan Marcotte .30 .75
13 Brian McCarthy .30 .75
14 Glen Mears .30 .75
15 Al Murphy .30 .75
16 Jay Neal .30 .75
17 Zbynek Neckar .30 .75
18 Dan Reja .30 .75
19 Stephane St. Amour .40 1.00
20 Briane Thompson .30 .75
21 Peter Zurba .30 .75
22 Bakersfield Centennial Arena .02 .10
23 Kevin MacDonald HCO .02 .10
24 Colonel Claw'd Mascot .02 .10

1999-00 Bakersfield Condors

This set features the Condors of the WCHL. The set was issued as a promotional giveaway at a home game midway through the season. It was later offered for sale at home games and by mail order.

COMPLETE SET (24) 8.00 20.00
1 Cory Banika .40 1.00
2 Philippe Bergeron .40 1.00
3 Kevin Boyd .40 1.00
4 Jamie Cooke .40 1.00
5 Dan Currie .60 1.50
6 Chris Dearden .40 1.00
7 Steve Dowhy .40 1.00
8 Chris Droeske .40 1.00
9 Brad Guzda .40 1.00
10 Paul McInnis .40 1.00
11 Glen Mears .40 1.00
12 Zbynek Neckar .40 1.00
13 Jani Ojala .40 1.00
14 Brad Phillips .40 1.00
15 Clark Polglase .40 1.00
16 Jason Reesor .40 1.00
17 Paul Rosebush .40 1.00
18 Briane Thompson .40 1.00
19 Rhett Trombley .40 1.00
20 Paul Willett .40 1.00
21 Kevin MacDonald CO .08 .25
22 Bakersfield Centennial .08 .25
23 Colonel Claw'd MAS .08 .25
24 Michael Ropchan TR .08 .25

2000-01 Bakersfield Condors

This set features the Condors of the WCHL. The set was issued as a promotional giveaway at a game midway through the season. The cards are unnumbered and are listed below alphabetically.

COMPLETE SET (24) 8.00 20.00
1 Trevor Amundrud .30 .75
2 Cory Banika .30 .75
3 Karel Betik .60 1.50
4 Kevin Boyd .30 .75
5 Jamie Cooke .30 .75
6 Dan Currie .60 1.50
7 Jean-Paul Davis .30 .75
8 Chris Dearden .30 .75
9 Quinn Fair .30 .75
10 Ben Gustavson .30 .75
11 Denis Ivanov .30 .75
12 Bryan Lachance .30 .75
13 Peter MacKellar .30 .75
14 Craig Martin .40 1.00
15 Glen Mears .30 .75
16 Pavel Mikulchik .30 .75
17 Matt Mullin .60 1.50
18 Jason Reesor .30 .75
19 Paul Rosebush .30 .75
20 Paul Willett .60 1.50
21 Paul Willett MVP .60 1.50
22 Kevin MacDonald CO .10 .25
23 Centenial Gardens ARENA .10 .25
24 Coloney .10 .25
Cal MASCOTS

2001-02 Bakersfield Condors

COMPLETE SET (24) 10.00 20.00
1 Ken Baker .40 1.00
2 Peter Brearley .40 1.00
3 Luciano Caravaggio .40 1.00
4 Jamie Cooke .40 1.00
5 Mark Edmundson .40 1.00
6 Todd Esselmont .40 1.00
7 Quinn Fair .40 1.00
8 Chris Felix .40 1.00
9 Jason Firth .40 1.00
10 Jeff Goldie .40 1.00
11 Ryan Hartung .40 1.00
12 Scott Hay .60 1.50
13 Sasha Lakovic .60 1.50
14 Josh Maser .40 1.00
15 Glen Mears .40 1.00
16 David Milek .40 1.00
17 Jason Ralph .40 1.00
18 Paul Rosebush .40 1.00
19 John Vary .40 1.00
20 Paul Willett .40 1.00
21 Paul Kelly HCO .04 .10
22 Condors in the Community .04 .10
23 Baby Cal MASCOT .04 .10
24 Colonel Claw MASCOT .04 .10

2002-03 Bakersfield Condors

COMPLETE SET (24) 10.00 20.00
1 Nate Anderson .40 1.00
2 David Bell .40 1.00
3 Shawn Byram .40 1.00
4 Jamie Cooke .40 1.00
5 Danielle Dube .40 1.00
6 Guy Dupuis .40 1.00
7 Quinn Fair .40 1.00
8 Jeff Goldie .40 1.00
9 Jason Jackman .40 1.00
10 Denis Ladouceur .40 1.00
11 Jonas Lennartsson .40 1.00
12 Christoffer Norgren .40 1.00
13 Jason Ralph .40 1.00
14 Jordan Roach .40 1.00
15 Paul Rosebush .40 1.00
16 Christian Skoryna .40 1.00
17 Jonathan Sorg .40 1.00
18 Kevin St. Pierre .60 1.50
19 Paul Willett .40 1.00
20 J.J. Wrobel .40 1.00
21 Paul Kelly HCO .10 .25
22 Martin Raymond ACO .10 .25
23 Colonel Claw'd .04 .10
Baby Cal

2003-04 Bakersfield Condors

The 25-card main set was issued as a promotional giveaway. No production run was announced.

COMPLETE SET (25) 10.00 25.00
1 Todd Alexander .40 1.00
2 Johan Astrom .40 1.00
3 Jamie Cooke .40 1.00
4 Paul Kelly CO .10 .25
5 Martin Raymond ACO .10 .25
6 Andrew Ianiero .40 1.00
7 Jason Jackman .40 1.00
8 Peter Hirsch .40 1.00
9 Devin Francon .40 1.00
10 Paul Rosebush .40 1.00
11 Kevin Riehl .40 1.00
12 Mascot .02 .10
13 Vince Malts .40 1.00
14 Quinn Fair .40 1.00
15 Jimmy Drolet .40 1.00
16 Glen Mears .40 1.00
17 Jon Mirasty .40 1.00
18 Darren Shakotko .40 1.00
19 Jani Virtanen .40 1.00
20 Joe Watkins .60 1.50
21 Paul Willett .40 1.00
22 Randy Perry .40 1.00
23 Jason Ralph .40 1.00
24 Denis Ladouceur .40 1.00
25 Jonas Lennartsson .40 1.00

2004-05 Bakersfield Condors

COMPLETE SET (24) 15.00 30.00
1 Ryan Coole .40 1.00
2 Guy Dupuis .40 1.00
3 Yutaka Fukufuji 4.00 10.00
4 Ryan Gillis .40 1.00
5 Ty Hennes .40 1.00
6 Mike Hofstrand .40 1.00
7 Connor James .40 1.00
8 David Kudelka .40 1.00
9 Ashlee Langdone .40 1.00
10 Tony Lawrence .40 1.00
11 Brett Lutes .40 1.00
12 Brad Mehalko .40 1.00
13 Dylan Mills .40 1.00
14 Lars Peder Nagel .40 1.00
15 Paul Rosebush .40 1.00
16 Vlad Serov .40 1.00
17 Dennis Shiryaev .40 1.00
18 Kevin St. Jacques .40 1.00
19 Luis Tremblay .40 1.00
20 ChrisTwerdun .40 1.00
21 Jason Wolfe .60 1.50
22 Marty Raymond CO .04 .10
23 Paul Willet ACO .04 .10
24 Mascots .04 .10

2005-06 Bakersfield Condors

COMPLETE SET (23) 8.00 20.00
1 Marty Raymond .40 1.00
2 Kevin Kotyluk .40 1.00
3 Brian Collins .40 1.00
4 Scott Balan .40 1.00
5 Paul Rosebush .40 1.00
6 Reagan Leslie .40 1.00
7 Scott Basiuk .40 1.00
8 Alexandre Bolduc .40 1.00
9 Nick Economakos .40 1.00
10 Oriel McHugh .40 1.00
11 Dennis Shiryaev .40 1.00
12 Kevin St.Jacques .40 1.00
13 Ryan Munce .40 1.00
14 Mike Hofstrand .40 1.00
15 Dave Bonk .40 1.00
16 Scott Borders .40 1.00
17 Andrew Ianiero .40 1.00
18 Eric Neilson .40 1.00
19 Kevin Truelson .40 1.00
20 Sean Venedam .40 1.00
21 Mark Pederson .40 1.00
22 Joel Irving .40 1.00
23 Mathieu Brunelle .40 1.00

2006-07 Bakersfield Condors

1 Sean Venedam .40 1.00
2 Rane Carnegie .60 1.50
3 Steve Rodberg .40 1.00
4 Brett Lutes .40 1.00
5 Coaches .10 .25
6 Kevin Truelson .40 1.00
7 David Kudelka .40 1.00
8 Andrew Oke .40 1.00
9 Andrew Ianiero .40 1.00
10 Alex Kim .40 1.00
11 Danny Taylor .40 1.00
12 Scott Borders .40 1.00
13 Mike Hofstrand .40 1.00
14 Josh Libenow .40 1.00
15 Alexandre Bolduc .40 1.00

16 Alec Rogosheske .40 1.00
17 Tyler Scott .40 1.00
18 Tyler Liebel .40 1.00
19 Jamie Hodson .75 2.00
20 Kevin St. Jacques .40 1.00
21 Scotty Balan .40 1.00
22 Kevin Asselin .40 1.00
23 Todd Griffith .40 1.00
24 Reagan Leslie .40 1.00

2013-14 Bakersfield Condors

COMPLETE SET () 6.00 15.00
1 Spencer Bennett .30 .75
2 Collin Bowman .30 .75
3 Joel Broda .30 .75
4 Laurent Brossoit .30 .75
5 Tyler Bunz .30 .75
6 Erik Burgdoerfer .30 .75
7 Andrew Carroll .30 .75
8 Chris Collins .30 .75
9 Wes Cunningham .30 .75
10 Travis Gawryletz .30 .75
11 George Hughes .30 .75
12 Jordan Knackstedt .30 .75
13 Joey Leach .30 .75
14 Ryan Little .30 .75
15 Troy Mann CO .30 .75
16 Joe Marciano .30 .75
17 Greg Miller .30 .75
18 Ryan Murphy Asst. CO .30 .75
19 Michael Neal .30 .75
20 Nick Pageau .30 .75
21 Chet Pickard .30 .75
22 Chase Schaber .30 .75
23 Gary Steffes .30 .75
24 Matt Thurber .30 .75
25 Ryan Watson .30 .75
26 Baby Cal MASCOT .30 .75

2014-15 Bakersfield Condors

COMPLETE SET (32) 8.00 20.00
1 Cameron Abney .30 .75
2 Akim Aliu .40 1.00
3 Kevin Barrett CA .30 .75
4 Scott Borders CA .30 .75
5 Jamie Cooke CA .30 .75
6 Graeme Craig .30 .75
7 Josh Currie .30 .75
8 Steve Dowhy CA .30 .75
9 Scott Hay CA .30 .75
10 Mike Hotstrand CA .30 .75
11 Andrew Ianiero CA .30 .75
12 Joel Irving CA .30 .75
13 Connor Jones .30 .75
14 Kellen Jones .30 .75
15 Jordan Kremyr .30 .75
16 Jonathan Lessard .30 .75
17 C.J. Ludwig .30 .75
18 Nick MacNeil .30 .75
19 Joe Marciano .30 .75
20 Brian McCarthy CA .30 .75
21 Glen Mears CA .30 .75
22 Brendon Nash .30 .75
23 Nick Pageau .30 .75
24 Paul Rosebush CA .30 .75
25 Chase Schaber .30 .75
26 Sebastien Sylvestre .30 .75
27 Kevin Truelson CA .30 .75
28 Gabriel Verpaelst .30 .75
29 Joe Watkins CA .30 .75
30 Ryan Watson .30 .75
31 Paul Willett CA .30 .75
32 Josh Winquist .30 .75

1997-98 Bakersfield Fog

Little is known about this set, though it is believed that it was sold by the team throughout the season. Any additional information can be forwarded to hockeymag@beckett.com.

COMPLETE SET (24) 5.00 12.00
1 John Devereaux .25 .60
2 Steve Dowhy .25 .60
3 Igor Galkin .40 1.00
4 Jeff Gorman .25 .60
5 Kelly Hrycun .25 .60
6 Jeff Jubenville .25 .60
7 Don Lester .25 .60
8 Brian McCarthy .25 .60
9 Glen Mears .25 .60
10 Rob Milliken .40 1.00
11 Jodi Murphy .40 1.00
12 Jay Neal .25 .60
13 Jeff Pierce .25 .60
14 Andrew Plumb .25 .60
15 Iannique Renaud .25 .60
16 Eddy Skazyk .40 1.00
17 Lindsay Vallis .25 .60
18 Wade Welte .40 1.00
19 Jason White .25 .60
20 Keith Gretzky HCO .40 1.00
21 Tule Fog Mascot .02 .10
22 Bakersfield Arena .02 .10
23 Sponsor Card .02 .10
24 Dick Earle TR .02 .10

1991-92 Baltimore Skipjacks

This 15-card set was issued as a promotional giveaway in 3-card perforated strips. The set commemorated the team's 10th anniversary and was sponsored by Wendy's and Coca-Cola. The cards are numbered card "xx" of 15.

COMPLETE SET (15) 8.00 20.00
1 Tim Taylor .40 1.00
2 Brent Hughes .30 .75
3 Trevor Halverson .30 .75
4 Bobby Reynolds .30 .75
5 Ken Lovsin .30 .75
6 Olaf Kolzig 4.00 10.00
7 Reggie Savage .30 .75
8 Jim Mathieson .40 1.00
9 Todd Hlushko .40 1.00
10 Mark Ferner .30 .75
11 John Purves .30 .75
12 Steve Seftel .30 .75
13 Craig Duncanson .30 .75
14 Simon Wheeldon .40 1.00
15 Bob Babcock .30 .75

1995-96 Barrie Colts

This set features the expansion Colts of the OHL. These attractive cards feature full-bleed photos on the front, along with a dynamic chartreuse design element along the right side. The back's feature a head shot and commentary from coach Bert Templeton. The set was sold by the team at home games and is noteworthy for the inclusion of future NHLers Dan Tkaczuk, Jan Bulis and Jeff Cowan.

COMPLETE SET (28) 4.80 12.00
1 Mauricio Alvarez .20 .50
2 Brian Barker .20 .50
3 Brock Boucher .20 .50
4 Jan Bulis .30 .75
5 Jason Cannon .20 .50
6 Jeff Cowan .30 .75
7 Shane Delaronde .30 .75
8 Robert DuBois .20 .50
9 Shawn Frappier .20 .50
10 Chris George .20 .50
11 In Action .02 .10
12 In Action .02 .10
13 In Action .02 .10
14 In Action .02 .10
15 Gerry Lanigan .20 .50
16 Quade Lightbody .20 .50
17 Jeremy Miculinic .30 .75
18 Andrew Morrison .20 .50
19 Luch Nasato .30 .75
20 Bert Templeton CO .08 .25
21 Jeff Tetzlaff .20 .50
22 Chris Thompson .30 .75
23 Justin Robinson .20 .50
24 Daniel Tkaczuk .30 .75
25 Alexander Volchkov .20 .50
26 Caleb Ward .20 .50
27 Mike White .20 .50
28 Darrell Woodley .20 .50

1996-97 Barrie Colts

This set was produced and sold by the team at home games. It is notable for featuring future NHLers Martin Skoula, Brian Finley and Daniel Tkaczuk. The cards are unnumbered, and so are unnumbered and checklisted below in alphabetical order.

COMPLETE SET (30) 6.00 15.00
1 Brian Barker .20 .50
2 Brock Boucher .20 .50
3 Casey Burnette .20 .50
4 Michael Christian .20 .50
5 Keith Delaney .20 .50
6 Adam Deleeuw .20 .50
7 Chris Feil .20 .50
8 Brian Finley .40 1.00
9 Michael Henrich .30 .75
10 John Hultberg .20 .50
11 Richard Kazda .20 .50
12 Darren Keily TR .02 .10
13 Cody Leibel .20 .50
14 Mihajlo Martinovich .20 .50
15 Kevin McClelland ACO .02 .10
16 Walker McDonald .20 .50
17 Jeff McKercher .20 .50
18 Luch Nasato .25 .60
19 Ryan O'Keefe .20 .50
20 Jason Pinizzotto .20 .50
21 Ryan Shaver .20 .50
22 Martin Skoula .40 1.00
23 Nick Smith .20 .50
24 Brandon Sugden .25 .60
25 Bert Templeton CO .20 .50
26 Jeff Tetzlaff .20 .50
27 Daniel Tkaczuk .30 .75
28 Charlie Horse(Mascot) .02 .10
29 Barrie Colts Team Picture .20 .50
30 Checklist .02 .10

1997-98 Barrie Colts

This attractive set was produced by the team and sold at home games. The set is unnumbered and checklisted below in alphabetical order.

COMPLETE SET (27) 4.80 10.00
1 Brian Barker .15 .40
2 Brock Boucher .15 .40
3 Jan Bulis .30 .75
4 Casey Burnette .15 .40
5 Jason Cannon .15 .40
6 Keith Delaney .15 .40
7 Chris George .15 .40
8 Nick Grady .15 .40
9 Mike Henrich .30 .75
10 John Hultberg .20 .50
11 Marcel Kars .15 .40
12 Darren Keily TR .02 .10
13 Gerry Lanigan .15 .40
14 Kevin McClelland .02 .10
15 Walker McDonald .15 .40
16 Jeff McKercher .15 .40
17 Brad Morgan .15 .40
18 Luch Nasato .30 .75
19 Corey Neilson .15 .40
20 Nick Smith .15 .40
21 Bert Templeton CO .02 .10
22 Jeff Tetzlaff .15 .40
23 Chris Thompson .15 .40
24 Daniel Tkaczuk .30 .75
25 Alexandre Volchkov .20 .50
26 Darrell Woodley .15 .40
27 Charlie Horse MAS .02 .10

1998-99 Barrie Colts

Released by the Colts in conjunction with Coca-Cola, this 25-card set pictures the 1998-99 Barrie Colts. Base cards feature full color action photography, white borders, and a blue nameplate along with the Coca-Cola logo along the bottom of the card.

COMPLETE SET (25) 7.20 15.00
1 Ryan O'Keefe .20 .50
2 Andre Lakos .20 .50
3 Shawn Cation .20 .50
4 Ed Hill .20 .50
5 Joel Dezainde .20 .50
6 Daniel Tkaczuk .30 .75
7 Martin Skoula .30 .75
8 Jerry Connell .20 .50
9 Tim Verbeek .20 .50
10 Rick Hwodeky .20 .50
11 Scott Cameron .30 .75
12 Ryan Barnes .20 .50
13 Sheldon Keefe .30 .75
14 Jeff Tetzlaff .20 .50
15 Chris Feil .20 .50
16 Michael Henrich .30 .75
17 Mike Christian .20 .50
18 Nick Smith .20 .50
19 Mike Jefferson .40 1.00
20 Denis Shvidki .30 .75
21 Brian Finley .30 .75
22 Ben Vanderklok .20 .50
23 Bert Templeton HCO .02 .10
24 D.Keily .02 .10
G.Scott
25 Charlie Horse MASCOT .02 .10

2000-01 Barrie Colts

This set features the Colts of the OHL. The set was sponsored by the Colts and Cops foundation and was distributed by the team's booster club at home games.

COMPLETE SET (24) 4.00 10.00
1 Frantisek Bakrlik .14 .40
2 Tim Branham .20 .50
3 Jordan Brenner .14 .40
4 Dean Byvelds .14 .40
5 David Chant .40 1.00
6 Fraser Clair .14 .40
7 Mike D'Alessandro .30 .75
8 Blaine Down .14 .40
9 Matt Dzieduszycki .14 .40
10 Shayne Fryia .14 .40
11 Matt Grennier .14 .40
12 Bryan Hayes .14 .40
13 Tyler Hanchuck .20 .50
14 Mike Henderson .14 .40
15 Ed Hill .20 .35
16 Charlie Horse Mascot/CL .10 .10
17 Gregg Mizzi .14 .40
18 Stephen Morris .14 .40
19 Jan Platil .14 .40
20 Neil Posillico .14 .40
21 Aaron Power .14 .40
22 Erik Reitz .14 .40
23 Bud Stefanski CO .10 .10
24 Brent Sullivan .14 .40
25 Joey Tenute .14 .40

2001-02 Barrie Colts

This set is unnumbered and is listed below in the order it appears on the checklist.

COMPLETE SET (23) 5.00 10.00
1 David Chant .40 1.00
2 Ryan Stokes .20 .50
3 Rick Arnaldo .20 .50
4 Eric Reitz .30 .75
5 Aaron Powers .20 .50
6 Steven Morris .20 .50
7 Blaine Down .20 .50
8 Joey Tenute .20 .50
9 Nick Lees .20 .50
10 Tyler Hanchuck .20 .50
11 B.J. Crombeen .20 .50
12 Andrew Shennan .20 .50
13 Jeremy Swanson .20 .50
14 Simon Barg .20 .50
15 Frantisek Bakrlik .20 .50
16 Daniel Girardi .20 .50
17 Kevin Ambroski .20 .50
18 Steve Farquharson .20 .50
19 Jan Platil .20 .50
20 Shayne Fria .20 .50
21 Fraser Clair .20 .50
22 Mascot .04 .10
23 Arena Card .04 .10

2002-03 Barrie Colts

COMPLETE SET (24) 5.00 10.00
1 Evan Brophey .20 .50
2 Justin DaCosta .20 .50
3 Andrew Shennan .20 .50
4 Zach Tranmer .20 .50
5 Michael Tuomi .20 .50
6 Simon Barg .20 .50
7 Ryan Sharp .20 .50
8 Nick Lees .20 .50
9 Hunter Tremblay .20 .50
10 Riley Moher .20 .50
11 Eric Himelfarb .30 .75
12 Mark Langdon .20 .50
13 Luc Chiasson .20 .50
14 Jeremy Swanson .20 .50
15 Kenny Jung .20 .50
16 Tyler Lawson .20 .50
17 Daniel Girardi .20 .50
18 Michael Ouzas .30 .75
19 Paulo Colaiacovo .40 1.00
20 B.J. Crombeen .20 .50
21 Dan Speer .20 .50
22 Jan Platil .20 .50
23 Mascot .04 .10
24 Barrie Molson Centre .04 .10

2003-04 Barrie Colts

Cards are listed according to the order they appear on the checklist card.

COMPLETE SET (24) 6.00 15.00
1 Thomas Lee .20 .50
2 Steve Spade .30 .75
3 Evan Brophey .30 .75
4 Ryan Hamilton .30 .75
5 Andrew Shennan .30 .75
6 Chad Thompson .30 .75
7 Chris Morrison .30 .75
8 Chad Robinson .30 .75
9 Hunter Tremblay .30 .75
10 Bryan Little 1.50 4.00
11 Scott Hotham .40 1.00
12 Mark Langdon .30 .75
13 Jeremy Swanson .30 .75
14 Michael Root .30 .75
15 Travis Fuller .30 .75
16 Paolo Colaiacovo .60 1.50
17 Lukas Bolf .30 .75
18 B.J. Crombeen .30 .75
19 Georgy Ryazantsev .30 .75
20 Dan Speer .30 .75
21 Cory Stillman .30 .75
22 Andrew Dennis .30 .75
23 Mascot .04 .10
Checklist
24 Barrie Molson Centre .04 .10

2004-05 Barrie Colts

Unnumbered cards, listed below in checklist order.

COMPLETE SET (25) 5.00 10.00
1 Jeff Weber .20 .50
2 Nathan Martine .20 .50
3 Michael Lombardi .20 .50
4 Nicholas Plastino .20 .50
5 Ryan Hamilton .20 .50
6 Andrew Shennan .20 .50
7 Dan Speer .20 .50
8 Mike Roelofsen .20 .50
9 Chris Morrison .20 .50
10 Chad Robinson .20 .50
11 Hunter Tremblay .20 .50
12 Bryan Little .40 1.00
13 Scott Hotham .20 .50
14 Aaron Lewicki .20 .50
15 Michael Root .20 .50
16 Travis Fuller .20 .50
17 Michael Birner .20 .50
18 Francois Thuot .20 .50
19 Lukas Bolf .20 .50
20 B.J. Crombeen .30 .75
21 Andrew Marshall .20 .50
22 Jordan Shine .20 .50
23 Andrew Hotham .20 .50
24 Andrew Dennis .20 .50
25 Mascot .04 .10
Checklist

2004-05 Barrie Colts 10th Anniversary

COMPLETE SET (25) 5.00 12.00
1 Daniel Tkaczuk .20 .50
2 Bryan Little .40 1.00
3 Michael Henrich .20 .50
4 Martin Skoula .20 .50
5 Blaine Down .20 .50
6 Jan Bulis .20 .50
7 Erik Reitz .30 .75
8 Jeremy Swanson .20 .50
9 Luch Nasato .20 .50
10 B.J. Crombeen .30 .75
11 Jan Platil .20 .50
12 Denis Shvidki .20 .50
13 Joey Tenute .20 .50
14 Aaron Power .20 .50
15 Alexander Volchkov .20 .50
16 Mark Langdon .20 .50
17 Fraser Clair .20 .50
18 Nick Lees .20 .50
19 Cory Stillman .20 .50
20 Jeff Tetzlaff .20 .50
21 Tim Verbeek .20 .50
22 Matt Dzieduszycki .20 .50
23 Paulo Colaiacovo .30 .75
24 David Chant .30 .75
25 Brian Finley .30 .75

2006-07 Barrie Colts

1 Andrew Perugini .30 .75
2 Michael Hutchinson .20 .50
3 Kyle Van De Bospoort .20 .50
4 Brian Lashoff .20 .50
5 Thomas Marcinko .20 .50
6 Nicolas Plastino .20 .50
7 Shawn Franck .20 .50
8 Alex Hutchings .20 .50
9 Hunter Tremblay .20 .50
10 Bryan Little .60 1.50
11 Stefan Della Rovere .30 .75
12 Richard Clune .20 .50
13 Ryan Bellows .20 .50
14 Mike Webber .20 .50
15 Chris Purves .20 .50
16 Tyson Aitcheson .20 .50
17 Matthew Bragg .20 .50
18 Kris Sparre .20 .50
19 Ryan Gottschalk .20 .50
20 Andrew Marshall .20 .50
21 Cort McGillis .20 .50
22 Vladimir Nikiforov .20 .50
23 George Lovatsis .20 .50
24 Joe Pleckaitis .20 .50
25 Michael Lombardi .20 .50
26 T.J. Battani .20 .50
27 Checklist .02 .10
LE2 Andrew Perugini 2.00 5.00

2013-14 Barrie Colts

COMPLETE SET (24) 8.00 20.00
1 Liam Maaskant .30 .75
2 Jonathan Laser .30 .75
3 Jake Dotchin .30 .75
4 Aaron Ekblad 1.50 4.00
5 Josh Carrick .30 .75
6 Mac Clutsam .30 .75
7 C.J. Garcia .30 .75
8 Joseph Blandisi .30 .75
9 Not Issued
10 Nick Pastorious .30 .75
11 Kevin Labanc .30 .75
12 Tyson Fawcett .30 .75
13 Matthew Kreis .30 .75
14 Justin Scott .30 .75
15 Brendan Lemieux 1.25 3.00
16 Andreas Athanasiou .60 1.50
17 Mitchell Theoret .30 .75
18 Michael Webster .30 .75
19 Garrett Hooey .30 .75
20 Andrew Mangiapane .30 .75
21 Cordell James .30 .75
22 Zach Hall .30 .75
23 Mackenzie Blackwood .30 .75
24 Daniel Gibl .30 .75

1951-52 Bas Du Fleuve

This set features top players from the Quebec Senior League. The cards are similar in size to the Parkhurst set that was released this season. The key card in the set pictures Denis Brodeur.

COMPLETE SET (58) 350.00 700.00
1 Gordon Poirier 12.50 25.00
2 Denis Brodeur 25.00 50.00
3 Conrad Poitras 7.50 15.00
4 Clement Tremblay 7.50 15.00
5 Raymond Leduc 7.50 15.00
6 Jacques Armstrong 7.50 15.00
7 Joe Schmidt 7.50 15.00
8 Gilles Laroche 7.50 15.00
9 Frank Pearce 7.50 15.00
10 Wayne Stephenson 7.50 15.00
11 Guy Lapointe 7.50 15.00
12 Guy Delisle 7.50 15.00
13 Ossie Carnegie 10.00 20.00
14 Gilbert Girouard 7.50 15.00
15 Jean-Paul Vandal 7.50 15.00
16 Guy Lalonde 7.50 15.00
17 Roland Bilodeau 7.50 15.00
18 Gaetan Laliberte 7.50 15.00
19 Maurice Benoit 7.50 15.00
20 Thomas McDougall 7.50 15.00
21 Roger Guay 7.50 15.00
22 Bob Brault 7.50 15.00
23 Edouard Theberge 7.50 15.00
24 Paul Lessard 7.50 15.00
25 Lucien Gilbert 7.50 15.00
26 Real Lafreniere 7.50 15.00
27 Renald Limoges 7.50 15.00
28 Roger Ste. Marie 7.50 15.00
29 Arthur Leyte 7.50 15.00
30 Magella Laforest 7.50 15.00
31 Bill Leblanc 7.50 15.00
32 Pius Gaudet 7.50 15.00
33 Jean-Roch Bellavance 7.50 15.00
34 Gerard Lachance 7.50 15.00
35 Marcel St. Pierre 7.50 15.00
36 Pierre Brillant 7.50 15.00
37 Paul Provost 7.50 15.00
38 Maurice Lamirande 7.50 15.00
39 Roger Hayfield 7.50 15.00
40 Normand Bellavance 7.50 15.00
41 Marcel Houde 7.50 15.00
42 Dan Janelle 7.50 15.00
43 Roland Rossignol 7.50 15.00
44 Roger Gagne 7.50 15.00
45 Jacques Monette 7.50 15.00
46 Bernie Bernaquez 7.50 15.00
47 Paul Gagnon 7.50 15.00
48 Jean-Marie Fillion 7.50 15.00
49 Bert Scullion 7.50 15.00
50 Don Bellringer 7.50 15.00
51 Frank Cote 7.50 15.00
52 Eddy Bolan 7.50 15.00
53 Maurice Parr 7.50 15.00
54 Many McIntyre 7.50 15.00
55 Roger Jodoin 7.50 15.00
56 Mario Senecal 7.50 15.00
57 Denis Fillion 7.50 15.00
58 Marcel Fillion 12.50 25.00

1952-53 Bas Du Fleuve

This set features players from the Quebec Senior League. The cards are similar in size to the 1951-52 Parkhurst set. Noteworthy players include Denis Brodeur (father of Martin and former Canadian Olympic goalie) and Marcel Paille.

COMPLETE SET (65) 400.00 800.00
1 Roger Gagner 12.50 25.00
2 Martial Pruneau 7.50 15.00
3 Fernand Gladu 7.50 15.00
4 Joseph Lacoursiere 7.50 15.00
5 Maurice Lamirande 7.50 15.00
6 Denis Smith 7.50 15.00
7 Real Jacques 7.50 15.00
8 Roland Landry 7.50 15.00
9 Dan Janelle 7.50 15.00
10 Pete Gaudette 7.50 15.00
11 Normand Bellavance 7.50 15.00
12 Roger Hayfield 7.50 15.00
13 Bill LeBlanc 7.50 15.00
14 Victor Corbin 7.50 15.00
15 Gerard Lachance 7.50 15.00
16 Guy Labrie 7.50 15.00
17 Denis Brodeur 15.00 30.00
18 Gerard Paquin 7.50 15.00
19 Irene St. Hilaire 10.00 20.00
20 Guy Gervais 7.50 15.00
21 Marcel Benoit 7.50 15.00
22 Roger Dumas 7.50 15.00
23 Gaston Gervais 7.50 15.00
24 Maurice St. Jean 7.50 15.00
25 Frank Pearce 7.50 15.00
26 Fernand Bernaquez 7.50 15.00
27 Henri-Paul Gagnon 7.50 15.00
28 Jean-Jacques Pichette 7.50 15.00
29 Jim Hayes 7.50 15.00
30 Fernand Rancourt 7.50 15.00
31 Nils Tremblay 7.50 15.00
32 Clement Tremblay 7.50 15.00
33 Jacques Lalancette 7.50 15.00
34 Marcel Fillion 10.00 20.00
35 Jacques Monette 7.50 15.00
36 Frank Cote 7.50 15.00
37 Bernie Lemonde 7.50 15.00
38 Guildor Levesque 7.50 15.00
39 Hector Legris 7.50 15.00
40 Jacques Gagnon 7.50 15.00
41 Donat Deschesnes 7.50 15.00
42 Bertrand LePage 7.50 15.00
43 Paul Lavoie 7.50 15.00
44 Denis Fillion 7.50 15.00
45 Floyd Crawford 12.50 25.00
46 Paul Duchesne 7.50 15.00
47 Rene Pronovost 7.50 15.00
48 Roger Jodoin 7.50 15.00
49 Mario Senecal 7.50 15.00
50 Garry Plamondon 12.50 25.00
51 Marcel Paille 7.50 15.00
52 Rene Pepin 7.50 15.00
53 Gilles Desrosiers 7.50 15.00
54 Edgard Gendron 7.50 15.00
55 Roland Limoges 7.50 15.00
56 Roland Bilodeau 7.50 15.00
57 Leon Bouchard 7.50 15.00
58 Bob Leger 7.50 15.00
59 Conrad L'Heureux 7.50 15.00
60 Raymond Leduc 7.50 15.00
61 Bob Brault 7.50 15.00
62 Roger Ste. Marie 7.50 15.00
63 Real Lafreniere 7.50 15.00
64 Lucien Gilbert 7.50 15.00
65 Louis Desrosiers 12.50 25.00

1998-99 Baton Rouge Kingfish

This set features the Kingfish of the ECHL. The set was issued in five strips, each containing five cards, as a promotional giveaway at a home game.

COMPLETE SET (25) 8.00 20.00
1 Brett Abrahamson .40 1.00
2 Chris Aldous .40 1.00
3 Cam Brown .40 1.00
4 Jason Byrnes .40 1.00
5 Paul Croteau .40 1.00
6 Luke Curtin .40 1.00
7 Allan Hitchen .40 1.00
8 Scott Humeniuk .40 1.00
9 Trevor Jobe .40 1.00
10 Billy-Jay Johnston .40 1.00
11 Mike Josephson .40 1.00
12 Martin Laroche .40 1.00
13 Michel Massie .40 1.00
14 Eric Montreuil .40 1.00
15 Jon Rempel .40 1.00
16 Bryan Richardson .40 1.00
17 Dan Shermerhorn .40 1.00
18 Bob Westerby .40 1.00
19 Jordan Willis .60 1.50
20 Barry Smith CO .08 .25
21 Ron Hansis GM .02 .10
22 Bob McGill CO .08 .25
23 Huey P. Kingfish MAS .08 .25
24 Pat Loughlin TR .02 .10
25 Chris Kenyon .40 1.00

1998-99 BC Icemen

This set features the BC Icemen of the United Hockey League. Little else is known about this set at this time.

COMPLETE SET (22) 4.00 10.00
1 Mark Dutiaume .30 .75
2 Pete Vandermeer .30 .75
3 Patrice Robitaille .20 .50
4 Ales Dvorak .20 .50
5 Shane Dow .20 .50
6 Scott Ricci .20 .50
7 Doug Johnson .20 .50
8 Justin Kearns .30 .75
9 Justin Plamondon .20 .50
10 Jarno Mensonen .20 .50
11 Jamie Bird .20 .50
12 Greg Pajor .20 .50
13 Derek Knorr .20 .50
14 Chris Kavanagh .20 .50
15 Dallas Mann .20 .50
16 Jon Hillebrandt .30 .75
17 Dieter Kochan .75 2.00
18 Brad Jones HCO .08 .25
19 Brian Waselko TR .08 .25
20 Mike Thornton BR .08 .25
21 Phantom Mascot .08 .25
22 Bamboni Mascot .08 .25

1998-99 BC Icemen II

This set is numbered out of 25 and features the Iceman of the United Hockey League. It is believed that this set was offered as a promotional giveaway at a late-season home game.

COMPLETE SET (27) 8.00 20.00
1 Ales Dvorak .30 .75
2 Shane Dow .30 .75
3 Scott Ricci .30 .75
4 Pete Vandermeer .30 .75
5 Doug Johnson .30 .75
6 Mark Dutiaume .60 1.50
7 Justin Kearns .30 .75
8 Patrice Robitaille .30 .75
9 Justin Plamondon .40 1.00
10 Chris Greenville .30 .75
11 Jarno Mensonen .30 .75
12 Jamie Bird .30 .75
13 Greg Pajor .30 .75
14 Dmitri Deryabin .30 .75
15 Derek Knorr .30 .75
16 Peter Cermak .30 .75
17 Chris Kavanagh .30 .75
18 Jon Hillebrandt .75 2.00
19 Dieter Kochan 1.50 4.00
20 Brad Jones HCO .20 .50
21 Brian Weslro TR .08 .25
22 Dallas Mann .30 .75
23 Mike Thornton BR .08 .25
24 Phamton Mascot .08 .25
25 Bamboni Mascot .08 .25
NNO UHL Website .02 .10
NNO Checklist .08 .25

2001-02 BC Icemen

This set features the Icemen of the UHL. The set was issued as a promotional giveaway at a last-season home game. The cards are unnumbered and are listed below in alphabetical order.

COMPLETE SET (29) 8.00 20.00
1 Chris Allen .30 .75
2 Eric Andersen .30 .75
3 Alex Andreyev .30 .75
4 Keith Aucoin .30 .75
5 Martin Belanger .30 .75
6 Karel Betik .40 1.00
7 Glendon Cominetti .30 .75
8 Ross Dufresne .30 .75
9 R.J. Gates .30 .75
10 Chris Grenville .30 .75
11 Eric Heffler .30 .75
12 David Jesiolowski .40 1.00
13 Marc Lauzon .30 .75
14 Jim Nagle .30 .75
15 Ryan Pepperall .30 .75
16 Larry Pierce .30 .75
17 Justin Plamondon .30 .75
18 Sean Rowe .60 1.50
19 Erasmo Saltarelli .30 .75
20 Bryan Schoen .40 1.00
21 Trevor Shoaf .30 .75
22 Marc Tropper .30 .75
23 Rob Voltera .30 .75
24 Derek Wood .30 .75
25 Brad Jones CO .10 .25
26 Pedro Trindade MGR .04 .10
27 Bamboni MASCOT .10 .25
28 Phantom MASCOT .10 .25
29 Jason Weinstein PR .04 .10

1983-84 Belleville Bulls

This 30-card police set measures approximately 2 5/8" by 4 1/8" and was sponsored by the Board of Commissioners of Police and other local organizations. The fronts feature posed color player photos with white borders. The player's name and position appear at the bottom. The backs carry P.L.A.Y. (Police, Laws and Youth) Card Tips from The Bulls which consist of a hockey term and relate it to everyday life.

COMPLETE SET (30) 30.00 80.00
1 Belleville Bulls Logo .10 .25
2 Quinte Sports Centre .10 .25
3 Dan Quinn 1.00 2.50
4 Dave MacLean .20 .50
5 Scott Gardiner .20 .50
6 Mike Knuude .20 .50
7 Brian Martin .20 .50
8 R. Vaughan OWN .10 .25
9 John McDonald .30 .75
10 Brian Small .20 .50
11 Mike Savage .20 .50
12 Dunc MacIntyre .20 .50
13 Charlie Moore .20 .50
14 Jim Andanoff .20 .50
15 Mario Martini .20 .50
16 Rick Adolfi .20 .50
17 Mike Vellucci .20 .50
18 Scott McMichel .20 .50
19 Ali Butorac .20 .50
20 Al Iafrate 1.25 3.00
21 Rob Crocock .20 .50
22 Craig Coxe .60 1.50
23 Grant Robertson .20 .50
24 Craig Billington 1.25 3.00
25 Darren Gani .20 .50
26 Tim Bean .20 .50
27 Wayne Gretzky 30.00 75.00
28 Russ Soule TR .10 .25
29 Larry Mavety CO/GM .10 .25
30 Team Photo .40 1.00

1984-85 Belleville Bulls

This 31-card police set measures approximately 2 5/8" by 4 1/8" and was sponsored by the City of Belleville Police Force and other local organizations. The fronts feature posed color player photos with white borders. The player's name, position, and the season (1984-85) appear at the bottom. The backs carry P.L.A.Y. (Police, Laws and Youth) Card Tips from The Bulls which explain a hockey term and relate it to everyday life.

COMPLETE SET (31) 6.00 15.00
1 Team photo .20 .50
2 R. Vaughan OWN .02 .10
3 Larry Mavety CO/MG .02 .10
4 Dunc MacIntyre .20 .50
5 Belleville Bulls Logo .02 .10
6 Mike Knuude .20 .50
7 John Purves .40 1.00
8 Charlie Moore .20 .50
9 Stan Drulia .40 1.00
10 Craig Billington .75 2.00
11 Dave MacLean .20 .50
12 Darren Moxam .20 .50
13 Shane Doyle .20 .50
14 Larry VanHerzele .20 .50
15 Tim Bean .20 .50
16 Kent Brimmer .20 .50
17 Angelo Catenaro .20 .50
18 Steve Linesman .20 .50
19 Grant Robertson .20 .50
20 John Reid .20 .50
21 Dean Whyte .20 .50
22 Darren Gani .20 .50
23 Roger Robertson .20 .50
24 Gary Callaghan .20 .50
25 John Tamer .20 .50
26 Todd Hawkins .20 .50
27 Jim Andanoff .20 .50
28 Chris Rutledge TR .02 .10
29 Matt Taylor .20 .50
30 Mike Hartman .40 1.00
NNO Title Card .10 .25

2000-01 Belleville Bulls

This set features the Bulls of the OHL. The cards were produced by the team and sold at home games. The cards are instantly recognizable by virtue of having three colour headshots on the back.

COMPLETE SET (29) 5.00 12.00
1 Team Photo .20 .50
2 Paulo Colaiacovo .40 1.00
3 Nick Policelli .20 .50
4 Matt Coughlin .20 .50
5 Mike Jacobsen .20 .50
6 Malcolm Hutt .20 .50
7 Cody McCormick .20 .50
8 Mike Renzi .20 .50
9 Andrew Brown .20 .50
10 Andre Deveaux .20 .50
11 Matt Stajan .60 1.50
12 Alex White .20 .50
13 David Silverstone .20 .50
14 Randy Rowe .20 .50
15 Brad Efthimiou .20 .50
16 Dan Growden .20 .50
17 Adam Paiement .20 .50
18 Jan Chovan .30 .75
19 Branko Radivojevic .60 1.50
20 David Cornacchia .20 .50
21 Rob Dmytruk .20 .50
22 Nate Robinson .20 .50
23 Kyle Wellwood 1.00 2.50
24 In Action .20 .50
25 In Action .20 .50
26 In Action .20 .50
27 Jim Hulton CO .20 .50
28 Fan Pictures .02 .10
29 Directory .02 .10

2001-02 Belleville Bulls

This set features the Bulls of the OHL. The cards are slightly oversized, and were issued by the team. As they are unnumbered, they are listed below in alphabetical order.

COMPLETE SET (29) 5.00 12.00
1 Title card .04 .10
2 James Boyd ACO .04 .10
3 Andrew Brown .20 .50
4 Rane Carnegie .20 .50
5 Jan Chovan .30 .75
6 Paulo Colaiacovo .30 .75
7 Matt Coughlin .20 .50
8 Andre Deveaux .20 .50
9 Jake Gilmour .20 .50
10 Dan Growden .20 .50
11 Jim Hulton CO .20 .50
12 Malcolm Hutt .20 .50
13 Michael Knight .20 .50
14 Neill MacInnis .20 .50
15 Oliver Maron .20 .50
16 Cody McCormick .20 .50
17 Adam Paiement .20 .50
18 Marc Rancourt .20 .50
19 Michael Renzi .20 .50
20 Nathan Robinson .40 1.00
21 David Silverstone .20 .50
22 Matt Stajan .20 .50
23 Adam Sturgeon .20 .50
24 Kyle Wellwood .75 2.00
25 Alex White .20 .50
26 Celebration card .04 .10
27 Celebration card .04 .10
28 Michael Renzi .40 1.00
Matt Coughlin#Cody McCormick|#Kyle
29 Bullie Mascot .04 .10

2001-02 Belleville Bulls Update

This set features the Bulls of the OHL. The set was created late in the season simply to take advantage of the presence of hobby favorite Jason Spezza, who was traded to the Bulls from Windsor halfway through the season. The design is the same as that used for the main set issued earlier that season, but these cards are regulation sized. It is believed that as few as 500 of these sets were produced. The cards are unnumbered, so are listed below in alphabetical order.

COMPLETE SET (9) 4.00 10.00
1 David Clarkson .10 .25
2 Steve Cooke .10 .25
3 Michael Mole .40 1.00
4 Neil Smith .10 .25
5 Jason Spezza 1.25 3.00
6 Jason Spezza 1.25 3.00
7 Jason Spezza 1.25 3.00
8 Glenn Ridler .10 .25
9 Lubos Velebny .10 .25

2002-03 Belleville Bulls

COMPLETE SET (30) 6.00 15.00
1 Blake Allan .20 .50
2 Andrew Brown .20 .50
3 Rane Carnegie .20 .50
4 Steve Cooke .20 .50
5 Andre Deveaux .20 .50
6 Jake Gilmour .20 .50
7 Todd Griffith .20 .50
8 Malcolm Hutt .20 .50
9 Mike Knight .20 .50
10 Josh Manning .20 .50
11 Oliver Maron .20 .50
12 Cody McCormick .30 .75
13 Michael Mole .30 .75
14 Adam Paiement .20 .50
15 Marc Rancourt .20 .50
16 Neil Smith .20 .50
17 Matt Stajan .60 1.50
18 Ivan Svarny .20 .50
19 Cody Thornton .20 .50
20 Eric Tobia .30 .75
21 Darcy Tuplin .20 .50
22 Patrick Turcotte .20 .50
23 Jordon Watson .20 .50
24 Coaches .04 .10
25 Michael Mole .30 .75
Eric Tobia
26 Matt Stajan .60 1.50
27 Andre Deveaux .20 .50
28 Rookies .20 .50
29 Defencemen .04 .10
30 Team Captains .04 .10

2003-04 Belleville Bulls

eated by Extreme Sportscards, this 22-card set was ld a home games and by Cartes Timbres Ste-Foy. rds are unnumbered and are listed below by jersey mber.

MPLETE SET (22) 5.00 10.00
Rane Carnegie .20 .50
Cody Thornton .20 .50
Matt Kelly .20 .50
Dan Rogers .20 .50
Marc Rancourt .20 .50
Eric Tobia .30 .75
Ryan Berard .20 .50
Josh Francis .20 .50
Andrew Brown .20 .50
Michael Knight .20 .50
Aaron Lewicki .20 .50
Geoff Patton .20 .50
Jake Gilmour .20 .50
Ivan Svarny .20 .50
Todd Griffith .20 .50
David Edgeworth .20 .50
Josh Manning .20 .50
Milan Hluchy .20 .50
Mike Roelofsen .20 .50
Shaun Clinton .20 .50
Andrew Brown TL .20 .50
Rane Carnegie TL .20 .50

2004-05 Belleville Bulls

total of 400 team sets were produced.

OMPLETE SET (24) 5.00 12.00
Andrew Maksym .20 .50
Bobby Davey .20 .50
Cody Thornton .20 .50
Connor Cameron .20 .50
Jeff Leavitt .20 .50
Eric Tobia .20 .50
Evan Brophey .20 .50
Geoff Killing .20 .50
John Hughes .20 .50
Kevin Lalande .20 .50
Kyle Sonnenberg .20 .50
Lubomir Stach .20 .50
Mark Rancourt .20 .50
Marc Johnson .20 .50
Martin Novak .20 .50
Matt Beleskey .20 .50
Matt Kelly .20 .50
Pat Sutton .20 .50
Ryan Berard .20 .50
Ryan Rorabeck .20 .50
Scott Baker .20 .50
Shawn Matthias .40 1.00
Steve Spade .20 .50
NO Marc Rancourt CAP .75 2.00

2005-06 Belleville Bulls

OMPLETE SET (24) 8.00 15.00
Matt Beleskey .30 .75
Ryan Rorabeck .30 .75
Sebastian Dahm .30 .75
Kyle Jukosky .30 .75
Matt Smyth .30 .75
P.K. Subban 2.00 5.00
Michael Neal .30 .75
Scott Baker .30 .75
Bryan Cameron .30 .75
10 Bobby Davey .30 .75
11 Bud Kelly .30 .75
12 Geoff Killing .30 .75
13 Nicholas Pageau .30 .75
14 John Hughes .30 .75
15 Bryan Cameron .30 .75
16 Steve Spade .30 .75
17 Kevin Lalande .30 .75
18 Ryan Berard .30 .75
19 Andrew Maksym .30 .75
20 Jeff Leavitt .30 .75
21 Shawn Matthias .40 1.00
22 Cory Tanaka .30 .75
23 Andrew Gibbons .30 .75
24 Andrew Self .30 .75

2006-07 Belleville Bulls

COMPLETE SET (23) 5.00 12.00
1 Matt Pelech .20 .50
2 Bryan Cameron .20 .50
3 Matt Beleskey .20 .50
4 Stephen Blunden .30 .75
5 Erik Caladi .20 .50
6 Tyler Donati .20 .50
7 Andrew Gibbons .20 .50
8 Jeff Leavitt .20 .50
9 Shawn Matthias .30 .75
10 Michael Neal .20 .50
11 Aaron Snow .20 .50
12 Cory Tanaka .20 .50
13 Eric Tangradi .20 .50
14 Matthew Tipoff .20 .50
15 Paul Cianfrini .20 .50
16 Geoff Killing .20 .50
17 Shawn Lalonde .20 .50
18 Nicholas Pageau .20 .50
19 P.K. Subban 1.00 2.50
20 Steven Whitely .20 .50
21 Kevin Lalande .20 .50
22 Mike Murphy .20 .50
LE2 Shawn Matthias 1.00 2.50

1981-82 Billings Bighorns

We've confirmed one single from this early WHL set to date and it is believed that many others exist as well, possibly including former first overall pick Gord Kluzak. Any additional information can be forwarded to hockeymag@beckett.com.

NNO Harry Mahood 4.00 10.00

1992-93 Binghamton Rangers

Issued by the team, these cards are printed on thin card stock. The cards themselves are not numbered, but numbers are assigned to each on the checklist card. The front is a full bleed photo with the player name appearing only on the back.

COMPLETE SET (24) 4.00 10.00
1 Team Card .15 .40
2 Mike Hurlbut .15 .40
3 Michael Stewart .15 .40
4 Craig Duncanson .15 .40
5 Rick Bennett .15 .40
6 Dave Thomlinson .15 .40
7 Mike Stevens .15 .40
8 Rob Kenny .15 .40
9 Chris Cichocki .15 .40
10 Sergei Zubov .40 1.00
11 Don Biggs .15 .40
12 Joby Messier .15 .40
13 Steven King .15 .40
14 Dave Archibalc .15 .40
15 Brian McReynolds .15 .40
16 Dave Marcinyshyn .15 .40
17 Jean-Yves Roy .15 .40
18 Peter Fiorentino .15 .40
19 Daniel Lacroix .15 .40
20 Per Djoos .15 .40
21 Boris Rousson .30 .75
22 Corey Hirsch .30 .75
23 Rockey Ranger Mascot .08 .25
24 Ranger Victory .15 .40

1994-95 Binghamton Rangers

This 22-card standard-size set was manufactured and distributed by Jessen Associates, Inc. for Classic. The fronts display color action player photos with a dark blue marbleized inner border and a black outer border. The player's name, jersey number, and position appear in the teal border on the right edge. Inside a black border on a marbleized background, the backs present biography, statistics, and sponsor logos. The cards are unnumbered and checklisted below in alphabetical order.

COMPLETE SET (22) 4.00 10.00
1 Eric Cairns .30 .75
2 Craig Duncanson .15 .40
3 Peter Fiorentino .15 .40
4 Ken Gernander .15 .40
5 Jim Hiller .15 .40
6 Corey Hirsch .30 .75
7 Rob Kenny .15 .40
8 Andrei Kudinov .15 .40
9 Darren Langdon .30 .75
10 Scott Malone .15 .40
11 Shawn McCosh .15 .40
12 Mike McLaughlin .15 .40
13 Joby Messier .15 .40
14 Jeff Nielsen .15 .40
15 Mattias Norstrom .30 .75
16 Jamie Ram .30 .75
17 Barry Richter .20 .50
18 Jean Yves Roy .15 .40
19 Brad Rubachuk .15 .40
20 Dave Smith .15 .40
21 Dmitri Starostenko .15 .40
22 Michael Stewart .15 .40
23 Darcy Werenka .15 .40

1995-96 Binghamton Rangers

This 25-card set of the AHL Binghamton Rangers was manufactured and distributed by SplitSecond. The fronts feature color action player photos, while the backs carry player information. The cards are unnumbered and checklisted below in alphabetical order.

COMPLETE SET (25) 4.00 10.00
1 Sylvain Blouin .20 .50
2 George Burnett CO .02 .10
3 Mike Busniuk ACO .02 .10
4 Eric Cairns .30 .75
5 Chris Ferraro .30 .75
6 Peter Ferraro .40 1.00
7 Maxim Galanov .20 .50
8 Ken Gernander .20 .50
9 Brad Jones .15 .40
10 Pavel Komarov .15 .40
11 Andrei Kudinov .15 .40
12 Daniel Lacroix .20 .50
13 Steve Larouche .15 .40
14 Jon Hillebrandt .20 .50
15 Scott Malone .15 .40
16 Cal McGowan .15 .40
17 Jeff Nielsen .15 .40
18 Jamie Ram .20 .50
19 Shawn Reid .15 .40
20 Barry Richter .20 .50
21 Andy Silverman .15 .40
22 Lee Sorochan .20 .50
23 Dmitri Starostenko .15 .40
24 Ryan Vandenbussche .30 .75
25 Rick Willis .15 .40

1996-97 Binghamton Rangers

This 24-card set features the Binghamton Rangers of the AHL. The cards were produced by SplitSecond and distributed by the team. The cards feature an action photo on the front, along with player name, number and team logo. The backs feature limited stats. The unnumbered cards are listed below alphabetically.

COMPLETE SET (24) 4.00 10.00
1 Micah Aivazoff .20 .50
2 Sylvain Blouin .15 .40
3 George Burnett .02 .10
4 Mike Busniuk .02 .10
5 Ed Campbell .15 .40
6 Dan Cloutier 1.00 2.50
7 Chris Ferraro .20 .50
8 Peter Ferraro .20 .50
9 Peter Fiorentino .15 .40
10 Eric Flinton .15 .40
11 Maxim Golanov .15 .40
12 Ken Gernander .15 .40
13 Mike Martin .15 .40
14 Bob Maudie .15 .40
15 Jeff Nielsen .15 .40
16 Rocky Raccoon .02 .10
17 Ken Shepard .15 .40
18 Andy Silverman .15 .40
19 Adam Smith .15 .40
20 Lee Sorochan .20 .50
21 Ryan VandenBussche .30 .75
22 Vladimir Vorobiev .15 .40
23 Rick Willis .15 .40
24 AHL Hockey Card .02 .10

2003-04 Binghamton Senators

This set was sold by the team at home games.

COMPLETE SET (24) 6.00 15.00
1 Steve Bancroft .20 .50
2 Dennis Bonvie .40 1.00
3 Daniel Corso .20 .50
4 Ray Emery .40 1.00
5 Alexandre Giroux .20 .50
6 Denis Hamel .40 1.00
7 Andy Hedlund .20 .50
8 Jody Hull .20 .50
9 David Hymovitz .20 .50
10 Chris Kelly .40 1.00
11 Brooks Laich .20 .50
12 Josh Langfeld .20 .50
13 Chris Leinweber .20 .50
14 Brian McGrattan .40 1.00
15 Sorge Payer .20 .50
16 Jan Platil .20 .50
17 Christoph Schubert .20 .50
18 Peter Smrek .20 .50
19 Billy Thompson .40 1.00
20 Tony Tuzzolino .20 .50
21 Julien Vauclair .20 .50
22 Antoine Vermette .40 1.00
23 Greg Watson .20 .50
24 Mascot .04 .10

2003-04 Binghamton Senators Postcards

According to minor league expert Ralph Slate, these cards were issued as a promotional giveaway. A single card was given out each week that a fan bought a newspaper at a Quickway gas station. The cards are numbered on the front, card x of 12, and a bonus 13th card exists of the mascot.

COMPLETE SET (13) 15.00 30.00
1 Chris Kelly 1.25 3.00
2 Josh Langfeld .75 2.00
3 Julien Vauclair .75 2.00
4 Daniel Corso .75 2.00
5 Dennis Bonvie 1.25 3.00
6 David Hymovitz .75 2.00
7 Brooks Laich .75 2.00
8 Brian McGrattan 1.25 3.00
9 Alexandre Giroux .75 2.00
10 Denis Hamel 1.25 3.00
11 Antoine Vermette 1.25 3.00
12 Ray Emery 1.50 4.00
NNO Mascot .75 2.00

2004-05 Binghamton Senators

COMPLETE SET (26) 6.00 15.00
1 Brandon Bochenski .30 .75
2 Danny Bois .20 .50
3 Ray Emery .40 1.00
4 Jesse Fibiger .20 .50
5 Denis Hamel .40 1.00
6 Andy Hedlund .20 .50
7 Pat Kavanagh .20 .50
8 Chris Kelly .30 .75
9 Neil Komadoski .20 .50
10 Josh Langfeld .20 .50
11 Brian McGrattan .40 1.00
12 Arpad Mihaly .20 .50
13 Jan Platil .20 .50
14 Brian Pothier .20 .50
15 Grant Potulny .20 .50
16 Christoph Schubert .20 .50
17 Jason Spezza .75 2.00
18 Charlie Stephens .20 .50
19 Billy Thompson .30 .75
20 Antoine Vermette .30 .75
21 Anton Volchenkov .20 .50
22 Greg Watson .20 .50
23 David Cameron CO .04 .10
24 John Paddock CO .04 .10
25 Mike Busniuk ACO .04 .10
26 Max MASCOT .04 .10

2004-05 Binghamton Senators Hess

Given away one at a time at local gas stations with the purchase of a newspaper. They measure approximately 3 7/8 by 4 7/8.

COMPLETE SET (14) 20.00 35.00
1 Chris Kelly 1.25 3.00
2 Denis Hamel 1.50 4.00
3 Brian Pothier .75 2.00
4 Christoph Schubert .75 2.00
5 Pat Kavanagh .75 2.00
6 Antoine Vermette 1.25 3.00
7 Brandon Bochenski 1.25 3.00
8 Andy Hedlund .75 2.00
9 Brian McGrattan 1.25 3.00
10 Josh Langfeld .75 2.00
11 Anton Volchenkov .75 2.00
12 Jason Spezza 4.00 10.00
13 Ray Emery 1.50 4.00
NNO Cover card .10 .25

2005-06 Binghamton Senators

COMPLETE SET (22) 10.00 25.00
1 Denis Hamel .75 2.00
2 Danny Bois .40 1.00
3 Jeff Heerema .40 1.00
4 Unknown
5 Jan Platil .40 1.00
6 Charlie Stephens .40 1.00
7 Steve Martins .40 1.00
8 Brad Norton .40 1.00
9 Filip Novak .40 1.00
10 Billy Thompson .75 2.00
11 Grant Potulny .40 1.00
12 Patrick Eaves 1.25 3.00
13 Brett Clouthier .40 1.00
14 Tomas Malec .40 1.00
15 Kelly Guard .75 2.00
16 Neil Petruic .40 1.00
17 Brandon Bochenski .75 2.00
18 Brennan Evans .40 1.00
19 Gregg Johnson .40 1.00
20 Jeff Glass .75 2.00
21 Lance Ward .40 1.00
22 Sponsor Card .02 .10
23 Joe Cullen .40 1.00
24 Neil Komadoski .40 1.00
25 Billy Thompson .40 1.00
26 Greg Watson .40 1.00
27 Max The Mascot .20 .50
28 Dave Cameron .20 .50
29 Mike Busniuk .20 .50
30 Domenic Nicoletta .20 .50
31 Tom Severance .20 .50

2005-06 Binghamton Senators Quickway

COMPLETE SET (22) 10.00 25.00
1 Denis Hamel .40 1.00
2 Danny Bois .40 1.00
3 Jeff Heerema .40 1.00
4 Joe Cullen .40 1.00
5 Jan Platil .40 1.00
6 Charlie Stephens .40 1.00
7 Steve Martins .40 1.00
8 Brad Norton .40 1.00
9 Filip Novak .40 1.00
10 Billy Thompson .75 2.00
11 Grant Potulny .40 1.00
12 Patrick Eaves 1.25 3.00
13 Brett Clouthier .40 1.00
14 Tomas Malec .40 1.00
15 Kelly Guard .75 2.00
16 Neil Petruic .40 1.00
17 Brandon Bochenski .75 2.00
18 Brennan Evans .40 1.00
19 Gregg Johnson .40 1.00
20 Jeff Glass .75 2.00
21 Lance Ward .40 1.00
22 .04 .10

2006-07 Binghamton Senators

1 Jamie Allison .30 .75
2 Michal Barinka .30 .75
3 Danny Bois .30 .75
4 Charlie Cook .30 .75
5 Andrew Ebbett .30 .75
6 Chanse Fitzpatrick .30 .75
7 Jeff Glass .60 1.50
8 Kelly Guard .60 1.50
9 Andy Hedlund .30 .75
10 Jeff Heerema .30 .75
11 Josh Hennessy .60 1.50
12 Neil Komadoski .30 .75
13 Arttu Luttinen .30 .75
14 Tomas Malec .30 .75
15 Brian Maloney .30 .75
16 Serge Payer .30 .75
17 Cory Pecker .30 .75
18 Neil Petruic .30 .75
19 Grant Potulny .30 .75
20 Bobby Robins .30 .75
21 Ryan Vesce .30 .75
22 Mike Busniuk .30 .75
23 Dave Cameron CO .10 .25
24 Dom Nicoletta TR .02 .10
25 Tom Severance EQ .02 .10
26 Grady Whittenburg ANN .02 .10
27 Maximus MASCOT .02 .10

2006-07 Binghamton Senators 5th Anniversary

COMPLETE SET (35) 10.00 25.00
1 Steve Bancroft .30 .75
2 Cody Bass .30 .75
3 Brandon Bochenski .60 1.50
4 Danny Bois .30 .75
5 Dennis Bonvie .60 1.50
6 Patrick Eaves .60 1.50
7 Ray Emery .60 1.50
8 Alexandre Giroux .30 .75
9 Jeff Glass .40 1.00
10 Kelly Guard .40 1.00
11 Denis Hamel .40 1.00
12 Andy Hedlund .30 .75
13 Jeff Heerema .30 .75
14 David Hymovitz .30 .75
15 Chris Kelly .30 .75
16 Josh Langfeld .30 .75
17 Steve Martins .30 .75
18 Brian McGrattan .60 1.50
19 Joe Murphy .30 .75
20 Filip Novak .30 .75
21 Serge Payer .30 .75
22 Cory Pecker .30 .75
23 Jan Platil .30 .75
24 Brian Pothier .30 .75
25 Grant Potulny .30 .75
26 Bobby Robins .30 .75
27 Christoph Schubert .30 .75
28 Brad Smyth .30 .75
29 Jason Spezza .75 2.00
30 Charlie Stephens .30 .75
31 Billy Thompson .30 .75
32 Julien Vauclair .30 .75
33 Antoine Vermette .40 1.00
34 Anton Volchenkov .40 1.00
35 Max MASCOT .02 .10

2007-08 Binghamton Senators

COMPLETE SET (30) 10.00 20.00
1 Greg Amadio .30 .75
2 Cody Bass .30 .75
3 Danny Bois .30 .75
4 Matt Carkner .30 .75
5 Niko Dimitrakos .30 .75
6 Tyler Donati .30 .75
7 Brian Elliott .40 1.00
8 Ray Emery .40 1.00
9 Nick Foligno .40 1.00
10 Jeff Glass .40 1.00
11 Denis Hamel .30 .75
12 Josh Hennessy .30 .75
13 Matt Kinch .30 .75
14 Tomas Kudelka .30 .75
15 Brian Lee .60 1.50
16 Justin Mapletoft .30 .75
17 Greg Mauldin .30 .75
18 Scott May .30 .75
19 Alexander Nikulin .30 .75
20 Lawrence Nycholat .30 .75
21 Derek Smith .30 .75
22 Geoff Waugh .30 .75
23 Shawn Weller .40 1.00
24 Jeremy Yablonski .40 1.00
25 Ilya Zubov .40 1.00
26 Cory Clouston HC .02 .10
27 Mike Busniuk AC .02 .10
28 Tom Severance EQ .02 .10
29 Domenic Nicoletta TR .02 .10
NNO Max MASCOT Checklist .02 .10

2013-14 Binghamton Senators

COMPLETE SET (29) 10.00 25.00
1 Ben Blood .30 .75
2 Mark Borowiecki .30 .75
3 Cody Ceci .50 1.25
4 Fredrik Claesson .30 .75
5 Corey Cowick .30 .75
6 Jakub Culek .30 .75
7 Stephane Da Costa .30 .75
8 David Dziurzynski .30 .75
9 Tyler Eckford .30 .75
10 Derek Grant .30 .75
11 Wacey Hamilton .30 .75
12 Andrew Hammond .75 2.00
13 Mike Hoffman .75 2.00
14 Ludwig Karlsson .30 .75
15 Darren Kramer .30 .75
16 Nathan Lawson .30 .75
17 Jim O'Brien .30 .75
18 Jean-Gabriel Pageau .30 .75
19 Andre Petersson .30 .75
20 Shane Prince .30 .75
21 Matt Puempel .30 .75
22 Buddy Robinson .30 .75
23 Troy Rutkowski .30 .75
24 Cole Schneider .30 .75
25 Michael Sdao .30 .75
26 Steve Stirling Asst. CO Luke Richardson CO .30 .75
27 Mark Stone .75 2.00
28 Chris Wideman .30 .75
29 Mika Zibanejad .50 1.25

2014-15 Binghamton Senators

COMPLETE SET (30) 8.00 20.00
1 Fredrik Claesson .30 .75
2 Michael Sdao .30 .75
3 Chris Wideman .30 .75
4 Daniel New .30 .75
5 Matt Puempel .40 1.00
6 Buddy Robinson .30 .75
7 Carter Camper .30 .75
8 Danny Hobbs .30 .75
9 Patrick Mullen .30 .75
10 Cole Schneider .30 .75
11 Garrett Thompson .30 .75
12 Max McCormick .30 .75
13 Shane Prince .40 1.00
14 Brad Mills .30 .75
15 Alex Grant .30 .75
16 David Dziurzynski .40 1.00
17 Alex Guptill .30 .75
18 Darren Kramer .30 .75
19 Jakub Culek .30 .75
20 Ryan Dzingel .30 .75
21 Jean-Gabriel Pageau .40 1.00
22 Derek Grant .30 .75
23 Aaron Johnson .30 .75
24 Andrew Hammond 2.00 5.00
25 Chris Driedger .30 .75
26 Scott Greenham .30 .75
27 Luke Richardson CO .30 .75
28 Steve Stirling Asst. CO .30 .75
29 Tim Marks Video CO .30 .75
30 Tom Severance Equip. Mgr. .30 .75

1992-93 Birmingham Bulls

The cards are larger than the standard size, and are numbered on the back. The set is sponsored by Fox-21, Coca-Cola and radio station WJOX-FM.

COMPLETE SET (23) 3.00 8.00
1 Logo Card .02 .10
2 Jim Larkin .15 .40
3 Brett Barnett .15 .40
4 Joe Flanagan .15 .40
5 Butch Kaebel .15 .40
6 Scott Matusovich .15 .40
7 Chuck Hughes .15 .40
8 Dave Craievich .15 .40
9 Alexander Khavanov .15 .40
10 Paul Marshall .15 .40
11 Jim Peters .15 .40
12 Chris Marshall .15 .40
13 Jerome Bechard .15 .40
14 Jean-Alain Schneider .15 .40
15 Kevin Kerr .15 .40
16 Rob Krauss .15 .40
17 Greg Burke .15 .40
18 Mark Romaine .15 .40
19 Bruce Garber CO .02 .10
20 Phil Roberto ASST CO .08 .25
21 Dave Cavaliere TR .02 .10
22 Tim Woodburn ANN .02 .10
NNO Team Logo/CL .02 .10

1993-94 Birmingham Bulls

Sponsored by Coca-Cola, Fox 21 TV and WJOX AM 690, this 23-card set measures approximately 2 5/8" by 3 5/8" and features the 1993-94 Birmingham Bulls of the East Coast Hockey League. On a white card face, the fronts have posed color player photos. The team name and logo are printed above the photo, while the player's name, his position and sponsor logos appear below the picture. The horizontal backs carry player biography, profile and sponsor logos.

COMPLETE SET (23) 4.00 10.00
1 Logo Card .02 .10
2 Jim Larkin .20 .50
3 Brett Barnett .20 .50
4 Joe Flanagan .20 .50
5 Butch Kaebel .20 .50
6 Scott Matusovich .20 .50
7 Chuck E. Hughes .20 .50
8 Dave Craievich .20 .50
9 Alexander Khavanov .75 2.00
10 Paul Marshall .20 .50
11 Jim Peters .20 .50
12 Chris Marshall .20 .50
13 Jerome Bechard .20 .50
14 Jean-Alain Schneider .20 .50
15 Kevin Kerr .20 .50
16 Rob Krauss .20 .50
17 Greg Burke .20 .50
18 Mark Romaine .20 .50
19 Bruce Garber CO .02 .10
20 Phil Roberto ACO .20 .50
21 Dave Cavaliere TR .02 .10
22 Tim Woodburn ANN .02 .10
NNO Title Card CL .02 .10

1993-94 Birmingham Bulls Birmingham News

This set features the Bulls of the ECHL. It is believed that these were offered as a promotional giveaway. Unlike the other issue available this season, the cards feature an image of the Birmingham News on the front and back.

COMPLETE SET (27) 4.80 12.00
1 Phil Roberto CO .07 .20
2 Phil Roberto CO .07 .20
3 Jerome Bechard .20 .50
4 Marc Beran .20 .50
5 Dave Craievich .20 .50
6 Murray Duval .20 .50
7 Dan Fournel .30 .75
8 Jon Duval .20 .50
9 Joe Flanagan .20 .50
10 Todd Harris .20 .50
11 Bill Kovacs .20 .50
12 Jim Larkin .20 .50
13 Paul Marshall .20 .50
14 Jim Mill .30 .75
15 Brad Mullahy .20 .50
16 Tom Neziol .20 .50
17 Darcy Norton .20 .50
18 Jay Schiavo .20 .50
19 J.A. Schneider .20 .50
20 Brad Smyth .30 .75
21 Rick Girhiny .20 .50
22 Sandy Galuppo .20 .50
23 Jamie Linden .30 .75
24 Ed Krayer ACO .02 .10
25 Joel Stern ANN .02 .10
26 Mark Mills EQM .02 .10
27 Header Card/CL .02 .10

1994-95 Birmingham Bulls

Sponsored by Chevron, WBMG 45, and The New Mix 94.5 FM, this 22-card set measures approximately 2 3/4" by 3 3/4" and features the 1994-95 Birmingham Bulls of the ECHL. On a white card face, the fronts have posed color player photos. The cards are unnumbered and checklisted below in alphabetical order.

COMPLETE SET (22) 3.00 8.00
1 Greg Bailey .15 .40
2 Norm Bazin .15 .40
3 Jerome Bechard .15 .40
4 Dave Boyd .15 .40
5 David Craievich .15 .40
6 Rob Donovan .15 .40
7 Jon Duval .15 .40
8 Sandy Galuppo .20 .50
9 Todd Harris .15 .40
10 Ian Hebert .15 .40
11 Craig Johnson .15 .40
12 John Joyce .15 .40
13 Chris Kerber ANN .02 .10
14 Olaf Kjenstad .20 .50
15 Mike Krassner EQMG .02 .10
16 Jim Larkin .15 .40
17 Craig Lutes .15 .40
18 Mark Michaud .15 .40
19 Jean-Marc Plante .15 .40
20 Phil Roberto CO .15 .40
21 Brad Smyth .15 .40
22 Title Card CL .02 .10

1995-96 Birmingham Bulls

This odd-sized (2 3/4" by 3 3/4") 29-card set features the Birmingham Bulls of the ECHL. The cards feature an action shot along with the team logo and player name on the front. The unnumbered backs contain player stats and sponsor logos. The set also contains a 6-card subset of WJOX DJs. The set was available through the team; apparently, no mail order was available.

COMPLETE SET (29) 4.00 10.00
1 Toro the Bull .02 .10
2 Phil Roberto CO .08 .25
3 Lance Brady .20 .50
4 Jeff Wells .20 .50
5 Brad Prefontaine .20 .50
6 Mark Raiter .20 .50
7 Rob Donovan .20 .50
8 Chris Grenville .20 .50
9 Colin Gregor .20 .50
10 Mike Latendresse .30 .75
11 John Morabito .20 .50
12 Brendan Creagh .20 .50
13 Chris Bergeron .20 .50
14 Jerome Bechard .20 .50
15 Craig Lutes .20 .50
16 Ian Hebert .20 .50
17 John Joyce .20 .50
18 Jeff Callinan .20 .50
19 Jason Dexter .20 .50
20 Olaf Kjenstad .20 .50
21 Chad Erickson .30 .75
22 Ray Pack EQMG .02 .10
23 Chris Kerber ANN .02 .10
24 M.Coulter S.Griffi DJs .02 .10
25 Doug Laxton DJ .02 .10
26 Randy Armstrong DJ .02 .10
27 Lee Davis DJ .02 .10
28 Herb Winches DJ .02 .10
29 Ben Cook DJ .02 .10

1982-83 Birmingham South Stars

This set is believed to have been issued in the form of perforated program pull-outs. It is not known if this checklist is complete.

COMPLETE SET (16) 24.00 60.00
1 Frank Beaton 1.25 3.00
2 Bob Bergloff 1.25 3.00
3 Bob Boileau 1.25 3.00
4 Rollie Boutin 1.25 3.00
5 Murray Brumwell 1.25 3.00
6 Steve Carlson 8.00 20.00
7 Dave Debol .75 2.00
8 Jim Dobson .75 2.00
9 Dave Richter 1.25 3.00
10 Keith Hanson .75 2.00
11 Peter Hayek .75 2.00
12 Glenn Hicks .75 2.00
13 Craig Homola .75 2.00
14 Wes Jarvis 1.25 3.00
15 Warren Young 2.00 5.00
16 Markus Mattsson 1.25 3.00

2013-14 Blainville-Boisbriand Armada

1 Aaron Hoyles .30 .75
2 Etienne Marcoux .30 .75
3 Marcus Hinds .30 .75
4 Frederic Bergeron .30 .75
5 Daniel Walcott .30 .75
6 Guillaume Beaudoin .30 .75
7 Nikita Jevpalovs .30 .75
8 Danick Martel .30 .75
9 Christopher Clapperton .30 .75
10 Samuel Montembeault .30 .75
11 Guillaume Decelles .30 .75
12 Samuel Tremblay .30 .75
13 Joseph Strong .30 .75
14 Antoine Dufort-Plante .30 .75
15 Ryan Tesink .30 .75
16 Julien Bahl .30 .75
17 Tyler Brown .30 .75
18 Philippe Sanche .30 .75
19 Marco Roy .30 .75
20 David Bedard .30 .75
21 Emil Aronsson .30 .75
22 Samuel Hodhod .30 .75
23 Nathanael Halbert .30 .75
24 Olivier Picard .30 .75

2015-16 Blainville-Boisbriand Armada

COMPLETE SET (23) 6.00 15.00
1 Morgan Adams-Moisan .30 .75
2 Guillaume Beaudoin .30 .75
3 Guillaume Bergeron-Charron .30 .75
4 Anthony Boucher .30 .75
5 Connor Bramwell .30 .75
6 Antoine Crete-Belzile .30 .75
7 Alexandre Delisle-Houde .30 .75
8 Mark Grametbauer .30 .75
9 Nathanael Halbert .30 .75
10 Brendan Hamelin .30 .75
11 Tyler Hylland .30 .75
12 Alexander Katerinakis .30 .75
13 T.J. Melancon .30 .75
14 Yvan-Gabriel Mongo .30 .75
15 Samuel Montembeault .30 .75
16 Miguel Picard .30 .75
17 Kristian Pospisil .30 .75
18 Charlie Roy .30 .75
19 Philippe Sanche .30 .75
20 Olivier Schingh-Gomez .30 .75
21 Joel Teasdale .30 .75
22 Matthew Thorpe .30 .75
23 Samuel Tremblay .30 .75

2006-07 Bloomington PrairieThunder

COMPLETE SET (24) 8.00 15.00
1 Mike Adamek .30 .75
2 Trevor Baker .30 .75
3 Jon Booras .30 .75
4 Jarad Bourassa .30 .75
5 Steffan Braunlich .30 .75
6 John Spoltore .30 .75
7 Mike Zbriger .30 .75
8 B.J. Gaustad .30 .75
9 Ryan Gillis .30 .75
10 Alex Goupil .30 .75
11 Dion Hyman .30 .75
12 Andrew Lackner .30 .75
13 Andre Niec .30 .75
14 Jason Payne .30 .75
15 Mark Phenow .30 .75
16 Tyler Rennette .30 .75
17 Jeff Reynaert .30 .75
18 Shawn Roed .30 .75
19 Tim Schneider .30 .75
20 Chip MASCOT .02 .10
21 Brad Thompson .30 .75
22 Derek Booth CO .10 .25
23 Clay Roffer EQ MGR .02 .10
24 Chris Walter TR .02 .10

2001-02 Bossier-Shreveport Mudbugs

This set features the Mudbugs of the WPHL. The set was sold by the team at home games. The cards are unnumbered, so they are listed in alphabetical order.

COMPLETE SET (24) 4.00 10.00
1 Tony Bergin .20 .50
2 Trevor Buchanan .20 .50
3 Jason Campbell .20 .50
4 Bob Case TR .04 .10
5 Greg Foster .20 .50
6 Tim Hill .20 .50
7 Mike Johnson .20 .50
8 Derek Kups .20 .50
9 Bill Lang .20 .50
10 Chad Lang .30 .75
11 Dave Lemay .20 .50
12 Forbes MacPherson .20 .50
13 David Mills .20 .50
14 Scott Muscutt CO .04 .10
15 Pat Powers .20 .50
16 Ryan Rintoul .20 .50
17 Mark Rupnow .20 .50
18 Corey Smith .20 .50
19 Jim Sprott .20 .50
20 Brandon Walker BR .04 .10
21 Billy Welker EQMG .04 .10
22 Dan Wildfong .20 .50
23 Clawed MASCOT .04 .10
24 Team Photo .10 .25

2002-03 Bossier-Shreveport Mudbugs

COMPLETE SET (24) 6.00 15.00
1 Jason Basile .30 .75
2 Tony Bergin .30 .75
3 Chris Brassard .30 .75
4 Trevor Buchanan .30 .75
5 Dru Burgess .30 .75
6 Jason Campbell .30 .75
7 Ken Carroll .30 .75
8 Chris Chelios .30 .75
9 Jonathan Forest .30 .75
10 Jeff Glowa .30 .75
11 Willie Hubloo .30 .75
12 Forbes MacPherson .30 .75
13 Craig Minard .30 .75
14 David Oliver .30 .75
15 Mark Rupnow .30 .75
16 Jim Sprott .30 .75
17 Chad Spurr .30 .75
18 Luc Theoret .30 .75
19 Dan Wildfong .30 .75
20 Scott Muscutt CO .04 .10
21 George Bullock Jr. TR .04 .10
21 Billy Welker EQM .04 .10
23 Team Photo .20 .50
24 Steve Mears ANN .04 .10

2003-04 Bossier-Shreveport Mudbugs

COMPLETE SET (25) 6.00 15.00
1 Jason Basile .40 1.00
2 Travis Bell .30 .75
3 Jeff Blair .30 .75
4 Wes Blevins .30 .75
5 Chris Brassard .30 .75
6 Trevor Buchanan .30 .75
7 Jason Campbell .30 .75
8 Ken Carroll .30 .75
9 Colin Kendall .30 .75
10 Quade Lightbody .40 1.00
11 Forbes MacPherson .30 .75
12 Ryan Manitowich .30 .75
13 Craig Minard .40 1.00
14 David Oliver .30 .75
15 Craig Soke .30 .75
16 Jim Sprott .30 .75
17 Chad Spurr .30 .75
18 Dan Wildfong .30 .75
19 Scott Muscutt CO .04 .10
20 John Madden OWN .04 .10
21 George Bullock Jr. TR .04 .10
22 Billy Welker EQM .04 .10
23 Mascot .04 .10
24 Team photo .20 .50
25 Steve Mears ANN .04 .10

2005-06 Bossier-Shreveport Mudbugs

COMPLETE SET (26) 6.00 15.00
1 Jason Basile .30 .75
2 Chris Brassard .30 .75
3 David Cacciola .30 .75
4 Jason Campbell .30 .75
5 Ken Carroll .30 .75
6 Jeremy Downs .30 .75
7 Chad Kemp .30 .75
8 Quade Lightbody .40 1.00
9 Dale Lupul .30 .75
10 Ryan Manitowich .30 .75
11 Blair Manning .30 .75
12 Craig Minard .30 .75
13 Shane Palahicky .30 .75
14 Chris Shaw .30 .75
15 Scott Sheppard .30 .75
16 Brett Smith .30 .75
17 Chad Spurr .30 .75
18 Martin Stuchlik .30 .75
19 Milan Vodrazka .30 .75
20 Dan Wildfong .30 .75
21 Scott Muscutt HC .02 .10
22 Trevor Buchanan AC .02 .10
23 Billy Welker EM .02 .10
24 Clawed & Lil' Bugger MASCOTS .02 .10
25 George Bullock Jr. TR .02 .10
26 Steve Mears ANNCR .02 .10

2003-04 Boston College Eagles

This set was issued as a promotional giveaway at a home game. It comes in a perforated strip and features the Eagles' six graduating seniors and a team photo.

COMPLETE SET (7) 5.00 10.00
1 Ben Eaves .75 2.00
2 Tony Voce .75 2.00
3 Brett Peterson .75 2.00
4 Ty Hennes .75 2.00

5 J.D. Forrest .75 2.00
6 Justin Dziama .75 2.00
7 Team Photo .40 1.00

2003-04 Boston University Terriers

This set was issued as a promotional giveaway at a late-season home game.

COMPLETE SET (27) 10.00 25.00
1 Mark Mullen .40 1.00
2 Stephen Siwiec .40 1.00
3 Gregg Johnson .40 1.00
4 John Laliberte .40 1.00
5 Thomas Morrow .40 1.00
6 Jack Parker HCO .40 1.00
7 Stephen Greeley .40 1.00
8 Brian McConnell .40 1.00
9 E.J. Solimine .40 1.00
10 Sean Fields .40 1.00
11 Bryan Miller .40 1.00
12 Jakabs Redlihs .40 1.00
13 Kevin Schaeffer .40 1.00
14 Brad Zancanaro .40 1.00
15 Sean Sullivan .40 1.00
16 Ryan Whitney 1.25 3.00
17 David Van Der Gulik .40 1.00
18 Eric Thomassian .40 1.00
19 Ken Roche .40 1.00
20 David Klema .40 1.00
21 Dan Spang .40 1.00
22 Ken Magowan .40 1.00
23 Matt Radoslovich .40 1.00
24 Harry Agganis Arena .04 .10
25 John Curry .40 1.00
26 Frantisek Skladany .60 1.50
27 Mascot .04 .10

2014-15 Boston University Terriers

COMPLETE SET (27) 25.00 50.00
1 Robbie Baillargeon .30 .75
2 J.D. Carrabino .30 .75
3 Brien Diffley .30 .75
4 Kevin Duane .30 .75
5 Jack Eichel 20.00 40.00
6 Brandon Fortunato .30 .75
7 A.J. Greer .30 .75
8 Matt Grzelcyk .30 .75
9 Brandon Hickey .30 .75
10 Cason Hohmann .30 .75
11 Tommy Kelley .30 .75
12 Connor LaCouvee .30 .75
13 Matthew Lane .30 .75
14 Dillon Lawrence .30 .75
15 Johnathan MacLeod .30 .75
16 Anthony Moccia .30 .75
17 Michael Moran .30 .75
18 Matt O'Connor .30 .75
19 Ahti Oksanen .30 .75
20 Nikolas Olsson .30 .75
21 Daniel O'Regan .30 .75
22 Chase Phelps .30 .75
23 J.J. Piccinich .30 .75
24 Nick Roberto .30 .75
25 Evan Rodrigues .30 .75
26 T.J. Ryan .30 .75
27 Doyle Somerby .30 .75

2003-04 Bowling Green Falcons

This 18-card set was issued in two series of 9 cards each. Cards in each series were issued on perforated sheets and feature current and former players. Series 1 9cards 1-9) were limited to 2000 sheets while Series 2 was limited to 1000. Both sets were sponsored by the Sentinel Tribune.

COMPLETE SET (18) 12.00 30.00
1 Brian Holzinger .75 2.00
2 Brian Escobedo .40 1.00
3 Alex Rogosheske .40 1.00
4 George McPhee .40 1.00
5 Garry Galley .75 2.00
6 D'Arcy McConvey .40 1.00
7 Rob Blake 2.00 5.00
8 Mark Wires .40 1.00
9 Jordan Sigalet 2.00 5.00
10 Steve Brudzewski .75 2.00
11 Erik Eaton .75 2.00
12 Dan Kane .75 2.00
13 Gary Kruzich .75 2.00
14 Dave Ellet .75 2.00
15 Kevin Bieksa .75 2.00
16 Ryan Minnabarriet .75 2.00
17 Gino Cavallini .75 2.00
18 John Samanski .75 2.00

1999-00 Brampton Battalion

This set pictures the second-year Brampton Battalions of the Ontario Hockey League. The set was available at the team's rink, and through the mail from sponsor Frozen Pond, a Toronto-based memorabilia dealer. The set is highlighted by 2000 NHL Entry Draft first rounders Raffi Torres and Rostislav Klesla. It also includes a card of 2001 second overall pick Jason Spezza, who played with the team during its inaugural season of 1998-99.

COMPLETE SET (27) 10.00 25.00
1 Header Card .02 .10
2 Team Photo .08 .25
3 David Chant .60 1.50
4 Scott Della Vedova .08 .25
5 Tyler Hanchuck .08 .25
6 Jason Maleyko .08 .25
7 Paul Flache .08 .25
8 Cam McLaughlin .08 .25
9 Rostislav Klesla .60 1.50
10 Brad Woods .08 .25
11 Raffi Torres .75 2.00
12 Matt Reynolds .08 .25
13 Chris Rowan .08 .25
14 Lukas Havel .08 .25
15 Mike Rice .08 .25
16 Tyler Dukelow .08 .25
17 Jay McClement .20 .50
18 Matt Grennier .08 .25
19 Kurt MacSweyn .08 .25
21 Chris Cook .08 .25
21 Aaron Van Leusen .08 .25
22 Jay Harrison .40 1.00
23 Richard Kearns .08 .25
24 Jeff Bateman .20 .50
25 Scott Thompson .08 .25
26 Blair McLaughlin .08 .25
27 Jason Spezza 4.00 10.00
28 Stan Butler CO .08 .25
29 Bobby Jones .08 .25
30 Raffi Torres .75 2.00
31 Jason Maleyko .08 .25
32 Inaugural Season .02 .10

2000-01 Brampton Battalion

COMPLETE SET (32) 6.00 15.00
1 Logo .02 .10
2 Team Picture .02 .10
3 2001 WJC Banner .02 .10
4 Brian Finley .30 .75
5•Travis Parent .20 .50
6 Jason Maleyko .20 .50
7 Paul Flache .20 .50
8 Corey LeClair .20 .50
9 Rostislav Klesla .60 1.50
10 Adam Henrich .20 .50
11 Raffi Torres .60 1.50
12 Chris Clayton .20 .50
13 Chris Rowan .20 .50
14 Lukas Havel .20 .50
15 Jonah Leroux .20 .50
16 Jay McClement .20 .50
17 Kurt MacSweyn .20 .50
18 Aaron Van Leusen .20 .50
19 Jay Harrison .30 .75
20 Ryan Bowness .20 .50
21 Jeff Bateman .20 .50
22 Scott Thompson .20 .50
23 Alex MacDonell .20 .50
24 Anthony Marshall .20 .50
25 Brad Topping .20 .50
26 Stan Butler HCO .02 .10
27 Derrick Smith ACO .02 .10
28 Rostislav Klesla All-Star .60 1.50
29 Raffi Torres All-Star .60 1.50
30 Jay Harrison/1998 First Round .30 .75
31 Jay McClement/1999 First Round .20 .50
32 Adam Henrich/2000 First Round .20 .50

2003-04 Brampton Batallion

The Kreps card was randomly inserted among the team sets.

COMPLETE SET (24) 5.00 12.00
1 Ryan Bowness .20 .50
2 Chris Clayton .20 .50
3 Kevin Couture .30 .75
4 Nick Duff .20 .50
5 Jamie Fraser .20 .50
6 Tyler Harrison .20 .50
7 Robert Heickert .20 .50
8 Adam Henrich .20 .50
9 Kamil Kreps .60 1.50
10 Aaron Lobb .20 .50
11 Martin Lojek .20 .50
12 Howie Martin .20 .50
13 Eliott McCormick .20 .50
14 Brock McPherson .20 .50
15 Geordie Michie .20 .50
16 Phil Oreskovic .20 .50
17 Ryan Oulahen .20 .50
18 Erik Schwanz .20 .50
19 John Seymour .20 .50
20 Stuart Simmons .20 .50
21 Rob Smith .20 .50
22 Patrick Sweeney .20 .50
23 Brad Topping .30 .75
24 Wojtek Wolski .60 1.50
NNO Kamil Kreps LTD .20 .50

2004-05 Brampton Battalion

A total of 300 team sets were produced.

COMPLETE SET (25) 12.00
1 Wojtek Wolski .60 1.50
2 Daren Machesney .20 .50
3 Kevin Couture .20 .50
4 Michael Vernace .20 .50
5 Stuart Simmons .20 .50
6 Phil Oreskovic .30 .75
7 Nick Duff .20 .50
8 Martin Lojek .20 .50
9 Tomas Stryncl .20 .50
10 Danny McDonald .20 .50
11 Aaron Snow .20 .50
12 Brock McPherson .20 .50
13 John de Gray .20 .50
14 Howie Martin .20 .50
15 Luke Lynes .20 .50
16 Graham McNabb .20 .50
17 Luch Aquino .20 .50
18 John Seymour .20 .50
19 Patrick Sweeney .20 .50
20 Tyler Harrison .20 .50
21 J.F. Houle .20 .50
22 Scott Boomsma .20 .50
23 Jason Cassidy .20 .50
24 Ryan Oulahen .20 .50
25 Kyle Sonnenberg .20 .50

2005-06 Brampton Battalion

COMPLETE SET (25) 5.00 12.00
1 Wojtek Wolski .60 1.50
2 Phil Oreskovic .20 .50
3 Nick Duff .20 .50
4 John de Gray .20 .50
5 Daren Machesney .20 .50
6 Bryan Pitton .20 .50
7 Michael Vernace .20 .50
8 Tomas Stryncl .20 .50
9 Stephane Chabot .20 .50
10 Aaron Snow .20 .50
11 Matt Smyth .20 .50
12 Howie Martin .20 .50
13 Luke Lynes .20 .50
14 Graham McNabb .20 .50
15 Justin Levac .20 .50
16 Luch Aquino .20 .50
17 John Seymour .20 .50
18 Nolan Waker .20 .50
19 Taylor Raszka .20 .50
20 Cody Smith .20 .50
21 Jason Cassidy .20 .50
22 Michal Kljna .20 .50
23 Kyle Sonnenburg .20 .50
24 Corey George .20 .50
25 Brock McPherson .20 .50

2006-07 Brampton Battalion

COMPLETE SET (23) 6.00 15.00
1 Sarge's Checklist .02 .10
2 Patrick Killeen .30 .75
3 Bryan Pitton .30 .75
4 Ken Peroff .30 .75
5 Dalyn Flatt .30 .75
6 Brad Albert .30 .75
7 Tomas Stryncl .30 .75
8 Stephane Chabot .30 .75
9 John De Gray .30 .75
10 Kyle Sonnenburg .30 .75
11 Conor O'Donnell .30 .75
12 Matt Smyth .30 .75
13 Thomas Stajan .30 .75
14 Luke Lynes .30 .75
15 Graham McNabb .30 .75
16 Jason Dale .30 .75
17 Justin Levac .30 .75
18 Cody Hodgson .75 2.00
19 John Seymour .30 .75
20 Mike Lomas .30 .75
21 John Hughes .30 .75
22 Kyle Decoste .30 .75
23 Michal Klejna .30 .75

1982-83 Brandon Wheat Kings

This 24-card set measures approximately 2 1/4" by 4" and features posed color player photos with thin yellow borders on a white card face. The player's name appears on the picture at the bottom. The backs carry P.L.A.Y. (Police, Laws and Youth) Tips From The Kings, which consist of a hockey term and relates it to a real life situation. Sponsor logos appear on the lower portion of the back.

COMPLETE SET (24) 12.00 30.00
1 Wheat Kings Logo .20 .50
2 Kevin Pylypow .30 .75
3 Dean Kennedy .40 1.00
4 Sonny Sodke .30 .75
5 Darren Schmidt .30 .75
6 Cam Plante .30 .75
7 Sid Cranston .30 .75
8 Bruce Thomson .30 .75
9 Dave McDowall CO .20 .50
10 Bill Vince .30 .75
11 Kelly Glowa .30 .75
12 Tom McMurchy .30 .75
13 Ed Palichuk .30 .75
14 Roy Caswell .30 .75
15 Allan Tarasuk .30 .75
16 Brent Jessiman .30 .75
17 Randy Slawson .30 .75
18 Gord Smith .30 .75
19 Mike Sturgeon .30 .75
20 Larry Bumstead .30 .75
21 Kirk Blomquist .30 .75
22 Ron Loustel .30 .75
23 Ron Hextall 6.00 15.00
24 Brandon Police Logo .08 .25

1983-84 Brandon Wheat Kings

This 24-card set measures approximately 2 1/4" by 4" and features color posed action player photos with thin yellow borders on a white card face. The player's name is printed on the picture at the bottom. The backs carry P.L.A.Y. (Police, Laws and Youth) Tips From The Kings. Sponsor logos appear in the lower portion of the card.

COMPLETE SET (24) 10.00 25.00
1 Bryan Wells .20 .50
2 Jim Agnew .40 1.00
3 Gord Paddock .20 .50
4 John Dzikowski .20 .50
5 Kelly Kozack .20 .50
6 Byron Lomow .20 .50
7 Pat Loyer .20 .50
8 Rob Ordman .20 .50
9 Brad Wells .20 .50
10 Dave Thomlinson .30 .75
11 Cam Plante .20 .50
12 Jay Palmer .30 .75
13 Boyd Lomow .20 .50
14 Brent Jessiman .20 .50
15 Paul More .20 .50
16 Stacy Prtt .20 .50
17 Brandon City Police .08 .25
18 Jack Sangster CO .20 .50
19 Derek Laxdal .30 .75
20 Ray Ferraro 2.00 5.00
21 Allan Tarasuk .20 .50
22 Randy Cameron .20 .50
23 Dave Curry .20 .50
24 Ron Hextall 4.00 10.00

1984-85 Brandon Wheat Kings

This 24-card set measures approximately 2 1/4" by 4" and features color posed action player photos with thin yellow borders on a white card face. The player's name is printed on the picture at the bottom. The backs carry P.L.A.Y. (Police, Laws and Youth) Tips From The Kings. Sponsor logos appear on the lower portion of the card.

COMPLETE SET (24) 4.80 12.00
1 Garnet Kazuik .20 .50
2 Brent Mireau .20 .50
3 Byron Lomow .20 .50
4 Dean Shaw .20 .50
5 Dean Sexsmith .20 .50
6 Brad Mueller .20 .50
7 John Dzikowski .20 .50
8 Artie Feher .20 .50
9 Pat Loyer .20 .50
10 Murray Rice .20 .50
11 Derek Laxdal .30 .75
12 Perry Fafard .20 .50
13 Lee Trim .20 .50
14 Dan Hart .20 .50
15 Trent Ciprick .20 .50
16 Jeff Waver .20 .50
17 Brandon Wheat Kings .20 .50
18 Jack Sangster CO .08 .25
19 Darwin McPherson .20 .50
20 Pokey Reddick .75 2.00
21 Boyd Lomow .20 .50
22 Dave Thomlinson .30 .75
23 Paul More .20 .50
24 Brent Severyn .40 1.00

1985-86 Brandon Wheat Kings

This 24-card set measures approximately 2 1/4" by 4" and features color posed action player photos with thin yellow borders on a white card face. The player's name is printed on the picture at the bottom. The backs carry P.L.A.Y. (Police, Laws and Youth) Tips From The Kings. Sponsor logos appear in the lower portion of the card.

COMPLETE SET (24) 4.80 12.00
1 Kelly Hitchins .20 .50
2 Brent Mireau .20 .50
3 Byron Lomow .20 .50
4 Bob Heeney .20 .50
5 Dean Sexsmith .20 .50
6 Dave Curry .20 .50
7 John Dzikowski .20 .50
8 Artie Feher .20 .50
9 Kevin Mayo .20 .50
10 Murray Rice .20 .50
11 Derek Laxdal .40 1.00
12 Al Cherniwchan .20 .50
13 Lee Trim .20 .50
14 Terry Yake .40 1.00
15 Trent Ciprick .20 .50
16 Jeff Waver .20 .50
17 Team Photo .20 .50
18 Jack Sangster CO .20 .50
19 Mike Morin .20 .50
20 Jason Phillips .20 .50
21 Rod Williams .20 .50
22 Dave Thomlinson .40 1.00
23 Shane Eirickson .20 .50
24 Randy Hoffart .20 .50

1988-89 Brandon Wheat Kings

This 24-card set measures approximately 2 1/4" by 4" and features posed, color player photos with a thin yellow border stripe against a white card face. The backs carry P.L.A.Y. (Police, Laws and Youth) Tips from the Kings and sponsor logos.

COMPLETE SET (24) 6.00 15.00
1 Kevin Cheveldayoff .20 .50
2 Bob Woods .20 .50
3 Dwayne Newman .20 .50
4 Mike Vandenberghe .20 .50
5 Brad Woods .20 .50
6 Gary Audette .20 .50
7 Mark Bassen .20 .50
8 Troy Frederick .20 .50
9 Troy Kennedy .20 .50
10 Barry Dreger .20 .50
11 Bill Whistle .20 .50
12 Jeff Odgers .40 1.00
13 Sheldon Kowalchuk .20 .50
14 Chris Robertson .20 .50
15 Don Laurin .20 .50
16 Curtis Folkett .20 .50
17 Team Photo .20 .50
18 Kelly McCrimmon ACO .20 .50
19 Doug Sauter CO .20 .50
20 Kelly Hitchins .20 .50
21 Trevor Kidd 1.25 3.00
22 Pryce Wood .20 .50
23 Cam Brown .20 .50
24 Greg Hutchings .20 .50

1989-90 Brandon Wheat Kings

This 24-card P.L.A.Y. (Police, Laws and Youth) set measures approximately 2 1/4" by 4". The fronts display color posed action photos inside of yellowish-orange borders. The player's name is printed in black across the bottom of the picture. In addition to sponsor logos, the backs carry "P.L.A.Y. Tips from the Kings" in the form of safety messages.

COMPLETE SET (24) 4.80 12.00
1 Trevor Kidd 1.25 3.00
2 Troy Frederick .20 .50
3 Kelly Thiessen .30 .75
4 Pryce Wood .20 .50
5 Mike Vandenberghe .20 .50
6 Chris Constant .20 .50
7 Hardy Sauter .20 .50
8 Cam Brown .20 .50
9 Bart Cote .20 .50
10 Jeff Hoad .20 .50
11 Kevin Robertson .20 .50
12 Dwayne Newman .20 .50
13 Calvin Flint .20 .50
14 Glen Webster .20 .50
15 Greg Hutchings .30 .75
16 Rob Puchniak .20 .50
17 Gary Audette .20 .50
18 Kevin Schmalz .20 .50
19 Dwayne Gylywoychuk .20 .50
20 Jeff Odgers .30 .75
21 Brian Purdy .20 .50
22 Merv Priest .20 .50
23 Doug Sauter CO .08 .25
24 Team Photo .20 .50

1990-91 Brandon Wheat Kings

This 24-card set measures approximately 2 1/4" by 4". The fronts feature posed color player photos with thin orange borders. The player's name appears on the picture at the bottom, while his uniform number and position are printed in the upper corners. On a white background, the backs carry P.L.A.Y. (Police, Laws and Youth) "Tips From The Kings". Sponsor logos and room for an autograph appear on the lower portion.

COMPLETE SET (24) 5.60 14.00
1 Jeff Hoad .20 .50
2 Merv Priest .20 .50
3 Mike Vandenberghe .20 .50
4 Bart Cote .20 .50
5 Hardy Sauter .20 .50
6 Mark Johnston ACO .08 .25
7 Kelly McCrimmon CO .08 .25
8 Team Photo .20 .50
9 Kevin Robertson .20 .50
10 Glen Webster .20 .50
11 Greg Hutchings .20 .50
12 Dan Kopec .20 .50
13 Dwayne Gylywoychuk .20 .50
14 Brian Purdy .20 .50
15 Trevor Kidd 1.25 3.00
16 Johan Skillgard .20 .50
17 Stu Scantlebury .20 .50
18 Byron Penstock .20 .50
19 Rob Puchniak .20 .50
20 Gary Audette .20 .50
21 Calvin Flint .20 .50
22 Jason White .20 .50
23 Chris Constant .20 .50
24 Glen Gulutzan .20 .50

1992-93 Brandon Wheat Kings

These 24 standard-size cards feature color player action shots on their fronts. Each picture is trimmed in white and has its corners blacked out, giving the impression of a mounted photograph. The cards are unnumbered and checklisted below in alphabetical order.

COMPLETE SET (24) 4.00 10.00
1 Aris Brimanis .15 .40
2 Colin Cloutier .20 .50
3 Chris Dingman .30 .75
4 Mike Dubinsky .20 .50
5 Todd Dutiaume .15 .40
6 Mark Franks .15 .40
7 Craig Geekie .15 .40
8 Dwayne Gylywoychuk .15 .40
9 Scott Hlady .15 .40
10 Jeff Hoad .15 .40
11 Bobby House .15 .40
12 Chris Johnston .15 .40
13 Mark Kolesar .20 .50
14 Scott Laluk .15 .40
15 Mike Maneluk .20 .50
16 Sean McFatridge .15 .40
17 Marty Murray .30 .75
18 Byron Penstock .20 .50
19 Darren Ritchie .15 .40
20 Trevor Robins .20 .50
21 Ryan Smith .15 .40
22 Jeff Staples .15 .40
23 Darcy Werenka .20 .50
24 Willie MASCOT .02 .10

1993-94 Brandon Wheat Kings

This set features the Wheat Kings of the WHL. The cards feature an action photo on the front, framed by black and gold borders. The cards were sold at home games.

COMPLETE SET (24) 6.00 15.00
1 Byron Penstock .30 .75
2 Craig Hordal .30 .75
3 Jeff Staples .20 .50
4 Scott Laluk .20 .50
5 Wade Redden .75 2.00
6 Justin Kurtz .30 .75
7 Sven Butenschon .20 .50
8 Adam Magarrell .20 .50
9 Dwayne Gylywoychuk .20 .50
10 Scott Hlady .20 .50
11 Joel Korenko .20 .50
12 Chris Johnston .20 .50
13 Bobby Brown .20 .50
14 Mark Kolesar .20 .50
15 Chris Low .20 .50
16 Dean Kletzel .20 .50
17 Darren Ritchie .20 .50
18 Mark Dutiaume .20 .50
19 Mike Dubinsky .20 .50
20 Chris Dingman .30 .75
21 Mike Maneluk .30 .75
22 Colin Cloutier .20 .50
23 Paul Bailley .20 .50
24 Marty Murray .30 .75

1994-95 Brandon Wheat Kings

This set features the Wheat Kings of the WHL and was sponsored by 7-Eleven and CKX Radio and was printed by Leech Printing. The set is not numbered and so is listed alphabetically.

COMPELTE SET (24) 6.00 15.00
1 Bobby Brown .20 .50
2 Sven Butenschon .20 .50
3 Colin Cloutier .20 .50
4 Chris Dingman .30 .75
5 Mike Dubinsky .20 .50
6 Mark Dutiaume .20 .50
7 Brian Elder .20 .50
8 Dean Kletzel .20 .50
9 Joel Korenko .20 .50
10 Justin Kurtz .30 .75
11 Scott Laluk .20 .50
12 Chris Low .20 .50
13 Adam Magarrell .20 .50
14 Marty Murray .20 .50
15 Byron Penstock .20 .50
16 Kevin Pozzo .20 .50
17 Wade Redden .75 2.00
18 Darren Ritchie .20 .50
19 Peter Schaefer .30 .75
20 Kelly Smart .20 .50
21 Jeff Staples .20 .50
22 Oleg Tverdovsky .40 1.00
23 Darren Van Oene .20 .50
24 Ian Walterson .20 .50

1995-96 Brandon Wheat Kings

This set was sponsored by 7-11 and was printed by Leech Printing. It is believed that it was sold in set-form by the team. The set is not numbered so the checklist appears below in alphabetical order.

COMPLETE SET (24) 6.00 15.00
1 Bobby Brown .20 .50
2 Sven Butenschon .20 .50
3 Stefan Cherneski .20 .50
4 Cory Cyrenne .30 .75
5 David Draguzas .20 .50
6 Chris Dingman .30 .75
7 Mark Dutiaume .20 .50
8 Brian Elder .20 .50
9 Burke Henry .20 .50
10 Vincent Jonasson .20 .50
11 Dean Kletzel .20 .50
12 Justin Kurtz .30 .75
13 Mike LeClerc .40 1.00
14 Andrei Lupandin .20 .50
15 Wade Redden .75 2.00
16 Ryan Robson .20 .50
17 Peter Schaefer .30 .75
18 Jason Skilnick .20 .50
19 Kelly Smart .20 .50
20 Daryl Stockham .20 .50
21 Jeff Temple .20 .50
22 Daniel Tetrault .20 .50
23 Gerhard Unterluggauer .20 .50
24 Darren Van Oene .30 .75

1996-97 Brandon Wheat Kings

COMPLETE SET (24) 7.00 12.00
1 Les Borsheim .20 .50
2 Daniel Tetrault .20 .50
3 Burke Henry .40 1.00
4 Darryl Stockham .20 .50
5 Gerhard Unterluggauer .20 .50
6 Josh Woitas .20 .50
7 Mark Dutiaume .20 .50
8 Johnathan Aitken .30 .75
9 Dorian Anneck .20 .50
10 Brian Elder .20 .50
11 Andrei Lupandin .20 .50
12 Brad Twordik .20 .50
13 Jeff Katcher .20 .50
14 Kelly Smart .20 .50
15 Peter Schaefer .40 1.00
16 Ryan Robson .20 .50
17 Cory Cyrenne .40 1.00
18 Jason Boyd .20 .50
19 Darren Van Oene .20 .50
20 Stefan Cherneski .20 .50
21 Aaron Goldade .20 .50
22 Justin Kurtz .20 .50
23 David Haun .20 .50
24 Bobby Leavins .20 .50

1997-98 Brandon Wheat Kings

This set features the Wheat Kings of the WHL. The set is sponsored by McDonald's and P.L.A.Y. The cards are unnumbered, so are listed in alphabetical order.

COMPLETE SET (26) 6.00 15.00
1 Alex Argyriou .20 .50
2 Johnathan Aitken .20 .50
3 Les Borsheim .20 .50
4 Stefan Cherneski .20 .50
5 Jomar Cruz .30 .75
6 Cory Cyrenne .30 .75
7 Brett Girard .20 .50
8 Aaron Goldade .20 .50
9 Bevin Guenther .20 .50
10 David Haun .20 .50
11 Burke Henry .20 .50
12 Jamie Hodson .40 1.00
13 Andrew Kaminsky .20 .50
14 Kirby Law .40 1.00
15 Bobby Leavins .20 .50
16 Andrei Lupandin .20 .50
17 Scott McCallum .20 .50
18 Brooks Paisley .20 .50
19 Randy Ponte .20 .50
20 Ryan Robson .20 .50
21 Wade Skolney .20 .50
22 Kelly Smart .20 .50
23 Daniel Tetrault .30 .75
24 Brent Twordik .20 .50
25 Darren Van Oene .20 .50
26 Josh Woitas .20 .50

1998-99 Brandon Wheat Kings

This set features the Wheat Kings of the WHL. The set was sold by the team at home games and was sponsored by McDonald's. The cards are unnumbered, and so are listed below alphabetically.

COMPLETE SET (24) 4.00 10.00
1 Alex Argyriou .20 .50
2 Ryan Craig .20 .50
3 Jomar Cruz .30 .75
4 Jan Fadrny .20 .50
5 Brett Girard .20 .50
6 Aaron Goldade .20 .50
7 Burke Henry .20 .50
8 Jamie Hodson .30 .75
9 Ryan Johnston .20 .50
10 J.D. Kehler .20 .50
11 Petr Kudrna .20 .50
12 Andrew Kaminsky .20 .50
13 Andrei Lupandin .20 .50
14 Scott McCallum .20 .50
15 Richard Mueller .20 .50
16 Randy Ponte .20 .50
17 Ryan Robson .20 .50
18 Wade Skolney .20 .50
19 Daniel Tetrault .20 .50
20 Brett Thurston .20 .50
21 Brad Twordik .20 .50
22 Cory Unser .20 .50
23 Mike Wirll .20 .50
24 Justin Yeoman .20 .50

1999-00 Brandon Wheat Kings

This set features the Wheaties of the WHL. The set was sold by the team at home games. The cards are unnumbered, so are listed below alphabetically.

COMPLETE SET (24) 6.00 25.00
1 Mark Ardelan .20 .50
2 Milan Bartovic .20 .50
3 Les Borsheim .20 .50
4 Ryan Craig .20 .50
5 Brett Dickie .20 .50
6 Ryan Diduck .20 .50
7 Jan Fadrny .20 .50
8 Brett Girard .20 .50
9 Aaron Goldade .20 .50
10 Kevin Harris .20 .50
11 Jamie Hodson .30 .75
12 J.D. Kehler .20 .50
13 Colin McRae .20 .50
14 Robert McVicar .30 .75
15 Richard Mueller .20 .50
16 Randy Ponte .20 .50
17 Bart Rushmer .20 .50
18 Wade Skolney .20 .50
19 Daniel Tetrault .20 .50
20 Brett Thurston .20 .50
21 Jordin Tootoo 6.00 15.00
22 Brad Twordik .20 .50
23 Cory Unser .20 .50
24 Mike Wirll .20 .50

2000-01 Brandon Wheat Kings

COMPLETE SET (24) 10.00 25.00
1 Jordin Tootoo 4.00 10.00
2 Jamie Hodson .30 .75
3 Mark Ardelan .20 .50
4 Reagan Leslie .20 .50
5 Brett Thurston .20 .50
6 Travis Young .20 .50
7 Brett Dickie .20 .50
8 Richard Mueller .20 .50
9 Nolan Yonkman .30 .75
10 Brett Girard .20 .50
11 James Marquis .20 .50
12 Colin McRae .20 .50
13 Aaron Goldade .20 .50
14 Milan Bartovic .20 .50
15 J.D. Kehler .20 .50
16 Lance Monych .40 1.00
17 Tim Konsorada .20 .50
18 Caine Pearpoint .20 .50
19 Ryan Craig 1.25 3.00
20 Randy Ponte .40 1.00
21 Kevin Harris .20 .50
22 Wade Skolney .20 .50
23 Jiri Jakes .20 .50
24 Robert McVicar .30 .75

2001-02 Brandon Wheat Kings

This set features the Wheaties of the WHL. The set was produced by the team and sponsored by McDonald's and was offered for sale at the team's souvenir shop. The cards are black bordered, and so are highly condition sensitive. As they are unnumbered, they are listed below alphabetically.

COMPLETE SET (24) 10.00 25.00
1 Andre Blanchette .20 .50
2 Dustin Bru .20 .50
3 Ryan Craig .20 .50
4 Brett Dickie .20 .50
5 Travis Eagles .20 .50
6 Eric Fehr .20 .50
7 Adrian Foster .40 1.00
8 Josh Garbutt .30 .75
9 Kevin Harris .20 .50
10 Jiri Jakes .30 .75
11 Tim Konsorada .20 .50
12 Reagan Leslie .20 .50
13 Geoff McIntosh .20 .50
14 Colin McRae .20 .50
15 Robert McVicar .20 .50
16 Lance Monych .20 .50
17 Caine Pearpoint .20 .50
18 Randy Ponte .40 1.00
19 Wade Skolney .20 .50
20 Ryan Stone .20 .50
21 Brett Thurston .20 .50
22 Jordin Tootoo .75 2.00
23 Willie MASCOT .04 .10
24 Travis Young .20 .50

2002-03 Brandon Wheat Kings

This 23-card set was sold at home games. An early card of Jordin Tootoo highlights this set.

COMPLETE SET (23) 10.00 25.00
1 Jonathan Webb .20 .50
2 Reagan Leslie .20 .50
3 Brett Thurston .20 .50
4 Bryan Nathe .20 .50
5 Brett Dickie .20 .50
6 Josh Garbutt .20 .50
7 Andre Blanchette .20 .50
8 Richard Jasovsky .20 .50
9 Tyler Dyck .20 .50
10 Derek Werenka .20 .50
11 Teegan Moore .20 .50
12 Eric Fehr 1.25 3.00
13 Ryan Stone .20 .50
14 Lance Monych .20 .50
15 Tim Konsorada .20 .50
16 Rick Kozak .20 .50
17 Jordin Tootoo 4.00 10.00
18 Greg Watson .40 1.00
19 Ryan Craig .20 .50
20 Ole-Kristian Tollefson .20 .50
21 Jeff Topilko .20 .50
22 Geoff McIntosh .30 .75
23 Robert McVicar .30 .75

2003-04 Brandon Wheat Kings

COMPLETE SET (24) 6.00 15.00
1 Josh Harding 1.25 3.00
2 Tyler Boldt .20 .50
3 Stephan Lenoski .20 .50
4 Erik Christensen .40 1.00
5 Lance Monych .40 1.00
6 Mark Derlago .20 .50
7 Corey Courchene .20 .50
8 Richard Jasovsky .20 .50
9 Tim Konsorada .20 .50
10 Codey Burki .20 .50
11 Teegan Moore .20 .50
12 Ryan Stone .40 1.00
13 Reagan Leslie .20 .50
14 Ole-Kristian Tollefsen .40 1.00
15 Steven Later .20 .50
16 Eric Fehr .75 2.00
17 Andre Blanchette .20 .50
18 Jeff Topilko .20 .50
19 Mark Louis .20 .50
20 Mark Shefchyk .20 .50
21 Jonathan Webb .20 .50
22 Tyler Dyck .20 .50
23 Derek LeBlanc .20 .50
24 Mike Nichol .20 .50

2004-05 Brandon Wheat Kings

COMPLETE SET (24) 8.00 20.00
1 Mike Nichol .30 .75
2 Jonathan Webb .30 .75
3 Corey Courchene .30 .75
4 Mike Cann .30 .75
5 Theran Yeo .30 .75
6 Steven Later .30 .75
7 Daryl Boyle .30 .75
8 Cole Hunter .30 .75
9 Sami Sandell .30 .75
10 Tyler Strautman .30 .75
11 Eric Fehr .75 2.00
12 Teegan Moore .30 .75
13 Ryan Stone .60 1.50
14 Lance Monych .40 1.00
15 Tim Konsorada .40 1.00
16 Jakub Sindel .30 .75
17 Riley Day .30 .75
18 Codey Burki .30 .75
19 Derek LeBlanc .30 .75
20 Ryan Reaves .30 .75
21 Jeff Topilko .30 .75
22 Mark Louis .30 .75
23 Stephan Lenoski .30 .75
24 Tyler Plante .30 .75

2005-06 Brandon Wheat Kings

COMPLETE SET (24) 10.00 18.00
1 Keith Aulie .30 .75
2 Daryl Boyle .30 .75
3 Codey Burki .30 .75
4 Andrew Clark .30 .75
5 Corey Courchene .30 .75
6 Riley Day .30 .75
7 Mark Derlago .30 .75
8 Tyler Dittmer .30 .75
9 Chad Erb .30 .75
10 Matt Hallick .30 .75
11 Cole Hunter .30 .75
12 Kurt Jory .30 .75
13 Bryan Kauk .30 .75
14 Dustin Kohn .30 .75
15 Stephan Lenoski .30 .75
16 Mark Louis .30 .75
17 Teegan Moore .30 .75
18 Tyler Plante .30 .75
19 Ryan Reaves .30 .75
20 Sami Sandell .30 .75
21 Tyler Strautman .30 .75
22 Jeff Topilko .30 .75
23 John Wikner .30 .75
24 Theran Yeo .30 .75

2013-14 Brandon Wheat Kings

COMPLETE SET (24) 6.00 15.00
1 Rihards Bukarts .30 .75
2 Tyler Coulter .30 .75
3 Jesse Gabrielle .30 .75
4 Taylor Green .30 .75
5 Jayce Hawryluk .30 .75
6 Curtis Honey .30 .75
7 Rene Hunter .30 .75
8 Brett Kitt .30 .75
9 Ryley Lindgren .30 .75
10 Quintin Lisoway .30 .75
11 Tim McGauley .30 .75
12 Jens Meilleur .30 .75
13 Richard Nejezchleb .30 .75
14 Kord Pankewicz .30 .75
15 Jordan Papirny .30 .75
16 Ryan Pilon .30 .75
17 Ryan Pulock .30 .75
18 John Quenneville .30 .75
19 Peter Quenneville .30 .75
20 Chad Robinson .30 .75
21 Eric Roy .30 .75
22 Braylon Shmyr .30 .75
23 Colton Waltz .30 .75
24 Willie MASCOT .30 .75

1983-84 Brantford Alexanders

This 30-card set measures approximately 2 3/4" by 3 1/2". The fronts feature posed color player photos inside a thin black picture frame and white outer borders. The player's name appears on the picture at the bottom. On a white background, the backs carry the player's name, number, and a short biography in the upper portion; P.L.A.Y. (Police, Laws and Youth) "Tips From The Alexanders And The Brantford and Area Police" in the middle; and sponsor logos in the lower portion.

COMPLETE SET (30) 12.00 30.00
1 Ken Gratton ACO .20 .50
2 Shayne Corson 2.00 5.00
3 Bob Probert 4.00 10.00
4 Bruce Bell .60 1.50
5 Warren Bechard ACO .20 .50

6 Jason Lafreniere .40 1.00
7 Rob Moffat .30 .75
8 Jack Calbeck PR .20 .50
9 Marc West .30 .75
10 Larry Van Herzele .30 .75
11 Doug Stewart .30 .75
12 Brian MacDonald .30 .75
13 Dave Draper CO .20 .50
GM
14 Jeff Jackson .60 1.50
15 Steve Linseman .30 .75
16 Steve Short .30 .75
17 Allan Bester .75 2.00
18 John Weir COP .20 .50
19 Chris Pusey .30 .75
20 Mike Millar .30 .75
21 Chris Glover .30 .75
22 Bob Pierson .30 .75
23 Phil Priddle .30 .75
24 Grant Anderson .30 .75
25 Ken Gagner .30 .75
26 Andy Alway TR .20 .50
27 Todd Francis .30 .75
28 John Meulenbroeks .30 .75
29 Mike Chettleburgh .30 .75
30 Bill Dynes TR .20 .50

1994-95 Brantford Smoke

Sponsored by Calbeck's Sports Centre and Davis Fuels, and printed by Slapshot Images Ltd., this 26-card set features the 1994-95 Brantford Smoke of the Colonial Hockey League.

COMPLETE SET (26) 3.00 8.00
1 Checklist .02 .10
2 Bob Delorimiere .15 .40
3 Todd Francis .15 .40
4 Pete Liptrott .15 .40
5 Lorne Knauft .15 .40
6 Paul Polillo .15 .40
7 Rob Arabski .15 .40
8 Derek Gauthier .15 .40
9 Joe Simon .15 .40
10 Brad Barton .15 .40
11 Terry Chitaroni .20 .50
12 Paul Mitton .15 .40
13 Wayne MacPhee .15 .40
14 Brian Blad .20 .50
15 John Laan .15 .40
16 Shane MacEachern .15 .40
17 Wayne Muir .15 .40
18 Ted Miskolczi .15 .40
19 Marc Delorme .15 .40
20 Mike Speer .15 .40
21 Bob Baird TR .02 .10
Ken Crabb
22 Ken Gratton CO .02 .10
23 Team Photo .20 .50
24 Craig Newton .02 .10
25 Joe Lowes .02 .10
NNO Ad Card .02 .10

2003-04 Bridgeport Sound Tigers

This set was issued as a promotional giveaway at several home games. The cards were issued in perforated strips, with one strip specific per game. The cards are numbered, but numbers 1-8 are repeated twice.

COMPLETE SET (20) 15.00 40.00
1A Wade Dubielewicz 2.00 5.00
1B Ryan Kraft .60 1.50
2A Ben Guite .60 1.50
2B Kevin Colley .60 1.50
3A Cole Jarrett .60 1.50
3B Rob Collins .60 1.50
4A Alan Letang .60 1.50
4B Jeff Hamilton .60 1.50
5A Dieter Kochan 2.00 5.00
5B Cail MacLean .60 1.50
6A Eric Manlow .60 1.50
6B Justin Mapletoft 1.25 3.00
7A Graham Belak .60 1.50
7B Alain Nasreddine .60 1.50
8A Martin Kariya 4.00 10.00
8B Tomi Pettinen .60 1.50
9 Brandon Smith .60 1.50
10 Derek Bekar .60 1.50
11 Blaine Down .60 1.50
12 Jody Robinson .60 1.50

2013-14 Bridgeport Sound Tigers

COMPLETE SET (8) 4.00 10.00
1 Johan Sundstrom .30 .75
2 Ryan Strome 1.00 2.50
3 Anders Lee 1.00 2.50
4 Mike Halmo .30 .75
5 Chris Bruton .30 .75
6 Scott Mayfield .30 .75
7 Aaron Ness .30 .75
8 Anders Nilsson 1.00 2.50

1991-92 British Columbia JHL

This 172-card standard-size set features players of the British Columbia Junior Hockey League The card design features action and posed color player photos. A border design that frames the picture is royal blue at the bottom and fades to pale blue and white at the top. Overlapping this frame at the top is a bar with a blue speckled pattern, which contains the player's name, team name, or card title. The team logo appears within a royal blue circle that is superimposed over the lower right corner of the picture. The backs carry a black-and-white close-up, statistics, and biographical information. Topical subsets featured are Stars of the Future (81, 91, 93, 106, 146-147, 164, 166, 168-169), Coastal All-Stars (151-154, 163), and Interior All-Stars (155-162). The cards are numbered on the back and checklisted below according to teams as follows: Vernon Lakers (1-17, 23-25), Kelowna Spartans (18-22, 26-41), Nanaimo Clippers (42-62, 79-80, 153), Merritt Centennials (63-78, 82, 107), Chilliwack Chiefs (81, 127-145), Surrey Eagles (83, 106, 108-117, 119-126), and Penticton Panthers (85-105, 118, 147).

COMPLETE SET (173) 40.00 100.00
1 Vernon Lakers .08 .25
Team Photo
2 Scott Longstaff .05 .15
3 Rick Crowe .05 .15
4 Sheldon Wolitski .05 .15
5 Kevan Rilcof .05 .15
6 Greg Buchanan .05 .15
7 Vernon Lakers .05 .15
Executives
8 Murray Caton .05 .15
9 Adrian Bubola .05 .15
10 Troy Becker .05 .15
11 Shawn Potyok .05 .15
12 John Morabito .05 .15
13 Peter Zurba .05 .15
14 Chad Schraeder .05 .15
15 Shawn Bourgeois .05 .15
16 Michal Sup .05 .15
17 Rick Eremenko .05 .15
18 David Lemanowicz .05 .15
19 Daniel Blasko .05 .15
20 Gary Audette .20 .50
21 Graham Harder .05 .15
22 Ryan Nessman .05 .15
23 Jason Switzer .05 .15
24 Roland Ramoser .05 .15
25 Dusty McLellan .05 .15
26 Dustin Green .05 .15
27 Steve Roberts .05 .15
28 Jason Lowe .05 .15
29 Brad Knight .05 .15
30 Pavel Suchanek .05 .15
31 Ken Crockett .05 .15
32 Adam Smith .08 .25
33 Glen Pullishy .05 .15
34 Mike Zambon .05 .15
35 Scott Chartier .08 .25
36 Donny Hearn .05 .15
37 Jeff Denham .05 .15
38 Jamie Marriott .05 .15
39 Silverio Mirao .05 .15
40 Darren Tymchyshyn .05 .15
41 Mark Basanta .05 .15
42 Trevor Prest .05 .15
43 Jim Lessard .05 .15
44 Jade Kersey .05 .15
45 Geordie Young .05 .15
46 Darren Holmes .05 .15
47 Wade Dayley .05 .15
48 Dan Murphy .05 .15
49 Paul Taylor .05 .15
50 Sjon Wynia .05 .15
51 Ryan Loxam .05 .15
52 Andy Faulkner .05 .15
53 Scott Kowalski .05 .15
54 Mickey McGuire .05 .15
55 Jason Disiewich .05 .15
56 Jim Ingram .05 .15
57 Ryan Keller .05 .15
58 Brian Schiebel .05 .15
59 Shawn York .05 .15
60 Sean Krause .05 .15
61 Casey Hungle .05 .15
62 Chris Jones .05 .15
63 Doug Stewart .05 .15
64 Jason Sirota .08 .25
65 Dave Dunnigan .05 .15
66 Aaron Hoffman .05 .15
67 Jason Timewell .05 .15
68 Pat Meehan .05 .15
69 Mike Leduc .05 .15
70 Brad Koopmans .05 .15
71 Guy Prince .05 .15
72 Dorel Gecse .05 .15
73 Scott Salmond .05 .15
74 Brian Zakall .05 .15
75 Mike Josephson .05 .15
76 Derek Harper .05 .15
77 John Graham .05 .15
78 Dan Morrissey .08 .25
79 Glenn Calder .05 .15
80 Jason Northard .05 .15
81 Chris Kerr .05 .15
82 Bill Muckalt .40 1.00
83 Greg Hunt .05 .15
84 Paul Kariya 10.00 25.00
1990-91 AS
85 Dean Rowland .05 .15
86 Paul Kariya 10.00 25.00
Skating
87 David Kilduff .05 .15
88 Jeff Tory .05 .15
89 Mike Newman .05 .15
90 Tyler Boucher .05 .15
91 Paul Kariya 10.00 25.00
Skating with stick
92 Phil Valk .05 .15
93 Paul Kariya 10.00 25.00
Passing
94 Bob Lewis .05 .15
95 Steve Williams .05 .15
96 James Pelzer .05 .15
97 Shawn Carter .05 .15
98 Ryan Erasmas .08 .25
99 John Dehart .05 .15
100 David Green .05 .15
101 Derek Gecse .05 .15
102 Brian Barnes .05 .15
103 Jason Given .05 .15
104 Jason Podollan .20 .50
105 Brian Veale .05 .15
106 Rob Tallas .30 .75
107 Bob McBurnie .05 .15
108 Paul McMillan .05 .15
109 Ryan Donovan .05 .15
110 Kevin Robertson .05 .15
111 Milt Mastad .08 .25
112 Kees Roodbol .05 .15
113 Carey Causey .05 .15
114 Patrick O'Flaherty .05 .15
115 Chad Vestergaard .05 .15
116 Tyler Quiring .08 .25
117 Loui Mellios .05 .15
118 Bob Bell .05 .15
119 Rob Tallas .30 .75
120 Clint MacDonald .05 .15
121 Bart Taylor .05 .15
122 Mark Basanta .05 .15
123 Don McCusker .05 .15
124 Jason Howse .05 .15
125 Mike McKinlay .05 .15
126 Trevor Pennock .05 .15
127 Dean Shmyr .08 .25
128 Chris Kerr .05 .15
129 Erin Thornton .05 .15
130 Dennis Archibald .05 .15
131 Brian McDonald .05 .15
132 Bob Quinnell .05 .15
133 Clint Black .05 .15
134 Jason Peters .05 .15
135 Doug Ast .05 .15
136 Jason Bilous .08 .25
137 Lee Schill .05 .15
138 Jason Sanford .05 .15
139 Jeff Hokanson .05 .15
140 Marc Gagnon .05 .15
141 Gunnar Henrikson .05 .15
142 Jamie Lund .05 .15
143 Jason White .05 .15
144 Jag Bal .05 .15
145 Brad Loring .05 .15
146 Marc Gagnon .05 .15
147 Brian Veale .05 .15
148 Checklist 1 .05 .15
149 Checklist 2 .05 .15
150 The Centennial Cup .08 .25
151 Brian Law .05 .15
152 Al Radke .05 .15
153 Andy Faulkner .08 .25
Jason Disiewich
Darren Holmes
Casey Hungle
Chris Jones
154 1982 Coastal Division .08 .25
Team Photo
155 Dusty McLellan .08 .25
Roland Ramoser
Rick Eremenko
Sheldon Wolitski
Shawn Potyok
Scott Longstaff
156 Hendrikson .08 .25
Anchikoski
Marc Gagnon
Jason White
157 John Graham .08 .25
Dave Dunnigan
158 Scott Chartier .08 .25
Mike Zambon
Paul Taylor
Jason Lowe
159 Jeff Tory .08 .25
Tyler Boucher
David Kilduff
Lee Davidson
John Dehart
Burns
160 Didmon .08 .25
Bentham
Marsh
Walsh
161 Lipsett .08 .25
McNeill
Klyn
Edgington
162 1991 Interior .08 .25
All-Stars Team
Photo
163 Johnson .08 .25
Meek
Welker
Fitzpatrick
Collins
Sofikitas
Hutson
Herman
164 John Dehart .05 .15
165 John Craighead .08 .25
166 Mike Josephson .05 .15
167 Wayne Anchikoski .20 .50
168 Paul Kariya 10.00 25.00
169 Jim Lessard .05 .15
170 Tommi Virkgunen .05 .15
NNO Wayne Anchikoski .20 .50
NNO John Craighead .08 .25
NNO Tommi Virkgunen .08 .25

1992-93 British Columbia JHL

This 246-card standard-size set showcases players in the British Columbia Junior Hockey League. The cards feature color, action player photos with white borders. The player's name and position appear at the top. The team name is at the bottom. The backs carry the team logo in orange and black, statistics, and biographical information. The cards are numbered on the back and are in team order as follows: Bellingham Ice Hawks (1-23), Chilliwack Chiefs (24-45), Kelowna Spartans (46-70), Merritt Centennials (71-92), Nanaimo Clippers (93-116, 240), Penticton Panthers (117-140), Powell River Paper Kings (141-163, 245), Surrey Eagles (164-188), Vernon Lakers (189-211), and Victoria Warriors (212-233). The set closes with an Alumni of the BCJHL subset (234-239, 241) and other miscellaneous cards (242-246).

COMPLETE SET (246) 10.00 50.00
1 Tom Wittenberg .08 .25
2 Kendel Kelly .08 .25
3 Gus Rettschlag .08 .25
4 Don Barr .08 .25
5 Dave Kirkpatrick .08 .25
6 Josh Flett .08 .25
7 Paul McKenna .08 .25
8 Brad Wingfield .08 .25
9 Derek Gesce .08 .25
10 Garry Gulash .08 .25
11 Tim Bell .08 .25
12 Dean Stork .08 .25
13 Wes Reusse .08 .25
14 Jason Peipmann .08 .25
15 Tyler Johnston .08 .25
16 Jason Delesoy .08 .25
17 The Ice Man .02 .10
18 Don Barr .08 .25
19 Brad Swain .08 .25
20 Wes Rudy .08 .25
21 Michael Sigouin .08 .25
22 Kevan Rilcof .08 .25
23 Brian Preston .08 .25
24 Doug Ast .08 .25
25 Knut Engqvist .08 .25
26 Zac George .08 .25
27 Clint Black .08 .25
28 Cameron Campbell .08 .25
29 Dan Davies .08 .25
30 Bryce Munro .08 .25
31 Ryan Dayman .08 .25
32 Kevin Kimura .08 .25
33 Paul Nicolls .08 .25
34 Thomas Kraft .08 .25
35 Erin Thornton .08 .25
36 Brad Loring .08 .25
37 Jag Bal .08 .25
38 Jeff Grabinsky .08 .25
39 Johan Ahrgren .08 .25
40 The Lethal Weapon .08 .25
41 Two Unidentified .08 .25
Players
42 Judd Lambert .08 .25
43 Brian Schiebel .08 .25
44 Dennis Archibald .08 .25
45 David Longbroek .08 .25
46 Silverio Mirao .08 .25
47 Jason Haakstad .08 .25
48 Lee Grant .08 .25
49 Ryan Esselmont .08 .25
50 Steve Roberts .08 .25
51 Curtis Fry .08 .25
52 David Dollard .08 .25
53 Diano Zol .08 .25
54 Bob Needham .08 .25
55 Dustin Green .08 .25
56 Darren Tymchyshyn .08 .25
57 Peter Arvanitis .08 .25
58 Don Hearn .08 .25
59 Title Card .10 .25
(Unnumbered)
60 Martin Masa .08 .25
61 Steffon Walby .20 .50
62 Joel Irwin .08 .25
63 Brent Bradford .08 .25
64 Dieter Kochan 2.00 5.00
65 Brendan Kenny .08 .25
66 Marty Craigdallie .08 .25
67 Graeme Harder .08 .25
68 Pavel Suchanek .08 .25
69 Shane Johnson .08 .25
70 Burt Henderson .08 .25
71 Tyler Willis .08 .25
72 Mike Olaski .08 .25
73 David Green .08 .25
74 Tom Mix .08 .25
75 Walter(Guy) Prince .08 .25
76 Joseph Rybar .40 1.00
77 Bill Muckalt .75 2.00
78 Jason Mansoff .08 .25
79 Duane Puga .08 .25
80 Aaron Hoffman .08 .25
81 Dan Blasko .08 .25
82 Rob Szatmary .08 .25
83 Mike Minnis .08 .25
84 Pat Meehan .08 .25
85 Andre Robichaud .08 .25
86 The Terminator .02 .10
87 Derrek Harper .08 .25
88 Dan Morrissey .08 .25
89 Joey Kennedy .08 .25
90 Derrek Harper .08 .25
91 Lawrence Klyne .08 .25
92 Ryan Beamin .08 .25
93 Sjon Wynia .08 .25
94 Jason Disiewich .08 .25
95 Jason Sanford .08 .25
96 Casey Hungle .08 .25
97 Brent Murcheson .08 .25
98 Glenn Calder .08 .25
99 Jade Kersey .08 .25
100 Shawn York .08 .25
101 Bob Quinnell .08 .25
102 Geordie Dunstan .08 .25
103 Cory Crowther .08 .25
104 Jason Hodson .08 .25
105 Chris Jones .08 .25
106 Cory Green .08 .25
107 Chris Buie .08 .25
108 Shaun Peet .08 .25
109 Jason Wood .08 .25
110 Dan Murphy .08 .25
111 Jason Disiewich .08 .25
112 Cory Dayley .08 .25
113 Brian Veale .08 .25
114 Jason Northard .08 .25
115 Phil Valk .08 .25
116 Wade Dayley .08 .25
117 Brendan Morrison 4.00 10.00
118 Marcel Sakac .08 .25
119 Tyler Boucher .08 .25
120 Ray Guze .08 .25
121 Brian Barnes .08 .25
122 Jason Given .08 .25
123 Michael Dairon .08 .25
124 Mike Newman .08 .25
125 Craig Fletcher .08 .25
126 Ty Davidson .08 .25
127 Miki Antonik .08 .25
128 Rob Pennoyer .08 .25
129 Dave Whitworth .08 .25
130 Steve Williams .08 .25
131 Robbie Trampuh .08 .25
132 Mark Filipenko .08 .25
133 Clint MacDonald .08 .25
134 Colin Ryder .08 .25
135 David Kilduff .08 .25
136 Mickey McGuire .08 .25
137 Randy Polacik .08 .25
138 Jeff Tory .08 .25
139 Chris Buckman .08 .25
140 Bill Moody .08 .25
141 Rick McLarren .08 .25
142 The Phantom .02 .10
143 Jason Zaichkowski .08 .25
144 Tony Hrycuik .08 .25
145 Cameron Knox .08 .25
146 Mike Warriner .08 .25
147 Robb Gordon .08 .25
148 Mike Pawluk .08 .25
149 Tim Harris .08 .25
150 Mike Bzdel .08 .25
151 Chad Wilson .08 .25
152 Andrew Plumb .08 .25
153 Andy MacIntosh .08 .25
154 Stefan Brannare .08 .25
155 Matt Sharrers .08 .25
156 Brent Berry .08 .25
157 Ryan Douglas .08 .25
158 Heath Dennison .08 .25
159 Chad Vizzutti .08 .25
160 Adam Lord .08 .25
161 Brad Klyn .08 .25
162 Andrew Young .08 .25
163 Casey Lemanski .08 .25
164 Mike McKinlay .08 .25
165 Derek Robinson .08 .25
166 Kees Roodbol .08 .25
167 Scott Boucher .08 .25
168 Shawn Gervais .08 .25
169 Ryan Schaffer .08 .25
170 Kevin Robertson .08 .25
171 Ryan Donovan .08 .25
172 Bart Taylor .08 .25
173 Greg Hunt .08 .25
174 Darcy George .08 .25
175 Shane Tidsbury .08 .25
176 Rob Smillie .08 .25
177 Chad Vestergaard .08 .25
178 Al Kinisky .08 .25
179 Patrick O'Flaherty .08 .25
180 Loui Mellios .08 .25
181 Lorin Murdock .08 .25
(Unnumbered)
182 Jason Genik .08 .25
183 Rob Herrington .08 .25
184 Loui Mellios .08 .25
185 Cal Benazic .08 .25
186 Richard Kraus .08 .25
187 Geoff White .08 .25
188 Kirk Buchanan .08 .25
189 Peter Zurba .08 .25
190 John Morabito .08 .25
191 Corey Kruchkowski .08 .25
192 Spencer Ward .08 .25
193 Danny Shermerhorn .08 .25
194 Mark Davies .08 .25
195 Jason Rushton .08 .25
196 Chad Buckle .08 .25
197 Serge Beauchesne .08 .25
198 Todd Kelman .08 .25
199 Jason Switzer .08 .25
200 Eon MacFarlane .08 .25
201 Terry Ryan .20 .50
202 Shawn Bourgeois .08 .25
203 Chad Schraeder .08 .25
204 Dusty McLellan .08 .25
205 The Predator .08 .25
206 Danny Shermerhorn .08 .25
207 Chris Godard .08 .25
208 Jason Chipman .08 .25
209 Christian Twomey .08 .25
210 Ryan Loxam .08 .25
211 Greg Buchanan .08 .25
212 Kees Roodbol .08 .25
213 Ryan Keller .08 .25
214 Kevin Paschal .08 .25
215 David Hebky .08 .25
216 Vince Devlin .08 .25
217 Mike Cole .08 .25
218 Daljit Takhar .08 .25
219 Scott Hall .08 .25
220 Derek Lawrence .08 .25
221 Mark Basanta .08 .25
222 Jan Kloboucek .08 .25
223 Randy Barker .08 .25
224 Kris Gailloux .08 .25
225 Tyson Scheuer .08 .25
226 Brent Wormald .08 .25
227 Vince Devlin .08 .25
228 Gus Miller .08 .25
229 Todd McKave .08 .25
230 Lawrence Oliver .08 .25
231 Scott Garvin .08 .25
232 Rob Milliken .08 .25
233 Roman Kobrc .08 .25
234 Dan Skene .08 .25
235 Blair Marsh .08 .25
236 Maco Balkovec .08 .25
237 Scott Kirton .08 .25
238 Blaine Moore .08 .25
239 Nigel Creightney .08 .25
240 Bill Zapt .08 .25
241 Jason Elders .08 .25
242 BCJHL Officials .02 .10
(Unidentified Referee)
243 Masks of the BCJHL .40 1.00
The
244 Masks of the BCJHL .40 1.00
The
245 Mike Pawluk .08 .25
BCJHL MVP
246 Steffon Walby .20 .50
Captains of the BCJHL

1987-88 Brockville Braves

This 25-card set is printed on thin card stock, measures 2 5/8" by 3 5/8", and features posed color player photos with red studio backgrounds. The pictures are set on a white card face and show the player's name, position, and season in the white margin below the photo.

COMPLETE SET (25) 4.00 10.00
1 Title Card .08 .25
2 Steve Harper TR .08 .25
3 Peter Kelly TR .08 .25
4 Mac MacLean CO .08 .25
MG
5 Mike McCourt .20 .50
6 Paul MacLean .20 .50
7 Mark Michaud .20 .50
8 Alain Marchessault .20 .50
9 Tom Roman .20 .50
10 Darren Burns .20 .50
11 Scott Halpenny .20 .50
12 Ray Gallagher .20 .50
13 Bob Lindsay .20 .50
14 Brett Harkins .40 1.00
15 Dave Hyrsky .20 .50
16 Richard Marchessault .20 .50
17 Scott Boston .20 .50
18 Steve Hogg .30 .75
19 Chris Webster .20 .50
20 Stuart Birnie .20 .50
21 Brett Dunk .20 .50
22 Charles Cusson .20 .50
23 Pat Gooley .20 .50
24 Andy Rodman .20 .50
25 Peter Radlein .20 .50

1988-89 Brockville Braves

This 25-card set is printed on thin card stock, measures 2 5/8" by 3 5/8", and features posed color player photos with pale blue studio backgrounds. The pictures are set on a white card face and show the player's name, position, and season in the white margin below the photo.

COMPLETE SET (25) 4.00 10.00
1 Ray Gallagher .20 .50
2 Peter Kelly TR .08 .25
3 Steve Harper TR .08 .25
4 Winston Jones ACO .08 .25
5 Mac MacLean CO/GM .08 .25
6 Kevin Doherty .20 .50
7 Stuart Birnie .20 .50
8 Charles Cusson .20 .50
9 Paul MacLean .20 .50
10 Bob Lindsay .20 .50
11 Darren Burns .20 .50
12 Rick Pracey .30 .75
13 Mike Malloy .20 .50
14 Dave Hyrsky .20 .50
15 Rob Percival .20 .50
16 Jarrett Eligh .20 .50
17 Pat Gooley .20 .50
18 Michael Bracco .30 .75
19 Ken Crook .20 .50
20 Brad Osborne .20 .50
21 Todd Reynolds .20 .50
22 Mike McCourt .20 .50
23 Chris Webster .20 .50
24 Kevin Lune .20 .50
25 Title Card .20 .50

1951-52 Buffalo Bison

This set features the Bison of the AHL. Little is known about this set, but it is believed to be oversized and distributed in set form by the team.

COMPLETE SET (19) 50.00 100.00
1 Team Photo 5.00 10.00
2 Don Ashbee 5.00 10.00
3 Frankie Christy 2.50 5.00
4 Gerry Couture 4.00 8.00
5 Lou Crowdis 2.50 5.00
6 Harry Dick 2.50 5.00
7 Lloyd Finkbeiner 2.50 5.00
8 Ab Demarco 5.00 10.00
9 Leroy Goldsworthy 2.50 5.00
10 Les Hickey 5.00 10.00
11 Vern Kaiser 2.50 5.00
12 Sam Lavitt 2.50 5.00
13 Stan Long 2.50 5.00
14 Cal Mackay 5.00 10.00
15 Ed Mazur 2.50 5.00
16 Sid McNabney 2.50 5.00
17 George Pargeter 2.50 5.00
18 Gordie Pennell 2.50 5.00
19 Grant Warwick 2.50 5.00

1995 Buffalo Stampedes RHI

This standard size, team issued set, features color borderless fronts with players name and "1994 World Champions" in gold along the left side of the card. Backs are grey and black on a white background and feature biographical information along with 1994 statistics. The set came boxed and was available at home games. Cards are unnumbered and checklisted below by jersey number, each of which is prominently displayed on the card back.

COMPLETE SET (21) 4.00 10.00
14 John Hendry .20 .50
16 Tom Nemeth .30 .75
19 John Vechiarelli .30 .75
19 John Vechiarelli IA .30 .75
20 Len Soccio .20 .50
24 Chris Bergeron .20 .50
32 Mark Major .20 .50
34 Jason Cirone .20 .50
36 Nick Vitucci .30 .75
37 Dave Lemay .20 .50
43 John Blessman .20 .50
44 Jay Neal .20 .50
61 Craig Martin .20 .50
72 Rick Corriveau .20 .50
94 Alex Hicks .30 .75
NNO1 Header Card .02 .10
NNO2 Title Card .02 .10
NNO3 Team Photo .02 .10
NNO4 Terry Buchwald .02 .10
NNO5 Stampede Cheerleaders .20 .50
NNO6 Claude the Trumpetor .08 .25

1998-99 Calgary Hitmen

This 26-card set was sold by the team in set form. It features early cards of several top prospects including Pavel Brendl, Jordan Krestanovich and Kris Beech.

COMPLETE SET (26) 8.00 20.00
1 Matt Kinch .30 .75
2 Ryan Shannon .20 .50
3 Jeff Feniak .20 .50
4 Kenton Smith .30 .75
5 Rod Sarich .20 .50
6 Pavel Brendl .60 1.50
7 Chris Nielsen .30 .75
8 Sean McAslan .20 .50
9 Jordan Krestanovich .60 1.50
10 Michael Bubnick .20 .50
11 Kris Beech .75 2.00
12 Ryan Geremia .20 .50
13 Wade Davis .20 .50
14 Brad Moran .30 .75
15 Lyle Steenbergen .20 .50
16 Curtis Rich .20 .50
17 Ryan Andres .20 .50
18 Brent Dodginghorse .20 .50
19 Jerred Smithson .20 .50
20 Peter Bergman .20 .50
21 Alexandre Fomitchev .30 .75
22 Eric Clark .20 .50
23 Donald Choukalos .30 .75
24 Dean Clark HCO .02 .10
25 Jeff Maher ACO .02 .10
26 Vulk MASCOT .02 .10

1998-99 Calgary Hitmen Autographs

This 26-card set resembles the regular set in every way other than carrying player autographs. Please note that Alexandre Fomitchev did not sign any of his cards though the sets were sold including that card in unsigned form.

COMPLETE SET (26) 40.00 80.00
1 Matt Kinch 1.25 3.00
2 Ryan Shannon 5.00 12.00
3 Jeff Feniak 1.25 3.00
4 Kenton Smith 1.25 3.00
5 Rod Sarich 1.25 3.00
6 Pavel Brendl 4.00 10.00
7 Chris Nielsen 1.25 3.00
8 Sean McAslan 1.25 3.00
9 Jordan Krestanovich 4.00 10.00
10 Michael Bubnick 1.25 3.00
11 Kris Beech 4.00 10.00
12 Ryan Geremia 1.25 3.00
13 Wade Davis 1.25 3.00
14 Brad Moran 1.25 3.00
15 Lyle Steenbergen 1.25 3.00
16 Curtis Rich 1.25 3.00
17 Ryan Andres 1.25 3.00
18 Brent Dodginghorse 1.25 3.00
19 Jerred Smithson 1.25 3.00
20 Peter Bergman 1.25 3.00
21 Alexandre Fomitchev .20 .50
UNSIGNED
22 Eric Clark 1.25 3.00
23 Donald Choukalos 1.25 3.00
24 Dean Clark HCO 2.00 5.00
25 Jeff Maher ACO 1.25 3.00
26 Vulk MASCOT .20 .50

1999-00 Calgary Hitmen

This team-issued set features the WHL's Hitmen. It was sold by the team at the rink and through its web site. The set is notable for featuring several first rounders, including Pavel Brendl, Kris Beech and Brent Krahn.

COMPLETE SET (25) 4.00 10.00
1 Kris Beech .60 1.50
2 Pavel Brendl .30 .75
3 Michael Bubnick .08 .25
4 Jared Carli .08 .25
5 Dean Clark CO .02 .10
6 Eric Clark .08 .25
7 Sean Connors .08 .25
8 Wade Davis .08 .25
9 Jeff Feniak .08 .25
10 Owen Fussey .08 .25
11 Robin Gomez .20 .50
12 Matt Kinch .30 .75
13 Brent Krahn .60 1.50
14 Jordan Krestanovich .40 1.00
15 Anders Lovdahl .15 .40
16 Jeff Maher ACO .08 .25
17 Sean McAslan .08 .25
18 Brad Moran .20 .50
19 Chris Nielsen .20 .50
20 Shaun Norrie .08 .25
21 Rod Sarich .08 .25
22 Brandon Segal .08 .25
23 Kenton Smith .15 .40
24 Jerred Smithson .08 .25
25 Vulk Mascot .02 .10
26 Calgary Herald .02 .10
27 Playstation Coupon .02 .10

1999-00 Calgary Hitmen Autographs

This 27-card set features the 1999-00 Calgary Hitmen of the Western Hockey League in an autographed parallel version of the main release. All players except Eric Clark and Jeff Feniak signed their cards, as the two players were dealt before the set was released. These cards are marked below as DNS. Cards are not numbered, so they appear alphabetically.

COMPLETE SET (27) 40.00 100.00
1 Kris Beech 4.00 10.00
2 Pavel Brendl 3.00 6.00
3 Michael Bubnick 1.25 3.00
4 Jared Carli 1.25 3.00
5 Dean Clark CO 1.25 3.00
6 Eric Clark DNS .08 .25
7 Sean Connors 1.25 3.00
8 Wade Davis 1.25 3.00
9 Jeff Feniak DNS .08 .25
10 Owen Fussey 1.25 3.00
11 Robin Gomez 2.00 5.00
12 Matt Kinch 3.00 6.00
13 Brent Krahn 4.00 8.00
14 Jordan Krestanovich 4.00 8.00
15 Anders Lovdahl 2.00 5.00
16 Jeff Maher ACO 1.25 3.00
17 Sean McAslan 1.25 3.00
18 Brad Moran 3.00 6.00
19 Chris Nielsen 3.00 6.00
20 Shaun Norrie 1.25 3.00
21 Rod Sarich 1.25 3.00
22 Brandon Segal 1.25 3.00
23 Kenton Smith 2.00 5.00
24 Jerred Smithson 1.25 3.00
25 Vulk Mascot .40 1.00
26 Calgary Herald .02 .10
27 Playstation Coupon .02 .10

2000-01 Calgary Hitmen

This set features the Hitmen of the WHL. The set was produced by the team, and sold at its souvenir stands at home games.

COMPLETE SET (28) 6.00 15.00
1 Toni Bader .20 .50
2 Kris Beech .50 1.25
3 Brady Block .20 .50
4 John Boychuk .40 1.00
5 Adam Breitkreuz .20 .50
6 Pavel Brendl .60 1.00
7 Michael Bubnick .20 .50
8 Jared Carli .20 .50
9 Dean Clark CO .10 .25
10 Wade Davis .20 .50
11 Mike Egener .20 .50
12 Dan Ehrman .20 .50
13 Owen Fussey .20 .50
14 Robin Gomez .20 .50
15 Matt Kinch .20 .50
16 Brent Krahn .40 1.00
17 Jordan Krestanovich .20 .50
18 Jeff Maher CO .10 .25
19 Sean McAslan .20 .50
20 Shaun Norrie .20 .50
21 Rod Sarich .20 .50
22 Brandon Segal .20 .50
23 Shaun Sutter .20 .50
24 David Vrbata .20 .50
25 The Vulk MASCOT .04 .10
26 Chad Wolkowski .20 .50
27 Calgary Herald .02 .10
28 Toys R Us .02 .10

2001-02 Calgary Hitmen

This set features the Hitmen of the WHL. The set was sold by the team at its souvenir stands. The set is noteworthy for including the first card of 2002 first-rounder Fredrik Sjostrom.

COMPLETE SET (26) 4.80 12.00
1 Paul Albers .20 .50
2 Kyle Annesley .20 .50
3 Tyler Beechey .30 .75
4 Johnny Boychuk .40 1.00
5 Adam Breitkreuz .20 .50
6 Michael Bubnick .20 .50
7 Jared Carli .20 .50
8 Wade Davis .20 .50
9 Mike Egener .20 .50
10 Dan Ehrman .20 .50
11 Owen Fussey .30 .75
12 Richard Kromm CO .10 .25
13 Sebastien LaPlante .20 .50
14 Jeff Maher ACO .10 .25
15 Ryan Martin .30 .75
16 Lance Morrison .20 .50
17 Ryan Papaioannou .20 .50
18 Wes Rypien .20 .50
19 Rod Sarich .20 .50
20 Brandon Segal .30 .75
21 Dennis Sergeyev .20 .50
22 Mark Shefchyk .20 .50
23 Fredrik Sjostrom .75 2.00
24 Rob Smith .20 .50
25 The Vulk MASCOT .10 .25
26 Chad Wolkowski .20 .50

2001-02 Calgary Hitmen Autographed

This set features the Hitmen of the WHL. The set was sold in autographed form at team souvenir stands. Unfortunately, the card of team mascot The Vulk is not autographed. The cards are unnumbered, and so are listed below in alphabetical order.

COMPLETE SET (26) 20.00 50.00
1 Paul Albers .75 2.00
2 Kyle Annesley .75 2.00
3 Tyler Beechey 1.25 3.00
4 Johnny Boychuk 1.60 5.00
5 Adam Breitkreuz .75 2.00
6 Michael Bubnick .75 2.00
7 Jared Carli .75 2.00
8 Wade Davis .75 2.00
9 Mike Egener .75 2.00
10 Dan Ehrman .75 2.00
11 Owen Fussey 1.50 4.00
12 Richard Kromm CO .40 1.00
13 Sebastien LaPlante .75 2.00
14 Jeff Maher ACO .40 1.00
15 Ryan Martin 1.25 3.00
16 Lance Morrison .75 2.00
17 Ryan Papaioannou .75 2.00
18 Wes Rypien .75 2.00
19 Rod Sarich .75 2.00
20 Brandon Segal 1.25 3.00
21 Dennis Sergeyev .75 2.00
22 Mark Shefchyk .75 2.00
23 Fredrik Sjostrom 4.00 10.00
24 Rob Smith .75 2.00

25 The Vulk MASCOT .04 .10
26 Chad Wolkowski .75 2.00

2002-03 Calgary Hitmen

COMPLETE SET (26) 8.00 18.00
1 Lance Morrison .20 .50
2 Michael Bubnick .20 .50
3 Gary Gladue .20 .50
4 Kris Deines .20 .50
5 Kyle Annesley .20 .50
6 Rob Smith .20 .50
7 Mark Shefchyk .20 .50
8 Bruno Campese ACO .04 .10
9 Richard Kromm HCO .04 .10
10 Mascot .04 .10
11 Fredrik Sjostrom .40 1.00
12 Wade Davis .20 .50
13 Paul Albers .20 .50
14 Patrick Wellar .20 .50
15 Marc Lesage .20 .50
16 Aaron Boogaard .20 .50
17 Jiri Cetkovsky .20 .50
18 Brandon Segal .20 .50
19 Owen Fussey .20 .50
20 Tyler Feakes .20 .50
21 Andy Rogers .20 .50
22 Steven Covington .20 .50
23 Johnny Boychuk .40 1.00
24 Michael Egener .40 1.00
25 Brent Krahn .40 1.00
26 Ryan Getzlaf 2.00 5.00

2003-04 Calgary Hitmen

COMPLETE SET (21) 6.00 15.00
1 Scott Bowles .30 .75
2 Brett Carson .20 .50
3 Dmitri Chupilkin .20 .50
4 Steve Covington .20 .50
5 Kris Deines .20 .50
6 Mike Egener .30 .75
7 Gerry Festa .30 .75
8 Paul Gentile .20 .50
9 Ryan Getzlaf 1.00 2.50
10 Dustin Kohn .20 .50
11 Andrew Ladd .75 2.00
12 Shaun Landolt .20 .50
13 Riley Merkley .20 .50
14 Andy Rogers .20 .50
15 Mark Rooneem .20 .50
16 Jeff Schultz .20 .50
17 Brandon Segal .20 .50
18 Tomas Troliga .20 .50
19 Patrick Wellar .20 .50
20 Darryl Yacboski .20 .50
21 Lee Zalasky .20 .50

2004-05 Calgary Hitmen

COMPLETE SET (25) 15.00 25.00
1 Karl Alzner .60 1.50
2 Brett Carlson .30 .75
3 Steven Covington .30 .75
4 Keegan Dansereau .30 .75
5 Brodie Dupont .30 .75
6 Ryan Getzlaf .75 2.00
7 Tyler Harder .30 .75
8 Dustin Kohn .30 .75
9 Andrew Ladd .60 1.50
10 Shaun Landolt .30 .75
11 Tyrel Lucas .30 .75
12 Riley Merkley .30 .75
13 Darryl Moscaluk .30 .75
14 Brett O'Malley .30 .75
15 Justin Pogge 2.00 5.00
16 Konstantin Pushkarev .40 1.00
17 Isaac Reid .30 .75
18 Jeff Schultz .40 1.00
19 Daniel Spence .30 .75
20 Ryan White .30 .75
21 Darryl Yacboski .30 .75
22 Dylan Yeo .30 .75
23 Dean Evason .04 .10
Kelly Kisio CO
24 Blaine Forsythe ACO .04 .10
Farley MASCOT
25 Ryan Getzlaf .60 1.50
Calgary Herald

2005-06 Calgary Hitmen

COMPLETE SET (28) 8.00 15.00
1 Karl Alzner .40 1.00
2 Brett Carson .30 .75
3 Steve Covington .30 .75
4 Keegan Dansereau .30 .75
5 Kris Deines .30 .75
6 Brodie Dupont .30 .75
7 Curtis Kelner .30 .75
8 Derek LeBlanc .30 .75
9 Ryan Letts .30 .75
10 Craig Lineker .30 .75
11 Carson McMillan .30 .75
12 Riley Merkley .30 .75
13 Shaden Moore .30 .75
14 Fredrik Pettersson .30 .75
15 Alexandre Plante .30 .75
16 Justin Pogge 1.25 3.00
17 Mike Reich .30 .75
18 Jeff Schultz .30 .75
19 Brett Sonne .40 1.00
20 Daniel Spence .30 .75
21 Lukas Vantuch .40 1.00
22 Ryan White .40 1.00
23 Dylan Yeo .30 .75
24 Kelly Kisio CO .10 .25
25 Blaine Forsythe ACO .10 .25
26 Dave Lowry ACO .10 .25
27 Farley the Fox MASCOT .10 .25
28 SPONSORS .01 .01

2013-14 Calgary Hitmen

COMPLETE SET (28) 8.00 20.00
1 Cal Babych .30 .75
2 Brady Brassart .30 .75
3 Greg Chase .30 .75
4 Terrell Draude .30 .75
5 Chris Driedger .30 .75
6 Radel Fazleev .30 .75
7 Colby Harmsworth .30 .75
8 Kenton Helgesen .30 .75
9 Brent Kisio Assoc. CO .30 .75
10 Chase Lang .30 .75
11 Joe Mahon .30 .75
12 Joel Otto Asst. CO .30 .75
13 Pavlo Padakin .30 .75
14 Linden Penner .30 .75
15 Elliot Peterson .30 .75
16 Connor Rankin .30 .75
17 Jaynen Rissling .30 .75
18 Alex Roach .30 .75
19 Travis Sanheim .50 1.25
20 Mack Shields .30 .75
21 Adam Tambellini .30 .75
22 Ben Thomas .30 .75
23 Jake Virtanen .30 .75
24 Landon Welykholowa .30 .75
25 Mike Williamson CO .30 .75
26 Mike Winther .30 .75
27 Michael Zipp .30 .75
28 Farley the Fox MASCOT .30 .75

2014-15 Calgary Hitmen

COMPLETE SET (28) 6.00 15.00
1 Jake Bean .30 .75
2 Layne Bensmiller .30 .75
3 Brendan Burke .30 .75
4 Terrell Draude .30 .75
5 Radel Fazleev .30 .75
6 Radel Fazleev TB Scorer .30 .75
7 Mark French CO .30 .75
8 Colby Harmsworth .30 .75
9 Kenton Helgesen .30 .75
10 Keegan Kanzig .30 .75
11 Pavel Karnaukhov .30 .75
12 Brent Kisio Asst. CO .30 .75
13 Chase Lang .30 .75
14 Beck Malenstyn .30 .75
15 Lochlan Morrison .30 .75
16 Joel Otto Asst. CO .30 .75
17 Elliot Peterson .30 .75
18 Connor Rankin .40 1.00
19 Taylor Sanheim .30 .75
20 Travis Sanheim .50 1.25
21 Mack Shields .30 .75
22 Jordan Stallard .30 .75
23 Adam Tambellini .30 .75
24 Ben Thomas .30 .75
25 Carsen Twarynski .30 .75
26 Jake Virtanen .75 2.00
27 Michael Zipp .30 .75
28 Farley the Fox MASCOT .30 .75

2007-08 Calgary Oval X-Treme

1 Lyndsay Baird .20 .50
2 Kelly Bechard .40 1.00
3 Delaney Collins .40 1.00
4 Meghan Corbett .20 .50
5 Gillian Ferrari .40 1.00
6 Kaley Hall .20 .50
7 Gina Kingsbury .40 1.00
8 Carla MacLeod .40 1.00
9 Stephanie Ramsay .20 .50
10 Rebecca Russell .20 .50
11 Colleen Sostorics .40 1.00
12 Laura St. Croix .20 .50
13 Amanda Tapp .20 .50
14 Meagan Walton .20 .50
15 Linuo Wang .20 .50
16 Samantha Watt .20 .50
17 Hayley Wickenheiser 1.00 2.50
18 Shi Yao .20 .50
19 Team Card .10 .25

2003-04 Camrose Kodiaks

Team-issued set from the Tier 2 BCJHL. The cards are not numbered. Checklist courtesy of collector Vinnie Montalbano.

COMPLETE SET (25) 6.00 15.00
1 Dan Bertram .40 1.00
2 Steve Bounds .30 .75
3 MacGregor Sharp .30 .75
4 Jared Veuger .30 .75
5 Jody Pederson .30 .75
6 Matt McKnight .30 .75
7 Travis Friedley .30 .75
8 Kyle Smith .30 .75
9 Rob MacIntyre .30 .75
10 Owen Langis .30 .75
11 Mason Raymond .30 .75
12 Ryan Muspratt .30 .75
13 Ryan Antoniuk .30 .75
14 Chance Olsen .30 .75
15 Logan Gorsalitz .30 .75
16 Ryan Armstrong .30 .75
17 Lee Jubinville .30 .75
18 Justin Taylor .30 .75
19 Chris Wanchulak .30 .75
20 Justin Blacklock .30 .75
21 Todd Steil .30 .75
22 Bob Graham .30 .75
23 David Thompson .30 .75
24 Ryan Muth .30 .75
25 Coaches .04 .10

2004-05 Camrose Kodiaks

The Kodiaks are a Tier 2 Alberta Junior Hockey League squad. This set may not be complete. Additional information can be forwarded to hockeymag@beckett.com.

COMPLETE SET (16) 4.00 10.00
1 Jody Pederson .40 1.00
2 Kirk Irving .40 1.00
3 Clark Thompson .40 1.00
4 Ryan Mayko .40 1.00
5 Logan Gorsalitz .40 1.00
6 Lee Jubinville .40 1.00
7 Todd Steil .40 1.00
8 Derek Wolbeck .40 1.00
9 Kyle Parkes .40 1.00
10 MacGregor Sharp .40 1.00
11 Chance Olsen .40 1.00
12 David Thompson .40 1.00
13 Mason Raymond .40 1.00
14 A.J. Nelson .40 1.00
15 Jason Roberts .40 1.00
16 Travis Friedley .40 1.00

2007-08 Camrose Kodiaks

COMPLETE SET (25) 6.00 15.00
1 David Anderson .30 .75
2 Jeremy Beirnes SP .30 .75
3 Scott Buchanan .30 .75
4 Nick Chartier .30 .75
5 Owen Chatwin .30 .75
6 Joe Colborne .75 2.00
7 Mike Connolly .30 .75
8 Nigel Dube .30 .75
9 Colin Dueck .30 .75
10 Wyatt Hamilton .30 .75
11 Jordan Heck .30 .75
12 Andre Herman SP .30 .75
13 David Jacobsen .30 .75
14 Clayton Jardine .30 .75
15 Mathieu Larochelle .30 .75
16 Alex Macleod SP .30 .75
17 Andrew MacWilliam .30 .75
18 Kyle Miller .30 .75
19 Dylan Olsen .30 .75
20 Shawn Ostrow .30 .75
21 Geoff Peet .30 .75
22 Dean Petiot .30 .75
23 Karl Stollery .30 .75
24 Jesse Todd .30 .75
25 Allen York .40 1.00

1994-95 Cape Breton Oilers

This 23-card standard-size set was manufactured and distributed by Jessen Associates, Inc. for Classic. The cards are unnumbered and checklisted below in alphabetical order.

COMPLETE SET (23) 5.00 12.00
1 Scott Allison .15 .40
2 Martin Bakula .15 .40
3 Ladislav Benysek .15 .40
4 Dennis Bonvie .30 .75
5 Jozef Cierny .15 .40
6 Duane Dennis .15 .40
7 Greg DeVries .30 .75
8 Joaquin Gage .30 .75
9 Ian Herbers .15 .40
10 Ralph Intranuovo .15 .40
11 Claude Jutras .15 .40
12 Marc LaForge .15 .40
13 Todd Marchant .60 1.50
14 Darcy Martini .15 .40
15 Roman Oksiuta .15 .40
16 David Oliver .30 .75
17 Steve Passmore .40 1.00
18 Nick Stajduhar .15 .40
19 John Van Kessel .15 .40
20 David Vyborny .15 .40
21 Peter White .15 .40
22 Tyler Wright .30 .75
23 Brad Zavisha .15 .40

2001-02 Cape Breton Screaming Eagles

This set features the Screaming Eagles of the QMJHL. The set was produced by CTM Ste-Foy and was sold at Eagles home games. It was reported that less than 1,000 sets were produced.

COMPLETE SET (23) 6.00 15.00
1 Steve Villeneuve .20 .50
2 Maxime Lessard .20 .50
3 Pierre-Luc Laprise .20 .50
4 David Cloutier .20 .50
5 Stuart MacRae .20 .50
6 Dominic Noel .20 .50
7 Jean-Philipe Cote .20 .50
8 Martin Kasik .20 .50
9 Steve Dixon .30 .75
10 Marc-Olivier Vary .20 .50
11 Justin Hawco .20 .50
12 Pierre-Luc Emond .20 .50
13 Guillaume Demers .20 .50
14 Rodrigue Boucher .20 .50
15 George Davis .20 .50
16 Andre Martineau .20 .50
17 Carl McLean .20 .50
18 Pascal Morency .20 .50
19 Mathieu Dumas .20 .50
20 Jean-Francois Dufort .20 .50
21 Marc-Andre Fleury 2.00 5.00
22 Jasen Awalt .20 .50
23 Kevin Asselin .20 .50

2002-03 Cape Breton Screaming Eagles

The cards are not numbered are are listed below in the order they appear on the checklist card.

COMPLETE SET (25) 6.00 15.00
1 Marc-Andre Fleury 1.25 3.00
2 Martin Houle .60 1.50
3 Maxime Lessard .15 .40
4 Nathan Veinot .30 .75
5 Maxime Robert .15 .40
6 Jean-Claude Sawyer .15 .40
7 Vincent Zaore-Vanie .15 .40
8 Stephen Dixon .30 .75
9 Martin Slovak .15 .40
10 Joel Maas .15 .40
11 Pierre-Luc Emond .15 .40
12 Guillaume Demers .15 .40
13 Gregory Hoffe .15 .40
14 Jonathan Labelle .15 .40
15 Kevin Asselin .15 .40
16 Jared Vokey .15 .40
17 Michel Charette .15 .40
18 Samuel Beland .15 .40
19 Jean-Francois Dufort .30 .75
20 Patrick Gilbert .15 .40
21 Martin Trempe .15 .40
22 Steeve Villeneuve .15 .40
23 Stuart McRae .15 .40
24 Jean-Philippe Cote .15 .40
25 George Davis .15 .40
26 Marc-Andre Fleury CL 1.25 3.00

2003-04 Cape Breton Screaming Eagles

COMPLETE SET (24) 6.00 15.00
2 Adam Pardy .20 .50
4 Steve Villeneuve .20 .50
6 Tim Ramholt .20 .50
8 Nathan Veinot .20 .50
11 Francois-Pierre Guenette .20 .50
12 Jean-Claude Sawyer .20 .50
13 Vincent Zaore-Vanie .20 .50
14 Stephen Dixon .30 .75
15 Alexandre Picard .40 1.00
18 Guillaume Demers .20 .50
19 Gregory Hoffe .20 .50
20 Neil Smith .20 .50
21 Michael Tessier .20 .50
22 Kevin Asselin .20 .50
23 Jean-Francois Cyr .20 .50
24 Charles Fontaine .20 .50
26 Samuel Beland .20 .50
27 Philippe Bertrand .20 .50
28 Vincent Lambert .20 .50
29 Marc-Andre Fleury 1.25 3.00
30 Francois Proteau .30 .75
31 Martin Houle .40 1.00
41 Marc-Andre Bernier .40 1.00
84 Nicolas Corbeil .30 .75

2004-05 Cape Breton Screaming Eagles

A total of 750 team sets were produced.

COMPLETE SET (23) 5.00 12.00
1 Martin Houle .40 1.00
2 Kevin Asselin .20 .50
3 Stephen Dixon .30 .75
4 Samuel Beland .20 .50
5 Philippe Bertrand .20 .50
6 Chris Culligan .20 .50
7 Guillaume Demers .20 .50
8 Charles Fontaine .20 .50
9 Luke Gallant .20 .50
10 Vladimir Kubus .20 .50
11 Vincent Lambert .20 .50
12 Brendon MacDonald .20 .50
13 Dean Ouellet .20 .50
14 Adam Pardy .20 .50
15 Leonard Puterman .20 .50
16 Jean-Claude Sawyer .20 .50
17 James Sheppard .60 1.50
18 Neil Smith .20 .50
19 Francois Theriault .20 .50
20 David Victor .20 .50
21 Tyler Whitehead .20 .50
22 Vincent Zaore .20 .50
23 David Davenport .20 .50

2005-06 Cape Breton Screaming Eagles

COMPLETE SET (25) 5.00 12.00
1 James Sheppard .50 1.25
2 Ondrej Pavelec .30 .75
3 Jason Swit .20 .50
4 David Victor .20 .50
5 Darrell Simich .20 .50
6 Chris Culligan .20 .50
7 Robert Slaney .20 .50
8 Dean Ouellet .20 .50
9 Vladimir Kubus .20 .50
10 Brad Gallant .20 .50
11 Jean-Claude Sawyer .20 .50
12 Francois Gauthier .20 .50
13 Philippe Bertrand .20 .50
14 Scott Brannon .20 .50
15 Etienne Breton .20 .50
16 Jeff Grenier .20 .50
17 Brendon MacDonald .20 .50
18 Kevin Asselin .20 .50
19 Francois Theriault .20 .50
20 Charles Fontaine .20 .50
21 Vincent Zaore .20 .50
22 David Davenport .20 .50
23 Paul McIlveen .20 .50
24 Cam Fergus .20 .50
25 Alexandre Blais .20 .50

2006-07 Cape Breton Screaming Eagles

COMPLETE SET (25) 8.00 15.00
1 James Sheppard .60 1.50
2 Etienne Breton .30 .75
3 Jason Swit .30 .75
4 Daniel Fazzalari .30 .75
5 Chris Culligan .30 .75
6 Robert Sanley .30 .75
7 Dean Ouellet .30 .75
8 Scott Brannon .30 .75
9 Brad Gallant .30 .75
10 Jean-Claude Sawyer .30 .75
11 Cam Fergus .30 .75
12 Jean-Christophe Gauthier .30 .75
13 Oskars Bartulis .30 .75
14 Alexandre Quesnel .30 .75
15 François Gauthier .30 .75
16 Stephen Ceccanese .30 .75
17 Brendon Macdonald .30 .75
18 Charlie Pens .30 .75
19 Mark Barberio .30 .75
20 Mickey Macdonald .30 .75
21 Nick Macneil .30 .75
22 Paul Mcilveen .30 .75
23 Ondrej Pavelec .40 1.00
24 David Davenport .30 .75
25 Screech MASCOT .02 .10

2003-04 Cape Fear Fire Antz

This set features the fearsome Fire Antz of the SEHL. According to minor league expert Ralph Slate, the cards seem to have been put together by hand, with two matte photo pieces of paper glued together.

COMPLETE SET (17) 15.00 30.00
1 David Bagley .75 2.00
2 Mike Bournazakis .75 2.00
3 Kevin Fines .75 2.00
4 Ryan Kiley .75 2.00
5 Matt Kohanskey .75 2.00
6 Dave Leger .75 2.00
7 Mike Maurice .75 2.00
8 Darren McLean .75 2.00
9 Chris Migliore .75 2.00
10 Marc Milburn .75 2.00
11 Glenn Ridler 1.00 2.50
12 Tim Rink .75 2.00
13 Matt Shannon .75 2.00
14 Aaron Shrieves .75 2.00
15 Rob Vessio .75 2.00
16 Scott Young .75 2.00
17 Scott Rex CO .10 .25

1996-97 Carolina Monarchs

This 30-card set was released by Multi-Ad services and sponsored by Taco Bell, whose logo appears on the front of the card. This set is not numbered so the cards appear alphabetically.

COMPLETE SET (30) 4.00 10.00
1 Checklist .02 .10
2 Chris Armstrong .15 .40
3 Drake Berehowsky .30 .75
4 Ashley Buckberger .15 .40
5 Chad Cabana .15 .40
6 Jon Christiano ACO .15 .40
7 Gilbert Dionne .30 .75
8 Trevor Doyle .15 .40
9 Ivan Droppa .15 .40
10 Craig Ferguson .20 .50
11 Craig Fisher .15 .40
12 Bob Halkidis .15 .40
13 Ryan Johnson .15 .40
14 Richard Kromm HCO .02 .10
15 Filip Kuba .15 .40
16 David Lemanowicz .08 .25
17 Craig Martin .20 .50
18 Eric Montreuil .15 .40
19 David Nemirovsky .15 .40
20 Jason Podollan .15 .40
21 Gaetan Poirier .15 .40
22 Garin Smith .15 .40
23 Geoff Smith .15 .40
24 Herbert Vasiljevs .15 .40
25 Steve Washburn .20 .50
26 Kevin Weekes .40 1.00
27 Dean Aayonce .15 .40
28 Monty MASCOT .02 .10
29 Prospect Card .15 .40
30 PHPA Web Site .01

2006-07 Cedar Rapids RoughRiders

COMPLETE SET (25) 10.00 20.00
1 Richard Bachman .40 1.00
2 Robin Bergman .40 1.00
3 David Boehm .40 1.00
4 Aaron Bogosian .40 1.00
5 Rob Bordson .40 1.00
6 Pat Cannone .40 1.00
7 Jacob Cepis .40 1.00
8 Brett Dickinson .40 1.00
9 Doug Jones .40 1.00
10 Sergei Kolosov .40 1.00
11 Scott Mathis .40 1.00
12 Kent Patterson .40 1.00
13 Mike Seidel .40 1.00
14 Ian Slater .40 1.00
15 Tomi Stahlhammer .40 1.00
16 Evan Stephens .40 1.00
17 Tyler Thompson .40 1.00
18 Matt Tomassoni .40 1.00
19 Kevin Wehrs .40 1.00
20 Casey Wellman .40 1.00
21 Scott Wietecha .40 1.00
22 Tommy Wingels .40 1.00
23 Mark Carlson CO .10 .25
24 Joe Exter ACO .10 .25
25 Ricochet MASCOT .02 .10

1994-95 Central Hockey League

This 127-card standard-size set features the seven teams of the Central Hockey League. Reportedly only 13,000 of each card were produced. The cards were available in pack form only, either at team rinks or from the league for 3.00 by mail. The fronts feature borderless color action player photos except on the left, where a gray bar edges the picture and carries the CHL logo, the player's name and number, and the team logo. On a white background with light gray team logos, the horizontal backs carry a short player biography, profile and stats. The cards are unnumbered, grouped alphabetically within teams and checklisted below alphabetically according to teams as follows: Dallas Freeze (1-18), Ft. Worth Fire (19-36), Memphis Riverkings (37-54), Oklahoma City Blazers (55-72), San Antonio Iguanas (73-90), Tulsa Oilers (91-108), and Wichita Thunder (109-126).

COMPLETE SET (127) 15.00 40.00
1 Jamie Adams .15 .40
2 Wayne Anchikoski .20 .50
3 Jeff Beaudin .15 .40
4 Troy Binnie .20 .50
5 Don Burke .15 .40
6 Derek Crawford .15 .40
7 Ray Desouza .15 .40
8 Ron Flockhart CO .15 .40
9 Jon Gustafson .20 .50
10 Jason Heiland .15 .40
11 James Jensen .15 .40
12 Frank LaScala .15 .40
13 Ryan Leschasin .15 .40
14 Rob Madia .15 .40
15 Rob McCaig .15 .40
16 Jim McGeough .20 .50
17 Doug Roberts .15 .40
18 Jason Taylor .15 .40
19 Scott Allen .15 .40
20 Bruce Bell .20 .50
21 Francois Bourdeau .15 .40
22 Troy Frederick .15 .40
23 Steve Harrison CO .15 .40
24 Alex Kholomeyev .20 .50
25 Dominic Maltals .20 .50
26 Martin Masa .20 .50
27 Jeff Massey .15 .40
28 Mike McCormick .15 .40
29 Pat McGarry .20 .50
30 Dwight Mullins .15 .40
31 Eric Ricard .15 .40
32 Sean Rowe .15 .40
33 Bryan Schoen .15 .40
34 Darren Srochenski .15 .40
35 Andy Stewart .15 .40
36 Stephen Tepper .15 .40
37 Denis Beauchamp .15 .40
38 Herb Boxer CO .15 .40
39 Nicolas Brousseau .15 .40
40 Scott Brower .20 .50
41 Dan Brown .15 .40
42 Brian Cook .15 .40
43 Brent Fleetwood .15 .40
44 Francois Gagon .15 .40
45 Dominic Grand-Maison .15 .40
46 Kyle Haviland .15 .40
47 Jamie Hearn .15 .40
48 Mike Jackson .20 .50
49 Paul Krake .20 .50
50 Layne LeBel .15 .40
51 Steve Magnusson .15 .40
52 Mark McGinn .15 .40
53 Darren Miciak .15 .40
54 Bobby Wallwork .20 .50
55 Ron Aubrey .20 .50
56 Joe Burton .20 .50
57 George Dupont .20 .50
58 Tom Gomes .15 .40
59 Sean Gorman .15 .40
60 Viktor Ignatjev .20 .50
61 Chris Laganas .15 .40
62 Michael McEwen CO .20 .50
63 Chris McMurtry .15 .40
64 Derry Menard .15 .40
65 Sergei Naumov .20 .50
66 Trent Pankewicz .15 .40
67 Alan Perry .30 .75
68 Eric Plante .15 .40
69 Dave Slifka .15 .40
70 Steve Simoni .15 .40
71 Michel St. Jacques .15 .40
72 Tom Thornbury .15 .40
73 Trevor Buchanan .15 .40
74 Link Gaetz .30 .75
75 Sean Goldsworthy .15 .40
76 Fred Goltz .15 .40
77 Sheldon Gorski .15 .40
78 Ross Harris .15 .40
79 Dale Henry .20 .50
80 Paul Jackson .30 .75
81 Scot Kelsey .15 .40
82 John Klaers .15 .40
83 Stu Kulak .20 .50
84 Ken Plaquin .15 .40
85 Brian Shantz .20 .50
86 Dean Shmyr .15 .40
87 Adam Thompson .15 .40
88 John Torchetti .15 .40
89 Ken Venis .15 .40
90 Mike Williams .15 .40
91 Colin Baustad .15 .40
92 Luc Beausoleil .20 .50
93 Mike Berger .15 .40
94 Mark Cavallin .15 .40
95 Shaun Clouston .15 .40
96 Michel Couvrette .15 .40
97 Taylor Hall .15 .40
98 Ryan Harrison .15 .40
99 Sasha Lakovic .30 .75
100 Chuck Loreto .15 .40
101 Tony Martino .20 .50
102 David Moore .15 .40
103 Sylvain Naud .20 .50
104 Dan O'Rourke .15 .40
105 Jody Praznik .15 .40
106 Andy Ross .15 .40
107 Mike Shea .15 .40
108 Garry Unger CO .30 .75
109 Bob Berg .15 .40
110 John DePourcq .20 .50
111 Dave Doucette .20 .50
112 Ron Handy .20 .50
113 Mark Hilton .15 .40
114 Darcy Kaminski .15 .40
115 Mark Karpen .15 .40
116 Jim Latos .15 .40
117 George Maneluk .20 .50
118 Greg Neish .15 .40
119 Brent Sapergia .30 .75
120 Doug Shedden CO .20 .50
121 Greg Smith .15 .40
122 Conrade Thomas .15 .40
123 John Vary .15 .40
124 Rob Weingartner .15 .40
125 Bryan Wells .15 .40
126 Jack Williams .15 .40
127 Title Card CL .15 .40

1995-96 Central Hockey League

This set features the players of the Central Hockey League. The cards feature action photography on the front ensconced in a gray marble border, highlighted by the team logo in the top left corner. The backs contain another photo, and player information. The cards are unnumbered, so they are listed alphabetically by team, and then by name. They were available in packs at CHL games.

COMPLETE SET (90) 15.00 30.00
1 Scott Allen .15 .40
2 Trevor Burgess .15 .40
3 Brian Caruso .15 .40
4 Trevor Converse .15 .40
5 Steve Dykstra .30 .75
6 Troy Frederick .15 .40
7 Phil Groeneveld .15 .40
8 Mark Hilton .20 .50
9 Jeff Massey .15 .40
10 Dennis Miller .15 .40
11 Dwight Mullins .15 .40
12 Steve Plouffe .30 .75
13 Vern Ray .15 .40
14 Kyle Reeves .30 .75
15 Troy Stephens .15 .40
16 Sean Whyte .20 .50
17 Scorch .02 .10
18 Bill McDonald .15 .40
19 Scott Brower .20 .50
20 Dan Brown .15 .40
21 Jamie Cooke .15 .40
22 Kevin Evans .15 .40
23 Brent Fleetwood .15 .40
24 Ron Fogarty .15 .40
25 Trent Gleason .15 .40
26 Derek Grant .15 .40
27 Mike Jackson .30 .75
28 Scot Kelsey .15 .40
29 Steve Magnusson .15 .40
30 Carl Menard .30 .75
31 Chris Morque .20 .50
32 Rick Robus .15 .40
33 Andy Ross .15 .40
34 Stephane Roy .30 .75
35 Doug Stromback .15 .40
36 Herb Boxer .15 .40
37 Kevin Barrett .15 .40
38 Carl Boudreau .30 .75
39 Joe Burton .30 .75
40 George Dupont .20 .50
41 Dominic Fafard .15 .40
42 Jean-Ian Filiatrault .15 .40
43 Tom Gomes .15 .40
44 Todd Harris .15 .40
45 Mervin Kopeck .15 .40
46 Doug Lawrence .30 .75
47 Kevin Lune .15 .40
48 Steve Moore .15 .40
49 Simon Olivier .15 .40
50 Darren Pengelly .15 .40
51 Steve Simoni .15 .40
52 Barkley Swenson .15 .40
53 Serge Tkachenko .20 .50
54 Doug Sauter .15 .40
55 Colin Baustad .15 .40
56 Mike Berger .15 .40
57 Mike Chase .15 .40
58 Trevor Ellerman .15 .40
59 Bryan Forslund .15 .40
60 Taylor Hall .15 .40
61 Craig Hamelin .15 .40
62 Ryan Harrison .15 .40
63 John Laan .15 .40
64 Glen Lang .15 .40
65 Dave Larouche .15 .40
66 Tony Martino .30 .75
67 Sylvain Naud .30 .75
68 Jim Peters .15 .40
69 Cory Peterson .15 .40
70 Chris Robertson .15 .40
71 Kyuin Shim .15 .40
72 Garry Unger .30 .75
73 Clint Black .15 .40
74 Mike Chighisola .15 .40
75 Leonard Devuono .15 .40
76 Ty Eigner .30 .75
77 Anton Fedorov .20 .50
78 Paul Krake .30 .75
79 Antonin Necas .15 .40
80 Ryan Pisiak .15 .40
81 Richard Roesler .15 .40
82 Jason Rushton .15 .40
83 Art Saran .15 .40
84 Stefan Simoes .15 .40
85 Greg Smith .15 .40
86 Dale Turnbull .15 .40
87 Rob Weingartner .15 .40
88 Bryan Wells .15 .40
89 Jack Williams .15 .40
90 Don Jackson .30 .75

1997-98 Central Texas Stampede

Little is known about this set other than the confirmed checklist. Additional information can be forwarded to hockeymag@beckett.com.

COMPLETE SET (20) 3.00 8.00
1 Matt Brenner .20 .50
2 Mike Dick .20 .50
3 Darren Duncalfe .20 .50
4 Larry Dyck .20 .50
5 Dwayne Gylywoychuk .20 .50
6 Ricky Jacob .20 .50
7 Peter Jas .20 .50
8 Dean Kolstad .30 .75
9 Jacques Mailhot .30 .75
10 Don McGrath .20 .50
11 Derek Nicolson .20 .50
12 Jeff Rask .20 .50
13 Layne Roland .20 .50
14 Alex Rummo .20 .50
15 Doug Smith .20 .50
16 Greg Smith .20 .50
17 Joe Tassone .20 .50
18 Jason Taylor .20 .50
19 Peter Zurba .20 .50
20 Wild Thing Mascot .02 .10

1996-97 Charlotte Checkers

This set was only available at the bakery department of a Charlotte Super Shop & Save grocery store, and thus is extremely difficult to find in the secondary market.

COMPLETE SET (20) 15.00 35.00
1 J.F. Aube .75 2.00
2 Eric Boulton 1.25 3.00
3 David Brosseau .75 2.00
4 Jeff Connolly .75 2.00
5 Kimbi Daniels .75 2.00
6 Mickey Elick .75 2.00
7 Eric Fenton .75 2.00
8 Mick Kempffer .75 2.00
9 Jay Kenney .75 2.00
10 Scott Kirton .75 2.00
11 Darcy Mitani .75 2.00
12 Darryl Norlen .75 2.00
13 Kevin Rappana .75 2.00
14 Matt Robbins .75 2.00
15 Evgeni Ryabchikov .75 2.00
16 Kurt Seher .75 2.00
17 Nick Vitucci .75 2.00
18 Shawn Wheeler .75 2.00
19 John Marks HCO .75 2.00
20 Chubby Checker Mascot .02 .10

1997-98 Charlotte Checkers

This 26-card set was given away by both the bakery of a Charlotte Hannaford grocery store and sold by the team. Note: three versions of card #25 exist.

COMPLETE SET (28) 15.00 30.00
1 Matt Alvey .40 1.00
2 Eric Boulton 1.25 3.00
3 David Brosseau .40 1.00
4 Paxton Schafer .60 1.50
5 Kurt Seher .40 1.00
6 Stephane Soulliere .40 1.00
7 Derek Crimin .40 1.00
8 Eric Flinton .40 1.00
9 Justin Gould .40 1.00
10 Jason Kelly .40 1.00
11 Mike Hartman .40 1.00
12 Jeff Heil .40 1.00
13 Jay Kenney .40 1.00
14 Milt Mastad .40 1.00
15 Dean Moore .40 1.00
16 Darryl Noren .40 1.00
17 Dale Purinton 1.25 3.00
18 Andre Roy 1.25 3.00
19 P.C. Drouin .60 1.50
20 Bill McCauley .40 1.00
21 Shawn Wheeler ACO .02 .10
22 John Marks HCO .02 .10
23 Chubby Checker Mascot .02 .10
24 Checklist .02 .10
25 Darryl Noren CAP .60 1.50
25 Eric Flinton CAP .60 1.50
25 Kurt Seher CAP .60 1.50
26 PHPA Web Site .02 .10

1998-99 Charlotte Checkers

This set was issued as a promotional giveaway through a local grocery store named Hannaford's. As such, it is extremely difficult to find on the secondary market.

COMPLETE SET (24) 10.00 25.00
1 J.F. Aube .60 1.50
2 Shannon Basaraba .40 1.00
3 Doug Battaglia .40 1.00
4 David Brosseau .40 1.00
5 Tom Brown .40 1.00
6 Pat Brownlee .40 1.00
7 Brooke Chateau .40 1.00
8 Jeff Heil .40 1.00
9 Boyd Kane .60 1.50
10 Kevin Kreutzer .40 1.00
11 Darryl Noren .60 1.50
12 Jason Norrie .40 1.00
13 Nikolai Pronin .40 1.00
14 Kurt Seher .60 1.50
15 Bob Sheehan .40 1.00
16 Ryan Sittler .40 1.00
17 Martin Sychra .40 1.00
18 Dean Zayonce .40 1.00
19 Shawn Wheeler CO .08 .25
20 Chubby Checker .08 .25
21 The Captains .40 1.00
22 Doug Battaglia .40 1.00
Pat Brownlee
23 J.F. Aube .40 1.00
Bob Sheehan
24 Checklist .02 .10

1999-00 Charlotte Checkers

This set features the Checkers of the ECHL. The cards were produced by Roox, and handed out as promotional giveaways over the course of several home games.

COMPLETE SET (38) 8.00 20.00
1 Jason Dailey .20 .50
2 Brooke Chateau .20 .50
3 Rocky Welsing .20 .50
4 Kurt Seher .20 .50
5 Kevin Hilton .20 .50
6 Reggie Brezeault .20 .50
7 Lee Hamilton .20 .50
8 Dave Risk .20 .50
9 Taras Lendzyk .20 .50
10 Kurt Mallett .20 .50
11 Tyler Deis .20 .50
12 Mike Rucinski .30 .75
13 Derek Wilkinson .40 1.00
14 Richard Scott .40 1.00
15 David Beauregard .30 .75
16 Mike Jaros .20 .50
17 Darryl Noren .20 .50
18 Marc Tropper .20 .50
19 Scott Bailey .40 1.00
20 Jeff Brown .20 .50
21 Boyd Kane .40 1.00
22 Chubby Checker MASCOT .02 .10
23 The Carolina Cup .02 .10
24 Marc Tropper .30 .75
24 Brooke Chateau .20 .50
25 Mark Burgess TR .02 .10
26 Don MacAdam CO .02 .10
27 Scott Bailey .40 1.00
28 Dean Mando .30 .75
29 Kevin Pozzo .20 .50
30 Martin Cerven .20 .50

arc Tropper AS	.30	.75
cott Bailey	.40	1.00
ike Rucinski	.40	1.00
yler Deis	.20	.50
avid Beauregard	.30	.75
arryl Noren	.20	.50
hecklist	.02	.10

2000-01 Charlotte Checkers

s set features the Checkers of the ECHL. It is eved that it was issued as a promotional giveaway r two home games, then later sold by the team at souvenir stands.

MPLETE SET (36)	10.00	25.00
ason Labarbera	.40	1.50
cott Bailey	.40	1.00
cott King	.40	1.00
arc Tropper	.30	.75
oyd Kane	.30	.75
ustin Harney	.30	.75
urt Seher	.30	.75
rad Mehalko	.30	.75
evin Hilton	.30	.75
Mathieu Benoit	.30	.75
David Oliver	.30	.75
Lee Hamilton	.30	.75
Wes Jarvis	.30	.75
Josh MacNevin	.30	.75
Kevin Pozzo	.30	.75
Don MacAdam HCO	.08	.25
Dave Baseggio CO	.08	.25
Chubby Checker MASCOT	.08	.25
Paul Ciblin	.30	.75
Tyler Deis	.30	.75
Mark Spence	.30	.75
Bob MacIsaac	.30	.75
Steve Duke	.30	.75
Andre Signoretti	.30	.75
Brandon Dietrich	.30	.75
Mike Derecola	.30	.75
Chris Plumhoff	.30	.75
Chubby Checker MASCOT	.08	.25
Richard Scott	.40	1.00
Vitali Yeremeyev	.60	1.50
Benjamin Carpentier	.30	.75
Francois Fortier	.30	.75
Scott Wray	.30	.75
Mark Moore	.30	.75
Bryce Wandler	.30	.75
Checklist	.08	.10

2002-03 Charlotte Checkers

MPLETE SET (18)	8.00	20.00
Nicholas Bilotto	.40	1.00
Kevin Caulfield	.40	1.00
Brandon Cullen	.60	1.50
Allan Egeland	.40	1.00
David Evans	.40	1.00
David Inman	.40	1.00
Dusty Jamieson	.40	1.00
Vince Malts	.40	1.00
Walker McDonald	.40	1.00
Konrad McKay	.60	1.50
Scott Meyer	.60	1.50
Eduard Pershin	.40	1.00
Kurt Seher	.40	1.00
Takahito Suzuki	.60	1.50
Craig Weller	.40	1.00
Chad Wilchynski	.40	1.00
Colin Zulianello	.40	1.00

2003-04 Charlotte Checkers

is set was produced by RBI Sports. The numbering low reflects the entire print run of the RBI ECHL set. has been reported that just 250 copies of this set re produced.

MPLETE SET (16)	6.00	15.00
Nicholas Bilotto	.40	1.00
Kevin Caulfield	.40	1.00
Doug Christiansen	.40	1.00
Ryan Cuthbert	.40	1.00
Allan Egeland	.40	1.00
Blaz Emersic	.40	1.00
Kengo Ito	.40	1.00
Steven MacIntyre	.40	1.00
Konrad McKay	.40	1.00
Scott Meyer	.60	1.50
Daisuke Obara	.40	1.00
Rory Rawlyk	.40	1.00
David St. Germain	.60	1.50
Marc St. Jean	.40	1.00
Jeff State	.40	1.00
Mike Wirll	.40	1.00

2013-14 Charlotte Checkers

OMPLETE SET ()	6.00	15.00
Header Card	.30	.75
Danny Biega	.30	.75
Nicolas Blanchard	.30	.75
Zach Boychuk	.30	.75
Philippe Cornet	.30	.75
Matt Corrente	.30	.75
Sean Dolan	.30	.75
Mark Flood	.30	.75
A.J. Jenks	.30	.75
0 Michal Jordan	.30	.75
1 Austin Levi	.30	.75
2 Keegan Lowe	.30	.75
3 Matt Marquardt	.30	.75
4 Mike Murphy	.30	.75
5 John Muse	.30	.75
6 Aaron Palushaj	.30	.75
7 Victor Rask	.30	.75
8 Rasmus Rissanen	.30	.75
9 Beau Schmitz	.30	.75
0 Justin Shugg	.30	.75
1 Jared Staal	.30	.75
2 Brett Sutter	.30	.75
3 Brody Sutter	.30	.75
4 Chris Terry	.30	.75
5 Brendan Woods	.30	.75

2002-03 Chicago Steel

his set features the Steel of the USHL.

OMPLETE SET (24)	8.00	20.00
Bill Bagron	.40	1.00
Jordan Black	.40	1.00
Dan Charleston	.40	1.00
Adam D'Alba	.60	1.50
Jeff Dunne	.40	1.00
Josh Elzinga	.40	1.00
Rene Gauthier	.40	1.00
Ben Geelan	.40	1.00
Brady Greco	.60	1.50
0 Michael Grenzy	.40	1.00
1 Eric Helstedt	.40	1.00
2 Mike Kennedy	.40	1.00
3 Vojtech Kloz	.40	1.00
4 Justin Lewandowski	.40	1.00
5 Travis Moran	.40	1.00
6 Joseph Pearce	1.00	2.50
17 Topher Scott	.40	1.00
18 Eric Slais	.40	1.00
19 Chad Solberg	.40	1.00
20 Alex Spezia	.40	1.00
21 Lee Sweatt	.40	1.00
22 Blake Williams	.40	1.00
23 A.J. Toews CO	.04	.10
24 Rusty Steel MASCOT	.04	.10

2003-04 Chicago Steel

This set features the Steel of the USHL. Little is known about the set beyond the checklist info.

COMPLETE SET (18)	6.00	15.00
1 Matt McIlvane	.60	1.50
2 Dan Marziani	.40	1.00
3 Shane Connelly	.60	1.50
4 Mike Van Wagner	.40	1.00
5 Jay Sprague	.40	1.00
6 Matt Clackson	.40	1.00
7 Justin Lewandowski	.40	1.00
8 Kevin Roeder	.40	1.00
9 David Marshall	.40	1.00
10 Chris Walsh	.40	1.00
11 Jeff Dunne	.40	1.00
12 Eric Lampe	.40	1.00
13 Ryan Kim	.40	1.00
14 John Kearns	.40	1.00
15 Ryan Hawkins	.40	1.00
16 T.J. Fox	.40	1.00
17 Alex Spezia	.40	1.00
18 Rene Gauthier	.40	1.00
19 Rusty Steel MASCOT	.04	.10

2004-05 Chicago Steel

We have confirmed a handful of cards from this USHL set. If you have additional information, please contact us at hockeymag@beckett.com.

COMPLETE SET (10)	4.00	10.00
1 Nathan Perkovich	.40	1.00
2 T.J. Fox	.40	1.00
3 Kevin Swallow	.40	1.00
4 Eric Slais	.40	1.00
5 Billy Sauer	.40	1.00
6 Shane Connelly	.40	1.00
7 Chris Clackson	.40	1.00
8 Sami Liimainen	.40	1.00
9 Ryan Oldis	.40	1.00
10 Joe Loprieno	.40	1.00

1998-99 Chicago Wolves

This set features the Wolves of the IHL. The set was handed out at a game in March as a promotional item.

COMPLETE SET (25)	8.00	20.00
1 Brent Gretzky	.40	1.00
2 Dan Plante	.30	.75
3 Tim Bergland	.30	.75
4 Steve Maltais	.75	2.00
5 Steve Gosselin	.40	1.00
6 Scott Pearson	.30	.75
7 Niklas Andersson	.40	1.00
8 Chris LiPuma	.30	.75
9 Pat Jablonski	.40	1.00
10 Skates MASCOT	.02	.10
11 Tim Breslin	.30	.75
12 Chris Marinucci	.30	.75
13 Steve Larouche	.30	.75
14 Wendell Young	.75	2.00
15 Glen Featherstone	.30	.75
16 Bob Nardella	.30	.75
17 Guy Larose	.30	.75
18 Dennis Vial	.40	1.00
19 Kevin Dahl	.30	.75
20 Jeremy Mylymok	.30	.75
21 Paul Koch	.30	.75
22 Tom Tilley	.30	.75
23 John Anderson HCO	.20	.50
24 Kevin Miller	.40	1.00
25 PHPA Web Site	.02	.10

1998-99 Chicago Wolves Turner Cup

This 24-card set was handed out at two separate games. It showcases players from the Turner Cup Championship team of 1997-98, although it was released in the 1998-99 season. Note: there at two different versions of card #3.

COMPLETE SET (25)	10.00	25.00
1 Wendell Young	.75	2.00
2 John Anderson	.20	.50
3 Ray LeBlanc	1.25	3.00
3 Dave Craievich	.20	.50
4 Paul Koch	.20	.50
5 Kevin Dahl	.20	.50
6 Jeremy Mylymok	.20	.50
7 Bob Nardella	.20	.50
8 Marc Rodgers	1.25	3.00
9 Marc Potvin	.75	2.00
10 Steve Larouche	.40	1.00
11 Steve Maltais	1.25	3.00
12 Doug Barrault	.20	.50
13 Jamie Baker	.20	.50
14 Chris Marinucci	.20	.50
15 Tim Breslin	.20	.50
16 Dennis Vial	1.25	3.00
17 Tom Tilley	.20	.50
18 Scott Pearson	.20	.50
19 Steve Martins	.30	.75
20 Matt Martin	.20	.50
21 Tim Bergland	.20	.50
22 Alexander Semak	.40	1.00
23 Ravil Gusmanov	.20	.50
24 Stephane Beauregard	.75	2.00

1999-00 Chicago Wolves

This set features the Wolves of the IHL. The set was issued as a promotional giveaway and was limited to 5,000 total sets.

COMPLETE SET (25)	8.00	20.00
1 Header Card/PHPA	.02	.10
2 Wendell Young	.75	2.00
3 Kevin Dahl	.30	.75
4 Dallas Eakins	.30	.75
5 Bob Nardella	.30	.75
6 Niklas Andersson	.30	.75
7 Steve Larouche	.75	2.00
8 Steve Maltais	.75	2.00
9 Chris Marinucci	.30	.75
10 Brian Noonan	.40	1.00
11 Guy Larose	.30	.75
12 Sean Berens	.30	.75
13 Glen Featherstone	.30	.75
14 Tom Tilley	.30	.75
15 Scott Pearson	.30	.75
16 Greg Andrusak	.30	.75
17 Dean Malkoc	.30	.75
18 David Mackey	.30	.75
19 Dan Plante	.30	.75
20 Chris LiPuma	.30	.75
21 Andrei Trefilov	.40	1.00
22 Daniel Lacroix	.30	.75
23 John Anderson CO	.08	.25
24 Marty Howe CO	.30	.75
25 Skates MASCOT	.08	.25

2000-01 Chicago Wolves

This set features the Wolves of the IHL. The set is noteworthy for the inclusion of Rick DiPietro, the first overall pick of the 2000 NHL Entry Draft. It is oversized, and is believed to have been handed out at a home game in February, 2001.

COMPLETE SET (25)	10.00	25.00
1 John Anderson	.20	.50
2 Niklas Anderson	.20	.50
3 Jesse Belanger	.40	1.00
4 Rob Brown	.40	1.00
5 Kevin Dahl	.20	.50
6 Rick DiPietro	4.00	10.00
7 Ted Drury	.20	.50
8 Dallas Eakins	.20	.50
9 Glen Featherstone	.20	.50
10 Eric Houde	.20	.50
11 Paul Kruse	.20	.50
12 Guy Larose	.20	.50
13 Steve Larouche	.40	1.00
14 Mark Lawrence	.30	.75
15 Chris LiPuma	.20	.50
16 Steve Maltais	.80	2.00
17 Dean Melanson	.20	.50
18 Bob Nardella	.30	.75
19 Brian Noonan	.40	1.00
20 Robert Petrovicky	.30	.75
21 Dan Plante	.20	.50
22 Tom Tilley	.40	1.00
23 Wendell Young	.40	1.00
24 Chicago Wolves	.20	.25
25 Skates MASCOT	.10	.25
NNO Header Card	.02	.10

2001-02 Chicago Wolves

This set features the Wolves of the AHL. It was issued as a promotional giveaway at a game in March 2002. The set is slightly oversized. Since the cards are unnumbered, they are listed below in alphabetical order.

COMPLETE SET (25)	10.00	25.00
1 Bryan Adams	.30	.75
2 Zdenek Blatny	.40	1.00
3 Rob Brown	.40	1.00
4 Frederic Cassivi	.40	1.00
5 Jeff Dessner	.30	.75
6 Dallas Eakins	.30	.75
7 Garnet Exelby	.60	1.50
8 Kurtis Foster	.30	.75
9 Darcy Hordichuk	.75	2.00
10 Derek MacKenzie	.30	.75
11 Steve Maltais	.40	1.00
12 Norm Maracle	.40	1.00
13 Bob Nardella	.30	.75
14 Pasi Nurminen	1.25	3.00
15 Kamil Piros	.40	1.00
16 Dan Plante	.30	.75
17 Brian Pothier	.40	1.00
18 Luke Sellars	.30	.75
19 Ben Simon	.30	.75
20 Jarrod Skalde	.40	1.00
21 Dan Snyder	.40	1.00
22 Brad Tapper	.40	1.00
23 J.P. Vigier	.40	1.00
24 Mike Weaver	.40	1.00
25 Skates MASCOT	.10	.25

2002-03 Chicago Wolves

This set was issued as a promotional giveaway at a late-season home game. The cards are unnumbered and are listed below in alphabetical order.

COMPLETE SET (25)	12.00	30.00
1 John Anderson CO	.10	.25
2 Zdenek Blatny	.60	1.50
3 Rob Brown	.40	1.00
4 Frederic Cassivi	.60	1.50
5 Joey DiPenta	1.25	3.00
6 Dallas Eakins	.40	1.00
7 Garnet Exelby	1.25	3.00
8 Jeff Farkas	.40	1.00
9 Kurtis Foster	.40	1.00
10 Simon Gamache	1.25	3.00
11 Mark Hartigan	.40	1.00
12 Milan Hnilicka	1.25	3.00
13 Andreas Karlsson	.40	1.00
14 Francis Lessard	.40	1.00
15 Derek MacKenzie	.40	1.00
16 Steve Maltais	1.25	3.00
17 Norm Maracle	1.25	3.00
18 Kamil Piros	.75	2.00
19 Kirill Safronov	.40	1.00
20 Luke Sellars	.40	1.00
21 Ben Simon	.40	1.00
22 Skates MASCOT	.04	.10
23 Ryan Tobler	.40	1.00
24 Libor Ustrnul	.40	1.00
25 J.P. Vigier	.75	2.00

2003-04 Chicago Wolves

COMPLETE SET (25)	15.00	30.00
1 Stephen Baby	.40	1.00
2 Zdenek Blatny	.40	1.00
3 Jim Campbell	.40	1.00
4 Frederic Cassivi	.60	1.50
5 Daniel Corso	.40	1.00
6 Joe DiPenta	.60	1.50
7 Kurtis Foster	.40	1.00
8 Michael Garnett	.60	1.50
9 Greg Hawgood	.40	1.00
10 Eric Healey	.40	1.00
11 Shawn Heins	.40	1.00
12 Kari Lehtonen	2.00	5.00
13 Derek MacKenzie	.40	1.00
14 Brian Maloney	.40	1.00
15 Steve Maltais	.60	1.50
16 Kamil Piros	.40	1.00
17 Tommi Santala	.40	1.00
18 Luke Sellars	.40	1.00
19 Karl Stewart	.40	1.00
20 Brian Swanson	.40	1.00
21 Libor Ustrnul	.40	1.00
22 Mike Weaver	.40	1.00
23 Brendan Yarema	.40	1.00
24 John Anderson HCO	.10	.25
25 Mascot	.04	.10

2004-05 Chicago Wolves

COMPLETE SET (25)	40.00	75.00
1 Kari Lehtonen	4.00	10.00
2 Brad Larsen	1.00	2.50
3 Travis Roche	1.00	2.50
4 Michael Garnett	1.25	3.00
5 Greg Hawgood	1.00	2.50
6 Joe Corvo	1.00	2.50
7 Libor Ustrnul	1.00	2.50
8 Paul Flache	1.00	2.50
9 Colin Stuart	1.00	2.50
10 Kyle Rossiter	1.00	2.50
11 Brian Maloney	1.00	2.50
12 J.P. Vigier	1.50	4.00
13 Ben Simon	1.00	2.50
14 Brian Sipotz	1.00	2.50
15 Tim Wedderburn	1.00	2.50
16 Lonny Bohonos	1.50	4.00
17 Cory Larose	1.00	2.50
18 Kip Brennan	1.50	4.00
19 Stephen Baby	1.00	2.50
20 Kevin Doell	1.00	2.50
21 Karl Stewart	1.00	2.50
22 Steve Maltais	2.00	5.00
23 Derek MacKenzie	1.00	2.50
24 Tommi Santala	1.00	2.50
25 Skates MASCOT	.40	1.00

2005-06 Chicago Wolves

COMPLETE SET (25)	10.00	25.00
1 Ramzi Abid	.40	1.00
2 Stephen Baby	.40	1.00
3 Scott Barney	.40	1.00
4 Braydon Coburn	.75	2.00
5 Kevin Doell	.40	1.00
6 Pat Dwyer	.40	1.00
7 Michael Garnett	.75	2.00
8 Tomas Kloucek	.40	1.00
9 Francis Lessard	.40	1.00
10 Derek MacKenzie	.40	1.00
11 Brian Maloney	.40	1.00
12 Kip Miller	.40	1.00
13 Justin Morrison	.40	1.00
14 Nick Naumenko	.40	1.00
15 Mark Popovic	.40	1.00
16 Travis Roche	.40	1.00
17 Jared Ross	.40	1.00
18 Brian Sipotz	.40	1.00
19 Karl Stewart	.40	1.00
20 Colin Stuart	.40	1.00
21 Tuomas Tarkki	.40	1.00
22 Billy Tibbetts	.40	1.00
23 Tim Wedderburn	.40	1.00
24 John Anderson HC	.02	.10
25 Skates MASCOT	.02	.10

2007-08 Chicago Wolves

COMPLETE SET (27)	6.00	15.00
1 Joey Crabb	.30	.75
2 Guillaume Desbiens	.30	.75
3 Andre Deveaux	.30	.75
4 Kevin Doell	.30	.75
5 Brian Fahey	.30	.75
6 Colton Fretter	.30	.75
7 Robert Gherson	.30	.75
8 Alexandre Giroux	.30	.75
9 Darren Haydar	.30	.75
10 Jason Krog	.30	.75
11 Joel Kwiatkowski	.30	.75
12 Jordan Lavallee	.30	.75
13 Scott Lehman	.30	.75
14 Grant Lewis	.30	.75
15 Bryan Little	.30	.75
16 Steve Martins	.30	.75
17 Nathan Oystrick	.30	.75
18 Chad Painchaud	.30	.75
19 Ondrej Pavelec	.75	2.00
20 Karel Pilar	.30	.75
21 Jesse Schultz	.30	.75
22 Brian Sipotz	.30	.75
23 Brett Sterling	.30	.75
24 Colin Stuart	.30	.75
25 Boris Valabik	.30	.75
26 John Anderson HC	.30	.75
27 Skates MASCOT	.30	.75

2013-14 Chicago Wolves

COMPLETE SET (31)	8.00	20.00
1 Cade Fairchild	.30	.75
2 Joel Edmundson	.30	.75
3 Taylor Chorney	.30	.75
4 Jani Hakanpaa	.30	.75
5 David Shields	.30	.75
6 Ty Rattie	.30	.75
7 Shane Harper	.30	.75
8 Chris Porter	.30	.75
9 Pat Cannone	.30	.75
10 Michael Davies	.30	.75
11 Mark Cundari	.30	.75
12 Sergei Andronov	.30	.75
13 Cody Beach	.30	.75
14 Tyler Shattock	.30	.75
15 Dmitrij Jaskin	.30	.75
16 Adam Cracknell	.30	.75
17 Mark Mancari	.30	.75
18 Nathan Longpre	.30	.75
19 Evan Oberg	.30	.75
20 Brent Regner	.30	.75
21 Keith Aucoin	.30	.75
22 Christian Hanson	.30	.75
23 Matt Climie	.30	.75
24 Jake Allen	.30	.75
25 Sebastian Wannstrom	.30	.75
26 Alexandre Bolduc	.30	.75
27 John Anderson CO	.30	.75
28 Scott Allen Asst. CO	.30	.75
29 Dave Allison Asst. CO	.30	.75
30 Wendell Young GM	.30	.75
31 Skates MASCOT	.30	.75

2014-15 Chicago Wolves

COMPLETE SET (30)	8.00	20.00
1 John Anderson CO	.30	.75
2 Cody Beach	.30	.75
3 Jordon Binnington	.30	.75
4 Rob Bordson	.30	.75
5 Terry Broadhurst	.30	.75
6 Mathieu Brodeur	.40	1.00
7 Adam Burish	.30	.75
8 Pat Cannone	.30	.75
9 Jake Chelios	.30	.75
10 Matt Climie	.30	.75
11 Adam Cracknell	.30	.75
12 Joel Edmundson	.40	1.00
13 Benn Ferriero	.30	.75
14 Colin Fraser	.30	.75
15 Jani Hakanpaa	.30	.75
16 Mark Hardy Asst. CO	.30	.75
17 Shane Harper	.30	.75
18 Petteri Lindbohm	.30	.75
19 Nathan Longpre	.30	.75
20 Phil McRae	.30	.75
21 Magnus Paajarvi-Svensson	.30	.75
22 Ty Rattie	.75	2.00
23 Brent Regner	.30	.75
24 David Shields	.30	.75
25 Brad Tapper Asst. CO	.30	.75
26 Yannick Veilleux	.30	.75
27 Sebastian Wannstrom	.30	.75
28 Jeremy Welsh	.30	.75
29 Wendell Young GM	.30	.75
30 Skates MASCOT	.30	.75

1984-85 Chicoutimi Sagueneens

This 24-card set sponsored by Mike's restaurants measures approximately 8 1/2" by 11" and features black-and-white player photos in a white-black-white-red frame. The complete set was issued in a protective folder. This folder is valued at $1. The card backs are blank. The cards are unnumbered and checklisted below in alphabetical order.

COMPLETE SET (24)	16.00	40.00
1 Mario Barbe	.40	1.00
2 Mario Bazinet	.40	1.00
3 Daniel Bedard	.40	1.00
Michel Boivin		
Guy Byatt		
Jean-Marc Couture		
Patrice Gosselin		
Jean-Yves Laberge		
Germain Munger		
Reginald Riverin		
4 Daniel Berthiaume	1.25	3.00
5 Francois Breault	.60	1.50
6 Gregg Choules	.40	1.00
7 Christian Duperron	.40	1.00
8 Luc Dufour	.40	1.00
9 Luc Duval	.40	1.00
10 Patrick Emond	.40	1.00
11 Marc Fortier	.60	1.50
12 Steven Gauthier	.40	1.00
13 Yves Heroux	.60	1.50
14 Daniel Jomphe	.40	1.00
15 Gilles Laberge	.40	1.00
16 Claude Lajoie	.40	1.00
17 Serge Lauzon	.40	1.00
18 Roch Marinier	.60	1.50
19 Pierre Millier	.40	1.00
20 Marc Morin	.40	1.00
21 Scott Rettew	.40	1.00
22 Jean-Marc Richard	.40	1.00
23 Stephane Richer	5.00	12.00
24 Pierre Sevigny	.40	1.00

2000-01 Chicoutimi Sagueneens

This set features the Sagueneens of the QMJHL. It was produced by CTM-Ste-Foy, and was sold by that company, as well as by the team at home games.

COMPLETE SET (23)	4.80	15.00
1 Olivier Dannel	.20	.50
2 Alex Turcotte	.20	.50
3 Mathieu Betournay	.20	.50
4 Michel Finn	.20	.50
5 Eric Betournay	.20	.50
6 Jonathan Francoeur	.20	.50
7 Sebastien Laprise	.20	.50
8 Sylvain Watt	.20	.50
9 Sebastien Lucier	.20	.50
10 Stanislav Hudec	.20	.50
11 Christian Larrivee	.20	.50
12 Francois Caron	.20	.50
13 Eric Beaudin	.20	.50
14 Alain Chenard	.20	.50
15 Karl St-Pierre	.20	.50
16 Michael Parent	.20	.50
17 David Ouellet Beaudry	.20	.50
18 Jean-Francois Demers	.20	.50
19 Dave Verville	.30	.75
20 Guillaume Karrer	.20	.50
21 Martin Beauchesne	.20	.50
22 Jean-Micheal Martin	.20	.50
23 Pierre-Marc Bouchard	2.00	5.00

2000-01 Chicoutimi Sagueneens Signed

This set is exactly the same as the base Sagueneens set from this season, save that every card has been hand signed by the player pictured. Each card also is serial numbered out of just 100.

COMPLETE SET (23)	18.00	50.00
1 Olivier Dannel	.80	2.00
2 Alex Turcotte	.80	2.00
3 Mathieu Betournay	.80	2.00
4 Michel Finn	.80	2.00
5 Eric Betournay	.80	2.00
6 Jonathan Francoeur	.80	2.00
7 Sebastien Laprise	.80	2.00
8 Sylvain Watt	.80	2.00
9 Sebastien Lucier	.80	2.00
10 Stanislav Hudec	.80	2.00
11 Christian Larrivee	.80	2.00
12 Francois Caron	.80	2.00
13 Eric Beaudin	.80	2.00
14 Alain Chenard	.80	2.00
15 Karl St-Pierre	.80	2.00
16 Michael Parent	.80	2.00
17 David Ouellet Beaudry	.80	2.00
18 Jean-Francois Demers	.80	2.00
19 Dave Verville	2.00	5.00
20 Guillaume Karrer	.80	2.00
21 Martin Beauchesne	.80	2.00
22 Jean-Micheal Martin	.80	2.00
23 Pierre-Marc Bouchard	10.00	25.00

2001-02 Chicoutimi Sagueneens

COMPLETE SET (23)	6.00	15.00
1 Team Card	.04	.10
2 Sebastien Lucier	.20	.50
3 Eric Betournay	.20	.50
4 Pierre-Alexandre Parenteau	.30	.75
5 Stanislav Hudec	.20	.50
6 Christian Larrivee	.20	.50
7 Patrick Tessier	.20	.50
8 Pierre-Luc Briere	.20	.50
9 Yvan Busque	.20	.50
10 Alexandre Blackburn	.30	.75
11 Jean-Francois Demers	.20	.50
12 Eric Tetrault	.20	.50
13 Jeff Drouin Deslauriers	.60	1.50
14 Eric Borbeau	.20	.50
15 Michael Lanthier	.20	.50
16 Nicolas Marcotte	.20	.50
17 Hugues Verpaelst	.20	.50
18 Francis Lemieux	.20	.50
19 Jean-Vincent Lachance	.20	.50
20 Martin Chabot	.20	.50
21 Rosario Ruggeri	.20	.50
22 Bruno Champagne	.20	.50
23 Pierre-Marc Bouchard	1.25	3.00

2004-05 Chicoutimi Sagueneens

A total of 1,100 team sets were produced.

COMPLETE SET (24)	5.00	12.00
1 Alexandre Lamarche	.20	.50
2 Alexandre Vincent	.20	.50
3 Bernard Elhokayen	.20	.50
4 Brandon Verge	.20	.50
5 Brent Macsween	.20	.50
6 David Desharnais	.20	.50
7 Francis Lemieux	.20	.50
8 Francis Verreault	.20	.50
9 Gabriel Houde-Brisson	.20	.50
10 Guillaume Lepine	.20	.50
11 Julien Brouillette	.20	.50
12 Louis-Etienne Leblanc	.20	.50
13 Marc-Andre Roy	.20	.50
14 Marek Zagrapan	.60	1.50
15 Mathieu Bolduc	.20	.50
16 Romy Elayoubi	.30	.75
17 Stanislav Lascek	.20	.50
18 Maxime Boisclair	.40	1.00
19 Nicolas Blanchard	.20	.50
20 Nicolas Marcotte	.20	.50
21 Ryan Spaulding	.20	.50
22 Shayne Tremblay	.20	.50
23 Travis Coles	.20	.50
24 Yan Gaudette	.20	.50

2005-06 Chicoutimi Sagueneens

COMPLETE SET (31)	6.00	15.00
1 David Desharnais	.20	.50
2 Stanislav Lascek	.20	.50
3 Marek Zagrapan	.40	1.00
4 Nicolas Blanchard	.20	.50
5 Maxime Boisclair	.40	1.00
6 Francis Verreault	.20	.50
7 Shayne Tremblay	.20	.50
8 Sylvain Michaud	.20	.50
9 Alexandre Vincent	.20	.50
10 Julien Brouillette	.20	.50
11 Geoff Oliver	.20	.50
12 Gabriel Carle	.20	.50
13 Marc Myre	.20	.50
14 Pierre-Luc Hunt	.20	.50
15 Maxime Tanguay	.20	.50
16 Mathieu Bolduc	.20	.50
17 Louis-Etienne Leblanc	.20	.50
18 Jean-Claude Milot	.20	.50
19 Brent MacSween	.20	.50
20 Guillaume Lepine	.20	.50
21 Oliver Lajeunesse	.20	.50
22 Bruno-Pierre Gosselin	.20	.50
23 Matthew Block	.20	.50
24 Ryan Lehr	.20	.50
25 Patrick Coulombe	.20	.50
26 Jean-Sebastien Adam	.20	.50
27 Gabriel Boies	.20	.50
28 Nicolas Lafontaine	.20	.50
29 Benoit Piche	.20	.50
30 Jean-Sebastien Cote	.20	.50
31 Sago MASCOT	.02	.10

2006-07 Chicoutimi Sagueneens

COMPLETE SET (23)	8.00	15.00
1 David Desharnais	.30	.75
2 Luc-Oliver Blain	.30	.75
3 Nicolas Blanchard	.30	.75
4 Mathieu Bolduc	.30	.75
5 Julien Brouillette	.30	.75
6 Patrick Campbell	.30	.75
7 Francois Chabot	.30	.75
8 Joel Champagne	.30	.75
9 Derek Famulare	.30	.75
10 Christopher Guay	.30	.75
11 Alexandre Imbeault	.30	.75
12 Dominic Jalbert	.30	.75
13 Marc-Andre Julien	.30	.75
14 Francois Levesque	.30	.75
15 Jurai Mikus	.30	.75
16 Bobby Nadeau	.40	1.00
17 Olivier Painchaud	.30	.75
18 Maxime Provencher	.30	.75
19 Antoine Roussel	.30	.75
20 Tommy Tremblay	.30	.75
21 Kirill Tulupov	.30	.75
22 Francois Verreault-Paul	.30	.75
23 Joel Rechlicz	.30	.75

2006-07 Chilliwack Bruins

COMPLETE SET (25)	15.00	25.00
1 Alex Archibald	.60	1.50
2 Matt Esposito	.60	1.50
3 Kevin Boutilier	.40	1.00
4 Dylan Chapman	.40	1.00
5 Cody Hobbs	.40	1.00
6 Nick Holden	.40	1.00
7 Craig Lineker	.40	1.00
8 Scott Maetche	.40	1.00
9 Cam Stevens	.40	1.00
10 Matt McCue	.40	1.00
11 Josh Aspenlind	.40	1.00
12 Patrick Bhungal	.40	1.00
13 Donnie Glennie	.40	1.00
14 Colton Graf	.40	1.00
15 Aki Kangasmaki	.40	1.00
16 Colby Kulhanek	.40	1.00
17 Matt Meropoulis	.40	1.00
18 Dillon Johnstone	.40	1.00
19 Oscar Moller	.75	2.00
20 Special Edition Oscar Moller	.75	2.00
21 Ken Petkau	.40	1.00
22 Mark Santorelli	.40	1.00
23 Cody Smuk	.40	1.00
24 Mike Proudley	.40	1.00
25 Bruiser MASCOT CL	.02	.10

1990-91 Cincinnati Cyclones

This 23-card set of the Cincinnati Cyclones of the ECHL was produced by 7th Inning Sketch. for distribution by the team. The cards are numbered 19-41 presumably because the company produced card sets for many ECHL teams this year.

COMPLETE SET (23)	3.00	8.00
19 Steve McGrinder	.15	.40
20 Steve Shaunessy	.15	.40
21 Jay Rose	.15	.40
22 Don Gagne	.15	.40
23 Mike Williams	.15	.40
24 Mike Chighisola	.15	.40
25 Daryl Harpe	.15	.40
26 Steve Cadieux	.15	.40
27 Jeff Salzbrunn	.15	.40
28 Rob Gador	.15	.40
29 Chris Marshall	.15	.40
30 Doug Melnyk	.15	.40
31 Mark Turner	.15	.40
32 Kevin Kerr	.15	.40
33 Rob Krauss	.15	.40
34 Mark Marentette	.15	.40
35 Jamie Kompon	.15	.40
36 Tom Neziol	.15	.40
37 John Fletcher	.15	.40
38 Dennis Desrosiers CO	.08	.25
39 Todd Harrison TR	.08	.25
40 Terry Ficorelli	.15	.40
41 Craig Daly	.15	.40

1991-92 Cincinnati Cyclones

The 1991-92 Cincinnati Cyclones of the East Coast Hockey League are represented in this 25-card set, which was sponsored by Cincinnati Bell Telephone and 19 XIX Fox. The cards measure 2 3/8" by 3 1/2" and feature posed color action shots enclosed by a white border. The team logo and year appear across the top of the card face, with the team name in silver outlined in red. The white front bottom portion of the card carries player information, the 19XIX Fox logo, and the Cincinnati Bell Telephone logo. Horizontally oriented backs carry biography and statistics in a white box surrounded by a gray border. The cards are unnumbered and checklisted below in alphabetical order.

COMPLETE SET (25)	3.00	8.00
1 Dan Beaudette	.20	.50
2 Steve Benoit TR	.02	.10
3 Steve Cadieux	.15	.40
4 Craig Charron	.15	.40
5 David Craievich	.15	.40
6 Doug Dadswell	.20	.50
7 Dennis Desrosiers CO	.02	.10
8 Terry Ficorelli ANN	.02	.10
9 Jeff Hogden	.15	.40
10 Kevin Kerr	.15	.40
11 Jaan Luik	.15	.40
12 Scott Luik	.15	.40
13 Chris Marshall	.15	.40
14 Daryn McBride	.15	.40
15 Doug Melnyk	.15	.40
16 David Moore	.15	.40
17 Tom Neziol	.15	.40
18 Mark Romaine	.15	.40
19 Jay Rose	.15	.40
20 Martin St. Amour	.20	.50
21 Kevin Scott	.15	.40
22 Peter Schure	.15	.40
23 Steve Shaunessy	.15	.40
24 Blaine Stoughton CO	.20	.50
25 Bobby Wallwork	.15	.40

1992-93 Cincinnati Cyclones

These standard-sized cards were released in set form and sold by the team. The set includes the logo of sponsor, Bell.

COMPLETE SET (30)	3.00	8.00
1 Bill Armstrong	.10	.30
2 Ralph Barahona	.15	.40
3 Mike Bodnarchuk	.15	.40
4 Craig Charron	.15	.40
5 Todd Copeland	.15	.40
6 Doug Dadswell	.30	.75
7 Mike Dagenais	.15	.40
8 Kevin Dean	.15	.40
9 Chad Erickson	.30	.75
10 Todd Flichel	.15	.40
11 Alan Hepple	.10	.30
12 Dennis Holland	.15	.40
13 Sergei Kharin	.15	.40
14 David Latta	.15	.40
15 Jeff Madill	.15	.40
16 Jon Morris	.15	.40
17 Dean Morton	.15	.40
18 Chris Nelson	.15	.40
19 Darcy Norton	.15	.40
20 Howie Rosenblatt	.20	.50
21 Scott Shaunessy	.15	.40
22 Mario Thyer	.15	.40
23 Al Tuer	.10	.30
24 Dennis Desrosiers HCO	.02	.10
25 Blaine Stoughton ACO	.20	.50
26 Alex Ochoa TR	.10	.30
27 Mr. Cyclone Mascot	.02	.10
28 Steve Benoit EM	.02	.10
29 Terry Ficorelli ANN	.15	.40
30 Wildman Walker ANN	.08	.25

1993-94 Cincinnati Cyclones

Little is known about this set beyond the confirmed checklist. Anyone with additional information should write hockeymag@beckett.com.

COMPLETE SET (32)	4.00	10.00
1 Doug Barrault	.15	.40
2 Len Barrie	.30	.75
3 Don Biggs	.15	.40
4 Chris Cichocki	.10	.30
5 Jason Cirone	.15	.40
6 Dallas Eakins	.20	.50
7 Daniel Gauthier	.15	.40
8 Jeff Greenlaw	.15	.40
9 Rick Hayward	.15	.40
10 Gord Hynes	.15	.40
11 Ian Kidd	.15	.40
12 Marc LaBelle	.15	.40
13 Paul Lawless	.15	.40
14 Jamie Leach	.15	.40
15 Patrick Lebeau	.20	.50
16 Ray LeBlanc	.30	.75
17 Jamie Linden	.15	.40
18 Jaroslav Nedved	.15	.40
19 Darcy Norton	.15	.40
20 Pokey Reddick	.30	.75
21 Stephane Richer	.15	.40
22 Jeff Serowik	.15	.40
23 Scott Shaunessy	.15	.40
24 Brad Smyth	.10	.30
25 Dennis Desrosiers HCO	.02	.10
26 Richard Kromm ACO	.02	.10
27 Wildman Walker ANN	.02	.10
28 Mr. Cyclone Mascot	.02	.10
29 Mike Spilman TR	.02	.10
30 Steve Benoit EQM	.02	.10
31 Terry Ficorelli ANN	.02	.10
NNO Header Checklist	.02	.10

1995-96 Cincinnati Cyclones

The set features the Cyclones of the IHL. The set was produced by Edge Ice and was sold by the team at its souvenir stands.

COMPLETE SET (25)	4.00	10.00
1 Don Biggs	.20	.50
2 Frederic Chabot	.40	1.00
3 Chris Cichocki	.20	.50
4 Chris Dahlquist	.20	.50
5 Dale DeGray	.20	.50
6 Brian Dobbin	.20	.50
7 Len Esau	.20	.50
8 Jeff Greenlaw	.20	.50
9 Todd Hawkins	.20	.50
10 Duane Joyce	.20	.50
11 Chris Kontos	.30	.75
12 Marc LaBelle	.20	.50
13 Paul Lawless	.30	.75
14 Danny Lorenz	.30	.75
15 Doug MacDonald	.20	.50
16 Dave Marcinyshyn	.20	.50
17 Scott Thomas	.20	.50
18 Dave Tomlinson	.20	.50
19 Jeff Wells	.20	.50
20 Bob Wilkie	.20	.50
21 Nick Kenney TR	.02	.10
22 Mark Mills TR	.02	.10
23 Al Hill CO	.02	.10
24 Ron Smith CO	.02	.10
25 Snowbird MAS	.02	.10

1996-97 Cincinnati Cyclones

This 25-card set was produced by Split Second and was sponsored by WGRR radio and WCPD TV. The unnumbered cards feature an action photo on the front, and stats package on the back. They are numbered below according to their sweater numbers, which are prominently featured on the backs.

COMPLETE SET (25) 4.00 10.00
1 Todd MacDonald .30 .75
3 Duane Joyce .20 .50
4 Ted Crowley .20 .50
5 Jeff Wells .20 .50
6 Myles O'Connor .20 .50
12 Todd Hawkins .20 .50
13 Paul Lawless .20 .50
17 Mike Casselman .20 .50
19 Scott Thomas .30 .75
22 Don Biggs .20 .50
24 Tony Horacek .20 .50
26 Marc Laniel .20 .50
27 Dave Marcinyshyn .20 .50
28 Scott Morrow .20 .50
29 Jeff Greenlaw .20 .50
31 Geoff Sarjeant .30 .75
33 Chris Cichocki .20 .50
37 Eric Dandenault .20 .50
44 Doug MacDonald .20 .50
51 Dale DeGray .20 .50
NNO Nick Kenney TR .02 .10
NNO Mark Mills (Equip MG) .02 .10
NNO Ron Smith CO .02 .10
NNO Al Hill ASST CO .02 .10
NNO Snowbird (Mascot) .02 .10

1997-98 Cincinnati Cyclones

This set features the Cyclones of the IHL. The cards were sponsored by Cincinnati Bell, and were issued as promotional giveaways.

COMPLETE SET (24) 4.80 12.00
1 Don Biggs .30 .75
2 Paul Broten .20 .50
3 Mike Casselman .20 .50
4 Eric Dandenault .20 .50
5 Gilbert Dionne .30 .75
6 Jeff Greenlaw .20 .50
7 Todd Hawkins .20 .50
8 Burt Henderson .20 .50
9 Steven King .20 .50
10 Marc LaBelle .20 .50
11 Doug MacDonald .20 .50
12 Todd MacDonald .20 .50
13 Pat MacLeod .20 .50
14 Scott Morrow .20 .50
15 Geoff Sarjeant .30 .75
16 Todd Simon .30 .75
17 Jeff Sirkka .20 .50
18 Jeff Wells .20 .50
19 David Williams .20 .50
20 Ron Smith CO .08 .25
21 Chris Cichocki CO .08 .25
22 Snowbird MAS .02 .10
23 Nick Kenney TR .02 .10
24 Mark Mills TR .02 .10

1998-99 Cincinnati Cyclones

Card fronts feature full color photos along with team name and position. Backs feature 1997-98 statistics and biographical information. Cards are unnumbered and checklisted below in alphabetical order.

COMPLETE SET (30) 6.00 10.00
1 Kaspars Astashenko .20 .50
2 Frederic Cassivi .30 .75
3 Phil Crowe .15 .40
4 Eric Dandenault .15 .40
5 Gilbert Dionne .30 .75
6 Todd Hawkins .15 .40
7 Jani Hurme .75 2.00
8 Burt Henderson .15 .40
9 Chris Joseph .15 .40
10 Ole Kjenstad .15 .40
11 Fred Knipscheer .15 .40
12 Doug Macdonald .15 .40
13 Pat Macleod .15 .40
14 Scott Morrow .15 .40
15 Tom Nemeth .15 .40
16 Kirk Nielsen .15 .40
17 Ed Patterson .15 .40
18 Rastislav Pavlikovsky .15 .40
19 Jeff Shevalier .15 .40
20 Todd Simon .15 .40
21 Geoff Smith .15 .40
22 Jeff Wells .15 .40
23 Snowbird Mascot .02 .10
24 Nick Kenney TR .02 .10
25 Mark Mills EQ .02 .10
26 Scott Macpherson ACO .02 .10
27 Chris Cichocki ACO .02 .10
28 Ron Smith CO .02 .10
29 Team Card .02 .10
30 Logo Card .02 .10

1998-99 Cincinnati Cyclones 2

This set features the Cyclones of the IHL. The set was issued as a promotional giveaway and was sponsored by Bell Telephone.

COMPLETE SET (30) 10.00 25.00
1 Todd Hawkins .40 1.00
2 Kirk Nielsen .40 1.00
3 Ed Patterson .40 1.00
4 Fred Knipscheer .40 1.00
5 Doug Macdonald .40 1.00
6 Todd Simon .40 1.00
7 Phil Crowe .40 1.00
8 Gilbert Dionne .40 1.00
9 Scott Morrow .40 1.00
10 Rastislav Pavlikovsky .40 1.00
11 Jeff Shevalier .40 1.00
12 Kaspars Astashenko .40 1.00
13 Eric Dandenault .40 1.00
14 Burt Henderson .40 1.00
15 Chris Joseph .40 1.00
16 Pat MacLeod .40 1.00
17 Geoff Smith .40 1.00
18 Jeff Wells .40 1.00
19 Frederic Cassivi .75 2.00
20 Jani Hurme .75 2.00
21 Tom Nemeth .40 1.00
22 Olaf Kjenstad .40 1.00
23 Team Photo Card .20 .50
24 Ron Smith CO .20 .50
25 Chris Cichocki CO .20 .50
26 Scott MacPherson CO .20 .50
27 Mark Mills EM .20 .50
28 Nick Kenney TR .02 .10
29 Snowbird MASCOT .02 .10
30 PHPA Card .01 .05

1999-00 Cincinnati Cyclones

This team set of the Cincinnati Cyclones of the IHL was sponsored by Cincinnati Bell. The cards show a color action photo of each player on front and individual stats on the card backs. The cards are not numbered and are listed below alphabetically.

COMPLETE SET (27) 4.80 10.00
1 Team Logo .10 .25
2 Craig Adams .20 .50
3 Steve Bancroft .20 .50
4 Eric Dandenault .20 .50
5 Gilbert Dionne .30 .75
6 Gilbert Dionne MVP .30 .75
7 Mark Fitzpatrick .30 .75
8 Len Esau .20 .50
9 Todd Hawkins .20 .50
10 David Karpa .20 .50
11 Greg Koehler .20 .50
12 Greg Kuznik .20 .50
13 Craig McDonald .30 .75
14 Pat McLeod .20 .50
15 Ian McNeil .20 .50
16 Randy Petruk .30 .75
17 Mike Rucinski .20 .50
18 Todd Simon .30 .75
19 Nikos Tselios .30 .75
20 Stefan Ustorf .30 .75
21 Shane Willis .40 1.00
22 Chris Cichocki CO .20 .50
23 Nick Kenney TR .02 .10
24 Mark Mills EM .02 .10
25 Ron Smith HCO .20 .50
26 Snowbird MASCOT .02 .10
27 PHPA Logo .02 .10

2000-01 Cincinnati Cyclones

This set features the Cyclones of the IHL. The cards were produced by Multi-Ad Sports, and were issued as a promotional giveaway.

COMPLETE SET (30) 8.00 20.00
1 Nikos Tselios .40 .75
2 Jeremiah McCarthy .30 .50
3 Greg Kuznik .30 .75
4 Byron Ritchie .40 1.00
5 Craig MacDonald .30 .75
6 Greg Koehler .20 .50
7 Stefan Ustorf .30 .50
8 Jeff Heerema .40 1.00
9 Mike Rucinski .40 1.00
10 Ian MacNeil .20 .50
11 Gilbert Dionne .40 1.00
12 Erik Cole 1.50 4.00
13 Reggie Berg .30 .50
14 Jon Rohloff .20 .50
15 Len Esau .20 .50
16 Brian Felsner .30 .75
17 Brad DeFauw .20 .50
18 Harlan Pratt .20 .50
19 Jaroslav Svoboda .75 1.00
20 Jean-Marc Pelletier .40 1.00
21 Corey Hirsch .30 .75
22 Marc Magliarditi .30 .75
23 Ron Smith CO .20 .50
24 Mark Mills EM .04 .10
25 Nick Kenney TR .04 .10
26 Snowbird MASCOT .04 .10
27 GMC Zamboni SPONSOR .10 .25
28 Team Photo .20 .50
29 The Firstar Center .02 .10
30 PHPA Web Site .02 .10

1998-99 Cincinnati Mighty Ducks

This 29-card set was handed out at a game in February. It is not thought that it was available through any other channels, and therefore is quite difficult to acquire.

COMPLETE SET (29) 8.00 20.00
1 Buster MASCOT .08 .25
2 Marc Andreozzi TR .02 .10
3 Gary Linquist EM .02 .10
4 John Walton .30 .75
5 Ed Johnstone ACO .08 .25
6 Moe Mantha HCO .08 .25
7 Frank Banham .40 1.00
8 Mike LeClerc 1.25 3.00
9 Byron Briske .30 .75
10 Eric Lecompte .30 .75
11 Terran Sandwith .30 .75
12 Jamie Ram .40 1.00
13 Craig Reichert .30 .75
14 Joel Kwiatkowski .30 .75
15 Mike Crowley .40 1.00
16 Matt Leon .30 .75
17 Jeremy Stevenson .30 .75
18 Dan Trebil .30 .75
19 Bob Wren .30 .75
20 Lloyd Shaw .30 .75
21 Igor Nikulin .30 .75
22 Jeff Winter .30 .75
23 Tony Mohagen .30 .75
24 Tony Tuzzolino .30 .75
25 Peter LeBoutillier .30 .75
26 Tom Askey .60 1.50
27 Marc Chouinard .40 1.00
28 Scott Ferguson .30 .75
29 PHPA Web Site .02 .10

1999-00 Cincinnati Mighty Ducks

This set features the Mighty Ducks of the AHL. The set was issued as a promotional giveaway at a home game during March of 2000.

COMPLETE SET (32) 12.00 30.00
1 Parent Clubs .08 .25
2 Moe Mantha CO .08 .25
3 Jason Payne .30 .75
4 Jeff Nielsen ALUM .30 .75
5 Antti Aalto ALUM .40 1.00
6 Ruslan Salei ALUM .30 .75
7 Joel Kwiatkowski .30 .75
8 Aren Miller .40 1.00
9 Dan Trebil .30 .75
10 Rastislav Pavlikovsky .30 .75
11 Frank Banham .40 1.00
12 Scott Ferguson .30 .75
13 Maxim Balmochnykh .60 1.50
14 Darryl Laplante .60 1.50
15 Johan Davidsson .60 1.50
16 Peter Leboutillier .30 .75
17 Jesse Wallin .40 1.00
18 Alexandre Jacques .30 .75
19 B.J. Young .30 .75
20 Ed Johnstone CO .08 .25
21 Ryan Hoople .30 .75
22 Matt Cullen ALUM .75 2.00
22 Mike LeClerc .75 2.00
22 Pavel Trnka ALUM .30 .75
23 Buster MASCOT .08 .25
24 Jeremy Stevenson .30 .75
25 Jay Legault .30 .75
26 Marc Chouinard .40 1.00
27 Torrey DiRoberto .40 1.00
28 Maxim Kuznetsov .40 1.00
29 Shane Hnidy .30 .75
30 Vitali Vishnevsky .40 1.00
31 Bob Wren .30 .75
32 Gregg Naumenko .60 1.50

2001-02 Cincinnati Mighty Ducks

This set features the Mighty Ducks of the AHL. The cards were issued as a promotional giveaway at a home game late in the season. As the cards are unnumbered, they are listed below in alphabetical order.

COMPLETE SET (28) 10.00 25.00
1 Sean Avery 1.00 2.50
2 Maxim Balmochnykh .40 1.00
3 Drew Bannister .30 .75
4 Ryan Barnes .30 .75
5 Travis Brigley .30 .75
6 Aris Brimanis .30 .75
7 Steve Brule .30 .75
8 Ilja Bryzgalov 1.00 2.50
9 Garrett Burnett .40 1.00
10 Yuri Butsayev .30 .75
11 Josh DeWolf .30 .75
12 Jason Elliott .60 1.50
13 Ryan Gaucher .30 .75
14 Andy McDonald 1.00 2.50
15 Antti-Jussi Niemi .40 1.00
16 Timo Parssinen .40 1.00
17 Peter Podhradsky .30 .75
18 Bruce Richardson .30 .75
19 Bert Robertsson .30 .75
20 David Roche .30 .75
21 Jonas Ronnqvist .40 1.00
22 Jarrett Smith .30 .75
23 Brian White .30 .75
24 Jason Williams .40 1.00
25 Dwayne Zinger .30 .75
26 Mike Babcock CO .10 .25
27 Kevin Kaminski ACO .10 .25
28 Buster the Duck MASCOT .04 .10

2002-03 Cincinnati Mighty Ducks

This set was given away over the course of two home games, Dec. 14, 2002 and March 23, 2003. The cards are unnumbered and listed below by series in alphabetical order.

COMPLETE SET (28) 15.00 30.00
A1 Mike Commodore 1.25 3.00
A2 Samuel Pahlsson .75 2.00
A3 Jean-Francois Damphousse .75 2.00
A4 Todd Reirden .40 1.00
A5 Jonathan Hedstrom .75 2.00
A6 Chris O'Sullivan .40 1.00
A7 Jarrett Smith .40 1.00
A8 Travis Brigley .40 1.00
A9 Brian Gornick .40 1.00
A10 Tony Martensson .40 1.00
A11 Cory Pecker .75 2.00
A12 Nick Smith .40 1.00
A13 Cam Severson 1.25 3.00
A14 Pete Podrasky .40 1.00
B1 Ilja Bryzgalov 1.25 3.00
B2 Darryl Williams ACO .20 .50
B3 Brad Shaw CO .20 .50
B4 Buster MASCOT .04 .10
B5 Puck Boy .04 .10
B6 Jan Tabacek .40 1.00
B7 Mark Popovic .75 2.00
B8 Rob Valicevic .40 1.00
B9 Ben Guite .75 2.00
B10 Francis Belanger .40 1.00
B11 Team Photo .40 1.00
B12 Josh DeWolf .40 1.00
B13 Jason Krog .75 2.00
B14 Alexei Smirnov .40 1.00

2003-04 Cincinnati Mighty Ducks

It's thought that these were issued as promotional giveaways at two Ducks home games. Anyone with additional information, please contact us at hockeymag@beckett.com.

COMPLETE SET (28) 10.00 25.00
A1 Keith Aucoin .40 1.00
A2 Eddie Ferhi .40 1.00
A3 Mike Mottau .40 1.00
A4 Pierre-Alexander Parenteau .40 1.00
A5 Cory Pecker .40 1.00
A6 Mark Popovic .40 1.00
A7 Todd Reirden .40 1.00
A8 Andy Reierson .40 1.00
A9 Cam Severson .40 1.00
A10 Alexei Smirnov .40 1.00
A11 Nick Smith .40 1.00
A12 Joel Stepp .40 1.00
A13 Darryl Williams ACO .10 .25
A14 Puck Boy .10 .25
B1 Juha Alen .40 1.00
B2 Chris Armstrong .40 1.00
B3 Sheldon Brookbank .40 1.00
B4 Ilja Bryzgalov .75 2.00
B5 Brian Gornick .40 1.00
B6 Casey Hankinson .40 1.00
B7 Mikael Holmqvist .40 1.00
B8 Chris Kunitz 1.00 2.50
B9 Tony Martensson .40 1.00
B10 Shane O'Brien .75 2.00
B11 Joel Perrault .40 1.00
B12 Igor Pohanka .40 1.00
B13 Brad Shaw CO .10 .25
B14 Mascot .04 .10

2004-05 Cincinnati Mighty Ducks

This set was produced by Choice Marketing and given away in two parts at different Mighty Ducks home games.

COMPLETE SET (30) 15.00 30.00
1 Brad Shaw CO .20 .50
2 Dan Bylsma ACO .20 .50
3 Aaron Rome .75 2.00
4 Juha Alen .40 1.00
5 Kurtis Foster .40 1.00
6 Shane O'Brien .75 2.00
7 Mark Popovic .40 1.00
8 Tim Brent .40 1.00
9 Buster MASCOT .04 .10
10 Joel Perrault .40 1.00
11 Zenon Konopka .40 1.00
12 Igor Pohanka .40 1.00
13 Sean O'Connor .40 1.00
14 Chris Kunitz .75 2.00
15 Joffrey Lupul 1.50 4.00
16 Joel Stepp .40 1.00
17 Sheldon Brookbank .40 1.00
18 Michael Holmqvist .40 1.00
19 Cory Pecker .40 1.00
20 Curtis Glencross .40 1.00
21 Sponsor card .04 .10
22 Alexei Smirnov .40 1.00
23 Stanislav Chistov .75 2.00
24 Dustin Penner 1.50 4.00
25 Pierre Parenteau .40 1.00
26 Checklist .04 .10
27 Tomas Malec .40 1.00
28 Eddie Ferhi .40 1.00
29 Ilja Bryzgalov .75 2.00
30 Frederic Cassivi .75 2.00

1992-93 Clarkson Knights

Issued in 1993 at the end of the hockey season, this 24-card standard-size set features the Clarkson Knights of the ECAC (Eastern Collegiate Athletic Conference). The cards feature on-ice player action and posed photos on the fronts. The pictures are on a white card face with the Clarkson hockey logo and name at the top and the player's name and position at the bottom. The horizontal backs carry biography, statistics for the 1991-92 and 1992-93 seasons, and career summary. The Clarkson hockey logo appears in the lower right. The cards are unnumbered and checklisted below in alphabetical order.

COMPLETE SET (24) 4.80 12.00
1 Josh Bartell .15 .40
2 Hugo Belanger .20 .50
3 Craig Conroy .60 1.50
4 Jason Currie .15 .40
5 Steve Dubinsky .20 .50
6 Shawn Fotheringham .15 .40
7 Dave Green .15 .40
8 Ed Henrich .15 .40
9 Chris Lipsett .15 .40
10 Todd Marchant .75 2.00
11 Brian Mueller .20 .50
12 Kevin Murphy .15 .40
13 Martin d'Orsonnens .15 .40
14 Steve Palmer .15 .40
15 Patrice Robitaille .15 .40
16 Chris Rogles .20 .50
17 Jerry Rosenheck .15 .40
18 Chris de Ruiter .15 .40
19 Guy Sanderson .15 .40
20 David Seitz .15 .40
21 Mikko Tavi .15 .40
22 Patrick Theriault .15 .40
23 Marko Tuomainen .20 .50
24 Men's Hockey 1992-93 .15 .40
Martin d'Orsonnens
Steve Du

1951-52 Cleveland Barons

This set was issued as a photo pack. The cards are printed on thin card stock, and measure 9 X 6 inches. The last card, Joe Lund, may be from the previous year's set, as he did not play for Cleveland in 1951-52.

COMPLETE SET (20) 75.00 150.00
1 Bun Cook CO 5.00 10.00
2 Fred Shero 10.00 20.00
3 Ed Reigle 3.00 6.00
4 Ike Hildebrand 3.00 6.00
5 Eddie Olson 3.00 6.00
6 Jerry Reid 3.00 6.00
7 Fred Thurier 3.00 6.00
8 Steve Wochy 3.00 6.00
9 Joe Carveth 4.00 8.00
10 Tom Williams 5.00 10.00
11 Johnny Bower 25.00 50.00
12 Jack Gordon 4.00 8.00
13 Ken Schultz 3.00 6.00
14 Fern Perreault 3.00 6.00
15 Ray Ceresino 3.00 6.00
16 Bob Bailey 3.00 6.00
17 Bob Chrystal 4.00 8.00
18 Phil Samis 3.00 6.00
19 Paul Gladu 3.00 6.00
20 Joe Lund 3.00 6.00

1960-61 Cleveland Barons

This 19-card set of oversized cards measures approximately 6 3/4" by 5 3/8". The set commemorates the Cleveland Barons 1959-60 season which ended with the team in fourth place after elimination in the Calder Cup Playoffs. The white-bordered fronts display action, black-and-white player photos. A facsimile autograph is printed near the bottom of the photo on all the cards except the team photo card. The backs are blank. Since the cards are unnumbered, they are checklisted below alphabetically.

COMPLETE SET (19) 60.00 120.00
1 Ron Attwell 3.00 6.00
2 Les Binkley 5.00 10.00
3 Bill Dineen 4.00 8.00
4 John Ferguson 10.00 20.00
5 Cal Gardner 4.00 8.00
6 Fred Glover 4.00 8.00
7 Jack Gordon 4.00 8.00
8 Aldo Guidolin 4.00 8.00
9 Greg Hicks 3.00 6.00
10 Wayne Larkin 3.00 6.00
11 Moe Mantha 4.00 8.00
12 Gil Mayer 3.00 6.00
13 Eddie Mazur 3.00 6.00
14 Jim Mikol 3.00 6.00
15 Bill Needham 3.00 6.00
16 Cal Stearns 3.00 6.00
17 Bill Sutherland 4.00 8.00
18 Tom Williams 4.00 8.00
19 Team Photo 5.00 10.00

1992-93 Cleveland Lumberjacks

Issued to commemorate the Lumberjacks' first season in Cleveland, these 25 cards feature on their fronts red-trimmed and white-bordered color player action shots and measure 2 3/8" by 3 1/2". The player's name, uniform number and position appear beneath the photo in the lower white margin. The team logo and season are displayed in the margin above the photo. The logos for the two sponsors, WKNR radio and Rusterminator, rest at the bottom. The horizontal backs display the player's name, uniform number, position, biography and stats within the central white rectangle. In the wide gray border, the logos for the team and the sponsors round out the card.

COMPLETE SET (25) 4.00 10.00
1 Title Card .02 .10
2 Larry Gordon GM .02 .10
3 Paul Laus .30 .75
4 Travis Thiessen .20 .50
5 Phil Russell CO .20 .50
6 Gilbert Delorme ACO .20 .50
7 Jamie Heward .20 .50
8 Greg Andrusak .20 .50
9 David Quinn .20 .50
10 Perry Ganchar .20 .50
11 George Zajankala UER .20 .50
Birthplace misspelled
Reve
12 Todd Nelson .20 .50
13 Dave Michayluk .20 .50
14 Bruce Racine .25 .60
15 Rob Dopson .25 .60
16 Bert Godin TR .02 .10
17 Ed Patterson .25 .60
18 Justin Duberman .20 .50
19 Sandy Smith .20 .50
20 Jason Smart .20 .50
21 Ken Priestlay .20 .50
22 Daniel Gauthier .20 .50
23 Robert Melanson .20 .50
24 Mark Major .20 .50
25 Paul Dyck .20 .50

1993-94 Cleveland Lumberjacks

These 24 black-bordered cards feature the 1993-94 Cleveland Lumberjacks of the IHL (International Hockey League). The cards measure approximately 2 3/8" by 3 1/2" and display on their fronts color player action shots framed by red lines. The player's name, uniform number, and position are shown in white lettering in the black margin below the photo. The logos for sponsors WKNR SportsRadio and RusTerminator Electronic Rust Control rest at the bottom. The gray and white horizontal back carries the player's uniform number, name, position, biography, and statistics.

COMPLETE SET (24) 4.00 10.00
1 Title Card .08 .25
2 Rick Paterson CO .08 .25
3 Gilbert Delorme ACO .08 .25
4 Paul Dyck .30 .75
5 Travis Thiessen .20 .50
6 Mike Dagenais .20 .50
7 Chris Tamer .20 .50
8 Greg Andrusak .20 .50
9 Todd Hawkins .20 .50
10 Jamie Black .20 .50
11 Justin Duberman .20 .50
13 Jock Callander UER .30 .75
(Misspelled Jack
on front)
14 Leonid Toropchenko .20 .50
15 Victor Gervais .20 .50
16 Perry Ganchar .20 .50
17 Ed Patterson .20 .50
18 Ladislav Karabin .20 .50
19 Dave Michayluk .20 .50
20 Jamie Heward .20 .50
21 Pat Neaton .20 .50
22 Rob Dopson .30 .75
23 Steve Bancroft .20 .50
24 Olie Sundstrom .20 .50
25 Grant Block .20 .50

1993-94 Cleveland Lumberjacks Postcards

These 21 black-bordered cards feature the 1993-94 Cleveland Lumberjacks of the IHL (International Hockey League). The white-bordered postcards measure approximately 3 1/2" by 5 1/2" and display on their fronts color player action shots. The player's name, uniform number, position, and biography are shown in yellow lettering within a black rectangle beneath the picture. Sponsor logos for WMMS Radio and The Peak (a sports medicine and injury rehab facility) also appear on the front. The white horizontal back carries a tip on how to treat a minor muscle sprain. The cards are unnumbered and checklisted below in alphabetical order.

COMPLETE SET (22) 4.00 10.00
1 Greg Andrusak .20 .50
2 Steve Bancroft .20 .50
3 Jamie Black .20 .50
4 Grant Block .20 .50
5 Jock Callander .30 .75
6 Mike Dagenais .20 .50
7 Gilbert Delorme ACO .08 .25
8 Rob Dopson .30 .75
9 Justin Duberman .20 .50
10 Paul Dyck .30 .75
11 Perry Ganchar .20 .50
12 Todd Hawkins .20 .50
13 Jamie Heward .20 .50
14 Ladislav Karabin .20 .50
15 Dave Michayluk .20 .50
16 Pat Neaton .20 .50
17 Rick Paterson CO .08 .25
18 Ed Patterson .20 .50
19 Olie Sundstrom .20 .50
20 Chris Tamer .20 .50
21 Travis Thiessen .20 .50
22 Leonid Toropchenko .20 .50

1994-95 Cleveland Lumberjacks

This set was a game-night giveaway and features many cards that are identical in appearance to those in the 1993-94 issue. The set is unnumbered.

COMPLETE SET (25) 4.80 12.00
1 Rick Paterson HCO .08 .25
2 Philippe DeRouville .30 .75
3 Paul Dyck .25 .60
4 Rick Hayward .20 .50
5 Mike Dagenais .20 .50
6 Chris Tamer .30 .75
7 Len Barrie .30 .75
8 Eric Murano .20 .50
9 Brad Lauer .20 .50
10 Ian Moran .20 .50
11 Brian Farrell .20 .50
12 Jock Callander .30 .75
13 Jeff Christian .20 .50
14 Larry DePalma .20 .50
15 Joe Dziedzic .20 .50
16 Victor Gervais .20 .50
17 Dominic Pittis .20 .50
18 Perry Ganchar .20 .50
19 Ed Patterson .30 .75
20 Ladislav Karabin .20 .50
21 Dave Michayluk ACO .20 .50
22 Michal Straka .20 .50
23 Corey Beaulieu .20 .50
24 Olie Sundstrom .25 .60
25 Dale DeGray .20 .50

1995-96 Cleveland Lumberjacks

This 24-card set of the Cleveland Lumberjacks was produced by SplitSecond for Collector's Edge. The set is sponsored by Huntington Banks and WKNR Radio. It features color player portraits on the fronts with player information and statistics on the backs. The cards are unnumbered and checklisted below in alphabetical order.

COMPLETE SET (24) 4.80 12.00
1 Peter Allen .15 .40
2 Bill Armstrong .15 .40
3 Len Barrie .30 .75
4 Dave Baseggio .15 .40
5 Oleg Belov .15 .40
6 Drake Berehowsky .15 .40
7 Stefan Bergkvist .15 .40
8 Jock Callander .30 .75
9 Jeff Christian .15 .40
10 Philippe DeRouville .30 .75
11 Rusty Fitzgerald .15 .40
12 Corey Foster .15 .40
13 Perry Ganchar ACO .02 .10
14 Victor Gervais .15 .40
15 Rick Hayward .15 .40
16 Patrick Lalime 1.25 3.00
17 Brad Lauer .15 .40
18 Dave McLlwain .20 .50
19 Dave Michayluk .15 .40
20 Mark Osborne .15 .40
21 Rick Paterson CO .02 .10
22 Dominic Pittis .15 .40
23 Ryan Savoia .15 .40
24 Mike Stevens .15 .40
25 Title Card .02 .10

1996-97 Cleveland Lumberjacks

This postcard set was sponsored by the Peak at Marymount, and was a game-night giveaway. Cards are checklisted below in alphabetical order.

COMPLETE SET (25) 10.00 20.00
1 Peter Allen .30 .75
2 Bill Armstrong .30 .75
3 Serge Aubin .40 1.00
4 Brian Bonin .40 1.00
5 Sven Butenschon .30 .75
6 Buzz MASCOT .08 .25
7 Jock Callendar .75 2.00
8 Jeff Christian .30 .75
9 Rusty Fitzgerald .30 .75
10 Corey Foster .30 .75
11 Rick Hayward .30 .75
12 Jan Hrdina .40 1.00
13 Petr Klima .40 1.00
14 Lane Lambert .30 .75
15 Brad Lauer .30 .75
16 Dave McLlwain .40 1.00
17 Dave Michayluk .40 1.00
18 Ian Moran .40 1.00
19 Mark Osborne .30 .75
20 Jim Paek .30 .75
21 Richard Park .30 .75
22 Rick Paterson CO .08 .25
23 Ed Patterson .30 .75
24 Mike Tamburro .30 .75
25 Derek Wilkinson .30 .75

1996-97 Cleveland Lumberjacks Multi-Ad

This set features the Lumberjacks of the IHL. The set was sponsored by Mult-Ad Services and was sold by the team at it souvenir stands.

COMPLETE SET (30) 6.00 15.00
1 Checklist .02 .10
2 Peter Allen .15 .40
3 Bill Armstrong .15 .40
4 Serge Aubin .40 1.00
5 Stefan Bergkvist .15 .40
6 Brian Bonin .20 .50
7 Sven Butenschon .15 .40
8 Jock Callander .30 .75
9 Jeff Christian .15 .40
10 Rusty Fitzgerald .15 .40
11 Corey Foster .15 .40
12 Perry Ganchar CO .02 .10
13 Rick Hayward .15 .40
14 Jan Hrdina .40 1.00
15 Patrick Lalime 1.25 3.00
16 Lane Lambert .15 .40
17 Brad Lauer .15 .40
18 Dave McLlwain .30 .75
19 Dave Michayluk .30 .75
20 Ian Moran .20 .50
21 Mark Osborne .15 .40
22 Jim Paek .15 .40
23 Richard Park .15 .40
24 Rick Paterson CO .02 .10
25 Ed Patterson .15 .40
26 Mike Tamburro .15 .40
27 Derek Wilkinson .20 .50
28 Buzz MAS .02 .10
29 Heritage Night .02 .10
30 Logo Card .02 .10

1997-98 Cleveland Lumberjacks

This standard-sized set was distributed by the team and sold at home games.

COMPLETE SET (30) 4.00 20.00
1 Team Photo .02 .10
2 Perry Ganchar HCO .02 .10
3 Mark Osborne ACO .02 .10
4 Dave Baseggio .10 .30
5 Stefan Bergkvist .10 .30
6 Jock Callander .40 1.00
7 Mark Cornforth .10 .30
8 John Craighead .10 .30
9 Joe Dziedzic .10 .30
10 Vadim Epantchinsev .10 .30
11 Rusty Fitzgerald .10 .30
12 Brett Harkins .10 .30
13 Rick Hayward .20 .50
14 Pat Jablonski .40 1.00
15 Alexei Krivchenkov .10 .30
16 Lane Lambert .10 .30
17 Brad Lauer .10 .30
18 Chris Longo .10 .30
19 Jason McBain .10 .30
20 Ryan Mougenel .10 .30
21 Jim Paek .10 .30
22 Rob Pearson .10 .30
23 Eric Perrin .75 2.00
24 Martin St. Louis 2.00 5.00
25 Mike Tamburro .10 .30
26 Darren Wetherill .10 .30
27 Derek Wilkinson .40 1.00
28 Martin St. Louis 2.00 5.00
Eric Perrin
29 Buzz Mascot .02 .10
30 PHPA Web site .02 .10

1997-98 Cleveland Lumberjacks Postcards

This set features the Lumberjacks of the AHL. The postcard-sized set was given away as a promotional item at a home game.

COMPLETE SET (25) 7.20 30.00
1 Perry Ganchar HCO .08 .25
2 Mark Osborne ACO .08 .25
3 Darren Wetherill .30 .75
4 Rick Hayward .30 .75
5 Jim Paek .30 .75
6 Dave Baseggio .30 .75
7 Martin St. Louis 4.00 10.00
8 John Craighead .30 .75
9 Eric Perrin 1.50 4.00
10 Rusty Fitzgerald .30 .75
11 Chris Longo .30 .7
12 Jock Callander .75 2.0
13 Joe Dziedzic .30 .7
14 Lane Lambert .30 .7
15 Mark Cornforth .30 .7
16 Vadim Epantchisev .30 .7
17 Rob Pearson .30 .7
18 Jason McBain .30 .7
19 Alexei Krivchenkov .30 .7
20 Derek Wilkinson .40 1.0
21 Brad Lauer .30 .7
22 Stefan Bergkvist .30 .7
23 Brett Harkins .30 .7
24 Mike Tamburro .30 .7
25 Buzz Mascot .08 .2

1998-99 Cleveland Lumberjacks

This set was sponsored by The Peak at Marymount, and was initially a game-night giveaway. It later was sold through the team's concession stands.

COMPLETE SET (24) 4.80 12.0
1 Header Card .02 .1
2 Perry Ganchar HCO .02 .1
3 Dave Baseggio .20 .5
4 Jesse Belanger .20 .5
5 Karel Betik .20 .5
6 Zac Bierk .75 2.0
7 Jason Bonsignore .20 .5
8 Jock Callander .40 1.0
9 John Cullen .40 1.0
10 Xavier Delisle .20 .5
11 Brett Harkins .20 .5
12 Lane Lambert .20 .5
13 Mario Larocque .20 .5
14 Eric Lavigne .15 .4
15 Chris Longo .20 .5
16 Jim Paek .20 .5
17 Eduard Pershin .15 .4
18 Brent Peterson .20 .50
19 Jason Ruff .20 .50
20 Corey Schwab .30 .75
21 Andrei Skopintsev .20 .50
22 Corey Spring .15 .40
23 Derek Wilkinson .30 .75
24 Buzz MASCOT .02 .10

1999-00 Cleveland Lumberjacks

This 24-card set pictures the 1999-00 Cleveland Lumberjacks. Cards feature full-color player photos o a non-glossy card stock. Since no number appears, cards are listed alphabetically. It is thought that this se might have been a promotional giveaway.

COMPLETE SET (24) 4.80 12.00
1 Radim Bicanek .08 .25
2 Buzz MASCOT .02 .10
3 Kyle Calder .75 2.00
4 Jock Callander .40 1.00
5 Jeff Christian .08 .25
6 Ted Crowley .08 .25
7 Casey Hankinson .08 .25
8 Brett Harkins .20 .50
9 Chris Herperger .08 .25
10 Ty Jones .20 .50
11 Marc Lamothe .20 .50
12 Eric Lavigne .08 .25
13 Chris Longo .08 .25
14 Evgeni Nabokov 2.00 5.00
15 Jim Paek .08 .25
16 Jeff Paul .08 .25
17 Nathan Perrott .30 .75
18 Geoff Peters .08 .25
19 Todd Rohloff .08 .25
20 Remi Royer .20 .50
21 Reid Simpson .20 .50
22 Dmitri Tolkunov .20 .50
23 Todd White .20 .50
24 Header Card .01

2000-01 Cleveland Lumberjacks

This set features the Lumberjacks of the IHL. It is believed that the set was issued as a promotional giveaway in January of 2001.

COMPLETE SET (25) 8.00 20.00
1 Christian Matte .40 1.00
2 Brian Bonin .40 1.00
3 Mike Matteucci .40 1.00
4 Eric Charron .30 .75
5 Nick Naumenko .30 .75
6 Brett McLean .30 .75
7 Pavel Patera .40 .75
8 Chris Longo .40 .75
9 Ian Herbers .40 1.00
10 Pascal Dupuis .30 .75
11 Kai Nurminen .40 1.00
12 David Brumby .30 .75
13 Zac Bierk .60 2.00
14 Jonathon Shockey .30 .75
15 Darryl Laplante .40 1.00
16 J.J. Daigneault .30 .75
17 Garrett Burnett .30 .75
18 Chris Armstrong .30 .75
19 Richard Park .40 1.00
20 Todd McLellan CO .20 .50
21 Jock Callander CO .40 1.00
22 Ray Schultz .30 .75
23 Steve Aronson .40 1.00
24 Derek Gustafson .60 1.50
25 Buzz MASCOT .10 .25

2001-02 Cleveland Barons

This set features the Barons of the AHL. The set was issued as a promotional giveaway, half at a time at two different home games. The cards are unnumbered and are listed in alphabetical order.

COMPLETE SET (24) 10.00 25.00
1 Steve Bancroft .30 .75
2 Matt Carkner .30 .75
3 Jonathan Cheechoo 1.20 5.00
4 Adam Colagiacomo .40 1.00
5 Mike Craig .30 .75
6 Rob Davison .30 .75
7 Jesse Fibiger .30 .75
8 Hannes Hyvonen .30 .75
9 Jeff Jillson .75 2.00
10 Seamus Kotyk .75 2.00
11 Ryan Kraft .30 .75
12 Eric Laplante .30 .75
13 Lynn Loyns .40 1.00
14 Andy Lundbohm .30 .75
15 Graig Mischler .30 .75
16 Robert Mulick .30 .75
17 Adam Nittel .40 1.00
18 Joel Prpic .30 .75
19 Brandon Smith .30 .75
20 Vesa Toskala 1.25 3.00
21 Chad Wiseman .30 .75
22 Miroslav Zalesak .30 .75
23 Roy Sommer CO .10 .25
24 Nick Fotiu ACO .10 .25

2002-03 Cleveland Barons

e cards are unnumbered and listed below in habetical order.

MPLETE SET (24) 10.00 25.00
Matt Carkner .40 1.00
David Cloutier .40 1.00
David Cunniff ACO .04 .10
Rob Davison .40 1.00
Niko Dimitrakos .60 1.50
Jesse Fibiger .40 1.00
Tavis Hansen .40 1.00
John Jakopin .40 1.00
Seamus Kotyk .60 1.50
Ryan Kraft .40 1.00
Eric Laplante .40 1.00
Willie Levesque .40 1.00
Lynn Loyns .40 1.00
Keith McCambridge .40 1.00
Graig Mischler .40 1.00
Yuri Moscevsky .40 1.00
Robert Mulick .40 1.00
Jeff Nelson .40 1.00
Pat Rissmiller .40 1.00
Roy Sommer CO .04 .10
Scott Thomas .40 1.00
Vesa Toskala 1.25 3.00
Chad Wiseman .40 1.00
Miroslav Zalesak .40 1.00

2003-04 Cleveland Barons

MPLETE SET (25) 5.00 12.00
Brad Boyes .40 1.00
Matt Carkner .20 .50
David Cloutier .20 .50
Ryan Clowe .20 .50
Jon DiSalvatore .20 .50
Niko Dimitrakos .30 .75
Christian Ehrhoff .30 .75
Jesse Fibiger .20 .50
Marcel Goc .40 1.00
Tavis Hansen .20 .50
Todd Harvey .30 .75
Seamus Kotyk .30 .75
Lynn Loyns .20 .50
Yuri Moscevsky .20 .50
Robert Mulick .20 .50
Doug Murray .20 .50
Dmitri Patzold .40 1.00
Tomas Plihal .20 .50
Pat Rissmiller .20 .50
Grant Stevenson .20 .50
Craig Valette .20 .50
Miroslav Zalesak .20 .50
Roy Sommer HCO .04 .10
David Cunniff ACO .04 .10
Mascot .04 .10

2004-05 Cleveland Barons

MPLETE SET (27) 6.00 15.00
Riley Armstrong .20 .50
Nick Bootland .30 .75
Matt Carkner .30 .75
Ryan Clowe .40 1.00
Tim Conboy .20 .50
Scott Dobben .20 .50
Christian Ehrhoff .30 .75
Jim Fahey .20 .50
Aaron Gill .20 .50
Marcel Goc .40 1.00
Josh Gorges .30 .75
Mike Hoffman .60 1.50
Shane Joseph .20 .50
Greg Labenski .20 .50
Doug Murray .20 .50
Glenn Olson .20 .50
Dimitri Patzold .30 .75
Tomas Plihal .20 .50
Josh Prudden .20 .50
Patrick Rissmiller .20 .50
Nolan Schaefer .30 .75
Garrett Stafford .20 .50
Grant Stevenson .20 .50
Craig Valette .20 .50
Roy Sommer CO .04 .10
David Cunniff ACO .04 .10
Slapshark MASCOT .04 .10

2005-06 Cleveland Barons

OMPLETE SET (28) 8.00 15.00
Riley Armstrong .20 .50
Steve Bernier .75 2.00
Matt Carkner .20 .50
Tom Cavanagh .20 .50
Ryan Clowe .30 .75
Tim Conboy .20 .50
Ray DiLauro .20 .50
Josh Gorges .20 .50
Josh Hennessy .20 .50
Jamie Holden .20 .50
Mike Iggulden .20 .50
Shane Joseph .20 .50
Lukas Kaspar .20 .50
Doug Murray .30 .75
Glenn Olson .20 .50
Dmitri Patzold .40 1.00
Tomas Plihal .20 .50
Joshua Prudden .20 .50
Pat Rissmiller .20 .50
Nolan Schaefer .40 1.00
Garrett Stafford .20 .50
Brad Staubitz .20 .50
Grant Stevenson .20 .50
Jonathan Tremblay .20 .50
Craig Valette .20 .50
Roy Sommer HC .02 .10
David Cunniff AC .02 .10
Jock Callander .02 .10

1998-99 Colorado Gold Kings

his set was handed out at a home game. Sets that eren't given away were later sold by the team at its ouvenir shop.

OMPLETE SET (24) 3.00 8.00
Nicholas Chabot .20 .50
Trevor Converse .20 .50
R.J. Enga .20 .50
Anton Federov .20 .50
Wade Fennig .20 .50
Mark Fox .20 .50
Jeff Grabinsky .20 .50
Shawn Harris .20 .50
Don Lester .20 .50
Kirk Llano .20 .50
Craig Lyons .20 .50
Rob McCaig .20 .50
Rusty McKie .20 .50
Kevin McKinnon .20 .50
Bryan McMullen .20 .50
Chad Penney .20 .50
Tom Perry .20 .50
18 Bob Revermann .20 .50
19 Bogdan Rudenko .20 .50
20 Jason Simon .20 .50
21 Jeff Sirkka .20 .50
22 Brad Toporowski .20 .50
23 Kirk Tomlinson CO .08 .25
24 King Midas Mascot .02 .10

1998-99 Colorado Gold Kings Postcards

This 5x7 set was issued with blank backs and is not numbered. It is believed they were used at player signings and were never issued in team set form, making a complete set quite difficult to compile.

COMPLETE SET (22) 8.00 20.00
1 Jason Simon .60 1.50
2 Brad Toporowski .60 1.50
3 Tom Perry .60 1.50
4 Jeff Sirkka .60 1.50
5 Chad Penney .60 1.50
6 Bryan McMullen .60 1.50
7 Bogdan Rudenko .60 1.50
8 Kevin McKinnon .60 1.50
9 Bob Revermann .60 1.50
10 Craig Lyons .60 1.50
11 Kirk Tomlinson HCO .20 .50
12 Trevor Converse .60 1.50
13 Jeff Grabinsky .60 1.50
14 R.J. Enga .60 1.50
15 Shawn Harris .60 1.50
16 Anton Fedorov .60 1.50
17 Hakan Jansson .60 1.50
18 Wade Fennig .60 1.50
19 Don Lester .60 1.50
20 Mark Fox .60 1.50
21 Kirk Llano .60 1.50
22 McDonald's Coupon .02 .10

1999-00 Colorado Gold Kings Taco Bell

This set features the Gold Kings of the WCHL. The set was sponsored by Taco Bell and sold by the team at home games.

COMPLETE SET (26) 5.00 12.00
1 Travis Thiessen .20 .50
2 R.J. Enga .20 .50
3 Tom Perry .20 .50
4 Corey Lyons .20 .50
5 Bogdan Rudenko .20 .50
6 Don Lester CO .08 .25
7 Stephane Madore .20 .50
8 Steve Dowhy .20 .50
9 Greg Eisler .20 .50
10 Jean-Francois Picard .20 .50
11 King Midas MAS .08 .25
12 Steve Vezina .30 .75
13 Kevin McKinnon .20 .50
14 Craig Lyons .20 .50
15 Aaron Schweitzer .20 .50
16 Carl LeBlanc .20 .50
17 Daniel Olers .20 .50
18 Dean Ewen .20 .50
19 Frederik Beaubien .30 .75
20 Kirk Tomlinson .20 .50
21 Wade Fennig .20 .50
22 Kristoffer Eriksson .20 .50
23 Rob McCaig .20 .50
24 Greg Gatto .20 .50
25 Colorado Gold Kings .08 .25
26 Taco Bell Logo .02 .10

1999-00 Colorado Gold Kings Wendy's

This set features the Gold Kings of the WCHL. The set features postcard-sized photos and a Wendy's ad on the back of each. The set was sold by the team at home games.

COMPLETE SET (22) 4.00 10.00
1 Jean-Francois Picard .20 .50
2 Corey Lyons .20 .50
3 Eric Long .20 .50
4 Wade Fennig .20 .50
5 R.J. Enga .20 .50
6 Travis Thiessen .20 .50
7 Daniel Olers .20 .50
8 Carl LeBlanc .20 .50
9 Greg Eisler .20 .50
10 Kevin McKinnon .20 .50
11 Dean Ewen .20 .50
12 Stephane Madore .20 .50
13 Darcy Anderson .20 .50
14 Tom Perry .20 .50
15 Rob McCaig .20 .50
16 Bogdan Rudenko .20 .50
17 Steve Vezina .30 .75
18 Aaron Schweitzer .20 .50
19 Craig Lyons .20 .50
20 Kirk Tomlinson CO .20 .50
21 Don Lester CO .08 .25
22 King Midas MAS .08 .25

2001-02 Colorado Gold Kings

COMPLETE SET (22) 10.00
1 Dwayne Blais .20 .50
2 Aaron Boh .20 .50
3 Zac Boyer .20 .50
4 Chad Cabana .20 .50
5 Colin Chaulk .20 .50
6 Kirk Daubenspeck .30 .75
7 R.J. Enga .20 .50
8 Mike Garrow .20 .50
9 Mark Gowan .20 .50
10 Brent Henley .20 .50
11 Darcy Johnson .20 .50
12 Jason Knox .20 .50
13 Cam Kryway .20 .50
14 Craig Lyons .20 .50
15 Mike Nicholishen .20 .50
16 Tom Perry .20 .50
17 Greg Schmidt .20 .50
18 Juraj Slovak .20 .50
19 Travis Thiessen .30 .75
20 Allen Pedersen HCO .04 .10
21 Kevin McKinnon ACO .04 .10
22 Mascot .04 .10

2003-04 Colorado Eagles

COMPLETE SET (25) 8.00 20.00
1 Lee Arnold .40 1.00
2 Ryan Bach .40 1.00
3 Gian Baldrica .40 1.00
4 Daniel Bohac .40 1.00
5 Igor Bonderev .40 1.00
6 Jesse Cook .40 1.00
7 Phil Crowe .60 1.50
8 Fraser Filipic .40 1.00
9 Aaron Grosul .40 1.00
10 Cam Kuzyk .40 1.00
11 Mike McGhan .40 1.00
12 Riley Nelson .40 1.00
13 Greg Pankewicz .40 1.00
14 Brad Patterson .40 1.00
15 Lee Ruff .40 1.00
16 Scott Swanson .40 1.00
17 Brent Thompson .60 1.50
18 Ryan Tobler .60 1.50
19 Brad Williamson .40 1.00
20 Karlis Zirnis .40 1.00
21 Chris Stewart CO .04 .10
22 Ralph Backstrom GM .04 .10
23 Mascot .04 .10
24 Team Photo .04 .10
25 Staff .04 .10

2004-05 Colorado Eagles

COMPLETE SET (24) 15.00
1 Team Card .04 .10
2 Ralph Backstrom .04 .10
3 Paulo Colaiacovo .40 1.00
4 Jesse Cook .30 .75
5 Matt Desrosiers .30 .75
6 Fraser Filipic .30 .75
7 Aaron Grosul .30 .75
8 Chris Hartsburg .30 .75
9 Mike Lephart .30 .75
10 Kris Mallette .30 .75
11 Kevin Marsh .30 .75
12 Kevin McDonald .30 .75
13 Riley Nelson .30 .75
14 Greg Pankewicz .30 .75
15 Sean Robertson .30 .75
16 Lee Ruff .30 .75
17 Chris Stewart CO .30 .75
18 David Svagrovsky .30 .75
19 Ryan Tobler .30 .75
20 Tyler Weiman .30 .75
21 Brad Williamson .30 .75
22 Karlis Zirnis .30 .75
23 Slapshot MASCOT .04 .10
24 Team Staff .04 .10

2005-06 Colorado Eagles

COMPLETE SET (26) 8.00 20.00
1 Erik Adams .40 1.00
2 Lee Arnold .40 1.00
3 Jeff Blair .40 1.00
4 Les Borsheim .40 1.00
5 Paulo Colaiacovo .60 1.50
6 Matt Desrosiers .40 1.00
7 Fraser Filipic .40 1.00
8 Aaron Grosul .40 1.00
9 Chris Hartsburg .40 1.00
10 Garrett Larson .40 1.00
11 Jason Lundmark .40 1.00
12 Ed McGrane .40 1.00
13 Riley Nelson .40 1.00
14 Greg Pankewicz .40 1.00
15 Nick Parillo .40 1.00
16 Scott Polaski .40 1.00
17 Sean Robertson .40 1.00
18 Ryan Tobler .40 1.00
19 Brad Williamson .40 1.00
20 Chris Stewart CO .02 .10
21 Phil Crowe AC .02 .10
22 Ralph Backstrom PRES GM .10 .25
23 Team Staff .02 .10
24 Eagles Chicks DANCERS .40 1.00
25 Slapshot MASCOT .02 .10
26 Colorado Eagles .20 .50

2006-07 Colorado Eagles

COMPLETE SET (31) 6.00 15.00
1 Team Card .10 .25
2 Erik Adams .30 .75
3 Lee Arnold .30 .75
4 Jay Birnie .30 .75
5 Tim Boron .30 .75
6 Les Borsheim .30 .75
7 Paulo Colaiacovo .40 1.00
8 Marco Emond .30 .75
9 Fraser Filipic .30 .75
10 Steve Haddon .30 .75
11 Chris Hartsburg .30 .75
12 Brent Hughes .30 .75
13 Seth Leonard .30 .75
14 Ed McGrane .30 .75
15 Riley Nelson .30 .75
16 Greg Pankewicz .30 .75
17 Scott Polaski .30 .75
18 Sean Robertson .30 .75
19 Aaron Schneekloth .30 .75
20 Craig Strain .30 .75
21 Ryan Tobler .30 .75
22 Brad Williamson .30 .75
23 Slapshot MASCOT .10 .25
24 Chris Stewart CO .10 .25
25 Phil Crowe ACO .10 .25
26 Ryan Bach ACO .10 .25
27 Ralph Backstrom PRES .10 .25
28 Tony Deynzer EQ MGR .10 .25
29 Chris Porowski TR .10 .25
30 Tori Holt ANN .10 .25
31 Eagles Chicks DANCERS .20 .50

2007-08 Colorado Eagles

COMPLETE SET (30) 6.00 15.00
1 Team Picture .30 .75
2 Erik Adams .30 .75
3 Jason Beatty .30 .75
4 Jay Birnie .30 .75
5 Les Borsheim .30 .75
6 Bryan Bridges .30 .75
7 Fraser Filipic .30 .75
8 Steve Haddon .30 .75
9 Chris Hartsburg .30 .75
10 Dave Iannazzo .30 .75
11 Sebastien Laplante .30 .75
12 Seth Leonard .30 .75
13 Ed McGrane .30 .75
14 Riley Nelson .30 .75
15 Greg Pankewicz .30 .75
16 Scott Polaski .30 .75
17 Aaron Schneekloth .30 .75
18 Brett Thurston .30 .75
19 Ryan Tobler .30 .75
20 Kris Wiebe .30 .75
21 Brad Williamson .30 .75
22 Chris Stewart HC .30 .75
23 Ryan Bach AC .30 .75
24 Tony Deynzer EQ .30 .75
25 Chris Porowski .30 .75
26 Ralph Backstrom .30 .75
27 Phil Crowe .30 .75
28 Tori Holt .30 .75
29 Eagles Chicks .20 .50
30 Slapshot MASCOT .20 .50

2013-14 Colorado Eagles

COMPLETE SET (25) 6.00 15.00
A01 Marc Cheverie .30 .75
A02 Kyle Ostrow .30 .75
A03 A.J. Hau .30 .75
A04 Daniel Johnston .30 .75
A05 Trent Daavettila .30 .75
B01 Kevin Ulanski .30 .75
B02 John Ryder .30 .75
B03 Kevin Young .30 .75
B04 Ryan Bach Goal. CO .30 .75
B05 Greg Gardner .30 .75
C01 Adam Brown .30 .75
C02 Arthur Bidwill .30 .75
C03 Chris Stewart CO .30 .75
C04 Isaac Smeltzer .30 .75
C05 Jesse Mychan .30 .75
D01 Aaron Schneekloth Asst. CO .30 .75
D02 Mark Nemec .30 .75
D03 Riley Nelson .30 .75
D04 Dylan Hood .30 .75
D05 Alex Hudson .30 .75
E01 Ralph Backstrom .30 .75
E02 Paul Phillips .30 .75
E03 Jason Beatty .30 .75
E04 Luke Fulghum .30 .75
E05 Jonathan Parker .30 .75

2014-15 Colorado Eagles

COMPLETE SET (20) 6.00 15.00
A01 Clarke Saunders .30 .75
A02 Mark Nemec .30 .75
A03 Jordan Kwas .30 .75
A04 Sean Zimmerman .30 .75
A05 Brock Nixon .30 .75
B01 Darryl Bootland .30 .75
B02 Curtis Gedig .30 .75
B03 Greg Gardner .30 .75
B04 Vitali Pavlov .30 .75
B05 Jonathan Parker .30 .75
C01 Trent Daavettila .30 .75
C02 Teigan Zahn .30 .75
C03 Brett Kulak .30 .75
C04 Chris Knowlton .30 .75
C05 Derek Rodwell .30 .75
D01 Kyle Kraemer .30 .75
D02 Collin Bowman .30 .75
D03 Doug Carr .30 .75
D04 Chris Duszynski .30 .75
D05 Nathan Moon .30 .75

2002-03 Columbia Inferno

COMPLETE SET (18) 10.00 25.00
97 Josh Blackburn .75 2.00
98 Paul Cabana .50 1.25
99 Robin Carruthers .50 1.25
100 Trevor Demmans .50 1.25
101 Regan Darby .50 1.25
102 Corey Hessler .50 1.25
103 Eric Labelle .75 2.00
104 Denis Martynyuk .50 1.25
105 Barrie Moore .50 1.25
106 Justin Morrison .50 1.25
107 Sean Owens .50 1.25
108 Chris Pittman .50 1.25
109 Tim Smith .50 1.25
110 Chris St. Croix .50 1.25
111 Rejean Stringer .50 1.25
112 Matt Ulwelling .50 1.25
113 Dennis Vial 1.25 3.00
114 Shawn Wansborough .50 1.25

2003-04 Columbia Inferno

This set was sold by the team at home games. The numbering reflects this set as part of the entire run of RBI Sports series this year. The production run was reported to be 250 sets.

COMPLETE SET (16) 10.00 25.00
97 Greg Amadio .60 1.50
98 Josh Blackburn .75 2.00
99 Alexandre Burrows .60 1.50
100 Paul Cabana .60 1.50
101 Robin Carruthers .60 1.50
102 Derek Eastman .60 1.50
103 Terry Harrison .60 1.50
104 Corey Hessler .60 1.50
105 Eric Labelle .60 1.50
106 Robert McVicar .75 2.00
107 Barrie Moore .60 1.50
108 Brandon Nolan .60 1.50
109 Chris Pittman .60 1.50
110 Tim Smith .75 2.00
111 Chris St. Croix .60 1.50
112 Dennis Vial .75 2.00

2003-04 Columbia Inferno Update

Produced by RBI Sports as a late season update, this was limited to 250 sets.

COMPLETE SET (6) 2.00 5.00
50 Mike Hanson .40 1.00
51 Sean Owens .40 1.00
52 Mike Roemensky .40 1.00
53 Marc-Andre Roy .40 1.00
54 Jesse Schultz .40 1.00
55 Matt Ulwelling .40 1.00

1966-67 Columbus Checkers

This 16-card set measures 4 x 7 1/4" and features a black and white photo on the front along with players name at the bottom. Backs are blank. Cards are unnumbered and checklisted below alphabetically.

COMPLETE SET (16) 35.00 70.00
1 John Bailey 2.50 5.00
2 Moe Bartoli 2.50 5.00
3 Kerry Bond 2.50 5.00
4 Andre Daoust 2.50 5.00
5 Bert Fizzell 2.50 5.00
6 Marcel Goudreau 2.50 5.00
7 Jim Graham 2.50 5.00
8 Paul Jackson 2.50 5.00
9 Ken Laidlaw 2.50 5.00
10 Noel Lirette 2.50 5.00
11 Gary Longman 2.50 5.00
12 Garry Macmillan 2.50 5.00
13 Gary Mork 2.50 5.00
14 Matt Thorpe 2.50 5.00
15 Jack Turner 2.50 5.00
16 Alton White 2.50 5.00

1967-68 Columbus Checkers

Little is known about this early team-issued photo set from the Checkers of the IHL. It is believed they were issued as a promotional item in response to mailed-in requests from fans. Any further information can be forwarded to hockeymag@beckett.com.

COMPLETE SET (16) 37.50 75.00
1 Team Photo 2.50 5.00
2 Moe Bartoli 2.50 10.00
3 Bill Bond 2.50 5.00
4 Serge Boudreault 2.50 5.00
5 Gord Dibley 2.50 10.00
6 Bert Fizzell 2.50 5.00
7 Chuck Kelly 2.50 5.00
8 Ken Saunders 2.50 5.00
9 Nelson Leclair 2.50 5.00
10 Real Paquette 2.50 5.00
11 Dick Proceviat 2.50 5.00
12 Hartley Estabrooks 2.50 5.00
13 Ken Sutyla 2.50 5.00
14 Nelson Tremblay 2.50 5.00
15 Jack Turner 2.50 5.00
16 Al White 2.50 5.00

1997-98 Columbus Cottonmouths

This 24-card set was handed out over the span of five games, and thus is extremely difficult to find in complete form.

COMPLETE SET (24) 8.00 20.00
1 Jerome Bechard .40 1.00
2 Chris Bergeron .40 1.00
3 Claude Fillion .40 1.00
4 Eric Germain .40 1.00
5 Brian Idalski .40 1.00
6 Mick Kempffer .40 1.00
7 Olaf Kienstadt .40 1.00
8 Doug Mann .40 1.00
9 Grady Manson .40 1.00
10 Derek Marchand .40 1.00
11 Bobby Marshall .40 1.00
12 Randy Murphy .40 1.00
13 Frankie Ouellette .60 1.50
14 Kevin Plager .40 1.00
15 Brad Prefontaine .40 1.00
16 Marcel Richard .40 1.00
17 John Sincinski .40 1.00
18 Greg Taylor .40 1.00
19 David Wainwright .40 1.00
20 Tom Wilson .40 1.00
21 Phil Roberto GM .08 .25
22 Bruce Garber HCO .08 .25
23 Charles B. Morrow .08 .25
24 Pete Carson .40 1.00

1998-99 Columbus Cottonmouths

This 24-card set was handed out at a home game in March of that season, and was later sold for at the team's souvenir stands for $5 per set.

COMPLETE SET (24) 3.60 9.00
1 Jerome Bechard .20 .50
2 Dan Brown .20 .50
3 Derek Crimin .20 .50
4 Claude Fillion .20 .50
5 Brian Idalski .20 .50
6 Mick Kempffer .20 .50
7 Grady Manson .20 .50
8 Roman Markhovski .20 .50
9 Mike Martens .20 .50
10 David Neilson .20 .50
11 Frankie Ouellette .20 .50
12 Kevin Plager .20 .50
13 Brad Prefontaine .20 .50
14 Marcel Richard .20 .50
15 Corwin Saurdiff .20 .50
16 Jean-Alain Schneider .20 .50
17 Robbie Sinclair .20 .50
18 Thomas Stewart .20 .50
19 Tom Wilson .20 .50
20 Derek Marchand ACO .02 .10
21 Phil Roberto GM .02 .10
22 Bruce Garber HCO .02 .10
23 Pete Carson HTR .02 .10
24 Martha Morrow .20 .50

1999-00 Columbus Cottonmouths

This set features the Cottonmouths of the CHL. The set was handed out as a promotional giveaway at home games, with one five-card strip being issued at each game. The complete set was later sold by the team for $5.

COMPLETE SET (28) 4.80 12.00
1 Aaron Vickar .20 .50
2 Kamil Kuriplach .20 .50
3 Mick Kempffer .20 .50
4 Kevin Plager .20 .50
5 Martha Morrow OWN .08 .25
6 Derek Crimin .20 .50
7 Jason Given .20 .50
8 Marcel Richard .20 .50
9 Ryan Aikia .20 .50
10 Phil Roberto GM .08 .25
11 Jerome Bechard .20 .50
12 Doug Mann .20 .50
13 Mark Martins .20 .50
14 Tommi Santala .30 .75
15 Bruce Garber HCO .08 .25
16 Mark Scott .20 .50
17 Kelly Van Hiltgen .20 .50
18 Frankie Ouellette .30 .75
19 Jaroslav Kerestes .20 .50
20 Brian Idalski ACO .08 .25
21 Per Fernhall .20 .50
22 Jackson Hegland .20 .50
23 Robert Frid .20 .50
24 Olaf Kjenstad .30 .75
25 Randy Scrimshire EQM .08 .25
26 Brodie Coffin .20 .50
27 Andy Powers .20 .50
28 Tonda Jackson AGM .08 .25

2000-01 Columbus Cottonmouths

This set features the Cottonmouths of the CHL. The cards were issued as giveaways over the course of five home dates, in the form of five-card perforated strips.

COMPLETE SET (25) 8.00 20.00
1 Jerome Bechard .40 1.00
2 Ryan Brown .40 1.00
3 Kris Cantu .40 1.00
4 Mick Kempffer .40 1.00
5 Jaroslav Kerestes .40 1.00
6 Doug Mann .40 1.00
7 Bobby Marshall .40 1.00
8 Mike Martens .40 1.00
9 Martin Menard .40 1.00
10 Riley Nelson .40 1.00
11 Frankie Ouellette .40 1.00
12 Daniel Payette .40 1.00
13 Andy Powers .40 1.00
14 Greg Quebec .40 1.00
15 Blaine Russell .40 1.00
16 Drew Schoneck .40 1.00
17 Kris Schultz .40 1.00
18 Rob Schweyer .40 1.00
19 Blake Sheane .40 1.00
20 Craig Stahl .40 1.00
21 Bruce Garber CO .10 .25
22 Phil Roberto GM .10 .25
23 Randy Scrimpshire EM .10 .25
24 Boomer MASCOT .10 .25
25 Teri LaSalle TR .10 .25

2002-03 Columbus Cottonmouths

COMPLETE SET (24) 8.00 20.00
1 Jerome Bechard .40 1.00
2 Phil Cole .40 1.00
3 Randy Copley .60 1.50
4 Brent Cullaton .40 1.00
5 Mitch Fritz .40 1.00
6 Chad Hamilton .40 1.00
7 J.J.Hunter .40 1.00
8 Matus Kostur .60 1.50
9 Mike Lee .60 1.50
10 Carlyle Lewis .60 1.50
11 Andrew Long .40 1.00
12 Sean McAslan .40 1.00
13 Darren McAusland .40 1.00
14 John Morlang .40 1.00
15 Mike Morrison .60 1.50
16 Ryan Risidore .40 1.00
17 Bart Rushmer .40 1.00
18 Darren Tiemstra .40 1.00
19 Jeff Zehr .60 1.50
20 Phil Roberto GM/CO .10 .25
21 Larry Kish ACO .10 .25
22 Randy Scrimpshire EQM .10 .25
23 Boomer Mascot .02 .10
24 Owners .02 .10

2003-04 Columbus Cottonmouths

This set was issued as a promotional giveaway over two home games. The cards were issued in perforated sheet form.

COMPLETE SET (30) 15.00 30.00
1 Salvador Diaz-Verson OWN .04 .10
2 Shelby Amos OWN .04 .10
3 Brian Curran CO .04 .10
4 Jerome Bechard ACO .04 .10
5 Heath Kaufman EQM .04 .10
6 Jason Stevens TR .04 .10
7 Rumun Ndur .75 2.00
8 Jason Tapp .75 2.00
9 Mitch Fritz .75 2.00
10 Marc-Andre Thinel .75 2.00
11 Ryan Davis .40 1.00
12 Joel Martin .75 2.00
13 Olivier Michaud .60 1.50
14 Tomas Micka .40 1.00
15 Mascot .04 .10
16 Brad Voth .40 1.00
17 Colin Pepperall .40 1.00
18 Dan Tudin .40 1.00
19 Matt Shasby .40 1.00
20 Mathieu Roy .75 2.00
21 Carlyle Lewis .40 1.00
22 John Morlang .40 1.00
23 Kenton Smith .40 1.00
24 Peter Hogan .40 1.00
25 Ryan Risidore .40 1.00
26 Christian Larrivee .75 2.00
27 Dan Tessier .75 2.00
28 Jean-Francois Plourde .40 1.00
29 Ray DiLauro .40 1.00
30 Matus Kostur .75 2.00

2004-05 Columbus Cottonmouths

Very little is known about this set featuring the Cottonmouths of the SPHL and no pricing is available. Please forward any additional info to hockeymag@beckett.com.

COMPLETE SET
1 Terry Friesen
2 Mick Kempffer
3 Joel Pullman
4 Chris Rook
5 Chad Rycroft
6 Brent Toews
7 Orrin Hergott
8 Tylor Keller
9 Ryan Haggerty
10 Tom McMonagle
11 Colby Will
12 Lorne Misita
13 Matt Mathias
14 Ryan Rutz
15 Craig Stahl
16 Ryan Aikia
17 Brock Johnson
18 Tim Green
19 Daryl Moor
20 Doug Mann
21 Jim Underwood
22 Jerome Bechard CO
23 Michael Slayton EQM
24 Jason Stevens TR

2003-04 Columbus Stars

This set features the Stars of the UHL. The set is labeled as a "youth season pass" on the front. The names of the players are not listed, but they can be identified by their jersey numbers. The back of each card lists the Stars schedule. Since the team folded midway through the season, only a handful of these cards were given out.

COMPLETE SET (5)
1 Tom Nemeth
2 Eric Naud
3 Greg Hewitt
4 Scott Levins
5 Chris Taliercio

2000-01 Connecticut Huskies

This set features the Huskies of the NCAA. It is believed that it was issued as a promotional giveaway as are all NCAA issues, but that has not been confirmed. The cards are printed on heavier card stock than usual and feature a swirling blue design along the bottom front.

COMPLETE SET (18) 15.00 30.00
1 Mike Anderson .75 2.00
2 Bret Bostock .75 2.00
3 Mike Boylan .75 2.00
4 Scott Brown .75 2.00
5 Ron D'Angelo .75 2.00
6 Eric Goclowski .75 2.00
7 Michael Goldkind .75 2.00
8 Matt Herhal .75 2.00
9 Anders Johnson .75 2.00
10 Kurt Kamienski .75 2.00
11 Trent Landry .75 2.00
12 Ciro Longobardi .75 2.00
13 Charles Ridolf .75 2.00
14 Evan Schwarz .75 2.00
15 Travis Wood .75 2.00
16 Bruce Marshall CO .20 .50
17 UCONN Huskies .20 .50
18 UCONN SCHEDULE .04 .10

1992-93 Cornell Big Red

This set features Cornell of the NCAA and is believed to be a promotional giveaway. The cards measure an oversized 2 3/4 by 3 3/4. They feature a posed color photo on the front with a white border and the words Cornell Hockey 92 93 on the front.The cards are listed below in alphabetical order.

COMPLETE SET (30) 6.00 15.00
1 Andrew Bandurski .40 1.00
2 Etienne Belzile .20 .50
3 Geoff Bumstead .30 .75
4 Brad Chartrand .20 .50
5 Rick Davis .20 .50
6 John DeHart .20 .50
7 Andre Doll .20 .50
8 P.C. Drouin .40 1.00
9 Dan Dufresne .20 .50
10 Blair Ettles .20 .50
11 Christian Felli .20 .50
12 Russ Hammond .20 .50
13 Shaun Hannah .20 .50
14 Steve Hayden .20 .50
15 Bill Holowatiuk .20 .50
16 Ryan Hughes .20 .50
17 Jake Karam .20 .50
18 Jiri Kloboucek .20 .50
19 Geoff Lopatka .20 .50
20 Joel McArter .20 .50
21 Tyler McManus .20 .50
22 Devon Nielsen .20 .50
23 Geoff Raynak .20 .50
24 Mike Sancimino .20 .50
25 Mark Scollan .20 .50
26 Tim Shean .20 .50
27 Greg Swenson .20 .50
28 Alex Vershinin .20 .50
29 Jason Vogel .20 .50
30 Mark Taylor ACO .02 .10

1993-94 Cornell Big Red

As typically is the case with NCAA sets, this series was issued as a promotional giveaway. The cards are unnumbered, so the set is checklisted below in alphabetical order.

COMPLETE SET (30) 4.80 12.00
1 Vincent Auger .15 .40
2 Andrew Bandurski .15 .40
3 Geoff Bumstead .15 .40
4 Brad Chartrand .15 .40
5 Matt Cooney .15 .40
6 John DeHart .15 .40
7 Andre Doll .15 .40
8 Dan Dufresne .15 .40
9 Blair Ettles .15 .40
10 Christian Felli .15 .40
11 Tony Fergin .15 .40
12 Shaun Hannah .15 .40
13 Bill Holowatiuk .15 .40
14 Jake Karam .15 .40
15 Jason Kendall .15 .40
16 Jiri Kloboucek .15 .40
17 Geoff Lopatka .15 .40
18 Joel McArter .15 .40
19 Tyler McManus .15 .40
20 Jamie Papp .15 .40
21 Mike Sancimino .15 .40
22 Mark Scollan .15 .40
23 Tim Shean .15 .40
24 Eddy Skazyk .15 .40
25 Alex Vershinin .15 .40
26 Jason Weber .15 .40
27 Steve Wilson .15 .40
28 Chad Wilson .15 .40
29 Jason Zubkus .15 .40
30 Mark Taylor ACO .02 .10

1991-92 Cornwall Royals

This 28-card set measures approximately 2 5/8" by 3 3/4". The fronts feature borderless posed color player photos. The player's name appears in the left upper corner, while the team logo is in the right upper corner. The Religious Hospitallers Of St. Joseph Health Centre Of Cornwall logo is printed in a white bar under the photo. On a white background, the backs carry "Royals Against Illegal Drug Tips from Cornwall Police Service" in the upper portion and sponsor logos below.

COMPLETE SET (29) 4.00 10.00
1 Jason Meloche .15 .40
2 Mark Desantis .15 .40
3 Richard Raymond .15 .40
4 Gord Pell .15 .40
5 Dave Lemay .15 .40
6 John Lovell CO .02 .10
7 Ryan Vandenbussche .40 1.00
8 David Babcock .15 .40
9 Sam Oliveira .15 .40
10 Jeremy Stevenson .20 .50
11 Todd Walker .15 .40
12 Jean-Alain Schneider .15 .40
13 Ilpo Kauhanen .20 .50
14 Guy Leveque .20 .50
15 Shayne Gaffar .15 .40
16 Rival Fullum .15 .40
17 Mike Prokopec .20 .50
18 Nathan LaFayette .20 .50
19 Larry Courville .20 .50
20 Chris Clancy .15 .40
21 Tom Nemeth .20 .50
22 Jeff Reid .15 .40
23 Paul Andrea .15 .40
24 John Slaney .40 1.00
25 Alan Letang .15 .40
26 Rob Dykeman .20 .50
27 Paul Fixter CO .02 .10
Brian O'Leary CO
28 Chief of Police .02 .10
29 Checklist .02 .10

1999-00 Cornwall Colts

This set features the Colts of the COHL, a tier 2 junior league. The listing below is not complete.

COMPLETE SET
1 Travis Albers
2 Joel Bergeron
3 Matt Collins
4 Jeff Legue
5 Kacey McDonell
6 Luc Paquin

2003-04 Cornwall Colts

The Colts play in the Central Junior Hockey League in Ontario, a Tier 2 circuit. Only two cards are confirmed to exist for this set so far. Information on others can be sent to hockeymag@beckett.com.

COMPLETE SET
1 Aaron Bogosian .40 1.00
2 Sean Flanagan .40 1.00

1999-00 Corpus Christi IceRays

This set features the IceRays of the WPHL. The set was produced by Grandstand and issued in two series. The second series was issued during the playoffs, so these contain complete 1999-2000 stats. The cards are unnumbered, and so are listed in alphabetical order.

COMPLETE SET (46) 8.00 20.00
1 Tyler Boucher .20 .50
2 Geoff Bumstead .30 .75
3 Paul Doherty .20 .50
4 Pat Dunn .20 .50
5 Jason Genik .20 .50
6 Regan Harper .20 .50
7 Brent Hoiness .20 .50
8 Trevor Janicki .20 .50
9 Cory Johnson .20 .50
10 Alex Kholomeyev .30 .75
11 Roger Lewis .20 .50
12 Dustin McArthur .20 .50
13 Darryl Olsen .20 .50
14 Jody Praznik .20 .50
15 Tobin Praznik .20 .50
16 Bob Quinnell .20 .50
17 Chris Robertson .20 .50
18 Layne Roland .20 .50
19 Andy Ross .20 .50
20 Dennis Shiryaev .20 .50
21 Eddy Skazyk .20 .50
22 Mike Tomlinson .20 .50
23 Phil Valk .20 .50
24 Quinten Van Horlick .20 .50
25 Mike Vandenberghe .20 .50
26 Kurt Wickenheiser .20 .50
27 Brad Wingfield .20 .50
28 Taylor Hall CO .20 .50
29 Jody Praznik .20 .50
30 Scott Brower .20 .50
31 Geoff Bumstead AS .30 .75
32 Jody Praznik .20 .50
32 Tobin Praznik .20 .50
33 Brad Wingfield .08 .25
33 Geoff Bumstead .30 .75
34 Kurt Wickenheiser .20 .50
34 Geoff Bumstead .30 .75
34 Tobin Praznik .08 .25
35 Radio Celebrities .02 .10
36 Home Opener .02 .10
37 Corpus Christi Icegirls .30 .75
38 Party Patrol .02 .10
39 SugarRay MASCOT .08 .25
40 Corpus Christi IceRays .20 .50
41 Best Fans in the WPHL .02 .10
42 ValueBank Texas .02 .10

1992-93 Dallas Freeze

This 20-card standard-size set features the Dallas Freeze of the Central Hockey League. White-bordered color player photos adorn the fronts of these cards. The Freeze logo appears on both sides of the card. In the border beneath the photo are the player's name and position. The cards are unnumbered and checklisted below in alphabetical order.

COMPLETE SET (20) 3.00 8.00
1 Wayne Anchikoski .20 .50
2 Gary Audette .20 .50
3 Jeff Beaudin .20 .50
4 Troy Binnie .20 .50
5 Brian Bruininks .20 .50
6 Derek Crawford .20 .50
7 Dave Doucette .20 .50
8 Don Dwyer .20 .50
9 Joe Eagan .20 .50
10 Ron Flockhart CO .30 .75
11 Frank Lascala .20 .50
12 Robert Lewis .20 .50
13 Joey Mittelsteadt .20 .50
14 Rico Rossi .20 .50
15 Dean Shmyr .20 .50
16 Doug Sinclair .20 .50
17 Greg Smith .20 .50
18 Jason Taylor .20 .50
19 Mike Zanier .30 .75
20 Team Photo .20 .50

1993-94 Dallas Freeze

These oddly shaped round cards are approximately the size of a hockey puck. They came in a plastic container with the team logo on the front and were available from the team's booster club at home games.

COMPLETE SET (18) 2.50 6.00
1 Wayne Anchikoski .20 .50
2 Jeff Beaudin .15 .40
3 Troy Binnie .20 .50
4 Brian Bruininks .15 .40
5 Derek Crawford .15 .40
6 Dave Doucette .20 .50
7 Don Dwyer .15 .40
8 Mark Holick .15 .40
9 Randy Jaycock .15 .40
10 Frank LaScala .15 .40
11 Robert Lewis .15 .40
12 Joey McTamney .15 .40
13 Joey Mittelsteadt .15 .40
14 Dean Shmyr .15 .40
15 Greg Smith .15 .40
16 Jason Taylor .15 .40
17 Jason White .15 .40
18 Ron Flockhart CO .20 .50

2005-06 Danbury Trashers

COMPLETE SET 5.00 12.00
1 Alex Goupil .20 .50
2 Donny Glover .20 .50
3 Eric Lind .20 .50
4 Drew Omicioli .20 .50
5 Danny Stewart .20 .50
6 Sergei Durden .20 .50
7 David Beauregard .20 .50
8 Frederic Belanger .20 .50
9 Jayme Platt .20 .50
10 Regan Kelly .20 .50
11 Sylvain Daigle .20 .50
12 Dave MacIsaac .20 .50
13 Mike Omicioli .20 .50
14 Luke Sellers .20 .50
15 Troy Smith .20 .50
16 Mario Larocque .20 .50
17 2005-06 UHL All-Stars .20 .50
18 Ryan Barnes .20 .50
19 Ed Campbell .20 .50
20 Jamie Thompson .20 .50
21 Jean-Michel Daoust .20 .50
22 Brad Wingfield .20 .50
23 Shawn Collymore .20 .50
24 Jeff Daw .20 .50
25 David Hymovitz .20 .50
26 Paul Gillis CO .04 .10
27 Paul Sacco .04 .10
28 A.J. Galante OWN .04 .10
29 Scrappy MASCOT .04 .10

1992-93 Dayton Bombers

This set features the Bombers of the ECHL. Just 2,500 sets were produced, with 2,300 given away as a game-night promotion and the remaining 200 sold for $5. The cards are unnumbered and checklisted below in alphabetical order.

COMPLETE SET (24) 4.00 10.00
1 John(B-Man) Beaulieu .02 .10
2 Steve Bogoyevac .20 .50
3 Christopher .02 .10
4 Darren Colbourne .20 .50
5 Derek Crawford .20 .50
6 Dan-O .02 .10
7 Derek Donald .20 .50
8 Ray Edwards .20 .50
9 Doug Evans .20 .50
10 Sandy Galuppo .30 .75
11 Shayne Green .20 .50
12 Rod Houk .20 .50
13 Peter Kasowski .20 .50
14 Steve Kerrigan .20 .50
15 Frank Kovacs .20 .50
16 Darren Langdon .30 .75
17 Denis Larocque .20 .50
18 Darwin McPherson .20 .50
19 Tom Nemeth .20 .50
20 Claude Noel CO .02 .10
21 Tony Peters .20 .50
22 Marshall Phillips .20 .50
23 Mike Reier .20 .50
24 Steve Wilson .20 .50

1993-94 Dayton Bombers

This set features the Bombers of the ECHL. 2,500 sets were produced and given away as a game-night promotion. Cards 19-28 feature radio disc jockeys.

COMPLETE SET (28) 3.00 8.00
1 Title Card CL .02 .10
2 Jeff Levy .15 .40
3 Steve Wilson .15 .40
4 Jason Downey .15 .40
5 Jim Peters .15 .40
6 Ondrej Kriz .15 .40
7 Steve Bogoyevac .15 .40
8 Jason Disiewich .15 .40
9 Marc Savard .15 .40
10 Dan O'Shea .15 .40
11 Tom Nemeth .15 .40
12 Guy Prince .15 .40
13 Ray Edwards .15 .40
14 Sergei Kharin .15 .40
15 Derek Donald .15 .40
16 Darwin McPherson .15 .40
17 Jeff Stolp .15 .40
18 Adam Bomber (Mascot) .02 .10
19 Kim .02 .10
20 Robby .02 .10
21 Lisa .02 .10
22 Marshall Phillips .02 .10
23 Dan-O .02 .10
24 John(B-Man) Beaulieu .02 .10
25 Christopher .02 .10
26 Steve Kerrigan .15 .40
27 Tony Peters .15 .40
28 Shaun Higgins .02 .10
Major Dic

1994-95 Dayton Bombers

This set features the Bombers of the ECHL. 5,000 sets were produced, 1,500 of which were given away as a game night promotion.

COMPLETE SET (24) 3.00 8.00
1 Title Card CL .02 .10
2 Paul Taylor .15 .40
3 Steve Wilson .15 .40
4 Jason Downey .15 .40
5 Craig Charron .15 .40
6 Jim Lessard .15 .40
7 Karson Kaebel .15 .40
8 Jamie Steer .15 .40
9 Rob Hartnell .15 .40
10 Mike Doers .15 .40
11 Sean Gagnon .20 .50
12 Kevin Brown .15 .40
13 John Brill .15 .40
14 Dean Fedorchuk .15 .40
15 Tony Gruba .15 .40
16 Steve Lingren .15 .40
17 Brandon Smith .15 .40
18 Jeff Stolp .20 .50
19 Mike Vandenberghe .15 .40
20 Jim Playfair .15 .40
21 Goal Celebration .15 .40
22 Jamie Steer AS .15 .40
23 Steve Wilson AW .15 .40
24 Jeff Stolp/1993-94 Top# .20 .50

1995-96 Dayton Bombers

This set features the Bombers of the ECHL. The cards are oversized (5 by 7 inches). The cards were limited in production to 500 copies each. One card was given away during each of 32 home games (3 games did not feature a card) inside the official game program. Purchase of a program was required to obtain a card.

COMPLETE SET (32) 10.00 25.00
1 Jim Playfair CO .30 .75
2 Sean Ortiz .30 .75
3 Derek Herlofsky .60 1.50
4 Paul Andrea .30 .75
5 Nick Poole .30 .75
6 Steve Lingren .40 1.00
7 Kevin Brown .30 .75
8 Jason Downey .30 .75
9 Sergei Kharin .40 1.00
10 Matt McElwee .30 .75
11 Mike Naylor .30 .75
12 Ted Russell .30 .75
13 Colin Miller .40 1.00
14 Brent Brekke .30 .75
15 John Brill .30 .75
16 Mike Murray .30 .75
17 Sean Gagnon .60 1.50
18 Brian Renfrew .40 1.00
19 Rob Peters .30 .75
20 Jeff Petruic .30 .75
21 Steve Roberts .30 .75
22 George Zajankala .30 .75
23 Adam Bomber MASCOT .20 .50
24 Steve Lingren AS .30 .75
25 Jim Playfair CO AS .30 .75
26 Jerry Buckley .40 1.00
27 Jeremy Stasiuk .30 .75
28 Greg Burke .30 .75
29 Chris Johnston .30 .75
30 Dwayne Gylywoychuk .30 .75
P1 Sean Gagnon .75 2.00
P2 Sergei Kharin .75 2.00

1996-97 Dayton Bombers

This set features the Bombers of the ECHL. The cards were issued as a promotional item within copies of the official game program. They were issued in 2-card strips, with the cards separated by a thin ad for sponsor WTUE radio. One strip was inserted during each of 12 home games over the course of the season. Purchase of the program was required to obtain the cards. The cards themselves were printed on thin stock, with color photos surrounded by a red border. Production was limited to 500 copies of each strip.

COMPLETE SET (24) 10.00 25.00
1 Steve Roberts .40 1.00
2 Chris Sullivan .40 1.00
3 Steve Lingren .40 1.00
4 Jordan Shields .40 1.00
5 Ildar Yubin .40 1.00
6 Dwight Parrish .40 1.00
7 Brian Ridolfi .40 1.00
8 Jordan Willis .75 2.00
9 Dale Hooper .40 1.00
10 Will Clarke .40 1.00
11 Tavis Morrison .40 1.00
12 Trent Schachle .40 1.00
13 John Emmons .60 1.50
14 Sam McKenney .40 1.00
15 Bryan Richardson .40 1.00
16 Ryan Gillis .40 1.00
17 Marty Flichel .60 1.50
18 Jason Downey .40 1.00
19 Troy Christensen .40 1.00
20 Derek Herlofsky .75 2.00
21 Sal Manganaro .40 1.00
22 Tom Nemeth .60 1.50
23 Evgeny Ryabchikov .75 2.00
24 Colin Miller .40 1.00

1998-99 Dayton Bombers

This set was handed out at a game late in the season, making it very difficult to acquire on the secondary market.

COMPLETE SET (25) 4.80 12.00
1 Frederic Bouchard .30 .75
2 Bobby Brown .20 .50
3 Norman Dezainde .30 .75
4 Travis Dillabough .20 .50
5 Ryan Furness .20 .50
6 Dan Hendrickson .20 .50
7 Trevor Koenig .20 .50
8 Justin Krall .20 .50
9 Aaron Kriss .20 .50
10 Jamie Ling .40 1.00
11 Jim Logan .20 .50
12 Colin Miller .20 .50
13 Tom Nemeth .30 .75
14 Brian Regan .20 .50
15 Brian Ridolfi .20 .50
16 Brian Secord .20 .50
17 Chris Wismer .20 .50
18 John Beaulieu ANN .02 .10
19 Dale Coulthard EQM .02 .10
20 Greg Ireland HCO .02 .10
21 Buddy Mascot .02 .10
22 Kerrigan & Christopher .02 .10
23 Team Photo .20 .50
24 Larry Thornton TR .02 .10
25 Lee Stieg .20 .50

1998-99 Dayton Bombers EBK

This 21-card set was different than the giveaway set from the same year, and was sold at games late in the season.

COMPLETE SET (22) 3.00 8.00
1 Frederic Bouchard .20 .50
2 Aaron Kriss .15 .40
3 Brian Secord .15 .40
4 Colin Miller .15 .40
5 Jamie Ling .30 .75
6 Bobby Brown .15 .40
7 Tom Nemeth .20 .50
8 Brian Ridolfi .15 .40
9 Travis Dillabough .15 .40
10 Justin Krall .15 .40
11 Dan Hendrickson .15 .40
12 Ed Gingher ACO .02 .10
13 Brian Regan .15 .40
14 Trevor Koenig .15 .40
15 Greg Ireland HCO .02 .10
16 Colin Miller .02 .10
Tom Nemeth ACO
17 Bucky Mascot .02 .10
18 Brandon Sugden .20 .50
19 Norman Dezainde .20 .50
20 Kiley Hill .15 .40
NNO Checklist .02 .10

2013-14 Dayton Demonz

COMPLETE SET (20) 5.00 12.00
1 Bonez MASCOT .30 .75
2 Trevor Karasiewicz CO .30 .75
3 Jack Collins Asst. CO .30 .75
4 Brandon Blair .30 .75
5 Brett Wall .30 .75
6 Jared Hicks .30 .75
7 August Aiken .30 .75
8 Casey Mignone .30 .75
9 Shaun Fisher .30 .75
10 Alex Norman .30 .75
11 Ahmed Mahfouz .30 .75
12 Jesse Felten .30 .75
13 Roger Tagoona .30 .75
14 Wehebe Darge .30 .75
15 Matt Kinsella .30 .75
16 Jeff Rose .30 .75
17 Len Pelletier .30 .75
18 Lee McClure .30 .75
19 Robert Vanwynsberghe .30 .75
20 Brian Marks .30 .75

1996-97 Dayton Ice Bandits

This set features the Ice Bandits of the ECHL. The set was initially given away as a promotional item, with remaining copies sold by the team at last-season home games.

COMPLETE SET (29) 4.00 10.00
1 Checklist .02 .10
2 Jesse Austin .20 .50
3 Mike Bajurny .20 .50
4 Dan Belisle HCO .02 .10
5 Dan Carter .20 .50
6 Cosmo Clarke .20 .50
7 Bob Clouston .20 .50
8 Tom Colasanto .20 .50
9 Brad Cook .20 .50
10 Richard Fatrola .20 .50
11 Jack Greig .20 .50
12 Kelly Melton .20 .50
13 Andrew Plumb .20 .50
14 Brian Renfrew .20 .50
15 Bobby Rapoza .20 .50
16 Jacque Rodrigue .20 .50
17 Fred Scott .20 .50
18 Troy Stevens .20 .50
19 Larry Thornton TR .02 .10
20 Mike Thornton .20 .50
21 Scott Vettraino .20 .50
22 Marty Wells .20 .50
23 Kevin Young .20 .50
24 The Phantom Mascot .02 .10
25 The Famous Chicken .02 .10
26 WTUE Employees .02 .10
27 WTUE Employees .02 .10
28 WTUE Employees .02 .10
29 WTUE Employees .02 .10

1996-97 Denver University Pioneers

This 10-card set features color action photos on the front and a team schedule on the back. It was issued as a game-night giveaway.

COMPLETE SET (10) 3.00 8.00
1 Travis Smith .40 1.00
2 Jim Mullin .30 .75
3 Mike Corbett .30 .75
4 Petri Gunther .30 .75
5 Garrett Buzan .30 .75
6 Antti Laaksonen .40 1.00
7 Charlie Host .30 .75
8 Erik Andersson .30 .75
9 Warren Smith .30 .75
10 Anders Bjork .30 .75

1999-00 Des Moines Buccaneers

This set features the Buccaneers of the USHL. The set was produced by Roox and sold by the team at home games.

COMPLETE SET (24) 4.00 12.00
1 Dominic Torretti .20 .50
2 Felipe Larranaga .20 .50
3 Paul Baumgartner .20 .50
4 Nathan Berry .20 .50
5 Matt Weber .20 .50
6 Troy Riddle .20 .50
7 Nick Dimella .20 .50
8 Jesse Lane .20 .50
9 Peter Sejna .75 2.00
10 Landon Bathe .20 .50
11 Travis Doan .20 .50
12 Mark Murphy .20 .50
13 Rob Novak .20 .50
14 Alex Kim .20 .50
15 Wade Chiodo .20 .50
16 Jerrid Reinholz .20 .50
17 Miroslav Durak .20 .50
18 Ryan Kirchhoff .20 .50
19 Mark Mullen .20 .50
20 Ryan Bennett .20 .50
21 Jeff Ronkoske .20 .50
22 Mike Mantua .20 .50
23 Paul Morrissey .20 .50
24 Winger MASCOT .02 .10

2007-08 Des Moines Buccaneers

COMPLETE SET (26) 5.00 12.00
1 Nielsson Arcibal .30 .75
2 Josh Balch .30 .75
3 Fredrik Bergman .30 .75
4 Brett Bruneteau .30 .75
5 Greg Burgdoerfer .30 .75
6 Rocco Carzo .30 .75
7 Alexander Denezhkin .30 .75
8 Nate Dewhurst .30 .75
9 Michael Dorr .30 .75
10 Derek Elliott .30 .75
11 Austin Handley .30 .75
12 Keith Kinkaid .30 .75
13 Chris Knowlton .30 .75
14 Cullen Lundholm .30 .75
15 J.P. Maley .30 .75
16 Taylor Matson .30 .75
17 Ryan McKiernan .30 .75
18 Andrew Panzarella .30 .75
19 Bobby Reiners .30 .75
20 Rody Selk .30 .75
21 Brad Walch .30 .75
22 Ryan Walters .30 .75
23 Matt White .30 .75
25 Todd Knott AC .30 .75
26 Rick Comley HC .30 .75
27 Bucky MASCOT .15 .40

1993-94 Detroit Jr. Red Wings

Sponsored by Compuware and printed by Slapshot Images Ltd., this standard size 26-card set features the 1993-94 Detroit Jr. Red Wings. On a geometrical red and white background, the fronts feature color action player photos with thin black borders.

COMPLETE SET (26) 4.00 10.00
1 Todd Harvey .40 1.00
2 Jason Saal .20 .50
3 Aaron Ellis .15 .40
4 Chris Mailloux .15 .40
5 Robin Lacour .15 .40
6 Mike Rucinski .15 .40
7 Eric Cairns .20 .50
8 Matt Ball .15 .40
9 Dale Junkin .15 .40
10 Bill McCauley .15 .40
11 Jeremy Meehan .15 .40
12 Mike Harding .15 .40
13 Brad Cook .15 .40
14 Jeff Mitchell .15 .40
15 Jamie Allison .15 .40
16 Dan Pawlaczyk .15 .40
17 Kevin Brown .15 .40
18 Duane Harmer .15 .40
19 Gerry Skrypec .15 .40
20 Shayne McCosh .15 .40
21 Sean Haggerty .15 .40
22 Nic Beaudoin .15 .40
23 Paul Maurice CO .20 .50
24 Pete DeBoer ACO .20 .50
25 Bob Wren .15 .40
NNO Slapshot Ad Card .01

1994-95 Detroit Jr. Red Wings

Sponsored by Compuware and printed by Slapshot Images Ltd., this 25-card set features the 1994-95 Detroit Jr. Red Wings. On a red and gray background, the fronts feature color action player photos with thin black borders.

COMPLETE SET (25) 4.00 10.00
1 Team Photo CL .15 .40
2 Darryl Foster .15 .40
3 Quade Lightbody .15 .40
4 Ryan MacDonald .15 .40
5 Mike Rucinski .15 .40
6 Murray Sheehan .15 .40
7 Matt Ball .15 .40
8 Gerry Lanigan .15 .40
9 Mike Morrone .15 .40
10 Tom Buckley .15 .40
11 Eric Manlow .30 .75
12 Bill McCauley .15 .40
13 Andrew Taylor .15 .40
14 Scott Blair .15 .40
15 Jeff Mitchell .15 .40
16 Jason Saal .25 .60
17 Jamie Allison .20 .50
18 Bryan Berard .40 1.00
19 Dan Pawlaczyk .15 .40
20 Milan Kostolny .15 .40
21 Duane Harmer .15 .40
22 Shayne McCosh .15 .40
23 Sean Haggerty .15 .40
24 Nic Beaudoin .15 .40
25 Paul Maurice CO .15 .40
GM

1994-95 Detroit Vipers Pogs

This set was handed out at a Vipers game. It was released in the form of a 6-inch circular disk which contains 5 player Pogs and one team logo Pog.

COMPLETE SET (6) .75 2.00
1 John Craighead .20 .50
2 Peter Ciavaglia .20 .50
3 Brad Tiley .20 .50
4 Al Conroy .20 .50
5 Daniel Shank .20 .50
6 Logo Pog .20 .50

1996-97 Detroit Vipers

This odd-sized set commemorates the Detroit Vipers of the IHL. The set was produced by the club as a game-night premium. The cards were issued one per night at twenty different home games, beginning January 3, 1997 and ending April 13. The giveaway dates for each card can be found on the backs of the cards, along with a mugs hot, player nickname and biographical data. The fronts feature an action photo, a reproduction of the player's autograph, and the logo of sponsor Ameritech. The unnumbered cards are listed below alphabetically. The set is noteworthy for the inclusion of 1997 draft pick Sergei Samsonov.

COMPLETE SET (20) 30.00 75.00
1 Darren Banks .75 2.00
2 Peter Ciavaglia .75 2.00
3 Yvon Corriveau .75 2.00
4 Phil Crowe .60 1.50
5 Mike Donnelly .75 2.00
6 Stan Drulia 1.25 3.00
7 Len Esau .75 2.00
8 Ian Herbers .60 1.50
9 Bobby Jay .60 1.50
10 Dan Kesa .60 1.50
11 Rich Parent 1.25 3.00
12 Jeff Parrott .60 1.50
13 Wayne Presley .60 1.50
14 Jeff Reese 1.25 3.00
15 Sergei Samsonov 15.00 40.00
16 Brad Shaw 1.25 3.00
17 Todd Simon .75 2.00
18 Patrice Tardif .75 2.00
19 Phil Von Steffenelli .60 1.50
20 Steve Walker .60 1.50

1997-98 Detroit Vipers

The cards in this oversized set was handed out by the team over the course of twenty different games and is nearly impossible in complete set form.

COMPLETE SET (20) 16.00 30.00
1 Peter Ciavaglia .75 2.00
2 Phil Crowe .40 1.00
3 Dan Kesa .40 1.00
4 Stan Drulia .75 2.00
5 Bob Jay .40 1.00
6 Ian Herbers .40 1.00
7 Brad Shaw .75 2.00
8 Steve Walker .75 2.00
9 Trent McCleary .40 1.00
10 Scott Thomas .75 2.00
11 Johan Hedberg 2.00 5.00
12 Jimmy Carson .75 2.00
13 Clayton Beddoes .40 1.00
14 Tim Murray .40 1.00
15 John Gruden .40 1.00
16 Jeff Reese .75 2.00
17 Keith Aldridge .40 1.00
18 Brent Fedyk .40 1.00
19 Darren Banks .75 2.00
20 Vipe-Bear Mascot .40 1.00

1998-99 Detroit Vipers

This set was produced by EBK Sports and was sold through its Web site, as well as at Vipers home games. Cards were numbered "XX of 27" on the card backs.

COMPLETE SET (26) 6.00 15.00
1 Keith Aldridge .20 .50
2 Brad Shaw .40 1.00
3 Tim Murray .15 .40
4 Brian Felsner .15 .40
5 Peter Ciavaglia .30 .75
6 Andy Bezeau .15 .40
7 Mike Gaffney .15 .40
8 Phil Crowe .15 .40
9 John Emmons .15 .40
10 Kory Karlander .15 .40
11 Mike Prokopec .15 .40
12 Stan Drulia .40 1.00
13 Bob Jay .20 .50
14 Darren Banks .20 .50
15 Jeff Whittle .15 .40
16 Steve Walker .15 .40
17 Ian Herbers .15 .40
18 Jani Hurme 1.50 4.00
19 John Gruden .15 .40
20 Kevin Weekes .75 2.00
21 Vipe-Bear Mascot .02 .10
22 Steve Ludzik HCO .02 .10
23 John Blum ACO .02 .10
24 Dave Boyer TR .02 .10
25 Mike Astalos EQM .02 .10
26 Checklist .02 .10
27 IHL
PHPA

1998-99 Detroit Vipers Freschetta

This set was issued as a giveaway late in the season in four different four-card strips. Each strip featured a different color background, and the four colors used are green (cards 1-4), yellow (cards 5-8), red (cards 9-12), and purple (cards 13-16). The cards were unnumbered.

COMPLETE SET (16) 12.00 30.00
1 Kevin Weekes 1.50 4.00
2 Peter Ciavaglia .75 2.00
3 Bob Jay .60 1.50
4 Keith Aldridge .60 1.50
5 Andy Bezeau .60 1.50
6 Stan Drulia 1.25 3.00
7 Ian Herbers .60 1.50
8 John Emmons .60 1.50
9 Mike Prokopec .60 1.50
10 Tim Murray .60 1.50
11 Brad Shaw 1.25 3.00
12 Steve Walker .60 1.50
13 John Gruden .60 1.50
14 Darren Banks .75 2.00
15 Brian Felsner .60 1.50
16 Geoff Sarjeant .75 2.00

1999-00 Detroit Vipers

Given out by the team over the span of 15 home games, this 15-card set features the 1999-2000 Detroit Vipers. The set is listed in the order that the players were given away. The dates are as follows: Jan. 15, Jan. 21, Jan. 22, Jan. 25, Jan. 27, Feb. 1, Feb. 6, Feb. 8, Feb. 15, Feb. 22, Feb. 24, Feb. 27, Mar. 12, Mar. 16, and Mar. 28.

COMPLETE SET (15) 14.00 35.00
1 Andy Bezeau 1.25 3.00
2 Nils Ekman 1.25 3.00
3 Mario Larocque 1.25 3.00
4 Steve Walker .75 2.00
5 Matt Elich 1.25 3.00
6 Jeff Shevalier .75 2.00
7 Peter Ciavaglia 1.25 3.00
8 Alek Stojanov .75 2.00
9 Dave Baseggio .75 2.00
10 Zac Bierk 1.50 4.00
11 Kyle Kos .75 2.00
12 Tim Thomas 5.00 12.00
13 Dale Rominski .75 2.00
14 Kyle Freadrich .75 2.00
15 Samuel St. Pierre .75 2.00

1999-00 Detroit Vipers Kid's Club

This 9-card set was given out free to members of the Detroit Vipers Kids Club. The set was issued as one three-by-three, 9-card panel, with perforations to allow the cards to be torn off. The set was sponsored by Keebler and Meijer. The cards are unnumbered and are standard-size. The fronts are full color with green borders. The backs are white with dark purple printing, containing player statistics. The final card in the set was intended to be a "membership card" for the Detroit Vipers Kids Club, containing a blank "name" spot on the card's front.

COMPLETE SET (9) 10.00 25.00
1 Team Logo Card .40 1.00
2 Peter Ciavaglia 2.00 5.00
3 Andy Bezeau 2.00 5.00
4 Stan Drulia 2.00 5.00
5 Steve Walker 2.00 5.00
6 Ian Herbers 2.00 5.00
7 Paulin Bordeleau HCO 2.00 5.00
8 Vipe-Bear Mascot .40 1.00
9 Kid's Club Membership Card .40 1.00

1996-97 Detroit Whalers

This 25-card set was produced by the team and available for sale at games and by mail order for $5. The standard-size cards feature a color action photo with a sea foam green border. The backs contain a headshot, bio and stats.

COMPLETE SET (25) 4.00 10.00
1 Jessie Boulerice .30 .75
2 Mark Cadotte .20 .50
3 Chad Cavanagh .15 .40
4 Harold Druken .40 1.00
5 Steve Dumonski .20 .50
6 Robert Esche .75 2.00
7 Sergei Fedotov .20 .50
8 Randy Fitzgerald .20 .50
9 Eric Gooldy .15 .40
10 Kevin Holdridge .15 .40
11 John Paul Luciuk .15 .40
12 Mike Morrone .15 .40
13 Pat Parthenais .20 .50
14 Julian Smith .15 .40
15 Troy Smith .15 .40
16 Andrew Taylor .15 .40
17 Anthony Terzo .15 .40
18 Jan Vodrazka .15 .40
19 Steve Wasylko .20 .50
20 Nathan West .15 .40
21 Peter DeBoer .08 .25
22 Luc Rioux .15 .40
23 Slapshot .02 .10
24 Checklist .02 .10
25 Discount Card .02 .10

1993-94 Drummondville Voltigeurs

This set features the Voltigeurs of the QMJHL. The set was printed by Slapshot Images and was sold at home games.

COMPLETE SET (28) 3.00 8.00
1 Title Card .02 .10
Checklist
2 Stephane Routhier .15 .40
3 Yannick Gagnon .15 .40
4 Sebastien Bety .15 .40
5 Martin Latulippe .15 .40
6 Nicolas Savage .15 .40
7 Sylvain Ducharme .15 .40
8 Yan St. Pierre .15 .40
9 Emmanuel Labranche .15 .40
10 Ian Laperriere .30 .75
11 Louis Bernard .15 .40
12 Stephane St. Amour .15 .40
13 Vincent Tremblay .15 .40
14 Denis Gauthier Jr. .30 .75
15 Eric Plante .15 .40
16 Christian Marcoux .15 .40
17 Patrice Charbonneau .15 .40
18 Raymond Delarosbil .15 .40
19 Patrick Livernoche .15 .40
20 Luc Decelles .15 .40
21 Francois Sasseville .15 .40
22 Steve Tardif .15 .40
23 Mathieu Sunderland .15 .40
24 Alexandre Duchesne .15 .40
25 Jean Hamel CO GM .02 .10
26 Mario Carrier ACO .02 .10
27 Me Andre Lepage TR .02 .10
28 Slapshot Ad Card .02 .10

2001-02 Drummondville Voltigeurs

This set features the Voltigeurs of the QMJHL. The set was produced by CTM Ste-Foy, and was sold at that shop as well as at home games. The production run is believed to be fewer than 1,000 sets.

COMPLETE SET (23) 4.00 10.00
1 Jean-Francois Racine .30 .75
2 Patrick Turbide .20 .50
3 Evgueni Nourislamov .20 .50
4 Jean-Philippe Glaude .20 .50
5 Thierry Kaszap .20 .50
6 Eric Jean .20 .50
7 Louis-Philippe Lessard .20 .50
8 Andre Vincent .20 .50
9 Steve Proulx .20 .50
10 Oliver Proulx .20 .50
11 Martin Autotte .20 .50
12 Yanick Riendeau .20 .50
13 Michael Stacey .20 .50
14 Frederic Faucher .20 .50
15 Benoit Paris .20 .50
16 Vincent Tougas .20 .50
17 Kirill Alexeev .20 .50
18 Jean-Francois Cyr .20 .50
19 Carl Zacharie .20 .50
20 Kevin Rainville .20 .50
21 Sylvain Michaud .20 .50
22 Maxime Bouchard .20 .50
NNO Title Card/CL .04 .10

2002-03 Drummondville Voltigeurs

COMPLETE SET (25) 5.00 12.00
1 Francis Breault CO .04 .10
2 Evgueni Nourislamov .20 .50
3 Todd Paul .20 .50
4 Andre Joaniss .20 .50
5 Jules Melanson .20 .50
6 Andre Vincent .20 .50
7 Dominic Fiset .20 .50
8 Kevin Lacombe .20 .50
9 Alexandre Demers .20 .50
10 Laurent Lanoie .20 .50
11 Yannick Riendeau .20 .50
12 Patrick Levesque .20 .50
13 Sebastien Laprise .20 .50
14 Benoit Duhamel .20 .50
15 Jonathan Dick .20 .50
16 Kevin Mailhiot .20 .50
17 Jason D'Ascanio .20 .50
18 Thomas Bellemare .20 .50
19 Samuel Villeneuve .20 .50
20 Kevin Duchaine .20 .50
21 Eric Dagenais .20 .50
22 Sylvain Michaud .40 1.00
23 Pierre Olivier Girouard .30 .75
24 Pier Olivier Begin .30 .75
25 Checklist/Logo .04 .10

2003-04 Drummondville Voltigeurs

COMPLETE SET (22) 6.00 15.00
1 Thomas Bellemare .20 .50
2 David Bouchard .20 .50
3 Maxim Chamberland .20 .50
4 Michel Charrette .20 .50
5 Alexandre Demers .20 .50
6 Keven Gagne .20 .50
7 Samuel Gibbons .20 .50
8 Gabriel Houde-Brisson .20 .50
9 Andre Joanisse .20 .50
10 Kevin Lacombe .20 .50
11 Guillaume Latendresse 2.00 5.00
12 Kevin Mailhiot .20 .50
13 Louis-Philippe Martin .20 .50
14 Jamie McCabe .20 .50
15 Jules Melanson .20 .50
16 Sylvain Michaud .30 .75
17 Pierre Morvan .20 .50
18 Ervins Mustukovs .30 .75
19 Jean-Francois Parent .20 .50
20 Yannick Riendeau .20 .50
21 Frederic St. Denis .20 .50
22 Andre Vincent .20 .50

2004-05 Drummondville Voltigeurs

A total of 330 sets were produced. The NNO cards do not appear in every sealed team bag.

COMPLETE SET (30) 6.00 20.00
1 Guillaume Latendresse .75 2.00
2 Philippe Roberge .20 .50
3 Pier-Olivier Pelletier .60 1.50
4 Derick Brassard 1.25 3.00
5 Chaz Johnson .20 .50
6 Henrick Lavoie .20 .50
7 Mathieu Ste-Marie .20 .50
8 Alexandre Demers .20 .50
9 Keven Gagne .20 .50
10 Andre Vincent .20 .50
11 Frederic St-Denis .20 .50
12 Andre Joanisse .20 .50
13 Louis-Philippe Martin .20 .50
14 Dave Bouchard .20 .50
15 Jules Melanson .20 .50
16 Steve Caccioti .20 .50
19 Romy Elayoubi .20 .50
20 Cedric Archambault .20 .50
21 Maxime Frechette .20 .50
22 Julien Beaulieu .20 .50
23 Maxime Aubut .20 .50
24 Jean-Philippe Cote .20 .50
25 Maxim Chamberland .20 .50
26 Kevin Mailhiot .20 .50
27 Gaby Roch .20 .50
28 Simon Archambault .20 .50
29 Sylvain Michaud .40 1.00
30 Jesse Arko .20 .50
NNO Derick Brassard 2.00 5.00
NNO Pier-Olivier Pelletier 2.00 5.00

2005-06 Drummondville Voltigeurs

COMPLETE SET (33) 6.00 15.00
1 Guillaume Latendresse .60 1.50
2 Derick Brassard .60 1.50
3 Pier-Olivier Pelletier .30 .75
4 Pierre-Alexandre Marion .15 .40
5 Jules Melanson .15 .40
6 Kevin Mailhiot .15 .40
7 Maxim Mallette .15 .40
8 Joey Pell .15 .40
9 Andre Joanisse .15 .40
10 Maxime Frechette .15 .40
11 Tomas Zohorna .15 .40
12 Dave Bouchard .15 .40
13 Nicolas Sigouin .15 .40
14 Steven Cacciotti .15 .40
15 Tomas Svoboda .15 .40
16 Gaby Roch .15 .40
17 Alexandre Demers .15 .40
18 Frederic St-Denis .15 .40
19 Vincent Beaulieu .15 .40
20 Keven Gagne .15 .40
21 Maxime Aubut .15 .40
22 Paul Yovanic .15 .40
23 Olivier Fortier .15 .40
24 Tirobut .02 .10
25 Bryan Wilson .15 .40
26 Olivier Legault .15 .40
27 Yanick Charron .15 .40
28 Nicolas D'Aoust .15 .40
29 Simon Bouchard .15 .40
30 Olivier Donovan .15 .40
31 Loic Lacasse .30 .75
32 Francis Charette .15 .40
33 Jean-Michel Bolduc .15 .40

2006-07 Drummondville Voltigeurs

MPLETE SET (26) 8.00 15.00
Derick Brassard .75 2.00
Bryan Wilson .20 .50
Mackenzie Micks .20 .50
Drew Paris .20 .50
Simon Bouchard .20 .50
Benoit Levesque .20 .50
Jonathan Duchesneau .20 .50
Tomas Zohorna .20 .50
Eric Campeau-Charron .20 .50
Steven Cacciotti .20 .50
Olivier Jannard .20 .50
Corey Garland .20 .50
Tomas Svoboda .20 .50
Gaby Roch .20 .50
Alexandre Demers .20 .50
Frederic St. Denis .20 .50
Stephen Valente .20 .50
Sebastien Bernier .20 .50
Etienne Bellavance-Martin .20 .50
Marc-Olivier Vachon .20 .50
Scott Howes .20 .50
Maxime Frechette .20 .50
Francis Charette .20 .50
Pier-Olivier Pelletier .30 .75
Maxime Gougeon .30 .75
Pierre-Alexandre Marion .20 .50

2006-07 Drummondville Voltigeurs Edition Limitee

1 Derick Brassard 1.50 4.00
2 Pier-Olivier Pelletier .60 1.50

1994-95 Dubuque Fighting Saints

his 29-card set measures the standard size. The fronts ature color action player photos with the player's me, jersey number, and team logo at the bottom. The am name runs down the left side of the front. The cks carry a black-and-white player portrait, the ayer's name, jersey number, biographical formation, statistics, career summary, and team logo. e cards are unnumbered and checklisted below in phabetical order.

OMPLETE SET (29) 4.00 10.00
Title Card .02 .10
Season schedule
Chris Addesa .20 .50
Matt Addesa .20 .50
Mark Allegrezza .15 .40
Todd Barclay .15 .40
Jay Boxer ACO .02 .10
Geoff Collard .15 .40
John Dwyer .15 .40
Jayme Filipowicz .20 .50
Zach Ham .15 .40
Mike Herrera .15 .40
2 Roger Holeczy .15 .40
3 Steve Holeczy .15 .40
4 John Hultberg .30 .75
5 Ryan Karasek .15 .40
6 Mike Kramer TR .02 .10
7 Chris Masters .15 .40
8 A.J. Melanson .15 .40
9 Mike Minichiello .15 .40
0 Berk Nelson .15 .40
1 Nik Patronas .15 .40
2 Andy Powers .15 .40
3 Matt Romaniski .15 .40
4 Tom Ryles .15 .40
5 John Sadowski .15 .40
6 Chris Showalter .15 .40
7 Dan Stepanek .15 .40
8 Trevor Tallackson .15 .40
9 Troy Ward GM .02 .10
CO

1997-98 Dubuque Fighting Saints

his set features the Fighting Saints of the USHL. The t was produced by the team and sold at home games. ard No. 30 was recently confirmed to be Josh ackburn. Thanks to collector Joseph Bonnett for this formation.

OMPLETE SET (30) 4.00 10.00
Dubuque Fighting Saints .15 .40
Justin Aufmann .15 .40
Travis Rotariu .15 .40
Marty Rychley .15 .40
Mario LeBlanc .15 .40
David Patch .15 .40
Evan Stensrud .15 .40
Josh Kern .15 .40
Christian Fletcher .15 .40
0 Scott Deopere .15 .40
1 Jeff Tarala .15 .40
2 Phil Lewandowski .15 .40
3 Joe Dudek .15 .40
4 Trent Landry .15 .40
5 Tom Rouleau .15 .40
6 Kris Harris .15 .40
7 Anders Johnson .15 .40
8 Matt Herhal .15 .40
9 Josh Myers .15 .40
0 David Brien .15 .40
1 Carl Hanson .15 .40
2 Scott Brown .15 .40
3 Adam Pobiak .15 .40
4 Todd Sanden CO .02 .10
5 Tom Hasenzahl CO .02 .10
6 Corey Courtney TR .02 .10
7 Sebastian St. Bernard MAS .02 .10
8 USHL Team Directory .02 .10
9 Schedule .02 .10
0 Josh Blackburn .30 .75

1998-99 ECHL All-Star Northern Conference

eleased by EBK Sports, this 21-card set was available r sale at the 1999 ECHL All-Star Game. It was later vailable for purchase through the PHPA web site.

OMPLETE SET (21) 15.00 40.00
Tom O'Connor .75 2.00
2 Duane Harmer 1.25 3.00
3 Jamie Ling 1.25 3.00
Darron Maloney .75 2.00
Bret Meyers .75 2.00
Jim Bermingham 1.25 3.00
Jamie Thompson .75 2.00
Andrew Williamson .75 2.00
Marc Tropper .75 2.00
0 Bobby Brown .75 2.00
1 Jakub Ficenec 1.25 3.00
2 Arturs Kupaks 1.25 3.00
3 Dru Burgess .75 2.00
4 Dan Ceman .75 2.00
5 Ryan Kraft 1.25 3.00
6 Joe Blaznek .75 2.00
17 Casey Kesselring .75 2.00
18 Matt Mullen 1.25 3.00
19 Maxime Gingras 1.50 4.00
20 Karl Infanger .75 2.00
21 Checklist .02 .10

1998-99 ECHL All-Star Southern Conference

Released by EBK Sports, this 21-card set was available for purchase at the All-Star Game, then later through the PHPA web site.

COMPLETE SET (21) 15.00 40.00
1 Jaroslav Obsut 1.25 3.00
2 Terry Lindgren .75 2.00
3 Kelly Hurd .75 2.00
4 Dana Mulvihill .75 2.00
5 Jonas Soling .75 2.00
6 Jamey Hicks .75 2.00
7 Patrick Rochon .75 2.00
8 John Varga 1.25 3.00
9 Dave Seitz .75 2.00
10 Jason Elders .75 2.00
11 Cail MacLean .75 2.00
12 Allan Sirois .75 2.00
13 Shane Calder .75 2.00
14 Chris Valicevic 1.25 3.00
15 J.F. Aube .75 2.00
16 Luke Curtin .75 2.00
17 Jan Kobezda .75 2.00
18 Bujar Amidovski 1.50 4.00
19 Chris Hynnes .75 2.00
20 Chris Wickenheiser 1.50 4.00
21 Checklist .02 .10

1999-00 ECHL All-Star Northern Conference

Released by EBK Sports, this 22-card set was available for purchase through the PHPA web site and at the rink during the 2000 ECHL All-Star Game.

COMPLETE SET (22) 8.00 20.00
1 Alexei Krovopuskov .30 .75
2 Andrew Williamson .30 .75
3 Blaine Fitzpatrick .30 .75
4 Bujar Amidovski .75 2.00
5 Calvin Elfring .30 .75
6 Chad Ackerman .30 .75
7 Chris Gignac .30 .75
8 Curtis Wilgosh .30 .75
9 Derek Walser .30 .75
10 Duane Harmer .30 .75
11 Jamie Ling .30 .75
12 Jan Lasak 1.00 2.50
13 Jason Lawmaster .30 .75
14 Jeff Mitchell .30 .75
15 Joel Irving .30 .75
16 Marc Tropper .30 .75
17 Mark Murphy .30 .75
18 Mike Perna .30 .75
19 Peter Vandermeer .75 2.00
20 Ryan Kraft .75 2.00
21 Sean Matile .30 .75
22 EBK Sports .02 .10

1999-00 ECHL All-Star Southern Conference

Released by EBK Sports, this 22-card set was available for purchase through the PHPA web site and at the rink during the 2000 ECHL All-Star Game.

COMPLETE SET (22) 8.00 20.00
1 Bobby Stewart .30 .75
2 Brad Dexter .30 .75
3 Buddy Smith .30 .75
4 Chris Valicevic .75 2.00
5 Dany Bousquet .40 1.00
6 David Brumby .30 .75
7 Eric Naud .30 .75
8 Greg Schmidt .30 .75
9 Jeff Lazaro .30 .75
10 Jeff Maund .75 2.00
11 John McNabb .30 .75
12 John Spoltore .75 2.00
13 Kelly Perrault .30 .75
14 Luke Curtin .30 .75
15 Marc Magliarditi .75 2.00
16 Neil Fewster .30 .75
17 Sean Venedam .60 1.50
18 Steve O'Brien .30 .75
19 Wes Mason .30 .75
20 Ryan Gaucher .30 .75
21 Olivier Morin .30 .75
22 EBK Sports .02 .10

2002-03 ECHL All-Star Northern

COMPLETE SET (20) 8.00 20.00
19 Kevin Colley .40 1.00
20 Pierre-Luc Courchesne .40 1.00
21 Ryan Gaucher .40 1.00
22 Jim Henkel .40 1.00
23 Jamie Herrington .40 1.00
24 Andrew Ianiero .40 1.00
25 Jason Jaffray .40 1.00
26 Zenon Konopka .60 1.50
27 Dan Lombard .40 1.00
28 Brian McCullough .40 1.00
29 Chris McNamara .40 1.00
30 Nick Parillo .40 1.00
31 Geno Parrish .40 1.00
32 Tyler Rennette .40 1.00
33 Brad Rooney .40 1.00
34 Mike Smith .40 1.00
35 Scott Stirling .40 1.00
36 Takahito Suzuki .60 1.50
37 Simon Tremblay .40 1.00
39 Dustin Wood .40 1.00
39 Jonathan Zion .40 1.00

2002-03 ECHL All-Star Southern

COMPLETE SET (21) 8.00 20.00
40 Jim Baxter .40 1.00
41 Kent Davyduke .40 1.00
42 Mike Glumac .40 1.00
43 Joe Guenther .40 1.00
44 Adam Hauser .75 2.00
45 Corey Hessler .40 1.00
46 J.J. Hunter .40 1.00
47 Marty Johnston .40 1.00
40 Judd Medak .40 1.00
49 Laurent Meunier .40 1.00
50 Justin Morrison .40 1.00
51 Ryan O'Keefe .40 1.00
52 Rod Sarich .40 1.00
53 Aaron Schneekloth .40 1.00
54 Bud Smith .40 1.00
55 Rejean Stringer .40 1.00
56 Matt Underhill .60 1.50
57 Steffon Walby .40 1.00
58 Brad Williamson .40 1.00
59 Patrick Yetman .40 1.00
60 Rob Zepp .75 2.00

2002-03 ECHL Update

COMPLETE SET (27) 8.00 20.00
U1 Rick Adduono HCO .10 .25
U2 Derrick Byfuglien .40 1.00
U3 Sebastien Centomo 1.25 3.00
U4 Jason Christie HCO .10 .25
U5 Pierre-Luc Courchesne .40 1.00
U6 Kent Davyduke .40 1.00
U7 Gord Dineen HCO .10 .25
U8 Gerry Fleming HCO .20 .50
U9 Joe Guenther .40 1.00
U10 Adam Hauser .60 1.50
U11 Jamie Hodson .60 1.50
U12 Zenon Konopka .60 1.50
U13 David Lohrei HCO .10 .25
U14 Don MacAdam HCO .10 .25
U15 Chris McNamara .40 1.00
U16 John Marks HCO .10 .25
U17 Ryan O'Keefe .40 1.00
U18 Mike Oliveira .40 1.00
U19 Davis Payne HCO .20 .50
U20 Bryan Richardson .40 1.00
U21 Rod Sarich .40 1.00
U22 Bud Smith .40 1.00
U23 Niklas Sundberg .40 1.00
U24 Mark Turner .40 1.00
U25 Scott White HCO .10 .25
U26 Dustin Wood .40 1.00
U27 Patrick Yetman .40 1.00

2003-04 ECHL All-Stars

This was actually issued as two separate team-bagged sets, one for the East and one for the West, but it is combined here. The numbering reflects that this as part of the full season's run of ECHL products released by RBI Sports.

COMPLETE SET (42) 50.00 100.00
241 Morten Ask 1.25 3.00
242 Alexandre Burrows 1.25 3.00
243 Cory Campbell 1.25 3.00
244 Brian Fahey 1.25 3.00
245 Chris Houle .75 2.00
246 Jason Jaffray .75 2.00
247 Dusty Jamieson 1.25 3.00
248 Nate Kiser .75 2.00
249 Shawn Limpright .75 2.00
250 Chris Lynch .75 2.00
251 Jason Maleyko 1.25 3.00
252 David Masse .75 2.00
253 Brian McCullough .75 2.00
254 Mark McRae .75 2.00
255 Jason Notermann .75 2.00
256 Sam Paolini .75 2.00
257 Tom Reimann .75 2.00
258 Randy Rowe .75 2.00
259 Kevin Spiewak .75 2.00
260 Scott Stirling .75 2.00
261 Jonathan Zion .75 2.00
262 Greg Barber .75 2.00
263 Greg Chambers .75 2.00
264 Frederic Cloutier 1.25 3.00
265 David Cornacchia .75 2.00
266 David Cousineau .75 2.00
267 Dan Ellis 2.00 5.00
268 Nick Ganga .75 2.00
269 Michael Garnett 1.50 4.00
270 Brent Gauvreau .75 2.00
271 Andrew Ianiero .75 2.00
272 Greg Jacina 1.25 3.00
273 Justin Kelly .75 2.00
274 Charles Linglet .75 2.00
275 Troy Milam .75 2.00
276 Corey Neilson .75 2.00
277 Jean-Francois Plourde .75 2.00
278 John Snowden .75 2.00
279 Ben Storey .75 2.00
280 Joe Talbot .75 2.00
281 Kevin Truelson .75 2.00
282 Steffon Walby 1.25 3.00

2003-04 ECHL Update RBI Sports

It's believed these cards were issued late in the season and limited to just 250 copies each, in three sets (A, B and C). Little else is known about their distribution.

COMPLETE SET (48) 30.00 60.00
49 Joe Talbot .40 1.00
56 Todd Alexander .40 1.00
57 Shane Bendera .75 2.00
58 Jon Mirasty .40 1.00
59 Joe Watkins .75 2.00
60 Lucas Lawson .40 1.00
61 Brett Clouthier .75 2.00
62 Phil Cole .40 1.00
63 Tyler Masters .40 1.00
64 Doug Teskey .40 1.00
113 Kristian Antila .40 1.00
114 Matus Kostur .75 2.00
115 Christian Larrivee .40 1.00
116 Olivier Michaud 1.50 4.00
117 Tomas Micka .40 1.00
118 Matt Shasby .40 1.00
119 Marc-Andre Thinel .75 2.00
120 Sean Connolly .40 1.00
121 Riley Cote .40 1.00
122 Jason Crain .40 1.00
123 Miguel Delisle .40 1.00
124 Janne Jokila .40 1.00
125 Andrew Penner .75 2.00
126 Olivier Proulx .40 1.00
127 Nicolas Corbeil .40 1.00
128 Daniel Boisclair .75 2.00
129 Mark Concannon .40 1.00
130 Brian Passmore .40 1.00
131 Michel Robinson .40 1.00
132 Russell Spence .40 1.00
133 Anthony Aquino .75 2.00
134 Wes Fox .40 1.00
135 Phil Lewandowski .40 1.00
136 Trevor Prior .75 2.00
137 Dan Ellis 1.50 4.00
138 Armands Berzins .40 1.00
139 Maxime Fortunus .40 1.00
140 Derek Gustafson .75 2.00
141 Jamie Johnson .40 1.00
142 Ed McGrane .40 1.00
143 Jean-Francois Soucy .75 2.00
144 Jeremy Van Hoof .40 1.00
283 Dustin Johner .40 1.00
284 Paul Ballantyne .40 1.00
285 Scott Kabotoff .40 1.00
286 Joe Exter 1.50 4.00
287 Tyler MacKay .40 1.00
288 Patrick Couture .75 2.00

1997-98 El Paso Buzzards

Little is known about this set beyond the confirmed checklist. Additional information can be forwarded to hockeymag@beckett.com.

COMPLETE SET (32) 4.00 10.00
1 Jamie Thompson .20 .50
2 Brent Scott .20 .50
3 Mark Sakala .20 .50
4 Jason Rose .20 .50
5 Corri Moffat .20 .50
6 Chris MacKenzie .20 .50
7 Trent Eigner .20 .50
8 Rusty McKie .30 .75
9 Jason Welch .20 .50
10 Martin Balleux .20 .50
11 Corey Heon .20 .50
12 Derek Riley .30 .75
13 Chris Gordon .20 .50
14 Bill Trew .20 .50
15 Jason Carey .20 .50
16 Sandy Lamarre .20 .50
17 Dan Carter .20 .50
18 Robert Haddock .20 .50
19 Mark Hilton .20 .50
20 Todd Brost CO .02 .10
21 Swoop Mascot .02 .10
22 Teresa Fernandez RG .02 .10
23 Greg Sieg TR .02 .10
24 KLAQ Morning Show .02 .10
25 KISS Morning Show .02 .10
26 KROD Morning Show .02 .10
27 Paul Strelzin ANNC .02 .10
28 DJ Card .02 .10
29 TV-7 Anchors .02 .10
30 TV-7 Sports Team .02 .10
31 DJ Card .02 .10
32 TV-7 Reporters .02 .10

1998-99 El Paso Buzzards

This set features the Buzzards of the WPHL. It was produced by the team and was sold at home games. The cards are not numbered, but are ordered by the listing on the checklist card.

COMPLETE SET (28) 20.00 40.00
1 Trent Eigner 1.25 3.00
2 Chris Gordon .75 2.00
3 Robert Haddock .75 2.00
4 Corey Heon .75 2.00
5 Alex Herbison .75 2.00
6 Bill Trew .75 2.00
7 Jeremy Vanin .75 2.00
8 Jason Welch .75 2.00
9 Deuce Wynes .75 2.00
10 Todd Brost CO .40 1.00
11 Steve Pottie .75 2.00
12 Mike Rees .75 2.00
13 Iannique Renaud .75 2.00
14 Jason Rushton .75 2.00
15 Blake Sheane .75 2.00
16 Mark Costea .75 2.00
17 Sandy Lamarre .75 2.00
18 Marc Labelle .75 2.00
19 Corri Moffat .75 2.00
20 Eric Peterson .75 2.00
21 McArthur/Palka .75 2.00
22 Warner/Casas .75 2.00
23 The Mike & Grace Show .02 .10
24 Cruz/Adams .02 .10
Keith/Steele
25 Garcia/Medina/Kaplowitz .02 .10
26 Dodson/Romano .02 .10
27 Paul Strelzin ANN .02 .10
28 Checklist .02 .10

2001-02 El Paso Buzzards

COMPLETE SET (20) 6.00 15.00
1 Trent Eigner .40 1.00
2 Van Burgess .40 1.00
3 Clint Collins .40 1.00
4 Rhett Dudley .40 1.00
5 Kelly Riou .40 1.00
6 Chris Zaleski .40 1.00
7 Jeremy Vanin .40 1.00
8 Derrell Upton .40 1.00
9 Mike Rees .40 1.00
10 Justin Van Parys .40 1.00
11 Trevor Hammer .40 1.00
12 Jason Tessier .40 1.00
13 Dory Tisdale .40 1.00
14 Rob Laurie .60 1.50
15 Troy Linna .40 1.00
16 Jeff Levy .40 1.00
17 Aaron Phillips .40 1.00
18 Kory Baker .40 1.00
19 Corey Waring .40 1.00
20 John Hanson .40 1.00

2002-03 El Paso Buzzards

This checklist is NOT complete. If you have any information about this set or the cards in it, please email hockeymag@beckett.com.

1 Jeff Levy .30 .75
2 Rhett Dudley .30 .75
3 Chris Zaleski .30 .75
4 John Hanson .30 .75
5 Aaron Phillips .30 .75
6 Rob Laurie .30 .75
7 Kory Baker .30 .75

2003-04 Elmira Jackals

COMPLETE SET (25) 12.00
1 Peter Aubry .30 .75
2 Cal Benazic .20 .50
3 J.F. Boutin .20 .50
4 Trevor Burgess .20 .50
5 Tom Clayton .20 .50
6 Carl Drakensjo .20 .50
7 Nathan Gillies .20 .50
8 Dean Jackson .20 .50
9 Greg Koehler .20 .50
Mike Thompson
10 Ed Lowe .20 .50
11 Kris Mallette .30 .75
12 Ryan McIntosh .30 .75
13 Randy Murphy .20 .50
14 Geoff O'Leary .20 .50
15 Matt Osborne .20 .50
16 Neil Posillico .20 .50
17 Michael Prochazka .20 .50
18 Trevor Segstro .20 .50
19 James Sheehan .20 .50
20 Don Smith .20 .50
21 Jamie Thompson .20 .50
23 Todd Brost HCO .08 .20
24 Spud Hamilton EQM .04 .10
25 Brandon Dionne TR .04 .10
26 Team Photo .20 .50

2013-14 Elmira Jackals

COMPLETE SET () 5.00 12.00
1 Jakub Culek .30 .75
2 Jean Bourbeau .30 .75
3 Jordan Pietrus .30 .75
4 Kyle Bushee .30 .75
5 Ludwig Karlsson .30 .75
6 Maxim Lamarche .30 .75
7 Mike Vaskivuo .30 .75
8 Neil Conway .30 .75
9 Nik Pokulok .30 .75
10 Patch Alber .30 .75
11 Rob Bellamy .30 .75
12 Scott Greenham .30 .75
13 Artem Demkov .30 .75
14 Corey Bellamy .30 .75
15 Dane Walters .30 .75
16 Daniel Koger .30 .75
17 Danny Hobbs .30 .75
18 Harry Young .30 .75

2003-04 Erie Otters

COMPLETE SET (24) 6.00 15.00
1 Derrick Bagshaw .20 .50
2 Michael Blunden .40 1.00
3 Brad Bonello .20 .50
4 Chris Campoli .30 .75
5 Sean Courtney .20 .50
6 Josh Disher .30 .75
7 Tomas Galasek .20 .50
8 Bryan Hamm .20 .50
9 Jacob Heller .20 .50
10 David Herring .20 .50
11 Rob Hisey .20 .50
12 Alex Karaulchuk .20 .50
13 Brian Lee .20 .50
14 Chad Loikets .20 .50
15 Matthew Lynn .20 .50
16 Mike Melinko .20 .50
17 Derek Merlini .20 .50
18 Sean O'Connor .20 .50
19 Ryan O'Marra .40 1.00
20 Josh Patterson .20 .50
21 Geoff Platt .40 1.00
22 Vince Scott .20 .50
23 Jhase Sniderman .30 .75
24 Jason Speight .20 .50

2004-05 Erie Otters

A total of 700 team sets were produced. The NNO cards are randomly inserted.

COMPLETE SET (25) 5.00 12.00
1 Michael Blunden .30 .75
2 Tomas Galasek .20 .50
3 Derek Merlini .20 .50
4 Brett MacLean .20 .50
5 Jhase Sniderman .30 .75
6 Geoff Platt .30 .75
7 Chris Greene .20 .50
8 Sean O'Connor .20 .50
9 Vince Scott .20 .50
10 Jake Heller .20 .50
11 Derrick Bagshaw .20 .50
12 Andrew Hotham .20 .50
13 Brian Lee .20 .50
14 Chad Loikets .20 .50
15 Peter Sergeant .20 .50
16 Josh Kidd .20 .50
17 Ryan O'Marra .40 1.00
18 Eric Regan .20 .50
19 Andrew Shennan .20 .50
20 Jason Speight .20 .50
21 Josh Disher .30 .75
22 David Herring .20 .50
23 Dave MacQueen CO .04 .10
24 Peter Sidorkiewicz ACO .10 .25
25 Shooter MASCOT .04 .10
NNO Ryan O'Marra LTD 2.00 5.00
NNO Geoff Platt LTD 1.50 4.00

2005-06 Erie Otters

COMPLETE SET (23) 5.00 12.00
1 Ryan O'Marra .40 1.00
2 Derrick Bagshaw .20 .50
3 Michael Blunden .40 1.00
4 Chris Greene .20 .50
5 Justin Hodgman .20 .50
6 Patrick Lee .20 .50
7 Jordan Nolan .20 .50
8 Sean O'Connor .20 .50
9 Vince Scott .20 .50
10 Christian Seest Olsen .20 .50
11 Nick Palmieri .20 .50
12 Anthony Peluso .20 .50
13 Josh Vatri .20 .50
14 Jake Heller .20 .50
15 Andrew Hotham .20 .50
16 Josh Kidd .20 .50
17 Chad Loikets .20 .50
18 Josh Disher .20 .50
19 Ryan Ludzik .20 .50
20 Adam Berti .20 .50
21 Bret Nasby .20 .50
22 Jonathan Hull .20 .50
23 Tyler McKinley .20 .50

2006-07 Erie Otters

COMPLETE SET (24) 8.00 15.00
1 Nick Palmieri .20 .50
2 Sean O'Connor .20 .50
3 Patrick Lee .20 .50
4 Derrick Bagshaw .20 .50
5 Mitchell Forbes .20 .50
6 Stanislav Polodna .20 .50
7 Luke Gazdic .20 .50
8 Justin Hodgman .20 .50
9 Josh Vatri .20 .50
10 Shayne Taylor .20 .50
11 Kelly Geoffrey .20 .50
12 Kyle Ramsay .20 .50
13 Zack Torquato .60 1.50
14 Ronny Rogers .20 .50
15 Josh Kidd .20 .50
16 Mitch Gaulton .20 .50
17 Andrew Hotham .20 .50
18 Anthony Peluso .20 .50
19 Brian Shaw .20 .50
20 Michael Liambas .20 .50
21 Ryan Henry .20 .50
22 Jonathan Laniel .40 1.00
23 Justin Garay .40 1.00
24 Ryan Ludzik .40 1.00

2012-13 Erie Otters

COMPLETE SET (24) 20.00 40.00
1 Connor McDavid 15.00 30.00

2013-14 Erie Otters Choice

COMPLETE SET (25) 8.00 20.00
1 Spencer Abraham .30 .75
2 Nick Betz .30 .75
3 Connor Brown .40 1.00
4 Andre Burakovsky .30 .75
5 Michael Curtis .30 .75
6 Oscar Dansk .30 .75
7 Travis Dermott .30 .75
8 Troy Donnay .30 .75
9 Jake Evans .30 .75
10 Justin Felker .30 .75
11 Dane Fox .30 .75
12 Brendan Gaunce .30 .75
13 Cory Genovese .30 .75
14 Kurtis MacDermid .30 .75
15 Quentin Maksimovich .30 .75
16 Connor McDavid 2.00 5.00
17 Patrick Murphy .30 .75
18 Adam Pelech .40 1.00
19 Kyle Pettit .30 .75
20 Darren Raddysh .30 .75
21 Dylan Strome .40 1.00
22 Joel Wigle .30 .75
23 Devin Williams .30 .75
24 Travis Wood .30 .75
25 Shooter [Mascot] .30 .75

2014-15 Erie Otters Choice

COMPLETE SET (16) 8.00 20.00
1 Nick Betz .30 .75
2 Shaun Bily .30 .75
3 Alex DeBrincat .30 .75
4 Daniel Dekoning .30 .75
5 Troy Donnay .30 .75
6 Patrick Fellows .30 .75
7 T.J. Fergus .30 .75
8 Kurtis MacDermid .30 .75
9 Kyle Maksimovich .30 .75
10 Quentin Maksimovich .30 .75
11 Jake Marchment .30 .75
12 Mason Marchment .30 .75
13 Connor McDavid 3.00 8.00
14 Patrick Murphy .30 .75
15 Kyle Pettit .30 .75
16 Dylan Strome .75 2.00

1994-95 Erie Panthers

Produced by CJ Sports, this 20-card standard-size set features the Erie Panthers of the East Coast Hockey League. The fronts display color action player photos with gray borders. The player's name, position, and sponsor's name are below. The team name and logo appear at the top. The backs are white, grey, and black with player biography and statistics.

COMPLETE SET (20) 3.00 8.00
1 Title Card .02 .10
2 Ron Hansis CO .02 .10
3 Barry Smith ACO .02 .10
4 Patrick Laughlin TR .02 .10
5 Larry Empey .20 .50
6 Vassili Demin .20 .50
7 Sergei Stas .20 .50
8 Brad Harrison .20 .50
9 Cam Brown .20 .50
10 Kevin McKinnon .20 .50
11 Andrei Kozlov .20 .50
12 Chris Tschupp .20 .50
13 Jason Smith .20 .50
14 Justin Peca .20 .50
15 Francis Ouellette .20 .50
16 Vern Guetens .30 .75
17 Scott Burfoot .30 .75
18 Vyacheslav Polikarkin .20 .50
19 Stephane Charbonneau .20 .50
20 Ian Decorby .20 .50

2003-04 Everett Silvertips

COMPLETE SET (28) 5.00 12.00
1 Checklist .04 .10
2 Bryan Nathe .20 .50
3 Marc Desloges .20 .50
4 Jovan Matic .20 .50
5 Mike Wall .30 .75
6 Michael Wuchterl .20 .50
7 Mark Kress .20 .50
8 Devin Wilson .20 .50
9 Martin Ruzicka .20 .50
10 Curtis Billsten .20 .50
11 Barry Horman .20 .50
12 Shaun Heshka .20 .50
13 Jeff Schmidt .20 .50
14 Cody Thoring .20 .50
15 Ryan Blatchford .20 .50
16 Torrie Wheat .20 .50
17 Mitch Love .20 .50
18 Devin Welsh .20 .50
19 Riley Armstrong .20 .50
20 Tyler Dietrich .20 .50
21 John Dahl .20 .50
22 Jeff Harvey .30 .75
23 Ivan Baranka .20 .50
24 Chad Bassen .20 .50
25 Doug Soetaert GM .04 .10
26 Kevin Constantine CO .04 .10
27 John Becanic ACO .04 .10
28 Jay Varady ACO .04 .10

2004-05 Everett Silvertips

COMPLETE SET 10.00 20.00
1 Header Card .04 .10
2 Tyler Dietrich .20 .50
3 Alex Leavitt .20 .50
4 Mitch Love .20 .50
5 Doug Soetaert .04 .10
6 Mike Wuchterl .20 .50
7 Cody Thoring .20 .50
8 Karel Hromas .20 .50
9 Ryan Blatchford .20 .50
10 Zach Sim .20 .50
11 Mark Kress .20 .50
12 Brennan Zasitko .20 .50
13 Torrie Wheat .20 .50
14 Michael Wall .40 1.00
15 Graham Potuer .20 .50
16 Matt Sawa .20 .50
17 Randy King .20 .50
18 Leland Irving 1.25 3.00
19 Shaun Heshka .20 .50
20 Jonathan Harty .20 .50
21 Zach Hamill 1.25 3.00
22 Taylor Ellington .20 .50
23 Jeremy Creurer .20 .50
24 Brady Calla .30 .75
25 Curtis Billsten .20 .50
26 Ivan Baranka .20 .50
27 Kyle Annesley .20 .50
28 Jay Varady .20 .50
29 John Becanic .20 .50
30 Kevin Constantine .04 .10

2005-06 Everett Silvertips

COMPLETE SET (30) 10.00 20.00
1 Damir Alic .30 .75
2 Brady Calla .30 .75
3 Zack Dailey .30 .75
4 Eric Doyle .30 .75
5 Taylor Ellington .30 .75
6 Matt Esposito .30 .75
7 Ondrej Fiala .40 1.00
8 Jason Fransoo .30 .75
9 Zach Hamill .75 2.00
10 Shane Harper .30 .75
11 Jonathon Harty .30 .75
12 Shaun Heshka .30 .75
13 Karel Hromas .30 .75
14 Leland Irving .75 2.00
15 Mark Kress .30 .75
16 John Lammers .30 .75
17 Jonathan Milhouse .30 .75
18 Peter Mueller 2.00 5.00
19 Graham Potuer .30 .75
20 Ryan Sawka .30 .75
21 Zach Sim .30 .75
22 Jesse Smyke .30 .75
23 Brennan Sonne .30 .75
24 Cody Thoring .30 .75
25 Torrie Wheat .30 .75
26 Kevin Constantine HC .02 .10
27 John Becanic AC .02 .10
28 Jay Varady AC .02 .10
29 Scott Scoville DPP .02 .10
30 Zoran Rajcic DO .02 .10

2013-14 Everett Silvertips

COMPLETE SET (28) 8.00 20.00
1 Logan Aasman .30 .75
2 Austin Adam .30 .75
3 Nik Amundrud .30 .75
4 Patrick Bajkov .30 .75
5 Kohl Bauml .30 .75
6 Ben Betker .30 .75
7 Kevin Constantine CO .30 .75
8 Kevin Davis .30 .75
9 Matt Fonteyne .30 .75
10 Manraj Hayer .30 .75
11 Zane Jones .30 .75
12 Noah Juulsen .30 .75
13 Jujhar Khaira .30 .75
14 Remi Laurencelle .30 .75
15 Dawson Leedahl .30 .75
16 Mark LeRose Asst. CO .30 .75
17 Austin Lotz .30 .75
18 Mitch Love Asst. CO .30 .75
19 Brayden Low .30 .75
20 Cole MacDonald .30 .75
21 Mirco Mueller .30 .75
22 Ivan Nikolishin .30 .75
23 Matthew Pufahl .30 .75
24 Tyler Sandhu .30 .75
25 Carson Stadnyk .30 .75
26 Jordan Wharrie .30 .75
27 Josh Winquist .30 .75
28 Header Card .30 .75

2005 Extreme Top Prospects Signature Edition

This 30-card set was sold only in set form and was limited to just 400 sets. Each card carried a certified player autograph. The Sidney Crosby stick/auto card was inserted in one out of 4 sets and was limited to 150 copies though only 100 copies were used in the sets. The other 50 cards were given to Crosby. Please note that there are two cards numbered S7 and that card S26 does not exist.

S1 Sidney Crosby 150.00 250.00
S2 Alex Bourret 6.00 15.00
S3 Guillaume Latendresse 12.00 30.00
S4 Marc-Antoine Pouliot 10.00 25.00
S5 Jean-Francois Jacques 6.00 15.00
S6 David Krejci 6.00 15.00
S7 Corey Perry 12.50 30.00
S7 Daren Machesney 6.00 15.00
S8 Rob Schremp 10.00 25.00
S9 Danny Syvret 6.00 15.00
S10 Petr Vrana 6.00 15.00
S11 Derick Brassard 10.00 25.00
S12 Stephen Dixon 6.00 15.00
S13 James Sheppard 8.00 20.00
S14 Marc Staal 8.00 20.00
S15 Benoit Pouliot 8.00 20.00
S16 Anthony Stewart 6.00 15.00
S17 Michael Ouzas 6.00 15.00
S18 Patrick O'Sullivan 8.00 20.00
S19 Lukas Kaspar 6.00 15.00
S20 Bobby Ryan 10.00 25.00
S21 Stanislav Lascek 6.00 15.00
S22 Marek Zagrapan 6.00 15.00
S23 Josh Hennessy 6.00 15.00
S24 Alexander Radulov 10.00 25.00
S25 Julien Ellis-Plante 8.00 20.00
S27 Wojtek Wolski 10.00 25.00
S28 Mike Richards 10.00 25.00
S29 Boris Valabik 6.00 15.00
S30 Ryan O'Marra 6.00 15.00
SS1 S.Crosby Stick AU/150 300.00 500.00

2013-14 Fargo Force

COMPLETE SET (26) 6.00 15.00
A01 Chris Buchanan .30 .75
A02 Andrew McDonald .30 .75
A03 C.J. Hayes .30 .75
A04 Michael Babcock .30 .75
A05 Hunter Warner .30 .75
A06 Butrus Ghafari .30 .75
B01 Christian Cakebread .30 .75
B02 Brendan Jensen .30 .75
B03 Alex Toscano .30 .75
B04 Garick Gray .30 .75
B05 Mason Morelli .30 .75
B06 Neal Goff .30 .75
C01 Tyler Hynes .30 .75
C02 Meirs Moore .30 .75
C03 Cody Longie .30 .75
C04 Tanner Jago .30 .75
C05 J.M. Piotrowski .30 .75
C06 Cam Ashley .30 .75
C07 Andrew Zerban .30 .75
C08 Mathias Israelsson .30 .75
D01 Kid Bobble MASCOT .30 .75
D02 Teemu Kivihalme .30 .75
D03 Cameron Johnson .30 .75
D04 John Baiocco .30 .75
D05 Alex Jackstadt .30 .75
D06 Mikey Eyssimont .30 .75

2014-15 Fargo Force

COMPLETE SET (21) 6.00 15.00
1 Colton Poolman .30 .75
2 Victor Bergstrom .30 .75
3 Brody Stevens .30 .75
4 Shane McMahan .30 .75
5 Christian Cakebread .30 .75
6 C.J. Hayes .30 .75
7 Zach Yon .30 .75
8 Denis Smirnov .30 .75
9 Michael Babcock .30 .75
10 Mikey Eyssimont .30 .75
11 Cole Bjugson .30 .75
12 Mason Morelli .30 .75
13 Mitch Slattery .30 .75
14 T.J. Roo .30 .75
15 Kyle Sylvester .30 .75
16 Chuck Bennis .30 .75
17 Mathias Israelsson .30 .75
18 Robbie Beydoun .30 .75

19 Justin Baudry .30 .75
20 Austin Pooley .30 .75
21 Matt McArdle .30 .75

1998-99 Fayetteville Force

Little is known about this Central Hockey League team set beyond the confirmed checklist. Any additional information can be forwarded to hockeymag@beckett.com.

COMPLETE SET (18) 3.60 9.00
1 David Lohrei HCO .20 .50
2 Darren McLean .20 .50
3 Rod Butler .20 .50
4 Steven Toll .20 .50
5 Justin Tomberlin .20 .50
6 Alexsandr Chunchukov .20 .50
7 Casey Hungle .20 .50
8 Jason Wright .20 .50
9 Roddy MacCormick .20 .50
10 Lon Hovland .20 .50
11 Chris Bernard .20 .50
12 Dan Dennis .20 .50
13 Chris Ford .20 .50
14 Ryan Guzior .20 .50
15 Chad Remackel .20 .50
16 Colin Muldoon .20 .50
17 Stephen Sangermano .20 .50
18 Tim Hill .20 .50

2006-07 Fayetteville FireAntz

COMPLETE SET (21) 20.00 40.00
1 Mike Clarke .75 2.00
2 Chad Collins• 1.25 3.00
3 Bryan Dobek .75 2.00
4 Chris Furguson .75 2.00
5 Gavin Hodgson .75 2.00
6 Garrett Kindred• 1.25 3.00
7 Nick Kormanyos .75 2.00
8 John Marks HC .20 .50
9 Rob Manchoff CO .20 .50
10 Adam Meyer .75 2.00
11 Marc Norrington .75 2.00
12 Josh Piro .75 2.00
13 Jarrett Robertson .75 2.00
14 Dylan Row .75 2.00
15 Pekka Saittakari .75 2.00
16 Rob Sich .75 2.00
17 B.J. Stephens .75 2.00
18 Josh Tataryn .75 2.00
19 Tim Velemirovich .75 2.00
20 Josh Welter .75 2.00
21 Chad Wilcox .75 2.00

1991-92 Ferris State Bulldogs

This 30-card standard-size set features the 1991-92 Ferris State Bulldogs. The cards were available in the Ferris State University Pro Shop at the arena. The cards are unnumbered and checklisted below in alphabetical order.

COMPLETE SET (30) 4.00 10.00
1 Aaron Asp .20 .50
2 Seth Appert .20 .50
3 J.J. Bamberger .20 .50
4 Kevin Beals ACO .02 .10
5 Scot Bell .20 .50
6 Brad Burnham .20 .50
7 Dan Chaput .20 .50
8 Tim Christian .20 .50
9 Bob Daniels .20 .50
10 Colin Dodunski .20 .50
11 Mick Dolan .20 .50
12 John Duff .20 .50
13 Daryl Filipek .20 .50
14 John Gruden .20 .50
15 Luke Harvey .20 .50
16 Jeff Jestadt .20 .50
17 Dave Karpa .30 .75
18 Gary Kitching .20 .50
19 Mike Kolenda .20 .50
20 Craig Lisko .20 .50
21 Mike May .20 .50
22 Pat Mazzoli .20 .50
23 Robb McIntyre .20 .50
24 Kevin Moore .20 .50
25 Greg Paine .20 .50
26 Dwight Parrish .20 .50
27 Val Passarelli .20 .50
28 Keith Sergott .20 .50
29 Doug Smith .20 .50
30 The Bulldog MASCOT .02 .10

1992-93 Ferris State Bulldogs

This set features the Bulldogs of the NCAA. The cards were issued as a giveaway and are unnumbered, so are listed below in alphabetical order.

COMPLETE SET (30) 8.00 20.00
1 Seth Appert .30 .75
2 Aaron Asp .30 .75
3 J.J. Bamberger .30 .75
4 Kevin Beals .30 .75
5 Scot Bell .30 .75
6 Brad Burnham .30 .75
7 Daniel Chaput .30 .75
8 Tim Christian .30 .75
9 Bob Daniels CO .08 .25
10 Colin Dodunski .30 .75
11 Mick Dolan .30 .75
12 John Duff .30 .75
13 Daryl Filipek .30 .75
14 John Gruden .40 1.00
15 Luke Harvey .30 .75
16 Jeff Jestadt .30 .75
17 Dave Karpa .40 1.00
18 Gary Kitching .30 .75
19 Mike Kolenda .30 .75
20 Craig Lisko .30 .75
21 Mike May .30 .75
22 Pat Mazzoli .30 .75
23 Robb McIntyre .30 .75
24 Kevin Moore .30 .75
25 Greg Paine .30 .75
26 Dwight Parrish .30 .75
27 Val Passarelli .40 1.00
28 Keith Sergott .30 .75
29 Doug Smith .30 .75
30 The Bulldog MASCOT .02 .10

1993-94 Flint Generals

This set of 20 cards features the Flint Generals of the Colonial Hockey League. It was produced for team distribution by Rising Star Sport Promotions. The fronts feature a posed photo, along with league logo and player information. The backs contain a smattering of biographical data and career numbers. The set is unnumbered.

COMPLETE SET (20) 40.00 75.00
1 Header Card .40 1.00
2 Brent Stickney 1.50 4.00
3 Brett Strot 1.50 4.00
4 Brian Sakic 2.00 5.00
5 Chris O'Rourke 1.50 4.00
6 Dan Elsener 1.50 4.00
7 Darcy Austin 1.50 4.00
8 Dominic Niro 1.50 4.00
9 Jim Duhart 1.50 4.00
10 John Heasty 1.50 4.00
11 Keith Whitmore 1.50 4.00
12 Ken Spangler 1.50 4.00
13 Kevin Kerr 1.50 4.00
14 Larry Bernard 1.50 4.00
15 Lorne Knauft 1.50 4.00
16 Marc Vachon 1.50 4.00
17 Mark Gowens 2.00 5.00
18 Peter Horachek 1.50 4.00
19 Stephane Brochu 1.50 4.00
20 Todd Humphrey 2.00 5.00

1994-95 Flint Generals

This 24-card set of the Flint Generals of the Colonial Hockey League was produced by and distributed through the team. The set's familiar look comes from its homage to the lamentable 1991-92 Pro Set issue. The card backs also ape the design, although they are in black and white, containing another photo and player stats.

COMPLETE SET (24) 20.00 50.00
1 Kevin Barrett .75 2.00
2 Larry Bernard .75 2.00
3 Ken Blum .75 2.00
4 Stephane Brochu .75 2.00
5 Keith Carney .75 2.00
6 Ryan Douglas .75 2.00
7 Jim Duhart .75 2.00
8 Ray Gallagher .75 2.00
9 Mark Gowens .75 2.00
10 Peter Horachek .75 2.00
11 Todd Humphrey .75 2.00
12 Fredrik Jax 1.00 2.50
13 Doug Jones .75 2.00
14 Kevin Kerr 1.00 2.50
15 Petr Leska .75 2.00
16 Stan Matwijiw 1.25 3.00
17 Glen Mears .75 2.00
18 Kyle Reeves 1.00 2.50
19 Brian Sakic 1.00 2.50
20 Stefan Simoes .75 2.00
21 Ken Spangler .75 2.00
22 Keith Whitmore .75 2.00
23 Jeff Whittle .75 2.00
24 Team Photo .75 2.00

1995-96 Flint Generals

This 25-card set features the Flint Generals of the CHL. The set was produced by, and available only through, the team's booster club. The fronts feature an action photo and team and booster club logos. The back includes another photo, player stats and a brief bio.

COMPLETE SET (25) 4.80 12.00
1 Erin Whitten 1.00 2.50
2 Kevin Kerr .30 .75
3 Sverre Sears .15 .40
4 Scott Burfoot .20 .50
5 John Batten .15 .40
6 Chad Grills .15 .40
7 Lady Generals .30 .75
8 General Rally Mascot .02 .10
9 Rob Nichols GM CO .02 .10
10 Mikhail Nemirovsky .15 .40
11 Robin Bouchard .15 .40
12 Dominic Grandmaison .15 .40
13 Andrei Mezin .30 .75
14 Steve Beadle .15 .40
15 Darryl Lafrance .15 .40
16 Chris Gotziaman .15 .40
17 Gerry St. Cyr .30 .75
18 Derek Knorr .15 .40
19 Chris Gordon .20 .50
20 Brett MacDonald .15 .40
21 Brian Sakic .20 .50
22 Jamie Hearn .15 .40
23 Jeff Whittle .15 .40
24 Stephane Brochu .15 .40
25 Jim Duhart .15 .40

1996-97 Flint Generals

This 28-card set was issued as a promotional giveaway over the span of several games. This set is not numbered so the cards appear in alphabetical order.

COMPLETE SET (28) 10.00 25.00
1 Steve Beadle .40 1.00
2 Pascal Belanger .40 1.00
3 Robin Bouchard .40 1.00
4 Stephane Brochu .40 1.00
5 Neil Eisenhut .40 1.00
6 Nick Forbes .40 1.00
7 Igor Galkin .40 1.00
8 Jason Glover .40 1.00
9 Chad Grills .40 1.00
10 John Heasty .40 1.00
11 Kevin Kerr .40 1.00
12 Lorne Knauft .40 1.00
13 Brett MacDonald .40 1.00
14 Andrei Mezin .60 1.50
15 Jason Payne .40 1.00
16 Jason Ralph .40 1.00
17 Dmitri Rodine .40 1.00
18 Zdenek Sikl .40 1.00
19 Ken Spangler .40 1.00
20 Matt Weder .40 1.00
21 Jeff Whittle .40 1.00
22 Ross Wilson .40 1.00
23 Rob Nichols HCO .20 .50
24 Karl Lawson .40 1.00
25 General Rally Mascot .20 .50
26 1996 Colonial Cup Champs .40 1.00
27 1996 Tarry Cup Champs .40 1.00
28 Checklist .20 .50

1997-98 Flint Generals

This set features the Generals of the UHL. The cards were issued as promotional giveaways in 10-card packs at three different games.

COMPLETE SET (30) 12.00 30.00
1 Steve Beadle .40 1.00
2 Stephane Brochu .60 1.50
3 Ian Crockford .40 1.00
4 Nick Forbes .40 1.00
5 Mark Giannetti .40 1.00
6 Jason Glover .40 1.00
7 Chad Grills .40 1.00
8 John Heasty .40 1.00
9 Raitis Ivanans .40 1.00
10 Kevin Kerr .60 1.50
11 Lorne Knauft .40 1.00
12 Ray LeBlanc .75 2.00
13 Brett MacDonald .40 1.00
14 Bryan McMullen .40 1.00
15 Andrei Mezin .75 2.00
16 Matt Mullin .60 1.50
17 Dmitri Rodine .40 1.00
18 Brian Sakic .60 1.50
19 Jeremy Sladovnik .40 1.00
20 Ken Spangler .40 1.00
21 Kahlil Thomas .40 1.00
22 Jeff Whittle .40 1.00
23 Ross Wilson .40 1.00
24 Rob Nichols CO .08 .25
25 General Rally MASCOT .08 .25
26 Mike Zanzarella TR .08 .25
27 Robert Roe STAFF .08 .25
28 Pam The Prize Lady .20 .50
29 Lady Generals .40 1.00
30 Flint Generals .40 1.00

1997-98 Flint Generals EBK

This set features the Generals of the UHL. The set was produced by ebk Sports and was sold by the team at home playoff games.

COMPLETE SET (23) 4.00 10.00
1 Checklist .02 .10
2 Kahlil Thomas .20 .50
3 Ken Spangler .20 .50
4 Stephane Brochu .30 .75
5 Lorne Knauft .20 .50
6 Janis Tomans .20 .50
7 Nick Forbes .20 .50
8 Trevor Jobe .20 .50
9 John Heasty .20 .50
10 Brian Sakic .30 .75
11 Kevin Kerr .30 .75
12 Chad Grills .20 .50
13 UHL All-Stars .20 .50
14 Jeremy Sladovnik .20 .50
15 Jeff Whittle .20 .50
16 Jason Glover .20 .50
17 Steve Beadle .20 .50
18 Bryan McMullen .20 .50
19 Emmanuel Labranche .20 .50
20 Brett MacDonald .20 .50
21 John Batten .20 .50
22 Ross Wilson .20 .50
23 Rob Nichols CO .08 .25

1998-99 Flint Generals

This set features the Generals of the UHL. The cards were issued in packs as a promotional giveaway at one home game. Reports conflict as to whether the packs contained four, six or eight cards. Anyone with additional information can forward it to hockeymag@beckett.com.

COMPLETE SET (22) 8.00 20.00
1 Logo Card .02 .10
2 Chad Grills .40 1.00
3 Jason Payne .40 1.00
4 Jeremy Sladovnik .40 1.00
5 Stephane Brochu .40 1.00
6 Jeff Whittle .40 1.00
7 Rob Nichols CO .08 .25
8 Brian Sakic .60 1.50
9 Checklist .02 .10
10 Nick Forbes .40 1.00
11 Mike Bondy .40 1.00
12 Peter Ambroziak .40 1.00
13 Luch Nasato .60 1.50
14 Mikhail Nemirovsky .40 1.00
15 Bobby Reynolds .40 1.00
16 Generals Staff .02 .10
17 Lorne Knauft .40 1.00
18 Rob Laurie .60 1.50
19 Ross Wilson .40 1.00
20 Jason Glover .40 1.00
21 Brett MacDonald .40 1.00
22 Kahlil Thomas .40 1.00

2001-02 Flint Generals

COMPLETE SET (24) 20.00
1 Joey Bastien .40 1.00
2 Sylvain Dufresne .40 1.00
3 Jim Duhart .40 1.00
4 Stu Dunn .60 1.50
5 Tim Findlay .40 1.00
6 Dale Greenwood .40 1.00
8 Lee Jelenic .40 1.00
9 Lorne Knauft .40 1.00
10 Corey Laniuk .40 1.00
11 Tom McKinnon .60 1.50
12 Frankie Nault .40 1.00
13 Eric Perricone .40 1.00
14 Jean-Francois Picard .40 1.00
15 Bobby Reynolds .40 1.00
16 Gary Roach .40 1.00
17 Mike Rutter .40 1.00
18 Jordan Trew .40 1.00
19 Mike Varhaug .60 1.50
20 Martin Woods .40 1.00
21 Vaclav Zavoral .40 1.00
22 Kirk Tomlinson HCO .20 .50
23 General Rally MASCOT .04 .10
24 The Lady Generals .04 .10

2007-08 Flint Generals

COMPLETE SET (21) 5.00 12.00
1 Team Checklist .15 .40
2 Jaroslav Cesky .30 .75
3 Eric Marvin .30 .75
4 Martin Ondrej .30 .75
5 Michel Beausoleil .30 .75
6 Greg Bullock .30 .75
7 Jared Dumba .30 .75
8 Brock Wilson .30 .75
9 Kris Mallette .30 .75
10 John DiPace .30 .75
11 Shaun Fisher .30 .75
12 Darren McCarty .30 .75
13 Ryan Jorde .30 .75
14 Josef Fojtik .30 .75
15 Mike Kinnie .30 .75
16 Jordan Fox .30 .75
17 Chad Alban .30 .75
18 Mike Alexiou .30 .75
19 Jonathan Duchesneau .30 .75
20 Nick Tuzzolino .30 .75
21 Justin Depretis .30 .75

1987-88 Flint Spirits

This 20-card standard-size set features white-bordered posed color player photos. The team name and the player's name edge the picture on the left and lower edges respectively. Team logos in the bottom border round out the front. The horizontal backs carry biography, player profile, and statistics.

COMPLETE SET (20) 4.80 12.00
1 Mario Chitaroni .20 .50
2 John Cullen .40 1.00
3 Bob Fleming .20 .50
4 Keith Gretzky .40 1.00
5 Todd Hawkins .20 .50
6 Mike Hoffman .20 .50
7 Curtis Hunt .20 .50
8 Dwaine Hutton .20 .50
9 Trent Kaese .20 .50
10 Tom Karalis .20 .50
11 Ray LeBlanc .40 1.00
12 Darren Lowe .20 .50
13 Brett MacDonald .20 .50
14 Chris McSorley .40 1.00
15 Mike Mersch .20 .50
16 Victor Posa .20 .50
17 Kevin Schamehorn .20 .50
18 Ron Stern .40 1.00
19 Don Waddell .20 .50
20 Dan Woodley .20 .50

1988-89 Flint Spirits

This 22-card standard-size features posed color player photos. The pictures are set at an angle on the card with green borders on the top and bottom. The player's name appears in the lower green border, while the team appears above. A thin blue line borders the front. The horizontal backs carry the player's name, biographical information, statistics, and career highlights. The cards are unnumbered and checklisted below in alphabetical order.

COMPLETE SET (22) 4.00 10.00
1 Dean Anderson .20 .50
2 Rob Bryden .20 .50
3 John Devereaux .20 .50
4 Stephane Giguere .20 .50
5 Steve Harrison .20 .50
6 Yves Heroux .30 .75
7 Mike Hoffman .20 .50
8 Peter Horachek .20 .50
9 Guy Jacob .20 .50
10 Bob Kennedy .20 .50
11 Gary Kruzich .20 .50
12 Lonnie Loach .40 1.00
13 Brett MacDonald .20 .50
14 Mike MacWilliam .20 .50
15 Moe Mansi .20 .50
16 Mike Mersch .20 .50
17 Michel Mongeau .40 1.00
18 Ken Spangler .20 .50
19 Three Amigos .30 .75
Steve Harrison
Mike Mersch
Mike Hoffman
20 Mark Vichorek .20 .50
21 Troy Vollhoffer .20 .50
22 Don Waddell GM .20 .50

2003-04 Florence Pride

COMPLETE SET (16) 15.00
145 Jack Baker .40 1.00
146 Craig Brunel .40 1.00
147 Adam Elzinga .40 1.00
148 Ryan Gaucher .40 1.00
149 Wes Goldie .40 1.00
150 Vladimir Gusev .40 1.00
151 Kyle Kidney .40 1.00
152 Dan Lombard .40 1.00
153 Mark McRae .40 1.00
154 Matt Reid .40 1.00
155 Bobby Russell .40 1.00
156 Allan Sirois .40 1.00
157 Jeff Szwez .40 1.00
158 Shaun Sutter .40 1.00
159 Mike Torney .40 1.00
160 Matt Underhill .60 1.50

1998-99 Florida Everblades

Little is known about this East Coast League team set beyond the confirmed checklist. Any additional information can be forwarded to hockeymag@beckett.com.

COMPLETE SET (27) 7.20 50.00
1 Brett Bruininks .75 2.00
2 Matt Brush .75 2.00
3 Nick Checco .75 2.00
4 Matt Demarski .75 2.00
5 Sergei Fedotov .75 2.00
6 Tim Ferguson .75 2.00
7 Bob Ferguson CO .02 .10
8 Hugh Hamilton .75 2.00
9 Mike Jickling .75 2.00
10 Gary Koehler .75 2.00
11 Greg Kuznik .75 2.00
12 Dane Litke .75 2.00
13 Marc Magliarditi 2.00 5.00
14 Kevin McDonald .75 2.00
15 Pat Mikesch .75 2.00
16 P.K. O'Handley ACO .02 .10
17 Josh Penn EQ .02 .10
18 Randy Petruk 2.00 5.00
19 Jason Prokepetz .75 2.00
20 Dan Keimann .75 2.00
21 Eric Ricard .75 2.00
22 Eric Rud .75 2.00
23 Steve Tardif .75 2.00
24 Andrew Taylor .75 2.00
25 Todd Wisocki .75 2.00
26 Mascot .02 .10
27 Title Card .02 .10

1999-00 Florida Everblades

This set features the Everblades of the ECHL. The set was produced by Roox and handed out as a promotional giveaway at a late-season home game.

COMPLETE SET (26) 8.00 20.00
1 Jeff Maund .60 1.50
2 Hugh Hamilton .30 .75
3 Greg Kuznik .30 .75
4 Dane Litke .30 .75
5 Peter Kasper .30 .75
6 Tim Ferguson .30 .75
7 Brent Cullaton .30 .75
8 Reggie Berg .40 1.00
9 Steve Moffatt .30 .75
10 Tom Buckley .30 .75
11 Eric Rud .30 .75
12 Jason Prokopetz .30 .75
13 Terry Lindgren .40 1.00
14 Matt Demarski .30 .75
15 Marc Magliarditi .60 1.50
16 Ty Jones .40 1.00
17 Harlan Pratt .30 .75
18 John Varga .40 1.00
19 Joe Cardarelli .30 .75
20 Steve Tardif .30 .75
21 Andy MacIntyre .30 .75
22 Jason Morgan .30 .75
23 Bob Ferguson CO .08 .25
24 P.K. O'Handley CO .08 .25
25 Swampy MAS .08 .25
26 Celluar One .02 .10

2000-01 Florida Everblades

This set features the Everblades of the ECHL. The set was produced by Roox as a promotional giveaway.

COMPLETE SET (26) 8.00 20.00
1 Bujar Amidovski .80 2.00
2 Reggie Berg .40 1.00
3 Sean Blanchard .40 1.00
4 Tom Buckley .40 1.00
5 Sandy Cohen .40 1.00
6 Randy Copley .40 1.00
7 Matt Demarski .30 .75
8 Bob Ferguson CO .20 .50
9 Hugh Hamilton .30 .75
10 Devin Hartnell .30 .75
11 Darrell Hay .40 1.00
12 Pete Hogan .30 .75
13 John Jennings EM .10 .25
14 Mike Jickling .30 .75
15 Terry Lindgren .40 1.00
16 Andy Macintyre .30 .75
17 Marc Magliarditi .60 1.50
18 Brent McDonald .30 .75
19 Jason Metcalfe .30 .75
20 Jason Morgan .30 .75
21 P.K. O'Handley CO .20 .50
22 Brent Pope .30 .75
23 Swampee MASCOT .20 .50
24 David Vallieres .30 .75
25 Todd Wisocki TR .10 .25
26 TTI Computers .01

2001-02 Florida Everblades

This set features the Everblades of the ECHL. The cards were produced by Choice Marketing and were issued as a giveaway. A total of 2,000 sets were produced. Each set also includes the ultimate whip, a card promoting a Pikachu cartoon.

COMPLETE SET (21) 8.00 20.00
1 Checklist .20 .50
2 Gerry Fleming CO .20 .50
3 P.K. O'Handley ACO .20 .50
4 Vince Williams .40 1.00
5 Terry Lindgren .60 1.50
6 Duane Harmer .40 1.00
7 Andrew Long .40 1.00
8 Reggie Berg .40 1.00
9 Brent McDonald .40 1.00
10 Tom Buckley .40 1.00
11 Briane Thompson .40 1.00
12 Mike Cirillo .40 1.00
13 Don Smith .40 1.00
14 Joe Blaznek .40 1.00
15 Peter Reynolds .40 1.00
16 Paul Spadafora .60 1.50
17 Keith Anderson .40 1.00
18 Shaun Fisher .40 1.00
19 Randy Petruk .60 1.50
20 Ryan Murphy .40 1.00
21 Swampee .20 .50

2002-03 Florida Everblades

This set was produced by Choice Marketing and given away at a home game.

COMPLETE SET (26) 10.00 25.00
1 Keith Anderson .40 1.00
2 George Awada .40 1.00
3 Anthony Battaglia .40 1.00
4 Joe Blaznek .40 1.00
5 Kevin Brown .40 1.00
6 Tom Buckley .40 1.00
7 Sean Curry .40 1.00
8 Brian Goudie .40 1.00
9 Duane Harmer .40 1.00
10 Ed Hill .40 1.00
11 Marty Johnston .40 1.00
12 Cam McCormick .60 1.50
13 Laurent Meunier .40 1.00
14 Ryan Murphy .40 1.00
15 Tom Nelson .40 1.00
16 Peter Reynolds .40 1.00
17 Lee Ruff .40 1.00
18 Don Smith .40 1.00
19 Ryan Stewart .40 1.00
20 Jimmy Verdule .75 2.00
21 Jon Insana .40 1.00
22 Rob Zepp .75 2.00
23 Gerry Fleming CO .20 .50
24 Terry Lindgren ACO .04 .10
25 Swampee MASCOT .04 .10
26 Checklist .04 .10

2002-03 Florida Everblades RBI

COMPLETE SET (18) 20.00
115 Keith Anderson .40 1.00
116 George Awada .40 1.00
117 Anthony Battaglia .40 1.00
118 Joe Blaznek .40 1.00
119 Tom Buckley .40 1.00
120 Brian Goudie .40 1.00
121 Duane Harmer .40 1.00
122 Marty Johnston .40 1.00
123 Cam McCormick .60 1.50
124 Brent McDonald .40 1.00
125 Laurent Meunier .40 1.00
126 Ryan Murphy .40 1.00
127 Tom Nelson .40 1.00
128 Jared Newman .40 1.00
129 Peter Reynolds .40 1.00
130 Don Smith .40 1.00
131 Jimmy Verdule .75 2.00
132 Rob Zepp .75 2.00

2003-04 Florida Everblades

This set was issued by Choice Marketing and given away at one home game.

COMPLETE SET (25) 8.00 20.00
1 Keith Anderson .40 1.00
2 Reggie Berg .40 1.00
3 Jim Brown .40 1.00
4 Brandon Coalter .40 1.00
5 Paul Esdale .40 1.00
6 Gerry Fleming CO .08 .20
7 Ian Forbes .40 1.00
8 Chris Heisten .40 1.00
9 Tom Buckley .40 1.00
10 Jon Insana .40 1.00
11 Chad Larose .40 1.00
12 Jay Legault .40 1.00
13 Terry Lindgren ACO .08 .20
14 Tim O'Connell .40 1.00
15 Jeff Maund .60 1.50
16 Brian McCullough .40 1.00
17 Brent McDonald .40 1.00
18 Jared Newman .40 1.00
19 Matt Pagnutti .40 1.00
20 Paul Vincent .40 1.00
21 Gray Shaneberger .40 1.00
22 Mascot .08 .20
23 Chris Thompson .40 1.00
24 Ryan Van Buskirk .40 1.00
25 Rob Zepp .75 2.00

2003-04 Florida Everblades RBI Sports

This set was issued by RBI Sports, and is limited to just 250 copies. The numbering sequence continues across all RBI Sports sets issued this season.

COMPLETE SET (16) 10.00 18.00
161 Reggie Berg .40 1.00
162 Brandon Coalter .40 1.00
163 Paul Esdale .40 1.00
164 Kevin Holdridge .40 1.00
165 Jon Insana .40 1.00
166 Chad Larose .40 1.00
167 Carl Mallette .50 1.25
168 Jeff Maund .60 1.50
169 Brian McCullough .40 1.00
170 Jared Newman .40 1.00
171 Stuart Pietersma .40 1.00
172 Peter Reynolds .40 1.00
173 Gray Shaneberger .40 1.00
174 Damian Surma .50 1.25
175 Ryan Van Buskirk .40 1.00
176 Rob Zepp .75 2.00

2004-05 Florida Everblades

COMPLETE SET (30) 20.00
1 Tyler MacKay .30 .75
2 Jared Newman .30 .75
3 Matt Pagnutti .30 .75
4 Shane Hnidy .30 .75
5 Simon Tremblay .30 .75
6 Reggie Berg .30 .75
7 Brent MacDonald .30 .75
8 Steve Saviano .30 .75
9 Ryan Brindley .30 .75
10 Tim Branham .30 .75
11 Brandon Coalter .30 .75
12 Matt Hendricks .30 .75
13 David Lundbohm .30 .75
14 Tim O'Connell .30 .75
15 Bryce Charpentier .30 .75
16 Kris Vernarsky .40 1.00
17 Brad Church .40 1.00
18 Greg Hornby .30 .75
19 Keith Anderson .30 .75
20 Damian Surma .30 .75
21 Rob Zepp .40 1.00
22 Craig Kowalski .30 .75
23 Chris Lee .30 .75
24 Jason Nobili .30 .75
25 Gerry Fleming .04 .10
26 Todd Wisocki .04 .10
27 John Jennings .04 .10
28 Swampee MASCOT .04 .10
29 Sponsor card .04 .10
30 Checklist .04 .10

2005-06 Florida Everblades

COMPLETE SET (25) 6.00 15.00
1 Jonathan Lehun .30 .75
2 Martin Tuma .30 .75
3 Paul Cabana .30 .75
4 Reggie Berg .30 .75
5 Swampee MASCOT .02 .10
6 Phil Aucoin .30 .75
7 Brandon Coalter .30 .75
8 Ernie Hartlieb .30 .75
9 Phil Osaer .30 1.00
10 Steve Saviano .30 .75
11 Ryan Brindley .30 .75
12 Bryce Charpentier .30 .75
13 Craig Kowalski .30 .75
14 Daniel Sisca .30 .75
15 Anders Strome .30 .75
16 Sean Stefanski .30 .75
17 Corey Neilson .30 .75
18 Grant McNeill .30 .75
19 Chris Lee .30 .75
20 Kevin Bergin .30 .75
21 John Adams .30 .75
22 Vince Bellissimo .30 .75
23 John Ronan .30 .75
24 Jeremy Swanson .30 .75
25 Gerry Fleming HC .02 .10

1990-91 Fort Saskatchewan Traders

This sheet contains 24 standard-size cards. Each card contains a color action player photo with his jersey number and name at the top on a white background. Above this are listed the player's position with the team name and years. At the lower right are the words "Next Generation Sport Cards." Each photo is framed by a thin red line and white border. The cards are unnumbered and checklisted below in alphabetical order.

COMPLETE SET (24) 2.50 6.00
1 Michael Buzak .15 .40
2 Wade Fennig .15 .40
3 Mark Goodkey .15 .40
4 Richard Groten .15 .40
5 Brett Gullion .15 .40
6 Keith Hill .15 .40
7 Justin Hocking .30 .75
8 Ian Kallay .15 .40
9 Scott Lindsay .15 .40
10 Faron Luchkow .15 .40
11 Wayne MacDonald .15 .40
12 Ted Oloriz .15 .40
13 Jason Plandowski .15 .40
14 Dory Reich .15 .40
15 Shawn Reich .15 .40
16 Darren Smith .15 .40
17 Mark Souch .15 .40
18 Bryan Stewart .15 .40
19 Paul Strand .15 .40
20 Tim Wiwchar .15 .40
21 Paul Wozney .15 .40
22 Allen Young .15 .40
23 Jason Yuzda .15 .40
24 Team Photo .20 .50

1993-94 Fort Wayne Komets

Cards are unnumbered and are listed below in alphabetical order.

COMPLETE SET (27) 6.00 15.00
1 Ian Boyce .30 .75
2 Colin Chin .30 .75
3 Lee Davidson .30 .75
4 Guy Dupuis .30 .75
5 Steve Fletcher .75 2.00
6 Sean Gauthier .30 .75
7 Darryl Gilmour .40 1.00
8 Kelly Hurd .30 .75
9 Carey Lucyk .30 .75
10 Kevin MacDonald .30 .75
11 Igor Malykhin .30 .75
12 Brian McKee .30 .75
13 Mitch Messier .40 1.00
14 Max Middendorf .40 1.00
15 John Purves .40 1.00
16 Grant Richison .30 .75
17 Darin Smith .30 .75
18 Dave Smith .30 .75
19 Shayne Stevenson .30 .75
20 David Tretowicz .30 .75
21 Vladimir Tsyplakov .30 .75
22 Doug Wickenheiser .40 1.00
23 Bruce Boudreau CO .20 .50
24 Derek Ray ACO .20 .50
25 Joe Franke TR .20 .50
26 Galen Head EQM .20 .50
27 Team Photo .20 .50

1995-96 Fort Wayne Komets

This set features the Komets of the IHL. The set was produced by Edge Ice and sold at the team's souvenir stands.

COMPLETE SET (25) 4.80 12.00
1 Andy Bezeau .20 .50
2 Colin Chin .20 .50
3 Shawn Cronin .20 .50
4 Guy Dupuis .20 .50
5 Pat Elynuik .20 .50
6 Bob Essensa .30 .75
7 Shawn Evans .20 .50
8 Steven Fletcher .20 .50
9 Peter Ing .20 .50
10 Andrew McBain .20 .50
11 Mitch Messier .20 .50
12 Rob Murphy .20 .50
13 Alex Nikolic .20 .50
14 Grant Richison .20 .50
15 Jeff Rohlicek .20 .50
16 Konstantin Shafronov .20 .50
17 Darin Smith .20 .50
18 Sergei Stas .20 .50
19 Brian Straub .20 .50
20 Chris Tok .20 .50
21 Paul Willett .20 .50
22 Kevin Wortman .20 .50
23 Oleg Yashin .20 .50
24 Derek Ray CO .08 .25
25 Icy MAS .02 .10

1997-98 Fort Wayne Komets

Little is known about this set beyond the confirmed checklist. Additional information can be forwarded to hockeymag@beckett.com.

COMPLETE SET (21) 4.00 10.00
1 Guy Dupuis .20 .50
2 Ian Boyce .20 .50
3 Lee Davidson .20 .50
4 Bruce Racine .30 .75
5 Dan Currie .20 .50
6 Robin Bawa .20 .50
7 Tom Nemeth .20 .50
8 Ed Campbell .20 .50
9 Vyacheslav Butsayev .20 .50
10 Steffon Walby .20 .50
11 Derek Eberle .20 .50
12 Chris Armstrong .20 .50
13 Norm Batherson .20 .50
14 Konstantin Shafronov .20 .50
15 Tom Pederson .20 .50
16 Andrei Bashkirov .20 .50
17 Carlin Nordstrom .20 .50
18 Trevor Doyle .20 .50
19 Eric Boguniecki .30 .75
20 Kevin Weekes .60 1.50
21 Icy D. Eagle Mascot .02 .10

1998-99 Fort Wayne Komets

Little is known about this team set beyond the confirmed checklist. Any additional information can be forwarded to hockeymag@beckett.com.

COMPLETE SET (29) 4.00 10.00
1 Ed Campbell .15 .40
2 Vyacheslav Butsayev .20 .50
3 Ian Boyce .15 .40
4 Eric Boguniecki .20 .50
5 Robin Bawa .15 .40
6 Gerard Gallant ACO .15 .40
7 Icy D. Eagle Mascot .02 .10
8 Guy Dupuis .15 .40
9 Dion Darling .15 .40
10 Bob Chase .15 .40
11 Brad Purdie .15 .40
12 Andrei Petrakov .15 .40
13 David Nemirovsky .20 .50
14 Mike Martin .15 .40
15 Tero Lehtera .20 .50
16 Oleg Shargorodsky .15 .40
17 Shawn Selmser .20 .50
18 Andre Roy .20 .50
19 Eldon Reddick .20 .50
20 Bruce Racine .20 .50
21 Memorial Coliseum .02 .10
22 Derek Wood .15 .40
23 Lee Sorochan .20 .50
24 Grant Sonier HCO .02 .10
25 Checklist .02 .10
26 Shawn Penn .15 .40
27 PHPA Web Site .02 .10
28 IHL Web Site .02 .10
29 Andrei Bashkirov .15 .40

1999-00 Fort Wayne Komets Points Leaders

This set was produced by the Komets of the UHL to honor their all-time leading scorers. However, since this was their first season in the league, the players pictured performed for the team during its IHL days. The cards are believed to have been issued as a promotional giveaway, but this has not been confirmed.

COMPLETE SET (16) 6.00 15.00
1 Header Card .02 .10
2 Len Thornson .40 1.00
3 Eddie Long .40 1.00
4 Terry McDougall .40 1.00
5 Colin Chin .40 1.00
6 John Goodwin .40 1.00
7 Reg Primeau .40 1.00
8 Merv Dubchek .40 1.00
9 Barry Scully .40 1.00
10 Rob Laird .40 1.00
11 Jim Burton .60 1.50
12 Lionel Repka .40 1.00
13 Norman Waslowski .40 1.00
14 Ron Leef .40 1.00
15 Bobby Rivard .40 1.00
16 Dale Baldwin .40 1.00

1999-00 Fort Wayne Komets Penalty Leaders

This set was produced by the Komets of the UHL to honor their all-time leading pugilists. However, since this was their first season in the league, the players pictured performed for the team during its IHL days. The cards are believed to have been issued as a promotional giveaway, but this has not been confirmed.

COMPLETE SET (16) 8.00 35.00
1 Header Card .02 .10
2 Steven Fletcher 1.25 3.00
3 Dale Baldwin .75 2.00
4 Cal Purinton 1.25 3.00
5 Rob Laird .75 2.00

Dave Norris .75 2.00
Robin Bawa 1.25 3.00
Terry Pembroke .75 2.00
Andy Bezeau 1.25 3.00
0 Eddie Long .75 2.00
1 Craig Channell .75 2.00
2 Steve Salvucci .75 2.00
3 Carey Lucyk .75 2.00
4 Lionel Repka .75 2.00
5 Scott Gruhl 1.25 3.00
6 Guy Dupuis .75 2.00

2000-01 Fort Wayne Komets

his set was produced by the team and sold at home ames throughout the season. The cards are unnumbered, and are listed below in alphabetical rder.

OMPLETE SET (24) 4.80 12.00
Frederic Bouchard .20 .50
Dave Butler .20 .50
Keli Corpse .30 .75
Derek Gauthier .30 .75
Jason Goulet .20 .50
Brent Gretzky .30 .75
Kelly Hurd .20 .50
Rick Judson .20 .50
Dave Lemay .20 .50
0 Jim Logan .20 .50
1 Igor Malykhin .20 .50
2 Darren Martens .20 .50
3 Mike McKay .20 .50
4 Geno Parrish .20 .50
5 Kevin Popp .20 .50
6 Sergei Radchenko .20 .50
7 Gary Ricciardi .20 .50
8 Dan Ronan .20 .50
9 Konstantin Simchuk .20 .50
20 Fred Slukynsky .20 .50
21 Doug Teskey .20 .50
22 Brad Twordik .20 .50
23 Greg Puhalski CO .10 .25
24 Ice Eagle MASCOT .04 .10

2000-01 Fort Wayne Komets Shoe Carnival

This set features the Komets of the UHL. The set was a promotional giveaway, sponsored by a local shoe store. The cards were released in five-card strips, featuring four players and a store coupon.

COMPLETE SET (16) 6.00 15.00
Rhett Trombley .40 1.00
Gary Ricciardi .40 1.00
Jason Goulet .40 1.00
Rick Judson .40 1.00
Igor Malykhin .40 1.00
Doug Teskey .40 1.00
Kelly Hurd .40 1.00
Mike McKay .40 1.00
Brent Gretzky .80 2.00
10 Geno Parrish .40 1.00
11 Dave Lemay .40 1.00
12 Jim Logan .40 1.00
13 Frederic Bouchard .40 1.00
14 Brad Twordik .40 1.00
15 Dan Ronan .40 1.00
16 Derek Gauthier .40 1.00

2001-02 Fort Wayne Komets

This set features the Komets of the UHL. It was produced by Choice Marketing and was sold by the team at its souvenir shop. The production was announced at 1,000 sets.

COMPLETE SET (22) 4.00 10.00
1 Doug Teskey .20 .50
2 Igor Bondarev .20 .50
3 Frederic Bouchard .30 .75
4 Christian Bragnalo .20 .50
5 Derek Gauthier .30 .75
6 Dustin Virag .20 .50
7 Chad Grills .20 .50
8 Kevin Holliday .20 .50
9 Icy D. Eagle Mascot .04 .10
10 Erik Landman .20 .50
11 Jim Logan .20 .50
12 Michael Massie .20 .50
13 David Mayes .20 .50
14 Mike McKay .20 .50
15 Kelly Miller .30 .75
16 Martin Fillion .20 .50
17 Kevin Schmidt .20 .50
18 Ryan Severson .20 .50
19 Matt Swain .20 .50
20 Kevin Bertram .20 .50
21 Steven Desjardins .20 .50
22 Brent Gretzky CO .30 .75

2001-02 Fort Wayne Komets Shoe Carnival

The set of the UHL's Fort Wayne franchise features players from both the current Komets team and former greats. The set was issued as a promotional giveaway, with four cards handed out per night at four different games.

COMPLETE SET (16) 6.00 15.00
1 Dustin Virag .40 1.00
2 Reg Primeau .40 1.00
3 Kevin Holliday .40 1.00
4 Steven Fletcher .75 2.00
5 Brent Gretzky .40 1.00
6 Len Thornson .40 1.00
7 Derek Gauthier .40 1.00
8 Robin Bawa .40 1.00
9 Frederic Bouchard .40 1.00
10 Lionel Repka .40 1.00
11 Michel Masse .40 1.00
12 Eddie Long .40 1.00
13 Doug Teskey .40 1.00
14 Chuck Adamson .40 1.00
15 Jim Logan .40 1.00
16 Ian Boyce .40 1.00

2002-03 Fort Wayne Komets

COMPLETE SET (25) 4.00 10.00
1 Marc Barlow .20 .50
2 David Beauregard .20 .50
3 Kevin Bertram .20 .50
4 Ken Boone .20 .50
5 Colin Chaulk .20 .50
6 Parris Duffus .30 .75
7 Joe Franke .20 .50
8 Kevin Kotyluk .30 .75
9 Tom Lawson .30 .75
10 Adam Lewis .20 .50
11 Michel Massie .20 .50
12 Troy Neumeier .20 .50
13 Jake Ortmeyer .20 .50
14 Kelly Perrault .20 .50
15 Eldon Reddick .30 .75
16 Kevin Schmidt .20 .50
17 Jason Selleke .20 .50
18 Ryan Severson .20 .50
19 Bart Stevens .20 .50
20 Bobby Stewart .20 .50
21 Sean Venedam .20 .50
22 Dustin Virag .20 .50
23 Icy D. Eagle MASCOT .04 .10
24 Greg Puhalski HCO .04 .10
NNO Checklist .04 .10

2002-03 Fort Wayne Komets Shoe Carnival

COMPLETE SET (16) 12.00 30.00
1 Kelly Perrault .75 2.00
2 David Beauregard .75 2.00
3 Jake Ortmeyer .75 2.00
4 Michel Massie .75 2.00
5 Tom Lawson .75 2.00
6 Bobby Stewart .75 2.00
7 Ryan Severson .75 2.00
8 Eldon Reddick 1.25 3.00
9 Sean Venedam .75 2.00
10 Kevin Bertram .75 2.00
11 Marc Barlow .75 2.00
12 Dustin Virag .75 2.00
13 Icy D. Eagle MASCOT .04 .10
14 Kevin Schmidt .75 2.00
15 Colin Chaulk .75 2.00
16 Adam Lewis .75 2.00

2003-04 Fort Wayne Komets

This series was produced by Choice Marketing and sold at home games.

COMPLETE SET (23) 4.00 10.00
1 Bobby Stewart .20 .50
2 Colin Chaulk .20 .50
3 David Beauregard .20 .50
4 Sean Venedam .20 .50
5 Dan Stewart .20 .50
6 Ryan Severson .20 .50
7 Michel Massie .20 .50
8 Dustin Virag .20 .50
9 Kevin Kotyluk .30 .75
10 Adam Lewis .20 .50
11 Dan Price .20 .50
12 Mascot .04 .10
13 Andy Townsend .20 .50
14 Kevin Schmidt .20 .50
15 Mark Cole .20 .50
16 Mike Perna .20 .50
17 Kelly Perrault .20 .50
18 Kevin Bertram .20 .50
19 Troy Neumeier .20 .50
20 Kelly Shields .30 .75
21 Kevin St. Pierre .30 .75
22 Ryan Coole .20 .50
23 Steve Rodberg .20 .50

2003-04 Fort Wayne Komets 2003 Champions

COMPLETE SET (21) 3.00 8.00
1 Colin Chaulk .20 .50
2 Kelly Perrault .20 .50
3 Dustin Virag .20 .50
4 Sean Venedam .20 .50
5 Tom Lawson .20 .50
6 Colin Chaulk .20 .50
7 Tom Lawson .20 .50
8 Parading the Cup .08 .20
9 Dustin Virag .20 .50
10 Kevin Bertram .20 .50
11 Greg Puhalski HCO .08 .20
12 Kelly Perrault .20 .50
13 Dustin Virag .20 .50
14 Michel Massie .20 .50
15 Marc Barlow .20 .50
16 Tom Lawson .20 .50
17 Team Photo .20 .50
17 Komets Fans .04 .10
18 Kelly Perrault .20 .50
19 Kevin Kotyluk .30 .75
20 Sponsor .04 .10

2003-04 Fort Wayne Komets Shoe Carnival

These were issued as a promotional giveaway over the course of four home games. The cards came in four-card perforated strips.

COMPLETE SET (16) 5.00 12.00
1 Kelly Perrault .40 1.00
2 Kevin Schmidt .40 1.00
3 Kevin Bertram .40 1.00
4 Adam Lewis .40 1.00
5 Troy Neumeier .40 1.00
6 Colin Chaulk .40 1.00
7 Kevin Kotyluk .60 1.50
8 Bobby Stewart .40 1.00
9 Kevin St. Pierre .60 1.50
10 David Beauregard .40 1.00
11 Michel Massie .40 1.00
12 Sean Venedam .40 1.00
13 Dan Price .40 1.00
14 Dan Stewart .40 1.00
15 Ryan Severson .40 1.00
16 Dustin Virag .40 1.00

2004-05 Fort Wayne Komets

This set was produced by Choice Marketing and sold at the pro shop.

COMPLETE SET (21) 3.00 8.00
1 Colin Chaulk .40 1.00
2 P.C. Drouin .30 .75
3 Jonathan Goodwin .20 .50
4 Chris Grenville .20 .50
5 Rob Guinn .20 .50
6 David Hukalo .20 .50
7 Jason Kean .20 .50
8 Shane Kenny .20 .50
9 Tyler Masters .30 .75
10 Tom Nelson .20 .50
11 Tom Nemeth .20 .50
12 Troy Nuemeier .20 .50
13 Steve Rodberg .20 .50
14 Kevin St. Pierre .30 .75
15 Danny Stewart .20 .50
16 Andy Townsend .20 .50
17 Sean Venedam .20 .50
18 Dustin Virag .20 .50
19 Jeff Worlton .20 .50
20 Team Checklist .04 .10
21 Mascot .04 .10
22 Sponsor Card .04 .10

2004-05 Fort Wayne Komets Shoe Carnival

This set was issued as a promotional giveaway at a home game.

COMPLETE SET (16) 10.00 25.00
1 Colin Chaulk 1.25 3.00
2 P.C. Drouin .75 2.00
3 Jonathan Goodwin .60 1.50
4 Chris Grenville .60 1.50
5 Rob Guinn .60 1.50
6 Jason Kean .60 1.50
7 Shane Kenny .60 1.50
8 Tim Krueckl .60 1.50
9 Corey Lucas .60 1.50
10 Tyler Masters .75 2.00
11 Troy Neumeier .60 1.50
12 Kevin St. Pierre .75 2.00
13 Dan Stewart .60 1.50
14 Sean Venedam .75 2.00
15 Dustin Virag .60 1.50
16 Jeff Worlton .60 1.50

2005-06 Fort Wayne Komets Choice

COMPLETE SET (25) 4.00 10.00
1 Kevin St. Pierre .20 .50
2 Jeff Worlton .20 .50
3 Jonathan Goodwin .20 .50
4 David Hukalo .20 .50
5 David Frawley .20 .50
6 David Carpentier .20 .50
7 Andrew Luciuk .20 .50
8 Brent Rumble .20 .50
9 Matt Hunter .20 .50
10 Kelly Miller .20 .50
11 Garrett Summerfield .20 .50
12 P.C. Drouin .20 .50
14 Lance Galbraith .20 .50
15 Mark Smith .20 .50
16 Kevin Kurk .20 .50
17 Guy Dupuis .20 .50
18 Jason Kean .20 .50
19 John Jarram .20 .50
20 A.J. Bozoian .20 .50
21 Rob Guinn .20 .50
22 Mark Lindsay .20 .50
23 Troy Neumeier .20 .50
24 Ryan Jorde .20 .50
25 Icy D. Eagle MASCOT .02 .10

2005-06 Fort Wayne Komets Sprint

COMPLETE SET (16) 8.00 20.00
1 A.J. Bozoian .60 1.50
2 David Carpentier .60 1.50
3 Colin Chaulk .60 1.50
4 P.C. Drouin .60 1.50
5 Guy Dupuis .60 1.50
6 Lance Galbraith .60 1.50
7 Lance Galbraith .60 1.50
8 Jonathan Goodwin .60 1.50
9 Rob Guinn .60 1.50
10 David Hukalo .60 1.50
11 John Jarram .60 1.50
12 Ryan Jorde .60 1.50
13 Mark Lindsay .60 1.50
14 Troy Neumeier .60 1.50
15 Brent Rumble .60 1.50
16 Kevin St. Pierre .60 1.50

2006-07 Fort Wayne Komets

COMPLETE SET (24) 10.00 20.00
1 A.J. Bozoian .40 1.00
2 Mike Dombkiewicz .40 1.00
3 Guy Dupuis .40 1.00
4 Martin Gascon .40 1.00
5 Daniel Goneau .40 1.00
6 Jonathan Goodwin .40 1.00
7 Kevin Hansen .40 1.00
8 Jani Honkanen .40 1.00
9 David Hukalo .40 1.00
10 Arthur Kiyaga .40 1.00
11 Jean-Francois Labarre .40 1.00
12 Mario Larocque .75 2.00
13 Dan McWhinney .60 1.50
14 Pascal Morency .40 1.00
15 Bruce Richardson .40 1.00
16 Bogdan Rudenko .40 1.00
17 J.C. Ruid .40 1.00
18 Kevin St. Pierre .60 1.50
19 Matt Syroczynski .40 1.00
20 Brent Henley .40 1.00
21 K.J. Voorhees .40 1.00
22 Pat Bingham .40 1.00
23 Icy D. Eagle MASCOT .02 .10
24 Nesquik SPONSOR .01 .01

2013-14 Fort Wayne Komets

COMPLETE SET (4) 1.00 2.50
1 Andrey Makarov .30 .75
2 Mike Embach .30 .75
3 Jordon Southorn .30 .75
4 Mickey Lang .30 .75

2013-14 Fort Wayne Komets Choice

COMPLETE SET (28) 8.00 20.00
1 Brandon Marino .30 .75
2 Chris Auger .30 .75
3 Jace Coyle .30 .75
4 Simon Danis-Pepin .30 .75
5 Scott Fleming .30 .75
6 Joe Hartman .30 .75
7 Bobby Hughes .30 .75
8 Mike Embach .30 .75
9 Nathan Martine .30 .75
10 Mickey Lang .30 .75
11 Andrey Makarov .30 .75
12 Phil Mangan .30 .75
13 Kenton Miller .30 .75
14 Nik Pokulok .30 .75
15 Cody Reichard .30 .75
16 Jordon Southorn .30 .75
17 Shawn Szydlowski .30 .75
18 Mike Vaskivuo .30 .75
19 Gary Graham CO .30 .75
20 Kaleigh Schrock .30 .75
21 Matt Carter .30 .75
22 Jeremy Gates .30 .75
23 William Lacasse .30 .75
24 Ben Meisner .30 .75
25 Sy Nutkevitch .30 .75
26 Christian Ouellet .30 .75
27 Dean Ouellet .30 .75
28 Jason Dale .30 .75

2014-15 Fort Wayne Komets

COMPLETE SET (6) 7.50 15.00
1 Kyle Thomas 1.25 3.00
2 Jean-Michel Rizk 1.25 3.00
3 Matthew Pistilli 1.25 3.00
4 Cody Sol 1.25 3.00
5 Pat Nagle 1.25 3.00
6 Roman Will 1.25 3.00

2014-15 Fort Wayne Komets Choice

COMPLETE SET (22) 8.00 20.00
1 Pat Nagle .30 .75
2 Ian Barteaux .30 .75
3 Mikael Tam .30 .75
4 Paul Crowder .30 .75
5 Drew Daniels .30 .75
6 Mike Embach .30 .75
7 Eric Faille .75 2.00
8 Thomas Frazee .30 .75
9 Mitchell Heard .30 .75
10 Matt Krug .30 .75
11 William Lacasse .30 .75
12 Joey Leach .30 .75
13 James Martin .30 .75
14 Garrett Meurs .30 .75
15 Christian Ouellet .30 .75
16 Brett Perlini .30 .75
17 Reid Petryk .75 2.00
18 Matthew Pistilli .30 .75
19 Kaleigh Schrock .30 .75
20 C.J. Severyn .75 2.00
21 Cody Sol .30 .75
22 Shawn Szydlowski .30 .75

1997-98 Fort Worth Brahmas

This 21-card set was sold at home games for $4. The cards do not bear numbers, so they are listed alphabetically.

COMPLETE SET (21) 4.00 10.00
1 Chris Albert .20 .50
2 Steve Carter .20 .50
3 Brian Caruso .20 .50
4 Cosmo DuPaul .20 .50
5 David Graff .20 .50
6 Craig Hayden .20 .50
7 Murray Hogg .20 .50
8 Alex Kholomeyev .30 .75
9 Stephane Larocque .30 .75
10 Rob Laurie .30 .75
11 Mike McCormick .20 .50
12 Nolan McDonald .20 .50
13 Terry Menard .20 .50
14 Max Middendorf .20 .50
15 Mark O'Donnell .20 .50
16 Adam Robbins .20 .50
17 Todd St. Louis .20 .50
18 Mark Strohack .20 .50
19 Gatis Tseplis .20 .50
20 Dwight Mullins ACO .20 .50
21 Bill McDonald CO .20 .50

1998-99 Fort Worth Brahmas

This 20-card set was handed out at a home game and is extremely scarce on the secondary market.

COMPLETE SET (20) 6.00 15.00
1 Terry Menard CO .20 .50
2 Steve Plouffe .60 1.50
3 Tim Green .40 1.00
4 Scott Shaunessy .40 1.00
5 Jim Dinneen .40 1.00
6 Martin Machacek .40 1.00
7 Francois Albert .40 1.00
8 Sean Brady .40 1.00
9 Murray Hogg .40 1.00
10 Ryan Black .40 1.00
11 Mark Strohack .40 1.00
12 Richie Walcott .40 1.00
13 Stephane Larocque .60 1.50
14 Barry Cummins .40 1.00
15 Phil Miaskowski .40 1.00
16 Martin Lamarche .40 1.00
17 Cosmo Dupaul .40 1.00
18 Jon Olotson .60 1.50
19 Craig Hayden .60 1.50
20 Steve Carter .40 1.00

1999-00 Fort Worth Brahmas

This 20-card set features the 1999-00 Fort Worth Brahmas on extra glossy card stock. In the upper left hand corner of each card appears "The Hockey Store" logo from a shop in Arlington, Texas. Cards are not numbered so they appear alphabetically. It is believed that they were issued as a promotional giveaway.

COMPLETE SET (20) 4.00 40.00
1 Louis Bernard .75 2.00
2 Bruiser MASCOT .02 .10
3 Jason Disher .75 2.00
4 Cosmo Dupaul .75 2.00
5 Cory Evans .75 2.00
6 Ross Harris .75 2.00
7 Murray Hogg .75 2.00
8 Alex Kholomeyev .75 2.00
9 Derek Kups .75 2.00
10 Martin Lamarche .75 2.00
11 Stephane Larocque .75 2.00
12 Terry Menard CO .20 .50
13 Jon Olotson 1.25 3.00
14 Steve Plouffe 2.00 5.00
15 Bobby Pochyly .75 2.00
16 Al Rooney .75 2.00
17 Mike Sanderson .75 2.00
18 Dennis Shiryaev .75 2.00
19 Mike Tilson .75 2.00
20 Gatis Tseplis .75 2.00

2000-01 Fort Worth Brahmas

This set features the Brahmas of the WPHL. The set was issued as a promotional giveaway in the form of a pair of unperforated nine-card sheets. The cards are not numbered so they appear below in alphabetical order.

COMPLETE SET (18) 4.80 12.00
1 Clint Cabana .30 .75
2 Justin Cardwell .30 .75
3 Jason Carey .30 .75
4 Steve Dowhy .30 .75
5 Ben Gorewich .30 .75
6 Jake Harney .30 .75
7 Ross Harris .30 .75
8 Casey Hungle .30 .75
9 Craig Johnson .30 .75
10 Todd Lalonde CO .08 .25
11 Rob Laurie .30 .75
12 Jason Pain .30 .75
13 Mike Rusk .30 .75
14 Ryan Shannon .30 .75
15 Mike Tilson .30 .75
16 Daniel Villeneuve .30 .75
17 Chad Woollard .30 .75
18 Mark Zacharias .30 .75

2001-02 Fort Worth Brahmas

This set features the Brahmas of the WPHL. The set was handed out at a game early in the season. Because the cards are unnumbered, they are listed below in alphabetical order.

COMPLETE SET (20) 8.00 20.00
1 Brady Austin .40 1.00
2 Jeff Bateman .60 1.50
3 Dave Bourque .40 1.00
4 Justin Cardwell .40 1.00
5 Jason Clarke .40 1.00
6 Kory Cooper .40 1.00
7 Dave Csumrik .40 1.00
8 Adam Davis .40 1.00
9 Sean Hughes .40 1.00
10 Craig Johnson .40 1.00
11 Chris Johnston .40 1.00
12 Cody Leibel .40 1.00
13 Todd Lalonde CO .20 .50
14 Cam MacDonald .40 1.00
15 Mike Tilson .60 1.50
16 Joe Van Volsen .60 1.50
17 Daniel Villeneuve .40 1.00
18 Chad Woollard .40 1.00
19 Scott Wray .40 1.00
20 Bruiser MASCOT .04 .10

2002-03 Fort Worth Brahmas

This set was issued as a promotional giveaway in two 10-card subsets at home games. The cards were printed on thin paper stock and are listed below in alphabetical order. Thanks to Ralph Slate for this checklist.

COMPLETE SET (20) 8.00 20.00
1 Adam Davis .40 1.00
2 Jason Fricker .60 1.50
3 David Fry .40 1.00
4 Rob Giffin .40 1.00
5 Chad Grills .40 1.00
6 Sean Hughes .40 1.00
7 Lee Jacobson .60 1.50
8 Lloyd Marks .40 1.00
9 Mike McKinnon .40 1.00
10 Jim Midgley .40 1.00
11 John Murphy .75 2.00
12 Jason Reesor .40 1.00
13 Mike Rusk .40 1.00
14 Joe Van Volsen .40 1.00
15 T.J. Warkus .40 1.00
16 Jeff Washbrook .40 1.00
17 Justin Williams .40 1.00
18 Chad Woollard .40 1.00
19 Bill Inglis CO .04 .10
20 Bruiser MASCOT .04 .10

2003-04 Fort Worth Brahmas

This set was issued as a promotional giveaway over the course of two home games.

COMPLETE SET (20) 6.00 15.00
1 Gary Baronick .40 1.00
2 Joey Bastien .40 1.00
3 Aaron Davis .40 1.00
4 Adam Davis .40 1.00
5 Scott English .60 1.50
6 Taras Foremsky .40 1.00
7 Chad Grills .40 1.00
8 Jan Jas .40 1.00
9 Jay McGee .40 1.00
10 Tyler Nilsson .60 1.50
11 Jason Reesor .40 1.00
12 Erasmo Saltarelli .60 1.50
13 Jeff Scharf .40 1.00
14 Peter Trumbley .40 1.00
15 Derrell Upton .40 1.00
16 Jeremy Vanin .40 1.00
17 Justin Williams .40 1.00
18 Chad Woollard .40 1.00
19 Al Sims HCO .20 .50
20 Mascot .04 .10

2004-05 Fort Worth Brahmas

Set was issued as a giveaway at two home games, 10 cards at a time.

COMPLETE SET (20) 12.00 30.00
1 Jay Banach .60 1.50
2 Brian Basner 1.00 2.50
3 Brandon Carper .60 1.50
4 Dave Csumrik .60 1.50
5 Aaron Davis .60 1.50
6 Adam Davis .60 1.50
7A Mark Hynes ERR .60 1.50
(Adam Davis back
7B Mark Hynes COR .60 1.50
8A Jan Jas ERR .60 1.50
(Mark Hynes back
8B Jan Jas COR .60 1.50
9 Brad Lukowich .75 2.00
10 Bryan Lundbohm .60 1.50
11 Dan Murphy .75 2.00
12 Sheldon Nedjelski .60 1.50
13 Martin Paquet .60 1.50
14 Larry Sterling .75 2.00
15 Nick Udovicic .60 1.50
16 Derrell Upton .60 1.50
17 Jorin Welsh .60 1.50
18 Chad Woollard .60 1.50
19 Al Sims CO .20 .50
20 Bruiser MASCOT .04 .10

1992-93 Fort Worth Fire

Sponsored by Whataburger, this 18-card set was issued as a cut set and also as a sheet. The sheet was rimmed on the left and right sides by a row of coupons redeemable at Whataburger. Card strips featuring three player cards sandwiched between two coupons were also produced. The cards measure the standard size and feature posed, color player photos with either a peach or a white studio background on white card stock. The picture is set off-center on a white area framed by a thin black line and shadow-bordered. The player's name and uniform number are printed above the photo, while "Whataburger" is printed in burnt orange below. The backs carry biographical information and career highlights. The cards are unnumbered and checklisted below in alphabetical order.

COMPLETE SET (18) 4.00 10.00
1 Ron Aubrey .20 .50
2 Roch Belley .40 1.00
3 Jason Brousseau .20 .50
4 Eric Brule .20 .50
5 Todd Drevitch .20 .50
6 Trevor Duhaime .20 .50
7 Steve Harrison ACO .08 .25
8 Ernest Hornak .20 .50
9 Alex Kholomeyev .30 .75
10 Curt Krolak .20 .50
11 Ryan Leschasin .20 .50
12 Peter Mahovlich CO .75 2.00
13 Mike McCormick .20 .50
14 Mike O'Hara .20 .50
15 Pat Penner .20 .50
16 Paolo Racicot .20 .50
17 Dan Rolfe .20 .50
18 Mike Sanderson .20 .50

1993-94 Fort Worth Fire

This 18-card set is similar in design to the Dallas Freeze issue of this year. The round cards are approximately the size of a hockey puck and came packaged in a plastic container with the team logo on the front. The sets were sold by the team's booster club at home games, and may have been made available through the mail.

COMPLETE SET (18) 2.40 75.00
1 Ron Aubrey 2.00 5.00
2 Derby Bognar 2.00 5.00
3 Reggie Brezeault 2.00 5.00
4 Jason Brousseau 2.00 5.00
5 Ty Eigner 2.00 5.00
6 Todd Huyber 2.00 5.00
7 Chris Jensen 2.00 5.00
8 Chad Johnson 2.00 5.00
9 Ryan Leschasin 2.00 5.00
10 Dominic Maltais 2.00 5.00
11 Mike McCormick 2.00 5.00
12 Patrick McGarry 2.00 5.00
13 Mike O'Hara 2.00 5.00
14 Sean Rowe 2.00 5.00
15 Mike Sanderson 2.50 6.00
16 Rob Striar 2.00 5.00
17 Scott Zygulski 2.00 5.00
18 Steve Harrison CO .75 2.00

1995-96 Fort Worth Fire

This 18-card team set features the Fort Worth Fire of the Central Hockey League. The set apparently was distributed by the booster club. In an unusual twist, the cards were not sold in team sets; instead, a 9-card assortment could be had for $3. Usually, it took three packs to assemble a complete set. The cards feature an action photo on the front, along with player bio and 1994-95 stats on the back.

COMPLETE SET (18) 4.00 10.00
1 Team Photo .30 .75
2 Bill McDonald CO .08 .25
3 Phil Groeneveld .20 .50
4 Vern Ray .20 .50
5 Steve Dykstra .30 .75
6 Trevor Burgess .20 .50
7 Scott Allen .20 .50
8 Sean Whyte .20 .50
9 Troy Frederick .20 .50
10 Troy Stephens .20 .50
11 Jeff Massey .20 .50
12 Dwight Mullins .20 .50
13 Kyle Reeves .40 1.00
14 Mike Gruttaduria .20 .50
15 Mark Hilton .20 .50
16 Brian Caruso .20 .50
17 Dennis Miller .20 .50
18 Steve Plouffe .30 .75

1996-97 Fort Worth Fire

This 18-card set features the CHL champion Fort Worth Fire. It was produced by the team and sold at the rink. The cards feature action photography surrounded by a condition sensitive black border. The player's name and number appear as well. The black and white back contains a player profile, but no numbering, hence the alphabetical listing below.

COMPLETE SET (18) 3.00 8.00
1 Malcolm Cameron .20 .50
2 Steve Carter .20 .50
3 Mike Sanderson .20 .50
4 Stephane Larocque .20 .50
5 Murray Hogg .20 .50
6 Bob Delorimiere .20 .50
7 Steve Plouffe .40 1.00
8 Glenn Painter .20 .50
9 Mark Strohack .20 .50
10 Brian Caruso .20 .50
11 Dwight Mullins .20 .50
12 Terry Menard .20 .50
13 Vern Ray .20 .50
14 Adam Robbins .20 .50
15 Mark O'Donnell .20 .50
16 Mike McCourt .20 .50
17 Ryan Black .20 .50
18 Bill McDonald CO .02 .10

1981-82 Fredericton Express

This 26-card set was issued by the team and endorsed by the Fredericton City Police, R.C.M.P., New Brunswick Highway Patrol, and New Brunswick Police Commission. The cards measure approximately 2 1/2" by 3 3/4" with a white border on the front. The fronts also carry a posed color player photo with the player's name printed below. The cards are numbered on the back.

COMPLETE SET (26) 8.00 20.00
1 Team Photo .30 .75
2 B.J. MacDonald .30 .75
3 Sylvain Cote .20 .50
4 Michel Bolduc .20 .50
5 Gary Lupul .20 .50
6 Clint Malarchuk .75 2.00
7 Tony Currie .20 .50
8 Tim Tookey .20 .50
9 Anders Eldebrink .40 1.00
10 Basil McRae .75 2.00
11 Kelly Elcombe .20 .50
12 Jacques Demers 1.25 3.00
13 Frank Caprice .40 1.00
14 Terry Johnson .20 .50
15 Grant Martin .20 .50
16 Andre Chartrain .20 .50
17 Marc Crawford 1.25 3.00
18 Gaston Therrien .20 .50
19 Andy Schliebener .20 .50
20 Christian Tanguay .20 .50
21 Art Rutland .20 .50
22 Jean MarcGaulin .20 .50
23 Neil Belland .20 .50
24 Andre Cote .20 .50
25 Jim MacRae .20 .50
26 Scott Beckingham .08 .25
Marty Flynn

1982-83 Fredericton Express

Sponsored by CFNB and Pepsi, this 26-card set measures approximately 2 1/2" by 3 3/4" and features posed, color player photos with white borders. The player's name and sponsor logos appear in the lower white margin.

COMPLETE SET (26) 8.00 20.00
1 Team Photo .40 1.00
2 B.J. MacDonald .30 .75
3 Sylvain Cote .30 .75
4 Michel Bolduc .20 .50
5 Gary Lupul .20 .50
6 Clint Malarchuk .75 2.00
7 Tony Currie .20 .50
8 Tim Tookey .20 .50
9 Anders Eldebrink .20 .50
10 Basil McRae 1.25 3.00
11 Kelly Elcombe .20 .50
12 Jacques Demers .75 2.00
13 Frank Caprice .60 1.50
14 Terry Johnson .20 .50
15 Grant Martin .20 .50
16 Andre Chartrain .20 .50
17 Marc Crawford .75 2.00
18 Gaston Therrien .20 .50
19 Andy Schliebener .20 .50
20 Christian Tanguay .20 .50
21 Art Rutland .20 .50
22 Jean-Marc Gaulin .20 .50
23 Neil Belland .20 .50
24 Andre Cote .20 .50
25 Jim MacRae .20 .50
26 Scott Beckingham TR .08 .25
Marty Flynn TR

1983-84 Fredericton Express

This 27-card set measures 2 1/2" by 3 3/4" and features posed action color player photos with white borders. The player's name, position, and NHL affiliation appear below the picture in the white margin. The horizontal backs are white and carry Police and Express Tips in French and English.

COMPLETE SET (27) 6.00 15.00
1 Team Photo .40 1.00
2 Frank Caprice .60 1.50
3 Michel Dufour .30 .75
4 Brian Ford .30 .75
5 Jean-Marc Lanthier .20 .50
6 Jim Dobson .20 .50
7 Mike Hough .40 1.00
8 Rick Lapointe .30 .75
9 Michel Bolduc .20 .50
10 Christian Tanguay .20 .50
11 Tony Currie .20 .50
12 Moe Lemay .40 1.00
13 Bruce Holloway .20 .50
14 Neil Belland .20 .50
15 Richard Turmel .20 .50
16 Claude Julien .30 .75
17 Andre Chartrain .20 .50
18 Grant Martin .20 .50
19 Rejean Vignola .20 .50
20 Andre Cote .20 .50
21 Jean-Marc Gaulin .20 .50
22 Andy Schliebener .20 .50
23 Stu Kulak .30 .75
24 Mike Eagles .60 1.50
25 Earl Jessiman CO .08 .25
GM
26 Marty Flynn TR .08 .25
Scott Beckingham TR
NNO Checklist .20 .50

1984-85 Fredericton Express

This 28-card set measures approximately 2 1/2" by 3 3/4" and features posed color player photos against a white card face. The player's name, biography, position, and NHL affiliation appear in black print below the picture. Sponsor logos are in the lower corners. The horizontal backs are white and carry Police and Express Tips in French and English.

COMPLETE SET (28) 6.00 15.00
1 Dave Morrison .20 .50
2 Dave Shaw .40 1.00
3 Bruce Holloway .20 .50
4 Roger Haegglund .20 .50
5 Neil Belland .20 .50
6 Gord Donnelly .40 1.00
7 David Bruce .20 .50
8 Claude Julien .20 .50
9 Dan Wood .20 .50
10 Clint Malarchuk .75 2.00
11 Jere Gillis .20 .50
12 Mike Hough .40 1.00
13 Michel Bolduc .20 .50
14 Peter Loob .20 .50
15 Steve Driscoll .20 .50
16 Newell Brown .20 .50
17 Jim Dobson .20 .50
18 Wendell Young .75 2.00
19 Mark Kumpel .30 .75
20 Mike Eagles .40 1.00
21 Tom Thornbury .20 .50
22 Grant Martin .20 .50
23 Marc Crawford .40 1.00
24 Andy Schliebener .20 .50
25 Earl Jessiman CO/GM .08 .25
26 Yvon Vautour .20 .50
27 Craig Coxe .40 1.00
28 Blake Wesley .20 .50

1985-86 Fredericton Express

This 28-card set measures 2 1/2" by 3 3/4" and features posed color player photos against a white card face. The player's name, biography, position, and NHL affiliation appear in black print below the picture. Sponsor logos are in the lower corners. The horizontal backs are white and carry Police and Express Tips in French and English.

COMPLETE SET (28) 4.80 12.00
1 Scott Tottle .20 .50
2 David Bruce .20 .50
3 Team Photo .30 .75
4 Marc Crawford .40 1.00
5 Mike Stevens .20 .50
6 Gary Lupul .20 .50
7 Alain Lemieux .30 .75
8 Mike Hough .40 1.00
9 Tony Currie .20 .50
10 Dunc MacIntyre .20 .50
11 Jere Gillis .20 .50
12 Wendell Young .60 1.50
13 Jean-Marc Lanthier .20 .50
14 Ken Quinney .30 .75
15 Claude Julien .30 .75
16 Michel Petit .40 1.00
17 Luc Guenette .20 .50
18 Andy Schliebener .20 .50
19 Mark Kirton .20 .50
20 Gord Donnelly .30 .75
21 Tom Karalis .20 .50
22 Daniel Poudrier .20 .50
23 Neil Belland .20 .50
24 Dale Dunbar .20 .50
25 Marty Flynn TR .08 .25
Scott Beckingham TR
26 Jean-Marc Gaulin .20 .50
27 Al MacAdam .30 .75
28 Andre Savard CO .20 .50
GM

1986-87 Fredericton Express

This 26-card set measures 2 1/2" by 3 3/4" and features posed color player photos against a white card face. The player's name, biography, position, statistics, and NHL affiliation appear in black print below the picture. Sponsor logos are in the lower corners. The horizontal backs are white and carry public service messages in French and English. The cards are unnumbered and checklisted below in alphabetical order.

COMPLETE SET (26) 4.00 10.00
1 Jim Agnew .20 .50
2 Brian Bertuzzi .20 .50
3 David Bruce .20 .50
4 Frank Caprice .30 .75
5 Marc Crawford .30 .75
6 Steven Finn .30 .75

7 Marty Flynn TR .08 .25
Scott Beckingham TR
8 Jean-Marc Gaulin .20 .50
9 Scott Gordon .30 .75
10 Taylor Hall .20 .50
11 Yves Heroux .20 .50
12 Mike Hough .30 .75
13 Tom Karalis .20 .50
14 Mark Kirton .20 .50
15 Jean-Marc Lanthier .20 .50
16 Jean LeBlanc .20 .50
17 Brett MacDonald .20 .50
18 Duncan MacIntyre .20 .50
19 Greg Malone .20 .50
20 Terry Perkins .20 .50
21 Daniel Poudrier .20 .50
22 Jeff Rohlicek .20 .50
23 Andre Savard CO .20 .50
24 Mike Stevens .20 .50
25 Trevor Stienburg .20 .50
26 Team Photo .30 .75

1992-93 Fredericton Canadiens

Printed on thin card stock, these 28 standard-size cards feature borderless color player action photos on the fronts. Each has the player's name and uniform number printed near the bottom and carries the Professional Hockey Player's Association logo. The white horizontal back displays a black-and-white posed player head shot in the upper left. The player's name, uniform number, and biography appear in a rectangle in the upper right, along with the Canadiens and Stay in School logos. A stat table is placed beneath, and the Pepsi, Village, and Ben's logos at the bottom round out the card. The cards are unnumbered and checklisted below in alphabetical order.

COMPLETE SET (28) 4.80 12.00
1 Jesse Belanger .30 .75
2 Paulin Bordeleau CO .20 .50
3 Donald Brashear .30 .75
4 Patrik Carnback .20 .50
5 Eric Charron .20 .50
6 Frederic Chabot .40 1.00
7 Alain Cote .20 .50
8 Paul DiPietro .30 .75
9 Craig Ferguson .20 .50
10 Gerry Fleming .20 .50
11 Luc Gauthier .20 .50
12 Robert Guillet .20 .50
13 Patric Kjellberg .30 .75
14 Les Kuntar .30 .75
15 Ryan Kuwabara .20 .50
16 Patrick Langlois TR .02 .10
17 Steve Larouche .20 .50
18 Jacques Parent TR .02 .10
19 Charles Poulin .20 .50
20 Oleg Petrov .20 .50
21 Yves Sarault .20 .50
22 Pierre Sevigny .20 .50
23 Darcy Simon .20 .50
24 Turner Stevenson .30 .75
25 Tricolo (Mascot) .02 .10
26 Lindsay Vallis .20 .50
27 Steve Veilleux .20 .50
28 Title card .08 .25

1993-94 Fredericton Canadiens

Printed on thin card stock, this 29-card standard-size features 1993-94 Fredericton Canadiens of the AHL. The fronts display color action player photos framed by red borders. The player's name and number are printed in the border beneath the picture. The horizontal backs carry a black-and-white close-up photo, biography, statistics, and sponsor logos (Ben's Bakery, Village, and Pepsi). The cards are unnumbered and checklisted below in alphabetical order.

COMPLETE SET (29) 4.80 12.00
1 Brent Bilodeau .20 .50
2 Paulin Bordeleau CO .08 .25
3 Donald Brashear .30 .75
4 Martin Brochu .40 1.00
5 Craig Darby .20 .50
6 Kevin Darby .20 .50
7 Mario Doyon .20 .50
8 Craig Ferguson .20 .50
9 Craig Fiander .20 .50
10 Gerry Fleming .20 .50
11 Luc Gauthier ACO .02 .10
12 Robert Guillet .20 .50
13 Les Kuntar .25 .60
14 Ryan Kuwabara .20 .50
15 Patrick Langlois .20 .50
16 Marc Laniel .20 .50
17 Christian Lariviere .20 .50
18 Kevin O'Sullivan .20 .50
19 Denis Ouellete .20 .50
20 Jacques Parent THER .02 .10
21 Oleg Petrov .30 .75
22 Charles Poulin .20 .50
23 Christian Proulx .20 .50
24 Tony Prpic .20 .50
25 Yves Sarault .20 .50
26 Turner Stevenson .30 .75
27 Tricolo (Mascot) .02 .10
28 Lindsay Vallis .20 .50
29 Title Card .02 .10

1994-95 Fredericton Canadiens

Printed on thin card stock, this 30-card standard-size set features the 1994-95 Fredericton Canadiens of the AHL. The fronts display borderless color action photos. The player's number and position, as well as his name, are printed vertically down the left and right sides respectively. The cards are unnumbered and checklisted below in alphabetical order.

COMPLETE SET (30) 4.80 12.00
1 Louis Bernard .15 .40
2 Brent Bilodeau .20 .50
3 Paulin Bordeleau CO .15 .40
4 Donald Brashear .40 1.00
5 Martin Brochu .40 1.00
6 Valeri Bure .60 1.50
7 Jim Campbell .20 .50
8 Paul Chagnon .15 .40
9 Craig Conroy .30 .75
10 Craig Darby .20 .50
11 Dion Darling .15 .40
12 Craig Ferguson .15 .40
13 Scott Fraser .15 .40
14 Luc Gauthier ACO .02 .10
15 Patrick Labrecque .20 .50
16 Marc Lamothe .30 .75
17 Patrick Langlois .15 .40
18 Brad Layzelle .15 .40
19 Derek Maguire .15 .40
20 Chris Murray .20 .50
21 Kevin O'Sullivan .15 .40
22 Jacques Parent THER .02 .10
23 Christian Proulx .15 .40
24 Craig Rivet .20 .50
25 Yves Sarault .15 .40
26 Turner Stevenson .20 .50
27 Martin Sychra .15 .40
28 Tim Tisdale .15 .40
29 Tricolo (Mascot) .02 .10
30 David Wilkie .15 .40

1995-96 Fredericton Canadiens

This 29-card set features color action player photos of the Fredericton Canadiens of the AHL. The backs carry biographical information and player statistics. The cards are unnumbered and checklisted below in alphabetical order.

COMPLETE SET (29) 4.80 12.00
1 Louis Bernard .15 .40
2 Paulin Bordeleau CO .08 .25
3 Sebastien Bordeleau .20 .50
4 Martin Brochu .40 1.00
5 Jim Campbell .20 .50
6 Paul Chagnon .15 .40
7 Craig Conroy .30 .75
8 Keli Corpse .15 .40
9 Dion Darling .15 .40
10 Rory Fitzpatrick .15 .40
11 Scott Fraser .15 .40
12 Gaston Gingras .20 .50
13 David Grenier .15 .40
14 Harold Hersh .20 .50
15 Patrick Labrecque .30 .75
16 Marc Lamothe .30 .75
17 Patrick Langlois .15 .40
18 Alan Letang .20 .50
19 Alexei Lojkin .15 .40
20 Xavier Majic .15 .40
21 Chris Murray .20 .50
22 Jacques Parent .15 .40
23 Craig Rivet .20 .50
24 Mario Roberge .15 .40
25 Pierre Sevigny .20 .50
26 Tricolo (Mascot) .02 .10
27 Darcy Tucker .40 1.00
28 Adam Wiesel .15 .40
29 Luc Gauthier ACO .02 .10

1996-97 Fredericton Canadiens

This set features the Canadiens of the AHL. The set was produced by the team and sold at home games, and is notable for containing one of the earliest and toughest issues of Jose Theodore.

COMPLETE SET (30) 30.00 80.00
1 Sebastien Bordeleau .15 .40
2 Brad Brown .40 1.00
3 Earl Cronan .15 .40
4 Dion Darling .15 .40
5 Jimmy Drolet .15 .40
6 Gerry Fleming .40 1.00
7 Scott Fraser .15 .40
8 Francois Groleau .15 .40
9 Miloslav Guren .15 .40
10 Harold Hersh .40 1.00
11 Eric Houde .15 .40
12 Alan Letang .15 .40
13 David Ling .20 .50
14 Alexei Lojkin .15 .40
15 Boyd Olson .15 .40
16 Tony Prpic .15 .40
17 Jesse Rezansoff .15 .40
18 Craig Rivet .40 1.00
19 Pierre Sevigny .20 .50
20 Todd Sparks .15 .40
21 Jose Theodore 20.00 40.00
22 Tomas Vokoun 8.00 20.00
23 Adam Wiesel .15 .40
24 Paulin Bordeleau CO .10 .25
25 Luc Gauthier CO .10 .25
26 Patrick Langlois TR .10 .25
27 Paul Chagnon TR .10 .25
28 Jacques Parent TR .10 .25
29 Tricolo MAS .02 .10
30 Jolly Rancher .02 .10

2000-01 Fresno Falcons

This set features the Falcons of the WCHL. It is believed that the set was a promotional giveaway sponsored by Carl's Jr. restaurants, but that has not been confirmed. The cards are unnumbered, however, and are listed below in alphabetical order.

COMPLETE SET (30) 8.00 20.00
1 Chris Albert .30 .75
2 Matt Alvey .40 1.00
3 Brad Both .30 .75
4 Brodie Coffin .30 .75
5 Kirk DeWaele .30 .75
6 Sheldon Flaman .40 1.00
7 Terry Friesen .40 1.00
8 Glen Gulutzan .30 .75
9 Don Malko .30 .75
10 Mike Mathers .30 .75
11 Mike McCourt .30 .75
12 David Mitchell .30 .75
13 Kory Mullin .40 1.00
14 Cory Murphy .30 .75
15 Kris Porter .30 .75
16 Chris Skoryna .30 .75
17 Adrian Smith .40 1.00
18 Greg Spenrath .30 .75
19 Rejean Stringer .30 .75
20 Darren Wetherill .30 .75
21 Terry Friesen SO .40 1.00
22 Blaine Moore CO .10 .25
23 Freddie Falcon MASCOT .04 .10
24 Mike Carey TR .04 .10
25 Fresno Falcons Celebration .20 .50
26 TV-47 ANCHORS .01 .05
27 Star-101 DJ's SPONSOR .01 .05
28 Mark Kuntz EM .04 .10
29 Brian Clark .30 .75
30 Team Photo .20 .50

2001-02 Fresno Falcons

This set features the Falcons of the WCHL. It was issued as a promotional giveaway at one home game in March, 2002.

COMPLETE SET (30) 8.00 20.00
1 Brad Both .40 1.00
2 Brodie Coffin .40 1.00
3 Kirk DeWaele .40 1.00
4 Joe Frederick .40 1.00
5 Terry Friesen .60 1.50
6 Glen Gulutzan .40 1.00
7 Dale Junkin .40 1.00
8 Dan Kerluke .40 1.00
9 Mike Mathers .40 1.00
10 Mike McCourt .40 1.00
11 David Mitchell .40 1.00
12 Kory Mullin .40 1.00
13 Cory Murphy .40 1.00
14 Kris Porter .40 1.00
15 Chris Skoryna .40 1.00
16 Adrian Smith .20 .50
17 Greg Spenrath .40 1.00
18 Ryan Tocher .40 1.00
19 Alex Todd .40 1.00
20 Jason Weaver .40 1.00
21 Darren Wetherill .40 1.00
22 Blaine Moore CO .10 .25
23 Game Winner Action Photo .10 .25
24 Mike Carey TR .04 .10
25 Mark Kuntz EQMG .04 .10
26 Freddie Falcon MASCOT .04 .10
27 Team Photo .20 .50
28 Carls Jr. .04 .10
29 Fresno Bee .04 .10
30 KRZR 103.7 .04 .10

2002-03 Fresno Falcons

COMPLETE SET (25) 8.00 20.00
1 Checklist .04 .10
2 Kevin Haupt .40 1.00
3 Chris Kenady .40 1.00
4 Cory Murphy .40 1.00
5 Mike Mathers .40 1.00
6 Alex Todd .40 1.00
7 Brad Both .60 1.50
8 Steve Lowe .40 1.00
9 Scott Borders .40 1.00
10 Jordan Landry .40 1.00
11 Colin Embley .40 1.00
12 Glen Gulutzan .40 1.00
13 Kirk DeWaele .40 1.00
14 Jason Weaver .40 1.00
15 Drew Schoneck .40 1.00
16 Mark Gowan .60 1.50
17 Terry Friesen .60 1.50
18 Joe Frederick .40 1.00
19 Kayle Short .40 1.00
20 Jason McBain .40 1.00
21 Kris Porter .40 1.00
22 Blaine Moore HCO .04 .10
23 Greg Spenrath ACO .04 .10
24 Happy Star .04 .10
25 KRZR-103.7 .04 .10

2003-04 Fresno Falcons

This set was produced by Choice Marketing and sold at home games.

COMPLETE SET (25) 10.00
1 Scott Borders .20 .50
2 Mike Brusseau .30 .75
3 Blair Clarance .20 .50
4 Terry Friesen .30 .75
5 Nathan Horne .20 .50
6 Mark Jackson .20 .50
7 Michael Kiesman .20 .50
8 Jordan Landry .20 .50
9 Mike Mathers .20 .50
10 Blaine Moore CO .20 .50
11 Kory Mullin .20 .50
12 Dominic Periard .20 .50
13 Kris Porter .20 .50
14 Boris Protsenko .20 .50
15 Riku Rahikainen .20 .50
16 Tapio Sammalkangas .20 .50
17 Mike Sandbeck .20 .50
18 Nolan Schaefer .30 .75
19 Drew Schoneck .20 .50
20 Greg Spenrath CO .20 .50
21 Adam Stefishen .20 .50
22 Kevin Truelson .20 .50
23 Jason Weaver .20 .50
24 John Wroblewski .20 .50
25 Mascot .04 .10
NNO Checklist .04 .10

2004-05 Fresno Falcons

COMPLETE SET (TBD) 10.00 25.00
1 David Brisson .40 1.00
2 Clint Cabana .40 1.00
3 John Dahl .40 1.00
4 Thierry Douville .40 1.00
5 Lanny Gare .40 1.00
6 Shawn Heaphy .40 1.00
7 Brett Jaegar .75 2.00
8 Tomas Jasko .40 1.00
9 Mike Kiesman .40 1.00
10 Derek Krestanovich .40 1.00
11 Simon Lajeunesse .75 2.00
12 Jim Lorentz .40 1.00
13 Matt O'Dette .40 1.00
14 Wes Rypien .40 1.00
15 Curtis Sheptak .40 1.00
16 Charles Simard .40 1.00
17 Greg Spenrath .40 1.00
18 Shaun Sutter .40 1.00
19 Dan Tessier .40 1.00
20 Kevin Truelson .40 1.00
21 Dustin VanBallegooie .40 1.00
22 Jason Weaver .40 1.00
23 John Wroblewski .40 1.00

2005-06 Fresno Falcons

COMPLETE SET (26) 6.00 15.00
1 P.O. Beaulieu .30 .75
2 Brad Both .30 .75
3 Fraser Clair .30 .75
4 Luke Curtin .30 .75
5 Matt Deschamps .30 .75
6 Peter Fregoe .30 .75
7 Brett Hammond .30 .75
8 Jamie Holden .30 .75
9 Brett Jaeger .30 .75
10 Derek Krestanovich .30 .75
11 Shawn Mather .30 .75
12 Rob McFeeters .30 .75
13 Kelsey Muench .30 .75
14 Cory Murphy .30 .75
15 Matt O'Dette .30 .75
16 Glenn Olson .30 .75
17 J.F. Plourde .30 .75
18 Dustin Vanballegooie .30 .75
19 Shawn Weiman .30 .75
20 John Wroblewski .30 .75
21 Ryan Mougenel .30 .75
22 Chris Burke .30 .75
23 Brian Clark .30 .75
24 Brad Jellis .30 .75
25 Matt Thomas .30 .75

2003-04 Gatineau Olympiques

COMPLETE SET (27) 5.00 12.00
1 Gabriel Bouthillette .30 .75
2 Scott Brophy .20 .50
3 Bruno Champagne .20 .50
4 Yanick Charron .20 .50
5 Dominic D'Amour .20 .50
6 Jean-Michel Daoust .20 .50
7 Philippe Dupuis .20 .50
8 Vincent Duriau .20 .50
9 Guillaume Fournier .20 .50
10 Martin Frechette .20 .50
11 Nick Fugere .20 .50
12 Derrick Kent .20 .50
13 Olivier Labelle .20 .50
14 Guillaume Labrecque .20 .50
15 Christian Laroche .20 .50
16 Doug O'Brien .20 .50
17 Keven Petit .20 .50
18 Petr Pohl .20 .50
19 Nicolas Ranger .20 .50
20 Maxime Robert .20 .50
21 Sam Roberts .20 .50
22 Maxime Rousseau .20 .50
23 Maxime Talbot .20 .50
24 David Tremblay .30 .75
25 Martin Vagner .30 .75
26 Francis Wathier .20 .50
27 Lance Woodman .20 .50

2004-05 Gatineau Olympiques

A total of 300 team sets were produced.

COMPLETE SET (24) 5.00 12.00
1 David Tremblay .30 .75
2 Martin Frechette .20 .50
3 Sam Roberts .20 .50
4 Scott Brophy .20 .50
5 Olivier Laliberte .30 .75
6 Francis Wathier .20 .50
7 Nicolas Ranger .20 .50
8 Keven Petit .20 .50
9 Jonathan Carrier .20 .50
10 Nick Fugere .20 .50
11 Olivier Labelle .20 .50
12 Maxime Rousseau .20 .50
13 Pierre-Luc Lessard .20 .50
14 Brett Morrison .20 .50
15 David Krejci .40 1.00
16 Petr Pohl .20 .50
17 Ryan Graham .20 .50
18 Guillaume Labrecque .20 .50
19 Cam Fergus .20 .50
20 Dave Starenky .20 .50
21 Bryan Wilson .20 .50
22 Geoffrey Walker .20 .50
23 Francis Gagnon .20 .50
24 Luke Pelham .20 .50

2005-06 Gatineau Olympiques

COMPLETE SET (28) 5.00 12.00
1 David Tremblay .20 .50
2 Olivier Laliberte .20 .50
3 Guillaume Labrecque .20 .50
4 Nick Fugere .20 .50
5 Keven Petit .20 .50
6 Maxime Rousseau .20 .50
7 Claude Giroux .50 1.25
8 David Krejci .40 1.00
9 Bryan Wilson .20 .50
10 Martin Frechette .20 .50
11 Jonathan Carrier .20 .50
12 Pierre-Luc Lessard .20 .50
13 Brad Tesink .20 .50
14 Michael Stinziani .20 .50
15 Colin Escott .20 .50
16 Benoit Gervais .20 .50
17 Maxime Malette .20 .50
18 Michel Champagne .20 .50
19 Maxime Langelier-Parent .20 .50
20 Brett Morrison .20 .50
21 Mathieu Curadeau .20 .50
22 Alexandre Boivin .20 .50
23 Bryan Main .20 .50
24 Darryl Smith .20 .50
25 Antonin Manavian .20 .50
26 Matthew Pistilli .20 .50
27 Philippi Cote .20 .50
28 Mascot .02 .10

2006-07 Gatineau Olympiques

COMPLETE SET (28) 8.00 15.00
1 Martin Frechette .20 .50
2 Olivier Laliberte .30 .75
3 Maxime Mallette .20 .50
4 Jonathan Carrier .20 .50
5 Viatcheslav Trukhno .20 .50
6 Steven Delisle .20 .50
7 Daniel Sauve .20 .50
8 Brad Tesink .20 .50
9 Keven Petit .20 .50
10 Brett Morrison .20 .50
11 Jean-Philipp Chabot .20 .50
12 Alexandre Boivin .20 .50
13 Claude Giroux .50 1.25
14 Bryan Main .20 .50
15 Paul Byron .20 .50
16 Benoit Gervais .20 .50
17 Matthew Pistilli .20 .50
18 Darryl Smith .20 .50
19 Travis Stacey .20 .50
20 Michael Stinziani .20 .50
21 Pierre-Marc Guilbault .20 .50
22 Alexandre Touchette .20 .50
23 Ken Dufresne .20 .50
24 Dave Bertrand-Duclos .20 .50
25 Chad Loikets .20 .50
26 David Kveton .20 .50
27 Ryan Mior .30 .75
28 Tyler Pugh .20 .50

1977-78 Granby Vics

This odd-sized (3 1/2 X7") black and white set features the Granby Vics of the LMJHQ. The card fronts are in a horizontal format, with the left half of the card containing a player photo, and the right featuring a player bio and an ad from a local business. The backs are blank and the cards are unnumbered. They are presented below alphabetically.

COMPLETE SET (20) 17.50 35.00
1 Mario Beauregard 1.00 2.00
2 Luc Breton 1.00 2.00
3 Daniel Caron 1.50 3.00
4 Mario Casavant 1.00 2.00
5 Marc Courtemanche 1.00 2.00
6 Yves Courtemanche 1.00 2.00
7 Sylvain d'Amour 1.00 2.00
8 Rene Delorme 1.00 2.00
9 Denis Dumas Jr. 1.00 2.00
10 Pierre Grondin 1.00 2.00
11 Andre Hebert 1.00 2.00
12 Marcel Lachance 1.00 2.00
13 Andre Lemieux 1.00 2.00
14 Pierre Lepage 1.00 2.00
15 Daniel Menard 1.00 2.00
16 Jacques Pomerleau 1.00 2.00
17 Mario Roy 1.00 2.00
18 Alain Tetrault 1.00 2.00
19 Paul Thibert 1.00 2.00
20 Luc Turgeon 1.00 2.00

1996-97 Grand Rapids Griffins

This odd-sized set (2 3/4" by 4") was produced by Meijer Exhibit Graphic Design and sponsored by Kodak and Jim Hill Photography. The set was released in five series of five cards each (plus one title card per series) over the course of the club's inaugural season. As the cards are unnumbered, they are listed below in alphabetical order.

COMPLETE SET (30) 20.00 50.00
1 Kevyn Adams 1.25 3.00
2 Dave Allison CO .40 1.00
3 Danton Cole .75 2.00
4 Keli Corpse .75 2.00
5 Pavol Demitra 4.00 10.00
6 Griff/Mascot .20 .50
7 Ben Hankinson .75 2.00
8 Stanislav Jasecko .75 2.00
10 Sean McCann .75 2.00
11 Cory Johnson .75 2.00
12 Jamie Linden .75 2.00
13 Don McSween .75 2.00
14 Tyler Moss 1.50 4.00
15 Jeff Nelson .75 2.00
16 Todd Nelson .75 2.00
17 Michel Picard .75 2.00
18 Bruce Ramsay .75 2.00
19 Pokey Reddick 1.50 4.00
20 Chad Remackel .75 2.00
21 Travis Richards .75 2.00
22 Matt Ruchty .75 2.00
23 Darcy Simon .75 2.00
24 1996 Inaugural Face-Off .20 .50
25 1996-97 Inaugural Team .75 2.00
26 Van Andel Arena .20 .50
NNO Title card 1 .08 .20
NNO Title card 2 .08 .20
NNO Title card 3 .08 .20
NNO Title card 4 .08 .20
NNO Title card 5 .08 .20

1997-98 Grand Rapids Griffins

Little is known about this set beyond the confirmed checklist. Additional information can be forwarded to hockeymag@beckett.com.

COMPLETE SET (24) 4.00 10.00
1 Michel Picard .30 .75
2 Tom Ashe .20 .50
3 Greg Clancy .20 .50
4 Danton Cole .20 .50
5 Ian Gordon .20 .50
6 Mark Greig .20 .50
7 Shane Hnidy .30 .75
8 Kerry Huffman .20 .50
9 Glen Metropolit .40 1.00
10 Todd Nelson .20 .50
11 Ed Patterson .20 .50
12 Bruce Ramsay .20 .50
13 Eldon Reddick .40 1.00
14 Travis Richards .20 .50
15 Matt Ruchty .20 .50
16 Darcy Simon .20 .50
17 Brian Sullivan .20 .50
18 Sean Tallaire .20 .50
19 Dean Trboyevich .20 .50
20 Jason Weaver .20 .50
21 Dave Allison HCO .10 .25
22 Curtis Hunt ACO .10 .25
23 Griff Mascot .02 .10
24 PHPA Web Site .02 .10

1998-99 Grand Rapids Griffins

Little is known about this IHL team set other than the confirmed checklist. It is believed, however, to be an oversized issue. Any additional information can be forwarded to hockeymag@beckett.com

COMPLETE SET (25) 5.00 12.00
1 Tom Ashe .20 .50
2 Jared Bednar .20 .50
3 Radim Bicanek .30 .75
4 Anders Bjork .20 .50
5 Aris Brimanis .20 .50
6 Danton Cole .20 .50
7 Jed Fiebelkorn .20 .50
8 Ian Gordon .20 .50
9 Todd Hlushko .20 .50
10 Kerry Huffman .20 .50
11 Neil Little .75 2.00
12 Glen Metropolit .40 1.00
13 Vaclav Nedomansky .20 .50
14 Robert Petrovicky .30 .75
15 Bruce Ramsay .20 .50
16 Travis Richards .20 .50
17 Gaetan Royer .20 .50
18 Darren Rumble .20 .50
19 Maxim Spiridonov .20 .50
20 Andrei Vasilyev .20 .50
21 Curtis Hunt ACO .10 .25
22 Guy Charron HCO .10 .25
23 Griff Mascot .02 .10
24 The Zone .02 .10
25 PHPA Web Site .02 .10

1999-00 Grand Rapids Griffins

This set features the Griffins of the IHL. The cards were produced by SplitSecond and were sold by the team at its souvenir stands.

COMPLETE SET (25) 6.00 15.00
1 Viacheslav Butsayev .20 .50
2 Guy Charron CO .08 .25
3 Ivan Ciernik .20 .50
4 Danton Cole CO .08 .25
5 John Emmons .20 .50
6 Mike Fountain .30 .75
7 Rick Goldman .20 .50
8 Konstantin Gorovikov .20 .50
9 John Gruden .20 .50
10 Curtis Hunt CO .08 .25
11 Jani Hurme 1.25 3.00
12 Derek King .20 .50
13 Kevin Miller .20 .50
14 Chris Neil .40 1.00
15 Todd Nelson .20 .50
16 Ed Patterson .20 .50
17 Michel Picard .20 .50
18 Phillippe Plante .20 .50
19 Karel Rachunek .30 .75
20 Travis Richards .20 .50
21 Yves Sarault .20 .50
22 Petr Schastlivy .60 1.50
23 Andrei Sryubko .20 .50
24 Chris Szysky .20 .50
25 Dave Van Drunen .20 .50

2000-01 Grand Rapids Griffins

This set features the Griffins of the IHL. The cards were produced by SplitSecond and were sold by the team at home games.

COMPLETE SET (25) 4.00 10.00
1 Keith Aldridge .14 .35
2 Sean Berens .14 .35
3 Vyacheslav Butsayev .14 .40
4 Mathieu Chouinard .40 1.00
5 Ivan Ciernik .14 .40
6 Ilja Demidov .14 .40
7 Mike Fountain .20 .50
8 Sean Gagnon .14 .40
9 Konstantin Gorovikov .14 .35
10 John Gruden .14 .35
11 Derek King .20 .50
12 Joel Kwiatkowski .14 .35
13 Marty McSorley .40 1.00
14 Kip Miller .20 .50
15 Chris Neil .40 1.00
16 David Oliver .15 .40
17 Ed Patterson .14 .40
18 Travis Richards .14 .40
19 David Roberts .14 .35
20 Petr Schastlivy .40 1.00
21 Chris Szysky .14 .35
22 Todd White .20 .50
23 Bruce Cassidy CO .10 .25
24 Danton Cole CO .10 .25
25 Griff MASCOT .04 .10

2001-02 Grand Rapids Griffins

This set features the Griffins of the AHL. The cards were created by Choice Marketing and were issued both as a promotional giveaway, and later were sold at the team's store. A total of 5,000 sets were produced.

COMPLETE SET (24) 4.80 12.00
1 Julien Vauclair .20 .50
2 John Gruden .20 .50
3 Wade Brookbank .20 .50
4 Kip Miller .20 .50
5 Alexandre Giroux .20 .50
6 Hugo Boisvert .20 .50
7 James Black .20 .50
8 Steve Martins .20 .50
9 David Hymovitz .20 .50
10 Chris Szysky .20 .50
11 Petr Schastlivy .40 1.00
12 Jeff Ulmer .20 .50
13 Josh Langfeld .20 .50
14 Chris Kelly .20 .50
15 Joe Murphy .20 .50
16 Travis Richards .20 .50
17 Martin Prusek .60 1.50
18 Chris Bala .20 .50
19 Dave Van Drunen .20 .50
20 Jason Doig .20 .50
21 Joel Kwiatkowski .20 .50
22 Mathieu Chouinard .60 1.50
23 Toni Dahlman .20 .50
24 Bruce Cassidy CO .04 .10
25 Gene Reilly ACO .04 .10
26 Griff MASCOT .04 .10

2002-03 Grand Rapids Griffins

This series was produced by Choice Marketing and, reportedly, was subject to a very odd distribution in which part of this set was given away as a game night promotion and the remaining cards were sold at the team's pro shop. The full set was never sold as a single unit. If anyone knows exactly how these were broken up, please write us at hockeymag@beckett.com.

COMPLETE SET (27) 5.00 12.00
1 Bryan Adams .30 .75
2 Sean Avery .75 2.00
3 Paul Ballantyne .30 .75
4 Ryan Barnes .30 .75
5 Gregor Baumgartner .30 .75
6 Patrick Boileau .30 .75
7 Hugo Boisvert .30 .75
8 Sheldon Brookbank .30 .75
9 Ed Campbell .30 .75
10 Danton Cole CO .04 .10
11 Rob Collins .30 .75
12 Nick Greenough .30 .75
13 Griff MASCOT .04 .10
14 Danny Groulx .30 .75
15 Derek King .30 .75
16 Tomas Kopecky .30 .75
17 Marc Lamothe .30 .75
18 Joey MacDonald .40 1.00
19 Mark Mowers .30 .75
20 Todd Nelson .30 .75
21 Michel Picard .30 .75
22 Travis Richards .30 .75
23 Nathan Robinson .30 .75
24 Stacy Roest .30 .75
25 Tim Skarperud .30 .75
26 Dave Van Drunen .30 .75
27 Shoe Carnival Ad .04 .10

2003-04 Grand Rapids Griffins

This set was issued as a promotional giveaway over the course of several home games. As a result, it is very difficult to find in complete set form. We've recently confirmed five additional cards in the checklist. Thanks to collector Dale Spengler.

COMPLETE SET (29) 20.00 30.40
1 Ryan Barnes .60 1.50
2 Hugo Boisvert .60 1.50
3 Darryl Bootland .75 2.00
4 David Brisson .60 1.50
5 Matt Ellis .60 1.50
6 Danny Groulx .60 1.50
7 Jiri Hudler 2.00 5.00
8 Derek King .60 1.50
9 Tomas Kopecky 1.25 3.00
10 Niklas Kronwall 2.00 5.00
11 Marc Lamothe .75 2.00
12 Joey MacDonald 1.25 3.00
13 Kevin Miller .75 2.00
14 Mark Mowers .75 2.00
15 Anders Myrvold .60 1.50
16 Michel Picard .60 1.50
17 Travis Richards .60 1.50
18 Nathan Robinson .75 2.00
19 Aaron Schneekloth .60 1.50
20 Tim Skarperud .60 1.50
21 David Van Drunen .60 1.50
22 Danton Cole CO .10 .25
23 Greg Ireland ACO .04 .10
24 Brad Thompson EQM .04 .10
25 Jiri Hudler 2.00 5.00
26 Kory Karlander .60 1.50
27 Jeff Nelson .60 1.50
28 Rob Snitzer TR .04 .10
29 Shoe Carnival Ad .04 .10

2013-14 Grand Rapids Griffins

COMPLETE SET (25) 6.00 15.00
1 Adam Almquist .30 .75
2 Mitch Callahan .30 .75
3 Patrick Eaves .30 .75
4 Cory Emmerton .30 .75
5 Brennan Evans .30 .75
6 Landon Ferraro .30 .75
7 Gleason Fournier .30 .75
8 Martin Frk .30 .75
9 Luke Glendening .30 .75
10 Triston Grant .30 .75
11 Jeff Hoggan .30 .75
12 Calle Jarnkrok .30 .75
13 Nick Jensen .30 .75
14 Tomas Jurco .30 .75
15 Alexey Marchenko .30 .75
16 Thomas McCollum .30 .75
17 David Mcintyre .30 .75
18 Petr Mrazek .30 .75
19 Andrej Nestrasil .30 .75
20 Xavier Ouellet .30 .75
21 Nathan Paetsch .30 .75
22 Teemu Pulkkinen .30 .75
23 Riley Sheahan .30 .75
24 Ryan Sproul .30 .75
25 Jordin Tootoo .30 .75

2004-05 Green Bay Gamblers

This set of the USHL Gamblers is noteworthy for including the first card of the fifth overall pick from 2003, Blake Wheeler.

COMPLETE SET (28) 10.00 25.00
1 Jeff Carlson .40 1.00
2 Corey Couturier .40 1.00
3 Derek Danowski .40 1.00
4 Jeremy Dehner .40 1.00
5 Spencer Dillon .40 1.00
6 Justin Johnson .40 1.00
7 Carl Lackey ACO .04 .10
8 Tyler Lehrke .40 1.00
9 Joe Long .40 1.00
10 Mark Magnowski .40 1.00
11 Mark Mazzoleni CO .04 .10
12 Andrew Meyer .40 1.00
13 Brad Miller .40 1.00
14 Ryan Peterson .40 1.00
15 Garren Reisweber .40 1.00
16 Daniel Rosen .40 1.00
17 Billy Smith .40 1.00
18 Chris Stansik .40 1.00
19 Mark Stockdale .40 1.00
20 Luke Strand ACO .04 .10
21 Dan Sturges .40 1.00
22 Garrett Suter .40 1.00
23 Blake Wheeler 1.25 3.00
24 Michael Zacharias .40 1.00
25 Suter .40 1.00
Dehner
Sturges
26 Missconducts .40 1.00
27 Mask Card .40 1.00
28 Mini Plan .04 .10

1991-92 Greensboro Monarchs

This set features the Monarchs of the ECHL. The cards feature borderless, posed and action color player photos. The player's name and position appear on a mustard-colored hockey stick design at the bottom. The backs are subdivided by a red stripe and carry a close-up picture with biographical information above the stripe, and statistics and career highlights below it. The cards are unnumbered and checklisted below in alphabetical order.

COMPLETE SET (19) 3.00 8.00
1 Rob Bateman .25 .60
2 Phil Berger .20 .50
3 Mike Butters .20 .50
4 John Devereaux .20 .50
5 Eric Dubois .20 .50
6 Todd Gordon .20 .50
7 Chris Laganas .20 .50
8 Eric LeMarque .20 .50
9 Timo Makela .20 .50
10 Greg Menges .20 .50
11 Daryl Noren .20 .50
12 Peter Sentner .20 .50
13 Boyd Sutton .20 .50
14 Nick Vitucci .25 .60
15 Shawn Wheeler .20 .50
16 Scott White .20 .50
17 Chris Wolanin .20 .50
18 Dean Zayonce .20 .50
19 Team Photo .20 .50

1992-93 Greensboro Monarchs

Sponsored by RBI Sports Cards Inc., this 19-card standard-size set features full-bleed, color, action player photos. The player's name and position appear in a blue and red stripe near the bottom. The backs display a close-up picture alongside biographical information. A red stripe below the photo divides the card in half and serves as a heading for statistics. A player profile appears below the statistics.

COMPLETE SET (19) 3.00 8.00
1 Team Photo .30 .75
2 Chris Wolanin .20 .50
3 Bill Horn .20 .50
4 Brock Woods .20 .50
5 Phil Berger .20 .50
6 Dan Bylsma .20 .50
7 Davis Payne .30 .75
8 Wayne Muir .20 .50
9 Andrei Iakovenko .20 .50
10 Roger Larche .20 .50
11 Jamie Nicolls .20 .50
12 Darryl Noren .20 .50
13 Todd Gordon .20 .50
14 Claude Maillet .20 .50
15 Dave Burke .20 .50
16 Jamie Steer .25 .60
17 Greg Capson .20 .50
18 Chris Lappin .20 .50
19 Greg Menges .20 .50

1993-94 Greensboro Monarchs

This 16-card set of the Greensboro Monarchs of the ECHL was produced by RBI Sportscards. It is similar in design to the Raleigh Icecaps issue from the same year. The cards feature an action photo on the front, while the backs include career stats.

COMPLETE SET (16) 2.00 5.00
1 Phil Berger .20 .50
2 Trevor Burgess .15 .40
3 Dan Bylsma .20 .50
4 Greg Capson .15 .40
5 Brendan Creagh .15 .40
6 Dan Gravelle .15 .40
7 Sebastien LaPlante .15 .40
8 Savo Mitrovic .15 .40
9 Tom Newman .15 .40
10 Jamie Nicolls .15 .40
11 Davis Payne .20 .50
12 Stig Salomonsson .15 .40
13 Sverre Sears .15 .40
14 Chris Valicevic .15 .40
15 John Young .15 .40
16 Dean Zayonce .15 .40

1994-95 Greensboro Monarchs

This 20-card set of the Greensboro Monarchs of the ECHL was again produced by RBI Sportscards. This year's set mimics the design used by Pinnacle in 1993-94, although the photography lacks somewhat in the area of clarity. The backs are numbered, and contain stats for 1993-94. The sets apparently were not sold by the team; speculation suggests the booster

ub was in charge of distribution.
OMPLETE SET (20) 4.00 10.00
Dean Zayonce .20 .50
Jeremy Stevenson .20 .50
Glenn Stewart .20 .50
Peter Skudra .40 1.00
Chad Seibel .20 .50
Sverre Sears .20 .50
Howie Rosenblatt .40 1.00
Hugo Proulx .20 .50
Davis Payne .20 .50
0 Ron Pasco .20 .50
1 Monte MASCOT .02 .10
2 Scott McKay .20 .50
3 Arturs Kupaks .20 .50
4 Bill Horn .20 .50
5 Dwayne Gylywoychuk .20 .50
6 Jeff Gabriel .20 .50
7 Doug Evans .20 .50
8 Mark DeSantis .20 .50
9 Brendan Creagh .20 .50
0 Phil Berger .20 .50

1999-00 Greensboro Generals

his set features the Generals of the ECHL. The cards ere produced by the team and sold at the souvenir tands.

OMPLETE SET (26) 4.00 10.00
Ian Walterson .15 .40
Clay Awe .15 .40
Sal Manganaro .15 .40
Oleg Timchenko .15 .40
David Whitworth .15 .40
T.J. Tanberg .15 .40
Keith O'Connell .15 .40
Tracy Egeland .15 .40
Igor Boiko .15 .40
0 Martin Galik .15 .40
1 Dean Shmyr .15 .40
2 Juraj Slovak .15 .40
3 Aniket Dhadphale .15 .40
4 Dean Zayonce .15 .40
5 Alexei Krovopuskov .15 .40
6 Van Burgess .15 .40
7 Matt Eisler .15 .40
8 Justin Cardwell .15 .40
9 Joel Irwin .15 .40
0 Wes Swinson .15 .40
1 Francis Larivee .30 .75
2 40th Anniversary Puck Drop .15 .40
3 Group Celebrates .15 .40
4 Settling Differences .75 2.00
5 Bill Flynn .15 .40
6 Greensboro Generals CL .08 .25

2001-02 Greensboro Generals

his set features the Generals of the ECHL. The sets ere only available to members of the Generals' Kids Club. Reportedly, just 250 sets were made, making it ne of the toughest minor league sets ever issued.

OMPLETE SET (20) 16.00 40.00
Daniel Passero .75 2.00
Rob Sandrock 1.25 3.00
Sal Manganaro .75 2.00
Vladislav Serov .75 2.00
Jarrett Thompson .75 2.00
Ryan Kummu .75 2.00
David Whitworth .75 2.00
Brian Loney .75 2.00
Chris Bell .75 2.00
0 Casey Kesselring .75 2.00
1 Shaun Peet .75 2.00
2 Jason Metcalfe .75 2.00
3 Chris Brassard .75 2.00
4 Dion Lassu .75 2.00
5 Jason Robinson .75 2.00
6 Jonathan Forest .75 2.00
7 Craig Stahl .75 2.00
8 Bujar Amidovski 1.25 3.00
9 Graeme Townshend CO .40 1.00
0 Sarge MASCOT .40 1.00

2002-03 Greensboro Generals RBI

OMPLETE SET (18) 6.00 15.00
Rod Aldoff .40 1.00
Chris Allen .40 1.00
Alex Andreyev .40 1.00
Chris Bell .40 1.00
Daniel Berthiaume .60 1.50
Shane Campbell .40 1.00
Matt Chandler .40 1.00
Kurt Drummond .40 1.00
Sam Ftorek .40 1.00
0 Pete Gardiner .40 1.00
1 Kevin Grimes .40 1.00
2 Olaf Kjenstad .40 1.00
3 Roman Marakhovski .40 1.00
4 Jay Murphy .40 1.00
5 Geno Parrish .40 1.00
6 Juraj Slovak .40 1.00
7 Matt Turek .40 1.00
8 David Whitworth .40 1.00

2003-04 Greensboro Generals

OMPLETE SET (16) 6.00 15.00
77 Alex Andreyev .40 1.00
78 Mike Bayrack .40 1.00
79 Daniel Berthiaume .60 1.50
80 Matt Chandler .40 1.00
81 Kurt Drummond .40 1.00
82 Matt Elich .40 1.00
83 Eric Fortier .40 1.00
84 Pete Gardiner .40 1.00
85 Joe Gerbe .40 1.00
86 Kevin Grimes .40 1.00
87 Jamie Hodson .60 1.50
88 Geno Parrish .40 1.00
89 Tom Reimann .40 1.00
90 Dean Shmyr .40 1.00
91 Matt Turek .40 1.00
92 Mark Turner .40 1.00

2001-02 Greenville Grrrowl

his set features the terribly named Grrrowl of the ECHL. The set was handed out as a promotional iveaway at a game in February, 2002. The cards are nnumbered, but they are numbered on a checklist ard. The listing below mirrors that checklist.

OMPLETE SET (24) 10.00 20.00
John Marks CO .20 .50
Nick Vitucci ACO .20 .50
Eric Lind .40 1.00
Judd Stauss .40 1.00
Eric Van Acker .40 1.00
Roger Trudeau .40 1.00
Jason Windle .40 1.00
Sean Venedam .75 2.00
Jay Langager .40 1.00
0 Steve Rymsha .40 1.00
1 Jonathan Roy .75 2.00
12 Colin Pepperall .40 1.00
13 Kevin Bergin .40 1.00
14 David Bell .40 1.00
15 Damon Whitten .40 1.00
16 Ryan Stewart .40 1.00
17 Martin Masa .40 1.00
18 David Kaczowka .40 1.00
19 Simon Gamache .75 2.00
20 Tyrone Garner .75 2.00
21 Jayme Platt .40 1.00
22 Chad Nelson .40 1.00
23 Grrruff MASCOT .10 .25
24 Greenville Grrrowl CL .10 .25

2002-03 Greenville Grrrowl

COMPLETE SET (23) 6.00 15.00
1 Michael Garnett .75 2.00
2 Paul Flache 1.00
3 Rico Fatticci .40 1.00
4 Matt Demarski .40 1.00
5 Tyler Deis .40 1.00
6 Alexandre Burrows .40 1.00
7 Josh Legge .40 1.00
8 David Kaczowka .40 1.00
9 Mike Henderson .40 1.00
10 Grrruff MASCOT .04 .10
11 Mark Gouett .40 1.00
12 Jonathan Gauthier .40 1.00
13 Judd Medak .40 1.00
14 Dan McIntyre .40 1.00
15 Martin Masa .40 1.00
16 John Marks HCO .04 .10
17 Chris Lynch .40 1.00
18 Eric Lind .40 1.00
19 Krzysztof Wieckowski .40 1.00
20 Nick Vitucci ACO .04 .10
21 Eric Van Acker .40 1.00
22 John Nail .40 1.00
23 Checklist .04 .10

2003-04 Greenville Grrrowl

We've recently confirmed the existence of a 24th card in the set of John Nail. Thanks to collector Dale Spengler.

COMPLETE SET (24) 10.00 25.00
1 Stacey Bauman .40 1.00
2 Daniel Boisclair 1.25 3.00
3 Steve Burgess .40 1.00
4 Michael Chin .40 1.00
5 Bob Cunningham .40 1.00
6 Randy Dagenais .40 1.00
7 Robin Delacoure .40 1.00
8 Matt Demarski .40 1.00
9 Mike Henderson .40 1.00
10 Troy Ilijow .40 1.00
11 Han-Sung Kim .75 2.00
12 Scott Kirton .40 1.00
13 Jeremy Kyte .40 1.00
14 Bryan Lachapelle .40 1.00
15 David Lizotte .40 1.00
16 Jason Metcalfe .40 1.00
17 Mike Nelson .40 1.00
18 Michel Robinson .75 2.00
19 Russell Spence .40 1.00
20 Ryan Stewart .40 1.00
21 Jonathan Zion .60 1.50
22 John Marks CO .20 .50
23 Team Photo .20 .50
24 John Nail .40 1.00

1993-94 Guelph Storm

Sponsored by Domino's Pizza and printed by Slapshot Images Ltd., this standard size 31-card set features the 1993-94 Guelph Storm. On a geometrical blue and grey background, the fronts feature color action player photos with thin black borders. The player's name, position and team name, as well as the producer's logo, appear on the front.

COMPLETE SET (31) 5.00 12.00
1 Title Card .15 .40
2 Jeff O'Neill .60 1.50
3 Mark McArthur .20 .50
4 Kayle Short .15 .40
5 Ryan Risidore .15 .40
6 Mike Rusk .15 .40
7 Regan Stocco .15 .40
8 Duane Harmer .15 .40
9 Sylvain Cloutier .15 .40
10 Eric Landry .15 .40
11 Jamie Wright .20 .50
12 Todd Norman .15 .40
13 Mike Pittman .15 .40
14 Ken Belanger .30 .75
15 Viktor Reuta .15 .40
16 Mike Prokopec .15 .40
17 Jeff Williams .20 .50
18 Chris Skoryna .15 .40
19 Stephane Lefebvre .15 .40
20 Jeff Cowan .20 .50
21 Murray Hogg .15 .40
22 Andy Adams .15 .40
23 Todd Bertuzzi 1.25 3.00
24 Grant Pritchett .15 .40
25 Rumun Ndur .20 .50
26 Jeff O'Neill .60 1.50
27 Paul Brydges ACO .10 .25
28 John Lovell CO .10 .25
29 Team Photo/CL .15 .40
30 Domino's Pizza .02 .10
NNO Slapshot Ad Card .02 .10

1994-95 Guelph Storm

Sponsored by Domino's Pizza and Burger King, and printed by Slapshot Images Inc., this 31-card standard-size set features the Storm of the OHL. The cards were sold in set form at the team's rink.

COMPLETE SET (31) 5.00 12.00
1 Team Photo/CL .15 .40
2 Mark McArthur .20 .50
3 Andy Adams .15 .40
4 Bryan McKinney .15 .40
5 Ryan Risidore .20 .50
6 Joel Cort .15 .40
7 Chris Hajt .20 .50
8 Regan Stocco .15 .40
9 Dwayne Hay .20 .50
10 Andrew Clark .15 .40
11 Neil Fewster .15 .40
12 Jamie Wright .20 .50
13 Jason Jackman .15 .40
14 Pat Barton .15 .40
15 Tom Johnson .15 .40
16 Brian Wesenberg .20 .50
17 Mike Pittman .15 .40
18 Jeff Williams .15 .40
19 Todd Norman .20 .50
20 Mike Rusk .15 .40
21 David Lylyk .15 .40
22 Todd Bertuzzi 1.00 2.50
23 Jeff Cowan .20 .50
24 Rumun Ndur .20 .50
25 Jeff O'Neill .40 1.00
26 Andrew Long .15 .40
27 Craig Hartsburg CO .20 .50
28 Paul Brydges ACO .10 .25
29 Sponsor Card/Burger King .02 .10
30 Sponsor Card/Domino's .02 .10
NNO Ad Card .02 .10

1995-96 Guelph Storm

This extremely attractive set was produced by Axiom Communications for distribution by the Storm at the club's pro shop. The set commemorates the team's fifth anniversary, and features strong action photography along with a dazzling design element along the right border. The back features a color mug shot, personal information and logos of sponsors.

COMPLETE SET (30) 4.00 10.00
1 Checklist .15 .40
2 Andrew Clark .15 .40
3 Dwayne Hay .20 .50
4 Jason Jackman .15 .40
5 Burger King Ad .02 .10
6 Nick Bootland .15 .40
7 Andrew Long .15 .40
8 Todd Norman .20 .50
9 Michael Pittman .15 .40
10 Herbert Vasilijevs .20 .50
11 Jeff Williams .15 .40
12 Joel Cort .20 .50
13 Chris Hajt .20 .50
14 Brian Willsie .20 .50
15 Brian Wesenberg .20 .50
16 Mike Lankshear .15 .40
17 Darryl McArthur .20 .50
10 Bryan McKinney .15 .40
19 Regan Stocco .15 .40
20 Ryan Risidore .20 .50
21 Mike Vellinga .15 .40
22 Dan Cloutier .40 1.00
23 Bryan McMullen .20 .50
24 Brett Thompson .20 .50
25 Ryan Robichaud .15 .40
26 Kid's Club .02 .10
27 Jamie Wright .20 .50
28 Guelph Police .02 .10
29 Mike Galati .15 .40
30 Domino's Pizza Ad .02 .10

1996-97 Guelph Storm

This 36 card set continues the tradition of high-quality sets from the Storm. The heavy-stock cards feature action photography on the front, alone with player name and number and team logo. The backs include a mug shot and personal information and a safety tip, but no playing stats. The set is noteworthy for the inclusion of Manny Malhotra, expected to be a high pick in 1998.

COMPLETE SET (36) 5.00 12.00
1 Checklist .02 .10
2 Brett Thompson .15 .40
3 David MacDonald .15 .40
4 John Zubyck .15 .40
5 Denis Ivanov .15 .40
6 Joel Cort .15 .40
7 Chris Hajt .20 .50
8 Manny Malhotra .30 .75
9 Mike Dombkiewicz .15 .40
10 Ryan Robichaud .15 .40
11 Kent McDonell .20 .50
12 Joe Gerbe .15 .40
13 Mike Christian .15 .40
14 Brian Wesenberg .15 .40
15 Todd Norman .20 .50
16 Darryl McArthur .15 .40
17 Richard Irwin .15 .40
18 Brian Willsie .15 .40
19 Mike Vellinga .15 .40
20 Jason Jackman .15 .40
21 Chris Madden .30 .75
22 Dwayne Hay .20 .50
23 Joey Bartley .15 .40
24 Mike Lankshear .20 .50
25 Andrew Long .15 .40
26 Matt Bell .15 .40
27 Nick Bootland .20 .50
28 E.J. McGuire .20 .50
29 Rick Allain .02 .10
30 Burger King Ad .02 .10
31 Burger King Kid's Club .02 .10
32 Guelph Police .15 .40
33 Domino's Pizza Ad .02 .10
34 Domino's Pizza Ad .02 .10
35 Chris Hajt .15 .40
Dwayne Hay
36 96-97 Team Picture :15 .40

1996-97 Guelph Storm Premier Collection

This odd-sized (4" X 6") collection was issued by the club along with game programs. The set is noteworthy for its outstanding photography and imaginative posing of the subjects; most appear out of hockey garb and in more expressive outfits and poses.

COMPLETE SET (12) 4.80 10.00
1 Todd Norman .40 1.00
2 Brian Wesenberg .40 1.00
3 Mike Vellinga .40 1.00
4 Brett Thompson .40 1.00
5 Joel Cort .40 1.00
6 Jason Jackman .40 1.00
7 Brian Willsie .40 1.00
8 Mike Lankshear .40 1.00
9 Dwayne Hay .40 1.00
10 Manny Malhotra .75 2.00
11 Chris Hajt .40 1.00
12 Nick Bootland .40 1.00

1997-98 Guelph Storm

Card fronts feature a black and white action photo, with players name and number on the bottom. Card backs feature biographical information and are numbered xx/34. Backs also feature sponsor logos and safety tips.

COMPLETE SET (34) 5.00 12.00
1 Header Card .02 .10
2 Chris Thompson .15 .40
3 Daniel Jacques .15 .40
4 Chris Madden .30 .75
5 Kevin Mitchell .15 .40
6 Joey Bartley .15 .40
7 Chris Hajt .20 .50
8 Manny Malhotra .30 .75
9 Mike Dombkiewicz .15 .40
10 Ian Forbes .15 .40
11 Joe Gerbe .15 .40
12 Mike Vellinga .15 .40
13 Lindsay Plunkett .15 .40
14 Kent McDonell .15 .40
15 Matt Lahey .15 .40
16 Bohuslav Subr .15 .40
17 Bob Crummer .15 .40
18 Andrew Long .15 .40
19 Brian McGrattan .15 .40
20 Darryl McArthur .30 .75
21 Brian Willsie .20 .50
22 John Zubyck .15 .40
23 Dusty Jamieson .30 .75
24 Eric Beaudoin .15 .40
25 Jason Jackman .15 .40
26 Nick Bootland .15 .40
27 George Burnett CO .15 .40
28 Rick Allain ACO .02 .10
29 Spyke .02 .10
30 Guelph Police .02 .10
31 Burger King .02 .10
32 Burger King .02 .10
33 Domino's .02 .10
34 Domino's .02 .10

1998-99 Guelph Storm

This set features the Storm of the OHL. The cards feature an action shot on the front, along with a full-color back. The cards were produced by the team and sold at home games.

COMPLETE SET (36) 5.00 12.00
1 Title Card/CL .02 .10
2 Mike D'Alessandro .30 .75
3 Chris Madden .40 1.00
4 Kevin Mitchell .20 .50
5 Jean Sebastien Larocque .20 .50
6 Kevin Dallman .30 .75
7 Matt Rock .20 .50
8 Ian Forbes .20 .50
9 Joe Gerbe .20 .50
10 Bo Subr .30 .75
11 Lindsay Plunkett .20 .50
12 Kent McDonell .20 .50
13 Garrett McAiney .20 .50
14 Nathan Herrington .20 .50
15 Bob Crummer .20 .50
16 Charlie Stephens .30 .75
17 Darryl Knight .20 .50
18 Darryl McArthur .30 .75
19 Ryan Davis .20 .50
20 Joey Bartley .20 .50
21 Frank Jolette .20 .50
22 Eric Beaudoin .20 .50
23 Lucas Nehrling .20 .50
24 Geoff Ward ACO .10 .25
25 Bart Crashley ACO .10 .25
26 Shane Mabey TR .02 .10
27 Russ Hammond ATR .02 .10
28 Spyke MASCOT .02 .10
29 Guelph Police .02 .10
30 1997-98 OHL Champs .20 .50
31 Robertson Cup .20 .50
32 Memorial Cup AS .08 .25
33 Burge King Ad .02 .10
34 Burger King Ad .02 .10
35 Domino's Ad .02 .10
36 Domino's Ad .02 .10

1999-00 Guelph Storm

Released in conjunction with Burger King and Domino's, this 36-card set features the 1999-00 Guelph Storm. Cards are black bordered and contain full color action photography. The last four cards of the set are coupons for Burger King and Domino's.

COMPLETE SET (36) 4.00 10.00
1 Header Card/CL .02 .10
2 Craig Andersson .60 1.50
3 Chris Madden .40 1.00
4 Kevin Mitchell .15 .40
5 Kevin Dallman .15 .40
6 Matt Rock .15 .40
7 Jon Hedberg .15 .40
8 Radek Matalik .15 .40
9 Joe Gerbe .15 .40
10 Bo Suba .15 .40
11 Lindsay Plunkett .15 .40
12 Kent McDonell .30 .75
13 Peter Flache .15 .40
14 Charlie Stephens .30 .75
15 Colt King .30 .75
16 Nick Jones .15 .40
17 Brent Kelly .15 .40
18 Jon Peters .15 .40
19 Derek Hennessey .15 .40
20 Andrew Brown .15 .40
21 Aran Myers .15 .40
22 Matt House .15 .40
23 Eric Beaudoin .15 .40
24 Ian Forbes .15 .40
25 Morgan McCormick .15 .40
26 Paul Gillis .15 .40
27 Bart Crashley .15 .40
28 Shane Mabey .15 .40
29 Russ Hammond .15 .40
30 Spyke Mascot .02 .10
31 Team Photo .15 .40
32 Guelph Police .02 .10
33 Burger King Coupon .02 .10
34 Burger King Coupon .02 .10
35 Domino's Coupon .02 .10
36 Domino's Coupon .02 .10

2000-01 Guelph Storm

We have confirmed this handful of cards to exist, thanks to collector Vinnie Montalbano.

1 Craig Anderson 1.50 4.00
2 Andrew Archer .40 1.00
3 Dustin Brown 1.50 4.00
4 Kevin Dallman .40 1.00

2001-02 Guelph Storm

COMPLETE SET (35) 8.00 20.00
1 Fedor Tyutin .40 1.00
2 Frank Burgio .20 .50
3 Kevin Dallman .30 .75
4 Leonid Zvachkin .20 .50
5 Tim Branham .20 .50
6 George Bradley .20 .50
7 Martin St. Pierre .20 .50
8 Malcolm MacMillan .20 .50
9 Michael Krelove .20 .50
10 Colin Power .20 .50
11 Aaron Lobb .20 .50
12 Daniel Paille .75 2.00
13 Alex Butkus .20 .50
14 Ryan Thompson .20 .50
15 Luc Chiasson .20 .50
16 Derek Hennessey .20 .50
17 Evan Kotsopoulos .20 .50
18 Matt Puntureri .20 .50
19 Andrew Archer .20 .50
20 Morgan McCormick .20 .50
21 Chris Beckford-Tseu 1.25 3.00
22 Andrew Penner .30 .75
23 Dustin Brown 1.50 4.00
24 Dwight LaBrosse .20 .50
25 Jeff Jackson CO .08 .20
26 Shawn Camp ACO .20 .50
27 Spyke MASCOT .04 .10
28 Shane Mabey TR .20 .50
29 Russ Hammond ATR .20 .50
30 Police Services .04 .10
31 Dominos .04 .10
32 Guelph Dominators .04 .10
33 Guelph Dominators .04 .10
34 M&T Printing Group .04 .10
35 Checklist .04 .10

2001-02 Guelph Storm Memorial Cup

Very similar to other Guelph set of this season, save for the addition of the Memorial Cup logo and a few other small changes in content.

COMPLETE SET (35) 8.00 20.00
1 Fedor Tyutin .60 1.50
2 Kevin Dallman .60 1.50
3 Leonid Zvachkin .30 .75
4 Tim Branham .30 .75
5 Eric Larochelle .30 .75
6 George Bradley .30 .75
7 Martin St. Pierre .30 .75
8 Malcolm MacMillan .30 .75
9 Michael Krelove .30 .75
10 Colin Power .30 .75
11 Aaron Lobb .30 .75
12 Daniel Paille 1.00 2.50
13 Alex Butkus .30 .75
14 Ryan Thompson .30 .75
15 Luc Chiasson .30 .75
16 Derek Hennessey .30 .75
17 Lou Dickenson .30 .75
18 Matt Puntureri .30 .75
19 Scott Rozendal .30 .75
20 Andrew Archer .30 .75
21 Morgan McCormick .30 .75
22 Andrew Penner .40 1.00
23 Dustin Brown 1.50 4.00
24 Dwight LaBrosse .30 .75
25 Jeff Jackson CO .04 .10
26 Shawn Camp ACO .04 .10
27 Spyke MASCOT .04 .10
28 Shane Mabey TR .04 .10
29 Russ Hammond ATR .04 .10
30 Sponsor .04 .10
31 Memorial Cup Card .04 .10
32 Team Photo .04 .10
33 Community .04 .10
34 Community .04 .10
35 Checklist .04 .10

2002-03 Guelph Storm

COMPLETE SET (36) 6.00 15.00
1 Andrew Penner .30 .75
2 Martin St. Pierre .20 .50
3 Andrew Archer .20 .50
4 Ryan Thompson .20 .50
5 Daniel Paille .60 1.50
6 Adam Dennis .30 .75
7 Dustin Brown .60 1.50
8 Eric Larochelle .20 .50
9 George Bradley .20 .50
10 Corey LeClair .20 .50
11 Geoff Patton .20 .50
12 Lou Dickenson .20 .50
13 Matt Ryan .20 .50
14 Colin Power .20 .50
15 Ryan Garlock .40 1.00
16 Steve Zmudczynski .20 .50
17 Leonid Zvachkin .20 .50
18 Brett Trudell .20 .50
19 Michael Okrzesik .20 .50
20 Ryan Callahan .40 1.00
21 Emil Bucic .20 .50
22 Aaron Lobb .20 .50
23 Tyler Haskins .20 .50
24 Malcolm MacMillan .20 .50
25 Matt Puntureri .20 .50
26 Jeff Jackson CO .10 .25
27 Shawn Camp ACO .10 .25
28 Jason Brooks ACO .10 .25
29 Shawn Mabey AT .10 .25
30 Russ Hammond ATR .04 .10
31 Spyke MASCOT .04 .10
32 Ad card .04 .10
33 Junior Storm .04 .10
34 Home Ice .04 .10
35 Guelph Police .04 .10
36 Team Photo/CL .04 .10

2003-04 Guelph Storm

COMPLETE SET (30) 6.00 15.00
1 Header Card .04 .10
2 Danny Taylor .20 .50
3 Mick Okrzesik .20 .50
4 Dan Girardi .40 1.00
5 Kevin Klein .40 1.00
6 Ryan Parent .75 2.00
7 George Bradley .20 .50
8 Marty St. Pierre .20 .50
9 Niko Tuomi .20 .50
10 Mark Lytwyn .20 .50
11 Nathan Spaling .20 .50
12 Steve Zmudczynski .20 .50
13 Daniel Paille .40 1.00
14 Brett Trudell .20 .50
15 Shane Hart .20 .50
16 Ryan Garlock .40 1.00
17 Ryan Card .20 .50
18 Matt Ryan .20 .50
19 Ryan Callahan .30 .75
20 Kyle Spurr .20 .50
21 Adam Dennis .40 1.00
22 Jakub Koreis .40 1.00
23 Dustin Brown 1.00 2.50
24 Shawn Camp CO .10 .25
25 Jason Brooks ACO .10 .25
26 Paul Brydges ACO .10 .25
27 Sponsor Card .04 .10
28 Sponsor Card .04 .10
29 Guelph Police .04 .10
30 Team Photo/CL .04 .10

2004-05 Guelph Storm

COMPLETE SET (31) 8.00 20.00
1 Danny Taylor .30 .75
2 Michael Caruso .30 .75
3 Shawn Haviland .30 .75
4 Michael Okrzesik .30 .75
5 Daniel Girardi .40 1.00
6 Josh Godfrey .30 .75
7 Ryan Parent .40 1.00
8 Brent Mackie .30 .75
9 Andy Hyvarinen .30 .75
10 Jaromir Florian .30 .75
11 Mark Versteeg-Lytwyn .40 1.00
12 Mark O'Leary .30 .75
13 Steve Zmudczynski .30 .75
14 Scot Zimmerman .30 .75
15 Ryan Kitchen .30 .75
16 Mike McLean .30 .75
17 Kyle Paige .30 .75
18 Matt Lyall .30 .75
19 Matt D'Agostini .30 .75
20 Ryan Card .30 .75
21 Darryl Smith .30 .75
22 Ryan Callahan .40 1.00
23 Kyle Spurr .30 .75
24 Tyler Doig .30 .75
25 Adam Dennis .40 1.00
26 Dave Barr CO .04 .10
27 Jason Brooks ACO .04 .10
28 Trent Cull ACO .04 .10
29 Spyke MASCOT .04 .10
30 Team Photo/CL .04 .10
31 Guelph Police .04 .10

2005-06 Guelph Storm

COMPLETE SET (32) 10.00 25.00
A01 Josh Godfrey .40 1.00
A02 Jamie Arniel .40 1.00
A03 Mark O'Leary .40 1.00
A04 Tyler Doig .40 1.00
A05 Ryan MacDonald .40 1.00
A06 Jason Brooks ACO .20 .50
A07 Guelph Police .02 .10
A08 Guelph Storm CL1 .10 .25
B01 Ryan Pottruff .40 1.00
B02 Ryan Parent 1.00 2.50
B03 Andy Hyvarinen .40 1.00
B04 Kelsey Wilson .40 1.00
B05 Matt D'Agostini .40 1.00
B06 Domino's Pizza SPONSOR .02 .10
B07 Dave Barr CO .20 .50
B08 Guelph Storm CL2 .02 .10
C01 Michael Caruso .40 1.00
C02 Drew Doughty 2.00 5.00
C03 Brandon Biggers .40 1.00
C04 Leigh Salters .40 1.00
C05 Rafael Rotter .40 1.00
C06 M&T Printing SPONSOR .02 .10
C07 Trent Cull ACO .10 .25
C08 Guelph Storm CL3 .02 .10
D01 Shawn Haviland .40 1.00
D02 Kyle Wharton .40 1.00
D03 Jason Pitton .40 1.00
D04 Mike McLean .40 1.00
D05 Harry Young .40 1.00
D06 Ryan Callahan .75 2.00
D07 Jason Guy .40 1.00
D08 Guelph Storm CL4 .02 .10

2006-07 Guelph Storm

COMPLETE SET (25) 6.00 15.00
1 Thomas McCollum .40 1.00
2 Ryan Pottruff .20 .50
3 Joe Underwood .20 .50
4 Brandon Buck .20 .50
5 Drew Doughty 1.25 3.00
6 Matt Kennedy .20 .50
7 Leigh Salters .20 .50
8 Anthony Nigro .20 .50
9 Jeff Hayes .20 .50
10 Tyler Melancon .20 .50
11 Tyler Doig .20 .50
12 Mike McLean .20 .50
13 Patrick Moran .20 .50
14 Anton Hedman .20 .50
15 Luke Pither .20 .50
16 Grant McGee .20 .50
17 Rafael Rotter .20 .50
18 Tim Priamo .20 .50
19 Jamie Arniel .20 .50
20 Ryan Parent .60 1.50
21 Corey Syvret .20 .50
22 Michael Caruso .20 .50
23 Cody St Jacques .20 .50
24 Dave Barr CO .10 .25
25 Rusty Hammond TR .02 .10

2013-14 Guelph Storm

COMPLETE SET (33) 8.00 20.00
A01 Series 1 Header .30 .75
A02 Justin Auger .30 .75
A03 Hunter Garlent .30 .75
A04 Tyler Bertuzzi .30 .75
A05 Ryan Horvat .30 .75
A06 Brody Milne .30 .75
A07 Jason Dickinson .30 .75
A08 Ben Harpur .30 .75
A09 Pius Suter .30 .75
A10 Zack Mitchell .30 .75
A11 Scott Kosmachuk .30 .75
A12 Chadd Bauman .30 .75
A13 Justin Nichols .30 .75
A14 Guelph Police Services .30 .75
A15 RBC Bank .30 .75
A16 M & T Printing Group .30 .75
B01 Series 2 Header .30 .75
B02 Steven Trojanovic .30 .75
B03 Matt Finn .30 .75
B04 Phil Baltisberger .30 .75
B05 Zac Leslie .30 .75
B06 Robby Fabbri .30 .75
B07 Nick Ebert .30 .75
B08 Adam Craievich .30 .75
B09 Marc Stevens .30 .75
B10 Kerby Rychel .30 .75
B11 Stephen Pierog .30 .75
B12 Brock McGinn .30 .75
B13 Garrett McFadden .30 .75
B14 Matthew Mancina .30 .75
B15 RBC Bank .30 .75
B16 Speedvale Dental Centre .30 .75
B17 Guelph Police Services .30 .75

2014-15 Guelph Storm

COMPLETE SET (33) 8.00 20.00
A01 Series 1 Header .30 .75
A02 Kyle Rhodes .30 .75
A03 Ben Harpur .30 .75
A04 Zac Leslie .30 .75
A05 Robby Fabbri .50 1.25
A06 Jason Dickinson .30 .75
A07 Adam Craievich .30 .75
A08 Marc Stevens .30 .75
A09 James McEwan .30 .75
A10 Pius Suter .30 .75
A11 Matthew Hotchkiss .30 .75
A12 Garrett McFadden .30 .75
A14 Bradley Van Schubert .30 .75
A15 Guelph Police Services .30 .75
A16 Royal Bank of Canada .30 .75
A17 M&T Printing Group .30 .75
B01 Series 2 Header .30 .75
B02 Noah Carroll .30 .75
B03 C.J. Garcia .30 .75
B04 Phil Baltisberger .30 .75
B05 Austin Hall .30 .75
B06 Tyler Hill .30 .75
B07 Tyler Boston .30 .75
B08 Ryan Foss .30 .75
B09 Tyler Bertuzzi .40 1.00
B10 Chris Marchese .30 .75
B11 Luke Cairns .30 .75
B12 Givani Smith .30 .75
B13 Luke Burghardt .30 .75
B14 Justin Nichols .30 .75
B15 Guelph Police Services .30 .75
B16 Royal Bank of Canada .30 .75
B17 Speedvale Dental .30 .75

2003-04 Gwinnett Gladiators

This set was sponsored by the Gwinnett Daily Post and was issued as a promotional giveaway at a home game. The oversized cards were issued on a perforated sheet.

COMPLETE SET (36) 12.00 30.00
1 Checklist .04 .10
2 Kevin Doell .40 1.00
3 Brad Peddle .40 1.00
4 Brandon Dietrich .40 1.00
5 Chris Durno .40 1.00
6 Rick Emmett .40 1.00
7 Anthony Aquino .60 1.50
8 Steve Slonina .40 1.00
9 Cam Brown .40 1.00
10 Wes Fox .40 1.00
11 Mike Buckley .60 1.50
12 Paul Flache .40 1.00
13 Joe Bourne .40 1.00
14 Blue Bennefield .60 1.50
15 Michael Garnett .60 1.50
16 Evan Nielsen .40 1.00
17 Jim Jackson .40 1.00
18 Troy Milam .40 1.00
19 Adam Munro .60 1.50
20 Kris Goodjohn .40 1.00
21 Mike Vigilante .40 1.00
22 Phil Lewandowski .40 1.00
23 J.P. O'Connor .40 1.00
24 Jeff Pyle CO .10 .25
25 Megan Guthrie TR .10 .25
26 Patrick Houlihan EQM .10 .25
27 Steve Chapman GM .10 .25
28 Dustin Bixby ANN .10 .25
29 Celebration Photo .20 .50
30 Mascot .10 .25
31 Gladiators first ever goal .20 .50
32 Gladiators win first game .20 .50
33 Opening Night .20 .50
34 Scramble in the crease .20 .50
35 Team Photo .20 .50
36 The Zamboni .10 .25

2003-04 Gwinnett Gladiators RBI Sports

This set was produced by RBI Sports, with a print run of 250 sets. The numbering sequence reflects the entire print run of RBI sets this season.

COMPLETE SET (16) 6.00 15.00
193 Blue Bennefield .60 1.50
194 Joe Bourne .40 1.00
195 Cam Brown .40 1.00
196 Brandon Dietrich .40 1.00
197 Kevin Doell .40 1.00
198 Chris Durno .40 1.00
199 Rick Emmett .40 1.00
200 Paul Flache .40 1.00
201 Michael Garnett .60 1.50
202 Kris Goodjohn .40 1.00
203 Jim Jackson .40 1.00
204 Troy Milam .40 1.00
205 Adam Munro .60 1.50
206 Evan Nielsen .40 1.00
207 Steve Slonina .40 1.00
208 Mike Vigilante .40 1.00

2004-05 Gwinnett Gladiators

COMPLETE SET (30) 8.00 20.00
1 T.J. Aceti .60 1.50
2 Adam Berkhoel .75 2.00
3 Dustin Bixby .30 .75
4 Joe Bourne .30 .75
5 Cam Brown .30 .75
6 Jeff Campbell .30 .75
7 Steve Champman GM .04 .10
8 Chris Durno .30 .75
9 Rick Emmett .30 .75
10 Brett Engelhardt .30 .75
11 Sean Fields .30 .75
12 Peter Flache .30 .75
13 Kris Goodjohn .30 .75
14 Megan Guthrie TR .04 .10
15 Patrick Houlihan EQMG .04 .10
16 Jim Jackson .30 .75
17 Lane Manson .30 .75
18 Dave McCullough .30 .75
19 Dr. Brian Morgan .04 .10
20 Chris Peterson .30 .75
21 Jeff Pyle CO .04 .10
22 Brad Schell .30 .75
23 Adam Smyth .30 .75
24 Mike Stathopoulos .30 .75
25 Kevin Truelson .30 .75
26 Ryan Van Buskirk .30 .75
27 Mike Vigilante .30 .75
28 Maximus MASCOT .04 .10
29 Team Picture .04 .10
30 Checklist .04 .10

1989-90 Halifax Citadels

This 26-card set measures approximately 2" by 4 1/4". The fronts feature full-bleed posed action color photos, except at the top where a gray stripe displays the logos of the Farmers Co-Operative Dairy Limited and 92/CJCH. The team logo in the form of a red star appears in the lower right corner, with the player's name in a blue bar that is printed over the team logo. The cards are unnumbered and checklisted below in alphabetical order.

COMPLETE SET (26) 4.80 12.00
1 Joel Baillargeon .20 .50
2 Jamie Baker .25 .60
3 Mario Brunetta .30 .75
4 Gerald Bzdel .20 .50
5 David Espe .20 .50
6 Bryan Fogarty .20 .50
7 Robbie Ftorek GM .20 .50
8 Scott Gordon .30 .75
9 Dean Hopkins .20 .50
10 Miroslav Ihnacak .20 .50
11 Claude Julien .20 .50
12 Kevin Kaminski .30 .75
13 Claude Lapointe .30 .75
14 Chris McQuaid EQ .08 .25
Brent Smith TR
15 Max Middendorf .20 .50
16 Stephane Morin .30 .75
17 Dave Pichette .20 .50
18 Ken Quinney .20 .50
19 Jean-Marc Richard .20 .50
20 Jean Marc Routhier .20 .50

21 Jaroslav Sevcik .20 .50
22 Brent Severyn .30 .75
23 Greg Smyth .20 .50
24 Trevor Steinburg .20 .50
25 Mark Vermette .20 .50
26 Ladislav Tresl .20 .50

1990-91 Halifax Citadels

This 28-card set measures approximately 2 3/4" by 4 1/4" and features color, posed-action player photos with white borders. The Farmers Co-Operative Dairy Limited and the 92/CJCH logo appear in the top border. The cards are unnumbered and checklisted below in alphabetical order.

COMPLETE SET (28) 4.80 12.00
1 Jamie Baker .20 .50
2 Mike Bishop .15 .40
3 Gerald Bzdel .15 .40
4 Daniel Dore .15 .40
5 Mario Doyon .15 .40
6 Dave Espe .15 .40
7 Stephane Fiset 1.25 3.00
8 Scott Gordon .30 .75
9 Stephane Guerard .15 .40
10 Dean Hopkins ACO .08 .25
11 Miroslav Ihnacak .20 .50
12 Jeff Jackson .20 .50
13 Clement Jodoin CO/MG .08 .25
14 Claude Lapointe .20 .50
15 Dave Latta .15 .40
16 Chris McQuaid EQ MG .08 .25
17 Kip Miller .20 .50
18 Stephane Morin .20 .50
19 Ken Quinney .15 .40
20 Jean-Marc Richard .15 .40
21 Serge Roberge .15 .40
22 Jaroslav Sevcik .15 .40
23 Brent Severyn .30 .75
24 Mike Shuman TR .08 .25
25 Greg Smyth .15 .40
26 Jim Sprott .15 .40
27 Trevor Stienburg .15 .40
28 Mark Vermette .15 .40

1995-96 Halifax Mooseheads

This set features the Mooseheads of the QMJHL. The set was produced by the team, and sold at its souvenir stands.

COMPLETE SET (25) 8.00 25.00
1 Harlin Hayes .20 .50
2 Jean-Sebastien Giguere 4.00 10.00
3 Patrick Lafleur .20 .50
4 Jamie Brown .20 .50
5 Elias Abrahamsson .20 .50
6 Didier Tremblay .20 .50
7 Chris Halverson .20 .50
8 Chris Peyton .20 .50
9 Frederic Belanger .20 .50
10 Joel Theriault .20 .50
11 Mark Lynk .20 .50
12 Derrick Pyke .20 .50
13 Steve Mongrain .20 .50
14 David Carson .20 .50
15 Jody Shelley 2.00 5.00
16 Daniel Payette .20 .50
17 Brian Surette .20 .50
18 Etienne Drapeau .30 .75
19 Billy Manley .20 .50
20 Jan Melichercik .20 .50
21 Nicolas Maheux .20 .50
22 Eric Houde .30 .75
23 Shawn MacKenzie CO .08 .25
24 Clement Jodoin CO .08 .25
25 Chris McQuaid TR .02 .10

1996-97 Halifax Mooseheads I

Series one pictures the team in their home uniforms. It was sold in team-set form early in the season.

COMPLETE SET (27) 12.00 30.00
1 Elias Abrahamsson .30 .75
2 Frederic Belanger .20 .50
3 Martin Bilodeau .20 .50
4 Jamie Brown .20 .50
5 Marc Chouinard .40 1.00
6 Benoit Dusablon .60 1.50
7 Jean-Sebastien Giguere 2.50 6.00
8 Andrew Gilby .20 .50
9 Alex Johnstone .20 .50
10 Eric Laplante .30 .75
11 Jean-Simon Lemay .20 .50
12 Mark Lynk .20 .50
13 Billy Manley .20 .50
14 Alexander Mathieu .20 .50
15 Todd Row .20 .50
16 Ryan Rowell .20 .50
17 Francois Sasseville .20 .50
18 Jody Shelley 1.50 4.00
19 Jeffrey Sullivan .20 .50
20 Alex Tanguay 4.00 10.00
21 Didier Tremblay .30 .75
22 Jason Troini .20 .50
23 Clark Udle .20 .50
24 Clement Jodoin HCO .02 .10
25 Shawn MacKenzie ACO .02 .10
26 Chris McQuaid TR .02 .10
27 Team Photo .20 .50

1996-97 Halifax Mooseheads II

Series 2 features the team in their away uniforms. According to various reports, it was issued later in the season and is considered slightly tougher to acquire.

COMPLETE SET (27) 14.22 35.56
1 Elias Abrahamsson .40 1.00
2 Frederic Belanger .30 .75
3 Martin Bilodeau .30 .75
4 Jamie Brown .30 .75
5 Marc Chouinard .50 1.25
6 Benoit Dusablon .75 2.00
7 Jean-Sebastien Giguere 4.00 10.00
8 Andrew Gilby .30 .75
9 Alex Johnstone .30 .75
10 Eric Laplante .40 1.00
11 Jean-Simon Lemay .30 .75
12 Mark Lynk .30 .75
13 Billy Manley .30 .75
14 Alexander Mathieu .30 .75
15 Todd Row .30 .75
16 Ryan Rowell .30 .75
17 Francois Sasseville .30 .75
18 Jody Shelley 2.00 5.00
19 Jeffrey Sullivan .30 .75
20 Alex Tanguay 5.00 12.00
21 Didier Tremblay .40 1.00
22 Jason Troini .30 .75
23 Clark Udle .30 .75
24 Clement Jodoin HCO .02 .10
25 Shawn MacKenzie ACO .02 .10
26 Chris McQuaid TR .02 .10
27 Team Photo .20 .50

1997-98 Halifax Mooseheads I

As with the previous year's set, Series 1 features the team in their home uniforms. The series was sold by the team at home games.

COMPLETE SET (27) 8.00 20.00
1 Frederic Belanger .20 .50
2 Martin Bilodeau .20 .50
3 Marc-Andre Binette .20 .50
4 Alexandre Couture .20 .50
5 Andrew Gilby .20 .50
6 Alex Johnstone .20 .50
7 Eric Laplante .30 .75
8 P.J. Lynch .20 .50
9 Mark Lynk .20 .50
10 Joey MacDonald .50 1.25
11 Ali MacEachern .20 .50
12 Billy Manley .20 .50
13 Alexander Mathieu .20 .50
14 Steve Mongrain .20 .50
15 Ryan Power .20 .50
16 Brandon Reid 1.25 3.00
17 Todd Row .20 .50
18 Dean Stock .20 .50
19 Jeffrey Sullivan .20 .50
20 Alex Tanguay 3.00 8.00
21 Didier Tremblay .30 .75
22 Jason Troini .20 .50
23 Dwight Wolfe .20 .50
24 Danny Grant HCO .20 .50
25 Shawn MacKenzie ACO .02 .10
26 Chris McQuaid TR .02 .10
27 Team Photo .20 .50

1997-98 Halifax Mooseheads II

Series 2 is unnumbered and listed alphabetically. The set features several players who were acquired by the team after the release of Series 1. It also was printed in lesser quantities than the first series.

COMPLETE SET (27) 12.00 30.00
1 Checklist .02 .10
2 Frederic Belanger .30 .75
3 Martin Bilodeau .30 .75
4 Marc-Andre Binette .30 .75
5 Alexandre Couture .30 .75
6 Mauro DiPaolo .30 .75
7 Alex Johnstone .30 .75
8 P.J. Lynch .30 .75
9 Joey MacDonald .40 1.00
10 Ali MacEachern .30 .75
11 Boris Majesky .30 .75
12 Billy Manley .30 .75
13 Alexander Mathieu .30 .75
14 Ryan Power .30 .75
15 Stephen Quirk .30 .75
16 Brandon Reid 1.50 4.00
17 A.J.Rivers .30 .75
18 Dean Stock .30 .75
19 Jeffrey Sullivan .30 .75
20 Alex Tanguay 4.00 10.00
21 Jason Troini .30 .75
22 Andrew Warr .30 .75
23 Dwight Wolfe .30 .75
24 Shawn MacKenzie ACO .10 .25
25 Danny Grant HCO .30 .75
26 Hal Mascot .02 .10
27 Alex Tanguay CAN 4.00 10.00
28 Chris McQuad TR .02 .10

1998-99 Halifax Mooseheads

COMPLETE SET (23) 12.00 20.00
1 Alexei Volkov .30 .75
2 Pascal Leclaire .75 2.00
3 Mathieu Paul .20 .50
4 Samuel Seguin .20 .50
5 Billy Manley .20 .50
6 Ladislav Nagy 1.25 3.00
7 Alex Tanguay 1.25 3.00
8 Mike Bray .20 .50
9 Carlyle Lewis .20 .50
10 Frederic Belanger .20 .50
11 David McCutcheon .20 .50
12 Jeff Sullivan .20 .50
13 Alexandre Mathieu .20 .50
14 Jason Troini .20 .50
15 Alex Johnstone .20 .50
16 Ali MacEachern .20 .50
17 Brandon Benedict .20 .50
18 Tyler Reid .20 .50
19 Jasmin Gelinas .20 .50
20 P.J. Lynch .20 .50
21 Mauro DiPaolo .20 .50
22 Brandon Reid .60 1.50
23 Marc-Andre Binette .20 .50
24 Jeff Towriss .20 .50
25 Rocco Anoia .20 .50
26 Daniel Villeneuve .20 .50
27 Alex Tanguay CL .75 2.00

1998-99 Halifax Mooseheads Second Edition

COMPLETE SET (27) 8.00 20.00
1 Tyler Reid .20 .50
2 Jasmin Gelinas .20 .50
3 Hal MASCOT .02 .10
4 Brandon Reid .40 1.00
5 Jeff Sullivan .20 .50
6 Alex Johnstone .20 .50
7 P.J. Lynch .20 .50
8 Mauro Dipaolo .20 .50
9 Marc-andre Binette .20 .50
10 Carlyle Lewis .20 .50
11 David McCutcheon .20 .50
12 Mike Bray .20 .50
13 Samuel Seguin .20 .50
14 Brandon Benedict .20 .50
15 Jason Troini .20 .50
16 Ali MacEachern .20 .50
17 Mathieu Paul .20 .50
18 Alexei Volkov .30 .75
19 Billy Manley .20 .50
20 Frederic Belanger .20 .50
21 Alex Tanguay 1.25 3.00
22 Pascal Leclaire .75 2.00
23 Ladislav Nagy 1.25 3.00
24 Alexandre Mathieu .30 .75
25 World Junior .40 1.00
26 Halifax Radio Team .02 .10
27 Team Card .02 .10

1999-00 Halifax Mooseheads

This 29-card set features the 1999-00 Halifax Mooseheads. Card fronts have white borders, and along the left side, a green status bar containing the player's name fades into a full color action photo. These cards are not numbered, therefore appear in order by the included checklist card.

COMPLETE SET (29) 7.20 18.00
1 Alexei Volkov .40 1.00
2 Pascal Leclaire 2.00 5.00
3 Carlos Sayde .08 .25
4 Joey Dipenta 1.25 3.00
5 Joe Groleau .08 .25
6 Jonathan Boone .08 .25
7 Nick Greenough .08 .25
8 Jason King .08 .25
9 Shawn Lewis .08 .25
10 Ramzi Abid .40 1.00
11 Jonathan St. Louis .08 .25
12 Darrell Jarrett .08 .25
13 Ryan Flinn .60 1.50
14 Robbie Sutherland .08 .25
15 Ali MacEachern .08 .25
16 Brandon Benedict .08 .25
17 Jules-Edy Laraque .40 1.00
18 Jasmin Gelinas .08 .25
19 Hugo Lehoux .08 .25
20 Gary Zinck .08 .25
21 Brandon Reid .75 2.00
22 Benoit Dusablon .40 1.00
23 Hal MASCOT .02 .10
24 Team Photo .08 .25
25 Cover Card 1 .02 .10
26 Cover Card 2 .02 .10
27 Cover Card 3 .02 .10
28 Cover Card 4 .02 .10
29 Cover Card 5 .02 .10

2000-01 Halifax Mooseheads

This attractive set features the Mooseheads of the QMJHL. The set was produced and sold by the team at its souvenir stands. The cards were sponsored by Sobey's and are unnumbered, therefore they are listed below in alphabetical order.

COMPLETE SET (26) 4.80 12.00
1 Brandon Benedict .15 .40
2 Jonathan Boone .15 .40
3 Michael Couch .15 .40
4 Dany Dallaire .30 .75
5 Bruce Gillis .15 .40
6 Nick Greenough .15 .40
7 Milan Jurcina .40 1.00
8 Derrick Kent .15 .40
9 Jason King .15 .40
10 Sergei Klyazmin .30 .75
11 Sebastien Laprise .15 .40
12 Jules-Edy Laraque .30 .75
13 Pascal Leclaire 1.25 3.00
14 Hugo Lehoux .15 .40
15 Ali MacEachern .15 .40
16 A.J. Maclean .15 .40
17 Ryan MacPherson .15 .40
18 Louis Mandeville .15 .40
19 Conor McGuire .15 .40
20 Jules Saulnier .15 .40
21 Giulio Scandella .15 .40
22 Robbie Sutherland .15 .40
23 Randy Upshall .15 .40
24 Ryan White .15 .40
25 Gary Zinck .15 .40
26 Team CL .01 .05

2001-02 Halifax Mooseheads

COMPLETE SET (26) 6.00 15.00
1 Dany Dallaire .40 1.00
2 Jonathan Boutin .30 .75
3 Milan Jurcina .40 1.00
4 Bobby Clarke .30 .75
5 Sergei Klyazmin .30 .75
6 Francois-Pierre Guenette .30 .75
7 A.J. MacLean .30 .75
8 Bruce Gillis .30 .75
9 Jason King .50 1.25
10 Derrick Kent .30 .75
11 Giulio Scandella .30 .75
12 Jean-Francois Cyr .30 .75
13 Michael Couch .30 .75
14 Robbie Sutherland .30 .75
15 Ryan White .30 .75
16 Randy Upshall .30 .75
17 Patrick Gilbert .30 .75
18 Brandon Benedict .30 .75
19 Marc-Andre Bernier .40 1.00
20 Louis-Philippe Lessard .30 .75
21 Alexandre Picard .30 .75
22 Louis Mandeville .30 .75
23 Action Shot 1 .10 .25
24 Action Shot 2 .10 .25
25 Action Shot 3 .10 .25
26 Checklist .04 .10

2002-03 Halifax Mooseheads

This set was issued by the Halifax Mooseheads of the QMJHL. The set is unnumbered and listed below in checklist order.

COMPLETE SET (22) 5.00 10.00
1 Chesklist .04 .10
2 Guillaume Lavallee .20 .50
3 Jonathan Boutin .20 .50
4 Milan Jurcina .40 1.00
5 Stuart McRae .20 .50
6 Francois-Pierre Guenette .20 .50
7 A.J. MacLean .20 .50
8 Kyle Doucet .20 .50
9 Thatcher Bell .20 .50
10 Derrick Kent .20 .50
11 Petr Vrana .60 1.50
12 Frederik Cabana .20 .50
13 Jean-Francois Cyr .20 .50
14 Jordie Preston .20 .50
15 George Davis .20 .50
16 Randy Upshall .20 .50
17 Brandon Benedict .20 .50
18 Marc-Andre Bernier .40 1.00
19 Colby MacIntyre .20 .50
20 Jimmy Sharrow .20 .50
21 Alexandre Picard .75 2.00
22 Steve Villeneuve .20 .50

2003-04 Halifax Mooseheads

COMPLETE SET (26) 6.00 15.00
1 Jimmy Sharrow .30 .75
2 Bobby Clarke .30 .75
3 James Pouliot .20 .50
4 Justin Munden .20 .50
5 Evan Jones .20 .50
6 Daniel Sparre .20 .50
7 Petr Vrana .40 1.00
8 George Davis .20 .50
9 Frederik Cabana .20 .50
10 Jared Vokey .20 .50
11 Jan Steber .20 .50
12 Justin Saulnier .20 .50
13 Jason Churchill .30 .75
14 Ryan Moore .20 .50
15 Randy Upshall .20 .50
16 Sebastien Nolet .30 .75
17 Federick Sonier .20 .50
18 Jean-Francois Brault .20 .50
19 Colby MacIntyre .20 .50
20 Franklin MacDonald .20 .50
21 David Brine .20 .50
22 Pierre-Olivier Beaulieu .20 .50
23 Luciano Lomanno .20 .50
24 Kenzie Sheppard .20 .50
NNO Petr Vrana TL .40 1.00
NNO Jimmy Sharrow TL .30 .75

2004-05 Halifax Mooseheads

A total of 900 team sets were produced. There is a variation of card #4. The first version featured David Brine with a full cage and a different sweater number. The card was pulled and replaced with an updated photo. A few of the original version made their way into packs, although these all are found with a large black X over the image.

COMPLETE SET (26) 6.00 15.00
1 Alexandre Picard .40 1.00
2 Bryce Swan .20 .50
3 Daniel Sparre .20 .50
4A David Brine full cage, X 8.00 20.00
4B David Brine common version .20 .50
5 Francois-Pierre Guenette .20 .50
6 Franklin MacDonald .20 .50
7 Frederik Cabana .20 .50
8 James Pouliot .20 .50
9 Jan Steber .20 .50
10 Jason Churchill .40 1.00
11 Jean-Francois Brault .20 .50
12 Jeff MacAuley .20 .50
13 Jimmy Sharrow .20 .50
14 Ryan Moore .20 .50
15 Justin Saulnier .20 .50
16 Kenzie Sheppard .20 .50
17 Kevin Cormier .20 .50
18 Luciano Lomanno .20 .50
19 Marc-Andre Bernier .40 1.00
20 Petr Vrana .40 1.00
21 Pierre-Olivier Beaulieu .20 .50
22 Rane Carnegie .30 .75
23 Roger Kennedy .40 1.00
24 Ryan Hillier .20 .50
25 Austin Corredato .20 .50
26 Jeremy Duchesne .40 1.00

2005-06 Halifax Mooseheads

COMPLETE SET (25) 8.00 20.00
1 Jeremy Duchesne .30 .75
2 Roger Kennedy .30 .75
3 Andrew Bodnarchuk .60 1.50
4 Jiri Suchy .30 .75
5 Luciano Lomanno .30 .75
6 Rane Carnegie .30 .75
7 James Pouliot .30 .75
8 Garrett Peters .30 .75
9 Kirk Forrest .30 .75
10 Bryce Swan .30 .75
11 Ryan Hillier .30 .75
12 Justin Saulnier .30 .75
13 Philippe Poirier .30 .75
14 Logan MacMillan .30 .75
15 Daniel Smith .30 .75
16 Ben Macaskill .30 .75
17 Kevin Cormier .30 .75
18 Brent Lynch .30 .75
19 Justin Pender .30 .75
20 Jean-Francois Brault .30 .75
21 Mikhail Aseev .30 .75
22 Franklin MacDonald .30 .75
23 David Brine .30 .75
24 Yuri Cheremetiev .30 .75
25 Frederik Cabana .30 .75

2006-07 Halifax Mooseheads

COMPLETE SET (21) 10.00 18.00
1 Jeremy Duchesne .40 1.00
2 Andrew Bodnarchuk .40 1.00
3 Roger Kennedy .40 1.00
4 Jiri Suchy .30 .75
5 Luciano Lomanno .30 .75
6 Ryan Seymour .30 .75
7 James Pouliot .30 .75
8 Garrett Peters .30 .75
9 Logan Macmillan .30 .75
10 Benjamin Chaisson .30 .75
11 Daniel Smith .30 .75
12 Bryce Swan .30 .75
13 Ryan Hillier .30 .75
14 Jakub Voracek 1.25 3.00
15 Andrew White .30 .75
16 Justin Pender .30 .75
17 Ben Macaskill .30 .75
18 Gabriel O'Connor .30 .75
19 Colby Pridham .30 .75
20 Yuri Cheremetiev .30 .75
21 Eric Louis-Seize .30 .75

2015-16 Halifax Mooseheads

COMPLETE SET (24) 6.00 15.00
1 Domenico Argento .30 .75
2 Kelly Bent .30 .75
3 Joel Bishop .30 .75
4 Dominik Blain-Dupuis .30 .75
5 Eric Brassard .30 .75
6 Brett Crossley .30 .75
7 Barrett Dachyshyn .30 .75
8 Cody Donaghey .30 .75
9 Arnaud Durandeau .30 .75
10 Cavan Fitzgerald .30 .75
11 Walter Flower .30 .75
12 Taylor Ford .30 .75
13 Maxime Fortier .30 .75
14 Cooper Jones .30 .75
15 Timo Meier .30 .75
16 Connor Moynihan .30 .75
17 Danny Moynihan .30 .75
18 Morgan Nauss .30 .75
19 Ilya Putintsev .30 .75
20 Kevin Resop .30 .75
21 Andrew Shewfelt .30 .75
22 Otto Somppi .30 .75
23 Jean-Sebastien Taillefer .30 .75
24 Vincent Watt .30 .75

1975-76 Hamilton Fincups

This 18-card standard-size set features sepia-tone player portraits. The player's name and position are printed in the lower border, which is also sepia-tone. The team name is superimposed over the picture at the bottom center. The backs are blank and grayish in color. The cards are unnumbered and checklisted below in alphabetical order.

COMPLETE SET (18) 15.00 30.00
1 Jack Anderson .75 1.50
2 Mike Clarke .75 1.50
3 Greg Clause .75 1.50
4 Joe Contini .75 1.50
5 Mike Fedorko .75 1.50
6 Paul Foley .75 1.50
7 Greg Hickey .75 1.50
8 Tony Horvath .75 1.50
9 Mike Keating .75 1.50
10 Archie King .75 1.50
11 Ted Long .75 1.50
12 Dale McCourt 2.50 5.00
13 Dave Norris .75 1.50
14 Greg Redquest .75 1.50
15 Glen Richardson .75 1.50
16 Ron Roscoe .75 1.50
17 Ric Seiling 1.25 2.50
18 Danny Shearer .75 1.50

1999-00 Hamilton Bulldogs

This set features the Bulldogs of the AHL. The cards were produced by SplitSecond and were sold at home games and by mail order.

COMPLETE SET (25) 4.00 10.00
1 Mike Minard .30 .75
2 Chris Hajt .15 .40
3 Brad Norton .15 .40
4 Walt Kyle CO .08 .25
5 Eric Houde .15 .40
6 Kevin Bolibruck .15 .40
7 Daniel Cleary .20 .50
8 Vladimir Vorobiev .20 .50
9 Dan LaCouture .20 .50
10 Brian Swanson .20 .50
11 Martin Laitre .15 .40
12 Peter Sarno .40 1.00
13 Alex Zhurik .15 .40
14 Chad Hinz .15 .40
15 Kevin Brown .15 .40
16 Matthieu Descoteaux .15 .40
17 Jason Chimera .40 1.00
18 Alex Henry .30 .75
19 Sean Selmser .20 .50
20 Ryan Risidore .15 .40
21 Michel Riesen .30 .75
22 Sergei Yerkovich .15 .40
23 Elias Abrahamsson .15 .40
24 Eric Heffler .15 .40
25 Bruiser MASCOT .08 .25

2000-01 Hamilton Bulldogs

This set features the Bulldogs of the AHL. The set was produced by the team and sold at its souvenir stands late in the season.

COMPLETE SET (28) 5.00 12.00
1 Chris Madden .30 .75
2 Terran Sandwith .15 .40
3 Ryan Risidore .15 .40
4 Kurt Drummond .15 .40
5 Chris Hajt .15 .40
6 Brad Norton .15 .40
7 Maxim Spiridonov .15 .40
8 Patrick Cote .30 .75
9 Alex Henry .30 .75
10 Paul Healey .15 .40
11 Jason Chimera .40 1.00
12 Peter Sarno .30 .75
13 Brian Urick .15 .40
14 Michael Henrich .30 .75
15 Brian Swanson .20 .50
16 Martin Laitre .15 .40
17 Chris Albert .15 .40
18 Fernando Pisani .40 1.00
19 Lloyd Shaw .15 .40
20 Scott Ferguson .15 .40
21 Michel Riesen .20 .50
22 Alain Nasreddine .15 .40
23 Chad Hinz .15 .40
24 Joaquin Gage .30 .75
25 Claude Julien CO .10 .25
26 Morey Gare CO .10 .25
27 Bruiser MASCOT .04 .10
28 Team CL .01 .05

2001-02 Hamilton Bulldogs

This set features the Bulldogs of the AHL. It was created by the well-known card shop CTM Ste-Foy, and was sold at that store, as well as by the team. Less than 1,000 sets were reportedly produced.

COMPLETE SET (26) 4.80 12.00
1 Ales Pisa .20 .50
2 Chris Hajt .20 .50
3 Alex Henry .30 .75
4 Jan Horacek .20 .50
5 Kevin Brown .20 .50
6 Jason Chimera .40 1.00
7 Peter Sarno .20 .50
8 Craig Reichert .20 .50
9 Greg Leeb .20 .50
10 Marc-Andre Bergeron .20 .50
11 Brian Swanson .20 .50
12 Jani Rita .40 1.00
13 Fernando Pisani .20 .50
14 Michael Henrich .20 .50
15 Sean Selmser .20 .50
16 Ty Conklin .40 1.00
17 Alain Nasreddine .20 .50
18 Alexei Semenov .30 .75
19 Adam Dewan .20 .50
20 Marc Lamothe .30 .75
21 Sven Butenschon .20 .50
22 Chad Hinz .20 .50
23 Claude Julien CO .04 .10
24 Geoff Ward ACO .04 .10
25 Bruiser Mascot .04 .10
NNO Title Card CL .04 .10

2002-03 Hamilton Bulldogs

COMPLETE SET (28) 8.00 20.00
1 Bobby Allen .20 .50
2 Ben Carpentier .20 .50
3 Ron Hainsey .40 1.00
4 Tony Salmelainen .20 .50
5 Chad Hinz .20 .50
6 Nate DiCasmirro .20 .50
7 Tomas Plekanec .40 1.00
8 Jason Ward .30 .75
9 Jarret Stoll .40 1.00
10 Matt O'Dette .20 .50
11 Marc-Andre Bergeron .20 .50
12 Jani Rita .30 .75
13 Francois Beauchemin .40 1.00
14 Fernando Pisani .30 .75
15 Michael Ryder 1.25 3.00
16 Michael Henrich .20 .50
17 Ty Conklin .30 .75
18 Eric Fichaud .30 .75
19 Alexei Semenov .20 .50
20 Adam Dewan .20 .50
21 Mathieu Garon .40 1.00
22 Benoit Gratton .20 .50
23 Francois Bouillon .30 .75
24 Mike Komisarek .30 .75
25 Jozef Balej .40 1.00
26 Marcel Hossa .40 1.00
27 Bruiser MASCOT .04 .10
28 Checklist .04 .10

2004-05 Hamilton Bulldogs

COMPLETE SET (30) 8.00 20.00
1 Andrew Archer .20 .50
2 Ben Carpentier .20 .50
3 JP Cote .20 .50
4 Trevor Daley .20 .50
5 Yann Danis .60 1.50
6 Benoit Dusablon .20 .50
7 Dan Ellis .60 1.50
8 Jonathan Ferland .20 .50
9 Dan Focht .20 .50
10 Ron Hainsey .40 1.00
11 Chris Higgins .40 1.00
12 Raitis Ivanans .20 .50
13 Dan Jancevski .20 .50
14 Doug Jarvis CO .20 .50
15 Andrei Kostitsyn 1.00 2.50
16 Michael Lambert .20 .50
17 Christian Larrivee .20 .50
18 Corey Locke .20 .50
19 Antti Miettinen .40 1.00
20 Duncan Milroy .20 .50
21 Gavin Morgan .20 .50
22 Steve Ott .60 1.50
23 Tomas Plekanec .40 1.00
24 Philippe Plante .20 .50
25 James Sanford .20 .50
26 Matt Shasby .20 .50
27 Marc-Andre Thinel .30 .75
28 Jason Ward .30 .75
29 Ron Wilson ACO .20 .50
30 Bruiser MASCOT .04 .10

2005-06 Hamilton Bulldogs

COMPLETE SET 6.00 15.00
1 Jonathan Aitken .20 .50
2 Andrew Archer .20 .50
3 Ryan Barnes .20 .50
4 Andre Benoit .20 .50
5 Jean-Philippe Cote .20 .50
6 Yann Danis .40 1.00
7 Jeff Drouin-Deslauriers .40 1.00
8 Jonathan Ferland .20 .50
9 Ron Hainsey .20 .50
10 Raitis Ivanans .40 1.00
11 Jean-Francois Jacques .20 .50
12 Andrei Kostitsyn .40 1.00
13 Michael Lambert .20 .50
14 Maxim Lapierre .20 .50
15 Francis Lemieux .20 .50
16 Corey Locke .20 .50
17 Olivier Michaud .40 1.00
18 Duncan Milroy .20 .50
19 Garth Murray .20 .50
20 Jeff Paul .20 .50
21 Marc-Antoine Pouliot .40 1.00
22 Mathieu Roy .75 2.00
23 James Sanford .20 .50
24 Dan Smith .20 .50
25 Danny Syvret .20 .50
26 Peter Vandermeer .40 1.00
27 Brad Winchester .20 .50
28 Don Lever .02 .10
29 Ron Wilson .02 .10
30 Bruiser .02 .10

2006-07 Hamilton Bulldogs

COMPLETE SET (26) 8.00 15.00
1 Andrew Archer .20 .50
2 Mathieu Aubin .20 .50
3 Ajay Baines .20 .50
4 Andre Benoit .20 .50
5 Kyle Chipchura .30 .75
6 Jean-Philippe Cote .20 .50
7 Matt D'Agostini .20 .50
8 Yann Danis .30 .75
9 Eric Manlow .20 .50
10 Jonathan Ferland .20 .50
11 Jon Gleed .20 .50
12 Mikhail Grabovsky .20 .50
13 Danny Groulx .20 .50
14 Jaroslav Halak .75 2.00
15 Dan Jancevski .20 .50
16 Andrei Kostitsyn .40 1.00
17 Michael Lambert .20 .50
18 Maxim Lapierre .30 .75
19 Francis Lemieux .20 .50
20 Corey Locke .20 .50
21 Duncan Milroy .20 .50
22 Ryan O'Byrne .20 .50
23 Mathieu Roy .40 1.00
24 Zach Stortini .40 1.00
25 Patrick Traverse .20 .50
26 Cory Urquhart .20 .50

2013-14 Hamilton Bulldogs

COMPLETE SET () 6.00 15.00
1 Greg Pateryn .30 .75
2 Jarred Tinordi .30 .75
3 Darren Dietz .30 .75
4 Nathan Beaulieu .30 .75
5 Justin Courtnall .30 .75
6 Nathan McIver .30 .75
7 Maxime Macenauer .30 .75
8 Mike Blunden .30 .75
9 Louis Leblanc .30 .75
10 Drew Schiestel .30 .75
11 Joonas Nattinen .30 .75
12 Jordan Owens .30 .75
13 Sven Andrighetto .30 .75
14 Robert Mayer .30 .75
15 Dustin Tokarski .30 .75
16 Patrick Holland .30 .75
17 Gabriel Dumont .30 .75
18 Morgan Ellis .30 .75
19 Stefan Fournier .30 .75
20 Joel Chouinard .30 .75
21 Nick Tarnasky .30 .75
22 Christian Thomas .30 .75
23 Martin St. Pierre .30 .75

2014-15 Hamilton Bulldogs

COMPLETE SET (25) 8.00 20.00
1 Gabriel Dumont .40 1.00
2 Joey MacDonald .30 .75
3 Magnus Nygren .30 .75
4 Michael Bournival .40 1.00
5 Sven Andrighetto .40 1.00
6 Joe Finley .30 .75
7 Eric Tangradi .40 1.00
8 Jack Nevins .30 .75
9 Connor Crisp .30 .75
10 Nick Sorkin .30 .75
11 Jacob De La Rose .75 2.00
12 Christian Thomas .30 .75
13 Jake Dowell .30 .75
14 T.J. Hensick .30 .75
15 Drayson Bowman .30 .75
16 Maxime Macenauer .30 .75
17 Daniel Carr .30 .75
18 Charles Hudon .30 .75
19 Mac Bennett .30 .75
20 Nathan Beaulieu .50 1.25
21 Darren Dietz .30 .75
22 Jarred Tinordi .40 1.00
23 Davis Drewiske .30 .75
24 Greg Pateryn .30 .75
25 Mike Condon .40 1.00

1992-93 Hamilton Canucks

Created by Diamond Memories Sportscards to commemorate the Canucks' inaugural season, these 30 standard-size cards feature black-bordered color player action photos on the fronts. The cards are unnumbered and checklisted below in alphabetical order.

COMPLETE SET (30) 4.00 10.00
1 Shawn Antoski .30 .75
2 Robin Bawa .15 .40
3 Jamie Carlson TR .02 .10
4 Jassen Cullimore .20 .50
5 Alain Deeks .15 .40
6 Neil Eisenhut .15 .40
7 Mike Fountain .30 .75
8 Troy Gamble .30 .75
9 Jason Herter .15 .40
10 Pat Hickey PR .02 .10
11 Dane Jackson .15 .40
12 Dan Kesa .15 .40
13 Jeff Lumby ANN .02 .10
14 Mario Marois UER .20 .50
Last name misspelled
Marios on back
15 Bob Mason .30 .75
16 Mike Maurice .15 .40
17 Jay Mazur .15 .40
18 Jack McIlhargey CO .02 .10
19 Sandy Moger .30 .75
20 Stephane Morin .15 .40
21 Eric Murano .15 .40
22 Troy Neumeier .15 .40
23 Matt Newsom GM .02 .10
24 Libor Polasek .15 .40
25 Phil von Stefenelli .15 .40
26 Doug Torrel .15 .40
27 Doug Tretiak TR .02 .10
28 Rick Vaive CO .15 .40
29 Opening Night .15 .40
Puck-Drop
Mario Marois
Pat Hickey
30 Team Photo .20 .50
(Checklist)

1961-62 Hamilton Red Wings

This oversized set features members of the top farm team of the Red Wings. They were sold as a set by the team.

COMPLETE SET (21) 37.50 75.00
1 Bud Blom 1.50 3.00
2 Eddie Bush 2.00 4.00
3 Bob Dean 1.50 3.00
4 John Gofton 1.50 3.00
5 Bob Hamilton 1.50 3.00
6 Bob Hamilton 1.50 3.00
7 Ron Harris 2.00 4.00
8 Earl Heiskala 2.00 4.00
9 Paul Henderson 7.50 15.00
10 Roger Lafreniere 1.50 3.00
11 Lowell Macdonald 4.00 8.00
12 Pit Martin 5.00 10.00
13 Jim Mclellan 1.50 3.00
14 Harvey Meisenheimer 1.50 3.00
15 Howie Menard 1.50 3.00
16 Wayne Rivers 4.00 8.00
17 Jim Peters 2.00 4.00
18 Bob Wall 1.50 3.00
19 Jack Wildfong 1.50 3.00
20 Terry Urkewicz 1.50 3.00
21 Larry Zilliotto 1.50 3.00

1989-90 Hampton Roads Admirals

This 21-card set of the Hampton Roads Admirals of the ECHL features color photos on the front. The cards are unnumbered, and are listed below in alphabetical order. We've recently learned that 19 of the 21 cards have variations, ie, one version showing a head shot, the other an action shot. We've listed them with letter suffixes detailing action (A) or head shot (H). A complete set includes only one version or the other. We cannot say which (if either) is more scarce, so we are showing no price difference between the two versions for the time being. The set, which last year was valued at $10, was the subject of fierce bidding wars each time it appeared on eBay in 2005 and earned one of the greatest value jumps in recent memory.

COMPLETE SET (21) 4.00 400.00
1A Mike Black 8.00 20.00
1H Mike Black 8.00 20.00
2 John Brophy CO 10.00 25.00
3A David Buckley 8.00 20.00
3H David Buckley 8.00 20.00
4A Pat Cavanagh 8.00 20.00
4H Pat Cavanagh 8.00 20.00
5A Mike Flanagan 8.00 20.00
5H Mike Flanagan 8.00 20.00
6A Frank Furlan 8.00 20.00
6H Frank Furlan 8.00 20.00
7A Don Gagne 8.00 20.00
7H Don Gagne 8.00 20.00
8A Steve Greenberg 8.00 20.00
8H Steve Greenberg 8.00 20.00
9A Murray Hood 8.00 20.00
9H Murray Hood 8.00 20.00
10A Trevor Jobe 8.00 20.00
10H Trevor Jobe 8.00 20.00
11A Trevor Kruger 8.00 20.00
11H Trevor Kruger 8.00 20.00
12A Chris Lukey 8.00 20.00
12H Chris Lukey 8.00 20.00
13A Brian Martin 8.00 20.00
13H Brian Martin 8.00 20.00
14A Dennis McEwen 8.00 20.00
14H Dennis McEwen 8.00 20.00
15A Bobby McGrath 8.00 20.00
15H Bobby McGrath 8.00 20.00
16A Darren Miciak 8.00 20.00
16H Darren Miciak 8.00 20.00
17A Al Murphy 8.00 20.00
17H Al Murphy 8.00 20.00
18A Jody Praznik 8.00 20.00
18H Jody Praznik 8.00 20.00
19A Alain Raymond 8.00 20.00
19H Alain Raymond 8.00 20.00
20A Wayne Stripp 8.00 20.00
20H Wayne Stripp 8.00 20.00
21 Scott Taylor 8.00 20.00

1990-91 Hampton Roads Admirals

is 20-card was issued by the Hampton Roads mirals of the ECHL. They feature color action otography on the front, along with another photo and tistical information on the back. The numbering of set is a mystery, as it clearly carries on from other issue. Interestingly, the previous year's mirals set is unnumbered. The set, therefore, may be mbered consecutively with other ECHL issues from same season.

MPLETE SET (20) 3.00 8.00
Scott King .20 .50
Greg Bignell .15 .40
David Buckley .15 .40
Jody Praznik .15 .40
John East .15 .40
Steve Greenberg .15 .40
Darcy Kaminski .15 .40
Glen Kehrer .15 .40
Murray Hood .15 .40
Dennis McEwen .15 .40
Billy Nolan .15 .40
Bill Thomas .15 .40
Pat Cavanagh .15 .40
Cory Banika .20 .50
Al Murphy .15 .40
Harry Mews .15 .40
Mark Bernard .15 .40
Brian Martin .15 .40
Curt Brackenbury ACO .08 .25
John Brophy CO .15 .40

1991-92 Hampton Roads Admirals

is 20-card set was produced by the team and ailable at the rink. The cards feature action photos on front, with stats and bio on the back. This set, ich features an early pro card of Olaf Kolzig, is numbered, and listed below alphabetically.

MPLETE SET (20) 4.00 50.00
Mark Bernard 1.25 3.00
Mike Chighisola .75 2.00
John East .75 2.00
Victor Gervais .75 2.00
Murray Hood .75 2.00
Scott Johnson .75 2.00
Olaf Kolzig 6.00 15.00
Paul Krepelka .75 2.00
Al MacIsaac .75 2.00
Brian Martin .75 2.00
Dennis McEwen .75 2.00
Dave Morissette .75 2.00
Billy Nolan .75 2.00
Randy Pearce .75 2.00
Steve Poapst 1.25 3.00
Pete Siciliano .75 2.00
Shawn Snesar .75 2.00
Keith Whitmore .75 2.00
John Brophy CO .40 1.00
Darcy Kaminski ACO .02 .10

1992-93 Hampton Roads Admirals

is set is unnumbered and was sponsored by Ward's rner Sporting Goods, Ogden Services, and radio ation WCMS. The set is listed by the order of the ayer's jersey number, which is listed on the back.

MPLETE SET (20) 3.00 8.00
Shawn Snesar .20 .50
Paul Krepelka .20 .50
Claude Barthe .20 .50
Steve Poapst .30 .75
Kelly Sorenson .20 .50
Trevor Duhaime .20 .50
Steve Mirabile .20 .50
Kurt Kabat .20 .50
Victor Gervais .25 .60
Jason Rathbone .20 .50
Rod Taylor .20 .50
Al MacIsaac CO .08 .25
Brian Martin .20 .50
Dave Morissette .20 .50
Harry Mews .20 .50
Mark Bernard .20 .50
Nick Vitucci .30 .75
Steve Martell .20 .50
Chris Scarlata TR .02 .10
John Brophy CO .20 .50

1993-94 Hampton Roads Admirals

is set features the Admirals of the ECHL. The set was onsored by Ward's Corner Sporting Goods, Ogden ervices and radio station WCMS. The set is nearly entical in design to the previous year's set. The cards e unnumbered, and so they are listed alphabetically.

MPLETE SET (20) 3.00 8.00
John Brophy CO .20 .50
Rick Burrill TR .02 .10
Daniel Chaput .20 .50
Brendan Curley .20 .50
Victor Gervais .20 .50
Brian Goudie .20 .50
Shamus Gregga .20 .50
Jason MacIntyre .20 .50
Al MacIsaac ACO .02 .10
Kevin Malgunas .20 .50
Dennis McEwen .20 .50
Mark Michaud .20 .50
Ron Pascucci .20 .50
Darren Perkins .20 .50
Steven Perkovic .20 .50
Shawn Snesar .20 .50
Kelly Sorenson .20 .50
Rod Taylor .20 .50
Richie Walcott .20 .50
Shawn Wheeler .20 .50

1994-95 Hampton Roads Admirals

is 23-card set measures the standard size. On a ite card face, the fronts feature color action player otos with a simulated blue marble frame and a thin llow, inner border. The player's name appears inside hockey stick on the bottom of the photo, with the am logo next to it.

MPLETE SET (23) 4.80 12.00
John Brophy CO .20 .50
Al MacIsaac ACO .02 .10
Patrick Lalime 2.00 5.00
Colin Gregor .15 .40
Ron Pascucci .15 .40
John Porco .15 .40
Trevor Halverson .20 .50
Rod Taylor .15 .40
Brian Goudie .15 .40
Chris Phelps .15 .40
Tom Menicci .15 .40
Anthony MacAulay .15 .40
13 Rick Kowalsky .15 .40
14 Dennis McEwen .15 .40
15 Kelly Sorenson .15 .40
16 Brendan Curley .15 .40
17 Jason MacIntyre .15 .40
18 Jim Brown .15 .40
19 Matt Mallgrave .15 .40
20 Ron Majic .15 .40
21 Corwin Saurdiff .15 .40
22 Rick Burrill TR .02 .10
23 Team Photo CL .15 .40
NNO Logo Card .02 .10

1995-96 Hampton Roads Admirals

This 25-card set showcases the Hampton Roads Admirals of the ECHL. The set was produced by Q-Cards, and distributed by Ward's Corner Sporting Goods; it may also have been sold through the team at games. The set features action photography on the front and an expanded player information section on the numbered back.

COMPLETE SET (25) 4.00 10.00
1 Team Photo .15 .40
2 John Brophy CO .15 .40
3 Al MacIsaac ACO .02 .10
4 Darryl Paquette .20 .50
5 Mark Bernard .15 .40
6 Ron Pascucci .15 .40
7 Dominic Maltais .15 .40
8 Jason MacIntyre .15 .40
9 Serge Aubin .40 1.00
10 Rick Kowalsky .08 .25
11 Claude Fillion .20 .50
12 Rod Taylor .15 .40
13 Alexei Krivchenkov .15 .40
14 David St. Pierre .15 .40
15 Steve Richards .15 .40
16 Trevor Halverson .30 .75
17 Chris Phelps .15 .40
18 Jeff Kostuch .15 .40
19 Sean Selmser .30 .75
20 Aaron Downey .40 1.00
21 Bob Woods .15 .40
22 Sergei Voronov .15 .40
23 Corwin Saurdiff .20 .50
24 Rick Burrell TR .02 .10
25 Gary Mansfield EQMG .02 .10

1997-98 Hampton Roads Admirals

This 24-card set was produced by a former player with the Ads and was handed out as a promotional giveaway at a home game.

COMPLETE SET (24) 7.20 18.00
1 Chad Ackerman .30 .75
2 Alexander Alexeev .30 .75
3 Rob Bonneau .30 .75
4 Dan Carney .30 .75
5 Dan Ceman .40 1.00
6 Sebastien Charpentier .40 1.00
7 Marty Clapton .30 .75
8 Victor Gervais .30 .75
9 Alexander Kharlamov .40 1.00
10 Rick Kowalsky .30 .75
11 Mike Larkin .30 .75
12 Bill Lincoln .30 .75
13 Ron Majic .30 .75
14 Jason Mansoff .30 .75
15 Chris Phelps .30 .75
16 Joel Poirier .30 .75
17 Jason Saal .60 1.50
18 Kayle Short .30 .75
19 Rod Taylor .30 .75
20 Joel Theriault .30 .75
21 Yuri Yuresko .30 .75
22 John Brophy HCO .20 .50
23 Al MacIsaac ACO .02 .10
24 Trainers .02 .10

1996-97 Hampton Roads Admirals

This 25-card set of the Hampton Roads Admirals of the ECHL was produced by Blueline Communications, and sponsored by Kline Chevrolet and The Score, 1310 AM. The cards feature action photos on the front, along with the player name. The backs include statistical and biographical data.

COMPLETE SET (25) 4.00 10.00
HRA1 Darryl Paquette .20 .50
HRA2 Mike Larkin .15 .40
HRA3 Chris Phelps .15 .40
HRA4 Alex Alexeev .15 .40
HRA5 Joel Theriault .15 .40
HRA6 Neal Martin .15 .40
HRA7 Ryan Mulhern .15 .40
HRA8 Darryl Shedden .15 .40
HRA9 Victor Gervais .15 .40
HRA10 Rod Taylor .15 .40
HRA11 Andy Weidenbach .15 .40
HRA12 Alain Savage .15 .40
HRA13 Randy Pearce .15 .40
HRA14 Chad Ackerman .15 .40
HRA15 Alexei Krivchenkov .15 .40
HRA16 Rick Kowalsky .15 .40
HRA17 Dominic Maltais .15 .40
HRA18 Joel Poirier .20 .50
HRA19 Marc Seliger .30 .75
HRA20 Aaron Downey .30 .75
HRA21 John Brophy CO .20 .50
HRA22 Al MacIsaac ACO .02 .10
HRA23 G.Mansfield EQMG .02 .10
K.Bender TR
HRA24 Salty (Mascot) .02 .10
NNO Team Photo .15 .40

1998-99 Hampton Roads Admirals

This 26-card set was handed out as a promotional giveaway at an Admirals game. Little else is known about the set, other than a confirmation that two versions of card #25 were released.

COMPLETE SET (26) 6.00 15.00
1 Mascot .08 .25
Checklist
2 John Brophy .20 .50
3 Al MacIsaac ACO .08 .25
4 Chris Phelps .20 .50
5 Trevor Johnson .20 .50
6 Jami Yoder .20 .50
7 Joel Poirier .30 .75
8 Alexander Kharlamov .30 .75
9 Bobby Russell .20 .50
10 Trever Fraser .20 .50
11 Jason Deleurme .20 .50
12 Henry Higdon .20 .50
13 Rod Taylor .20 .50
14 Jeff Corbett .20 .50
15 Derek Ernest .20 .50
16 Charlie Retter .20 .50
17 Chad Ackerman .20 .50
18 Boris Zelenko .20 .50
19 Dan Ceman .30 .75
20 Marty Clapton .20 .50
21 Milt Mastad .20 .50
22 Dominic Maltais .30 .75
23 Stephen Valiquette .75 2.00
24 Jason Saal .40 1.00
25 Stu Bender TR .08 .25
25 Scott Boggs EM .08 .25

1998-99 Hampton Roads Admirals 10th Anniversary

This 30-card set was handed out at a game in December, and features alumni of the Admirals, including several prominent NHLers. Because of the unique distribution method, the cards are quite scarce.

COMPLETE SET (30) 10.00 25.00
1 John Brophy HCO .20 .50
2 Rod Taylor .20 .50
3 Victor Gervais .20 .50
4 Brian Martin .20 .50
5 Dennis McEwen .20 .50
6 Chris Phelps .20 .50
7 Randy Pearce .20 .50
8 Murray Hood .20 .50
9 Olaf Kolzig 2.00 5.00
10 Kelly Sorenson .20 .50
11 Mark Bernard .20 .50
12 Andrew Brunette .40 1.00
13 Trevor Halverson .20 .50
14 Rick Kowalsky .20 .50
15 Aaron Downey .75 2.00
16 Patrick Lalime 1.50 4.00
17 Steve Poapst .30 .75
18 Alexander Alexeev .20 .50
19 Harry Mews .20 .50
20 Al MacIsaac .20 .50
21 John Parco .20 .50
22 Kent Hawley .20 .50
23 Dave Flanagan .20 .50
24 Billy Nolan .20 .50
25 Brendan Curley .20 .50
26 Ron Pascucci .20 .50
27 Mark Michaud .20 .50
28 Shawn Snesar .20 .50
29 Byron Dafoe 1.25 3.00
30 Sebastien Charpentier .40 1.00

1999-00 Hampton Roads Admirals

This set features the Admirals of the ECHL. The set was produced by Q-Cards and issued as a promotional giveaway at a home game, and later at Ragazzi's, a local restaurant.

COMPLETE SET (25) 8.00 20.00
1 Chad Ackerman .30 .75
2 Gerad Adams .30 .75
3 Louis Bedard .40 1.00
4 Brad Church .40 1.00
5 Marty Clapton .30 .75
6 Curtis Cruickshank .40 1.00
7 Derek Ernest .30 .75
8 Ryan Gillis .30 .75
9 Trevor Johnson .30 .75
10 Rick Kowalsky .30 .75
11 Jan Lasak 1.25 3.00
12 Dominic Maltais .40 1.00
13 Mike Omicioli .30 .75
14 John Parco .30 .75
15 Dwight Parrish .30 .75
16 Colin Pepperall .30 .75
17 Richard Pitirri .30 .75
18 Bobby Russell .30 .75
19 Mike Siklenka .30 .75
20 Dean Stork .30 .75
21 Rod Taylor .30 .75
22 John Brophy CO .08 .25
23 Al MacIsaac CO .08 .25
24 Stu Bender .08 .25
Scott Boggs TR
NNO Checklist .08 .25

1997-98 Hartford Wolf Pack

This set features the Wolf Pack of the AHL. The singles are postcard-sized, and were issued only to members of the team's Kid's Club.

COMPLETE SET (29) 12.00 35.00
1 Derek Armstrong .40 1.00
2 Sylvain Blouin .60 1.50
3 Eric Cairns .60 1.50
4 Dan Cloutier 1.50 4.00
5 Christian Dube .40 1.00
6 Peter Ferraro .60 1.50
7 Maxim Galanov .40 1.00
8 Ken Gernander .40 1.00
9 Daniel Goneau .40 1.00
10 Todd Hall .40 1.00
11 Johan Lindbom .40 1.00
12 Mike Martin .40 1.00
13 Jason Muzzatti .60 1.50
14 Dale Purinton .75 2.00
15 Marc Savard .75 2.00
16 Pierre Sevigny .40 1.00
17 Adam Smith .40 1.00
18 Geoff Smith .40 1.00
19 Brad Smyth .40 1.00
20 Lee Sorochan .40 1.00
21 Robb Stauber .60 1.50
22 P.J. Stock 1.50 4.00
23 Ronnie Sundin .40 1.00
24 Tim Sweeney .40 1.00
25 Brent Thompson .40 1.00
26 Ryan VandenBussche .75 2.00
27 Vladimir Vorobiev .40 1.00
28 Chris Winnes .40 1.00
29 Sonar MASCOT .08 .25

1998-99 Hartford Wolf Pack

This set features the Wolf Pack of the AHL. The set was given only to members of the team's Kid's Club. The cards bear the logos of Brigham's Ice Cream.

COMPLETE SET (28) 14.00 35.00
1 Derek Armstrong .40 1.00
2 Jeff Brown .40 1.00
3 Ed Campbell .40 1.00
4 Ben Carpentier .40 1.00
5 Christian Dube .40 1.00
6 Bob Errey .40 1.00
7 Jeff Finley .40 1.00
8 Ken Gernander .40 1.00
9 Daniel Goneau .40 1.00
10 Todd Hall .40 1.00
11 Boyd Kane .75 2.00
12 Jean-Francois Labbe .75 2.00
13 Mike Martin .40 1.00
14 Dale Purinton .60 1.50
15 Ryan Risidore .40 1.00
16 Marc Savard .75 2.00
17 Adam Smith .40 1.00
18 Lee Sorochan .60 1.50
19 P.J. Stock 3.00 8.00
20 Brent Thompson .40 1.00
21 Alexei Vasiliev .40 1.00
22 Vladimir Vorobiev .40 1.00
23 Kay Whitmore .60 1.50
24 Chris Winnes .40 1.00
25 Johan Witehall .40 1.00
26 Sonar MASCOT .08 .25
27 Rich Brennan .40 1.00
28 Stefan Cherneski .40 1.00

1999-00 Hartford Wolf Pack

This set features the Wolf Pack of the AHL. These cards were handed out to members of the team's Kid's Club at a special practice. The cards are blank-backed and unnumbered, and therefore are listed in alphabetical order.

COMPLETE SET (23) 12.00 30.00
1 Derek Armstrong .40 1.00
2 Drew Bannister .40 1.00
3 Ben Carpentier .40 1.00
4 Stefan Cherneski .40 1.00
5 Jason Doig .60 1.50
6 Francois Fortier .40 1.00
7 Ken Gernander .40 1.00
8 Daniel Goneau .40 1.00
9 Todd Hall .40 1.00
10 Mike Harder .40 1.00
11 Burke Henry .40 1.00
12 Milan Hnilicka 1.50 4.00
13 Chris Kenady .40 1.00
14 Tomas Kloucek .75 2.00
15 Alexander Korobolin .40 1.00
16 Jean-Francois Labbe .75 2.00
17 Dale Purinton .75 2.00
18 Brad Smyth .60 1.50
19 P.J. Stock 1.25 3.00
20 Tony Tuzzolino .60 1.50
21 Alexei Vasiliev .40 1.00
22 Terry Virtue .60 1.50
23 Johan Witehall .60 1.50

2000-01 Hartford Wolf Pack

This set features the Wolf Pack of the AHL. The set was a very tough giveaway item, available only to members of the team's youth fan club. The cards are unnumbered and blank-backed. Three of the cards (Grosek, Labarbera and Mehalko) do not feature names on the front.

COMPLETE SET (29) 10.00 25.00
1 Derek Armstrong .30 .75
2 Drew Bannister .30 .75
3 Ryan Bast .30 .75
4 Ben Carpentier .30 .75
5 Jason Dawe .30 .75
6 Brandon Dietrich .30 .75
7 Jason Doig .30 .75
8 Dave Duerden .30 .75
9 Ken Gernander .30 .75
10 Michal Grosek .30 1.00
11 Todd Hall .30 .75
12 Burke Henry .30 .75
13 Johan Holmqvist .80 2.00
14 Boyd Kane .40 1.00
15 Chris Kenady .30 .75
16 Tomas Kloucek .80 2.00
17 Jason Labarbera .80 2.00
18 Manny Malhotra .60 1.00
19 Brad Mehalko .30 .75
20 Mike Mottau .60 1.50
21 Dale Purinton .40 1.00
22 Bert Robertsson .30 .75
23 Richard Scott .40 1.00
24 Brad Smyth .30 .75
25 Tony Tuzzolino .30 .75
26 Jeff Ulmer .30 .75
27 Terry Virtue .40 1.00
28 Vitali Yeremeyev .60 1.50
29 Sonar MASCOT .10 .25

2001-02 Hartford Wolf Pack

This set features the Wolf Pack of the AHL. These very scarce cards were available only to members of the Wolf Pack Kids Club. The cards are blank backed and unnumbered, so they are listed below in alphabetical order. Minor league expert Ralph Slate reports that Igor Ulanov's card was most likely a late addition, as it is printed on thinner card stock than the rest of the set.

COMPLETE SET (26) 20.00 40.00
1 Benoit Dusablon .75 2.00
2 Jason Dawe .75 2.00
3 Rico Fata .75 2.00
4 Sean Gagnon .75 2.00
5 Ken Gernander .40 1.00
6 Christian Gosselin .40 1.00
7 Michal Grosek .40 1.00
8 Barrett Heisten .75 2.00
9 Johan Holmqvist .75 2.00
10 Wes Jarvis .40 1.00
11 Boyd Kane .75 2.00
12 Matt Kinch .40 1.00
13 Jason Labarbera .75 2.00
14 Jamie Lundmark 3.00 8.00
15 Dave MacIsaac .40 1.00
16 Brad Mehalko .40 1.00
17 Scott Meyer .40 1.00
18 Mike Mottau 1.25 3.00
19 Cam Severson .40 1.00
20 Peter Smrek .75 2.00
21 Brad Smyth .40 1.00
22 Chris St. Croix .40 1.00
23 John Tripp .40 1.00
24 Igor Ulanov 3.00 8.00
25 Terry Virtue .75 2.00
26 Sonar MASCOT .20 .50

2002-03 Hartford Wolf Pack

COMPLETE SET (30) 12.00 30.00
1 Bobby Andrews .40 1.00
2 Dean Arsene .40 1.00
3 Patrick Aufiero .40 1.00
4 Ryan Bast .40 1.00
5 Garrett Burnett .40 1.00
6 Ted Donato .40 1.00
7 Benoit Dusablon .75 2.00
8 Nils Ekman .40 1.00
9 Ken Gernander .40 1.00
10 Johan Holmqvist .75 2.00
11 Dave Karpa .40 1.00
12 Matt Kinch .40 1.00
13 Jason Labarbera .75 2.00
14 Bryce Lampman .40 1.00
15 Cory Larose .40 1.00
16 Janne Laukkanen .40 1.00
17 Roman Lyashenko .40 1.00
18 Garth Murray .40 1.00
19 Chris Pittman .40 1.00
20 Richard Scott .40 1.00
21 Billy Tibbetts 1.25 3.00
22 John Tripp .40 1.00
23 Layne Ulmer .40 1.00
24 Dixon Ward .40 1.00
25 Mike Wilson .40 1.00
26 Patrick Yetman .40 1.00
27 Damon Scott ANN .04 .10
28 Nick Fotiu ACO .20 .50
29 Ryan McGill HCO .20 .50
30 Sonar Mascot .04 .10

2003-04 Hartford Wolf Pack

This set was made available to members of the Wolf Pack Kids Club, according to minor league maven Ralph Slate. The cards are oversized, unnumbered, and are listed below in alphabetical order. The card of Jamie Pushor was most likely a late addition, since it is printed on larger card stock than the rest of the set. It was not included in every set distributed by the team and therefore is considered a short print.

COMPLETE SET (27) 25.00 50.00
1 Bobby Andrews .40 1.00
2 Brandon Cullen .40 1.00
3 Ryan Cuthbert .40 1.00
4 Benoit Dusablon .75 2.00
5 Jayme Filipowicz .40 1.00
6 Ken Gernander .40 1.00
7 Paul Healey .40 1.00
8 Jeff Heerema .75 2.00
9 John Jakopin .40 1.00
10 Matt Kinch .40 1.00
11 Jason Labarbera 1.25 3.00
12 Bryce Lampman .40 1.00
13 Cory Larose .40 1.00
14 Lucas Lawson .40 1.00
15 Jason MacDonald .40 1.00
16 Dominic Moore SP 4.00 10.00
17 Garth Murray .60 1.50
18 Lawrence Nycholat .40 1.00
19 Phil Osaer .40 1.00
20 Jamie Pushor SP 4.00 10.00
21 Richard Scott .75 2.00
22 Juris Stals .40 1.00
23 Jeff State .40 1.00
24 Fedor Tyutin 1.25 3.00
25 Layne Ulmer .60 1.50
26 Craig Weller .40 1.00
27 Chad Wiseman .40 1.00

2004-05 Hartford Wolf Pack

Available only to member's of the team's Kid's Club.

COMPLETE SET (26) 30.00 60.00
1 Jozef Balej 1.25 3.00
2 Blair Betts .75 2.00
3 Ken Gernander .75 2.00
4 Trevor Gillies 1.25 3.00
5 Alexandre Giroux 1.25 3.00
6 Martin Grenier .75 2.00
7 Jeff Hamilton .75 2.00
8 Dwight Helminen .75 2.00
9 Ryan Hollweg 1.25 3.00
10 Jason Labarbera 1.25 3.00
11 Bryce Lampman .75 2.00
12 Lucas Lofton .75 2.00
13 Dave Liffiton .75 2.00
14 Jamie Lundmark 1.25 3.00
15 Steven MacIntyre .75 2.00
16 Jeff MacMillan .75 2.00
17 Dominic Moore .75 2.00
18 Garth Murray .75 2.00
19 Lawrence Nycholat .75 2.00
20 Jed Ortmeyer 1.25 3.00
21 Thomas Pock 1.25 3.00
22 Jake Taylor .75 2.00
23 Layne Ulmer .75 2.00
24 Stephen Valiquette 1.25 3.00
25 Craig Weller .75 2.00
26 Chad Wiseman .75 2.00

2005-06 Hartford Wolf Pack

COMPLETE SET (28) 15.00 30.00
1 Ivan Baranka .40 1.00
2 Nigel Dawes .75 2.00
3 Lee Falardeau .40 1.00
4 Fedor Fedorov .40 1.00
5 Colby Genoway .40 1.00
6 Robert Gherson .40 1.00
7 Daniel Girardi .75 2.00
8 Alexandre Giroux .40 1.00
9 Bruce Graham .40 1.00
10 Martin Grenier .40 1.00
11 Dwight Helminen .40 1.00
12 Jarkko Immonen .40 1.00
13 Hugh Jessiman .40 1.00
14 Bryce Lampman .40 1.00
15 Dave Liffiton .40 1.00
16 Al Montoya .50 4.00
17 Thomas Pock .40 1.00
18 Dale Purinton .75 2.00
19 Joe Rullier .40 1.00
20 Martin Sonnenberg .40 1.00
21 Daniel Sparre .40 1.00
22 Jake Taylor .40 1.00
23 Craig Weller .40 1.00
24 Chad Wiseman .40 1.00
25 Jim Schoenfeld HC .02 .10
26 Ken Gernander AC .02 .10
27 Ulf Samuelsson AC .02 .10
28 Sonar & Torpedo MASCOTS .01 .01

2006-07 Hartford Wolf Pack

COMPLETE SET (28) 25.00 50.00
1 Ryan Constant .60 1.50
2 Hugh Jessiman .60 1.50
3 Mark Lee .60 1.50
4 Bryce Lampman .60 1.50
5 Corey Potter .60 1.50
6 Bruce Graham .60 1.50
7 Zdenek Bahensky .60 1.50
8 Lee Falardeau .60 1.50
9 Daniel Girardi 1.25 3.00
10 Darius Kasparaitis .60 1.50
11 Steve Valiquette .75 2.00
12 Brad Isbister .60 1.50
13 Jarkko Immonen 1.25 3.00
14 Marvin Degon .60 1.50
15 Lauri Korpikoski 1.25 3.00
16 Jake Taylor .60 1.50
17 Nigel Dawes 1.25 3.00
18 Dale Purinton .60 1.50
19 Dane Byers 1.25 3.00
20 Dwight Helminen .60 1.50
21 Greg Moore .60 1.50
22 Martin Richter .60 1.50
23 Craig Weller .60 1.50
24 Ryan Callahan 1.25 3.00
25 Dave Liffiton .60 1.50
26 Al Montoya 1.25 3.00
27 Francis Lessard .60 1.50
28 Brandon Dubinsky .60 1.50

2014-15 Hartford Wolf Pack

COMPLETE SET (30) 8.00 20.00
1 Dylan McIlrath .40 1.00
2 Mathew Bodie .30 .75
3 Ryan Bourque .40 1.00
4 Chris Bourque .40 1.00
5 Joey Crabb .30 .75
6 Cedrick Desjardins .30 .75
7 Jesper Fast .40 1.00
8 Ryan Haggerty .30 .75
9 Marek Hrivik .30 .75
10 Tommy Hughes .30 .75
11 Dallas Jackson .30 .75
12 Josh Nicholls .30 .75
13 Danny Kristo .30 .75
14 Oscar Lindberg 1.50 4.00
15 J.T. Miller .40 1.00
16 Chris Mueller .30 .75
17 Shawn O'Donnell .30 .75
18 Ryan Potulny .30 .75
19 Mackenzie Skapski .30 .75
20 Steve Spinell .30 .75
21 Mike Kostka .30 .75
22 Nick Tarnasky .30 .75
23 Justin Vaive .30 .75
24 Conor Allen .30 .75
25 Ryan Malone .30 .75
26 Ken Gernander CO .30 .75
27 Jeff Beukeboom Asst. CO .30 .75
28 Pat Boller Asst. CO .30 .75
29 Sonar MASCOT .30 .75
CL Header Card CL .30 .75

1992-93 Harvard Crimson

As with most NCAA sets, this product is believed to be a promotional giveaway of some kind. The cards are unnumbered and checklisted below in alphabetical order.

COMPLETE SET (31) 8.00 20.00
1 Brian Adams .30 .75
2 Chris Baird .30 .75
3 Lou Body .30 .75
4 Michel Breistroff .30 .75
5 Perry Cohagen .30 .75
6 Ben Coughlin .30 .75
7 Ted Drury .40 1.00
8 Brian Farell .30 .75
9 Steven Flomenhoft .30 .75
10 Eric Grahling .30 .75
11 Cory Gustafson .30 .75
12 Kevin Hampe ACO .02 .10
13 Steve Hermsdorf .30 .75
14 Tom Holmes .30 .75
15 Aaron Israel .30 .75
16 Jason Karmanos .30 .75
17 Ian Kennish .30 .75
18 Brad Konik .30 .75
19 Bryan Lonsinger .30 .75
20 Derek Maguire .40 1.00
21 Matt Mallgrave .30 .75
22 Geb Marett .30 .75
23 Steve Martins .40 1.00
24 Sean McCann .30 .75
25 Peter McLaughlin .30 .75
26 Keith McLean .30 .75
27 Kirk Nielsen .40 1.00
28 Jerry Pawloski ACO .02 .10
29 Ronn Tomassoni CO .02 .10
30 Tripp Tracy .60 1.50
31 Header Card .02 .10

1994-95 Hershey Bears

This 24-card set was handed out at the Bears charity carnival. The cards are blank-backed so they are listed in alphabetical order.

COMPLETE SET (24) 8.00 20.00
1 Vladislav Boulin .40 1.00
2 Aris Brimanis .40 1.00
3 Bruce Coles .40 1.00
4 Yanick Dupre .40 1.00
5 Tracy Egeland .40 1.00
6 Andre Faust .40 1.00
7 Jeff Finley .40 1.00
8 Milos Holan .40 1.00
9 Paul Jerrard .40 1.00
10 Dan Kordic .40 1.00
11 Les Kuntar .60 1.50
12 Mitch Lamoureux .60 1.50
13 Neil Little 1.25 3.00
14 Mike McHugh .40 1.00
15 Clayton Norris .40 1.00
16 Vaclav Prospal .75 2.00
17 Terran Sandwith .40 1.00
18 Ryan Sittler .40 1.00
19 Bob Wilkie .40 1.00
20 Chris Winnes .40 1.00
21 Mike Stothers ACO .02 .10
22 Brad Dibeler ATR .02 .10
23 Jay Leach HCO .02 .10

1998-99 Hershey Bears

This 40-card set was sponsored by the Lebanon Daily News and features players from the 1998-99 Hershey Bears as well as several cards of past players and teams from this AHL franchise. The team photos carry player checklists on the back of each card.

COMPLETE SET (40) 12.00 30.00
1 Evgeny Lazarev .30 .75
{Mitch Lamoureux
2 Marc Denis 1.50 4.00
3 Jeff Buchanan .15 .40
4 Ted Crowley .15 .40
5 Yuri Babenko .15 .40
6 Evgeny Lazarev .30 .75
7 Scott Parker 1.25 3.00
8 Mike Foligno CO .20 .50
9 Rob Shearer .20 .50
10 Brad Larsen .15 .40
11 1946-47 Team Photo .20 .50
12 Rick Berry .20 .50
13 Troy Crowder .15 .40
14 Dan Hinote .40 1.00
15 Serge Aubin .40 1.00
16 1957-58 Team Photo .20 .50
17 1958-89 Team Photo .20 .50
18 1968-69 Team Photo .20 .50
19 David Aebischer 2.00 5.00
20 Mitch Lamoureux .30 .75
21 Christian Matte .20 .50
22 Dan Smith .15 .40
23 Jay Wells CO .15 .40
24 1973-74 Team Photo .15 .40
25 Ville Nieminen .75 2.00
26 Nick Bootland .15 .40
27 1979-80 Team Photo .20 .50
28 Bruce Richardson .15 .40
29 Brian Willsie .15 .40
30 Hershey Park Arena .08 .25
31 Brian White .15 .40
32 1980-81 Team Photo .20 .50
33 1987-88 Team Photo .20 .50
34 Dan Stuck TR .08 .25
35 1996-97 Team Photo .20 .50
36 Frank Mathers .20 .50
37 Arnie Kullman .15 .40
38 Mike Nykoluk .15 .40
39 Tim Tookey .30 .75
40 Team Logo .08 .25

2000-01 Hershey Bears

This set features the Bears of the AHL. This set was produced as a giveaway with the purchase of a local newspaper. Collectors buying a paper at the game would get one card, making a complete set very difficult to piece together.

COMPLETE SET (20) 5.00 25.00
1 Yuri Babenko .20 1.00
2 Rick Berry .20 1.50
3 Nick Bootland .20 1.00
4 Frederic Cassivi .30 2.00
5 Mike Craig .20 1.00
6 Kelly Fairchild .20 1.00
7 Brad Larsen .20 1.00
8 Yevgeny Lazarev .20 1.50
9 Stewart Malgunas .20 1.00
10 Ville Nieminen .15 3.00
11 Joel Prpic .20 1.00
12 Alex Ryazantsev .30 1.50
13 Philippe Sauve .15 4.00
14 Matthew Scorsune .20 1.00
15 Rob Shearer .20 1.50
16 Dan Smith .20 1.00
17 Ben Storey .20 1.00
18 K.C. Timmons .20 1.00
19 Steffon Walby .20 1.00
20 Brian White .20 1.00

2001-02 Hershey Bears

This set features the Bears of the AHL. The cards were issued singlely as a promotional giveaway with the purchase of a Hershey Patriot News newspaper at each home game. The last eight cards were apparently issued as an update set. The series is very difficult to complete due to this distribution. Although the player's jersey number appears on the front and back, the cards are considered unnumbered, and thus are listed in alphabetical order.

COMPLETE SET (28) 20.00 40.00
1 Yuri Babenko .60 1.50
2 Frederic Cassivi .60 1.50
3 Mike Cirillo .60 1.50
4 Coco MASCOT .50 1.25
5 Larry Courville .60 1.50
6 Jeff Daw .60 1.50
7 Kelly Fairchild .60 1.50
8 Paul Fixter ACO .50 1.25
9 Mike Foligno CO .50 1.25
10 Riku Hahl .75 2.00
11 Matt Herr .60 1.50
12 Jordan Krestanovich .60 1.50
13 Mikhail Kuleshov .60 1.50
14 Yevgeny Lazarev .60 1.50
15 Dave MacIsaac .60 1.50
16 Steve Moore .60 1.50
17 Bryan Muir .60 1.50
18 Vaclav Nedorost .60 1.50
19 Brad Norton .60 1.50
20 Jaroslav Obsut .60 1.50
21 Jeff Paul .60 1.50
22 Alex Riazantsev .60 1.50
23 Phil Sauve .75 2.00
24 Matt Scorsune .60 1.50
25 Brent Thompson .60 1.50
26 Rocky Thompson .60 1.50
27 K.C. Timmons .60 1.50
28 Radim Vrbata .75 2.00

2002-03 Hershey Bears

COMPLETE SET (30) 12.00 30.00
1 Eric Bertrand .40 1.00
2 Nick Bootland .40 1.00
3 Steve Brule .40 1.00
4 Peter Budaj .75 2.00
5 Marc Busenburg .40 1.00
6 Brett Clark .40 1.00
7 Dale Clarke .40 1.00
8 Pierre-Luc Emond .40 1.00
9 Mark Freer .40 1.00
10 Riku Hahl .75 2.00
11 Jordan Krestanovich .40 1.00
12 Mikhail Kuleshov .40 1.00
13 Cail MacLean .40 1.00
14 Steve Moore .40 1.00
15 Bryan Muir .40 1.00
16 Jeff Paul .40 1.00
17 Alexander Ryazantsev .40 1.00
18 Philippe Sauve 1.25 3.00
19 Agris Saviels .40 1.00
20 Charlie Stephens .40 1.00
21 Marek Svatos 1.25 3.00
22 Brent Thompson .40 1.00
23 K.C.Timmons .40 1.00
24 Rob Voltera .40 1.00
25 Tim Wedderburn .40 1.00
26 Brian Willsie .40 1.00
27 Mike Foligno HCO .10 .25
28 Paul Fixter ACO .10 .25
29 Coco Mascot .04 .10
30 Giant Center Arena .04 .10

2003-04 Hershey Bears

This set was produced by Choice Marketing and sold as a set at home games.

COMPLETE SET (24) 4.00 10.00
1 Peter Budaj .40 1.00
2 Jeff Finger .20 .50
3 D.J. Smith .20 .50
4 Brett Clark .20 .50
5 Tomas Slovak .20 .50
6 Pascal Trepanier .20 .50
7 Jordan Krestanovich .20 .50
8 Gavin Morgan .20 .50
9 Eric Perrin .40 1.00
10 Ryan Craig .20 .50
11 Mikhail Kuleshov .20 .50
12 Shane Willis .20 .50
13 Rob Voltera .20 .50
14 Steve Brule .20 .50
15 Bruce Richardson .20 .50
16 Sheldon Keefe .20 .50
17 Agris Saviels .20 .50
18 Charlie Stephens .20 .50
19 Marc Busenburg .20 .50
20 Mark Jerant .20 .50
21 Evgeny Artyukhin .30 .75
22 Tom Lawson .20 .50
23 Paul Fixter HCO .10 .25
24 Paul Jerrard ACO .10 .25

2003-04 Hershey Bears Patriot News

Singles from this set could be acquired only with the purchase of a Patriot News newspaper at select home games, making these cards, and this set, one of the season's toughest to acquire.

COMPLETE SET (30) 15.00 40.00
1 Evgeny Artyukhin .60 1.50
2 Dennis Bonvie .75 2.00
3 Steve Brule .60 1.50
4 Peter Budaj .75 2.00
5 Marc Busenburg .60 1.50
6 Brett Clark .60 1.50
7 Ryan Craig .60 1.50
8 Jeff Finger .60 1.50
9 Mark Jerant .60 1.50
10 Sheldon Keefe .60 1.50
11 Jordan Krestanovich .60 1.50
12 Mikhail Kuleshov .60 1.50
13 Brad Larsen .60 1.50
14 Tom Lawson .75 2.00
15 Steve Moore .60 1.50
16 Gavin Morgan .60 1.50
17 Eric Perrin 1.25 3.00
18 Bruce Richardson .60 1.50
19 Darren Rumble .60 1.50
20 Agris Saviels .60 1.50
21 Tomas Slovak .60 1.50
22 D.J. Smith .60 1.50
23 Charlie Stephens .60 1.50
24 Pascal Trepanier .60 1.50
25 Mikko Viitanen .60 1.50
26 Rob Voltera .60 1.50
27 Shane Willis .60 1.50
28 Paul Fixter HCO .10 .25
29 Paul Jerrard ACO .10 .25
30 Mascot .10 .25

2004-05 Hershey Bears Patriot News

Cards were available individually with the purchase of a Patriot News newspaper.

COMPLETE SET (31) 15.00 40.00
1 Dean Arsene .40 1.00
2 Chris Bala .40 1.00
3 Greg Barber .40 1.00
4 Dennis Bonvie 1.50 4.00
5 Johnny Boychuk .40 1.00
6 Peter Budaj .75 2.00
7 Brett Clark .40 1.00
8 Carl Corrazzini .75 2.00
9 Mathieu Darche .75 2.00
10 Jeff Finger .40 1.00
11 Paul Fixter CO .20 .50
12 Martin Hlinka .40 1.00
13 Paul Jerrard ACO .20 .50
14 Sergei Klyazmin .40 1.00
15 Tom Lawson .75 2.00
16 David Masse .40 1.00
17 Frank Mathers .75 2.00
18 Frank Mathers .75 2.00
19 Cody McCormick .75 2.00
20 Cail MacLean .40 1.00
21 Eric Perrin 1.25 3.00
22 Jamie Rivers .40 1.00
23 Agris Saviels .40 1.00
24 Frantisek Skladany .40 1.00
25 Mike Souza .40 1.00
26 Ryan Steeves .40 1.00
27 Marek Svatos 1.25 3.00
28 Jeff Ulmer .40 1.00
29 Mikko Viitanen .75 2.00
30 Martin Wilde .75 2.00
31 Coco MASCOT .04 .10

2005-06 Hershey Bears

COMPLETE SET (28) 8.00 20.00
1 Dean Arsene .30 .75
2 Jared Aulin .30 .75
3 Chris Bourque .60 1.50
4 Frederic Cassivi .60 1.50
5 Jakub Cutta .30 .75
6 Eric Fehr .30 .75
7 Tomas Fleischmann .30 .75
8 Owen Fussey .30 .75
9 Mike Green .30 .75
10 Jonas Johansson .30 .75
11 Boyd Kane .30 .75
12 Jakub Klepis .30 .75
13 Graham Mink .60 1.50
14 Lawrence Nycholat .30 .75
15 Dave Steckel .30 .75
16 Joey Tenute .30 .75
17 Martin Wilde .30 .75
18 Bruce Boudreau HC .02 .10
19 Bob Woods AC .02 .10
20 Coco the Bear MASCOT .02 .10
21 Kirk Daubenspeck .40 1.00
22 Deryk Engelland .30 .75
23 Colin Forbes .30 .75
24 J.F. Fortin .30 .75
25 Brooks Laich .30 .75
26 Louis Robitaille .75 2.00
27 Mark Wotton .30 .75
28 Dwayne Zinger .30 .75

2013-14 Hershey Bears

COMPLETE SET () 8.00 20.00
1 Team Photo .30 .75
2 Patrick Wellar .30 .75
3 Steven Oleksy .30 .75
4 Tomas Kundratek .30 .75
5 Nate Schmidt .30 .75
6 Coco the Bear MASCOT .30 .75
7 Peter Leblanc .30 .75
8 Dustin Gazley .30 .75
9 Chay Genoway .30 .75
10 Grant Potulny .30 .75
11 David Kolomatis .30 .75
12 Nicolas Deschamps .30 .75
13 Patrick Wey .30 .75
14 Tyson Strachan .30 .75
15 Matt Watkins .30 .75
16 Nathan Walker .30 .75
17 Jeff Taffe .30 .75
18 Josh Brittain .30 .75
19 Casey Wellman .30 .75
20 Julien Brouillette .30 .75
21 Cameron Schilling .30 .75
22 Ryan Stoa .30 .75
23 Michael Latta .30 .75
24 Joel Rechlicz .30 .75
25 Philipp Grubauer .30 .75
26 Brandon Segal .30 .75
27 Dane Byers .30 .75
28 Garrett Mitchell .30 .75
29 Dmitri Orlov .30 .75
30 Derek Whitmore .30 .75

2014-15 Hershey Bears

COMPLETE SET (30) 8.00 20.00
1 Joel Broda .30 .75
2 Chris Brown .30 .75
3 Erik Burgdoerfer .30 .75
4 Dane Byers .30 .75
5 Michal Cajkovsky .30 .75
6 Connor Carrick .40 1.00
7 Chris Conner .30 .75
8 Pheonix Copley .30 .75
9 Philippe Cornet .40 1.00
10 Stanislav Galiev .40 1.00
11 Dustin Gazley .30 .75
12 Philipp Grubauer .30 .75
13 Bryan Helmer .30 .75
14 Tim Kennedy .30 .75
15 Tomas Kundratek .30 .75
16 Jon Landry .30 .75
17 Troy Mann CO .30 .75
18 Garrett Mitchell .30 .75
19 Mike Moore .30 .75
20 Kris Newbury .30 .75
21 Jim O'Brien .30 .75
22 Liam O'Brien .30 .75
23 Steven Oleksy .30 .75
24 Cameron Schilling .30 .75
25 Tim Spencer .30 .75
26 Chandler Stephenson .30 .75
27 Nathan Walker .30 .75
28 Casey Wellman .40 1.00
29 Coco the Bear MASCOT .30 .75
30 Team Photo .30 .75

1995-96 Houston Aeros

This set features the Aeros of the IHL. The cards were produced by Edge Ice and sold at the team's souvenir stands.

COMPLETE SET (25) 4.80 12.00
1 Scott Arniel .30 .75
2 Al Conroy .20 .50
3 Paul DiPietro .20 .50
4 Gord Donnelly .20 .50
5 Rob Dopson .30 .75
6 Mark Freer .20 .50
7 Troy Gamble .30 .75
8 Kevin Grant .20 .50
9 Curtis Hunt .20 .50
10 Steve Jaques .20 .50
11 Gord Kruppke .20 .50
12 Mark Lamb .30 .75
13 Marc Laniel .30 .75
14 Kevin Malgunas .20 .50
15 Mike Maurice .20 .50
16 Scott McCrory .20 .50
17 Myles O'Connor .20 .50
18 Jim Paek .20 .50
19 Vadim Slivchenko .20 .50
20 Graeme Townshend .20 .50
21 Sylvain Turgeon .20 .50
22 Carl Valimont .20 .50
23 Mike Yeo .20 .50
24 Dave Tippett .20 .50
25 Terry Ruskowski CO .20 .50

1999-00 Houston Aeros

Created by ebk Sports, this standard size set was created specifically for the 2000 IHL All-Star Game, which featured the defending Turner Cup champion Aeros against the best players from the rest of the league. The set was sold at the Aeros home rink, although production problems delayed its release. The set features color action photos on a plastic-type stock. The cards are prone to poor centering and cutting.

COMPLETE SET (29) 10.00 25.00
1 Paul Dyck .40 1.00
2 Marty Wilford .40 1.00
3 Matt Swanson .40 1.00
4 Mark Lamb .60 1.50
5 Jeff Daw .40 1.00
6 Brian Wiseman .60 1.50
7 Lane Lambert .60 1.50
8 Brian Felsner .40 1.00
9 Terry Marchant .40 1.00
10 Lee Jinman .40 1.00
11 Rudy Poeschek .60 1.50
12 David Oliver .40 1.00
13 Brad Williamson .40 1.00
14 Mark Major .40 1.00
15 David Wilkie .40 1.00
16 Maxime Gingras .75 2.00
17 Greg Pankewicz .40 1.00
18 Gregg Walters .40 1.00
19 Sandy Moger .60 1.50
20 Frederic Chabot 1.25 3.00
21 Ron Low CO .40 1.00
22 Dave Barr ACO .20 .50
25 Mascot .08 .25
NNO Steve Sumner EQ .02 .10
NNO Jerry Meins TR .02 .10
NNO Checklist .08 .25
NNO Header Card .02 .10

2003-04 Houston Aeros

COMPLETE SET (20) 10.00
1 Chris Bala .20 .50
2 Jason Beckett .20 .50
3 Dan Cavanaugh .20 .50
4 Marc Cavosie .20 .50
5 Mark Cullen .20 .50
6 Josh DeWolf .20 .50
7 Chris Dyment .20 .50
8 Matthew Foy .20 .50
9 Mika Hannula .20 .50
10 Chris Heid .20 .50
11 Jeff Hoggan .20 .50
12 Johan Holmqvist .30 .75
13 Jason Marshall .20 .50
14 Zbynek Michalek .20 .50
15 Kevin Mitchell .20 .50
16 Bill Muckalt .20 .50
17 Eric Reitz .20 .50
18 Stephane Veilleux .20 .50
19 Rickard Wallin .20 .50
20 Kyle Wanvig .20 .50

2004-05 Houston Aeros

This set was handed out in 10-card increments at two different Aeros home games. The cards are unnumbered and so are listed below in alphabetical order.

COMPLETE SET (20) 12.00 30.00
1 Derek Boogaard .75 2.00
2 Pierre-Marc Bouchard 1.25 3.00
3 Brent Burns 1.25 3.00
4 Dan Cavanaugh .40 1.00
5 Mark Cullen .40 1.00
6 John Erskine .60 1.50
7 Matt Foy .40 1.00
8 Ray Giroux .40 1.00
9 Josh Harding 1.25 3.00
10 Mikko Koivu 1.25 3.00
11 Kirby Law .40 1.00
12 Junior Lessard .75 2.00
13 Zbynek Michalek .40 1.00
14 Todd Reirden .40 1.00
15 Eric Reitz .40 1.00
16 Mike Smith .75 2.00
17 Patrick Traverse .75 2.00
18 Stephane Veilleux .40 1.00
19 Rickard Wallin .40 1.00
20 Kyle Wanvig .40 1.00

2006-07 Houston Aeros Retro

COMPLETE SET (10) 5.00 10.00
1 Frederic Chabot .75 2.00
2 Mark Freer .30 .75
3 Cam Stewart .30 .75
4 Brian Wiseman .30 .75
5 Derek Boogaard 1.25 3.00
6 Jeff Christian .30 .75
7 Manny Fernandez .40 1.00
8 Curtis Murphy .30 .75
9 Todd McLellan .30 .75
10 Dave Tippett CO .30 .75

1987-88 Hull Olympiques

This set features a rare card of Wayne Gretzky, who was pictured as a result of buying the team.

COMPLETE SET (24) 35.00 75.00
1 Header Card .08 .25
2 Joe Aloi .40 1.00
3 Joel Blain .40 1.00
4 Christian Breton .40 1.00
5 Benoit Brunet .75 2.00
6 Guy Dupuis .40 1.00
7 Martin Gelinas 1.25 3.00
8 Jason Glickman .60 1.50
9 Wayne Gretzky OWN 25.00 60.00
10 Herbert Hohenberger .60 1.50
11 Ken MacDermid .40 1.00
12 Craig Martin .75 2.00
13 Mark McLane .40 1.00
14 Stephane Matteau .75 2.00
15 Kelly Nester .40 1.00
16 Marc Saumier .40 1.00
17 Claude-Charles Sauriol .40 1.00
18 Daniel Shank 1.00 2.50
19 Joe Suk .40 1.00
20 Alain Vigneault .40 1.00
21 George Wilcox .40 1.00
22 Team Card .20 .50
23 Team Card .20 .50
24 Team Card .20 .50

1999-00 Hull Olympiques

Released by Hull Olympiques in conjunction with the Banque Nationale, this 24-card set features the 1999-00 team. Base cards have gray borders, feature full-color photos, and have both the team logo and the Banque Nationale logo on the card front.

COMPLETE SET (24) 5.00 12.00
1 Erich Paroshy .15 .40
2 Andrew Carver .15 .40
3 Bobby Clarke .15 .40
4 Donald Johnstone .15 .40
5 Bruno Lemire .15 .40
6 Derrick Martin .15 .40
7 Alexandre Giroux .30 .75
8 Dustin Russell .15 .40
9 Daniel Hudgin .15 .40
10 Roberto Bissonnette .15 .40
11 Daniel Clermont .15 .40
12 Radim Vrbata .40 1.00
13 Mario Joly .15 .40
14 Jason Lehoux .15 .40
15 Brock Boucher .15 .40
16 Philippe Lacasse .15 .40
17 Paul Spadafora .15 .40
18 Ryan Lauzon .15 .40
19 Michael Ryder 1.25 3.00
20 Adam Rivet .15 .40
21 Patrick Lafreniere .15 .40
22 Eric Lafrance .20 .50
23 Philippe Sauve .40 1.00
24 Team Photo/CL .15 .40
NNO Luc Robitaille .60 1.50

1999-00 Hull Olympiques Signed

This 24-card set parallels the base Hull Olympiques set in an autographed version. The cards are signed on the front in a ghosted area of the photo, while the backs are serial numbered out of 100. The Luc Robitaille card in the set is limited to 100 copies, but it is not signed.

COMPLETE SET (24) 30.00 80.00
1 Erich Paroshy .75 2.00
2 Andrew Carver .75 2.00
3 Bobby Clarke .75 2.00
4 Donald Johnstone .75 2.00
5 Bruno Lemire .75 2.00
6 Derrick Martin .75 2.00
7 Alexandre Giroux 2.00 5.00
8 Dustin Russell .75 2.00
9 Daniel Hudgin .75 2.00
10 Roberto Bissonnette .75 2.00
11 Daniel Clermont .75 2.00
12 Radim Vrbata 6.00 15.00
13 Mario Joly .75 2.00
14 Jason Lehoux .75 2.00
15 Brock Boucher .75 2.00
16 Philippe Lacasse .75 2.00
17 Paul Spadafora .75 2.00
18 Ryan Lauzon .75 2.00
19 Michael Ryder 15.00 30.00
20 Adam Rivet .75 2.00
21 Patrick Lafreniere .75 2.00
22 Eric Lafrance 1.25 3.00
23 Philippe Sauve 6.00 15.00
24 Team Photo/CL .08 .25
NNO Luc Robitaille 6.00 15.00

2000-01 Hull Olympiques

This set features the Olympiques of the QMJHL. The set was produced by CTM-Ste-Foy and was sold by that card shop, as well as by the team at home games.

COMPLETE SET (24) 6.00 20.00
1 Chris Moher .20 .50
2 Andrew Carver .20 .50
3 Bobby Clarke .20 .50
4 Doug O'Brien .20 .50
5 Bruno Lemire .20 .50
6 John Cilladi .20 .50
7 Derrick Martin .20 .50
8 Roberto Bissonnette .20 .50
9 Ales Hemsky 4.00 10.00
10 Phillippe Chainlere .20 .50
11 Jonathan Labelle .20 .50
12 Mario Joly .20 .50
13 Jason Kostadine .20 .50
14 Carl Rochon .20 .50
15 Philippe Lacasse .20 .50
16 Maxime Talbot .75 2.00
17 Jean-Michel Daoust .20 .50
18 Brent G. Roach .20 .50
19 Dale Sullivan .20 .50
20 Adam Rivet .30 .75
21 Eric Lafrance .20 .50
22 Olivier Dannel .30 .75
23 Ian Courville .20 .50
NNO Team CL .01 .05

2000-01 Hull Olympiques Signed

This set is exactly the same as the base Olympiques set from this season, save that every card has been hand signed by the player pictured. Each card also is serial numbered out of just 100. The team CL is not signed.

COMPLETE SET (24) 24.00 60.00
1 Chris Moher .80 2.00
2 Andrew Carver .80 2.00
3 Bobby Clarke .80 2.00
4 Doug O'Brien .80 2.00
5 Bruno Lemire .80 2.00
6 John Cilladi .80 2.00
7 Derrick Martin 1.20 3.00
8 Roberto Bissonnette .80 2.00
9 Ales Hemsky 6.00 30.00
10 Phillippe Chainlere .80 2.00
11 Jonathan Labelle .80 2.00
12 Mario Joly .80 2.00
13 Jason Kostadine .80 2.00
14 Carle Rochon .80 2.00
15 Philippe Lacasse .75 2.00
16 Maxime Talbot .80 2.00
17 Jean-Michel Daoust .80 2.00
18 Brent G. Roach .80 2.00
19 Dale Sullivan .80 2.00
20 Adam Rivet 2.00 5.00
21 Eric Lafrance .80 2.00
22 Olivier Dannel 2.00 5.00
23 Ian Courville .80 2.00
NNO Team CL .10 .25

2001-02 Hull Olympiques

This set features the Olympiques of the QMJHL. The set was produced by CTM Ste-Foy and was sold at Olympiques home games. There were 1,000 copies produced of this set.

COMPLETE SET (23) 4.80 12.00
1 Chris Moher .20 .50
2 Bryan Riddell .20 .50
3 Charles Fontaine .20 .50
4 Dominic D'Amour .20 .50
5 Doug O'Brien .20 .50
6 Francis Wathier .20 .50
7 Derrick Martin .20 .50
8 Philippe Dupuis .20 .50
9 Scott Gibson .20 .50
10 Ales Hemsky 2.00 5.00
11 Nick Fugere .20 .50
12 Jonathan Labelle .20 .50
13 Martin Vagner .40 1.00
14 Jason Kostadine .20 .50
15 Jesse Lane .30 .75
16 Philippe Lacasse .20 .50
17 Brent Roach .20 .50
18 Maxime Talbot .20 .50
19 Jean-Michel Daoust .20 .50
20 Dale Sullivan .20 .50
21 Eric Lafrance .30 .75
22 Michael Dilorenzo .30 .75
23 Jean-Junior Morin .20 .50

2002-03 Hull Olympiques

COMPLETE SET (24) 5.00 12.00
1 Christopher Pottie .20 .50
2 Jeff Smith .20 .50
3 Charles Fontaine .20 .50
4 Dominic D'Amour .20 .50
5 Doug O'Brien .20 .50
6 Sam Roberts .20 .50
7 Francis Wathier .20 .50
8 Jonathan Bellemare .20 .50
9 Phillipe Dupuis .20 .50
10 Guillaume Labrecque .20 .50
11 Nick Fugere .20 .50
12 Olivier Labelle .20 .50
13 Martin Vagner .30 .75
14 Renaud des Alliers .20 .50
15 Andrew Hayes .20 .50
16 Brent Roach .20 .50
17 Maxime Talbot .20 .50
18 Jean Michel Daoust .20 .50
19 Dale Sullivan .20 .50
20 Mathieu Brunelle .20 .50
21 Eric Lafrance .30 .75
22 David Tremblay .30 .75
23 Tyler Reid .20 .50
24 Checklist/Logo .04 .10

2003 Hull Olympiques Memorial Cup

COMPLETE SET (20) 15.00
1 Jonathan Bellemare .30 .75
2 Mathieu Brunelle .30 .75
3 Dominic D'Amour .30 .75
4 Jean-Michel D'Aoust .30 .75
5 Renaud DesAlliers .30 .75
6 Philippe Dupuis .30 .75
7 Nick Fugere .30 .75
8 Olivier Labelle .30 .75
9 Guillaume Labrecque .30 .75
10 Eric Lafrance .40 1.00
11 Doug O'Brien .30 .75
12 Tyler Reid .30 .75
13 Sam Roberts .30 .75
14 Brent Roach .30 .75
15 Jeff Smith .30 .75
16 Dale Sullivan .30 .75
17 Maxime Talbot .30 .75
18 David Tremblay .40 1.00
19 Martin Vagner .40 1.00
20 Francis Wathier .30 .75

1993-94 Huntington Blizzard

Sponsored by WCHS-TV8, this 27-card standard-size set commemorates the 1993-94 inaugural season of the Huntington Blizzard (ECHL). Just 2,500 sets were produced and each was hand-numbered "X of 2,500" on the title card. One thousand sets were given away on trading card night, with the rest being sold at the souvenir shops in the arena. The fronts feature borderless color action and posed player photos. The player's name and the team logo appear on the front. The cards are unnumbered and checklisted below in alphabetical order.

COMPLETE SET (27) 3.00 8.00
1 Ray Alcindor .15 .40
2 Shayne Antoski .15 .40
3 Greg Bailey .15 .40
4 Jared Bednar .15 .40
5 Andy Borggaard .15 .40
6 Malcolm Cameron .15 .40
7 Dave Dimitri .15 .40
8 Mark Franks .15 .40
9 Ray Gallagher .15 .40
10 Murray Garbutt .15 .40
11 Brad Harrison .15 .40
12 Henry's Blizzard Babes .20 .50
13 Todd Huyber .15 .40
14 Klondike The Bear .02 .10
(Masc
15 Ron Majic .15 .40
16 Bob May .15 .40
17 Jim Mill .15 .40
18 Jim Mirabello ANN .02 .10
19 Dan Persigehl ANN .02 .10
20 Paul Pickard CO .02 .10
21 Scott Roberts .02 .10
(TV ancho
22 Greg Scott .15 .40
23 Geoff Simpson .15 .40
24 Doug Stromback .15 .40
25 Dave Weekley .02 .10
(TV Sports
26 Misty Zambito .20 .50
27 Title Card .02 .10

1994-95 Huntington Blizzard

This set features the Blizzard of the ECHL. Approximately 3,000 sets were produced; 1,000 were given away on trading card night, while the others were sold at the souvenir shops in the arena.

COMPLETE SET (32) 4.00 10.00
1 Title Card CL .02 .10
2 Steve Barnes .20 .50
3 Jared Bednar .20 .50
4 Jim Bermingham .20 .50
5 Todd Brost .30 .75
6 Alan Brown .20 .50
7 Ray Edwards .20 .50
8 Trent Eigner .20 .50
9 Dan Fournel .20 .50
10 Mark Franks .20 .50
11 Gord Frantti .20 .50
12 Chris Gordon .20 .50
13 Kelly Harper .20 .50
14 J.C. Ihrig TR .02 .10
EQMG
15 Mitch Kean .20 .50
16 Jeff Levy .20 .50
17 Chris Morque .20 .50
18 Derek Schooley .20 .50
19 Jim Solly .20 .50
20 Mike Stone .20 .50
21 Jason Weinrich .20 .50
22 Mark Woolf .20 .50
23 Paul Pickard CO .02 .10
24 Klondike MASCOT .02 .10
25 Blizzard Babes .30 .75
26 Jim Mirabello ANN .02 .10
27 Dan Persigehl ANN .02 .10
28 Jeff Crawford DJ .02 .10
Van Ma
29 Russell T. Hill DJ .02 .10
Sara
30 Jeff Ramsey DJ .02 .10
Teresa N
31 Melanie Shafer .02 .10
(TV anch
32 Title Card .02 .10

1998-99 Huntington Blizzard

Little is known about this ECHL team set beyond the confirmed checklist. Any additional information can be forwarded to hockeymag@beckett.com.

COMPLETE SET (27) 3.20 50.00
1 Bill Baaki .75 2.00
2 Mike Perna .75 2.00
3 Chad Lang 1.50 4.00
4 Jamie Sokolsky .75 2.00
5 D.J. Harding .75 2.00
6 Jan Slavik .75 2.00
7 Karson Kaebel 1.50 4.00
8 Jason Bermingham .75 2.00
9 Kelly Harper .75 2.00
10 Derek Smith .75 2.00
11 Jim Bermingham 1.50 4.00
12 Tracy Egeland .75 2.00
13 Brodie Coffin 1.50 4.00
14 Rob Stanfield .75 2.00
15 Kevin Paden .75 2.00
16 Mike Schultz .75 2.00
17 Rich Bronilla .75 2.00
18 Jake Deadmarsh 1.50 4.00
19 Butch Kaebel .75 2.00
20 Blaine Russell .75 2.00
21 Ray Edwards HCO .02 .10
22 Chris Plumhoff EM .02 .10
23 Dave Allen .02 .10
24 Klondike Mascot .02 .10
25 Checklist .02 .10
26 Blizzard Pro Shop .02 .10
27 PHPA .02 .10
ECHL

1999-00 Huntington Blizzard

This set features the Blizzard of the ECHL. The set was produced by Roox and sold by the team at home games.

COMPLETE SET (24) 30.00 50.00
1 Anthony Cappelletti 1.25 3.00
2 Mike Perna 1.25 3.00
3 Jamie Pegg 1.25 3.00
4 Jamie Sokolsky 1.25 3.00
5 Andrew Pearsall 1.25 3.00
6 Jason Bermingham 1.25 3.00
7 Peter Brearley 1.25 3.00
8 Jim Bermingham 1.25 3.00
9 Jim Moss 1.25 3.00
10 Bill Baaki 1.25 3.00
11 Anthony Terzo 1.25 3.00
12 David Oliver 1.25 3.00
13 Keith Cassidy 1.25 3.00
14 Mark Spence 1.25 3.00
15 Ryan Hoople 1.50 4.00
16 Butch Kaebel 1.25 3.00
17 Blaine Russell 1.50 4.00
18 WRVC AM390 .02 .10
19 Huntington Blizzard .15 .40
20 Klondike MAS .02 .10
21 Ray Edwards CO .40 1.00
22 Dave Allen .02 .10
23 Kelly Harper .02 .10
24 Curtis Bois .02 .10

1998-99 Huntsville Channel Cats

This 22-card set was given out an early season game. The set contains a message card from the president of the Channel Cats that is dated December 25, 1998.

COMPLETE SET (22) 6.00 15.00
1 Chris Stewart HCO .02 .10
2 John Gibson .40 1.00
3 Igor Bonderev .40 1.00
4 Jonathan Dubois .40 1.00
5 Phil Daigle .40 1.00
6 Pat Bingham ACO .02 .10
7 Mike Degurse .40 1.00
8 Ryan Wood .40 1.00
9 Tyler Quiring .40 1.00
10 Greg Lakovic .40 1.00
11 Wade Gibson .40 1.00
12 Josh Erdman .40 1.00
13 Ken Richardson .40 1.00
14 Todd Dougherty .40 1.00
15 Finnley Mascot .02 .10
16 Clint Collins .40 1.00
17 Mike Gamble .40 1.00
18 Marc Vachon .40 1.00
19 Chris George .40 1.00
20 Derek Puppa .40 1.00
21 Schedule Card .02 .10
22 Message Card .02 .10

2003-04 Huntsville Channel Cats

COMPLETE SET (18) 5.00 12.00
1 Claude Amstutz .30 .75
2 Joel Bresciani .30 .75
3 Dan Buccella .30 .75
4 Dave Cadarette .30 .75
5 Matt Carmichael .40 1.00
6 Allan Carr .30 .75
7 Jason Deguehery .30 .75
8 Mike Degurse .40 1.00
9 Scott Graham .40 1.00
10 Daniel Kletke .30 .75
11 Shawn Martin .30 .75
12 Jessi Otis .30 .75
13 James Patterson .30 .75
14 Luke Phillips .40 1.00
15 Greg Snitowsky .30 .75
16 Joe Urbanik .30 .75
17 John Gibson CO .20 .50
18 Finnley MASCOT .04 .10

2004-05 Huntsville Havoc

Features the Havoc of the SPHL. Was issued as a giveaway at the last home game of the season.

COMPLETE SET (27) 8.00 20.00
1 Chaos MASCOT .04 .10
2 John Gibson CO .20 .50
3 Adam MacLean .60 1.50
4 Steve Howard .40 1.00
5 Jason Deguehery .60 1.50
6 Tim Plett .40 1.00
7 Aaron Lewis .40 1.00
8 Jeremy Law .40 1.00
9 Jeff Dams .40 1.00
10 Brandon Doria .40 1.00
11 James Patterson .40 1.00
12 Josh Liebenow .40 1.00
13 Brad McDonald .40 1.00
14 Mark Cole .40 1.00
15 Jason Simon .40 1.00
16 Doug Merrill .40 1.00
17 Matt Carmichael .75 2.00
18 Mike Degurse .40 1.00
19 Derek McKinlay .40 1.00
20 Luke Phillips .40 1.00
21 Dan Bucella .40 1.00
22 DeWayne Manning TR .04 .10
23 Chad Daniels TR .04 .10
24 John Markushewski DR .04 .10
25 Brian Carter DR .04 .10
26 John Greco DR .04 .10
27 Stanton Davis DR .04 .10

1997-98 Idaho Steelheads

Little is known about this set. It is believed that it was issued as a promotional giveaway at one home game, which would explain its scarcity on the secondary market.

COMPLETE SET (22) 12.00 30.00
1 Rob Dumas .60 1.50
2 Frederik Beaubien .75 2.00
3 Patrick Moreau .60 1.50
4 Bill McGuigan .60 1.50
5 Alain Savage .60 1.50
6 Mario Therrien .60 1.50
7 Kevin Deschambeault .60 1.50
8 Sean Farmer .60 1.50
9 Scott Davis .60 1.50
10 Lee Svangstu .60 1.50
11 Troy Edwards .60 1.50
12 Andreas Sjolund .60 1.50
13 Pat O'Connell .60 1.50
14 Patrick Gallagher .60 1.50
15 Sam Fields .60 1.50
16 Marco Pietroniro .60 1.50
17 Dmitri Leonov .75 2.00
18 Jamie Cooke .60 1.50
19 Todd Dougherty .60 1.50
20 Carl Menard .60 1.50
21 Bart Hull .75 2.00
22 Dave Langevin HCO .60 1.50

1998-99 Idaho Steelheads

This set features the Steelheads of the WCHL. It was issued as a promotional giveaway at a late-season home game.

COMPLETE SET (23) 10.00 25.00
1 Alex Alepin .40 1.00
2 Frederik Beaubien .60 1.50
3 Francois Bourdeau .40 1.00
4 Scott Davis .40 1.00
5 Rob Dumas .40 1.00
6 Troy Edwards .40 1.00
7 Christian Friberg .40 1.00
8 Marc Genest .40 1.00
9 Cal Ingraham .75 2.00
10 Jason Lammers .40 1.00
11 Dmitri Leonov .60 1.50
12 Sebastian Parent .40 1.00
13 Marco Pietroniro .40 1.00
14 Tony Prpic .40 1.00
15 Bryan Randall .40 1.00
16 Alain Savage .40 1.00
17 Jonathon Shockey .40 1.00
18 Andreas Sjolund .40 1.00
19 Mario Thierren .40 1.00
20 Jeff Trigg .40 1.00
21 All-Star Trio .60 1.50
22 Clint Malarchuk HCO .60 1.50
23 Bonk Mascot .08 .25

1999-00 Idaho Steelheads

This set features the Steelheads of the WCHL. The cards were first issued as a promotional giveaway. Later, remaining copies were sold by the team.

COMPLETE SET (22) 4.00 10.00
1 Cal Ingraham .30 .75
2 Nicolas Chabot .30 .75
3 Troy Edwards .20 .50
4 Todd Robinson .20 .50
5 Dan Marcotte .20 .50
6 Bryan Randall .20 .50
7 Tom Menicci .20
8 Roy Mitchell .20
9 Scott Davis .20
10 Andrei Lupandin .20
11 Gavin Morgan .20
12 Jeff Petruic .20
13 Clint Malarchuk CO .20
14 Marc Genest .20
15 Darcy Loewen .20
16 Rob Dumas .20
17 Rob Hartnell .20
18 Ryan Johnston .20
19 Matt Garver .20
20 Andreas Sjolund .30
21 Kory Cooper .30
22 Bonk MAS .08

2000-01 Idaho Steelheads

This set features the Steelheads of the WCHL. The cards were produced by Grandstand and issued in fi[ve] card strips at five separate home games. The strips a[re] not perforated, making it difficult to acquire cards in single form.

COMPLETE SET (25) 6.00 20.0
1 Chad Alban .40 1.0
2 Colin Anderson .24 .7
3 Adam Borzecki .24 .7
4 Scott Burt .24 .7
5 Rob Concannon .24 .7
6 Thom Cullen .24 .7
7 Bobby Hayes .24 .7
8 Cal Ingraham .40 1.5
9 Kevin Knopp .24 .7
10 Arturs Kupaks .24 .7
11 Mike Legg .24 .7
12 Darcy Loewen .24 .7
13 Matt Martin .24 .7
14 Roy Mitchell .24 .7
15 Jeremy Mylymok .40 1.0
16 Vladimir Nemec .24 .7
17 Barry Potomski .40 1.5
18 Eric Rud .24 .7
19 Dan Shermerhorn .24 .7
20 Kendall Sidoruk .24 .7
21 Shawn Wansborough .24 .7
22 Cal Ingraham AS .40 1.0
23 Jeremy Mylymok AS .40 1.0
24 Todd Hine TR .04 .1
25 Khris Bestel EQM .04 .1

2001-02 Idaho Steelheads

COMPLETE SET (24) 10.00 25.0
1 Blair Allison .60 1.5
2 Scott Burt .40 1.0
3 Adam Copeland .40 1.0
4 Jason Cugnet .60 1.5
5 Thom Cullen .40 1.0
6 Wes Dorey .40 1.0
7 Cal Ingraham .60 1.5
8 Dan Kerluke .40 1.0
9 Jeremy Mylymok .40 1.0
10 Matt Oates .40 1.0
11 Zdenek Ondrej .40 1.0
12 Derek Paget .40 1.0
13 Eric Rud .40 1.0
14 Terry Ryan .40 1.0
15 Dan Shermerhorn .40 1.0
16 Jeff Shevalier .40 1.0
17 Kevin Smyth .40 1.0
18 Bobby Stewart .40 1.0
19 Petr Suchanek .40 1.0
20 Scott Swanson .40 1.0
21 Garry Toor .40 1.0
22 Jeremy Yablonski .60 1.5
23 Edgars Zaltkovskis .40 1.0
24 John Oliver HCO .10 .2

2004-05 Idaho Steelheads

This ECHL set was originally offered as a game-night giveaway, but the team later sold the few remaining sets for $5 at its pro shop.

COMPLETE SET (27) 6.00 15.0
1 Mascot .04 .1
2 John Oliver CO .10 .2
3 Blair Allison ACO .40 1.0
4 Frank Doyle .40 1.0
5 Jeremy Mylymok .20 .5
6 Petr Suchanek .20 .5
7 Billy Tibbetts .60 1.5
8 Ben Keup .20 .5
9 Scott Burt .20 .5
10 Darren McLachlan .40 1.0
11 Jim Leger .20 .5
12 Dan Vandermeer .20 .5
13 David Morrisett .40 1.0
14 Frank Lukes .20 .5
15 Jonathan Zion .20 .5
16 Bobby Russell .20 .5
17 Peter Metcalf .20 .5
18 Warren Peters .20 .5
19 Matt Elich .20 .5
20 Landon Bathe .20 .5
21 Colin Zulianello .40 1.0
22 Tim Verbeek .20 .5
23 Brett Draney .20 .5
24 David Cornacchia .20 .5
25 Darrell Hay .20 .5
26 Marty Flichel .20 .5
27 Lance Galbraith .40 1.0

2005-06 Idaho Steelheads

COMPLETE SET (26) 10.00 25.0
1 David Bararuk .60 1.5
2 Garrett Bembridge .60 1.5
3 Jarad Bourassa .40 1.0
4 Scott Burt .40 1.0
5 Justin Cox .40 1.0
6 Brian Fahey .40 1.0
7 Marty Flichel .40 1.0
8 Blake Forsyth .40 1.0
9 Mike Gabinet .40 1.0
10 Kevin Gardner .40 1.0
11 Dan Hacker .40 1.0
12 Jim Hakewill .40 1.0
13 Greg Hornby .40 1.0
14 Kurt MacSweyn .40 1.0
15 D'Arcy McConvey .40 1.0
16 Tyrell Moulton .40 1.0
17 Jeremy Mylymok .60 1.5
18 Matt Reid .40 1.0
19 Steve Silverthorn .40 1.0
20 Mike Stutzel .40 1.0
21 Brad Thompson .40 1.0
22 Janos Vas .40 1.0
23 Matthew Yeats .40 1.0
24 Jonathan Zion .40 1.0
25 Derek Laxdal HC .02 .1
26 Bonk MASCOT .02 .1

2006-07 Idaho Steelheads

MPLETE SET (27) 10.00 20.00
daho Steelheads .02 .10
yle Bruce .40 1.00
Scott Burt .40 1.00
aggart Desmet .40 1.00
Marty Flichel .40 1.00
ance Galbraith .75 2.00
Charlie Johnson .40 1.00
'Arcy McConvey .40 1.00
uomas Mikkonen .40 1.00
Derek Nesbitt .40 1.00
Greg Rallo .40 1.00
Francis Wathier .40 1.00
Jeremy Yablonski .75 2.00
Cody Blanshan .40 1.00
Blake Forsyth .40 1.00
Mike Gabinet .40 1.00
Darrell Hay .40 1.00
Jared Nightingale .40 1.00
Colin Peters .40 1.00
Kory Scoran .40 1.00
Travis Wight .40 1.00
John Daigneau .60 1.50
Steve Silverthorn .40 1.00
Derek Laxdal CO .10 .25
Khris Bestel EQ MGR .02 .10
Dennis Brogna TR .02 .10
Blue MASCOT .02 .10

2013-14 Idaho Steelheads

MPLETE SET (20) 6.00 15.00
Dmitri Leonov .30 .75
Frederik Beaubien .30 .75
Bill McGuigan .30 .75
Kendall Sidoruk .30 .75
Cal Ingraham .30 .75
Bobby Stewart .30 .75
im Gattolliat .30 .75
Andrei Vasilyev .30 .75
Tyler Kindle .30 .75
Lance Galbraith .30 .75
Dan Ellis .30 .75
Steve Silverthorn .30 .75
Greg Rallo .30 .75
John-Scott Dickson .30 .75
Dustin Friesen .30 .75
Jorry Kuhn .30 .75
Andrew Carroll .30 .75
David de Kastrozza .30 .75
Josh Robinson .30 .75
Header Card CL .30 .75

2013-14 Idaho Steelheads Choice

MPLETE SET (21) 6.00 15.00
Blair Allison .30 .75
Richard Bachman .30 .75
Scott Burt .30 .75
Matt Case .30 .75
Mark Derlago .30 .75
Rob Dumas .30 .75
Dan Ellis .30 .75
Marty Flichel .30 .75
Lance Galbraith .30 .75
Darrell Hay .30 .75
Cal Ingraham .30 .75
Zenon Konopka .30 .75
Jerry Kuhn .30 .75
Kael Mouillierat .30 .75
Jeremy Mylymok .30 .75
Alain Savage .30 .75
Kory Scoran .30 .75
Dan Shermerhorn .30 .75
Steve Silverthorn .30 .75
Jeremy Yablonski .30 .75
O Header Card .30 .75

1998-99 IHL All-Star Eastern Conference

leased by EBK Sports, this 25-card set was available purchase at the 1999 IHL All-Star Game, then later ough the PHPA web site.

MPLETE SET (25) 14.00 35.00
Guy Dupuis .20 .50
Viacheslav Butsayev .20 .50
Zac Bierk .40 1.00
Brian Noonan .20 .50
Dave Hymovitz .20 .50
Marty Turco 8.00 20.00
on Sim .60 1.50
Brad Shaw .75 2.00
Pat Neaton .20 .50
Peter Ciavaglia .40 1.00
Mike Prokopec .20 .50
Stan Drulia .40 1.00
Steve Walker .75 2.00
Todd Richards .20 .50
Maxim Spiridonov .20 .50
Robert Petrovicky .20 .50
Curtis Murphy .20 .50
Mark Beaufait .40 1.00
Gilbert Dionne .40 1.00
Brad Lukowich .40 1.00
Bruce Cassidy ACO .08 .25
Steve Ludzik HCO .20 .50
Keith Aldridge .30 .75
IHL Logo .02 .10
Checklist .02 .10

1998-99 IHL All-Star Western Conference

leased by EBK Sports, this 24-card set was available purchase at the 1999 IHL All-Star Game, then later ough the PHPA web site.

MPLETE SET (24) 8.00 20.00
Richard Shulmistra .40 1.00
Brett Hauer .20 .50
Bill Bowler .60 1.50
Pat Jablonski .60 1.50
Niklas Andersson .20 .50
Steve Maltais .75 2.00
Tom Tilley .20 .50
Dan Ratushny .20 .50
Andy Roach .20 .50
Rob Valicevic .75 2.00
Jeff Tory .20 .50
Patrik Augusta .20 .50
Kimmo Timonen .75 2.00
Mark Mowers .60 1.50
Patrice Lefebvre .60 1.50
Cam Stewart .20 .50
Brian Wiseman .40 1.00
Greg Hawgood .40 1.00
John Purves .75 2.00
Scott Thomas .75 2.00
Randy Carlyle ACO .08 .25
Dave Tippett HCO .08 .25
IHL Logo .02 .10
Checklist .02 .10

1999-00 IHL All-Stars

The set was created by ebk Sports to commemorate the members of the 2000 IHL All-Star team. In an unusual scenario, the game pitted the league champion Houston Aeros against the best players from the rest of the IHL. The set was sold only at the Compaq Center in Houston. Production problems led to many cards being off-centered or poorly cut.

COMPLETE SET (24) 16.00 50.00
1 Mike Crowley .75 2.00
2 Nils Ekman .60 1.50
3 Rich Parent .75 2.00
4 Shane Willis 1.25 3.00
5 John Purves .75 2.00
6 Kevin Miller .75 2.00
7 Mike Prokopec .40 1.00
8 Petr Schastlivy 1.25 3.00
9 Marty Turco 10.00 25.00
10 Stewart Malgunas .40 1.00
11 Curtis Murphy .40 1.00
12 Todd White .60 1.50
13 Brett Hauer .40 1.00
14 David Gosselin .40 1.00
15 David Ling .60 1.50
16 Gilbert Dionne .75 2.00
17 Jeff Sharples .40 1.00
18 John Gruden .40 1.00
19 Jarrod Skalde .75 2.00
20 Steve Maltais .75 2.00
21 Bob Bourne .40 1.00
22 Al Sims .40 1.00
NNO Checklist Card .08 .25
NNO Header Card .08 .25

1981-82 Indianapolis Checkers

Sponsored by Pizza Hut, this 20-card standard-size set features the Indianapolis Checkers of the CHL. The cards were available singly at Pizza Hut restaurants and Checkers games on alternate weeks. On a blue background, the fronts have color action player photos with thin white borders. The team name appears above the photo in an orange border that extends down the right side. The player's name, position, and number are printed above the photo. The cards are unnumbered and checklisted below in alphabetical order.

COMPLETE SET (20) 12.00 30.00
1 Bruce Andres .40 1.00
2 Frank Beaton .40 1.00
3 Kelly Davis .40 1.00
4 Kevin Devine .40 1.00
5 Glen Duncan .40 1.00
6 Mats Hallin .60 1.50
7 Neil Hawryliw .40 1.00
8 Bob Holland .40 1.00
9 Mike Hordy .40 1.00
10 Kelly Hrudey 4.00 10.00
11 Randy Johnston .40 1.00
12 Red Laurence .40 1.00
13 Tim Lockridge .40 1.00
14 Garth MacGuigan .40 1.00
15 John Marks .60 1.50
16 Darcey Regier .75 2.00
17 Charlie Skjodt .40 1.00
18 Lorne Stamler .40 1.00
19 Steve Stoyanovich .40 1.00
20 Monty Trottier .40 1.00

1982-83 Indianapolis Checkers

Sponsored by Pizza Hut, this 21-card standard-size set features the Indianapolis Checkers of the CHL. The cards were available singly at Pizza Hut restaurants and Checkers games on alternate weeks. On a red-orange background, the fronts have color action player photos with thin white borders. The team name appears above the photo in an orange border that extends down the right side. The player's name, position, and number are printed above the photo. The cards are unnumbered and checklisted below in alphabetical order.

COMPLETE SET (21) 16.00 40.00
1 Kelly Davis .40 1.00
2 Kevin Devine .40 1.00
3 Gord Dineen .60 1.50
4 Glen Duncan .40 1.00
5 Greg Gilbert .75 2.00
6 Mike Gredder .40 1.00
7 Mats Hallin .75 2.00
8 Dave Hanson 4.00 10.00
9 Rob Holland .40 1.00
10 Scott Howson .40 1.00
11 Kelly Hrudey 3.00 8.00
12 Randy Johnston .40 1.00
13 Red Laurence .40 1.00
14 Tim Lockridge .40 1.00
15 Garth MacGuigan .40 1.00
16 Darcey Regier .60 1.50
17 Dan Revell .40 1.00
18 Dave Simpson .40 1.00
19 Lorne Stamler .40 1.00
20 Steve Stoyanovich .40 1.00
21 Monty Trottier .40 1.00

1992-93 Indianapolis Ice

This 26-card set measures the standard size. On a light blue background, the fronts feature posed, color action photos with a thin red border. The team logo appears on the bottom left side, while the player's number, name and position appear in black letters on the right side. The cards are unnumbered and checklisted below in alphabetical order.

COMPLETE SET (26) 4.00 10.00
1 Alexandr Andrievski .15 .40
2 Steve Bancroft .15 .40
3 Zac Boyer .15 .40
4 Rod Buskas .20 .50
5 Shawn Byram .15 .40
6 Joe Cleary .15 .40
7 Rob Conn .15 .40
8 Joe Crowley .15 .40
9 Trevor Dam .15 .40
10 Ivan Droppa .15 .40
11 Tracy Egeland .15 .40
12 Dave Hakstol .15 .40
13 Kevin Hodson .30 .75
14 Tony Horacek .15 .40
15 Tony Hrkac .30 .75
16 Sergei Krivokrasov .30 .75
17 Brad Lauer .20 .50
18 Ray LeBlanc .30 .75
19 Owen Lessard .15 .40
20 Jim Playfair ACO .02 .10
John M
21 Kevin St. Jacques .15 .40
22 Michael Speer .15 .40
23 Milan Tichy .15 .40
24 Kerry Toporowski .15 .40
25 Sean Williams .15 .40
26 Craig Woodcroft .15 .40

1993-94 Indianapolis Ice

Set was produced by MJ's Collectibles and features cards that are slightly narrower than standard size. Thanks to Dale Spengler for the complete checklist.

COMPLETE SET (25) 6.00 15.00
1 Hugo Belanger .30 .75
2 Zac Boyer .30 .75
3 Shawn Byram .30 .75
4 Rob Cimetta .30 .75
5 Rob Conn .30 .75
6 Joe Crowley .30 .75
7 Ivan Droppa .30 .75
8 Steve Dubinsky .30 .75
9 Karl Dykhuis .30 .75
10 Dino Grossi .30 .75
11 Dave Hakstol .30 .75
13 Bobby House .30 .75
14 Tony Horacek .30 .75
15 Bob Kellogg .30 .75
16 Jeff Ricciardi .30 .75
17 Sergei Krivokrasov .30 .75
18 Chris Rogles .60 1.50
19 Kevin St. Jacques .30 .75
20 Christian Soucy .60 1.50
21 Yves Heroux .30 .75
21 Michael Speer .30 .75
22 Kerry Toporowski .60 1.50
23 Duane Sutter CO .40 1.00
24 Gene Parfet TR .02 .10
25 Polar Bear MASCOT .02 .10

1994-95 Indianapolis Ice

Manufactured and distributed by Jessen Associates, Inc. for Classic, this 26-card standard-size set features the Ice of the IHL. Sets were sold by the team at home games. The cards are unnumbered and checklisted below in alphabetical order.

COMPLETE SET (26) 4.00 10.00
1 Hugo Belanger .15 .40
2 Bruce Cassidy .15 .40
3 Rob Conn .20 .50
4 Ivan Droppa .15 .40
5 Steve Dubinsky .20 .50
6 Karl Dykhuis .20 .50
7 Craig Fisher .15 .40
8 Daniel Gauthier .15 .40
9 Tony Horacek .15 .40
10 Bobby House .15 .40
11 Bob Kellogg .15 .40
12 Sergei Klimovich .15 .40
13 Sergei Krivokrasov .30 .75
14 Andy MacIntyre .15 .40
15 Dean Malkoc .20 .50
16 Matt Oates .15 .40
17 Mike Pomichter .15 .40
18 Mike Prokopec .15 .40
19 Jeff Ricciardi .15 .40
20 Chris Rogles .30 .75
21 Bogdan Savenko .15 .40
22 Jeff Shantz .30 .75
23 Christian Soucy .30 .75
24 Duane Sutter CO .20 .50
25 Travis Thiessen .15 .40
26 Team Photo .15 .40

1995-96 Indianapolis Ice

This 23-card set was produced by SplitSecond for Collector's Edge. The cards featured the standard design element for that season, with the color schemes adapted for that of the team. As they are unnumbered, the cards are listed below alphabetically.

COMPLETE SET (23) 4.00 10.00
1 Bill Armstrong .15 .40
2 James Black .15 .40
3 Jeff Buchanan .15 .40
4 Bruce Cassidy .15 .40
5 Ivan Droppa .15 .40
6 Steve Dubinsky .15 .40
7 Dmitri Filimonov .15 .40
8 Daniel Gauthier .15 .40
9 Ryan Huska .15 .40
10 Sergei Klimovich .15 .40
11 Eric Lecompte .20 .50
12 Andy MacIntyre .15 .40
13 Eric Manlow .15 .40
14 Steve McLaren .15 .40
15 Kip Miller .30 .75
16 Ethan Moreau .30 .75
17 Mike Prokopec .20 .50
18 Andre Racicot .30 .75
19 Jeff Serowik .20 .50
20 Christian Soucy .30 .75
21 Jimmy Waite .30 .75
22 Brad Werenka .20 .50
23 Bob Ferguson .15 .40

1997-98 Indianapolis Ice

Little is known about this set beyond the confirmed checklist. Additional information can be forwarded to hockeymag@beckett.com.

COMPLETE SET (30) 6.00 15.00
1 Bob Ferguson HCO .02 .10
2 Chris Mizer HTR .02 .10
3 Jim Stuckey EM .02 .10
4 Kory Cooper .20 .50
5 Kirk Daubenspeck .30 .75
6 Glen Featherstone .20 .50
7 Brian Felsner .20 .50
8 Martin Gendron .20 .50
9 Jani Hurme 1.25 3.00
10 Ryan Huska .20 .50
11 Marc Hussey .20 .50
12 David Hymovitz .20 .50
13 Marc Lamothe .40 1.00
14 Eric Lecompte .20 .50
15 Eric Manlow .20 .50
16 Steve McLaren .20 .50
17 Kevin Miller .20 .50
18 Craig Mills .20 .50
19 Frank Musil .20 .50
20 Dmitri Nabokov .20 .50
21 Alain Nasreddine .20 .50
22 Ryan Risidore .20 .50
23 Michal Sykora .20 .50
24 Steve Tardif .20 .50
25 Allie Turcotte .20 .50
26 Petri Varis .20 .50
27 Todd White .20 .50
28 Marty Wilford .20 .50
29 M.J.'s Collectibles .02 .10
30 PHPA Web Site .02 .10

1998-99 Indianapolis Ice

Little is known about this set beyond the confirmed checklist. Any additional information can be forwarded to hockeymag@beckett.com.

COMPLETE SET (29) 4.00 10.00
1 Brian Noonan .20 .50
2 Matt Cooney .15 .40
3 Ryan VandenBussche .30 .75
4 Marty Wilford .15 .40
5 Nathan Perrott .40 1.00
6 Mike Vukonich .15 .40
7 Remi Royer .20 .50
8 Marc Dupuis .15 .40
9 Mike Hall .15 .40
10 Sylvain Cloutier .15 .40
11 Andrei Trefilov .20 .50
12 Andrei Kozyrev .15 .40
13 Chris Herperger .15 .40
14 Marc Lamothe .30 .75
15 Erik Andersson .15 .40
16 Bryan Fogarty .15 .40
17 Slapshot MASCOT .02 .10
18 Bob Lachance .15 .40
19 Kirk Daubenspeck .30 .75
20 Barrie Moore .15 .40
21 Bruce Cassidy HCO .15 .40
22 David Hymovitz .15 .40
23 Justin Hocking .15 .40
24 King Team .02 .10
25 Dale DeGray .15 .40
26 Jeff Paul .15 .40
27 IHL Web Site .02 .10
28 MJ Collectibles .02 .10
29 PHPA Web Site .02 .10

1999-00 Indianapolis Ice

This set features the Ice of the CHL. The set was produced by Roox and sold by the team at home games.

COMPLETE SET (21) 90.00 150.00
1 Mike Berger 3.00 8.00
2 Ken Boone 4.00 10.00
3 Jason Carriere 3.00 8.00
4 Yvan Corbin 3.00 8.00
5 Dan Cousineau 3.00 8.00
6 Robert Davidson 3.00 8.00
7 Jay Hern 3.00 8.00
8 Peler Jas 3.00 8.00
9 Bernie John 3.00 8.00
10 Lubos Krajcovic 3.00 8.00
11 Eric Landry 3.00 8.00
12 Chris MacKenzie 3.00 8.00
13 Jason Mansoff 3.00 8.00
14 Jamie Morris 4.00 10.00
15 Sebastian Pajerski 3.00 8.00
16 Tom Stewart 3.00 8.00
17 Benoit Thibert 4.00 10.00
18 Steven Toll 3.00 8.00
19 M.J. Collectibles .40 1.00
20 Rod Davidson CO 2.00 5.00
21 Joe Trotta CO 2.00 5.00
22 Slapshot MAS 2.00 5.00

2000-01 Indianapolis Ice

This set features the Ice of the CHL. The cards were sold in team set form at the rink and at a shop called MJ's Collectibles. The latter version actually included an extra card, which featured a swatch of Yvan Corbin's jersey.

COMPLETE SET (23) 4.00 10.00
COMPLETE MJ SET (24) 8.00 20.00
1 Ryan Aho .20 .50
2 Dan Back .20 .50
3 Ken Boone .20 .50
4 Brandon Christian .20 .50
5 Yvan Corbin .20 .50
5GJ Yvan Corbin 4.00 10.00
6 Dan Cousineau .20 .50
7 Robert Davidson .20 .50
8 Casey Harris .20 .50
9 Jan Jas .20 .50
10 Peter Jas .20 .50
11 David Jesiolowski .20 .50
12 Bernie John .20 .50
13 Lubos Krajcovic .20 .50
14 Marc Laforge .20 .50
15 Chris MacKenzie .20 .50
16 Aigars Mironovics .20 .50
17 Jamie Morris .20 .50
18 Chris Richards .20 .50
19 Kevin Schmidt .20 .50
20 Jason Selleke .20 .50
21 Rod Davidson CO .10 .25
22 Slapshot MASCOT .04 .10
23 MJ's Collectibles .04 .10

2001-02 Indianapolis Ice

This set features the Ice of the UHL. The set was sold at home games as a 22-card version, at and MJ's Collectibles, which sold a 23-card version featuring a game jersey card of Bernie John. The latter set is priced below. The cards are unnumbered and are listed in alphabetical order.

COMPLETE SET (23) 8.00 20.00
1 Ryan Aikia .20 .50
2 Mike Berger ACO .04 .10
3 Peter Bournazakis .20 .50
4 Dan Cousineau .20 .50
5 Robert Davidson .20 .50
6 Rod Davidson CO .04 .10
7 Charlie Elezi .20 .50
8 Chris George .20 .50
9 Casey Harris .20 .50
10 Jay Hern .20 .50
11 Bernie John .20 .50
12 Bernie John GJ 4.00 10.00
13 Justin Kearns .30 .75
14 Chris MacKenzie .20 .50
15 Don Malko .20 .50
16 Jamie Morris .20 .50
17 Kevin Popp .20 .50
18 Jason Selleke .20 .50
19 Jonathan Sorg .20 .50
20 Dylan Taylor .20 .50
21 J.C. Wells .20 .50
22 Slapshot MASCOT .10 .25
23 MJs Collectibles .04 .10

2002-03 Indianapolis Ice

COMPLETE SET (23) 4.00 10.00
1 Ryan Aikia .20 .50
2 Jason Baird .20 .50
3 Ryan Carter .20 .50
4 Bryce Classen .20 .50
5 Jared Dumba .20 .50
6 Nate Elliott .20 .50
7 Randy Holmes .20 .50
8 Bernie John .20 .50
9 Justin Kearns .30 .75
10 Scott Lewis .20 .50
11 Etienne Morin .20 .50
12 Jamie Morris .20 .50
13 Greg Olsen .20 .50
14 Byron Pool .20 .50
15 Kevin Popp .20 .50
16 Shawn Silver .30 .75
17 Kevin St. Jacques .20 .50
18 Kevin St. Jacques .20 .50
19 Andrew Taylor .20 .50
20 Ken McRae CO .10 .25
21 Darrin Flinchem EQM .04 .10
22 Mascot .04 .10
23 Todd Champlin TR .04 .10

2003-04 Indianapolis Ice

COMPLETE SET (24) 10.00
1 Ryan Aikia .20 .50
2 Jason Baird .20 .50
3 Ken Boone .20 .50
4 Ryan Carter .20 .50
5 Philippe Choiniere .20 .50
6 Mario Doyon .20 .50
7 Jared Dumba .20 .50
8 Nate Elliott .20 .50
9 Dave Gilmore .20 .50
10 Joe Guenther .20 .50
11 Russ Guzior .20 .50
12 Bernie John .20 .50
13 Steve Lecuyer .20 .50
14 Chad McIver .20 .50
15 Adam Redmond .20 .50
16 Remi Royer .20 .50
17 Jeff Sanger .30 .75
18 Jason Selleke .20 .50
19 Mike Zeibaq .20 .50
20 Brent Zelenewich .30 .75
21 Ken McRae CO .10 .25
22 Darren Flinchem EQM .04 .10
23 Mascot .04 .10
24 Marc Schlichtenmyer TR .04 .10

2014-15 Indy Fuel

COMPLETE SET (26) 6.00 15.00
1 Anders Franzon .30 .75
2 Nick Bruneteau .30 .75
3 Nick Jones .30 .75
4 Dean Chelios .30 .75
5 Rhett Bly .30 .75
6 Dan Ford .30 .75
7 Kyle Stroh .30 .75
8 Evan Vossen .30 .75
9 Mike Duco .30 .75
10 Saverio Posa .30 .75
11 Pete Massar .30 .75
12 Jamie Wise .30 .75
13 Nicklas Lindberg .30 .75
14 Matt White .30 .75
15 Johnny McGuire .30 .75
16 Dillon Fournier .30 .75
17 Kirill Gotovets .30 .75
18 Justin Holl .30 .75
19 Vincent Arseneau .30 .75
20 Chris DeSousa .30 .75
21 Mac Carruth .30 .75
22 Garett Bembridge .30 .75
23 Shane Owen .30 .75
24 Garrett Klotz .30 .75
25 Scott Hillman CO .30 .75
26 Header Card CL .30 .75

2006-07 Iowa Stars

COMPLETE SET (27) 8.00 15.00
1 Greg Amadio .20 .50
2 Mark Ardelan .20 .50
3 Krys Barch .30 .75
4 Chris Conner .40 1.00
5 Dan Ellis .30 .75
6 Loui Eriksson .60 1.50
7 Mark Fistric .30 .75
8 Mike Green .20 .50
9 Nicklas Grossman .20 .50
10 Dan Hacker .20 .50
11 Yared Hagos .20 .50
12 Marius Holtet .20 .50
13 John Lammers .20 .50
14 Junior Lessard .40 1.00
15 Joel Lundqvist .40 1.00
16 Matt Nickerson .40 1.00
17 Toby Petersen .20 .50
18 Vojtech Polak .20 .50
19 Mario Scalzo .20 .50
20 Marty Sertich .40 1.00
21 Tobias Stephan .40 1.00
22 Janos Vas .20 .50
23 Francis Wathier .20 .50
24 Marty Wilford .20 .50
25 Dave Allison CO .02 .10
26 Paul Jerrard ACO .02 .10
27 Shooter MASCOT .02 .10

2000-01 Jackson Bandits

This set features the Bandits of the ECHL. The set was sold at home games late in the 2000-01 season. The singles are over-sized and numbered on the back.

COMPLETE SET (25) 4.80 12.00
1 Mike Tamburro .20 .50
2 Jeff Helperl .20 .50
3 Derek Gustafson .30 .75
4 Randy Fitzgerald .20 .50
5 Milt Mastad .20 .50
6 Jonathon Shockey .20 .50
7 Chris Wismer .20 .50
8 J.P. O'Connor .20 .50
9 Bobby Russell .20 .50
10 Cory Larose .20 .50
11 Brendan Walsh .20 .50
12 Ryan Mougenel .20 .50
13 Chris Peyton .20 .50
14 Brian Callahan .20 .50
15 Jim Bermingham .20 .50
16 Dan Carney .20 .50
17 Dave Stewart .20 .50
18 Brad Peddle .20 .50
19 Denny Felsner .30 .75
20 Steve Wilson .20 .50
21 Quintin Laing .20 .50
22 J.P. Tessier .20 .50
23 Lee Jinman .30 .75
24 Derek Clancey .20 .50
25 Tim Green .20 .50

2000-01 Jackson Bandits Promos

This set features the Bandits of the ECHL. The cards were issued prior to the main set (which is listed below) as a test of the popularity of trading cards as a promotional item. Apparently, the test went well. Any further info on this set can be forwarded to hockeymag@beckett.com.

COMPLETE SET (8) 3.20 8.00
1 David Brumby .40 1.00
2 Derek Gustafson .60 1.50
3 Denny Felsner .60 1.50
4 Brian Callahan .40 1.00
5 Bobby Russell .40 1.00
6 Dave Stewart .40 1.00
7 Mike Tamburro .40 1.00
8 Brendan Walsh .40 1.50

1999-00 Jacksonville Lizard Kings

This set features the Lizard Kings of the ECHL. This set was handed out as a promotional giveaway at a home game early in the season. It is believed that an update set was issued later in the year. Any information on this set can be forwarded to hockeymag@beckett.com.

COMPLETE SET (15) 4.80 12.00
1 Jean-Philippe Soucy .40 1.00
2 Alex Podalinski .30 .75
3 Rich Bronilla .30 .75
4 Brad Federenko .30 .75
5 Dan Reja .40 1.00
6 Ray LeBlanc .60 1.50
7 Mark Giannetti .30 .75
8 Patrick Gingras .30 .75
9 Derek Eberle .40 1.00
10 Eric Naud .40 1.00
11 Bryan Forslund .30 .75
12 Ryan Cirillo .30 .75
13 Lenny the Lizard MAS .20 .50
14 Alain Lemieux CO .20 .50
15 Jacksonville Lizard Kings .20 .50

1989-90 Johnstown Chiefs

This 18-card set of the Johnstown Chiefs of the ECHL was produced by Big League Cards. The set is believed to have been issued by the team, but that is not a certainty. The set's numbering begins with 19, leading to speculation that a 1988-89 set exists as well. The fronts feature a posed photo, with the player seated beside a prominent logo of sponsor Sheetz convenience store.

COMPLETE SET (18) 6.00 50.00
19 Rick Burchill 1.25 3.00
20 Bob Goulet .75 2.00
21 John Messuri .75 2.00
22 Darren Servatius .75 2.00
23 Rick Boyd .75 2.00
24 Bob Kennedy .75 2.00
25 Mike Rossetti .75 2.00
26 Dan Williams .75 2.00
27 Mark Bogoslowski .75 2.00
28 Dean Hall .75 2.00
29 Mitch Molloy .75 2.00
30 Darren Schwartz 1.25 3.00
31 Doug Weiss .75 2.00
32 Marc Vachon .75 2.00
33 Mike Jeffrey 1.25 3.00
34 Frank Dell ANN .08 .25
35 Sean Finn .75 2.00
36 Steve Carlson CO 6.00 15.00

1991-92 Johnstown Chiefs

This 20-card set features the Johnstown Chiefs of the ECHL. The set was sponsored by Ponderosa Steakhouse and KB Card Company and likely was sold by the team at home games. The fronts feature a posed photo along with team and sponsor logos.

COMPLETE SET (20) 4.00 10.00
1 Steve Carlson CO .75 2.00
2 Dana Heinze TR .02 .10
3 John Fletcher .20 .50
4 Mark Krys .20 .50
5 Doug Sinclair .20 .50
6 Bruce Coles .20 .50
7 Doug Weiss .20 .50
8 Dave MacIntyre .20 .50
9 Bob Woods .20 .50
10 Mike Roberts .20 .50
11 Jeff Beaudin .20 .50
12 Brian Ferreira .20 .50
13 Christian Lariviere .20 .50
14 Ted Miskolczi .20 .50
15 Rob Hrytsak .20 .50
16 Mark Green .20 .50
17 Matt Glennon .20 .50
18 Mike Rossetti .30 .75
19 Stan Reddick .30 .75
20 Perry Florio .20 .50

1993-94 Johnstown Chiefs

This 22-card set features the Johnstown Chiefs of the ECHL. The set was sponsored by Ponderosa Steakhouse and KB Card Company and likely was sold by the team at home games. The fronts feature a posed photo along with team and sponsor logos.

COMPLETE SET (22) 3.00 8.00
1 John Bradley .15 .40
2 Campbell Blair .15 .40
3 Francois Bourdeau .15 .40
4 Bob Woods .15 .40
5 Ted Dent .15 .40
6 Matt Hoffman .15 .40
7 Gord Christian .15 .40
8 Tim Hanus .15 .40
9 Phil Soukoroff .15 .40
10 Jason Jennings .15 .40
11 Dusty McLellan .15 .40
12 Dennis Purdie .20 .50
13 Chuck Wiegand .15 .40
14 Jamie Adams .15 .40
15 Jan Beran .15 .40
16 Rob Laurie .20 .50
17 Cory Banika .15 .40
18 Perry Florio .15 .40
19 Rob Leask .15 .40
20 Ed Johnstone CO .08 .25
21 John Daley GM .02 .10
22 Matt Koeck TR .02 .10
NNO Header Card .02 .10

1994-95 Johnstown Chiefs

This 24-card set features the Johnstown Chiefs of the ECHL. The set was likely sold by the team at home games. The fronts feature a posed photo along with team and sponsor logos.

COMPLETE SET (24) 3.00 8.00
1 Cover Card CL .02 .10
2 Jason Brousseau .15 .40
3 Brandon Christian .15 .40
4 Gord Christian .15 .40
5 Bruce Coles .15 .40
6 Ted Dent .15 .40
7 Martin D'Orsonnens .15 .40
8 Perry Florio .15 .40
9 Rod Hinks .15 .40
10 Matt Hoffman .15 .40
11 Aaron Israel .15 .40
12 Jason Jennings .15 .40
13 Rob Laurie .15 .40
14 Rob Leask .15 .40
15 Dennis Purdie .40 1.00
16 Kevin Quinn .15 .40
17 Jason Richard .15 .40
18 Dan Sawyer .15 .40
19 Ben Wyzansky .15 .40
20 Matt Yingst .15 .40
21 Training Staff .02 .10
22 Ed Johnstone .02 .10
23 WMTZ-FM Personalities .02 .10
24 WMTZ-FM Personalities .02 .10

1996-97 Johnstown Chiefs

This set was produced by Big League Sports and sponsored by Burger King. The set could only be acquired through the team's Kids Club. Note: There are two versions of card #26, both of which are short printed.

COMPLETE SET (31) 15.00 40.00
1 Greg Callahan .75 2.00
2 Brandon Christian .75 2.00
3 Alexsandr Chunchukov .75 2.00
4 Trevor Converse .75 2.00
5 Chad Dameworth .75 2.00
6 Carl Fleury 1.25 3.00
7 Dan Harrison .75 2.00
8 Jim Krayer .75 2.00
9 Denis Lamoureux .75 2.00
10 Kelly Leroux .75 2.00
11 Martin Masa .75 2.00
12 Klemen Mohoric .75 2.00
13 Sean Perry .75 2.00
14 Ryan Petz .75 2.00
15 Dan Reimann .75 2.00
16 Beau Riedel .75 2.00
17 Ted Russell .75 2.00
18 Ryan Savoia .75 2.00
19 Marc Siegel .75 2.00
20 Lukas Smital .75 2.00
21 Olie Sundstrom .75 2.00
22 Kam White .75 2.00
23 Martin Woods .75 2.00
24 Nick Fotiu HCO .40 1.00
25 Scott Allen ACO .20 .50
26 Mic Midderhoff EM .08 .25
26 Dana Heinze TR .08 .25
27 Chief's Office Staff .08 .25
28 The Iron Dog Mascot .08 .25
29 Home Schedule .08 .25
30 Logo Card .02 .10

1997-98 Johnstown Chiefs

This set features the Chiefs of the ECHL. The cards were issued primarily to members of the team's kid's club. It is believed that local police officers may also have given singles away to local children through other venues. Anyone with additional information may forward it to hockeymag@beckett.com.

COMPLETE SET (29) 30.00 60.00
1 Schedule Card .02 .10
2 Logo Card .02 .10
3 10th Anniversary Logo Card .02 .10
4 The Iron Dog Mascot .02 .10
5 Staff .10 .25
6 Scott Allen ACO .40 1.00
7 Nick Fotiu HCO .75 2.00
8 Martin Masa 1.50 4.00
9 Harold Hersh 1.50 4.00
10 Lukas Smital 1.50 4.00
11 Steve Plouffe 3.00 8.00
12 Jonathan Sorg 1.00 2.50
13 Dan Harrison 1.00 2.50
14 Carl Fleury 3.00 8.00
15 Martin Woods 1.00 2.50
16 Mark Yannetti 1.00 2.50
17 Garrett Burnett 1.00 2.50
18 Greg Callahan 1.00 2.50
19 Ivo Jan 1.00 2.50
20 Kelly Leroux 1.00 2.50
21 Brian Scott 1.00 2.50
22 Scott Stephens 1.00 2.50
23 Marcus Draxler 1.00 2.50
24 Brian Callahan 1.00 2.50
25 Francois Archambault 1.00 2.50
26 Dan Dennis 1.00 2.50
27 Reg Cardinal 1.00 2.50
28 Ian Smith 1.00 2.50
29 Yuri Krivokhija 1.00 2.50

1998-99 Johnstown Chiefs

This set was produced by Big League Sports and, like other Johnstown sets, could only be acquired through the Chiefs' Kid's Club.

COMPLETE SET (23) 8.00 20.00
1 Schedule Card .02 .10
2 Logo Card .02 .10
3 Iron Dog Mascot .02 .10
4 Scott Allen HCO .02 .10
5 Galen Head ACO .02 .10
6 Training Staff .02 .10
7 Office Staff .02 .10
8 Etienne Drapeau .40 1.00
9 Jody Shelley 2.00 5.00
10 Jeremy Thompson .40 1.00
11 Carl Fleury .60 1.50
12 Lukas Smital .40 1.00
13 Jonathan Sorg .40 1.00
14 Matt Eisler .40 1.00
15 Martin Masa .40 1.00
16 Shawn Frappier .40 1.00
17 E.J. Bradley .40 1.00
18 Joel Irving .40 1.00
19 Pavel Nestak .40 1.00
20 Kent Simpson .40 1.00
21 Steve Duke .40 1.00
22 Brad Englehart .40 1.00
23 Eric Normandin .40 1.00

1999-00 Johnstown Chiefs

This set features the Chiefs of the ECHL. The cards were issued as promotional giveaways. Police officers attended each game and handed out cards to children, one per night, making the set very difficult to complete.

COMPLETE SET (28) 10.00 25.00
1 Johnstown Chiefs Schedule .08 .25
2 Johnstown Chiefs .40 1.00
3 Iron Dog MASCOT .08 .25
4 Staff Card .08 .25
5 Scott Allen HCO .08 .25
6 Jason Spence .40 1.00
7 Ryan Chaytors .40 1.00
8 Jeffrey Sullivan .40 1.00
9 Andrew Dale .40 1.00
10 Derrick Walser .40 1.00
11 Dmitri Tarabrin .40 1.00
12 Carl Fleury .60 1.50
13 Joel Irving .40 1.00
14 Shawn Frappier .40 1.00
15 John Tripp .40 1.00
16 Chuck Mindel .40 1.00
17 Andrew Clark .40 1.00
18 Jody Shelley 2.00 5.00
19 Brent Bilodeau .40 1.00
20 Mike Vellinga .40 1.00
21 E.J. Bradley .40 1.00
22 Bryan McKinney .40 1.00
23 Mike Thompson .40 1.00
24 Frederic Deschenes .60 1.50
25 Kevin Kellett .40 1.00

26 Tyrone Garner .60 1.50
27 Training Staff .08 .25
28 Frank Cislo DRVR .08 .25

2000-01 Johnstown Chiefs

This set features the Chiefs of the ECHL The singles were handed out a designated games, one card at a time, to members of the kid's club, making the complete set very difficult to acquire.

COMPLETE SET (28) 12.00 30.00
1 Schedule Card .04 .10
2 Johnstown Chiefs .40 1.00
3 Scott Allen HCO .10 .25
4 Galen Head ACO .10 .25
5 Toby O'Brien .60 1.50
6 Training Staff .04 .10
7 Radio Guys .04 .10
8 Frank Cislo DRVR .04 .10
9 Front Office Staff .04 .10
10 Iron Dog MASCOT .04 .10
11 Frederic Deschenes .80 2.00
12 Dorian Anneck .60 1.50
13 Maxim Potapov .60 1.50
14 Eric Schneider .60 1.50
15 Jason Spence .60 1.50
16 Michael Kiesman .60 1.50
17 Mikko Kuparinen .80 2.00
18 Brent Bilodeau .80 2.00
19 Mike Vellinga .60 1.50
20 Jeffrey Sullivan .60 1.50
21 Andrew Clark .60 1.50
22 Jan Sulc .60 1.50
23 Dany Sabourin .60 2.00
24 Ryan Tocher .60 1.50
25 Dmitri Tarabrin .60 1.50
26 Mike Rodrigues .60 1.50
27 Mark Thompson .60 1.50
28 Andrew Dale .60 1.50

2001-02 Johnstown Chiefs

This set features the Chiefs of the ECHL. The cards were given away to members of the Chiefs' Kids Club at a rate of one card per game over the course of the season. According to minor league expert Ralph Slate, the card fronts can be misleading. Cards No. 1-10 have no season listed, cards No. 11-15 mistakenly read 2000-01, while cards No. 16-29 read 2001-02. Because of the nature of the distribution, this set is extremely difficult to compile.

COMPLETE SET (29) 20.00 50.00
1 Header Card .04 .10
2 Home Schedule .10 .25
3 Toby & James PRES/GM .20 .50
4 Brent Bilodeau 1.25 3.00
5 Jeffrey Sullivan .75 2.00
6 Kevin Baker .75 2.00
7 Dan Carlson .75 2.00
8 Kevin Clauson .75 2.00
9 Frank Cislo DR .20 .50
10 Staff .10 .25
11 Jim Leger .75 2.00
12 Dany Sabourin 1.25 3.00
13 Lukas Smital .75 2.00
14 J.F. Boutin .75 2.00
15 David Gove 1.25 3.00
16 Frederic Deschenes 1.25 3.00
17 Jason Spence .75 2.00
18 Andrew Clark 1.25 3.00
19 Blair Stayzer 1.25 3.00
20 Mike Rodrigues .75 2.00
21 Philippe Roy .75 2.00
22 Eric Schneider .75 2.00
23 Jim Shepherd .75 2.00
24 Ryan Townsend .75 2.00
25 Chad Onufrechuk .75 2.00
26 Vladimir Nemec .75 2.00
27 Mark White .75 2.00
28 Training Staff .10 .25
29 Mascots .20 .50

2002-03 Johnstown Chiefs

Listed below in alphabetical order.

COMPLETE SET (23) 20.00 40.00
1 Peter Aubry .75 2.00
2 Brent Bilodeau 1.00 2.50
3 J.F. Boutin .75 2.00
4 Pierre-Luc Courchesne .75 2.00
5 Andy Doktorchik .75 2.00
6 Dominic Forget .75 2.00
7 Steve Hildenbrand .75 2.00
8 Jay Langager .75 2.00
9 Jim Leger .75 2.00
10 Vladimir Nemec .75 2.00
11 Toby O'Brien .75 2.00
12 Mike Rodrigues .75 2.00
13 Philippe Roy .75 2.00
14 Mark Scally .75 2.00
15 Lukas Smital .75 2.00
16 Jason Spence .75 2.00
17 Sam St. Pierre .75 2.00
18 Jeff Sullivan .75 2.00
19 Dmitri Tarabrin .75 2.00
20 Ryan Townsend .75 2.00
21 Anniversary Logo .04 .10
22 Mascots .10 .25
23 Training Staff .04 .10

2003-04 Johnstown Chiefs

This set was produced by Big League Cards to be given away to members of the team's kids club. Because they were issued one card per game over the course of the season, it is an incredibly difficult set to complete. It's possible the checklist below is not complete. Please forward additional information to hockeymag@beckett.com. As we have no market information, the cards cannot be priced.

COMPLETE SET (19)
1 Brent Bilodeau
2 Jeffrey Sullivan
3 Dmitri Tarabrin
4 Dominic Forget
5 Ian Manzano
6 Steve Hildenbrand
7 Jay Langager
8 Shawn Mather
9 Josh Piro
10 Cory Campbell
11 Dan Growden
12 Mike James
13 Pierre-Luc Courchesne
14 David Currie
15 Jason Notermann
16 Chad Cavanagh
17 Richard Paul
18 Larry Courville
19 Brent Kelly

2003-04 Johnstown Chiefs RBI Sports

This set was produced by RBI Sports and was limited to 250 copies. The numbering sequence reflects the entire run of RBI series that season.

COMPLETE SET (16) 6.00 15.00
209 Brent Bilodeau .40 1.00
210 Chad Cavanagh .40 1.00
211 Pierre-Luc Courchesne .40 1.00
212 Larry Courville .40 1.00
213 David Currie .60 1.50
214 Dominic Forget .40 1.00
215 Steve Hildenbrand .40 1.00
216 Mike James .40 1.00
217 Brent Kelly .40 1.00
218 Jay Langager .40 1.00
219 Chris Leinweber .40 1.00
220 Ian Manzano .40 1.00
221 Shawn Mather .40 1.00
222 Jason Notermann .40 1.00
223 Dmitri Patzold .60 1.50
224 Dmitri Tarabrin .40 1.00

2004-05 Johnstown Chiefs

An album to store these cards was also produced.

COMPLETE SET (21) 6.00 15.00
1 Brent Bilodeau .40 1.00
2 David Bowman .30 .75
3 David Cann .40 1.00
4 Chad Cavanagh .30 .75
5 P.L. Courchesne .30 .75
6 David Currie .40 1.00
7 Jean Desrochers .30 .75
8 Steve Hildenbrand .30 .75
9 Mike James .60 1.50
10 Brent Kelly .30 .75
11 Chris Leinweber .30 .75
12 Ian Manzano .30 .75
13 Shawn Mather .30 .75
14 Dennis Packard .30 .75
15 Matt J. Reid .30 .75
16 Jeff Sullivan .30 .75
17 Joe Tallari .30 .75
18 Dmitri Tarabrin .30 .75
19 Johnathan Tremblay .30 .75
20 Jeremy Van Hoof .30 .75
21 Toby O'Brien CO .04 .10

2005-06 Johnstown Chiefs

COMPLETE SET (20) 6.00 15.00
1 Doug Andress .30 .75
2 J.B. Bittner .30 .75
3 Jonathan Boutin .30 .75
4 Morgan Cey .30 .75
5 Steve Cygan .30 .75
6 Jean Desrochers .30 .75
7 Gerard Dicaire .30 .75
8 Mike Egener .30 .75
9 Brandon Elliott .30 .75
10 Brady Greco .30 .75
11 Adam Henrich .30 .75
12 Justin Kelly .30 .75
13 Ian Manzano .30 .75
14 Brett Peterson .30 .75
15 Randy Rowe .30 .75
16 Jason Spence .30 .75
17 Joe Tallari .30 .75
18 Dmitri Tarabrin .30 .75
19 John Toffey .30 .75
20 Ben Wallace .30 .75

1971-72 Johnstown Jets Acme

This set features the Jets of the EHL. The oversized cards measure 3.5" x 5 " and feature black and white photos. The cards are blank backed and unnumbered, and so are listed below in alphabetical order.

COMPLETE SET (16) 40.00 80.00
1 Dave Birch 2.00 5.00
2 Vern Campigatto 2.00 5.00
3 Len Cunning 2.00 5.00
4 Guy Delparte 2.00 5.00
5 Wynne Dempster 2.00 5.00
6 Ron Docken 2.00 5.00
7 Galen Head 2.00 5.00
8 Eddie Kachur 2.00 5.00
9 Reg Kent(Taschuk) 2.00 5.00
10 Jerry MacDonald 2.00 5.00
11 Gene Peacosh 2.50 6.00
12 Dick Roberge 2.00 5.00
13 Jim Trewin 2.00 5.00
14 Brian Vescio 2.00 5.00
15 Bob Vroman 2.50 6.00
16 Gary Wood 2.00 5.00

1972-73 Johnstown Jets

This set features the Jets of the EHL. The cards reportedly were included as a premium in game day programs and measure an oversized 3 1/2 by 5 inches. The photos on the front are black and white, while the backs are blank.

COMPLETE SET (18) 50.00 100.00
1 Ron Docken 2.50 6.00
2 Brian Coughlin 2.00 5.00
3 Tony McCarthy 2.00 5.00
4 Tom Steeves 2.00 5.00
5 Kevin Collins 2.00 5.00
6 Jerry MacDonald 2.00 5.00
7 Wynne Dempster 2.00 5.00
8 Ted Lanyon 2.00 5.00
9 Brian Vescio 2.00 5.00
10 Denis Erickson 2.50 6.00
11 Vern Campigatto 2.00 5.00
12 Gary Wood 2.00 5.00
13 Dave Birch 2.00 5.00
14 Galen Head 2.50 6.00
15 Reg Kent(Taschuk) 2.00 5.00
16 Tom McVie 2.50 6.00
17 Bill McEwan 2.00 5.00
18 Doug Anderson 2.00 5.00

2014-15 Johnstown Tomahawks

COMPLETE SET (24) 6.00 15.00
1 Mike Letizia [Head Coach] .30 .75
2 Jacob Gwillim .30 .75
3 Jake Houston .30 .75
4 Ian Spencer .30 .75
5 Steven Quagliata .30 .75
6 Logan Hudson .30 .75
7 Collin Montgomery .30 .75
8 Lane Valimont .30 .75
9 Joe Drabin .30 .75
10 Andrew Romano .30 .75
11 Joe Delandro .30 .75
12 Brady Bender .30 .75
13 Zac Robbins .30 .75
14 Dalton Hunter .30 .75
15 Alex Alger .30 .75
16 Nick Le Sage .30 .75
17 Tanner Barnes .30 .75
18 Josh Bowes .30 .75
19 Casey Linkenheld .30 .75
20 Filips Buncis .30 .75
21 Alex Jaeckle .30 .75
22 Trevor Recktenwald .30 .75
23 Luke Lynch .30 .75
24 Ryan Bednard .30 .75

1952-53 Juniors Blue Tint

The 1952-53 Junior set contains 182 cards measuring approximately 2" by 3". The cards have a blue tint and are numbered on the back. It is not known at this time who sponsored this set. Key cards in this set are "Pre-Rookie Cards" of Al Arbour, Don Cherry, Charlie Hodge, John Muckler, Henri Richard, and Harry Sinden.

COMPLETE SET (182) 1250.00 2500.00
1 Dennis Riggin 8.00 20.00
2 Joe Zorica 5.00 10.00
3 Larry Hillman 10.00 25.00
4 Edward(Ted) Reid 5.00 10.00
5 Al Arbour 35.00 75.00
6 Marlin McAlendin 5.00 10.00
7 Ross Graham 5.00 10.00
8 Cumming Burton 5.00 10.00
9 Ed Palamar 5.00 10.00
10 Elmer Skov 6.00 15.00
11 Eddie Louttit 5.00 10.00
12 Gerry Price 5.00 10.00
13 Lou Dietrich 5.00 10.00
14 Gaston Marcotte 5.00 10.00
15 Bob Brown 5.00 10.00
16 Archie Burton 5.00 10.00
17 Marv Edwards 15.00 40.00
18 Norman Defelice 6.00 15.00
19 Pete Kamula 5.00 10.00
20 Charles Marshall 5.00 10.00
21 Alex Leslie 5.00 10.00
22 Minpy Roberts 5.00 10.00
23 Danny Poliziani 5.00 10.00
24 Allen Kellogg 5.00 10.00
25 Brian Cullen 15.00 40.00
26 Ken Schinkel 6.00 15.00
27 W. Hass 5.00 10.00
28 Don Nash 5.00 10.00
29 Robert Maxwell 5.00 10.00
30 Eddie Mateka 5.00 10.00
31 Joe Kastelic 5.00 10.00
32 Hank Ciesla 6.00 15.00
33 Hugh Barlow 5.00 10.00
34 Claude Roy 5.00 10.00
35 Jean-Guy Gamache 5.00 10.00
36 Leon Michelin 5.00 10.00
37 Gerard Bergeron 5.00 10.00
38 Herve Lalonde 5.00 10.00
39 J.M. Cossette 5.00 10.00
40 Jean-Guy Gendron 10.00 25.00
41 Gamill Bedard 5.00 10.00
42 Alfred Soucy 5.00 10.00
43 Jean Leclerc 5.00 10.00
44 Raymond St.Cyr 6.00 15.00
45 Lester Lahaye 5.00 10.00
46 Yvan Houle 5.00 10.00
47 Louis Desrosiers 5.00 10.00
48 Douglas Lessor 5.00 10.00
49 Irvin Scott 5.00 10.00
50 Danny Blair 5.00 10.00
51 Jim Connelly 6.00 15.00
52 William Chalmers 5.00 10.00
53 Frank Bettiol 5.00 10.00
54 James Holmes 5.00 10.00
55 Birley Dimme 5.00 10.00
56 Donald Beattie 5.00 10.00
57 Terrance Chattington 5.00 10.00
58 Bruce Wallace 5.00 10.00
59 William McCreary 6.00 15.00
60 Fred Brady 5.00 10.00
61 Ronald Murphy 6.00 15.00
62 Lavi Purola 5.00 10.00
63 George Whyte 5.00 10.00
64 Marcel Paille 25.00 50.00
65 Maurice Collins 5.00 10.00
66 Gerard(Butch) Houle 6.00 15.00
67 Gilles Laperriere 5.00 10.00
68 Robert Chevalier 5.00 10.00
69 Bertrand Lepage 5.00 10.00
70 Michel Labadie 5.00 10.00
71 Gabriel Alain 5.00 10.00
72 Jean-Jacques Pichette 6.00 15.00
73A Camille Henry (Citadelles) 12.00 30.00
73B Camille Henry (New York 100.00 200.00
74 Jean-Guy Gignac 5.00 10.00
75 Leo Amadio 6.00 15.00
76 Gilles Thibault 6.00 15.00
77 Gaston Pelletier 6.00 15.00
78 Adolph Kukulowicz 6.00 15.00
79 Roland Leclerc 5.00 10.00
80 Phil Watson CO 20.00 40.00
81 Raymond Cyr 6.00 15.00
82 Jacques Marcotte 5.00 10.00
83 Floyd Hillman 6.00 15.00
84 Bob Attersley 5.00 10.00
85 Harry Sinden 35.00 75.00
86 Stan Parker 5.00 10.00
87 Bob Mader 5.00 10.00
88 Roger Maisonneuve 5.00 10.00
89 Phil Chapman 5.00 10.00
90 Don McIntosh 5.00 10.00
91 Jack Armstrong 5.00 10.00
92 Carlo Montemurro 5.00 10.00
93 Ken Courtney 5.00 10.00
94 Bill Stewart 6.00 15.00
95 Gerald Casey 5.00 10.00
96 Fred Etcher 5.00 10.00
97 Orrin Carver 5.00 10.00
98 Ralph Willis 5.00 10.00
99 Kenneth Robertson 5.00 10.00
100 Don Cherry 175.00 350.00
101 Fred Pletsch 5.00 10.00
102 Larry Thibault 5.00 10.00
103 James Robertson 5.00 10.00
104 Orval Tessier 10.00 25.00
105 Jack Higgins 5.00 10.00
106 Robert White 5.00 10.00
107 Doug Mohns 15.00 40.00
108 William Sexton 5.00 10.00
109 John Martan 5.00 10.00
110 Tony Poeta 6.00 15.00
111 Don McKenney 10.00 25.00
112 Bill Harrington 5.00 10.00
113 Allen Peal 5.00 10.00
114 John Ford 5.00 10.00
115 Kenneth Collins 6.00 15.00
116 Marc Boileau 6.00 15.00
117 Doug Vaughan 5.00 10.00
118 Gilles Boisvert 5.00 10.00
119 Buddy Horne 5.00 10.00
120 Graham Joyce 5.00 10.00
121 Gary Collins 5.00 10.00
122 Roy Greenan 5.00 10.00
123 Beryl Klynck 5.00 10.00
124 Grieg Hicks 5.00 10.00
125 Jack Novak 5.00 10.00
126 Ken Tennant 5.00 10.00
127 Glen Cressman 5.00 10.00
128 Curly Davies 5.00 10.00
129 Charlie Hodge 37.50 75.00
130 Bob McCord 6.00 15.00
131 Gordie Hollinworth 5.00 10.00
132 Ronald Pilon 5.00 10.00
133 Brian Mackay 5.00 10.00
134 Yvon Chasle 5.00 10.00
135 Denis Boucher 6.00 15.00
136 Claude Boileau 5.00 10.00
137 Claude Vinet 5.00 10.00
138 Claude Provost 20.00 40.00
139 Henri Richard 150.00 300.00
140 Les Lilley 5.00 10.00
141 Phil Goyette 15.00 40.00
142 Guy Rousseau 5.00 10.00
143 Paul Knox 5.00 10.00
144 Bill Lee 5.00 10.00
145 Ted Topazzini 6.00 15.00
146 Marc Reaume 6.00 15.00
147 Bill Dineen 15.00 40.00
148 Ed Plata 5.00 10.00
149 Noel Price 6.00 15.00
150 Mike Ratchford 5.00 10.00
151 Jim Logan 5.00 10.00
152 Art Clune 5.00 10.00
153 Jerry MacNamara 5.00 10.00
154 Jack Caffery 6.00 15.00
155 Les Duff. 5.00 10.00
156 Murray Costello 6.00 15.00
157 Ed Chadwick 40.00 80.00
158 Mike Desilets 5.00 10.00
159 Ross Watson 5.00 10.00
160 Roger Landry 5.00 10.00
161 Terry O'Connor 5.00 10.00
162 Ovila Gagnon 5.00 10.00
163 Dave Broadbelt 5.00 10.00
164 Sandy Monrisson 5.00 10.00
165 John MacGillvray 5.00 10.00
166 Claude Beaupre 5.00 10.00
167 Eddie Eustache 5.00 10.00
168 Stan Rodek 5.00 10.00
169 Maurice Mantha 6.00 15.00
170 Hector Lalande 8.00 20.00
171 Bob Wilson 5.00 10.00
172 Frank Bonello 5.00 10.00
173 Peter Kowalchuch 5.00 10.00
174 Les Binkley 25.00 50.00
175 John Muckler 20.00 40.00
176 Ken Wharram 15.00 40.00
177 John Sleaver 5.00 10.00
178 Ralph Markarian 5.00 10.00
179 Ken McMeekin 5.00 10.00
180 Ron Boomer 5.00 10.00
181 Kenneth (Red) Crawford 5.00 10.00
182 Jim McBurney 8.00 20.00

2001-02 Kalamazoo K-Wings

This set features the K-Wings of the UHL. It was produced by Choice Marketing and sold at the team's souvenir stands.

COMPLETE SET (24) 4.00 10.00
1 Andrew Huggett .20 .50
2 Michael Goldkind .20 .50
3 Sergei Deshevyy .20 .50
4 Randy Holmes .20 .50
5 Michael Ford .20 .50
6 Jeff Scharf .20 .50
7 Mathieu Paul .20 .50
8 Jim Brown .20 .50
9 Darcy Anderson .20 .50
10 Harry Schwefel .20 .50
11 Greg Dupre .20 .50
12 Benoit Beausoleil .20 .50
13 Craig Patterson .20 .50
14 Jeff Foster .20 .50
15 Mark Lawrence .30 .75
16 Steve Moore .20 .50
17 Tim Knudsen .30 .75
18 Scott Langkow .30 .75
19 Brad Cook .20 .50
20 Sandy Lamarre .20 .50
21 Ted Laviolette .20 .50
22 Dennis Desrosiers CO .04 .10
23 Scott Allison TR .04 .10
24 Slappy MASCOT .04 .10
NNO Team CL .04 .10

1977-78 Kalamazoo Wings

These standard size cards, sponsored by ISB bank, feature black and white photos with a white border. Backs feature players name, position, and card number.

COMPLETE (15) 15.00 30.00
1 George Klsons 1.00 2.00
2 Ron Wilson 1.00 2.00
3 Bob Lemieux 1.00 2.00
4 Len Ircandia 1.00 2.00
5 Ron Kennedy 1.00 2.00
6 Daniel Poulin 1.00 2.00
7 Terry Evans 1.00 2.00
8 Yvon Douris 1.00 2.00
9 Tom Milani 1.00 2.00
10 Mike Wanchuk 1.00 2.00
11 Steve Lee 1.00 2.00
12 Yves Guilmette 1.00 2.00
13 Al Genovy 1.00 2.00
15 Jim Baxter 1.00 2.00
18 Alvin White 1.00 2.00

2002-03 Kalamazoo Wings

COMPLETE SET (29) 8.00 20.00
1 Checklist .04 .10
2 Kirill Alexeev .40 1.00
3 Tyson Turgeon .40 1.00
4 Eric Lawson .40 1.00
5 Quade Lightbody .40 1.00
6 Herman Hultgren .40 1.00
7 Bryan Farquhar .40 1.00
8 Mike Ford .40 1.00
9 Peter Roed .40 1.00
10 Joe Pecoraro .40 1.00
11 Jordan Trew .40 1.00
12 Glendon Cominetti .40 1.00
13 Pete Pierman .40 1.00
14 Kurt Miller .40 1.00
15 Mark Phenow .40 1.00
16 Craig Bilick .40 1.00
17 Mark Lawrence .40 1.00
18 Justin Cardwell .40 1.00
19 Richard Keyes .40 1.00
20 Chad Dameworth .40 1.00
21 Chad Alban .60 1.50
22 Brian Rogers .40 1.00
23 Jeff Reynaert .40 1.00
24 Mark Kaufman CO .04 .10
25 Mike Modugno ANN .04 .10
26 Scott Allison TR .04 .10
27 Slappy Mascot .04 .10
28 Shoe Carnival .04 .10
29 Burger King .04 .10

2003-04 Kalamazoo Wings

COMPLETE SET (32) 4.00 10.00
1 Checklist .04 .10
2 Mark Reeds CO .04 .10
3 Mark Vilneff .15 .40
4 Guy Dupuis .15 .40
5 Tyson Turgeon .15 .40
6 Jim Dube .15 .40
7 Kevin Caudill .15 .40
8 Daniel Carriere .15 .40
9 Steve Doherty .15 .40
10 Tyler Willis .30 .75
11 Jeff Turner .15 .40
12 Kurt Miller .15 .40
13 Marty Flichel .15 .40
14 Tim Turner .15 .40
15 David Hukalo .15 .40
16 Yannick Carpentier .15 .40
17 Pat O'Leary .15 .40
18 Josh Akright .15 .40
19 Andrew Luciuk .15 .40
20 Dan Watson .15 .40
21 Chad Alban .30 .75
22 Brock McGillis .30 .75
23 Brent Rumble .15 .40
24 Nick Bootland .30 .75
25 Joe Ritson .15 .40
26 Team Staff .04 .10
27 Mike Modugno ANN .04 .10
28 Mascot .04 .10
29 Ad Card .04 .10
30 Ad Card .04 .10
31 Ad Card .04 .10
32 Ad Card .04 .10

2004-05 Kalamazoo Wings

COMPLETE SET (30) 5.00 12.00
1 Checklist .04 .10
2 Mark Reeds CO .04 .10
3 Josh Elzinga .20 .50
4 Mark Vilneff .20 .50
5 Kevin Holdridge .20 .50
6 Tyson Turgeon .20 .50
7 Shaun Fisher .20 .50
8 Daniel Carriere .20 .50
9 Greg Labenski .20 .50
10 Tyler Willis .20 .50
11 Tom Ditzer .20 .50
12 Steve Doherty .20 .50
13 Tim Turner .20 .50
14 Matt Noga .20 .50
15 Tim Krueckl .20 .50
16 Yannick Carpentier .20 .50
17 Ryan Crane .20 .50
18 Gray Shaneberger .20 .50
19 Andrew Luciuk .20 .50
20 Sean Starke .20 .50
21 Kevin Kotyluk .20 .50
22 Chad Alban .40 1.00
23 Joel Martin .20 .50
24 Mike Manley .20 .50
25 Daniel Carriere AS Greg Labenski AS .20 .50
26 Trainers .04 .10
27 Slappy MASCOT .04 .10
28 Announcer .04 .10
29 Rocker Morning Show .04 .10
30 WKFR Morning Show .04 .10

2005-06 Kalamazoo Wings

COMPLETE SET (30) 8.00 20.00
1 Kalamazoo Wings CL .02 .10
2 Mark Reeds HC .02 .10
3 Josh Elzinga .40 1.00
4 Mark Vilneff .40 1.00
5 Mike Dombkiewicz .40 1.00
6 Jason Deitsch .40 1.00
7 Daniel Carriere .40 1.00
8 Tyler Willis .40 1.00
9 Damian Surma .40 1.00
10 Tim Turner .40 1.00
11 Lucas Drake .40 1.00
12 Tyler Rennette .40 1.00
13 Dustin Virag .40 1.00
14 Adam Elzinga .40 1.00
15 Lee Ruff .40 1.00
16 Brad Church .40 1.00
17 Greg Labenski .40 1.00
18 Kory Karlander .40 1.00
19 Jeff Reynaert .40 1.00
20 Mike Manley .40 1.00
21 Joel Martin .40 1.00
22 Nick Bootland .40 1.00
23 K-Wings Alumni .40 1.00
24 Mike Plandowski TR .02 .10
25 Eric Bechtol EQM .02 .10
26 Slappy MASCOT .02 .10
27 Mike Modugno ANN .02 .10
28 The Rocker Morning Show .02 .10
29 The KFR Morning Show .02 .10
30 Scoopie MASCOT .02 .10

1984-85 Kamloops Blazers

This set features color action photos on the front along with team name, position, and number. Backs feature safety tips and sponsor logos. Cards are unnumbered and checklisted below in alphabetical order.

COMPLETE SET (24) 8.00 20.00
1 Will Anderson .30 .75
2 Brian Benning .30 .75
3 Brian Bertuzzi .30 .75
4 Rob Brown .60 1.50
5 Todd Carnelley .30 .75
6 Dean Clark .40 1.00
7 Rob Dimaio .75 2.00
8 Greg Evtushevski .30 .75
9 Mark Ferner .30 .75
10 Greg Hawgood .60 1.50
11 Ken Hitchcock CO .75 2.00
12 Mark Kachowski .30 .75
13 Bob Labrier ACO .08 .25
14 Pat Mangold .30 .75
15 Gord Mark .30 .75
16 Len Mark .30 .75
17 Rob McKinley .40 1.00
18 Mike Nottingham .30 .75
19 Neil Pilon .30 .75
20 Rudy Poeschek .75 2.00
21 Daryl Reaugh .75 2.00
22 Ryan Stewart .30 .75
23 Mark Thietke .30 .75
24 Gord Walker .30 .75

1985-86 Kamloops Blazers

This standard size set features full color fronts along with sponsor logs and hockey tips on the backs. Cards are unnumbered and checklisted below in alphabetical order.

COMPLETE SET (26) 12.00 30.00
1 Robin Bawa .75 2.00
2 Craig Berube 2.00 5.00
3 Pat Bingham .40 1.00
4 Rob Brown .75 2.00
5 Todd Carnelly .40 1.00
6 Randy Hansch .75 2.00
7 Greg Hawgood .75 2.00
8 Ken Hitchcock CO 2.00 5.00
9 Mark Kachowski .40 1.00
10 Troy Kennedy .40 1.00
11 R.T. Labrier ACO .20 .50
12 Dave Marcinyshyn .40 1.00
13 Len Mark .40 1.00
14 Rob McKinley .40 1.00
15 Ken Morrison .40 1.00
16 Pat Nogier .40 1.00
17 Mike Nottingham .40 1.00
18 Doug Pickell .40 1.00
19 Rudy Poeschek 2.00 5.00
20 Mike Ragot .40 1.00
21 Don Schmidt .40 1.00
22 Ron Shudra .40 1.00
23 Peter Soberlak .40 1.00
24 Lonnie Spink .40 1.00
25 Chris Tarnowski .40 1.00
26 Greg Wallace TR .07 .20

1986-87 Kamloops Blazers

This 24-card sheet was issued in nine four-card sheets. Six of the panels feature two cards and an advertisement, while the other three panels feature four cards per panel. The sheets are perforated vertically but not horizontally, which produces two-card stripes. If cut, the cards would measure the standard size. On a white card face, the fronts display posed action photos inside a bright blue border. The cards are unnumbered and checklisted below in alphabetical order.

COMPLETE SET (24) 12.00 30.00
1 Warren Babe .20 .50
2 Robin Bawa .20 .50
3 Rob Brown .60 1.50
4 Dean Cook .40 1.00
5 Scott Daniels .20 .50
6 Mario Desjardines .20 .50
7 Bill Harrington .20 .50
8 Greg Hawgood .40 1.00
9 Serge Lajoie .20 .50
10 Dave Marcinyshyn .20 .50
11 Len Mark .20 .50
12 Rob McKinley .40 1.00
13 Casey McMillan .20 .50
14 Darcy Norton .20 .50
15 Kelly Para .20 .50
16 Doug Pickell .20 .50
17 Rudy Poeschek .60 1.50
18 Mark Recchi 6.00 15.00
19 Don Schmidt .20 .50
20 Ron Shudra .20 .50
21 Chris Tarnowski .20 .50
22 Steve Wienke .20 .50
23 Rich Wiest .20 .50
24 Team Photo .20 .50

1987-88 Kamloops Blazers

This 24-card set was issued in three-card perforated strips each consisting of two player cards and one advertisement or coupon card. (As listed below, two of these advertisement cards display team logos on the front). The strips measure 7 1/2" by 3 1/2", and if cut, the individual cards would measure the standard size. The front features a color posed-action player photo with thin blue borders on a white card face. The cards are unnumbered and checklisted below in alphabetical order.

COMPLETE SET (24) 12.00 30.00
1 Warren Babe .30 .75
2 Paul Checknita .30 .75
3 Dave Chyzowski .40 1.00
4 Dean Cook .40 1.00
5 Greg Davies .30 .75
6 Kim Deck .30 .75
7 Todd Decker .30 .75
8 Bill Harrington .30 .75
9 Phil Huber .30 .75
10 Steve Kloepzig .30 .75
11 Willie MacDonald .40 1.00
12 Pat MacLeod .30 .75
13 Glenn Mulvenna .40 1.00
14 Mike Needham .30 .75
15 Darcy Norton .30 .75
16 Devon Oleniuk .30 .75
17 Doug Pickell .30 .75
18 Garth Premak .30 .75
19 Mark Recchi 6.00 15.00
20 Don Schmidt .30 .75
21 Alec Sheflo .30 .75
22 Team Photo .20 .50
23 Logo Card .08 .25
24 Logo Card .08 .25

1988-89 Kamloops Blazers

This 36-card set was issued in three-card perforated strips that measure approximately 7 1/2" by 3 1/2". After perforation, the individual cards measure approximately 2 1/2" by 3 1/2". One of the cards on each three-card strip has the Kamloops logo in blue and orange on the front and the back contains a coupon. The regular player cards have white borders with an inner royal blue line surrounding a posed player photo. The cards are unnumbered and are checklisted below in alphabetical order.

COMPLETE SET (36) 8.00 20.00
COMMON AD CARD (25-36) .02 .10
1 Cory Anderson .20 .50
2 Pat Bingham .20 .50
3 Ed Bertuzzi .20 .50
4 Zac Boyer .20 .50
5 Trevor Buchanan .20 .50
6 Dave Chyzowski .30 .75
7 Dean Cook .30 .75
8 Cory Crichton .20 .50
9 Kim Deck .20 .50
10 Ryan Harrison .20 .50
11 Brad Heschuk .20 .50
12 Corey Hirsch 1.25 3.00
13 Phil Huber .20 .50
14 Len Jorgenson .20 .50
15 Paul Kruse .30 .75
16 Dave Linford .20 .50
17 Pat MacLeod .20 .50
18 Darwin McClelland .20 .50
19 Cal McGowan .20 .50
20 Mike Needham .20 .50
21 Don Schmidt .20 .50
22 Brian Shantz .20 .50
23 Darryl Sydor 1.50 3.50
24 Steve Yule .20 .50
25 Hasty Market Ad .02 .10
26 McDonalds Ad .02
27 Mr. Mike's Ad .02
28 Yellow Submarine Ad .02
29 Blazers Logo .02
30 Blazers Logo .02
31 Blazers Logo .02
32 Blazers Logo .02
33 Blazers Logo .02
34 Blazers Logo .02
35 Blazers Logo .02
36 Blazers Logo .02

1989-90 Kamloops Blazers

This 24-card set is believed to have been released in three-card panel form, as were previous Blazers issu[illegible] It is noteworthy for featuring the first card of All-Star defender Scott Niedermayer.

COMPLETE SET (24) 6.00 15.[illegible]
1 Len Barrie .20
2 Craig Bonner .20
3 Jarrett Bousquet .20
4 Zac Boyer .25
5 Murray Duval .20
6 Shea Essolmont .20
7 Todd Esselmont .20
8 Todd Harris .20
9 Corey Hirsch .60
10 Phil Huber .20
11 Lance Johnson .20
12 Paul Kruse .25
13 Dean Malkoc .20
14 Dale Mason .20
15 Cal McGowan .20
16 Joey Mittelsteadt .20
17 Mike Needham .25
18 Scott Niedermayer 1.50
19 Brian Shantz .20
20 Trevor Sim .20
21 Darryl Sydor .75
22 Jeff Waatchorn .20
23 Clayton Young .20
24 Steve Yule .20

1993-94 Kamloops Blazers

This 24-card set was issued on three-card perforated strips each consisting of two player cards and one advertisement or coupon card. The strips measure 7 1/2" by 3 1/2", and if cut, the individual cards would measure the standard size. The fronts feature a color posed-action player photo with thin blue borders on white background. The cards are unnumbered and checklisted below in alphabetical order.

COMPLETE SET (24) 12.00
1 Nolan Baumgartner .30
2 Rod Branch .20
3 Jarrett Deuling .20
4 Shane Doan 2.00
5 Hnat Domenichelli .30
6 Scott Ferguson .20
7 Greg Hart .20
8 Jason Holland .20
9 Ryan Huska .20
10 Jarome Iginla 6.00
11 Mike Josephson .20
12 Aaron Keller .20
13 Mike Krooshoop .20
14 Scott Loucks .20
15 Brad Lukowich .40
16 Bob Maudie .20
17 Chris Murray .20
18 Tyson Nash 1.25
19 Steve Passmore .60
20 Rod Stevens .20
21 Jason Strudwick .30
22 Darcy Tucker 1.50
23 Bob Westerby .20
24 David Wilkie .20

1994-95 Kamloops Blazers

This set features the Blazers of the WHL. It is believe[illegible] that it was issued as a promotional giveaway.

COMPLETE SET (24) 12.00
1 Darcy Tucker .75
2 Jarome Iginla 4.00
3 Nolan Baumgartner .40
4 Jeff Oldenborger .20
5 Ivan Vologjaninov .20
6 Shawn McNeil .20
7 Donnie Kinney .20
8 Bob Maudie .20
9 Jason Holland .20
10 Greg Hart .20
11 Shane Doan 1.25
12 Brad Lukowich .40
13 Randy Petruk .40
14 Jason Strudwick .40
15 Jeff Ainsworth .20
16 Aaron Keller .20
17 Rod Branch .20
18 Bob Westerby .20
19 Tyson Nash 1.25
20 Hnat Domenichelli .40
21 Ryan Huska .20
22 Jeff Henkelman .20
23 Cam Severson .20
24 Kamloops Arena .04

1995-96 Kamloops Blazers

This set features the Blazers of the WHL. Although th[illegible] checklist is confirmed, little else is known about the distribution of this set. Additional information can be forwarded to hockeymag@beckett.com.

COMPLETE SET (31) 8.00
1 Jarome Iginla 2.00
2 Nolan Baumgartner .20
3 Jake Deadmarsh .20
4 Scott Reid .20
5 Randy Petruk .30
6 Brad Lukowich .40
7 Shawn McNeil .30
8 Ed Dempsey CO .08
9 Peter Bergman .20
10 Greg Hart .20
11 Hnat Domenichelli .40
12 Al Glendenning CO .08
13 Digger MAS .02
14 Rob Skrlac .20
15 Donnie Kinney .20
16 Chris St. Croix .20
17 Jeff Oldenborger .20
18 Steve Albrecht .20
19 Bob Maudie .20
20 Blair Rota .20
21 Brian Henderson CO .08
22 Aaron Keller .20
23 Ryan Rishaug .20
24 Steve Gainey .40
25 Jeff Ainsworth .20
26 Ajay Baines .20
27 Jordan Landry .20
28 Jason Holland .20

Kamloops Arena .08 .25
Cadrin Smart .20 .50
Konrad Brand .20 .50

1996-97 Kamloops Blazers

s 28-card set was distributed in 3-panel strips, each which contained two player cards and one ad card a local business. When separated the cards are ndard size and feature color photos with player ne, number and position at the top, while the bottom corner is dominated by a flame-like element and an n identifying the set as the '96-97 Limited Edition. e cards are unnumbered and are listed below in habetical order.

MPLETE SET (28) 8.00 20.00
eff Ainsworth .30 .75
teve Albrecht .30 .75
ils Antons .30 .75
jay Baines .30 .75
onrad Brand .30 .75
Vade Burt .30 .75
ake Deadmarsh .30 .75
d Dempsey CO .08 .25
igger MAS .02 .10
Micki DuPont .40 1.00
Steve Gainey .40 1.00
Jonathan Hobson .30 .75
Drew Kehler .30 .75
Donnie Kinney .30 .75
Alan Manness .30 .75
Shawn McNeil .30 .75
Randy Petruk .40 1.00
Clayton Pool .40 1.00
Gennady Razin .30 .75
Robyn Regehr .60 1.50
Blair Rota .30 .75
Thomas Scantlebury .30 .75
Steve Shrum .30 .75
Rob Skrlac .30 .75
Darcy Smith .30 .75
Chris St. Croix .30 .75
Spike Wallace .08 .25
Darren Wright .30 .75

1998-99 Kamloops Blazers

ese cards are unnumbered and so are listed below in habetical order.

MPLETE SET (24) 12.00 20.00
ared Aulin .40 1.00
jay Baines .40 1.00
nton Borodkin .30 .75
Mike Brown .30 .75
aul Deniset .30 .75
dam Dombrowski .30 .75
rett Draney .30 .75
Micki Dupont .40 1.00
enric Exner .40 1.00
Jordon Flodell .30 .75
Steve Gainey .40 1.00
Aaron Gionet .30 .75
Gable Gross .30 .75
Jonathan Hobson .30 .75
Donnie Kinney .30 .75
David Klatt .30 .75
Kevin MacKie .30 .75
Alan Manness .30 .75
Konstantin Panov .30 .75
Robyn Regehr .75 2.00
Steve Shrum .30 .75
Chris St. Croix .30 .75
Chad Starling .30 .75
Ryan Thorpe .30 .75

1999-00 Kamloops Blazers

s set features the Blazers of the WHL. The set was duced by the team and sold at its souvenir stands. e cards are unnumbered, so are listed below habetically.

MPLETE SET (24) 6.00 15.00
ared Aulin .75 2.00
ason Bone .30 .75
nton Borodkin .20 .50
rik Christensen .20 .50
aul Deniset .20 .50
laine Depper .20 .50
rett Draney .20 .50
Micki DuPont .40 1.00
aron Gionet .30 .75
Gable Gross .20 .50
Jonathan Hobson .20 .50
Kyle Ladobruk .20 .50
Kevin Mackie .20 .50
Grant McCune .30 .75
Shaone Morrisonn .60 1.50
Mike Munro .20 .50
Konstantin Panov .30 .75
Davis Parley .30 .75
Mark Rooneem .20 .50
Chad Schockenmaier .20 .50
Steve Shrum .20 .50
Chad Starling .20 .50
Jordan Walker .20 .50
Digger MASCOT .08 .25

2000-01 Kamloops Blazers

MPLETE SET (24) 6.00 15.00
yan Cuthbert .20 .50
teve Belanger .40 1.00
yler Boldt .20 .50
osh Bonar .20 .50
at Brandreth .20 .50
rik Christensen .40 1.00
aul Elliott .20 .50
aron Gionet .40 1.00
able Gross .20 .50
Jonathan Hobson .20 .50
Nikita Korovkin .20 .50
Derek Krestanovich .20 .50
Kyle Ladobruk .20 .50
Jarret Lukin .20 .50
Shaone Morrisonn .40 1.00
Colton Orr 1.25 3.00
Konstantin Panov .20 .50
Davis Parley .40 1.00
Mark Rooneem .20 .50
Chad Shockenmaier .20 .50
Conlan Seder .20 .50
Tyler Sloan .20 .50
Scottie Upshall .75 2.00
Digger MASCOT .02 .10

2002-03 Kamloops Blazers

ed on previous Kamloops issues, it's possible this cklist is NOT complete.

e Coaches .10 .25
ascot .04 .10
evan Dubnyk 1.25 3.00
ul Brown .30 .75
ade Davis .30 .75
eid Jorgensen .30 .75
son Lloyd .30 .75

8 Moises Gutierrez .30 .75
9 Cam Cunning .30 .75
10 Grant Jacobsen .30 .75
11 Josh Morrow .30 .75
12 Davis Parley .60 1.50
13 Jonas Johansson .60 1.50
14 Nikita Korovkin .30 .75
15 Tyler Boldt .30 .75
16 Scottie Upshall .60 1.50
17 Erik Christensen .60 1.50
18 Aaron Gionet .30 .75
19 Kris Hogg .30 .75

2003-04 Kamloops Blazers

COMPLETE SET (24) 8.00 20.00
1 Geoff McIntosh .30 .75
2 Roman Tesliuk .30 .75
3 Kalvin Sagert .30 .75
4 Max Gordichuk .30 .75
5 Josh Garbutt .30 .75
6 Grant Jacobsen .30 .75
7 Jonas Johansson .60 1.50
8 Nathan Grochmal .30 .75
9 Cam Cunning .30 .75
10 Kris Hogg .30 .75
11 Kyle Sheen .30 .75
12 Brock Nixon .30 .75
13 Rick Kozak .30 .75
14 Paul Brown .40 1.00
15 Conlan Seder .30 .75
16 Codey Becker .30 .75
17 Ryan Bender .30 .75
18 Ray Macias .30 .75
19 Moises Gutierrez .30 .75
20 Devan Dubnyk 1.00 2.50
21 Jarret Lukin .30 .75
22 Reid Jorgensen .30 .75
23 Derek Werenka .30 .75
24 Checklist .04 .10

2004-05 Kamloops Blazers

We have confirmed only a handful of cards from this set. It was issued in 12 strips of three, and contains 36 cards.

1 Checklist
2 Bryan Kauk
3 Reid Jorgensen
4 Devan Dubnyk
5 Ray Macias
6 Adam Chorneyko

2005-06 Kamloops Blazers

COMPLETE SET (25) 6.00 15.00
1 Checklist .02 .10
2 Michael Maniago .30 .75
3 Roman Tesliuk .30 .75
4 Garrett Thiessen .30 .75
5 Keaton Ellerby .30 .75
6 Ryan White .40 1.00
7 Victor Bartley .30 .75
8 Ashton Rome .40 1.00
9 Janick Steinmann .30 .75
10 C.J. Stretch .30 .75
11 Travis Dunstall .30 .75
12 Scott Skrudland .30 .75
13 T.J. Mulock .30 .75
14 Brady Mason .30 .75
15 Brock Nixon .30 .75
16 Matt Kassian .30 .75
17 Kevin Hayman .30 .75
18 Terrance Delaronde .30 .75
19 Ryan Bender .30 .75
20 Ray Macias .30 .75
21 Moises Gutierrez .30 .75
22 Devan Dubnyk .60 1.50
23 Joel Eisenkirch .30 .75
24 Reid Jorgensen .30 .75
25 911 Digger MASCOT .02 .10

2006-07 Kamloops Blazers

COMPLETE SET (25) 10.00 18.00
1 Victor Bartley .30 .75
2 Ryan Bender .30 .75
3 Dustin Butler .40 1.00
4 Terrance Delaronde .30 .75
5 Brenden Dowd .30 .75
6 Travis Dunstall .30 .75
7 Keaton Ellerby .30 1.25
8 Dalyn Flette .40 1.00
9 Sasha Golin .30 .75
10 Mark Hall .30 .75
11 Reid Jorgensen .30 .75
12 Matt Kassian .30 .75
13 Kevin Kraus .30 .75
14 Raymond Macias .30 .75
15 Brady Mason .30 .75
16 Brock Nixon .30 .75
17 Juuso Puustinen .30 .75
18 Alex Rodgers .30 .75
19 Ivan Rohac .30 .75
20 Jordan Rowley .30 .75
21 Tyler Shattock .30 .75
22 C.J. Stretch .30 .75
23 Ryan White .30 .75
24 Kamloops Blazers CL .01 .05
25 Digger MASCOT .02 .10

2007-08 Kamloops Blazers

COMPLETE SET (25) 5.00 12.00
1 Kurt Torbohm .25 .60
2 Spencer Fraipont .25 .60
3 Ivan Rohac .25 .60
4 Mark Hall .25 .60
5 Brady Calla .25 .60
6 CJ Stretch .25 .60
7 Scott Wasden .25 .60
8 Kenton Dulle .25 .60
9 Tyler Shattock .25 .60
10 Juuso Puustinen .25 .60
11 Matt Wray .25 .60
12 Devon Kalinski .25 .60
13 Jimmy Bubnick .25 .60
14 Alex Rodgers .25 .60
15 Sasha Golin .25 .60
16 Jordan Rowley .25 .60
17 Darcy Huisman .25 .60
18 Nick Ross .25 .60
19 Mark Schneider .25 .60
20 James Priestner .25 .60
21 Justin Leclerc .25 .60
22 Mike Gauthier .25 .60
23 Shayne Wiebe .25 .60
24 Digger .15 .40
25 Kamloops Blazers Checklist .15 .40

2014-15 Kamloops Blazers

COMPLETE SET (25) 6.00 15.00
1 Quinn Benjafield .30 .75
2 Matthew Campese .30 .75
3 Nick Chyzowski .30 .75
4 Dawson Davidson .30 .75
5 Michael Fora .30 .75
6 Brady Gaudet .30 .75
7 Joel Hamilton .30 .75
8 Luke Harrison .30 .75
9 Connor Ingram .30 .75
10 Cole Kehler .30 .75
11 Jake Kryski .30 .75
12 Jermaine Loewen .30 .75
13 Patrik Maier .30 .75
14 Marc McNulty .30 .75
15 Logan McVeigh .30 .75
16 Matt Needham .30 .75
17 Cam Reagan .30 .75
18 Ryan Rehill .30 .75
19 Matt Revel .30 .75
20 Collin Shirley .30 .75
21 Deven Sideroff .30 .75
22 Cole Ully .30 .75
23 Travis Verveda .30 .75
24 Jesse Zaharichuk .30 .75
25 Header Card .30 .75

1990-91 Kansas City Blades

This 20-card standard-size set features posed, color player photos on a black card face. The pictures are bordered on three sides by a red design similar to a shadow border. Player information appears below the photo in the red border. The year and team name are printed at the upper left corner.

COMPLETE SET (20) 4.00 10.00
1 Claudio Scremin .20 .50
2 Jeff Odgers .30 .75
3 Wade Flaherty .30 .75
4 Rick Barkovich .20 .50
5 Ron Handy .20 .50
6 Kevin Sullivan .20 .50
7 Randy Exelby .30 .75
8 Darin Smith .20 .50
9 Stu Kulak .20 .50
10 Andrew Akervik .20 .50
11 Scott White .20 .50
12 Claude Julien .20 .50
13 Mike Hiltner .20 .50
14 Michael Colman .20 .50
15 Kurt Semandel .20 .50
16 Mike Kelfer .20 .50
17 Mark Karpen .20 .50
18 Lee Giffin .20 .50
19 Cam Plante .20 .50
20 Jim Latos .30 .75

1991-92 Kansas City Blades

This set features the Blades of the IHL. It is believed the set was sold by the team at its souvenir stands. The set is noteworthy as Kansas City won the Turner Cup that year. It also features an early card goaltender Arturs Irbe, who in 1991-92 was an IHL First Team All-Star. The checklist was provided by collector Jeff Barak.

COMPLETE SET (20) 4.80 12.00
1 Pat McLeod .20 .50
2 Rick Lessard .20 .50
3 Duane Joyce .20 .50
4 David Williams .20 .50
5 Arturs Irbe 1.25 3.00
6 Murray Garbutt .20 .50
7 Gary Emmons .20 .50
8 Jeff Madill .20 .50
9 Ron Handy .20 .50
10 Peter Lappin .20 .50
11 Mike Colman .20 .50
12 Ed Courtenay .20 .50
13 Mikhail Kravets .20 .50
14 Claudio Scremin .20 .50
15 Dale Craigwell .20 .50
16 Wade Flaherty .30 .75
17 Kevin Evans .20 .50
18 Larry DePalma .20 .50
19 Dean Kolstad .20 .50
20 Gord Frantti .20 .50

1992-93 Kansas City Blades

Little is known about this set beyond confirmation of the checklist and some recent sales. Any additional information should be forwarded to hockeymag@beckett.com.

COMPLETE SET (20) 4.00 10.00
1 Wade Flaherty .30 .75
2 David Williams .20 .50
3 Duane Joyce .20 .50
4 Jeff Sharples .20 .50
5 Victor Ignatjev .20 .50
6 Jeff McLean .20 .50
7 Brian Lawton .20 .50
8 Troy Frederick .20 .50
9 Jaroslav Otevrel .20 .50
10 Gary Emmons .20 .50
11 Dody Wood .20 .50
12 Ed Courtenay .20 .50
13 Mark Beaufait .20 .50
14 J.F. Quintin .20 .50
15 Dale Craigwell .20 .50
16 Mikhail Kravets .20 .50
17 John Weisbrod .20 .50
18 Mike Colman .20 .50
19 Claudio Scremin .20 .50
20 Dean Kolstad .20 .50

1993-94 Kansas City Blades

Little is known about this set beyond the confirmed checklist. Any additional information should be forwarded to hockeymag@beckett.com.

COMPLETE SET (20) 4.00 10.00
1 Duane Joyce .20 .50
2 Sean Gorman .20 .50
3 Victor Ignatjev .20 .50
4 Jeff McLean .20 .50
5 Kip Miller .30 .75
6 Jaroslav Otevrel .20 .50
7 David Bruce .20 .50
8 Gary Emmons .20 .50
9 Dody Wood .20 .50
10 Lee Leslie .20 .50
11 Alexander Cherbayev .20 .50
12 J.F. Quintin .20 .50
13 Ed Courtenay .20 .50
14 Andrei Nazarov .30 .75
15 Mikhail Kravets .20 .50
16 Mike Colman .20 .50
17 Vlastimil Kroupa .20 .50
18 Andrei Buschan .20 .50
19 Trevor Robins .20 .50
20 Wade Flaherty .30 .75

1994-95 Kansas City Blades

This set features the Blades of the IHL. Beyond the confirmed checklist, we don't have too many details to offer. Anyone up on this set is encouraged to contact us.

COMPLETE SET (20) 4.00 10.00
1 Duane Joyce .20 .50
2 Ken Hammond .20 .50
3 Michal Sykora .20 .50
4 Kevin Wortman .20 .50
5 Andrei Buschan .20 .50
6 Chris Tancill .20 .50
7 Ken Hodge .20 .50
8 David Bruce .20 .50
9 Jan Caloun .30 .75
10 Gary Emmons .20 .50
11 Dody Wood .20 .50
12 Lee Leslie .20 .50
13 Alexander Cherbayev .20 .50
14 J.F. Quintin .20 .50
15 Claudio Scremin .20 .50
16 Dean Grillo .20 .50
17 Andrei Nazarov .30 .75
18 Todd Holt .20 .50
19 Vlastimil Kroupa .20 .50
20 Trevor Robins .20 .50

1995-96 Kansas City Blades

Little is known about this set beyond the confirmed checklist. Additional information should be forwarded to hockeymag@beckett.com.

COMPLETE SET (25) 4.00 10.00
1 Larry Dyck .15 .40
2 Paul Dyck .15 .40
3 Jeff Batters .15 .40
4 David Bruce .15 .40
5 Jan Caloun .30 .75
6 Alexander Cherbayev .20 .50
7 Gary Emmons .15 .40
8 Dean Ewens .15 .40
9 Pat Ferschweiler .15 .40
10 Dean Grillo .15 .40
11 Ken Hammond .15 .40
12 Alexander Osadchy .15 .40
13 Jeff McLean .15 .40
14 Fredrik Nilsson .20 .50
15 Fredrik Oduya .15 .40
16 J.F. Quintin .15 .40
17 Geoff Sarjeant .20 .50
18 Claudio Scremin .15 .40
19 Chris Tancill .20 .50
20 Alexi Yegorov .20 .50
21 Viktor Kozlov .40 1.00
22 Sergei Bautin .15 .40
23 Vasily Tikhonov HCO .02 .10
24 Drew Remenda ACO .02 .10
25 Chilly MASCOT .02 .10

1996-97 Kansas City Blades

Little is known about this set beyond confirmation of the checklist. Additional information can be forwarded to hockeymag@beckett.com.

COMPLETE SET (25) 4.80 12.00
1 Ian Boyce .20 .50
2 David Bruce .30 .75
3 Jason Cirone .20 .50
4 Dale Craigwell .30 .75
5 Brent Cullaton .20 .50
6 Philippe DeRouville .30 .75
7 Larry Dyck .20 .50
8 Paul Dyck .20 .50
9 Gary Emmons .20 .50
10 Dean Ewen .20 .50
11 Bryan Fogarty .20 .50
12 Jason Herter .20 .50
13 Jim Kyte .20 .50
14 Jeff Madill .20 .50
15 Jeff McLean .20 .50
16 John Purves .30 .75
17 J.F. Quintin .20 .50
18 Normand Rochefort .20 .50
19 Claudio Scremin .20 .50
20 Brian Stacey .20 .50
21 Dean Sylvester .30 .75
22 Don Jackson HCO .02 .10
23 Lucien DeBlois ACO .20 .50
24 KC Blades .02 .10
25 PHPA Web Site .02 .10

1997-98 Kansas City Blades Magnets

These magnets were released as promotional giveaways over a series of five games.

COMPLETE SET (5) 4.00 10.00
1 Claudio Scremin .75 2.00
2 Gary Emmons .75 2.00
3 David Bruce .75 2.00
4 Jan Caloun .75 2.00
5 Dean Grillo .75 2.00

1998-99 Kansas City Blades

Little is known about this set beyond the checklist. Any additional information can be forwarded to hockeymag@beckett.com.

COMPLETE SET (30) 6.00 15.00
1 Title Card .02 .10
2 Brian Leitza .20 .50
3 Dan Ratushny .20 .50
4 Trevor Sherban .20 .50
5 Eric Rud .20 .50
6 Tuomas Gronman .20 .50
7 Eric Perrin .20 .50
8 Brendan Yarema .20 .50
9 Brian Bonin .20 .50
10 Pat Ferschweiler .20 .50
11 Dody Wood .40 1.00
12 David Ling .40 1.00
13 Rocky Weising .20 .50
14 Jean-Guy Trudel .30 .75
15 Vlastimil Kroupa .20 .50
16 Steven Low .20 .50
17 Ryan Mulhern .20 .50
18 Brent Bilodeau .20 .50
19 Grant Richison .20 .50
20 Dave Chyzowski .20 .50
21 David Vallieres .20 .50
22 Patrick Lalime .75 2.00
23 Jean Sebastien Aubin .75 2.00
24 Jason Cirone .20 .50
25 Paul MacLean CO .02 .10
26 Gary Emmons ACO .02 .10
27 John Doolan EQ .02 .10
28 Jeff Kreuser TR .02 .10
29 Scrapper Mascot .02 .10
30 Logo Card .02 .10

1999-00 Kansas City Blades

These two oversized cards are likely part of a larger set offered to fans at public autograph signing sessions. Information on others can be forwarded to hockeymag@beckett.com.

COMPLETE SET (2) .75 2.00
1 Gary Emmons .40 1.00
2 Wade Flaherty .40 1.00

1999-00 Kansas City Blades Supercuts

This 29-card set was sponsored by Supercuts and featured an action photo of each player with a small bio on back of each card. The cards are not numbered and are listed below in alphabetical order. It is believed that the cards were offered as a promotional giveaway.

COMPLETE SET 6.00 15.00
1 Tom Askey .40 1.00
2 Joe Blaznek .20 .50
3 Aris Brimanis .20 .50
4 Dave Chyzowski .20 .50
5 Jason Cirone .20 .50
6 Pat Ferschweiler .20 .50
7 Forrest Gore .20 .50
8 Sean Haggerty .20 .50
9 David Ling .40 1.00
10 Steve Lingren .20 .50
11 Tyler Moss .40 1.00
12 Nick Naumenko .20 .50
13 Eric Perrin .20 .50
14 Michal Pivonka .40 1.00
15 Bruce Racine .40 1.00
16 Grant Richison .20 .50
17 Jon Rohloff .20 .50
18 Ray Schultz .20 .50
19 David Valliers .20 .50
20 Jan Vodrazka .20 .50
21 Dody Wood .40 1.00
22 Brendan Yarema .20 .50
23 Scrapper MASCOT .08 .25
24 Jeff Kreuser TR .08 .25
25 John Doolan MGR .08 .25
26 Gary Emmons CO .08 .25
27 Paul MacLean HCO .08 .25
28 PHPA Logo .01
20 Supercuts Coupon .01

2000-01 Kansas City Blades

This set features the Blades of the IHL. The set was issued as a promotional giveaway early in the season and was sponsored by Dick's Sporting Goods.

COMPLETE SET (27) 6.00 15.00
1 Ryan Bonni .30 .75
2 Jan Vodrazka .20 .50
3 Bryan Allen .30 .75
4 Zenith Komarniski .20 .50
5 Sean Tallaire .20 .50
6 Ryan Ready .20 .50
7 Regan Darby .20 .50
8 Dody Wood .30 .75
9 Harold Druken .30 .75
10 Darrell Hay .20 .50
11 Vadim Sharifijanov .30 .75
12 Steve Lingren .20 .50
13 Josh Holden .40 1.00
14 Mike Brown .30 .75
15 Jeff Scissons .20 .50
16 Jarkko Ruutu .30 .75
17 Pat Kavanagh .20 .50
18 Brad Leeb .20 .50
19 Bryan Helmer .20 .50
20 Artem Chubarov .30 .50
21 Corey Schwab .30 .75
22 Alfie Michaud .30 .75
23 Stan Smyl CO .20 .50
24 Barry Smith CO .20 .50
25 Ryno SPONSOR .02 .10
26 Dick's SPONSOR .02 .10
27 PHPA SPONSOR .02 .10

1998-99 Kelowna Rockets

This 28-card set features the Kelowna Rockets of the Western Hockey League. Among the players featured are 2001 first-round pick Kiel McLeod and San Jose Sharks defender Scott Hannan.

COMPLETE SET (28) 6.00 15.00
1 Ryan Cuthbert .20 .50
2 Jan Dusanek .20 .50
3 B.J. Fehr .20 .50
4 Vernon Fiddler .30 .75
5 Mitch Fritz .20 .50
6 Carsen Germyn .20 .50
7 Scott Hannan .40 1.00
8 Bruce Harrison .20 .50
9 Trevor Hitchings .20 .50
10 J.J. Hunter .20 .50
11 Justin Jack .20 .50
12 Clint Keichinger .20 .50
13 Kevin Korol .20 .50
14 Corey Koski .20 .50
15 Quintin Laing .20 .50
16 Lindsey Materi .20 .50
17 Rory McDade .20 .50
18 Brett McLean .30 .75
19 Gavin McLeod .20 .50
20 Kiel Mcleod .40 1.00
21 Lubomir Pistek .20 .50
22 Robby Sandrock .20 .50
23 David Selthun .20 .50
24 Joe Suderman .20 .50
25 Kevin Swanson .20 .50
26 Ryan Wade .20 .50
27 Nolan Yonkman .30 .75
28 Rocky Racoon MASCOT .02 .10

2000-01 Kelowna Rockets

This set features the Rockets of the WHL. It was originally issued in the form of two-card perforated strips as a promotional giveaway. The cards are unnumbered, and so are listed alphabetically.

COMPLETE SET (22) 6.00 15.00
1 Kiel McLeod .40 1.00
2 Rory McDade .30 .75
3 Tomas Oravec .30 .75
4 Carsen Germyn .40 1.00
5 Chris Di Ubaldo .30 .75
6 Ryan Cuthbert .30 .75
7 Randall Gelech .30 .75
8 Blaine Depper .30 .75
9 Gavin McLeod .30 .75
10 Bart Rushmer .30 .75
11 Tyler Mosienko .30 .75
12 Josh Gorges .30 .75
13 Jason Stone .30 .75
14 Brett Palin .30 .75
15 Richie Regehr .40 1.00
16 David Selthun .30 .75
17 Seth Leonard .30 .75
18 Jan Fadrny .30 .75
19 Joe Suderman .30 .75
20 Kevin Swanson .30 .75
21 Rocky Raccoon MASCOT .02 .10
22 Marc Habscheid CO .10 .25
23 Paul Hurd .20 .50
24 Cam Paddock .20 .50
25 Richard Kelly .20 .50
26 Travis Moen .40 1.00

2001-02 Kelowna Rockets

The cards were issued as a promotional giveaway. As they are unnumbered, they are listed in alphabetical order.

COMPLETE SET (28) 8.00 20.00
1 Shane Bendera .40 1.00
2 Jeff Coulter .30 .75
3 Ryan Cuthbert .30 .75
4 Jesse Ferguson .30 .75
5 Randall Gelech .30 .75
6 Josh Gorges .40 1.00
7 Richard Kelly .30 .75
8 Chuck Kobasew 1.25 3.00
9 Seth Leonard .30 .75
10 Josh Lepp .30 .75
11 Nick Marach .30 .75
12 Ryan Mayko .30 .75
13 Kiel McLeod .40 1.00
14 Travis Moen .40 1.00
15 Tyler Mosienko .30 .75
16 Tomas Oravec .30 .75
17 Cam Paddock .30 .75
18 Brett Palin .30 .75
19 Bart Rushmer .30 .75
20 Tomas Slovak .30 .75
21 Stephen Sunderman .30 .75
22 Kevin Young .30 .75
23 Marc Habscheid HCO .08 .20
24 Larry Keating ACO .04 .10
25 Jeff Truitt ACO .04 .10
26 Scott Hoyer TR .04 .10
27 Regan Bartel PA .04 .10
28 Mascot .04 .10

2002-03 Kelowna Rockets

COMPLETE SET (28) 6.00 15.00
1 Josh Lepp .30 .75
2 Cam Paddock .20 .50
3 Kiel McLood .40 1.00
4 Joel Henituik .20 .50
5 Brett Palin .20 .50
6 Richard Kelly .20 .50
7 Stephen Sunderman .20 .50
8 Tyler Spurgeon .20 .50
9 Joni Lindolf .20 .50
10 Darren Deschamps .20 .50
11 Shea Weber 1.50 4.00
12 Randall Gelech .20 .50
13 David Jacobson .20 .50
14 Jesse Schultz .20 .50
15 Blake Comeau .20 .50
16 Ryan Mayko .20 .50
17 Mike Card .20 .50
18 Josh Gorges .40 1.00
19 Tomas Slovak .30 .75
20 Kelly Guard .40 1.00
21 Troy Bodie .20 .50
22 Ryan Cuthbert .20 .50
23 Tyler Mosienko .20 .50
24 Mark Olafson .20 .50
25 Nick Tarnasky .20 .50
26 Marc Habscheid HCO .20 .50
27 Jeff Truitt ACO .10 .25
28 Mascot .04 .10

2003 Kelowna Rockets Memorial Cup

Cards are unnumbered and listed below in alphabetical order.

COMPLETE SET (20) 6.00 15.00
1 Troy Brodie .30 .75
2 Mike Card .30 .75
3 Blake Comeau .30 .75
4 Ryan Cuthbert .30 .75
5 Simon Ferguson .30 .75
6 Randall Gelech .30 .75
7 Josh Gorges .40 1.00
8 Kelly Guard .30 1.50
9 Duncan Keith 1.00 2.50
10 Josh Lepp .40 1.00
11 Joni Lindolf .30 .75
12 Kiel McLeod .40 1.00
13 Tyler Mosienko .30 .75
14 Mark Olafson .30 .75
15 Cam Paddock .30 .75
16 Brett Palin .30 .75
17 Jesse Schultz .40 1.00
18 Tomas Slovak .40 1.00
19 Tyler Spurgeon .30 .75
20 Shea Weber 1.00 2.50

2003-04 Kelowna Rockets

COMPLETE SET (28) 10.00 25.00
1 Michael Blanar .40 1.00
2 Troy Bodie .40 1.00
3 Mike Card .40 1.00
4 Blake Comeau .75 2.00
5 Kyle Cumiskey .40 1.00
6 Darren Deschamps .40 1.00
7 Simon Ferguson .40 1.00
8 Randall Gelech .40 1.00
9 Josh Gorges .75 2.00
10 Kelly Guard .75 2.00
11 Brent Howarth .40 1.00
12 Justin Keller .40 1.00
13 Joni Lindlof .40 1.00
14 Tyler Mosienko .40 1.00
15 Mark Olafson .40 1.00
16 Cam Paddock .40 1.00
17 Brett Palin .40 1.00
18 Chris Ray .40 1.00
19 Kevin Reinholt .40 1.00
20 Tyler Spurgeon .40 1.00
21 Nolan Waker .40 1.00
22 Shea Weber 1.25 3.00
23 Derek Yeomans .40 1.00
24 Marc Habscheid CO .04 .10
25 Jeff Truitt ACO .04 .10
26 Regan Bartel ANN .04 .10
27 Scott Hoyer TR .04 .10
28 Rocky Raccoon MASCOT .04 .10

2004-05 Kelowna Rockets

COMPLETE SET (28) 8.00 20.00
1 Troy Bodie .30 .75
2 Shea Weber 1.25 3.00
3 Justin Keller .30 .75
4 Craig Cuthbert .30 .75
5 Darren Deschamps .30 .75
6 Kristofer Westblom .30 .75
7 Brett Palin .30 .75
8 Kyle Cumiskey .30 .75
9 Chris Ray .30 .75
10 Lauris Darzins .30 .75
11 Rockey Raccoon .04 .10
12 Jeff Truitt .30 .75
13 Colin Joe .30 .75
14 Tyler Mosienko .30 .75
15 Blake Comeau .50 1.25
16 Tyler Spurgeon .30 .75
17 Derek Yeomans .30 .75
18 Ryan Huska .30 .75
19 Scott Hoyer .30 .75
20 Regan Bartel .30 .75
21 Gary Sylvester .30 .75
22 Troy Ofukany .30 .75
23 Kirt Hill .30 .75
24 Brent Howarth .30 .75
25 Clayton Bauer .30 .75
26 Michal Blanar .30 .75
27 Mike Card .30 .75
28 Kevin Reinholt .30 .75

2005-06 Kelowna Rockets

COMPLETE SET (28) 8.00 20.00
1 Cody Almond .30 .75
2 Josiah Anderson .30 .75
3 Clayton Bauer .30 .75
4 Troy Bodie .30 .75
5 Mike Card .30 .75
6 Blake Comeau .60 1.50
7 Liam Couture .30 .75
8 Kyle Cumiskey .30 .75
9 Craig Cuthbert .30 .75
10 Lauris Darzins .30 .75
11 Tysen Dowzak .30 .75
12 Alexander Edler .30 .75
13 Kirt Hill .30 .75
14 Brent Howarth .30 .75
15 Colin Joe .30 .75
16 Justin Keller .30 .75
17 Colin Long .30 .75
18 Myles MacRae .30 .75
19 Troy Ofukany .30 .75
20 Chris Ray .30 .75
21 Kevin Reinholt .30 .75
22 Rob Roteliuk .30 .75
23 Luke Schenn .30 .75
24 Tyler Spurgeon .30 .75
25 Kristofer Westblom .30 .75
26 Derek Yeomans .30 .75
27 Jeff Truitt HC .02 .10
28 Rocky Raccoon MASCOT .02 .10

2014-15 Kelowna Rockets

COMPLETE SET (32) 8.00 20.00
1 Header Card CL .30 .75
2 Riley Stadel .30 .75
3 Madison Bowey .30 .75
4 Mitch Wheaton .30 .75
5 Lucas Johansen .30 .75
6 Cole Martin .30 .75
7 Tanner Wishnowski .30 .75
8 Nick Merkley .30 .75
9 Tyrell Goulbourne .30 .75
10 Rourke Chartier .30 .75
11 Tomas Soustal .30 .75
12 Rodney Southam .30 .75
13 Tate Coughlin .30 .75
14 Dillon Dube .30 .75
15 Gage Quinney .30 .75
16 Devante Stephens .30 .75
17 Chance Braid .30 .75
18 Justin Kirkland .30 .75
19 Tyson Baillie .50 1.25
20 Cole Linaker .30 .75
21 Josh Morrissey .30 .75
22 Joe Gatenby .30 .75
23 Leon Draisaitl 2.00 5.00
24 Jackson Whistle .30 .75
25 Michael Herringer .30 .75
26 Jake Morrissey .30 .75
27 Dan Lambert CO .30 .75
28 Kim Gellert Skills Ins. .30 .75
29 Travis Crickard Goalie CO .30 .75
30 Kris Mallette Asst. CO .30 .75
31 Scott Hoyer Trainer .30 .75
32 Rocky MASCOT .30 .75

1984-85 Kelowna Wings

This 56-card safety standard-size set was sponsored by A and W, Pizza Patio, CKIQ (a radio station), and the Kelowna Wings. The cards feature black-and-white posed and action player photos. The words "Kelowna Wings 1984-85" are at the top of card numbers 2-22, while the words "Junior Hockey Grads" appear at the top of card numbers 1 and 23-56. The player's name, position, and the card number are at the bottom. The cards are numbered on the front in the lower right corner.

COMPLETE SET (56) 32.00 80.00
1 Checklist .20 .50
2 Darcy Wakaluk .60 1.50
3 Stacey Nickel .20 .50
4 Jeff Sharples .30 .75
5 Greg Zuk .20 .50
6 Daryn Sivertson .20 .50
7 Randy Cameron .20 .50
8 Mark Fioretti .20 .50
9 Ron Viglasi .20 .50
10 Ian Herbers .20 .50
11 Mike Wegleitner .20 .50
12 Terry Zaporzan .20 .50
13 Dwaine Hutton .20 .50
14 Rod Williams .20 .50
15 Jeff Rohlicek .20 .50
16 Brent Gilchrist .60 1.50
17 Rocky Dundas .20 .50
18 Grant Delcourt .20 .50
19 Cam Laroruk .20 .50
20 Tony Horacek .20 .50
21 Mark Wingerter .20 .50
22 Mick Vukota .30 .75
23 Danny Gare .60 1.50
24 Rich Sutter .40 1.00
25 Alfie Turcotte .20 .50
26 Bryan Trottier 4.00 10.00
27 Bill Derlago .40 1.00
28 Stan Smyl .75 2.00
29 Brent Sutter .75 2.00
30 Mel Bridgman .40 1.00
31 Paul Cyr .30 .75
32 Gary Lupul .20 .50
33 Ray Neufeld .30 .75
34 Brian Propp .75 2.00
35 Bob Nystrom .75 2.00
36 Ryan Walter .40 1.00
37 Russ Courtnall .75 2.00
38 Larry Playfair .20 .50
39 Ron Delorme .20 .50
40 Ron Sutter .40 1.00
41 Bobby Clarke 4.00 10.00
42 Bob Bourne .40 1.00
43 Cam Neely 15.00 40.00
44 Murray Craven .40 1.00
45 Clark Gillies 1.25 3.00
46 Ron Flockhart .40 1.00
47 Harold Snepsts 1.25 3.00
48 Duane Sutter .40 1.00
49 Garth Butcher .40 1.00
50 Bill Hajt .20 .50
51 Jim Benning .20 .50
52 Ray Allison .20 .50
53 Ken Wregget .75 2.00
54 Phil Russell .30 .75
55 Brad McCrimmon .60 1.50
56 Dan Hodgson .20 .50

1996-97 Kentucky Thoroughblades

This set was sold at the Kentucky team store, and featured an SRP of $3.00. Set features color action photos on the front, with statistics and biographical information on the back.

COMPLETE SET (26) 5.00 12.00
1 Ken Belanger .30 .75
2 Alexandre Boikov .20 .50
3 Jan Caloun .30 .75
4 Denis Chervyakov .20 .50
5 Jarrett Deuling .20 .50
6 Iain Fraser .20 .50
7 Dean Grillo .20 .50
8 Steve Guolla .30 .75
9 Sean Haggerty .20 .50
10 Jason Holland .20 .50
11 Lance Leslie .20 .50
12 Chris Lipuma .20 .50
13 Pat Mikesch .20 .50
14 Fredrik Oduya .20 .50
15 Jamie Ram .30 .75
16 Chris Tancill .30 .75
17 Jason Strudwick .30 .75
18 Steve Webb .30 .75
19 Jason Widmer .20 .50
20 Jim Wiley .20 .50
21 Alexei Yegorov .30 .75
NNO Ad Card-In Your Face .02 .10
NNO Ad Card-PHPA .02 .10
NNO Lucky the Mascot .02 .10
NNO Rupp Arena .20 .50
NNO Team Photo .08 .25

1997-98 Kentucky Thoroughblades

Little is known about this set beyond the confirmed checklist. Additional information can be forwarded to hockeymag@beckett.com.

COMPLETE SET (25) 8.00 20.00
1 Team Photo .10 .25
2 Peter Allen .20 .50
3 Niklas Andersson .20 .50
4 Alexandre Boikov .20 .50
5 Zdeno Chara 1.25 3.00
6 Steve Guolla .25 .60
7 Sean Haggerty .20 .50
8 Jason Holland .20 .50
9 Alexander Korolyuk .30 .75
10 Evgeni Nabokov 4.00 10.00
11 Fredrik Oduya .20 .50
12 Chad Penney .20 .50
13 Jamie Ram .30 .75
14 Peter Roed .20 .50
15 Jason Strudwick .20 .50
16 Tony Tuzzolino .30 .75
17 Steve Webb .30 .75
18 Jason Widmer .20 .50
19 Brendan Yarema .20 .50
20 Alexei Yegorov .25 .60
21 Andrei Zyuzin .30 .75
22 Jim Wiley HCO .10 .25
23 Lucky Mascot .02 .10
24 PHPA Web Site .02 .10
25 AHL Web Site .02 .10

1998-99 Kentucky Thoroughblades

This 25-card set was released after the regular season had ended. It was produced by Split Second. All cards are unnumbered, and are listed in alphabetical order.

COMPLETE SET (25) 8.00 20.00
1 Peter Allen .15 .40
2 Eric Boulton .75 2.00
3 Dan Boyle .30 .75
4 Matt Bradley .20 .50
5 Mike Craig .15 .40
6 Jarrett Deuling .15 .40
7 Curtis Doell .15 .40
8 Dave Duerden .15 .40
9 Sean Gauthier .15 .40
10 Christian Gosselin .15 .40
11 Steve Guolla .20 .50
12 Harold Hersh .20 .50
13 Alexander Korolyuk .20 .50
14 Filip Kuba .20 .50
15 Steve Lingren .15 .40
16 Andy MacIntyre .10 .30
17 Evgeni Nabokov 4.00 10.00
Nickname John on card front
18 Jarrod Skalde .30 .75
19 Mark Smith .60 1.50
20 Herbert Vasiljevs .15 .40
21 Eric Veilleux .15 .40
22 Andrei Zyuzin .30 .75
23 Roy Sommer HCO .10 .25
24 Lucky Mascot .02 .10
25 AHL Web Site .02 .10

1999-00 Kentucky Thoroughblades

This set features the Thoroughblades of the AHL. The slightly oversized set was produced by the team and sold at home games.

COMPLETE SET (25) 8.00 20.00
1 Kentucky Thoroughblades .08 .25
2 Coaching Staff .08 .25
3 Chris Armstrong .20 .50
4 Matt Bradley .20 .50
5 Garrett Burnett .20 .50
6 Adam Colagiacomo .30 .75
7 Jon Coleman .20 .50
8 Larry Courville .20 .50
9 Mike Craig .20 .50
10 Jarrett Deuling .20 .50
11 Doug Friedman .20 .50
12 Christian Gosselin .20 .50
13 Scott Hannan .30 .75
14 Johan Hedberg 2.00 5.00
15 Shawn Heins .30 .75
16 Robert Jindrich .30 .75
17 Miikka Kiprusoff 2.00 5.00
18 Eric Landry .20 .50
19 Chris Lipsett .20 .50
20 Andy Lundbohm .20 .50
21 Robert Mulick .20 .50
22 Adam Nittel .40 1.00
23 Peter Roed .20 .50
24 Mark Smith .30 .75
25 Lucky MASCOT .08 .25

2000-01 Kentucky Thoroughblades

This set features the Thoroughblades of the AHL. It is believed that the set was sold by the team, but this is not confirmed. It's also believed that the final five cards were available as redemptions at an area business, which accounts for their scarcity. Any additional information can be forwarded to hockeymag@beckett.com.

COMPLETE SET (30) 30.00 80.00
1 Greg Andrusak .14 .35
2 Steve Bancroft .14 .40
3 Zoltan Batovsky .14 .40
4 Matt Bradley .14 .40
5 Jonathan Cheechoo 4.00 10.00
6 Adam Colagiacomo .20 .50
7 Larry Courville .20 .50
8 Rob Davison .20 .50
9 Jarrett Deuling .14 .35
10 Christian Gosselin .14 .40
11 Robert Jindrich .20 .50
12 Miikka Kiprusoff 4.00 10.00
13 Ryan Kraft .14 .50
14 Eric Laplante .14 .40
15 Chris Lipsett .14 .35
16 Andy Lundbohm .14 .35
17 Dave MacIsaac .14 .35
18 Jim Montgomery .20 .50
19 Robert Mulick .14 .40
20 Adam Nittel .40 1.00
21 Mikael Samuelsson .20 .50
22 Mark Smith .30 .75
23 Vesa Toskala 2.00 5.00
24 Miroslav Zalesak .10 .25
25 Roy Sommer CO .10 .25
Nick Fotiu CO
L1 Kentucky Thoroughblades .40 1.00
P1 Adam Nittel 1.00 2.50
P2 Jonathan Cheechoo 10.00 25.00
SP1 Ryan Kraft .60 2.00
SP2 Evgeni Nabokov 10.00 25.00

1981-82 Kingston Canadians

This 25-card set measures approximately 2 5/8" by 4" and features posed, color player photos on thin white card stock. The player's name, position, and the team logo are printed in black below the picture.

COMPLETE SET (25) 12.00 30.00
1 Canadians Logo .20 .50
2 Scott MacLellan .20 .50
3 Dave Courtemanche .20 .50
4 Mark Reade .20 .50
5 Shawn Babcock .20 .50
6 Phil Bourque .40 1.00
7 Ian MacInnis .20 .50
8 Neil Trineer .20 .50
9 Syl Grandmaitre .20 .50
10 Carmine Vani .30 .75
11 Chuck Brimmer .20 .50
12 Mike Linseman .20 .50
13 Steve Seguin .20 .50
14 Dan Wood .20 .50
15 Kirk Muller 6.00 15.00
16 Jim Aldred .20 .50
17 Rick Wilson .60 1.50
18 Mike Siltala .20 .50
19 Howie Scruton .20 .50
20 Mike Stothers .40 1.00
21 Dennis Smith .20 .50
22 Steve Richey .20 .50
23 Mike Moffat .75 2.00
24 Jim Morrison CO/MG .20 .50
25 Randy Plumb .20 .50

1982-83 Kingston Canadians

This 27-card set measures approximately 2 5/8" by 4 1/8" and features posed action, color player photos with white borders on thin card stock. The player's name, position, and year of issue appear below the picture between the team logo and the Kingston Police Force insignia.

COMPLETE SET (27) 6.00 15.00
1 Jim Morrison MG .08 .25
2 Dennis Smith .30 .75
3 Curtis Collin .30 .75
4 Joel Brown .30 .75
5 Ron Handy .30 .75
6 Carmine Vani .30 .75
7 Al Andrews .40 1.00
8 Mike Siltala .30 .75
9 Syl Grandmaitre .30 .75
10 Steve Seguin .30 .75
11 Brian Dobbin .40 1.00
12 Mark Reade .30 .75
13 John Kemp .40 1.00
14 Dan Mahon .30 .75
15 Keith Knight .30 .75
16 Ron Sanko .30 .75
17 John Landry .30 .75
18 Chris Brant .30 .75
19 Dave Simurda .30 .75
20 Mike Lafoy .30 .75
21 Scott MacLellan .30 .75
22 Brad Walcot .30 .75
23 Steve Richey .30 .75
24 Rod Graham CO .08 .25
25 Ben Levesque .30 .75
26 Canadians Logo .08 .25
27 International Hockey .20 .50
Hall of Fame

1983-84 Kingston Canadians

This 30-card set measures slightly larger than standard at 2 5/8" by 3 5/8" and features posed color player photos with white borders on thin card stock. The player's name, position, and year appears below the picture between the Canadians logo and the Kingston Police Force insignia.

COMPLETE SET (30) 6.00 15.00
1 Kingston Police Crest .08 .25
2 Dennis Smith .20 .50
3 Ben Levesque .20 .50
4 Const. Arie Moraal .08 .25
5 Tom Allen .20 .50
6 Mike Plesh .20 .50
7 Roger Belanger .20 .50
8 Jeff Chychrun .40 1.00
9 Mike King .20 .50
10 Scott Metcalfe .30 .75
11 David Lundmark .20 .50
12 Tim Salmon .20 .50
13 Ted Linesman .20 .50
14 Chris Clifford .30 .75
15 Todd Elik .40 1.00
16 Kevin Conway .20 .50
17 Barry Burkholder .20 .50
18 Joel Brown .20 .50
19 Steve King .20 .50
20 Craig Kales .20 .50
21 John Humphries TR .08 .25
22 David James .20 .50
23 Dave Simurda .20 .50
24 Allen Bishop .20 .50
25 Jeff Hogg .30 .75
26 Rick Cornacchia CO .30 .75
27 Ken Slater .08 .25
28 Bill Dextater .08 .25
29 Canadians Crest .08 .25
30 IHHOF logo .08 .25

1984-85 Kingston Canadians

This 30-card features the Canadians of the OHL. It measures 2 5/8" by 3 5/8" and features color, posed action player photos with white borders. The player's name, position, and year appear at the bottom.

COMPLETE SET (30) 6.00 15.00
1 Kingston Police Force .08 .25
2 Rick Cornacchia CO .20 .50
3 Const. Arie Moraal .08 .25
4 Ken Slater/DPP .08 .25
5 Kingston Crest .08 .25
6 Scott Metcalfe .30 .75
7 Chris Clifford .30 .75
8 Todd Elik .30 .75
9 Len Spratt .30 .75
10 Mike Plesh .20 .50
11 Marc Lyons .20 .50
12 Barry Burkholder .20 .50
13 Rick Fera .20 .50
14 David Hoover .20 .50
15 Andy Rivers .20 .50
16 Marc Laforge .30 .75
17 Peter Viscovich .20 .50
18 Jeff Chychrun .30 .75
19 Wayne Erskine .20 .50
20 Todd Clarke .20 .50
21 Darren Wright .20 .50
22 Tony Rocca .20 .50
23 Brian Verbeek .20 .50
24 Herb Raglan .30 .75
25 Daril Holmes .20 .50
26 Len Coyle TR .08 .25
27 Ted Linesman .20 .50
28 IHHOF logo .08 .25
29 Troy MacNevin .20 .50
30 Peter Campbell TR .08 .25

1985-86 Kingston Canadians

This 30-card measures approximately 2 5/8" by 3 5/8" and features color, posed action player photos with white borders. The player's name and position appear at the bottom.

COMPLETE SET (30) 5.00 12.00
1 Kingston Police Crest .08 .25
2 Dale Sandles ACO .08 .25
3 Const. Arie Moraal .08 .25
4 Fred O'Donnell GM/CO .08 .25
5 Kingston Crest .08 .25
6 Scott Metcalfe .20 .50
7 Chris Clifford .30 .75
8 Steve Seftel .20 .50
9 Andy Pearson .20 .50
10 Jeff Cornelius .20 .50
11 Marc Lyons .20 .50
12 Barry Burkholder .20 .50
13 Bryan Fogarty .30 .75
14 Jeff Sirkka .20 .50
15 Scott Pearson .30 .75
16 Marc Laforge .20 .50
17 Peter Viscovich .20 .50
18 Jeff Chychrun UER .30 .75
Name misspelled Chycren
19 Wayne Erskine .20 .50
20 Todd Clarke .20 .50
21 Darren Wright .20 .50
22 Mike Maurice .20 .50
23 Brian Verbeek .20 .50
24 Mike Fiset .20 .50
25 Daril Holmes .20 .50
26 Len Coyle TR .08 .25
27 Ted Linesman .20 .50
28 IHHOF logo .08 .25
29 Troy MacNevin .20 .50
30 Peter Campbell TR .08 .25

1986-87 Kingston Canadians

This 30-card set measures approximately 2 5/8" by 3 5/8" and features color, posed player portraits with blue studio backgrounds set on a white card face. The player's name, position, and year appear at the bottom.

COMPLETE SET (30) 4.00 10.00
1 Kingston Crest .08 .25
2 Fred O'Donnell GM/CO .02 .10
3 Arie Moraal COP .02 .10
4 Dale Sandles CO .02 .10
5 Kingston Police Crest .02 .10
6 Brian Tessier .30 .75
7 Franco Giammarco .30 .75
8 Peter Liptrott .20 .50
9 Chris Clifford .30 .75
10 Scott Metcalfe .20 .50
11 Scott Pearson .30 .75
12 Bryan Fogarty .30 .75
13 Daril Holmes .20 .50
14 Andy Rivers .20 .50
15 Troy MacNevin .20 .50
16 Marc Laforge .20 .50
17 Wayne Erskine .20 .50
18 Peter Viskovich .20 .50
19 Mike Maurice .20 .50
20 Steve Seftel .20 .50
21 Chad Badaway .20 .50
22 Marc Lyons .20 .50
23 Jeff Sirkka .20 .50
24 Mike Fiset .20 .50
25 John Battice .20 .50
26 Len Coyle TR .02 .10
27 Sloan Torti .20 .50
28 Alain Laforge .20 .50
29 Ted Linesman .20 .50
30 Peter Campbell TR .02 .10

1987-88 Kingston Canadians

This 30-card P.L.A.Y. (Police, Laws and Youth) set measures approximately 2 3/4" by 3 5/8" and features color player portraits with blue studio backgrounds. The fronts are accented by white borders.

COMPLETE SET (30) 4.80 12.00
1 Arie Moraal COP .02 .10
2 Gord Wood GM .02 .10
3 Kingston Police Crest .08 .25
4 Jacques Tremblay CO .08 .25
5 Rhonda Sheridan PR .02 .10
6 Jeff Wilson .30 .75
7 Franco Giammarco .30 .75
8 Peter Liptrott .20 .50
9 David Weiss .30 .75
10 Joel Morin .20 .50
11 Mark Turner .20 .50
12 Jeff Sirkka .20 .50
13 James Henckle .20 .50
14 Mike Bodnarchuk .20 .50
15 Mike Cavanaugh .20 .50
16 Darcy Cahill .20 .50
17 Kevin Falesy .20 .50
18 Dean Pella .20 .50
19 Brad Gratton .20 .50
20 Steve Seftel .20 .50
21 Bryan Fogarty .20 .50
22 Scott Pearson .20 .50
23 Tyler Pella .20 .50
24 Mike Fiset .20 .50
25 John Battice .20 .50
26 Len Coyle TR .02 .10
27 Geoff Schneider .20 .50
28 Chris Lukey .20 .50
29 Trevor Smith .20 .50
30 Peter Campbell TR .02 .10

1993-94 Kingston Frontenacs

Printed by Slapshot Images Ltd., this standard size 25-card set features the 1993-94 Kingston Frontenacs. On a team color-coded background with black stripes, the fronts feature color action player photos with thin black borders. The team name is printed diagonally in the upper left corner of the photo, while the player's name and number appear in a yellow bar in the bottom edge of the photo.

COMPLETE SET (25) 4.00 10.00
1 Greg Lovell .15 .40
2 Marc Lamothe .15 .40
3 Tyler Moss .20 .50
4 Marc Moro .15 .40
5 Trevor Doyle .15 .40
6 Jeff Dacosta .15 .40
7 Gord Walsh .15 .40
8 Brian Scott .15 .40
9 Jason Disher .15 .40
10 Alexander Zhurik .15 .40
11 Ken Boone .15 .40
12 Cail MacLean .15 .40
13 Bill Maranduik .15 .40
14 Martin Sychra .15 .40
15 Duncan Fader .15 .40
16 David Ling .30 .75
17 Chad Kilger .30 .75
18 Greg Kraemer .15 .40
19 Trent Cull .15 .40
20 Steve Parson .15 .40
21 Craig Rivet .15 .40
22 Keli Corpse .15 .40
23 Brett Lindros .30 .75
24 David Allison CO .02 .10
Michae
NNO Slapshot Ad Card .02 .10

1998-99 Kingston Frontenacs

The set features the Frontenacs of the OHL. Sponsored by the Community Sport and Activity News, this team-issued set features color action photos on the front of each card with a headshot and stats of each player on the back. The cards are unnumbered, so they are listed alphabetically.

COMPLETE SET (25) 4.80 12.00
1 Eric Braff .20 .50
2 Brett Clouthier .20 .50
3 Curtis Cruickshank .20 .50
4 Matt Elich .30 .75
5 Aaron Fransen .20 .50
6 Sean Griffin .20 .50
7 Kevin Grimes .20 .50
8 Andrew Ianiero .20 .50
9 Chad Lynch .20 .50
10 D.J. Maracle .20 .50
11 Larry Mavety HCO .08 .25
12 Morgan McCormick .20 .50
13 Walker McDonald .20 .50
14 Matt Price .20 .50
15 Mike Oliveira .20 .50
16 Brett Ormond .20 .50
17 Ryan Rivard .20 .50
18 Jonathan Schill .20 .50
19 Colin Scotland .20 .50
20 Nathan Tennant .20 .50
21 Darryl Thomson .20 .50
22 Ian Turner .20 .50
23 Jamie Young .20 .50
24 Mike Zigomanis .40 1.00
25 Checklist .02 .10

1999-00 Kingston Frontenacs

This set features the Frontenacs of the OHL. The slightly oversized cards were produced by the team and sold at home games. The set is noteworthy for an early appearance of goalie Andrew Raycroft and forwards Cory Stillman and Mike Zigomanis.

COMPLETE SET (23) 6.00 15.00
1 Checklist .02 .10
2 Sean Avery .60 1.50
3 Eric Braff .20 .50
4 Brett Clouthier .30 .75
5 Chris Cook .20 .50
6 Sean Griffin .20 .50
7 Brad Horan .20 .50
8 Andrew Ianiero .20 .50
9 Matt Junkins .20 .50
10 Darryl Knight .20 .50
11 Travis Lisabeth .20 .50
12 Doug MacIver .20 .50
13 Shaun Peet .20 .50
14 Jason Polera .20 .50
15 Andrew Raycroft 1.00 2.50
16 Johnathan Schill .20 .50
17 J-F Seguin .20 .50
18 Tomas Skvaridlo .20 .50
19 Mike Smith .20 .50
20 Cory Stillman .40 1.00
21 Nathan Tennant .30 .75
22 Darryl Thomson .20 .50
23 Michael Zigomanis .40 1.00

2000-01 Kingston Frontenacs

This set features the Frontenacs of the OHL. The set was produced by the team and sold at its souvenir stands. The cards are unnumbered, and so are listed below in alphabetical order.

COMPLETE SET (23) 4.80 10.00
1 Eric Braff .15 .40
2 Derek Campbell .15 .40
3 Brett Clouthier .30 .75
4 Chris Cook .15 .40
5 Count Frontenac MASCOT .04 .10
6 Peter Hamerlik .40 1.00
7 Brad Horan .15 .40
8 Andrew Ianiero .15 .40
9 Travis Lisabeth .15 .40
10 Doug MacIver .15 .40
11 The Coaches .04 .10
12 Justin McCutcheon .15 .40
13 Sean McMorrow .20 .50
14 Shane O'Brien .60 1.50
15 Glenn Ridler .30 .75
16 Corey Sabourin .15 .40
17 J.F. Seguin .15 .40
18 Tomas Skvaridlo .15 .40
19 Cory Stillman .30 .75
20 Nathan Tennant .15 .40
21 Darryl Thomson .15 .40
22 Brody Todd .15 .40
23 Mike Zigomanis .40 1.00
NNO Coca Cola .01 .05
NNO Title Card .01 .05

2001-02 Kingston Frontenacs

This set features the Frontenacs of the OHL. The cards were sold by the team at its souvenir stands.

COMPLETE SET (25) 5.00 12.00
1 Header Card .04 .10
2 Chris Cook .20 .50
3 Lou Dickenson .30 .75
4 Josh Gratton .20 .50
5 Peter Hamerlik .40 1.00
6 Chris Hardill .20 .50
7 Brad Horan .20 .50
8 Andrew Ianiero .30 .75
9 Drew Kivell .20 .50
10 Sean Langdon .20 .50
11 Doug MacIver .20 .50
12 Brandon McBride .20 .50
13 Justin McCutcheon .20 .50
14 Kyle Neufeld .20 .50
15 Shane O'Brien .20 .50
16 Scott Sheppard .20 .50
17 Mike Smith .20 .50
18 Sean Stefanski .20 .50
19 Anthony Stewart 1.25 3.00
20 Cory Stillman .30 .75
21 Justin Suda .20 .50
22 Nathan Tennant .30 .75
23 Ed Van Herpt .20 .50
24 Nick Van Herpt .20 .50
25 Coca-Cola Ad .04 .10

2002-03 Kingston Frontenacs

COMPLETE SET (25) 5.00 12.00
1 Header Card .04 .10
2 Chris Cook .20 .50
3 Austin Corredato .20 .50
4 Miguel Delisle .20 .50
5 Drew Fata .20 .50
6 Peter Hamerlik .30 .75
7 Brad Horan .20 .50
8 Bill Kinkel .20 .50
9 Drew Kivell .20 .50
10 Dwight LaBrosse .20 .50
11 Scott Maher .20 .50
12 Brandon McBride .20 .50
13 Justin McCutcheon .20 .50
14 Danny McDonald .20 .50
15 Clay McFadden .20 .50
16 Richard Power .20 .50
17 Bryan Rodney .20 .50
18 Ryan Stephenson .20 .50
19 Anthony Stewart .75 2.00
20 Cory Stillman .20 .50
21 Justin Suda .20 .50
22 Dan Turple .20 .50
23 Nick Van Herpt .20 .50
24 The Count MASCOT .04 .10
25 Ad card .04 .10

2004-05 Kingston Frontenacs

A total of 500 team sets were produced.

COMPLETE SET (24) 5.00 12.00
1 Evan Kotsopoulos .20 .50
2 Anthony Stewart .40 1.00
3 Bobby Bolt .20 .50
4 Chris Stewart .20 .50
5 Dayne Davis .20 .50
6 David Edgeworth .20 .50
7 Cory Emmerton .20 .50
8 Shawn Futers .20 .50
9 Todd Griffith .20 .50
10 Bobby Hughes .20 .50
11 Michael Kolarz .20 .50
12 Derek Lyons .20 .50
13 Phil Mangan .20 .50
14 Adam Nemeth .20 .50
15 Chris Petrow .20 .50
16 Blake Pronk .20 .50
17 Dany Revelle .20 .50
18 Ben Shutron .20 .50
19 Radek Smolenak .40 1.00
20 Justin Suda .20 .50
21 Justin Wallingford .20 .50
22 Tony Rizzi .20 .50
23 Greg Williams .20 .50
24 Brady Morrison .20 .50

2005-06 Kingston Frontenacs

COMPLETE SET (23) 12.00 30.00
1 Cory Emmerton 1.00 2.50
2 Chris Stewart 1.00 2.50
3 Ben Shutron .50 1.25
4 Shawn Connors .50 1.25
5 Adam Nemeth .50 1.25
6 Matt Reis .50 1.25
7 Blake Pronk .50 1.25
8 Radek Smolenak 1.00 2.50
9 Luke Pither .50 1.25
10 Andrew Kizito .50 1.25
11 Tony Rizzi .50 1.25
12 Andrew Wilson .50 1.25
13 Bobby Hughes .50 1.25
14 Justin Wallingford .50 1.25
15 Todd Griffith .50 1.25
16 Michael Kolarz .50 1.25
17 Bobby Bolt .50 1.25
18 Connor Cameron .50 1.25
19 Mike Looby .50 1.25
20 Peder Skinner .50 1.25
21 J.F. Houle .50 1.25
22 Danny Taylor .60 1.50
23 Daryl Borden .60 1.50

2006-07 Kingston Frontenacs

COMPLETE SET (23) 8.00 15.00
1 Chris Stewart .40 1.00
2 Kyle Bochek .30 .75
3 Bobby Mignardi .30 .75
4 Nathan Moon .30 .75
5 Peder Skinner .30 .75
6 Matt Auffrey .30 .75
7 Matthew Kang .30 .75
8 Bobby Nyholm .30 .75
9 Jesse Biduke .30 .75
10 Bobby Hughes .30 .75
11 Josh Brittain .30 .75
12 Bobby Bolt .30 .75
13 Cory Emmerton .40 1.00
14 Peter Stevens .30 .75
15 Michael Kolarz .30 .75
16 Ben Shutron .40 1.00
17 Kevin Mole .40 1.00
18 Adam Nemeth .30 .75
19 Jonathan Sciacca .30 .75
20 Andrew Kizito .30 .75
21 Justin Wallingford .30 .75
22 Daryl Borden .30 .75
23 Jason Guy .30 .75

1982-83 Kitchener Rangers

This 30-card set measures approximately 2 3/4" by 3 1/2" and features posed action color player photos with black inner borders and white outer borders.

COMPLETE SET (30) 16.00 40.00
1 Waterloo Regional .08 .25
Police Crest
2 Harold Basse .08 .25
Chief of Police
3 Sponsors' Card .08 .25
4 Joe Crozier GM .20 .50
5 Checklist .08 .25
6 Kerry Kerch .30 .75
7 Tom St. James .20 .50
8 Wendell Young .75 2.00
9 David Shaw .60 1.50
10 Darryl Boudreau .30 .75
11 David Bruce .40 1.00
12 Wayne Presley .60 1.50
13 Garnet McKechney .20 .50
14 Kevin Petendra .20 .50
15 Brian Wilks .20 .50
16 Jim Quinn .20 .50
17 Al MacInnis 8.00 20.00
18 Dave Nicholls .20 .50
19 Mike Eagles .60 1.50
20 Mike Hough .60 1.50
21 Greg Puhalski .20 .50
22 Darren Wright .20 .50
23 Todd Steffen .20 .50
24 John Tucker .60 1.50
25 Kent Paynter .20 .50
26 Andy O'Brien .20 .50
27 Les Bradley TR .08 .25
28 Scott Biggs .20 .50
29 Chris Martin TR .08 .25
30 Dave Webster .20 .50

1983-84 Kitchener Rangers

The Kitchener Rangers of the OHL are featured in this 30-card P.L.A.Y. (Police, Law and Youth) set, which was sponsored by the Waterloo Regional Police in conjunction with several company sponsors. The cards measure approximately 2 3/4" by 3 1/2" and are printed on thin card stock. The fronts feature color photos with the players posed in action stances. The photos are framed by black and white borders, and a facsimile autograph is inscribed across the bottom of the picture.

COMPLETE SET (30) 6.00 15.00
1 Joe Mantione .40 1.00
2 Jim Quinn .20 .50
3 Kitchener Rangers logo .08 .25
Checklist
4 Rob MacInnis .20 .50
5 Louie Berardicurti .20 .50
6 Neil Sandilands .20 .50
7 Darren Wright .20 .50
8 Tom Barrett CO .08 .25
GM
9 Brian Wilks .20 .50
10 Garnet McKechney .20 .50
11 David Bruce .40 1.00
12 Kent Paynter .20 .50
13 Sponsor's card .08 .25
P.L.A.Y.
14 Scott Kerr .20 .50
15 Greg Puhalski .20 .50
16 Wayne Presley .40 1.00
17 Carmine Vani .20 .50
18 Shawn Burr .75 2.00
19 Dave Latta .30 .75
20 John Tucker .60 1.50
21 Mike Stevens .20 .50
22 Harold Basse .08 .25
Chief of Police
23 Waterloo Regional .08 .25
Police
24 Peter Bakovic .20 .50
25 Brian Ross .20 .50
26 Brad Balshin .20 .50
27 David Shaw .40 1.00
28 Chris Trainer TR .08 .25
29 Les Bradley TR .08 .25
30 Ray LeBlanc .75 2.00

1984-85 Kitchener Rangers

The Kitchener Rangers of the OHL are featured in this 30-card P.L.A.Y. (Police, Law and Youth) set, which was sponsored by the Waterloo Regional Police in conjunction with several company sponsors. The cards measure approximately 2 3/4" by 3 1/2" and are printed on thin card stock. The fronts feature color photos with the players posed in action stances. The photos are framed by black and white borders, and a facsimile autograph is inscribed across the bottom of the picture.

COMPLETE SET (30) 4.80 12.00
1 Waterloo Regional .08 .25
Police Crest
2 Harold Basse .08 .25
Chief of Police
3 Garnet McKechney .20 .50
4 Tom Barrett GM/CO .08 .25
5 Kitchener Rangers logo .08 .25
6 Mike Bishop .30 .75
7 Craig Wolanin .40 1.00
8 Steve Marcolini .20 .50
9 Peter Langlois .20 .50
10 Dave Weiss .30 .75
11 Ken Alexander .20 .50
12 Ian Pound .20 .50
13 Doug Stromback .20 .50
14 Joel Brown .20 .50
15 Brian Wilks .20 .50
16 Robin Rubic .20 .50
17 Kent Paynter .20 .50
18 Jon Helinski .20 .50
19 Greg Puhalski .20 .50
20 Wayne Presley .40 1.00
21 Dave McIlwain .40 1.00
22 Shawn Burr .40 1.00
23 Dave Latta .25 .60
24 John Keller .20 .50
25 Mike Stevens .20 .50
26 Sponsors' Card .08 .25
27 Richard Adolfi .20 .50
28 Grant Sanders .20 .50
29 Les Bradley TR .08 .25
30 Sponsors' Card .08 .25

1985-86 Kitchener Rangers

This 30-card set measures approximately 2 3/4" by 3 1/2" and is printed on thin card stock. The fronts feature posed, color player photos with thin black borders on a white card face. A facsimile autograph is inscribed across the picture. The cards are numbered on the front and back.

COMPLETE SET (30) 5.00 12.00
1 Waterloo Regional Police .08 .25
2 Harold Basse .08
Chief of Police
3 Sponsors' Card .08
4 Tom Barrett GM/CO .08
5 Kitchener Rangers logo .20
Checklist
6 Dave Weiss .30
7 Steve Marcolini .20
8 Kevin Gant .20
9 Ken Alexander .20
10 Mike Volpe .30
11 Ian Pound .20
12 Brett MacDonald .20
13 Scott Taylor .20
14 Greg Hankkio .20
15 Mike Morrison .20
16 Mike Wolak .20
17 Craig Booker .20
18 Jeff Noble .20
19 Shawn Tyers .20
20 Peter Lisy .20
21 Shawn Burr .40 1
22 David Latta .20
23 Ron Sanko .20
24 Doug Jones .20
25 Paul Penelton .20
26 Blair MacPherson .20
27 Richard Hawkins .20
28 Brad Sparkes .20
29 Ron Goodall .20
30 Kevin Duguay TR .08

1986-87 Kitchener Rangers

The Kitchener Rangers of the OHL are featured in th 30-card P.L.A.Y. (Police, Law and Youth) set, which was sponsored by the Waterloo Regional Police in conjunction with several corporate sponsors. The c measure approximately 2 3/4" by 3 1/2" and are printed on thin card stock. The fronts feature color photos with the players posed in action stances. Th photos are framed by black and white borders. The player's name appears in the lower right corner. The cards are numbered on both sides.

COMPLETE SET (30) 4.00 10
1 Waterloo Police Crest .02
2 Harold Basse COP .02
3 Sponsor's Card .02
4 Tom Barrett GM/CO .02
5 Checklist .08
6 Dave Weiss .30
7 Darren Rumble .20
8 Kevin Grant .20
9 Len Fawcett .20
10 Darren Beals .30
11 Ed Kister .20
12 Scott Taylor .20
13 Darren Moxam .20
14 Paul Epoch .20
15 Richard Borgo .20
16 Allan Lake .20
17 Jeff Noble .20
18 Mark Montanari .20
19 Jim Hulton .20
20 Kelly Cain .20
21 Craig Booker .20
22 David Latta .20
23 Doug Jones .20
24 Gary Callahan .20
25 Bruno Lapensee .20
26 Scott Montgomery TR .02
27 Ron Goodall .20
28 Discount Card .02
29 Steve Ewing .20
30 Joe McDonnell ACO .08

1987-88 Kitchener Rangers

This 30-card set measures approximately 2 3/4" by 1/2" and was sponsored by Waterloo Region Optim Clubs. The cards, which are printed on thin card st feature color posed action player photos with white borders. The card number, the player's name, and th season year appear in black print across the bottom the photo The cards are numbered on both sides.

COMPLETE SET (30) 4.00 10
1 Waterloo Regional .02
Police
2 Harold Basse .02
Chief of Police
3 Children's Bonus Card .02
4 Joe McDonnell GM/CO .02
5 Kitchener Ranger logo .08
6 Gus Morschauser .30
7 Rick Allain .20
8 Kevin Grant .20
9 Rob Thiel .20
10 Darren Beals .30
11 Cory Keenan .20
12 Rival Fullum .20
13 Tony Crisp .20
14 Tyler Ertel .20
15 Richard Borgo .20
16 Steven Rice .20
17 Rob Sangster .20
18 Jeff Noble .20
19 Mark Montanari .20
20 Jim Hulton .20
21 Craig Booker .20
22 Doug Jones .20
23 Randy Pearce .20
24 Darren Rumble .20
25 Joe Ranger .20
26 Optimist's Sponsor Card .02
27 Ron Goodall .20
28 Allan Lake .20
29 Scott Montgomery TR .02
30 Optimist's Sponsor .02
Card

1988-89 Kitchener Rangers

The Kitchener Rangers of the OHL are featured in th 30-card P.L.A.Y. (Police, Law and Youth) set, which was sponsored by the Waterloo Regional Police in conjunction with several area Optimist Clubs. The cards measure approximately 2 3/4" by 3 1/2" and a printed on thin card stock. The fronts feature color photos with the players posed in action stances. Th photos are framed by black and white borders. The cards are numbered on both sides.

COMPLETE SET (30) 4.00 10
1 Waterloo Regional .02
Police Crest
2 Harold Basse .02
Chief of Police
3 Children's Bonus Card .02
4 Joe McDonnell GM/CO .02
5 Kitchener Rangers logo .20
Checklist
6 Mike Torchia .30
7 Rick Allain .20
8 John Uniac .20

9 Rob Thiel .20 .50
10 Gus Morschauser .30 .75
11 Cory Keenan .20 .50
12 Rival Fullum .20 .50
13 Jason Firth .20 .50
14 Joey St. Aubin .20 .50
15 Richard Borgo .20 .50
16 Steven Rice .20 .50
17 Rob Sangster .20 .50
18 Gilbert Dionne .30 .75
19 Mark Montanari .20 .50
20 Shayne Stevenson .30 .75
21 Pierre Gagnon .20 .50
22 Kirk Tomlinson .20 .50
23 Randy Pearce .20 .50
24 Brad Barton .20 .50
25 Chris LiPuma .20 .50
26 Optimist's Sponsor's Card A-K .02 .10
27 Steve Herniman .20 .50
28 Darren Rumble .20 .50
29 Rick Chambers TR .02 .10
30 Optimist's Sponsor's Card L-W .02 .10

1989-90 Kitchener Rangers

The Kitchener Rangers of the OHL are featured in this 30-card P.L.A.Y. (Police, Law and Youth) set, which was sponsored by the Waterloo Regional Police in conjunction with several area Optimist Clubs. The cards measure approximately 2 3/4" by 3 1/2" and are printed on thin card stock. The fronts feature posed color player photos inside a black picture frame and white outer borders. Most cards are numbered on both sides.

COMPLETE SET (30) 4.80 12.00
1 Waterloo Police Crest .02 .10
2 Harold Basse COP .02 .10
3 Children's Bonus Card .02 .10
4 Joe McDonnell GM/CO .02 .10
5 Logo/Checklist .08 .25
6 Mike Torchia .30 .75
7 Rick Allain .20 .50
8 John Uniac .20 .50
9 Jack Williams .20 .50
10 Dave Schill .30 .75
11 John Copley .20 .50
12 Cory Keenan .20 .50
13 Rival Fullum .20 .50
14 Jason Firth .20 .50
15 Joey St. Aubin .20 .50
16 Richard Borgo .20 .50
17 Steven Rice .20 .50
18 Rob Sangster .20 .50
19 Gilbert Dionne .30 .75
20 Jamie Israel .20 .50
21 Shayne Stevenson .30 .75
22 Gib Tucker .20 .50
23 Randy Pearce .20 .50
24 Brad Barton .20 .50
25 Chris Li Puma .20 .50
26 Optimist's Sponsors Card A-L .02 .10
27 Kevin Falesy .20 .50
28 Steve Smith .20 .50
29 Rick Chambers TR .02 .10
30 Optimist's Sponsors Card M-W .02 .10

1990-91 Kitchener Rangers

The Kitchener Rangers of the OHL are featured in this 30-card P.L.A.Y. (Police, Law and Youth) set, which was sponsored by the Waterloo Regional Police in conjunction with several area Optimist Clubs. The cards measure approximately 2 3/4" by 3 1/2" and are printed on thin card stock. The fronts feature color photos with the players posed in action stances. The photos are framed by black and red borders The cards are numbered on both sides.

COMPLETE SET (30) 3.00 8.00
1 Waterloo Regional Police Crest .02 .10
2 Harold Basse Chief of Police .02 .10
3 Joe McDonnell GM/CO .02 .10
4 Rick Chambers TR .02 .10
5 Kitchener Rangers logo Checklist .08 .25
6 Mike Torchia .20 .50
7 Len DeVuono .10 .30
8 John Uniac .10 .30
9 Steve Smith .10 .30
10 Rob Stopar .10 .30
11 Tony McCabe .10 .30
12 Jason Firth .10 .30
13 Joey St. Aubin .10 .30
14 Richard Borgo .10 .30
15 Norm Dezainde .10 .30
16 Jeff Szeryk .10 .30
17 Derek Gauthier .10 .30
18 Jamie Israel .10 .30
19 Shayne McCosh .10 .30
20 Gib Tucker .10 .30
21 Paul McCallion .10 .30
22 Mike Allen .10 .30
23 Brad Barton .10 .30
24 Chris LiPuma .15 .40
25 Justin Cullen .10 .30
26 Optimist's Sponsors Card (A-K) .02 .10
27 Rod Saarinen .10 .30
28 Jack Williams .10 .30
29 Steven Rice .20 .50
30 Optimist's Sponsors Card (K-W) .02 .10

1993-94 Kitchener Rangers

Sponsored by Domino's Pizza and printed by Slapshot Images Ltd., this standard size 31-card set features the Kitchener Rangers of the OHL. On a geometrical blue and red background, the fronts feature color action player photos with thin grey borders. The player's name, position and team name, as well as the producer's logo, appear on the front.

COMPLETE SET (31) 3.60 9.00
1 Eric Manlow .15 40
Jason Gladney
Tim Spitig
Checklist
2 David Belitski .20 .50
3 Darryl Whyte .20 .50
4 Greg McLean .15 .40
5 Jason Hughes .15 .40
6 Gord Dickie .15 .40
7 Travis Riggin .15 .40
8 Norm Dezainde .15 .40
9 Tim Spitzig .15 .40
10 Trevor Gallant .15 .40
11 Chris Pittman .15 .40
12 Ryan Pawluk .15 .40
UER (Name m
13 Jason Morgan .15 .40
14 James Boyd .15 .40
15 Todd Warriner .30 .75
16 Mark Donahue .15 .40
17 Peter Brearley .15 .40
18 Andrew Taylor .15 .40
19 Jason Gladney .15 .40
20 Wes Swinson .15 .40
21 Matt O'Dette .15 .40
22 Darren Schmidt .15 .40
23 Jason Johnson .15 .40
24 Eric Manlow .15 .40
25 Jeff Lillie .15 .40
26 Sergei Olympiev .15 .40
27 Joe McDonnell CO .02 .10
28 Rick Chambers TR .02 .10
29 Andrew Taylor .15 .40
Travis Riggin
David Belitski
Top
30 Sponsor Card .02 .10
Domino's P
NNO Slapshot Ad Card .02 .10

1994-95 Kitchener Rangers

Sponsored by Domino's Pizza and printed by Slapshot Images Ltd., this 31-card set features the Rangers of the OHL. The sets were sold by the team at home games.

COMPLETE SET (31) 3.00 8.00
1 Checklist .02 .10
2 David Belitski .20 .50
3 Darryl Whyte .20 .50
4 Daniel Godbout .15 .40
5 Greg McLean .15 .40
6 Jason Hughes .15 .40
7 Jason Byrnes .15 .40
8 Paul Traynor .15 .40
9 Travis Riggin .15 .40
10 Tim Spitzig .15 .40
11 Trevor Gallant .15 .40
12 Chris Pittman .20 .50
13 Rick Emmett .15 .40
14 Jason Morgan .15 .40
15 Luch Nasato .30 .75
16 Ryan Pepperall .20 .50
17 Keith Welsh .15 .40
18 Bill McGuigen .15 .40
19 Chris Brassard .15 .40
20 Andrew Taylor .15 .40
21 Rob Deciantis .15 .40
22 Wes Swinson .20 .50
23 Lucas Miller .15 .40
24 Sergei Olympiev .15 .40
25 Rob Maric .15 .40
26 Eric Manlow .20 .50
27 Geoff Ward CO .02 .10
28 Bob Ertel GM .02 .10
29 Rick Chambers TR .02 .10
Dave N
30 Sponsor Card .02 .10
Domino's P
NNO Ad Card .02 .10

1994-95 Kitchener Rangers Update

This update set has the same design as the 1994-95 Kitchener Rangers set and features players that were traded to the Rangers during the 1994-95 season. It was sold separately and also included a Slapshot ad card with a 1995 calendar on the back. The numbering is a continuation of the regular set.

COMPLETE SET (7) .75 2.00
31 Brian Scott .20 .50
32 Robin LaCour .15 .40
33 Jim Ensom .20 .50
34 Dylan Seca .15 .40
35 Garrett Burnett .15 .40
NNO Craig Bignell ACO .15 .40
Mike Wright ACO
NNO Ad Card .02 .10

1996-97 Kitchener Rangers

This set was sold by the team at home games. The cards are unnumbered and so are listed in alphabetical order.

COMPLETE SET (30) 4.00 15.00
1 Jeff Ambrosio .20 .50
2 David Belitski .40 1.00
3 Jason Byrnes .20 .50
4 Peter Bureaux .20 .50
5 Vratislav Cech .20 .50
6 Rob DeCiantis .20 .50
7 Shawn Degagne .20 .50
8 Boyd Devereaux .60 1.50
9 Boyd Devereaux .60 1.50
10 Bryan Duce .20 .50
11 Michal Dvorak .20 .50
12 Darcy Harris .20 .50
13 Bryan Hayton ACO .02 .10
14 Wes Jarvis .20 .50
15 Dan Lebold TR .02 .10
16 Adam Lewis .20 .50
17 Rob Marc .20 .50
18 Mark McMahon .20 .50
19 Ryan Milanovic .30 .75
20 Ryan Mougenel .20 .50
21 Serge Payer .20 .50
22 Ryan Pepperall .20 .50
23 Alan Rourke .20 .50
24 Rob Stanfield .20 .50
25 Paul Traynor .20 .50
26 Tim Verbeek .20 .50
27 Geoff Ward CO .02 .10
28 Keith Welsh .20 .50
29 Header Card .02 .10
30 Checklist .02 .10

1999-00 Kitchener Rangers

This 30-card set features the 1999-00 Kitchener Rangers. Base cards have white and gray borders with a red nameplate along the right side of the card. The set was sold by the team at its souvenir stands.

COMPLETE SET (30) 4.00 10.00
1 John Eminger .15 .40
2 Matt Armstrong .15 .40
3 Serge Payer .20 .50
4 Steve Eminger .60 1.50
5 Andrew Peters .40 1.00
6 Mike Amodeo .15 .40
7 Bill Browne .15 .40
8 Maxim Sharifijanov .20 .50
9 Tex Mascot .02 .10
10 Dan Lebold .15 .40
11 Michael Wehrstedt .15 .40
12 Jeff Snyder .15 .40
13 Ryan Held .20 .50
14 John Dunphy .15 .40
15 Rusian Akhmadulin .15 .40
16 Bobby Naylor .15 .40
17 Jimmy Gagnon .15 .40
18 Brandon Merli .15 .40
19 Chris Brannen .15 .40
20 Alan Rourke .15 .40
21 Sean McMorrow .30 .75
22 Mike Mazzuca .15 .40
23 Reg Bourcier .20 .50
24 Scott Dickie .20 .50
25 Kevin Bloch .15 .40
26 Jeff McGee .15 .40
27 Derek Roy .75 2.00
28 Header Card/CL .02 .10
29 Kinsmen Club .02 .10
30 Kinsmen Club .02 .10

2000-01 Kitchener Rangers

This set features the Rangers of the OHL. The set was produced by the team and sold at its souvenir stands during home games. The cards are unnumbered, so are listed in alphabetical order.

COMPLETE SET (30) 4.80 10.00
1 Team CL .15 .40
2 Matt Armstrong .15 .40
3 Josh Bennett .15 .40
4 Andre Benoit .15 .40
5 Vasily Bizyayev .15 .40
6 Kevin Bloch CO .04 .10
7 Chris Brannen .15 .40
8 Chris Cava .20 .50
9 Travis Chapman .15 .40
10 Scott Dickie .30 .75
11 John Dunphy .15 .40
12 Steve Eminger .40 1.00
13 Jimmy Gagnon .15 .40
14 Mike Hough .20 .50
15 Jeff Johnston .30 .75
16 Brad Larter .15 .40
17 Dan Lebold TR .02 .10
18 Jamie Minchella .15 .40
19 Steve Richards .15 .40
20 Matt Rock .15 .40
21 Derek Roy .60 1.50
22 Derrick Shultz .30 .75
23 Scott Sheppard .15 .40
24 Sam Skwarchuk .15 .40
25 Marcus Smith .15 .40
26 Jeff Snyder CO .02 .10
27 Tex MASCOT .02 .10
28 Brock Yates .15 .40
29 Kinsmen Club .02 .10
30 Kinsmen Club 2 .02 .10

2001-02 Kitchener Rangers

COMPLETE SET (22) 12.00
1 Scott Dickie .30 .75
2 Nick Policelli .20 .50
3 Thomas Harrison .20 .50
4 Ryan Ramsay .20 .50
5 Steve Eminger .30 .75
6 Peter Kanko .40 1.00
7 Mike Amodeo .20 .50
8 Matt Grennier .20 .50
9 Derek Roy .30 .75
10 Andre Benoit .20 .50
11 Mike Richards .60 1.50
12 Petr Hemsky .20 .50
13 John Osborne .20 .50
14 Rafal Martynowski .20 .50
15 Marcus Smith .20 .50
16 T.J. Eason .20 .50
17 Adam Keefe .20 .50
18 Matt Harpwood .30 .75
19 Bill Kinkel .20 .50
20 Jeff Szwez .20 .50
21 Chad McCaffrey .20 .50
22 Checklist .04 .10

2002-03 Kitchener Rangers

COMPLETE SET(19) 12.00
1 Andre Benoit .20 .50
2 Jesse Boucher .20 .50
3 Greg Campbell .40 1.00
4 David Clarkson .20 .50
5 Carlo DiRienzo .20 .50
6 Scott Dickie .30 .75
7 T.J. Eason .20 .50
8 Steve Eminger .40 1.00
9 Matt Grennier .20 .50
10 George Halkidis .20 .50
11 Peter Kanko .40 1.00
12 Adam Keefe .20 .50
13 Rafal Martynowski .20 .50
14 Chad McCaffrey .20 .50
15 Evan McGrath .20 .50
16 Nathan O'Nabigon .20 .50
17 Mike Richards .60 1.50
18 Derek Roy .40 1.00
19 Marcus Smith .20 .50

2002-03 Kitchener Rangers Postcards

These five singles were recently confirmed. If you have any additional information about this set, please contact us at hockeymag@beckett.com.

COMPLETE SET
1 Steve Eminger .75 2.00
2 Petr Kanko .75 2.00
3 Mike Richards .75 2.00
4 Derek Roy .75 2.00
5 Evan McGrath .75 2.00

2003-04 Kitchener Rangers

COMPLETE SET (24) 12.00
1 Andre Benoit .20 .50
2 Jesse Boucher .20 .50
3 Mike Chmielewski .20 .50
4 David Clarkson .20 .50
5 Patrick Davis .20 .50
6 Carlo DiRienzo .30 .75
7 Nick Duff .20 .50
8 Cam Fergus .20 .50
9 Peter Franchin .20 .50
10 Chris Gravelding .20 .50
11 Thomas Harrison .20 .50
12 Devereaux Heshmatpour .20 .50
13 Petr Kanko .30 .75
14 Adam Keefe .20 .50
15 Tyson Kellerman .30 .75
16 Matt Lashoff .20 .50
17 Rafal Martynowski .20 .50
18 Paul McFarland .20 .50
19 Evan McGrath .20 .50
20 Nathan O'Nabigon .20 .50
21 Anthony Pototschnik .20 .50
22 Mike Richards .40 1.00
23 Marcus Smith .20 .50
24 Boris Valabik .30 .75

2003 Kitchener Rangers Memorial Cup

Cards are unnumbered and are listed below in alphabetical order.

COMPLETE SET (19) 6.00 15.00
1 Andre Benoit .30 .75
2 Jesse Boucher .30 .75
3 Gregory Campbell .40 1.00
4 David Clarkson .30 .75
5 Scott Dickie .40 1.00
6 Carlo Dirienzo .40 1.00
7 T.J. Eason .30 .75
8 Steve Eminger .30 1.50
9 Matt Grennier .30 .75
10 George Halkidis .30 .75
11 Petr Kanko .40 1.00
12 Adam Keefe .30 .75
13 Rafal Martynowski .30 .75
14 Chad McCaffrey .30 .75
15 Evan McGrath .30 .75
16 Nathan O'Nabigon .30 .75
17 Mike Richards 1.00 2.50
18 Derek Roy .60 1.50
19 Marcus Smith .30 .75

2004-05 Kitchener Rangers

A total of 600 team sets were produced.

COMPLETE SET (24) 6.00 15.00
2 Andre Benoit .20 .50
2 Mike Richards .60 1.50
3 Boris Valabik .30 .75
4 Mark Packwood .20 .50
5 Craig Voakes .20 .50
6 Dan Turple .20 .50
7 Dan Cyenes .20 .50
8 David Clarkson .20 .50
9 Eric Pfligler .20 .50
10 Evan McGrath .40 1.00
11 Jack Combs .20 .50
12 Jakub Kindl .30 .75
13 Joe McCann .20 .50
14 Justin Azevedo .20 .50
15 Justin Piquette .20 .50
16 Kevin Henderson .20 .50
17 Mark Fraser .20 .50
18 Matt Lashoff .40 1.00
19 Matt Pepe .20 .50
20 Adam Keefe .20 .50
21 Michael Duco .20 .50
22 Myles Applebaum .20 .50
23 Patrick Davis .20 .50
24 Paul McFarland .20 .50

2005-06 Kitchener Rangers

COMPLETE SET (27) 6.00 15.00
1 Dan Turple .40 1.00
2 Julien Machabee .30 .75
3 Mark Packwood .40 1.00
4 Matt Lashoff .40 1.00
5 Patrick Davis .30 .75
6 Justin Azevedo .30 .75
7 Evan McGrath .40 1.00
8 Sean Smyth .30 .75
9 Dan Gyenes .30 .75
10 Boris Valabik .40 1.00
11 Kevin Henderson .30 .75
12 Matt Thomson .30 .75
13 Mark Fraser .30 .75
14 Jakub Kindl .30 .75
15 Nick Spaling .30 .75
16 Mike Duco .30 .75
17 Yves Bastien .30 .75
18 Matt Pepe .30 .75
19 Craig Voakes .30 .75
20 Michael Pelech .30 .75
21 Jean-Michel Rizk .30 .75
22 Ryan Donally .30 .75
23 Myles Applebaum .30 .75
24 Matt Auffrey .30 .75
25 Cory Konecny .30 .75
26 David Lomas .30 .75
27 Victor Oreskovich .30 .75

2006-07 Kitchener Rangers

COMPLETE SET (25) 8.00 15.00
1 Jakub Kindl .30 .75
2 Steve Tarasuk .30 .75
3 Nick Spaling .30 .75
4 Scott Timmins .30 .75
5 Mike Duco .30 .75
6 Justin Azevedo .30 .75
7 Yves Bastien .30 .75
8 Mike Mascioli .30 .75
9 Matt Halischuk .30 .75
10 Nazem Kadri .50 1.25
11 Matt Pepe .30 .75
12 Robert Bortuzzo .30 .75
13 Dan Gyenes .30 .75
14 Denver Manderson .30 .75
15 Mark Packwood .40 1.00
16 John Murray .40 1.00
17 Jean-Michel Rizk .30 .75
18 Adam Zamec .30 .75
19 Kevin Henderson .30 .75
20 Victor Oreskovich .30 .75
21 Yannick Weber .30 .75
22 Brian Soso .30 .75
23 Phil Varone .30 .75
24 Dan Kelly .30 .75
LE1 Justin Azevedo 1.25 3.00

2007-08 Kitchener Rangers

COMPLETE SET (24) 5.00 12.00
1 Josh Unice .25 .60
2 Mavric Parks .25 .60
3 Alex Dzielski .25 .60
4 Yannick Weber .25 .60
5 Steve Jensen .25 .60
6 Phil Varone .25 .60
7 Dan Kelly .25 .60
8 Steve Tarasuk .25 .60
9 Nick Spaling .25 .60
10 Myles Barbieri .25 .60
11 Scott Timmins .25 .60
12 Mike Duco .25 .60
13 Justin Azevedo .25 .60
14 Mike Mascioli .25 .60
15 Matt Halischuk .25 .60
16 Nazem Kadri .40 1.00
17 Matt Pepe .25 .60
18 Robert Bortuzzo .25 .60
19 Brandon Mashinter .25 .60
20 Spencer Anderson .25 .60
21 T.J. Battani .25 .60
22 Doug Clarkson .25 .60
23 Alexei Dostoinov .25 .60
24 Mikkel Boedker .25 .60

2014-15 Kitchener Rangers

COMPLETE SET () 6.00 15.00
1 Justin Bailey .30 .75
2 Doug Blaisdell .30 .75
3 Connor Bunnaman .30 .75
4 Mark Bzowey .30 .75
5 Dawson Carty .30 .75
6 Mike Davies .30 .75
7 Dylan DiPerna .30 .75
8 Gustaf Franzen .30 .75
9 Matthew Greenfield .30 .75
10 Frank Hora .30 .75
11 Max Iafrate .30 .75
12 Mason Kohn .30 .75
13 Darby Llewellyn .30 .75
14 Liam Maaskant .30 .75
15 Ryan MacInnis .40 1.00
16 Nick Magyar .30 .75
17 Adam Mascherin .40 1.00
18 Curtis Meighan .30 .75
19 Brent Pedersen .30 .75
20 Brandon Robinson .30 .75
21 Logan Schmidt .30 .75
22 Dmitrii Sergeev .30 .75

2015-16 Kitchener Rangers

COMPLETE SET (23) 6.00 15.00
1 Doug Blaisdell .30 .75
2 Jeremy Bracco .30 .75
3 Brian Brosnan .30 .75
4 Connor Bunnaman .30 .75
5 Dawson Carty .30 .75
6 Dylan Di Perna .30 .75
7 Gustaf Franzen .30 .75
8 Joseph Garreffa .30 .75
9 Connor Hall .30 .75
10 Jake Henderson .30 .75
11 Frank Hora .30 .75
12 Mason Kohn .30 .75
13 Darby Llewellyn .30 .75
14 Ryan MacInnis .30 .75
15 Nick Magyar .30 .75
16 Adam Mascherin .30 .75
17 Nick McHugh .30 .75
18 David Miller .30 .75
19 Luke Opilka .30 .75
20 Luke Richardson .30 .75
21 Elijah Roberts .30 .75
22 Brandon Robinson .30 .75
23 Dmitrii Sergeev .30 .75

1990-91 Knoxville Cherokees

This 19-card set of the Knoxville Cherokees of the ECHL was produced by 7th Inning Sketch, and offered for sale by the team at home games. Interestingly, the set is numbered 101-119, suggesting it is the continuation of a larger (all ECHL?) set. The fronts feature a posed shot, while the backs offer limited player information and logos for the club and the Knoxville News-Sentinel.

COMPLETE SET (19) 3.60 9.00
101 David Williams .25 .60
102 Paul Laus .40 1.00
103 Don Jackson CO .08 .25
104 Steve Ryding .20 .50
105 Jeff Lindsay .20 .50
106 Daniel Gauthier .20 .50
107 Stan Drulia .25 .60
108 Mike Murray .20 .50
109 Tom Sasso .20 .50
110 Butch Kaebel .20 .50
111 Don McClennan .20 .50
112 Jamie Hanlon .20 .50
113 Troy Mick .20 .50
114 Brett Strot .20 .50
115 Dean Anderson .20 .50
116 Quinton Brickley .20 .50
117 Greg Batters .20 .50
118 Alex Daviault .20 .50
119 Mike Greenlay .30 .75

1991-92 Knoxville Cherokees

This 20-card set of the ECHL's Knoxville Cherokees was sponsored by the News-Sentinel, and offered for sale by the team at home games. The cards feature posed shots on the front; the unnumbered backs include vital statistics and a brief career history.

COMPLETE SET (20) 3.60 9.00
1 Bill Nyrop CO .20 .50
2 Galen Head TR .02 .10
3 Mike Greenlay .30 .75
4 Karl Clauss .30 .75
5 Steve Ryding .20 .50
6 Mike Gober .20 .50
7 Chad Thompson .20 .50
8 Trevor Forsythe .20 .50
9 Greg Pankewicz .20 .50
10 David Shute .20 .50
11 Jamie Dabanovich .20 .50
12 Shawn Lillie .20 .50
13 Joel Gardner .20 .50
14 Roman Hubalek .20 .50
15 Bruno Villeneuve .20 .50
16 Troy Mick .20 .50
17 Dean McDonald .20 .50
18 Brett Lawrence .20 .50
19 Dean Anderson .20 .50
20 Robert Melanson .20 .50

1993-94 Knoxville Cherokees

This 20-card standard-size set features the Knoxville Cherokees. On a black background with white borders, the fronts have color action and posed player photos with thin teal borders. The team name appears above the photo, while the player's name, position, and the team logo are under the photo. The cards are unnumbered and checklisted below in alphabetical order.

COMPLETE SET (20) 6.00 15.00
1 Scott Boston .15 .40
2 Cory Cadden .15 .40
3 Tim Chase .15 .40
4 Steven Flomenhoft .15 .40
5 Scott Gordon .20 .50
6 Jon Larson .15 .40
7 Carl LeBlanc .15 .40
8 Kim Maier .15 .40
9 Wes McCauley .15 .40
10 Scott Metcalfe .15 .40
11 Mike Murray .15 .40
12 Hayden O'Rear .15 .40
13 Jeff Reid .15 .40
14 Manon Rheaume 3.00 8.00
15 Marc Rodgers .15 .40
16 Doug Searle .15 .40
17 Barry Smith CO .08 .25
18 Martin Tanguay .15 .40
19 Nicholas Vachon .20 .50
20 Bruno Villeneuve .15 .40

1994-95 Knoxville Cherokees

This 24-card set of the Knoxville Cherokees of the ECHL was issued by the team and available at home games.

COMPLETE SET (24) 3.00 8.00
1 Checklist .02 .10
2 Barry Smith CO .08 .25
3 Aaron Fackler TR .02 .10
4 Andy Davis Broadcaster .02 .10
5 Stephane Menard .15 .40
6 Doug Searle .15 .40
7 Hayden O'Rear .15 .40
8 Sean Brown .15 .40
9 Mike Murray .15 .40
10 Jon Jenkins .15 .40
11 Sean Pronger .30 .75
12 Steven Flomenhoft .15 .40
13 David Neilson .15 .40
14 Jack Callahan .15 .40
15 Carl LeBlanc .15 .40
16 Alain Deeks .20 .50
17 George Zajankala .15 .40
18 Chris Fess .15 .40
19 Michel Gaul .15 .40
20 Pat Murray .15 .40
21 Robb McIntyre .15 .40
22 Vaclav Nedomansky .15 .40
23 Cory Cadden .15 .40
24 Michael Burman .15 .40

1996-97 Knoxville Cherokees

The 22-card base set was sold in team set form at home games. Cards numbered P1 and P2 were available one night-only giveaways at two Cherokee home games. The designs are the same as those of the base set. Because of the unique distribution of these two cards, they are not considered part of the complete set.

COMPLETE SET (20) 4.00 10.00
1 Knoxville Cherokees .20 .50
2 Barry Smith HCO .20 .50
3 Sean Halifax .20 .50
4 Daniel Chaput .20 .50
5 Jamie Bird .20 .50
6 Matt Turek .20 .50
7 Chris Fees .20 .50
8 Kelly Hollingshead .20 .50
9 Darren Johnson .20 .50
10 Vaclav Nedomansky .20 .50
11 Kent Fearns .20 .50
12 Martin Tanguay .20 .50
13 Wayne Anchikoski .20 .50
14 Jim Brown .20 .50
15 Garrett Burnett .40 1.00
16 Stephane Soulliere .20 .50
17 Dean Moore .20 .50
18 David Neilson .20 .50
19 Mike Vandenberghe .20 .50
20 Brad Guzda .40 1.00
21 Olaf Kjenstad .20 .50
22 PHPA Web Site .02 .10
P1 Brad Guzda LL 2.00 5.00
P2 Jim Brown LL 2.00 5.00

2004-05 Knoxville Ice Bears

COMPLETE SET (24) 10.00 20.00
1 K.C. Caudill .25 .60
2 Chris Bodnar .25 .60
3 Kevin Swider .25 .60
4 Todd MacIsaac .25 .60
5 Marcus Forsberg .25 .60
6 Civic Colisseum .20 .50
7 Chilly MASCOT .20 .50
8 TCS card .25 .60
9 Doug Serle .25 .60
10 Craig Desjarlais .25 .60
11 Mike Cragen .25 .60
12 Darren Caine .25 .60
13 Curtis Menzul .25 .60
14 Terry Dunbar .25 .60
15 Free Kid's Ticket .20 .50
16 David Bagley .25 .60
17 Matt Moore .25 .60
18 Jeff Hansen .25 .60
19 James Ronayne .25 .60
20 Miss Icebear .25 .60
21 Liam McCarthy .25 .60
22 Jim Bermingham .25 .60
23 Rob Miller .25 .60
24 K.J. Voorhees .25 .60

2005-06 Knoxville Ice Bears

COMPLETE SET (24) 6.00 15.00
1 Jason Bermingham .30 .75
2 Patrick Carriere .30 .75
3 Kevin Caudill .30 .75
4 Mike Craigen .30 .75
5 Nathan Daly .30 .75
6 Marcus Forsberg .30 .75
7 Aaron Lewis .30 .75
8 Ben Manny .30 .75
9 Liam McCarthy .30 .75
10 Curtis Menzul .30 .75
11 Rob Miller .30 .75
12 Matt Moore .30 .75
13 Ryan Person .30 .75
14 Bob Rangus .30 .75
15 Jamie Ronayne .30 .75
16 Doug Searle .30 .75
17 Kevin Swider .30 .75
18 K.J. Voorhees .30 .75
19 Jim Bermingham HC .02 .10
20 Dance Team .02 .10
21 Drew Kitts EM .02 .10
22 Chilly MASCOT .02 .10
23 Tim Douglas TP .02 .10
24 Knoxville Ice Bears .20 .50

1999-00 Knoxville Speed

This set features the Speed of the UHL. The cards were issued as a promotional giveaway, with the first 15 cards going on one night, followed by a second set of 15 (a sponsor card was doubled up).

COMPLETE SET (29) 6.00 15.00
1 Sponsor Card .02 .05
2 Sponsor Card .02 .05
3 Bradley Denis .30 .75
4 Hockey History .02 .05
5 UHL History .02 .05
6 Trevor Jobe .40 1.00
7 Cam Law .30 .75
8 Rusty McKie .40 1.00
9 Eric Mohntreuil .30 .75
10 Mike Murray .30 .75
11 Dan Myre .30 .75
12 Sergei Radchenko .30 .75
13 Bill Russell .30 .75
14 Eric Schneider .30 .75
15 Mike Schultz .30 .75
16 Doug Searle .30 .75
17 Jordan Shaw .30 .75
18 Konstantin Simchuk .40 1.00
19 Jeff Suggitt .30 .75
20 Jeremy Thompson .30 .75
21 Andrew Tortorella .30 .75
22 Dmitry Ustyuzhanin .30 .75
23 Team on the Bench .20 .50
24 Mike Wilhelm EM .02 .10
25 Terry Ruskowski CO .30 .75
26 Tim Douglas TR .02 .10
27 Hersheys Pilot .02 .05
28 Hersheys Pilot .02 .05
29 Eyewitness Sports .02 .05

2000-01 Knoxville Speed

This set features the Speed of the UHL. The set was released as a promotional giveaway, with a different mixture of cards being given away at various home games to allow collectors to trade amongst themselves to complete sets.

COMPLETE SET (29) 10.00 30.00
1 Alex Alepin .30 1.00
2 Bradley Denis .60 1.50
3 Craig Desjarlais .60 1.50
4 Brad Guzda .40 1.50
5 Tom Lawson .30 1.00
6 David Mayes .30 1.00
7 Alain Savage .30 1.00
8 Mike Schultz .30 1.00
9 Dean Shmyr .40 1.50
10 Mike Vandenberghe .30 1.00
11 Mike Wilhelm EM .04 .10
12 Nick Paranjape (Fox 43) .04 .10
13 Brad Domonsky .80 2.00
14 Dmitry Ustyuzhanin .30 1.00
15 Yannick Latour .30 1.00
16 Sergei Petrov .60 1.50
17 Iannique Renaud .30 1.00
18 Mikko Sivonen .40 1.50
19 Mike Henderson .80 2.00
20 Geno Parrish .30 1.00
21 Andrew Tortorella .60 1.50
22 Mark Karpen .30 1.00
23 Dan Myre .30 1.00
24 Mike Murray .30 1.00
25 Mike Green .30 1.00
26 Oleg Kuzmin .30 1.00
27 Terry Ruskowski CO .20 .50
28 Tim Douglas TR .04 .10
29 JBG SPONSOR .04 .10

1998-99 Kootenay Ice

This set features the Ice of the WHL. Each card measures approximately 3" x 6" and is unnumbered. The cards were sold by the team at home games.

COMPLETE SET (24) 6.00 15.00
1 Clayton Pool .20 .50
2 Scott Roles .20 .50
3 Dean Arsene .20 .50
4 Jesse Ferguson .20 .50
5 Dion Lassu .20 .50
6 Mark Thompson .20 .50
7 Steve McCarthy .75 2.00
8 Rod Leroux .20 .50
9 Mike Green .20 .50
10 Wade Burt .20 .50
11 Nick Marach .20 .50
12 Jaroslav Svoboda .40 1.00
13 Trevor Wasyluk .40 1.00
14 Jarret Stoll 1.25 3.00
15 Jason Jaffray .20 .50
16 Trevor Johnson .20 .50
17 Kyle Wanvig .75 2.00
18 Tyler Beechey .20 .50
19 Stanislav Gron .40 1.00
20 Colin Sinclair .20 .50
21 Jeremy Yablonski .20 .50
22 Graham Belak .20 .50
23 B.J. Boxma .20 .50
24 Brad Tutschek .20 .50

2000-01 Kootenay Ice

This set features the Ice of the WHL. The cards are oversized by about 1/2 inch in height and width, and were sold by the team at home games. The cards are unnumbered, so are listed below in alphabetical order.

COMPLETE SET (24) 8.00 20.00
1 Dean Arsene .20 .50
2 Tyler Beechey .20 .50
3 Dan Blackburn .75 2.00
4 Zdenek Blatny .80 1.00
5 Eric Bowen .20 .50
6 Bret DeCecco .40 1.00
7 Brennan Evans .20 .50
8 Cole Fischer .20 .50
9 Richard Hamula .20 .50
10 Jeff Harvey .20 .50
11 Pat Iannone .20 .50
12 Jason Jaffray .20 .50
13 Trevor Johnson .20 .50
14 Mike Lee .20 .50
15 Steve Makway .20 .50
16 Lance Morrison .20 .50
17 Aaron Rome .20 .50
18 Mascot Shivers .04 .10
19 Colin Sinclair .20 .50
20 Jarret Stoll 1.25 3.00
21 Marek Svatos 2.00 5.00
22 Adam Taylor .20 .50
23 Andy Thompson .20 .50
24 Craig Weller .20 .50

2002-03 Kootenay Ice

We have confirmed a handful of singles from this set.

1 Gerard Dicaire .30 .75
2 Duncan Milroy .30 .75
3 Tomas Plihal .30 .75
4 Adam Taylor .30 .75

2003-04 Kootenay Ice

COMPLETE SET (25) 8.00 20.00
1 Taylor Dakers .30 .75
2 Jeff Glass 2.00 5.00
3 Derek Price .30 .75
4 Donny Lloyd .30 .75
5 James Cherewyk .30 .75
6 Brad Zanon .30 .75
7 Brad Cole .30 .75
8 Travis Featherstone .30 .75
9 Nigel Dawes .75 2.00
10 Mike Boxma .30 .75
11 Glenn Olson .30 .75
12 Josh Morrow .30 .75
13 Adam Taylor .30 .75
14 Igor Agarunov .30 .75
15 Adam Cracknell .30 .75
16 Jeremy Schenderling .30 .75
17 Dale Mahovsky .30 .75
18 Ryan Russell .30 .75
19 Aaron Bader .30 .75
20 Sean Affleck .30 .75
21 Martin Sagat .30 .75
22 Brett Sutter .60 1.50
23 Checklist .04 .10
24 Shivers MASCOT .04 .10
25 Sponsor .04 .10

2004-05 Kootenay Ice

COMPLETE SET (25) 8.00 20.00
1 Laine Allen .30 .75
2 Andy Bossence .30 .75
3 Michael Busto .30 .75
4 James Cherewyk .30 .75
5 Brad Cole .30 .75
6 Adam Cracknell .30 .75
7 Steven DaSilva .30 .75
8 Taylor Dakers .30 .75
9 Nigel Dawes .60 1.50
10 Joshua Fauth .30 .75
11 Jeff Glass 1.25 3.00
12 Chad Greenan .30 .75
13 Casey Lee .30 .75
14 Dale Mahovsky .30 .75
15 Ben Maxwell .30 .75
16 Roman Polak .30 .75
17 Derek Price .30 .75
18 Ryan Russell .30 .75
19 Martin Sagat .30 .75
20 Josh Saywell .30 .75
21 Brett Sutter .40 1.00
22 Adam Taylor .30 .75
23 Devin Welsh .30 .75
24 Commitment .04 .10
25 Sponsor Card .04 .10

2005-06 Kootenay Ice

COMPLETE SET (25) 6.00 15.00
1 Andrew Bailey .30 .75
2 Curtis Billsten .30 .75
3 Lukas Bohunicky .30 .75
4 Michael Busto .30 .75
5 Adam Cracknell .30 .75
6 Steven DaSilva .30 .75
7 Taylor Dakers .30 .75
8 Dalyn Flatt .30 .75
9 Trent Fussi .30 .75
10 Chad Greenan .30 .75
11 Paul Kurceba .30 .75
12 Kris Lazaruk .30 .75
13 Casey Lee .30 .75
14 Paul MacDonald .30 .75
15 Dale Mahovsky .30 .75
16 Ben Maxwell .30 .75
17 John Negrin .30 .75
18 Michal Psurny .30 .75
19 Ryan Russell .30 .75
20 Dustin Sylvester .30 .75
21 Devin Welsh .30 .75
22 Luke Wiens .30 .75
23 Shivers MASCOT .02 .10
24 Concord Pacific SPONSOR .01 .01
25 Kootenay Ice .20 .50

1991-92 Lake Superior State Lakers

This set features the Lakers of the NCAA. The cards are unnumbered and so are listed in alphabetical order.

COMPLETE SET (28) 8.00 20.00
1 1991 CCHA Champs .08 .25
2 Dan Angelelli .30 .75
3 Mark Astley .30 .75
4 Mike Bachusz .30 .75
5 Steve Barnes .30 .75
6 Clayton Beddoes .30 .75
7 Paul Constantin .30 .75
8 Vincent Faucher .30 .75
9 David Gartshore .30 .75
10 Tim Hanley .30 .75
11 John Hendry .30 .75
12 Dean Hulett .30 .75
13 Jeff Jackson CO .20 .50
14 Blaine Lacher .40 1.00
15 Darrin Madeley .40 1.00
16 Kurt Miller .30 .75
17 Sandy Moger .40 1.00
18 Mike Morin .30 .75
19 Jay Ness .30 .75
20 Jim Peters .30 .75
21 Brian Rolston .75 2.00
22 Michael Smith .30 .75
23 Wayne Strachan .30 .75
24 Jason Trzcinski .30 .75
25 Rob Valicevic .60 1.50
26 Darren Wetherill .30 .75
27 Brad Willner .30 .75
28 Jason Welch .30 .75

1992-93 Lake Superior State Lakers

This 33-card standard-size set features the 1992 NCAA Champion Lake Superior State Lakers. The cards feature color, action player photos with gradated blue borders. The player's name and the Lakers logo appears below the picture. The backs carry black-and-white close-up photos along with biographical information, quick facts, and statistics. The cards are unnumbered and checklisted below in alphabetical order.

COMPLETE SET (33) 6.00 15.00
1 Team Photo/1992 NCAA Ch .20 .50
2 Team Photo/1992 CCHA Champions .20 .50
3 Keith Aldridge .20 .50
4 Dan Angelelli .15 .40
5 Mark Astley .20 .50
6 Mike Bachusz .15 .40
7 Steven Barnes .15 .40
8 Clayton Beddoes .15 .40
9 David Gartshore .15 .40
10 Tim Hanley .15 .40
11 Matt Hansen .15 .40
12 John Hendry .15 .40
13 Dean Hulett .15 .40
14 Jeff Jackson .20 .50
15 Blaine Lacher .40 1.00
16 Darrin Madeley .20 .50
17 Mike Matteucci .15 .40
18 Scott McCabe .15 .40
19 Kurt Miller .15 .40
20 Mike Morin .15 .40
21 Jay Ness .15 .40
22 Gino Pulente .15 .40
23 Brian Rolston .75 2.00
24 Paul Sass .15 .40
25 Michael Smith .15 .40
26 Wayne Strachan .15 .40
27 Sean Tallaire .15 .40
28 Adam Thompson .15 .40
29 Jason Trzcinski .15 .40
30 Rob Valicevic .60 1.50
31 Jason Welch .15 .40
32 Darren Wetherill .15 .40
33 Brad Willner .15 .40

2004-05 Lakehead University Thunderwolves

These cards, featuring the CIAU Thunderwolves, were available individually from Quality Markets, making the sets extremely difficult to piece together. The set features Drew Kivell, who appeared in the TV show Making The Cut.

COMPLETE SET (27) 8.00 20.00
1 Joel Scherban .30 .75
2 Chris Shaffer .30 .75
3 Jeff Richards .30 .75
4 Erik Lodge .30 .75
5 Murray Magill .30 .75
6 Jason Lange .30 .75
7 Robert Hillier .30 .75
8 Francis Walker .30 .75
9 Andrew Brown .30 .75
10 Kris Callaway .30 .75
11 Jouni Kuokkanen .30 .75
12 Leon Cooper .30 .75
13 Hugo Lehoux .30 .75
14 Michael Wehrstedt .30 .75
15 Mike Self .30 .75
16 Austin Wycisk .30 .75
17 Steve Rawski .30 .75
18 Grant McCune .30 .75
19 Sean Stefanski .30 .75
20 Drew Kivell .30 .75
21 Jesse Baraniuk .30 .75
22 Dene Poulin .30 .75
23 Tobias Whelan .30 .75
24 Chris Whitley .30 .75
25 Peter Cava .40 1.00
26 Mark Robinson .30 .75
27 Brad Priestlay .30 .75

1993-94 Lakeland Ice Warriors

This set consists of player photos with photocopied biographies glued to the backs. There are variations of several players in this set.

COMPLETE SET (25) 10.00 25.00
1 Lakeland Ice Warriors .75 2.00
2 Chief Mascot .40 1.00
3 Chris Babkirk .40 1.00
4 Chris Baxter .40 1.00
5 Pat Bingham .40 1.00
6 Ian Collins .40 1.00
7 Ian Collins .40 1.00
8 Eric Daoust .40 1.00
9 Eric Daoust .40 1.00
10 Derek Edgerly .40 1.00
11 Andrew Ernst .40 1.00
12 John Finnie .40 1.00
13 John Finnie .40 1.00
14 Sean Gabriele .40 1.00
15 John Grand .40 1.00
16 Manny Hawkins .40 1.00
17 Jules Jardine .40 1.00
18 John Labenski .40 1.00
19 Francois Michaud .40 1.00
20 Bob Nicholls .40 1.00
21 Ed Sabo .40 1.00
22 Brent Selman .40 1.00
23 Gary Thomas .40 1.00
24 Dean Turgeon .40 1.00
25 Dave Wright .40 1.00

2004-05 Langley Hornets

This set features the Hornets of the BCJHL. The cards feature an Upper Deck logo as they were produced by the company's personalized card division.

COMPLETE SET (22) 10.00 25.00
1 Matt Allen .40 1.00
2 Aaron Berman .40 1.00
3 Justin Binab .40 1.00
4 Tyler Boice .40 1.00
5 Marcel Bruinsma .40 1.00
6 Gary Butler .40 1.00
7 Tyson Chernask .40 1.00
8 Steve Christie .75 2.00
9 Tyson Daniels .60 1.50
10 Gord Edmondson .40 1.00
11 Brian Harris .40 1.00
12 Steve Matic .40 1.00
13 Taylor Moore .75 2.00
14 Robert Pritchard .40 1.00
15 Graham Sheppard .40 1.00
16 Luke Shier .75 2.00
17 Justin Taylor .40 1.00
18 Chris Vassos .40 1.00
19 Nathan Westover .40 1.00
20 Mike Wilson .40 1.00
21 Jason Wright .40 1.00
22 Robert Pritchard#)Brian Harris AS .40 1.00

2003-04 Laredo Bucks

According to minor league afficionado Ralph Slate, this set was released by the team's booster club, which limited production to just 200 sets and charged a whopping $50 a set to raise funds.

COMPLETE SET (23) 30.00 60.00
1 Mike Amodeo 1.50 4.00
2 Jeff Bes 1.25 3.00
3 Max Birbraer 1.50 4.00
4 Brent Cullaton 1.25 3.00
5 Jean-Francois David 1.25 3.00
6 Serge Dube 1.25 3.00
7 Marco Emond 1.50 4.00
8 Chris Grenville 1.25 3.00
9 David Guerrera 1.50 4.00
10 James Hiebert 1.25 3.00
11 Dion Hyman 1.25 3.00
12 Mark Matier 1.25 3.00
13 Bobby-Chad Mitchell 1.25 3.00
14 Patrik Nilson 1.25 3.00
15 Adam Paiement 1.25 3.00
16 Gabriel Proulx 1.25 3.00
17 Steve Simoes 1.25 3.00
18 Jason Spence 1.25 3.00
19 Mike Vellinga 1.25 3.00
20 Steve Weidlich 1.25 3.00
21 Terry Ruskowski CO .40 1.00
22 Derek Craft EQM .20 .50
23 Bobby Moore TR .20 .50

1998-99 Las Vegas Coyotes RHI

This 20-card set was handed out as a promotional giveaway at a home game in late July of that season. The cards are not numbered, so they are listed in alphabetical order.

COMPLETE SET (20) 3.00 8.00
1 Konstantin Simchuk .20 .50
2 Jay Neal .20 .50
3 Mike Ciolli .20 .50
4 Jakub Ficenec .20 .50
5 Blake Knox .20 .50
6 Darren Meek .20 .50
7 Mike Jorgensen .20 .50
8 Kirk Llano .20 .50
9 Jamie Cooke .20 .50
10 Tom Perry .20 .50
11 Don Parsons .20 .50
12 Rich Bronilla .20 .50
13 Gerry St. Cyr .30 .75
14 Brad Guzda .20 .50
15 Rob Pallin .20 .50
16 Dan Reja .20 .50
17 Chris McSorley CO .20 .50
18 Howl N. Coyote Mascot .02 .10
19 KOMP Morning Crew .02 .10
20 1999 Las Vegas Coyotes .02 .10

1993-94 Las Vegas Thunder

Sponsored by Saturn, bc and More, and KVBC (Channel 3), this 32-card standard-size set features the 1993-94 Las Vegas Thunder of the IHL. On a black card face, the fronts have posed color player photos with thin white borders. The player's name and number appear under the picture. The team and sponsor logos are printed in the four corners. The cards are unnumbered and checklisted below in alphabetical order. This set may also have been issued as a perforated sheet.

COMPLETE SET (32) 3.00 8.00
1 Brent Ashton .15 .40
2 Boom Boom (Mascot) .02 .10
3 Bob Bourne CO .15 .40
4 Rod Buskas .08 .25
5 Lyndon Byers .30 .75
6 Rich Campbell TR .02 .10
7 Colin Cowherd ANN .02 .10
8 Butch Goring CO .15 .40
9 Steve Gotaas .08 .25
10 Marc Habscheid .08 .25
11 Brett Hauer .08 .25
12 Shawn Heaphy .08 .25
13 Scott Hollis .08 .25
14 Peter Ing .20 .50
15 Steve Jaques .08 .25
16 Bob Joyce .08 .25
17 Jim Kyte .08 .25
18 Patrice Lefebvre .30 .75
19 Clint Malarchuk .20 .50
20 Ken Quinney .08 .25
21 Jean-Marc Richard .08 .25
22 Todd Richards .08 .25
23 Marc Rodgers .08 .25
24 Jeff Sharples .08 .25
25 Randy Smith .08 .25
26 Greg Spenrath .08 .25
27 Bob Strumm GM .02 .10
28 Kirk Tomlinson .08 .25
29 Kerry Toporowski .15 .40
30 Mark Vermette .08 .25
31 Steve Wissman EQMG .02 .10
32 Title Card .02 .10

1994-95 Las Vegas Thunder

This 29-card standard-size set was manufactured and distributed by Jessen Associates, Inc. for Classic. The fronts display color action player photos with a teal marbleized inner border and a black outer border. The player's name, jersey number, and position appear in the teal border on the right edge. The cards are unnumbered and checklisted below in alphabetical order.

COMPLETE SET (29) 4.80 12.00
1 James Black .08 .25
2 Radek Bonk .40 1.00
3 Boom Boom MASCOT .02 .10
4 Rich Campbell Athletic .02 .10
5 Frank Evans .08 .25
6 Marc Habscheid .20 .50
7 Alex Hicks .20 .50
8 Bob Joyce .20 .50
9 Jim Kyte .08 .25
10 Lark & Craig Morning Ra .02 .10
11 Patrice Lefebvre .40 1.00
12 Darcy Loewen .20 .50
13 Sal Lombardi EQMG .02 .10
14 Clint Malarchuk .20 .50
15 Andrew McBain .20 .50
16 Chris McSorley CO .20 .50
17 David Neilson .08 .25
18 Jerry Olenyn .08 .25
19 Ken Quinney .20 .50
20 Pokey Reddick .20 .50
21 Jeff Reid .08 .25
22 Manon Rheaume 2.00 5.00
23 Jean-Marc Richard .20 .50
24 Todd Richards .08 .25
25 Marc Rodgers .08 .25
26 Jeff Sharples .08 .25
27 Jarrod Skalde .20 .50
28 Bob Strumm GM CO .02 .10
29 Kerry Toporowski .20 .50

1995-96 Las Vegas Thunder

This 26-card set of the Las Vegas Thunder of the IHL was produced by Split Second for Collector's Edge Ice. The set was available through the team at home games and by mail. The cards are unnumbered, so are listed alphabetically. The set is notable for containing 1996 Anaheim first rounder Ruslan Salei, as well as bright NHL prospect Bill Bowler.

COMPLETE SET (26) 4.80 12.00
1 Bill Bowler .30 .75
2 Peter Fiorentino .15 .40
3 Greg Hawgood .30 .75
4 Sasha Lakovic .15 .40
5 Patrice Lefebvre .40 1.00
6 Darcy Loewen .15 .40
7 Gord Marx .15 .40
8 Blaine Moore .15 .40
9 Vaclav Nedomansky .15 .40
10 Pokey Reddick .30 .75
11 Jeff Ricciardi .15 .40
12 Jean-Marc Richard .15 .40
13 Marc Rodgers .40 1.00
14 Chris Rogles .30 .75
15 Ken Quinney .20 .50
16 Ruslan Salei .20 .50
17 Jeff Sharples .20 .50
18 Daniel Shank .20 .50
19 Todd Simon .20 .50
20 Rhett Trombley .15 .40
21 Vladimir Tsyplakov .20 .50
22 Sergei Zholtok .30 .75
23 Chris McSorley CO .08 .25
24 Clint Malarchuk AGM .20 .50
25 Bob Strumm GM .02 .10
26 BoomBoom .02 .10

1996-97 Las Vegas Thunder

This 24-card set of the Las Vegas Thunder of the IHL was produced by Multi-Ad Services and sponsored by Heineken and U.S. Home, among others. The cards were sold by the team at the rink or through the mail. The cards are unnumbered, and are listed below alphabetically.

COMPLETE SET (24) 4.80 12.00
1 Egor Bashkatov .20 .50
2 Boom Boom (Mascot) .02 .10
3 Kevin Dahl .20 .50
4 Chris Dahlquist .20 .50
5 Pavol Demitra .60 1.50
6 Parris Duffus .30 .75
7 Martin Gendron .20 .50
8 Brent Gretzky .20 .50
9 Kerry Huffman .20 .50
10 Igor Karpenko .30 .75
11 Don Larner .20 .50
12 Patrice Lefebvre .40 1.00
13 Darcy Loewen .20 .50
14 Clint Malarchuk AGM .20 .50
15 Chris McSorley CO .02 .10
16 Blaine Moore .20 .50
17 Ken Quinney .30 .75
18 Jeff Serowik .20 .50
19 Jason Simon .20 .50
20 Bob Strumm GM .02 .10
21 Rhett Trombley .20 .50
22 Sergei Yerkovich .20 .50
23 Sergei Zholtok .30 .75
24 Logo Card .02 .10

1997-98 Las Vegas Thunder

This set features the Thunder of the IHL and was sold by the team at home games. The cards are standard-sized and are numbered on the back.

COMPLETE SET (28) 4.80 12.00
1 Ken Quinney .30 .75
2 Manny Legace .60 1.50
3 Jesse Belanger .20 .50
4 Joe Day .20 .50
5 Darcy Loewan .20 .50
6 Trevor Roenick .20 .50
7 Steve Bancroft .20 .50
8 Thom Cullen .20 .50
9 John Slaney .20 .50
10 Sergei Yerkovich .20 .50
11 Bob Strumm GM .02 .10
12 Chris McSorley HCO .08 .25
13 Doug Tretiak EQM .02 .10
14 KKLZ .02 .10
15 Patrice Lefebvre .40 1.00
16 Tim Cheveldae .40 1.00
17 Jeff Christian .20 .50
18 Sergei Klimovich .20 .50
19 Rob Pattison .20 .50
20 Dan Shermerhorn .20 .50
21 Ilya Byakin .20 .50
22 Justin Kurtz .20 .50
23 Radoslav Suchy .20 .50
24 Boom Boom MASCOT .02 .10
25 Clint Malarchuk AGM .20 .50
26 Van Parfet TR .02 .10
27 Dave McCann TV .02 .10
28 PHPA Web Site .02 .10

1998-99 Las Vegas Thunder

Little is known about this set beyond the confirmed checklist. Any additional information can be forwarded to hockeymag@beckett.com.

COMPLETE SET (30) 4.00 10.00
1 Drew Bannister .15 .40
2 Sean Berens .15 .40
3 Dampy Brar .15 .40
4 Dean Ewen .15 .40
5 Petr Franek .15 .40
6 Brad Guzda .15 .40
7 Sami Helenius .30 .75
8 Bryan Helmer .20 .50
9 Scott Hollis .15 .40
10 Kevin Kaminski .30 .75
11 Patrice Lefebvre .30 .75
12 Jason McBain .15 .40
13 Taj Melson .15 .40
14 Brad Miller .15 .40
15 Nick Naumenko .20 .50
16 Petr Nedved .30 .75
17 Trevor Roenick .20 .50
18 Russ Romaniuk .20 .50
19 Konstantin Simchuk .15 .40
20 Andrei Sryubko .15 .40
21 Stefan Ustorf .20 .50
22 Shawn Wansborough .15 .40
23 Mike Wilson .15 .40
24 Bob Strumm GM .02 .10
25 Bob Bourne CO .02 .10
26 Rod Buskas ACO .02 .10
27 Van Parfet TR .02 .10
28 Bubba Kennedy Richard Krouse EQ .02 .10
29 BoomBoom Mascot .02 .10
30 Logo Card .02 .10

2003-04 Las Vegas Wranglers

COMPLETE SET (24) 4.00 10.00
1 Jeff Attard .20 .50
2 Blaine Bablitz .20 .50
3 Cam Bristow .20 .50
4 Ryan Christie .20 .50
5 David Cousineau .20 .50
6 Greg Day .20 .50
7 Deryk Engelland .20 .50
8 Justin Kelly .20 .50
9 Chris Kenady .20 .50
10 Brent Krahn .40 1.00
11 Marc Magliarditi .30 .75
12 Jason McBain .20 .50
13 Mike McBain .20 .50
14 Tom Nelson .20 .50
15 Kevin O'Flaherty .20 .50
16 Eric Schneider .20 .50
17 Jonathon Shockey .20 .50
18 Kayle Short .20 .50
19 Riku Varjamo .20 .50
20 Chris Wheaton .20 .50
21 Doug Wright .20 .50
22 Glen Gulutzan GM CO .20 .50
23 Mascot .04 .10
24 Checklist .04 .10

2003-04 Las Vegas Wranglers RBI

This set was produced by RBI Sports and was limited to 250 copies. The set numbering reflects the entire run of RBI sets that season.

COMPLETE SET (16) 6.00 15.00
225 Jeff Attard .40 1.00
226 Cam Bristow .40 1.00
227 Ryan Christie .40 1.00
228 David Cousineau .40 1.00
229 Greg Day .40 1.00
230 Deryk Engelland .40 1.00
231 Chris Kenady .40 1.00
232 Brent Krahn .75 2.00
233 Marc Magliarditi .60 1.50
234 Jason McBain .40 1.00
235 Mike McBain .40 1.00
236 Tom Nelson .40 1.00
237 Kevin O'Flaherty .40 1.00
238 Eric Schneider .40 1.00
239 Jonathon Shockey .40 1.00
240 Doug Wright .40 1.00

2004-05 Las Vegas Wranglers

COMPLETE SET (24) 8.00 20.00
1 Mike McBain .40 1.00
2 Jon Krall .40 1.00
3 Deryk Engelland .40 1.00
4 Jason McBain .40 1.00
5 Dustin Johner .40 1.00
6 Christian Chartier .40 1.00
7 Chris Stanley .40 1.00
8 Adam Huxley .40 1.00
9 Dana Lattery .40 1.00
10 Dan Tudin .40 1.00
11 Jeff Attard .40 1.00
12 Marc Magliarditi .60 1.50
13 Regan Darby .40 1.00
14 Shawn Limpright .40 1.00
15 Darren Lynch .40 1.00
16 Doug Wright .40 1.00
17 Jason Spence .40 1.00
18 Sebastien Centomo .75 2.00
19 Ryan Gaucher .40 1.00
20 Glen Gulutzan CO .04 .10
21 Drew Schoneck ACO .04 .10
22 Joe Frederick ACO .04 .10
23 Jeff Sharples ACO .04 .10
24 The Duke MASCOT .04 .10

2005-06 Las Vegas Wranglers

COMPLETE SET (25) 6.00 15.00
1 Todd Alexander .30 .75
2 Nick Anderson .30 .75
3 Thomas Bellemare .30 .75
4 Christian Chartier .30 .75
5 Steven Crampton .30 .75
6 Matt Dzieduszycki .30 .75
7 Derek Edwardson .30 .75
8 Lee Green .30 .75
9 Tim Hambly .30 .75
10 Shawn Limpright .30 .75
11 Darren Lynch .30 .75
12 Marc Magliarditi .40 1.00
13 Mike McBain .30 .75
14 Mike McKenna .30 .75
15 Chris Neiszner .30 .75
16 Sean O'Connor .30 .75
17 Adam Pardy .30 .75
18 Marco Peluso .30 .75
19 Scott Schoneck .30 .75
20 Tyler Sloan .30 .75
21 Chris Stanley .30 .75
22 Dan Tudin .30 .75
23 Glen Gulutzan CO .02 .10
24 Brent Bilodeau ACO .02 .10
25 The Duke MASCOT .02 .10

2006-07 Las Vegas Wranglers

COMPLETE SET (25) 10.00 20.00
1 Nick Anderson .30 .75
2 Ryan Bonni .30 .75
3 Adam Cracknell .30 .75
4 Steve Crampton .60 1.50
5 Kelly Czuy .30 .75
6 Ryan Donally .30 .75
7 Derek Edwardson .30 .75
8 Jason Jozsa .30 .75
9 Jason Krischuk .30 .75
10 Shawn Limpright .30 .75
11 Marc Magliarditi .60 1.50
12 Mike McBain .30 .75
13 Mike McKenna .30 .75
14 Arpad Mihaly .30 .75
15 Tyler Mosienko .30 .75
16 Kevin Nastiuk .60 1.50
17 Chris Neiszner .30 .75
18 Marco Peluso .30 .75
19 Aaron Power .30 .75
20 Scott Schoneck .30 .75
21 Aki Seitsonen .30 .75
22 Joe Tallari .30 .75
23 Bryce Thoma .30 .75
24 Brent Bilodeau ACO .10 .25
25 Glen Gulutzan CO .10 .25

1951-52 Laval Dairy Lac St. Jean

The 1951-52 Laval Dairy Lac St. Jean set includes 59 green-and-white tinted cards measuring approximately 1 3/4" by 2 1/2". The backs are blank. The cards are numbered on the front.

COMPLETE SET (59) 750.00 1500.00
1 Eddy Daoust 25.00 50.00
2 Guy Gareau 20.00 40.00
3 Gilles Desrosiers 20.00 40.00
4 Robert Desbiens 20.00 40.00
5 James Hayes 20.00 40.00
6 Paul Gagnon 20.00 40.00
7 Gerry Perreault 20.00 40.00
8 Marcel Dufour 20.00 40.00
9 Armand Bourdon 20.00 40.00
10 Jean-Marc Pichette 25.00 50.00
11 Gerry Gagnon 20.00 40.00
12 Jules Racette 20.00 40.00
13 Real Marcotte 20.00 40.00
14 Gerry Theberge 20.00 40.00
15 Rene Harvey 20.00 40.00
16 Joseph Lacoursiere 20.00 40.00
17 Fernand Benaquez 20.00 40.00
18 Andre Boisvert 20.00 40.00
19 Claude Chretien 20.00 40.00
20 Norbert Clark 20.00 40.00
21 Sylvio Lambert 20.00 40.00
22 Lucien Roy 20.00 40.00
23 Gerard Audet 20.00 40.00
24 Jacques Lalancette 20.00 40.00
25 Maurice St.Jean 20.00 40.00
26 Camille Lupien 20.00 40.00
27 Rodrigue Pelchat 20.00 40.00
28 Conrad L'Heureux 20.00 40.00
29 Paul Tremblay 20.00 40.00
30 Robert Vincent 20.00 40.00
31 Charles Lamirande 20.00 40.00
32 Leon Gaudreault 20.00 40.00
33 Maurice Thiffault 20.00 40.00
34 Marc-Aurele Tremblay 20.00 40.00
35 Rene Pronovost 20.00 40.00
36 Victor Corbin 20.00 40.00
37 Tiny Tamminen 25.00 50.00
38 Guildor Levesque 20.00 40.00
39 Gaston Lamirande 20.00 40.00
40 Guy Gervais 20.00 40.00
41 Rayner Makila 25.00 50.00
42 Jules Tremblay 20.00 40.00
43 Roland Girard 20.00 40.00
44 Germain Bergeron 20.00 40.00
45 Paul Duchesne 20.00 40.00
46 Roger Beaudoin 20.00 40.00
47 Georges Archibal 20.00 40.00
48 Claude Basque 20.00 40.00
49 Roger Sarda 20.00 40.00
50 Edgard Gendron 20.00 40.00
51 Gaston Labossiere 20.00 40.00
52 Roland Clantara 20.00 40.00
53 Florian Gravel 20.00 40.00
54 Jean-Guy Thompson 20.00 40.00
55 Yvan Forton 20.00 40.00
56 Yves Laporte 20.00 40.00
57 Claude Germain 20.00 40.00
58 Gerry Brunet 20.00 40.00
59 Maurice Courteau 25.00 50.00

1951-52 Laval Dairy QSHL

The 1951-52 Laval Dairy QSHL set includes 109 black and white blank-back cards measuring approximately 1 3/4" by 2 1/2". These cards were issued in the province of Quebec and the Ottawa region. The cards are numbered and dated on the front. Key cards in this set are "Pre-Rookie Cards" of Jean Beliveau and Jacques Plante. The card numbering is organized by team as follows: Aces de Quebec (1-18 and 37), Chicoutimi (19-36), Sherbrooke (38-51), Shawinigan Falls (52-67), Valleyfield (68-84), Royals de Montreal (85-100), and Ottawa (101-109).

COMPLETE SET (109) 1000.00 2000.00
1 Jean Beliveau 375.00 750.00
2 Jean Marois 5.00 10.00
3 Joe Crozier 12.50 25.00
4 Jack Gelineau 5.00 10.00
5 Murdo McKay 6.00 12.00
6 Arthur Leyte 5.00 10.00
7 Bill LeBlanc 5.00 10.00
8 Robert Hayes 5.00 10.00
9 Yogi Kraiger 6.00 12.00
10 Frank King 5.00 10.00
11 Ludger Tremblay 6.00 12.00
12 Jackie Leclair 20.00 40.00
13 Martial Pruneau 5.00 10.00
14 Armand Gaudreault 5.00 10.00
15 Marcel Bonin 20.00 40.00
16 Herbie Carnegie 37.50 75.00
17 Claude Robert 5.00 10.00
18 Phil Renaud 5.00 10.00
19 Roland Hebert 5.00 10.00
20 Donat Duschene 5.00 10.00
21 Jacques Gagnon 5.00 10.00
22 Normand Dussault 6.00 12.00
23 Stan Smrke 10.00 20.00
24 Louis Smrke 6.00 12.00
25 Floyd Crawford 5.00 10.00
26 Germain Leger 5.00 10.00
27 Delphis Franche 5.00 10.00
28 Dick Wray 5.00 10.00
29 Guildor Levesque 7.50 15.00
30 Georges Roy 5.00 10.00
31 J.P. Lamirande 5.00 10.00
32 Gerard Glaude 5.00 10.00
33 Marcel Pelletier 10.00 20.00
34 Pete Tkachuck 5.00 10.00
35 Sherman White 5.00 10.00
36 Jimmy Moore 5.00 10.00
37 Punch Imlach 50.00 100.00
38 Alex Sandalax 5.00 10.00
39 William Kyle 5.00 10.00
40 Kenneth Biggs 5.00 10.00
41 Peter Wright 5.00 10.00
42 Rene Pepin 5.00 10.00
43 Tod Campeau 6.00 12.00
44 John Smith 5.00 10.00
45 Thomas McDougall 5.00 10.00
46 Jos. Lepine 5.00 10.00
47 Guy Labrie 5.00 10.00
48 Roger Bessette 5.00 10.00
49 Yvan Dugre 6.00 12.00
50 James Planche 5.00 10.00
51 Nils Tremblay 5.00 10.00
52 Bill MacDonagh 5.00 10.00
53 Georges Ouellet 5.00 10.00
54 Billy Arcand 5.00 10.00
55 Johnny Mahaffy 6.00 12.00
56 Bucky Buchanan 10.00 20.00
57 Al Miller 5.00 10.00
58 Don Penniston 5.00 10.00
59 Spike Laliberte 5.00 10.00
60 Ernie Oakley 5.00 10.00
61 Jack Bownass 5.00 10.00
62 Ted Hodgson 5.00 10.00
63 Lyall Wiseman 5.00 10.00
64 Erwin Grosse 5.00 10.00
65 Mel Read 5.00 10.00
66 Lloyd Henchberger 5.00 10.00
67 Jack Taylor 5.00 10.00
68 Marcel Bessette 5.00 10.00
69 Jack Schmidt 5.00 10.00
70 Paul Saindon 5.00 10.00
71 J.P. Bisaillon 5.00 10.00
72 Eddie Redmond 5.00 10.00
73 Larry Kwong 10.00 20.00
74 Andre Corriveau 5.00 10.00
75 Kitoute Joanette 5.00 10.00
76 Toe Blake 75.00 150.00
77 Georges Bougie 5.00 10.00
78 Jack Irvine 5.00 10.00
79 Paul Larivee 5.00 10.00
80 Paul Leclerc 5.00 10.00
81 Bertrand Bourassa 5.00 10.00
82 Jacques Deslauriers 5.00 10.00
83 Bingo Ernst 5.00 10.00
84 Gaston Gervais 5.00 10.00
85 Gerry Plamondon 6.00 12.00
86 Glen Harmon 5.00 10.00
87 Bob Friday 5.00 10.00
88 Rolland Rousseau 5.00 10.00
89 Billy Goold 5.00 10.00
90 Lloyd Finkbeiner 5.00 10.00
91 Cliff Malone 5.00 10.00
92 Jacques Plante 375.00 750.00
93 Gerard Desaulniers 6.00 12.00
94 Arthur Rose 5.00 10.00
95 Jacques Locas 5.00 10.00
96 Walter Clune 5.00 10.00
97 Louis Denis 5.00 10.00
98 Fernand Perreault 5.00 10.00
99 Douglas McNeil 6.00 12.00
100 Les Douglas 5.00 10.00
101 Howard Riopelle 10.00 20.00
102 Vic Grigg 5.00 10.00
103 Bobby Roberts 5.00 10.00
104 Legs Fraser 5.00 10.00
105 Butch Stahan 5.00 10.00
106 Fritz Frazer 5.00 10.00
107 Bill Robinson 5.00 10.00
108 Eddie Emberg 5.00 10.00
109 Leo Gravelle 12.50 25.00

1951-52 Laval Dairy Subset

The 1951-52 Laval Dairy Subset includes 66 skip-numbered black and white blank-back cards measuring approximately 1 3/4" by 2 1/2". Apparently, this set was intended to update the QSHL set and was issued after the QSHL set perhaps even as late as the 1952-53 season. The card numbering is organized by team as follows: Aces de Quebec (7-15 and 117), Chicoutimi (25-38), Sherbrooke (39-57), Shawinigan Falls (59-67, 89-90, 94-95, 115, 118, and 120), Valleyfield (68-84 and 116), Royals de Montreal (85-86, 92-93, and 96-97), and Ottawa (98-114, 119, and 121).

COMPLETE SET (66) 750.00 1500.00
4 Jack Gelineau SP 25.00 50.00
7 Al Miller 10.00 20.00
8 Walter Pawlyshyn 10.00 20.00
9 Yogi Kraiger SP 25.00 50.00
10 Al Baccari 10.00 20.00
12 Denis Smith 10.00 20.00
13 Pierre Brillant 10.00 20.00
14 Frank Mario 10.00 20.00
15 Danny Nixon 10.00 20.00
25 Leon Bouchard 10.00 20.00
26 Pete Taillefer 10.00 20.00
29 Bucky Buchanan 12.50 25.00
36 Marius Groleau 10.00 20.00
38 Fernand Perreault 10.00 20.00
39 Robert Drainville 10.00 20.00
40 Ronnie Matthews 10.00 20.00
44 Roger Roberge 10.00 20.00
46 Pete Wywrot 10.00 20.00
50 Gilles Dube 10.00 20.00
51 Nils Tremblay SP 25.00 50.00
52 Bob Pepin 10.00 20.00
53 Dewar Thompson 10.00 20.00
55 Irene St.Hilaire 10.00 20.00
56 Martial Pruneau 10.00 20.00
57 Jacques Locas 10.00 20.00
59 Nelson Podolsky 10.00 20.00
60 Bert Giesebrecht 10.00 20.00
61 Steve Brklaicich 10.00 20.00
65 Jack Hamilton 10.00 20.00
66 Dave Gatherum 10.00 20.00
67 Jean-Marie Plante 10.00 20.00
68 Gordie Haworth 12.50 25.00
69 Jack Schmidt SP 25.00 50.00
70 Bruce Cline 12.50 25.00
72 Phil Vitale 10.00 20.00
81 Carl Smelle 10.00 20.00
84 Tom Smelle 10.00 20.00
85 Gerry Plamondon 12.50 25.00
86 Glen Harmon 10.00 20.00
89 Frank Bathgate 10.00 20.00
90 Bernie Lemonde 10.00 20.00
92 Jacques Plante 375.00 750.00
93 Gerard Desaulniers 10.00 20.00
94 J.C. Lebrun 10.00 20.00
95 Bob Leger 10.00 20.00
96 Walter Clune 10.00 20.00
97 Louis Denis 10.00 20.00
98 Jackie Leclair 15.00 30.00
99 John Arundel 10.00 20.00
100 Les Douglas 10.00 20.00
103 Bobby Robertson 10.00 20.00
104 Ray Fredericks 10.00 20.00
106 Emile Dagenais 10.00 20.00
108 Al Kuntz 10.00 20.00
110 Red Johnson 10.00 20.00
111 John O'Flaherty 10.00 20.00
112 Jack Giesebrecht 12.50 25.00
113 Bill Richardson 10.00 20.00
114 Bep Guidolin 20.00 40.00
115 Roger Bedard 10.00 20.00
116 Renald Lacroix 10.00 20.00
117 Gordie Hudson 10.00 20.00
118 Dick Wray 10.00 20.00
119 Ronnie Hurst 10.00 20.00
120 Eddie Joss 10.00 20.00
121 Lyall Wiseman 10.00 20.00

2014-15 Laval Predateurs

COMPLETE SET (25) 6.00 15.00
1 Steve Bosse .30 .75
2 Mathieu Brisson .30 .75
3 Mathieu Brunelle .30 .75
4 Mathieu Corbeil-Theriault .30 .75
5 Frederick Cote .30 .75
6 Nicolas D'Aoust .30 .75
7 Joshua Desmarais .30 .75
8 Chris Doyle .30 .75
9 Manuel Frechette .30 .75
10 Francis Gourdeau .30 .75
11 Alexandre Imbeault .30 .75
12 Jeremi Janneteau .30 .75
13 Juraj Kolnik .30 .75
14 Jean-Francois LaPlante .30 .75
15 David Lacroix .30 .75
16 Louis-Philip Lacroix .30 .75
17 Eric Lajeunesse .30 .75
18 Dannick Lessard Asst. CO .30 .75
19 David Masse .30 .75
20 Pierre-Luc O'Brien .30 .75
21 Jonathan Oligny .30 .75
22 Steven Oligny .30 .75
23 Vincent Richer .30 .75
24 Joe Rullier .30 .75
25 Curtis Tidball .30 .75

1988-89 Lethbridge Hurricanes

This 24-card set was issued in 12 strips of three perforated cards with the third card on each strip being an ad or coupon card. The strips measure approximately 7 1/2" by 3 1/2". The fronts feature color posed player photos with a heavy black line framing the edge of the card leaving white space between the line and the picture. The team name, player's name, jersey number, and position appear in the white margin at the bottom. The cards are unnumbered and checklisted below in alphabetical order.

COMPLETE SET (24) 4.80 12.00
1 Mark Bassen .20 .50
2 Pete Berthelsen .20 .50
3 Bryan Bosch .20 .50
4 Paul Checknita .20 .50
5 Kelly Ens .20 .50
6 Jeff Ferguson .30 .75
7 Scott Fukami .20 .50
8 Colin Gregor .20 .50
9 Mark Greig .30 .75
10 Rob Hale .20 .50
11 Ted Hutchings .20 .50
12 Dusty Imoo .30 .75
13 Ivan Jessey .20 .50
14 Mark Kuntz .20 .50
15 Corey Lyons .20 .50
16 Shane Mazutinec .20 .50
17 Casey McMillan .20 .50
18 Pat Pylypuik .20 .50
19 Brad Rubachuk .20 .50
20 Jason Ruff .20 .50
21 Chad Seibel .20 .50
22 Wes Walz .60 1.50
23 Jim Wheatcroft .20 .50
24 Team Picture .20 .50

989-90 Lethbridge Hurricanes

›wing signs of perforation, this 24-card set was ued in strips of several cards each. The cards asure the standard size when separated and feature ed, color player photos. The photos are set on a te card face with a heavy black line framing the e of the card, leaving white space between the line the picture. The player's name, jersey number, and ition appear in the white margin at the bottom. The ks carry "Tips from the Hurricanes," which are key tips and public service messages. The cards unnumbered and checklisted below in alphabetical er.

MPLETE SET (24) 8.00 20.00
oug Barrault .30 .75
eter Berthelsen .30 .75
ryan Bosch .30 .75
elly Ens .30 .75
lark Greig .30 .75
on Gunville .30 .75
ob Hale .30 .75
eil Hawryluk .30 .75
avid Holzer .30 .75
Dusty Imoo .60 1.50
Darcy Kaminski ACO .08 .25
Bob Loucks CO .08 .25
Corey Lyons .30 .75
Duane Maruschak .30 .75
Jamie McLennan 1.25 3.00
Shane Peacock .30 .75
Pat Pylypuik .30 .75
Gary Reilly .30 .75
Brad Rubachuk .30 .75
Jason Ruff .30 .75
Kevin St. Jacques .30 .75
Wes Walz .60 1.50
Darcy Werenka .40 1.00
Brad Zimmer .30 .75

993-94 Lethbridge Hurricanes

s 24-card set was issued on three-card perforated ps each consisting of two player cards and one ertisement or coupon card. The strips measure 7 " by 3 1/2", and if cut, the individual cards would asure the standard size. The fronts of each card ure a color posed player photo with thin red ders on a white background. The cards are umbered and checklisted below in alphabetical er.

MPLETE SET (24) 4.80 12.00
ob Daum CO .08 .25
irk DeWaele .20 .50
erek Diener .20 .50
cott Grieco .20 .50
avid Jesiolowski .20 .50
odd MacIsaac .20 .50
an Matwijiw .40 1.00
arry McMorran .20 .50
rad Mehalko .20 .50
Shane Peacock .20 .50
Randy Perry .20 .50
Domenic Pittis .30 .75
Byron Ritchie .25 .60
Bryce Salvador .40 1.00
Ryan Smith .20 .50
Lee Sorochan .30 .75
Mark Szoke .20 .50
Scott Townsend .20 .50
David Trofimenkoff .20 .50
Twister (Mascot) .02 .10
van Vologjaninov .20 .50
Jason Widmer .20 .50
Derek Wood .20 .50
Aaron Zarowny .20 .50

995-96 Lethbridge Hurricanes

: 25-card set was issued on three-card perforated ps measuring approximately 7 1/2" by 3 1/2". Each consists of two player cards and one ertisement card. The cards include player jersey nbers on the front, but are checklisted below habetically.

MPLETE SET (25) 8.00 20.00
ike Bayrack .40 1.00
hn Bradley .40 1.00
avis Brigley .40 1.00
avid Brumby .40 1.00
erek Diener .40 1.00
cott Grieco .40 1.00
e Hamilton .40 1.00
evor Hanas .40 1.00
an Hoople .40 1.00
Mike Josephson .40 1.00
Kirby Law .40 1.00
Bryan Maxwell CO .02 .10
Doyle McMorris .40 1.00
Brad Mehalko .40 1.00
Dennis Mullen .40 1.00
iri Novotny .40 1.00
Mike O'Grady .40 1.00
Randy Perry .40 1.00
Byron Ritchie .40 1.00
Bryce Salvador .60 1.50
Darren Shakotko .40 1.00
Mark Smith .40 1.00
Dave Taylor .40 1.00
uc Theoret .40 1.00
Windy MASCOT .02 .10

996-97 Lethbridge Hurricanes

24-card set features color player photos with the 's nickname serving as a design element along the border. The player's name and number, along the team's anniversary logo also are featured. The umbered cards are checklisted below abetically.

MPLETE SET (24) 4.80 12.00
avis Brigley .20 .50
vid Cameron .20 .50
att Demarski .20 .50
ul Elliott .20 .50
son Hegberg .20 .50
artin Hohenberger .20 .50
an Hoople .20 .50
rk Ivan .20 .50
ke Josephson .20 .50
irby Law .30 .75
Mike O'Grady .20 .50
ale Purinton .75 2.00
yron Ritchie .30 .75
ryce Salvador .30 .75
ichard Seeley .20 .50
am Severson .20 .50
arren Shakotko .20 .50
es Schneider .20 .50
arry Shockey CO .08 .25
an Maxwell GM
ark Smith .20 .50
ave Taylor .20 .50
uc Theoret .20 .50
23 Evgeni Tsybouk .25 .60
24 Shane Yellowhorn .20 .50

1997-98 Lethbridge Hurricanes

This set features the Hurricanes of the WHL. Little else is known about this set beyond the confirmed checklist. Additional information can be forwarded to hockeymag@beckett.com.

COMPLETE SET (25) 4.80 12.00
1 Derrick Atkinson .20 .50
2 Brady Block .20 .50
3 Scott Borders .20 .50
4 Jeff Church .20 .50
5 Jason Hegberg .20 .50
6 Derek Holland .20 .50
7 Curtis Huppe .20 .50
8 Dustin Kazak .20 .50
9 Chad Kletzel .20 .50
10 Vladislav Klochkov .20 .50
11 Charlie Mattersdorfer .20 .50
12 Jason McLean .20 .50
13 Sean Robertson .20 .50
14 Bart Rushmer .20 .50
15 Thomas Scantlebury .20 .50
16 Darren Shakotko .20 .50
17 Mark Smith .40 1.00
18 Shaun Sutter .40 1.00
19 Luc Theoret .20 .50
20 Kaleb Toth .20 .50
21 Evgeni Tsybouk .30 .75
22 Mike Varhaug .20 .50
23 Trevor Wasyluk .20 .50
24 Shane Willis .40 1.00
25 Lethbridge Power .02 .10

1999-00 Lethbridge Hurricanes

This set features the Hurricanes of the WHL. The set was produced by the team and sold at home games. The cards are unnumbered, and thus are listed alphabetically.

COMPLETE SET (25) 4.80 12.00
1 Derek Atkinson .20 .50
2 Brian Ballman .20 .50
3 Nathan Barrett .20 .50
4 Brady Block .30 .75
5 Scott Borders .20 .50
6 Phil Cole .20 .50
7 Radek Duda .30 .75
8 Simon Ferguson .20 .50
9 Jordon Flodell .20 .50
10 Eric Godard .30 .75
11 Jason Hegberg .20 .50
12 Brandon Janes .20 .50
13 Ryan Jorde .20 .50
14 Dustin Kazak .20 .50
15 Angel Krstev .20 .50
16 Petr Kudrna .20 .50
17 Darren Lynch .20 .50
18 Warren McCutheon .20 .50
19 Justin Ossachuk .20 .50
20 Derek Parker .20 .50
21 Brian Patterson .20 .50
22 Derrick Ruck .20 .50
23 Thomas Scantlebury .20 .50
24 Eric Sonnenberg .20 .50
25 Chad Yaremko .20 .50

2000-01 Lethbridge Hurricanes

This set features the Hurricanes of the WHL. The set was produced by the team and sold at home games.

COMPLETE SET (25) 4.80 40.00
1 Brian Ballman .60 1.50
2 Nathan Barrett 2.00 5.00
3 Scott Borders .60 1.50
4 Phil Cole .60 1.50
5 Simon Ferguson .60 1.50
6 Matt Fetzner .60 1.50
7 Mark Forth .60 1.50
8 Tim Green .60 1.50
9 Matt Jacques .60 1.50
10 Adam Johnson .60 1.50
11 Andrew Jungwirth .60 1.50
12 Tomas Kopecky 2.00 5.00
13 Ryley Layden .60 1.50
14 Darren Lynch .60 1.50
15 Joel Martin .75 2.00
16 Warren McCutcheon .60 1.50
17 Brett O'Malley .60 1.50
18 Brian Patterson .60 1.50
19 Martin Podlesak .75 2.00
20 Derek Ruck .60 1.50
21 Thomas Scantlebury .60 1.50
22 Blake Ward .75 2.00
23 Twister MASCOT .02 .10
24 Header Card .02 .10
25 Sponsor Card .02 .10

2001-02 Lethbridge Hurricanes

COMPLETE SET (23) 5.00 12.00
1 Matthew Berger .20 .50
2 Simon Ferguson .20 .50
3 Stewart Thiessen .20 .50
4 Tim Green .20 .50
5 Braden Appleby .20 .50
6 Tomas Kopecky .30 .75
7 Paul McBrien .20 .50
8 Nathan Barrett .30 .75
9 Martin Podlesak .20 .50
10 Kris Callaway .20 .50
11 Brian Patterson .20 .50
12 Ryley Layden .20 .50
13 D.J. King .20 .50
14 Logan Koopmans .30 .75
15 Brett O'Malley .20 .50
16 Scott Borders .20 .50
17 David Selthun .20 .50
18 Clay Plume .20 .50
19 Blake Ward .30 .75
20 Brent Seabrook .20 .50
21 Jeremy Jackson .20 .50
22 Nick Chibi .20 .50
23 Tyrell Moulton .20 .50

2003-04 Lethbridge Hurricanes

We have confirmed a handful of singles from this set.

1 Joel Andresen .75 2.00
2 John Lammers .75 2.00
3 Jake Riddle .75 2.00
4 Brent Seabrook 1.50 4.00
5 Nick Tarnasky .75 2.00
6 Kris Versteeg 2.00 5.00

2004-05 Lethbridge Hurricanes

Cards are not numbered.

COMPLETE SET (24) 10.00 25.00
1 Mark Ashton .40 1.00
2 Shawn Mezei .40 1.00
3 Brennan Chapman .40 1.00
4 Brent Seabrook .40 1.00
5 Tyler Redenbach .40 1.00
6 Kris Versteeg 2.00 5.00
7 Mark Olafson .40 1.00
8 John Lammers .40 1.00
9 Martin Ruzicka .40 1.00
10 Colton Yellow Horn .60 1.50
11 Kyle Pess .40 1.00
12 Michael Kaye .40 1.00
13 Kenny Petkau .40 1.00
14 Jon Filewich .40 1.00
15 Chase Hentuik .40 1.00
16 Neil Kodman .40 1.00
17 Rob Klinkhammer .40 1.00
18 Michal Gulasi .40 1.00
19 Mike Ulrich .40 1.00
20 Lenny Thunderchild .40 1.00
21 Jesse Dudas .40 1.00
22 Aaron Sorochan .60 1.50
23 Scott Bolland .60 1.50
24 MASCOT .04 .10

2005-06 Lethbridge Hurricanes

COMPLETE SET (24) 8.00 20.00
1 Mark Ashton .40 1.00
2 Andrew Bentz .40 1.00
3 Zach Boychuk .40 1.00
4 Ryan Bryce .40 1.00
5 Mike Cann .40 1.00
6 Jacob Dietrich .40 1.00
7 Mitch Fadden .40 1.00
8 Yashar Farmanara .40 1.00
9 Kris Hogg .40 1.00
10 Michael Kaye .40 1.00
11 Ryan Kerr .40 1.00
12 Dwight King .40 1.00
13 Randy King .40 1.00
14 Tomas Kudelka .40 1.00
15 Justin Leclerc .40 1.00
16 Gavin McHale .40 1.00
17 Mark Olafson .40 1.00
18 Isaac Reid .40 1.00
19 Brad Riege .40 1.00
20 Roman Wick .40 1.00
21 Ben Wright .40 1.00
22 Michael Wuchterl .40 1.00
23 Colton Yellowhorn .75 2.00
24 Twister MASCOT .02 .10

2014-15 Lethbridge Hurricanes

COMPLETE SET (22) 6.00 15.00
1 Scott Allan .30 .75
2 Carter Amson .30 .75
3 Florian Baltram .30 .75
4 Brayden Burke .30 .75
5 Giorgio Estephan .30 .75
6 Devan Fafard .30 .75
7 Carter Folk .30 .75
8 Kade Jensen .30 .75
9 Brandon Kennedy .30 .75
10 Ryley Lindgren .30 .75
11 Andrew Nielsen .30 .75
12 Kord Pankewicz .30 .75
13 Brady Reagan .30 .75
14 Jayden Sittler .30 .75
15 Stuart Skinner .30 .75
16 Pavel Skumatov .30 .75
17 Nick Walters .30 .75
18 Jamal Watson .30 .75
19 John Wesley .30 .75
20 Jaeger White .30 .75
21 Mike Winther .30 .75
22 Tyler Wong .30 .75

2003-04 Lewiston Maineiacs

COMPLETE SET (28) 12.00 20.00
1 Mathieu Aubin .30 .75
2 Gabriel Balasescu .30 .75
3 Vladislav Balaz .30 .75
4 Alex Bourret .60 1.50
5 Marc-Andre Cliché .60 1.50
6 Nicolas Cowan .30 .75
7 Matthew Davis .30 .75
8 Chad Denny .30 .75
9 Pierre-Luc Faubert .30 .75
10 Karl Fournier .30 .75
11 Bobby Gates .30 .75
12 Olivier Legault .30 .75
13 Travis Mealey .30 .75
14 Ryan Murphy .30 .75
15 Jonathan Paiement .30 .75
16 Alexandre Picard .75 2.00
17 Brandon Roach .30 .75
18 Maxime Robert .30 .75
19 Richard Stehlik .30 .75
20 Francis Trudel .30 .75
21 Kevin Turgeon .30 .75
22 Brandon Verge .30 .75
23 Sheldon Wenzel .30 .75
24 Mario Durocher CO .04 .10
25 Jeff Guay ACO .04 .10
26 Ed Harding ACO .04 .10
27 Lewy MASCOT .04 .10
28 Team Photo CL .10 .25

2002-03 Lexington Men O'War

COMPLETE SET (26) 8.00 20.00
1 Team Photo .20 .50
2 Jim Wiley .30 .75
3 Justin Van Parys .30 .75
4 Mike Smith .30 .75
5 Marc-Andre Thinel .30 .75
6 Jared Smyth .30 .75
7 Jesse Cook .30 .75
8 Ben Storey .30 .75
9 Mark Smith .60 1.50
10 Dan Murphy .60 1.50
11 Daryl Moor .30 .75
12 Alexander Mathieu .30 .75
13 Dominic Periard .30 .75
14 Chris Dirkes .30 .75
15 Van Burgess .30 .75
16 Fraser Clair .30 .75
17 Terry Craven .30 .75
18 Brett Draney .30 .75
19 Joe Vandermeer .30 .75
20 Aaron Miskovich .30 .75
21 Jay Banach .30 .75
22 Ryan Fultz .30 .75
23 Mike Sgroi .30 .75
24 Josh Mizerek .30 .75
25 Kevin Knopp .30 .75
26 Mow MASCOT .04 .10

2000-01 Lincoln Stars

This set featured the Lincoln Stars of the USHL. Cards are numbered XX of 28 on the card backs.

COMPLETE SET (28)
1 Nick Fouts .30 .75
2 Ken Scruderi .15 .40
3 Tom Watkins .15 .40
4 Andy Schneider .15 .40
5 Matt Wavra .15 .40
6 Chris Fournier .15 .40
7 Mike Fournier .15 .40
8 John Snowden .15 .40
9 Nick Fuher .15 .40
10 Preston Callander .15 .40
11 Bobby John Byfuglien .15 .40
12 Josh Magnuson .15 .40
13 Brandon Polich .15 .40
14 Chad Hontvet .15 .40
15 Billy Hengen .15 .40
16 Ryan Young .15 .40
17 Matthew Trojovsky .15 .40
18 Lee Marvin .15 .40
19 Brandon Bochenski .15 .40
20 Trevor Frischmon .15 .40
21 Marco Peluso .15 .40
22 Jake Brandt .30 .75
23 Justin Johnson .30 .75
24 Beau Fritz .30 .75
25 Steve Johnson HCO .10 .25
26 Steve Ross ACO .10 .25
27 Corey Courtney TR .10 .25
28 Mascot .10 .25

2001-02 Lincoln Stars

This 28-card set features the Lincoln Stars of the USHL.

COMPLETE SET (28) 5.00 12.00
1 Ben Assenmacher .20 .50
2 David Backes .40 1.00
3 Josh Budish .20 .50
4 Jamie Dowhatko .20 .50
4 Mike Eickman .20 .50
6 Luke Erickson .20 .50
7 Matt Erickson .20 .50
8 Mike Fournier .20 .50
9 Trevor Frischmon .20 .50
10 Beau Fritz .30 .75
11 Ethan Graham .20 .50
12 Billy Hengen .20 .50
13 Chad Hontvet .20 .50
14 Dan Irmen .20 .50
15 Patrick Knutson .20 .50
16 Philippe Lamoureux .30 .75
17 Lee Marvin .20 .50
18 T.J. McElroy .20 .50
19 Ryan Potulny .20 .50
20 John Snowden .20 .50
21 Dirk Southern .20 .50
22 Ryan Swanson .20 .50
23 Matt Wavra .20 .50
24 Nate Ziegelmann .30 .75
25 Steve Johnson HCO .04 .10
26 Mark Pivetz ACO .04 .10
27 Corey Courtney TR .04 .10
28 Mascot .04 .10

2002-03 Lincoln Stars

This series was issued in two parts. Cards 31-48 were issued as a supplemental set.

COMPLETE SET (48) 8.00 20.00
1 Philippe Lamoureux .20 .50
2 Ethan Graham .20 .50
3 David Backes .40 1.00
4 Mike Eickman .20 .50
5 Chris Porter .20 .50
6 Ryan Potulny .20 .50
7 Danny Irmen .20 .50
8 Mike Fournier .20 .50
9 Tyler Magura .20 .50
10 John Snowden .20 .50
11 Ben Gordon .20 .50
12 Jamison Orr .20 .50
13 Mick Berge .20 .50
14 Mike Nesdill .20 .50
15 Brent Borgen .20 .50
16 Matt Hayek .20 .50
17 David Carlisle .20 .50
18 Luke Erickson .20 .50
19 Jesse Lindenberg .20 .50
20 Keith Rodger .20 .50
21 Robbie Bina .20 .50
22 Joel Gasper .20 .50
23 Ross Cherry .20 .50
24 Nate Ziegelmann .20 .50
25 Steve Johnson .20 .50
26 Mark Pivetz .20 .50
27 Rob Facca .20 .50
28 Corey Courtney .20 .50
29 Starzan MASCOT .04 .10
30 Checklist .04 .10
31 Mark Schwamberger .20 .50
32 Jeff McFarland .20 .50
33 Per Mars .20 .50
34 David Backes AS .40 1.00
35 Chris Porter AS .20 .50
36 Ryan Potulny AS .20 .50
37 Dan Irmen AS .20 .50
38 John Snowden AS .20 .50
39 Nate Ziegelmann AS .20 .50
40 Philippe Lamoureux .20 .50
41 Ethan Graham .20 .50
42 David Backes .40 1.00
43 Mike Eickman .20 .50
44 Ryan Potulny .20 .50
45 Dan Irmen .20 .50
46 John Snowden .20 .50
47 Nate Ziegelmann .20 .50
48 Update Checklist .04 .10

2003-04 Lincoln Stars

COMPLETE SET (29) 12.00
1 Philippe Lamoureux .20 .50
2 Morgan Simonson .20 .50
3 Kaj Kallarsson .20 .50
4 Jared Boll .20 .50
5 Evan Rankin .20 .50
6 Nick Tuzzolino .20 .50
7 Garrett Raboin .20 .50
8 Tyler Magura .20 .50
9 Ben Gordon .20 .50
10 Mick Berge .20 .50
11 Michael Nesdill .20 .50
12 Brent Borgen .20 .50
13 Alexcei McAvoy .20 .50
14 Matt Hayek .20 .50
15 David Carlisle .20 .50
16 Andrew Guyer .20 .50
17 Jesse Lindenberg .20 .50
18 Chris Tarkir .20 .50
19 Keith Rodger .20 .50
20 Adam Bartholomay .20 .50
21 Michael Waidlich .20 .50
22 Dan Comrie .20 .50
23 Aaron Walski .20 .50
24 Aaron McCloy .20 .50
25 Steve Johnson CO .04 .10
26 Rob Facca ACO .04 .10
27 Corey Courtney TR .04 .10
28 Mascot .04 .10
29 Checklist .04 .10

2003-04 Lincoln Stars Update

COMPLETE SET (18) 3.00 8.00
30 Checklist .04 .10
31 John Vadnais .20 .50
32 Dan Riedel .20 .50
33 Derek Whitmore .20 .50
34 Jered Bye .20 .50
35 Chris Robinson .20 .50
36 John Swanson .20 .50
37 Matt Weir .20 .50
38 Checklist .04 .10
39 Philippe Lamoureux .20 .50
Tyler Magura
40 Ben Gordon .20 .50
Mick Berge
41 Mike Nesdill .20 .50
Brent Borgen
42 Matt Hayek .20 .50
David Carlisle
43 Philippe Lamoureux RB .20 .50
44 Philippe Lamoureux AS .20 .50
45 Evan Rankin AS .20 .50
46 Nick Tuzzolino AS .20 .50
47 David Carlisle AS .20 .50

2004-05 Lincoln Stars

This USHL set was sold at home games. Reportedly, there were certified autographs included in some sets. We have yet to confirm their existence. If you can help, write us at hockeymag@beckett.com.

COMPLETE SET (30) 5.00 12.00
1 Jordan Pearce .40 1.00
2 Brian Bina .20 .50
3 John Vadnais .20 .50
4 Jared Boll .40 1.00
5 Dillon Duncan .20 .50
6 Dan Riedel .20 .50
7 Garrett Raboin .20 .50
8 Erik Condra .20 .50
9 Eli Vlaisavljevich .20 .50
10 J.J. Koehler .20 .50
11 Ryan Hohl .20 .50
12 Shawn Gawrys .20 .50
13 Chris Nugent .20 .50
14 David Carlisle .20 .50
15 Mike Kramer .20 .50
16 Mick Berge .20 .50
17 Tom Sawatske .20 .50
18 Brock Trotter .20 .50
19 Chris Robinson .20 .50
20 John Swanson .20 .50
21 Steve Jakiel .20 .50
22 Patrik Valcak .20 .50
23 Linus Klasen .20 .50
24 Steve Johnson CO .04 .10
25 Ryan Bencurik ACO .04 .10
26 Derek Reynolds ACO .04 .10
27 Corey Courtney TR .04 .10
28 Starzan MASCOT .04 .10
29 Checklist .04 .10
30 contest card .04 1.00

2004-05 Lincoln Stars Update

Issued on Feb. 21, 2005 as an update to the team set issued earlier in the season. It has been reported that just 350 copies of the Update series were produced. The set is noteworthy for the inclusion of Brian Lee, the ninth overall pick in 2005.

COMPLETE SET (18) 5.00 12.00
31 Brian Lee 1.50 4.00
32 Kyle Hardwick .20 .50
33 Chris Vande Velde .40 1.00
34 Russ Sinkewich .20 .50
35 Ryan Salvis .20 .50
36 Chris Murphy .20 .50
37 Ryan Kelly .20 .50
38 Taylor Raszka .20 .50
39 Jared Boll .40 1.00
40 Dan Riedel .20 .50
41 Garrett Raboin .20 .50
42 David Carlisle .20 .50
43 Mick Berge .20 .50
44 Chris Robinson .20 .50
45 Jordan Pearce AS .40 1.00
46 Jared Boll AS .40 1.00
47 Dan Riedel AS .20 .50
48 Tom Sawatske AS .20 .50

2006-07 Lincoln Stars

COMPLETE SET (29) 10.00 18.00
1 Lincoln Stars .10 .25
2 David Brack .30 .75
3 Chad Langlais .30 .75
4 Rick Carden .30 .75
5 Eric Lake .30 .75
6 Chris Stansik .30 .75
7 Jared Brown .30 .75
8 Matt Bartkowski .30 .75
9 Stephen Schultz .30 .75
10 Ryan Ruikka .30 .75
11 Jason Gregoire .40 1.00
12 Brandon Bollig .30 .75
13 Danny Baco .30 .75
14 Ross Henry .30 .75
15 Mike Kramer .30 .75
16 Ryan Lowery .30 .75
17 Colby Cohen .30 .75
18 Kyle O'Kane .30 .75
19 Pat McAuley .30 .75
20 Jon Morrow .40 1.00
21 Kyle Follmer .30 .75
22 Bryan Hogan .40 1.00
23 Anthony Principato .30 .75
24 Carter Camper .30 .75
25 Steve Johnson CO .10 .25
26 Ryan Bencurik ACO .02 .10
27 Jim McGroarty ACO .02 .10
28 Corey Courtney TR .02 .10
29 Starzan MASCOT .02 .10

2006-07 Lincoln Stars Traded

COMPLETE SET (18) 5.00 12.00
1T Checklist .02 .10
2T Patrick Johnson .30 .75
3T Joey Miller .30 .75
4T J.J Crew .30 .75
5T Mike Hull .30 .75
6T Dan Lawson .30 .75
7T Bryce Christianson .30 .75
8T Chad Langlais .30 .75
9T Chris Stansik .30 .75
10T Jared Brown .30 .75
11T Brandon Bollig .30 .75
12T Danny Baco .30 .75
13T Mike Kramer .30 .75
14T Bryan Hogan .30 .75
15T Chad Langlais .30 .75
16T Stephen Schultz .30 .75
17T Colby Cohen .30 .75
18T Cartor Campor .40 1.00

2006-07 Lincoln Stars Upper Deck Signature Series

Each card is signed and serial numbered out of 9, except for the cards of O'Kane and McAuley, who were traded prior to the cards being issued.

1 Danny Baco 20.00 50.00
2 Matt Bartowski 20.00 50.00
3 Brandon Bollig 25.00 60.00
4 David Brack 20.00 50.00
5 Jared Brown 20.00 50.00
6 Carter Camper 20.00 50.00
7 Rick Carden 20.00 50.00
8 Bryce Christianson 20.00 50.00
9 Colby Cohen 20.00 50.00
10 J.J. Crew 20.00 50.00
11 Kyle Follmer 20.00 50.00
12 Jason Gregoire 25.00 60.00
13 Ross Henry 20.00 50.00
14 Bryan Hogan 25.00 60.00
15 Mike Hull 20.00 50.00
16 Patrick Johnson 20.00 50.00
17 Mike Kramer 20.00 50.00
18 Eric Lake 20.00 50.00
19 Chad Langlais 20.00 50.00
20 Dan Lawson 20.00 50.00
21 Pat McAuley 4.00 10.00
22 Joey Miller 20.00 50.00
23 Kyle O'Kane 4.00 10.00
24 Stephen Schultz 20.00 50.00
25 Chris Stansik 20.00 50.00

2007-08 Lincoln Stars

COMPLETE SET (57) 10.00 25.00
1 Kevin Murdock .25 .60
2 Mike Dalhuisen .25 .60
3 Jake Newton .25 .60
4 Dennis Brown .25 .60
5 Michael Sdao .25 .60
6 Rick Carden .25 .60
7 Mike Henderson .25 .60
8 Kyle Follmer .25 .60
9 Jared Festler .25 .60
10 Matt Bartkowski .25 .60
11 Ryan Kretzer .25 .60
12 Kyle Verbeek .25 .60
13 Jason Gregoire .25 .60
14 Brandon Bollig .25 .60
15 Danny Baco .25 .60
16 Ross Henry .25 .60
17 P.J. Tatum .25 .60
18 Travis Erstad .25 .60
19 J.J. Crew .25 .60
20 Kyle Delaurell .25 .60
21 Tyler Brickler .25 .60
22 Tyler Kieffer .25 .60
23 Nick Hopper .25 .60
24 Jimmy McGroarty .25 .60
25 Nick Fuher .25 .60
26 Nick Fouts .25 .60
27 Corey Courtney .25 .60
28 I.C. Starz (Mascot) .15 .40
29 Lincoln Stars CL .15 .40
30 Checklist .15 .40
31 Kevin Murdock .25 .60
32 Mike Dalhuisen .25 .60
33 Lyon Messier .25 .60
34 Jake Newton .25 .60
35 Taylor Kuypers .25 .60
36 Michael Sdao .25 .60
37 Rick Carden .25 .60
38 Kyle Follmer .25 .60
39 Jared Festler .25 .60
40 Matt Bartkowski .25 .60
41 Ryan Kretzer .25 .60
42 Jimmy Hayes .25 .60
43 Jason Gregoire .25 .60
44 Brandon Bollig .25 .60
45 Danny Baco .25 .60
46 Ross Henry .25 .60
47 Chris Forfar .25 .60
48 Travis Erstad .25 .60
49 J.J Crew .25 .60
50 Eric Meland .25 .60
51 Josh Myers .25 .60
52 Tyler Brickler .25 .60
53 David Reekie .25 .60
54 Jared Festler .25 .60
55 Matt Bartkowski .25 .60
56 Jason Gregoire .25 .60
57 Ross Henry .25 .60

2014-15 Lincoln Stars

COMPLETE SET (36) 10.00 25.00
1 Header Card CL .30 .75
2 Cam Hackett .30 .75
3 Connor Frantti .30 .75
4 James LaDouce .30 .75
5 Dylan Woolf .30 .75
6 Ryan Cook .30 .75
7 Chris Klack .30 .75
8 Dominick Sacco .30 .75
9 Miguel Fidler .30 .75
10 Christopher Dodero .30 .75
11 Max Humitz .30 .75
12 Joe Lappin .30 .75
13 August Von Ungern-Sternberg .30 .75
14 Michael Gillespie .30 .75
15 Ludvig Hoff .30 .75
16 Wyatt Kalynuk .30 .75
17 Angus Scott .30 .75
18 Tye Ausmus .30 .75
19 Ryan Jones .30 .75
20 Cam Lee .30 .75
21 Grant Jozefek .30 .75
22 Biagio Lerario .30 .75
23 Patrick Polino .30 .75
24 Blake Christensen .30 .75
25 Peyton Jones .30 .75
26 Chris Hartsburg CO .30 .75
27 Mick Berge Asst. CO .30 .75
28 Corey Courtney Trainer .30 .75
29 John Hull GM .30 .75
30 Southside Auto Tech Ad .30 .75
1T Luke Jaycox .30 .75
2T Ethan Price .30 .75
3T Waltteri Hopponen .30 .75
4T Jack Badini .30 .75
5T Chris Gambardella .30 .75
6T Sean MacTavish .30 .75

2015-16 Lincoln Stars

COMPLETE SET (30) 6.00 15.00
1 Checklist .30 .75
2 Dylan Woolf .30 .75
3 Christian Hausinger .30 .75
4 Luke Jaycox .30 .75
5 Liam Schioler .30 .75
6 Anthony Wyse .30 .75
7 Will D'Orsi .30 .75
8 Carson Gicewicz .30 .75
9 Joachim Weber .30 .75
10 Henry Bowlby .30 .75
11 Christian Evers .30 .75
12 Sam Kauppila .30 .75
13 Ludvig Hoff .30 .75
14 Nate Pionk .30 .75
15 Adam Brady .30 .75
16 Tye Ausmus .30 .75
17 Jack Badini .30 .75
18 Ryan Jones .30 .75
19 Grant Jozefek .30 .75
20 Biagio Lerario .30 .75
21 Patrick Polino .30 .75
22 Dominick Mersch .30 .75
23 Peyton Jones .30 .75
24 Patrik Virtanen .30 .75
25 Ethen Frank .30 .75
26 Chris Hartsburg CO .30 .75
27 Mick Berge Asst. CO .30 .75
28 Clay Adams .30 .75
29 Corey Courtney .30 .75
30 Cayden Primeau UCS .30 .75

1985-86 London Knights

The London Knights of the OHL are featured in this 30-card P.L.A.Y. (Police, Law and Youth) set, which was sponsored by the London Crime Prevention Committee in conjunction with area businesses. The cards measure approximately 2 3/4" by 3 1/2" and are printed on thin card stock. The fronts feature color photos with the players posed in action stances. A facsimile autograph is inscribed at the bottom of the picture.

COMPLETE SET (30) 20.00 50.00
1 LaVerne Shipley CoP .08 .25
2 Joe Ranger .20 .50
3 Kellogg's Ad CL .08 .25
4 Don Boyd GM/CO .08 .25
5 Harry E. Sparling COP .08 .25
6 Murray Nystrom .20 .50
7 Bob Halkidis .30 .75
8 Morgan Watts .20 .50
9 Brendan Shanahan 15.00 40.00
10 Brian Dobbin .30 .75
11 Ed Kister .20 .50
12 Darin Smith .20 .50
13 Greg Puhalski .20 .50
14 Dave Haas .20 .50
15 Pete McLeod .20 .50
16 Frank Tremblay .20 .50
17 Matthew Smyth .20 .50
18 Glen Leslie .20 .50
19 Mike Zombo .20 .50
20 Jamie Groke .20 .50
21 Brad Schlegel .30 .75
22 Kelly Cain .20 .50
23 Tom Allen .20 .50
24 Rod Gerow .20 .50
25 Pat Vachon .20 .50
26 Paul Cook ACO .08 .25
27 Jeff Reese .60 1.50
28 Fred Kean PR .08 .25
29 Scott Cumming .30 .75
30 John Williams ACO .08 .25

1986-87 London Knights

The London Knights of the OHL are featured in this 30-card P.L.A.Y. (Police, Law and Youth) set, which was sponsored by the London Crime Prevention Committee in conjunction with area businesses. The cards measure approximately 2 3/4" by 3 1/2" and are printed on thin card stock. The fronts feature color photos with the players posed in action stances. The set is noteworthy for featuring a card of Brendan Shanahan issued prior to his RC.

COMPLETE SET (30) 14.00 35.00
1 LaVerne Shipley CoP .08 .25
2 Tom Gosnell Mayor .08 .25
3 Kellogg's Ad CL .08 .25
4 Wayne Maxner CO/GM .20 .50
5 Harry E. Sparling COP .08 .25
6 Brendan Shanahan 10.00 25.00
7 Pat Vachon .20 .50
8 Brad Schlegel .20 .50
9 Barry Earhart .20 .50
10 Jean Marc MacKenzie .20 .50
11 Jason Simon .20 .50
12 Jim Sprott .20 .50
13 Bill Long VP .08 .25
14 Murray Nystrom .20 .50
15 Shayne Stevenson .30 .75
16 Don Martin .20 .50
17 Ian Pound .20 .50
18 Peter Lisy .20 .50
19 Steve Marcolini .20 .50
20 Craig Majaury .20 .50
21 Trevor Dam .20 .50
22 Dave Akey .20 .50
23 Dennis McEwen .20 .50
24 Shane Whelan .20 .50
25 Greg Hankkio .20 .50
26 Pat Kelly TR .08 .25
27 Stephen Titus .30 .75
28 Fred Kean PR .08 .25
29 Chris Somers .30 .75
30 Gord Clark MD .08 .25

1993-94 London Knights

This standard size set was issued at home games during the 1993-94 season. Card fronts feature posed, color photos. Card backs feature statistics and biographical information. Cards are unnumbered and checklisted below alphabetically.

COMPLETE SET (29) 4.80 12.00
1 Jason Allison 2.00 5.00
2 Ryan Appel .15 .40
3 Tim Bacik .08 .25
4 Ryan Black .08 .25
5 Chris Brassard .08 .25
6 Ryan Burgoyne .08 .25
7 Brodie Coffin .08 .25
8 Rob Frid .08 .25
9 David Gilmore .08 .25
10 Roy Gray .08 .25
11 John Guirestante .08 .25
12 Brent Holdsworth .08 .25
13 Don Margettie .08 .25
14 Dan Reja .08 .25
15 Daryl Rivers .00 .25
16 Gord Ross .08 .25
17 Kevin Slota .08 .25
18 Brian Stacey .08 .25
19 Nick Stajduhar .08 .25
20 Bill Tibbetts .40 1.00
21 Ben Walker .08 .25
22 Jordan Willis .15 .40
23 Chris Zanutto .08 .25
24 Knights Top Picks .08 .25
Ryan Appel
Ben Walker

Den Reja
Roy Gray
25 Knights Future Stars .40 1.00
Nick Stajduhar
Jason Allison
John Guirestante
Ryan Black
Jordan Willis
26 Gary Agnew CO .02 .10
27 Steve Stoyanovich ACO .02 .10
Tom Hedican CO
28 Murray Nystrom ACO .02 .10
29 Title Card .02 .10

2000-01 London Knights

This series features a 27-card main set and an eight-card "update." The series also features the first junior cards of Rick Nash.

COMPLETE SET (35) 25.00 50.00
1 Mark Hunter .20 .50
Dale Hunter
2 Bobby Turner .20 .50
3 Matt Cooper .20 .50
4 Aaron Lobb .20 .50
5 Lou Dickenson .20 .50
6 Lindsay Hofford ACO .02 .10
7 Kyle Neufeld .20 .50
8 Petr Hemsky .20 .50
9 Rick Nash 8.00 20.00
10 Brent Varty .20 .50
11 Danny Bois .30 .75
12 Joel Scherban .20 .50
13 Brian Dobbin .20 .50
14 Aaron Molnar .30 .75
15 Mike Clarke .20 .50
16 Ian Turner .20 .50
17 John Eminger .20 .50
18 Dan Jancevski .40 1.00
19 Jason Davies .20 .50
20 Logan Hunter .40 1.00
21 Checklist card .01 .01
22 Don Brankley TR .01 .01
23 Josh Chambers .20 .50
24 Chris Kelly .20 .50
25 Matt Albiani .20 .50
26 Matt Junkins .20 .50
27 Mike Stathopoulos .20 .50
U1 Chris Kelly .40 1.00
U2 Mark Hunter ACO .10 .25
U3 Dan Jancevski .40 1.00
U4 Logan Hunter .40 1.00
U5 Dale Hunter CO .20 .50
U6 Danny Bois .40 1.00
U7 Scorch MASCOT .02 .10
U8 Rick Nash 10.00 25.00

2001-02 London Knights

This set features the Knights of the OHL. The set was produced by the team and was sold at its souvenir stands. It's believed that 1,000 total sets were produced. The set is noteworthy for the inclusion of a card of Rick Nash, the first-overall pick in 2002, and Dale Hunter, owner of the Knights.

COMPLETE SET (30) 10.00 25.00
1 Title Card CL .04 .10
2 Sean Dixon .20 .50
3 Dennis Wideman .30 .75
4 Patrick Barbieri .20 .50
5 Bryan Thompson .20 .50
6 Chris Bain .20 .50
7 Mike Stathopoulos .20 .50
8 Danny Bois .20 .50
9 Matt Iannetta .20 .50
10 Charlie Stephens .30 .75
11 Dylan Hunter .20 .50
12 Logan Hunter .20 .50
13 Sean McMorrow .30 .75
14 Chad Thompson .20 .50
15 Rick Steadman .20 .50
16 Matt Junkins .20 .50
17 Dan Buccella .20 .50
18 Rick Nash 6.00 15.00
19 Robbie Colangelo .20 .50
20 Matt Iorianni .20 .50
21 Ian Turner .20 .50
22 Corey Perry 1.50 4.00
23 Jan Chovan .30 .75
24 Matt Weir .20 .50
25 Alex White .20 .50
26 Jacques Beaulieu ACO .04 .10
27 Lindsay Hofford ACO .04 .10
28 Dale Hunter CO .20 .50
29 Don Brankley TR .04 .10
NNO Mission Hockey AD .04 .10

2002-03 London Knights

COMPLETE CHECKLIST 8.00 20.00
1 Team Picture .04 .10
CL
2 Dennis Wideman .30 .75
3 Logan Hunter .30 .75
4 Corey Perry .75 2.00
5 Mike Stathopoulos .20 .50
6 Danny Bois .30 .75
7 Ryan Hare .20 .50
8 Dylan Hunter .40 1.00
9 Rick Steadman .20 .50
10 Matt Weir .20 .50
11 David Bolland .75 2.00
12 Kyle Piwowarczyk .20 .50
13 Brandon Prust .30 .75
14 Chris Bain .20 .50
15 Adam Nemeth .20 .50
16 Zach Trammer .20 .50
17 Danny Syvret .30 .75
18 Jimmy Ball .20 .50
19 Kyle Quincey .40 1.00
20 Marc Methot .30 .75
21 Gerald Coleman .40 1.00
22 Chris Houle .20 .50
23 Jayme Helmer .20 .50
24 Robbie Drummond .20 .50
25 Tomas Linhart .20 .50
26 Matt Iorianni .20 .50
27 Dale Hunter CO .20 .50
28 Don Brankley TR .04 .10
29 Jacques Beaulieu ACO .04 .10
30 Opening Night .04 .10

2003-04 London Knights

This 26-card set was sponsored by Remax and created by Extreme Sports cards. The set was sold at home games. The Perry team leader card at the end of the checklist is not considered part of the set and the set is complete without it.

COMPLETE SET (26) 10.00 20.00
1 Rob Schremp 1.25 3.00
2 Corey Perry .60 1.50
3 Adam Nemeth .30 .75
4 Danny Syvret .30 .75
5 Ivan Khomutov .20 .50
6 Jacques Beaulieu ACO .04 .10
7 Don Brankley TR .04 .10
8 Trevor Kell .20 .50
9 Dennis Wideman .30 .75
10 Marc Methot .20 .50
11 Vadim Karaga .20 .50
12 Scott Sheppard .20 .50
13 Dale Hunter CO .20 .50
14 Logan Hunter .30 .75
15 Rick Steadman .20 .50
16 Ryan MacDonald .40 1.00
17 Danny Bois .20 .50
18 David Bolland .40 1.00
19 Tommy Mannino .20 .50
20 Gerald Coleman .40 1.00
21 Dylan Hunter .40 1.00
22 Josh Beaulieu .20 .50
23 Robbie Drummond .20 .50
24 Ryan Pottruff .20 .50
25 Brandon Prust .30 .75
26 Danny Richmond .40 1.00
27 Corey Perry TL 2.50 6.00

2004-05 London Knights

Note: there is no card #24. Two cards bear the #25. A total of 2,600 team sets were produced.

COMPLETE SET (26) 15.00
1 Ryan MacDonald .30 .75
2 Rick Steadman .20 .50
3 Steve Ferry .20 .50
4 Rob Schremp .40 1.00
5 Trevor Kell .20 .50
6 Robbie Drummond .20 .50
7 Bryan Rodney .20 .50
8 Brandon Prust .20 .50
9 Corey Perry .75 2.00
10 Frank Rediker .20 .50
11 Danny Syvret .30 .75
12 Gerald Coleman .30 .75
13 David Bolland .40 1.00
14 Josh Beaulieu .20 .50
15 Dylan Hunter .40 1.00
16 Drew Larman .20 .50
17 Jordan Foreman .20 .50
18 Ryan Pottruff .20 .50
19 Kelly Thomson .20 .50
20 Shawn Futers .20 .50
21 Marc Methot .30 .75
22 Jeff Whitfield .20 .50
23 Dale Hunter CO .20 .50
25 Don Brankley TR .04 .10
25 Jacques Beaulieu ACO .04 .10
NNO Re .04 .10
Max Sponsor Card

2005-06 London Knights

COMPLETE SET (26) 5.00 12.00
1 Rob Schremp .60 1.50
2 Dylan Hunter .40 1.00
3 Trevor Kell .20 .50
4 Kris Belan .20 .50
5 Matt Clarke .20 .50
6 Jamie Vanderveeken .20 .50
7 Sergei Kostitsyn .40 1.00
8 Jordan Foreman .20 .50
9 Adam Perry .20 .50
10 David Bolland .40 1.00
11 Frank Rediker .20 .50
12 Matt McCready .20 .50
13 Scott Aarssen .20 .50
14 Steve Ferry .20 .50
15 Robbie Drummond .20 .50
16 Andrew Wilkins .20 .50
17 Ryan Martinelli .20 .50
18 Corey Syvret .20 .50
19 Josh Beaulieu .20 .50
20 Adam Dennis .40 1.00
21 Steve Mason .60 1.50
22 Dale Hunter CO .02 .10
23 Jaques Beaulieu ACO .02 .10
24 Jeff Perry ACO .02 .10
25 Don Brankley WATERBOY .01 .01
26 Chris Maton .02 .10

2006-07 London Knights

COMPLETE SET (26) 12.00 20.00
1 Sam Gagner 1.25 4.00
2 Patrick Kane 5.00 12.00
3 Steve Mason .40 1.00
4 Todd Perry .30 .75
5 Kevin Bodker .20 .50
6 Scott Aarssen .20 .50
7 David Jarram .20 .50
8 Josh Beaulieu .20 .50
9 Matt Clarke .20 .50
10 Philip Mcrae .20 .50
11 Robbie Drummond .20 .50
12 Tony Dehart .20 .50
13 Sergei Kostitsyn .40 1.00
14 Andrew Wilkins .20 .50
15 Ryan Martinelli .20 .50
16 Jordan Shine .20 .50
17 Adam Hasani .20 .50
18 Stephane Cesar .20 .50
19 Luke Vanmoerkerke .20 .50
20 David Meckler .20 .50
21 Jordan Foreman .20 .50
22 Corey Syvret .20 .50
23 Adam Perry .20 .50
24 Dale Hunter .20 .50
25 Dave Gagner .20 .50
26 Todd Bidner .10 .25

2007-08 London Knights

COMPLETE SET (26) 5.00 12.00
1 Steve Mason .25 .60
2 Stephen Heming .25 .60
3 Michael Zador .25 .60
4 Scott Aarssen .25 .60
5 Matt Ashmann .25 .60
6 Jadran Beljo .25 .60
7 Matt Clarke .25 .60
8 Tucker Hunter .25 .60
9 Garett Hunter .25 .60
10 Tony DeHart .25 .60
11 Kevin Montgomery .25 .60
12 Vladimir Roth .25 .60
13 Andrew Wilkins .25 .60
14 Kale Kerbashian .25 .60
15 Jordan Shine .25 .60
16 Patrick Maroon .25 .60
17 Akim Aliu .25 .60
18 Adam Perry .25 .60
19 Philip McRae .25 .60
20 Tony Romano .25 .60
21 Justin Taylor .25 .60
22 Sean O'Connor .25 .60
23 Dale Hunter .25 .60
24 Dave Gagne .25 .60
25 Pat Curcio .25 .60
26 Don Brankley .25 .60

2015-16 London Knights

COMPLETE SET (25) 6.00 15.00
1 Aaron Berisha .30 .75
2 Evan Bouchard .30 .75
3 Brandon Crawley .30 .75
4 Christian Dvorak .30 .75
5 Eric Henderson .30 .75
6 Jack Hidi .30 .75
7 Aiden Jamieson .30 .75
8 Max Jones .30 .75
9 Olli Juolevi .30 .75
10 Owen MacDonald .30 .75
11 Mitchell Marner 1.25 3.00
12 Chris Martenet .30 .75
13 Nicolas Mattinen .30 .75
14 Victor Mete .30 .75
15 Sam Miletic .30 .75
16 Tyler Parsons .30 .75
17 J.J. Piccinich .30 .75
18 Cliff Pu .40 1.00
19 Kole Sherwood .30 .75
20 Robert Thomas .30 .75
21 Matthew Tkachuk .30 .75
22 Ryan Valentini .30 .75
23 Emanuel Vella .30 .75
24 C.J. Yakimowicz .30 .75
25 Header Card CL .30 .75

1997-98 Long Beach Ice Dogs

Little is known about this set beyond the confirmed checklist. Additional information can be forwarded to hockeymag@beckett.com.

COMPLETE SET (20) 4.00 10.00
1 Doug Ast .20 .50
2 Patrik Augusta .20 .50
3 Collin Bauer .20 .50
4 Mike Buzak .20 .50
5 John Byce .20 .50
6 Brian Chapman .20 .50
7 Mark Ferner .20 .50
8 Victor Ignatjev .20 .50
9 Rob Kenny .20 .50
10 Dan Lambert .40 1.00
11 Mike Matteucci .20 .50
12 Joby Messier .20 .50
13 Stephane Morin .20 .50
14 Shawn Penn .20 .50
15 Russ Romaniuk .20 .50
16 Nicholas Vachon .20 .50
17 Andrei Vasilyev .20 .50
18 Kay Whitmore .40 1.00
19 Darryl Williams .20 .50
20 Spike MASCOT .02 .10

1998-99 Long Beach Ice Dogs

Little is known about this set beyond the confirmed checklist. Any additional information can be forwarded to hockeymag@beckett.com.

COMPLETE SET (20) 6.00 15.00
1 Doug Ast .20 .50
2 Patrik Augusta .20 .50
3 John Byce .20 .50
4 Dan Bylsma .20 .50
5 Mark Ferner .20 .50
6 Mike Jickling .20 .50
7 Frederick Jobin .20 .50
8 Claude Jutras .20 .50
9 Dan Lambert .30 .75
10 Manny Legace .60 1.50
11 Jocelyn Lemieux .20 .50
12 Mike Matteucci .20 .50
13 Sacha Molin .20 .50
14 Jan Nemecek .20 .50
15 Andy Roach .20 .50
16 Pavel Rosa .20 .50
17 Patrik Stefan 2.00 5.00
18 Darryl Williams .20 .50
19 John Van Boxmeer HCO .08 .25
20 Spike MASCOT .02 .10

1998-99 Long Beach Ice Dogs Promo

This single card of 1999 first-overall pick Patrik Stefan was given out to fans who attended a Long Beach Ice Dogs game during the 1998-99 season. The card was sponsored by Ice Breakers gum and was licensed by the Ice Dogs and the IHL.

NNO Patrik Stefan 2.00 5.00

1999-00 Long Beach Ice Dogs

This 10-card set was given away one card per home game during the 1999-2000 season. As such, complete sets are nearly impossible to find.

COMPLETE SET (10) 6.00 15.00
1 Rene Chapdelaine .75 2.00
2 Pavel Rosa .75 2.00
3 Mike Crowley .75 2.00
4 Mike O'Neill .75 2.00
5 Len Barrie .75 2.00
6 Mike Matteucci .40 1.00
7 Scott Thomas .75 2.00
8 Doug Ast .40 1.00
9 Spike Mascot .40 1.00
10 John Van Boxmeer HCO .40 1.00

1994-95 Los Angeles Blades RHI

This set features the Blades of Roller Hockey International. The cards were sold in set form by the team at home games.

COMPLETE SET (20) 3.00 8.00
1 Checklist .02 .10
2 Chris Nelson .20 .50
3 Mike Burman .20 .50
4 Steve Wilson .20 .50
5 Vaclav Nedomansky, Jr. .20 .50
6 Rob Hartnell .20 .50
7 Kraig Nienhuis .30 .75
8 Eric LeMarque .20 .50
9 Peter Kasowski .20 .50
10 Brett Kurtz .20 .50
11 Terran Sandwith .20 .50
12 Brad Sholl .20 .50
13 Mike Doers .20 .50
14 Steve Bogoyevac .20 .50
15 Sean Gauthier .20 .50
16 Eric Lavigne .20 .50
17 Mike Callahan .20 .50
18 Bobby Hull Jr. CO .20 .50
19 Jeanie Buss .02 .10
20 Los Angeles Blades Logo .02 .10

1995-96 Louisiana Ice Gators

This 21-card set of the Louisiana Ice Gators of the ECHL features borderless color player photos with the player's name, position, and jersey number printed in a green bar across the bottom. The backs carry player information. The cards are unnumbered and checklisted below in alphabetical order. This is the first of two sets released by the Ice Gators in 1995-96, their inaugural season.

COMPLETE SET (21) 4.80 12.00
1 Bob Berg .20 .50
2 John Depourcq .20 .50
3 Wade Fournier .20 .50
4 Fred Goltz .20 .50
5 Ron Handy .20 .50
6 Mike Heany .20 .50
7 Dean Hulett .20 .50
8 Jim Latos .20 .50
9 George Maneluk .30 .75
10 Rob McCaig .20 .50
11 Jason McQuat .20 .50
12 Rod Pasma .30 .75
13 Sean Rowe .20 .50
14 Bryan Schoen .30 .75
15 Darryl Shedden .20 .50
16 Doug Shedden CO .20 .50
17 Fred Spoltore .20 .50
18 Chris Valicevic .20 .50
19 Rob Valicevic .75 2.00
20 John Vary .20 .50
21 Marty Yewchuk .20 .50

1995-96 Louisiana Ice Gators Playoffs

This 21-card set features borderless color player photos with the player's name and jersey number printed in a black bar across the bottom. The backs carry player information. A note on the card back reveals no more than 2,500 sets were produced. The cards are unnumbered and checklisted below in alphabetical order.

COMPLETE SET (21) 4.00 10.00
1 Bob Berg .20 .50
2 Aaron Boh .20 .50
3 Eric Cloutier .20 .50
4 John DePourcq .20 .50
5 Wade Fournier .20 .50
6 Ron Handy .25 .60
7 Mike Heaney .20 .50
8 Dean Hulett .20 .50
9 Jim Latos .20 .50
10 George Maneluk .25 .60
11 Rob McCaig .20 .50
12 Jason McQuat .20 .50
13 Chad Nelson .20 .50
14 Dan O'Rourke .20 .50
15 Rod Pasma .30 .75
16 Darryl Shedden .20 .50
17 Doug Shedden CO .25 .60
18 John Spoltore .25 .60
19 Chuck Thuss .25 .60
20 Rob Valicevic .40 1.00
Chris Valicevic
21 John Vary .20 .50

1995 Louisiana Ice Gators Glossy

We have confirmed the existence of five cards in what might be a larger series of Ice Gators cards. These singles have a laminated finish, unlike the larger base set of Ice Gators cards this season. The cards are unnumbered and listed below in alphabetical order. If you have additional information, please contact us at hockeymag@beckett.com

COMPLETE SET (?)
1 Aaron Boh 4.00 10.00
2 Eric Cloutier 4.00 10.00
3 Chad Nelson 4.00 10.00
4 Dan O'Rourke 4.00 10.00
5 Chuck Thuss 5.00 12.00

1996-97 Louisiana Ice Gators

This set features the Ice Gators of the ECHL. It is believed that this set was issued by the team early in the season. Any additional information can be forwarded to hockeymag@beckett.com.

COMPLETE SET (23) 4.80 12.00
1 Bujar Amidovski .40 1.00
2 Doug Bonner .30 .75
3 Eric Cloutier .20 .50
4 Mark DeSantis .20 .50
5 Louis Dumont .20 .50
6 Blair Manning .20 .50
7 Roger Maxwell .20 .50
8 Jason McQuat .20 .50
9 Stan Melanson .20 .50
10 Jay Murphy .20 .50
11 Michael Murray .20 .50
12 Matt Pagnutti .20 .50
13 Don Parsons .20 .50
14 Team Photo .20 .50
15 Gary Roach .20 .50
16 Ryan Shanahan .20 .50
17 John Spoltore .30 .75
18 Chris Valicevic .30 .75
19 John Varga .30 .75
20 Rob Weingartner .20 .50
21 Billy Thurlow .20 .50
Bruce Livin
22 Doug Shedden HCO .08 .25
23 Alphonse MAS .02 .10

1996-97 Louisiana Ice Gators II

This set was issued by the team later in the season (or during the playoffs) and includes players acquired through the course of the season.

COMPLETE SET (22) 4.00 10.00
1 Aaron Boh .20 .50
2 John DePourcq .20 .50
3 Mark Delmore .20 .50
4 Louis Dumont .20 .50
5 Ron Handy .20 .50
6 Mikhail Kravets .20 .50
7 James Latos .20 .50
8 Rob McCaig .20 .50
9 Jason McQuat .20 .50
10 Stan Melanson .20 .50
11 Joey Mittelsteadt .30 .75
12 Chad Nelson .20 .50
13 Dan O'Rourke .20 .50
14 Ken Ruddick .20 .50
15 Dean Seymour .20 .50
16 Ryan Shanahan .20 .50
17 Darryl Shedden .20 .50
18 Sergei Tkachenko .20 .50
19 Chris Valicevic .30 .75
20 Rob Weingartner .20 .50
21 Jack Williams .20 .50
22 Doug Shedden HCO .08 .25

1997-98 Louisiana Ice Gators

This set features the Ice Gators of the ECHL. Little is known about this set beyond the confirmed checklist. Additional information can be forwarded to hockeymag@beckett.com.

COMPLETE SET (22) 4.00 10.00
1 Louis Dumont .20 .50
2 Jason McQuat .20 .50
3 Alphonse MAS .02 .10
4 Matt Pagnutti .20 .50
5 Richard Smit .20 .50
6 John Varga .30 .75
7 Jay Murphy .20 .50
8 Darrel Woodley .20 .50
9 Scott McKay .20 .50
10 Jack Williams .20 .50
11 Stan Melanson .20 .50
12 Brad Toporowski .20 .50
13 John Jennings EM .02 .10
14 Eric Cloutier .20 .50
15 Ryan Pisiak .20 .50
16 John Spoltore .30 .75
17 Mikhail Kravets .20 .50
18 Paul Rushforth .20 .50
19 Doug Bonner .30 .75
20 Chad Nelson .20 .50
21 Doug Shedden HCO .08 .25
22 Don Parsons .20 .50

1998-99 Louisiana Ice Gators

This set features the Ice Gators of the ECHL. The set was produced by Starz Cards and was sold by the team at home games.

COMPLETE SET (26) 4.00 10.00
1 Mascot .15 .40
2 Bujar Amidovski .30 .75
3 Doug Bonner .30 .75
4 Eric Cloutier .15 .40
5 Mark Desantis .15 .40
6 Louis Dumont .15 .40
7 Blair Manning .15 .40
8 Roger Maxwell .15 .40
9 Jason McQuat .15 .40
10 Stan Melanson .15 .40
11 Jay Murphy .30 .75
12 Mike P. Murray .20 .50
13 Matthew Pagnutti .15 .40
14 Don Parsons .15 .40
15 Gary Roach .15 .40
16 Ryan Shanahan .30 .75
17 Doug Shedden CO .15 .40
18 John Spoltore .02 .10
19 Billy Thurlow .30 .75
Bruce Livin CO
20 Chris Valicevic .30 .75
21 John Varga .20 .50
22 Rob Weingartner .15 .40
23 Team Card .02 .10

1999-00 Louisiana Ice Gators

This set features the Ice Gators of the ECHL. This set was produced by Roox, and sold by the team at home games. The numbering system of the set is less than ideal, as there are two versions of both card No. 1 and 2. It is believed that cards No 21-23 also exist, but they have not yet been confirmed. Anyone with additional information should contact hockeymag@beckett.com.

COMPLETE SET (25) 4.80 12.00
1 Vaclav Nedomansky .20 .50
1 Sean Gauthier .20 .50
2 Michael Murray .20 .50
2 Mike Oliveira .20 .50
3 Matt Pagnutti .20 .50
4 Jesse Rezansoff .20 .50
5 Mike Kucsulain .20 .50
6 Stan Melanson .20 .50
7 Shawn McNeil .20 .50
8 Ryan Shanahan .20 .50
9 John DePourcq .30 .75
10 Hugo Marchand .20 .50
11 Corey Neilson .20 .50
12 Chris Bogas .20 .50
13 Jason McQuat .30 .75
14 John Spoltore .30 .75
15 Dave Arsenault .20 .50
16 Chris Valicevic .30 .75
17 Jason Sessa .20 .50
18 Mark Cadotte .20 .50
19 Jay Murphy .20 .50
20 John Jennings TR .02 .10
24 Dennis Holland CO .02 .10
25 Don Murdoch CO .02 .10
26 Claw'd MAS .08 .25

2000-01 Louisiana Ice Gators

This set features the Ice Gators of the ECHL. The set was sponsored by the Tamahka Trails Golf Club and was sold by the team at its souvenir stands.

COMPLETE SET (25) 4.00 10.00
1 Stan Melanson .16 .40
2 Jay Murphy .16 .40
3 Nathan Borega .16 .40
4 Shawn McNeil .16 .40
5 Ryan Shanahan .16 .40
6 Roman Marakhovski .16 .40
7 Mike Kucsulain .16 .40
8 Dalen Hrooshkin .16 .40
9 Kevin Karlander .16 .40
10 Corey Neilson .16 .40
11 Bruce Richardson .16 .40
12 Jason Saal .30 .75
13 Michael Murray .16 .40
14 Jason McQuat .16 .40
15 John Spoltore .30 .75
16 Mike Valley .16 .40
17 Magnus Nilsson .30 .75
18 Dan Tessier .30 .75
19 Matt Pagnutti .16 .40
20 Roger Maxwell .16 .40
21 Dave Farrish HCO .10 .25
22 John DePourcq ACO .10 .25
23 Johnny Gomez TR .04 .10
24 Greg Sieg EM .04 .10
25 Andy Davis DOB .04 .10

2001-02 Louisiana Ice Gators

This set features the Ice Gators of the ECHL. The set was produced by Starz Sports and was sold by the team at home games.

COMPLETE SET (26) 4.00 10.00
1 Header Card .04 .10
2 Steve Aronson .20 .50
3 Frederic Cloutier .20 .50
4 Cory Cyrenne .30 .75
5 Andy Davis DBR .04 .10
6 John DePourcq ACO .04 .10
7 Dave Farrish CO .10 .25
8 Dominic Forget .30 .75
9 Russell Hewson .20 .50
10 Konstantin Kalmikov .30 .75
11 Branislav Kvetan .20 .50
12 Greg Labenski .20 .50
13 Marc Magliarditi .30 .75
14 Ryan Marsh .20 .50
15 Shawn McNeil .20 .50
16 Kevin Mitchell .20 .50
17 Jay Murphy .20 .50
18 Corey Neilson .20 .50
19 Dennis Shiryaev .20 .50
20 Randy Perry .20 .50
21 Nathan Rempel .20 .50
22 Ryan Shanahan .20 .50
23 Ricky Casataneda TR .04 .10
Greg Sieg EQMG
24 Chris Valicevic .30 .75
25 Alphonse MASCOT .04 .10

2002-03 Louisiana Ice Gators

COMPLETE SET (25) 5.00 12.00
1 Header Card .04 .10
2 Semir Ben-Amor .20 .50
3 Cal Benazic .20 .50
4 Bobby Brown .20 .50
5 Frederic Cloutier .30 .75
6 Kenny Corupe .20 .50
7 John DePourcq .30 .75
8 Daniel Goneau .30 .75
9 Kyle Kettles .20 .50
10 Branislav Kvetan .20 .50
11 Louis Mass .20 .50
12 Shawn McNeil .20 .50
13 Kevin Mitchell .20 .50
14 J.P. Morin .20 .50
15 Nathan Rempel .20 .50
16 Bruce Richardson .20 .50
17 Rod Sarich .20 .50
18 Dennis Shiryaev .20 .50
19 Shawn Skiehar .20 .50
20 Chris Taliercio .20 .50
21 Tony Tuzzolino .20 .50
22 Jeff Worlton .20 .50
23 Dave Farrish HCO .04 .10
24 Andy Davis ANN .04 .10
25 Greg Sieg EQM .04 .10

2003-04 Louisiana Ice Gators

COMPLETE SET (25) 5.00 12.00
1 Armands Berzins .20 .50
2 Bobby Brown .20 .50
3 Frederic Cloutier .30 .75
4 Kenny Corupe .20 .50
5 Maxime Fortunus .20 .50
6 Derek Gustafson .30 .75
7 Jason Hamilton .30 .75
8 Brian Herbert .20 .50
9 Jamie Johnson .20 .50
10 Konstantin Kalmikov .20 .50
11 Ben Kilgour .20 .50
12 Martin Masa .20 .50
13 Milt Mastad .20 .50
14 Alex Materukhin .20 .50
15 Ed McGrane .20 .50
16 Kevin Mitchell .20 .50
17 Josh Mizerek .20 .50
18 Rod Sarich .20 .50
19 Dennis Shiryaev .30 .75
20 Ben Storey .20 .50
21 Jim Vickers .20 .50
22 Dave Farrish CO .04 .10
23 Team Photo .20 .50
24 Checklist .04 .10
25 Mascot .04 .10

2004-05 Louisiana Ice Gators

COMPLETE SET (26) 6.00 15.00
1 David Bararuk .75 2.00
2 Josh Barker .40 1.00
3 Ricky Castaneda TR .04 .10
4 Randy Dagenais .30 .75
5 John Evangelista .30 .75
6 Maxime Fortunus .40 1.00
7 Jody Green EQMG .04 .10
8 Todd Gordon CO .04 .10
9 Kyle Kettles .30 .75
10 Roger Leonard .30 .75
11 Doug Maciver .30 .75
12 Nathan Marsters .30 .75
13 Wes Mason .30 .75
14 Alex Materukhin .30 .75
15 Mike Omicioli .30 .75
16 Jake Ortmeyer .40 1.00
17 Pascal Pelletier .30 .75
18 Bryan Perez .30 .75
19 Mark Rooneem .30 .75
20 Shawn Skiehar .30 .75
21 Troy Smith .30 .75
22 Chris Thompson .30 .75
23 Gator Girls .10 .25
24 Gator Girls .10 .25
25 Mascots .04 .10
26 Announcers .04 .10

1999-00 Louisville Panthers

This set features the Panthers of the AHL. The cards were produced by Roox and issued as a promotional giveaway at a late-season home game.

COMPLETE SET (33) 8.00 20.00
1 Craig Ferguson .30 .75
2 Brent Thompson .30 .75
3 Craig Reichert .30 .75
4 Eric Boguniecki .60 1.50
5 Dan Boyle .40 1.00
6 Ivan Novoseltsev .40 1.00
7 Dave Duerden .30 .75
8 Curtis Doell .30 .75
9 Sean Gauthier .40 1.00
10 Peter Ratchuk .30 .75
11 John Jakopin .30 .75
12 Marcus Nilson .40 1.00
13 Paws MASCOT .08 .25
14 Chris Wells .30 .75
15 Kirby Law .40 1.00
16 Chris Allen .30 .75
17 Chad Cabana .30 .75
18 Richard Shulmistra .40 1.00
19 Dwayne Hay .30 .75
20 Joey Tetarenko .60 1.50
21 Paul Brousseau .30 .75
22 Nick Smith .40 1.00
23 Brad Ference .40 1.00
24 Lance Ward .30 .75
25 Jeff Ware .30 .75
26 Paul Harvey .08 .25
27 Andrew Long .30 .75
28 Joe Paterson CO .08 .25
29 Gerard Gallant CO .08 .25
30 Tamer Afr PRES .08 .25
31 Chuck Fletcher GM .08 .25
32 UPS Zamboni .08 .25
33 Indiana Casino Zamboni .08 .25

2000-01 Louisville Panthers

This set features the Panthers of the AHL. The cards were issued as promotional giveaways at two separate games, in two sets of 12-cards apiece.

COMPLETE SET (24) 7.20 18.00
1 Team CL .10 .25
2 Brent Thompson .40 1.00
3 Paul Brousseau .30 .75
4 David Emma .30 .75
5 Joey Tetarenko .40 1.00
6 Peter Ratchuk .40 .75
7 Dave Duerden .30 .75
8 Sean Gauthier .30
9 Kyle Rossiter .30
10 Rocky Thompson .30
11 Denis Shvidki .60
12 Brad Ference .40
13 Joe Paterson CO .20
14 Gord Dineen ACO .20
15 Travis Brigley .40
16 Ryan Bach .40
17 Andrei Podkonicky .40
18 Mike Harder .40
19 Evgeny Korolev .30
20 Eric Godard .30
21 Mike Cirillo .30
22 Eric Beaudoin .30
23 Paul Harvey .30
24 Paws Mascot .10

1996-97 Louisville Riverfrogs

This 30-card set of the Louisville Riverfrogs of the ECHL was sponsored by Winn-Dixie, Surge and Fox 41. The cards feature action photography on the front with '95-96 stats on the back. The cards were sold by the club at the rink and through the mail.

COMPLETE SET (30) 4.00
1 Checklist .02
2 Sandy Allan .60
3 Gino Santerre .30
4 Pete Liptrott .30
5 Jason Hanchuk .30
6 Adam Young .30
7 Dan Reja .30
8 Terry Lindgren .30
9 Sheldon Gorski .30
10 Jeff Kostuch .30
11 Randy Stevens .30
12 Chris Rowland .30
13 Chris DeProfio .30
14 Mike Sancimino .30
15 Dean Seymour .30
16 Stephane Madore .30
17 Chet Cullic .30
18 Tim Chase .30
19 Jack Kowal .30
20 Tom MacDonald .30
21 Jimmy Provencher .30
22 Lance Leslie .30
23 Warren Young CO .08
24 R.J. Romero TR .02
25 Mark Shepherd EQMG .02
26 David Wilson ANN .02
27 Rowdy the Riverfrog .02
28 Sandy Allan AS .60
29 Warren Young .08
Future Riverfrog Brett Young
30 Team Photo .30

1997-98 Louisville Riverfrogs

Little is known about this set beyond the confirmed checklist. Additional information can be forwarded to hockeymag@beckett.com.

COMPLETE SET (29) 4.00
1 Title Card .02
2 Craig Nelson .15
3 P.J. Lepler .15
4 Jason Pain .15
5 Terry Lindgren .15
6 Michael Flynn .15
7 Sheldon Gorski .15
8 Jeff Kostuch .15
9 Steve Ferranti .15
10 Bob Gohde .15
11 Marko Makinen .15
12 Mike Sancimino .15
13 Tobias Ablad .15
14 Jeff Kikesch .15
15 Stephane Madore .15
16 Chris DeProfio .15
17 Danny Reja .15
18 Jack Kowal .15
19 Dan Reimann .15
20 Rob Frid .15
21 Deiter Kochan .60
22 Lance Leslie .15
23 Warren Young CO .15
24 R.J. Romeiro TR .02
25 Mark Miller EQ .02
26 Matt Gorsky BR .02
27 Rowdy Mascot .02
28 Sheldon Gorski .15
29 Team Photo .15

1999-00 Lowell Lock Monsters

This set features the Lock Monsters of the AHL. This set was issued in the form of a perforated album, with four pages of cards. The album/set was issued as a promotional giveaway at a game in Feb. 2000.

COMPLETE SET (27) 6.00
1 Ray Giroux .30
2 Dave MacIsaac .20
3 Richard Seeley .20
4 Nathan LaFayette .20
5 Rich Brennan .30
6 Petr Mika .20
7 Donald MacLean .20
8 Cody Bowtell .20
9 Vladimir Chebaturkin .20
10 David Hymovitz .20
11 Sean Blanchard .20
12 Eric Belanger .20
13 Dmitri Nabokov .20
14 Vladimir Orszagh .40
15 Greg Phillips .20
16 Jason Krog .40
17 Eric Brewer .75
18 Travis Scott .40
19 Evgeny Korolev .20
20 Stephen Valiquette .60
21 Jason Podollan .20
22 Jack Baldwin .20
23 Lowell Lock Monsters .08
24 Louie MASCOT .02
25 Bruce Boudreau CO .08
26 Steve Stirling CO .08
27 Tom Rowe GM .08

2000-01 Lowell Lock Monsters

This set features the Lock Monsters of the AHL. The cards were issued as a promotional giveaway in the form of an album with perforatable images. They were distributed at a game in December, 2000.

COMPLETE SET (30) 7.20
1 Joe Corvo .30
2 Andreas Lilja .30
3 Joe Rullier .30
4 Jeff Daw .20
5 Petr Mika .30
6 Rich Brennan .20
7 Brad Chartrand .20
8 Marko Tuomainen .30
9 Eric Veilleux .20

0 Eric Belanger .40 1.00
1 Peter Leboutillier .20 .50
2 David Hymovitz .20 .50
3 Juraj Kolnik .40 1.00
4 Chris Schmidt .20 .50
5 Kevin Baker .20 .50
6 Steve Passmore .40 1.00
7 Richard Seeley .20 .50
8 Jason Krog .30 1.00
9 Travis Scott .30 1.00
0 Marcel Cousineau .30 1.00
1 Nate Miller .20 .50
2 Branislav Mezei .40 1.00
3 Mathieu Biron .30 .75
4 Kip Brennan .40 1.00
5 Greg Phillips .20 .50
6 Louie MAS .04 .10
7 Mike Pudlick .20 .50
8 Bruce Boudreau CO .10 .25
9 Steve Stirling CO .10 .25
0 Tom Rowe GM .04 .10

2002-03 Lowell Lock Monsters

OMPLETE SET (25) 8.00 20.00
Igor Knyazev .40 1.00
Nikos Tselios .40 1.00
Sean Curry .40 1.00
Ed Hill .40 1.00
Mike Zigomanis .40 1.00
Ryan Bayda .40 1.00
Craig MacDonald .40 1.00
Jeff Daw .40 1.00
Steve Halko .40 1.00
0 Jeff Heerema .40 1.00
1 Brent McDonald .40 1.00
2 Mike Watt .40 1.00
3 Tomas Kurka .40 1.00
4 Damian Surma .40 1.00
5 Kaspars Astashenko .40 1.00
6 Greg Kuznik .40 1.00
7 Tommy Westlund .40 1.00
8 Randy Petruk .60 1.50
9 Brett Lysak .40 1.00
0 Ryan Bast .40 1.00
1 Jean-Marc Pelletier .60 1.50
2 Brad DeFauw .40 1.00
3 Tomas Malec .40 1.00
Lowell Lock Monsters AU .04 .10
5 Lowell Lock Monsters AU .04 .10

2003-04 Lowell Lock Monsters

is set was produced by Choice Marketing and sold home games.
OMPLETE SET (25) 4.00 10.00
Alan Rourke .15 .40
Brad DeFauw .15 .40
Brad Fast .15 .40
Brennan Evans .15 .40
Brent Krahn .30 .75
Brett Lysak .15 .40
Damian Surma .15 .40
Dany Sabourin .30 .75
Dan Sullivan .15 .40
Jason Morgan .15 .40
Jesse Wallin .15 .40
Joey Tetarenko .15 .40
Josh Green .15 .40
Martin Sonnenberg .15 .40
Matt Davidson .15 .40
Mike Commodore .15 .40
Mike Zigomanis .15 .40
Patrick DesRochers .30 .75
Pavel Brendl .15 .40
Robert Dome .15 .40
Ryan Bayda .15 .40
Sean Curry .15 .40
Tomas Kurka .15 .40
Tomas Malec .15 .40
Checklist .04 .10

2003-04 Lowell Lock Monsters Photo Album

is was issued as a promotional item in Nov. 2003. e cards came in a perforated album format.
MPLETE SET (25) 8.00 20.00
Mike Commodore .30 .75
Jesse Wallin .30 .75
Sean Curry .30 .75
Ryan Bayda .30 .75
Jason Morgan .30 .75
Mike Zigomanis .30 .75
Tomas Kurka .30 .75
Damian Surma .30 .75
Brad Fast .30 .75
Martin Sonnenberg .30 .75
Allan Rourke .30 .75
Josh Green .30 .75
Autograph Card .04 .10
Dan Sullivan .30 .75
Brett Lysak .30 .75
Joey Tetarenko .40 1.00
Robert Dome .30 .75
Brad DeFauw .30 .75
Pavel Brendl .30 .75
Matt Davidson .30 .75
Brennan Evans .30 .75
Tomas Malec .30 .75
Autograph Card .04 .10
Dany Sabourin .60 1.50
Patrick DesRochers .60 1.50

2004-05 Lowell Lock Monsters

MPLETE SET (24) 6.00 15.00
yan Bayda .20 .50
Mike Commodore .20 .50
ean Curry .20 .50
ordie Dwyer .40 1.00
rennan Evans .20 .50
rad Fast .30 .75
olin Forbes .20 .50
arsen Germyn .20 .50
lark Giordano .20 .50
Jim Henkel .20 .50
Chuck Kobasew .40 1.00
Brent Krahn .40 1.00
Chad Larose .20 .50
Lynn Loyns .20 .50
Craig MacDonald .20 .50
Brantt Myhres .60 1.50
Richie Regehr .20 .50
Danny Richmond .20 .50
Allan Rourke .20 .50
Eric Staal .75 2.00
Bruno St. Jacques .40 1.00
Justin Taylor .20 .50
Cam Ward .40 1.00
Mike Zigomanis .20 .50

2004-05 Lowell Lock Monsters Photo Album

s set was issued as a game night giveaway in January of 2005. The cards were distributed in an album format with perforations.
COMPLETE SET (25) 12.00 30.00
1 Ryan Bayda .40 1.00
2 Mike Commodore .40 1.00
3 Sean Curry .40 1.00
4 Gordie Dwyer .75 2.00
5 Brennan Evans .40 1.00
6 Brad Fast .60 1.50
7 Colin Forbes .40 1.00
8 Carsen Germyn .40 1.00
9 Mark Giordano .40 1.00
10 Jim Henkel .40 1.00
11 Chuck Kobasew .75 2.00
12 Brent Krahn .75 2.00
13 Chad Larose .40 1.00
14 Lynn Loyns .40 1.00
15 Craig MacDonald .40 1.00
16 Brantt Myhres 1.25 3.00
17 Richie Regehr .40 1.00
18 Danny Richmond .40 1.00
19 Allan Rourke .40 1.00
20 Bruno St. Jacques .75 2.00
21 Eric Staal 1.50 4.00
22 Justin Taylor .40 1.00
23 Cam Ward .75 2.00
24 Mike Zigomanis .40 1.00
25 Logo Card .04 .10

2000-01 Lubbock Cotton Kings

This set features the Cotton Kings of the WPHL. It was produced by the team and sold at its souvenir stands.
COMPLETE SET (20) 4.00 10.00
1 Kyle Reeves .30 .75
2 Tracy Egeland .20 .50
3 Jan Melichercik .20 .50
4 Peter Cava .20 .50
5 Dave MacIntyre .20 .50
6 Patrick Brownlee .20 .50
7 Chris Rowland .20 .50
8 Bill McDonald HCO .10 .25
9 Neil Savary .30 .75
10 Lance Leslie .20 .50
11 Mike Hiebert .20 .50
12 Ryan Shmyr .20 .50
13 Brandon Carper .20 .50
14 Trevor Burgess .20 .50
15 Tom Menicci .20 .50
16 Derek Holland .20 .50
17 Walker McDonald .20 .50
18 Cosmo DuPaul .30 .75
19 Adam Robbins .20 .50
20 Lubbock Cotton Kings .20 .25

2003-04 Lubbock Cotton Kings

This set was produced by Choice Marketing and sold at home games.
COMPLETE SET (20) 3.00 8.00
1 Checklist .04 .10
2 Craig Binns .20 .50
3 Steve Birch .20 .50
4 Joe Blaznek .20 .50
5 Mike Brusseau .30 .75
6 Jeff Dewar .20 .50
7 Chris Duggan .20 .50
8 Kevin Fines .30 .75
9 Paul Fioroni .20 .50
10 Derek Holland .20 .50
11 Jean-Francois Labarre .20 .50
12 Dave MacIntyre .20 .50
13 Jan Melichercik .20 .50
14 Mathieu Paul .20 .50
15 Sebastien Roy .20 .50
16 Jim Shepherd .20 .50
17 Jeremy Symington .30 .75
18 Rob Vessio .20 .50
19 Kirk Tomlinson HCO .04 .10
20 Mascot .04 .10
NNO Sponsor .04 .10
NNO Sponsor .04 .10

2002-03 Macon Trax

This set features the Trax of the Atlantic Coast league. It was sponsored by Applebees and sold at home games.
COMPLETE SET (20) 3.00 8.00
1 Corey Smith .20 .50
2 Dan Welch .20 .50
3 David Deeves .20 .50
4 Landon Bathe .20 .50
5 Tom Stewart .20 .50
6 Corey Lucas .20 .50
7 Rick Emmett .20 .50
8 Jeremy Kyte .20 .50
9 Brad Rice .20 .50
10 Nolan Weir .20 .50
11 Brad Bourhis .20 .50
12 Stephane Desjardins .20 .50
13 Luke Murphy .20 .50
14 Steve Howard .20 .50
15 Geoff Faulkner .20 .50
16 Dennis Brogna TR .04 .10
17 Brian Curran HCO .04 .10
18 Dave Monteiro ACO .04 .10
19 Todd MacGowan EM .04 .10
20 Mascot .04 .10
NNO Checklist .04 .10

1997-98 Macon Whoopee

This 18-card set was produced and sold by the Macon Whoopee Booster Club at home games for $10 each. This set was also available in an autographed version and in uncut sheets.
COMPLETE SET (18) 3.60 9.00
1 Steve Vezina .30 .75
2 Martin Belanger .20 .50
3 John Paris HCO .02 .10
4 Sebastien Parent .20 .50
5 Gary Golczewski .20 .50
6 Jocelyn Langlois .20 .50
7 Joe Letendre .20 .50
8 Martin LaChaine .20 .50
9 Todd MacIsaac .20 .50
10 Patrice Charbonneau .30 .75
11 Marc Genest .20 .50
12 Claude Fillion .20 .50
13 Craig Willard .20 .50
14 Raymond Delarosbil .20 .50
15 Francois Loroux .20 .50
16 Trent Cavicchi .20 .50
17 Alexei Deev .30 .75
18 Alain Cote .20 .50

1997-98 Macon Whoopee Autographs

This 18-card set is the same as the base 1997-98 Macon Whoopee set, but with each card autographed. Autographed uncut sheets were available also. This set was originally sold at the arena for $20.
COMPLETE SET (18) 14.00 35.00
1 Steve Vezina 1.50 4.00
2 Martin Belanger .75 2.00
3 John Paris HCO .75 2.00
4 Sebastien Parent 1.50 4.00
5 Gary Golczewski .75 2.00
6 Jocelyn Langlois .75 2.00
7 Joe Letendre .75 2.00
8 Martin LaChaine .75 2.00
9 Todd MacIsaac .75 2.00
10 Patrice Charbonneau 1.25 3.00
11 Marc Genest .75 2.00
12 Claude Fillion .75 2.00
13 Craig Willard .75 2.00
14 Raymond Delarosbil .75 2.00
15 Francois Leroux .75 2.00
16 Trent Cavicchi .75 2.00
17 Alexei Deev 1.25 3.00
18 Alain Cote .75 2.00

2001-02 Macon Whoopee

This set features the Whoopee of the CHL. The set was produced by Choice Marketing and was issued by the team as a promotional giveaway. The production was limited to 1,000 copies.
COMPLETE SET (21) 8.00 20.00
1 Checklist .40 1.00
2 Andrew Allen .75 2.00
3 Krikor Arman .40 1.00
4 Nic Beaudoin .40 1.00
5 David Brosseau .40 1.00
6 Travis Dillabough .40 1.00
7 Gord Dineen CO .40 1.00
8 Rick Emmett .40 1.00
9 Paul Giblin .40 1.00
10 Mike Green .40 1.00
11 Mike Josefowicz .40 1.00
12 Chris Madden .75 2.00
13 Milt Mastad .40 1.00
14 Luke Murphy .40 1.00
15 Johan Olsson .40 1.00
16 Michel Periard .40 1.00
17 Doug Schueller .40 1.00
18 Kris Waltze .60 1.50
19 Alex Zinevych .40 1.00
20 Casey Kesselring .40 1.00
21 Header Card CL .04 .10

1995-96 Madison Monsters

This 24-card set features the Madison Monsters of the Colonial Hockey League and was sponsored by Z-104 and Electrolarm. The cards, which apparently were a game night giveaway, feature a color shot on the front, along with the player name and team logo. The backs feature one of the most comprehensive player information packages ever seen on cardboard, including career stats and personal biography. The cards are unnumbered.
COMPLETE SET (24) 8.00 25.00
1 Duane Derksen .75 2.00
2 Brian Downey .40 1.00
3 Dmitri Alekhin .40 1.00
4 Monster MASCOT .02 .10
5 Sean Wilmert .40 1.00
6 Corey Grassel .40 1.00
7 Dan Ruoho .40 1.00
8 Billy Brown TR .02 .10
9 Kent Hawley .40 1.00
10 Dan Laughlin .40 1.00
11 Vyacheslav Polikarkin .40 1.00
12 Todd Dvorak .40 1.00
13 Brian Idalski .40 1.00
14 Gunnar Kroseberg .40 1.00
15 Brett Larson .40 1.00
16 Paul Clatney .40 1.00
17 Matt Loen .40 1.00
18 Stanislav Tkach .60 1.50
19 Glenn Painter .40 1.00
20 Joe Bonvie .60 1.50
21 Mark Johnson CO .60 1.50
22 Justin Morrison .60 1.50
23 Marcel Richard .60 1.50
24 Sponsor card .01 .05

1996-97 Madison Monsters

This 24-card set was given away over the course of four card nights, and was sold later in the season. The cards are not numbered and so they are listed in the order in which they were distributed.
COMPLETE SET (24) 8.00 20.00
1 Electroalarm Services .02 .10
2 Dave Schultz HCO .60 1.50
3 Kent Hawley .40 1.00
4 Alexander Galchenyuk .40 1.00
5 Jeremie Legault .40 1.00
6 Randy Holmes .40 1.00
7 Fran Reed .40 1.00
8 Chris Markstrom .40 1.00
9 Team Photo .40 1.00
10 Duane Derksen .60 1.50
11 Brian Downey .40 1.00
12 Matt Loen .40 1.00
13 Justin Morrison .40 1.00
14 Dave Rowe .40 1.00
15 Colby Van Tassel .40 1.00
16 Dan Ruoho .40 1.00
17 ElectroAlarm Security Sys .02 .10
18 Brian Idalski .40 1.00
19 Brian LaVack .40 1.00
20 Todd Passini .40 1.00
21 Stas Tkatch .40 1.00
22 Joakin Wiberg .40 1.00
23 Jeff Winter .40 1.00
24 Jose Ortiz TR .20 .50

1998-99 Madison Monsters

This set features the Monsters of the UHL. The cards were produced by Roox, and intended as a season-long promotional giveaway. Apparently there was a problem at some point and the promotion was cancelled after the distribution of just 16 cards. If anyone knows of any other cards in this set, please write hockeymag@beckett.com.
COMPLETE SET (16) 8.00 20.00
1 Kent Hawley CO .08 .25
2 Andrew Wilhelm OWN .08 .25
3 Dana Doll TR .08 .25
4 Jason Disher .60 1.50
5 Kelly Stephens .60 1.50
6 Derek Beuselinck .60 1.50
7 Cory Holland .60 1.50
8 Mike Maurice .60 1.50
9 Luke Strand .60 1.50
10 Brian Downey .60 1.50
11 David Fletcher .60 1.50
12 Andy Faulkner .60 1.50
13 Jim Duhart .60 1.50
14 Jay Wilson .60 1.50
15 Ed Corwin .60 1.50
16 Monster Madness .40 1.00

1986-87 Maine

This 14-card set of Maine Black Bears is part of a "Kids and Kops" promotion, and one card was printed each Saturday in the Bangor Daily News. The cards measure approximately 2 1/2" by 4". The cards were to be collected from any participating plice officer. Once five cards had been collected (including card number 1), they could be turned in at a police station for a University of Maine ID card, which permitted free admission to selected university activities. When all 14 cards had been collected, they could be turned in at a police station to register for the Grand Prize drawing (bicycle) and to pick up a free "Kids and Kops" tee-shirt. The backs have tips in the form of an anti-drug or alcohol message and logos of Burger King, University of Maine and Pepsi across the bottom. With the exception of the rules card, the cards are numbered on the back.
COMPLETE SET (14) 6.00 15.00
2 Jack Capuano HK .40 1.00
11 Eric Weinrich HK 1.60 4.00

1987-88 Maine

This 14-card set of Maine Black Bears is part of a "Kids and Kops" promotion, and one card was printed each Saturday in the Bangor Daily News. The cards measure approximately 2 1/2" by 4". The cards were to be collected from any participating police officer. Once five cards had been collected (including card number 1), they could be turned in at a police station for a University of Maine ID card, which permitted free admission to selected university activities. When all 14 cards had been collected, they could be turned in at a police station to register for the Grand Prize drawing (bicycle) and to pick up a free "Kids and Kops" tee-shirt. The backs have tips in the form of an anti-drug or alcohol message and logos of Burger King, University of Maine, and Pepsi across the bottom. With the exception of the rules card, the cards are numbered on the back. Sports represented in this set include hockey (2), basketball (3, 9, 13), tennis (4), baseball (5), swimming (6), soccer (7), track (8), football (10), field hockey (11), and softball (12).
COMPLETE SET (14) 6.00 15.00
2 Mike McHugh HK .80 2.00

1992-93 Maine Black Bears

This set features the Black Bears of the NCAA. The set was issued as two series (1-16 and 17-36). This set includes one of the first cards of NHL superstar Paul Kariya.
COMPLETE SET (36) 20.00 50.00
1 Title Card .10 .25
2 Mike Dunham 1.25 3.00
3 Andy Silverman .20 .50
4 Matt Martin .20 .50
5 Chris Imes .20 .50
6 Jason Weinrich .20 .50
7 Scott Pellerin .30 .75
8 Dan Murphy .20 .50
9 Dave LaCouture .20 .50
10 Patrice Tardif .40 1.00
11 Eric Fenton .20 .50
12 Jim Montgomery .40 1.00
13 Kent Salfi .20 .50
14 Jean-Yves Roy .40 1.00
15 Garth Snow .40 1.00
16 Cal Ingraham .40 1.00
17 Title Card .10 .25
18 Mike Dunham 1.25 3.00
19 Chris Imes .20 .50
20 Paul Kariya 15.00 40.00
21 Mike Latendresse .20 .50
22 Dan Murphy .20 .50
23 Dave MacIsaac .20 .50
24 Dave LaCouture .20 .50
25 Chris Ferraro .40 1.00
26 Peter Ferraro .40 1.00
27 Jim Montgomery .40 1.00
28 Brad Purdie .20 .50
29 Lee Saunders .20 .50
30 Justin Tomberlin .20 .50
31 Chuck Texeira .20 .50
32 Martin Mercier .20 .50
33 Garth Snow .40 1.00
34 Cal Ingraham .40 1.00
35 Greg Hirsch .20 .50
36 Jamie Thompson .20 .50

1993-94 Maine Black Bears

Measuring the standard size, this 26-card set features the Maine Black Bears. The fronts feature color action player photos with light blue, dark blue, and white borders. A black stripe near the bottom carries the player's name and position in white print. The team logo is superimposed on the picture. The backs carry biographical information, career highlights, and statistics along with a small black-and-white player headshot. The numbering continues where the previous year's numbering left off.
COMPLETE SET (25) 24.00 60.00
37 Paul Kariya 4.00 10.00
Leo Wlasow#
38 Andy Silverman .20 .50
39 Jason Weinrich .20 .50
40 Jason Mansoff .20 .50
41 Paul Kariya 8.00 20.00
42 Mike Latendresse .20 .50
43 Barry Clukey .20 .50
44 Wayne Conlan .20 .50
45 Dave MacIsaac .20 .50
46 Patrice Tardif .30 .75
47 Brad Purdie .20 .50
48 Dan Shermerhorn .20 .50
49 Lee Saunders .20 .50
50 Justin Tomberlin .20 .50
51 Chuck Texeira .20 .50
52 Tim Lovell .20 .50
53 Cal Ingraham .20 .50
54 Leo Wlasow .20 .50
55 Blair Allison .20 .50
56 Blair Marsh .20 .50
57 Marcel Pineau .20 .50
58 Trevor Roenick .20 .50
59 Reg Cardinal .20 .50
60 Paul Kariya 8.00 20.00
61 Jim Montgomery 4.00 10.00
Paul Kar

2004-05 Maine Black Bears

Issued as a promotional giveaway.
COMPLETE SET (32) 25.00 50.00
1 Mike Lundin .75 2.00
2 Tom Zabkowicz .75 2.00
3 Steve Mullin .75 2.00
4 Travis Wight .75 2.00
5 Troy Barnes .75 2.00
6 Matt Deschamps .75 2.00
7 John Ronan .75 2.00
8 Michel Leveille .75 2.00
9 Keith Johnson .75 2.00
10 Keenan Hopson .75 2.00
11 Billy Ryan .75 2.00
12 Greg Moore .75 2.00
13 Robert Bellamy .75 2.00
14 Ben Murphy .75 2.00
15 Josh Soares .75 2.00
16 Tim Maxwell .75 2.00
17 Mike Hamilton .75 2.00
18 Jon Jankus .75 2.00
19 Wes Clark .75 2.00
20 Travis Ramsey .75 2.00
21 Derek Damon .75 2.00
22 Brent Shepheard .75 2.00
23 Matt Lundin .75 2.00
24 Jim Howard 1.25 3.00
25 Matt Greyeyes .75 2.00
26 Ryan Shelley .75 2.00
27 Bret Tyler .75 2.00
28 Jeff Mushaluk .75 2.00
29 Staff .04 .10
30 Erik Soltys ACO .04 .10
31 Tim Whitehead CO .04 .10
32 Team Picture .20 .50

2005-06 Maine Black Bears

COMPLETE SET (32) 10.00 25.00
1 Rob Bellamy .30 .75
2 Ben Bishop .75 2.00
3 Wes Clark .30 .75
4 Derek Damon .30 .75
5 Simon Danis-Pepin .60 1.50
6 Matt Duffy .30 .75
7 Chris Hahn .30 .75
8 Mike Hamilton .30 .75
9 John Hopson .30 .75
10 Keenan Hopson .30 .75
11 Jon Jankus .30 .75
12 Keith Johnson .30 .75
13 Vince Laise .30 .75
14 Michel Leveille .30 .75
15 Matt Lundin .40 1.00
16 Mike Lundin .30 .75
17 Jeff Marshall .30 .75
18 Greg Moore .30 .75
19 Steve Mullin .30 .75
20 Brian Plasszcz .30 .75
21 Travis Ramsey .30 .75
22 Billy Ryan .30 .75
23 Ryan Shelley .30 .75
24 Brent Shepheard .30 .75
25 Josh Soares .30 .75
26 Bret Tyler .30 .75
27 Travis Wight .30 .75
28 Tim Whitehead HC .20 .50
29 Campbell Blair AC .20 .50
30 Dan Kerluke AC .20 .50
31 Grant Standbrook AC .20 .50
32 Maine Black Bears .20 .50

2007-08 Maine Black Bears

COMPLETE SET (32) 6.00 15.00
1 Mike Banwell .25 .60
2 Rob Bellamy .25 .60
3 Glenn Belmore .25 .60
4 Ben Bishop .25 .60
5 Nolan Boike .25 .60
6 Brett Carriere .25 .60
7 Wes Clark .25 .60
8 Simon Danis-Pepin .25 .60
9 David de Kastrozza .25 .60
10 Robby Dee .25 .60
11 Jeff Dimmen .25 .60
12 Matt Duffy .25 .60
13 Shane Foley .25 .60
14 Chris Hahn .25 .60
15 Keenan Hopson .25 .60
16 Tanner House .25 .60
17 Vince Laise .25 .60
18 Jeff Marshall .25 .60
19 Keif Orsini .25 .60
20 Nick Payson .25 .60
21 Travis Ramsey .25 .60
22 Lem Randall .25 .60
23 Billy Ryan .25 .60
24 Kevin Swallow .25 .60
25 Andrew Sweetland .25 .60
26 Bret Tyler .25 .60
27 Josh Van Dyk .25 .60
28 Dave Wilson .25 .60
29 Tim Whitehead HC .15 .40
30 Guy Perron AHC .15 .40
31 Dan Kerluke AC .10 .25
32 Grant Standbrook AC .10 .25

2001-02 Manchester Monarchs

This set features the Monarchs of the AHL. The set was released in two series of 15 cards each and was sold at the team's souvenir stands. Each series was limited to 1,000 copies. As the cards from both series are numbered 1-15, we have added an A and B suffix to differentiate between them.
COMPLETE SET (30) 8.00 20.00
1A Randy Robitaille .25 .60
1B Dane Jackson .25 .60
2A Derek Bekar .25 .60
2B Travis Scott .30 .75
3A Brad Chartrand .25 .60
3B Ted Donato .25 .60
4A Nate Miller .25 .60
4B Joe Rullier .25 .60
5A Andre Payette .25 .60
5B Rich Brennan .25 .60
6A Brett Hauer .25 .60
6B Eric Healey .25 .60
7A Chris Schmidt .25 .60
7B Jason Holland .25 .60
8A Mike Pudlick .25 .60
8B Richard Seeley .25 .60
9A Kip Brennan .30 .75
9B Jaroslav Bednar .40 1.00
10A Tomas Zizka .25 .60
10B Ryan Flinn .60 1.50
11A Jerred Smithson .25 .60
11B Rob Valicevic .60 1.50
12A Joe Corvo .25 .60
12B Steve Kelly .25 .60
13A Stephane Fiset .60 1.50
13B Dan Riva .25 .60
14A Marcel Cousineau .30 .75
14B Scott Thomas .25 .60
15A Bruce Boudreau CO .04 .10
15B Maximillian MASCOT .04 .10

2002-03 Manchester Monarchs

COMPLETE SET (30) 10.00 25.00
1 Chris Aldous .20 .50
2 Scott Barney .20 .50
3 Bruce Boudreau HCO .30 .75
4 Kip Brennan .30 .75
5 Mike Cammalleri 1.00 2.50
6 Joe Corvo .20 .50
7 Eric Healey .20 .50
8 Steve Heinze .20 .50
9 Dane Jackson .20 .50
10 Steve Kelly .30 .75
11 Yanick Lehoux .30 .75
12 Mike Pudlick .20 .50
13 Joe Rullier .20 .50
14 Travis Scott .30 .75
15 Richard Seeley .20 .50
16 Derek Armstrong .20 .50
17 Jared Aulin .60 1.50
18 Derek Bekar .20 .50
19 Chris Bogas .20 .50
20 Ryan Flinn .40 1.00
21 Jeff Giuliano .20 .50
22 Jason Holland .20 .50
23 Cristobal Huet .75 2.00
24 Maximillian MASCOT .04 .10
25 Dan Riva .20 .50
26 Pavel Rosa .20 .50
27 Chris Schmidt .20 .50
28 Jerred Smithson .20 .50
29 Mat Snesrud .20 .50
30 Tomas Zizka .30 .75

2003-04 Manchester Monarchs

This set was produced by Choice Marketing and sold at home games.
COMPLETE SET (25) 6.00 15.00
1 Scott Barney .20 .50
2 Noah Clarke .30 .75
3 Ryan Flinn .30 .75
4 Jeff Giuliano .20 .50
5 Denis Grebeshkov .20 .50
6 Adam Hauser .30 .75
7 Leon Hayward .20 .50
8 Steve Kelly .20 .50
9 Yanick Lehoux .20 .50
10 Bryan Muir .20 .50
11 Doug Nolan .20 .50
12 George Parros .20 .50
13 Pavel Rosa .20 .50
14 Joe Rullier .20 .50
15 Chris Schmidt .20 .50
16 Richard Seeley .20 .50
17 Jerred Smithson .20 .50
18 John Tripp .20 .50
19 Dan Welch .20 .50
20 Tomas Zizka .20 .50
21 Mascot .04 .10
22 Bruce Boudreau HCO .20 .50
23 Jim Hughes ACO .04 .10
24 Verizon Wireless Arena .04 .10
25 Checklist .04 .10

2003-04 Manchester Monarchs Team Issue

This set was given away at a game in Jan. 2004. The set was sponsored by the New Hampshire Tobacco Prevention/Control program. The cards are unnumbered and are listed below in alphabetical order.

COMPLETE SET (20) 8.00 20.00
1 Scott Barney .40 1.00
2 Mathieu Chouinard .60 1.50
3 Noah Clarke .60 1.50
4 Ryan Flinn .60 1.50
5 Jeff Giuliano .40 1.00
6 Denis Grebeshkov .40 1.00
7 Milan Hnilicka .60 1.50
8 Steve Kelly .40 1.00
9 Yanick Lehoux .40 1.00
10 Bryan Muir .40 1.00
11 Doug Nolan .40 1.00
12 George Parros .40 1.00
13 Pavel Rosa .40 1.00
14 Joe Rullier .40 1.00
15 Chris Schmidt .40 1.00
16 Richard Seeley .40 1.00
17 Jerred Smithson .40 1.00
18 John Tripp .40 1.00
19 Dan Welch .40 1.00
20 Tomas Zizka .40 1.00

2004-05 Manchester Monarchs

Produced by Choice Marketing.
COMPLETE SET (26) 6.00 15.00
1 Adam Hauser .40 1.00
2 Brad Smyth .40 1.00
3 Chris Schmidt .15 .40
4 Dan Welch .15 .40
5 Dave Steckel .30 .75
6 Denis Grebeshkov .15 .40
7 Doug Nolan .15 .40
8 Dustin Brown .40 1.00
9 George Parros .15 .40
10 Greg Hogeboom .15 .40
11 Jeff Giuliano .15 .40
12 Joe Rullier .30 .75
13 Mathieu Garon .60 1.50
14 Matt Ryan .15 .40
15 Michael Cammalleri .40 1.00
16 Mike Weaver .15 .40
17 Noah Clarke .40 1.00
18 Petr Kanko .40 1.00
19 Ryan Flinn .40 1.00
20 Scott Barney .15 .40
21 Tim Gleason .30 .75
22 Tom Kostopoulos .30 .75
23 Troy Milam .15 .40
24 Yanick Lehoux .30 .75
25 Maximillian MASCOT .04 .10
NNO Checklist .04 .10

2004-05 Manchester Monarchs Tobacco

These cards were issued as a promotional giveaway.
COMPLETE SET (25) 12.00 30.00
1 Mathieu Garon 1.25 3.00
2 Adam Hauser .75 2.00
3 Brad Smyth .75 2.00
4 Chris Schmidt .30 .75
5 Dan Welch .30 .75
6 Dave Steckel .60 1.50
7 Denis Grebeshkov .30 .75
8 Doug Nolan .30 .75
9 Dustin Brown .75 2.00
10 George Parros .30 .75
11 Greg Hogeboom .30 .75
12 Jeff Guiliano .30 .75
13 Joe Rullier .60 1.50
14 Matt Ryan .30 .75
15 Mike Cammalleri .75 2.00
16 Mike Weaver .30 .75
17 Noah Clarke .75 2.00
18 Petr Kanko .75 2.00
19 Ryan Flinn .75 2.00
20 Scott Barney .30 .75
21 Tim Gleason .60 1.50
22 Tom Kostopoulos .60 1.50
23 Troy Milam .30 .75
24 Yanick Lehoux .60 1.50
25 Mascot .04 .10

2005-06 Manchester Monarchs

This set was issued in two series. The fist series included (1-24), while series 2 had (25-48).
COMPLETE SET (48) 12.00 30.00
COMPLETE SER. 2 (24) 6.00 15.00
COMPLETE SER. 1 (24) 6.00 15.00
1 Barry Brust .40 1.00
2 Noah Clarke .25 .60
3 Brad Fast .25 .60
4 Ryan Flinn .40 1.00
5 Jeff Giuliano .25 .60
6 Denis Grebeshkov .25 .60
7 Adam Hauser .40 1.00
8 Connor James .25 .60
9 Petr Kanko .25 .60
10 Joey Mormina .25 .60
11 Ryan Murphy .25 .60
12 Doug Nolan .25 .60
13 Richard Petiot .25 .60
14 Konstantin Pushkarev .25 .60
15 Dany Roussin .25 .60
16 Matt Ryan .25 .60
17 Richard Seeley .25 .60
18 Brad Smyth .25 .60
19 Jeff Tambellini .40 1.00
20 Lauri Tukonen .60 1.50
21 Marty Wilford .40 1.00
22 Derek Clancey AC .02 .10
23 Jim Hughes HC .02 .10
24 Maximillian MASCOT .10 .25
25 Brendan Bernakevitch .25 .60
26 Dustin Brown .75 2.00
27 Michael Cammalleri .40 1.00
28 Noah Clarke .25 .60
29 Ryan Flinn .40 1.00
30 Yutaka Fukufuji 1.25 3.00
31 Mathieu Garon .40 1.00
32 Jeff Giuliano .25 .60
33 Tim Gleason .25 .60
34 Denis Grebeshkov .25 .60
35 Adam Hauser .40 1.00
36 Greg Hogeboom .25 .60
37 Connor James .25 .60
38 Petr Kanko .25 .60
39 Tom Kostopoulos .25 .60
40 Yanick Lehoux .25 .60
41 George Parros .60 1.50
42 Richard Petiot .25 .60
43 Reagan Rome .25 .60
44 Dany Roussin .25 .60
45 Matt Ryan .25 .60
46 Jeff Tambellini .40 1.00
47 Mike Weaver .25 .60
48 Eric Werner .25 .60

2006-07 Manchester Monarchs

COMPLETE SET (24) 7.00 12.00
1 Barry Brust .30 .75
2 Brendan Buckley .20 .50
3 Bryan Schmidt .20 .50
4 Dany Roussin .30 .75
5 Doug Nolan .20 .50
6 Eric Werner .20 .50
7 Jason Labarbera .30 .75
8 Jeff Giuliano .30 .75
9 Joey Mormina .20 .50
10 John Zeiler .20 .50
11 Konstantin Pushkarev .20 .50
12 Lauri Tukonen .40 1.00
13 Matt Moulson .20 .50
14 Matt Ryan .20 .50
15 Ned Lukacevic .20 .50
16 Noah Clarke .20 .50
17 Peter Harrold .20 .50
18 Petr Kanko .20 .50
19 Ryan Murphy .20 .50
20 Shay Stephenson .20 .50
21 Tim Jackman .20 .50
22 Mark Morris CO .02 .10
23 Scott Pellerin ACO .02 .10
24 Max MASCOT .02 .10

2014-15 Manchester Monarchs

COMPLETE SET (25) 6.00 15.00
1 Justin Auger .30 .75
2 Sean Backman .30 .75
3 Patrik Bartosak .30 .75
4 Jean-Francois Berube .50 1.25
5 Andrew Bodnarchuk .30 .75
6 Andrew Crescenzi .30 .75
7 Nic Dowd .30 .75
8 Nick Ebert .30 .75
9 Derek Forbort .30 .75
10 Josh Gratton .30 .75
11 Kevin Gravel .30 .75
12 Ryan Horvat .30 .75
13 Vincent LoVerde .30 .75
14 Michael Mersch .40 1.00
15 Colin Miller .40 1.00
16 Zach O'Brien .40 1.00
17 Brian O'Neill .30 .75
18 Kevin Raine .30 .75
19 Scott Sabourin .30 .75
20 Jeff Schultz .30 .75
21 Nick Shore .30 .75
22 David Van Der Gulik .30 .75
23 Jordan Weal .50 1.25
24 Max MASCOT .30 .75
25 Header Card CL .30 .75

1992-93 Manitoba Junior League

Only one card from this set has been confirmed.
COMPLETE SET (?)
181 Dane Litke

1997-98 Manitoba Moose

These oversized cards were inserted in game programs in two series. Cards 7 and 8 in each series were only available at Grapes Leon's Centre with any kid's menu purchase.
COMPLETE SET (16) 15.00 40.00
A1 Ralph Intranuovo .75 2.00
A2 Russ Romaniuk .75 2.00
A3 Randy Gilhen .75 2.00
A4 Dave Thomlinson .75 2.00
A5 Fred Brathwaite 2.00 5.00
A6 Mick E. Moose Mascot .40 1.00
A7 Scott Arniel 2.00 5.00
A8 Randy Carlyle HCO 2.00 5.00
B1 Brian Chapman .75 2.00
B2 Radim Bicanek .75 2.00
B3 Michael Stewart .75 2.00
B4 Jason Christie .75 2.00
B5 Greg Pankewicz .75 2.00
B6 Brad Purdie .75 2.00
B7 Kont Foarns 2.00 5.00
B8 Mike Ruark 2.00 5.00

1998-99 Manitoba Moose

This oversized set was issued in two series, with each card inserted into various game programs. The series are numbered C and D which continues the numbering from the previous season. Cards 7 and 8 in each series are much tougher as they were only available at Grapes Leon's Centre with a food purchase.

COMPLETE SET (16)	16.00	40.00
C1 Scott Arniel	1.25	3.00
C2 Bill Bowler	1.25	3.00
C3 Kent Fearns	.75	2.00
C4 Brett Hauer	.75	2.00
C5 Ralph Intranuovo	.75	2.00
C6 Mike Ruark	.75	2.00
C7 Michael Stewart	2.00	5.00
C8 Scott Thomas	2.00	5.00
D1 Jason MacDonald	1.25	3.00
D2 Christian Bronsard	1.25	3.00
D3 Jeff Parrott	.75	2.00
D4 Brian Chapman	.75	2.00
D5 Richard Shulmistra	1.25	3.00
D6 Jimmy Roy	.75	2.00
D7 Rhett Gordon	2.00	5.00
D8 Patrice Tardif	2.00	5.00

1999-00 Manitoba Moose

Released in conjunction with Grapes, Husky, and Mohawk, this 22-card set pictures the 1999-00 Manitoba Moose. Each card measures 6.25x9.5" and comes complete with two perforated coupons on the bottom.

COMPLETE SET (22)	10.00	25.00
1 Manny Legace	1.25	3.00
2 Michael Stewart	.40	1.00
3 Vladislav Serov	.40	1.00
4 Lonny Bohonos	.75	2.00
5 Mike Prokopec	.75	2.00
6 Jeff Parrott	.40	1.00
7 Bill Bowler	.75	2.00
8 Mike Ruark	.40	1.00
9 Eric Veilleux	.40	1.00
10 Brett Hauer	.40	1.00
11 Jason Elliott	.75	2.00
12 Cory Cyrenne	.60	1.50
13 Justin Kurtz	.40	1.00
14 Patrice Tardif	.75	2.00
15 Jimmy Roy	.40	1.00
16 Jason MacDonald	.40	1.00
17 Larry Shapley	.40	1.00
18 Brian Chapman	.40	1.00
19 Marc Rodgers	.75	2.00
20 Jim Montgomery	.40	1.00
21 M2K Header Card	.20	.50
22 Checklist	.20	.50

2000-01 Manitoba Moose

This set features the Moose of the IHL. The set was oversized and was sold by the team at home games and through its Web site. The set is noteworthy for the card of Johan Hedberg, who became a huge hobby star after being acquired by the Penguins during this season.

COMPLETE SET	6.00	12.00
1 Mel Angelstad	.30	.75
2 Doug Ast	.20	.50
3 Cal Benazic	.20	.50
4 Philippe Boucher	.20	.50
5 Steve Brule	.20	.50
6 Brian Chapman	.20	.50
7 Dion Darling	.20	.50
8 Bobby Dollas	.20	.50
9 Rusty Fitzgerald	.20	.50
10 Daniel Goneau	.20	.50
11 Brett Hauer	.20	.50
12 Johan Hedberg	2.00	3.00
13 Dan Kesa	.20	.50
14 Justin Kurtz	.20	.75
15 Dmitri Leonov	.20	.50
16 John MacLean	.30	.75
17 Sean Pronger	.20	.50
18 Bruce Richardson	.20	.50
19 Jimmy Roy	.20	.75
20 Mike Ruark	.20	.50
21 Scott Thomas	.20	.50
22 Ken Wregget	.30	.75
23 Mick E. Moose MASCOT	.02	.10

2001-02 Manitoba Moose

This set features the Moose of the AHL. The set was sold by the team at its souvenir stand for $15. The cards are slightly oversized. Since they are unnumbered, the cards are listed alphabetically.

COMPLETE SET (23)	6.00	15.00
1 Header Card	.04	.10
2 Bryan Allen	.30	.75
3 Ryan Bonni	.30	.75
4 Brian Chapman	.30	.75
5 Artem Chubarov	.30	.75
6 Jason Cipolla	.30	.75
7 Regan Darby	.30	.75
8 Fedor Fedorov	.30	.75
9 Darrell Hay	.30	.75
10 Bryan Helmer	.30	.75
11 Josh Holden	.30	.75
12 Steve Kariya	.40	1.00
13 Pat Kavanagh	.30	.75
14 Zenith Komarniski	.30	.75
15 Justin Kurtz	.30	.75
16 Brad Leeb	.30	.75
17 Alfie Michaud	.40	1.00
18 Justin Morrison	.30	.75
19 Ryan Ready	.30	.75
20 Brandon Reid	.40	1.00
21 Jimmy Roy	.30	.75
22 Andre Savage	.30	.75
23 Mick E. Moose MASCOT	.10	.25

2002-03 Manitoba Moose

COMPLETE SET (26)	6.00	15.00
1 Header Card	.04	.10
2 Mick E. Moose Mascot	.04	.10
3 Zenith Komarniski	.20	.50
4 Bryan Helmer	.20	.50
5 Ryan Ready	.20	.50
6 Steve Kariya	.60	1.50
7 Nolan Baumgartner	.20	.50
8 Regan Darby	.20	.50
9 Jimmy Roy	.20	.50
10 Fedor Fedorov	.40	1.00
11 Jaroslav Obsut	.20	.50
12 Jason King	.20	.50
13 Darrell Hay	.20	.50
14 Tyler Moss	.30	.75
15 Herbert Vasilijevs	.20	.50
16 Nathan Smith	.20	.50
17 Alex Auld	.40	1.00
18 Bryan Allen	.20	.50
19 Brandon Reid	.60	1.50
20 Jason Goulet	.20	.50
21 Justin Kurtz	.20	.50
22 Brian Chapman	.20	.50
23 Pat Kavanagh	.20	.50
24 Rene Vydareny	.20	.50
25 Tyler Bouck	.20	.50
26 Jason Shmyr	.20	.50

2003-04 Manitoba Moose

This set was sold by the team at home games.

COMPLETE SET (24)	6.00	15.00
1 Checklist	.04	.10
2 Autograph Card	.04	.10
3 Mascot	.04	.10
4 Tomas Mojzis	.25	.60
5 Mikko Jokela	.25	.60
6 Nolan Baumgartner	.25	.60
7 Chris Nielsen	.25	.60
8 Tyler Bouck	.25	.60
9 Nathan Smith	.25	.60
10 Ryan Ready	.25	.60
11 Pat Kavanagh	.25	.60
12 Ryan Kesler	.75	2.00
13 Sean Pronger	.25	.60
14 Rene Vydareny	.25	.60
15 Jimmy Roy	.25	.60
16 Justin Morrison	.25	.60
17 Martin Grenier	.25	.60
18 Tyler Moss	.40	1.00
19 Alex Auld	.40	1.00
20 Dallas Eakins	.25	.60
21 Jaroslav Obsut	.25	.60
22 Kirill Koltsov	.25	.60
23 Brandon Reid	.40	1.00
24 Fedor Fedorov	.40	1.00

2004-05 Manitoba Moose

COMPLETE SET (24)	8.00	20.00
1 Kevin Bieksa	.40	1.00
2 Tomas Mojzis	.40	1.00
3 Joey DiPenta	.60	1.50
4 Kent Huskins	.40	1.00
5 Nolan Baumgartner	.40	1.00
6 Justin Morrison	.40	1.00
7 Jeff Heerema	.40	1.00
8 Ryan Kesler	.60	1.50
9 Peter Sarno	.60	1.50
10 Nathan Smith	.40	1.00
11 Jimmy Roy	.40	1.00
12 Jesse Schultz	.40	1.00
13 Brandon Nolan	.40	1.00
14 Jason King	.60	1.50
15 Wade Flaherty	.60	1.50
16 Alex Auld	.60	1.50
17 Josh Green	.40	1.00
18 Lee Goren	.60	1.50
19 Wade Brookbank	.40	1.00
20 Johnathan Aitken	.40	1.00
21 Autograph Card	.04	.10
22 MTS Centre 1st Goal	.04	.10
23 Inaugural Season	.04	.10
24 Mick E. Moose MASCOT	.04	.10

2005-06 Manitoba Moose

COMPLETE SET (27)	5.00	12.00
1 Jozef Balej	.20	.50
2 Ryan Bayda	.20	.50
3 Kevin Bieksa	.20	.50
4 Mike Brown	.20	.50
5 Alexandre Burrows	.40	1.00
6 Sven Butenschon	.20	.50
7 Craig Darby	.20	.50
8 Wade Flaherty	.40	1.00
9 Maxime Fortunus	.20	.50
10 Josh Green	.20	.50
11 Jason Jaffray	.20	.50
12 Mike Keane	.20	.50
13 Nathan McIver	.20	.50
14 Tomas Mojzis	.20	.50
15 Yuri Moscevsky	.20	.50
16 Maxime Ouellet	.60	1.50
17 Jimmy Roy	.20	.50
18 Prestin Ryan	.20	.50
19 Rick Rypien	.20	.50
20 Jesse Schultz	.40	1.00
21 Brett Skinner	.20	.50
22 Nathan Smith	.20	.50
23 AHL All-Star Classic	.02	.10
24 Autograph Card	.02	.10
25 The Home of Hockey	.02	.10
26 Manitoba Moose CL	.02	.10
27 Mick E. Moose MASCOT	.02	.10

2006-07 Manitoba Moose

COMPLETE SET (27)	12.00	20.00
1 Mick E. Moose MASCOT	.10	.25
2 Drew McIntyre	.40	1.00
3 Alexander Edler	.30	.75
4 Prestin Ryan	.30	.75
5 Joe Rullier	.30	.75
6 Nathan McIver	.30	.75
7 Brandon Reid	.40	1.00
8 Mike Keane	.30	.75
9 Mike Brown	.30	.75
10 Jason Jaffray	.30	.75
11 Jannik Hansen	.60	1.50
12 J.J. Hunter	.30	.75
13 Nathan Smith	.30	.75
14 Brad Moran	.30	.75
15 Jesse Schultz	.30	.75
16 Dustin Wood	.30	.75
17 Adam Keefe	.30	.75
18 Maxime Fortunus	.30	.75
19 Marc-Andre Bernier	.30	.75
20 Tyler Bouck	.30	.75
21 Wade Flaherty	.40	1.00
22 Julien Ellis	.40	1.00
23 Lee Goren	.40	1.00
24 Yannick Tremblay	.30	.75
25 Patrick Coulombe	.30	.75
26 Shaun Heshka	.30	.75
27 Alexandre Bolduc	.30	.75

2007-08 Manitoba Moose

COMPLETE SET (29)	6.00	15.00
1 Mike E. Moose MASCOT	.15	.40
2 Drew MacIntyre	.50	1.25
3 Luc Bourdon	.50	1.25
4 Mason Raymond	.50	1.25
5 Nathan McIver	.20	.50
6 Jozef Balej	.20	.50
7 Rick Rypien	.20	.50
8 Mike Keane	.20	.50
9 Mike Brown	.20	.50
10 Jason Jaffray	.20	.50
11 Jannik Hansen	.50	1.25
12 Zack Fitzgerald	.20	.50
13 Greg Classen	.20	.50
14 Brad Moran	.20	.50
15 Ryan Shannon	.20	.50
16 Juraj Simek	.20	.50
17 Shaun Heshka	.20	.50
18 Maxime Fortunis	.20	.50
19 Colby Genoway	.20	.50
20 Pierre-Cedric Labrie	.20	.50
21 Cory Schneider	.50	1.25
22 Michael Grabner	.20	.50
23 Jimmy Sharrow	.20	.50
24 Danny Groulx	.20	.50
25 Alexandre Bolduc	.20	.50
26 Team Checklist	.10	.25
27 Scott Arniel HC	.15	.40
28 Brad Berry AC	.10	.25
29 Autograph Card	.10	.25

1982-83 Medicine Hat Tigers

These 21 blank-backed cards measure approximately 3" by 4" and feature white-bordered, black-and-white posed studio head shots of the WHL Tigers on the left halves of the cards. The player's name, jersey number and biography, along with a space for an autograph, appear on the right half. The cards are unnumbered and checklisted below in alphabetical order.

COMPLETE SET (21)	8.00	20.00
1 Al Conroy	.60	1.50
2 Murray Craven	.75	2.00
3 Mark Frank	.40	1.00
4 Kevan Guy	.40	1.00
5 Jim Hougen	.40	1.00
6 Ken Jorgenson	.40	1.00
7 Matt Kabayama	.40	1.00
8 Brent Kisilivich	.40	1.00
9 Mark Lamb	1.25	3.00
10 Mike Lay	.40	1.00
11 Dean McArthur	.40	1.00
12 Brent Meckling	.40	1.00
13 Shawn Nagurny	.40	1.00
14 Kodie Nelson	.40	1.00
15 Al Pedersen	.60	1.50
16 Todd Pederson	.40	1.00
17 Jay Reid	.40	1.00
18 Gord Shmyrko	.40	1.00
19 Brent Steblyk	.40	1.00
20 Rocky Trottier	.40	1.00
21 Dan Turner	.40	1.00

1983-84 Medicine Hat Tigers

This 23-card P.L.A.Y. (Police, Laws and Youth) set measures approximately 2 3/4" by 5" and features color player portraits with a wide white bottom border. The border contains the player's jersey number and name. The team logo is also printed in this area. The backs carry sponsor logos and public service "Tips From The Tigers."

COMPLETE SET (23)	12.00	40.00
1 Murray Craven	.75	2.00
2 Shane Churla	2.00	5.00
3 Don Herczeg	.60	1.50
4 Gary Johnson	.60	1.50
5 Brent Kisilivich	.60	1.50
6 Blair MacGregor	.60	1.50
7 Terry Knight	.60	1.50
8 Mark Lamb	1.25	3.00
9 Al Pedersen	.75	2.00
10 Trevor Semeniuk	.60	1.50
11 Dan Turner	.60	1.50
12 Brent Steblyk	.60	1.50
13 Rocky Trottier	.75	2.00
14 Kevan Guy	.75	2.00
15 Bobby Bassen	.75	2.00
16 Brent Meckling	.60	1.50
17 Matt Kabayama	.60	1.50
18 Gord Hynes	.75	2.00
19 Daryl Henry	.60	1.50
20 Jim Kambeitz	.60	1.50
21 Mike Lay	.75	2.00
22 Gord Shmyrko	.60	1.50
23 Al Conroy	.75	2.00

1985-86 Medicine Hat Tigers

This 24-card set measures approximately 2 1/4" by 4" and features posed, color player photos on white card stock. The player's name and the team logo are printed in the larger white margin at the bottom. The player's jersey number and position are printed on the picture in the upper corners. A thin red line encloses the picture, player's name, and logo. The backs display P.L.A.Y. (Police, Laws, and Youth) tips and sponsor logos.

COMPLETE SET (24)	8.00	20.00
1 Mike Claringbull	.30	.75
2 Doug Houda	.40	1.00
3 Mark Kuntz	.30	.75
4 Guy Phillips	.30	.75
5 Rob DiMaio	.75	2.00
6 Al Conroy	.40	1.00
7 Craig Berube	.75	2.00
8 Doug Sauter CO	.20	.50
9 Dean Chynoweth	.40	1.00
10 Scott McCrady	.30	.75
11 Neil Brady	.30	.75
12 Dale Kushner	.30	.75
13 Jeff Wenaas	.30	.75
14 Wayne Hynes	.30	.75
15 Troy Gamble	.75	2.00
16 Bryan Maxwell ACO	.20	.50
17 Gord Hynes	.30	.75
18 Wayne McBean	.40	1.00
19 Mark Pederson	.40	1.00
20 Darren Cota	.30	.75
21 Randy Siska	.30	.75
22 Dave Mackey	.30	.75
23 Mark Fitzpatrick	1.25	3.00
24 Doug Ball TR	.08	.25

1995-96 Medicine Hat Tigers

This 21-card set features color player photos of the Medicine Hat Tigers of the WHL and was sponsored by Pizza Hut. The black front border is highly susceptible to dings, and thus the set is considered condition sensitive. Although the cards feature player jersey numbers on the fronts, they are unnumbered, and thus the set is checklisted below in alphabetical order.

COMPLETE SET (21)	6.00	15.00
1 Johnathan Aitken	.30	.75
2 Brady Austin	.30	.75
3 Cal Benazic	.30	.75
4 Scott Buhler	.30	.75
5 Clint Cabana	.30	.75
6 Mike Eley	.30	.75
7 Josh Green	.40	1.00
8 Curtis Huppe	.30	.75
9 Henry Kuster	.30	.75
10 Aaron Millar	.30	.75
11 Mark Polak	.30	.75
12 Bryan Randall	.30	.75
13 Chad Reich	.30	.75
14 Kyle Ronan	.30	.75
15 Rroary MASCOT	.02	.10
16 Blair St. Martin	.30	.75
17 Paxton Schafer	.30	.75
18 Derek Senkow	.30	.75
19 Darcy Smith	.30	.75
20 Rocky Thompson	.40	1.00
21 Trevor Wasyluk	.40	1.00

1996-97 Medicine Hat Tigers

This 25-card set features posed color player photos surrounded by an orange/yellow border. The player's name, number and position are listed along the left border, while the logos of the team and Canadian Tire can be found along the bottom. The top reads "Medicine Hat News Collector's Edition", leading to speculation that the set was issued as a premium either through the paper, or at a game night sponsored by the paper. The backs contain a large Canadian Tire logo, along with biographical info for the player. The cards are unnumbered, and are checklisted below in alphabetical order.

COMPLETE SET (25)	6.00	15.00
1 Berkeley Buchko	.30	.75
2 Scott Buhler	.30	.75
3 Jason Chimera	.60	1.50
4 Michael Dyck ACO	.02	.10
5 Mike Eley	.30	.75
6 Josh Green	.30	.75
7 Derek Holland	.30	.75
8 Curtis Huppe	.30	.75
9 Henry Kuster	.30	.75
10 Kurt Lackten CO	.02	.10
11 Kevin McDonald	.30	.75
12 Aaron Millar	.30	.75
13 Doug Mosher GM	.02	.10
14 Jaroslav Obsut	.30	.75
15 Colin O'Hara	.30	.75
16 Mark Polak	.30	.75
17 Rroary MASCOT	.02	.10
18 Blair St. Martin	.30	.75
19 Rob Sandrock	.30	.75
20 Dustin Schwartz	.30	.75
21 Lee Svangstu	.30	.75
22 Jeff Temple	.30	.75
23 Rocky Thompson	.30	.75
24 Trevor Wasyluk	.30	.75
25 Chad Wilchynski	.30	.75

1997-98 Medicine Hat Tigers

This set features the Tigers of the WHL. The set was sponsored by the Medicine Hat News and was sold at home games. The cards are unnumbered, and so are listed below in alphabetical order.

COMPLETE SET (25)	4.80	12.00
1 Steve Albrecht	.20	.50
2 James Boyd	.20	.50
3 Konrad Brand	.20	.50
4 Berkeley Buchko	.20	.50
5 Scott Buhler	.40	1.00
6 Rick Carriere CO	.04	.10
7 Jason Chimera	.75	2.00
8 Randall Dyck	.20	.50
9 Shaun Hill	.20	.50
10 Derek Holland	.20	.50
11 Henry Kuster	.20	.50
12 Kevin McDonald	.20	.50
13 Aaron Millar	.20	.50
14 Derek Rupprecht	.20	.50
15 Rob Sandrock	.20	.50
16 Brett Scheffelmaier	.30	.75
17 Justin Schwartz	.30	.75
18 Blair Simpson	.20	.50
19 Blair St. Martin	.20	.50
20 Jeff Temple	.20	.50
21 Brad Voth	.20	.50
22 Trevor Wasyluk	.20	.50
23 Travis Willie	.20	.50
24 Randy Wong ACO	.02	.10
25 Rroary MASCOT	.02	.10

1998-99 Medicine Hat Tigers

This set features the Tigers of the WHL. The set was sponsored by the Medicine Hat News and was sold at home games. The cards are unnumbered, and so are listed below in alphabetical order.

COMPLETE SET (25)	4.80	12.00
1 Brady Austin	.20	.50
2 James Boyd	.20	.50
3 Konrad Brand	.20	.50
4 Berkeley Buchko	.20	.50
5 Scott Buhler	.30	.75
6 Rick Carriere CO	.02	.10
7 Jason Chimera	.60	1.50
8 Martin Cibak	.40	1.00
9 Frazer Donahue	.20	.50
10 Paul Elliott	.20	.50
11 Kris Graf	.20	.50
12 Shaun Hill	.20	.50
13 Denny Johnston	.20	.50
14 Tyson Kentel	.20	.50
15 Cody Lyseng	.20	.50
16 Aaron Millar	.20	.50
17 Derek Rupprecht	.20	.50
18 Brett Scheffelmaier	.30	.75
19 Justin Schwartz	.30	.75
20 Blair Simpson	.20	.50
21 Ben Thompson	.20	.50
22 Brad Voth	.20	.50
23 Kevin Young	.20	.50
24 Randy Wong ACO	.02	.10
25 Rroary MASCOT	.02	.10

1999-00 Medicine Hat Tigers

This set was produced on very thin card stock and is highly susceptible to damage. The cards were sold by the team at its souvenir stands. The set is noteworthy for featuring the first card of 2002 first-rounder Jay Bouwmeester.

COMPLETE SET (25)	10.00	25.00
1 Header Card	.02	.10
2 Chris Ferguson	.20	.50
3 Jay Bouwmeester	6.00	15.00
4 Josh Morrow	.20	.50
5 Paul Elliott	.20	.50
6 Tyson Mulock	.20	.50
7 Kevin Labbe	.20	.50
8 Ryan Hollweg	.30	.75
9 Berkeley Buchko	.20	.50
10 Chris St. Jacques	.20	.50
11 Cody Jensen	.20	.50
12 Ben Thompson	.20	.50
13 Brad Voth	.20	.50
14 Martin Cibak	.20	.50
15 Denny Johnston	.20	.50
16 Konrad Brand	.20	.50
17 Shaun Sutter	.30	.75
18 Ken Davis	.20	.50
19 Ryan Kinasewich	.20	.50
20 Brett Scheffelmaier	.30	.75
21 Justin Taylor	.20	.50
22 Vladimir Sicak	.20	.50
23 Ben McMullin	.30	.75
24 Kyle Kettles	.30	.75
25 Josh Maser	.20	.50
27 Brett Scheffelmaier	.20	.50
28 Justin Taylor	.20	.50
29 Vladimir Sicak	.20	.50
30 Ben McMullin	.20	.50
31 Kyle Kettles	.20	.50
32 Jash Maser	.20	.50

2000-01 Medicine Hat Tigers

This set features the Tigers of the WHL. The set was sold by the team at its souvenir stands. The cards are unnumbered and is listed below alphabetically. The set features an early card of top prospect Jay Bouwmeester.

COMPLETE SET (26)	8.00	25.00
1 Jay Bouwmeester	4.00	8.00
2 Ryan Chieduch	.16	.40
3 Petr Chivojka	.16	.40
4 Ken Davis	.16	.40
5 Brett Draney	.16	.40
6 Bryan Ellerman ACO	.04	.10
7 B.J. Fehr	.16	.40
8 Vernon Fiddler	.16	.40
9 Jeremy Goetzinger	.16	.40
10 Ryan Hollweg	.30	.75
11 Denny Johnston	.16	.40
12 Kyle Kettles	.16	.40
13 Ryan Kinasewich	.16	.40
14 Bob Loucks HCO	.04	.10
15 Joffrey Lupul	2.00	10.00
16 Ben McMullin	.20	.50
17 Josh Morrow	.16	.40
18 Tyson Mulock	.16	.40
19 Ryan Olynyk	.16	.40
20 Brett Scheffelmaier	.30	.75
21 Chris St. Jacques	.16	.40
22 Ben Thompson	.16	.40
23 David Ullmann	.16	.40
24 Brad Voth	.16	.40
26 Mascot	.04	.10
26 Randy Wong ACO	.04	.10

2002-03 Medicine Hat Tigers

These cards are unnumbered and are listed below in alphabetical order.

COMPLETE SET (25)	8.00	20.00
1 Curtis Austring	.20	.50
2 Cam Barker	.60	1.50
3 Chad Bassen	.20	.50
4 Kieran Block	.20	.50
5 Brenden Cuthbert	.20	.50
6 Riley Day	.20	.50
7 Tyler Dietrich	.20	.50
8 Nick Harsulla	.20	.50
9 Ryan Hollweg	.30	.75
10 Daniel Idema	.20	.50
11 Martin Kubaliak	.20	.50
12 Joffrey Lupul	2.00	5.00
13 Steve Marr	.20	.50
14 Tommy Maxwell	.20	.50
15 Stefan Meyer	.20	.50
16 Clarke MacArthur	.40	1.00
17 Kevin Nastiuk	.60	1.50
18 Kyle Pess	.20	.50
19 Adam Redmond	.20	.50
20 Steven Regier	.20	.50
21 Darren Reid	.20	.50
22 Mark Vodden	.20	.50
23 Chris St. Jacques	.20	.50
24 Ryan Stempfle	.20	.50
25 Ben Thomson	.20	.50

2003-04 Medicine Hat Tigers

This checklist is incomplete, but the cards below have been confirmed to exist.

COMPLETE SET
1 Cam Barker
2 Riley Day
3 Ryan Hollweg
4 Clarke MacArthur
5 Stefan Meyer
6 Kevin Nastiuk
7 Darren Reid
8 Yannick Seidenberg

2004-05 Medicine Hat Tigers

COMPLETE SET (25)	8.00	20.00
1 Gord Baldwin	.30	.75
2 Cam Barker	.60	1.50
3 Jordan Bendfeld	.30	.75
4 Cody Blanshan	.30	.75
5 Kieran Block	.30	.75
6 Derek Dorsett	.30	.75
7 Nathan Exner	.30	.75
8 Trevor Glass	.30	.75
9 Darren Helm	.30	.75
10 Matt Keetley	.30	.75
11 Jarret Lukin	.30	.75
12 Clarke MacArthur	.40	1.00
13 Steve Marr	.30	.75
14 Tommy Maxwell	.30	.75
15 Stefan Meyer	.30	.75
16 Kevin Nastiuk	.60	1.50
17 Roman Psurny	.30	.75
18 Brett Robertson	.30	.75
19 Kris Russell	.30	.75
20 David Schlemko	.30	.75
21 Daine Todd	.30	.75
22 Devyn Tremblay	.30	.75
23 Kevin Undershute	.30	.75
24 Willie Desjardins CO	.04	.10
25 Shaun Clouston ACO	.04	.10

2005-06 Medicine Hat Tigers

COMPLETE SET (25)	8.00	20.00
1 Gord Baldwin	.30	.75
2 Cam Barker	.60	1.50
3 Jason Battershill	.30	.75
4 Jordan Bendfeld	.30	.75
5 Kieran Block	.30	.75
6 Brennan Bosch	.30	.75
7 Shayne Brown	.30	.75
8 Marek Curilla	.30	.75
9 Derek Dorsett	.30	.75
10 Tyler Ennis	.50	1.25
11 Trevor Glass	.30	.75
12 Darren Helm	.30	.75
13 Matt Keetley	.30	.75
14 Tommy Maxwell	.30	.75
15 Blaine Neufeld	.30	.75
16 Roman Psurny	.30	.75
17 Brett Robertson	.30	.75
18 Kris Russell	.30	.75
19 Jerrid Sauer	.30	.75
20 David Schlemko	.30	.75
21 Matt Sokol	.30	.75
22 Chris Stevens	.30	.75
23 Daine Todd	.30	.75
24 Kevin Undershute	.30	.75
25 Scott Wasden	.30	.75

2006-07 Medicine Hat Tigers

COMPLETE SET (25)	12.00	20.00
1 Gord Baldwin	.30	.75
2 Jordan Bendfeld	.30	.75
3 Brennan Bosch	.30	.75
4 Shayne Brown	.30	.75
5 Derek Dorsett	.30	.75
6 Tyler Ennis	.50	1.25
7 Trevor Glass	.30	.75
8 Colton Grant	.30	.75
9 Darren Helm	.30	.75
10 Jordan Hickmott	.30	.75
11 Ryan Holfeld	.40	1.00
12 Mark Isherwood	.30	.75
13 Matt Keetley	.40	1.00
14 Matt Lowry	.30	.75
15 Jakub Rumpel	.30	.75
16 Kris Russell	.75	2.00
17 Jerrid Sauer	.30	.75
18 Michael Sauer	.30	.75
19 David Schlemko	.30	.75
20 Chris Stevens	.30	.75
21 Tyler Swystun	.30	.75
22 Daine Todd	.30	.75
23 Kevin Undershute	.30	.75
24 Scott Wasden	.30	.75
25 Willie Desjardins CO	.10	.25

1993-94 Memphis RiverKings

Like most of the CHL sets issued that season, these round cards are approximately the size of a hockey puck. They came in a plastic container with the team logo on the front, and were sold by the booster club for $5..

COMPLETE SET (18)	3.60	9.00
1 Rocco Amonte	.20	.50
2 Peter D'Amario	.20	.50
3 Roydon Gunn	.20	.50
4 Kyle Haviland	.20	.50
5 Mike Jackson	.20	.50
6 Scot Johnston	.20	.50
7 Robert Kelley	.20	.50
8 Mark McGinn	.20	.50
9 Antoine Mindjimba	.30	.75
10 David Moore	.20	.50
11 Glenn Painter	.20	.50
12 Scott Phillips	.20	.50
13 Mike Roberts	.20	.50
14 Andy Ross	.20	.50
15 Steve Shaunessy	.20	.50
16 Ken Venis	.20	.50
17 Bobby Wallwork	.20	.50
18 Randy Boyd CO	.08	.25

1994-95 Memphis RiverKings

Available in 14-card CHL packs that contained an assortment of teams, this 18-card set featured players of the RiverKings.

COMPLETE SET (18)	3.00	8.00
1 Denis Beauchamp	.20	.50
2 Nicolas Brousseau	.20	.50
3 Scott Bower	.30	.75
4 Dan Brown	.20	.50
5 Brian Cook	.20	.50
6 Brent Fleetwood	.20	.50
7 Francois Gagnon	.20	.50
8 Dominic Grand'maison	.20	.50
9 Kyle Haviland	.20	.50
10 Jamie Hearn	.20	.50
11 Mike Jackson	.30	.75
12 Paul Krake	.30	.75
13 Layne LeBel	.20	.50
14 Steve Magnusson	.20	.50
15 Darren Miciak	.20	.50
16 Mark McGinn	.20	.50
17 Bobby Wallwork	.20	.50
18 Herb Boxer CO	.08	.25

1999-00 Memphis RiverKings All-Time

This set features the RiverKings of the CHL. Rather than commemorate the current roster, it features the best players ever to don the River Kings sweater. The set was originally issued as a promotional giveaway, but later was sold by the team as well.

COMPLETE SET (20)	4.00	10.00
1 Tom Mutch	.20	.50
2 Doug Stromback	.20	.50
3 Mike Jackson	.30	.75
4 Mark McGinn	.20	.50
5 Antoine Mindjimba	.30	.75
6 Andrew Miller	.20	.50
7 Dan Brown	.20	.50
8 Hugo Hamelin	.20	.50
9 Derek Grant	.20	.50
10 Steve Thorpe	.20	.50
11 Bobby Wallwork	.20	.50
12 Peter D'Amario	.20	.50
13 John Batten	.20	.50
14 Andy Ross	.20	.50
15 Kyle Haviland	.20	.50
16 Scot Kelsey	.20	.50
17 Scott Brower	.20	.50
18 Jamie Cooke	.30	.75
19 Craig Lindsay	.20	.50
20 Riverthing MAS	.08	.25

2001-02 Memphis RiverKings

This set features the RiverKings of the CHL. The set was sold by the team at home games late in the season, after goalie Sebastien Centomo had moved on to the AHL and later, the NHL. The cards are unnumbered, although they are listed on a checklist. The set is listed in the order it appears on the checklist.

COMPLETE SET (21)	6.00	15.00
1 Team CL Centomo	.30	.75
2 Kahlil Thomas	.20	.50
3 Brad Mueller	.20	.50
4 Kevin Fricke	.20	.50
5 Anthony DiPalma	.20	.50
6 Michal Stastny	.30	.75
7 Jean-Francois Picard	.20	.50
8 Jay Neal	.20	.50
9 Jacques Lariviere	.30	.75
10 Rob Palahnuk	.20	.50
11 Kevin Ryan	.20	.50
12 Sebastien Centomo	2.00	5.00
13 Don Parsons	.20	.50
14 Luch Nasato	.30	.75
15 Mark Richards	.20	.50
16 Brian Tucker	.20	.50
17 Don Martin	.20	.50
18 Ben Gorewich	.20	.50
19 A.J. Aitken	.20	.50
20 Jonathan Gagnon	.20	.50
21 Doug Shedden CO	.20	.50

2003-04 Memphis RiverKings

COMPLETE SET	6.00	15.00
1 Jeremy Cornish	.40	1.00
2 Trent Dickson	.30	.75
3 Juraj Durco	.30	.75
4 Jonathan Gagnon	.30	.75
5 Jasmin Gelinas	.30	.75
6 Jerry Gernander	.30	.75
7 Jeremy Goetzinger	.30	.75
8 Chad Grills	.30	.75
9 Derek Landmesser	.40	1.00
10 Stephen Margeson	.30	.75
11 Alexandre Mathieu	.40	1.00
12 Mike Minard	.40	1.00
13 Brad Mueller	.30	.75
14 Jay Neal	.30	.75
15 Brent Ozarowski	.30	.75
16 Don Parsons	.40	1.00
17 Jean-Francois Racine	.60	1.50
18 Mark Richards	.30	.75
19 Tim Schneider	.30	.75
20 Brian Tucker	.30	.75
21 David Turon	.30	.75

2004-05 Memphis RiverKings

COMPLETE SET (22)	6.00	15.00
1 Header Card	.04	.10
2 Aaron Lewis	.20	.50
3 Allan Carr	.20	.50
4 Brad Mueller	.20	.50
5 David Lemanowicz	.60	1.50
6 Derek Landmesser	.20	.50
7 Don Parsons	.30	.75
8 J.F. Racine	.60	1.50
9 Jeremy Goetzinger	.20	.50
10 Jeremy Wray	.20	.50
11 Ken Goetz	.60	1.50
12 Mark Richards	.20	.50
13 Peter Robertson	.20	.50
14 Phil Aucoin	.20	.50
15 Ryan Rome	.20	.50
16 Scott English	.75	2.00
17 Stephen Margeson	.20	.50
18 Ted Crowley	.20	.50
19 Tim Plett	.20	.50
20 Travis Banga	.20	.50
21 Tyson Gajda	.20	.50
22 Wayne Hall	.20	.50

1991-92 Michigan Falcons

This set features the Falcons of the UHL. According to minor league expert Ralph Slate, the set wasn't widely distributed until 1994-95, but based on the players involved and the fact that the manufacturer -- 7th Inning Sketch -- actually went out of business in 1992 this set must have been intended for distribution during that season.

COMPLETE SET (21)	8.00	20.00
1 Christian LaLonde	.40	1.00
2 Victor Posa	.40	1.00
3 Al Murphy	.40	1.00
4 Bill Horn	.40	1.00
5 Rich Sewell	.40	1.00
6 Dan Fowler	.40	1.00
7 Kip Noble	.40	1.00
8 Ange Guzzo	.40	1.00
9 Dean Morton	.40	1.00
10 Jeff Lindsay	.40	1.00
11 Mike Vellucci	.60	1.50
12 Brett Strot	.40	1.00
13 Rick Berens	.40	1.00
14 Kevin Clayton	.40	1.00
15 Todd Humphrey	.40	1.00
16 Ray De Grendel ACO	.08	.25
16 Terry Christensen CO	.08	.25
16 Tom Viggiano ACO	.08	.25
17 Bill Gutenberg	.40	1.00
18 Jamie Stewart	.40	1.00
19 Bob McKillop	.40	1.00
20 Clayton Young	.40	1.00
21 Steve Beadle	.40	1.00

1996-97 Michigan K-Wings

This set features the K-Wings of the IHL. The set was sponsored by BJ Sports, and sold by the team at home games.

COMPLETE SET (27)	4.80	10.0
1 Dan Keczmer	.15	.4
2 Dennis Smith	.15	.4
3 Brad Berry	.15	.4
4 Shane Peacock	.15	.4
5 Jason Lafreniere	.15	.4
6 Collin Bauer	.15	.4
7 Sergei Gusev	.15	.4
8 Igor Korolev	.15	.4
9 Brent Fedyk	.15	.4
10 Pat Elynuik	.15	.4
11 Jamie Wright	.15	.4
12 Lee Jinman	.15	.4
13 Jeff Mitchell	.15	.4
14 Brad Lukowich	.20	.5
15 Derrick Smith	.15	.4
16 Petr Buzek	.15	.4
17 Patrick Cote	.20	.5
18 Mark Lawrence	.15	.4
19 Jim Storm	.15	.4
20 Roman Turek	.40	1.0
21 Neil Brady	.15	.4
22 Manny Fernandez	.75	2.0
23 Claude Noel CO	.02	.1
24 Jim Playfair CO	.02	.1
25 Checklist	.01	.0
26 PHPA Web Site	.01	.0
27 BJ Sports	.01	.0

1998-99 Michigan K-Wings

This 21-card set features the K-Wings of the IHL on an extra glossy card stock. The cards are not numbered they appear in the order that was released on the checklist card.

COMPLETE SET (21)	8.00	25.0
1 Mel Angelstad	.40	1.0
2 Jason Botterill	.15	.4
3 Ryan Christie	.15	.4
4 Doug Doull	.75	2.0
5 Kelly Fairchild	.15	.4
6 Marty Flichel	.15	.4
7 Aaron Gavey	.30	.7
8 Greg Leeb	.15	.4
9 Jeff Mitchell	.15	.4
10 Dave Roberts	.15	.4
11 Jon Sim	.30	.7
12 Brad Berry	.15	.4
13 Petr Buzek	.30	
14 Richard Jackman	.30	
15 Brad Lukowich	.30	
16 Matt Martin	.15	
17 Evgueni Tsybouk	.15	
18 Mike Bales	.30	
19 Marty Turco	6.00	15.0
20 IHL Logo card	.02	
21 Header Checklist	.02	

1999-00 Michigan K-Wings

This set features the K-Wings of the IHL. The set was produced by EBK Sports and was sold by the team at its souvenir stands. Each card also is serial numbered out of 1,000.

COMPLETE SET (21)	14.00	40.
1 Jamie Wright	.30	

Aldridge .30 .75
Gainey .30 .75
than Sim .40 1.00
Martin .20 .50
an Royer .20 .50
MacMillan .20 .50
n Gavey .20 .50
ny Tsybouk .20 .50
ty Turco 8.00 20.00
t Martin .20 .50
n Christie .20 .50
g Leeb .20 .50
k Wotton .20 .50
y Fairchild .20 .50
gor Baumgartner .20 .50
nden Morrow 4.00 10.00
Angelstad .75 2.00
e Bales .30 .75
hard Jackman .30 .75
nan Lyashenko .40 1.00

0-91 Michigan Tech Huskies

-card standard-size set was sponsored by The Mining Gazette and showcases the Michigan uskies of the WCHA. Reportedly only 500 sets roduced. The cards are printed on thin ard stock. Borderless high gloss player photos he fronts, with the jersey number, team name, name, and position given in a black stripe at the of the card face. On a black and pale yellow ound, each back has a black and white head iography, statistics, and career summary. A es Hockey Quick Fact" completes the card back. rds are unnumbered and checklisted below in etical order.

LETE SET (31) 6.00 15.00
Bonner .20 .50
ll Brown CO .08 .25
ht DeGiacomo .20 .50
Ewacha .20 .50
Grant .20 .50
Hartnett .20 .50
Hauswirth .20 .50
Hurd .20 .50
Hurd .20 .50
Wings
ne Lebel .20 .50
Hill
dy Lewis .20 .50
Luknowsky .20 .50
Martel CO .08 .25
Leach CO
cy Martini .20 .50
l McDonald .20 .50
h McEwen .30 .75
Storm
Manninen
Osborne .20 .50
g Parnell .20 .50
is Payne .20 .50
y Perrault .20 .50
n Brkic
Plaquin .20 .50
hian Rhodes .75 2.00
ff Sarjeant .30 .75
ie Steer .20 .50
Tustian .20 .50
tt Vettraino .30 .75
e Ram
Watters b/w .20 .50
n Young .20 .50
n Young .20 .50
Hurd
1 MacInnes Cup .20 .50
5 NCAA Champions .20 .50

1-92 Michigan Tech Huskies

-card standard-size set features the 1992-93 an Tech Huskies. Reportedly approximately ets were produced. The fronts features full- olor action player photos. A gray and yellow t the bottom contains the player's name. The s logo overlaps the picture and the stripe. Some have two cards, the second of which is uished by a subtitle. The cards are unnumbered ecklisted below in alphabetical order.

LETE SET (36) 6.00 15.00
Bonner .20 .50
n Brkic .20 .50
Ewacha .20 .50
Hartnett .20 .50
Hauswirth .20 .50
Hill .20 .50
e LeBel .20 .50
y Lewis .20 .50
y Lewis .20 .50
quad
n MacInnes CO .02 .10
cy Martini .20 .50
cy Martini .20 .50
Blaster
McDonald .20 .50
h McEwen .20 .50
Olson ANN .02 .10
Osborne .20 .50
Parnell .20 .50
s Payne .20 .50
y Perrault .20 .50
Plaquin .20 .50
ie Ram .30 .75
ff Sarjeant .30 .75
ff Sarjeant .30 .75
A Student-Athlete
ie Steer .20 .50
ie Steer .20 .50
Runner
Storm .20 .50
t Vettraino .20 .50
Young .20 .50
its (Team .20 .50
ing on ice)
hman .20 .50
Peca
Garvey
Stevens
Peterson
Seale
t Lakes .02 .10
ional
e Ice .02 .10
nes Student Ice Arena
n Photo .20 .50
Draft .20 .50
Martini
Payne
Sarjeant
laquin
torm
Ram
Steer

Jim Bonner
35 Pep Band .02 .10
36 Michigan Tech Univ. .02 .10

1993-94 Michigan Tech Huskies

The set features the Huskies of the NCAA. As is the case with most collegiate sets, this is believed to have been issued as a promotional giveaway. Any additional information can be forwarded to hockeymag@beckett.com.

COMPLETE SET (25) 4.80 12.00
1 Pat Mikesch .20 .50
2 Eric Jensen .20 .50
3 Kyle Peterson .20 .50
4 Jay Storm .20 .50
5 Jason Hanchuk .20 .50
6 Mike Figliomeni .20 .50
7 Randy Stevens .20 .50
8 Brent Peterson .20 .50
9 Kirby Perrault .20 .50
10 Brian Hunter .20 .50
11 Travis Seale .20 .50
12 Jamie Ram .30 .75
13 Jeff Hill .20 .50
14 Justin Peca .20 .50
15 Layne LeBel .20 .50
16 Jeff Mikesch .20 .50
17 John Kisil .20 .50
18 Liam Garvey .20 .50
19 Kyle Ferguson .20 .50
20 Jason Wright .20 .50
21 Luciano Caravaggio .20 .50
22 Mitch Lane .20 .50
23 Randy Wakeham .20 .50
24 Martin Machacek .20 .50
25 Winter Carnival .02 .10

2001-02 Michigan Tech Huskies

This set features the Huskies of the NCAA. The set was issued as a promotional giveaway. As the cards are unnumbered, they are listed below in alphabetical order.

COMPLETE SET (33) 8.00 20.00
1 Greg Amadio .30 .75
2 Justin Brown .30 .75
3 Paul Cabana .30 .75
4 Tony DeLorenzo .30 .75
5 Jaron Doetzel .30 .75
6 Chris Durno .30 .75
7 Cam Ellsworth .40 1.00
8 Brett Engelhardt .30 .75
9 Chuck Fabry .30 .75
10 Brady Greco .30 .75
11 John Hartman .30 .75
12 Blizzard T. Husky .04 .10
13 Tom Kaiman .30 .75
14 Bryan Konkel .30 .75
15 Tim Laurila .40 1.00
16 Ryan Lenton .30 .75
17 MacInnes Arena .04 .10
18 Ryan Markham .30 .75
19 Pep Band .04 .10
20 Colin Murphy .30 .75
21 Bob Olson ANN .04 .10
22 Brad Patterson .30 .75
23 Bryan Perez .30 .75
24 Phil Pietila .30 .75
25 Jon Pittis .30 .75
26 Bob Rangus .30 .75
27 Rob Rankin .30 .75
28 Brian Rogers .40 1.00
29 Mike Sertich CO .10 .25
30 Josh Singer .30 .75
31 Brad Sullivan .30 .75
32 Frank Werner .30 .75
33 Clay Wilson .30 .75

1991 Michigan

This 56-card multi-sport standard-size set was issued by College Classics. The fronts feature a mix of color or black and white player photos. This set features a card of Gerald Ford, center for the Wolverine football squad from 1932-34. Ford autographed 200 of his cards, one of which was to be included in each of the 200 cases of 50 sets. The Ford autographs were printed on linen card stock, feature a hand serial number on the front and have a different player image than card #21. A letter of authenticity (containing a matching serial number) on Gerald Ford stationery accompaned each Ford autographed card. Some Ford autographs, also on the linen stock, surfaced later missing the serial numbering. The cards are unnumbered and we have checklisted them below according to alphabetical order.

COMPLETE SET (56) 6.00 15.00
3 Red Berenson H .08 .25
4 John Blum H .02 .10
22 Wally Grant H .02 .10
29 Brad Jones H .02 .10
35 Wilf Martin H .02 .10
38 Jeff Norton H .02 .10
44 Steve Richmond H .02 .10
48 Warren Sharples H .02 .10

1991-92 Michigan Wolverines

Little is known about this set beyond confirmation of the checklist. These cards are unnumbered and checklisted below in alphabetical order. Additional info can be forwarded to hockeymag@beckett.com

COMPLETE SET (25) 6.00 15.00
1 Doug Evans .20 .50
2 Denny Felsner .20 .50
3 Anton Fedorov .20 .50
4 Chris Gordon .20 .50
5 David Harlock .20 .50
6 Mike Helber .20 .50
7 Tim Hogan .20 .50
8 Mike Knuble .30 .75
9 Ted Kramer .20 .50
10 Pat Neaton .20 .50
11 David Oliver .30 .75
12 David Roberts .20 .50
13 Marc Ouimet .20 .50
14 Ron Sacka .20 .50
15 Mark Sakala .20 .50
16 Steve Shields 1.25 3.00
17 Alan Sinclair .20 .50
18 Cam Stewart .30 .75
19 Dan Stiver .20 .50
20 Mike Stone .20 .50
21 Chris Tamer .25 .60
22 Aaron Ward .30 .75
23 Rick Willis .20 .50
24 Brian Wiseman .20 .50
25 Team Card .02 .10

1993-94 Michigan Wolverines

This set features the Wolverines of the NCAA. As is the case with most collegiate sets, this is believed to have been a promotional giveaway. The cards are unnumbered and checklisted below in alphabetical order.

COMPLETE SET (28) 8.00 20.00
1 John Arnold .20 .50
2 Jason Botterill .30 .75
3 Peter Bourke .20 .50
4 Drew Denzin .20 .50
5 Anton Fedorov .20 .50
6 Chris Frescoln .20 .50
7 Chris Gordon .20 .50
8 Steve Halko .20 .50
9 Kevin Hilton .20 .50
10 Tim Hogan .20 .50
11 Mike Knuble .30 .75
12 Mike Legg .20 .50
13 Al Loges .20 .50
14 Warren Luhning .20 .50
15 John Madden 1.50 4.00
16 Brendan Morrison .75 2.00
17 David Oliver .20 .50
18 Ron Sacka .20 .50
19 Mark Sakala .20 .50
20 Harold Schock .20 .50
21 Steve Shields .60 1.50
22 Alan Sinclair .20 .50
23 Ryan Sittler .20 .50
24 Blake Sloan .40 1.00
25 Mike Stone .20 .50
26 Rick Willis .20 .50
27 Brian Wiseman .20 .50
28 Team Photo .20 .50

2002-03 Michigan Wolverines

COMPLETE SET (30) 15.00 35.00
1 Billy Powers ACO .04 .10
2 Danny Richmond .75 2.00
3 Mike Roemensky .40 1.00
4 David Wyzgowski .40 1.00
5 Charlie Henderson .40 1.00
6 Jed Ortmeyer .75 2.00
7 Jeff Tambellini 1.25 3.00
8 David Moss .40 1.00
9 Gordon Berenson HCO .40 1.00
10 NCAA Frozen Four .10 .25
11 Eric Nystrom 1.25 3.00
12 John Shouneyia .40 1.00
13 Andrew Ebbett .40 1.00
14 Michael Woodford .40 1.00
15 Mel Pearson ACO .10 .25
16 Brandon Rogers .40 1.00
17 Joe Kautz .40 1.00
18 Mark Mink .40 1.00
19 Nick Martens .40 1.00
20 2002 CCHA Champions .10 .25
21 Jason Ryznar .40 1.00
22 Andy Burnes .40 1.00
23 Dwight Helminen .40 1.00
24 Milan Gajic .40 1.00
25 Yost Arena .04 .10
26 2002 CCHA Tournament Champs .10 .25
27 J.J. Swistak .40 1.00
28 Al Montoya 3.00 8.00
29 Brandon Kaleniecki .40 1.00
30 Eric Werner .40 1.00

2003-04 Michigan Wolverines

This set was issued as a promotional giveaway.

COMPLETE SET (30) 20.00 40.00
1 Jeff Tambellini 1.25 3.00
2 Mike Mayhew .40 1.00
3 David Moss .75 2.00
4 Red Berenson CO .40 1.00
5 Endowed Scholarships .04 .10
6 Jason Ryznar .40 1.00
7 Andy Burnes .40 1.00
8 Dwight Helminen .40 1.00
9 Milan Gajic .40 1.00
10 Reilly Olson .40 1.00
11 Brandon Rogers .40 1.00
12 Joe Kautz .40 1.00
13 Tim Cook .40 1.00
14 Nick Martens .40 1.00
15 T.J. Hensick .75 2.00
16 Eric Werner .40 1.00
17 Brandon Kaleniecki .40 1.00
18 Al Montoya 3.00 8.00
19 Mike Brown .40 1.00
20 Noah Ruden .40 1.00
21 David Rohlfs .40 1.00
22 Eric Nystrom 1.25 3.00
23 Andrew Ebbett .40 1.00
24 Michael Woodford .40 1.00
25 Mel Pearson ACO .04 .10
26 Charlie Henderson .40 1.00
27 David Wyzgowski .40 1.00
28 Jason Dest .40 1.00
29 Matt Hunwick .75 2.00
30 Billy Powers ACO .04 .10

2004-05 Michigan Wolverines

This set was given out at home games in five strips of five cards.

COMPLETE SET (25) 12.00 30.00
1 David Rohlfs .40 1.00
2 Andrew Ebbett .40 1.00
3 Brandon Kaleniecki .40 1.00
4 Al Montoya 2.00 5.00
5 Gameday .04 .10
6 Chad Kolarik .40 1.00
7 Kevin Porter .40 1.00
8 Mike Brown .60 1.50
9 Tim Cook .40 1.00
10 Yost Arena .04 .10
11 Jason Dest .40 1.00
12 Matt Hunwick .60 1.50
13 T.J. Hensick .75 2.00
14 Mike Mayhew .40 1.00
15 Endowed Scholarships .04 .10
16 Nick Martens .40 1.00
17 David Moss 1.25 3.00
18 Eric Nystrom 1.25 3.00
19 Reilly Olson .40 1.00
20 Mel Pearson ACO .04 .10
21 Noah Ruden .40 1.00
22 Jeff Tambellini 1.25 3.00
23 Milan Gajic .40 1.00
24 Charlie Henderson .40 1.00
25 Billy Powers .40 1.00

2007-08 Michigan Wolverines

COMPLETE SET (28) 4.00 10.00
1 Louie Caporusso .15 .40
2 Anthony Ciraulo .15 .40
3 Eric Elmblad .15 .40
4 Danny Fardig .15 .40
5 Chris Fragner .15 .40
6 Carl Hagelin .15 .40
7 Bryan Hogan .15 .40
8 Shawn Hunwick .15 .40
9 Steve Kampfer .15 .40
10 Chad Kolarik .15 .40
11 Chad Langlais .15 .40
12 Brian Lebler .15 .40
13 Tristin Llewellyn .15 .40
14 Tim Miller .15 .40
15 Mark Mitera .15 .40
16 Brandon Naurato .15 .40
17 Max Pacioretty .15 .40
18 Aaron Palushaj .15 .40
19 Kevin Porter .15 .40
20 Kevin Quick .15 .40
21 Matt Rust .15 .40
22 Billy Sauer .15 .40
23 Chris Summers .15 .40
24 Travis Turnbull .15 .40
25 Scooter Vaughn .15 .40
26 Ben Winnett .15 .40
27 Red Berenson HC .10 .25
28 Yost Arena .15 .40

1990-91 Michigan State Collegiate Collection 200

This 200-card standard-size set was produced by Collegiate Collection. The fronts feature black and white shots for earlier players or color shots for later players, with borders in the team's colors white and green. Since most cards are football, we've noted below which cards feature other sports. Although some players were famous in others sports, like Kirk Gibson and Steve Garvey, they do have football cards in this set.

COMPLETE SET (200) 6.00 15.00
52 Don(Zippy) Thompson HK .05 .15
55 Doug Roberts HK .05 .15
64 Tom Ross HK .05 .15
69 John Chandik HK .05 .15
75 Weldon Olson HK .05 .15
84 Joe Selinger HK .05 .15
95 Norm Barnes HK .05 .15
97 Craig Simpson HK .07 .20
125 Craig Simpson .05 .15
137 Bob Essensa HK .08 .25
197 Rod Brind'Amour HK .20 .50

1990-91 Michigan State Collegiate Collection Promos

This ten-card standard size set features some of the great athletes from Michigan State History. Most of the cards in the set feature an action photograph on the front of the card along with either statistical or biographical information on the back of the card. Since this set involves more than one sport we have put a two-letter abbreviation to indicate the sport played.

COMPLETE SET (10) 1.50 4.00
1 Ron Scott HK .08 .25

1992-93 Michigan State Spartans

This set features the Spartans of the NCAA. The cards are unnumbered and so are listed below in alphabetical order. The cards were issued as a promotional giveaway.

COMPLETE SET (30) 15.00 40.00
1 Team Photo .60 1.50
2 Ron Mason HCO .60 1.50
3 Matt Albers .60 1.50
4 Michael Burkett .60 1.50
5 Mike Buzak .60 1.50
6 Anson Carter 2.50 6.00
7 Brian Clifford .60 1.50
8 Scott Dean .60 1.50
9 Ryan Fleming .60 1.50
10 Ryan Folkening .60 1.50
11 Steve Guolla 1.25 3.00
12 Kelly Harper .60 1.50
13 Eric Kruse .60 1.50
14 James Lambros .60 1.50
15 Mike Mattis .60 1.50
16 Wes McCauley .60 1.50
17 Rem Murray 1.25 3.00
18 Steve Norton .60 1.50
19 Nicolas Perreault .60 1.50
20 Bill Shalawylo .60 1.50
21 Chris Smith .60 1.50
22 Bryan Smolinski 1.25 3.00
23 Steve Suk .60 1.50
24 Chris Sullivan .60 1.50
25 Bart Turner .60 1.50
26 Bart Vanstaalduinen .60 1.50
27 Mike Ware .60 1.50
28 John Weidenbach .60 1.50
29 Rob Woodward .60 1.50
30 Scott Worden .60 1.50

1993-94 Michigan State Spartans

This set features the Spartans of the NCAA. The cards were produced by Phipps Sports Marketing, Inc and were issued as a promotional giveaway. The cards are unnumbered and checklisted below in alphabetical order.

COMPLETE SET (32) 15.00 40.00
1 Matt Albers .40 1.00
2 Michael Burkett .40 1.00
3 Mike Buzak .40 1.00
4 Anson Carter 2.00 5.00
5 Brian Clifford .75 2.00
6 Brian Crane .40 1.00
7 Steve Ferranti .40 1.00
8 Ryan Fleming .40 1.00
9 Steve Guolla .75 2.00
10 Kelly Harper .40 1.00
11 Eric Kruse .40 1.00
12 Ron Mason CO .40 1.00
13 Mike Mattis .40 1.00
14 Rem Murray .75 2.00
15 Steve Norton .40 1.00
16 Nicolas Perreault .40 1.00
17 Tom Ross .75 2.00
Spartan Great
18 Chris Slater .40 1.00
19 Chris Smith .40 1.00
20 Bryan Smolinski 1.25 3.00
21 Sparty (Mascot) .02 .10
22 Chris Sullivan .40 1.00
23 Steve Suk .40 1.00
24 Bart Turner .40 1.00
25 Tony Tuzzolino 1.25 3.00
26 Bart Vanstaalduinen .40 1.00
27 Mike Ware .40 1.00
28 John Weidenbach .40 1.00
29 Josh Wiegand .40 1.00
30 Scott Worden .40 1.00
31 Munn Arena .02 .10
32 Title Card .02 .10

2000-01 Michigan State Spartans

This set features the Spartans of the NCAA. It was handed out as a promotional giveaway at a pair of home games in 2000. The set is noteworthy for including an early card of hot prospect Ryan Miller.

COMPLETE SET (21) 10.00 35.00
1 Joe Blackburn .75 2.00
2 Andrew Bogle .40 1.00
3 Steve Clark .40 1.00
4 Rustyn Dolyny .40 1.00
5 Brad Fast .40 1.00
6 Troy Ferguson .40 1.00
7 Joe Goodenow .40 1.00
8 Adam Hall 2.00 5.00
9 Andrew Hutchinson .75 2.00
10 Jon Insana .40 1.00
11 Steve Jackson .40 1.00
12 Kris Koski .40 1.00
13 John-Michael Liles 2.00 5.00
14 Brian Maloney .40 1.00
15 Ryan Miller 6.00 15.00
16 John Nail .40 1.00
17 Sean Patchell .40 1.00
18 Damon Whitten .40 1.00
19 Ron Mason CO .40 1.00
20 White Out Game 3/2/01 .10 .25
21 Chevy Fans.Com .02 .10

1981-82 Milwaukee Admirals

This 15-card standard-size set was produced by TCMA and features the members of the Milwaukee Admirals. The cards are made of thick card stock. On the front, a black-and-white player photo with thin black borders is framed in bright yellow. The team name appears in the yellow border above the photo, while the player's name, jersey number, and position appear below. The horizontal backs carry biography and statistics.

COMPLETE SET (15) 6.00 15.00
1 Pat Rabbitt .40 1.00
2 Real Paiement .40 1.00
3 Fred Berry .40 1.00
4 Blaine Peerless .40 1.00
5 John Flesch .40 1.00
6 Yves Preston .40 1.00
7 Bruce McKay .40 1.00
8 Dale Yakiwchuk .40 1.00
9 Lorne Bokshowan .40 1.00
10 Danny Lecours .40 1.00
11 Sheldon Currie .40 1.00
12 Doug Robb .40 1.00
13 Rob Polman Tuin .60 1.50
14 Bob Collyard .40 1.00
15 Tim Ringler TR .20 .50

1994-95 Milwaukee Admirals

This 28-card standard-size set was manufactured and distributed by Jessen Associates, Inc. for Classic. The fronts display color action player photos with a dark blue marbleized inner border and a black outer border. The player's name, jersey number, and position appear in the teal border on the right edge. The cards are unnumbered and checklisted below in alphabetical order.

COMPLETE SET (28) 3.00 8.00
1 Doug Agnew TR .02 .10
2 Peter Bakovic ACO .02 .10
3 Matt Block .08 .25
4 Gino Cavallini .15 .40
5 Sylvain Couturier .15 .40
6 Brian Dobbin .15 .40
7 Shawn Evans .08 .25
8 Fabulous Fritz .02 .10
9 Chris Govedaris .20 .50
10 Jim Hrivnak .30 .75
11 Tony Hrkac .20 .50
12 Fabian Joseph .20 .50
13 Mark Laforest .20 .50
14 Don MacAdam ACO .02 .10
15 Dave Mackey .08 .25
16 Pat MacLeod .15 .40
17 Dave Marcinyshyn .08 .25
18 Bob Mason .30 .75
19 Mike McNeill .20 .50
20 Kent Paynter .08 .25
21 Ken Sabourin .08 .25
22 Trevor Sim .08 .25
23 Martin Simard .08 .25
24 Mike Tomlak .08 .25
25 Steve Tuttle .08 .25
26 Randy Velischek .15 .40
27 Brad Werenka .15 .40
28 Phil Wittliff CO .02 .10

1995-96 Milwaukee Admirals

This high-quality 25-card set was produced for the team by Collector's Edge and sponsored by Bank One. The card fronts feature color action photography, along with the logos of the club, the bank and the manufacturer. The last card in the set, entitled Dream Ride, features on the back the lyrics to the song of the same name, which apparently is near and dear to the hearts of Admirals fans everywhere. This marks what could be the first ever appropriation of song lyrics for the edification of card collectors. As they cards are unnumbered, they are listed below alphabetically.

COMPLETE SET (25) 4.00 10.00
1 Shawn Anderson .20 .50
2 Jergus Baca .20 .50
3 Gino Cavallini .30 .75
4 Joe Cirella .20 .50
5 Sylvain Couturier .20 .50
6 Tom Draper .30 .75
7 Robert Guillet .20 .50
8 Tony Hrkac .30 .75
9 Fabian Joseph .20 .50
10 Mark LaForest .30 .75
11 Dave MacIsaac .20 .50
12 Mike McNeill .20 .50
13 Dave Mackey .20 .50
14 Kent Paynter .20 .50
15 Ken Sabourin .20 .50
16 Andrew Shier .20 .50
17 Tom Tilley .20 .50
18 Mike Tomlak .20 .50
19 Steve Tuttle .20 .50
20 Terry Yake .30 .75
21 Phil Wittliff CO .02 .10
22 Peter Bakovic ASST CO .02 .10
23 Rob Irsch ASST CO .02 .10
24 Doug Agnew TR .02 .10
25 Dream Ride .02 .10

1995-96 Milwaukee Admirals Postcards

Postcard series measures 3 1/2" x 5 1/2" and was sponsored by Sports Medicine Institute.

COMPLETE SET (21) 10.00 25.00
1 Dave MacIsaac .40 1.00
2 Kent Paynter .40 1.00
3 Garry Gulash .40 1.00
4 Jergus Baca .40 1.00
5 Fabian Joseph .40 1.00
6 Sylvain Couturier .40 1.00
7 Mike McNeill .40 1.00
8 Terry Yake .40 1.00
9 David Mackey .40 1.00
10 Bruce Ramsay .40 1.00
11 Tony Hrkac .75 2.00
12 Robert Guillet .40 1.00
13 Shawn Anderson .40 1.00
14 Andrew Shier .40 1.00
15 Steve Tuttle .40 1.00
16 Mike Tomlak .40 1.00
17 Tom Draper .75 2.00
18 Mark Laforest .75 2.00
19 Mikhail Kravets .40 1.00
20 Gino Cavallini .75 2.00
21 Ken Sabourin .40 1.00

1996-97 Milwaukee Admirals

This odd-sized (2 1/2" X 4") 27-card set features the Milwaukee Admirals of the IHL. The cards were produced by the club and sponsored by Bank One as a promotional item. The cards feature action photography on the front surrounded by a thin white border. The logos of Bank One and the PHPA are in the top corners, while the player's name, position and uniform number are listed along the bottom. The cards are unnumbered, and are listed in alphabetical order.

COMPLETE SET (27) 4.00 10.00
1 Doug Agnew TR .02 .10
2 Peter Bakovic ACO .02 .10
3 Sylvain Couturier .15 .40
4 Larry DePalma .15 .40
5 Peter Douris .15 .40
6 Denny Felsner .15 .40
7 Eric Fenton .15 .40
8 Shannon Finn .15 .40
9 Tony Hrkac .30 .75
10 Fabian Joseph ASST CO .15 .40
11 Jacques Joubert .15 .40
12 Rick Knickle .30 .75
13 Brad Layzell .15 .40
14 Danny Lorenz .30 .75
15 Chris Luongo .15 .40
16 Dave Mackey .15 .40
17 Mike McNeill .15 .40
18 Michel Mongeau .30 .75
19 Kent Paynter .15 .40
20 Christian Proulx .15 .40
21 Patrice Robitaille .15 .40
22 Ken Sabourin .15 .40
23 Steve Strunk .15 .40
24 Tom Tilley .15 .40
25 Mike Tomlak .15 .40
26 Steve Tuttle .15 .40
27 Phil Wittliff CO .02 .10

1997-98 Milwaukee Admirals

Little is known about this set beyond the confirmed checklist. Additional information can be forwarded to hockeymag@beckett.com.

COMPLETE SET (25) 4.00 10.00
1 Jason Cipolla .15 .40
2 Kerry Clark .15 .40
3 Jarrett Deuling .15 .40
4 Kelly Fairchild .20 .50
5 Eric Fenton .15 .40
6 Shannon Finn .15 .40
7 Martin Gendron .30 .75
8 Mike Harder .15 .40
9 Marc Hussey .15 .40
10 Danny Lorenz .30 .75
11 Dave MacIntyre .15 .40
12 Mike McNeill .15 .40
13 Don McSween .15 .40
14 Jeff Nelson .15 .40
15 Brent Peterson .15 .40
16 Christian Proulx .15 .40
17 Ken Sabourin .15 .40
18 Mike Tomlak .15 .40
19 Mike Torchia .20 .50
20 Steve Tuttle .15 .40
21 Mark Visheau .15 .40
22 Al Sims HCO .02 .10
23 Peter Bakovic ACO .02 .10
24 Fabian Joseph ACO .02 .10
25 Doug Agnew TR .02 .10

1998-99 Milwaukee Admirals

Little is known about this set beyond the confirmed checklist. Additional information can be forwarded to hockeymag@beckett.com.

COMPLETE SET (24) 4.00 10.00
1 Al Sims CO .02 .10
2 Jeff Daniels .15 .40
3 Sergei Klimentiev .15 .40
4 Chris Mason .20 .50
5 Eric Fenton .15 .40
6 Shannon Finn .15 .40
7 Jason Cipolla .15 .40
8 Jeff Kealty .15 .40
9 Bobby Russell .15 .40
10 David Gosselin .30 .75
11 Richard Lintner .30 .75
12 Jeff Nelson .20 .50
13 Kay Whitmore .25 .60
14 Claude Noel ACO .02 .10
15 Karlis Skrastins .20 .50
16 Mark Mowers .20 .50
17 Craig Darby .20 .50
18 Roscoe MASCOT .02 .10
19 Doug Friedman .15 .40
20 Matt Henderson .15 .40
21 Marc Moro .30 .75
22 Petr Sykora .30 .75
23 Jeff Staples .15 .40
24 Marian Cisar .40 1.00

1998-99 Milwaukee Admirals Postcards

This set features the Admirals of the IHL. These postcard-sized issues were given out at autograph sessions and other promotional ventures.

COMPLETE SET (11) 4.00 10.00
1 Doug Friedman .20 .50
2 Brad Smyth .20 .50
3 Jeff Staples .20 .50
4 Matt Henderson .20 .50
5 Petr Sykora .40 1.00
6 Jeff Kealty .20 .50
7 Jason Cipolla .20 .50
8 Richard Lintner .30 .75
9 Kimmo Timonen .30 .75
10 Vitali Yachmenev .30 .75
11 Tomas Vokoun 1.25 3.00

1999-00 Milwaukee Admirals Keebler

This set was issued in sheet form as a promotional giveaway.

COMPLETE SET (20) 6.00 15.00
1 Corey Hirsch .40 1.00
2 Marian Cisar .40 1.00
3 Chris Mason .40 1.00
4 Jayme Filipowicz .40 1.00
5 Bubba Berenzweig .40 1.00
6 Mark Mowers .40 1.00
7 Brent Peterson .40 1.00
8 Phil Crowe .40 1.00
9 Dan Keczmer .40 1.00
10 Jason Dawe .40 1.00
11 Eric Fenton .40 1.00
12 Matt Eldred .40 1.00
13 Alexandre Boikov .40 1.00
14 Marc Moro .40 1.00
15 Paul Healey .40 1.00
16 Daniel Riva .40 1.00
17 Ryan Tobler .40 1.00
18 David Gosselin .40 1.00
19 Al Sims CO .40 1.00
20 Claude Noel ACO .40 1.00

2000-01 Milwaukee Admirals Keebler

This 20-card set features players from the 2000-01 Milwaukee Admirals of the IHL. The cards were issued in perforated sheets of five which consisted of 4 player cards and one coupon for Keebler products. The card fronts carry an action photo with a Keebler logo in the top left corner, the backs carry biographical information, career stats and accomplishments. The cards are not numbered and are listed below in alphabetical order.

COMMON CARD (20) 8.00 20.00
1 Jonas Andersson .60 1.50
2 Denis Arkhipov .60 2.00
3 Bubba Borenzweig .30 .75
4 Greg Classen .30 1.00
5 Mark Eaton .30 .75
6 Jayme Filipowicz .30 .75
7 Sean Haggerty .30 .75
8 Jan Lasak .40 2.00
9 Chris Mason .40 1.00
10 Marc Moro .40 1.00
11 Mark Mowers .30 1.00
12 John Namestnikov .30 .75
13 Ville Peltonen .40 1.00
14 Daniel Riva .30 .75
15 Petr Sachl .30 .75
16 Pavel Skrbek .30 1.00
17 Jeremy Stevenson .30 1.00
18 Ryan Tobler .30 .75
19 Alexei Vasiliev .30 .75
20 Mike Watt .30 .75

2000-01 Milwaukee Admirals Postcards

This set features the Admirals of the IHL. These postcard-like issues were handed out a various games in conjunction with player autograph sessions. They are not numbered and are listed below in alphabetical order.

COMPLETE SET (18) 6.00 15.00
1 Jonas Andersson .60 1.50
2 Andrew Berenzweig .30 .75
3 Alexandre Boikov .30 .75
4 Jayme Filipowicz .30 .75
5 David Gosselin .60 1.50
6 Jason Goulet .30 .75
7 Sean Haggerty .30 .75
8 Jan Lasak .80 2.00
9 Chris Mason .40 1.00
10 Mark Mowers .40 1.00
11 Ville Peltonen .40 1.00
12 Dan Riva .30 .75
13 Petr Sachl .30 .75
14 Pavel Skrbek .40 1.00
15 Ryan Tobler .30 .75
16 Alexei Vasiliev .30 .75
17 Mike Watt .30 .75
18 Alex Westlund .30 .75

2001-02 Milwaukee Admirals

This set features the Admirals of the AHL. The set was issued as a promotional giveaway in the form of five six-card strips. Each strip contains five player cards and one coupon for a product of Keebler, the sponsor of the set. The cards are unnumbered, so they are listed in alphabetical order.

COMPLETE SET (25) 8.00 20.00
1 Erik Anderson .30 .75
2 Jonas Andersson .30 .75
3 Martin Bartek .30 .75
4 Bubba Berenzweig .30 .75
5 Alexandre Boikov .30 .75
6 Frederic Bouchard .30 .75
7 Marian Cisar .40 1.00
8 Kevin Dean .30 .75
9 Steve Dubinsky .30 .75
10 David Gosselin .40 1.00
11 Jason Goulet .30 .75
12 Chris Mason .40 1.00
13 Brett Hauer .30 .75
14 Timo Helbling .30 .75
15 Jan Lasak .75 2.00
16 Jay Legault .30 .75
17 Bryan Lundbohm .30 .75
18 Marc Moro .60 1.50
19 Mark Mowers .40 1.00
20 Konstantin Panov .30 .75
21 Nathan Perrott .60 1.50
22 Petr Sachl .30 .75
23 Yves Sarault .30 .75
24 Robert Schnabel .30 .75
25 Jeremy Stevenson .30 .75

2001-02 Milwaukee Admirals Postcards

This set features the Admirals of the AHL. These cards were given out individually at player autograph sessions, making set building difficult. This checklist is not believed to be complete. If you have information on other singles, please forward it to hockeymag@beckett.com..

COMPLETE SET (11) 2.00 5.00
1 Robert Schnabel .20 .50
2 Bryan Lundbohm .20 .50
3 Yves Sarault .20 .50
4 Timo Helbling .20 .50
5 Martin Bartek .20 .50
6 Kevin Dean .20 .50
7 David Gosselin .30 .75
8 Marc Moro .40 1.00
9 Jason Goulet .20 .50
10 Jonas Andersson .20 .50
11 Roscoe MASCOT .10 .25

2002-03 Milwaukee Admirals

These cards were issued as promotional giveaways in five-card strips over the course of five home games. They were sponsored by Keebler.

COMPLETE SET (25) 15.00 40.00
1 Tomas Kloucek 1.25 3.00
2 Chris Madden 1.25 3.00
3 Wyatt Smith .40 1.00
4 Brian Finley 1.25 3.00
5 Dan Hamhuis 1.25 3.00
6 Andrew Hutchinson .75 2.00

7 Robert Schnabel .40 1.00
8 Bob Wren .40 1.00
9 Reid Simpson .40 1.00
10 Jan Lasak 1.25 3.00
11 Cameron Mann .75 2.00
12 Domenic Pittis .75 2.00
13 Martin Erat .75 2.00
14 Jonas Andersson .40 1.00
15 Greg Koehler .40 1.00
16 Bubba Berenzweig .40 1.00
17 Konstantin Panov .40 1.00
18 Peter Smrek .40 1.00
19 Vernon Fiddler .40 1.00
20 Jason Beckett .40 1.00
21 Greg Classen .40 1.00
22 Timo Helbling .40 1.00
23 Darren Haydar .75 2.00
24 Pascal Trepanier .40 1.00
25 Bryan Lundbohm .40 1.00

2002-03 Milwaukee Admirals Postcards

These postcards were issued as singles at player signing sessions. It's likely the checklist is incomplete. Please forward any additional information to hockeymag@beckett.com

COMPLETE SET (15) 6.00 15.00
1 Jonas Andersson .30 .75
2 Jason Beckett .30 .75
3 Bubba Berenzweig .30 .75
4 Greg Classen .30 .75
5 Martin Erat .60 1.50
6 Vern Fiddler .30 .75
7 Dan Hamhuis .75 2.00
8 Darren Haydar .40 1.00
9 Tomas Kloucek .75 2.00
10 Jan Lasak .75 2.00
11 Chris Madden .75 2.00
12 Cameron Mann .40 1.00
13 Konstantin Panov .20 .50
14 Robert Schnabel .20 .50
15 Pascal Trepanier .20 .50

2003-04 Milwaukee Admirals

COMPLETE SET (30) 6.00 15.00
1 Kirill Safronov .20 .50
2 Jay Henderson .20 .50
3 Brian Finley .30 .75
4 Timo Helbling .20 .50
5 Cheerleaders .04 .10
6 Darren Haydar .30 .75
7 Curtis Murphy .20 .50
8 Tony Hrkac .20 .50
9 Andrew Hutchinson .30 .75
10 Mascot .04 .10
11 Brad Tiley .20 .50
12 Timofei Shishkanov .20 .50
13 Vernon Fiddler .20 .50
14 Scott Upshall .75 2.00
15 Claude Noel CO .04 .10
16 Raitis Ivanans .20 .50
17 Mathieu Darche .20 .50
18 Wade Flaherty .30 .75
19 Brandon Segal .20 .50
20 Arena .04 .10
21 Greg Zanon .20 .50
22 Simon Gamache .40 1.00
23 Greg Classen .20 .50
24 Wyatt Smith .20 .50
25 Team Photo .10 .25
26 Ray Schultz .20 .50
27 Mike Farrell .20 .50
28 Bryan Lundbohm .20 .50
29 Libor Pivko .20 .50
30 Todd Richards ACO .04 .10

2003-04 Milwaukee Admirals Postcards

These oversized cards were issued at team events in singles form.

COMPLETE SET (23) 8.00 20.00
1 Greg Classen .30 .75
2 Mathieu Darche .30 .75
3 Mike Farrell .30 .75
4 Vernon Fiddler .30 .75
5 Brian Finley .40 1.00
6 Wade Flaherty .40 1.00
7 Simon Gamache .60 1.50
8 Darren Haydar .40 1.00
9 Timo Helbling .30 .75
10 Jay Henderson .30 .75
11 Tony Hrkac .30 .75
12 Andrew Hutchinson .40 1.00
13 Raitis Ivanans .30 .75
14 Bryan Lundbohm .30 .75
15 Curtis Murphy .30 .75
16 Libor Pivko .30 .75
17 Kirill Safronov .30 .75
18 Ray Schultz .30 .75
19 Timofei Shishkanov .30 .75
20 Wyatt Smith .30 .75
21 Brad Tiley .30 .75
22 Scott Upshall 1.00 2.50
23 Greg Zanon .30 .75

2004-05 Milwaukee Admirals

These cards were issued as promotional giveaways on various nights throughout the season in five-card strips.

COMPLETE SET (30) 20.00 50.00
1 Brian Finley 1.25 3.00
2 Jeremy Yablonski .40 1.00
3 Brad Tiley .40 1.00
4 Cam Severson .75 2.00
5 Roscoe MASCOT .04 .10
6 Seamus Kotyk .75 2.00
7 Paul Brown .40 1.00
8 Burke Henry .40 1.00
9 Libor Pivko .40 1.00
10 Brendan Yarema .40 1.00
11 Jerred Smithson .40 1.00
12 Bryan Lundbohm .75 2.00
13 Ryan Suter 1.25 3.00
14 Brandon Segal .40 1.00
15 Calder Cup Winners .40 1.00
16 Jordin Tootoo 4.00 10.00
17 Scottie Upshall 1.25 3.00
18 Dan Hamhuis .75 2.00
19 Andrew Hutchinson .75 2.00
20 Admirals Ice Angels .40 1.00
21 Greg Zanon .40 1.00
22 Simon Gamache .75 2.00
23 Kevin Klein .40 1.00
24 Wyatt Smith .40 1.00
25 Todd Richards .40 1.00
26 Darren Haydar .40 1.00
27 Timofei Shishkanov .40 1.00
28 Vernon Fiddler .40 1.00
29 Tony Hrkac .40 1.00
30 Claude Noel .40 1.00

2005-06 Milwaukee Admirals Choice

COMPLETE SET (19) 4.00 10.00
1 Kris Beech .20 .50
2 Sheldon Brookbank .20 .50
3 Paul Brown .20 .50
4 Greg Classen .20 .50
5 Vern Fiddler .20 .50
6 Brian Finley .30 .75
7 Darren Haydar .20 .50
8 Kevin Klein .20 .50
9 Libor Pivko .20 .50
10 T.J. Reynolds .20 .50
11 Pekka Rinne .60 1.50
12 Marco Rosa .20 .50
13 Brandon Segal .20 .50
14 Timofei Shishkanov .20 .50
15 Jordin Tootoo .75 2.00
16 Shea Weber .20 .50
17 Jeremy Yablonski .20 .50
18 Greg Zanon .20 .50
19 Claude Noel HC .02 .10

2005-06 Milwaukee Admirals Pepsi

COMPLETE SET (26) 10.00 25.00
1 Kris Beech .40 1.00
2 Rick Berry .40 1.00
3 Sheldon Brookbank .40 1.00
4 Paul Brown .40 1.00
5 Greg Classen .40 1.00
6 Chris Durno .40 1.00
7 Brian Finley .60 1.50
8 Simon Gamache .40 1.00
9 Darren Haydar .40 1.00
10 Kevin Klein .40 1.00
11 Nathan Lutz .40 1.00
12 Scott May .40 1.00
13 Rich Peverley .40 1.00
14 Libor Pivko .40 1.00
15 T.J. Reynolds .40 1.00
16 Pekka Rinne 1.25 3.00
17 Brandon Segal .40 1.00
18 Zach Stortini .40 1.00
19 Jordin Tootoo 1.25 3.00
20 Scottie Upshall .75 2.00
21 Shea Weber .40 1.00
22 Jeremy Yablonski .40 1.00
23 Greg Zanon .40 1.00
24 Claude Noel HC .02 .10
25 Todd Richards AC .02 .10
26 Roscoe MASCOT .02 .10

2006-07 Milwaukee Admirals

COMPLETE SET (24) 8.00 20.00
1 Ramzi Abid .30 .75
2 Sheldon Brookbank .40 1.00
3 Chris Durno .30 .75
4 Karl Goehring• .40 1.00
5 Jason Guerriero .30 .75
6 Alex Henry .30 .75
7 Bracken Kearns .30 .75
8 Kevin Klein .30 .75
9 Ville Koistinen .30 .75
10 John Laliberte .30 .75
11 Patrick Leahy .30 .75
12 Cal O'Reilly .30 .75
13 Rich Peverley .30 .75
14 T.J. Reynolds .30 .75
15 Pekka Rinne• .40 1.00
16 Brandon Segal .30 .75
17 Kim Staal .30 .75
18 Victor Uchevatov .30 .75
19 John Vigilante .30 .75
20 Kelsey Wilson .60 1.50
21 Nolan Yonkman .30 .75
22 Claude Noel CO .10 .25
23 Lane Lambert ACO .10 .25
24 Roscoe MASCOT .02 .10

2007-08 Milwaukee Admirals

COMPLETE SET (24) 4.00 10.00
1 Dov Grumet-Morris .50 1.25
2 Bryan Schmidt .15 .40
3 Cody Franson• .50 1.25
4 Ryan Maki .15 .40
5 Mike Santorelli .15 .40
6 John Vigilanti .15 .40
7 Andreas Thuresson .15 .40
8 Jason Guerriero .15 .40
9 John Laliberti .15 .40
10 Cal O'reilly .15 .40
11 Kelsey Wilson .15 .40
12 Mark Matheson .15 .40
13 Matt Ellison .15 .40
14 Josh Langfeld .15 .40
15 Kevin Ulanski .15 .40
16 Janne Niskala .15 .40
17 Alex Henry .15 .40
18 Pekka Rinne .15 .40
19 Rich Peverley .15 .40
20 Antti Pihlstrom .15 .40
21 Nolan Yonkman .15 .40
22 Alexander Sulzer .15 .40
23 Lane Lambert• .15 .40
24 Brad Lauer .15 .40

2014-15 Milwaukee Admirals

COMPLETE SET (25) 6.00 15.00
1 Pontus Aberg .30 .75
2 Johan Alm .30 .75
3 Taylor Aronson .30 .75
4 Viktor Arvidsson .30 .75
5 Anthony Bitetto .30 .75
6 Zach Budish .30 .75
7 Patrick Cehlin .30 .75
8 Richard Clune .30 .75
9 Jonathan-Ismael Diaby .30 .75
10 Frederick Gaudreau .30 .75
11 Felix Girard .30 .75
12 Triston Grant .30 .75
13 Magnus Hellberg .30 .75
14 Brendan Leipsic .30 .75
15 Michael Liambas .30 .75
16 Marek Mazanec .40 1.00
17 Garrett Noonan .30 .75
18 Jimmy Oligny .30 .75
19 Joseph Pendenza .30 .75
20 Joe Piskula .30 .75
21 Miikka Salomaki .30 .75
22 Josh Shalla .30 .75
23 Colton Sissons .30 .75
24 Mark Van Guilder .30 .75
25 Austin Watson .30 .75

1984-85 Minnesota-Duluth Bulldogs

This set features the Bulldogs of the NCAA and was confirmed to exist in 2002 by Ralph Slate of hockeydb.com reknown. The set was produced by Tim and Larry's Sportscards and features the first card of Brett Hull. It is believed that as few as 250 sets were produced.

COMPLETE SET (33) 35.00 75.00
1 Ben Duffey .40 1.00
2 Brett Hull 25.00 50.00
3 Danny May .40 1.00
4 Dave Morrow .40 1.00
5 Joe Delisle .40 1.00
6 Brian Nelson .40 1.00
7 Jon Downing .40 1.00
8 Brian Nelson .40 1.00
9 Sean Toomey .40 1.00
10 Brian Durand .40 1.00
11 Jim Plankers .40 1.00
12 Mark Odnokon .40 1.00
13 Jim Sprenger .40 1.00
14 Tom Lorentz .40 1.00
15 Darin Illikainen .40 1.00
16 Rick Kosti .40 1.00
17 Norm Maciver .75 2.00
18 Guy Gosselin .40 1.00
19 Matt Christensen .40 1.00
20 Jim Johnson .75 2.00
21 Mark Baron .40 1.00
22 Bill Watson .40 1.00
23 Bruce Fishback .40 1.00
24 Dave Cowan .40 1.00
25 Mike Cortes .40 1.00
26 Jim Toninato .40 1.00
27 Skeeter Moore .40 1.00
28 Mike DeAngelis .40 1.00
29 Tom Herzig .40 1.00
30 Mike Sertich CO .08 .25
31 Bulldog Cheerleaders .40 1.00
32 Bulldogs Assistants .08 .25
33 Team Photo .08 .25

1985-86 Minnesota-Duluth Bulldogs

This 36-card standard-size set features color action player photos with rounded corners and black borders against a white card face. An oval inset at the lower right shows a head shot. The player's name is printed in black at the bottom. The cards are numbered on the back. It has been reported that this set may have been reprinted to take advantage of the popularity of Brett Hull.

COMPLETE SET (36) 12.00 30.00
1 Skeeter Moore .30 .75
2 Terry Shold .20 .50
3 Mike DeAngelis .20 .50
4 Rob Pallin .20 .50
5 Norm Maciver .30 .75
6 Wayne Smith .20 .50
7 Dave Cowan .20 .50
8 Darin Illikainen .20 .50
9 Rick Hayko .20 .50
10 Guy Gosselin .30 .75
11 Paul Roff .20 .50
12 Jim Toninato .20 .50
13 Tom Hanson .20 .50
14 Mike Cortes .20 .50
15 Matt Christensen .20 .50
16 Bruce Fishback .20 .50
17 Mark Odnokon .20 .50
18 Brian Johnson .20 .50
19 Bob Alexander .20 .50
20 Tom Lorentz .20 .50
21 Roman Sindelar .20 .50
22 Jim Sprenger .20 .50
23 Dan Tousignant .20 .50
24 Sean Toomey .20 .50
25 Brian Durand .20 .50
26 John Hyduke .20 .50
27 Brian Nelson .20 .50
28 Brett Hull 8.00 20.00
29 Joe DeLisle .20 .50
30 Pat Janostin .20 .50
31 Ben Duffy .20 .50
32 Sean Krakiwsky .20 .50
33 Mike Sertich .20 .50
34 Coaching Staff .08 .25
Jim Knapp ACO
Glenn Kulyk ACO
Tim McDonald ACO
Mike Valesano ACO
Rick Menz EQUIP
Dale Hoganson EQUIP
Betty Fleissner TR
35 Cheerleaders .40 1.00
36 Jay Jackson (Mascot) .08 .25

1993-94 Minnesota-Duluth Bulldogs

These 30 standard-size cards feature on their fronts white-bordered color player action shots. The player's name and position, along with the Minnesota Bulldog logo, appear within the brown stripe across the bottom of the photo. The back carries the player's name, position, biography, and statistics on the left. His career highlights appear on the right. The set was produced by Collect-A-Sport and features a card of Chris Marinucci, 1993-94 Hobey Baker winner. The cards are unnumbered and checklisted below in alphabetical order.

COMPLETE SET (30) 4.00 10.00
1 Rod Aldoff .15 .40
2 Niklas Axelson .15 .40
3 David Buck .15 .40
4 Jerome Butler .15 .40
5 Brian Caruso .20 .50
6 Matt Christian .20 .50
Chet Culic
7 Marc Christian .15 .40
8 Joe Ciccarello .15 .40
9 Kyle Erickson .15 .40
Adam Roy
10 Brad Federenko .20 .50
11 Rusty Fitzgerald .20 .50
12 Jason Garatti .15 .40
13 Greg Hanson .20 .50
14 Don Jablonic .15 .40
15 Kraig Karakas .15 .40
16 Brett Larson .20 .50
17 Taras Lendzyk .15 .40
18 Derek Locker .15 .40
19 Chris Marinucci .20 .50
20 Todd Mickolajak .20 .50
Chris Snell
21 Rod Miller .15 .40
22 Rick Mrozik .20 .50
23 Aaron Novak .15 .40
24 Corey Osmak .15 .40
25 Sergei Petrov .15 .40
26 Jeff Romfo .15 .40
27 Mike Sertich CO .02 .10
28 Chris Sittlow .15 .40
29 Joe Tamminen .15 .40
30 Title Card .08 .25
Roster

1993-94 Minnesota-Duluth Commemorative

These four standard-size cards feature black-and-white fronts with color photos on the backs. The set was produced by Collect-A-Sport to commemorate the 1992-93 WCHA champs.

COMPLETE SET (4) 1.50 4.00
1 Chris Marinucci .40 1.00
2 Derek Plante .75 2.00
3 Brett Hauer .40 1.00
4 Jon Rohloff .40 1.00

2004-05 Minnesota-Duluth Bulldogs

The cards came in three packs of seven cards and two packs of six cards and were handed out over five different home games.

COMPLETE SET (33) 12.00 30.00
1 Nick Anderson .40 1.00
2 Tyler Brosz .40 1.00
3 T. J. Caig .40 1.00
4 Dan Carlson .40 1.00
5 Mike Curry .40 1.00
6 Steve Czech .40 1.00
7 Travis Gawryletz .40 1.00
8 Ryan Garis .40 1.00
9 Tim Hambly .40 1.00
10 Brett Hammond .40 1.00
11 Josh Johnson .60 1.50
12 Blair Lefebvre .40 1.00
13 Jeff McFarland .40 1.00
14 Bryan McGregor .40 1.00
15 Matt McKnight .60 1.50
16 Josh Miskovich .40 1.00
17 Marco Peluso .40 1.00
18 Neil Petruic .40 1.00
19 Isaac Reichmuth .60 1.50
20 Jay Rosehill .40 1.00
21 Evan Schwabe .60 1.50
22 Todd Smith .40 1.00
23 Tim Stapleton .40 1.00
24 Luke Stauffacher .40 1.00
25 Ryan Swanson .40 1.00
26 Justin Williams .40 1.00
27 Lee Davidson ACO .04 .10
Scott Sandelin CO
Steve Rohlik
28 Tom Kurvers .40 1.00
29 Junior Lessard .75 2.00
30 Chris Marinucci .75 2.00
31 Bill Watson .40 1.00
32 Mascots .04 .10
33 Sponsor .04 .10

1991-92 Minnesota Golden Gophers

Sponsored by MCI, this 26-card standard-size set features the 1991-92 Minnesota Golden Gophers. On a maroon background, the horizontal and vertical fronts have color action player photos along with the player's name and the name of the high school he attended. The white backs carry the player's name, number, biography, and profile. The cards are unnumbered and checklisted below in alphabetical order.

COMPLETE SET (26) 6.00 15.00
1 Scott Bell .20 .50
2 Tony Bianchi .20 .50
3 John Brill .20 .50
4 Jeff Callinan .20 .50
5 Joe Dziedzic .30 .75
6 Sean Fabian .20 .50
7 Jed Fiebelkorn .20 .50
8 Nick Gerebi .20 .50
9 Darby Hendrickson .30 .75
10 Craig Johnson .30 .75
11 Trent Klatt .40 1.00
12 Cory Laylin .20 .50
13 Steve Magnusson .30 .75
14 Chris McAlpine .30 .75
15 Justin McHugh .20 .50
16 Eric Means .20 .50
17 Mike Muller .20 .50
18 Tom Newman .20 .50
19 Jeff Nielsen .20 .50
20 John O'Connell .20 .50
21 Larry Olimb .20 .50
22 Travis Richards .20 .50
23 Brandon Steege .20 .50
24 Jeff Stolp .20 .50
25 Todd Westlund .20 .50
26 Doug Zmolek .30 .75

1992-93 Minnesota Golden Gophers

Featuring the 1992-93 Minnesota Golden Gophers hockey team (WCHA), this 25-card measures the standard-size. The fronts feature full-bleed, posed, color player photos. A gray bar at the top (or right edge) displays the school name, while the player's name is printed in maroon lettering in a yellow bar at the bottom. The cards are unnumbered and checklisted below in alphabetical order.

COMPLETE SET (25) 4.00 10.00
1 Scott Bell .15 .40
2 Jesse Bertogliat .40 1.00
Brian Bonin
3 Tony Bianchi .15 .40
4 John Brill .15 .40
5 Jeff Callinan .15 .40
6 Bobby Dustin .15 .40
Dave Larson
7 Joe Dziedzic .20 .50
8 Jed Fiebelkorn .15 .40
9 Darby Hendrickson .20 .50
10 Craig Johnson .15 .40
11 Steve Magnusson .20 .50
12 Chris McAlpine .20 .50
13 Justin McHugh .15 .40
14 Eric Means .15 .40
15 Jeff Moen .15 .40
16 Tom Newman .15 .40
17 Jeff Nielsen .20 .50
18 Travis Richards .15 .40
19 Brandon Steege .15 .40
20 Matt Stelljes .15 .40
Ryan Alstead
21 Dan Trebil .02 .10
Greg Zwakman
22 Charlie Wasley .15 .40
Mike McAlpine
23 Todd Westlund .15 .40
24 Dan Woog .08 .25
Jim Hillman
25 Doug Woog CO .08 .25

1993-94 Minnesota Golden Gophers

This set features the Golden Gophers of the NCAA. The cards were printed by the team and issued as a promotional giveaway. On a maroon background, the fronts feature posed, color action player photos and portraits with a thin yellow border. The player's name is printed in yellow letters with a maroon outline on the bottom of the photo. The cards are unnumbered and checklisted below in alphabetical order.

COMPLETE SET (30) 6.00 100.00
1 Brett Abrahamson 1.50 4.00
2 Jesse Bertogliat 1.50 4.00
3 Tony Bianchi 1.50 4.00
4 Brian Bonin 2.00 5.00
5 Andy Brink 1.50 4.00
6 Jeff Callinan 1.50 4.00
7 Nick Checco 1.50 4.00
8 Bobby Dustin 1.50 4.00
9 Joe Dziedzic 2.00 5.00
10 Jed Fiebelkorn 1.50 4.00
11 Brent Godbout 1.50 4.00
12 Dan Hendrickson 1.50 4.00
13 Jim Hillman 1.50 4.00
14 John Hillman 1.50 4.00
15 Brian LaFleur 1.50 4.00
16 Dave Larson 1.50 4.00
17 Steve Magnusson 1.50 4.00
18 Chris McAlpine 2.00 5.00
19 Mike McAlpine 1.50 4.00
20 Justin McHugh 1.50 4.00
21 Eric Means 1.50 4.00
22 Jeff Moen 1.50 4.00
23 Jeff Nielsen 2.00 5.00
24 Brandon Steege 1.50 4.00
25 Dan Trebil 1.50 4.00
26 Charlie Wasley 1.50 4.00
27 Dan Woog ACO .40 1.00
28 Doug Woog CO .75 2.00
29 Greg Zwakman 1.50 4.00
30 Title Card .02 .10

1994-95 Minnesota Golden Gophers

This set features the Golden Gophers of the NCAA. The cards were sponsored by SuperAmerica and EverReady and issued as a promotional giveaway. On a white card face with team color-coded stripes in the background, the fronts display action shots or water color portraits by artist M.L. Sahlberg. The cards are unnumbered and checklisted below in alphabetical order.

COMPLETE SET (31) 10.00 25.00
1 Will Anderson .30 .75
2 Scott Bell .30 .75
3 Jesse Bertogliat .30 .75
4 Brian Bonin .40 1.00
5 Andy Brink .30 .75
6 Aaron Broten .75 2.00
Neal Brote
7 Jeff Callinan .30 .75
8 Nick Checco .30 .75
9 Mike Crowley .75 2.00
10 Steve DeBus .30 .75
11 Bobby Dustin .30 .75
12 Jed Fiebelkorn .30 .75
13 Brent Godbout .30 .75
14 Jason Godbout .30 .75
15 Casey Hankinson .30 .75
16 Dan Hendrickson .30 .75
17 Ryan Kraft .30 .75
18 Brian LaFleur .30 .75
19 Dave Larson .30 .75
20 Justin McHugh .30 .75
21 Jeff Moen .30 .75
22 Jay Moser .30 .75
23 Lou Nanne .40 1.00
24 Joe Pankratz .30 .75
25 Jason Seils .30 .75
26 Brandon Steege .30 .75
27 Dan Trebil .40 1.00
28 Charlie Wasley .30 .75
29 Dan Woog .08 .25
30 Doug Woog CO .08 .25
31 Greg Zwakman .30 .75

1995-96 Minnesota Golden Gophers

This set was issued by the team as a promotional giveaway. The cards are unnumbered so the set is checklisted in alphabetical order.

COMPLETE SET (30) 100.00 175.00
1 Checklist .40 1.00
2 Doug Woog CO .75 2.00
3 Brett Abrahamson 3.00 6.00
4 Mike Anderson 3.00 6.00
5 Reggie Berg 3.00 6.00
6 Jesse Bertogliat 3.00 6.00
7 Brian Bonin 5.00 10.00
8 Andy Brink 3.00 6.00
9 Nick Checco 3.00 6.00
10 Nick Crowley 3.00 6.00
11 Steve Debus 3.00 6.00
12 Bobby Dustin 3.00 6.00
13 Jason Godbout 3.00 6.00
14 Casey Hankinson 3.00 6.00
15 Dan Hendrickson 3.00 6.00
16 Clint Johnson 3.00 6.00
17 Bill Kohn 3.00 6.00
18 Ryan Kraft 3.00 6.00
19 Brian LaFleur 3.00 6.00
20 Dave Larson 3.00 6.00
21 Jeff Moen 3.00 6.00
22 Jay Moser 3.00 6.00
23 Tom Nevers 3.00 6.00
24 Erik Rasmussen 5.00 10.00
25 Jason Seils 3.00 6.00
26 Wyatt Smith 3.00 6.00
27 Dan Trebil 3.00 6.00
28 Charlie Wasley 3.00 6.00
29 Dan Woog ACO .75 2.00
30 Greg Zwakman 3.00 6.00

1996-97 Minnesota Golden Gophers

Little is known about this set beyond the confirmed checklist and the fact that it was issued as a promotional giveaway. Any additional information can be forwarded to hockeymag@beckett.com.

COMPLETE SET (27) 25.00 50.00
1 Checklist .02 .10
2 Doug Woog CO .02 .10
3 Brett Abrahamson .60 1.50
4 Mike Anderson .60 1.50
5 Reggie Berg 1.25 3.00
6 Nick Checco 1.25 3.00
7 Ben Clymer 1.25 3.00
8 Mike Crowley 1.25 3.00
9 Eric Day .60 1.50
10 Steve DeBus .60 1.50
11 Brent Godbout .60 1.50
12 Jason Godbout .60 1.50
13 Casey Hankinson 1.25 3.00
14 Dan Hendrickson 1.25 3.00
15 Bill Kohn .60 1.50
16 Ryan Kraft 1.25 3.00
17 Brian LaFleur .60 1.50
18 Mike Lyons .60 1.50
19 Willy Marvin .60 1.50
20 Cory Miller .60 1.50
21 Nate Miller .60 1.50
22 Rico Pagel .60 1.50
23 Erik Rasmussen 1.25 3.00
24 Wyatt Smith 1.25 3.00
25 Dave Spehar .60 1.50
26 Ryan Trebil .60 1.50
27 Dan Woog .02 .10

1997-98 Minnesota Golden Gophers

This set was handed out as a promotional giveaway at one home game, making it quite scarce on the secondary market.

COMPLETE SET (26) 15.00 30.00
1 Checklist .08 .25
2 Doug Woog HCO .20 .50
3 Mike Anderson .40 1.00
4 Stev Debus .40 1.00
5 Ryan Kraft .60 1.50
6 Nate Miller .40 1.00
7 Brett Abrahamson .40 1.00
8 Erik Day .40 1.00
9 Bill Kohn .40 1.00
10 Cory Miller .40 1.00
11 Ben Clymer .75 2.00
12 Casey Hankinson .40 1.00
13 Willy Marvin .40 1.00
14 Reggie Berg .40 1.00
15 Jason Godbout .40 1.00
16 Mike Lyons .40 1.00
17 Ryan Trebil .40 1.00
18 Dylan Mills .40 1.00
19 Dave Spehar .40 1.00
20 Erik Westrum .75 2.00
21 Wyatt Smith .60 1.50
22 Aaron Miskovich .40 1.00
23 Rico Pagel .40 1.00
24 Matt Leimbeck .40 1.00
25 Stuart Senden .40 1.00
26 Goldy Gopher Mascot .20 .50

1998-99 Minnesota Golden Gophers

This set features the Golden Gophers of the NCAA. Like most NCAA issues, this set was handed out as a promotional giveaway at a single home game.

COMPLETE SET (30) 20.00 35.00
1 Header Card .02 .10
2 Doug Woog HCO .20 .50
3 Mark Nenovich .40 1.00
4 Erik Wendell .75 2.00
5 Dylan Mills .40 1.00
6 Nate Miller .40 1.00
7 Rob LaRue .40 1.00
8 Reggie Berg .40 1.00
9 Bill Kohn .40 1.00
10 Mike Lyons .40 1.00
11 Cory Miller .40 1.00
12 Mike Anderson .40 1.00
13 Jordon Leopold 1.50 4.00
14 Ryan Westrum .40 1.00
15 Doug Meyer .40 1.00
16 Rico Pagel .40 1.00
17 Stuart Senden .40 1.00
18 Nick Angell .40 1.00
19 Dave Spehar .40 1.00
20 Pat O'Leary .40 1.00
21 Ryan Trebil .40 1.00
22 Adam Hauser .75 2.00
23 Wyatt Smith .75 2.00
24 Brad Timmons .40 1.00
25 Matt Leimbeck .40 1.00
26 Aaron Miskovich .40 1.00
27 Erik Daly .40 1.00
28 Erik Westrum .75 2.00
29 John Pohl .75 2.00
30 Goldy Gopher Mascot .08 .25

1998-99 Minnesota Golden Gophers Women

Issued as a giveaway at a late-season home game.

COMPLETE SET (25) 10.00 25.00
1 Angela Borek .40 1.00
2 Winny Brodt .40 1.00
3 Emily Buchholz .40 1.00
4 Tracy Donaghue .40 1.00
5 Tracy Engstrom .40 1.00
6 Lacey Franzmeier .40 1.00
7 Laura Halldorson CO .08 .25
8 Amber Hegland .40 1.00
9 David Horn ACO .08 .25
10 Courtney Kennedy .40 1.00
11 Shannon Kennedy .40 1.00
12 Erica Killewald .40 1.00
13 Betsey Kukowski .40 1.00
14 Megan Milbert .40 1.00
15 Nadine Muzerall .40 1.00
16 Crystal Nicholas .40 1.00
17 Kelly Olson .40 1.00
18 Sarma Pone .40 1.00
19 Brittny Ralph .40 1.00
20 Jenny Schmidgall 1.25 3.00
21 Kris Scholz .40 1.00
22 Laura Slominski .40 1.00
23 Ambria Thomas .40 1.00
24 Tai Thorsheim .40 1.00
25 Libby Witchger ACO .08 .25

1999-00 Minnesota Golden Gophers

This set features the Golden Gophers of the NCAA. The cards were issued as a promotional giveaway at a late-season game. The cards are unnumbered, and so are listed in alphabetical order.

COMPLETE SET (30) 8.00 20.00
1 Nick Angell .20 .50
2 Nick Anthony .20 .50
3 Matt DeMarchi .20 .50
4 Goldy Gopher MAS .08 .25
6 Ben Hamilton .20 .50
7 Adam Hauser .75 2.00
8 Matt Leimbeck .20 .50
9 Jordan Leopold 1.25 3.00
10 Don Lucia CO .08 .25
11 Mike Lyons .20 .50
12 Doug Meyer .20 .50
13 Nate Miller .20 .50
14 Dylan Mills .20 .50
15 Aaron Miskovich .20 .50
16 Mark Nenovich .20 .50
17 Pat O'Leary .20
18 Rico Pagel .20
19 John Pohl 1.25
20 Chad Roberge .20
21 Pete Samargia .20
22 Stuart Senden .20
23 Dave Spehar .20
24 Jeff Taffe 2.00
25 Ben Tharp .20
26 Ryan Trebil .20
27 University of Minnesota .08
28 Dan Welch .20
29 Erik Wendell .30
29 Erik Young .20
30 Erik Westrum .40

2000-01 Minnesota Golde

This set features the Golden Gophers of the NCA cards were issued as a promotional giveaway lat the season. The cards are unnumbered, so are lis below in alphabetical order.

COMPLETE SET (28) 15.00
1 Header Card .02
2 Nick Angell .30
3 Nick Anthony .30
4 Matt DeMarchi .30
5 Goldy Gopher MASCOT .04
6 Adam Hauser .75
7 Rod Johnson FOOTBALL .30
8 Matt Koalska .30
9 Matt Leimbeck .30
10 Jordan Leopold 1.25
11 Don Lucia CO .10
12 Joey Martin .30
13 Paul Martin .30
14 Dylan Mills .30
15 Aaron Miskovich .30
16 Mark Nenovich .30
17 Pat O'Leary .30
18 John Pohl .75
19 Grant Potulny .40
20 Troy Riddle .30
21 Chad Roberge .30
22 Pete Samargia .30
23 Stuart Senden .30
24 Jeff Taffe 1.25
25 Ben Tharp .30
26 Jon Waibel .30
27 Erik Wendell .30
28 Erik Westrum .75

2001-02 Minnesota Golde

This set features the Golden Gophers of the NCA their championship season. The set was issued a promotional giveaway at a game in January, 200

COMPLETE SET (29) 12.00
1 Header Card .10
2 Don Lucia CO .10
3 Goldy Gopher MASCOT .04
4 Nick Anthony .40
5 Mike Erickson .40
6 Chad Roberg .60
7 Keith Ballard .60
8 Erik Wendell .60
9 Paul Martin .40
10 John Pohl .60
11 Judd Stevens .40
12 Jon Waibel .40
13 Jordan Leopold 1.25
14 Mark Nenovich .40
15 Adam Hauser .40
16 Garrett Smaagaard .40
17 Grant Potulny .40
18 Matt DeMarchi .40
19 Joey Martin .40
20 Troy Riddle .40
21 Jeff Taffe 1.25
22 Matt Koalska .40
23 Pat O'Leary .40
24 Nick Angell .40
25 Barry Tallackson .40
26 Brett MacKinnon .40
27 Jake Fleming .40
28 Travis Weber .40
29 Justin Johnson .40

2002-03 Minnesota Golde Gophers

COMPLETE SET (31) 20.00
1 Nick Anthony .40
2 P.J. Atherton .40
3 Keith Ballard 1.00
4 Matt DeMarchi .40
5 Mike Erickson .40
6 Jake Fleming .40
7 Gino Guyer .60
8 Chris Harrington .40
9 Tyler Hirsch .40
10 Justin Johnson .40
11 Peter Kennedy .40
12 Matt Koalska .40
13 Brett MacKinnon .40
14 Joey Martin .40
15 Paul Martin .75
16 Grant Potulny .60
17 Jerrid Reinholz .40
18 Troy Riddle .40
19 Chad Roberg .40
20 Andrew Sertich .40
21 Garrett Smaagaard .40
22 Dustin Smieja .40
23 Judd Stevens .40
24 Barry Tallackson .75
25 Thomas Vanek 6.00
26 Jon Waibel .40
27 Travis Weber .40
28 Dan Welch .40
29 Don Lucia HCO .10
30 Goldy Gopher Mascot .04
31 NCAA Champs .20

2003-04 Minnesota Golde Gophers

This set was issued as a promotional giveaway course of four home games in the form of four s card strips.

COMPLETE SET (28) 20.00
1 Barry Tallackson .75
2 Jake Taylor .50
3 Thomas Vanek 3.00
4 Mike Vannelli .50
5 Jon Waibel .50
6 Dustin Smieja .50
7 Championship Team Photo .10
8 Don Lucia CO .04
9 P.J. Atherton .50
10 Keith Ballard 1.00
11 Kellen Briggs .75

12 Jake Fleming	.50	1.25
13 Gino Guyer	1.00	2.50
14 Chris Harrington	.50	1.25
15 Tyler Hirsch	.50	1.25
16 Dan Irmen	.75	2.00
17 Justin Johnson	.75	2.00
18 Peter Kennedy	.50	1.25
19 Matt Koalska	.60	1.50
20 Brett MacKinnon	.50	1.25
21 Joey Martin	.50	1.25
22 Grant Potulny	.50	1.25
23 Ryan Potulny	1.25	3.00
24 Jerrid Reinholz	.50	1.25
25 Troy Riddle	.50	1.25
26 Andy Sertich	.60	1.50
27 Garrett Smaagaard	.50	1.25
28 Judd Stevens	.50	1.25

2004-05 Minnesota Golden Gophers

COMPLETE SET (27)	10.00	25.00
1 PJ Atherton	.40	1.00
2 Brent Borgen	.40	1.00
3 Kellen Briggs	.60	1.50
4 Kris Chucko	.75	2.00
5 Jake Fleming	.40	1.00
6 Alex Goligoski	1.25	3.00
7 Ben Gordon	.40	1.00
8 Gino Guyer	.40	1.00
9 Nate Hagemo	.40	1.00
10 Chris Harrington	.40	1.00
11 Tyler Hirsch	.40	1.00
12 Mike Howe	.40	1.00
13 Danny Irmen	.40	1.00
14 Justin Johnson	.60	1.50
15 Evan Kaufman	.40	1.00
16 Peter Kennedy	.40	1.00
17 Don Lucia	.40	1.00
18 Derek Peltier	.40	1.00
19 Tom Pohl	.40	1.00
20 Ryan Potulny	.40	1.00
21 Jerrid Reinholz	.40	1.00
22 Andy Sertich	.75	2.00
23 Garrett Smaagaard	.40	1.00
24 Brent Solei	.40	1.00
25 Judd Stevens	.40	1.00
26 Barry Tallackson	.40	1.00
27 Mike Vannelli	.40	1.00

2004-05 Minnesota Golden Gophers Women

COMPLETE SET (14)	6.00	15.00
1 Natalie Darwitz	1.00	2.50
2 Krissy Wendell	1.00	2.50
3 Anya Miller	.40	1.00
4 Erica McKenzie	.40	1.00
5 Natalie Lamme	.40	1.00
6 Krista Johnson	.40	1.00
7 Jody Horak	.40	1.00
8 Stacy Troumbly	.40	1.00
9 Becky Wacker	.40	1.00
10 Lyndsay Wall	.40	1.00
11 Whitney Graft	.40	1.00
12 Chelsey Brodt	.40	1.00
13 Ashley Albrecht	.40	1.00
14 Laura Halldorson CO	.04	.10

2005-06 Minnesota Golden Gophers

COMPLETE SET (27)	15.00	30.00
1 R.J. Anderson	.30	.75
2 P.J. Atherton	.30	.75
3 Brent Borgen	.30	.75
4 Justin Bostrom	.30	.75
5 Kellen Briggs	.30	.75
6 Kris Chucko	.60	1.50
7 Jeff Frazee	1.25	3.00
8 Alex Goligoski	.75	2.00
9 Ben Gordon	.30	.75
10 Gino Guyer	.40	1.00
11 Nate Hagemo	.40	1.00
12 Chris Harrington	.30	.75
13 Mike Howe	.30	.75
14 Danny Irmen	.40	1.00
15 Evan Kaufmann	.30	.75
16 Peter Kennedy	.30	.75
17 Phil Kessel	4.00	10.00
18 Derek Peltier	.30	.75
19 Tom Pohl	.30	.75
20 Ryan Potulny	1.25	3.00
21 Andy Sertich	.30	.75
22 Brent Solei	.30	.75
23 Ryan Stoa	.60	1.50
24 Mike Vannelli	.30	.75
25 Blake Wheeler	.75	2.00
26 Don Lucia HC	.02	.10
27 Goldy Gopher MASCOT	.02	.10

2006-07 Minnesota Golden Gophers

COMPLETE SET (25)	25.00	35.00
1 R.J. Anderson	.40	1.00
2 Jay Barriball	.60	1.50
3 Justin Bostrom	.40	1.00
4 Kellen Briggs	.40	1.00
5 Mike Carman	.40	1.00
6 David Fischer	.40	1.00
7 Ryan Flynn	.40	1.00
8 Jeff Frazee	.75	2.00
9 Alex Goligoski	.75	2.00
10 Ben Gordon	.40	1.00
11 Mike Howe	.40	1.00
12 Erik Johnson	2.00	5.00
13 Evan Kaufmann	.40	1.00
14 Tony Lucia	.40	1.00
15 Jim O'Brien	.75	2.00
16 Kyle Okposo	2.00	5.00
17 Derek Peltier	.40	1.00
18 Tom Pohl	.40	1.00
19 Brian Schack	.40	1.00
20 Brent Solei	.40	1.00
21 Ryan Stoa	.75	2.00
22 Mike Vannelli	.40	1.00
23 Blake Wheeler	.75	2.00
24 Don Lucia CO	.10	.25
25 Goldy Gopher MASCOT	.10	.25

2007-08 Minnesota Golden Gophers

COMPLETE SET (25)	4.00	10.00
1 R.J. Anderson	.15	.40
2 Jay Barriball	.15	.40
3 Stu Bickel	.30	.75
4 Justin Bostrom	.15	.40
5 Mike Carman	.15	.40
6 Cade Fairchild	.15	.40
7 David Fischer	.15	.40
8 Drew Fisher	.15	.40
9 Ryan Flynn	.15	.40
10 Jeff Frazee	.15	.40
11 Ben Gordon	.15	.40
12 Mike Hoeffel	.15	.40
13 Mike Howe	.15	.40
14 Alex Kangas	.15	.40
15 Evan Kaufmann	.15	.40
16 Tony Lucia	.15	.40
17 Derek Peltier	.15	.40
18 Tom Pohl	.15	.40
19 Brian Schack	.15	.40
20 Brent Solei	.15	.40
21 Ryan Stor	.15	.40
22 Kevin Wehrs	.15	.40
23 Blake Wheeler	.15	.40
24 Patrick White	.15	.40
25 Don Lucia HC	.10	.40

1994-95 Minnesota Moose

This set features the Moose of the IHL. The set was issued as a promotional giveaway in the form of four, four-card perforated strips. It is believed that all were issued on the same night, but that is not yet verified.

COMPLETE SET (16)	8.00	20.00
1 Dave Christian	.60	1.50
2 Kris Miller	.60	1.50
3 John Young	.60	1.50
4 Tom Draper	.75	2.00
5 Daniel Shank	.60	1.50
6 Dean Kolstad	.60	1.50
7 Yvon Corriveau	.60	1.50
8 Frank Serratore CO	.20	.50
9 Dave Snuggerud	.60	1.50
10 Mark Osiecki	.60	1.50
11 Brad Miller	.60	1.50
12 Frank Pietrangelo	.75	2.00
13 Stephane Morin	.60	1.50
14 Sean Williams	.60	1.50
15 Dave Hakstol	.60	1.50
16 Mick E. Moose MAS	.20	.50

1995-96 Minnesota Moose

This set features the Moose of the IHL. It is believed to have been issued as a promotional giveaway, but that has not been confirmed. Any additional information can be forwarded to hockeymag@beckett.com

COMPLETE SET (16)	6.00	15.00
1 Dave Christian	.40	1.00
2 Chris Jensen	.40	1.00
3 Sandy Smith	.60	1.50
4 Stephane Morin	.60	1.50
5 Dave Gagnon	.60	1.50
6 Sean Williams	.40	1.00
7 Yvon Corriveau	.40	1.00
8 Chris Govedaris	.40	1.00
9 Mike Hurlbut	.40	1.00
10 Dave Hakstol	.40	1.00
11 Bryan Fogarty	.40	1.00
12 Dave Morissette	.40	1.00
13 Brad Miller	.40	1.00
14 Kris Miller	.40	1.00
15 Frank Serratore CO	.20	.50
16 Mick E. Moose MASCOT	.20	.50

2003-04 Minnesota State Mavericks

This set was issued as a promotional giveaway. The cards are unnumbered and so are listed below in alphabetical order.

COMPLETE SET (20)	8.00	20.00
1 Cole Bassett	.40	1.00
2 Brock Becker	.40	1.00
3 Jake Brenk	.40	1.00
4 Chad Clower	.40	1.00
5 Jon Dubel	.40	1.00
6 Aaron Forsythe	.40	1.00
7 Adam Gerlach	.40	1.00
8 Jon Hart	.40	1.00
9 Steven Johns	.50	1.25
10 Shane Joseph	.40	1.00
11 Rick Kisskeys	.40	1.00
12 Jeff Marler	.40	1.00
13 Ryan McKelvie	.40	1.00
14 Nate Metcalf	.40	1.00
15 Kyle Nixon	.60	1.50
16 Matt Paluczak	.40	1.00
17 Dana Sorensen	.40	1.00
18 Brad Thompson	.40	1.00
19 Christian Toll	.40	1.00
20 Jon Volp	.60	1.50

2000-01 Mississauga Ice Dogs

This set features the Ice Dogs of the OHL. The set was produced by the team and sold at its souvenir shop. The cards are unnumbered, so the set is listed in alphabetical order. It is noteworthy for including an early card of top prospect Jason Spezza.

COMPLETE SET (28)	8.00	20.00
1 Team CL	.04	.10
2 Brett Angel	.20	.50
3 Blue and Baby Blue MASCOT	.10	.25
4 Grant Buckley	.15	.40
5 Don Cherry OWN	.75	2.00
6 Steve Cherry CO	.04	.10
7 Fraser Clair	.15	.40
8 Mark Cranley	.15	.40
9 David Dalliday	.15	.40
10 Andrew Davis	.15	.40
11 Justin Dumont	.15	.40
12 Omar Ennaffati	.15	.40
13 John Jarram	.15	.40
14 Patrick Jarrett	.40	1.00
15 Brent Labre	.15	.40
16 Brian McGrattan	.15	.40
17 Sean McMorrow	.40	1.00
18 Michael Mole	.40	1.00
19 Chris Osborne	.15	.40
20 Jeff Paisley	.15	.40
21 Brandon Robinson	.15	.40
22 Adam Solnik	.15	.40
23 Jason Spezza	4.00	10.00
24 Dan Sullivan	.15	.40
25 Chris Thaler	.15	.40
26 Rick Vaive CO	.10	.25
27 Mike Wehrstedt	.15	.40
28 Chad Wiseman	.15	.40

2001-02 Mississauga Ice Dogs

COMPLETE SET (26)	5.00	12.00
1 Team card	.04	.10
2 Matt Tanel	.15	.40
3 T.J. Reynolds	.15	.40
4 Travis Parent	.15	.40
5 Nathan O'Nabigon	.15	.40
6 Patrick O'Sullivan	.60	1.50
7 Chris Churran	.15	.40
8 Dan Rudisuela	.15	.40
9 Mike Wehrstedt	.15	.40
10 Tyler Eady	.15	.40
11 John Kozoriz	.15	.40
12 Adam Sturgeon	.15	.40
13 Chris Hawley	.15	.40
14 Alexander Skorohod	.15	.40
15 Miguel Beaudry	.15	.40
16 Andrew Smale	.15	.40
17 Bobby Turner	.15	.40
18 John Eminger	.15	.40
19 Igor Radulov	.75	2.00
20 Greg Jacina	.15	.40
21 Mike Barrett	.15	.40
22 Daniel Sisca	.15	.40
23 Don Cherry OWN	.75	2.00
24 Steve Cherry GM	.04	.10
25 Joel Washkurak ACO	.04	.10
26 Blue MASCOT	.04	.10

2002-03 Mississauga Ice Dogs

COMPLETE SET (31)	6.00	15.00
1 Checklist	.04	.10
2 Travis Parent	.20	.50
3 Ian Maracle	.20	.50
4 Scott Hotham	.20	.50
5 Derek Lyons	.20	.50
6 Chris Curran	.20	.50
7 Dan Rudisuela	.20	.50
8 Tyler Eady	.20	.50
9 Tomas Linhart	.30	.75
10 Chris Hawley	.20	.50
11 Pavel Voroshin	.30	.75
12 Wes Rypien	.20	.50
13 Miguel Beaudry	.30	.75
14 Matt Harpwood	.30	.75
15 Daniel Buccella	.20	.50
16 Rob Schremp	1.25	3.00
17 Salvatore Malandrino	.20	.50
18 Greg Jacina	.20	.50
19 Ryan Stokes	.20	.50
20 Patrick O'Sullivan	.60	1.50
21 Dany Revelle	.20	.50
22 Blair Jarrett	.20	.50
23 Daniel Sisca	.20	.50
25 Matt Harpwood	.20	.50
26 Steve Ludzik	.20	.50
27 Mark Osborne	.20	.50
28 Wayne Crawford	.20	.50
29 Dave Sweetman	.20	.50
30 Kevin Elliot	.20	.50
31 Blue the mascot	.10	.25

2003-04 Mississauga Ice Dogs

COMPLETE SET (24)	5.00	12.00
1 Adam Abraham	.20	.50
2 Chris Bain	.30	.75
3 Cody Bass	.20	.50
4 Anthony Butera	.20	.50
5 Rick Caughell	.20	.50
6 Chris Chimienti	.20	.50
7 Chris Curran	.20	.50
8 Brad Efthimiou	.20	.50
9 Brandon Elliott	.20	.50
10 Lukas Grauwiler	.20	.50
11 Doug Groenestege	.30	.75
12 Blair Jarrett	.20	.50
13 Daryl Knowles	.20	.50
14 Mark O'Leary	.20	.50
15 Patrick O'Sullivan	.30	.75
16 Chad Painchaud	.20	.50
17 Kyle Quincey	.20	.50
18 Dany Revelle	.20	.50
19 Dan Rudisuela	.20	.50
20 David Shantz	.60	1.50
21 Ryan Stokes	.20	.50
22 Nick Van Herpt	.20	.50
23 Tom Zanoski	.20	.50
24 Scott Zimmerman	.20	.50

2004-05 Mississauga Ice Dogs

A total of 300 team sets were produced.

COMPLETE SET (24)	6.00	15.00
1 Anthony Butera	.30	.75
2 Bradley Snetsinger	.20	.50
3 Adam Abraham	.20	.50
4 Cody Bass	.20	.50
5 David Shantz	.60	1.50
6 Dustin Jeffrey	.20	.50
7 Kyle Quincey	.30	.75
8 Michael Swift	.20	.50
9 Gianluc Caputi	.20	.50
10 Craig Cescon	.20	.50
11 Tom Zanoski	.20	.50
12 Vladimir Svacina	.20	.50
13 Patrick O'Sullivan	.60	1.50
14 Daniel Carcillo	.20	.50
15 John Hecimovic	.20	.50
16 Paul Merchese	.20	.50
17 Michael Ouzas	.20	.50
18 David Pszenyczny	.20	.50
19 Frankie Santini	.20	.50
20 Justin DaCosta	.40	1.00
21 Stefan Legein	.20	.50
22 Nathan Hooper	.20	.50
23 Jordan Owens	.20	.50
24 Aaron Barton	.20	.50

2005-06 Mississauga Ice Dogs

COMPLETE SET (24)	6.00	15.00
1 Cody Bass	.30	.75
2 Vladimir Svacina	.30	.75
3 Jordan Owens	.30	.75
4 Drew Schiestel	.30	.75
5 Michael Smift	.30	.75
6 Keith Wynn	.30	.75
7 Lucas Lobsinger	.40	1.00
8 Luca Caputi	.30	.75
9 Kyle Lamb	.30	.75
10 Justin Gvora	.30	.75
11 Jordan Skellett	.30	.75
12 Andrew Marcoux	.30	.75
13 Andrew Merrett	.30	.75
14 Oskar Osala	.30	.75
15 Brett Oliphante	.30	.75
16 Justin Dacosta	.30	.75
17 Kyle Knechtel	.30	.75
18 Joshua Day	.30	.75
19 Franck Santini	.30	.75
20 Nathan Martine	.30	.75
21 Drew McAvoy	.30	.75
22 Stefan Legein	.30	.75
23 Jadran Beljo	.30	.75
24 Chris Lawrence	.30	.75

2006-07 Mississauga Ice Dogs

COMPLETE SET (23)	8.00	15.00
1 Cody Bass	.25	.60
2 Alex Pietrangelo	.25	.60
3 Stephan Legein	.25	.60
4 Jadran Beljo	.25	.60
5 Chris Lawrence	.25	.60
6 Jordan Owens	.25	.60
7 Brett Oliphant	.25	.60
8 Michael Swift	.25	.60
9 Luca Caputi	.25	.60
10 Barry Sanderson	.25	.60
11 Jordan Skellett	.25	.60
12 Andrew Merrett	.25	.60
13 Travis Fuller	.25	.60
14 Oskar Osala	.25	.60
15 Steven Manojlovic	.25	.60
16 Josh Day	.25	.60
17 Franck Santini	.25	.60
18 Nathan Martine	.25	.60
19 Drew Mcavoy	.25	.60
20 Drew Schiestel	.25	.60
21 Kyle Lamb	.25	.60
22 Lucas Lobsinger	.40	1.00
23 Andrew Loverrock	.40	1.00

2014-15 Mississauga Steelheads

COMPLETE SET (25)	6.00	15.00
1 Sam Babintsev	.30	.75
2 Nathan Bastian	.30	.75
3 Justin Bean	.30	.75
4 Damian Bourne	.30	.75
5 Jacob Brennan	.30	.75
6 Josh Burnside	.30	.75
7 Bryson Cianfrone	.30	.75
8 Everett Clark	.30	.75
9 Sean Day	.30	.75
10 Brandon Devlin	.30	.75
11 Marcus Dickerson	.30	.75
12 Adam Donnelly	.30	.75
13 Austin Gerhart	.30	.75
14 Stephen Gibson	.30	.75
15 Leif Hertz	.30	.75
16 Stefan Leblanc	.30	.75
17 Jimmy Lodge	.30	.75
18 Bobby MacIntyre	.30	.75
19 Spencer Martin	.30	.75
20 Michael McLeod	.30	.75
21 Jason Smith	.30	.75
22 Cody Thompson	.30	.75
23 Jared Walsh	.30	.75
24 Cameron Zanussi	.30	.75
25 Nick Zottl	.30	.75

1996-97 Mississippi Sea Wolves

This set was sold by the team at home games and was sponsored by Play It Again Sports.

COMPLETE SET (22)	4.00	10.00
1 Frederik Beaubien	.30	.75
2 Alexei Budayev	.20	.50
3 Sylvain Daigle	.20	.50
4 Kevin Evans	.20	.50
5 Quinn Fair	.20	.50
6 Shawn Frappier	.20	.50
7 Kevin Hilton	.20	.50
8 Kelly Hurd	.20	.50
9 Derek Innanen	.20	.50
10 Yanick Jean	.20	.50
11 John Kosobud	.20	.50
12 Troy Mann	.20	.50
13 Roger Maxwell	.20	.50
14 Mike Muller	.30	.75
15 Simon Oliver	.20	.50
16 Patrick Rochon	.20	.50
17 Jeff Rohlicek	.30	.75
18 Mark Rupnow	.20	.50
19 Joaikin Wassberger	.20	.50
20 Steven Yule	.20	.50
21 Bruce Boudreau HCO	.08	.25
22 Hook Mascot	.02	.10

1997-98 Mississippi Sea Wolves

Little is known about this set beyond the confirmed checklist. Additional information can be forwarded to hockeymag@beckett.com.

COMPLETE SET (22)	4.00	10.00
1 Sinuhe Wallinheimo	.40	1.00
2 Neal Martin	.20	.50
3 Don Chase	.20	.50
4 John Kosobud	.20	.50
5 Jeff Rohlicek	.20	.50
6 Kelly Hurd	.20	.50
7 Chad Dameworth	.20	.50
8 Bruce Boudreau HCO	.02	.10
9 Teemu Numminen	.20	.50
10 Dan Back	.20	.50
11 Dean Hulett	.20	.50
12 Mark Rupnow	.20	.50
13 Hook Mascot	.02	.10
14 Patrick Rochon	.20	.50
15 Troy Mann	.20	.50
16 Quinn Fair	.20	.50
17 Shawn Frappier	.20	.50
18 Brian Farrell	.20	.50
19 Steve Yule	.20	.50
20 Kevin Evans	.20	.50
21 Brad Guzda	.20	.50
22 Forbes MacPherson	.20	.50

1999-00 Mississippi Sea Wolves

This set features the Sea Wolves of the ECHL. The set was produced by Roox and was sold by the team at home games.

COMPLETE SET (25)	20.00	50.00
1 Rob Flahiff EQM	.02	.10
2 Marc Potvin HCO	.75	2.00
3 Hook MAS	.02	.10
4 Team Photo	.75	2.00
5 Cynthia Dedeaux TR	.02	.10
6 Trevor Gillies	.75	2.00
7 Steve Duke	.75	2.00
8 Sean Gillam	.75	2.00
9 Bob Woods	.75	2.00
10 Cody Bowtell	.75	2.00
11 Patrick Rochon	.75	2.00
12 Jonathan Weaver	.75	2.00
13 John Kosobud	.75	2.00
14 Brad Essex	1.25	3.00
15 Scott King	.75	2.00
16 Ryan Gaucher	.75	2.00
17 Brad Goulet	.75	2.00
18 Mike Martone	.75	2.00
19 J.F. Aube	.75	2.00
20 Dave Paradise	.75	2.00
21 John Evangelista	.75	2.00
22 Mikhail Kravets	.75	2.00
23 Chuck Thuss	1.25	3.00
24 Sylvain Daigle	1.25	3.00
25 Mark Rupnow	.75	2.00

1999-00 Mississippi Sea Wolves Kelly Cup

This set features the Sea Wolves of the ECHL. The set was produced by the team and features players from the previous season to honor their league championship win. The set was sold by the team at home games for $10.

COMPLETE SET (25)	4.00	10.00
1 Bruce Boudreau CO	.20	.50
2 Hook MAS	.02	.10
3 James Carey TR	.02	.10
4 Cynthia Dedeaux TR	.02	.10
5 Karl Infanger	.20	.50
6 Sean Blanchard	.20	.50
7 Bob Woods	.20	.50
8 Cody Bowtell	.20	.50
9 Vaclav Nedomansky	.20	.50
10 Patrick Rochon	.20	.50
11 John Kosobud	.20	.50
12 Brad Essex	.30	.75
13 Andrew Dale	.20	.50
14 Dean Mando	.20	.50
15 Kevin Hilton	.20	.50
16 Quinn Fair	.20	.50
17 Chris Schmidt	.20	.50
18 Mike Martone	.20	.50
19 Kelly Hurd	.20	.50
20 Mikhail Kravets	.20	.50
21 Travis Scott	.30	.75
22 Mark Rupnow	.20	.50
23 Troy Mann	.20	.50
24 Chuck Thuss	.30	.75
25 Mississippi Sea Wolves	.20	.50

2003-04 Mississippi Sea Wolves

These cards were given away as promotional items at several home games. It's believed that other cards exist in this series.

COMPLETE SET (17)
1 Anthony Battaglia
2 Brent Gauvreau
3 Louis Dumont
4 Greg Gardner
5 Jeff Hutchins
6 Andrei Lupandin
7 Austin Miller
8 Steve O'Rourke
9 John Evangelista
10 Travis Lisabeth
11 Sean Matile
12 Roger Maxwell
13 Patrick Rochon
14 Kerry Ellis-Toddingto
15 Steffon Walby
16 Mascot
17 Checklist

1999-00 Missouri River Otters

This set features the River Otters of the UHL. The cards were printed by Roox and sold by the team. They are not numbered, so they are listed below in alphabetical order.

COMPLETE SET (29)	4.00	10.00
1 Team Photo	.20	.50
2 Tomas Baluch	.15	.40
3 Chris Bernard	.15	.40
4 Charles Blyth	.15	.40
5 Colin Chaulk	.15	.40
6 Randy Gallatin	.15	.40
7 Forrest Gore	.15	.40
8 Ben Gorewich	.15	.40
9 Jay Hebert	.15	.40
10 Kiley Hill	.15	.40
11 Jan Kobezda	.15	.40
12 Lonnie Loach	.30	.75
13 Jeremiah McCarthy	.20	.50
14 Jeremy Rebek	.15	.40
15 Brian Regan	.15	.40
16 Allan Roulette	.15	.40
17 Alain St. Hilaire	.15	.40
18 Curtis Sayler	.15	.40
19 Trevor Sherban	.15	.40
20 Marty Standish	.15	.40
21 Michal Stastny	.30	.75
22 Chris Tok	.15	.40
23 Dan Tompkins	.15	.40
24 Mark Reeds HCO	.15	.40
25 Scott Bell CO	.15	.40
26 Oscar MASCOT	.08	.25
27 Otter Mobile	.08	.25
28 Checklist	.08	.25
29 Cover Card	.08	.25

2000-01 Missouri River Otters

This set features the River Otters of the UHL. The cards were issued as promotional giveaways, apparently on three separate occasions, and in subsets of nine cards. Collectors needed to attend all three games to compile the entire set.

COMPLETE SET (27)	7.20	18.00
1 Team CL #1	.04	.10
2 Lonnie Loach	.40	1.00
3 Chris Tok	.30	.75
4 Colin Chaulk	.40	1.00
5 Kiley Hill	.40	1.00
6 Jeremy Rebek	.30	.75
7 Trevor Sherban	.30	.75
8 Jay Hebert	.30	.75
9 Randy Gallatin	.30	.75
10 Team CL #2	.04	.10
11 Darin Kimble	.40	1.00
12 Troy Michalski	.30	.75
13 Benoit Thibert	.30	.75
14 Eric Murano	.40	1.00
15 Lee Cole	.30	.75
16 Robert Starke	.30	.75
17 Ryan Johnston	.30	.75
18 Mark Reeds CO	.10	.25
19 Team CL #3	.04	.10
20 Kevin Plager	.30	.75
21 Mike Bayrack	.30	.75
22 Jay Woodcroft	.30	.75
23 Jared Reigstad	.30	.75
24 Anthony Cappelletti	.30	.75
25 Kiley Hill AS	.30	.75
26 Colin Chaulk AS	.30	.75
27 Jim Jeans EM	.04	.10
27 John Sheehan TR	.04	.10

1999-00 Missouri River Otters Sheet

This set features the River Otters of the UHL. The cards were issued as a promotional giveaway in the form of a three-panel perforated sheet. The set was sponsored by a local pub and by Disney.

COMPLETE SET (25)	7.20	18.00
1 Tomas Baluch	.30	.75
2 Charlie Blythe	.30	.75
3 Colin Chaulk	.30	.75
4 Randy Gallatin	.30	.75
5 Yuri Gerasimov	.30	.75
6 Ben Gorewich	.30	.75
7 Jay Hebert	.30	.75
8 Kiley Hill	.30	.75
9 Jan Kobezda	.30	.75
10 Lonnie Loach	.40	1.00
11 Jeremiah McCarthy	.30	.75
12 Jeremy Rebek	.30	.75
13 Brian Regan	.30	.75
14 Alan Roulette	.30	.75
15 Alain St. Hilaire	.30	.75
16 Curtis Sayler	.30	.75
17 Trevor Sherban	.30	.75
18 Marty Standish	.30	.75
19 Michal Stastny	.40	1.00
20 Jason Stewart	.30	.75
21 Chris Tok	.30	.75
22 Dan Tompkins	.30	.75
23 Mark Reeds CO	.08	.25
24 Scott Bell	.30	.75
25 Oscar the Otter MASCOT	.02	.10

2001-02 Missouri River Otters

This set features the River Otters of the UHL. The set was issued as a promotional giveaway in two 15-card series, and then was later sold by the team as a complete 30-card issue.

COMPLETE SET (30)	8.00	20.00
1 Missouri River Otters Logo	.04	.10
2 Aaron Vickar	.30	.75
3 Lonnie Loach	.40	1.00
4 Dustin Whitecotton	.30	.75
5 Troy Mann	.30	.75
6 Anthony Cappelletti	.30	.75
7 Casey VanSchagen	.30	.75
8 Ben White	.30	.75
9 Curtis Voth	.40	1.00
10 Charlie Blyth	.30	.75
11 Scott Perry	.30	.75
12 Kelvin Solari	.30	.75
13 Mark Reeds CO	.30	.75
14 Oscar the River Otter MASCOT	.04	.10
15 Checklist I	.04	.10
16 Missouri River Otters	.30	.75
17 Brian Regan	.30	.75
18 Darin Kimble	.60	1.50
19 Eric Murano	.40	1.00
20 Jason Gudmundson	.30	.75
21 Mike Jaros	.30	.75
22 Joe Ritson	.30	.75
23 Tony White	.30	.75
24 Simon Poirier	.30	.75
25 Vaclav Pazourek	.30	.75
26 Joe Pecoraro	.30	.75
27 Kevin Chabbert	.30	.75
28 John Sheehan TR	.04	.10
29 Team Photo	.30	.75
30 Checklist 2	.04	.10

2003-04 Missouri River Otters

This set was issued in two series as a promotional giveaway.

COMPLETE SET (24)	8.00	20.00
1 Checklist	.04	.10
2 Anthony Cappelletti	.40	1.00
3 Charlie Blyth	.40	1.00
4 Jesse Heerema	.40	1.00
5 Jeff Cameron	.40	1.00
6 Jeff Petruic	.40	1.00
7 Colin Embley	.40	1.00
8 Bobby Rapoza	.40	1.00
9 Troy Mann	.40	1.00
10 Tony White	.40	1.00
11 Chad Moore	.40	1.00
12 Team Photo	.10	.25
13 Checklist	.04	.10
14 Ben White	.40	1.00
15 Kevin Chabbert	.40	1.00
16 Forrest Gore	.40	1.00
17 Joe Ritson	.40	1.00
18 Brian Regan	.60	1.50
19 George Cantrall	.60	1.50
20 River Otters Kids Club	.04	.10
21 Ryan Gillis	.40	1.00
22 Tim Knudsen	.60	1.50
23 Rob Davidson	.40	1.00
24 Lonnie Loach HCO	.10	.25

2004-05 Missouri River Otters

This set was issued in two parts by the River Otters of the UHL. Each 16-card series was sold for $4 at the team's merchandise shop.

COMPLETE SET (32)	5.00	12.00
1 Header	.04	.10
2 Charlie Blyth	.20	.50
3 Jason Tapp	.20	.50
4 B.J. Heckendorn	.20	.50
5 Barrie Moore	.20	.50
6 Mike Dombkiewicz	.20	.50
7 Cole Bassett	.20	.50
8 Ryan Johnson	.30	.75
9 Riku Varjamo	.20	.50
10 Mat Snesrud	.20	.50
11 Quinten Van Horlick	.30	.75
12 Jim Montgomery	.30	.75
13 Kevin Kaminski CO	.20	.50
14 Ice Zone	.04	.10
15 Prize Card	.04	.10
16 Checklist Series 1	.04	.10
17 Header	.04	.10
18 Bob Rapoza	.20	.50
19 Josh Legge	.20	.50
20 Kevin Reiter	.20	.50
21 Lars Pettersen	.20	.50
22 Mark Odut	.20	.50
23 George Cantrall	.20	.50
24 Justin Quenneville	.20	.50
25 Glen Detulleo	.20	.50
26 Rod Sundquist	.20	.50
27 Brad MacMillan	.20	.50
28 Barret Jackman	.60	1.50
29 Team Photo	.20	.50
30 Sponsor Card	.04	.10
31 Prize Card	.04	.10
32 Checklist Series 2	.04	.10

2005-06 Missouri River Otters

COMPLETE SET (24)	8.00	20.00
1 Missouri River Otters	.04	.10
2 Kevin Kaminski HC	.04	.10
3 Richard Paul	.40	1.00
4 Dave Stewart	.40	1.00
5 Martin Vasut	.40	1.00
6 Jim Murphy	.40	1.00
7 J.P. Beilsten	.40	1.00
8 Lars Pettersen	.40	1.00
9 B.J. Heckendorn	.40	1.00
10 Tyler Butler	.40	1.00
11 Mark Lindsay	.40	1.00
12 Brenden Cuthbert	.40	1.00
13 Missouri River Otters	.04	.10
14 Brad Church	.40	1.00
15 Tim O'Connell	.40	1.00
16 Jimmy Callahan	.40	1.00
17 Frank Littlejohn	.40	1.00
18 Mark Odut	.40	1.00
19 Brad MacMillan	.40	1.00
20 Kevin Reiter	.40	1.00
21 Damian Surma	.40	1.00
22 Oscar [Mascot]	.04	.10
23 Matt Suderman	.40	1.00
24 Scott Horvath	.40	1.00

1997-98 Mobile Mysticks

This set features the Mysticks of the ECHL. The cards were produced by Starzsports, and were sold by the team at home games.

COMPLETE SET (21)	4.00	10.00
1 Chuck Thuss	.20	.50
2 Mike Mayhew	.20	.50
3 Matt Shaw CO	.08	.25
4 Dave Craievich	.20	.50
5 Jim Jensen	.20	.50
6 Anton Fedorov	.20	.50
7 Russell Monteith	.20	.50
8 Yanick Jean	.20	.50
9 Dave Larson	.20	.50
10 Chris Brooks	.20	.50
11 Brandon Carper	.20	.50
12 Phil Valk	.20	.50
13 Patrice Paquin	.20	.50
14 Kevin Hilton	.20	.50
15 Fredrick Nasvall	.20	.50
16 Andrew Will	.20	.50
17 Steve Suk	.20	.50
18 Mike Lenarduzzi	.30	.75
19 Neil Donovan	.20	.50
20 Hugues Gervais	.20	.50
21 Chad Remackel	.20	.50

1997-98 Mobile Mysticks Kellogg's

This set features the Mysticks of the ECHL. These cards were issued as a promotional giveaway in four-card strips at seven different home games. Each strip contained three player cards and one Kellogg's ad card. The players on cards No. 2 and 4 are not known at this time. Identification should be sent to hockeymag@beckett.com.

COMPLETE SET (21)	6.00	15.00
1 Andrew Will	.40	1.00
2 unknown		
3 Neil Donovan	.40	1.00
4 unknown		
5 Dave Larson	.40	1.00
6 Jim Jensen	.40	1.00
7 Mike Mayhew	.40	1.00
8 Matt Shaw HCO	.15	.40
9 Yanick Jean	.40	1.00
10 Steve Suk	.40	1.00
11 Chad Remackel	.40	1.00
12 Tom Neziol ACO	.08	.25
13 Dave Craievich	.40	1.00
14 Chris Brooks	.40	1.00
15 Fredrick Nasvall	.40	1.00
16 Puck MAS	.08	.25
17 Anton Fedorov	.40	1.00
18 Hugues Gervais	.40	1.00
19 Phil Valk	.40	1.00
20 Mike Lenarduzzi	.60	1.50
21 Russell Monteith	.40	1.00

1998-99 Mobile Mysticks

This 22-card set was handed out as a promotional giveaway at five different home games, making it an extremely difficult set to acquire. The cards were distributed in perforated strips.

COMPLETE SET (22)	6.00	15.00
1 Russell Monteith	.40	1.00
2 Slapshot Mascot	.02	.10
3 Tom Neziol ACO	.02	.10
4 Kevin Kerr	.40	1.00
5 Steve Debus	.40	1.00
6 Steve Chapman GM	.02	.10
7 Puck Mascot	.02	.10
8 Yanick Jean	.40	1.00
9 Dave Craievich	.40	1.00
10 Jason Elders	.40	1.00
11 Alain Savage	.40	1.00
12 Joel Theriault	.40	1.00
13 Chad Alban	.60	1.50
14 John McCabe	.40	1.00
15 Simmons Jeffreys Young	.20	.50
16 Hughes Gervais	.40	1.00
17 Brandon Carper	.40	1.00
18 Craig Binns	.40	1.00
19 Jeff Pyle HCO	.08	.25
20 Jim Shepherd	.40	1.00
21 Andrew Will	.40	1.00
22 Francois Page	.40	1.00

1999-00 Mobile Mysticks

This set features the Mysticks of the ECHL. The set was issued as a promotional giveaway at an early-season game.

COMPLETE SET (23)	6.00	50.00
1 Dave Craievich	1.00	2.50
2 David Van Drunen	1.00	2.50
3 Mitch Vig	1.00	2.50
4 Benoit Cotnoir	1.00	2.50
5 Bobby Stewart	1.00	2.50
6 John McCabe	1.00	2.50
7 Hugues Gervais	1.00	2.50
8 Tom Nolan	1.00	2.50
9 Chad Onufrechuk	1.00	2.50
10 Jason Elders	1.00	2.50
11 B.J. Kilbourne	1.00	2.50
12 Mark Turner	1.00	2.50
13 Jeff Kozakowski	1.00	2.50
14 Josh Harrold	1.00	2.50
15 Russ Guzior	1.00	2.50
16 Anders Sorensen	1.00	2.50
17 Jason Clarke	1.00	2.50
18 Chad Alban	2.00	5.00
19 Steve Debus	2.00	5.00
20 Scott Cherrey	1.00	2.50
21 Jeff Pyle CO	1.00	2.50
22 Tom Neziol CO	.08	.25
23 Southern Ford Dealers		.01

1983-84 Moncton Alpines

The Moncton Alpines are featured in this 28-card P.L.A.Y. (Police, Law and Youth) set, which was sponsored by the Moncton Police in conjunction with several company sponsors. The cards measure approximately 2 1/2" by 3 3/4" and are printed on thin card stock. The fronts feature color photos with the players posed in action stances. The photos are framed by white borders. The player's name and position are printed below the picture between Coke and Hostess logos. The backs have biography, statistics, and safety tips in English and French.

COMPLETE SET (28)	6.00	15.00
1 Doug Messier CO	.20	.50
2 Chris Smith	.20	.50
3 Marco Baron	.40	1.00
4 Mike Zanier	.40	1.00
5 Dwayne Boettger	.20	.50
6 Lowell Loveday	.20	.50
7 Joe McDonnell	.20	.50
8 Peter Dineen	.20	.50
9 John Blum	.30	.75
10 Steve Smith	.75	2.00
11 Reg Kerr	.30	.75
12 Tom Rowe	.20	.50

13 Ross Lambert .20 .50
14 Pat Conacher .40 1.00
15 Paul Miller .20 .50
16 Bert Yachimel .20 .50
17 Tom Gorence .30 .75
18 Jeff Crawford .20 .50
19 Serge Boisvert .30 .75
20 Todd Strueby .30 .75
21 Todd Bidner .20 .50
22 Dean Dachyshyn .20 .50
23 Ray Cote .20 .50
24 Shawn Babcock .20 .50
25 Shawn Dineen .20 .50
26 Marc Habscheid .40 1.00
27 Charlie Lavalee TR .08 .25
Kevin Ferris TR
NNO Checklist Card .20 .50

1984-85 Moncton Golden Flames

The Moncton Golden Flames are featured in this 26-card P.L.A.Y. (Police, Law and Youth) set, which was sponsored by the Moncton Police in conjunction with several company sponsors. The cards measure approximately 2 1/2" by 3 3/4" and are printed on thin card stock. The fronts feature color photos with the players posed in action stances.

COMPLETE SET (26) 10.00 25.00
1 Brian Patafie TR .08 .25
2 Mike Bianni TR .08 .25
3 Pierre Page CO .20 .50
4 Neil Sheehy .40 1.00
5 George White .20 .50
6 Mark Lamb .40 1.00
7 Dan Kane .20 .50
8 Dan Bolduc .40 1.00
9 Lou Kiriakou .20 .50
10 Joel Otto .75 2.00
11 Dale Degray .40 1.00
12 Mike Clayton .20 .50
13 Mickey Volcan .20 .50
14 Ted Pearson .20 .50
15 Mario Simioni .20 .50
16 Keith Hanson .20 .50
17 Yves Courteau .20 .50
18 Dan Cormier .20 .50
19 Todd Hooey .20 .50
20 Mike Vernon 4.00 10.00
21 Dave Meszaros .20 .50
22 Bruce Eakin .20 .50
23 Ed Kastelic .40 1.00
24 Tony Stiles .20 .50
25 Pierre Rioux .20 .50
26 Gino Cavallini .40 1.00

1985-86 Moncton Golden Flames

The Moncton Golden Flames are featured in this 28-card P.L.A.Y. (Police, Law and Youth) set, which was sponsored by the Moncton Police in conjunction with several company sponsors. The cards measure approximately 2 1/2" by 3 3/4" and are printed on thin card stock. The fronts feature color photos with the players posed in action stances. The photos are framed by white borders. The player's name and position are printed below the picture between Coke and Hostess logos. The backs have biography, statistics, and safety tips in English and French.

COMPLETE SET (28) 8.00 20.00
1 Terry Crisp GM/CO .40 1.00
2 Dan Bolduc ACO .08 .25
3 Terry Crisp GM/CO .40 1.00
Dan Bolduc ACO
4 Al Pedersen .30 .75
5 Dave Meszaros .20 .50
6 George White .20 .50
7 Mark Lamb .60 1.50
8 Doug Kostynski .20 .50
9 Brian Bradley .75 2.00
10 Rob Kivell .20 .50
11 Geoff Courtnall 1.25 3.00
12 Tony Stiles .20 .50
13 Jim Buettgen .20 .50
14 Cleon Daskalakis .40 1.00
15 Rick Kosti .20 .50
16 Kevan Guy .20 .50
17 John Blum .20 .50
18 Brian Patafie .08 .25
Mike Baiani
Jamie Druet
19 Greg Johnston .30 .75
20 Dale Degray .20 .50
21 John Meulenbroeks .20 .50
22 Dave Reid .40 1.00
23 Jay Miller 1.25 3.00
24 Yves Courteau .20 .50
25 Robin Bartel .20 .50
26 Benoit Doucet .20 .50
27 Pete Bakovic .20 .50
28 Team Photo .40 1.00

1986-87 Moncton Golden Flames

The Moncton Golden Flames are featured in this 28-card P.L.A.Y. (Police, Law and Youth) set, which was sponsored by the Moncton Police in conjunction with several company sponsors. The cards measure approximately 2 1/2" by 3 3/4" and are printed on thin card stock. The fronts feature color photos with the players posed in action stances. This set includes first pro cards of Brett Hull, Gary Roberts, Bill Ranford, and Lyndon Byers.

COMPLETE SET (28) 30.00 75.00
1 Terry Crisp CO/GM .40 1.00
2 Danny Bolduc ACO .08 .25
3 Doug Dadswell .40 1.00
4 Doug Kostynski .20 .50
5 Bill Ranford 6.00 15.00
6 Brian Patafie TR .08 .25
7 Dave Pasin .30 .75
8 Darwin McCutcheon .20 .50
9 Team Photo .40 1.00
10 Kevan Guy .20 .50
11 Kraig Nienhuis .30 .75
12 Gary Roberts 2.00 5.00
13 Ken Sabourin .30 .75
14 Marc D'Amour .40 1.00
15 Don Mercier .20 .50
16 Wade Campbell .20 .50
17 Mark Paterson .20 .50
18 Cleon Daskalakis .40 1.00
19 Lyndon Byers 2.00 5.00
20 Brett Hull 15.00 40.00
21 Bob Sweeney .40 1.00
22 Gord Hynes .20 .50
23 Peter Bakovic .20 .50
24 Dave Reid .40 1.00
25 Mike Rucinski .20 .50
26 Ray Podloski .20 .50
27 Bob Bodak .20 .50
28 John Carter .30 .75

1987-88 Moncton Hawks

Sponsored by Coke, Shoppers Drug Mart, and CKCW, this 25-card set measures approximately 2 1/2" by 3 3/4" and features posed, color player photos with white studio backgrounds. The fronts have white borders with sponsor names printed in red above and below the picture. The player's name and position are printed in black just below the photo. The cards are unnumbered and checklisted below in alphabetical order.

COMPLETE SET (25) 4.80 12.00
1 Joel Baillargeon .20 .50
2 Rick Bowness CO .20 .50
3 Rick Carrano TR .08 .25
Wayne Fleming EQ
4 Bobby Dollas .30 .75
5 Peter Douris .30 .75
6 Iain Duncan .20 .50
7 Bob Essensa .75 2.00
8 Todd Flichel .20 .50
9 Rob Fowler .20 .50
10 Randy Gilhen .30 .75
11 Matt Hervey .20 .50
12 Brent Hughes .30 .75
13 Jamie Husgen .20 .50
14 Mike Jeffrey .20 .50
15 Guy Larose .20 .50
16 Chris Levasseur .20 .50
17 Len Nielson .20 .50
18 Roger Ohman .20 .50
19 Dave Quigley .20 .50
20 Ron Pesetti .20 .50
21 Steve Penney .40 1.00
22 Scott Schneider .20 .50
23 Ryan Stewart .20 .50
24 Gord Whitaker .20 .50
25 Team Photo .40 1.00

1990-91 Moncton Hawks

These 25 cards measure approximately 2 7/16" by 3 5/8" and feature on their fronts white-bordered posed-on-ice color shots of the '90-91 Moncton Hawks. The player's name and position appear at the lower left. The logos for the set's sponsors, Hostess, Frito Lay, and CKCW Radio, also appear on the front. The cards are unnumbered and checklisted below in alphabetical order.

COMPLETE SET (25) 4.00 10.00
1 Larry Bernard .15 .40
2 Lee Davidson .15 .40
3 Iain Duncan .15 .40
4 Craig Duncanson .15 .40
5 Dallas Eakins .20 .50
6 Dave Farrish CO/GM .02 .10
7 Wayne Flemming EQMG .02 .10
8 Todd Flichel .15 .40
9 Peter Hankinson .15 .40
10 Matt Hervey .15 .40
11 Brent Hughes .20 .50
12 Anthony Joseph .15 .40
13 Sergei Kharin .15 .40
14 Denis Larocque .15 .40
15 Guy Larose .20 .50
16 Scott Levins .20 .50
17 Bryan Marchment .40 1.00
18 Chris Norton .15 .40
19 Mike O'Neill .30 .75
20 Grant Richison .15 .40
21 Scott Schneider .15 .40
22 Rob Snitzer TR .02 .10
23 Rick Tabaracci .40 1.00
24 Simon Wheeldon .20 .50
25 Team Card .20 .50

1991-92 Moncton Hawks

This 28-card set measures approximately 2 1/2" by 3 5/8" and was sponsored by the Moncton Police Force, the Sackville Police Force, and the Hostess/Frito Lay company. The fronts feature color photos with the players posed in action stances. The photos are framed by white borders. The player's name and position appear in the lower left corner, while the Hostess/Frito Lay logo is in the lower right corner.The cards are unnumbered and checklisted below in alphabetical order.

COMPLETE SET (28) 4.00 10.00
1 Luciano Borsato .15 .40
2 Jason Cirone .15 .40
3 Rob Cowie .15 .40
4 Lee Davidson .15 .40
5 Kris Draper .40 1.00
6 Dallas Eakins .20 .50
7 Dave Farrish GM/CO .02 .10
8 Wayne Flemming EQMG .02 .10
9 Sean Gauthier .20 .50
10 Ken Gernander .20 .50
11 Tod Hartje .15 .40
12 Bob Joyce .20 .50
13 Claude Julien .15 .40
14 Chris Kiene .15 .40
15 Mark Kumpel P/ACO .15 .40
16 Derek Langille .15 .40
17 Tyler Larter .15 .40
18 John LeBlanc .15 .40
19 Scott Levins .15 .40
20 Rob Murray .15 .40
21 Kent Paynter .15 .40
22 Rudy Poeschek .20 .50
23 Dave Prior CO .02 .10
24 Warren Rychel .20 .50
25 Rob Snitzer TR .02 .10
26 Rick Tabaracci .40 1.00
27 The Hawk (Mascot) .02 .10
28 Darren Veitch .20 .50

2001-02 Moncton Wildcats

This set features the Wildcats of the QMJHL. The cards were produced by CTM Ste-Foy and were sold at that shop, as well as at the team's home games. It was reported that less than 1,000 sets were produced.

COMPLETE SET (26) 6.00 15.00
1 Bill Ruggiero .30 .75
2 Andrew Carver .20 .50
3 James Sanford .20 .50
4 Kyle Murnaghan .20 .50
5 Daniel Hudgin .20 .50
6 Mathieu Betournay .20 .50
7 Karl Gagne .20 .50
8 Ian Seguin .20 .50
9 Michel Dube .20 .50
10 Francois Caron .20 .50
11 Nathan Saunders .20 .50
12 Brad Larter .20 .50
13 Teddy Kyres .20 .50
14 Kevin Glode .20 .50
15 David Philpott .20 .50
16 Ryan Salvis .20 .50
17 Collin Circelli .20 .50
18 Corey Crawford .30 .75
19 Matt Davis .30 .75
20 Patrick Thoreson .75 2.00
21 Maxime Desruisseaux .20 .50
22 Julien Lavoie .20 .50
23 Scott English .20 .50
24 Luke Pelham .20 .50
25 Steve Bernier 1.00 2.50
NNO Title Card .04 .10
CL

2002-03 Moncton Wildcats

COMPLETE SET (26) 8.00 15.00
1 Nathan Saunders .20 .50
2 Matt Davis .20 .50
3 Francois Caron .20 .50
4 Evgeni Artukhin .30 .75
5•Evgeni Artukhin WJC .30 .75
6 Corey Crawford .40 1.00
7 Bruce Graham .30 .75
8 James Sanford .30 .75
9 Patrick Sampson .20 .50
10 Mathieu Betournay .20 .50
11 Ryan Salvis .20 .50
12 Kevin Glode .20 .50
13 Luke Pelham .20 .50
14 Maxime Desruisseaux .20 .50
15 Kevin Hamel .20 .50
16 Josh Hepditch .20 .50
17 Jonathan Favreau .20 .50
18 Kyle Murnaghan .20 .50
19 Daniel Hudgin .20 .50
20 Michel Dube .20 .50
21 Sebastien Strozynski .20 .50
22 Yannick Searles .20 .50
23 Carl McLean .20 .50
24 Karl Gagne .20 .50
25 Steve Bernier 1.25 3.00
26 Team Picture .10 .25

2003-04 Moncton Wildcats

COMPLETE SET (25) 5.00 12.00
1 James Sanford .15 .40
2 Yan Ouimet .15 .40
3 Bruce Graham .40 1.00
4 Mathieu Betournay .15 .40
5 Karl Gagne .15 .40
6 Christian Gaudet .15 .40
7 Martin Karsums .40 1.00
8 Francois Caron .15 .40
9 Kevin Hamel .15 .40
10 Nathan Saunders .15 .40
11 Kevin Glode .15 .40
12 Thierry Douville .15 .40
13 Cody Doucette .15 .40
14 Joshua Hepditch .15 .40
15 Mathieu Wathier .15 .40
16 Ryan Salvis .15 .40
17 Bobby Mazerolle .15 .40
18 Konstantin Zakharov .15 .40
19 Corey Crawford .30 .75
20 Ryan Papaioannou .30 .75
21 Luke Pelham .15 .40
22 Maxime Desruisseaux .15 .40
23 Steve Bernier .40 1.00
NNO Steve Bernier TL .40 1.00
NNO James Sanford TL .15 .40

2004-05 Moncton Wildcats

A total of `1,050 team sets were produced.

COMPLETE SET (25) 5.00 12.00
1 Wesley Welcher .20 .50
2 Oskars Bartulis .20 .50
3 Corey Crawford .40 1.00
4 Charles Bergeron .20 .50
5 Kevin Glode .20 .50
6 Brad Marchand .20 .50
7 Adam Blanchette .20 .50
8 Charles Tanguay .20 .50
9 Luke Pelham .20 .50
10 Christian Gaudet .20 .50
11 Jean-Sebastien Adam .20 .50
12 Stephane Goulet .20 .50
13 Jason Demers .20 .50
14 Ryan Salvis .20 .50
15 Adam Pineault .20 .50
16 Yan Ouimet .20 .50
17 Jean-Christophe Blanchard .40 1.00
18 Stanson Donovan .20 .50
19 Martins Karsums .40 1.00
20 Bruce Graham .30 .75
21 Steve Bernier .40 1.00
22 Jerome Samson .20 .50
23 Josh Hepditch .20 .50
24 Guillaume Veilleux .20 .50
25 Nathan Saunders .20 .50

2005-06 Moncton Wildcats

COMPLETE SET (30) 8.00 20.00
1 Adam Pineault .40 1.00
2 Stephane Goulet .30 .75
3 Jean Christophe Blanchard .30 .75
4 Matt Eagles .30 .75
5 Brad Marchand .30 .75
6 Christian Gaudet .30 .75
7 Guillaume Blouin .30 .75
8 Oskars Bartulis .30 .75
9 Keith Yandle .30 .75
10 Josh Hepditch .30 .75
11 Maxime Belanger .30 .75
12 Tim Spencer .30 .75
13 Martins Karsums .60 1.50
14 Jerome Samson .30 .75
15 Jean Sebastien Adam .30 .75
16 Andrew MacDonald .30 .75
17 Philippe Dupuis .30 .75
18 Nathan Welton .30 .75
19 Nick Emanuele .30 .75
20 Jason Demers .30 .75
21 Ian-Mathieu Girard .30 .75
22 Jean-Philip Chabot .30 .75
23 Matt Marquardt .30 .75
24 Chris Morehouse .30 .75
25 Brad Ouskun .30 .75
26 Brad Smith .30 .75
27 Jhase Sniderman .30 .75
28 Josh Tordjman .60 1.50
29 Luc Bourdon .60 1.50
30 David MacDonald .30 .75

2006-07 Moncton Wildcats

COMPLETE SET (24) 8.00 15.00
1 Nicola Riopel .40 1.00
2 Andrew Macdonald .25 .60
3 Rooppertti Martikainen .25 .60
4 Matthew Brenton .25 .60
5 Randy Cameron .25 .60
6 Jason Lepage .25 .60
7 Jerome Samson .25 .60
8 Pierre-Marc Lessard .25 .60
9 Matt Marquardt .25 .60
10 Matt Eagles .25 .60
11 Nathan Welton .25 .60
12 Murdock Maclellan .25 .60
13 Jhase Sniderman .40 1.00
14 Nick Emanuele .25 .60
15 Alexi Pianosi .25 .60
16 Brad Smith .25 .60
17 Marc-Andre Labelle .25 .60
18 Chris Morehouse .25 .60
19 Brad Ouskun .25 .60
20 Patrick Campbell .25 .60
21 Igor Voroshilov .25 .60
22 Matt Boyle .25 .60
23 Kelan Herr .25 .60
24 Christian Gaudet .25 .60

2015-16 Moncton Wildcats

COMPLETE SET (23) 6.00 15.00
1 Cameron Askew .30 .75
2 William Bower .30 .75
3 Lane Cormier .30 .75
4 Noah Corson .30 .75
5 Ethan Crossman .30 .75
6 Sebastien Dupre .30 .75
7 Conor Garland .30 .75
8 Maximilian Glaessl .30 .75
9 Adam Holwell .30 .75
10 Stephen Johnson .30 .75
11 Matthew Klebanskyj .30 .75
12 Kevin Klima .30 .75
13 Kelly Klima .30 .75
14 Austin Kosack .30 .75
15 Eric Leger .30 .75
16 Zack MacEwen .30 .75
17 Zachary Malatesta .30 .75
18 Blade Mann-Dixon .30 .75
19 Liam Murphy .30 .75
20 Will Smith .30 .75
21 Jacob Sweeney .30 .75
22 Marcus Tesink .30 .75
23 Mauel Wiederer .30 .75

1997-98 Moose Jaw Warriors

COMPLETE SET (19) 5.00 12.00
1 Jay Ewasiuk .40 1.00
2 Jordon Flodell .30 .75
3 Justin Hansen .30 .75
4 Cory Hintz .30 .75
5 Chad Hinz .30 .75
6 Brent Hobday .30 .75
7 Marek Ivan .30 .75
8 Trevor Johnson .30 .75
9 Tim McEachen .30 .75
10 Donavan Nunweiler .40 1.00
11 Dustin Paul .30 .75
12 Nathan Read .30 .75
13 Scott Schoneck .30 .75
14 Shawn Skolney .30 .75
15 Dave Taylor .30 .75
16 Chris Twerdun .30 .75
17 Dreu Volk .30 .75
18 Jason Weitzel .30 .75
19 Dayle Wilcox .30 .75

2001-02 Moose Jaw Warriors

This set features the Warriors of the WHL. The set was produced by CTM Ste-Foy and was sold at Warriors home games. The production run for the set was 1,000 copies.

COMPLETE SET (22) 4.80 12.00
1 Ryan Jorde .20 .50
2 Jarad Bourassa .20 .50
3 Deryk Engelland .20 .50
4 Nathan Paetsch .40 1.00
5 Bobby-Chad Mitchell .20 .50
6 Kyle Brodziak .20 .50
7 Derek Krestanovich .40 1.00
8 Steve Crampton .20 .50
9 Sean O'Connor .20 .50
10 Brian Sutherby .60 1.50
11 Tim Plett .20 .50
12 Shawn Limpright .20 .50
13 Lee Zalasky .20 .50
14 Harlan Anderson .20 .50
15 Tyler Johnson .20 .50
16 David Bararuk .20 .50
17 Mark Kitts .20 .50
18 Craig Olynick .30 .75
19 Lane Manson .20 .50
20 Shaun Landolt .20 .50
21 Kyle Kettles .20 .50
22 Blake Grenier .20 .50

2002-03 Moose Jaw Warriors

COMPLETE SET (22) 5.00 12.00
1 John Boychuk .40 1.00
2 Jarad Bourassa .20 .50
3 Deryk Engelland .20 .50
4 Nathan Paetsch .40 1.00
5 Michael Busto .20 .50
6 Kyle Brodziak .20 .50
7 Tomas Fleischmann .75 2.00
8 Derek Krestanovich .30 .75
9 Owen Fussey .30 .75
10 Petr Jelinek .20 .50
11 Jon Kress .20 .50
12 Harlan Anderson .20 .50
13 Tyler Johnson .20 .50
14 David Bararuk .20 .50
15 Troy Brouwer .20 .50
16 Ashton Rome .20 .50
17 Lane Manson .20 .50
18 Dustin Boyd .20 .50
19 Cam Lilley .20 .50
20 Blake Grenier .30 .75
21 Steve Belanger .30 .75
22 Checklist Logo .04 .10

2004-05 Moose Jaw Warriors

COMPLETE SET (24) 8.00 20.00
1 Greg Park .30 .75
2 Jordan Henry .30 .75
3 Cole Simpson .30 .75
4 Cole Butterfield .30 .75
5 Dan Ehrman .30 .75
6 Dylan Chapman .30 .75
7 Jacob Dietrich .30 .75
8 Justin Scott .30 .75
9 Kenndal McArdle 1.25 3.00
10 Blair Jones .30 .75
11 Garrett Robinson .30 .75
12 Dustin Boyd .30 .75
13 Andre Hermanson .30 .75
14 Brennen Wray .30 .75
15 Masi Marjamaki .40 1.00
16 Stuart Kerr .30 .75
17 Riley Holzapfel .30 .75
18 Troy Brouwer .30 .75
19 Steven Gillen .30 .75
20 Ian McKenzie .30 .75
21 Carter Smith .30 .75
22 Joey Perricone .30 .75
23 Josh Lepp .40 1.00
24 Checklist .04 .10

2005-06 Moose Jaw Warriors

COMPLETE SET (25) 6.00 15.00
1 Jason Bast .25 .60
2 Dustin Boyd .60 1.50
3 Troy Brouwer .25 .60
4 Dylan Chapman .25 .60
5 Travis Ehrhardt .25 .60
6 Kyle Fecho .25 .60
7 Steven Gillen .25 .60
8 Martin Grundling .25 .60
9 Matthew Hansen .25 .60
10 Andre Herman .25 .60
11 Riley Holzapfel .25 .60
12 Blair Jones .25 .60
13 Andrew Leslie .20 .50
14 Kendall McArdle .60 1.50
15 Ian McKenzie .25 .60
16 Joey Perricone .40 1.00
17 Garrett Robinson .25 .60
18 Cole Simpson .25 .60
19 Carter Smith .25 .60
20 Bjorn Svensson .25 .60
21 Brennen Wray .25 .60
22 Jesse Zetariuk .25 .60
23 Old Dutch Foods SPONSOR .04 .10
24 Boston Pizza SPONSOR .04 .10
25 Air Waves SPONSOR .04 .10

2006-07 Moose Jaw Warriors

COMPLETE SET (24) 10.00 18.00
1 Jock Sutter .30 .75
2 Travis Hamonic .30 .75
3 Ryan Stanton .30 .75
4 Chad Suer .30 .75
5 Travis Ehrhardt .30 .75
6 Martin Grundling .30 .75
7 Keith Voytechek .30 .75
8 Neal Prokop .30 .75
9 Brady Calla .30 .75
10 Matt Isbister .30 .75
11 Garrett Robinson .30 .75
12 Brad Riege .30 .75
13 Ryley Grantham .30 .75
14 Jordan Knackstedt .30 .75
15 Jason Bast .30 .75
16 Riley Holzaphel .40 1.00
17 Michael Hengen .30 .75
18 Steven Gillen .30 .75
19 Jason Reese .30 .75
20 Cody Thoring .30 .75
21 Jason Grecica .30 .75
22 Joey Perricone .40 1.00
23 Kurt Jory .40 1.00
24 Giffen Nyren .30 .75

1990-91 Montreal-Bourassa AAA

The 25 cards in this oversized set measure approximately 3" by 3 3/4" and feature players from the AAA Midget squad based in Bourassa, a suburb of Montreal. The cards feature a posed color photo on the front, with an anti-drug inscription written in French along the bottom. The crudely designed backs have biographical data, along with the logo celebrating the 15th anniversary of the club.

COMPLETE SET (25) 2.00 5.00
1 Team Card .02 .10
2 Police Card .02 .10
3 Coach Card .02 .10
4 Coach Card .02 .10
5 Coach Card .02 .10
6 Peter Arvanitis .08 .25
7 Luc Bilodeau .08 .25
8 Luc Corriveau .08 .25
9 David Desnoyers .08 .25
10 Alexandre Duchesne .08 .25
11 Dominic Gagne .08 .25
12 Benoit Goyer .08 .25
13 Serge Kiopini .08 .25
14 Ted Laviolette .08 .25
15 Ian McIntyre .08 .25
16 Nathan Morin .08 .25
17 Valentino Passarelli .08 .25
18 Jean-Sebastien Perras .08 .25
19 Sylvain Pinel .08 .25
20 Sebastien Plouffe .15 .40
21 Simon Roy .08 .25
22 Erasmo Saltarelli .15 .40
23 Alain Savage .08 .25
24 Christian Sbrocca .08 .25
25 Patrick Traverse .30 .75

1979-80 Montreal Juniors

This oversized set (approximately 4X6) features black and white images.

1 Jeff Barratt 2.00 5.00
2 Andre Begin 2.00 5.00
3 Dennis Champagne 2.00 5.00
4 Denis Cyr 2.00 5.00
5 Ghyslain Cyr 2.00 5.00
6 Roland Diotte 2.00 5.00
7 Pierre Dubois 2.00 5.00
8 Sylvain Gagne 2.00 5.00
9 Guy Jacob 2.00 5.00
10 Mike Krushelnyski 2.00 5.00
11 Ron Lapointe 2.00 6.00
12 Richard Lavallee 2.00 5.00
13 Daniel Laxton 2.00 5.00
14 Francois Laxton 2.00 5.00
15 Francois Lecompte 2.00 5.00
16 Eikke Leime 2.00 5.00
17 Pierre Martin 2.00 5.00
18 Bill Mulcahey 2.00 5.00
19 Gates Orlando 2.00 5.00
20 Patrice Pare 2.00 5.00
21 Mario Patry 2.00 5.00
22 Fabian Pavlin 2.00 5.00
23 Roger Poitras 2.00 5.00
24 Constant Prindolo 2.00 5.00
25 Denis Savard 5.00 10.00
26 Eric Taylor 2.00 5.00
27 Denis Tremblay 2.50 6.00
28 J.J. Vezina 2.00 5.00
29 Taras Zytynsky 2.00 5.00

1955-56 Montreal Royals

This set features the Royals, Montreal's top farm team. Cards measure 5 1/4" x 4 1/2" and were issued by Hygrade Franks. Card fronts are black and white and card backs feature an ad for Hygrade Franks that encourages purchasers to collect all six cards.

COMPLETE SET (6) 50.00 350.00
1 Walter Cline 6.00 50.00
2 Andre Corriveau 6.00 50.00
3 Jacques Deslauriers 6.00 50.00
4 Cec Hoekstra 10.00 60.00
5 Gerry McNeil 20.00 100.00
6 Guy Rousseau 10.00 60.00

1993-94 Muskegon Fury

This 20-card set of the Muskegon Fury of the Colonial Hockey League was produced by Rising Star Sports Promotions. The cards feature action photography on the front inside a teal border, along with league logo and player name, number and position. the backs have complete stats but are unnumbered.

COMPLETE SET (20) 10.00 25.00
1 Header Card .08 .25
2 Steve Ludzik CO .50 1.25
3 Bob Jones .50 1.25
4 Darrel Newman .50 1.25
5 Brett Seguin .50 1.25
6 Dan Woodley .75 2.00
7 Jodi Murphy .50 1.25
8 Mark Karpen .50 1.25
9 Robert Melanson .50 1.25
10 Paul Kelly .50 1.25
11 Joey Simon .50 1.25
12 Scott Feasby .50 1.25
13 Scott Campbell .50 1.25
14 Joe Hawley .50 1.25
15 Justin Morrison .50 1.25
16 Roch Belley 1.25 3.00
17 Todd Charlesworth .75 2.00
18 Kevin Barrett .50 1.25
19 Mark Turner .50 1.25
20 Steve Herniman .50 1.25

1994-95 Muskegon Fury

This 18-card set of the Muskegon Fury of the CHL was produced by Rising Star Sports Promotions and sponsored by McDonald's. The cards feature and action photo inside a teal border. The logos of Rising Star and the CHL are prominently displayed alongside the player's name and position. Card backs contain complete career and personal stats, but are unnumbered. These cards are very similar in design to other Muskegon sets; check the stats on the back to determine the year of your set.

COMPLETE SET (18) 3.00 8.00
1 Header Card .02 .10
2 Rich Parent .40 1.00
3 Grant Block .20 .50
4 Justin Morrison .20 .50
5 Scott Feasby .20 .50
6 Scott Campbell .20 .50
7 Mark Vilneff .20 .50
8 Brett Seguin .20 .50
9 Todd Charlesworth .20 .50
10 Marc Saumier .20 .50
11 Norm Krumpschmid .20 .50
12 Darryl Gilmour .30 .75
13 Paul Kelly .20 .50
14 Steve Walker .20 .50
15 Wes McCauley .20 .50
16 Steve Herniman .20 .50
17 Andy Bezeau .20 .50
18 Jamie Black .20 .50

1995-96 Muskegon Fury

This 20-card set produced by Rising Star Promotions and sponsored by McDonald's features the Muskegon Fury of the Colonial Hockey League. The card fronts have a color action photo within a teal border. The league logo is in the lower left, with player name, number and position along the bottom. The back contains career information for each player. The cards are unnumbered. The design for this set is eerily similar to the previous two years: collectors should check the stats on the back to ascertain which year their set is from.

COMPLETE SET (20) 4.00 10.00
1 Team Photo .20 .50
2 Mark Vilneff .20 .50
3 Kyle Haviland .20 .50
4 Brett Seguin .20 .50
5 Rick Girhiny .20 .50
6 Cory Johnson .20 .50
7 Paul Kelly .20 .50
8 Mark Turner .20 .50
9 Scott Feasby .20 .50
10 Stephen Webb .30 .75
11 Bobby Wallwork .20 .50
12 Richard Fatrola .20 .50
13 Steve Walker .20 .50
14 Robert Melanson .20 .50
15 Rich Parent .60 1.50
16 Jamie Hearn .20 .50
17 Brian Greer .20 .50
18 Steve Herniman .20 .50
19 Terry Ficorelli ANN .02 .10
20 McDonald's .02 .10
Sponsor

1998-99 Muskegon Fury

This set features the Fury of the UHL. The cards were issued as promotional giveaways over the course of several home games, making the set difficult to complete.

COMPLETE SET (30) 12.00 30.00
1 Terry Ficorelli ANN .02 .10
2 Jason Pain .60 1.50
3 Furious Fred MAS .02 .10
4 Lubos Krajcovic .60 1.50
5 Chris Maillet .60 1.50
6 Robin Bouchard .60 1.50
7 Randy Cantu TR .02 .10
8 Francis Nault .60 1.50
9 Checklist .02 .10
10 Richard Kromm CO .02 .10
11 Joe Dimaline .60 1.50
12 Richard Kromm CO .02 .10
13 David Bouskill .60 1.50
14 Cory Banika .75 2.00
15 Rob Melanson .60 1.50
16 John Vary .60 1.50
17 Ginman Tire AD .01 .05
18 Andy Bezeau .75 2.00
18 Steve Webb .75 2.00
19 Paul Willett .60 1.50
20 Mike Feasby .60 1.50
21 Sergei Kharin .75 2.00
22 Denis Khlopotnov .75 2.00
23 David Beauregard .75 2.00
24 Dmitri Emilyantsev .60 1.50
25 Mark Vilneff .60 1.50
26 Scott Feasby .60 1.50
27 Andrei Petrunin .75 2.00
28 Vadim Podrezov .60 1.50
29 Grant Richison .60 1.50
30 Tony Lisman GM .02 .10

1999-00 Muskegon Fury

This set features the Fury of the UHL. The set was produced by Roox and issued as a promotional giveaway over the course of several games throughout the season.

COMPLETE SET (36) 8.00 20.00
1 Sergei Kharin .30 .75
2 Vadim Podrezov .30 .75
3 Andrei Petrunin .40 1.00
4 Scott Feasby .30 .75
5 Joe Dimaline .40 1.00
6 Rob Melanson .30 .75
7 Robin Bouchard .30 .75
8 Muskegon Fury .30 .75
9 Quinn Hancock .30 .75
10 Francis Nault .30 .75
11 Alex Vasilevski .30 .75
12 Mark Vilneff .30 .75
13 Andrew Luciuk .30 .75
14 Bob Janosz .40 1.00
15 Chris Maillet .30 .75
16 Tomas Kapusta .30 .75
17 Mike McCourt .30 .75
18 Brian Tucker .30 .75
19 Aaron Porter .30 .75
20 Jason Rose .30 .75
21 Alain LaPlante .30 .75
22 Mike Feasby .08 .25
23 Terry Ficorelli .08 .25
24 Furious Fred MAS .08 .25
25 Richard Kromm CO .08 .25
26 Phil Kopinski TR .08 .25
27 Mikhail Nemirovsky .30 .75
28 Don McSween .30 .75
29 Dalen Hrooshkin .30 .75
30 Lucas Nehrling .30 .75
31 1999-00 Fury AS .30 .75
32 Tony Lisman GM .08 .25
33 Checklist .08 .25
34 Rob Hutson .30 .75
35 Joel Gardner .30 .75
36 Muskegon Fury .20 .50

2000-01 Muskegon Fury

This set features the Fury of the UHL. The cards were handed out as promotional giveaways over the course of several games, and were sponsored by a local tire store.

COMPLETE SET (30) 15.00 30.00
1 Robin Bouchard .40 1.00
2 Philippe Roy .60 1.50
3 Alain O'Driscoll .40 1.00
4 Todd Robinson .60 1.50
5 J.F. Tremblay .40 1.00
6 Ed Kowalski .40 1.00
7 Dean Mayrand .40 1.00
8 Glenn Crawford .60 1.50
9 Sergei Kharin .40 1.00
10 Andrew Luciuk .40 1.00
11 Sylvain Daigle .60 1.50
12 Maxim Linnik .60 1.50
13 Andrew Merrick .40 1.00
14 Mark Vilneff .40 1.00
15 Rob Melanson .40 1.00
16 Scott Feasby .60 1.50
17 Quinn Hancock .40 1.00
18 Francis Nault .40 1.00
19 Krikor Arman .40 1.00
20 Richard Kromm CO .40 1.00
21 Joe Dimaline .40 1.00
22 Justin Martin .40 1.00
23 Alexei Krovopuskov .40 1.00
24 Rob Hutson .40 1.00
25 Furious Fred MAS .04 .10
26 Scott Hlady .40 1.00
27 Phil Kopinski TR .04 .10
28 Rick Emmett .40 1.00
29 Scott Myers .40 1.00
30 Terry Ficorelli ANN .04 .10

2002-03 Muskegon Fury

COMPLETE SET (27) 4.00 10.00
1 Brant Blackned .20 .50
2 Robin Bouchard .20 .50
3 Josh Burk .20 .50
4 Mike Busniuk HCO .04 .10
5 Sylvain Daigle .30 .75
6 Rustyn Dolyny .20 .50
7 Terry Ficorelli ANN .04 .10
8 John Glavota .20 .50
9 Shane Glover .20 .50
10 Scott Hollis .20 .50
11 Rob Kennedy EQM .04 .10
12 Jeff Kozakowski .20 .50
13 Tony Lisman OWNER .04 .10
14 Andrew Luciuk .20 .50
15 Jeff Lukasak .20 .50
16 Mike Feasby ACO .04 .10
17 Steven MacIntyre .20 .50
18 Philippe Plante .20 .50
19 Chris Porowski TR .04 .10
20 Billy Pugliese .20 .50
21 Gary Ricciardi .20 .50
22 Todd Robinson .20 .50
23 Scott Feasby .20 .50
24 Brandon Snee .20 .50
25 Travis Thiessen .20 .50
26 Furious Fred Mascot .04 .10
NNO Checklist .04 .10

2003-04 Muskegon Fury

COMPLETE SET (23) 4.00 10.00
1 David Ambler .20 .50
2 Brant Blackned .20 .50
3 Robin Bouchard .20 .50
4 Sylvain Daigle .30 .75
5 Rustyn Dolyny .20 .50
6 Scott Feasby .20 .50
7 B.J. Gaustad .20 .50
8 Brian Haaland .30 .75
9 Scott Hollis .20 .50
10 Jason Jaworski .20 .50
11 Trevor Johnson .20 .50
12 Jason Lawmaster .30 .75
13 Jeff Nelson .20 .50
14 Dave Noel-Bernier .20 .50
15 Tyler Palmer .20 .50
16 Michal Pinc .20 .50
17 Billy Pugliese .20 .50
18 Todd Robinson .20 .50
19 Petr Suchanek .20 .50
20 Garry Toor .20 .50
21 Todd Nelson CO .04 .10
22 Chris Davidson-Adams EQM .04 .10
23 Brad Chavis TR .04 .10

2005-06 Muskegon Fury

COMPLETE SET (24) 6.00 15.00
1 Brett Angel .40 1.00
2 Robin Bouchard .30 .75
3 Bill Collins .30 .75
4 Rustyn Dolyny .30 .75
5 Ken Fels .40 1.00
6 Nigel Hawryliw .30 .75
7 Jon Insana .30 .75
8 Trevor Johnson .30 .75
9 Ryan Keller .30 .75
10 Kevin LaPointe .40 1.00
11 Jason Lawmaster .40 1.00
12 Jeff Nelson .30 .75
13 Steve O'Rourke .30 .75
14 Jeff Petruic .30 .75

15 Joe Pomaranski .30 .75
16 Clayton Pool .40 1.00
17 Todd Robinson .30 .75
18 David Van Drunen .30 .75
19 Clay Wilson .30 .75
20 David Wrigley .30 .75
21 Bill Zalba .30 .75
22 Todd Nelson CO .04 .10
23 Furious Fred MASCOT .04 .10
24 Terry Ficorelli VPC .04 .10

1984-85 Nanaimo Clippers

Thi set features the Clippers of the BCJHL. The cards are oversized (3 X 5) and feature posed shots on the ice. The set was sponsored by the RCMP and local businesses. The cards are unnumbered and so are listed in alphabetical order. Checklist provided by the good folks at Ab. D Cards.

COMPLETE SET (22) 8.00 20.00
1 Team Picture .20 .50
2 Jay Barner .40 1.00
3 Dale Brisco .40 1.00
4 Chris Calverley .40 1.00
5 Jamie Cayford .40 1.00
6 Carey Coroy .40 1.00
7 Brian Deleeuw .40 1.00
8 Frank Furlan .60 1.50
9 Bill Hardy .40 1.00
10 Rick Hunt .40 1.00
11 Rob Jack .60 1.50
12 Al Johnson .40 1.00
13 Gery Keremidschieff .40 1.00
14 Wade Michalenko .40 1.00
15 Mitch Poulin .40 1.00
16 Kevin Rabbitt .40 1.00
17 Rob Schmidt .40 1.00
18 Ron Sparks .40 1.00
19 Joe Stanley .40 1.00
20 Rod Summers .40 1.00
21 Kevin Thorlakson .40 1.00
22 Darren Wourns .60 1.50

1991-92 Nanaimo Clippers

This oversized set features the Nanaimo Clippers of the British Columbia JHL. The cards measure approximately 3 1/2 x 5 and are full color. They were produced by DEC.

COMPLETE SET (22) 3.00 8.00
1 Glenn Calder .15 .40
2 Wade Dayley .15 .40
3 Jason Disiewich .15 .40
4 Andy Faulkner .15 .40
5 Darren Holme .15 .40
6 Casey Hungle .15 .40
7 Jim Ingram .15 .40
8 Chris Jones .15 .40
9 Ryan Keller .15 .40
10 Jade Kersey .15 .40
11 Scott Kowalski .15 .40
12 Sean Krause .15 .40
13 Jim Lessard .15 .40
14 Ryan Loxam .15 .40
15 Mickey McGuire .15 .40
16 Dan Murphy .15 .40
17 Jason Northand .15 .40
18 Trevor Post .15 .40
19 Brian Schiebel .15 .40
20 Sjon Wynia .15 .40
21 Shawn York .15 .40
22 Geordie Young .15 .40

1989-90 Nashville Knights

This 23-card standard-size set was sponsored by Lee's Famous Recipe Country Chicken (a restaurant chain). The fronts feature color photos with the players in a variety of action and still poses. White borders enhance the front, and the player's name appears in the border below the picture. The cards are unnumbered and checklisted below in alphabetical order.

COMPLETE SET (23) 3.00 8.00
1 Pat Bingham .15 .40
2 Andre Brassard .15 .40
3 Mike Bukta .15 .40
4 Chris Cambio .15 .40
5 Chick-E-Lee (Mascot) .08 .25
6 Glen Engevik .15 .40
7 Matt Gallagher .08 .25
Dir. Player Development
Scott Greer AGM
8 Archie Henderson CO .20 .50
9 Billy Huard .30 .75
10 Craig Jenkins ANN .08 .25
Dave Cavaliere TR
11 Todd Jenkins .15 .40
12 Brock Kelly .15 .40
13 Paul Krayer .15 .40
14 Garth Lamb .15 .40
15 Rob Levasseur .15 .40
16 Dan O'Brien .15 .40
17 Bob Polk OWN .08 .25
Ron Fuller
18 John Reid (In action) .15 .40
19 John Reid (Portrait) .15 .40
20 Jeff Salzbrunn .15 .40
21 Mike Schwalb .20 .50
22 Ron Servatius .15 .40
23 Jason Simon .20 .50

1991-92 Nashville Knights

This 24-card set of the Nashville Knights of the East Coast Hockey League was issued as a game premium. The set is unnumbered; the cards are listed by order of the player's jersey number, which is listed on the front of the card. It was sponsored by TV station WZTV, whose logo is garishly emblazoned across the card fronts.

COMPLETE SET (25) 2.80 50.00
1 Header Card .02 .10
2 San Jose Sharks .40 1.00
3 Chris Harvey 1.25 3.00
4 Chris Grassie .75 2.00
5 Daryll Mitchell .75 2.00
6 Ron Majic .75 2.00
7 Daniel Rolfe .75 2.00
8 Mark Hilton .75 2.00
9 Angelo Russo .75 2.00
10 Jeff Jablonski .75 2.00
11 Rob Dumas .75 2.00
12 Chuck Wiegand .75 2.00
13 Steve Chelios .75 2.00
14 Kevin Sullivan .75 2.00
15 Mike Hiltner .75 2.00
16 Brock Kelly 1.25 3.00
17 Paul Cohen 1.25 3.00
18 Scott Taylor .75 2.00
19 Mike DeCarle .75 2.00
20 Jim Ritchie .75 2.00
21 Michael Seaton .75 2.00
22 Frank Anzalone CO .08 .25
23 Dave Cavaliere TR .02 .10
24 Mike Eruzione 2.00 5.00
Part Owner
25 Sean Tomalty .75 2.00

1992-93 Nashville Knights

This 25-card set of the Nashville Knights of the ECHL was sponsored by WZTV and issued as a game premium. The cards feature posed photos on the front and cursory stats on the back, along with card number.

COMPLETE SET (25) 3.00 8.00
1 Header Card .08 .25
2 Nick Fotiu CO .20 .50
3 George Kozak ACO .02 .10
4 Tom Cole .15 .40
5 Scott Matusovich .15 .40
6 Chris Grassie .15 .40
7 Bob Creamer .15 .40
8 Ray DeSouza .20 .50
9 Stanislav Tkach .15 .40
10 Don Parsons .15 .40
11 Steve Sullivan .15 .40
12 Brian Ferreira .15 .40
13 Rob Dumas .15 .40
14 Michael Seaton .15 .40
15 Mike DeCarle .15 .40
16 Trevor Jobe .15 .40
17 Brian Horan .15 .40
18 Andrey Dylevsky .15 .40
19 Rob Pallante .15 .40
20 Bryan Krygier .15 .40
21 Troy Mick .20 .50
22 Darcy Kaminski .15 .40
23 Olie Sundstrom .20 .50
24 Dale King TR .02 .10
25 Kevin Krueger .02 .10
Sports Medicine

1995-96 Neepewa Natives

This blank backed set features color photos of each player along with their name and the team logo.

COMPLETE SET (24) 4.00 10.00
1 Ryan Anderson .20 .50
2 Ryan Brunel .20 .50
3 Jeff Hudson .20 .50
4 Darren Kirk .20 .50
5 Dwayne Ripley .20 .50
6 Trevor Angus .20 .50
7 Mike Baranyk .20 .50
8 Duane Hoey .20 .50
9 Spencer Platt .20 .50
10 Jeremy Robinson .20 .50
11 Ryan Ogilvie .20 .50
12 Angelo Kokanas .20 .50
13 Craig Anderson .20 .50
14 Dale Isfeld .20 .50
15 Derek Henkelman .20 .50
16 Darcy Pengelly .20 .50
17 Kori Pearson .20 .50
18 Brett Hagberg .20 .50
19 Keith Carson .20 .50
20 Todd Barth .20 .50
21 Craig Martin .20 .50
22 Jason Glover .20 .50
23 Danny Senff .20 .50
24 Billy Joe Stasiuk HCO .08 .25

1996-97 New Hampshire Wildcats

This set was handed out in conjunction with the local DARE program. The cards below are the only ones known to exist, but the numbering suggests that others were released at some point.

COMPLETE SET (10) 10.00 25.00
21 Derek Bekar .75 2.00
22 Eric Boguniecki 2.00 5.00
23 Christian Bragnalo .75 2.00
24 Eric Fitzgerald .75 2.00
25 Jason Krog 1.50 4.00
26 Mark Mowers 1.50 4.00
27 Eric Nickulas 1.50 4.00
28 Tim Murray .75 2.00
29 Tom Nolan .75 2.00
30 Steve O'Brien .75 2.00

1997-98 New Hampshire Wildcats

This set features the Wildcats of the NCAA. The cards were produced by the team and handed out to kids by members of the local police force. The odd numbering suggests other cards might exist in this series.

13 Steve O'Brien .40 1.00
14 Dan Enders .40 1.00
15 Jason Krog 1.25 3.00
16 Dylan Dellezay .40 1.00
17 Sean Matile .60 1.50
18 Chad Onufrechuk .40 1.00
19 Tim Walsh .40 1.00
20 Tom Nolan .40 1.00
21 Derek Bekar .60 1.50
22 Erik Johnson .40 1.00
23 Ryan Harris .40 1.00
24 Christian Bragnalo .40 1.00

1998-99 New Hampshire Wildcats

This set features the Wildcats of the NCAA. The singles were handed out to kids by local police officers. The set is noteworthy for including members of the school's men's and women's teams.

COMPLETE SET (18) 10.00 25.00
1 John Sadowski .40 1.00
2 Chad Onufrechuk .40 1.00
3 Dan Enders .40 1.00
4 Jason Krog 1.25 3.00
5 Sean Matile .60 1.50
6 Michelle Thornton .75 2.00
7 Kim Knox .75 2.00
8 Tina Carrabba .75 2.00
9 Megan Hales .75 2.00
10 Allicia Roberts .75 2.00
11 Samantha Holmes .75 2.00
12 Steve O'Brien .40 1.00
13 Ryan Harris .40 1.00
14 Jay Shipulski .40 1.00
15 Tim Walsh .40 1.00
16 Jayme Filipowicz .75 2.00
17 Mike Souza .40 1.00
18 Christian Bragnalo .40 1.00

1998-99 New Haven Beast

This set features the Beast of the AHL. The cards were produced by the team and sold at its souvenir stands.

COMPLETE SET(20) 4.00 8.00
1 Craig Ferguson .15 .40
2 Ian MacNeil .15 .40
3 Marek Malik .15 .40
4 Craig MacDonald .15 .40
5 Byron Ritchie .15 .40
6 Steve Halko .15 .40
7 Shane Willis .40 1.00
8 Todd MacDonald .15 .40
9 Scott Levins .15 .40
10 Dwayne Hay .15 .40
11 Chad Cabana .15 .40
12 Tom Buckley .15 .40
13 Ryan Johnson .15 .40
14 Mike Fountain .30 .75
15 Ashlin Halfnight .15 .40
16 John Jakopin .15 .40
17 Chris Allen .15 .40
Peter Ratchuk
18 Lance Ward .40 1.00
Joey Tetarenko
19 Greg Koehler .15 .40
Andrw Long
20 Marcus Nilsson .30 .75
Tommy Westlund

1989-90 New Haven Nighthawks

This black-and-white set was issued on the 20th anniversary of the Nighthawks of the ECHL. It commemorates the best players of the team's past. The set was sponsored by Casio. It is unnumbered and is listed alphabetically by player name.

COMPLETE SET (15) 4.80 12.00
1 Ken Baumgartner .75 2.00
2 John Bednarski .20 .50
3 Tom Colley .20 .50
4 Daryl Evans .30 .75
5 Ed Johnstone .30 .75
6 Alain Langlais .20 .50
7 Mark Lofthouse .30 .75
8 Hubie McDonough .60 1.50
9 Bill Plager .75 2.00
10 Ron Scott .30 .75
11 Bobby Sheehan .40 1.00
12 Doug Soetaert .60 1.50
13 Jim Wiemer .30 .75
14 Rick Dudley CO .40 1.00
15 Parker McDonald GM/CO .30 .75

1990-91 Newmarket Saints

This 26-card set features the 1990-91 Newmarket Saints of the AHL (American Hockey League). Measuring approximately 2 1/2" by 3 3/4", the fronts feature on-ice color posed action shots framed by white borders. The cards are unnumbered and checklisted below in alphabetical order.

COMPLETE SET (26) 4.00 10.00
1 Frank Anzalone CO .08 .25
2 Tim Bean .15 .40
3 Brian Blad .15 .40
4 Bryan Cousineau COP .02 .10
5 Alan Hepple .15 .40
6 Donald Hillock COP .02 .10
7 Robert Horyna .15 .40
8 Kent Hulst .15 .40
9 Mike Jackson .15 .40
10 Greg Johnston .20 .50
11 Eldred King MAYOR .02 .10
12 Frank Kovacs COP .02 .10
13 Derek Langille .15 .40
14 Lanny the dog .02 .10
15 Mike Millar .15 .40
16 Mike Moes .15 .40
17 Bill Purcell ACO .02 .10
18 Bobby Reynolds .15 .40
19 Damian Rhodes .60 1.50
20 Bill Root .20 .50
21 Joe Sacco .30 .75
22 Darryl Shannon .30 .75
23 Doug Shedden .30 .75
24 Mike Stevens .20 .50
25 Darren Veitch .20 .50
26 Greg Walters .15 .40

1997-98 New Mexico Scorpions

Little is known about this set beyond the confirmed checklist. It is believed that this set was sold by this WPHL team early in the season. Additional information can be forwarded to hockeymag@beckett.com.

COMPLETE SET (30) 4.80 12.00
1 Team Photo .15 .40
2 Regan Harper .15 .40
3 Eric Ricard .15 .40
4 Darren Wright .15 .40
5 Derek Crawford .15 .40
6 Sylvain Naud .30 .75
7 Mike Sanderson .15 .40
8 Brian Barnes .15 .40
9 Craig Hamelin .15 .40
10 Darcy Pengelly .15 .40
11 Todd Marcellus .15 .40
12 George Dupont .15 .40
13 Jordan Shields .15 .40
14 Francois Chaput .15 .40
15 Nick Hriczov .15 .40
16 Frederik Beaubien .30 .75
17 David Lessard .15 .40
18 Hugh Bertrand .15 .40
19 Kelly Morel .15 .40
20 Derek Shybunka .15 .40
21 Tony Martino .20 .50
22 Marc Sigel .15 .40
23 Brad Wingfield .15 .40
24 Tyler Boucher .15 .40
25 Carl Paradis .15 .40
26 Aldo Iaquinta .15 .40
27 Garry Unger CO .20 .50
28 Spencer MAS .02 .10
29 Team shot .15 .40
30 New Year's Celebration .02 .10

1997-98 New Mexico Scorpions II

This 12-card set was a late-season release, and contains multiple photos of a few of the team's key players.

COMPLETE SET (12) 2.50 6.00
1 Center Ice .08 .25
2 Eric Ricard .20 .50
3 Sylvain Naud .30 .75
4 Sylvain Naud .30 .75
5 Tony Martino .30 .75
6 Tony Martino .30 .75
7 Tyler Boucher .20 .50
8 Tyler Boucher .20 .50
9 Tyler Boucher .20 .50
10 George Dupont .20 .50
11 Aldo Iaquinta .20 .50
12 Spencer the Scorpion .08 .25

2001-02 New Mexico Scorpions

This set features the Scorpions of the WPHL. The set was produced by Choice Marketing and was issued as a promotional giveaway in March, 2002. A total of 2,000 sets were produced.

COMPLETE SET (23) 40.00 80.00
1 Sergei Radchenko .60 1.50
2 Trevor Hammer .60 1.50
3 Jay Banach .60 1.50
4 Shaun Fairweather .60 1.50
5 Mike O'Malley .60 1.50
6 Peter Ambroziak 2.00 5.00
7 Chris Richards .60 1.50
8 Yann Joseph .60 1.50
9 Jonathan St. Louis .60 1.50
10 Tyler Baines .60 1.50
11 Alek Stojanov 2.00 5.00
12 Jonathan Delisle .60 1.50
13 Scott Myers .60 1.50
14 Travis Van Tighem .60 1.50
15 Arturs Kupaks 1.50 4.00
16 David Cornacchia .60 1.50
17 Donald Choukalos 2.00 5.00
18 Steve Zoryk .60 1.50
19 Gatis Tseplis .60 1.50
20 Tony Martino CO .20 .50
21 Robert Haddock ACO .20 .50
22 The Scorpion MASCOT .20 .50
NNO Header Card .04 .10

2002-03 New Mexico Scorpions

COMPLETE SET (23) 8.00 20.00
1 Peter Ambroziak .40 1.00
2 Tyler Baines .40 1.00
3 Peter Brearley .40 1.00
4 Luciano Caravaggio .60 1.50
5 Leigh Dean .40 1.00
6 Mario Dumoulin .40 1.00
7 Arturs Kupaks .40 1.00
8 Stephen Margeson .40 1.00
9 Nate Mauer .40 1.00
10 Scott Myers .60 1.50
11 Mike O'Malley .40 1.00
12 Shaun Peet .40 1.00
13 Neil Breen .40 1.00
14 Tobin Praznik .40 1.00
15 Chris Richards .40 1.00
16 Craig Stahl .40 1.00
17 Dave Bourque .40 1.00
18 Bill McDonald HCO .04 .10
19 Mike Payne .40 1.00
21 Travis Van Tighem ACO .04 .10
22 Stanley the Scorpion Mascot .04 .10
NNO Checklist .04 .10

2003-04 New Mexico Scorpions

This set was produced by Choice Marketing and sold at home games.

COMPLETE SET (22) 4.00 10.00
1 Checklist .04 .10
2 Erik Adams .20 .50
3 Jeff Alcombrack .20 .50
4 Ben Gorewich .20 .50
5 Brian Barker .20 .50
6 Chris Richards .20 .50
7 Clint Wensley .20 .50
8 Danny Lorenz .30 .75
9 Vladimir Hartinger .20 .50
10 Jaroslav Kerestes .20 .50
11 Kevin Edgar .20 .50
12 Arturs Kupaks .20 .50
13 Matt Mathias .20 .50
14 Miguel Beaudry .30 .75
15 Mike Oliveira .20 .50
16 Mike Possin .20 .50
17 Shaun Peet .20 .50
18 Peter Ambroziak .20 .50
19 Craig Stahl .20 .50
20 Walker McDonald .20 .50
21 Bill McDonald HCO .04 .10
22 Mascot .04 .10

2004-05 New Mexico Scorpions

These cards were issued in strips of five as stadium giveaways at several home games.

COMPLETE SET (25) 12.00 30.00
1 Peter Ambroziak .40 1.00
2 Miguel Beaudry .75 2.00
3 Jordan Bianchin .40 1.00
4 Vladimir Hartinger .40 1.00
5 Mike Possin .40 1.00
6 Ladislav Kouba .40 1.00
7 Alexandre Piche .40 1.00
8 Aaron Schneekloth .40 1.00
9 Guy St. Vincent .40 1.00
10 Matt Weber .40 1.00
11 Erik Adams .40 1.00
12 Trevor Hammer .40 1.00
13 Andrew Katzburg .75 2.00
14 Konrad McKay .40 1.00
15 Ivan Svarny .40 1.00
16 Shawn Legault 1.00 2.50
17 Daryl Moor .40 1.00
18 Randy Murphy .40 1.00
19 Mike Oliveira .40 1.00
20 Daniel Tetrault .40 1.00
21 Ladislav Kouba .40 1.00
22 Alexandre Piche .40 1.00
23 Aaron Schneekloth .40 1.00
24 Guy St. Vincent .75 2.00
25 Matt Weber .40 1.00

2006-07 New Mexico Scorpions

COMPLETE SET (21) 20.00 35.00
1 Ray Edwards CO .10 .25
2 Randy Murphy ACO .10 .25
3 Stanley The Scorpion MASCOT .02 .10
4 Chris Robertson .60 1.50
5 Mike Falk .60 1.50
6 Scott Reid .75 2.00
7 Dave Cacciola .75 2.00
8 Andrew Smale .60 1.50
9 Ryan McLeod .60 1.50
10 Rob Guinn .60 1.50
11 Konrad Reeder .60 1.50
12 Mike Prpich .75 2.00
13 Kevin Harvey .60 1.50
14 Craig MacDonald .60 1.50
15 Jamie Herrington .60 1.50
16 Lance Herauf .60 1.50
17 Josh Garbutt .60 1.50
18 Matt Frick .60 1.50
19 Peter Kennedy .60 1.50
20 Aaron MacInnis .60 1.50
21 Vladimir Hartinger .60 1.50

1997-98 New Orleans Brass

Little is known about this set beyond the confirmed checklist. Additional information can be forwarded to hockeymag@beckett.com.

COMPLETE SET (21) 4.00 10.00
1 Jeff Lazaro .30 .75
2 Darryl LaFrance .20 .50
3 Eric Montreuil .20 .50
4 Steve Cheredaryk .30 .75
5 Brad Symes .20 .50
6 Bill McKay .20 .50
7 Martin Villeneuve .20 .50
8 Martin Woods .20 .50
9 Joe Seroski .20 .50
10 Russ Guzior .20 .50
11 Scratch Mo Mascot .02 .10
12 Kevin Pozzo .20 .50
13 Pierre Gendron .20 .50
14 Mike Minard .30 .75
15 Scott Allegrino TR .02 .10
16 Mikhail Nemirovsky .20 .50
17 Kyle Peterson .20 .50
18 Ted Sator HCO .02 .10
19 Scott King .30 .75
20 Jason Downey .20 .50
21 Eric Brule .30 .75

1988-89 Niagara Falls Thunder

This 25-card set measures approximately 2 5/8" by 4 1/8" and was sponsored by the Niagara Falls Fire Department and area businesses. The cards are printed on thin card stock. The fronts have a white card face and feature color action player photos with two thin black lines forming a border.

COMPLETE SET (25) 8.00 20.00
1 Title Card .08 .25
2 Brad May .75 2.00
3 Paul Wolanski .20 .50
4 Keith Primeau 3.00 8.00
5 Mark Lawrence .20 .50
6 Mike Rosati .40 1.00
7 Dennis Vial .30 .75
8 Shawn McCosh .20 .50
9 Jason Soules .20 .50
10 Rob Fournier .20 .50
11 Scott Pearson .20 .50
12 Jamie Leach .20 .50
13 Colin Miller .20 .50
14 Bryan Fogarty .20 .50
15 Keith Osborne .20 .50
16 Stan Drulia .40 1.00
17 Paul Laus .40 1.00
18 Adrian Van Der Sloot .20 .50
19 Greg Allen .20 .50
20 Don Pancoe .20 .50
21 Alain LaForge .20 .50
22 Bill LaForge GM .08 .25
CO
23 Steve Locke .20 .50
24 Benny Rogano ACO .08 .25
25 Heavy Evason ACO .08 .25

1989-90 Niagara Falls Thunder

Sponsored by local Arby's and Pizza Pizza stores, these 25 cards measure approximately 2 5/8" by 4 1/8" and feature on their fronts white-bordered posed-on-ice color shots of the 1989-90 Niagara Falls Thunder. The player's name appears in red lettering within the white bottom margin. The cards are unnumbered and checklisted below in alphabetical order.

COMPLETE SET (25) 6.00 15.00
1 Greg Allen .20 .50
2 Roch Belley .30 .75
3 David Benn .20 .50
4 Andy Bezeau .20 .50
5 George Burnett CO .20 .50
6 Todd Coopman .20 .50
7 Randy Hall ACO .08 .25
8 John Johnson .20 .50
9 Paul Laus .40 1.00
10 Mark Lawrence .20 .50
11 Brad May .40 1.00
12 Don McConnell .20 .50
13 Brian Mueggler .20 .50
14 Don Pancoe .20 .50
15 Keith Primeau 2.00 5.00
16 Geoff Rawson .20 .50
17 Ken Ruddick .20 .50
18 Greg Suchan .20 .50
19 Trainers .08 .25
Paul Bruneau
Dennis Scott
20 Steve Udvari .30 .75
21 Jeff Walker .20 .50
22 Jason Winch .20 .50
23 Paul Wolanski .20 .50
24 Title Card .08 .25
25 Checklist Card .20 .50

1993-94 Niagara Falls Thunder

Printed by Slapshot Images Ltd., this 29-card set features the 1993-94 Niagara Falls Thunder. The cards measure standard size (2 1/2" by 3 1/2"). On a geometrical purple and green background, the fronts feature color action player photos with thin grey borders.

COMPLETE SET (29) 4.00 10.00
1 Title Card .02 .10
Checklist
2 Jimmy Hibbert .15 .40
3 Darryl Foster .15 .40
4 Gerry Skrypec .15 .40
5 Greg de Vries .30 .75
6 Tim Thompson .15 .40
7 Joel Yates .15 .40
8 Yianni Ioannou .15 .40
9 Steve Nimigon .15 .40
10 Jeff Johnstone .15 .40
11 Brandon Convery .15 .40
12 Dale Junkin .15 .40
13 Ethan Moreau .30 .75
14 Derek Grant .15 .40
15 Neil Fewster .15 .40
16 Jason Reesor .15 .40
17 Tom Moores .15 .40
18 Matthew Mayo .15 .40
19 Bogdan Savenko .15 .40
20 Corey Bricknell .15 .40
21 Derek Sylvester .15 .40
22 Anatoli Filatov .15 .40
23 Jason Bonsignore .15 .40
24 Mike Perna .15 .40
25 Manny Legace .40 1.00
26 Randy Hall CO GM .02 .10
27 Chris Johnstone CO .02 .10
28 Jason Bonsignore .20 .50
Ethan Moreau
Brandon Convery
Towering Prospects
NNO Slapshot Ad Card .01 .05

2001-02 Norfolk Admirals

This set features the Admirals of the AHL. It is believed that this set was produced by the team and sold at home games.

COMPLETE SET (27) 4.80 12.00
1 Ajay Baines .20 .50
2 Bill Bowler .30 .75
3 Bobby Russell .15 .35
4 Casey Hankinson .30 .75
5 Chris McAlpine .15 .35
6 Craig Andersson .60 1.50
7 Dmitri Tolkunov .14 .35
8 Jean-Yves Leroux .15 .35
9 Jeff Helperl .15 .35
10 Jim Campbell .15 .35
11 Kent Huskins .15 .35
12 Matt Henderson .15 .35
13 Michael Leighton .75 2.00
14 Mike Peluso .30 .75
15 Mike Souza .15 .35
16 Nolan Baumgartner .15 .35
17 Peter White .15 .35
18 Quintin Laing .15 .35
19 Rumun Ndur .15 .35
20 Shawn Thornton .15 .35
21 Steve McCarthy .20 .50
22 Ty Jones .20 .50
23 Tyler Arnason .30 .75
24 Valeri Zelepukin .15 .35
25 Vladimir Chebaturkin .15 .35
26 Trent Yawney CO .04 .10
NNO Team CL .04 .10

2002-03 Norfolk Admirals

COMPLETE SET (26) 15.00
1 Johnathan Aitken .20 .50
2 Craig Andersson .40 1.00
3 Ajay Baines .20 .50
4 Scotty Balan .20 .50
5 Cam Bristow .20 .50
6 Brandin Cote .20 .50
7 Louie DeBrusk .20 .50
8 Casey Hankinson .20 .50
9 Jeff Helperl .20 .50
10 Matt Henderson .20 .50
11 Burke Henry .20 .50
12 Kent Huskins .20 .50
13 Quintin Laing .20 .50
14 Mike Leighton .60 1.50
15 Steve McCarthy .30 .75
16 Brett McLean .20 .50
17 Travis Moen .30 .75
18 Mike Peluso .20 .50
19 Igor Radulov .75 2.00
20 Shawn Thornton .40 1.00
21 Dmitri Tolkunov .20 .50
22 Yorick Treille .20 .50
23 Marty Wilford .20 .50
24 Mikhail Yakubov .40 1.00
25 Trent Yawney CO .04 .10
NNO Checklist .04 .10

2003-04 Norfolk Admirals

COMPLETE SET (24) 5.00 12.00
1 Johnathan Aitken .30 .75
2 Craig Andersson .40 1.00
3 Anton Babchuk .20 .50
4 Ajay Baines .20 .50
5 Michal Barinka .20 .50
6 Blake Bellefeuille .30 .75
7 Brandin Cote .20 .50
8 Matt Ellison .20 .50
9 Carsen Germyn .30 .75
10 Burke Henry .20 .50
11 Duncan Keith .30 .75
12 Matt Keith .20 .50
13 Lasse Kukkonen .20 .50
14 Quintin Laing .40 1.00
15 Adam Munro .40 1.00
16 Steve Passmore .40 1.00
17 Bobby Russell .20 .50
18 Shawn Thornton .20 .50
19 Yorick Treille .20 .50
20 Pavel Vorobiev .20 .50
21 Marty Wilford .20 .50
22 Mikhail Yakubov .20 .50
23 Trent Yawney CO .04 .10
24 Checklist .04 .10

2004-05 Norfolk Admirals

COMPLETE SET (26) 6.00 15.00
1 Craig Anderson .40 1.00
2 Anton Babchuk .20 .50
3 Ajay Baines .20 .50
4 Michal Barinka .20 .50
5 Rene Bourque .40 1.00
6 Mike Brown .20 .50
7 Brandin Cote .20 .50
8 Matt Ellison .20 .50
9 Duncan Keith .20 .50
10 Matt Keith .20 .50
11 Nick Kuiper .20 .50
12 Quintin Laing .30 .75
13 Michael Leighton .40 1.00
14 Travis Moen .20 .50
15 Jason Morgan .20 .50
16 Eric Nickulas .30 .75
17 Igor Radulov .20 .50
18 Shawn Thornton .40 1.00
19 Jim Vandermeer .40 1.00
20 Pavel Vorobiev .20 .50
21 Marty Wilford .30 .75
22 James Wisniewski .20 .50
23 Mikhail Yakubov .20 .50
24 Trent Yawney CO .04 .10
25 Training Staff .04 .10
NNO Checklist .04 .10

2005-06 Norfolk Admirals

COMPLETE SET (30) 6.00 15.00
1 Norfolk Admirals .04 .10
2 Steve Munn .20 .50
3 Michal Barinka .20 .50
4 Brian Lee .20 .50
5 Carl Corazzini .20 .50
6 Anton Babchuk .20 .50
7 Martin St. Pierre .20 .50
8 Milan Bartovic .20 .50
9 Mark Cullen .20 .50
10 Colin Fraser .30 .75
11 Dustin Byfuglien 2.00 5.00
12 Jason Morgan .20 .50
13 Nathan Barrett .20 .50
14 James Wisniewski .20 .50
15 Mike Brown .20 .50
16 Matt Keith .20 .50
17 Nick Kuiper .20 .50
18 Eric Meloche .20 .50
19 Quintin Laing .20 .50
20 Corey Crawford .40 1.00
21 Ajay Baines .20 .50
22 Adam Munro .40 1.00
23 Mikhail Yakubov .20 .50
24 Shawn Thornton .40 1.00
25 Mike Haviland HC .04 .10
26 Rick Kowalsky AC .04 .10
27 McClung .04 .10
Bender TR
28 Cinq-Mars .04 .10
Holden EQM
29 Al MacIsaac GM .04 .10
30 Pascal Bedard .20 .50

2006-07 Norfolk Admirals

COMPLETE SET (28) 6.00 15.00
1 Patrick Lalime .30 .75
2 Corey Crawford .30 .75
3 Steve Munn .20 .50
4 David Koci .20 .50
5 Brandon Rogers .20 .50
6 Cam Barker .20 .50
7 Jordan Hendry .20 .50
8 Carl Corazzini .20 .50
9 Bruno St. Jacques .20 .50
10 Martin St. Pierre .20 .50
11 Craig MacDonald .20 .50
12 Troy Brouwer .30 .75
13 David Bolland 1.25 3.00
14 Colin Fraser .20 .50
15 Dustin Byfuglien 2.00 5.00
16 Bryan Bickell .20 .50
17 Adam Burish .20 .50
18 Jonas Nordqvist .20 .50
19 Michael Blunden .30 .75
20 Pierre Parenteau .20 .50
21 Reed Low .30 .75
22 Adam Berti .20 .50
23 Brandon Bochenski .20 .50
24 Danny Richmond .20 .50
25 Al Macisaac GM .05 .10
26 Mike Haviland CO .10 .25
27 Ted Dent ACO .05 .10
28 Trainers .05 .10

2007-08 Norfolk Admirals

COMPLETE SET (30) 6.00 15.00
1 Jonathan Boutin .40 1.00
2 Marc Denis .40 1.00
3 Karri Ramo .40 1.00
4 Jay Leach .20 .50
5 Matt Smaby .20 .50
6 Mario Scalzo .20 .50
7 David Schneider .20 .50
8 Vladimir Mihalik .20 .50
9 Jay Rosehill .20 .50
10 Andy Rogers .20 .50
11 Justin Keller .20 .50
12 Adam Henrich .20 .50
13 Kyle Wanvig .20 .50
14 Norm Milley .20 .50
15 Chris Lawrence .20 .50
16 Junior Lessard .20 .50
17 Paul Szczechura .20 .50
18 Karl Stewart .20 .50
19 Radek Smolenak .40 1.00
20 Rob Klinkhammer .20 .50
21 Bracken Kearns .20 .50
22 Blair Jones .20 .50
23 Justin Fletcher .20 .50
24 Zbynek Hrdel .20 .50
25 Marek Kvapil .20 .50
26 Stanislav Lascek .20 .50
27 Shawn Collymore .20 .50
28 Steve Stirling HC .04 .10
29 Darren Rumble AC .04 .10
30 T.Alva/P.Henderson TR .04 .10

2014-15 Norfolk Admirals

COMPLETE SET (33) 8.00 20.00
1 Yann Danis .50 1.25
2 Josh Manson .30 .75
3 Kevin Gagne .30 .75
4 Nathan McIver .30 .75
5 Matt Bailey .30 .75
6 Brandon Yip .40 1.00
7 Louis Leblanc .50 1.25
8 Antoine Laganiere .30 .75
9 Steve MacIntyre .30 .75
10 Jarrod Skalde CO .30 .75
11 John Gibson .75 2.00
12 Matt Clark .30 .75
13 Nicolas Kerdiles .30 .75
14 Emerson Etem .50 1.25
15 Charles Sarault .30 .75
16 Joseph Cramarossa .30 .75
17 William Karlsson .50 1.25
18 Andrew O'Brien .30 .75
19 Dave Steckel .30 .75
20 Eric Veilleux Asst. CO .30 .75
21 Jason Labarbera .30 .75
22 Mark Fistric .30 .75
23 Brendan Bell .30 .75
24 Stefan Noesen .30 .75
25 John Kurtz .30 .75
26 Max Friberg .50 1.25
27 Brad Winchester .40 1.00
28 Chris Wagner .30 .75
29 Colby Robak .30 .75
30 Jaycob Megna .30 .75
31 Shea Theodore .40 1.00
32 Dany Heatley .50 1.25
33 Marty Wilford Asst. CO .30 .75

1982-83 North Bay Centennials

This 24-card set was printed on thick card stock. The fronts feature a mix of action poses and portraits bordered in white. The backs carry biographical information and sponsor logos, Aunt May's City Bakery (Northern) Limited and CFCH-600 Radio. The cards are unnumbered and checklisted below in alphabetical order.

COMPLETE SET (24) 8.00 20.00
1 Allen Bishop .30 .75
2 John Capel .30 .75
3 Rob Degagne .30 .75
4 Phil Drouillard .30 .75
5 Jeff Eatough .30 .75
6 Tony Gilliard .30 .75
7 Paul Gillis .60 1.50
8 Pete Handley .30 .75
9 Mark Hatcher .30 .75
10 Tim Helmer .30 .75
11 Craig Kales .30 .75
12 Bob LaForest .30 .75
13 Mark LaForest .75 2.00
14 Bill Maguire .30 .75
15 Andrew McBain .60 1.50
16 Ron Meighan .30 .75
17 Rick Morocco .30 .75
18 Alain Raymond .30 .75
19 Joe Reekie .75 2.00
20 Joel Smith .40 1.00
21 Bert Templeton CO .30 .75
22 Kevin Vescio .30 .75
23 Peter Woodgate .30 .75
24 Don Young .30 .75

1983-84 North Bay Centennials

This 25-card set measures approximately 2 1/2" by 4" and is printed on thin card stock. The fronts carry color, posed action player photos with white borders. The player's name appears in a butterscotch-colored plaque that is superimposed over the picture.The cards are unnumbered and checklisted below in alphabetical order.

COMPLETE SET (25) 8.00 20.00
1 Sponsor's Card .08 .25

2 Peter Abric .30 .75
3 Richard Benoit .30 .75
4 Scott Birnie .30 .75
5 John Capel .30 .75
6 Curtis Collin .30 .75
7 Rob Degagne .30 .75
8 Kevin Hatcher 1.25 3.00
9 Mark Hatcher .30 .75
10 Tim Helmer .30 .75
11 Jim Hunter .30 .75
12 Kevin Kerr .30 .75
13 Nick Kypreos .60 1.50
14 Mike Larouche .30 .75
15 Greg Larsen .30 .75
16 Mark Lavarre .30 .75
17 Brett MacDonald .30 .75
18 Wayne Macphee .30 .75
19 Peter McGrath .30 .75
20 Rob Nichols .30 .75
21 Ron Sanko .30 .75
22 Kevin Vescio .30 .75
23 Mike Webber .30 .75
24 Peter Woodgate .30 .75
25 Bert Templeton CO/GM .30 .75

1993-94 North Bay Centennials

Co-sponsored by MCTV and Collectors Corner and printed by Slapshot Images Ltd., this standard size 26-card set features the 1993-94 North Bay Centennials. On a geometrical yellow and black background, the fronts feature color action player photos with thin grey borders. The player's name, position and team name, as well as the producer's logo, appear on the front.

COMPLETE SET (26) 4.00 10.00
1 Brad Brown .20 .50
2 Sandy Allan .20 .50
3 Rob Lave .15 .40
4 Steve McLaren .15 .40
5 Andy Delmore .40 1.00
6 Corey Neilson .15 .40
7 Jason Campeau .15 .40
8 Jim Ensom .15 .40
9 Bill Lang .15 .40
10 Ryan Gillis .15 .40
11 Michael Burman .15 .40
12 Stefan Rivard .15 .40
13 B.J. MacPherson .15 .40
14 Lee Jinman .15 .40
15 Scott Cherrey .15 .40
16 Damien Bloye .15 .40
17 Denis Gaudet .15 .40
18 Bob Thornton .15 .40
19 John Guirestante .15 .40
20 Jeff Shevalier .15 .40
21 Scott Roche .20 .50
22 Vitali Yachmenev .30 .75
23 Bert Templeton CO .15 .40
24 Rob Kirsch ACO .02 .10
25 Brad Brown .15 .40
Vitali Yachmenev
Top Prospects
NNO Slapshot Ad Card .01 .05

1994-95 North Bay Centennials

Sponsored by MCTV, Guardian and Wingate Lottery, and printed by Slapshot Images Ltd., this 26-card set features the 1994-95 North Bay Centennials. On a yellow and black background, the fronts feature color action player photos with thin gray borders. The player's name, position and team name, as well as the producer's logo, appear on the front.

COMPLETE SET (26) 4.00 10.00
1 Joel Gagnon .15 .40
2 Scott Roche .20 .50
3 Derek Lahnalampi .15 .40
4 Brad Brown .20 .50
5 Steve McLaren .15 .40
6 Kam White .15 .40
7 Corey Neilson .15 .40
8 Jason Campeau .15 .40
9 Stephen Carpenter .15 .40
10 Trevor Gallant .15 .40
11 Alex Matvichuk .15 .40
12 Ryan Gillis .15 .40
13 Kris Cantu .15 .40
14 Stefan Rivard .15 .40
15 Brian Whitley .15 .40
16 Dustin Virag .15 .40
17 Lee Jinman .20 .50
18 Scott Cherrey .15 .40
19 Damien Bloye .15 .40
20 Justin Robinson .15 .40
21 Kody Grigg .15 .40
22 John Guirestante .15 .40
23 Gary Roach .15 .40
24 Vitali Yachmenev .30 .75
25 Shane Parker CO/GM .02 .10
Tom
NNO Ad Card .01 .05

1991-92 North Dakota

COMPLETE SET (12) 6.00 12.00
13 Hockey Team Photo .20 .50
14 Dixon Ward 1.00 2.50
Marty Schriner
Greg Johnson
hockey players
15 Russ Romaniuk .20 .50
Jeff McLean
Jason Herter
hockey players
16 Donny Riendeau .20 .50
Chad Johnson
Dane Jackson
hockey players
17 The Roseau Connection .20 .50
Chris Gotziaman
Corey Howe
Jon Larson
hockey play
18 Darren Bear .20 .50
Jamie Burt
Brad Bombardir
hockey players
19 Brad Pascall .20 .50
Dave Hakstol
Justin Duberman
hockey players
20 Jeff Lembke .20 .50
Todd Jones
Corey Cadden
Checklist

1992-93 North Dakota Fighting Sioux

This scarce promotional giveaway set features North Dakota of the NCAA. The cards are unnumbered and checklisted below alphabetically. Thirteen additional cards in this series (28-40) were recently confirmed by collector Dale Sprenger. Cards #28-32, including a key issue of Ed Belfour, were apparently included with the base set. The remaining eight cards feature ND alumni and a design similar to the Belfour and Casey base set cards. These final eight cards were available only with a purchase at local Subway sandwich shops. We have no pricing info on these cards.

COMPLETE SET (32) 8.00 20.00
1 Akil Adams .30 .75
2 Darren Bear .30 .75
3 Sean Beswick .30 .75
4 Brad Bombardir .40 1.00
5 Joby Bond .30 .75
6 Troy Davis .30 .75
7 Chris Gotziaman .30 .75
8 Dean Grillo .30 .75
9 Corey Howe .30 .75
10 Brett Hryniuk .30 .75
11 Greg Johnson .75 2.00
12 Chad Johnson .30 .75
13 Corey Johnson .30 .75
14 Todd Jones .30 .75
15 Scott Kirton .30 .75
16 Page Klostreich .30 .75
17 Jon Larson .30 .75
18 Jeff Lembke .30 .75
19 John McCoy .30 .75
20 Kevin McKinnon .30 .75
21 Darcy Mitani .30 .75
22 Keith Murphy .30 .75
23 Nick Naumenko .40 1.00
24 Jarrod Olson .30 .75
25 Lars Oxholm .30 .75
26 Kevin Powell .30 .75
27 Kevin Rappana .30 .75
28 Don Riendeau
29 Marty Schriner
30 Teeder Wynne
31 Ed Belfour ALUM
32 Jon Casey ALUM
33 Dave Christian ALUM
34 Tony Hrkac ALUM
35 Bob Joyce ALUM
36 Troy Murray ALUM
37 James Patrick ALUM
38 Russ Romaniuk ALUM
39 Garry Valk ALUM
40 Dixon Ward ALUM

2003-04 North Dakota Fighting Sioux

These cards were issued over the course of six home games. A five-card pack was given to the first 1,000 attendees who asked for them at each game. Thanks to collector Dale Sprenger for the info.

COMPLETE SET (30) 20.00 50.00
1 Brandon Bochenski 1.25 3.00
2 Nate Ziegelmann .40 1.00
3 James Massen .40 1.00
4 Quinn Fylling .40 1.00
5 Mike Prpich .40 1.00
6 Ryan Hale .40 1.00
7 Tyler Palmiscno .40 1.00
8 Matt Jones .75 2.00
9 Brad Berry ACO .20 .50
10 Chris Porter .40 1.00
11 Zach Parise 8.00 20.00
12 Drew Stafford 2.00 5.00
13 Colby Genoway .75 2.00
14 Lee Marvin .40 1.00
15 Team Logo .04 .10
16 Andy Schneider .40 1.00
17 Brady Murray 1.25 3.00
18 Engelstad Arena .04 .10
19 Rory McMahon .40 1.00
20 Matt Smaby 1.25 3.00
21 Jordan Parise 1.25 3.00
22 Brian Canady .40 1.00
23 Robbie Bina .40 1.00
24 Jake Brandt .40 1.00
25 Dean Blais CO .20 .50
26 Matt Greene 1.25 3.00
27 Erik Fabian .40 1.00
28 David Lundholm .40 1.00
29 Dave Hakstol .75 2.00
30 Nick Fuher .40 1.00

2004-05 North Dakota Fighting Sioux

These were issued as a stadium giveaway. They were handed out in five-card perforated strips only on Friday night games and only at certain doors. It was stated on the UND website that only the first 1,000 people would receive the cards so there is a potential of just 1,000 sets.

COMPLETE SET (30) 15.00 40.00
1 Header Card .04 .10
2 Robbie Bina .40 1.00
3 Jake Brandt .75 2.00
4 Brian Canady .40 1.00
5 Erik Fabian .40 1.00
6 Scott Foyt .40 1.00
7 Nick Fuher .40 1.00
8 Quinn Fylling .40 1.00
9 Colby Genoway .40 1.00
10 Matt Greene 1.25 3.00
11 Matt Jones .75 2.00
12 Rylan Kaip .40 1.00
13 Philippe Lamoureux .75 2.00
14 Lee Marvin .40 1.00
15 James Massen .40 1.00
16 Rory McMahon .40 1.00
17 Brady Murray .75 2.00
18 Jordan Parise 1.25 3.00
19 Chris Porter .40 1.00
20 Mike Prpich .40 1.00
21 Kyle Radke .40 1.00
22 Andy Schneider .40 1.00
23 Matt Smaby .75 2.00
24 Rastislav Smirko .75 2.00
25 Drew Stafford 1.25 3.00
26 Travis Zajac 1.25 3.00
27 Brad Berry ACO .20 .50
28 Carey Eades ACO .20 .50
29 Dave Hakstol CO .20 .50
30 Team Photo .20 .50

1995-96 North Iowa Huskies

This 34-card set features color action player photos on the fronts with player information on the backs. The set contains a 1995-96 season schedule of games listed below as card number 33. The cards are unnumbered and so are checklisted below in alphabetical order.

COMPLETE SET (34) 20.00 50.00
1 Dave Boehm .75 2.00
2 Mike Cerniglia .75 2.00
3 Lionel Crump .75 2.00
4 Peter Cullen .75 2.00
5 Nate Dicasmirro .75 2.00
6 D.J. Drayna .75 2.00
7 Andy Fermoyle .75 2.00
8 Matt Fetterman .75 2.00
9 Mike Fryar 1.25 3.00
10 Shane Fukushima .75 2.00
11 Bucky Gruber .75 2.00
12 Jason Helgeson TR .02 .10
13 Mark Hicks ACO .02 .10
14 Huskies CL .02 .10
15 Furlin Husky (Mascot) .02 .10
16 Ryan James .75 2.00
17 Tom Lund .75 2.00
18 Kevin Mackey .75 2.00
19 Erik Macy .75 2.00
20 Josh Mizerek .75 2.00
21 Joe Mussey ACO .02 .10
22 Gregg Naumenko 2.00 5.00
23 Matt Noga .75 2.00
24 P.K. O'Handley CO .02 .10
25 Mark Pannitto 1.25 3.00
26 Matt Romaniski .75 2.00
27 Mike Romano .75 2.00
28 Mike Rucinski 1.25 3.00
29 R.J. Schriefer .75 2.00
30 Mike Skogland .75 2.00
31 Matt Snesrud .75 2.00
32 Team Media/ .02 .10
33 Season Schedule .02 .10
34 Title Card .02 .10

1992-93 Northern Michigan Wildcats

Little is known about this set beyond the confirmed checklist. Any additional information can be forwarded to hockeymag@beckett.com.

COMPLETE SET (32) 4.80 12.00
1 Brian Barker .20 .50
2 Steve Carpenter .20 .50
3 Chad Dameworth .20 .50
4 Dustin Fahl .20 .50
5 Joe Frederick .20 .50
6 Bryan Ganz .20 .50
7 Scott Green .20 .50
8 Greg Hadden .20 .50
9 Steve Hamilton .20 .50
10 Mike Harding .20 .50
11 Jason Hehr .20 .50
12 Dave Huettl .20 .50
13 Troy Johnson .20 .50
14 Karson Kaebel .20 .50
15 Kory Karlander .20 .50
16 Rob Kruhlak .20 .50
17 Garett MacDonald .20 .50
18 Bill MacGillivray .20 .50
19 Don McCusker .20 .50
20 Brent Riplinger .20 .50
21 Dan Ruoho .20 .50
22 Corwin Saurdiff .20 .50
23 Kyuin Shim .20 .50
24 Geoff Simpson .20 .50
25 Scott Smith .20 .50
26 Paul Taylor .20 .50
27 Steve Woog .20 .50
28 Rick Comley CO .02 .10
29 Pat Ford ACO .02 .10
30 Morey Gare ACO .02 .10
31 Dave Shyiak .20 .50
32 Wildcat Willy .02 .10

1993-94 Northern Michigan Wildcats

This 32-card set was issued at one home game as a promotional giveaway. Any additional information can be forwarded to hockeymag@beckett.com.

COMPLETE SET (32) 6.00 15.00
1 Brian Barker .20 .50
2 Keith Bartholomaus .20 .50
3 Steve Carpenter .20 .50
4 Darcy Dallas .20 .50
5 Chad Dameworth .20 .50
6 Bryan Ganz .20 .50
7 Justin George .20 .50
8 Scott Green .20 .50
9 Greg Hadden .20 .50
10 Steve Hamilton .20 .50
11 Patrick Hansson .20 .50
12 Mike Harding .20 .50
13 Jason Hehr .20 .50
14 Mike Hillock .20 .50
15 Trevor Janicki .20 .50
16 Karson Kaebel .20 .50
17 Kory Karlander .20 .50
18 Dieter Kochan .40 1.00
19 Roger Lewis .20 .50
20 Garett MacDonald .20 .50
21 Bill MacGillivray .20 .50
22 Don McCusker .20 .50
23 Brent Riplinger .20 .50
24 Dean Seymour .20 .50
25 Scott Smith .20 .50
26 Paul Taylor .20 .50
27 Shayne Tomlinson .20 .50
28 Jason Welch .20 .50
29 Steve Woog .20 .50
30 Pat Ford ACO .02 .10
31 Morey Gare ACO .02 .10
32 Rick Comley CO .02 .10

2004-05 Northern Michigan Wildcats

This set was given away over the course of several NMU home games.

COMPLETE SET (27) 12.00 30.00
1 Pat Bateman .40 1.00
2 Matt Ciancio .40 1.00
3 Dusty Collins .40 1.00
4 Andrew Contois .40 1.00
5 Blake Cosgrove .40 1.00
6 Kevin Gardner .40 1.00
7 Tim Hartung .40 1.00
8 Josh Hatinger .40 1.00
9 Bob Helminen .40 1.00
10 Clayton Lainsbury .40 1.00
11 Rob Lehtinen .40 1.00
12 Matt Maunu .40 1.00
13 Jamie Milam .40 1.00
14 John Miller .40 1.00
15 Patrick Murphy .40 1.00
16 Dan Olver .75 2.00
17 Nathan Oystrick .40 1.00
18 Mike Santorelli .40 1.00
19 Andrew Sarauer .40 1.00
20 Bobby Selden .40 1.00
21 Matt Siddall .40 1.00
22 Dirk Southern .40 1.00
23 Alan Swanson .40 1.00
24 Zach Tarkir .40 1.00
25 Tuomas Tarkki .75 2.00
26 Geoff Waugh .40 1.00
27 Bill Zaniboni .75 2.00

1988 Notre Dame Smokey

This 14-card standard size set was sponsored by the U. S. Forestry Service. The front features a color action photo, with orange and green borders on a purple background. The back has biographical information (or a schedule) and a fire prevention cartoon starring Smokey the Bear. These unnumbered cards are ordered alphabetically within type for convenience. Ricky Watters is featured in this set.

COMPLETE SET (14) 14.00 35.00
12 Men's Hockey .60 1.50

2001-02 Notre Dame Fighting Irish

This set features the Fighting Irish of the NCAA. Little is known about this set, its distribution or if this is a full checklist. If you have any additional information, please forward it to hockeymag@beckett.com. Thanks to Vinnie Montalbano for updating this information.

COMPLETE SET 15.00 30.00
1 Jeremiah Kimento .75 2.00
2 David Inman .75 2.00
3 Jon Maruk .75 2.00
4 Sam Cornelius .75 2.00
5 Rob Globke 1.25 3.00
6 Neil Komadoski .75 2.00
7 Brett Lebda .75 2.00
8 Connor Dunlop 1.25 3.00
9 Evan Neilsen .75 2.00
10 T.J. Mathieson .75 2.00
11 Brad Wanchulak .75 2.00
12 Ryan Mundt .75 2.00
13 Paul Harris .75 2.00
14 Aaron Gill .75 2.00
15 John Wroblewski .75 2.00
16 Derek Smith .75 2.00
17 Cory McLean .75 2.00
18 Michael Chin .75 2.00

2002-03 Notre Dame Fighting Irish

COMPLETE SET (16) 8.00 20.00
1 Jake Wiegand .60 1.50
2 Connor Dunlop .75 2.00
3 Michael Chin .60 1.50
4 Tony Zasowski .60 1.50
5 John Wroblewski .60 1.50
6 Ad card .04 .10
7 Evan Nielsen .60 1.50
8 team card .04 .10
9 Ad card .04 .10
10 Kyle Dolder .60 1.50
11 Tom Galvin .60 1.50
12 Neil Komadoski .60 1.50
13 Brett Lebda 1.25 3.00
14 Rob Globke .75 2.00
15 Aaron Gill .60 1.50
16 T.J. Mathieson .75 2.00

2003-04 Notre Dame Fighting Irish

These cards were issued as a promotional giveaway. It's believed there could be more cards in this series. Please forward any information to hockeymag@beckett.com.

1 Joe Zurenko .40 1.00
2 Derek Smith .40 1.00
3 Cory McLean .40 1.00
4 Brad Wanchulak .40 1.00
5 Morgan Cey .60 1.50
6 T.J. Mathieson .40 1.00
7 Brett Lebda .40 1.00
8 Rob Globke 1.25 3.00
9 Neil Komadoski .40 1.00
10 Tom Galvin .40 1.00
11 Aaron Gill .60 1.50

2004-05 Notre Dame Fighting Irish

This set was issued as a promotional giveaway. It's possible the checklist is not complete. Please forward additional info to hockeymag@beckett.com.

COMPLETE SET (25) 10.00 25.00
1 Wes O'Neill .75 2.00
2 David Brown .75 2.00
3 Bryan D'Arcy .40 1.00
4 Mark Van Guilder .40 1.00
5 Victor Oreskovich .40 1.00
6 Evan Rankin .40 1.00
7 Brock Sheahan .40 1.00
8 Andrew Eggert .40 1.00
9 Luke Lucyk .40 1.00
10 Dave Venard .40 1.00
11 Michael Bartlett .40 1.00
12 T.J. Jindra .40 1.00
13 Matt Williams-Kovacs .40 1.00
14 Josh Sciba .40 1.00
15 Noah Babin .40 1.00
16 Jason Paige .40 1.00
17 Rory Walsh .75 2.00
18 Tim Wallace .40 1.00
19 Tony Gill .40 1.00
20 Mike Walsh .40 1.00
21 Matt Amado .40 1.00
22 Chris Trick .40 1.00
23 Joe Zurenko .40 1.00
24 Cory McLean .40 1.00
25 Morgan Cey .75 2.00

2005-06 Notre Dame Freshmen

COMPLETE SET (5) 2.00 5.00
1 Eric Condra .40 1.00
2 Justin White .40 1.00
3 Garrett Regan .40 1.00
4 Jordan Pierce .40 1.00
5 Christian Hanson .40 1.00

2014-15 Notre Dame Fighting Irish

COMPLETE SET () 6.00 15.00
1 Joe Aiken .30 .75
2 Anders Bjork .30 .75
3 Bo Brauer .30 .75
4 Tony Bretzman .30 .75
5 Dawson Cook .30 .75
6 Thomas DiPauli .30 .75
7 Jake Evans .30 .75
8 Steven Fogarty .30 .75
9 Jordan Gross .30 .75
10 Sam Herr .30 .75
11 Vince Hinostroza .30 .75
12 Connor Hurley .30 .75
13 Eric Johnson .30 .75
14 Chad Katunar .30 .75
15 Mario Lucia .30 .75
16 Ben Ostlie .30 .75
17 Cal Petersen .30 .75
18 Luke Ripley .30 .75
19 Robbie Russo .30 .75
20 Andy Ryan .30 .75
21 Peter Schneider .30 .75
22 Nick Stasack .30 .75
23 Ali Thomas .30 .75
24 Justin Wade .30 .75
25 Austin Wuthrich .30 .75

1984-85 Nova Scotia Oilers

This 26-card police set features the Nova Scotia Oilers of the American Hockey League. The cards measure approximately 2 1/2" by 3 3/4" and were sponsored by Q104 (an FM radio station), Coca-Cola, Hostess, and the Bedford Town Police, and the Halifax City Police. The cards display posed color player photos on a white card face. The player's name and position appear at the bottom.

COMPLETE SET (26) 6.00 15.00
1 Mark Holden .30 .75
2 Dave Allison .20 .50
3 Dwayne Boettger .20 .50
4 Lowell Loveday .20 .50
5 Rejean Cloutier .20 .50
6 Ray Cote .20 .50
7 Pat Conacher .40 1.00
8 Ken Berry .40 1.00
9 Steve Graves .20 .50
10 Todd Strueby .40 1.00
11 Steve Smith .75 2.00
12 Archie Henderson .30 .75
13 Dean Dachyshyn .20 .50
14 Marc Habscheid .40 1.00
15 Larry Melnyk .30 .75
16 Raimo Summanen .40 1.00
17 Jim Playfair .20 .50
18 Mike Zanier .40 1.00
19 Ian Wood .20 .50
20 Dean Hopkins .20 .50
21 Norm Aubin .20 .50
22 Tony Currie .20 .50
23 Ross Lambert .20 .50
24 Terry Martin .20 .50
25 Ed Chadwick CO .40 1.00
Larry Kish CO
Bob Boucher CO
26 Lou Christian TR .08 .25
Kevin Farris TR

1985-86 Nova Scotia Oilers

This 28-card police set features the Nova Scotia Oilers. The cards measure approximately 2 1/2" by 3 3/4" and were sponsored by Coca-Cola, Hostess, Q104 (an FM radio station), IGA food stores, and the Halifax City Police. The fronts display color action photos on a white card face. The sponsor logos appear across the top and in the lower corners. The player's name and position is below the picture.

COMPLETE SET (28) 6.00 15.00
1 Dean Hopkins .20 .50
2 Jeff Larmer .20 .50
3 Mike Moller .20 .50
4 Dean Dachyshyn .20 .50
5 Bruce Boudreau .30 .75
6 Ken Solheim .20 .50
7 Jeff Beukeboom .30 .75
8 Mark Lavarre .20 .50
9 John Ollson .20 .50
10 Lou Crawford .20 .50
11 Warren Skorodenski .40 1.00
12 Dwayne Boettger .20 .50
13 Daryl Reaugh 1.25 3.00
14 John Miner .20 .50
15 Jim Ralph 1.25 3.00
16 Wayne Presley .30 .75
17 Steve Graves .20 .50
18 Tom McMurchy .20 .50
19 Darin Sceviour .20 .50
20 Kent Paynter .20 .50
21 Larry Kish GM/CO .08 .25
22 Jim Playfair .20 .50
23 Kevin Farris TR .08 .25
Ralph Mosher TR
24 Mickey Volcan .20 .50
25 Ron Low ACO .40 1.00
26 Don Biggs .20 .50
27 Bruce Eakin .20 .50
28 Team Photo .30 .75

1976-77 Nova Scotia Voyageurs

Set was sponsored by Farmers Twin Cities Co-op Dairy Ltd. Cards measure 4"x 6". Cards are listed below in alphabetical order.

COMPLETE SET (?)
1 Bruce Baker
2 Mike Busniuk
3 Jim Cahoon
4 Cliff Cox
5 Dave Elenbaas
6 Brian Engblom
7 Don Howse
8 Pat Hughes
9 Peter Lee
10 Chuck Luksa
11 Gilles Lupien
12 Al MacNeil CO
13 Gord McTavish
14 Pierre Mondou
15 Hal Phillipoff
16 Mike Polich
17 Rod Schutt
18 Ed Walsh
19 Ron Wilson
20 Paul Woods

1977-78 Nova Scotia Voyageurs

Sponsored by the Farmers Twin Cities Co-op Dairy Ltd., this 24-card set measures approximately 3 1/4" by 6" and features the Nova Scotia Voyageurs of the American Hockey League. The fronts feature posed action player photos bordered in white. In the top border appears "Nova Scotia Voyageurs 1977-78," while the player's name, facsimile autograph, sponsor name and logo, and team logo are printed below the picture. The backs are blank. The cards are unnumbered and checklisted below in alphabetical order.

COMPLETE SET (24) 15.00 30.00
1 Bruce Baker .50 1.00
2 Maurice Barrette .50 1.00
3 Barry Borrett .50 1.00
4 Tim Burke .50 1.00
5 Jim Cahoon .50 1.00
6 Norm Dupont .75 1.50
7 Greg Fox .75 1.50
8 Mike Hobin .50 1.00
9 Bob Holland .50 1.00
10 Don Howse .50 1.00
11 Pat Hughes 1.00 2.00
12 Chuck Luksa .50 1.00
13 Dave Lumley 1.00 2.00
14 Al MacNeil CO .75 1.50
15 Gord McTavish .50 1.00
16 Rick Meagher 1.50 3.00
17 Mike Polich .50 1.00
18 Moe Robinson .50 1.00
19 Gaeton Rochette .50 1.00
20 Pierre Roy .50 1.00
21 Frank St.Marseille 1.00 2.00
22 Derrick St.Marseille TR .25 .50
23 Rod Schutt .50 1.00
24 Ron Wilson 1.00 2.00

1983-84 Nova Scotia Voyageurs

This 24-card police set features the Nova Scotia Oilers of the American Hockey League. The cards measure approximately 2 1/2" by 3 3/4" and were sponsored by Q104 (an FM radio station), Coca-Cola, and Hostess. The cards display posed color player photos on a white card face. The player's name and jersey number appear at the top. The three sponsors' logos are in the bottom white border.

COMPLETE SET (24) 6.00 15.00
1 Mark Holden .40 1.00
2 Bill Kitchen .20 .50
3 Dave Allison .20 .50
4 Stephane Lefebvre .20 .50
5 Stan Hennigar .20 .50
6 Steve Marengere .20 .50
7 John Goodwin .20 .50
8 John Newberry .20 .50
9 Bill Riley .30 .75
10 Norman Baron .30 .75
11 Brian Skrudland .75 2.00
12 Mike Lalor .40 1.00
13 Blair Barnes .20 .50
14 Remi Gagne .20 .50
15 Steve Penney .75 2.00
16 Michel Therrien .30 .75
17 Dave Stoyanovich .20 .50
18 Brian Patafie TR .08 .25
Lou Christian TR
19 Mike McPhee .75 2.00
20 Wayne Thompson .20 .50
21 Ted Fauss .20 .50
22 Jeff Teal .20 .50
23 Larry Landon .20 .50
24 Greg Moffett .20 .50

1996-97 OCN Blizzard

COMPLETE SET (25) 4.00 10.00
1 Rick Gregory .20 .50
2 Reynold Monias .20 .50
3 Dave Patenaude .20 .50
4 Clint Miller .20 .50
5 Alec Durocher .20 .50
6 Peter Bird .20 .50
7 Steve Ford .20 .50
8 Devin Salisbury .20 .50
9 John Brass .20 .50
10 Barrett Labossiere .20 .50
11 Cliff Duchesne .20 .50
12 Mike Stevenson .20 .50
13 Wally Wuttunee .20 .50
14 Don Boyer .20 .50
15 Jay Seymour .20 .50
16 Darren Kirk .20 .50
17 Tobias Hall .20 .50
18 John O'Toole .20 .50
19 Chad Ramsay .20 .50
20 Clayton Debray .20 .50
21 Konrad Mckay .20 .50
22 Ryan Belbas .20 .50
23 John McCusker .20 .50
24 Ryan Person .20 .50
25 Patrick Herman .20 .50

1997-98 OCN Blizzard

COMPLETE SET (24) 20.00
1 Team Picture .20 .50
2 Tucker Madder .20 .50
3 Kevin Wilson .20 .50
4 Larry Willerton .20 .50
5 Terence Tootoo 4.00 10.00
6 Clayton Quinn .20 .50
7 Shaun Rose .20 .50
8 Brad Hicks .20 .50
9 Barrett Labossiere .20 .50
10 Curtis Baldwin .20 .50
11 Jimmie Ronnback .20 .50
12 Wally Wuttunee .20 .50
13 Don Boyer .20 .50
14 Aaron Porter .20 .50
15 Alec Durocher .20 .50
16 Cliff Duchesne .20 .50
17 Devin Salisbury .20 .50
18 Cory Dittmer .20 .50
19 Derek Ernest .20 .50
20 Konrad Mckay .20 .50
21 Ryan Belbas .20 .50
22 John McCusker .20 .50
23 Ryan Person .20 .50
24 Tyler Love .20 .50

1998-99 OCN Blizzard

This set features the first card of the extremely popular Inuit star, Jordin Tootoo.

COMPLETE SET (24) 20.00 40.00
1 Team Picture .40 1.00
2 Terence Tootoo 4.00 10.00
3 Kevin Wilson .20 .50
4 Larry Willerton .20 .50
5 Morris Elderkin .20 .50
6 Darcy Johnson .20 .50
7 Shaun Rose .20 .50
8 Brad Hicks .20 .50
9 Barrett Labossiere .20 .50
10 Kevin Stoneman .20 .50
11 Jamie Vossen .20 .50
12 Jordin Tootoo 10.00 25.00
13 Aaron Porter .20 .50
14 Chad Ryan .20 .50
15 Cliff Duchesne .20 .50
16 Devin Salisbury .20 .50
17 Jimmie Ronnback .20 .50
18 Tom Herman .20 .50
19 Konrad Mckay .20 .50
20 Ryan Belbas .20 .50
21 John McCusker .20 .50
22 Ryan Person .20 .50
23 Preston McKay .20 .50
24 Brian Tucker .20 .50

1999-00 OCN Blizzard

COMPLETE SET (24)
1 Team Picture .20 .50
2 Rob Hrabec .20 .50
3 Justin Relland .20 .50
4 Cory Sawatzky .20 .50
5 Justin Seaborg .20 .50
6 Gary Lafreniere .20 .50
7 Darcy Johnson .20 .50
8 Darryl Crumb .20 .50
9 Kirk Ziefflie .20 .50
10 Jamie Muswagon .20 .50
11 Michael Young .20 .50
12 Ryan Braun .20 .50
13 Mike Glover .20 .50
14 Dustin Rogers .20 .50
15 Phillip Albert .20 .50
16 Justin Williams .20 .50
17 Dave Splawinski .20 .50
18 Steve Reid .20 .50
19 Clifford Scatch .20 .50
20 Tom Herman .20 .50
21 Terence Tootoo 4.00 10.00
22 Dwayne Twerdin .20 .50
23 Jeff Grandfield .20 .50
24 Preston McKay .20 .50

2000-01 OCN Blizzard

COMPLETE SET (25) 8.00 20.00
1 Team Picture .20 .50
2 Marc-Andre Leclerc .20 .50
3 Garrett Hildebrandt .20 .50
4 Matko Malbasa .20 .50
5 Jared Lang .20 .50
6 Darcy Johnson .20 .50
7 Alton Jackson .20 .50
8 Kirk Ziefflie .20 .50
9 Jamie Muswagon .20 .50
10 Michael Young .20 .50
11 Ryan Braun .20 .50
12 Shayne Emmons .20 .50
13 Derek Sharp .20 .50
14 Phillip Albert .20 .50
15 Justin Williams .20 .50
16 Curtis Campbell .20 .50
17 Clifford Scatch .20 .50
18 Trevor Len .20 .50
19 Terence Tootoo 4.00 10.00
20 Justin Tetrault .20 .50
21 Jeff Grandfield .20 .50
22 Dan Joyal .20 .50
23 Steve Macintyre .20 .50
24 Tim Haun .20 .50
25 Dave Splawinski .20 .50

2001-02 OCN Blizzard

COMPLETE SET (27) 5.00 12.00
1 Header Card .04 .10
2 Team Picture .10 .25
3 Louis Chabot .20 .50
4 Mike Gooch .20 .50
5 Garrett Hildebrandt .20 .50
6 Jeff Froese .20 .50
7 Cody Reynolds .20 .50
8 Andy Coates .20 .50
9 Aaron Starr .20 .50
10 Alton Jackson .20 .50
11 Kirk Ziefflie .20 .50
12 Jamie Muswagon .20 .50
13 Michael Young .20 .50
14 Ryan Braun .20 .50
15 Russell Spence .20 .50
16 Phillip Albert .20 .50
17 Justin Williams .20 .50
18 Justin Seaborg .20 .50
19 Leighton Alexson .20 .50
20 Trevor Len .20 .50
21 Mark Wallmann .20 .50
22 Justin Tetrault .20 .50
23 Mike Ouellet .20 .50
24 Everett Bear .20 .50
25 Dylan Rochon .20 .50
26 Marc-Andre Leclerc .20 .50
27 Dave Splawinski .20 .50

2002-03 OCN Blizzard

COMPLETE SET (27) 5.00 12.00
1 Team Picture .10 .25
2 Andrew Gallant .20 .50
3 Mike Gooch .20 .50
4 Garrett Hildebrandt .20 .50
5 Dallas Jackson .20 .50
6 Paul Wallmann .20 .50
7 Andy Coates .20 .50
8 Aaron Starr .20 .50
9 Alton Jackson .20 .50
10 Jared Lang .20 .50
11 Michael Young .20 .50
12 Ryan Braun .20 .50
13 Kiel Wilgosh .20 .50
14 Daniel Mayer .20 .50
15 Jason Kowalski .20 .50
16 Mike Kaluzny .20 .50
17 Ryan Weistche .20 .50
18 Trevor Len .20 .50
19 Tyler Rhyorchuk .20 .50
20 Jason Marin .20 .50
21 Everett Bear .20 .50
22 Chop Melnyk .20 .50
23 Dylan Rochon .20 .50
24 Ryan Constant .20 .50
25 Jonathon Meyer .20 .50
26 Mark Wallmann .20 .50
27 League Champs .04 .10

2003-04 OCN Blizzard

COMPLETE SET (27) 4.00 10.00
1 Header Card .04 .10
2 Everett Bear .20 .50
3 Jason Butler .20 .50
4 Ryan Constant .20 .50
5 Pierre-Olivier Girouard .20 .50
6 Mike Gooch .20 .50
7 Tim Hammell .20 .50
8 Cole Hunter .20 .50
9 Dallas Jackson .20 .50
10 Travis Kotyk .20 .50
11 Jared Lang .20 .50
12 Daniel Mayer .20 .50
13 Lyle McKay .20 .50
14 Don Melnyk .20 .50
15 Jonathon Meyer .20 .50
16 Brett Needham .20 .50
17 Lem Randell .20 .50
18 Jonathon Romic .20 .50
19 Aaron Starr .20 .50
20 Matt Summers .20 .50
21 Stephen Sunderman .20 .50
22 David Victor .20 .50
23 Mark Wallmann .20 .50
24 Paul Wallmann .20 .50
25 Kiel Wilgosh .20 .50
26 Michael Young .20 .50
27 Team Photo .04 .10

1998-99 Odessa Jackalopes

This 22-card set of the WPHL Jackalopes was handed out as a promotional giveaway at a home game in November, 1998.

COMPLETE SET (22) 10.00 25.00
1 Jacque Rodrigue .40 1.00
2 Rob Lukacs .75 2.00
3 Ryan Equale .40 1.00
4 Rick Girhiny .75 2.00

5 Terry Flynn .40 1.00
6 Paul Fioroni .40 1.00
7 Mike Ross .60 1.50
8 Johan Hagman .40 1.00
9 Sami Laine .60 1.50
10 Anders Lindberg .75 2.00
11 Dan Lavergne .40 1.00
12 Bo Anderson .40 1.00
13 Shayne LeBreton .40 1.00
14 Michael Tornquist .60 1.50
15 Christian Wibner .75 2.00
16 Chris Morque .40 1.00
17 Bill Pye .75 2.00
18 Martin Ohestedt .75 2.00
19 Joe Clark CO .02 .10
20 Pat Kerin EM .02 .10
21 Greg Andis TR .02 .10
22 Golden Corral .02 .10

1999-00 Odessa Jackalopes

This set featuring the Jackalopes of the WPHL was issued as a promotional giveaway at a home game in December of 1999.

COMPLETE SET (21) 5.60 20.00
1 Michael Tornquist .40 1.00
2 Paul Vincent .40 1.00
3 Chris Morque .40 1.00
4 Fredrick Lindh .40 1.00
5 Bill Pye .75 2.00
6 Sami Laine .75 2.00
7 Jason Pellerin .40 1.00
8 Eric Perricone .40 1.00
9 Karson Kaebel .40 1.00
10 Roy Gray .40 1.00
11 Rick Girhiny .40 1.00
12 Mark Smith .40 1.00
13 John Bossio .40 1.00
14 Mike Vandenberghe .40 1.00
15 Gary Coupal .75 2.00
16 Jacque Rodrigue .40 1.00
17 Savo Mitrovic .40 1.00
18 George Umunna .40 1.00
19 Greg Andis TR .02 .10
20 Joe Harrell EQM .02 .10
21 Kentucky Fried Chicken .02 .10

2001-02 Odessa Jackalopes

This set features the Jackalopes of the WPHL. The set was issued as a promotional giveaway at a home game. The cards are unnumbered, so they are listed in alphabetical order.

COMPLETE SET (21) 12.00 30.00
1 Trevor Allman .60 1.50
2 Jeffrey Ambrosio .75 2.00
3 John Bossio .60 1.50
4 Kenny Corupe .75 2.00
5 Matt Cressman .60 1.50
6 Adam Doyle .60 1.50
7 Robert Frid .60 1.50
8 Mike Gorman .60 1.50
9 Joe Harris .60 1.50
10 Jeff Haydar .60 1.50
11 Scott Hillman .60 1.50
12 Doug Johnson .60 1.50
13 Derek Laxdal ACO .10 .25
14 Alexander Lyubimov .60 1.50
15 Don Margettie .60 1.50
16 Don McKee CO .10 .25
17 Jacque Rodrigue .60 1.50
18 Mike Sanderson .75 2.00
19 Mark Smith .60 1.50
20 Tim Stay .60 1.50
21 Team Photo .20 .50

2002-03 Odessa Jackalopes

COMPLETE SET (24) 8.00 20.00
1 John Bossio .40 1.00
2 Matt Carney .60 1.50
3 Matt Cressman .40 1.00
4 Jerry Cunningham .40 1.00
5 Denis Desmarais .40 1.00
6 Adam Doyle .40 1.00
7 Ryan Edwards .40 1.00
8 David Francis .40 1.00
9 Robert Frid .40 1.00
10 Greg Gatto .40 1.00
11 Mike Gorman .60 1.50
12 Scott Green .40 1.00
13 Kevin Hansen .40 1.00
14 Scott Hillman .40 1.00
15 Don Margettie .40 1.00
16 Mike Rutter .40 1.00
17 Sebastien Thinel .40 1.00
18 Greg Willers .40 1.00
19 Jami Yoder .40 1.00
20 Don McKee HCO .10 .25
21 Derek Laxdal ACO .10 .25
22 Joe Harrell EQM .04 .10
23 Greg Andis TR .04 .10
24 Sonic Ad .04 .10

2003-04 Odessa Jackalopes

Produced by Grandstand Cards, this set was sold by the team at home games. The cards are unnumbered and are listed in alphabetical order.

COMPLETE SET (22) 4.00 10.00
1 Header Card .04 .10
2 John Bossio .20 .50
3 Mark Cairns .30 .75
4 Matt Cressman .20 .50
5 Adam Doyle .20 .50
6 Shaun Fairweather .20 .50
7 Jeff Goldie .20 .50
8 Mike Gorman .30 .75
9 Scott Green .20 .50
10 Wayne Hall .20 .50
11 Scott Hillman .20 .50
12 Jaroslav Kerestes .20 .50
13 Sal Lettieri .20 .50
14 Joel Martin .30 .75
15 Matt Price .20 .50
16 Mike Rutter .20 .50
17 Pat Stachniak .30 .75
18 Sebastien Thinel .30 .75
19 Danny Williams .20 .50
20 Jami Yoder .20 .50
21 Don McKee HCO .04 .10
22 Greg Gatto ACO .04 .10

2004-05 Odessa Jackalopes

This team set was issued as a stadium giveaway at a late-season home game.

COMPLETE SET (21) 8.00 20.00
1 B.J. Adams .40 1.00
2 Pascal Bedard .40 1.00
3 Matt Cressman .40 1.00
4 Paul Davies .40 1.00
5 Derek Dolson .75 2.00
6 Adam Doyle .60 1.50
7 Mike Gorman .75 2.00
8 Mike Hanson .40 1.00
9 Scott Hillman .40 1.00
10 Joel Irving .40 1.00
11 Tom Kotsopolous .75 2.00
12 John Kozoriz .40 1.00
13 R.C. Lyke .40 1.00
14 Don Margettie .40 1.00
15 Chris Paradise .40 1.00
16 Mike Rutter .75 2.00
17 Sebastien Thinel .75 2.00
18 Ben Wallace .40 1.00
19 Don McKee CO .20 .50
20 Slappy MASCOT .04 .10
21 Midland Memorial Hospital .04 .10

2005-06 Odessa Jackalopes

COMPLETE SET (19) 6.00 15.00
1 Pascal Bedard .30 .75
2 Chris Brannen .30 .75
3 Mike Carter .30 .75
4 Matt Cressman .30 .75
5 Paul Davies .30 .75
6 Andrew Davis .30 .75
7 Derek Dolson .60 1.50
8 Jeff Ewasko .30 .75
9 Mike Gorman .60 1.50
10 Scott Hillman .30 .75
11 John Kozoriz .30 .75
12 Josh Legge .30 .75
13 Dominic Leveille .30 .75
14 Adam Loncan .60 1.50
15 Jamie Lovell .30 .75
16 Don Margettie .30 .75
17 Mike Rutter .30 .75
18 Sebastien Thinel .30 .75
19 Don McKee HC .10 .25

2006-07 Odessa Jackalopes

COMPLETE SET (21) 15.00 30.00
1 Blaine Bablitz .60 1.50
2 Pascal Bedard .60 1.50
3 Chris Brannen .60 1.50
4 Matt Cressman .60 1.50
5 Andrew Davis .60 1.50
6 Derek Dolson 1.00 2.50
7 Alex Dunn .60 1.50
8 Jeff Ewasko 1.25 3.00
9 Mike Gorman 1.00 2.50
10 Scott Hillman .60 1.50
11 John Kozoriz .60 1.50
12 Jay Latulippe .60 1.50
13 Josh Legge .60 1.50
14 Don Margettie .60 1.50
15 Mike Ramsay .60 1.50
16 Mike Rutter .60 1.50
17 Steve Shrum .60 1.50
18 Brian Swiniarski .60 1.50
19 Nathan Ward .60 1.50
20 Don McKee CO .20 .50
21 Doug Johnson ACO .20 .50

1997-98 Ohio State

This 22-card set is unnumbered and listed below in alphabetical order. The cards feature top athletes from both men's and women's sports at Ohio State.

COMPLETE SET (22) 4.00 10.00
15 Chad Power HK .20 .50

1999-00 Ohio State Buckeyes

This set features the Buckeyes of the NCAA. The set was issued as a promotional giveaway at a home game.

COMPLETE SET (20) 6.00 20.00
1 Ray Aho .60 1.50
2 Peter Broccoli .40 1.00
3 Louie Colsant .40 1.00
4 Jason Crain .40 1.00
5 Yan DesGagne .40 1.00
6 Jean-Francois Dufour .40 1.00
7 Jaisen Freeman .40 1.00
8 Nick Ganga .40 1.00
9 Ryan Jestadt .40 1.00
10 Miguel LaFleche .40 1.00
11 Mike McCormick .40 1.00
12 Eric Meloche .40 1.00
13 Luke Pavlas .60 1.50
14 Jason Selleke .40 1.00
15 Andre Signoretti .40 1.00
16 Ryan Skaleski .40 1.00
17 Ryan Smith .40 1.00
18 Scott Titus .40 1.00
19 Benji Wolke .40 1.00
20 Brutus Buckeye MASCOT .08 .25

2000-01 Ohio State Buckeyes

This set features the Buckeyes of the NCAA. The set was issued as a promotional giveaway in Jan. 2001. The set is noteworthy for featuring the first cards of 2001 first-rounders Dave Steckel and R. J Umberger.

COMPLETE SET (20) 8.00 20.00
1 Andre Signoretti .30 .75
2 Jean-Francois Dufour .30 .75
3 Jaisen Freeman .30 .75
4 Jason Crain .30 .75
5 Mike McCormick .30 .75
6 Scott Titus .30 .75
7 Nick Ganga .30 .75
8 Yan DesGagne .30 .75
9 Miguel LaFleche .30 .75
10 Ryan Smith .30 .75
11 Peter Broccoli .30 .75
12 Luke Pavlas .40 1.00
13 Peter Wishloff .30 .75
14 Mike Betz .30 .75
15 R.J. Umberger 2.00 5.00
16 Dave Steckel 1.20 3.00
17 Scott May .30 .75
18 Doug Andress .30 .75
19 Brutus Buckeye MASCOT .10 .25
20 John Markell CO .10 .25

2001-02 Ohio State Buckeyes

This set features the Buckeyes of the NCAA. It was issued as a promotional giveaway at a last-season home game. The cards, which are slightly smaller than standard size, are unnumbered, and thus are listed in alphabetical order.

COMPLETE SET (20) 12.00 30.00
1 Doug Andress .60 1.50
2 Daymen Bencharski .60 1.50
3 Mike Betz .60 1.50
4 Peter Broccoli .60 1.50
5 Paul Caponigri .60 1.50
6 Jason Crain .60 1.50
7 Yan DesGagne .60 1.50
8 Miguel LaFleche .60 1.50
9 T.J. Latorre .60 1.50
10 Scott May .60 1.50
11 Mike McCormick .60 1.50
12 Chris Olsgard .60 1.50
13 Luke Pavlas .75 2.00
14 Eric Skaug .60 1.50
15 Ryan Smith .60 1.50
16 Dave Steckel 1.25 3.00
17 Scott Titus .60 1.50
18 R.J. Umberger 1.25 3.00
19 Reed Whiting .60 1.50
20 Brutus Buckeye MASCOT .10 .25

2002-03 Ohio State Buckeyes

COMPLETE SET (20) 8.00 20.00
1 Doug Andress .40 1.00
2 Daymen Bencharski .40 1.00
3 Mike Betz .60 1.50
4 J.B. Bittner .40 1.00
5 Peter Broccoli .40 1.00
6 Paul Caponigri .40 1.00
7 Miguel LaFleche .40 1.00
8 Scott May .40 1.00
9 Chris Olsgard .40 1.00
10 Luke Pavlas .40 1.00
11 Eric Skaug .40 1.00
12 Lee Spector .40 1.00
13 Dave Steckel .60 1.50
14 Scott Titus .40 1.00
15 R.J. Umberger 1.00 2.50
16 Thomas Welsh .40 1.00
17 Reed Whiting .40 1.00
18 John Markell HCO .10 .25
19 Brutus Buckeye .04 .10
20 Nathan Guenin .20 .50
Ryan Kesler
Dan Knapp{#Rod Pelley#

2003-04 Ohio State Buckeyes

This set was given away to the first 5,000 fans at the Jan. 17, 2004 home game, The cards are smaller than standard size. They are unnumbered and so are listed below in alphabetical order.

COMPLETE SET (20) 8.00 20.00
1 Doug Andress .40 1.00
2 Daymen Bencharski .40 1.00
3 Mike Betz .60 1.50
4 J.B. Bittner .40 1.00
5 Paul Caponigri .40 1.00
6 Dave Caruso .60 1.50
7 Nathan Guenin .40 1.00
8 Kelly Holowaty .40 1.00
9 Dan Knapp .40 1.00
10 Scott May .40 1.00
11 Chris Olsgard .40 1.00
12 Rod Pelley .40 1.00
13 Lee Spector .40 1.00
14 Dave Steckel .75 2.00
15 Thomas Welsh .40 1.00
16 Reed Whiting .40 1.00
17 Sean Collins .40 1.00
Andrew Schembri
18 Matt Beaudoin .40 1.00
Kenny Bernard
Matt Waddell
19 Bryce Anderson .40 1.00
Tyson Strachan
Dave Barton
20 Mascot .10 .25

2004-05 Ohio State Buckeyes

COMPLETE SET (20) 10.00 25.00
1 Bryce Anderson .40 1.00
2 Dave Barton .40 1.00
3 Matt Beaudoin .40 1.00
4 Kenny Bernard .40 1.00
5 J.B. Bittner .40 1.00
6 Dave Carusa .75 2.00
7 Sean Collins .40 1.00
8 Nate Guenin .75 2.00
9 Dan Knapp .40 1.00
10 Rod Pelley .40 1.00
11 Andrew Schembri .40 1.00
12 Lee Spector .40 1.00
13 Tyson Strachan .40 1.00
14 Matt Waddell .40 1.00
15 Thomas Welsh .40 1.00
16 Ian Keserich .75 2.00
Johan Krull
17 Matt McIlvane .40 1.00
Domenic Maiani
18 Tom Fritsche .75 2.00
Kyle Hood
19 John Dingle .40 1.00
Jason DeSantis
20 Sam Campbell .40 1.00
Phil Lauderdale
Zach Pelletier

2004-05 Ohio State Buckeyes Women

This set was issued as a promotional giveaway. The design mirrors that of the men's set from the same season.

COMPLETE SET (20) 8.00 20.00
1 Melissa Glasser .75 2.00
2 Jennifer Desson .40 1.00
3 Jeni Creary .40 1.00
4 Jaclyn Haines .40 1.00
5 Meaghan Mulvaney .40 1.00
6 Jana Harrigan .40 1.00
7 Crystal Sayther .40 1.00
8 Katie Sershen .40 1.00
9 Tessa Bonhomme .40 1.00
10 Amber Bowman .40 1.00
11 Katie Maroney .40 1.00
12 Lacey Schultz .40 1.00
13 Krysta Skarda .40 1.00
14 Erika Vanderweer .75 2.00
15 Shelby Aldous .75 2.00
Lisa Chesson
16 Jody Heywood .40 1.00
Erin Keyes
17 Jill Mauch .75 2.00
Pamela Patterson
18 Mallory Peckels .40 1.00
Rachel Vanscoy
19 Jackie Barto CO .04 .10
20 Buckeye MASCOT .04 .10

2005-06 Ohio State Buckeyes

COMPLETE SET (25) 8.00 20.00
1 Bryce Anderson .30 .75
2 Dave Barton .30 .75
3 Matt Beaudoin .30 .75
4 Kenny Bernard .30 .75
5 Dave Caruso .60 1.50
6 Sean Collins .30 .75
7 Tom Fritsche .60 1.50
8 Nate Guenin .30 .75
9 Kyle Hood .30 .75
10 Dan Knapp .30 .75
11 Domenic Maiani .30 .75
12 Rod Pelley .60 1.50
13 Andrew Schembri .30 .75
14 Tyson Strachan .30 .75
15 Matt Waddell .30 .75
16 Ian Keserich SO .60 1.50
17 Zach Pelletier SO .30 .75
18 Jason DeSantis SO .30 .75
19 Phil Lauderdale SO .30 .75
20 Johann Kroll SO .30 .75
21 Sam Campbell SO .30 .75
22 Matt McIlvane SO .30 .75
23 John Dingle SO .30 .75
24 Corey Elkins FR .30 .75
25 Nick Biondo FR .30 .75

2006-07 Ohio State Buckeyes

COMPLETE SET (25) 15.00 25.00
1 Bryce Anderson .40 1.00
2 Dave Barton .40 1.00
3 Matt Beaudoin .40 1.00
4 Kenny Bernard .40 1.00
5 Sean Collins .40 1.00
6 Jason DeSantis .40 1.00
7 John Dingle .40 1.00
8 Tommy Goebel .40 1.00
9 Johann Kroll .40 1.00
10 Domenic Maiani .40 1.00
11 Matt McIlvane .40 1.00
12 Andrew Schembri .40 1.00
13 Tyson Strachan .40 1.00
14 Matt Waddell .40 1.00
15 Phil Lauderdale .40 1.00
16 Nick Filion .60 1.50
17 Corey Elkins .40 1.00
18 Nick Biondo .40 1.00
19 Tom Fritsche .60 1.50
20 Zach Pelletier .40 1.00
21 Kyle Hood .40 1.00
22 Sam Campbell .40 1.00
23 Joe Palmer .60 1.50
24 Mathieu Picard .40 1.00
25 Brutus Buckeye MASCOT .10 .25

2006-07 Ohio State Buckeyes Women

COMPLETE SET (20) 15.00 25.00
1 Mallory Peckels .50 1.25
2 Katie Maroney .50 1.25
3 Jody Heywood .50 1.25
4 Tessa Bonhomme .50 1.25
5 Erika Vanderveer .50 1.25
6 Whitney Miller .50 1.25
7 Hayley Klassen .50 1.25
8 Lisa Chesson .50 1.25
9 Liana Bonanno .50 1.25
10 Krysta Skarda .50 1.25
11 Jill Mauch .50 1.25
12 Erin Keys .50 1.25
13 Kelly Cahill .50 1.25
14 Olivia Antognoli .50 1.25
15 Lacey Schultz .50 1.25
16 Morgan Marziali .50 1.25
17 Megan Hostasek .50 1.25
18 Amber Bowman .50 1.25
19 Shelby Aldous .50 1.25
20 The Freshmen .50 1.25

2007-08 Ohio State Buckeyes

1 Nick Biondo .15 .40
2 Jason DeSantis .15 .40
3 John Dingle .15 .40
4 Corey Elkins .15 .40
5 Nick Filion .15 .40
6 Tom Fritsche .15 .40
7 Tommy Goebel .15 .40
8 Kyle Hood .15 .40
9 Johann Kroll .15 .40
10 Phil Lauderdale .15 .40
11 Matt McIlvane .15 .40
12 Joseph Palmer .15 .40
13 Zach Pelletier .15 .40
14 Mathieu Picard .15 .40
15 J.Albert/E.Belanger .15 .40
16 Boyd/Carlson/Gorham .15 .40
17 Markell/Reed/Reed .15 .40
18 Rudasill/Schafer/Severyn .15 .40
19 Sims/Somma/Toy .15 .40
20 Brutus Buckeye MASCOT .10 .40

2005-06 OHL Bell All-Star Classic

COMPLETE SET (38) 8.00 20.00
1 Kevin Lalande .20 .50
2 David Bolland .20 .50
3 Wojtek Wolski .40 1.00
4 Bobby Ryan .40 1.00
5 Matt Lashoff .20 .50
6 John Vigilante .20 .50
7 Cory Emmerton .20 .50
8 Derek Joslin .20 .50
9 Andrej Sekera .20 .50
10 Marc Staal .20 .50
11 Chris Stewart .20 .50
12 Jonathan D'Aversa .20 .50
13 Ryan Parent .20 .50
14 Peter Aston .20 .50
15 Benoit Pouliot .40 1.00
16 Dan Lacosta .20 .50
17 Jordan Owens .40 1.00
18 Patrick McNeill .20 .50
19 Peter Tsimikalis .20 .50
20 Andrew Marshall .20 .50
21 Bobby Sanguinetti .20 .50
22 Michael Blunden .40 1.00
23 Ryan Callahan .20 .50
24 Adam Dennis .40 1.00
25 Justin Donati .20 .50
26 Steve Downie .75 2.00
27 Tyler Haskins .20 .50
28 Dylan Hunter .20 .50
29 Tyler Kennedy .20 .50
30 Scott Lehman .20 .50
31 Bryan Little .40 1.00
32 Ryan MacDonald .20 .50
33 Evan McGrath .40 1.00
34 Ryan O'Marra .40 1.00
35 Chad Painchaud .20 .50
36 Tommy Pyatt .20 .50
37 Robbie Schremp .40 1.00
38 Jordan Staal 1.25 3.00
39 Matt Kelly .20 .50
40 Jamie Tardif .20 .50

1992-93 Oklahoma City Blazers

This 18-card standard-size set was sponsored by TD's Sports Cards (a Tulsa baseball card store) and Planters Nuts and Snacks. Ten thousand sets were produced. Randomly inserted throughout the sets were 350 autographed cards of each player. The cards feature color action player photos with white borders. The player's name is superimposed on the photo at the bottom. The cards are unnumbered and checklisted below in alphabetical order.

COMPLETE SET (18) 3.00 8.00
1 Title Card .08 .25
2 Carl Boudreau .20 .50
3 Joe Burton .20 .50
4 Sylvain Fleury .20 .50
5 Brendan Garvey .20 .50
6 Guy Girouard .20 .50
7 Sean Gorman .20 .50
8 Jamie Hearn .20 .50
9 Craig Johnson .20 .50
10 Paul Krake .30 .75
11 Chris Laganas .20 .50
12 Daniel Larin .20 .50
13 Mark McGinn .20 .50
14 Alan Perry .30 .75
15 Steve Simoni .20 .50
16 Jim Solly .20 .50
17 Boyd Sutton .20 .50
18 Team Photo .20 .50

1993-94 Oklahoma City Blazers

Like each of the CHL sets issued that year, these are round cards approximately the size of a hockey puck. They come in a plastic container with the team logo on the front, and were sold at home games by the booster club for about $5.

COMPLETE SET (18) 3.00 8.00
1 Kent Anderson .20 .50
2 Carl Boudreau .20 .50
3 Joe Burton .20 .50
4 Mike Ciolli .20 .50
5 Guy Girouard .20 .50
6 Jules Jardine .20 .50
7 Craig Johnson .20 .50
8 Chris Laganas .20 .50
9 Jeff Massey .20 .50
10 Derry Menard .20 .50
11 Trent Pankewicz .20 .50
12 Alan Perry .30 .75
13 James Richmond .20 .50
14 Bruce Shoebottom .20 .50
15 Steve Simoni .20 .50
16 Jim Solly .20 .50
17 Mike Williams .20 .50
18 Mike McEwen CO .07 .20

1998-99 Oklahoma City Blazers

This 23-card set of the CHL Blazers was sold by the team late in the season at its souvenir stands.

COMPLETE SET (23) 4.00 10.00
1 Peter Arvanitis .20 .50
2 Dan Fournel .20 .50
3 Dominic Fafard .20 .50
4 Craig Willard .20 .50
5 Simon Olivier .20 .50
6 Joe Burton .30 .75
7 Craig Johnson .20 .50
8 Tom Gomes .20 .50
9 Steve Moore .20 .50
10 Jim Jensen .20 .50
11 Brad Preston .20 .50
12 Rod Butler .20 .50
13 Michael Pozzo .20 .50
14 Chris Johnston .20 .50
15 Hardy Sauter .20 .50
16 Jean-Ian Filiatrault .30 .75
17 Mike Williams .20 .50
18 Doug Sauter HCO .02 .10
19 Corey MacIntyre .20 .50
20 Daniel Larin .20 .50
21 Brandon Rose TR .02 .10
22 Team Photo .20 .50
23 Checklist .02 .10

2003-04 Oklahoma City Blazers

This set was sold at home games. The cards are unnumbered and listed in alphabetical order.

COMPLETE SET (24) 4.00 10.00
1 Header Card .04 .10
2 Peter Arvanitis .20 .50
3 Boyd Ballard .30 .75
4 Les Borsheim .20 .50
5 Ryan Campbell .20 .50
6 Sean Connors .30 .75
7 Qamil Charlie Elezi .30 .75
8 Tyler Fleck .20 .50
9 Bryan Forslund .20 .50
10 Brad Herauf .20 .50
11 Stefan Katalina .20 .50
12 Justin Kot .20 .50
13 Tim Laurila .20 .50
14 Mike Lucci .20 .50
15 Blair Manning .20 .50
16 Peter Robertson .20 .50
17 Jesse Saltmarsh .20 .50
18 Hardy Sauter .20 .50
19 Doug Sheppard .20 .50
20 Marty Standish .30 .75
21 Ryan Watson .20 .50
22 Doug Sauter HCO .04 .10
23 Sponsor .04 .10
24 Sponsor .04 .10

2004-05 Oklahoma City Blazers

COMPLETE SET (24) 10.00 25.00
1 B.J. Ballas .40 1.00
2 Jarad Bourassa .40 1.00
3 Michel Beausoleil .60 1.50
4 Brenden Morrow 4.00 10.00
5 Hardy Sauter .60 1.50
6 Pat Hallett .40 1.00
7 Tyler Fleck .40 1.00
8 Brad Herauf .40 1.00
9 Scott Selig .40 1.00
10 Cody Loughlean .40 1.00
11 Bryan Forslund .40 1.00
12 Garrett Prosofsky .60 1.50
13 Boyd Ballard .60 1.50
14 Jason Goulet .60 1.50
15 Sean Connors .60 1.50
16 Kevin Harris .40 1.00
17 Kahlil Thomas .40 1.00
18 Shawn Weiman .40 1.00
19 Doug Sauter CO .04 .10
20 Team Photo .04 .10
21 Clyde S. Dale MASCOT .04 .10
22 Crash Test Dummies .04 .10
23 Sponsor .04 .10
NNO Header Card .04 .10

1995-96 Oklahoma Coyotes RHI

This set features the Coyotes of Roller Hockey Intl. Only 500 of these 18 card sets were printed. They were available through the Coyotes Booster Club over a several game span at the end of the season. The cards are not numbered, and therefore are listed alphabetically.

COMPLETE SET (18) 6.00 15.00
1 Kevin Barrett .30 .75
2 Joe Burton .40 1.00
3 Scott Drevitch .30 .75
4 George Dupont .30 .75
5 Jason Elders .30 .75
6 Jean-Ian Filiatrault .40 1.00
7 Johan Finnstrom .30 .75
8 Tom Gomes .30 .75
9 Radek Hamr .30 .75
10 Ross Harris .40 1.00
11 Jason Knox .30 .75
12 Perry Neufeld .30 .75
13 Darcy Pengelly .30 .75
14 Trevor Sherban .30 .75
15 Peter Skudra .75 2.00
16 Darren Stolk .30 .75
17 Rob Weingartner .30 .75
18 Guy Gadowsky CO .08 .25

2006-07 Okotoks Oilers

COMPLETE SET (24) 12.00 20.00
1 Nathan Brummit .40 1.00
2 Jesse Budkins .40 1.00
3 Derrick Burnett .40 1.00
4 David Civitarese .40 1.00
5 Dan Conacher .40 1.00
6 Justin Daigle .40 1.00
7 Bradley Eidsness .40 1.00
8 Mark Jensen .40 1.00
9 Curtis Leinweber .40 1.00
10 Zack MacKinnon .40 1.00
11 Spencer Mcelhinney .40 1.00
12 Carter Madsen .40 1.00
13 Jeff Matheson .40 1.00
14 Andrew Owsiak .40 1.00
15 Jesse Perrin .40 1.00
16 Jeff Sapisha .40 1.00
17 Brian Schmautz .40 1.00
18 Kyle Schussler .40 1.00
19 Elliott Sheen .40 1.00
20 Everett Sheen .40 1.00
21 Devin Welsh .40 1.00
22 Garry Vanhereweghe•CO• .10 .25
23 Trevor McFarlane•ACO• .10 .25
24 Jeff Totz•ACO• .10 .25

2007-08 Okotoks Oilers

COMPLETE SET (20) 4.00 10.00
1 James Bannister .25 .60
2 David Civitarese .25 .60
3 Dan Conacher .25 .60
4 Mason Conway .25 .60
5 Justin Daigle .25 .60
6 Brian Doust .25 .60
7 Chris Duszynsky .25 .60
8 Brad Eidsness .25 .60
9 Corbin Gavin .25 .60
10 Brandon Hoogenboom .25 .60
11 Jesse Hudkins .25 .60
12 Curtis Leinweber .25 .60
13 Zak MacKinnon .25 .60
14 Carter Madsen .25 .60
15 Amory Mudrewich .25 .60
16 Jesse Perrin .25 .60
17 Derek Rodwell .25 .60
18 Kyle Schussler .25 .60
19 Elliot Sheen .25 .60
20 Braely Torris .25 .60

1993-94 Omaha Lancers

This set features the Lancers of the USHL. The set was available at hobby shops in the Omaha area and at AK-SAR-BEN arena where the Lancers play. The fronts feature posed action shots inside borders. The team name and player information appears in two stripes immediately below the picture. The cards are unnumbered and checklisted below in alphabetical order.

COMPLETE SET (28) 4.00 10.00
1 Ryan Bencurik .15 .40
2 Jeff Borders .15 .40
3 Sean Bowman .15 .40
4 Doc Del Castillo ACO .02 .10
5 Jeff Edwards .15 .40
6 Tony Gasparini .15 .40
7 Mike Guentzel CO .02 .10
8 Scott Haig .15 .40
9 Ken Hemenway .15 .40
10 Bill Hubbard .15 .40
11 Klage Kaebel .15 .40
12 Rob Klasnick .15 .40
13 Tony Kolozsy .15 .40
14 Tom Kowal .15 .40
15 Charlie Lentz .15 .40
16 Justin Lyle .15 .40
17 Chris Marvel .15 .40
18 Mike Peluso .15 .40
19 Scott Pionk ACO .02 .10
20 Dan Riva .15 .40
21 Nathan Rocheleau .15 .40
22 Eric Runyan .15 .40
23 Joe Russo .15 .40
24 Brian Swanson .40 1.00
25 Scott Swanson .15 .40
26 Justin Theel .15 .40
27 Jamie Thompson .15 .40
28 Brendan Walsh .15 .40

2002-03 Orlando Seals

It's possible this checklist is incomplete.

COMPLETE SET 6.00 15.00
1 B.J. Stephens .40 1.00
2 Mike Correia .40 1.00
3 Stan Drulia HCO .40 1.00
4 Mascot .04 .10
5 Todd Bennett .40 1.00
6 Chris LiPuma .40 1.00
7 Louis Goulet .40 1.00
8 Zac Boyer .40 1.00
9 David Goverde .60 1.50
10 Mark White .40 1.00
11 Jad Ramsay .40 1.00
12 Joe Spencer .40 1.00
13 Sponsor Card .04 .10
14 Ethan Burnes .40 1.00
15 Ryan Anderson .40 1.00
16 Mascot .04 .10
17 Chris Cerrella .40 1.00
18 Todd Nowicki .40 1.00
19 Joe Seroski .40 1.00

1998-99 Orlando Solar Bears

This set features the Solar Bears of the IHL. This issue was sold in team set form at home games and is much easier to find than the giveaway cards issued later that season.

COMPLETE SET (19) 4.00 10.00
1 Checklist .02 .10
Logo card
2 Patrick Neaton .20 .50
3 Sean McCann .20 .50
4 Clayton Norris .20 .50
5 Hubie McDonough .30 .75
6 Shawn Carter .20 .50
7 Grigori Panteleyev .30 .75
8 Todd Richards .30 .75
9 Shawn Wansborough .20 .50
10 Mark Beaufait .40 1.00
11 Scott Hollis .20 .50
12 David Mackey .20 .50
13 David Littman .30 .75
14 Grigori Panteleyev AS .30 .75
15 Mark Beaufait AS .40 1.00
16 Curt Fraser CO .20 .50
17 Peter Horachek ACO .20 .50
18 Orlando Arena .20 .50
19 Shades MASCOT .20 .50

1998-99 Orlando Solar Bears II

This set was given away at two different home games. The cards were issued in perforated sheets and are unnumbered. They are extremely difficult to find in complete set form.

COMPLETE SET (22) 10.00 25.00
1 David Littman .60 1.50
2 Mark Beaufait .75 2.00
3 Shawn Carter .40 1.00
4 David Mackey .40 1.00
5 Sean McCann .40 1.00
6 Hubie McDonough .60 1.50
7 Patrick Neaton .40 1.00
8 Clayton Norris .40 1.00
9 Grigori Panteleyev .60 1.50
10 Todd Richards .60 1.50
11 Curt Fraser HCO .40 1.00
12 Scott Bailey .60 1.50
13 Rob Bonneau .40 1.00
14 Allan Egeland .40 1.00
15 Todd Krygier .40 1.00
16 Kirby Law .40 1.00
17 Curtis Murphy .40 1.00
18 Mike Nicholishen .40 1.00
19 Frederik Oduya .40 1.00
20 Ken Sabourin .40 1.00
21 Pierre Sevigny .40 1.00
22 Peter Horachek ACO .40 1.00

1980-81 Oshawa Generals

This 25-card P.L.A.Y. (Police, Laws and Youth) set measures approximately 2 5/8" by 4 1/8" and features color posed action player photos and is bordered by white borders accented by a thin red line. The player's name, position, and team are superimposed in white letters on the picture.

COMPLETE SET (25) 62.50 125.00
1 Generals Logo .40 1.00
2 Ray Flaherty .40 1.00
3 Craig Kitchener .40 1.00
4 Dan Revell .40 1.00
5 Bob Kucheran .40 1.00
6 Pat Poulin .40 1.00
7 Dave Andreychuk 7.50 15.00
8 Barry Tabobondung .40 1.00
9 Steve Konroyd 1.25 3.00
10 Paul Edwards .40 1.00
11 Dale Degray 1.25 3.00
12 Joe Cirella 1.25 3.00
13 Norm Schmidt .40 1.00
14 Markus Lehto .60 1.50
15 Mitch Lamoureux .60 1.50
16 Tony Tanti 1.50 4.00
17 Bill Laforge .40 1.00
18 Greg Gravel .40 1.00
19 Mike Lekun .40 1.00
20 Chris Smith .40 1.00
21 Peter Sidorkiewicz 1.50 4.00
22 Greg Stefan 1.50 4.00
23 Tom McCarthy 1.50 4.00
24 Rick Lanz 1.50 4.00
25 Bobby Orr 40.00 80.00

1981-82 Oshawa Generals

This 25-card P.L.A.Y. (Police, Laws and Youth) set measures approximately 2 5/8" by 4 1/8" and features color posed action player photos. The backs carry "Tips from the Generals" that include a hockey tip and its application to a life situation.

COMPLETE SET (25) 24.00 60.00
1 Generals Logo .40 1.00
2 Chris Smith .60 1.50
3 Peter Sidorkiewicz 1.50 4.00
4 Ali Butorac .60 1.50
5 Dan Revell .60 1.50
6 Mitch Lamoureux .75 2.00
7 Norm Schmidt .60 1.50
8 Paul Edwards .60 1.50
9 Dan Nicholson .60 1.50
10 John Hutchings .60 1.50
11 Dave Gans .60 1.50
12 Dave Andreychuk 6.00 15.00
13 Mike Stern .60 1.50
14 Dale Degray .75 2.00
15 Mike Lekun .60 1.50
16 Greg Gravel .60 1.50
17 Dave MacLean .60 1.50
18 Tony Tanti 1.25 3.00
19 John MacLean 6.00 15.00
20 Jim Uens .60 1.50
21 Guy Jacob .60 1.50
22 Jeff Steffan .60 1.50
23 Paul Theriault .60 1.50
24 Sherry Bassin .60 1.50
25 Durham Regional .20 .50
Police Logo

1982-83 Oshawa Generals

This 25-card set measures approximately 2 5/8" by 4 1/8" and features color, posed action player photos framed by thin red border lines that rest on a white card face. The player's name, position, and the team logo are superimposed across the top of the picture in white lettering.

COMPLETE SET (25) 14.00 35.00
1 Generals Logo .20 .50
2 Jeff Hogg .60 1.50
3 Peter Sidorkiewicz 1.25 3.00
4 Dale Degray .60 1.50
5 Joe Cirella .60 1.50
6 Todd Smith .40 1.00
7 Scott Brydges .40 1.00
8 Jeff Steffen .40 1.00
9 Don Biggs .40 1.00
10 Todd Hooey .40 1.00
11 Tony Tanti .75 2.00
12 Danny Gratton .40 1.00
13 Steve King .40 1.00
14 Dan Defazio .40 1.00
15 John MacLean 3.00 8.00
16 Tim Burgess .40 1.00
17 Mike Stern .40 1.00
18 Dan Nicholson .40 1.00
19 David Gans .40 1.00
20 John Hutchings .40 1.00
21 Norm Schmidt .40 1.00
22 Todd Charlesworth .40 1.00
23 Paul Theriault CO .30 .75
24 Sherry Bassin GM .40 1.00
25 Durham Regional .20 .50
Police Logo

1983-84 Oshawa Generals

This 30-card P.L.A.Y. (Police, Laws and Youth) set measures approximately 2 5/8" by 4 1/8" and features color posed action player photos. The backs carry "Tips from the Generals" that include a hockey tip and its application to a life situation.

COMPLETE SET (30) 12.00 30.00
1 Peter Sidorkiewicz .75 2.00
2 Kirk McLean 4.00 10.00
3 Todd Charlesworth .40 1.00
4 Ian Ferguson .30 .75
5 John Hutchings .30 .75
6 Generals Logo .08 .25
7 Mark Haarmann .30 .75
8 Joel Curtis .30 .75
9 Dan Gratton .30 .75
10 Steve Hedington .30 .75
11 Scott Brydges .30 .75
12 CKAR Radio .08 .25
13 Brad Walcot .30 .75
14 Paul Theriault CO .30 .75
15 Jon Jenkins .08 .25
Chief of Police
16 Sherry Bassin GM .40 1.00
17 Craig Morrison .30 .75
18 Bolahood's .08 .25
19 Bruce Melanson .30 .75
20 Mike Stern .30 .75
21 Gary McColgan .30 .75
22 Lee Giffin .40 1.00
23 Brent Maki .30 .75
24 Ronald McDonald .20 .50
25 Jeff Steffen .30 .75
26 John Stevens .30 .75
27 David Gans .30 .75
28 Don Biggs .40 1.00
29 Chip Crandall .30 .75
30 Durham Police Logo .08 .25

1989-90 Oshawa Generals

These over-sized cards (approximately 2 5/8 X 4 1/8 inches) feature color action photos on the front and sponsor logos on the back. Cards were printed by Whitby Business Forms. The Lindros single has been widely counterfeited. Collectors should be wary when purchasing that card in single form. Your best bet is to purchase the complete set if you want a legitimate copy.

COMPLETE SET (35) 10.00 25.00
1 Corey Banika .20 .50
2 David Craievich .20 .50
3 Scott Hollis .20 .50
4 Mike Decoff .20 .50
5 Joe Busillo .20 .50
6 Matt Hoffman .20 .50
7 Craig Donaldson .20 .50
8 Jason Denomme .20 .50
9 Brian Grieve .20 .50
10 Wade Simpson .20 .50
11 Dale Craigwell .40 1.00
12 Mike Lenarduzzi .20 .50
13 Rick Cornacchia CO .04 .10
14 David Edwards .20 .50
15 Kevin Butt .40 1.00
16 Team Photo .08 .20
17 Clair Cornish .20 .50
18 Jarrod Skalde .40 1.00
19 Mark Deazeley .20 .50
20 Jean Paul Davis .20 .50
21 Todd Coopman .04 .10
22 Trevor McIvor .20 .50
23 Mike Craig .40 1.00
24 Paul O'Hagan .20 .50
25 Iain Fraser .20 .50
26 Brent Grieve .20 .50
27 Lions International .04 .10
28 National Sports Centre .04 .10
29 Durham Regional Police .04 .10
30 Oshawa Generals .04 .10
31 Eric Lindros 6.00 15.00
32 Bill Armstrong .20 .50
33 Chris Vanclief .20 .50
34 Scott Luik .20 .50
35 Fred Brathwaite 1.25 3.00

1989-90 Oshawa Generals 7th Inning Sketch

This set of the 1989-90 Oshawa Generals of the OHL was released by 7th Inning Sketch in advance of its full 1989-90 OHL issue. The cards, numbered 1-23, are the same as those found in the larger set. Card #1, featuring Eric Lindros, has been widely counterfeited. Collectors should exercise caution when purchasing this card as a single. Your best precaution is to use a jeweler's loupe to carefully study the print pattern on the front of the card.

COMPLETE SET (23) 6.00 15.00
1 Eric Lindros 2.00 5.00
2 Jarrod Skalde .30 .75
3 Joe Busillo .20 .50
4 Dale Craigwell .30 .75
5 Clair Cornish .20 .50
6 Jean-Paul Davis .20 .50
7 Craig Donaldson .20 .50
8 Wade Simpson .20 .50
9 Mike Craig .20 .50
10 Mark Deazeley .20 .50
11 Scott Hollis .20 .50
12 Brian Grieve .20 .50
13 Dave Craievich .20 .50
14 Paul O'Hagan .20 .50
15 Matt Hoffman .20 .50
16 Trevor McIvor .20 .50
17 Cory Banika .20 .50
18 Kevin Butt .30 .75
19 Iain Fraser .20 .50
20 Bill Armstrong .20 .50
21 Scott Luik .20 .50
22 Brent Grieve .20 .50
23 Fred Brathwaite .60 1.50

1991-92 Oshawa Generals

This 32-card standard-size set was sponsored by Coca-Cola and Domino's Pizza. The cards feature color action player photos framed by a royal blue double line. A white circle at the lower right corner carries the player's jersey number or the season year '91-'92.

COMPLETE SET (32) 8.00 20.00
1 Mike Fountain .30 .75
2 Brian Grieve .15 .40
3 Trevor Burgess .15 .40
4 Wade Simpson .15 .40
5 Ken Shepard .15 .40
6 Stephane Yelle .30 .75
7 Matt Hoffman .15 .40
8 Neil Iserhoff .15 .40
9 Rob Leask .15 .40
10 Kevin Spero .15 .40
11 Scott Hollis .15 .40
12 Sean Brown .20 .50
13 Todd Bradley .15 .40
14 Darryl LaFrance .15 .40
15 Markus Brunner .20 .50
16 B.J. MacPherson .15 .40
17 Jason Campeau .15 .40
18 Jason Weaver .15 .40
19 Jan Benda .20 .50
20 Jason Arnott 1.50 4.00
21 Eric Lindros 3.00 8.00
22 Wayne Daniels .02 .10
Dir. of Operations
23 Joe Cook .15 .40
24 Can't Beat the Real .02 .10
Thing (Coke Ad)
25 Experience the .02 .10
Domino's Effect/(Pizza Ad)
26 Mark Deazeley .15 .40
27 Jean-Paul Davis .15 .40
28 Brian Grieve .15 .40
29 Oshawa Generals .40 1.00
Team Photo
30 Ian Young CO .02 .10
Larry Marson CO5
Rick Cornacchia CO
31 Sponsor Ads .02 .10
Checklist
32 Prosport's Action .02 .10

1991-92 Oshawa Generals Sheet

This 18" by 12" sheet was sponsored by the 8th Annual United Way Face-Off Breakfast. The front features posed, color player cards with the players' names printed in a black stripe that appears below each picture. The center of the sheet carries the words "8th Annual United Way Face-Off Breakfast" in sky blue print. The team name also appears in the center, along with the year, the individual sheet number, and the production run (5,000). The players are checklisted below as they appear from left to right. Although these typically are found in sheet form, we are listing values for singles below as well as the complete sheet price.

COMPLETE SHEET (26) 8.00 20.00
1 Scott Hollis .15 .40
2 Jan Benda .20 .50
3 Joe Cook .15 .40
4 Wade Simpson .15 .40
5 B.J. MacPherson .15 .40
6 David Anderson .15 .40
7 Stephane Yelle .30 .75
8 Troy Sweet .15 .40
9 Matt Hoffman .15 .40
10 Trevor Burgess .15 .40
11 Jason Weaver .15 .40
12 Craig Lutes .15 .40
13 Darryl LaFrance .15 .40
14 Jason Arnott 1.50 4.00
15 Eric Lindros 3.00 8.00
16 Brian Grieve .15 .40
17 Mark Deazeley .15 .40
18 Mike Cote .15 .40
19 Markus Brunner .20 .50
20 Kevin Spero .15 .40
21 Todd Bradley .15 .40
22 Mike Fountain .30 .75
23 Fred Brathwaite .30 .75
24 Jean-Paul Davis .15 .40
25 Jason Campeau .15 .40
26 Neil Iserhoff .15 .40

1992-93 Oshawa Generals Sheet

This 18" by 12" sheet was sponsored by the 9th Annual United Way Face-Off Breakfast. The front features posed, color player cards with the players' names printed in a black stripe that appears below each picture. The center of the sheet carries the words "9th Annual United Way Face-Off Breakfast" in black print. The team name also appears in the center, along with the year, the individual sheet number, and the production run (5,000). Although these typically are found in sheet form, we are listing values for singles below as well as the complete sheet price.

COMPLETE SHEET (26) 6.00 15.00
1 Wade Simpson .20 .50
2 Jamie Kress .20 .50
3 Sean Brown .25 .60
4 Jason Arnott 1.25 3.00
5 Mark Brooks .20 .50
6 Rob McQuat .20 .50
7 Joe Cook .20 .50
8 Chris Hall .20 .50
9 Jason McQuat .20 .50
10 Jason Julian .20 .50
11 Kevin Spero .20 .50
12 Steve Haight .20 .50
13 B.J. MacPherson .20 .50
14 Billy-Jay Johnston .20 .50
15 Stephane Soulliere .20 .50
16 Todd Bradley .20 .50
17 Darryl Lafrance .20 .50
18 Aaron Albright .20 .50
19 Trevor Burgess .20 .50
20 Scott Hollis .20 .50
21 Serge Dunphy .20 .50
22 Joel Gagnon .30 .75
23 Brian Kent .30 .75
24 Stephane Yelle .40 1.00
25 Jason Campeau .20 .50
26 Neil Iserhoff .20 .50

1993-94 Oshawa Generals

Printed by Slapshot Images Ltd., this standard size 27-card set features the 1993-94 Oshawa Generals. Reportedly only 3,000 of these sets were produced; the title card also serves as a Certificate of Authenticity and has the number 3,000 printed in the lower right corner. On a geometrical team color-coded background, the fronts feature color action player photos with thin black borders. The player's name, position and team name, as well as the producer's logo, appear on the front.

COMPLETE SET (27) 4.00 10.00
1 Title Card .02 .10
Checklist
2 Joel Gagnon .20 .50
3 Ken Shepard .20 .50
4 Jan Snopek .20 .50
5 David Froh .15 .40
6 Brandon Gray .15 .40
7 Damon Hardy .15 .40
8 Sean Brown .25 .60
9 Jeff Andrews .15 .40
10 Stephane Yelle .30 .75
11 Stephane Soulliere .15 .40
12 Andrew Power .15 .40
13 Todd Bradley .15 .40
14 Darryl Lafrance .20 .50
15 Darryl Moxam .15 .40
16 Robert Dubois .15 .40
17 Kevin Vaughan .15 .40
18 Rob McQuat .20 .50
19 B.J. Johnston .15 .40
20 Paul Doherty .15 .40
21 Eric Boulton .40 1.00
22 Marc Savard .40 1.00
23 Chris Hall .15 .40
24 Jason McQuat .15 .40
25 Ryan Lindsay .15 .40
26 Rick Cornacchia CO .02 .10
Wayne Daniels DIR
Brian Drumm
NNO Slapshot Ad Card .02 .10

2003-04 Oshawa Generals

COMPLETE SET (26) 5.00 12.00
1 Dan Turple .30 .75
3 John Neal .20 .50
4 Chris Petrow .20 .50
6 Bret Nasby .20 .50
7 Clay McFadden .20 .50
8 Fred Hatziioannou .20 .50
10 Tyler Donati .20 .50
11 Andrew Gibbons .20 .50
12 Justin Donati .20 .50
14 Andy Reiss .20 .50
15 Aaron Lobb .20 .50
16 Mike McLean .20 .50
17 Chris Hulit .20 .50
19 Jordan Beirnes .20 .50
20 Justin Wallingford .20 .50
21 Adam Berti .20 .50
22 Mike Kavanagh .20 .50
23 Brandon McBride .20 .50
24 Ryan Kitchen .20 .50
25 Ben Eager .40 1.00
26 Paul Ranger .20 .50
27 Gary Friesen .20 .50
28 Tobias Whelan .20 .50
31 Ryan Gibb .30 .75
NNO Paul Ranger TL .75 2.00
NNO Ben Eager TL .75 2.00

2004-05 Oshawa Generals

COMPLETE SET (22) 5.00 12.00
1 Carlo Di Rienzo .40 1.00
2 Ryan Gibb .40 1.00
3 John Neal .60 1.50
4 Trevor Waddell .20 .50
5 Bret Nasby .20 .50
6 Brett Trudell .20 .50
7 Justin Allen .20 .50
8 Peter Tsimikalis .20 .50
9 Tom Jefferson .20 .50
10 Cal Clutterbuck .40 1.00
11 Matt Piva .20 .50
12 Matt Puntureri .20 .50
13 Jesse Biduke .20 .50
14 Devereaux Heshmatpour .30 .75
15 Adam Berti .40 1.00
16 Mike Kavanaugh .20 .50
17 Brandon McBride .20 .50
18 Chad Thompson .20 .50
19 James DeLory .20 .50
20 David Halasz .20 .50
21 Gary Friesen .20 .50
22 Checklist .04 .10

2006-07 Oshawa Generals

COMPLETE SET (24) 12.00 20.00
1 John Tavares 3.00 8.00
2 Dale Mitchell .40 1.00
3 Tyler Taylor .20 .50
4 Igor Gongalsky .20 .50
5 Cal Clutterbuck .20 .50
6 Dean Howard .20 .50
7 Kory Nagy .20 .50
8 Brett Maclean .40 1.00
9 Corey Cowick .20 .50
10 Kyle Paige .20 .50
11 Kody Musselman .20 .50
12 Shea Kewin .20 .50
13 Brett Parnham .20 .50
14 Ziga Pance .20 .50
15 Trevor Koverko .20 .50
16 Michael Del Zotto .60 1.50
17 Matt Seegmiller .20 .50
18 Peter Aston .20 .50
19 Eric Regan .20 .50
20 Billy Siekris .20 .50
21 James Delory .20 .50
22 Loic Lacasse .30 .75
23 Mark Packwood .30 .75
24 Oshawa Generals .10 .25

2014-15 Oshawa Generals

COMPLETE SET (24) 6.00 15.00
1 Ken Appleby .30 .75
2 Jeremy Brodeur .30 .75
3 Josh Brown .30 .75
4 Chris Carlisle .30 .75
5 Cole Cassels .30 .75
6 Anthony Cirelli .30 .75
7 Michael Dal Colle .30 .75
8 Stephen Desrocher .30 .75
9 Sam Harding .30 .75
10 Sonny Hertzberg .30 .75
11 Kenny Huether .30 .75
12 Bradley Latour .30 .75
13 Tobias Lindberg .30 .75
14 Joe Manchurek .30 .75
15 Will Petschenig .30 .75
16 Cliff Pu .40 1.00
17 Daniel Robertson .30 .75
18 Hunter Smith .30 .75
19 Josh Sterk .30 .75
20 Stephen Templeton .30 .75
21 Michael Turner .30 .75
22 Mitchell Vande-Sompel .30 .75
23 Aidan Wallace .30 .75
24 Header Card CL .30 .75

1981-82 Ottawa 67's

The cards measure approximately 5 1/2" by 8 1/2" and feature black-and-white player portraits in white borders. A facsimile autograph and player's jersey number are printed in the wide bottom margin. The backs are blank. The cards are unnumbered and checklisted below in alphabetical order. Thanks to collector Stan Mendes for providing additional checklist information.

COMPLETE SET (25) 12.00 30.00
1 James Allison .30 .75
2 John Boland .30 .75
3 Randy Boyd .30 .75
4 Adam Creighton 1.25 3.00
5 Bill Dowd .30 .75
6 Dwayne Davison .30 .75
7 Alan Hepple .30 .75
8 Mike James .30 .75
9 Brian Kilrea CO .75 2.00
10 Moe Lemay .60 1.50
11 Benny Longe .30 .75
12 Paul Louttit .30 .75
12 Doug Stewart .30 .75
13 Fraser Wood .30 .75
13 Don McLaren .30 .75
14 John Ollson .30 .75
15 Brian Patafie TR .20 .50
16 Mark Paterson .40 1.00
17 Phil Patterson .30 .75
18 Larry Power .30 .75
19 Jim Ralph 2.00 5.00
20 Darcy Roy .40 1.00
21 Brad Shaw 1.25 3.00
22 Brian Small .30 .75
23 Doug Stewart .30 .75
24 Jeff Vaive .30 .75
25 Fraser Wood .30 .75

1982-83 Ottawa 67's

Sponsored by Coke and Channel 12, this 25-card set measures approximately 2 5/8" by 4 1/8" and features posed, color player photos with white borders. The player's name and jersey number are printed in black across the bottom of the picture.The cards are unnumbered and checklisted below in alphabetical order.

COMPLETE SET (25) 12.00 30.00
1 Bruce Cassidy .30 .75
2 Greg Coram .30 .75
3 Adam Creighton .75 2.00
4 Bill Dowd .30 .75
5 Gord Hamilton ACO .20 .50
6 Scott Hammond .30 .75
7 Alan Hepple .30 .75
8 Alan Hepple .30 .75
9 Jim Jackson TR .20 .50
10 Mike James .30 .75
11 Brian Kilrea CO .75 2.00
12 Paul Louttit .30 .75
13 Brian McKinnon .30 .75
14 Don McLaren .30 .75
15 John Ollson .30 .75
16 Darren Pang 2.00 5.00
17 Mark Paterson .30 .75
18 Phil Patterson .30 .75
19 Larry Power .30 .75
20 Gary Roberts 3.00 8.00
21 Brian Rome .30 .75
22 Darcy T. Roy .30 .75
23 Brad Shaw 1.00 2.50
24 Doug Stewart .30 .75
25 Jeff Vaive .30 .75
26 Larry MacAndrew .30 .75
27 Gord Hamilton Jr. .30 .75

1983-84 Ottawa 67's

Sponsored by Coke and Channel 12, this 27-card set measures approximately 2 5/8" by 4 1/8". The fronts feature posed, color player photos with white borders. The player's name and jersey number are printed in black across the bottom of the picture. The cards are unnumbered and checklisted below in alphabetical order.

COMPLETE SET (27) 10.00 25.00
1 Richard Adolfi .20 .50
2 Bill Bennett .20 .50
3 Bruce Cassidy .30 .75
4 Todd Clarke .20 .50
5 Greg Coram .30 .75
6 Adam Creighton .75 2.00
7 Bob Giffin .20 .50
8 Gord Hamilton ACO .08 .25
9 Gord Hamilton Jr. TR .08 .25
10 Scott Hammond .20 .50
11 John Hanna .20 .50
12 Tim Helmer .20 .50
13 Steve Hrynewich .20 .50
14 Jim Jackson TR .08 .25
15 Mike James .20 .50
16 Brian Kilrea CO/MG .40 1.00
17 Larry MacAndrew TR .08 .25
18 Brian McKinnon .20 .50
19 Don McLaren .30 .75
20 Roy Myllari .20 .50
21 Darren Pang 1.50 4.00
22 Mark Paterson .30 .75
23 Phil Patterson .20 .50
24 Gary Roberts 2.00 5.00
25 Darcy Roy .20 .50
26 Brad Shaw .75 2.00
27 Steve Simoni .20 .50

1984-85 Ottawa 67's

This 28-card set was sponsored by Coca-Cola and Focus Photographic Services Commercial Photography. The cards measure approximately 2 5/8" by 4 1/8" and feature color, full-length, posed player photos with white borders. The player's name and jersey number are superimposed on the bottom of the picture. The cards are unnumbered and checklisted below in alphabetical order.

COMPLETE SET (28) 8.00 20.00
1 Tom Allen .30 .75
2 Graydon Almstedt .30 .75
3 Bill Bennett .30 .75
4 Bruce Cassidy .30 .75
5 Greg Coram .40 1.00
6 Bob Ellett CO .08 .25
7 Tony Geesink .30 .75
8 Bob Giffin .30 .75
9 John Hanna .30 .75
10 Tim Helmer .30 .75
11 Andy Helmuth .30 .75
12 Steve Hrynewich .30 .75
13 Rob Hudson .30 .75
14 Jim Jackson TR .08 .25
15 Steve Kayser .30 .75
16 Bill Kuchma .30 .75
17 Mike Larouche .30 .75
18 Tom Lawson MG .08 .25
19 Richard Lessard .30 .75
20 Gary Roberts 1.50 4.00
21 Jerry Scott .30 .75
22 John Shepherd PR .08 .25
23 Steve Simoni .30 .75
24 Greg Sliz .30 .75
25 Gord Thomas TR .08 .25
26 Chris Vickers .30 .75
27 Bert Weir .30 .75
28 Dennis Wigle .30 .75

1992-93 Ottawa 67's

Celebrating the 25th anniversary of the Ottawa 67's, this 24-card standard-size set features color posed and action player photos with purple borders. The player's name, position, and jersey number appear in a black vertical stripe on the left side of the card. The phrase "25th Anniversary" is printed at the bottom in large red and blue letters. The cards are unnumbered and checklisted below in alphabetical order.

COMPLETE SET (24) 4.80 12.00
1 Ken Belanger .30 .75
2 Curt Bowen .20 .50
3 Rich Bronilla .20 .50
4 Mathew Burnett .20 .50
5 Shawn Caplice .20 .50
6 Mike Carr .20 .50
7 Chris Coveny .20 .50
8 Howard Darwin (Founder) .08 .25
9 Shean Donovan .40 1.00
10 Mark Edmundson .20 .50
11 Billy Hall .20 .50
12 Mike Johnson .20 .50
13 Brian Kilrea GM .20 .50
CO
14 Grayson Lafoley .20 .50
15 Grant Marshall .40 1.00
16 Cory Murphy .20 .50
17 Mike Peca 1.25 3.00
18 Greg Ryan .20 .50
19 Jeff Salajko .20 .50
20 Gerry Skrypec .20 .50
21 Sean Spencer .20 .50
22 Steven Washburn .25 .60
23 Mark Yakabuski .20 .50
24 Title Card .08 .25

1999-00 Ottawa 67's

Released in 1999 by JOGO Incorporated, this full-color set features the Ottawa 67's of the OHL. Card backs contain black and white portraits and a short blurb about each player highlighting his career. The checklist card features a shot of the Memorial Cup winning 1998-99 Ottawa 67's.

COMPLETE SET (30) 4.80 12.00
1 Mark Bell .60 1.50
2 Matt Zultek .20 .50
3 Adam Chapman .08 .25
4 Miguel Delisle .30 .75
5 Randy Davidson .08 .25
6 Lance Galbraith .20 .50
7 Ian Jacobs .08 .25
8 Mike James .08 .25
9 Zenon Konopka .20 .50
10 Marc Lefebvre .08 .25
11 Joe Talbot .08 .25
12 Josh Tataryn .08 .25
13 Dan Tessier .20 .50
14 Vincent Grant .20 .50
15 Brendan Bell .08 .25
16 Chris Cava .08 .25
17 Kevin Malcolm .08 .25
18 Mike Gresdal .08 .25
19 Russ Moyer .08 .25
20 Luke Sellars .20 .50
21 Jeremy Van Hoof .20 .50
22 Jon Zion .30 .75
23 Seamus Kotyk .40 1.00
24 Lavente Szuper .40 1.00
25 Jeff Hunt .08 .25
26 Brian Kilrea HCO .20 .50
27 Bert O'Brien ACO .02 .10
28 Vince Mallette ACO .02 .10
29 Jeff Keech TR .02 .10
30 Checklist .02 .10

2000-01 Ottawa 67's

This thick-stock set was produced by Jogo, and sold by the team at its gift shop for $5. Production was limited to 3,000 copies. There are at least two spelling errors on the checklist card, neither of which were corrected.

COMPLETE SET (30) 4.80 12.00
1 Joe Talbot .20 .50
2 Lance Galbraith .20 .50
3 Jeremy Van Hoof .20 .50
4 Jon Zion .20 .50
5 Russ Moyer .15 .40
6 Pierre Mitsou .15 .40
7 Brendan Bell .20 .50
8 Adam Smyth .15 .40
9 Marc Lefebvre .15 .40
10 Sean Scully .15 .40
11 Brett McGrath .15 .40
12 Zenon Konopka .20 .50
13 Rodney Bauman .15 .40
14 Luke Sellars .20 .50
15 Miguel Delisle .20 .50
16 Vadim Sozinov .20 .50
17 Adam Chapman .15 .40
18 Bryan Rodney .15 .40
19 Sebastien Savage .15 .40
20 Seamus Kotyk .30 .75
21 John Ceci .15 .40
22 Vince Mallette CO .10 .25
23 Bert O'Brien CO .10 .25
24 Brian Kilrea CO .20 .50
25 Jeff Hunt OWN .04 .10
26 Riley & Killer Puck MASCOT .04 .10
27 Brian Kilrea 900 .20 .50
28 Doug Wilson .20 .50
29 Team Photo .10 .25
30 Team CL .10 .25

2001-02 Ottawa 67's

This set features the 67's of the OHL. The set was produced by Jogo and sold at the team's souvenir stand.

COMPLETE SET (30) 4.80 12.00
1 J.F. Perras .30 .75
2 Jon Ceci .20 .50
3 Karol Sloboda .20 .50
4 Carter Trevisani .20 .50
5 Jon Zion .30 .75
6 Russ Moyer .20 .50
7 Pierre Mitsou .20 .50
8 Adam Smyth .20 .50
9 Brendan Bell .30 .75
10 Matthew Albiani .20 .50
11 Lane Moodie .20 .50
12 Sean Scully .20 .50
13 Brett McGrath .20 .50
14 Zenon Konopka .30 .75
15 Rodney Bauman .20 .50
16 Miguel Delisle .20 .50
17 Jeremy Akeson .20 .50
18 Mark Mancari .20 .50
19 Adam Chapman .20 .50
20 Bryan Rodney .20 .50
21 Corey Locke .20 .50
22 Vince Malette ACO .04 .10
23 Bert O'Brien ACO .04 .10
24 Brian Kilrea CO .20 .50
25 Jeff Hunt OWN .04 .10
26 Banner Ceremony .04 .10
27 Brad Marsh .20 .50
28 Riley and Riley Jr. .04 .10
29 Killer Puck .04 .10
30 Dance Team .20 .50
CL

2002-03 Ottawa 67's

COMPLETE SET 5.00 12.00
1 Chris Hardill .30 .75
2 Karol Sloboda .20 .50
3 Carter Trevisani .20 .50
4 Will Colbert .20 .50
5 Russ Moyer .20 .50
6 Pierre Mitsou .20 .50
7 Adam Smyth .20 .50
8 Brendan Bell .30 .75
9 Matthew Albiani .20 .50
10 Lou Dickenson .20 .50
11 Scott Sheppard .20 .50
12 Bryan Bickell .20 .50
13 Sean Scully .20 .50
14 Peter Tsimikalis .20 .50
15 Rodney Bauman .20 .50
16 Kyle Wharton .20 .50
17 Jeremy Akeson .20 .50
18 Mark Mancari .20 .50
19 Julian Talbot .20 .50
20 Lukas Mensator .40 1.00
21 Matthew Foy .30 .75
22 Corey Locke .60 1.50
23 Jeff Hunt Owner .04 .10
24 Brian Kilrea HCO .10 .25
25 Bert O'Brien ACO .04 .10
26 Vince Malette ACO .04 .10
27 Mascot .04 .10
28 XFM Girls .10 .25
29 Mike Peca .20 .50
Brian Kilrea
30 Girl Guides of Canada .04 .10

2003-04 Ottawa 67's

COMPLETE SET (25) 6.00 15.00
1 Tyson Aitcheson .20 .50
2 Jeremy Akeson .20 .50
3 Matthew Albiani .20 .50
4 Danny Battochio .30 .75
5 Rodney Bauman .20 .50
6 Brodie Beard .20 .50
7 Bryan Bickell .20 .50
8 Will Colbert .20 .50
9 Greg Goodnough .20 .50
10 David Halasz .20 .50
11 Brad Hartley .20 .50
12 Robbie Lawrance .20 .50
13 Corey Locke .40 1.00
14 Mark Mancari .20 .50
15 Phil Mangan .20 .50
16 Lukas Mensator .40 1.00
17 Pierre Mitsou .20 .50
18 Elgin Reid .20 .50
19 Julian Talbot .20 .50
20 Brody Todd .20 .50
21 Peter Tsimikalis .20 .50
22 Kyle Wharton .20 .50
NNO Lukas Mensator TL .75 2.00
NNO Brian Kilrea CO .04 .10
NNO Corey Locke TL .75 2.00

2004-05 Ottawa 67's

A total of 1,000 team sets were produced.

COMPLETE (23) 5.00 12.00
1 Lukas Kaspar .20 .50
2 Anthony Guadagnolo .40 1.00
3 Bryan Bickell .20 .50
4 Brodie Beard .20 .50
5 Pat Ouellette .20 .50
6 Robbie Lawrance .20 .50
7 Jeremy Akeson .20 .50
8 Mark Mancari .20 .50
9 Julian Talbot .20 .50
10 Brad Bonello .20 .50
11 Nick Van Herpt .20 .50
12 Danny Battochio .60 1.50
13 Will Colbert .20 .50
14 David Jarram .20 .50
15 Brad Staubitz .40 1.00
16 Jamie Vanderveeken .20 .50
17 Arron Alphonso .20 .50
18 Derek Joslin .20 .50
19 Elgin Reid .20 .50
20 Jamie McGinn .20 .50
21 Chris Hulit .40 1.00
22 Jakub Petruzalek .20 .50
23 Matt Lahey .20 .50

2005-06 Ottawa 67's

COMPLETE SET (25) 8.00 15.00
1 Julian Talbot .20 .50
2 Brodie Beard .20 .50
3 Bryan Bickell .20 .50
4 Pat Campbell .20 .50
5 Shea Kewin .20 .50
6 Thomas Kiriakou .20 .50
7 Robbie Lawrence .20 .50
8 Pat Ouellette .20 .50
9 Sean Ryan .20 .50
10 Jakub Vojta .20 .50
11 Brent Mackie .20 .50
12 Danny Battochio .40 1.00
13 Arron Alphonso .20 .50
14 Logan Couture 1.00 2.50
15 Pat Daley .20 .50
16 Chris Hulit .20 .50
17 Brady Morrison .40 1.00
18 Derek Joslin .20 .50
19 Matt Lahey .20 .50
20 Jamie McGinn .30 .75
21 Joe Pleckaitis .20 .50
22 Tibor Radulay .20 .50
23 Elgin Reid .20 .50
24 Joe Grimaldi .20 .50
25 Brett Liscomb .20 .50

2006-07 Ottawa 67's

COMPLETE SET (22) 8.00 15.00
1 Logan Couture .60 1.50
2 Scott Cowie .25 .60
3 Thomas Kiriakou .25 .60
4 Matt Lahey .25 .60
5 Cody Lindsay .25 .60
6 Brett Liscomb .40 1.00
7 Jamie Mcginn .40 1.00
8 Matthieu Methot .25 .60
9 Thomas Nesbitt .25 .60
10 Matt Ribeiro .25 .60
11 Brodie Beard .25 .60
12 Tyler Cuma .25 .60
13 Julien Demers .25 .60
14 Joe Grimaldi .25 .60
15 Derek Joslin .25 .60
16 Sean Ryan .25 .60
17 Jakub Vojta .25 .60
18 Arron Alphonso .25 .60
19 Jason Bailey .25 .60
20 Julian Cimadamore .25 .60
21 Lukas Flueler .40 1.00
22 Brady Morrison .40 1.00

2000-01 Owen Sound Attack

This set features the Attack of the OHL. The cards were produced by the team and sold at its souvenir stands. The cards are unnumbered and so are listed below in alphabetical order.

COMPLETE SET (26) 4.80 12.00
1 Michael Barrett .20 .50
2 Trevor Blanchard .20 .50
3 Luc Chiasson .20 .50
4 Richard Colwill .20 .50
5 Justin Day .30 .75
6 Kris Fraser .20 .50
7 Justin Hodgins .20 .50
8 Greg Jacina .20 .50
9 Bryan Kazarian .30 .75
10 Josh Legge .20 .50
11 Paul MacDermid CO .10 .25
12 Jason Nobili CO .10 .25
13 Brian O'Leary CO .10 .25
14 Dene Poulin .20 .50
15 Richard Power .20 .50
16 Corey Roberts .30 .75
17 Agris Saviels .30 .75
18 Ryan Sharp .20 .50
19 Daniel Sisca .20 .50
20 Shawn Snider .20 .50
21 Dan Sullivan .20 .50
22 Brandon Verner .20 .50
23 Nick Vukovic .20 .75
24 Joel Ward .20 .50
25 Bill Zalba .20 .50
26 Team Photo .20 .25

2001-02 Owen Sound Attack

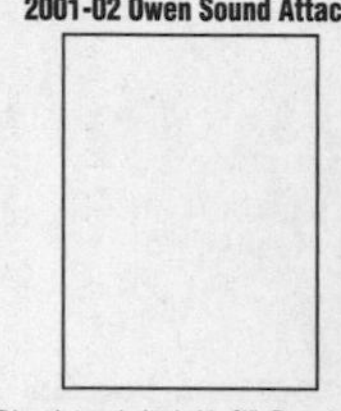

This set features the Attack of the OHL. The cards were produced by the team and sold at its souvenir shop. The cards are unnumbered, and are listed below in alphabetical order.

COMPLETE SET (24) 4.80 12.00
1 Robert Chapman .20 .50
2 Richard Colwill .20 .50
3 Ryan Courtney .20 .50
4 David Dalliday .20 .50
5 Justin Day .30 .75
6 Jesse Gimblett .20 .50
7 Fred Hatziioannou .20 .50
8 Greg Jacina .30 .75
9 Michael Jacobsen .20 .50
10 Ladislav Kolda .20 .50
11 Jeff MacDermid .20 .50
12 Kyle McAllister .30 .75
13 Richard Power .20 .50
14 Justin Renner .30 .75
15 Brad Richardson .20 .50
16 Cory Roberts .30 .75
17 Dan Rogers .20 .50
18 Agris Saviels .30 .75
19 Ryan Sharp .20 .50
20 Daniel Sisca .20 .50
21 Sean Stefanski .20 .50
22 Dan Sullivan .20 .50
23 John Wheaton .20 .50
24 Tom Zanoski .20 .50

2002-03 Owen Sound Attack

COMPLETE SET (26) 5.00 12.00
1 Mascot .04 .10
2 Brett Howden .20 .50
3 Pat Sutton .20 .50
4 Jiri Paska .20 .50
5 Mark Giordano .20 .50
6 Patrick Jarrett .40 1.00
7 Dan Rogers .20 .50
8 Matt Passfield .20 .50
9 Tom Zanoski .20 .50
10 Jesse Gimblett .20 .50
11 Michael Gough .20 .50
12 Brad Richardson .20 .50
13 Andrew Maksym .20 .50
14 Steve Henwood .20 .50
15 Brett McGrath .20 .50
16 Justin Renner .20 .50
17 Ladislav Kolda .20 .50
18 John Weathon .20 .50
19 Fred Hatziioannou .20 .50
20 Jeff McDermid .20 .50
21 Miguel Delisle .20 .50
22 David Edgeworth .20 .50
23 Mike Angelidis .20 .50
24 Dan LaCosta .30 .75
25 Marty Magers .30 .75
26 Checklist .04 .10

2003-04 Owen Sound Attack

COMPLETE SET (25) 6.00 15.00
1 The Bear Cubby .04 .10
2 Matt Smyth .20 .50
3 Wes Cunningham .20 .50
4 Pat Sutton .20 .50
5 Justin Dacosta .20 .50

6 Mark Giordano .20 .50
7 Patrick Jarrett .30 .75
8 Bobby Ryan 1.50 4.00
9 Andrew Maksym .20 .50
10 Richard Hornseth .20 .50
11 Brad Richardson .20 .50
12 Kevin Baker .20 .50
13 Kevin Harvey .20 .50
14 Jonathan Lehun .20 .50
15 Pavel Voroshnin .30 .75
16 Andre Deveaux .20 .50
17 Jim Kehoe .20 .50
18 Stefan Ruzicka .40 1.00
19 Jeff MacDermid .20 .50
20 John Wires .20 .50
21 Adam Smyth .20 .50
22 Mike Angelidis .20 .50
23 Dan LaCosta .30 .75
24 Robert Gherson .30 .75
25 Checklist .04 .10

2004-05 Owen Sound Attack

A total of 500 team sets were produced.

COMPLETE SET (24) 6.00 15.00
1 Mike Angelidis .20 .50
2 Neil Conway .40 1.00
3 Igor Gongalsky .20 .50
4 Derek Brochu .20 .50
5 Brad Richardson .20 .50
6 Kevin Baker .20 .50
7 Matthew Kang .20 .50
8 Colin Hanley .20 .50
9 Jonathan Lehun .20 .50
10 Matt Smyth .20 .50
11 Bob Sanguinetti .40 1.00
12 Stefan Ruzicka .40 1.00
13 Theo Peckham .20 .50
14 Payton Liske .20 .50
15 Robin Big Snake .60 1.50
16 Andrej Sekera .20 .50
17 Dan Lacosta .20 .50
18 Wes Cunningham .20 .50
19 Trevor Koverko .40 1.00
20 Justin Dacosta .20 .50
21 Scott Giles .20 .50
22 Patrick Jarrett .30 .75
23 Bobby Ryan 1.50 4.00
24 Cubby MASCOT .04 .10

2005-06 Owen Sound Attack

COMPLETE SET (24) 8.00 15.00
1 Bobby Ryan .75 2.00
2 Neil Conway .40 1.00
3 Andrej Sekera .20 .50
4 Kyle Lamb .20 .50
5 Trevor Koverko .20 .50
6 Jeff Moor .20 .50
7 Scott Giles .20 .50
8 Igor Gongalsky .20 .50
9 Derek Brochu .20 .50
10 Scott Tregunna .20 .50
11 Josh Catto .20 .50
12 Jeff Kyrzakos .20 .50
13 Matthew Kang .20 .50
14 Zach McCullough .20 .50
15 Joshua Bailey .20 .50
16 Marcus Carroll .20 .50
17 Bob Sanguinetti .40 1.00
18 Theo Peckham .40 1.00
19 Marek Bartanus .20 .50
20 Payton Liske .20 .50
21 Mike Angelidis .20 .50
22 Miles Cope .20 .50
23 Justin Allen .20 .50
24 Kyle Knechtel .40 1.00

2006-07 Owen Sound Attack

COMPLETE SET (22) 8.00 15.00
1 Theo Peckham .20 .50
2 Michael D'orazio .20 .50
3 Neil Conway .40 1.00
4 Dalyn Flatt .20 .50
5 Andrew Shorkey .20 .50
6 David Kolomatis .20 .50
7 Guy Carteciano .20 .50
8 Bobby Ryan .75 2.00
9 Derek Brochu .20 .50
10 Scott Tregunna .20 .50
11 Lane Macdermid .20 .50
12 Thomas Stajan .20 .50
13 Wayne Simmonds .20 .50
14 Zach Mccullough .20 .50
15 Josh Bailey .20 .50
16 Michael Farrell .20 .50
17 Marcus Carroll .20 .50
18 Bobby Sanguinetti .40 1.00
19 Marek Bartanus .20 .50
20 Anton Hedman .20 .50
21 Trevor Lewis .60 1.50
22 Scott Bowles .40 1.00

1993-94 Owen Sound Platers

Sponsored by Domino's Pizza, The Eastwood Network, and The Sport Stop, this 36-card set measures the standard size. The fronts feature posed and action color player photos with white borders. The player's name and number appears in a black bar under the picture. The cards are unnumbered and checklisted below in alphabetical order.

COMPLETE SET (36) 8.00 20.00
1 Craig Binns .15 .40
2 Jim Brown .15 .40
3 Andrew Brunette .60 1.50
4 Luigi Calce .15 .40
5 Jason Campbell .15 .40
6 Draft Veterans .15 .40
Rod Hinks
Jason MacDonald
Kevin
7 Paddy Flynn ACO .02 .10
8 Kirk Furey .15 .40
9 Jerry Harrigan CO .02 .10
10 Joe Harris .15 .40
11 Rod Hinks .15 .40
12 Marian Kacir .15 .40
13 Shane Kenny .15 .40
14 Jeff Kostuch .15 .40
15 Dave Lemay .15 .40
16 Jason MacDonald .20 .50
17 Rick Mancini TR .02 .10
18 Kirk Maltby .40 1.00
19 Brian Medeiros .15 .40
20 Mike Morrone .15 .40
21 Ryan Mougenel .15 .40
22 Scott Penton .15 .40
23 Wayne Primeau .40 1.00
24 Jeremy Rebek .15 .40
25 Rob Schweyer .15 .40
26 Willie Skilliter .15 .40
27 Jamie Storr .60 1.50
28 Jamie Storr .60 1.50
Pure Gold
29 Jamie Storr's Mask .60 1.50
30 Jamie Storr .60 1.50
Wayne Prime
31 Scott Walker .40 1.00
32 Kevin Weekes .60 1.50
33 Kevin Weekes' Mask .40 1.00
34 Shayne Wright .15 .40
35 Title Card .02 .10
Domino's Ad
36 Title Card .02 .10
Eastwood Ad

1994-95 Owen Sound Platers

This set features the Platers of the OHL and was sponsored by Domino's Pizza. Frankly, that's about all we know on this one. Have any additional info? Send it to hockeymag@beckett.com.

COMPLETE SET (36) 6.00 15.00
1 Shawn Silver .20 .50
2 Shane Kenny .15 .40
3 Kevin Young .15 .40
4 Kirk Furey .15 .40
5 Peter MacKellar .15 .40
6 Willie Skilliter .15 .40
7 Joe Harris .15 .40
8 Brian Medeiros .15 .40
9 David Zunic .15 .40
10 Jeff Kostuch .15 .40
11 Jason Campbell .15 .40
12 Scott Smith .15 .40
13 Rob Schweyer .15 .40
14 Shayne Wright .15 .40
15 Scott Seiling .15 .40
16 Jeremy Rebek .15 .40
17 Rob Fitzgerald .15 .40
18 Ryan Mougenel .15 .40
19 John Argiropoulos .15 .40
20 Wayne Primeau .20 .50
21 Chris Wismer .15 .40
22 Matt Osborne .15 .40
23 Murray Hogg .15 .40
24 Brent Johnson 2.00 5.00
25 Jamie Storr (Jersey #31) .40 1.00
26 Jamie Storr (Jersey #92 .40 1.00
27 Jamie Storr (King Tut Mask) .40 1.00
28 Jamie Storr Draft .40 1.00
28 Wayne Primeau Draft .20 .50
28 Shayne Wright Draft .15 .40
29 Wayne Primeau Prime Time .20 .50
30 Coaching Staff .04 .10
31 Larry Gibson SB .04 .10
32 Joel Traplin TR .04 .10
33 Broadcast Team .04 .10
34 Ed Schambers Bus Dr. .04 .10
35 Domino's Pizza .01 .02
36 Jim Gardhouse Motors .01 .02

1995-96 Owen Sound Platers

This set features the Platers of the OHL. The set was produced by the team and sold at its souvenir stands.

COMPLETE SET (36) 4.80 12.00
1 Team Photo Card .15 .40
2 Ric Seiling CO .02 .10
3 Gus Eyers CO .02 .10
4 Brian Warrilow CO .02 .10
5 Rick Mancini TR .02 .10
6 Wayne Primeau .20 .50
7 Shawn Gallant .15 .40
8 Shane Kenny .15 .40
9 Chris Biagini .15 .40
10 Marek Babic .15 .40
11 Oleg Tsirkounov .15 .40
12 Peter MacKellar .15 .40
13 Ryan Davis .15 .40
14 John Argiropoulos .15 .40
15 Jason Campbell .15 .40
16 Dan Snyder .40 1.00
17 Steve Gallace .15 .40
18 Scott Seiling .15 .40
19 Jeremy Rebek .15 .40
20 Adam Mair .20 .50
21 Ryan Christie .20 .50
22 Larry Paleczny .20 .50
23 Wayne Primeau .20 .50
24 Chris Wismer .15 .40
25 Matt Osborne .15 .40
26 Mike Loach .15 .40
27 Brent Johnson .75 2.00
28 Jim Ensom .15 .40
29 Brent Johnson .75 2.00
30 Mike Loach .15 .40
31 Jim Ensom .15 .40
32 Wayne Primeau .20 .50
33 Shane Kenny .15 .40
34 Sun Times News .01 .05
35 Jim Gardhouse Motors .01 .05
36 Domino's Pizza .01 .05

1996-97 Owen Sound Platers

This set features the Platers of the OHL. The set was produced by the team and sold at its souvenir stands.

COMPLETE SET (27) 6.00 15.00
1 John Lovell CO .02 .10
2 Brian O'Leary CO .02 .10
3 Curtis Sanford .60 1.50
4 Shawn Gallant .15 .40
5 Brent Johnson .75 2.00
6 Joel Dezainde .15 .40
7 Kyle Dafoe .15 .40
8 Kyle Flaxey .15 .40
9 Matt Osborne .15 .40
10 Jamie Sokolsky .15 .40
11 Kurt Walsh .15 .40
12 Andrew Williamson .15 .40
13 Ryan Davis .15 .40
14 Sean Avery .75 2.00
15 Pascal Daze .15 .40
16 Dan Snyder .40 1.00
17 Steve Gallace .15 .40
18 Scott Wray .15 .40
19 Adam Mair .30 .75
20 Larry Paleczny .20 .50
21 Ryan Christie .15 .40
22 Chris Wismer .15 .40
23 Todd Miller .15 .40
24 Adam Campbell .15 .40
25 Jason Doyle .30 .75
26 Wes Goldie .15 .40
27 Owen Sound Platers .15 .40

1997-98 Owen Sound Platers

This set features the Platers of the OHL. The set was produced by the team and sold at home games.

COMPLETE SET (26) 4.80 12.00
1 Owen Sound Platers .20 .50
2 Curtis Sanford .30 .75
3 Adam Campbell .20 .50
4 Kyle Dafoe .20 .50
5 Kyle Flaxey .20 .50
6 Chris Hopiavuori .20 .50
7 Jamie Sokolsky .20 .50
8 Colin Beardsmore .20 .50
9 Dave Stephenson .20 .50
10 Ryan Davis .20 .50
11 Ryan Rivard .20 .50
12 Sean Avery .75 2.00
13 Dan Snyder .40 1.00
14 Wes Goldie .20 .50
15 Adam Mair .30 .75
16 Larry Paleczny .20 .50
17 Ryan Christie .20 .50
18 Randy Davidson .20 .50
19 Joel Ward .20 .50
20 Chris Wismer .20 .50
21 Jason Doyle .30 .75
22 Brendan Brooks .20 .50
23 Adam Collins .20 .50
24 Eoin McInerney .40 1.00
25 Brian O'Leary CO .08 .25
26 Kirk Maltby .30 .75

1998-99 Owen Sound Platers

This set features the Platers of the OHL. It is believed that the set was produced by the team and sold at its souvenir stands.

COMPLETE SET (28) 4.80 12.00
1 Owen Sound Platers .08 .25
2 Curtis Sanford .40 1.00
3 Mike Barrett .15 .40
4 Kyle Flaxey .15 .40
5 Chris Hopiavuori .20 .50
6 Mike Dombkiewicz .15 .40
7 Jeff Kaufman .15 .40
8 Dave Stephenson .15 .40
9 Chris Minard .30 .75
10 Stephane Savage .15 .40
11 Sean Avery .40 1.00
12 Peter Campbell .15 .40
13 Dan Snyder .40 1.00
14 Jan Sulc .15 .40
15 Wes Goldie .30 .75
16 Adam Mair .30 .75
17 Chad Woollard .20 .50
18 Stephen Lafleur .20 .50
19 Randy Davidson .20 .50
20 Joel Ward .20 .50
21 Juri Golicic .20 .50
22 Bryan Kazarian .20 .50
23 Nick Vukovic .30 .75
24 Brent Sullivan .15 .40
25 Adam Campbell .15 .40
26 Corey Roberts .15 .40
27 Adam Mair .30 .75
28 Coaches .02 .10

1999-00 Owen Sound Platers

This 31-card set features the OHL's Platers. Cards feature full color action shots and a black border along the bottom that contains the player's name, position, number, and team logo. These cards are not numbered, therefore they appear in the order they came out of the sealed set.

COMPLETE SET (31) 4.00 10.00
1 Brian O'Leary ACO .02 .10
2 Dave Siciliano HCO .02 .10
3 Michael Barrett .15 .40
4 Kenny Corupe .20 .50
5 Tim Hamel .15 .40
6 Curtis Sanford .40 1.00
7 Agris Saviels .20 .50
8 Joel Ward .15 .40
9 Bill Zalba .15 .40
10 Matt Rock .15 .40
11 Mike Lymer .15 .40
12 Adam Campbell .15 .40
13 Chris Hopiavuori .15 .40
14 Mike Dombkiewicz .15 .40
15 Cory Roberts .20 .50
16 Greg Jacina .15 .40
17 Wes Goldie .20 .50
18 Dave Stephenson .15 .40
19 Daniel Sisca .15 .40
20 Bryan Kazarian .30 .75
21 Kyle McAllister .30 .75
22 Shawn Snider .15 .40
23 Trevor Blanchard .15 .40
24 Derek Campbell .15 .40
25 Jason Kowalski .15 .40
26 Brent Sullivan .15 .40
27 Alexei Salaschenko .15 .40
28 Nick Vukovic .15 .40
29 Kris Fraser .15 .40
30 Chris Minard .15 .40
31 Team Photo .02 .10

2003-04 Pacific AHL Prospects

COMPLETE SET (100) 15.00 40.00
1 Ari Ahonen .40 1.00
2 Adrian Foster .20 .50
3 Tuomas Pihlman .20 .50
4 Aleksander Suglobov .20 .50
5 Ray Emery .75 2.00
6 Alexandre Giroux .20 .50
7 Chris Kelly .20 .50
8 Julien Vauclair .20 .50
9 Wade Dubielewicz .40 1.00
10 Jeff Hamilton .20 .50
11 Justin Mapletoft .20 .50
12 Mattias Weinhandl .20 .50
13 Kari Lehtonen 2.00 5.00
14 Tommi Santala .20 .50
15 Karl Stewart .20 .50
16 Ilja Bryzgalov .40 1.00
17 Chris Kunitz .75 2.00
18 Tony Martensson .20 .50
19 Brad Boyes .40 1.00
20 Marcel Goc .30 .75
21 Seamus Kotyk .40 1.00
22 Garrett Stafford .20 .50
23 Miroslav Zalesak .30 .75
24 Jiri Hudler .75 2.00
25 Niklas Kronwall .75 2.00
26 Marc Lamothe .40 1.00
27 Nathan Robinson .20 .50
28 Benoit Gratton .20 .50
29 Alexander Perezhogin .40 1.00
30 Tomas Plekanec .40 1.00
31 Eero Somervuori .20 .50
32 Jozef Balej .40 1.00
33 Jason LaBarbera .60 1.50
34 Dominic Moore .30 .75
35 Fedor Tyutin .30 .75
36 Layne Ulmer .20 .50
37 Chad Wiseman .20 .50
38 Peter Budaj .60 1.50
39 Eric Perrin .40 1.00
40 Dan Cavanaugh .20 .50
41 Kyle Wanvig .40 1.00
42 Patrick DesRochers .30 .75
43 Dany Sabourin .40 1.00
44 Mike Zigomanis .20 .50
45 Scott Barney .20 .50
46 Mathieu Chouinard .40 1.00
47 Noah Clarke .20 .50
48 Denis Grebeshkov .20 .50
49 Adam Hauser .75 2.00
50 Steve Kelly .20 .50
51 Yanick Lehoux .20 .50
52 Pavel Rosa .20 .50
53 Fedor Fedorov .40 1.00
54 Kirill Koltsov .20 .50
55 Brandon Reid .40 1.00
56 Simon Gamache .40 1.00
57 Darren Haydar .40 1.00
58 Andrew Hutchinson .20 .50
59 Timofei Shishkanov .20 .50
60 Scottie Upshall SP 6.00 15.00
61 Anton Babchuk .20 .50
62 Matt Ellison .20 .50
63 Kirby Law .20 .50
64 Antero Niittymaki .40 1.00
65 Graham Mink .20 .50
66 Maxime Ouellet .40 1.00
67 Pat Leahy .20 .50
68 Colton Orr .75 2.00
69 Hannu Toivonen .75 2.00
70 Ryan Miller 1.25 3.00
71 Jason Pominville .75 2.00
72 Eric Beaudoin .20 .50
73 Mike Green .40 1.00
74 Lukas Krajicek .20 .50
75 Denis Shvidki .20 .50
76 Petr Taticek .20 .50
77 David LeNeveu .40 1.00
78 Fredrik Sjostrom .20 .50
79 Jeff Taffe .20 .50
80 Brendan Bell .20 .50
81 Sebastien Centomo .40 1.00
82 Mikael Tellqvist .60 1.50
83 Kyle Wellwood .40 1.00
84 Tim Jackman .20 .50
85 Aaron Johnson .20 .50
86 Pascal Leclaire .40 1.00
87 Brad Moran .20 .50
88 Doug Lynch .20 .50
89 Mike Morrison .40 1.00
90 Jani Rita .20 .50
91 Steve Valiquette .40 1.00
92 Jason Bacashihua .40 1.00
93 Dan Jancevski .20 .50
94 Colby Armstrong .40 1.00
95 Andy Chiodo .40 1.00
96 Michel Ouellet .40 1.00
97 Michal Sivek .20 .50
98 Jay McClement .20 .50
99 Johnny Pohl .20 .50
100 Peter Sejna .20 .50

2003-04 Pacific AHL Prospects Gold

*GOLD/925: 2X TO 5X BASIC CARDS
STATED PRINT RUN 925 SER.#'d SETS

2003-04 Pacific AHL Prospects Autographs

PRINT RUN 500 SER.#'d SETS
1 Kari Lehtonen 15.00 40.00
2 Ryan Miller 12.50 30.00
3 Wade Dubielewicz 12.50 30.00
4 David LeNeveu 12.50 30.00
5 Ari Ahonen 15.00 40.00
6 Pascal Leclaire 12.50 30.00

2003-04 Pacific AHL Prospects Crease Lightning

STATED ODDS 1:10
1 Ari Ahonen 1.50 4.00
2 Kari Lehtonen 3.00 8.00
3 Phil Sauve 1.50 4.00
4 Alex Auld 1.50 4.00
5 Rastislav Stana 2.50 6.00
6 Andrew Raycroft 3.00 8.00
7 Ryan Miller 2.50 6.00
8 Pascal Leclaire 2.00 5.00

2003-04 Pacific AHL Prospects Destined for Greatness

COMMON CARD (1-10) 1.25 3.00
STATED ODDS 1:5
1 Jason Spezza 3.00 8.00
2 Antoine Vermette 1.25 3.00
3 Rick DiPietro 1.25 3.00
4 Trent Hunter 2.50 6.00
5 Jonathan Cheechoo 3.00 8.00
6 Jiri Hudler 1.50 4.00
7 Michael Ryder 2.00 5.00
8 Jason King 1.25 3.00
9 Carlo Colaiacovo 1.25 3.00
10 Peter Sejna 1.25 3.00

2003-04 Pacific AHL Prospects Jerseys

STATED ODDS ONE PER HOBBY BOX
1 Wade Dubielewicz 10.00 25.00
2 Jeff Hamilton 6.00 15.00
3 Tomas Plekanec 5.00 12.00
4 Denis Shvidki 5.00 12.00
5 David LeNeveu 8.00 20.00
6 Matt Murley 8.00 20.00

1995-96 PEI Senators

This set features the Senators of the AHL. These postcard-sized (5X7) collectibles are blank backed and are believed to have been issued as a promotional giveaway.

COMPLETE SET (24) 6.00 15.00
1 Scott Allison .20 .50
2 Radim Bicanek .20 .50
3 Patrick Charbonneau .20 .50
4 Pavol Demitra 1.25 3.00
5 Cosmo Dupaul .20 .50
6 Daniel Guerard .20 .50
7 Steve Guolla .30 .75
8 Shawn Heaphy .20 .50
9 Justin Hocking .20 .50
10 Martin Lamarche .20 .50
11 Eric Lavigne .20 .50
12 Kaj Linna .30 .75
13 Darrin Madeley .30 .75
14 Chad Penney .20 .50
15 Michel Picard .20 .50
16 Lance Pitlick .30 .75
17 Jean-Yves Roy .30 .75
18 Claude Savoie .20 .50
19 Darcy Simon .20 .50
20 Steve Strunk .20 .50
21 Patrick Traverse .20 .50
22 Jason Zent .20 .50
23 Coaching Staff .08 .25
24 Brutus MAS .02 .10

2003-04 P.E.I. Rocket

COMPLETE SET (24) 5.00 12.00
1 Julien Beaulieu .20 .50
2 Jimmy Bonneru .20 .50
3 Jonathan Boutin .30 .75
4 Pierre-Andre Bureau .20 .50
5 Yanick Charron .20 .50
6 Marc-Andre Gragnani .20 .50
7 Tyler Hawes .20 .50
8 Milan Hruska .20 .50
9 David Laliberte .20 .50
10 Michael Lambert .20 .50
11 Mark Lee .20 .50
12 Fabien Laniel .20 .50
13 Maxim Lapierre .20 .50
14 Jeff Macauley .20 .50
15 Tyler Noye .20 .50
16 Brent Maclellan .20 .50
17 Ryan Mior .30 .75
18 Sebastien Nolet .30 .75
19 Steve Pelletier .20 .50
20 Jonathan Persson .20 .50
21 Jean-Francois Roux .20 .50
22 Dominic Soucy .20 .50
23 Steve Tilley .20 .50
24 Cory Urquhart .20 .50

2004-05 P.E.I. Rocket

A total of 400 team sets were produced. Card #23 does not exist.

COMPLETE SET (30) 5.00 12.00
1 Alexandre Boivin .15 .40
2 Anthony Pototschnik .15 .40
3 Billy Bezeau .15 .40
4 Connor MacDonald .15 .40
5 David Laliberte .15 .40
6 David MacDonald .15 .40
7 Dominic Soucy .15 .40
8 Greg O'Brien .15 .40
9 Jimmy Bonneau .15 .40
10 Jonathan Boutin .40 1.00
11 Julien Beaulieu .15 .40
12 Kris MacDonald .15 .40
13 Marc-Andre Gragnani .15 .40
14 Maxim Lapierre .15 .40
15 Michael Dubuc .15 .40
16 Michel Charette .15 .40
17 Pierre-Andre Bureau .15 .40
18 Riku Korpinen .15 .40
19 Ryan Mior .40 1.00
20 Tyler Hawes .15 .40
21 Viatcheslav Trukhno .30 .75
22 Yanick Charron .15 .40
24 Kevin Hamel .15 .40
25 Alexander Ennaffati .15 .40
26 Pierre Bergeron .15 .40
27 Jean-Francois Boucher .15 .40
28 Jean-Francois Bernard .40 1.00
29 Fabien Laniel .15 .40
30 Louis-Philippe Lachance .15 .40
31 Alain Vigneault CO .15 .40

2005-06 P.E.I. Rocket

COMPLETE SET (29) 6.00 15.00
1 Ryan Mior .40 1.00
2 Stephen Lund .20 .50
3 Louis-Philippe LaChance .20 .50
4 Travis Mealy .20 .50
5 Nathan Snowie .20 .50
6 Alexandre Boivin .20 .50
7 Geoff Walker .20 .50
8 Slava Trukhno .40 1.00
9 Greg O'Brien .20 .50
10 Stanson Donovan .20 .50
11 David Laliberte .20 .50
12 Devan Praught .20 .50
13 Olivier Gauthier .20 .50
14 Tyler Hawes .20 .50
15 Anton Skorykh .20 .50
16 Lucasz Steciuk .20 .50
17 Nicolas Leduc .20 .50
18 Jean-Claude Milot .20 .50
19 Joseph Haddad .20 .50
20 Michael Dubuc .20 .50
21 Chad Locke .20 .50
22 Steve Natywary .20 .50
23 Matthew LaChaine .20 .50
24 Antoine Lafleur .40 1.00
25 Simon Bolduc .20 .50
26 David MacDonald .20 .50
27 Pascal Lebel .20 .50
28 Marc-Andre Gragnani .20 .50
29 Danny Stewart .20 .50

2006-07 P.E.I. Rocket

COMPLETE SET (23) 8.00 15.00
1 David Laliberte .25 .60
2 Geoff Walker .25 .60
3 Ryan Mior .30 .75
4 Antoine Lafleur .50 1.25
5 Stephen Lund .25 .60
6 Pierre-Marc Guilbault .25 .60
7 Jordon Southorn .25 .60
8 Pierre-Luc Lessard .25 .60
9 Marc-Andre Gragnani .40 1.00
10 Pascal Boutin .25 .60
11 Chris Doyle .25 .60
12 Martin Latal .25 .60
13 Guillaume Doucet .25 .60
14 Lucas Mckinley .25 .60
15 Devan Praught .25 .60
16 Benoit Levesque .25 .60
17 Tyles Hawes .25 .60
18 Peter Cmorej .25 .60
19 Matthew Lachaine .25 .60
20 Maxim Cliché .25 .60
21 Joey Haddad .25 .60
22 Chad Locke .25 .60
23 Gregory Paynter .25 .60

2002-03 Pee Dee Pride RBI

COMPLETE SET (18) 8.00 20.00
133 B.J. Adams .40 1.00
134 Daniel Carriere .40 1.00
135 Aaron Gates .40 1.00
136 Mike Glumac .60 1.50
137 Wes Goldie .40 1.00
138 Derek Halldorson .40 1.00
139 Kyle Kidney .40 1.00
140 Gregor Krajnc .40 1.00
141 Ryan Knox .40 1.00
142 Eric Naud .40 1.00
143 Jason Metcalfe .40 1.00
144 Matt Reid .40 1.00
145 Jason Robinson .40 1.00
146 Greg Schmidt .40 1.00
147 Allan Sirois .40 1.00
148 Mike Torney .40 1.00
149 Matt Underhill .40 1.00
150 Ron Vogel .75 2.00

1996-97 Pensacola Ice Pilots

This set features the Ice Pilots of the ECHL. The standard-sized cards were produced by DLUX printing and sold by the team at home games.

COMPLETE SET (24) 4.00 10.00
1 Craig Brown .15 .40
2 Stephane Julien .15 .40
3 David Borrozino .15 .40
4 Jeremy Mylymok .15 .40
5 Patrik Alvin .15 .40
6 Rostislav Saglo .15 .40
7 Glen Metropolit .40 1.00
8 Chad Quenneville .15 .40
9 Trevor Buchanan .15 .40
10 Brandon Gray .15 .40
11 Jon Pirrong .30 .75
12 Brent Gretzky .30 .75
13 Martin LaChaine .15 .40
14 Brian Secord .15 .40
15 Hugo Belanger .15 .40
16 Christian Sbrocca .15 .40
17 Tony Prpic .15 .40
18 Shane Calder .15 .40
19 Nick Stajduhar .15 .40
20 Brendan Concannon .15 .40
21 Sean Gauthier .20 .50
22 Al Pederson CO .15 .40
23 George Kozak .15 .40
NNO Header Card .02 .10

1997-98 Pensacola Ice Pilots

This 25-card set features the Ice Pilots of the ECHL. The set apparently was handed out at as a promotional item at several late-season games.

COMPLETE SET (25) 5.00 10.00
1 Team Photo .20 .50
2 J.F. Aube .30 .75
3 Craig Brown .20 .50
4 Michael Burkett .20 .50
5 Shane Calder .20 .50
6 Martin Chouinard .20 .50
7 Brendan Concannon .20 .50
8 Jon Dunmar .20 .50
9 Sean Gauthier .20 .50
10 Christian Gosselin .20 .50
11 Brian LaFleur .20 .50
12 Steven Low .20 .50
13 Scott Malone .20 .50
14 Mike Mayhew .20 .50
15 Keith O'Connell .20 .50
16 Val Passarelli .30 .75
17 Mark Polak .20 .50
18 Chad Quenneville .20 .50
19 Andrew Rodgers .20 .50
20 Nick Stajduhar .20 .50
21 Mike Sullivan .20 .50
22 Kelly Hultgren .20 .50
23 George Kozak ACO .20 .50
24 Allen Pedersen HCO .20 .50
25 D-Lux Printing .20 .50

1998-99 Pensacola Ice Pilots

This set features the Ice Pilots of the ECHL. According to various sources, the sets were intended to be issued as a promotional giveaway, but legal or financial issues forced cancellation of those plans. Several players and team officials were given sets, however, and some have made their way into the secondary market. They are checklisted below.

1 Shane Calder 2.00 5.00
2 Nick Stajduhar 2.00 5.00
3 Etienne Beaudry 2.00 5.00
4 Bob Wilkie 2.00 5.00
5 Don Chase 2.00 5.00
6 Stephen Naughton 2.00 5.00
7 Chad Quenneville 2.00 5.00
8 Keith O'Connell 2.00 5.00
9 Brendan Concannon 2.00 5.00
10 Keli Corpse 2.00 5.00
11 Andrew Rodgers 2.00 5.00
12 Dave Ivaska 2.00 5.00
13 Rob Phillips 2.00 5.00
14 Mark Polak 2.00 5.00
15 Craig Brown 2.00 5.00
16 Tom Noble 2.00 5.00
17 Eon MacFarlane 2.00 5.00
18 Allen Pedersen CO 2.00 5.00
19 George Kosak CO 2.00 5.00
20 Iceman MAS 2.00 5.00
21 Pensacola Ice Pilots 2.00 5.00
22 The Hangar 2.00 5.00
23 Pensacola Ice Pilots 2.00 5.00
24 Kelly Hultgren 2.00 5.00
25 Mike Sullivan 2.00 5.00
26 Pensacola Ice Pilots CL 2.00 5.00
27 PHPA Web Site 2.00 5.00

2003-04 Pensacola Ice Pilots

This set was produced by RBI Sports with a production run limited to 250 copies. The numbering sequence reflects the entire run of RBI sets that season.

COMPLETE SET (16) 8.00 20.00
337 Tyler Beechey .40 1.00
338 Greg Chambers .40 1.00
339 Brian Collins .40 1.00
340 Brad Cruikshank .40 1.00
341 Brian Eklund .75 2.00
342 Brandon Fleenor .40 1.00
343 Brett Gibson .40 1.00
344 Jade Galbraith .40 1.00
345 Aaron Gionet .40 1.00
346 Dwayne Hay .40 1.00
347 Andreas Holmqvist .40 1.00
348 Evgeny Konstantinov .75 2.00
349 Wes Mason .40 1.00
350 Corey Neilson .75 2.00
351 Aaron Phillips .40 1.00
352 Kent Sauer .40 1.00

2004-05 Penticton Vees

The Vees play in the BC Tier 2 Junior League.

COMPLETE SET (25) 6.00 15.00
1 History Card .04 .10
2 Checklist .04 .10
3 Josh Brown .30 .75
4 Aaron Agnew .30 .75
5 Ben Robinson .30 .75
6 Brian Lobler .30 .75
7 Shaun MacDonald .30 .75
8 Ryan Coghlan .60 1.50
9 Jon Cara .30 .75
10 Colin Williams .30 .75
11 Mike Towns .30 .75
12 Jason Harding .30 .75
13 Kevin Borba .60 1.50
14 Cody Collins .30 .75
15 Alex MacLeod .30 .75
16 Chris Rengert .30 .75
17 Peter Farrell .30 .75
18 Justin Coutu .30 .75
19 John Kopp .30 .75
20 Adrian Jack .30 .75
21 Brad Thiessen .75 2.00
22 Corey Milan .60 1.50
23 Bruno Campese CO .04 .10
24 Ken Law ACO .04 .10
25 Dan Marshall ANN .04 .10

2005-06 Penticton Vees

COMPLETE SET (24) 10.00 20.00
1 Brennan Barker .40 1.00
2 Jordan Cheveldave .40 1.00
3 Ryan Costanzo .40 1.00
4 Deron Cousens .40 1.00
5 Peter Farrell .40 1.00
6 Tanner House .40 1.00
7 John Kopp .40 1.00
8 Justin Krueger .40 1.00
9 Brian Lebler .40 1.00
10 Alex MacLeod .40 1.00
11 Corey Milan .40 1.00
12 T.J. Miller .40 1.00
13 Ivo Musa .40 1.00
14 Lee Pagee .40 1.00
15 Ben Robinson .40 1.00
16 Robert Skinner .40 1.00
17 Gary Sylvester .40 1.00
18 Mike Towns .40 1.00
19 Evan Trupp .40 1.00
20 Ryan Wagner .40 1.00
21 Mark Walters .40 1.00
22 Jordan White .40 1.00
23 Bruno Campese CO .10 .25
24 1986 Penticton Knights .10 .25

2006-07 Penticton Vees

COMPLETE SET (25) 12.00 20.00
1 Jeremy Beller .30 .75
2 Travis Briard .30 .75
3 Steve Cameron .30 .75
4 Deron Cousens .30 .75
5 Brad Davis .30 .75
6 Dustin Donaghy .30 .75
7 Nigel Dube .30 .75
8 Joel Eisenkirch .30 .75
9 Jordan Funk .30 .75
10 Elias Grossmann .30 .75
11 Michael Guzzo .30 .75
12 Brett Hextall .30 .75
13 Tanner House .30 .75
14 Alex MacLeod .30 .75
15 Kyle McMurphy .30 .75
16 Corey Milan .30 .75
17 Bryant Molle .40 1.00
18 Robert Skinner .30 .75
19 Evan Smith .30 .75
20 Gary Sylvester .30 .75
21 Mike Towns .30 .75
22 Evan Trupp .30 .75
23 Ryan Wagner .30 .75
24 Bruno Campese HC .30 .75
25 72-73 Penticton Broncos Team Photo .30 .75

2007-08 Penticton Vees

COMPLETE SET (21) 5.00 12.00
1 James Bettauer .25 .60
2 Zak Dalpe .25 .60
3 Alex Evin .25 .60
4 Elias Grossmann .25 .60
5 Michael Guzzo .25 .60
6 Michael Hengen .25 .60
7 Brett Hextall .25 .60
8 Zack Josepher .25 .60
9 Nic Knudsen .25 .60
10 Devon Krogh .25 .60
11 Eric Kroshus .25 .60
12 Mitch Labreche .25 .60
13 Denver Manderson .25 .60
14 Kyle McMurphy .25 .60
15 Bryan Mountain .25 .60
16 Trevor Nill .25 .60
17 Cory Schneider .50 1.25
18 Austin Smith .25 .60
19 Ryan Wagner .25 .60
20 Nathan Westover .25 .60
21 Fred Harbinson HC .15 .40

1992-93 Peoria Rivermen

Sponsored by Coca-Cola and Kroger, this 30-card set measures the standard size. The fronts feature color player photos with a white border. The team logo, the player's name, and position appear in a gray bar under the photo, while "1992" is printed in white letters on a blue triangle in the top right corner of the photo. The cards are unnumbered and checklisted below in alphabetical order.

COMPLETE SET (30) 4.00 10.00
1 Jeff Batters .15 .40
2 Parris Duffus .20 .50
3 Greg Eberle TR .02 .10
4 John Faginkrantz MG .02 .10
5 Denny Felsner .15 .40
6 Derek Frenette .15 .40
7 Ron Handy .15 .40
8 Joe Hawley .15 .40
9 Terry Hollinger .15 .40
10 Ron Hoover .15 .40
11 Daniel Laperriere .20 .50
12 Lee J. Leslie .15 .40
13 Dave Mackey .15 .40
14 Jason Marshall .20 .50
15 Brian McKee .15 .40
16 Rick Meagher CO .15 .40
17 Kevin Miehm .15 .40
18 Brian Pellerin ACO .02 .10
19 Mark Reeds .15 .40
20 Kyle Reeves .15 .40
21 Rob Robinson .15 .40
22 Jason Ruff .15 .40
23 Geoff Sarjeant .30 .75
24 Richard Pion .15 .40
25 Darren Veitch .15 .40
26 Doug Wickenheiser .15 .40
27 Shawn Wheeler .15 .40
28 Checklist .02 .10
29 Coca Cola Coupon .02 .10
30 Title Card .02 .10

1993-94 Peoria Rivermen

Produced by 1993 Hat Tricks, Inc., this 31-card D.A.R.E. (Drug Abuse Resistance Education) set measures approximately 2 3/8" by 3 1/4" and celebrates the tenth anniversary of the Peoria Rivermen (International Hockey League). The fronts feature full-bleed color action photos, except at the bottom where an orange stripe separates a thicker blue stripe carrying player information. The 10th anniversary logo in the lower right corner completes the front. The cards are unnumbered and checklisted below in alphabetical order.

COMPLETE SET (31) 4.00 10.00

1 Mark Bassen .15 .40
2 Jeff Batters .15 .40
3 Rene Chapdelaine .15 .40
4 Doug Crossman .20 .50
5 Parris Duffus .30 .75
6 Greg Eberle TR .02 .10
7 Doug Evans .15 .40
8 Kevin Evans .15 .40
9 John Faginkrantz EQ MG .02 .10
10 Denny Felsner .15 .40
11 Derek Frenette .15 .40
12 Terry Hollinger .15 .40
13 Ron Hoover .15 .40
14 Butch Kaebel .15 .40
15 Nathan Lafayette .15 .40
16 Dan Laperriere .20 .50
17 Dave Mackey .15 .40
18 Paul MacLean CO .15 .40
19 Michel Mongeau .20 .50
20 Brian Pellerin .15 .40
21 Rick Pion .15 .40
22 Vitali Prokhorov .15 .40
23 Mark Reeds ACO .02 .10
24 John Roderick .15 .40
25 Geoff Sarjeant .30 .75
26 Steve Staios .20 .50
27 Darren Veitch .15 .40
28 Nick Vitucci .30 .75
29 Title card .02 .10
(Team history on back)
30 Checklist .02 .10
31 Alcohol is its own .02 .10
puni

1995-96 Peoria Rivermen

This standard-sized, 24-card set was produced by the Rivermen and offered for sale through the club at games and by mail. The cards are unnumbered and listed below in alphabetical order.

COMPLETE SET (24) 4.00 10.00
1 Jon Casey .30 .75
2 Rene Chapdelaine .20 .50
3 Doug Evans .20 .50
4 Eric Fenton .20 .50
5 Shannon Finn .15 .40
6 Martin Hamrlik .15 .40
7 Ron Hoover .15 .40
8 Jacques Joubert .15 .40
9 Lee J. Leslie .20 .50
10 Dave MacIntyre .20 .50
11 Jason Miller .15 .40
12 Michel Mongeau .30 .75
13 Glenn Mulvenna .20 .50
14 Eric Murano .15 .40
15 Keith Osborne .20 .50
16 Greg Paslawski .20 .50
17 Jon Pratt .15 .40
18 Dan Ratushny .20 .50
19 Patrice Robitaille .20 .50
20 Paul Taylor .15 .40
21 Travis Thiessen .15 .40
22 Steve Thornton .15 .40
23 Kirk Tomlinson .20 .50
24 Steve Wilson .15 .40

1996-97 Peoria Rivermen

This 25-card set marks the debut of the Rivermen as a member club of the ECHL, but continues the tradition of fine sets. The cards feature action photos on the front, and full stats and bio on the reverse. The unnumbered cards are listed below in alphabetical order.

COMPLETE SET (25) 4.00 10.00
1 Mike Barrie .20 .50
2 Doug Bonner .30 .75
3 Greg Eberle .02 .10
John Krouse
4 Brad Essex .15 .40
5 Doug Evans ASST CO .02 .10
6 Liam Garvey .15 .40
7 Trevor Hanas .15 .40
8 Jon Hillebrandt .30 .75
9 Dan Hodge .20 .50
10 Butch Kaebel .15 .40
11 Karson Kaebel .15 .40
12 Justin Krall .15 .40
13 Jeff Kungle .15 .40
14 Kevin Lune .15 .40
15 Darren Maloney .15 .40
16 Dustin McArthur .15 .40
17 Jon Pratt .15 .40
18 Brad Purdie .15 .40
19 Mark Reeds CO .02 .10
20 Jason Saal .30 .75
21 Jan Slavik .15 .40
22 Marc Terris .15 .40
23 Jean-Guy Trudel .20 .50
24 Paul Vincent .20 .50
25 Title Card .02 .10

1996-97 Peoria Rivermen Photo Album

This 24-card set was released in perforated album form as a game night promotional giveaway. The cards are unnumbered and therefore are listed below in alphabetical order.

COMPLETE SET (24) 8.00 20.00
1 Mike Barrie .30 .75
2 Doug Bonner .60 1.50
3 Greg Eberle TR .20 .50
4 Brad Essex .30 .75
5 Doug Evans ASST CO .20 .50
6 Liam Garvey .30 .75
7 Trevor Hanas .30 .75
8 Jon Hillebrandt .60 1.50
9 Dan Hodge .30 .75
10 Butch Kaebel .30 .75
11 Karson Kaebel .30 .75
12 Justin Krall .30 .75
13 John Krouse EQUIP .20 .50
14 Jeff Kungle .30 .75
15 Kevin Lune .30 .75
16 Darren Maloney .30 .75
17 Dustin McArthur .30 .75
18 Jon Pratt .30 .75
19 Brad Purdie .30 .75
20 Jason Saal .60 1.50
21 Jan Slavik .30 .75
22 Marc Terris .30 .75
23 Jean-Guy Trudel .40 1.00
24 Paul Vincent .30 .75

1997-98 Peoria Rivermen

Little is known about this set beyond the confirmed checklist. Additional information can be forwarded to hockeymag@beckett.com.

COMPLETE SET (29) 4.00 10.00
1 Garry Gruber .15 .40
2 Derek Diener .15 .40
3 Samy Nasreddine .20 .50
4 Doug Evans .15 .40
5 Darren Maloney .15 .40
6 Joe Craigen .20 .50
7 Rob Phillips .15 .40
8 Brian Clifford .15 .40
9 Darcy Smith .15 .40
10 Butch Kaebel .20 .50
11 Jean Guy Trudel .20 .50
12 Brad Essex .15 .40
13 Justin Krall .15 .40
14 John Dance .15 .40
15 Marc Terris .15 .40
16 Trevor Hanas .15 .40
17 Dave Paradise .15 .40
18 David Vallieres .15 .40
19 Scott Roche .30 .75
20 Marcel Kuris .15 .40
21 Jon Pratt .15 .40
22 Rob Giffin .20 .50
23 Mark Reeds .20 .50
24 Greg Eberle .15 .40
25 John Krouse EQ .02 .10
26 Mascot .02 .10
27 Title Card .02 .10
28 Header Card .02 .10

1998-99 Peoria Rivermen

This set features the Rivermen of the ECHL. The set was produced by ebk Sports and was sold by the team at home games.

COMPLETE SET (27) 4.80 12.00
1 Darren Maloney .15 .40
2 Dan Hodge .15 .40
3 Doug Evans .15 .40
4 Dan Carney .15 .40
5 Chris Coveny .15 .40
6 Alexandre Couture .15 .40
7 Jamie Thompson .15 .40
8 Jay Kenney .15 .40
9 J.F. Boutin .15 .40
10 Joe Craigen .30 .75
11 Darcy Smith .15 .40
12 Dan Murphy .15 .40
13 Quinn Hancock .15 .40
14 Mark Reeds CO .02 .10
15 Marek Ivan .15 .40
16 Kory Karlander .15 .40
17 Ken Boone .15 .40
18 Jeff Trembecky .15 .40
19 Steve MacKinnon .15 .40
20 Joe Rybar .30 .75
21 Peoria Rivermen .15 .40
22 Scott Roche .30 .75
23 Chad Lang .30 .75
24 Kevin Paden .20 .50
25 Blaine Fitzpatrick .15 .40
26 Mike Schultz .15 .40
27 Darren Maloney AS .02 .10
28 Jamie Thompson AS .15 .40

1999-00 Peoria Rivermen

This set features the Rivermen of the ECHL. The set was produced by Roox and was issued as a promotional giveaway at a home game.

COMPLETE SET (36) 40.00 80.00
1 Rocky MAS .08 .25
2 Don Granato CO .40 1.00
3 Greg Eberle TR .02 .10
4 Jamie Healy TR .02 .10
5 Trevor Baker 1.50 4.00
6 Duane Derksen 2.00 5.00
7 Darren Clark 1.50 4.00
8 Jason Christie 1.50 4.00
9 Blaine Fitzpatrick 1.50 4.00
10 John Gurskis 1.50 4.00
11 Alexandre Couture 1.50 4.00
12 Darren Maloney 1.50 4.00
13 Blaz Emersic 1.50 4.00
14 Cody Rudkowsky 2.00 5.00
15 J.F. Boutin 1.50 4.00
16 Joe Rybar 2.00 5.00
17 Matt Smith 1.50 4.00
18 Tomaz Razinger 1.50 4.00
19 Craig Anderson 1.50 4.00
20 Jason Lawmaster 1.50 4.00
21 Bret Meyers 1.50 4.00
22 Sean Farmer 1.50 4.00
23 Darin Kimble 3.00 8.00
24 Dan Hodge 1.50 4.00
25 Luke Gruden 1.50 4.00
26 Tyler McMillan 1.50 4.00
27 Kenzie Homer 1.50 4.00
28 James Desmarais 1.50 4.00
29 John Butler PRES .02 .10
30 Mike Nelson VP .02 .10
31 Bart Rogers GM .02 .10
32 Michael Sauers GM .02 .10
33 Jim Small GM .02 .10
34 Norm Ulrich DOB .02 .10
35 Manda Girard SALES .02 .10
36 B.J. Stone SALES .02 .10

2001-02 Peoria Rivermen

This set features the Rivermen of the UHL. We have no additional information besides the checklist. If you can shed some light on this issue, please write to hockeymag@beckett.com.

COMPLETE SET (24) 8.00 20.00
1 Checklist .04 .10
2 Jason Christie CO .04 .10
3 Curtis Sanford .75 2.00
4 Bob Gassoff Jr. .40 1.00
5 Chad Starling .40 1.00
6 Blake Evans .40 1.00
7 Kevin Tucker .40 1.00
8 Trevor Baker .40 1.00
9 Jonathan Fauteux .40 1.00
10 Randy Rowe .40 1.00
11 Dustin Kuk .40 1.00
12 Bret Meyers .40 1.00
13 Kevin Granato .40 1.00
14 Dan Hodge .40 1.00
15 Tyler Rennette .40 1.00
16 Ryan Finnerty .40 1.00
17 Brad Voth .40 1.00
18 Joe Rybar .60 1.50
19 Darren Clark .40 1.00
20 Matt Golden .40 1.00
21 Phil Osaer .40 1.00
22 Jason Lawmaster .40 1.00
23 Arvid Rekis .40 1.00
24 Kevin Cloutier .40 1.00

2000-01 Peoria Rivermen

This set features the Rivermen of the ECHL. The set was produced by Roox and sold by the team at its souvenir stands.

COMPLETE SET (21) 4.00 10.00
1 Curtis Sanford .30 2.00
2 Didier Tremblay .20 .50
3 Luke Gruden .20 .50
4 J.F. Boutin .20 .50
5 Lauri Kinos .20 .50
6 Darren Maloney .20 .50
7 Trevor Baker .20 .50
8 Tyler Willis .20 .50
9 Bret Meyers .20 .50
10 Dustin Kuk .20 .50
11 Dan Hodge .20 .50
12 Joe Rybar .20 .50
13 Blaine Fitzpatrick .20 .50
14 Darren Clark .20 .50
15 Matt Golden .20 .50
16 Kenric Exner .40 1.00
17 Jason Lawmaster .20 .50
18 Arvid Rekis .20 .50
19 Tomaz Razinger .20 .50
20 Joe Trotta ACO .10 .25
21 Jason Christie HCO .10 .25

2002-03 Peoria Rivermen

COMPLETE SET (25) 5.00 12.00
1 Jason Christie HCO .10 .25
2 Simon Lajeunesse .40 1.00
3 Trevor Gillies .20 .50
4 Lauri Kinos .20 .50
5 Darren Clark .20 .50
6 Trevor Baker .20 .50
7 Greg Day .20 .50
8 Brett DeCecco .20 .50
9 Randy Rowe .20 .50
10 Randy Copley .20 .50
11 Duane Derksen .40 1.00
12 Kevin Granato .20 .50
13 Tyler Rennette .20 .50
14 Ryan Finnerty .20 .50
15 Brad Voth .20 .50
16 Brendan Brooks .20 .50
17 Derek Booth .20 .50
18 Scott Crawford .20 .50
19 Jeremy Yablonski .20 .50
20 Jason Lawmaster .20 .50
21 Josh Kern .20 .50
22 Arvid Rekis .20 .50
23 Anthony Belza .20 .50
24 Alfie Michaud .40 1.00
NNO Checklist .04 .10

2002-03 Peoria Rivermen Photo Pack

These oversized (11X14) photos were sold in set form by the team. Each card in the set is autographed in black Sharpie and is serial numbered out of 100. The cards are unnumbered and so are listed below in alphabetical order.

COMPLETE SET (8) 25.00 50.00
1 Trevor Baker 2.50 6.00
2 Brendan Brooks 2.50 6.00
3 Darren Clark 2.50 6.00
4 Duane Derksen 4.00 10.00
5 Ryan Finnerty 2.50 6.00
6 Jason Lawmaster 2.50 6.00
7 Alfie Michaud 4.00 10.00
8 Tyler Rennette 2.50 6.00

2002-03 Peoria Rivermen RBI Sports

COMPLETE SET (18) 8.00 20.00
151 Trevor Baker .40 1.00
152 Anthony Belza .40 1.00
153 Derek Booth .40 1.00
154 Brendan Brooks .40 1.00
155 Darren Clark .40 1.00
156 Randy Copley .40 1.00
157 Scott Crawford .40 1.00
158 Greg Day .40 1.00
159 Duane Derksen .75 2.00
160 Trevor Gillies .40 1.00
161 Josh Kern .40 1.00
162 Jason Lawmaster .75 2.00
163 Alfie Michaud .75 2.00
164 Arvid Rekis .40 1.00
165 Tyler Rennette .40 1.00
166 Randy Rowe .40 1.00
167 Rod Taylor .40 1.00
168 Brad Voth .40 1.00

2003-04 Peoria Rivermen

This set was produced by Choice Marketing and sold at home games.

COMPLETE SET (24) 4.00 10.00
1 Adam Edinger .15 .40
2 Brendan Brooks .15 .40
3 Bret DeCecco .15 .40
4 Brett Scheffelmaier .15 .40
5 Chad Starling .15 .40
6 Colin Hemingway .15 .40
7 Craig Olynick .15 .40
8 Doug MacIver .15 .40
9 George Halkidis .15 .40
10 Greg Black .15 .40
11 Joe Pereira .15 .40
12 Joe Vandermeer .15 .40
13 Ken Goetz .30 .75
14 Levente Szuper .40 1.00
15 Malcolm Hutt .15 .40
16 Malcolm MacMillan .15 .40
17 Marty Johnston .15 .40
18 Mike Valley .30 .75
19 Randy Rowe .15 .40
20 Scott Crawford .15 .40
21 Scott Turner .15 .40
22 Trevor Baker .30 .75
23 Tyler Rennette .15 .40
24 Jason Christie HCO .04 .10
NNO Checklist .04 .10

2004-05 Peoria Rivermen

COMPLETE SET (25) 5.00 12.00
1 Chad Starling .20 .50
2 Warren Toews .20 .50
3 Mark Jarant .20 .50
4 Chris Bogas .20 .50
5 Brian McCullough .20 .50
6 Randy Rowe .20 .50
7 Trevor Baker .20 .50
8 Justin Maiser .20 .50
9 Travis Rycroft .20 .50
10 Scott Turner .20 .50
11 Alfie Michaud .40 1.00
12 Chris Beckford-Tseu .40 1.00
13 Kris Kasper .40 1.00
14 Ed Hill .20 .50
15 Jake Riddle .20 .50
16 James Sanford .20 .50
17 Patrick Wellar .20 .50
18 David Kaczowka .20 .50
19 Tyler Rennette .20 .50
20 Joe Pereira .20 .50
21 Rejean Stringer .04 .10
22 Stringer MASCOT .04 .10
23 Colin Hemingway .20 .50
24 Trevor Byrne .20 .50
25 Jason Christie CO .04 .10

2005-06 Peoria Rivermen

1 Curtis Sanford .40 1.00
2 Mike Mottau .30 .75
3 Rocky Thompson .20 .50
4 Trevor Byrne .20 .50
5 Brendan Buckley .20 .50
6 Gavin Morgan .20 .50
7 Colin Hemingway .20 .50
8 Jon DiSalvatore .20 .50
9 Mike Stuart .20 .50
10 Blake Evans .20 .50
11 Mike Glumac .20 .50
12 D.J. King .20 .50
13 Aaron MacKenzie .20 .50
14 Troy Riddle .20 .50
15 Trent Whitfield .20 .50
16 Peter Sejna .20 .50
17 Brendan Brooks .20 .50
18 Ryan Ramsay .20 .50
19 Chris Beckford-Tseu .75 2.00
20 Doug Lynch .20 .50
21 Jason Bacashihua .40 1.00
22 Patrick Lalime .40 1.00
23 Jeff Woywitka .20 .50
24 Steve Pleau CO .02 .10

2006-07 Peoria Rivermen

COMPLETE SET (25) 8.00 15.00
1 Chris Beckford-Tseu .60 1.50
2 Michal Birner .20 .50
3 Jon DiSalvatore .20 .50
4 Zack Fitzgerald .20 .50
5 Mike Glumac .30 .75
6 Cam Keith .20 .50
7 D.J. King .20 .50
8 Charles Linglet .20 .50
9 Doug Lynch .20 .50
10 Aaron MacKenzie .20 .50
11 Ryan MacMurchy .20 .50
12 Tomas Mojzis .20 .50
13 Gavin Morgan .20 .50
14 Roman Polak .20 .50
15 Ryan Ramsay .30 .75
16 Marek Schwarz .60 1.50
17 Peter Sejna .20 .50
18 Mike Stuart .20 .50
19 Rocky Thompson .20 .50
20 Trent Whitfield .20 .50
21 Stephen Wood .20 .50
22 Jeff Woywitka .20 .50
23 Konstantin Zakharov .20 .50
24 Dave Baseggio .20 .50
25 Checklist .02 .10

2007-08 Peoria Rivermen

COMPLETE SET (26) 5.00 12.00
1 Dave Baseggio HC .15 .40
2 Chris Beckford-Tseu .25 .60
3 Hans Benson .25 .60
4 Alex Brooks .25 .60
5 Nicholas Drazenovic .25 .60
6 Micki DuPont .25 .60
7 Ryan Glenn .25 .60
8 Mike Glumac .25 .60
9 Alexander Hellstrom .25 .60
10 Martin Kariya .25 .60
11 Cam Keith .25 .60
12 Neil Komadoski .25 .60
13 Nikolay Lemtyugov .25 .60
14 Charles Linglet .25 .60
15 Aaron MacKenzie .25 .60
16 Roman Polak .25 .60
17 Chris Porter .25 .60
18 Ryan Reaves .25 .60
19 Marek Schwarz .25 .60
20 Yan Stastny .25 .60
21 Julian Talbot .25 .60
22 Jean-Guy Trudel .25 .60
23 Steve Wagner .25 .60
24 Trent Whitfield .25 .60
25 Jeff Woywitka .25 .60
NNO Checklist .10 .25

1989-90 Peterborough Petes

This 25-card set paralleled the 7th Inning Sketch OHL league set but featured players of the Peterborough club. The card stock was thicker than the league set and the pictures were sharper.

COMPLETE SET (26) 10.00 25.00
98 Troy Stephens .40 1.00
99 Dan Brown .40 1.00
100 Mike Ricci 1.25 3.00
101 Brent Pope .40 1.00
102 Mike Dagenais .40 1.00
103 Scott Campbell .40 1.00
104 Jamie Pegg .40 1.00
105 Joe Hawley .40 1.00
106 Jason Dawe .40 1.00
107 Paul Mitton .40 1.00
108 Mike Tomlinson .40 1.00
109 Dave Lorentz .40 1.00
110 Dale McTavish .40 1.00
111 Willie McGarvey .40 1.00
112 Don O'Neill .40 1.00
113 Mark Myles .40 1.00
114 Chris Longo .40 1.00
115 Tom Hopkins .40 1.00
116 Jassen Cullimore .40 1.00
117 Geoff Ingram .40 1.00
118 Twohey .40 1.00
Bovair TR
119 Doug Searle .40 1.00
120 Bryan Gendron .40 1.00
121 Andrew Verner .60 1.50
122 Todd Bocjun .60 1.50
123 Dick Todd CO .20 .50

1991-92 Peterborough Petes

This 30-card P.L.A.Y. (Police, Laws and Youth) set measures approximately 2 1/2" by 3 3/4" and features posed, color player photos with bright blue and white borders. The player's name is printed on the picture in white letters in the upper left corner. The team logo appears in the upper right corner.

COMPLETE SET (30) 8.00 20.00
1 Jason Dawe .30 .75
2 Chris Pronger 3.00 8.00
3 Scott Turner .20 .50
4 Chad Grills .20 .50
5 Brent Tully .20 .50
6 Mike Harding .20 .50
7 Chris Longo .20 .50
8 Slapshot MASCOT .02 .10
9 Doug Searle .20 .50
10 Mike Tomlinson .20 .50
11 Bryan Gendron .20 .50
12 Andrew Verner .30 .75
13 Ryan Black .20 .50
14 Don O'Neill .20 .50
15 Jeff Twohey MG .02 .10
CO
16 Dale McTavish .20 .50
17 Jeff Walker .20 .50
18 Matt St. Germain .20 .50
19 Dave Roche .20 .50
20 Colin Wilson .20 .50
21 Jassen Cullimore .20 .50
22 Chad Lang .30 .75
23 Dick Todd MG .20 .50
CO
24 Geordie Kinnear .20 .50
25 Shawn Heins .25 .60
26 John Johnson .20 .50
27 Kelly Vipond .20 .50
NNO Police Crest .02 .10
NNO Kiwanis Sponsor Card .02 .10
NNO Quaker Sponsor Card .02 .10

1993-94 Peterborough Petes

Sponsored by Cardboard Heroes and printed by Slapshot Images Ltd., this standard-size 31-card set features the 1993-94 Peterborough Petes. Only 3,000 of these sets have been produced; the first card also serves as a Certificate of Authenticity and has the individual set number printed in the upper left corner. On a grey background, the fronts feature color action player photos with thin maroon borders. The player's name, position and team name, as well as the producer's logo, appear on the front.

COMPLETE SET (31) 6.00 15.00
1 1992-93 OHL Champions .15 .40
2 Jonathan Murphy .15 .40
3 Dave Roche .15 .40
4 Rob Giffin .15 .40
5 Mike Harding .15 .40
6 Tim Hill .15 .40
7 Darryl Moxam .15 .40
8 Pat Paone .15 .40
9 Brent Tully .15 .40
10 Zac Bierk .30 .75
11 Chad Grills .15 .40
12 Matt St. Germain .15 .40
13 Henrik Eppers .15 .40
14 Rick Emmett .15 .40
15 Chad Lang .20 .50
16 Cameron Mann .40 1.00
17 Steve Hogg .15 .40
18 Mike Williams .15 .40
19 Ryan Nauss .15 .40
20 Jamie Langenbrunner .40 1.00
21 Ryan Douglas .15 .40
22 Matt Johnson .30 .75
23 Kelvin Solari .15 .40
24 Dan Delmonte .15 .40
25 Quayde Lightbody .15 .40
26 Adrian Murray .15 .40
27 Jason Dawe .15 .40
28 Mike Harding .15 .40
29 Chris Pronger 2.00 5.00
30 Sponsor Card .02 .10
Cardboard
NNO Slapshot Ad Card .02 .10

2001-02 Peterborough Petes

This set features the Petes of the OHL. The cards are an oversized 4X6, and feature blurred colour photos on front, with a Gatorade logo upper left and player name and number along the bottom. The cards are not numbered, but are listed in order of jersey number, as they were released. It is believed they were issued as a promotional giveaway by the team.

COMPLETE SET (20) 8.00 20.00
1 Cody Spicer .60 1.50
2 Dustin Wood .40 1.00
3 Bryan Hamm .40 1.00
4 Mark Flood .40 1.00
5 Trevor Hendrix .40 1.00
6 James Edgar .40 1.00
7 Jason Penner .40 1.00
8 Jon Howse .40 1.00
9 Ryan Card .40 1.00
10 Eric Staal 4.00 10.00
11 Josh Patterson .40 1.00
12 Jim Gagnon .40 1.00
13 Brad Self .40 1.00
14 Matt Herneisen .40 1.00
15 Adam Elzinga .40 1.00
16 Greg Chambers .40 1.00
17 Jamie Tardif .40 1.00
18 Matt Armstrong .40 1.00
19 David Currie .60 1.50
20 Lukas Krajicek .75 2.00

2002-03 Peterborough Petes

COMPLETE SET (24) 6.00 15.00
1 Rick Allain CO .04 .10
2 Steve Smith ACO .04 .10
3 Aaron Dawson .20 .50
4 Mark Flood .20 .50
5 Shawn Futers .20 .50
6 Trevor Hendrix .20 .50
7 Jordan Morrison .20 .50
8 Jon Howse .20 .50
9 Ryan Card .20 .50
10 Eric Staal 2.00 5.00
11 Evgeny Kadatskiy .20 .50
12 Josh Patterson .20 .50
13 Jason Penner .20 .50
14 Greg Williams .20 .50
15 Chad Robinson .20 .50
16 Mike Ramsay .20 .50
17 Patrick Kaleta .20 .50
18 Adam Elzinga .20 .50
19 Greg Chambers .20 .50
20 Jamie Tardif .20 .50
21 Mike McKeown .20 .50
22 Jeff MacDougald .20 .50
23 David Currie .20 .50
24 Lukas Krajicek .40 1.00

2004-05 Peterborough Petes Postcards

This set of 5X7 postcard-sized singles were sold in set form by the team.

COMPLETE SET (25) 10.00 25.00
1 Jordan Staal 1.25 3.00
2 Liam Reddox .40 1.00
3 Daniel Ryder .40 1.00
4 Jamie Tardif .40 1.00
5 Eero Kilpelainen .75 2.00
6 Patrick Kaleta .40 1.00
7 Jordan Morrison .40 1.00
8 Trevor Henrikx .40 1.00
9 Mark Flood .40 1.00
10 Niko Vainio .40 1.00
11 Justin Carauna .40 1.00
12 Mike Montgomery .40 1.00
13 Aaron Barton .40 1.00
14 Patrick Kaleta .40 1.00
15 Aaron Dawson .40 1.00
16 Scott Cowie .40 1.00
17 Justin Soryal .40 1.00
18 Darryl Flowers .40 1.00
19 Bryan Young .40 1.00
20 Peter Aston .40 1.00
21 Jadran Baljo .40 1.00
22 Greg Stewart .40 1.00
23 Greg Williams .40 1.00
24 Corey Gault .40 1.00
25 Jeff MacDougald .40 1.00

2002-03 Philadelphia Phantoms

COMPLETE SET (26) 6.00 15.00
1 Antero Niittymaki .75 2.00
2 Bruno St. Jacques .20 .50
3 Dan Peters .20 .50
4 Mark Greig .20 .50
5 Kirby Law .30 .75
6 Peter White .30 .75
7 Eric Betournay .20 .50
8 Jack Baker .20 .50
9 Patrick Sharp .30 .75
10 Guillaume Lefebvre .30 .75
11 Pete Vandermeer .30 .75
12 Andre Savage .20 .50
13 Jim Vandermeer .30 .75
14 Mike Siklenka .30 .75
15 Ian MacNeil .20 .50
16 Ben Stafford .20 .50
17 John Slaney .20 .50
18 Mike Lephart .20 .50
19 Brad Tiley .20 .50
20 Wade Skolney .20 .50
21 Neil Little .40 1.00
22 David Harlock .20 .50
23 John Stevens CO .04 .10
24 Phlex Mascot .04 .10
25 Subway Coupon .04 .10
NNO Checklist .04 .10

2003-04 Philadelphia Phantoms

This set was produced by Choice Marketing and sold at home games.

COMPLETE SET (26) 5.00 12.00
1 Checklist .04 .10
2 Antero Niittymaki .60 1.50
3 Ben Stafford .15 .40
4 Boyd Kane .15 .40
5 Craig Berube .15 .40
6 Dennis Seidenberg .15 .40
7 Freddy Meyer .15 .40
8 Ian MacNeil .15 .40
9 Jeff Woywitka .20 .50
10 Joey Hope .15 .40
11 John Slaney .15 .40
12 Kirby Law .30 .75
13 Mark Murphy .15 .40
14 Mike Peluso .15 .40
15 Mike Siklenka .15 .40
16 Neil Little .40 1.00
17 Nick Deschenes .15 .40
18 P.J. Stock .40 1.00
19 Patrick Sharp .15 .40
20 Pete Vandermeer .30 .75
21 Peter White .15 .40
22 Randy Jones .15 .40
23 Wade Skolney .15 .40
24 John Stevens .15 .40
25 Mascot .04 .10
26 Sponsor .04 .10

2004-05 Philadelphia Phantoms

COMPLETE SET (25) 6.00 15.00
1 Riley Cote .20 .50
2 Ben Eager .30 .75
3 Todd Fedoruk .40 1.00
4 Josh Gratton .60 1.50
5 Joey Hope .20 .50
6 Randy Jones .20 .50
7 Boyd Kane .30 .75
8 Neil Little .40 1.00
9 Eric Meloche .20 .50
10 Freddy Meyer .30 .75
11 Mark Murphy .20 .50
12 Antero Niittymaki .75 2.00
13 Joni Pitkanen .40 1.00
14 David Printz .20 .50
15 Ryan Ready .20 .50
16 Dennis Seidenberg .20 .50
17 Patrick Sharp .30 .75
18 Jon Sim .30 .75
19 Wade Skolney .20 .50
20 John Slaney .20 .50
21 Jeff Smith .20 .50
22 Ben Stafford .20 .50
23 R.J. Umberger .60 1.50
24 Tony Voce .20 .50
NNO Checklist .04 .10

2005-06 Philadelphia Phantoms

COMPLETE SET (26) 5.00 12.00
1 Philadelphia Phantoms CL .01 .01
2 B.J. Abel .20 .50
3 Rejean Beauchemin .40 1.00
4 Marc Cavosie .20 .50
5 Eric Chouinard .20 .50
6 Charlie Cook .20 .50
7 Riley Cote .20 .50
8 Ben Eager .20 .50
9 Triston Grant .20 .50
10 Josh Gratton .40 1.00
11 Joey Hope .20 .50
12 Randy Jones .20 .50
13 Pat Kavanagh .20 .50
14 Eric Meloche .20 .50
15 Freddy Meyer .20 .50
16 Alexandre Picard .20 .50
17 David Printz .20 .50
18 Ryan Ready .20 .50
19 Stefan Ruzicka .20 .50
20 Wade Skolney .20 .50
21 John Slaney .20 .50
22 Jamie Storr .30 .75
23 R.J. Umberger .40 1.00
24 Tony Voce .20 .50
25 John Stevens HC .02 .10
26 Phlex MASCOT .02 .10

2005-06 Philadelphia Phantoms All-Decade Team

COMPLETE SET (12) 8.00 15.00
1 Patrick Sharp .40 1.00
2 Frank Bialowas .75 2.00
3 Mark Greig .40 1.00
4 John Slaney .40 1.00
5 John Stevens .40 1.00
6 Neil Little .75 2.00
7 Peter White .40 1.00
8 Mike Maneluk .40 1.00
9 Kirby Law .40 1.00
10 Freddy Meyer .40 1.00
11 Dennis Seidenberg .40 1.00
12 Antero Niittymaki .75 2.00

2006-07 Philadelphia Phantoms

COMPLETE SET (30) 10.00 18.00
1 Joe Mullen ACO .10 .25
2 Kjell Samuelsson CO .10 .25
3 Ryan Potulny .60 1.50
4 Niko Dimitrakos .30 .75
5 Lars Jonsson .20 .50
6 Denis Tolpeko .20 .50
7 Eric Meloche .20 .50
8 John Slaney .20 .50
9 Martin Houle .40 1.00
10 Rejean Beauchemin .40 1.00
11 Scott Munroe .20 .50
12 Tony Voce .20 .50
13 Triston Grant .40 1.00
14 David Printz .30 .75
15 Nate Guenin .30 .75
16 Ben Eager .30 .75
17 Martin Grenier .20 .50
18 Riley Cote .20 .50
19 Matt Ellison .20 .50
20 Alexandre Picard .20 .50
21 Nolan Baumgartner .20 .50
22 Stefan Ruzicka .30 .75
23 Mark Cullen .20 .50
24 Matt Davis .20 .50
25 Don Morrison .20 .50
26 Jussi Timonen .20 .50
27 Darren Reid .20 .50
28 Frederik Cabana .20 .50
29 Peter Zingoni .20 .50
30 Gino Pisellini .20 .50

1993-94 Phoenix Cobras RHI

This set features the Cobras of Roller Hockey Intl. The set was produced by the team and sold at home games.

COMPLETE SET (20) 3.00 8.00
1 Header Card .02 .10
2 Lee Kasper .20 .50
3 Stuart Silver .20 .50
4 Lou Franceschetti HCO .02 .10
5 Aaron Boh .20 .50
6 Todd Brost .30 .75
7 Michel Couvrette .20 .50
8 Wade Gibson .20 .50
9 Rickard Gronborg .20 .50
10 Hugo Hamelin .20 .50
11 Daniel Larin .20 .50
12 Mike O'Hara .20 .50
13 Sergei Olympiev .20 .50
14 John Redinger .20 .50
15 Brent Sapergia .30 .75
16 Daniel Shank .30 .75
17 Troy Stephens .20 .50
18 Boyd Sutton .20 .50
19 Mike Vukonich .20 .50
20 Alex Zhurik .20 .50

1992-93 Phoenix Roadrunners

Sponsored by Safeway, this 28-card standard-size set features color action photos on the front edged by a blue border on the top and left margins, with full bleed on the bottom and right. The IHL logo is in the top right corner. The player's name and jersey number are printed in red at the bottom while the team name is printed in white immediately above. The team logo is in the lower right and the player's position is printed in red inside a hockey puck in the lower left. The cards are unnumbered and checklisted below in alphabetical order.

COMPLETE SET (28) 4.00 10.00
1 Tim Bothwell CO .15 .40
2 Frank Breault .15 .40
3 Tim Breslin .15 .40
4 Rene Chapdelaine .15 .40
5 Sylvain Couturier .20 .50
6 Phil Crowe .20 .50
7 Darryl Gilmour .20 .50
8 David Goverde .20 .50
9 Ed Kastelic .15 .40
10 Rick Kozuback ACO .02 .10
11 Ted Kramer .15 .40
12 Robert Lang .30 .75
13 Guy Leveque .15 .40
14 Jim Maher .15 .40
15 Brad McCaughey .15 .40
16 Shawn McCosh .15 .40
17 John Mokosak .15 .40
18 Keith Redmond .15 .40
19 Mike Ruark .15 .40
20 Brandy Semchuk .15 .40
21 Dave Stewart .15 .40
22 Brad Tiley .15 .40
23 Dave Tretowicz .15 .40
24 Mike Vukonich .15 .40
25 Tim Watters .20 .50
26 Sean Whyte .15 .40
27 Darryl Williams .15 .40
28 Rocky Roadrunner .02 .10
(Masco

1993-94 Phoenix Roadrunners

This 25-card set measures the standard size. On a black and white marbleized background, the fronts feature color action player photos with rounded corners and a thin blue border. The player's name, position, and number appear under the photo, along with the team logo. The cards are unnumbered and checklisted below in alphabetical order.

COMPLETE SET (25) 4.00 10.00
1 Tim Breslin .15 .40
2 Brian Chapman .15 .40
3 Stephane Charbonneau .15 .40
4 Dan Currie .20 .50
5 Rick Dudley CO .20 .50
6 Marc Fortier .20 .50
7 David Goverde .20 .50
8 Kevin Grant .15 .40
9 Mark Hardy Player/Coach .15 .40
10 Dean Hulett .15 .40
11 Pauli Jaks .20 .50
12 Bob Jay .15 .40
13 Rick Knickle .30 .75
14 Guy Leveque .20 .50
15 Eric Lavigne .20 .50
16 Dominic Lavoie .15 .40
17 Jim Maher .15 .40
18 Brian McReynolds .15 .40
19 Rob Murphy .15 .40
20 Keith Redmond .15 .40
21 Dave Stewart .15 .40
22 Dave Thomlinson .15 .40
23 Brad Tiley .15 .40
24 Jim Vesey .15 .40
25 Darryl Williams .15 .40

1995-96 Phoenix Roadrunners
This 24-card set was produced by Jessen Associates for Collector's Edge. The full colour cards were available as a free promotional item at a game; they also were sold through the team's pro shop for $6. Approximately 8,000 sets were made. The cards are unnumbered and are checklisted below in alphabetical order.

COMPLETE SET (24) 4.80 12.00
1 Ruslan Batyrshin .15 .40
2 Frederik Beaubien .30 .75
3 John Blue .30 .75
4 Mike Boback .15 .40
5 Kevin Brown .20 .50
6 Jim Burton .15 .40
7 Dan Bylsma .20 .50
8 Brian Chapman .15 .40
9 Rob Cowie .15 .40
10 Devin Edgerton .15 .40
11 Ken McRae .15 .40
12 Barry Potomski .30 .75
13 Daniel Rydmark .15 .40
14 Jeff Shevalier .20 .50
15 Gary Shuchuk .20 .50
16 Chris Snell .20 .50
17 Jamie Storr .75 2.00
18 Dave Thomlinson .15 .40
19 Nicholas Vachon .15 .40
20 Jan Vopat .20 .50
21 Steve Wilson .15 .40
22 S.Green .02 .10
S.Wissman
J.Adams
23 Rob Laird CO .02 .10
24 Rocky Roadrunner .02 .10

1998-99 Phoenix Mustangs
This oversized set was issued in perforated strip form. It was handed out at a home game as a promotional giveaway, and most of the singles were sponsored by local doctors.

COMPLETE SET (25) 60.00 150.00
1 Hugo Belanger 3.00 8.00
2 David Goverde 3.00 8.00
3 Dana G. Seltzer MD .08 .25
4 Iannique Renaud 2.50 6.00
5 Mark Spence 2.50 6.00
6 Daniel Shank 8.00 20.00
7 Stu Kulak 3.00 8.00
8 Rusty McKie 2.50 6.00
9 Gene Bono 2.50 6.00
10 Jamie Allan 2.50 6.00
11 Michel Couvrette 2.50 6.00
12 Sebastien Fortier 2.50 6.00
13 Corey Laniuk 2.50 6.00
14 Doug McCarthy 2.50 6.00
15 Tom Menicci 2.50 6.00
16 Savo Mitrovic 2.50 6.00
17 Matt Oliver 2.50 6.00
18 Teemu Numminen 3.00 8.00
19 Bobby Rapoza 2.50 6.00
20 Jason Rose 2.50 6.00
21 Darren Veitch 2.50 6.00
22 Sean Whyte 2.50 6.00
23 Brad McCaughey HCO .08 .25
24 Dick Earle TR .08 .25
25 Rusty the Wrangler Mascot .08 .25

1983-84 Pinebridge Bucks
These card are unnumbered and measure 4 1/8" by 2 3/8". There are reports that there may be as many as 20 cards in this set, this checklist represents the 12 that are confirmed.

COMPLETE SET (12) 6.00 15.00
1 Dave Burke .60 1.50
2 Dan Burrows .60 1.50
3 Kim Collins .60 1.50
4 Bob Fleming .60 1.50
5 Rick Harris .60 1.50
6 Steve Heittola .60 1.50
7 Ken Latta .60 1.50
8 Tom Madsen .60 1.50
9 Larry Mollard .60 1.50
10 Kelly Rissling .60 1.50
11 Frank Perkins CO .20 .50
12 Frank Juror TR .20 .50

2001-02 Plymouth Whalers
COMPLETE SET (33) 15.00 30.00
1 Libor Ustrnul .30 .75
2 Jared Newman .30 .75
3 Stephen Weiss 1.25 3.00
4 Nathan Tennant .30 .75
5 Damian Surma .30 .75
6 Chad LaRose .60 1.50
7 Jeff Phillips .30 .75
8 Kyle Neufeld .30 .75
9 Brad Yeo .30 .75
10 Paul Drew .30 .75
11 Cole Jarrett .30 .75
12 Nate Kiser .30 .75
13 Karl Stewart .60 1.50
14 John Mitchell .30 .75
15 Greg Campbell .60 1.50
16 George Nistas .30 .75
17 Tim Sestito .30 .75
18 Kris Vernarsky .30 .75
19 James Wisniewski .30 .75
20 Danny McDonald .30 .75
21 Jason Bacashihua 1.25 3.00
22 Jonas Fiedler .30 .75
23 David Liffiton .60 1.50
24 Roberts ACO .04 .10
25 Mike Vellucci CO .04 .10
26 Dan Reed .30 .75
27 Bryan Thompson .30 .75
28 Stephen Weiss AS 1.25 3.00
29 Jason Bacashihua AS 1.25 3.00
30 Chad LaRose AS .60 1.50
31 Greg Campbell TP .40 1.00
32 James Wisniewski TP .30 .75

2002-03 Plymouth Whalers
COMPLETE SET (30) 5.00 12.00
1 Cole Jarrett .15 .40
2 Nate Kiser .15 .40
3 Karl Stewart .30 .75
4 John Mitchell .15 .40
5 Jimmy Gagnon .15 .40
6 Sean Thompson .15 .40
7 Chad LaRose .40 1.00
8 John Vigilante .15 .40
9 Taylor Raszka .15 .40
10 Ryan Ramsay .15 .40
11 Mike Letizia .15 .40
12 Steve Phillips .15 .40
13 Paul Drew .30 .75
14 Jonas Fielder .15 .40
15 Brent Mahon .15 .40
16 Cole Jarrett AS .15 .40
17 Tim Sestito .15 .40
18 Martin Cizek .15 .40
19 Chad LaRose AS .40 1.00
20 Chris Thorburn .30 .75
21 James Wisniewski .30 .75
22 Mike Nelson .15 .40
23 Nick Vernelli .15 .40
24 Jeff Weber .30 .75
25 Erik Lundmark .15 .40
26 David Liffiton .30 .75
27 David Liffiton .30 .75
Top Prospect
28 Mascot .04 .10
29 Pat Peake RET .10 .25
30 Team Photo .10 .25

2003-04 Plymouth Whalers
COMPLETE SET (28) 6.00 15.00
1 Rane Carnegie .30 .75
2 Dan Collins .20 .50
3 Jonas Fiedler .20 .50
4 Jordan Grant .20 .50
5 Brent Mahon .20 .50
6 Mike Martinelli .20 .50
7 Vaclav Meidl .20 .50
8 John Mitchell .20 .50
9 Gino Pisellini .20 .50
10 Ryan Ramsay .20 .50
11 Tim Sestito .20 .50
12 Sean Thompson .20 .50
13 Nick Vernelli .20 .50
14 John Vigilante .20 .50
15 Craig Cescon .20 .50
16 Mike Knight .20 .50
17 David Liffiton .30 .75
18 Erik Lundmark .20 .50
19 Ryan McGinnis .20 .50
20 Richard Power .20 .50
21 James Wisniewski .30 .75
22 Paul Drew .20 .50
23 Dan Miller .20 .50
24 Ryan Nie .20 .50
25 Michael Vellucci CO .04 .10
26 Coaching Staff .04 .10
27 Alex Roberts .20 .50
28 Mascot .04 .10

2005-06 Plymouth Whalers
COMPLETE SET (29) 8.00 15.00
A01 John Vigilante .20 .50
A02 John Armstrong .20 .50
A03 Jared Boll .30 .75
A04 Steve Ward .20 .50
A05 Cory Tanaka .20 .50
A06 Tom Sestito .20 .50
A07 Gino Pisellini .30 .75
A08 Ryan Nie .20 .50
A09 James Neal .50 1.25
A10 Vaclav Meidl .30 .75
A11 Ryan McGinnis .20 .50
A12 Mike Letizia .20 .50
A13 Andrew Fournier .20 .50
A14 Dan Collins .20 .50
B01 Justin Peters .30 .75
B02 Justin Garay .20 .50
B03 Jeremy Smith .60 1.50
B04 Ondrej Otcenas .20 .50
B05 Wes Cunningham .20 .50
B06 Derek Merlini .20 .50
B07 Zack Shepley .20 .50
B08 Joe McCann .20 .50
B09 Brett Bellemore .20 .50
B10 Leo Jenner .20 .50
B11 Chris Terry .20 .50
B12 Joe Gaynor .20 .50
B13 Ryan Stephenson .20 .50
B14 Evan Brophey .20 .50
B15 Plymouth Whalers CL .01 .01

2006-07 Plymouth Whalers
COMPLETE SET (29) 12.00 20.00
1 John Armstrong .20 .50
2 Brett Bellemore .20 .50
3 Jared Boll .20 .50
4 Evan Brophey .20 .50
5 Dan Collins .20 .50
6 Vern Cooper .30 .75
7 Wes Cunningham .20 .50
8 Andrew Fournier .20 .50
9 Joe Gaynor .20 .50
10 Kaine Geldart .20 .50
11 A.J. Jenks .20 .50
12 Leo Jenner .20 .50
13 Joe McCann .20 .50
14 Ryan McGinnis .20 .50
15 James Neal 1.00 2.50
16 Michal Neuvirth .60 1.50
17 Sean O'Connor .20 .50
18 Dan Ryder .40 1.00
19 Tom Sestito .40 1.00
20 Zack Shepley .20 .50
21 Jozef Sladok .20 .50
22 Jeremy Smith .60 1.50
23 Chris Terry .40 1.00
24 Brett Valliquette .20 .50
25 Steve Ward .20 .50
26 Steven Whitely .20 .50
27 James Neal 1.00 2.50
28 Plymouth Whalers .10 .25
29 Shooter MASCOT .02 .10

2014-15 Plymouth Whalers
COMPLETE SET (32) 8.00 20.00
1 Header Card .30 .75
2 Alex Peters .30 .75
3 Alex DiCarlo .30 .75
4 Sean Callaghan .30 .75
5 Tyler Sensky .30 .75
6 Mitch Jones .30 .75
7 Frankie Vilardi .30 .75
8 Nicholas Caamano .30 .75
9 Connor Chatham .30 .75
10 Viktor Crus-Rydberg .30 .75
11 Bryce Yetman .30 .75
12 Danny Vanderwiel .30 .75
13 Cullen Mercer .30 .75
14 Joshua Wesley .30 .75
15 Ryan Moore .40 1.00
16 Connor Sills .30 .75
17 Mathieu Henderson .30 .75
18 Yannick Rathgeb .30 .75
19 Zach Bowman .30 .75
20 Glanluca Curcuruto .30 .75
21 Vincent Scognamiglio .30 .75
22 Alex Nedeljkovic .30 .75
23 William Bitten .30 .75
24 Jacob Collins .30 .75
25 Sonny Milano .30 .75
26 Mathew Campagna .40 1.00
27 Overage Players .30 .75
28 Shooter MASCOT .30 .75
29 Tyler Seguin AL .50 1.25
30 James Neal AL .40 1.00
31 David Legwand AL .40 1.00
32 Team Photo .30 .75

2003-04 Port Huron Beacons
This set was issued as a promotional giveaway at several Beacons home games. The cards were issued in perforated strip form.

COMPLETE SET (23) 10.00 25.00
1 Michel Beausoleil .40 1.00
2 David Bell .40 1.00
3 Aaron Brand .40 1.00
4 Kory Cooper .60 1.50
5 Mike Corneau .40 1.00
6 Adam Dewan .40 1.00
7 Stu Dunn .60 1.50
8 Ken Fels .40 1.00
9 Jason Firth .60 1.50
10 Benoit Genesse .40 1.00
11 Matt Goody .40 1.00
12 Brent Gretzky .40 1.00
13 Casey Harris .40 1.00
14 Ian Jacobs .40 1.00
15 Trevor Karasiewicz .40 1.00
16 Barry McKinlay .40 1.00
17 Sam Miller .40 1.00
18 Simon Poirier .40 1.00
19 Michael Prochazka .40 1.00
20 Joey Sewell .40 1.00
21 Josh Tataryn .40 1.00
22 John Vary .40 1.00
23 Wade Winkler .40 1.00

1998-99 Port Huron Border Cats
This set features the Border Cats of the UHL. The set was produced by ebk Sports, and sold by the team at its souvenir stands.

COMPLETE SET (26) 4.80 12.00
1 Wayne Muir .30 .75
2 Mike O'Grady .20 .50
3 Adam Robbins .20 .50
4 Curtis Sayler .20 .50
5 Olie Sundstrom .20 .50
6 Bob McKillop .20 .50
7 Chris Bergeron .20 .50
8 Lee Cole .20 .50
9 Chad Dameworth .20 .50
10 Mike Zanzarella TR .02 .10
11 Bernie John .20 .50
12 Matt Carmichael .20 .50
13 Kevin Brown .20 .50
14 Kevin Boyd .20 .50
15 Jeff Blum .20 .50
16 Bruce Watson .20 .50
17 Andrei Sryubko .20 .50
18 Paul Polillo .20 .50
19 Kraig Nienhuis .30 .75
20 Brock Myles EM .02 .10
21 Nikolai Syrtsov .20 .50
22 Greg Puhalski CO .08 .25
23 Bridges MASCOT .02 .10
24 Fedor Fedorov .75 2.00
25 Konstantin Simchuk .30 .75
26 Team CL .02 .10

2006-07 Port Huron Flags
COMPLETE SET (25) 12.00 20.00
1 Team Photo .10 .25
2 Craig Mahon .30 .75
3 Pat Sutton .30 .75
4 Mike Olynyk .30 .75
5 Bobby Kukulka .30 .75
6 Kris Vernarsky .30 .75
7 Robert Snowball .75 2.00
8 Jeremy Tucker .30 .75
9 Mike James .30 .75
10 B.J. Adams .30 .75
11 Mark Cadotte .30 .75
12 Ben Gustovson .30 .75
13 Greg Bullock .30 .75
14 Ryan Markham .30 .75
15 Scott Wray .30 .75
16 Trevor Edwards .30 .75
17 John Doherty .30 .75
18 Dustin Traylen .40 1.00
19 Noah Ruden .40 1.00
20 Shayne Tomlinson .30 .75
21 Steve Hildebrand .30 .75
22 Chris Bogas .30 .75
23 Colt King .75 2.00
24 Garett Cameron .30 .75
25 Slapshot MASCOT .02 .10

1993-94 Portland Pirates
This 24-card set of the Portland Pirates of the American Hockey League was sponsored by Pepsi. The glossy cards were available at home games and through the mail. The glossy cards are numbered on the back.

COMPLETE SET (24) 4.80 12.00
1 Randy Pearce .15 .40
2 Crackers MASCOT .02 .10
3 Barry Trotz CO .08 .25
4 Paul Gardner ASST CO .02 .10
5 Chris Jensen .08 .25
6 Ken Klee .20 .50
7 Steve Poapst .15 .40
8 Jason Woolley .20 .50
9 Jim Mathieson .15 .40
10 Michel Picard .15 .40
11 Jeff Nelson .15 .40
12 Kent Hulst .15 .40
13 Eric Fenton .15 .40
14 Martin Jiranek .15 .40
15 Mike Boback .15 .40
16 Darren McAusland .15 .40
17 Chris Longo .15 .40
18 Kerry Clark .15 .40
19 Jeff Sirkka .15 .40
20 John Slaney .20 .50
21 Kevin Kaminski .20 .50
22 Byron Dafoe .75 2.00
23 Olaf Kolzig 1.25 3.00
24 Todd Nelson .15 .40
NNO Header Card .02 .10

1994-95 Portland Pirates
This 23-card standard-size set was manufactured and distributed by Jessen Associates, Inc. for Classic. The fronts display color action player photos with a red marbleized inner border and a black outer border. The player's name, jersey number, and position appear in the teal border on the right edge.The cards are unnumbered and checklisted below in alphabetical order.

COMPLETE SET (23) 4.00 10.00
1 Norm Batherson .15 .40
2 Mike Boback .15 .40
3 Andrew Brunette .40 1.00
4 Jim Carey .30 .75
5 Jason Christie .15 .40
6 Kerry Clark .15 .40
7 Brian Curran .15 .40
8 Martin Gendron .30 .75
9 Sergei Gonchar .40 1.00
10 Kent Hulst .15 .40
11 Chris Jensen .15 .40
12 Kevin Kaminski .20 .50
13 Ken Klee .15 .40
14 Chris Longo .15 .40
15 Jim Mathieson .15 .40
16 Darren McAusland .15 .40
17 Jeff Nelson .20 .50
18 Todd Nelson .15 .40
19 Mike Parson .20 .50
20 Steve Poapst .15 .40
21 Andre Racicot .20 .50
22 Sergei Tertyshny .15 .40
23 Stefan Ustorf .20 .50

1995-96 Portland Pirates
This 24-card set of the Portland Pirates was sponsored by Dunkin' Donuts and features color action player photos framed in red and shades of gray. The backs carry a small black-and-white player head photo with biographical information and player statistics. The cards are unnumbered and checklisted below in alphabetical order.

COMPLETE SET (24) 6.00 15.00
1 Alexander Alexeev .15 .40
2 Jason Allison .75 2.00
3 Norm Batherson .15 .40
4 Frank Bialowas .40 1.00
5 Patrick Boileau .15 .40
6 Andrew Brunette .60 1.50
7 Stephane Charbonneau .15 .40
8 Jason Christie .15 .40
9 Crackers MASCOT .02 .10
10 Brian Curran .08 .25
11 Martin Gendron .20 .50
12 Kent Hulst .15 .40
13 Alexander Kharlamov .15 .40
14 Jim Mathieson .20 .50
15 Darren McAusland .15 .40
16 Jeff Nelson .15 .40
17 Darryl Paquette .20 .50
18 Rob Pearson .20 .50
19 Steve Poapst .15 .40
20 Joel Poirier .15 .40
21 Sergei Tertyshny .15 .40
22 Barry Trotz CO .08 .25
23 Ron Tugnutt .60 1.50
24 Stefan Ustorf .20 .50

1996-97 Portland Pirates
This 25-card set was produced by Split Second. The set features action photos on the front and a statistical package on the reverse. The unnumbered cards feature the player's sweater number prominently on the back, and are numbered thusly below.

COMPLETE SET (25) 5.00 12.00
1 Robb Stauber .30 .75
3 Steve Poapst .20 .50
4 Stewart Malgunas .20 .50
5 Nolan Baumgartner .20 .50
6 Ron Pascucci .20 .50
7 Norm Batherson .20 .50
9 Marc Potvin .30 .75
10 Kent Hulst .20 .50
12 Brad Church .20 .50
14 Richard Zednik .40 1.00
15 Jaroslav Svejkovsky .30 .75
16 Darren McAusland .20 .50
19 Andrew Brunette .40 1.00
20 Miika Elomo .20 .50
21 Jason Christie .20 .50
22 Alexander Kharlamov .20 .50
24 Daniel Laperriere .20 .50
25 Benoit Gratton .20 .50
27 Patrick Boileau .20 .50
28 Trevor Halverson .20 .50
30 Martin Brochu .40 1.00
33 Anson Carter .60 1.50
NNO Paul Gardner ACO .10 .25
NNO AHL Hockey Card .01 .05
NNO Barry Trotz CO .20 .50

1996-97 Portland Pirates Shop N' Save
This set features the Pirates of the AHL. The cards were issued as promotional giveaways at a local grocery store.

COMPLETE SET (10) 4.00 10.00
1 Robb Stauber .50 1.25
2 Steve Poapst .40 1.00
3 Nolan Baumgartner .40 1.00
4 Norm Batherson .40 1.00
5 Kent Hulst .40 1.00
6 Jaroslav Svejkovsky .40 1.00
7 Andrew Brunette .75 2.00
8 Miika Elomo .75 2.00
9 Jason Christie .40 1.00
10 Benoit Gratton .40 1.00

1997-98 Portland Pirates
Little is known about this set beyond the confirmed checklist, but it is believed that the cards were sold in team set form at home games. Additional information can be forwarded to hockeymag@beckett.com.

COMPLETE SET (26) 5.00 12.00
1 Nolan Baumgartner .20 .50
2 Jan Benda .15 .40
3 Patrick Boileau .15 .40
4 Martin Brochu .40 1.00
5 Andrew Brunette .40 1.00
6 Sebastien Charpentier .30 .75
7 Jason Christie .15 .40
8 Brad Church .15 .40
9 Miika Elomo .20 .50
10 Benoit Gratton .30 .75
11 David Harlock .20 .50
12 Dwayne Hay .20 .50
13 Kent Hulst .15 .40
14 Kevin Kaminski .30 .75
15 Mark Major .15 .40
16 Stewart Malgunas .15 .40
17 Rick Mrozik .15 .40
18 Ryan Mulhern .15 .40
19 Mike O'Neill .30 .75
20 Steve Poapst .20 .50
21 Kayle Short .15 .40
22 Alexandre Volchkov .20 .50
23 Jay Wells ACO .15 .40
24 Bryan Trottier HCO .40 1.00
25 PHPA Web Site .01 .05
26 AHL Web Site .01 .05

1998-99 Portland Pirates
This set features the Pirates of the AHL. The set was produced and sold by the team. Research has determined that two versions exist of card #19.

COMPLETE SET (26) 5.00 12.00
1 J-P Dumont .75 2.00
2 Patrick Boileau .15 .40
3 Martin Brochu .30 .75
4 Trevor Halverson .15 .40
5 Matt Herr .20 .50
6 Benoit Gratton .20 .50
7 Nolan Baumgartner .15 .40
8 Casey Hankinson .15 .40
9 Kent Hulst .15 .40
10 Rick Kowalsky .15 .40
11 Daniel Cleary .30 .75
12 Todd Rohloff .15 .40
13 Jeff Toms .15 .40
14 Steve Poapst .15 .40
15 Mike Peluso .30 .75
16 Young/Soutuyo .15 .40
17 Mike Rosati .30 .75
18 Trent Whitfield .30 .75
19 Mark Kumpel HCO .02 .10
19 Neil Belland ACO .02 .10
20 Craig Mills .20 .50
21 Stewart Malgunas .15 .40
22 Rick Mrozik .15 .40
23 Dwight Parrish .15 .40
24 Mark Major .15 .40
25 AHL Web Site .01 .05

1999-00 Portland Pirates
This 25-card set features the Pirates of the AHL. The series was produced by Split Second and sold by the team at home games. Since the cards are not numbered, they are listed below in alphabetical order.

COMPLETE SET (25) 4.00 10.00
1 Nolan Baumgartner .20 .50
2 Alexei Tezikov .30 .75
3 Patrick Boileau .15 .40
4 Martin Brochu .40 1.00
5 Sebastien Charpentier .40 1.00
6 Miika Elomo .20 .50
7 Jakub Ficenec .15 .40
8 J.F. Fortin .20 .50
9 Matt Herr .20 .50
10 Kent Hulst .15 .40
11 Jamie Huscroft .15 .40
12 M.Kumpel/G.Hanlon .15 .40
13 Mascot .02 .10
14 Glen Metropolit .30 .75
15 Barrie Moore .15 .40
16 Ryan Mulhern .15 .40
17 Jeff Nelson .15 .40
18 Mike Peluso .20 .50
19 Steve Poapst .15 .40
20 Steve Shirreffs .15 .40
21 Jason Shmyr .15 .40
22 Trainer Card .02 .10
23 Alexandre Volchkov .15 .40
24 Trent Whitfield .30 .75
25 Rob Zettler .15 .40

2000-01 Portland Pirates
This set features the Pirates of the AHL. The set was produced by Choice Marketing and issued initially as a kid's club giveaway. Later, it was available with purchase at a local sub shop.

COMPLETE SET (20) 5.00 12.00
1 Kent Hulst .20 .50
2 Jeff Nelson .20 .50
3 Krys Barch .30 .75
4 Mark Murphy .20 .50
5 Patrick Boileau .20 .50
6 Todd Rohloff .20 .50
7 Jean-Francois Fortin .20 .50
8 Sebastien Charpentier .40 1.00
9 Glen Metropolit .30 .75
10 Remi Royer .20 .75
11 Derek Bekar .20 .50
12 Martin Hlinka .20 .50
13 Corey Hirsch .40 1.00
14 Alexei Tezikov .40 1.00
15 Rob Zettler .20 .50
16 Mike Farrell .20 .50
17 Jakub Ficenec .20 .50
18 Matt Pettinger .40 1.00
19 Jason Shmyr .20 .50
20 Brad Church .30 .75

2004-05 Portland Pirates
Set was given out in 12-card segments at two home games.

COMPLETE SET (12) 12.00
1 Steve Eminger .20 .50
2 Brian Sutherby .30 .75
3 Boyd Gordon .20 .50
4 Owen Fussey .20 .50
5 Jason Ulmer .20 .50
6 Justin Eddy .20 .50
7 Jeff Paul .20 .50
8 Jared Aulin .30 .75
9 Michel Periard .20 .50
10 Graham Mink .40 1.00
11 Chris Hajt .20 .50
Mike Amodeo
12 Cam McCaffrey .20 .50
Jonas Johansson
13 Jakub Cutta .20 .50
14 Brooks Laich .30 .75
15 Carlyle Lewis .20 .50
16 Shaone Morrisonn .20 .50
17 Maxime Ouellet .40 1.00
18 Louis Robitaille .20 .50
19 Garrett Stroshein .40 1.00
20 Darcy Verot .40 1.00
21 Trent Whitfield .40 1.00
22 Nolan Yonkman .20 .50
23 Dwayne Zinger .20 .50
24 Jakub Klepis .40 1.00
Tomas Fleischmann

2005-06 Portland Pirates
COMPLETE SET (24) 8.00 15.00
1 Geoff Peters .20 .50
2 Aaron Rome .40 1.00
3 Shane O'Brien .20 .50
4 Tim Brent .20 .50
5 Aaron Gavey .20 .50
6 Pierre Parenteau .20 .50
7 Corey Perry .60 1.50
8 Curtis Glencross .20 .50
9 Jordan Smith .20 .50
10 Kenny Smith .20 .50
11 Dieter Kochan .60 1.50
12 Ryan Shannon .20 .50
13 Joel Perrault .20 .50
14 Nathan Saunders .20 .50
15 Ryan Getzlaf .60 1.50
16 Ladislav Smid .40 1.00
17 Igor Pohanka .20 .50
18 Kent Huskins .20 .50
19 Bruno St. Jaques .20 .50
20 Dustin Penner .40 1.00
21 Simon Ferguson .20 .50
22 Nathan Marsters .40 1.00
23 Shane Hynes .20 .50
24 Trevor Gillies .60 1.50

2006-07 Portland Pirates
COMPLETE SET (24) 10.00 18.00
1 Bruce Crowder ACO .10 .25
2 Eric Weinrich ACO .10 .25
3 Zenon Konopka .30 .75
4 Aaron Rome .30 .75
5 Nathan Marsters .30 .75
6 Tim Brent .30 .75
7 Clay Wilson .30 .75
8 Brian Salcido .30 .75
9 Curtis Glencross .30 .75
10 Chris Durno .30 .75
11 Colby Genoway .30 .75
12 Simon Ferguson .30 .75
13 Geoff Peters .30 .75
14 Brett Skinner .30 .75
15 Drew Miller .60 1.50
16 Matt Keith .30 .75
17 Shawn Thornton .40 1.00
18 Petteri Wirtanen .30 .75
19 Bjorn Melin .30 .75
20 Trevor Gillies .40 1.00
21 Ryan Carter .40 1.00
22 Kent Huskins .30 .75
23 Mike Wall .40 1.00
24 Kevin Dineen CO .10 .25

2007-08 Portland Pirates
COMPLETE SET (24) 6.00 15.00
1 Crackers and Salty Pete MASCOTS .30 .75
2 Brendan Mikkelson .30 .75
3 Stephen Dixon .30 .75
4 Darryl Bootland .30 .75
5 Tyler Bouck .30 .75
6 Simon Ferguson .30 .75
7 Brandon Segal .30 .75
8 Joe Callahan .30 .75
9 Bobby Ryan .30 .75
10 Mike McKenna .30 .75
11 Matt Christie .30 .75
12 Drew Miller 1.00 2.50
13 Eric Weinrich .30 .75
14 Jason King .30 .75
15 Bruno St. Jacques .30 .75
16 Mike Hoffman .50 1.25
17 Geoff Platt .30 .75
18 Andrew Ebbett .30 .75
19 Brian Salcido .30 .75
20 Michal Birner .30 .75
21 Petteri Wirtanen .30 .75
22 Gerald Coleman .30 .75
23 Brett Festerling .30 .75
24 Andy Schneider .30 .75

1986-87 Portland Winter Hawks
Sponsored by AM-PM Mini-Market, this 24-card set measures the standard size. The white-bordered fronts feature posed-on-ice color player photos. The player's name, number, and position appear in black lettering within the white margin beneath the picture, while the team name is printed vertically along the left border. The sponsor's logo appears at the upper right. The cards are unnumbered and checklisted below in alphabetical order.

COMPLETE SET (24) 15.00 40.00
1 Dave Archibald 1.00 2.50
2 Bruce Basken .60 1.50
3 Thomas Bjuhr .60 1.50
4 Shaun Clouston .60 1.50
5 Jeff Finley .60 1.50
6 Bob Foglietta .60 1.50
7 Brian Gerrits .60 1.50
8 Darryl Gilmour 1.00 2.50
9 Dennis Holland .60 1.50
10 Steve Kloepzig .60 1.50
11 Jim Latos .60 1.50
12 Dave McLay .60 1.50
13 Scott Melnyk .60 1.50
14 Troy Mick .60 1.50
15 Roy Mitchell .60 1.50
16 Jamie Nicolls .60 1.50
17 Trevor Pohl .60 1.50
18 Troy Pohl .60 1.50
19 Glen Seymour 1.00 2.50
20 Jeff Sharples .60 1.50
21 Jay Stark .60 1.50
22 Jim Swan .60 1.50
23 Glen Wesley 2.00 5.00
24 Dan Woodley .60 1.50

1987-88 Portland Winter Hawks
Sponsored by Fred Meyer and Pepsi, this 21-card standard-size set features the 1987-88 Portland Winter Hawks of the Western Hockey League. Inside white borders, the fronts feature posed color player photos shot on the ice at the stadium. The wider left border carries the team name, while the upper right corner of the picture has been cut off to allow space for the sponsor logo. The cards are unnumbered and checklisted below in alphabetical order.

COMPLETE SET (21) 4.80 12.00
1 Wayne Anchikoski .20 .50
2 Eric Badzgon .30 .75
3 Chad Biafore .20 .50
4 James(Hamish) Black .20 .50
5 Terry Black .20 .50
6 Shaun Clouston .20 .50
7 Byron Dafoe 1.25 3.00
8 Brent Fleetwood .20 .50
9 Rob Flintoft .20 .50
10 Bryan Gourlie .20 .50
11 Mark Greyeyes .20 .50
12 Dennis Holland .20 .50
13 Kevin Jorgenson .20 .50
14 Greg Leahy .20 .50
15 Troy Mick .20 .50
16 Roy Mitchell .20 .50
17 Joey Mittelsteadt .20 .50
18 Mike Moore .20 .50
19 Scott Mydan .20 .50
20 Calvin Thudiun .20 .50
21 Pepsi Ad Card .02 .10

1988-89 Portland Winter Hawks
Sponsored by Pepsi and Fred Meyer, this 21-card set measures the standard size. On a white background, the fronts feature posed color player photos with a facsimile autograph in the bottom part of the picture. The player's name, number, and position appear under the picture, while the team name is printed alongside the left border. The cards are unnumbered and checklisted below in alphabetical order.

COMPLETE SET (21) 4.80 12.00
1 Wayne Anchikoski .20 .50
2 Eric Badzgon .30 .75
3 Chad Biafore .20 .50
4 James(Hamish) Black .20 .50
5 Terry Black .20 .50
6 Shaun Clouston .20 .50
7 Byron Dafoe 1.25 3.00
8 Brent Fleetwood .20 .50
9 Rob Flintoft .20 .50
10 Bryan Gourlie .20 .50
11 Mark Greyeyes .20 .50
12 Dennis Holland .20 .50
13 Kevin Jorgenson .20 .50
14 Greg Leahy .20 .50
15 Troy Mick .20 .50
16 Roy Mitchell .20 .50
17 Joey Mittelsteadt .20 .50
18 Mike Moore .20 .50
19 Scott Mydan .20 .50
20 Calvin Thudiun .20 .50
21 Pepsi Coupon .02 .10

1989-90 Portland Winter Hawks
Sponsored by Pepsi and Fred Meyer, this 21-card set measures the standard size. The fronts feature posed color player photos inside a black picture frame and white outer borders. A facsimile autograph is inscribed across the picture. The player's name, number, and position appear under the photo, while the team name is printed alongside the left border. The cards are unnumbered and checklisted below in alphabetical order.

COMPLETE SET (21) 4.80 12.00
1 Jamie Black .20 .50
2 Vince Cocciolo .20 .50
3 Byron Dafoe .75 2.00
4 Cam Danyluk .20 .50
5 Kim Deck .20 .50
6 Dean Dorchak .20 .50
7 Brent Fleetwood .20 .50
8 Rick Fry .20 .50
9 Bryan Gourlie .20 .50
10 Brad Harrison .20 .50
11 Judson Innes .20 .50
12 Dean Intwert .30 .75
13 Kevin Jorgenson .20 .50
14 Todd Kinniburgh .20 .50
15 Greg Leahy .20 .50
16 Jamie Linden .20 .50
17 Scott Mydan .20 .50
18 Mike Ruark .20 .50
19 Jeff Sebastian .20 .50
20 Brandon Smith .25 .60
21 Steve Young .20 .50

1993-94 Portland Winter Hawks
This is a tough team-issued set from the Winter Hawks of the WHL. The cards are unnumbered and are checklisted below in alphabetical order.

COMPLETE SET (27) 8.00 15.00
1 Mike Arbulic .10 .30
2 Lonny Bohonos .20 .50
3 Shannon Briske .10 .30
4 Dave Cammock .10 .30
5 Shawn Collins .10 .30
6 Matt Davidson .10 .30
7 Adam Deadmarsh 1.25 3.00
8 Adam Deadmarsh GM 1.25 3.00
9 Jake Deadmarsh .10 .30
10 Brett Fizzell .10 .30
11 Colin Foley .10 .30
12 Brad Isbister .60 1.50
13 Scott Langkow .40 1.00
14 Mike Little .10 .30
15 Dmitri Markovsky .10 .30
16 Jason McBain .10 .30
17 Scott Nichol .10 .30
18 Brent Peterson .10 .30
19 Nolan Pratt .20 .50
20 Scott Rideout .10 .30
21 Layne Roland .10 .30
22 Dave Scatchard .30 .75
23 Brandon Smith .20 .50
24 Brad Swanson .10 .30
25 Brad Symes .10 .30
26 Jason Wiemer .75 2.00
27 Mike Williamson .10 .30

1997-98 Portland Winter Hawks
This set of standard-sized cards was sold in set form by the team. It features early cards of hobby heroes Marian Hossa and Brenden Morrow.

COMPLETE SET (27) 16.00 40.00
1 Checklist .02 .10
2 Brent Belecki .15 .40
3 Mike Muzechka .15 .40
4 Marian Hossa 6.00 15.00
5 Ken Davis .15 .40
6 Jerad Smith .15 .40
7 Josh Green .40 1.00
8 Bobby Russell .15 .40
9 Kyle Chant .15 .40
10 Brenden Morrow 4.00 10.00
11 Derek MacLean .40 1.00
12 Todd Hornung .15 .40
13 Andrej Podkonicky .30 .75
14 Bobby Duncan .15 .40
15 Todd Robinson .15 .40
16 Chris Jacobson .15 .40
17 Shon Jones-Parry .15 .40
18 Kevin Haupt .15 .40
19 Ryan Thrussell .15 .40
20 Marty Standish .15 .40
21 Jason Labarbera .75 2.00
22 Matt Walker .15 .40
23 Andrew Ference .40 1.00
24 Joey Tetarenko 1.25 3.00
25 Brent Peterson HCO .08 .25
26 Mike Williamson ACO .02 .10
27 Julius Supler ACO .02 .10

2003-04 Portland Winter Hawks
This set was sold by the team at home games.

COMPLETE SET (29) 5.00 12.00
1 Dustin Butler .30 .75
2 Tomas Fojtik .15 .40
3 Taylor Sutherlin .15 .40
4 Michael Funk .15 .40
5 Richie Regehr .30 .75
6 Brendan Mikkelson .15 .40
7 Cody McLeod .15 .40
8 Aaron Roberge .15 .40
9 Brian Woolger .15 .40
10 C.J. Jackson .15 .40
11 Chad Wolkowski .15 .40
12 Shane Halifax .15 .40
13 Robin Big Snake .30 .75
14 Alex Aldred .15 .40
15 Brandon Dubinsky 1.25 3.00
16 Ivan Dornic .15 .40
17 Dan Da Silva .15 .40
18 Braydon Coburn .15 .40
19 Frazer McLaren .15 .40
20 Derek Poplawski .15 .40

21 Kyle Bailey .15 .40
22 Kevin Opsahl .30 .75
23 Krister Toews .30 .75
24 Ivan Dornic Draft .15 .40
25 Braydon Coburn Draft .60 1.50
26 Mike Williamson HCO .10 .25
27 Blake Wesley ACO .10 .25
28 Mascot .04 .10
29 Checklist .04 .10

2004-05 Portland Winter Hawks

We've confirmed the existence of a handful of cards from this set. If you know of others, please contact us at hockeymag@beckett.com. The three unnumbered bonus cards were available outside of the team set. The Coburn was available only at the Mock Crest Tavern, whose ad is on the back. The other two were available only at the booster club's table.

COMPLETE SET (25) 4.00 10.00
1 Dustin Butler .20 .50
2 Cameron Cepek .20 .50
3 Braydon Coburn .50 1.25
4 Dan DaSilva .20 .50
5 Brandon Dubinsky .75 2.00
6 Michael Funk .20 .50
7 Frazer McLaren .75 2.00
8 Mike Sauer .75 2.00
9 Brian Woolger .20 .50
10 Paul Gaustad .20 .50
11 Richie Regehr .20 .50
12 Cody McLeod .20 .50
13 Robin Big Snake .20 .50
NNO Braydon Coburn MCT .40 1.00
NNO R. Regehr/P. Gaustad .10 .25
NNO C. McLeod/R. Big Snake .10 .25

1984-85 Prince Albert Raiders Stickers

This set of 22 stickers was sponsored by Autotec Oil and Saskatchewan Ronald McDonald House. Each sticker measures 2" by 1 3/4" and could be pasted on a 17" by 11" poster printed in thin glossy paper. The stickers display a black-and-white head shot; the uniform number is also printed on the front. The stickers are unnumbered and checklisted below in alphabetical order.

COMPLETE SET (22) 10.00 25.00
1 Ken Baumgartner 1.25 3.00
2 Brad Bennett .40 1.00
3 Dean Braham .40 1.00
4 Rod Dallman .40 1.00
5 Neil Davey .40 1.00
6 Pat Elynuik .60 1.50
7 Collin Feser .40 1.00
8 Dave Goertz .40 1.00
9 Steve Gotaas .40 1.00
10 Tony Grenier .40 1.00
11 Roydon Gunn .40 1.00
12 Doug Hobson .40 1.00
13 Dan Hodgson .60 1.50
14 Curtis Hunt .40 1.00
15 Kim Issel .40 1.00
16 Ward Komonosky .40 1.00
17 David Manson .40 1.00
18 Dale McFee .40 1.00
19 Ken Morrison .40 1.00
20 Dave Pasin .60 1.50
21 Don Schmidt .40 1.00
22 Emanuel Viveiros .40 1.00

1990-91 Prince Albert Raiders

Sponsored by the High Noon Optimist Club, these 25 standard-size cards of the WHL's Prince Albert Raiders are printed on thin card stock and feature on their fronts color posed-on-ice player photos with white outer borders and yellow and green inner borders. The player's name, jersey number, and position appear in white lettering within the green inner border beneath the picture. The cards are unnumbered and checklisted below in alphabetical order.

COMPLETE SET (25) 4.00 10.00
1 Scott Allison .15 .40
2 Laurie Billeck .15 .40
3 Jeff Gorman .15 .40
4 Donevan Hextall .20 .50
5 Troy Hjertaas .15 .40
6 Dan Kesa .20 .50
7 Jason Kwiatkowski .15 .40
8 Travis Laycock .15 .40
9 Lee J. Leslie .20 .50
10 Jamie Linden .15 .40
11 Dean McAmmond .30 .75
12 Dave Neilson .15 .40
13 Jeff Nelson .20 .50
14 Troy Neumeier .15 .40
15 Pat Odnokon .15 .40
16 Brian Pellerin .15 .40
17 Darren Perkins .15 .40
18 Curt Regnier .20 .50
19 Chad Seibel .15 .40
20 Mark Stowe .15 .40
21 Darren Van Impe .30 .75
22 Shane Zulyniak .15 .40
23 Title Card .02 .10
24 Info Card (Strangers) .02 .10
25 Info Card (Vandalism) .02 .10

1991-92 Prince Albert Raiders

Sponsored by the High Noon Optimist Club, these 24 standard-size cards of the WHL's Prince Albert Raiders are printed on thin card stock and feature on their fronts color posed-on-ice player photos enclosed by green borders. The player's name, jersey number, and position appear in white lettering within the green border near the bottom. The cards are unnumbered and checklisted below in alphabetical order.

COMPLETE SET (24) 3.00 8.00
1 Mike Fedorko CO .02 .10
2 Jeff Gorman .15 .40
3 Merv Haney .15 .40
4 Donevan Hextall .20 .50
5 Troy Hjertaas .15 .40
6 Dan Kesa .20 .50
7 Jason Klassen .15 .40
8 Jason Kwiatkowski .15 .40
9 Jeff Lank .15 .40
10 Travis Laycock .15 .40
11 Lee J. Leslie .15 .40
12 Stan Matwijiw .20 .50
13 Dean McAmmond .20 .50
14 David Neilson .15 .40
15 Jeff Nelson .15 .40
16 Mark Odnokon ACO .02 .10
17 Darren Perkins .15 .40
18 Ryan Pisiak .15 .40
19 Nick Polychronopoulos .15 .40
20 Curt Regnier .20 .50
21 Jason Renard .15 .40
22 Barkley Swenson .15 .40
23 Darren Van Impe .20 .50
24 Shane Zulyniak .15 .40

1993-94 Prince Albert Raiders

This 22-card standard-size set was sponsored by High Noon Prince Albert Optimists and "Stay in School Canada." On a white card face, the fronts feature color action player photos inside a black picture frame. The player's name appears in a yellow bar under the picture. The cards are unnumbered and checklisted below in alphabetical order.

COMPLETE SET (22) 4.00 10.00
1 Ryan Bast .15 .40
2 Rodney Bowers .15 .40
3 Van Burgess .15 .40
4 Brad Church .30 .75
5 Joaquin Gage .30 .75
6 Jeff Gorman .15 .40
7 Merv Haney .15 .40
8 Greg Harvey .15 .40
9 Paul Healey .15 .40
10 Shane Hnidy .30 .75
11 Russell Hogue .15 .40
12 Jason Issel .15 .40
13 Steve Kelly .30 .75
14 Jeff Lank .15 .40
15 Mike McGhan .15 .40
16 Denis Pederson .30 .75
17 Mitch Shawara .15 .40
18 Shayne Toporowski .15 .40
19 David Van Drunen .15 .40
20 Dean Whitney .15 .40
21 Darren Wright .15 .40
22 Shane Zulyniak .15 .40

1994-95 Prince Albert Raiders

This 23-card set of the Prince Albert Raiders of the WHL was sponsored by the Prince Albert Optimists and "Stay in School Canada." The design mirrors that of the 1993-94 set. The set is noteworthy for the inclusion of several NHL first rounders, including Brad Church, Steve Kelly and Dennis Pederson. The cards are unnumbered, and are checklisted below alphabetically.

COMPLETE SET (23) 4.80 12.00
1 Sandy Allan .20 .50
2 Ryan Bast .20 .50
3 Brad Church .30 .75
4 Kris Fizzell .15 .40
5 Paul Healey .15 .40
6 Rob Hegberg .15 .40
7 Shane Hnidy .30 .75
8 Russell Hogue .15 .40
9 Craig Hordal .20 .50
10 Jason Issel .15 .40
11 Neil Johnston .15 .40
12 Steve Kelly .30 .75
13 Jeff Lank .15 .40
14 Mike McGhan .15 .40
15 Denis Pederson .60 1.50
16 Sean Robertson .15 .40
17 Mitch Shawara .15 .40
18 Shayne Toporowski .20 .50
19 Kaleb Toth .15 .40
20 Dave Van Drunen .20 .50
21 Shane Willis .60 1.50
22 Darren Wright .15 .40
23 Shane Zulyniak .15 .40

1995-96 Prince Albert Raiders

This 22-card set of the Prince Albert Raiders of the WHL was sponsored by the Prince Albert Optimists and features color action player photos in a thin back border on a white background. The player's name is printed in a yellow bar with his position in a white star below the picture. This set includes several first round selections, including 1996 first overall selection Chris Phillips. The cards are unnumbered and checklisted below in alphabetical order.

COMPLETE SET (22) 4.80 25.00
1 Rod Branch .40 1.00
2 Curtis Brown .75 2.00
3 Brad Church .40 1.00
4 Kris Fizzell .40 1.00
5 Dallas Flaman .40 1.00
6 Don Halverson .40 1.00
7 Shane Hnidy .40 1.00
8 Russell Hogue .40 1.00
9 Jason Issel .40 1.00
10 Garnet Jacobson .40 1.00
11 Kevin Kellett .40 1.00
12 Steve Kelly .60 1.50
13 Dylan Kemp .40 1.00
14 Michael McGhan .40 1.00
15 Marian Menhart .40 1.00
16 Chris Phillips .75 2.00
17 Blaine Russell .40 1.00
18 Mitch Shawara .40 1.00
19 Dave Van Drunen .40 1.00
20 Roman Vopat .40 1.00
21 Shane Willis .60 1.50
22 Darren Wright .40 1.00

1996-97 Prince Albert Raiders

Sponsored by the Prince Albert Optimists Clubs, this 23-card set features color player photos and jersey numbers on the front, and is checklisted below alphabetically.

COMPLETE SET (23) 4.80 12.00
1 Trevor Baker .20 .50
2 Scott Botterill .20 .50
3 Craig Brunel .20 .50
4 Marco Cefalo .20 .50
5 Dallas Flaman .20 .50
6 Jeremy Goetzinger .20 .50
7 Don Halverson .20 .50
8 Russell Hogue .20 .50
9 Jason Issel .20 .50
10 Garnet Jacobson .20 .50
11 Kevin Kellett .20 .50
12 Dylan Kemp .20 .50
13 Evan Lindsay .30 .75
14 Marian Menhart .20 .50
15 Cory Morgan .20 .50
16 Derek Paget .20 .50
17 Chris Phillips .60 1.50
18 Harlan Pratt .20 .50
19 Blaine Russell .15 .40
20 Adam Stewart .20 .50
21 Dave Van Drunen .30 .75
22 Steve Wilejto .20 .50
23 Shane Willis .40 1.00

1997-98 Prince Albert Raiders

This set features the Raiders of the WHL. The set was sponsored by the Prince Albert Optimists Club and was sold at home games. The cards are unnumbered, and so are listed below in alphabetical order.

COMPLETE SET (21) 4.00 10.00
1 Scott Botterill .20 .50
2 Derek Brandon .20 .50
3 Craig Brunel .20 .50
4 David Cameron .20 .50
5 Clayton Chartrand .20 .50
6 Dallas Flaman .20 .50
7 Jeremy Goetzinger .20 .50
8 Don Halverson .20 .50
9 Trevor Hitchings .20 .50
10 Kevin Kellett .20 .50
11 Evan Lindsay .30 .75
12 Ross Lupaschuk .40 1.00
13 Brady Magneson .20 .50
14 Grant McCune .30 .75
15 Cory Morgan .20 .50
16 Derek Paget .20 .50
17 Harlan Pratt .30 .75
18 Richard Seeley .20 .50
19 Cam Severson .20 .50
20 Brad Swanson .20 .50
21 Steve Wilejto .20 .50

1998-99 Prince Albert Raiders

This 22-card set was produced by Action Printing LTD and is not numbered. The set is listed in alphabetical order

COMPLETE SET (22) 12.00 20.00
1 Derek Brandon .20 .50
2 Marc Brown .20 .50
3 Craig Brunel .20 .50
4 Clayton Chartrand .20 .50
5 Riley Cote .20 .50
6 Todd Fedoruk .75 2.00
7 Dallas Flaman .20 .50
8 Jeremy Goetzinger .20 .50
9 Scott Hartnell 2.00 5.00
10 Shaun Hill .20 .50
11 Cody Jensen .20 .50
12 Kevin Kellet .20 .50
13 Milan Kraft .75 2.00
14 Evan Lindsay .30 .75
15 Ross Lupachuk .40 1.00
16 Grant McCune .20 .50
17 Cory Morgan .20 .50
18 Kerry Nice .20 .50
19 Derek Paget .20 .50
20 Garrett Prosofsky .20 .50
21 Nick Schultz .75 2.00
22 Richard Seeley .20 .50

2000-01 Prince Albert Raiders

This set features the Raiders of the WHL. The cards were sold by the team at home games. Because they are unnumbered, they are listed below alphabetically.

COMPLETE SET (25) 4.80 12.00
1 Jay Batchelor .20 .50
2 Anton Borodkin .20 .50
3 Kyle Bruce .20 .50
4 Jordan Clarke .20 .50
5 Riley Cote .20 .50
6 Cary Grant TR .04 .11
7 Ryan Haggarty .20 .50
8 J.J. Hunter .20 .50
9 Dustin Kazak .20 .50
10 Jon Kress .20 .50
11 Landon Lillejord .20 .50
12 Connor Lowe .20 .50
13 Grant McCune .31 .78
14 Grant McNeill .20 .50
15 Scott McQueen .20 .50
16 Jon Mirasty .20 .50
17 Chris Harper .20 .50
18 Igor Pohanka .20 .50
19 Garett Prosofsky .31 .78
20 Riley MASCOT .04 .11
21 Jeff Schmidt .20 .50
22 Nick Schultz .80 2.00
23 Aaron Sorochan .31 .78
24 Blain Stowards .20 .50
25 Greg Watson .31 .78

2001-02 Prince Albert Raiders

This set features the Raiders of the WHL. The cards are slightly taller than standard-size and feature a pair of photos on the front, accentuated by a red and yellow border. The black and white backs feature stats. It's believed the cards were sold by the team at home games.

COMPLETE SET (24) 6.00 15.00
1 Jay Batchelor .30 .75
2 Kyle Bruce .30 .75
3 Jeremy Colliton .60 1.50
4 Riley Cote .30 .75
5 Justin Cruse .30 .75
6 James Demone .30 .75
7 Paul Deniset .30 .75
8 Perry Faul .30 .75
9 Luke Fritshaw .30 .75
10 Jon Kress .30 .75
11 Wade Klippenstein CO .10 .25
12 Landon Lillejord .30 .75
13 Rastislav Lipka .30 .75
14 Grant McNeill .30 .75
15 Brett Novak .30 .75
16 Igor Pohanka .30 .75
17 Jeff Schmidt .30 .75
18 Drew Schoneck ACO .10 .25
19 Jesse Schultz .30 .75
20 Aaron Sorochan .40 1.00
21 Joe Suderman .30 .75
22 Thomas Vicars .40 1.00
23 Greg Watson .40 1.00
24 Mike Wirll .30 .75

2002-03 Prince Albert Raiders

COMPLETE SET (23) 8.00 20.00
1 Rejean Beauchemin 1.25 3.00
2 Kyle Bruce .30 .75
3 Dane Byers .60 1.50
4 Kyle Chipchura .75 2.00
5 Jeremy Colliton .75 2.00
6 Mark Cress .30 .75
7 Justin Cruse .30 .75
8 Chris Di Ubaldo .30 .75
9 Perry Faul .30 .75
10 Luke Fritshaw .30 .75
11 Kevin Harris .30 .75
12 Jon Kress .30 .75
13 Colin Lafreniere .30 .75
14 Seth Leonard .30 .75
15 Rastislav Lipka .30 .75
16 Grant McNeill .30 .75
17 Brett Novak .30 .75
18 Igor Pohanka .30 .75
19 Rory Rawlyk .30 .75
20 Evan Schafer .30 .75
21 Aaron Sorochan .30 .75
22 Greg Watson .30 .75
23 Andy Zulyniak .30 .75

2003-04 Prince Albert Raiders

This checklist may be incomplete. Please forward additional info to hockeymag@beckett.com.

COMPLETE SET (25) 6.00 15.00
1 Aki Seitsonen .30 .75
2 Brandon Peet .20 .50
3 Brant Hilton .20 .50
4 Brett Novak .20 .50
5 Caine Pearpoint .20 .50
6 Colin Lafreniere .20 .50
7 Dane Byers .60 1.50
8 Dave Manson .20 .50
9 Evan Schafer .20 .50
10 Garth Collins .20 .50
11 Jeff May .20 .50
12 Jeremy Colliton .60 1.50
13 Jordan Morgan .20 .50
14 Justin Cruse .20 .50
15 Kyle Chipchura .60 1.50
16 Luke Fritshaw .20 .50
17 Mark Ardelan .20 .50
18 Michal Polak .20 .50
19 Mike Gauthier .20 .50
20 Mike Hellyer .20 .50
21 Perry Faul .20 .50
22 Peter Anholt .20 .50
23 Rejean Beauchemin .60 1.50
24 Seth Leonard .20 .50
25 Travis Young .20 .50

2004-05 Prince Albert Raiders

COMPLETE SET (24) 8.00 20.00
1 Alex Archibald .30 .75
2 Mike Gauthier .30 .75
3 Jeff May .30 .75
4 Evan Schafer .30 .75
5 Luke Fritshaw .40 1.00
6 Landon Jones .30 .75
7 Scott Doucet .30 .75
8 Mike Hellyer .30 .75
9 Brandon Peet .30 .75
10 Brad Erickson .30 .75
11 Brett Ottmann .30 .75
12 Nolan Waker .30 .75
13 Kyle Chipchura .60 1.50
14 Aki Seitsonen .40 1.00
15 Ryan Depape .30 .75
16 Brett Novak .30 .75
17 Jeremy Colliton .60 1.50
18 Josh Elder .30 .75
19 Caine Pearpoint .30 .75
20 Chris Schlenker .30 .75
21 Dane Byers .60 1.50
22 Garth Collins .30 .75
23 Rejean Beauchemin .75 2.00
24 Peter Anholt CO .04 .10

2005-06 Prince Albert Raiders

COMPLETE SET (26) 8.00 20.00
1 Alex Archibald .40 1.00
2 Dane Byers .60 1.50
3 Kyle Chipchura .60 1.50
4 Peter Cmorej .30 .75
5 Ryan DePape .30 .75
6 Jesse Deckert .40 1.00
7 Scott Doucet .30 .75
8 Jarrid Dowhay .30 .75
9 Josh Elder .30 .75
10 Brad Erickson .30 .75
11 Mike Gauthier .30 .75
12 Mike Hellyer .30 .75
13 Ashton Hewson .30 .75
14 Kyle Howarth .30 .75
15 Jeff May .30 .75
16 Brett Novak .30 .75
17 Brent Ottmann .30 .75
18 Justin Palazzo .30 .75
19 Evan Schafer .30 .75
20 Aki Seitsonen .40 1.00
21 A.J. Thelen .60 1.50
22 Kevin Tipper .30 .75
23 Peter Anholt CO .02 .10
24 Dave Manson ACO .20 .50
25 Mark Odnokon ACO .02 .10
26 Duane Bartley AT .02 .10

2006-07 Prince Albert Raiders

COMPLETE SET (26) 12.00 20.00
1 David Aime .40 1.00
2 Jesse Deckert .40 1.00
3 Mike Gauthier .40 1.00
4 Jeff May .30 .75
5 A.J. Thelen .60 1.50
6 Blaine Tendler .30 .75
7 Cody Vann .30 .75
8 Scott Doucet .30 .75
9 Mike Hellyer .30 .75
10 Jarrid Dowhay .30 .75
11 Matthew Robertson .30 .75
12 Brent Ottmann .30 .75
13 Milan Jurik .30 .75
14 Lukas Zeliska .30 .75
15 Jordan Trach .30 .75
16 Ryan DePape .30 .75
17 Cody Gross .30 .75
18 Andy Smith .40 1.00
19 Josh Elder .30 .75
20 Ashton Hewson .30 .75
21 Justin Palazzo .30 .75
22 Bryce Lamb .30 .75
23 Shane Malone .30 .75
24 Peter Anholt CO .10 .25
25 Dave Manson ACO .20 .50
26 Kris Knoblauch ACO .10 .25

1998-99 Prince George Cougars

This set features the Cougars of the WHL. The set was sponsored by Sight and Sound Music and was sold at home games. The cards are unnumbered and so are listed below in alphabetical order.

COMPLETE SET (27) 15.00 40.00
1 Header card .02 .10
2 Mike Bayrack .40 1.00
3 Blair Betts .75 2.00
4 Tyler Bouck .75 2.00
5 Eric Brewer 4.00 10.00
6 Tyler Brough .40 1.00
7 Justin Cox .40 1.00
8 Travis Eagles .40 1.00
9 Dan Hamhuis 4.00 10.00
10 Trent Hunter 4.00 10.00
11 Michael Kiesman .40 1.00
12 Petr Kubos .40 1.00
13 Adam Loncan .40 1.00
14 Jozef Mrena .40 1.00
15 Scott Myers .75 2.00
16 Mike Olynyk .40 1.00
17 Jonathan Parker .40 1.00
18 Owen Richey .40 1.00
19 Jarrett Smith .75 2.00
20 Kevin Swanson .75 2.00
21 Curtis Tipler .75 2.00
22 Gary Toor .40 1.00
23 Jordan Walker .40 1.00
24 Ian Walterson .40 1.00
25 Tim Wedderburn .40 1.00
26 Jeff Zorn .40 1.00
27 Cougar Coaches .02 .10

1999-00 Prince George Cougars

This set features the Cougars of the WHL. It is believed that the cards were produced by the team and sold at its souvenir stands. The set includes the first card of 2001 first-rounder Dan Hamhuis.

COMPLETE SET (25) 6.00 15.00
1 Scott Meyers .20 .50
2 Tim Wedderburn .20 .50
3 Ryan Chieduch .20 .50
4 Jeff Zorn .20 .50
5 Dan Hamhuis .75 2.00
6 Kevin Seibel .20 .50
7 Gary Toor .20 .50
8 Devin Wilson .20 .50
9 Jozef Mrena .20 .50
10 Aaron Foster .20 .50
11 Tyler Bouck .30 .75
12 Jonathan Parker .20 .50
13 Shon Jones-Parry .20 .50
14 Roman Takac .20 .50
15 Chris Falloon .20 .50
16 Justin Hansen .20 .50
17 Trent Hunter .75 2.00
18 Blair Betts .40 1.00
19 Travis Eagles .20 .50
20 Ed Dempsey CO .02 .10
21 Dallas Thompson CO .02 .10
22 Paul Valaitis .20 .50
23 Billy Thompson .20 .50
24 Justin Cox .30 .75
25 Dan Baum .20 .50

2000-01 Prince George Cougars

This set features the Cougars of the WHL. It is believed that the cards were sponsored by Dairy Queen and sold by the team, but that has not been confirmed. The set is noteworthy for including an early card of 2001 first rounder Dan Hamhuis.

COMPLETE SET (25) 4.80 12.00
1 Team Card .10 .25
2 Billy Thompson .16 .75
3 Tim Wedderburn .16 .40
4 David Koci .16 .40
5 Dan Hamhuis 1.20 2.00
6 Gary Gladue .16 .40
7 Joey Hope .16 .40
8 Devin Wilson .16 .40
9 Chris Falloon .16 .40
10 Nathan Brice .16 .40
11 Christian Chartier .30 .75
12 Berkeley Buchko .30 .75
13 Scott Lynch .16 .40
14 Aaron Foster .16 .40
15 Jon Filewich .16 .40
16 Tomas Tesarek .16 .40
17 Dan Baum .16 .40
18 Adam Stefishen .16 .40
19 Mark Kitts .16 .40
20 Willy Glover .16 .40
21 Brett Allan .16 .40
22 Travis Eagles .16 .40
23 Justin Cox .16 .40
24 Duane Perillat .16 .40
25 Derek Boogaard .16 .50

2001-02 Prince George Cougars

We have confirmed the existence of only two cards in this set.

COMPLETE SET
1 Jon Filewich
2 Dan Hamhuis

2003-04 Prince George Cougars

COMPLETE SET (25) 10.00 25.00
1 Header Card .04 .10
2 Justin Pogge 3.00 8.00
3 Devin Featherstone .20 .50
4 Curtis Cooper .20 .50
5 Dustin Byfuglien 4.00 10.00
6 Brett Dickie .20 .50
7 Mike Fogolin .20 .50
8 Dennis Rehak .20 .50
9 Chris Falloon .20 .50
10 Nicholas Drazenovic .20 .50
11 Stanislav Bolshakov .20 .50
12 Dylan Yeo .30 .75
13 Brad Priestlay .20 .50
14 Jon Filewich .20 .50
15 Joshua Aspenlind .20 .50
16 Eric Hunter .20 .50
17 Greg Gardiner .20 .50
18 Danny Lapointe .20 .50
19 Myles Zimmer .30 .75
20 Steven Later .20 .50
21 Colin Patterson .20 .50
22 Tyrell Moulton .30 .75
23 Brett Parker .20 .50
24 Todd Ford .20 .50
25 Team Photo .20 .50

1988-89 ProCards AHL

This set of 348 cards features the 14 teams of the American Hockey League. The cards measure the standard size, 2 1/2" by 3 1/2". The fronts feature color player photos accented by a beige-colored hockey stick superimposed on the right and lower sides of the picture. The AHL logo appears in the lower left corner, and the photo is bordered on all sides by red. The cards are unnumbered and checklisted below alphabetically according to teams as follows (teams in alphabetical order and players listed alphabetically within each team): Adirondack Red Wings (1-25), Baltimore Skipjacks (26-48), Binghamton Whalers (49-72), Cape Breton Oilers (73-96), Halifax Citadels (97-119), Hershey Bears (120-147), Maine Mariners (148-169), Moncton Hawks (170-190), New Haven Nighthawks (191-222), Newmarket Saints (223-244), Rochester Americans (245-268), Sherbrooke Canadiens (269-299), Springfield Indians (300-324), and Utica Devils (325-348). Although the team sets were originally packaged individually, they are listed below as one giant set.

COMPLETE SET (348) 32.00 80.00
1 Rob Nichols .07 .20
2 Bill Dineen CO .08 .25
3 Tim Paris Asst.TR .01 .05
4 Glenn Merkosky .05 .15
5 Mike Gober .07 .20
6 Dave Casey TR .01 .05
7 Sam St.Laurent .30 .75
8 Mark Reimer .08 .25
9 Dennis Smith .07 .20
10 Lou Crawford .07 .20
11 John Mokosak .07 .20
12 Murray Eaves .07 .20
13 Dave Korol .07 .20
14 Miroslav Ihnacak .20 .50
15 Dale Krentz .07 .20
16 Brent Fedyk .20 .50
17 Dean Morton .07 .20
18 Jeff Brubaker .15 .40
19 Tim Cheveldae .60 1.50
20 Randy McKay .40 1.00
21 Peter Dineen .07 .20
22 Rob Doyle .07 .20
23 Daniel Shank .40 1.00
24 Joe Ferras .07 .20
25 John Blum .08 .25
26 Tim Bergland .07 .20
27 Robin Bawa .07 .20
28 Shawn Simpson .07 .20
29 Chris Felix .08 .25
30 Jeff Greenlaw .07 .20
31 Frank Dimuzio .07 .20
32 Tyler Larter .07 .20
33 Rob Whistle .07 .20
34 Dallas Eakins .07 .20
35 Mark Hatcher .07 .20
36 Dave Farrish .08 .25
37 Bill Houlder .20 .50
38 Doug Keans .30 .75
39 Lou Franceschetti .08 .25
40 Rob Murray .05 .15
41 Terry Murray GM/CO .20 .50
42 Steve Seftel .07 .20
43 J.P. Mattingly TR .01 .05
44 Mike Richard .07 .20
45 Shawn Cronin .20 .50
46 Scott McCrory .07 .20
47 Mike Millar .07 .20
48 Dave Sherrid TR .01 .05
49 Marc Laforge .07 .20
50 David O'Brien .07 .20
51 Dave Rowbotham .07 .20
52 Kay Whitmore .40 1.00
53 Richard Brodeur .20 .50
54 Mike Vellucci .07 .20
55 Terry Yake .20 .50
56 Roger Kortko .07 .20
57 Jon Smith TR .01 .05
58 Lindsay Carson UER .07 .20
Misspelled Lindsy
59 Chris Brant .07 .20
60 Claude Larose CO .08 .25
61 Dallas Gaume .07 .20
62 Charlie Bourgeois .07 .20
63 Todd Krygier .20 .50
64 Gary Callahan .07 .20
65 Mark Reeds .07 .20
66 Al Tuer .07 .20
67 Brian Chapman .07 .20
68 Mark Lavarre .07 .20
69 Mark Dumas .07 .20
70 Jim Culhane .07 .20
71 Larry Trader .07 .20
72 Tom Mitchell GM .01 .05
73 Rob MacInnis .07 .20
74 John B. Hanna .07 .20
75 Dan Currie .20 .50
76 Dave Roach .07 .20
77 Jamie Nicolls .07 .20
78 Alan May .08 .25
79 David Haas .07 .20
80 Daryl Reaugh .60 1.50
81 Mike Ware .07 .20
82 Mike Glover .07 .20
83 Nick Beaulieu .07 .20
84 Mario Barbe .07 .20
85 Darren Beals .07 .20
86 Kim Issel .07 .20
87 Shaun Van Allen .20 .50
88 Jim Ennis .07 .20
89 Mark Lamb .40 1.00
90 Larry Floyd .07 .20
91 Ron Shudra .07 .20
92 Fabian Joseph .08 .25
93 Selmar Odelein .08 .25
94 Don Martin .07 .20
95 Jim Wiemer .08 .25
96 Brad MacGregor .07 .20
97 Gerald Bzdel .07 .20
98 Mike Hough .20 .50
99 Ken McRae .08 .25
100 Bobby Dollas .08 .25
101 Joel Baillargeon .07 .20
102 Ladislav Tresl .05 .15
103 Jacques Mailhot .20 .50
104 Dean Hopkins .07 .20
105 Claude Julien .07 .20
106 Brent Severyn .30 .75
107 Keith Miller .07 .20
108 Scott Shaunessy .07 .20
109 Jaroslav Sevcik .07 .20
110 Darin Kimble .20 .50
111 Jean-Marc Routhier .07 .20
112 Ken Quinney .07 .20
113 Max Middendorf .07 .20
114 Marc Fortier .15 .40
115 Jean-Marc Richard .07 .20
116 Mike Natyshak .07 .20
117 Ron Tugnutt 1.25 3.00
118 Scott Gordon .20 .50
119 Doug Carpenter CO/GM .02 .10
120 Jeff Harding .07 .20
121 Jocelyn Perrault .07 .20
122 Darryl Gilmour .20 .50
123 John Stevens .07 .20
124 Warren Harper .07 .20
125 Chris Jensen .07 .20
126 Mark Freer .08 .25
127 Gordon Paddock .07 .20
128 Bruce Randall .07 .20
129 Glen Seabrooke .07 .20
130 Mike Stothers .07 .20
131 Dave Fenyves .08 .25
132 Mark Lofthouse .07 .20
133 Marc D'Amour .20 .50
134 Shaun Sabol .07 .20
135 Craig Kitteringham .07 .20
136 J.J. Daigneault .20 .50
137 Don Biggs .08 .25
138 Kent Hawley .07 .20
139 Tony Horacek .07 .20
140 Al Hill .08 .25
141 Don Nachbaur .07 .20
142 John Paddock CO .07 .20
143 Kevin McCarthy CO .07 .20
144 Dan Stuck TR .01 .05
145 Doug Yingst .07 .20
146 Frank Mathers PR/GM .07 .20
147 Brian Bucciarelli TR .01 .05
148 Terry Taillefer .07 .20
149 Paul Beraldo .07 .20
150 Jeff Lamb .07 .20
151 Mitch Molloy .07 .20
152 Darren Lowe .07 .20
153 Stephane Quintal .40 1.00
154 Norm Foster .08 .25
155 Jean-Marc Lanthier .07 .20
156 Carl Mokosak .07 .20
157 Mike Neill .07 .20
158 Mike Jeffrey .07 .20
159 Steve Tsujiura .07 .20
160 Scott Drevitch .07 .20
161 Paul Guay .08 .25
162 Scott Wykoff ANN .01 .05
163 John Carter .08 .25
164 Phil Degaetano .07 .20
165 Doug Foerster PB .01 .05
166 Bruce Shoebottom .08 .25
167 Ray Podloski .07 .20
168 Greg Hawgood .20 .50
169 Joe Flaherty .07 .20
170 Todd Flichel .07 .20
171 Steven Fletcher .08 .25
172 Len Nielson .07 .20
173 Neil Meadmore .07 .20
174 Gilles Hamel .08 .25
175 Ron Wilson .20 .50
176 Stu Kulak .08 .25
177 Scott Schneider .07 .20
178 Mike Warus .07 .20
179 Jamie Husgen .07 .20
180 Tom Draper .20 .50
181 Guy Gosselin .07 .20
182 Guy Larose .08 .25
183 Stephane Beauregard .30 .75
184 Brent Hughes .15 .40
185 Sean Clement .07 .20
186 Matt Hervey .05 .15
187 Chris Norton .07 .20
188 Rob Snitzer THER .01 .05
189 Rick Bowness CO .20 .50
190 Wayne Flemming MG .01 .05
191 Tim Tookey .08 .25
192 Ken Baumgartner .40 1.00
193 John English .07 .20
194 Darryl Williams .07 .20
195 Hubie McDonough .20 .50
196 Brad Hyatt .07 .20
197 Phil Sykes .05 .15
198 Mario Chitaroni .07 .20
199 Tom Pratt .07 .20
200 Sal Lombardi TR .01 .05
201 Rick Dudley CO .08 .25
202 John Tortorella CO .01 .05
203 Chris Panek .07 .20
204 Scott Green TR .01 .05
205 Eric Germain .07 .20
206 Bob Kudelski .20 .50
207 Joe Paterson .07 .20
208 Al Loring .07 .20
209 Mark Fitzpatrick 1.25 3.00
210 Dan Gratton .07 .20
211 Sylvain Couturier .07 .20
212 Pat Hickey DIR .01 .05
213 Petr Prajsler .05 .15
214 Lyle Phair .07 .20
215 Bob Logan .07 .20
216 Francois Breault .07 .20
217 Paul Kelly .07 .20
218 Steve Richmond .07 .20
219 Denis Larocque .07 .20
220 Brian Wilks .07 .20
221 Dave Pasin .08 .25
222 Gordie Walker .07 .20
223 Marty Dallman .07 .20
224 Jim Ralph .60 1.50
225 Mike Blaisdell .20 .50
226 Sean McKenna .07 .20
227 Mark Kirton .08 .25
228 Greg Hotham .07 .20
229 Bill Root .08 .25
230 Wes Jarvis .07 .20
231 Daryl Evans .07 .20
232 Jack Capuano .07 .20
233 Tim Armstrong .07 .20
234 Alan Hepple .07 .20
235 Brian Blad .07 .20
236 Ken Yaremchuk .08 .25
237 Paul Gagne .15 .40
238 Doug Shedden .20 .50
239 Brian Hoard .07 .20
240 Greg Terrion .15 .40
241 Trevor Jobe .01 .05
242 Jeff Reese .40 1.00
243 Darryl Shannon .20 .50
244 Tim Bernhardt .30 .75
245 The Moose Mascot .02 .10
246 Paul Brydges .07 .20
247 Ken Priestlay .08 .25
248 Jacques Cloutier .20 .50
249 Steve Smith .07 .20
250 Jim Jackson .08 .25
251 Grant Tkachuk .07 .20
252 Kevin Kerr .07 .20
253 Mark Ferner .08 .25
254 Jeff Parker .07 .20
255 Don McSween .08 .25
256 Jim Hofford .07 .20
257 Darcy Wakaluk .60 1.50
258 Scott Metcalfe .07 .20
259 Richie Dunn .07 .20
260 Wayne Van Dorp .15 .40
261 Shawn Anderson .08 .25
262 Jeff Capello .07 .20
263 Mike Donnelly .20 .50
264 Mikael Anderson .20 .50
265 Robert Ray 1.50 4.00
266 Jody Gage .30 .75
267 Francois Guay .05 .15
268 John Van Boxmeer CO .08 .25
269 Jim Nesich .07 .20
271 J.J. Daigneault .20 .50
272 Randy Exelby .08 .25
273 Jyrki Lumme .60 1.50
275 Francois Gravel .07 .20
276 Jacques Parent THER .01 .05
277 Bobby Boulanger MG .01 .05
278 Benoit Brunet .40 1.00
279 Martin Nicoletti .07 .20
280 Mark Pederson .08 .25
281 Stephan Lebeau .40 1.00
282 Claude Larose CO .08 .25
283 Steve Bisson .07 .20
284 Scott Sandelin .07 .20
285 Rocky Dundas .07 .20
286 Serge Roberge .07 .20
287 Rob Bryden .07 .20
288 Marc Saumier .07 .20
289 Jean Hamel CO .07 .20
290 Mario Roberge .08 .25
291 Jocelyn Lemieux .20 .50
292 Ron Chyzowski .07 .20
293 Martin Desjardins .07 .20
294 Steven Martinson .07 .20

295 Jose Charbonneau .08 .25
296 Stephane J.G. Richer .05 .15
297 Sylvain Lefebvre .30 .75
298 Donald Dufresne .08 .25
299 Luc Gauthier .07 .20
300 Shawn Evans .05 .15
301 Mike Stevens .07 .20
302 Bruce Boudreau .20 .50
303 Todd McLellan .07 .20
304 Jeff Hackett 1.50 4.00
305 Bill Berg .20 .50
306 Stu Burnie .07 .20
307 Duncan McPherson .07 .20
308 Jeff Finley .08 .25
309 Ralph Calvanese MG .01 .05
310 Rob DiMaio .40 1.00
311 Chris Pryor .07 .20
312 Jim Roberts CO .07 .20
313 Vern Smith .07 .20
314 Mike Walsh .07 .20
315 Ed Tyburski TR .01 .05
316 Rod Dallman .07 .20
317 George Maneluk .08 .25
318 Richard Kromm .08 .25
319 Kerry Clark .07 .20
320 Hank Lammens .08 .25
321 Tom Fitzgerald .20 .50
322 Dale Henry .07 .20
323 Shawn Byram .07 .20
324 Doug Weiss .07 .20
325 John Walker .07 .20
326 Paul Ysebaert .30 .75
327 Chris Cichocki .07 .20
328 Marc Laniel .07 .20
329 Kevin Todd .20 .50
330 Dan Delianedls .07 .20
331 Robert Bill TR .01 .05
332 Jeff Croop TR .01 .05
333 Craig Billington .75 2.00
334 Alan Stewart .07 .20
335 Jeff Madill .08 .25
336 Scott Moon TR .01 .05
337 Neil Brady .08 .25
338 Murray Brumwell .07 .20
339 Anders Carlsson .07 .20
340 Dan Dorion .07 .20
341 Tom McVie CO .08 .25
342 David Marcinyshyn .07 .20
343 John Blessman .07 .20
344 Chris Terreri .75 2.00
345 Eric Weinrich .30 .75
346 Janne Ojanen .20 .50
347 Tim Lenardon .07 .20
348 Jamie Huscroft .20 .50

1988-89 ProCards IHL

This set of 119 cards features players from the teams of the International Hockey League. The cards measure the standard size 2 1/2" by 3 1/2". The fronts feature color player photos accented by a beige-colored hockey stick superimposed on the right and lower sides of the picture. The cards are unnumbered and checklisted below alphabetically according to teams as follows: Indianapolis Ice (1-22), Kalamazoo Wings (23-42), Muskegon Lumberjacks (43-65), Peoria Rivermen (66-94), and Saginaw Hawks (95-119). Although the team sets were originally sold with a suggested retail price of 3.00 per team set and packaged individually, they are listed below as one giant set. In many cases that was the way they were advertised and sold, i.e., as a complete set of all the teams in the IHL.

COMPLETE SET (119) 20.00 50.00
1 Bob Lakso .07 .20
2 Rick Boyd .07 .20
3 Alan Perry .20 .50
4 Mark Teevens .07 .20
5 Gary Stewart .07 .20
6 Randy Taylor .07 .20
7 Scott Clements .07 .20
8 Chris McSorley .20 .50
9 Dave Allison .07 .20
10 Shane Doyle .07 .20
11 Darwin McCutcheon .07 .20
12 Geoff Benic .07 .20
13 Rich Oberlin TR .01 .05
14 Glen Johannesen .07 .20
15 Graeme Bonar .07 .20
16 Ron Handy .07 .20
17 Archie Henderson .08 .25
18 Brent Sapergia .07 .20
19 Brad Beck .07 .20
20 Paul Houck .07 .20
21 Jimmy Mann .20 .50
22 Rick Barkovich .07 .20
23 Scott McCrady .07 .20
24 Andy Akervik .07 .20
25 Rob Zettler .20 .50
26 Jarmo Myllys .40 1.00
27 D'Arcy Norton .07 .20
28 Ken Hodge Jr. .20 .50
29 Emanuel Viveiros .07 .20
30 Scott Bjugstad .07 .20
31 Mike Berger .07 .20
32 Joe Lockwood .07 .20
33 Stephane Roy .08 .25
34 Randy Smith .08 .25
35 Mike McHugh .07 .20
36 Warren Babe .07 .20
37 Gary McColgan .07 .20
38 Darin Baker .07 .20
39 Neil Wilkinson .20 .50
40 Kirk Tomlinson .07 .20
41 Larry Dyck .15 .40
42 Dave Schofield .07 .20
43 Brad Aitken .07 .20
44 Jock Callander .40 1.00
45 Todd Charlesworth .07 .20
46 Jeff Cooper .07 .20
47 Jeff Daniels .20 .50
48 Greg Davies .07 .20
49 Lee Giffin .07 .20
50 Dave Goertz .07 .20
51 Steve Gotaas .07 .20
52 Scott Gruhl .40 1.00
53 Doug Hobson .07 .20
54 Kevin MacDonald .07 .20
55 Pat Mayer .07 .20
56 Dave McLlwain .20 .50
57 Dave Michayluk .07 .20
58 Glenn Mulvenna .07 .20
59 Jim Paek .20 .50
60 Frank Pietrangelo .30 .75
61 Bruce Racine .20 .50
62 Mark Recchi 3.00 8.00
63 Troy Vollhoffer .07 .20
64 Jeff Waver .07 .20
65 Mitch Wilson .07 .20
66 Mitch Messier .08 .25
67 Dave Lowry .20 .50
68 Tim Bothwell .08 .25
69 Sheryl Reeves ADM .01 .05
70 Shane MacEachern .08 .25
71 Glen Featherstone .20 .50
72 Charlie Thompson MGR .01 .05
73 Wayne Thomas CO .08 .25
74 Dominic Lavoie .08 .25
75 Team Photo .20 .50
Peoria Rivermen
76 Scott Paluch .07 .20
77 Wayne Gagne .07 .20
78 Dave Thomlinson .20 .50
79 Tony Twist 2.00 5.00
80 Brad McCaughey .07 .20
81 Kelly Chase 1.25 3.00
82 Scott Harlow .07 .20
83 Peter Douris .20 .50
84 Cliff Ronning 1.00 2.50
85 Lyle Odelein .40 1.00
86 Terry MacLean .07 .20
87 Darin Smith .07 .20
88 Skip Probst .07 .20
89 Ed McMurray MGR .01 .05
90 Greg Eberle TR .01 .05
91 Jim Vesey .07 .20
92 Toby Ducolon .07 .20
93 Pat Jablonski .60 1.50
94 Darrell May .07 .20
95 Ed Belfour 10.00 25.00
96 Bruce Cassidy .08 .25
97 Chris Clifford .20 .50
98 Mario Doyon .07 .20
99 Bill Gardner .07 .20
100 Mark Kurzawski .07 .20
101 Lonnie Loach .20 .50
102 Steve Ludzik .08 .25
103 David Mackey .07 .20
104 Dale Marquette .07 .20
105 Gary Moscaluk .07 .20
106 Marty Nanne .07 .20
107 Brian Noonan .40 1.00
108 Mark Paterson .07 .20
109 Kent Paynter .07 .20
110 Guy Phillips .07 .20
111 John Reid .07 .20
112 Mike Rucinski .07 .20
113 Warren Rychel .30 .75
114 Everett Sanipass .20 .50
115 Mike Stapleton .08 .25
116 Darryl Sutter .40 1.00
117 Jari Torkki .07 .20
118 Bill Watson .08 .25
119 Sean Williams .08 .25

1989-90 ProCards AHL

This set of 360 standard-size cards features the 14 teams of the American Hockey League. Although the team sets were originally sold with a suggested retail price of 3.00 per team set and packaged individually, they are listed below as one giant set. In many cases that was the way they were advertised and sold, i.e., as a complete set of all the teams in the AHL. The set is constructed in team order.

COMPLETE SET (360) 36.00 90.00
1 New Haven Checklist .01 .05
2 Francois Breault .08 .25
3 Paul Kelly .08 .25
4 Phil Sykes .15 .40
5 Ron Scott .15 .40
6 Micah Aivazoff .15 .40
7 Sylvain Couturier .08 .25
8 Carl Repp .08 .25
9 Murray Brumwell .08 .25
10 Todd Elik .20 .50
11 Darwin Bozek .08 .25
12 Eric Germain .08 .25
13 Scott Young .40 1.00
14 Chris Kontos .20 .50
15 Scott Bjugstad .15 .40
16 Eric Ricard .08 .25
17 Ross Wilson .08 .25
18 Graham Stanley .08 .25
19 Chris Panek .10 .25
20 Nick Fotiu .40 1.00
21 Rene Chapdelaine .08 .25
22 Gordie Walker .08 .25
23 Tim Bothwell .15 .40
24 Kevin MacDonald .08 .25
25 Darryl Williams .08 .25
26 John Van Kessel .08 .25
27 Paul Brydges .08 .25
28 Moncton Checklist .01 .05
29 Guy Larose .15 .40
30 Danton Cole .15 .40
31 Brent Hughes .15 .40
32 Larry Bernard .08 .25
33 Stu Kulak .08 .25
34 Bob Essensa .75 2.00
35 Luciano Borsato .15 .40
36 Guy Gosselin .08 .25
37 Todd Flichel .08 .25
38 Brian Hunt .08 .25
39 Neil Meadmore .08 .25
40 Matt Hervey .08 .25
41 Dallas Eakins .08 .25
42 Brad Jones .08 .25
43 Chris Norton .08 .25
44 Bryan Marchment .40 1.00
45 Rick Tabaracci .60 1.50
46 Grant Richison .08 .25
47 Brian McReynolds .08 .25
48 Tony Joseph .08 .25
49 Dave Farrish .15 .40
50 Rob Snitzer .01 .05
51 Ron Wilson .15 .40
52 Scott Schneider .08 .25
53 Maine Checklist .01 .05
54 Dave Buda .08 .25
55 Paul Beraldo .08 .25
56 Lou Crawford .08 .25
57 Mark Montanari .08 .25
58 Don Sweeney .40 1.00
59 Jeff Sirkka .08 .25
60 Norm Foster .20 .50
61 Greg Poss .08 .25
62 Gord Cruickshank .08 .25
63 Bruce Shoebottom .08 .25
64 Mark Ziliotto .08 .25
65 Ron Hoover .08 .25
66 Scott Harlow .08 .25
67 Mike Millar .08 .25
68 Bob Beers .20 .50
69 Ray Neufeld .15 .40
70 Graeme Townshend .20 .50
71 Billy O'Dwyer .08 .25
72 Frank Caprice .20 .50
73 John Blum .08 .25
74 Jerry Foster .08 .25
75 Bill Sutherland .08 .25
Rick Bowness
76 Scott Drevitch .08 .25
77 Baltimore Checklist .01 .05
78 John Purves .08 .25
79 Jeff Greenlaw .08 .25
80 Jim Taylor .08 .25
81 Alfie Turcotte .08 .25
82 Dan Redmond .01 .05
83 Chris Felix .08 .25
84 Bobby Babcock .08 .25
85 Steve Maltais .08 .25
86 Mike Richard .08 .25
87 Team Picture .08 .25
88 Bob Mason .30 .75
89 Mark Ferner .15 .40
90 Steve Seftel .08 .25
91 Brian Tutt .08 .25
92 Terry Murray .15 .40
93 Jim Hrivnak .20 .50
94 Tyler Larter .08 .25
95 Tim Bergland .08 .25
96 Dennis Smith .08 .25
97 Steve Hollett .08 .25
98 Shawn Simpson .08 .25
99 Robin Bawa .08 .25
100 John Druce .20 .50
101 Kent Paynter .08 .25
102 Alain Cote .15 .40
103 J.P. Mattingly .01 .05
104 Newmarket Checklist .01 .05
105 Dean Anderson .08 .25
106 Wes Jarvis .08 .25
107 Brian Blad .08 .25
108 Derek Laxdal .08 .25
109 Kent Hulst .08 .25
110 Tim Bernhardt .20 .50
111 Brian Hoard .08 .25
112 Bill Root .15 .40
113 Paul Gardner .08 .25
114 Tim Armstrong .08 .25
115 Sean McKenna .08 .25
116 Tim Bean .08 .25
117 Alan Hepple .08 .25
118 Greg Hotham .08 .25
119 Scott Pearson .20 .50
120 Peter Ihnacak .15 .40
121 John McIntyre .08 .25
122 Paul Gagne .08 .25
123 Darren Veitch .15 .40
124 Mark LaForest .15 .40
125 Doug Shedden .15 .40
126 Bobby Reynolds .08 .25
127 Tie Domi 3.00 8.00
128 Ken Hammond .15 .40
129 Cape Breton Checklist .01 .05
130 Wade Campbell .08 .25
131 Chris Joseph .15 .40
132 Mario Barbe .08 .25
133 Mike Greenlay .20 .50
134 Peter Soberlak .08 .25
135 Bruce Bell .15 .40
136 Dan Currie .08 .25
137 Fabian Joseph .15 .40
138 Stan Drulia .20 .50
139 Todd Charlesworth .08 .25
140 Norm Maciver .20 .50
141 David Haas .08 .25
142 Tim Tisdale .08 .25
143 Eldon Reddick .20 .50
144 Alexander Tyznych .08 .25
145 Kim Issel .08 .25
146 Corey Foster .08 .25
147 Tomas Kapusta .08 .25
148 Brian Wilks .08 .25
149 John LeBlanc .08 .25
150 Ivan Matulik .08 .25
151 Shaun Van Allen .30 .75
152 Halifax Checklist .01 .05
153 Scott Gordon .20 .50
154 Trevor Steinburg .08 .25
155 Miroslav Ihnacak .15 .40
156 Jamie Baker .15 .40
157 Robbie Ftorek .20 .50
158 C. McQuaid .01 .05
B.Smith
159 Mario Brunetta .20 .50
160 Jean-Marc Routhier .08 .25
161 David Espe .08 .25
162 Ken Quinney .08 .25
163 Mark Vermette .08 .25
164 Dean Hopkins .08 .25
165 Claude Julien .08 .25
166 Claude Lapointe .20 .50
167 Stephane Morin .20 .50
168 Bryan Fogarty .20 .50
169 Dave Pichette .08 .25
170 Kevin Kaminski .15 .40
171 Brent Severyn .40 1.00
172 Max Middendorf .08 .25
173 Jean-Marc Richard .08 .25
174 Gerald Bzdel .08 .25
175 Ladislav Tresl .08 .25
176 Jaroslav Sevcik .08 .25
177 Greg Smyth .15 .40
178 Joel Baillargeon .08 .25
179 Sherbrooke Checklist .01 .05
180 Andre Racicot .20 .50
181 Jean-Claude Bergeron .20 .50
182 Jim Nesich .08 .25
183 Todd Richards .08 .25
184 Francois Gravel .08 .25
185 Lyle Odelein .40 1.00
186 Benoit Brunet .30 .75
187 Mario Roberge .15 .40
188 Marc Saumier .08 .25
189 Norman Desjardins .08 .25
190 Dan Woodley .08 .25
191 Andrew Cassels .30 .75
192 Roy Mitchell .08 .25
193 Guy Darveau .08 .25
194 Ed Cristofoli .08 .25
195 Stephane J.G. Richer .08 .25
196 Jacques Parent .01 .05
197 Luc Gauthier .08 .25
198 John Ferguson .08 .25
199 Mathieu Schneider .40 1.00
200 Serge Roberge .08 .25
201 Jean Hamel .08 .25
202 Utica Checklist .01 .05
203 Jason Simon .08 .25
204 Jeff Madill .08 .25
205 Kevin Todd .20 .50
206 Myles O'Connor .08 .25
207 Jon Morris .15 .40
208 Bob Hoffmeyer .08 .25
209 Paul Ysebaert .30 .75
210 Steve Rooney .15 .40
211 Claude Vilgrain .20 .50
212 Paul Guay .08 .25
213 Roland Melanson .30 .75
214 Tom McVie .15 .40
215 David Marcinyshyn .08 .25
216 Perry Anderson .08 .25
217 Jamie Huscroft .20 .50
218 Bob Woods .08 .25
219 Pat Conacher .20 .50
220 Jean-Marc Lanthier .08 .25
221 Chris Kiene .08 .25
222 Eric Weinrich .20 .50
223 Brian Fitzgerald .01 .05
224 Craig Billington .60 1.50
225 Jim Thomson .15 .40
226 Tim Budy .08 .25
227 Marc Laniel .08 .25
228 Robert Bill .01 .05
229 Springfield Checklist .01 .05
230 Mike Walsh .08 .25
231 Dale Henry .08 .25
232 Bill Berg .20 .50
233 Hank Lammens .08 .25
234 Rob DiMaio .40 1.00
235 Shawn Byram .08 .25
236 Jeff Hackett .75 2.00
237 Wayne McBean .15 .40
238 Tim Hanley .08 .25
239 Tom Fitzgerald .15 .40
240 Mike Stevens .08 .25
241 George Maneluk .08 .25
242 Dean Ewen .08 .25
243 Dale Kushner .08 .25
244 Shawn Evans .08 .25
245 Rod Dallman .08 .25
246 Mike Kelfer .08 .25
247 Sean LeBrun .08 .25
248 Kerry Clark .08 .25
249 Ed Tyburski .01 .05
250 Derek King .40 1.00
251 Marc Bergevin .20 .50
252 Jeff Finley .15 .40
253 Jim Roberts .08 .25
254 Chris Pryor .08 .25
255 Rochester Checklist .01 .05
256 Robert Ray 2.00 5.00
257 Ken Priestlay .15 .40
258 Darcy Wakaluk .30 .75
259 Richie Dunn .08 .25
260 Ken Sutton .20 .50
261 Terry Martin .08 .25
262 Scott Metcalfe .08 .25
263 Joel Savage .08 .25
264 Brad Miller .08 .25
265 Donald Audette .75 2.00
266 John Van Boxmeer .08 .25
267 The Moose .01 .05
268 Brian Ford .08 .25
269 Darcy Loewen .08 .25
270 Bob Halkidis .15 .40
271 Steve Ludzik .15 .40
272 Steve Smith .08 .25
273 Francois Guay .08 .25
274 Mike Donnelly .20 .50
275 Darrin Shannon .30 .75
276 Jody Gage .40 1.00
277 Dave Baseggio .08 .25
278 Bob Corkum .30 .75
279 Jim Jackson .08 .25
280 Don McSween .08 .25
281 Jim Hofford .08 .25
282 Scott McCrory .08 .25
283 Binghamton Checklist .01 .05
284 Raymond Saumier .08 .25
285 Mike Berger .08 .25
286 Corey Beaulieu .08 .25
287 Doug McKay .08 .25
288 Blair Atcheynum .08 .25
289 Al Tuer .08 .25
290 Chris Lindberg .15 .40
291 Daryl Reaugh .75 2.00
292 James Black .08 .25
293 Vern Smith .08 .25
294 Todd Krygier .20 .50
295 Bob Bodak .08 .25
296 Jon Smith .01 .05
297 Michel Picard .15 .40
298 Jim Culhane .08 .25
299 Brian Chapman .08 .25
300 Jim Ennis .08 .25
301 Jacques Caron .08 .25
302 Jim McKenzie .15 .40
303 Kay Whitmore .40 1.00
304 Terry Yake .15 .40
305 Mike Moller .08 .25
306 Adirondack Checklist .01 .05
307 Bob Wilkie .08 .25
308 Chris McRae .08 .25
309 Chris Kotsopoulos .15 .40
310 Steve Sumner .01 .05
311 Timothy Abbott .01 .05
312 Gord Kruppke .08 .25
313 Mike Gober .08 .25
314 Al Conroy .08 .25
315 Sam St.Laurent .15 .40
316 Dave Casey .01 .05
317 Yves Racine .20 .50
318 Randy McKay .20 .50
319 Dale Krentz .08 .25
320 Sheldon Kennedy .30 .75
321 Barry Melrose 1.25 3.00
322 Dennis Holland .08 .25
323 Glenn Merkosky .08 .25
324 Murray Eaves .08 .25
325 Mark Reimer .15 .40
326 Tim Cheveldae .40 1.00
327 Peter Dineen .08 .25
328 Dean Morton .08 .25
329 Derek Mayer .15 .40
330 Hershey Checklist .01 .05
331 Don Biggs .08 .25
332 Scott Sandelin .08 .25
333 Shaun Sabol .08 .25
334 Murray Baron .15 .40
335 Dave Fenyves .08 .25
336 Glen Seabrooke .08 .25
337 Mark Freer .15 .40
338 Ray Allison .08 .25
339 Chris Jensen .08 .25
340 Ross Fitzpatrick .08 .25
341 Brian Dobbin .08 .25
342 Darren Rumble .08 .25
343 Mike Stothers .08 .25
344 Jiri Latal .08 .25
345 Don Nachbaur .08 .25
346 John Stevens .08 .25
347 Steven Fletcher .08 .25
348 Kent Hawley .08 .25
349 Bill Armstrong .08 .25
350 Bruce Hoffort .15 .40
351 Gordon Paddock .08 .25
352 Marc D'Amour .20 .50
353 Tim Tookey .08 .25
354 Reid Simpson .08 .25
355 Mark Bassen .08 .25
356 Rocky Trottier .08 .25
357 Harry Bricker .01 .05
358 Dan Stuck .01 .05
359 Al Hill .08 .25
360 Kevin McCarthy .08 .25

1989-90 ProCards IHL

This set of 208 standard-size cards features the nine teams of the International Hockey League. Although the team sets were originally sold with a suggested retail price of 3.00 per team set and packaged individually, they are listed below as one giant set. In many cases that was the way they were advertised and sold, i.e., as a complete set of all the teams in the IHL.

COMPLETE SET (208) 28.00 70.00
1 Peoria Checklist .01 .05
2 Darwin McPherson .08 .25
3 Pat Jablonski .30 .75
4 Scott Paluch .08 .25
5 Guy Hebert 2.00 5.00
6 Rich Pilon .15 .40
7 Curtis Joseph 8.00 20.00
8 Robert Dirk .20 .50
9 Darin Smith .08 .25
10 Terry McLean .08 .25
11 Kevin Miehm .15 .40
12 Toby Ducolon .08 .25
13 Mike Wolak .08 .25
14 Adrien Plavsic .20 .50
15 Dave Thomlinson .15 .40
16 Jim Vesey .08 .25
17 Michel Mongeau .20 .50
18 Tom Nash .01 .05
19 David O'Brien .08 .25
20 Dominic Lavoie .20 .50
21 Keith Osborne .08 .25
22 Rob Robinson .08 .25
23 Wayne Thomas .15 .40
24 Flint Checklist .01 .05
25 Jason Lafreniere .15 .40
26 Rick Knickle .30 .75
27 Jerry Tarrant .08 .25
28 Paul Broten .20 .50
29 Kevin Miller .40 1.00
30 Jim Latos .08 .25
31 Daniel Lacroix .15 .40
32 Dennis Vial .40 1.00
33 Denis Larocque .08 .25
34 Mike Golden .08 .25
35 Mike Hurlbut .08 .25
36 Scott Brower .08 .25
37 Lee Giffin .08 .25
38 Jeff Bloemberg .08 .25
39 Simon Wheeldon .20 .50
40 Rob Zamuner .40 1.00
41 Joe Paterson .08 .25
42 Barry Chyzowski .08 .25
43 Peter Laviolette .08 .25
44 Corey Millen .20 .50
45 Darren Lowe .08 .25
46 Peter Fiorentino .08 .25
47 Soren True .08 .25
48 Mike Richter 4.00 10.00
49 Ice Checklist .01 .05
50 Sean Williams .08 .25
51 Bruce Cassidy .08 .25
52 Mark Kurawski .08 .25
53 Bob Bassen .20 .50
54 Marty Nanne .08 .25
55 Jari Torkki .08 .25
56 Ryan McGill .15 .40
57 Mike Peluso .60 1.50
58 Darryl Sutter .40 1.00
59 Dan Vincelette .08 .25
60 Lonnie Loach .15 .40
61 Mike Rucinski .08 .25
62 Jim Playfair .08 .25
63 Everett Sanipass .08 .25
64 Dale Marquette .08 .25
65 Gary Moscaluk .08 .25
66 Mario Doyon .08 .25
67 Ray LeBlanc .40 1.00
68 Mike Eagles .15 .40
69 Warren Rychel .20 .50
70 Jim Johannson .15 .40
71 Cam Russell .20 .50
72 Mike McNeil .08 .25
73 Jimmy Waite .30 .75
74 Kalamazoo Checklist .01 .05
75 Kevin Schamehorn .08 .25
76 Kevin Evans .08 .25
77 D'Arcy Norton .08 .25
78 Scott Robinson .08 .25
79 Larry DePalma .08 .25
80 Ed Courtenay .15 .40
81 Rob Zettler .20 .50
82 Dusan Pasek .08 .25
83 Gary Emmons .08 .25
84 Peter Lappin .08 .25
85 Mario Thyer .08 .25
86 Mike McHugh .08 .25
87 Randy Smith .15 .40
88 Link Gaetz .40 1.00
89 Ken Hodge Jr. .15 .40
90 Pat MacLeod .20 .50
91 Neil Wilkinson .20 .50
92 Brett Barnett .08 .25
93 Larry Dyck .15 .40
94 Dean Kolstad .08 .25
95 Jarmo Myllys .30 .75
96 Paul Jerrard .08 .25
97 Jean-Francois Quintin .15 .40
98 Mitch Messier .08 .25
99 Phoenix Checklist UER .01 .05
110 Jeff Lamb not listed
100 Bryant Perrier .08 .25
101 Keith Gretzky .40 1.00
102 Don Martin .08 .25
103 David Littman .15 .40
104 Mike DeCarle .08 .25
105 Grant Tkachuk .08 .25
106 Richard Novak .08 .25
107 Chris Luongo .08 .25
108 Bruce Boudreau .15 .40
109 Nick Beaulieu .08 .25
110 Jeff Lamb .08 .25
111 Rob Nichols .08 .25
112 Garry Unger .20 .50
113 Larry Floyd .08 .25
114 Brent Sapergia .08 .25
115 Randy Exelby .20 .50
116 Jim McGeough .08 .25
117 Tom Karalis .08 .25
118 Ken Spangler .08 .25
119 Jacques Mailhot .08 .25
120 Shawn Dineen .08 .25
121 Dave Korol .08 .25
122 Fort Wayne Checklist .01 .05
123 Colin Chin .08 .25
124 Scott Shaunessy .08 .25
125 Bob Lakso .08 .25
126 Duane Joyce .08 .25
127 Joe Stephan .08 .25
128 Ron Shudra .08 .25
129 Bob Fowler .08 .25
130 Steve Bisson .08 .25
131 Craig Endean .08 .25
132 Carl Mokosak .08 .25
133 Carey Lucyk .08 .25
134 Craig Channell .08 .25
135 Frederic Chabot .75 2.00
136 Brian Hannon .08 .25
137 Keith Miller .08 .25
138 Al Sims .20 .50
139 Stephane Beauregard .30 .75
140 Ron Handy .08 .25
141 Byron Lomow .08 .25
142 Muskegon Checklist .01 .05
143 Jamie Leach .08 .25
144 Chris Clifford .08 .25
145 Dave Capuano .15 .40
146 Jeff Daniels .08 .25
147 Dave Goertz .08 .25
148 Perry Ganchar .08 .25
149 Mitch Wilson .08 .25
150 Scott Gruhl .30 .75
151 Randy Taylor .08 .25
152 Bruce Racine .20 .50
153 Dave Michayluk .15 .40
154 Richard Zemlak .15 .40
155 Brad Aitken .08 .25
156 Paul Stanton .15 .40
157 Darren Stolk .08 .25
158 Jim Paek .15 .40
159 Mark Kachowski .08 .25
160 Dan Frawley .08 .25
161 Mike Mersch .08 .25
162 Glenn Mulvenna .08 .25
163 Phil Russell .15 .40
164 Blair McDonald .08 .25
165 Milwaukee Checklist .01 .05
166 Shaun Clouston .08 .25
167 Steve Veilleux .08 .25
168 Peter Bakovic .08 .25
169 Peter DeBoer .20 .50
170 Ernie Vargas .08 .25
171 Keith Street .08 .25
172 Rob Murphy .15 .40
173 David Bruce .20 .50
174 Shannon Travis .08 .25
175 Jeff Rohlicek .08 .25
176 Jay Mazur .08 .25
177 Kevan Guy .08 .25
178 Troy Gamble .40 1.00
179 Ronnie Stern .20 .50
180 Jim Revenberg .08 .25
181 Jose Charbonneau .08 .25
182 Ian Kidd .08 .25
183 Todd Hawkins .08 .25
184 Carl Valimont .08 .25
185 Jim Agnew .08 .25
186 Curtis Hunt .08 .25
187 Dean Cook .08 .25
188 Ron Wilson .15 .40
189 Ron Lapointe .08 .25
190 Salt Lake City .01 .05
Checklist
191 Brian Glynn .15 .40
192 Stephane Matteau .30 .75
193 Rick Barkovich .08 .25
194 Jeff Wenaas .08 .25
195 Darryl Olsen .08 .25
196 Rick Lessard .08 .25
197 Kevin Grant .08 .25
198 Rich Chernomaz .08 .25
199 Stu Grimson 1.25 3.00
200 Jamie Hislop .08 .25
Bob Francis
201 Doug Pickell .08 .25
202 Chris Biotti .08 .25
203 Tim Sweeney .20 .50
204 Ken Sabourin .15 .40
205 Randy Bucyk .08 .25
206 Wayne Cowley .15 .40
207 Rick Hayward .08 .25
208 Marc Bureau .20 .50

1990-91 ProCards AHL/IHL

This 629-card standard-size set features players who started or were expected to start the 1990-91 season in the minors. Players from the American Hockey League and the International Hockey League are included in this set. This set features red borders with a yellow hockey stick on the left side of the card diagonally framing a full-color picture of the player while the backs of the cards feature the basic factual information about the player as well as a complete statistical history. There are two number 99's: and the set is arranged by teams: Binghamton Rangers (1-25), Hershey Bears (26-53), Fredericton Canadiens (54-75), Peoria Rivermen (76-99) Kalamazoo Wings (99-122), Maine Mariners (123-145), Newmarket Saints (146-170), Springfield Indians (171-194), Baltimore Skipjacks (195-219), Cape Breton Oilers (220-242), Moncton Hawks (243-264, 343-344), Rochester Americans (265-295), San Diego Gulls (296-321), Milwaukee Admirals (322-342), Phoenix Roadrunner (345-369), Muskegon Lumberjacks (370-392), Indianapolis Ice (393-414), New Haven Nighthawks (415-441), Halifax Citadels (442-468), Adirondack Red Wings (469-493), Capital District Islanders (494-514), Albany Choppers (515-535), Fort Wayne Komets (536-556), Utica Devils (557-581), Kansas City Blades (582-602), and Salt Lake City Golden Eagles (603-628). Each team has its own team checklist (TC) card as the last card in the team's numbering sequence. Although the team sets were originally sold with a suggested retail price of 4.00 per team set and packaged individually, we've listed the cards below as one comprehensive set.

COMPLETE SET (632) 40.00 100.00
1 Rob Zamuner .30 .75
2 Todd Charlesworth .05 .15
3 Bob Bodak .05 .15
4 Len Hachborn .08 .25
5 Peter Fiorentino .05 .15
6 Kord Cernich .05 .15
7 Daniel Lacroix .20 .50
8 Joe Paterson .05 .15
9 Sam St.Laurent .20 .50
10 Jeff Bloemberg .05 .15
11 Mike Golden .05 .15
12 Mike Hurlbut .08 .25
13 Mark LaForest .20 .50
14 Chris Cichocki .05 .15
15 John Paddock .08 .25
16 Peter Laviolette .20 .50
17 Martin Bergeron .05 .15
18 Rudy Poeschek .40 1.00
19 Eric Germain .05 .15
20 Al Hill ACO .05 .15
21 Rick Bennett .08 .25
22 Tie Domi 2.00 5.00
23 Ross Fitzpatrick .05 .15
24 Brian McReynolds .08 .25
25 Binghampton Rangers CL .01 .05
26 Mike Eaves CO .05 .15
27 Lance Pitlick .15 .40
28 Dale Kushner .05 .15
29 Reid Simpson .05 .15
30 Craig Fisher .08 .25
31 Dominic Roussel .30 .75
32 Dave Fenyves .05 .15
33 Brian Dobbin .05 .15
34 Darren Rumble .15 .40
35 Murray Baron .15 .40
36 Bruce Hoffort .08 .25
37 Steve Beadle .05 .15
38 Chris Jensen .05 .15
39 Mike Stothers .05 .15
40 Kent Hawley .05 .15
41 Scott Sandelin .05 .15
42 Guy Phillips .05 .15
43 Mark Bassen .05 .15
44 Steve Scheifele .05 .15
45 Bill Armstrong .05 .15
46 Shaun Sabol .05 .15
47 Mark Freer .05 .15
48 Claude Boivin .08 .25
49 Len Barrie .08 .25
50 Bill Armstrong .05 .15
51 Tim Tookey .08 .25
52 Harry Bricker ACO .01 .05
53 Hershey Bears TC .01 .05
54 Alain Cote .08 .25
55 Luc Gauthier .05 .15
56 Eric Charron .05 .15
57 Mario Roberge .05 .15
58 Tom Sagissor .05 .15
59 Brent Bobyck .05 .15
60 John Ferguson .05 .15
61 Jim Nesich .05 .15
62 Gilbert Dionne .15 .40
63 Herbert Hohenberger .05 .15
64 Dan Woodley .05 .15
65 Roy Mitchell .05 .15
66 Frederic Chabot .60 1.50
67 Andre Racicot .20 .50
68 Paul DiPietro .20 .50
69 Norman Desjardins .05 .15
70 Martin St.Amour .05 .15
71 Jesse Belanger .20 .50
72 Ed Cristofoli .05 .15
73 Patrick Lebeau .08 .25
74 Paulin Bordeleau CO .05 .15
75 Fredericton Canadiens TC .01 .05
76 Keith Osborne .05 .15
77 Rich Pilon .15 .40
78 Alain Raymond .05 .15
79 Rob Robinson .05 .15
80 Andy Rymsha .05 .15
81 Randy Skarda .08 .25
82 Dave Thomlinson .08 .25
83 Tom Tilley .15 .40
84 Steve Tuttle .05 .15
85 Tony Twist 1.50 4.00
86 David Bruce .08 .25
87 Kelly Chase .40 1.00
88 Nelson Emerson .75 2.00
89 Guy Hebert 1.25 3.00
90 Tony Hejna .05 .15
91 Michel Mongeau .15 .40
92 David O'Brien .05 .15
93 Kevin Miehm .08 .25
94 Darwin McPherson .05 .15
95 Dominic Lavoie .05 .15
96 Yves Heroux .05 .15
97 Pat Jablonski .30 .75
98 Bob Plager CO .20 .50
99A Peoria Rivermen TC .01 .05
99B Jayson More .08 .25
100 Kevin Evans .05 .15
101 Warren Babe .05 .15
102 Mitch Messier .05 .15
103 John Blue .20 .50
104 Larry Dyck .08 .25
105 Duane Joyce .05 .15
106 Kari Takko .15 .40
107 Brett Barnett .05 .15
108 Pat MacLeod .08 .25
109 Peter Lappin .05 .15
110 Link Gaetz .40 1.00
111 Larry DePalma .05 .15
112 Steve Gotaas .05 .15
113 Mike McHugh .05 .15
114 Dan Keczmer .08 .25
115 Jackson Penney .05 .15
116 Ed Courtenay .15 .40
117 Jean-Francois Quintin .05 .15
118 Scott Robinson .05 .15
119 Mario Thyer .05 .15
120 Enrico Ciccone .30 .75
121 Kevin Constantine .15 .40
John Marks
122 Kalamazoo Wings TC .01 .05
123 Shayne Stevenson .20 .50
124 Jeff Lazaro .08 .25
125 Matt DelGuidice .20 .50
126 Ron Hoover .05 .15
127 John Mokosak .05 .15
128 John Blum .05 .15
129 Mike Parson .20 .50
130 Bruce Shoebottom .05 .15
131 Dave Donnelly .05 .15
132 Ralph Barahona .05 .15
133 Graeme Townshend .40 1.00
134 Ken Hodge Jr. .15 .40
135 Norm Foster .20 .50
136 Greg Poss .05 .15
137 Brad James .05 .15
138 Lou Crawford .05 .15
139 Rick Allain .05 .15
140 Bob Beers .15 .40
141 Ken Hammond .08 .25
142 Mark Montanari .05 .15
143 Rick Bowness CO .08 .25
144 Bob Gould PLAYER/COACH .05 .15
145 Maine Mariners TC .01 .05
146 Mike Stevens .05 .15
147 Greg Walters .05 .15
148 Mike Moes .05 .15
149 Kent Hulst .05 .15

150 Len Esau .05 .15
151 Darryl Shannon .15 .40
152 Bobby Reynolds .05 .15
153 Derek Langille .05 .15
154 Jeff Serowik .08 .25
155 Darren Veitch .15 .40
156 Joe Sacco .15 .40
157 Alan Hepple .05 .15
158 Doug Shedden .15 .40
159 Steve Bancroft .05 .15
160 Greg Johnston .15 .40
161 Trevor Jobe .05 .15
162 Bill Root .15 .40
163 Tim Bean .05 .15
164 Brian Blad .05 .15
165 Robert Hornya .05 .15
166 Dean Anderson .05 .15
167 Damian Rhodes .75 2.00
168 Mike Millar .05 .15
169 Mike Jackson .05 .15
170 Newmarket Saints .01 .05
171 Cal Brown .05 .15
172 Michel Picard .15 .40
173 Cam Brauer .05 .15
174 Jim Burke .05 .15
175 Jim McKenzie .15 .40
176 Mike Tomlak .05 .15
177 Ross McKay .05 .15
178 Blair Atcheynum .20 .50
179 Chris Tancill .08 .25
180 Mark Greig .08 .25
181 Joe Day .05 .15
182 Jim Roberts CO .05 .15
183 Emanuel Viveiros .05 .15
184 Daryl Reaugh .75 2.00
185 Tommie Eriksen .05 .15
186 Terry Yake .15 .40
187 Chris Govedaris .05 .15
188 Chris Bright .05 .15
189 John Stevens .05 .15
190 Brian Chapman .05 .15
191 James Black .08 .25
192 Scott Daniels .05 .15
193 Kelly Ens .05 .15
194 Springfield Indians TC .01 .05
195 Ken Lovsin .05 .15
196 Kent Paynter .05 .15
197 Jim Mathieson .20 .50
198 Bob Mendel .05 .15
199 Reggie Savage .08 .25
200 Alfie Turcotte .05 .15
201 Victor Gervais .05 .15
202 Todd Hlushko .20 .50
203 Steve Seftel .05 .15
204 Thomas Sjogren .05 .15
205 Steve Maltais .08 .25
206 Bob Joyce .15 .40
207 Tyler Larter .05 .15
208 Mark Ferner .08 .25
209 Bobby Babcock .05 .15
210 Jeff Greenlaw .05 .15
211 Tim Taylor .30 .75
212 John Purves .05 .15
213 Chris Felix .15 .40
214 Jiri Vykoukal .05 .15
215 Shawn Simpson .05 .15
216 Jim Hrivnak .20 .50
217 Rob Laird CO/GM .01 .05
218 Barry Trotz Asst.CO .20 .50
219 Baltimore Skipjacks TC .01 .05
220 David Haas .05 .15
221 Wade Campbell .05 .15
222 Dan Currie .05 .15
223 Shaun Van Allen .15 .40
224 Norm Maciver .20 .50
225 Mike Greenlay .20 .50
226 Peter Soberlak .05 .15
227 Tim Tisdale .05 .15
228 Mario Barbe .05 .15
229 Shjon Podein .40 1.00
230 Trevor Sim .05 .15
231 Corey Foster .08 .25
232 Mike Ware .05 .15
233 Marc Laforge .05 .15
234 Bruce Bell .08 .25
235 Tomas Kapusta .05 .15
236 Alexander Tyjynch .05 .15
237 Tomas Srsen .05 .15
238 Collin Bauer .05 .15
239 Francois Leroux .20 .50
240 Don MacAdam CO .01 .05
241 Norm Ferguson ACO .01 .05
242 Cape Breton Oilers TC .01 .05
243 Tony Joseph .05 .15
244 Brent Hughes .15 .40
245 Larry Bernard .05 .15
246 Simon Wheeldon .05 .15
247 Todd Flichel .05 .15
248 Craig Duncanson .05 .15
249 Iain Duncan .05 .15
250 Bryan Marchment .20 .50
251 Matt Hervey .05 .15
252 Chris Norton .05 .15
253 Dallas Eakins .05 .15
254 Peter Hankinson .05 .15
255 Grant Richison .05 .15
256 Lee Davidson .05 .15
257 Denis Larocque .05 .15
258 Scott Levins .15 .40
259 Guy Larose .08 .25
260 Scott Schneider .05 .15
261 Sergei Kharin .05 .15
262 Hawk .01 .05
263 Dave Farrish CO .05 .15
264 Moncton Hawks TC .01 .05
265 Kevin Haller .20 .50
266 Joel Savage .05 .15
267 Scott Metcalfe .05 .15
268 Ian Boyce .05 .15
269 David Littman .20 .50
270 Dave Baseggio .05 .15
271 Ken Sutton .15 .40
272 Brad Miller .05 .15
273 Bill Houlder .20 .50
274 Dan Frawley .15 .40
275 Scott McCrory .05 .15
276 Steve Ludzik .15 .40
277 Robert Ray 1.50 4.00
278 Darrin Shannon .20 .50
279 Dale Degray .05 .15
280 Bob Corkum .30 .75
281 Grant Tkachuk .05 .15
282 Kevin Kerr .05 .15
283 Mitch Molloy .05 .15
284 Darcy Loewen .08 .25
285 Jody Gage .20 .50
286 Jiri Sejba .05 .15
287 Steve Smith .05 .15
288 Darcy Wakaluk .20 .50
289 Donald Audette .60 1.50
290 Don McSween .08 .25
291 Francois Guay .05 .15
292 Terry Martin ACO .01 .05
293 Don Lever CO .05 .15
294 The Moose .01 .05
295 Rochester Americans TC .01 .05
296 Mike O'Connell CO .15 .40
297 Paul Marshall .05 .15
298 Darin Bannister .05 .15
299 Rob Nichols .05 .15
300 Charlie Simmer P/CO .20 .50
301 Bob Jones .05 .15
302 Scott Brower .05 .15
303 Taylor Hall .05 .15
304 Carl Mokosak .05 .15
305 Glen Hanlon .20 .50
306 Peter Dineen .05 .15
307 Mike Sullivan .20 .50
308 Steven Martinson .05 .15
309 Dave Korol .05 .15
310 Darren Lowe .05 .15
311 Mark Reimer .08 .25
312 Mike Gober .05 .15
313 Al Tuer .05 .15
314 Dean Morton .05 .15
315 Jim McGeough .05 .15
316 Clark Donatelli .05 .15
317 Steven Dykstra .05 .15
318 Brent Sapergia .05 .15
319 Lloyd Floyd .05 .15
320 D'Arcy Norton .05 .15
321 San Diego Gulls TC .01 .05
322 Garry Valk .20 .50
323 Ian Kidd .05 .15
324 Todd Hawkins .05 .15
325 Carl Valimont .05 .15
326 Peter DeBoer .05 .15
327 Curt Fraser ACO .15 .40
328 David Mackey .05 .15
329 Jim Benning .20 .50
330 Peter Bakovic .08 .25
331 Steve Weeks .20 .50
332 Steve Veilleux .05 .15
333 Shaun Clouston .05 .15
334 Gino Odjick .75 2.00
335 Mike Murphy CO .08 .25
336 Cam Brown .05 .15
337 Patrice LeFebvre .08 .25
338 Eric Murano .05 .15
339 Jim Revenberg .05 .15
340 Don Gibson .05 .15
341 Steve McKichan .05 .15
342 Milwaukee Admirals TC .01 .05
343 Rick Tabaracci .30 .75
344 Mike O'Neill .20 .50
345 Rick Hayward .05 .15
346 Sean Whyte .05 .15
347 Petr Prajsler .05 .15
348 John Van Kessel .05 .15
349 Mario Gosselin .20 .50
350 Kyosti Karjalainen .05 .15
351 Mikael Lindholm .05 .15
352 David Goverde .08 .25
353 Graham Stanley .05 .15
354 Stephane J.G. Richer .05 .15
355 Brian Lawton .15 .40
356 Jerome Bechard .05 .15
357 Jeff Rohlicek .05 .15
358 Steve Jacques .06 .15
359 Chris Kontos .20 .50
360 Sylvain Couturier .05 .15
361 Peter Sentner .05 .15
362 Steve Graves .05 .15
363 Daryn McBride .05 .15
364 Steve Rooney .15 .40
365 Mickey Volcan .05 .15
366 Kevin MacDonald .05 .15
367 Ralph Backstrom CO .20 .50
368 Garry Unger ACO .20 .50
369 Phoenix Roadrunners TC .01 .05
370 Rob Dopson .20 .50
371 Jock Callander .40 1.00
372 Chris Clifford .20 .50
373 Sandy Smith .05 .15
374 Jim Kyte .15 .40
375 Mike Needham .15 .40
376 Mitch Wilson .05 .15
377 Dave Goertz .05 .15
378 Mark Kachowski .05 .15
379 Perry Ganchar .05 .15
380 Mark Major .08 .25
381 Joel Gardner .05 .15
382 Scott Gruhl .30 .75
383 Todd Nelson .05 .15
384 Darren Stolk .05 .15
385 Scott Shaunessy .05 .15
386 Mike Mersch .05 .15
387 Glenn Mulvenna .05 .15
388 Brad Aitken .05 .15
389 Dave Michayluk .05 .15
390 Blair MacDonald CO .05 .15
391 Phil Russell ACO .08 .25
392 Muskegon Lumberjacks TC .01 .05
393 Sean Williams .05 .15
394 Ryan McGill .05 .15
395 Mike Eagles .15 .40
396 Jim Johannson .15 .40
397 Marty Nanne .05 .15
398 Jim Playfair .05 .15
399 Warren Rychel .30 .75
400 Cam Russell .20 .50
401 Jimmy Waite .20 .50
402 Mike Stapleton .05 .15
403 Trevor Dam .05 .15
404 Tracy Egeland .05 .15
405 Owen Lessard .05 .15
406 Jeff Sirkka .05 .15
407 Mike Dagenais .05 .15
408 Alex Roberts .05 .15
409 Dominik Hasek 10.00 25.00
410 Martin Desjardins .05 .15
411 Frantisek Kucera .15 .40
412 Carl Mokosak .05 .15
413 Dave McDowell .05 .15
414 Indianapolis Ice TC .01 .05
415 Paul Saundercock .05 .15
416 Darryl Williams .05 .15
417 Micah Aivazoff .05 .15
418 Robb Stauber .20 .50
419 Tom Martin .05 .15
420 Billy O'Dwyer .05 .15
421 Scott Harlow .05 .15
422 Jim Thomson .05 .15
423 Jim Pavese .05 .15
424 Ron Scott .05 .15
425 Dave Pasin .05 .15
426 Serge Roy .05 .15
427 Darryl Gilmour .15 .40
428 Mike Donnelly .20 .50
429 Rene Chapdelaine .05 .15
430 Brandy Semchuk .05 .15
431 Paul Holden .05 .15
432 Bob Berg .05 .15
433 Ladislav Tresl .05 .15
434 Eric Ricard .05 .15
435 Murray Brumwell .05 .15
436 Shawn McCosh .05 .15
437 Ross Wilson .05 .15
438 Scott Young .40 1.00
439 David Moylan .05 .15
440 Marcel Comeau CO .05 .15
441 New Haven Nighthawks TC .01 .05
442 David Espe .05 .15
443 Mario Doyon .05 .15
444 Gerald Bzdel .05 .15
445 Claude Lapointe .20 .50
446 Dean Hopkins .05 .15
447 Clement Jodoin .05 .15
448 Kevin Kaminski .40 1.00
449 Jamie Baker .15 .40
450 Mark Vermette .05 .15
451 Iiro Jarvi .15 .40
452 Kip Miller .40 1.00
453 Greg Smyth .08 .25
454 Serge Roberge .05 .15
455 Stephane Morin .20 .50
456 Brent Severyn .40 1.00
457 Jean-Marc Richard .05 .15
458 Ken Quinney .05 .15
459 Jeff Jackson .15 .40
460 Jaroslav Sevcik .05 .15
461 David Latta .05 .15
462 Trevor Steinburg .05 .15
463 Miroslav Ihnacak .05 .15
464 Jim Sprott .05 .15
465 Mike Bishop .05 .15
466 Stephane Fiset .75 2.00
467 Scott Gordon .20 .50
468 Halifax Citadels TC .01 .05
469 Gord Kruppke .05 .15
470 Glenn Merkosky .15 .40
471 Dennis Holland .05 .15
472 Chris McRae .05 .15
473 Al Conroy .05 .15
474 Yves Racine .20 .50
475 Jim Nill P/CO .05 .15
476 Barry Melrose CO .75 2.00
477 Bob Wilkie .05 .15
478 Guy Dupuis .05 .15
479 Doug Houda .15 .40
480 Tom Bissett .05 .15
481 Bill McDougall .08 .25
482 Glen Goodall .05 .15
483 Kory Kocur .05 .15
484 Chris Luongo .05 .15
485 Serge Anglehart .05 .15
486 Marc Potvin .40 1.00
487 Stewart Malgunas .05 .15
488 John Chabot .20 .50
489 Daniel Shank .20 .50
490 Randy Hansch .20 .50
491 Dave Gagnon .08 .25
492 Scott King .05 .15
493 Adirondack Red Wings TC .01 .05
494 Derek Laxdal .05 .15
495 Sean LeBrun .05 .15
496 Shawn Bryan .05 .15
497 Wayne Doucet .05 .15
498 Rich Kromm .05 .15
499 Chris Pryor P/CO .05 .15
500 George Maneluk .05 .15
501 Brad Lauer .08 .25
502 Wayne McBean .08 .25
503 Jeff Finley .15 .40
504 Jim Culhane .05 .15
505 Paul Cohen .05 .15
506 Brent Grieve .08 .25
507 Kevin Cheveldayoff .05 .15
508 Dennis Vaske .08 .25
509 Dave Chyzowski .05 .15
510 Travis Green .75 2.00
511 Dean Chynoweth .20 .50
512 Rob DiMaio .30 .75
513 Paul Guay .05 .15
514 Capital District Islanders TC .01 .05
515 Rick Knickle .20 .50
516 Curtis Hunt .05 .15
517 Bruce Racine .20 .50
518 Yves Heroux .05 .15
519 Joe Stefan .05 .15
520 Torrie Robertson .20 .50
521 Nick Beaulieu .05 .15
522 Dave Richter .08 .25
523 Jeff Waver .05 .15
524 Gordon Paddock .05 .15
525 Darryl Noren .05 .15
526 Byron Lomow .05 .15
527 Ivan Matulik .05 .15
528 Dan Woodley .05 .15
529 Dale Henry .05 .15
530 Soren True .05 .15
531 Stuart True .05 .15
532 Rob MacInnis .05 .15
533 Vern Smith .05 .15
534 Paul Laus .40 1.00
535 Albany Choppers TC .01 .05
536 Robin Bawa .05 .15
537 Steven Fletcher .05 .15
538 Lonnie Loach .08 .25
539 Al Sims CO .08 .25
540 Colin Chin .05 .15
541 Bruce Boudreau P/CO .05 .15
542 Bob Lakso .05 .15
543 John Anderson .15 .40
544 Kevin Kaminski .40 1.00
545 Bruce Major .05 .15
546 Stephane Brochu .05 .15
547 Peter Hankinson .05 .15
548 Carey Lucyk .05 .15
549 Tom Karalis .05 .15
550 Bob Jay .05 .15
551 Mike Butters .05 .15
552 Brian McKee .05 .15
553 Ray LeBlanc .30 .75
554 Tom Draper .15 .40
555 Steve Laurin .05 .15
556 Fort Wayne Komets TC .01 .05
557 Sergei Starikov .05 .15
558 Claude Vilgrain .15 .40
559 Jeff Sharples .08 .25
560 Bob Woods .05 .15
561 Perry Anderson .08 .25
562 Brennan Maley .05 .15
563 Mike Posma .05 .15
564 Tom McVie GM/CO .05 .15
565 Chris Palmer .05 .15
566 Bill Huard .15 .40
567 Marc Laniel .05 .15
568 Neil Brady .05 .15
569 Jason Simon .08 .25
570 Kevin Todd .20 .50
571 Jeff Madill .08 .25
572 Jeff Christian .05 .15
573 Todd Copeland .05 .15
574 Mike Bodnarchuk .05 .15
575 Chris Kiene .05 .15
576 Myles O'Connor .08 .25
577 Jamie Huscroft .15 .40
578 Mark Romaine .05 .15
579 Rollie Melanson .20 .50
580 Utica Devils Team .08 .25
581 Utica Devils TC .01 .05
582 Ron Handy .05 .15
583 Cam Plante .05 .15
584 Lee Giffin .08 .25
585 Jim Latos .05 .15
586 Stu Kulak .08 .25
587 Claude Julien .05 .15
588 Rick Barkovich .05 .15
589 Randy Exelby .20 .50
590 Mark Vichorek .05 .15
591 Darin Smith .05 .15
592 Mike Kelfer .05 .15
593 Andy Akervik .05 .15
594 Mike Hiltner .05 .15
595 Kevin Sullivan .05 .15
596 Troy Frederick .05 .15
597 Claudio Scremin .05 .15
598 Kurt Semandel .05 .15
599 Mike Colman .05 .15
600 Jeff Odgers .40 1.00
601 Wade Flaherty .20 .50
602 Kansas City Blades TC .01 .05
603 Marc Bureau .20 .50
604 Darryl Olsen .05 .15
605 Rick Lessard .05 .15
606 Kevin Grant .05 .15
607 Rich Chernomaz .05 .15
608 Randy Bucyk .05 .15
609 Wayne Crowley .05 .15
610 Ken Sabourin .05 .15
611 Bob Francis CO .01 .05
612 Jamie Hislop CO .05 .15
613 Kevan Melrose .05 .15
614 Scott McCrady .05 .15
615 Corey Lyons .05 .15
616 Martin Simard .05 .15
617 C.J. Young .08 .25
618 Mark Osiecki .08 .25
619 Bryan Deasley .05 .15
620 Kerry Clark .05 .15
621 Paul Kruse .15 .40
622 Darren Banks .40 1.00
623 Richard Zemlak .08 .25
624 Todd Harkins .05 .15
625 Warren Sharples .05 .15
626 Andrew McKim .15 .40
627 Steve Guenette .08 .25
628 Salt Lake City Golden Eagles TC .01 .05
NNO Bobby Boulanger .05 .15
NNO Ray Dudley Mariners mascot .05 .15
NNO Jerry Foster Mariners TR .05 .15
NNO Patrick Langlois .05 .15
NNO Jacques Parent .05 .15

1991-92 ProCards

This 620-card standard-size set was produced by ProCards and features players from the American, International and Colonial Leagues. Fronts feature a posed color photo enclosed by a white border. The player's name is in black within a gold bar at the top and the team name appears beneath in a yellow bar. The photo appears in a red and black speckled "frame" enclosed by a small blue border. The respective league logo (American Hockey League, Colonial Hockey League, or International Hockey League) appears in the lower right corner. The cards are numbered on the back and checklisted below according to teams as follows: Rochester Americans (1-24), Peoria Rivermen (25-47), Maine Mariners (48-69), Fredericton Canadiens (70-92), Springfield Indians (93-117), Adirondack Red Wings (118-142), Kalamazoo Wings (143-163), Moncton Hawks (164-189), Binghamton Rangers (190-214), Cape Breton Oilers (215-238), Fort Wayne Komets (239-262), Hershey Bears (263-287), Muskegon Lumberjacks (288-310), San Diego Gulls (311-334), St. John's Maple Leafs (335-359), New Haven Nighthawks (360-383), Phoenix Roadrunners (384-407), Utica Devils (408-428), Flint Bulldogs of the Colonial Hockey League (429-451), Capital District Islanders (452-476), Indianapolis Ice (477-504), Kansas City Blades (505-527), Halifax Citadels (528-546), Baltimore Skipjacks (547-573), Salt Lake City Golden Eagles (574-594), and Milwaukee Admirals (595-620). Although the team sets were originally sold with a suggested retail price of 4.00 per team set and packaged individually, they are listed below as one giant set.

COMPLETE SET (620) 40.00 100.00
1 Bill Houlder .15 .40
2 Brian Curran .08 .25
3 Dan Frawley .08 .25
4 Darcy Loewen .08 .25
5 Jiri Sejba .08 .25
6 Lindy Ruff .08 .25
7 Chris Snell .08 .25
8 Bob Corkum .20 .50
9 Dave Baseggio .05 .15
10 Sean O'Donnell .05 .15
11 Brad Rubachuk .05 .15
12 Peter Ciavaglia .08 .25
13 Joel Savage .05 .15
14 Jason Winch .05 .15
15 Steve Ludzik .08 .25
16 Don McSween .08 .25
17 David DaVita .05 .15
18 Greg Brown .08 .25
19 David Littman .20 .50
20 Tom Draper .20 .50
21 Jody Gage .40 1.00
22 Terry Martin .07 .20
23 Don Lever .08 .25
24 Rochester Checklist .01 .05
25 Jason Marshall .08 .25
26 Michel Mongeau .08 .25
27 Derek Frenette .05 .15
28 Kevin Miehm .08 .25
29 Guy Hebert .75 2.00
30 Greg Poss .05 .15
31 Dave Mackey .08 .25
32 Dan Fowler .05 .15
33 Mark Bassen .07 .20
34 Yves Heroux .08 .25
35 Harold Snepsts .40 1.00
36 Bruce Shoebottom .07 .20
37 Jaan Luik .05 .15
38 Alain Raymond .05 .15
39 Kyle Reeves .05 .15
40 Brian McKee .05 .15
41 Steve Tuttle .08 .25
42 Rob Tustian .05 .15
43 Richard Pion .08 .25
44 Joe Hawley .05 .15
45 Brian Pellerin .05 .15
46 Jason Ruff .08 .25
47 Rivermen Checklist .01 .05
48 Wes Walz .30 .75
49 Steve Bancroft .05 .15
50 John Blue .20 .50
51 Rick Allain .05 .15
52 Mike Walsh .08 .25
53 Dave Thomlinson .08 .25
54 Dennis Smith .05 .15
55 Jack Capuano .08 .25
56 Mike Rossetti .05 .15
57 Petr Prajsler .08 .25
58 Matt Glennon .05 .15
59 John Byce .08 .25
60 Howie Rosenblatt .08 .25
61 Brad Tiley .05 .15
62 Lou Crawford .05 .15
63 Matt Hervey .08 .25
64 Peter Douris .08 .25
65 Jeff Lazaro .08 .25
66 David Reid .20 .50
67 E.J. McGuire .05 .15
68 Frank Bathe .07 .20
69 Maine Checklist .01 .05
70 Paul DiPietro .08 .25
71 Darcy Simon .05 .15
72 Patrick Lebeau .20 .50
73 Gilbert Dionne .20 .50
74 John Ferguson .08 .25
75 Norman Desjardins .05 .15
76 Luc Gauthier .07 .20
77 Jean-Claude Bergeron .20 .50
78 Andre Racicot .15 .40
79 Steve Veilleux .05 .15
80 Patrice Brisebois .20 .50
81 Tom Sagissor .05 .15
82 Lindsay Vallis .05 .15
83 Steve Larouche .08 .25
84 Sean Hill .20 .50
85 Jesse Belanger .20 .50
86 Stephane J.G. Richer .08 .25
87 Marc Labelle .05 .15
88 Pierre Sevigny .08 .25
89 Eric Charron .08 .25
90 Ed Ronan .08 .25
91 Paulin Bordeleau .08 .25
92 Fredericton Checklist .01 .05
93 Daryl Reaugh .75 2.00
94 Jergus Baca .08 .25
95 Karl Johnston .05 .15
96 Shawn Evans .05 .15
97 Scott Humeniuk .05 .15
98 Cam Brauer .05 .15
99 Scott Eichstadt .05 .15
100 Paul Cyr .08 .25
101 James Black .08 .25
102 Chris Govedaris .08 .25
103 Joe Day .08 .25
104 Chris Tancill .08 .25
105 Kerry Russell .07 .20
106 Denis Chalifoux .05 .15
107 Blair Atcheynum .08 .25
108 John Stevens .05 .15
109 Brian Chapman .05 .15
110 Chris Bright .05 .15
111 Jim Burke .05 .15
112 Scott Daniels .08 .25
113 Kelly Ens .05 .15
114 Mike Tomlak .08 .25
115 Mario Gosselin .20 .50
116 Jay Leach .05 .15
117 Springfield Checklist .01 .05
118 Allan Bester .20 .50
119 Daniel Shank .20 .50
120 Lonnie Loach .08 .25
121 Mark Reimer .08 .25
122 Kirk Tomlinson .05 .15
123 Stewart Malgunas .08 .25
124 Serge Anglehart .05 .15
125 Chris Luongo .08 .25
126 Keith Primeau 1.25 3.00
127 Ken Quinney .08 .25
128 Dave Flanagan .05 .15
129 Pete Stauber .05 .15
130 Mike Sillinger .20 .50
131 Micah Aivazoff .08 .25
132 Gary Schuchuk .08 .25
133 Bill McDougall .08 .25
134 Sheldon Kennedy .20 .50
135 Derek Mayer .05 .15
136 Darin Bannister .05 .15
137 Guy Dupuis .05 .15
138 Gord Kruppke .05 .15
139 Jason York .20 .50
140 Barry Melrose .40 1.00
141 Glenn Merkosky .08 .25
142 Adirondack Checklist .01 .05
143 Larry Dyck .08 .25
144 Roy Mitchell .05 .15
145 Greg Spenrath .05 .15
146 Steve Herniman .05 .15
147 Brad Berry .08 .25
148 Jim Nesich .05 .15
149 Tim Lenardon .05 .15
150 Steve Guenette .08 .25
151 Paul Jerrard .05 .15
152 Cal McGowan .08 .25
153 Scott Robinson .05 .15
154 Mitch Messier .08 .25
155 Tony Joseph .05 .15
156 Steve Maltais .40 1.00
157 Steve Gotaas .05 .15
158 Doug Barrault .08 .25
159 Dave Moylan .05 .15
160 Mario Thyer .08 .25
161 Bob Hoffmeyer .05 .15
162 Wade Dawson .05 .15
163 Wings Checklist .01 .05
164 Rob Murray .07 .20
165 Chris Kiene .05 .15
166 Lee Davidson .05 .15
167 Rudy Poeschek .40 1.00
168 Kent Paynter .05 .15
169 John LeBlanc .07 .20
170 Dallas Eakins .05 .15
171 Claude Julien .05 .15
172 Bob Joyce .08 .25
173 Derek Langille .05 .15
174 Rob Cowie .08 .25
175 Warren Rychel .40 1.00
176 Tom Karalis .05 .15
177 Kris Draper .40 1.00
178 Ken Gernander .05 .15
179 Tod Hartje .08 .25
180 Sean Gauthier .05 .15
181 Tyler Larter .05 .15
182 Scott Levins .08 .25
183 Jason Cirone .05 .15
184 Mark Kumpel .08 .25
185 Rick Tabaracci .40 1.00
186 Luciano Borsato .08 .25
187 Dave Farrish .08 .25
188 Dave Prior .05 .15
189 Moncton Checklist .01 .05
190 Peter Fiorentino .05 .15
191 Glen Goodall .05 .15
192 John Mokosak .05 .15
193 Sam St.Laurent .20 .50
194 Daniel Lacroix .20 .50
195 Guy Larose .08 .25
196 Mike Hurlbut .08 .25
197 Peter Laviolette .08 .25
198 Eric Bennett .05 .15
199 Steven King .08 .25
200 Boris Rousson .40 1.00
201 Jody Hull .15 .40
202 Shaun Sabol .05 .15
203 Joe Paterson .05 .15
204 Rob Zamuner .30 .75
205 Don Biggs .08 .25
206 Chris Cichocki .07 .20
207 Ross Fitzpatrick .05 .15
208 Mark LaForest .08 .25
209 Brian McReynolds .07 .20
210 Jeff Bloemberg .08 .25
211 Kord Cernich .05 .15
212 Ron Smith .05 .15
213 Al Hill .08 .25
214 Binghamton Checklist .01 .05
215 Francois Leroux .15 .40
216 Marc Laforge .05 .15
217 Max Middendorf .07 .20
218 Shjon Podein .30 .75
219 Jason Soules .07 .20
220 Collin Bauer .05 .15
221 Shaun Van Allen .15 .40
222 Eldon Reddick .20 .50
223 Eygeny Belosheiken .20 .50
224 David Haas .05 .15
225 Norm Foster .20 .50
226 Greg Hawgood .20 .50
227 Steven Rice .15 .40
228 Dan Currie .08 .25
229 Peter Soberlak .05 .15
230 Martin Rucinsky .40 1.00
231 Tomas Kapusta .08 .25
232 Dean Antos .05 .15
233 Craig Fisher .07 .20
234 Tomas Srsen .05 .15
235 Don McAdam .05 .15
236 Norm Ferguson .05 .15
237 Coaching Staff .01 .05
238 Cape Breton Checklist .01 .05
239 Peter Hankinson .05 .15
240 Chris McRae .05 .15
241 Craig Martin .08 .25
242 Carey Lucyk .05 .15
243 Jean-Marc Richard .05 .15
244 Grant Richison .05 .15
245 Mark Turner .05 .15
246 Todd Flichel .05 .15
247 Scott Shaunessy .05 .15
248 Darin Smith .05 .15
249 Ian Boyce .05 .15
250 Colin Chin .07 .20
251 Bob Jones .05 .15
252 Bob Jay .07 .20
253 Kelly Hurd .05 .15
254 Scott Gruhl .40 1.00
255 Kory Kocur .07 .20
256 Steven Fletcher .05 .15
257 Bob Lakso .07 .20
258 Dusty Imoo .20 .50
259 Mike O'Neill .20 .50
260 Bruce Boudreau .08 .25
261 Al Sims .15 .40
262 Komets Checklist .01 .05
263 Ray Letourneau .05 .15
264 Marc D'Amour .20 .50
265 Dominic Roussel .30 .75
266 Bill Armstrong (LW) .07 .20
267 Al Conroy .08 .25
268 Dale Kushner .08 .25
269 Toni Porkka .05 .15
270 Mike Stothers .05 .15
271 Darren Rumble .08 .25
272 Reid Simpson .05 .15
273 Claude Boivin .08 .25
274 Len Barrie .08 .25
275 Chris Jensen .08 .25
276 Pat Murray .08 .25
277 Eric Dandenault .05 .15
278 Rod Dallman .05 .15
279 Mark Freer .08 .25
280 Bill Armstrong (D) .08 .25
281 Tim Tookey .08 .25
282 Jamie Cooke .05 .15
283 Dave Fenyves .08 .25
284 Steve Morrow .05 .15
285 Martin Hostak .08 .25
286 Mike Eaves .08 .25
287 Hershey Checklist .01 .05
288 Dave Michayluk .20 .50
289 Glenn Mulvenna .07 .20
290 Jean Blouin .05 .15
291 Jock Callander .40 1.00
292 Perry Ganchar .05 .15
293 Paul Laus .30 .75
294 Mark Major .05 .15
295 Bruce Racine .20 .50
296 Daniel Gauthier .05 .15
297 Mike Needham .08 .25
298 Jeff Daniels .08 .25
299 Sandy Smith .05 .15
300 Gilbert Delorme .08 .25
301 Rob Dopson .20 .50
302 Eric Brule .05 .15
303 Alain Morissette .05 .15
304 Paul Dyck .05 .15
305 Jason Smart .05 .15
306 Gord Dineen .08 .25
307 Todd Nelson .08 .25
308 Jamie Heward .05 .15
309 Paul Russell .05 .15
310 Lumberjack Checklist .01 .05
311 Soren True .05 .15
312 Murray Duval .05 .15
313 Dmitri Kvartalnov .15 .40
314 Larry Floyd .05 .15
315 Alan Legett .05 .15
316 Alan Hepple .05 .15
317 Ron Duguay .20 .50
318 Len Hachborn .08 .25
319 Steve Martinson .08 .25
320 Rick Knickle .30 .75
321 Darcy Norton .05 .15
322 Keith Gretzky .20 .50
323 Brian Straub .05 .15
324 Denny Lambert .08 .25
325 Jason Prosofsky .08 .25
326 Bruce Hoffort .08 .25
327 Sergei Starikov .07 .20
328 Dave Korol .05 .15
329 Robbie Nichols .05 .15
330 Kord Cernich .05 .15
331 Brent Sapergia .08 .25
332 Don Waddell .05 .15
333 Charlie Simmer .20 .50
334 San Diego Checklist .01 .05
335 Rob Mendel .05 .15
336 Curtis Hunt .05 .15
337 Jeff Serowik .08 .25
338 Bruce Bell .08 .25
339 Yanic Perreault .30 .75
340 Brad Aitken .05 .15
341 Keith Osborne .05 .15
342 Todd Hawkins .05 .15
343 Andrew McKim .08 .25
344 Kevin McClelland .08 .25
345 Mike Stevens .08 .25
346 Dave Tomlinson .08 .25
347 Kevin Maguire .08 .25
348 Mike MacWilliams .05 .15
349 Greg Walters .05 .15
350 Guy Lehoux .05 .15
351 Todd Gillingham .05 .15
352 Len Esau .05 .15
353 Greg Johnston .08 .25
354 Felix Potvin 2.00 5.00
355 Damian Rhodes .40 1.00
356 Joel Quenneville .05 .15
357 Marc Crawford .30 .75
358 Mike Eastwood .08 .25
359 St.Johns Checklist .01 .05
360 Lou Franceschetti .08 .25
361 John Murray Anderson .05 .15
362 Scott Schneider .05 .15
363 Jerome Bechard .05 .15
364 Mario Doyon .07 .20
365 Jeff Jackson .08 .25
366 John Tanner .08 .25
367 Al Tuer .05 .15
368 Paul Willett .05 .15
369 Darryl Williams .05 .15
370 George Maneluk .08 .25
371 Eric Ricard .05 .15
372 Trevor Stienburg .05 .15
373 Jerry Tarrant .05 .15
374 Michael McEwen .08 .25
375 Brian Dobbin .08 .25
376 David Latta .05 .15
377 Jim Sprott .05 .15
378 Trevor Pochipinski .05 .15
379 Stan Drulia .20 .50
380 Kent Hulst .05 .15
381 Brad Turner .05 .15
382 Doug Carpenter .08 .25
383 New Haven Checklist .01 .05
384 Bob Berg .05 .15
385 Steve Jaques .05 .15
386 Chris Norton .05 .15
387 Vern Smith .05 .15
388 Kevin MacDonald .05 .15
389 Ross Wilson .05 .15
390 Shawn McCosh .05 .15
391 Mike Vukonich .05 .15
392 Marc Saumier .05 .15
393 Mike Ruark .05 .15
394 Kris Miller .05 .15
395 Tim Breslin .05 .15
396 Paul Holden .05 .15
397 Jeff Rohlicek .05 .15
398 Kyosti Karjalainen .08 .25
399 David Goverde .20 .50
400 John Van Kessel .05 .15
401 Sean Whyte .05 .15
402 Brent Thompson .08 .25
403 Darryl Gilmour .20 .50
404 Scott Bjugstad .07 .20
405 Ralph Backstrom .15 .40
406 Rick Kozuback .05 .15
407 Roadrunner Checklist .01 .05
408 Brent Severyn .40 1.00
409 Dean Malkoc .08 .25
410 Matt Ruchty .05 .15
411 Jarrod Skalde .20 .50
412 Brian Sullivan .05 .15
413 Ben Hankinson .08 .25
414 Bill Huard .15 .40
415 Jeff Christian .05 .15
416 Corey Schwab .20 .50
417 Kevin Dean .05 .15
418 Todd Copeland .05 .15
419 Mike Bodnarchuk .05 .15
420 Jason Miller .05 .15
421 Chad Erickson .20 .50
422 David Craievich .05 .15
423 Jim Dowd .20 .50
424 Jamie Huscroft .15 .40
425 Myles O'Connor .08 .25
426 Jon Morris .08 .25
427 Valeri Zelepukin .20 .50
428 Utica Checklist .01 .05
429 Brad Beck .05 .15
430 Brett MacDonald .05 .15
431 Jacques Mailhot .08 .25
432 Francois Ouellette .05 .15
433 Ron Kinghorn .05 .15
434 Dennis Miller .05 .15
435 Darren Miciak .05 .15
436 Tom Sasso .05 .15
437 Peter Corbett .05 .15
438 Brian Horan .05 .15
439 John Messuri .05 .15
440 E.J. Sauer .05 .15
441 Tom Mutch .05 .15
442 Jason Simon .05 .15
443 Steve Sullivan .05 .15
444 Scott Allen .05 .15
445 Stephane Brochu .08 .25
446 Ken Spangler .08 .25
447 Lee Odelein .05 .15
448 Antti Autere .05 .15
449 John Reid .05 .15
450 Skip Probst CO .01 .05

451 Flint Checklist .05 .15
452 Dean Ewen .05 .15
453 Brent Grieve .15 .40
454 Jim Culhane .05 .15
455 Joni Lehto .05 .15
456 Graeme Townshend .08 .25
457 Danny Lorenz .08 .25
458 Phil Huber .05 .15
459 Kevin Cheveldayoff .07 .20
460 Dennis Vaske .15 .40
461 Wayne Doucet .05 .15
462 Greg Parks .07 .20
463 Dean Chynoweth .05 .15
464 Lee Giffin .08 .25
465 Richard Kromm .08 .25
466 Derek Laxdal .08 .25
467 Travis Green .40 1.00
468 Iain Fraser .08 .25
469 Rick Hayward .08 .25
470 Jeff Finley .08 .25
471 Dave Chyzowski .07 .20
472 Mark Fitzpatrick .40 1.00
473 Hubie McDonough .08 .25
474 Sean LeBrun .05 .15
475 Chris Pryor .05 .15
476 Capital District CL .01 .05
477 Jeff Sirkka .05 .15
478 Owen Lessard .05 .15
479 Jim Playfair .05 .15
480 Dan Vincelette .07 .20
481 Tracey Egeland .05 .15
482 Shawn Byram .05 .15
483 Trevor Dam .05 .15
484 Martin Desjardins .05 .15
485 Milan Tichy .08 .25
486 Cam Russell .15 .40
487 Mike Speer .05 .15
488 Sean Williams .05 .15
489 Paul Gillis .08 .25
490 Brad Lauer .08 .25
491 Trent Yawney .15 .40
492 Craig Woodcroft .08 .25
493 Justin LaFayette .05 .15
494 Rob Conn .08 .25
495 Frantisek Kucera .08 .25
496 Mike Peluso .40 1.00
497 Roch Belley .20 .50
498 Ryan McGill .07 .20
499 Kerry Toporowski .08 .25
500 Dominik Hasek 4.00 8.00
501 Adam Bennett .07 .20
502 Ray LeBlanc .20 .50
503 John Marks .07 .20
504 Ice Checklist .01 .05
505 Mikhail Kravets .07 .20
506 Gary Emmons .05 .15
507 Ed Courtenay .08 .25
508 Claudio Scremin .05 .15
509 Jarmo Myllys .40 1.00
510 Mike Colman .05 .15
511 Kevin Evans .08 .25
512 Troy Frederick .05 .15
513 Ron Handy .05 .15
514 Murray Garbutt .05 .15
515 Gordon Frantti .05 .15
516 Dale Craigwell .20 .50
517 Wade Flaherty .30 .75
518 Dean Kolstad .08 .25
519 Rick Lessard .08 .25
520 Craig Coxe .40 1.00
521 Jeff Madill .08 .25
522 Peter Lappin .08 .25
523 Duane Joyce .05 .15
524 Larry DePalma .08 .25
525 Pat MacLeod .08 .25
526 Andy Akervik .05 .15
527 Blades Checklist .01 .05
528 Mike Dagenais .05 .15
529 Gerald Bzdel .05 .15
530 Stephane Fiset .40 1.00
531 David Espe .05 .15
532 Patrick Labrecque .20 .50
533 Niclas Andersson .08 .25
534 Jon Klemm .30 .75
535 Denis Chasse .20 .50
536 Stephane Charbonneau .05 .15
537 Ivan Matulik .05 .15
538 Serge Roberge .05 .15
539 Daniel Dore .05 .15
540 Sergei Kharin .08 .25
541 Jamie Baker .08 .25
542 Ken McRae .08 .25
543 David Marcinyshyn .07 .20
544 Clement Jodoin .05 .15
545 Dean Hopkins .05 .15
546 Checklist .01 .05
547 Jeff Greenlaw .07 .20
548 Byron Dafoe .40 1.00
549 Jim Hrivnak .20 .50
550 Olaf Kolzig 1.25 3.00
551 John Purves .07 .20
552 Bobby Reynolds .05 .15
553 Simon Wheeldon .20 .50
554 Jim Mathieson .20 .50
555 Trevor Halverson .08 .25
556 Steve Seftel .05 .15
557 Ken Lovsin .08 .25
558 Victor Gervais .05 .15
559 Steve Martell .08 .25
560 Chris Clarke .05 .15
561 Brent Hughes .08 .25
562 Jiri Vykoukal .05 .15
563 Tim Taylor .20 .50
564 Richie Walcott .05 .15
565 Harry Mews .05 .15
566 Craig Duncanson .08 .25
567 Todd Hlushko .08 .25
568 Mark Ferner .08 .25
569 Bobby Babcock .07 .20
570 Reggie Savage .08 .25
571 Rob Laird .05 .15
572 Barry Trotz .01 .05
573 Baltimore Checklist .01 .05
574 Kevan Melrose .05 .15
575 Kevin Grant .05 .15
576 Kevan Guy .08 .25
577 Darryl Olsen .05 .15
578 Kevin Worthman .05 .15
579 Darren Stolk .05 .15
580 Bryan Deasley .05 .15
581 Paul Kruse .08 .25
582 Darren Banks .40 1.00
583 Corey Lyons .05 .15
584 Kenny Clark .05 .15
585 Todd Strueby .08 .25
586 Rich Chernomaz .05 .15
587 Tim Harris .05 .15
588 Shawn Heaphy .05 .15
589 Todd Harkins .08 .25
590 Richard Zemlak .08 .25
591 Warren Sharples .08 .25
592 Jason Muzzatti .20 .50
593 Dennis Holland .05 .15
594 Salt Lake City CL .01 .05
595 Shawn Antoski .15 .40
596 Peter Bakovic .05 .15
597 Robin Bawa .07 .20
598 Cam Brown .05 .15
599 Neil Eisenhut .08 .25
600 Jason Herter .07 .20
601 Ian Kidd .05 .15
602 Troy Neumeier .05 .15
603 Carl Valimont .05 .15
604 Phil Von Stefenelli .08 .25
605 Andrew McBain .08 .25
606 Eric Murano .08 .25
607 Rob Murphy .08 .25
608 Brian Blad .05 .15
609 Randy Boyd .05 .15
610 Don Gibson .05 .15
611 Paul Guay .08 .25
612 Jay Mazur .08 .25
613 Jeff Larmer .08 .25
614 Ladislav Tresl .08 .25
615 Dennis Snedden .05 .15
616 Corrie D'Alessio .08 .25
617 Bob Mason .20 .50
618 Jack McIlhargey .08 .25
619 Curt Fraser .08 .25
620 Admirals Checklist .01 .05

1996-97 Providence Bruins

This 25-card set was produced by SplitSecond for sale by the club at the team shop. It was originally offered for sale for $5. The cards feature the standard SplitSecond design. The cards are listed below according to jersey number, which is displayed prominently on the card.

COMPLETE SET (25) 4.00 10.00
2 Mark Cornforth .15 .40
3 Charles Paquette .15 .40
4 John Gruden .15 .40
6 Peter Laviolette .20 .50
8 Jean-Yves Roy .15 .40
9 Justin Gould .15 .40
10 David Emma .15 .40
11 Davis Payne .20 .50
13 Martin Simard .20 .50
14 Kirk Nielsen .15 .40
17 P.C. Drouin .20 .50
18 Jay Moser .15 .40
19 Bill McCauley .15 .40
21 Tim Sweeney LL .15 .40
22 Mitch Lamoureux .20 .50
23 Yevgeny Shaldybin .15 .40
25 Kevin Sawyer .30 .75
27 Brad Konik .15 .40
28 Milt Mastad .15 .40
29 Rob Tallas .30 .75
34 Bob Beers .20 .50
44 Brett Harkins .15 .40
49 Andre Roy .20 .50
NNO Bob Francis CO .10 .25
NNO AHL Web Site .01 .05

1997-98 Providence Bruins

This set features the Bruins of the AHL. The set was produced by the team and sold at home games for $8.

COMPLETE SET (26) 5.00 12.00
1 Rob Tallas .30 .75
2 Elias Abrahamsson .15 .40
3 Bill Armstrong .15 .40
4 Dean Chynoweth .15 .40
5 Aaron Downey .60 1.50
6 Hal Gill .30 .75
7 John Grahame .60 1.50
8 Antti Laaksonen .20 .50
9 Cameron Mann .20 .50
10 Anders Myrvold .20 .50
11 Eric Naud .15 .40
12 Kirk Nielsen .15 .40
13 Charles Paquette .15 .40
14 Joel Prpic .15 .40
15 Barry Richter .20 .50
16 Randy Robitaille .30 .75
17 Jon Rohloff .15 .40
18 Andre Roy .30 .75
19 Jean-Yves Roy .15 .40
20 Yevgeny Shaldybin .15 .40
21 Landon Wilson .20 .50
22 Andrei Yakhanov .15 .40
23 Tom McVie HCO .02 .10
24 Rod Langway ACO .02 .10
25 PHPA Web Site .01 .05
26 AHL Web Site .01 .05

1998-99 Providence Bruins

This set features the Bruins of the AHL. The set was produced by Split Second and sold by the team at its souvenir stands.

COMPLETE SET (25) 5.00 10.00
1 Peter Laviolette .25 .60
2 Elias Abrahamsson .15 .40
3 Johnathan Aitken .15 .40
4 Bill Armstrong .15 .40
5 Steve Bancroft .15 .40
6 Shawn Bates .30 .75
7 Jim Carey .30 .75
8 Aaron Downey .60 1.50
9 John Grahame .60 1.50
10 Joe Harney .15 .40
11 Jay Henderson .20 .50
12 Antti Laaksonen .30 .75
13 Cameron Mann .20 .50
14 Marquis Mathieu .20 .50
15 Eric Nickulas .20 .50
16 Peter Nordstrom .15 .40
17 Joel Prpic .15 .40
18 Randy Robitaille .20 .50
19 Andre Savage .30 .75
20 Brandon Smith .20 .50
21 Mattias Timander .15 .40
22 Joel Trottier .15 .40
23 Terry Virtue .20 .50
24 Landon Wilson .20 .50
25 AHL Web Site .01 .05

1999-00 Providence Bruins

This set features the Bruins of the AHL. The set was produced by SplitSecond and was sold by the team at home games.

COMPLETE SET (25) 5.00 12.00
1 Elias Abrahamsson .15 .40
2 Johnathan Aitken .15 .40
3 Shane Belter .15 .40
4 Nick Boynton .40 1.00
5 Jeremy Brown .15 .40
6 Vratislav Cech .15 .40
7 Jassen Cullimore .15 .40
8 Aaron Downey .60 1.50
9 Peter Ferraro .15 .40
10 Maxime Gingras .30 .75
11 John Grahame .60 1.50
12 Jay Henderson .30 .75
13 Joe Hulbig .15 .40
14 Antti Laaksonen .15 .40
15 Tim Lovell .15 .40
16 Cameron Mann .30 .75
17 Marquis Mathieu .20 .50
18 Keith McCambridge .15 .40
19 Eric Nickulas .30 .75
20 Joel Prpic .15 .40
21 Andre Savage .20 .50
22 Brandon Smith .20 .50
23 Denis Timofeev .15 .40
24 Jeff Wells .15 .40
25 Kay Whitmore .20 .50

2000-01 Providence Bruins

This set features the Bruins of the AHL. The set was produced by Choice Marketing and sold by the team at its souvenir stands.

COMPLETE SET (22) 6.00 10.00
1 Kay Whitmore .30 .75
2 Keith McCambridge .20 .50
3 Nick Boynton .40 1.00
4 Eric Manlow .20 .50
5 Zdenek Kutlak .20 .50
6 Cameron Mann .30 .75
7 Eric Nickulas .30 .50
8 Pavel Kolarik .20 .50
9 Jay Henderson .20 .50
10 Lee Goren .40 .75
11 Peter Vandermeer .20 .75
12 Marquis Mathieu .30 .50
13 Ivan Huml .60 1.00
14 Terry Hollinger .20 .50
15 Elias Abrahamsson .20 .50
16 Jeremy Brown .20 .50
17 Brandon Smith .20 .50
18 Mattias Karlin .20 .50
19 Jon Coleman .20 .50
20 Jonathan Girard .40 1.00
21 Peter Ferraro .20 .50
22 Kay Whitmore .30 .75
NNO Team CL .10 .25

2001-02 Providence Bruins

This set features the Bruins of the AHL. The 21-card set was produced by Choice Marketing and sold by the team at its souvenir shop. It is known that 1,000 of these sets were produced.

COMPLETE SET (21) 5.00 12.00
1 Andrew Raycroft .75 2.00
2 Jeff Maund .20 .50
3 Keith McCambridge .15 .35
4 Bobby Allen .15 .35
5 Chris Kelleher .15 .35
6 Eric Manlow .15 .35
7 Zdenek Kutlak .20 .50
8 Tony Tuzzolino .20 .50
9 Pavel Kolarik .15 .35
10 Lee Goren .40 1.00
11 John Emmons .15 .35
12 Andy Hilbert .40 1.00
13 Joe Hulbig .15 .35
14 Carl Corazzini .15 .35
15 Ivan Huml .40 1.00
16 Sean Haggerty .15 .35
17 Dennis Bonvie .20 .50
18 Mattias Karlin .20 .50
19 Martin Wilde .15 .35
20 Greg Crozier .20 .50
21 Jonathan Girard .40 1.00
NNO Title Card/CL .02 .10

2002-03 Providence Bruins

COMPLETE SET (21) 5.00 12.00
1 Andrew Raycroft .75 2.00
2 Kevin Dallman .20 .50
3 Chris Kelleher .20 .50
4 Keith Aucoin .20 .50
5 Rich Brennan .20 .50
6 Zdenek Kutlak .20 .50
7 Matt Herr .20 .50
8 Martin Samuelsson .40 1.00
9 Kris Vernarsky .30 .75
10 Jay Henderson .20 .50
11 Chris Paradise .20 .50
12 Andy Hilbert .30 .75
13 Shaone Morrisonn .40 1.00
14 Darren Van Oene .20 .50
15 Peter Metcalf .20 .50
16 Lee Goren .30 .75
17 Mike Gellard .20 .50
18 Brantt Myhres .20 .50
19 Pat Leahy .30 .75
20 Tim Thomas .75 2.00
NNO Checklist .04 .10

2003-04 Providence Bruins

This set was produced by Choice Marketing and sold at home games.

COMPLETE SET (24) 5.00 12.00
1 Rich Brennan .15 .40
2 Ed Campbell .15 .40
3 Carl Corazzini .15 .40
4 Kevin Dallman .15 .40
5 Mike Gellard .15 .40
6 Matt Herr .15 .40
7 Andy Hilbert .30 .75
8 Ivan Huml .15 .40
9 Milan Jurcina .30 .75
10 Zdenek Kutlak .15 .40
11 Pat Leahy .30 .75
12 Robert Liscak .15 .40
13 Peter Metcalf .15 .40
14 Brett Nowak .15 .40
15 Colton Orr .40 1.00
16 Martin Samuelsson .15 .40
17 Andre Savage .15 .40
18 Tim Thomas .60 1.50
19 Hannu Toivonen 1.25 3.00
20 Darren Van Oene .15 .40
21 Kris Vernarsky .15 .40
22 Brendan Walsh .15 .40
23 Brian White .15 .40
24 Martin Wilde .15 .40
NNO Checklist .04 .10

2004-05 Providence Bruins

This set was sold by the team at home games.

COMPLETE SET (25) 5.00 12.00
1 Pat Aufiero .20 .50
2 Patrice Bergeron .60 1.50
3 Brad Boyes .40 1.00
4 Carl Corazzini .20 .50
5 Kevin Dallman .20 .50
6 Chris Dyment .20 .50
7 Jayme Filipowicz .20 .50
8 David Gove .20 .50
9 Ben Guite .20 .50
10 Jay Henderson .20 .50
11 Andy Hilbert .20 .50
12 Milan Jurcina .20 .50
13 Pat Leahy .20 .50
14 Steve Munn .20 .50
15 Colton Orr .40 1.00
16 Martin Samuelsson .20 .50
17 Brent Thompson .20 .50
18 Yorick Treille .20 .50
19 Kris Vernarsky .20 .50
20 Brendan Walsh .20 .50
21 Peter Hamerlik .30 .75
22 Hannu Toivonen .75 2.00
23 Scott Gordon CO .04 .10
24 Rob Murray ACO .04 .10
25 Checklist .04 .10

2005-06 Providence Bruins

COMPLETE SET (25) 6.00 15.00
1 Zdenek Blatny .20 .50
2 Sean Curry .20 .50
3 Chris Dyment .20 .50
4 Scott Ford .30 .75
5 Ben Guite .20 .50
6 Eric Healey .20 .50
7 Jay Leach .20 .50
8 David Lundbohm .20 .50
9 Jason MacDonald .20 .50
10 Eric Nickulas .20 .50
11 Pascal Pelletier .30 .75
12 Tyler Redenbach .20 .50
13 Jeremy Reich .20 .50
14 Nathan Robinson .40 1.00
15 Michael Schutte .20 .50
16 Jonathan Sigalet .40 1.00
17 Jordan Sigalet .75 2.00
18 Garret Stroshein .40 1.00
19 Mark Stuart .40 1.00
20 Tim Thomas .60 1.50
21 Nate Thompson .20 .50
22 Ben Walter .20 .50
23 Scott Gordon HC .02 .10
24 Rob Murray AC .02 .10
NNO Providence Bruins CL .02 .10

2006-07 Providence Bruins

COMPLETE SET (25) 8.00 15.00
1 Bobby Allen .20 .50
2 Chris Collins .30 .75
3 Sean Curry .20 .50
4 Nathan Dempsey .20 .50
5 Nate DiCasmirro .20 .50
6 Brian Finley .30 .75
7 Petr Kalus .30 .75
8 Martin Karsums .20 .50
9 David Krejci .30 .75
10 Matt Lashoff .30 .75
11 Jay Leach .20 .50
12 Dennis Packard .20 .50
13 Pascal Pelletier .20 .50
14 Wacey Rabbit .60 1.50
15 Jeremy Reich .30 .75
16 Jonathan Sigalet .40 1.00
17 Jordan Sigalet .75 2.00
18 Yan Stastny .20 .50
19 Mark Stuart .40 1.00
20 Philippe Sauve .30 .75
21 Nate Thompson .30 .75
22 T.J. Trevelyan .40 1.00
23 Kris Versteeg 2.00 5.00
24 Ben Walter .20 .50
25 Dwayne Zinger .20 .50

2014-15 Providence Bruins

COMPLETE SET (28) 8.00 20.00
1 Christopher Breen .30 .75
2 Anthony Camara .30 .75
3 Chris Casto .30 .75
4 Andrew Cherniwchan .30 .75
5 Tommy Cross .30 .75
6 Steve Eminger .40 1.00
7 Brian Ferlin .30 .75
8 Rob Flick .30 .75
9 Justin Florek .30 .75
10 Seth Griffith .40 1.00
11 Cory Kane .30 .75
12 Alexander Khokhlachev .30 .75
13 Jared Knight .30 .75
14 Matt Lindblad .40 1.00
15 Joseph Morrow .30 .75
16 Tyler Randell .30 .75
17 Bobby Robins .30 .75
18 Ben Sexton .30 .75
19 Jeremy Smith .30 .75
20 Ryan Spooner .50 1.25
21 Colin Stuart .40 1.00
22 Malcolm Subban .75 2.00
23 Niklas Svedberg .40 1.00
24 Zach Trotman .30 .75
25 David Warsofsky .30 .75
26 Ethan Werek .30 .75
27 Ben Youds .30 .75
28 Header Card CL .30 .75

1936-37 Providence Reds

Printed on thin card stock, this 10-card set measures approximately 2 1/4" by 3 1/2". The fronts feature black-and-white player photos bordered in white. The player's name and position are printed beneath the picture, along with the statement "A New 'Reds' Picture Every Amateur Hockey Night". Unlike the other nine cards, the name of the player on card 10 is not printed beneath his picture. From his facsimile autograph on the picture, his first name may be "Jacques," but his last name remains unidentified. The backs are blank. The cards are unnumbered and checklisted below in alphabetical order.

COMPLETE SET (10) 200.00 400.00
1 Bobby Bauer 37.50 75.00
2 Paddy Byrne 12.50 25.00
3 Woody Dumart 37.50 75.00
4 Jackie Keating 12.50 25.00
5 Art Lesieur 12.50 25.00
6 Bert McInenly 12.50 25.00
7 Gus Rivers 12.50 25.00
8 Milt Schmidt 75.00 150.00
9 Jerry Shannon 12.50 25.00
10 Player Unidentified 12.50 25.00

2000 QMJHL All-Star Program Inserts

These oversized cards were issued as perforated inserts inside the 2000 QMJHL All-Star Game program.

COMPLETE SET (46) 20.00 50.00
1 Guy Chouinard CO .20 .50
2 Maxime Ouellet .60 1.50
3 Sebastien Caron .75 2.00
4 Joe Rullier .40 1.00
5 Marc-Andre Bergeron .75 2.00
6 Chris Lyness .40 1.00
7 Jonathan Gautier .40 1.00
8 Francois Beauchemin 1.25 3.00
9 Michel Periard .40 1.00
10 Mike Ribeiro .75 2.00
11 Wesley Scanzano .40 1.00
12 Jonathan Roy .40 1.00
13 Carl Malette .40 1.00
14 Ramzi Abid .40 1.00
15 Simon Gamache .40 1.00
16 Marco Charpentier .40 1.00
17 Marc-Andre Thinel .40 1.00
18 Jerome Tremblay .40 1.00
19 Brandon Reid .75 2.00
20 Benoit Dusablon .40 1.00
21 Eric Chouinard .40 1.00
22 Claude Julien CO .40 1.00
23 Alexei Volkov .40 1.00
24 Drew MacIntyre .40 1.00
25 Joey DiPenta .75 2.00
26 Kirill Safronov .40 1.00
27 Alexander Riazantsev .40 1.00
28 Daniel MacLeod .40 1.00
29 Roustam Bakhriddinov .40 1.00
30 Adam Rivet .40 1.00
31 Miroslav Zalesak .40 1.00
32 Edo Terglav .40 1.00
33 Maxim Potapov .40 1.00
34 Thatcher Bell .40 1.00
35 Radim Vrbata 1.25 3.00
36 Jan-Philippe Cadieux .40 1.00
37 Dmitri Afanassenkov .40 1.00
38 Michael Ryder 2.00 5.00
39 Artem Rybin .40 1.00
40 Andrei Shefer .40 1.00
41 Brad Richards 4.00 10.00
42 Juraj Kolnik .40 1.00
43 Danny Bowie .40 1.00
44 All-Star Game Logo .02 .10
45 Team World Logo .02 .10
46 Team Quebec Logo .02 .10

1996-97 Quad-City Mallards

This 22-card set is circular in design. It was initially released as a giveaway only promotion with two cards inserted in Whitey's Ice Cream Bars, and other cards handed out at the games. Later in the season the entire set was sold at Whitey's.

COMPLETE SET (22) 8.00 20.00
1 Todd Newton .40 1.00
2 Brad Barton .40 1.00
3 Travis Tucker .40 1.00
4 Stephen Sangermano .40 1.00
5 Dave Larson .40 1.00
6 Jim Ensom .40 1.00
7 Justin McHugh .40 1.00
8 Fredrick Nasvall .40 1.00
9 Hugo Proulx .40 1.00
10 Carl LeBlanc .40 1.00
11 Glenn Stewart .40 1.00
12 Brett Strot .40 1.00
13 Andy Faulkner .40 1.00
14 Mark McFarlane .40 1.00
15 Howie Rosenblatt .60 1.50
16 Rick Emmett .40 1.00
17 Sergei Zvyagin .40 1.00
18 David Fletcher .40 1.00
19 John Batten .40 1.00
20 John Anderson HCO .40 1.00
21 Matt Shaw ACO .40 1.00
22 Mo Mallard Mascot .20 .50

1997-98 Quad-City Mallards

This set features the Mallards of the UHL. The cards were produced by Roox, and sold by the team at its souvenir stands.

COMPLETE SET (23) 4.80 12.00
1 Glenn Stewart .20 .50
2 Rick Emmett .20 .50
3 Sergei Zvyagin .20 .50
4 Howie Rosenblatt .30 .75
5 Brad Barton .20 .50
6 Kirk Llano .20 .50
7 Wayne Muir .30 .75
8 Hugo Proulx .20 .50
9 Mark McFarlane .20 .50
10 Steve Chelios .30 .75
11 Travis Tucker .20 .50
12 Carl LeBlanc .20 .50
13 Stas Tkatch .20 .50
14 Andy Faulkner .20 .50
15 Steve Gibson .20 .50
16 Tom Perry .20 .50
17 Matt Mullin .30 .75
18 Bogdan Rudenko .30 .75
19 Ryan Gelinas .30 .75
20 Jim Brown .20 .50
21 Kerry Toporowski .30 .75
22 Corey Neilson .20 .50
23 Quad City Mallards CL .02 .10

1998-99 Quad-City Mallards

This set features the Mallards of the UHL. The set was produced by Roox and was sold by the team at home games.

COMPLETE SET (24) 4.00 10.00
1 Sergei Zvyagin .20 .50
2 Brendan Brooks .20 .50
3 Scott Burfoot .02 .10
4 Matt Carey .20 .50
5 Rick Emmett .20 .50
6 Martin Fillion .20 .50
7 Rusty Fitzgerald .20 .50
8 Chad Ford .20 .50
9 Robert Frid .20 .50
10 Steve Gibson .20 .50
11 Garry Gulash .20 .50
12 Kevin Kerr .30 .75
13 Brian LaFleur .20 .50
14 Carl LeBlanc .30 .75
15 Mark McFarlane .20 .50
16 Stephanie Madore .20 .50
17 Mike Melas .20 .50
18 Hugo Proulx .20 .50
19 Bruce Richardson .20 .50
20 Howie Rosenblatt .30 .75
21 Scott Thompson .20 .50
22 Bill Weir .20 .50
23 Glenn Stewart .20 .50
24 Team CL .02 .10

1999-00 Quad-City Mallards

This set features the Mallards of the UHL. The set was produced by Roox and sold at home games. There are two number one cards in the set.

COMPLETE SET (24) 4.00 10.00
1 Iannique Renaud .20 .50
1 Moe Mallard MAS .02 .10
2 Yannick Latour .20 .50
3 Steve Gibson .20 .50
4 Garry Gulash .20 .50
5 Mike Melas .20 .50
6 Rick Emmett .20 .50
7 Ryan Lindsay .20 .50
8 Patrick Nadeau .20 .50
9 Hugo Proulx .20 .50
10 Paul Johnson .20 .50
11 Brendan Buckley .20 .50
12 Martin Hlinka .20 .50
13 Brendan Brooks .20 .50
14 Rusty Fitzgerald .20 .50
15 Kelly Hultgren .20 .50
16 Mark McFarlane .20 .50
17 Glenn Stewart .20 .50
18 Martin Villeneuve .30 .75
19 Brian LaFleur .20 .50
20 Robert DeCiantis .20 .50
21 Kevin Kerr .30 .75
22 Scott Buhler .30 .75
24 Quad City Mallards CL .02 .10

2000-01 Quad-City Mallards

This set features the Mallards of the UHL. The cards were produced by Roox and sold by the team at its souvenir stands.

COMPLETE SET (27) 4.00 10.00
1 Team CL .04 .10
2 Andy Fermoyle .15 .40
3 Garry Gulash .15 .40
4 Frederick Jobin .15 .40
5 Vlad Serov .15 .40
6 Dan Bjornlie .15 .40
7 Peter Armbrust .15 .40
8 Patrick Nadeau .15 .40
9 Ryan Lindsay .15 .40
10 Jason Ulmer .15 .40
11 Hugo Proulx .15 .40
12 Mike Sim .15 .40
13 Chad Power .15 .40
14 Paul Johnson .15 .40
15 Kelly Perrault .15 .40
16 Mark McFarlane .15 .40
17 Etienne Drapeau .20 .50
18 Martin Hlinka .15 .40
19 Rick Emmett .20 .50
20 Martin Villeneuve .15 .40
21 Scott Myers .15 .40
22 Cam Severson .15 .75
23 Steve Gibson .15 .40
24 Kerry Toporowski .20 .50
25 Paul MacLean CO .10 .25
26 Mo Mallard MASCOT .04 .10
27 Ima Duck MASCOT .04 .10

2001-02 Quad-City Mallards

This set features the Mallards of the UHL. The set was sold by the team at home games. The cards are unnumbered and so are listed below in alphabetical order.

COMPLETE SET (24) 4.80 12.00
1 Peter Armbrust .20 .50
2 Dan Bjornlie .20 .50
3 Keli Corpse .30 .75
4 Joe Dimaline .20 .50
5 Andy Fermoyle .20 .50
6 Nick Ganga .20 .50
7 Steve Gibson .30 .75
8 Garry Gulash .20 .50
9 Frederick Jobin .20 .50
10 Kyle Kidney .20 .50
11 Sanny Lindstrom .20 .50
12 Brian McCullough .20 .50
13 Mark McFarlane .20 .50
14 Paul MacLean CO .20 .50
15 Dylan Mills .20 .50
16 Aaron Miskovich .30 .75
17 Patrick Nadeau .20 .50
18 Brant Nicklin .20 .50
19 Hugo Proulx .30 .75
20 Jesse Rooney .20 .50
21 Brandon Sampair .20 .50
22 Kerry Toporowski .30 .75
23 Jason Ulmer .30 .75
24 Mo and Ima MASCOTS .04 .10

2005-06 Quad City Mallards

COMPLETE SET (25) 6.00 12.00
1 Anthony Blumer .20 .50
2 Tom Clayton .20 .50
3 Glenn Detulleo .20 .50
4 Terry Friesen .40 1.00
5 Tom Galvin .20 .50
6 Jason Jaworski .20 .50
7 Andrei Lupandin .20 .50
8 Rafal Martynowski .20 .50
9 Patrick Nadeau .20 .50
10 Samy Nasreddine .40 1.00
11 Mike Olynyk .20 .50
12 Joe Pace .20 .50
13 Joel Pullman .20 .50
14 Matt Radoslovich .20 .50
15 Jesse Rycroft .20 .50
16 Jason Tapp .40 1.00
17 Jonathan Tremblay .20 .50
18 Noah Whyte .20 .50
19 Chad Wollard .20 .50
20 J. J. Wrobel .20 .50
21 Jami Yoder .20 .50
22 Brian Curran CO .04 .10
23 Larry Easter TR .04 .10
24 Jason Rivera TR .04 .10
25 Aaron Roof ANN .04 .10

2006-07 Quad City Mallards

COMPLETE SET (20) 12.00 20.00
1 Justin Chwedoruk .40 1.00
2 Brian Curran CO .20 .50
3 Brent Currie .75 2.00
4 Sergei Durdin .40 1.00
5 Travis Granbois .40 1.00
6 Nick Harloff .40 1.00
7 Andrei Lupandin .40 1.00
8 Patrick Nadeau .40 1.00
9 Don Parsons .40 1.00
10 Jeff Petruic .40 1.00
11 Brett Pilkington .40 1.00
12 Matt Radoslovich .40 1.00
13 Zach Sikich .60 1.50
14 Sean Starke .40 1.00
15 Luke Stauffacher .75 2.00
16 Blake Stewart .40 1.00
17 Jason Tapp .75 2.00
18 Mathieu Wathier .40 1.00
19 Chad Woollard .40 1.00
20 Jami Yoder .40 1.00

2007-08 Quad City Flames

COMPLETE SET (25) 5.00 12.00
1 Ryan McGill HC .15 .40
2 David van der Gulik .25 .60
3 Brett Sutter .25 .60
4 Grant Stevenson .25 .60
5 Brandon Prust .25 .60
6 Warren Peters .25 .60
7 Matt Pelech .25 .60
8 Eric Nystrom .25 .60
9 Dustin Boyd .25 .60
10 Brent Krahn .25 .60
11 Adam Pardy .25 .60
12 Brett Palin .25 .60
13 Tomi Maki .25 .60
14 Krys Kolanos .25 .60
15 Matt Keetley .25 .60
16 Tim Hambly .25 .60
17 Carsen Germyn .25 .60
18 Cam Cunning .25 .60
19 Derek Couture .25 .60
20 Kris Chucko .25 .60
21 Gord Baldwin .25 .60
22 Curtis McElhinney .25 .60
23 Kevin Lalande .25 .60
24 Tim Ramholt .25 .60
25 Team Card .10 .25

2007-08 Quad City Flames Franchise Firsts

COMPLETE SET (5) 2.00 5.00
A Dustin Boyd .40 1.00
B Matt Keetley .40 1.00
C Grant Stevenson .40 1.00
D Eric Nystrom .40 1.00
E Curtis McElhinney .40 1.00

1956-57 Quebec Aces

The set was also issued on a limited basis as a factory set in a black presentation box. This 15-card set measures approximately 5" by 7" and features black-and-white posed action player photos with a white border. The player's name is inscribed across the lower portion of the photo. On a white background, the backs carry the sponsor (Maurice Pollack Limitee) and team logos. The cards are unnumbered and checklisted below in alphabetical order.

COMPLETE SET (16) 75.00 150.00
1 Gene Achtynichuk 3.00 6.00
2 Bob Beckett 6.00 12.00
3 Marcel Bonin 7.50 15.00
4 Joe Crozier 10.00 20.00
5 Jacque Gagne 3.00 6.00
6 Dick Garnelle 3.00 6.00
7 Floyd Hillman 6.00 12.00
8 Jean Paul Lamonde 3.00 6.00
9 Jean-Marie Loisette 3.00 6.00
10 Brent MacNab 3.00 6.00
11 Al Millar 3.00 6.00
12 Willie O'Ree 15.00 30.00
13 Nick Tabuchie 3.00 6.00
14 Skip Teal 3.00 6.00
15 Orval Tessier 7.50 15.00
16 Judges Tremblay 5.00 10.00

1962-63 Quebec Aces

This 21-card set features the Quebec Aces of the Quebec Senior Hockey League. The cards measure approximately 3 1/2" by 5 1/2" and have black and white posed action photos with white borders. The player's name is printed in black at the bottom. The backs are blank. The cards are unnumbered and checklisted below in alphabetical order. The existence of a corrected version of the Bill Dineen card recently has been confirmed. The set is considered complete with either version.

COMPLETE SET (21) 50.00 100.00
1 Ronald Attwell 2.00 4.00
2 Serge Aubry 3.00 6.00
3 Guy Black 2.00 4.00
4 Skippy Burchell 2.00 4.00
5 Jean Marie Cossette 2.00 4.00
6 Robert Courcy 2.00 4.00
7A Bill Dineen UER 6.00 12.00
(Misspelled Dinenn
7B Bill Dineen COR 7.50 15.00
8 Terry Gray 5.00 10.00
9 Reggie Grigg 2.00 4.00
10 John Hanna 2.00 4.00
11 Michel Harvey 2.00 4.00
12 Charlie Hodge 12.50 25.00
13 Ed Hoekstra 3.00 6.00
14 Michel Labadie 2.00 4.00
15 Claude Labrosse 2.00 4.00
16 Danny Lewicki 4.00 8.00
17 Frank Martin 2.00 4.00
18 Jim Morrison 3.00 6.00
19 Guy Rousseau 2.00 4.00
20 Dollard St. Laurent 5.00 10.00
21 Bill Sutherland 3.00 6.00

1963-64 Quebec Aces

This 23-card set features the Quebec Aces of the Quebec Senior Hockey League. The cards measure approximately 3 1/2" by 5 1/2" and have black and white posed action photos with white borders. The player's name is printed in black at the bottom. The backs are blank. The cards are unnumbered and checklisted below in alphabetical order.

COMPLETE SET (23) 75.00 150.00
1 Gilles Banville 1.50 3.00
2 Don Blackburn 1.50 3.00
3 Skippy Burchell 1.50 3.00
4 Billy Carter 1.50 3.00
5 Floyd Curry CO 5.00 10.00
6 Bill Dineen 5.00 10.00
7 Wayne Freitag 1.50 3.00
8 Jean Gauthier 1.50 3.00
9 Terry Gray 2.50 5.00
10 John Hanna 1.50 3.00
11 Doug Harvey 15.00 30.00
12 Wayne Hicks 1.50 3.00
13 Charlie Hodge 7.50 15.00
14 Charlie Hodge 7.50 15.00
15 Ed Hoekstra 2.50 5.00
16 Frank Martin 1.50 3.00
17 Rene LaCasse 1.50 3.00
18 Cleland Mortson 1.50 3.00
19 Gerry O'Drowski 2.50 5.00
20 Rino Robazzo 2.50 5.00
21 Leon Rochefort 1.50 3.00
22 Cliff Pennington 2.50 5.00
23 Lorne Worsley 17.50 35.00

1964-65 Quebec Aces

This 19-card set features the Quebec Aces of the Quebec Senior Hockey League. The cards measure approximately 3 1/2" by 5 1/2". The fronts have posed black-and-white player photos with white borders. The player's name is printed in black at the bottom. The backs are blank. The cards are unnumbered and checklisted below in alphabetical order.

COMPLETE SET (19) 62.50 125.00
1 Gilles Banville 1.50 3.00
2 Red Berenson 5.00 10.00
3 Don Blackburn 1.50 3.00
4 Jean Guy Gendron 4.00 8.00

5 Bernard Geoffrion 15.00 30.00
6 Terry Gray 4.00 8.00
7 John Hanna 1.50 3.00
8 Doug Harvey 12.50 25.00
9 Wayne Hicks 1.50 3.00
10 Edward Hoekstra 2.50 5.00
11 Rene Lacasse 1.50 3.00
12 Raymond Larose 1.50 3.00
13 Jimmy Morrison 2.50 5.00
14 Cleland Mortson 1.50 3.00
15 Leon Rochefort 4.00 8.00
16 Guy Rousseau 1.50 3.00
17 Bill Sutherland 2.00 4.00
18 Brian Watson 2.00 4.00
19 Lorne Worsley 12.50 25.00

1965-66 Quebec Aces

This 19-card set measures 3 1/2" by 5 1/2". The fronts feature white-bordered posed action shots. The player's name is printed in the wider white border at the bottom. The backs are blank. The cards are unnumbered and checklisted below in alphabetical order.

COMPLETE SET (19) 37.50 75.00
1 Gilles Banville 1.50 3.00
2 Gary Bauman 1.50 3.00
3 Don Blackburn 1.50 3.00
4 Jean-Guy Gendron 2.50 5.00
5 Bernard Geoffrion CO 12.50 25.00
6 Terry Gray 2.50 5.00
7 John Hanna 1.50 3.00
8 Wayne Hicks 1.50 3.00
9 Ed Hoekstra 2.50 5.00
10 Don Johns 1.50 3.00
11 Gordon Labossiere 2.50 5.00
12 Yvon Lacoste 1.50 3.00
13 Jimmy Morrison 2.50 5.00
14 Cleland Mortson 1.50 3.00
15 Simon Nolet 4.00 8.00
16 Noel Price 2.50 5.00
17 Rino Robazzo 2.50 5.00
18 Leon Rochefort 2.50 5.00
19 Bill Sutherland 2.00 4.00

1950 Quebec Citadelles

These 20 blank-backed photos of the Quebec Citadelles measure 4" by 6" and feature cream-bordered sepia tones of the suited-up players posed on the ice. The players' facsimile autographs appear near the bottom of the pictures. The photos are unnumbered and checklisted below in alphabetical order. These photos were sent as a complete set by the team via postal envelopes. Blue-tinted variations of these cards exist. More difficult to locate, they command a premium of up to two times. This set includes the earliest known card-like element of all-time great, Jean Beliveau.

COMPLETE SET (20) 200.00 400.00
1 Neil Amadio 5.00 10.00
2 Jean Beliveau 125.00 250.00
3 Georges Bergeron CO 4.00 8.00
4 Bruce Cline 6.00 12.00
5 Norm Diviney 4.00 8.00
6 Guy Gervais 4.00 8.00
7 Bernard Guay 4.00 8.00
8 Gord Haworth 5.00 10.00
9 Camille Henry 12.50 25.00
10 Gordie Hudson 4.00 8.00
11 Claude Larochelle 6.00 12.00
12 Bernie Lemonde 4.00 8.00
13 Paul-Emile Legault 4.00 8.00
14 Copper Leyte 4.00 8.00
15 Rainer Makila 5.00 10.00
16 Marcel Paille 12.50 25.00
17 Jean-Marie Plante 4.00 8.00
18 Claude Senechal 4.00 8.00
19 Jean Tremblay 12.50 25.00
20 Alphonses Gagnon CO 4.00 8.00

1999-00 Quebec Citadelles

This set features the Citadelles of the AHL. The set was produced by card shop CTM-Ste-Foy and was sold at that store and home games as well.

COMPLETE SET (26) 4.80 12.00
1 Mike McBain .15 .40
2 Gennady Razin .15 .40
3 Chris Albert .15 .40
4 Xavier Delisle .15 .40
5 Darcy Harris .15 .40
6 Marc Beaucage .15 .40
7 Stephane Robidas .15 .40
8 Jason Ward .30 .75
9 Francois Groleau .15 .40
10 Jonathan Delisle .15 .40
11 Stephane Roy .15 .40
12 Patrice Tardif .30 .75
13 Pierre Sevigny .30 .75
14 Jesse Belanger .15 .40
15 Eric Fichaud .30 .75
16 Andre Bashkirov .15 .40
17 Mathieu Garon .60 1.50
18 Dave Morissette .15 .40
19 Miloslav Guren .15 .40
20 Matthieu Descoteaux .15 .40
21 Jeff Shevalier .15 .40
22 Josh DeWolf .15 .40
23 Boyd Olson .15 .40
24 Matt Higgins .15 .40
25 Arron Asham .20 .50
NNO Quebec Citadelles .08 .25

2000-01 Quebec Citadelles

This set features the Citadelles of the AHL. The cards were produced by CTM-Ste-Foy and sold by that card shop, as well as by the team.

COMPLETE SET (24) 6.00 15.00
1 Gennady Razin .20 .50
2 Eric Chouinard .40 1.00
3 Francois Beauchemin .20 .50
4 Xavier Delisle .20 .50
5 Marc Beaucage .20 .50
6 Jason Ward .30 .75
7 Matt Higgins .20 .50
8 Mike McBain .20 .50
9 Miloslav Guren .20 .50
10 Pierre Sevigny .20 .50
11 Michael Ryder .75 2.00
12 Jonathan Delisle .20 .50
13 Eric Fichaud .30 .75
14 Andrei Bashkirov .30 .75
15 Mathieu Garon .60 1.50
16 Matt O'Dette .20 .50
17 Mathieu Raby .20 .50
18 Barry Richter .20 .50
19 Matthieu Descoteaux .20 .50
20 Josh DeWolf .20 .50
21 Eric Bertrand .20 .50
22 Arron Asham .30 .75
23 Mike Ribeiro .40 1.00
NNO Team CL .10 .25

2000-01 Quebec Citadelles Signed

This set is exactly the same as the base Citadelles set from this season, save that every card has been hand signed by the player pictured. Each card also is serial numbered out of just 100. The team CL is not signed.

COMPLETE SET (24) 30.00 75.00
1 Gennady Razin 1.20 3.00
2 Eric Chouinard 4.00 10.00
3 Francois Beauchemin 1.20 3.00
4 Xavier Delisle 1.20 3.00
5 Marc Beaucage 1.20 3.00
6 Jason Ward 2.00 5.00
7 Matt Higgins 1.20 3.00
8 Mike McBain 1.20 3.00
9 Miloslav Guren 1.20 3.00
10 Pierre Sevigny 1.20 3.00
11 Michael Ryder 2.00 20.00
12 Jonathan Delisle 1.20 3.00
13 Eric Fichaud 1.20 3.00
14 Andrei Bashkirov 1.20 3.00
15 Mathieu Garon 6.00 15.00
16 Matt O'Dette 1.20 3.00
17 Mathieu Raby 1.20 3.00
18 Barry Richter 1.20 3.00
19 Matthieu Descoteaux 1.20 3.00
20 Josh DeWolf 1.25 3.00
21 Eric Bertrand 1.20 3.00
22 Arron Asham 1.20 3.00
23 Mike Ribeiro 4.00 10.00
NNO Team CL .10 .25

2001-02 Quebec Citadelles

This set features the Citadelles of the AHL. The set was produced by CTM Ste-Foy and was sold at home games. Production of the set was limited to 1,000 copies.

COMPLETE SET (28) 8.00 20.00
1 Gennady Razin .20 .50
2 Eric Chouinard .30 .75
3 Eric Landry .20 .50
4 Ron Hainsey .40 1.00
5 Jason Ward .20 .50
6 Craig Darby .20 .50
7 Marc-Andre Thinel .30 .75
8 Martti Jarventie .30 .75
9 Francois Bouillon .30 .75
10 Francis Belanger .20 .50
11 Francois Beauchemin .20 .50
12 Pierre Sevigny .20 .50
13 Michael Ryder .40 1.00
14 Jonathan Delisle .20 .50
15 Vadim Tarasov .40 1.00
16 Mathieu Garon .40 1.00
17 Matt O'Dette .20 .50
18 Luc Belanger .30 .75
19 Jayme Filipowicz .20 .50
20 Mathieu Descoteaux .20 .50
21 Benoit Gratton .20 .50
22 Timo Vertala .20 .50
23 Arron Asham .20 .50
24 Andrei Markov .20 .50
25 Xavier Delisle .20 .50
26 Mike Ribeiro .30 .75
27 Marcel Hossa 1.50 4.00
28 Title Card/CL .04 .10

1992 Quebec Pee-Wee Tournament

This set features the best 12 and 13-year-old teams in the world that participated in the annual Quebec Pee-Wee Tournament. Though there are more than 1,900 cards in the set, we list only those players that might be familiar to the average collector.

COMPLETE SET (1903) 50.00 125.00
495 Daniel Tkaczuk .75 2.00
560 J-P Dumont 1.25 3.00
777 J.F. Damphousse .75 2.00
836 Steve Begin .75 2.00
1002 Bobby Allen .75 2.00
1120 Chris Bala .75 2.00
1403 David Aebischer 2.00 5.00
1464 Dainius Zubrus .40 1.00
1576 Mike York 1.25 3.00
1741 Robert Dome .40 1.00
1776 Sergei Samsonov 4.00 10.00

1993 Quebec Pee-Wee Tournament

This 1808-card set measures the standard size (2 1/2" by 3 1/2") and features posed, color player photos of participants at the Quebec International Pee-Wee Tournament. The pictures are framed by a wide stripe that is purple at the top and blends to a pinkish-purple shade toward the bottom. The player's name is printed in white in the purple border above the photo, while the team name is printed below. The player's country is printed on both sides of the photo. The backs have the same purple color scheme and carry a small, close-up photo along with biographical information and the appropriate national flag. The series was available only as one giant set boxes in acrylic, making singles somewhat difficult to acquire. Because of the vast numbers of players never to be heard from again, we only list players of some note in the book. Card numbers 1446, 1499, 1570, 1736, 1738, 1741, 1744, 1746, 1747, 1757, 1780, 1807 are missing. Card 1758 Donald Pierce is listed as 1757 on the checklist card.

COMPLETE SET (1808) 80.00 200.00
COMMON CARD (1-1808) .02 .10
15 Sebastien Caron 1.25 3.00
116 Eric Chouinard .60 1.50
301 Frederic Brindamour .40 1.00
342 Simon Gagne 10.00 25.00
348 Jean-Francois Damphousse 1.25 3.00
432 Sebastien Caron 1.25 3.00
523 Alex Tanguay 8.00 20.00
562 Daniel Tkaczuk .75 2.00
565 Peter Sarno .40 1.00
597 Paul Mara 1.25 3.00
664 Tim Connolly 2.00 5.00
704 Niklos Tselios .30 .75
877 Brian Gionta 3.00 8.00
903 Jonathan Girard .40 1.00
911 Eric Bertrand .20 .50
1053 Philippe Sauve 2.50 6.00
1152 Mike Comrie 2.00 5.00
1227 Jason Labarbera .75 2.00
1391 Mike Ribeiro 2.50 6.00
1398 Patrick Desrosiers .75 2.00
1408 Adam Colagiacomo .75 2.00
1417 Michael Ryder 2.00 5.00
1529 Gregor Baumgartner .20 .50
1554 Marian Hossa 12.00 30.00
1560 Robert Dome .40 1.00
1704 Ladislav Nagy 2.00 5.00
1717 Jan Lasak .75 2.00
1775 Sascha Goc 2.00 5.00
NNO Manon Rheaume 2.00 5.00

1993 Quebec Pee-Wee Tournament Gold

This three-card insert standard-size set features color player photos with metallic-gold borders on white card stock. The player's name is printed in the border at the top, while the card title is printed below the picture. The backs carry a player profile against a metallic-gold background with white borders. Two of the cards are numbered, while one is not. The listing below reflects this numbering.

COMPLETE SET (3) 4.80 12.00
1 Brad Park .75 2.00
2 Manon Rheaume 4.00 10.00
NNO Guy Chouinard .40 1.00

1994 Quebec Pee Wee Tournament

This set features the best 12 and 13-year-old teams in the world that participated in the annual Quebec Pee-Wee Tournament. Though there are more than 1,800 cards in the set, we list only those players who might be familiar to the average collector.

COMPLETE SET (1853) 60.00 150.00
COMMON CARD (1-1853) .01 .05
11 Vincent Lecavalier 10.00 25.00
46 Tony Voce
246 John-Michael Liles 1.50 4.00
345 Eric Chouinard .40 1.00
418 Ramzi Abid .40 1.00
497 Mathieu Chouinard .40 1.00
512 Phillipe Sauve 1.25 3.00
565 Seamus Kotyk .40 1.00
573 Rico Fata .40 1.00
617 Jonathan Girard .40 1.00
628 Martin Grenier .40 1.00
649 Tim Connolly .75 2.00
806 Justin Papineau .60 1.50
888 David Legwand 1.25 3.00
902 Junior Lessard 1.50 4.00
934 Marcel Rodman .40 1.00
1025 Norm Milley .75 2.00
1077 Simon Gagne 4.00 10.00
1148 Maxime Ouellet 1.25 3.00
1169 Jordan Krestanovich .40 1.00
1182 Brian Eklund .75 2.00
1202 Freddy Meyer .75 2.00
1211 Rick DiPietro 4.00 10.00
1256 Michael Ryan .40 1.00
1269 Michael Ayers
1607 Dominic Moore .75 2.00
1717 Sheldon Keefe .40 1.00
1752 Mathieu Biron .40 1.00
1846 Jeff Dwyer

1995 Quebec Pee Wee Tournament

This set features the best 12 and 13-year-old teams in the world that participated in the annual Quebec Pee-Wee Tournament. Though there are more than 1,800 cards in the set, we list only those players who might be familiar to the average collector.

COMPLETE SET (1825) 50.00 125.00
COMMON CARD (1-1825) .01 .05
1 Jozef Balej .40 1.00
109 Brandon Reid 1.25 3.00
234 Simon Gamache .75 2.00
278 Antoine Vermette 2.00 5.00
378 Maxime Ouellet .75 2.00
448 Marc-Andre Thinel .75 2.00
516 Tim Connolly .75 2.00
552 Zenon Konopka .40 1.00
607 Dusty Jamieson .40 1.00
608 Michael Leighton 1.25 3.00
617 Jamie Chamberlain .40 1.00
692 Justin Williams 1.50 4.00
762 Andy Hilbert .75 2.00
764 Damian Surma .40 1.00
834 Luke Sellars .40 1.00
1054 Craig Andersson .75 2.00
1153 Alexandre Giroux .40 1.00
1205 Luca Cereda .40 1.00
1243 Ron Hainsey 1.25 3.00
1318 Jason Pominville 2.00 5.00
1438 Jamie Lundmark .75 2.00

1996 Quebec Pee Wee Tournament

This set features the best 12 and 13-year-old teams in the world that participated in the annual Quebec Pee-Wee Tournament. Though there are more than 1,400 cards in the set, we list only those players who might be familiar to the average collector. It is worth noting, however, that there are a number of female players in this set. Although they are not worth listing individually, we have confirmed sales for some of these cards anywhere from $1 to $5.

COMPLETE SET (1474) 50.00 125.00
COMMON CARD (1-1474) .01 .05
1 Jozef Balej .40 1.00
2 Michal Barinka .40 1.00
16 Daniel Boisclair .75 2.00
23 Bobby Goeppert 1.50 4.00
32 Ryan Shannon .75 2.00
166 Brett Lebda .75 2.00
245 Jared Aulin 1.25 3.00
328 Pascal Leclaire 2.00 5.00
333 Yanick Lehoux .75 2.00
335 Jason Pominville 1.50 4.00
531 Rob Globke 1.00 2.50
560 J-F Racine 1.25 3.00
578 Gregory Campbell 1.25 3.00
668 Tim Gleason 1.50 4.00
678 Jim Slater .75 2.00
680 Kris Vernarsky .75 2.00
720 Jay Bouwmeester 6.00 15.00
899 Michael Komisarek 2.00 5.00
975 Sean McMorrow .75 2.00
992 Alexandre Vermette 1.50 4.00
1174 Michael Cammalleri 2.00 5.00
1227 M-A Pouliot 2.00 5.00
1288 Charline Labonte 2.00 5.00
1406 Scottie Upshall 2.00 5.00

1997 Quebec Pee Wee Tournament

This set features the best 12 and 13-year-old teams in the world that participated in the annual Quebec Pee-Wee Tournament. Though there are nearly 1,400 cards in the set, we list only those players who might be familiar to the average collector.

COMMON CARD .05
284 Stephen Werner .40 1.00
290 Scottie Upshall 1.50 4.00
820 Eric Nystrom 2.00 5.00
831 Chris Higgins 2.00 5.00
835 Bobby Goeppert 1.00 2.50
1113 Oliver Setzinger .40 1.00
1118 Thomas Vanek 10.00 25.00
1126 Tobias Stephan 1.50 4.00
1165 Ryan Whitney 2.00 5.00
1234 Sean Collins .40 1.00
1384 Marcel Goc 1.25 3.00

1998 Quebec Pee Wee Tournament

This mammoth set features the best 12 and 13-year-old teams in the world. Several players have achieved some notoriety in the intervening years. We list only those players.

157 Ryan Kesler 3.00 10.00
544 Danny Richmond .40 1.00
1032 Igor Mirnov .40 1.00
1225 Christopher Campoli 1.50 4.00

1999 Quebec Pee Wee Tournament Collection Souvenir

Sponsored by Compuware, this set features color action photos of many current NHL superstars who played in the Quebec Pee Wee Hockey World Championships before they were famous.

COMPLETE SET (30) 16.00 40.00
1 Brad Park .40 1.00
2 Guy Chouinard .08 .25
3 Manon Rheaume 1.25 3.00
4 Patrick Roy 4.00 10.00
5 Joe Juneau .20 .50
6 Sergei Samsonov 1.25 3.00
7 Dainius Zubrus .20 .50
8 Robert Dome .08 .25
9 Daniel Tkaczuk .20 .50
10 Alex Tanguay 1.25 3.00
11 Jean-Marc Pelletier .40 1.00
12 Oleg Kvasha .20 .50
13 Steve Begin .08 .25
14 Daniel Corso .20 .50
15 Sacha Goc .20 .50
16 Marian Hossa 2.00 5.00
17 Paul Mara .40 1.00
18 J-F Damphousse .40 1.00
19 Philippe Sauve .75 2.00
20 Gregor Baumgartner .08 .25
21 Ladislav Nagy .75 2.00
22 Vincent Lecavalier 2.00 5.00
23 David Legwand .75 2.00
24 Rico Fata .40 1.00
25 Mathieu Chouinard .40 1.00
26 Eric Chouinard .40 1.00
27 Mathieu Biron .20 .50
28 Simon Gagne 1.50 4.00
29 Mike Ribeiro .40 1.00
30 Jonathan Girard .40 1.00

2000 Quebec Pee Wee Tournament

COMPLETE SET
1276 Evan McGrath .75 2.00
1347 Robbie Schremp 4.00 10.00

1980-81 Quebec Remparts

This 22-card set measures approximately 2" by 3" and features posed color player photos. The cards were issued as part of a contest. The pictures are full-bleed except for a white bottom border that contains the team logo, player's name, and jersey number. The backs are blank. The collector who obtained the entire set and turned it in became eligible to enter a contest in which the grand prize was a trip to Disney World. The cards are unnumbered and checklisted below in alphabetical order.

COMPLETE SET (22) 10.00 20.00
1 Marc Bertrand .30 .75
2 Jacques Chouinard .30 .75
3 Roger Cote .30 .75
4 Gaston Drapeau CO .20 .50
5 Claude Drouin .30 .75
6 Gaetan Duchesne .75 2.00
7 Scott Fraser .40 1.00
8 Jean-Marc Lanthier .40 1.00
9 Jean-Paul Lariviere .30 .75
10 Andre Larocque .30 .75
11 Roberto Lavoie .30 .75
12 Marc Lemay .30 .75
13 Stephane Lessard .30 .75
14 Paul Levesque .30 .75
15 Richard Linteau .30 .75
16 Patrice Masse .30 .75
17 David Pretty .30 .75
18 Guy Riel .30 .75
19 Daniel Rioux .30 .75
20 Roberto Romano .75 2.00
21 Michel Therrien .75 2.00
22 Gilles Tremblay .60 1.50

1998-99 Quebec Remparts

This 25-card set was produced by Cartes Timbres Monnaies in conjunction with the Quebec Remparts of the QMJHL. It features several top prospects, including Eric Chouinard and Maxime Ouellet.

COMPLETE SET (25) 16.00 40.00
1 David Archambault .20 .50
2 David Bernier .20 .50
3 Nicholas Bilotto .20 .50
4 Tommy Bolduc .20 .50
5 Eric Chouinard .75 2.00
6 Ray Dalton .20 .50
7 Joey Fetta .20 .50
8 Simon Gagne 6.00 15.00
9 Martin Grenier .40 1.00
10 Eric Laplante .20 .50
11 Jeff Leblanc .20 .50
12 Pierre Loiselle .20 .50
13 Jerome Marois .20 .50
14 Andre Martineau .20 .50
15 Martin Moise .20 .50
16 Alexandre Morel .20 .50
17 Maxime Ouellet 4.00 10.00
18 Sylvain Plamondon .20 .50
19 Wesley Scanzano .20 .50
20 Simon Tremblay .20 .50
21 Dmitri Tolkunov .75 2.00
22 Antoine Vermette 1.25 3.00
23 Jonathan Wilhelmy .20 .50
24 Travis Zachary .20 .50
25 Title Card .02 .10

1998-99 Quebec Remparts Signed

This 25-card set was produced by Cartes Timbres Monnaies in conjunction with the Quebec Ramparts. Production was limited to just 100 serial #'d sets and the entire set is signed (except for Joey Fetta who was traded). Set is unnumbered and checklisted below in alphabetical order.

COMPLETE SET (25) 40.00 100.00
1 David Archambault 1.25 3.00
2 David Bernier 1.25 3.00
3 Nicholas Bilotto 1.25 3.00
4 Tommy Bolduc 1.25 3.00
5 Eric Chouinard 4.80 10.00
6 Ray Dalton 1.25 3.00
7 Joey Fetta 1.25 3.00
8 Simon Gagne 15.00 40.00
9 Martin Grenier 2.00 5.00
10 Eric Laplante 1.25 3.00
11 Jeff Leblanc 1.25 3.00
12 Pierre Loiselle 1.25 3.00
13 Jerome Marois 1.25 3.00
14 Andre Martineau 1.25 3.00
15 Martin Moise 1.25 3.00
16 Alexandre Morel 1.25 3.00
17 Maxime Ouellet 10.00 25.00
18 Sylvain Plamondon 1.25 3.00
19 Wesley Scanzano 1.25 3.00
20 Simon Tremblay 1.25 3.00
21 Dmitri Tolkunov 2.00 5.00
22 Antoine Vermette 4.00 10.00
23 Jonathan Wilhelmy 1.25 3.00
24 Travis Zachary 1.25 3.00
25 Title Card .08 .25

1999-00 Quebec Remparts

This 25-card set pictures the Remparts of the QMJHL. Base cards feature full-color action photography and a red border along the right edge and bottom of the card which contains player names and the team logo.

COMPLETE SET (25) 5.00 12.00
1 Jean Mallette .15 .40
2 Patrick Chouinard .15 .40
3 Kirill Safronov .30 .75
4 Eric Chouinard .40 1.00
5 Patrick Grandmaitre .15 .40
6 Eric Laplante .15 .40
7 Wesley Scanzano .15 .40
8 Chris Lyness .15 .40
9 Tommy Bolduc .15 .40
10 Jean-Francois Touchette .15 .40
11 Philippe Paris .15 .40
12 Karl Morin .15 .40
13 Andre Martineau .15 .40
14 Sylvain Plamondon .15 .40
15 Martin Moise .15 .40
16 Martin Grenier .30 .75
17 Andre Hart .15 .40
18 Maxime Ouellet 1.25 3.00
19 Martin Pare .15 .40
20 Eric Cloutier .15 .40
21 Kristian Kudroc .30 .75
22 Casey Leggett .15 .40
23 Shawn Collymore .20 .50
24 Mike Ribeiro .75 2.00
25 Header Card/CL .02 .10

1999-00 Quebec Remparts Signed

This 25-card set parallels the base Quebec Remparts set in an autographed version. The cards are signed on a unique ghosted area on the card front, while the backs are serial numbered out of 100. The header card remains in the set, but it is not signed.

COMPLETE SET (25) 30.00 75.00
1 Jean Mallette .75 2.00
2 Patrick Chouinard .75 2.00
3 Kirill Safronov 2.00 5.00
4 Eric Chouinard 4.00 10.00
5 Patrick Grandmaitre .75 2.00
6 Eric Laplante .75 2.00
7 Wesley Scanzano .75 2.00
8 Chris Lyness .75 2.00
9 Tommy Bolduc .75 2.00
10 Jean-Francois Touchette .75 2.00
11 Philippe Paris .75 2.00
12 Karl Morin .75 2.00
13 Andre Martineau .75 2.00
14 Sylvain Plamondon .75 2.00
15 Martin Moise .75 2.00
16 Martin Grenier 2.00 5.00
17 Andre Hart .75 2.00
18 Maxime Ouellet 8.00 20.00
19 Martin Pare .75 2.00
20 Eric Cloutier .75 2.00
21 Kristian Kudroc 2.00 5.00
22 Casey Leggett .75 2.00
23 Shawn Collymore 1.25 3.00
24 Mike Ribeiro 6.00 15.00
25 Header Card/CL .08 .25

2000-01 Quebec Remparts

This set features the Remparts of the QMJHL. The cards were produced by CTM-Ste-Foy and sold by that shop, as well as by the team.

COMPLETE SET (24) 4.80 12.00
1 Jean Mallette .20 .50
2 Sebastian Bourgon .20 .50
3 Richard Paul .20 .50
4 David Boilard .20 .50
5 Jeff Hadley .20 .50
6 Remi Bergeron .20 .50
7 Sebastian Morissette .20 .50
8 Philippe Paris .20 .50
9 Justin Stewart .20 .50
10 Yannick Searles .20 .50
11 Mike Bray .20 .50
12 Guillaume Fournier .20 .50
13 Robert Pearce .20 .50
14 Petr Preucil .20 .50
15 Philippe Parent .20 .50
16 Didier Bochatay .20 .50
17 Scott Della Vedova .30 .75
18 Alexandre Reuben .20 .50
19 David Masse .20 .50
20 Shawn Collymore .20 .75
21 Guillaume Berube .20 .50
22 Kevin Lachance .30 .75
23 Cory Urquhart .20 .50
NNO Team CL .04 .10

2000-01 Quebec Remparts Signed

This set is exactly the same as the base Remparts set from this season, save that every card has been hand signed by the player pictured. Each card also is serial numbered out of just 100. The team CL is not signed.

COMPLETE SET (24) 14.00 35.00
2 Sebastian Bourgon .80 2.00
3 Richard Paul .80 2.00
5 Jeff Hadley .80 2.00
6 Remi Bergeron .80 2.00
7 Sebastian Morissette .80 2.00
8 Philippe Paris .80 2.00
9 Justin Stewart .80 2.00
10 Yannick Searles .80 2.00
11 Mike Bray .80 2.00
12 Guillaume Fournier .80 2.00
13 Robert Pearce .80 2.00
14 Petr Preucil .80 2.00
15 Philippe Parent .80 2.00
17 Scott Della Vedova 2.00 5.00
20 Shawn Collymore .80 5.00
21 Guillaume Berube .80 2.00
22 Kevin Lachance 2.00 5.00
NNO Team CL .04 .25

2001-02 Quebec Remparts

This set features the Remparts of the QMJHL. The set was produced by CTM Ste-Foy and was sold at Remparts home games. It is believed that less than 1,000 sets were produced.

COMPLETE SET (24) 5.00 12.00
1 Jean-Michel Bolduc .20 .50
2 Sebastien Bourgon .20 .50
3 Yan Turcotte .20 .50
4 Jeff Hadley .20 .50
5 Josh Hennessy .20 .50
6 Mark Hurtubise .20 .50
7 Mathieu Dery .20 .50
8 Robert Pearce .20 .50
9 Yannick Searles .20 .50
10 Mike Bray .20 .50
11 Tomas Spila .20 .50
12 Samuel Duplain .20 .50
13 Petr Preucil .20 .50
14 Daniel Houle .20 .50
15 Didier Bochatay .20 .50
16 Denis Berube .20 .50
17 Jeff MacAulay .20 .50
18 Mario Joly .20 .50
19 David Masse .20 .50
20 Shawn Collymore .20 .50
21 Guillaume Berube .20 .50
22 Kevin Lachance .20 .50
23 Sebastien Thinel .20 .50
24 Cory Urquhart .20 .50

2002-03 Quebec Remparts

Cards U12-U23 available as an update set.

COMPLETE SET (23) 8.00 20.00
1 Jean-Michel Bolduc .30 .75
2 Sebastien Bourgon .20 .50
3 Colin Ledaire .20 .50
4 Josh Hennessy .20 .50
5 Mark Hurtubise .20 .50
6 Vladimir Kutny .20 .50
7 Robert Pearce .20 .50
8 Jordan LaVallee .20 .50
9 Timofei Shishkanov .40 1.00
10 Jason Kostadine .20 .50
11 Curtis Tidball .20 .50
12 Frederic Faucher .20 .50
13 Karl St. Pierre .20 .50
14 Didier Bochatay .20 .50
15 Ben McMullin .30 .75
16 David Masse .20 .50
17 Shawn Collymore .30 .75
18 Guillaume Berube .20 .50
19 Steve Pelletier .20 .50
20 Kevin Lachance .30 .75
21 Pierre-Olivier Beaulieu .20 .50
22 Chris Montgomery .20 .50
U12 Evan Shaw .20 .50
U14 Jean-Michel Filiatrault .75 2.00
U15 Alexandre Rouleau .30 .75
U16 Aaron Johnson .20 .50
U17 Pierre Morvan .20 .50
U20 Benoit Beauchemin .20 .50
U21 Remy Tremblay .20 .50
U22 Checklist/Logo .04 .10
U23 Jamie McCabe .20 .50
NNO Checklist .04 .10

2003 Quebec Remparts Memorial Cup

Cards are unnumbered and thus are listed in alphabetical order.

COMPLETE SET (21) 6.00 15.00
1 Guillaume Berube .30 .75
2 Jean-Michel Bolduc .40 1.00
3 Sebastien Bourgon .30 .75
4 Frederic Faucher .30 .75
5 Jean-Michel Filiatrault 1.00 2.50
6 Josh Hennessy .30 .75
7 Aaron Johnson .30 .75
8 Jason Kostadine .30 .75
9 Vladimir Kutny .30 .75
10 Kevin Lachance .40 1.00
11 Jordan Lavallee .30 .75
12 David Masse .30 .75
13 Jamie McCabe .30 .75
14 Chris Montgomery .30 .75
15 Pierre Morvan .30 .75
16 Robert Pearce .30 .75
17 Alexandre Rouleau .40 1.00
18 Evan Shaw .30 .75
19 Timofei Shishkanov .30 1.25
20 Karl St.Pierre .30 .75
21 Curtis Tidball .30 .75

2003-04 Quebec Remparts

COMPLETE SET (28) 5.00 12.00
1 Andrew Andricopoulos .20 .50
2 Adam Blanchette .20 .50
3 Christian Brideau .20 .50
4 Tyler Chambers .20 .50
5 Jean-Michel Cote .30 .75
6 Kevin Coughlin .20 .50
7 Simon Courcelles .20 .50
8 Jean-Michel Filiatrault .40 1.00
9 Ian Girard .20 .50
10 Stephane Goulet .20 .50
11 Josh Hennessy .30 .75
12 Alexandre Imbeault .20 .50
13 Alexandre Kojevnikov .20 .50
14 Louis-Phillipe Lachance .20 .50
15 Jordan LaVallee .20 .50
16 Justin Laverdiere .20 .50
17 Maxime Lincourt .20 .50
18 Eric L'Italien .20 .50
19 Mathieu Melanson .20 .50
20 Corey Pastershank .20 .50
21 Robert Pearce .20 .50
22 Joey Ryan .20 .50
23 Evan Shaw .20 .50
24 Alexei Shkotov .20 .50
25 Brandon Tidball .20 .50
26 Marc-Edouard Vlasic .60 1.50
27 Nathan Welton .20 .50
28 Checklist .04 .10
Title Card

2004-05 Quebec Remparts

A total of 400 team sets were produced.

COMPLETE SET (25) 6.00 15.00
1 Gennady Churilov .20 .50
2 Jordan LaVallee .20 .50
3 Karl Gagne .20 .50
4 Maxime Lacroix .20 .50
5 Maxime Lincourt .20 .50
6 Simon Courcelles .20 .50
7 Andrew Andricopoulos .20 .50
8 Ian Girard .20 .50
9 Maxime Joyal .20 .50
10 Alexander Radulov 1.50 4.00
11 Brandon Tidball .40 1.00
12 Marc-Edouard Vlasic 1.25 3.00
13 Max Gratchev .20 .50
14 Josh Hennessy .40 1.00
15 Mathieu Melanson .20 .50
16 Drew Paris .20 .50
17 Jonathan Alain-Rochette .20 .50
18 Joey Ryan .20 .50
19 Sebastien Bernier .20 .50
20 Kevin Coughlin .20 .50
21 Jonathan Boutin .30 .75
22 Alexandre Mineault .20 .50
23 Michael Tessier .20 .50
24 Guillaume Veilleux .20 .50
25 Evan Shaw .20 .50

2005-06 Quebec Remparts

COMPLETE SET (25) 10.00 18.00
1 Angelo Esposito 2.00 5.00
2 Alexander Radulov .75 2.00
3 Stephen Valente .20 .50
4 Joey Ryan .20 .50
5 Drew Paris .20 .50
6 Michal Sersen .20 .50
7 Simon Coucelles .20 .50
8 Felix Petit .20 .50
9 Maxime Lacroix .20 .50
10 Alexandre Mineault .20 .50
11 Max Gratchev .20 .50
12 Andrew Andricopoulos .20 .50
13 Jordan Lavallee .20 .50
14 Cedrick Desjardins .30 .75
15 Kevin Desfosses .20 .50
16 Kenzie Sheppard .20 .50
17 Nicolas Robillard .20 .50
18 Pierre Bergeron .20 .50
19 Brent Aubin .20 .50
20 Christophe Poirier .20 .50
21 Guillaume Veilleux .20 .50
22 Marc-Edouard Vlasic .20 .50
23 Todd Chinova .20 .50
24 Yan Ouimet .20 .50
25 Mathieu Melanson .20 .50

2006-07 Quebec Remparts

COMPLETE SET (27) 12.00 20.00
1 Angelo Esposito 2.00 5.00
2 Andrew Andricopoulos .20 .50
3 Joey Ryan .20 .50
4 Pierre Bergeron .20 .50
5 Kelsey Tessier .40 1.00
6 Roman Bashkirov .40 1.00
7 Hubert Genest .20 .50
8 Felix Petit .20 .50
9 Brent Aubin .40 1.00
10 Maxime Sauve .20 .50
11 Loic Lacasse .20 .50
12 Alexandre Mineault .20 .50
13 Ruslan Bashkirov .40 1.00
14 Billy Bezeau .20 .50
15 Kevin Desfosses .40 1.00
16 Boby Fugere .20 .50
17 Maxime Lacroix .20 .50
18 Christophe Poirier .20 .50
19 Philippe Poirier .20 .50
20 Joel Roch .20 .50
21 Benjamin Rubin .20 .50
22 Kenzie Sheppard .20 .50
23 Matthew Smith .40 1.00
24 Marc-Olivier Vallerand .20 .50
25 Guillaume Veilleux .20 .50
26 Mathieu Lavoie .20 .50
EL2 Brent Aubin .20 .50

2015-16 Quebec Remparts

COMPLETE SET (26) 6.00 15.00
1 Bronson Beaton .30 .75
2 Callum Booth .30 .75
3 Matthew Boucher .30 .75
4 Nikolas Brouillard .30 .75
5 Massimo Carozza .30 .75
6 Alexandre Drapeau .30 .75
7 Aaron Dutra .30 .75
8 Julian Galloway .30 .75
9 Olivier Garneau .30 .75
10 Derek Gentile .30 .75
11 Charley Graaskamp .30 .75
12 Christian Huntley .30 .75
13 Auguste Impase .30 .75
14 Ross MacDougall .30 .75
15 Raphael Maheux .30 .75
16 Austin McEneny .30 .75
17 Ryan McReynolds .30 .75
18 Zachery Moody .30 .75
19 Matt Murphy .30 .75
20 Sean O'Brien .30 .75
21 Mikael Robidoux .30 .75
22 Jesse Sutton .30 .75
23 Lucas Thierus .30 .75
24 Dmytro Timashov .30 .75
25 Yanick Turcotte .30 .75
26 Dakotah Woods .30 .75

1992-93 Raleigh Icecaps

This 38-card standard-size set features the Raleigh Icecaps of the ECHL. Inside a blue-and-white border design, the fronts feature on-ice posed color player photos with rounded corners. The player's name and position appear under the photo, while the words "1992-93 Raleigh IceCaps" are printed above the photo. The backs carry biography, stats, and a player profile. The cards were issued in two separate series. The first series cards, produced by Sportsprint (Atlanta, GA), are unnumbered and checklisted below in alphabetical order, whereas the second series cards, produced by RBI Sports Cards Inc. (Greensboro, North Carolina), are numbered on the back.

COMPLETE SET (38) 6.00 15.00
1 Cappy Bear (Mascot) .02 .10
2 Sean Cowan .20 .50
3 Joel Gardner .20 .50
4 Bill Kovacs .20 .50
5 Alan Leggett .20 .50
6 Kirby Lindal .20 .50
7 Derek Linnell .20 .50
8 Jim Mill .20 .50
9 Kris Miller .20 .50
10 Todd Person .20 .50
11 Chic Pojar .20 .50
12 Jim Powers .20 .50
13 Stan(Smokey) Reddick .30 .75
14 Doug Roberts .20 .50
15 Jeff Robison .20 .50
16 Jeff Tomlinson .20 .50
17 Brian Tulik .20 .50
18 Bruno Villeneuve .20 .50
19 Lyle Wildgoose .20 .50
20 Team Photo DP .15 .40
21 Bruno Villeneuve .20 .50

22 Jeff Robison .20 .50
23 Jim Powers .20 .50
24 Derek Linnell .20 .50
25 Chris Marshall .20 .50
26 Kris Miller .20 .50
27 Joel Gardner .20 .50
28 Stan(Smokey) Reddick .30 .75
29 Jim Mill .20 .50
30 Alan Leggett .20 .50
31 Brian Tulik .20 .50
32 Kirby Lindal .20 .50
33 Sean Cowan .20 .50
34 Lyle Wildgoose .20 .50
35 Todd Person .20 .50
36 Chic Pojar .20 .50
37 Mike Lappin .20 .50
38 Doug Bacon .20 .50

1993-94 Raleigh Icecaps

Produced by RBI Sports Cards, this 20-card standard-size set features the Raleigh Icecaps of the ECHL. On a white card face, the fronts feature color action player photos inside purple borders. The player's name appears under the photo.

COMPLETE SET (20) 3.00 8.00
1 Ralph Barahona .15 .40
2 Rick Barkovich .15 .40
3 Matt Delguidice .20 .50
4 Martin D'Orsonnens .15 .40
5 Jamie Erb .15 .40
6 Chad Erickson .20 .50
7 Donevan Hextall .20 .50
8 Shaun Kane .15 .40
9 Al Leggett .15 .40
10 Derek Linnell .15 .40
11 Joe McCarthy .15 .40
12 Chris Nelson .15 .40
13 Barry Nieckar .15 .40
14 Jim Powers .15 .40
15 Stan Reddick .20 .50
16 Kevin Riehl .15 .40
17 Jeff Robison .15 .40
18 David Shute .15 .40
19 Lyle Wildgoose .15 .40
20 Kurt Kleinendorst CO .08 .25

1994-95 Raleigh Icecaps

Produced by RBI Sports Cards, this 19-card standard-size set features the Raleigh Icecaps of the ECHL. Just 1,000 sets were produced. On a black card face, the fronts feature color action and posed player photos inside a white frame. The player's name appears under the photo, while the team name is printed above the photo. There are several production errors in this set. Card number 12 was not produced. Card numbers 9 and 18 were mistakenly duplicated and explains the absence of card numbers 10 and 19.

COMPLETE SET (19) 3.00 8.00
1 John Blessman .20 .50
2 Rick Barkovich CO .08 .25
3 Alexsandr Chunchukov .20 .50
4 Frank Cirone .20 .50
5 Brett Duncan .20 .50
6 Anton Fedorov .20 .50
7 Todd Hunter .20 .50
8 Rodrigo Lavinsh .30 .75
9 Derek Linnell .20 .50
10 Eric Long UER .20 .50
11 Scott MacNair .20 .50
13 Brad Mullahy .20 .50
14 Lenny Pereira .20 .50
15 Jimmy Powers .20 .50
16 Chic Pojar .20 .50
17 Kevin Riehl .20 .50
18 Todd Reirden .30 .75
19 Justin Tomberlin UER .20 .50
20 Lyle Wildgoose .20 .50

1989-90 Rayside-Balfour Jr. Canadians

This 20-card set is printed on thin card stock and measures approximately 2 3/8" by 3 3/8." The cards feature full-bleed, color, posed player photos. The player's name and jersey number are printed in black at the bottom. The team logo and name are printed at the top. The cards are unnumbered and checklisted below in alphabetical order.

COMPLETE SET (20) 3.00 8.00
1 Team Photo .40 1.00
2 Dave Barrett .20 .50
3 Dan Baston .20 .50
4 Rick Chartrand .20 .50
5 Simon Chartrand .20 .50
6 Ron Clark .20 .50
7 Brian Dickinson .20 .50
8 Trevor Duncan .20 .50
9 Don Gauthier .20 .50
10 Shawn Hawkins .20 .50
11 Roy Hildebrandt .20 .50
12 Al Laginski .20 .50
13 Eric Lanteigne .20 .50
14 Mike Leblanc .20 .50
15 Kevin MacDonald .20 .50
16 Mike Mooney .20 .50
17 Rick Potvin .20 .50
18 Rick Poulin .20 .50
19 Steve Prior .20 .50
20 Scott Sutton .20 .50

1990-91 Rayside-Balfour Jr. Canadians

This 23-card set is printed on thin card stock and measures approximately 2 3/8" by 3 1/4." The cards feature full-bleed, color, posed player photos. The player's name and jersey number are printed in black at the bottom. The team logo and name are printed at the top. The cards are unnumbered and checklisted below in alphabetical order.

COMPLETE SET (23) 3.00 8.00
1 Dan Baston .15 .40
2 Jon Boeve .15 .40
3 Jordan Boyle .15 .40
4 Serge Coulombe .15 .40
5 Mike Dore .15 .40
6 Denis Gosselin .15 .40
7 Mike Gratton .15 .40
8 Jason Hall .15 .40
9 Grant Healey .15 .40
10 Marc Lafreniere .15 .40
11 Alain Leclair .15 .40
12 Mike Longo .15 .40
13 Troy Mallette .30 .75
1985-86 rookie photo
14 Matthew Mooney .15 .40
15 Virgil Nose .15 .40
16 Trevor Oystrick .15 .40
17 Steve Proceviat .15 .40
18 Chris Puskas .15 .40
19 Yvon Quenneville .15 .40
20 Michael Sullivan .20 .50
21 Trevor Tremblay .15 .40
22 Sean Van Amburg .15 .40
23 Title Card .02 .10

1991-92 Rayside-Balfour Jr. Canadians

This 23-card set measures approximately 2 3/8" by 3 5/16" and is printed on thin card stock. The fronts feature color, full-bleed, posed action player photos. The player's name and jersey number are printed in black at the bottom. The team logo appears in either red or white at the upper left corner. The cards are unnumbered and checklisted below in alphabetical order.

COMPLETE SET (23) 3.00 8.00
1 Dan Baston .20 .50
2 Don Cucksey .20 .50
3 Dean Cull .20 .50
4 Mike Dore .20 .50
5 Denis Gosselin .20 .50
6 Jason Hall .20 .50
7 Grant Healey .20 .50
8 Marc Lafreniere .20 .50
9 Mike Longo .20 .50
10 Scott Maclellan .20 .50
11 Matt Mooney .20 .50
12 Rob Moxness .20 .50
13 Virgil Nose .20 .50
14 Trent Oystrick .20 .50
15 Jon Stewart .20 .50
16 Jon Stos .20 .50
17 Dave Sutton .20 .50
18 Scott Sutton .20 .50
19 Trevor Tremblay .20 .50
20 Jaak Valiots .20 .50
21 Sean Van Amburg .20 .50
22 Jason Young .02 .10
Stickboy
23 Title Card .02 .10

2002-03 Reading Royals

COMPLETE SET (32) 10.00 25.00
1 Series 1 Header Card .04 .10
2 Francois Drainville .40 1.00
3 David Lohrei CO .20 .50
4 Matt Snesrud .40 1.00
5 Ray DiLauro .40 1.00
6 Chris Bogas .40 1.00
7 Simon Tremblay .40 1.00
8 Jim Dube .40 1.00
9 Series 2 Header Card .04 .10
10 Jonathon Shockey .40 1.00
11 Colin Pepperall .40 1.00
12 Brad Rooney .40 1.00
13 Brandon Dietrich .40 1.00
14 Kris Waltze .40 1.00
15 Hunter Lahache .40 1.00
16 Jeff Giuliano .40 1.00
17 Series 3 Header Card .20 .50
18 Sean Gauthier .40 1.00
19 Steve Rymsha .40 1.00
20 Tom Rouleau .40 1.00
21 Geoff Peters .40 1.00
22 Duilio Grande .40 1.00
23 Keegan McAvoy .40 1.00
24 Brian McCullough .40 1.00
25 Series 4 Header Card .04 .10
26 Steve Shirreffs .40 1.00
27 Ryan Flinn .60 1.50
28 Scott Fankhouser .60 1.50
29 Jeff Sanger .40 1.00
30 Antoine Bergeron .40 1.00
31 Alex Kim .40 1.00
32 Dan Riva .40 1.00

2002-03 Reading Royals RBI Sports

COMPLETE SET (18) 8.00 20.00
169 Antoine Bergeron .40 1.00
170 Craig Brunel .40 1.00
171 Brandon Dietrich .40 1.00
172 Ray DiLauro .40 1.00
173 Jim Dube .40 1.00
174 Jeff Giuliano .40 1.00
175 Duilio Grande .40 1.00
176 Alex Kim .40 1.00
177 Brian McCullough .40 1.00
178 Colin Pepperall .40 1.00
179 Dan Riva .40 1.00
180 Brad Rooney .40 1.00
181 Remi Royer .75 2.00
182 Tom Rouleau .40 1.00
183 Steve Rymsha .40 1.00
184 Jeff Sanger .75 2.00
185 Mat Snesrud .40 1.00
186 Simon Tremblay .40 1.00

2003-04 Reading Royals

This set was issued in four mini-sets as a promotional giveaway over the course of the 2003-04 season.

COMPLETE SET (30) 12.00 30.00
1 Header Card Series One .04 .10
2 Derek Clancey .40 1.00
3 Adam Hauser 1.25 3.00
4 Mat Snesrud .40 1.00
5 Jason Maleyko .40 1.00
6 Tomas Slovak .40 1.00
7 Jonathan Zion .40 1.00
8 Leon Hayward .40 1.00
9 Header Card Series Two .04 .10
10 Judd Medak .40 1.00
11 David Masse .40 1.00
12 Nick Lent .40 1.00
13 Jeff Finger .40 1.00
14 Francis Nault .40 1.00
15 Graig Mischler .40 1.00
16 Header Card Series Three .04 .10
17 Peter Hay .40 1.00
18 Ian Turner .40 1.00
19 Kent Davyduke .40 1.00
20 Dean Arsene .40 1.00
21 Darryl Laplante .40 1.00
22 Dave Stewart .75 2.00
23 Header Card Series Four .04 .10
24 Mascot .04 .10
25 Reading Royals .04 .10
26 Brad Church .40 1.00
27 Cody Rudkowsky .75 2.00
28 Terry Denike .75 2.00
29 Matt Passfield .40 1.00
30 Doug Nolan .40 1.00

2003-04 Reading Royals RBI Sports

This set was produced by RBI Sports and limited to just 250 copies. The numbering sequence reflects the entire run of RBI sets over the course of the season.

COMPLETE SET (18) 6.00 15.00
289 Brad Church .40 1.00
290 Kent Davyduke .40 1.00
291 Peter Hay .40 1.00
292 Leon Hayward .40 1.00
293 Nick Lent .40 1.00
294 Jason Maleyko .40 1.00
295 Judd Medak .40 1.00
296 Graig Mischler .40 1.00
297 Francis Nault .40 1.00
298 Doug Nolan .40 1.00
299 Matt Passfield .40 1.00
300 Cody Rudkowsky .60 1.50
301 Tomas Slovak .40 1.00
302 Scooter Smith .40 1.00
303 Mat Snesrud .40 1.00
304 Ian Turner .40 1.00
305 David Belitski .60 1.50
306 Josh Barker .40 1.00

2005-06 Reading Royals

COMPLETE SET (19) 8.00 15.00
1 Chris Bala .30 .75
2 Doug Christiansen .30 .75
3 Larry Courville .30 .75
4 Jon Francisco .30 .75
5 Yutaka Fukufuji .75 2.00
6 Tyler Hanchuck .30 .75
7 T.J. Kemp .30 .75
8 Mike Kompon .30 .75
9 Malcolm MacMillan .30 .75
10 John Morlang .30 .75
11 Reagan Rome .30 .75
12 Dany Roussin .60 1.50
13 Cody Rudkowsky .60 1.50
14 Jeff State .30 .75
15 Shay Stephenson .30 .75
16 Eric Werner .30 .75
17 Karl Taylor HC .02 .10
18 Slapshot MASCOT .02 .10
19 Reading Royals .02 .10

2006-07 Reading Royals

COMPLETE SET (18) 15.00 30.00
1 Rob Lalonde .75 2.00
2 Shawn German .60 1.50
3 Taylor Christie .60 1.50
4 Reagan Rome .60 1.50
5 Jason Becker .60 1.50
6 Malcolm Macmillan 1.00 2.50
7 Shawn Collymore .60 1.50
8 Joe Zappala .60 1.50
9 John Snowden .60 1.50
10 Jon Francisco .60 1.50
11 Dany Roussin .60 1.50
12 Ned Lukacevic .60 1.50
13 Kevin Saurette .60 1.50
14 Greg Hogeboom .60 1.50
15 Chris Bala .60 1.50
16 Jeff Pietrasiak .75 2.00
17 Yutaka Fukufuji 2.00 5.00
18 Karl Taylor CO .20 .50

2007-08 Reading Royals

COMPLETE SET (22) 4.00 10.00
1 Terry Denike .25 .60
2 Rob LaLonde .25 .60
3 Patrik Hersley .25 .60
4 Shawn Germain .25 .60
5 Victor Uchevatov .25 .60
6 Steven Later .25 .60
7 Ned Lukacevic .25 .60
8 Malcolm MacMillan .25 .60
9 Joe Zappala .25 .60
10 Chris Blight .25 .60
11 Patrick Jarrett .25 .60
12 Dany Roussin .25 .60
13 Brock Hooton .25 .60
14 Mike Salekin .25 .60
15 Kevin Saurette .25 .60
16 Matt Herneisen .25 .60
17 Marc Cavosie .25 .60
18 Brian Boulay .25 .60
19 Charlie Kronschnabel .25 .60
20 Jon Quick .25 .60
21 PJ Atherton .25 .60
22 Karl Taylor .25 .60

2014-15 Reading Royals

COMPLETE SET (27) 8.00 20.00
1 Brandon Alderson .30 .75
2 Michael Caruso .40 1.00
3 Willie Coetzee .30 .75
4 Adam Comrie .30 .75
5 Larry Courville CO .30 .75
6 Ryan Cruthers .30 .75
7 Zach Davies .30 .75
8 Brett Flemming .30 .75
9 Matt Hatch .30 .75
10 Jordan Heywood .30 .75
11 Adam Hughesman .30 .75
12 Andrew Johnston .30 .75
13 Connor Knapp .30 .75
14 Olivier Labelle .30 .75
15 Maxim Lamarche .30 .75
16 Mike Marcou .30 .75
17 David Marshall .30 .75
18 Derek Mathers .30 .75
19 Bryant Molle .30 .75
20 Pat Mullane .30 .75
21 Martin Ouellette .30 .75
22 Cam Reid .30 .75
23 Kevin Walrod .30 .75
24 Ian Watters .30 .75
25 Sean Wiles .30 .75
26 Slapshot MASCOT .30 .75
27 Tiara MASCOT .30 .75

1993-94 Red Deer Rebels

This 30-card set measures the standard size. The fronts feature posed action on-ice player photos with hatched borders. The player's name and number are printed in white letters inside a silver bar above the picture, while the team name appears alongside the left side. The cards are unnumbered and checklisted below in alphabetical order.

COMPLETE SET (30) 4.00 10.00
1 Peter Anholt CO .02 .10
2 Byron Briske .15 .40
3 Curtis Cardinal .15 .40
4 Jason Clague .15 .40
5 Dale Donaldson .15 .40
6 Dave Greenway .15 .40
7 Scott Grimwood TR .02 .10
8 Sean Halifax .15 .40
9 Chris Kibormanis .15 .40
10 Pete LeBoutillier .15 .40
11 Pete LeBoutillier .15 .40
In Ac
12 Terry Lindgren .15 .40
13 Chris Maillet .15 .40
14 Eddy Marchant .15 .40
15 Mike McBain .15 .40
16 Mike Moller ACO .02 .10
17 Andy Nowicki ACO .02 .10
18 Berkley Pennock .15 .40
19 Tyler Quiring .15 .40
20 Craig Reichert .15 .40
21 Ken Richardson .15 .40
22 Sean Selmser .15 .40
23 Vaclav Slansky .15 .40
24 Mark Toljanich .15 .40
25 Darren Van Impe .20 .50
26 Pete Vandermeer .30 .75
27 Chris Wickenheiser .20 .50
28 Brad Zimmer .15 .40
29 Jonathan Zukiwsky .15 .40
30 The Centrum .02 .10

1995-96 Red Deer Rebels

This 24-card set of the Red Deer Rebels of the WHL features extremely blurry color player photos in gray and black borders. The backs carry a player profile. The cards are unnumbered and checklisted below in alphabetical order.

COMPLETE SET (24) 4.00 10.00
1 Arron Asham .15 .40
2 Bryan Boorman .15 .40
3 Aleksei Boudaev .15 .40
4 Mike Broda .15 .40
5 Mike Brown .20 .50
6 Jay Henderson .30 .75
7 David Hruska .15 .40
8 Chris Kibermanis .15 .40
9 Brad Leeb .30 .75
10 Terry Lindgren .15 .40
11 Mike McBain .20 .50
12 Brent McDonald .15 .40
13 Ken McKay .15 .40
14 Harlan Pratt .15 .40
15 Greg Schmidt .15 .40
16 Pete Vandermeer .30 .75
17 Jesse Wallin .20 .50
18 Lance Ward .20 .50
19 Mike Whitney .15 .40
20 Chris Wickenheiser .30 .75
21 B.J. Young .15 .40
22 Jonathan Zukiwsky .20 .50
23 Drug Awareness Team .02 .10
24 Team Picture .15 .40

1996-97 Red Deer Rebels

Sold by the team at home games. Sponsored by RCMP and Parkland Colour Press.

COMPLETE SET (29) 6.00 15.00
1 Collector Series Card .01 .05
2 Team Photo .08 .25
3 Mike McBain .20 .50
4 Jesse Wallin .20 .50
5 Arron Asham .40 1.00
6 Kyle Kos .20 .50
7 Jonathan Zukiwsky .20 .50
8 Stephen Peat .75 2.00
9 Brent McDonald .20 .50
10 Greg Schmidt .20 .50
11 Chris Ovington .20 .50
12 Martin Tomasek .20 .50
13 Brad Rohrig .20 .50
14 Devin Francon .20 .50
15 B.J. Young .20 .50
16 Mike Broda .20 .50
17 Matt Van Horlick .20 .50
18 Mike Brown .20 .50
19 Lance Ward .20 .50
20 Kris Knoblauch .20 .50
21 Brad Leeb .20 .50
22 Garnet Stevenson .20 .50
23 Lloyd Shaw .20 .50
24 Mike Whitney .20 .50
25 Jesse Wallin .20 .50
26 Lance Ward .20 .50
27 The Centrum .02 .10
28 Drug Awareness .02 .10
29 Rowdy MASCOT .02 .10

1997-98 Red Deer Rebels

This set features the Rebels of the WHL. The set was produced by the team and sold at home games. The cards are unnumbered, and so are listed alphabetically.

COMPLETE SET (25) 5.00 12.00
1 Team photo .15 .40
2 Arron Asham .30 .75
3 Andrew Bergen .15 .40
4 Joel Boschman .15 .40
5 Chris Cederstrand .15 .40
6 Devin Francon .15 .40
7 John Kachur .15 .40
8 Kyle Kos .15 .40
9 Brad Leeb .15 .40
10 Justin Mapletoft .60 1.50
11 Brent McDonald .15 .40
12 Shawn McNeil .15 .40
13 Scott McQueen .15 .40
14 Frank Mrazek .20 .50
15 Cam Ondrik .15 .40
16 Chris Ovington .15 .40
17 Stephen Peat .60 1.50
18 Brad Rohrig .15 .40
19 Robert Schnabel .20 .50
20 Jesse Wallin .30 .75
21 Lance Ward .30 .75
22 Mike Whitney .15 .40
23 Jon Zukiwsky .20 .50
24 Woolly Bully MASCOT .02 .10
25 Drug Awareness .01 .05

1998-99 Red Deer Rebels

This set features the Rebels of the WHL. The cards were sold by the team at home games. They are unnumbered, so they are listed below in alphabetical order.

COMPLETE SET (24) 5.00 12.00
1 Jay Batchelor .20 .50
2 Lukas Bednarik .20 .50
3 Andrew Bergen .20 .50
4 Michael Clague .30 .75
5 Andrew Coates .20 .50
6 Devin Francon .20 .50
7 Kyle Kos .20 .50
8 Brad Leeb .20 .50
9 Justin Mapletoft .60 1.50
10 Kevin Marsh .20 .50
11 Brett McDonald .20 .50
12 Shawn McNeil .20 .50
13 Scott McQueen .20 .50
14 Frank Mrazek .20 .50
15 Rhett Nevill .20 .50
16 Chris Ovington .20 .50
17 Stephen Peat .60 1.50
18 Dustin Schwartz .30 .75
19 Jeff Smith .20 .50
20 Jim Vandermeer .20 .50
21 Justin Wallin .20 .50
22 Jordan Watt .30 .75
23 Wooly Bully MASCOT .02 .10
24 Drug Awareness Card .01 .05

2000-01 Red Deer Rebels

This set features the Rebels of the WHL. The set is noteworthy for capturing the team during its Memorial Cup-winning season. The cards were sold by the team and are unnumbered, so they are listed below in alphabetical order.

COMPLETE SET (24) 4.80 15.00
1 Checklist .04 .10
2 Colby Armstrong .40 1.50
3 Shane Bendera .40 1.00
4 Andrew Bergen .16 .40
5 Devin Francon .16 .40
6 Michael Garnett .16 .40
7 Boyd Gordon .16 .40
8 Shane Grypiuk .16 .40
9 Diarmuid Kelly .16 .40
10 Ladislav Kouba .16 .40
11 Ross Lupaschuk .30 .75
12 Doug Lynch .30 .75
13 Justin Mapletoft .60 1.50
14 Derek Meech .16 .40
15 Donovan Rattray .16 .40
16 Jeff Smith .16 .40
17 Shay Stephenson .16 .40
18 Joel Stepp .16 .40
19 Bryce Thoma .16 .40
20 Jim Vandermeer .16 .75
21 Martin Vymazal .16 .40
22 Justin Wallin .16 .40
23 Kyle Wanvig .60 1.50
24 Jeff Woywitka .40 1.50

2000-01 Red Deer Rebels Signed

This set is exactly the same as the base Rebels set from this season, save that every card has been hand signed by the player pictured. Amazingly, this set was originally made available by the team for the bargain price of $10.

COMPLETE SET (24) 24.00 60.00
1 Checklist .04 .10
2 Colby Armstrong 3.00 8.00
3 Shane Bendera 2.00 5.00
4 Andrew Bergen .80 2.00
5 Devin Francon .80 2.00
6 Michael Garnett .80 2.00
7 Boyd Gordon .80 2.00
8 Shane Grypiuk .80 2.00
9 Diarmuid Kelly .80 2.00
10 Ladislav Kouba .80 2.00
11 Ross Lupaschuk 2.00 5.00
12 Doug Lynch 2.00 5.00
13 Justin Mapletoft 3.00 7.50
14 Derek Meech .80 2.00
15 Donovan Rattray .80 2.00
16 Jeff Smith .80 2.00
17 Shay Stephenson .80 2.00
18 Joel Stepp .80 2.00
19 Bryce Thoma .80 2.00
20 Jim Vandermeer .80 3.00
21 Martin Vymazal .80 2.00
22 Justin Wallin .80 2.00
23 Kyle Wanvig 3.00 7.50
24 Jeff Woywitka 2.00 8.00

2001-02 Red Deer Rebels

COMPLETE SET (21) 6.00 15.00
1 Cover Card .04 .10
2 Colby Armstrong .40 1.00
3 Shane Bendera .40 1.00
4 Andrew Bergen .20 .50
5 Derek Endicott .20 .50
6 Jason Ertl .20 .50
7 Colin Fraser .20 .50
8 Boyd Gordon .40 1.00
9 Diarmuid Kelly .20 .50
10 Ladislav Kouba .20 .50
11 Doug Lynch .30 .75
12 Derek Meech .30 .75
13 Chris Neiszner .20 .50
14 Joel Rupprecht .20 .50
15 Jeff Smith .20 .50
16 Shay Stephenson .20 .50
17 Joel Stepp .20 .50
18 Bryce Thoma .20 .50
19 Cam Ward 4.00 10.00
20 Mikhail Yakubov .40 1.00
21 Woolly Bully MAS .04 .10

2002-03 Red Deer Rebels

This set features the Rebels of the WHL. The cards are listed in the order they appear on the checklist card.

COMPLETE SET (26) 15.00 40.00
1 Cam Ward 2.00 5.00
CL
2 Derek Meech .40 1.00
3 Dion Phaneuf 6.00 15.00
4 Bryce Thoma .20 .50
5 Jeff Woywitka .40 1.00
6 Cody Holzapfel .20 .50
7 Masi Marjamaki .40 1.00
8 Matt Ellison .20 .50
9 Joel Stepp .20 .50
10 Colin Fraser .30 .75
11 Blair Jones .20 .50
12 Jason Ertl .20 .50
13 Jared Walker .20 .50
14 Derek Endicott .20 .50
15 Carsen Germyn .20 .50
16 Boyd Gordon .40 1.00
17 Stuart Kerr .20 .50
18 Ladislav Kouba .20 .50
19 Matt Keith .20 .50
20 Diarmuid Kelly .20 .50
21 Shay Stephenson .20 .50
22 Nathan Brice .20 .50
23 Jesse Zetariuk .20 .50
24 Chris Neiszner .20 .50
25 Cam Ward 2.00 5.00
26 Adam Jennings .30 .75

2003-04 Red Deer Rebels

COMPLETE SET (24) 10.00 25.00
1 Derek Meech .30 .75
2 Dion Phaneuf 6.00 15.00
3 Paul Kurceba .20 .50
4 Dan Mercer .20 .50
5 Mikko Kuukka .20 .50
6 Andre Herman .20 .50
7 Colin Fraser .30 .75
8 Kyle Ross .20 .50
9 Jason Ertl .20 .50
10 Jared Walker .20 .50
11 Derek Endicott .20 .50
12 Justin Taylor .20 .50
13 Ted Vandermeer .20 .50
14 Stuart Kerr .30 .75
15 Blair Jones .20 .50
16 Shay Stephenson .20 .50
17 Nathan Brice .20 .50
18 Jesse Zetariuk .20 .50
19 Chris Neiszner .20 .50
20 Cam Ward 1.50 4.00
21 Trevor Peeters .30 .75
22 Wooly Bully MASCOT .04 .10
23 Brent Sutter CO .20 .50
24 Team Photo .20 .50

2005-06 Red Deer Rebels

COMPLETE SET (25) 8.00 15.00
1 Brennan Chapman .20 .50
2 Matthew Cline .20 .50
3 Luke Egener .20 .50
4 Eric Frere .20 .50
5 Tanner Gillies .20 .50
6 Matthew Hansen .20 .50
7 Garrett Klotz .20 .50
8 Jordan Knackstedt .20 .50
9 Pierre-Paul Lamoureux .20 .50
10 Devon LeBlanc .20 .50
11 Andrew Leslie .40 1.00
12 Vladimir Mihalik .20 .50
13 Karey Pieper .20 .50
14 Alex Poulter .20 .50
15 James Reimer .20 .50
16 Justin Scott .20 .50
17 Jonathon Smith .20 .50
18 Brandon Sutter 1.00 2.50
19 Brett Sutter .40 1.00
20 Ted Vandermeer .20 .50
21 Kris Versteeg 2.00 5.00
22 Roman Wick .20 .50
23 Mike Berube .20 .50
24 Josh Bray .20 .50
25 Red Deer Rebels CL .01 .01

2014-15 Red Deer Rebels

1 Conner Bleackley .30 .75
2 Brayden Burke .30 .75
3 Taz Burman .30 .75
4 Nick Charif .30 .75
5 Brett Cote .30 .75
6 Kolton Dixon .30 .75
7 Kayle Doetzel .30 .75
8 Devan Fafard .30 .75
9 Scott Feser .30 .75
10 Haydn Fleury .50 1.25
11 Mario Grman .30 .75
12 Wyatt Johnson .30 .75
13 Presten Kopeck .30 .75
14 Josh Mahura .30 .75
15 Brooks Maxwell .30 .75
16 Mason McCarty .30 .75
17 Adam Musil .30 .75
18 Meyer Nell .30 .75
19 Grayson Pawlenchuk .30 .75
20 Evan Polei .30 .75
21 Tyler Sandhu .30 .75
22 Austin Shmoorkoff .30 .75
23 Austin Strand .30 .75
24 Rylan Toth .30 .75
25 Jeff de Wit .30 .75
26 Header Card .30 .75

1981-82 Regina Pats

This 25-card set measures approximately 2 5/8" by 4 1/8" and is printed on thin card stock. The fronts feature color, posed action player photos with white borders accented by a thin red line. The player's jersey number, name, and position appear in black print across the bottom of the picture. The cards are unnumbered and checklisted below in alphabetical order.

COMPLETE SET (25) 12.00 30.00
1 Pats Logo .20 .50
2 Garth Butcher .75 2.00
3 Lyndon Byers 2.00 5.00
4 Jock Callander 1.50 4.00
5 Marc Centrone .40 1.00
6 Dave Goertz .40 1.00
7 Evans Dobni .40 1.00
8 Dale Derkatch .40 1.00
9 Jeff Crawford .40 1.00
10 Jim Clarke .40 1.00
11 Jayson Meyer .40 1.00
12 Gary Leeman .75 2.00
13 Bruce Holloway .40 1.00
14 Ken Heppner .40 1.00
15 Taylor Hall .40 1.00
16 Wally Schreiber .60 1.50
17 Kevin Pylypow .40 1.00
18 Ray Plamondon .40 1.00
19 Brent Pascal .40 1.00
20 Dave Michayluk .60 1.50
21 Barry Trotz .40 1.00
22 Al Tuer .60 1.50
23 Tony Vogel .40 1.00
24 Martin Wood .40 1.00
25 Regina Police Logo .20 .50

1982-83 Regina Pats

This 25-card set measures approximately 2 5/8" by 4 1/8" and features color, posed action player photos on white card stock. The pictures are framed by a thin red line. The player's name, jersey number, and position are printed in black on the photo.

COMPLETE SET (25) 10.00 25.00
1 Regina Pats and .08 .25
Police Logo
2 Todd Lumbard .40 1.00
3 Jamie Reeve .40 1.00
4 Dave Goertz .30 .75
5 John Miner .30 .75
6 Doug Trapp .30 .75
7 R.J. Dundas .30 .75
8 Stu Grimson 1.50 4.00
9 Al Tuer .30 .75
10 Rick Herbert .30 .75
11 Tony Vogel .30 .75
12 John Bekkers .30 .75
13 Dale Derkatch .60 1.50
14 Gary Leeman .75 2.00
15 Nevin Markwart .40 1.00
16 Kurt Wickenheiser .30 .75
17 Jeff Frank .30 .75
18 Marc Centrone .30 .75
19 Taylor Hall .30 .75
20 Lyndon Byers 1.50 4.00
21 Jayson Meyer .30 .75
22 Jeff Crawford .30 .75
23 Don Boyd CO .20 .50
24 Barry Trapp ACO .20 .50
25 K-9 Big Blue (Mascot) .08 .25

1983-84 Regina Pats

This 25-card set measures approximately 2 5/8" by 4 1/8" and features color, posed action player photos with white borders accented by a thin red line. The player's name is superimposed at the bottom of the picture.

COMPLETE SET (25) 8.00 20.00
1 Title Card .08 .25
2 Todd Lumbard .40 1.00
3 Jamie Reeve .40 1.00
4 Dave Goertz .30 .75
5 John Miner .30 .75
6 Doug Trapp .30 .75
7 R.J. Dundas .30 .75
8 Stu Grimson 1.25 3.00
9 Al Tuer .30 .75
10 Rick Herbert .30 .75
11 Tony Vogel .30 .75
12 John Bekkers .30 .75
13 Dale Derkatch .40 1.00
14 Gary Leeman .60 1.50
15 Nevin Markwart .40 1.00
16 Kurt Wickenheiser .30 .75
17 Jeff Frank .30 .75
18 Marc Centrone .30 .75
19 Taylor Hall .30 .75
20 Lyndon Byers 1.25 3.00
21 Jayson Meyer .30 .75
22 Jeff Crawford .30 .75
23 Don Boyd CO .20 .50
24 Barry Trapp ACO .20 .50
25 K-9 Big Blue (Mascot) .08 .25

1986-87 Regina Pats

Produced by Royal Studios, this 30-card set measures the standard size. The fronts feature color posed action player photos with red and white borders. The player's name and number are printed in red in the bottom white margin along with the team name and year, which are printed in black. The cards are unnumbered and checklisted below in alphabetical order.

COMPLETE SET (30) 6.00 15.00
1 Troy Bakogeorge .20 .50
2 Grant Chorney .20 .50
3 Gary Dickie .20 .50
4 Milan Dragicevic .20 .50
5 Mike Dyck .20 .50
6 Craig Endean .20 .50
7 Mike Gibson .20 .50
8 Erin Ginnell .20 .50
9 Brad Hornung .20 .50
10 Mark Janssens .30 .75
11 K-9 (Mascot) .08 .25
12 Trent Kachur .20 .50
13 Craig Kalawsky .20 .50
14 Dan Logan .20 .50
15 Jim Mathieson .20 .50
16 Darin McInnes .20 .50
17 Darrin McKechnie .20 .50
18 Rob McKinley .30 .75
19 Brad Miller .20 .50
20 Stacy Nickel .20 .50
21 Cregg Nicol .20 .50
22 Len Nielsen .20 .50
23 Darren Parsons .20 .50
24 Doug Sauter .20 .50
25 Ray Savard .20 .50
26 Dennis Sobchuk .30 .75
27 Chris Tarnowski .20 .50
28 Mike Van Slooten .20 .50
29 Brian Wilkie .20 .50
30 Rod Williams .20 .50

1987-88 Regina Pats

Produced by Royal Studios, this 28-card standard-size set features color, posed action player photos with red and white borders. The player's name is printed in red in the bottom white margin along with the team name and year, which are printed in black. The cards are unnumbered and checklisted below in alphabetical order.

COMPLETE SET (28) 4.80 12.00
1 Kevin Clemens .20 .50
2 Gary Dickie .20 .50
3 Milan Dragicevic .20 .50
4 Mike Dyck .20 .50
5 Craig Endean .20 .50
6 Kevin Gallant PR .08 .25
7 Jamie Heward .20 .50
8 Rod Houk .30 .75
9 Mark Janssens .30 .75
10 Trent Kachur .20 .50
11 Craig Kalawsky .20 .50
12 K-9 (Mascot) .08 .25
13 Frank Kovacs .20 .50
14 Darren Kwiatkowski .20 .50
15 Brian Leibel .20 .50
16 Tim Logan .20 .50
17 Jim Mathieson .20 .50
18 Darrin McKechnie .20 .50
19 Rob McKinley .20 .50
20 Brad Miller .20 .50
21 Cregg Nicol .20 .50
22 Doug Sauter CO .08 .25
23 Dan Sexton .20 .50
24 Mike Sillinger .40 1.00
25 Dennis Sobchuk .30 .75
26 Stanley Szumlak TR .08 .25
27 Mike Van Slooten .20 .50
28 Team Photo .20 .50

1988-89 Regina Pats

This 25-card standard-size set features color, posed action player photos with red and white borders. The player's name is printed in red in the bottom white margin along with the team name and year, which are printed in black. The cards are unnumbered and checklisted below in alphabetical order.

COMPLETE SET (24) 4.80 12.00
1 Shane Bogden .20 .50
2 Cam Brauer .20 .50
3 Scott Daniels .25 .60
4 Gary Dickie .20 .50
5 Mike Dyck .20 .50
6 Dave Gerse .20 .50
7 Kevin Haller .25 .60
8 Jamie Heward .20 .50
9 Terry Hollinger .20 .50
10 Rod Houk .20 .50
11 Frank Kovacs .20 .50
12 Brian Leibel .20 .50
13 Bernie Lynch CO .20 .50
14 Kelly Markwart .20 .50
15 Jim Mathieson .30 .75
16 Brad Mcginnis .20 .50
17 Brad Miller .20 .50
18 Dwayne Montieth TR .08 .25
19 Curtis Nykyforuk .20 .50
20 Darren Parsons .20 .50
21 Cory Paterson .20 .50
22 Jeff Sebastian .20 .50
23 Mike Sillinger .30 .75
24 Chad Silver .20 .50
25 Jamie Splett .20 .50

1989-90 Regina Pats

Sponsored by Mr. Lube, this 22-card set measures approximately 4" by 6" and is printed on thin card stock. The fronts feature black-and-white posed action photos with royal blue borders. The player's jersey number and name are printed in white in the bottom margin along with the team and sponsor logo.The cards are unnumbered and checklisted below in alphabetical order.

COMPLETE SET (21) 4.00 10.00
1 Kelly Chotowetz .20 .50
2 Hal Christiansen .20 .50
3 Scott Daniels .25 .60
4 Wade Fennig .20 .50
5 Jason Glickman .20 .50
6 Kevin Haller .30 .75
7 Jamie Heward .30 .75
8 Terry Hollinger .20 .50
9 Frank Kovacs .20 .50
10 Mike Kirby .20 .50
11 Kelly Markwart .20 .50
12 Jim Mathieson .30 .75
13 Cam McLellan .20 .50
14 Troy Mick .20 .50
15 Greg Pankewicz .20 .50
16 Cory Paterson .20 .50
17 Garry Pearce .20 .50
18 Mike Risdale .20 .50
19 Colin Ruck .20 .50
20 Mike Sillinger .30 .75
21 Jamie Splett .20 .50
22 Heath Weenk .20 .50

1996-97 Regina Pats

This 25-card set features the Regina Pats of the WHL. The cards were produced by the team and offered for sale for $7 at the team shop. The fronts feature a color action photo superimposed over a cutaway rink shot. The player's name and number appear at the top, with the team logo in the bottom right. The set includes several prominent prospects, including NHL first rounders Josh Holden, Dmitri Nabokov, Derek Morris, Kyle Calder and Brad Stuart.

COMPLETE SET (25) 7.20 15.00
1 Josh Holden .30 .75
2 Curtis Tipler .15 .40
3 Shane Lanigan .15 .40
4 Brad Stuart 1.25 3.00
5 David Maruca .15 .40
6 Perry Johnson .15 .40
7 Chad Mercier .15 .40
8 Kyle Calder .40 1.00
9 Josh Dobbyn .15 .40
10 Aaron Mori .15 .40
11 Gerad Adams .15 .40
12 Boyd Kane .20 .50
13 Lars Pattersen .15 .40
14 Dean Arsene .15 .40
15 Andy Adams .15 .40
16 Derek Morris .75 2.00
17 Kyle Freadrich .20 .50
18 Bryan Randall .15 .40
19 Clint Orr .15 .40
20 Brett Lysak .30 .75
21 Joey Bouvier .15 .40
22 Cody Jensen .15 .40
23 Rich Preston CO .08 .25
24 Team Photo .15 .40
25 Dmitri Nabokov .15 .40

1997-98 Regina Pats

This set features the Pats of the WHL. The set was sponsored by local police, and was handed out by officers to kids.

COMPLETE SET (25) 7.20 20.00
1 Gerad Adams .20 .50
2 Kyle Calder .75 2.00
3 Boyd Kane .30 .75
4 Brett Lysak .30 .75
5 Kevin Saurette .20 .50
6 Travis Churchman .20 .50
7 Dean Arsene .20 .50
8 Barret Jackman 2.00 5.00
9 Scott Roles .20 .50
10 John Cirjak .20 .50
11 Ronald Petrovicky .30 .75
12 Kyle Freadrich .30 .75
13 David Maruca .20 .50
14 Drew Kehler .20 .50
15 Bryan Randall .20 .50
16 Joey Bouvier .20 .50
17 Cody Jensen .20 .50
18 Shane Lanigan .20 .50
19 Mark Thompson .20 .50
20 Dennis Bassett .20 .50
21 Chris Kwas .20 .50
22 Derek Morris .75 2.00
23 Aaron Mori .20 .50
24 Brad Stuart 1.25 3.00
25 Josh Holden .40 1.00

2001-02 Regina Pats

This set was produced by the Pats of the WHL. It's uncertain how they were distributed, but it's believed they were issued as a promotional giveaway, based on the wealth of sponsor logos. The set we obtained was signed by every player, save for Bassen and Yacboski. It's not known whether they were widely issued signed, or if this was a limited edition that was made available. Any additional information can be forwarded to hockeymag@beckett.com. The cards are unnumbered, and so are listed in alphabetical order.

COMPLETE SET (24) 10.00 25.00
1 Curtis Austring .40 1.00
2 Chad Bassen .40 1.00
3 Corey Becker .40 1.00
4 Dean Beuker .40 1.00
5 Drew Callender ACO .04 .10
6 Brennan Chapman .40 1.00
7 Chad Davidson .75 2.00
8 Jeff Feniak .40 1.00
9 Josh Harding .75 2.00
10 Grant Jacobsen .40 1.00
11 Kevin Korol .40 1.00
12 Kyle Ladobruk .40 1.00
13 Bob Lowes CO .10 .25
14 David McDonald .40 1.00
15 Chad Mercier ACO .04 .10
16 Tyson Moulton .40 1.00
17 Garth Murray .75 2.00
18 Filip Novak .75 2.00
19 Zach Roe .40 1.00
20 Chris Schlenker .40 1.00
21 Eric Sonnenberg .40 1.00
22 Matej Trojovsky .40 1.00
23 Daniel Waschuk .40 1.00
24 Darryl Yacboski .40 1.00

2002-03 Regina Pats

COMPLETE SET (23) 8.00 20.00
1 Grant Jacobsen .30 .75
2 Matt Trojovsky .30 .75
3 Petr Dvorak .30 .75
4 Matt Hubbauer .30 .75
5•Darryl Yacboski .30 .75
6 Jesse Deckert .30 .75
7 Todd Davison .30 .75
8 Rick Rypien .40 1.00
9 David Graden .30 .75
10 Wade Davis .30 .75
11 Britt Dougherty .30 .75
12 Curtis Austring .30 .75
13 Kyle Ladobruk .30 .75
14 Codey Becker .30 .75
15 Chris Schlenker .30 .75
16 Tyson Mulock .30 .75
17 Daniel Waschuk .30 .75
18 David McDonald .30 .75
19 Jordan McGillivary .30 .75
20 Brennan Chapman .30 .75
21 Tyson Moulton .40 1.00
22 Kyle Fecho .30 .75
23 Josh Harding 1.25 3.00

2003-04 Regina Pats

COMPLETE SET (24) 5.00 12.00
1 Paul Albers .20 .50
2 Craig Lineker .20 .50
3 Kyle Deck .20 .50
4 Derek Reinhart .20 .50
5 Landon Jones .20 .50
6 Tanner Stockwell .20 .50
7 Lance Morrison .20 .50
8 Rick Rypien .30 .75
9 David McDonald .20 .50
10 Kyle Lamb .20 .50
11 Dan Waschuk .20 .50
12 Ivo Kratena .20 .50
13 Kamil Vavra .20 .50
14 Kyle Nason .20 .50
15 Chris Schlenker .20 .50
16 Codey Becker .20 .50
17 Jonathan Bubnick .20 .50
18 Mike O'Dwyer .20 .50
19 Jordan McGillivray .20 .50
20 Andrew DeSousa .20 .50
21 Nick Olynyk .20 .50
22 Jesse Deckert .20 .50
23 Josh Harding .75 2.00
24 Britt Dougherty .20 .50

2004-05 Regina Pats

COMPLETE SET (24) 5.00 12.00
1 Regina Pats CL .04 .10
2 Paul Albers .20 .50
3 Craig Lineker .20 .50
4 Kyle Deck .20 .50
5 Derek Reinhart .20 .50
6 Logan Pyett .20 .50
7 Rick Rypien .30 .75
8 Kyle Ross .20 .50
9 Justin Bernhardt .20 .50
10 Braden Appleby .20 .50
11 Dan Waschuk .20 .50
12 Ryan McDonald .20 .50
13 Ian Duval .20 .50
14 Kyle Nason .20 .50
15 Terrance Delaronde .20 .50
16 Brent Hill .20 .50
17 Jonathan Bubnick .20 .50
18 Jordan McGillivray .20 .50
19 Jan Zapletal .20 .50
20 David Reekie .20 .50
21 Jordan Fuder .20 .50
22 Dustin Slade .20 .50
23 Craig Schira .20 .50
24 Preston Mosewich .20 .50

2005-06 Regina Pats

COMPLETE SET (28) 8.00 15.00
1 Justin Bernhardt .20 .50
2 Kyle Deck .20 .50
3 Ian Duval .20 .50
4 Garrett Festerling .20 .50
5 Spencer Fraipont .20 .50
6 Jordan Fuder .20 .50
7 Shane Halifax .20 .50
8 Petr Kalus .60 1.50
9 Brett Leffler .20 .50
10 Levi Lind .20 .50
11 Jason MacDonald .20 .50
12 Jordan McGillivray .20 .50
13 Curtis Patterson .20 .50
14 Logan Pyett .20 .50
15 David Reekie .40 1.00
16 Derek Reinhart .20 .50
17 Matt Robinson .20 .50
18 Kyle Ross .20 .50
19 Nick Ross .20 .50
20 Linden Rowatt .40 1.00
21 Andy Schenn .20 .50
22 Craig Schira .20 .50
23 Michael Senseman .20 .50
24 Tyson Sievert .20 .50
25 Denis Tolpeko .20 .50
26 Ryan McDonald .20 .50
27 Matt MacDermott .20 .50
28 Joshua Fauth .20 .50

2006-07 Regina Pats

COMPLETE SET (23) 12.00 20.00
1 Justin Bernhardt .40 1.00
2 Scott Brownlee .40 1.00
3 Kyle Deck .40 1.00
4 Matt Delahey .40 1.00
5 Ian Duval .40 1.00
6 Jordan Eberle .75 2.00
7 Garrett Festerling .40 1.00
8 Derek Hulak .40 1.00
9 Jared Jagow .40 1.00
10 Brett Leffler .40 1.00
11 Levi Lind .40 1.00
12 Jason MacDonald .40 1.00
13 Ryan McDonald .40 1.00
14 Logan Pyett .40 1.00
15 Derek Reinhart .40 1.00
16 Kyle Ross .40 1.00
17 Nick Ross .40 1.00
18 Linden Rowatt .60 1.50
19 Craig Schira .40 1.00
20 Justin Scott .40 1.00
21 Niko Snellman .40 1.00
22 Colten Teubert .40 1.00
23 Regina Pats .10 .25

2014-15 Regina Pats

COMPLETE SET (22) 6.00 15.00
1 Adam Brooks .30 .75
2 Tyler Brown .30 .75
3 Braden Christoffer .30 .75
4 Rykr Cole .30 .75
5 Taylor Cooper .30 .75
6 Patrick D'Amico .30 .75
7 Jesse Gabrielle .30 .75
8 Carter Hansen .30 .75
9 Chase Harrison .30 .75
10 James Hilsendager .30 .75
11 Connor Hobbs .40 1.00
12 Colton Kroeker .30 .75
13 Ryan Krushen .30 .75
14 Jared McAmmond .30 .75
15 Nathyn Mortlock .30 .75
16 Pavlo Padakin .30 .75
17 Luc Smith .30 .75
18 Sam Steel .30 .75
19 Austin Wagner .30 .75
20 Daniel Wapple .30 .75
21 Colby Williams .30 .75
22 Sergey Zborovskiy .30 .75

1996 RHI Inaugural Edition

This nineteen-card Roller Hockey International set features the logos of all the teams from the hip, new game on the front, with franchise information on the back.

COMPLETE SET (19) 1.25 3.00
1 Los Angeles Blades .08 .25
2 Long Island Jaws .08 .25
3 Empire State Cobras .08 .25
4 Denver DareDevils .08 .25
5 Anaheim Bullfrogs .08 .25
6 Orlando Jackals .08 .25
7 Ottawa Loggers .08 .25
8 Oklahoma Coyotes .08 .25
9 Oakland Skates .08 .25
10 New Jersey Rockin Rollers .08 .25
11 Montreal Roadrunners .08 .25
12 Minnesota Arctic Blast .08 .25
13 Vancouver VooDoo .08 .25
14 St. Louis Vipers .08 .25
15 San Jose Rhinos .08 .25
16 San Diego Barracudas .08 .25
17 Sacramento River Rats .08 .25
18 Philadelphia Bulldogs .08 .25
NNO Checklist .02 .10

1984-85 Richelieu Riverains

This 19-card set of the Richelieu Riverains of the Quebec Midget AAA league measures approximately 4" by 5 1/2". The fronts feature black-and-white posed player portraits with a facsimile autograph and jersey number on the left. The backs are blank. The cards are unnumbered and checklisted below in alphabetical order.

COMPLETE SET (19) 4.80 12.00
1 Miguel Baldris .30 .75
2 Nicolas Beaulieu .30 .75
3 Martin Cote .30 .75
4 Sylvain Coutourier .40 1.00
5 Dominic Edmond .30 .75
6 Yues Gaucher .30 .75
7 Eric Gobel .30 .75
8 Carl Lemieux .30 .75
9 Michel Levesque .30 .75
10 Brad Loi .30 .75
11 Eric Primeau .30 .75
12 Stephane Quintal .60 1.50
13 Jean-Michel Ray .30 .75
14 Serge Richard .30 .75
15 Stephane Robinson .30 .75
16 Danny Rochefort .30 .75
17 Martin Savaria .30 .75
18 Sylvain Senecal .30 .75
19 Eric Sharron .30 .75

1988-89 Richelieu Riverains

Cards measure approximately 3" x 4" with card fronts featuring color posed photos. Card backs have players name and number along with safety tips in French.

COMPLETE SET (30) 4.80 12.00
1 Header Card .07 .20
2 Marc Beaurivage .20 .50
3 Denis Benoit .20 .50
4 Jonathan Black .20 .50
5 Richard Boisvert .20 .50
6 Hugues Bouchard .20 .50
7 Francois Bourdeau .20 .50
8 Guy Caplette .20 .50
9 Bertrand Cournoyer .20 .50
10 Yves Cournoyer .20 .50
11 Michel Deguise .20 .50
12 Patrick Grise .20 .50
13 Robert Guillet .20 .50
14 Jimmy Lachance .20 .50
15 Roger Laporte .20 .50
16 Frederic Lefebvre .20 .50
17 Frederic Maltais .20 .50
18 Andre Kid Millette .20 .50
19 Joseph Napolitano .20 .50
20 Remy Patoine .20 .50
21 Jean Plamondon .20 .50
22 Steve Plasse .20 .50
23 Jean Francois Poirier .20 .50
24 Jacques Provencal .20 .50
25 Alain Rancourt .20 .50
26 Francois St.Germain .20 .50
27 Frederic Savard .20 .50
28 Martin Tanguay .20 .50
29 Richard Valois .20 .50
30 Stephane Valois .20 .50

1910 Richmond College Silks S23

These colorful silks were issued around 1910 by Richmond Straight Cut Cigarettes. Each measures roughly 4" by 5 1/2" and are often called "College Flag, Seal, Song, and Yell" due to the content found on each one. More importantly to most sports collectors is the image found in the lower right hand bottom corner. A few feature a mainstream sports' subject such as a generic player or piece of equipment, while most include a realistic image of the school's mascot or image of the founder or the school's namesake.

10 Cornell HK Stick 60.00 120.00

1990-91 Richmond Renegades

Produced by 7th Inning Sketch and sponsored by Richmond Comix and Cardz Inc., this 18-card standard-size set features posed color player photos with red borders. The player's name appears at the bottom.

COMPLETE SET (18) 3.00 8.00
1 Brad Turner .20 .50
2 Victor Posa .20 .50
3 Antti Autere .20 .50
4 Phil Huber .20 .50
5 Steve Spott .20 .50
6 Kelly Mills .20 .50
7 Paul Cain .20 .50
8 Shawn Lillie .20 .50
9 Kirby Lindal .20 .50
10 Dave Aiken .20 .50
11 Terry McCutcheon .20 .50
12 Jordan Fois .20 .50
13 Brad Beck .20 .50
14 Doug Pickell .20 .50
15 Frank Lascala .20 .50
16 John Haley .20 .50
17 Peter Harris .20 .50
18 Chris McSorley CO .30 .75

1991-92 Richmond Renegades

Sponsored by "Bleacher Bums" Sports Cards Inc. and Domino's Pizza, this 20-card set was issued as a trifold sheet, one 12 1/2" by 7" team photo and two sheets with ten standard-size player cards per sheet. The fronts feature color action player photos accented by a border design that shades from orange at the top to black at the bottom. The player's name and position appear below the picture, as do sponsor names.

COMPLETE SET (20) 3.60 9.00
1 Rob Vanderydt .20 .50
2 Larry Rooney .15 .40
3 Brendan Flynn .15 .40
4 Scott Drevitch .15 .40
5 Joni Lehto .15 .40
6 Todd Drevitch .15 .40
7 Paul Rutherford .15 .40
8 Dave Aiken .15 .40
9 Pat Bingham .15 .40
10 Trevor Jobe .15 .40
11 Bob Berg .15 .40
12 Mark Kuntz .15 .40
13 Joe Capprini .15 .40
14 Trevor Converse .15 .40
15 Steve Scheifele .15 .40
16 Jon Gustafson .20 .50
17 Marco Fuster .15 .40
18 Guy Gadowsky .15 .40
19 Dave Allison CO .08 .25
20 Jamie McLennan .40 1.00
NNO Large Team Photo .75 2.00

1992-93 Richmond Renegades

Sponsored by "Bleacher Bums" Sports Cards Inc. and Kellogg's, this 20-card set was issued as a trifold sheet, one 12 1/2" by 7" team photo and two sheets with ten standard-size player cards per sheet. The fronts feature color action player photos accented by a black and orange border design. The picture itself is rimmed by an orange and white frame. Outside the frame is an orange design with varying sizes of stripes against a black background. The player's name and position appear below the picture as do sponsor names. The cards are unnumbered and checklisted below in alphabetical order.

COMPLETE SET (20) 3.00 8.00
1 Will Averill .15 .40
2 Frank Bialowas .20 .50
3 Scott Drevitch .15 .40
4 Brendan Flynn .15 .40
5 Guy Gadowsky ACO .02 .10
6 Jon Gustafson .20 .50
7 Phil Huber .15 .40
8 Mike James .15 .40
9 Jeffery Kampersal .15 .40
10 Mark Kuntz .15 .40
11 Sean LeBrun .15 .40
12 Kevin Malgunas .15 .40
13 Jim McGeough .20 .50
14 Ed Sabo .15 .40
15 Jeff Saterdalen .15 .40
16 Alan Schuler .15 .40
17 Martin Smith .15 .40
18 Roy Sommer CO .02 .10
19 Jeff Torrey .15 .40
20 Ben Wyzansky .15 .40
NNO Large Team Photo 1.00 2.50

1993-94 Richmond Renegades

Sponsored by "Bleacher Bum" Collectibles, Inc., radio station XL102, and Kellogg's, this 20-card set features the 1993-94 Richmond Renegades. The standard-size cards are printed on thin card stock. On a team color-coded background, the fronts feature color action player photos with purple borders, along with the player's name, position and team name.

COMPLETE SET (20) 3.00 8.00
1 Ken Weiss .15 .40
2 Guy Phillips .15 .40
3 Alexander Zhdan .15 .40
4 Alan Schuler .15 .40
5 John Craighead .15 .40
6 Colin Gregor .15 .40
7 Rob MacInnis .15 .40
8 Devin Derksen .20 .50
9 Jason Renard .15 .40
10 Peter Allen .15 .40
11 Roy Sommer CO .08 .25
12 Milan Hnilicka .60 1.50
13 Oleg Santurian .15 .40
14 Brendan Flynn .15 .40
15 Ken Blum .15 .40
16 Steve Bogoyevac .15 .40
17 Eric Germain .15 .40
18 Chris Foy .15 .40
19 Darren Colbourne .15 .40
20 Jon Gustafson .20 .50

1994-95 Richmond Renegades

This 20-card set produced by Bleacher Bums and sponsored by Q-94 features the Richmond Renegades of the ECHL. The sets were available through the team. The fronts feature dynamic action shots over a blurred background, while the backs include player stats. The cards are unnumbered and are listed below as they came out of the team bag. Reportedly, production was significantly shorter for this set than the previous two Richmond issues.

COMPLETE SET (20) 4.00 10.00
1 Andrew Shier .20 .50
2 Shane Henry .20 .50
3 Shawn Snesar .20 .50
4 Steve Bogoyevac .20 .50
5 Chris Foy .20 .50
6 Scott Gruhl .30 .75
7 Blaine Moore .20 .50
8 Don Lester .20 .50
9 Kurt Mallett .20 .50
10 Garett MacDonald .20 .50
11 Jay Murphy .20 .50
12 Darren Wetherill .20 .50
13 Grant Sjerven .20 .50
14 Jan Benda .30 .75
15 Lou Body .20 .50
16 Mike Taylor .20 .50
17 Sean O'Brien .20 .50
18 Chris Tucker .20 .50
19 Jason Currie .20 .50
20 Roy Sommer CO .08 .25

1995-96 Richmond Renegades

This 25-card set of the Richmond Renegades of the ECHL was produced by Bleacher Bum and was supported by a wealth of sponsors. The cards were originally issued in a strip, thus single cards will have perforated edges. The cards feature a dynamic front design including an action photo and the Riley Cup Championship logo in the bottom right. The cards are unnumbered, and are ordered as they appeared on the strips.

COMPLETE SET (25) 3.60 9.00
1 Greg Hadden .15 .40
2 Mike Taylor .15 .40
3 Jay Murphy .15 .40
4 Todd Sparks .15 .40
5 Lou Body .15 .40
6 Sandy Allan .30 .75
7 Darren Wetherill .15 .40
8 Brian Goudie .15 .40
9 Brendan Flynn .15 .40
10 Kurt Mallett .15 .40
11 Dmitri Pankov .15 .40
12 Steve Carpenter .15 .40
13 Jason Mallon .15 .40
14 Scott Gruhl .40 1.00
15 Trevor Senn .15 .40
16 Garett MacDonald .15 .40
17 Martin Roy .15 .40
18 Michael Burman .15 .40
19 Grant Sjerven .15 .40
20 Mike Morin .15 .40
21 Andy Davis Broadcaster .02 .10
22 The Gade Mascot .02 .10
23 Rob Jones TR .02 .10
24 Roy Sommer CO .02 .10
25 C.Laughlin GM H.Feuerstein CEO .02 .10

1996-97 Richmond Renegades

These cards feature full-color fronts with statistical information and a profile photo on the back. Cards are unnumbered and checklisted below in alphabetical order.

COMPLETE SET (25) 3.00 8.00
1 Scott Burfoot .20 .50
2 Taylor Clarke .15 .40
3 David Dartsch .15 .40
4 Freezer .02 .10
5 Gade .02 .10
6 Matt Garzone .15 .40
7 Brian Goudie .15 .40
8 Scott Gruhl CO .20 .50
9 Garry Gulash .15 .40
10 Mike Harding .15 .40
11 Tommy Holmes .15 .40
12 Rod Langway ACO .20 .50
13 Paul Lepler .15 .40
14 Jay McNeill .15 .40
15 Craig Paterson .15 .40
16 Chris Pittman .15 .40
17 Mike Rucinski .15 .40
18 Brian Secord .15 .40
19 Trevor Senn .15 .40
20 Grant Sjerven .15 .40
21 Andrew Shier .15 .40
22 Mike Taylor .15 .40
23 Tripp Tracy .30 .75
24 Jason Wright .15 .40
25 Title Card .02 .10

2000-01 Richmond Renegades

This set features the Renegades of the ECHL. The set was produced as a promotional giveaway and was handed out after the All-Star break. The cards are slightly oversized and are printed on very thin cardstock. The cards are unnumbered, and so are listed below in alphabetical order.

COMPLETE SET (19) 8.00 20.00
1 Gerad Adams .40 1.00
2 Brian Goudie .40 1.00
3 Nathan Forster .40 1.00
4 Joe Blaznek .40 1.00
5 Bob Thornton .40 1.00
6 Forrest Gore .40 1.00
7 Dan Vandermeer .40 1.00
8 Joe Vandermeer .40 1.00
9 Rod Taylor .40 1.00
10 Richard Pitirri .40 1.00
11 George Awada .40 1.00
12 Ryan Skaleski .40 1.00
13 Derek Schutz .40 1.00
14 Frank Novock .40 1.00
15 Matt Noga .40 1.00
16 Mike Siklenka .40 1.00
17 Sean Matile .60 1.50
18 Rastislav Stana .80 2.00
19 Brian McCullough .40 1.00

2006-07 Richmond Renegades

COMPLETE SET (20) 8.00 15.00
1 Jay Chrapala .40 1.00
2 Scott Corbett .30 .75
3 Brett Cross .30 .75
4 Andre Gill .30 .75
5 Mat Goody .75 2.00
6 Brian Goudie .30 .75
7 Doug Groenestege .40 1.00
8 Dean Jackson .30 .75
9 Don Melnyk .30 .75
10 David Mitchell .30 .75
11 Mike Owens .30 .75
12 Joe Pace .30 .75
13 Richard Reichenbach .30 .75
14 Tyler Schremp .30 .75
15 Danny White .30 .75
16 Duane Whitehead .30 .75
17 J.J. Wrobel .30 .75
18 Phil Youngclaus .30 .75
19 John Brophy CO .10 .25
20 Graffiti Ink Gallery SPONSOR .01 .01

2004-05 Richmond Riverdogs

This set features the Riverdogs of the UHL.

COMPLETE SET (28) 5.00 12.00
1 Checklist .04 .10
2 Donny Martin CO .04 .10
3 Glenn Morelli OWN .04 .10
4 Jim Duhart .40 1.00
5 Simo Pulkki .20 .50
6 Brian Goudie .20 .50
7 Ivan Curic .40 1.00
8 Francis Belanger .40 1.00
9 Ryan Prentice .20 .50
10 David Hymovitz .40 1.00
11 Mark Turner .20 .50
12 Mark Langdon .20 .50
13 David Brosseau .20 .50
14 Luch Nasato .20 .50
15 Trevor Senn .20 .50
16 Brian Herbert .20 .50
17 J.J. Wrobel .20 .50
18 Dennis Vial .40 1.00
19 Derek Shutz .20 .50
20 Brett Cross .20 .50
21 Anthony Dipalma .20 .50
22 Brent Belecki .20 .50
23 Dan McIntyre .20 .50
24 Semir Ben-Amor .20 .50
25 Razz MASCOT .04 .10
26 Team Photo .04 .10
27 Zamboni .04 .10
28 Richmond Coliseum .04 .10

1996-97 Rimouski Oceanic

This 28-card set was the first of two this season to feature the Oceanic of the QMJHL. The cards featured a color action photo and jersey number on the front, with a head shot and statistical data on the back. It was sold through the team and at convenience stores in the region. The set is unnumbered, and listed in alphabetical order. The most noteworthy player in the set is Vincent Lecavalier, a forward looked upon as an early favorite for the top pick in the 1998 NHL Entry Draft. Less than 3,000 of these sets were produced.

COMPLETE SET (28) 12.00 25.00
1 Jonathan Beaulieu .15 .40
2 Martin Bedard .15 .40
3 Eric Belzile .15 .40
4 Denis Boily .15 .40
5 Dave Bolduc .15 .40
6 Yan Bouchard .20 .50
7 Nicolas Chabot .20 .50
8 Eryc Collin .15 .40
9 Eric Drouin .15 .40
10 Yannick Dupont .15 .40
11 Frederic Girard .15 .40
12 Jimmy Grondin .15 .40
13 Bobby Lebel .08 .25
14 Vincent Lecavalier 7.50 15.00
15 Frederic Levac .15 .40
16 Francois Levesque .15 .40
17 Philippe Lord .15 .40
18 Dave Malenfant .15 .40
19 Eric Normandin .20 .50
20 Mathieu Normandin .15 .40
21 Philippe Plante .15 .40
22 Martin Poitras .20 .50
23 Saison 1996-1997 .08 .25
24 Philippe Sauve 1.25 3.00
25 Sebastien Simard .15 .40
26 David St-Onge .15 .40
27 Mathieu Sunderland .20 .50
28 Gaston Therrien CO .08 .25

1996-97 Rimouski Oceanic Quebec Provincial Police

Card fronts feature color photos, along with players jersey number and the Rimouski logo. Card backs feature statistical information and all text is in French. Each card also bears a serial number. Cards are unnumbered and checklisted below alphabetically.

COMPLETE SET (26) 16.00 40.00
1 Jonathan Beaulieu .20 .50
2 Martin Bedard .20 .50
3 Eric Belzile .20 .50
4 Maxime Blouin .20 .50
5 Denis Boily .20 .50
6 Yan Bouchard .20 .50
7 Nicolas Chabot .20 .50
8 Eryc Collin .20 .50
9 Eric Drouin .20 .50
10 Yannick Dupont .20 .50
11 Frederic Girard .20 .50
12 Jimmy Grondin .20 .50
13 Vincent Lecavalier 12.00 25.00
14 Frederic Levac .20 .50
15 Francois Levesque .20 .50
16 Philipe Lord .20 .50
17 Dave Malenfant .20 .50
18 Eric Normandin .20 .50
19 Mathieu Normandin .20 .50
20 Philippe Plante .20 .50
21 Martin Poitras .20 .50
22 Philippe Sauve 2.00 5.00
23 Nicola Spaccucci .20 .50
24 David St-Onge .20 .50
25 Sebastien Tremblay .20 .50
26 Title Card .02 .10

1996-97 Rimouski Oceanic Update

This 10-card set was produced as a companion set to the basic Rimouski series issued earlier in the season. The design for both series is identical. The players featured in the update were late arrivals due to trades. Less than 1200 of these sets were produced. The cards are unnumbered and thus are listed in alphabetical order.

COMPLETE SET (10) 2.50 6.00
1 Eric Belanger (LW) .20 .50
2 Eric Belanger (C) .60 1.50
3 Philippe Grondin .20 .50
4 Jason Lehoux .20 .50
5 Jonathan Levesque .20 .50
6 Louki MASCOT .08 .25
7 Guillaume Rodrigue .20 .50
8 Joe Rullier .40 1.00
9 Russell Smith .20 .50
10 Derrick Walser .30 .75

1997-98 Rimouski Oceanic

This set was produced by the team and sold at home games. It is noteworthy for including early cards of Vincent Lecavalier and Brad Richards.

COMPLETE SET (25) 10.00 25.00
4 Vincent Lecavalier 4.00 10.00
7 Joe Rullier .30 .75
9 Jonathan Beaulieu .15 .40
10 David Bilodeau .15 .40
11 Jimmy Grondin .15 .40
14 Dave Malenfant .15 .40
17 Kevin Bolduc .15 .40
19 Eric Normandin .15 .40
20 Francois Drainville .15 .40
21 Eric Belanger .30 .75
22 Eric Drouin .15 .40
24 Julien Desrosiers .15 .40
25 David St-Onge .15 .40
27 Phillippe Grondin .15 .40
33 Phillippe Sauve 1.25 3.00
35 Jean-Marc Pelletier .60 1.50
36 Jonathan St-Louis .15 .40
39 Brad Richards 5.00 12.00
44 Guillaume Couture .15 .40
45 Chad Gagnon .15 .40
55 Casey Leggett .15 .40
79 Denis Boily .15 .40
91 Derrick Walser .30 .75
98 Adam Borzecki .15 .40
NNO Team Card .15 .40

1999-00 Rimouski Oceanic

This 24-card set features the QMJHL's Oceanic, the Memorial Cup winners for that season. Base cards contain full color action photography and have purple borders along the top and the right hand side which feature the player's name and team logo.

COMPLETE SET (24) 6.00 15.00
1 Nicolas Pilote .15 .40
2 Joe Rullier .30 .75
3 Jonathan Beaulieu .15 .40
4 Nicolas Poirier .15 .40
5 Thatcher Bell .20 .50
6 Brent Maclellan .15 .40
7 Alexandre Tremblay .15 .40
8 Jean-Francois Babin .15 .40
9 Benoit Martin .15 .40
10 Jan Philippe Cadieux .15 .40
11 Jean-Philippe Briere .15 .40
12 Alexis Castonguay .15 .40
13 Rene Vydareny .15 .40
14 Ronnie Decontie .15 .40
15 Shawn Scanzano .15 .40
16 Michel Ouellet .15 .40
17 Jacques Lariviere .15 .40
18 Eric Salvail .15 .40
19 Sebastien Caron .40 1.00
20 Brad Richards 2.00 5.00
21 Aaron Johnson .15 .40
22 Juraj Kolnik .60 1.50
23 Michel Periard .30 .75
24 Header Card/CL .02 .10

1999-00 Rimouski Oceanic Signed

This set of 23 cards parallels the base Rimouski Oceanic Set. The main differences are that the cards are signed on a specially imprinted area on the front of the card, while the backs are serial numbered out of 100.

COMPLETE SET (24) 30.00 75.00
1 Nicolas Pilote .75 2.00
2 Joe Rullier 1.50 4.00
3 Jonathan Beaulieu .75 2.00
4 Nicolas Poirier .75 2.00
5 Thatcher Bell 1.50 4.00
6 Brent Maclellan .75 2.00
7 Alexandre Tremblay .75 2.00
8 Jean-Francois Babin .75 2.00
9 Benoit Martin .75 2.00
10 Jan Philippe Cadieux .75 2.00
11 Jean-Philippe Briere .75 2.00
12 Alexis Castonguay .75 2.00
13 Rene Vydareny .75 2.00
14 Ronnie Decontie .75 2.00
15 Shawn Scanzano .75 2.00
16 Michel Ouellet .75 2.00
17 Jacques Lariviere .75 2.00
18 Eric Salvail .75 2.00
19 Sebastien Caron 2.00 5.00
20 Brad Richards 10.00 25.00
21 Aaron Johnson .75 2.00
22 Juraj Kolnik 3.00 8.00
23 Michel Periard 1.50 4.00
24 Header Card/CL .08 .25

2000-01 Rimouski Oceanic

This set features the Oceanic of the QMJHL. The set was produced by CTM-Ste-Foy, and was sold both by that card shop, as well as by the team.

COMPLETE SET (26) 5.00 12.00
1 Phillippe Lauze .20 .75
2 Tim Sinasac .20 .50
3 Jonathan Beaulieu .20 .50
4 Nichola Pilote .20 .50
5 Nicolas Poirier .20 .50
6 Thatcher Bell .20 .50
7 Tomas Malec .20 .50
8 Brent MacLellan .20 .50
9 Jean-Francois Plourde .20 .50
10 Jean-Francois Babin .20 .50
11 Benoit Martin .20 .50
12 Daniel Petiguay .30 .75
13 Jean-Phillippe Briere .20 .50
14 Ryan Clowe .75 2.00
15 Mathieu Fournier .20 .50
16 Gabriel Balasescu .20 .50
17 Mathieu Simard .20 .50
18 Samuel Gibbons .20 .50
19 Michel Ouellet .20 .50
20 Jonathan Pelletier .30 .75
21 Eric Salvail .30 .75
22 Aaron Johnson .20 .50
23 Sebastien Bolduc .30 .75
24 Louky MASCOT .04 .10
25 Doris Labonte CO .04 .10
NNO Team CL .04 .10

2000-01 Rimouski Oceanic Signed

This set is exactly the same as the base Oceanic set from this season, save that every card has been hand signed by the player pictured. Each card also is serial numbered out of just 100.

COMPLETE SET (26) 15.00 40.00
1 Phillippe Lauze .80 4.00
2 Tim Sinasac .80 2.00
3 Jonathan Beaulieu .80 2.00
4 Nichola Pilote .80 2.00
5 Nicolas Poirier .80 2.00
6 Thatcher Bell 1.20 3.00
7 Tomas Malec .80 2.00
8 Brent MacLellan .80 2.00
9 Jean-Francois Plourde .80 2.00
10 Jean-Francois Babin .80 2.00
11 Benoit Martin .80 2.00
12 Daniel Petiguay .80 4.00
13 Jean-Phillippe Briere .80 2.00
14 Ryan Clowe 4.00 10.00
15 Mathieu Fournier .80 2.00
16 Gabriel Balasescu .80 2.00
17 Mathieu Simard .80 2.00
18 Samuel Gibbons .80 2.00
19 Michel Ouellet .80 2.00
20 Jonathan Pelletier 1.20 4.00
21 Eric Salvail 1.20 4.00
22 Aaron Johnson .80 2.00
23 Sebastien Bolduc .80 4.00
24 Louky MASCOT .04 .10
25 Doris Labonte CO .04 .10
NNO Team CL .04 .10

2001-02 Rimouski Oceanic

This set features the Oceanic of the QMJHL. The set was produced by CTM Ste-Foy and was sold at Oceanic home games. It was reported that less than 1,000 sets were produced.

COMPLETE SET (23) 5.00 12.00
1 Chaz Johnson .20 .50
2 Philippe Lauze .20 .50
3 Dany Stewart .20 .50
4 Michael Gavalier .20 .50
5 Nicolas Poirier .40 1.00
6 Thatcher Bell .30 .75
7 Thomas Malec .30 .75
8 Brent Maclellan .20 .50
9 Jean-Francois Plourde .20 .50
10 Benoit Martin .20 .50

aniel Petiquay .20 .50
an-Philippe Briere .20 .50
an Clowe .30 .75
athieu Fournier .20 .50
abriel Balasescu .20 .50
amuel Gibbons .20 .50
ichel Ouellet .20 .50
ic Neilson .20 .50
atrick Lepage .40 1.00
ic Salvail .40 1.00
aron Johnson .40 1.00
ebastien Bolduc .40 1.00
arc-Antoine Pouliot 1.25 3.00

2002-03 Rimouski Oceanic

PLETE SET (22) 5.00 12.00
illaume Chicoine .20 .50
trick Coulombe .20 .50
son D'Ascanio .20 .50
ancois Gauthier .20 .50
chel Gavalier .20 .50
ynek Hrdel .20 .50
nick Jasmin-Riel .20 .50
ilippe Lauze .20 .50
attews Lemaire .20 .50
ric Neilson .20 .50
ebastien Nolet .20 .50
aniel Petiquay .20 .50
Marc-Antoine Pouliot .75 2.00
onathan Robert .20 .50
Dany Roussin .40 1.00
ric Salvail .20 .50
Christopher Sorensen .20 .50
Dany Stewart .20 .50
Mark Tobin .20 .50
Erick Tremblay .20 .50
Jeremy Turgeon .20 .50
Alexander Vachon .40 1.00

2003-04 Rimouski Oceanic

s regulation-sized set was produced by CTM Ste- and Extreme Cards and features the first two nsed cards of Sidney Crosby. Not every set udes the NNO cards, so the set is considered nplete without them.

MPLETE SET (26) 30.00 60.00
enoit Arsenault .20 .50
harles Bergeron .20 .50
ancois Bolduc .20 .50
ean-Michael Bolduc .20 .50
ean-Sebastien Cote .20 .50
atrick Coulombe .20 .50
idney Crosby 8.00 20.00
edrick Desjardins .40 1.00
livier Didier .20 .50
Zbynek Hrdel .20 .50
Danick Jasmin-Riel .20 .50
Philippe Lauze .30 .75
Guillaume Lavallee .20 .50
Mattews Lemaire .20 .50
Eric Neilson .20 .50
Marc-Antoine Pouliot .40 1.00
Dany Roussin .20 .50
Michal Sersen .20 .50
Danny Stewart .20 .50
Mark Tobin .20 .50
Erick Tremblay .20 .50
Alexandre Vachon .20 .50
Guillaume Veilleux .20 .50
Hubert Veilleux .20 .50
Sidney Crosby TL SP 12.00 30.00
Marc-Antoine Pouliot TL SP .75 2.00

2003-04 Rimouski Oceanic Sheets

is team issued set of 5 sheets featured players of the eanic from the 2003-04 season. Sheets measured proximately 17" x 6".

MPLETE SET (5) 20.00 40.00
Mattews Lemaire 2.00 5.00
Charles Bergeron
Eric Nelson
Olivier Didier
Danick Jasmin Riel
Erick Tremblay 2.00 5.00
Dany Roussin
Philippe Lauze
Jean-Sebastien Cote
Michal Sersen
Mark Tobin 2.00 5.00
Patrick Coulombe
Marc-Antone Pouliot
Francois Bolduc
Cedrick Desjardins
Guillame Veilleux 10.00 25.00
Sidney Crosby
Guillame Lavallee
Alexandre Vachon
Jean-Michal Bolduc 2.00 5.00
Hubert Veilleux
Zbynek Hrdel
Dany Stewart
Benoit Arsenault

2004-05 Rimouski Oceanic

total of 5,000 team sets were produced, with dditional cards being available in wax form. The imited Edition cards of Crosby and Pouliot were vailable in random team sets.

OMPLETE SET (23) 10.00 25.00
Sidney Crosby 4.00 10.00
Alexandre Vachon .40 1.00
Dany Roussin .40 1.00
Graham Bona .20 .50
Sebastien Aspirot .20 .50
Nicolas Bachand .20 .50
Jamie Blom .20 .50
Francois Bolduc .20 .50
Francis Charette .20 .50
0 Jean-Sebastien Cote .20 .50
1 Patrick Coulombe .20 .50
2 Cedrick Desjardins .40 1.00
3 Maxime Desruisseaux .20 .50
4 Zbynek Hrdel .20 .50
5 Sebastien Laferriere .20 .50
6 Eric Neilson .40 1.00
7 Marc-Antoine Pouliot .40 1.00
8 Michal Sersen .20 .50
9 Danny Stewart .20 .50
0 Mark Tobin .20 .50
1 Erick Tremblay .20 .50
2 Jean-Michel Filiatrault .75 2.00
3 Jean-Michel Bolduc .20 .50
E1 Sidney Crosby LTD/300 15.00 40.00
E2 Marc-Antoine Pouliot LTD/300 4.00 10.00

2004-05 Rimouski Oceanic Season Ticket

This set of six cards was available only to purchasers of season tickets to the 2004-05 Oceanic. The cards are printed on clear plastic, are horizontally oriented, and have a serial number on the back. They are unnumbered, and so are listed below in alphabetical order.

COMPLETE SET (6) 25.00 60.00
1 Jonathan Beaulieu .75 2.00
2 Sebastien Caron 1.50 4.00
3 Sidney Crosby 15.00 40.00
4 Vincent Lecavalier 4.00 10.00
5 Brad Richards 4.00 10.00
6 Allan Sirois .75 2.00

2005-06 Rimouski Oceanic

COMPLETE SET (30) 6.00 15.00
1 Patrick Coulombe .20 .50
2 Erick Tremblay .20 .50
3 Jean-Michel Bolduc .20 .50
4 Jamie Blom .20 .50
5 Mark Tobin .20 .50
6 Sebastien Aspirot .20 .50
7 Francois Bolduc .20 .50
8 Jean-Sebastien Cote .20 .50
9 Sebastien Laferriere .20 .50
10 Graham Bona .20 .50
11 Francis Charette .20 .50
12 Maxime Lincourt .20 .50
13 Philippe Roberge .40 1.00
14 David Skokan .40 1.00
15 Pierre-Alexandre Joncas .20 .50
16 Maxime Macenauer .20 .50
17 David Bouchard .40 1.00
18 Jason Caron .20 .50
19 Nicholas Goyens .20 .50
20 Guillaume Mailloux .20 .50
21 Dave Plante .20 .50
22 Michael Chiasson .20 .50
23 Marc-Andre Laroche .20 .50
24 Guillaume Letourneau .20 .50
25 Olivier Fortier .20 .50
26 Philippe Garnier .20 .50
27 Drew Paris .20 .50
28 Max Gratchev .20 .50
29 Maxime Tanguay .20 .50
30 Tommy Legault .20 .50

2006-07 Rimouski Oceanic

COMPLETE SET (24) 8.00 15.00
1 Olivier Fortier .25 .60
2 Maxime Tanguay .40 1.00
3 Philippe Garnier .25 .60
4 Maxime Gratchev .40 1.00
5 François Bolduc .25 .60
6 Graham Bona .25 .60
7 David Skokan .25 .60
8 Pierre-Alexandre Joncas .25 .60
9 David Bouchard .25 .60
10 Nicholas Goyens .25 .60
11 Dave Plante .25 .60
12 Marc-André Laroche .25 .60
13 Philippe Cornet .25 .60
14 Patrice Cormier .25 .60
15 Alexandre Néron .25 .60
16 Jordan Caron .25 .60
17 Alexandre Brunet .25 .60
18 Louis-Philippe Lachance .25 .60
19 Christopher Stevens .25 .60
20 Frédéric Desrochers .25 .60
21 Michal Frolik .60 1.50
22 Kevin Cormier .25 .60
23 Tommy Legault .40 1.00
24 Michael Chiasson .40 1.00

1993-94 Roanoke Express

Sponsored by Advance Auto Parts, First Virginia Bank, radio station J93.5 FM and WJPR TV 27, this 25-card standard-size set commemorates the inaugural season of the Roanoke Express. The fronts feature borderless color action player photos. The team logo appears on the bottom left with the player's name, position and number in two red bars next to it. The cards are unnumbered and checklisted below in alphabetical order.

COMPLETE SET (25) 3.00 8.00
1 Frank Anzalone CO .08 .25
2 Will Averill .15 .40
3 Claude Barthe .15 .40
4 Lev Berdichevsky .15 .40
5 Hughes Bouchard .15 .40
6 Reggie Brezeault .15 .40
7 Ilja Dubkov .15 .40
8 Pat Ferschweiler .15 .40
9 Kyle Galloway .15 .40
10 Jeff Jestadt .15 .40
11 Roger Larche .15 .40
12 Dana McGuane TR .02 .10
13 Jim Mill .15 .40
14 Dave Morissette .15 .40
15 Chris Potter .15 .40
16 Dan Ryder .15 .40
17 Gairin Smith .15 .40
18 Michael Smith .15 .40
19 Tony Szabo .15 .40
20 Stephen Tepper .15 .40
21 Oleg Yashin .15 .40
22 Team Photo .15 .40
23 Dave Morissette .02 .10
First F
24 Sponsor Card .02 .10
Advance Au
25 Sponsor Card .02 .10
First Virg

1994-95 Roanoke Express

This 24-card set features the Roanoke Express of the ECHL. The cards -- which were printed on extremely thin paper -- were available through the team, and possibly offered as a game night promotion. The fronts feature a blurry action photo, with team logo and player name and position. The unnumbered backs include stats and the logos of several sponsors.

COMPLETE SET (24) 4.00 10.00
1 Team Photo .20 .50
2 Dave Gagnon .30 .75
3 Chris Potter .20 .50
4 Dave Stewart .20 .50
5 Michael Smith .20 .50
6 Jon Larson .20 .50
7 Carl Fleury .20 .50
8 Jeff Jestadt .20 .50
9 Marty Schriner .20 .50
10 Rouslan Toujikov .20 .50
11 Jason Clarke .20 .50
12 Stephane Desjardins .20 .50
13 Robin Bouchard .20 .50
14 Oleg Yashin .20 .50
15 Ilja Dubkov .20 .50
16 Derek Laxdal .30 .75
17 Mark Luger .20 .50
18 Pat Ferschweiler .20 .50
19 Dan Ryder .20 .50
20 Frank Anzalone CO .08 .25
21 Dana McGuane TR .02 .10
22 Loco/Mascot .02 .10
23 Board of Directors .02 .10
24 Fan Card .01 .05

1995-96 Roanoke Express

This 25-card set of the Roanoke Express of the ECHL was a team-produced issue, and available only through the club. The fronts feature sharp, pseudo-action shots with the player's name in a red border along the left, and position and number in a green border along the top. A gold foil Express logo graces the lower right corner.

COMPLETE SET (25) 6.00 15.00
1 Jeff Jestadt .15 .40
2 Dave Stewart .15 .40
3 Matt DelGuidice .30 .75
4 Dave Holum .15 .40
5 Mike Stacchi .15 .40
6 Paul Croteau .15 .40
7 Marty Schriner .15 .40
8 L.P. Charbonneau .15 .40
9 Michael Smith .15 .40
10 Ilja Dubkov .20 .50
11 Tim Christian .15 .40
12 Brian Gallentine .15 .40
13 Jeff Jablonski .15 .40
14 Daniel Berthiaume .40 1.00
15 Duane Harmer .15 .40
16 Jason Clarke .15 .40
17 Tim Hanley .15 .40
18 Jon Larson .15 .40
19 Nick Jones .15 .40
20 Chris Potter .15 .40
21 Craig Herr .15 .40
22 Frank Anzalone CO .08 .25
23 Chris Pollack TR .02 .10
24 Loco .02 .10
Mascot
25 Team Photo .02 .10

1996-97 Roanoke Express

This 24-card set of the Roanoke Express of the ECHL was team issued. The cards feature action photography on the front, along with a comprehensive stats package on the reverse. The cards prominently feature the player's jersey number on the back, and are listed below thusly.

COMPLETE SET (24) 8.00 20.00
1 Dave Gagnon .20 .50
2 Dave Stewart .15 .40
3 Eric Landry .15 .40
5 Michael Smith .15 .40
7 Jeff Loder .15 .40
8 Duane Harmer .15 .40
10 Bobby Brown .15 .40
11 J.F. Tremblay .15 .40
12 Ryan Equale .15 .40
14 Doug Searle .15 .40
15 Jeff Jablonski .15 .40
17 Jeff Cowan .20 .50
18 Sean Brown .20 .50
21 Ilya Dubkov .15 .40
22 Matt O'Dette .15 .40
23 Chris Lipsett .15 .40
24 Tim Christian .15 .40
35 Larry Moberg .20 .50
NNO Mike Holden TR .02 .10
NNO Checklist .02 .10
NNO Frank Anzalone CO .02 .10
NNO Loco the Railyard Dog .02 .10
NNO Team Photo .15 .40
NNO Elmer the Engine .02 .10

1998-99 Roanoke Express

These card were handed out at Express home games. They are numbered on the back on the lower left hand corner in small print. Card #7 is unconfirmed to date, but is believed to exist. Anyone with additional information is urged to forward it to the publisher.

COMPLETE SET (26) 10.00 25.00
1 Tony Mancuso GM .20 .50
2 Scott Gordon HCO .20 .50
3 Perry Florio ACO .20 .50
4 Darren Abbott DOB .20 .50
5 Dave Gagnon .60 1.50
6 Daniel Berthiaume .75 2.00
7 Unknown .40 1.00
8 Doug Searle .40 1.00
9 Jason Dailey .40 1.00
10 Duane Harmer .40 1.00
11 Mike Peron .40 1.00
12 Kris Cantu .40 1.00
13 Travis Smith .40 1.00
14 J.C. Ruid .40 1.00
15 Ben Schust .40 1.00
16 Jeremy Schaefer .40 1.00
17 J.F. Tremblay .40 1.00
18 Mike Mader .40 1.00
19 Nicholas Windsor .40 1.00
20 Peter Brearley .40 1.00
21 Nic Beaudoin .40 1.00
22 Chris Lipsett .40 1.00
23 Tim Christian .40 1.00
24 Dru Burgess .40 1.00
25 Chris Wismer .40 1.00
26 Loco Mascot .20 .50

2000-01 Roanoke Express

This set features the Express of the ECHL. The set was issued as a promotional giveaway. Local police officers attended several games, handing out a different card to children at each one. That makes accumulating a complete set a difficult task, indeed.

COMPLETE SET (22) 8.00 20.00
1 Roanoke Express .20 .50
2 Mike Peron .40 1.00
3 Joe Dusbabek .40 1.00
4 Troy Lake .40 1.00
5 Jeff Burgoyne .40 1.00
6 Ben Schust .40 1.00
7 Dave Gagnon .60 1.50
8 Calvin Elfring .40 1.00
9 Colin Anderson .40 1.00
10 Todd Compeau .40 1.00
11 Daniel Berthiaume .60 1.50
12 Loco MASCOT .10 .25
13 Aaron Gates .40 1.00
14 Travis Smith .40 1.00
15 John Sadowski .40 1.00
16 Perry Florio CO .10 .25
17 Nate Handrahan .40 1.00
18 Jeff Sproat .40 1.00
19 Jay Shipulski .40 1.00
20 Doug Sheppard .40 1.00
21 George McMillan SHERIFF .04 .10
22 Adam Dewan .40 1.00

2001-02 Roanoke Express

This set features the Express of the ECHL. The cards were handed out to children, one card at a time, from police officers at Express games. Because of this, complete sets are nearly impossible to compile.

COMPLETE SET (24) 20.00 50.00
1 Daniel Berthiaume 1.25 3.00
2 Chris Cava .75 2.00
3 Steve Chabbert .75 2.00
4 Duncan Dalmao .75 2.00
5 Brett DeCecco 1.25 3.00
6 Joe Dusbabek .75 2.00
7 Brad Essex .75 2.00
8 Vernon Fiddler .75 2.00
9 Pete Gardiner .75 2.00
10 Jeff Helperl .75 2.00
11 Marty Hughes .75 2.00
12 Rick Kowalsky .75 2.00
13 Troy Lake .75 2.00
14 Frank Novock .75 2.00
15 Mike Omicioli 1.25 3.00
16 Mike Peron .75 2.00
17 Gary Ricciardi 1.25 3.00
18 Travis Smith .75 2.00
19 Jeff Sproat .75 2.00
20 Terence Tootoo 2.00 5.00
21 Jordan Willis 1.50 4.00
22 Perry Florio CO .20 .50
23 Mark Bernard ACO .20 .50
24 George McMillan .75 2.00

2002-03 Roanoke Express

COMPLETE SET (25) 15.00 40.00
1 Sebastien Laplante .75 2.00
2 Sheriff McMillan .10 .25
3 Dan Sullivan .75 2.00
4 Loco Mascot .10 .25
5 Cole Fischer .75 2.00
6 Perry Florio HCO .10 .25
7 Tony MacAulay ACO .10 .25
8 Scotty Balan .75 2.00
9 Josh Barker .75 2.00
10 Dan Carlson .75 2.00
11 Adam Colagiacomo .75 2.00
12 Duncan Dalmao .75 2.00
13 Joe Dusbabek .75 2.00
14 Brad Essex .75 2.00
15 Dylan Gyori 1.25 3.00
16 Jason Jaffray .75 2.00
17 Rick Kowalsky .75 2.00
18 Shawn Limpright .75 2.00
19 Evan Lindsay .75 2.00
20 Chad Mazurak .75 2.00
21 Frank Novock .75 2.00
22 Mike Peron .75 2.00
23 Doug Schueller .75 2.00
24 David Silverstone .75 2.00
25 Tim O'Connell .75 2.00

2002-03 Roanoke Express RBI Sports

COMPLETE SET (18) 10.00 18.00
187 Josh Barker .40 1.00
188 Scotty Balan .40 1.00
189 Cam Bristow .40 1.00
190 Dan Carlson .40 1.00
191 Duncan Dalmao .40 1.00
192 Joe Dusbabek .40 1.00
193 Brad Essex .40 1.00
194 Cole Fisher .40 1.00
195 Dylan Gyori .60 1.50
196 Jason Jaffray .40 1.00
197 Rick Kowalsky .40 1.00
198 Sebastien Laplante .60 1.50
199 Chad Mazurak .40 1.00
200 Frank Novock .40 1.00
201 Tim O'Connell .40 1.00
202 Mike Peron .40 1.00
203 Doug Schueller .40 1.00
204 David Silverstone .40 1.00

2003-04 Roanoke Express

COMPLETE SET (16) 6.00 15.00
305 Josh Barker .40 1.00
306 David Belitski .60 1.50
307 Kevin Bergin .40 1.00
308 Dan Carlson .40 1.00
309 Dan Carney .40 1.00
310 Duncan Dalmao .40 1.00
311 Joe Dusbabek .40 1.00
312 Rick Kowalsky .40 1.00
313 Shawn Limpright .40 1.00
314 Andrew McPherson .40 1.00
315 Andrew Oke .40 1.00
316 Bryan Perez .40 1.00
317 Doug Scatchard .40 1.00
318 Robert Snowball .40 1.00
319 Blair Stayzer .40 1.00
320 Jason Wolfe .60 1.50

1963-64 Rochester Americans

Printed on thin paper stock, this set of twenty photos, was issued in two series and measures approximately 4" by 6". This set features borderless black-and-white posed or action shots of the AHL (American Hockey League) Amerks. The white back carries the player's name, age, height, weight, and statistics from previous years in the minors. The cards are unnumbered and checklisted below in alphabetical order.

COMPLETE SET (20) 100.00 200.00
1 Lou Angotti 4.00 8.00
2 Al Arbour 10.00 20.00
3 Norm Armstrong 2.50 5.00
4 Ed Babiuk 2.50 5.00
5 Wally Boyer 4.00 8.00
6 Arnie Brown 4.00 8.00
7 Gerry Cheevers UER 25.00 50.00
8 Don Cherry 30.00 60.00
9 Mike Corbett 2.50 5.00
10 Joe Crozier CO 2.50 5.00
11 Jack Curran TR 2.50 5.00
12 Les Duff 2.50 5.00
13 Gerry Ehman 2.50 5.00
14 Dick Gamble 4.00 8.00
15 Larry Hillman 2.50 5.00
16 Bronco Horvath 7.50 15.00
17 Eddie Lawson 2.50 5.00
18 Jim Pappin 4.00 8.00
19 Darryl Sly 2.50 5.00
20 Stan Smrke 3.00 6.00

1971-72 Rochester Americans

Cards measure 5" x 7" and feature black and white glossy photos on the front, along with a facsimile autograph. Backs are blank. Cards are unnumbered and checklisted below alphabetically.

COMPLETE SET (18) 30.00 80.00
1 Red Armstrong 2.00 5.00
2 Guy Burrowes 2.00 5.00
3 Gaye Cooley 2.00 5.00
4 Bob Craig 2.00 5.00
5 Bob Ellett 2.00 5.00
6 Ron Fogal 2.00 5.00
7 Rod Graham 2.00 5.00
8 Dave Hrechkosy 2.50 6.00
9 Herman Karp 2.00 5.00
10 Bob Kelly 4.00 10.00
11 Larry McKillop 2.00 5.00
12 Bob Malcolm 2.00 5.00
13 Barry Merrell 2.00 5.00
14 Wayne Morusyk 2.00 5.00
15 Rick Pagnutti 2.00 5.00
16 Gerry Sillers 2.00 5.00
17 Gene Sobchuk 2.00 5.00
18 Lynn Zimmerman 2.00 5.00

1977-78 Rochester Americans

These cards feature black and white front photos with a facsimile autograph. Front also features players name, position, biographical information, and statistics. Cards are unnumbered and checklisted below in alphabetical order.

COMPLETE SET (24) 12.50 25.00
1 Team Photo .50 1.00
2 Duane Rupp .75 1.50
3 Nate Angelo TR .25 .50
4 Earl Anderson .75 1.50
5 Bill Bennett .50 1.00
6 Daryl Drader .50 1.00
7 Rene Drolet .50 1.00
8 Rene Drolet .50 1.00
9 Darryl Edestrand .75 1.50
10 Ron Garwasiuk .50 1.00
11 Rod Graham .50 1.00
12 Rod Graham .50 1.00
13 Doug Halward .75 1.50
14 Bjorn Johansson .50 1.00
15 Steve Langdon .50 1.00
16 Ray Maluta .50 1.00
17 Brian McGregor .50 1.00
18 Clayton Pachal .50 1.00
19 Dave Parro .75 1.50
20 Jim Pettie .50 1.00
21 Sean Shanahan .50 1.00
22 Al Sims 1.00 2.00
23 Barry Smith .75 1.50

1979-80 Rochester Americans

These cards are oversized, measuring 8-by-10.5 inches. They are blank backed and unnumbered. The set was sponsored by Wendy's.

1 Mike Boland 2.00 5.00
2 Mike Breen 2.00 5.00
3 Paul Crowley 2.00 5.00
4 Daryl Drader 2.00 5.00
5 Ron Garwasiuk 2.00 5.00
6 Chris Halyk 2.00 5.00
7 Bill Inglis CO 1.50 4.00
8 Randy Ireland 2.00 5.00
9 Joe Kowal 2.00 5.00
10 Normand Lefebvre 2.00 5.00
11 Bob Mongrain 2.00 5.00
12 Wayne Ramsey 2.00 5.00
13 Jacques Richard 3.00 8.00
14 Geordie Robertson 2.00 5.00
15 Andre Savard 3.00 10.00
16 Ron Schock 3.00 8.00
17 Dave Schultz 12.00 30.00
18 Barry Smith 2.00 5.00
19 Bill Stewart 2.00 5.00
20 Richard Suwek 2.00 5.00
21 Mark Toffolo 2.00 5.00
22 Jim Turkiewicz 2.00 5.00
23 Ed Walsh 2.00 5.00
24 Jim Walsh 2.00 5.00

1991-92 Rochester Americans Dunkin' Donuts

Sponsored by Dunkin' Donuts, this 20-card set measures the standard size. It was issued in four perforated strips, each consisting of four player cards and a Dunkin' Donuts coupon. On white card stock, the fronts feature color action player photos. Blue and red border stripes edge the picture on the bottom and half way on each side. The player's name is printed in a red-lined box above the picture, while logos and additional player information appear beneath it. In black print on a white background, the backs carry biography, statistics, and sponsor logo. The cards are unnumbered and checklisted below in alphabetical order.

COMPLETE SET (20) 4.00 10.00
1 Greg Brown .20 .50
2 Peter Ciavaglia .30 .75
3 Bob Corkum .30 .75
4 Brian Curran .20 .50
5 David DiVita .20 .50
6 Tom Draper .30 .75
7 Jody Gage .40 1.00
8 Dan Frawley .20 .50
9 Dave Littman .30 .75
10 Darcy Loewen .20 .50
11 Don McSween .30 .75
12 Brad Rubachuk .20 .50
13 Lindy Ruff .40 1.00
14 Joel Savage .20 .50
15 Jiri Sejba .20 .50
16 Chris Snell .20 .50
17 Coupon Dunkin' Donuts .01 .05
18 Coupon Dunkin' Donuts .01 .05
19 Coupon Dunkin' Donuts .01 .05
20 Coupon Dunkin' Donuts .01 .05

1991-92 Rochester Americans Kodak

The 1991-92 Rochester American Team Photo and Trading Card Set was co-sponsored by Kodak and Wegmons Photo Center. It consists of three 11 1/4" by 9 1/2" sheets joined together and tri-folded. The first sheet displays a team photo of the players dressed in street clothes. The second and third sheets consist of 15 cards each arranged in three rows of five cards. The last four slots of the third sheet display sponsor coupons. After perforation, the cards would measure approximately 2 1/4" by 3 1/8". The player photos on the fronts have rounded corners and are poses shot from the waist up against a studio background. Team color-coded (red and blue) stripes edge the pictures on the bottom and each side. The player's name, position, and the team logo are above the picture, while sponsor logos and the uniform number are below it. In red and blue print, the backs carry biography and statistics. The cards are checklisted below as they are arranged in the album, with coaches presented first and then the players in alphabetical order.

COMPLETE SET (26) 5.00 12.00
1 Don Lever CO .20 .50
2 Torry Martin ACO .08 .25
3 Ian Boyce .20 .50
4 John Bradley .20 .50
5 Greg Brown .20 .50
6 Keith Carney .20 .50
7 Peter Ciavaglia .20 .50
8 Bob Corkum .30 .75
9 Brian Curran .20 .50
10 David DiVita .20 .50
11 Lou Franceschetti .30 .75
12 Dan Frawley .20 .50
13 Jody Gage .40 1.00
14 Kevin Haller .30 .75
15 Dave Littman .25 .60
16 Darcy Loewen .20 .50
17 Steve Ludzik .20 .50
18 Don McSween .20 .50
19 Brad Miller .20 .50
20 Sean O'Donnell .30 .75
21 Brad Rubachuk .20 .50
22 Lindy Ruff .40 1.00
23 Joel Savage .20 .50
24 Jiri Sejba .20 .50
25 Chris Snell .20 .50
26 Jason Winch .20 .50

1991-92 Rochester Americans Postcards

Sponsored by Genny Light, this 21-card set measures approximately 3 1/2" by 5 1/2" and features the 1991-92 Rochester Americans of the American Hockey League. The fronts have black-and-white action player photos with rounded corners and black borders. The player's name, uniform number, position, biography and last amateur club appear beneath the photo, along with the team logo. The backs are in postcard format and carry the sponsor's logo along with the words "STOP DWI. Don't Drink and Drive". The cards are unnumbered and checklisted below in alphabetical order.

COMPLETE SET (21) 4.00 10.00
1 Dave Basoggio .20 .50
2 John Bradley .20 .50
3 Greg Brown .20 .50
4 Keith Carney .20 .50
5 Peter Ciavaglia .20 .50
6 Bob Corkum .30 .75
7 David DiVita .20 .50
8 Tom Draper .30 .75
9 Lou Franceschetti .30 .75
10 Dan Frawley .20 .50
11 Bill Houlder .30 .75
12 Don Lever CO .08 .25
13 David Littman .30 .75
14 Terry Martin ACO .08 .25
15 Don McSween .20 .50
16 Sean O'Donnell .30 .75
17 Lindy Ruff .20 .50
18 Joel Savage .20 .50
19 Jiri Sejba .20 .50
20 Chris Snell .20 .50
21 Ed Zawatsky .20 .50

1992-93 Rochester Americans Dunkin' Donuts

Sponsored by Dunkin' Donuts, this 20-card set measures the standard size. It was issued in four perforated strips, each consisting of five player cards. On white card stock, the fronts feature color action player photos framed by team color-coded (red and blue) border stripes. Logos, jersey number, and position are printed above the picture, while the player's name is printed on the wider blue stripe beneath the picture. In black print on a white background, the backs carry biography, statistics, and sponsor logo. The cards are unnumbered and checklisted below in alphabetical order.

COMPLETE SET (20) 6.00 15.00
1 Peter Ambroziak .20 .50
2 Greg Brown .20 .50
3 Peter Ciavaglia .25 .60
4 Jozef Cierny .20 .50
5 David DiVita .20 .50
6 Dan Frawley .20 .50
7 Jody Gage .30 .75
8 Andrei Jakovenko .20 .50
9 Olaf Kolzig 2.00 5.00
10 Doug Macdonald .20 .50
11 Mike McLaughlin .20 .50
12 Sean O'Donnell .30 .75
13 Bill Pye .30 .75
14 Brad Rubachuk .20 .50
15 Bruce Shoebottom .20 .50
16 Todd Simon .20 .50
17 Jeff Sirkka .20 .50
18 Chris Snell .20 .50
19 Scott Thomas .30 .75
20 Jason Young .20 .50

1992-93 Rochester Americans Kodak

The 1992-93 Rochester American Team Photo and Trading Card Set was co-sponsored by Kodak and Wegmons Photo Center. It consists of three 11 1/4" by 9 1/2" sheets joined together and tri-folded. The first sheet displays a team photo of the players in uniform. The second and third sheets consist of 15 cards each arranged in three rows of five cards. (The last four slots of the third sheet display sponsor coupons.) After perforation, the cards would measure approximately 2 1/4" by 3 1/8". The player photos on the fronts have rounded corners and are poses shot from the waist up against a studio background. The player's name, position, and the team logo are above the picture, while sponsor logos and the uniform number are below it. In red and blue print, the backs carry biography and statistics. The cards are checklisted below as they are arranged in the album, with coaches presented first and then the players in alphabetical order.

COMPLETE SET (26) 15.00 40.00
1 John Van Boxmeer CO .40 1.00
2 Terry Martin ACO .08 .25
3 Peter Ambroziak .40 1.00
4 Greg Brown .40 1.00
5 Peter Ciavaglia .40 1.00
6 Jozef Cierny .40 1.00
7 David DiVita .40 1.00
8 Dan Frawley .40 1.00
9 Jody Gage 1.00 2.50
10 The Moose (mascot) .08 .25
11 Tony Iob .40 1.00
12 Olaf Kolzig 4.00 10.00
13 Doug MacDonald .40 1.00
14 Mike McLaughlin .40 1.00
15 Sean O'Donnell 1.00 2.50
16 Brad Pascall 1.00 2.50
17 Bill Pye 1.00 2.50
18 Brad Rubachuk .40 1.00
19 Joel Savage .40 1.00
20 Bruce Shoebottom .75 2.00
21 Todd Simon .40 1.00
22 Jeff Sirkka .40 1.00
23 Chris Snell .40 1.00
24 Scott Thomas 1.00 2.50
25 Jason Winch .40 1.00
26 Jason Young .40 1.00

1993-94 Rochester Americans Kodak

This 25-card set of the Rochester Americans of the AHL was sponsored by Kodak and distributed by the team's booster club. The set was issued in sheet form, with each card measuring 2 1/2" by 3 1/4". The card fronts carry a posed photo, player name and position and logos of the club and sponsors. The backs are unnumbered, but carry comprehensive stats.

COMPLETE SET (25) 4.80 12.00
1 John Van Boxmeer CO .20 .50
2 Terry Martin ASST CO .08 .25
3 Peter Ambroziak .25 .60
4 Mike Bavis .25 .60
5 James Black .25 .60
6 Derek Booth .25 .60
7 Philippe Boucher .25 .60
8 David Cooper .25 .60
9 Todd Flichel .25 .60
10 Jody Gage .40 1.00
11 Viktor Gordiouk .25 .60
12 Bill Horn .25 .60
13 Markus Ketterer .30 .75
14 Mark Krys .25 .60
15 Doug MacDonald .25 .60
16 Dean Melanson .25 .60
17 Moose .08 .25
Mascot
18 Sean O'Donnell .30 .75
19 Brad Pascall .25 .60
20 Sergei Petrenko .25 .60
21 Brad Rubachuk .25 .60
22 Todd Simon .25 .60
23 Scott Thomas .30 .75
24 Mikhail Volkov .25 .60
25 Jason Young .25 .60

1995-96 Rochester Americans

This 25-card set of the Rochester Americans of the AHL was produced for the team by Split Second. The sets were available at games and by mail through the club. The set features a blurry action photo on the front and complete stats on the back. As they are unnumbered, the cards are presented in alphabetical order.

COMPLETE SET (25) 6.00 15.00
1 Craig Charron .20 .50
2 David Cooper .20 .50
3 Dan Frawley .20 .50
4 Jody Gage .40 1.00
5 Terry Hollinger .25 .60
6 Dane Jackson .20 .50
7 Ladislav Karabin .20 .50
8 Sergei Klimentiev .20 .50
9 Jamie Leach .20 .50
10 Jay Mazur .20 .50
11 Dean Melanson .20 .50
12 Scott Metcalfe .20 .50
13 Barrie Moore .20 .50
14 Scott Nichol .20 .50
15 Rumun Ndur .25 .60
16 Scott Pearson .20 .50
17 Serge Roberge .20 .50
18 Steve Shields .75 2.00
19 Robb Stauber .30 .75
20 Mikhail Volkov .20 .50
21 Dixon Ward .30 .75
22 Bob Westerby .20 .50
23 Mike Wilson .20 .50
24 Shayne Wright .20 .50
25 John Tortorella CO .08 .25

1996-97 Rochester Americans

This set features the Americans of the AHL. The set was produced by SplitSecond and was sold at home games for $5.

COMPLETE SET (26) 4.00 10.00
1 Rochester Americans .15 .40
2 Sergei Klimentiev .15 .40
3 Craig Charron .15 .40
4 Craig Millar .15 .40
5 Scott Metcalfe .15 .40
6 Ed Ronan .15 .40
7 Terry Hollinger .15 .40
8 Shayne Wright .15 .40
9 Barrie Moore .15 .40
10 Scott Nichol .15 .40
11 Charlie Huddy .15 .40
12 Vaclav Varada .20 .50
13 Wayne Primeau .30 .75
14 Terry Yake .15 .40
15 Dan Frawley .15 .40
16 Frederic Deschenes .15 .40
17 Steve Shields .40 1.00
18 Paul Rushforth .15 .40
19 Dane Jackson .15 .40
20 Rumun Ndur .20 .50
21 Greg Walters .15 .40
22 Eric Lavigne .15 .40
23 John Tortorella CO .40 1.00
24 Moose MAS .02 .10
25 AHL Web Site .01 .05
26 PHPA Web Site .01 .05

1997-98 Rochester Americans

This set features the Amerks of the AHL. The cards were sponsored by Pepsi and issued as a promotional giveaway. The cards came in five-card sheets, and were given out at five different games.

COMPLETE SET (25) 8.00 20.00
1-1 Dane Jackson .30 .75
1-2 Scott Metcalfe .30 .75
1-3 Denis Hamel .30 .75
1-4 Mark Dutiaume .30 .75
1-5 Daniel Bienvenue .30 .75
2-1 Craig Charron .30 .75
2-2 Scott Nichol .30 .75
2-3 Martin Menard .30 .75
2-4 Erik Rasmussen .40 1.00
2-5 Mike Zanutto .30 .75
3-1 Vaclav Varada .40 1.00
3-2 Dan Frawley .30 .75
3-3 Patrice Tardif .40 1.00
3-4 Greg Walters .30 .75
3-5 Matt Davidson .30 .75
4-1 Mike Hurlbut .30 .75
4-2 Shayne Wright .30 .75
4-3 Jay McKee .30 .75
4-4 Dean Melanson .30 .75
4-5 Eric Lavigne .30 .75
5-1 Martin Biron 2.00 5.00
5-2 Sergei Klimentiev .30 .75
5-3 Mike Bales .40 1.00
5-4 Rumun Ndur .30 .75
5-5 Jean-Luc Grand-Pierre .30 .75

1998-99 Rochester Americans

This set features the Amerks of the AHL. The set was issued in five-card strips at five home games late in the season.

COMPLETE SET (25) 6.00 15.00
1 Craig Fisher .20 .50
2 Greg Walters .20 .50
3 Matt Davidson .20 .50
4 Randy Cunneyworth .20 .50
5 Martin Biron 1.25 3.00
6 Mike Hurlbut .20 .50
7 Tom Draper .30 .75
8 Mike Harder .20 .50
9 Denis Hamel .20 .50
10 Jean-Luc Grand-Pierre .20 .50
11 Scott Nichol .20 .50
12 Francois Methot .20 .50
13 Dean Melanson .20 .50
14 Jason Mansoff .20 .50
15 Jason Holland .20 .50
16 Darren Van Oene .20 .50
17 Dean Sylvester .30 .75
18 Cory Sarich .20 .50
19 Erik Rasmussen .30 .75
20 Dominic Pittis .20 .50
21 The Moose MAS .02 .10
22 Darwin McCutcheon CO .02 .10
23 Jody Gage .30 .75
24 Shane Kenny .20 .50
25 Steffon Walby .20 .50

2000-01 Rochester Americans

This set features the Americans of the AHL. The set was produced by Choice Marketing, and sold by the team at its souvenir stands.

COMPLETE SET (29) 4.80 12.00
1 Jeremy Adduono .15 .40
2 Tom Askey .20 .50
3 Martin Biron .75 2.00
4 Kevin Bolibruck .15 .40
5 Craig Brunel .15 .40
6 Brian Campbell .20 .50
7 Craig Charron .15 .40
8 Jason Cipolla .15 .40
9 Jason Holland .15 .40
10 Doug Houda .15 .40
11 Mike Hurlbut .15 .40
12 Dane Jackson .15 .40
13 Jaroslav Kristek .20 .50
14 Mike Mader .15 .40
15 Francois Methot .15 .40
16 Norm Milley .30 .75
17 Joe Murphy .15 .40
18 Todd Nelson .15 .40
19 Mika Noronen .60 1.50
20 Andrew Peters .40 1.00
21 Chris Taylor .15 .40
22 Paul Traynor .15 .40
23 Darren Van Oene .15 .40
24 Randy Cunneyworth CO .10 .25
25 Jon Christiano CO .04 .10
26 Dave A. Williams EM .04 .10
27 Kent Weisbeck TR .04 .10
28 The Moose MASCOT .04 .10
NNO Team CL .04 .10

2002-03 Rochester Americans

COMPLETE SET (26) 8.00 20.00
1 Tom Askey .30 .75
2 Milan Bartovic .20 .50
3 Jason Botterill .20 .50
4 Rory Fitzpatrick .20 .50
5 Paul Gaustad .30 .75
6 Denis Hamel .20 .50
7 Radoslav Hecl .20 .50
8 Doug Houda .20 .50
9 Doug Janik .20 .50
10 Ryan Jorde .20 .50
11 Jaroslav Kristek .30 .75
12 Sean McMorrow .30 .75
13 Francois Methot .20 .50
14 Ryan Miller 2.00 5.00
15 Norm Milley .20 .50
16 Karel Mosovsky .20 .50
17 Jiri Novotny .30 .75
18 Andrew Peters .60 1.50
19 Jason Pominville .60 1.50
20 Peter Ratchuk .20 .50
21 Chris Taylor .20 .50
22 Ryan Miller 2.00 5.00
23 Randy Cunneyworth HCO .04 .10
24 Jon Christiano ACO .04 .10
25 The Moose Mascot .04 .10
NNO Checklist .04 .10

2003-04 Rochester Americans

This set was produced by Choice Marketing and sold at home games.

COMPLETE SET (29) 6.00 15.00
1 Doug Houda ACO .04 .10
2 Tom Askey .30 .75
3 Milan Bartovic .12 .30
4 Jason Botterill .12 .30
5 Brian Chapman .12 .30
6 David Cullen .12 .30
7 Randy Cunneyworth .12 .30
8 Pete Gardiner .12 .30
9 Paul Gaustad .20 .50
10 Doug Janik .12 .30
11 Ryan Jorde .12 .30
12 Steve Lingren .12 .30
13 Sean McMorrow .30 .75
14 Ryan Miller 1.25 3.00
15 Jason Dawe .12 .30
16 Norm Milley .30 .75
17 Karel Mosovsky .12 .30
18 Rick Mrozik .12 .30
19 Jiri Novotny .30 .75
20 Nathan Paetsch .30 .75
21 Geoff Peters .30 .75
22 Domenic Pittis .20 .50
23 Jason Pominville .75 2.00
24 Scott Ricci .12 .30
25 Derek Roy .75 2.00
26 Derek Roy .75 2.00
27 Michael Ryan .20 .50
28 Mascot .04 .10
29 Chris Thorburn .12 .30
NNO Checklist .04 .10

2004-05 Rochester Americans

COMPLETE SET (30) 8.00 20.00
1 Checklist .04 .10
2 Tom Askey .30 .75
3 Milan Bartovic .20 .50
4 Jason Botterill .20 .50
5 David Cullen .20 .50
6 Paul Gaustad .20 .50
7 Doug Janik .20 .50
8 Jeff Jillson .20 .50
9 Ryan Jorde .20 .50
10 Steve Lingren .20 .50
11 Sean McMorrow .30 .75
12 Ryan Miller .75 2.00
13 Norm Milley .20 .50
14 Jiri Novotny .20 .50
15 Nathan Paetsch .20 .50
16 Daniel Paille .40 1.00
17 Geoff Peters .60 1.50
18 Jason Pominville .40 1.00
19 Todd Rohloff .20 .50
20 Derek Roy .40 1.00
21 Michael Ryan .20 .50
22 Brandon Smith .20 .50
23 Chris Taylor .20 .50
24 Chris Thorburn .20 .50
25 Thomas Vanek .75 2.00
26 The Moose MASCOT .04 .10
27 Ryan Miller .75 2.00
28 Derek Roy .40 1.00
29 Thomas Vanek .75 2.00
30 Randy Cunneyworth CO .04 .10
Doug Houda CO

2014-15 Rochester Americans

COMPLETE SET (25) 6.00 15.00
1 Joel Armia .30 .75
2 Brady Austin .30 .75
3 Drew Bagnall .30 .75
4 William Carrier .30 .75
5 Chadd Cassidy CO .30 .75
6 Daniel Catenacci .30 .75
7 Jerry D'Amigo .40 1.00
8 Zac Dalpe .30 .75
9 Matt Ellis .30 .75
10 Mikhail Grigorenko .50 1.25
11 Brayden Irwin .30 .75
12 Justin Kea .30 .75
13 Johan Larsson .30 .75
14 Jerome Gauthier-Leduc .30 .75
15 Nathan Lieuwen .30 .75
16 Matt Mackenzie .30 .75
17 Andrey Makarov .30 .75
18 Jake McCabe .40 1.00
19 Nick Petrecki .30 .75
20 Mark Pysyk .40 1.00
21 Chad Ruhwedel .30 .75
22 Jordan Samuels-Thomas .30 .75
23 Tim Schaller .30 .75
24 Kevin Sundher .30 .75
25 Philip Varone .30 .75

1999-00 Rockford IceHogs

This set features the IceHogs of the UHL. The set was produced by Roox and was sold by the team at home games. Because of the obtuse numbering system on the card backs, they have been listed below in alphabetical order.

COMPLETE SET (26) 20.00 40.00
1 Brant Blackned .75 2.00
2 Peter Cava 1.25 3.00
3 Patrice Charbonneau .75 2.00
4 Mike Correia .75 2.00
5 Dan Davies .75 2.00
6 Raymond Delarosbil .75 2.00
7 Mike Figliomeni 1.25 3.00
8 Jason Firth 1.25 3.00
9 Sheldon Gorski 1.25 3.00
10 Jeff Kostuch .75 2.00
11 Evgeny Krivomaz .75 2.00
12 Derek Landmesser .75 2.00
13 Alexandre Makombo 1.25 3.00
14 Barry McKinley .75 2.00
15 Normand Paquet .75 2.00
16 Jean-Francois Rivard .75 2.00
17 Shawn Smith .75 2.00
18 Carlos Soke .75 2.00
19 Wayne Strachan .75 2.00
20 Curtis Tipler .75 2.00
21 Jesse Welling .75 2.00
22 Scott Burfoot CO .08 .25
23 Dale DeGray CO .08 .25
24 Hamilton E. Hog MASCOT .02 .10
25 Mike Figliomeni AS 1.25 3.00
26 Jason Firth AS 1.25 3.00

2000-01 Rockford IceHogs

This set features the IceHogs of the UHL. The set was produced by the team and sold at its souvenir stands. The cards are unnumbered and are listed below alphabetically.

COMPLETE SET (25) 4.00 10.00
1 Curtis Bois .20 .50
2 Patrice Charbonneau .20 .50
3 Nick Checco .20 .50
4 Curtis Cruickshank .30 .75
5 Jeff DaCosta .20 .50
6 Dan Davies .20 .50
7 Steve Dumonski .20 .50
8 Chris Fattey .20 .50
9 Mike Figliomeni .20 .50
10 Justin Kearns .30 .75
11 Evgeny Krivomaz .20 .50
12 Jocelyn Langlois .20 .50
13 Michel Periard .20 .50
14 Jean-Francois Rivard .20 .50
15 David Runge .20 .50
16 Francois Sasseville .20 .50
17 Shawn Smith .20 .50
18 Mike Tobin .20 .50
19 Yan Turgeon .20 .50
20 Eduard Zankovets .20 .50
21 Dale DeGray CO .10 .25
22 Scott Burfoot CO .10 .25
23 Hamilton E. Hog MASCOT .10 .25
24 Logo Card .04 .10
25 Header Card .04 .10

2001-02 Rockford IceHogs

COMPLETE SET (25) 8.00 20.00
1 Ben Christopherson .40 1.00
2 Clint Wensley .40 1.00
3 Dan Davies .40 1.00
4 Darwin Murray .40 1.00
5 David Hoogsteen .40 1.00
6 Ernie Thorp .40 1.00
7 Forrest Gore .40 1.00
8 Hamilton E. Hog .40 1.00
9 Harold Hersh .10 .25
10 J.F. Rivard .40 1.00
11 Jared Reigstad .40 1.00
12 Jeff Antonovich .40 1.00
13 Jeff Dacosta .40 1.00
14 Jeremy Vokes .40 1.00
15 Joe Statkus .40 1.00
16 Mike Sgroi .40 1.00
17 Nick Checco .40 1.00
18 Oak Hewer .40 1.00
19 Quinten Van Horlick .40 1.00
20 Scott Bell CO .10 .25
21 Sergei Petrov .40 1.00
22 Steve Debus .40 1.00
23 T.J. Guidarelli .40 1.00
24 Wes Blevins .40 1.00
NNO Team CL .40 1.00

2002-03 Rockford IceHogs

COMPLETE SET (25) 8.00 20.00
1 Scott Bell CO .04 .10
2 Darwin Murray .40 1.00
3 Raitis Ivanans .40 1.00
4 Kenzie Homer .40 1.00
5 Alexander Alexeev .40 1.00
6 Oak Hewer .40 1.00
7 Erik Wendell .40 1.00
8 Jeff Antonovich .40 1.00
9 Matt Loen .40 1.00
10 Jeremy Rebek .40 1.00
11 Steve Cygan .40 1.00
12 Clint Wensley .40 1.00
13 Quinten Van Horlick .40 1.00
14 Steve Dumonski .40 1.00
15 Nick Angell .40 1.00
16 Joe Statkus .40 1.00
17 Jay Hebert .40 1.00
18 Dan Davies .40 1.00
19 Brad Olsen .40 1.00
20 Jeff Dacosta .40 1.00
21 Brant Nicklin .40 1.00
22 Ryan McIntosh .40 1.00
23 Mascot .04 .10
24 Mascot .04 .10
25 Team card/CL .04 .10

2003-04 Rockford IceHogs

This set was produced by Choice Marketing and sold at home games. Minor league collector Ralph Slate reports just 300 sets were produced.

COMPLETE SET (20) 6.00 15.00
1 B.J. Adams .30 .75
2 Justin Cardwell .30 .75
3 Steve Cygan .30 .75
4 Dan Davies .30 .75
5 Jeff Ewasko .40 1.00
6 John Glavota .30 .75
7 Kenzie Homer .30 .75
8 Dale Junkin .30 .75
9 Nathan Lutz .30 .75
10 Don Margettie .40 1.00
11 Kelly Miller .30 .75
12 Bob Nardella .30 .75
13 Dave Paradise .30 .75
14 Gary Ricciardi .30 .75
15 Paul Schonfelder .40 1.00
16 Adam Solnik .30 .75
17 Ron Vogel .40 1.00
18 Owen Walter .30 .75
19 Maris Ziedins .30 .75
20 Mark Bernard HCO .10 .25

2005-06 Rockford IceHogs

COMPLETE SET (27) 8.00 15.00
1 Greg Barber .20 .50
2 Robin Big Snake .75 2.00
3 Dan Boeser .20 .50
4 Ryan Carrigan .20 .50
5 Matt Gens .20 .50
6 Corey Hessler .20 .50
7 Chaz Johnson .40 1.00
8 Nathan Lutz .20 .50
9 Preston Mizzi .20 .50
10 Bob Nardella .20 .50
11 Jason Notermann .40 1.00
12 Steve Pelletier .20 .50
13 Olivier Proulx .20 .50
14 Jason Ralph .40 1.00
15 Billy Tibbetts .40 1.00
16 Yannick Tifu .20 .50
17 Rob Voltera .20 .50
18 Bruce Watson .40 1.00
19 Steve Yetman .20 .50
20 Tom Zabkowicz .20 .50
21 Josh Mizerek .20 .50
22 Ron Vogel .40 1.00
23 Michel Robinson .20 .50
24 Steve Martinson .20 .50
25 Hammer Hog MASCOT .02 .10
26 Hamilton E. Hog MASCOT .02 .10
NNO Rockford Ice Hogs CL .02 .10

2006-07 Rockford IceHogs

COMPLETE SET (27) 12.00 20.00
1 Jesse Bennefield .30 .75
2 Kaleb Betts .40 1.00
3 Robin Big Snake .75 2.00
4 Dan Boeser .30 .75
5 Paul Brown .30 .75
6 Frederic Cloutier• .60 1.50
7 Bryce Cockburn .30 .75
8 Nicolas Corbeil .30 .75
9 Mike Doyle .30 .75
10 Luke Fritshaw .30 .75
11 Matt Gens .30 .75
12 Corey Hessler .30 .75
13 Chaz Johnson .30 .75
14 Mike Letizia .30 .75
15 Erik Lizon .30 .75
16 Nathan Lutz .30 .75
17 Preston Mizzi .40 1.00
18 Jake Moreland .40 1.00
19 Jason Notermann .30 .75
20 Jason Ralph .30 .75
21 Kevin Ulanski .30 .75
22 Bruce Watson .30 .75
23 Tim Wedderburn .30 .75
24 Steve Martinson CO .20 .50
25 Hammer Hog MASCOT .02 .10
26 Hamilton E. Hog MASCOT .02 .10
27 Team Card .10 .25

2014-15 Rockford IceHogs

COMPLETE SET () 10.00 25.00
1 Header Card .30 .75
2 Ted Dent CO .30 .75
3 Adam Clendening .50 1.25
4 Zach Miskovic .30 .75
5 Stephen Johns .30 .75
6 T.J. Brennan .40 1.00
7 Viktor Svedberg .50 1.25
8 Klas Dahlbeck .30 .75
9 Peter Regin .30 .75
10 Dennis Rasmussen .30 .75
11 Drew LeBlanc .30 .75
12 Kyle Cumiskey .30 .75
13 Cody Bass .40 1.00
14 Phillip Danault .30 .75
15 Teuvo Teravainen 1.25 3.00
16 Pierre-Cedric Labrie .30 .75
17 Joakim Nordstrom .50 1.25
18 Ryan Hartman .40 1.00
19 Alex Broadhurst .30 .75
20 Garret Ross .30 .75
21 Matt Carey .30 .75
22 Mark McNeill .30 .75
23 Ville Pokka .30 .75
24 Scott Darling .40 1.00
25 Mac Carruth .30 .75
26 Ryan Schnell .30 .75
27 Mike Leighton .30 .75
28 Brandon Mashinter .30 .75

1995-96 Roller Hockey Magazine RHI

This 6-card set was inserted as a promotional enticement into the September 1996 issue of Roller Hockey Magazine.

COMPLETE SET (6) 2.00 5.00
1 Oleg Yashin .40 1.00
2 Frankie Ouellette .40 1.00
3 Nick Vitucci .60 1.50
4 Mike Martens .40 1.00
5 Alain Morissette .40 1.00
6 Simon Roy .40 1.00

1999-00 Rouyn-Noranda Huskies

This set features the Huskies of the QMJHL. The set was produced by card shop CTM-Ste-Foy and was sold at the store and at home games.

COMPLETE SET (26) 4.80 12.00
1 Kyrill Alexeev .15 .40
2 Marc-Andre Binette .15 .40
3 Maxime Bouchard .15 .40
4 Bruno Cadieux .15 .40
5 Sebastien Centomo .60 1.50
6 Kevin Cloutier .15 .40
7 Jonathan Gauthier .15 .40
8 Patrick Gilbert .15 .40
9 Andre Hart .15 .40
10 Robert Horak .15 .40
11 Eric L'Italien .15 .40
12 Mathieu Leclerc .15 .40
13 Jason Lehoux .15 .40
14 Jonathan Pelletier .15 .40
15 Bertrand-Pierre Plouffe .15 .40
16 Matthew Quinn .15 .40
17 Mike Ribeiro .60 1.50
18 Shawn Scanzano .15 .40
19 Jason Tessier .15 .40
20 Jerome Tremblay .15 .40
21 Alain Turcotte .15 .40
22 Steve Vandal .15 .40
23 Guy Boucher CO .02 .10
24 Andre Parke CO .02 .10
25 Jean Pronovost CO .15 .40
26 Michel Maroux TR .02 .10

2000-01 Rouyn-Noranda Huskies

This set features the Huskies of the QMJHL. The cards were produced by CTM-Ste-Foy, and were sold both by that card shop and by the team.

COMPLETE SET (26) 6.00 15.00
1 Dominic D'Amour .20 .50
2 Jonathan Gauthier .20 .50
3 Matthew Quinn .20 .50
4 Kirill Alexeev .20 .50
5 Sebastian Strozynski .20 .50
6 Bertrand Pierre Plouffe .20 .50
7 Maxime Talbot .20 .50
8 Guillaume Lefebvre .40 1.00
9 Alexandre Morel .20 .50
10 Michal Pinc .20 .50
12 Mathieu Leclerc .20 .50
13 Jerome Marois .20 .50
14 Patrice Theriault .20 .50
15 Patrick Gilbert .20 .50
16 Maxime Ouellet .75 2.00
17 Louis Mandeville .20 .50
18 Wesley Scanzano .30 .75
19 Sebastien Centomo .40 1.00
20 Maxime Bouchard .20 .50
21 Bruno Cadieux .20 .50
22 Jean-Philippe Hamel .20 .50
23 Shawn Scanzano .20 .50
24 Jonathan Gagnon .20 .50
25 Marc-Andre Binette .20 .50
26 Jean Pronovost CO .10 .25
NNO Lappy MASCOT .04 .10

2000-01 Rouyn-Noranda Huskies Signed

This set is exactly the same as the base Huskies set from this season, save that every card has been hand signed by the player pictured. Each card also is serial numbered out of just 100.

COMPLETE SET (26) 24.00 60.00
1 Dominic D'Amour .80 2.00
2 Jonathan Gauthier .80 2.00
3 Matthew Quinn .80 2.00
4 Kirill Alexeev .80 2.00
5 Sebastian Strozynski .80 2.00
6 Bertrand Pierre Plouffe .80 2.00
7 Maxime Talbot .80 2.00
8 Guillaume Lefebvre 2.00 5.00
9 Alexandre Morel .75 2.00
10 Michal Pinc .80 2.00
12 Mathieu Leclerc .80 2.00
13 Jerome Marois .80 2.00
14 Patrice Theriault .80 2.00
15 Patrick Gilbert .80 2.00
16 Maxime Ouellet 4.00 10.00
17 Louis Mandeville .80 2.00
18 Wesley Scanzano 1.20 3.00
19 Sebastien Centomo 6.00 8.00
20 Maxime Bouchard .80 2.00
21 Bruno Cadieux .80 2.00
22 Jean-Philippe Hamel .75 2.00
23 Shawn Scanzano .80 2.00
24 Jonathan Gagnon .80 2.00
25 Marc-Andre Binette .80 2.00
26 Jean Pronovost CO .80 2.00
NNO Lappy MASCOT .04 .10

1993-94 RPI Engineers

This 31-card set of the RPI Engineers was produced by Collect-A-Sport. Reportedly, production was limited to 2,000 sets, all of which were offered for sale at the arena on game nights.

COMPLETE SET (31) 4.00 10.00
1 Kelly Askew .15 .40
2 Adam Bartell .15 .40
3 Kobie Boykins .15 .40
4 Jeff Brick .15 .40
5 Tim Carvel .15 .40
6 Wayne Clarke .15 .40
7 Cam Cuthbert .15 .40
8 Steve Duncan ACO .02 .10
9 Dan Fridgen ACO .02 .10
10 Jeff Gabriel .15 .40
11 Craig Hamelin .15 .40
12 Chris Kiley .15 .40
13 Ken Kwasniewski .15 .40
14 Brad Layzell .15 .40
15 Neil Little .30 .75
16 Xavier Majic .20 .50
17 Jeff Matthews .15 .40
18 Chris Maye .15 .40
19 Jeff O'Connor .15 .40
20 Ron Pasco .15 .40
21 Eric Perardi .15 .40
22 Jon Pirrong .15 .40
23 Buddy Powers CO .02 .10
24 Tim Regan .15 .40
25 Bryan Richardson .15 .40
26 Patrick Rochon .15 .40
27 Mike Rolanti .15 .40
28 Tim Spadafore .15 .40
29 Mike Tamburro .15 .40
30 1993-94 Team .15 .40
31 Checklist .02 .10

1976-77 Saginaw Gears

This set features black and white player photos on slightly oversized stock. It's possible that the checklist is not complete. If you have additional information, please forward it to hockeymag@beckett.com.

COMPLETE SET (13) 17.50 35.00
1 Rick Chinnink 1.50 3.00
2 Marcel Comeau 1.50 3.00
3 Michel DeGuise 1.50 3.00
4 Marc Gaudreault 1.50 3.00
5 Greg Hotham 1.50 3.00
6 Stu Irving 1.50 3.00
7 Kevin Kemp 1.50 3.00
8 Mario Lessard 1.50 3.00
9 Gord Malinoski 1.50 3.00
10 Mike Ruest 1.50 3.00
11 D'Arcy Ryan 1.50 3.00
12 Dave Westner 1.50 3.00
13 Wayne Zuk 1.50 3.00

1978-79 Saginaw Gears

This 20-card set features black-and-white posed player photos. The team name and year appear in the top white border with the player's name printed in the bottom border. The player's position is listed on a puck at the bottom left of the photo. The backs are blank. The cards are unnumbered and checklisted below in alphabetical order. This set was the subject of a number of fierce bidding wars over the past two years, leading to a tremendous value increase in this edition.

COMPLETE SET (20) 175.00 300.00
1 Wren Blair 6.00 15.00
2 Marcel Comeau 6.00 15.00
3 Dennis Desrosiers 6.00 15.00
4 Jon Fontas 6.00 15.00
5 Bob Froese 12.50 25.00
6 Gunnar Garrett TR 4.00 10.00
7 Bob Gladney 6.00 15.00
8 Warren Holmes 6.00 15.00
9 Stu Irving 6.00 15.00
10 Larry Hopkins 6.00 15.00
11 Scott Jessee 6.00 15.00
12 Lynn Jorgenson 6.00 15.00
13 Doug Keans 12.50 25.00
14 Claude Larochelle 7.50 15.00
15 Paul McIntosh 6.00 15.00
16 Don Perry 6.00 15.00
17 Greg Steel 6.00 15.00
18 Mark Suzor 6.00 15.00
19 Mark Toffolo 6.00 15.00
20 Dave Westner 6.00 15.00

1999-00 Saginaw Gears

This set features the Gears of the UHL. Little is known about this set, other than that is was produced by Roox as part of a series of promotional giveaways. The Loder issue is actually a magnet, while the others are traditional cards. Any additional information can be forwarded to hockeymag@beckett.com.

COMPLETE SET (4) 2.00 5.00
1 Brian Mueller .40 1.00
2 Derek Pinfold .40 1.00
3 Jeff Loder .75 2.00
4 Keith Osborne .40 1.00

2003-04 Saginaw Spirit

COMPLETE SET (28) 5.00 12.00
1 Patrick Asselin .20 .50
2 Paul Bissonnette .20 .50
3 Daniel Borges .20 .50
4 Mike Brown .30 .75
5 Chase Crowder .20 .50
6 Steve Dix .20 .50
7 Adam Gibson .20 .50
8 Jesse Gimblett .20 .50
9 Jesse Jenish .20 .50
10 Phil Kozak .20 .50
11 Nick Lees .20 .50
12 Justin McCutcheon .20 .50
13 Patrick McNeill .20 .50
14 Georgi Misharin .20 .50
15 Mike Pain .20 .50
16 Eric Pfligler .20 .50
17 Geoff Platt .20 .50
18 Tom Pyatt .30 .75
19 Taylor Raszka .20 .50
20 Jean-Michel Rizk .30 .75
21 Marc-Andre Rizk .20 .50
22 Adam Sturgeon .20 .50
23 Mike Suggs .20 .50
24 Stephen Sunderman .20 .50
25 Team Card .04 .10
26 Rizk Brothers .20 .50
27 Moe Mantha CO .04 .10
28 Bryan and Jose .04 .10

2004-05 Saginaw Spirit

COMPLETE SET (24) 5.00 12.00
1 Patrick McNeill .20 .50
2 Marek Kvapil .20 .50
3 Jean-Michel Rizk .20 .50
4 Paul Bissonnette .20 .50
5 Patrick Asselin .20 .50
6 Peter Franchin .20 .50
7 Rick Caughell .20 .50
8 Kevin Tuckey .20 .50
9 Gary Klapkowski .20 .50
10 Scott Fletcher .20 .50
11 Daniel Borges .20 .50
12 Jamie Klie .20 .50
13 Chris Ferguson .20 .50
14 Taylor Raszka .20 .50
15 Dan Idema .20 .50
16 Chase Crowder .20 .50
17 Tom Pyatt .30 .75
18 Thomas Harrison .20 .50
19 Sean Courtney .20 .50
20 Aaron Rock .20 .50
21 Jesse Gimblett .20 .50
22 Matt Corrente .40 1.00
23 Mike Brown .30 .75
24 Mascot .04 .10

2005-06 Saginaw Spirit

COMPLETE SET (24) 6.00 12.00
1 Patrick Asselin .20 .50
2 Michal Birner .20 .50
3 Chris Chappell .20 .50
4 Jack Combs .20 .50
5 Matt Corrente .40 1.00
6 Tom Craig .20 .50
7 Ryan Daniels .20 .50
8 Chris Ferguson .20 .50
9 Scott Fletcher .20 .50
10 Jesse Gimblett .20 .50
11 Tyson Gimblett .20 .50
12 Jamie Klie .20 .50
13 Erik Lundmark .20 .50
14 Tom Mannino .20 .50
15 Joe McCann .20 .50
16 Ryan McDonough .20 .50
17 Patrick McNeill .20 .50
18 Tim Priamo .20 .50
19 Tom Pyatt .40 1.00
20 Garrett Sinfield .20 .50
21 Anthony Soboczynski .20 .50
22 Francois Thuot .40 1.00
23 Zack Torquato .20 .50
24 Steven Whitely .20 .50

2006-07 Saginaw Spirit

COMPLETE SET (25) 8.00 15.00
1 Tom Pyatt .40 1.00
2 Patrick Mcneill .30 .75
3 Garrett Sinfield .20 .50
4 Curtis Cooper .20 .50
5 Nick Crawford .20 .50
6 Tommy Mannino .20 .50
7 Christopher Breen .20 .50
8 Tomas Zaborsky .20 .50
9 Jan Mursak .20 .50
10 Matt Corrente .30 .75
11 Tyler Haskins .20 .50
12 Andrew Cloutier .20 .50
13 Tom Craig .20 .50
14 Chris Chappell .20 .50
15 Ryan Daniels .40 1.00
16 Jack Combs .20 .50
17 Zack Torquato .40 1.00
18 Patrick Asselin .20 .50
19 Jovica Zelenbaba .20 .50
20 T.J. Brodie .20 .50
21 Ryan Berard .20 .50
22 Ryan McDonough .20 .50
23 Sammy Spirit MASCOT .10 .25
24 Steagle Colbeagle MASCOT .40 1.00
LE1 Patrick Mcneill .75 2.00

2014-15 Saginaw Spirit

COMPLETE SET (24) 6.00 15.00
1 Nick Moutrey .30 .75
2 Artem Artemov .30 .75
3 Jacob Ringuette .30 .75
4 Blake Clarke .30 .75
5 Tye Felhaber .30 .75
6 Jake Paterson .30 .75
7 Keaton Middleton .30 .75
8 Luke Cairns .30 .75
9 David Ovsjannikov .30 .75
10 Nikita Serebryakov .30 .75
11 Mitchell Stephens .30 .75
12 Jack Webb .30 .75
13 Jimmy Lodge .30 .75
14 Connor Brown .30 .75
15 Adam McPhail .30 .75
16 Devon Paliani .30 .75
17 Mitchell Webb .30 .75
18 Michael Holmes .30 .75
19 Kris Bennett .30 .75
20 Dylan Sadowy .30 .75
21 Ryan Orban .30 .75
22 Marcus Crawford .30 .75
23 Sean Callaghan .30 .75
CL Header Card CL .30 .75

1994-95 Saint John Flames

This 26-card standard-size set was manufactured and distributed by Jessen Associates, Inc. for Classic. The fronts display color action player photos with a red marbleized inner border and a black outer border. The player's name, jersey number, and position appear in the teal border on the right edge. The cards are unnumbered and checklisted below in alphabetical order.

COMPLETE SET (26) 3.00 8.00
1 Joel Bouchard .20 .50
2 Rick Carriere ACO .02 .10
3 Ryan Duthie .08 .25
4 Neil Eisenhut .08 .25
5 Leonard Esau .08 .25
6 Bob Francis CO .02 .10
7 Mark Greig .08 .25
8 Francois Groleau .08 .25
9 Sami Helenius .30 .75
10 Todd Hlushko .20 .50
11 Dale Kushner .08 .25
12 Bobby Marshall .08 .25
13 Scott Morrow .08 .25
14 Michael Murray .08 .25
15 Jason Muzzatti .30 .75
16 Barry Nieckar .08 .25
17 Nicolas Perreault .08 .25
18 Jeff Perry .08 .25
19 Dwayne Roloson .30 .75
20 Todd Simpson .08 .25
21 Harbour Station .02 .10
22 Cory Stillman .30 .75
23 David Struch .08 .25
24 Niklas Sundblad .08 .25
25 Andrei Trefilov .20 .50
26 Vesa Viitakoski .08 .25

1996-97 Saint John Flames

This set features the Flames of the AHL. The cards were produced by SplitSecond and sold at home games. The cards are unnumbered, and so are listed below alphabetically.

COMPLETE SET (26) 4.00 10.00
1 Jamie Allison .15 .40
2 Chris Dingman .20 .50
3 Scott Fraser .15 .40
4 Denis Gauthier .15 .40
5 Ian Gordon .15 .40
6 Patrik Haltia .20 .50
7 Sami Helenius .30 .75
8 Marc Hussey .15 .40
9 Marko Jantunen .20 .50
10 Ladislav Kohn .15 .40
11 Martin Lamarche .15 .40
12 Jesper Mattsson .20 .50
13 Keith McCambridge .15 .40
14 Dale McTavish .15 .40
15 Burke Murphy .15 .40
16 Marty Murray .30 .75
17 Paxton Schulte .15 .40
18 Jarrod Skalde .30 .75
19 Jason Smith .30 .75
20 Clarke Wilm .20 .50
21 Ravil Yakubov .15 .40
22 Paul Baxter CO .08 .25
23 Jeff Perry CO .08
24 Fleaburn MAS .02
25 AHL Web Site .01
26 PHPA Web Site .01

1995-96 Saint John Flames

This 25-card set features borderless color action pl[...] photos of the Saint John Flames of the AHL. The ba[...] carry player information and statistics. The cards a[...] unnumbered and checklisted below in alphabetical order.

COMPLETE SET (25) 15.00 40
1 Jamie Allison .60 1
2 Paul Baxter CO .60 1
3 Joel Bouchard .60 1
4 Tom Coolen CO .60 1
5 Brett Duncan .60 1
6 Ian Gordon .60 1
7 Sami Helenius 1.25 3
8 Todd Hlushko .60 1
9 Marc Hussey .60 1
10 Ladislav Kohn .60 1
11 Frank Kovacs .60 1
12 David Ling .75 2.
13 Jesper Mattsson .60 1.
14 Keith McCambridge .60 1.
15 Marty Murray .75 2
16 Michael Murray .60
17 David Neilson .60 1.
18 Jeff Perry .60 1.
19 Darren Ritchie .60 1.
20 Dwayne Roloson 6.00 15.
21 Todd Simpson .60 1.
22 Jarrod Skalde .75 2.
23 David Struch .60 1.
24 Niklas Sundblad .75 2.
25 Vesa Viitakoski .60 1.

1997-98 Saint John Flames

This set features the Flames of the AHL. The cards w[...] produced by the team and sold at home games and [...] mail.

COMPLETE SET (25) 8.00 15.
1 Jamie Allison .15
2 Erik Andersson .15
3 Ryan Bast .15
4 Travis Brigley .15
5 Eric Charron .15
6 Jeff Cowan .30
7 Hnat Domenichelli .20
8 Jim Dowd .20
9 Denis Gauthier .30
10 Jean-Sebastien Giguere 2.00 5.
11 Sami Helenius .30
12 Ladislav Kohn .15
13 Eric Landry .15
14 Jesper Mattsson .15
15 Keith McCambridge .15
16 Tyler Moss .20
17 Burke Murphy .15
18 Marty Murray .20
19 Chris O'Sullivan .15
20 Paxton Schulte .20
21 Rocky Thompson .15
22 John Tripp .20
23 Clarke Wilm .15
24 Bill Stewart HCO .08
25 Jeff Perry CO .08

2005-06 Saint John Sea Dogs

COMPLETE SET (24) 6.00 12.0
1 Jason Churchill .40 1.0
2 Alex Grant .20 .5
3 Alexandre Monahan .20 .5
4 Alexandre Labonte .20 .5
5 Brett Gallant .20 .5
6 Cedric Archambault .20 .5
7 Charles Bergeron .40 1.0
8 Felix Schutz .40 1.0
9 Jean-Philippe Cote .20 .5
10 Jeff Caron .20 .5
11 Jevin Maclellan .20 .5
12 Jonathan Laberge .20 .5
13 Kevin Coughlin .20 .5
14 Martin Bartos .20 .5
15 Maxime Dubuc .20 .5
16 Mike Neil .20 .5
17 Patrick Leask .20 .5
18 Riley Whitlock .40 1.0
19 Ryan Moore .20 .50
20 Ryan Sparling .20 .50
21 Sebastien Rioux .20 .50
22 Vincent Lambert .20 .50
23 Matthew Block .20 .50
24 Luc Melanson .20 .50

2006-07 Saint John Sea Dogs

COMPLETE SET (25) 8.00 15.00
1 Alex Grant .40 1.00
2 Mike Noyers .25 .60
3 Ryan Sparling .25 .60
4 Felix Schutz .40 1.00
5 David Macdonald .25 .60
6 Dave Bouchard .25 .60
7 Bruce Crawford .25 .60
8 Sebastien Rioux .25 .60
9 Jonathan Laberge .25 .60
10 Mike Thomas .25 .60
11 Charles Bergeron .25 .60
12 Shayne Tremblay .25 .60
13 Maxime Dubuc .25 .60
14 Alexandre Labonte .25 .60
15 Olivier Painchaud .25 .60
16 David Stich .25 .60
17 Chris Didomenico .25 .60
18 Alexandre Monohan .25 .60
19 Anthony Bergin .25 .60
20 Maxime Joyal .40 1.00
21 Aaron Barton .40 1.00
22 Pascal Amyot .25 .60
23 Brett Gallant .25 .60
24 Yann Sauve .25 .60
LE1 Alex Grant .75 2.00

2015-16 Saint John Sea Dogs

COMPLETE SET (25) 6.00 15.00
1 Adam Bateman .30 .75
2 Jason Bell .30 .75
3 Alex Bishop .30 .75
4 Thomas Chabot .30 .75
5 Austin Clapman .30 .75
6 Daniel Del Paggio .30 .75
7 Samuel Dove-Mcfalls .30 .75
8 Oliver Felixson .30 .75
9 Matt Green .30 .75
10 Luke Green .30 .75
11 Matthew Highmore .30 .75
12 Bokondji Imana .30 .75
13 Mathieu Joseph .30 .75
14 Adam Marsh .30 .75
15 Nathan Noel .30 .75

16 Sam Povoroznlouk .30 .75
17 Spencer Smallman .30 .75
18 Julien Tessier .30 .75
19 Dawson Theede .30 .75
20 Marc-Antoine Turcotte .30 .75
21 Joe Veleno .30 .75
22 Joe Veleno FG .30 .75
23 Kyle Ward .30 .75
24 Bailey Webster .30 .75
25 Jakub Zboril .30 .75

2003-04 Salmon Arm Silverbacks

The set features the Silverbacks of the BCJHL, including two 2004 first rounders in Chucko and Zajac. The set is unnumbered and listed in alphabetical order.

COMPLETE SET (25) 8.00 20.00
1 Evan Barlow .20 .50
2 Jay Birnie .40 1.00
3 Steve Christie .40 1.00
4 Kris Chucko 1.25 3.00
5 Rick Cleaver .20 .50
6 Spencer Dillon .20 .50
7 Bryn Gagnon .20 .50
8 Trevor Geiger .20 .50
9 Blaine Jarvis .20 .50
10 Jaye Judd .20 .50
11 Patrick Lepage .40 1.00
12 Julian Marcuzzi .20 .50
13 Tyrell Mason .20 .50
14 Ryan McLeod .20 .50
15 Jason Miller .20 .50
16 Travis Ramsey .20 .50
17 Chris Shudo .20 .50
18 Kiel Sonne .40 1.00
19 Ben Street .20 .50
20 Craig Switzer .20 .50
21 Travis Zajac 2.00 5.00
22 Header Card .04 .10
23 Award Winners .40 1.00
24 Header Card .04 .10
25 Team Photo .20 .50

2004-05 Salmon Arm Silverbacks

COMPLETE SET (24) 5.00 12.00
1 Jamie Silverson .30 .75
2 Brendon Nash .30 .75
3 Dustin Degagne .30 .75
4 Robbie Rodgers .30 .75
5 Mark Santorelli .30 .75
6 Brodie Sheahan .30 .75
7 Ben Street .30 .75
8 Tyrell Mason .30 .75
9 Darcy Zajac .40 1.00
10 Bryn Gagnon .30 .75
11 Trevor Geiger .30 .75
12 Luke Cain .30 .75
13 Ryan Duncan .30 .75
14 Ernie Stewart .30 .75
15 Kiel Sonne .30 .75
16 Jesse Deckert .30 .75
17 Brad Atkinson .30 .75
18 Evan Barlow .30 .75
19 Julian Marcuzzi .30 .75
20 Jesse Griffith .30 .75
21 Kong MASCOT .04 .10
22 Team Card .04 .10
23 Logo Card .04 .10
24 Logo Card .30 .75

2005-06 Salmon Arm Silverbacks

COMPLETE SET (25) 10.00 20.00
1 Logo .01 .01
2 Logo .01 .01
3 August Aiken .40 1.00
4 Billy Blase .40 1.00
5 Luke Cain .40 1.00
6 Dustin Degagne .40 1.00
7 Matt Dyck .40 1.00
8 Jesse Griffith .40 1.00
9 Travis Holloway .40 1.00
10 Damon Kipp .40 1.00
11 Josh Lund .40 1.00
12 Cam Macintyre .40 1.00
13 Brendon Nash .40 1.00
14 Evan Pighin .40 1.00
15 Chris Rawlings .40 1.00
16 Rob Rodgers .40 1.00
17 Brodie Sheahan .40 1.00
18 Erik Spady .40 1.00
19 Ernie Stewart .40 1.00
20 Justin Taylor .40 1.00
21 Ben Winnet .40 1.00
22 Shaun Witschen .40 1.00
23 Darcy Zajac .40 1.00
24 Kong ♦MASCOT• .01 .01
25 Ad Card .01 .01

2014-15 Salmon Arm Silverbacks

COMPLETE SET (20) 5.00 12.00
1 Angus Redmond .30 .75
2 Phillip Middleton .30 .75
3 Andrew Farny .30 .75
4 Chase Priskie .30 .75
5 Ryley Booth .30 .75
6 Damian Chrcek .30 .75
7 Logan Mick .30 .75
8 Nick Hutchison .30 .75
9 Carson Bolduc .30 .75
10 Thomas Plese .30 .75
11 Josh Blanchard .30 .75
12 Taro Hirose .30 .75
13 Jack Berezan .30 .75
14 Colton Thibault .30 .75
15 Shane Danyluk .30 .75
16 Ross Heidt .30 .75
17 Bryden Marsh .30 .75
18 Taylor Maruya .30 .75
19 Josh Laframboise .30 .75
20 Zach Dyment .30 .75

1988-89 Salt Lake Golden Eagles

Commemorating the 20th anniversary of the Salt Lake Golden Eagles, this 24-card standard-size set features color close-up shots against a light blue background. The player's name and position are printed diagonally in black across the front. The set was sponsored by the USDA Forest Service and Utah State Lands and Forestry agency. Card number 10 was never issued.

COMPLETE SET (24) 12.00 30.00
1 Rick Barkovich .20 .50
2 Michael Dark .20 .50
3 Terry Perkins .20 .50
4 Peter Lappin .20 .50
5 Wayne Cowley .20 .50
6 Rich Chernomaz .20 .50
7 Steve Smith .40 1.00
8 Theo Fleury 8.00 20.00
9 Dave Reierson .20 .50
10 Not Issued .20 .50
11 Martin Simard .20 .50
12 Stu Grimson 1.25 3.00
13 Darwin McCutcheon .20 .50
14 Doug Clarke .20 .50
15 Doug Pickell .20 .50
16 Randy Bucyk .20 .50
17 Jim Johannson .20 .50
18 Rick Lessard .20 .50
19 Ken Sabourin .20 .50
20 Chris Biotti .20 .50
21 Jeff Wenaas .20 .50
22 Mark Holmes .20 .50
23 Bob Bodak .20 .50
24 Marc Bureau .40 1.00
NNO Smokey the Bear .20 .50

1992-93 Salt Lake Golden Eagles

Little is known about this set beyond the confirmed checklist. Any additional information should be forwarded to hockeymag@beckett.com.

COMPLETE SET (26) 4.00 10.00
1 Todd Brost .15 .40
2 Rod Buskas .15 .40
3 Rich Chernomaz .15 .40
4 Kerry Clark .15 .40
5 Tomas Forslund .15 .40
6 Todd Gillingham .15 .40
7 Todd Harkins .15 .40
8 Tim Harris .15 .40
9 Shawn Heaphy .15 .40
10 Paul Holden .15 .40
11 Trevor Kidd .40 1.00
12 Paul Kruse .20 .50
13 Patrick Lebeau .20 .50
14 Sandy McCarthy .30 .75
15 Kris Miller .15 .40
16 Jason Muzzatti .20 .50
17 Alex Nikolic .15 .40
18 Ken Sabourin .15 .40
19 David St. Pierre .15 .40
20 Darren Stolk .15 .40
21 David Sturch .15 .40
22 Andrei Trefilov .20 .50
23 Kevin Wortman .15 .40
24 Bob Francis CO .08 .25
25 Brian Patafie TR .02 .10
26 Team card .15 .40

1998-99 San Angelo Outlaws

This 27-card set was handed out early in the season over the span of several home games.

COMPLETE SET (27) 7.20 18.00
1 Jason Abel .30 .75
2 Jean Blouin .30 .75
3 Carl Boudreau .40 1.00
4 Daniel Chaput .30 .75
5 Ryan Connolly .30 .75
6 Brad Cook .30 .75
7 Marty Diamond .30 .75
8 Chad Erickson .40 1.00
9 Sandis Girvitch .30 .75
10 Ross Harris .40 1.00
11 Kevin McKinnon .30 .75
12 Aigars Mironovics .30 .75
13 Skeeter Moore .30 .75
14 Carl Paradis .40 1.00
15 Ryan Reid .30 .75
16 Al Rooney .30 .75
17 Shayne Stevenson .40 1.00
18 Mike Vandenberghe .30 .75
19 Kris Waltze .30 .75
20 Tom Nurre .30 .75
21 Rich Van Patten EM .08 .25
22 Shaun Clouston CO .08 .25
23 Ransom Mascot .08 .25
24 Rusty Mascot .08 .25
25 Jay Willman ANNC .08 .25
26 Jonathan Luce .30 .75
27 Joe Briley TR .08 .25

1999-00 San Angelo Outlaws

This 31-card set was sold by the team a the rink and through the mail. The set is numbered on the back up to 35, however, card numbers 16,20,25,and 30 do not exist.

COMPLETE SET (31) 30.00 75.00
1 Mike Bajurny 1.50 4.00
2 Scott Chartier 1.25 3.00
3 Jamie Garrick 1.25 3.00
4 Sandis Girvitch 1.25 3.00
5 Corey Isen 1.25 3.00
6 Ed Kowalski 1.25 3.00
7 Kevin Kreutzer 1.50 4.00
8 Adam Lord 1.50 4.00
9 Dave Lylyk 1.25 3.00
10 Kevin McKinnon 1.25 3.00
11 Skeeter Moore 1.25 3.00
12 Erik Noack 1.25 3.00
13 Carl Paradis 1.50 4.00
14 Pavel Evstigneev 1.25 3.00
15 Robby Sandrock 1.25 3.00
17 Kris Waltze 1.50 4.00
18 Dion Wandler 1.25 3.00
19 Darren Wright 1.25 3.00
21 San Angelo Coliseum .40 1.00
22 Frank Froio EQM .40 1.00
23 Jeff Smith 1.25 3.00
24 Harvard .40 1.00
Henry
26 Mike Collins CO .40 1.00
27 Off-Ice Officials .40 1.00
28 Ransom Mascot .40 1.00
29 Rusty Mascot .40 1.00
31 Inflatable Rusty .40 1.00
32 Side Rink Action .40 1.00
33 Team Photo .40 1.00
34 Jay Willman 1.25 3.00
35 Booster Club .40 1.00

1998-99 San Antonio Iguanas

This 21-card set was sold by the team at games and via mail order. The Jason MacIntyre card may have been pulled from some of the sets due to his lifetime ban from the WCHL that was issued during this season.

COMPLETE SET (21) 4.80 12.00
1 Ken Shepard .20 .50
2 John Hultberg .40 1.00
3 Brian Shantz .40 1.00
4 Paul Jackson .40 1.00
5 Iggy Mascot .02 .10
6 Jason MacIntyre .75 2.00
7 Pat Caron .20 .50
8 Mike Tobin .20 .50
9 Dave Doucette .20 .50
10 Marc Laforge .20 .50
11 Kevin Lune .20 .50
12 Jay Pylypuik .20 .50
13 Johnny Brdarovic .20 .50
14 Roy Gray .20 .50
15 Ricky Jacob .20 .50
16 Blair Rota .20 .50
17 Cheyne Lazar .20 .50
18 Trevor Matschke .20 .50
19 Fred Goltz .20 .50
20 Todd Gordon HCO .02 .10
21 Iguanas Cheerleaders .40 1.00

1999-00 San Antonio Iguanas

This set features the Iguanas of the CHL. The set was produced and sold by the team at home games.

COMPLETE SET (25) 4.00 10.00
1 San Antonio Iguanas .20 .50
2 Church's Chicken .10 .25
3 Jason MacIntyre .20 .50
4 Trevor Matschke .20 .50
5 Johnny Brdarovich .20 .50
6 Scott Green .20 .50
7 Brian Shantz .30 .75
8 Henry Kuster .30 .75
9 Bob Westerby .30 .75
10 Blair Rota .20 .50
11 Garnet Jacobson .20 .50
12 Ricky Jacob .20 .50
13 Jeff Boettger .20 .50
14 Wade Gibson .20 .50
15 Sam Fields .20 .50
16 Marc Laforge .30 .75
17 Trevor Anderson .20 .50
18 Corwin Saurdiff .30 .75
19 Mitch Shawara .20 .50
20 Chris Stewart CO .08 .25
21 Craig Coxe CO .30 .75
22 Manny Sanchez TR .02 .10
23 Chad Daniels TR .02 .10
24 Iggy MAS .02 .10
25 San Antonio Iguanas CL .02 .10

2003-04 San Antonio Rampage

COMPLETE SET (24) 5.00 12.00
1 Scott Allen HCO .04 .10
2 Ian Herbers ACO .04 .10
3 Lukas Krajicek .30 .75
4 Daryl Andrews .30 .75
5 Mascot .04 .10
6 Kent Huskins .20 .50
7 Paul Elliott .20 .50
8 Grant McNeill .20 .50
9 Vaclav Nedorost .20 .50
10 Greg Campbell .30 .75
11 Sean O'Connor .20 .50
12 Ryan Jardine .20 .50
13 Brent Cullaton .20 .50
14 Denis Shvidki .20 .50
15 Josh Olson .20 .50
16 Eric Beaudoin .20 .50
17 Matt Dzieduszycki .20 .50
18 Petr Taticek .40 1.00
19 Michel Periard .20 .50
20 Simon Lajeunesse .40 1.00
21 Kristian Kudroc .20 .50
22 Lee Goren .30 .75
23 Travis Scott .30 .75
24 Sponsor .04 .10

2004-05 San Antonio Rampage

These cards are not numbered. Issued as a stadium giveaway.

COMPLETE SET (22) 10.00 25.00
1 Mascot .04 .10
2 Lukas Krajicek .40 1.00
3 T.J. Reynolds .40 1.00
4 Jay Bouwmeester .75 2.00
5 Filip Novak .40 1.00
6 Joel Kwiatkowski .40 1.00
7 Serge Payer .40 1.00
8 Stephen Weiss .75 2.00
9 Chris Nielsen .40 1.00
10 Gregory Campbell .75 2.00
11 Joe Cullen .40 1.00
12 Ryan Jardine .40 1.00
13 Rob Globke .75 2.00
14 Nathan Horton .75 2.00
15 Juraj Kolnik .40 1.00
16 Jeff Brown .40 1.00
17 Petr Taticek .40 1.00
18 Kamil Kreps .40 1.00
19 Patrick DesRochers .75 2.00
20 Victor Uchevatov .40 1.00
21 Travis Scott .40 1.00
22 Greg Jacina .40 1.00

1995-96 San Diego Barracudas RHI

This 14-card set is blank-backed, and features card fronts with varying border colours. Any additional information can be forwarded to hockeymag@beckett.com.

COMPLETE SET (14) 2.00 5.00
1 Dan Elsener .20 .50
2 Sandy Gasseau .20 .50
3 Brad Belland .20 .50
4 Stephen Grogg .20 .50
5 Frankie Ouellette .30 .75
6 Alan Leggett .20 .50
7 Soren True .20 .50
8 John Spoltore .30 .75
9 Ralph Barahona .20 .50
10 Oleg Yashin .20 .50
11 Stephane St. Amour .20 .50
12 Max Middendorf .30 .75
13 Clark Polgase .20 .50
14 Steve Martinson HCO .08 .25

1992-93 San Diego Gulls

This 24-card standard-size set features full-bleed, color player photos. The player's name is superimposed on the picture in red lettering. The player's position appears in a black circle in the lower left corner. The cards are unnumbered and checklisted below in alphabetical order.

COMPLETE SET (24) 4.00 10.00
1 John Anderson .20 .50
2 Perry Anderson .15 .40
3 Scott Arniel .20 .50
4 Michael Brewer .15 .40
5 Dale DeGray .15 .40
6 Gord Dineen .15 .40
7 Rick Dudley CO .15 .40
8 Larry Floyd .15 .40
9 Keith Gretzky .20 .50
10 Peter Hankinson .15 .40
11 Bill Houlder .20 .50
12 Andrei Iakovenko .15 .40
13 Rick Knickle .30 .75
14 Denny Lambert .20 .50
15 Mitch Lamoureux .20 .50
16 Clint Malarchuk .30 .75
17 Steve Martinson .15 .40
18 Huble McDonough .20 .50
19 Don McSween .15 .40
20 Mitch Molloy .15 .40
21 Robbie Nichols .15 .40
22 Lindy Ruff .20 .50
23 Daniel Shank .30 .75
24 Sergei Starikov .15 .40

1999-00 San Diego Gulls

This set features the Gulls of the WCHL. The unnumbered cards were handed out in two different packs of 10 at a single home game late in the season.

COMPLETE SET (20) 6.00 15.00
1 Rod Aldoff .20 .50
2 Brad Belland .20 .50
3 Jamie Black .30 .75
4 Frederick Jobin .20 .50
5 Olaf Kjenstadt .30 .75
6 Brett Larson .20 .50
7 Steven Low .20 .50
8 B.J. MacPherson .20 .50
9 Petr Marek .20 .50
10 Taj Melson .20 .50
11 Sergei Naumov .60 1.50
12 Barry Potomski .60 1.50
13 Dennis Purdie .60 1.50
14 Martin St. Amour .30 .75
15 Stephane St. Amour .30 .75
16 Mark Woolf .30 .75
17 Steve Martinson HCO .30 .75
18 Gulls Win .20 .50
19 Goal Celebration .20 .50
20 Gulls Girls Cheerleaders .40 1.00

2000-01 San Diego Gulls

This set features the Gulls of the WCHL. The set was produced by Grandstand Cards and was sold by the team at its souvenir stands.

COMPLETE SET (22) 3.60 10.00
1 Jamie Black .16 .40
2 Cris Classen .16 .75
3 Serge Crochetiere .16 .40
4 Dan Gravelle .16 .40
5 Trevor Koenig .16 .75
6 Ashley Langdone .16 1.00
7 Brett Larson .16 .40
8 Cory Laylin .16 .40
9 B.J. MacPherson .16 .40
10 Kevin Mackie .16 .40
11 Petr Marek .16 .40
12 Taj Melson .16 .40
13 Brian Morrison .16 .40
14 Samy Nasreddine .16 .40
15 Jeff Petruic .16 .40
16 Dennis Purdie .30 .75
17 Mark Stitt .16 .40
18 Mike Taylor .16 .40
19 Chad Wagner .16 .40
20 Mark Woolf .16 .40
21 Gulls Score! .10 .25
22 San Diego Gulls Bench .16 .40

2001-02 San Diego Gulls

This set features the Gulls of the WCHL. These cards were handed out at a game on December 28, 2001. The set is unnumbered and is listed in alphabetical order.

COMPLETE SET (24) 10.00 25.00
1 Boyd Ballard .40 1.00
2 Jamie Black .40 1.00
3 Clint Cabana .40 1.00
4 Serge Crochetiere .40 1.00
5 Jaisen Freeman .40 1.00
6 Dan Gravelle .40 1.00
7 Trevor Koenig .40 1.00
8 Ashley Langdone .40 1.00
9 Shawn Mansoff .40 1.00
10 Petr Marek .40 1.00
11 Taj Melson .40 1.00
12 Brian Morrison .40 1.00
13 Samy Nasreddine .60 1.50
14 Billy Pugliese .40 1.00
15 Dennis Purdie .75 2.00
16 Trevor Sherban .40 1.00
17 John Spoltore .75 2.00
18 Mark Stitt .40 1.00
19 Mark Woolf .75 2.00
20 B.J. MacPherson .60 1.50
21 Gulls Girls .75 2.00
22 Sandy MASCOT .04 .10
23 Gulls Bench .04 .10
24 Gulls Score! .20 .50

1994-95 San Jose Rhinos RHI

This set features the Rhinos of Roller Hockey Intl. The cards were sold in set form by the team at home games.

COMPLETE SET (16) 3.00 8.00
1 Rocky Mascot .08 .25
2 Ken Blum .20 .50
3 Steve Carpenter .20 .50
4 Will Clarke .20 .50
5 Darren Colbourne .20 .50
6 Bart Cote .20 .50
7 Brian Goudie .20 .50
8 Jon Gustafson .30 .75
9 Greg Hadden .20 .50
10 Blaine Moore .20 .50
11 Jay Murphy .20 .50
12 Dennis Purdie .40 1.00
13 Roy Sommer CO .08 .25
14 Mike Taylor .20 .50
15 Darren Wetherill .20 .50
16 Mark Woolf .30 .75

1994-95 Sarnia Sting

Sponsored by Big V Drug Stores and Pizza Hut and printed by Slapshot Images Ltd., this 31-card set commemorates the Sting's inaugural year. On a black and silver background, the fronts feature color action player photos with thin grey borders. The player's name, position and team name, as well as the producer's logo, also appear on the front.

COMPLETE SET (31) 4.00 10.00
1 Checklist .02 .10
2 Ken Carroll .10 .30
3 Scott Hay .10 .30
4 Kam White .10 .30
5 Joe Doyle .10 .30
6 Tom Brown .10 .30
7 Jeremy Miculinic .10 .30
8 Darren Mortier .10 .30
9 Aaron Brand .20 .50
10 Chris George .10 .30
11 Stephane Soulliere .10 .30
12 Paul McInnes .10 .30
13 Trevor Letowski .40 1.00
14 Dustin McArthur .10 .30
15 Rob Massa .10 .30
16 Brendan Yarema .10 .30
17 Dan DelMonte .10 .30
18 B.J. Johnston .10 .30
19 Wes Mason .10 .30
20 Rob Guinn .10 .30
21 Jeff Brown .10 .30
22 Dennis Maxwell .10 .30
23 Damon Hardy .10 .30
24 Alan Letang .20 .50
25 Matt Hogan .10 .30
26 Sasha Cucuz .10 .30
27 Rich Brown CO .02 .10
28 Gord Hamilton TR .02 .10
29 Dino Ciccarelli .20 .50
Shawn Burr
30 Buzz MASCOT .02 .10
NNO Ad Card .02 .10

1995-96 Sarnia Sting

COMPLETE SET (25) 5.00 12.00
1 Jeff Salajko .20 .50
2 Patrick DesRochers .30 .75
3 Gerald Moriarity .20 .50
4 Allan Carr .20 .50
5 Tom Brown .20 .50
6 Andy Delmore .30 .75
7 Darren Mortier .20 .50
8 Aaron Brand .20 .50
9 Eric Boulton .60 1.50
10 Jonathan Sim .30 .75
11 Trevor Letowski .30 .75
12 Mike Hanson .20 .50
13 Todd Miller .20 .50
14 Brendan Yarema .20 .50
15 Brad Simms .20 .50
16 David Nemirovsky .20 .50
17 Jeff Brown .20 .50
18 Andrew Proskurnicki .20 .50
19 Wes Mason .20 .50
20 Scott Corbett .20 .50
21 Dave Bourque .20 .50
22 Sean Brown .20 .50
23 Marcin Snita .20 .50
24 Rich Brown ACO .02 .10
25 Mark Hunter HCO .08 .25

1996-97 Sarnia Sting

This attractive 31-card set was produced by Haines Printing for the Sting and was distributed by the club at the rink. The cards feature action photography on the front, with the player's name and number, and the insignia of the sponsor, Bayview Chrysler, along the bottom. The set is noteworthy for the inclusion of a special card of captain Trevor Letowski as a member of the Canadian National Junior team.

COMPLETE SET (31) 6.00 10.00
1 Bill Abercrombie ACO .10 .25
2 Louie Blackbird .15 .40
3 Bryan Blair .15 .40
4 Dave Bourque .15 .40
5 Joe Canale CO .10 .25
6 Scott Corbett .15 .40
7 Andy Delmore .30 .75
8 Patrick DesRochers .30 .75
9 Michael Hanson .15 .40
10 Abe Herbst .20 .50
11 Shane Kenny .15 .40
12 Darryl Knight .15 .40
13 Trevor Letowski .40 1.00
14 Trevor Letowski .40 1.00
15 Wes Mason .20 .50
16 Darren Mortier .15 .40
17 Kevin Mota .15 .40
18 Eoin McInerney .30 .75
19 Lucas Nehrling .15 .40
20 Dan Pawlaczyk .15 .40
21 Andrew Proskurnicki .15 .40
22 Richard Rochefort .15 .40
23 Bogdan Rudenko .15 .40
24 Jon Sim .40 1.00
25 Brad Simms .15 .40
26 Marcin Snita .15 .40
27 Casey Wolak .15 .40
28 Season Line-Up .02 .10
29 Title Card .10 .25
30 Team Logo .10 .25
31 Calendar Card .02 .10

2000-01 Sarnia Sting

This set features the Sting of the OHL. The set was produced by the team and sold at home games. The cards are unnumbered, and are listed below alphabetically.

COMPLETE SET (24) 4.80 12.00
1 Header Card .04 .10
2 Larry Bernard CO .10 .25
3 Chris Berti .20 .50
4 Cory Brekelmans .20 .50
5 Rick Brown CO .10 .25
6 Alex Buturlin .20 .50
7 Adam Campbell .20 .50
8 Tyler Coleman .20 .50
9 Ryan Fraser .20 .50
10 Robert Gherson .40 1.00
11 Julius Halfkenny .20 .50
12 Ryan Hare .20 .50
13 John Hecimovic .20 .50
14 Scott Heffernan .20 .50
15 Eric Himelfarb .40 1.00
16 Dusty Jamieson .30 .75
17 Jeff Luckovitch .20 .50
18 Preston Mizzi .20 .50
19 Kris Newbury .30 .75
20 Robb Palahnuk .20 .50
21 Jason Penner .30 .75
22 Tom Rogerson .20 .50
23 Maxim Rybin .30 .75
24 Reg Thomas .20 .50

2003-04 Sarnia Sting

COMPLETE SET (23) 5.00 12.00
1 Charles Amodeo .20 .50
2 John Barrow .30 .75
3 Marco Caprara .30 .75
4 Daniel Carcillo .75 2.00
5 Marek Chvatal .20 .50
6 Richard Clune .20 .50
7 Craig Foster .20 .50
8 Dan Fritsche .75 2.00
9 Micheal Haley .20 .50
10 John Hecimovic .20 .50
11 Anton Kadeykin .20 .50
12 Colt King .30 .75
13 Drew Larman .20 .50
14 Matt Manias .20 .50
15 Ryan Munce .60 1.50
16 Matt Pelech .20 .50
17 David Pszenyczny .20 .50
18 Daniel Sisca .20 .50
19 Trevor Solomon .20 .50
20 Joey Tenute .30 .75
21 Steve Ward .20 .50
22 Jeff Whitfield .20 .50
23 Kelsey Wilson .20 .50

2006-07 Sarnia Sting

COMPLETE SET (22) 12.00 20.00
1 Steven Stamkos 4.00 10.00
2 Trevor Kell .30 .75
3 Tomas Pospisil .30 .75
4 Steven Reese .30 .75
5 Steve Ferry .30 .75
6 Sebastian Dahm .40 1.00
7 Ryan Wilson .30 .75
8 Parker Van Buskirk .40 1.00
9 Mike Roelofsen .30 .75
10 Matt Martin .30 .75
11 Mark Katic .50 1.25
12 Kyle Tront .30 .75
13 Justin Dibenedetto .30 .75
14 Jared Gomes .30 .75
15 Harrison Reed .30 .75
16 Danny Anger .30 .75
17 Daniel Lombardi .30 .75
18 Dalton Prout .30 .75
19 Christian Steingraber .30 .75
20 Chris Mifflen .30 .75
21 Brandon Mashinter .30 .75
22 Bobby Davey .30 .75

2007-08 Sarnia Sting

COMPLETE SET (25) 5.00 12.00
1 Tomi Karhunen .15 .40
2 Peter DiSalvo .15 .40
3 Ryan Berard .15 .40
4 Justin DiBenedetto .15 .40
5 Devin Didiomete .15 .40
6 Steve Ferry .15 .40
7 Jared Gomes .15 .40
8 Jordan Hill .15 .40
9 Marek Indra .15 .40
10 Mark Katic .15 .40
11 Colt Kennedy .15 .40
12 Dan Lombardi .15 .40
13 Matt Martin .15 .40
14 Brett Oliphant .15 .40
15 Ben O'Quinn .15 .40
16 Dalton Prout .15 .40
17 Harrison Reed .15 .40
18 Steve Reese .15 .40
19 Joe Rogalski .15 .40
20 Matt Smyth .15 .40
21 Steven Stamkos 1.00 2.50
22 Steve Whitely .15 .40
23 Ryan Wilson .15 .40
24 Aaron Snow .15 .40
25 Jamie Arniel .15 .40

1992-93 Saskatchewan JHL

This 168-card set features players in the Saskatchewan Junior Hockey League. The cards are slightly larger than standard size, measuring 2 9/16" by 3 9/16." The fronts feature color action player photos with team color-coded borders at the top and bottom. The player's name and position appear in the top border. The team name and logo appear in the wider bottom border.

COMPLETE SET (168) 8.00 20.00
1 Troy Edwards .05 .15
2 Simon Oliver .05 .15
3 Gerald Tallaire .05 .15
4 Blair Allison .05 .15
5 Mads True .05 .15
6 Steve Brent .05 .15
7 Jay Dobrescu .05 .15
8 Dave Debusschere .05 .15
9 Bryan Cossette .05 .15
10 Brooke Battersby .05 .15
11 Kyle Niemegeers .05 .15
12 Darren McLean .05 .15
13 Carson Cardinal .05 .15
14 Bill McKay .05 .15
15 Chris Hatch .05 .15
16 Nolan Weir .05 .15
17 Karl Johnson .05 .15
18 Jason Brown .05 .15
19 Tyler Kuhn .05 .15
20 Daniel Dennis .05 .15
21 Wally Spence .05 .15
22 Rob Beck .05 .15
23 Aaron Cain .20 .50
24 Darryl Dickson .05 .15
25 Travis Cheyne .05 .15
26 Mark Leoppky .05 .15
27 Jason Ahenakew .05 .15
28 Kyle Paul .05 .15
29 Dean Normand .05 .15
30 Brett Kinaschuk .05 .15
31 Darren Schmidt .05 .15
32 Chris Schinkel .05 .15
33 David Foster .05 .15
34 Jason Zimmerman .05 .15
35 Tom Perry .05 .15
36 Kent Kinaschuk .05 .15
37 Colin Froese .05 .15
38 Shawn Zimmerman .05 .15
39 Larry Empey .05 .15
40 Curtis Knight .05 .15
41 Blake Shipley .05 .15
42 Cory Heon .05 .15
43 Steve Pashulka .05 .15
44 Rob Kinch .05 .15
45 Dean Gerard .05 .15
46 Matt Desmarais .05 .15
47 Chad Rusnak .05 .15
48 Brad Bagu .05 .15
49 Cam Bristow .05 .15
50 Derek Simonson .05 .15
51 Ken Ruddock .05 .15
52 Tyler Deis .05 .15
53 Steve Tansowny .05 .15
54 Bill Stait .05 .15
55 Garfield Henderson .05 .15
56 Lonny Deobald .05 .15
57 Lyle Ehrmantraut .05 .15
58 Layne Humenny .05 .15
59 Darren Balcombe .05 .15
60 Jeff McCutheon .05 .15
61 Trevor Wathen .05 .15
62 Derek Wynne .05 .15
63 Matt Russo .05 .15
64 Bruce Matatall .05 .15
65 Derek Crimin .05 .15
66 Chad Crumley .05 .15
67 Mike Hillock .05 .15
68 Art Houghton .05 .15
69 Lee Materi .05 .15
70 Nick Dyhr .05 .15
71 Darren Maloney .05 .15
72 Kurtise Souchotte .05 .15
73 Noel Kamel .05 .15
74 Trent Harper .05 .15
75 Ted Grayling .05 .15
76 Keith Harris .05 .15
77 Corri Moffat .05 .15
78 Travis Vantighem .05 .15
79 Darren Houghton .05 .15
80 Wade Welte .05 .15
81 Dave Doucet .05 .15
82 Jason Prokopetz .05 .15
83 Gordon McCann .05 .15
84 Clint Hooge .05 .15
85 Glen McGillvary .05 .15
86 Regan Simpson .05 .15
87 Mike Masse .05 .15
88 Jeremy Procyshyn .05 .15
89 Jim Nellis .05 .15
90 Todd Kozak .05 .15
91 Brent Hoiness .05 .15
92 Josh Welter .05 .15
Jason Welter
93 Eldon Barker .05 .15
94 Duane Vandale .05 .15
95 Brad McEwen .05 .15
96 Trent Tibbatts .05 .15
97 Jody Reiter .05 .15
98 Greg Moore .05 .15
99 Jon Rowe .05 .15
100 Mike Evans .05 .15
101 Jason Krug .05 .15
102 Jon Bracco .05 .15
103 Ryan Sandholm .05 .15
104 Darryl Sangster .05 .15
105 Brett Colborne .05 .15
106 Dean Moore .05 .15
107 Chris Dechaine .05 .15
108 Steve McKenna .05 .15
109 Tony Bergin .05 .15
110 Tim Murray .05 .15
111 Casey Kesselring .05 .15
112 Todd Barth .05 .15
113 Ryan McConnell .05 .15
114 Ian Adamson .05 .15
115 Warren Pickford .05 .15
116 Todd Murphy .05 .15
117 Rob Phillips .05 .15
118 Trevor Demmans .05 .15
119 Jeff Greenwood .05 .15
120 Kevin Messer .05 .15
121 Dion Johnson .05 .15
122 Rejean Stringer .05 .15
123 Scott Mead .05 .15
124 Jeff Lawson .05 .15
125 Scot Newberry .05 .15
126 Bill Reid .05 .15
127 Chris Winkler .05 .15
128 Kyle Girgan .05 .15
129 Trevor Warrener .05 .15
130 Richard Boscher .05 .15
131 Tom Thomson .05 .15
132 Mike Wevers .05 .15
133 Barton Holt .05 .15
134 Kent Rogers .05 .15
135 Richard Gibbs .05 .15
136 Jared Witt .05 .15
137 Jamie Stelmak .05 .15
138 Greg Wahl .05 .15
139 J. Sotropa .05 .15
140 Mark Pivetz .05 .15
141 Travis Kirby .05 .15
142 Jason Scanzano .05 .15
143 Tyson Balog .05 .15
144 Daryl Krauss .05 .15
145 Mike Harder .05 .15
146 Tyler McMillan .05 .15
147 Darcy Herlick .05 .15
148 Dave Zwyer .05 .15
149 Craig McKechnie .05 .15
150 Cam Cook .05 .15
151 Derek Bruselinck .05 .15
152 Travis Smith .05 .15
153 Daryl Jones .05 .15
154 Mike Savard .05 .15
155 Jeremy Matthies .05 .15
156 Michel Cook .05 .15
157 Leigh Brookbank .05 .15
158 Christian Dutil .05 .15
159 Scott Heshka .05 .15
160 Danny Galarneau .05 .15
161 Jamie Dunn .05 .15
162 Nigel Werenka .05 .15
163 Steve Sabo .05 .15
164 Tony Toth .05 .15
165 Sebastien Moreau .05 .15
166 Tim Slukynsky .05 .15
167 Sheldon Bylsma .05 .15
168 Stacy Prevost .10 .30

1981-82 Saskatoon Blades

This 25-card P.L.A.Y. (Police, Laws and Youth) set was sponsored by the Saskatoon Police Department and area businesses. The cards measure approximately 2 1/2" by 3 3/4" and are printed on thin card stock. The fronts feature white-bordered color photos with the player's posed in action stances. The player's name, biographical information, and position appear in the bottom white margin. The team logo appears in the lower left corner.

COMPLETE SET (25) 10.00 25.00
1 Blades Team Photo .75 2.00
2 Daryl Stanley .30 .75
3 Leroy Gorski .30 .75
4 Donn Clark .30 .75
5 Brad Duggan .30 .75
6 Dave Chartier .30 .75
7 Dave Brown 1.25 3.00
8 Adam Thompson .30 .75
9 Bruce Eakin .30 .75
10 Brian Skrudland 1.25 3.00
11 Roger Kortko .30 .75
12 Ron Dreger .30 .75
13 Daryl Lubiniecki .30 .75
14 Marc Habscheid .75 2.00
15 Saskatoon Police Logo .20 .50
16 Todd Strueby .40 1.00
17 Craig Hurley .30 .75
18 Bill Hlynsky .30 .75
19 Lane Lambert .75 2.00
20 Mike Bloski .30 .75
21 Bruce Gordon .30 .75
22 Perry Ganchar .40 1.00
23 Ron Loustel .30 .75
24 Blades Logo .20 .50
25 Checklist Card .20 .50

1983-84 Saskatoon Blades

This set contains 24 P.L.A.Y. (Police, Law and Youth) cards and features the Saskatoon Blades of the Western Hockey League. The cards measure approximately 2 7/16" by 3 3/4". The fronts feature a color posed action shot with white borders. The team logo appears in the lower left corner, with player information to the right in black lettering.

COMPLETE SET (24) 12.00 30.00
1 Team Photo .40 1.00
2 Trent Yawney .40 1.00
3 Grant Jennings .40 1.00
4 Duncan MacPherson .20 .50
5 Greg Holtby .20 .50
6 Dan Leier .20 .50
7 Dwaine Hutton .20 .50

8 Wendel Clark 6.00 15.00
9 Kerry Laviolette .20 .50
10 Dave Chartier .20 .50
11 Dale Henry .20 .50
12 Randy Smith .20 .50
13 Kevin Kowalchuk .20 .50
14 Todd McLellan .20 .50
15 Title Card .08 .25
Saskatoon Police
16 Larry Korchinkski .20 .50
17 Curtis Chamberlain .20 .50
18 Greg Lebsack .20 .50
19 Ron Dreger .20 .50
20 Doug Kyle .20 .50
21 Rick Smith .20 .50
22 Joey Kocur 2.00 5.00
23 Allan Larochelle .20 .50
24 Mark Thietke .20 .50

1984-85 Saskatoon Blades Stickers

This set of 20 stickers was sponsored by Autotec Oil and Saskatchewan Ronald McDonald House. Each sticker measures approximately 2" by 1 3/4" and could be pasted on a 17" by 11" poster printed in thin glossy paper. The stickers display a black-and-white head shot; the uniform number is also printed on the front. The stickers are unnumbered and checklisted below in alphabetical order.

COMPLETE SET (20) 10.00 25.00
1 Jack Bowkus .30 .75
2 Curtis Chamberlain .30 .75
3 Wendel Clark 6.00 15.00
4 Ron Dreger .30 .75
5 Randy Hoffart .30 .75
6 Mark Holick .30 .75
7 Greg Holtby .30 .75
8 Grant Jennings .40 1.00
9 Kevin Kowalchuk .30 .75
10 Bryan Larkin .30 .75
11 James Latos .30 .75
12 Duncan MacPherson .30 .75
13 Rod Matechuk .30 .75
14 Todd McLellan .30 .75
15 Darren Moren .30 .75
16 Mike Morin .30 .75
17 Devon Oleniuk .30 .75
18 Grant Tkachuk .30 .75
19 Troy Vollhoffer .30 .75
20 Trent Yawney .40 1.00

1986-87 Saskatoon Blades Photos

This set is comprised of 25 photos of members of the WHL's Saskatoon Blades. The photos measure a large 8 X 11.5 inches, and bear the mark of sponsor Shell Oil.

COMPLETE SET (24) 14.00 35.00
1 Blair Atcheynum .75 2.00
2 Colin Bayer .40 1.00
3 Jack Bowkus .40 1.00
4 Mike Butkas .40 1.00
5 Kelly Chase 2.00 5.00
6 Tim Cheveldae .75 2.00
7 Blaine Chrest .40 1.00
8 Kerry Clark .40 1.00
9 Brian Glynn .40 1.00
10 Mark Holick .40 1.00
11 Kevin Kaminski .75 2.00
12 Tracey Katelnikoff .40 1.00
13 Kory Kocur .40 1.00
14 Bryan Larkin .40 1.00
15 Curtis Leschyshyn .75 2.00
16 Dan Logan .40 1.00
17 Todd MacLellan .40 1.00
18 Devon Oleniuk .40 1.00
19 Marty Prazma .40 1.00
20 Marty Weimer .40 1.00
21 Walter Shutter .40 1.00
22 Grant Tkachuk .40 1.00
23 Tony Twist 2.00 5.00
24 Shaun Van Allen .75 2.00

1988-89 Saskatoon Blades

This standard size set features posed color photos on the front, and safety tips and logos on the back. Cards are numbered as seen below.

COMPLETE SET (25) 4.00 10.00
1 Joe Penkala .20 .50
2 Saskatoon Police Emblem .07 .20
3 Marcel Comeau .20 .50
4 Dean Kuntz .20 .50
5 Mike Greenlay .20 .50
6 Jody Praznik .20 .50
7 Ken Sutton .20 .50
8 Sawn Snesar .20 .50
9 Shane Langager .20 .50
10 Dean Holdien .20 .50
11 Rob Lelacheur .20 .50
12 David Struch .20 .50
13 Collin Bauer .20 .50
14 Kevin Yellowaga .20 .50
15 Drew Sawtell .20 .50
16 Brian Gerrits .20 .50
17 Kirk Roworth .20 .50
18 Tracey Katelnikoff .20 .50
19 Scott Scissons .20 .50
20 Jason Smart .20 .50
21 Jason Christie .20 .50
22 Daren Bader .20 .50
23 Kevin Kaminski .20 .50
24 Kory Kocur .20 .50
25 Darwin McPherson .20 .50

1989-90 Saskatoon Blades

These standard-sized cards feature the Blades of the Western Hockey League. It is believed that they were issued individually by members of the local police, rather than issued in team set form.

COMPLETE SET (25) 6.00 15.00
1 Terry Ruskowski .30 .75
2 Cam Moon .20 .50
3 Damon Kustra .20 .50
4 Trevor Robins .20 .50
5 Mark Raiter .20 .50
6 Mark Wotton .30 .75
7 Shawn Snesar .20 .50
8 Trevor Sherban .20 .50
9 Shane Langager .20 .50
10 Dean Holdien .20 .50
11 Rob Lelacheur .20 .50
12 David Struch .20 .50
13 Derek Tibbatts .20 .50
14 Drew Sawtell .20 .50
15 Richard Matvichuk .60 1.50
16 Trent Coghill .20 .50
17 Jeff Buchanan .20 .50
18 Grant Chorney .20 .50
19 Shawn Yakimishyn .20 .50
20 Scott Scissons .20 .50
21 Jason Smart .20 .50
22 Jason Christie .20 .50
23 Darin Bader .20 .50
24 Dean Rambo .20 .50
25 Collin Bauer .20 .50

1990-91 Saskatoon Blades

This 27-card P.L.A.Y. (Police, Laws and Youth) set was sponsored by the Saskatoon Police Department and area businesses. The cards measure approximately 2 1/2" by 3 3/4" and are printed on thin card stock. On a blue card face, the fronts feature white-bordered posed action color photos. The player's name, position, and biographical information appear in the bottom blue margin. The yellow and blue team logo appears in the lower right corner.

COMPLETE SET (27) 4.80 12.00
1 Terry Ruskowski CO .25 .60
2 Trevor Robins .20 .50
3 Cam Moon .20 .50
4 Jeff Buchanan .20 .50
5 Mark Raiter .20 .50
6 Trevor Sherban .20 .50
7 Jason Knox .20 .50
8 Dean Rambo .20 .50
9 Rob LeLacheur .20 .50
10 David Struch .20 .50
11 Greg Leahy .20 .50
12 Derek Tibbatts .20 .50
13 Shane Calder .20 .50
14 Richard Matvichuk .40 1.00
15 Trent Coghill .20 .50
16 Mark Wotton .25 .60
17 Kelly Markwart .20 .50
18 Mark Franks .20 .50
19 Scott Scissons .20 .50
20 Tim Cox .20 .50
21 Gaetan Blouin .20 .50
22 Darin Bader .20 .50
23 Shawn Yakimishyn .20 .50
24 Ryan Strain .20 .50
25 Jason Peters .20 .50
26 Team Card .20 .50
27 Title Card .20 .50

1991-92 Saskatoon Blades

This 25-card P.L.A.Y. (Police, Laws and Youth) set was issued as a sheet measuring approximately 12 1/2" by 17 1/2", with five rows of five cards each. If cut, the individual cards would measure the standard size. On a black card face, the fronts feature posed color player photos with thin white borders. The player's name and biography along with the team's 25th anniversary logo appear below the picture.

COMPLETE SET (25) 4.80 12.00
1 Lorne Molleken CO .08 .25
2 Trevor Robins .20 .50
3 Norm Maracle .40 1.00
4 Jeff Buchanan .20 .50
5 Mark Raiter .20 .50
6 Bryce Goebel .20 .50
7 Rhett Trombley .30 .75
8 Chad Rusnak .20 .50
9 Jason Knight .20 .50
10 David Struch .20 .50
11 Shane Calder .20 .50
12 Derek Tibbatts .20 .50
13 Glen Gulutzan .20 .50
14 Richard Matvichuk .60 1.50
15 Chad Michalchuk .20 .50
16 Mark Wotton .30 .75
17 Mark Franks .20 .50
18 Andy MacIntyre .20 .50
19 Ryan Fujita .20 .50
20 Sean McFatridge .20 .50
21 Jason Becker .20 .50
22 Shawn Yakimishyn .20 .50
23 James Startup .20 .50
24 Paul Buczkowski .20 .50
NNO McGruff .02 .10

1993-94 Saskatoon Blades

Sponsored by Coca-Cola, this is an oversized 24-card set measuring approximately 8 1/2" by 5 1/2". The borderless fronts feature posed color player photos on the ice surrounded by a Coca-Cola advertising display. The player's name and number in black letters appear in the lower left corner. The words "Best on Ice - Blades and Coca-Cola" are printed over the top of the photo in red, white, and blue. The backs are blank. The cards are unnumbered and checklisted below in alphabetical order.

COMPLETE SET (24) 4.80 12.00
1 Chad Allan .20 .50
2 Frank Banham .25 .60
3 Frank Banham .25 .60
Mark Deyel
4 Wade Belak .20 .50
5 Paul Buczkowski .20 .50
6 Shane Calder .25 .60
7 Mark Deyell .30 .75
8 Jason Duda .20 .50
9 Trevor Ethier .20 .50
10 Mike Gray .20 .50
11 Trevor Hanas .20 .50
12 Devon Hanson .20 .50
13 Andrew Kemper .20 .50
14 Kirby Law .20 .50
15 Andy Macintyre .20 .50
16 Norm Maracle .40 1.00
17 Ivan Salon .20 .50
18 Todd Simpson .20 .50
19 Derek Tibbatts .20 .50
20 Derek Tibbatts .20 .50
Clarke W
21 Rhett Warrener .30 .75
22 Clarke Wilm .30 .75
23 Mark Wotton .25 .60
24 Team Photo .20 .50

1995-96 Saskatoon Blades

The 27 oversized (2 1/2" by 4 1/2") cards set feature the Saskatoon Blades of the WHL. Apparently, the cards were issued as a promotional giveaway at PW Pharmacies in Saskatoon. The front displays a color action photo, along with the player's name and number and the Blades logo. A Carlton cards logo appears in the upper right. The backs contain biographical information as well as the logos of all participating sponsors. Complete cards also included a coupon for savings on various products at PW. The cards are worth 50 percent of the value below without the coupon. The cards are unnumbered and thus are checklisted below in alphabetical order.

COMPLETE SET (27) 4.80 12.00
1 Chad Allan .20 .50
2 Frank Banham .30 .75
3 Dennis Bassett .20 .50
4 Wade Belak .30 .75
5 Ryan Bonni .30 .75
6 Paul Buczkowski .20 .50
7 Don Clark CO .20 .50
8 Mattieu Cusson .20 .50
9 Mark Deyell .30 .75
10 Pavel Kriz .20 .50
11 Jeromie Kufflick .20 .50
12 Laird Laluk .20 .50
13 Erik Leefe .20 .50
14 Richard Peacock .20 .50
15 Greg Phillips .20 .50
16 Garrett Prosofsky .30 .75
17 Nathan Rempel .20 .50
18 Cory Sarich .40 1.00
19 Jeremy Schaefer .20 .50
20 Mark Smith .20 .50
21 Martin Sonnenberg .20 .50
22 Randy Weinberger .20 .50
23 Clark Wilm .30 .75
24 Team Logo CL .02 .10
25 Crime Stoppers Logo .02 .10
26 Celebration 30 Years .02 .10
27 Assistant Coaches .02 .10
Chartier
Engele
Federke

1996-97 Saskatoon Blades

This set of the Saskatoon Blades features 28 oversized (2 1/2" X 4 1/2") cards. The fronts display color photos, with the player's name, jersey number and Blades logo inscribed along the bottom. The backs feature biographical data, a safety tip, and the locations of every PW Pharmacy in Saskatoon. PW sponsored the set as a promotional giveaway at local stores. Interestingly, the backs exhort fans to collect all 27 cards, but the set contains 28. The cards come attached to money-saving coupons from PW; if the coupon is removed, the value is 50 percent that listed below. The unnumbered cards are checklisted below alphabetically.

COMPLETE SET (28) 5.00 12.00
1 Stewart Bacharuk .20 .50
2 Jon Barkman .20 .50
3 Justin Bekkering .20 .50
4 Derek Bjornson .20 .50
5 Ryan Bonni .20 .50
6 Christian Chartier .30 .75
7 Matt Cockell .20 .50
8 Mathieu Cusson .20 .50
9 Jared Dumba .20 .50
10 Ryan Gaucher .20 .50
11 Ryan Henderson .20 .50
12 Ryan Johnston .20 .50
13 Vladislav Klochkov .20 .50
14 Laird Laluk .20 .50
15 Tyler Love .20 .50
16 Sheldon Nedielski .20 .50
17 Greg Phillips .20 .50
18 Garrett Prosofsky .20 .50
19 Nathan Rempel .20 .50
20 Cory Sarich .20 .50
21 Brian Skrudland .20 .50
22 Martin Sonnenberg .20 .50
23 Lyle Steenbergen .20 .50
24 Rhett Warrener .30 .75
25 Kyle Werner .20 .50
26 Team Logo CL .08 .25
27 Action/Goal .08 .25
28 Team(Reebok) .08 .25

1997-98 Saskatoon Blades

Released by the Blades in conjunction with Coca-Cola, this 27-card set features oversized cards with full color action photography and blank backs. The fronts also feature a ghosted area to facilitate autographing. The set is not numbered, therefore it appears in alphabetical order.

COMPLETE SET (27) 5.00 12.00
1 Jon Barkman .20 .50
2 Garett Bembridge .20 .50
3 Derek Bjornson .20 .50
4 Ryan Bonni .30 .75
5 Christian Chartier .30 .75
6 Matt Cockell .20 .50
7 Mathieu Cusson .20 .50
8 Chad Elmy .20 .50
9 Ryan Gaucher .20 .50
10 Derek Halldorson .20 .50
11 Ryan Johnston .20 .50
12 Dylan Kemp .20 .50
13 Tyler Mackay .20 .50
14 Kevin McKay .30 .75
15 Matt Miller .20 .50
16 Dennis Mullen .20 .50
17 Greg Phillips .20 .50
18 Petja Pietilainen .20 .50
19 Garrett Prosofsky .30 .75
20 Nathan Rempel .20 .50
21 Darcy Robinson .20 .50
22 Cory Sarich .30 .75
23 Martin Sonnenberg .30 .75
24 Header Card .08 .25
25 Mascot - Hermutt .08 .25
26 Price Watchers .08 .25
27 Team Photo .20 .50

2000-01 Saskatoon Blades

This set features the Blades of the WHL. The cards were sold at the team's home games.

COMPLETE SET (32) 4.80 12.00
1 Logo Card .04 .11
2 Team Photo .16 .40
3 Kevin Dickie CO .10 .25
4 Bruno Baseotto ACO .10 .25
5 Tim Cheveldae ACO .16 .40
6 Jason Goulet .16 .40
7 Matt Suderman .16 .40
8 Scotty Balan .16 .40
9 Ryan Stempfle .16 .40
10 Kane Ludwar .16 .40
11 Adrian Foster .40 1.00
12 Martin Erat .40 1.00
13 Garrett Bembridge .16 .40
14 Davin Heintz .16 .40
15 Justin Wallin .16 .40
16 Trent Adamus .16 .40
17 Jeff Coulter .16 .40
18 Chris Manchakowski .16 .40
19 Justin Kanigan .16 .40
20 David Cameron .16 .40
21 Derek Halldorson .16 .40
22 Aaron Starr .16 .40
23 Ryan Kehrig .16 .40
24 Rob Woods .16 .40
25 Warren Peters .16 .40
26 Petr Prochazka .16 .40
27 Justin Kelly .16 .40
28 Michael Garnett .16 .40
29 Tony Kolewaski .16 .40
30 Martin Vymazal .16 .40
31 Helmutt MASCOT .04 .11
32 Jay Richards DJ .04 .11

2001-02 Saskatoon Blades

This set features the Blades of the WHL. Little has been confirmed to date regarding this set, but it is believed that they were sold at home games.

COMPLETE SET (32) 6.00 15.00
1 Header .04 .10
2 Derek Couture .20 .50
3 Paul Gentile .20 .50
4 Willy Glover .20 .50
5 Kyle Harris .20 .50
6 Davin Heintz .20 .50
7 Adam Huxley .20 .50
8 Justin Keller .20 .50
9 Ryan Keller .75 2.00
10 Justin Kelly .20 .50
11 Richard Mueller .20 .50
12 Warren Peters .20 .50
13 Tim Preston .20 .50
14 Daniel Volrab .20 .50
15 Trent Adamus .20 .50
16 Tiger Williams .40 1.00
Kelly Hrudey
17 Scotty Balan .20 .50
18 Mike Green .60 1.50
19 Kane Ludwar .20 .50
20 Stephen Mann .20 .50
21 Sean Moir .20 .50
22 Ryan Stempfle .20 .50
23 Matt Suderman .20 .50
24 Rob Woods .20 .50
25 Michael Garnett .40 1.00
26 Ryan Senft .20 .50
27 Helmutt .04 .10
28 Steve Hildebrand TR .04 .10
29 Kevin Dickie CO .04 .10
30 Bruno Baseotto .04 .10
31 Wendel Clark Night .40 1.00
32 Team Photo .20 .50

2002-03 Saskatoon Blades

COMPLETE SET (30) 4.00 10.00
1 Evan Haw .20 .50
2 Sean Moir .20 .50
3 Matt Suderman .20 .50
4 Matt Bergen .20 .50
5 Steven Later .20 .50
6 Denny Johnston .20 .50
7 Trent Adamus .20 .50
8 Michael Bubnick .20 .50
9 Marcus Paulsson .20 .50
10 Adam Houle .20 .50
11 Daniel Volrab .20 .50
12 Wacey Rabbit .20 .50
13 Derek Couture .20 .50
14 Joe Barnes .20 .50
15 Rob Woods .20 .50
16 Warren Peters .20 .50
17 Adam Huxley .30 .75
18 Mike Green .40 1.00
19 John Dahl .20 .50
20 Stephen Mann .20 .50
21 Adam Ward .30 .75
22 Brett Jaeger .30 .75
23 Ryan Keller .20 .50
24 Tanner Shultz .20 .50
25 Jack Brodsky PRES .04 .10
26 Brent McEwan GM .04 .10
27 Kevin Dickie CO .04 .10
28 Bruno Baseotto ACO .04 .10
29 Stev Hildebrand TR .04 .10
30 Team Photo .04 .10
CL

2003-04 Saskatoon Blades

COMPLETE SET (23) 6.00 15.00
1 Mascot .04 .10
2 Team Photo .04 .10
3 Boris Lekovic .30 .75
4 Adam Ward .30 .75
5 Joel Eisenkirch .30 .75
6 Dane Crowley .30 .75
7 Evan Haw .30 .75
8 Nicolaus Knudsen .30 .75
9 Ben Van Lare .30 .75
10 Richard Kelly .30 .75
11 Rob Woods .30 .75
12 Matt Fetzner .30 .75
13 Mike Green .40 1.00
14 Bjorn Svensson .30 .75
15 Ryan Cyr .30 .75
16 Dayln Flatt .30 .75
17 Joe Barnes .30 .75
18 Trent Adamus .30 .75
19 Derek Couture .30 .75
20 Tanner Shultz .30 .75
21 Wacey Rabbit .75 2.00
22 Devin Setoguchi .75 2.00
23 Ryan Keller .30 .75

2004-05 Saskatoon Blades

This set was issued in two parts: a 12-card first series and a 10-card second series.

COMPLETE SET (22) 8.00 20.00
1 Nicolaus Knudsen .30 .75
2 Joel Eisenkirch .30 .75
3 Justin McCrae .30 .75
4 Russell Monette .30 .75
5 Tyson Sievert .30 .75
6 Aaron Bader .30 .75
7 Daniel Waschuk .30 .75
8 Chris Cloud .30 .75
9 Ben Van Lare .30 .75
10 Tyler Boldt .30 .75
11 Mike Green .40 1.00
12 Zdenek Bahensky .40 1.00
13 Ryan Cyr .30 .75
14 Ryan Keller .30 .75
15 Devin Setoguchi .75 2.00
16 Joe Barnes .30 .75
17 Dayln Flatt .40 1.00
18 Dane Crowley .30 .75
19 Evan Haw .30 .75
20 Wacey Rabbit .75 2.00
21 Ryan Menei .30 .75
22 Bjorn Svensson .30 .75

2005-06 Saskatoon Blades

COMPLETE SET (24) 10.00 20.00
1 Aaron Bader .30 .75
2 Zdenek Bahensky .30 .75
3 Joe Barnes .30 .75
4 Chris Cloud .30 .75
5 Brad Cole .30 .75
6 Ryan Funk .30 .75
7 Adam Geric .30 .75
8 Colton Gillies .30 .75
9 Michael Hengen .30 .75
10 Anton Khudobin .40 1.00
11 Chad Klassen .30 .75
12 Joe Logan .30 .75
13 Michael MacAngus .30 .75
14 Blair MacAulay .30 .75
15 Justin McCrae .30 .75
16 Ryan Menei .30 .75
17 Todd Panchyson .30 .75
18 Derek Price .30 .75
19 Wacey Rabbit .60 1.50
20 David Schulz .30 .75
21 Devin Setoguchi .60 1.50
22 Brett Ward .30 .75
23 Jim Watt .40 1.00
24 Brennan Zasitko .30 .75

2006-07 Saskatoon Blades

COMPLETE SET (24) 8.00 15.00
1 Dustin Cameron .25 .60
2 Chris Cloud .25 .60
3 Brad Cole .25 .60
4 Troy Crowley .25 .60
5 Craig Cuthbert .25 .60
6 Kenton Dulle .25 .60
7 Ryan Funk .25 .60
8 Adam Geric .25 .60
9 Colton Gillies .25 2.00
10 Braden Holtby .25 .60
11 Derek Hulak .25 .60
12 Sam Klassen .25 .60
13 Garrett Klotz .25 .60
14 Rastislav Konecny .25 .60
15 Joe Logan .25 .60
16 Blair MacAulay .25 .60
17 Justin McCrae .25 .60
18 Ryan Menei .25 .60
19 Gaelan Patterson .25 .60
20 Bohdan Visnak .25 .60
21 Brett Ward .25 .60
22 Walker Wintoneak .25 .60
23 Teigan Zahn .25 .60
24 Garrett Zemlak .25 .60

1980-81 Sault Ste. Marie Greyhounds

Sponsored by Blue Bird Bakery Limited and Coke, this 25-card set captures the 1980-81 Soo Greyhounds of the OHL. The cards measure approximately 2 1/2" by 4" and feature posed, color player photos. Of interest to collectors are the first cards of current NHL stars John Vanbiesbrouck and Ron Francis.

COMPLETE SET (25) 37.50 75.00
1 Ken Porteous .30 .75
2 Brian Petterle .30 .75
3 Gord Dineen .40 1.00
4 Tony Cella .30 .75
5 Doug Shedden .60 1.50
6 Terry Tait .30 .75
7 Greyhounds Logo .20 .50
8 Steve Smith .30 .75
9 Huey Larkin .30 .75
10 Steve Gatzos .30 .75
11 Tim Zwijack .30 .75
12 Vic Morin .30 .75
13 John Vanbiesbrouck 12.50 25.00
14 Ron Francis 12.50 25.00
15 Tony Butorac .30 .75
16 John Goodwin .30 .75
17 Ron Handy .30 .75
18 Jim Pavese .40 1.00
19 Sault Ste. Marie .20 .50
Police Logo
20 Rick Morocco .30 .75
21 Ken Latta .30 .75
22 Kirk Rueter .30 .75
23 OMJHL Logo .20 .50
24 Terry Crisp 1.00 2.50
25 Marc D'Amour .75 2.00

1981-82 Sault Ste. Marie Greyhounds

Sponsored by Blue Bird Bakery Limited, Coke, 920 CKCY radio, and Canadian Tire, this 28-card set measures approximately 2 1/8" by 4 1/8" and features posed, color player photos with white borders. The player's name is printed in white on the picture, above the player's head. His position and the team name are printed in fuchsia at the bottom. The cards are unnumbered and checklisted below in alphabetical order. This set contains early cards of Rick Tocchet, John Vanbiesbrouck and Ron Francis.

COMPLETE SET (28) 32.00 80.00
1 Jim Aldreda .30 .75
2 Dave Andreoli .30 .75
3 Richard Beaulne .30 .75
4 Bruce Bell .30 .75
5 Chuck Brimmer .30 .75
6 Tony Cella .30 .75
7 Kevin Conway .30 .75
8 Terry Crisp CO .75 2.00
9 Marc D'Amour .60 1.50
10 Gord Dineen .40 1.00
11 Chris Felix .40 1.00
12 Ron Francis 10.00 25.00
13 Steve Graves .30 .75
14 Wayne Groulx .30 .75
15 Huey Larkin .30 .75
16 Ken Latta .30 .75
17 Mike Lococo .30 .75
18 Jim Pavese .40 1.00
19 Dirk Rueter .30 .75
20 Steve Smith .30 .75
21 Terry Tait .30 .75
22 Rick Tocchet 8.00 20.00
23 John Vanbiesbrouck 10.00 25.00
24 Harry Wolfe ANN .20 .50
25 J.D. Yari .02 .10
26 Bluebird Bakery .02 .10
Limited Logo
27 Canadian Tire Logo .02 .10
28 Coca-Cola Ad .02 .10

1982-83 Sault Ste. Marie Greyhounds

Sponsored by Blue Bird Bakery Limited and 920 CKCY radio station, this 25-card set measures approximately 2 1/2" by 4" and feature color, posed player photos with white borders. The player's name is superimposed on the photo in white lettering. His position is in black at the bottom. The cards are unnumbered and checklisted below in alphabetical order.

COMPLETE SET (25) 16.00 40.00
1 Jim Aldred .30 .75
2 John Armelin .30 .75
3 Richard Beaulne .30 .75
4 Jeff Beukeboom .60 1.50
5 Tony Cella .30 .75
6 Kevin Conway .30 .75
7 Terry Crisp .60 1.50
8 Chris Felix .40 1.00
9 Steve Graves .30 .75
10 Gus Greco .30 .75
11 Wayne Groulx .30 .75
12 Sam Haidy .30 .75
13 Tim Hoover .30 .75
14 Pat Lahey .30 .75
15 Huey Larkin .30 .75
16 Mike Lococo .30 .75
17 Mike Neill .30 .75
18 Ken Sabourin .30 .75
19 Steve Smith .30 .75
20 Terry Tait .30 .75
21 Rick Tocchet 4.00 10.00
22 John Vanbiesbrouck 6.00 15.00
23 Harry Wolfe ANN .20 .50
24 Station Mall Sponsor .02 .10
25 Bluebird Bakery Ltd. .02 .10

1983-84 Sault Ste. Marie Greyhounds

Sponsored by 920 CKCY radio, Coke, and IGA, the cards in this 25-card set measure approximately 2 1/2" by 4" and feature color, posed player photos with white borders. The player's name appears in an orange bar at the bottom of the picture. The cards are unnumbered and checklisted below in alphabetical order.

COMPLETE SET (25) 8.00 20.00
1 Jeff Beukeboom .40 1.00
2 Graeme Bonar .20 .50
3 Chris Brant .20 .50
4 John English .20 .50
5 Chris Felix .40 1.00
6 Rick Fera .20 .50
7 Marc Tournier .20 .50
8 Steve Graves .20 .50
9 Gus Greco .20 .50
11 Wayne Groulx .20 .50
11 Sam Haidy .20 .50
12 Tim Hoover .20 .50
13 Jerry Iuliano .20 .50
14 Pat Lahey .20 .50
15 Mike Lococo .20 .50
16 Jean-Marc MacKenzie .20 .50
17 Mike Oliverio .20 .50
18 Brit Peer .20 .50
19 Joey Rampton .20 .50
20 Ken Sabourin .40 1.00
21 Jim Samec .20 .50
22 Rick Tocchet 3.00 8.00
23 Harry Wolfe ANN .20 .50
24 IGA Sponsor Card .02 .10
25 Coke Sponsor Card .02 .10

1984-85 Sault Ste. Marie Greyhounds

Sponsored by 920 CKCY radio, Coke, and IGA, this 25-card set measures approximately 2 1/2" by 4" and features white-bordered, posed, color photos of the players on ice with a blue studio background. The player's name appears on a bright red plaque near the bottom. The cards are unnumbered and checklisted below in alphabetical order.

COMPLETE SET (25) 8.00 20.00
1 Marty Abrams .20 .50
2 Jeff Beukeboom .30 .75
3 Graeme Bonar .20 .50
4 Chris Brant .20 .50
5 Terry Crisp CO .40 1.00
6 Chris Felix .40 1.00
7 Scott Green .20 .50
8 Wayne Groulx .20 .50
9 Steve Hollett .20 .50
10 Tim Hoover .20 .50
11 Derek King .60 1.50
12 Tyler Larter .20 .50
13 Jean-Marc MacKenzie .20 .50
14 Scott Mosey .20 .50
15 Mike Oliverio .20 .50
16 Brit Peer .20 .50
17 Wayne Presley .40 1.00
18 Bob Probert 3.00 8.00
19 Brian Rome .20 .50
20 Ken Sabourin .30 .75
21 Rob Veccia .20 .50
22 Harry Wolfe ANN .08 .25
23 Rob Zettler .40 1.00
24 IGA Ad .08 .25
25 Coca-Cola Ad .08 .25

1987-88 Sault Ste. Marie Greyhounds

Printed on thin card stock, this 35-card set features players from the 1987-88 season of the Sault Ste. Marie Greyhounds and also past Greyhounds players who have gone on to NHL fame, such as Wayne Gretzky. The fronts feature white-bordered posed-on-ice color player photos. The player's name appears in white lettering near the top; his position and the team name appear in blue lettering near the bottom.

COMPLETE SET (35) 50.00 125.00
1 Barry King .08 .25
Chief of Police
2 Dan Currie .20 .50
3 Mike Glover .20 .50
4 Tyler Larter .20 .50
5 Bob Jones .20 .50
6 Lyndon Slewidge .08 .25
Anthem Singer
7 Brad Jones .20 .50
8 Ron Francis 3.00 8.00
9 Dale Turnbull .20 .50
10 Don McConnell .20 .50
11 Chris Felix .30 .75
12 Steve Udvari .20 .50
13 Shawn Simpson .20 .50
14 Rob Zettler .40 1.00
15 Phil Esposito 6.00 15.00
Co-owner
16 John Vanbiesbrouck 6.00 15.00
17 Mike Oliverio .20 .50
18 Colin Ford .20 .50
19 Steve Herniman .20 .50
20 Troy Mallette .40 1.00
21 Craig Hartsburg .40 1.00
22 Don Boyd CO .08 .25
GM
23 Peter Fiorentino .20 .50
24 Jeff Columbus .20 .50
25 Brad Stepan .20 .50
26 Rick Tocchet 2.00 5.00
27 Shane Sargant .20 .50
28 Wayne Muir .20 .50
29 Wayne Gretzky 40.00 100.00
30 Gary Luther .20 .50
31 Harry Wolfe ANN .08 .25
32 Rod Thacker .20 .50
33 Coaches Card .08 .25
Terry Tait
Ted Nolan
Mark Pavoni
34 Brian Hoard .20 .50
35 Glen Johnston .20 .50

1989-90 Sault Ste. Marie Greyhounds

This 30-card P.L.A.Y. (Police, Law and Youth) set measures 2 3/4" by 3 1/2". The fronts feature posed on-ice player photos with black and white borders. The player's name and number appear on the bottom. The backs carry sponsor logos at the bottom and "Tips from the Hounds."

COMPLETE SET (30) 8.00 20.00
1 Barry King CL .08 .25
Chief of Police
2 Sault Ste. Marie .08 .25
Police Logo
3 Ted Nolan CO .30 .75
4 Team Logo .20 .50
5 Sherry Bassin GM .20 .50
6 Jim Ritchie .20 .50
7 Bob Boughner .30 .75
8 Denny Lambert .40 1.00
9 Doug Minor .20 .50
10 Rick Pracey .20 .50
11 Colin Miller .20 .50
12 Kevin King .20 .50
13 Ron Francis 2.00 5.00
14 Rick Kowalsky .20 .50
15 Adam Foote .75 2.00
16 Wade Whitten .20 .50
17 Dale Turnbull .20 .50
18 Bob Jones .20 .50
19 David Carrie .20 .50
20 Brad Tiley .20 .50
21 Wayne Muir .20 .50
22 Dave Babcock .20 .50
23 David Matsos .20 .50
24 Dan Ferguson .20 .50
25 Jeff Szeryk .20 .50
26 Mike Zuke ACO .08 .25
27 Dave Doucette .20 .50
28 John Campbell .08 .25
Constable
29 Graeme Harvey .20 .50
30 John Fuselli ACO .08 .25

1993-94 Sault Ste. Marie Greyhounds

Sponsored by Pino's Food Trunk Road and Sault Ste. Marie Public Utilities Commission, and printed by Slapshot Images Ltd., this standard-size 30-card set features the 1993-94 Sault Ste. Marie Greyhounds. On a geometrical team color-coded background, the fronts feature color action player photos with thin black borders. The player's name, position and team name, as well as the producer's logo, also appear on the front.

COMPLETE SET (30) 4.80 10.00
1 Andrea Carpano .15 .40
2 Ryan Douglas .15 .40
3 Dan Cloutier .75 2.00
4 Oliver Pastinsky .15 .40
5 Scott King .25 .60
6 Drew Bannister .25 .60
7 Sean Gagnon .15 .40
8 Andre Payette .15 .40
9 Peter MacKellar .15 .40
UER Name spelled
Mackellar on fr
10 Richard Uniacke .15 .40
11 Steve Zoryk .15 .40
12 Brad Baber .15 .40
13 Gary Roach .15 .40
14 Jeff Gies .15 .40
15 Tom MacDonald .15 .40
16 Rhett Trombley .15 .40
17 Joe VanVolsen .15 .40
18 Andrew Clark .15 .40
19 Briane Thompson .15 .40
20 Aaron Gavey .25 .60
21 Wade Gibson .15 .40
22 Chad Grills .15 .40
23 Jeff Toms .15 .40
24 Steve Sullivan .60 1.50
25 Jeremy Stevenson .15 .40
26 Corey Moylan .15 .40
27 Steve Spina .15 .40
28 Dave Mayville GM .02 .10
29 Ted Nolan CO .30 .75
30 Dan Flynn ACO .02 .10
Mike Zuke ACO

1993-94 Sault Ste. Marie Greyhounds Memorial Cup

This 32-card standard-size set was printed by Precision Litho. The fronts feature color action player photos with rounded corners and gray-and-red team color-coded borders. The team name and logo are printed above the photos, while the player's name and number appear below. The backs present biography, 1992-93 statistics, an anti-drug or alcohol slogan, and sponsor logos.

COMPLETE SET (32) 6.00 15.00
1 Memorial Cup .40 1.00
2 Dan Tanevski .15 .40
3 Mark Matier .15 .40
4 Oliver Pastinsky .15 .40
5 Peter MacKellar .15 .40
6 Drew Bannister .20 .50
7 Sean Gagnon .20 .50
8 Joe Clarke .15 .40
9 Chad Penney .15 .40
10 Neal Martin .15 .40
11 Perry Pappas .15 .40
12 David Matsos .15 .40
13 Rick Kowalsky .15 .40
14 Gary Roach .15 .40
15 Jarret Reid .15 .40
16 Steve Sullivan .60 1.50
17 Tom MacDonald .15 .40
18 Jodie Murphy .15 .40
19 Ralph Intranuovo .15 .40
20 Brad Baber .15 .40
21 Briane Thompson .15 .40
22 Aaron Gavey .20 .50
23 Wade Gibson .15 .40
24 Kiley Hill .15 .40
25 Jeff Toms .15 .40
26 Joe Van Volsen .15 .40
27 Dan Cloutier .75 2.00
28 Kevin Hodson .60 1.50
29 David Mayville DIR .02 .10
Sher
30 Ted Nolan CO .20 .50
Danny Flyn
31 Executive and Office .02 .10
St
32 Mike Zuke ACO .02 .10
Forrest V

1995-96 Sault Ste. Marie Greyhounds

This 30-card set was produced by the Greyhounds for distribution at the rink, by mail, and through the team's web page. The cards feature action photography on the front, with player name, number and bio superimposed over a Hounds logo on the back. The cards are unnumbered, and are listed below alphabetically. The set is noteworthy for including the first cards ever of several outstanding prospects, including Joe Thornton, Rico Fata and Richard Jackman.

COMPLETE SET (30) 10.00 25.00
1 Peter Cava .15 .40
2 Scott Cherrey .15 .40
3 Dan Cloutier .60 1.50
4 Lee Cole .15 .40
5 Jason Doyle .20 .50
6 Rico Fata .30 .75
7 Blaine Fitzpatrick .15 .40
8 Jeff Gies .15 .40
9 Richard Jackman .30 .75
10 Steve Lowe .15 .40
11 Dave Mayville Director of Oper. .02 .10
12 Robert Mulick .15 .40
13 Kevin Murnaghan .15 .40
14 Cory Murphy .15 .40
15 Joe Paterson .02 .10
Head Coach
16 Andre Payette .15 .40
17 Michal Podolka .30 .75
18 Ben Schust .15 .40
19 Brian Stacey .15 .40
20 Brian Stewart .15 .40
21 Joe Thornton 6.00 15.00
22 Trevor Tokarczyk .15 .40
23 Richard Uniacke .20 .50
24 Joe Vanvolsen .15 .40
25 Jamie Wentzell .15 .40
26 M.Zuke .02 .10
B.Jones ACO
27 Greyhounds Staff .02 .10
28 Toronto Bank and Trust .02 .10
29 Greyhounds and .02 .10
Toronto School of Business
30 Team Photo .02 .10

1996-97 Sault Ste. Marie Greyhounds

This 30-card set may stand as the top junior issue of the year. The cards feature color action photography, along with the player's name and number. The backs feature comprehensive stats, but are unnumbered, hence the alphabetical listing below. The set is noteworthy for the inclusion of two cards of Joe Thornton, the top pick in the '97 NHL draft. The second card features him as a member of the Canadian National Junior Team.

COMPLETE SET (30) 10.00 25.00
1 Wes Booker .15 .40
2 Bill Browne .15 .40
3 Peter Cava .15 .40
4 Justin Davis .15 .40
5 J.J. Dickie .15 .40
6 Oak Hewer .15 .40
7 Richard Jackman .20 .50
8 Richard Jackman .20 .50
Team Canada 1997
9 Matt Lahey .15 .40
10 David Mayville .02 .10
Director of Operations
11 Jake McCracken .30 .75
12 Marc Moro .30 .75
13 Robert Mulick .15 .40
14 Joe Paterson CO .02 .10
15 Daniel Passero .15 .40
16 Nathan Perrott .30 .75
17 Michael Podolka .30 .75
18 Nick Robinson .15 .40
19 Ben Schust .15 .40
20 Joe Seroski .15 .40
21 Chad Spurr .15 .40
22 Brian Stewart .15 .40
23 Joe Thornton 4.00 10.00
24 Joe Thornton 4.00 10.00
Team Canada 1997
25 Trevor Tokarczyk .15 .40
26 Richard Uniacke .15 .40
27 David Wight .15 .40
28 Chad Woollard .15 .40
29 Mike Zuke ACO .02 .10
B.Jones ACO
30 Team Photo .02 .10

1996-97 Sault Ste. Marie Greyhounds Autographed

Along with the regular version of the team set, the Hounds also offered a completely signed version for $15. This set includes two signed cards from 1997 top pick Joe Thornton. The cards do not bear any authenticating marks, so it is possible that an autographed set could be compiled individually.

COMPLETE SET (24) 40.00 100.00
1 Wes Booker .75 2.00
2 Bill Browne .75 2.00
3 Peter Cava .75 2.00
4 Justin Davis .75 2.00
5 J.J. Dickie .75 2.00
6 Oak Hewer .75 2.00
7 Richard Jackman 1.25 3.00
8 Richard Jackman 1.25 3.00
Team Canada 1997
9 Matt Lahey .75 2.00
11 Jake McCracken 1.50 4.00
12 Marc Moro 2.00 5.00
13 Robert Mulick .75 2.00
14 Joe Paterson CO .75 2.00
15 Daniel Passero .75 2.00
16 Nathan Perrott 2.00 5.00
17 Michael Podolka 1.50 4.00
18 Nick Robinson .75 2.00
19 Ben Schust .75 2.00
20 Joe Seroski 1.25 3.00
21 Chad Spurr .75 2.00
22 Brian Stewart .75 2.00
23 Joe Thornton 15.00 40.00
24 Joe Thornton 15.00 40.00
Team Canada 1997
25 Trevor Tokarczyk .75 2.00
26 Richard Uniacke 1.25 3.00
27 David Wight .75 2.00
28 Chad Woollard .75 2.00
29 Mike Zuke ACO .75 2.00
B.Jones ACO

2002-03 Sault Ste. Marie Greyhounds

COMPLETE SET (23) 8.00 20.00
1 Adam Munro .40 1.00
2 Joey Biasucci .30 .75
3 Trevor Daley .40 1.00
4 Jeff Carter 3.00 8.00
5 Michael Krelove .20 .50
6 Matt Herneisen .20 .50
7 Jeff Doyle .20 .50
8 Mike Moher .20 .50
9 Tyler Kennedy .20 .50
10 Tyler Dutchyshen .20 .50
11 Brian Rempel .20 .50
12 Petr Taticek .40 1.00
13 Jeff Larsh .20 .50
14 Sean Stefanski .20 .50
15 Jordan Smith .20 .50
16 Mike Amodeo .20 .50
17 Jiri Drtina .20 .50
18 Niko Tuomi .20 .50
19 Ryan Kitchen .20 .50
20 Scott Dobben .20 .50
21 Brad Staubitz .20 .50
22 Jordan Kennedy .20 .50
23 Ryan McKay .20 .50

2003-04 Sault Ste. Marie Greyhounds

COMPLETE SET (32) 6.00 15.00
1 Jakub Cechs .30 .75
2 Travis Chapman .20 .50
3 Brett Connolly .20 .50
4 Andrew Desjardins .20 .50
5 Scott Dobben .20 .50
6 Jeffrey Doyle .20 .50
7 Kevin Druce .30 .75
8 Brad Good .20 .50
9 Jeff Carter 1.50 4.00
10 David Jarram .20 .50
11 Tyler Kennedy .20 .50
12 Jacob King .20 .50
13 Jeff Larsh .20 .50
14 Chris Lawrence .20 .50
15 Matt Leszczynski .20 .50
16 Aaron Lewicki .20 .50
17 Mike Looby .20 .50
18 Jason Pitton .20 .50
19 Matt Puntureri .20 .50
20 Jordan Smith .20 .50
21 Brad Staubitz .20 .50
22 Reg Thomas .20 .50
23 Martin Tuma .20 .50
24 Marty Abrams CO .04 .10
25 Denny Lambert ACO .04 .10
26 Terry Barbeau ACO .04 .10
27 Andy Martin EQM .04 .10
28 Dave Torrie GM .04 .10
29 Rod Bogart TR .04 .10
30 Header Card .04 .10
31 Header Card .04 .10
32 Checklist .04 .10

2004-05 Sault Ste. Marie Greyhounds

COMPLETE SET (25) 6.00 15.00
1 Jakub Cech .20 .50
2 Kyle Gajewski .20 .50
3 Brad Good .20 .50
4 David Jarram .20 .50
5 Joshua Day .20 .50
6 Jeff Carter 1.25 3.00
7 Tyler Cuthbert .20 .50
8 Chris Lawrence .20 .50
9 Ryan McInerny .20 .50
10 Brandon MacLean .20 .50
11 Tyler Kennedy .20 .50
12 Tyler McKinley .20 .50
13 Jason Pitton .20 .50
14 Jeff Larsh .20 .50
15 Jordan Smith .20 .50
16 Jacob King .20 .50
17 Andrew Desjardins .20 .50
18 Matt Puntureri .30 .75
19 Matthew Leszczynski .20 .50
20 Blair Jarrett .20 .50
21 Brad Staubitz .20 .50
22 Martin Tuma .20 .50
23 Jacob Lalonde .20 .50
24 Reg Thomas .20 .50
25 Checklist .04 .10

1993-94 Seattle Thunderbirds

This 30-card standard-size set features the 1993-94 Seattle Thunderbirds of the Western Hockey League (WHL). On a white card face, the fronts display posed color player photos. The pictures are edged by a row of blue stars on the left and by "Thunderbirds" in green print on the right. At the top left corner appears the team logo, while the player's name and position are printed in black beneath the photo.

COMPLETE SET (30) 4.80 12.00
1 Mike Barrie .20 .50
2 Doug Bonner .20 .50
3 Davie Carson .20 .50
4 Jeff Dewar .20 .50
5 Brett Duncan .20 .50
6 Shawn Gervais .20 .50
7 Chris Herperger .30 .75
8 Troy Hyatt .20 .50
9 Curt Kamp TR .02 .10
10 Olaf Kjenstadt .20 .50
11 Walt Kyle CO .02 .10
12 Milt Mastad .20 .50
13 Larry McMorran .20 .50
14 Jim McTaggart ACO .02 .10
15 Regan Mueller .20 .50
16 Kevin Mylander .20 .50
17 Drew Palmer .20 .50
18 Jeff Peddigrew .20 .50
19 Darryl Plandowski ACO .02 .10
20 Deron Quint .30 .75
21 Darrell Sandback .20 .50
22 Chris Schmidt .20 .50
23 Lloyd Shaw .20 .50
24 Alexandre Matvichuk .20 .50
25 Darcy Smith .20 .50
26 Rob Tallas .30 .75
27 Paul Vincent .20 .50
28 Chris Wells .20 .50
29 Brendan Witt .30 .75
30 Team photo .20 .50

1995-96 Seattle Thunderbirds

This 32-card set was produced and sold by the club. The fronts feature action photography, while the backs include a headshot, stats and bio. The set is noteworthy for including the first appearance of Patrick Marleau, the second player selected in the 1997 Entry Draft. The cards are unnumbered and are listed below in alphabetical order.

COMPLETE SET (32) 10.00 30.00
1 Perry Andrusiak ACO .02 .10
2 Shane Belter .20 .50
3 Rick Berry .30 .75
4 Jeff Blair .20 .50
5 Doug Bonner .30 .75
6 Kevin Borris .15 .40
7 Torrey DiRoberto .20 .50
8 Michal Divisek .15 .40
9 Paul Ferone .15 .40
10 Shawn Gervais .15 .40
11 Jan Hrdina .75 2.00
12 Curt Kamp TR .02 .10
13 Greg Kuznik .15 .40
14 Blair Manning .15 .40
15 Patrick Marleau 8.00 20.00
16 Jim McTaggart ACO .02 .10
17 Tony Mohagen .15 .40
18 Don Nachbaur CO .02 .10
19 Jason Norrie .15 .40
20 Drew Palmer .15 .40
21 Tyler Perry .15 .40
22 Jame Pollock .15 .40
23 Kevin Popp .15 .40
24 Jeremy Reich .20 .50
25 Cody Rudkowsky .40 1.00
26 Chris Schmidt .15 .40
27 Lloyd Shaw .15 .40
28 Chris Thompson .15 .40
29 Dan Tompkins .15 .40
30 Cool Bird MASCOT .02 .10
32 Seattle Key Arena .02 .10
NNO Title Card .02 .10

1996-97 Seattle Thunderbirds

This 28-card set was produced by S&H Ltd. The cards were available through the team at the rink or through the mail. The cards feature action photos on the front, and statistical analysis on the backs. The player's sweater number is displayed in the lower right hand corner. As the cards themselves are unnumbered, they are listed below according to the sweater number. The set is noteworthy for the inclusion of Patrick Marleau, the second overall pick in the 1997 NHL Entry Draft.

COMPLETE SET (28) 8.00 20.00
1 Jeff Blair .20 .50
3 Rod LeRoux .20 .50
4 Nathan Forster .20 .50
5 Brad Swanson .20 .50
6 Rick Berry .30 .75
7 Paul Ferone .20 .50
8 Jame Pollock .20 .50
9 Tyler Willis .20 .50
11 Chris Thompson .20 .50
12 Patrick Marleau 3.00 8.00
13 Jouni Kuokkanen .20 .50
14 Martin Cerven .20 .50
15 Jeremy Reich .30 .75
16 Bret DeCecco .40 1.00
17 Tony Mohagen .20 .50
18 Torrey DiRoberto .20 .50
19 Nick Szadkowski .20 .50
21 Brian Ballman .20 .50
22 Greg Kuznik .20 .50
23 Randy Perry .20 .50
24 Shawn Skolney .20 .50
30 Cody Rudkowsky .40 1.00
31 Kris Cantu .20 .50
32 Shane Belter .20 .50
NNO Rob Sumner ASST CO .02 .10
NNO Thunderbirds .02 .10
Through the Years
NNO Don Nachbaur CO .02 .10
NNO Cool Bird MASCOT .02 .10

1997-98 Seattle Thunderbirds

This set features the Thunderbirds of the WHL. It was sold in set form by the team. It features early cards of NHL young star Mark Parrish.

COMPLETE SET (1-27) 7.20 15.00
1 Header Card .02 .10
2 Cool Bird Mascot .02 .10
3 Rod Leroux .20 .50
4 Nathan Forster .20 .50
5 Jason Beckett .20 .50
6 Rick Berry .30 .75
7 Chris Thompson .20 .50
8 Jame Pollock .20 .50
9 David Morisset .30 .75
10 Jeff Blair .20 .50
11 Jouni Kuokkanen .20 .50
12 Scott Kelman .30 .75
13 Jeremy Reich .30 .75
14 Brett DeCecco .30 .75
15 Tim Preston .20 .50
16 Torrey DiRoberto .30 .75
17 Petr Vala .20 .50
18 Ryan Tresk .20 .50
19 Greg Kuznik .20 .50
20 Matt Demarski .20 .50
21 Mark Parrish .75 2.00
22 Stanislav Gron .60 1.50
23 Cody Rudkowsky .40 1.00
24 A.J. Van Bruggen .20 .50
25 Don Nachbaur HCO .08 .25
26 Rob Sumner ACO .04 .10
27 Curt Kamp TR .02 .10

2014-15 Seattle Thunderbirds

COMPLETE SET (30) 8.00 20.00
1 Header Card .30 .75
2 Danny Mumaugh .30 .75
3 Jerret Smith .30 .75
4 Turner Ottenbreit .30 .75
5 Sahvan Khaira .30 .75
6 Scott Eansor .30 .75
7 Justin Hickman .30 .75
8 Kaden Elder .30 .75
9 Ryan Gropp .50 1.25
10 Mathew Barzal .75 2.00
11 Lane Pederson .30 .75
12 Alexander True .30 .75
13 Shea Theodore .40 1.00
14 Donovan Neuls .30 .75
15 Cory Millette .30 .75
16 Florian Baltram .30 .75
17 Calvin Spencer .30 .75
18 Ethan Bear .30 .75
19 Nolan Volcan .30 .75
20 Evan Wardley .30 .75
21 Keegan Kolesar .30 .75
22 Roberts Lipsbergs .30 .75
23 Logan Flodell .30 .75
24 Jared Hauf .30 .75
25 Luke Osterman .30 .75
26 Taran Kozun .30 .75
27 Nick Holowko .30 .75
28 Steve Konowalchuk CO .30 .75
29 Cool Bird MASCOT .30 .75
30 Header Card .30 .75

1969-70 Seattle Totems

This set features the Totems of the old WHL. A White Front Stores exclusive at stores in Aurora, Tacoma, Burien, and Bellevue, this set of 20 team photos measures approximately 8" by 10". Printed on thin paper, the front features a posed color player photo with a studio background. The pictures have white borders, and the player's signature is inscribed in the lower right corner. In black print on white, the backs present biography and statistics from the past season.

COMPLETE SET (20) 60.00 150.00
1 Don Head 8.00 20.00
2 Chuck Holmes 3.00 8.00
3 Bob Courcy 3.00 8.00
4 Marc Boileau 3.00 8.00
5 Gerry Leonard 3.00 8.00
6 Art Stratton 3.00 8.00
7 Gary Kilpatrick 3.00 8.00
8 Don Ward 3.00 8.00
9 Jack Michie 3.00 8.00
10 Ronald Ingram 3.00 8.00
11 John Hanna 3.00 8.00
12 Ray Larose 3.00 8.00
13 Jack Dale 3.00 8.00
14 Tom McVie 3.00 8.00
15 Gerry Meehan 6.00 15.00
16 Chris Worthy 3.00 8.00
17 Bobby Schmautz 8.00 20.00
18 Dwight Carruthers 3.00 8.00
19 Patrick Dunn TR .75 2.00
20 Bill MacFarland CO .75 2.00

1989-90 7th Inning Sketch OHL

This 200-card standard-size set was issued by 7th Inning Sketch featuring members of the Ontario Hockey League. The fronts of the cards have yellow borders which surround the player's photo and on the bottom of the front is the player's name. In the upper right hand corner, the team's name is featured. The set has been popular with collectors since it features early cards of Eric Lindros. The set was also issued on a limited basis (a numbered edition of 3000) as a factory set; however, the factory set only included 167 cards as 33 cards were dropped for unspecified reasons.

COMPLETE SET (200) 12.00 30.00
COMPLETE FACT.SET (167) 12.00 30.00
1 Eric Lindros 1.50 4.00
(Beware counterfeits)
2 Jarrod Skalde .20 .50
3 Joe Busillo .02 .10
4 Dale Craigwell .08 .25
5 Clair Cornish .02 .10
6 Jean-Paul Davis .02 .10
7 Craig Donaldson .02 .10
8 Wade Simpson .02 .10
9 Mike Craig .08 .25
10 Mark Deazeley .02 .10
11 Scott Hollis .02 .10
12 Brian Grieve .02 .10
13 Dave Craievich .02 .10
14 Paul O'Hagan .02 .10
15 Matt Hoffman .02 .10
16 Trevor McIvor .02 .10
17 Cory Banika .02 .10
18 Kevin Butt .07 .20
19 Iain Fraser .02 .10
20 Bill Armstrong .07 .20
21 Scott Luik .02 .10
22 Brent Grieve .02 .10
23 Fred Brathwaite .40 1.00
24 Paul Holden .02 .10
25 Trevor Dam .02 .10
26 Chris Taylor .02 .10
27 Mark Guy .02 .10
28 Louie DeBrusk .30 .75
29 John Battice .02 .10
30 Chris Crombie .02 .10
31 Sean Basilio .07 .20
32 Aaron Nagy .02 .10
33 Greg Ryan .02 .10
34 Steve Martell .02 .10
35 Scott MacKay .02 .10
36 Dennis Purdie .30 .75
37 Steve Boyd .02 .10
38 John Tanner .08 .25
39 David Anderson .02 .10
40 Rick Corriveau .02 .10
41 Todd Hlushko .08 .25
42 Doug Synish .02 .10
43 Dan LeBlanc .07 .20
44 Dave Noseworthy .02 .10
45 Karl Taylor .02 .10
46 Jeff Hodgen .02 .10
47 Mike Kelly .01 .05
Gary Agnew
48 Wayne Maxner .02 .10
49 Brett Seguin .02 .10
50 Greg Walters .02 .10
51 Chris Snell .02 .10
52 Troy Binnie .02 .10
53 Joni Lehto .02 .10
54 Steve Kluczkowski .02 .10
55 Ryan Kuwabara .07 .20
56 Chris Simon .40 1.00
57 Jerrett DeFazio .07 .20
58 Rob Sangster .02 .10
59 Greg Clancy .02 .10
60 Peter Ambroziak .02 .10
61 Jeff Ricciardi .02 .10
62 John East .02 .10
63 Joey McTamney .02 .10
64 Dan Poirier .02 .10
65 Gairin Smith .02 .10
66 Wade Gibson .02 .10
67 Checklist Card .01 .05
68 Andrew Brodie .02 .10
69 Craig Wilson .02 .10
70 Peter McGlynn .02 .10
71 George Dourian .02 .10
72 Bob Berg .07 .20
73 Richard Fatrola .02 .10
74 Craig Fraser .02 .10
75 Brent Gretzky .20 .50
76 Jake Grimes .02 .10
77 Darren McCarty .75 2.00
78 Ted Miskolczi .02 .10
79 Rob Pearson .08 .25
80 Gordon Pell .02 .10
81 John Porco .02 .10
82 Ken Rowbotham .02 .10
83 Scott Thornton .20 .50
84 Shawn Way .02 .10
85 Steve Bancroft .02 .10
86 Greg Bignell .02 .10
87 Scott Boston .02 .10
88 Scott Feasby .02 .10
89 Derek Morin .07 .20
90 Sean O'Reilly .07 .20
91 Jason Skelet .02 .10
92 Greg Dreveny .02 .10
93 Jeff Fife .02 .10
94 Rob Stopar .02 .10
95 Joe Desrosiers .01 .05
96 Danny Flynn .02 .10
97 Dr. R.L. Vaughan .01 .05
98 Troy Stephens .02 .10
99 Dan Brown .02 .10
100 Mike Ricci .40 1.00
101 Brent Pope .02 .10
102 Mike Dagenais .07 .20
103 Scott Campbell .02 .10
104 Jamie Pegg .02 .10
105 Joe Hawley .02 .10
106 Jason Dawe .08 .25
107 Paul Mitton .02 .10
108 Mike Tomlinson .02 .10
109 Dave Lorentz .02 .10
110 Dale McTavish .02 .10
111 Willie McGarvey .02 .10
112 Don O'Neill .02 .10
113 Mark Myles .02 .10
114 Chris Longo .07 .20
115 Tom Hopkins .02 .10
116 Jassen Cullimore .02 .10
117 Geoff Ingram .02 .10
118 Twohey .01 .05
Bovair TR
119 Doug Searle .02 .10
120 Bryan Gendron .02 .10
121 Andrew Verner .08 .25
122 Todd Bocjun .07 .20
123 Dick Todd .02 .10
124 George Burnett .02 .10
125 Brad May .30 .75
126 David Benn .02 .10
127 Brian Mueggler .02 .10
128 Todd Coopman .02 .10
129 Geoff Rawson .02 .10
130 Keith Primeau .75 2.00
131 Mark Lawrence .07 .20
132 Randy Hall .02 .10
133 Greg Suchan .02 .10
134 Ken Ruddick .02 .10
135 Jason Winch .07 .20
136 Paul Wolanski .02 .10
137 Dennis Scott .01 .05
138 Steve Udvari .02 .10
139 Rich Beley .07 .20
140 Don Pancoe .02 .10
141 Paul Bruneau .01 .05
142 Paul Laus .20 .50
143 Mike St. John .02 .10
144 John Johnson .02 .10
145 Greg Allen .02 .10
146 Don McConnell .02 .10
147 Andy Bezeau .02 .10
148 Jeff Walker .02 .10
149 John Spoltore .02 .10
150 Derek Switzer .07 .20
151 Tyler Ertel .02 .10
152 Shawn Antoski .08 .25
153 Jason Corrigan .02 .10
154 Derian Hatcher .30 .75
155 John Vary .02 .10
156 Jamie Caruso .02 .10
157 Trevor Halverson .02 .10
158 Robert Deschamps .02 .10
159 Jeff Gardiner .07 .20
160 Gary Miller .02 .10
161 Shayne Antoski .08 .25
162 John Van Kessel .02 .10
163 Colin Austin .02 .10
164 Tom Purcell .02 .10
165 Joel Morin .02 .10
166 Tim Favot .02 .10
167 Checklist Card .01 .05
168 Jason Beaton .02 .10
169 Chris Ottmann .02 .10
170 Mike Matuszek .02 .10
171 Rob Fournier .02 .10
172 Ron Bertrand .07 .20
173 Bert Templeton .02 .10
174 Casey Jones .01 .05
175 Robert Frayn .02 .10
176 Claude Noel .02 .10
177 Sean Basilio Award .02 .10
178 Chris Longo Rookie .02 .10
179 Cory Keenan AS .02 .10
180 Owen Nolan Award .40 1.00
181 Steven Rice AS .08 .25
182 Shayne Stevenson .08 .25
Scorer
183 Mike Ricci Award .20 .50
184 Jason Firth Award .02 .10
185 John Slaney Award .02 .10
186 Iain Fraser Award .02 .10
187 Steven Rice Star .08 .25
188 Eric Lindros Scorer 1.25 3.00
189 Keith Primeau Scorer .40 1.00
190 Mike Ricci Award .20 .50
191 Mike Torchia AS .08 .25
192 Mike Torchia Star .07 .20
193 Jarrod Skalde Champs .08 .25
194 Paul O'Hagan Award .02 .10
195 Eric Lindros 1.25 3.00
(Where in 1991)
196 Eric Lindros AS 1.25 3.00
197 Jeff Fife Award .02 .10
198 Iain Fraser MVP .02 .10
199 Bill Armstrong Winner .02 .10
200 Checklist Card .01 .05

1990-91 7th Inning Sketch OHL

The 7th Inning Sketch OHL Hockey set contains 400 standard-size cards. The front features a full color photo, enframed by different color borders. The player's position appears in a star at the lower left hand corner, with his name and "OHL" in the bar below the picture. The back has another color photo, with biographical information and career summary in a box running the length of the card. This set features a regular card (1) as well as a promo card of hockey star Eric Lindros. The promo version has the same front as Lindros' card number 1 but has an asterisk in the card number position on the card back. Players from the following teams are represented in this set: Oshawa Generals (1, 325-339, 341-345, 347-350), Belleville Bulls (2-10, 12-21, 23, 340, 346), Kingston Frontenacs (11, 51-75), Cornwall Royals (22, 24-50), Ottawa 67's (76-100, 230), Detroit Compuware Ambassadors (101-121, 123-125), North Bay Centennials (122, 301-324), London Knights (126-149), Sault Ste. Marie Greyhounds (150-173, 175-176), Windsor Spitfires (174, 177-200), Dukes of Hamilton (201-225), Kitchener Rangers (226-229, 231 250, 370), Niagara Falls Thunder (251-275), Owen Sound Platers (276-299), Peterborough Petes (351-369, 371-376), and Sudbury Wolves (377-400). First round picks (1991 NHL Draft) in this set include Eric Lindros (1), Alex Stojanov (7), Pat Peake (14), Glen Murray (18), and Trevor Halverson (21). First round picks (1992 NHL Draft rank indicated in parenthesis) in this set include Todd Warriner (4), Cory Stillman (6), Brandon Convery (8), Curtis Bowen (22), and Grant Marshall (23). A factory set, a numbered edition of 9000 sets, was produced and marketed separately.

COMPLETE SET (400) 8.00 20.00
COMPLETE FACT.SET (400) 10.00 25.00
1 Eric Lindros 1.50 4.00
2 Greg Dreveny .02 .10
3 Belleville Checklist UER .01 .05
4 Richard Fatrola .02 .10
5 Craig Fraser .02 .10
6 Robert Frayn .02 .10
7 Brent Gretzky .15 .40
8 Jake Grimes .02 .10
9 Darren Hurley .02 .10
10 Rick Marshall .02 .10
11 Checklist UER .01 .05
12 Darren McCarty .75 2.00
13 Derek Morin .02 .10
14 Sean O'Reilly .02 .10
15 Rob Pearson UER .08 .25
16 John Porco .02 .10
17 Ken Rowbotham .02 .10
18 Ken Ruddick .02 .10
19 Jim Sonmez .02 .10
20 Brad Teichmann .02 .10
21 Chris Varga .02 .10
22 Checklist Card .01 .05
23 Larry Mavety CO .01 .05
24 Rival Fullum .02 .10
25 Nathan Lafayette .02 .10
26 Darren Bell .02 .10
27 Craig Brocklehurst .02 .10
28 Shawn Caplice .02 .10
29 Mike Cavanaugh .02 .10
30 Jason Cirone .02 .10
31 Chris Clancy .02 .10
32 Mark DeSantis .02 .10
33 Rob Dykeman .02 .10
34 Shayne Gaffar .02 .10
35 Ilpo Kauhanen .02 .10
36 Rob Kinghan .02 .10
37 Dave Lemay .02 .10
38 Guy Leveque .02 .10
39 Matt McGuffin .02 .10
40 Marcus Middleton .02 .10
41 Thomas Nemeth .02 .10
42 Rod Pasma .02 .10
43 Richard Raymond .02 .10
44 Jeff Reid .02 .10
45 Jerry Ribble .02 .10
46 Jean-Alain Schneider .02 .10
47 John Slaney .02 .10
48 Jeremy Stevenson .02 .10
49 Ryan VandenBussche .40 1.00
50 Marc Crawford CO .20 .50
51 Tony Bella .02 .10
52 Drake Berehowsky .20 .50
53 Jason Chipman .02 .10
54 Tony Cimellaro .02 .10
55 Keli Corpse .02 .10
56 Mike Dawson .02 .10
57 Sean Gauthier UER .02 .10
58 Fred Goltz .02 .10
59 Gord Harris .02 .10
60 Tony Iob .02 .10
61 John Bernie .02 .10
62 Dale Junkin .02 .10
63 Nathan Lafayette .02 .10
64 Blake Martin .02 .10
65 Mark McCague .02 .10
66 Bob McKillop .02 .10
67 Justin Morrison .02 .10
68 Bill Robinson .02 .10
69 Joel Sandie .02 .10
70 Kevin King .02 .10
71 Dave Stewart .02 .10
72 Joel Washkurak .02 .10
73 Brock Woods .02 .10
74 Randy Hall CO .02 .10
75 John Vary .02 .10
76 Peter Ambroziak .02 .10
77 Troy Binnie .02 .10
78 Curt Bowen .02 .10
79 Andrew Brodie .02 .10
80 Ottawa Checklist .02 .10
81 Greg Clancy .02 .10
82 Jerrett DeFazio .02 .10
83 Kris Draper .40 1.00
84 Wade Gibson .02 .10
85 Ryan Kuwabara .02 .10
86 Joni Lehto .02 .10
87 Donald MacPherson .02 .10
88 Grant Marshall .20 .50
89 Peter McGlynn .02 .10
90 Maurice O'Brien .02 .10
91 Jeff Ricciardi .02 .10
92 Brett Seguin .02 .10
93 Len DeVuono .02 .10
94 Gerry Skrypec .02 .10
95 Chris Snell .02 .10
96 Jason Snow .02 .10
97 Sean Spencer .02 .10
98 Brad Spry .02 .10
99 Matt Stone .02 .10
100 Brian Kilrea CO .02 .10
101 Kevin Butt .08 .25
102 Glen Craig .02 .10
103 Paul Doherty .02 .10
104 Mark Donahue .02 .10
105 Jeff Gardiner .02 .10
106 Trent Gleason .02 .10
107 Troy Gleason .02 .10
108 Mark Lawrence .08 .25
109 Trevor McIvor .02 .10
110 Paul Mitton .02 .10
111 David Myles .02 .10
112 Jeffery Nolan .02 .10
113 Rob Papineau .02 .10
114 Pat Peake .02 .10
115 Chris Phelps .02 .10
116 John Pinches .02 .10
117 James Shea .02 .10
118 James Sheehan .02 .10
119 John Stos .02 .10
120 Tom Sullivan .02 .10
121 John Wynne .02 .10
122 Robert Thorpe .02 .10
123 David Benn .02 .10
124 Andy Weidenbach CO UER .01 .05
125 Detroit Checklist .01 .05
126 David Anderson .02 .10
127 Sean Basilio .08 .25
128 Brent Brownlee .02 .10
129 Rick Corriveau .02 .10
130 Derrick Crane .02 .10
131 Chris Crombie .02 .10
132 Louie DeBrusk .40 1.00
133 Mark Guy .02 .10
134 Brett Marrietti .02 .10
135 Steve Martell .02 .10
136 Scott McKay .02 .10
137 Aaron Nagy .02 .10
138 Brett Nicol .02 .10
139 Barry Potomski .40 1.00
140 Dennis Purdie .40 1.00
141 Kelly Reed .02 .10
142 Gregory Ryan .02 .10
143 Brad Smyth .02 .10
144 Nick Stajduhar .02 .10
145 John Tanner .08 .25
146 Chris Taylor .02 .10
147 Mark Visheau .02 .10
148 Gary Agnew CO .08 .25
149 London Checklist .02 .10
150 Sault Ste. Marie .02 .10
Checklist
151 David Babcock .02 .10
152 Drew Bannister .02 .10
153 Bob Boughner .30 .75
154 Joe Busillo .02 .10
155 Mike DeCoff .02 .10
156 Jason Denomme .02 .10
157 Adam Foote .75 2.00
158 Kevin Hodson .30 .75
159 Shaun Imber .02 .10
160 Ralph Intranuovo .02 .10
161 Kevin King .02 .10
162 Rick Kowalsky .02 .10
163 Chris Kraemer .02 .10
164 Dan Lambert .08 .25
165 Mike Lenarduzzi .08 .25
166 Tom MacDonald .02 .10
167 Mark Matier .02 .10
168 David Matsos .02 .10
169 Colin Miller .02 .10
170 Perry Pappas .02 .10
171 Jarrett Reid .02 .10
172 Kevin Reid .02 .10
173 Brad Tiley UER .02 .10
174 Windsor Checklist .01 .05
175 Wade Whitten .02 .10
176 Ted Nolan CO .20 .50
177 Sean Burns .02 .10
178 Jason Cirone .02 .10
179 John Copley .02 .10
180 Tyler Ertel .02 .10
181 Brian Forestell .02 .10
182 Rival Fullum .02 .10
183 Steve Gibson .02 .10
184 Leonard MacDonald .02 .10
185 Mike Speer .02 .10
186 Kevin MacKay .02 .10
187 Ryan Merritt .02 .10
188 Doug Minor .02 .10
189 Rick Morton .02 .10
190 Sean O'Hagan .08 .25
191 Mike Polano .02 .10
192 Cory Stillman .20 .50
193 Jason Stos .02 .10
194 Trevor Walsh .02 .10
195 Todd Warriner .20 .50
196 Jeff Wilson .02 .10
197 Jason York .20 .50
198 Jason Zohil .02 .10
199 Steve Smith .02 .10
200 Brad Smith CO .02 .10
201 Jeff Bes .02 .10
202 Mike Blum .02 .10
203 Sean Brown .02 .10
204 Darcy Cahill .02 .10
205 Dale Chokan .02 .10
206 Chris Code .02 .10
207 George Dourion .02 .10
208 Todd Gleason .02 .10
209 Hamilton Checklist UER .01 .05
210 Michael Hartwick .02 .10
211 Scott Jenkins .02 .10
212 Rob Leask .02 .10
213 Gordon Pell .02 .10
214 Michael Reier .02 .10
215 Kayle Short .02 .10
216 Jason Skellett .02 .10
217 Gairin Smith .02 .10
218 Jeff Smith .02 .10
219 Jason Soules .02 .10
220 Alex Stojanov .02 .10
221 Dan Tanevski .02 .10
222 Gary Taylor .02 .10
223 Brent Watson .02 .10
224 Steve Woods .02 .10
225 Jay Johnston CO UER .01 .05
226 Mike Allen .02 .10
227 Brad Barton .02 .10
228 Richard Borgo .02 .10
229 Justin Cullen .02 .10
230 Lenny DeVuono .02 .10
231 Norman Dezainde .02 .10
232 Jason Firth .02 .10
233 Derek Gauthier .02 .10
234 Jamie Israel .02 .10
235 Chris LiPuma .02 .10
236 Tony McCabe .02 .10
237 Paul McCallion .02 .10
238 Shayne McCosh .02 .10
239 Rod Saarinen .02 .10
240 Steve Smith .02 .10
241 Joey St.Aubin .02 .10
242 Rob Stopar .02 .10
243 Jason Zohil UER .02 .10
244 Mike Torchia .08 .25
245 Gib Tucker .02 .10
246 John Uniac .02 .10
247 Jack Williams .02 .10
248 Joe McDonnell CO .02 .10
249 Steven Rice .02 .10
250 Mike Polano .02 .10
251 Greg Allen .02 .10
252 Roch Belley .08 .25
253 Andy Bezeau .02 .10
254 Derek Booth .02 .10
255 Kevin Brown .02 .10
256 Mark Cardiff .02 .10
257 Jason Coles .02 .10
258 Todd Coopman .02 .10
259 Richard Girhiny .02 .10
260 Brian Holk .02 .10
261 John Johnson .02 .10
262 Dan Krisko .02 .10
263 Manny Legace .75 2.00
264 Brad May .30 .75
265 Don McConnell .02 .10
266 Niagara Falls CL .01 .05
267 Aaron Morrison .02 .10
268 Cory Pageau .02 .10
269 Geoff Rawson .02 .10
270 Todd Simon .02 .10

271 Steve Staios .08 .25
272 Jeff Walker .02 .10
273 Todd Wetzel .02 .10
274 Jason Winch .02 .10
275 Paul Wolanski .02 .10
276 Owen Sound Checklist .01 .05
277 Andrew Brunette .40 1.00
278 Wyatt Buckland .02 .10
279 Jason Buetow .02 .10
280 Jason Castellan .02 .10
281 Trent Cull .02 .10
282 Robert Deschamps .02 .10
283 Chris Driscoll .02 .10
284 Bryan Drury .02 .10
285 Todd Hunter .02 .10
286 Troy Hutchinson .02 .10
287 Kirk Maltby .30 .75
288 Geordie Maynard .02 .10
289 Kevin McDougall .02 .10
290 Ted Miskolczi .02 .10
291 Steve Parson .02 .10
292 Jeff Perry .02 .10
293 Grayden Reid .02 .10
294 Mike Speer .02 .10
295 Mark Strohack .02 .10
296 Mark Vilneff .02 .10
297 Keith Whitmore .02 .10
298 Jim Brown .02 .10
299 Len McNamara CO .01 .05
300 David Branch COMM .02 .10
301 Shayne Antoski .02 .10
302 Jason Beaton .02 .10
303 Ron Bertrand .02 .10
304 Michael Burman .02 .10
305 Jamie Caruso .02 .10
306 Allan Cox .02 .10
307 Tim Favot .02 .10
308 Trevor Halverson .02 .10
309 Derian Hatcher .40 1.00
310 Bill Lang .02 .10
311 Jason MacDonald .02 .10
312 Gary Miller .02 .10
313 Chris Ottmann .02 .10
314 Chad Penney .02 .10
315 Rick Pollard .02 .10
316 Bradley Shepard .02 .10
317 John Spoltore .08 .25
318 Derek Switzer .02 .10
319 Karl Taylor .02 .10
320 John Vary .02 .10
321 Kevin White .02 .10
322 Billy Wright .02 .10
323 Bert Templeton CO .02 .10
324 North Bay Checklist .01 .05
325 Oshawa Checklist UER .01 .05
326 Jan Benda .02 .10
327 Fred Brathwaite .40 1.00
328 Markus Brunner .02 .10
329 Trevor Burgess .02 .10
330 Clair Cornish .02 .10
331 Mike Cote .02 .10
332 Dave Craievich .02 .10
333 Dale Craigwell .20 .50
334 Jean-Paul Davis .02 .10
335 Mark Deazeley .02 .10
336 Mike Fountain .08 .25
337 Brian Grieve .02 .10
338 Matt Hoffman .02 .10
339 Scott Hollis .02 .10
340 Scott Boston .02 .10
341 Scott Luik .02 .10
342 Craig Lutes .02 .10
343 William MacPherson .02 .10
344 Paul O'Hagan .02 .10
345 Wade Simpson .02 .10
346 Jarrod Skalde UER .20 .50
347 Troy Sweet .02 .10
348 Jason Weaver .02 .10
349 Rick Cornacchia CO .02 .10
350 The Trophy .02 .10
351 Greg Bailey .02 .10
352 Ryan Black .02 .10
353 Todd Bocjun UER .08 .25
354 Toby Burkitt .02 .10
355 Scott Campbell .02 .10
356 Jassen Cullimore .02 .10
357 Jason Dawe .08 .25
358 Dan Ferguson .02 .10
359 Bryan Gendron .02 .10
360 Michael Harding .02 .10
361 Joe Hawley .02 .10
362 Peterborough CL .01 .05
363 Geordie Kinnear .02 .10
364 Chris Longo UER .02 .10
365 Dale McTavish .02 .10
366 Mark Myles .02 .10
367 Don O'Neill .02 .10
368 Jamie Pegg .02 .10
369 Brent Pope .02 .10
370 Kitchener CL .01 .05
371 Doug Searle .02 .10
372 Troy Stephens .02 .10
373 Mike Tomlinson .02 .10
374 Brent Tully .02 .10
375 Andrew Verner .08 .25
376 Dick Todd CO .02 .10
377 John Tanner .08 .25
378 Adam Bennett .02 .10
379 Kyle Blacklock .02 .10
380 Terry Chitaroni .02 .10
381 Brandon Convery .02 .10
382 J.D. Eaton .02 .10
383 Derek Etches .02 .10
384 Rod Hinks .02 .10
385 Bill Kovacs .02 .10
386 Alain Laforge .02 .10
387 Jamie Matthews .02 .10
388 Glen Murray .75 2.00
389 Dean Cull .02 .10
390 Sean O'Donnell .20 .50
391 Sudbury Checklist UER .01 .05
392 Mike Peca .75 2.00
393 Shawn Rivers .02 .10
394 Dan Ryder .02 .10
395 Alastair Still .02 .10
396 Michael Yeo .02 .10
397 Barry Young .02 .10
398 Jason Young .02 .10
399 Ken MacKenzie CO .02 .10
400 Bob Berg UER .02 .10
NNO Eric Lindros promo 2.00 5.00

1990-91 7th Inning Sketch QMJHL

This 268-card standard-size set was produced by 7th Inning Sketch featuring players from the Quebec Major Junior Hockey League. First round picks (1991 NHL Draft) in this set include Patrick Poulin (9), Martin Lapointe (10), and Philippe Boucher (13). The best known players in the set, however, are 1990 second-rounder Felix Potvin and 1991 first-rounder Martin Brodeur. A factory set, a numbered edition of 4,800, was produced and marketed separately.

COMPLETE SET (268) 8.00 20.00
COMPLETE FACT.SET (268) 10.00 25.00
1 Patrick Poulin .08 .25
2 Steve Lupien .08 .25
3 Pierre Gagnon .08 .25
4 Eric Plante .02 .10
5 Stephane Desjardins .02 .10
6 Peter Valenta .02 .10
7 Alexander Legault .02 .10
8 Patrice Brisebois .20 .50
9 Martin Charrois .02 .10
10 Eric Dandenault .02 .10
11 Claude Juiras Jr. .02 .10
12 David Pekarek .02 .10
13 Denis Chasse .08 .25
14 Ian Laperriere .08 .25
15 Roger Larche .02 .10
16 Dave Paquet .02 .10
17 Pascal Lebrasseur .02 .10
18 Eric Meloche .02 .10
19 The Face Off .01 .05
20 Sylvain Rodrigue .08 .25
21 Dary Giarard .02 .10
22 Eric Rochette .02 .10
23 Steve Gosselin .02 .10
24 Martin Lavalle .02 .10
25 Martin Lapointe .75 2.00
26 Eric Brule .02 .10
27 Richard Boivin .02 .10
28 Patrice Martineau .02 .10
29 Dave Tremblay .02 .10
30 Steve Larouche .02 .10
31 Danny Beauregard .02 .10
32 Francois Belanger .02 .10
33 Michel St.Jacques .02 .10
34 Patric Sissillan .02 .10
35 Felix Potvin 1.50 4.00
36 Sebastien Parent .02 .10
37 Eric Duchesne .02 .10
38 Gilles Bouchard .02 .10
39 Martin Gagne .02 .10
40 Stephane Charbonneau .02 .10
41 Martin Beaupre .02 .10
42 Daniel Paradis .02 .10
43 Joe Canale .02 .10
44 Georges Vezina Arena .02 .10
45 Francois Leblanc .08 .25
46 Martin Chaput .02 .10
47 Marc Beaucage .02 .10
48 Carl Mantha .02 .10
49 Jim Bermingham .02 .10
50 Philippe Boucher .08 .25
51 Denis Chalifoux .02 .10
52 Sylvain Naud .02 .10
53 Jean Roberge .02 .10
54 Sandy McCarthy .40 1.00
55 Eric Dubois .02 .10
56 Jean Blouin .02 .10
57 Jason Brousseau .02 .10
58 Pierre Sandke .02 .10
59 Benoit Larose .02 .10
60 Yanick Frechette .02 .10
61 Pierre Calder .02 .10
62 Patric Grise .02 .10
63 Martin Balfeux .02 .10
64 Boris Rousson .40 1.00
65 Martin Trudeli .02 .10
66 Carl Leblanc .02 .10
67 Martin Brochu .40 1.00
68 Benoit Terrien .02 .10
69 QMJHL Action .02 .10
70 Pascal Vincent .02 .10
71 Christian Tardi .02 .10
72 Christian Campeau .02 .10
73 Eric Raymond .08 .25
74 John Kovacs .02 .10
75 Steve Areas .02 .10
76 Pascal Dufalt .02 .10
77 Greg MacEachern .02 .10
78 Remi Belliveau .02 .10
79 Jocelyn Langlois .02 .10
80 Carl Menard .02 .10
81 Sebastein Foneir .02 .10
82 Jean-Franco Gregoire .02 .10
83 Normand Demers .02 .10
84 Nicolas Lefebvre .02 .10
85 Dominic Maltais .02 .10
86 Mario Therrien .02 .10
87 Daniel Thibault .02 .10
88 Jean-Francois Labbe .40 1.00
89 Alain Cote .02 .10
90 Eric Prillo .02 .10
91 Patrick Nadeau .02 .10
92 Claude Poner .02 .10
93 Stephane Julier .02 .10
94 Patrice Rene .02 .10
95 Francis Coutineir .02 .10
96 Guy Lefebvre .02 .10
97 Carl Boudreau .02 .10
98 Jacques Parent .02 .10
99 Stephane Bouquet .02 .10
100 Yanic Perreault .20 .50
101 Yvan Bergeron .02 .10
102 Jean-Francois Rivard .08 .25
103 Daniel Laflamme .02 .10
104 Francois Bourdeau .02 .10
105 Yvan Charrois .02 .10
106 Patric Genest .02 .10
107 Herve Lapointe .02 .10
108 Jean-Francois Jomphe .08 .25
109 Marc Tardif .02 .10
110 Eric Cardinal .02 .10
111 Denis Cloutier .02 .10
112 QMJHL Action .02 .10
113 Alain Samscartier .01 .05
114 Marquis Mathieu .08 .25
115 Stephan Tartari .02 .10
116 QMJHL Action .02 .10
117 QMJHL Action .02 .10
118 Martin Ray .02 .10
119 David Boudreault .02 .10
120 Mario Durroulin .02 .10
121 Jean-Francis Dieard .02 .10
122 QMJHL Action .02 .10
123 QMJHL Action .02 .10
124 Mausime Gagne .02 .10
125 Stephane Guellet .02 .10
126 Steven Paiement .02 .10
127 Francois Olympique .02 .10
128 Eric Coci .02 .10
129 Simon Toupin .02 .10
130 Shane Doirrin .02 .10
131 Todd Sparks .02 .10
132 Bruno Lajeunesse .02 .10
133 Marcel Cousineau .20 .50
134 Claude-Charl Sauirol .02 .10
135 Eric Bellerose .02 .10
136 QMJHL Action .02 .10
137 QMJHL Action .02 .10
138 Martin Lepage .02 .10
139 Michael Langauer .02 .10
140 Fredric Boivin .02 .10
141 Steven Dion .02 .10
142 QMJHL Action .02 .10
143 QMJHL Action .02 .10
144 Dan Paolucci .02 .10
145 Bruno Villeneuve .02 .10
146 Yanic Perreault CL .08 .25
147 Checklist Card .01 .05
148 Stefan Simoes .02 .10
149 Joel Blain .02 .10
150 Eric Lavigne .02 .10
151 Checklist Card .01 .05
152 Patrick Poulin CL .02 .10
153 Robert Melanson .02 .10
154 Brian Rogger .02 .10
155 Checklist Card .01 .05
156 Checklist Card .01 .05
157 Francois Ouellette .08 .25
158 QMJHL Action .02 .10
159 Felix Potvin CL .75 2.00
160 Checklist Card .01 .05
161 Checklist Card .01 .05
162 Checklist Card .01 .05
163 QMJHL Action .02 .10
164 QMJHL Action .02 .10
165 Checklist Card .01 .05
166 Checklist Card .01 .05
167 QMJHL Action .02 .10
168 QMJHL Action .02 .10
169 Pierre Fillon .02 .10
170 Yanick Degrace .08 .25
171 Paul Daigneault .02 .10
172 Stacy Dellaire .02 .10
173 Steve Searles .02 .10
174 Todd Gillingham .02 .10
175 Yves Sarault .02 .10
176 Jason Downey .02 .10
177 Paul Brousseau .02 .10
178 Raymond Delarosbi .02 .10
179 Yvan Corbin .02 .10
180 Gaston Drapeau .02 .10
181 Celebration .02 .10
182 Reginald Brezeault .02 .10
183 Eric Lafrance .02 .10
184 Martin Lavalle .08 .25
185 Sebastein Lavallere .02 .10
186 Martin Lefebvre .02 .10
187 Richard Hamelin .02 .10
188 Eric Beauvois .02 .10
189 Hughes Mongeon .02 .10
190 Alaine Cole .02 .10
191 Eric Desrochers .08 .25
192 Eric Joyal .02 .10
193 Steve Dortigny .02 .10
194 Fredrick Lefebvre .02 .10
195 Patrick Hebert .02 .10
196 Johnny Lorenzo .08 .25
197 Sylvain Cornier .02 .10
198 QMJHL Action .02 .10
199 Dave Morissette .02 .10
200 Yanick Dupre .02 .10
201 Eric Marcoux .02 .10
202 Bruno Ducharme .02 .10
203 Martin Caron .02 .10
204 Yves Meunier .02 .10
205 Eric Bissonette .02 .10
206 Jason Underhill .02 .10
207 Dave Belliveau .02 .10
208 Steve Lapointe .02 .10
209 Dean Melanson .02 .10
210 Trevor Dehaime .02 .10
211 Jacques Leblanc .02 .10
212 Normand Pacquet .02 .10
213 Huges Laliberte .02 .10
214 Craig Prior .02 .10
215 Patrick Labrecque .08 .25
216 Patrick Cloutier .02 .10
217 Michael Bazinet .02 .10
218 Christian Proulx .02 .10
219 QMJHL Action .02 .10
220 Charles Poulin .02 .10
221 Christian Larivierre .02 .10
222 Martin Brodeur 3.00 8.00
223 Yanick Lemay .02 .10
224 Dennis Leblanc .02 .10
225 Francois Groleau .02 .10
226 Pierre Sevigny .02 .10
227 Pierre Allard .02 .10
228 Craig Martin .02 .10
229 Karl Dykhuis .08 .25
230 Etienne Lavoie .02 .10
231 Stan Melanson .02 .10
232 Dominic Rheaume .02 .10
233 Mario Nobili .02 .10
234 Martin Gendron .08 .25
235 Stephane Menard .02 .10
236 David St.Pierre .02 .10
237 Yan Arsenault .02 .10
238 Norman Flynn .01 .05
239 QMJHL Action .02 .10
240 David Chouinard .02 .10
241 Robert Guilliet .02 .10
242 Martin Lajeunesse .02 .10
243 Nichol Cloutier .02 .10
244 Joel Brouchard .08 .25
245 Donald Brashear .40 1.00
246 Sebastien Tremblay .02 .10
247 Dominique Grandmaison .02 .10
248 Nicolas Lefebvre .02 .10
249 Joseph Napolitano .02 .10
250 Marc Savard .02 .10
251 Alain Gauthier .02 .10
252 Patrick Cole .02 .10
253 Richard Aimonette .02 .10
254 Martin Laitre .02 .10
255 Carl Lamonthe .02 .10
256 QMJHL Action .02 .10
257 Andre Durocher .02 .10
258 Jocelyn Martel .02 .10
259 Jeanot Ferlard .02 .10
260 Claude Savoie .02 .10
262 Denis Beauchamp .02 .10
263 Jean-Francois Gagnon .02 .10
264 Andre Boulaine .02 .10
265 Paul-Emile Exantus .02 .10
266 Danny Nolet .02 .10
267 Jean Lebreau .02 .10
268 Claude Barthe .02 .10

1990-91 7th Inning Sketch WHL

The 7th Inning Sketch WHL Hockey set contains 347 standard-size cards. The front features a full color photo, framed by different color borders, with the player's name and "WHL" in the bar below the picture. The set includes noteworthy cards of Scott Niedermayer and, Chris Osgood. A factory set, (a numbered edition of 6,000), was produced and marketed separately. Card number 120 was never issued.

COMPLETE SET (347) 7.20 18.00
COMPLETE FACT.SET (347) 8.00 20.00
1 Brent Bilodeau .08 .25
2 Craig Chapman .02 .10
3 Jeff Jubenville .02 .10
4 Al Kinisky .02 .10
5 Kevin Malgunas .02 .10
6 Andy MacIntyre .02 .10
7 Darren McAusland .02 .10
8 Mike Seaton .02 .10
9 Turner Stevenson .20 .50
10 Lindsay Valis .02 .10
11 Dave Wilkie .08 .25
12 Jesse Wilson .02 .10
13 Dody Wood .02 .10
14 Bradley Zavisha .02 .10
15 Vince Boe .02 .10
16 Scott Davis .02 .10
17 Troy Hyatt .02 .10
10 Trevor Pennook .02 .10
19 Corey Schwab .20 .50
20 Scott Bellefontaine .08 .25
21 Travis Kelln .02 .10
22 Peter Anholt CO/GM .01 .05
23 Sonny Mignacca UER .08 .25
24 Chris Osgood .75 2.00
25 Murray Garbutt .02 .10
26 Kalvin Knibbs .02 .10
27 Jason Krywulak .02 .10
28 Jason Miller .02 .10
29 Rob Niedermayer .30 .75
30 Clayton Norris .02 .10
31 Jason Prosofsky .02 .10
32 Dana Rieder .02 .10
33 Kevin Riehl .02 .10
34 Tyler Romanchuk .02 .10
35 Dave Shute .02 .10
36 Lorne Toews .02 .10
37 Scott Townsend .02 .10
38 David Cooper .02 .10
39 Jon Duval .02 .10
40 Dan Kordic .08 .25
41 Mike Rathje .20 .50
42 Tim Bothwell CO .02 .10
43 Brent Thompson .08 .25
44 Jeff Knight .02 .10
45 Van Burgess .02 .10
46 Kimbi Daniels .08 .25
47 Curtis Friesen .02 .10
48 Todd Holt .02 .10
49 Blake Knox .02 .10
50 Trent McCleary .02 .10
51 Mark McFarlane .02 .10
52 Eddie Patterson .02 .10
53 Lloyd Pellitier .02 .10
54 Geoff Sanderson .30 .75
55 Andrew Schneider .02 .10
56 Tyler Wright .08 .25
57 Joel Dyck .02 .10
58 Len MacAusland .02 .10
59 Evan Marble .02 .10
60 David Podlubny .02 .10
61 Kurt Seher .02 .10
62 Jason Smith .02 .10
63 Justin Burke .08 .25
64 Kelly Thiessen .08 .25
65 Todd Esselmont .02 .10
66 Graham James CO/GM .01
67 Chris Herperger .02 .10
68 Mark McCoy .02 .10
69 Dean Malkoc .08 .25
70 Dennis Sproxton .08 .25
71 Centennial Civic Center .02 .10
72 Kimbi Daniels .08 .25
73 Shane Calder .02 .10
74 Mark Franks .02 .10
75 Greg Leahy .02 .10
76 Dean Rambo .02 .10
77 Scott Scissons .02 .10
78 David Struch .02 .10
79 Derek Tibbatts .02 .10
80 Shawn Yakimishyn .02 .10
81 Trent Coghill .02 .10
82 Robert Lelacheur .02 .10
83 Richard Matvichuk .30 .75
84 Mark Raiter .02 .10
85 Trevor Sherban .02 .10
86 Mark Wotton .08 .25
87 Cam Moon .08 .25
88 Trevor Robins .08 .25
89 Jeff Buchanan .02 .10
90 Ryan Strain .02 .10
91 Tim Cox .02 .10
92 Terry Ruskowski CO .02 .10
93 Saskatchewan Place .02 .10
94 Darin Bader .02 .10
95 Gaetan Blouin .02 .10
96 Rick Kozuback CO/GM .01 .05
97 Jason Bowen .02 .10
98 Fran Deferenza .02 .10
99 Terry Degner .02 .10
100 Devin Derksen .02 .10
101 Martin Svetlik .02 .10
102 Jeremy Warring .08 .25
103 Corey Jones .08 .25
104 Dean Tiltgen UER .02 .10
105 Ryan Fujita .02 .10
106 Jeff Fancy .02 .10
107 Terry Virtue .20 .50
108 Dennis Pinfold .02 .10
109 Kyle Reeves .02 .10
110 Steve McNutt UER .02 .10
111 Todd Klassen .02 .10
112 Darren Hastman .02 .10
113 Bill Lindsay .20 .50
114A Brian Sakic ERR .02 .10
114B Brian Sakic COR .02 .10
115 Dan Sherstenka .02 .10
116 Don Blishen .08 .25
117 Jason Marshall .02 .10
118 Dean Zayonce .02 .10
119 Brad Loring .02 .10
121 Darcy Austin UER .08 .25
122 Darcy Werenka .02 .10
123 Shane Peacock .02 .10
124 Rob Hartnell UER .02 .10
125 Brad Zimmer .02 .10
126 Allan Egeland .02 .10
127 Brad Rubachuk .02 .10
128 Jamie Pushor .20 .50
129 Jamie McLennan UER .30 .75
130 Lance Burns .02 .10
131 Ryan Smith .02 .10
132 Jason McBain .02 .10
133 Duane Maruschak UER .02 .10
134 Kevin St.Jacques .02 .10
135 Jason Sorochan .02 .10
136 Jason Widmer .02 .10
137 Bob Loucks CO .02 .10
138 Jason Ruff .02 .10
139 Pat Pylypuik .02 .10
140 Scott Adair .02 .10
141 Radek Sip .02 .10
142 Russ West .02 .10
143 Scott Thomas .02 .10
144 Kent Staniforth .02 .10
145 Travis Thiessen .02 .10
146 Mark Hussey .02 .10
147 Kevin Masters .02 .10
148 Todd Johnson .02 .10
149 Bob Loucks .02 .10
150A Rob Reimer ERR .02 .10
150B Rob Reimer COR .02 .10
151 Jeff Petruic .02 .10
152 Chris Schmidt .02 .10
153 Scott Barnstable .02 .10
154 Ian Layton .02 .10
155 Kevin Smyth .02 .10
156 Kim Deck .02 .10
157 Jason White .02 .10
158 Peter Cox .02 .10
159 Jeff Calvert UER .08 .25
160 Paul Dyck UER .02 .10
161 Derek Kletzel .02 .10
162 Jason Fitzsimmons UER .08 .25
163 Darcy Jerome .02 .10
164 Hal Christiansen .02 .10
165 Terry Hollinger .02 .10
166 Mike Risdale .08 .25
167 Jamie Heward .02 .10
168 Louis Dumont .02 .10
169 Cory Dosdall .02 .10
170 Terry Bendera .02 .10
171 Jamie Hayden .02 .10
172 Kelly Chotowetz .02 .10
173 Brad Scott .02 .10
174 Jeff Shantz .30 .75
175 Kelly Markwart .02 .10
176 Gary Pearce .02 .10
177 Kerry Biette .02 .10
178 Jamie Splett .02 .10
179 Frank Kovacs .02 .10
180 Greg Pankewicz .02 .10
181 Colin Ruck .02 .10
182 Brad Tippett CO .02 .10
183 Dusty Imoo .08 .25
184 Derek Eberle .02 .10
185 Heath Weenk .02 .10
186 Mike Sillinger .20 .50
187 Erin Thornton .02 .10
188 Mike Chrun .02 .10
189 Pat Falloon .20 .50
190 Bobby House UER .02 .10
191 Mike Jickling .02 .10
192 Trevor Tovall UER .02 .10
193 Steve Junker .02 .10
194 Shane Maitland .02 .10
195 Chris Lafrèniere .02 .10
196 Frank Evans .02 .10
197 Jon Klemm .30 .75
198 Shawn Dietrich UER .08 .25
199 Dennis Saharchuk UER .02 .10
200 Mark Woolf .02 .10
201 Ray Whitney .20 .50
202 Scott Bailey .08 .25
203 Mark Ruark .02 .10
204 Brent Thurston .02 .10
205 Dan Faassen .02 .10
206 Kerry Toporowski .02 .10
207 Des Christopher .08 .25
208 Geoff Grandberg .02 .10
209 Bryan Maxwell CO .02 .10
210 Cam Danyluk .02 .10
211 Bram Vanderkracht .02 .10
212 Calvin Thudium .02 .10
213 Mark Szoke UER .02 .10
214 Kelly McCrimmon CO/GM .02 .10
215 Kevin Robertson UER .02 .10
216A Brian Purdy ERR .02 .10
216B Brian Purdy COR .02 .10
217 Hardy Sauter .02 .10
218 Dwayne Gylywoychuk .02 .10
219 Bart Cote .02 .10
220 Merv Priest .02 .10
221 Jeff Hoad .02 .10
222 Glen Gulutzan .02 .10
223 Johan Skillgard .02 .10
224 Byron Penstock .08 .25
225A Mike Vadenberghe ERR .02 .10
225B Mike Vadenberghe COR .02 .10
226 Trevor Kidd .40 1.00
227 Dan Kopec .02 .10
228 Greg Hutchings .02 .10
229 Chris Constant .02 .10
230 Glen Webster .02 .10
231 Rob Puchniak .02 .10
232 Calvin Flint .02 .10
233 Stuart Scantlebury .02 .10
234 Jason White .02 .10
235 Gary Audette .02 .10
236 Kevin Schmalz .02 .10
237 Dwayne Newman .02 .10
238 Chris Catellier .02 .10
239 Todd Harris .02 .10
240 Mike Shemko .02 .10
241 John Badduke .02 .10
242 Mark Cipriano .02 .10
243 Brad Bagu .02 .10
244 Ross Harris .02 .10
245 Dino Caputo .02 .10
246 Cam Bristow .02 .10
247 Jarret Zukiwsky UER .02 .10
248 Jason Knox .02 .10
249 Gerry St.Cyr .02 .10
250 Larry Woo .02 .10
251 Jason Peters .02 .10
252 Shane Stangby .02 .10
253 Dave McMillen .02 .10
254 Colin Gregor UER .02 .10
255 Steve Passmore .40 1.00
256 Shayne Green UER .02 .10
257 Kevin Koopman .08 .25
258 Larry Watkins UER .02 .10
259 Scott Fukami UER .02 .10
260 Rick Hopper CO .01 .05
261 Laurie Billeck .02 .10
262 Rob Daum CO/GM UER .01 .05
263 Mark Stowe .02 .10
264 Curtis Regnier .02 .10
265 David Neilson .02 .10
266 Brian Pellerin .02 .10
267 Dean McAmmond .20 .50
268 Darren Van Impe .15 .40
269 Troy Neumeier .02 .10
270 Mike Langen .08 .25
271 Dan Kesa .02 .10
272 Travis Laycock .08 .25
273 Scott Allison .02 .10
274 Jeff Gorman .02 .10
275 Lee J. Leslie .02 .10
276 Jason Kwiatkowski .02 .10
277 Donevan Hextall UER .02 .10
278 Shane Zulyniak .02 .10
279 Darren Perkins .02 .10
280 Chad Seibel .02 .10
281 Jeff Nelson .02 .10
282 Troy Hjertas .02 .10
283 Jamie Linden .02 .10
284 Zac Boyer .02 .10
285 Jarret Bousquet .02 .10
286 Steven Yule .02 .10
287 Tommy Renney CO UER .08 .25
288 Lance Johnson .02 .10
289 Scott Niedermayer .75 2.00
290 Ryan Harrison .02 .10
291 Ed Patterson .08 .25
292 Jeff Watchorn .02 .10
293 Cal McGowan .02 .10
294 Dale Masson .08 .25
295 Joey Mittelsteadt UER .02 .10
296 Scott Loucks .02 .10
297 Shea Esselmont .02 .10
298 Craig Bonner .02 .10
299 Mike Mathers .02 .10
300 Fred Hettle .02 .10
301 Craig Lyons .02 .10
302 Murray Duval .02 .10
303 Jamie Barnes .02 .10
304 Bryan Gourlie .02 .10
305 Chad Berezniuk .02 .10
306 Corey Hirsch .20 .50
307 Darryl Sydor .30 .75
308 Jarrett Deuling .02 .10
309 Cory Stock .02 .10
310 Chris Rowland .02 .10
311 Mike Ruark .02 .10
312 Steve Konowalchuk .30 .75
313 Jeff Sebastian .02 .10
314 Brandon Smith .08 .25
315 Greg Gatto .02 .10
316 Brad Harrison .02 .10
317 Brantt Myhres .40 1.00
318 Jamie Black .02 .10
319 Colin Foley .02 .10
320 Cam Danyluk .02 .10
321 Dean Dorchak .02 .10
322 Ryan Slemko .02 .10
323 Kim Deck .02 .10
324 Kelly Harris .02 .10
325 Murray Bokenfohr .02 .10
326 Dean Intwert .08 .25
327 Dennis Saharchuk UER .02 .10
328 Shane Seiker UER .02 .10
329 Terry Virtue .20 .50
330 Josh Erdman .02 .10
331 Layne Roland .02 .10
332 Michel Michon .02 .10
333 Scott Mydan UER .02 .10
334 Brandon Wheat Kings .01 .05
335 Moose Jaw Warriors .01 .05
336 Swift Current Broncos .01 .05
337 Regina Pats UER .01 .05
338 Saskatoon Blades .01 .05
339 Medicine Hat Tigers .01 .05
340 The Goalmouth .01 .05
341 Portland Winter Hawks .01 .05
342 Kamloops Blazers UER .01 .05
343 Victoria Cougars .01 .05
344 Tri City Americans .01 .05
345 Spokane Chiefs .01 .05
346 Seattle Thunderbirds .01 .05
347 Lethbridge Hurricanes .01 .05
348 Prince Albert Raiders .01 .05

1990 7th Inning Sketch Memorial Cup

The 7th Inn. Sketch Memorial Cup Hockey set consists of 100 standard-size cards. The front features a borderless color posed photo of the player against an aqua blue background. The upper right corner of the picture is cut off and various hockey league logos are placed there. The set features players from the four semi-final teams in the 1990 Memorial Cup playoffs, Kamloops Blazers (1-25), Kitchener Rangers (26-49), Laval Titans (50-74), and Oshawa Generals (75-100). These cards were only issued as factory sets, with a numbered edition of 3,000 sets. The set features cards of future NHL players Corey Hirsch, Eric Lindros, Martin Lapointe, Scott Niedermayer, and Darryl Sydor.

COMPLETE SET (100) 30.00 50.00
1 Len Barrie .20 .50
2 Zac Boyer .20 .50
3 Dave Chyzowski .20 .50
4 Shea Esselmont .20 .50
5 Todd Esselmont .20 .50
6 Phil Huber .20 .50
7 Lance Johnson .20 .50
8 Paul Kruse .20 .50
9 Cal McGowan .20 .50
10 Mike Needham .20 .50
11 Brian Shantz .20 .50
12 Darryl Sydor .75 2.00
13 Jeff Watchorn .20 .50
14 Jarrett Bousquet .20 .50
15 Todd Harris .20 .50
16 Deen Malkoc .20 .50
17 Joey Mittelstadt .20 .50
18 Scott Niedermayer 1.25 3.00
19 Clayton Young .20 .50
20 Trevor Sim .20 .50
21 Murray Duval .20 .50
22 Steve Yule .20 .50
23 Craig Bonner .20 .50
24 Dale Masson .20 .50
25 Corey Hirsch .40 1.00
26 Joe McDonnell .20 .50
27 Rick Chambers .20 .50
28 John Finnie .20 .50
29 Randy Pearce .20 .50
30 Mark Montanari .20 .50
31 Mike Torchia .20 .50
32 Jason York .30 .75
33 Jason Firth .20 .50
34 Jamie Israel .20 .50
35 Richard Borgo .20 .50
36 John Uniac .20 .50
37 Steve Smith .20 .50
38 Steven Rice .20 .50
39 Gilbert Dionne .30 .75
40 Cory Keenan .20 .50
41 Rick Allain .20 .50
42 John Copley .20 .50
43 Gib Tucker .20 .50
44 Chris LiPuma .20 .50
45 Brad Barton .20 .50
46 Rival Fullum .20 .50
47 Joey St.Aubin .20 .50
48 Jack Williams .20 .50
49 Shayne Stevenson .20 .50
50 Pierre Creamer .20 .50
51 Carl Mantha .20 .50
52 Julien Cameron .20 .50
53 Sandy McCarthy .75 2.00
54 Gino Odjick .40 1.00
55 Eric Raymond .20 .50
56 Carl Boudreau .20 .50
57 Greg MacEachern .20 .50
58 Allen Kerr .20 .50
59 Patrice Brisebois .30 .75
60 Eric Bissonette .20 .50
61 Martin Lapointe 1.25 3.00
62 Michel Gingras .20 .50
63 Sylvain Naud .20 .50
64 Pat Caron .20 .50
65 Regis Tremblay .20 .50
66 Francois Pelletier .20 .50
67 Jason Brousseau .20 .50
68 Eric Dubois .20 .50
69 Claude Boivin .20 .50
70 Denis Chalifoux .20 .50
71 Jim Bermingham .20 .50
72 Daniel Arsenault .20 .50
73 Normand Demers .20 .50
74 Serge Anglehart .20 .50
75 Rick Cornacchia .20 .50
76 Kevin Butt .20 .50
77 Fred Brathwaite 1.25 3.00
78 Paul O'Hagan .20 .50
79 Craig Donaldson .20 .50
80 Jean-Paul Davis .20 .50
81 Brian Grieve .20 .50
82 Bill Armstrong .20 .50
83 Wade Simpson .20 .50
84 Dave Craievich .20 .50
85 Dale Craigwell .30 .75
86 Joe Busillo .20 .50
87 Cory Banika .20 .50
88 Eric Lindros 10.00 20.00
89 Iain Fraser .20 .50
90 Mike Craig .20 .50
91 Jarrod Skalde .30 .75
92 Brent Grieve .20 .50
93 Scott Luik .20 .50
94 Matt Hoffman .20 .50
95 Trevor McIvor .20 .50
96 Scott Hollis .20 .50
97 Mark Deazeley .20 .50
98 Clair Cornish .20 .50
99 Oshawa Wins 2.00 5.00
(Eric Lindros w/Memorial Cup
100 Checklist Card .02 .10

1991-92 7th Inning Sketch OHL

This 384-card standard-size set was issued by 7th Inning Sketch and features players of the Ontario Hockey League. The production run was limited to 9,000 for factory sets, with each set individually numbered "X of 9,000." On a white card face, the fronts feature color action player photos enclosed by different color frames. The player's name, the year and league, and the team name appear below the picture. The cards are numbered on the back and checklisted below according to teams. Cards numbered 98, 147, 293 and 360 were never produced.

COMPLETE SET (384) 8.00 20.00
1 John Slaney .07 .20
2 Jason Meloche .02 .10
3 Mark DeSantis .02 .10
4 Richard Raymond .02 .10
5 Dave Lemay .02 .10
6 Matt McGuffin .02 .10
7 Sam Oliveira .02 .10
8 Jeremy Stevenson .05 .15
9 Todd Walker .02 .10
10 Jean-Alain Schneider .02 .10
11 Guy Leveque .05 .15
12 Shayne Gaffar .02 .10
13 Mike Prokopec .05 .15
14 Nathan LaFayette .07 .20
15 Larry Courville .08 .25
16 Chris Clancy .02 .10
17 Tom Nemeth .05 .15
18 Jeff Reid .02 .10
19 Ilpo Kauhanen .08 .25
20 Rob Dykeman .08 .25
21 Rival Fullum .05 .15
22 Ryan VandenBussche .08 .25
23 Gordon Pell .05 .15
24 Paul Andrea UER .02 .10
Team affiliation says Generals
25 John Lovell CO UER .01 .05
Team affiliation says Generals
26 Alan Letang .02 .10
27 Chris Phelps .02 .10
28 John Wynne .02 .10
29 Rob Kinghan .02 .10
30 Glen Craig .02 .10
31 Eric Cairns .40 1.00
32 John Pinches .02 .10
33 Todd Harvey .20 .50
34 Craig Fraser .02 .10
35 Pat Peake .08 .25
36 Chris Skoryna .02 .10
37 Bob Wren .05 .15
38 Chris Varga .02 .10
39 David Benn .02 .10
40 Mark Lawrence .05 .15
41 Jeff Kostuch .02 .10
42 J.D. Eaton .02 .10
43 Derek Etches .02 .10
44 Jeff Gardiner .02 .10
45 James Shea .08 .25
46 Brad Teichmann .08 .25
47 Jim Rutherford CO .05 .15
48 Derek Wilkinson .05 .15
49 OHL Action .02 .10
50 OHL Action .02 .10
51 Sandy Allan .08 .25
52 Ron Bertrand .08 .25
53 Brad Brown .08 .25
54 Dennis Bonvie .40 1.00
55 Bradley Shepard .02 .10
56 Allan Cox .02 .10
57 Jack Williams .05 .15
58 Chad Penney .02 .10
59 Jason Firth .02 .10
60 Bill Lang .02 .10
61 Ryan Merritt .02 .10
62 Michael Burman .02 .10
63 Billy Wright .02 .10

64 Dave Szabo .02 .10
65 James Sheehan .02 .10
66 John Spoltore .02 .10
67 Paul Rushforth .02 .10
68 Jeff Shevalier .07 .20
69 Robert Thorpe .02 .10
70 Drake Berehowsky .08 .25
71 Patrick Barton .02 .10
72 Bert Templeton CO .05 .15
73 Wade Gibson .02 .10
74 C.J. Denomme UER .08 .25
Name spelled C. Jay
on back
75 Mike Torchia .08 .25
76 Mike Polano .02 .10
77 Tony McCabe .02 .10
78 Chris Kraemer .02 .10
79 Tim Spitzig .02 .10
80 Trevor Gallant .02 .10
81 Yvan Corbin .02 .10
82 Norman Dezainde .05 .15
83 Marc Robillard .02 .10
84 Derek Gauthier .02 .10
85 Gib Tucker .02 .10
86 Paul McCallion .02 .10
87 Eric Manlow .05 .15
88 Jamie Caruso .05 .15
89 Gary Miller .02 .10
90 Jason Stevenson .02 .10
91 Shayne McCosh .02 .10
92 Jason Gladney .02 .10
93 Brad Barton .02 .10
94 Chris LiPuma .07 .20
95 Justin Cullen .02 .10
96 Bill Smith SCOUT .01 .05
97 Joe McDonnell CO .01 .05
99 Brent Gretzky .08 .25
100 Gairin Smith .02 .10
101 Blair Scott .02 .10
102 Daniel Godbout .02 .10
103 Dan Preston .02 .10
104 Ian Keiller .02 .10
105 Rick Marshall .02 .10
106 Aaron Morrison .02 .10
107 Dominic Belanger .02 .10
108 Kevin Brown .05 .15
109 Tony Cimellaro .02 .10
110 Larry Mavety CO .01 .05
111 Jake Grimes .05 .15
112 Greg Dreveny .08 .25
113 Darren McCarty .75 2.00
114 Doug Doull .02 .10
115 Scott Boston .05 .15
116 Dale Chokan .02 .10
117 Darren Hurley .02 .10
118 Brian Mielko UER .02 .10
Card misnumbered 61
119 Richard Gallace UER .02 .10
Card misnumbered 65
120 Shayne Antoski .08 .25
121 Greg Bailey .02 .10
122 Keith Redmond .02 .10
123 Dick Todd CO .05 .15
124 Scott Turner .02 .10
125 Colin Wilson .02 .10
126 Mike Tomlinson .02 .10
127 Dale McTavish .02 .10
128 Chris Longo .02 .10
129 Chad Lang .08 .25
130 Brent Tully .05 .15
131 Shawn Heins .05 .15
132 Geordie Kinnear .05 .15
133 Jeff Walker .02 .10
134 Chris Pronger 1.25 3.00
135 Chad Grills .02 .10
136 Michael Harding .02 .10
137 Matt St.Germain .02 .10
138 Don O'Neill .02 .10
139 Dave Roche .08 .25
140 Doug Searle .02 .10
141 Bryan Gendron .02 .10
142 Kelly Vipond .05 .15
143 Andrew Verner .08 .25
144 Ryan Black .05 .15
145 Jason Dawe .08 .25
146 Jassen Cullimore .08 .25
148 Jason Arnott .40 1.00
149 Jan Benda .05 .15
150 Todd Bradley .02 .10
151 Markus Brunner .05 .15
152 Jason Campeau .02 .10
153 Mark Deazeley .02 .10
154 Matt Hoffman .02 .10
155 Scott Hollis .02 .10
156 Neil Iserhoff .02 .10
157 Darryl Lafrance .02 .10
158 B.J. MacPherson .05 .15
159 Troy Sweet .02 .10
160 Jason Weaver .02 .10
161 Stephane Yelle .20 .50
162 Trevor Burgess .02 .10
163 Joe Cook .02 .10
164 Jean-Paul Davis .02 .10
165 Brian Grieve .02 .10
166 Rob Leask .07 .20
167 Wade Simpson .02 .10
168 Kevin Spero .02 .10
169 Fred Brathwaite .40 1.00
170 Mike Fountain .08 .25
171 Rick Cornacchia .05 .15
172 Checklist 1-98 .01 .05
173 Todd Warriner .08 .25
174 Reuben Castella .02 .10
175 Cory Stillman .20 .50
176 Steve Gibson .02 .10
177 Trent Cull .02 .10
178 John Copley .02 .10
179 Craig Binns .02 .10
180 Ryan O'Neill .02 .10
181 Matthew Mullin .08 .25
182 Todd Hunter .02 .10
183 Jason Stos .02 .10
184 Robert Frayn .02 .10
185 Leonard MacDonald .02 .10
186 Tom Sullivan .02 .10
187 Steve Smith .02 .10
188 Bill Bowler .08 .25
189 James Allison .02 .10
190 Kevin MacKay .02 .10
191 David Myles .02 .10
192 Wayne Maxner GM CO .02 .10
193 Dave Prpich CO UER .01 .05
Windsor on front
194 Brady Blain .02 .10
195 Eric Stamp UER .02 .10
Windsor on front
196 OHL Action .02 .10
197 David Babcock .02 .10
198 Brad Love .02 .10
199 Dale Junkin .02 .10
200 Rick Corriveau .02 .10
201 Scott Campbell .02 .10
202 Jason Clarke .02 .10
203 George Burnett .02 .10
204 Ryan Tocher .02 .10
205 Dennis Maxwell .08 .25
206 Greg Scott .02 .10
207 Mark Tardiff .05 .15
208 Neil Fewster .02 .10
209 Jason Coles .02 .10
210 Randy Hall CO .01 .05
211 Todd Simon .05 .15
212 Ethan Moreau .30 .75
213 Todd Wetzel .02 .10
214 Tom Moores .02 .10
215 Geoff Rawson .02 .10
216 Dan Krisko .02 .10
217 Manny Legace .40 1.00
218 Kevin Brown .05 .15
219 Steve Staios .07 .20
220 Checklist 99-196 .01 .05
221 Checklist 197-290 .01 .05
222 Tony Bella .02 .10
223 Shawn Caplice .02 .10
224 Keli Corpse .05 .15
225 Chris Gratton .40 1.00
226 Gord Harris .02 .10
227 Cory Johnson .02 .10
228 Kevin King .02 .10
229 Justin Morrison .05 .15
230 Alastair Still .02 .10
231 Chris Scharf .02 .10
232 Brian Stagg .02 .10
233 Mike Dawson .02 .10
234 Rod Pasma .02 .10
235 Craig Rivet .08 .25
236 Dave Stewart .02 .10
237 John Vary .02 .10
238 Jason Wadel .02 .10
239 Joel Yates .02 .10
240 Marc Lamothe .08 .25
241 Pete McGlynn .02 .10
242 OHL Action .02 .10
243 Checklist 291-383 .01 .05
244 Joel Sandie .05 .15
245 Glen Murray .40 1.00
246 Derek Armstrong .02 .10
247 Michael Peca .40 1.00
248 Barry Young .08 .25
249 Bernie John .02 .10
250 Terry Chitaroni .05 .15
251 Jason Young .05 .15
252 Rod Hinks .02 .10
253 Michael Yeo .02 .10
254 Kyle Blacklock .08 .25
255 Dan Ryder .08 .25
256 Doug Mason CO .01 .05
257 Jamie Rivers .08 .25
258 Brandon Convery .07 .20
259 Barrie Moore .02 .10
260 Shawn Rivers .05 .15
261 Jamie Matthews .07 .20
262 Tim Favot .02 .10
263 Bob MacIsaac .02 .10
264 Sean Gagnon .02 .10
265 Ken MacKenzie GM CO .01 .05
266 George Dourion .02 .10
267 Brian MacKenzie .02 .10
268 Jason Zohil .02 .10
269 Rick Tarasuk .02 .10
270 Jamie Storr .30 .75
271 Sean Basilio .08 .25
272 Rick Morton .02 .10
273 Jason Hughes .02 .10
274 Scott Walker .40 1.00
275 Willie Skilliter .02 .10
276 Shawn Krueger .02 .10
277 Jason MacDonald .02 .10
278 Kirk Maltby .20 .50
279 Brock Woods .02 .10
280 Troy Hutchinson .02 .10
281 Geordie Maynard .02 .10
282 Luigi Calce .02 .10
283 Steven Parson .02 .10
284 Andrew Brunette .20 .50
285 Robert MacKenzie .02 .10
286 Jason Buetow .02 .10
287 Wyatt Buckland .02 .10
288 Jim Brown .02 .10
289 Gord Dickie .02 .10
290 Jeff Smith .02 .10
291 Peter Ambroziak .05 .15
292 Mark O'Donnell UER .02 .10
Name spelled
O'donnell on back
294 Grayden Reid .05 .15
295 Sean Spencer .08 .25
296 Gerry Skrypec .02 .10
297 Billy Hall .02 .10
298 Sean Gawley .02 .10
299 Grant Marshall .08 .25
300 Michael Johnson .02 .10
301 Brett Seguin .02 .10
302 Chris Coveny .02 .10
303 Ryan Kuwabara .05 .15
304 Jeff Ricciardi .02 .10
305 Curt Bowen .05 .15
306 Zbynek Kukacka .02 .10
307 Chris Gignac .02 .10
308 Steve Washburn .08 .25
309 Brian Kilrea CO .05 .15
310 Mike Lenarduzzi .08 .25
311 Matt Stone .02 .10
312 Ken Belanger .02 .10
313 Chris Simon .20 .50
314 Kiley Hill .02 .10
315 Chris Grenville .02 .10
316 Aaron Gavey .08 .25
317 Briane Thompson .02 .10
318 Ted Nolan CO .08 .25
319 Perry Pappas .02 .10
320 Kevin Hodson .20 .50
321 Colin Miller .02 .10
322 Tom MacDonald .02 .10
323 Shaun Imber .02 .10
324 Jarret Reid .02 .10
325 Tony Iob .02 .10
326 Mark Matier .02 .10
327 Drew Bannister .07 .20
328 Jason Denomme .02 .10
329 David Matsos .05 .15
330 Rick Kowalsky .02 .10
331 Tim Bacik .02 .10
332 Ralph Intranuovo .07 .20
333 Jonas Rudberg .02 .10
334 Jeff Toms .02 .10
335 Jason Julian .02 .10
336 Brian Goudie .02 .10
337 Gary Roach .02 .10
338 Brad Baber .02 .10
339 Todd Gleason UER .05 .15
Team affiliation says
Greyhound
340 Chris McMurtry .02 .10
341 Matt Turek .02 .10
342 Shane Johnson .02 .10
343 Grant Pritchett .02 .10
344 Mike Cote .02 .10
345 Duane Harmer .02 .10
346 Jeff Bes .05 .15
347A Wade Whitten .02 .10
347B Dan Tanevski UER .02 .10
(Should be number 360)
348 Bill Kovacs .05 .15
349 Kayle Short .02 .10
350 Sylvain Cloutier .07 .20
351 Brent Watson .02 .10
352 Brent Pope .02 .10
353 Craig Lutes .02 .10
354 Michael Hartwick .02 .10
355 Kevin Reid .02 .10
356 Toby Burkitt .02 .10
357 Todd Bertuzzi .75 2.00
358 Angelo Amore .08 .25
359 Jeff Pawluk .02 .10
361 Gordon Ross .02 .10
362 Dennis Purdie .30 .75
363 Dave Gilmore .02 .10
364 Brent Brownlee .08 .25
365 Aaron Nagy .02 .10
366 Barry Potomski .40 1.00
367 Steve Smillie .02 .10
368 Kelly Reed .02 .10
369 Gary Agnew CO .01 .05
370 Chris Taylor .05 .15
371 Brett Marietti .02 .10
372 Cory Evans .02 .10
373 Brian Stacey .02 .10
374 Chris Crombie .02 .10
375 Derrick Crane .02 .10
376 Scott McKay .05 .15
377 Gregory Ryan .02 .10
378 Mark Visheau .02 .10
379 Gerry Arcella .02 .10
380 Nick Stajduhar .05 .15
381 Jason Allison .75 2.00
382 Sean O'Reilly .02 .10
383 Paul Wolanski .02 .10
XXX Chris Schushack .05 .15

1991-92 7th Inning Sketch QMJHL

This 298-card standard-size set was issued by 7th Inning Sketch and features players of the Quebec Major Junior Hockey League. The production run was limited to 4,000 factory sets, with each set individually numbered "X of 4,000." On a white card face, the fronts feature color action player photos enclosed by different color frames. The corners of the picture are cut out to permit space for gold stars. The player's name, the year and league, and the team name appear below the picture. In a horizontal format, the backs have biography, statistics, and player profile in French and English. The cards are numbered on the back and checklisted below according to teams as follows: St. Hyacinthe Laser (1-28), Granby Bisons (29-52), Shawinigan Cataractes (53-77), Chicoutimi Sagueneens (78-101), Trois Rivieres Draveurs (102-125), Verdun College Francais (126-150), St. Jean Lynx (151-172), Beauport Harfangs (173-198), Hull Olympiques (199-223), Laval Titan (224-248), Victoriaville Tigres (249-273), and Drummondville Voltigeurs (274-298). Card number 256 was never produced.

COMPLETE SET (297) 6.00 15.00
1 Martin Brodeur 1.50 4.00
2 Normand Paquet .02 .10
3 David Desnoyers .02 .10
4 Carlo Colombi .02 .10
5 Stephane Menard .08 .25
6 Sebastien Berube .02 .10
7 Marc Desgagne .02 .10
8 Mil Sukovic .02 .10
9 Patrick Belisle .02 .10
10 Patrick Poulin .08 .25
11 Martin Trudel .02 .10
12 Charles Poulin .05 .15
13 Etienne Thibault .02 .10
14 Pierre Allard .02 .10
15 Francois Gagnon .02 .10
16 Stephane Huard .02 .10
17 Yannik Lemay .02 .10
18 Dany Fortin .02 .10
19 Carl Menard .02 .10
20 Serge Labelle .02 .10
21 Dean Melanson .02 .10
22 Yves Meunier .02 .10
23 Pierre Petroni CO .01 .05
24 Mario Pouliot CO .01 .05
25 Alain Cote .05 .15
26 Hugues Laliberte .02 .10
27 Martin Gendron .08 .25
28 Stan Melanson .02 .10
29 Carl Leblanc .05 .15
30 Patrick Grise .02 .10
31 Yves Charron .05 .15
32 Hughes Mongeon .02 .10
33 Christian Tardif .02 .10
34 Patrick Tessier .08 .25
35 Christian Campeau .02 .10
36 Mario Therrien .02 .10
37 Martin Balleux .02 .10
38 Joel Brassard .02 .10
39 Sebastien Fortier .20 .50
40 Jocelyn Langlois .02 .10
41 Giuseppe Argentos .02 .10
42 Sylvain Brisson .08 .25
43 Philippe Boucher .08 .25
44 Martin Brochu .40 1.00
45 Marc Rodgers .02 .10
46 Pascal Gagnon .20 .50
47 Benoit Therrien .02 .10
48 Robin Bouchard .02 .10
49 Michel Savoie .02 .10
50 Jean-Sebastien Boileau .02 .10
51 Patrick Lamoureux .02 .10
52 Stephane Giard .08 .25
53 Daniel Laflamme .02 .10
54 Alain Cote .05 .15
55 Francois Groleau .05 .15
56 Richard Hamelin .05 .15
57 Eric Beauvis UER .05 .15
(Name misspelled
Beavis on back
58 Steve Laplante .02 .10
59 Yves Meunier .02 .10
60 Steve Dontigny .02 .10
61 Simon Roy .02 .10
62 Jean-Francois Laroche .02 .10
63 Patrick Traverse .08 .25
64 Eric Joyal .02 .10
65 Jean-Francois .02 .10
Gregoire UER/(Name misspelled
Jean-Fracois on front)
66 Jocelyn Charbonneau .05 .15
67 Jean Imbeau .05 .15
68 Francois Bourdeau .02 .10
69 Alain Savage Jr. .02 .10
70 Johnny Lorenzo .08 .25
71 Patrick Lalime .75 2.00
72 Patrick Melfi .02 .10
73 Marc Tardif .02 .10
74 Marc Savard .02 .10
75 Alain Sanscartier CO .01 .05
76 Pascal Lebrasseur .05 .15
77 Checklist 1-101 .01 .05
78 Dany Girard .02 .10
79 Eddy Gervais .02 .10
80 Dave Tremblay .02 .10
81 Dany Larochelle .02 .10
82 Michel St.Jacques .02 .10
83 Rodney Petawabano .02 .10
84 Eric Duchesne .02 .10
85 Patrick Clement .02 .10
86 Steve Gosselin .02 .10
87 Patrick Lacombe .02 .10
88 Patrice Martineau .02 .10
89 Danny Beauregard .02 .10
90 Martin Lamarche .02 .10
91 Sebastien Parent .02 .10
92 Christian Caron .02 .10
93 Sylvain Careau .08 .25
94 Martin Beaupre .02 .10
95 Daniel Paradis .02 .10
96 Sylvain Rodrigue .08 .25
97 Joe Canale CO .01 .05
98 Patrick Lampron .02 .10
99 Carl Blondin .02 .10
100 Carl Wiseman .02 .10
101 Hugo Hamelin .08 .25
102 Claude Poirier .02 .10
103 Charles Paquette .02 .10
104 Carl Fleury UER .05 .15
(Name spelled FLeury
on front)
105 Paolo Racicot .02 .10
106 Sebastien Moreau .02 .10
107 Pascal Trepanier .02 .10
108 Dominic Maltais .05 .15
109 Steve Ares .08 .25
110 Daniel Thibault .02 .10
111 Eric Messier .20 .50
112 Stephane Julien .02 .10
113 Dave Paquet .02 .10
114 Nicolas Turmel .02 .10
115 Pascal Rheaume .20 .50
116 Carl Boudreau .02 .10
117 Dave Boudreault .02 .10
118 Eric Bellerose .05 .15
119 Steve Searles .05 .15
120 Patrick Nadeau .05 .15
121 Stephan Viens .02 .10
122 Jean-Francois Labbe .40 1.00
123 Jocelyn Thibault 1.25 3.00
124 Gaston Drapeau CO .01 .05
125 Checklist 102-198 .01 .05
126 Martin Lajeunesse .02 .10
127 Etienne Lavoie .02 .10
128 Dominic Rheaume .02 .10
129 Robert Guillet .02 .10
130 Francois Rivard .02 .10
131 Phillippe DeRouville .15 .40
132 Andrej Dobrota .02 .10
133 Pierre Gendron .02 .10
134 Dave Chouinard .02 .10
135 Martin Tanguay .05 .15
136 Jacques Blouin .02 .10
137 Martin Larochelle .02 .10
138 Jean-Martin Morin .02 .10
139 Donald Brashear .40 1.00
140 Stephane Paradis .02 .10
141 Jan Simcik .02 .10
142 Yan Arsenault .02 .10
143 Joel Bouchard .08 .25
144 Jean-Sebastien .02 .10
Lefebvre
145 David St. Pierre UER .05 .15
(Name misspelled
St-Pierre on front)
146 Mario Nobili .02 .10
147 Stacy Dallaire .02 .10
148 Carl Lamothe .02 .10
149 Andre Bouliane .08 .25
150 Simon Arial .02 .10
151 Stephane Madore .02 .10
152 Hughes Bouchard .02 .10
153 Steve Decaen .02 .10
154 Jason Downey .02 .10
155 Raymond Delarosbil .02 .10
156 Lino Salvo .02 .10
157 Reginald Brezeault .02 .10
158 Nathan Morin .02 .10
159 Samuel Groleau .02 .10
160 Patrick Carignan .02 .10
161 Stephane St-Amour .02 .10
162 Marquis Mathieu .05 .15
163 Yves Sarault .05 .15
164 Dave Belliveau .02 .10
165 Trevor Duhaime .02 .10
166 Eric O'Connor .02 .10
167 Christian Proulx .05 .15
168 Martin Lavallee .08 .25
169 Jean-Francois Gagnon .08 .25
170 Eric Lafrance .02 .10
171 Enrico Scardocchio .02 .10
172 David Bergeron .02 .10
173 Guillaume Morin .08 .25
174 Charlie Boucher .08 .25
175 Martin Rozon .02 .10
176 Brandon Piccarreto .02 .10
177 Simon Toupin .05 .15
178 Jamie Bird .02 .10
179 Herve Lapointe .02 .10
180 Ian MacIntyre .02 .10
181 Jean-Francois Rivard .08 .25
182 Alain Chainey CO .01 .05
183 Daniel Laflamme .02 .10
184 Patrice Paquin .02 .10
185 Patrick Deraspe .02 .10
186 Martin Roy .02 .10
187 Jeannot Ferland .02 .10
188 Patrick Genest .02 .10
189 Matthew Barnaby .40 1.00
190 Jean-Guy Trudel .02 .10
191 Eric Moreau .02 .10
192 Eric Cool .05 .15
193 Alexandre Legault .02 .10
194 Gregg Pineo .02 .10
195 LHJMQ Action .02 .10
196 Radoslav Balaz .02 .10
197 Stefan Simoes .02 .10
198 LHJMQ Action .02 .10
199 Francois Paquette .02 .10
200 Paul Macdonald .02 .10
201 Shane Doiron .02 .10
202 Michal Longauer .02 .10
203 Joe Crowley .02 .10
204 Joey Deliva .02 .10
205 Pierre-Francois .02 .10
Lalonde
206 Paul Brousseau .05 .15
207 Martin Lepage .02 .10
208 Yanick DeGrace .08 .25
209 Jim Campbell .08 .25
210 Sebastien Bordeleau .02 .10
211 Marc Legault .08 .25
212 Joel Blain .02 .10
213 Claude Jutras .02 .10
214 Eric Lavigne .05 .15
215 Todd Sparks .02 .10
216 Sylvain Lapointe .02 .10
217 Eric Lecompte .08 .25
218 Thierry Mayer .02 .10
219A Harold Hersh ERR .08 .25
(Jim Campbell photo
on back)
219B Harold Hersh COR .02 .10
220 Frederic Boivin .02 .10
221 Steven Dion .02 .10
222 Alain Vigneault .15 .40
223 Checklist 199-298 .01 .05
224 Petr Valenta .02 .10
225 LHJMQ Action .02 .10
226 Jim Bermingham .02 .10
227 Yanick Dube .08 .25
228 Sandy McCarthy .40 1.00
229 Dany Michaud .02 .10
230 Jason Brousseau .02 .10
231 Marc Beaucage .02 .10
232 Eric Cardinal .02 .10
233 Martin Chaput .02 .10
234 Jean Roberge .02 .10
235 Philip Gathercole .02 .10
236 Michael Gaul .02 .10
237 Yannick Frechette .02 .10
238 Sylvain Blouin .02 .10
239 David Pekarek .02 .10
240 John Kovacs .02 .10
241 Eric Raymond .08 .25
242 Emmanuel Fernandez 1.25 3.00
243 Yan St. Pierre .02 .10
244 Brant Blackned .02 .10
245 Eric Veilleux .02 .10
246 Pascal Vincent .02 .10
247 Benoit Larose .02 .10
248 Olivier Guillaume .02 .10
249 Alain Gauthier .08 .25
250 Bruno Ducharme .08 .25
251 Patrick Charbonneau .08 .25
252 Daniel Germain .02 .10
253 Pascal Chiasson .02 .10
254 Marc Thibeault .02 .10
255 Martin Woods .02 .10
257 Dominic Grand'maison .02 .10
258 Carl Poirer .02 .10
259 Stephane Larocque .02 .10
260 Mario Dumoulin .02 .10
261 Yan Laterreur .02 .10
262 Claude Savoie .05 .15
263 Denis Beauchamp .02 .10
264 Patrick Bisaillon .02 .10
265 Pascal Bernier .02 .10
266 Nicolas Lefebvre .02 .10
267 LHJMQ Action .02 .10
268 Joseph Napolitano .05 .15
269 Sebastien Tremblay .02 .10
270 Alexandre Daigle .20 .50
271 Pierre Pillion .02 .10
272 Yves Lambert .40 1.00
273 Pierre Aubry CO .01 .05
274 Yves Loubier .08 .25
275 Pierre Sandke UER .02 .10
(First name Peter
on back)
276 Louis Bernard .02 .10
277 Alain Nasreddine .05 .15
278 Sylvain Ducharme .02 .10
279 Jeremy Caissie .02 .10
280 Eric Meloche .02 .10
281 Ian Laperriere .20 .50
282 Hugo Proulx .07 .20
283 Dave Whittom .02 .10
284 Yanick Dupre .05 .15
285 Eric Plante .02 .10
286 Stephane Desjardins .02 .10
287 Rene Corbet .20 .50
288 David Lessard .02 .10
289 Eric Marcoux .02 .10
290 Alexandre Duchesne .02 .10
291 Maxime Petitclerc UER .02 .10
(Name misspelled
Peticlerc on front)
292 Pierre Gagnon .08 .25
293 Roger Larche UER .02 .10
(Name misspelled
Larache on front)
294 Jean Hamel .02 .10
295 Alexandre Gaumond .02 .10
296 Paul-Emile Exentus .02 .10
297 LHJMQ Action .02 .10
298 LHJMQ Action .02 .10

1991-92 7th Inning Sketch WHL

This 361-card standard-size set was issued by 7th Inning Sketch and features players of the Western Hockey League. The production run was limited to 7,000 for factory sets, with each set individually numbered "X of 7,000." Wax boxes featuring 36 packs were also issued. On a white card face, the fronts feature color action player photos enclosed by different color frames. The corners of the picture are cut out to permit space for gold stars. The player's name, the year and league, and the team name appear below the picture. The cards are numbered on the back and checklisted below according to team order.

COMPLETE SET (361) 6.00 15.00
1 Valeri Bure .30 .75
2 Hardy Sauter .02 .10
3 Bryan Maxwell CO .02 .10
4 Scott Bailey .08 .25
5 Mike Gray .02 .10
6 Mark Szoke .40 1.00
7 Mike Jickling .02 .10
8 Frank Evans .02 .10
9 Steve Junker .07 .20
10 Greg Gatto .02 .10
11 Jared Bednar .02 .10
12 Justin Hocking .07 .20
13 Paxton Schulte .07 .20
14 Brad Toporowski .02 .10
15 Shane Maitland .02 .10
16 Aaron Boh .02 .10
17 Ryan Duthie .05 .15
18 Craig Reichert .05 .15
19 Danny Faassen .02 .10
20 Randy Toye .02 .10
21 Geoff Grandberg .02 .10
22 Jeremy Warring .08 .25
23 Tyler Romanchuck .02 .10
24 Jamie Linden .05 .15
25 1990-91 Champs .02 .10
26 Corey Jones .08 .25
27 Brandon Smith .02 .10
28 Mike Williamson .02 .10
29 Adam Murray .02 .10
30 Steve Konowalchuk .20 .50
31 Shawn Stone .02 .10
32 Adam Deadmarsh .40 1.00
33 Rick Mearns .02 .10
34 Chris Rowland .02 .10
35 Brandon Coates .02 .10
36 Dave Cammock .02 .10
37 Colin Foley .02 .10
38 Dennis Saharchuk .02 .10
39 Jiri Beranek .02 .10
40 Chad Seibel .02 .10
41 Kelly Harris .02 .10
42 Layne Roland .02 .10
43 Cale Hulse .05 .15
44 Ken Hodge CO .02 .10
45 Peter Cox .02 .10
46 Joaquin Gage .20 .50
47 Brent Peterson CO .02 .10
48 Jason McBain .02 .10
49 John Badduke .02 .10
50 Rick Hopper .01 .05
51 Dave Hamilton .08 .25
52 Dwayne Newman .02 .10
53 Chris Catellier .02 .10
54 Fran Defrenza .02 .10
55 Randy Chadney .02 .10
56 David Hebky .02 .10
57 Craig Fletcher .02 .10
58 Kane Chaloner .02 .10
59 Ross Harris .02 .10
60 Mike Barrie .02 .10
61 Steve Lingren .02 .10
62 Shea Esselmont .02 .10
63 Matt Smith .02 .10
64 Gerry St.Cyr .05 .15
65 Andrew Laming .02 .10
66 Jeff Fancy .02 .10
67 Ryan Pellaers .02 .10
68 Steve Passmore .40 1.00
69 Scott Fukami .02 .10
70 Darcy Mattersdorfer .02 .10
71 Chris Hawes .02 .10
72 The Goalies I .05 .15
73 Checklist 1-97 .01 .05
74 Riverside Coliseum .02 .10
75 Tom Renney .07 .20
76 Corey Hirsch .20 .50
77 Scott Ferguson .02 .10
78 Steve Yule .02 .10
79A Todd Johnson Warriors .02 .10
79B Todd Johnson Blazers .02 .10
80 Jarrett Bousquet .02 .10
81 Mike Mathers .02 .10
82 Rod Stevens .02 .10
83 Lance Johnson .02 .10
84 Zac Boyer .02 .10
85 Craig Lyons .05 .15
86 Dale Masson .08 .25
87 Scott Loucks .20 .50
88 Darcy Tucker .20 .50
89 Shayne Green .05 .15
90 Michal Sup .02 .10
91 Craig Bonner .02 .10
92 Jeff Watchorn .02 .10
93 Jarrett Dueling .02 .10
94 Ed Patterson .07 .20
95 David Wilkie .08 .25
96 The Goalies III .05 .15
97 A Goal .02 .10
98 Andy MacIntyre .02 .10
99 Rhett Trombley .07 .20
100 Lorne Molleken CO .01 .05
101 Trevor Robins .08 .25
102 Jeff Buchanan .02 .10
103 Mark Raiter .02 .10
104 Bryce Goebel .02 .10
105 Paul Buczkowski .02 .10
106 James Startup .02 .10
107 Chad Rusnak .02 .10
108 Sean McFatridge .02 .10
109 Shane Calder .05 .15
110 Ryan Fujita .02 .10
111 Derek Tibbatts .02 .10
112 Glen Gulutzan .02 .10
113 Richard Matvichuk .20 .50
114 Chad Michalchuk .02 .10
115 Mark Wotton .07 .20
116 Mark Franks .20 .50
117 Norm Maracle .20 .50
118 Jason Becker .02 .10
119 Shawn Yakimishyn .02 .10
120 Ed Chynoweth PRES .05 .15
121 Checklist 98-195 .01 .05
122 Craig Chapman .02 .10
123 Jeff Jubenville .02 .10
124 George Zajankala .02 .10
125 Turner Stevenson .20 .50
126 Rob Tallas .20 .50
127 Ryan Brown .02 .10
128 Andrew Kemper .02 .10
129 Brendan Witt .20 .50
130 Troy Hyatt .02 .10
131 Mike Kennedy .08 .25
132 Jesse Wilson .02 .10
133 Kurt Seher .05 .15
134 Dody Wood .05 .15
135 Darren McAusland .02 .10
136 Jeff Sebastian .02 .10
137 Eric Bouchard .02 .10
138 Joel Dyck .02 .10
139 Blake Knox .02 .10
140 Peter Anholt CO .01 .05
141 Chris Wells .08 .25
142 Andrew Reimer .07 .20
143 Along the Boards .02 .10
144 Which Way Is Up .01 .05
145 Checklist 196-287 .01 .05
146 Tacoma Dome .02 .10
147 Opening Ceremonies .02 .10
148 Marcel Comeau CO .02 .10
149 Donn Clark CO .01 .05
150 John Varga .05 .15
151 Joey Young .02 .10
152 Laurie Billeck .02 .10
153 Jeff Calvert .08 .25
154 Tuomas Gronman .08 .25
155 Jason Knox .02 .10
156 Kevin Malgunas .02 .10
157 Dave McMillen .02 .10
158 Darryl Onofrychuk .08 .25
159 Mike Piersol .02 .10
160 Lasse Pirjeta .02 .10
161 Drew Schoneck .02 .10
162 Corey Stock .02 .10
163 Ryan Strain .02 .10
164 Michal Sykora .05 .15
165 Scott Thomas .05 .15
166 Toby Weishaar .02 .10
167 Jeff Whittle .05 .15
168 The Rockettes .05 .15
169 Allan Egeland .05 .15
170 Van Burgess .02 .10
171 Trever Fraser .02 .10
172 Jamie Black .05 .15
173 WHL Action .02 .10
174 Andy Schneider .05 .15
175 John McMulkin .02 .10
176 Rick Girard .05 .15
177 Shane Hnidy .05 .15
178 Jason Krywulak .05 .15
179 Jeremy Riehl .05 .15
180 Brent Bilodeau .08 .25
181 Mark McCoy .02 .10
182 Matt Young .02 .10
183 Dan Sherstenka .02 .10
184 Jarrod Daniel .08 .25
185 Lennie MacAusland .02 .10
186 Keith McCambridge .02 .10
187 Jason Horvath .02 .10
188 Kevin Koopman .08 .25
189 Chris Herperger .05 .15
190 Trent McCleary .08 .25
191 Tyler Wright .08 .25
192 Todd Holt .05 .15
193 Ashley Buckberger .05 .15
194 Bram Vanderkracht .02 .10
195 Ken Zilka .02 .10
196 Chris Osgood .75 2.00
197 Rob Puchniak .02 .10
198 Todd Dutiaume .02 .10
199 Mike Maneluk .07 .20
200 Shawn Dietrich .08 .25
201 Chris Johnston .02 .10
202 Brian Purdy .05 .15
203 Mike Chrun .02 .10
204 Dan Kopec .02 .10
205 Ryan Smith .05 .15
206 Marty Murray .08 .25
207 Merv Priest .02 .10
208 Bobby House .05 .15
209 Chris Constant .05 .15
210 Dwayne Gylywoychuk .02 .10
211 Stu Scantlebury .02 .10
212 Mark Kolesar .07 .20
213 Craig Geekie .02 .10
214 Terran Sandwith .02 .10
215 Jeff Hoad .02 .10
216 Kelly McCrimmon .02 .10
217 Carlos Bye .02 .10
218 Trevor Hanas .02 .10
219 Jeff Shantz .20 .50
220 Heath Weenk .02 .10
221 Nathan Dempsey .02 .10
222 Louis Dumont .02 .10
223 Garry Pearce .02 .10
224 Terry Bendera .02 .10
225 Hal Christiansen .02 .10
226 Jason Smith .20 .50
227 Kerry Biette .02 .10
228 Barry Becker .08 .25
229 Derek Eberle .02 .10
230 Ken Richardson .02 .10
231 Niklas Barklund .02 .10
232 Frank Kovacs .02 .10
233 Not Issued .01 .05
234 Not Issued .01 .05
235 Lloyd Pelletier .08 .25
236 Dale Vossen .01 .05
237 A.J. Kelham .02 .10
238 Mike Risdale .08 .25
239 Brad Bagu .02 .10
240 Niko Ovaska .02 .10
241 Brad Tippett CO .01 .05
242 The Goalies II .05 .15
243 Lee J. Leslie .05 .15
244 Darren Perkins .02 .10
245 Jason Kwiatkowski .02 .10
246 Jason Renard .02 .10
247 Dan Kesa .07 .20
248 Jason Klassen .02 .10
249 Nick Polychronopoulus .02 .10
250 David Neilson .02 .10
251 Merv Haney .02 .10
252 Troy Hjertaas .02 .10
253 Curt Regnier .07 .20
254 Dean McAmmond .20 .50
255 Travis Laycock .08 .25
256 Jeff Lank .02 .10
257 Barkley Swenson .02 .10
258 Darren Van Impe .08 .25
259 Ryan Pisiak .02 .10
260 Jeff Gorman .02 .10
261 Stan Matwijiw .08 .25
262 Mike Fedorko .02 .10
263 Mark Odnokon .01 .05
264 Shane Zulyniak .02 .10
265 Jeff Nelson .07 .20
266 Donevan Hextall .07 .20
267 Kevin Masters .02 .10
268 Chris Schmidt .02 .10
269 Jeff Budai .02 .10
270 Bill Hooson .02 .10
271 Fred Hettle .02 .10
272 Kent Staniforth .02 .10
273 Travis Stevenson .05 .15
274 David Jesiolowski .02 .10
275 Mike Babcock CO .01 .05
276 Scott Allison .02 .10
277 Travis Thiessen .02 .10
278 Marc Hussey .02 .10
279 Kevin Smyth .05 .15
280 Jason Fitzsimmons .08 .25
281 Jeff Petruic .02 .10
282 Russ West .02 .10
283 Derek Kletzel .02 .10
284 Jarret Zukiwsky .05 .15
285 Jason Carey .02 .10
286 Close Checking .02 .10

287 Checklist 288-360 .01 .05
288 Jason Bowen .05 .15
289 Dean Tiltgen .05 .15
290 Terry Degner .07 .20
291 Jodie Murphy .02 .10
292 Brian Sakic .05 .15
293 Jamie Barnes .02 .10
294 Darren Hastman .02 .10
295 Todd Klassen .05 .15
296 Mirsad Mujcin .02 .10
297 Trevor Sherban .02 .10
298 Chadden Cabana .02 .10
299 Adam Rettschlag .02 .10
300 Mark Toljanich .02 .10
301 Kory Mullin .02 .10
302 Byron Penstock .08 .25
303 Vladimir Vujtek .07 .20
304 Bill Lindsay .08 .25
305 Jeff Cej .02 .10
306 Mike Busniak CO .02 .10
307 Todd Harris .02 .10
308 Cory Dosdall .02 .10
309 Jason Smith .20 .50
310 Mark Dawkins .08 .25
311 Dan O'Rourke .02 .10
312 Darby Walker .02 .10
313 Olaf Kjenstadt .05 .15
314 Sonny Mignacca .08 .25
315 Jon Duval .02 .10
316 Lorne Toews .02 .10
317 Dana Rieder .02 .10
318 Clayton Norris .05 .15
319 David Cooper .07 .20
320 Larry Watkins .02 .10
321 Evan Marble .02 .10
322 Scott Lindsay .05 .15
323 Ryan Petz .02 .10
324 Jeramie Heistad .02 .10
325 Scott Townsend .02 .10
326 Stacy Roest .20 .50
327 Rob Niedermayer .30 .75
328 Tim Bothwell CO .05 .15
329 Kevin Riehl .07 .20
330 Mike Rathje .08 .25
331 Bryan McCabe .20 .50
332 MHT Tiger MASCOT .02 .10
333 Dean Intwert .08 .25
334 Mike Vandenberghe .02 .10
335 Cam Danyluk .02 .10
336 Darcy Austin .08 .25
337 Jason Knight .02 .10
338 Lee Sorochan .08 .25
339 Al Kinisky .02 .10
340 Rob Hartnell .02 .10
341 Radek Sip .02 .10
342 Jamie Pushor .08 .25
343 Shane Peacock .02 .10
344 Cadrin Smart .02 .10
345 Maurice Meagher .02 .10
346 Lance Burns .02 .10
347 Dominic Pittis .20 .50
348 Todd MacIsaac .02 .10
349 Brad Zimmer .02 .10
350 Jason Sorochan .02 .10
351 Darcy Werenka .07 .20
352 Kevin St.Jacques .05 .15
353 David Trofimenkoff .02 .10
354 Terry Hollinger .05 .15
355 Travis Munday .02 .10
356 Slade Stephenson .02 .10
357 Jason Widmer .07 .20
358 Brad Zavisha .05 .15
359 Bob Loucks CO .01 .05
360 Brantt Myhres .40 1.00
0 Garfield Henderson .05 .15

1991 7th Inning Sketch CHL Award Winners

This 30-card boxed standard-size set features Canadian Hockey League Award Winners. Each box has on its back a checklist and the set serial number. The cards feature action color player photos with gray borders against a black card face. The player's specific achievement is printed in gray in the black margin at the top. His name and team appear in white at the bottom.

COMPLETE SET (30) 4.00 10.00
1 Eric Lindros .75 2.00
2 Dale Craigwell .08 .25
3 Nathan Lafayette .07 .20
4 Chris Snell .08 .25
5 Cory Stillman .20 .50
6 Mike Torchia .20 .50
7 George Burnett .07 .20
8 Eric Lindros .75 2.00
9 Sherwood Bassin .07 .20
10 Eric Lindros .75 2.00
11 Scott Niedermayer .20 .50
12 Pat Falloon .08 .25
13 Scott Niedermayer .20 .50
14 Darryl Sydor .20 .50
15 Donevan Hextall .07 .20
16 Jamie McLennan .15 .40
17 Tom Renney .08 .25
18 Frank Evans .07 .20
19 Bob Brown .07 .20
20 Ray Whitney .20 .50
21 Philippe Boucher .07 .20
22 Yanic Perreault .15 .40
23 Benoit Larose .07 .20
24 Patrice Brisebois .08 .25
25 Philippe Boucher .07 .20
26 Felix Potvin .40 1.00
27 Joe Canale .07 .20
28 Christian Lariviere .07 .20
29 Roland Janelle .07 .20
30 Yanic Perreault .15 .40

1991 7th Inning Sketch Memorial Cup

The 1991 7th Inn. Sketch Memorial Cup Hockey set captures the four teams that participated in the Canadian junior hockey championship, with one team each from the OHL and WHL, and two from the QMJHL (the host league). The cards measure the standard size and feature on the fronts color action player photos enclosed by silver borders. The upper right and lower left corners are cut off to permit space for the CHL and '91 Memorial Cup logos, respectively. The player's name in the bottom silver border rounds out the card face. The set is skip-numbered due to the fact that several cards were withdrawn from the set after only a few sets had been released. These 17 card numbers are 21, 36 (Rob Dykeman), 96 (Eric Lindros), 106 (Pat Peake), 107 (Steve Staios), 110 (Alex Stojanov), 111 (Glen Murray), 113 (Jason Dawe), 114 (Nathan Lafayette), 116 (Guy Leveque), 118 (Shayne Antoski), 119 (Eric Lindros), 120 (Dennis Purdie), 121 (Terry Chitaroni), and 124 (Jamie Matthews).

COMPLETE SET (130) 50.00 100.00
COMPLETE SHORT SET (113) 6.00 15.00
1 Mike Lenarduzzi .10 .25
2 Kevin Hodson .20 .50
3 OHL Action .05 .15
Sault Ste. Marie
vs. Oshawa
4 Bob Boughner .20 .50
5 Adam Foote .30 .75
6 Brad Tiley .05 .15
7 Brian Goudie .05 .15
8 Wade Whitten .05 .15
9 Jason Denomme .05 .15
10 David Matsos .05 .15
11 Rick Kowalsky .05 .15
12 Jarret Reid .05 .15
13 Perry Pappas .05 .15
14 Tom MacDonald .05 .15
15 Mike DeCoff .05 .15
16 Joe Busillo .05 .15
17 Denny Lambert .10 .30
18 Mark Matier .05 .15
19 Shaun Imber .05 .15
20 Ralph Intranuovo .08 .25
21 Chris Snell SP .75 2.00
22 Tony Iob .05 .15
23 Colin Miller .05 .15
24 Ted Nolan .20 .50
25 Sylvain Rodrigue .05 .15
26 Felix Potvin 1.50 4.00
27 Martin Lavallee .05 .15
28 Eric Brule .05 .15
29 Steve Larouche .05 .15
30 Michel St-Jacques .05 .15
31 Patrick Clement .05 .15
32 Patrick Bisaillon .05 .15
33A Checklist 62-131 SP .75 2.00
33B Checklist 62-131 .08 .25
(Withdrawn numbers omitted)
34 Gilles Bouchard .05 .15
35 Eric Rochette .05 .15
36 Rob Dykeman SP .75 2.00
37A Checklist 1-61 SP .75 2.00
37B Checklist 1-61 .08 .25
(Withdrawn numbers omitted)
38 Patrice Martineau .05 .15
39 Danny Beauregard .05 .15
40 Francois Belanger .05 .15
41 Sebastien Parent .08 .25
42 Martin Gagne .05 .15
43 Stephane Charbonneau .05 .15
44 Martin Beaupre .05 .15
45 Daniel Paradis .05 .15
46 Joe Canale .05 .15
47 OHL Action .05 .15
Sault Ste. Marie
vs. Oshawa
48 Jubilation .05 .15
49 Steve Lupien .05 .15
50 Pierre Gagnon .05 .15
51 Alexandre Legault .05 .15
52 Martin Charrois .05 .15
53 Eric Dandenault .05 .15
54 Denis Chasse .08 .25
55 Guy Lehoux .05 .15
56 Ian Laperriere .20 .50
57 Hugo Proulx .05 .15
58 Dave Whittom .05 .15
59 Yanick Dupre UER .08 .25
60 Eric Plante .05 .15
61 Stephane Desjardins .08 .25
62 Patrice Brisebois .08 .25
63 Rene Corbet .20 .50
64 Marc Savard .05 .15
65 Claude Jutras Jr. .05 .15
66 David Pekarek .05 .15
67 Roger Larche UER .05 .15
(Name misspelled
Larohe on front)
68 Dave Paquet .08 .25
69 Eric Meloche .05 .15
70 CHL Action .05 .15
Spokane vs. Lethbridge
71 Celebration .15 .40
Ed Chynoweth PRES
Jon Klemm
72 Felix Potvin MVP 1.50 4.00
73 Scott Bailey .20 .50
74 Trevor Kidd .30 .75
75 Chris Lafreniere .05 .15
76 Frank Evans .05 .15
77 Jon Klemm .20 .50
78 Brent Thurston .05 .15
79 Jamie McLennan .20 .50
80 Steve Junker .05 .15
81 Mark Szoke .05 .15
82 Ray Whitney .40 1.00
83 Geoff Grandberg .05 .15
84 Cam Danyluk .05 .15
85 Kerry Toporowski .05 .15
86 Trevor Tovell .05 .15
87 Pat Falloon .20 .50
88 Bram Vanderkracht .05 .15
89 Mike Jickling .05 .15
90 Murray Garbutt .05 .15
91 Calvin Thudium .05 .15
92 Mark Woolf .05 .15
93 Shane Maitland .05 .15
94 Bart Cote .05 .15
95 Bryan Maxwell .05 .15
96 Eric Lindros SP 12.00 25.00
97 Scott Niedermayer .40 1.00
98 Patrick Poulin .08 .25
99 Brent Bilodeau .08 .25
100 Pat Falloon .20 .50
101 Darcy Werenka .08 .25
102 Martin Lapointe .60 1.50
103 Philippe Boucher .08 .25
104 Jeff Nelson .08 .25
105 Rene Corbet .20 .50
106 Pat Peake SP .75 2.00
107 Steve Staios SP .75 2.00
108 Richard Matvichuk .20 .50
109 Dean McAmmond .20 .50
110 Alex Stojanov SP .75 2.00
111 Glen Murray SP 1.50 4.00
112 Tyler Wright .08 .25
113 Jason Dawe SP 1.25 3.00
114 Nathan Lafayette SP .75 2.00
115 Yanic Perreault .20 .50
116 Guy Leveque SP .75 2.00
117 Darren Van Impe .08 .25
118 Shawn Antoski SP .75 2.00
119 Eric Lindros SP 12.00 25.00
120 Dennis Purdie SP .75 2.00
121 Terry Chitaroni SP .75 2.00
122 Jamie Pushor .08 .25
123 Chris Osgood 1.50 4.00
124 Jamie Matthews SP .75 2.00
125 Yves Sarault .05 .15
126 Yanic Dupre UER .08 .25
127 Brad Zimmer .05 .15
128 Copps Coliseum .05 .15
129 Jason Widmer .08 .25
130 Marc Savard .05 .15
131 Mike Torchia .08 .15
132 Andrew Verner .10 .25

1999-00 Shawinigan Cataractes

This 24-card set features the QMJHL Cataractes. Base cards feature full-color action photography and have green borders along the right side and the bottom of the card where the team logo is also pictured.

COMPLETE SET (24) 4.00 10.00
1 Jonathan Lessard .15 .40
2 Philippe Gelinas .15 .40
3 Jonathan Bellemare .15 .40
4 Anthony Quessy .20 .50
5 Alexandre Blackburn .15 .40
6 Pascal Dupuis .15 .40
7 Marc-Andre Bergeron .20 .50
8 Francis Desaluriers .15 .40
9 Jean-Sebastien Trudelle .15 .40
10 Jean-Philippe Pare .20 .50
11 Jean-Francois David .15 .40
12 Phillppe Deblois .15 .40
13 Dave Verville .15 .40
14 Mathieu Chouinard .60 1.50
15 Gilbert Lefrancois .15 .40
16 Denis Desmarais .15 .40
17 Yannick Noiseux .15 .40
18 Dominic Forget .15 .40
19 Conor McGuire .15 .40
20 Jean-Francois Dufort .15 .40
21 Andre Landry .15 .40
22 David Chicoine .15 .40
23 Jason Pominville .60 1.50
24 Header Card/CL .02 .10

1999-00 Shawinigan Cataractes Signed

This 24-card set parallels the base Shawinigan Cataractes set in an autographed version. The fronts feature autographs on a ghosted-out portion of the photo, while the backs are serial numbered out of 100.

COMPLETE SET (24) 20.00 50.00
1 Jonathan Lessard .75 2.00
2 Philippe Gelinas .75 2.00
3 Jonathan Bellemare .75 2.00
4 Anthony Quessy .75 2.00
5 Alexandre Blackburn .75 2.00
6 Pascal Dupuis .75 2.00
7 Marc-Andre Bergeron 1.50 4.00
8 Francis Desaluriers .75 2.00
9 Jean-Sebastien Trudelle .75 2.00
10 Jean-Philippe Pare 1.50 4.00
11 Jean-Francois David .75 2.00
12 Philippe Deblois .75 2.00
13 Dave Verville .75 2.00
14 Mathieu Chouinard 4.00 10.00
15 Gilbert Lefrancois .75 2.00
16 Denis Desmarais .75 2.00
17 Yannick Noiseux .75 2.00
18 Dominic Forget .75 2.00
19 Conor McGuire .75 2.00
20 Jean-Francois Dufort .75 2.00
21 Andre Landry .75 2.00
22 David Chicoine .75 2.00
23 Jason Pominville 4.00 10.00
24 Header Card/CL .20 .50

2000-01 Shawinigan Cataractes

This set features the Cataractes of the QMJHL. The set was produced by CTM Ste-Foy and was sold both by that card shop and by the team.

COMPLETE SET (24) 6.00 15.00
1 Denis Desmarais .16 .40
2 Zbynek Michalek .16 .40
3 Jonathan Beaulieu .16 .40
4 Jonathan Lessard .16 .40
5 Jonathan Bellemare .16 .40
6 Patrick Bolduc .16 .40
7 Anthony Quessy .16 .40
8 David Chicoine .16 .40
9 Gilbert Lefrancois .16 .40
10 Radim Vrbata .60 1.00
11 Yannick Noiseux .16 .40
12 Marc-Andre Bergeron .16 .50
13 Jimmy Cuddihy .20 1.00
14 Kevin Bergin .16 .40
15 Francois Gagnon .16 .40
16 Olivier Michaud 2.00 3.00
17 Frederic Cloutier .16 1.00
18 Jean-Francois David .16 .40
19 Alexandre Menard Burrows .16 .40
20 Jason Pominville .40 1.50
21 Dominic Forget .16 .40
22 Trevor Ettinger .16 .40
23 Jean-Francois Dufort .16 .40
NNO Coaches .10 .25

2000-01 Shawinigan Cataractes Signed

This set is exactly the same as the base Cataractes set from this season, save that every card has been hand signed by the player pictured. Each card also is serial numbered out of just 100.

COMPLETE SET (24) 24.00 60.00
1 Denis Desmarais .80 2.00
2 Zbynek Michalek .80 2.00
3 Jonathan Beaulieu .80 2.00
4 Jonathan Lessard .80 2.00
5 Jonathan Bellemare .80 2.00
6 Patrick Bolduc .80 2.00
7 Anthony Quessy .80 2.00
8 David Chicoine .80 2.00
9 Gilbert Lefrancois .80 2.00
10 Radim Vrbata 3.20 8.00
11 Yannick Noiseux .80 2.00
12 Marc-Andre Bergeron .80 4.00
13 Jimmy Cuddihy 1.20 5.00
14 Kevin Bergin .80 2.00
15 Francois Gagnon .80 2.00
16 Olivier Michaud 4.00 10.00
17 Frederic Cloutier .80 5.00
18 Jean-Francois David .80 2.00
19 Alexandre Menard Burrows .80 2.00
20 Jason Pominville 2.00 10.00
21 Dominic Forget .80 2.00
22 Trevor Ettinger .75 2.00
23 Jean-Francois Dufort .80 2.00
NNO Coaches .10 .25

2001-02 Shawinigan Cataractes

This set features les Cataractes of the QMJHL. The set was produced by well-known card store CTM Ste-Foy, and was sold by that shop and at the team's souvenir stand. Production was limited to no more than 1,000 sets.

COMPLETE SET (24) 6.00 15.00
1 Denis Desmarais .20 .50
2 Zbynek Michalek .20 .50
3 Paul-Andre Bourgoin .20 .50
4 Jimmy Fillion .30 .75
5 Jonathan Lessard .20 .50
6 Jonathan Bellemore .20 .50
7 Mathieu Gravel .20 .50
8 Jonathan Villeneuve .20 .50
9 David Chicoine .20 .50
10 Armands Berzins .20 .50
11 Philippe Bastarache .20 .50
12 Jimmy Cuddihy .40 1.00
13 Chris Hodgson .20 .50
14 Thiery Poudrier .20 .50
15 Olivier Michaud 2.00 5.00
16 Guillaume Lavallee .20 .50
17 David Leroux .20 .50
18 Jean-Francois David .20 .50
19 Jonathan Boutin .20 .50
20 Alexandre Burrows .20 .50
21 Mathieu Payette .20 .50
22 Jason Pominville .30 .75
23 Jean-Francois Dufort .20 .50
NNO Title Card/CL .04 .10

2002-03 Shawinigan Cataractes

COMPLETE SET (25) 5.00 12.00
1 Julien Ellis .30 .75
2 Dave Grenier .20 .50
3 Paul-Andre Bourgouin .20 .50
4 Frederic Gariepy .20 .50
5 Mathieu Gravel .20 .50
6 Karl Morin .20 .50
7 Armands Berzins .20 .50
8 Danick Bouchard .20 .50
9 Jimmy Cuddihy .30 .75
10 Mathieu Fournier .20 .50
11 Kevin Deslauriers .20 .50
12 Thiery Poudrier .20 .50
13 David Leroux .20 .50
14 Sebastien Gauthier .20 .50
15 Jonathan Villeneuve .20 .50
16 Michel Bergevin-Robinson .30 .75
17 Jonathan Boutin .20 .50
18 Justin Vienneau .20 .50
19 Marek Hascak .20 .50
20 Simon-Pierre Sauve .20 .50
21 Dominic Plante .20 .50
22 Benoit Mondou .30 .75
23 Nicolas Desilets .20 .50
24 Charles Gauthier .20 .50
25 Checklist .04 .10

2003-04 Shawinigan Cataractes

COMPLETE SET (23) 5.00 12.00
1 Eric Begin .20 .50
2 Steve Bellefleur .20 .50
3 Danick Bouchard .20 .50
4 Jonathan Boutin .20 .50
5 Ben Chaisson .20 .50
6 Jimmy Cuddihy .30 .75
7 Marty Doyle .30 .75
8 Nicolas Desilets .20 .50
9 Julien Ellis .30 .75
10 Charles Gauthier .20 .50
11 Sebastien Gauthier .20 .50
12 Michal Gavalier .20 .50
13 Marc-Olivier Gignac .30 .75
14 Mathieu Gravel .20 .50
15 Pierre-Marc Guilbault .20 .50
16 Marek Hascak .20 .50
17 Jonathan Jolette .20 .50
18 Benoit Mondou .30 .75
19 Jean-Philippe Paquet .20 .50
20 Pascal Pelletier .30 .75
21 Thiery Poudrier .20 .50
22 Simon-Pierre Sauve .20 .50
23 Justin Vienneau .20 .50

2005-06 Shawinigan Cataractes

COMPLETE SET (23) 6.00 12.00
1 Julien Ellis .30 .75
2 Ben MacFarlane .20 .50
3 Alex Bourret .40 1.00
4 Benoit Mondou .30 .75
5 Jean-Philippe Paquet .20 .50
6 Justin Vienneau .20 .50
7 Eric Begin .20 .50
8 Steve Bellefleur .20 .50
9 Patrick Bernier .20 .50
10 Danick Bouchard .20 .50
11 Nicolas Desilets .20 .50
12 Guillaume Durand .20 .50
13 Pierre-Marc Guilbault .20 .50
14 Kyell Henegan .20 .50
15 Cedric Lalonde-McNicoll .20 .50
16 Triston Manson .20 .50
17 Francis Pare .20 .50
18 Mathieu Petrin .20 .50
19 Egor Egorov .20 .50
20 Charles Milette .20 .50
21 Guillaume Labreque .20 .50
22 Jan Danecek .20 .50
23 Sean Smyth .20 .50

1986-87 Sherbrooke Canadiens

This 30-card set of the Sherbrooke Canadiens of the AHL was produced by Graphique Estrie, Inc. The cards feature action photos on the front, surrounded by a white border. The team logo, player name and sweater name appear along the bottom, along with the position in French. These unnumbered cards are listed below in alphabetical order.

COMPLETE SET (30) 4.00 10.00
1 Entraineurs 1986-87 .02 .10
2 Soigneurs 1986-87 .02 .10
3 Coupe Stanley 1986 .20 .50
4 Joel Baillargeon .15 .40
5 Daniel Berthiaume .30 .75
6 Serge Boisvert .15 .40
7 Graeme Bonar .15 .40
8 Randy Bucyk .15 .40
9 Bill Campbell .15 .40
10 Jose Charbonneau .15 .40
11 Rejean Cloutier .15 .40
12 Bobby Dollas .15 .40
13 Peter Douris .15 .40
14 Steven Fletcher .15 .40
15 Perry Ganchar .15 .40
16 Luc Gauthier .15 .40
17 Randy Gilhen .15 .40
18 Scott Harlow .15 .40
19 Rick Hayward .15 .40
20 Kevin Houle .15 .40
21 Rick Knickle .30 .75
22 Vincent Riendeau .30 .75
23 Guy Rouleau .15 .40
24 Scott Sandelin .15 .40
25 Karel Svoboda .15 .40
26 Peter Taglianetti .15 .40
27 Gilles Thibaudeau .15 .40
28 Ernie Vargas .15 .40
29 Andre Villeneuve .15 .40
30 Brian Williams .15 .40

2000-01 Sherbrooke Castors

This set features the Castors of the QMJHL and was produced by CTM- Ste-Foy. They were made available through that card shop, as well as at the team's home games. Although the set is numbered to 23, it apparently contains just 19 cards. It's not known whether certain cards were pulled, or never produced.

COMPLETE SET (19) 3.60 10.00
1 Drew MacIntyre .20 .75
2 Sebastien Courcelles .20 .50
3 Simon Tremblay .20 .50
4 Eric Lavigne .20 .50
5 Patrick Gosselin .20 .50
6 Steve Morency .20 .50
7 Francis Trudel .20 .50
9 Jonathan Robert .20 .50
11 Eric Dagenais .20 .50
12 Louis-Philip Lemay .20 .75
13 Artem Trmavski .20 .50
14 Joey Neale .20 .50
15 Benoit Genesse .20 .50
16 Pierre-Luc Courchesne .20 .50
17 Mathieu Thibodeau .20 .50
18 Nicolas Corbeil .40 1.00
21 Francois Belanger .20 .50
22 Cajou MAS .04 .10
23 Jos Canale CO .20 .50

2000-01 Sherbrooke Castors Signed

This set is exactly the same as the base Castors set from this season, save that every card has been hand signed by the player pictured. Each card also is serial numbered out of just 100.

COMPLETE SET (19) 16.00 40.00
1 Drew MacIntyre 1.00 5.00
2 Sebastien Courcelles 1.00 2.50
3 Simon Tremblay 1.00 2.50
4 Eric Lavigne 1.00 2.50
5 Patrick Gosselin 1.00 2.50
6 Steve Morency 1.00 2.50
7 Francis Trudel 1.00 2.50
9 Jonathan Robert 1.00 2.50
11 Eric Dagenais 1.00 2.50
12 Louis-Philip Lemay 1.00 5.00
13 Artem Trmavski 1.00 2.50
14 Joey Neale 1.00 2.50
15 Benoit Genesse 1.00 2.50
16 Pierre-Luc Courchesne 1.00 2.50
17 Mathieu Thibodeau 1.00 2.50
18 Nicolas Corbeil 2.00 5.00
21 Francois Belanger 1.00 2.50
22 Cajou MAS .04 .10
23 Jos Canale CO 1.00 2.50

2001-02 Sherbrooke Castors

This set features the Castors of the QMJHL. The set was produced by CTM Ste-Foy and was sold at Castors home games. It was reported that less than 1,000 sets were produced.

COMPLETE SET (21) 4.80 12.00
1 Drew MacIntyre .30 .75
2 Eric Dagenais .20 .50
3 Dany Roussin .20 .50
4 Juha-Pekka Ketola .20 .50
5 Patrik Levesque .20 .50
6 David Chicoine .20 .50
7 Jonathan Paiement .20 .50
8 Cedrick Duhamel .20 .50
9 Yan Gaudette .20 .50
10 Francis Trudel .20 .50
11 Maxime Boisclair .30 .75
12 Jonathan Robert .20 .50
13 Mathieu Wathier .20 .50
14 Louis-Philip Lemay .30 .75
15 Bertrand-Pierre Plouffe .30 .75
16 Sebastien Courcelles .20 .50
17 Patrick Mbaraga .20 .50
18 Pierre-Luc Courchesne .20 .50
19 Nicolas Corbeil .40 1.00
20 Bruno D'Amico .20 .50
21 Francois Belanger .20 .50

1993-94 Sherbrooke Faucons

Recently confirmed set features unnumbered cards. They are listed below by jersey number.

COMPLETE SET 6.00 15.00
1 Jocelyn Thibault 2.00 5.00
2 Mathieu Dandenault .40 1.00
3 Christian Dube .20 .50
4 Luc Belanger .20 .50
5 Dany Larochelle .20 .50
6 Charles Paquette .20 .50
7 Daniel Villeneuve .20 .50
8 Etienne Beaudry .20 .50
9 Jean-Francois Boutin .20 .50
10 Lachlan Coombe .20 .50
11 Pascal Trepanier .30 .75
12 Dave Douville .20 .50
13 Stephane Larocque .20 .50
14 Eric Messier .30 .75
15 Francois Archambault .20 .50
16 Stephane Julien .20 .50
17 Dave Belliveau .20 .50
18 Hugo Turcotte .20 .50
19 Rocco Anoia .20 .50
20 Carl Fleury .30 .75
21 Mirko Langlois .20 .50
22 Hugo Hamelin .20 .50
23 Steven Low .20 .50
24 Atoucou MASCOT .02 .10
25 Guy Chouinard HCO .08 .25
26 Mario Durocher ACO .02 .10

1974-75 Sioux City Musketeers

This 20-card set is printed on yellow stock. According to the producer, the cards were intended to be standard size but actually came out a little larger. The fronts feature bordered, posed player photos that have a dark green tint to them. In dark green lettering, the team name is printed above the picture while the player's name is printed below it. The cards are unnumbered and checklisted below in alphabetical order. Reportedly only 250 sets were made and they were originally sold at home games for $2.50.

COMPLETE SET (20) 50.00 100.00
1 Steve Boyle 2.50 5.00
2 Dave Davies 2.50 5.00
3 Steve Desloges 2.50 5.00
4 Greg Gilbert 2.50 5.00
5 Barry Head 2.50 5.00
6 Steve Heathwood 2.50 5.00
7 Dave Kartio 2.50 5.00
8 Ralph Kloiber 2.50 5.00
9 Pete Maxwell 2.50 5.00
10 Randy McDonald 2.50 5.00
11 Terry Mulroy 2.50 5.00
12 Sam Nelligan 2.50 5.00
13 Julian Nixon 2.50 5.00
14 Mike Noel 2.50 5.00
15 Jim Peck 2.50 5.00
16 Bogdan Podwysocki 2.50 5.00
17 John Saville P/CO 2.50 5.00
18 Alex Shibicky Jr. 5.00 10.00
19 Bob Thomerson 2.50 5.00
20 Jim White 5.00 10.00

1998-99 Sioux City Musketeers

This set features the Musketeers of the USHL. The oversized (5X6) cards feature an action photo and bio info on the front, along with a blank back. They were issued by the team and sold at the rink. The set is noteworthy for featuring top prospects Rostislav Klesla, David Hale and Ruslan Fedotenko. The set is unnumbered and listed below alphabetically.

COMPLETE SET (25) 8.00 15.00
1 Lee Arnold .20 .50
2 Michael Betz .20 .50
3 Mark Bry .20 .50
4 Chad Dahlen .20 .50
5 Ruslan Fedotenko .75 2.00
6 Cullen Flaherty .20 .50
7 David Hale .40 1.00
8 Tim Judy .20 .50
9 Rostislav Klesla 2.00 5.00
10 Nathan Kotewa .20 .50
11 A.J. Kratofil .20 .50
12 Jordan Lashmett .20 .50
13 Brendan McCartin .20 .50
14 Jake Moreland .20 .50
15 Trent Mozak .20 .50
16 Chad Nordhagen .20 .50
17 Pat O'Leary .20 .50
18 Chris Olsgard .20 .50
19 Tyler Palmiscno .20 .50
20 Luke Pavlas .30 .75
21 Morgan Roach .20 .50
22 Tim Skarperud .20 .50
23 Jeff Van Dyke .20 .50
24 Adam Wallace .20 .50
25 B.J. Willis .20 .50

1999-00 Sioux City Musketeers

This set features the Musketeers of the USHL. It is believed the set was produced by the team and sold at its souvenir stands. The set is noteworthy for including the first card of David Hale, a 2000 first-round choice of the New Jersey Devils.

COMPLETE SET (21) 4.00 10.00
1 Mike Betz .20 .50
2 Max Bull .20 .50
3 Matt Ciancio .20 .50
4 Chad Dahlen .20 .50
5 Henry Dryden .20 .50
6 Lukas Fiala .20 .50
7 David Hale .40 1.00
8 Eric Helstedt .20 .50
9 Justin Hillier .20 .50
10 Steve Jones .20 .50
11 Tim Judy .20 .50
12 A.J. Kratofil .20 .50
13 Brendan McCartin .20 .50
14 John Miller .20 .50
15 Trent Mozak .20 .50
16 Chad Nordhagen .20 .50
17 Chris Olsgard .20 .50
18 Tyler Palmiscno .20 .50
19 Scott Palaski .20 .50
20 Brandon Schmitt .20 .50
21 Jeff Van Dyke .20 .50

2000-01 Sioux City Musketeers

This set features the Musketeers of the USHL. Little is known about the set beyond the confirmed checklist. Additional information can be forwarded to hockeymag@beckett.com.

COMPLETE SET (30) 8.00 20.00
1 Cover Card .04 .10
2 Casey Beauvais .30 .75
3 Matt Ciancio .30 .75
4 Dan Cohen .30 .75
5 Jeff Van Dyke .30 .75
6 Dan Fallon .30 .75
7 Arthur Femenella .30 .75
8 Matt Fetzer .30 .75
9 Justin Fletcher .30 .75
10 Ryan Geris .30 .75
11 Brent Halverson .30 .75
12 Fred Harbinson CO .10 .25
13 Tim Judy .30 .75
14 Erik Johnson .30 .75
15 Brian Kerr .30 .75
16 Zechariah Klann .30 .75
17 Patrick Knutson .30 .75
18 Jack Kowal CO .10 .25
19 Brendan McCartin .30 .75
20 Trent Mozak .30 .75
21 Brian Panik .30 .75
22 Scott Polaski .30 .75
23 Brandon Schmitt .30 .75
24 Brandon Schwartz .30 .75
25 Dave Siciliano CO .10 .25
26 Bryan Smith .30 .75
27 Mitch Thortsen .30 .75
28 Aaron Venasky .30 .75
29 David Vychodil .30 .75
30 John Zeiler .30 .75

2004-05 Sioux City Musketeers

COMPLETE SET (30) 8.00 20.00
1 Brian Bales .30 .75
2 Justin Bostrom .30 .75
3 Kent Bostrom .30 .75
4 Chris Butler .30 .75
5 John Cartera .30 .75
6 Joe Charlebois .30 .75
7 Adam Davis .30 .75
8 Phil DeSimone .30 .75
9 Corey Elkins .30 .75
10 Steve Kampfer .30 .75
11 Nick Kemp .30 .75
12 Tim Kennedy .30 .75
13 Peter Lenes .30 .75
14 Louis Liotti .30 .75
15 Blake Martin .30 .75
16 Dennis McCauley .60 1.50
17 Josh Meyers .30 .75
18 Christian Minella UER .30 .75
19 Jon Ralph .30 .75
20 Chris Spicer .30 .75
21 Jimmy Spratt .60 1.50
22 Travis Turnbull .30 .75
23 Jeff Zatkoff .60 1.50
24 Team Picture .30 .75
25 Schedule .04 .10
26 Mascot .04 .10
27 Dave Siciliano CO .04 .10
28 Marty Quarters ACO .04 .10
29 Chris Brandenberger TR .04 .10
30 Bill Danderand EQM .04 .10

2000-01 Sioux Falls Stampede

Set was produced by the team and sponsored by Wells Fargo Bank. The cards are oversized (5" X 6"). The cards are unnumbered and are listed alphabetically. The checklist may be incomplete. If you know of other cards, please contact us at hockeymag@beckett.com.

COMPLETE SET (21) 10.00 25.00
1 Robbie Barker .30 .75
2 J.B. Bittner .30 .75
3 Jon Booras .30 .75
4 Kellen Briggs .30 .75
5 Jeff Corey .30 .75
6 Donny DeMars .30 .75
7 Mike Doyle .30 .75
8 Jon Dubel .30 .75
9 John Funk .30 .75
10 Dave Iannazzo .30 .75
11 Joe Jensen .30 .75
12 Josh Grahn .30 .75
13 Dustan Lick .30 .75
14 James Massen .30 .75
15 Jamie Mattie .30 .75
16 Zach Sikich .30 .75
17 Dinos Stamoulis .30 .75
18 Thomas Vanek 4.00 10.00
19 Eric Werner .30 .75
20 Tom Zaleski .30 .75
21 Stomp MASCOT .02 .10

2001-02 Sioux Falls Stampede

These cards are unnumbered. They measure 5 X 6. The set features the first card of Marty Sertich, the 2005 Hobey Baker winner.

COMPLETE SET (19) 10.00 25.00
1 Cody Blanshan .30 .75
2 Kellen Briggs .75 2.00
3 Mike Forconi .30 .75
4 Alex Foster .30 .75
5 Quinn Fylling .60 1.50
6 Joe Jensen .30 .75
7 Jacob Micflikier .30 .75
8 Jason Moul .30 .75
9 Eric Przepiorka .30 .75
10 Layne Sedevie .40 1.00
11 Marty Sertich 1.50 4.00
12 Jeremy Smith .30 .75
13 Jesse Stokke .30 .75
14 Kelly Sullivan .30 .75
15 Thomas Vanek 3.00 8.00
16 Mike Vannelli .30 .75
17 Merit Waldrop .30 .75
18 Jake Wilkens .30 .75
19 Chris Wothe .30 .75

2004-05 Sioux Falls Stampede

Set features the Stampede of the USHL. They measure 3"x 4" and are unnumbered. They were issued on four six-card perforated sheets. Set includes 2005 first-rounder T. J. Oshie and Patrick Mullen, son of HOFer Joe Mullen. Thanks to collector Dale Spengler for the list.

COMPLETE SET (24) 15.00 30.00
1-1 Andrew Carroll .40 1.00
1-2 Tom Gorowsky .40 1.00
1-3 Nate Prosser .40 1.00
1-4 Greg Barrett .75 2.00
1-5 Ryan Thang .40 1.00
1-6 T.J. Oshie 2.00 5.00
2-1 Chris Peluso .40 1.00
2-2 Stewart Carlin .40 1.00
2-3 Aleksanders Jerofejevs .40 1.00
2-4 Joe Vitale .40 1.00
2-5 Justin White .40 1.00
2-6 Andreas Nodl .40 1.00
3-1 Evan Stephens .40 1.00
3-2 Warren Byrne .40 1.00
3-3 Joe Finley .75 2.00
3-4 John Murray .75 2.00
3-5 Ben Holmstrom .40 1.00
3-6 Blake Friesen .40 1.00
4-1 Justin Milo .40 1.00
4-2 Jacob Hipp .40 1.00
4-3 Jon Globke .40 1.00
4-4 Patrick Mullen .75 2.00
4-5 Buffalo Wild Wings ad .04 .10
4-6 Brandon Harrington .40 1.00

2006-07 Sioux Falls Stampede

COMPLETE SET (24) 12.00 20.00
1 Brad Malone .40 1.00
2 Patrick Tiesling .40 1.00
3 Drew Fisher .40 1.00
4 Ryan Guentzel .40 1.00
5 David Grun .40 1.00
6 Matt Lundin .75 2.00
7 Joey Miller .40 1.00
8 David Solway .40 1.00
9 Eric Peterson .40 1.00
10 Robbie Vrolyk .40 1.00
11 Doug Schueller ACO .10 .25
12 Nick Dineen .40 1.00
13 Stu Bickel .40 1.00
14 Jake Bauer .40 1.00
15 Sam Zabkowicz .40 1.00
16 Zach Redmond .40 1.00
17 Chris Huxley .40 1.00
18 Zach Hansen .40 1.00
19 Dan Sexton .40 1.00
20 Stomp Mascot .02 .10
21 Alexi Dostoinov .40 1.00
22 Jake Drewiske .40 1.00
23 Kevin Hartzell CO .10 .25
24 Corey Tropp .75 2.00

2001-02 Sorel Royaux

This set features the Royaux of the Quebec Senior League. The cards are standard sized and, because they are unnumbered, are listed below alphabetically. Note: the Patrick Roy listed below is not the famous NHL goaltender.

COMPLETE SET (28) 4.80 12.00
1 Daniel Archambault .20 .50
2 Francois Bourdeau .20 .50
3 Michel Caron .20 .50
4 L.P. Charbonneau .20 .50
5 Georges-Etienne Cote .20 .50
6 Dany Couette .20 .50
7 Christian Deschenes .20 .50
8 Stephane Groleau .20 .50
9 Eric Joyal .20 .50
10 Patrick Labrecque .40 1.00
11 Martin Lacroix .20 .50
12 Stephane Larocque .20 .50
13 Jamie Leinhos .20 .50
14 Justin Leinhos .20 .50
15 Yanick Levesque GM .04 .10
16 Dominic Maltais .40 1.00
17 Francois Paquette .20 .50

Guillaume Rodrigue .20 .50
Patrick Roy .20 .50
Carl St. Germain .20 .50
Yannick Theriault .20 .50
Dan Tice .20 .50
Steve Vincent .20 .50
Sponsor Card .04 .10
Coaching Staff .04 .10
Rink Staff .04 .10
Team Photo .20 .50
History Card .20 .50

1991 South Carolina Collegiate Collection

is 200-card set measures standard sized and atures cards of all-time great South Carolina athletes. e fronts have a black border with color action shots each one. The school name and logo are found ross the top border of the card. The featured player's me is found along the bottom border set against a d background. The backs carry a small bio of the ayer and his/her statistics.

OMPLETE SET (200) 5.00 12.00
Chris Boyle HK .05 .15

1995-96 South Carolina Stingrays

is 24-card set of the South Carolina Stingrays of the CHL was produced for the team by Multi-Ad Services. e set was distributed through the team as well. The onts feature a blurry action photo, along with team d player name. The numbered backs include a rtrait and stats.

OMPLETE SET (24) 3.60 9.00
Rick Vaive CO .20 .50
Dan Wiebe ASST CO .02 .10
Joseph Cramp TR .02 .10
Aaron Fackler .02 .10
Equipment Manager
Mikhail Volkov .15 .40
Jason Cipolla .15 .40
Mike Ross .15 .40
Rob Concannon .15 .40
Dan Fournel .15 .40
0 Mark Bavis .15 .40
1 Darren Ritchie .15 .40
2 Mike Barrie .15 .40
3 Marc Tardif .15 .40
4 Chris Foy .15 .40
5 Scott Boston .20 .50
6 Carl LeBlanc .15 .40
7 Brett Marietti .15 .40
8 Jared Bednar .15 .40
9 Paul Rushforth .15 .40
0 Kevin Knopp .15 .40
1 Todd Sullivan .20 .50
2 Justin Duberman .15 .40
3 Sean Gauthier .20 .50
4 Mark Rupnow .15 .40
NO Header Card .02 .10

1996-97 South Carolina Stingrays

his 27-card set features the South Carolina Stingrays f the ECHL, and was produced by the team, in onjunction with Marvin Foy Marketing, Inc. The cards eature action photography on the front, complemented y a pair of Stingrays logos on the left side, and the layer's name along the lower right border. The back ontains two more photos, as well as statistical and iographical data. The set is noteworthy for the rare nclusion of a card depicting a fight in progress (Dan ournel). The cards boldly feature the player's sweater umber on the back of the card, precipitating their umbering thusly below.

COMPLETE SET (28) 4.00 10.00
Mike Ross .15 .40
0 Marc Genest .15 .40
1 Dan Fournel .40 1.00
2 David Mayes .15 .40
4 David Seitz .15 .40
5 Jeff Romfo .15 .40
6 Kyle Ferguson .15 .40
7 Marc Tardif .15 .40
8 Steve Parson .15 .40
9 Doug Wood .15 .40
20 Scott Boston .30 .75
21 Rob Concannon .15 .40
22 Rob Butler .15 .40
24 Brett Marietti .15 .40
25 Jared Bednar .15 .40
27 Ed Courtenay .20 .50
28 Kevin Knopp .15 .40
29 Jay Moser .15 .40
30 Corey Cadden .15 .40
31 Jason Fitzsimmons .15 .40
33 Chris Hynnes .15 .40
35 Taras Lendzyk .15 .40
NNO Header card
NNO Kenny Snider(Medical Trainer) .02 .10
NNO Rick Vaive CO .20 .50
NNO Aaron Fackler (Equipment Manager) .02 .10
NNO Rick Adduono ASST CO .02 .10
NNO Randy Page(Radio Broadcaster) .02 .10

2001-02 South Carolina Stingrays

This set features the Stingrays of the ECHL. The set was handed out over the course of several games during the season. The cards are unnumbered and are listed below in alphabetical order.

COMPLETE SET (20) 12.00 30.00
1 Rick Adduono CO .20 .50
2 Jared Bednar .75 2.00
3 Ryan Brindley .60 1.50
4 Adam Calder .60 1.50
5 Marty Clapton .60 1.50
6 Jason Fitzsimmons ACO .20 .50
7 Alan Fyfe .60 1.50
8 Zach Ham .60 1.50
9 Jamie Hodson .75 2.00
10 Joel Irving .60 1.50
11 Trevor Johnson .60 1.50
12 Jody Lehman .60 1.50
13 Hugo Marchand .60 1.50
14 Brett Marietti .60 1.50
15 David Seitz .60 1.50
16 Jason Sessa .75 2.00
17 Paul Traynor .75 2.00
18 Buddy Wallace .60 1.50
19 Chris Wheaton .60 1.50
20 Brad Williamson .60 1.50

2002-03 South Carolina Stingrays

This set was sponsored by Mills Printing and was issued as a promotional giveaway at a Stingrays home game.

COMPLETE SET (24) 8.00 20.00
1 Peter Armbrust .40 1.00
2 Jeff Boulanger .40 1.00
3 Ryan Brindley .40 1.00
4 Adam Calder .40 1.00
5 Marty Clapton .40 1.00
6 Kirk Daubenspeck .60 1.50
7 Matt Desrosiers .40 1.00
8 Robin Gomez .60 1.50
9 Brent Henley .60 1.50
10 Curtis Huppe .40 1.00
11 Joel Irving .40 1.00
12 Mike Jickling .40 1.00
13 Trevor Johnson .40 1.00
14 Brett Marietti .40 1.00
15 Andy Powers .40 1.00
16 Aaron Schneekloth .40 1.00
17 David Seitz .40 1.00
18 Rod Taylor .40 1.00
19 Dean Weasler .40 1.00
20 Brad Williamson .40 1.00
21 Jason Fitzsimmons CO .10 .25
22 Jared Bednar ACO .10 .25
23 DJ Church TR .04 .10
24 Jocko Cayer EQM .10 .25

2002-03 South Carolina Stingrays RBI

COMPLETE SET (18) 8.00 20.00
205 Ryan Brinkley .40 1.00
206 David Brumby .60 1.50
207 Adam Calder .40 1.00
208 Marty Clapton .40 1.00
209 Matt Desrosiers .40 1.00
210 Kirk Daubenspeck .60 1.50
211 Robin Gomez .60 1.50
212 Brent Henley .60 1.50
213 Curtis Huppe .40 1.00
214 Joel Irving .40 1.00
215 Mike Jickling .40 1.00
216 Trevor Johnson .40 1.00
217 Brett Marietti .40 1.00
218 Andy Powers .40 1.00
219 Aaron Schneekloth .40 1.00
220 David Seitz .40 1.00
221 Rod Taylor .40 1.00
222 Brad Williamson .40 1.00

2003-04 South Carolina Stingrays

COMPLETE SET (16) 6.00 15.00
321 Chris Allen .40 1.00
322 Jeff Boulanger .40 1.00
323 David Brumby .60 1.50
324 Ed Courtenay .40 1.00
325 Kirk Daubenspeck .60 1.50
326 Robin Gomez .60 1.50
327 Curtis Huppe .40 1.00
328 Mike Jickling .40 1.00
329 Colin Johnson .40 1.00
330 Trevor Johnson .60 1.50
331 Jim Lorentz .40 1.00
332 Aaron Power .40 1.00
333 David Seitz .40 1.00
334 Shawn Skiehar .40 1.00
335 Steven Spencer .40 1.00
336 Kevin Spiewak .40 1.00

2005-06 South Carolina Stingrays

COMPLETE SET (16) 10.00 20.00
1 Matt Reid .75 2.00
2 Jeff Legue .75 2.00
3 Chick-Fil-A Cow .01 .01
4 Ticket Voucher Card .01 .01
5 Trevor Johnson .75 2.00
6 Robin Gomez .75 2.00
7 Maxime Daigneault 1.50 4.00
8 Ticket Voucher Card .01 .01
9 Cail McLean .75 2.00
10 Marty Clapton .75 2.00
11 Steve Spencer .75 2.00
12 Ticket Voucher Card .01 .01
13 Brad Parsons .75 2.00
14 Nate Kiser .75 2.00
15 Aaron Power .75 2.00
16 Ticket Voucher Card .01 .01

1989-90 Spokane Chiefs

Sponsored by the Spokane Teachers Credit Union, this 20-card standard-size set of the 1989-90 Spokane Chiefs features color posed-on-ice player photos on its fronts. The photos are bordered in team colors (red, white, and blue). The player's name, uniform number, and position appear within the blue border below the picture. The cards are unnumbered and checklisted below in alphabetical order. Reportedly only 3,600 sets were made.

COMPLETE SET (20) 6.00 15.00
1 Mike Chrun .20 .50
2 John Colvin .20 .50
3 Shawn Dietrich .20 .50
4 Milan Dragicevic .20 .50
5 Frank Evans .20 .50
6 Pat Falloon .40 1.00
7 Scott Farrell .20 .50
8 Jeff Ferguson .20 .50
9 Travis Green 1.25 3.00
10 Mike Hawes .20 .50
11 Bobby House .20 .50
12 Mike Jickling .20 .50
13 Steve Junker .20 .50
14 Jon Klemm .40 1.00
15 Chris Rowland .20 .50
16 Dennis Saharchuk .20 .50
17 Kerry Toporowski .20 .50
18 Trevor Tovell .20 .50
19 Bram Vanderkracht .20 .50
20 Ray Whitney 1.25 3.00

1993-94 Spokane Chiefs

This set features the Chiefs of the WHL. The set was produced by the team and sold at home games for $5. The cards are unnumbered and so are listed below in alphabetical order.

COMPLETE SET (30) 6.00 15.00
1 Barry Becker .30 .75
2 Maxim Bets .20 .50
3 Valeri Bure .75 2.00
4 Shaun Byrne .20 .50
5 Joe Cardarelli .20 .50
6 John Cirjak .20 .50
7 Dion Darling .20 .50
8 Derek Descoteau .20 .50
9 Ryan Duthie .20 .50
10 Randy Favaro .20 .50
11 Craig Geekie .20 .50
12 Sean Gillam .20 .50
13 Hugh Hamilton .20 .50
14 David Jesiolowski .20 .50
15 Dmitri Leonov .20 .50
16 Bryan Maxwell CO .02 .10
17 Bryan McCabe .40 1.00
18 Memorial Cup Champs .20 .50
19 Rick More TR .02 .10
20 Jason Podollan .20 .50
21 Kevin Popp .20 .50
22 Kevin Sawyer .75 2.00
23 Trevor Shoaf .20 .50
24 Darren Sinclair .20 .50
25 Darren Smadis .30 .75
26 Jeremy Stasiuk .20 .50
27 Scott Townsend .20 .50
28 Spokane Coliseum .02 .10
29 Checklist .02 .10
30 Clover Club Cheerleaders .20 .50

1994-95 Spokane Chiefs

This set features the Chiefs of the WHL. The cards are standard-sized and were sold at home games. Any additional information can be forwarded to hockeymag@beckett.com.

COMPLETE SET (32) 6.00 15.00
1 Randy Favaro .20 .50
2 Jarrod Daniel .20 .50
3 Jason Podollan .40 1.00
4 Trent Whitfield .40 1.00
5 Greg Leeb .20 .50
6 Jay Bertsch .20 .50
7 Joe Cardarelli .20 .50
8 Robby Sandrock .20 .50
9 Kevin Sawyer .40 1.00
10 Sean Gillam .20 .50
11 Ryan Berry .20 .50
12 Mike Haley .20 .50
13 John Cirjak .20 .50
14 Jared Hope .20 .50
15 Joel Boschman .20 .50
16 Derek Descoteau .20 .50
17 Jeremy Stasiuk .20 .50
18 Tomas Pisa .20 .50
19 Darren Sinclair .20 .50
20 Paul Bailley .20 .50
21 Dmitri Leonov .20 .50
22 Bryan McCabe .40 1.00
23 Hugh Hamilton .20 .50
24 Scott Fletcher .20 .50
25 David Lemanowicz .40 1.00
26 Mike Babcock CO .04 .10
27 Parry Schockey CO .04 .10
28 T.D. Forbes EQMG .04 .10
29 Ted Schott EQMG .04 .10
30 Veterans Memorial .04 .10
31 Veterans Memorial .04 .10
32 Veterans Memorial .04 .10

1995-96 Spokane Chiefs

This 30-card set features color player photos in a thin red border on a silver background. The backs carry player information.

COMPLETE SET (30) 4.80 12.00
1 David Lemanowicz .30 .75
2 Scott Fletcher .20 .50
3 Hugh Hamilton .20 .50
4 Chris Lane .20 .50
5 Dmitri Leonov .20 .50
6 Darren Sinclair .20 .50
7 Ty Jones .30 .75
8 Kris Graf .20 .50
9 Trent Whitfield .30 .75
10 Martin Cerven .30 .75
11 Randy Favaro .20 .50
12 Jason Podollan .30 .75
13 Joel Boschman .20 .50
14 Jared Hope .20 .50
15 Greg Leeb .20 .50
16 John Cirjak .20 .50
17 Mike Haley .20 .50
18 Ryan Berry .20 .50
19 Sean Gillam .20 .50
20 Derek Schutz .20 .50
21 Joe Cardarelli .20 .50
22 Adam Magarrell .20 .50
23 Jay Bertsch .20 .50
24 John Shockey .20 .50
25 Mike Babcock CO .15 .40
26 Parry Shockey ACO .02 .10
27 T.D. Forss EQMG .02 .10
28 Ted Schott AEQMG .02 .10
29 Dan Mitchell .02 .10
30 Aren Miller .30 .75

1996-97 Spokane Chiefs

This set features the Chiefs of the WHL. It is believed to have been produced and distributed by the team. Any additional information pertinent to this set can be forwarded to hockeymag@beckett.com.

COMPLETE SET (30) 6.00 15.00
1 Aren Miller .30 .75
2 Brad Ference .40 1.00
3 Hugh Hamilton .20 .50
4 Chris Lane .20 .50
5 Yegor Mikhailov .20 .50
6 Ty Jones .30 .75
7 Kris Graf .20 .50
8 Trent Whitfield .30 .75
9 Blake Evans .20 .50
10 Jared Smyth .20 .50
11 Joel Boschman .20 .50
12 Greg Leeb .30 .75
13 John Cirjak .20 .50
14 Mike Haley .20 .50
15 Kyle Rossiter .30 .75
16 Derek Schutz .40 1.00
17 Marian Cisar .40 1.00
18 Joe Cardarelli .20 .50
19 Adam Magarrell .20 .50
20 Jay Bertsch .20 .50
21 Curtis Suter .20 .50
22 Marc Brown .20 .50
23 Marc Magliarditi .30 .75
24 Boomer Mascot .02 .10
25 Mike Babcock HCO .30 .75
26 Brett Cox ACO .02 .10
27 T.D. Forss TR .02 .10
28 Ted Schott EM .02 .10
29 Dan Mitchell DRM .02 .10
30 Spokane All-Star Game .02 .10

1997-98 Spokane Chiefs

This set features the Chiefs of the WHL. It is believed to have been produced and distributed by the team. Any additional information pertinent to this set can be forwarded to hockeymag@beckett.com.

COMPLETE SET (30) 6.00 15.00
1 Aren Miller .30 .75
2 Brad Ference .40 1.00
3 Perry Johnson .20 .50
4 Mark Forth .20 .50
5 Zenith Komarniski .30 .75
6 Justin Ossachuk .20 .50
7 Cole Fischer .20 .50
8 Brandin Cote .20 .50
9 Ty Jones .30 .75
10 Kris Graf .20 .50
11 Trent Whitfield .30 .75
12 Jared Smyth .20 .50
13 Marc Brown .20 .50
14 Greg Leeb .30 .75
15 Justin Kelly .20 .50
16 Ben Johnson .20 .50
17 Kyle Rossiter .30 .75
18 Derek Schutz .30 .75
19 Marian Cisar .40 1.00
20 Lynn Loyns .40 1.00
21 Kris Waltze .20 .50
22 Curtis Suter .20 .50
23 Josh Maser .20 .50
24 Ron Grimard .20 .50
25 Dan Vandermeer .20 .50
26 Shaun Fleming .20 .50
27 Mike Babcock HCO .02 .10
28 Mike Pelino ACO .02 .10
29 T.D. Forss TR .02 .10
30 Dan Mitchell DRM .02 .10

1998-99 Spokane Chiefs

COMPLETE SET (28) 6.00 15.00
1 Mike Babcock CO .20 .50
2 Daniel Bohac .20 .50
3 Kris Callaway .20 .50
4 Brandin Cote .20 .50
5 Jeremy Farr .20 .50
6 Brad Ference .30 .75
7 Cole Fischer .20 .50
8 Mark Forth .20 .50
9 David Hajek .20 .50
10 Chris Harper .20 .50
11 David Haun .20 .50
12 Simon Jones .20 .50
13 Ty Jones .30 .75
14 Tim Krymusa .20 .50
15 Bobby Leavins .20 .50
16 Mike Lencucha .20 .50
17 Lynn Loyns .30 .75
18 Josh Maser .20 .50
19 Mike Pelino .20 .50
20 Kyle Rossiter .20 .50
21 Derek Schutz .20 .50
22 Cam Severson .40 1.00
23 Tim Smith .20 .50
24 Jared Smyth .20 .50
25 Curtis Suter .20 .50
26 Shawn Thompson .20 .50
27 Dan Vandermeer .20 .50
28 Mason Wallin .20 .50

1999-00 Spokane Chiefs

This set features the Chiefs of the WHL. It is believed that the cards were sold in set form by the team. The cards are unnumbered, and are listed below in alphabetical order.

COMPLETE SET (30) 5.00 12.00
1 Mike Babcock CO .40 1.00
2 Chris Barr .20 .50
3 Daniel Bohac .20 .50
4 David Boychuk .20 .50
5 Kris Callaway .20 .50
6 Brandin Cote .20 .50
7 Jeremy Farr .20 .50
8 T.D. Forss EQMG .02 .10
9 Chris Heid .20 .50
10 Matt Keith .20 .50
11 Tim Krymusa .20 .50
12 Mike Lencucha .30 .75
13 Lynn Loyns .30 .75
14 Jeff Lucky .20 .50
15 Tyler MacKay .20 .50
16 Brent McDonald .20 .50
17 Dan Mitchell STAFF .02 .10
18 Bill Peters ACO .02 .10
19 Scott Roles .20 .50
20 Kyle Rossiter .40 1.00
21 Kurt Sauer .30 .75
22 Beau Schott EQMG .02 .10
23 Derek Schutz .20 .50
24 Tim Smith .20 .50
25 Shawn Thompson .20 .50
26 Ryan Thorpe .20 .50
27 Roman Tvrdon .20 .50
28 Mason Wallin .20 .50
29 Boomer MASCOT .02 .10
30 Spokane Arena .02 .10

2000-01 Spokane Chiefs

This set features the Chiefs of the WHL. It is believed that the cards were sold in set form by the team. The cards are unnumbered and so are listed below in alphatetical order.

COMPLETE SET (30) 4.80 12.00
1 Chris Barr .20 .50
2 David Boychuk .20 .50
3 Barry Brust .30 .75
4 Brandin Cote .20 .50
5 Jevon Desautels .20 .50
6 T.D. Forss EQMG .04 .10
7 Perry Ganchar CO .04 .10
8 Chris Heid .20 .50
9 Barry Horman .20 .50
10 Joff Kehler .20 .50
11 Matt Keith .20 .50
12 Justin Keller .20 .50
13 Tim Krymusa .20 .50
14 Ratislav Lipka .20 .50
15 Lynn Loyns .20 1.00
16 Jeff Lucky .20 .50
17 Tyler MacKay .30 .75
18 Stephen Mann .20 .50
19 Dan Mitchell STAFF .04 .10
20 Chris Ovington .20 .50
21 Craig Perry .20 .50
22 Bill Peters ACO .04 .10
23 Kurt Sauer .20 .75
24 Brad Schell .20 .50
25 Tim Smith .20 .50
26 Shawn Thompson .20 .50
27 Ryan Thorpe .20 .50
28 Roman Tvrdon .20 .50
29 Mason Wallin .20 .50
30 Boomer MASCOT .04 .10

2001-02 Spokane Chiefs

COMPLETE SET (28) 5.00 12.00
1 Header Card .04 .10
2 Chris Barr .20 .50
3 David Boychuk .20 .50
4 Barry Brust .40 1.00
5 Jordan Clarke .20 .50
6 Brandin Cote .20 .50
7 Curtis Darling .40 1.00
8 Jevon Desautels .20 .50
9 Ivan Garcia .20 .50
10 Chris Heid .20 .50
11 Barry Horman .20 .50
12 Joff Kehler .20 .50
13 Matt Keith .30 .75
14 Stuart Kerr .20 .50
15 Chad Klassen .20 .50
16 Tim Krymusa .20 .50
17 Jeff Lucky .20 .50
18 Jeff Lynch .20 .50
19 Kurt Sauer .30 .75
20 Brad Schell .20 .50
21 Scott Scherger .20 .50
22 Mason Wallin .20 .50
23 Perry Ganchar CO .04 .10
24 Bill Peters ACO .04 .10
25 Dan Mitchell TR .04 .10
26 Darcy Bishop TR .04 .10
27 Boomer MASCOT .04 .10
28 Overagers .20 .50

2002-03 Spokane Chiefs

COMPLETE SET (30) 5.00 12.00
1 Chris Barr .20 .50
2 Ryan Blatchford .20 .50
3 Barry Brust .40 1.00
4 Liam Couture .20 .50
5 Andrew DeSousa .20 .50
6 Jevon Desautels .20 .50
7 Chris Heid .20 .50
8 Barry Horman .20 .50
9 Joff Kehler .20 .50
10 Chad Klassen .20 .50
11 Tim Krymusa .20 .50
12 Jakub Langhammer .20 .50
13 Darren Lefebvre .20 .50
14 Jeff Lucky .20 .50
15 Ned Lukacevic .20 .50
16 Doug Lynch .30 .75
17 Jeff Lynch .20 .50
18 Joel Rupprecht .20 .50
19 Brad Schell .20 .50
20 Andy Schenn .20 .50
21 Scott Scherger .20 .50
22 Miroslav Stolc .20 .50
23 Mason Wallin .20 .50
24 Jim Watt .20 .50
25 Colby Zavisha .20 .50
26 Al Conroy CO .04 .10
27 Jamie Huscroft ACO .04 .10
28 Dan Mitchell TR .04 .10
29 Boomer MASCOT .04 .10
30 Darcy Bishop TR .04 .10

2004-05 Spokane Chiefs Magnets

These cards have magnetic backs and were handed out one per night at Wednesday home games.

1 Gary Gladue .75 2.00
2 Jevon Desautels .75 2.00
3 Scott Lynch .75 2.00
4 Chad Klassen .75 2.00
5 Jim Watt .75 2.00
6 Ned Lukacevic .75 2.00
7 Gustav Engman .75 2.00
8 Jeff Lynch .75 2.00

1996-97 Springfield Falcons

This 21-card set was produced by Split Second. These unnumbered cards feature an action photo on the front with a stats package on the reverse. The cards were available through the club at the rink or by mail order.

COMPLETE SET (21) 4.00 10.00
3 Brent Thompson .30 .75
4 Deron Quint .30 .75
5 Steve Cheredaryk .15 .40
10 Kent Manderville .15 .40
11 Hnat Domenichelli .30 .75
12 Steve Martins .30 .75
14 Tom Buckley .15 .40
15 Juha Ylonen .30 .75
16 Chris Longo .15 .40
17 Rhett Gordon .15 .40
19 Tavis Hansen .15 .40
20 Steve Halko .15 .40
22 Scott Levins .15 .40
23 Rob Murray .15 .40
25 Jason McBain .15 .40
27 Jeff Daniels .15 .40
28 Ryan Risidore .20 .50
30 Manny Legace .60 1.50
33 Reggie Savage .15 .40
34 Nolan Pratt .20 .50
35 Scott Langkow .30 .75
44 Kevin Brown .15 .40
NNO AHL Hockey Card .02 .10

1997-98 Springfield Falcons

This set features the Falcons of the AHL. The set was produced by SplitSecond and was sold by the team at home games.

COMPLETE SET (26) 5.00 15.00
1 Daniel Briere 1.00 2.50
2 Ruslan Batyrshin .15 .40
3 Ted Crowley .15 .40
4 Sylvain Daigle .15 .40
5 Andrew Dale .15 .40
6 Shane Doan 1.00 2.50
7 Jason Doig .20 .50
8 Dan Focht .15 .40
9 Sean Gagnon .15 .40
10 Rhett Gordon .15 .40
11 Tavis Hansen .15 .40
12 Chad Kilger .30 .75
13 Scott Langkow .30 .75
14 Trevor Letowski .40 1.00
15 Scott Levins .20 .50
16 Richard Lintner .20 .50
17 Jason Morgan .15 .40
18 Rob Murray .15 .40
19 Mike Pomichter .15 .40
20 Jeff Shevalier .15 .40
21 Martin Simard .15 .40
22 Brad Tiley .15 .40
23 Dave Farrish CO .08 .25
24 Ron Wilson CO .08 .25
25 PHPA Web Site .01 .05
26 AHL Web Site .01 .05

2002-03 Springfield Falcons

COMPLETE SET (24) 6.00 15.00
1 Ramzi Abid .30 .75
2 Dmitry Afanasenkov .30 .75
3 Nikita Alexeev .40 1.00
4 Frank Banham .20 .50
5 Goran Bezina .20 .50
6 Zac Bierk .40 1.00
7 Jason Bonsignore .20 .50
8 Martin Cibak .20 .50
9 Dan Focht .20 .50
10 Corey Foster .20 .50
11 Martin Grenier .30 .75
12 Jason Jaspers .20 .50
13 Boyd Kane .40 1.00
14 Evgeny Konstantinov .30 .75
15 Kristian Kudroc .20 .50
16 Norm Maciver ACO .04 .10
17 Marty McSorley HCO .20 .50
18 Rob Murray .20 .50
19 Darren Rumble .20 .50
20 Michael Schutte .20 .50
21 Dan Smith .20 .50
22 Jeff Taffe .40 1.00
23 Erik Westrum .40 1.00
24 Shane Willis .20 .50

2003-04 Springfield Falcons Postcards

These singles were recently confirmed. If you have any additional information about this set, please contact us at hockeymag@beckett.com.

COMPLETE SET (28) 15.00 30.00
1 Goran Bezina .40 1.00
2 Trevor Gillies .40 1.00
3 Kiel McLeod .40 1.00
4 Erik Westrum .75 2.00
5 Dustin Wood .40 1.00
6 Igor Knyazev .40 1.00
7 Nikos Tselios .40 1.00
8 Martin Podlesak .40 1.00
9 Darren McLachlin .40 1.00
10 Frederik Sjostrom .40 1.00
11 Jason Jaspers .40 1.00
12 Bryan Helmer .40 1.00
13 Mike Stutzel .40 1.00
14 Peter Ferraro .40 1.00
15 Gary Shuchuk .40 1.00
16 Frank Lukes .40 1.00
17 Chris Ferraro .40 1.00
18 Chris Dyment .40 1.00
19 Frank Banham .75 2.00
20 Jean-Marc Pelletier .75 2.00
21 Mike Wilson .40 1.00
22 Ladislav Kouba .40 1.00
23 Jeremiah McCarthy .40 1.00
24 David LeNeveu .75 2.00
25 Michael Schutte .40 1.00
26 Marty McSorley CO .40 1.00
27 Gord Dineen ACO .20 .50
28 MASCOT .04 .10

2004-05 Springfield Falcons

COMPLETE SET (27) 6.00 15.00
1 Adam Henrich .20 .50
2 Andre Deveaux .20 .50
3 Andreas Holmqvist .20 .50
4 Brian Chapman .20 .50
5 Brian Eklund .30 .75
6 Craig Darby .20 .50
7 Darren Reid .20 .50
8 Dennis Packard .20 .50
9 Derek Bekar .20 .50
10 Doug O'Brien .20 .50
11 Evgeny Artukhin .20 .50
12 Gerard DiCaire .20 .50
13 Harlan Pratt .20 .50
14 Jamie Storr .30 .75
15 Jason Jaspers .20 .50
16 Marc Busenburg .20 .50
17 Mike Egener .20 .50
18 Mitch Fritz .40 1.00
19 Nick Tarnasky .40 1.00
20 Nikita Alexeev .20 .50
21 Nikos Tselios .20 .50
22 Paul Ranger .20 .50
23 Ryan Craig .75 2.00
24 Shane Willis .20 .50
25 Steve McLaren .20 .50
26 Phil Russell ACO .04 .10
27 Dirk Graham CO .04 .10

2005-06 Springfield Falcons

COMPLETE SET (27) 8.00 15.00
1 Adam Henrich .20 .50
2 Andre Deveaux .20 .50
3 Brad Tiley .20 .50
4 Brian Eklund .30 .75
5 Darren Reid .20 .50
6 Dennis Packard .20 .50
7 Doug O'Brien .20 .50
8 Evgeny Artyukhin .20 .50
9 Gerald Coleman .40 1.00
10 Gerard Dicaire .20 .50
11 Harlan Pratt .20 .50
12 Jason Jaspers .20 .50
13 Jim Campbell .20 .50
14 Marek Kvapil .20 .50
15 Mike Egener .40 1.00
16 Mitch Fritz .40 1.00
17 Nick Tarnasky .30 .75
18 Norm Milley .20 .50
19 Paul Ranger .20 .50
20 Steve McLaren .20 .50
21 Ryan Craig .40 1.00
22 Ryan Vesce .20 .50
23 Timo Helbling .20 .50
24 Todd Rohloff .20 .50
25 Dirk Graham HC .02 .10
26 Phil Russell ACO .02 .10
27 Darren Rumble ACO .02 .10

2006-07 Springfield Falcons

COMPLETE SET (28) 8.00 15.00
1 Sean Burke .40 1.00
2 Doug O'Brien .20 .50
3 Dan Cavanaugh .20 .50
4 Andy Delmore .20 .50
5 Eric Healey .20 .50
6 Blair Jones .20 .50
7 Sylvain Dufresne .20 .50
8 Mitch Fritz .30 .75
9 Jay Rosehill .20 .50
10 Karri Ramo .40 1.00
11 Zdenek Blatny .20 .50
12 Justin Keller .20 .50
13 Mike Egener .30 .75
14 Darren Reid .20 .50
15 David Spina .20 .50
16 Marek Kvapil .20 .50
17 Norm Milley .20 .50
18 Andy Rogers .20 .50
19 Matt Smaby .40 1.00
20 Jonathan Boutin .40 1.00
21 Zbynek Hrdel .20 .50
22 Steve Stirling HC .10 .25
23 Darren Rumble CO .10 .25
24 Jared Aulin .20 .50
25 Andre Deveaux .20 .50
26 Adam Henrich .20 .50
27 Geoff Waugh .20 .50
28 Screech MASCOT .02 .10

2014-15 Springfield Falcons

COMPLETE SET (25) 6.00 15.00
1 Anton Forsberg .30 .75
2 Hubert Labrie .30 .75
3 Will Weber .30 .75
4 Austin Madaisky .30 .75
5 Dennis Urban .30 .75
6 Marko Dano .50 1.25
7 Mike Hoeffel .30 .75
8 Ryan Craig .30 .75
9 Trent Vogelhuber .30 .75
10 Dana Tyrell .40 1.00
11 Kerby Rychel .30 .75
12 Sean Collins .30 .75
13 T.J. Tynan .30 .75
14 Nathan Oystrick .30 .75
15 Lukas Sedlak .30 .75
16 Brett Ponich .30 .75
17 Mathieu Gagnon .30 .75
18 Jaime Sifers .30 .75
19 Oscar Dansk .40 1.00
20 Frederic St. Denis .30 .75
21 Corey Cowick .30 .75
22 Thomas Larkin .30 .75
23 Domenic Monardo .30 .75
24 Josh Anderson .30 .75
25 Jared Bednar CO .30 .75

1983-84 Springfield Indians

Produced by Card Collectors Closet (Springfield, MA), this 25-card standard-size set features black-and-white player portraits on a white card face. The team name and year are printed in black at the top. The player's name and position appear at the bottom.

COMPLETE SET (25) 7.20 18.00
1 Gil Hudon .30 .75
2 Jim Ralph 1.25 3.00
3 Todd Bergen .30 .75
4 Len Hachborn .40 1.00
5 John Ollson .20 .50
6 Steve Tsujiura .40 1.00
7 Gordie Williams .20 .50
8 Dave Brown 1.25 3.00
9 Dan Frawley .20 .50
10 Tom McMurchy .20 .50
11 Dave Michayluk .30 .75
12 Bob Mormina .20 .50
13 Perry Pelensky .20 .50
14 Andy Brickley .40 1.00
15 Ross Fitzpatrick .20 .50
16 Florent Robidoux .20 .50
17 Jeff Smith .20 .50
18 Rod Willard .20 .50
19 Darrell Anholt .20 .50
20 Steve Blyth .20 .50
21 Don Dietrich .20 .50
22 Steve Smith .20 .50
23 Daryl Stanley .40 1.00
24 Taras Zytynsky .20 .50
25 Doug Sauter CO .20 .50

1984-85 Springfield Indians

Produced by Card Collectors Closet (Springfield, MA), this 25-card standard-size set features black-and-white player portraits on a white card face. The team name and year are printed in black at the top. The player's name and position appear at the bottom. The pictures are framed by a royal blue border while a red border encloses the photo and the text.

COMPLETE SET (25) 6.00 15.00
1 Mike Sands .40 1.00
2 Lorne Molleken .20 .50
3 Todd Lumbard .20 .50
4 Randy Velischek .30 .75
5 David Jensen .30 .75
6 Ken Leiter .20 .50
7 Vern Smith .20 .50
8 Alan Kerr .30 .75
9 Scott Howson .20 .50
10 Tim Coulis .20 .50
11 Terry Tait .20 .50
12 Tim Trimper .20 .50
13 Rob Flockhart .30 .75
14 Ron Handy .20 .50
15 Jiri Poner .20 .50
16 Chris Pryor .20 .50
17 Dale Henry .20 .50
18 Mark Hamway .20 .50
19 Monty Trottier .20 .50
20 Miroslav Maly .20 .50
21 Dirk Graham 1.25 3.00
22 Roger Kortko .20 .50
23 Bob Bodak .20 .50
24 Lorne Henning CO .30 .75
25 Checklist Card .20 .50

1957-58 St. Catharines Tee Pees Murray's Chips

This set features the Tee Pees of the old OHA. The set features players who were in the Chicago Blackhawks farm system. The set is also known as the Murray's Potato Chips set, due to that name appearing on top of these undersized, black and white issues. The cards apparently were distributed in conjunction with the purchase of a bag of chips. The checklist is known to be incomplete, so no set price is listed. While the cards are numbered, we have yet to be able to confirm the numbering for all of the card so we have listed them alphabetically below with the card's number listed after the player's name.

1 Bob Corupe 18 25.00 50.00
2 Don Cosburn 25.00 50.00
3 Roy Edwards 1 40.00 80.00
4 Don Grosso 17 25.00 50.00
5 Ed Hoekstra 30.00 60.00
6 Chico Maki 16 40.00 80.00
7 John McKenzie 50.00 100.00
8 Stan Mikita 200.00 400.00
9 Matt Ravlich 30.00 60.00

1993-94 St. Cloud State Huskies

This set features the Huskies of the NCAA. The set was issued as a promotional giveaway at a single home game in the form of a large perforated sheet. The cards have traded hands in both complete and singles form, so both values are listed.

COMPLETE SHEET (30) 6.00 15.00
1 Randy Best .20 .50
2 Chad Brennan .20 .50
3 Neil Cooper .20 .50
4 Chris Dopp .20 .50
5 Marc Gagnon .20 .50
6 Sandy Gasseau .20 .50
7 Jay Geisbaur .20 .50
8 Tony Gruba .20 .50
9 Dave Holum .20 .50
10 Kelly Hultgren .20 .50
11 Jason Jiskra .20 .50
12 Eric Johnson .20 .50
13 P.J. Lepler .20 .50
14 Brett Lievers .20 .50
15 Billy Lund .20 .50
16 Mike Maristuen .20 .50
17 Chris Markstrom .20 .50
18 Taj Melson .20 .50

19 Brad Nelson .20 .50
20 Mike O'Connell .20 .50
21 Dave Paradise .20 .50
22 Dan Reimann .20 .50
23 Kelly Rieder .20 .50
24 Adam Rodak .20 .50
25 Gino Santerre .20 .50
26 Jeff Schmidt .20 .50
27 Grant Sjerven .20 .50
28 Coaching Staff .20 .50
29 Marc Gagnon IA .20 .50
30 Kelly Rieder IA .20 .50

2000-01 St. Cloud State Huskies

COMPLETE SET (31) 4.00 10.00
1 Keith Anderson .15 .40
2 Tyler Arnason .30 .75
3 Lee Brooks .15 .40
4 Jon Cullen .15 .40
5 Nate DiCasmirro .15 .40
6 Derek Eastman .15 .40
7 Jeff Finger .15 .40
8 Brian Gaffaney .15 .40
9 Mark Hartigan .15 .40
10 Matt Hendricks .15 .40
11 Ryan Johnson .15 .40
12 Ryan LaMere .15 .40
13 Ritchie Larson .15 .40
14 Andy Lundbohm .15 .40
15 Ryan Malone .15 .40
16 Jim McNamara .15 .40
17 Scott Meyer .15 .40
18 Jake Moreland .15 .40
19 Joe Motzko .15 .40
20 Joel Peterson .15 .40
21 Chris Purslow .15 .40
22 Brandon Sampair .15 .40
23 Brian Schuster .15 .40
24 Mike Walsh .15 .40
25 Dean Weasler .15 .40
26 Duvie Westcott .15 .40
27 Craig Dahl .15 .40
28 Doc DelCastillo .15 .40
29 Brad Willner .15 .40
30 Dog Pound .15 .40
31 Chuck Clausen .15 .40

2003-04 St. Cloud State Huskies

These cards were issued as a promotional giveaway at a late-season home game.

COMPLETE SET (31) 8.00 20.00
1 Casey Borer .30 .75
2 Tim Boron .40 1.00
3 Grant Clafton .30 .75
4 Tim Conboy .30 .75
5 Adam Coole .40 1.00
6 Mike Doyle .30 .75
7 Justin Fletcher .30 .75
8 Matt Gens .30 .75
9 Matt Hendricks .30 .75
10 Billy Hengen .30 .75
11 Brock Hooton .30 .75
12 Gary Houseman .30 .75
13 Dave Iannazzo .30 .75
14 Joe Jensen .30 .75
15 Ryan LaMere .30 .75
16 Garrett Larson .30 .75
17 Bille Luger .30 .75
18 Andy Lundbohm .30 .75
19 Brian McCormack .30 .75
20 T.J. McElroy .30 .75
21 Jason Montgomery .40 1.00
22 Colin Peters .30 .75
23 Nate Raduns .30 .75
24 Konrad Reeder .30 .75
25 Peter Szabo .30 .75
26 Nate Wright .30 .75
27 Craig Dahl CO .04 .10
28 Brad Willner ACO .04 .10
29 Fred Harbinson ACO .04 .10
30 Mascot .04 .10
31 Team Photo .10 .25

2004-05 St. Cloud State Huskies

Issued as a promotional giveaway. Cards are unnumbered so are listed below in alphabetical order.

COMPLETE SET (32) 10.00 25.00
1 Chris Anderson .40 1.00
2 Casey Borer .40 1.00
3 Tim Boron .40 1.00
4 Aaron Brocklehurst .40 1.00
5 Grant Clafton .40 1.00
6 Nate Dey .40 1.00
7 Mike Doyle .40 1.00
8 Justin Fletcher .40 1.00
9 Matt Francis .40 1.00
10 Sean Garrity .40 1.00
11 Matt Gens .40 1.00
12 Andrew Gordon .40 1.00
13 Matt Hartman .40 1.00
14 Billy Hengen .40 1.00
15 Brock Hooton .40 1.00
16 Gary Houseman .40 1.00
17 Dave Iannazzo .40 1.00
18 Joe Jensen .40 1.00
19 Ethan Lyerly .40 1.00
20 T.J. McElroy .40 1.00
21 Marty Mjelleli .40 1.00
22 Jason Montgomery .40 1.00
23 Nate Radums .40 1.00
24 Konrad Reeder .40 1.00
25 Josh Singer .40 1.00
26 Matt Stephenson .40 1.00
27 Peter Szabo .40 1.00
28 Craig Dahl CO .10 .25
29 Fred Harbinson ACO .10 .25
30 Brad Willner ACO .10 .25
31 Sean Donley TR .10 .25
32 Jeremiah Minkel EQM .10 .25

2005-06 St. Cloud State Huskies

COMPLETE SET (33) 10.00 20.00
1 Chris Anderson .30 .75
2 Casey Borer .30 .75
3 Tim Boron .30 .75
4 Aaron Brocklehurst .30 .75
5 David Carlisle .30 .75
6 Grant Clafton .30 .75
7 Nate Dey .30 .75
8 Justin Fletcher .30 .75
9 Matt Francis .30 .75
10 Sean Garrity .30 .75
11 Bobby Goepfert .60 1.50
12 Andrew Gordon .30 .75
13 Matt Hartman .30 .75
14 Billy Hengen .30 .75
15 Brock Hooton .30 .75
16 Gary Houseman .30 .75
17 Joe Jensen .30 .75
18 Dan Kronick .30 .75
19 T.J. McElroy .30 .75
20 Marty Mjelleli .30 .75
21 Jason Montgomery .30 .75
22 Michael Olson .30 .75
23 Nate Raduns .30 .75
24 Konrad Reeder .30 .75
25 Josh Singer .30 .75
26 Matt Stephenson .30 .75
27 John Swanson .30 .75
28 Bob Motzko CO .02 .10
29 Fred Harbinson ACO .02 .10
30 Eric Rud ACO .02 .10
31 Bryan Demaine TR .02 .10
32 Jeremiah Minkel EQM .02 .10
33 Blizzard MASCOT .02 .10

2003-04 St. Francis Xavier X-Men

St. Francis is a Canadian University.

COMPLETE SET (30) 5.00 12.00
1 Ryan White .20 .50
2 Ryan Armstrong .20 .50
3 Stuart MacRae .20 .50
4 Wes Jarvis .20 .50
5 Mike Martone .20 .50
6 Bobby Reed .20 .50
7 Blake Robson .20 .50
8 Ben Berthiaume .20 .50
9 Troy Smith .20 .50
10 Mike Smith .20 .50
11 Danny White .20 .50
12 Graham Power .20 .50
13 Patrick Grandmaitre .20 .50
14 Dustin Russell .20 .50
15 Darren MacMillan .20 .50
16 Alan Dwyer .20 .50
17 Colin Circelli .20 .50
18 Dwayne Bateman .20 .50
19 Ryan Walsh .20 .50
20 Omar Ennaffati .20 .50
21 Eric Braff .20 .50
22 Mike Mole .30 .75
23 Shawn Snider .20 .50
24 Chris Brannen .20 .50
25 Dallas Flaman .20 .50
26 Todd Norman .20 .50
27 Danny Flynn CO .04 .10
28 Greg MacDonald ACO .04 .10
29 John Kibyuk ACO .04 .10
30 Kyle MacIsaac ACO .04 .10

2004-05 St. Francis Xavier X-Men

COMPLETE SET (24) 5.00 12.00
1 Ryan Armstrong .20 .50
2 Eric Braff .20 .50
3 Collin Circelli .20 .50
4 Alan Dwyer .20 .50
5 Tyler Dyck .20 .50
6 Omar Ennaffati .20 .50
7 Patrick Grandmaitre .20 .50
8 Wes Jarvis .30 .75
9 Jim Kehoe .20 .50
10 Tyson Kellerman .20 .50
11 Matthew Lynn .20 .50
12 Ryan MacKay .20 .50
13 Stuart MacRae .20 .50
14 Darren McMillan .20 .50
15 Michael Mole .40 1.00
16 Graham Power .20 .50
17 Bobby Reed .20 .50
18 Blake Robson .20 .50
19 Mike Smith .20 .50
20 Shawn Snider .20 .50
21 Niko Tuomi .20 .50
22 Ryan Walsh .20 .50
23 Danny White .20 .50
24 Ryan White .20 .50

2003-04 St. Georges de Beauce Garaga

This set was produced by Extreme Sports Cards. The Shantz card is incorrectly identified as Daniel Shank.

COMPLETE SET (20) 4.00 10.00
1 Philippe Audet .20 .50
2 Kevin Cloutier .20 .50
3 Philippe Deblois .20 .50
4 Raymond Delarosbil .20 .50
5 Jonathan Delisle .20 .50
6 Carl Fleury .20 .50
7 Francois Garand .20 .50
8 Steve Gosselin .20 .50
9 Jason Groleau .20 .50
10 Jean-Francois Labbe .20 .50
11 Daniel Laflamme .20 .50
12 Jean-Yves Leroux .20 .50
13 Dannick Lessard .20 .50
14 Claude Morin .20 .50
15 Normand Rochefort .20 .50
16 Paul Shantz UER .20 .50
17 Steve Tardif .20 .50
18 Hugo Turcotte .20 .50
19 Mathieu Vachon .20 .50
20 Frederic Vermette .20 .50

2004-05 St. Georges de Beauce Garaga

COMPLETE SET (24) 6.00 15.00
1 Steve Tardif .30 .75
2 Jonathan Forest .30 .75
3 Paul Shantz .30 .75
4 Nicolas Poirier .30 .75
5 Claude Morin .30 .75
6 Raymond Delarosbil .30 .75
7 Martin Fillion .30 .75
8 Eric Bertrand .30 .75
9 David Lessard .30 .75
10 Jonathan Delisle .30 .75
11 Mathieu Vachon .30 .75
12 Tommy Bolduc .30 .75
13 Daniel Laflamme .30 .75
14 Kevin Cloutier .30 .75
15 Jean-Philippe Soucy .40 1.00
16 Mike Bajurny .60 1.50
17 Carl Paradis .30 .75
18 John Murphy .30 .75
19 Hugo Levesque .30 .75
20 Jason Rushton .30 .75
21 Didier Tremblay .30 .75
22 Rejean Dufour .30 .75
23 Brandon Christian .30 .75
24 Randy Copley .30 .75

2014-15 St. Georges Cool 103.5FM

COMPLETE SET (25) 7.50 15.00
1 David Starenky .30 .75
2 Robin Lemay .30 .75
3 Jean-Philippe Pare .30 .75
4 Mike Novosad .30 .75
5 Michel Leveille .30 .75
6 Keven Dupont .30 .75
7 Dany Roussin .30 .75
8 Alex Gagne .30 .75
9 Mikael Bedard .30 .75
10 Pascal Lariviere .30 .75
11 Martin Nolet .30 .75
12 Charles Bety .30 .75
13 Jean-Philipp Paquet .30 .75
14 Jeremy Duchesne .30 .75
15 Michel Robinson .30 .75
16 Tommy Gauthier .30 .75
17 Hubert Morin .30 .75
18 Stephane Goulet .30 .75
19 Jean-Francois St. Laurent .30 .75
20 Maxime Levesque .30 .75
21 Philippe Lauze .30 .75
22 Samuel Grenache .30 .75
23 Hubert Poulin .30 .75
24 Guillaume Parenteau .30 .75
25 Mario Boilard .30 .75

2003-04 St. Jean Mission

The Mission played in the LNAH, the Quebec semi-pro circuit. The cards were sold at home games.

COMPLETE SET (28) 6.00 15.00
1 Luc Bilodeau .20 .50
2 Murray Cobb .20 .50
3 Alain Cote .20 .50
4 Greg Davis .20 .50
5 Mario DeBenedictis .20 .50
6 Martin Dicaire .20 .50
7 Bobby Dollas .20 .50
8 Corey Foster .20 .50
9 Link Gaetz .75 2.00
10 Pierre Gendron .20 .50
11 Victor Gervais .20 .50
12 Daniel Guerard .20 .50
13 Hugo Hamelin .20 .50
14 Eric Lachapelle .20 .50
15 Steven Low .20 .50
16 Dominique Maltais .20 .50
17 Eric McIntyre .20 .50
18 Rob Murphy .20 .50
19 Charles Paquette .30 .75
20 Pierre Pelletier .20 .50
21 Jean-Francois Piche .20 .50
22 Guillaume Richard .20 .50
23 Sebastien Roger .20 .50
24 Christian Sbrocca .20 .50
25 Dan Tice .20 .50
26 Ronny Valenti .20 .50
27 Steve Vezina .30 .75
28 Dan Zimmerman .20 .50

2015-16 St. John's IceCaps

COMPLETE SET (28) 8.00 20.00
1 Josiah Didier .30 .75
2 Morgan Ellis .30 .75
3 Dalton Thrower .30 .75
4 Darren Dietz .30 .75
5 Mark Barberio .30 .75
6 Mac Bennett .30 .75
7 Charles Hudson .30 .75
8 Daniel Carr .30 .75
9 Ryan Johnston .30 .75
10 Brett Lernout .30 .75
11 Joel Hanley .30 .75
12 Mark MacMillan .30 .75
13 Nikita Scherbak .30 .75
14 Christian Thomas .30 .75
15 Jacob de la Rose .50 1.25
16 Bud Holloway .30 .75
17 Connor Crisp .30 .75
18 Brandon McNally .30 .75
19 Michael McCarron .60 1.50
20 Eric Neilson .30 .75
21 Sven Andrighetto .40 1.00
22 Tim Bozon .30 .75
23 Zachary Fucale .75 2.00
24 Dustin Tokarski .40 1.00
25 Jeremy Gregoire .30 .75
26 Markus Eisenschmid .30 .75
27 Gabriel Dumont .30 .75
NNO Header Card CL .30 .75

1992-93 St. John's Maple Leafs

Measuring approximately 2 1/2" by 3 3/4", this 25-card set features the St. John's Maple Leafs of the American Hockey League. The fronts display color action player photos framed by white borders. In the wider bottom border, the player's name, uniform number, position, and logos are printed in black. The cards are unnumbered and checklisted below in alphabetical order.

COMPLETE SET (25) 4.00 10.00
1 Patrik Augusta .15 .40
2 Drake Berehowsky .20 .50
3 Robert Cimetta .15 .40
4 Marc Crawford CO .20 .50
5 Ted Crowley .15 .40
6 Mike Eastwood .30 .75
7 Todd Hawkins .15 .40
8 Curtis Hunt .15 .40
9 Eric Lacroix .20 .50
10 Guy Lehoux .15 .40
11 Kent Manderville .20 .50
12 Kevin McClelland .15 .40
13 Ken McRae .15 .40
14 Brad Miller .15 .40
15 Yanic Perreault .40 1.00
16 Rudy Poeschek .30 .75
17 Joel Quenneville ACO .08 .25
18 Damian Rhodes .40 1.00
19 Joe Sacco .15 .40
20 Jeff Serowik .15 .40
21 Scott Sharples .15 .40
22 Dave Tomlinson .15 .40
23 Nick Wohlers .15 .40
24 Team Photo .15 .40
25 Buddy (Mascot) .02 .10

1993-94 St. John's Maple Leafs

This 25-card standard-size set features the St. John's Maple Leafs of the American Hockey League. The fronts feature color action player photos with white borders and a gray shadow border. The team name "Leafs" in blue lettering edges the left side of the picture. The cards are unnumbered and checklisted below in alphabetical order.

COMPLETE SET (25) 4.00 10.00
1 Patrik Augusta .15 .40
2 Frank Bialowas .20 .50
3 Buddy (Mascot) .02 .10
4 Rich Chernomaz .15 .40
5 Terry Chitaroni .15 .40
6 Marcel Cousineau .20 .50
7 Marc Crawford CO .20 .50
8 Todd Gillingham .15 .40
9 Chris Govedaris .15 .40
10 Paul Holden .15 .40
11 Curtis Hunt .15 .40
12 Alexei Kudashov .15 .40
13 Eric Lacroix .40 1.00
14 Guy Lehoux .15 .40
15 Matt Mallgrave .15 .40
16 Grant Marshall .20 .50
17 Ken McRae .15 .40
18 Yanic Perreault .30 .75
19 Bruce Racine .20 .50
20 Damian Rhodes .40 1.00
21 Chris Snell .15 .40
22 Dan Stiver .15 .40
23 Andy Sullivan .15 .40
24 Ryan Vandenbussche .20 .50
25 Steffon Walby .15 .40

1994-95 St. John's Maple Leafs

This 24-card standard-size set was manufactured and distributed by Jessen Associates, Inc. for Classic. The fronts display color action player photos with a dark blue marbleized inner border and a black outer border. The player's name, jersey number, and position appear in the teal border on the right edge. The cards are unnumbered and checklisted below in alphabetical order.

COMPLETE SET (24) 3.60 9.00
1 Patrik Augusta .08 .25
2 Ken Belanger .20 .50
3 Frank Bialowis .40 1.00
4 Rich Chernomaz .08 .25
5 Brandon Convery .08 .25
6 Marcel Cousineau .20 .50
7 Trent Cull .08 .25
8 Nathan Dempsey .20 .50
9 Kelly Fairchild .20 .50
10 Janne Gronvall .08 .25
11 David Harlock .08 .25
12 Darby Hendrickson .08 .25
13 Marc Hussey .08 .25
14 Kenny Jonsson .40 1.00
15 Mark Kolesar .08 .25
16 Alexei Kudashov .08 .25
17 Guy Lehoux .08 .25
18 Guy Leveque .08 .25
19 Matt Martin .08 .25
20 Robb McIntyre .08 .25
21 Bruce Racine .20 .50
22 Ryan Vandenbussche .30 .75
23 Steffon Walby .08 .25
24 Todd Warriner .20 .50

1995-96 St. John's Maple Leafs

This 25-card set of the St. John's Maple Leafs of the AHL was produced by Split Second for distribution by the team at home games and via mail order.

COMPLETE SET (25) 4.00 10.00
1 Team Photo .15 .40
2 Ken Belanger .30 .75
3 Rob Butz .15 .40
4 Brandon Convery .20 .50
5 Marcel Cousineau .20 .50
6 Trent Cull .15 .40
7 Nathan Dempsey .15 .40
8 Kelly Fairchild .15 .40
9 Brent Gretzky .20 .50
10 Janne Gronvall .15 .40
11 David Harlock .20 .50
12 Jamie Heward .15 .40
13 Mark Kolesar .15 .40
14 Guy Lehoux .15 .40
15 Kent Manderville .30 .75
16 Kory Mullin .15 .40
17 Jason Saal .20 .50
18 Shayne Toporowski .15 .40
19 Paul Vincent .15 .40
20 Steffon Walby .15 .40
21 Mike Ware .15 .40
22 Todd Warriner .30 .75
23 Tom Watt CO .02 .10
24 Mike Foligno CO .08 .25
25 Buddy .02 .10
Mascot

1996-97 St. John's Maple Leafs

This standard size set features color action photos on the front and backs are loaded with biographical information. The players name and position are featured in a triangle in the lower right corner of the card front. Cards are unnumbered and checklisted below in alphabetical order. This set was sponsored in part by the Royal Canadian Mounted Police.

COMPLETE SET (25) 4.00 10.00
1 Don Beaupre .30 .75
2 Jared Bednar .15 .40
3 Aaron Brand .20 .50
4 Rich Brown CO .15 .40
5 Buddy MAS .02 .10
6 Greg Bullock .15 .40
7 Rob Butz .15 .40
8 Shawn Carter .15 .40
9 Jason Cipolla .15 .40
10 Brandon Convery .20 .50
11 David Cooper .15 .40
12 John Craighead .30 .75
13 Trent Cull .15 .40
14 Nathan Dempsey .20 .50
15 Mark Deyell .20 .50
16 Jamie Heward .15 .40
17 Mark Hunter CO .15 .40
18 Mark Kolesar .20 .50
19 Guy Lehoux .20 .50
20 Sgt. Randy Mercer .15 .40
21 Jason Saal .30 .75
22 Greg Smyth .15 .40
23 Shayne Toporowski .15 .40
24 Yannick Tremblay .20 .50
25 Brian Wiseman .15 .40

1997-98 St. John's Maple Leafs

This set features the Leafs of the AHL. It was produced by the team and sold at home games.

COMPLETE SET (25) 4.00 10.00
1 Kevyn Adams .30 .75
2 Lonny Bohonos .20 .50
3 Aaron Brand .15 .40
4 Rich Brown ACO .02 .10
5 Buddy .02 .10
6 Shawn Carter .15 .40
7 David Cooper .15 .40
8 Marcel Cousineau .30 .75
9 Nathan Dempsey .15 .40
10 Mark Deyell .20 .50
11 Todd Gillingham .15 .40
12 Per Gustafsson .15 .40
13 Mike Kennedy .15 .40
14 Francis Larivee .30 .75
15 Al MacAdam CO .02 .10
16 Daniil Markov .30 .75
17 Zdenek Markov .15 .40
18 Clayton Norris .15 .40
19 Warren Norris .15 .40
20 Ryan Pepperall .15 .40
21 Jason Podoll .15 .40
22 D.J. Smith .20 .50
23 Greg Smyth .15 .40
24 Shawn Thornton .15 .40
25 Jeff Ware .15 .40

1999-00 St. John's Maple Leafs

This 25-card set features players of the St. John's Maple Leafs of the AHL. The front of the card features an action photo with the left edge colored purple and carrying the players last name and the team logo.

COMPLETE SET (25) 4.00 10.00
1 Kevyn Adams .30 .75
2 Vladimir Antipov .15 .40
3 Syl Apps .15 .40
4 Jason Bonsignore .20 .50
5 Aaron Brand .15 .40
6 Craig Charron .15 .40
7 Nathan Dempsey .30 .75
8 Tyler Harlton .15 .40
9 Justin Hocking .15 .40
10 Bobby House .15 .40
11 Konstantin Kalmikov .20 .50
12 Alan MacAdam CO .08 .25
13 Dennis Maxwell .15 .40
14 David Nemirovsky .20 .50
15 Adam Mair .20 .50
16 Ryan Pepperall .15 .40
17 Marek Posmyk .20 .50
18 Marc Robitaille .15 .40
19 Terry Ryan .20 .50
20 Terran Sandwith .15 .40
21 Darrin Shannon .15 .40
22 D.J. Smith .20 .50
23 Shawn Thornton .15 .40
24 Jimmy Waite .30 .75
25 Dimitri Yakushin .15 .40

2000-01 St. John's Maple Leafs

This set features the Maple Leafs of the AHL. The set was produced by the team and sold at home games. The set also features five former AHL All-Stars who once toiled on the Rock.

COMPLETE SET (30) 4.80 12.00
1 Chad Allan .14 .40
2 Syl Apps .14 .40
3 Patrik Augusta .20 .50
4 Buddy The Puffin MASCOT .04 .10
5 Rich Chernomaz .20 .50
6 David Cooper .14 .40
7 Lou Crawford CO .10 .25
8 Nathan Dempsey .30 .75
9 Jeff Farkas .30 .75
10 Mikael Hakanson .14 .40
11 Tyler Harlton .14 .40
12 Bobby House .14 .40
13 Konstantin Kalmikov .30 .75
14 Jacques Lariviere .14 .35
15 Don MacLean .20 .50
16 Adam Mair .20 .50
17 Kevin McClelland CO .10 .25
18 Mike Minard .20 .50
19 Frank Mrazek .14 .35
20 Yanic Perreault .30 .75
21 Alexei Ponikarovsky .30 .75
22 Felix Potvin .40 1.00
23 Alan Rourke .14 .35
24 D.J. Smith .20 .75
25 Chris Snell .14 .35
26 Shawn Thornton .14 .75
27 Michal Travnicek .14 .35
28 Jimmy Waite .20 .75
29 Morgan Warren .14 .40
30 Dmitri Yakushin .14 .35

2001-02 St. John's Maple Leafs

This set features the Leafs of the AHL. The set was sold by the team at its souvenir stands. The set included a contest card that would allow winners to enjoy a special weekend at the AHL All-Star Game, held that season in St. John's. The cards are unnumbered, and are listed alphabetically.

COMPLETE SET (30) 7.20 18.00
1 Russ Adam ACO .04 .10
2 Nikolai Antropov .40 1.00
3 Francois Bouchard .20 .50
4 Luca Cereda .40 1.00
5 Christian Chartier .20 .50
6 Lou Crawford CO .10 .25
7 Nathan Dempsey .30 .75
8 Doug Doull .20 .50
9 Jeff Farkas .40 1.00
10 Paul Healey .20 .50
11 Bobby House .20 .50
12 Jacques Lariviere .20 .50
13 Donald MacLean .20 .50
14 Kevin McClelland ACO .10 .25
15 Craig Mills .20 .50
16 Mike Minard .30 .75
17 Frank Mrazek .20 .50
18 Karel Pilar .40 1.00
19 Alexei Ponikarovsky .40 1.00
20 Alan Rourke .20 .50
21 D.J. Smith .40 1.00
22 Petr Svoboda .20 .50
23 Mikael Tellqvist 1.25 3.00
24 Michal Travnicek .30 .75
25 Morgan Warren .20 .50
26 Marty Wilford .30 .75
27 Bob Wren .30 .75
28 Mile One Stadium .04 .10
29 Buddy the Puffin MASCOT .04 .10
30 All-Star Game PROMO .04 .10

2001-02 St. John's Maple Leafs Police

Each card features a player and a local police officer. Banner across the top reads 'Clarenville Area Citizens' Crime Prevention'. These cards were given out one at a time at a sick childrens hospital about 175 miles from St.John's. Reportedly, just 100 of each card were produced.

COMPLETE SET (16) 15.00 30.00
1 Luca Cereda .75 2.00
2 Christian Chartier .75 2.00
3 Nathan Dempsey 1.25 3.00
4 Doug Doull 2.00 5.00
5 Jeff Farkas .75 2.00
6 Paul Healey .75 2.00
7 Bobby House .75 2.00
8 Donald MacLean .75 2.00
9 Craig Mills .75 2.00
10 Mike Minard .75 2.00
11 Alexei Ponikarovsky 1.25 3.00
12 Allan Rourke .75 2.00
13 D.J.Smith 1.25 3.00
14 Petr Svoboda .75 2.00
15 Morgan Warren .75 2.00
16 Marty Wilford .75 2.00

2002-03 St. John's Maple Leafs Aliant

The cards in this oversized set appear similar to a bookmark. The checklist is possibly incomplete. If you have additional info, please forward to hockeymag@beckett.com.

COMPLETE SET (6) 4.00 10.00
1 Doug Doull .75 2.00
2 Aaron Gavey .40 1.00
3 Mikael Tellqvist UER 2.00 5.00
(Misspelled Mikeal
4 Brad Boyes .75 2.00
5 Josh Holden .40 1.00
6 Craig Mills .40 1.00

1996-97 St. Louis Vipers RHI

This 16-card set was originally supposed to be a 3-series issue, but printer problems forced the third series to be cancelled. The set (except for checklists and headers) is serial numbered out of 500.

COMPLETE SET (16) 75.00 125.00
1 Frank LaScala 4.00 10.00
2 Russ Parent 4.00 10.00
3 Jeff Beaudin 4.00 10.00
4 Perry Turnbull HCO 2.00 5.00
5 Chris Skoryna 4.00 10.00
6 Chris Rogles 6.00 15.00
7 Kevin Plager 4.00 10.00
8 Wayne Anchikoski 6.00 15.00
9 Vipers Record Holders 4.00 10.00
10 Frank Cirone 4.00 10.00
11 C.J. Yoder 4.00 10.00
12 Victor Viper Mascot 2.00 5.00
13 Series 1 Checklist 2.00 5.00
14 Series 2 Checklist 2.00 5.00
15 Series 1 Header 2.00 5.00
16 Series 2 Header 2.00 5.00

1952-53 St. Lawrence Sales

This 108-card black and white set put out by St. Lawrence Sales Agency featured members of the QSHL. The card backs are written in French. The cards measure approximately 1 15/16" by 2 15/16" and are numbered on the back. The key cards in the set are those of future (at that time) NHL greats Jean Beliveau and Jacques Plante. The complete set price includes both versions of card number 17.

COMPLETE SET (108) 700.00 1400.00
1 Jacques Plante 175.00 350.00
2 Glen Harmon 5.00 10.00
3 Jimmy Moore 5.00 10.00
4 Gerard Desaulniers 5.00 10.00
5 Les Douglas 5.00 10.00
6 Fred Burchell 6.00 12.00
7 Ed Litzenberger 7.50 15.00
8 Rollie Rousseau 5.00 10.00
9 Roger Leger 5.00 10.00
10 Phil Samis 5.00 10.00
11 Paul Masnick 6.00 12.00
12 Walter Clune 5.00 10.00
13 Louis Denis 5.00 10.00
14 Gerry Plamondon 6.00 12.00
15 Cliff Malone 5.00 10.00
16 Pete Morin 6.00 12.00
17A Jack Schmidt 6.00 12.00
17B Aldo Guidolin 10.00 20.00
18 Paul Leclerc 5.00 10.00
19 Larry Kwong 6.00 12.00
20 Rosario Joanette 5.00 10.00
21 Tom Smelle 5.00 10.00
22 Gordie Haworth 6.00 12.00
23 Bruce Cline 6.00 12.00
24 Andre Corriveau 5.00 10.00
25 Jacques Deslauriers 5.00 10.00
26 Bingo Ernst 5.00 10.00
27 Jacques Chartrand 5.00 10.00
28 Phil Vitale 5.00 10.00
29 Renald Lacroix 5.00 10.00
30 J.P. Bisaillon 5.00 10.00
31 Jack Irvine 5.00 10.00
32 Georges Bougie 5.00 10.00
33 Paul Larivee 5.00 10.00
34 Carl Smelle 5.00 10.00
35 Walter Pawlyschyn 5.00 10.00
36 Jean Marois 5.00 10.00
37 Jack Gelineau 5.00 10.00
38 Danny Nixon 5.00 10.00
39 Jean Beliveau 200.00 400.00
40 Phil Renaud 5.00 10.00
41 Leon Bouchard 5.00 10.00
42 Dennis Smith 5.00 10.00
43 Joe Crozier 7.50 15.00
44 Al Bacari 5.00 10.00
45 Murdo MacKay 6.00 12.00
46 Gordie Hudson 5.00 10.00
47 Claude Robert 5.00 10.00
48 Yogi Kraiger 6.00 12.00
49 Ludger Tremblay 6.00 12.00
50 Pierre Brillant 5.00 10.00
51 Frank Mario 5.00 10.00
52 Copper Leyth 5.00 10.00
53 Herbie Carnegie 20.00 50.00
54 Punch Imlach 20.00 40.00
55 Howard Riopelle 5.00 10.00
56 Ken Laufman 5.00 10.00
57 Jackie Leclair 7.50 15.00
58 Bill Robinson 5.00 10.00
59 George Ford 5.00 10.00
60 Bill Johnson 5.00 10.00
61 Leo Gravelle 5.00 10.00
62 Jack Giesebrecht 5.00 10.00
63 John Arundel 5.00 10.00
64 Vic Gregg 5.00 10.00
65 Bep Guidolin 7.50 15.00
66 Al Kuntz 5.00 10.00
67 Emile Dagenais 5.00 10.00
68 Bill Richardson 5.00 10.00
69 Bob Robertson 5.00 10.00
70 Ray Fredericks 5.00 10.00
71 James O'Flaherty 5.00 10.00
72 Butch Stahan 5.00 10.00
73 Roger Roberge 5.00 10.00
74 Guy Labrie 5.00 10.00
75 Gilles Dube 5.00 10.00
76 Pete Wywrot 5.00 10.00
77 Tod Campeau 6.00 12.00
78 Roger Bessette 5.00 10.00
79 Martial Pruneau 5.00 10.00
80 Nils Tremblay 5.00 10.00
81 Jacques Locas 5.00 10.00
82 Rene Pepin 5.00 10.00
83 Bob Pepin 5.00 10.00
84 Tom McDougall 5.00 10.00
85 Peter Wright 5.00 10.00
86 Ronnie Matthews 5.00 10.00
87 Irene St-Hilaire 5.00 10.00
88 Dewar Thompson 5.00 10.00
89 Bob Dainville 5.00 10.00
90 Marcel Pelletier 5.00 10.00
91 Delphis Franche 5.00 10.00
92 Georges Roy 5.00 10.00
93 Andy McCallum 5.00 10.00
94 Lou Smrke 5.00 10.00
95 J.P. Lamirande 5.00 10.00
96 Normand Dussault 5.00 10.00
97 Stan Smrke 6.00 12.00
98 Jack Bownass 5.00 10.00
99 Billy Arcand 5.00 10.00
100 Lyall Wiseman 5.00 10.00
101 Jack Hamilton 5.00 10.00
102 Bob Leger 5.00 10.00
103 Larry Regan 6.00 12.00
104 Erwin Grosse 5.00 10.00
105 Roger Bedard 5.00 10.00
106 Ted Hodgson 5.00 10.00
107 Dave Gatherum 7.50 15.00

2000-01 St. Michaels Majors

This set features the Majors of the OHL. The set was produced by the team and sold at its souvenir stands. The cards are unnumbered, so are listed in alphabetical order.

COMPLETE SET (27) 4.80 12.00
1 Team CL .04 .10
2 Team Photo .16 .40
3 Majors Review .10 .25
4 Matt Bacon .16 .40
5 Matt Bannan .16 .40
6 Darryl Bootland .16 .75
7 Chris Boucher .16 .40
8 Tim Brent .30 .75
9 Peter Budaj .60 1.50
10 Dave Cameron CO .10 .25
11 Andy Chiodo .40 2.00
12 Tyler Cook .16 .40
13 Adam Deleeuw .30 .75
14 Matt Ellis .16 .40
15 Steve Farquharson .16 .40
16 Drew Fata .30 .75
17 Michael Gough .16 .40
18 Bob Jones CO .04 .10
19 Kevin Klein .16 1.00
20 Frantisek Lukes .16 .40
21 Lorne Misita .16 .40
22 Lindsay Plunkett .16 .40
23 Mark Popovic .40 1.00
24 T.J. Reynolds .16 .40
25 Ryan Robert .16 .40
26 Mike Sellan .16 .40
27 Ryan Walsh .16 .40

2001-02 St. Michaels Majors

Set was produced and sold by the team. The cards are unnumbered, and so are listed in order of jersey number.

COMPLETE SET (28) 6.00 15.00
1 Logo Checklist .04 .10
2 Team Photo .04 .10
3 Geoff Patton .20 .50
4 Scott Heffernan .20 .50
5 Tyson Gimblett .20 .50
6 Steven Rawski .20 .50
7 Kevin Klein .30 .75
8 Mark Popovic .30 .75
9 Tim Brent .40 1.00
10 Drew Fata .20 .50
11 Jordan Freeland .20 .50
12 Jerrod Smith .20 .50
13 Michael Gouch .20 .50
14 Kyle Spurr .20 .50
15 Ryan Rorabeck .20 .50
16 Matt Bacon .20 .50
17 Frantisek Lukes .20 .50
18 Matt Ellis .20 .50
19 Darryl Boyce .20 .50
20 Daryl Knowles .20 .50
21 Matt Seymour .20 .50
22 Joe Guenther .20 .50
23 Darryl Bootland .30 .75
24 Peter Budaj .60 1.50
25 Andy Chiodo .75 2.00
26 Dave Cameron .20 .50
27 Bob Jones .20 .50
28 Mascot .04 .10

2002-03 St. Michaels Majors

COMPLETE SET (28) 5.00 12.00
1 Justin Peters .30 .75
2 Ted Perry .15 .40
3 Martin Karafiat .15 .40
4 Tyson Gimblett .15 .40
5 Steven Rawski .15 .40
6 Kevin Klein .40 1.00
7 Nathan McIver .15 .40
8 Tim Brent .40 1.00
9 Drew Fata .40 1.00
10 Scott Lehman .15 .40
11 Scott Horvath .15 .40
12 Chris Rebernik .15 .40
13 Kyle Spurr .15 .40
14 Ryan Rorabeck .15 .40
15 Matt Bacon .15 .40
16 Frantisek Lukes .15 .40
17 Connor Cameron .15 .40
18 Darryl Boyce .15 .40
19 Alan Nolan .15 .40
20 Matt Seymour .15 .40
21 Cory Vitarelli .15 .40
22 Darryl Knowles .15 .40
23 Sal Peralta .15 .40
24 Andy Chiodo .75 2.00
25 Dave Cameron CO .04 .10
26 Bob Jones CO .04 .10
27 Mascot .04 .10
28 Logo/CL .04 .10

2003-04 St. Michael's Majors

Cards are unnumbered, so they're listed below in the order they appear on the checklist card.

COMPLETE SET (27) 5.00 12.00
1 Justin Peters .30 .75
2 Ted Perry .20 .50
3 Jamie Vanderveeken .20 .50
4 Ryan Wilson .20 .50
5 Nathan McIver .20 .50
6 Tim Brent .30 .75
7 Ryan Rorabeck .20 .50
8 Chris Cunningham .20 .50
9 Scott Lehman .20 .50
10 Cal Clutterbuck .40 1.00
11 Colin Power .30 .75
12 Tyler Haskins .20 .50
13 Brent Small .20 .50
14 Ian Maracle .20 .50
15 Conner Cameron .20 .50
16 Richard Kelly .20 .50
17 Thomas Waugh .20 .50
18 Darryl Boyce .20 .50
19 Joe Rand .20 .50
20 Cory Vitarelli .20 .50

Dustin Vanballegoole	.20	.50
Sal Peralta	.20	.50
Michael Ouzas	.30	.75
Dave Cameron CO	.04	.10
Bob Jones ACO	.04	.10
Mikey MASCOT	.04	.10
Checklist	.04	.10

2004-05 St. Michael's Majors

ards are unnumbered and so are listed below in hecklist order.

OMPLETE SET (24)	5.00	12.00
Justin Peters	.30	.75
Steve Whitely	.20	.50
Jamie Vanderveeken	.20	.50
Ryan Wilson	.20	.50
Dale Good	.20	.50
Nathan McIver	.20	.50
Matt Halischuk	.20	.50
John Adamsa	.20	.50
Chris Cunningham	.20	.50
Scott Lehman	.20	.50
Cal Clutterbuck	.30	.75
Colin Power	.20	.50
Tyler Haskins	.20	.50
Cassidy Preston	.20	.50
Justin DiBenedetto	.20	.50
Alexei Ivanov	.20	.50
Scott Levigne	.20	.50
Travis Elder	.20	.50
Darryl Boyce	.20	.50
Joe Rand	.20	.50
Cory Vitarelli	.20	.50
Jaroslav Mrazek	.20	.50
Wayne Savage	.20	.50
Checklist	.04	.10

2005-06 Stockton Thunder

OMPLETE SET (25)	6.00	15.00
Likit Andersson	.30	.75
Casey Bartzen	.30	.75
Landon Bathe	.30	.75
Derek Campbell	.30	.75
Aaron Foster	.30	.75
Nick Greenough	.30	.75
Joel Irwin	.30	.75
Tony Johnson	.30	.75
Jason Kostadine	.30	.75
Mike Lalonde	.30	.75
Aaron MacInnis	.30	.75
Nathan Martz	.30	.75
Dave McCulloch	.30	.75
Jason Metcalfe	.30	.75
Jake Moreland	.30	.75
Geno Parrish	.30	.75
Steve Slonina	.30	.75
Dean Stork	.30	.75
Jeff Weber	.30	.75
Maris Ziedins	.30	.75
21 Opening Night		.10
22 Chris Cichocki HC	.02	.10
23 Stockton Arena	.02	.10
24 Thor MASCOT	.02	.10
NNO Stockton Thunder CL	.02	.10

2006-07 Stockton Thunder

COMPLETE SET (25)	15.00	30.00
1 Jason Beckett	.75	2.00
2 Devan Dubnyk•	.75	2.00
3 Stephane Goulet	.40	1.00
4 Jeff Lang	.40	1.00
5 Fans Tribute Card	.02	.10
6 Beau Geisler	.40	1.00
7 Mike Lalonde	.40	1.00
8 Tim Sestito	.40	1.00
9 Tyler Spurgeon	.40	1.00
10 Thor MASCOT	.02	.10
16 Tim Verbeek	.75	2.00
17 Eric Main	.40	1.00
18 Bryan Young	.40	1.00
19 Jim Dahl	.40	1.00
20 Adam Huxley	.40	1.00
11a Troy Bodie	.40	1.00
11b Stephen Slonina	.40	1.00
12a Cam Ellsworth•	.40	1.00
12b Liam Reddox	.40	1.00
13a Brendon Hodge	.40	1.00
13b Mark Adamek	.40	1.00
14a Nathan Martz	.40	1.00
14b Frank Rediker	.40	1.00
15a Chris Cichoki CO	.40	1.00
15b Tim O'Connell	.02	.10

2014-15 Stockton Thunder

COMPLETE SET (15)	4.00	10.00
1 Ryan Constant	.30	.75
2 Ryan Hayes	.30	.75
3 James Henry	.30	.75
4 Garet Hunt	.30	.75
5 Loic Leduc	.30	.75
6 Jack MacLellan	.30	.75
7 Tyler Maxwell	.30	.75
8 Michael Pereira	.30	.75
9 Shane Owen	.30	.75
10 Adam Phillips	.30	.75
11 Peter Sivak	.30	.75
12 Brad Stebner	.30	.75
13 Lukas Sutter	.30	.75
14 Shane Owen	.30	.75
15 Garet Hunt	.30	.75

1962-63 Sudbury Wolves

These 22 blank-backed cards measure approximately 4" by 6" and feature white-bordered, posed black-and-white studio head shots of Wolves players (Eastern Professional Hockey League). The player's name and position appear above the team name within the broad white bottom border. The imprint, "Crown Life Hockey School," rounds out the card at the bottom. The cards are unnumbered and checklisted below in alphabetical order.

COMPLETE SET (22)	40.00	100.00
1 Paul Andrea	2.50	5.00
2 Norm Armstrong	1.50	3.00
3 Ed Babiuk	2.00	5.00
4 Hub Beaudry ANN	.75	1.50
5 Vern Buffey REF	1.50	3.00
6 Murph Chamberlain CO	1.50	3.00
7 Gerry Cheevers UER	20.00	50.00
8 Wally Chevrier	1.50	3.00
9 Marc Dufour	2.00	4.00
10 Edgar Ehrenverth	1.50	3.00
11 Bill Friday REF	2.50	5.00
12 Jim Johnson	1.50	3.00
13 Chico Kozurok TR	.75	1.50
14 Gord Labossiere	2.00	4.00
15 Dunc McCallum	4.00	8.00
16 Dave McComb	1.50	3.00
17 Hugh McLean REF	1.50	3.00
18 Mike McMahon	1.50	3.00
19 Dave Richardson	1.50	3.00

20 Joe Spence ANN	.75	1.50
21 Ted Taylor	1.50	3.00
22 Bob Woytowich	4.00	8.00

1984-85 Sudbury Wolves

This 16-card set measures approximately 3 1/2" by 6" and features color, action player photos accented by a hockey stick graphic design in white, green, gray, and red. The player's name and sponsor logos are printed on the design. A discount coupon for 2.50 off any children's admission to a game is attached at the bottom and can be torn along perforations. The card measures approximately 5 1/4" tall when the coupon is removed. The backs carry biographical information and sponsor logos. The cards are numbered on the front near the right edge.

COMPLETE SET (16)	6.00	15.00
1 Andy Spruce CO	.20	.50
2 Sean Evoy	.60	1.50
3 Mario Martini	.40	1.00
4 Brent Daugherty	.40	1.00
5 Mario Chitaroni	.40	1.00
6 Dan Chiasson	.40	1.00
7 Jeff Brown	.75	2.00
8 Todd Sepkowski	.40	1.00
9 Brad Belland	.40	1.00
10 Glenn Greenough	.40	1.00
11 John Landry	.40	1.00
12 Max Middendorf	.40	1.00
13 David Moylan	.40	1.00
14 Jamie Nadjiwan	.40	1.00
15 Warren Rychel	.75	2.00
16 Ed Smith	.40	1.00

1985-86 Sudbury Wolves

This 26-card set measures approximately 2 3/4" by 4" and features color, posed player photos with white borders. A facsimile autograph is inscribed across the bottom of the picture.

COMPLETE SET (26)	4.80	12.00
1 Sudbury Police Crest	.10	.25
2 Sponsor Card	.10	.25
3 Logo Checklist	.20	.50
4 R. Zanibbi Chief of Police	.02	.10
5 Wayne Maxner CO	.20	.50
6 Sean Evoy	.20	.50
7 Todd Lalonde	.20	.50
8 Costa Papista	.20	.50
9 Robin Rubic	.20	.50
10 Dave Moylan	.20	.50
11 Brent Daugherty	.20	.50
12 Glenn Greenough	.20	.50
13 Mario Chitaroni	.30	.75
14 Ken McRae	.30	.75
15 Mike Hudson	.40	1.00
16 Andy Paquette	.20	.50
17 Ed Lemaire	.20	.50
18 Mark Turner	.20	.50
19 Craig Duncanson	.20	.50
20 Jeff Brown	.40	1.00
21 Team Photo	.40	1.00
22 Max Middendorf	.20	.50
23 Keith Van Rooyen	.20	.50
24 Brad Walcot	.20	.50
25 Rob Wilson	.20	.50
26 Bill White	.20	.50

1986-87 Sudbury Wolves

Cards measure approximately 3" x 4" and feature color action photos and a facsimile autograph on the front. The card backs feature biographical information along with P.L.A.Y. public service messages.

COMPLETE SET (33)	4.80	12.00
1 Ted Mielczarek	.30	.75
2 Todd Lalonde	.20	.50
3 Costa Papista	.20	.50
4 Justin Corbeil	.20	.50
5 Dave Moylan	.20	.50
6 Brent Daugherty	.20	.50
8 Mario Chitaroni	.30	.75
9 Jim Way	.20	.50
10 Dean Jalbert	.20	.50
11 Joe Dragon	.20	.50
12 Ken McRae	.20	.50
14 Steve Hedington	.20	.50
15 Mike Hudson	.30	.75
16 Pierre Gagnon	.20	.50
17 Peter Hughes	.20	.50
18 Mark Turner	.20	.50
19 Sudbury Police Logo	.08	.25
20 Wayne Doucet	.20	.50
21 Paul Dipietro	.25	.60
22 Max Middendorf	.30	.75
23 Phil Paquette	.20	.50
25 Rob Wilson	.20	.50
26 Checklist	.08	.25
27 Chief of Police	.08	.25
28 Claude D'Amour	.20	.50
29 Guy Blanchard	.20	.50
30 Joe Desrosiers	.20	.50
31 Jake Disschops	.20	.50
33 Bill White	.30	.75
34 Anders Hogberg	.20	.50

1987-88 Sudbury Wolves

This 26-card set measures approximately 3" by 4 1/8" and features color, posed action player photos with white borders. The player's name, jersey number, and position are superimposed on the photo at the bottom.

COMPLETE SET (26)	4.00	10.00
1 Checklist Card	.08	.25
2 Ted Mielczarek	.30	.75
3 Dan Gatenby	.20	.50
4 Todd Lalonde	.20	.50
5 Justin Corbeil	.20	.50
6 Jordan Fois	.20	.50
7 Rodney Lapointe	.20	.50
8 Dave Akey	.20	.50
9 Jim Smith	.20	.50
10 Fred Pennell	.20	.50
11 Joey Simon	.20	.50
12 Luciano Fagioli	.20	.50
13 Robb Graham	.20	.50
14 John Uniac	.20	.50
15 Dave Carrie	.20	.50
16 Pierre Gagnon	.20	.50
17 Peter Hughes	.20	.50
18 Scott McCullough	.20	.50
19 Dean Guitard	.20	.50
20 Pat Holley	.20	.50
21 Chad Badaway	.20	.50
22 Paul DiPietro	.20	.50
23 Derek Thompson	.20	.50
24 Scott Luce	.20	.50
25 Rob Wilson	.20	.50
26 R. Zanibbi Chief of Police	.02	.10

1988-89 Sudbury Wolves

This 26-card set measures approximately 3" by 4 1/8" and features color, posed action player photos with white borders. The player's name, jersey number, and position are superimposed on the photo at the bottom.

COMPLETE SET (26)	4.00	10.00
1 Checklist	.08	.25
2 David Goverde	.30	.75
3 Ted Mielczarek	.30	.75
4 Adam Bennett	.20	.50
5 Kevin Grant	.20	.50
6 Jordan Fois	.20	.50
7 Sean O'Donnell	.30	.75
8 Kevin Meisner	.20	.50
9 Jim Smith	.20	.50
10 Red Pennell	.20	.50
11 Tyler Pella	.20	.50
12 Dean Pella	.20	.50
13 Darren Bell	.20	.50
14 Derek Thompson	.20	.50
15 Terry Chitaroni	.20	.50
16 Sean Stansfield	.20	.50
17 Alastair Still	.20	.50
18 Jim Sonmez	.20	.50
19 Shannon Bolton	.20	.50
20 Andy Paquette	.20	.50
21 Mark Turner	.20	.50
22 Paul DiPietro	.20	.50
23 Robert Knesaurek	.20	.50
24 Todd Lalonde	.20	.50
25 Scott Herniman	.20	.50
26 R. Zanibbi Chief of Police	.08	.25

1989-90 Sudbury Wolves

This 25-card set measures approximately 3" by 4 1/8" and features color, posed action player photos with white borders. The player's name, jersey number, and position are superimposed on the photo at the bottom.

COMPLETE SET (25)	4.80	12.00
1 Checklist NNO	.08	.25
2 Alastair Still	.20	.50
3 Bill Kovacs	.20	.50
4 Darren Bell	.20	.50
5 Scott Mahoney	.20	.50
6 Glen Murray	.75	2.00
7 Alain Laforge	.20	.50
8 Jamie Matthews	.20	.50
9 Jon Boeve	.30	.75
10 Adam Bennett	.20	.50
11 Derek Etches	.20	.50
12 Marcus Middleton	.20	.50
13 Jim Sonmez	.20	.50
14 Leonard MacDonald	.20	.50
15 Paul DiPietro	.30	.75
16 Neil Ethier	.20	.50
17 Sean O'Donnell	.20	.50
18 Andy MacVicar	.20	.50
19 David Goverde	.30	.75
20 Jason Young	.20	.50
21 Wade Bartley	.20	.50
22 Barry Young	.20	.50
23 R. Zanibbi Chief of Police	.08	.25
24 Terry Chitaroni	.20	.50
25 Rob Knesaurek	.20	.50

1990-91 Sudbury Wolves

This 25-card P.L.A.Y. (Police, Law and Youth) set measures approximately 3" by 4 1/8" and features color posed action player photos with white borders. The player's name and position is superimposed on the picture at the bottom. For the most part, the cards are numbered on both sides after the player's jersey number (except for card number 7 and 18).

COMPLETE SET (25)	4.80	12.00
1 Darryl Paquette	.25	.60
2 Adam Bennett	.20	.50
3 Barry Young	.20	.50
4 Jon Boeve	.20	.50
5 Kyle Blacklock	.20	.50
6 Sean O'Donnell	.25	.60
7 Dan Ryder	.25	.60
8 Wade Bartley	.20	.50
9 Jamie Matthews	.20	.50
10 Rod Hinks	.20	.50
11 Derek Etches	.20	.50
12 Brandon Convery	.20	.50
13 Glen Murray	.75	2.00
14 Bill Kovacs	.20	.50
15 Terry Chitaroni	.20	.50
16 Jason Young	.20	.50
17 Alastair Still	.20	.50
18 Shawn Rivers	.20	.50
19 Alain Laforge	.20	.50
20 J.D. Eaton	.20	.50
21 Mike Peca	.75	2.00
22 Howler (Mascot)	.02	.10
23 Mike Yeo	.20	.50
24 L'il Rookie Checklist	.02	.10
25 R. Zanibbi Chief of Police	.02	.10

1991-92 Sudbury Wolves

This 25-card set measures approximately 3" by 4 1/8" and features color, posed action player photos with white borders. The player's name, jersey number, and position are superimposed on the photo at the bottom.

COMPLETE SET (25)	4.80	12.00
1 R. Zanibbi Chief of Police	.02	.10
2 Howler (Mascot)	.02	.10
3 Team Photo	.20	.50
4 Kyle Blacklock	.15	.40
5 Sean Gagnon	.20	.50
6 Bernie John	.15	.40
7 Bob MacIsaac	.15	.40
8 Jamie Rivers	.20	.50
9 Shawn Rivers	.15	.40
10 Joel Sandie	.15	.40
11 Barry Young	.15	.40
12 George Dourian	.15	.40
13 Dan Ryder	.30	.75
14 Derek Armstrong	.15	.40
15 Terry Chitaroni	.15	.40
16 Brandon Convery	.20	.50
17 Tim Favot	.15	.40
18 Rod Hinks	.15	.40
19 Jamie Matthews	.20	.50
20 Barrie Moore	.20	.50
21 Glen Murray	.40	1.00
22 Michael Peca	.75	2.00
23 Michael Yeo	.15	.40
24 Jason Young	.15	.40
25 Jason Zohil	.15	.40

1992-93 Sudbury Wolves

These 27 oversized bilingual cards measure approximately 3" by 4 3/16" and feature on their fronts white-bordered color posed-on-ice player photos. The player's name, jersey number, and position are displayed on each card in white lettering at the bottom of the photo.

COMPLETE SET (27)	4.80	12.00
1 Howler and Lil Rookie	.02	.10
2 Sudbury Regional Police	.02	.10
3 Bob MacIsaac	.20	.50
4 Joel Sandie	.20	.50
5 Rory Fitzpatrick	.20	.50
6 Mike Wilson	.20	.50
7 Shawn Frappier	.20	.50
8 Bernie John	.20	.50
9 Jamie Rivers	.30	.75
10 Jamie Matthews	.20	.50
11 Zdenek Nedved	.20	.50
12 Ryan Shanahan	.20	.50
13 Corey Crane	.20	.50
14 Matt Kiereck	.20	.50
15 Rick Bodkin	.20	.50
16 Derek Armstrong	.20	.50
17 Barrie Moore	.20	.50
18 Rod Hinks	.20	.50
19 Kayle Short	.20	.50
20 Michael Yeo	.20	.50
21 Gary Coupal	.20	.50
22 Dennis Maxwell	.20	.50
23 Steve Potvin	.20	.50
24 Joel Poirier	.20	.50
25 Greg Dreveny	.20	.50
26 Mark Gowan	.30	.75
27 Steve Staios	.25	.60

1993-94 Sudbury Wolves

Sponsored by The Sudbury Star, CoverStory, and Sudbury Sports North, and printed by Slapshot Images Ltd., this standard-size 25-card set features the 1993-94 Sudbury Wolves. On a geometrical team color-coded background, the fronts feature color action player photos with thin grey borders. The player's name, position and team name, as well as the producer's logo, also appear on the front.

COMPLETE SET (25)	4.00	10.00
1 Shawn Silver	.20	.50
2 Jeff Melnechuk	.15	.40
3 Jay McKee	.30	.75
4 Chris McMurtry	.15	.40
5 Rory Fitzpatrick	.20	.50
6 Mike Wilson	.20	.50
7 Shawn Frappier	.15	.40
8 Jamie Rivers	.30	.75
9 Zdenek Nedved	.20	.50
10 Ryan Shanahan	.20	.50
11 Sean Venedam	.20	.50
12 Andrew Dale	.15	.40
13 Mark Giannetti	.15	.40
14 Rick Bodkin	.20	.50
15 Barrie Moore	.20	.50
16 Jamie Matthews	.20	.50
17 Gary Coupal	.15	.40
18 Ilya Lysenko	.15	.40
19 Simon Sherry	.15	.40
20 Steve Potvin	.15	.40
21 Joel Poirier	.20	.50
22 Mike Yeo	.15	.40
23 Bob MacIsaac	.15	.40
24 Paul DiPietro	.20	.50
NNO Slapshot Ad Card	.02	.10

1993-94 Sudbury Wolves Police

This traditional over-sized issue was released in conjunction with the Sudbury Police. It features color photos on the front, with safety tips and player info on the back.

COMPLETE SET (26)	4.00	10.00
1 Chief of Police	.07	.20
2 The Howler	.07	.20
3 Jay McKee	.30	.75
4 Chris McMurtry	.15	.40
5 Rory Fitzpatrick	.20	.50
6 Mike Wilson	.20	.50
7 Shawn Frappier	.15	.40
8 Jamie Rivers	.30	.75
9 Jamie Matthews	.20	.50
10 Zdenek Nedved	.20	.50
11 Ryan Shanahan	.20	.50
12 Andrew Dale	.15	.40
13 Mark Giannetti	.15	.40
14 Rick Bodkin	.20	.50
15 Barrie Moore	.20	.50
16 Gary Coupal	.15	.40
17 Ilya Lysenko	.15	.40
18 Simon Sherry	.15	.40
19 Steve Potvin	.15	.40
20 Joel Poirier	.20	.50
21 Shawn Silver	.20	.50
22 Micheal Yeo	.15	.40
23 Jeff Melnechuk	.15	.40
24 Sean Venedam	.20	.50
25 Bob Macisaac	.15	.40
26 Sudbury Police	.07	.20

1994-95 Sudbury Wolves

Sponsored by The Sudbury Star CoverStory, Sudbury Sports North and Nick's Sports Cards, and printed by Slapshot Images Ltd., this 26-card set features the 1994-95 Sudbury Wolves. On a silver and blue background, the fronts feature color action player photos with thin black borders. The player's name, position and team name, as well as the producer's logo, also appear on the front.

COMPLETE SET (26)	4.00	10.00
1 Checklist	.02	.10
2 Dave MacDonald	.15	.40
3 Rory Fitzpatrick	.15	.40
4 Mike Wilson	.15	.40
5 Neal Martin	.15	.40
6 Shawn Frappier	.15	.40
7 Jamie Rivers	.20	.50
8 Zdenek Nedved	.15	.40
9 Ryan Shanahan	.15	.40
10 Sean Venedam	.20	.50
11 Andrew Dale	.15	.40
12 Rick Bodkin	.15	.40
13 Luc Gagne	.15	.40
14 Barrie Moore	.15	.40
15 Richard Rochefort	.15	.40
16 Krystof Secemski	.15	.40
17 Jason Bonsignore	.15	.40
18 Liam MacEachern	.15	.40
19 Simon Sherry	.15	.40
20 Ethan Moreau	.30	.75
21 Matt Mullin	.20	.50
22 Aaron Starnyski	.15	.40
23 Ron Newhook	.30	.75
24 Glenn Merkosky CO/GM/To	.02	.10
25 Dan Lebold TR/Jason All	.02	.10
NNO Ad Card	.02	.10

1994-95 Sudbury Wolves Police

Card fronts feature a posed color photo surrounded by a white border. The card number is located in a star in the upper left corner. Card backs contain hockey and safety tips in French and English.

COMPLETE SET (27)	4.80	12.00
1 Chief of Police	.02	.10
2 The Howler	.02	.10
3 Rick Bodkin	.15	.40
4 Gary Coupal	.15	.40
5 Andrew Dale	.15	.40
6 Luc Gagne	.15	.40
7 Chester Gallant	.02	.10
8 Kiley Hill	.15	.40
9 Liam MacEachern	.15	.40
10 Barrie Moore	.15	.40
11 Zdenek Nedved	.20	.50
12 Ron Newhook	.40	1.00
13 Richard Rochefort	.15	.40
14 Krysztof Secemski	.15	.40
15 Ryan Shanahan	.15	.40
16 Simon Sherry	.15	.40
17 Sean Venedam	.40	1.00
18 Rory Fitzpatrick	.15	.40
19 Shawn Frappier	.15	.40
20 Gregg Lalonde	.15	.40
21 Neal Martin	.15	.40
22 Jay McKee	.40	1.00
23 Jamie Rivers	.20	.50
24 Mike Wilson	.20	.50
25 Dave Macdonald	.15	.40
26 Matt Mullin	.30	.75
27 Steve Valiquette	.40	1.00

1995-96 Sudbury Wolves

This 25-card set was one of two produced to commemorate the '95-96 Wolves. This one was released by the team, in conjunction with sponsors Four Star Sports and Belanger's. The set is standard size with an action photo on the front, while the backs contain a player bio.

COMPLETE SET (25)	4.00	10.00
1 Sean Venedam	.20	.50
2 Brad Domonsky	.20	.50
3 Joe Lombardo	.15	.40
4 Tyson Flinn	.15	.40
5 Luc Gagne	.15	.40
6 Ryan Shanahan	.15	.40
7 Simon Sherry	.15	.40
8 Kevin Hansen	.15	.40
9 Gregg Lalonde	.15	.40
10 Liam MacEachern	.15	.40
11 Jeremy Adduono	.20	.50
12 Ron Newhook	.30	.75
13 Noel Burkitt	.15	.40
14 Neal Martin	.15	.40
15 Tim Swartz	.15	.40
16 Rob Butler	.15	.40
17 Darryl Moxam	.15	.40
18 Steve Valiquette	.30	.75
19 Ryan Sly	.15	.40
20 Dave MacDonald	.20	.50
21 Andrew Dale	.15	.40
22 Belanger's All-Star Team	.02	.10
23 Four Star Sports	.02	.10
24 Richard Rochefort	.15	.40
25 Title Card	.02	.10

1995-96 Sudbury Wolves Police

This 24-card P.L.A.Y. set measures approximately 3" by 4 1/8" and features color posed player photos augmented by a white border. The player's name and position is superimposed on the photo along the bottom.

COMPLETE SET (24)	4.00	10.00
1 Chief Alex McCauley	.02	.10
2 The Howler Mascot	.02	.10
3 Jeremy Adduono	.20	.50
4 Noel Burkitt	.15	.40
5 Rob Butler	.15	.40
6 Andrew Dale	.15	.40
7 Brad Domonsky	.20	.50
8 Tyson Flinn	.15	.40
9 Luc Gagne	.15	.40
10 Kevin Hansen	.15	.40
11 Gregg Lalonde	.15	.40
12 Joe Lombardo	.15	.40
13 Dave MacDonald	.20	.50
14 Liam MacEachern	.15	.40
15 Neal Martin	.15	.40
16 Darryl Moxam	.15	.40
17 Ron Newhook	.30	.75
18 Richard Rochefort	.15	.40
19 Ryan Shanahan	.15	.40
20 Simon Sherry	.15	.40
21 Ryan Sly	.15	.40
22 Shawn Sobush	.15	.40
23 Stephen Valiquette	.30	.75
24 Sean Venedam	.20	.50

1996-97 Sudbury Wolves

One of two sets issued to commemorate the Wolves' 25th anniversary season, this 27-card standard sized issue was produced by the team and sponsored by Play It Again Sports, The Great Canadian Card. Co. and the Sudbury Star. The cards were produced by the team and sold through arena concessions. The cards feature action photography on the front complemented by a black border containing the player's name and the team logo on the left.

COMPLETE SET (27)	4.80	12.00
1 Title card	.08	.25
2 Jeremy Adduono	.20	.50
3 Louie Blackbird	.15	.40
4 Tom Brown	.20	.50
5 Peter Campbell	.15	.40
6 Brad Domonsky	.15	.40
7 Jason Gaggi	.20	.50
8 Luc Gagne	.15	.40
9 Kevin Hansen	.15	.40
10 Jason Hurlbut	.15	.40
11 Konstantin Kalmikov	.20	.50
12 Robin LaCour	.15	.40
13 Paul Mara	.40	1.00
14 Norm Milley	.60	1.50
15 Gerald Moriarty	.15	.40
16 Scott Page	.15	.40
17 Steve Reid	.15	.40
18 Richard Rochefort	.15	.40
19 Brian Scott	.15	.40
20 Chris Shanahan	.15	.40
21 Ryan Sly	.15	.40
22 Jonas Soling	.15	.40
23 Steve Valiquette	.60	1.50
24 Sean Venedam	.20	.50
25 Great Canadian Card Co.	.02	.10
26 LaSalle Court Plaza	.02	.10
27 Derek Chartrand	.08	.25

1996-97 Sudbury Wolves Police

This oversized (3" by 4 3/16"), 26-card set was issued in conjunction with the Sudbury Police Department. The card fronts feature a posed color photo surrounded by a white border. The player's name, number and position are along the bottom, with the card number is displayed in a star in the upper left corner.

COMPLETE SET (26)	4.80	12.00
1 Chief Alex McCauley	.02	.10
2 The Howler MASCOT	.02	.10
3 Sudbury Wolves 25th	.02	.10
4 Jeremy Adduono	.20	.50
5 Louie Blackbird	.15	.40
6 Tom Brown	.20	.50
7 Peter Campbell	.15	.40
8 Brad Domonsky	.15	.40
9 Tyson Flinn	.15	.40
10 Jason Gaggi	.15	.40
11 Luc Gagne	.15	.40
12 Kevin Hansen	.15	.40
13 Konstantin Kalmikov	.20	.50
14 Robin Lacour	.15	.40
15 Joe Lombardo	.15	.40
16 Paul Mara	.40	1.00
17 Norm Milley	.60	1.50
18 Scott Page	.15	.40
19 Richard Rochefort	.15	.40
20 Brian Scott	.15	.40
21 Chris Shanahan	.15	.40
22 Ryan Sly	.15	.40
23 Jonas Soling	.15	.40
24 Tim Swartz	.15	.40
25 Steve Valiquette	.60	1.50
26 Sean Venedam	.15	.40

1997-98 Sudbury Wolves Police

Card fronts feature a posed color photo surrounded by a white border. The card number is located in a star in the upper left corner. Card backs contain hockey and safety tips in French and English.

COMPLETE SET (25)	8.00	20.00
1 Chief of Police	.02	.10
2 Jeremy Adduono	.15	.40
3 Ryan Barnes	.15	.40
4 Peter Campbell	.15	.40
5 Konstantin Kalmikov	.20	.50
6 Tom Watt	.15	.40
7 Norm Milley	.60	1.50
8 Scott Page	.15	.40
9 Jonas Soling	.15	.40
10 Mike Fisher	.75	2.00
11 Taylor Pyatt	.40	1.00
12 Derek MacKenzie	.40	1.00
13 Nevin Patterson	.15	.40
14 Jason Sands	.15	.40
15 Colin Scotland	.15	.40
16 Paul Mara	.40	1.00
17 David Cornacchia	.15	.40
18 Ryan McKie	.15	.40
19 Michael Tilson	.15	.40
20 Brad Morgan	.15	.40
21 Matthew Hodges	.15	.40
22 Brad Simms	.15	.40
23 Steve Valiquette	.60	1.50
24 Andrew Raycroft	1.50	4.00
25 The Howler	.02	.10

1998-99 Sudbury Wolves

This set features the Wolves of the OHL. The slightly oversized cards were handed out by local police officers.

COMPLETE SET (25)	7.20	18.00
1 Alex McCauley POLICE	.02	.10
2 Ken MacKenzie CO	.02	.10
3 Alexei Salashchenko	.20	.50
4 Kevin Beaumont	.20	.50
5 Norm Milley	.40	1.00
6 Derek MacKenzie	.40	1.00
7 Reg Higgs CO	.02	.10
8 Matt Barnhardt	.20	.50
9 Mike Fisher	.60	1.50
10 Tom Kotsopoulos	.40	1.00
11 Marc Long	.20	.50
12 Kyle Dafoe	.20	.50
13 Jason Jaspers	.40	1.00
14 Glenn Crawford	.20	.50
15 Ryan McKie	.20	.50
16 Corey Sabourin	.20	.50
17 Kip Brennan	.75	2.00
18 Serge Dube	.20	.50
19 Brad Morgan	.20	.50
20 Brian McGrattan	.20	.50
21 Taylor Pyatt	.40	1.00
22 Abe Herbst	.20	.50
23 Kevin Mota	.20	.50
24 Mark Aggio	.20	.50
25 Andrew Raycroft	1.25	3.00

1999-00 Sudbury Wolves

This slightly oversized set features the Wolves of the OHL. The set was sold by the team at the rink, and features 1999 first-rounders Taylor Pyatt and Mike Fisher.

COMPLETE SET (26)	4.80	12.00
1 Chief Alex McCauley	.02	.10
2 Bert Templeton CO	.08	.25
3 Darren Keily ACO	.02	.10
4 Corey Sabourin	.15	.40
5 Kyle Dafoe	.15	.40
6 Abe Herbst	.15	.40
7 Dennis Wideman	.15	.40
8 Kevin Mota	.15	.40
9 Norm Milley	.40	1.00
10 Taylor Pyatt	.40	1.00
11 Mike Fisher	.60	1.50
12 Alexei Semenov	.40	1.00
13 Alexei Salashcenko	.15	.40
14 Derek MacKenzie	.40	1.00
15 Steve Ellis	.15	.40
16 Warren Hefford	.15	.40
17 Jason Jaspers	.40	1.00
18 Brian Mcgrattan	.15	.40
19 Drew Kivell	.15	.40
19B Tom Kotsopoulos	.40	1.00
21 Brad Morgan	.15	.40
22 Scott Smith	.15	.40
23 R.A. Mobile	.02	.10
24 Mike Vaillancourt	.15	.40
25 Mike Gorman	.15	.40
26 Miguel Beaudry	.15	.40

2000-01 Sudbury Wolves

This set features the Wolves of the OHL. The cards are slightly oversized and were produced as part of the P.L.A.Y. series. They were apparently distributed primarily by police officers to school-aged children.

COMPLETE SET (26)	8.00	20.00
1 Chief Alex McCauley	.04	.10
2 Bert Templeton CO	.20	.50
3 Darren Keily CO	.10	.25
4 T.J. Warkus	.30	.75
5 Dave Csumrik	.30	.75
6 Jason Hicks	.30	.75
7 Wally Prawdzik	.30	.75
8 Dennis Wideman	.30	.75
9 Mike Vaillancourt	.30	.75
10 Troy Duncan	.30	.75
11 Ladislav Reznicek	.30	.75
12 Alexei Semenov	.60	1.50
13 Chad Starling	.30	.75
14 Nathan Harrington	.30	.75
15 Derek MacKenzie	.40	1.00
16 Jerry Connell	.30	.75
17 Steve Ellis	.30	.75
18 Adam Keefe	.30	.75
19 Jason Jaspers	.40	1.00
20 Jason Bone	.30	.75
21 Drew Kivell	.30	.75
22 Tom Kotsopoulos	.40	1.00
23 Fedor Fedorov	.60	1.50
24 Mike Smith	.30	.75
25 Miguel Beaudry	.30	.75
26 Howler MASCOT	.04	.10

2001-02 Sudbury Wolves

This set features the Wolves of the OHL. It measures the standard size and was sold by the team at home games. It is believed that less than 1,000 sets were produced.

COMPLETE SET (30)	6.00	15.00
1 Shandor Alphonso	.25	.60
2 Trevor Blanchard	.25	.60
3 Travis Chapman	.25	.60
4 Bob Chaumont	.25	.60
5 Jerry Connell	.25	.60
6 Ryan Hastings	.25	.60
7 Jim Kehoe	.25	.60
8 Darren Keily ACO	.04	.10
9 Josh Legge	.25	.60
10 Tyler Leggo	.25	.60
11 Andrei Mikhnov	.60	1.50
12 Dene Poulin	.25	.60
13 Jean-Francois Seguin	.25	.60
14 Jeff Shaw	.25	.60
15 Rob Shilton	.25	.60
16 Sam Skwarchuk	.25	.60
17 Mike Smith	.40	1.00
18 Shawn Snider	.25	.60
19 Dan Speer	.25	.60
20 Zach Stortini	.25	.60
21 Bert Templeton CO	.20	.50
22 Brody Todd	.25	.60
23 Joel Whitmarsh	.40	1.00
24 John Winstanley	.25	.60
25 Sudbury Wolves Card	.10	.25
26 Wolves Season Line-Up	.10	.25
27 Randy Carlyle No. Retired	.20	.50
28 Sudbury Carpetland	.04	.10
29 Sudbury City Centre	.04	.10
30 Sudbury King Sportswear	.04	.10

2001-02 Sudbury Wolves Police

This set features the Wolves of the OHL. The cards are slightly oversized, and were issued as promotional giveaways by the team and the Sudbury Police. It is believed that less than 1,000 sets exist.

COMPLETE SET (26)	6.00	15.00
1 Chief Alex McCauley	.04	.10
2 Bert Templeton CO	.04	.10
3 Darren Keily ACO	.04	.10
4 Brody Todd	.30	.75
5 Travis Chapman	.30	.75
6 Jim Kehoe	.30	.75
7 Josh Legge	.30	.75
8 J.F. Seguin	.30	.75
9 Andrei Mikhnov	.40	1.00
10 John Winstanley	.30	.75
11 Shawn Snider	.30	.75
12 Jeff Shaw	.30	.75
13 Bobby Chaumont	.30	.75
14 Rob Shilton	.30	.75
15 Tyler Leggo	.30	.75
16 Shandor Alphonso	.30	.75
17 Jerry Connell	.30	.75
18 Zack Stortini	.30	.75
19 Dan Speer	.30	.75
20 Trevor Blanchard	.30	.75
21 Sam Skwarchuk	.30	.75
22 Dene Poulin	.30	.75
23 Ryan Hastings	.30	.75
24 Mike Smith	.40	1.00
25 Joel Whitmarsh	.40	1.00
26 Howler MASCOT	.04	.10

2003-04 Sudbury Wolves

COMPLETE SET (25)	6.00	15.00
1 Header Card	.04	.10
2 Shandor Alphonso	.25	.60
3 Kevin Beech	.40	1.00
4 Stefan Blaho	.25	.60
5 Bobby Chaumont	.25	.60
6 Jonathan D'Aversa	.25	.60
7 Luke Dubbin	.25	.60
8 Alexander Eaton	.30	.75
9 Patrick Ehelechner	.60	1.50
10 Chanse Fitzpatrick	.25	.60
11 Ryan Hastings	.25	.60
12 Kyle Lamb	.25	.60
13 Sean Langdon	.25	.60
14 Eric Larochelle	.25	.60
15 Matt Maccarone	.25	.60
16 Rafal Martynowski	.25	.60
17 Adam McQuaid	.25	.60
18 Mike Mills	.25	.60
19 Dene Poulin	.25	.60
20 Jordan Prevost	.25	.60
21 Chris Robertson	.25	.60
22 Marc Staal	.75	2.00
23 Sean Stefanski	.25	.60
24 Zach Stortini	.25	.60
25 Mike Foligno HCO	.10	.25

2004-05 Sudbury Wolves

A total of 1,000 team sets were produced.

COMPLETE SET (26)	8.00	20.00
1 Luke Dubbin	.30	.75
2 Bobby Chaumont	.40	1.00
3 Tomas Sample	.30	.75
4 Marc Staal	.75	2.00
5 Nick Foligno	.75	2.00
6 Kevin Beech	.30	.75
7 Zach Stortini	.30	.75
8 Stefan Blaho	.30	.75
9 Devin Didiomete	.30	.75
10 Kyle Musselman	.30	.75
11 Patrick Ehelechner	.60	1.50
12 Alexander Eaton	.30	.75
13 Stephen Miller	.30	.75
14 Ryan Hastings	.30	.75
15 Adam McQuaid	.30	.75
16 Ryan McDonough	.30	.75
17 Benoit Pouliot	1.25	3.00
18 Mike Mills	.30	.75
19 Jonathan D'Aversa	.30	.75
20 Rafal Martynowski	.30	.75

21 Troy Murray .30 .75
22 Kevin Baker .30 .75
23 Mike Foligno CO .04 .10
24 Bob Jones ACO .04 .10
25 Bryan Verrault ACO .04 .10
26 Howler MASCOT .04 .10

2005-06 Sudbury Wolves

COMPLETE SET (26) 8.00 15.00
1 Marc Staal .60 1.50
2 Kevin Beech .20 .50
3 Chris Abbey .20 .50
4 Ryan Hastings .20 .50
5 Adam McQuaid .20 .50
6 Troy Murray .20 .50
7 Jonathan D'Aversa .20 .50
8 Ryan Crouch .20 .50
9 Kevin Baker .20 .50
10 Matt Dias .20 .50
11 Nick Foligno .60 1.50
12 Devin Didiomete .20 .50
13 Anton Hedman .20 .50
14 Akim Aliu .20 .50
15 Mike Mills .20 .50
16 Mark Versteeg-Lytwyn .20 .50
17 Gary Friesen .20 .50
18 Ryan Donally .20 .50
19 Nicholas Tuzzolino .20 .50
20 Justin Allen .20 .50
21 Gerome Giudice .20 .50
22 Mike Foligno .10 .25
23 Bob Jones .20 .50
24 Bryan Verreault .20 .50
25 Howler .02 .10
26 Benoit Pouliot .60 1.50

2006-07 Sudbury Wolves

COMPLETE SET (27) 8.00 20.00
1 Marc Staal .60 1.50
2 Andrew Self .20 .50
3 J.K. Gill .20 .50
4 Matt Dias .20 .50
5 Nick Foligno .60 1.50
6 Gerome Giudice .20 .50
7 Kyle Tarini .20 .50
8 Gary Friesen .20 .50
9 Geoff Guimond .20 .50
10 Devin Didiomete .20 .50
11 Jared Staal 2.00 5.00
12 Patrik Lusnak .20 .50
13 Justin Larson .20 .50
14 Akim Aliu .60 1.50
15 Justin Donati .20 .50
16 Kevin Baker .20 .50
17 Ryan Crouch .20 .50
18 Stephen Miller .20 .50
19 Zach Mccullough .20 .50
20 Adam Mcquaid .40 1.00
21 Tyler Arps .20 .50
22 Jonathan D'Aversa .20 .50
23 Sebastien Dahm .40 1.00
24 Michael Swick .40 1.00
25 Mike Foligno CO .20 .50
26 Bob Jones .10 .25
27 Bryan Verreault .10 .25

1995-96 Swift Current Broncos

This 20-card set features color player photos on a blue-and-green background. The backs carry player information. The cards are unnumbered and so are checklisted below in alphabetical order.

COMPLETE SET (20) 3.00 8.00
1 Derek Arbez .15 .40
2 Chad Beagle .15 .40
3 Kurt Drummond .15 .40
4 Terry Friesen .30 .75
5 Ryan Geremia .15 .40
6 Jeff Henkelman .15 .40
7 Jeff Kirwan .15 .40
8 Brad Larsen .30 .75
9 Aaron MacDonald .20 .50
10 Craig Millar .15 .40
11 Jaroslav Obsut .20 .50
12 Colin O'Hara .15 .40
13 Jeff Schaeffer .15 .40
14 Brent Sopel .30 .75
15 Josh St. Louis .15 .40
16 Chris Szysky .15 .40
17 Jesse Rezansoff .15 .40
18 Jeremy Rondeau .15 .40
19 Sergei Varlamov .30 .75
20 Tyler Willis .15 .40

1996-97 Swift Current Broncos

This 24-card set was produced by the club for distribution at the rink and by mail. The cards feature an action photograph surrounded by a blue, white and green borders. The black and white backs feature a mug shot, team logo, personal stats and bio and an anti-drug tip.

COMPLETE SET (24) 4.00 10.00
1 Terry Friesen .30 .75
2 Lindsey Materi .20 .50
3 Kevin Mackie .15 .40
4 Jeff Henkelman .15 .40
5 Michal Rozsival .30 .75
6 Brent Sopel .30 .75
7 Lawrence Nycholat .15 .40
8 Chad Beagle .15 .40
9 Jeff Schaeffer .15 .40
10 Tyler Shybunka .15 .40
11 Josh St. Louis .15 .40
12 Chris Szysky .20 .50
13 Tyler Perry .15 .40
14 Dreu Volk .15 .40
15 Nathan Strueby .15 .40
16 Kurt Drummond .15 .40
17 Brad Larsen .30 .75
18 Ryan Tobler .30 .75
19 Jeremy Rondeau .15 .40
20 Jeff Kirwan .15 .40
21 Brett Allan .15 .40
22 Andrew Milne .15 .40
23 Sergei Varlamov .30 .75
24 Derek Arbez .20 .50

1997-98 Swift Current Broncos

This set features the Broncos of the WHL. It is believed to have been produced and distributed by the team. Any additional information pertinent to this set can be forwarded to hockeymag@beckett.com.

COMPLETE SET (22) 4.80 12.00
1 Terry Friesen .30 .75
2 Lindsey Materi .20 .50
3 Tyson Motz .20 .50
4 Jeffrey Beatch .20 .50
5 Jeff Henkelman .20 .50
6 Michal Rozsival .30 .75
7 Dan Hulak .20 .50
8 Lawrence Nycholat .20 .50
9 Toni Bader .20 .50
10 Chad Beagle .20 .50
11 Jeff Schaeffer .20 .50
12 Tyler Shybunka .20 .50
13 Tyler Murray .20 .50
14 Tony Mohagen .20 .50
15 Layne Ulmer .30 .75
16 Dean Serdachny .20 .50
17 Brent Twordik .20 .50
18 Quinn Sherdahl .20 .50
19 Jeff Kirwan .20 .50
21 Brett Allan .20 .50
22 Sergei Varlamov .30 .75

1998-99 Swift Current Broncos

This set features the Chiefs of the WHL. It is believed to have been produced and distributed by the team. Because of the players featured, it is though to have been sold late in the season. Any additional information pertinent to this set can be forwarded to hockeymag@beckett.com.

COMPLETE SET (24) 4.80 12.00
1 Chad Beagle .20 .50
2 Brett Allan .20 .50
3 Quinn Sherdahl .20 .50
4 Bryce Wandler .20 .50
5 Dean Serdachny .20 .50
6 Danis Zaripov .20 .50
7 Kurt Drummond .20 .50
8 Tyler Murray .20 .50
9 Toni Bader .20 .50
10 Brent Twordik .20 .50
11 Nathan Smith .20 .50
12 Jakub Cutta .40 1.00
13 Lawrence Nycholat .20 .50
14 Ben Ondrus .20 .50
15 Tyson Motz .20 .50
16 Jay Langager .20 .50
17 Brad Rohrig .20 .50
18 Jeremy Reich .30 .75
19 Layne Ulmer .40 1.00
20 Chris Sotiropolous .20 .50
21 Josh Maser .20 .50
22 Dan Hulak .20 .50
23 Dustan Heintz .20 .50
24 Jeremy Rondeau .20 .50

1999-00 Swift Current Broncos

This set features the Broncos of the WHL. The set features standard-sized cards with a purple border. The cards are unnumbered, and so are listed below in alphabetical order.

COMPLETE SET (25) 6.00 15.00
1 Brett Allan .20 .50
2 Jay Batchelor .20 .50
3 Jakub Cutta .30 .75
4 Houston Hair .20 .50
5 Scott Henkelman .20 .50
6 James Hiebert .20 .50
7 Todd Hornung .20 .50
8 Dan Hulak .20 .50
9 Jay Langager .20 .50
10 Duncan Milroy .40 1.00
11 Tyson Motz .40 1.00
12 Lawrence Nycholat .20 .50
13 Ben Ondrus .20 .50
14 Colton Orr .40 1.00
15 Craig Priestlay .20 .50
16 Jeremy Reich .20 .50
17 Dean Serdachny .20 .50
18 Nathan Smith .30 .75
19 Matt Sommerfield .20 .50
20 Clay Thoring .20 .50
21 Brent Twordik .20 .50
22 Layne Ulmer .40 1.00
23 Igor Valeev .20 .50
24 Brendan Vanthuyne .20 .50
25 Bryce Wandler .30 .75

2000-01 Swift Current Broncos

This set features the Broncos of the WHL. The cards were issued by the team and sold at home games. As they are unnumbered, they are listed below in alphabetical order.

COMPLETE SET (24) 4.80 15.00
1 B.J. Boxma .40 1.00
2 Ales Cerny .20 .50
3 Jakub Cutta .40 1.00
4 John Dahl .20 .50
5 Paul Deniset .20 .50
6 Adam Dumbrowski .20 .50
7 Todd Ford .40 1.00
8 Dustin Friesen .30 .75
9 Scott Henkelman .20 .50
10 James Hiebert .20 .50
11 Jay Langager .20 .50
12 Duncan Milroy .60 1.50
13 Tyson Motz .40 1.00
14 Ben Ondrus .20 .50
15 Craig Priestlay .20 .50
16 Kevin Seibel .20 .50
17 Dean Serdachny .20 .50
18 Nathan Smith .30 .75
19 Mat Sommerfeld .20 .50
20 Clay Thoring .20 .50
21 Ian White .20 2.00
22 Header Card .04 .10
23 Checklist .04 .10
24 Charlie MASCOT .04 .10

2001-02 Swift Current Broncos

COMPLETE SET (24) 5.00 12.00
1 Steven Spencer .20 .50
2 Ales Cerny .20 .50
3 Kevin Seibel .20 .50
4 Travis Friedley .20 .50
5 Ian White .40 1.00
6 Aaron Richards .20 .50
7 James Hiebert .20 .50
8 Nathan Smith .20 .50
9 Tim Smith .20 .50
10 Dustin Friesen .20 .50
11 Jason Roberts .20 .50
12 Ben Ondrus .40 1.00
13 John Dahl .20 .50
14 Luke Hunter .20 .50
15 Mitch Love .20 .50
16 Brent Twordik .20 .50
17 Torrie Wheat .20 .50
18 Colin Slobodian .20 .50
19 Ivan Usenko .20 .50
20 Duncan Milroy .40 1.00
21 Mat Sommerfeld .20 .50
22 Todd Ford .20 .50
23 B.J. Boxma .20 .50
24 Mascot .04 .10

2002-03 Swift Current Broncos

COMPLETE SET (24) 5.00 12.00
1 John Dahl .20 .50
2 Todd Ford .20 .50
3 Travis Friedlay .20 .50
4 Dustin Friesen .20 .50
5 Jeff Harvey .20 .50
6 Marian Havel .20 .50
7 James Hiebert .20 .50
8 Luke Hunter .20 .50
9 Alex Lentowich .20 .50
10 Mitch Love .20 .50
11 Darryl Moscaluk .20 .50
12 Ben Ondrus .20 .50
13 Derek Poplawski .20 .50
14 Aaron Richards .20 .50
15 Jason Roberts .20 .50
16 Aaron Rome .40 1.00
17 David Schulz .20 .50
18 Dennis Sergeyev .20 .50
19 Steven Spencer .20 .50
20 Colin Stone .20 .50
21 Torrie Wheat .20 .50
22 Ian White .40 1.00
23 Jeremy Williams .40 1.00
24 Charlie Horse MASCOT .04 .10

2003-04 Swift Current Broncos

COMPLETE SET (24) 6.00 15.00
1 Bryn Brucks .20 .50
2 Jason Fransoo .20 .50
3 Dustin Friesen .20 .50
4 Davin Heintz .20 .50
5 Michael Hengen .20 .50
6 Luke Hunter .20 .50
7 Alex Leavitt .20 .50
8 Alex Lentowich .20 .50
9 Kyle Moir .30 .75
10 Ty Morris .20 .50
11 Darryl Moscaluk .20 .50
12 Tyler Redenbach .30 .75
13 Aaron Richards .20 .50
14 Aaron Rome .30 .75
15 Myles Rumsey .20 .50
16 Jerrid Sauer .20 .50
17 David Schulz .20 .50
18 Colin Stone .20 .50
19 Michael Szczachor .20 .50
20 Matej Trojovsky .30 .75
21 Brent Walker .30 .75
22 Ian White .40 1.00
23 Bobby Williams .20 .50
24 Jeremy Williams .40 1.00

2004-05 Swift Current Broncos

COMPLETE SET (24) 8.00 15.00
1 Travis Brisebois .30 .75
2 Marc Defoe .30 .75
3 Marc Desloges .30 .75
4 Tyler Feakes .30 .75
5 Jason Fransoo .30 .75
6 Michael Hengen .30 .75
7 Barry Horman .30 .75
8 Luke Hughson .30 .75
9 Luke Hunter .30 .75
10 Marek Knebl .30 .75
11 Brady Leavold .30 .75
12 Andrew Leslie .30 .75
13 Don Lloyd .30 .75
14 Kyle Moir .40 1.00
15 Tyler Redenbach .40 1.00
16 Myles Rumsey .30 .75
17 Jerrid Sauer .30 .75
18 Jeremy Schenderling .30 .75
19 David Schulz .30 .75
20 Blair Stengler .30 .75
21 Colin Stone .30 .75
22 Michael Szczachor .30 .75
23 Matej Trojovsky .40 1.00
24 Andrew Wasmuth .30 .75

2005-06 Swift Current Broncos

COMPLETE SET (24) 8.00 15.00
1 Karl Benke .30 .75
2 Michael Hengen .30 .75
3 Derek Price .30 .75
4 Thomas Raffl .30 .75
5 Andrew Wasmuth .30 .75
6 Daniel Rakos .30 .75
7 R.J. Larochelle .30 .75
8 Travis Yonkman .30 .75
9 Kyle Bortis .30 .75
10 Kyle Moir .30 .75
11 Luke Hunter .30 .75
12 Spencer McAvoy .30 .75
13 Donny Lloyd .30 .75
14 Josh Aspenlind .30 .75
15 Levi Nelson .40 1.00
16 Grant Toulmin .30 .75
17 Dale Weise .30 .75
18 Charlie Horse .02 .10
19 Paul Postma .30 .75
20 Jeremy Schenderling .30 .75
21 Myles Rumsey .30 .75
22 Ned Lukacevic .30 .75
23 Marc Desloges .30 .75
24 Zack Smith .30 .75

2006-07 Swift Current Broncos

COMPLETE SET (24) 12.00 20.00
1 Travis Yonkman .60 1.50
2 Kyle Moir .60 1.50
3 David Stieler .30 .75
4 Grant Toulmin .30 .75
5 R.J Larochelle .30 .75
6 Ryan Molle .30 .75
7 Levi Nelson .60 1.50
8 Geordie Wudrick .30 .75
9 Dale Weise .30 .75
10 Kyle Bortis .30 .75
11 Phil Gervais .30 .75
12 Michael Wilson .30 .75
13 Daniel Rakos .30 .75
14 Brady Leavold .30 .75
15 Spencer Mcavoy .30 .75
16 Matt Tassone .30 .75
17 Paul Postma .30 .75
18 Derek Claffey .30 .75
19 Zack Smith .30 .75
20 Myles Rumsey .30 .75
21 Dane Crowley .30 .75
22 Jeremy Schenderling .30 .75
23 L.Nelson .60 1.50
D.Crowley
24 Charlie Horse .10 .25

2007-08 Swift Current Broncos

COMPLETE SET (24) 12.00 20.00
1 Mike Brown .30 .75
2 Derek Claffey .30 .75
3 Ian Curtis .60 1.50
4 Jan Dalecky .30 .75
5 Keegan Dansereau .30 .75
6 Justin Dowling .30 .75
7 Eric Doyle .30 .75
8 Cody Eakin .30 .75
9 Erik Felde .30 .75
10 Brad Hoban .30 .75
11 R.J. LaRochelle .30 .75
12 Spencer McAvoy .30 .75
13 Ryan Molle .30 .75
14 Levi Nelson .60 1.50
15 Joel Rogers .30 .75
16 Zack Smith .30 .75
17 Dave Stieler .30 .75
18 Matt Tassone .30 .75
19 Dale Weise .30 .75
20 Michael Wilson .30 .75
21 George Wudrick .30 .75
22 Travis Younkman .60 1.50
23 Charlie Horse MASCOT .02 .10
24 Team Checklist .02 .10

2014-15 Swift Current Broncos

COMPLETE SET (24) 6.00 15.00
1 Header Card .35 .75
2 Colby Cave .35 .75
3 Jay Merkley .35 .75
4 Cavin Leth .35 .75
5 Kristian Ferletak .35 .75
6 Glenn Gawdin .35 .75
7 Tyler Steenbergen .35 .75
8 Colo Johnson .35 .75
9 Jake DeBrusk .35 .75
10 Carter Rigby .35 .75
11 Zac MacKay .35 .75
12 Andreas Schumacher .35 .75
13 Coda Gordon .35 .75
14 Tanner Lesann .35 .75
15 Dillon Heatherington .35 .75
16 Jordan Harris .35 .75
17 Brett Lernout .35 .75
18 Brycen Martin .35 .75
19 Ayrton Nikkel .35 .75
20 Max Lajoie .35 .75
21 Jaydan Gordon .35 .75
22 Landon Bow .35 .75
23 Travis Child .35 .75
24 Charlie Horse MASCOT .35 .75

1996-97 Syracuse Crunch

This 25-card set was produced by Split Second and sponsored by Y94 radio and Healthsource. The set features action photos on the front, and statistical information on the back. The cards were sold by the club at the rink or through the mail. The unnumbered cards are listed below according to their sweater numbers, which are displayed prominently in the upper left hand corner of each card back.

COMPLETE SET (25) 4.80 12.00
1 Mike Fountain .30 .75
4 Mark Wotton .15 .40
5 Mark Krys .15 .40
9 Robb Gordon .30 .75
10 Darren Sinclair .15 .40
11 Ian McIntyre .15 .40
14 John Badduke .15 .40
16 Doug Ast .15 .40
17 Brian Loney .15 .40
18 Tyson Nash .60 1.50
19 Lonny Bohonos .20 .50
21 Dave Scatchard .30 .75
23 Chad Allan .15 .40
25 Bogdan Savenko .15 .40
26 John Namestnikov .15 .40
27 Bert Robertsson .20 .50
28 Chris McAllister .20 .50
30 Frederic Cassivi .30 .75
35 Larry Courville .20 .50
37 Rick Girard .15 .40
38 Rod Stevens .15 .40
44 Brent Tully .15 .40
NNO AHL Ad Card .02 .10
NNO Jack McIlhargey CO .02 .10
NNO Crunchman (Mascot) .02 .10

1999-00 Syracuse Crunch

This set features the Crunch of the AHL. The set was released as a promotional giveaway. Sixteen of the cards were given out in sets of eight at two Crunch home games. The remaining cards were available at Tully's Restaurant.

COMPLETE SET (25) 10.00 25.00
1 Harold Druken .40 1.00
2 Matt Cooke .75 2.00
3 Brian Bonin .40 1.00
4 Zenith Komarniski .40 1.00
5 Chad Allan .40 1.00
6 Crunchman MASCOT .08 .25
7 Ryan Ready .40 1.00
8 Brad Leeb .40 1.00
9 Reggie Savage .40 1.00
10 Trent Klatt .40 1.00
11 Martin Gendron .40 1.00
12 Lubomir Vaic .40 1.00
13 Ryan Bonni .40 1.00
14 Brent Sopel .60 1.50
15 Christian Bronsard .60 1.50
16 Barry Smith CO .20 .50
17 Stan Smyl CO .40 1.00
18 Alfie Michaud .60 1.50
19 Trevor Doyle .40 1.00
20 Jarkko Ruutu .40 1.00
21 Chris O'Sullivan .40 1.00
22 Ryan Shannon .40 1.00
23 Pat Kavanagh .40 1.00
24 Mike Brown .40 1.00
25 Tully's Restaurant .02 .10

2000-01 Syracuse Crunch

This set features the Crunch of the AHL. The set was produced by Choice Marketing and apparently was distributed in two 12-card subsets at a pair of home games.

COMPLETE SET (24) 10.00 25.00
1 Marc Lamothe .80 1.50
2 Jean-Francois Labbe .60 1.50
3 Andrei Sryubko .40 1.00
4 Jonas Junkka-Andersson .40 1.00
5 Mike Gaul .40 1.00
6 Dan Watson .40 1.00
7 Bill Bowler .60 1.50
8 Chris Nielsen .40 1.00
9 Jody Shelley 2.00 5.00
10 Mathieu Darche .80 1.50
11 Blake Bellefeuille .60 1.50
12 Jeremy Reich .40 1.00
13 Jeff Williams .40 1.00
14 Martin Spanhel .60 1.50
15 Brad Moran .40 1.00
16 Scott Hollis .40 1.00
17 Jeff Ware .40 1.00
18 Matt Davidson .40 1.00
19 Sean Selmser .40 1.00
20 Radim Bicanek .40 1.00
21 Reggie Savage .40 1.00
22 Gary Agnew CO .10 .25
23 Ross Yates CO .10 .25
24 Al MASCOT .04 .10

2001-02 Syracuse Crunch

This set features the Crunch of the AHL. The cards were produced by Choice Marketing and were sold at home games.

COMPLETE SET (25) 6.00 15.00
1 Jean-Francois Labbe .30 .75
2 Andrei Sryubko .20 .50
3 Dan Watson .20 .50
4 Paul Manning .20 .50
5 Matt Davidson .30 .75
6 Duvie Westcott .30 .75
7 Jody Shelley .60 1.50
8 Mathieu Darche .30 .75
9 Blake Bellefeuille .30 .75
10 Jeremy Reich .20 .50
11 Martin Spanhel .30 .75
12 David Ling .30 .75
13 Sean Pronger .20 .50
14 Brad Moran .30 .75
15 Derrick Walser .30 .75
16 Jeff Ware .20 .50
17 Martin Paroulek .20 .50
18 Darrel Scoville .20 .50
19 Kent McDonell .20 .50
20 Adam Borzecki .20 .50
21 Andrej Nedorost .30 .75
22 Brett Harkins .20 .50
23 Jonathan Schill .20 .50
24 Tully's Ad Card .04 .10
25 Al MASCOT .04 .10

2002-03 Syracuse Crunch

COMPLETE SET (25) 12.00
1 Karl Goehring .30 .75
2 Pascal Leclaire .60 1.50
3 Tyler Sloan .20 .50
4 Dan Watson .20 .50
5 Paul Manning .20 .50
6 Matt Davidson .20 .50
7 Mathieu Darche .30 .75
8 Blake Bellefeuille .20 .50
9 Jeremy Reich .20 .50
10 Tim Jackman .20 .50
11 David Ling .20 .50
12 Jonathan Schill .20 .50
13 Brad Moran .20 .50
14 Pauli Levokari .20 .50
15 Darrel Scoville .20 .50
16 Kent McDonell .20 .50
17 Adam Borzecki .20 .50
18 Andrej Nedorost .20 .50
19 Radim Bicanek .20 .50
20 Trevor Ettinger .20 .50
21 Matt Dzieduszycki .20 .50
22 Mike Pandolfo .20 .50
23 Trent Cull .20 .50
24 Al the Gorilla Mascot .04 .10
NNO Quickway Ad .04 .10

2003-04 Syracuse Crunch

This set was produced by Choice Marketing and sold at home games.

COMPLETE SET (24) 4.00 10.00
1 Karl Goehring .30 .75
2 Jamie Pushor .15 .40
3 Mark Hartigan .20 .50
4 Darrel Scoville .15 .40
5 Zenith Komarniski .15 .40
6 Ben Knopp .15 .40
7 Todd Rohloff .15 .40
8 Paul Traynor .15 .40
9 Donald MacLean .15 .40
10 Jeremy Reich .20 .50
11 Tim Jackman .15 .40
12 Joe Motzko .15 .40
13 Brad Moran .15 .40
14 Derrick Walser .15 .40
15 Pauli Levokari .15 .40
16 Aaron Johnson .15 .40
17 Kent McDonell .15 .40
18 Tyler Sloan .15 .40
19 Brandon Sugden .30 .75
20 Pascal Leclaire .40 1.00
21 Anders Eriksson .15 .40
22 Mike Pandolfo .15 .40
23 Trent Cull .15 .40
24 Mascot .04 .10

2004-05 Syracuse Crunch

Produced by Choice Marketing and sold at home games.

COMPLETE SET (25) 5.00 12.00
1 Header .04 .10
Checklist
2 Karl Goehring .30 .75
3 Jamie Pushor .20 .50
4 Mark Hartigan .20 .50
5 Zenith Komarniski .20 .50
6 Ole-Kristian Tollefsen .20 .50
7 Prestin Ryan .20 .50
8 Matthias Trattnig .20 .50
9 Jeremy Reich .20 .50
10 Tim Jackman .20 .50
11 Steven Goertzen .20 .50
12 Alexander Svitov .20 .50
13 Joe Motzko .20 .50
14 Brad Moran .20 .50
15 Andre Lakos .20 .50
16 Aaron Johnson .20 .50
17 Francois Beauchemin .30 .75
18 Brandon Sugden .40 1.00
19 Raffaele Sannitz .20 .50
20 Pascal Leclaire .40 1.00
21 Greg Mauldin .20 .50
22 Jeff Panzer .20 .50
23 Mike Pandolfo .20 .50
24 Al MASCOT .04 .10
25 Sponsor card .04 .10

2005-06 Syracuse Crunch

COMPLETE SET (26) 8.00 15.00
1 Mike Ayers .20 .50
2 Marc Methot .30 .75
3 Mark Hartigan .20 .50
4 Darcy Verot .20 .50
5 Ben Simon .20 .50
6 Geoff Platt .30 .75
7 Andrew Murray .20 .50
8 Tyler Kolarik .20 .50
9 Steven Goertzen .20 .50
10 Peter Sarno .30 .75
11 Joe Motzko .20 .50
12 Brett Nowak .20 .50
13 Alexandre Picard .60 1.50
14 Jeff MacMillan .20 .50
15 Jamie Pushor .20 .50
16 Andy Canzanello .20 .50
17 Ole-Kristian Tollefsen .20 .50
18 Brandon Sugden .40 1.00
19 Martin Prusek .30 .75
20 Tim Konsorada .20 .50
21 Andrew Penner .40 1.00
22 Joakim Lindstrom .30 .75
23 Greg Mauldin .20 .50
24 Aaron Johnson .20 .50
25 Andy Delmore .20 .50
26 Al MASCOT .02 .10

2006-07 Syracuse Crunch

COMPLETE SET (26) 8.00 15.00
1 Tomas Popperle .30 .75
2 Marc Methot .20 .50
3 Mark Hartigan .20 .50
4 Filip Novak .20 .50
5 Darcy Verot .30 .75
6 Ben Simon .20 .50
7 Geoff Platt .30 .75
8 Andrew Murray .20 .50
9 Adam Pineault .30 .75
10 Philippe Dupuis .20 .50
11 Steven Goertzen .20 .50
12 Janne Hauhtonen .20 .50
13 Joe Motzko .20 .50
14 Alexandre Picard .30 .75
15 Tomas Kloucek .20 .50
16 Jeff Szwez .20 .50
17 Ryan Caldwell .20 .50
18 Jamie Pushor .20 .50
19 Andy Canzanello .20 .50
20 Derrick Walser .20 .50
21 Dan LaCosta .20 .50
22 Jekabs Redlihs .20 .50
23 Ty Conklin .30 .75
24 Joakim Lindstrom .30 .75
25 Olivier Labelle .20 .50
26 Al MASCOT .02 .10

1992-93 Tacoma Rockets

This 30-card standard-size set features hatch-bordered, posed-on-ice color player photos. In a white field under the photo are the player's name, and in the right corner, the team logo of crossed red rockets. The team name appears in a diagonal across the top left corner of the photo and the player's position is in blue letters across the top. The cards are unnumbered and checklisted below in alphabetical order.

COMPLETE SET (30) 4.00 10.00
1 Alexander Alexeev .15 .40
2 Jamie Black .20 .50
3 Jamie Butt .20 .50
4 Jeff Calvert .15 .40
5 Don Clark ACO .02 .10
6 Marcel Comeau CO .15 .40
7 Duane Crouse TR .02 .10
8 Allan Egeland .15 .40
9 Marty Flichel .15 .40
10 Trever Fraser .15 .40
11 Jason Kwiatkowski .15 .40
12 Todd MacDonald .15 .40
13 Dave McMillen .15 .40
14 Tony Pechthalt TR .02 .10
15 Ryan Phillips .15 .40
16 Mike Piersol .15 .40
17 Dennis Pinfold .15 .40
18 Kevin Powell .15 .40
19 Tyler Prosofsky .15 .40
20 Stu Scantlebury .15 .40
21 Drew Schoneck .15 .40
22 Adam Smith .15 .40
23 Corey Stock .15 .40
24 Barkley Swenson .15 .40
25 Michal Sykora .20 .50
26 Dallas Thompson .15 .40
27 John Varga .15 .40
28 Toby Weishaar .15 .40
29 Michal Sykora IA .20 .50
30 Cover Card (Team Logo) .08 .25

1993-94 Tacoma Rockets

This 30-card standard-size set features the 1993-94 Tacoma Rockets. The set is printed on thin card stock. The fronts have hatch-bordered color action player photos, with the player's name and position printed in white letters in a dark turquoise shadowed border above the photo. The team name also appears in a dark turquoise shadowed bar to the left of the photo. The cards are unnumbered and checklisted below in alphabetical order.

COMPLETE SET (30) 4.80 12.00
1 Alexander Alexeev .20 .50
2 Jamie Butt .20 .50
3 Trevor Cairns .15 .40
4 Jeff Calvert .15 .40
5 Marcel Comeau CO .15 .40
6 Jason Deleurme .15 .40
7 Allan Egeland .20 .50
8 Marty Flichel .15 .40
9 Trever Fraser .15 .40
10 Michal Grosek .40 1.00
11 Lada Hampeis .15 .40
12 Tavis Hansen .20 .50
13 Burt Henderson .15 .40
14 Jeff Jubenville .15 .40
15 Todd MacDonald .20 .50
16 Kyle McLaren .60 1.50
17 Kory Mullin .15 .40
18 Steve Oviatt TR .02 .10
19 Ryan Phillips .15 .40
20 Mike Piersol .15 .40
21 Dennis Pinfold .15 .40
22 Tyler Prosofsky .20 .50
23 Jamie Reeve ACO .02 .10
24 Adam Smith .15 .40
25 Corey Stock .15 .40
26 Dallas Thompson .15 .40
27 John Varga .20 .50
28 Team Photo .20 .50
29 The Tacoma Dome .02 .10
30 The Tacoma Rockets .15 .40
In Action
Marty Flichel

1998-99 Tacoma Sabercats

This set of the WCHL Sabercats was handed out as a promotional giveaway at one home game, making it extremely difficult to find on the secondary market.

COMPLETE SET (25) 8.00 20.00
1 Blair Allison .30 .75
2 Jergis Bertins .30 .75
3 Scott Boston .60 1.50
4 Dampy Brar .30 .75
5 Jamie Butt .60 1.50
6 Scott Drevitch .60 1.50
7 Brett Duncan .30 .75
8 Jim Gattolliat .30 .75
9 Scott Green .30 .75
10 Casey Hungle .30 .75
11 Tim Lovell .60 1.50
12 Kim Maier .30 .75
13 Trevor Matter .30 .75
14 Brad Mehalko .40 1.00
15 Alex Mukhanov .40 1.00
16 Chris Nelson .30 .75
17 Alex Podalinski .30 .75
18 Chad Richard .30 .75
19 Kevin Smyth .30 .75
20 Paul Taylor .30 .75
21 Edgar Zaltkovskis .30 .75
22 John Oliver HCO .20 .50
23 Sponsor Card .02 .10
24 Mike Carey TR .08 .25
25 Sponsor Card .02 .10

1999-00 Tacoma Sabercats

This set features the Sabercats of the WCHL. The set was produced by Grandstand and issued as a promotional giveaway at one home game.

COMPLETE SET (25) 6.00 15.00
1 Scott Boston .40 1.00
2 Alexander Alexeev .40 1.00
3 Pavel Mikulchik .30 .75
4 Trever Fraser .30 .75
5 Chad Richard .30 .75
6 Cory Morgan .30 .75
7 Brian Leitza .30 .75
8 Alexander Kharlamov .40 1.00
9 Craig Chapman .30 .75
10 Ashley Buckberger .30 .75
11 Trevor Roenick .30 .75
12 Scott Drevitch .30 .75
13 Jim Gattolliat .30 .75
14 Dampy Brar .30 .75
15 Blair Allison .30 .75
16 Brandon Fleenor .30 .75
17 Kim Maier .30 .75
18 Edgars Zaltkovskis .30 .75
19 Shayne Green .30 .75
20 Brett Duncan .30 .75
21 Local Electrician .02 .10
22 Local Electrician .02 .10
23 Local Electrician .02 .10
24 John Olver CO .08 .25
25 Mike Carey TR .08 .25

2000-01 Tacoma Sabercats

This set features the Sabercats of the WCHL. The set was produced by Grandstand and was used as a promotional giveaway at a late-season game.

COMPLETE SET (24) 8.00 20.00
1 Cory Morgan .40 1.00
2 Scott Boston .50 1.25
3 Trever Fraser .40 1.00
4 Jarrett Whidden .40 1.00
5 Charlie Blyth .40 1.00
6 Rob Dumas .40 1.00
7 Alexei Deev .40 1.00
8 Danny Lorenz .50 1.25
9 Alexander Alexeev .40 1.00
10 Ashley Buckberger .50 1.25
11 Brandon Fleenor .40 1.00
12 Luke Curtin .40 1.00
13 Gavin Hodgson .40 1.00
14 Dampy Brar .40 1.00
15 Steve Lowe .40 1.00
16 Dennis Pinfold .40 1.00
17 Scott Drevitch .40 1.00
18 Curtis Menzul .40 1.00
19 Phil Husak .40 1.00
20 Robert Dirk CO .10 .25
21 Jason Kirkman TR .04 .10
22 Sponsor .04 .10
23 Sponsor .04 .10
24 Sponsor .04 .10

2001-02 Tacoma Sabercats

This set features the Sabercats of the WCHL. It was handed out at a game in late February, 2002 and is very difficult to find on the secondary market.

COMPLETE SET (24) 8.00 20.00
1 Alexander Alexeev .40 1.00
2 Eric Bowen .40 1.00
3 Dampy Brar .60 1.50
4 Mike Brusseau .40 1.00
5 Etienne Drapeau .40 1.00
6 Scott Drevitch .60 1.50
7 Marty Flichel .60 1.50
8 Trever Fraser .40 1.00
9 David Goverde .60 1.50
10 Nathan Horne .40 1.00
11 Yannick Latour .40 1.00
12 Matt Loen .40 1.00
13 Casson Masters .40 1.00
14 Dennis Pinfold .40 1.00
15 Clayton Read .40 1.00
16 Francois Sasseville .40 1.00
17 Brian Stacey .40 1.00
18 Jarrett Whidden .40 1.00
19 Jeff Winter .40 1.00
20 Dampy Brar .60 1.50
21 Scott Drevitch .60 1.50
22 Robert Dirk CO .10 .25
23 Fang MASCOT .10 .25
24 Saberkitty MASCOT .10 .25

1995-96 Tallahassee Tiger Sharks

This 27-card set of the Tallahassee Tiger Sharks of the ECHL was sponsored by Burger King and features color action player photos. The backs carry player information.

COMPLETE SET (27) 3.00 8.00
1 Rodrigo Lavinsh .15 .40
2 Jon Engter .15 .40
3 Rod Aldoff .15 .40
4 Aaron Kriss .15 .40
5 Ron Pasco .15 .40
6 Mark Deazley .20 .50
7 Sean O'Brien .20 .50
8 Kevin Paden .15 .40
9 Darren Schwartz .15 .40
10 Jim Paradise .15 .40
11 John Uniac .15 .40
12 Cal Ingraham .15 .40
13 Matt Osiecki .15 .40
14 Greg Geldart .15 .40
15 Alexander Savchenkov .15 .40
16 Casey Hungle .15 .40
17 Mark Richards .20 .50
18 Bob Bell .20 .50
19 Frenzy (Mascot) .02 .10
20 Jim Mirabello ANN .02 .10
21 Mark Richards .20 .50
Bob Bell
22 Terry Christensen CO .02 .10
23 Jack Capuano ACO .02 .10
24 Jerry Hilker TR .02 .10
25 Walter Edwards VP .02 .10
GM
26 Tony Mancuso AGM .02 .10
27 John Summers ANN .02 .10

1999-00 Tallahassee Tiger Sharks

set features the Tiger Sharks of the ECHL. The set produced by the team and issued as a promotional way.

PLETE SET (26) 6.00 15.00
in Kellett .25 .60
ek Paget .25 .60
on Reid .25 .60
ren McAusland .25 .60
m Copeland .25 .60
id Thibeault .25 .60
t Oates .25 .60
l Buczkowski .25 .60
xandre LaPorte .25 .60
ike Thompson .25 .60
mbi Daniels .25 .60
n Perkins .25 .60
ris Wickenheiser .40 1.00
rry Shapley .25 .60
ad Hinz .30 .75
ent Cullaton .25 .60
an-Francois Houle .25 .60
son Weinrich .25 .60
axim Spiridonov .30 .75
vel Smirnov .25 .60
arc-Andre Gaudet .25 .60
rry Christensen CO .08 .25
m Paradise CO .08 .25
le Schultz .25 .60
ory Paterson .25 .60
enzy MAS .08 .25

1994 Tampa Bay Tritons RHI

set features the Tritons of Roller Hockey Intl. The s were sold in an oversized package featuring team mation. The set is noteworthy for featuring what is f the scarcest cards of Mark Messier, who was owner of the club.

PLETE SET (21) 7.20 25.00
ul Messier HCO .08 .25
rk Messier 6.00 15.00
ke Jickling .15 .40
n Spoltore .40 1.00
dd Goodwin .15 .40
ig Streu .15 .40
nis Sproxton .15 .40
rman Dezainde .40 1.00
er Esdale ACO .08 .25
evor Sherban .15 .40
uane Dennis .15 .40
rret Zukiwsky .15 .40
on Darling .40 1.00
ean Basilio .40 1.00
eff MacLeod .15 .40
heerleaders .20 .50
ean Rowe .20 .50
eorge Dupont .15 .40
eam Photo .15 .40
oug Messier ACO .08 .25
rad Woods .15 .40

2009-10 Texas Stars

PLETE SET (24) 4.00 8.00
ndon Wilson .20 .50
n Jancevski .20 .50
xime Fortunus .20 .50
rrett Stafford .20 .50
ancis Wathier .20 .50
ron Gagnon .20 .50
rttu Lindgren .20 .50
rgei Korostin .20 .50
tt Beaudoin .20 .50
uke Gazdic .20 .50
revor Ludwig .20 .50
cott McCulloch .20 .50
olton Sceviour .20 .50
Matt Stephenson .20 .50
Mathieu Tousignant .20 .50
Warren Peters .20 .50
Matt Climie .20 .50
Brent Krahn .20 .50
aymond Sawada .20 .50
Greg Rallo .20 .50
ravis Morin .20 .50
ndrew Hutchinson .20 .50
Glen Gulutzan .20 .50
Checklist .20 .50

2010-11 Texas Stars

MPLETE SET (28) 4.00 8.00
ler Beskorowany .20 .50
n Spang .20 .50
verin Blindenbacher .20 .50
olton Sceviour .20 .50
rdie Benn .30 .75
ron Gagnon .20 .50
cott McCulloch .20 .50
ymond Sawada .20 .50
ean Backman .20 .50
Tomas Vincour .30 .75
Maxime Fortunus .20 .50
Ondrej Roman .20 .50
Travis Morin .20 .50
Trevor Ludwig .20 .50
Matt Stephenson .20 .50
Cody Chupp .20 .50
Greg Rallo .20 .50
Fabian Brunnstrom .20 .50
Richard Bachman .20 .50
Luke Gazdic .20 .50
Philip Larsen .20 .50
Brad Lukowich .20 .50
Francis Wathier .20 .50
Mathieu Tousignant .20 .50
Brent Krahn .20 .50
Glen Gulutzan .20 .50
Paul Jerrard .20 .50
0 Checklist .20 .50

2014-15 Texas Stars

MPLETE SET (27) 8.00 20.00
ack Campbell .40 1.00
illiam Wrenn .30 .75
mie Oleksiak .40 1.00
ulius Honka .30 .75
evin Henderson .30 .75
erek Meech .30 .75
ustin Dowling .30 .75
randen Troock .30 .75
emel Smith .30 .75
Scott Glennie .30 .75
Curtis McKenzie .40 1.00
Maxime Fortunus .30 .75
Brendan Ranford .30 .75
Brett Ritchie .40 1.00
Scott Valentine .30 .75
Travis Morin .30 .75
Cameron Gaunce .30 .75
Taylor Peters .30 .75
19 Matt Mangene .30 .75
20 Greg Rallo .30 .75
21 Matej Stransky .30 .75
22 Radek Faksa .40 1.00
23 Derek Hulak .30 .75
24 Jussi Rynnas .40 1.00
25 Karl Taylor Asst. CO .30 .75
26 Derek Laxdal CO .30 .75
27 Header Card CL .30 .75

2006-07 Texas Tornados

COMPLETE SET (25) 15.00 25.00
1 Thomas Murphy .40 1.00
2 Lyon Messier 2.00 5.00
3 Troy Puente .40 1.00
4 Jake Newton .40 1.00
5 Nielsson Arcibal .40 1.00
6 Dylan Cooper .40 1.00
7 Justin King .40 1.00
8 Julian Mikola .40 1.00
9 Ryan Fuller .40 1.00
10 Colin Long .40 1.00
11 Tom Brooks .40 1.00
12 Sean Roadhouse .40 1.00
13 Adam Flink .40 1.00
14 John Bullis .40 1.00
15 Brendan Brickley .40 1.00
16 Ben Miller .40 1.00
17 Rob Blanchette .40 1.00
18 Brian Reagan .40 1.00
19 Stephane Da Costa .40 1.00
20 Paul Yovanic .40 1.00
21 Mike Cifelli .40 1.00
22 Corson Cramer .40 1.00
23 Thomas Tragust .60 1.50
24 Tony Curtale CO .02 .10
25 Tom Murphy ACO .02 .10

1998-99 Thetford Mines Coyotes

This set features players from the Thetford Mines Coyotes of the Quebec Semi-Professional Hockey League, one of the most entertaining leagues in all of hockey.

COMPLETE SET (23) 4.00 10.00
1 Steven Paiement .20 .50
2 Marco Sevigny .20 .50
3 Stephane Nepveu .20 .50
4 Jean-Pierre Tardif .20 .50
5 Eric Roy .20 .50
6 Eric Deblois .20 .50
7 Nick Perreault .20 .50
8 Sebastian Vallee .20 .50
9 Yohan Bedard .20 .50
10 Francois Allaire .20 .50
11 Bernard Bouffard .20 .50
12 Philippe Morin .20 .50
13 Pierre Perron .20 .50
14 Michel Dodier .20 .50
15 Frederic Barbeau .20 .50
16 Yves Loubier .20 .50
17 Michel Bisson .20 .50
18 David Desnoyers .20 .50
19 Dominic Cote .20 .50
20 Jean Roberge .20 .50
21 Pierre Marcoux .20 .50
22 Nathan Morin .20 .50
23 Marc Rodrigue .20 .50

2001-02 Thetford Mines Coyotes

This set features the Coyotes of the Quebec Senior League. The set sold by the team at home games. The set we received did not include card #14, but the checklist indicates this card pictures Daniel Payette. If anyone has a set and can verify this, please contact us at hockeymag@beckett.com

COMPLETE SET (25) 10.00 25.00
1 Sebastien Bety .60 1.50
2 Louis Bernard .40 1.00
3 Terry Bartlett .40 1.00
4 Stephane Thivierge .40 1.00
5 Mathieu Gagne .40 1.00
6 Frederic Barbeau .40 1.00
7 Jean-Francois Brunelle .40 1.00
8 Martin Fillion .40 1.00
9 Pierre Perron .40 1.00
10 Eric Roy .40 1.00
11 Francois Page .40 1.00
12 Eric Drouin .40 1.00
13 Jean Roberge .40 1.00
14 Daniel Payette .40 1.00
15 Marc-Andre Gaudet .40 1.00
16 Denis Desbiens .40 1.00
17 Yves Loubier .40 1.00
18 Daniel Poudrier .40 1.00
19 Pierre Marcoux .40 1.00
20 Hugo Poulin .40 1.00
21 Patrice Tardif .75 2.00
22 Bryan Faucher .40 1.00
23 David Thibeault .40 1.00
24 Martin Lamarche .40 1.00
NNO Checklist .10 .25

2002-03 Thetford Mines Coyotes

COMPLETE SET (23) 5.00 12.00
1 Benoit Beausoleil .20 .50
2 Louis Bernard .20 .50
3 Sebastien Bety .30 .75
4 Jean-Francois Brunelle .20 .50
5 Christian Caron .20 .50
6 Denis Desbiens .20 .50
7 Frederic Deschenes .20 .50
8 Jason Disher .20 .50
9 Eric Drouin .20 .50
10 Martin Fillion .20 .50
11 Marc-Andre Gaudet .20 .50
12 Guy Loranger .20 .50
13 Pierre Marcoux .20 .50
14 Andre Martineau .20 .50
15 Francois Page .20 .50
16 Daniel Payette .20 .50
17 Daniel Poudrier .20 .50
18 Hugo Poulin .20 .50
19 Jean Roberge .20 .50
20 Eric Roy .20 .50
21 Claude Savoie .20 .50
22 Patrice Tardif .30 .75
23 David Thibeault .20 .50

2003-04 Thetford Mines Prolab

COMPLETE SET (24) 4.00 10.00
1 Benoit Beausoleil .20 .50
2 Louis Bernard .20 .50
3 Eric Betournay .20 .50
4 Sebastien Bety .20 .50
5 Patrick Bolduc .20 .50
6 Denis Desbiens .20 .50
7 Frederic Deschenes .20 .50
8 Martin Fillion .20 .50
9 Marc-Andre Gaudet .20 .50
10 Eric Lavigne .20 .50
11 David Lessard .20 .50
12 Pierre Marcoux .20 .50
13 Andre Martineau .20 .50
14 Simon Olivier .20 .50
15 Francois Page .20 .50
16 Daniel Poudrier .20 .50
17 Hugo Poulin .20 .50
18 Christian Proulx .20 .50
19 Jean Roberge .20 .50
20 Eric Roy .20 .50
21 Claude Savoie .20 .50
22 Pierre Sevigny .20 .50
23 Patrice Tardif .20 .50
24 David Thibeault .20 .50

2004-05 Thetford Mines Prolab

COMPLETE SET (24) 6.00 15.00
1 David Thibeault .20 .50
2 Benoit Deschamps .20 .50
3 Marc-Andre Gaudet .20 .50
4 Dany Lavoie .20 .50
5 Patrice Tardif .20 .50
6 Michel Picard .30 .75
7 Frederic Deschenes .30 .75
8 Andre Martineau .20 .50
9 Serge Poudrier .20 .50
10 Marquis Mathieu .40 1.00
11 Francois Page .20 .50
12 Eric Lavigne .20 .50
13 Samuel Groleau .20 .50
14 Yves Racine .20 .50
15 Hugo Poulin .20 .50
16 Glen Kjernisted .20 .50
17 Frederic Henry .20 .50
18 Jean-Francois Beliveau .20 .50
19 Samuel Gagnon .20 .50
20 Simon Olivier .20 .50
21 Mathieu Biron .20 .50
22 Matt Holmes .20 .50
23 Dennis Leblanc .20 .50
24 Benoit Beausoleil .20 .50
25 Ryan Pisiak .20 .50
26 Link Gaetz .75 2.00
27 Gaetan Royer .20 .50
28 Frederic Deschenes .30 .75

2014-15 Thetford Mines Isothermic

COMPLETE SET (24) 6.00 15.00
1 Sylvain Dufresne .30 .75
2 Guillaume Letourneau .40 1.00
3 Matthew Medley .30 .75
4 Sebastien Courcelles .30 .75
5 Gabriel Lemieux .30 .75
6 Alexandre Neron .30 .75
8 Philippe Pepin .30 .75
9 Tommy Bolduc .30 .75
10 Isothermic 2012 Champs .30 .75
11 Joel Theriault .40 1.00
12 Jean-Philippe Levasseur .30 .75
13 Kevin Bolduc .30 .75
14 Gabriel Girard .30 .75
15 Eric Fortier .30 .75
16 Simon Courcelles .30 .75
17 Andrzej Sandrzyk .30 .75
18 Michel Ouellet .40 1.00
19 Keven Veilleux .30 .75
20 Martin Lariviere .30 .75
21 Maxime Villemaire .30 .75
22 Simon Gamache .30 .75
23 Marc-Antoine Desnoyers .30 .75
24 Pierre-Luc Sleigher .30 .75
25 Bobby Baril CO .30 .75

1993-94 Thunder Bay Senators

This 19-card set of the Thunder Bay Senators of the Colonial Hockey League was produced for the team by Rising Star Sports Promotions. The set was available through the club, and may have been offered as a game night premium.

COMPLETE SET (19) 4.00 10.00
1 Jean-Francois Labbe .40 1.00
2 Jamie Hayden .20 .50
3 Llew NcWana .20 .50
4 Chris Hynnes .20 .50
5 Trent McCleary .40 1.00
6 Richard Borgo .20 .50
7 Bryan Wells .20 .50
8 Don Osborne .20 .50
9 Todd Howarth .20 .50
10 Bruce Ramsay .20 .50
11 Brian Downey .20 .50
12 Barry McKinley .20 .50
13 Ron Talakowki .20 .50
14 Tom Warden .20 .50
15 Mel Angelstad .30 .75
16 Tommi Hietala .20 .50
17 Vern Ray .20 .50
18 Gerry St. Cyr .20 .50
19 Terry Menard .20 .50

1994-95 Thunder Bay Senators

This 20-card set of the Thunder Bay Senators of the CHL was produced for the team by Rising Star Sports Promotions. The cards were available through the team and may have been issued as a game night giveaway.

COMPLETE SET (20) 3.00 8.00
1 Todd Howarth .15 .40
2 Darren Perkins .15 .40
3 Derek Scanlan .15 .40
4 Pat Szturm .20 .50
5 Barry McKinley .15 .40
6 Jake Grimes .15 .40
7 Alain Cote .15 .40
8 Rival Fullum .15 .40
9 Terry Menard .20 .50
10 Mike McCourt .15 .40
11 Mel Angelstad .40 1.00
12 Jason Firth .15 .40
13 Llew NcWana .15 .40
14 Lance Leslie .15 .40
15 Neal Purdon .15 .40
16 Steve Parson .15 .40
17 Chris Rowland .15 .40
18 Bruce Ramsay .15 .40
19 Don Osborne .15 .40
20 Jean Blouin .15 .40

1995-96 Thunder Bay Senators

This 20-card set of the Thunder Bay Senators of the Colonial Hockey League was produced by Rising Star Sports Promotions. The cards were only available through Shoppers Drug Mart stores in Thunder Bay, making hobby acquisition difficult. The cards feature a blurry action photo on the front, an complete stats on the back, along with the Shoppers logos. The cards are unnumbered and so are listed below alphabetically.

COMPLETE SET (20) 6.00 15.00
1 Team Photo .30 .75
2 Mel Angelstad .40 1.00
3 Omer Belisle .30 .75
4 Frederic Cassivi .60 1.50
5 Brandon Christian .30 .75
6 Jason Disher .30 .75
7 Jason Firth .30 .75
8 Rival Fullum .30 .75
9 Todd Howarth .30 .75
10 Chris Hynnes .30 .75
11 Barry McKinley .30 .75
12 Terry Menard .30 .75
13 Derek Nicolson .30 .75
14 Llew NcWana .30 .75
15 Steve Parson .30 .75
16 Darren Perkins .30 .75
17 Dan Poirier .30 .75
18 Neal Purdon .30 .75
19 Bruce Ramsay .30 .75
20 Pat Szturm .40 1.00

1998-99 Thunder Bay Thunder Cats

This set features the Thunder Cats of the UHL. The singles were given away with issues of the local paper. There also have been reports that the complete set could be purchased directly through the paper at the end of the season.

COMPLETE SET (21) 4.00 10.00
1 Jason Lehman .20 .50
2 Barry McKinlay .20 .50
3 David Mayes .20 .50
4 Darrin Szczygiel .20 .50
5 Allan Roulette .20 .50
6 Normand Paquet .20 .50
7 Wayne Strachan .20 .50
8 Kevin Holliday .20 .50
9 Dan Brenzavich .20 .50
10 Mike Henderson .20 .50
11 Neal Purdon .20 .50
12 Nikolai Pronin .20 .50
13 Dan Myre .20 .50
14 Derek Landmesser .30 .75
15 Jason Firth .30 .75
16 Shawn Smith .20 .50
17 Jean-Francois Rivard .20 .50
18 Brant Blackned .20 .50
19 Darrell Clarke TR .02 .10
20 Tom Warden CO .02 .10
21 Sean McEachran .20 .50

1992-93 Thunder Bay Thunder Hawks

This set features the Thunder Hawks of the UHL. The cards were sold by the team at its souvenir stands, and are notable for being slightly smaller than typical cards.

COMPLETE SET (30) 6.00 15.00
1 Checklist .02 .10
2 Bill McDonald CO .02 .10
3 Larry Wintoneak ACO .02 .10
4 Mark Michaud .20 .50
5 Marc Lyons .20 .50
6 Jamie Hayden .20 .50
7 Llew Ncwana .20 .50
8 Marc LaBelle .20 .50
9 Gary Callaghan .20 .50
10 Jason Firth .30 .75
11 Mike Martens .30 .75
12 Gerry St. Cyr .30 .75
13 Everton Blackwin .20 .50
14 Bryan Wells .20 .50
15 Brian Downey .20 .50
16 Todd Howarth .20 .50
17 Bruce Rendall .20 .50
18 Vern Ray .20 .50
19 Bruce Ramsay .20 .50
20 Chris Rowland .20 .50
21 Barry McKinlay .20 .50
22 Vincent Faucher .20 .50
23 Tom Warden .20 .50
24 Brock Shyiak .20 .50
25 Mel Angelstad .40 1.00
26 Harijs Vitolinsh .20 .50
27 Steve Hogg .30 .75
28 Terry Menard .30 .75
29 Mark Woolf .30 .75
30 Darrell Clarke TR .02 .10

1992-93 Toledo Storm

This 25-card set features the Toledo Storm of the ECHL. The set features action photography -- which often suffers from the poor quality -- on the front, with stats and bio on the back. The cards were offered for sale by the club at the rink on game nights.

COMPLETE SET (25) 3.00 8.00
1 Checklist .02 .10
2 Chris McSorley CO .20 .50
3 Scott Luhrmann EQMG .02 .10
4 Barry Soskin GM .02 .10
5 Tim Mouser PR .02 .10
6 Jeff Gibbons PR .02 .10
7 Claude Scott .02 .10
The Happy Trumpeter
8 Scott King .20 .50
9 Andy Suhy .15 .40
10 Pat Pylypuik .15 .40
11 Alex Roberts .15 .40
12 Mark Deazley .15 .40
13 John Johnson .15 .40
14 Jeff Rohlicek .15 .40
15 Dan Wiebe .15 .40
16 Jeff Jablonski .15 .40
17 Greg Puhalski .15 .40
18 Bruce MacDonald .15 .40
19 Iain Duncan .15 .40
20 Rick Judson .15 .40
21 Alex Hicks .20 .50
22 Barry Potomski .20 .50
23 Derek Booth .15 .40
24 Rick Corriveau .15 .40
25 Mark Richards .15 .40

1992-93 Toledo Storm Team Issue

Little is known about this set beyond the confirmed checklist. Any additional information can be forwarded to hockeymag@beckett.com.

COMPLETE SET (30) 3.00 8.00
1 Logo Card .02 .10
2 Chris McSorley CO .20 .50
3 Scott Luhrmann EQMG .02 .10
4 Barry Soskin GM .20 .50
5 Tim Mouser PR .02 .10
6 Jeff Gibbons PR .15 .40
7 Mike Williams .15 .40
8 Scott King .20 .50
9 Alex Hicks .20 .50
10 Rick Judson .15 .40
11 Brent Sapergia .08 .25
12 Iain Duncan .15 .40
13 Mark Deazeley .15 .40
14 Jeff Jablonski .15 .40
15 Bruce MacDonald .15 .40
16 Rick Corriveau .15 .40
17 Pat Pylypuik .15 .40
18 Alex Roberts .15 .40
19 Derek Booth .15 .40
20 Andy Suhy .15 .40
21 Jason Stos .15 .40
22 Greg Puhalski .15 .40
23 Wade Bartley .08 .25
24 Distillery Crew .02 .10
25 The Dawnbusters .02 .10
26 Becky Shock .02 .10
27 Don Davis .02 .10
28 Beth Daniels .02 .10
29 Dennis O'Brien .02 .10
30 Will Worster .02 .10

1993-94 Toledo Storm

This 29-card standard-size set features the 1992-93 Riley Cup Champions Toledo Storm of the ECHL (East Coast Hockey League). Inside a white and a thin red border, the fronts feature color action player photos with the player's name and position in a red border at the bottom of the card. The team logo also appears at the bottom. The Erin Whitten First Win card reportedly was issued at a later date.

COMPLETE SET (29) 4.00 10.00
1 Checklist Card .02 .10
2 Chris McSorley CO .20 .50
3 Barry Soskin PRES .02 .10
4 Tim Mouser MG .02 .10
5 Jeff Gibbons ANN .02 .10
6 Scott Luhrmann TR .02 .10
7 Nick Vitucci .20 .50
8 Andy Suhy .08 .25
9 Pat Pylypuik .08 .25
10 Chris Belanger .08 .25
11 Mike Markovich .08 .25
12 Darren Perkins .08 .25
13 Dennis Snedden .08 .25
14 Mark Deazeley .20 .50
15 Mark McCreary .08 .25
16 Jeff Rohlicek .08 .25
17 Chris Bergeron .08 .25
18 John Hendry .08 .25
19 Greg Puhalski .08 .25
20 Bruce MacDonald .08 .25
21 Marc Lyons .08 .25
22 Rick Judson .08 .25
23 Alex Hicks .20 .50
24 Barry Potomski .30 .75
25 Rick Corriveau .20 .50
26 Kyle Reeves .20 .50
27 Erin Whitten 1.25 3.00
28 Brian Schoen .08 .25
29 Riley Cup Champions .08 .25
30 Erin Whitten First Win 1.25 3.00

1994-95 Toledo Storm

This 24-card standard-size set features the 1993-94 Riley Cup Champion Storm of the ECHL. The borderless fronts have color action player photos with the player's name, number and position across the bottom. The words "Toledo Hockey" are printed vertically down the right edge, while the team logo appears in the upper left corner. The cards are unnumbered and checklisted below in alphabetical order.

COMPLETE SET (24) 3.00 8.00
1 Dave Bankoske .15 .40
2 Wyatt Buckland .15 .40
3 Rick Corriveau .15 .40
4 Norm Dezainde .20 .50
5 Iain Duncan .15 .40
6 Jeff Gibbons .15 .40
7 Alain Harvey .20 .50
8 John Hendry .15 .40
9 Ed Henrich .15 .40
10 Rick Judson .15 .40
11 Mike Latendresse .15 .40
12 Scott Luhrmann TR .02 .10
13 B.J. MacPherson .15 .40
14 Jim Maher .15 .40
15 Jay Neal .15 .40
16 Marquis Mathieu .15 .40
17 Shawn Penn .15 .40
18 Darren Perkins .15 .40
19 Greg Puhalski CO .02 .10
20 Barry Soskin PR/GM .02 .10
21 Gerry St. Cyr .15 .40
22 Rhett Trombley .20 .50
23 Nick Vitucci .20 .50
24 1993-94 Riley Cup Champ .20 .50

1995-96 Toledo Storm

This 26-card set of the Toledo Storm of the ECHL was sponsored by Frito-Lay and available through the team and its booster club. The fronts feature an action photo along with team, league and sponsor logos. The unnumbered backs contain player analysis and stats.

COMPLETE SET (26) 3.00 8.00
1 Rob Laurie .15 .40
2 Nicolas Perreault .20 .50
3 Brandon Carper .15 .40
4 Paul Koch .15 .40
5 Glen Mears .15 .40
6 Dan Carter .15 .40
7 Patrick Gladu .15 .40
8 Todd Wetzel .15 .40
9 B.J. MacPherson .15 .40
10 Mark Stitt .15 .40
11 Dennis Purdie .20 .50
12 Rick Judson .15 .40
13 Mike Whitton .15 .40
14 Norman Dezainde .15 .40
15 Jason Gladney .15 .40
16 Wade Bartley .15 .40
17 Jason Smart .15 .40
18 Mike Kolenda .15 .40
19 Shawn Penn .15 .40
20 David Goverde .20 .50
21 Barry Soskin .02 .10
Owner
22 Greg Puhalski CO .02 .10
23 Chuck Imburgia .02 .10
Director of Players
24 Scott Luhrmann .02 .10
Equipment Manager
25 Mark Kelly .02 .10
Broadcaster
26 Raging Color Classics .02 .10
Sponsor

1996-97 Toledo Storm

This 24-card set was produced by Split Second. The unnumbered cards feature an action photo on the front, with a brief statistical package on the back. The club offered them for sale at games and through the mail.

COMPLETE SET (24) 3.00 8.00
1 Ryan Bach .30 .75
5 Paul Koch .15 .40
6 Ryan Bast .15 .40
8 Andrei Srubko .15 .40
11 Brian Clifford .15 .40
14 Mike Sullivan .15 .40
17 Alex Matvichuk .15 .40
18 Arturs Kupaks .15 .40
19 Dennis Purdie .20 .50
20 Rick Judson .15 .40
22 Norm Dezainde .15 .40
23 Jason Gladney .15 .40
24 Chris Bergeron .15 .40
25 Mike Whitton .15 .40
27 Mike Kolenda .15 .40
28 Dan Pawlaczyk .15 .40
29 Jeremy Mylymok .15 .40
32 Don Larner .15 .40
33 Rob Thorpe .15 .40
35 David Goverde .30 .75
NNO Mark Kelly ANN .02 .10
NNO Scott Luhrmann TR .02 .10
NNO Greg Puhalski CO .02 .10
NNO Barry Soskin PRES .02 .10

1997-98 Toledo Storm

This set was made by Grandstand and were sold by the team at home games. The cards are unnumbered, and are listed below in the order they were inserted in the pack.

COMPLETE SET (30) 3.00 8.00
1 Louis Bernard .10 .30
2 Robert Thorpe .10 .30
3 Greg Lakovic .10 .30
4 Alexandre Jacques .10 .30
5 Gordy Hunt .10 .30
6 Andrei Sryubko .10 .30
7 Sean Venedam .10 .30
8 Jeremy Rebek .10 .30
9 Sean Ortiz .10 .30
10 Tony Prpic .10 .30
11 Brian Blad .10 .30
12 Ron Newhook .20 .50
13 Nick Vitucci .20 .50
14 Dennis Holland .10 .30
15 Mark Deazeley .10 .30
16 Rick Judson .10 .30
17 Lee Cole .10 .30
18 Mike Kolenda .10 .30
19 Dave Arsenault .10 .30
20 Jason Gladney .10 .30
21 Bruce MacDonald .10 .30
22 Kevin Brown .10 .30
23 Andrew Williamson .10 .30
24 Shawn Maltby .10 .30
25 Mike Loach .10 .30
26 Greg Puhalski HCO .02 .10
27 Barry Soskin PR .02 .10
28 Team Staff .02 .10
29 Mark Kelly .02 .10
30 Matt Bresnan EM .02 .10

2003-04 Toledo Storm

These cards were issued as promotional giveaways throughout the 2003-04 season. The cards came in four-card perforated strips. It's believed this checklist is incomplete. If you have further info, please email us at hockeymag@beckett.com.

COMPLETE SET (12) 4.00 10.00
1 Toledo Storm .04 .10
2 Doug Teskey .60 1.50
3 Mike Nelson .40 1.00
4 Josh Legge .40 1.00
5 Morten Ask .40 1.00
6 Nick Parillo .40 1.00
7 Tom Nemeth .40 1.00
8 Alexandre Jacques .40 1.00
9 Rick Judson .40 1.00
10 Landon Bathe .40 1.00
11 Kris Waltze .40 1.00
12 Jim Abbott .40 1.00

2006-07 Toledo Storm

COMPLETE SET (26) 8.00 15.00
1 Andrew Martin .30 .75
2 Jamie Tardif .30 .75
3 Jason Maleyko .30 .75
4 Tim Songin .30 .75
5 P.J. Martin .30 .75
6 Paul Crosty .40 1.00
7 Jon Sitko .30 .75
8 Jason Schweinsberg EQ MGR .02 .10
9 Mike Brodeur .40 1.00
10 Dominic Vicari .40 1.00
11 Scooter Smith .30 .75
12 Chris Blight .30 .75
13 Logan Koopmans .40 1.00
14 Mike James .30 .75
15 Taylor Raszka .30 .75
16 Ken Magowan .30 .75
17 Nick Parillo .30 .75
18 Jeff Attard .30 .75
19 Gerry Burke .30 .75
20 Dan Watson .30 .75
21 Mike Walsh .30 .75
22 Matt Zultek .30 .75
23 Nick Vitucci CO .10 .25
24 Rick Judson CO .02 .10
25 Barry Soskin PRES .02 .10
26 Dukes MASCOT .02 .10

2014-15 Toledo Walleye

COMPLETE SET (24) 6.00 15.00
1 Tyler Barnes .30 .75
2 Shane Berschbach .30 .75
3 Kyle Bonis .30 .75
4 Joel Chouinard .30 .75
5 Kevin Clare .30 .75
6 Jared Coreau .30 .75
7 Scott Czarnowczan .30 .75
8 Tyler Elbrecht .30 .75
9 A.J. Jenks .30 .75
10 Derek Lalonde CO .30 .75
11 Cody Lampl .30 .75
12 Jeff Lerg .30 .75
13 Anthony Luciani .30 .75
14 Justin Mercier .30 .75
15 Jared Nightingale .30 .75
16 Kyle Rogers .30 .75
17 Troy Schwab .30 .75
18 Shane Sims .30 .75
19 Marek Tvrdon .30 .75
20 Dane Walters .30 .75
21 Dan Watson Asst. CO .30 .75
22 Cattrick MASCOT .30 .75
23 Spike MASCOT .30 .75
24 Header Card CL .30 .75

1998-99 Topeka Scarecrows

This 23-card set of the WPHL Scarecrows was sold at home games. Note: there are two versions of card #21. It is not known whether either version is scarcer than the other.

COMPLETE SET (23) 4.00 10.00
1 Topeka Scarecrows CL .02 .10
2 Michal Podolka .30 .75
3 Shawn Randall .20 .50
4 Mike Rusk .20 .50
5 Brett Seguin .20 .50
6 Tom Stewart .20 .50
7 Andy Adams .20 .50
8 Chad Antonishyn .20 .50
9 Chris Bowen .20 .50
10 Joe Coombs .20 .50
11 Scott Dickson .20 .50
12 Troy Frederick .20 .50
13 Dave Gregory .20 .50
14 Trevor Hanas .20 .50
15 Kyle Haviland .20 .50
16 Haywire Mascot .02 .10
17 Kevin Lune .20 .50
18 Sergei Olympiev .20 .50
19 Ryan Phillips .20 .50
20 Paul Kelly HCO .02 .10
21 Michael Podolka NM .40 1.00
21 Andy Adams NM .40 1.00
22 Team Photo .20 .50

1999-00 Topeka Scarecrows

This set features the Scarecrows of the CHL. The set was produced by Roox and was sold by the team at home games.

COMPLETE SET (21) 4.00 10.00
1 Topeka Scarecrows .20 .50
2 John Vary .20 .50
3 Oleg Tsirkounov .20 .50
4 Bill Monkman .20 .50
5 Sergei Deschevvy .20 .50
6 Randy Best .20 .50
7 Blair Manning .20 .50
8 Steve Moore .20 .50
9 Kirk Llano .20 .50
10 Joey Beaudry .20 .50
11 Trevor Hanas .20 .50
12 David Bouskill .20 .50
13 Rod Branch .20 .50
14 Joe Coombs .20 .50
15 Mike Rusk .20 .50
16 Scot Bell .20 .50
17 Michal Podolka .30 .75
18 Brett Seguin .30 .75
19 Haywire MAS .08 .25
20 Paul Kelly CO .08 .25
21 Topeka Scarecrows .20 .50

2002-03 Topeka Scarecrows

COMPLETE SET (30) 10.00 25.00
1 Layne Sedevie .40 1.00
2 Slavomir Tomko .40 1.00
3 Tony Gliniany .40 1.00
4 Phil Angell .40 1.00
5 Jeff Balvin .40 1.00
6 Ryan Peterson .40 1.00
7 Nick Pernula .40 1.00
8 J.P. Platisha .40 1.00
9 Justin White .40 1.00
10 Luke Erickson .40 1.00
11 Wade Harstad .40 1.00
12 James Unger .40 1.00
13 Steve Eastman .40 1.00
14 Ryan Miller .40 1.00
15 Erik Fabian .40 1.00
16 Eric Vesely .40 1.00
17 Brent Cummings .40 1.00
18 Nick Miller .40 1.00
19 Rob Rankin .40 1.00
20 Mark Buchholz .40 1.00
21 Adam Bartholomay .40 1.00
22 Michael Zacharias .40 1.00
23 Mascots .04 .10
24 Zambeauty-Taumi .20 .50
25 Zambeauty-Janea .20 .50
26 Zambeauty-Audrey .20 .50
27 Zambeauty-Tara .20 .50
28 Zambeauty-Melissa .20 .50
29 Zambeauty-Amanda .20 .50
30 Scarecrows logo .04 .10

2006-07 Toronto Marlies

COMPLETE SET (34) 12.00 20.00
1 J.S. Aubin .30 .75
2 Bates Battaglia .20 .50
3 Brendan Bell .20 .50
4 Brad Brown .20 .50
5 Carlo Colaiacovo .20 .50
6 Jeff Corey .20 .50
7 Dominic D'Amour .20 .50
8 Duke The Dog MASCOT .02 .10
9 Robbie Earl .40 1.00
10 Brett Engelhardt .20 .50
11 Alex Foster .20 .50
12 Owen Fussey .20 .50
13 Greg Gilbert CO .02 .10
14 Jay Harrison .20 .50
15 Staffan Kronwall .20 .50
16 Brad Leeb .20 .50
17 John Mitchell .20 .50
18 Marc Moro .30 .75
19 Colin Murphy .20 .50
20 Kris Newbury .20 .50
21 Ben Ondrus .20 .50
22 Justin Pogge .75 2.00
23 John Pohl .30 .75
24 J.F. Racine .30 .75
25 Martin Sagat .20 .50
26 Justin Sawyer .20 .50
27 Jamie Sifers .20 .50
28 Chris St. Jacques .20 .50
29 Alexander Suglobov .20 .50
30 Jiri Tlusty .40 1.00
31 Erik Westrum .40 1.00
32 Ian White .20 .50
33 Jeremy Williams .20 .50
34 Andy Wozniewski .20 .50

2007-08 Toronto Marlies

COMPLETE SET (23) 15.00 25.00
1 Justin Pogge 2.00 5.00
2 Bryan Muir .75 2.00
3 Chris Harrington .40 1.00
4 Anton Stralman .60 1.50
5 Simon Gamache .40 1.00
6 Robbie Earl .60 1.50
7 Kris Newbury .40 1.00
8 David Ling .75 2.00
9 Brent Aubin .40 1.00
10 Jeremy Williams .40 1.00
11 Jay Harrison .40 1.00
12 Alex Foster .40 1.00
13 Ben Ondrus .40 1.00
14 Jaime Sifers .40 1.00
15 Scott Clemmensen .60 1.50
16 Michel Leveille .40 1.00
17 Derrick Walser .40 1.00
18 Colin Murphy .40 1.00

19 Darryl Boyce .40 1.00
20 John Mitchell .10 .25
21 Greg Gilbert .10 .25
22 Dance Park .02 .10
23 Duke The Dog MASCOT .02 .10

2003-04 ITG Toronto Star

Available through select retailers in late October 2003, fans could purchase packs consisting of four random cards from the 100-card base set plus the special foil insert card for that day. The cost of each pack was $3.49 (Canadian funds) plus taxes. A coupon was inserted into each daily issue of the Toronto Star offering one dollar off on a pack of cards. Each coupon was specific to the day's special pack. The promotion ran for 30 days. The cards were produced by In the Game,Inc for the paper.

COMPLETE SET (100) 10.00 25.00
1 Jean-Sebastien Giguere .20 .50
2 Petr Sykora .08 .20
3 Stanislav Chistov .08 .20
4 Dany Heatley .30 .75
5 Ilya Kovalchuk .40 1.00
6 Glen Murray .08 .20
7 Joe Thornton .40 1.00
8 Sergei Samsonov .20 .50
9 Martin Biron .20 .50
10 Miroslav Satan .08 .20
11 Ryan Miller .40 1.00
12 Rod Brind'Amour .08 .20
13 Jeff O'Neill .08 .20
14 Ron Francis .08 .20
15 Rick Nash .40 1.00
16 Rostislav Klesla .08 .20
17 Jarome Iginla .40 1.00
18 Eric Daze .08 .20
19 Jocelyn Thibault .20 .50
20 Alex Tanguay .20 .50
21 Joe Sakic .50 1.25
22 Milan Hejduk .20 .50
23 Patrick Roy 1.50 4.00
24 Peter Forsberg .60 1.50
25 Rob Blake .08 .20
26 Bill Guerin .08 .20
27 Marty Turco .20 .50
28 Mike Modano .25 .60
29 Brendan Shanahan .25 .60
30 Brett Hull .30 .75
31 Chris Chelios .20 .50
32 Dominik Hasek .40 1.00
33 Henrik Zetterberg .20 .50
34 Nicklas Lidstrom .20 .50
35 Pavel Datsyuk .20 .50
36 Steve Yzerman 1.25 3.00
37 Mike Comrie .08 .20
38 Ryan Smyth .20 .50
39 Jay Bouwmeester .08 .20
40 Kristian Huselius .08 .20
41 Roberto Luongo .25 .60
42 Olli Jokinen .08 .20
43 Alexander Frolov .08 .20
44 Jason Allison .08 .20
45 Zigmund Palffy .08 .20
46 Marian Gaborik .40 1.00
47 Manny Fernandez .20 .50
48 Jose Theodore .25 .60
49 Saku Koivu .20 .50
50 Jeff Friesen .08 .20
51 Martin Brodeur 1.00 2.50
52 Patrik Elias .08 .20
53 Scott Niedermayer .08 .20
54 Scott Stevens .08 .20
55 Jamie Langenbrunner .08 .20
56 Alexei Yashin .08 .20
57 Rick DiPietro .20 .50
58 Alexei Kovalev .08 .20
59 Anson Carter .08 .20
60 Eric Lindros .25 .60
61 Mark Messier .25 .60
62 Mike Dunham .20 .50
63 Pavel Bure .25 .60
64 Daniel Alfredsson .08 .20
65 Jason Spezza .25 .60
66 Marian Hossa .20 .50
67 Martin Havlat .20 .50
68 Patrick Lalime .20 .50
69 Jeremy Roenick .25 .60
70 John LeClair .08 .20
71 Simon Gagne .08 .20
72 Tony Amonte .08 .20
73 Sean Burke .20 .50
74 Mario Lemieux 1.50 4.00
75 Evgeni Nabokov .25 .60
76 Pavol Demitra .08 .20
77 Al MacInnis .08 .20
78 Barret Jackman .08 .20
79 Chris Pronger .08 .20
80 Doug Weight .08 .20
81 Keith Tkachuk .20 .50
82 Brad Richards .25 .60
83 Nikolai Khabibulin .25 .60
84 Vincent Lecavalier .25 .60
85 Martin St.Louis .25 .60
86 Owen Nolan .08 .20
87 Alexander Mogilny .08 .20
88 Carlo Colaiacovo .08 .20
89 Nikolai Antropov .08 .20
90 Ed Belfour .25 .60
91 Gary Roberts .08 .20
92 Mats Sundin .25 .60
93 Tie Domi .08 .20
94 Tomas Kaberle .08 .20
95 Ed Jovanovski .08 .20
96 Markus Naslund .08 .20
97 Todd Bertuzzi .08 .20
98 Jaromir Jagr .40 1.00
99 Olaf Kolzig .20 .50
100 Peter Bondra .08 .20

2003-04 ITG Toronto Star Foil

These foil cards were inserted one per pack and the available card changed each day of the promotion.

ONE PER PACK
1 Mario Lemieux 2.00 5.00
2 Steve Yzerman 1.50 4.00
3 Peter Forsberg 1.25 3.00
4 Marian Gaborik .75 2.00
5 Dominik Hasek .75 2.00
6 Joe Thornton .75 2.00
7 Henrik Zetterberg .40 1.00
8 Mike Modano .75 2.00
9 Ed Belfour .40 1.00
10 Marian Hossa .40 1.00
11 Owen Nolan .40 1.00
12 Pavel Bure .75 2.00
13 Jose Theodore .75 2.00
14 Mike Comrie .40 1.00
15 Tie Domi .40 1.00
16 Roberto Luongo .75 2.00
17 Saku Koivu .40 1.00
18 Jarome Iginla .75 2.00
19 Brett Hull .75 2.00
20 Markus Naslund .40 1.00
21 Jaromir Jagr 1.25 3.00
22 Jason Spezza .75 2.00
23 Rick Nash 1.25 3.00
24 Jean-Sebastien Giguere .40 1.00
25 Mats Sundin .75 2.00
26 Ilya Kovalchuk 1.25 3.00
27 Dany Heatley .75 2.00
28 Joe Sakic 1.25 3.00
29 Martin Brodeur 1.50 4.00
30 Patrick Roy 2.00 5.00

2000-01 Trenton Titans

This set features the Titans of the ECHL. The cards were actually distributed in the form of two 12-card sets at different points of the season. Each set had a retail price of $15.

COMPLETE SET (24) 12.00 30.00
1 Scott Bertoli .60 1.50
2 Sandy Cohen .80 2.00
3 Aniket Dhadphale .60 1.50
4 Mike Hall .60 1.50
5 Cail MacLean .60 1.50
6 Steve O'Brien .60 1.50
7 Alain St. Hilaire .60 1.50
8 Scott Stirling .60 1.50
9 Jed Whitchurch .60 1.50
10 Vince Williams .60 1.50
11 Mike Haviland ACO .10 .25
12 Troy Ward HCO .10 .25
13 Dennis Bassett .60 1.50
14 Shane Belter .60 1.50
15 Sasha Cucuz .60 1.50
16 Ian Forbes .60 1.50
17 Butch Kaebel .60 1.50
18 Sean Molina .60 1.50
19 Benoit Morin .60 1.50
20 Jeff Potter .60 1.50
21 Paul Spadafora .60 1.50
22 Kam White .60 1.50
23 David Whitworth .60 1.50
24 Clash MASCOT .10 .25

2001-02 Trenton Titans

This set features the Titans of the ECHL. The set was sold by the team at home games in two 12-card series. The first was released in Jan. 2002, the second in March. Both series retailed for $15 each. The cards are unnumbered and so they are listed alphabetically by 12-card series.

COMPLETE SET (24) 12.00 30.00
1-1 Syl Apps .75 2.00
1-2 Marco Charpentier .60 1.50
1-3 Aniket Dhadphale .60 1.50
1-4 Kirk Lamb .60 1.50
1-5 Matt Libby .60 1.50
1-6 Cail MacLean .60 1.50
1-7 John Nail .60 1.50
1-8 Geoff Peters .60 1.50
1-9 Scott Ricci .60 1.50
1-10 David St. Germain .60 1.50
1-11 Chuck Weber ACO .10 .25
1-12 Matt Zultek .75 2.00
2-1 Graham Belak .75 2.00
2-2 Scott Bertoli .60 1.50
2-3 Ian Forbes .60 1.50
2-4 Peter Horachek CO .20 .50
2-5 Pat Leahy .60 1.50
2-6 Andreas Moborg .60 1.50
2-7 Dan Murphy .60 1.50
2-8 Steve O'Brien .60 1.50
2-9 Alain St. Hilaire .75 2.00
2-10 Ben Stafford .60 1.50
2-11 Kam White .60 1.50
2-12 Rivet MASCOT .10 .25

2002-03 Trenton Titans

COMPLETE SET (24) 20.00
A1 Scott Bertoli .40 1.00
A2 Adam Edinger .40 1.00
A3 Andy Hedlund .40 1.00
A4 Yann Joseph .40 1.00
A5 B.J. Kilbourne .40 1.00
A6 John Nail .40 1.00
A7 Cody Rudkowsky 1.25 3.00
A8 Kam White .40 1.00
A9 Dustin Wood .40 1.00
A10 Matt Zultek .60 1.50
A11 Bill Armstrong CO .04 .10
A12 Rivet MASCOT .04 .10
B1 Syl Apps .40 1.00
B2 Tyler Beechey .40 1.00
B3 Sean Connolly .40 1.00
B4 Shaun Fisher .40 1.00
B5 Ian Forbes .40 1.00
B6 Mike Hurley .40 1.00
B7 Steve O'Brien .40 1.00
B8 David St. Germain .40 1.00
B9 Jeff Smith .40 1.00
B10 Daniel Tetrault .40 1.00
B11 Vince Williams .40 1.00
B12 Clash MASCOT .04 .10

2003-04 Trenton Titans

This set was produced by RBI Sports and reportedly limited to just 250 copies. The number sequencing includes all sets produced by RBI that season.

COMPLETE SET (16) 6.00 15.00
353 B.J. Abel .40 1.00
354 Andrew Allen .50 1.25
355 Scott Bertoli .40 1.00
356 Mathieu Brunelle .40 1.00
357 Bill Cass .40 1.00
358 Bryce Cockburn .40 1.00
359 Nick Deschenes .40 1.00
360 Peter Fregoe .40 1.00
361 Jay Leach .40 1.00
362 P.J. Martin .40 1.00
363 Devin Rask .40 1.00
364 Dan Riva .40 1.00
365 Jeff Smith .50 1.25
366 Pete Summerfelt .40 1.00
367 Vince Williams .40 1.00
368 Matt Zultek .60 1.50

1994-95 Tri-City Americans

This unusual series was produced by Summit. Four of the cards (#4-7) are standard size, while the other four are slightly oversized, suggesting that they may have been released at different times, or in two separate series. The larger four cards also have a slightly darker blue border around the posed studio shot. All of the cards appear to be laminated, or made strictly from a plastic-type material. The checklist below may be incomplete. Additional information from the readership would be appreciated.

COMPLETE SET (8) 10.00 25.00
1 Dorian Anneck .40 1.00
2 Brent Ascroft .20 .50
3 Brian Boucher 6.00 15.00
4 Rob Butz .20 .50
5 Chad Cabana .30 .75
6 Daymond Langkow 2.00 5.00
7 Ryan Marsh .20 .50
8 Terry Ryan .75 2.00

1995-96 Tri-City Americans

This 31-card set was produced by S&H Ltd. The cards feature action photos on the front, with a mug shot and bio on the back. Unnumbered, the cards are listed below in alphabetical order. The set is noteworthy for the inclusion of three first round selections from the 1995 Entry Draft: Daymond Langkow (TB), Terry Ryan (MTL) and Brian Boucher (PHI).

COMPLETE SET (31) 8.00 20.00
1 Chris Anderson .15 .40
2 Dorian Anneck .20 .50
3 Brent Ascroft .15 .40
4 Aaron Baker .20 .50
5 Alexandre Boikov .15 .40
6 Brian Boucher 2.00 5.00
7 Byron Briske .20 .50
8 Bob Brown GM .02 .10
9 Jerry Fredericksen TR .02 .10
10 Dan Focht .20 .50
11 Dylan Gyori .30 .75
12 Mark Hurley .15 .40
13 Mike Hurley .15 .40
14 Zenith Komarniski .20 .50
15 Daymond Langkow .75 2.00
16 Jody Lapeyre .15 .40
17 Bob Loucks CO .02 .10
18 Scott McCallum .15 .40
19 Boyd Olson .15 .40
20 Warren Renden ACO .02 .10
21 Terry Ryan .30 .75
22 Eric Schneider .15 .40
23 Dan Smith .15 .40
24 Craig Stahl .15 .40
25 Jaroslav Svejkovsky .30 .75
26 Jeremy Thompson .15 .40
27 Gary Toor .15 .40
28 Tom Zavediuk .15 .40
29 Eddie the Eagle (Mascot) .02 .10
30 Brian Boucher 1.25 3.00
(Daymond Langkow
Terry Ryan
31 Logo Card .02 .10

1998-99 Tri-City Americans

This set of the WHL Americans was issued by the team and sold at its souvenir stands. It features several promising NHLers including Josef Melichar, Jaroslav Kristek and 1999 Rookie of the Year Scott Gomez.

COMPLETE SET (28) 8.00 20.00
1 Jeff Blair .20 .50
2 Josef Melichar .40 1.00
3 Andrew DeSousa .30 .75
4 Darrell Hay .40 1.00
5 Jeff Katcher .20 .50
6 Toni Bader .20 .50
7 Jaroslav Kristek .40 1.00
8 Ken McKay .20 .50
9 Eric Johannson .20 .50
10 Scott Gomez 1.25 3.00
11 Ryley Layden .20 .50
12 Tim Green .20 .50
13 Blake Evans .20 .50
14 K.C. Timmons .20 .50
15 Jordan Landry .20 .50
16 Dylan Gyori .40 1.00
17 Brad Ference .60 1.50
18 Mike Muzechka .20 .50
19 Stephen Peat .60 1.50
20 Curtis Huppe .30 .75
21 Mike Lee .20 .50
22 Jody Lapeyre .20 .50
23 Andrew Guindon .20 .50
24 Blake Ward .30 .75
25 Terry Bangen ACO .02 .10
AGM
26 Training Staff .02 .10
27 Don Hay HCO .20 .50
GM
28 Craig West BR .02 .10

2002-03 Tri-City Stormfront

COMPLETE SET (25) 20.00 40.00
1 Cover Card .10 .25
2 Stormy MASCOT .10 .25
3 Brian Kilburg .75 2.00
4 Nick Klaren .75 2.00
5 Luke Lucyk 1.25 3.00
6 Mark Agnew .75 2.00
7 Tim Madsen .75 2.00
8 Geoff Paukovich .75 2.00
9 Chris Nathe .75 2.00
10 Ryan Dingle .75 2.00
11 Josh Leddy .75 2.00
12 Matt Scherer .75 2.00
13 Bill Thomas .75 2.00
14 Scott Parse .75 2.00
15 Steve Wagner .75 2.00
16 Tom Pohl .75 2.00
17 David Boguslawski .75 2.00
18 James Martin .75 2.00
19 Chad Anderson .75 2.00
20 Mark Van Guilder .75 2.00
21 T.J. Dahl .75 2.00
22 Casey Mapes .75 2.00
23 Eric Aarnio .75 2.00
24 Tom Kowal .75 2.00
25 Regg Simon .75 2.00

2014-15 Trois-Rivieres Blizzard

COMPLETE SET () 6.00 15.00
1 Etienne Archambault .30 .75
2 Pierre-Olivier Beaulieu .30 .75
3 Michael Belanger .30 .75
4 Thomas Bellemare .30 .75
5 Jonathan Bellemarre .30 .75
6 Stephane Boileau .30 .75
7 Gabriel Boutin-Gagnon .30 .75
8 Marco Cousineau .30 .75
9 Marco Cousineau .30 .75
10 Marc-Andre Daneau .30 .75
11 Jean-Francois David .30 .75
12 Nicolas Dumoulin .30 .75
13 Nicolas Dumoulin .30 .75
14 Boby Fugere .30 .75
15 Carl Gelinas .30 .75
16 Marc-Antoine Gelinas .30 .75
17 Mathieu Guertin .30 .75
18 Marc-Andre Huot .30 .75
19 Yann Joseph .30 .75
20 Tommy Lafontaine .30 .75
21 Benjamin Lecomte .30 .75
22 Marc-Antoine Moisan .30 .75
23 Francois Ouimet .30 .75
24 Hubert Poulin .30 .75
25 Christophe Rodrigue .30 .75

1997-98 Tucson Gila Monsters

This set features the Gila Monsters of the WCHL. These postcard-sized singles are blank backed, and were issued by the team as a promotional giveaway.

COMPLETE SET (10) 4.00 10.00
1 Jon Rowe .40 1.00
2 Dan Marcotte .40 1.00
3 David Piirto .40 1.00
4 Peter Romeo .40 1.00
5 Patrick Bisaillon .40 1.00
6 Jason Crane .40 1.00
7 Chris Everett .40 1.00
8 Sam Fields .40 1.00
9 Pierre Gagnon .40 1.00
10 Aigars Mironovics .40 1.00

1966-67 Tulsa Oilers

Little is known about this set featuring the Oilers of the old CHL beyond the confirmed checklist. The cards were oversized black and white images and likely were issued in photo-pack form. Any additional information can be forwarded to hockeymag@beckett.com.

COMPLETE SET (12) 25.00 50.00
1 Ken Campbell 1.50 3.00
2 Andrew Champagne 1.50 3.00
3 Doug Dunville 1.50 3.00
4 Bill Flett 5.00 10.00
5 Nick Harbaruk 1.50 3.00
6 Lowell MacDonald 5.00 10.00
7 Jim McKenny 2.50 5.00
8 Al Millar 1.50 3.00
9 Marc Reaume 2.00 4.00
10 Harry Shaw 1.50 3.00
11 Gary Venneruzzo 2.50 5.00
12 Ron Ward 2.00 4.00

1992-93 Tulsa Oilers

This 18-card standard-size set was sponsored by Crown Auto World. Ten thousand were sets were reportedly produced. Randomly inserted throughout the sets were 350 autographed cards of each player. The cards feature color photos of players in action and still poses. The pictures have white borders, and the player's name is printed in black on the photo at the bottom. The cards are unnumbered and checklisted below in alphabetical order.

COMPLETE SET (18) 3.00 8.00
1 Mike Berger .20 .50
2 Pat Cavanagh .20 .50
3 Shaun Clouston .20 .50
4 Brian Fiatt .20 .50
Tony Martin
5 Tony Fiore .20 .50
6 Taylor Hall .30 .75
7 Tom Karalis .20 .50
8 Greg MacEachern .20 .50
9 Terry MacLean .20 .50
10 Al Murphy .20 .50
11 Sylvain Naud .30 .75
12 Mario Nobili .20 .50
13 Jody Praznik .20 .50
14 E.J. Sauer .20 .50
15 Craig Shepherd .20 .50
16 Garry Unger .40 1.00
17 Team Photo .20 .50
18 Title Card .20 .50

1993-94 Tulsa Oilers

As with the other teams sets issued throughout the Central Hockey League this season, these are round cards approximately the size of a hockey puck. They come in a plastic container with the team logo on the front, and were sold by the booster club at home games for $5 per set.

COMPLETE SET (18) 3.00 8.00
1 Luc Beausoleil .30 .75
2 Mike Berger .20 .50
3 Shaun Clouston .20 .50
4 Craig Coxe .30 .75
5 Brian Flatt .20 .50
6 Taylor Hall .20 .50
7 Tom Karalis .20 .50
8 Doug Lawrence .30 .75
9 Jamie Loewen .20 .50
10 Mike MacWilliam .20 .50
11 Al Murphy .20 .50
12 Sylvain Naud .30 .75
13 Jody Praznik .20 .50
14 Chad Seibel .20 .50
15 Brian Shantz .20 .50
16 Sean Whyte .20 .50
17 Garry Unger CO .30 .75
18 Crown Auto World .02 .10
Sponsor

2003-04 Tulsa Oilers

These cards are unnumbered and thus are listed below in alphabetical order.

COMPLETE SET (24) 4.00 10.00
1 Header Card .04 .10
2 Jason Bermingham .20 .50
3 Rod Branch .30 .75
4 Anthony D'Arpino .20 .50
5 Jordon Flodell .20 .50
6 Dan Gravelle .20 .50
7 Regan Harper .20 .50
8 Tim Kelleher .30 .75
9 Cam Kuzyk .20 .50
10 Branislav Kvetan .20 .50
11 Todd Marcellus .20 .50
12 Rob Meanchoff .20 .50
13 Aaron Millar .20 .50
14 Chris Page .20 .50
15 Derek Reynolds .20 .50
16 Jordan Roach .20 .50
17 Shawn Scanzano .20 .50
18 Wes Scanzano .20 .50
19 Lukas Sedlacek .20 .50
20 Butch Kaebel CO .04 .10
21 Steve Enlow EQM .04 .10
22 Ad card .04 .10
23 Ad card .04 .10
24 Stuart Nichols TR .04 .10

2004-05 Tulsa Oilers

Cards are listed below in alphabetical order. Set is noteworthy for inclusion of Angela Ruggiero, the member of the American women's team who played briefly with the Oilers. The print run was reported to be 2,500 copies.

COMPLETE SET (24) 6.00 15.00
1 Cover Card .04 .10
2 Jason Birmingham .30 .75
3 Cameron Breitkreuz .30 .75
4 Mike Brusseau .30 .75
5 Jeff Cameron .30 .75
6 Jaroslav Cesky .30 .75
7 Lucas Dora .30 .75
8 Steve Enlow .30 .75
9 John Glavota .30 .75
10 Dan Gravelle .30 .75
11 Malcolm Hutt .30 .75
12 Mario Joly .30 .75
13 Butch Kaebel CO .04 .10
14 Klage Kaebel .30 .75
15 Justin Laird .30 .75
16 Todd Marcellus .30 .75
17 Justin Ossachuk .30 .75
18 Todd Paul .30 .75
19 Chris Pelletier .30 .75
20 Doug Pirnak .30 .75
21 Angela Ruggiero 1.25 3.00
22 Bill Ruggiero .40 1.00
23 Dallas Steward .30 .75
24 Oklahoma Trooper .04 .10

1999-00 Tupelo T-Rex

This set features the T-Rex of the WPHL. The cards were produced by SuperCard and were sold by the team at $2 each or a complete set for $30. The cards are very low quality, with a computer-generated bio glued to the back.

COMPLETE SET (19) 12.00 30.00
1 Drent Scott 1.25 3.00
2 Trevor Amundrud 1.25 3.00
3 Bob Brandon 1.25 3.00
4 Jay Pecora .75 2.00
5 Marc Vachon .75 2.00
6 Dave Szabo .75 2.00
7 Joe Van Volsen .75 2.00
8 Regan Harper .75 2.00
9 Jeff Mercer .75 2.00
10 Dave Wilejto .75 2.00
11 Clint Black .75 2.00
12 Pat Powers .75 2.00
13 Roby Gropp 1.25 3.00
14 Casey Hungle .75 2.00
15 Mike Mayhew .75 2.00
16 Jason Dexter .75 2.00
17 Kevin Evans .75 2.00
18 Martin Belanger .75 2.00
19 Ryan Rintoul .75 2.00

1998-99 UHL All-Stars

This set features players who earned a spot in the 1999 UHL All-Star Game. The cards were produced by ebk Sports and were supposed to be sold at the rink the day of the game. Apparently, that was not the case, but a few sets have leaked out onto the secondary market.

COMPLETE SET (22) 16.00 40.00
1 Ross Wilson .75 2.00
2 Stephane Brochu .75 2.00
3 Brian Downey .75 2.00
4 Mark Bultje .75 2.00
5 David Beauregard .75 2.00
6 Joe Dimaline .75 2.00
7 John Vary .75 2.00
8 Paul Willett .75 2.00
9 Vadim Podrezov .75 2.00
10 Wayne Muir .75 2.00
11 Brian Mueller .75 2.00
12 Alexei Deev .75 2.00
13 Lindsay Vallis .75 2.00
14 Patrice Robitaille .75 2.00
15 Jean-Francois Rivard .75 2.00
16 Jason Firth .75 2.00
17 Wayne Strachan .75 2.00
18 Brian LaFleur .75 2.00
19 Kevin Kerr .75 2.00
20 Garry Gulash .75 2.00
21 Mike Melas .75 2.00
22 Glenn Stewart .75 2.00

1999-00 UHL All-Stars East

This set, produced by ebk Sports, was sold at the rink during the 2000 UHL All-Star Game. Due to various production problems, #6T was also released as #2T, #15T released as #6T and #18T released as #1T. It is not known whether any variation is printed in shorter quantities than the others.

COMPLETE SET (22) 4.80 12.00
1T Yevgeny Shaldybin .20 .50
2T Stephan Brochu .20 .50
3T Nick Stajduhar .20 .50
4T Sam Myre .20 .50
5T Mike Maurice .20 .50
6T Chris Palmer .20 .50
7T Chris Grenville .20 .50
8T Gary Roach .20 .50
9T David Mayes .20 .50
10T John Vecchiarelli .40 1.00
11T Nic Beaudoin .20 .50
12T Peter Cermak .20 .50
13T Jay Neal .20 .50
14T Alexei Deev .20 .50
15T Chad Grills .20 .50
16T Dieter Kochan .75 2.00
17T Mark Richards .20 .50
18T Lindsay Vallis .20 .50
19T Ross Wilson .20 .50
20T Doug Searle .20 .50
21T Brent Gretzky .40 1.00
22T Header .08 .25
Checklist

1999-00 UHL All-Stars West

This set was produced by ebk Sports and was offered for sale during the 2000 UHL All-Star Game.

COMPLETE SET (22) 4.80 12.00
1T Kelly Hurd .20 .50
2T Frederic Bouchard .20 .50
3T Jim Durhart .20 .50
4T Jeff Winter .20 .50
5T Lonnie Loach .40 1.00
6T Brian Regan .30 .75
7T Ryan Lindsay .20 .50
8T Jeremy Rebek .20 .50
9T Colin Chaulk .20 .50
10T Scott Feasby .20 .50
11T Joe Dimaline .20 .50
12T Quinn Hancock .20 .50
13T Mike McCourt .20 .50
14T Keith Osborne .30 .75
15T Jeff Loder .20 .50
16T Garry Gulash .20 .50
17T Hugo Proulx .20 .50
18T Glenn Stewart .20 .50
19T Kevin Kerr .40 1.00
20T Jason Firth .30 .75
21T Mike Figliomeni .20 .50
22T Header .08 .25
Checklist

1990 UMD Hull Collection

This 12-card standard-size set (The Brett Hull Collection), was issued by University Minnesota-Duluth in conjunction with World Class Marketing and Collect-A-Sport. The cards have maroon and gold borders on the top and the bottom and are borderless on the side. Cards numbered 10 and 11 are in black and white while the rest of the set was issued with color photos. The set was issued in a special white box with a photo of Brett Hull on the front as well. The sets are numbered (out of 5,000) on the backs of the number 1 card.

COMPLETE SET (12) 6.00 15.00
COMMON CARD (1-12) .60 1.50
1 Hull Portrait 1.25 3.00

1999-00 Utah Grizzlies

This set features the Grizzlies of the IHL. The set was produced by the team and handed out as a promotional giveaway in the form of seven cards at five different home games.

COMPLETE SET (36) 8.00 20.00
1 Volkswagon Golf .04 .10
2 Rich Parent .75 2.00
3 Richard Park .30 .75
4 John Purves .75 2.00
5 Jarrod Skalde .75 2.00
6 Bob Bourne CO .20 .50
7 Checklist .04 .10
8 Volkswagon Jetta .04 .10
9 Gord Dineen .08 .25
10 Sean Tallaire .30 .75
11 Micah Aivazoff .75 2.00
12 Shawn Penn .30 .75
13 Larry Ness TR .08 .25
14 Utah Grizzlies .08 .25
15 Volkswagon New Beetle .04 .10
16 Joe Frederick .30 .75
17 Stewart Malgunas .30 .75
18 Mick Vukota .30 .75
19 Patrick Neaton .30 .75
20 Dean Chynoweth .30 .75
21 Micah Aivazoff .75 2.00
21 Gord Dineen .08 .25
22 Volkswagon Passat .04 .10
23 Rob Bonneau .30 .75
24 Ian Gordon .30 .75
25 Brad Lauer .30 .75
26 Neil Brady .30 .75
27 Grizbee MAS .08 .25
28 Mick Vukota .30 .75
29 Volkswagon GTI .04 .10
30 Brad Miller .30 .75
31 Jeff Sharples .30 .75
32 Darcy Werenka .30 .75
33 Zarley Zalapski .30 .75
34 Greg Payette TR .08 .25
35 Utah Freezz Indoor Soccer .04 .10

2000-01 Utah Grizzlies

This set features the Grizzlies of the IHL. The set was issued as a promotional giveaway at three home games. The cards were issued in perforated strips.

COMPLETE SET (37) 10.00 25.00
1 Volkswagon GTI SPONSOR .04 .10
2 Mike Bales .40 1.50
3 Steve Gainey .80 1.50
4 Brad Lauer .30 1.00
5 Jeff MacMillan .30 1.00
6 Bob Bourne CO .20 .50
7 Utah Grizzlies CL .04 .10
8 Passat SPONSOR .04 .10
9 Patrick Neaton .30 1.00
10 John Erskine .80 2.00
11 John Purves .40 1.50
12 Greg Leeb .40 1.00
13 Jason Taylor CO .10 .25
14 Team Photo .30 1.00
15 New Beetle SPONSOR .04 .10
16 Rick Tabaracci .40 1.50
17 Chris Wells .30 1.00
18 Ryan Christie .60 1.00
19 Alan Letang .30 1.00
20 Craig Ludwig CO .30 1.00
21 1997-98 Team Photo .10 .25
22 Jetta SPONSOR .04 .10
23 Evgeny Tsybouk .40 1.00
24 Eric Houde .40 1.00
25 David Ling .40 1.50
26 Gavin Morgan .30 1.00
27 Payette .04 .10
Ness
Lund STAFF
28 1996-97 Team Photo .10 .25
29 Golf SPONSOR .04 .10
30 Richard Jackman .40 1.00
31 Gregor Baumgartner .40 1.00
32 Jamie Wright .40 1.00
33 Mark Wotton .30 1.00
34 Grizzbee MASCOT .04 .10
35 1995-96 Team Photo .10 .25
36 1998-99 Team Photo .04 .10
37 1999-00 Team Photo .04 .10

2001-02 Utah Grizzlies

This set features the Grizzlies of the AHL. The cards were handed out over the course of the season in 6-card strips, one strip at different games. Each strip featured five player cards and one ad card featuring a Volkswagen car. The series features several former Grizzlies, as well as current players.

COMPLETE SET (35) 14.22 35.56
1 Paul Elliott .40 1.00
2 John Erskine .75 2.00
3 Gregor Baumgartner .40 1.00
4 Jon Sim .60 1.50
5 Tommy Salo 1.25 3.00
6 Mascot .04 .10
7 The New Beetle .04 .10
8 Greg Hawgood .40 1.00
9 John Purves .75 2.00
10 Steve Gainey .75 2.00
11 Serge Payer .40 1.00
12 Zigmund Palffy 1.25 3.00
13 Equipment Assistants .04 .10
14 The Cabrino GL .04 .10
15 Mark Wotton .40 1.00
16 Marc Kristoffersson .60 1.50
17 Eric Beaudoin .40 1.00
18 Roman Lyashenko .60 1.50
19 Vladimir Orszagh .40 1.00
20 Bob Bassen ACO .04 .10
21 The GTI .04 .10
22 Jeff MacMillan .40 1.00
23 Cameron Mann .60 1.50
24 Ryan Jardine .60 1.50
25 Jim Montgomery .60 1.50
26 Chad Alban .75 2.00
27 EQMG and TR .04 .10
28 The New Passat .04 .10
29 Dan Jancevski .60 1.50
30 Justin Cox .40 1.00
31 Kyle Rossiter .60 1.50
32 Gavin Morgan .40 1.00
33 Wade Flaherty .60 1.50
34 Don Hay CO .04
35 The Jetta Wagon .04

2002-03 Utah Grizzlies

COMPLETE SET (30) 15.00
1 Jonathan Sim .60
2 Steve Ott 3.00
3 Dan Jancevski .40
4 Eric Chouinard .40
5 Justin Cox .40
6 Checklist .04
7 John Erskine .40
8 Corey Hirsch .60
9 Barrett Heisten .40
10 David Gosselin .40
11 Jim Montgomery .40
12 Don Hay HCO .04
13 Steve Gainey .40
14 Marc-Andre Thinel .40
15 Jeff Bateman .40
16 Greg Hawgood .40
17 David Oliver .40
18 Bob Bassen ACO .04
19 Jason Bacashihua 2.00
20 Marc Kristoffersson .60
21 Jeff MacMillan .40
22 Alexei Komarov .40
23 Matthieu Descoteaux .40
24 Richard Krouse EM .04
25 Gavin Morgan .40
26 Mark Wotton .40
27 Mike Smith .40
28 Eric Landry .40
29 Mascot .04
30 Greg Payette .40

1998-99 Val d'Or Foreurs

Card measure 8 1/2 x 11 and feature color action photos on the front and stats and biographical information on the back. Back also features a white to obtain autographs. Card #S3 features a complete checklist with the dates the cards were made availa[ble] at Val d'Or Foreurs games.

COMPLETE SET (29) 16.00
1 Christian Daigle .40
2 Benoit Dusablon 1.25
3 Guillaume Lamoureux .40
4 Danny Groulx .40
5 Alain Charbonneau .40
6 Jonathan Fauteux .40
7 Didier Tremblay .40
8 Dynamit MASCOT .40
9 Roberto Luongo 6.00
10 Nick Greenough .40
11 Lucio DeMartinis .40
12 Gaston Therien .40
13 Francois Hardy .40
14 David St.Germain .40
15 Sebastien Laprise .40
16 Luc Girard .40
17 Simon Gamache 1.50
18 Steve Morency .40
19 Seneque Hyacinthe .40
20 Dave Verville .40
21 Alexandre Page .40
22 Denis Boily .40
23 Dwight Wolfe .40
24 Jerome Petit .40
25 Eric Dubois .40
26 Jonathan Charron .40
S1 Anthony Quessy .40
S2 Mathieau Lendick .40
S3 Philippe Ouellette .40

2000-01 Val d'Or Foreurs

This set features les Foreurs of the QMJHL. The set was produced by CTM-Ste-Foy, and was sold by th[e] card shop, as well as by the team.

COMPLETE SET (25) 6.00
1 Mathieu Roy .15
2 Yan Hallee .15
3 Chris Lyness .15
4 Hugo Levesque .15
5 Luc Girard .15
6 David Cloutier .15
7 Tomas Psenka .15
8 Nicolas Pelletier .30
9 Kory Baker .15
10 Steve Pelletier .15
11 Alex Turcotte .15
12 Simon Gamache 1.25
13 Simon Lajeunesse .75
14 Alexandre Rouleau .15
15 Samuel Duplain .15
16 Pierre Morvan .15
17 Brandon Reid 1.25
18 Mathieu Bastien .15
19 Maxime Daigneault .75
20 Jerome Bergeron .15
21 Frederic Bedard .15
22 Eric Fortier .15
23 Stephane Veilleux .15
24 Seneque Hyacinthe .15
NNO Team CL .04

2000-01 Val d'Or Foreurs Signe[d]

This set is exactly the same as the base Foreurs set from this season, save that every card has been hand signed by the player pictured. Each card also is seria[l] numbered out of just 100.

COMPLETE SET (25) 30.00
1 Mathieu Roy .80
2 Yan Hallee .80
3 Chris Lyness .80
4 Hugo Levesque .80
5 Luc Girard .80
6 David Cloutier .80
7 Tomas Psenka .80
8 Nicolas Pelletier 1.60
9 Kory Baker .80
10 Steve Pelletier .80
11 Alex Turcotte .80
12 Simon Gamache 4.00
13 Simon Lajeunesse 4.00
14 Alexandre Rouleau .80
15 Samuel Duplain .80
16 Pierre Morvan .80
17 Brandon Reid 4.00
18 Mathieu Bastien .80
19 Maxime Daigneault 6.00
20 Jerome Bergeron .80
21 Frederic Bedard .80
22 Eric Fortier .80
23 Stephane Veilleux .80
24 Seneque Hyacinthe .80
NNO Team CL .04

2001-02 Val d'Or Foreurs

This set features the Foreurs of the QMHJL. The set was produced by CTM Ste-Foy and was sold at Foreurs home games. There were 1,000 copies produced of this set.

COMPLETE SET (24) 4.80 12.00
1 Philippe Seguin .20 .50
2 Hugo Levesque .20 .50
3 Chaz Johnson .20 .50
4 Remy Tremblay .20 .50
5 Steve Richards .20 .50
6 Jonathan Gautier .20 .50
7 Vincent Duriau .20 .50
8 Jeff Cotton .20 .50
9 Patrice Bilodeau .20 .50
10 Frederic Bedard .20 .50
11 Nicolas Pelletier .20 .50
12 Francois Gagnon .20 .50
13 Alexandre Rouleau .20 .50
14 Pierre Morvan .20 .50
15 Mathieu Roy .20 .50
16 Samuel Gibbons .20 .50
17 Jonathan Charette .20 .50
18 Kyle Schutte .20 .50
19 Steve Pelletier .20 .50
20 Maxime Daigneault .40 1.00
21 Eric Fortier .30 .75
22 Mathieu Simard .20 .50
23 Adam Morneau .20 .50
24 David Rodman .20 .50

2002-03 Val d'Or Foreurs

COMPLETE SET (24) 5.00 12.00
1 Eric Glaude .20 .50
2 Pierre-Luc Laprise .20 .50
3 Patrice Bilodeau .20 .50
4 Vincent Durlau .20 .50
5 Mark Hurtubise .20 .50
6 Frederic Bedard .20 .50
7 Artem Kozitsyn .20 .50
8 Mathieu Curadeau .20 .50
9 Francois Gagnon .20 .50
10 Erik Lajoie .20 .50
11 Mathieu Dumas .20 .50
12 Denis Berube .30 .75
13 Olivier Latendresse .30 .75
14 Mathieu Roy .60 1.50
15 Benoit Genesse .20 .50
16 Jonathan Charette .20 .50
17 Shawn Collymore .30 .75
18 Didier Bochatay .20 .50
19 Maxime Daigneault .30 .75
20 Jeff Cotton .20 .50
21 Dominic Lachaine .20 .50
22 David Rodman .20 .50
23 Chaz Johnson .20 .50
24 Checklist .04 .10

2003-04 Val d'Or Foreurs

Created by Extreme Sportscards, this 23-card set was sold a home games and by Cartes Timbres Ste-Foy. Cards are unnumbered and are listed below iby jersey number.

COMPLETE SET (23) 5.00 12.00
1 Benoit Lessard .20 .50
2 Etienne Grandmont .20 .50
3 Dominic Lachaine .20 .50
4 Patrice Bilodeau .20 .50
5 Mark Hurtubise .20 .50
6 Luc Bourdon .75 2.00
7 Vladimir Kutny .20 .50
8 Artem Kozitsyn .20 .50
9 Jonathan Charette .20 .50
10 Francois Gagnon .20 .50
11 Erik Lajoie .20 .50
12 Mathieu Dumas .20 .50
13 Francois Thuot .30 .75
14 Olivier Latendresse .20 .50
15 Benoit Piche .20 .50
16 Shawn Collymore .20 .50
17 Guillaume Chicoine .20 .50
18 Maxime Daigneault .40 1.00
19 Jeff Cotton .20 .50
20 Patrick Bordeleau .20 .50
21 Mathieu Curadeau .20 .50
22 Sebastien Bisaillon .20 .50
23 Chaz Johnson .20 .50

1973-74 Vancouver Blazers

This set features the Blazers of the WHA. The cards are actually oversized black and white photos and were issued as a promotional item by the team. The Archambault and Cardiff cards were recently confirmed by collector M.R. LaFleche. No pricing information is available for these singles at this time.

COMPLETE SET (21) 25.00 50.00
1 Jim Adair 1.50 3.00
2 Yves Archambault 1.50 3.00
3 Don Burgess 2.00 4.00
4 Bryan Campbell 2.00 4.00
5 Colin Campbell 2.50 6.00
6 Jim Cardiff 1.50 3.00
7 Mike Chernoff 1.50 3.00
8 Peter Donnelly 1.50 3.00
9 George Gardner 1.50 3.00
10 Sam Gellard 1.50 3.00
11 Ed Hatoum 1.50 3.00
12 Dave Hutchison 2.00 4.00
13 Danny Lawton 1.50 3.00
14 Ralph MacSweyn 1.50 3.00
15 Denis Meloche 1.50 3.00
16 John Migneault 1.50 3.00
17 Murray Myers 1.50 3.00
18 Michel Plante 1.50 3.00
19 Ron Plumb 2.00 4.00
20 Claude St. Sauveur 1.50 3.00
21 Irv Spencer 2.00 4.00

2001-02 Vancouver Giants

This set features the expansion Giants of the WHL. The cards were produced by the team and sold at souvenir stands for $10 per set. The cards came in a sealed wrapper with an image that emulates the title card. The cards themselves feature an action photo on the front, and black and white player data on the back. Although jersey numbers appear on the front, the cards are unnumbered and thus are listed below alphabetically.

COMPLETE SET (25) 4.80 12.00
1 Title Card .10 .25
2 Mark Ardelan .20 .50
3 Mark Ashton .20 .50
4 Chad Bassen .20 .50
5 Jeff Beatch .20 .50
6 Robin Big Snake .40 1.00
7 Josh Bonar .20 .50
8 Pat Brandreth .20 .50
9 Jeff Coulter .20 .50
10 Don Choukalos .30 .75
11 Andrew Davidson .20 .50
12 Andrew DeSousa .20 .50
13 Marian Havel .30 .75
14 Jeremy Jackson .20 .50
15 Brett Jaeger .20 .50
16 Robin Kovar .20 .50
17 Darren Lynch .30 .75
18 Nick Marach .20 .50
19 Tyson Marsh .20 .50
20 T.J. Mulock .20 .50
21 Jack Redlick .20 .50
22 Dave Selthun .20 .50
23 Chris Stubel .20 .50
24 Ryan Thomas .20 .50
25 Clay Thoring .20 .50

2003-04 Vancouver Giants

COMPLETE SET (25) 10.00 25.00
1 Title Card .04 .10
2 Jordan McLaughlin .20 .50
3 Aaron Sorochan .20 .50
4 Ryan Mayko .20 .50
5 Chad Scharff .20 .50
6 Mark Fistric .30 .75
7 Brennan Chapman .20 .50
8 Joe Logan .20 .50
9 Marcin Kolusz .20 .50
10 Adam Courchaine .20 .50
11 Triston Grant .20 .50
12 Kyle Bruce .20 .50
13 Darrell May .20 .50
14 Gilbert Brule 6.00 15.00
15 Kevin Hayman .20 .50
16 Mitch Bartley .20 .50
17 Braden Appleby .20 .50
18 Matt Kassian .20 .50
19 Tyson Marsh .30 .75
20 Darren Lynch .20 .50
21 Tim Kraus .20 .50
22 Ty Morris .20 .50
23 Lukas Pulpan .20 .50
24 Dean Evason HCO .04 .10
25 Team Photo .20 .50

2004-05 Vancouver Giants

COMPLETE SET 8.00 20.00
1 Luke Egener .20 .50
2 Mark Fistric .30 .75
3 Cody Franson .20 .50
4 Stewart Thiessen .20 .50
5 Jason Reese .20 .50
6 Matt Robinson .20 .50
7 J.D. Watt .20 .50
8 Adam Courchaine .20 .50
9 Triston Grant .20 .50
10 Keith Voytechek .20 .50
11 Shaun Vey .20 .50
12 Andrej Meszaros .40 1.00
13 Gilbert Brule 2.00 5.00
14 Mitch Bartley .20 .50
15 Matt Kassian .20 .50
16 Max Gordichuk .20 .50
17 Garet Hunt .20 .50
18 Paul Albers .20 .50
19 Kyle Lamb .20 .50
20 Tim Kraus .20 .50
21 Chad Scharff .20 .50
22 Marek Schwarz .75 2.00
23 Conlan Seder .20 .50
24 Adam Jennings .20 .50

2005-06 Vancouver Giants

COMPLETE SET (25) 8.00 20.00
1 Paul Albers .30 .75
2 Mitchell Bartley .30 .75
3 Mario Bliznak .30 .75
4 Jonathon Blum .30 .75
5 Gilbert Brule 2.00 4.00
6 Mitch Czibere .30 .75
7 Brett Festerling .30 .75
8 Mark Fistric .50 1.25
9 John Flatters .30 .75
10 Cody Franson .30 .75
11 Garet Hunt .30 .75
12 Tim Kraus .30 .75
13 Kyle Lamb .30 .75
14 Milan Lucic 2.00 5.00
15 Spencer Machacek .30 .75
16 Brendan Mikkelson .40 1.00
17 Jason Reese .30 .75
18 Michal Repik .30 .75
19 David Rutherford .30 .75
20 Chad Scharff .30 .75
21 Tyson Sexsmith .30 .75
22 Dustin Slade .30 .75
23 Tommy Tartaglione .30 .75
24 J.D. Watt .30 .75
25 Vancouver Giants .04 .10

1995 Vancouver VooDoo RHI

This 25-card set from Slapshot Images features the Vancouver VooDoo of Roller Hockey International. The cards feature color player photos in a thin gray frame on a black background with a purple zigzag stripe down the left. The backs carry player information.

COMPLETE SET (25) 3.00 8.00
1 Title Card CL .02 .10
2 Tiger Williams .40 1.00
3 James Jenson .20 .50
4 Laurie Billeck .15 .40
5 Doug McCarthy .15 .40
6 Jason Knox .15 .40
7 Brent Thurston .15 .40
8 Dave Cairns CO .02 .10
9 Jason Jennings .15 .40
10 Shayne Green .15 .40
11 Rob Dumas .15 .40
12 Ivan Matulik .15 .40
13 Rob Stewart .15 .40
14 Doug Ast .20 .50
15 Chris Morrison .15 .40
17 Kevin Hoffman .15 .40
17 Ryan Harrison .15 .40
18 Ken Kinney .20 .50
19 Merv Priest .15 .40
20 Steve Brown .15 .40
21 Ryan Harrison/1994 All Star Card .15 .40
22 VooDoo Dolls .15 .40
23 1995 Season Schedules .02 .10
24 VooDoo Merchandise Card .02 .10
25 Titan (Mascot) .02 .10

2003-04 Vernon Vipers

This set features the Vipers of the BCJHL.

COMPLETE SET (22) 4.00 10.00
1 Checklist .04 .10
2 Steve Belanger .20 .50
3 David Boudreau .20 .50
4 Cole Byers .20 .50
5 Dustin Claffey .20 .50
6 Dallas Costanzo .20 .50
7 Scott Dafoe .20 .50
8 Ryan Kindret .20 .50
9 Reed Kipp .20 .50
10 Andrew Lord .20 .50
11 Mark Nelson .20 .50
12 Luke Pierce .20 .50
13 Les Reaney .20 .50
14 Mike Santorelli .20 .50
15 Mark Sibbald .20 .50
16 Aaron Volpatti .20 .50
17 Jake Wilkens .20 .50
18 Mark Wilson .20 .50
19 Andy Zulyniak .20 .50
20 Mike Vandekamp CO .04 .10
21 Bob Dever ACO .04 .10
22 Shawn Bourgeois ACO .04 .10

2004-05 Vernon Vipers

This set features the Vipers from the BCJHL.

COMPLETE SET (25) 6.00 15.00
1 Checklist Card .04 .10
2 Mark Nelson .30 .75
3 Mark Sibbald .30 .75
4 Dean Strong .30 .75
5 Matt Watkins .30 .75
6 History Card .04 .10
7 Sssniper MASCOT .04 .10
8 Andy Zulyniak .30 .75
9 Ryan Whitfield .30 .75
10 Scott Wallace .30 .75
11 Aaron Volpatti .30 .75
12 Mike Ullrich .30 .75
13 Rob Turville .30 .75
14 Lyle Tassone .30 .75
15 Matt Swerhone .30 .75
16 Aaron Schepers .30 .75
17 Mick McCrimmon .30 .75
18 Reed Kipp .30 .75
19 Corey Gannon .30 .75
20 Jeff Fedyk .30 .75
21 Wade Davison .30 .75
22 Dallas Costanzo .30 .75
23 Kurtis Colling .30 .75
24 Troy Cherwinski .30 .75
25 Matt Bourdreau .30 .75

2005-06 Vernon Vipers

COMPLETE SET (25) 6.00 15.00
1 Vernon Vipers CL .02 .10
2 David Arduin .30 .75
3 Hunter Bishop .30 .75
4 Travis Brisebois .30 .75
5 Patrick Cey .30 .75
6 Troy Cherwinski .30 .75
7 Andrew Coburn .30 .75
8 Chris Crowell .30 .75
9 Wade Davison .30 .75
10 Korey Gannon .30 .75
11 Chay Genoway .30 .75
12 Jerry Holden .30 .75
13 Kevyn Kirbyson .30 .75
14 Mickey McCrimmon .30 .75
15 Cody McMullin .30 .75
16 Mike Nichol .30 .75
17 Jon Olthuis .30 .75
18 Shawn Overton .30 .75
19 Matt Swerhone .30 .75
20 Mike Ullrich .30 .75
21 Aaron Volpatti .30 .75
22 Chad Wren .30 .75
23 Andy Zulyniak .30 .75
24 Viper History .02 .10
25 Sniper MASCOT .02 .10

2007-08 Vernon Vipers

COMPLETE SET (25) 10.00 20.00
1 History Card .02 .10
2 Kyle Bigos .40 1.00
3 Hunter Bishop .40 1.00
4 Travis Brisebois .40 1.00
5 Bryce Christianson .40 1.00
6 Chris Crowell .40 1.00
7 Matt Cumming .40 1.00
8 John Digness .40 1.00
9 Trent Dorais .40 1.00
10 Dallas Goodrunning .40 1.00
11 Lucas Gore .40 1.00
12 Cody Ikkala .40 1.00
13 Conner Jones .40 1.00
14 Kellen Jones .40 1.00
15 Ryan Kakoske .40 1.00
16 Brock Palasty .40 1.00
17 Braden Pimm .40 1.00
18 Eliot Raibl .40 1.00
19 Patrick Raley .40 1.00
20 Patrick Rogan .40 1.00
21 Rob Short .40 1.00
22 Evan Witt .40 1.00
23 Scott Zurevinski .40 1.00
24 SS Sniper MASCOT .02 .10
25 Checklist .02 .10

2014-15 Vernon Vipers

COMPLETE SET (22) 6.00 15.00
1 Thomas Aldworth .30 .75
2 Mackenzie Bauer .30 .75
3 Riley Brandt .30 .75
4 Blaine Caton .30 .75
5 Ken Citron .30 .75
6 Johny Coughlin .30 .75
7 Liam Coughlin .30 .75
8 T.J. Dumonceaux .30 .75
9 Brandon Egli .30 .75
10 Liam Finlay .30 .75
11 Riley Guenther .30 .75
12 Linden Hora .30 .75
13 Anthony Latina .30 .75
14 Colton McCarthy .30 .75
15 Mitch Meek .30 .75
16 Mitchell Oliver .30 .75
17 Nicholas Rasovic .30 .75
18 Jarrod Schamerhorn .30 .75
19 Luke Shiplo .30 .75
20 Danny Todosychuk .30 .75
21 Luke Voltin .30 .75
22 Jagger Williamson .30 .75

1981-82 Victoria Cougars

This 16-card set was sponsored by the West Coast Savings Credit Union and Saanich Police Department Community Services. The cards measure approximately 3" by 5" and feature posed, color player photos with white borders. The player's name, position, and biographical information appear at the bottom. The cards are unnumbered and checklisted below in alphabetical order.

COMPLETE SET (16) 8.00 20.00
1 Bob Bales .40 1.00
2 Greg Barber .40 1.00
3 Ray Benik .40 1.00
4 Rich Chernomaz .60 1.50
5 Daryl Coldwell .40 1.00
6 Geoff Courtnall 3.00 8.00
7 Paul Cyr .75 2.00
8 Wade Jenson .40 1.00
9 Stu Kulak .60 1.50
10 Peter Martin .40 1.00
11 John Mokosak .40 1.00
12 Mark Morrison .40 1.00
13 Bryant Seaton .40 1.00
14 Jack Shupe .40 1.00
15 Eric Thurston .40 1.00
16 Randy Wickware .40 1.00

1982-83 Victoria Cougars

Featuring current and past players, this 24-card set features the Cougars of the WHL. The cards measure approximately 3" by 5" and feature color player portraits with red and blue borders on a white card face. Past player cards have the words "Graduation Series" stamped in the lower right corner of the picture (card numbers 7, 8, 13, 20-21). The cards are unnumbered and checklisted below in alphabetical order. The Doug Hannesson card has recently been confirmed. It apparently was pulled from the set before release and most copies destroyed. Because we have not yet confirmed one of these cards ever actually appearing in a team set, we no longer recognize it as part of the complete set.

COMPLETE SET (23) 25.00 50.00
1 Steve Bayliss .20 .50
2 Ray Benik .20 .50
3 Rich Chernomaz .40 1.00
4 Geoff Courtnall 1.50 4.00
5 Russ Courtnall 2.50 6.00
6 Paul Cyr .40 1.00
7 Curt Fraser .60 1.50
8 Grant Fuhr 10.00 25.00
9 Shawn Green .20 .50
10 Fabian Joseph .40 1.00
11 Stu Kulak .40 1.00
12 Brenn Leach .20 .50
13 Gary Lupul .20 .50
14 Jack MacKeigan .20 .50
15 Dave Mackey .40 1.00
16 Mark McLeary .20 .50
17 Dan Moberg .20 .50
18 John Mokosak .20 .50
19 Mark Morrison .20 .50
20 Brad Palmer .40 1.00
21 Barry Pederson .75 2.00
22 Eric Thurston .20 .50
23 Ron Viglasi .20 .50
24 Doug Hannesson 10.00 25.00

1983-84 Victoria Cougars

Featuring current and past players, this 24-card set was sponsored by the West Coast Savings Credit Union, CFAX 1070 Radio, and the Greater Victoria Police Departments. The cards measure approximately 3" by 5" and feature color player portraits with red and blue borders on a white card face. The player's name, position, and biographical information appear at the bottom. Past player cards have the words "Graduation Series" stamped in the lower right corner of the picture (card number 2 and 20). The cards are unnumbered and checklisted below in alphabetical order.

COMPLETE SET (24) 8.00 20.00
1 Misko Antisin .40 1.00
2 Murray Bannerman .75 2.00
3 Steve Baylis .20 .50
4 Paul Bifano .20 .50
5 Russ Courtnall 2.00 5.00
6 Greg Davies .20 .50
7 Dean Drozdiak .20 .50
8 Jim Gunn .20 .50
9 Richard Hajdu .20 .50
10 Randy Hansch .40 1.00
11 Matt Hervey .20 .50
12 Fabian Joseph .40 1.00
13 Rob Kivell .20 .50
14 Brenn Leach .20 .50
15 Jack Mackeigan .20 .50
16 Dave Mackey .20 .50
17 Tom Martin .20 .50
18 Darren Moren .30 .75
19 Adam Morrison .20 .50
20 Gord Roberts .20 .50
21 Dan Sexton .20 .50
22 Randy Siska .20 .50
23 Eric Thurston .20 .50
24 Simon Wheeldon .40 1.00

1984-85 Victoria Cougars

Featuring current and past players, this 24-card set was sponsored by the West Coast Savings Credit Union, CFAX 1070 Radio, and the Greater Victoria Police Departments. The cards measure approximately 3" by 5" and feature color player portraits with red and blue borders on a white card face. The player's name, position, and biographical information appear at the bottom. Past player cards have the words "Graduation Series" stamped in the lower right corner of the picture (card numbers 6 and 20). The cards are unnumbered and checklisted below in alphabetical order.

COMPLETE SET (24) 6.00 15.00
1 Misko Antisin .30 .75
2 Greg Batters .20 .50
3 Mel Bridgman .60 1.50
4 Chris Calverley .20 .50
5 Darin Choquette .20 .50
6 Geoff Courtnall .75 2.00
7 Russ Courtnall 1.25 3.00
8 Rick Davidson .20 .50
9 Bill Gregoire .20 .50
10 Richard Hajdu .30 .75
11 Randy Hansch .30 .75
12 Rob Kivell .20 .50
13 Brad Melin .20 .50
14 Jim Mentis .20 .50
15 Adam Morrison .20 .50
16 Mark Morrison .20 .50
17 Kodie Nelson .20 .50
18 Ken Priestlay .30 .75
19 Bruce Pritchard .20 .50
20 Torrie Robertson .40 1.00
21 Trevor Semeniuk .20 .50
22 Dan Sexton .20 .50
23 Randy Siska .20 .50
24 Chris Tarnowski .20 .50

1989-90 Victoria Cougars

Sponsored by Safeway and Romeo's, this 21-card set measures approximately 2 3/4" by 4" and was sponsored by Flynn Printing and other area businesses. The cards feature color, posed action player photos with rounded corners on a yellow card face. The lower right corner of the picture is cut off and the words "Keeper Card" are written diagonally. The cards are unnumbered and checklisted below in alphabetical order.

COMPLETE SET (21) 4.00 10.00
1 John Badduke .20 .50
2 Terry Bendera .20 .50
3 Trevor Buchanan .20 .50
4 Jaret Burgoyne .30 .75
5 Dino Caputo .20 .50
6 Chris Catellier .20 .50
7 Mark Cipriano .20 .50
8 Milan Drag .20 .50
9 Dean Dyer .20 .50
10 Shayne Green .20 .50
11 Ryan Harrison .20 .50
12 Corey Jones .30 .75
13 Terry Klapstein .20 .50
14 Jason Knox .20 .50
15 Curtis Nykyforuk .20 .50
16 Jason Peters .20 .50
17 Blair Scott .20 .50
18 Mike Seaton .20 .50
19 Rob Sumner .20 .50
20 Larry Woo .20 .50
21 Jarret Zukiwsky .20 .50

2014-15 Victoria Royals

COMPLETE SET () 6.00 15.00
1 Axel Blomqvist .30 .75
2 Travis Brown .30 .75
3 Austin Carroll .30 .75
4 Greg Chase .30 .75
5 Taylor Crunk .30 .75
6 Jared Dmytriw .30 .75
7 Logan Fisher .30 .75
8 Brandon Fushimi .30 .75
9 Ryan Gagnon .30 .75
10 Dante Hannoun .30 .75
11 Joe Hicketts .30 .75
12 Marsel Ibragimov .30 .75
13 Ralph Jarratt .30 .75
14 Brandon Magee .30 .75
15 Regan Nagy .30 .75
16 Jack Palmer .30 .75
17 Chaz Reddekopp .30 .75
18 Jayden Sittler .30 .75
19 Mitch Skapski .30 .75
20 Evan Smith .30 .75
21 Tyler Soy .30 .75
22 Coleman Vollrath .30 .75
23 Jack Walker .30 .75
24 Marty the Marmot MASCOT .30 .75

2015-16 Victoria Royals

COMPLETE SET (24) 6.00 15.00
1 Keith Anderson .30 .75
2 Vladimir Bobylev .30 .75
3 Jared Dmytriw .30 .75
4 Matt Dykstra .30 .75
5 Logan Fisher .30 .75
6 Alex Forsberg .40 1.00
7 Ryan Gagnon .30 .75
8 Dante Hannoun .30 .75
9 Joe Hicketts .30 .75
10 Marsel Ibragimov .30 .75
11 Ralph Jarratt .30 .75
12 Regan Nagy .30 .75
13 Griffen Outhouse .30 .75
14 Brayden Pachel .30 .75
15 Ryan Peckford .30 .75
16 Matthew Phillips .30 .75
17 Ethan Price .30 .75
18 Chaz Reddekopp .30 .75
19 Tyler Soy .30 .75
20 Tyler Thompson .30 .75
21 Coleman Vollrath .30 .75
22 Scott Walford .30 .75
23 Jack Walker .30 .75
24 Jordan Wharrie .30 .75

2000-01 Victoriaville Tigres

This set features les Tigres of the QMJHL. The set was produced by CTM-Ste-Foy and was sold by that card shop, as well as by the team.

COMPLETE SET (24) 4.80 12.00
1 James Sanford .20 .50
2 Carl Mallette .30 .75
3 Matthew Lombardi .20 .50
4 Teddy Kyres .20 .50
5 Martin Autotte .20 .50
6 Simon St-Pierre .20 .50
7 Pierre-Luc Daneau .20 .50
8 Antoine Vermette .40 1.00
9 Marc-Andre Thinel .40 1.00
10 Mathieu Wathier .20 .50
11 Pierre-Luc Sleigher .20 .50
12 Sandro Sbrocca .20 .50
13 Jonathan Fauteux .20 .50
14 Sergei Kaltygen .20 .50
15 Adam Wojcik .20 .50
16 Jean-Francois Nogues .30 .75
17 Richard Paul .20 .50
18 David Masse .20 .50
19 Luc Levesque .20 .50
20 Mathieu Brunelle .20 .50
21 Sebastien Morissette .20 .50
22 Sebastien Thinel .20 .50
23 Danny Groulx .20 .50
24 Mario Durocher CO .10 .25

2000-01 Victoriaville Tigres Signed

This set is exactly the same as the base Tigres set from this season, save that every card has been hand signed by the player pictured. Each card also is serial numbered out of just 100.

COMPLETE SET (24) 20.00 50.00
1 James Sanford .80 2.00
2 Carl Mallette 1.20 3.00
3 Matthew Lombardi .80 2.00
4 Teddy Kyres .80 2.00
5 Martin Autotte .80 2.00
6 Simon St-Pierre .80 2.00
7 Pierre-Luc Daneau .80 2.00
8 Antoine Vermette 2.00 5.00
9 Marc-Andre Thinel 2.00 5.00
10 Mathieu Wathier .80 2.00
11 Pierre-Luc Sleigher .80 2.00
12 Sandro Sbrocca .80 2.00
13 Jonathan Fauteux .80 2.00
14 Sergei Kaltygen .80 2.00
15 Adam Wojcik .80 2.00
16 Jean-Francois Nogues 1.20 3.00
17 Richard Paul .80 2.00
18 David Masse .80 2.00
19 Luc Levesque .80 2.00
20 Mathieu Brunelle .80 2.00
21 Sebastien Morissette .80 2.00
22 Sebastien Thinel .80 2.00
23 Danny Groulx .80 2.00
24 Mario Durocher CO .80 2.00

2003-04 Victoriaville Tigres

COMPLETE SET (29) 6.00 15.00
1 Matthew Augustine .20 .50
2 Justin Belanger .20 .50
3 Gabriel Boies .20 .50
4 Francis Charland .20 .50
5 Renaud Des Alliers .20 .50
6 Benoit Doucet .20 .50
7 Kyle Doucet .20 .50
8 Jeremy Duchesne .30 .75
9 Cole Fetzner .20 .50
10 Benoit Fournier .20 .50
11 Guillaume Fournier .20 .50
12 Scott Gibson .20 .50
13 Ryan Jenner .20 .50
14 Martin Kasik .20 .50
15 Arthur Kiyaga .20 .50
16 Tommy Lafontaine .20 .50
17 Christian Laroche .20 .50
18 Daniel Manzato .30 .75
19 Olivier Plouffe .20 .50
20 Michael Ramsay .20 .50
21 Robin Richards .20 .50
22 Jonathan Ryan .20 .50
23 Mario Scalzo .40 1.00
24 Daniel Sparre .20 .50
25 Simon St-Pierre .20 .50
26 Josh Tordjman .60 1.50
27 Guillaume Trudel .20 .50
NNO Francis Charland TL .20 .50
NNO Mario Scalzo TL .20 .50

2004-05 Victoriaville Tigres

A total of 350 team sets were produced.

COMPLETE SET (30) 6.00 15.00
1 Maxim Noreau .20 .50
2 Jeremy Duchesne .20 .50
3 Justin Belanger .20 .50
4 Jan Danecek .20 .50
5 Gabriel Boies .20 .50
6 Pierre-Olivier Dupere .20 .50
7 Danny Hollet .20 .50
0 Alexandre Imbeault .20 .50
9 Josh Tordjman .60 1.50
10 Jason Legault .20 .50
11 Tommy Lafontaine .20 .50
12 Bruce Noivo .20 .50
13 Mike Ramsay .20 .50
14 Arthur Kiyaga .20 .50
15 Matt Nickerson .40 1.00
16 Renaud Des Alliers .20 .50
17 Mario Scalzo Jr .40 1.00
18 Samuel Hounsell .20 .50
19 Benoit Doucet .20 .50
20 Francis Guerette-Charland .20 .50
21 Kyle Doucet .20 .50
22 Trevor Mock .20 .50
23 Erick Lizon .20 .50
24 Ryan Jenner .20 .50
25 Maxime Desruisseaux .20 .50
26 Brant Miller .20 .50
27 Nicolas Laplante .20 .50
28 Gabriel Houde-Brisson .20 .50
29 Toby Lafrance .20 .50
30 Alexandre Vachon .20 .50

2005-06 Victoriaville Tigres

COMPLETE SET (22) 6.00 15.00
1 Keven Guerette-Charland .30 .75
2 Jason Legault .30 .75
3 Ryan Jenner .30 .75
4 Benoit Doucet .30 .75
5 Josh Tordjman .60 1.50
6 Benoit Massicotte .30 .75
7 Toby Lafrance .30 .75
8 Gabriel Boies .30 .75
9 Jan Danecek .30 .75
10 Renaud Des Alliers .30 .75
11 Philippe Brisebois .30 .75
12 Alexandre Imbeault .30 .75
13 Maxim Noreau .30 .75
14 Brant Miller .60 1.50
15 Carl Chamberland .30 .75
16 Pierre-Olivier Duperre .30 .75
17 Matthew David .30 .75
18 Erick Lizon .30 .75
19 Trevor Mock .30 .75
20 Francis Guerette-Charland .30 .75
21 Adam Ross .30 .75
22 Stephan Lebeau .30 .75

2006-07 Victoriaville Tigres

COMPLETE SET (24) 5.00 12.00
1 Morten Madsen .40 1.00
2 Keven Veilleux .40 1.00
3 Jean-Christophe Blanchard .20 .50
4 Kevin Poulin .20 .50
5 Maxim Noreau .20 .50
6 Carl Chamberland .20 .50
7 Erick Tremblay .20 .50
8 Jan Kolarik .20 .50
9 Sansdrick Lavoie .20 .50
10 Dave Nolin .20 .50
11 Maxime Robichaud .20 .50
12 Jason Demers .20 .50
13 Jason Legault .20 .50
14 David Foucher .20 .50
15 Keven Guerette-Charland .20 .50
16 Dany Roch .20 .50
17 Adam Ross .20 .50
18 Vincent Zaore-Vanie .20 .50
19 Philippe-Michael Devos .20 .50
20 Kyle Kelly .20 .50
21 Kyle Mcneil .20 .50
22 Benoit Doucet .20 .50
23 Francis Guerette-Charland .20 .50
24 Toby Lafrance .20 .50

1993-94 Waterloo Black Hawks

This 27-card standard-size set features the Waterloo Black Hawks of the USHL. The fronts feature color action player photos, with the team name and logo in a red border above the photo, and the player's name, number, and position beneath it. The cards are unnumbered and checklisted below in alphabetical order.

COMPLETE SET (27) 3.60 9.00
1 Brent Bessey .15 .40
2 Jason Blake .30 .75
3 Scott Brand GM .02 .10
4 Eric Brown .15 .40
5 Rod Butler .15 .40
6 Chris Coakley .15 .40
7 Austin Crawford .15 .40
8 Doug Dietz ACO .02 .10
9 Jon Garver .15 .40
10 Brian Folden .15 .40
11 Bobby Hayes .15 .40
12 Jake Jacoby .15 .40
13 Terry Jarkowsky .15 .40
14 Jeff Kozakowski UER .15 .40
(Misspelled
Kozakowski on fr
15 Josh Lampman .15 .40
16 Marty Laurila .15 .40
17 Steve McCall ANN .02 .10
18 Bill McNelis .15 .40
19 Rich Metro .15 .40
20 Scott Mikesch CO .02 .10
21 Barry Soskin PR .02 .10
22 Ben Stadey .15 .40
23 Ed Stanek .15 .40
24 Todd Steinmetz .15 .40
25 Scott Swanjord .20 .50
26 Miles Van Tassel .15 .40
27 Supporting Staff .02 .10
Dave Christians
Mike Christians

1995-96 Waterloo Black Hawks

COMPLETE SET (26) 25.00 50.00
1 Jayme Adduono 1.00 2.50
2 Chris Cerrella 1.00 2.50
3 Mark Eaton 1.25 3.00
4 Jason Furness 1.00 2.50
5 Joe Gray UER .08 .25
6 Zach Ham 1.00 2.50
7 Trevor Hanger 1.00 2.50
8 Kris Harris 1.00 2.50
9 Steve Holeczy 1.00 2.50
10 Lubos Krajcovic 1.00 2.50
11 Jeff Melnechuk 1.00 2.50
12 Jimmy Mroz 1.00 2.50
13 Bobby Owen 1.00 2.50
14 Anthony Perardi 1.00 2.50
15 Chad Poliquin 1.00 2.50
16 Dan Ragusett 1.00 2.50
17 Ryan Rentz 1.00 2.50
18 Ryan Sarazin 1.00 2.50
19 Doug Schmidt 1.00 2.50
20 Andrew Tortorella 1.00 2.50
21 Roger Trudeau 1.00 2.50
22 Mark Wilkinson 1.00 2.50
23 Scott Mikesch CO• .08 .25
24 Barry Soskin Owner .08 .25
25 Scott Brand GM .08 .25
26 Jason Shaver PR .08 .25

2003-04 Waterloo Black Hawks

Team-issued set features the Blackhawks of the USHL. The checklist below may not be complete. The cards are unnumbered. Checklist courtesy of collector Vinnie Montalbano.

COMPLETE SET (21) 8.00 20.00
1 Joel Hanson .40 1.00
2 Joe Pavelski 4.00 10.00
3 Matt Fornataro .40 1.00
4 Kevin Regan .75 2.00
5 Garrett Regan .40 1.00
6 Zach Bearson .40 1.00
7 Dan Sturges .40 1.00
8 Tim Filangieri .40 1.00
9 Mike Radja .40 1.00
10 Michael Annett .40 1.00
11 Andrew Thomas .40 1.00
12 Aaron Johnson .75 2.00
13 John Vadnais .40 1.00
14 Jesse Vesel .40 1.00
15 Jake Schwan .40 1.00
16 Josh Duncan .40 1.00
17 Jon-Paul Testwuide .40 1.00
18 Mike Dagenais .40 1.00
19 Dustin Molle .40 1.00
20 David Meckler .40 1.00
21 Peter MacArthur .40 1.00

2005-06 Waterloo Black Hawks

COMPLETE SET (30) 6.00 15.00
1 Ricky Akkerman .20 .50
2 Matt Arhontas .20 .50
3 Zach Bearson .20 .50
4 Eric Bennett .20 .50
5 Andy Bohmbach .20 .50
6 Mike Borisnok .20 .50
7 Cody Chupp .20 .50
8 Kurt Davis .20 .50
9 Drew Dobson .20 .50
10 Tim Gilbert .20 .50
11 Joe Grossman .20 .50
12 Brad Hoelzer .20 .50
13 Christian Jensen .20 .50
14 Vincent LeVerde .20 .50
15 James Marcou .20 .50
16 Clark Oliver .20 .50
17 Kyle Reeds .20 .50
18 Mitch Ryan .40 1.00
19 Pasko Skarica .20 .50
20 Joe Sova .20 .50
21 Jeremy Tejchma .20 .50
22 Mike Testwuide .20 .50
23 Isak Tranvik .20 .50
24 Kenny Wochele .40 1.00
25 P K O'Handley CO .20 .50
26 Chris Tok ACO .20 .50
27 Zac Headrick ACO .20 .50
28 Derrick Johnson ACO .20 .50
29 Dave Graham EQM .20 .50
30 Todd Klein TR .20 .50

2014-15 Waterloo Black Hawks

COMPLETE SET (25) 6.00 15.00
1 Philip Beaulieu .30 .75
2 Kris Carlson .30 .75
3 Max Coatta .30 .75
4 Jeremy Davies .30 .75
5 Marcel Godbout .30 .75
6 Niko Hildenbrand .30 .75
7 Steve Howard Asst. CO .30 .75
8 Larry Jungwirth .30 .75
9 Craig Laue Announ. .30 .75
10 Hayden Lavigne .30 .75
11 Sean MacTavish .30 .75
12 Alec McCrea .30 .75
13 Tyson McLellan .30 .75
14 George Mika .30 .75
15 P.K. O'Handley CO .30 .75
16 Nick Olczyk .30 .75
17 Rem Pitlick .30 .75
18 Alex Robert .30 .75
19 Henrik Rommel .30 .75
20 Sam Rossini .30 .75
21 Brendan Shane .30 .75
22 Hayden Shaw .30 .75
23 Tyler Sheehy .30 .75
24 John Wiitala .30 .75
25 Waterloo Black Hawks Champs .30 .75

1992-93 Western Michigan Broncos

These 30 standard-size cards feature color player photos on their fronts, some are action shots, others are posed. These photos are borderless on the sides. The player's name and position appear in a brown bar upon a yellow stripe across the bottom. His uniform number appears within a brown stripe across the top. The cards are unnumbered and checklisted below in alphabetical order.

COMPLETE SET (30) 4.80 12.00
1 Chris Belanger .20 .50
2 Joe Bonnett .15 .40
3 Brent Brekke .20 .50
4 Chris Brooks .15 .40
5 Craig Brown .15 .40
6 Jeremy Brown .15 .40
7 Tom Carriere .15 .40
8 Scott Chartier .20 .50
9 Ryan D'Arcy .15 .40
10 Pat Ferschweiler .15 .40
11 Brian Gallentine .15 .40
12 Jim Holman .15 .40
13 Derek Innanen .15 .40
14 Jason Jennings .20 .50
15 Mikhail Lapin .20 .50
16 Francois Leroux .20 .50
17 Jamal Mayers .60 1.50
18 Kevin McCaffrey ACO .02 .10
19 Dave Mitchell .15 .40
20 Brian Renfrew .15 .40
21 Mike Schafer ACO .02 .10
22 Derek Schooley .15 .40
23 Neil Smith .20 .50
WMU Hall of Fame
24 Colin Ward .15 .40
25 Dave Weaver .15 .40
26 Mike Whitton .15 .40
27 Bill Wilkinson CO .02 .10
28 Peter Wilkinson .15 .40
29 Byron Witkowski .15 .40
30 Lawson Arena .02 .10

1993-94 Western Michigan Broncos

These 30 standard-size cards feature color player photos on their fronts, some are action shots, others are posed. These photos are borderless on three sides. The player's name and uniform number appear vertically in the brown left margin. The cards are unnumbered and checklisted below in alphabetical order.

COMPLETE SET (30) 6.00 15.00
1 David Agnew .20 .50
2 Brent Brekke .30 .75
3 Chris Brooks .20 .50
4 Craig Brown .20 .50
5 Jeremy Brown .20 .50
6 Justin Cardwell .20 .50
7 Tom Carriere .20 .50
8 Tony Code .20 .50
9 Matt Cressman .20 .50
10 Jim Culhane ACO .02 .10
11 Ryan D'Arcy .20 .50
12 Brian Gallentine .20 .50
13 Matt Greene .20 .50
14 Rob Hodge .20 .50
WMU Hall of Fame
15 Jim Holman .20 .50
16 Derek Innanen .20 .50
17 Mark Jodoin .20 .50
18 Brendan Kenny .20 .50
19 Misha Lapin .20 .50
20 Darren Maloney .20 .50
21 Jamal Mayers .75 2.00
22 Dave Mitchell .20 .50
23 Brian Renfrew .20 .50
24 Mike Schafer ACO .02 .10
25 Derek Schooley .20 .50
26 Colin Ward .20 .50
27 Mike Whitton .20 .50
28 Bill Wilkinson CO .02 .10
29 Peter Wilkinson .20 .50
30 Shawn Zimmerman .20 .50

2001-02 Western Michigan Broncos

This set features the Broncos of the NCAA. Little is known about the set and its distribution, or even if the checklist is complete. If you have any additional information, please forward it to hockeymag@beckett.com.

COMPLETE SET (10) 4.00 10.00
1 Anthony Battaglia .40 1.00
2 Mike Bishai .40 1.00
3 Ryan Crane .40 1.00
4 Bryan Farquhar .40 1.00
5 Chad Kline .40 1.00
6 Austin Miller .40 1.00
7 Jeff Reynaert .40 1.00
8 Wayne Gagne ATG .40 1.00
9 Harry Lawson CO .40 1.00
10 Team Photo .40 1.00

2006-07 Westside Warriors

COMPLETE SET (21) 6.00 15.00
1 The General MASCOT .02 .10
2 Mark Howell CO .02 .10
3 Stephen Caple .30 .75
4 Eric Fraser .30 .75
5 Brock Meadows .30 .75
6 Joel Wozniakoski .30 .75
7 Chris Santiago .30 .75
8 Denis Semenov .30 .75
9 Craig Eisenhut .30 .75
10 Kevin Walrod .30 .75
11 Tommy Grant .30 .75
12 Micah Anderson .30 .75
13 Chris Vassos .30 .75
14 Ron Kelly .30 .75
15 Brad Plumton .30 .75
16 Trevor Bailey .30 .75
17 Brendan Ellis .30 .75
18 August Aiken .30 .75
19 Konrad Becker .30 .75
20 Bryce Kakoske .30 .75
21 Sam Huston .30 .75
22 Milrod Kos .30 .75
23 Marcel Bruinsma .30 .75
24 Mark Howell CO .02 .10

1996-97 Wheeling Nailers

This 23-card set of the Wheeling Nailers of the ECHL was produced by Split Second. The cards feature action photography on the front, along with the player's name and number and the team logo. The backs have a brief stats package, along with a larger interpretation of the player's number. As these cards are unnumbered otherwise, they are listed alphabetically below.

COMPLETE SET (23) 3.00 8.00
1 Scotty Allegrino TR .02 .10
2 John Badduke .20 .50
3 Frederic Barbeau .15 .40
4 John Blessman .15 .40
5 Francois Bouillon .15 .40
6 Greg Callahan .15 .40
7 Don Chase .15 .40
8 Jason Clark .15 .40
9 Keli Corpse .15 .40
10 Chad Dameworth .15 .40
11 Ryan Haggerty .20 .50
12 Martin LePage .15 .40
13 Ian McIntyre .15 .40
14 Greg McLean .15 .40
15 Mike Minard .20 .50
16 Perry Pappas .15 .40
17 Eric Royal .15 .40
18 Brad Symes .15 .40
19 John Tanner .20 .50
20 Rob Trumbley .15 .40
21 John Varga .30 .75
22 Tom McVie CO .15 .40
23 Spike Mascot .02 .10

1997-98 Wheeling Nailers

This 25-card set was given out at games as a sheet of perforated cards in a photo pack. The cards measure 2x3". The set was sponsored by TV-WTOV, Nickles, and Undo's. The cards are listed in the order they appear on the sheet.

COMPLETE SET (25) 3.00 8.00
1 J.F. Boutin .15 .40
2 Chris Jensen .15 .40
3 Dan Jablonic .15 .40
4 Dmitri Tarabrin .15 .40
5 Matt Garzone .15 .40
6 Jeremy Brown .15 .40
7 Joe Harney .15 .40
8 Scott Kirton .15 .40
9 Patrick Charbonneau .15 .40
10 Matt Van Horlick .15 .40
11 Mike Latendresse .20 .50
12 Karl Infanger .15 .40
13 Olie Sundstrom .20 .50
14 Stefan Brannare .15 .40
15 Fredrik Svensson .15 .40
16 Marquis Mathieu .30 .75
17 Sergei Radchenko .20 .50
18 Alex Matvichuk .15 .40
19 Kurt Brown .15 .40
20 Quinten Van Horlick .15 .40
21 Nailers Logo .02 .10
22 Swaze Armstrong TR .02 .10
23 Vinny Ferraiuolo EM .02 .10
24 Spike Mascot .02 .10
25 Peter Laviolette HCO .20 .50

1997-98 Wheeling Nailers Photo Pack

This 25-card set measures 2 1/8" X 3 1/8". It was a game-night giveaway sponsored by Nickles Bread. The set is attached as a single sheet. The set is not numbered so the cards appear in sheet order.

COMPLETE SET (25) 4.80 12.00
1 J.F. Boutin .20 .50
2 Chris Jensen .20 .50
3 Dan Jablonic .20 .50
4 Dmitri Tarabrin .30 .75
5 Matt Garzone .20 .50
6 Jeremy Brown .20 .50
7 Joe Harney .20 .50
8 Scott Kirton .20 .50
9 Patrick Charbonneau .20 .50
10 Matt Van Horlick .20 .50
11 Mike Latendresse .30 .75
12 Karl Infanger .20 .50
13 Olie Sundstrom .30 .75
14 Stefane Brannare .20 .50
15 Fredrik Svensson .20 .50
16 Marquis Mathieu .40 1.00
17 Sergei Radchenko .30 .75
18 Alex Matvichuk .20 .50
19 Kurt Brown .20 .50
20 Quinten Van Horlick .20 .50
21 Nailers History Card .02 .10
22 Swaze Armstrong TR .02 .10
23 Vinny Ferraiuolo MGR .02 .10
24 Spike Mascot .02 .10
25 Peter Laviolette HCO .20 .50

2003-04 Wheeling Nailers

COMPLETE SET (16) 8.00 20.00
81 Nick Boucher .75 2.00
82 Steven Crampton .50 1.25
83 Jean-Francois Dufour .50 1.25
84 Drew Fata .60 1.50
85 Brendon Hodge .50 1.25
86 Jason Jaffray .50 1.25
87 Mark Kosick .50 1.25
88 Kamil Kuriplach .50 1.25
89 Mario Larocque .50 1.25
90 Brad Mehalko .50 1.25
91 Jake Ortmeyer .50 1.25
92 Eduard Pershin .50 1.25
93 T.J. Reynolds .75 2.00
94 Alexandre Rouleau .50 1.25
95 Bogdan Rudenko .50 1.25
96 J.C. Ruid .50 1.25

2004-05 Wheeling Nailers Riesbeck's

This set was available with a minimum food purchase at Riesbeck's Food Market in Wheeling.

COMPLETE SET (20) 8.00 20.00
1 Team Card .20 .50
2 Alexandre Rouleau .40 1.00
3 Armands Berzins .40 1.00
4 Team Staff .20 .50
5 Cam Paddock .40 1.00
6 Cliff Loya .40 1.00
7 Curtiss Patrick .40 1.00
8 Dany Sabourin 1.25 3.00
9 Ed McGrane .40 1.00
10 Evgeny Lazarev .40 1.00
11 Brendon Hodge .40 1.00
12 James Laux .40 1.00
13 Joe Exter .40 1.00
14 Kenny Corupe .75 2.00
15 Pascal Morency .40 1.00
16 Randy Perry .40 1.00
17 Ray DiLauro .40 1.00
18 Steve Crampton .40 1.00
19 Kraft Sponsor .04 .10
20 FritoLay Sponsor .04 .10

2014-15 Wheeling Nailers

COMPLETE SET (23) 6.00 15.00
1 Derek Army .30 .75
2 Shane Bakker .30 .75
3 Riley Brace .30 .75
4 Jarrett Burton .30 .75
5 Paul Cianfrini .30 .75
6 Morgan Ellis .30 .75
7 Tyler Fernandez .30 .75
8 Stefan Fournier .30 .75
9 David Gilbert .30 .75
10 Sahir Gill .30 .75
11 Eric Hartzell .30 .75
12 Chaz Johnson .30 .75
13 Nicholas Kugali .30 .75
14 Tristin Llewellyn .30 .75
15 David Makowski .30 .75
16 Patrick McGrath .30 .75
17 Frank Palazzese .30 .75
18 Mike Ratchuk .30 .75
19 Harrison Ruopp .30 .75
20 Clark Seymour .30 .75
21 Bobby Shea .30 .75
22 Shawn Skelly .30 .75
23 Zack Torquato .30 .75

1992-93 Wheeling Thunderbirds

This 24-card standard-size set features color, posed action player photos. The pictures are set on a gray card face with a red banner above the photo that contains the year and the manufacturer name (Those Guys Productions). The player's name, position, and team name are printed below the picture.

COMPLETE SET (24) 3.00 8.00
1 Title Card .02 .10
2 Claude Barthe .15 .40
3 Joel Blain .15 .40
4 Derek DeCosty .15 .40
5 Marc Deschamps .15 .40
6 Tom Dion .15 .40
7 Devin Edgerton .15 .40
8 Pete Heine .15 .40
9 Kim Maier .15 .40
10 Mike Millham .20 .50
11 Cory Paterson .15 .40
12 Trevor Pochipinski .15 .40
13 Tim Roberts .15 .40
14 Mark Rodgers .15 .40
15 Darren Schwartz .15 .40
16 Trevor Senn .15 .40
17 Tim Tisdale .15 .40
18 John Uniac .20 .50
19 Denny Magruder MG .02 .10
20 Chuck Greenwood .02 .10
Jim Smi
21 Larry Kish VP/MG .02 .10
22 Doug Sauter CO .02 .10
23 T-Bird (Mascot) .02 .10
24 Doug Bacon .15 .40

1993-94 Wheeling Thunderbirds

Minor league expert Ralph Slate reports that these cards were distributed in three different manners: Cards 1-21 were the standard team set, available all season long at home games. Cards PC1-PC4 were handed out as premiums at games. Cards UD1-UD10 comprise a late-season update set which was sold separately. The three are combined here for cataloguing purposes, but may be found on the market as separate entities.

COMPLETE SET (21) 10.00 25.00
1 Header Card CL .02 .10
2 Darren Schwartz .15 .40
3 Cory Paterson .15 .40
4 Derek DeCosty .15 .40
5 Jim Bermingham .15 .40
6 Brock Woods .15 .40
7 Tim Roberts .15 .40
8 Eric Raymond .15 .40
9 Brett Abel .15 .40
10 Sebastien Fortier .15 .40
11 John Johnson .15 .40
12 Brent Pope .15 .40
13 Marquis Mathieu .30 .75
14 Terry Virtue .20 .50
15 Vadim Slivchenko .20 .50
16 Clayton Gainer .15 .40
17 Sylvain LaPointe .15 .40
18 Doug Sauter CO .02 .10
19 Larry Kish VP GM .02 .10
20 Denny Magruder GM .02 .10
21 Bill Cordery ASST TR .02 .10
PC1 Wheeling Thunderbirds 2.00 5.00
PC2 Darren Schwartz 2.00 5.00
PC3 Tim Tisdale 2.00 5.00
PC4 Cory Paterson 2.00 5.00
UD1 Update Checklist .02 .10
UD2 Tim Tisdale .40 1.00
UD3 John Van Kessel .40 1.00
UD4 Rival Fullum .40 1.00
UD5 Steve Gibson .40 1.00
UD6 Dave Goucher .02 .10
Director of Communication
UD7 Gary Zearott .02 .10
Photographer
UD8 Darren Schwartz .02 .10
T-Bird Leader
UD9 Vadim Slivchenko .40 1.00
T-Bird Leader
UD10 Brock Woods .40 1.00
T-Bird Leader

1994-95 Wheeling Thunderbirds

This 25-card set of the Wheeling Thunderbirds of the ECHL was produced by Those Guys for the team. The set was available through the club at games. The stylish fronts featured a player photo, name, number and position, along with team logo.

COMPLETE SET (25) 2.00 5.00
1 Checklist .08 .25
2 Tim Tisdale .20 .50
3 Brock Woods .20 .50
4 Vadim Slivchenko .20 .50
5 Tim Roberts .20 .50
6 Derek DeCosty .20 .50
7 Steve Gibson .20 .50
8 Xavier Majic .25 .60
9 Peter Marek .20 .50
10 Greg Louder .20 .50
11 Gairin Smith .20 .50
12 Darren McAusland .20 .50
13 Brent Pope .08 .25
14 Dominic Fafard .08 .25
15 Pat Barton .08 .25
16 Patrick Labrecque .08 .25
17 Lorne Toews .08 .25
18 Scott Matusovich .08 .25
19 Louis Bernard .08 .25
20 Doug Sutter .08 .25
21 Scott Allegrino TR .08 .25
22 Bill Cordery .08 .25
23 Mark Landini .08 .25
PC1 Xavier Majic .30 .75
PC2 Vadim Slivchenko .30 .75

1995-96 Wheeling Thunderbirds

Sponsored by Nickles Bread, this 24-card set was produced by Zee Productions. The cards measure 2 1/8" X 3 1/8" and were released as part of a perforated sheet, with a large team photo at the top of the set.

COMPLETE SET (24) 4.00 10.00
1 Rob Trumbley .15 .40
2 Geoff Finch .15 .40
3 Samuel Groleau .15 .40
4 Keli Corpse .15 .40
5 Tomas Vokoun .60 1.50
6 Steve Gibson .15 .40
7 Eric Royal .15 .40
8 Brock Woods .15 .40
9 Derek Decosty .15 .40
10 Lorne Toews .15 .40
11 Gairin Smith .15 .40
12 Tony Prpic .20 .50
13 Brent Pope .15 .40
14 Martin Sychra .15 .40
15 Martin LePage .15 .40
16 John Blessman .15 .40
17 Louis Dumont .15 .40
18 Pat Barton .15 .40
19 Ron Wilson .15 .40
20 Martin Brochu .40 1.00
21 Tim Tisdale .15 .40
22 Larry Kish HCO .02 .10
23 Scott Allegrino TR .02 .10
24 T Bird Mascot .02 .10

1995-96 Wheeling Thunderbirds Series II

Sponsored by Nickles Bread, this 20-card set was produced by Zee Productions. The cards measure 2 1/8" X 3 1/8" and came attached with large photos of the two goalies Geoff Finch and Tomas Vokoun.

COMPLETE SET (20) 3.00 8.00
1 John Badduke .20 .50
2 Pat Barton .15 .40
3 John Blessman .15 .40
4 Keli Corpse .15 .40
5 Louis Dumont .15 .40
6 Geoff Finch .30 .75
7 Steve Gibson .15 .40
8 Samuel Groleau .15 .40
9 Martin LePage .15 .40
10 Kevin Lune .15 .40
11 Brent Pope .15 .40
12 Tim Roberts .15 .40
13 Eric Royal .15 .40
14 Gairin Smith .15 .40
15 Lorne Toews .15 .40
16 Tim Tisdale .15 .40
17 Rob Trumbley .15 .40
18 Tomas Vokoun .60 1.50
19 Ron Wilson .15 .40
20 Brock Woods .15 .40

1993-94 Wichita Thunder

As with all CHL sets issued this season, these are round cards approximately the size of a hockey puck. They come in a plastic container with the team logo on the front, and were sold by the team's booster club for about $5 per set.

COMPLETE SET (18) 3.00 8.00
1 Bob Berg .20 .50
2 Mark Bourgeois .20 .50
3 Steve Chelios .20 .50
4 Robert Desjardins .20 .50
5 Paul Dukovac .20 .50
6 Yannick Gosselin .20 .50
7 Ron Handy .20 .50
8 Jamie Hearn .20 .50
9 Roger Hunt .20 .50
10 Paul Jackson .20 .50
11 James Latos .20 .50
12 Greg Neish .20 .50
13 Brent Sapergia .20 .50
14 Darren Srochenski .20 .50
15 Stephane Venne .20 .50
16 Rob Weingartner .20 .50
17 Jack Williams .20 .50
18 Doug Shedden CO .07 .20

1998-99 Wichita Thunder

This 25-card set was given out at a game late in the season and then was sold at the merchandise stand.

COMPLETE SET (25) 4.80 12.00
1 Checklist .02 .10
2 Vernon Beardy .20 .50
3 Travis Clayton .20 .50
4 Chris Dashney .20 .50
5 Mike Donaghue .20 .50
6 Jason Duda .20 .50
7 Rhett Dudley .20 .50
8 Trevor Folk .20 .50
9 Todd Howarth .20 .50
10 John Kachur .20 .50
11 Mark Karpen .20 .50
12 Lance Leslie .30 .75
13 Brad Link .20 .50
14 Mark Macera .30 .75
15 Walker McDonald .20 .50
16 John McGeough .20 .50
17 Thomas Migdal .20 .50
18 Aaron Novak .20 .50
19 Sean O'Reilly .30 .75
20 Kevin Powell .20 .50
21 Greg Smith .30 .75
22 Travis Tipler .20 .50
23 Troy Yarosh .20 .50
24 Bryan Wells HCO .04 .10
25 Goodwrench Dealer Logo .04 .10

1999-00 Wichita Thunder

This set features the Thunder of the CHL. The cards feature full color fronts with name and position on the lower front of the card. Backs feature statistical and biographical information. The cards are unnumbered and checklisted below in alphabetical order.

COMPLETE SET (25) 4.00 10.00
1 Vern Beardy .15 .40
2 Travis Clayton .30 .75
3 Chris Dashney .15 .40
4 Mike Donaghue .15 .40
5 Jason Duda .15 .40
6 Rhett Dudley .15 .40
7 Trevor Folk .15 .40
8 Todd Howarth .15 .40
9 John Kachur .15 .40
10 Mark Karpen .15 .40
11 Lance Leslie .30 .75
12 Brad Link .15 .40
13 Mark Macera .15 .40
14 Walker McDonald .15 .40
15 Jim McGeough .15 .40
16 Thomas Migdal .15 .40
17 Aaron Novak .15 .40
18 Sean O'Reilly .15 .40
19 Kevin Powell .15 .40
20 Greg Smith .30 .75
21 Travis Tipler .15 .40
22 Troy Yarosh .15 .40
23 Bryan Wells .15 .40
24 Title Card .02 .10
25 Dealer Logo Card .02 .10

2000-01 Wichita Thunder

This set features the Thunder of the CHL. Little is known about the set beyond the confirmed checklist. Any additional information can be forwarded to hockeymag@beckett.com.

COMPLETE SET (22) 6.00 15.00
1 Jerod Bina .30 .75
2 Troy Caley .30 .75
3 Travis Clayton .30 .75
4 Trevor Converse .30 .75
5 Mike Donaghue .30 .75
6 Jason Duda .30 .75
7 Rhett Dudley .30 .75
8 Rocky Florio .30 .75
9 Trevor Folk .30 .75
10 Dwayne Gylywoychuk .30 .75
11 Derrek Harper .30 .75
12 Mike Hiebert .30 .75
13 Mark Karpen .30 .75
14 Lance Leslie .30 .75
15 Jim McGeough .30 .75
16 Aaron Novak .30 .75
17 Sean O'Reiley .30 .75
18 Kevin Powell .30 .75
19 Kris Schultz .30 .75
20 Greg Smith .30 .75
21 Mark Strohack .30 .75
22 Checklist .02 .10

2000-01 Wilkes-Barre Scranton Penguins

This set features the Penguins of the AHL. The set was produced by Choice Marketing and handed out as a game night promotion late in the season.

COMPLETE SET (28) 5.00 20.00
1 Dennis Bonvie .60 1.50
2 Brendan Buckley .30 .75
3 Sven Butenschon .30 .75
4 Sebastien Caron .60 1.50
5 Greg Crozier .40 1.00
6 Trent Cull .30 .75
7 Andrew Ference .40 1.00
8 Dylan Gyori .40 1.00
9 Chris Kelleher .30 .75
10 Tom Kostopoulos .40 1.00
11 Joel Laing .30 .75
12 Jim Leger .30 .75
13 Jason MacDonald .30 .75
14 Alexandre Mathieu .30 .75
15 Josef Melichar .30 .75
16 Eric Meloche .30 .75
17 Rich Parent .40 1.00
18 Glenn Patrick HCO .10 .25
19 Toby Petersen .40 1.00
20 John Slaney .30 .75
21 Martin Sonnenberg .30 .75
22 Jean-Philippe Soucy .40 1.00
23 Billy Tibbetts .60 1.50
24 Darcy Verot .30 .75
25 Mike Yeo ACO .02 .10
26 Alexander Zevakhin .30 .75
27 Tux MASCOT .02 .10
28 Checklist .02 .10

2001-02 Wilkes-Barre Scranton Penguins

This set features the Penguins of the AHL. The set was produced by Choice Marketing and was sold at home games.

COMPLETE SET (26) 4.80 12.00
1 Robbie Tallas .30 .75
2 Robert Scuderi .20 .50
3 David Koci .20 .50
4 Brooks Orpik .30 .75
5 Darcy Robinson .20 .50
6 Mike Wilson .20 .50
7 Darcy Verot .20 .50
8 Ross Lupaschuk .20 .50
9 Martin Sonnenberg .20 .50
10 Jan Fadrny .20 .50
11 Alexander Zevakhin .20 .50
12 Shane Endicott .40 1.00
13 Brendan Buckley .20 .50
14 Jason MacDonald .20 .50
15 Tomas Surovy .20 .50
16 Tom Kostopoulos .20 .50
17 Alexandre Mathieu .20 .50
18 Peter Ratchuk .20 .50
19 Sebastien Caron .30 .75
20 Steve Parsons .30 .75
21 Robert Dome .30 .75
22 Eric Meloche .30 .75
23 Glenn Patrick CO .04 .10
24 Mike Yeo ACO .04 .10
25 Tux MASCOT .04 .10
NNO Checklist .04 .10

2002-03 Wilkes-Barre Scranton Penguins

COMPLETE SET (27) 5.00 12.00
1 Rob Scuderi .40 1.00
2 Brooks Orpik .40 1.00
3 Darcy Robinson .20 .50
4 Mike Wilson .20 .50
5 Michel Ouellet .20 .50
6 Ross Lupaschuk .20 .50
7 Matt Hussey .20 .50
8 Milan Kraft .30 .75
9 Alexander Zevakhin .20 .50
10 Kris Beech .30 .75
11 Shane Endicott .20 .50
12 Toby Petersen .20 .50
13 Colby Armstrong .30 .75
14 Michal Sivek .20 .50
15 Matt Murley .20 .50
16 Brendan Buckley .20 .50
17 Jason MacDonald .20 .50
18 Tomas Surovy .20 .50
19 Francois Leroux .20 .50
20 Konstantin Koltsov .30 .75
21 Tom Kostopoulos .20 .50
22 Rob Tallas .20 .50
23 Sebastien Caron .30 .75
24 Eric Meloche .20 .50
25 Glen Patrick HCO .04 .10
26 Mike Yeo ACO .04 .10
NNO Checklist .04 .10

2003-04 Wilkes-Barre Scranton Penguins

This set was produced by Choice Marketing and sold at home games.

COMPLETE SET (30) 4.00 10.00
1 Checklist .04 .10
2 Colby Armstrong .30 .75
3 Jean-Sebastien Aubin .30 .75
4 Kris Beech .30 .75
5 Patrick Boileau .15 .40
6 Martin Brochu .30 .75
7 Brendan Buckley .15 .40
8 Andy Chiodo .60 1.50
9 Shane Endicott .15 .40
10 Drew Fata .15 .40
11 Matt Hussey .15 .40
12 David Koci .30 .75
13 Tom Kostopoulos .15 .40
14 Guillaume Lefebvre .15 .40
15 Ross Lupaschuk .15 .40
16 Marquis Mathieu .15 .40
17 Eric Meloche .15 .40
18 Matt Murley .15 .40
19 Michel Ouellet .15 .40
20 Toby Petersen .15 .40
21 Darcy Robinson .15 .40
22 Alexandre Rouleau .15 .40
23 Rob Scuderi .30 .75
24 Reid Simpson .15 .40
25 Michal Sivek .15 .40
26 Tomas Surovy .15 .40
27 Steve Webb .15 .40
28 Michel Therrien CO .04 .10
29 Mike Yeo ACO .04 .10
30 Mascot .04 .10

2004-05 Wilkes-Barre Scranton Penguins

COMPLETE SET (30) 6.00 15.00
1 Checklist .04 .10
2 Rob Scuderi .20 .50
3 David Koci .20 .50
4 Chris Kelleher .20 .50
5 Darcy Robinson .20 .50
6 Ryan Whitney .30 .75
7 Michel Ouellet .20 .50
8 Ross Lupaschuk .20 .50
9 Colby Armstrong .30 .75
10 Kris Beech .20 .50
11 Ben Eaves .20 .50
12 Shane Endicott .20 .50
13 Cam Paddock .20 .50
14 Erik Christensen .30 .75
15 Guillaume Lefebvre .20 .50
16 Ramzi Abid .20 .50
17 Mike Sgroi .20 .50
18 Maxime Talbot .30 .75
19 Matt Murley .20 .50
20 Tomas Surovy .20 .50
21 Drew Fata .20 .50
22 Matt Hussey .20 .50
23 Marc-Andre Fleury 1.00 2.50
24 Alain Nasreddine .20 .50
25 Dany Sabourin .40 1.00
26 Andy Chiodo .40 1.00
27 Tux MASCOT .04 .10
28 Michel Therrien CO .04 .10
29 Mike Yeo ACO .04 .10
30 Wachovia Arena .04 .10

2005-06 Wilkes-Barre Scranton Penguins

COMPLETE SET (29) 6.00 15.00
1 Colby Armstrong .40 1.00
2 Dennis Bonvie .40 1.00
3 Daniel Carcillo .20 .50
4 Sebastien Caron .40 1.00
5 Erik Christensen .40 1.00
6 Kenny Corupe .20 .50
7 Stephen Dixon .20 .50
8 Ben Eaves .20 .50
9 Rico Fata .20 .50
10 Daniel Fernholm .20 .50
11 Jon Filewich .20 .50
12 Marc-Andre Fleury .75 2.00
13 Matt Hussey .20 .50
14 Chris Kelleher .20 .50
15 David Koci .20 .50
16 Konstantin Koltsov .20 .50
17 Ryan Lannon .20 .50
18 Guillaume Lefebvre .20 .50
19 Arpad Mihaly .20 .50
20 Alain Nasredinne .20 .50
21 Michel Ouellet .40 1.00
22 Dany Sabourin .40 1.00
23 Andy Schneider .20 .50
24 Ryan Stone .20 .50
25 Tomas Surovy .20 .50
26 Noah Welch .20 .50
27 Ryan Whitney .40 1.00
28 Joe Mullen ACO .20 .50
29 Al Sims CO .07 .20

2006-07 Wilkes-Barre Scranton Penguins

COMPLETE SET (25) 5.00 12.00
1 Alain Nasreddine .30 .75
2 Alexei Mikhnov .20 .50
3 Andrew Penner .30 .75
4 Connor James .20 .50
5 Daniel Carcillo .30 .75
6 Dennis Bonvie .40 1.00
7 Erik Christensen .30 .75
8 Jeff Deslauriers .30 .75
9 Jon Filewich .30 .75
10 Kyle Brodziak .30 .75
11 Marc-Antoine Pouliot .30 .75
12 Matt Carkner .20 .50
13 Maxime Talbot .30 .75
14 Micki DuPont .20 .50
15 Noah Welch .30 .75
16 Rob Schremp .40 1.00
17 Ryan Lannon .20 .50
18 Ryan Stone .40 1.00
19 Stephen Dixon .20 .50
20 Tom Gilbert .20 .50
21 Tyler Kennedy .30 .75
22 Wade Skolney .20 .50
23 Dan Bylsma ACO .02 .10
24 Todd Richards CO .02 .10
NNO Checklist .01 .01

2006-07 Wilkes-Barre Scranton Penguins Jerseys

COMPLETE SET (22) 125.00 300.00
1 Jeff Deslauriers 8.00 20.00
2 Andrew Penner 8.00 20.00
3 Micki DuPont 6.00 15.00
4 Kyle Brodziak 6.00 15.00
5 Jon Filewich 6.00 15.00
6 Ryan Lannon 6.00 15.00
7 Connor James 6.00 15.00
8 Noah Welch 6.00 15.00
9 Tom Gilbert 6.00 15.00
10 Stephen Dixon 6.00 15.00
11 Tyler Kennedy 6.00 15.00
12 Daniel Carcillo 8.00 20.00
13 Dennis Bonvie 10.00 25.00
14 Tim Sesito 6.00 15.00
15 Erik Christensen 10.00 25.00
16 Maxime Talbot 10.00 25.00
17 Matt Carkner 6.00 15.00
18 Ryan Stone 10.00 25.00
19 Marc Antoine Pouliot 10.00 25.00
20 Wade Skolney 6.00 15.00
21 Alain Nasreddine 6.00 15.00
22 Rob Schremp 10.00 25.00

2007-08 Wilkes-Barre Scranton Penguins

COMPLETE SET (29) 10.00 20.00
1 Mark Ardelan .30 .75
2 Dennis Bonvie .60 1.50
3 Aaron Boogaard .40 1.00
4 Tim Brent .30 .75
5 Ty Conklin .40 1.00
6 John Curry .30 .75
7 Jon D'Aversa .30 .75
8 Deryk Engelland .30 .75
9 Jon Filewich .30 .75
10 Alex Goligoski .60 1.50
11 Ned Havern .40 1.00
12 Connor James .30 .75
13 Joe Jensen .30 .75
14 Tyler Kennedy .30 .75
15 Ryan Lannon .30 .75
16 Kris Letang .30 .75
17 Mark Letestu .30 .75
18 Ben Lovejoy .30 .75
19 Kurtis McLean .30 .75
20 Chris Minard .30 .75
21 Alain Nasreddine .30 .75
22 Nathan Smith .30 .75
23 Ryan Stone .30 .75
24 Jeff Taffe .30 .75
25 Tim Wallace .30 .75
26 Dan Bylsma ACO .02 .10
27 Todd Richards CO .02 .10
28 Tux MASCOT .02 .10
29 Team Photo .02 .10

2007-08 Wilkes-Barre Scranton Penguins Jersey Edition

1 Ryan Lannon 3.00 8.00
2 Deryk Engelland 3.00 8.00
3 Ben Lovejoy 3.00 8.00
4 Nathan Smith 3.00 8.00
5 Tim Brent 3.00 8.00
6 Connor James 3.00 8.00
7 Tyler Kennedy 4.00 10.00
8 Mark Ardelan 3.00 8.00
9 Alex Goligoski 5.00 12.00
10 Chris Minard 3.00 8.00
11 Joe Jensen 3.00 8.00
12 Kurtis McLean 3.00 8.00
13 Jon Filewich 3.00 8.00
14 Jeff Taffe 3.00 8.00
15 Ryan Stone 3.00 8.00
16 Tim Wallace 3.00 8.00
17 Dennis Bonvie 6.00 15.00
18 Alain Nasreddine 3.00 8.00
19 Ty Conklin 5.00 12.00
20 Karl Goehring 5.00 12.00
21 Kris Letang 5.00 12.00
27 Dennis Bonvie LE 8.00 20.00

2014-15 Wilkes-Barre Scranton Penguins

COMPLETE SET (25) 6.00 15.00
1 Josh Archibald .30 .75
2 Taylor Chorney .30 .75
3 Jean-Sebastien Dea .30 .75
4 Nick Drazenovic .30 .75
5 Brian Dumoulin .30 .75
6 Andrew Ebbett .30 .75
7 Bobby Farnham .30 .75
8 Barry Goers .30 .75
9 Scott Harrington .30 .75
10 Jayson Megna .30 .75
11 Tom Kostopoulos .30 .75
12 Tom Kuhnhackl .30 .75
13 Pierre-Luc Letourneau-Leblond .40 1.00
14 Reid McNeill .30 .75
15 Matt Murray .50 1.25
16 Adam Payerl .30 .75
17 Derrick Pouliot .40 1.00
18 Carter Rowney .30 .75
19 Bryan Rust .30 .75
20 Conor Sheary 2.00 5.00
21 Dominik Uher .30 .75
22 Scott Wilson .30 .75
23 Jeff Zatkoff .30 .75
24 Tux MASCOT .30 .75
CL Header Card CL .30 .75

2004-05 Williams Lake Timberwolves

Set from the BCJHL is noteworthy for the inclusion of the first card of Fabio Luongo, younger brother of NHL All-Star Roberto Luongo.

COMPLETE SET (28) 8.00 20.00
1 Andrew Braithwaite .40 1.00
2 Cody Brookwell .30 .75
3 Matt Crowell .30 .75
4 Bryce Dale .30 .75
5 Mark Ehl .30 .75
6 Kevin Galan .30 .75
7 Zach Gieszler .30 .75
8 Alex Greenlay .30 .75
9 Dustin Honing .30 .75
10 Dave Krisky .30 .75
11 Mike Leidl .30 .75
12 Fabio Luongo 1.25 3.00
13 Trent Manchur .30 .75
14 Tyler Mazzei .30 .75
15 Josh Murray .30 .75
16 Brad Reaney .30 .75
17 Les Reaney .40 1.00
18 Trever Turner .30 .75
19 Steve Van Oosten .30 .75
20 Duane Whitehead .30 .75
21 Shaun Witschen .30 .75
22 Josh Murray .30 .75
23 Dave Krisky .30 .75
24 Rick Pitta CO .04 .10
25 Peter Martin ACO .04 .10
26 Zamboni .04 .10
27 Action photo .04 .10
28 T.H. Wolf MASCOT .04 .10

1989-90 Windsor Spitfires

This 22-card standard-size set features members of the 1989-90 Windsor Spitfires of the Ontario Hockey league (OHL). The fronts feature posed shots of the players in front of their lockers. The cards are unnumbered and checklisted below in alphabetical order.

COMPLETE SET (22) 4.00 10.00
1 Sean Burns .20 .50
2 Glen Craig .20 .50
3 Brian Forestell .20 .50
4 Chris Fraser .20 .50
5 Trent Gleason .20 .50

6 Jon Hartley .20 .50
7 Ron Jones .20 .50
8 Bob Leeming .20 .50
9 Kevin MacKay .20 .50
10 Kevin McDougall .20 .50
11 Ryan Merritt .20 .50
12 David Myles .20 .50
13 Sean O'Hagan .30 .75
14 Mike Polano .20 .50
15 Jason Snow .20 .50
16 Brad Smith CO .30 .75
17 Jason Stos .20 .50
18 Jon Stos .20 .50
19 Jamie Vargo .20 .50
20 Trevor Walsh .20 .50
21 K.J. White .20 .50
22 Jason Zohl .20 .50

1992-93 Windsor Spitfires

Sponsored by the Devonshire Mall, these 31 cards measure approximately 2 5/8" by 3 5/8" and feature on their fronts posed-on-ice color shots of the 1992-93 Windsor Spitfires bordered in red, white, and blue. The player's name and the Spitfires logo appear in the white area above the photo.

COMPLETE SET (31) 4.80 12.00
1 Team Card .08 .25
Checklist
2 Mike Martin .15 .40
3 Luke Clowes .15 .40
4 Jason Haelzle .15 .40
5 Adam Graves 1.25 3.00
6 Craig Lutes .15 .40
7 David Pluck .15 .40
8 Colin Wilson .15 .40
9 Bill Bowler .30 .75
10 Ryan O'Neill .15 .40
11 Adam Young .15 .40
12 Gerrard Masse .15 .40
13 Daryl Lavoie .15 .40
14 Peter Allison .15 .40
15 Ernie Godden RET .15 .40
16 Brady Blain .15 .40
17 Todd Warriner .30 .75
18 Rick Marshall .15 .40
19 Craig Johnson .15 .40
20 Kelly Vipond .15 .40
21 Devy Bear MASCOT .02 .10
22 Stephen Webb .20 .50
23 Scott Miller RET .15 .40
24 Dennis Purdie .20 .50
25 Steve Gibson .15 .40
26 Mike Hartwick .15 .40
27 Shawn Heins .30 .75
28 David Benn .15 .40
29 Matt Mullin .20 .50
30 David Mitchell .15 .40
31 The Dynamic Duo .20 .50
Todd Wa

1993-94 Windsor Spitfires

Co-sponsored by Pizza Hut and radio station CKLW AM 800, and printed by Slapshot Images Ltd., this 27-card standard-size set features the 1993-94 Windsor Spitfires. On a geometrical team color-coded background, the fronts feature color action player photos with thin grey borders. The player's name, position and team name, as well as the producer's logo, also appear on the front.

COMPLETE SET (27) 4.80 12.00
1 Ed Jovanovski .75 2.00
2 Shawn Silver .20 .50
3 Travis Scott .20 .50
4 Mike Martin .20 .50
5 Daryl Lavoie .15 .40
6 Craig Lutes .15 .40
7 David Pluck .15 .40
8 Bill Bowler .20 .50
9 David Green .15 .40
10 Adam Young .15 .40
11 Mike Loach .15 .40
12 Brady Blain .15 .40
13 Shayne McCosh .15 .40
14 Rob Shearer .20 .50
15 Joel Poirier .15 .40
16 Cory Evans .15 .40
17 Vladimir Kretchine .15 .40
18 Dave Roche .20 .50
19 Ryan Stewart .15 .40
20 Dave Geris .15 .40
21 Dan West .15 .40
22 Luke Clowes .15 .40
23 John Cooper .15 .40
24 Akil Adams .15 .40
25 Sponsor Card .02 .10
Pizza Hut
26 Sponsor Card .02 .10
Steve Bell
NNO Slapshot Ad Card .02 .10

1994-95 Windsor Spitfires

Sponsored by Pizza Hut, Mr. Lube, CKLW AM 800, and printed by Slapshot Images Ltd., this 29-card set features the 1994-95 Windsor Spitfires. On a red and blue background, the fronts feature color player action photos with thin black borders. The player's name, position and team name, as well as the producer's logo, also appear on the front.

COMPLETE SET (29) 6.00 15.00
1 Checklist .04 .10
2 Jamie Storr .30 .75
3 Travis Scott .20 .50
4 Paul Beazley .15 .40
5 Mike Martin .15 .40
6 Chris Van Dyk .15 .40
7 Denis Smith .20 .50
8 Glenn Crawford .15 .40
9 David Pluck .15 .40
10 Bill Bowler .30 .75
11 David Green .15 .40
12 Adam Young .15 .40
13 Wes Ward .15 .40
14 Ed Jovanovski 1.25 3.00
15 Kevin Paden .15 .40
16 Rob Shearer .20 .50
17 Joel Poirier .15 .40
18 Cory Evans .15 .40
19 Vladimir Kretchine .15 .40
20 David Roche .20 .50
21 Rick Emmett .15 .40
22 David Goris .15 .40
23 Caleb Ward .15 .40
24 Luke Clowes .15 .40
25 John Cooper .15 .40
26 Tim Findlay .20 .50
27 Pizza Hut .10
28 Sponsor Card .04 .10
Steve Bell
NNO Ad Card .04 .10

1998-99 Windsor Spitfires

This set features the Spitfires of the OHL. It is believed that they were issued as part of a fire safety program, and may only have been available to school children. Additional information can be forwarded to us at hockeymag@beckett.com.

COMPLETE SET (9) 3.00 8.00
1 Fire Chief .04 .10
2 Coaches .04 .10
3 Duke MASCOT .04 .10
4 Michael Hanson .40 1.00
5 Jeff Kapitanchuk .40 1.00
6 Michael Leighton 1.25 3.00
7 Jason Polera .40 1.00
8 Blair Stayzer .75 2.00
9 Curtis Watson .40 1.00

2002-03 Windsor Spitfires

This oversized set was sold at Spitfires home games. The cards are unnumbered, but are listed in the order they were issued in (roughly by jersey number, with non-team members interspersed throughout.)

COMPLETE SET (30) 8.00 20.00
1 Title Card .04 .10
Checklist
2 Ryan Aschaber .40 1.00
3 Frank Rediker .40 1.00
4 David Lomas .15 .40
5 Iain McPhee .15 .40
6 Mitchell Maunu .60 1.50
7 Tim Gleason .75 2.00
8 Mike James .15 .40
9 David Bowman .15 .40
10 Chief of Police .04 .10
11 Jason Dixon .15 .40
12 Rob Honnigar .30 .75
13 Craig Kennedy .30 .75
14 Elmer Mascot .04 .10
15 Ahren Nittel .20 .50
17 Phil Gibson .15 .40
18 Ryan Donnally .30 .75
19 Paul Giallonardo .15 .40
20 Josh Gratton .15 .40
21 Alexander Shevchenko .15 .40
22 Darryl Lloyd .15 .40
23 Jeff Leavitt .15 .40
24 Duke Mascot .04 .10
25 Ryan Dickie .15 .40
26 Matt Anthony .15 .40
27 John-Scott Dickson .15 .40
28 Denis Khudyakov .40 1.00
29 Mike Self .15 .40
30 Kyle Wellwood .60 1.50
116 Cam Janssen .75 2.00

2007-08 Windsor Spitfires

This set includes two 2008 first rounders (Josh Bailey and Greg Nemisz) and likely top-10 pick in 2009, Taylor Hall.

COMPLETE SET (30) 3.00 10.00
1 Team Checklist .02 .10
2 Joshua Bailey 1.25 3.00
3 Ryan Baldwin .40 1.00
4 Marek Biro .40 1.00
5 Jesse Blacker .40 1.00
6 Matthew Bragg .40 1.00
7 Mark Cundari .40 1.00
8 Ryan Ellis .40 1.00
9 Andrew Engelage .60 1.50
10 Richard Greenop .40 1.00
11 Taylor Hall 1.50 4.00
12 Adam Henrique .40 1.00
13 Tom Kane .40 1.00
14 Greg Nemisz .60 1.50
15 Michal Neuvirth .75 2.00
16 Jordan Nolan .60 1.50
17 Blake Parlett .40 1.00
18 Elgin Reid .40 1.00
19 Mickey Renaud .75 2.00
20 Bradley Snetsinger .40 1.00
21 Eric Wellwood .40 1.00
22 Andrew Yogan .40 1.00
23 Harry Young .40 1.00
24 Bob Boughner PRES .10 .25
25 Warren Rychel VP/GM .10 .25
26 Bob Jones AC .02 .10
27 D.J. Smith AC .02 .10
28 Bomber Spitfire MASCOT .02 .10
29 Glenn Stannard CHIEF OF POLICE .02 .10
30 Elmer Windsor POLICE MASCOT .02 .10

2003-04 Wisconsin Badgers

Two cards from this set were handed out at Badger home games over the course of the 2003-04 season. The cards are unnumbered and thus are listed below in alphabetical order.

COMPLETE SET (30) 20.00 40.00
1 Dan Boeser .30 .75
2 Rene Bourque 1.50 4.00
3 Andy Brandt .75 2.00
4 Bernd Bruckler .60 1.50
5 Adam Burish .75 2.00
6 A.J. Degenhardt .30 .75
7 Jake Dowell .30 .75
8 Robbie Earl 1.25 3.00
9 John Eichelberger .30 .75
10 Brian Elliott .60 1.50
11 John Funk .30 .75
12 Brent Gibson .30 .75
13 Tom Gilbert 1.25 3.00
14 Mark Heatley .75 2.00
15 Andrew Joudrey .30 .75
16 Chris Julka .30 .75
17 Luke Kohtala .60 1.50
18 Jon Krall .30 .75
19 Nick Licari .30 .75
20 Jeff Likens .30 .75
21 Ryan MacMurchy .30 .75
22 Joey McElroy .30 .75
23 Matt Olinger .30 .75
24 Ken Rowe .30 .75
25 Tom Sawatske .30 .75
26 Ryan Suter 1.50 4.00
27 Pete Talafous .30 .75
28 Andy Wozniewski .60 1.50
29 Mike Eaves HCO .20 .50
30 Mascot .04 .10

2004-05 Wisconsin Badgers

Set was issued as a promotional giveaway at a home game. The cards are not numbered.

COMPLETE SET (28) 15.00 30.00
1 Brian Elliott .40 1.00
2 Matt Olinger .40 1.00
3 Matt Auffrey .40 1.00
4 Robbie Earl 1.25 3.00
5 Pete Talafous .40 1.00
6 Matt Ford .75 2.00
7 Davis Drewiske .40 1.00
8 Bernd Bruckler .75 2.00
9 Ken Rowe .40 1.00
10 Jeff Likens .40 1.00
11 John Funk .40 1.00
12 Andy Brandt .40 1.00
13 Jake Dowell .40 1.00
14 Kyle Klubertanz .40 1.00
15 Joe Pavelski .40 1.00
16 Mike Eaves CO .20 .50
17 Joe Piskula .40 1.00
18 Ryan MacMurchy .40 1.00
19 Ross Carlson .40 1.00
20 A.J. Degenhardt .40 1.00
21 Josh Engel .40 1.00
22 Tom Gilbert 1.25 3.00
23 Andrew Joudrey .40 1.00
24 Nick Licari .40 1.00
25 Jeff Slinde .40 1.00
26 Luke Kohtala .75 2.00
27 Mark Heatley .75 2.00
28 Adam Burish .75 2.00

2004-05 Wisconsin Badgers Women

Issued as a promotional giveaway.

COMPLETE SET (24) 10.00 25.00
1 Sara Bauer .40 1.00
2 Nikki Burish .40 1.00
3 Sharon Cole .40 1.00
4 Vicki Davis .40 1.00
5 Christine Dufour .40 1.00
6 Molly Engstrom .40 1.00
7 Jackie Friesen .40 1.00
8 Meghan Horras .40 1.00
9 Grace Hutchins .40 1.00
10 Mark Johnson CO .40 1.00
11 Cyndy Kenyon .40 1.00
12 Heidi Kletzien .40 1.00
13 Carla MacLeod .75 2.00
14 Lindsay Macy .40 1.00
15 Meaghan Mikkelson .40 1.00
16 Phoebe Monteleone .40 1.00
17 Emily Morris .40 1.00
18 Mikka Nordby .40 1.00
19 Bobbi-Jo Slusar .40 1.00
20 Nicole Uliasz .40 1.00
21 Amy Vermeulen .40 1.00
22 Jesse Vetter .40 1.00
23 Kristen Witting .40 1.00
24 Jinelle Zaugg .40 1.00

2005-06 Wisconsin Badgers

COMPLETE SET (27) 15.00 30.00
1 Andy Brandt .40 1.00
2 Adam Burish .40 1.00
3 Ross Carlson .40 1.00
4 Shane Connelly .75 2.00
5 A.J. Degenhardt .40 1.00
6 Jake Dowell .40 1.00
7 Davis Drewiske .40 1.00
8 Robbie Earl .75 2.00
9 Brian Elliott .75 2.00
10 Josh Engel .40 1.00
11 Matthew Ford .40 1.00
12 Tom Gilbert .40 1.00
13 Tom Gorowsky .40 1.00
14 Ryan Jeffery .40 1.00
15 Andrew Joudrey .40 1.00
16 Kyle Klubertanz .40 1.00
17 Nick Licari .40 1.00
18 Jeff Likens .40 1.00
19 Ryan MacMurchy .40 1.00
20 Matt Olinger .40 1.00
21 Joe Pavelski .40 1.00
22 Joe Piskula .40 1.00
23 Jack Skille 2.00 5.00
24 Jeff Slinde .40 1.00
25 Ben Street .40 1.00
26 Mike Eaves HC .20 .50
27 Bucky Badger MASCOT .02 .10

2007-08 Wisconsin Badgers

These cards were given away at three separate home games. The cards were issued in perforated strips. The first had 10 cards, the others nine. The cards are standard size and have color fronts and black and white backs. The fronts also feature the logo of the set sponsor, Quaker Steak and Lube Restaurant. The set features three 2007 NHL first rounders, including the third overall Pick, Kyle Turris. The cards are not numbered and are listed below alphabetically.

COMPLETE SET (27) 25.00 40.00
1 Tom Bardis .60 1.50
2 Zach Bearson .60 1.50
3 Aaron Bendickson .60 1.50
4 Andy Bohmbach .60 1.50
5 Shane Connelly .60 1.50
6 Michael Davies .60 1.50
7 Sean Dolan .60 1.50
8 Davis Drewiske .60 1.50
9 Josh Engel .60 1.50
10 Matthew Ford .60 1.50
11 Blake Geoffrion 1.00 2.50
12 Cody Goloubef .60 1.50
13 Tom Gorowsky .60 1.50
14 Ben Grotting .60 1.50
15 Scott Gudmandson .60 1.50
16 Jeff Henderson .60 1.50
17 Ryan Jeffery .60 1.50
18 Craig Johnson .60 1.50
19 Patrick Johnson .60 1.50
20 Kyle Klubertanz .60 1.50
21 Jamie McBain .75 2.00
22 Ryan McDonagh 1.00 2.50
23 John Mitchell .60 1.50
24 Brendan Smith .60 1.50
25 Podge Turnbull .60 1.50
26 Kyle Turris 4.00 10.00
27 Mike Eaves HC .60 1.50

2014-15 Wisconsin Badgers

COMPLETE SET (28) 7.50 15.00
1 Grant Besse .30 .75
2 Jake Bunz .30 .75
3 Aiden Cavallini .30 .75
4 Tim Davison .30 .75
5 Jack Dougherty .30 .75
6 Chase Drake .30 .75
7 Mike Eaves CO .30 .75
8 Jason Ford .30 .75
9 Gabe Grunwald .30 .75
10 Cameron Hughes .30 .75
11 Cullen Hurley .30 .75
12 Joseph Labate .30 .75
13 Jake Linhart .30 .75
14 Corbin McGuire .30 .75
15 Adam Miller .30 .75
16 Brad Navin .30 .75
17 Matt Paape .30 .75
18 Landon Peterson .30 .75
19 Adam Rockwood .30 .75
20 Joel Rumpel .30 .75
21 Kevin Schulze .30 .75
22 Alex Shuchuk .30 .75
23 Jedd Soleway .30 .75
24 Matt Ustaski .30 .75
25 Ryan Wagner .30 .75
26 Eddie Wittchow .30 .75
27 Morgan Zulinick .30 .75
28 Bucky Badger MASCOT .30 .75

2000-01 Worcester IceCats

This set features the IceCats of the AHL. The set was produced by Choice Marketing and was handed out over the course of two games as a promotional giveaway.

COMPLETE SET (30) 8.00 20.00
1 Ed Campbell .20 .50
2 Daniel Corso .40 1.00
3 Justin Papineau .40 1.00
4 Jaroslav Obsut .20 .50
5 Ladislav Nagy .75 2.00
6 Marc Brown .20 .50
7 Pascal Rheaume .20 .50
8 Mike Van Ryn .40 1.00
9 Cody Rudkowsky .60 1.50
10 Andrei Troschinsky .20 .50
11 Mark Rycroft .40 1.00
12 Matt Walker .20 .50
13 Jamie Thompson .20 .50
14 Darren Rumble .30 .75
15 Scratch MASCOT .04 .10
16 Team CL .04 .10
17 Dwayne Roloson .75 2.00
18 Jame Pollock .20 .50
19 Eric Boguniecki .60 1.50
20 Chris Murray .40 1.00
21 Tyler Rennette .20 .50
22 Marty Reasoner .40 1.00
23 Dale Clarke .30 .75
24 Tyler Willis .30 .75
25 Jan Horacek .30 .75
26 Peter Smrek .30 .75
27 Mike Peluso .30 .75
28 Doug Friedman .30 .75
29 Shawn Mamane .20 .50
30 Don Granato CO .10 .25

2001-02 Worcester IceCats

This set features the Icecats of the AHL and actually features two separately released series of cards. The sets -- one issued early in the season, another late -- were produced by Choice Marketing and was sold by the team at its souvenir shop. Each series was limited to 2,000 copies.

COMPLETE SET (15) 10.00 25.00
1 Darren Rumble .30 .75
2 Marc Brown .30 .75
3 Ed Campbell .30 .75
4 Jeff Panzer .30 .75
5 Cody Rudkowsky .40 1.00
6 Igor Valeev .30 .75
7 Dale Clarke .30 .75
8 Mike Van Ryn .40 1.00
9 Barret Jackman .75 2.00
10 Jame Pollock .30 .75
11 Daniel Tkaczuk .30 .75
12 Greg Davis .30 .75
13 Jamie Thompson .30 .75
14 Tyson Nash .60 1.50
15 Scratch MASCOT .04 .10
16 Team Photo/CL .10 .25
17 Reinhard Divis .60 1.50
18 Andrei Troschinsky .30 .75
19 Steve Halko .30 .75
20 Matt Walker .30 .75
21 Eric Boguniecki .40 1.00
22 Justin Papineau .40 1.00
23 Christian Laflamme .30 .75
24 Brad Voth .30 .75
25 Mark Rycroft .30 .75
26 Steve McLaren .30 .75
27 Eric Nickulas .30 .75
28 Justin Papineau (# Jeff Panzer .30 .75
(# Eric Boguniecki
29 Brent Johnson .75 2.00
30 Don Granato CO .10 .25

2002-03 Worcester IceCats

COMPLET SET (28) 6.00 15.00
1 Checklist .04 .10
2 Terry Virtue .20 .50
3 Steve Bancroft .20 .50
4 Aris Brimanis .20 .50
5 John Pohl .75 2.00
6 Jame Pollock .20 .50
7 Eric Nickulas .20 .50
8 Jason Dawe .20 .50
9 Blake Evans .20 .50
10 Greg Davis .20 .50
11 Marc Brown .20 .50
12 Steve Dubinsky .20 .50
13 Steve McLaren .20 .50
14 Brett Scheffelmaier .20 .50
15 Mark Rycroft .20 .50
16 Christian Laflamme .20 .50
17 Justin Papineau .20 .50
18 Igor Valeev .20 .50
19 Matt Walker .20 .50
20 Jeff Panzer .20 .50
21 Sergei Varlamov .20 .50
22 Christian Backman .20 .50
23 Curtis Sanford .60 1.50
24 Phil Osaer .20 .50
25 Reinhard Divis .40 1.00
26 Eric Boguniecki MVP .20 .50
27 Don Granato HCO .04 .10
28 Scratch Mascot .04 .10

2003-04 Worcester IceCats

This set was produced by Choice Marketing and sold at home games.

COMPLETE SET (28) 4.00 10.00
1 Checklist .04 .10
2 Curtis Sanford .40 1.00
3 Joe Vandermeer .15 .40
4 Terry Virtue .15 .40
5 Jon Coleman .15 .40
6 Trevor Byrne .15 .40
7 Aris Brimanis .15 .40
8 Johnny Pohl .40 1.00
9 Tom Koivisto .15 .40
10 Jame Pollock .15 .40
11 Grog Black .15 .40
12 Mike Stuart .15 .40
13 Blake Evans .15 .40
14 Mike Glumac .15 .40
15 Chris Corrinet .15 .40
16 Marc Brown .15 .40
17 Jay McClement .15 .40
18 Steve McLaren .30 .75
19 Aaron MacKenzie .15 .40
20 Colin Hemingway .15 .40
21 Ernie Hartlieb .15 .40
22 Steve Martins .15 .40
23 Brett Scheffelmaier .15 .40
24 Jeff Panzer .15 .40
25 Sergei Varlamov .15 .40
26 Reinhard Divis .30 .75
27 Don Granato CO .04 .10
28 Steve Pleau ACO .04 .10

2003-04 Worcester IceCats 10th Anniversary

This special set was produced by Choice Marketing to commemorate the team's anniversary and was sold at home games.

COMPLETE SET (20) 4.00 10.00
1 Checklist .04 .10
2 Dwayne Roloson .40 1.00
3 Brent Johnson .40 1.00
4 Barret Jackman .30 .75
5 Bryce Salvador .15 .40
6 Terry Virtue .30 .75
7 Matt Walker .15 .40
8 Ed Campbell .15 .40
9 Rory Fitzpatrick .15 .40
10 Ricard Persson .15 .40
11 Eric Boguniecki .15 .40
12 Justin Papineau .15 .40
13 Marty Reasoner .15 .40
14 Ladislav Nagy .30 .75
15 Jeff Panzer .15 .40
16 Stephane Roy .15 .40
17 Jochen Hecht .15 .40
18 Johnny Pohl .30 .75
19 Michal Handzus .15 .40
20 Reed Low .15 .40

2004-05 Worcester IceCats

COMPLETE SET (26) 5.00 12.00
1 Curtis Sanford .40 1.00
2 Mike Mottau .20 .50
3 Trevor Byrne .20 .50
4 Aris Brimanis .20 .50
5 Brendan Buckley .20 .50
6 Johnny Pohl .40 1.00
7 Jon DiSalvatore .20 .50
8 Mike Stuart .20 .50
9 Blake Evans .20 .50
10 Mike Glumac .20 .50
11 Erkki Rajamaki .20 .50
12 Jay McClement .20 .50
13 D.J. King .20 .50
14 Aaron MacKenzie .20 .50
15 Alexei Shkotov .20 .50
16 Peter Sejna .20 .50
17 Dennis Wideman .20 .50
18 Brendan Brooks .20 .50
19 Jason Bacashihua .60 1.50
20 Jeff Hoggan .40 1.00
21 Ryan Ramsay .20 .50
22 Robin Gomez .20 .50
23 Don Granato CO .04 .10
24 Steve Pleau ACO .04 .10
25 Mascots .04 .10
NNO Checklist .04 .10

2007-08 Worcester Sharks

COMPLETE SET (27) 12.00 20.00
1 Riley Armstrong .30 .75
2 Marc Busenburg .30 .75
3 Tom Cavanagh .30 .75
4 Taylor Dakers .60 1.50
5 Brennan Evans .30 .75
6 T.J. Fox .30 .75
7 Thomas Greiss .60 1.50
8 Mike Iggulden .30 .75
9 Derek Joslin .30 .75
10 Lukas Kaspar .30 .75
11 Graham Mink .60 1.50
12 Mike Morris .30 .75
13 Dennis Packard .30 .75
14 Dimitri Patzold .60 1.50
15 Tomas Plihal .30 .75
16 Nate Raduns .30 .75
17 Ashton Rome .30 .75
18 Devin Setoguchi .75 2.00
19 Dan Spang .30 .75
20 Brad Staubitz .30 .75
21 Patrick Traverse .30 .75
22 Jonathan Tremblay .30 .75
23 Craig Valette .30 .75
24 Tom Walsh .30 .75
25 Roy Sommer HC .02 .10
26 David Cunniff AC .02 .10
27 Finz MASCOT .02 .10

2003-04 Yarmouth Mariners

COMPLETE SET (31) 4.00 10.00
1 Checklist .04 .10
2 Travis Antler .20 .50
3 Todd Ballah .20 .50
4 Jamie Barbour .20 .50
5 Brent Boardman .20 .50
6 Jarrett Bottomley .20 .50
7 Tim Clayton .20 .50
8 Georges d'Entremont .20 .50
9 Justin d'Entremont .20 .50
10 Jason Hedges .20 .50
11 Steve Holland .20 .50
12 Grant Kenny .20 .50
13 Brad Larter .20 .50
14 Jordan McMullen .20 .50
15 Jody Mosher .20 .50
16 Matt Oxtoby .20 .50
17 David Philpott .20 .50
18 Mark Plenzich .20 .50
19 Jason Robichaud .20 .50
20 Curtis Thorne .20 .50
21 Michael Dilorenzo .20 .50
22 Josh Vanderbreggen .20 .50
23 Sean Wadden .20 .50
24 Steve Yetman .20 .50
25 Paul Currie CO .04 .10
26 Laurie Barron ACO .04 .10
27 Mark Muise EQM .04 .10
28 Mark Wheeler TR .04 .10
29 One Team One Goal .04 .10
30 Mariner Pressure .04 .10
31 Hard to the Net .04 .10

1991 Arena Draft Picks

The 1991 Arena Draft Picks boxed set consists of 33 standard-size cards. The set was produced in English as well as French versions, with both versions currently carrying the same values. One thousand cards (numbered out of 667 for the English version, 333 for the French) signed by each player were randomly inserted throughout the sets with one autograph per approximately ten sets or two per case. Moreover, a Pat Falloon hologram was produced in conjunction with this set, although its release came much later. The Falloon hologram is not included in the complete set price below. The production run was reported to be 198,000 English and 99,000 French sets, and each set was issued with a numbered certificate of authenticity. The full-bleed fronts have a white background and show the hockey player in an action pose wearing a tuxedo.

COMPLETE SET (33) 1.25 3.00
1 Pat Falloon .02 .10
2 Scott Niedermayer .08 .25
3 Scott Lachance .01 .05
4 Peter Forsberg UER .40 1.00
5 Alek Stojanov .01 .05
6 Richard Matvichuk .02 .10
7 Patrick Poulin .01 .05
8 Martin Lapointe .20 .50
9 Tyler Wright .01 .05
10 Philippe Boucher .01 .05
11 Pat Peake .01 .05
12 Markus Naslund UER .20 .50
13 Brent Bilodeau .01 .05
14 Glen Murray .20 .50
15 Niklas Sundblad .01 .05
16 Trevor Halverson .01 .05
17 Dean McAmmond .02 .10
18 Rene Corbet .01 .05
19 Eric Lavigne .01 .05
20 Steve Staios .01 .05
21 Jim Campbell .02 .10
22 Jassen Cullimore .01 .05
23 Jamie Pushor .02 .10
24 Donevan Hextall .01 .05
25 Andrew Verner .02 .10
26 Jason Dawe .01 .05
27 Jeff Nelson .01 .05
28 Darcy Werenka .01 .05
29 Francois Groleau .01 .05
30 Guy Leveque .01 .05
31 Yanic Perreault .05 .15
32 Pat Falloon .02 .10
Scott Lachance
NNO Checklist Card .02 .10
HOLO Pat Falloon .08 .25
Hologram

1991 Arena Draft Picks Autographs

The 1991 Arena Draft Picks autographs consists of 33 standard-size cards. One thousand cards (numbered out of 667 for the English version, 333 for the French) signed by each player were randomly inserted throughout the sets with one autograph per approximately ten sets or two per case. The full-bleed fronts have a white background and show the hockey player in an action pose wearing a tuxedo.

COMPLETE SET (33) 75.00 125.00
1 Pat Falloon 2.00 5.00
2 Scott Niedermayer 6.00 15.00
3 Scott Lachance 1.25 3.00
4 Peter Forsberg UER 30.00 75.00
5 Alek Stojanov 1.25 3.00
6 Richard Matvichuk 2.00 5.00
7 Patrick Poulin 1.25 3.00
8 Martin Lapointe 6.00 15.00
9 Tyler Wright 1.25 3.00
10 Philippe Boucher 1.25 3.00
11 Pat Peake 1.25 3.00
12 Markus Naslund UER 6.00 15.00
13 Brent Bilodeau 1.25 3.00
14 Glen Murray 6.00 15.00
15 Niklas Sundblad 1.25 3.00
16 Trevor Halverson 1.25 3.00
17 Dean McAmmond 2.00 5.00
18 Rene Corbet 2.00 5.00
19 Eric Lavigne 1.25 3.00
20 Steve Staios 1.25 3.00
21 Jim Campbell 1.25 3.00
22 Jassen Cullimore 1.25 3.00
23 Jamie Pushor 1.25 3.00
24 Donevan Hextall 1.25 3.00
25 Andrew Verner 2.00 5.00
26 Jason Dawe 1.25 3.00
27 Jeff Nelson 1.25 3.00
28 Darcy Werenka 1.25 3.00
29 Francois Groleau 1.25 3.00
30 Guy Leveque 1.25 3.00
31 Yanic Perreault 2.00 5.00

1991 Arena Holograms 12th National

These standard-size cards have on their fronts a 3-D silver-colored emblem on a white background with orange borders. Though the back of each card salutes a different superstar, the players themselves are not pictured; instead, one finds pictures of a football; hockey stick and puck; basketball; and baseball in glove respectively. The cards are numbered on the front.

COMPLETE SET (4) 4.00 10.00
2 Wayne Gretzky 1.25 3.00

1994-95 Assets

Produced by Classic, the 1994 Assets set features stars from basketball, hockey, football, baseball, and auto racing. The set was released in two series of 50 cards each. 1,994 cases were produced of each series. This standard-sized card set features a player photo with his name in silver letters on the lower left corner and the Assets logo on the upper right. The back has a color photo on the left side along with a biography on the right side of the card. A Sprint phone card is randomly inserted in each five-card pack.

COMPLETE SET (100) 6.00 15.00
8 Ed Jovanovski .05 .15
20 Radek Bonk .08 .25
21 Manon Rheaume .50 1.25
33 Ed Jovanovski .05 .15
45 Radek Bonk .08 .25
46 Manon Rheaume .50 1.25
57 Jeff O'Neill .05 .15
60 Petr Sykora .08 .25
62 Eric Fichaud .07 .20
72 Manon Rheaume .50 1.25
82 Jeff O'Neill .05 .15
85 Petr Sykora .08 .25
87 Eric Fichaud .07 .20
97 Manon Rheaume .50 1.25

1994-95 Assets Silver Signature

This 48-card standard-size set was randomly inserted at a rate of four per box. The cards are identical to the first twenty-four cards in the each series, except that these show a silver facsimile autograph on their fronts. The first 24 cards correspond to cards 1-24 in the first series while the second 24 cards correspond to cards 51-74 in the second series.

*SILVER SIGS: 1.2X TO 3X BASIC CARDS

1994-95 Assets Die Cuts

This 25-card standard-size set was randomly inserted into packs. DC1-10 were included in series one while DC11-25 were included in series two packs. These cards feature the player on the card and the ability to separate the player's photo. The back contains information about the player on the section of the card that is separable.

COMPLETE SET (25) 30.00 80.00
DC9 Ed Jovanovski .60 1.50
DC10 Manon Rheaume 4.00 10.00
DC24 Eric Fichaud .60 1.50

1994-95 Assets Phone Cards $2000

These rounded-corner cards measuring 2" by 3 1/4" were randomly inserted into second series packs. Just four of each of these cards were produced. The front features the player's photo, with "Two Thousand Dollars" written in cursive script along the left edge. In the bottom left corner is the Assets logo. The back gives instructions on how to use the phone card. Two different Emmitt Smith promo cards were also issued to promote the product. The cards are unnumbered and checklisted below in alphabetical order. The cards expired on March 31, 1996.

1994-95 Assets Phone Cards $5

These cards measure 2" by 3 1/4", have rounded corners and were randomly inserted into packs. Cards 1-5 were inserted into first series packs while 6-15 were in second series packs. The front features the player's photo, with "Five Dollars" written in cursive script along the left edge. In the bottom left corner is the Assets logo. The back gives instructions on how to use the phone card. Series one cards expired on December 1, 1995 while second series cards expired on March 31, 1996.

COMPLETE SET (15) 8.00 20.00
*PIN NUMBER REVEALED: .2X TO .5X
14 Manon Rheaume .75 1.50

1994-95 Assets Phone Cards One Minute

Measuring 2" by 3 1/4", these cards have rounded corners and were inserted one per pack. Cards 1-24 were in first series packs while 25-48 were included with second series packs. The front features the player's photo and on the side is how long the card is good for. The Assets logo is in the bottom left corner. The back gives instructions on how to use the phone card. The first series cards expired on December 1, 1995 while the second series cards expired on March 31, 1996. The cards with a $2 logo are worth a mulitple of the regular cards. Please refer to the values below for these cards.

COMPLETE SET (48) 7.50 20.00
*PIN NUMB.REVEALED: .2X TO .5X BASIC INS.
*TWO DOLLAR: .5X TO 1.2X BASIC INSERTS
4 Radek Bonk .15 .40
10 Ed Jovanovski .15 .40
18 Manon Rheaume .60 1.50
28 Eric Fichaud .15 .40
41 Jeff O'Neill .15 .40
42 Manon Rheaume .60 1.50
48 Petr Sykora .20 .50

1995 Assets Gold

This 50-card set measures the standard size. The fronts feature borderless player action photos with the player's name printed in gold at the bottom. The backs carry a portrait of the player with his name, career highlights, and statistics. The Dale Earnhardt card was pulled from circulation early in the product's release. It is considered a Short Print (SP) but is not included in the complete set price.

COMPLETE SET (49) 6.00 15.00
2 Jeff O'Neill .05 .15
3 Jeff Friesen .07 .20
4 Aki-Petteri Berg .05 .15
5 Todd Marchant .07 .20
6 Blaine Lacher .07 .20
7 Petr Sykora .08 .25
8 David Oliver .05 .15
9 Manon Rheaume .20 .50
10 Ed Jovanovski .07 .20

1995 Assets Gold Printer's Proofs

These parallel cards were randomly seeded at the rate of 1:18 packs. They feature the words "Printer's Proof" on the cardfronts.

*PRINT PROOF: 2X TO 5X BASIC CARDS

1995 Assets Gold Silver Signatures

These parallel cards were inserted one per pack. They feature a silver foil facsimile signature on the cardfronts.

COMP. SILVER SIG SET (50) 15.00 40.00
*SILVER SIGS: .8X TO 2X BASIC CARDS

1995 Assets Gold Die Cuts Silver

This 20-card set was randomly inserted in packs at a rate of one in 18. The fronts feature a borderless player color action photo with a diamond-shaped top and the player's action taking place in front of the card name. The backs carry the card name, player's name and career highlights. The cards are numbered on the backs. Gold versions were inserted at a rate of one in 72 packs.

COMPLETE SET (20) 10.00 25.00
*GOLDS: .8X TO 2X SILVERS
GOLD STATED ODDS 1:72
SDC13 Manon Rheaume .75 2.00

1995 Assets Gold Phone Cards $2

This 47-card set was randomly inserted in packs and measures 2 1/8" by 3 3/8". The fronts feature color action player photos with the player's name below. The $2 calling value is printed vertically down the left. The backs carry the instructions on how to use the cards which expired on 7/31/96. The cards are unnumbered.

COMPLETE SET (47) 15.00 40.00
*PIN NUMBER REVEALED: HALF VALUE
2 Jeff O'Neill .30 .75
3 Jeff Friesen .40 1.00
4 Aki-Petteri Berg .30 .75
5 Todd Marchant .30 .75
6 Blaine Lacher .30 .75
7 Petr Sykora .60 1.50
8 David Oliver .30 .75
9 Manon Rheaume .75 2.00
10 Ed Jovanovski .30 .75

1995 Assets Gold Phone Cards $5

This 16-card set measures 2 1/8" by 3 3/8" and was randomly inserted in packs. The fronts feature color action player photos with the player's name below. The $5 calling value is printed vertically down the left. The backs carry the instructions on how to use the cards which expired on 7/31/96. The cards are unnumbered. The Microlined versions are inserted at a rate of one in 18 packs versus one in six packs for the basic $5 card.

COMPLETE SET (16) 25.00 60.00
*MICROLINED: .6X TO 1.5X BASIC INSERTS
STATED ODDS 1:18
*PIN NUMBER REVEALED: HALF VALUE
3 Manon Rheaume 1.00 2.50

1996 Assets

The 1996 Classic Assets was issued in one set totalling 50 cards. This 50-card premium set has a tremendous selection of the top athletes in the world headlines. Each card features action photos, up-to-date statistics and is printed on high-quality, foil-stamped stock. Hot Print cards are parallel cards randomly inserted in Hot Packs and are valued at a multiple of the regular cards below.

COMPLETE SET (50) 5.00 10.00
8 Radek Dvorak .05 .15
14 Brian Holzinger .05 .15
17 Ed Jovanovski .05 .15
45 Petr Sykora .05 .15

1996 Assets A Cut Above

The even cards were randomly inserted in retail packs at a rate of one in eight, and the odd cards were inserted in clear asset packs at a rate of one in 20, this 20-card die-cut set is composed of 10 phone cards and 10 trading cards. The cards have rounded corners except for one which is cut in a straight corner design. The fronts feature a color action player cut-out superimposed over a gray background with the words "cut above" printed throughout and resembled to be cut so it displays a basketball game behind it. The backs carry a color action player photo with the player's name and a short career summary.

COMPLETE SET (20) 20.00 50.00
CA4 Brian Holzinger .50 1.25

1996 Assets Hot Prints

These parallel cards were randomly seeded in 1996 Assets Hot Packs. Each card is marked Hot Print on the cardfront.

*HOT PRINTS: .8X TO 2X BASIC CARDS

1996 Assets Phone Cards $2

This 30-card set was inserted in retail packs at a rate of 1 per pack with a minimum value of $2 per phone card. The cards measure approximately 2 1/8" by 3 3/8" with rounded corners. The fronts display color aciton player photos with the player's name in a red bar below. The backs carry the instructions on how to use the cards and the expiration date of 1/31/97. Hot Print Cards parallel cards were randomly inserted in Hot Packs. These cards are valued as a mulitple of the cards below.

COMPLETE SET (30) 12.50 30.00
*$2 CARDS: .6X TO 1.5X $1 CARDS
*PIN NUMBER REVEALED: HALF VALUE

1997 Bowman CHL

The 1997-98 Bowman CHL set was issued in one series totaling 165 cards and was distributed in eight-card packs with a suggested retail price of $1.89. It marks Topps first venture into minor league hockey. The set features color photos of established CHL stars as well as 40 NHL 1997 Draft Prospects. The 40 Draft Prospects each autographed cards that were distributed at the rate of one in 24 to form the Bowman CHL Prospects Autographs insert set. Each of these cards is authenticated by the Topps Certified Autograph Issue stamp.

COMPLETE SET (160) 10.00 25.00
1 Jan Bulis .15 .40
2 Daniel Cleary .15 .40
3 Dave Duerden .07 .20
4 Cameron Mann .07 .20
5 Alyn McCauley .15 .40
6 Tyler Rennette .07 .20
7 Marc Savard .20 .50
8 Daniel Tkaczuk .15 .40
9 John Tripp .07 .20
10 Joel Trottier .07 .20
11 Sean Yenedam .07 .20
12 Alexander Volchkov .07 .20
13 Sean Blanchard .07 .20
14 Kevin Bolibruck .07 .20
15 Nick Boynton .20 .50
16 Paul Mara .15 .40
17 Marc Moro .07 .20
18 Marty Wilford .07 .20
19 Zac Bierk .20 .50
20 Kory Cooper .07 .20
21 Richard Rochefort .07 .20
22 Matt Cooke .20 .50
23 Boyd Devereaux .20 .50
24 Rico Fata .15 .40
25 Dwayne Hay .07 .20
26 Trevor Letowski .07 .20
27 Ryan Mougenel .07 .20
28 Todd Norman .07 .20
29 Larry Paleczny .07 .20
30 Colin Pepperall .07 .20
31 Jonathan Sim .07 .20
32 Joe Thornton 1.50 4.00
33 Brian Wesenberg .07 .20
34 Andy Delmore .07 .20
35 Chris Hajt .07 .20
36 Richard Jackman .07 .20
37 Denis Smith .07 .20
38 Jamie Sokolsky .07 .20
39 Paul Traynor .07 .20
40 Patrick DesRochers .15 .40
41 Robert Esche .40 1.00
42 Roberto Luongo 1.50 4.00
43 Frederic Henry .07 .20
44 Marc Oliver Roy .07 .20
45 Samy Nasreddine .07 .20
46 Jean-Francois Fortin .07 .20
47 Martin Ethier .07 .20
48 Jason Doig .07 .20
49 Dominic Perna .07 .20
50 Daniel Briere .30 .75
51 Pavel Rosa .07 .20
52 Philippe Audet .07 .20
53 Gordie Dwyer .07 .20
54 Martin Menard .07 .20
55 Jonathan Delisle .07 .20
56 Peter Worrell .20 .50
57 Francois Methot .07 .20
58 Steve Begin .07 .20
59 Karol Bartanus .07 .20
60 J-P Dumont .40 1.00
61 Marc Denis .40 1.00
62 Jean-Sebastien Giguere .75 2.00
63 Jason Gorleau .07 .20
64 Radoslav Suchy .07 .20
65 Stephane Robidas .07 .20
66 Marc-Andre Gaudet .07 .20
67 Eric Drouin .07 .20
68 Derrick Walser .07 .20
69 Vincent Lecavalier 1.25 3.00
70 Denis Hamel .07 .20
71 Daniel Corso .07 .20
72 Martin Moise .07 .20
73 Eric Belanger .07 .20
74 Olivier Morin .07 .20
75 Jerome Tremblay .07 .20
76 Jody Shelley .30 .75
77 Eric Normandin .07 .20
78 David Thibeault .07 .20
79 Christian Daigle .15 .40
80 Alexandre Jacques .07 .20
81 Brian Boucher .40 1.00
82 Randy Petruk .15 .40
83 Hugh Hamilton .07 .20
84 Joel Kwiatkowski .07 .20
85 Zenith Komarniski .07 .20
86 Joey Tetarenko .20 .50
87 Tyler Willis .07 .20
88 Patrick Marleau 1.00 2.50
89 Trent Whitfield .07 .20
90 Martin Cerven .07 .20
91 Donnie Kinney .07 .20
92 Brad Isbister .15 .40
93 Todd Robinson .07 .20
94 Greg Leeb .07 .20
95 John Cirjak .07 .20
96 Randy Perry .07 .20
97 Derek Schutz .07 .20
98 Brenden Morrow .40 1.00
99 Shawn McNeil .07 .20
100 Brad Ference .07 .20
101 Ryan Hoople .07 .20
102 Brian Elder .07 .20
103 Mike McBain .07 .20
104 Jesse Wallin .07 .20
105 Chris Phillips .20 .50
106 Kelly Smart .07 .20
107 Arron Asham .07 .20
108 Byron Ritchie .07 .20
109 Derek Morris .20 .50
110 Travis Brigley .07 .20
111 Justin Kurtz .07 .20
112 B.J. Young .07 .20
113 Shane Willis .07 .20
114 Josh Holden .07 .20
115 Cory Sarich .07 .20
116 Brad Larsen .07 .20
117 Stefan Cherneski .07 .20
118 Peter Schaefer .07 .20
119 Dmitri Nabokov .07 .20
120 Sergei Varlamov .20 .50
121 Daniel Cleary TP .07 .20
122 Jarrett Smith TP .07 .20
123 Alexandre Mathieu TP .07 .20
124 Matt Elich TP .07 .20
125 Joe Thornton TP .75 2.00
126 Mike Brown TP .07 .20
127 Derek Schutz TP .07 .20
128 Benoit Cote TP .07 .20
129 Jason Ward TP .07 .20
130 Karol Bartanus TP .07 .20
131 Tyler Rennette TP .07 .20
132 Matt Zultek TP .15 .40
133 Brad Ference TP .15 .40
134 Daniel Tetrault TP .07 .20
135 Ray Bonni TP .07 .20
136 Kevin Grimes TP .07 .20
137 Paul Mara TP .15 .40
138 Nikos Tselios TP .07 .20
139 Curtis Cruickshank TP .07 .20
140 Pierre-Luc Therrien TP .07 .20
141 Patrick Marleau TP .50 1.50
142 Ty Jones TP .07 .20
143 Jeremy Reich TP .07 .20
144 Adam Mair TP .15 .40
145 Adam Colagiacomo TP .07 .20
146 Harold Druken TP .15 .40
147 Brenden Morrow TP .30 .75
148 Jay Legault TP .07 .20
149 Jeff Zehr TP .07 .20
150 Scott Barney TP .07 .20
151 Gregor Baumgartner TP .07 .20
152 Daniel Tkaczuk TP .20 .50
153 Eric Brewer TP .20 .50
154 Nick Boynton TP .20 .50
155 Vratislav Cech TP .07 .20
156 Kyle Kos TP .07 .20
157 Jean-Francois Fortin TP .07 .20
158 Wes Jarvis TP .07 .20
159 Roberto Luongo TP .75 2.00
160 Jean-Francois Damphousse TP .07 .20
NNO B.B.Redempt. .40 1.00
NNO Ref.Redempt. .40 1.00
NNO Ato.Ref.Redempt. .40 1.00
NNO Auto.Redempt. .40 1.00

1997 Bowman CHL OPC

Randomly inserted in packs at the rate of 1:6, this 160 card set is an O-Pee-Chee parallel version of the basic Bowman CHL issue.

COMPLETE SET (160) 300.00 600.00
*STARS: 4X TO 10X BASIC CARDS

1997 Bowman CHL Autographs

Randomly inserted at the rate of 1:46, this 37-card set features cards signed by the top NHL draft picks. Each of these cards is authenticated by the Topps Certified Autograph Issue stamp.

COMPLETE SET (40) 150.00 200.00
2 Jarrett Smith 2.00 5.00
3 Alexandre Mathieu 2.00 5.00
4 Matt Elich 2.00 5.00
10 Karol Bartanus 2.00 5.00
11 Tyler Rennette 2.00 5.00
13 Brad Ference 2.00 5.00
14 Daniel Tetrault 2.00 5.00
15 Ray Bonni 2.00 5.00
16 Kevin Grimes 2.00 5.00
18 Nikos Tselios 2.00 5.00
19 Curtis Cruickshank 2.00 5.00
20 Pierre-Luc Therrien 2.00 5.00
22 Ty Jones 2.00 5.00
23 Jeremy Reich 2.00 5.00
24 Adam Mair 2.00 5.00
25 Adam Colagiacomo 2.00 5.00
26 Harold Druken 2.00 5.00
28 Jay Legault 2.00 5.00
29 Jeff Zehr 4.00 10.00
30 Scott Barney 2.00 5.00
31 Gregor Baumgartner 2.00 5.00
33 Eric Brewer 5.00 12.00
34 Nick Boynton 5.00 12.00
35 Vratislav Cech 2.00 5.00
36 Kyle Kos 2.00 5.00
37 Jean Francois Fortin 2.00 5.00
38 Wes Jarvis 2.00 5.00
39 Roberto Luongo 8.00 20.00
121 Daniel Cleary 2.00 5.00
125 Joe Thornton 20.00 40.00
126 Mike Brown 2.00 5.00
127 Derek Schutz 2.00 5.00
128 Benoit Cote 2.00 5.00
129 Jason Ward 4.00 10.00
132 Matt Zultek 2.00 5.00
147 Brenden Morrow 10.00 20.00
160 Jean-Francois Damphousse 5.00 12.00
149 Jeff Zehr

1997 Bowman CHL Bowman's Best

This 20-card set was randomly inserted in packs at the rate of one in 12 and features color player photos printed on laser-cut cards using chromium technology. Refractor and atomic refractor parallels were also created and randomly inserted. Refractors were inserted at a rate of 1:24 and atomic refractors at 1:48.

COMPLETE SET (20) 25.00 35.00
*REF.STARS: 1.5X TO 3X BASIC BOWMAN'S BEST
*ATOMIC REF: 2.5X TO 5X BASIC BOWMAN'S BEST
1 Joe Thornton 4.00 10.00
2 Patrick Marleau 2.00 5.00
3 Paul Mara .60 1.50
4 Daniel Tkaczuk .60 1.50
5 Jason Ward .60 1.50
6 Nick Boynton .75 2.00
7 Daniel Cleary .60 1.50
8 Eric Brewer .75 2.00
9 Brad Ference .60 1.50
10 Stefan Cherneski .60 1.50
11 Ryan Bonni .60 1.50
12 Adam Colagiacomo .60 1.50
13 Mike Brown .60 1.50
14 Scott Barney .60 1.50
15 Jarrett Smith .60 1.50
16 Brenden Morrow 1.25 3.00
17 Jean-Francois Fortin .60 1.50
18 Roberto Luongo 4.00 10.00
19 Curtis Cruickshank .60 1.50
20 Pierre-Luc Therrien .60 1.50

1998 Bowman CHL

The 1998 Bowman CHL set was issued in one series totaling 165 cards and was distributed in eight-card packs with a suggested retail price of $1.89. The set features action color photos of established CHL stars as well as 40 NHL 1998 Draft Prospects. The backs carry player information and statistics.

COMPLETE SET (165) 20.00 50.00
1 Robert Esche .20 .50
2 Chris Hajt .07 .20
3 Mark McMahon .07 .20
4 Jeff Brown .07 .20
5 Richard Jackman .07 .20
6 Greg Labenski .07 .20
7 Marek Posmyk .07 .20
8 Brian Willsie .07 .20
9 Jason Ward .07 .20
10 Manny Malhotra .07 .20
11 Matt Cooke .40 1.00
12 Mike Gorman .07 .20
13 Rodney Richard .07 .20
14 David Legwand .40 1.00
15 Jon Sim .07 .20
16 Peter Sarno .07 .20
17 Andrew Long .07 .20
18 Peter Cava .07 .20
19 Colin Pepperall .07 .20
20 Jay Legault .07 .20
21 Brian Finley .15 .40
22 Martin Skoula .07 .20
23 Brian Campbell .07 .20
24 Sean Blanchard .07 .20
25 Bryan Allen .07 .20
26 Peter Hogan .07 .20
27 Nick Boynton .30 .75
28 Matt Bradley .07 .20
29 Jeremy Adduono .07 .20
30 Mike Henrich .07 .20
31 Justin Papineau .20 .50
32 Bujar Amidovski .30 .75
33 Robert Mailloux .07 .20
34 Daniel Tkaczuk .07 .20
35 Sean Avery .40 1.00
36 Mark Bell .20 .50
37 Kevin Colley .07 .20
38 Norm Milley .30 .75
39 Scott Barney .07 .20
40 Joel Trottier .07 .20
41 Brent Belecki .07 .20
42 Randy Petruk .20 .50
43 Brad Ference .07 .20
44 Perry Johnson .07 .20
45 Joel Kwiatkowski .07 .20
46 Zenith Komarniski .07 .20
47 Greg Kuznik .07 .20
48 Andrew Ference .07 .20
49 Jason Deleurme .07 .20
50 Trent Whitfield .07 .20
51 Dylan Gyori .07 .20
52 Todd Robinson .07 .20
53 Marian Hossa .40 1.00
54 Mike Hurley .07 .20
55 Greg Leeb .07 .20
56 Andrej Podkonicky .20 .50
57 Quinn Hancock .07 .20
58 Marian Cisar .07 .20
59 Bret DeCecco .07 .20
60 Brenden Morrow .20 .50
61 Evan Lindsay .20 .50
62 Terry Friesen .20 .50
63 Ryan Shannon .07 .20
64 Michal Rozsival .07 .20
65 Luc Theoret .07 .20
66 Brad Stuart .40 1.00
67 Burke Henry .07 .20
68 Cory Sarich .07 .20
69 Martin Sonnenberg .07 .20
70 Mark Smith .20 .50
71 Shawn McNeil .07 .20
72 Brad Moran .07 .20
73 Josh Holden .07 .20
74 Cory Cyrenne .07 .20
75 Shane Willis .07 .20
76 Stefan Cherneski .07 .20
77 Jay Henderson .07 .20
78 Ronald Petrovicky .07 .20
79 Sergei Varlamov .07 .20
80 Chad Hinz .07 .20
81 Mathieu Garon .20 .50
82 Mathieu Chouinard .20 .50
83 Dominic Perna .07 .20
84 Didier Tremblay .07 .20
85 Mike Ribeiro .20 .50
86 Marty Johnston .07 .20
87 Remi Royer .07 .20
88 Patrick Pelchat .07 .20
89 Daniel Corso .07 .20
90 Francois Fortier .07 .20
91 Marc-Andre Gaudet .07 .20
92 Francois Beauchemin .07 .20
93 Michel Tremblay .07 .20
94 Jean-Philippe Pare .07 .20
95 Francois Methot .07 .20
96 David Thibeault .07 .20
97 Jonathan Girard Jr. .20 .50
98 Karol Bartanus .07 .20
99 Peter Ratchuk .07 .20
100 Pierre Dagenais .20 .50
101 Philippe Sauve .40 1.00
102 Remi Bergeron .07 .20
103 Vincent Lecavalier .20 .50
104 Eric Chouinard .40 1.00
105 Oleg Timchenko .07 .20
106 Sebastien Roger .07 .20
107 Simon Gagne .40 1.00
108 Alex Tanguay .40 1.00
109 David Gosselin .07 .20
110 Ramzi Abid .20 .50
111 Eric Drouin .07 .20
112 Dominic Auger .07 .20
113 Martin Moise .07 .20
114 Randy Copley .07 .20
115 Alexandre Mathieu .07 .20
116 Brad Richards .20 .50
117 Dmitri Tolkunov .07 .20
118 Alexei Tezikov .07 .20
119 Derrick Walser .07 .20
120 Adam Borzecki .07 .20
121 Ramzi Abid .20 .50
122 Brett Allan .07 .20
123 Mark Bell .20 .50
124 Blair Betts .07 .20
125 Randy Copley .07 .20
126 Simon Gagne .40 1.00
127 Mike Henrich .07 .20
128 Vincent Lecavalier .20 .50
129 Norm Milley .40 1.00
130 Chris Neilsen .07 .20
131 Rico Fata .20 .50
132 Mike Ribeiro .20 .50
133 Bryan Allen .07 .20
134 John Erskine .20 .50
135 Jonathan Girard Jr. .20 .50
136 Stephen Peat .40 1.00
137 Robyn Regehr .30 .75
138 Brad Stuart .40 1.00
139 Patrick Desrochers .20 .50
140 Jason Labarbera .20 .50
141 David Cameron .07 .20
142 Jonathan Cheechoo .40 1.00
143 Eric Chouinard .40 1.00
144 Brent Gauvreau .07 .20
145 Scott Gomez .20 .50
146 Jeff Heerema .07 .20
147 David Legwand .40 1.00
148 Manny Malhotra .20 .50
149 Justin Papineau .07 .20
150 Andrew Peters .07 .20
151 Michael Rupp .40 1.00
152 Alex Tanguay .40 1.00
153 Francois Beauchemin .07 .20
154 Mathieu Biron .07 .20
155 Jiri Fischer .40 1.00
156A Alex Henry ERR Jer #26 .20 .50
156B Alex Henry COR Jer #68 .20 .50
157 Kyle Rossiter .07 .20
158 Martin Skoula .07 .20
159 Mathieu Chouinard .20 .50
160 Philippe Sauve .40 1.00
161 Brian Finley .15 .40
162 Brent Belecki .07 .20
163A Dominic Perna ERR IHMQ .07 .20
163B Dominic Perna COR MVP .07 .20
164 Jonathan Cheechoo .40 1.00
165 Checklist .07 .20

1998 Bowman CHL Golden Anniversary

Randomly inserted in packs at the rate of 1:57, this 165-card set is a gold-foil parallel version of the base set and is sequentially numbered to 50 in honor of the 50 years of Bowman cards.

*STARS: 12.5X TO 30X BASIC CARDS

1998 Bowman CHL OPC International

Inserted one in every pack, this 165-card set is parallel to the base set and features color player photos with a national indication in the background by way of a map printed on 16 pt. mirror board. Each back is written in the language of that player's native country.

*STARS: .75X TO 2X BASIC CARDS

1998 Bowman CHL Autographs Blue

Randomly inserted in packs at the rate of 1:39, this 40-card set features cards signed by the top 40 NHL draft prospects and authenticated by a blue foil "Topps Certified Issue" stamp. Silver and blue variations were also created and inserted randomly. Silver autos were inserted at a rate of 1:157 and gold at 1:470.

*SILVER AU's: .75X TO 2X BASIC AU
*GOLD AU's: 2X TO 5X BASIC AU
A1 Justin Papineau 2.50 6.00
A2 Jason Labarbera 4.00 10.00
A3 Michael Rupp 8.00 8.00
A4 Stephen Peat 3.00 8.00
A5 Manny Malhotra 2.50 6.00
A6 Michael Henrich 2.50 6.00
A7 Kyle Rossiter 2.50 6.00
A8 Mark Bell 3.00 8.00
A9 Mathieu Chouinard 4.00 10.00
A10 Vincent Lecavalier 10.00 25.00
A11 David Legwand 4.00 10.00
A12 Bryan Allen 2.50 6.00
A13 Francois Beauchemin 2.50 6.00
A14 Robyn Regehr 5.00 12.00
A15 Eric Chouinard 8.00 8.00
A16 Norman Milley 8.00 8.00
A17 Alex Henry 2.50 6.00
A18 Ramzi Abid 3.00 8.00
A19 Jiri Fischer 5.00 12.00
A20 Patrick Desrochers 8.00 8.00
A21 Mathieu Biron 2.50 6.00
A22 Brad Stuart 5.00 12.00
A23 Philippe Sauve 8.00 20.00
A24 John Erskine 8.00 8.00
A25 Jonathan Cheechoo 10.00 25.00
A26 Brett Allan 2.50 6.00
A27 Scott Gomez 6.00 15.00
A28 Chris Neilsen 2.50 6.00
A29 David Cameron 2.50 6.00
A30 Jonathan Girard Jr. 4.00 10.00
A31 Jeff Heerema 2.50 6.00
A32 Blair Betts 2.50 6.00
A33 Andrew Peters 2.50 6.00
A34 Randy Copley 8.00 8.00
A35 Alex Tanguay 6.00 15.00
A36 Simon Gagne 8.00 20.00
A37 Brent Gauvreau 2.50 6.00
A38 Mike Ribeiro 5.00 12.00
A39 Martin Skoula 2.50 6.00
A40 Rico Fata 4.00 10.00

1998 Bowman CHL Scout's Choice

Randomly inserted in packs at the rate of 1:12, this 21-card set features color photos of players picked by Bowman Hockey Scouts and printed on borderless, double-etched foil cards.

COMPLETE SET (21) 8.00 20.00
SC1 Bryan Allen .40 1.00
SC2 Manny Malhotra .40 1.00
SC3 Daniel Tkaczuk .40 1.00
SC4 Bujar Amidovski .40 1.00
SC5 Patrick Desrochers .40 1.00
SC6 Brad Ference .40 1.00
SC7 Marian Hossa .60 1.50
SC8 Brad Stuart .40 1.00
SC9 Sergei Varlamov .40 1.00
SC10 Randy Petruk .40 1.00
SC11 Karol Bartanus .40 1.00
SC12 Vincent Lecavalier .50 1.25
SC13 Jonathan Girard .40 1.00
SC14 Peter Ratchuk .40 1.00
SC15 Alex Tanguay .60 1.50
SC16 Rico Fata .40 1.00
SC17 Brian Finley .50 1.25
SC18 Jonathan Cheechoo .40 1.00
SC19 Scott Gomez .40 1.00
SC20 Michal Rozsival .40 1.00
SC21 Mathieu Garon .40 1.00

1998 Bowman Chrome CHL

The 1998-99 Bowman Chrome CHL hobby-only set was issued in one series totaling 165 cards. The 4-card packs retail for $3.00 each. The fronts feature color action photography on chromium technology. The Bowman Rookie Card stamp appears on all cards for players making their first appearance in the set. The scheduled release date was September, 1998.

COMPLETE SET (165) 30.00 60.00
1 Robert Esche .60 1.50
2 Chris Hajt .15 .40
3 Mark McMahon .15 .40
4 Jeff Brown .15 .40
5 Richard Jackman .15 .40
6 Greg Labenski .15 .40
7 Marek Posmyk .15 .40
8 Brian Willsie .15 .40
9 Jason Ward .15 .40
10 Manny Malhotra .15 .40
11 Matt Cooke .75 2.00
12 Mike Gorman .15 .40
13 Rodney Richard .15 .40
14 David Legwand .75 2.00
15 Jon Sim .15 .40
16 Peter Sarno .60 1.50
17 Andrew Long .15 .40
18 Peter Cava .15 .40
19 Colin Pepperall .15 .40
20 Jay Legault .15 .40
21 Brian Finley .60 1.50
22 Martin Skoula .15 .40
23 Brian Campbell .15 .40
24 Sean Blanchard .15 .40
25 Bryan Allen .15 .40
26 Peter Hogan .15 .40
27 Nick Boynton .75 2.00
28 Matt Bradley .15 .40
29 Jeremy Adduono .15 .40
30 Mike Henrich .15 .40
31 Justin Papineau .15 .40
32 Bujar Amidovski .60 1.50
33 Robert Mailloux .15 .40
34 Daniel Tkaczuk .15 .40
35 Sean Avery .75 2.00
36 Mark Bell .75 2.00
37 Kevin Colley .15 .40
38 Norm Milley .60 1.50
39 Scott Barney .15 .40
40 Joel Trottier .15 .40
41 Brent Belecki .15 .40
42 Randy Petruk .60 1.50
43 Brad Ference .15 .40
44 Perry Johnson .15 .40
45 Joel Kwiatkowski .15 .40
46 Zenith Komarniski .15 .40
47 Greg Kuznik .15 .40
48 Andrew Ference .60 1.50
49 Jason Deleurme .15 .40
50 Trent Whitfield .15 .40
51 Dylan Gyori .15 .40
52 Todd Robinson .15 .40
53 Marian Hossa .75 2.00
54 Mike Hurley .15 .40
55 Greg Leeb .15 .40
56 Andrej Podkonicky .15 .40
57 Quinn Hancock .15 .40
58 Marian Cisar .15 .40
59 Bret DeCecco .15 .40
60 Brenden Morrow .60 1.50
61 Evan Lindsay .60 1.50
62 Terry Friesen .60 1.50
63 Ryan Shannon .15 .40
64 Michal Rozsival .15 .40
65 Luc Theoret .15 .40
66 Brad Stuart .75 2.00
67 Burke Henry .15 .40
68 Cory Sarich .15 .40
69 Martin Sonnenberg .15 .40
70 Mark Smith .60 1.50
71 Shawn McNeil .15 .40
72 Brad Moran .15 .40
73 Josh Holden .15 .40
74 Cory Cyrenne .15 .40
75 Shane Willis .15 .40
76 Stefan Cherneski .15 .40
77 Jay Henderson .15 .40
78 Ronald Petrovicky .15 .40
79 Sergei Varlamov .15 .40
80 Chad Hinz .15 .40
81 Mathieu Garon .40 1.00
82 Mathieu Chouinard .60 1.50
83 Dominic Perna .15 .40
84 Didier Tremblay .15 .40
85 Mike Ribeiro .40 1.00
86 Marty Johnston .15 .40
87 Remi Royer .15 .40
88 Patrick Pelchat .15 .40
89 Daniel Corso .15 .40
90 Francois Fortier .15 .40
91 Marc-Andre Gaudet .15 .40
92 Francois Beauchemin .15 .40
93 Michel Tremblay .15 .40
94 Jean-Philippe Pare .15 .40
95 Francois Methot .15 .40
96 David Thibeault .15 .40
97 Jonathan Girard Jr. .60 1.50
98 Karol Bartanus .15 .40
99 Peter Ratchuk .15 .40
100 Pierre Dagenais .60 1.50
101 Philippe Sauve .75 2.00
102 Remi Bergeron .15 .40
103 Vincent Lecavalier .60 1.50
104 Eric Chouinard .60 1.50
105 Oleg Timchenko .15 .40
106 Sebastien Roger .15 .40
107 Simon Gagne .75 2.00
108 Alex Tanguay .75 2.00
109 David Gosselin .15 .40
110 Ramzi Abid .15 .40
111 Eric Drouin .15 .40
112 Dominic Auger .15 .40
113 Martin Moise .15 .40
114 Randy Copley .15 .40
115 Alexandre Mathieu .15 .40
116 Brad Richards .60 1.50
117 Dmitri Tolkunov .15 .40
118 Alexei Tezikov .15 .40
119 Derrick Walser .15 .40
120 Adam Borzecki .15 .40
121 Ramzi Abid .15 .40
122 Brett Allan .15 .40
123 Mark Bell .40 1.00
124 Blair Betts .15 .40
125 Randy Copley .60 1.50
126 Simon Gagne .75 2.00
127 Mike Henrich .15 .40
128 Vincent Lecavalier .60 1.50
129 Norm Milley .60 1.50
130 Chris Nielsen .15 .40
131 Rico Fata .60 1.50
132 Mike Ribeiro .40 1.00
133 Bryan Allen .15 .40
134 John Erskine .60 1.50
135 Jonathan Girard Jr. .60 1.50
136 Stephen Peat .75 2.00
137 Robyn Regehr .60 1.50
138 Brad Stuart .75 2.00
139 Patrick Desrochers .60 1.50
140 Jason Labarbera .60 1.50
141 David Cameron .15 .40
142 Jonathan Cheechoo 1.25 3.00
143 Eric Chouinard .60 1.50
144 Brent Gauvreau .15 .40
145 Scott Gomez .40 1.00
146 Jeff Heerema .15 .40
147 David Legwand .75 2.00
148 Manny Malhotra .15 .40
149 Justin Papineau .15 .40
150 Andrew Peters .15 .40
151 Michael Rupp .60 1.50
152 Alex Tanguay .75 2.00
153 Francois Beauchemin .15 .40
154 Mathieu Biron .15 .40
155 Jiri Fischer .75 2.00
156 Alex Henry .15 .40
157 Kyle Rossiter .15 .40
158 Martin Skoula .15 .40
159 Mathieu Chouinard .60 1.50
160 Philippe Sauve .75 2.00
161 Brian Finley .60 1.50
162 Brent Belecki .15 .40
163 Dominic Perna .15 .40
164 Jonathan Cheechoo .75 2.00
165 Checklist .15 .40
NNO Puck Redemption .15 .40

1998 Bowman Chrome CHL Golden Anniversary

Randomly inserted in packs at a rate of 1:39, this 165-card parallel offers the same players as in the Bowman Chrome CHL base set. The set is sequentially numbered to 50. Cards are randomly inserted into packs. A refractor variation was also created and inserted randomly. Refractors were serial numbered to just 5 and are not priced due to scarcity.

*STARS: 10X TO 25X BASIC CARDS

1998 Bowman Chrome CHL OPC International

Randomly inserted in packs at a rate of 1:8, this 165-card parallel features the same players as in the Bowman Chrome CHL base set. The set also offers background map designs of the player's homeland and vital statistics written in that player's native language. A refractor variation was also created and inserted at a rate of 1:48.

*STARS: 2.5X TO 5X BASIC CARD
*REF.STARS: 8X TO 20X BASIC CARDS

1998 Bowman Chrome CHL Refractors

Randomly inserted in packs at a rate of 1:12, this 165-card parallel offers a refractive version of the same players as in the Bowman Chrome CHL base set.

REF.STARS: 4X TO 10X BASIC CARD

1999 Bowman CHL

Released as a 165-card set, 1999 Bowman CHL set features 122 CHL superstars, 40 NHL draft prospects, two dual player cards of stars from the WHL, OHL, QMJHL and Prospects All-Star Game, and one checklist.

COMPLETE SET (165) 20.00 50.00
1 Alex Auld .30 .75
2 Maxime Ouellet .40 1.00
3 Nolan Yonkman .07 .20
4 Jeff Beatch .07 .20
5 Pavel Brendl .20 .50
6 Jamie Chamberlain .07 .20
7 Kyle Wanvig .07 .20
8 Chris Kelly .07 .20
9 Scott Kelman .07 .20
10 Derek MacKenzie .07 .20
11 Tim Connolly .20 .50
12 Alexandre Giroux .07 .20
13 Oleg Saprykin .20 .50
14 Sheldon Keefe .20 .50
15 Branislav Mezei .20 .50
16 Brett Lysak .07 .20
17 Peter Reynolds .07 .20
18 Ross Lupaschuk .07 .20
19 Mirko Murovic .07 .20
20 Steve McCarthy .20 .50
21 Radim Vrbata .20 .50
22 Dusty Jamieson .07 .20
23 Matt Carkner .07 .20
24 Denis Shvidki .20 .50
25 Jonathan Fauteux .07 .20
26 Martin Grenier .07 .20
27 Marc-Andre Thinel .20 .50
28 Luke Sellars .07 .20
29 Brad Ralph .07 .20
30 Scott Cameron .07 .20
31 Charlie Stephens .07 .20
32 Jamie Lundmark .20 .50
33 Justin Mapletoft .20 .50
34 Kristopher Beech .20 .50
35 Taylor Pyatt .20 .50
36 Michael Zigomanis .20 .50
37 Edward Hill .07 .20
38 Barret Jackman .40 1.00
39 Simon LaJeunesse .30 .75
40 Brian Finley .30 .75
41 Maxime Ouellet .40 1.00
42 Alexei Volkov .30 .75
43 Roberto Luongo .60 1.50
44 Chris Lyness .07 .20
45 Simon Tremblay .07 .20
46 Eric Tremblay .07 .20
47 Jonathan Girard .20 .50
48 Dimitri Tolkunov .07 .20
49 Philippe Plante .07 .20
50 Eric Chouinard .20 .50
51 Wesley Scanzano .07 .20
52 Vincent Dionne .07 .20
53 Sebastien Roger .07 .20
54 Ladislav Nagy .40 1.00
55 Alex Tanguay .40 1.00
56 Martin Moise .07 .20
57 Brad Richards .40 1.00
58 Juraj Kolnik .20 .50
59 Simon Gagne .40 1.00
60 Gregor Baumgartner .07 .20
61 Mathieu Benoit .07 .20
62 Pierre-Luc Therrien .07 .20
63 Danny LaVoie .07 .20
64 Mathieu Chouinard .07 .20
65 Andrew Carver .07 .20
66 Jiri Fischer .20 .50
67 Alexander Ryazantsev .07 .20
68 Didier Tremblay .07 .20
69 Mathieu Biron .07 .20
70 Michel Periard .07 .20
71 Mike Ribeiro .30 .75
72 Francois Fortier .07 .20
73 Benoit Dusablon .07 .20
74 Jerome Tremblay .07 .20
75 Samuel St.Pierre .07 .20
76 Marc-Andre Thinel .20 .50
77 Alexandre Tremblay .07 .20
78 Patrick Grandmaitre .07 .20
79 Christian Daigle .07 .20
80 David Thibeault .07 .20
81 Dominic Forget .07 .20
82 James Desmarais .07 .20
83 Pavel Brendl .20 .50
84 Kyle Calder .20 .50
85 Jason Chimera .20 .50
86 Chad Hinz .07 .20
87 Curtis Huppe .07 .20
88 Milan Kraft .20 .50
89 Brad Leeb .07 .20
90 Jamie Lundmark .20 .50
91 Brett Lysak .07 .20
92 Brad Moran .20 .50
93 Frantisek Mrazek .07 .20
94 Brad Twordik .07 .20
95 Kurt Drummond .07 .20
96 Burke Henry .07 .20
97 Steve McCarthy .20 .50
98 Richard Seeley .07 .20
99 Brad Stuart .30 .75
100 Luc Theoret .07 .20
101 Alexandre Fomitchev .07 .20
102 Brady Block .07 .20
103 Ajay Baines .07 .20
104 Blair Betts .20 .50
105 Tyler Bouck .20 .50
106 Mike Brown .07 .20
107 Bret DeCecco .07 .20
108 Scott Gomez .30 .75
109 Dylan Gyori .07 .20
110 Donnie Kinney .07 .20
111 Ken McKay .07 .20
112 Brett McLean .07 .20
113 Brenden Morrow .30 .75
114 Marty Standish .07 .20
115 Andrew Ference .20 .50
116 Brad Ference .07 .20
117 Scott Hannan .30 .75
118 Darrell Hay .07 .20
119 Robyn Regehr .30 .75
120 Chris St. Croix .07 .20
121 Kenric Exner .20 .50
122 Cody Rudkowsky .20 .50
123 Scott Barney .07 .20
124 Kevin Colley .07 .20
125 Sheldon Keefe .20 .50
126 Norman Milley .20 .50
127 Scott Page .07 .20
128 Justin Papineau .20 .50
129 Ryan Ready .07 .20
130 Denis Shvidki .20 .50
131 Chris Stanley .07 .20
132 Dan Tessier .07 .20
133 Daniel Tkaczuk .07 .20
134 Michael Zigomanis .20 .50
135 Jim Baxter .07 .20
136 Branislav Mezei .20 .50
137 Brian Campbell .07 .20
138 Greg Labenski .07 .20
139 Jeff McKercher .07 .20
140 Martin Skoula .20 .50
141 Brian Finley .20 .50
142 Seamus Kotyk .20 .50
143 Adam Colagiacomo .07 .20
144 Tim Connolly .30 .75
145 Harold Druken .20 .50
146 Rico Fata .20 .50
147 David Legwand .30 .75
148 Adam Mair .07 .20
149 Kent McDonell .07 .20
150 Ivan Novoseltsev .20 .50
151 Peter Sarno .20 .50
152 Dan Snyder .40 1.00
153 Jason Spezza 1.50 4.00
154 Jason Ward .07 .20
155 Alex Henry .07 .20
156 Wes Jarvis .07 .20
157 Paul Mara .20 .50
158 Kevin Mitchell .07 .20
159 Dan Passero .07 .20
160 Dan Watson .07 .20
161 Gene Chiarello .07 .20
162 Chris Madden .30 .75
163 Maxime Ouellet .30 .75
B.DeCecco

Barney .07 .20
hinel
hecklist .07 .20

1999 Bowman CHL Gold

omly inserted in packs, this 165-card set parallels se Bowman CHL set on cards enhanced with a nan Gold" stamp on the card front. Each card is mly inserted at a rate of one in eight packs and ntially numbered to 99.
RS: 6X TO 15X BASIC CARDS

1999 Bowman CHL OPC International

omly seeded in packs, this 165-card set parallels se Bowman CHL set on cards with enhanced rounds featuring a monument from the player's province or country. Card backs contain relevant written in the featured player's native language.
PLETE SET (165) 50.00 100.00
RS: .75X TO 2X BASIC CARDS

99 Bowman CHL Autographs

omly inserted in packs at the rate of 1:16, this 40-set features authentic autographs coupled with photography. Each card contains the gold foil nan Certified Autograph" stamp in the upper right corner. Silver and gold variations were also d and inserted randomly, Silver autos were ed at a rate of 1:43 and gold at 1:128. Note: Card 9, long thought not to exist, has been confirmed. o not have any pricing information, however.
ER: 1X TO 2X BASIC CARDS
D: 2.5X TO 5X BASIC CARDS
Brian Finley 2.50 6.00
Simon Lajeunesse 3.00 8.00
Barret Jackman 4.00 10.00
Edward Hill 2.00 5.00
Michael Zigomanis 2.50 6.00
Taylor Pyatt 4.00 10.00
Kristopher Beech 4.00 10.00
Justin Mapletoft 3.00 8.00
Jamie Lundmark 4.00 10.00
Charlie Stephens 2.00 5.00
Scott Cameron 2.00 5.00
Brad Ralph 2.00 5.00
Luke Sellars 2.00 5.00
Marc-Andre Thinel 2.50 6.00
Martin Grenier 3.00 8.00
Jonathan Fauteux 2.00 5.00
Denis Shvidki 2.00 5.00
Matt Carkner 2.00 5.00
Dusty Jamieson 2.00 5.00
Radim Vrbata 4.00 10.00
Alex Auld 5.00 12.00
Maxime Ouellet 6.00 15.00
Nolan Yonkman 2.00 5.00
Jeff Beatch 2.00 5.00
Pavel Brendl 3.00 8.00
Jamie Chamberlain 2.00 5.00
Kyle Wanvig 4.00 10.00
Chris Kelly 2.00 5.00
Scott Kelman 2.00 5.00
Derek MacKenzie 2.00 5.00
Tim Connolly 4.00 10.00
Alexandre Giroux 2.00 5.00
Oleg Saprykin 3.00 8.00
Sheldon Keefe 2.00 5.00
Branislav Mezei 2.00 5.00
Brett Lysak 3.00 8.00
Peter Reynolds 2.50 6.00
Ross Lupaschuk 2.00 5.00
Mirko Murovic 2.00 5.00
Steve McCarthy 2.00 5.00

1999 Bowman CHL Scout's Choice

omly inserted in packs at the rate of 1:12, this 21-set double-etched foil and identifies top ranked players. Card backs carry an "SC" prefix.
Tim Connolly 1.25 3.00
Scott Kelman .75 2.00
Pavel Brendl .75 2.00
Maxime Ouellet 1.25 3.00
Brian Finley 1.25 3.00
Denis Shvidki .75 2.00
Michael Zigomanis .75 2.00
Taylor Pyatt .75 2.00
Kris Beech .75 2.00
Jamie Lundmark .75 2.00
Jason Spezza 2.00 5.00
Rico Fata .75 2.00
David Legwand 1.25 3.00
Daniel Tkaczuk .75 2.00
Brad Stuart .75 2.00
Jiri Fischer .75 2.00
Simon Gagne 1.50 4.00
Alex Tanguay 1.25 3.00
Scott Gomez .75 2.00
Ladislav Nagy .75 2.00
Roberto Luongo 1.50 4.00

1991 Classic

set features 50 of the top 60 NHL draft picks. The as issued in a run of 360,000 factory sets and ded an individually numbered certificate of enticity. The cards were issued in both English French and carry the same value.
PLETE SET (50) 1.25 3.00
NCH: SAME VALUE
c Lindros .60 1.50
t Falloon .02 .10
ott Niedermayer .30 .75
ott Lachance .02 .10
er Forsberg .75 2.00
k Stojanov .02 .10
chard Matvichuk .02 .10
rick Poulin .02 .10
rtin Lapointe .08 .25
ler Wright .02 .10
hilippe Boucher .02 .10
at Peake .02 .10
larkus Naslund .30 .75
rent Bilodeau .02 .10
len Murray .15 .40
iklas Sundblad .02 .10
lartin Rucinsky .08 .25
revor Halverson .02 .10
ean McAmmond .02 .10
ay Whitney .08 .25
ene Corbet .02 .10
ric Lavigne .02 .10
gmund Palffy .15 .40
teve Staios .02 .10
m Campbell .02 .10
assen Cullimore .02 .10
artin Hamrlik .02 .10
amie Pushor .02 .10
onevan Hextall .02 .10
ndrew Verner .02 .10
ason Dawe .02 .10
32 Jeff Nelson .02 .10
33 Darcy Werenka .02 .10
34 Jozef Stumpel .08 .25
35 Francois Groleau .02 .10
36 Guy Leveque .02 .10
37 Jamie Matthews .02 .10
38 Dody Wood .02 .10
39 Yanic Perreault .08 .25
40 Jamie McLennan .08 .25
41 Yanic Dupre UER .02 .10
42 Sandy McCarthy .08 .25
43 Chris Osgood .30 .75
44 Fredrik Lindquist .02 .10
45 Jason Young .02 .10
46 Steve Konowalchuk .08 .25
47 Michael Nylander UER .08 .25
48 Shane Peacock .02 .10
49 Yves Sarault .02 .10
50 Marcel Cousineau .08 .25
NNO Patrick Poulin AU/1100 .75 2.00
NNO Rocket Ismail .08 .25

1991 Classic Promos

The two standard size promo cards were issued by Classic to show collectors and dealers the style of their new hockey draft picks set.
COMPLETE SET (2) 1.20 3.00
1 Eric Lindros 1.25 3.00
2 Pat Falloon .08 .25

1992 Classic

The 1992 Classic Hockey Draft Picks set consists of 120 standard-size cards. The production run for the regular issue cards was reportedly 9,966 ten-box cases. Classic also issued the 1992 Draft Pick set in a Gold version. The Gold factory sets were packaged in a walnut display case. The Gold sets also included an individually numbered card signed by Valeri and Pavol Bure. The set included the first card of female goaltender Manon Rheaume.
COMPLETE SET (120) 5.00 10.00
1 Roman Hamrlik .02 .10
2 Alexei Yashin .02 .10
3 Mike Rathje .02 .10
4 Darius Kasparaitis .02 .10
5 Cory Stillman .02 .10
6 Robert Petrovicky .02 .10
7 Andrei Nazarov .02 .10
8 Cory Stillman CL .02 .10
9 Jason Bowen .02 .10
10 Jason Smith .02 .10
11 David Wilkie .02 .10
12 Curtis Bowen .02 .10
13 Grant Marshall .02 .10
14 Valeri Bure .10 .30
15 Jeff Shantz .02 .10
16 Justin Hocking .02 .10
17 Mike Peca .20 .50
18 Marc Hussey .02 .10
19 Sandy Allan .10 .30
20 Kirk Maltby .10 .30
21 Cale Hulse .02 .10
22 Sylvain Cloutier .10 .30
23 Martin Gendron .02 .10
24 Kevin Smyth .02 .10
25 Jason McBain .02 .10
26 Lee J. Leslie .02 .10
27 Ralph Intranuovo .02 .10
28 Martin Reichel .02 .10
29 Stefan Ustorf .02 .10
30 Jarkko Varvio .02 .10
31 Jere Lehtinen .15 .40
32 Janne Gronvall .02 .10
33 Martin Straka .15 .40
34 Libor Polasek .02 .10
35 Jozef Cierny .02 .10
36 Jan Vopat .02 .10
37 Ondrej Steiner .02 .10
38 Jan Caloun .02 .10
39 Petr Hrbek .02 .10
40 Richard Smehlik .02 .10
41 Sergei Gonchar CL .02 .10
42 Sergei Krivokrasov .02 .10
43 Sergei Gonchar .10 .30
44 Boris Mironov .02 .10
45 Denis Metlyuk .02 .10
46 Sergei Klimovich .02 .10
47 Sergei Brylin .02 .10
48 Andrei Nikolishin .02 .10
49 Alexander Cherbayev .02 .10
50 Sergei Zholtok .02 .10
51 Vitali Prokhorov .02 .10
52 Nikolai Borschevsky .02 .10
53 Vitali Tomilin .02 .10
54 Alexander Alexeyev .02 .10
55 Roman Zolotov .02 .10
56 Konstantin Korotkov .02 .10
57 Laperriere Family .02 .10
58 Lacroix Family .02 .10
59 Manon Rheaume 1.50 4.00
60 Hamrlik .02 .10
Yashin
Rathje CL
61 Viktor Kozlov CL .02 .10
62 Viktor Kozlov .10 .30
63 Denny Felsner CL .02 .10
64 Denny Felsner .02 .10
65 Darrin Madeley .02 .10
66 Mario Lemieux FLB .60 1.50
67 Sandy Moger .02 .10
68 Dave Karpa .02 .10
69 Martin Jiranek .02 .10
70 Dwayne Norris .02 .10
71 Michael Stewart .02 .10
72 Joby Messier .02 .10
73 Mike Bales .10 .30
74 Scott Thomas .02 .10
75 Dan Laperriere .02 .10
76 Mike Lappin .02 .10
77 Eric Lacroix .02 .10
78 Martin Lacroix .02 .10
79 Scott LaGrand .02 .10
80 Jean-Yves Roy .02 .10
81 Scott Pellerin .02 .10
82 Rob Gaudreau .02 .10
83 Mike Boback .02 .10
84 Dixon Ward .02 .10
85 Jeff McLean .02 .10
86 Dallas Drake .02 .10
87 Bret Hedican .02 .10
88 Doug Zmolek .02 .10
89 Trent Klatt .02 .10
90 Larry Olimb .02 .10
91 Duane Derksen .10 .30
92 Doug MacDonald .02 .10
93 Dmitri Kvartalnov CL .02 .10
94 Jim Cummins .02 .10
95 Lonnie Loach .02 .10
96 Keith Jones .02 .10
97 Jason Woolley .02 .10
98 Rob Zamuner .10 .30
99 Brad Werenka .02 .10
100 Brent Grieve .02 .10
101 Sean Hill .10 .30
102 Keith Carney .02 .10
103 Peter Ciavaglia .02 .10
104 David Littman .10 .30
105 Bill Guerin .25 .60
106 Mikhail Kravets .02 .10
107 J.F. Quintin .02 .10
108 Mike Needham .02 .10
109 Jason Ruff .02 .10
110 Mike Vukonich .02 .10
111 Shawn McCosh .02 .10
112 Dave Tretowicz .02 .10
113 Todd Harkins .02 .10
114 Jason Muzzatti .02 .10
115 Paul Kruse .02 .10
116 Kevin Wortman .02 .10
117 Sean Burke .10 .30
118 Keith Gretzky .02 .10
119 Ray Whitney .10 .30
120 Dmitri Kvartalnov .02 .10
SP1 Mario Lemieux FLB 2.00 5.00
AU1 M.Lemieux AU/2000 40.00 80.00
AU2 Bure Brothers AU/6000 10.00 20.00

1992 Classic Gold

Classic also issued the 1992 Draft Picks set in a Gold version. The singles sell for between three and eight times the corresponding regular cards. Reportedly only 6,000 sets and 7,500 uncut sheets were produced. The sets were packaged in a walnut display case. The Gold factory sets also included an individually numbered card signed by Valeri and Pavel Bure.
*GOLD STARS: 1.5X TO 4X BASIC CARDS

1992 Classic Autographs

Cards have a pre-printed statement of authenticity on back.
COMPLETE SET
NNO Mike Peca 3.00 8.00
NNO Petr Hrbek 2.50 6.00
NNO Eric Lacroix 2.50 6.00
NNO Jeff McLean 2.50 6.00
NNO David Wilkie 2.50 6.00

1992 Classic Gold Promo

The front features a black-and-white action player photo bordered in white. The player's name is printed in a gold foil stripe beneath the picture, with the position given on a short black bar. On a gold background, the back has draft information, statistics, player profile, and a second black-and-white photo that is horizontally oriented. The card is unnumbered and has the disclaimer "For Promotional Purposes Only" printed on the back.
NNO Mario Lemieux 3.00 8.00

1992 Classic LPs

This ten-card standard-size set features hockey draft picks. The cards are numbered on the back with an "LP" prefix. The cards were random inserts in packs of 1992 Classic Hockey Draft Picks.
COMPLETE SET (10) 2.50 6.00
LP1 Roman Hamrlik .20 .50
LP2 Alexei Yashin .20 .50
LP3 Mike Rathje .20 .50
LP4 Darius Kasparaitis .20 .50
LP5 Cory Stillman .20 .50
LP6 Dmitri Kvartalnov .20 .50
LP7 David Wilkie .20 .50
LP8 Curtis Bowen .20 .50
LP9 Valeri Bure .40 1.00
LP10 Joby Messier .20 .50

1992 Classic Promos

These three cards measure the standard size and feature color action player photos with white borders, except for the Lemieux card, which has a black and white picture with the words "Flash Back 92" printed at the top. The player's name is printed in a gold stripe at the bottom, which intersects the Classic logo at the lower left corner. The gold backs have horizontally oriented player photos, again the Lemieux being black and white and the others color. The text on the back is vertically oriented, except for the biography, and includes draft information, career highlights, and the words "For Promotional Purposes Only". The cards are unnumbered and checklisted below in alphabetical order.
COMPLETE SET (3) 3.00 8.00
1 Roman Hamrlik 1.25 3.00
2 Mario Lemieux 2.00 5.00
(Flash Back 92)
3 Ray Whitney .40 1.00

1992 Classic Show Promos 20

This 20-card standard-size set was issued one card at a time at the various shows throughout the year where Classic maintained a presence or booth. Typically the cards were given out free to attendees while supplies lasted. The cards all read "Promo Card x of 20" prominently on the card back. The cards are done in several different styles depending on the Classic issue that was being promoted by that particular card.
COMPLETE SET (20) 15.00 30.00
15 Roman Hamrlik .20 .50
(1992 Tri-Star St. Louis)

1992-93 Classic C3

Limited to only 25,000 members, the Classic Collectors Club (also known as C3) featured two types of memberships: 1) the Presidential Charter membership (5,000), and 2) the Charter membership (20,000). As a bonus, the first 10,000 members received three packs of the bilingual edition of the 1991 Classic Draft Picks Collection. Exclusive to Presidential members were the following: a Brien Taylor autograph card (hand numbered "X/5,000"); an uncut sheet of either 1992 baseball, football, or hockey draft picks; and three special promo cards. In addition to other items (promo cards, T-shirt, newsletter, membership card, and posters), all members received a 30-card standard-size multi-sport set featuring tomorrow's future stars. Each set was accompanied by a certificate of limited edition, giving the set serial number and total production run (25,000). The sports represented are baseball (1-7, 25-27), basketball (8-13), football (14-20), hockey (21-24), track and field (28), and swimming (29).
COMP.FACT SET (30) 6.00 15.00
21 Roman Hamrlik .20 .50
22 Mike Rathje .20 .50
23 Manon Rheaume .75 2.00
24 Viktor Kozlov .40 1.00

1992-93 Classic Manon Rheaume C3 Presidential

This standard-size card pictures Rheaume holding a hockey stick and carrying an equipment bag over her shoulder. The picture is bordered in white, and her name and position are printed on the wider right border. The Classic "C3 Presidential" logo is gold foil stamped across the top of the picture. The back has a color close-up photo and a player quote. Reportedly only 5,000 of these cards were produced.
1 Manon Rheaume 4.00 10.00

1992-93 Classic Manon Rheaume Promo

Manon Rheaume, professional hockey's first female player, signed her trading card for fans before the Atlanta Braves playoff game Wednesday, October 7, 1992. Fans who brought a jar of pennies or a 10.00 donation were given the autographed Rheaume promotional card; close to 1,000 cards were signed and about 2,500 promo bags were given away. The words "A Classic First" are printed in gold at the upper right corner of the picture. "For Promotional Purposes Only" is printed twice on the card back.
NNO Manon Rheaume 4.00 10.00

1993 Classic

The 1993 Classic Hockey Draft set consists of 150 standard-size cards. Production was reported to be 14,500 sequentially-numbered ten-box cases. More than 15,000 autographed cards from Manon Rheaume, Doug Gilmour, Mark Recchi, Mike Bossy, Jeff O'Neill and other hockey stars were randomly inserted throughout the packs. Subsets featuring foil-stamped cards are Top 10, The Class of '94, The Daigle File, Flashbacks, College Champions, Manon Rheaume, and Hockey Art.
COMPLETE SET (150) 4.00 10.00
1 Alexandre Daigle .02 .10
2 Chris Pronger .20 .50
3 Chris Gratton .08 .25
4 Paul Kariya .40 1.00
5 Rob Niedermayer .02 .10
6 Viktor Kozlov .08 .25
7 Jason Arnott .20 .50
8 Niklas Sundstrom .02 .10
9 Todd Harvey .02 .10
10 Jocelyn Thibault .20 .50
11 Checklist 1 .02 .10
Top Draft Picks
12 Pat Peake .02 .10
1993 CHL POY
13 Jason Allison .25 .60
14 Todd Bertuzzi .20 .50
15 Maxim Bets .02 .10
16 Curtis Bowen .02 .10
17 Kevin Brown .02 .10
18 Valeri Bure .08 .25
19 Jason Dawe .02 .10
20 Adam Deadmarsh .02 .10
21 Aaron Gavey .02 .10
22 Nathan Lafayette .02 .10
23 Eric Lecompte .02 .10
24 Manny Legace .20 .50
25 Mike Peca .20 .50
26 Denis Pederson .02 .10
27 Jeff Shantz .02 .10
28 Nick Stadjuhar .02 .10
29 Cory Stillman .02 .10
30 Michal Sykora .02 .10
31 Brent Tully .02 .10
32 Mike Wilson .02 .10
33 K.Brown .02 .10
P.Peake
B.Wren
34 Daigle/Yashin .02 .10
35 Antti Aalto .02 .10
36 Radim Bicanek .02 .10
37 Vladimir Chebaturkin .02 .10
38 Alexander Cherbayev .02 .10
39 Markus Ketterer .02 .10
40 Saku Koivu .20 .50
41 Vladimir Kretchine .02 .10
42 Alexei Kudashov .02 .10
43 Janne Laukkanen .02 .10
44 Janne Niinimaa .02 .10
45 Juha Riihijarvi .02 .10
46 Nikolai Tsulygin .02 .10
47 Vesa Viitakoski .02 .10
48 David Vyborny .02 .10
49 Nikolai Zavarukhin .02 .10
50 Alexandre Daigle .02 .10
51 Alexandre Daigle .02 .10
52 Alexandre Daigle .02 .10
53 Alexandre Daigle .02 .10
54 Alexandre Daigle .02 .10
55 Jim Montgomery .02 .10
56 Mike Dunham .02 .10
57 Matt Martin .02 .10
58 Garth Snow .08 .25
59 Shawn Walsh .02 .10
60 Mark Bavis .02 .10
Mike Bavis
61 Scott Chartier .02 .10
62 Craig Darby .02 .10
63 Ted Drury .02 .10
64 Steve Dubinsky .02 .10
65 Joe Frederick .02 .10
66 Cammi Granato .20 .50
67 Brett Hauer .02 .10
68 Jon Hillebrandt .02 .10
69 Ryan Hughes .02 .10
70 Dean Hulett .02 .10
71 Kevin O'Sullivan .02 .10
72 Dan Plante .02 .10
73 Derek Plante .02 .10
74 Travis Richards .02 .10
75 Barry Richter .02 .10
76 David Roberts .02 .10
77 Chris Rogles .02 .10
78 Jon Rohloff .02 .10
79 Brian Rolston .02 .10
80 David Sacco .02 .10
81 Brian Savage .08 .25
82 Mike Smith .02 .10
83 Chris Tamer .02 .10
84 Chris Therien .02 .10
85 Aaron Ward .02 .10
86 Russian Celebration .02 .10
87 Vyacheslav Butsayev .02 .10
88 Jan Kaminsky .02 .10
89 Alexander Karpovtsev .02 .10
90 Valeri Karpov .02 .10
91 Sergei Petrenko .02 .10
92 Andrei Sapozhnikov .02 .10
93 Sergei Sorokin .02 .10
94 German Titov .02 .10
95 Andrei Trefilov .02 .10
96 Alexei Yashin .02 .10
97 Dimitri Yushkevich .02 .10
98 Radek Bonk .02 .10
99 Jason Bonsignore .02 .10
100 Brad Brown .02 .10
101 Chris Drury .40 1.00
102 Jeff Friesen .02 .10
103 Sean Haggerty .02 .10
104 Jeff Kealty .02 .10
105 Alexander Kharlamov .02 .10
106 Stanislav Neckar .02 .10
107 Tom O'Connor .02 .10
108 Jeff O'Neill .20 .50
109 Deron Quint .02 .10
110 Vadim Sharifianov .02 .10
111 Oleg Tverdovsky .08 .25
112 Manon Rheaume COMIC .30 .75
113 Paul Kariya COMIC .20 .50
114 Alexandre Daigle COMIC .02 .10
115 Jeff O'Neill COMIC .02 .10
116 Mike Bossy .20 .50
117 Pavel Bure .20 .50
118 Chris Chelios .20 .50
119 Doug Gilmour .08 .25
120 Roman Hamrlik .08 .25
121 Jari Kurri .20 .50
122 Alexander Mogilny .08 .25
123 Felix Potvin .20 .50
124 Teemu Selanne .40 1.00
125 Tommy Soderstrom .08 .25
126 Mike Bales .02 .10
127 Jozef Cierny .02 .10
128 Ivan Droppa .02 .10
129 Anders Eriksson .02 .10
130 Anatoli Fedotov .02 .10
131 Martin Gendron .02 .10
132 Daniel Guerard .02 .10
133 Corey Hirsch .02 .10
134 Milos Holan .02 .10
135 Kenny Jonsson .02 .10
136 Steven King .02 .10
137 Alexei Kovalev .20 .50
138 Sergei Krivokrasov .02 .10
139 Mats Lindgren .02 .10
140 Grant Marshall .02 .10
141 Jesper Mattsson .02 .10
142 Sandy McCarthy .02 .10
143 Dean Melanson .02 .10
144 Robert Petrovicky .02 .10
145 Mike Rathje .02 .10
146 Manon Rheaume .40 1.00
147 Claude Savoie .02 .10
148 Mikhail Shtalenkov .08 .25
149 Manon Rheaume .40 1.00
150 Manon Rheaume .40 1.00
MR1 M.Rheaume Acetate 10.00 25.00

1993 Classic Autographs

AU1 M.Bossy AU/975 12.50 30.00
AU2 P.Bure AU/900 20.00 50.00
AU3 C.Chelios AU/1800 15.00 40.00
AU4 D.Gilmour AU/1850 15.00 40.00
AU5 A.Mogilny/950 12.50 30.00
AU6 J.Montgomery AU/1800 2.00 5.00
AU7 R.Niedermayer AU/2500 12.50 30.00
AU8 J.O'Neill AU/2225 8.00 20.00
AU9 P.Peake AU/790 2.00 5.00
AU10 M.Recchi AU/1725 12.00 30.00
AU11 M.Rheaume AU/1500 15.00 40.00
AU12 G.Sanderson AU/875 2.00 5.00

1993 Classic Class of '94

These standard size cards were randomly inserted throughout the foil packs. The cards are acetates and the player's last name is in capital letters in the clear potion. The fronts also have a color action photo of the player. The backs have player statistics. The cards are numbered on the back with a "CL" prefix.
COMPLETE SET (7) 3.00 8.00
CL1 Jeff O'Neill .60 1.50
CL2 Jason Bonsignore .40 1.00
CL3 Jeff Friesen .40 1.00
CL4 Radek Bonk .40 1.00
CL5 Deron Quint .40 1.00
CL6 Vadim Sharifianov .40 1.00
CL7 Tom O'Connor .40 1.00

1993 Classic Crash Numbered

This 10-card standard-size set was randomly inserted throughout the foil packs and 15,000 individually numbered copies were made of each. The fronts have a color action photo with the player's name at the bottom in the icy border. The backs have a color photo on the right-side and player information and statistics on the left. The cards are numbered on the back with a "N" prefix.
COMPLETE SET (10) 30.00 80.00
N1 Alexandre Daigle 2.00 5.00
N2 Paul Kariya 6.00 15.00
N3 Jeff O'Neill 1.25 3.00
N4 Jason Bonsignore 2.00 5.00
N5 Teemu Selanne 6.00 15.00
N6 Pavel Bure 2.00 5.00
N7 Alexander Mogilny 2.00 5.00
N8 Manon Rheaume 5.00 12.00
N9 Felix Potvin 2.00 5.00
N10 Radek Bonk 1.25 3.00

1993 Classic Manon Rheaume Promo

This standard-size promo card features then-Atlanta Knights goaltender, Manon Rheaume. Inside a light gray border, the fronts features Rheaume in a sleeveless white blouse. The horizontal back has player information on the left and a second picture on the right with Rheaume dressed in black. The disclaimer "For Promotional Purposes Only" appears on the left beneath the text. The card is unnumbered.
NNO Manon Rheaume 2.00 5.00
Up Close

1993 Classic Previews

These five standard-size cards were inserted on an average of three per case of 1993 Classic Basketball Draft Picks. The fronts have a color action photo with the player's name at the bottom in the icy border. The backs say "preview" and tells that it is one of 17,500 preview cards of that player. The cards are unnumbered.
COMPLETE SET (5) 2.00 5.00
HK1 Alexandre Daigle .20 .50
HK2 Manon Rheaume 1.50 4.00
HK3 Barry Richter .20 .50
HK4 Teemu Selanne .75 2.00
HK5 Alexei Yashin .20 .50

1993 Classic Promos

These four standard-size promo cards feature gray-bordered glossy color player action shots on the fronts. The player's name and position appears in blue lettering within the bottom border. The back carries another color player action shot, but bordered in white. The player's biography and draft status are printed in black lettering within the broad lower border. The unnumbered Paul Kariya card was distributed at the San Francisco Labor Day Sports Collectors Convention, held in September 1993. The cards are numbered on the back with a "PR" prefix.
COMPLETE SET (4) 8.00 20.00
1 Alexandre Daigle 2.00 5.00
2 Jeff O'Neill 2.00 5.00
Jason Bonsignore
Jeff Friesen
The
3 Pavel Bure 2.00 5.00
NNO Paul Kariya 2.00 5.00

1993 Classic Team Canada

This seven-card standard size set was randomly inserted throughout the foil packs. These acetate cards have a color action photo on the left clear portion with player name at the bottom. The right-side has a letter so the complete set spells Canada. The backs have the player's name and statistics. The cards are numbered on the back with a "TC" prefix.
COMPLETE SET (7) 7.50 15.00
TC1 Greg Johnson .75 2.00
TC2 Paul Kariya 2.00 5.00
TC3 Brian Savage .75 2.00
TC4 Bill Ranford .75 2.00
TC5 Mark Recchi .75 2.00
TC6 Geoff Sanderson .75 2.00
TC7 Adam Graves .75 2.00

1993 Classic Top Ten

Measuring the standard-size, these ten acetate cards were randomly inserted throughout the foil packs. The cards have a color action photo, visible on both sides. the backs also have player statistics. The cards are numbered on the back with a "DP" prefix.
COMPLETE SET (10) 10.00 20.00
DP1 Alexandre Daigle .40 1.00
DP2 Chris Pronger 1.00 2.50
DP3 Chris Gratton .40 1.00
DP4 Paul Kariya 2.00 5.00
DP5 Rob Niedermayer .40 1.00
DP6 Viktor Kozlov .40 1.00
DP7 Jason Arnott .40 1.00
DP8 Niklas Sundstrom .40 1.00
DP9 Todd Harvey .40 1.00
DP10 Jocelyn Thibault 1.00 2.50

1993 Classic Superheroes

This purple-bordered three-card standard-size subset features the art work of Neal Adams, who has produced sports and comics fantasy cards of various athletes. It is one of two insert sets included (randomly inserted) in Classic's Deathwatch 2,000 110-card set. The horizontal backs carry a color action player photo with a player profile on a purple background.
COMPLETE SET (3) 8.00 20.00
SS2 Manon Rheaume 2.00 5.00

1993-94 Classic C3 Gold Crown Cut Lasercut

Along with the 20-card set checklisted below, the 10,000 members of the 1994 Classic Collectors Gold Crown Club received a 1994 C3 T-shirt, a TONX milk caps collectible sheet, a Classic Games magnet, and a 1994 C3 membership card. In later mailings they also received a 1993 Basketball Draft uncut sheet, a Chris Webber poster, and an autographed card of Jamal Mashburn, along with two promo cards. The sports represented are basketball (1-6), football (7-13), baseball (14-17), and hockey (18-20). The unnumbered checklist carries the set's production number out of the 10,000 produced.
COMPLETE SET (21) 10.00 25.00
18 Alexandre Daigle .40 1.00
19 Chris Pronger .40 1.00
20 Chris Gratton .40 1.00

1994 Classic

The 1994 Classic Hockey set consists of 120 standard-size cards. Production was reported at 6,000 U.S. and 2,000 Canadian 10-box foil cases. The Jason Arnott Canada World Champs card (numbered TC1) was randomly inserted into Canadian packs. Classic also offered a redemption program in which a collector sending in wrappers received various prizes. For each 216 wrappers redeemed a collector received either a Cam Neely or a Doug Gilmour autographed card. For each 360 wrappers redeemed, a Manon Rheaume autograph card was sent by Classic.
COMPLETE SET (120) 4.00 10.00
1 Ed Jovanovski .02 .10
2 Oleg Tverdovsky .01 .05
3 Radek Bonk .01 .05
4 Jason Bonsignore .01 .05
5 Jeff O'Neill .01 .05
6 Ryan Smyth .08 .25
7 Jamie Storr .02 .10
8 Jason Wiemer .01 .05
9 Nolan Baumgartner .01 .05
10 Jeff Friesen .01 .05
11 Wade Belak .01 .05
12 Ethan Moreau .02 .10
13 Alexander Kharlamov .01 .05
14 Eric Fichaud .02 .10
15 Wayne Primeau .01 .05
16 Brad Brown .01 .05
17 Chris Dingman .01 .05
18 Evgeni Ryabchikov .01 .05
19 Yan Golubovsky .01 .05
20 Chris Wells .01 .05
21 Vadim Sharifjanov .01 .05
22 Dan Cloutier .08 .25
23 Checklist .01 .05
24 Jamie Langenbrunner .01 .05
25 Kenny Jonsson .01 .05
26 Curtis Bowen .01 .05
27 Sergei Gonchar .02 .10
28 Stefan Bergqvist .01 .05
29 Vaclav Prospal .01 .05
30 Valeri Bure .01 .05
31 Richard Shulmistra .01 .05
32 Chris Armstrong .01 .05
33 Brian Farrell .01 .05
34 Brian Savage .02 .10
35 Blaine Lacher .01 .05
36 Kevin Brown .01 .05
37 Joe Dziedzic .01 .05
38 Peter Ferraro .01 .05
39 Chris Ferraro .01 .05
40 Todd Harvey .02 .10
41 Eric Lecompte .01 .05
42 Dean Grillo .01 .05
43 Valeri Karpov .01 .05
44 Andrew Shier .01 .05
45 Vesa Viitakoski .01 .05
46 Xavier Majic .01 .05
47 Kevin Smyth .01 .05
48 Jeff Nelson .01 .05
49 Cory Stillman .01 .05
50 Clayton Beddoes .01 .05
51 Craig Conroy .01 .05
52 Dean Fedorchuk .01 .05
53 John Gruden .01 .05
54 Chris McAlpine .01 .05
55 Sean McCann .01 .05
56 Derek Maguire .01 .05
57 David Oliver .01 .05
58 Mike Pomichter .01 .05
59 Jamie Ram .01 .05
60 Shawn Reid .01 .05
61 Dwayne Roloson .01 .05
62 Steve Shields .08 .25
63 Brian Wiseman .01 .05
64 Drew Bannister .01 .05
65 Matt Johnson .01 .05
66 Scott Malone .01 .05
67 Sergei Berezin .01 .05
68 Chad Penney .01 .05
69 Ian Laperriere .01 .05
70 Andrei Nikolishin .01 .05
71 Kelly Fairchild .01 .05
72 Jere Lehtinen .08 .25
73 Ravil Gusmanov .01 .05
74 Checklist .01 .05
75 Neil Little .01 .05
76 Brian Rolston .02 .10
77 David Vyborny .01 .05
78 Nikolai Tsulygin .01 .05
79 Niklas Sundstrom .01 .05
80 Patrik Juhlin .01 .05
81 Dan Plante .01 .05
82 Brandon Convery .01 .05
83 Nick Stajduhar .01 .05
84 Garth Snow .02 .10
85 Corey Hirsch .02 .10
86 Craig Darby .01 .05
87 Andrei Nazarov .01 .05
88 Todd Marchant .01 .05
89 Jeff Neilson .01 .05
90 Brendan Witt .01 .05
91 Denis Metlyuk .01 .05
92 Maxim Bets .01 .05
93 Sean Pronger .01 .05
94 Chris Tamer .01 .05
95 Saku Koivu .08 .25
96 Mattias Norstrom .02 .10
97 Ville Peltonen .02 .10
98 Rene Corbet .01 .05
99 Brent Gretzky .01 .05
100 Chris Marinucci .01 .05
101 Ian Moran .01 .05
102 Janne Laukkanen .01 .05
103 Todd Bertuzzi .08 .25
104 Darby Hendrickson .01 .05
105 Janne Niinimaa .01 .05
106 David Roberts .01 .05
107 Pat Neaton .01 .05
108 Mats Lindgren .01 .05
109 Todd Warriner .01 .05
110 Jason Allison .08 .25
111 Radim Bicanek .01 .05
112 Denis Pederson .02 .10
113 Viktor Kozlov .02 .10
114 Mike Murray .01 .05
115 Aaron Gavey .01 .05
116 Mike Peca .08 .25
117 Jason Zent .01 .05
118 Jason MacDonald .01 .05
119 Aaron Israel .01 .05
120 Manon Rheaume .60 1.50
TC1 Jason Arnott CWC .75 2.00
AU1 Doug Gilmour AU 8.00 20.00
AU2 Cam Neely AU 12.50 30.00
AU3 Manon Rheaume AU 12.50 30.00

1994 Classic Gold

Each of the 120 regular issue cards was issued as a parallel set with a gold-foil stamp and inserted at a rate of one gold card per pack. The card design is identical to the regular issue, except that the city name is printed in gold-foil stamped letters. In addition, collectors could acquire gold cards by mail. If Classic received either 36 or 54 wrappers in their redemption program from any collector, the collector received 10 gold cards. If a collector mailed in 108 wrappers, there were 25 gold cards sent from Classic. Also, a complete gold factory set was available to collectors who redeemed the Field card from the "Rookie of the Year?" insert set/contest.
*STARS: 1.25X TO 3X BASIC CARDS

1994 Classic All-Americans

Found only in U.S. cases and inserted at a rate of one card per box, this ten-card standard-size set spotlights first team NCAA All-Americans. The cards are serially numbered out of 6,000 on the back.
COMPLETE SET (10) 3.00 8.00
AA1 Craig Conroy .40 1.00
AA2 John Gruden .40 1.00
AA3 Chris Marinucci .40 1.00
AA4 Chris McAlpine .40 1.00
AA5 Sean McCann .40 1.00
AA6 David Oliver .40 1.00
AA7 Mike Pomichter .40 1.00
AA8 Jamie Ram .40 1.00
AA9 Shawn Reid .40 1.00
AA10 Dwayne Roloson .75 2.00

1994 Classic All-Rookie Team

Inserted in both U.S. and Canadian cases at a rate of one card per box. Each card is serially numbered out of 13,500.
COMPLETE SET (6) 4.00 10.00
AR1 Martin Brodeur 4.00 10.00
AR2 Jason Arnott .20 .50
AR3 Alexei Yashin .20 .50
AR4 Oleg Petrov .08 .25
AR5 Chris Pronger .75 2.00
AR6 Alexander Karpovtsev .08 .25

1994 Classic Autographs

Inserted at a rate of one card per box, this 36-card set measures the standard size. The backs carry a congratulatory message which serves to authenticate the signature. The autograph cards that correspond to the regular draft cards are listed in numerical order. In addition to the insertion of one per box, these cards were redeemable on a random basis in exchange for sending 72 wrappers to Classic.
3 Radek Bonk/4940 1.50 4.00
4 Jason Bonsignore/4300 .75 2.00
5 Jeff O'Neill/5380 1.50 4.00
10 Jeff Friesen/6145 4.00 10.00
34 Brian Savage/4930 1.50 4.00
38 Peter Ferraro/4875 .75 2.00
39 Chris Ferraro/4770 .75 2.00
76 Brian Rolston/2400 1.50 4.00
86 Craig Darby/1915 .75 2.00
94 Chris Tamer/1900 .75 2.00
106 David Roberts/1970 .75 2.00

NNO Rob Niedermayer/950 8.00 20.00
NNO Mike Dunham/1955 4.00 10.00
NNO Chris Marinucci .75 2.00
NNO Doug Gilmour/1950 15.00 30.00
120 Manon Rheaume/2280 15.00 40.00
NNO Chris Gratton/2000 6.00 15.00
NNO Dan Plante .75 2.00
NNO Dallas Drake/960 .75 2.00
NNO Dean Hulett/1955 .75 2.00
NNO Aaron Ward/1965 .75 2.00
NNO Jon Rohloff/2010 .75 2.00
NNO Mike Bavis/1955 4.00 10.00
NNO Ryan Hughes/1940 .75 2.00
NNO Brett Hauer/1930 .75 2.00
NNO Travis Richards/1950 .75 2.00
NNO Jim Storm/1950 .75 2.00
NNO Scott Chartier/1930 .75 2.00
NNO Ted Drury/1920 .75 2.00
NNO Brett Harkins/1885 .75 2.00
NNO Fred Knipscheer/1945 .75 2.00
NNO Stanislav Neckar/4645 .75 2.00
NNO Chris Rogles/1920 .75 2.00
NNO Jon Hillebrandt/1570 .75 2.00
NNO Cam Stewart/970 .75 2.00
NNO Barry Richter/1935 .75 2.00
NNO David Sacco/1975 .75 2.00
NNO Eric Fenton/1845 .75 2.00
NNO John Lilley/2460 .75 2.00
NNO Derek Plante/1970 1.50 4.00

1994 Classic CHL All-Stars

This 10-card standard-size set was randomly inserted in Canadian foil packs only. The fronts have a color action photo with the player's name at the top along with the CHL emblem. The backs have a full-color action photo with player information and the number printed out of 2,000. The cards are numbered on the back with a "C" prefix.

COMPLETE SET (10) 7.50 20.00
C1 Jason Allison 1.25 3.00
C2 Yanick Dube .40 1.00
C3 Eric Fichaud .75 2.00
C4 Jeff Friesen .40 1.00
C5 Aaron Gavey .40 1.00
C6 Ed Jovanovski .75 2.00
C7 Jeff O'Neill 1.25 3.00
C8 Ryan Smyth 1.25 3.00
C9 Jamie Storr .75 2.00
C10 Brendan Witt .40 1.00

1994 Classic CHL Previews

Randomly inserted in Canadian foil packs only, this six-card standard-size set was created to preview Classic's 1995 CHL set. Unfortunately, the company was unable to complete negotiations with the league, and the full set was never created.

COMPLETE SET (6) 15.00 25.00
CP1 Wayne Primeau 1.25 3.00
CP2 Eric Fichaud 2.50 6.00
CP3 Wade Redden 2.50 5.00
CP4 Jason Doig 1.25 3.00
CP5 Vitali Yachmenev 1.25 3.00
CP6 Nolan Baumgartner 1.25 3.00

1994 Classic Draft Day

Issued in a ten-card cello pack, these cards were issued on the occasion of the NHL draft, which took place on June 28-29, 1994. The cards measure the standard size, and were available through a wrapper redemption offer. The fronts feature borderless color action player photos; the player's name is printed in a bar at the bottom that intersects the Classic logo at the lower left corner. The city (or state) of the teams that were likely to draft the player is printed vertically in block lettering along the right edge. The backs carry the "Draft Day 94" logo superimposed over a color painting of a hockey player. A tagline at the bottom rounds out the back and gives the production figures "1 of 10,000". The cards are unnumbered and checklisted below in alphabetical order.

COMPLETE SET (10) 12.50 30.00
1 Radek Bonk 1.50 4.00
2 Radek Bonk 1.50 4.00
3 Radek Bonk 1.50 4.00
4 Jason Bonsignore 1.50 4.00
5 Ed Jovanovski 1.50 4.00
6 Ed Jovanovski 1.50 4.00
7 Ed Jovanovski 1.50 4.00
8 Jeff O'Neill 1.50 4.00
9 Jeff O'Neill 1.50 4.00
10 Jeff O'Neill 1.50 4.00

1994 Classic Draft Prospects

Found only in U.S. cases and inserted at a rate of one card per box, this ten-card standard-size set features players expected to be selected early in the 1995 NHL entry draft. The fronts feature the player's name in capital letters on the top with a small notation underneath that he is a 1995 Draft Prospect. The majority of the card is devoted to the player's photo. The reverse of the card features the player's photo on the left side of the cards with a biography on the right side. The cards are numbered in the top left corner. Each card is serially numbered out of 6,000 on the bottom.

COMPLETE SET (10) 5.00 12.00
DP1 Bubba Berenzweig .40 1.00
DP2 Aki Berg .40 1.00
DP3 Chad Kilger .40 1.00
DP4 Daymond Langkow .75 2.00
DP5 Alyn McCauley .75 2.00
DP6 Igor Melyakov .40 1.00
DP7 Erik Rasmussen .40 1.00
DP8 Marty Reasoner .75 2.00
DP9 Scott Roche .75 2.00
DP10 Petr Sykora 2.00 5.00

1994 Classic Enforcers

Featured in both U.S. and Canadian cases and inserted on average of three cards per box, this ten-card standard-size set captures the toughest players in the minor leagues. The horizontal fronts feature color action player photos with the player's name in a black bar at the bottom. The set name also appears at the bottom. On a background consisting of a crude drawing of the front photo, the back carries a player profile.

COMPLETE SET (10) 7.50 15.00
E1 Donald Brashear 1.25 3.00
E2 Daniel Lacroix .60 1.50
E3 Dale Henry .60 1.50
E4 John Badduke .60 1.50
E5 Corey Schwab 1.25 3.00
E6 Craig Martin .60 1.50
E7 Kerry Clark .60 1.50
E8 Kevin Kaminski .60 1.50
E9 Jim Kyte .60 1.50
E10 Mark DeSantis .60 1.50

1994 Classic Enforcers Promo

This standard-size card was issued to promote the 1994 Classic hockey series. The horizontal front features Richard Zemlak preparing to fight another player. On a background consisting of a crude drawing of the front photo, the back presents an advertisement for Classic hockey cards. The card is numbered on the back in the upper right corner.

PR1 Richard Zemlak .40 1.00

1994 Classic Picks

This five-card standard-size set was randomly inserted in packs. The fronts feature color action photos with the player's name and the Classic logo at the bottom. The backs carry the player's name in the upper left, card number in the upper right, career and biographical information, logos, and a small color player photo.

COMPLETE SET (5) 6.00 15.00
CP11 Ed Jovanovski 2.00 5.00
CP12 Oleg Tverdovsky .75 2.00
CP13 Radek Bonk .75 2.00
CP14 Jason Allison 2.00 5.00
CP15 Manon Rheaume 2.00 5.00

1994 Classic Previews

Randomly inserted in 1994 Classic basketball packs, this 5-card set measures the standard-size. The fronts feature full-bleed color action photos, except at the bottom where a color stripe carries the player's name. The word "PREVIEW" is printed vertically in large block letters running down the right edge. On a purple-tinted action photo, the backs display the Classic logo and a short congratulatory message. The cards are unnumbered and checklisted below in alphabetical order.

COMPLETE SET (5) 10.00 20.00
HK1 Jason Allison 1.50 4.00
HK2 Radek Bonk .75 2.00
HK3 Xavier Majic .75 2.00
HK4 Manon Rheaume 7.50 15.00
HK5 Oleg Tverdovsky 1.50 4.00

1994 Classic ROY Sweepstakes

This 20-card standard-size set was featured in U.S. and Canadian cases and inserted on average of five cards per case. Holders of the winning Field Card could redeem it for a complete set of 1994 Classic Hockey Gold cards. The fronts feature a color action player cutout superimposed over a large hockey puck. The words "Rookie of the Year?" and the player's name appear along the right. The backs carry the checklist, along with information on how to claim the prize. The deadline for redeeming cards was September 1, 1995.

COMPLETE SET (20) 4.00 10.00
R1 Jason Allison .60 1.50
R2 Radek Bonk .20 .50
R3 Jason Bonsignore .08 .25
R4 Valeri Bure .20 .50
R5 Jeff Friesen .20 .50
R6 Aaron Gavey .08 .25
R7 Todd Harvey .20 .50
R8 Kenny Jonsson .20 .50
R9 Ed Jovanovski .60 1.50
R10 Patrik Juhlin .08 .25
R11 Valeri Karpov .08 .25
R12 Viktor Kozlov .20 .50
R13 Blaine Lacher .20 .50
R14 Andrei Nikolishin .08 .25
R15 Jeff O'Neill .40 1.00
R16 David Oliver .08 .25
R17 Garth Snow .20 .50
R18 Jamie Storr .20 .50
R19 Oleg Tverdovsky .20 .50
R20 Field Card WIN G .08 .25

1994 Classic Tri-Cards

Featured in both U.S. and Canadian cases and inserted at a rate of two cards per box, this 26-card standard-size set showcases the top three prospects from each NHL city. The horizontal fronts feature three borderless color player photos next to each other, with the player's name in a black bar under each photo, and the team name in a purple bar directly below. The backs carry three small color player portraits with a brief player profile. The cards are arranged alphabetically by city name. Each card has three numbers.

COMPLETE SET (26) 30.00 60.00
T1 Karpov/2 Tsul/3 Tverdovsky 1.25 3.00
T4 Knip/5 Lacher/6 Ryabchikov 1.25 3.00
T7 David CooperT8 .75 2.00
Wayne Primeau
T9Steve Shields
T10 Chris Dingman .75 2.00
T11Cory Stillman
T12Vesa Vii
T13 Eric Lecompte .75 2.00
T14Ethan Moreau
T15Mike Pomichter
T16 Harvey/17 Langen/18 Lehtin 1.25 3.00
T19 Curtis Bowen .75 2.00
T20Yan Golubovsky
T21Kevin Hodson
T22 Bonsignore/23 Lind/24 Oliver 1.25 3.00
T25 Arms/26 Jovanovski/27 Podo 1.50 4.00
T28 Andrei Nikolishin .75 2.00
T29}Jeff O'Neill
T30}Kevin Smyth
T31 Brown/32 Johnson/33 Storr 1.25 3.00
T34 Bure/35 Koivu/36 Savage 3.00 8.00
T37 Denis Pederson .75 2.00
T38}Brian Rolston
T39}Vadim
T40 Todd Bertuzzi .75 2.00
T41} Chris Marinucci
T42}Dan
T43 Corey Hirsch .75 2.00
T44Niklas Sundstrom#}T45Scott Malone
T46 Bicanek/47 Bonk/48 Penney 1.25 3.00
T49 Patrik Juhlin .75 2.00
50Denis Metlyuk
T51Janne Niinimaa
T52 Greg Andrusak .75 2.00
T53Pat Neaton
T54Chris Wells
T55 Rene Corbet .75 2.00
T56Adam Deadmarsh
T57Garth Snow
T58 David Roberts .75 2.00
T59Ian Laperriere
T60Patrice Tardiff
T61 Friesen/62 Kozlov/63 Pelton 1.50 4.00
T64 Aaron Gavey .75 2.00
T65Brent Gretzky
T66Jason Weimer
T67 Conv/68 Fichaud/69 Jonsson 1.50 4.00
T70 Mike Fountain .75 2.00
T71Rick Girard
T72Mike Peca
T73 Jason Allison .75 2.00
T74Alexander Kharlamov
T75Brendan Witt
T76 Mika Alatalo .75 2.00
T77Ravil Gusmanov
T78Deron Quint

1994 Classic Women of Hockey

Inserted in both U.S. and Canadian product at a rate of one card per pack, this 40-card standard-size set features female hockey players who represented Canada (1-21) and the U.S.A. (22-40) at the 1994 World Women's Ice Hockey Championships. The fronts have color action player cutouts superimposed over a Canadian or American flag with a metallic sheen. The words "Team Canada Women" or "Team USA Women" appear alongside the right, while the player's name is printed at the bottom. The backs carry a close-up color player photo, along with stats from the tournament (won by Canada) and player profile.

COMPLETE SET (40) 8.00 20.00
W1 Manon Rheaume 1.25 3.00
W2 France St. Louis .20 .50
W3 Cheryl Pounder .20 .50
W4 Therese Brisson .20 .50
W5 Cassie Campbell .75 2.00
W6 Angela James .20 .50
W7 Danielle Goyette .40 1.00
W8 Jane Robinson .20 .50
W9 Stacy Wilson .20 .50
W10 Margot Page .20 .50
W11 Laura Leslie .20 .50
W12 Judy Diduck .20 .50
W13 Hayley Wickenheiser 2.00 5.00
W14 Nathalie Picard .20 .50
W15 Leslie Reddon .20 .50
W16 Marianne Grnak .20 .50
W17 Andria Hunter .20 .50
W18 Nancy Drolet .40 1.00
W19 Geraldine Heaney .20 .50
W20 Karen Nystrom .20 .50
W21 Manon Rheaume CL .40 1.00
W22 Kelly Dyer .20 .50
W23 Vicki Movsessian .20 .50
W24 Lisa Brown .20 .50
W25 Shawna Davidson .20 .50
W26 Colleen Coyne .20 .50
W27 Karyn Bye .75 2.00
W28 Suzanne Merz .20 .50
W29 Gretchen Ulion .20 .50
W30 Sandra Whyte .20 .50
W31 Cindy Curley .20 .50
W32 Michele DiFronzo .20 .50
W33 Stephanie Boyd .20 .50
W34 Shelley Looney .20 .50
W35 Jeanine Sobek .20 .50
W36 Beth Beagan .20 .50
W37 Cammi Granato .75 2.00
W38 Christina Bailey .20 .50
W39 Kelly O'Leary .20 .50
W40 Erin Whitten .30 .75

1994 Classic International Promos

This four-card standard-size set was given away during the International Sportscard and Memorabilia Expo at the Anaheim Convention Center July 19-24, 1994. The fronts display full-bleed color action shots. The player's name appears in red print on a black bar near the bottom. On a dark screened background, the backs carry the logo for the card show. The cards are unnumbered and checklisted below in alphabetical order.

COMPLETE SET (4) 3.00 8.00
2 Radek Bonk BK .40 1.00

1994 Classic National Promos

This five-card standard-size set was issued to promote the 15th National Sports Collectors Convention in Houston August 4-7, 1994. The fronts display full-bleed color action shots. The player's name appears in red print on a black bar near the bottom. On a dark screened background, the backs carry a gold foil National Convention logo. The Hill card was given out on Exhibitor Preview Night, as noted on its back. The cards are unnumbered and checklisted below in alphabetical order.

COMPLETE SET (5) 6.00 15.00
1 Jason Arnott HK .75 2.00

1995 Classic

This 100-card standard-size set marked the conclusion of the fifth (and so far, final) set Classic issued featuring hockey prospects. 3,990 sequentially numbered American cases and 999 Canadian cases were issued with 12 boxes in a case, 36 packs in a box and 10 cards in a pack. There were also a special Manon Rheaume autograph card issued on the average of one per case. One Hot Box, containing nothing but inserts, was inserted one every five cases.

COMPLETE SET (100) 3.00 8.00
1 Bryan Berard .05 .15
2 Wade Redden .01 .05
3 Aki Berg .01 .05
4 Chad Kilger .01 .05
5 Daymond Langkow .05 .15
6 Steve Kelly .01 .05
7 Shane Doan .08 .25
8 Terry Ryan .01 .05
9 Mike Martin .01 .05
10 Radek Dvorak .08 .25
11 Jarome Iginla .08 .25
12 Teemu Riihijarvi .01 .05
13 Jean-Sebastien Giguere .08 .25
14 Peter Schaefer .01 .05
15 Jeff Ware .01 .05
16 Martin Biron .60 1.50
17 Brad Church .01 .05
18 Petr Sykora .08 .25
19 Denis Gauthier .01 .05
20 Sean Brown .01 .05
21 Brad Isbister .20 .50
22 Miikka Elomo .01 .05
23 Mathieu Sunderland .01 .05
24 Marc Moro .01 .05
25 Jan Hlavac .08 .25
26 Brian Wesenberg .01 .05
27 Mike McBain .01 .05
28 Georges Laraque .08 .25
29 Marc Chouinard .08 .25
30 Donald MacLean .01 .05
31 Jason Doig .01 .05
32 Aaron MacDonald .01 .05
33 Patrick Cote .01 .05
34 Christian Dube .01 .05
35 Chris McAllister .01 .05
36 Denis Smith .01 .05
37 Mark Dutiaume .01 .05
38 Dwayne Hay .01 .05
39 Nathan Perrott .01 .05
40 Christian Laflamme .01 .05
41 Paxton Schafer .01 .05
42 Shane Kenny .01 .05
43 Nic Beaudoin .01 .05
44 Philippe Audet .01 .05
45 Brad Larsen .01 .05
46 Ryan Pepperall .01 .05
47 Mike Leclerc .05 .15
48 Shane Willis .10 .30
49 Darryl Laplante .01 .05
50 Larry Courville .01 .05
51 Mike O'Grady .01 .05
52 Petr Buzek .01 .05
53 Alyn McCauley .01 .05
54 Scott Roche .01 .05
55 John Tripp .01 .05
56 Johnathan Aitken .01 .05
57 Blake Bellefeuille .01 .05
58 Daniel Briere .20 .50
59 Josh DeWolf .01 .05
60 Josh Green .01 .05
61 Chris Hajt .01 .05
62 Josh Holden .01 .05
63 Henry Kuster .01 .05
64 Dan Lacouture .01 .05
65 Oleg Orekhovsky .01 .05
66 Andrei Petrunin .01 .05
67 Tom Poti .01 .05
68 Peter Ratchuk .01 .05
69 Andrei Zyuzin .01 .05
70 George Breen .01 .05
71 Greg Bullock .01 .05
72 Kent Fearns .01 .05
73 Eric Flinton .01 .05
74 Brian Holzinger .01 .06
75 Chris Kenady .01 .05
76 Kaj Linna .01 .05
77 Brian Mueller .01 .05
78 Brent Peterson .01 .05
79 Chad Quenneville .01 .05
80 Randy Stevens .01 .05
81 Adam Wiesel .01 .05
82 Barrie Colts .01 .05
83 Belleville Bulls .01 .05
84 Detroit Jr. Whalers .01 .05
85 Guelph Storm .01 .05
86 Kingston Frontenacs .01 .05
87 Kitchener Rangers .01 .05
88 London Knights .01 .05
89 Niagara Falls Thunder .01 .05
90 North Bay Centennials .01 .05
91 Oshawa Generals .08 .25
92 Ottawa 67's .01 .05
93 Owen Sound Platers .01 .05
94 Peterborough Petes .01 .05
95 S.S. Marie Greyhounds .50 1.25
96 Sarnia Sting .01 .05
97 Sudbury Wolves .01 .05
98 Windsor Spitfires .01 .05
99 Bryan Berard CL .01 .05
100 Wade Redden CL .01 .05

1995 Classic Gold

This 100 card set is a parallel to the regular Classic issue. The cards are inserted one per American pack.

COMPLETE SET (100) 20.00 40.00
*GOLD: 1.2X TO 3X BASIC CARDS

1995 Classic Printer's Proofs

These cards were inserted approximately one per box. The cards carry an announced print run of 749.

COMPLETE SET (100) 150.00 300.00
*PRINT.PROOF/749: 8X TO 20X BASIC CARDS

1995 Classic Printer's Proofs Gold

These 100 cards are a parallel to the Classic Gold set. The cards were inserted one every three boxes and are numbered out of 249.

GOLD/249: 12X TO 30X BASIC CARDS

1995 Classic Silver

This 100 card standard-size set is a parallel to the regular Classic issue. The cards were inserted one per Canadian pack.

COMPLETE SET (100) 20.00 40.00
*SILVER: .6X TO 1.5X BASIC CARDS

1995 Classic Autographs

These 24 standard-size cards were inserted on the average of one per box. Classic guaranteed that there would be one autographed card in each box. The front is a picture of the card along with the signature. The back is a congratulatory message that you have received an authentic signed card.

1 George Breen/2400 .75 2.00
2 Greg Bullock/2485 .75 2.00
3 Petr Buzek/3978 1.50 4.00
4 Radek Dvorak/4022 2.00 5.00
5 Kent Fearns/4034 .75 2.00
6 Eric Flinton/2495 .75 2.00
7 Josh Green/4293 .75 2.00
8 Josh Holden/4994 .75 2.00
9 B.Holzinger/2599 .75 2.00
10 Ed Jovanovski/2584 1.50 4.00
11 Chris Kenady/2500 .75 2.00
12 Henry Kuster/2490 .75 2.00
13 Josef Marha/2584 .75 2.00
14 Brian Mueller/2488 .75 2.00
15 Angel Nikolov/2500 .75 2.00
16 Oleg Orekhovsky/5090 .75 2.00
17 Brent Peterson/2468 .75 2.00
18 A.Petrunin/4764 .75 2.00
19 Chad Quenneville/2500 .75 2.00
20 M.Satan/2487 12.50 30.00
21 Randy Stevens/2591 .75 2.00
22 Petr Sykora/792 12.50 30.00
23 Adam Wiesel/2511 .75 2.00
24 Andrei Zyuzin/5076 .75 2.00
NNO Manon Rheaume/6300 12.50 30.00

1995 Classic CHL All-Stars

These cards feature all-stars of the CHL. They were inserted into Canadian packs at a ratio of 1:72. The cards are hand serial numbered to 849.

COMPLETE SET (18) 25.00 50.00
AS1 Nolan Baumgartner .75 2.00
AS2 Wade Redden 1.50 4.00
AS3 Henry Kuster .75 2.00
AS4 Daymond Langkow 1.50 4.00
AS5 Shane Doan 2.00 5.00
AS6 Steve Kelly .75 2.00
AS7 Tyler Moss .75 2.00
AS8 Bryan Berard 1.50 4.00
AS9 Ed Jovanovski 1.50 4.00
AS10 Chad Kilger .75 2.00
AS11 Daniel Cleary .75 2.00
AS12 Ethan Moreau .75 2.00
AS13 Jean-Sebastien Giguere 1.50 4.00
AS14 Denis Gauthier .75 2.00
AS15 Jason Doig .75 2.00
AS16 Etienne Drapeau .75 2.00
AS17 Daniel Briere 1.50 4.00
AS18 Mark Chouinard .75 2.00

1995 Classic Ice Breakers

These cards were randomly inserted into packs at a ratio of approximately one every other box. The cards are numbered "1 of 1,649". The cards feature some of the leading prospects which included Bryan Berard, Nolan Baumgartner and Wade Redden. A die-cut Ice Breakers version of these cards were issued as well. These cards were sequentially numbered to 495. The cards are numbered with a "BK" prefix.

COMPLETE SET (20) 15.00 40.00
*DIE CUT/495: 1X TO 2.5X BASIC INSERT
BK1 Bryan Berard 1.25 3.00
BK2 Wade Redden 1.25 3.00
BK3 Aki Berg 1.00 2.50
BK4 Chad Kilger 1.00 2.50
BK5 Daymond Langkow 1.25 3.00
BK6 Steve Kelly 1.00 2.50
BK7 Shane Doan 1.50 4.00
BK8 Terry Ryan 1.00 2.50
BK9 Radek Dvorak 1.50 4.00
BK10 Miikka Elomo 1.00 2.50
BK11 Teemu Riihijarvi 1.00 2.50
BK12 Jean-Sebastien Giguere 1.25 3.00
BK13 Martin Biron 1.50 4.00
BK14 Jeff Ware 1.00 2.50
BK15 Brad Church 1.00 2.50
BK16 Petr Sykora 1.50 4.00
BK17 Jason Bonsignore 1.00 2.50
BK18 Brian Holzinger 1.00 2.50
BK19 Ed Jovanovski 1.25 3.00
BK20 Nolan Baumgartner 1.00 2.50

1995 Classic Five Sport

The 1995 Classic Five Sport set was issued in one series of 200 standard-size cards. Cards were issued in 10-card regular packs (SRP $1.99). Boxes contained 36 packs. One autographed card was guaranteed in each pack and one certified autographed card (with an embossed logo) appeared in each box. There were also memorabilia redemption cards included in some packs and were guaranteed in at least one pack per box. The cards are numbered and divided into the five sports as follows: Basketball (1-42), Football (43-92), Baseball (93-122), Hockey (123-160), Racing (161-180), Alma Maters (181-190), Picture Perfect (191-200).

COMPLETE SET (200) 6.00 15.00
123 Bryan Berard .05 .15
124 Wade Redden .05 .15
125 Aki-Petteri Berg .05 .15
126 Nolan Baumgartner .05 .15
127 Jason Bonsignore .05 .15
128 Steve Kelly .05 .15
129 George Breen .05 .15
130 Terry Ryan .05 .15
131 Greg Bullock .05 .15
132 Jarome Iginla .30 .75
133 Petr Buzek .05 .15
134 Brad Church .05 .15
135 Jay McKee .05 .15
136 Jan Hlavac .08 .25
137 Petr Sykora .15 .40
138 Ed Jovanovski .05 .15
139 Chris Kenady .05 .15
140 Marc Moro .05 .15
141 Kaj Linna .05 .15
142 Aaron MacDonald .05 .15
143 Chad Kilger .05 .15
144 Tyler Moss .05 .15
145 Christian Laflamme .05 .15
146 Brian Mueller .05 .15
147 Daymond Langkow .15 .40
148 Brent Peterson .05 .15
149 Chad Quenneville .05 .15
150 Chris Van Dyk .05 .15
151 Kent Fearns .05 .15
152 Adam Wiesel .05 .15
153 Marc Chouinard .05 .15
154 Jason Doig .05 .15
155 Denis Smith .05 .15
156 Radek Dvorak .05 .15
157 Donald MacLean .05 .15
158 Shane Kenny .05 .15
159 Brian Holzinger .05 .15
160 Eric Flinton .05 .15
189 E.Williams .05 .15
Breen

1995 Classic Five Sport Printer's Proofs

*PRINTER PROOF/75: 4X TO 10X BASIC CARDS
STATED PRINT RUN 795 SETS

1995 Classic Five Sport Red Die Cuts

*RED DIE CUT: 1.2X TO 3X BASIC CARDS
RED DIE CUT STATED ODDS 1:8

1995 Classic Five Sport Silver Die Cuts

These cards are identical to the regular set with the exception of a die-cut around the balls that are printed on the right side. They were inserted one per regular pack.

COMPLETE SET (200) 12.00 30.00
*SILVER DC: .8X TO 2X BASIC CARDS

1995 Classic Five Sport Autographs

This set was randomly inserted into packs and is a signed version of the basic issue cards. The backs carry a "Congratulations" message stating that it is an autographed 1995 Five Sport Autograph Edition Card with the sport's ball pictured at the bottom. The cards are unnumbered. Many of these autographed cards were later re-issued in 1995-96 Classic Five Sport Signings witha a slightly different cardback that reads "...Received a Limited-Edition Autographed Card." This message is the same one used on the Hot Box Autographs but these Five Sport Signings Autographs are not serial numbered on the back.

*SIGNINGS VERSION: .4X TO 1X
126 Nolan Baumgartner 2.00 5.00
127 Jason Bonsignore 2.00 5.00
128 Steve Kelly 2.00 5.00
129 George Breen 2.00 5.00
131 Greg Bullock 2.00 5.00
132 Jarome Iginla 10.00 20.00
133 Petr Buzek 2.00 5.00
135 Jay McKee 2.00 5.00
136 Jan Hlavac 2.00 5.00
137 Petr Sykora SP 10.00 20.00
138 Ed Jovanovski 2.50 6.00
139 Chris Kenady 2.00 5.00
140 Marc Moro 2.00 5.00
141 Kaj Linna 2.00 5.00
142 Aaron MacDonald 2.00 5.00
144 Tyler Moss 2.00 5.00
145 Christian Laflamme 2.00 5.00
146 Brian Mueller 2.00 5.00
148 Brent Peterson 2.00 5.00
149 Chad Quenneville 2.00 5.00
150 Chris Van Dyk SP 2.00 5.00
151 Kent Ferns 2.00 5.00
152 Adam Wiesel 2.00 5.00
153 Marc Chouinard SP 3.00 8.00
154 Jason Doig 2.00 5.00
155 Denis Smith 2.00 5.00
156 Radek Dvorak 2.00 5.00
157 Don MacLean 2.00 5.00
158 Shane Kenny 2.00 5.00

1995 Classic Five Sport Autographs Numbered

Cards in this set were issued primarily in 1995-96 Classic Five Sport Signings packs and are essentially a parallel verson of the basic 1995 Classic Five Sport Autographs insert. The only differences are in the hand serial numbering on the cardbacks (of 225 or 295) and the embossing crimp on the card's corner.

137 Petr Sykora/225 5.00 12.00

1995 Classic Five Sport Classic Standouts

Randomly inserted in regular packs at a rate of one in 216, this 10-card standard-size set features both the hot new stars and the established elite of all five sports. Fronts have full-color action player cutouts set against a gold and black foil background. The player's name is printed in gold foil at the top. Backs contain a full-color action shot with the player's name printed in yellow and a career highlights box. The cards are numbered with a "CS" prefix.

COMPLETE SET (10) 15.00 40.00
C35 Dryan Derard .76 2.00

1995 Classic Five Sport Fast Track

Randomly inserted in retail packs, this 20-card standard-size set spotlights the young stars of sports who are fast becoming major stars. Borderless fronts contain a player in full-color action while the rest of the shot is printed in colored foil. Backs have a color action shot in one box and two color separted boxes with the rest of the photo. A player profile appears underneath the photo. The cards are numbered with a "FT" prefix.

COMPLETE SET (20) 15.00 40.00
FT5 Bryan Berard .40 1.00
FT14 Petr Sykora 1.00 2.50

1995 Classic Five Sport On Fire

Ten of the 20-cards in this set were released in Hobby Hot Packs while the other ten were released in retail Hot packs. Fronts have full-color player cutouts set against a flame background with the On Fire logo printed at the bottom. The player's name is printed vertically in white type on the left side. backs feature biography and players's statistics.

COMPLETE SET (20) 30.00 80.00
R9 Bryan Berard 2.00 5.00

1995 Classic Five Sport Phone Cards $3

The five-card set of $3 Foncards were found one per 72 retail packs. The credit-card size plastic pieces have a borderless front with a full-color action player photo and the $3 emblem printed on the upper right in blue. The player's name is printed in white type vertically on the lower left. The Sprint logo appears on the bottom also. White backs carry information of how to place calls using the card.

COMPLETE SET (5) 4.00 8.00
3 Brian Holzinger .40 1.00

1995 Classic Five Sport Phone Cards $4

These cards were inserted randomly into packs at a rate of one in 72 and featured the five top prospects or performers of the individual sports. The borderless fronts feature full-color action photos with the athlete's name printed in white across the bottom. The Sprint logo and $4 are printed along the top. White backs contain information about placing calls using the card.

COMPLETE SET (5) 6.00 15.00
3 Wade Redden .50 1.25

1995 Classic Five Sport Record Setters

This 10-card standard-size set was inserted in retail packs and feature the stars and rookies of the five sports. The fronts display full-bleed color action photos; the set title "Record Setters" iin prismatic block lettering appears toward the bottom. On a sepia-tone photo, the backs carry a player profile. The cards are numbered on the back with an "RS" prefix and hand-numbered out of 1250.

COMPLETE SET (10) 12.00 30.00
RS2 Bryan Berard .60 1.50

1995 Classic Five Sport Strive For Five

This interactive game card set consists of 65 cards to be used like playing cards. Collector's gained a full suit of cards to redeem prizes. The odds of finding the card in packs were one in 10. Fronts are bordered in metallic silver foil and picture the player in full-color action. The cards are numbered on both top and bottom in silver foil and the player's name is printed vertically in silver foil. Backs have green backgrounds with the game rules printed in white type.

COMPLETE SET (65) 12.00 30.00
HK1 Wade Redden .20 .50
HK2 Jan Hlavac .20 .50
HK3 Brad Church .20 .50
HK4 Steve Kelly .20 .50
HK5 Radek Dvorak .20 .50
HK6 Jason Bonsignore .20 .50
HK7 Petr Sykora .20 .50
HK8 Daymond Langkow .20 .50
HK9 Chad Kilger .20 .50
HK10 Nolan Baumgartner .20 .50
HK11 Brian Holzinger .20 .50
HK12 Aki-Petteri Berg .20 .50
HK13 Ed Jovanovski .20 .50

1995 Classic Five Sport Previews

Randomly inserted in Classic hockey packs, this five-card standard-size set salutes the leaders and the up-and-coming rookies of the five sports. Borderless fronts have a full-color action shot with gold foil stamp of "preview" and the player's name, school and position printed vertically on the right side of the card. The player's sport's ball (or tire) is printed in a montage on the right. Backs have another full-color action shot and also a biography, statistics and profile. The cards are numbered with a "SP" prefix.

COMPLETE SET (5) 3.00 8.00
SP4 Bryan Berard .40 1.00

1995-96 Classic Five Sport Signings

COMPLETE SET (100) 6.00 15.00
70 Bryan Berard .07 .20
71 Wade Redden .07 .20
72 Aki-Petteri Berg .07 .20
73 Nolan Baumgartner .07 .20
74 Jason Bonsignore .07
75 Ed Jovanovski .07
76 Radek Dvorak .07
77 Brian Holzinger .07
78 Brad Church .07

1995-96 Classic Five Sport Signings Blue Signature

The Blue Signature parallels were randomly inser regular Classic Five Sport Hot Boxes and are ider to the regular card with the exception of a blue foi facsimile signature on the front (basic cards featu silver foil signatures).

*BLUE SIGN: 1.5X TO 4X BASIC CARDS

1995-96 Classic Five Sport Signings Die Cuts

These parallel cards were randomly inserted into every four packs. The cards feature a die cut desig the front right edge.

*DIE CUT: .8X TO 2X BASIC CARDS
STATED ODDS 1:4

1995-96 Classic Five Sport Signings Red Signature

The Red Signature parallels were randomly insert regular Classic Five Sport Hot Boxes and are iden to the regular cards with the exception of a red foi facsimile signature on the front (basic cards featu silver foil signatures).

*RED SIGN: 1.5X TO 4X BASIC CARDS

1995-96 Classic Five Sport Signings Freshly Inked

This 30-card set was randomly inserted in 1995 Classic Five Sport Signings packs. The fronts fea borderless player color action photos with the pla name printed in gold foil across the bottom. The b carry an artist's drawing of the player with the play name at the top.

COMPLETE SET (30) 12.00 3
STATED ODDS 1:10
FS23 Brian Holzinger .40
FS24 Radek Dvorak .40
FS25 Petr Sykora .60
FS26 Daymond Langkow .40

1991 Classic Four Sport

This 230-card multi-sport standard-size set incluc all 200 draft picks players from the four Classic D Picks sets (football, baseball, basketball, and hock plus an additional 30 draft picks not previously fo in these other sets. A subset within the 230 cards consists of five cards highlighting the publicized c on-one game between Billy Owens and Larry John As an additional incentive to collectors, Classic randomly inserted over 60,000 autographed cards the 15-card foil packs; it is claimed that each case should contain two or more autographed cards. T autographed cards feature 61 different players, approximately two-thirds of whom were hockey players. The production run for the English versio 25,000 cases, and a bilingual (French) version of set was also produced at 20 percent of the English production.

COMPLETE SET (230) 5.00 1
1 Future Superstars .15
2 Pat Falloon .05
3 Scott Niedermayer .08
4 Scott Lachance .05
5 Peter Forsberg .60
6 Alek Stojanov .05
7 Richard Matvichuk .05
8 Patrick Poulin .05
9 Martin Lapointe .05
10 Tyler Wright .05
11 Philippe Boucher .05
12 Pat Peake .05
13 Markus Naslund .05
14 Brent Bilodeau .05
15 Glen Murray .05
16 Niklas Sundblad .05
17 Martin Rucinsky .05
18 Trevor Halverson .05
19 Dean McAmmond .05
20 Ray Whitney .07
21 Rene Corbet .05
22 Eric Lavigne .05
23 Zigmund Palffy .20
24 Steve Staios .05
25 Jim Campbell .05
26 Jassen Cullimore .05
27 Martin Hamrlik .05
28 Jamie Pushor .05
29 Donevan Hextall .05
30 Andrew Verner .05
31 Jason Dawe .05
32 Jeff Nelson .05
33 Darcy Werenka .05
34 Jozef Stumpel .07
35 Francois Groleau .05
36 Guy Leveque .05
37 Jamie Matthews .05
38 Dody Wood .05
39 Yanic Perreault .05
40 Jamie McLennan .05
41 Yanick Dupre UER .05
Yanic misspelled
on both sides)
42 Sandy McCarthy .05
43 Chris Osgood .30
44 Fredrik Lindqvist .05
45 Jason Young .05
46 Steve Konowalchuk .05
47 Michael Nylander UER .05
48 Shane Peacock .05
49 Yves Sarault .05
50 Marcel Cousineau .05
NNO Pat Falloon PROMO .10

1991 Classic Four Sport Autographs

The 1991 Classic Draft Collection Autograph set consists of 61 standard-size cards. They were randomly inserted throughout the foil packs. Listed after the player's name is how many cards were autographed by that player. An "A" suffix after card number is used here for convenience.

2A Pat Falloon/1100 2.50
3A Scott Niedermayer/1250 6.00
4A Scott Lachance/1100 2.00
6A Alek Stojanov/950 2.00
8A Patrick Poulin/1100 2.00
10A Tyler Wright/950 2.00
11A Philippe Boucher/1150 2.00
12A Pat Peake/1100 2.50
14A Brent Bilodeau/1000 2.00
15A Glen Murray/1100 2.00
16A Niklas Sundblad/900 2.00
17A Martin Rucinsky/1100 2.00
18A Trevor Halverson/1100 2.00

9A Dean McAmmond/1100 2.00 5.00
0A Ray Whitney/2600 2.50 6.00
1A Rene Corbet/950 2.00 5.00
2A Eric Lavigne/1100 2.00 5.00
4A Steve Staios/1100 2.00 5.00
5A Jim Campbell/1100 2.50 6.00
6A Jassen Cullimore/1000 2.00 5.00
8A Jamie Pushor/1050 2.00 5.00
9A Donevan Hextall/1100 2.50 6.00
0A Andrew Verner/1200 2.00 5.00
1A Jason Dawe/950 2.00 5.00
2A Jeff Nelson/1100 2.00 5.00
3A Darcy Werenka/1150 2.00 5.00
5A Francois Groleau/1150 2.00 5.00
6A Guy Leveque/1150 2.00 5.00
7A Jamie Matthews/1100 2.00 5.00
8A Dody Wood/1050 2.00 5.00
9A Yanic Perreault/1100 2.00 5.00
0A Jamie Matthews/1100 2.00 5.00
1A Yanick Dupre/1050 2.00 5.00
2A Sandy McCarthy/1150 2.50 6.00
3A Chris Osgood/1100 8.00 20.00
4A F.Lindqvist/1100 3.00 8.00
5A Jason Young/1200 2.00 5.00
6A S.Konowalchuk/1350 2.50 6.00
7A Michael Nylander/1100 2.00 5.00
8A Shane Peacock/1150 2.00 5.00
9A Yves Sarault/1150 2.00 5.00
0A Marcel Cousineau/1100 2.00 5.00

1991 Classic Four Sport French

:OMPLETE SET (230) 6.00 15.00
FRENCH VERSION: .4X TO 1X

1992 Classic Four Sport

he 1992 Classic Draft Picks Collection consists of 25 standard-size cards, featuring the top picks from ootball, basketball, baseball, and hockey drafts. ccording to Classic, 40,000 12-box foil cases were roduced. Randomly inserted in the 12-card packs ere over 100,000 autograph cards from over 50 of the p draft picks from basketball, football, baseball, and ockey, including cards autographed by Shaquille 'Neal, Desmond Howard, Roman Hamrlik, and Phil evin. Also inserted in the packs were "Instant Win iveway Cards" that entitled the collector to the 00,000.00 sports memorabilia giveway that Classic ffered in this contest. There was also a factory set roduced with gold parallel cards.

OMPLETE SET (326) 6.00 15.00
51 Roman Hamrlik .05 .15
52 Alexei Yashin .05 .15
53 Mike Rathje .05 .15
54 Darius Kasparaitis .05 .15
55 Cory Stillman .05 .15
56 Robert Petrovicky .05 .15
57 Andrei Nazarov .05 .15
58 Jason Bowen .05 .15
59 Jason Smith .05 .15
60 David Wilkie .05 .15
61 Curtis Bowen .05 .15
62 Grant Marshall .05 .15
63 Valeri Bure .08 .25
64 Jeff Shantz .05 .15
65 Justin Hocking .05 .15
66 Mike Peca .25 .60
67 Marc Hussey .05 .15
68 Sandy Allan .05 .15
69 Kirk Maltby .05 .15
70 Cale Hulse .05 .15
71 Sylvain Cloutier .05 .15
72 Martin Gendron .05 .15
73 Kevin Smyth .05 .15
74 Jason McBain .05 .15
75 Lee J. Leslie .05 .15
76 Ralph Intranuovo .05 .15
77 Martin Reichel .05 .15
78 Stefan Ustorf .05 .15
79 Jarkko Varvio .05 .15
80 Martin Straka .20 .50
81 Libor Polasek .05 .15
82 Jozef Cierny .05 .15
83 Sergei Krivokrasov .15 .40
84 Sergei Gonchar .15 .40
85 Boris Mironov .05 .15
86 Denis Metlyuk .05 .15
87 Sergei Klimovich .05 .15
88 Sergei Brylin .05 .15
89 Andrei Nikolishin .05 .15
90 Alexander Cherbayev .05 .15
91 Vitali Tomilin .05 .15
92 Sandy Moger .05 .15
93 Darrin Madeley .05 .15
94 Denny Felsner .05 .15
95 Dwayne Norris .05 .15
96 Joby Messier .05 .15
97 Michael Stewart .05 .15
98 Scott Thomas .05 .15
99 Daniel Laperriere .05 .15
:00 Martin Lacroix .05 .15
:01 Scott LaGrand .05 .15
:02 Scott Pellerin .05 .15
:03 Jean-Yves Roy .05 .15
:04 Rob Gaudreau .05 .15
:05 Jeff McLean .05 .15
:06 Dallas Drake .05 .15
:07 Doug Zmolek .05 .15
:08 Duane Derksen .05 .15
:09 Jim Cummins .05 .15
:10 Lonnie Loach .05 .15
:11 Rob Zamuner .05 .15
:12 Brad Werenka .05 .15
:13 Brent Grieve .05 .15
:14 Sean Hill .05 .15
:15 Peter Ciavaglia .05 .15
:16 Jason Ruff .05 .15
:17 Shawn McCosh .05 .15
:18 Dave Tretowicz .05 .15
:19 Mike Vukonich .05 .15
:20 Kevin Wortman .05 .15
:21 Jason Muzzatti .05 .15
:22 Dmitri Kvartalnov .05 .15
:23 Ray Whitney .07 .20
:24 Manon Rheaume .40 1.00
:25 Viktor Kozlov .08 .25

1992 Classic Four Sport Gold

ssued in factory set form, these cards parallel the asic Classic Four-Sport set. Each cards features gold oil highlights and are valued as a multiple of the basic our-Sport cards. The factory sealed set also included n additional "Future Superstars" autographed card.)nly 9,500 sequentially numbered factory sets were roduced and each was packaged in a walnut display ase.

:OMP.FACT.SET (326) 60.00 120.00
GOLD: 1.2X TO 3X BASIC CARDS
U Future Superstars AU 30.00 60.00

1992 Classic Four Sport Autographs

The 1992 Classic Four Sport Autograph set consists of base cards hand signed by the featured player with a congratulatory message on the backs. They were randomly inserted throughout the foil packs. Each card also included a hand written serial number on the front and the checklist below reflects the quantity of cards each player signed. We've assigned card number according to the player's base card. Jan Caloun and Jan Vopat were not included in the regular set and hence are listed as unnumbered.

151 Roman Hamrlik/1550 2.50 6.00
153A Mike Rathje/2075 2.00 5.00
155 Cory Stillman/2125 2.00 5.00
158 Jason Bowen/2075 2.00 5.00
159 Jason Smith/2075 2.00 5.00
165 Justin Hocking/2075 2.00 5.00
170 Cale Hulse/1850 2.00 5.00
181 Libor Polasek/1950 2.00 5.00
185 Boris Mironov/2075 2.00 5.00
192 Sandy Moger/1075 2.00 5.00
195 Dwayne Norris/1075 2.00 5.00
196 Joby Messier/1075 2.00 5.00
207 Doug Zmolek/1075 2.00 5.00
224 Manon Rheaume/1992 12.50 30.00
NNO Jan Caloun/1975 2.00 5.00
NNO Jan Vopat/1775 2.00 5.00

1992 Classic Four Sport BCs

Inserted one per jumbo pack, these 20 bonus cards measure the standard size. The cards are numbered on the dark gray stripe and arranged according to sport as follows: basketball (1-6), hockey (7-12), football (13-17), and baseball (18-20). A randomly inserted Future Superstars card has a picture of all four players on its front, shot against a horizon with dark clouds and lightning; the back indicates that just 10,000 of these cards were produced.

COMPLETE SET (20) 3.00 8.00
BC7 Roman Hamrlik .08 .25
BC8 Valeri Bure .08 .25
BC9 Dallas Drake .08 .25
BC10 Dmitri Kvartalnov .08 .25
BC11 Manon Rheaume .75 2.00
BC12 Viktor Kozlov .08 .25

1992 Classic Four Sport LPs

Randomly inserted in foil packs, this 25-card standard-size insert set features full-bleed glossy color action player photos on the fronts. The sports represented are football (1-7, 16), basketball (8-14), baseball (17-21), and hockey (22-25). An 8 1/2" by 11" version of Shaquille O'Neal is known to exist.

LP15 Future Superstars 1.50 4.00
LP22 Roman Hamrlik .20 .50
LP23 Mike Rathje .20 .50
LP24 Valeri Bure .20 .50
LP25 Alexei Yashin .30 .75
LP15P Phil Nevin 2.00 5.00
Shaquille O'Neal
Roman Hamrlik
Desmond Howard
(Super Bowl Show promo)

1992 Classic Four Sport Previews

These five preview standard-size cards were randomly inserted in baseball and hockey draft picks foil packs. According to the backs, just 10,000 of each card were produced. The fronts display the full-bleed glossy color player photos. At the upper right corner, the word "Preview" surmounts the Classic logo. This logo overlays a black stripe that runs down the left side and features the player's name and position. The gray backs have the word "Preview" in red lettering at the top and are accented by short purple diagonal stripes on each side. Between the stripes are a congratulations and an advertisement. The cards are numbered on the back with a "CC" prefix.

COMPLETE SET (5) 6.00 15.00
CC3 Roman Hamrlik .40 1.00

1992 Classic Four Sport Promos

These five promo cards were packaged in a cello pack and distributed to dealers. The cards measure the standard size (2 1/2" by 3 1/2"). The fronts display the same full-bleed glossy color player photos as the above-mentioned preview cards. They differ in that the Classic logo at the upper left corner is not surmounted by the word Preview." The promo backs have a different design than the preview backs, displaying a second color player photo on the right side as well as biography and player profile in black print on a silver background. The cards are numbered on the back.

COMPLETE SET (5) 6.00 15.00
PR3 Roman Hamrlik .40 1.00

1993 Classic Four Sport

The 1993 Classic Four-Sport Draft Pick Collection set consists of 325 standard-size cards of the top 1993 draft picks from football, basketball, baseball, and hockey. Just 49,500 sequentially numbered 12-box cases were produced. The set includes two topical subsets: John R. Wooden Award (310-314) and All-Rookie Basketball Team (315-319).

COMPLETE SET (325) 4.00 10.00
185 Alexandre Daigle .05 .15
186 Chris Pronger .20 .50
187 Chris Gratton .05 .15
188 Paul Kariya .40 1.00
189 Rob Niedermayer .08 .25
190 Viktor Kozlov .08 .25
191 Jason Arnott .20 .50
192 Niklas Sundstrom .05 .15
193 Todd Harvey .05 .15
194 Jocelyn Thibault .20 .50
195 Kenny Jonsson .05 .15
196 Denis Pederson .05 .15
197 Adam Deadmarsh .08 .25
198 Mats Lindgren .05 .15
199 Nick Stajduhar .05 .15
200 Jason Allison .08 .25
201 Jesper Mattsson .05 .15
202 Saku Koivu .20 .50
203 Anders Eriksson .05 .15
204 Todd Bertuzzi .05 .15
205 Eric Lecompte .05 .15
206 Nikolai Tsulygin .05 .15
207 Janne Niinimaa .05 .15
208 Maxim Bets .05 .15
209 Rory Fitzpatrick .05 .15
210 Eric Manlow .05 .15
211 David Roche .05 .15
212 Vladimir Chebaturkin .05 .15
213 Bill McCauley .05 .15
214 Chad Lang .05 .15
215 Cosmo DuPaul .05 .15
216 Bob Wren .05 .15
217 Chris Simon .05 .15
218 Ryan Brown .05 .15
219 Mikhail Shtalenkov .05 .15
220 Vladimir Krechine .05 .15
221 Jason Saal .05 .15
222 Dion Darling .05 .15
223 Chris Helleher .05 .15
224 Antti Aalto .05 .15
225 Alain Nasreddine .05 .15
226 Paul Vincent .05 .15
227 Manny Legace .05 .15
228 Igor Chibirev .05 .15
229 Tom Noble .05 .15
230 Mike Bales .05 .15
231 Jozef Cierny .05 .15
232 Ivan Droppa .05 .15
233 Anatoli Fedotov .05 .15
234 Martin Gendron .05 .15
235 Daniel Guerard .05 .15
236 Corey Hirsch .07 .20
237 Steven King .05 .15
238 Sergei Krivokrasov .05 .15
239 Darrin Madeley .05 .15
240 Grant Marshall .05 .15
241 Sandy McCarthy .07 .20
242 Bill McDougall .05 .15
243 Dean Melanson .05 .15
244 Roman Oksiuta .05 .15
245 Robert Petrovicky .05 .15
246 Mike Rathje .05 .15
247 Eldon Reddick .05 .15
248 Andrei Trefilov .05 .15
249 Jiri Slegr .05 .15
250 Leonid Toropchenko .05 .15
251 Dody Wood .05 .15
252 Kevin Paden .05 .15
253 Manon Rheaume .30 .75
254 Cammi Granato .08 .25
255 Patrick Charbonneau .05 .15
256 Curtis Bowen .05 .15
257 Kevin Brown .05 .15
258 Valeri Bure .08 .25
259 Janne Laukkanen .05 .15

1993 Classic Four Sport Gold

This parallel issue to the 1993 Classic Four Sport set consists of 325 Gold foil versions of the regular set, plus four player autograph cards that were inserted into each factory gold set. Each of the four players autographed 3900 cards. Aside from the special gold-foil highlights (such as the ghosted stripe carrying the player's name being offset by gold-foil lines) the cards are identical to the regular 1993 Classic Four Sport base cards.

COMP.FACT.SET (332) 150.00 250.00
*GOLD: 1.5X TO 4X BASIC CARDS
AU2 Chris Gratton AU/3900 4.00 10.00

1993 Classic Four Sport Acetates

Randomly inserted throughout the 1993 Classic Four-Sport foil packs, this 12-card standard-size acetate set features on its fronts clear-bordered color player action cutouts set on basketball, football, baseball, or hockey stick backgrounds. The cards are unnumbered but carry letter designations. They are checklisted in the order that spells '93 Rookie Class.

COMPLETE SET (12) 6.00 15.00
11 Alexandre Daigle .40 1.00
12 Chris Pronger .40 1.00

1993 Classic Four Sport Autographs

Randomly inserted in '93 Classic Four-Sport packs, these standard-size cards feature on their fronts borderless color player action shots. The back carries a congratulatory message. The cards are listed below by their corresponding regular card numbers, except for Jennings and Klippenstein, which are shown as unnumbered cards (NNO) at the end of the checklist since they are not in the regular set. The number of cards each player signed is shown. The Rider card may have been autopenned.

189A Rob Niedermayer/4500 2.00 5.00
196A Denis Pederson/2050 1.50 4.00
197A Adam Deadmarsh/4250 2.00 5.00
218A Ryan Brown/900 1.50 4.00
222A Dion Darling/1500 1.50 4.00
253A Manon Rheaume/1250 30.00 60.00
NNO Jason Jennings/1475 1.50 4.00
NNO Wade Klippenstein/800 1.50 4.00

1993 Classic Four Sport Chromium Draft Stars

Inserted one per jumbo pack, these 20 standard-size cards feature color player action cutouts on their borderless metallic fronts. The player's name, along with the production number (1 of 80,000), appear vertically in gold foil at the lower left. The cards are numbered on the back with a "DS" prefix.

COMPLETE SET (20) 8.00 20.00
DS58 Alexandre Daigle .40 1.00
DS59 Chris Pronger .40 1.00
DS60 Chris Gratton .40 1.00

1993 Classic Four Sport LP Jumbos

Random inserts in hobby boxes, these five oversized cards measure approximately 3 1/2" by 5" and feature on their fronts borderless color player action shots. The player's name, statistics, biography, and career highlights, along with the card's production number out of 8,000 produced, appear on a gray lithic background to the left. The cards are numbered on the back as "X of 5."

COMPLETE SET (5) 12.00 30.00
2 Alexandre Daigle 1.25 3.00

1993 Classic Four Sport LPs

Randomly inserted throughout the 1993 Classic Four-Sport foil packs, this 25-card standard-size set features the hottest draft pick players in 1993. The borderless fronts feature color player action shots. The player's name appears vertically at the lower left. The production number (1 of 63,400) appears in gold foil at the lower right. The cards are numbered on the back with an "LP" prefix.

COMPLETE SET (25) 20.00 40.00
LP1 Four in One 1.50 4.00
LP22 Alexandre Daigle .40 1.00
LP23 Chris Pronger .60 1.50
LP24 Chris Gratton .40 1.00
LP25 Paul Kariya .75 2.00

1993 Classic Four Sport MBNA Promos

This two-card set uses Classic's designs from its Four-Sport LPs "Four in One" insert number LP1. Card number 1 reproduces the Chris Wehher/Alex Rodriguez side of LP1, card number 2 reproduces the Drew Bledsoe/Alexandre Daigle side. This set was issued exclusively to cardholders of the MBNA/ScoreBoard VISA. The backs contain congratulatory messages, information about the players depicted, and a notation than 10,000 sets were issued. Although the design and copyright reads 1993, these cards probably were first issued in 1994.

2 D.Bledsoe 2.00 5.00
A.Daigle

1993 Classic Four Sport McDonald's

Classic produced this 35-card four-sport standard-size set for a promotion at McDonald's restaurants in central and southeastern Pennsylvania, southern New Jersey, Delaware, and central Florida. The cards were distributed in five-card packs. A five-card "limited production" subset was randomly inserted throughout these packs. The promotion also featured instant win cards awarding 2,000 pieces of autographed Score Board memorabilia. An autographed Chris Webber card was also randomly inserted in the packs on a limited basis. The set is arranged according to sports as follows: football (1-10), baseball (11, 26, 31-35), hockey (12-20), and basketball (21-25, 27-30). The cards are numbered on the back in the upper left, and the McDonald's trademark is gold foil stamped toward the bottom.

COMPLETE SET (35) 4.00 10.00
13 Kevin Dineen .05 .15
14 Andre Faust .05 .15
15 Roman Hamrlik .08 .25
16 Mark Recchi .20 .50
17 Manon Rheaume .50 1.25
18 Dominic Roussel .10 .30
19 Teemu Selanne .40 1.00
20 Tommy Soderstrom .10 .30

1993 Classic Four Sport McDonald's LPs

Measuring the standard size, these five limited production cards were randomly inserted in 1993 Classic McDonald's five-card packs. Chris Webber, the number one pick in the NBA draft, autographed 1,250 of his cards. Printed vertically, and parallel and next to the gold foil band, "1 of 16,750" appears in gold foil. The Classic Four Sport logo appears in the upper right. The cards are numbered on the back in gold foil with an "LP" prefix.

COMPLETE SET (5) 3.00 8.00
LP4 Manon Rheaume 1.50 4.00

1993 Classic Four Sport Power Pick Bonus

Issued one per jumbo sheet, these 20 standard-size cards feature on their borderless fronts color player action shots, the backgrounds for which are faded to black-and-white. The player's name and the sets production number (1 of 80,000) appear in green-foil cursive lettering near the bottom. The cards are numbered on the back with a "PP" prefix.

COMPLETE SET (20) 10.00 25.00
PP18 Alexandre Daigle .40 1.00
PP19 Chris Pronger .60 1.50
PP20 Chris Gratton .40 1.00
NNO Four in One/60,000 1.50 4.00

1993 Classic Four Sport Tri-Cards

Randomly inserted throughout the 1993 Classic Four-Sport foil packs, this set features five standard-size cards with three players on each card separated by perforations. The cards are numbered on the back with a "TC" prefix.

COMPLETE SET (5) 10.00 25.00
TC4 Daigle/9 Pronger/14 Gratton 1.50 4.00

1993 Classic Four Sport Previews

Issued as unnumbered inserts in '93 Classic hockey packs, these five cards measure the standard size. The fronts are similar in design to regular 1993 Classic Four-Sport cards. The backs carry a congratulatory message.

COMPLETE SET (5) 2.50 6.00
CC1 Alexandre Daigle .30 .75

1994 Classic Four Sport

Featuring top rookies from basketball, baseball, football and hockey, the 1994 Classic Four-Sport set consists of 200 standard-size cards. No more than 25,000 cases were produced. Over 100 players signed 100,000 cards that were randomly inserted four per case. Collectors who found one of 100 Glenn Robinson Instant Winner Cards received a complete Classic Four-Sport autographed card set. Also inserted on an average of one in every five cases were 4,695 hand-numbered 4-in-1 cards featuring all four number 1 picks. Classic's wrapper redemption program offered four levels of participation: 1) bronze-collect 20 wrappers and receive a 4-card Classic Player of the Year set, featuring Grant Hill, Shaquille O'Neal, Emmitt Smith, and Steve Young; 2) silver-collect 30 wrappers and receive the Classic Player of the Year set and a random autograph card; 3) gold-collect 144 wrappers and receive the Classic Player of the Year set and an autograph card by Muhammad Ali; and 4) platinum-collect 216 wrappers and receive the Classic Player of the Year set plus an autograph card by Shaquille O'Neal. The cards are numbered on the back and checklisted below by sport.

COMPLETE SET (200) 6.00 15.00
115A Ed Jovanovski ERR .08 .25
115B Ed Jovanovski COR .08 .25
116 Oleg Tverdovsky .08 .25
117 Radek Bonk .08 .25
118 Jason Bonsignore .05 .15
119 Jeff O'Neill .07 .20
120 Ryan Smyth .05 .15
121 Jamie Storr .15 .40
122 Jason Wiemer .05 .15
123 Evgeny Ryabchikov .05 .15
124 Nolan Baumgartner .05 .15
125 Jeff Friesen .10 .30
126 Wade Belak .05 .15
127 Maxim Bets .05 .15
128 Ethan Moreau .05 .15
129 Alexander Kharlamov .05 .15
130 Eric Fichaud .05 .15
131 Wayne Primeau .05 .15
132 Brad Brown .05 .15
133 Chris Dingman .05 .15
134 Craig Darby .05 .15
135 Darby Hendrickson .05 .15
136 Yan Golubovsky .05 .15
137 Chris Wells .05 .15
138 Vadim Sharifijanov .05 .15
139 Dan Cloutier .05 .15
140 Todd Marchant .08 .25
141 David Roberts .05 .15
142 Brian Rolston .05 .15
143 Garth Snow .15 .40
144 Cory Stillman .05 .15
145 Chad Penney .05 .15
146 Jeff Nelson .05 .15
147 Michael Stewart .05 .15
148 Mike Dunham .08 .25
149 Joe Frederick .05 .15
150 Mark DeSantis .05 .15
151 David Cooper .05 .15
152 Andrei Buschan .05 .15
153 Mike Greenlay .05 .15
154 Geoff Sarjeant .05 .15
155 Pauli Jaks .05 .15
156 Greg Andrusak .05 .15
157 Denis Metlyuk .05 .15
158 Mike Fountain .05 .15
159 Brent Gretzky .05 .15
160 Jason Allison .20 .50
F01 4-in-1 1.00 2.50
Glenn Robinson
Dan Wilkinson
Paul Wilson
Ed Jovanovski
Number One Draft Picks

1994 Classic Four Sport Gold

Seeded one per pack and featuring top rookies from basketball, baseball, football and hockey, the 1994 Classic Four-Sport gold set consists of 200 standard-size cards. The player's name and the Classic Four-Sport logo is on the right side of the picture along with the information that this is a gold card.

COMPLETE SET (200) 12.00 30.00
*GOLD: .8X TO 2X BASIC CARDS

1994 Classic Four Sport Printer's Proofs

Randomly inserted in packs and featuring top rookies from basketball, baseball, football and hockey, the 1994 Classic Four-Sport Printer's Proofs set consists of 200 standard-size cards. The information that this is a printer's proof card is directly above the player's name. Both the printer's proof logo and the name of the player are in red.

*PRINT PROOFS: 2.5X TO 6X BASIC CARDS

1994 Classic Four Sport Autographs

Randomly inserted in packs at a rate of one in 103, this standard-size set features players from the 1994 Classic Four-Sport set who autographed cards within the set. The fronts feature full-bleed color action player photos. The player's name is gold-foil stamped across the bottom of the picture. The backs have a congratulatory message about receiving an autographed card. Though the cards are unnumbered, we have assigned them the same number as their four-sport regular issue counterpart.

115A Ed Jovanovski/1180 6.00 15.00
119A Jeff O'Neill/3000 3.00 8.00
124A Nolan Baumgartner/2900 2.00 5.00
134A Craig Darby/2990 2.00 5.00
139A Dan Cloutier/2980 2.50 6.00
140A Todd Marchant/3100 2.50 6.00
143A Garth Snow/3050 2.50 6.00
144A Cory Stillman/3000 2.00 5.00
148A Mike Dunham/2960 3.00 8.00
149A Joe Frederick/3000 2.00 5.00
150A Mark DeSantis/3000 2.00 5.00
154A Geoff Sarjeant/3000 2.00 5.00
156A Greg Andrusak/2970 2.00 5.00
157A Denis Metlyuk/2960 2.00 5.00
158A Mike Fountain/3000 2.00 5.00

1994 Classic Four Sport BCs

This 20-card bonus standard-size set was inserted one per '94 Classic Four-Sport jumbo packs. The fronts feature full color player photos. The backs carry biographical and statistical information about the player.

COMPLETE SET (20) 6.00 15.00
BC17 Ed Jovanovski .20 .50
BC18 Radek Bonk .20 .50
BC19 Jeff O'Neill .20 .50
BC20 Ethan Moreau .20 .50

1994 Classic Four Sport Classic Picks

This 10-card standard-size set was randomly inserted in packs at rate of one in 72. The fronts feature full-color action player photos with the player's name and card title below. The backs carry a small player photo, the player's name, biographical information, and career highlights printed over a ghosted photo of the same player.

COMPLETE SET (10) 6.00 15.00
25 Ethan Moreau .40 1.00

1994 Classic Four Sport High Voltage

This 20-card sequentially-numbered standard-size set features the top draft picks. The cards are printed on holographic foil board with a striking design. 2,995 of each even-numbered card and 5,495 of each odd-numbered cards were produced. The cards were inserted on an average of 3 per case and had stated odds of one in 144 hobby packs. The fronts feature the players against a background of lightning while the backs feature a biography on the left side of the card. The right side shows more lightning and the player's photo.

COMPLETE SET (20) 40.00 100.00
HV4 Ed Jovanovski SP 2.50 6.00
HV8 Oleg Tverdovsky SP 2.00 5.00
HV12 Radek Bonk SP 4.00 10.00
HV16 Jason Bonsignore SP 2.00 5.00
HV19 Jeff O'Neill .75 2.00

1994 Classic Four Sport Phone Cards $1

This set of eight phone cards was randomly inserted in Four-Sport packs. Printed on hard plastic, each card measures 2 1/8" by 3 3/8" and has rounded corners. The fronts display full-bleed color action photos, with the phone time value ($1, $2, $3, $4 or $5) and the player's name printed vertically in red along the right edge. The horizontal backs carry instructions for use of the cards. The cards are unnumbered and checklisted below in alphabetical order. The $3 and $5 cards were inserted into retail packs. The phone cards could be used until November 30, 1995.

COMPLETE SET (8) 3.00 8.00
*TWO DOLLAR: .5X TO 1.2X $1 CARDS
*THREE DOLLAR: .6X TO 1.5X $1 CARDS
*FOUR DOLLAR: .8X TO 2X $1 CARDS
*FIVE DOLLAR: 1X TO 2.5X $1 CARDS
*PIN NUMBER REVEALED: HALF VALUE
4 Ed Jovanovski .20 .50
6 Jeff O'Neill .20 .50

1994 Classic Four Sport Tri-Cards

Inserted one in every three cases, this five-card standard-size set features three top running backs, linebackers, hockey centers, pitchers and basketball guards and compares their individual skills. Every card is sequentially-numbered out of 2,695. The horizontal fronts feature the three players equally while the backs gives a brief biography of why the three players are grouped together.

COMPLETE SET (5) 4.00 10.00
TC4 Bonk .40 1.00
Wells
O'Neill

1994 Classic Four Sport Previews

Randomly inserted in 1994-95 Classic hockey foil packs at a rate of three per case, these five standard-size preview cards show the design of the 1994-95 Classic Four-Sport series. The full-bleed color action photos are gold-foil stamped with the "4-Sport Preview" emblem and the player's name. The backs feature another full-bleed closeup photo, with biography and statistics displayed on a ghosted panel.

COMPLETE SET (5) 6.00 15.00
P1 Jeff O'Neill .40 1.00

1993 Classic Pro Prospects

The 1993 Classic Pro Hockey Prospects set features 150 standard-size cards. The production run was 6,500 sequentially numbered cases, and female hockey phenom Manon Rheaume autographed 6,500 cards for random insertion into the foil packs.

COMPLETE SET (150) 4.00 10.00
1 Manon Rheaume .40 1.00
2 Manon Rheaume .40 1.00
3 Manon Rheaume .40 1.00
4 Manon Rheaume .40 1.00
5 Manon Rheaume .40 1.00
6 Manon Rheaume .40 1.00
7 Manon Rheaume .40 1.00
8 Oleg Petrov .01 .05
9 Shjon Podein .01 .05
10 Alexei Kovalev AS .08 .25
11 Roman Oksiuta .01 .05
12 Dave Tomlinson .01 .05
13 Jason Miller .01 .05
14 Andrew McKim .01 .05
15 Dallas Drake .01 .05
16 Rob Gaudreau .01 .05
17 Darrin Madeley .01 .05
18 Scott Pellerin .01 .05
19 Scott Thomas .01 .05
20 Chris Tancill AS .01 .05
21 Patrick Kjellberg .01 .05
22 Jim Dowd .01 .05
23 Daniel Gauthier .01 .05
24 Mark Beaufait .01 .05
25 Milan Tichy AS .01 .05
26 Chris Osgood .50 1.25
27 Charles Poulin .01 .05
28 Patrick Lebeau .01 .05
29 Chris Govedaris .01 .05
30 Andrei Trefilov AS .01 .05
31 Kevin Stevens MLG .08 .25
32 Dmitri Kvartalnov MLG .01 .05
33 Patrick Roy MLG .60 1.50
34 Mark Recchi MLG .20 .50
35 Adam Oates MLG .20 .50
36 Patrick Augusta .01 .05
37 Gerry Fleming .01 .05
38 Sergei Krivokrasov .01 .05
39 Mike O'Neill .01 .05
40 Darrin Madeley AS .01 .05
41 Lindsay Vallis .01 .05
42 Todd Nelson .01 .05
43 Keith Jones .01 .05
44 Howie Rosenblatt .01 .05
45 Jason Ruff AS .01 .05
46 Robert Lang .01 .05
47 Andre Faust .01 .05
48 Steve Bancroft .01 .05
49 Iain Fraser .01 .05
50 Roman Hamrlik AS .01 .05
51 Pierre Sevigny .01 .05
52 Jeff Levy .01 .05
53 Len Barrie .01 .05
54 David Goverde .01 .05
55 Vladimir Malakhov AS .01 .05
56 Scott White .01 .05
57 Dmitri Motkov .01 .05
58 Jason Herter .01 .05
59 Drake Berehowsky .01 .05
60 Steve King AS .01 .05
61 Doug Barrault .01 .05
62 Martin Hamrlik .01 .05
63 Kevin Miehm .01 .05
64 Shaun Van Allen .01 .05
65 Corey Hirsch AS .01 .05
66 Dwayne Norris .01 .05
67 Petr Hrbek .01 .05
68 Philippe Boucher .01 .05
69 Denis Chervyakov .01 .05
70 Sergei Zubov AS .01 .05
71 Geoff Sarjeant .01 .05
72 Les Kuntar .01 .05
73 Byron Dafoe .20 .50
74 Checklist .01 .05
Alexei Kovalev
Sergei Zubov
Steve King
Corey Hirsch
75 Alexander Andrievski AS .01 .05
76 Checklist .01 .05
Joby Messier
Mitch Messier
77 Brian Sullivan .01 .05
78 Steve Larouche .01 .05
79 Denis Chasse .01 .05
80 Felix Potvin AS .20 .50
81 Josef Beranek .01 .05
82 Ken Klee .01 .05
83 Jozef Stumpel .08 .25
84 Andrew Verner .01 .05
85 Keith Osborne AS .01 .05
86 Igor Malykhin .01 .05
87 Gilbert Dionne .01 .05
88 Viktor Gordiouk .01 .05
89 Glen Murray .01 .05
90 Scott Pellerin AS .01 .05
91 Tommy Soderstrom .08 .25
92 Terry Chitaroni .01 .05
93 Viktor Kozlov .08 .25
94 Mikhail Shtalenkov .08 .25
95 Leonid Toropchenko .01 .05
96 Alexander Galchenyuk .01 .05
97 Anatoli Fedotov .01 .05
98 Igor Chibirev .01 .05
99 Keith Gretzky .01 .05
100 Manon Rheaume .60 1.50
101 Sean Whyte .01 .05
102 Steve Konowalchuk .08 .25
103 Richard Borgo .01 .05
104 Paul DiPietro .01 .05
105 Patrik Carnback AS .01 .05
106 Mike Fountain .01 .05
107 Jamie Heward .01 .05
108 David St. Pierre .01 .05
109 Sean O'Donnell .01 .05
110 Greg Andrusak AS .01 .05
111 Damian Rhodes .08 .25
112 Ted Crowley .01 .05
113 Chris Taylor .01 .05
114 Terran Sandwith .01 .05
115 Jesse Belanger AS .01 .05
116 Justin Duberman .01 .05
117 Arturs Irbe .20 .50
118 Chris LiPuma .01 .05
119 Mike Torchia .01 .05
120 Niclas Andersson AS .01 .05
121 Rick Knickle .01 .05
122 Scott Gruhl .01 .05
123 Dave Michayluk .01 .05
124 Guy Leveque .01 .05
125 Scott Thomas AS .01 .05
126 Travis Green .01 .05
127 Joby Messier .01 .05
128 Victor Ignatjev .01 .05
129 Brad Tiley .01 .05
130 Grigori Panteleyev AS .01 .05
131 Vyatcheslav Butsayev .01 .05
132 Danny Lorenz .01 .05
133 Marty McInnis .01 .05
134 Ed Ronan .01 .05
135 Slava Kozlov AS .20 .50
136 Kevin St. Jacques .01 .05
137 Pavel Kostichkin .01 .05
138 Mike Hurlbut .01 .05
139 Tomas Forslund .01 .05
140 Rob Gaudreau AS .01 .05
141 Shawn Heaphy .01 .05
142 Radek Hamr .01 .05
143 Jaroslav Otevrel .01 .05
144 Keith Redmond .01 .05
145 Tom Pederson AS .01 .05
146 Jaroslav Modry .01 .05
147 Darren McCarty .01 .05
148 Terry Yake .01 .05
149 Ivan Droppa .01 .05
150 S.Van Allen .01 .05
D.Currie
S.Rice
AU1 D.Kvartalnov AU/4000 2.00 5.00
AU2 M.Rheaume AU/6500 20.00 40.00

1993 Classic Pro Prospects BCs

One BC card was inserted in each jumbo pack. The cards are numbered on the back with a "BC" prefix.

COMPLETE SET (20) 15.00 30.00
BC1 Alexei Kovalev .40 1.00
BC2 Andrei Trefilov .20 .50
BC3 Roman Hamrlik .20 .50
BC4 Vladimir Malakhov .20 .50
BC5 Corey Hirsch .30 .75
BC6 Sergei Zubov .20 .50
BC7 Felix Potvin .40 1.00
BC8 Tommy Soderstrom .30 .75
BC9 Viktor Kozlov .30 .75
BC10 Manon Rheaume 1.50 4.00
BC11 Jesse Belanger .20 .50
BC12 Rick Knickle .20 .50
BC13 Joby Messier .20 .50
BC14 Vyacheslav Butsayev .20 .50
BC15 Tomas Forslund .20 .50
BC16 Jozef Stumpel .30 .75
BC17 Dmitri Kvartalnov MLG .20 .50
BC18 Adam Oates MLG .40 1.00
BC19 Dallas Drake .20 .50
BC20 Mark Recchi MLG .40 1.00

1993 Classic Pro Prospects LPs

The cards are numbered on the back with an "LP" prefix.

COMPLETE SET (5) 12.50 25.00
LP1 Manon Rheaume 6.00 15.00
LP2 Alexei Kovalev 1.25 3.00
LP3 Rob Gaudreau .75 2.00
LP4 Viktor Kozlov 1.25 3.00
LP5 Dallas Drake .75 2.00

1993 Classic Pro Prospects Prototypes

These three standard-size promo cards were issued to show the design of the 1993 Classic Pro Hockey Prospects set. Inside white borders, the fronts display color action player photos. A color bar edges the top of each picture and carries the player's name, team, and position. Also a black bar edges the bottom of each picture. On a gray background, the backs feature a color close-up photo, logos, biographical information, statistics, and career summary. A black bar that accents the top carries the card number and the disclaimer "For Promotional Purposes Only".

COMPLETE SET (3) 3.00 8.00
PR1 Steve King .60 1.50
PR2 Manon Rheaume 2.50 6.00
PR3 Rob Gaudreau .60 1.50

1994 Classic Pro Prospects

This 250-card set includes more than 100 foil-stamped subset cards. Randomly inserted throughout the foil packs were 25 limited print clear acetate cards and over 10,000 randomly inserted autographed cards of Radek Bonk, Alexei Yashin, Chris Pronger, Manon Rheaume, Joe Juneau, and more.

COMPLETE SET (250) 3.00 8.00
1 Radek Bonk .01 .05
2 Radek Bonk .01 .05
3 Radek Bonk .01 .05
4 Vlastimil Kroupa .01 .05
5 Mattias Norstrom .01 .05
6 Jaroslav Nedved .01 .05
7 Steve Dubinsky .01 .05
8 Christian Proulx .01 .05
9 Michal Grosek .01 .05
10 Pat Neaton .01 .05
11 Jason Arnott .01 .05
12 Martin Brodeur .40 1.00
13 Alexandre Daigle .01 .05
14 Ted Drury .01 .05
15 Iain Fraser .01 .05
16 Chris Gratton .08 .25
17 Greg Johnson .01 .05
18 Paul Kariya .40 1.00
19 Alexander Karpovtsev .01 .05
20 Chris Lipuma .01 .05
21 Kirk Maltby .01 .05
22 Sandy McCarthy .01 .05
23 Darren McCarty .01 .05

24 Jaroslav Modry .01 .05
25 Jim Montgomery .01 .05
26 Markus Naslund .20 .50
27 Rob Niedermayer .08 .25
28 Chris Osgood .30 .75
29 Pat Peake .01 .05
30 Derek Plante .01 .05
31 Chris Pronger .20 .50
32 Mike Rathje .01 .05
33 Mikael Renberg .08 .25
34 Damian Rhodes .08 .25
35 Garth Snow .08 .25
36 Cam Stewart .01 .05
37 Jim Storm .01 .05
38 Michal Sykora .01 .05
39 Jocelyn Thibault .20 .50
40 Alexei Yashin .01 .05
41 Checklist 1 .01 .05
42 Vesa Viitakoski .01 .05
43 Jake Grimes .01 .05
44 Jim Dowd .01 .05
45 Craig Ferguson .01 .05
46 Mike Boback .01 .05
47 Francois Groleau .01 .05
48 Juha Riihijarvi .01 .05
49 Mikhail Shtalenkov .08 .25
50 Zigmund Palffy .08 .25
51 Felix Potvin .20 .50
52 Alexei Kovalev .08 .25
53 Larry Robinson .08 .25
54 John LeClair .30 .75
55 Dominic Roussel .08 .25
56 Geoff Sanderson .08 .25
57 Greg Pankewicz .01 .05
58 Brent Bilodeau .01 .05
59 Brandon Convery .01 .05
60 Fred Knipscheer .01 .05
61 Igor Chibirev .01 .05
62 Anatoli Fedotov .01 .05
63 Bob Kellogg .01 .05
64 Mike Maurice .01 .05
65 Chad Penney .01 .05
66 Mike Bavis .01 .05
67 Eric Veilleux .01 .05
68 Parris Duffus .01 .05
69 Daniel Lacroix .01 .05
70 Milos Holan .01 .05
71 Mike Muller .01 .05
72 Micah Aivazoff .01 .05
73 Krzysztof Oliwa .01 .05
74 Ryan Hughes .01 .05
75 Christian Soucy .01 .05
76 Keith Redmond .01 .05
77 Mark De Santis .01 .05
78 Craig Martin .01 .05
79 Mike Kennedy .01 .05
80 Pauli Jaks .01 .05
81 Colin Chin .01 .05
82 Jody Gage .01 .05
83 Don Biggs .01 .05
84 Tim Tookey .01 .05
85 Clint Malarchuk .08 .25
86 Jozef Cierny .01 .05
87 Radek Hamr .01 .05
88 Jason Dawe .01 .05
89 Chris Longo .01 .05
90 Brian Rolston .08 .25
91 Mike McKee .01 .05
92 Vitali Prokhorov .01 .05
93 Chris Snell .01 .05
94 Martin Brochu .08 .25
95 Dan Plante .01 .05
96 Darcy Werenka .01 .05
97 Steffon Walby .01 .05
98 David Emma .01 .05
99 Dan Stiver .01 .05
100 Radek Bonk .01 .05
101 Mark Visheau .01 .05
102 Dean Melanson .01 .05
103 Vladimir Tsyplakov .01 .05
104 Mikhail Volkov .01 .05
105 Aaron Miller .01 .05
106 Alexei Kudashov .01 .05
107 Shawn Rivers .01 .05
108 Ladislav Karabin .01 .05
109 Matt Mallgrave .01 .05
110 Craig Darby .01 .05
111 Marcel Cousineau .01 .05
112 Jamie McLennan .08 .25
113 Yanic Perreault .08 .25
114 Zac Boyer .01 .05
115 Sergei Zubov .01 .05
116 Dan Kesa .01 .05
117 Jim Hiller .01 .05
118 Dmitri Starostenko .01 .05
119 Chris Tamer .01 .05
120 Aaron Ward .01 .05
121 Claude Savoie .01 .05
122 Jamie Black .01 .05
123 Jean-Francois Jomphe .01 .05
124 Paxton Schulte .01 .05
125 Jarkko Varvio .01 .05
126 Jaroslav Otevrel .01 .05
127 Dane Jackson .01 .05
128 Brent Grieve .01 .05
129 Rheaumes CL .30 .75
130 Rene Corbet .01 .05
131 Joe Frederick .01 .05
132 Martin Tanguay .01 .05
133 Fredrik Jax .01 .05
134 Jamie Linden .01 .05
135 Jason Smith .01 .05
136 Rick Kowalsky .01 .05
137 Dino Grossi .01 .05
138 Aris Brimanis .01 .05
139 Jeff McLean .01 .05
140 Tyler Wright .01 .05
141 Roman Gorev .01 .05
142 Dean Hulett .01 .05
143 Niklas Sundblad .01 .05
144 Jeff Bes .01 .05
145 Pascal Rheaume .01 .05
146 Donald Brashear .01 .05
147 Hugo Belanger .01 .05
148 Blair Scott .01 .05
149 Steve Staios .01 .05
150 Matt Martin .01 .05
151 Richard Matvichuk .01 .05
152 Paul Brousseau .01 .05
153 Evgeny Namestnikov .01 .05
154 Mike Peca .20 .50
155 Jeff Nelson .01 .05
156 Greg Andrusak .01 .05
157 Norm Batherson .01 .05
158 Martin Bakula .01 .05
159 Ed Patterson .01 .05
160 Steve Larouche .01 .05
161 Libor Polasek .01 .05
162 Jon Hillebrandt .01 .05
163 Guy Leveque .01 .05
164 Eric Lacroix .01 .05
165 Scott Walker .01 .05
166 Robert Burakovsky .01 .05
167 Markus Ketterer .01 .05
168 Mike Speer .01 .05
169 Martin Jiranek .01 .05
170 Andy Schneider .01 .05
171 Terry Hollinger .01 .05
172 Mark Lawrence .01 .05
173 Martin Lapointe .20 .50
174 Vaclav Prospal .01 .05
175 Mike Fountain .01 .05
176 Alexander Kerch .01 .05
177 Oleg Petrov .01 .05
178 Derek Armstrong .01 .05
179 Matthew Barnaby .01 .05
180 Andrei Nazarov .01 .05
181 Andrei Trefilov .01 .05
182 Jean-Yves Roy .01 .05
183 Boris Rousson .01 .05
184 Dan Laperriere .01 .05
185 Yan Kaminsky .01 .05
186 Ralph Intranuovo .01 .05
187 Sandy Moger .01 .05
188 Grant Marshall .01 .05
189 Denny Felsner .01 .05
190 Cory Stillman .01 .05
191 Eric Lavigne .01 .05
192 Jarrod Skalde .01 .05
193 Steve Junker .01 .05
194 Alexander Cherbayev .01 .05
195 Nathan Lafayette .01 .05
196 Ed Ward .01 .05
197 Harijs Vitolinsh .01 .05
198 Jarmo Kekalainen .01 .05
199 Neil Eisenhut .01 .05
200 Radek Bonk .01 .05
201 Jason Bonsignore .01 .05
202 Jeff Friesen .01 .05
203 Ed Jovanovski .08 .25
204 Brett Lindros .01 .05
205 Jeff O'Neill .20 .50
206 Deron Quint .01 .05
207 Vadim Sharifjanov .01 .05
208 Oleg Tverdovsky .01 .05
209 Friesen .01 .05
O'Neill CL
210 David Cooper .01 .05
211 Doug McDonald .01 .05
212 Leonid Toropchenko .01 .05
213 Chris Rogles .01 .05
214 Slava Kozlov .08 .25
215 Denis Metlyuk .01 .05
216 Scott McKay .01 .05
217 Brian Loney .01 .05
218 Kevin Hodson .01 .05
219 Bobby House .01 .05
220 Sergei Krivokrasov .01 .05
221 Brett Harkins .01 .05
222 Cale Hulse .01 .05
223 Marc Tardif .01 .05
224 Jon Rohloff .01 .05
225 Kevin Smyth .01 .05
226 Jason Young .01 .05
227 Sergei Zholtok .01 .05
228 Todd Simon .01 .05
229 Jerome Bechard .01 .05
230 Matt Robbins .01 .05
231 Joe Cook .01 .05
232 John Brill .01 .05
233 Dan Goldie .01 .05
234 Dan Gravelle .01 .05
235 Shawn Wheeler .01 .05
236 Brad Harrison .01 .05
237 Joe Dragon .01 .05
238 Jason Jennings .01 .05
239 Manon Rheaume .75 2.00
240 Jamie Steer .01 .05
241 Scott Rogers .01 .05
242 Lyle Wildgoose .01 .05
243 Darren Colbourne .01 .05
244 Mike Smith .01 .05
245 Chris Bright .01 .05
246 Chris Belanger .01 .05
247 Darren Schwartz .01 .05
248 Cammi Granato .60 1.50
249 Erin Whitten .20 .50
250 Manon Rheaume .75 2.00
NNO Arnott .40 1.00
Yashin ROY

1994 Classic Pro Prospects Autographs

This 9-card set includes over 10,000 randomly inserted autographed cards of Radek Bonk, Alexei Yashin, Chris Pronger, Manon Rheaume, Joe Juneau, and more.

AU1 R.Bonk AU/2400 5.00 10.00
AU2 J.Bonsignore AU/2450 5.00 10.00
AU3 J.Friesen AU/2450 10.00 25.00
AU4 J.Juneau AU/1370 8.00 20.00
AU5 A.Kovalev AU/1900 5.00 10.00
AU6 C.Pronger AU/1400 12.50 30.00
AU7 M.Rheaume AU/1900 30.00 80.00
AU8 E.Whitten AU/1800 12.50 30.00
AU9 A.Yashin AU/1400 6.00 15.00

1994 Classic Pro Prospects Ice Ambassadors

This standard-size set features young players from all over the world. The cards were inserted one per jumbo sheet in a late-season, retail-only repackaging configuration. The fronts feature a player photo with a stripe down the right side carrying the player's name. On the bottom of the card in gold lettering is the identification of the team. The reverse of the card features a player photo on the top half with statistical information on the bottom half.

COMPLETE SET (20) 3.00 8.00
IA1 Adrian Aucoin .08 .25
IA2 Corey Hirsch .15 .40
IA3 Paul Kariya 1.00 2.50
IA4 David Harlock .08 .25
IA5 Manny Legace .30 .75
IA6 Chris Therien .08 .25
IA7 Todd Warriner .08 .25
IA8 Todd Marchant .08 .25
IA9 Matt Martin .08 .25
IA10 Peter Ferraro .08 .25
IA11 Brian Rolston .15 .40
IA12 Jim Campbell .08 .25
IA13 Mike Dunham .30 .75
IA14 Craig Johnson .08 .25
IA15 Saku Koivu 1.00 2.50
IA16 Jere Lehtinen .30 .75
IA17 Viktor Kozlov .15 .40
IA18 Andrei Nikolishin .08 .25
IA19 Sergei Gonchar .15 .40
IA20 Valeri Karpov .08 .25

1994 Classic Pro Prospects International Heroes

Randomly inserted through the foil packs, these 25 clear acetate standard-size cards predominantly feature the U.S. and Canadian National Teams. The cards are numbered on the back with an "LP" prefix. The nationalities of the players are as follows: U.S. (1-10); Canadian (11-20, 24); Czech (21); Russian (22, 25); and Finnish (23).

COMPLETE SET (25) 20.00 40.00
LP1 Jim Campbell .75 2.00
LP2 Ted Drury .75 2.00
LP3 Mike Dunham 1.25 3.00
LP4 Chris Ferraro .75 2.00
LP5 Peter Ferraro .75 2.00
LP6 Darby Hendrickson .75 2.00
LP7 Craig Johnson .75 2.00
LP8 Todd Marchant .75 2.00
LP9 Matt Martin .75 2.00
LP10 Brian Rolston .75 2.00
LP11 Adrian Aucoin .75 2.00
LP12 Martin Gendron .75 2.00
LP13 David Harlock .75 2.00
LP14 Corey Hirsch .75 2.00
LP15 Paul Kariya 3.00 8.00
LP16 Manny Legace 1.25 3.00
LP17 Brett Lindros .75 2.00
LP18 Brian Savage .75 2.00
LP19 Chris Therien .75 2.00
LP20 Todd Warriner .75 2.00
LP21 Radek Bonk .75 2.00
LP22 Pavel Bure 1.25 3.00
LP23 Teemu Selanne 3.00 8.00
LP24 Mark Recchi 1.50 4.00
LP25 Alexei Yashin 1.50 4.00

1994 Classic Pro Prospects Promo

This standard-size promo card was issued to show the design of the 1994 Classic Pro Hockey Prospects set. Inside white borders, the front displays a color action player photo. The player's name, team, and position appear in a black bar at the bottom of the card. Also inside white borders, the back features another color player photo, logos, biographical information, and scoring totals. The disclaimer "For Promotional Purposes Only" is printed on the back.

NNO Radek Bonk PROMO 1.50 4.00

1994 Classic Pro Prospects Prototype

Given away at the 1994 National Sports Convention in Houston, this prototype card measures the standard size. The front features a borderless color action player photo, with the player's name on the bottom. The word "PROTOTYPE" is written vertically in red block lettering along the right edge. On a screened background, the back carries an advertisement for the convention in gold foil lettering. The card is unnumbered.

NNO Jason Arnott 2.00 5.00

1996 Clear Assets

The 1996 Clear Assets set was issued in one series totaling 70 cards. The set features 75 upscale acetate cards of the most collectible athletes from baseball, basketball, football, hockey and auto racing. Also included is the debut appearance by many of the top players entering the 1996 football draft. Release date was April 1996.

COMPLETE SET (70) 6.00 15.00
51 Manon Rheaume .20 .50
56 Bryan Berard .08 .25
57 Petr Sykora .10 .30
58 Ed Jovanovski .10 .30
59 Radek Dvorak .08 .25

1996 Clear Assets Phone Cards $1

COMPLETE SET (30) 5.00 12.00
*PIN NUMBER REVEALED: HALF VALUE
$1 CARDS ONE PER RETAIL PACK
*$2 CARDS: .6X TO 1.5X $1 CARDS
ONE PER HOBBY PACK
CARDS EXPIRED 10/1/97
5 Wade Redden .10 .30
11 Manon Rheaume .30 .75
22 Petr Sykora .15 .40

1996 Clear Assets Phone Cards $5

Inserted at a rate of 1:10 packs, this 20-card set of acetate phone cards features many of the biggest names in sports. The Sprint phone cards carry expiration dates of 10/1/97.

COMPLETE SET (20) 12.00 30.00
*PIN NUMBER REVEALED: HALF VALUE
16 Petr Sykora .40 1.00

1996 Collector's Edge Future Legends

This set features top performers from the AHL and IHL. The cards were sold in wax pack form and featured thin card stock with stylized metallic etching on the front.

COMPLETE SET (50) 6.00 15.00
1 Brad Bombardir .07 .20
2 Niklas Andersson .07 .20
3 Mike Dunham .20 .50
4 Anders Eriksson .07 .20
5 Kelly Fairchild .07 .20
6 Chris Ferraro .07 .20
7 Peter Ferraro .07 .20
8 Eric Fichaud .15 .40
9 Manny Legace .20 .50
10 David Ling .07 .20
11 Jim Montgomery .07 .20
12 Chris Murray .07 .20
13 Rob Brown .07 .20
14 Rem Murray .07 .20
15 Rob Murray .07 .20
16 Jan Caloun .07 .20
17 Frederic Chabot .15 .40
18 Craig Fisher .07 .20
19 Dwayne Roloson .15 .40
20 Brad Smyth .07 .20
21 Steve Sullivan .20 .50
22 Petr Sykora .07 .20
23 Darcy Tucker .15 .40
24 Landon Wilson .15 .40
25 Greg Hawgood .07 .20
26 Stephane Beauregard .15 .40
27 Aki Berg .07 .20
28 Matt Johnson .07 .20
29 Curtis Joseph .20 .50
30 Dan Lambert .07 .20
31 Eric LeCompte .07 .20
32 Brett Lievers .07 .20
33 Mark McArthur .15 .40
34 Ethan Moreau .15 .40
35 Marty Murray .07 .20
36 Wayne Primeau .07 .20
37 John Purves .07 .20
38 Manon Rheaume 1.00 2.50
39 Barry Richter .07 .20
40 Jamie Rivers .07 .20
41 Tommy Salo .20 .50
42 Jamie Storr .20 .50
43 Tom Tilley .07 .20
44 Derek Wilkinson .15 .40
45 Mike Wilson .07 .20
46 Sandis Ozolinsh .07 .20
47 Andrew Brunette .15 .40
48 James Black .07 .20
49 Terry Yake .07 .20
50 Mike Prokopec .07 .20

1996 Collector's Edge Future Legends Autographed Hot Picks

Randomly inserted at 2 per box, these cards carry full color photos and autographs of the featured player.

COMPLETE SET (4) 10.00 20.00
1 Chris Phillips/6000 2.00 5.00
2 Boyd Devereaux/6000 2.00 5.00
3 Richard Jackman/5000 2.00 5.00
4 Marcus Nilsson/6000 2.00 5.00

1996 Collector's Edge Ice

This 200 card standard-size set features members of the America Hockey League and the International Hockey League: The cards are sequenced in alphabetical order within alphabetical team order A parallel prismatic version of these cards were issued, they are valued as a multiple of the regular cards.

COMPLETE SET (200) 15.00 30.00
1 Curtis Bowen .02 .10
2 Anders Eriksson .02 .10
3 Kevin Hodson .08 .25
4 Martin Lapointe .20 .50
5 Aaron Ward .02 .10
6 Mike Dunham .20 .50
7 Chris McAlpine .02 .10
8 Brian Rolston .20 .50
9 Corey Schwab .08 .25
10 Steve Sullivan .20 .50
11 Petr Sykora .20 .50
12 Darren Van Impe .02 .10
13 Mike Maneluk .02 .10
14 David Sacco .02 .10
15 Jarrod Skalde .08 .25
16 Nikolai Tsulygin .02 .10
17 Peter Ferraro .02 .10
18 Chris Ferraro .02 .10
19 Corey Hirsch .08 .25
20 Mattias Norstrom .08 .25
21 Jamie Ram .08 .25
22 Chris Armstrong .02 .10
23 Alexei Kudashov .02 .10
24 Todd MacDonald .02 .10
25 Steve Washburn .02 .10
26 Kevin Weekes .20 .50
27 Rene Corbet .02 .10
28 Janne Laukkanen .02 .10
29 Aaron Miller .02 .10
30 Landon Wilson .08 .25
31 Fred Brathwaite .20 .50
32 Ryan Haggerty .02 .10
33 Ralph Intranuovo .02 .10
34 Todd Marchant .20 .50
35 David Oliver .02 .10
36 Marko Tuomainen .02 .10
37 Peter White .02 .10
38 Sebastien Bordeleau .02 .10
39 Martin Brochu .08 .25
40 Valeri Bure .08 .25
41 Craig Conroy .08 .25
42 Darcy Tucker .20 .50
43 David Wilkie .02 .10
44 Paul Healey .02 .10
45 Chris Herperger .02 .10
46 Jim Montgomery .02 .10
47 Chris Therien .02 .10
48 Pavol Demitra .20 .50
49 Michel Picard .02 .10
50 Jason Zent .02 .10
51 Patrick Boileau .02 .10
52 Jim Carey .08 .25
53 Sergei Gonchar .08 .25
54 Jeff Nelson .02 .10
55 Stefan Ustorf .02 .10
56 Alexander Kharlamov .02 .10
57 Ron Tugnutt .20 .50
58 Scott Bailey .08 .25
59 Clayton Beddoes .02 .10
60 Andre Roy .08 .25
61 Evgeny Ryabchikov .08 .25
62 Mark Astley .02 .10
63 Jody Gage .08 .25
64 Sergei Klimentiev .02 .10
65 Barrie Moore .02 .10
66 Mike Wilson .02 .10
67 Shayne Wright .02 .10
68 Michal Grosek .08 .25
69 Tavis Hansen .02 .10
70 Nikolai Khabibulin .30 .75
71 Scott Langkow .08 .25
72 Jason McBain .02 .10
73 Dwayne Roloson .08 .25
74 Cory Stillman .08 .25
75 Jamie Allison .02 .10
76 Jesper Mattson .02 .10
77 David Ling .02 .10
78 Brandon Convery .02 .10
79 Darby Hendrickson .02 .10
80 Janne Gronvall .02 .10
81 Jason Saal .02 .10
82 Brent Gretzky .02 .10
83 Kent Manderville .02 .10
84 Shayne Toporowski .02 .10
85 Paul Vincent .02 .10
86 Mark Kolesar .02 .10
87 Lonny Bohonos .02 .10
88 Larry Courville .02 .10
89 Jassen Cullimore .02 .10
90 Scott Walker .08 .25
91 Mike Buzak .02 .10
92 Craig Darby .02 .10
93 Eric Fichaud .08 .25
94 Andreas Johansson .02 .10
95 Jamie Rivers .02 .10
96 Jason Strudwick .02 .10
97 Patrice Tardif .02 .10
98 Alex Vasilevskii .02 .10
99 Drew Bannister .02 .10
100 Stan Drulia .08 .25
101 Aaron Gavey .02 .10
102 Reggie Savage .02 .10
103 Derek Wilkinson .08 .25
104 Rob Brown .02 .10
105 Dan Currie .02 .10
106 Kevin MacDonald .02 .10
107 Steve Maltais .08 .25
108 Shawn Rivers .02 .10
109 Wendell Young .08 .25
110 Don Biggs .02 .10
111 Dale DeGray .02 .10
112 Paul Lawless .02 .10
113 Danny Lorenz .02 .10
114 Dave Tomlinson .02 .10
115 Jock Callander .08 .25
116 Phillipe DeRouville .02 .10
117 Ryan Savoia .02 .10
118 Mike Stevens .02 .10
119 Chris Tamer .08 .25
120 Peter Bondra .20 .50
121 Peter Ciavaglia .02 .10
122 Rick Knickle .02 .10
123 Lonnie Loach .02 .10
124 Michal Pivonka .02 .10
125 Andy Bezeau .02 .10
126 Bob Essensa .08 .25
127 Andrew McBain .02 .10
128 Kevin Miehm .02 .10
129 Scott Arniel .02 .10
130 Kevin Dineen .08 .25
131 Rob Dopson .08 .25
132 Mark Freer .02 .10
133 Troy Gamble .08 .25
134 Ethan Moreau .08 .25
135 Sergei Klimovich .02 .10
136 Eric Lecompte .02 .10
137 Eric Manlow .02 .10
138 Kip Miller .02 .10
139 Manny Fernandez .20 .50
140 Mike Kennedy .02 .10
141 Jamie Langenbrunner .20 .50
142 Derrick Smith .02 .10
143 Jordan Willis .08 .25
144 Jan Caloun .02 .10
145 Viktor Kozlov .08 .25
146 Andrei Nazarov .02 .10
147 Geoff Sarjeant .02 .10
148 Patrik Augusta .02 .10
149 Viktor Gordiouk .02 .10
150 Dave Littman .08 .25
151 Todd Gillingham .02 .10
152 Greg Hawgood .02 .10
153 Patrice Lefebvre .02 .10
154 Pokey Reddick .08 .25
155 Manon Rheaume .75 2.00
156 Jeff Sharples .02 .10
157 Todd Simon .02 .10
158 Radek Bonk .20 .50
159 Gino Cavallini .02 .10
160 Tom Draper .08 .25
161 Tony Hrkac .08 .25
162 Fabian Joseph .02 .10
163 Mark Laforest .02 .10
164 Dave Christian .02 .10
165 Bryan Fogarty .02 .10
166 Chris Govedaris .02 .10
167 Mike Hurlbut .02 .10
168 Chris Imes .02 .10
169 Stephane Morin .02 .10
170 Allan Bester .08 .25
171 Kerry Clark .02 .10
172 Neil Eisenhut .02 .10
173 Craig Fisher .02 .10
174 Patrick Neaton .02 .10
175 Todd Richards .02 .10
176 Jon Casey .08 .25
177 Doug Evans .02 .10
178 Michel Mongeau .02 .10
179 Greg Paslawski .02 .10
180 Darren Veitch .02 .10
181 Frederick Beaubien .02 .10
182 Kevin Brown .02 .10
183 Rob Cowie .02 .10
184 Yanic Perreault .08 .25
185 Chris Snell .02 .10
186 Jan Vopat .02 .10
187 Robin Bawa .02 .10
188 Stephane Beauregard .08 .25
189 Dale Craigwell .02 .10
190 John Purves .08 .25
191 Jeff Madill .02 .10
192 Gord Dineen .02 .10
193 Chris Marinucci .08 .25
194 Mark McArthur .02 .10
195 Zigmund Palffy .20 .50
196 Tommy Salo .20 .50
197 Checklist .02 .10
198 Checklist .02 .10
199 Checklist .02 .10
200 Checklist .02 .10
P155 Manon Rheaume Promo
(Toronto Fall Expo '95)

1996 Collector's Edge Ice Crucibles

This 25 card standard-size set was randomly inserted into packs. The fronts feature the players photo along with the word "Crucible" on the top and his name on the bottom. The cards are numbered with a "C" prefix. The backs include a player head shot as well as recent stats.

COMPLETE SET (25) 15.00 30.00
C1 David Roberts .40 1.00
C2 Ian Laperriere .40 1.00
C3 Kevin Dineen .40 1.00
C4 Kenny Jonsson .40 1.00
C5 Jim Carey .75 2.00
C6 Todd Marchant .40 1.00
C7 David Oliver .40 1.00
C8 Yanic Perreault .75 2.00
C9 Chris Therien .40 1.00
C10 Viktor Kozlov .75 2.00
C11 Valeri Bure .40 1.00
C12 Nikolai Khabibulin 1.00 2.50
C13 Steven Rice .40 1.00
C14 Mike Kennedy .40 1.00
C15 Peter Bondra .75 2.00
C16 Sergei Zubov .40 1.00
C17 Slava Kozlov .75 2.00
C18 Chris Osgood .75 2.00
C19 Darren McCarty .40 1.00
C20 Jason Dawe .40 1.00
C21 Trevor Kidd 1.00 2.50
C22 Tommy Salo 1.00 2.50
C23 Michal Pivonka .40 1.00
C24 Zigmund Palffy .75 2.00
NNO Checklist .40 1.00

1996 Collector's Edge Ice Livin' Large

This set was randomly inserted into packs. The cards feature top players. The cards are numbered with a "L" prefix.

COMPLETE SET (11) 20.00 40.00
L1 Adam Graves .75 2.00
L2 Marty McSorley .75 2.00
L3 Adam Oates 1.25 3.00
L4 Keith Primeau .75 2.00
L5 Bill Ranford 1.25 3.00
L6 Curtis Joseph 1.50 4.00
L7 Felix Potvin 1.50 4.00
L8 Mike Vernon 1.25 3.00
L9 Theo Fleury .75 2.00
L10 Kevin Stevens .75 2.00
L11 Martin Brodeur 8.00 20.00
NNO Checklist .75 2.00

1996 Collector's Edge Ice Future Legends Hot Picks Autographs

1 Chris Phillips/6000 1.25 3.00
3 Richard Jackman/5000 1.25 3.00

1996 Collector's Edge Ice Future Legends Platinum Club

Random inserts in packs of Collectors Edge Ice.

COMPLETE SET (8) 10.00 25.00
1 Mike Dunham 2.00 5.00
2 Eric Fichaud .75 2.00
3 Manny Legace 2.00 5.00
4 Steve Sullivan .75 2.00
5 Darcy Tucker .75 2.00
6 Jamie Langenbrunner .75 2.00
7 Ethan Moreau .75 2.00
8 Jamie Storr .75 2.00

1996 Collector's Edge Ice Prism

This 200-card set was issued as a parallel to the base set. They weren't issued as inserts, however. Instead, they were sold in team set form on a localized basis across the AHL and IHL. These cards are actually quite scarce, and provide a real challenge for player collectors.

*PRISM CARDS: 2X to 5X BASIC CARDS

1996 Collector's Edge Ice Promos

This 7-card set was issued as a promotional device to entice dealers to purchase the upcoming Collector's Edge Ice set of minor league stars. The cards mirror the design of the regular issue cards, save for the numbering, which comes with a PR-prefix.

COMPLETE SET (7) .75 2.00
PR1 Todd Marchant .08 .25
PR2 Tommy Salo .20 .50
PR3 Michael Dunham .20 .50
PR4 Viktor Kozlov .15 .40
PR5 Dwayne Roloson .15 .40
PR6 Tony Hrkac .08 .25
NNO Title Card .20 .50

1996 Collector's Edge Ice Quantum Motion

This 13 card set was randomly inserted into packs. The full-bleed cards feature a player photo over most of it. The words "Quantum Motion" are located in the lower right corner.

COMPLETE SET (13) 15.00 30.00
1 Manny Fernandez 1.50 4.00
2 Pokey Reddick .75 2.00
3 Yanic Perreault .75 2.00
4 Rob Brown .75 2.00
5 Hubie McDonough .75 2.00
6 Stan Drulia .75 2.00
7 Michel Picard .75 2.00
8 Jim Carey 1.25 3.00
9 Martin Lapointe 1.25 3.00
10 Valeri Bure .75 2.00
11 Martin Brochu 1.25 3.00
12 Corey Schwab 1.25 3.00

1996 Collector's Edge Ice Future Legends Signed, Sealed and Delivered

This 8-card set highlights youngsters set to make their power known in the NHL.

COMPLETE SET (8) 8.00 20.00
1 Alexandre Volchkov/5000 1.25 3.00
2 Chris Allen/4000 1.25 3.00
3 Brian Bonin 1.25 3.00
4 Josh Green/6000 1.25 3.00
5 Chris Hajt/4000 1.25 3.00
6 Josh Holden 1.25 3.00
8 Andrei Zyuzin/6000 1.25 3.00
P1 Alexandre Volchkov Proto Unsigned 1.00 2.50

1996 Collector's Edge Ice The Wall

This 13 card die-cut set was inserted as a set in each sealed foil box. The cards feature goaltenders and their masks are on the front. The backs are devoted to a player photo. Also on the backs are vital statistics, and a brief biography. The cards are numbered with a "TW" prefix.

COMPLETE SET (12) 6.00 12.00
TW1 Ray LeBlanc .40 1.00
TW2 Manny Fernandez .75 2.00
TW3 Rick Knickle .40 1.00
TW4 Troy Gamble .40 1.00
TW5 Pokey Reddick .40 1.00
TW6 Wendell Young .40 1.00
TW7 Jim Carey .40 1.00
TW8 Dwayne Roloson .40 1.00
TW9 Les Kuntar .40 1.00
TW10 Mike Dunham .75 2.00
TW11 Eric Fichaud .40 1.00
TW12 Kevin Hodson .40 1.00

1995 Images

This 100-card set features top NHL prospects currently playing in the juniors, minors or overseas. The standard-sized cards feature full-bleed color photography over a metallic sheen background. The Classic logo is in the upper left corner, while the Images logo, player name and position rest on a blue and silver bar near the bottom. The backs feature another color photo, stats and the logos of the licensing bodies. One autographed card was found in each box. A total of 1995 individually numbered 12-box cases were produced.

COMPLETE SET (100) 5.00 12.00
1 Bryan Berard .07 .20
2 Jeff Friesen .02 .10
3 Tommy Salo .25 .60
4 Jim Carey .07 .20
5 Wade Redden .07 .20
6 Jocelyn Thibault .15 .40
7 Ian Laperriere .02 .10
8 Todd Marchant .02 .10
9 Blaine Lacher .02 .10
10 Pavel Bure .15 .40
11 Alex Vasilevskii .02 .10
12 Jason Doig .02 .10
13 Eric Fichaud .07 .20
14 Eric Daze .07 .20
15 Ed Jovanovski .07 .20
16 Alexander Selivanov .02 .10
17 Brent Gretzky .02 .10
18 Terry Ryan .02 .10
19 Chris Wells .02 .10
20 Wade Belak .02 .10
21 Kevin Dineen .02 .10
22 Craig Fisher .02 .10
23 Jan Caloun .02 .10
24 Manny Fernandez .15 .40
25 Radek Bonk .02 .10
26 Dave Christian .02 .10
27 Patrice Tardif .02 .10
28 Kevin Brown .02 .10
29 Hubie McDonough .02 .10
30 Yan Golubovsky .02 .10
31 Steve Larouche .02 .10
32 Chris Therien .02 .10
33 Craig Darby .02 .10
34 Dwayne Norris .02 .10
35 Roman Oksiuta .02 .10
36 Steve Washburn .02 .10
37 Todd Bertuzzi .15 .40
38 Cory Stillman .07 .20
39 Steve Kelly .02 .10
40 Nathan LaFayette .02 .10
41 Dwayne Roloson .07 .20
42 Nikolai Khabibulin .15 .40
43 Radim Bicanek .02 .10
44 Jeff O'Neill .02 .10
45 Jason Bonsignore .02 .10
46 Shean Donovan .02 .10
47 Wayne Primeau .02 .10
48 Jamie Langenbrunner .02 .10
49 Dan Cloutier .15 .40
50 Ethan Moreau .07 .20
51 Brad Bombardir .02 .10
52 Jason Muzzatti .02 .10
53 Jassen Cullimore .02 .10
54 Jason Zent .02 .10
55 Sergei Gonchar .07 .20
56 Steve Rucchin .02 .10
57 Rob Cowie .02 .10
58 Miroslav Satan .40 1.00
59 Kenny Jonsson .07 .20
60 Adam Deadmarsh .02 .10
61 Mike Dunham .15 .40
62 Corey Hirsch .02 .10
63 Janne Laukkanen .02 .10
64 Craig Conroy .02 .10
65 Ryan Sittler .02 .10
66 Jeff Nelson .02 .10
67 Michel Picard .02 .10
68 Mark Astley .02 .10
69 Lonny Bohonos .02 .10
70 Evgeny Ryabchikov .02 .10
71 Chris Osgood .07 .20
72 Manon Rheaume 1.00 2.50
73 Mike Kennedy .02 .10
74 Deron Quint .02 .10
75 Jamie Storr .07 .20
76 Aris Brimanis .02 .10
77 Valeri Bure .02 .10
78 Rene Corbet .02 .10
79 David Oliver .02 .10
80 Chris McAlpine .02 .10
81 Petr Sykora .15 .40
82 Brad Church .07 .20
83 Daymond Langkow .15 .40
84 Chad Kilger .02 .10
85 Shane Doan .20 .50
86 Jeff Ware .02 .10
87 Christian Laflamme .02 .10
88 Cory Cross .02 .10
89 Al Secord .02 .10
90 Jason Woolley .02 .10
91 Bryan McCabe .02 .10
92 Travis Richards .02 .10
93 Andrei Nazarov .02 .10
94 Mike Pomichter .02 .10
95 Chris Marinucci .02 .10
96 Jean-Yves Roy .02 .10
97 Brian Rolston .07 .20
98 Aaron Ward .02 .10
99 Jim Carey CL .02 .10
100 Pavel Bure CL .07 .20

1995 Images Gold

These 100 standard-size cards were issued as a one-per-pack parallel to the Images set. The card design is identical to the standard Images card, except for the metallic background being a golden tone rather than the standard silver.

*STARS: 1.25X TO 2.5X BASIC CARDS

1995 Images Autographs

These 22 standard-size cards were random inserts throughout the packs. The card design is identical to the standard Images card except for the facsimile autograph inscribed across the picture. The number of cards signed is indicated in parenthesis.

2A J.Friesen/1500 4.00 10.00
6A J.Thibault/1185 4.00 10.00
9A B.Lacher/1500 2.00 5.00
25A R.Bonk/970 3.00 8.00
30A Yan Golubovsky/1500 .75 2.00
36A Steve Washburn/1500 .75 2.00
41A Dwayne Roloson/1115 .75 2.00
45A Jason Bonsignore/1500 2.00 5.00
46A Shean Donovan/1500 .75 2.00
48A J.Langenbrunner/1500 5.00 12.00
54A Jason Zent/1125 .75 2.00
59A K.Jonsson/1180 2.00 5.00
60A A.Deadmarsh/1500 6.00 15.00
64A Craig Conroy/1170 .75 2.00
74A D.Quint/1500 .75 2.00
76A Aris Brimanis/1500 .75 2.00
79A David Oliver/1500 .75 2.00
80A Chris McAlpine/1185 .75 2.00
81A P.Sykora/1500 3.00 8.00
94A Mike Pomichter/1175 .75 2.00
95A Chris Marinucci/1500 .75 2.00
98A Aaron Ward/1190 .75 2.00

1995 Images Clear Excitement

This 20-card standard-size set was randomly inserted only in Hot boxes. Essentially, the odds of finding one of these cards was 1, 152 packs. Each pack in a Hot box has 3 cards from any of the five insert sets. These clear cards feature color player action cutouts on their fronts. The player's name appears in a blue bar on the left. The backs carry the reverse image as a shadow with the player's name in an oval across it. The blue bar on the left contains information about the player and the card number at the top.

MPLETE SET (20) 75.00 150.00
1 Bryan Berard 2.50 6.00
2 Jeff Friesen 2.00 5.00
3 Tommy Salo 3.00 8.00
4 Jim Carey 2.50 6.00
5 Wade Redden 2.50 6.00
6 Jocelyn Thibault 3.00 8.00
7 Ian Laperriere 2.00 5.00
8 Todd Marchant 2.00 5.00
9 Blaine Lacher 2.00 5.00
10 Pavel Bure 3.00 8.00
11 Petr Sykora 3.00 8.00
12 Daymond Langkow 2.50 6.00
13 Radek Bonk 2.00 5.00
14 Patrice Tardif 2.00 5.00
15 Jeff Nelson 2.00 5.00
16 Jeff O'Neill 2.00 5.00
17 Ed Jovanovski 2.50 6.00
18 Jason Doig 2.00 5.00
19 Chris Marinucci 2.00 5.00
20 Manon Rheaume 12.50 30.00

1995 Images Platinum Players

e cards in this 10 card standard-size set were ndomly inserted at a rate of one per 36 packs. The nts have a color action photo with a green and silver background. The word "Images" is at the top and atinum Player" is at the bottom. The backs have a or action photo with a green tint in the background. yer information appears at the bottom and each card numbered out of 1,995.

MPLETE SET (10) 10.00 20.00
1 Pavel Bure 1.50 4.00
2 Tony Granato .40 1.00
3 Kevin Dineen .40 1.00
4 Ron Hextall 1.25 3.00
5 Claude Lemieux .40 1.00
6 Mark Recchi 1.50 4.00
7 Benoit Hogue .40 1.00
8 Tim Cheveldae .40 1.00
9 Darcy Wakaluk .40 1.00
10 Todd Gill .40 1.00

1995 Images Premier Draft Choice

e card from this 10 standard-size set was randomly serted in every 48 packs. The card of Bryan Berard, e no. 1 draft choice, was redeemable for a $25 anon Rheaume autographed phone card. The offer pired 12/31/95. The fronts feature a player action oto on a borderless blue and silver background with e player's name printed vertically down the left side. e backs carry the card number and players name in a arble blue stripe at the top with the redemption ections below. A checklist of the 10 cards is printed the bottom. The announced print run was 2250 sets.

MPLETE SET (10) 10.00 20.00
1 Bryan Berard 1.00 2.50
2 Wade Redden 1.00 2.50
3 Steve Kelly .40 1.00
4 Petr Sykora 3.00 8.00
5 Brad Church .40 1.00
6 Daymond Langkow 1.50 4.00
7 Chad Kilger .40 1.00
8 Terry Ryan .40 1.00
9 Jason Doig .40 1.00
10 Field Card .40 1.00

95 Images Platinum Prospects

e ten cards in this set (found 1:36 packs) feature e of the top prospects for NHL stardom. The cards ture a color player photo over a diagonally split ver and blue metallic background. The Images logo in the top left corner, while the Platinum Prospects go rests in the bottom right, beside the player's name stylized script. The backs feature another color photo d a blurb assessing the player's chances. Each card serially numbered out of 1,995 at the bottom left rner.

MPLETE SET (10) 10.00 20.00
1 Jeff Nelson .40 1.00
2 Jim Carey 1.25 3.00
3 Ian Laperriere .40 1.00
4 Chris Osgood 1.25 3.00
5 Todd Marchant .40 1.00
6 Radek Bonk .40 1.00
7 Chris Marinucci .40 1.00
8 Tommy Salo 2.50 5.00
9 Manny Fernandez 1.50 4.00
10 Jan Caloun .40 1.00

1993-94 Images Four Sport

ese 150 standard-size cards feature on their rderless fronts color player action shots with ckgrounds that have been thrown out of focus. On e white background to the left, career highlights, graphy and statistics are displayed. Just 6,500 of ch card were produced. The set closes with Classic adlines (128-147) and checklists (148-150). A demption card inserted one per case entitled the llector to one set of basketball draft preview cards. is offered expired 9/30/94.

MPLETE SET (150) 6.00 15.00
Alexandre Daigle .10 .30
Chris Pronger .20 .50
Jim Montgomery .08 .25
Todd Marchant .08 .25
Mike Dunham .08 .25
Garth Snow .10 .30
Barry Richter .08 .25
Rob Niedermayer .15 .50
Jesse Belanger .08 .25
Peter Ferraro .08 .25
Ted Drury .08 .25
Derek Plante .08 .25
Jim Campbell .08 .25
Chris Osgood .60 1.50
Jason Arnott .15 .40
Jocelyn Thibault .10 .30
Chris Gratton .08 .25
Mike Rathje .08 .25
Martin Brodeur .40 1.00
6 Paul Kariya .60 1.50
1 Manon Rheaume .40 1.00
1 Felix Potvin .20 .50
5 Alexei Yashin .10 .30
0 Alexei Yashin B/W .08 .25
5 Chris Pronger B/W .08 .25
8 Chris Gratton B/W .08 .25
2 Jason Arnott B/W .10 .30
7 Manon Rheaume B/W .25 .60

1993-94 Images Four Sport Chrome

ndomly inserted one in every fourteen 1994 Classic ages packs, these 20 limited print (9,750 of each) rds measure the standard size and feature color yer action shots on their borderless metallic fronts. e cards are numbered on the back with a "CC" prefix. is set was also available in uncut sheet form as a deemed prize for the Marshall Faulk M5 card.

COMPLETE SET (20) 15.00 40.00
CC12 Cammi Granato .75 2.00
CC13 Alexei Yashin .50 1.25
CC14 Alexandre Daigle .60 1.50
CC15 Manon Rheaume 1.25 3.00
CC16 Radek Bonk .40 1.00
NNO Uncut Sheet 30.00 80.00

1993-94 Images Four Sport Sudden Impact

Inserted one per '94 Classic Images pack, these 20 gold foil-board cards measure the standard-size. The gold metallic fronts feature borderless color player action shots on backgrounds that have been thrown out of focus. The player's name and position appear in vertical lettering within a black strip across the card near the right edge. The backs carry a color player action shot at the top, followed below by career highlights on a white panel. The player's name appears in vertical black lettering within a ghosted action strip at the left edge. The cards are numbered on the back with an "SI" prefix.

COMPLETE SET (20) 4.00 10.00
SI5 Alexandre Daigle .40 1.00
SI6 Rob Niedermayer .30 .75
SI7 Jocelyn Thibault .30 .75
SI8 Derek Plante .20 .50

1995 Images Four Sport

Printed on 18-point micro-lined foil board, the 1995 Classic Images set consists of 120 standard-size cards, featuring the top draft picks from the four major sports. Classic produced 1,995 sequentially-numbered 16-box hobby cases. This series also features one "Hot Box" in every four cases; each pack in it included at least one card from five insert sets, plus the special Clear Excitement chase cards not found anywhere else, for a total of 24 inserts per Hot Box. There was a promotional card issued, not inserted into '94-95 Assets packs, for Grant Hill numbered HP1. The front is the same as the card in the set, but the back has an orange background and describes the product's features.

COMPLETE SET (120) 6.00 15.00
94 Ed Jovanovski .15 .40
95 Oleg Tverdovsky .10 .30
96 Radek Bonk .20 .50
97 Jason Bonsignore .10 .30
98 Jeff O'Neill .10 .30
99 Ryan Smyth .30 .75
100 Jamie Storr .20 .50
101 Jason Wiemer .10 .30
102 Nolan Baumgartner .10 .30
103 Jeff Friesen .20 .50
104 Wade Belak .10 .30
105 Ethan Moreau .10 .30
106 Alexander Kharlamov .10 .30
107 Eric Fichaud .20 .50
108 Wayne Primeau .10 .30
109 Brad Brown .10 .30
110 Chris Dingman .10 .30
111 Chris Wells .10 .30
112 Vadim Sharifijanov .10 .30
113 Dan Cloutier .10 .30
114 Jason Allison .20 .50
115 Todd Marchant .10 .30
116 Brent Gretzky .10 .30
117 Petr Sykora .30 .75
118 Manon Rheaume .20 .50
120 Marshall Faulk CL .15 .40

1995 Images Four Sport Classic Performances

Randomly inserted in hobby boxes at a rate of one in every 12 packs, this 20-card standard-size set relives great moments from the careers of 20 top athletes. Each card is numbered out of 4,495. The fronts feature the player against a gold background. The back contains on the left side a description of the great moment and on the right side a color player photo. The cards are numbered with a "CP" prefix.

COMPLETE SET (20) 20.00 50.00
CP19 Ed Jovanovski .40 1.00
CP20 Eric Fichaud .50 1.25

1995 Images Four Sport Clear Excitement

Randomly inserted at a rate of one in every 24 packs in hobby and retail hot boxes (1:1536 over the product run), these two five-card acetate sets each feature five notable athletes from different sports. Cards with the prefix "E" were inserted in hobby hot boxes, while cards with the prefix "C" were found in retail hot boxes. The cards are numbered out of 300.

COMPLETE SET (10) 60.00 150.00
E5 Manon Rheaume 5.00 12.00

1995 Images Four Sport Previews

Randomly inserted one per 24 packs in second-series '94-95 Assets packs, this five-card standard-size set was issued to promote the Classic Images series. Just 5,000 of each card were produced. The fronts display the player's photo showcased against a metallic background. The backs are devoted on the left side to the player's identification and a note saying you have received a limited edition preview card. The right side of the reverse has a full-color photo of the player and the card is numbered at the upper right corner. The cards are numbered with an "IP" prefix.

COMPLETE SET (5) 6.00 15.00
IP4 Manon Rheaume .75 2.00

2015 ITG CHL Draft

COMPLETE SET (30) 10.00 25.00
*BLACK/50: .6X TO 1.5X BASIC CARDS
*BLUE/25: 1X TO 2.5X BASIC CARDS
*GOLD/100: .5X TO 1.2X BASIC CARDS
*PINK/200: .5X TO 1.2X BASIC CARDS
*RED/10: 1.2X TO 3X BASIC CARDS
*SILVER/500: .4X TO 1X BASIC CARDS
1 Connor McDavid 1.50 4.00
2 Mathew Barzal 1.00 2.50
3 Dylan Strome .60 1.50
4 Jeremy Roy .30 .75
5 Travis Konecny .50 1.25
6 Mitchell Marner 1.00 2.50
7 Daniel Sprong .40 1.00
8 Lawson Crouse .30 .75
9 Nick Merkley .50 1.25
10 Pavel Zacha .50 1.25
11 Connor McDavid CB 1.50 4.00
12 Mathew Barzal CB 1.00 2.50
13 Dylan Strome CB .60 1.50
14 Jeremy Roy CB .30 .75
15 Travis Konecny CB .50 1.25
16 Mitchell Marner CB 1.00 2.50
17 Daniel Sprong CB .40 1.00
18 Lawson Crouse CB .30 .75
19 Nick Merkley CB .50 1.25
20 Pavel Zacha CB .50 1.25
21 Connor McDavid YS 1.50 4.00
22 Mathew Barzal YS 1.00 2.50
23 Dylan Strome YS .60 1.50
24 Jeremy Roy YS .30 .75
25 Travis Konecny YS .50 1.25
26 Mitchell Marner YS 1.00 2.50
27 Daniel Sprong YS .40 1.00
28 Lawson Crouse YS .30 .75
29 Nick Merkley YS .50 1.25
30 Pavel Zacha YS .50 1.25

1996-97 Score Board All Sport PPF

The 1996-97 All Sport Past Present and Future set was issued in two series in six-card packs. The product contains original vintage and rookie cards of the top athletes from baseball, basketball, football and hockey as well as new cards of tomorrow's stars from each sport. Release date for series one was October 1996; series two was February 1997. There was also a gold parallel produced for this set. Series one gold cards were inserted 1:10 packs while series two had gold cards inserted at a 1:5 ratio.

COMPLETE SET (200) 6.00 15.00
71 Ed Jovanovski .07 .20
72 Chris Phillips .07 .20
73 Alexander Volchkov .07 .20
74 Adam Colagiacomo .07 .20
75 Jonathan Aitken .07 .20
76 Rico Fata .07 .20
77 Andrei Zyuzin .07 .20
78 Josh Holden .07 .20
79 Boyd Devereaux .07 .20
97 Bryan Berard .07 .20
98 Dainius Zubrus .07 .20
99 Radek Dvorak .07 .20
170 Dainius Zubrus .07 .20
171 Joe Thornton .15 .40
172 Daniel Briere .07 .20
173 Radek Dvorak .07 .20
174 Richard Jackman .07 .20
175 Robert Dome .07 .20
176 Sergei Samsonov .15 .40
177 Jarome Iginla .15 .40
178 Dan Cleary .07 .20
199 Andrei Zyuzin .07 .20

1996-97 Score Board All Sport PPF Gold

*GOLDS: 1.2X TO 3X BASIC CARDS
GOLD STATED ODDS SER.1 1:10/SER.2 1:5

1996-97 Score Board Autographed Collection

Each box of Score Board Autographed Collection contains 16 packs containing six cards. The 50-card regular set includes top athletes from all four major team sports. According to Score Board, a total of 1,500 sequentially numbered cases were produced.

COMPLETE SET (50) 5.00 12.00
45 Joe Thornton .15 .40
46 Dan Cleary .07 .20
47 Robert Dome .07 .20
48 Alexander Volchkov .07 .20
49 Adam Colagiacomo .07 .20
50 Andrei Zyuzin .07 .20

1996-97 Score Board Autographed Collection Autographs

Each box of Autographed Collection contains an average of four autographed cards. There are two different varieties: silver foil stamped cards with no individual serial numbering inserted at a rate of 1:7 packs, and Gold foil serial numbered autographs inserted at a rate of 1:16 packs.

9 Dan Cleary 1.50 4.00
10 Adam Colagiacomo 1.50 4.00
13 Robert Dome 1.50 4.00
40 Sergei Samsonov 5.00 12.00
45 Joe Thornton 6.00 15.00
53 Dainius Zubrus 2.00 5.00
54 Andrei Zyuzin 1.50 4.00

1996-97 Score Board Autographed Collection Autographs Gold

These Gold foil parallel signed cards were seeded at the rate of 1:16 packs. They are Score Board Certified and individually numbered out of 250, 300 or 350 except for Steptret Williams.

*UNLISTED GOLD: .6X TO 1.5X BASIC AU

1996-97 Score Board Autographed Collection Game Breakers

This 30-card insert set was printed on metallic stock and has two versions-- regular and gold. The insertion ratio is 1:10 packs for regular inserts and 1:50 for the gold foil version.

COMPLETE SET (30) 25.00 60.00
*GOLD: .8X TO 2X BASIC INSERTS
GB29 Joe Thornton 1.25 3.00
GB30 Alexander Volchkov .60 1.50

1997-98 Score Board Autographed Collection

The 1998 Autographed Collection set was issued in one series totalling 50 cards with players from baseball, basketball, football and hockey. The product's major draw was an average of five autographed cards and one memorabilia redemption card per 18-pack box. The regular autographs were inserted 1:4.5 packs, the Blue Ribbon autographs were inserted 1:18 packs. The one-per box memorabilia redemption cards were not all redeemed due to the fact that Score Board, Inc. filed for bankruptcy a few months after the product's release. Score Board also released a "Strongbox Collection" that original retailed for around $125. Each Strongbox also included a parallel of this 50 card set, one star player autographed baseball with holder, one star player autographed 8" x 10", one Athletic Excellence card and One Sports City USA card.

COMPLETE SET (50) 5.00 12.00
4 Joe Thornton .07 .20
27 Robert Dome .07 .20
36 Sergei Samsonov .10 .30

1997-98 Score Board Autographed Collection Athletic Excellence

These 3 1/2" x 5" cards, were inserted one per Score Board "Strongbox Collection" box that originally retailed for around $125. Each Strongbox also included a parallel of the 1998 Autograph Collection 50 card set, one star player autographed baseball with holder, one star player autographed 8" x 10" and one Sports City USA card. Each card is sequentially numbered out of 750.

COMPLETE SET (12) 10.00 25.00
AE2 Joe Thornton .75 2.00

1997-98 Score Board Autographed Collection Autographs

One autographed card was available in one in every 4.5 Score Board Autograph Collection packs. The cards have a circular player photograph in the middle with a white oval below that includes a player's autograph. The card backs read, "Congratulations! You have received an authentic Score Board autographed card." There were also Kerry Wood and Greg Jones cards produced that appear on the marketplace later, although not inserted into packs. The cards are unnumbered and listed below in alphabetical order.

4 Daniel Briere HK 1.50 4.00
5 Dan Cleary HK 1.50 4.00
7 Robert Dome HK 1.50 4.00
11 Richard Jackman HK 1.50 4.00

1997-98 Score Board Autographed Collection Blue Ribbon Autographs

One Blue Ribbon autographed card was available in one in every 18 Score Board Autograph Collection packs. The cards have a circular player photograph with a blue ribbon border in the middle with a white oval below that includes a player's autograph. The cards are hand numbered out of the amounts listed below in the upper right hand corner. The card backs read, "Congratulations! You have received an authentic Score Board autographed card." The cards are unnumbered and listed below in alphabetical order. A Warrick Dunn card was later released through a home shopping network show. Some Kobe Bryant cards have surfaced in un-signed form and can often be found with forged autographs on the front. No authentic Kobe signed and numbered cards are known although the Congratulations Score Board message is included on the cardbacks.

14 Joe Thornton/1950 4.00 10.00

1997-98 Score Board Autographed Collection Sports City USA

These multi-player, city-themed cards were inserted one in nine Autographed Collection packs. There is also a Strongbox parallel found one per Score Board "Strongbox Collection" box that originally retailed for around $125. Each Strongbox also included a parallel of the 1998 Autograph Collection 50 card set, one star player autographed baseball with holder, one star player autographed 8" x 10"and one Athletic Excellence jumbo card.

COMPLETE SET (15) 10.00 25.00
SC10 E.Smith/Aikm/Jackman 1.50 4.00
SC11 K.Stewart/R.Dome .50 1.25

1997-98 Score Board Autographed Collection Sports City USA Strongbox

*STRONGBOX/600: .8X TO 2X BASIC INSERTS

1997-98 Score Board Autographed Collection Strongbox

*STRONGBOX: .8X TO 2X BASIC CARDS

1997 Score Board Players Club

The 70 cards that make-up this set are a grouping from baseball, basketball, football and hockey players. Card fronts are full colored action shots, with professional team names air-brushed out. The card backs contain 1997 projected statistics and biographical information. Along with the number 1 Die-Cuts and Play Back inserts, vintage cards were the major draw to this product. One in 32 packs contained a vintage card from 1909-1979 from any of the four sports. An original Honus Wagner T206 card was offered as a redemption in 1:153,600 packs. Also, one vintage wax pack was available via redemption card in one in every 32 packs.

COMPLETE SET (70) 5.00 12.00
6 Robert Dome .07 .20
12 Daniel Briere .07 .20
22 Joe Thornton .07 .20
32 Dainius Zubrus .07 .20
42 Sergei Samsonov .15 .40
57 Dan Cleary .07 .20
60 Richard Jackman .07 .20
65 Alexander Volchkov .07 .20

1997 Score Board Players Club #1 Die-Cuts

Each player in this 20 card set, inserted one in 32 packs, was at one time selected as a first round selection in the professional draft. The cards are die-cut in the shape of a "1" and have gold foil on the left border. The backs contain pre-professional biographical information and (if applicable) statistics from their last college or minor league season. The card numbers have a "D" prefix.

COMPLETE SET (20) 25.00 60.00
D4 Joe Thornton 1.50 4.00

1997 Score Board Players Club Play Backs

This 15-card set highlights stars form all four major U.S. sports. The card fronts have a player photo superimposed on a photo of the player's jersey. To the left is a movie reel design with individual action shots. The backs have another player photograph and biographical information. The cards are numbered with a "PB" prefix.

COMPLETE SET (15) 30.00 80.00
STATED ODDS 1:32
PB8 Dainius Zubrus 1.25 3.00

1997 Score Board Talk N' Sports

This product features phone cards with a couple twists, including trivia contests to win memorabilia and to check current sports scores. The 50-card regular set includes stars and prospects from all four major team sports. According to Score Board, a total of 1,500 sequentially numbered cases were produced.

COMPLETE SET (50) 4.00 10.00
46 Dainius Zubrus .07 .20
47 Sergei Samsonov .20 .50
48 Jay McKee .07 .20
49 Marcus Nilsson .07 .20
50 Joe Thornton .20 .50

1997 Score Board Talk N' Sports Essentials

These 10 plastic acetate cards were randomly inserted at a rate of 1:24 Talk N' Sports packs.

COMPLETE SET (10) 25.00 60.00
E10 Dainius Zubrus 1.50 4.00

1997 Score Board Talk N' Sports Phone Cards $1

The $1 phone cards were inserted one per pack. The checklist of this 50-card set parallels the regular set. The phone time on these $1 phone cards could be combined. They expired on 7/31/1998.

COMPLETE SET (50) 8.00 20.00
*PIN NUMBER REVEALED: HALF VALUE

1997 Score Board Talk N' Sports Phone Cards $20

These $20 phone cards allow users to choose sports updates in lieu of the phone time. The time on the card can be used interchangably for either phone calls or sports updates. The $20 cards were inserted at a rate of 1:36 packs and expired on 7/31/1998. Each card is sequentially numbered out of 1,440.

COMPLETE SET (10) 25.00 60.00
*PIN NUMBER REVEALED: HALF VALUE
10 Dainius Zubrus 2.00 5.00

1995 Signature Rookies

This 70-card standard-size set features a number of NHL draft picks from 1994 as well as several future draft prospects. With a suggested retail price of 5.00, each foil pack contained five regular cards, a mail-in offer or a chase card, and an autographed card. Each player signed 7,750 of their cards. The fronts feature borderless color action player cut-outs on a colorful, computerized background. The player's name in gold-foil appears in a black bar at the bottom, while the production number "1 of 45,000" is printed in a gold-foil bar at the left. The backs carry a small color player photo, along with a short biography and player profile. 1,995 cases were produced; 1,000 cases were supposedly sold out of the country, with the remaining 995 cases available in the U.S. Several error cards exist in the set. Limited numbers of corrected versions exist for four of them, as noted below.

COMPLETE SET (70) 5.00 12.00
1 Vaclav Varada .02 .10
2 Roman Vopat .02 .10
3 Yanick Dube UER .02 .10
4 Colin Cloutier .02 .10
5 Scott Cherrey .02 .10
6 Johan Finnstrom .02 .10
7 Fredrik Modin .20 .50
8 Stephane Roy .02 .10
9 Yevgeni Ryabchikov .02 .10
10 Jose Theodore .50 1.25
11 Jason Holland .02 .10
12 Richard Park .02 .10
13 Jason Podollan .02 .10
14 Mattias Ohlund .20 .50
15 Chris Wells .02 .10
16 Hugh Hamilton .02 .10
17 Edvin Frylen .02 .10
18 Wade Belak .02 .10
19 Sebastien Bety .02 .10
20 Chris Dingham .02 .10
21 Peter Nylander .02 .10
22 Daymond Langkow .40 1.00
23 Kelly Fairchild .02 .10
24 Norm Dezainde .02 .10
25 Nolan Baumgartner .02 .10
26 Deron Quint .02 .10
27 Sheldon Souray .02 .10
28 Stefan Ustorf .02 .10
29 Juha Vuorivirta UER .02 .10
30 Mark Seliger .02 .10
31 Ryan Smyth .50 1.25
32 Dimitri Tabarin .02 .10
33 Nikolai Tsulygin .02 .10
34 Paul Vincent .02 .10
35 Rhett Warrener .02 .10
36 Jamie Rivers .02 .10
37 Rumun Ndur .02 .10
38 Phil Huber .02 .10
39 Radek Dvorak .20 .50
40 Mike Barrie .02 .10
41 Chris Hynnes .02 .10
42 Mike Dubinsky .02 .10
43 Steve Cheredaryk .02 .10
44 Jim Carey .08 .25
45A Dorian Anneck ERR .02 .10
45B Dorian Anneck COR .02 .10
46 Jorgen Jonsson .02 .10
47 Alyn McCauley .02 .10
48 Corey Nielson .02 .10
49 Daniel Tjarnqvist .08 .25
50 Vadim Yepanchintsev .02 .10
51 Sean Haggerty .02 .10
52A Milan Hejduk ERR 1.00 2.50
52B Milan Hejduk COR 1.00 2.50
53 Adam Magarrell .02 .10
54 Dave Scatchard .08 .25
55 Sebastien Vallee .02 .10
56 Milos Guren .02 .10
57 Johan Davidsson .02 .10
58 Byron Briske .02 .10
59 Sylvain Blouin .02 .10
60 Bryan Berard UER .60 1.50
61 Tim Findlay .02 .10
62 Doug Bonner .02 .10
63 Curtis Brown .08 .25
64A Brad Symes ERR .02 .10
64B Brad Symes COR .02 .10
65 Andrew Taylor .02 .10
66 Brad Bombardir .02 .10
67 Joe Dziedzic .02 .10
68 Valentin Morozov .02 .10
69A Mark McArthur ERR .02 .10
69B Mark McArthur COR .02 .10
70 Checklist .02 .10
CS1 Martin Brodeur

1995 Signature Rookies Auto-Phonex

This 41-card set measures standard size. The fronts feature a color action player photo made to look as if breaking out of a blue background. The backs carry a small close-up photo of the player with the team name, position, biographical information and statistics. Each 6-card pack consisted of five regular cards and one hand-signed phone card.

COMPLETE SET (41) 2.00 5.00
1 Mika Alatalo .02 .10
2 Chad Allan UER .02 .10
3 J. Andersson-Junkka .02 .10
4 Serge Aubin .08 .25
5 David Belitski .05 .15
6 Aki Berg .08 .25
7 Zac Bierk .08 .25
8 Lou Body .02 .10
9 Kevin Bolibruck .02 .10
10 Brian Boucher .30 .75
11 Jack Callahan .02 .10
12 Jake Deadmarsh .02 .10
13 Andy Delmore .02 .10
14 Shane Doan .30 .75
15 Daniel Cleary .02 .10
16 Ian Gordon .02 .10
17 Jochen Hecht .08 .25
18 Martin Hohenberger .02 .10
19 Thomas Holmstrom .30 .75
20 Cory Keenan .02 .10
21 Shane Kenny .02 .10
22 Pavel Kriz .02 .10
23 Justin Kurtz .02 .10
24 Jan Labraaten .02 .10
25 Brad Larsen .02 .10
26 Donald MacLean .02 .10
27 Tavis MacMillan .02 .10
28 Mike Martin .02 .10
29 Bryan Berard .08 .25
30 Dmitri Nabokov .02 .10
31 Todd Norman .02 .10
32 Cory Peterson .02 .10
33 Johan Ramstedt .02 .10
34 Wade Redden .08 .25
35 Kevin Riehl .02 .10
36 David Roberts .02 .10
37 Terry Ryan .02 .10
38 Brian Scott .02 .10
39 Alexander Selivanov .08 .25
40 Peter Wallin .02 .10
NNO Checklist .02 .10

1995 Signature Rookies Auto-Phonex Beyond 2000

Inserted 1:6 packs, this set features five players who were thought to have a great shot at excelling well into the 21st century. The fronts feature the player's photo against a futuristic background. The back has a player portrait along with his position, his '93-94 stats and a quote about that player's abilities. 5,000 sets were produced, and each player signed 200 cards. Signed versions are worth 10X to 20X basic cards.

COMPLETE SET (5) 2.00 5.00
B1 Jamie Rivers .20 .50
B2 Terry Ryan .20 .50
B3 Ryan Smyth .75 2.00
B4 Nolan Baumgartner .20 .50
B5 Jose Theodore 1.25 3.00

1995 Signature Rookies Auto-Phonex Jaromir Jagr

Inserted 1:6 packs, this 5-card standard-size set showcases Jaromir Jagr. 5,000 sets were produced, and Jagr signed 500 of each card. The front features color photos picturing Jagr in action; the irregular fuchsia borders mimic the effect of water splattering on a surface. The back has a photo of Jagr along with biographical details and personal information located at the upper right corner.

COMPLETE SET (5) 3.00 8.00
COMMON JAGR (JJ1-JJ5) .75 2.00
JAGR SIGNATURE (JJ1-JJ5) 40.00 100.00

1995 Signature Rookies Auto-Phonex Phone Cards

Inserted one per pack, this 39-phone card set features a number of top NHL prospects. Each phone card bears an authentic signature and is serially numbered on the front. Shane Doan, card 14, did not sign. The backs explain how to use the card. Values below are for unused $3 cards. Scratching the back to reveal the PIN number decreases the value by 50 percent. The higher value NNO phone cards listed at the bottom were random inserts at indeterminate odds.

COMPLETE SET (40) 60.00 120.00
1 Mika Alatalo 1.50 4.00
2 Chad Allan .75 2.00
3 Jonas Andersson-Junkka .75 2.00
4 Serge Aubin 1.50 4.00
5 David Belitski .75 2.00
6 Aki Berg 1.25 3.00
7 Zac Bierk 1.25 3.00
8 Lou Body .75 2.00
9 Kevin Bolibruck .75 2.00
10 Brian Boucher 8.00 20.00
11 Jack Callahan .75 2.00
12 Jake Deadmarsh .75 2.00
13 Andy Delmore 1.25 3.00
14 Shane Doan 2.00 5.00
15 Daniel Cleary 1.25 3.00
16 Ian Gordon .75 2.00
17 Jochen Hecht 3.00 8.00
18 Martin Hohenberger .75 2.00
19 Thomas Holmstrom 2.00 5.00
20 Cory Keenan .75 2.00
21 Shane Kenny .75 2.00
22 Pavel Kriz .75 2.00
23 Justin Kurtz .75 2.00
24 Jan Labraaten .75 2.00
25 Brad Larsen .75 2.00
26 Donald MacLean .75 2.00
27 Tavis MacMillan .75 2.00
28 Mike Martin .75 2.00
29 Bryan Berard 1.50 4.00
30 Dmitri Nabokov .75 2.00
31 Todd Norman .75 2.00
32 Cory Peterson .75 2.00
33 Johan Ramstedt .75 2.00
34 Wade Redden 1.25 3.00
35 Kevin Riehl .75 2.00
36 David Roberts .75 2.00
37 Terry Ryan .75 2.00
38 Brian Scott .75 2.00
39 Alexander Selivanov .75 2.00
40 Peter Wallin .75 2.00
NNO Nolan Baumgartner $6 1.50 4.00
NNO Daymond Langkow $30 1.50 4.00
NNO Wade Redden $6 1.50 4.00
NNO Terry Ryan $6 1.50 4.00

1995 Signature Rookies Auto-Phonex Prodigies

Inserted 1:6 packs, this five-card standard-size set features five young guns. The front features the player showcased in action. The player's name is in red while the word "Prodigies" is printed in big, black bold letters against a yellow background on the bottom. The back features biographical information in the upper left corner. The rest of the reverse features a black-and-white player photo with his '93-94 stars and a quote about the player also placed on the bottom half. 5,000 sets were produced, and each player signed 200 of his cards. Signed versions are worth 5X to 8X basic cards.

COMPLETE SET (5) 2.00 5.00
P1 Bryan Berard UER .40 1.00
P2 Daymond Langkow .75 2.00
P3 Daniel Cleary .40 1.00
P4 Aki Berg .40 1.00
P5 Wade Redden .75 2.00

1995 Signature Rookies Club Promos

These five standard-size cards were sent to members of the Signature Rookies Club. The fronts feature the players photo occupying most of the right side of the card. The player's are identified underneath the photos. The cards are autographed just above the player's name while the sequential autograph number is under the player's name. The words Club Promo go vertically down the left side of the card while the Signature Rookies Hockey logo is in the lower left corner. The backs have a smaller duplication of the front photo on the left side while all relevant vital stats and biographical information are on the right side. The Signature Rookies authentic signature sticker is right above their logo on the back. Reports suggest that unsigned versions of these cards exist as well. These cards are marked PROMO, and are numbered One of 2,000. As these are rarely seen, no values have been tracked. It is fair to suggest, however, that they are worth considerably less than the signed versions.

COMPLETE SET (5) 20.00 20.00
1 Sergei Luchinkin 2.00 5.00
2 Stefan Ustorf 2.00 5.00
3 Brad Brown 2.00 5.00
4 Yanick Dube 2.00 5.00
5 Vitali Yachmenev 2.00 5.00

1995 Signature Rookies Cool Five

The five cards in this standard-size set were randomly inserted into packs. The left side of the front identifies the card as being 1 of 7,000, with the Cool Five logo in the lower left corner. The remainder is devoted to a full-color player photo which bleeds to the corner. The back has a head-and-shoulders portrait on the left side along with his biography on the right side. Signatures from this 5-card set were randomly inserted throughout the packs.

COMPLETE SET (5) 10.00 10.00
CF1 Radek Bonk .20 .50
CF2 Brad Park .75 2.00
CF3 Brian Leetch .75 2.00
CF4 Maurice Richard 2.00 5.00
CF5 Henri Richard .75 2.00

1995 Signature Rookies Cool Five Signatures

The five cards in this standard-size set were randomly inserted into packs. The left side of the front identifies the set as 1 of 7,000 and the Cool Five logo is in the lower left corner. The card is autographed over the player's photo and the serial number of the autograph is on the bottom. The remainder of the card is devoted to a full-color player photo that bleeds to the corner. In the middle of the back is the Signature Rookies authentic signature logo. The remainder of the back features a head-and-shoulders player portrait on the left side along with his biography on the right side. The card is numbered in the upper right corner.

CF1 Radek Bonk 2.00 5.00
CF2 Brad Park 6.00 15.00
CF3 Brian Leetch 5.00 10.00
CF4 Maurice Richard 40.00 80.00
CF5 Henri Richard 10.00 25.00

1995 Signature Rookies Fame and Fortune #1 Pick

Randomly inserted in packs at a rate of three in 16, this five-card set features the No. 1 pick in the NHL, the NFL, The NBA and Major leagues. The No. 5 card pictures all four of the picks. Fronts have a psychedelic background and feature the player in a full-color action cutout. "#1 Pick" appears in a sky blue and green type at the top and the bottom has a gold foil strip that contains the player's name, or names in the case of the #5 card, in raised white letters. Backs continue with the psychedelic background and picture the player or players in action. Player stats and biographies also appear on the back.

COMPLETE SET (5) 1.00 2.50
P1 Bryan Berard .20 .50
P5 Berard .30 .75
Carter
Erstad
J.Smith

1995 Signature Rookies Future Flash

The ten cards in this standard-size set were randomly inserted into packs. The left side of the front identifies the card as being one of 7,000, with the Future Flash logo in the lower left corner. The remainder of the card is devoted to a full-color player photo with a multiple exposure effect that bleeds to the corner. The back has a head-and-shoulders player portrait on the left side along with his biography on the right side. The card is numbered in the upper right corner. Signatures from this 10-card set were randomly inserted throughout the packs.

COMPLETE SET (10) 2.00 5.00
FF1 Jeff Ambrosio .40 1.00
FF2 Brad Brown .40 1.00
FF3 Patrick Juhlin .40 1.00
FF4 Sergei Gorbachev .40 1.00
FF5 Vasili Kamenev 1.50 4.00
FF6 Oleg Orekhovski .40 1.00
FF7 Maxim Kuznetsov .40 1.00
FF8 Sergei Luchinkin .40 1.00
FF9 Scott Roche .75 2.00
FF10 Alexei Morozov .75 2.00

1995 Signature Rookies Future Flash Signatures

The ten cards in this standard-size set were randomly inserted into packs. The left side of the front identifies the card as being 1 of 2,100, with the Future Flash logo in the lower left corner. The autograph is on the player's photo and is sequentially identified underneath the player's name. The remainder of the card is devoted to a full-color player photo with a multiple exposure effect that bleeds to the corner. The Signature Rookies Authentic Signature Logo is on the right side near the bottom. Other aspects of the back include a head-and-shoulders player portrait on the left side along with his biography on the right side. The cards are numbered in the upper right corner.

COMPLETE SET (10) 60.00 120.00
FF1 Jeff Ambrosio 6.00 15.00
FF2 Brad Brown 6.00 15.00
FF3 Patrick Juhlin 6.00 15.00
FF4 Sergei Gorbachev 6.00 15.00
FF5 Vasili Kamenev 6.00 15.00
FF6 Oleg Orekhovski 6.00 15.00
FF7 Maxim Kuznetsov 8.00 20.00
FF8 Sergei Luchinkin 6.00 15.00
FF9 Scott Roche 8.00 20.00
FF10 Alexei Morozov 8.00 20.00

1995 Signature Rookies Miracle on Ice

This 50-card standard-size set features 20 players, two coaches, and special action shots. Just 299 cases were produced, and each six-card pack contained an autograph card. The fronts display color action player photos that are edged on the left and bottom by a red, white and blue American flag design. Also the lower left corner of each card has a small oblique photo of the American team celebrating. The production run ("1 of 24,000"), a special "Miracle On Ice, 1980" emblem, and the player's name are gold foil-stamped on the front. On a ghosted red, white and blue flag design, the backs carry a color close-up photo, biography, and player profile.

COMPLETE SET (50)	10.00	20.00
1 Bill Baker	.07	.20
2 Bill Baker	.07	.20
3 Neal Broten	.30	.75
4 Neal Broten	.30	.75
5 Dave Christian	.20	.50
6 Dave Christian	.20	.50
7 Steve Christoff	.07	.20
8 Steve Christoff	.07	.20
9 Jim Craig	.60	1.50
10 Jim Craig	.60	1.50
11 Miko Eruzione	.60	1.50
12 Mike Eruzione	.60	1.50
13 John Harrington	.07	.20
14 John Harrington	.07	.20
15 Steve Janaszak	.07	.20
16 Steve Janaszak	.07	.20
17 Mark Johnson	.07	.20
18 Mark Johnson	.07	.20
19 Rob McClanahan	.07	.20
20 Rob McClanahan	.07	.20
21 Ken Morrow	.20	.50
22 Ken Morrow	.20	.50
23 Jack O'Callahan	.07	.20
24 Jack O'Callahan	.07	.20
25 Mark Pavelich	.07	.20
26 Mark Pavelich	.07	.20
27 Mike Ramsey	.08	.25
28 Mike Ramsey	.08	.25
29 Buzz Schneider	.07	.20
30 Buzz Schneider	.07	.20
31 Dave Silk	.07	.20
32 Dave Silk	.07	.20
33 Bob Suter	.07	.20
34 Bob Suter	.07	.20
35 Eric Strobel	.07	.20
36 Eric Strobel	.07	.20
37 Phil Verchota	.07	.20
38 Phil Verchota	.07	.20
39 Marc Wells	.07	.20
40 Marc Wells	.07	.20
41 Herb Brooks CO	.60	1.50
42 Herb Brooks CO	.60	1.50
43 Craig Patrick ACO	.20	.50
44 Craig Patrick ACO	.20	.50
45 Clinching The Gold	.20	.50
46 Do You Believe In Miracles	.20	.50
47 Eruzione Decides It	.20	.50
48 Celebration	.20	.50
49 A Dream Becomes Reality	.20	.50
50 Checklist	.07	.20
P1 Jim Craig Promo	1.00	2.50

1995 Signature Rookies Miracle on Ice Signatures

This 43-card standard-size set features 20 players, two coaches, and special action shots. The cards are identical to the regular issue with the addition of authentic signatures inscribed across the fronts. Card numbers 41 and 45-50 were not issued in signed form. Cards are numbered out of 2,000 on front.

COMPLETE SET (43)	175.00	350.00
1 Bill Baker	5.00	12.00
2 Bill Baker	5.00	12.00
3 Neal Broten	5.00	12.00
4 Neal Broten	5.00	12.00
5 Dave Christian	5.00	12.00
6 Dave Christian	5.00	12.00
7 Steve Christoff	5.00	12.00
8 Steve Christoff	5.00	12.00
9 Jim Craig	12.00	30.00
10 Jim Craig	12.00	30.00
11 Mike Eruzione	20.00	50.00
12 Mike Eruzione	20.00	50.00
13 John Harrington	5.00	12.00
14 John Harrington	5.00	12.00
15 Steve Janaszak	5.00	12.00
16 Steve Janaszak	5.00	12.00
17 Mark Johnson	10.00	25.00
18 Mark Johnson	10.00	25.00
19 Rob McClanahan	5.00	12.00
20 Rob McClanahan	5.00	12.00
21 Ken Morrow	4.00	10.00
22 Ken Morrow	4.00	10.00
23 Jack O'Callahan	12.50	30.00
24 Jack O'Callahan	12.50	30.00
25 Mark Pavelich	5.00	12.00
26 Mark Pavelich	5.00	12.00
27 Mike Ramsey	5.00	12.00
28 Mike Ramsey	5.00	12.00
29 Buzz Schneider	10.00	25.00
30 Buzz Schneider	10.00	25.00
31 Dave Silk	4.00	10.00
32 Dave Silk	4.00	10.00
33 Bob Suter	6.00	15.00
34 Bob Suter	6.00	15.00
35 Eric Strobel	10.00	25.00
36 Eric Strobel	10.00	25.00
37 Phil Verchota	5.00	12.00
38 Phil Verchota	6.00	15.00
39 Marc Wells	5.00	12.00
40 Marc Wells	5.00	12.00
42 Herb Brooks CO	90.00	150.00
43 Craig Patrick ACO	4.00	10.00
44 Craig Patrick ACO	4.00	10.00
P1 Celebration Promo Herb Brooks/7500	30.00	80.00
P2 Celebration Promo Mike Eruzione/60		

1995 Signature Rookies Signatures

Inserted one per foil pack, this 69-card issue is a parallel set and features the same design as the regular issue. Each player signed 7,750 of his cards which are hand numbered. The fronts feature borderless color action player cut-outs on a colorful, computerized background. The player's name in gold-foil appears in a black bar at the bottom. The backs carry a small color player photo, along with a short biography and player profile. Because several players could not fulfill their signing commitments in time for packaging, Signature Rookies inserted some redemption cards which specifically identified the player for whom the card could be redeemed. Once the redemption period expires, these cards will have limited market value.

COMPLETE SET (69)	75.00	150.00
1 Vaclav Varada	1.25	3.00
2 Roman Vopat	1.25	3.00
3 Yanick Dube	1.25	3.00
4 Colin Cloutier	1.25	3.00
5 Scott Cherrey	1.25	3.00
6 Johan Finnstrom	1.25	3.00
7 Fredrik Modin	2.00	5.00
8 Stephane Roy	1.25	3.00
9 Evgeni Ryabchikov	1.25	3.00
10 Jose Theodore	6.00	15.00
11 Jason Holland	1.25	3.00
12 Richard Park	1.25	3.00
13 Jason Podollan	1.25	3.00
14 Mattias Ohlund	2.00	5.00
15 Chris Wells	1.25	3.00
16 Hugh Hamilton	1.25	3.00
17 Edvin Frylen	1.25	3.00
18 Wade Belak	5.00	12.00
19 Sebastien Bety	1.25	3.00
20 Chris Dingman	1.25	3.00
21 Peter Nylander	1.25	3.00
22 Daymond Langkow	2.00	5.00
23 Kelly Fairchild	1.25	3.00
24 Norm Dezainde	1.25	3.00
25 Nolan Baumgartner	1.25	3.00
26 Deron Quint	1.25	3.00
27 Sheldon Souray	1.25	3.00
28 Stefan Ustorf	1.25	3.00
29 Juha Vuorivirta UER	1.25	3.00
30 Marc Seliger	1.50	4.00
31 Ryan Smyth	4.00	10.00
32 Dimitri Tabarin	1.25	3.00
33 Nikolai Tsulygin	1.25	3.00
34 Paul Vincent	1.25	3.00
35 Rhett Warrener	1.25	3.00
36 Jamie Rivers	1.25	3.00
37 Rumun Ndur	1.50	4.00
38 Phil Huber	1.25	3.00
39 Radek Dvorak	2.00	5.00
40 Mike Barrie	1.25	3.00
41 Chris Hynnes	1.25	3.00
42 Mike Dubinsky	1.25	3.00
43 Steve Cheredaryk	1.25	3.00
44 Jim Carey	2.00	5.00
45 Brad Symes	1.25	3.00
46 Jorgen Jonsson	1.25	3.00
47 Alyn McCauley	1.25	3.00
48 Corey Nielson	1.25	3.00
49 Daniel Tjarnqvist	1.50	4.00
50 Vadim Epanchintsev	1.25	3.00
51 Sean Haggerty	1.25	3.00
52 Mark McArthur	1.25	3.00
53 Adam Magarrell	1.25	3.00
54 Dave Scatchard	1.50	4.00
55 Sebastien Vallee	1.25	3.00
56 Milos Guren	1.25	3.00
57 Johan Davidsson	1.25	3.00
58 Byron Briske	1.25	3.00
59 Sylvain Blouin	1.25	3.00
60 Bryan Berard UER	1.50	4.00
61 Tim Findlay	1.25	3.00
62 Doug Bonner	1.50	4.00
63 Curtis Brown	1.25	3.00
64 Dorian Anneck	1.25	3.00
65 Andrew Taylor	1.25	3.00
66 Brad Bombardir	1.25	3.00
67 Joe Dziedzic	1.25	3.00
68 Valentin Morozhov	1.25	3.00
69 Milan Hejduk	6.00	15.00

1994 Signature Rookies Gold Standard

This multi-sport set consists of 100 standard-size cards. The fronts feature color action players photos with a circular gold foil seal at the upper left corner. The player's name appears on a diagonal black stripe edged by yellow. The horizontal backs carry a narrowly-cropped closeup photo and, on a ghosted panel, biography and player profile. The set is subdivided according to sport as follows: basketball (1-25), football (26-50), baseball (51-75), and hockey (76-100). Each sport is sequenced in alphabetical order.

COMPLETE SET (100)	5.00	12.00
76 Nolan Baumgartner	.07	.20
77 Wade Belak	.07	.20
78 Radek Bonk	.10	.30
79 Brad Brown	.07	.20
80 Dan Cloutier	.10	.30
81 Johan Davidsson	.07	.20
82 Yanick Dube	.07	.20
83 Eric Fichaud	.10	.30
84 Johann Finnstrom	.07	.20
85 Edvin Frylen	.07	.20
86 Patrik Juhlin	.07	.20
87 Valeri Karpov	.07	.20
88 Nikolai Khabibulin	.30	.75
89 Mattias Ohlund	.10	.30
90 Jason Podollan	.07	.20
91 Vadim Sharifjanov	.10	.30
92 Ryan Smyth	.20	.50
93 Dimitri Tabarin	.07	.20
94 Nikolai Tsulygin	.07	.20
95 Stefan Ustorf	.07	.20
96 Paul Vincent	.07	.20
97 Roman Vopat	.07	.20
98 Rhett Warrener	.07	.20
99 Vitali Yachmenev	.07	.20
100 Vadim Yepenchinstev	.07	.20

1994 Signature Rookies Gold Standard Facsimile

This 20-card standard-size set was inserted one per pack. The fronts display full-bleed color player photos. A facsimile autograph, the "Gold Standard" seal, and another emblem are gold-foil stamped on the fronts. Also a diagonal line carrying the player's name (also in gold foil) is edged by gold foil stripes. On the left side, the horizontal backs show a narrowly-cropped closeup of the front photo. The remainder of the backs carry biography, statistics, and player profile, all on a ghosted background. In addition to card number, each back carries a serial number.

COMPLETE SET (20)	5.00	12.00
GS3 Radek Bonk	.30	.75
GS4 Nolan Baumgartner	.30	.75
GS7 Valeri Karpov	.30	.75
GS18 Ryan Smyth	.40	1.00

1994 Signature Rookies Gold Standard HOF

COMPLETE SET (24)	8.00	20.00
STATED PRINT RUN 20,000 SETS		
ISSUED VIA MAIL REDEMPTION		
HOF3 Mike Bossy	.60	1.50
HOF7 Tony Esposito	.50	1.25

1994 Signature Rookies Gold Standard HOF Autographs

Inserted at a rate of one per box, this 24-card standard-sized set is identical to the regular set except for the signatures inscribed across the front and the expression "Hall of Fame" gold-foil stamped at the upper left. Each card is numbered out of 2500. The collector could obtain unsigned versions by mailing in a redemption card that was randomly inserted in packs. These redemption cards are valued at 1/10 the value of the signed cards. The cards are numbered with an "HOF" prefix.

3 Mike Bossy	10.00	25.00
7 Tony Esposito	12.00	30.00

1994 Signature Rookies Gold Standard Legends

This five-card standard size set was randomly inserted into packs. This set has great athletes past and presents from all sports. The fronts have the word "Legends" on the top and the player's name on the bottom printed in silver ink against a black background. Meanwhile, the player's photo is shown against a gold background. The backs contains the player's photo on the left quarter with a biography about that player on the remainder of the card.

COMPLETE SET (5)	3.00	8.00
L5 Brian Leetch	.40	1.00

1996 Signature Rookies Super Stars

COMPLETE SET (6)	3.00	8.00
SS1 Jim Carey HK	.60	1.50

1994 Signature Rookies Tetrad

These 120 standard-size cards feature borderless color player action shots on their fronts. The player's name appears in gold-foil lettering near the bottom. The words "1 of 45,000" appear in vertical gold-foil lettering within a simulated marble column near the left edge. The cards of this four-sport set are numbered on the back in Roman numerals and organized as follows: Football (1-40), Basketball (41-83), Baseball (84-103), and Hockey (104-118).

COMPLETE SET (120)	3.00	8.00
104 Sven Butenschon	.07	.20
105 Dan Cloutier	.10	.30
106 Pat Jablonski	.07	.20
107 Valeri Karpov	.07	.20
108 Nikolai Khabibulin	.20	.50
109 Sergei Klimentiev	.07	.20
110 Krzysztof Oliwa	.07	.20
111 Dmitri Riabykin	.07	.20
112 Ryan Risidore	.07	.20
113 Shawn Rivers	.07	.20
114 Vadim Sharifjanov	.10	.30
115 Mika Stromberg	.07	.20
116 Tim Taylor	.07	.20
117 Vitali Yachmenev	.07	.20
118 Wendell Young	.07	.20

1994 Signature Rookies Tetrad Autographs

Inserted one card (or trade coupon) per pack, these 117 standard-size autographed cards comprise a parallel set to the regular '94 Tetrad set. Aside from the autographs and each card's numbering out of 7,750 produced, they are identical in design to their regular issue counterparts. The cards of this four-sport set are numbered on the back in Roman numerals and organized as follows: Football (1-40), Basketball (41-83), Baseball (84-103), and Hockey (104-118). Bernard Williams (card number 11) did not sign his cards.

104 Sven Butenschon	1.50	4.00
105 Dan Cloutier	2.50	6.00
106 Pat Jablonski	1.50	4.00
107 Valeri Karpov	1.50	4.00
108 Nikolai Khabibulin	3.00	8.00
109 Sergei Klimentiev	1.50	4.00
110 Krzysztof Oliwa	1.50	4.00
111 Dmitri Riabykin	1.50	4.00
112 Ryan Risidore	1.50	4.00
113 Shawn Rivers	1.50	4.00
114 Vadim Sharifjanov	2.50	6.00
115 Mika Stromberg	1.50	4.00
116 Tim Taylor	1.50	4.00
117 Vitali Yachmenev	1.50	4.00
118 Wendell Young	1.50	4.00

1994 Signature Rookies Tetrad Previews

Randomly inserted in Signature Rookies Football packs, these seven standard-size cards feature borderless color player action shots on their fronts. The player's name and position appear in gold-foil lettering near the bottom. The words "Promo, 1 of 10,000" appear in vertical gold-foil lettering within a simulated marble column near the left edge. On a ghosted background drawing of a Greek temple, the back carries the player's name, position, team, height and weight, and career highlights. The cards of this multisport set are numbered on the back with a "T" prefix.

COMPLETE SET (7)	1.25	3.00
T2 Tim Taylor	.08	.25

1994 Signature Rookies Tetrad Titans

Randomly inserted in packs, these 12 standard-size cards feature borderless color player action shots on their fronts. The player's name appears in gold-foil lettering near the bottom. The words "1 of 10,000" appear in vertical gold-foil lettering within a simulated marble column near the left edge. On a ghosted background drawing of a Greek temple, the back carries the player's name, position, team, height and weight, and career highlights. The cards of this multisport set are numbered on the back in Roman numerals.

COMPLETE SET (12)	3.00	8.00
122 Bobby Hull	.60	1.50

1994 Signature Rookies Tetrad Titans Autographs

Randomly inserted in packs, these 12 standard-size autographed cards comprise a parallel set to the regular 1994 Tetrad Titans set. Aside from the autographs (some cards issued as redemptions in packs) and each card's numbering out of 1,050 produced (except the 2,500 signed O.J. cards), they are identical in design to their regular issue counterparts. The cards of this multisport set are numbered on the back in Roman numerals.

COMPLETE SET (12)	125.00	250.00
122 Bobby Hull/1050	20.00	40.00

1995 Signature Rookies Tetrad

This 76-card standard-size set features borderless fronts with color action player photos. The named player stands out on a faded background with his name printed in gold below. The backs carry an elongated color action player photo on one side while a head photo, biographical information, position, college, and career statistics round out the backs.

COMPLETE SET (76)	5.00	12.00
61 Alexei Morozov	.15	.40
62 Radek Dvorak	.05	.15
66 Terry Ryan	.05	.15
67 Shane Doan	.15	.40
68 Brad Church	.05	.15
69 Brian Boucher	.40	1.00
70 Dmitri Nabokov	.05	.15

1995 Signature Rookies Tetrad Autographs

SIGS NUMBERED OUT OF 5000		
61 Alexei Morozov	1.25	3.00
62 Radek Dvorak	1.25	3.00
66 Terry Ryan	1.25	3.00
67 Shane Doan	1.50	4.00
68 Brad Church	1.25	3.00
69 Brian Boucher	2.50	6.00
70 Dmitri Nabokov	1.25	3.00

1995 Signature Rookies Tetrad Mail-In

This five-card standard size set was available through the mail from Signature Rookies. The set highlights the 1995 first overall draft picks in basketball, football, baseball and hockey. The fronts picture color action photos blended with a fractal-swirling design. In a gold foil stamp, the players name is found vertically on the right, "Mail In" and "#1 Pick" adorn the top and bottom respectively on the left. The back has another color action photo in the upper-right corner. The rest is devoted to a player biography and statistics set on top of the same fractal-swirling design. The cards are numbered with a "P" prefix (P1-P5).

COMPLETE SET (5)	1.50	4.00
P4 Bryan Berard	.40	1.00
P5 Joe Smith Ki-Jana Carter Darin Erstad Bryan Berard	.60	1.50

1995 Signature Rookies Tetrad Previews

This five-card standard-size set was randomly inserted in SR BK autobilia packs. The fronts display borderless color action player photos. The named player stands out on a faded background with his name printed in gold below. The backs carry an elongated color action player photo on one side while a head photo, biographical information, position, college, and career statistics round out the backs.

COMPLETE SET (5)	1.00	2.50
2 Jim Carey	.20	.50

1995 Signature Rookies Tetrad SR Force

This 35-card standard-size set features color action player photos on the front on a white background. Pictures of one foot, the head, and one arm are set out as separate photos on the side of the main picture. The words, "SR Force," are printed in the white border at the top, while the player's name is in gold at the bottom of the picture. The backs carry the same photo as a faded background with photos of the head and parts of one leg. The player's name, position, team, biographical information, and statistics round out the back. The cards are numbered with an "F" prefix.

COMPLETE SET (35)	6.00	15.00
F1 Nolan Baumgartner	.10	.30
F2 Bryan Berard	.10	.30
F3 Aki-Petteri Berg	.15	.40
F4 Daymond Langkow	.20	.50
F5 Wade Redden	.10	.30
F6 Martin Brodeur	.60	1.50
F7 Jim Carey	.20	.50
F8 Jaromir Jagr	.75	2.00
F9 Maxim Kuznetsov	.10	.30
F10 Terry Ryan	.10	.30

1995 Signature Rookies Tetrad SR Force Autographs

RANDOM INSERTS IN PACKS		
F1 Nolan Baumgartner	1.25	3.00
F2 Bryan Berard	1.50	4.00
F3 Aki-Petteri Berg	1.50	4.00
F4 Daymond Langkow	1.25	3.00
F5 Wade Redden	1.25	3.00
F6 Martin Brodeur	6.00	15.00
F7 Jim Carey	4.00	10.00
F8 Jaromir Jagr	10.00	25.00
F9 Maxim Kuznetsov	1.25	3.00
F10 Terry Ryan	1.25	3.00

1995 Signature Rookies Tetrad Autobilia

The 1995 Signature Rookies Tetrad Autobilia set was issued in one series with a total of 100 cards. The fronts feature a color action player cut-out on a background of a repeated action player photo with the player's name printed in a gold bar at the bottom. The words" Club Set" are printed in gold foil on the fronts as well. The backs carry two player photos with the player's name, position, biographical information, career statistics, and a player fact.

COMPLETE SET (100)	10.00	25.00
*SILVER: .4X TO 1X GOLD		
38 Nolan Baumgartner	.08	.25
39 Bryan Berard	.15	.40
40 Aki-Petteri Berg	.10	.30
41 Dan Cleary	.08	.25
42 Radek Dvorak	.08	.25
43 Patrick Juhlin	.08	.25
44 Jan Labraaten	.08	.25
45 Daymond Langkow	.15	.40
46 Sergei Luchinkin	.08	.25
47 Cameron Mann	.15	.40
48 Alexei Morozov	.15	.40
49 Oleg Tverdovsky	.15	.40
50 Johan Ramstedt	.08	.25
51 Wade Redden	.15	.40
52 Sami-Ville Salomaa	.08	.25
53 Alexei Vasiljev	.08	.25
54 Peter Wallin	.08	.25
94 Brian Boucher	.60	1.50
95 Martin Brodeur	.50	1.25
96 Brad Church	.08	.25
97 Shane Doan	.30	.75
98 Terry Ryan	.08	.25
99 Ryan Smyth	.15	.40

1995 Signature Rookies Tetrad Autobilia Auto-Phonex Test

This 3-card set was issued in packs of 1995 Signature Rookies Autobilia packs. Each card follows a similar design to the base cards except for the addition of the words 'Auto-Phonex Test Issue' on the left hand side of the cardfronts. The title 'Autobilia' at the top was also replaced with the word Tetrad.

COMPLETE SET (3)	1.25	3.00
T1 Jim Carey	.50	1.25

1995 Signature Rookies Tetrad Autobilia Autographed Cards

These cards are an autographed parallel to the base set. Signature Rookies reported that players signed the following items: 1000 cards, 3000 photos, 500 pennants, 500 hats, 3000 baseballs, 550 basketballs, 1000 footballs. Special items included 100 Darin Erstad signed bats and an undisclosed amount of the following issues: Muhammad Ali signed boxing glove, Joe DiMaggio signed cards, Jaromir Jagr signed hockey stick, Jaromir Jagr signed practice jersey, and Jim Carey signed mask.

38 Nolan Baumgartner	1.25	3.00
39 Bryan Berard	2.00	5.00
40 Aki-Petteri Berg	1.50	4.00
41 Dan Cleary	1.50	4.00
42 Radek Dvorak	1.25	3.00
43 Patrick Juhlin	1.25	3.00
44 Jan Labraaten	1.25	3.00
45 Daymond Langkow	1.25	3.00
46 Sergei Luchinkin	1.25	3.00
47 Cameron Mann	1.25	3.00
48 Alexei Morozov	1.25	3.00
49 Oleg Tverdovsky	1.25	3.00
50 Johan Ramstedt	1.25	3.00
51 Wade Redden	1.25	3.00
52 Sami-Ville Salomaa	1.25	3.00
53 Alexei Vasiljev	1.25	3.00
54 Peter Wallin	1.25	3.00
94 Brian Boucher	2.50	6.00
95 Martin Brodeur	6.00	15.00
96 Brad Church	1.25	3.00
97 Shane Doan	1.50	4.00
98 Terry Ryan	1.25	3.00
99 Ryan Smyth	4.00	10.00

1995 Signature Rookies Tetrad Autobilia Autographed Photos

ANNOUNCED PRINT RUN 3000		
38 Nolan Baumgartner	1.25	3.00
39 Bryan Berard	2.00	5.00
40 Aki-Petteri Berg	1.50	4.00
41 Dan Cleary	1.50	4.00
42 Radek Dvorak	1.25	3.00
43 Patrick Juhlin	1.25	3.00
44 Jan Labraaten	1.25	3.00
45 Daymond Langkow	1.25	3.00
46 Sergei Luchinkin	1.25	3.00
47 Cameron Mann	1.25	3.00
48 Alexei Morozov	1.25	3.00
49 Oleg Tverdovsky	1.25	3.00
50 Johan Ramstedt	1.25	3.00
52 Sami-Ville Salomaa	1.25	3.00
53 Alexei Vasiljev	1.25	3.00
54 Peter Wallin	1.25	3.00
94 Brian Boucher	2.50	6.00
95 Martin Brodeur	6.00	15.00
96 Brad Church	1.25	3.00
97 Shane Doan	2.50	6.00
98 Terry Ryan	1.25	3.00
99 Ryan Smyth	4.00	10.00

1995 Slapshot Memorial Cup

Produced by Slapshot Images Ltd., this 110-card standard-size set commemorates the 1995 Memorial Cup of the Canadian Hockey League. The set includes the champions of the three member leagues (Detroit/OHL; Hull/LMJHQ; Kamloops/WHL) as well as the host team (Brandon). On a simulated wood background, the fronts feature color action photos inside a jagged black or blue picture frame. The player's name is printed above the photo, while the team name is printed vertically running down the left edge. The backs have biography, a color headshot, and a player profile. The set is arranged according to teams as follows: Kamloops Blazers (1-25), Brandon Wheat Kings (26-50), Hull Olympiques (51-75), and Detroit Jr. Red Wings (76-100).

COMPLETE SET (110)	12.00	30.00
1 Rod Branch	.07	.20
2 Jeff Oldenborger	.07	.20
3 Jason Holland	.07	.20
4 Nolan Baumgartner	.15	.40
5 Keith McCambridge	.07	.20
6 Ivan Vologjaninov	.07	.20
7 Aaron Keller	.07	.20
8 Greg Hart	.07	.20
9 Jarome Iginla	2.00	5.00
10 Ryan Huska	.07	.20
11 Jeff Ainsworth	.07	.20
12 Darcy Tucker	.40	1.00
13 Hnat Domenichelli	.15	.40
14 Tyson Nash	.75	2.00
15 Shane Doan	1.25	3.00
16 Jeff Antonovich	.07	.20
17 Bonnie Kinney	.07	.20
18 Ashley Buckberger	.07	.20
19 Brad Lukowich	.30	.75
20 Bob Westerby	.07	.20
21 Jason Strudwick	.15	.40
22 Bob Maudie	.07	.20
23 Randy Petruk	.20	.50
24 Shawn McNeil	.07	.20
25 Don Hay CO	.07	.20
26 Bryon Penstock	.07	.20
27 Brian Elder	.07	.20
28 Jeff Staples	.07	.20
29 Scott Laluk	.07	.20
30 Kevin Pozzo	.07	.20
31 Wade Redden	.40	1.00
32 Justin Kurtz	.15	.40
33 Sven Butenschon	.07	.20
34 Bryan McCabe	.20	.50
35 Kelly Smart	.07	.20
36 Bobby Brown	.07	.20
37 Mike Dubinsky	.07	.20
38 Mike LeClerc	.30	.75
39 Dean Kletzel	.07	.20
40 Darren Ritchie	.07	.20
41 Mark Dutiaume	.07	.20
42 Ryan Robson	.07	.20
43 Chris Dingman	.15	.40
44 Darren Van Oene	.07	.20
45 Colin Cloutier	.07	.20
46 Darryl Stockham	.07	.20
47 Peter Schaefer	.20	.50
48 Marty Murray	.20	.50
49 Alex Vasilevski	.07	.20
50 Bob Lowes CO	.07	.20
51 Michael Coveny	.07	.20
52 Jan Nemecek	.15	.40
53 Chris Hall	.07	.20
54 Jason Groleau	.07	.20
55 Alex Rodrigue	.07	.20
56 Jamie Bird	.07	.20
57 Harold Hersh	.07	.20
58 Carl Prud'Homme	.07	.20
59 Sean Farmer	.07	.20
60 Carl Beaudoin	.07	.20
61 Gordie Dwyer	.07	.20
62 Richard Safarik	.07	.20
63 Carl Charland	.07	.20
64 Jean-Guy Trudel	.15	.40
65 Francois Cloutier	.07	.20
66 Roddie MacKenzie	.07	.20
67 Colin White	.30	.75
68 Martin Menard	.07	.20
69 Sebastien Bordeleau	.07	.20
70 Jonathan Delisle	.07	.20
71 Peter Worrell	.40	1.00
72 Louis-Philippe Charbonn	.15	.40
73 Jose Theodore	2.00	5.00
74 Neil Savary	.15	.40
75 Michael McKay	.15	.40
76 Darryl Foster	.07	.20
77 Quade Lightbody	.07	.20
78 Ryan MacDonald	.07	.20
79 Mike Rucinski	.07	.20
80 Murray Sheehan	.07	.20
81 Matt Ball	.07	.20
82 Gerry Lanigan	.07	.20
83 Mike Morrone	.07	.20
84 Tom Buckley	.07	.20
85 Eric Manlow	.07	.20
86 Bill McCauley	.07	.20
87 Andrew Taylor	.07	.20
88 Scott Blair	.07	.20
89 Jeff Mitchell	.07	.20
90 Jason Saal	.15	.40
91 Jamie Allison	.15	.40
92 Bryan Berard	.20	.50
93 Dan Pawlaczyk	.07	.20
94 Milan Kostolny	.07	.20
95 Duane Harmer	.07	.20
96 Shayne McCosh	.07	.20
97 Sean Haggerty	.07	.20
98 Nic Beaudoin	.07	.20
99 Paul Maurice CO/GM	.07	.20
100 Pete Deboer ACO	.07	.20
101 Kamloops Checklist	.07	.20
102 Brandon Checklist	.07	.20
103 Hull Checklist	.07	.20
104 Detroit Checklist	.07	.20
105 OHL Champions Detroit J	.07	.20
106 WHL Champions Kamloops	.07	.20
107 LHJMQ Champions Hull OI	.07	.20
NNO OHL Playoff Summary	.07	.20
NNO LHJMQ Playoff Summary	.07	.20
NNO WHL Playoff Summary	.07	.20

1991 Star Pics

This 72 card standard-size set contained 18 1991 first round draft picks. The cards have glossy action color player photos, with a thin white border on a background picturing a hockey mask. The player's name appears in a white lettering below the picture. The print run was supposed to be 225, 000 individually numbered sets. Autographed cards were randomly inserted into the sets. The autograph cards are valued at 20X to 100X the prices below for Flashback cards and 20X to 50X for the other cards.

SEALED SET (72)	2.00	10.00
1 Al Morganti	.02	.10
2 Pat Falloon	.02	.10
3 Jamie Pushor	.02	.10
4 Jean Beliveau FLB	.08	.25
5 Martin Lapointe	.20	.50
6 Jamie Matthews	.02	.10
7 Rod Gilbert FLB	.08	.25
8 Niklas Sundblad	.02	.10
9 Steve Konowalchuk	.02	.10
10 Alex Delvecchio FLB	.08	.25
11 Donevan Hextall	.02	.10
12 Dody Wood	.02	.10
13 Scott Niedermayer	.20	.50
14 Trevor Halverson	.02	.10
15 Terry Chitaroni	.02	.10
16 Tyler Wright	.02	.10
17 Andrei Lomakin UER	.02	.10
18 Martin Hamrlik	.02	.10
19 Dimitri Filimonov UER	.02	.10
20 Ed Belfour FLB	.20	.50
21 Andrew Verner	.02	.10
22 Yanic Perreault	.02	.10
23 Michael Nylander	.02	.10
24 Scott Lachance	.02	.10
25 Pavel Bure	.60	1.50
26 Mike Torchia	.02	.10
27 Frank Mahovlich FLB	.08	.25
28 Philippe Boucher	.02	.10
29 Jiri Slegr	.02	.10
30 Sergei Fedorov FLB	.30	.75
31 Rene Corbet	.02	.10
32 Jamie McLennan	.02	.10
33 Shane Peacock	.02	.10
34 Mario Nobili	.02	.10
35 Peter Forsberg	.75	2.00
36 All-Rookie Team Pat Falloon Tyler Wright Philippe Boucher Andrew Verner Scott Lachance	.02	.10
37 Arturs Irbe	.20	.50
38 Alexei Zhitnik	.02	.10
39 Pat Peake	.02	.10
40 Adam Oates FLB	.08	.25
41 Markus Naslund	.20	.50
42 Eric Lavigne	.02	.10
43 Jeff Nelson	.02	.10
44 Yanic Dupre UER	.02	.10
45 Justin Morrison	.02	.10
46 Alek Stojanov	.02	.10
47 Marcel Cousineau	.02	.10
48 Alexei Kovalev	.08	.25
49 Andrei Trefilov	.02	.10
50 Mats Sundin FLB	.20	.50
51 Steve Staios	.02	.10
52 Glenn Hall FLB	.08	.25
53 Brent Bilodeau	.02	.10
54 Darcy Werenka	.02	.10
55 Chris Osgood	.40	1.00
56 Nathan Lafayette	.02	.10
57 Richard Matvichuk	.02	.10
58 Dimitri Mironov UER	.02	.10
59 Jason Dawe	.02	.10
60 Mike Ricci FLB	.02	.10
61 Gerry Cheevers FLB	.08	.25
62 Jim Campbell	.02	.10
63 Francois Groleau	.02	.10
64 Glen Murray	.20	.50
65 Jason Young	.02	.10
66 Dean McAmmond	.02	[illegible]
67 Guy Leveque	.02	[illegible]
68 Patrick Poulin	.02	[illegible]
69 Bobby House	.02	[illegible]
70 Jaromir Jagr FLB	.40	1.
71 Jassen Cullimore	.02	[illegible]
72 Checklist Card	.02	[illegible]

2000-01 UD CHL Prospects

This 100-card base set was released in March 2001 with a SRP of $2.49 for a 5-card pack. There was a subset of 10 Draft Prospects included in the base se

COMPLETE SET (100)	10.00	25.
1 Jay Harrison	.25	[illegible]
2 Jay McClement	.20	[illegible]
3 Adam Henrich	.25	[illegible]
4 Carlo Colaiacovo	.25	[illegible]
5 Nikita Alexeev	.20	[illegible]
6 Brad Boyes	.40	1.
7 Peter Hamrlik	.25	[illegible]
8 Cory Stillman	.20	[illegible]
9 Derek Roy	.30	[illegible]
10 Michael Zigomanis	.25	[illegible]
11 Jason Spezza	1.00	2.
12 Chad Wiseman	.20	[illegible]
13 Patrick Jarrett	.25	.6
14 Chris Thornburn	.25	.6
15 John Kozoriz	.20	[illegible]
16 Brandon Cullen	.20	[illegible]
17 Jonathan Zion	.20	[illegible]
18 Miguel Delisle	.20	[illegible]
19 Ryan Ramsay	.20	[illegible]
20 Marcel Rodman	.20	[illegible]
21 Stephen Weiss	.40	1.(
22 Libor Ustrnul	.20	[illegible]
23 Rob Zepp	.25	.6
24 Kris Vernarsky	.25	.6
25 Jason Penner	.20	[illegible]
26 Trevor Daley	.25	.6
27 Alexei Semenov	.25	.6
28 Mark Popovic	.20	[illegible]
29 Tim Gleason	.30	[illegible]
30 Craig Kennedy	.20	[illegible]
31 Steve Ott	.30	.7
32 Brian Finley	.25	.6
33 Kyle Wellwood	.30	.7
34 Raffi Torres	.30	.7
35 Chris Kelly	.20	[illegible]
36 Scott Cameron	.20	[illegible]
37 Cole Jarrett	.20	[illegible]
38 Maxim Rybin	.20	[illegible]
39 Derek MacKenzie	.20	[illegible]
40 Ryan Held	.20	[illegible]
41 Colt King	.20	[illegible]
42 Rick Nash	1.25	3.(
43 Greg Jacina	.20	[illegible]
44 Branko Radivojevic	.25	.6
45 Jordin Tootoo	.60	1.5
46 Pavel Brendl	.20	[illegible]
47 Ryan Craig	.20	[illegible]
48 Owen Fussey	.20	[illegible]
49 Brent Krahn	.25	.6
50 Erik Christensen	.20	.5
51 Jared Aulin	.25	.6
52 Kiel McLeod	.20	.5
53 Dan Blackburn	.25	.6
54 Jeff Woywitka	.25	.6
55 Ryan Hollweg	.25	.6
56 Jay Bouwmeester	.50	1.2
57 Ben Knopp	.20	.5
58 Marcel Hossa	.25	.6
59 Greg Watson	.20	.5
60 Justin Mapletoft	.25	.6
61 Matt Hubbauer	.20	.5
62 Garth Murray	.20	.5
63 Matthew Spiller	.25	.6
64 Barrett Heisten	.30	.7
65 Gerard Dicaire	.20	.5
66 Jamie Lundmark	.30	.7
67 Duncan Milroy	.20	.5
68 Nathan Smith	.20	.5
69 Konstantin Panov	.20	.5
70 Mike Comrie	.50	1.2
71 Tomas Kopecky	.30	.7
72 Jozef Balej	.30	.7
73 Shane Bendera	.25	.6
74 Blake Evans	.20	.5
75 Igor Pohanka	.20	.5
76 Robin LeBlanc	.20	.5
77 Yanick Lehoux	.25	.6
78 Jean-Francois Racine	.25	.6
79 Pascal LeClaire	.30	.7
80 Chris Montgomery	.20	.5
81 Brent MacLellan	.20	.5
82 Thatcher Bell	.20	.5
83 Antoine Vermette	.30	.7
84 Carl Mallette	.20	.5
85 Nicolas Poirier	.20	.5
86 Radim Vrbata	.25	.6
87 Maxime Ouellet	.30	.7
88 Brandon Reid	.30	.7
89 Jason Spezza	1.00	2.5
90 Pascal LeClaire	.30	.7
91 Dan Blackburn	.25	.6
92 Stephen Weiss	.40	1.0
93 Tim Gleason	.30	.7
94 Duncan Milroy	.20	.5
95 Kiel McLeod	.20	.5
96 Jay McClement	.20	.5
97 Jay Harrison	.25	.6
98 Greg Watson	.20	.5
99 Jason Spezza	1.00	2.5
100 Jay Bouwmeester	.50	1.2

2000-01 UD CHL Prospects Autographs

Randomly inserted at a rate of 1:107, this 9-card set features some of the hottest prospects from the CHL i full color photos and player autographs.

STATED ODDS 1:107		
ABK Brent Krahn	4.00	10.0
ABO Bobby Orr	100.00	200.0
ADB Dan Blackburn	5.00	12.0
AJB Jay Bouwmeester	10.00	25.0
AJS Jason Spezza	12.50	30.0
APB Pavel Brendl	4.00	10.0
APL Pascal LeClaire	5.00	12.0
ART Raffi Torres	5.00	12.0
ARZ Rob Zepp	6.00	15.0

2000-01 UD CHL Prospects CHL Class

Inserted at a rate of 1:17, this 10-card set featured elit CHL performers on silver foil card stock. The card fronts carry the player's name and jersey number in re foil.

COMPLETE SET (10)	12.50	25.0
CC1 Brian Finley	.75	2.0
CC2 Michael Zigomanis	.40	1.0
CC3 Jason Spezza	3.00	8.0

CC4 Jay Bouwmeester 2.00 5.00
CC5 Rob Zepp .75 2.00
CC6 Pavel Brendl .40 1.00
CC7 Dan Blackburn 1.25 3.00
CC8 Mike Comrie .75 2.00
CC9 Pascal LeClaire .75 2.00
CC10 Maxime Ouellet .75 2.00

2000-01 UD CHL Prospects Destination the Show

Inserted at a rate of 1:33, this 6-card set features players who are considered locks for the NHL. Each card carries a color action photo and is highlighted by silver and red foil accents.

COMPLETE SET (6) 8.00 20.00
D1 Jason Spezza 4.00 8.00
D2 Dan Blackburn 1.50 3.00
D3 Pavel Brendl .50 1.00
D4 Jay Bouwmeester 2.50 5.00
D5 Zdenek Blatny .50 1.00
D6 Pascal LeClaire 1.00 2.00

2000-01 UD CHL Prospects Future Leaders

Inserted at 1:17, this 10-card set features player's of the CHL considered to be the future of the NHL. Each card is printed on silver foil card stock with red foil highlights.

COMPLETE SET (10) 6.00 15.00
FL1 Jason Spezza 3.00 5.00
FL2 Raffi Torres .75 2.00
FL3 Brad Boyes .75 2.00
FL4 Stephen Weiss .75 2.00
FL5 Michael Zigomanis .40 1.00
FL6 Jamie Lundmark .60 1.50
FL7 Mike Comrie .75 2.00
FL8 Nathan Smith .40 1.00
FL9 Radim Vrbata .40 1.00
FL10 Brandon Reid .40 1.00

2000-01 UD CHL Prospects Game Jerseys

Inserted a rate of 1:18, these cards carry game-worn jersey swatches of some of the biggest names in the CHL. Card fronts carry a color action photo on mostly white stock, the player's name appears vertically on the right side and his jersey number is in grey at the bottom right. The swatch is in the shape of a maple leaf in the center of the card. Autographed parallels were also inserted and numbered to 100 sets.

DBL.JSY STAT.PRINT RUN 250 SER.#'d SETS
BK Brent Krahn 6.00 15.00
DB Dan Blackburn 8.00 20.00
JA Jason Spezza Win 8.00 20.00
JB Jay Bouwmeester 6.00 15.00
JL Jamie Lundmark 5.00 12.00
JS Jason Spezza Mis 8.00 20.00
NE Nikita Alexeev 4.00 10.00
PB Pavel Brendl 5.00 12.00
RT Raffi Torres 6.00 15.00
RZ Rob Zepp 5.00 12.00
BB D.Blackburn B.Krahn 10.00 25.00
BZ D.Blackburn R.Zepp 8.00 20.00
LB J.Lundmark D.Blackburn 10.00 25.00
LK J.Lundmark B.Krahn 6.00 15.00
SB J.Spezza J.Bouwmeester 20.00 50.00
SL J.Spezza J.Lundmark 15.00 40.00
SS J.Spezza J.Spezza 20.00 50.00
ST J.Spezza R.Torres 15.00 40.00
SZ J.Spezza R.Zepp 12.50 30.00
TZ R.Torres R.Zepp 6.00 15.00

2000-01 UD CHL Prospects Great Desire

Inserted at a rate of 1:33, this 6-card set features a small color action photo in the top right hand corner, and a larger photo of the player's eyes in the center surrounded by the words "Great Desire" in red foil. The player's jersey number is in the left bottom corner in silver foil.

COMPLETE SET (6) 10.00 25.00
GD1 Jason Spezza 4.00 8.00
GD2 Jay Bouwmeester 2.50 5.00
GD3 Mike Comrie 1.25 3.00
GD4 Raffi Torres .75 2.00
GD5 Brandon Reid .75 2.00
GD6 Pascal LeClaire 1.25 3.00

2000-01 UD CHL Prospects Supremacy

Randomly inserted at 1:17, this 10-card set features elite players of the CHL on silver foil stock. The player's name and jersey number on the card front in red foil.

COMPLETE SET (10) 10.00 25.00
CS1 Jason Spezza 3.00 8.00
CS2 Brian Finley .75 2.00
CS3 Raffi Torres 1.00 2.50
CS4 Rob Zepp .75 2.00
CS5 Pavel Brendl .60 1.50
CS6 Justin Mapletoft .75 2.00
CS7 Barrett Heisten 1.00 2.50
CS8 Mike Comrie 1.50 4.00
CS9 Jay Bouwmeester 1.50 4.00
CS10 Pascal LeClaire 1.00 2.50

1999-00 UD Prospects

The 1999-00 Upper Deck Prospects set was released as a 90-card set that featured 67 NHL prospects, 22 Canada's Best, and 1 checklist card. Each pack contained 5-cards and carried a suggested retail price of $1.99.

COMPLETE SET (90) 12.50 30.00
1 Wayne Gretzky 1.25 3.00
2 Jason Spezza 1.25 3.00
3 Sheldon Keefe .08 .25
4 Mark Bell .20 .50
5 Justin Papineau .15 .40
6 Denis Shvidki .15 .40
7 Darryl Bootland .20 .50
8 Michael Zigomanis .15 .40
9 Chris Eade .08 .25
10 Brad Boyes .60 1.50
11 Michael Henrich .08 .25
12 Nikita Alexeev .08 .25
13 Libor Ustrnul .08 .25
14 Brian Finley .15 .40
15 Chris Berti .08 .25
16 Agris Saviels .08 .25
17 Kris Newbury .08 .25
18 Jared Newman .08 .25
19 Samu Isosalo .08 .25
20 Mike Van Ryn .15 .40
21 Miguel Delisle .08 .25
22 Rostislav Klesla .20 .50
23 Raffi Torres .20 .50
24 Kurtis Foster .08 .25
25 Lou Dickenson .08 .25
26 Milan Kraft .15 .40
27 Jamie Lundmark .20 .50
28 Scott Hartnell .50 1.25
29 Ben Knopp .08 .25
30 Mike Wirll .08 .25
31 Ryan Craig .08 .25
32 Kris Beech .15 .40
33 Pavel Brendl .15 .40
34 Blake Robson .08 .25
35 Jarret Stoll .15 .40
36 Oleg Saprykin .15 .40
37 Eric Johannson .08 .25
38 Warren Peters .08 .25
39 Marcel Hossa .30 .75
40 Shane Endicott .08 .25
41 Craig Olynick .08 .25
42 Brent Krahn .30 .75
43 Matt Pettinger .15 .40
44 Jaroslav Kristek .08 .25
45 Milan Bartovic .08 .25
46 Jared Aulin .15 .40
47 Jakub Cutta .15 .40
48 Blake Ward .08 .25
49 Lynn Lyons .15 .40
50 Jay Bouwmeester .75 2.00
51 Nick Schultz .15 .40
52 Filip Novak .08 .25
53 Michael Bubnick .08 .25
54 Charline Labonte .75 2.00
55 Thatcher Bell .08 .25
56 Yanick Lehoux .08 .25
57 Antoine Vermette .20 .50
58 Alexei Volkov .15 .40
59 Michal Sivek .15 .40
60 Carl Mallette .08 .25
61 Maxime Ouellet .30 .75
62 Simon Lagace-Daigle .08 .25
63 Andrei Shefer .08 .25
64 Mathieu Chouinard .15 .40
65 Philippe Sauve .20 .50
66 Daniel Sedin .30 .75
67 Henrik Sedin .30 .75
68 Thatcher Bell .08 .25
69 Brad Boyes .60 1.50
70 Jared Aulin .15 .40
71 Dany Heatley 1.25 3.00
72 Ryan Hare .08 .25
73 Scott Hartnell .75 2.00
74 Jay Bouwmeester .75 2.00
75 Kiel McLeod .08 .25
76 Kris Newbury .08 .25
77 Blake Robson .08 .25
78 Jarret Stoll .15 .40
79 Antoine Vermette .20 .50
80 Mike Wirll .08 .25
81 Jason Spezza 1.25 3.00
82 Jay Harrison .08 .25
83 Brandon Janes .08 .25
84 Craig Olynick .08 .25
85 Mark Popovic .08 .25
86 Nick Schultz .15 .40
87 Karl St. Pierre .08 .25
88 Pascal Leclaire .30 .75
89 Blake Ward .08 .25
90 Checklist .08 .25

1999-00 UD Prospects CHL Class

Randomly inserted in packs at 1:4, this 10-card insert set showcases ten of the hottest talents in the CHL. Card backs carry a "C" prefix.

COMPLETE SET (10) 6.00 15.00
C1 Jason Spezza 2.00 5.00
C2 Justin Papineau .60 1.50
C3 Mark Bell .60 1.50
C4 Kris Beech .60 1.50
C5 Jay Bouwmeester 1.25 3.00
C6 Denis Shvidki .60 1.50
C7 Pavel Brendl .60 1.50
C8 Brian Finley .60 1.50
C9 Jamie Lundmark .75 2.00
C10 Thatcher Bell .60 1.50

1999-00 UD Prospects Destination the Show

Randomly inserted in packs at 1:17, this 10-card insert set features ten prospects that are preparing for their trip to "The Show". Card backs carry a "DS" prefix.

COMPLETE SET (10) 20.00 35.00
DS1 Jason Spezza 4.00 10.00
DS2 Pavel Brendl 1.25 3.00
DS3 Henrik Sedin 1.50 4.00
DS4 Daniel Sedin 1.50 4.00
DS5 Jamie Lundmark 1.50 4.00
DS6 Taylor Pyatt 1.25 3.00
DS7 Brian Finley 1.50 4.00
DS8 Kris Beech 1.50 4.00
DS9 Denis Shvidki 1.25 3.00
DS10 Jay Bouwmeester 2.00 5.00

1999-00 UD Prospects Game Jerseys

Randomly inserted in packs at 1:215, this 12-card insert features twelve of some of the most collectable phenoms in the game. Card backs are numbered using the players initials.

CL Charline Labonte 25.00 60.00
HS Henrik Sedin 15.00 30.00
JB Jay Bouwmeester 40.00 50.00
JS Jason Spezza 60.00 100.00
KB Kris Beech 15.00 30.00
LD Lou Dickenson 10.00 20.00
PB Pavel Brendl 10.00 20.00
TB Thatcher Bell 10.00 20.00
DSD Daniel Sedin 15.00 30.00

1999-00 UD Prospects International Stars

Randomly inserted in packs at 1:9, this 10-card insert set features the next generation of international superstars. Card backs carry an "IN" prefix.

COMPLETE SET (10) 20.00 40.00
IN1 Daniel Sedin .75 2.00
IN2 Henrik Sedin .75 2.00
IN3 Pavel Brendl .60 1.50
IN4 Alexei Volkov .75 2.00
IN5 Denis Shvidki .60 1.50
IN6 Milan Kraft .75 2.00
IN7 Nikita Alexeev .60 1.50
IN8 Oleg Saprykin .75 2.00
IN9 Jaroslav Kristek .60 1.50
IN10 Marcel Hossa .75 2.00

1999-00 UD Prospects Signatures of Tradition

Randomly inserted in packs at 1:17, this 30-card insert set features autographed cards of future NHL stars. Card backs are numbered using the player's initials.

AV Alexei Volkov 6.00 15.00
BF Brian Finley 6.00 15.00
BM Branislav Mezei 4.00 10.00
CL Charline Labonte 8.00 20.00
DS Daniel Sedin 10.00 25.00
HS Henrik Sedin 6.00 15.00
JB Jay Bouwmeester 8.00 20.00
JL Jamie Lundmark 6.00 15.00
JS Jason Spezza 6.00 15.00
KB Kris Beech 6.00 15.00
MB Mark Bell 6.00 15.00
MC Mathieu Chouinard 6.00 15.00
MO Maxime Ouellet 6.00 15.00
MV Mike Van Ryn 4.00 10.00
PB Pavel Brendl 4.00 10.00
TP Taylor Pyatt 4.00 10.00
WG Wayne Gretzky 250.00 400.00
DSH Denis Shvidki 4.00 10.00

2001-02 UD Prospects

Released in mid-August 2001, this 45-card set focused on young prospects of the CHL.

COMPLETE SET (45) 12.50 30.00
1 Jason Spezza 1.25 3.00
2 Dan Blackburn .30 .75
3 Daniel Boisclair .30 .75
4 Jeff Woywitka .30 .75
5 Matthew Spiller .25 .60
6 Nathan Paetsch .25 .60
7 Mark Popovic .25 .60
8 Jay McClement .25 .60
9 Garth Murray .25 .60
10 Aaron Lobb .25 .60
11 Derek Roy .40 1.00
12 Jean-Francois Soucy .30 .75
13 Nicolas Corbeil .25 .60
14 Colt King .25 .60
15 Robin Leblanc .25 .60
16 Jay Harrison .25 .60
17 Jiri Jakes .25 .60
18 Lukas Krajicek .25 .60
19 Jason Pominville .60 1.50
20 Shawn Collymore .25 .60
21 Michael Garnett .30 .75
22 Adam Munro .40 1.00
23 Dan Hamhuis .30 .75
24 Doug Lynch .25 .60
25 Shaone Morrisonn .30 .75
26 Carlo Colaiacovo .30 .75
27 Stephen Weiss .60 1.50
28 Joel Stepp .25 .60
29 Jeff Lucky .25 .60
30 Cory Stillman .25 .60
31 Chris Thorburn .25 .60
32 Colby Armstrong .30 .75
33 Brent Maclellan .25 .60
34 Jordin Tootoo .75 2.00
35 Greg Watson .25 .60
36 Martin Podlesak .25 .60
37 Duncan Milroy .25 .60
38 Frantisek Bakrlik .25 .60
39 Brendan Bell .25 .60
40 Kiel McLeod .25 .60
41 Jason Spezza 1.25 3.00
42 Jason Spezza 1.25 3.00
43 Jason Spezza 1.25 3.00
44 Jason Spezza 1.25 3.00
45 2001 Top Prospects Summary .25 .50

2001-02 UD Prospects Autographs

Randomly inserted at 1:6 packs, this 23-card set featured authentic player autographs.

AAM Adam Munro 8.00 20.00
ABK Brent Krahn 6.00 15.00
ABO Bobby Orr 125.00 250.00
ACK Colt King 4.00 10.00
ACS Cory Stillman 4.00 10.00
ACT Chris Thorburn 4.00 10.00
ADB Dan Blackburn 6.00 15.00
ADH Dan Hamhuis 8.00 20.00
ADM Duncan Milroy 4.00 10.00
AGW Greg Watson 4.00 10.00
AJB Jay Bouwmeester 12.50 25.00
AJH Jay Harrison 4.00 10.00
AJL Jamie Lundmark 6.00 15.00
AJM Jay McClement 4.00 10.00
AJS Jason Spezza 12.50 30.00
AKM Kiel McLeod 4.00 10.00
AMG Michael Garnett 6.00 15.00
AMP Mark Popovic 4.00 10.00
APL Pascal Leclaire 6.00 15.00
ARK Rostislav Klesla 6.00 15.00
ART Raffi Torres 8.00 20.00
ASW Stephen Weiss 8.00 20.00
AWG Wayne Gretzky 125.00 300.00

2001-02 UD Prospects Jersey Autographs

Limited to just 30 serial-numbered copies each, this 17-card set featured both game-worn jersey swatches and authentic player autographs.

SAM Adam Munro 20.00 50.00
SCK Colt King 15.00 40.00
SCS Cory Stillman 15.00 40.00
SCT Chris Thorburn 15.00 40.00
SDB Dan Blackburn 15.00 40.00
SDH Dan Hamhuis 30.00 80.00
SDM Duncan Milroy 15.00 40.00
SGW Greg Watson 15.00 40.00
SJH Jay Harrison 15.00 40.00
SJM Jay McClement 15.00 40.00
SJS Jason Spezza 60.00 150.00
SKM Kiel McLeod 15.00 40.00
SMG Michael Garnett 20.00 50.00
SMP Mark Popovic 15.00 40.00
SSW Stephen Weiss 25.00 60.00
SWA Jason Spezza 60.00 150.00
SWH Jason Spezza 60.00 150.00

2001-02 UD Prospects Jerseys

Inserted at overall odds of 1 per pack, this 62 card set featured swatches of jerseys worn by the pictured player(s) during the 2001 CHL Top Prospects Game. Dual jersey cards were serial-numbered to 125 copies each. A gold parallel of this set was also created and each card was serial-numbered out of 75.

JAL Aaron Lobb 4.00 10.00
JAM Adam Munro 5.00 12.00
JBB Brendan Bell 4.00 10.00
JBM Brent Maclellan 4.00 10.00
JBO Daniel Boisclair 5.00 12.00
JCA Colby Armstrong 4.00 10.00
JCK Colt King 4.00 10.00
JCS Cory Stillman 4.00 10.00
JCT Chris Thorburn 4.00 10.00
JDB Dan Blackburn 6.00 15.00
JDH Dan Hamhuis 5.00 12.00
JDL Doug Lynch 4.00 10.00
JDM Duncan Milroy 4.00 10.00
JDR Derek Roy 5.00 12.00
JFB Frantisek Bakrlik 4.00 10.00
JGM Garth Murray 4.00 10.00
JGW Greg Watson 4.00 10.00
JJF Jean-Francois Soucy 5.00 12.00
JJH Jay Harrison 4.00 10.00
JJJ Jiri Jakes 4.00 10.00
JJL Jeff Lucky 4.00 10.00
JJM Jay McClement 4.00 10.00
JJP Jason Pominville 8.00 20.00
JJS Jason Spezza 8.00 20.00
JJT Jordin Tootoo 15.00 40.00
JJW Jeff Woywitka 5.00 12.00
JKM Kiel McLeod 4.00 10.00
JLK Lukas Krajicek 5.00 12.00
JMG Michael Garnett 4.00 10.00
JMP Mark Popovic 4.00 10.00
JMS Matthew Spiller 4.00 10.00
JNC Nicolas Corbeil 4.00 10.00
JNP Nathan Paetsch 4.00 10.00
JPO Martin Podlesak 4.00 10.00
JRL Robin Leblanc 4.00 10.00
JSC Shawn Collymore 4.00 10.00
JSM Shaone Morrisonn 5.00 12.00
JST Joel Stepp 4.00 10.00
JSW Stephen Weiss 4.00 10.00
JWA Jason Spezza 8.00 20.00
JWH Jason Spezza 8.00 20.00
CBD D.Blackburn/D.Milroy 8.00 20.00
CBG D.Boisclair/M.Garnett 8.00 20.00
CBM D.Blackburn/A.Munro 8.00 20.00
CBS D.Blackburn/J.Spezza 15.00 40.00
CBW D.Blackburn/S.Weiss 10.00 25.00
CHM J.Harrison/K.McLeod 8.00 20.00
CHW D.Hamhuis/S.Weiss 8.00 20.00
CKP L.Krajicek/M.Podlesak 6.00 15.00
CKW C.King/G.Watson 8.00 20.00
CMS J.McClement/C.Stillman 8.00 20.00
CMT G.Murray/C.Thorburn 8.00 20.00
CPM M.Popovic/D.Milroy 8.00 20.00
CRT D.Roy/J.Tootoo 50.00 125.00
CSA Jason Spezza Dual 15.00 40.00
CSB Jason Spezza Dual 15.00 40.00
CSH J.Spezza/D.Hamhuis 12.50 30.00
CSM J.Spezza/D.Milroy 10.00 25.00
CSS Jason Spezza Dual 15.00 40.00
CSW J.Spezza/S.Weiss 15.00 40.00
CWA J.Woywitka/C.Armstrong 8.00 20.00
CWM S.Weiss/D.Milroy 10.00 25.00

1991 Ultimate Draft

The 1991 Ultimate/Smokey's Draft Picks hockey set contains 90 standard-size cards. The front design has glossy, color action player photos, bordered in white. The upper left corner of the picture is cut off to allow space for a logo with the words "Sportscards Ultimate Hockey". The player's name, position, and team appear in white lettering in a blue-gray rectangle near the card bottom. Reportedly production quantities were as follows: 6,000 American set cases equaling 120,000 sets, 750 French set cases equaling 15,000 sets, 5,000 American ten-box wax cases, 1,500 French ten-box wax cases, and 500 autographed sets.

COMPLETE SET (90) 3.00 8.00
*FRENCH: .4X TO 1X BASIC CARDS
1 Ultimate Preview .01 .05
2 Pat Falloon .02 .10
3 Scott Niedermayer .02 .10
4 Scott Lachance .01 .05
5 Peter Forsberg .40 1.00
6 Alek Stojanov .01 .05
7 Richard Matvichuk .02 .10
8 Patrick Poulin .01 .05
9 Martin Lapointe .08 .25
10 Tyler Wright .01 .05
11 Philippe Boucher .01 .05
12 Pat Peake .01 .05
13 Markus Naslund .08 .25
14 Brent Bilodeau .01 .05
15 Glen Murray .08 .25
16 Niklas Sundblad .01 .05
17 Trevor Halverson .01 .05
18 Dean McAmmond UER .01 .05
19 Jim Campbell .01 .05
20 Rene Corbet .01 .05
21 Eric Lavigne .01 .05
22 Steve Staios .01 .05
23 Jassen Cullimore .01 .05
24 Jamie Pushor .01 .05
25 Donevan Hextall .01 .05
26 Andrew Verner .02 .10
27 Jason Dawe .01 .05
28 Jeff Nelson .01 .05
29 Darcy Werenka .01 .05
30 Francois Groleau .01 .05
31 Guy Leveque .01 .05
32 Jamie Matthews .01 .05
33 Dody Wood .02 .10
34 Yanic Perreault .01 .05
35 Jamie McLennan UER .02 .10
36 Yanic Dupre .01 .05
37 1st Round Checklist .01 .05
38 Chris Osgood .40 1.00
39 Fredrik Lindquist .01 .05
40 Jason Young .01 .05
41 Steve Konowalchuk .02 .10
42 Michael Nylander .02 .10
43 Shane Peacock .01 .05
44 Yves Sarault .01 .05
45 Marcel Cousineau .02 .10
46 Nathan Lafayette .01 .05
47 Bobby House .01 .05
48 Kerry Toporowski .01 .05
49 Terry Chitaroni .01 .05
50 Mike Torchia .02 .10
51 Mario Nobili .01 .05
52 Justin Morrison .01 .05
53 Grayden Reid .01 .05
54 Yanic Perreault Underdog .01 .05
55 2nd Round Checklist .01 .05
56 Scott Niedermayer Pat Falloon Scott Lachance .02 .10
57 The Goalies .02 .10
58 Pat Falloon FDP .02 .10
59 Scott Niedermayer FDP .02 .10
60 Scott Lachance FDP .01 .05
61 Peter Forsberg FDP .40 1.00
62 Alek Stojanov FDP .01 .05
63 Richard Matvichuk FDP .02 .10
64 Patrick Poulin FDP .01 .05
65 Martin Lapointe FDP .08 .25
66 Tyler Wright FDP .01 .05
67 Philippe Boucher FDP .01 .05
68 Pat Peake FDP .01 .05
69 Markus Naslund FDP .08 .25
70 Brent Bilodeau FDP .01 .05
71 Glen Murray FDP .08 .25
72 Niklas Sundblad FDP .01 .05
73 Trevor Halverson FDP .01 .05
74 Dean McCammond FDP .01 .05
75 Award Winners Philippe Boucher Jeff Nelson Scott Niedermayer .01 .05
76 The Swedes Markus Naslund Peter Forsberg .08 .25
77 3rd and 4th Round Checklist .01 .05
78 Pat Falloon BW .02 .10
79 Scott Niedermayer BW .02 .10
80 Falloon/Niedermayer BW .02 .10
81 Scott Lachance BW .01 .05
82 Philippe Boucher BW .01 .05
83 Markus Naslund BW .08 .25
84 Glen Murray BW .08 .25
85 Niklas Sundblad BW .01 .05
86 Jason Dawe BW .01 .05
87 Yanic Perreault BW .02 .10
88 Offensive Threats Yanic Dupre Mikael Nylander .01 .05
89 Group Shot/Overview .01 .05
90 Face the Future .01 .05

1991 Ultimate Draft Promos

This three-card standard-size set was given out to dealers and collectors to promote the new Ultimate hockey draft picks cards. The front design is basically the same as the regular issue. The Torchia card displays a different player photo, while the Stojanov card is cropped differently. Also the promos have the team name below the player's name rather than city name as with their regular issue. The backs of the promos differ from those of the regular issue in that the photos on the back are more ghosted and the word "Sample" is stenciled over them. Also the player information on the Stojanov card back is arranged differently on the promo. The cards are unnumbered and checklisted below in alphabetical order.

COMPLETE SET (3) .40 1.00
1 Pat Falloon .20 .50
2 Alex Stojanov .08 .25
3 Mike Torchia .08 .25

1991-92 Ultimate Promo Panel

1 6-card strip 1.25 3.00

2014-15 Upper Deck AHL

COMPLETE SET (150) 40.00 80.00
COMP.SET w/o SPs (100) 15.00 40.00
101-150 ISSUED ONE PER PACK
1 J.C. Lipon .30 .75
2 Seth Griffith .50 1.25
3 Igor Bobkov .30 .75
4 Alex Petrovic .30 .75
5 Troy Bourke .40 1.00
6 Brody Sutter .25 .60
7 Markus Granlund .60 1.50
8 Ryan Haggerty .30 .75
9 Andreas Athanasiou .50 1.25
10 Derek Forbort .30 .75
11 Philipp Grubauer .40 1.00
12 Jujhar Khaira .50 1.25
13 Phil Varone .30 .75
14 Michael Chaput .25 .60
15 Tyler Pitlick .30 .75
16 T.J. Tynan .40 1.00
17 Johan Gustafsson .30 .75
18 Taylor Leier .40 1.00
19 Landon Ferraro .25 .60
20 Sven Baertschi .25 .60
21 Nick Cousins .30 .75
22 Gabriel Dumont .30 .75
23 Sebastian Collberg .40 1.00
24 Cedrick Desjardins .25 .60
25 David Pastrnak 1.50 4.00
26 Mark McNeill .30 .75
27 Slater Koekkoek .25 .60
28 Connor Hellebuyck .50 1.25
29 Connor Brown .40 1.00
30 Radek Faksa .50 1.25
31 Jeff Zatkoff .30 .75
32 Freddie Hamilton .25 .60
33 Christopher Gibson .60 1.50
34 Mike Zalewski .30 .75
35 Brendan Leipsic .30 .75
36 Nic Dowd .40 1.00
37 Kris Newbury .25 .60
38 Anthony Stolarz .50 1.25
39 Trevor Carrick .25 .60
40 Keegan Lowe .25 .60
41 Michael Sgarbossa .25 .60
42 Joey MacDonald .50 1.25
43 Joni Ortio .50 1.25
44 Jared Staal .40 1.00
45 Max Reinhart .30 .75
46 Chris Bourque .30 .75
47 Zack Mitchell .50 1.25
48 Marek Mazanec .30 .75
49 Anton Lander .25 .60
50 Jean-Francois Berube .40 1.00
51 Calvin Pickard .30 .75
52 Ryan Bourque .30 .75
53 Rocco Grimaldi .40 1.00
54 T.J. Brennan .25 .60
55 Ryan Dzingel .25 .60
56 Daniil Tarasov .30 .75
57 Jacob Markstrom .30 .75
58 Sean Collins .25 .60
59 Nick Petrecki .25 .60
60 Phoenix Copley .50 1.25
61 Jacob de la Rose .30 .75
62 Keith Kinkaid .25 .60
63 Ryan Sproul .40 1.00
64 Pat Cannone .40 1.00
65 Gustav Olofsson .30 .75
66 Pontus Aberg .25 .60
67 Greg McKegg .30 .75
68 Michael Leighton .40 1.00
69 Brenden Kichton .25 .60
70 Brendan Gaunce .50 1.25
71 Troy Grosenick .40 1.00
72 Curtis McKenzie .30 .75
73 Eric O'Dell .25 .60
74 Joe Morrow .50 1.25
75 Chris Wagner .40 1.00
76 Cameron Schilling .25 .60
77 Yannick Veilleux .25 .60
78 Corban Knight .40 1.00
79 David Shields .25 .60
80 Michael Mersch .30 .75
81 Andrey Makarov .40 1.00
82 Max Friberg .30 .75
83 Cedric Paquette .40 1.00
84 Petter Granberg .30 .75
85 Philip Samuelsson .25 .60
86 Adam Clendening .40 1.00
87 Anton Zlobin .30 .75
88 Joe Whitney .25 .60
89 Drew MacIntyre .40 1.00
90 Michael Houser .30 .75
91 Travis Morin .25 .60
92 Ryan Spooner .30 .75
93 Kevin Poulin .30 .75
94 Jordan Szwarz .25 .60
95 Andrew Agozzino .30 .75
96 Austin Watson .25 .60
97 Carl Klingberg .25 .60
98 Brian Dumoulin .25 .60
99 Martin Marincin .30 .75
100 Andrew Hammond .60 1.50
101 Joel Armia .75 2.00
102 Ty Rattie 1.00 2.50
103 Joey Hishon 1.00 2.50
104 Nicolas Kerdiles .75 2.00
105 Reid Boucher .50 1.25
106 Alexander Khokhlachev .75 2.00
107 Jack Campbell 1.00 2.50
108 Zack Phillips .50 1.25
109 Kerby Rychel .60 1.50
110 Jean-Gabriel Pageau .60 1.50
111 Josh Leivo .50 1.25
112 Jordan Weal .60 1.50
113 Teemu Pulkkinen 1.00 2.50
114 Chandler Stephenson .50 1.25
115 Laurent Brossoit .75 2.00
116 Stefan Matteau .50 1.25
117 Josh Archibald .50 1.25
118 Quinton Howden .50 1.25
119 Henrik Samuelsson .60 1.50
120 Shayne Gostisbehere 3.00 8.00
121 Ryan Pulock .60 1.50
122 Mitchell Moroz .50 1.25
123 Colton Sissons .75 2.00
124 Oscar Lindberg 2.00 5.00
125 Matt Puempel .50 1.25
126 Brandon Gormley .75 2.00
127 Jordan Binnington .75 2.00
128 Stefan Noesen .60 1.50
129 Anders Lee .75 2.00
130 Scott Kosmachuk .50 1.25
131 Ryan Hartman .75 2.00
132 Scott Laughton .50 1.25
133 Nick Shore .75 2.00
134 Sven Andrighetto 1.00 2.50
135 Hunter Shinkaruk 1.25 3.00
136 Konrad Abeltshauser .50 1.25
137 Malcolm Subban 1.25 3.00
138 Charles Hudon .75 2.00
139 Brock McGinn .60 1.50
140 Mikhail Grigorenko .75 2.00
141 Anthony Mantha 1.25 3.00
142 Oscar Dansk 1.25 3.00
143 Teuvo Teravainen 1.25 3.00
144 Andrei Vasilevskiy 2.50 6.00
145 Duncan Siemens .50 1.25
146 Danny Kristo .60 1.50
147 Nicklas Jensen .50 1.25
148 William Nylander 2.00 5.00
149 Vincent Trocheck 1.00 2.50
150 Brett Ritchie .75 2.00

2014-15 Upper Deck AHL Autographs

STATED ODDS 1:8 PACKS
1 J.C. Lipon 2.50 6.00
2 Seth Griffith 4.00 10.00
11 Philipp Grubauer 3.00 8.00
13 Phil Varone 2.50 6.00
14 Michael Chaput 2.00 5.00
17 Johan Gustafsson 2.50 6.00
21 Nick Cousins 2.50 6.00
22 Gabriel Dumont 2.50 6.00
24 Cedrick Desjardins 2.00 5.00
27 Slater Koekkoek 2.00 5.00
28 Connor Hellebuyck 4.00 10.00
30 Radek Faksa 4.00 10.00
31 Jeff Zatkoff 2.50 6.00
32 Freddie Hamilton 2.00 5.00
33 Christopher Gibson 5.00 12.00
35 Brendan Leipsic 2.50 6.00
37 Kris Newbury 2.00 5.00
38 Anthony Stolarz 4.00 10.00
39 Trevor Carrick 2.00 5.00
40 Keegan Lowe 2.00 5.00
41 Michael Sgarbossa 2.00 5.00
42 Joey MacDonald 4.00 10.00
43 Joni Ortio 4.00 10.00
44 Jared Staal 3.00 8.00
45 Max Reinhart 2.50 6.00
47 Zack Mitchell 4.00 10.00
48 Marek Mazanec 2.50 6.00
49 Anton Lander 2.00 5.00
50 Jean-Francois Berube 3.00 8.00
53 Rocco Grimaldi 3.00 8.00
54 T.J. Brennan 2.00 5.00
55 Ryan Dzingel 2.00 5.00
58 Sean Collins 2.00 5.00
59 Nick Petrecki 2.00 5.00
60 Phoenix Copley 4.00 10.00
61 Jacob de la Rose 2.50 6.00
62 Keith Kinkaid 2.00 5.00
63 Ryan Sproul 3.00 8.00
64 Pat Cannone 3.00 8.00
65 Gustav Olofsson 2.50 6.00
66 Pontus Aberg 2.00 5.00
67 Greg McKegg 2.50 6.00
69 Brenden Kichton 2.00 5.00
70 Brendan Gaunce 4.00 10.00
71 Troy Grosenick 3.00 8.00
72 Curtis McKenzie 2.50 6.00
73 Eric O'Dell 2.00 5.00
74 Joe Morrow 4.00 10.00
75 Chris Wagner 3.00 8.00
76 Cameron Schilling 2.00 5.00
77 Yannick Veilleux 2.00 5.00
78 David Shields 2.00 5.00
83 Cedric Paquette 3.00 8.00
84 Petter Granberg 2.50 6.00
85 Philip Samuelsson 2.00 5.00
86 Adam Clendening 3.00 8.00
89 Drew MacIntyre 3.00 8.00
91 Travis Morin 2.00 5.00
92 Ryan Spooner 2.50 6.00
94 Jordan Szwarz 2.00 5.00
100 Andrew Hammond 25.00 50.00
102 Ty Rattie 4.00 10.00
103 Joey Hishon 4.00 10.00
104 Nicolas Kerdiles 3.00 8.00
106 Alexander Khokhlachev 3.00 8.00
108 Zack Phillips 2.00 5.00
109 Kerby Rychel 2.50 6.00
110 Jean-Gabriel Pageau 2.50 6.00
111 Josh Leivo 2.00 5.00
113 Teemu Pulkkinen 4.00 10.00
114 Chandler Stephenson 2.00 5.00
116 Stefan Matteau 2.00 5.00
117 Josh Archibald 2.00 5.00
118 Quinton Howden 2.00 5.00
119 Henrik Samuelsson 2.50 6.00
120 Shayne Gostisbehere 12.00 30.00
121 Ryan Pulock 2.50 6.00
122 Mitchell Moroz 2.00 5.00
123 Colton Sissons 3.00 8.00
124 Oscar Lindberg 8.00 20.00
125 Matt Puempel 2.00 5.00
127 Jordan Binnington 3.00 8.00
128 Stefan Noesen 2.50 6.00
129 Anders Lee 3.00 8.00
130 Scott Kosmachuk 2.00 5.00
132 Scott Laughton 2.00 5.00
134 Sven Andrighetto 4.00 10.00
135 Hunter Shinkaruk 5.00 12.00
136 Konrad Abeltshauser 2.00 5.00
137 Malcolm Subban 5.00 12.00
138 Charles Hudon 3.00 8.00
139 Brock McGinn 2.50 6.00
141 Anthony Mantha 10.00 25.00
142 Oscar Dansk 5.00 12.00
144 Andrei Vasilevskiy 10.00 25.00
146 Danny Kristo 2.50 6.00
147 Nicklas Jensen 2.00 5.00
150 Brett Ritchie 3.00 8.00

2014-15 Upper Deck AHL Logo Patches

STATED ODDS 1:60 HOBBY
1 Adirondack Flames 8.00 20.00
2 Albany Devils 8.00 20.00
3 Binghamton Senators 8.00 20.00
4 Bridgeport Sound Tigers 8.00 20.00
5 Charlotte Checkers 8.00 20.00
6 Chicago Wolves 8.00 20.00
7 Grand Rapids Griffins 8.00 20.00
8 Hamilton Bulldogs 8.00 20.00
9 Hartford Wolf Pack 8.00 20.00
10 Hershey Bears 8.00 20.00
11 Iowa Wild 8.00 20.00
12 Lake Erie Monsters 8.00 20.00
13 Lehigh Valley Phantoms 8.00 20.00
14 Manchester Monarchs 8.00 20.00
15 Milwaukee Admirals 8.00 20.00
16 Norfolk Admirals 8.00 20.00
17 Oklahoma City Barons 8.00 20.00
18 Portland Pirates 8.00 20.00
19 Providence Bruins 8.00 20.00
20 Rochester Americans 8.00 20.00
21 Rockford IceHogs 8.00 20.00
22 San Antonio Rampage 8.00 20.00
23 Springfield Falcons 8.00 20.00
24 St. John's IceCaps 8.00 20.00
25 Syracuse Crunch 8.00 20.00
26 Texas Stars 8.00 20.00
27 Toronto Marlies 8.00 20.00
28 Utica Comets 8.00 20.00
29 Wilkes-Barre/Scranton 8.00 20.00
30 Worcester Sharks 8.00 20.00
31 Adirondack Flames Alt. 10.00 25.00
32 Albany Devils Alt. 10.00 25.00
33 Binghamton Senators Alt. 10.00 25.00
34 Bridgeport Sound Tigers Alt. 10.00 25.00
35 Charlotte Checkers Alt. 10.00 25.00
36 Chicago Wolves Alt. 10.00 25.00
37 Grand Rapids Griffins Alt. 10.00 25.00
38 Hamilton Bulldogs Alt. 10.00 25.00
39 Hartford Wolf Pack Alt. 10.00 25.00
40 Hershey Bears Alt. 10.00 25.00
41 Iowa Wild Alt. 10.00 25.00
42 Lake Erie Monsters Alt. 10.00 25.00
43 Lehigh Valley Phantoms Alt. 10.00 25.00
44 Manchester Monarchs Alt. 10.00 25.00
45 Milwaukee Admirals Alt. 10.00 25.00
46 Norfolk Admirals Alt. 10.00 25.00
47 Oklahoma City Barons Alt. 10.00 25.00
48 Portland Pirates Alt. 10.00 25.00
49 Providence Bruins Alt. 10.00 25.00
50 Rochester Americans Alt. 10.00 25.00
51 Rockford IceHogs Alt. 10.00 25.00
52 San Antonio Rampage Alt. 10.00 25.00
53 Springfield Falcons Alt. 10.00 25.00
54 St. John's IceCaps Alt. 10.00 25.00
55 Syracuse Crunch Alt. 10.00 25.00
56 Texas Stars Alt. 10.00 25.00
57 Toronto Marlies Alt. 10.00 25.00
58 Utica Comets Alt. 10.00 25.00
59 Wilkes-Barre/Scrntn Alt. 10.00 25.00
60 Worcester Sharks Alt. 10.00 25.00

2014-15 Upper Deck AHL Logo Stickers

PRIMARY STATED ODDS 1:7
ALTERNATE STATED ODDS 1:14
VINTAGE STATED ODDS 1:40
1 Adirondack Flames Primary 1.25 3.00
2 Albany Devils Primary 1.25 3.00
3 Binghamton Senators Primary 1.25 3.00
4 Bridgeport Sound Tigers Primary 1.25 3.00
5 Charlotte Checkers Primary 1.25 3.00
6 Chicago Wolves Primary 1.25 3.00
7 Grand Rapids Griffins Primary 1.25 3.00
8 Hamilton Bulldogs Primary 1.25 3.00
9 Hartford Wolf Pack Primary 1.25 3.00
10 Hershey Bears Primary 1.25 3.00
11 Iowa Wild Primary 1.25 3.00
12 Lake Erie Monsters Primary 1.25 3.00
13 Lehigh Valley Phantoms Primary 1.25 3.00
14 Manchester Monarchs Primary 1.25 3.00
15 Milwaukee Admirals Primary 1.25 3.00
16 Norfolk Admirals Primary 1.25 3.00
17 Oklahoma City Barons Primary 1.25 3.00
18 Portland Pirates Primary 1.25 3.00
19 Providence Bruins Primary 1.25 3.00
20 Rochester Americans Primary 1.25 3.00
21 Rockford IceHogs Primary 1.25 3.00
22 San Antonio Rampage Primary 1.25 3.00
23 Springfield Falcons Primary 1.25 3.00
24 St. John's IceCaps Primary 1.25 3.00
25 Syracuse Crunch Primary 1.25 3.00

26 Texas Stars Primary 1.25 3.00
27 Toronto Marlies Primary 1.25 3.00
28 Utica Comets Primary 1.25 3.00
29 Wilkes-Barre Scranton Penguins Primary 1.25 3.00
30 Worcester Sharks Primary 1.25 3.00
31 Adirondack Flames Alternate 2.00 5.00
32 Albany Devils Alternate 2.00 5.00
33 Binghamton Senators Alternate 2.00 5.00
34 Bridgeport Sound Tigers Alternate 2.00 5.00
35 Charlotte Checkers Alternate 2.00 5.00
36 Chicago Wolves Alternate 2.00 5.00
37 Grand Rapids Griffins Alternate 2.00 5.00
38 Hamilton Bulldogs Alternate 2.00 5.00
39 Hartford Wolf Pack Alternate 2.00 5.00
40 Hershey Bears Alternate 2.00 5.00
41 Iowa Wild Alternate 2.00 5.00
42 Lake Erie Monsters Alternate 2.00 5.00
43 Lehigh Valley Phantoms Alternate 2.00 5.00
44 Manchester Monarchs Alternate 2.00 5.00
45 Milwaukee Admirals Alternate 2.00 5.00
46 Norfolk Admirals Alternate 2.00 5.00
47 Oklahoma City Barons Alternate 2.00 5.00
48 Portland Pirates Alternate 2.00 5.00
49 Providence Bruins Alternate 2.00 5.00
50 Rochester Americans Alternate 2.00 5.00
51 Rockford IceHogs Alternate 2.00 5.00
52 San Antonio Rampage Alternate 2.00 5.00
53 Springfield Falcons Alternate 2.00 5.00
54 St. John's IceCaps Alternate 2.00 5.00
55 Syracuse Crunch Alternate 2.00 5.00
56 Texas Stars Alternate 2.00 5.00
57 Toronto Marlies Alternate 2.00 5.00
58 Utica Comets Alternate 2.00 5.00
59 Wilk-Bre/Scrntn Pegns Alt 2.00 5.00
60 Worcester Sharks Alternate 2.00 5.00
61 New Haven Nighthawks Vintage 3.00 8.00
62 Iowa Chops Vintage 3.00 8.00
63 Kentucky Thoroughblades Vintage 3.00 8.00
64 Lowell Monsters Vintage 3.00 8.00
65 Manitoba Moose Vintage 3.00 8.00
66 St. John's Maple Leafs Vintage 3.00 8.00
67 Nova Scotia Voyagers Vintage 3.00 8.00
68 Quebec Aces Vintage 3.00 8.00
69 Saint John Flames Vintage 3.00 8.00
70 Springfield Kings Vintage 3.00 8.00

2015-16 Upper Deck AHL

1 Stefan Noesen .30 .75
2 Petteri Lindbohm .25 .60
3 Blake Coleman .25 .60
4 Jeremy Langlois .25 .60
5 Connor Hellebuyck 1.00 2.50
6 Michael Keranen .30 .75
7 Zack Mitchell .25 .60
8 Marek Hrivik .25 .60
9 Nick Baptiste .25 .60
10 Michael Mersch .40 1.00
11 Rocco Grimaldi .25 .60
12 Chad Ruhwedel .25 .60
13 Devin Shore .40 1.00
14 Riley Barber .25 .60
15 Adam Erne .25 .60
16 Andrew Miller .30 .75
17 Justin Shugg .25 .60
18 Stephon Williams .25 .60
19 Brady Skjei .30 .75
20 Chris Driedger .30 .75
21 Nikita Scherbak .25 .60
22 Yanni Gourde .75 2.00
23 Christopher Gibson .25 .60
24 Calvin Pickard .30 .75
25 Antoine Bibeau .40 1.00
26 Bryan Rust 1.25 3.00
27 Zachary Fucale .40 1.00
28 Jordan Schmaltz .25 .60
29 Oliver Bjorkstrand .25 .60
30 Kevin Fiala .40 1.00
31 Joe Cannata .25 .60
32 Hunter Shinkaruk .40 1.00
33 Byron Froese .30 .75
34 Julius Honka .25 .60
35 Brendan Ranford .30 .75
36 Anthony DeAngelo .25 .60
37 Scott Wilson .25 .60
38 Chris Bigras .25 .60
39 Markus Hannikainen .30 .75
40 Brock McGinn .40 1.00
41 Ryan Graves .25 .60
42 Ivan Barbashev .25 .60
43 Markus Granlund .30 .75
44 Mattias Plachta .25 .60
45 Alexandre Grenier .30 .75
46 Kasperi Kapanen .25 .60
47 Brendan Gaunce .50 1.25
48 Garnet Hathaway .25 .60
49 Tanner Richard .25 .60
50 Curtis McKenzie .25 .60
51 Jean-Sebastien Dea .25 .60
52 Josh Leivo .25 .60
53 Kenny Agostino .25 .60
54 Colin Smith .25 .60
55 Max Friberg .25 .60
56 Mirco Mueller .25 .60
57 Bill Arnold .25 .60
58 Jacob de la Rose .40 1.00
59 Louis Domingue .40 1.00
60 Ryan Hartman .50 1.25
61 Garrett Wilson .25 .60
62 Tim Schaller .25 .60
63 Phil Varone .25 .60
64 Garret Sparks .50 1.25
65 Adrian Kempe .25 .60
66 Joel Armia .25 .60
67 Anthony Stolarz .40 1.00
68 T.J. Tynan .25 .60
69 Greg McKegg .25 .60
70 Ryan Sproul .30 .75
71 Trevor Carrick .25 .60
72 Frank Vatrano .75 2.00
73 Jordan Schroeder .25 .60
74 Raman Hrabarenka .30 .75
75 Leon Draisaitl .40 1.00
76 Matt O'Connor .30 .75
77 Jon Gillies .25 .60
78 Mitch Callahan .25 .60
79 Paul Thompson (NHL) .50 1.25
80 Brad Hunt .25 .60
81 Aaron Ness .25 .60
82 Brody Sutter .25 .60
83 Anthony Mantha .25 .60
84 Magnus Hellberg .25 .60
85 Connor Carrick .25 .60
86 Colton Sissons .40 1.00
87 Taylor Leier .40 1.00
88 Chandler Stephenson .40 1.00
89 John Albert .25 .60
90 Max Reinhart .25 .60
91 Reid Boucher .25 .60
92 Henrik Samuelsson .30 .75
93 Remi Elie .25 .60
94 Gabriel Dumont .25 .60
95 Joey Hishon .25 .60
96 Tyler Bertuzzi .25 .60
97 Daniel Carr .30 .75
98 Troy Grosenick .25 .60
99 Nick Ritchie .40 1.00
100 Marek Mazanec .25 .60
101 Brendan Shinnimin .50 1.25
102 Cole Cassels .50 1.25
103 Kristers Gudlevskis .60 1.50
104 Cole Ully .50 1.25
105 Conor Sheary 2.00 5.00
106 Matt Puempel .60 1.50
107 Charles Hudon .75 2.00
108 John Gibson .75 2.00
109 Madison Bowey .60 1.50
110 Tobias Lindberg .50 1.25
111 Petr Straka .60 1.50
112 Morgan Klimchuk .50 1.25
113 Jonathan Marchessault .75 2.00
114 Jordan Binnington .60 1.50
115 Mike Reilly .50 1.25
116 Nicolas Kerdiles .50 1.25
117 Shane Harper .50 1.25
118 Anton Forsberg .50 1.25
119 Ryan Pulock .50 1.25
120 Alexander Khokhlachev .50 1.25
121 Darnell Nurse .75 2.00
122 Sonny Milano .60 1.50
123 Sergey Tolchinsky .50 1.25
124 Cole Schneider .50 1.25
125 Andrew Agozzino .50 1.25
126 Mark McNeill .50 1.25
127 Jason Dickinson .50 1.25
128 Nikolay Goldobin .75 2.00
129 Adam Tambellini .50 1.25
130 Derrick Pouliot .60 1.50
131 Matt Murray 4.00 10.00
132 Connor Brown .50 1.25
133 Garret Ross .50 1.25
134 Shea Theodore .75 2.00
135 Marko Dano .60 1.50
136 Sven Andrighetto .50 1.25
137 Kerby Rychel .50 1.25
138 Emile Poirier .75 2.00
139 Ryan Bourque .60 1.50
140 Linden Vey .50 1.25
141 Brendan Leipsic .50 1.25
142 Alan Quine .50 1.25
143 Ty Rattie .60 1.50
144 Laurent Brossoit .50 1.25
145 Jared Coreau .50 1.25
146 Valentin Zykov .50 1.25
147 Malcolm Subban 2.00 5.00
148 Nick Cousins .75 2.00
149 Josh Morrissey .75 2.00
150 William Nylander .50 1.25

2015-16 Upper Deck AHL Autographs

STATED ODDS 1:8 PACKS
1 Stefan Noesen 3.00 8.00
2 Petteri Lindbohm 2.50 6.00
3 Blake Coleman 2.50 6.00
4 Jeremy Langlois 2.50 6.00
5 Connor Hellebuyck 10.00 25.00
6 Michael Keranen 3.00 8.00
8 Marek Hrivik 2.50 6.00
11 Rocco Grimaldi 2.50 6.00
13 Devin Shore 4.00 10.00
15 Adam Erne 2.50 6.00
16 Andrew Miller 3.00 8.00
17 Justin Shugg 2.50 6.00
18 Stephon Williams 2.50 6.00
20 Chris Driedger 3.00 8.00
21 Nikita Scherbak 2.50 6.00
22 Yanni Gourde 8.00 20.00
23 Christopher Gibson 2.50 6.00
25 Antoine Bibeau 4.00 10.00
27 Zachary Fucale 4.00 10.00
31 Joe Cannata 2.50 6.00
32 Hunter Shinkaruk 4.00 10.00
33 Byron Froese 3.00 8.00
34 Julius Honka 2.50 6.00
35 Brendan Ranford 3.00 8.00
36 Anthony DeAngelo 2.50 6.00
37 Scott Wilson 2.50 6.00
39 Markus Hannikainen 3.00 8.00
41 Ryan Graves 2.50 6.00
43 Markus Granlund 3.00 8.00
44 Mattias Plachta 2.50 6.00
45 Alexandre Grenier 3.00 8.00
47 Brendan Gaunce 5.00 12.00
48 Garnet Hathaway 2.50 6.00
50 Curtis McKenzie 2.50 6.00
51 Jean-Sebastien Dea 2.50 6.00
52 Josh Leivo 2.50 6.00
56 Mirco Mueller 2.50 6.00
57 Bill Arnold 2.50 6.00
61 Garrett Wilson 2.50 6.00
67 Anthony Stolarz 4.00 10.00
69 Greg McKegg 2.50 6.00
70 Ryan Sproul 3.00 8.00
73 Jordan Schroeder 2.50 6.00
76 Matt O'Connor 3.00 8.00
81 Aaron Ness 2.50 6.00
82 Brody Sutter 2.50 6.00
83 Anthony Mantha 2.50 6.00
85 Connor Carrick 2.50 6.00
86 Colton Sissons 4.00 10.00
87 Taylor Leier 4.00 10.00
88 Chandler Stephenson 4.00 10.00
93 Remi Elie 2.50 6.00
94 Gabriel Dumont 2.50 6.00
95 Joey Hishon 2.50 6.00
96 Tyler Bertuzzi 2.50 6.00
101 Brendan Shinnimin 2.50 6.00
104 Cole Ully 2.50 6.00
106 Matt Puempel 3.00 8.00
107 Charles Hudon 4.00 10.00
110 Tobias Lindberg 2.50 6.00
112 Morgan Klimchuk 2.50 6.00
113 Jonathan Marchessault 4.00 10.00
114 Jordan Binnington 3.00 8.00
116 Nicolas Kerdiles 2.50 6.00
119 Ryan Pulock 2.50 6.00
120 Alexander Khokhlachev 2.50 6.00
122 Sonny Milano 5.00 12.00
123 Sergey Tolchinsky 2.50 6.00
124 Cole Schneider 2.50 6.00
125 Andrew Agozzino 2.50 6.00
127 Jason Dickinson 2.50 6.00
128 Nikolay Goldobin 4.00 10.00
129 Adam Tambellini 2.50 6.00
130 Derrick Pouliot 3.00 8.00
134 Shea Theodore 4.00 10.00
135 Marko Dano 3.00 8.00
136 Sven Andrighetto 2.50 6.00
137 Kerby Rychel 2.50 6.00
139 Ryan Bourque 3.00 8.00
142 Alan Quine 2.50 6.00
143 Ty Rattie 3.00 8.00
144 Laurent Brossoit 2.50 6.00
145 Jared Coreau 2.50 6.00
147 Malcolm Subban 10.00 25.00
148 Nick Cousins 4.00 10.00
149 Josh Morrissey 4.00 10.00

2015-16 Upper Deck AHL Logo Stickers

1 Albany Devils 1.25 3.00
2 Bakersfield Condors 1.25 3.00
3 Binghamton Senators 1.25 3.00
4 Bridgeport Sound Tigers 1.25 3.00
5 Charlotte Checkers 1.25 3.00
6 Chicago Wolves 1.25 3.00
7 Grand Rapids Griffins 1.25 3.00
8 Hartford Wolf Pack 1.25 3.00
9 Hershey Bears 1.25 3.00
10 Iowa Wild 1.25 3.00
11 Lake Erie Monsters 1.25 3.00
12 Lehigh Valley Phantoms 1.25 3.00
13 Manitoba Moose 1.25 3.00
14 Milwaukee Admirals 1.25 3.00
15 Ontario Reign 1.25 3.00
16 Portland Pirates 1.25 3.00
17 Providence Bruins 1.25 3.00
18 Rochester Americans 1.25 3.00
19 Rockford IceHogs 1.25 3.00
20 San Antonio Rampage 1.25 3.00
21 San Diego Gulls 1.25 3.00
22 San Jose Barracuda 1.25 3.00
23 Springfield Falcons 1.25 3.00
24 St. John's IceCaps 1.25 3.00
25 Stockton Heat 1.25 3.00
26 Syracuse Crunch 1.25 3.00
27 Texas Stars 1.25 3.00
28 Toronto Marlies 1.25 3.00
29 Utica Comets 1.25 3.00
30 Wilkes-Barre/Scranton Penguins 1.25 3.00

2015-16 Upper Deck AHL Logo Tattoos

1 Albany Devils 1.25 3.00
2 Bakersfield Condors 1.25 3.00
3 Binghamton Senators 1.25 3.00
4 Bridgeport Sound Tigers 1.25 3.00
5 Charlotte Checkers 1.25 3.00
6 Chicago Wolves 1.25 3.00
7 Grand Rapids Griffins 1.25 3.00
8 Hartford Wolf Pack 1.25 3.00
9 Hershey Bears 1.25 3.00
10 Iowa Wild 1.25 3.00
11 Lake Erie Monsters 1.25 3.00
12 Lehigh Valley Phantoms 1.25 3.00
13 Manitoba Moose 1.25 3.00
14 Milwaukee Admirals 1.25 3.00
15 Ontario Reign 1.25 3.00
16 Portland Pirates 1.25 3.00
17 Providence Bruins 1.25 3.00
18 Rochester Americans 1.25 3.00
19 Rockford IceHogs 1.25 3.00
20 San Antonio Rampage 1.25 3.00
21 San Diego Gulls 1.25 3.00
22 San Jose Barracuda 1.25 3.00
23 Springfield Falcons 1.25 3.00
24 St. John's IceCaps 1.25 3.00
25 Stockton Heat 1.25 3.00
26 Syracuse Crunch 1.25 3.00
27 Texas Stars 1.25 3.00
28 Toronto Marlies 1.25 3.00
29 Utica Comets 1.25 3.00
30 Wilkes-Barre/Scranton Penguins 1.25 3.00

2015-16 Upper Deck AHL Upper Deck Logo Stickers

UD1 Upper Deck Logo 1.25 3.00
UD2 Upper Deck Logo 1.25 3.00
UD3 Upper Deck Logo 1.25 3.00
UD4 Upper Deck Logo 1.25 3.00
UD5 Upper Deck Logo 1.25 3.00

2015-16 Upper Deck AHL Upper Deck Logo Tattoos

UD1 Upper Deck Logo 1.25 3.00
UD2 Upper Deck Logo 1.25 3.00
UD3 Upper Deck Logo 1.25 3.00
UD4 Upper Deck Logo 1.25 3.00
UD5 Upper Deck Logo 1.25 3.00

2016-17 Upper Deck AHL

1 Chris Bourque .40 1.00
2 Scott Wedgewood .60 1.50
3 Danny Kristo .40 1.00
4 Cole Schneider .40 1.00
5 Taylor Beck .40 1.00
6 Trevor Carrick .40 1.00
7 Matthew Lorito .40 1.00
8 Bracken Kearns .40 1.00
9 Justin Dowling .30 .75
10 Mac Carruth .30 .75
11 JC Lipon .40 1.00
12 Jake Guentzel 1.50 4.00
13 Jordan Schmaltz .30 .75
14 Matthew Ford .30 .75
15 Jordan Binnington .30 .75
16 T.J. Tynan .30 .75
17 Daniel Zaar .30 .75
18 Casey Bailey .30 .75
19 Jared Coreau .50 1.25
20 Mathew Bodie .40 1.00
21 Eric Tangradi .30 .75
22 Stanislav Galiev .30 .75
23 Mackenzie Skapski .40 1.00
24 Vitek Vanacek .30 .75
25 Derek Ryan .30 .75
26 Zack Mitchell .40 1.00
27 Taylor Leier .30 .75
28 Nick Baptiste .40 1.00
29 Quinton Howden .40 1.00
30 Vincent Loverde .30 .75
31 Justin Bailey .40 1.00
32 Tanner Kero .30 .75
33 Evan Rodrigues .50 1.25
34 Greg Carey .30 .75
35 Pat Cannone .30 .75
36 Chris Conner .30 .75
37 Marko Dano .30 .75
38 Eric Comrie .30 .75
39 Yanni Gourde .50 1.25
40 Malcolm Subban .60 1.50
41 Sean Backman .40 1.00
42 Cal O'Reilly .30 .75
43 Griffin Reinhart .30 .75
44 Barclay Goodrow .30 .75
45 Cameron Schilling .40 1.00
46 Max Friberg .30 .75
47 Emile Poirier .30 .75
48 Brett Sterling .30 .75
49 Brad Hunt .30 .75
50 Matt Hackett .30 .75
51 Tom Kostopoulos .30 .75
52 T.J. Hensick .30 .75
53 Tanner Richard .30 .75
54 Mike McKenna .30 .75
55 Mark McNeill .40 1.00
56 Mike Zalewski .30 .75
57 Andy Miele .30 .75
58 Brendan Ranford .30 .75
59 Michael Bournival .30 .75
60 Jakub Vrana .40 1.00
61 Ville Pokka .40 1.00
62 Jordan Weal .30 .75
63 Maxime Lagace .30 .75
64 Mike Sislo .30 .75
65 Ryan Hamilton .30 .75
66 Andrew Copp .25 .60
67 Colton Hargrove .40 1.00
68 Curtis Lazar .25 .60
69 Mirco Mueller .30 .75
70 Aaron Palushaj .30 .75
71 Craig Cunningham .30 .75
72 Sven Andrighetto .30 .75
73 Linden Vey .40 1.00
74 Brandon Defazio .40 1.00
75 Michael Sgarbossa .40 1.00
76 Connor Brickley .40 1.00
77 Jack Campbell .30 .75
78 Kenny Agostino .30 .75
79 Carter Rowney .30 .75
80 Michael Leighton .40 1.00
81 Anton Forsberg .40 1.00
82 Alexandre Grenier .30 .75
83 Jeremy Smith .30 .75
84 Colin Smith .30 .75
85 Colin Greening .30 .75
86 Mike Kostka .30 .75
87 Juuse Saros .40 1.00
88 Chris Mueller .30 .75
89 Travis Morin .40 1.00
90 Adam Erne .60 1.50
91 Corey Tropp .30 .75
92 Austin Watson .30 .75
93 Justin Peters .30 .75
94 Antoine Bibeau .30 .75
95 Tanner Glass .30 .75
96 Michael Latta .30 .75
97 Landon Ferraro .30 .75
98 Danick Martel .30 .75
99 Erik Condra .30 .75
100 Tobias Lindberg 1.25 3.00
101 Michael Dal Colle .75 2.00
102 Sergey Tolchinsky .60 1.50
103 Thatcher Demko 1.50 4.00
104 Jordan Subban .75 2.00
105 Nicolas Petan .60 1.50
106 Chase De Leo .75 2.00
107 Cristoval Nieves 1.00 2.50
108 Zachary Fucale 1.00 2.50
109 Rourke Chartier .75 2.00
110 Brandon Montour .75 2.00
111 Anthony Mantha 2.00 5.00
112 Charles Hudon .60 1.50
113 Timo Meier .75 2.00
114 Jon Gillies .60 1.50
115 Oliver Kylington .60 1.50
116 Mike McCarron .75 2.00
117 Jack Roslovic .75 2.00
118 Chris Bigras .60 1.50
119 John Quenneville .75 2.00
120 Anthony DeAngelo .75 2.00
121 Kasperi Kapanen 1.50 4.00
122 Christian Fischer .75 2.00
123 Alex Tuch .75 2.00
124 Brendan Leipsic .75 2.00
125 Alexander Nylander .75 2.00
126 Nick Paul 1.00 2.50
127 Nikita Scherbak .75 2.00
128 Tyler Bertuzzi 1.00 2.50
129 Vladislav Kamenev .60 1.50
130 Brendan Lemieux .60 1.50
131 Christian Djoos .75 2.00
132 Joel Eriksson Ek .75 2.00
133 Tristan Jarry 1.50 4.00
134 Kevin Labanc .75 2.00
135 Madison Bowey .60 1.50
136 Joe Hicketts .60 1.50
137 Evgeny Svechnikov .75 2.00
138 Sonny Milano 1.00 2.50
139 Travis Sanheim .60 1.50
140 Oskar Sundqvist .75 2.00
141 Hunter Shinkaruk .75 2.00
142 Adrian Kempe .75 2.00
143 Joseph Blandisi .60 1.50
144 Ivan Barbashev .75 2.00
145 Haydn Fleury .75 2.00
146 Nikita Soshnikov .50 1.25
147 Kyle Wood .60 1.50
148 Riley Barber .60 1.50
149 Shea Theodore .60 1.50
150 Pontus Aberg 1.00 2.50

2016-17 Upper Deck AHL Autographs

1 Chris Bourque 4.00 10.00
2 Scott Wedgewood 6.00 15.00
3 Danny Kristo 4.00 10.00
6 Trevor Carrick 4.00 10.00
7 Matthew Lorito 4.00 10.00
8 Bracken Kearns 4.00 10.00
9 Justin Dowling 3.00 8.00
10 Mac Carruth 3.00 8.00
11 JC Lipon 4.00 10.00
14 Matthew Ford 3.00 8.00
18 Casey Bailey 3.00 8.00
19 Jared Coreau 5.00 12.00
20 Mathew Bodie 4.00 10.00
21 Eric Tangradi 3.00 8.00
22 Stanislav Galiev 3.00 8.00
23 Mackenzie Skapski 4.00 10.00
24 Vitek Vanacek 3.00 8.00
25 Derek Ryan 3.00 8.00
27 Taylor Leier 3.00 8.00
28 Nick Baptiste 4.00 10.00
30 Vincent Loverde 3.00 8.00
32 Tanner Kero 3.00 8.00
33 Evan Rodrigues 5.00 12.00
34 Greg Carey 3.00 8.00
36 Chris Conner 3.00 8.00
37 Marko Dano 3.00 8.00
38 Eric Comrie 3.00 8.00
39 Yanni Gourde 5.00 12.00
41 Sean Backman 4.00 10.00
43 Griffin Reinhart 3.00 8.00
44 Barclay Goodrow 3.00 8.00
45 Cameron Schilling 4.00 10.00
47 Emile Poirier 3.00 8.00
48 Brett Sterling 3.00 8.00
49 Brad Hunt 3.00 8.00
50 Matt Hackett 3.00 8.00
51 Tom Kostopoulos 3.00 8.00
52 T.J. Hensick 3.00 8.00
53 Tanner Richard 3.00 8.00
54 Mike McKenna 3.00 8.00
55 Mark McNeill 4.00 10.00
56 Mike Zalewski 3.00 8.00
57 Andy Miele 3.00 8.00
60 Jakub Vrana 4.00 10.00
61 Ville Pokka 4.00 10.00
63 Maxime Lagace 3.00 8.00
64 Mike Sislo 3.00 8.00
65 Ryan Hamilton 3.00 8.00
67 Colton Hargrove 4.00 10.00
69 Mirco Mueller 3.00 8.00
70 Aaron Palushaj 3.00 8.00
74 Brandon Defazio 4.00 10.00
75 Michael Sgarbossa 4.00 10.00
78 Kenny Agostino 3.00 8.00
79 Carter Rowney 3.00 8.00
80 Michael Leighton 4.00 10.00
81 Anton Forsberg 4.00 10.00
82 Alexandre Grenier 3.00 8.00
83 Jeremy Smith 3.00 8.00
84 Colin Smith 3.00 8.00
87 Juuse Saros 4.00 10.00
88 Chris Mueller 3.00 8.00
89 Travis Morin 4.00 10.00
90 Adam Erne 6.00 15.00
91 Corey Tropp 3.00 8.00
94 Antoine Bibeau 3.00 8.00
103 Thatcher Demko 8.00 20.00
106 Chase De Leo 4.00 10.00
108 Zachary Fucale 5.00 12.00
109 Rourke Chartier 4.00 10.00
112 Charles Hudon 3.00 8.00
116 Mike McCarron 4.00 10.00
119 John Quenneville 4.00 10.00
122 Christian Fischer 4.00 10.00
123 Alex Tuch 4.00 10.00
124 Brendan Leipsic 4.00 10.00
128 Tyler Bertuzzi 5.00 12.00
129 Vladislav Kamenev 3.00 8.00
131 Christian Djoos 4.00 10.00
133 Tristan Jarry 8.00 20.00
134 Kevin Labanc 4.00 10.00
136 Joe Hicketts 3.00 8.00
137 Evgeny Svechnikov 4.00 10.00
138 Sonny Milano 5.00 12.00
139 Travis Sanheim 3.00 8.00
140 Oskar Sundqvist 4.00 10.00
141 Hunter Shinkaruk 4.00 10.00
143 Joseph Blandisi 3.00 8.00
145 Haydn Fleury 4.00 10.00
148 Riley Barber 3.00 8.00

2016-17 Upper Deck AHL Team Mascots

TM1 Devil Dawg 1.00 2.50
TM2 Coloniel Claw'd 1.00 2.50
TM3 Max 1.00 2.50
TM4 Storm 1.00 2.50
TM5 Chubby 1.00 2.50
TM6 Skates The Grey Wolf 1.00 2.50
TM7 Sully 1.00 2.50
TM8 Griff 1.00 2.50
TM9 Crash 1.00 2.50
TM10 Sonar The Wolf 1.00 2.50
TM11 Coco The Bear 1.00 2.50
TM12 meLVin 1.00 2.50
TM13 Mick E. Moose 1.00 2.50
TM14 Roscoe 1.00 2.50
TM15 Kingston 1.00 2.50
TM16 Samboni 1.00 2.50
TM17 Mioose 1.00 2.50
TM18 Hammy Hog 1.00 2.50
TM19 T-Bone 1.00 2.50
TM20 Gulliver 1.00 2.50
TM21 Frenzy 1.00 2.50
TM22 Boomer 1.00 2.50
TM23 Frankie The Firebird 1.00 2.50
TM24 Buddy The Puffin 1.00 2.50
TM25 Crunchman 1.00 2.50
TM26 Dusty The Roadrunner 1.00 2.50
TM27 Duke The Dog 1.00 2.50
TM28 Audie 1.00 2.50
TM29 Tux The Penguin 1.00 2.50
TM30 Mulllet Brothers 1.00 2.50

2016-17 Upper Deck AHL Wordmark Logo Window Cling

1 Albany Devils 1.50 4.00
2 Bakersfield Condors 1.50 4.00
3 Binghamton Senators 1.50 4.00
4 Bridgeport Sound Tigers 1.50 4.00
5 Charlotte Checkers 1.50 4.00
6 Chicago Wolves 1.50 4.00
7 Cleveland Monsters 1.50 4.00
8 Grand Rapids Griffins 1.50 4.00
9 Iowa Wild 1.50 4.00
10 Hartford Wolf Pack 1.50 4.00
11 Hershey Bears 1.50 4.00
12 Lehigh Valley Phantoms 1.50 4.00
13 Manitoba Moose 1.50 4.00
14 Milwaukee Admirals 1.50 4.00
15 Ontario Reign 1.50 4.00
16 Providence Bruins 1.50 4.00
17 Rochester Americans 1.50 4.00
18 Rockford IceHogs 1.50 4.00
19 San Antonio Rampage 1.50 4.00
20 San Diego Gulls 1.50 4.00
21 San Jose Barracuda 1.50 4.00
22 Springfield Thunderbirds 1.50 4.00
23 Stockton Heat 1.50 4.00
24 St. John's IceCaps 1.50 4.00
25 Syracuse Crunch 1.50 4.00
26 Texas Stars 1.50 4.00
27 Tucson Roadrunners 1.50 4.00
28 Toronto Marlies 1.50 4.00
29 Utica Comets 1.50 4.00
30 Wilkes-Barre/Scranton Penguins 1.50 4.00

2017-18 Upper Deck AHL

1 Cameron Schilling .40 1.00
2 Ville Husso .40 1.00
3 Nick Paul .30 .75
4 Joey LaLeggia .30 .75
5 Nick Lappin .30 .75
6 Colin White .40 1.00
7 Jordan Schmaltz .50 1.25
8 Travis Boyd .30 .75
9 Gage Quinney .30 .75
10 Samuel Blais .40 1.00
11 Adin Hill .40 1.00
12 Roope Hintz .30 .75
13 Linus Ullmark .30 .75
14 Adam Erne .30 .75
15 Noah Juulsen .40 1.00
16 Anders Lindback .30 .75
17 Rudolfs Balcers .30 .75
18 Ryan Graves .30 .75
19 Ville Pokka .30 .75
20 Daniel Audette .30 .75
21 Kon Appleby .30 .75
22 Matiss Kivlenieks .30 .75
23 Nick Ellis .30 .75
24 Lawson Crouse .30 .75
25 Alex Nedeljkovic .30 .75
26 Michael Bournival .30 .75
27 Brendan Guhle .30 .75
28 Matt Lorito .40 1.00
29 Mike McKenna .30 .75
30 Connor Ingram .40 1.00
31 Paul LaDue .30 .75
32 Andreas Johnsson .30 .75
33 Cal Petersen .30 .75
34 Hunter Miska .30 .75
35 Jeremy Bracco .30 .75
36 Ivan Barbashev .40 1.00
37 Darren Raddysh .30 .75
38 Reid Boucher .30 .75
39 Samuel Montembeault .30 .75
40 Peter Cehlarik .40 1.00
41 Dean Kukan .30 .75
42 Kevin Roy .40 1.00
43 Chris Nell .30 .75
44 Niklas Svedberg .30 .75
45 Mason Appleton .30 .75
46 Morgan Klimchuk .30 .75
47 Oskar Lindblom .30 .75
48 Charlie Lindgren .30 .75
49 Spencer Foo .30 .75
50 Mike Vecchione .30 .75
51 Teemu Pulkkinen .30 .75
52 Carter Bancks .30 .75
53 Julien Gauthier .40 1.00
54 Tyler Moy .30 .75
55 Mike Reilly .30 .75
56 Devon Toews .30 .75
57 Andy Welinski .30 .75
58 T.J. Tynan .30 .75
59 Brendan Lemieux .40 1.00
60 Tommy Cross .30 .75
61 Scott Eansor .30 .75
62 Dominic Turgeon .30 .75
63 Eric Comrie .30 .75
64 Ty Rattie .30 .75
65 Adam Helewka .30 .75
66 Austin Ortega .30 .75
67 Adam Carlson .30 .75
68 Nikita Soshnikov .25 .60
69 Sergey Tolchinsky .30 .75
70 Lane Pederson .30 .75
71 Maxime Lagace .40 1.00
72 Jean-Francois Berube .30 .75
73 Casey DeSmith .30 .75
74 Jared Coreau .30 .75
75 Emil Pettersson .30 .75
76 Kevin Boyle .30 .75
77 Mark Jankowski .30 .75
78 Chris Bourque .30 .75
79 Tom Kostopoulos .30 .75
80 Juho Lammikko .30 .75
81 Alex Broadhurst .30 .75
82 Lucas Johansen .30 .75
83 Michael Amadio .40 1.00
84 Travis Morin .30 .75
85 Andrew Hammond .30 .75
86 Nicolas Aube-Kubel .30 .75
87 Austin Czarnik .40 1.00
88 Christopher Gibson .30 .75
89 Kyle Rau .30 .75
90 Axel Holmstrom .30 .75
91 Maxim Mamin .30 .75
92 Kyle Baun .30 .75
93 Adam Tambellini .30 .75
94 Kevin Porter .30 .75
95 Garret Sparks .30 .75
96 Antoine Bibeau .30 .75
97 Guillaume Brisebois .40 1.00
98 Alex Lyon .30 .75
99 Garnet Hathaway .30 .75
100 Nathan Bastian .30 .75
101 Mitchell Stephens SP .75 2.00
102 Daniel O' Regan SP 1.25 3.00
103 Michael Dal Colle SP .75 2.00
104 Michael Mersch SP .75 2.00
105 Thatcher Demko SP .75 2.00
106 Daniel Sprong SP .75 2.00
107 Denis Gurianov SP .75 2.00
108 Filip Chytil SP .75 2.00
109 Jon Gillies SP .75 2.00
110 Klim Kostin SP .75 2.00
111 Chandler Stephenson SP .75 2.00
112 Luke Kunin SP .75 2.00
113 Philippe Myers SP .60 1.50
114 Anthony Cirelli SP .60 1.50
115 Tage Thompson SP 1.25 3.00
116 Laurent Dauphin SP 1.25 3.00
117 Jesse Puljujarvi SP 1.00 2.50
118 Josh Ho-Sang SP 1.00 2.50
119 Vladislav Kamenev SP 1.25 3.00
120 Kasperi Kapanen SP .75 2.00
121 Shea Theodore SP .60 1.50
122 Nikita Scherbak SP 1.50 4.00
123 Ethan Bear SP .75 2.00
124 Alex Tuch SP 2.00 5.00
125 Lucas Wallmark SP .75 2.00
126 Jayce Hawryluk SP .75 2.00
127 Nick Merkley SP .75 2.00
128 Filip Chlapik SP .75 2.00
129 Timothy Liljegren SP .75 2.00
130 Nikolay Goldobin SP .75 2.00
131 Jack Roslovic SP 1.00 2.50
132 Zane Mcintyre SP .75 2.00
133 Andrew Mangiapane SP .75 2.00
134 Tyler Motte SP .75 2.00
135 Mike McCarron SP .75 2.00
136 Jason Dickinson SP .75 2.00
137 Evgeny Svechnikov SP 1.50 4.00
138 Kyle Connor SP .75 2.00
139 Jacob Larsson SP .75 2.00
140 Matthew Highmore SP .75 2.00
141 Dylan Strome SP .75 2.00
142 Thomas Chabot SP 1.25 3.00
143 Nick Baptiste SP .75 2.00
144 Nicolas Kerdiles SP .75 2.00
145 Valentin Zykov SP .75 2.00
146 C.J. Smith SP .60 1.50
147 Danick Martel SP .75 2.00
148 John Quenneville SP .60 1.50
149 Danton Heinen SP .75 2.00
150 Dominik Simon SP .75 2.00

2017-18 Upper Deck AHL Autographs

1 Cameron Schilling A 4.00 10.00
2 Ville Husso A 4.00 10.00
3 Nick Paul A 3.00 8.00
4 Joey LaLeggia B 3.00 8.00
7 Jordan Schmaltz B 5.00 12.00
8 Travis Boyd A 3.00 8.00
11 Adin Hill A 4.00 10.00
12 Roope Hintz A 3.00 8.00
13 Linus Ullmark B 3.00 8.00
14 Adam Erne B 3.00 8.00
17 Rudolfs Balcers B 3.00 8.00
18 Ryan Graves B 3.00 8.00
19 Ville Pokka A 3.00 8.00
21 Ken Appleby A 3.00 8.00
22 Matiss Kivlenieks A 3.00 8.00
23 Nick Ellis A 3.00 8.00
25 Alex Nedeljkovic A 3.00 8.00
26 Michael Bournival B 3.00 8.00
27 Brendan Guhle B 3.00 8.00
28 Matt Lorito B 4.00 10.00
29 Mike McKenna B 3.00 8.00
33 Cal Petersen A 3.00 8.00
35 Jeremy Bracco A 3.00 8.00
36 Ivan Barbashev A 4.00 10.00
37 Darren Raddysh A 3.00 8.00
40 Peter Cehlarik A 4.00 10.00
41 Dean Kukan A 3.00 8.00
43 Chris Nell B 3.00 8.00
44 Niklas Svedberg B 3.00 8.00
46 Morgan Klimchuk B 3.00 8.00
47 Oskar Lindblom A 3.00 8.00
48 Charlie Lindgren A 3.00 8.00
51 Teemu Pulkkinen A 3.00 8.00
52 Carter Bancks A 3.00 8.00
53 Julien Gauthier A 4.00 10.00
54 Tyler Moy A 3.00 8.00
55 Mike Reilly A 3.00 8.00
56 Devon Toews A 3.00 8.00
60 Tommy Cross A 3.00 8.00
61 Scott Eansor B 3.00 8.00
62 Dominic Turgeon A 3.00 8.00
63 Eric Comrie A 3.00 8.00
64 Ty Rattie B 3.00 8.00
66 Austin Ortega A 3.00 8.00
67 Adam Carlson B 3.00 8.00
70 Lane Pederson B 3.00 8.00
71 Maxime Lagace A 4.00 10.00
72 Jean-Francois Berube B 3.00 8.00
73 Casey DeSmith A 3.00 8.00
74 Jared Coreau A 3.00 8.00
76 Kevin Boyle A 3.00 8.00
78 Chris Bourque A 3.00 8.00
79 Tom Kostopoulos B 3.00 8.00
80 Juho Lammikko B 3.00 8.00
81 Alex Broadhurst B 3.00 8.00
82 Lucas Johansen A 3.00 8.00
83 Michael Amadio A 4.00 10.00
84 Travis Morin B 3.00 8.00
86 Nicolas Aube-Kubel A 3.00 8.00
87 Austin Czarnik A 4.00 10.00
88 Christopher Gibson B 3.00 8.00
89 Kyle Rau B 3.00 8.00
92 Kyle Baun A 3.00 8.00
93 Adam Tambellini B 3.00 8.00
94 Kevin Porter B 3.00 8.00
95 Garret Sparks A 3.00 8.00
96 Antoine Bibeau A 3.00 8.00
97 Guillaume Brisebois A 4.00 10.00
98 Alex Lyon B 3.00 8.00
100 Nathan Bastian A 3.00 8.00
103 Michael Dal Colle SP 6.00 15.00
104 Michael Mersch SP 6.00 15.00
107 Denis Gurianov SP 6.00 15.00
110 Klim Kostin SP 6.00 15.00
111 Chandler Stephenson SP 6.00 15.00
112 Luke Kunin SP 6.00 15.00
113 Philippe Myers SP 5.00 12.00
114 Anthony Cirelli SP 5.00 12.00
115 Tage Thompson SP 10.00 25.00
119 Vladislav Kamenev SP 10.00 25.00
123 Ethan Bear SP 6.00 15.00
126 Jayce Hawryluk SP 6.00 15.00
127 Nick Merkley SP 6.00 15.00
129 Timothy Liljegren SP 6.00 15.00
132 Zane Mcintyre SP 6.00 15.00
135 Mike McCarron SP 6.00 15.00
137 Evgeny Svechnikov SP 12.00 30.00
139 Jacob Larsson SP 6.00 15.00
140 Matthew Highmore SP 6.00 15.00
144 Nicolas Kerdiles SP 6.00 15.00
145 Valentin Zykov SP 6.00 15.00
147 Danick Martel SP 6.00 15.00
149 Danton Heinen SP 6.00 15.00

2017-18 Upper Deck AHL Team Logo Mini Posters

1 Bakersfield Condors 1.25 3.00
2 Belleville Senators 1.25 3.00
3 Binghamton Devils 1.25 3.00
4 Bridgeport Sound Tigers 1.25 3.00
5 Charlotte Checkers 1.25 3.00
6 Chicago Wolves 1.25 3.00
7 Cleveland Monsters 1.25 3.00
8 Grand Rapids Griffins 1.25 3.00
9 Hartford Wolf Pack 1.25 3.00
10 Hershey Bears 1.25 3.00
11 Iowa Wild 1.25 3.00
12 Laval Rocket 1.25 3.00
13 Lehigh Valley Phantoms 1.25 3.00
14 Manitoba Moose 1.25 3.00
15 Milwaukee Admirals 1.25 3.00
16 Ontario Reign 1.25 3.00
17 Providence Bruins 1.25 3.00
18 Rochester Americans 1.25 3.00

19 Rockford IceHogs 1.25 3.00
20 San Antonio Rampage 1.25 3.00
21 San Diego Gulls 1.25 3.00
22 San Jose Barracuda 1.25 3.00
23 Springfield Thunderbirds 1.25 3.00
24 Stockton Heat 1.25 3.00
25 Syracuse Crunch 1.25 3.00
26 Texas Stars 1.25 3.00
27 Toronto Marlies 1.25 3.00
28 Tucson Roadrunners 1.25 3.00
29 Utica Comets 1.25 3.00
30 Wilkes-Barre/Scranton Penguins 1.25 3.00

2017-18 Upper Deck AHL Team Standouts

TS1 Ty Rattie .50 1.25
TS2 Colin White .60 1.50
TS3 Nick Lappin .50 1.25
TS4 Christopher Gibson .50 1.25
TS5 Lucas Wallmark .60 1.50
TS6 Teemu Pulkkinen .50 1.25
TS7 Tyler Motte .60 1.50
TS8 Matt Puempel .50 1.25
TS9 Cole Schneider .50 1.25
TS10 Chris Bourque .50 1.25
TS11 Zack Mitchell .50 1.25
TS12 Daniel Carr .40 1.00
TS13 Danick Martel .60 1.50
TS14 Jack Roslovic .75 2.00
TS15 Emil Pettersson .50 1.25
TS16 Cal Petersen .50 1.25
TS17 Jakob Forsbacka-Karlsson .60 1.50
TS18 C.J. Smith .50 1.25
TS19 Vincent Hinostroza .40 1.00
TS20 Klim Kostin .60 1.50
TS21 Giovanni Fiore .60 1.50
TS22 Rudolfs Balcers .50 1.25
TS23 Alexandre Grenier .50 1.25
TS24 Andrew Mangiapane .60 1.50
TS25 Anthony Cirelli .50 1.25
TS26 Jason Dickinson .60 1.50
TS27 Garret Sparks .50 1.25
TS28 Dylan Strome .60 1.50
TS29 Nikolay Goldobin .60 1.50
TS30 Casey DeSmith .50 1.25

2014-15 Upper Deck AHL Box Set

COMP.FACT.SET (105) 35.00 50.00
COMPLETE SET (100) 4.00 10.00
1 Sven Baertschi .12 .30
2 Max Reinhart .15 .40
3 Markus Granlund .30 .75
4 Corban Knight .20 .50
5 Joni Ortio .25 .60
6 Jason Akeson .12 .30
7 Nick Cousins .15 .40
8 Tye McGinn .12 .30
9 Stefan Matteau .12 .30
10 Keith Kinkaid .12 .30
11 Scott Wedgewood .15 .40
12 David Wohlberg .15 .40
13 Joe Whitney .12 .30
14 Mike Hoffman .15 .40
15 Shane Prince .15 .40
16 Anders Lee .20 .50
17 Scott Mayfield .15 .40
18 Zach Boychuk .12 .30
19 Brett Sutter .12 .30
20 Aaron Palushaj .25 .60
21 Victor Rask .20 .50
22 Jake Allen .25 .60
23 Dmitrij Jaskin .15 .40
24 Ty Rattie .25 .60
25 Cory Emmerton .12 .30
26 Tomas Jurco .20 .50
27 Tom McCollum .15 .40
28 Alexey Marchenko .12 .30
29 Dustin Tokarski .12 .30
30 Nathan Beaulieu .15 .40
31 Louis Leblanc .15 .40
32 Oscar Lindberg .50 1.25
33 Jesper Fast .15 .40
34 Danny Kristo .15 .40
35 Philipp Grubauer .20 .50
36 Nate Schmidt .12 .30
37 Ryan Stoa .12 .30
38 Patrick Wey .12 .30
39 Johan Gustafsson .15 .40
40 Josh Caron .12 .30
41 Calvin Pickard .15 .40
42 Michael Sgarbossa .12 .30
43 Jordan Weal .15 .40
44 Martin Jones .20 .50
45 Linden Vey .15 .40
46 Derek Forbort .15 .40
47 Maxim Kitsyn .12 .30
48 Calle Jarnkrok .20 .50
49 Austin Watson .12 .30
50 Magnus Hellberg .20 .50
51 Colton Sissons .20 .50
52 Emerson Etem .15 .40
53 John Gibson .25 .60
54 Rickard Rakell .15 .40
55 Max Friberg .15 .40
56 Will Acton .12 .30
57 Oscar Klefbom .40 1.00
58 David Musil .12 .30
59 Chet Pickard .12 .30
60 Andy Miele .12 .30
61 Brandon Yip .12 .30
62 Mark Visentin .20 .50
63 Matt Fraser .12 .30
64 Alexander Khokhlachev .20 .50
65 Andrey Makarov .20 .50
66 Phil Varone .15 .40
67 Jeremy Morin .12 .30
68 Brandon Pirri .12 .30
69 Adam Clendening .20 .50
70 Quinton Howden .12 .30
71 Jacob Markstrom .15 .40
72 Michael Houser .15 .40
73 Frederic St. Denis .12 .30
74 Cody Goloubef .12 .30
75 Mike McKenna .12 .30
76 Jonathan Marchessault .20 .50
77 Kael Mouillierat .15 .40
78 Patrice Cormier .12 .30
79 Brenden Kichton .12 .30
80 Edward Pasquale .12 .30
81 Brett Connolly .12 .30
82 Kristers Gudlevskis .20 .50
83 Cedric Paquette .20 .50
84 Jack Campbell .25 .60
85 Travis Morin .12 .30
86 Curtis McKenzie .15 .40
87 Colton Sceviour .12 .30
88 T.J. Brennan .12 .30
89 Josh Leivo .12 .30
90 Greg McKegg .15 .40
91 Benn Ferriero .12 .30
92 Pascal Pelletier .12 .30
93 Joe Cannata .12 .30
94 Nicklas Jensen .12 .30
95 Brian Gibbons .12 .30
96 Eric Hartzell .12 .30
97 Harry Zolnierczyk .12 .30
98 Freddie Hamilton .12 .30
99 Konrad Abeltshauser .12 .30
100 Brodie Reid .12 .30

2014-15 Upper Deck AHL Box Set Autographs

FOUR AUTO PER FACTORY SET
1 Sven Baertschi 5.00 12.00
2 Max Reinhart 3.00 8.00
3 Markus Granlund 6.00 15.00
4 Corban Knight 4.00 10.00
5 Joni Ortio 5.00 12.00
6 Jason Akeson 2.50 6.00
7 Nick Cousins 3.00 8.00
8 Tye McGinn 2.50 6.00
9 Stefan Matteau 2.50 6.00
10 Keith Kinkaid 2.50 6.00
11 Scott Wedgewood 3.00 8.00
12 David Wohlberg 3.00 8.00
13 Joe Whitney 2.50 6.00
14 Mike Hoffman 3.00 8.00
15 Shane Prince 3.00 8.00
16 Anders Lee 4.00 10.00
17 Scott Mayfield 3.00 8.00
18 Zach Boychuk 2.50 6.00
19 Brett Sutter 2.50 6.00
20 Aaron Palushaj 5.00 12.00
21 Victor Rask 4.00 10.00
22 Jake Allen 5.00 12.00
23 Dmitrij Jaskin 3.00 8.00
24 Ty Rattie 5.00 12.00
25 Cory Emmerton 2.50 6.00
26 Tomas Jurco 4.00 10.00
27 Tom McCollum 3.00 8.00
28 Alexey Marchenko 2.50 6.00
29 Dustin Tokarski 2.50 6.00
30 Nathan Beaulieu 3.00 8.00
31 Louis Leblanc 3.00 8.00
32 Oscar Lindberg 10.00 25.00
33 Jesper Fast 3.00 8.00
34 Danny Kristo 3.00 8.00
35 Philipp Grubauer 4.00 10.00
36 Nate Schmidt 2.50 6.00
37 Ryan Stoa 2.50 6.00
38 Patrick Wey 2.50 6.00
39 Johan Gustafsson 3.00 8.00
40 Josh Caron 2.50 6.00
41 Calvin Pickard 3.00 8.00
42 Michael Sgarbossa 2.50 6.00
43 Jordan Weal 3.00 8.00
44 Martin Jones 6.00 15.00
45 Linden Vey 3.00 8.00
46 Derek Forbort 3.00 8.00
47 Maxim Kitsyn 2.50 6.00
48 Calle Jarnkrok 4.00 10.00
49 Austin Watson 2.50 6.00
50 Magnus Hellberg 4.00 10.00
51 Colton Sissons 4.00 10.00
52 Emerson Etem 3.00 8.00
53 John Gibson 5.00 12.00
54 Rickard Rakell 3.00 8.00
55 Max Friberg 3.00 8.00
56 Will Acton 2.50 6.00
57 Oscar Klefbom 8.00 20.00
58 David Musil 2.50 6.00
59 Chet Pickard 2.50 6.00
60 Andy Miele 2.50 6.00
61 Brandon Yip 2.50 6.00
62 Mark Visentin 4.00 10.00
63 Matt Fraser 2.50 6.00
64 Alexander Khokhlachev 4.00 10.00
65 Andrey Makarov 4.00 10.00
66 Phil Varone 3.00 8.00
67 Jeremy Morin 2.50 6.00
68 Brandon Pirri 2.50 6.00
69 Adam Clendening 4.00 10.00
70 Quinton Howden 2.50 6.00
71 Jacob Markstrom 3.00 8.00
72 Michael Houser 3.00 8.00
73 Frederic St. Denis 2.50 6.00
74 Cody Goloubef 2.50 6.00
75 Mike McKenna 4.00 10.00
76 Jonathan Marchessault 4.00 10.00
77 Kael Mouillierat 3.00 8.00
78 Patrice Cormier 2.50 6.00
79 Brenden Kichton 2.50 6.00
80 Edward Pasquale 2.50 6.00
81 Brett Connolly 2.50 6.00
82 Kristers Gudlevskis 4.00 10.00
83 Cedric Paquette 4.00 10.00
84 Jack Campbell 5.00 12.00
85 Travis Morin 2.50 6.00
86 Curtis McKenzie 3.00 8.00
87 Colton Sceviour 2.50 6.00
88 T.J. Brennan 2.50 6.00
89 Josh Leivo 2.50 6.00
90 Greg McKegg 3.00 8.00
91 Benn Ferriero 2.50 6.00
92 Pascal Pelletier 2.50 6.00
93 Joe Cannata 2.50 6.00
94 Nicklas Jensen 2.50 6.00
95 Brian Gibbons 2.50 6.00
96 Eric Hartzell 2.50 6.00
97 Harry Zolnierczyk 4.00 10.00
98 Freddie Hamilton 2.50 6.00
99 Konrad Abeltshauser 2.50 6.00
100 Brodie Reid 2.50 6.00

2017-18 Upper Deck CHL

1 Joseph Veleno .30 .75
2 Carter Hart .40 1.00
3 Max Jones .25 .60
4 Lucas Chiodo .25 .60
5 Ondrej Vala .25 .60
6 Kyle Maksimovich .25 .60
7 Kale Clague .30 .75
8 Jeffrey Truchon-Viel .25 .60
9 Garrett Pilon .25 .60
10 Jake Bean .30 .75
11 Dylan Wells .25 .60
12 William Bitten .25 .60
13 Ryan Moore .25 .60
14 Jakob Stukel .25 .60
15 Jordan Martel .25 .60
16 Vince Loschiavo .25 .60
17 Zach Magwood .25 .60
18 David Quenneville .25 .60
19 Jack Studnicka .25 .60
20 Vitalii Abramov .25 .60
21 Beck Malenstyn .25 .60
22 Sam Steel .30 .75
23 Alexander Chmelevski .25 .60
24 Brady Gilmour .25 .60
25 Cody Glass .40 1.00
26 Ty Smith .30 .75
27 Davis Koch .25 .60
28 Ivan Lodnia .25 .60
29 Matteo Gennaro .25 .60
30 Dillon Dube .30 .75
31 Nicholas Chyzowski .25 .60
32 Jordan Sambrook .25 .60
33 Mason Shaw .25 .60
34 Anthony Salinitri .25 .60
35 Juuso Valimaki .25 .60
36 Jake Leschyshyn .25 .60
37 Michael DiPietro .25 .60
38 Calen Addison .25 .60
39 Jaret Anderson-Dolan .40 1.00
40 Morgan Frost .25 .60
41 Jayden Halbgewachs .25 .60
42 Ryan McGregor .25 .60
43 Maxime Comtois .40 1.00
44 Cale Fleury .25 .60
45 Noel Hoefenmayer .25 .60
46 Arnaud Durandeau .25 .60
47 Logan Stanley .25 .60
48 Dmitry Sokolov .40 1.00
49 Trent Fox .25 .60
50 Jordan Kyrou .30 .75
51 Nicolas Hague .25 .60
52 Macauley Carson .25 .60
53 Elijah Brown .25 .60
54 Ben Jones .25 .60
55 Stuart Skinner .25 .60
56 Ryan McLeod .30 .75
57 Pascal Corbeil .25 .60
58 Parker Kelly .25 .60
59 Evan Bouchard .40 1.00
60 Evan Fitzpatrick .25 .60
61 Matthew Struthers .25 .60
62 Tanner Kaspick .25 .60
63 Ben Hawerchuk .25 .60
64 Cedric Pare .25 .60
65 D'Artagnan Joly .25 .60
66 Zachary Lauzon .25 .60
67 Tim Gettinger .25 .60
68 Isaac Ratcliffe .30 .75
69 Drake Batherson .25 .60
70 Brett Howden .30 .75
71 Givani Smith .25 .60
72 Peter Abbandonato .25 .60
73 Connor Hall .25 .60
74 Matthew Boucher .25 .60
75 Taylor Raddysh .40 1.00
76 Mitchell Balmas .25 .60
77 Jonah Gadjovich .25 .60
78 Ryan Peckford .25 .60
79 Jacob Paquette .25 .60
80 Aleksi Heponiemi .25 .60
81 Tyler Benson .25 .60
82 Jett Woo .30 .75
83 Benoit-Olivier Groulx .25 .60
84 Nick Suzuki .30 .75
85 Nate Schnarr .30 .75
86 Travis Barron .25 .60
87 Cal Foote .25 .60
88 Olivier Garneau .25 .60
89 Riley Stillman .25 .60
90 Adam Mascherin .25 .60
91 Jared McIsaac .30 .75
92 Zach Gallant .25 .60
93 Cliff Pu .25 .60
94 Matthew Timms .25 .60
95 Ryan Merkley .25 .60
96 Bailey Webster .25 .60
97 Matthew Strome .30 .75
98 Markus Phillips .25 .60
99 Kole Lind .25 .60
100 Michael Rasmussen .25 .60
101 David Levin .25 .60
102 Connor Bunnaman .25 .60
103 Maxime Fortier .25 .60
104 Tyler Steenbergen .25 .60
105 Derek Gentile .25 .60
106 Maurizio Colella .25 .60
107 Hudson Elynuik .25 .60
108 Matthew Phillips .25 .60
109 Liam Hawel .30 .75
110 Hugo Roy .25 .60
111 Brett McKenzie .25 .60
112 Nicolas Beaudin .25 .60
113 Jake Durham .25 .60
114 Dominic Cormier .25 .60
115 Aaron Hyman .25 .60
116 Jonathan Ang .25 .60
117 Nicholas Caamano .25 .60
118 Jeffrey Durocher .25 .60
119 Brady Hinz .25 .60
120 Anthony Popovich .25 .60
121 Trenton Bourque .25 .60
122 Glenn Gawdin .25 .60
123 Pierre-Olivier Joseph .25 .60
124 Justin Fazio .25 .60
125 Nolan Volcan .25 .60
126 Alexandre Alain .25 .60
127 Griffen Outhouse .25 .60
128 Adam Thilander .25 .60
129 Brayden Gorda .25 .60
130 Stephen Dhillon .25 .60
131 Patrick Bajkov .25 .60
132 MacKenzie Entwistle .30 .75
133 Otto Somppi .25 .60
134 Robert Thomas .25 .60
135 Thomas Gregoire .25 .60
136 Kyle Jessiman .25 .60
137 Christopher Paquette .25 .60
138 Stelio Mattheos .30 .75
139 Evan Cormier .25 .60
140 Brody Willms .25 .60
141 Shawn Boudrias .25 .60
142 Adam Marsh .25 .60
143 Carson Mackinnon .25 .60
144 Austen Keating .25 .60
145 Artyom Minulin .25 .60
146 Jacob McGrath .30 .75
147 Marc-Olivier Duquette .25 .60
148 Keaton Middleton .25 .60
149 Giorgio Estephan .25 .60
150 Isaac Nurse .25 .60
151 Noah Gregor .25 .60
152 Boris Katchouk .25 .60
153 Morgan Geekie .25 .60
154 Josh Brook .30 .75
155 Jason Robertson .25 .60
156 Aaron Luchuk .25 .60
157 Ian Scott .30 .75
158 Tyler Soy .25 .60
159 Conor Timmins .25 .60
160 Antoine Morand .25 .60
161 Kody McDonald .25 .60
162 Jack Kopacka .25 .60
163 Mathieu Boucher .25 .60
164 Sean Day .25 .60
165 Libor Hajek .25 .60
166 Domenic Commisso .25 .60
167 Antoine Samuel .25 .60
168 Etienne Montpetit .25 .60
169 Riley Sutter .25 .60
170 Jeremy Helvig .25 .60
171 Jocktan Chainey .30 .75
172 Jared Bethune .25 .60
173 Logan Flodell .25 .60
174 Ty Ronning .25 .60
175 Alex Barre-Boulet .25 .60
176 James Phelan .25 .60
177 Jordy Bellerive .30 .75
178 Gabe Vilardi .25 .60
179 Samuel Asselin .25 .60
180 James Malm .25 .60
181 Cole Fonstad .25 .60
182 Jordan-Tyler Fournier .25 .60
183 Samuel Blier .25 .60
184 Adam Cheezo .25 .60
185 Nikita Popugaev .25 .60
186 Brandon Hagel .25 .60
187 Scott Walford .25 .60
188 Cole Kehler .25 .60
189 Vojtech Budik .25 .60
190 David Noel .30 .75
191 Reilly Pickard .25 .60
192 Brendan De Jong .25 .60
193 Mikhail Denisov .25 .60
194 Skyler McKenzie .25 .60
195 Pascal Laberge .25 .60
196 Lane Zablocki .25 .60
197 Ty Lewis .25 .60
198 Josh Mahura .25 .60
199 Josh Paterson .25 .60
200 Kyle Olson .30 .75
201 Will Warm .25 .60
202 Matt Fonteyne .25 .60
203 Jordan Hollett .25 .60
204 Dmitri Zaitsev .25 .60
205 Kevin Hancock .25 .60
206 Joseph Garreffa .25 .60
207 Johnny Corneil .25 .60
208 Matt Bradley .25 .60
209 Akil Thomas .30 .75
210 Connor Dewar .25 .60
211 Noah Dobson .25 .60
212 Christian Girhiny .25 .60
213 Matthew Grouchy .25 .60
214 Dawson Davidson .25 .60
215 Luke Boka .25 .60
216 Tye Felhaber .25 .60
217 Liam Murphy .25 .60
218 Olivier Rodrigue .25 .60
219 Logan DeNoble .25 .60
220 Peter Stratis .25 .60
221 Denis Mikhnin .25 .60
222 Alexis Gravel .30 .75
223 Pavel Koltygin .25 .60
224 Dmitri Samorukov .25 .60
225 Mark Rubinchik .25 .60
226 Mark Grametbauer .25 .60
227 Allan McShane .25 .60
228 Ivan Kosorenkov .25 .60
229 Grayson Pawlenchuk .25 .60
230 Brad Morrison .25 .60
231 Leon Gawanke .25 .60
232 Kade Landry .25 .60
233 Adam Ruzicka .25 .60
234 Jeremy McKenna .25 .60
235 Rafael Harvey-Pinard .25 .60
236 Jason Willms .25 .60
237 Felix Bibeau .25 .60
238 Brett Davis .25 .60
239 Austin McEneny .25 .60
240 Jordy Stallard .25 .60
241 Yaroslav Alexeyev .25 .60
242 Anderson MacDonald .25 .60
243 Sean Durzi .25 .60
244 Curtis Douglas .25 .60
245 Jacob Friend .25 .60
246 Danil Antropov .25 .60
247 Jordan Ernst .25 .60
248 Michael Pezzetta .25 .60
249 Garrett McFadden .25 .60
250 Serron Noel .25 .60
251 Samuel Dove-McFalls .25 .60
252 Nicholas Welsh .25 .60
253 Zachary Bouthillier .25 .60
254 Ivan Chekhovich .25 .60
255 Michael McLeod 1.25 3.00
256 Jake Smith .25 .60
257 Samuel L'Italien .25 .60
258 Charle-Edouard D'Astou .25 .60
259 Jack Flaman .25 .60
260 Nick Henry .25 .60
261 Felix Robert .25 .60
262 Maksim Sushko .25 .60
263 Justin Brazeau .25 .60
264 Daniel Hardie .25 .60
265 Cam Dineen .25 .60
266 Linus Nyman .25 .60
267 Pavel Gogolev .25 .60
268 Riley Woods .25 .60
269 Nicolas Ouellet .25 .60
270 Jacob Moverare .25 .60
271 Drake Rymsha .25 .60
272 Aidan Dudas .25 .60
273 Adam Capannelli .25 .60
274 Kevin Bahl .25 .60
275 Simon Lafrance .25 .60
276 Jared Legien .25 .60
277 Mason McCarty .25 .60
278 Maxim Mizyurin .25 .60
279 Chase Harwell .25 .60
280 Nicolas Guay .25 .60
281 Riley Lamb .25 .60
282 Marek Zachar .25 .60
283 Sami Moilanen .25 .60
284 Dante Hannoun .25 .60
285 Jake Henderson .25 .60
286 Bradley Lalonde .25 .60
287 Yvan Mongo .25 .60
288 Joachim Blichfeld .25 .60
289 Renars Krastenbergs .25 .60
290 Adam Timleck .25 .60
291 Mark Rassell .25 .60
292 Barrett Hayton .25 .60
293 Brayden Burke .25 .60
294 Robert Lynch .25 .60
295 Trey Fix-Wolansky .25 .60
296 Nathan Dunkley .25 .60
297 Tyler Hinam .25 .60
298 Julien Tessier .25 .60
299 Kirill Maksimov .25 .60
300 Mika Cyr .25 .60
301 Ryan Suzuki 3.00 8.00
302 Brandon Coe 1.25 3.00
303 Nolan Hutcheson 1.25 3.00
304 Ben Badalamenti 1.25 3.00
305 Giovanni Vallati 1.25 3.00
306 Bowen Byram 1.25 3.00
307 Alexey Lipanov 1.25 3.00
308 Nick Wong 3.00 8.00
309 Reece Vitelli 1.25 3.00
310 Blake Murray 1.25 3.00
311 Ostap Safin 3.00 8.00
312 Jake Lee 1.25 3.00
313 Luke Bignell 1.25 3.00
314 Peyton Krebs 1.25 3.00
315 Philip Tomasino 1.25 3.00
316 Bastian Eckl 1.25 3.00
317 Alex Beaucage 1.25 3.00
318 Ethan Keppen 1.25 3.00
319 Jackson Van De Leest 1.25 3.00
320 Cedric Desruisseaux 1.25 3.00
321 Riley Stotts 1.25 3.00
322 Raphael Lavoie 1.25 3.00
323 Liam Kindree 1.25 3.00
324 Merrick Rippon 1.25 3.00
325 Josh Williams 1.25 3.00
326 Mathew MacDougall 1.25 3.00
327 Graeme Clarke 1.25 3.00
328 Zach Cox 1.25 3.00
329 Kieffer Bellows 4.00 10.00
330 Nicholas Porco 1.25 3.00
331 Dylan Cozens 1.25 3.00
332 Xavier Bouchard 1.25 3.00
333 Jan Drozg 1.25 3.00
334 Dawson Barteaux 1.25 3.00
335 Hunter Holmes 1.25 3.00
336 Justin Barron 1.25 3.00
337 Pier-Olivier Lacombe 1.25 3.00
338 Nick Robertson 3.00 8.00
339 Maxim Golod 1.25 3.00
340 Milos Roman 1.25 3.00
341 Eemeli Rasanen 1.25 3.00
342 Nico Gross 1.25 3.00
343 Xavier Simoneau 1.25 3.00
344 Nathan Allensen 3.00 8.00
345 Filip Zadina 1.25 3.00
346 Braden Schneider 1.25 3.00
347 Matthew Villalta 1.25 3.00
348 Alexey Toropchenko 1.25 3.00
349 German Rubtsov 1.25 3.00
350 Emil Oksanen 1.25 3.00
351 Egor Sokolov 1.25 3.00
352 Cameron Hillis 1.25 3.00
353 Rhett Rhinehart 1.25 3.00
354 Jakob Pelletier 1.25 3.00
355 Gabriel Denis 1.25 3.00
356 Kirill Nizhnikov 1.25 3.00
357 Jonny Hooker 1.25 3.00
358 Justin Ducharme 1.25 3.00
359 Dmitry Zavgorodniy 1.25 3.00
360 Ty Dellandrea 1.25 3.00
361 Carl Stankowski 1.25 3.00
362 Ryan Roth 1.25 3.00
363 Liam Foudy 1.25 3.00
364 Dawson Baker 1.25 3.00
365 Egor Zudilov 1.25 3.00
366 Kristian Reichel 1.25 3.00
367 Isaac Johnson 1.25 3.00
368 Daemon Hunt 1.25 3.00
369 Filip Kral 1.25 3.00
370 Andrei Svechnikov 1.25 3.00
371 Samuel Poulin 1.25 3.00
372 Vladislav Kotkov 1.25 3.00
373 Martin Bodak 1.25 3.00
374 Gabriel Fortier 1.25 3.00
375 Cody Morgan 1.25 3.00
376 Sasha Mutala 1.25 3.00
377 Cole Reinhardt 1.25 3.00
378 Oleg Sosunov 1.25 3.00
379 Arthur Kaliyev 1.25 3.00
380 Nolan Foote 1.25 3.00
381 Damien Giroux 1.25 3.00
382 Jacob Ingham 1.25 3.00
383 Dennis Cholowski 1.25 3.00
384 Brodi Stuart 1.25 3.00
385 Philipp Kurashev 1.25 3.00
386 Xavier Parent 1.25 3.00
387 Luke Henman 1.25 3.00
388 Ryan Francis 1.25 3.00
389 Libor Zabransky 1.25 3.00
390 Alexis Lafreniere 25.00 60.00
391 Kirby Dach 1.25 3.00
392 Henri Jokiharju 1.25 3.00
393 Nikita Okhotyuk 1.25 3.00
394 Maxence Guenette 1.25 3.00
395 Mason Primeau 1.25 3.00
396 Riley Damiani 1.25 3.00
397 Blade Jenkins 1.25 3.00
398 Cole Schwindt 1.25 3.00
399 Samuel Bitten 1.25 3.00
400 Igor Martynov 1.25 3.00

2017-18 Upper Deck CHL Autographs

3 Max Jones B 6.00 15.00
7 Kale Clague B 8.00 20.00
8 Jeffrey Truchon-Viel B 6.00 15.00
10 Jake Bean B 8.00 20.00
11 Dylan Wells B 6.00 15.00
12 William Bitten B 6.00 15.00
18 David Quenneville B 6.00 15.00
19 Jack Studnicka B 6.00 15.00
22 Sam Steel A 8.00 20.00
25 Cody Glass A 10.00 25.00
26 Ty Smith A 8.00 20.00
27 Davis Koch B 6.00 15.00
31 Nicholas Chyzowski B 6.00 15.00
35 Juuso Valimaki B 6.00 15.00
36 Jake Leschyshyn B 6.00 15.00
37 Michael DiPietro B 6.00 15.00
39 Jaret Anderson-Dolan B 10.00 25.00
40 Morgan Frost A 6.00 15.00
41 Jayden Halbgewachs B 6.00 15.00
42 Ryan McGregor B 6.00 15.00
44 Cale Fleury B 6.00 15.00
46 Arnaud Durandeau B 6.00 15.00
47 Logan Stanley B 6.00 15.00
48 Dmitry Sokolov B 10.00 25.00
50 Jordan Kyrou A 8.00 20.00
51 Nicolas Hague B 6.00 15.00
54 Ben Jones B 6.00 15.00
56 Ryan McLeod A 8.00 20.00
58 Parker Kelly B 6.00 15.00
59 Evan Bouchard A 10.00 25.00
60 Evan Fitzpatrick B 6.00 15.00
62 Tanner Kaspick B 6.00 15.00
63 Ben Hawerchuk B 6.00 15.00
66 Zachary Lauzon B 6.00 15.00
68 Isaac Ratcliffe B 8.00 20.00
69 Drake Batherson B 6.00 15.00
70 Brett Howden B 8.00 20.00
71 Givani Smith B 6.00 15.00
74 Matthew Boucher B 6.00 15.00
75 Taylor Raddysh B 10.00 25.00
76 Mitchell Balmas B 6.00 15.00
78 Ryan Peckford B 6.00 15.00
81 Tyler Benson B 6.00 15.00
82 Jett Woo B 8.00 20.00
83 Benoit-Olivier Groulx A 6.00 15.00
84 Nick Suzuki A 8.00 20.00
87 Cal Foote A 6.00 15.00
90 Adam Mascherin A 6.00 15.00
91 Jared McIsaac A 8.00 20.00
95 Ryan Merkley A 6.00 15.00
97 Matthew Strome B 8.00 20.00
99 Kole Lind B 6.00 15.00
100 Michael Rasmussen A 6.00 15.00
301 Ryan Suzuki A 20.00 50.00
302 Brandon Coe B 8.00 20.00
308 Nick Wong B 20.00 50.00
310 Blake Murray B 8.00 20.00
311 Ostap Safin B 20.00 50.00
316 Bastian Eckl B 8.00 20.00
320 Cedric Desruisseaux B 8.00 20.00
325 Josh Williams B 8.00 20.00
329 Kieffer Bellows A 25.00 60.00
332 Xavier Bouchard B 8.00 20.00
333 Jan Drozg B 8.00 20.00
336 Justin Barron B 8.00 20.00
338 Nick Robertson B 20.00 50.00
339 Maxim Golod B 8.00 20.00
340 Milos Roman B 8.00 20.00
341 Eemeli Rasanen B 8.00 20.00
343 Xavier Simoneau B 8.00 20.00
345 Filip Zadina A 8.00 20.00
346 Braden Schneider B 8.00 20.00
347 Matthew Villalta B 8.00 20.00
349 German Rubtsov B 8.00 20.00
351 Egor Sokolov B 8.00 20.00
352 Cameron Hillis B 8.00 20.00
354 Jakob Pelletier B 8.00 20.00
355 Gabriel Denis B 8.00 20.00
358 Justin Ducharme B 8.00 20.00
359 Dmitry Zavgorodniy B 8.00 20.00
360 Ty Dellandrea B 8.00 20.00
361 Carl Stankowski B 8.00 20.00
366 Kristian Reichel B 8.00 20.00
370 Andrei Svechnikov A 8.00 20.00
371 Samuel Poulin B 8.00 20.00
372 Vladislav Kotkov B 8.00 20.00
374 Gabriel Fortier B 8.00 20.00
376 Sasha Mutala B 8.00 20.00
380 Nolan Foote B 8.00 20.00
381 Damien Giroux B 8.00 20.00
383 Dennis Cholowski B 8.00 20.00
384 Brodi Stuart B 8.00 20.00
385 Philipp Kurashev B 8.00 20.00
387 Luke Henman B 8.00 20.00
388 Ryan Francis A 8.00 20.00
390 Alexis Lafreniere A 30.00 80.00
391 Kirby Dach B 8.00 20.00
392 Henri Jokiharju B 8.00 20.00
394 Maxence Guenette B 8.00 20.00
396 Riley Damiani B 8.00 20.00
397 Blade Jenkins B 8.00 20.00

2017-18 Upper Deck CHL Promising Futures

PF1 Cody Glass 1.00 2.50
PF2 Vitalii Abramov .60 1.50
PF3 Kole Lind .60 1.50
PF4 Andrei Svechnikov .75 2.00
PF5 Filip Zadina .75 2.00
PF6 Ryan Merkley .60 1.50
PF7 Jordan Kyrou .75 2.00
PF8 Ryan McLeod .75 2.00
PF9 Jared McIsaac .75 2.00
PF10 Ty Smith .75 2.00
PF11 Cal Foote .60 1.50
PF12 Carter Hart 1.00 2.50
PF13 Nick Suzuki .75 2.00
PF14 Robert Thomas .60 1.50
PF15 Joseph Veleno .75 2.00
PF16 Akil Thomas .75 2.00
PF17 Maxime Comtois 1.00 2.50
PF18 Taylor Raddysh 1.00 2.50
PF19 Sam Steel .75 2.00
PF20 Kieffer Bellows 2.50 6.00

2017-18 Upper Deck CHL Top Prospects Game

TP1 Jake Leschyshyn .50 1.25
TP2 Nikita Popugaev .50 1.25
TP3 Henri Jokiharju .60 1.50
TP4 Jacob Paquette .50 1.25
TP5 MacKenzie Entwistle .60 1.50
TP6 Michael DiPietro .50 1.25
TP7 Nick Suzuki .60 1.50
TP8 Juuso Valimaki .50 1.25
TP9 Robert Thomas .50 1.25
TP10 Cody Glass .75 2.00
TP11 Gabe Vilardi .50 1.25
TP12 Michael Rasmussen .50 1.25
TP13 Ian Scott .60 1.50
TP14 Morgan Frost .50 1.25
TP15 Isaac Ratcliffe .60 1.50
TP16 Kole Lind .50 1.25
TP17 Antoine Morand .50 1.25
TP18 Stelio Mattheos .60 1.50
TP19 Maxime Comtois .75 2.00
TP20 Alexander Chmelevski .50 1.25

1996 Visions

The 1996 Classic Visions set consists of 150 standard-size cards. The fronts feature full-bleed color action player photos. The player's position and name are presented in blue foil, while the Classic logo and set title "96 Visions" are stamped in gold foil. The back carries a second color photo, college statistics, biography, and a player fact.

COMPLETE SET (150) 6.00 15.00
82 Bryan Berard .15 .40
83 Jeff Friesen .15 .40
84 Petr Buzek .15 .40
85 Nolan Baumgartner .08 .25
86 Jason Bonsignore .08 .25
87 Jan Hlavac .15 .40
88 Ethan Moreau .08 .25
89 Radek Dvorak .08 .25
90 Brian Holzinger .08 .25
91 Petr Sykora .20 .50
92 Ed Jovanovski .15 .40
93 Jeff O'Neill .08 .25
94 Manon Rheaume .20 .50
123 Petr Sykora .20 .50

1996 Visions Signings

The 1996 Visions Signings set consists of 100 standard-size cards. The fronts feature full-bleed color action player photos. The player's position and name are stamped in prismatic foil along with the Classic logo and set title "96 Visions Signings." This set contains standouts from five sports grouped together in this order: basketball, football, hockey, baseball and racing. Cards were distributed in six-card packs. Release date was June 1996. The main allure to this product, in addition to the conventional inserts, were autographed memorabilia redemption cards inserted one per 10 packs.

COMPLETE SET (100) 6.00 15.00
61 Boyd Devereaux .08 .25
62 Alexandre Volchkov .08 .25
63 Trevor Wasyluk .08 .25
64 Luke Curtin .08 .25
65 Richard Jackman .08 .25
66 Jonathan Zukiwsky .08 .25
67 Geoff Peters .08 .25
68 Daniel Briere .30 .75
69 Chris Allen .08 .25
70 Jason Sweitzer .08 .25
71 Steve Nimigon .08 .25
72 Jay McKee .08 .25
73 Henry Kuster .08 .25
74 Johnathan Aitken .08 .25
75 Ed Jovanovski .08 .25
76 Petr Sykora .15 .40
77 Bryan Berard .08 .25
78 Manon Rheaume .20 .50
79 Radek Dvorak .08 .25

1996 Visions Signings Artistry

This 10-card insert set was printed on thick 24-point stock. Cards were inserted at a rate of 1:60 Vision Signings packs.

COMPLETE SET (10) 20.00 50.00
6 Petr Sykora 2.00 5.00

1996 Visions Signings Autographs Gold

Certified autographed cards were inserted in Visions Signings packs at an overall rate of 1:12. Some players signed only the silver version while others signed both gold and silver cards. The Gold foil cards were not individually serial numbered. The quantity signed is unknown but assumed to be significantly higher than the corresponding number signed for the silver foil cards. We've listed the unnumbered cards alphabetically.

2 Jonathan Aitken 1.50 4.00
4 Chris Allen 1.50 4.00
8 Daniel Briere 4.00 10.00
14 Luke Curtin 1.50 4.00
17 Boyd Devereaux 2.00 5.00
31 Richard Jackman 2.00 5.00
33 Ed Jovanovski 3.00 8.00
35 Henry Kuster 1.50 4.00
37 Jay McKee 1.50 4.00
44 Steve Nimigon 1.50 4.00
50 Geoff Peters 1.50 4.00
63 Jason Sweitzer 1.50 4.00
67 Alexandre Volchkov 2.00 5.00
69 Trevor Wasyluk 1.50 4.00
74 Jonathan Zukiwsky 1.50 4.00

1996 Visions Signings Autographs Silver

Certified autographed cards were inserted in Visions Signings packs at an overall rate of 1:12. Some players signed only silver cards while others signed gold and silver foil cards. The Silver cards were individually serial numbered as noted below. We've listed the unnumbered cards alphabetically.

3 Jonathan Aitken/360 2.00 5.00
5 Chris Allen/385 2.00 5.00
11 Daniel Briere/390 3.00 8.00
17 Luke Curtin/370 2.00 5.00
20 Boyd Devereaux/350 2.00 5.00
36 Richard Jackman/400 2.00 5.00
38 Ed Jovanovski/405 4.00 10.00
40 Henry Kuster/415 2.00 5.00
43 Jay McKee/385 2.00 5.00
50 Steve Nimigon/380 2.00 5.00
56 Geoff Peters/390 2.00 5.00
71 Jason Sweitzer/355 2.00 5.00
76 Alexandre Volchkov/375 2.00 5.00
79 Trevor Wasyluk/365 2.00 5.00
85 Jonathan Zukiwsky/375 2.00 5.00

1997 Visions Signings

Score Board's follow-up to the 1996 Visions Signings debut product was released in June 1997. The second-year product had more of a memorabilia emphasis. According to Score Board, 1,700 sequentially numbered cases were produced with five cards per pack, 16 packs per box and 10 boxes per case. Each pack contains either an autographed card or an insert card. The 50-card regular set includes stars and prospects from all four major team sports. Also, one in every two packs contained a gold parallel card to the base set.

COMPLETE SET (50) 5.00 10.00
40 Dainius Zubrus .05 .15
41 Joe Thornton .15 .40
42 Dan Cleary .05 .15
43 Sergei Samsonov .08 .25

1997 Visions Signings Gold

COMPLETE SET (50) 10.00 25.00
*GOLD: .8X TO 2X BASIC CARDS
GOLD STATED ODDS 1:2

1997 Visions Signings Artistry

The cards in this 20-card set feature Score Board's "exclusive printing technology" and were inserted at a rate of 1:6 Vision Signings packs.

COMPLETE SET (20) 20.00 40.00
A20 Dainius Zubrus .40 1.00

1997 Visions Signings Artistry Autographs

These certified autographed cards feature Score Board's "exclusive printing technology" and were inserted at a rate of 1:18 packs. These 20 cards are autographed parallels of the Artistry insert set.

A20 Dainius Zubrus 2.50 6.00

1997 Visions Signings Autographs

Each 1997 Visions Signings pack contained either an autographed card or an insert card. One in six packs contain a regular autograph card. Four cards, Troy Aikman, Brett Favre, Allen Iverson, and Emmitt Smith were never issued although they appeared on early checklists. One additional key card, Tony Gonzalez, surfaced long after the manufacturer ceased operations.

28 Josh Holden 1.50 4.00
51 Sergei Samsonov 4.00 10.00
55 Joe Thornton 3.00 8.00
65 Dainius Zubrus 2.00 5.00
66 Andrei Zyuzin 1.50 4.00

Acknowledgments

A great deal of diligence, hard work, and dedicated effort went into this year's volume. The high standards to which we hold ourselves, however, could not have been met without the expert input and generous amount of time contributed by many people. Our sincere thanks are extended to each and every one of you.

Each year we refine the process of developing the most accurate and up-to-date information for this book. I believe this year's Price Guide is our best yet. Thanks again to all of the contributors nationwide as well as to our staff worldwide since the success of the Beckett Price Guides has always been the result of a team effort.

For more than two decades now, many individuals have provided price input, illustrative material, checklist verifications, errata, and/or background information. Jim Beckett began this project in the early 1990s and his steadfast leadership and dedication to excellence can still be felt and seen in every page. Our company and the hobby as a whole extends to Dr. Beckett a sincere "Thank You."

At the risk of inadvertently overlooking or omitting these many contributors, we should like to personally thank: AbD Cards (Dale Wesolewski), Jerry Adamic, Pete Adauto, Bren Adams, Murray Akbart, Applegate, Neil Armstrong, Mike Aronstein, Alan Roland J. Atlas, Art Baker, Brent Barnes, Frank and Vivian Barning, Robert Beaudoin, Al Beharrell, Pete Belanger, Todd Bellerose, Gary Benton, Beulah Sports (Jeff Blatt), Ki Billy, Chad Blick, Michel Bolduc, Joseph Bonett, Peter Borkowski, Erwin Borau, Bill Bossert, Luc Boucher, B. Jack Bourland III, Tony Bouwman, Jim Boyne, Elio Brandelli, Tim Brahmer, John Brenner Marco Brizuela, Douglas Brown, Bob Bruner, Dan Bruner, Jacey Buel, Dave Bullis, Eric Burgoyne, Scott Burke, Jason Caines, Jim Cappello, Danny Cariseo, Cartomania (Joseph E. Filion), Greg Caskey, Rick Chambers, Dwight Chapin, Jeff Chapman, Michael Chark, Steve Chiaramonte, Susan Christensen, Larry Ciancone, Scott Coates, Allan E. Cohen, Shane Cohen (Grand Slam), Barry Colla, Collection de Sport AZ (Ronald Villanueve), Matt Collett, Ken Collins, Shelby Colson, Joe Conte, Dan Conway, Ryan Cope, Michael J. Cox, Taylor Crane, Wil Curtis, Allen Custer, Kenneth Daniels, Steven Danver, Leo Davis, Scott Dean, Jim Decorso, Mary Dempster, Deerquotes Baseball Cards, Normand Desroches, Larry DeTienne, Dave Deveney, Karlos Diego, Leon Dill, Mario DiPastena, Marc Dixon, Bill Dodge, Gerard Dolci, Benoit Doyon, Michel Dubois, Charles Dugre, John Duplisea, Denny W. Eckes (Mr. Sport Americana), Don Ellis, Danny Ellwood, Michael Esposito, Bryan Epstein, Doak Ewing, Dave Feltham, Gean Paul Figari, Larry Fleming, Gervise Ford, Don Forsey, Frank Fox, Craig Frank, Mark Franke, Steve Freedman, Kathryn Friedlander, Bob Friedman, Larry and Jeff Fritsch, Bob Frye, James Funke Jr., John Furniss, Gary Gagen, Tom Galanis, Jim Galusha, Richard, Gariepy, Neil Garvey, Ron and Dave Gibara, Dick Gilkeson, Michael R. Gionet, Dave Giove, Mike Gogal, Harvey Goldfarb, Brian Goldstein, Jeff Goldstein, Renvel Gonsalves, Rynel Gonsalves, Mike and Howard Gordon, Seth Gordon, John Gosney, George Grauer, Erik Gravel, Pierre-Luc Gravel, Great Canadian Sportcard Co., Gene Guarnere, Hall's Nostalgia, Gerald Hamelin, Tom Harrett, Ron Heller, Bill Henderson, Tom Hendrickson, Wayne Hepburn, Jerry and Etta Hersh, Mike Hersh, Chick Hershberger, Gerald Higgs, Clay Hill, Dan Hitt, Gary Hlady, Shawn Hoagland, Keith Holtzmann, Joseph Horgan, Dan Horton, Teresa Horton, D. Howery Jr., In The Game, Richard Irving, Sean Isaacs, Torstein H. Jacobsen, John James, Robert Jansing, Cliff Janzen, Peter Jeffrey, Leslie Jezuit, Scott Jugan, Dennis Kannokko, Paul and Anna Kannokko, Robert Kantor, Jay and Mary Kasper, Sam Kassam, John Kelly, Rick Keplinger, Larry Kerrigan, John Killan, Rich Klein, Dean Konieczka, Bob Krawetz, Chuck Kucera, George Kumagai, Rob Kuhlman, Thomas Kunnecke, Roger Lampert, Ted Larkins, Brent Lee, Scott LeLievre, Irv Lerner, Howie Levy, Mike Lewandoski, Lew Lipset, Stephane Lizotte, Nicholas LoCasto, The Locker Room, Tim Loop, Frank Lopez, Karoline K. Lowry, Doug Lowther, Steven J. Loy, Thierry Lubenec, Jim Macie, Paul Marchant, Joe Marasco, Adam Martin, Jason Martin, Chris Mayhew, Michael McDonald, Blake Meyer, John Meyer, Dick Millerd, Ben Mitchell, Paul V. Mohrle, Tony Moore, Joe Morano, Michael Moretto, Michel Morin, Brian Morris, Kevin Mudrak, Al Muir, Larry Murray, Todd Nelkin, Rob Nicholls, Dave Nicklas, Paul Noble, Leandre Normand, David Nystrom, John O'Hara, John O' Mara, Glenn Olson, Nelson Paine, Andrew Pak, David Paolicelli, Tom Parker, Clay Pasternack, Alan Peace, Joe Pellicio, Alan Philpot, Jean-Guy Pichette, Dale Pinney, Richard Plett, Jack Pollard, Len Pottie, Scott Prusha, Red River Coins and Cards, Randall Reese, Tom Reid, Dave and Shawn Redden, Paula Reinke, Ralph Reitsma, Ron Ressler, Dorothy Reznik, Owen Ricker, Gavin Riley, Mark Rogers, John Wayne Roman, Paul Romero, Charles Rooke, Francis Rose, Rotman Productions, Jim Routly, Grant Rowland, Joe Rubert II, John Rumierz, Terry Sack, Joe Sak, Grant Sandground, Linda Santiago, Cheryl Sauve, Kevin Savage Cards, Angelo Savelli, Mike Schechter (MSA), Mike Shafer, Richard Sherman, Brad Shrabin, Gary Silkstone, Chris Sklener, Lyle Skrapek, Slapshot Sports Collectibles, Steve Smith, Gerry Sobie, Don Spagnola, John Spalding, Carl Specht, Phil and Joan Spector, Nigel Spill, Dave Stallings, Cary Stephenson, Murvin Sterling, Dan Stickney, Andy Stoltz, Ray Stonehouse, Cheryl Suave, Mark Suchawericz, Dave Sularz, Walt Suski, Fred Suzman, Danny Tarquini, Paul S. Taylor, Lee Temanson, Teresa Tewell, Chuck Thomas, Tim Thompson, Joe Tomasik, Topps, Darren Turcotte, Rob Unlus, Upper Deck, Michel Vaillancourt, Variete Sports, Rob Veres, Verville Enr., Ernie Vickers, Clayton Vigent, Shirl Volk, Jonathan Waldman, Jonathan Watts, David Weiner, Andrew B. Weisenfeld, Kermit B. Wells, Brian Wentz, Bill Wesslund, Frank and Jason Wilder, Kelly Wionzek, Brian Wobbeking, Ted Woo, Pete Wooten, Thomas L. Wujek, Andre Yip Hoi, Yaz's Sports Memorabilia, Gerard Yodice, Kit Young, Robert Zanze, Christina Zawadzki, and Bill Zimpleman.

A special thanks also goes out to those who graciously donated their knowledge and expertise (and their card images) in adding to the comprehensiveness of the minor league and foreign issues sections: Ralph Slate (Whose web site www.hockeydb.com is one of the hobby's great minor league resources), Benny Kurz (European issues), Vinnie Montalbano and Dale Sprenger (for their efforts in improving the scope of our minor league and college coverage), Caspar Friberg (Finnish issues), Marek Pandoscak (Slovakian issues), Jiri Kuca and Jiri Peterka (Czech issues), Holger Petersen (German issues), Hockey Heaven, Christian Olander, and Per Vedin (Swedish issues), Joe Bonnett, Stewart Etlinger, Dino Fazio, Steve Fraser, CTM Ste-Foy, Gerry Garland, Gary Giovane, Ian Green (Armchair Sports UK), John Ignato, Chad Kitzman, Troy Moore, Jeremy Poclitar, J.D. Porter, Gus Saunders, Andre Yip Hoi (Time-Out Sportscards).

Every year we make active solicitations for expert input. We are particularly appreciative of the help (however extensive or cursory) provided for this volume. We receive many inquiries, comments and questions regarding material within this book. In fact, each and every one is read and digested. Time constraints, however, prevent us from personally replying - but please keep sharing your knowledge. Even though we cannot respond to each letter, you are making significant contributions to the hobby through your interest and comments.

The Beckett hockey specialist is Eric Norton. His pricing analysis and careful proofreading were key to the accuracy of this annual. The team effort was led by Brian Fleischer (Manager – Collectibles Data Publishing). They were ably assisted by the rest of the Market Analysts: Jeff Camay, Arsenio Tan, Lloyd Almonguera, Kristian Redulla, Justin Grunert, Matt Bible, Irish Desiree Serida, Paul Wirth, Ian McDaries, Steve Dalton and Badz Mercader.

The price gathering and analytical talents of this fine group of hobbyists have helped make our Beckett team stronger, while making this guide and its companion monthly Price Guide more widely recognized as the hobby's most reliable and relied upon sources of pricing information. Surajpal Singh Bisht, Munesh Kumar and Hritik Godara were responsible for layout of the book. The reason this book looks as good as it does is due to their hard work and expertise.

In the years since this guide debuted, Beckett Media has grown beyond any rational expectation. Many talented and hardworking individuals have been instrumental in this growth and success. Our whole team is to be congratulated for what we have accomplished.